Who's Who of American Women

**Biographical Reference Works
Published by Marquis Who's Who**

Who's Who
of American Women.

**9th edition
1975-1976**

**MARQUIS
Who's Who**

Marquis Who's Who, Inc.
200 East Ohio Street
Chicago, Illinois 60611 U.S.A.

Library of Congress Catalog Card Number 58-13264
ISBN 0-8379-0409-9

Distributed in the United Kingdom by
George Prior Associated Publishers
Rugby Chambers, 2 Rugby Street
London WC 1N 3 QU

Manufactured in the United States of America by
Kingsport Press, Inc., Kingsport, Tennessee 37662

Table of Contents

Preface

The Ninth Edition of *Who's Who of American Women* represents the efforts of Marquis editors to keep pace with the steadily expanding role of women in American life. It reflects the significant progress that women have made in all fields of human endeavor, and it seeks to call attention to women whose achievements have not, heretofore, been recognized on this scale.

The names recorded on these pages are the result of the combined efforts of Marquis' highly skilled staff of researchers, writers, and editors. The editors have compiled this present listing through continuing examination of newspapers, magazines and journals, books by and about women, and the output of all other communications media; and through correspondence with research associations, national organizations, and other institutions and individuals who know best the most eminent women in current world affairs.

In the majority of cases, the women listed in *Who's Who of American Women* have furnished their own data. This information is reviewed by the Marquis staff before being written in sketch form. A prepublication proof of the sketch is then sent back to the biographee for final verification.

The verified sketch, when returned to Marquis Who's Who, is rechecked and put into final form. In many cases where individuals fail to furnish their own data, the Marquis staff completes the information through careful original research. Sketches compiled in this way are indicated by an asterisk.

Marquis Who's Who editors exercise the utmost care in preparing each biographical sketch for publication. Occasionally, however, errors do occur, despite all precautions taken to minimize such occurrences. All users of this directory are requested to draw the attention of the publisher to any errors found, so that corrections can be made in a later edition.

The task of putting together this volume demands a keen knowledge of all aspects of human activity. Marquis Who's Who is uniquely qualified to provide this knowledge as publishers of *Who's Who in America* (thirty-eight editions in seventy-seven years); *Who Was Who in America; Who's Who in the World;* and other specialized reference works of national or international scope.

The question is often asked, "How do people get into any Who's Who volume?" Name selection is based on one principle: reference value.

Many individuals are eligible by virtue of position achieved through election or appointment to office; others have distinguished themselves in business, the professions, the arts, science, politics, entertainment, and athletics. Therefore, in the editorial evaluation that resulted in the ultimate selection of the names for *Who's Who of American Women,* an individual's desire to be listed was not a determining criterion for inclusion; rather it was the individual's demonstrated merit that ruled. Similarly, wealth or social position does not guarantee selection; only occupational stature or demonstrated ability in some particular field earn recognition. It is a fact that many of the biographees are engaged in fields marked far more by service than by monetary reward.

Thus the Ninth Edition of *Who's Who of American Women* carries on the tradition of excellence established with the publication of the First Edition of *Who's Who in America.* The essence of that tradition is Marquis' unceasing effort to produce reference works responsive to the needs of their users throughout the world.

Standards of Admission

The foremost consideration in determining who will be admitted to the pages of *Who's Who of American Women* is the extent of an individual's reference value throughout the world. Such reference interest is judged on either or both of two factors: (1) The position of responsibility held and (2) the level of achievement attained by the individual.

Admissions based on the factor of position include:

Pre-eminent governmental figures.

Ambassadors and ministers plenipotentiary.

Administrators at important diplomatic posts.

High ranking military officers.

High ranking legal officials.

Prominent figures from business, the professions, and the arts.

Heads of leading philanthropic, educational, and scientific societies.

Chief scientists.

Outstanding educators from major universities and colleges.

Other individuals similarly chosen because of incumbency or membership.

Admission based on individual achievement, on the other hand, must be decided by a judicious process of evaluating qualitative factors. To be selected on this basis, a person must have accomplished some conspicuous achievement—something that distinguishes her from the vast majority of her contemporaries. She may scarcely be known in the local community but may be widely recognized in some special field of endeavor. Such a person often is one whose work is better known than she is herself.

Key to Information in this Directory

(1) **BROUGHTON, Aloise Walton** (Mrs. Lester Broughton), (2) home economist; (3) b. Elyria, O., July 28, 1923; (4) d. Jason William and Velma (Ross) Walton; (5) B.S., Wooster Coll., 1944; M.S., Ohio State U., 1946, Ph.D., 1950; (6) m. Lester Broughton, May 21, 1947; (7) children—Barbara Lorraine, William Lawrence and Lester Ross (twins). (8) Tchr. Johnstown (O.) High Sch., 1946-48; research asst. Ohio State Agrl. Expt. Sta., Columbus, 1948-50; consumer service rep. East Ohio Gas Co., Columbus, 1955-61; dir. home econs. bur. Warden Packaging Co., Cleve., 1961—. (9) Cons. home econs. Dept. Health, Edn. and Welfare, 1966—. (10) Active Greater Cleve. United Fund; treas. Hudson (O.) Civic Assn., 1968-69. (11) Mem. Hudson Bd. Edn., 1970—. (12) Trustee Wooster (O.) Coll. (14) Named Bus. Woman of Year, Hudson Women's Club, 1969. (15) Mem. Am. Home Econs. Assn., Home Economists in Bus. (treas. Cleve. chpt. 1965-66), Alpha Xi Delta. (16) Republican. (17) Methodist. (18) Mem. Order Eastern Star. (19) Club: Hudson Country. (20) Author: The Working Woman's Cook Book, 1967. (21) Home: 40 College Rd Hudson OH 44236 (22) Office: 1103 Spring St Cleveland OH 44106

Key

1. Name
2. Position
3. Vital statistics
4. Parents
5. Education
6. Marital status
7. Children
8. Career
9. Career related activities
10. Civic activities
11. Political activities
12. Non-professional directorships
13. Military record (where applicable)
14. Decorations and awards
15. Professional and other memberships
16. Political affiliation
17. Religion
18. Lodges
19. Clubs
20. Writings
21. Home address
22. Office address

The biographical listings in *Who's Who of American Women* are arranged in alphabetical order according to the first letter of the last name of the biographee. Each sketch is presented in a uniform order as in the sample sketch above. The many abbreviations used in the sketches are explained in the Table of Abbreviations.

Table of Abbreviations

The following abbreviations and symbols are frequently used in this Directory

* Following a sketch indicates that it was researched and written by the Marquis Who's Who editorial staff and has not been verified by the biographee.

A.A., Associate in Arts.
A.A.A., Agricultural Adjustment Administration; Anti-Aircraft Artillery.
A.A.A.S., American Association for the Advancement of Science.
AAC, Army Air Corps.
A. and M., Agricultural and Mechanical.
AAF, Army Air Force.
A.A.H.P.E.R., American Association for Health, Physical Education, and Recreation.
AB, Alberta.
A.B., Bachelor of Arts.
ABC, American Broadcasting Company.
A.,B.&C.R.R., Atlanta, Birmingham & Coast R.R.
AC, Air Corps.
acad., academy; academic.
A.C.L.R.R., Atlantic Coast Line R.R.
A.C.P., American College of Physicians.
A.C.S., American College of Surgeons.
a.d.c., aide-de-camp.
adj., adjutant; adjunct.
adm., admiral.
adminstr., administrator.
adminstrn., administration.
adminstrv., administrative.
adv., advocate; advisory.
advt., advertising.
A.E., Agricultural Engineer.
A.E. and P., Ambassador Extraordinary and Plenipotentiary.
AEC, Atomic Energy Commission.
AEF, American Expeditionary Forces.
aero., aeronautical, aeronautic.
AFB, Air Force Base.
A.F.D., Doctor of Fine Arts.
AFL (or **A.F. of L**), American Federation of Labor.
A.F.T.R.A., American Federation TV and Radio Artists.
agr., agriculture.
agrl., agricultural.
agt., agent.
agy., agency.
A.I.A., American Institute of Architects.
AID, Agency for International Development.
A.I.M., American Institute of Management.
AK, Alaska.
AL, Alabama.
Ala., Alabama.
A.L.A., American Library Association.
Alta., Alberta.
Am., American, America.
A.M., Master of Arts.
A.M.A., American Medical Association.
A.M.E., African Methodist Episcopal.
Am. Inst. E.E., American Institute of Electrical Engineers.
Am. Soc. C.E., American Society of Civil Engineers.
Am. Soc. M.E., American Society of Mechanical Engineers.
A.N.A., Associate National Academician.
anat., anatomical.
ann., annual.
ANTA, American National Theatre and Academy.
anthrop., anthropological.
A.P., Associated Press.
apptd., appointed.

apt., apartment.
AR, Arkansas.
A.R.C., American Red Cross.
archeol., archaeological.
archtl., architectural.
Ariz., Arizona.
Ark., Arkansas.
ArtsD., Doctor of Arts.
arty., artillery.
AS, Air Service.
A.S.C.A.P., American Society of Composers, Authors and Publishers.
ASF, Air Service Force.
assn., association.
asso., associate; associated.
asst., assistant.
astron., astronomical.
astrophys., astrophysical.
ATSC, Air Technical Service Command.
A., T. & S. F. Ry., Atchison, Topeka & Santa Fe Ry.
atty., attorney.
AUS, Army of the United States.
Aux., Auxiliary.
Av., Avenue.
AZ, Arizona.

b., born.
B., Bachelor.
B.A., Bachelor of Arts.
B.Agr., Bachelor of Agriculture.
Balt., Baltimore.
Bapt., Baptist.
B. Arch., Bachelor of Architecture.
B. & A. R.R., Boston & Albany R.R.
B.A.S., Bachelor of Agricultural Science.
B.B.A., Bachelor of Business Administration.
BBC, British Broadcasting Corp.
BC, British Columbia.
B.C., British Columbia.
B.C.E., Bachelor of Civil Engineering.
B.Chir., Bachelor of Surgery.
B.C.L., Bachelor of Civil Law.
B.C.S., Bachelor of Commercial Science.
bd., Board.
B.D., Bachelor of Divinity.
B.Di., Bachelor of Didactics.
B.E., Bachelor of Education.
B.E.E., Bachelor of Electrical Engineering.
BEF, British Expeditionary Force.
B.F.A., Bachelor of Fine Arts.
bibl., biblical.
bibliog., bibliographical.
biog., biographical.
biol., biological.
B.J., Bachelor of Journalism.
Bklyn., Brooklyn.
B.L., Bachelor of Letters.
bldg., building.
B.L.S., Bachelor of Library Science.
Blvd., Boulevard.
B. & M. R.R., Boston & Maine R.R.
Bn., Battalion.
B.O., Bachelor of Oratory.
B. & O. R.R., Baltimore & Ohio R.R.
bot., Botanical.
B.P., Bachelor of Painting.
B.P.E., Bachelor of Physical Education.
B.Pd., Bachelor of Pedagogy.
B.Py., Bachelor of Pedagogy.
br., branch.
B.R.E., Bachelor of Religious Education.
brig. gen., brigadier general.
Brit., British; Britannica.

Bro., Brother.
B.S., Bachelor of Science.
B.S.A., Bachelor of Agricultural Science.
B.S.D., Bachelor of Didactic Science.
B.S.T., Bachelor of Sacred Theology.
B.Th., Bachelor of Theology.
bull., bulletin.
bur., bureau.
bus., business.
B.W.I., British West Indies.

CA, California.
Cal., California.
C.Am., Central America.
CAA, Civil Aeronautics Adminstrn.
CAB, Civil Aeronautics Board.
CAC, Coast Artillery Corps.
Can., Canada.
capt., captain.
Cath., Catholic.
cav., cavalry.
CBI, China, Burma, India Theatre of Operations.
C.B. & Q. R.R., Chicago, Burlington & Quincy R.R. Co.
CBS, Columbia Broadcasting System.
CCC, Commodity Credit Corporation.
C.,C.,C. & St.L. Ry., Cleveland, Cincinnati, Chicago & St. Louis Ry.
C.E., Civil Engineer, Corps of Engineers.
CEF, Canadian Expeditionary Force.
C. & E.I. R.R., Chicago & Eastern Illinois R.R.
C.G.W. R.R., Chicago Great Western Ry.
ch., church.
Ch.D., Doctor of Chemistry.
chem., chemical.
Chem.E., Chemical Engineer.
Chgo., Chicago.
Chirurg., Chirurgical.
chmm., Chairman.
chpt., Chapter.
Cia. (Spanish), Company.
CIA, Central Intelligence Agency.
CIC, Counter Intelligence Corps.
C.,I. & L. Ry., Chicago, Indianapolis & Louisville Ry.
Cin., Cincinnati.
CIO, Congress of Industrial Organizations.
Cleve., Cleveland.
climatol., Climatological.
clin., clinical.
clk., clerk.
C.L.U., Chartered Life Underwriter.
C.M., Master in Surgery.
C.M., St.P. & P. R.R., Chicago, Milwaukee, St. Paul & Pacific R.R. Co.
C. & N.-W. Ry., Chicago & Northwestern Ry.
CO, Colorado.
Co., Company.
C. of C., Chamber of Commerce.
C.O.F., Catholic Order of Foresters.
C. of Ga. Ry., Central of Georgia Ry.
col., colonel.
coll., college.
Colo., Colorado.
com., committee.
comd., commanded.
comdg., commanding.
comdr., commander.
comdt., commandant.
commd., commissioned.
comml., commercial.
commn., commission.
commr., commissioner.
condr., conductor.

conf., conference.
Congl., Congregational; Congressional.
Conglist., Congregationalist.
Conn., Connecticut.
cons., consulting, consultant.
consol., consolidated.
constl., constitutional.
constn., constitution.
constrn., construction.
contbd., contributed.
contbg., contributing.
contbn., contribution.
contbr., contributor.
conv., convention.
coop. (or **co.op**), cooperative.
corp., corporation.
corr., correspondent; corresponding; corre-
spondence.
C. & O. Ry., Chesapeake & Ohio Ry. Co.
C.P.A., Certified Public Accountant.
C.P.C.U., Chartered Property and Casualty
Underwriter.
C.P.H., Certificate of Public Health.
cpl., corporal.
C.P. Ry., Canadian Pacific Ry. Co.
C.,R.I. & P. Ry., Chicago, Rock Island & Pacific
Ry. Co.
C.R.R. of N.J., Central Railroad Co. of New Jersey.
C.S., Christian Science.
C.S.B., Bachelor of Christian Science.
C.S.D., Doctor of Christian Science.
C. & S. Ry. Co., Colorado & Southern Ry. Co.
C.,St.P.,M. & O. Ry., Chicago, St. Paul, Min-
neapolis & Omaha Ry. Co.
CT, Connecticut.
ct., court.
C.T., Candidate in Theology.
C.Vt. Ry., Central Vermont Ry.
C. & W.I. R.R., Chicago & Western Indiana R.R. Co.
CWS, Chemical Warfare Service.
cyclo., cyclopedia.
C.Z., Canal Zone.
CZ., Canal Zone.
d., daughter.
D., Doctor.
D.Agr., Doctor of Agriculture.
D.A.R., Daughters of the American Revolution.
dau., daughter.
D.A.V., Disabled American Veterans.
D.C., District of Columbia.
DC, District of Columbia.
D.C.L., Doctor of Civil Law.
D.C.S., Doctor of Commercial Science.
D.D., Doctor of Divinity.
D.D.S., Doctor of Dental Surgery.
DE, Delaware.
dec., deceased.
Def., Defense.
Del., Delaware.
del., delegate.
Dem., Democratic; Democrat.
D.Eng., Doctor of Engineering.
denom., denominational.
dep., deputy.
dept., department.
dermatol., dermatological.
desc., descendant.
devel., development.
D.F.C., Distinguished Flying Cross.
D.H.L., Doctor of Hebrew Literature.
D. & H. R.R., Delaware & Hudson R.R. Co.
dir., director.
disch., discharged.

dist., district.
distbg., distributing.
distbn., distribution.
distbr., distributor.
div., division; divinity; divorce proceedings.
D.Litt., Doctor of Literature.
D., L. & W. R.R., Delaware, Lackawanna &
Western R.R. Co.
D.M.D., Doctor of Dental Medicine.
D.M.S., Doctor of Medical Science.
D.O., Doctor of Osteopathy.
DPA, Defense Production Administration.
D.P.H., Diploma in Public Health.
Dr., Doctor, Drive.
D.R., Daughters of the Revolution.
D.R.E., Doctor of Religious Education.
D. & R.G.W. R.R. Co., Denver & Rio Grande
Western R.R. Co.
Dr.P.H., Doctor of Public Health, Doctor of Public
Hygiene.
D.Sc., Doctor of Science.
D.S.C., Distinguished Service Cross.
D.S.M., Distinguished Service Medal.
D.S.T., Doctor of Sacred Theology.
D.T.M., Doctor of Tropical Medicine.
D.V.M., Doctor of Veterinary Medicine.
D.V.S., Doctor of Veterinary Surgery.

E., East.
E. and P., Extraordinary and Plenipotentiary.
ECA, Economic Cooperation Administration.
eccles., ecclesiastical.
ecol., ecological.
econ., economic.
ECOSOC, Economic and Social Council (of the
UN).
ed., educated.
E.D., Doctor of Engineering.
Ed.B., Bachelor of Education.
Ed.D., Doctor of Education.
edit., edition.
Ed.M., Master of Education.
edn., education.
ednl., educational.
E.E., Electrical Engineer.
E.E. and M.P., Envoy Extraordinary and Minister
Plenipotentiary.
Egyptol., Egyptological.
elec., electrical.
electrochem., electrochemical.
electrophys., electrophysical.
E. M., Engineer of Mines.
ency., encyclopaedia.
Eng., England.
engr., engineer.
engring., engineering.
entomol., entomological.
ethnol., ethnological.
ETO, European Theater of Operations.
Evang., Evangelical.
exam., examination; examining.
exec., executive.
exhbn., exhibition.
expdn., expedition.
expn., exposition.
expt., experiment.
exptl., experimental.

F.A., Field Artillery.
FAA, Federal Aviation Agency.
FAO, Food and Agriculture Organization (of
the UN).
FBI, Federal Bureau of Investigation.

FCA, Farm Credit Administration.
FCC, Federal Communications Commission.
FCDA, Federal Civil Defense Administration.
FDA, Food and Drug Administration.
FDIA, Federal Deposit Insurance Administration.
F.E., Forest Engineer.
Fed., Federal.
Fedn., Federation.
Fgn., Foreign.
FHA, Federal Housing Administration.
FL, Florida.
Fla., Florida.
FOA, Foreign Operations Administration.
Found., Foundation.
frat., fraternity.
FSA, Federal Security Agency.
Ft., Fort.
FTC, Federal Trade Commission, Federal Tariff
Commission.

G.-1 (or other number), Division of General Staff.
GA, Georgia.
Ga., Georgia.
gastroent., gastroenterological.
GATT, General Agreement on Tariffs and Trade.
G.,C. & S.F. Ry., Gulf, Colorado & Santa Fe Ry. Co.
G.D., Graduate in Divinity.
gen., general.
geneal., genealogical.
geod., geodetic.
geog., geographical; geographic.
geol., geological.
geophys., geophysical.
G.H.Q., General Headquarters.
G.,M. & N. R.R., Gulf, Mobile & Northern R.R. Co.
G.,M. & O. R.R., Gulf, Mobile & Ohio R.R. Co.
G.N. Ry., Great Northern Ry. Co.
gov., Governor.
govt., government.
govtl., governmental.
grad., graduated; graduate.
Gt., Great.
G.T. Ry., Grand Trunk Ry. System.
GU, Guam.
G.W. Ry. of Can., Great Western Ry. of Canada.
gynecol., genecological.

Hdqrs., Headquarters.
H.H.D., Doctor of Humanities.
HHFA, Housing and Home Finance Agency.
HI, Hawaii.
H.I., Hawaiian Islands.
H.M., Master of Humanics.
hist., Historical.
HOLC, Home Owners Loan Corporation.
homeo., homeopathic.
hon., honorary; honorable.
Ho. of Dels., House of Delegates.
Ho. of Reps., House of Representatives.
Hort., Horticultural.
hosp., hospital.
H.T., Territory of Hawaii.
Hwy., Highway.
hydrog., hydrographic.

IA, Iowa.
Ia., Iowa.
IAEA, International Atomic Energy Agency.
IBM, International Business Machines Corp.
ICA, International Cooperation Administration.
ICC, Interstate Commerce Commn.
I.C. R.R., Illinois Central R.R. System.
ID, Idaho.

Ida., Idaho.
I.E.E.E., Institute of Electrical and Electronics Engineers.
IFC, International Finance Corp.
I.G.N. R.R., International–Great Northern R.R.
IGY, International Geophysical Year.
IL, Illinois.
Ill., Illinois.
illus., illustrated.
ILO, International Labor Orgn.
IMF, International Monetary Fund.
IN, Indiana.
Inc., Incorporated.
Ind., Indiana.
ind., independent.
Indpls., Indianapolis.
indsl., industrial.
inf., infantry.
ins., insurance.
insp., inspector.
inst., institute.
instl., institutional.
instn., institution.
instr., instructor.
instrn., instruction.
internat., international.
intro., introduction.
I.R.E., Institute of Radio Engineers.

J.B., Jurum Baccalaureus.
J.C.B., Juris Canonici Bachelor.
J.C.L., Juris Canonici Lector.
J.D., Doctor of Jurisprudence.
j.g., junior grade.
jour., journal.
jr., junior.
J.S.D., Doctor of Juristic Science.
jud., Judicial.
J.U.D., Juris Utriusque Doctor: Doctor of Both (Canon and Civil) Laws.

Kan., Kansas.
K.C., Knight of Columbus.
K.P., Knight of Pythias.
K.C.S. Ry., Kansas City Southern Ry.
KS, Kansas.
K.T., Knight Templar.
KY, Kentucky.
Ky., Kentucky.

LA, Louisiana.
lab., laboratory.
lang., language.
laryngol., laryngological.
LB, Labrador.
lectr., lecturer.
L.H.D., Doctor of Humane Letters.
L.I., Long Island.
L.I. R.R., Long Island R.R. Co.
lit., literary; literature.
Litt.B., Bachelor of Letters.
Litt.D., Doctor of Letters.
LL.B., Bachelor of Laws.
LL.D., Doctor of Laws.
LL.M., Master of Laws.
L. & N. R.R., Louisville & Nashville R.R.
L.R.C.P., Licentiate Royal Coll. Physicians.
L.R.C.S., Licentiate Royal Coll. Surgeons.
L.S., Library Science.
lt., lieutenant.
Ltd., Limited.
Luth., Lutheran.
L.V. R.R., Lehigh Valley R.R. Co.

m., marriage ceremony.
M., Master.
MA, Massachusetts.
M.A., Master of Arts.
mag., magazine.
M.Agr., Master of Agriculture.
maj., major.
Man., Manitoba.
M.Arch., Master in Architecture.
Mass., Massachusetts.
math., mathematical, mathematics.
MB, Manitoba.
M.B., Bachelor of Medicine.
M.B.A., Master of Business Administration.
MBS, Mutual Broadcasting System.
M.C., Medical Corps.
M.C.S., Master of Commercial Science.
M.C.E., Master of Civil Engineering.
mcht., merchant.
M.C. R.R., Michigan Central R.R.
MD, Maryland.
Md., Maryland.
M.D., Doctor of Medicine.
M.Di., Master of Didactics.
M.Dip., Master in Diplomacy.
mdse., merchandise.
M.D.V., Doctor of Veterinary Medicine.
ME, Maine.
Me., Maine.
M.E., Mechanical Engineer.
mech., mechanical.
M.E. Ch., Methodist Episcopal Church.
M.Ed., Master of Education.
med., medical.
Med. O.R.C., Medical Officers' Reserve Corps.
Med. R.C., Medical Reserve Corps.
M.E.E., Master of Electrical Engineering.
mem., member.
Meml., Memorial.
merc., mercantile.
met., metropolitan.
metall., metallurgical.
Met.E., Metallurgical Engineer.
meteorol., meteorological.
Meth., Methodist.
metrol., metrological.
M.F., Master of Forestry.
M.F.A., Master of Fine Arts (carries title of Dr.).
mfg., manufacturing.
mfr., manufacturer.
mgmt., management.
mgr., manager.
M.H.A., Master of Hospital Administration.
MI, Michigan.
M.I., Military Intelligence.
Mich., Michigan.
micros., microscopical.
mil., military.
Milw., Milwaukee.
mineral., mineralogical.
Minn., Minnesota.
M.-K.-T. R.R., Missouri-Kansas-Texas R.R. Co.
M.L., Master of Laws.
M.L.D., Magister Legnum Diplomatic.
M.Litt., Master of Literature.
Minn., Minnesota.
Miss., Mississippi.
Mlle., Mademoiselle.
M.L.S., Master of Library Science.
Mme., Madame.
M.M.E., Master of Mechanical Engineering.
MN, Minnesota.
mng., managing.

MO, Missouri.
Mo., Missouri.
Moblzn., Mobilization.
Mont., Montana.
M.P., Member of Parliament.
M.Pd., Master of Pedagogy.
M.P.E., Master of Physical Education.
M.P.H., Master of Public Health.
M.P.L., Master of Patent Law.
Mpls., Minneapolis.
M.P. R.R., Missour Pacific R.R.
M.R.E., Master of Religious Education.
MS, Mississippi.
M.S., Master of Science.
M.Sc., Master of Science.
M.S.F., Master of Science of Forestry.
M.S.T., Master of Sacred Theology.
M. & St. L. R.R., Minneapolis & St. Louis R.R. Co.
M.,St.P. & S.S.M. Ry., Minneapolis, St. Paul & Sault Ste. Marie Ry.
M.S.W., Master of Social Work.
MT, Montana.
Mt., Mount.
MTO, Mediterranean Theater of Operations.
mus., museum; musical.
Mus.B., Bachelor of Music.
Mus.D., Doctor of Music.
Mus. M., Master of Music.
Mut., Mutual.
mycol., mycological.

N., North.
N.A., National Academician; National Army.
N.A.A.C.P., National Association for the Advancement of Colored People.
NACA, National Advisory Committee for Aeronautics.
N.A.D., National Academy of Design.
N.Am., North America.
N.A.M., National Association of Manufacturers.
NASA, National Aeronautics and Space Administration.
nat., national.
NATO, North Atlantic Treaty Organization.
NATOUSA, North African Theater of Operations, U.S. Army.
nav., navigation.
NB, New Brunswick.
N.B., New Brunswick.
NBC, National Broadcasting Company.
NC, North Carolina.
N.C., North Carolina.
N.,C. & St.L. Ry., Nashville, Chattanooga & St. Louis Ry.
ND, North Dakota.
N.D., North Dakota.
NDRC, National Defense Research Committee.
NE, Nebraska.
N.E., Northeast.
N.E.A., National Education Association.
Neb., Nebraska.
neurol., neurological.
Nev., Nevada.
New Eng., New England.
NF, Newfoundland.
Nfld., Newfoundland.
N.G., National Guard.
NH, New Hampshire.
N.H., New Hampshire.
NIH, National Institutes of Health.
NJ, New Jersey.
N.J., New Jersey.
NLRB, National Labor Relations Bd.
NM, New Mexico.

N.M., New Mexico.
No., Northern.
NPA, National Production Authority.
N.P. Ry., Northern Pacific Ry.
nr., near.
NRA, National Recovery Administrn.
NRC, National Research Council.
NS, Nova Scotia.
N.S., Nova Scotia.
NSC, National Security Council.
NSF, National Science Foundation.
NSRB, National Security Resources Board.
NT, Northwest Territories.
N.T., New Testament.
numis., numismatic.
NV, Nevada.
N.W., Northwest.
N. & W. Ry., Norfolk & Western Ry.
N.W.T., Northwest Territories.
NY, New York.
N.Y., New York.
N.Y.C., New York City.
N.Y.C. RR., New York Central R.R. Co.
N.Y.,C. & St.L. R.R., New York, Chicago & St. Louis R.R. Co.
N.Y.,N.H. & H. R.R., New York, New Haven & Hartford R.R. Co.
N.Y.,O. & W. Ry., New York, Ontario & Western Ry.

O., Ohio.
OAS, Organization of American States.
O.B., Bachelor of Oratory.
obs., observatory.
obstet., obstetrical.
OCDM, Office of Civil and Defense Mobilization.
ODM, Office of Defense Mobilization.
OECD, Organization European Cooperation and Development.
OEEC, Organization European Economic Co-operation.
ofcl., official.
OH, Ohio.
OK, Oklahoma.
Okla., Oklahoma.
ON, Ontario.
Ont., Ontario.
OPA, Office of Price Administration.
ophthal., ophthalmological.
OPM, Office of Production Management.
OPS, Office of Price Stabilization.
O.Q.M.G., Office of Quartermaster General.
OR, Oregon.
O.R.C., Officers' Reserve Corps.
orch., orchestra.
Ore., Oregon.
orgn., organization.
ornithol., ornithological.
O.S.L. R.R., Oregon Short Line R.R.
OSRD, Office of Scientific Research and Development.
OSS, Office of Strategic Services.
osteo., osteopathic.
O.T., Old Testament.
O.T.C., Officers Training Camp.
otol., Otological.
otolaryn., otolaryngological.
O.T.S., Officers Training School.

O.U.A.M., Order United American Mechanics.
OWI, Office of War Information.
O.-W. R.R. & N. Co., Oregon-Washington R.R. & Navigation Co.

PA, Pennsylvania.
Pa., Pennsylvania.
paleontol., paleontological.
Pa. R.R., Pennsylvania R.R.
path., pathological.
Pd.B., Bachelor of Pedagogy.
Pd.D., Doctor of Pedagogy.
Pd.M., Master of Pedagogy.
PE, Prince Edward Island.
P.E., Protestant Episcopal.
Pe.B., Bachelor of Pediatrics.
P.E.I., Prince Edward Island.
P.E.N., Poets, Playwrights, Editors, Essayists and Novelists (Internat. Assn.).
penol., penological.
pfc., private first class.
PHA, Public Housing Administration.
pharm., pharmaceutical.
Pharm.D., Doctor of Pharmacy.
Pharm.M., Master of Pharmacy.
Ph.B., Bachelor of Philosophy.
Ph.C., Pharmaceutical Chemist.
Ph.D., Doctor of Philosophy.
Ph.G., Graduate in Pharmacy.
Phila., Philadelphia.
philol., philological.
philos., philosophical.
photog., photographic.
phys., physical.
Phys. and Surg., Physicians and Surgeons (College at Columbia U.).
physiol., physiological.
P.I., Philippine Islands.
Pitts., Pittsburgh.
Pkwy., Parkway.
Pl., Place.
P. & L.E. R.R., Pittsburgh & Lake Erie R.R.
P.M. R.R., Pere Marquette R.R. Co.
P.O., Post Office.
polit., political.
poly., polytechnic; polytechnical.
pomol., pomological.
PQ, Quebec (province).
PR, Puerto Rico.
P.R., Puerto Rico.
prep., preparatory.
pres., president.
Presbyn., Presbyterian.
presdl., presidential.
prin., principal.
proc., proceedings.
prod., produced (play production).
prodn., production.
prof., professor.
profl., professional.
prog., progressive.
propr., proprietor.
pros. atty., prosecuting attorney.
pro tem, pro tempore (for the time being).
psychiat., psychiatric.
psychol., psychological.
P.T.A., Parent-Teacher Association.
PTO, Pacific Theater of Operations.
pub., public; publisher; publishing; published.
publ., publication.
pvt., private.
PWA, Public Works Administration.

q.m., quartermaster.
Q.M.C., Quartermaster Corps.
Q.M.O.R.C., Quartermaster Officers' Reserve Corps.
quar., quarterly.
Que., Quebec (province).

radiol., Radiological.
RAF, Royal Air Force.
R.C., Roman Catholic.
RCA, Radio Corporation of America.
RCAF, Royal Canadian Air Force.
Rd., Road.
R.D., Rural Delivery.
R.E., Reformed Episcopal.
rec., recording.
ref., reformed.
regt., regiment.
regtl., regimental.
rehab., rehabilitation.
Rep., Republican.
rep., representative.
Res., Reserve.
ret., retired.
rev., review, revised.
RFC, Reconstruction Finance Corp.
R.F.D., Rural Free Delivery.
rhinol., rhinological.
RI, Rhode Island.
R.I., Rhode Island.
R.N., Registered Nurse.
roentgenol., roentgenological.
R.O.S.C., Reserve Officers' Sanitary Corps.
R.O.T.C., Reserve Officers' Training Corps.
R.P., Reformed Presbyterian.
R.R., Railroad.
R.T.C., Reserve Training Corps.
Ry., Railway.

s., son.
S., South.
S.A., (Spanish) Sociedad Anonima: (French) societe Anonyme.
SAC, Strategic Air Command.
S.A.L. Ry., Seaboard Air Line Ry.
S.Am., South America.
san., sanitary.
S.A.R., Sons of the Am. Revolution.
Sask., Saskatchewan.
S.A.T.C., Student's Army Training Corps.
Sat. Eve. Post, Saturday Evening Post.
savs., savings.
S.B., Bachelor of Science.
SC, South Carolina.
S.C., South Carolina.
SCAP, Supreme Command Allies Pacific.
Sc.B., Bachelor of Science.
Sc.D., Doctor of Science.
S.C.D., Doctor of Commercial Science.
sch., school.
sci., science; scientific.
S.C.V., Sons of Confederate Veterans.
SD, South Dakota.
S.D., South Dakota.
S.E., Southeast.
SEATO, Southeast Asia Treaty Organization.
SEC, Securities and Exchange Commn.
sec., secretary.
sect., section.
seismol., seismological.
sem., seminary.
sgt., sergeant.
SHAEF, Supreme Headquarters, Allied Expeditionary Forces.
SHAPE, Supreme Headquarters Allied Powers in Europe.
S.I., Staten Island.
S.J., Society of Jesus (Jesuit).
SK, Saskatchewan.
S.J.D., Doctor Juristic Science.

S.M., Master of Science.
So., Southern.
soc., society.
sociol., sociological.
SOS, Service of Supply.
S.P. Co., Southern Pacific Co.
spl., special.
splty., specialty.
Sq., Square.
sr., senior.
S.R., Sons of the Revolution.
S.S., Steamship.
SSS, Selective Service System.
St., Saint; Street.
sta., station.
statis., statistical.
S.T.B., Bachelor of Sacred Theology.
Stblzn., Stabilization.
S.T.D., Doctor of Sacred Theology.
S.T.L., Licentiate in Sacred Theology; Lector of Sacred Theology.
St.L.-S.F. R.R., St. Louis-San Francisco Ry. Co.
supr., supervisor.
supt., superintendent.
surg., surgical.
S.W., Southwest.

T.A.P.P.I., Technical Association Pulp and Paper Industry.
Tb, Tuberculosis.
tchr., teacher.
tech., technical, technology.
technol., technological.
Tel. & Tel., Telephone and Telegraph.
temp., temporary.
Tenn., Tennessee.
Ter., Territory.
Tex., Texas.
T.H., Territory of Hawaii.
Th.D., Doctor of Theology.
Th.M., Master of Theology.
theol., theological.
TN, Tennessee.
tng., training.
topog., topographical.
T. & P. Ry., Texas & Pacific Ry. Co.
trans., transactions; transferred.
transl., transition.
transp., transportation.
treas., treasurer.

TV, Television.
TVA, Tennessee Valley Authority.
Twp., Township.
TX, Texas.
Ty., Territory.
typog., typographical.

U., University.
UAR, United Arab Republic.
U.A.W., International Union United Automobile, Aircraft, and Agricultural Implement Workers of American-AFL-CIO.
U.B., United Brethren in Christ.
U.D.C., United Daughters of the Confederacy.
U.K., United Kingdom.
UN, United Nations.
UNESCO, United Nations Educational, Scientific and Cultural Organization.
UNICEF, United Nations International Childrens Emergency Fund.
univ., university.
UNRRA, United Nations Relief and Rehabilitation Administration.
U.P., United Presbyterian.
U.P.I., United Press International.
U.P. R.R., Union Pacific R.R.
urol., urological.
U.S., United States.
U.S.A., United States of America.
USAAF, United States Army Air Force.
USAC, United States Air Corps.
USAF, United States Air Force.
USCG, United States Coast Guard.
USCGR, U.S. Coast Guard Reserve.
USES, United States Employment Service.
USIA, United States Information Agency.
USIS, United States Information Service.
USMC, United States Marine Corps.
USMCR, U.S. Marine Corps Reserve.
USMHS, United States Marine Hospital Service.
USN, United States Navy.
U.S.N.A., United States National Army.
U.S.N.G., United States National Guard.
USNR, United States Naval Reserve.
USNRF, United States Naval Reserve Force.
U.S.O., United Service Organizations.
USOM, United States Operations Mission.
USPHS, United States Public Health Service.
U.S.S., United States Ship.

USSR, Union of Soviet Socialist Republics.
U.S.V., United States Volunteers.
UT, Utah.

VA, Virginia.
Va., Virginia.
VA, Veterans Administration.
vet., Veteran; veterinary.
V.F.W., Veterans of Foreign Wars.
VI, Virgin Islands.
V.I., Virgin Islands.
vice pres., vice president.
vis., visiting.
vol., volunteer; volume.
v.p., vice president.
vs., versus.
VT, Vermont.
Vt., Vermont.

W., West.
WA, Washington.
WAC, Women's Army Corps.
Wash., Washington (state).
WAVES, Womens Reserve, U.S. Naval Reserve.
W.C.T.U., Women's Christian Temperance Union.
WHO, World Health Organization (of the UN).
WI, Wisconsin.
W.I., West Indies.
Wis., Wisconsin.
W. & L.E. Ry., Wheeling & Lake Erie Ry. Co.
WPA, Works Progress Administration.
WPB, War Production Board.
W.P.R.R. Co., Western Pacific R.R. Co.
WSB, Wage Stabilization Board.
WV, West Virginia.
W. Va., West Virginia.
WY, Wyoming.
Wyo., Wyoming.

YMCA, Young Men's Christian Assn.
YMHA, Young Men's Hebrew Assn.
YM and YWHA, Young Men's and Young Women's Hebrew Assn.
Y. & M.V. R.R., Yazoo & Mississippi Valley R.R.
YT, Yukon Territory.
Y.T., Yukon Territory.
YWCA, Young Women's Christian Assn.

zool., zoological.

Alphabetical Practices

Names are arranged alphabetically according to the surnames, and under identical surnames according to the first given name. If both surnames and first given names are identical, names are arranged alphabetically according to the second given name. Where full names are identical, they are arranged in order of age—those of the elder being put first.

Surnames beginning with De, Des, Du, etc., however capitalized or spaced, are recorded with the prefix preceding the surname and arranged alphabetically, under the letter D.

Surnames beginning with Mac are arranged alphabetically under M. This also holds for names beginning with Mc, that is, all names beginning Mc will be found in alphabetical order after those beginning Mac.

Surnames beginning with Saint or St. all appear after names that would begin Sains, and such surnames are arranged according to the second part of the name, e.g., St. Clair would come before Saint Dennis.

Surnames beginning with prefix Van are arranged alphabetically under letter V.

Surnames containing the prefix Von or von are usually arranged alphabetically under letter V; any exceptions are noted by cross reference (Von Kleinsmid, Rufus Bernhard; see Kleinsmid, Rufus Bernhard von).

Compound hyphenated surnames are arranged according to the first member of the compound.

Compound unhyphenated surnames common in Spanish are not rearranged but are treated as hyphenated names.

Since Chinese names have the family name first, they are so arranged, but without comma between family name and given name (as Lin Yutang).

Parentheses used in connection with a name indicate which part of the full name is usually deleted in common usage. Hence Abbott, W(illiam) Lewis indicates that the usual form of the given name is W. Lewis. In alphabetizing this type, the parentheses are not considered.

Who's Who of American Women

AAGAARD, EARLA GARDNER (MRS. CARL AAGAARD), psychiatrist; b. Bandung, Java, Dec. 5, 1922; d. J. Earl and Ethel (Swing) Gardner; B.A., Pacific Union Coll., 1942; M.D., Coll. Med. Evangelists, 1945; m. Carl M. J. Aagaard, Mar. 13, 1943; children—Carla, Earl, Victor, Lola. Intern Los Angeles County Gen. Hosp., 1945-46; resident Children's Hosp., San Francisco, 1947-48; staff physician Mendocino State Hosp., Talmage, Cal., 1949-52; resident in psychiatry Langley Porter Clinic, San Francisco, 1952-53, staff psychiatrist, 1954; pvt. practice psychiatry, Ukiah, Cal., 1955—. Trustee Pacific Union Coll., Angwin, Cal. Mem. A.M.A., Cal., Mendocino-Lake Counties med. socs., Am. Psychiat. Assn. Home: 1101 W Clay St Ukiah CA 95482 Office: 215 W Standley St Ukiah CA 95482

AAMODT, MARGARET DORA, author; b. Crow Wing County, Minn., Dec. 14, 1910; d. Roy J. and Effie Louise (Thomson) Cunningham; m. Henry Oscar Aamodt, May 15, 1930; children—Myrna (Mrs. Duane Langerud), Bonnie (Mrs. Verdell Schmalle). News corr. Mason City (Ia.) Globe Gazette, 1927—, Des Moines Register and Tribune, 1942—, Northwood (Ia.) Anchor, 1942-46, Forest City (Ia.) Summit, 1947-66; news corr. Albert Lea (Minn.) Tribune, 1947-69, 71—, farm editor, 1969-71; news corr. Lake Mills (Ia.) Graphic, 1950-66, editor, 1966-69. Recipient numerous poetry and press awards. Founding fellow Internat. Poetry Soc.; mem. Midwest Fedn. Chaparral Poets (regent Ia. 1972—, asso. editor mag.). Author: (poetry) Through Country Lanes, 1963. Home: 106 S Lincoln St Lake Mills IA 50450

AARON, EVALYN WILHELMINA KEISLER (MRS. PAUL AARON), artist; b. N.Y.C.; d. John J. and Anna (Horowitz) Keisler; student Art Students League; pvt. student in watercolor and Sumi-e; m. Paul Aaron, Nov. 14, 1937; children—L. Neil, Barry. Exhibited in one-man show Unitarian Ch., Plandome, N.Y., 1968; exhibited in group shows Nippon Club N.Y., Japan Soc., Internat. Platform Assn., Sumi-e Soc. shows, 1963-71, Community Synagogue, Sands Point, N.Y., 1966-67; represented in permanent collections. Pres., Workshops for Art, Port Washington, N.Y., 1967—; instr. adult edn. in Sumi-e, Great Neck, Port Washington, N.Y., 1964—; award judge Sumi-e Exhbn., 1971; lectr., demonstrator Sumi-e art before civic and ch. groups. Recipient 1st prize for Sumi-e Nippon Club exhibit, 1964, cup Consul Gen. Japan, 1966, 1st prize for Sumi-e, N.Y. Bd. Trade exhibit, 1970. Mem. Sumi-e Soc. Am. (a founder, pres.), Water Color Soc. Am. (asso.), Japan Soc. (asso., former coordinator, adminstr. service program for Japanese students in U.S.), Nat. Women's Com. Brandeis U., Am. Jewish Congress, Internat. Platform Assn., Art League Nassau County. Home: 60 Richards Rd Port Washington NY 11050 Office: Workshops for Art 301 Main St Port Washington NY 11050

AASEN, DOREEN ELIZABETH, nursing exec.; b. Turner Valley, Oct. 13, 1931; d. Angus Wellington and Kitty Bell (Kerr) McLeod; R.N., Edmonton Gen. Hosp.; m. Mr. Aasen, Nov. 2, 1956; children—Miles Emmerson, Sharon Lee, Rena Bell. Registered nurse, dir. nursing, Elk Point, Alta., 1954-58; part time registered nurse, 1958-68; dir. nursing small hosps. in Mayerthorpe, Slave Lake, Alta., N.W.T., Bashaw and Whitecourt Gen. Hosp., 1968—. Sec. of body to form Registered Nurses Assn. in N.W.T. Mem. Joint Health Planning Com., Bashaw; pres. Mental Health Com., Whitecourt. Mem. Alta. Assn. Registered Nurses. Home: PO Box 787 Whitecourt AB Canada Office: Whitecourt Gen Hosp Whitecourt AB Canada

ABBATE, CELESTE GLENAKOPULOS (MRS. ARTHUR ABBATE), educator; b. Chgo., July 1, 1915; d. Peter Christopher and Madalen Coarl (Calamarl) Glanakopulos; B.S., Northwestern U., 1937, M.A. with honors, 1944; m. Arthur Abbate, Mar. 24, 1940. Tchr. Northbrook (Ill.) High Sch., 1942-49, pub. schs., Phoenix, 1949-57; supr. field operations Artco Distbrs., Inc., Glendale, Ariz., 1957—. Guest speaker Nat. Conf. Use Pesticides and Insecticides, 1973, Teamsters Union on Western Farm Labor, Hawaii, 1974. Contbr. Nat. Sch. Bd. Jour., 1944—. Home: PO Box 15128 Phoenix AZ 85018 Office: PO Box 1287 Glendale AZ 85301

ABBATE, GRACE MCLEAN, physician; b. Bklyn., 1905; M.D., L.I. Coll. Medicine, 1932. Intern, Cumberland Hosp., Bklyn., 1932-33; intern Middletown State Hosp. (N.Y.), 1934-36, asst. physician, 1936; practice medicine, specializing in psychiatry; asst. physician Pilgrim State Hosp., Brentwood, L.I., N.Y., 1936-38; Commonwealth Fund fellow Cleve. Guidance Center, 1938-39; sch. psychiatrist in charge of unit Bur. Child Guidance, N.Y.C. Bd. Edn., Bklyn., 1939-48; psychiat. cons. Ednl. Inst. Learning and Research, 1948-72; instr. N.Y. Psychoanalytic Inst. Diplomate Am. Bd. Psychiatry and Neurology. Fellow Am. Orthopsychiat. Assn.; mem. A.M.A., Am. Psychiat. Assn., Am. Psychoanalytic Assn. Office: 9 Garden Pl Brooklyn NY 11201

ABBE, JEAN SKOGLUND (MRS. ROBERT REED ABBE), pediatrician; b. Kansas City, Kan., Feb. 14, 1939; d. John Egnar and Daisy Winifred (Nelson) Skoglund; B.A., Linfield Coll., 1959; M.D., U. Rochester, 1963; m. Robert Reed Abbe, June 11, 1960; children—Ruth Christine, Jennifer Linnea. Intern, Upstate Med. Center, Syracuse, N.Y., 1963-64; resident children's Meml. Hosp., Chgo., 1966-68; pediatrician Third Ward Med. Center, Rochester, N.Y., 1970-71, Near North Children's Center, Chgo., 1971—. Recipient fellowship in infectious diseases Nat. Insts. Allergy and Infectious Diseases, 1968-70. Mem. Am. Med. Women's Assn. Club: Great Lakes Officers' Wives. Home: 2158 Hawaii Av Great Lakes IL 60088 Office: 1441 N Cleveland St Chicago IL 60088

ABBOTT, BETTY LORRAINE CONDON (MRS. DOUGLAS HUNT ABBOTT), city ofcl.; b. Council Bluffs, Ia., Feb. 16, 1923; d. Willis Madill and Dorothy (Sargent) Condon; student Drake U., 1941-43; m. Douglas Hunt Abbott, Sept. 26, 1950; children—Gwen Annette, Diana Ray. Copywriter, broadcaster, staff musician Radio Sta. KVFD, Ft. Dodge, Ia., 1943-44, KSWI, Council Bluffs, Ia., 1947-49; copywriter Buchanan-Thomas Advt. Agy., Omaha, 1949-51; free-lance advt., pub. relations, broadcasting, Omaha, 1951—; mem. Omaha City Council, 1965—; mem. aux. faculty John F. Kennedy Coll., 1969—. Mem. Omaha-Douglas County Health Bd., 1967-70, Mayor's Traffic Safety Adv. Com., 1967—, Omaha Zoning Revision Com., 1967—, Service Sta. Environmental Adv. Com., 1969—, Sr. Citizens Adv. Com., 1970-72, Nat. Security Forum, 1970; mem. Def. Adv. Com. on Women in Services, 1972—, exec. com., 1974—; mem. United Community Services Budget Com., 1961-67; mem. pub. information, pub. relations com. Regional Red Cross Blood Program, 1964-66; accompanist, choral dir. Omaha Civic Opera, 1958; cellist Des Moines Symphony, 1941-43; vice chmn. Neb. Environmental Control Council, 1971-72, chmn, 1972—; mem. Mayor's Commn. on Status Women, 1972—. Vice chmn. Douglas County Republican com., 1962-63; mem. Omaha City Council, 1974—. Bd. dirs., mem. exec. bd. Douglas/Sarpy County Red Cross; women's adv. bd. Island Hope, 1971—; mem. exec. bd. Neb. League Municipalities, 1970—, v.p., 1973-74; pres. Omaha YWCA, 1963-66; mem. exec. bd. Mid Am. council Boy Scouts Am., 1974—; mem. Mayor's Traffic Safety Adv. Com., 1967—; trustee Neb. Humane Soc. Mem. Omaha Zool. Soc. (dir.), Am. Fedn. Musicians, Omaha Musicians Assn., League Women Voters (dir. 1956-57), Omaha C. of C. (mil. relations com. 1973—), Neighborhood Devel. Assn. (dir. 1965-67), Good Govt. Assn. (dir., 1961-62), Omaha Woman's Town Hall (dir. 1965-66), Air Force Assn. Club: Quota (dir. 1955-57). Home: 6751 Leavenworth St Omaha NE 68106 Office: City Hall 108 S 18th St Omaha NE 68102

ABBOTT, CHARLOTTE MACAULAY, librarian; b. Stratford, Ont., Can., Apr. 13, 1913; d. Charles Christopher and Frances Hamilton (Macaulay) Abbott; B.A., Queen's U., 1937; B.L.S., U. Toronto, 1938. Librarian, Joint Intelligence Bur., Def. Research Bd., Ottawa, Ont., 1946-50; library asst., chief cataloger Oshawa (Ont.) Pub. Library, 1950-62; librarian, med. staff library Oshawa (Ont.) Gen. Hosp., 1963—. Curator Henry House Museum, Oshawa, 1963-70. Served with Women's Royal Canadian Naval Service, 1943-46. Mem. Canadian, Ont., Med. library assns., Inst. Profl. Librarians Ont., Ont. Hist. Soc., N.Y. State Hist. Assn.; Am. Assn. for State and Local History, Council of Women. Home: 738 Simcoe St N Oshawa ON L1G 4V8 Canada Office: 24 Alma St Oshawa ON L1G 2B9 Canada

ABBOTT, DOROTHY ISABEL, sculptor; b. Thibadoux, La., Apr. 19, 1932; d. Argyle Campbell and Doris Edith (Beihoff) Abbott; student Temple U., 1949-50, Parsons Sch. Design, 1950-52, N.Y. U., 1950-55; B.A., San Francisco State Coll., 1956; M.A., Columbia U., 1962. Exhibited in one-woman shows East Hampton Guild Hall, East Hampton, N.Y., 1967, So. Vermont Art Center, Manchester, 1968, Southold (N.Y.) Gallery, 1969, Gallery Madison 90, N.Y.C., 1973, Hays Gallery, Silvermine Guild, New Canaan, Conn., 1974, Easthampton Guild Hall, 1975, Mickelson Gallery, 1975; exhibited in group shows, Easthampton (N.Y.) Guild Halls Annuals, 1964, 65, Parrish Art Mus., Southampton, N.Y., 1965, Jersey City Mus., 1967, Nat. Arts Club Exhibition, N.Y.C., 1968, Nat. Arts Club, N.Y.C., 1970, Nat. Sculpture Soc., N.Y.C., 1972, Columbia U. Club, N.Y.C., 1972, Nat. Acad. Gallery, N.Y.C., 1972, 73, N.A.D. Ann. Exhn., 1972, Gallery Madison 90, N.Y.C., Mem. Audubon Artists, Sculptors League, Silvermine Guild. Home and studio: PO Box 369 Cutchogue NY 11935

ABBOTT, KATHARINE ELIZABETH (MRS. RAYMOND C. ABBOTT), univ. adminstr.; b. Indpls., May 26, 1934; d. Hugh Harold and Ruth Marion (Folger) Neff; A.B., Ind. U., 1956; M.A., Ohio State U., 1964; postgrad. George Williams Coll., 1972—; m. Raymond C. Abbott, June 16, 1957; children—Robert C., Richard C. Reporter, Louisville Courier Jour., 1954-56, Indpls. Star, 1955; asst. editor McCall Corp. Employee mag., Dayton, O., 1956; copywriter Hutzler and Long Advt., Dayton, 1957; pub. information writer Ohio Dept. Hwy. Safety, Columbus, 1958-59; reporter Garfieldian Publs., Chgo., 1960; pub. relations asst. Ill. Soc. C.P.A.'s, Chgo., 1963-68; asso. adminstr. pub. relations Ill. Nurses Assn., 1963-68; dir. pub. relations George Williams Coll., Downers Grove, Ill., 1968—. Recipient Golden Trumpet awards Publicity Club Chgo., 1965, 71; Helen Cody Baker awards Welfare Pub. Relations Forum Chgo., 1970, 71, 72. Mem. Pub. Relations Soc. Am., Ill. Coll. Relations Assn. (pres. 1972-73), Women in Communications (mem. and chmn. various coms.), DuPage Press Assn., Welfare Pub. Relations Forum, Am. Assn. U. Women. Club: Publicity of Chicago (mem. various coms.). Home: 1526 Cleveland St LaGrange Park IL 60525 Office: 555 31st St Downers Grove IL 60515

ABBOTT, LORETTA, dancer, singer, actress; d. Alfred Bruce and Agatha (Alexander) Abbott; B.S., M.S. Soloist with dance companies of Paul Sanasardo, 1966, Donald McKayle, 1969, Louis Johnson, 1969, Alvin Ailey Am. Dance Theatre, 1967; singer, dancer, actress in Hallelujah Baby, 1968, Peer Gynt, 1969, La Strada, 1969, Purlie, 1970, Two Gentlemen of Verona, 1971-72; appearance on Swedish TV spl. Riedaiglia, 1967; panelist Creative Artists Pub. Services, 1972; a founder Loretta Abbott-Al Perryman Dynamic Dance Duo, 1972; featured dancer Broadway prodn. Raisin, 1973; appeared as singer, dancer on Liza with a Z; guest artist Harkness Ballet, also with Robert de Cormier Chorale; guest instr. master classes Hofstra U., Nyack (N.Y.) Acad. Classical Ballet. Address: 33 Mt Morris Park W New York City NY 10027

ABBOTT, LORRAINE, sports found. exec.; b. Toledo, Dec. 9, 1937; d. Russell Ward and Georgianna (Conklin) Abbott; B.A., Rollins Coll., 1959; B.S. in Edn., Bowling Green State U., 1961, M.Ed., 1962. Grad. asst. Bowling Green (O.) State U., 1962-65; tchr. phys. edn. Kansas City pub. schs., 1961-64; instr. phys. edn. U. Ill., Urbana, 1965-66; ednl. cons. Nat. Golf Found., Chgo., 1966-70, dir. ednl. services, 1971—. Profl. golfer, 1965—. Vol. golf instr. Toledo YMCA, spring 1962. Recipient Woman Athlete of Yr. award Toledo Times, 1960. Mem. Ladies Profl. Golf Assn., A.A.H.P.E.R., Nat., Midwest assns. phys. edn. for coll. women, Kappa Alpha Theta. Club: Sylvania (O.) Country. Contbr. to publs. in field. Home: 2237 N 74th Av Elmwood Park IL 60635 Office: 707 Merchandise Mart Chicago IL 60654

ABBOTT, MARY DEVLIN (MRS. J. ALLAN ABBOTT), exec. sec.; b. Trenton, N.J., May 27, 1923; d. Peter James and Margaret (Duffy) Devlin; student pub. schs., Trenton; m. George N. Simko, May 27, 1943 (div. 1958); 1 son, Michael Devlin; m. 2d, Clarence Anderson Chafey, Aug. 15, 1960 (dec. Mar. 1970; m. 3d, J. Allan Abbott. Exec. sec. to pres. and chmn. bd. Trenton Trust Co., 1948-60; exec. social sec. N.J. Gov.'s Residence, Princeton, 1961-70. Mem. New Jersey adv. council Small Business Administration, 1966—. Mem. bd. Mercer County Girl Scouts. Democrat. Roman Catholic. Clubs: Trenton Country; Farmington Country (Charlottesville, Va.); Ridgewood (N.J.) Country; Pine Tree Country (Delray Beach, Fla.); Boca Raton (Fla.) Hotel, Royal Palm Yacht and Country; Innis Arden Golf and Country (Greenwich, Conn.). Home: 2 Jill Lane Lawrence Twp Trenton NJ 08638 also 251 Dogwood Lane Stamford CT also 2301 Spanish River Rd Boca Raton FL

ABBOTT, MILDRED JANE HALE (MRS. W. ROGERS ABBOTT), civic worker; b. Purcell, Okla.; d. Jesse J. and Minnie (Walk) Hale; B.F.A., U. Okla., 1927; m. William Rogers Abbott, June 1, 1924; 1 son, William Rogers II. Prin. grade sch., Lindsay, Okla., 1923-24; tchr. Dundee Sch., Wirt, Okla., 1924-26; tchr. music, and English, high sch., Comanche, Okla., 1926-27; tchr. music elementary and high sch. Norfolk Sch., Yale, Okla., 1927-30; tchr. pub. sch. music Oklahoma City, 1930-31; piano instr., Oklahoma City, 1931-56. Mem. state bd. Okla. Congress Parents and Tchrs., 1952—, program chmn., 1952-55, publs. chmn., 1955-58, 60-61, v.p. S.W. region, 1958-60, 2d v.p., 1961-64, 1st v.p., 1964-67, pres., 1967-70; bd. mgrs. Nat. P.T.A., 1967-70, vice chmn. State Presidents' Conf., 1969-70, Sec. State President's Club, 1970-71; mem. Women's Symphony Soc., 1950-62; vice chmn. Okla. Commn. on Ednl. Adminstrn.; mem. legislative council Okla. Edn. Assn.; mem. adv. com. home econs. div. Okla. Dept. Pub. Instrn.; mem. profl. standards bd. Okla. Dept. Edn., 1969-70; chmn. joint com. Okla. Edn. Assn.-Okla. State Sch. Bds. Assn.-Oklahoma PTA, 1969-70; 1st v.p. Okla. Fedn. Music Clubs, 1971-73, pres., 1973—; pres. Oklahoma City Council of P.T.A.'s, 1973—; mem. commn. Oklahoma City Housing Authority, 1973—. Bd. dirs. YWCA, Inspiration Point Fine Arts Colony, Eureka Springs, Ark., 1971—. Named Byline Honoree, Theta Sigma Phi, 1972. Mem. Oklahoma City Citizens Financial Study Com., 1972—. Mem. Soon-Airs (pres. 1962-64), Ninety-Nines (chmn. Okla. chpt. 1963-65), League Women Voters, Okla. Flying Farmers, Aviation Club Oklahoma City, Aircraft Owners and Pilots Assn., Am. Assn. U. Women, recipient W.T. Piper achievement award, 1962; Sigma Alpha Iota Patronesses (sec.-treas., scholarship chmn.). Mem. Christian Ch. Mem. Kiwanis Ladies (v.p., sec., program chmn., yearbook editor). Clubs: MacDowell of Allied Arts (pres. 1948-50), Ladies Music of Oklahoma (pres. 1955-56), Women's Dinner, Redbud Women's (Oklahoma City). Editor Okla. Flying Farmer News; asso. editor Okla. Parent-Tchr. mag., 1967-70. Home: Route 12 Box 570 Oklahoma City OK 73115 Office: 512 Robert S Kerr Av Oklahoma City OK 73102

ABBOTT, MURIEL MACPHERSON, psychologist; b. Montclair, N.J.; d. Graham and Muriel Margaret (Burleigh) Macpherson; B.A., Brown; M.A., Newark State Coll., 1961; Ph.D., Columbia U., 1968. Jr. economist Standard Oil Co., N.Y.C., 1946-53; research psychologist Harcourt Brace Jovanovich Co., N.Y.C., 1965-70, div. head, test dept., N.Y.C., 1970—. Lectr. Tchrs. Coll., Columbia U., N.Y.C., 1965-73. Nat. Defense Edn. Act fellow, 1962-64; Ednl. Testing Service fellow, 1963. Mem. Am. Psychol. Assn., Am. Ednl. Research Assn., Nat. Council on Measurement in Edn., Fla. Ednl. Research Assn., Brown U. Alumni Assn., Columbia U. Alumni Assn., Tchrs. Coll. Alumni Assn., Sigma Xi. Contbr. articles to profl. jours. Home: 249 E 48th St New York City NY 10017 Office: 757 3d Av New York City NY 10017

ABBOTT, ROSE MARIE S(AVELKOUL), educator, scientist; b. Chaska, Minn., Feb. 7, 1931; B.A., U. Minn., 1953, M.S., 1955; Ph.D. (univ. fellow 1955-56; NSF fellow 1956-57), Cornell U., 1959; m. 1956; 4 children. Instr. biology Smith Coll., 1957-58; plant morphologist U. Minn. at Morris, 1964—, geneticist, 1966—. Mem. Bot. Soc. Am. Address: Div Sci and Math U Minnesota Morris MN 56267

ABBOTT, SIGRID (MRS. W. ROGERS ABBOTT II), journalist; b. Munich, Germany, Sept. 30, 1941; came to U.S., 1967; naturalized, 1970; d. Heinz and Gertraud (Becker) Raecke; student U. Catolica Andres Bello, Caracas, Venezuela, 1964-67; B.A., U. Okla., 1970; m. W. Rogers Abbott II, Feb. 6, 1965; 1 son, James Alexander. Translator Inst. Venezolano de Investigaciones Cientificas, Caracas, Venezuela, 1956-59; sec. Chrysler de Venezuela, 1959-61; hostess VIASA, Venezuelan airlines, 1961-64; sec. Coca-Cola Export Corp., Caracas, 1965-66; reporter Oklahoma City Times and Daily Oklahoman, 1970—. Mem. Okla. Partners of the Ams., Theta Sigma Phi, Phi Beta Kappa, Kappa Tau Alpha. Kiwanian. Club: Twin Hills Golf and Country (Oklahoma City). Contbr. Young Students Ency., 1973. Home: 3512 E Maxwell Dr Forest Park OK 73121 Office: 500 N Broadway Oklahoma City OK 73102

ABBOTT, VIRGINIA DOLORES (MRS. FRANK RANDOLPH ABBOTT), horse trainer, driver; b. Cambridge, Md., Apr. 9, 1941; d. Anthony Felix and Pellie John (Barnett) Nardone; grad. high sch.; m. Frank Randolph Abbott, June 18, 1967; children—Frank Randolph, Mary Dolores. Clk., J. McKenny Willis & Son, Easton, Md., 1959-60; key punch operator Md. State Dept., Annapolis, 1960-62, Service Bur., Birmingham, Ala., 1962; skeiner Delmarva Narrow Fabrics, Easton, 1962-63; sec., kennelwoman Tred-Avon Kennels, Royal Oak, Md., 1963; camshaft refacer Noble Motor Rebuilders, Easton, 1964-65; horse trainer John Green Stables, Easton, 1964-65, Wye Plantation, Queenstown, Md., 1965-68, horsetrainer, farrier, horse driver, Federalsburg, Md., 1965—. Mem. U.S. Trotting Assn. Democrat. Mem. Ch. of Jesus Christ of Latter-day Saints. Address: Route 4 Box 434 Seaford DE 19973

ABDELLAH, FAYE GLENN, nurse researcher, govt. ofcl.; b. N.Y.C., Mar. 13, 1919; d. H.B. and Margaret (Glenn) Abdellah; R.N. summa cum laude, Ann May Sch. Nursing, N.J., 1942; B.S., Columbia, 1945, M.A., 1947, Ed.D., 1955; LL.D., Case-Western Res. U., 1967, Rutgers U., 1973. Dir. health edn. Child Edn. Found., N.Y.C., 1943-45; faculty Yale Sch. Nursing, 1945-48; research fellow, mem. faculty Tchrs. Coll., Columbia, 1948-49; chief nursing edn. br. div. nursing resources USPHS, Dept. Health, Edn. and Welfare, Washington, 1949-59, chief research grants and fellowship br., sr. cons. nursing research 1959-69, chief research grants and fellowship br., 1969-70, chief nurse officer USPHS, asst. surgeon gen., 1970—; acting dep. dir. Nat. Center Health Services Research and Devel., Dept. Health, Edn. and Welfare, 1970, dir. Office Nursing Home Affairs, 1973—; also chief nurse officer USPHS. Cons., Western Interstate Commn. for Higher Edn. Nurse dir. (rear adm.) Commd. Corps, USPHS. Recipient Fed. Nursing Service awards, 1964; Alumni award for research and scholarship, Columbia U., 1969, Centennial award Ohio State U., 1970, Meritorious Service medal USPHS, 1971, Helen Evans award, 1971, D.S.M., 1973, Tchrs. Coll. distinguished service medal, 1974. Fellow Am. Psychol. Assn., Am. Acad. Nursing (charter); mem. Am. Nurses Assn., Nat. League for Nursing, Am.

Pub. Health Assn., Am. Edn. Assn., A.A.A.S., N.Y. Acad. Scis., Sigma Theta Tau, Pi Lambda Theta. Author: Patient-Centered Approaches to Nursing, 1960; Better Patient Care Through Nursing Research, 1965; Intensive Care, Concepts and Practices for Clinical Nurse Specialists, 1969; New Directions in Nursing Service, 1973; New Directions in Patient Centered Care, 1973; also articles in field. Home: 3713 Chanel Rd Annandale VA 22003 Office: Office of Asst Secretary Dept Health Edn and Welfare Washington DC 20201

ABEL, DOROTHEA MARGARET HOEBELT (MRS. WALTER JOHN ABEL), city ofcl.; b. Moccasin, Mont., Nov. 16, 1921; d. Walter Richard and Selma Minna (Tippner) Hoebelt; grad. high sch.; m. Walter John Abel, June 3, 1946; 1 dau., Bernadette Josephine (Mrs. Russell Lloyd Dunnington). Stenographer, Welfare Dept., Stanford, Mont., 1940-41; with accounting dept. U.S. Army, Ft. Peck, Mont., 1941-43, Douglas Aircraft, Long Beach, Cal., 1943-45; stenographer First Nat. Bank, Lewistown, Mont., 1945-48; city clk. City of Lewistown, 1953—. Elk, Moose. Home: 119 E Lake Av Lewistown MT 59457 Office: 308 4th Av S Lewistown MT 59457

ABEL, ELIZABETH ANN (MRS. BARTON LANE), dermatologist; b. Hartford, Conn., Mar. 16, 1940; d. Frederick A. and Rose (Borovicka) Abel; B.S. in Med. Tech., Colby Jr. Coll., 1961; B.S., U. Md., 1965, M.D. cum laude, 1967; m. Barton Lane, Dec. 17, 1967; children—Barton Frederick, Geoffrey Woodward. Intern, San Francisco Gen. Hosp., 1967-68; USPHS trainee in oncology, resident in medicine Cancer Research Inst., U. Cal. Med. Center, San Francisco, 1968-69; resident dermatology N.Y. U. Med. Center, N.Y.C., 1969-72, chief resident dermatology, 1971-72, teaching asst. dermatology, 1971-73, USPHS research trainee in dermatology, 1972-73; dep. chief dermatology USPHS Hosp., S.I., N.Y., 1973—. Diplomate Am. Bd. Dermatology. Fellow Am. Acad. Dermatology; mem. A.M.A., Alpha Omega Alpha. Home: 439 Flint St Staten Island NY 10306 Office: Dept Dermatology USPHS Hospital Staten Island NY 10304

ABELL, ALICE VIRGINIA SIMS (MRS. NORMAN ABELL), civic worker; b. Elizabethtown, Ky., June 29, 1902; d. Francis Leroy and Antoinette (Freeman) Sims; student N.Y. Sch. Design, Otis Art Inst., Cal. Sch. Fine Arts; student U. Ariz., 1921-22; m. Norman Abell, Mar. 19, 1927; children—Norman, Virginia Frances (Mrs. James Langdon Blake), Arlene Alice (Mrs. Francis Bruce Robertson). Pres., Abell Enterprises, Long Beach, Cal., 1954—. Gray Lady A.R.C., Long Beach, Cal., 1942-45; chmn. arts and crafts, 1945; mem. Pan Hellenic Bd., Long Beach, 1961; vol. Meml. Hosp. Aux., Long Beach, 1960—, occupational therapy chmn., 1960-62; organizer minimal universal lang. project, 1958; mem. Regional Arts Council. Recipient first prize Santa Ana (Cal.) Art Exhibit, 1941. Mem. D.A.R., Art Mus. Assn., Los Angeles World Affairs Council, Internat. Platform Assn., Town Hall of Cal., Gamma Phi Beta. Episcopalian. Clubs: Pacific Coast (Long Beach), Otis Art Associates (Los Angeles); Queen Mary. Home: 4022 Pacific Av Long Beach CA 90807

ABELL, ELAINE DURBIN, lawyer; b. Baton Rouge, La., Mar. 21, 1942; d. Gilbert Joseph and Rachel Wallice (O'Quin) Durbin; B.S. in Bus. Adminstrn., La. State U., 1964, J.D., 1969; m. Edward Charles Abell, Jr., July 3, 1971. Admitted to La. bar, 1969; law clk. to justice La. Supreme Ct., 1969-71; practiced in Lafayette, La., 1971—. Mem. Gov.'s Task Force to Study Women and Credit in La., 1973—. Bd. dirs. Lafayette Day Nursery. Pres. Lafayette Women's Republican Club, 1972-73. Mem. Am., La., Lafayette bar assns., La. State U. Alumni Assn. (exec. council), Jr. League, Pi Beta Phi. Address: 413 E Glynndale Av Lafayette LA 70501

ABELL, HELEN CAROLINE, educator; b. Medicine Hat., Alta., Can., Jan. 28, 1917; d. John Lambert and Caroline (Nowack) Abell; B.H.Sc., U. Toronto, 1941; M.S., Cornell U., 1947, Ph.D., 1951. Head rural sociology research unit, econ. div. Can. Dept. Agr., 1951-62; prof. sociology U. Guelph, 1962-67, U. Waterloo, (Ont., Can.), 1967-72; dean Coll. Home Econs., U. Sask., Saskatoon, 1972—; on leave as tech. expert Jamaica, 1954-55, No. Nigeria, 1961; research Govt. of Can. and UNESCO, Ghana, 1964-65; social affairs officer community devel. group UN, 1957-58; cons. rural devel. research, Colombia, summers 1969, 70, Indonesia, 1973; rural sociologist E. Indonesia Regional Devel. Study, 1974—. Served with Canadian Women's Army Corps, World War II. Mem. Canadian Council Rural Devel. (vice chmn. 1972—), Rural Sociol. Soc. (past v.p.), Canadian Sociology and Anthropology Assn. (exec. com.), Canadian Agrl. Econs. Soc., Internat. Assn. Agrl. Economists, Canadian Soc. Rural Extension, Community Planning Assn. Can., Canadian Assn. Consumers, Canadian Home Econs. Assn. Contbr. articles to profl. jours. Home: PO Box 7 Stouffville ON Canada

ABELLA, ROSA MARGARITA, librarian; b. Havana, Cuba, Feb. 13, 1920; d. Faustino and Rosa Abella; Ph.D., Filosofia y Letras, Universidad de la Havana Tecnica Bibliotecaria, 1956. Came to U.S., 1961, naturalized, 1969. Librarian, Havana Inst., 1952-59; head librarian Circulation Dept., Jose Marti Nat. Library, Havana, 1959-61; asso. prof., librarian U. Miami Library, Coral Gables, 1962—. Mem. Sigma Delta Pi. Roman Catholic. Home: 335 SW 47th Av Miami FL 33134 Office: University Miami Library Coral Gables FL 33124

ABELSON, HOPE (MRS. LESTER S. ABELSON), theatrical producer; b. Chgo.; d. Gilbert and Sadie (Lesem) Altman; student Northwestern U., Chgo. Art Inst., spl. tng. dance, dramatics; m. Lester S. Abelson, Jan. 15, 1939; children—Stuart R., Katherine A. Asso. producer Chevy Chase Summer Theatre, Ill., 1949-50; producer, mng. dir. Highland Park (Ill.) Music Theatre, 1950-52; prodn. asst. play Camino Real, N.Y.C., 1952; asst. to dir. play Madame Will You Walk, 1953; asst. to producers play Golden Apple, 1954; asso. producer The Rainmaker, 1954-55; producer The Egghead, 1957; dir. community relations Vivian Beaumont Theatre, Lincoln Center; co-producer Royal Hunt of the Sun, 1965. Mem. Goodman Theatre com. Art Inst. Chgo.; chmn. theatre com. Ravinia Festival Assn.; founding chmn. Stratford (Ont.) Festival-Chgo. Season, 1969; mem. regional com. for Met. Auditions; charter mem., exec. com. Joseph Jefferson Awards Com. for local profl. theatre artists; mem. Ill. Gov.'s Adv. Commn. on Financing Arts in Ill.; mem. governing bd. Urban Gateways, Chgo. Friends of Am. Ballet Theatre; mem. Theatre panel Ill. Arts Council. Recipient Stratford Festival Shakespeare Quadricentennial medal; citations Canadian Sec. State, Friends of Lit.; named Laureate for services to Chgo. performing arts Cliff Dwellers Club. Club: Arts. Home: 1040 Lake Shore Dr Chicago IL 60611

ABELSON, NEVA MARTIN (MRS. PHILIP H. ABELSON), pathologist; b. Lamar, Miss., Nov. 19, 1910; d. Virgil and Mary Elizabeth (Parr) Martin; B.S., Wash. State U., 1934; M.D., Johns Hopkins, 1942; m. Philip H. Abelson, Dec. 30, 1936; 1 dau., Ellen (Mrs. John C. Cherniavsky). Intern, Johns Hopkins Hosp., Balt., 1942-43, resident-asst. in pediatrics, 1944; instr. pediatrics U. Pa., Phila., 1944-48, asst. prof., 1950-55, asso. prof., 1955-58; dir. serum exchange div. Children's Hosp. of Phila., 1954-57, asso. prof. clin. pathology in medicine, 1957-71, prof. pathology, 1971—. Recipient Emily Cooley award Am. Assn. Blood Banks, 1971. Mem. Internat. Soc. Blood Transfusion, Phi Beta Kappa. Contbr. articles to med. jours. Research in physicochem. characteristics of blood group antibodies and pathogenesis of rheumatoid joint inflammation. Home: 4244 50th NW Washington DC 20016 Office: 3400 Spruce St Philadelphia PA 19104

ABERG, BLOSSOM ZELDA (MRS. GILBERT S. ABERG), ednl. adminstr.; b. Chgo., Dec. 11, 1923; d. Alex and Helen (Siegel) Fisher; B.A., U. Wis., 1946, M.A., 1947; m. Gilbert S. Aberg, July 17, 1943; children—Miriam, Jerrold, Steven, Ethan, Rachel. Chief psychologist Ill. Children's Hosp. Sch., Chgo., 1948-51; psychologist N. Shore Mental Health Clinic, Highland Park, Ill., 1952-54; instr. Pa. State U., University Park, 1959-62; psychologist The Counseling Service, Inc., Bellefonte, Pa., 1963-67; clin. psychologist Centre County Schs. and Central Intermediate Unit, Philipsburg, Pa., 1968-73; dir. pupil personnel services State College (Pa.) Area Sch. Dist., 1973—. Mem. Am., Pa. Psychol. assns., Jewish Community Council. Home: 704 McKee St State College PA 16801 Office: 131 W Nittany Av State College PA 16801

ABERLE, SOPHIE BLEDSOE D., physician; b. Schenectady; d. Albert Bledsoe and Clara Sidney (White) Herrick; A.B., Stanford, 1923, A.M., 1925, Ph.D., 1927; M.D. (Alexander Brown Cox fellow), Yale, 1930; m. William A. Brophy, Sept. 20, 1940 (dec., 1962). Teaching, research fellow Stanford, 1924-26; instr. anthropology Inst. Human Relations, Yale, 1927-30, instr., intern Sch. Medicine, 1930-34; research medicine specializing in endocrinology; asso. Carnegie Inst., 1934; gen. supt. United Pueblos Indian Agy. U.S. Dept. Interior, 1935-44; with div. med. scis. NRC, 1944-49; spl. research dir. U. N.M., 1949-54; mem. staff Bernalillo County Med. Center, 1953—; exec. dir. Com. on Rights, Liberties and Responsibilities of Am. Indian, Fund for Republic, 1957-63; dir. ednl. survey Bur. Indian Affairs, 1963-67; faculty dept. psychiatry U. N.M. Med. Sch., 1966-68; field work among Pueblo Indians under grant from Com. for Research in Problems of Sex of NRC and from Carnegie Corp. N.Y., 1927-35; mem. White House Conf. Children in a Democracy, 1940-46. Mem. exec. com. Nat. Sci. Bd. NSF, 1953-56. Sec., S.W. Supt. Council U.S. Indian Service, 1935-44; mem. Upper Rio Grande Drainage Basin Com., Nat. Resources Planning Bd., 1935-41; mem. N.M. Nutrition Com., 1940—; mem. Def. Savs. Com. State N.M., 1941-44; chief Emergency Med. Service N.M. Office Civilian Def., 1942-44; chmn. Bernalillo County Hosp. Com., 1949-50; cons. nutrition Bernalillo County Med. Center, 1954—; mem. N.M. Commn. on Indian Affairs, 1966—; cons. on Indian edn. Inst. for Math. Studies in Social Scis., Stanford, 1971—; social studies cons. U. N.M. Sch. Law, 1971—. Bd. dirs. Albuquerque YWCA, 1964-69, World Population-Planned Parenthood, Interstate Indian Council; mem. adv. bd. Am. Indian Traveling Coll. Mem. expansion and policy com. U. N.M. Sch. Medicine Ednl. Programs for Disadvantaged, 1969—. Named Greek of Month Panhellenic, 1967. Sterling fellow, 1930-31. Fellow Am. Anthrop. Assn.; mem. Albuquerque Acad. Medicine, A.A.A.S., A.M.A., Am. Assn. Anatomists, Bernalillo County Heart Assn., N.M. Acad. Sci., N.M. and County Med. Soc., Albuquerque C. of C., Sigma Si, Alpha Omega Alpha, Iota Sigma Pi. Club: Cosmos (Washington). Author: Primate Malaria, 1946; (with W. B. Corner) Twenty-Five Years of Sex Research, 1953; A Program for Indian Citizens, 1961; The Indian: America's Unfinished Business, 1966. Contbr. articles to profl. jours. Home and office: Route 3 Box 3030 Albuquerque NM 87120

ABERNATHY, JO ANNE, educator; b. Pineville, Miss., Mar. 18, 1936; d. Enos Christopher and Gladys (Sorey) Abernathy; student Miss. State Coll. Women, 1954-55; B.A. in Elementary Edn., Millsaps Coll., 1957; M.A. in Elementary Edn. and Sch. Principalship, Miss. Coll., 1967; certificate in elementary edn. (Delta Kappa Gamma Zeta State scholar), Miss. State U., 1973; Tchr. pub. elementary schs. Natchez, Miss., 1957-59, Jackson, Miss., 1959-64, 65—, 1st grade J.L. Power Elementary Sch., 1965—; tchr. pub. schs. Memphis, Tenn., 1964-65. Curriculum adv. tchr. lang. arts Miss. Instructional TV Curriculum Lab., Miss. Authority Ednl. TV, 1968—; cons. Scott Foresman Co. for 14th Pre-school Tchrs. Workshop, 1969; adviser Officer Friendly unit Jackson Police Dept., 1970. Mem. P.T.A. NSF scholar, 1963. Mem. Nat., Miss. (chmn. childhood edn. sect.), Jackson (2d v.p. 1973-74) edn. assns., Assn. Childhood Edn. Internat., Delta Kappa Gamma (rec. sec., 1st v.p., pres. Tau chpt.), Kappa Delta Pi. Methodist. Home: 513 Pennsylvania Av Jackson MS 39216 Office: 1120 Riverside Dr Jackson MS 39202

ABERNETHY, ROSE LORETTA (MRS. ROBERT TATE IRVINE JR.), educator; b. Kingston, N.Y., Nov. 14, 1924; d. William Francis and Julia (Flynn) Abernethy; B.A., Coll. of St. Rose, Albany, N.Y., 1945; M.A., Columbia, 1946; Ph.D., Northwestern U., 1964; m. Robert Tate Irvine, Jr., Dec. 18, 1965 (dec. June 24, 1968). Tchr. English and speech Croton-Harmon High Sch., 1947-48; with State U. N.Y. at New Paltz, 1949—, instr., asst. prof. speech 1949-56, asso. prof., 1957-64, prof., 1964—. Lectr. on internat. communication Yonsei U., Seoul, Korea; lectr. state, regional, nat. speech confs. Active Jr. League of Kingston. Named Outstanding Educator of Am., 1971. Mem. Am. Speech and Hearing Assn., Speech Communication Assn., Eastern States, N.Y. speech assns. Am. Assn. U. Profs., Kappa Delta Pi, Pi Lambda Theta, Zeta Phi Eta. Contbr. numerous articles to profl. publs. Address: 164 Huguenot St New Paltz NY 12561

ABISCH, ROSLYN KROOP (MRS. HOWARD R. ABISCH), author; b. Bklyn., Mar. 2, 1927; d. Benjamin and Frieda (Steinberg) Kroop; B.A., Bklyn. Coll., 1948; m. Howard R. Abisch, Dec. 25, 1946; children—Janet, Ellen, Susan. Tchr. pub. schs., N.Y.C., 1948-49; free-lance copywriter, 1949-56. Tchr., therapist United Cerebral Palsy of Queen's, 1954-56; adminstr., curriculum coordinator Merrick Enrichment Program, 1959-61. Mem. Child Study Assn. (mem. speaker's bur.). Author: (with Boche Kaplan) Open Your Eyes, 1964, Anywhere in the World, 1966, Art is For You, 1967, Do You Know What Time It Is?, 1969, 'Twas in the Moon of Wintertime, 1969, Mai-Ling and the Mirror, 1969, The Shoe For Your Left Foot Won't Fit on the Right, 1970, Sweet Betsy From Pike, 1970, Let's Find Out About Butterflies, 1971, Around the House That Jack Built, 1971; (pseudonymn A.K. Roche) I Can Be, 1967, The Pumpkin Heads, 1968, The Onion Maidens, 1968, The Clever Turtle, 1969, Even the Promise of Freedom, 1970, The City, 1970, Easy-To-Make Holiday Gift Things, 1973, Mixed Bag of Magic Tricks, 1973, also filmstrips; (pseudonymn Mr. McGillicuddy) Spring, Summer, Fall, Winter, 1970; (pseudonymn Mr. Sniff) Wishes, Whiffs, and Birthday Gifts, Circus Tents and Circus Scents, Scented Rhymes for Story Times, Scents and Sun and Picnic Fun, 1971; If I Could, I Would; Silly Street, 1971; Smile If You Meet a Crocodile, Blast Off!; Out in the Woods; Under the Ocean, Under the Sea, 1971; Big, Little, Tall, Short, 1974; others. Home: 1095 Verbena Av N North Merrick NY 11566

ABLES, BILLIE SUE, educator, psychologist; b. Columbus, Miss., July 14, 1925; d. James Victor and Mary Truma (Walters) Talantis; B.A., U. Ala., 1946, M.A., 1949; Ph.D., Purdue U., 1954; m. Murray French Ables, Dec. 22, 1932; children—Scott Carlton Mandl, Amy Katherine. Psychologist Beatty Meml. Hosp., Westville, Inc., 1956; post-doctoral fellow Menninger Found., Topeka, 1956-57; asst. prof. psychology Washburn U., Topeka, Kan., 1957-60; chief psychologist Family Service and Guidance Center, Topeka, Kan., 1960-64; attending clin. psychology U. Ky. Coll. Medicine, 1964-66, asst. prof. psychiatry, 1966-71, asso. prof. psychiatry, 1971—, interviewer Coll. Medicine Admissions Com., 1971—, mem. doctoral coms. dept. psychology, 1971—; cons. V.A. Hosp., Lexington, Ky., 1966—. Diplomate Am. Bd. Examiners Profl. Psychology in clin. psychology. Mem. Am. Psychol. Assn., Orthopsychiat. Assn. Contbr. articles in field. Research in dyslexia, childhood psychosis, teaching psychiatry, child devel. Home: 417 Lakeshore Dr Lexington KY 40502

ABLON, JOAN (MRS. JOAN DEKORNE), anthropologist, educator; b. Dallas, Oct. 21, 1934; d. Dave and Bessie (Suloway) Ablon; B.A., U. Tex., 1955; M.A., U. Chgo., 1958, Ph.D., 1963. Research anthropologist U. Cal. Sch. Criminology, Berkeley, 1963-66, N.M. State Dept. Pub. Health, Santa Fe, 1966-67; asso. prof. med. anthropology in residence Dept. Psychiatry, U. Cal. Med. Sch., San Francisco, 1968—. Fellow Am. Anthropol. Assn., Soc. for Applied Anthropology (exec. com. 1973—); mem. S.W. Anthropol. Assn. (sec.-treas. 1969-70), Soc. for Med. Anthropology (exec. com. 1973—). Home: 1329 Cole St San Francisco CA 94117

ABRAHAM, GRACEY MOLLY PHILIP (MRS. KOTHOOR ABRAHAM), physician; b. Trivandrum, Kerala State, South India, Aug. 7, 1934; d. Philip and Sarah (Cherian) Philip; B.Sc., Women's Coll. Trivandrum, 1954; M.B.B.S., Christian Med. Coll. and Hosp., Vellore, 1960; diploma phys. medicine and rehab. Royal No. Hosp., London, 1968; m. Kothoor Abraham, June 4, 1962; children—Mary, Sarah, Neena. Intern, Christian Med. Coll. Hosp., Vellore, S. India, 1960-61, house officer, 1961-62; resident South and West Middlesex Hosp., London, Stoke Mandiville Hosp., U.K., 1962-63; registrar Central Middlesex, Royal No. and Hyland Gen. Hosps., London, U.K., 1963-68; lectr. Inst. Rehab. Medicine, 1969-71; provicincial dir. rehab. medicine, New Brunswick, Can., 1971—; med. dir. Forest Hill Rehab. Centre, 1971—; cons. Victoria Pub. Hosp., Fredericton, N.B., Can., 1971—. Mem. Canadian Assn. Phys. Medicine and Rehab., Canadian Arthritis and Rheumatism Soc., British Assn. Phys. Medicine and Rheumatology, Internat. Med. Soc. Paraplegia, Canadian, N.B. med. assns. Home: 221 University Av Fredericton NB E3B 4H8 Canada Office: Forest Hill Rehab Centre Woodbridge St Fredericton NB Canada

ABRAHAM, PATRICIA ANN GALLAGHER (MRS. HAROLD ALLEN ABRAHAM), ednl. adminstr.; b. Dayton, O., Dec. 25, 1937; d. Joseph Thomas and Helen Louise (Tullis) Gallagher; B.A. in Psychology, U. Mich., 1959; M.S., State U. N.Y., 1969; postgrad. Harvard Summer Inst. Arts, 1972; m. Harold Allen Abraham, Nov. 3, 1962. Tchr. St. Agnes Sch., Loudonville, N.Y., 1960-62; mem. faculty Castleton (Vt.) State Coll., 1964—, asso. prof. theatre arts, 1974—, dir. fine arts div., 1972—. Vice pres., dir. programs Crossroads Arts Council, 1971—. Bd. dirs. Rutland Community Center Assn., 1973—. Vt. Council Arts grantee, 1969-74. Mem. Alliance for Arts in Edn., Vt. Assn. Health, Phys. Edn. and Recreation (dance chmn. 1965-68), Phi Mu. Home: RD 1 N Grove St Rutland VT 05701 Office: Fine Arts Center Castleton State Coll Castleton VT 05735

ABRAHAMSON, SHIRLEY SCHLANGER (MRS. SEYMOUR ABRAHAMSON), lawyer; b. N.Y.C., Dec. 17, 1933; d. Leo and Ceil (Sauerteig) Schlanger; A.B., N.Y.U., 1953; J.D., Ind. U., 1956; S.J.D., U. Wis., 1962; m. Seymour Abrahamson, Aug. 26, 1953; 1 son, Daniel Nathan. Asst. dir. Legislative Drafting Research Fund, Columbia U. Law Sch., 1957-60; admitted to Wis. bar, 1962, since practiced in Madison; mem. firm Lafollette, Sinykin, Anderson & Abrahamson, 1962—; prof. U. Wis. Sch. Law, 1966—. Mem. Mayor's Adv. Com., Madison, 1968-70; mem. Gov.'s Study Com. on Jud. Orgn., 1970-73; mem. Wis. Bd. Bar Commrs., 1973—. Bd. dirs. League Women Voters, Madison, 1963-65, Union council Wis. Union, U. Wis., 1970-71; bd. dirs. Wis. Civil Liberties Union, 1968—, chmn. Capital Area chpt., 1969. Mem. Am., Wis. Dane County bar assns., Order of Coif, Phi Beta Kappa. Editor: Constitutions of the United States (National and State) 2 vols., 1962. Home: 2012 Waunona Way Madison WI 53713 Office: 222 W Washington Av Madison WI 53703

ABRAMOVITZ, ANITA ZELTNER BROOKS (MRS. MAX ABRAMOVITZ), author; b. L.I., N.Y., Jan. 7, 1914; d. Charles Frederick and Amelia (Koch) Zeltner; B.A., Sarah Lawrence Coll., 1934; m. Thomas Vall Brooks, Sept. 25, 1937 (div. July 1957); children—Antoinette (Mrs. Thomas Stucklen), Cora Vall (Mrs. Donald A. Metz, Jr.), Henry Stanford Brooks II; m. 2d, Max Abramovitz, Feb. 29, 1964. Editorial asst. New Yorker mag., N.Y.C., 1943-46; editor alumni mag. Sarah Lawrence Coll., 1947-48; tchr. remedial reading, 1950; asst. to prof. history Sarah Lawrence Coll., 1958-60, asst. in writing to lectr. courses, 1960-62; asst. to dir. Sarah Lawrence Paris Summer Sch., 1963. Democratic Party Insp. 18th Dist. Hastings-on-Hudson, N.Y., 1958-61; founding mem. Village League, 1950. Mem. Am. Civil Liberties Union, League Women Voters, Authors Guild. Author series Picture Aids to World Geography: Picture Book of Fisheries, 1961; Picture Book of Tea and Coffee, 1962; Picture Book of Grains, 1963; Picture Book of Salt, 1964; Picture Book of Oil, 1965; Picture Book of Timber, 1966; A Small Bird Sang, 1967; Winifred, 1970; Picture Book of Metals, 1972; also articles and children's stories. Home: 418 E 50th St New York City NY 10022

ABRAMS, BERENDA WEINBERG (MRS. WILLIAM BERNARD ABRAMS), occupational therapist; b. Atlantic City, Oct. 12, 1925; d. Samuel Gladstone and Sophie (Tucker) Weinberg; student Pa. State Coll., 1942-43; B.S., U. Pa., 1945; Occupational Therapist, Registered, Phila. Sch. Occupational Therapy, 1946; m. William Bernard Abrams, Mar. 4, 1945; children—James Coleman, Andrew Paul, Joseph Todd, Julie Ann. Dir. occupational therapy Betty Bacharach Home, Longport, N.J., 1946-48; with Dept. Pub. Assistance, Phila., 1948-49; attendance officer Bd. Edn. Phila., 1949-50; pvt. practice occupational therapist, specializing in children with perceptual motor dysfunction, South Orange, N.J., 1967—. Chmn. Leisure Time Facilities Directory of Essex and Hudson Counties, 1968—; chmn. Am. Art at Mid-Century, West Orange, N.J., 1962-63; pres. Elementary P.T.A., South Orange, 1962-63, Columbia High Sch. P.T.A., Maplewood, N.J., 1969-70; v.p. Friends of Library of South Orange, 1959-66; chmn. Know Your Town, South Orange, 1959-60, Orange, 1954-55. Bd. dirs. Garden State Concerts Guild, 1960-63. Mem. Am., N.J. occupational therapy assns., Nat. Council Jewish Women (v.p. Essex County sect. 1964-66), League Women Voters (pres. South Orange, 1955-56). Home: 416 N Ridgewood Rd South Orange NJ 07079

ABRAMS, PEARL BILSKY (MRS. GEORGE J. ABRAMS), artist; b. New Bedford, Mass.; d. Morris and Rose (Kestenbaum) Bilsky; student Swain Sch. Design, 1928-32, Pratt Inst., 1935; m. George J. Abrams, June 19, 1941; children—Robert Edward, Marjorie Susan. Artist with Buzza Co., 1938-40, Pollack Co., 1940-42; chmn. art dept. Am. Women's Voluntary Services, 1941-43; exhibited in group shows at L.I. Art League, N.Y., North Shore Community Arts Center, Manhasset Art League, Lincoln House Found., Glen Cove, N.Y., Juried Am. Artists Assn.-Pratt Internat. Miniature Graphics Exhbn., 1971, Ann. Exhbn. Nat. Arts Club, 1972. Bd. dirs. North Shore Community Arts Center; mem. exec. bd. Roslyn Civic Assn., 1962-63; Am. Women's Vol. Services, 1942. Recipient Grumbacher award, L.I. Art League, 1954; 1st prize for graphic drawing Manhasset Art Assn., 1972. Home: 31 Pine Drive N Roslyn NY 11576

ABRAMS, ROSALIE SILBER (MRS. WILLIAM ABRAMS), state senator; b. Balt., June 2, 1916; d. Isaac and Dora (Rodbell) Silber; grad. with honors Sinai Hosp. Sch. Nursing, 1938; B.S., Johns Hopkins, 1963, M.A. in Polit. Sci., 1969; m. William Abrams, Oct. 14, 1953; 1 dau., Elizabeth Joan. Instr., supr. operating room Sinai Hosp., Balt., 1938-40; pub. health nurse Balt. City Dept. Edn., 1941-45; bus. mgr. Sequoia Med. Group, Redwood City, Cal., 1946-47; asst. bus. mgr. Silber's Bakery, Inc., Balt., 1947-53; mem. Md. Ho. of Dels., 1967-70, Md. Senate, 1970—, mem. finance com. mem. Mayor's Mem. health com. Md. Conf. Social Welfare, 1968-69; founder, dir. Cross Country Improvement Assn., 1969—; dir. Md. Food Com., Inc., 1969—; mem. adv. com. cost containment Hosp. Cost Analysis Service, Inc., 1969—; Health Services Adv. and Planning Council, 1968; mem. comprehensive health planning com. Balt. Regional Planning Council, 1967—; mem. Gov.'s Adv. Council Comprehensive Health Planning, 1968—, Md. Commn. on Status Women, 1968—; legislative chmn. Balt. area Council on Alcoholism; chmn. legislative com. Balt. Area Council Alcoholism, 1970—; chmn. Md. Humane Practices Commn., 1973—; mem. Md. adv. com. Traffic Safety and Alcoholism Project, 1970—; mem. exec. com. Md. Health Maintenance Orgn., 1971-73. Bd. dirs. Sinai Hosp., 1971—. Served as ensign USNR, 1945-46. Recipient Louise Waterman Wise community service award Am. Jewish Congress, 1969, Am. Assn. for Comprehensive Health Planning award, 1971, Safety Crusader plaque Safety First Club of Md., 1971. Mem. Md. Order Women Legislators (pres. 1973), Nat. Women's Polit. Caucus. Home: 6205 Wirt Av Baltimore MD 21215

ABRAMS, RUTH IDA, judge; b. Boston, Dec. 26, 1930; d. Samuel and Matilda (Bortman) Abrams; A.B., Radcliffe Coll., 1953; LL.B., Harvard, 1956. Admitted to Mass. bar, 1957, U.S. Supreme Ct. bar; partner Abrams, Abrams and Abrams, Boston, 1957-60; asst. dist. atty No. Dist., Middlesex County, Mass., 1961-69; asst. atty. gen., chief appellate sect. Criminal div., 1969-71; spl. counsel Mass. Supreme Jud. Ct., 1971-72; asso. justice Superior Ct., Boston, 1972—. Tchr. law enforcement personnel, Middlesex County, 1961-72. Mem. Am., Mass., Cambridge, Middlesex bar assns. Home: 100 Memorial Dr Cambridge MA 02142 Office: 11th Floor New Courthouse Boston MA 02108

ABRAMSON, HILARY ELLEN, journalist; b. Passaic, N.J., May 28, 1945; d. Bernard and Gertrude (Simmons) Abramson; B.A., Ohio Wesleyan U., 1967; postgrad. Radcliffe Coll., 1967. Mem. coll. bd. Mademoiselle mag., 1967; editorial asst., picture research asst. Am. Heritage Pub. Co., N.Y.C., 1967-68; sr. editor, travel writer, researcher Frommer/Pasmantier Pub. Corp., N.Y.C., 1968; asst. editor Broadcast, mgmt.-engring. mag., N.Y.C., 1968-70; reporter, feature writer, photographer Daily Democrat, Woodland, Cal., 1970-72; reporter, feature writer The Sacramento Union, 1972—. Recipient Youth Scholarship, United Synagogue, 1961. Mem. Pi Delta Epsilon. Democrat. Jewish religion. Home: PO Box 16042 Sacramento CA 95816 Office: 301 Capitol Mall Sacramento CA 95814

ABRAMSON, JOAN FREULICH (MRS. NORMAN ABRAMSON), univ. ofcl.; b. Los Angeles, Oct. 7, 1932; d. Roman and Katherine (Merkin) Freulich; A.B., U. Cal. at Los Angeles, 1954, M.S., 1955; m. Norman Abramson, July 4, 1954; children—Mark, Caren. Reporter, Palo Alto Times, Redwood City Tribune, 1955-58; editor Ravenwood Post, 1958; corr. Time mag., 1965-66, Time-Life Books, 1966-71; instr. U. Hawaii, Honolulu, 1967-72, asst. dir. New Coll., 1972-73, dir., 1973—; pres., Pacific Writing Service, 1969—. Trustee, v.p. Pacific Ecol. Inst., 1970-71. Mem. Kappa Tau Alpha. Author: The Hill of Life, 1968; Forty Years in Hollywood, 1971; Faces of Israel, 1972. Home: 2545 Manoa Rd Honolulu HI 96822 Office: 2001 Vancouver St Honolulu HI 96822

ABRAVANEL, DIANE (MRS. BEN DON ABRAVANEL), hosp. pub. relations dir.; b. Pitts., Aug. 26, 1921; d. Nicholas W. and Etta (Hazen) Rosenberg; student Bus. Tng. Coll., Pitts., 1938-39, U. Pitts., 1971-74; m. Ben Don Abravanel, Sept. 29, 1946; children—Lynn, Nicki Ann. Asst. to pub. relations dir. United Jewish Fedn. Pitts., 1961-62; pub. relations and advt. firm account exec. William H. Mazefsky Assos., Pitts., 1957-62; dir. pub. relations Montefiore Hosp., Pitts., 1962—. Mem. Pub. Relations Soc. Western Pa. Hosps. (pres. 1967-68), Pub. Relations Soc. Am. (bd. mem. Pitts. chpt. 1971-72, 2d v.p. 1973, 1st v.p. 1974), Pub. Relations Soc. Hosp. Assn. Pa. (chmn. edn. com. 1971), Assn. Am. Med. Colls. (pub. relations sect.), Montefiore Hosp. Ladies Hosp. Aid Soc., Nat. Council Jewish Women, Women's Am. Orgn. for Rehab. Through Tng., Ladies Aux. Jewish Home and Hosp. for the Aged, Women's Aux. Am. Cancer Soc. Jewish religion (mem. temple sisterhood). Club: Pittsburgh Press. Home: 2770 Fernwald Rd Pittsburgh PA 15217 Office: 3459 5th Av Pittsburgh PA 15213

ABROMSON, MARIAN FLEMING (MRS. JAMES J. ABROMSON), civic leader; b. Portland, Ind., Sept. 18, 1907; d. James R. and Jennie (Adair) Fleming; student DePauw U., 1926; m. James J. Abromson, July 15, 1933; 1 dau., Suzanne Fleming (Mrs. William C. H. Joiner). Dir. Ft. Wayne Jour.-Gazette. Co-chmn. vol. blood service program A.R.C., Portland, 1947—; pres. Jay County Bd. Pub. Welfare, Portland, 1964—; sec. Earlham Coll. Parents Assn., Richmond, Ind., 1957-58; mem. Jay County Com. Aging, 1951-59; Jay County rep. to N.E. Ind. Dist. Com. Aging, 1959-60; bd. dirs. Jay County Mental Health Assn., 1958—; v.p. Jay County A.R.C.; mem. Jay County Hosp. Aux.; chmn. Adopt-a-Patient Program, 1961-73; mem. Ind. Mental Health Bd., 1971—. Del. Democratic Nat. Conv., 1964. Recipient Achievement Service Award Jay County, 1960. Mem. D.A.R., Daus. Am. Colonists, Delta Theta Tau, Alpha Chi Omega. Presbyn. (deaconess, trustee ch. 1969-72). Club: Portland Country. Home: 301 W Race St Portland IN 47371

ABZUG, BELLA SAVITZKY (MRS. MAURICE M. ABZUG), congresswoman; b. N.Y.C., July 24, 1920; d. Emanuel and Esther Savitzky; B.A., Hunter Coll., 1942; LL.B., Columbia, 1945; m. Maurice M. Abzug, June 4, 1944; children—Eve Gail, Isobel Jo. Admitted to N.Y. bar, 1947; pvt. practice, N.Y.C., 1944-70; legislative dir. Women Strike for Peace, 1961-70; mem. 92-93d Congresses, 19th and 20th Dist. N.Y. Mem. Women Strike for Peace, Nat. Urban League, Women's Prison Assn., Members of Congress for Peace Through Law, Democratic Study Group, Nat. Orgn. Women, Nat. Women's Polit. Caucus, Women's Action Alliance, Hadassah, Am. Civil Liberties Union, UN Assn. U.S., B'nai B'rith. Home: 37 Bank St New York City NY 10014 Office: Longworth Office Bldg Washington DC 20515

ACE VEDO, CAROLYN LEA LIND, assn. exec.; b. Duluth, Minn., Sept. 5, 1940; d. Ralph G. and Myrtle T. (Erickson) Lind; B.A., U. Minn., 1962; postgrad. Phoenix Coll., 1965-66; m. William Ace Vedo, Nov. 24, 1968 (div.); children—Angela, Lea. Mem. staff Cactus Pine council Girl Scouts U.S.A., Phoenix, 1962-67, St. Croix Valley council, St. Paul, Minn., 1967-72; exec. dir. YWCA, Duluth, Minn., 1972—. James Wright Hunt scholar, 1958-59. Mem. Am. Camping Assn., Nat. Forensic League. Democrat. Home: 123 W Toledo St Duluth MN 55811 Office: 202 W 2d St Duluth MN 55802

ACHEY, DOROTHY MAIE, textile co. exec.; b. Bethlehem, Pa., Oct. 8, 1914; d. William C. and Sadie (Stine) Achey; grad. high sch. Lab. technician, clk. Queen City Textile Co., Allentown, Pa., 1933-39; supt. dyeing Blue Ridge Textile Co., Bangor, Pa., 1939-49, supt. dyeing and finishing, 1949-56; exec. asst., 1956-59; tech. dir., tech. asst. to pres. Blue Ridge-Winkler Textiles div. Lehigh Valley Industries Inc., Bangor, 1959-66, product mgr. automotive and indsl., 1966-71; supt. dyeing and finishing Timme Fabrics, Inc., Rio Grande, N.J., 1971—. Mem. Am. Assn. Textile Colorists & Chemists. Home: 3045 Center St Bethlehem PA 18017 Office: Timme Fabrics Inc Cape May County Indsl Park Rio Grande NJ 08242

ACHILLES, EDITH MULHALL, psychologist; b. Boston, Aug. 6; d. Henry Pope and Ida Frances (Munro) Mulhall; student Barnard Coll.; Ph.D., Columbia 1918; m. Paul Achilles, Oct. 23, 1917; 1 child, Frances. Psychologist Barnard Coll., Vassar Coll. Lectr. embroidery. Bd. dirs. Aux. Neurol. Inst., N.Y.C.; past alumnae trustee Barnard Coll. Address: 417 Park Av New York City NY 10022

ACHS, RUTH, physician; b. N.Y.C., Feb. 2, 1920; d. Benjamin and Yetta (Sklar) Sibowitz; B.A., Hunter Coll., 1942; M.D., L.I. Coll. Medicine, 1945; m. Samuel Achs, Jan. 1, 1942 (div. Jan. 1966); children—Naomi (Mrs. Eric Foner), Robert. Intern Bklyn. Jewish Hosp., 1945-46, resident, 1946-48; practice medicine specializing in pediatrics, Bklyn., 1948-60; dir. out-patient dept. Kings County Hosp., 1960—; asso. prof. pediatrics State U. N.Y. Downstate Med. Center, Bklyn., 1960. Diplomate Am. Bd. Pediatrics. Mem. Am. Acad. Pediatrics, Phi Beta Kappa. Home: 160 Parkside Av Brooklyn NY 11226 Office: State U NY Downstate 450 Clarkson Av Brooklyn NY 11226

ACHTEN, ESTHER (MRS. ALFRED FRIEDMAN), physician; b. Dchurin, Russia, Nov. 27, 1919; d. Jacob and Lifsa (Lernerman) Achten; M.S., Excuela Preparatoria de Mexico, 1937; M.D. cum laude, Nat. U. Mex., 1943; m. Alfred Friedman, Dec. 3, 1944; children—Jack, Frank, Stanley, Melvin. Came to U.S., 1945, naturalized, 1950. Intern, Orange County Gen. Hosp., Orange, Cal., 1947-49; mem. Ross-Loos Med. Group, Los Angeles, 1951; gen. practice medicine, Los Angeles, 1951—. Active Farband Labor Zionist Group. Mem. Am. Israel Med. Assn., Los Angeles County Med. Assn. Home: 1222 S Genesee Av Los Angeles CA 90019 Office: 947 W 8th St Los Angeles CA 90019

ACKER, GERALDINE ENOD, home economist; b. Fargo, N.D.; d. Edward Louis and Inga (Johanson) Acker; B.S., N.D. State U., 1937; M.S., Kan. State U., 1949. Tchr. home econs. high schs., Gardner, N.D., 1937-40, Oakes, N.D., 1941-43; asst. supr. prodn. projects WPA, Fargo, 1940-41; instr. Baker and Cooks Sch., Ft. Sheridan, Ill., 1946-47; mem. staff Coop. Extension Service, U. Ill. at Urbana, 1949—, specialist in food and nutrition, 1949—, prof. food and nutrition, 1967—. Chmn. Ill. Nutrition Com., 1964-66. Served with WAC, 1943-45. Mem. A.A.A.S., Am. Home Econs. Assn. (chmn. food and nutrition sect. 1967-69), Am. Dietetic Assn., Gamma Sigma Delta, Epsilon Sigma Phi. Home: 605 W Vermont St Urbana IL 61801

ACKER, NANCY JANE, educator; b. Cambridge Springs, Pa., Oct. 22, 1934; d. George David and Mildred Marie (Lilly) Acker; B.S., Slippery Rock State U., 1956; M.S. in Phys. Edn., Ind. U., 1962, postgrad., 1964. Tchr. phys. edn. Oil City (Pa.) Area High Sch., 1956-59; mem. faculty health and phys. edn., Edinboro (Pa.) State Coll., 1959—, asso. prof., 1970—, asst. dept. chmn., 1974—. Dir., Girl Scouts Am. camp, Meadville, Pa., 1956-57. Mem. Venango (Pa.) Boro Sch. Bd., 1966-72. Mem. Assn. Pa. State Coll. and Univ. Faculty, Am., Pa. State (mem. membership com. 1972-74, mem. profl. preparation and certification com. 1969—, chmn., 1973—, treas. Erie County chpt. 1971—), assns. health, phys. edn., and recreation, 600 Bowling Club, Delta Kappa Gamma (treas. 1966-71). Mem. Order Eastern Star. Home: Erie St Venango PA 16440 Office: 103 Crawford Gym Edinboro PA 16412

ACKERMAN, ANNE RUTH (MRS. STEVEN CHARLES ACKERMAN), educator; b. Wichita, Kan., Feb. 11, 1947; d. James Charles and Winifred Irene (McCoy) Copeland; B.A. cum laude in Journalism, Trinity Coll., 1969; m. Steven Charles Ackerman, Dec. 5, 1970. Pub. relations asst. Paseo del Rio Assn., 1969-70; pub. relations dir. San Antonio Homebuilders Assn., 1970; communications coordinator San Antonio Conv. and Visitors Bur., 1971—; tchr. Northside Ind. Sch. Dist., 1972—. Mem. Women in Communications (v.p. 1972-73), Alamo Indsl. Editors Assn. (sec. 1971). Home: 214 W Silver Sands San Antonio TX 78216 Office: 1400 Cedarhurst San Antonio TX 78227

ACKERMAN, CAROLINE IVERSON (MRS. LESLIE ACKERMAN), educator; b. Milw., Mar. 6, 1918; d. Jacob Engval and Ella Dorothy (Schmidt) Iverson; B.A., U. Wis., 1939; M.S., Boston U., 1969; m. Leslie Ackerman, Dec. 31, 1949; children—Karin (Mrs. Ronald Field), Terrell Iver, Jon Frederic. Reporter, Janesville (Wis.) Daily Gazette, 1939; advt. Milw. Jour., 1940; aviation ground instr., publicity dir. U. Wis., Milw. and others, 1941; aviation researcher, editor Life mag., N.Y.C., 1942-47; women's travel dir. Shell Oil Co., N.Y.C., 1947-50; free lance and community vol., R.I., Mass., 1950-71; instr. journalism Northeastern U., Boston, 1971-73, asst. prof. journalism, 1973—. Charter mem. Wis. Civil Air Patrol; pub. relations chmn. Warwick (R.I.) council Girl Scouts U.S.A., 1953-57, R.I. Council, 1958-59, also troop leader; pres. Rhodes P.T.A., 1961-62. Recipient Headliner award Theta Sigma Phi, 1949. Mem. Women in Communications (pres. Boston chpt. 1973-74, chmn. jury award, nat. Bernays award 1975), Aviation Writers Assn., 99's Women Pilots Assn. (founder, 1st pres. Milw. chpt. 1941-42), Am. Assn. U. Women, Theta Sigma Phi (chpt. pres. Milw. 1941-42, N.Y.C. 1946-47, Eastern Alumnae-at-large chmn. 1950-52). Lutheran (sec. to bd. parish 1970-71, Sunday sch. tchr.). Life story, Suzy Z, the Fightingest Flying Fortress, included in Best 100 True Stories of World War II, biography featured in New Wings for Women, also pub. in Am. mag., Flying, Coronet, McCall's, Travel, Matrix mag., Milw. Jour., Providence Jour. First woman to fly a small plane from U.S. to Alaska and Mexico City. Home: 14 Indian Ridge Rd South Natick MA 01760 Office: Northeastern U UR 214 Boston MA 02115

ACKERMAN, ELLA LAURETTA (MRS. HENRY JACKSON APPLE), veterinarian; b. Columbus, O., Apr. 29, 1909; d. Christian and Iva May (Pace) Ackerman; B.S. in Edn., Ohio State U., 1930, M.A., 1931, Ph.D., 1934, D.V.M., 1948; m. Henry Jackson Apple, Aug. 10, 1935; children—Christine Adella, Adam Dewey. Practice vet. medicine, specializing in small animals and birds, Columbus, 1948—. Mem. Women's Vet. Med. Assn., Pi Lambda Theta. Home: 1037 Chambers Rd Columbus OH 43212 Office: 1600 W 5th Av Columbus OH 43212

ACKERMAN, FLORENCE S. GOLDSTEIN (MRS. AARON ACKERMAN), edn. counselor; b. Plainfield, N.J.; d. Strul and Betty (Abish) Goldstein; B.S., N.Y.U., M.A., 1948; postgrad. Rutgers U., 1959-61; m. Aaron Ackerman, Dec. 25, 1952. Tchr. pub. schs., Plainfield, 1959; dir. guidance Maxson Jr. High Sch., Plainfield, 1959-68; counselor Plainfield High Sch., 1968-69; counselor Lab. Psychol. Studies, Stevens Inst. Tech., Hoboken, N.J., 1969—. Coordinator human relations workshops, Denver U., Columbia U., Rutgers U., 1949-54; chmn. No. N.J. Council Vocational Service, 1971-74. Mem., sec. Plainfield Mayor's Commn. on Civil Rights, 1947-58; mem. Edn. Commn. on Human Relations, 1947-50. Mem. N.E.A., N.J. Edn. Assn., Am., N.J. personnel and guidance assns., Nat. Vocational Guidance Assn. Mem. B'nai B'rith Women (pres. 1968). Home and office: 14 Lockwood Dr Roselle NJ 07203

ACKERMAN, HELEN RUTH PENNER (MRS. ROSS SCOTT ACKERMAN), ednl. adminstr., psychologist; b. N.Y.C., Mar. 5, 1939; d. Isacc William and Sylvia Celia (Katz) (dec.) Penner; B.A., Hofstra U., 1960; M.A., George Washington U., 1962; Ed.D. (Univ. fellow) U. Md., 1967; m. Ross Scott Ackerman, Feb. 8, 1960; children—Eric Scott, Ruth Dara. Instr., Army Edn. Center, Bad Kissingen, Germany, 1961-63; lectr. psychology U. Md., Schweinfurt, Bad Kissengen, 1962-63; psychologist Crownsville (Md.) State Hosp., 1963-65, Balt. County Bd. Edn., 1966-68, Mills Sch., Ft. Lauderdale, Fla., 1968-69; research psychologist Johns Hopkins, 1965; asst. prof. psychology Anne Arundel Community Coll., Arnold, Md., 1968; cons. Hosp. Mgmt. and Planning Assn., Miami, Fla., 1968-73; adminstr., founder Ross Acad., Plantation, Fla., 1972—. Co-chmn. Plantation Golf Estates Beautification, 1968-69; mem. com. aircraft noise pollution FAA, Ft. Lauderdale, 1973-74. Mem. Am., Fla., Md., Canadian, Southeastern psychol. assns., Nat., Fla. assns. sch. psychologists, Am. Assn. U. Women. Address: 5921 Almond Terrace Plantation FL 33317

ACKERMANN, BARBARA (MRS. PAUL ACKERMANN), city ofcl.; b. Stockholm, Sweden, Mar. 1, 1925 (parents Am. citizens); d. Benjamin Mayham and Joan Margaret (Carrington), Hulley; B.A., Smith Coll., 1945; m. Paul Kurt Ackermann, Dec. 31, 1945; children—Richard Paul, Joan Barbara. Mem. Cambridge (Mass.) Sch. Com., 1962-67; mem. City Council, 1968—, mayor (1st woman), 1972—. Active Peace Movement, 1966—. Home: 41 Gibson St Cambridge MA 02138 Office: City Hall Cambridge MA 02139

ACOSTA-RUA, MARIA VICTORIA, psychiatrist; b. Madrid, Spain, Nov. 28, 1939; d. Antonio and Maria (Gimenez) Pol; B.S., St. Louis des Français Sch., 1956; M.D., U. Madrid, 1963; m. Gaston J. Acosta-Rua, June 7, 1964; children—Gaston, Fernando, Antonio. Came to U.S., 1964, naturalized, 1971. Intern Marymount Hosp., Cleve., 1966-67; resident Ia. U. Hosp., Iowa City, 1968-72; practice medicine specializing in child psychiatry, Jacksonville, Fla., 1972—; chief child psychiatry sect. Jacksonville Children's Hosp., 1973—; med. dir. Children's Day Treatment Center, St. Vincent's Hosp., Jacksonville, 1973—. Cons. psychiatrist Jacksonville Full Year Head Start Program. Mem. Am. Acad. Child Psychiatrists, Fla. Psychiat. Soc., Am. Psychiat. Assn., Am. Orthopsychiat. Assn., Am. Group Psychotherapy Assn., A.M.A. Home: 5026 Long Bow Rd Jacksonville FL 32210 Office: 1717 Barrs St Suite 518 Jacksonville FL 32204

ACTON, JEANNE VIRGINIA (MRS. GEORGE ANDREW ACTON III), real estate broker; b. San Francisco; d. Randolph Martin and Ella Myrtle (Hendrickson) Lipelt; student Stockton Coll., 1948-49; m. George Andrew Acton III, May 1, 1954; children—Kelly Jeanne, George Andrew IV, Leslie Ella. Legal sec. firm Mertz, Adams, Horstmann and Funke, Lodi, Cal., 1962-66; owner Acton Realty, Lodi, Cal., 1969—. Mem. Nat. Assn. Realtors, Cal. Real Estate Assn., Lodi Bd. Realtors. Republican. Lutheran. Home: 2525 E Acampo Rd Acampo CA 95220 Office: 225 N California St Lodi CA 95240

ACUFF, MARY BETH SCHAUB (MRS. MARK DOUGLAS ACUFF), publisher; b. Balt., Apr. 14, 1941; d. Ernest John and Mary Elizabeth (Chambers) Schaub; B.A., Bryn Mawr Coll., 1964; postgrad. U. N.M., 1964-65; m. Mark Douglas Acuff, June 8, 1964. Internat. adminstr. Nat. Student Assn., Phila., 1962-63; adminstr. grant in internat. edn., Casework, N.M., 1965; counselor Job Corps, Omaha, 1967-68, Am. Field Service, N.Y.C., 1969; co-publisher Ind. Pub. Co., Albuquerque, 1971—, also dir. Mem. exec. bd. N.M. Regional Med. Program, 1973-74. Mem. N.M. Civil Liberties Union (dir., co-chmn. 1973-74). Office: PO Box 429 Albuquerque NM 87103

ADAIR, DORIS MARIE, former social worker; b. Gastonia, N.C., Aug. 12, 1932; d. Otto Grady and Willie (Gibbons) Adair; A.A., Gardner-Webb Jr. Coll., 1952; B.S. cum laude, Carson-Newman Coll., 1954; M.A., Carver Sch. Missions and Social Work, 1959; M.S. in Social Work, U. Tenn., 1965. Chem. aide TVA, Sheffield, Ala., 1954-55, analytical chemist, 1955-56, Chattanooga, 1956-57; prof. biology physics Brewton-Parker Coll., Mt. Vernon, Ga., 1959-60; chief coagulation technician Vanderbilt U. Hosp., Nashville, 1962-64; psychiat. social worker Central State Psychiat. Hosp., Nashville, 1965-69; asso. dir. rehab. Samaritans, Inc., Nashville, 1969; social work supr. Mecklenburg County Health Dept., Charlotte, N.C., 1970-73. Cons. social work Peabody Coll., Nashville, 1967-68; cons., therapist for pilot program Nat. Council Alcoholism, Nashville, 1968. Mem. Nat. Assn. Social Workers, Acad. Certified Social Workers, Phi Alpha. Democrat. Home: 2434 Vail Av Charlotte NC 28207

ADAIR, PERRY SHEEHAN (MRS. J. CARLTON ADAIR), actress; b. N.Y.C., Aug. 17, 1921; d. Joseph Vincent and Emily (Carey) Sheehan; student Bklyn. Coll., 1939-40, Grace Inst., 1940-41, Detroit Conservatory Music, 1948-49; m. J. Carlton Adair, June 3, 1957; children—Susan Esther, Valerie Perry. Photog. model John Robert Powers, N.Y.C., 1942-45; motion picture model Jam Handy Pictures, Detroit, 1948-49; radio network actress MBS, Hollywood, 1950-51; freelance motion picture actress R.K.O., Columbia, Hollywood, 1950-51; motion picture actress Metro-Goldwyn-Mayer, Culver City, Cal., 1951-56; women's editor, broadcaster, producer Sta. KLAS-TV, Las Vegas, 1956-61; dir., asst. sec.-treas. Lake Adair Corp., Nev., 1959—. Past chmn., treas. Thrift Shop Aux. of Assistance League So. Cal. Mem. Clark County Republican Central Com., 1960-62; vice chmn. Nev. Rep. Com., 1960-62; mem. Nev. Rep. Exec. Com., 1960-62. Mem. Screen Actors Guild, Las Vegas Press Club, Nev. Fedn. Rep. Women (adviser 1960-62), So. Nev. Hist. Soc. (sec.-treas., 1960-63), Women's Aux. Variety Internat., Gen. Fedn. Women's Clubs, St. Anne's Hosp. Aux. Los Angeles (pres. 1967), Los Angeles Social Service Aux., Los Angeles Orphanage Guild, Motion Picture Country Home Aux., St. Jude's Ranch for Children Aux. (dir. 1973—), Las Vegas Opportunity Village for Retarded Citizens (dir. 1972—), Beta Sigma Phi. Roman Catholic. Clubs: Los Angeles Athletic; Hollywood (Cal.) Yacht; Mesquite (Las Vegas). Home: 2505 Mason Av Las Vegas NV 89102

ADAM, DONNA MAE, city ofcl.; b. Odgen, Utah, Jan. 3, 1926; d. Frederick Herbert and Bessie Pearl (Scott) Adam; student Weber State Coll., 1959-60. Dep. county clk. of dist. Odgen, 1952-69; city recorder, 1970—. Sec., Young Democrats, 1954-55. Mem. Ch. Jesus Christ of Latter-day Saints. Club: Altrusa Women's. Home: 875 26th St Ogden UT 84401 Office: Municipal Bldg Ogden UT 84401

ADAMO, EVELYN FELEPPA (MRS. IDO ADAMO), psychologist; b. Mt. Vernon, N.Y., Aug. 18, 1936; d. Alfred E. and Anna E. (Foresti) Feleppa; B.S., Boston U., 1958; M.A., Fordham U., 1961, Ph.D., 1965; m. Ido Adamo, June 20, 1964; children—Sonya, Alisa. Research asst. Child Devel. Centre, N.Y.C., 1961-62; clin. interne Norwich (Conn.) Hosp., 1962-64; research psychologist Douglas Hosp., Montreal, Que., Can., 1964-65; cons. psychologist Clifton T. Perkins Hosp., Jessup, Md., 1967—, Mental Health,

Cheverly, Md., 1968—; pvt. practice psychotherapy, Laurel, Md., 1971—, Bowie, Md., 1973—. Fellow Md. Psychol. Assn.; mem. Am. Psychol. Assn., Sigma Xi. Contbr. articles to profl. jours. Home: 8705 Crystal Rock Lane Laurel MD 20811

ADAMS, ANN ELIZABETH, journalist; b. Guthrie, Okla., Jan. 29, 1948; d. Jack Paul and Billie Elizabeth (May) Adams; B.A. (McMahon Journalism scholar), U. Okla., 1970, M.A., 1971. Supr. teleshopper advt. program KOCO-TV, Oklahoma City, 1971; pub. information officer Okla. County Libraries, Oklahoma City, 1972—. Mem. Am. Advt. Fedn., Library Pub. Relations Council, Women in Communications, Okla. Library Assn., Oklahoma City Advt. Club, ADS, Kappa Tau Alpha. Democrat. Home: Apt 421 5336 Willow Cliff Oklahoma City OK 73122 Office: 131 NW 3d St Oklahoma City OK 73102

ADAMS, ARLEEN PENNY, state ofcl.; b. Bridgeport, Conn., Sept. 28, 1927; B.A., Tufts U., 1950; m. John Adams; 4 children. Mem. Vt. Gov.'s Com. Children and Youth, Vt. Spl. Edn. Adv. Council. mem. Springfield, Vt. Sch. Bd. Edn. Mem. League Women Voters, Vt. Assn. Children with Learning Disabilities, Springfield Assn. Retarded Children. Unitarian-Universalist. Address: Route 1 Box 54 Springfield VT 05156

ADAMS, BEATRICE ANN, librarian; b. Owosso, Mich., May 23, 1940; d. Edwin Hayes and Dorothy Lavinia (Guenther) Adams; B.A., Albion Coll., 1962; M.A., Western Mich. U., 1963. Children's librarian Niles (Mich.) Pub. Library, 1963-65, Grosse Pointe (Mich.) Pub. Library, 1965-71, St. Clair Shores (Mich.) Pub. Library, 1972—. Mem. mag. staff Detroit Soc. Geneal. Research, 1974. Bd. dirs. Detroit Council Am. Youth Hostels, 1972-74, rec. sec., 1972-73. Mem. Am. Assn. U. Women, Mich. Library Assn. (sec. children's services roundtable 1969-70), N.E.A., Mich. Edn. Assn., Beta Phi Mu. Methodist. Home: 26301 Jefferson St St Clair Shores MI 48081 Office: 22500 Eleven Mile St St Clair Shores MI 48081

ADAMS, BEEJAY SEABURY (MRS. MERLIN F. ADAMS), civic worker, pub. relations exec.; b. Jefferson Barracks, Mo.; d. Alden Humphrey and Louise Marion (Banta) Seabury; A.B., Bradley U., 1942; m. Merlin F. Adams, July 10, 1948; children—Stephen Kent, Mark Francis. Service editor Peoria (Ill.) Jour. Transcript, 1942-46; record reveille program radio sta. WMBD, Peoria, 1943; profl. lectr. Hillis-Folks Bur., Peoria, also Sch. Assembly Service, Chgo., 1942-49; womans program dir. radio sta. WEEK, Peoria, 1946-47; Nancy Dixon program radio sta. KSD, St. Louis, 1948, field supr. Bur. Census, 1970; pres. B.J. Adams Agy., Quincy, Ill. Territorial chmn. Community Projects, Am. Cancer Soc., Quincy, Ill., 1952, Community Chest, 1958, Heart Fund, 1959, A.R.C., 1960. Bd. dirs. Quincy Community Little Theatre; life pres. Quincy Jr. Theatre, 1956—; pres. Quincy Panhellenic Soc., 1964-66; bd. dirs. Quincy chpt. A.R.C.; asso. gov. region Childrens Theatre Conf. and Secondary Sch. Theatre Conf., 1967-68. Dir. Ill. Fedn. Republican Women, 1969—. Mem. Am. Ednl. Theatre Assn., Pi Beta Phi, Theta Alpha Phi. Episcopalian. Clubs: Quincy Art (dir.), Atlantis Study (1st v.p. 1968-70; pres. 1970-72). Home: 424 S 16th St Quincy IL 62301

ADAMS, BETTY, writer, reporter, TV producer, performer; b. Cranston, R.I.; d. Ernest Ernest S. and Alice (Giles) Calder; A.B. cum laude, Smith Coll.; M.A. (hon.), R.I. Coll. Edn., 1959; m. David McKey Adams, Sept. 10, 1949 (dec.) children—Holly, John McKey. Engaged as news reporter and writer; appeared on TV program News at Nine, 1960, Sunday program Dimensions, 1960, also documentary films; lectr. News Analysis World in Your Home, Glamor on a Budget, Travel Is a Family Affair; corr. broadcaster with the ABC Network, N.Y.C.; producer, writer, reporter WABC-TV News; news corr., producer N.J. Pub. Broadcasting Authority, Trenton, 1971—, bur. chief N. Jersey News Bur., 1974—. Publicity chmn. R.I. Cancer Soc. Fund Drive; mem. Jr. League of Providence, Inc. Recipient Gabriel award Confraternity of Christian Doctrine, 1960; McCall's Golden Mike award, 1961. Mem. New Eng. Press Women's Assn. (1st v.p. 1962). Club: Overseas Press (N.Y.C.). Home: 620 Pkwy Mamaroneck NY 10543 Office: 40 Rector St Newark NJ 07102

ADAMS, BEULAH GRACE JENKINS (MRS. ADDISON FRANK ADAMS), abstract co. exec.; b. Bastrop, Tex., Nov. 29, 1909; d. Hartford and Beulah Alice (Hemphill) Jenkins; B.A., Baylor U., 1930; postgrad. U. Tex., 1933, 39, U. Colo., 1934; m. Addison Frank Adams, Dec. 26, 1938; children—Forrest Jenkins, Alice Ann (Mrs. Charles Woodrow Miller). Tchr., Bastrop (Tex.) Pub. Schs., 1930-41; v.p., mgr. Bastrop County Abstract Co., Inc., Tex., 1942—. Mem. Am. Assn. U. Women, Tex. State Geneal. Soc., Am., Tex. land title assns., Am. Assn. Petroleum Landmen, Delta Kappa Gamma. Baptist. Home: 1707 Pecan St Bastrop TX 78602 Office: 901 Main St PO Box 550 Bastrop TX 78602

ADAMS, BLANCHE HALL (MRS. CLIFFORD ADAMS), educator; b. Laporte, Ind.; d. Earl Cranston and Catherine W. (Shannon) Hall; A.B., Hanover Coll., 1936; M.A., U. Ia., 1942; postgrad. U. Chgo. Sch. Social Adminstrn., 1937-38, dept. anthropology Ind. U., 1967-71; m. Clifford Adams, Dec. 24, 1938. Med. social worker social service Dept. State U. Ia. Hosps., Iowa City, 1940-42; asst. dir. social service dept. King County Hosp. System, Seattle, 1942-45; teaching fellow U. Wash. Grad. Sch. Social Work, 1944-45; instr. dept. sociology Hanover Coll., 1945-48; med. social cons. Ind. Dept. Pub. Welfare, Indpls., 1948-53; instr., coordinator family health program Dept. Community Health, U. Louisville Sch. Medicine, 1953-57; prof. Kent Sch. Social Work, U. Louisville, 1957—. Bd. dirs. Louisville and Jefferson County Planned Parenthood Center. Mem. Nat. Assn. Social Workers, Acad. Certified Social Workers, Am. Assn. U. Profs. Am. Anthropol. Assn. Home: Box 217 Hanover IN 47243 Office: Belknap Campus University of Louisville Louisville KY 40208

ADAMS, CARMEN BOITEL, poetess; b. Bklyn., Apr. 3, 1920; d. Ringgold Raphael and Emma May (Phillips) Boitel; student Katherine Gibbs Secretarial Sch., N.Y.C., 1934; m. Hugh Thomas Adams, Aug. 11, 1950. Pvt. sec. Arnold Serton Export Co., N.Y.C., 1938-46, Anglo-Cal. Nat. Bank, Modesto, 1947-50. Worked with Cuban refugee children, Portland, Ore., 1962; tchr. class in Am. naturalization to Mexicans in Phoenix. Mem. Am. Poetry League, Ariz. Poetry Soc., Maj. Poets. Author: Twenty Little Lyrics, 1970; Quiet Reflections, 1971; (poem) The Greatest of These. Contbr. to poetry mags. Home: 345 W Cambridge Av Phoenix AZ 85003

ADAMS, ELEANOR, newspaper editor; student Butler U., 1932-34; A.B. in Journalism, Ind. U., 1936; M.A. in Journalism, U. Mo., 1941. Club editor Indpls. Times, 1948-52, society and women's editor, 1952-56; asst. society editor, columnist Cin. Enquirer, 1959-69, columnist, society editor, 1969—. Mem. Ohio Newspaper Women's Assn., Women in Communications (pres. Cin. chpt. 1963; Indpls. chpt. 1964), Nat. Soc. Arts and Letters, Ohio Press Women, Nat. Fedn. Press Women, Kappa Alpha Theta. Home: 1071 Celestial St Apt 1103 Cincinnati OH 45202 Office: 617 Vine St Cincinnati OH 45202

ADAMS, ERNESTINE, editor; b. Hartville, Mo., Apr. 14, 1905; d. Ernest James and Betty (Cottengim) Adams; B.J., U. Mo., 1926; postgrad. New Sch. Social Research, Columbia, 1929, N.Y. U., 1938, So. Meth. U., 1943-45. Pub., owner Logan County News, Crescent, Okla., 1930-37; advt. dept. Neiman Marcus, Dallas, 1943; editor Petroleum Engrs. Pub. Co., Dallas, 1943—, dir. Search Enterprises subsidiary, 1969—. Named 1st Oil Woman of Yr., Internat. Petroleum Expn., 1953; recipient Editorial Achievement award, Am. Bus. Press, 1963; Matrix award, Theta Sigma Phi, 1964. Mem. Women in Communication, Chi Omega, Pi Epsilon Tau. Presbyn. (deacon). Clubs: Press (Dallas); Downtown Republican Women's (Dallas). Home: 2818 Fondrew Dallas TX 75205 Office: 800 Davis Bldg Dallas TX 75202

ADAMS, EVA B(ERTRAND), former dir. U.S. Mint, lawyer, cons.; b. Wonder, Nev.; d. Verner Lauer and Cora (Varble) Adams; B.A., U. Nev., LL.D., 1967; M.A., Columbia, 1937; J.D., Washington Coll. Law, 1968; LL.M., George Washington U., 1950; LL.D., U. Portland, 1966. Tchr., Las Vegas High Sch.; asst. dean women, instr. English, U. Nev., 1937-40; adminstrv. asst. to Senator Pat McCarran, 1940-54, Senator Ernest Brown, 1954, Senator Alan Bible, 1954-61; admitted to Nev. bar, 1950, D.C. bar, 1950; dir. Bur. Mint, Teasury Dept., 1961-66, 66-69; now cons., atty., Washington. Dir. Tele-Trip Corp., Medallic Art Corp. Trustee Graham-Eckes Sch., Palm Beach, Fla.; bd. dirs. Med. Coll. Pa., Interlochen Center for Arts. Mem. Reno C. of C., Senate Secs. Assn. (pres. 1943-44), Sales and Marketing Execs., Bus. and Profl. Women, Am. Newspaper Women's Assn., Am. Women in Radio and Television, Cap and Scroll, Kappa Alpha Theta, Phi Kappa Phi, Kappa Delta Pi. Clubs: 1925 F Street, Soroptimist. Home: 701 Skyline Blvd Reno NV 89502 Office: Mutual of Omaha 1700 Pennsylvania Av NW Washington DC 20006

ADAMS, FAE MARGARET, physician, educator; b. San Jose, Cal., June 13, 1918; d. Earl Samuel and Emily Isabella (Seymour) Adams; student U. Cal. at Berkeley, 1937-40; M.D., Woman's Med. Coll. Pa., 1951. Commd. 1st lt. M.C., U.S. Army, 1952, advanced through grades to capt., 1961; intern, Woman's Med. Coll. Pa. Hosp., Phila., 1951-52; resident Walter Reed Army Hosp., Washington, 1953-56; asst. chief, chief obstetrics, gynecology Tokyo Army Hosp., 1956-58; chief obstetrics and gynecology McClellan Army Hosp., 1958-59, Fort Devens Army Hosp., 1959-61, resigned, 1961; practiced medicine specializing in obstetrics and gynecology, Littleton, Mass., 1961-68; chief obstetrics and gynecology Ayer-Groton Community Hosp., 1966-68; mem. staff Ayer and Groton Hosps., 1961-68; mem. staff Hosp. Med. Coll. Pa., also mem. faculty, 1968—, research asst. prof. obstetrics-gynecology, 1968-69, asst. prof., 1969-70, asso. prof., 1969—. Diplomate Am. Bd. Obstetrics and Gynecology, Nat. Bd. Med. Examiners. Mem. A.M.A., Am. Med. Womens Assn., Assn. Mil. Surgeons, Mass., Phila. County med. socs., Am. Coll. Obstetrics and Gynecology, Obstet. Soc. Phila. Home: 3600 Conshohocken Av Philadelphia PA 19131 Office: 3300 Henry Av Philadelphia PA 19131

ADAMS, GEORGIA SACHS (MRS. JOSEPH JOHN ADAMS), educator, author; b. Ortonville, Minn., May 23, 1913; d. John Frederick and Ella (Merry) Wein; A.B., U. So. Cal., 1933, M.S., 1935, Ph.D., 1941; postgrad. U. Chgo., Claremont Grad. Sch.; m. Joseph John Adams, Sept. 7, 1946; children—Margaret (Mrs. Lawrence Cross), Jo-Ann, Joseph, Mary. Research asst., research dir. Pasadena City Schs., 1936-51; instr. Muir Coll., 1951-52, 53-54; lectr. Claremont Grad. Sch., 1953—; asst. prof. edn. Cal. State U., Los Angeles, 1954-58, asso. prof. edn., 1958-62, prof. edn., 1962—. Research cons. Orientation and Mobility Skills for Blind, 1965-67, Reading Program for Mexican-Am. Children, 1965-68. Fellow Am. Psychol. Assn.; mem. Am. Ednl. Research Assn., Phi Beta Kappa, Pi Lambda Theta (nat. v.p. 1963-67; 1st v.p. 1969-70; pres. 1970-73). Author: Exploring the World of Work, 1937; Evaluating Group Guidance in Secondary Schools, 1945; California Tests in Social and Related Sciences, 1947, 54; Measurement and Evaluation for the Elementary School Teacher, 1954; Measurement and Evaluation for the Secondary School Teacher, 1956; Measurement and Evaluation in Education, Psychology and Guidance, 1964, Spanish edit., 1970; co-author Studying Social Relationships in the Classroom, 1959; California Survey Tests, 1959. Home: 2772 N Lake Av Altadena CA 91001 Office: 5151 State University Dr Los Angeles CA 90032

ADAMS, GLADYS BURGESS (MRS. OZIE L. ADAMS), educator; b. Algood, Tenn., July 23, 1922; d. James Robert and Ida Belle (Roberts) Burgess; B.S., Tenn. Agr. and Indsl. State Coll., 1943, M.S., 1949; postgrad. U. Utah, 1956, Ore. State Coll., 1959, Purdue U., 1963; m. Ozie L. Adams, Jan. 28, 1950; children—Eula Gaynelle, Sara Michelle. Math. and sci. tchr. Cook High Sch., Athens, Tenn., 1943-47; grad. asst. biology Tenn. State U., 1947-49; asst. prof. biology, 1950—, coordinator alumni affairs, 1963—, initial dir. econ. opportunity grant program, 1966. Mem. Nashville Opportunity for Industrialization Corp. Aux., 1972-73, Nashville Urban League. Recipient Alumni Citation, Tenn. State U., 1962, Alumni Service awards Tenn. State U. Nat. Alumni Assn., 1965. NSF grantee, 1962. Mem. Nat. Council Negro Women, Am. Inst. Biol. Scis., Am. Alumni Council (dist. pub. instn. chmn. 1971-72), Tenn. Acad. Sci., Tenn. State U. Nat. Alumni Assn. (exec. sec. 1957—), Alpha Kappa Mu, Beta Kappa Chi, Alpha Kappa Alpha. Methodist. Club: Jack and Jill (Nashville). Editor Tenn. State U. Alumni Newsletter, 1970—. Office: Tenn State U Nashville TN

ADAMS, HARRIET DYER, coll. librarian; b. Champaign, Ill.; d. Charles Christopher and Alice L. (Norton) Adams; A.B., U. Mich., 1933; A.M., Inst. Fine Arts N.Y.U., 1937; M.S. in L.S., State U. N.Y., 1960. Curator, Person Hall Art Gallery; instr. art dept. U. N.C., Chapel Hill, 1940-44; curator Mus. Cranbrook Acad. Art, Bloomfield Hills, Mich., 1945-48; research asst. dept. painting Art Inst. Chgo., 1949; dir. Jr. Art Gallery, Louisville, 1950-52; lectr., docent Montclair (N.J.) Art Mus., 1952-55; instr. art history Russell Sage Coll., Troy, N.Y., also N.Y. State Tchrs. Coll., Albany, N.Y., 1956-59; reference librarian Skidmore Coll., Saratoga Springs, N.Y., 1960-65; asst. librarian Pierce Library, State U. N.Y., Albany, 1965-71, asso. librarian rare books Univ. Library, 1971—. Vice pres. in charge of civic affairs City Club, Albany, 1958. Mem. Soc. Archtl. Historians, A.L.A., N.Y., Hudson-Mohawk library assns., Soc. Bibliophiles (sec.), Typophiles, Guild Book Workers, William Morris Soc. (Eng.), Capitol Dist. Library Council (chmn. preservation com. 1973—). Home: 149 Manning Blvd Albany NY 12203 Office: 1400 Washington Av Albany NY 12222

ADAMS, HAZEL GREENLEE REDFEARN (MRS. PAYTON F. ADAMS II), educator; b. Monroe, N.C., Nov. 12, 1905; d. Ephraim Eugene and Rebecca (Laney) Redfearn; student Radford Coll., 1924; A.B., U. Ky., 1940, M.A., 1953; postgrad. U. Neb., 1955; m. Payton F. Adams II, July 11, 1928; children—Payton F. III, Juliette Greenlee (Mrs. J. B. Hawk). Elementary tchr. Larchmont Sch., Norfolk, Va., 1924-28, Winchester (Ky.) City Schs., 1943-53; supr. Clark County (Ky.) Schs., 1953-61; supr. student tchrs. Ky. Wesleyan Coll., 1945-48; instr. Wesleyan Coll., Macon, Ga., 1960; asst. prof. edn. Dakota Wesleyan U., Mitchell, S.D., asso. prof. edn.; now asso. prof. early childhood edn. Pfeiffer Coll., Misenheimer, N.C., supr. student tchrs., 1969-73. Chmn., Clark County Council, 1950-52, Clark County Recreation Bd., 1955-60; supr. Teen-Town Winchester, 1954-60. Mem. Am. Assn. U. Women, Am. Assn. U. Profs., N.E.A., S.D. Edn. Assn., D.A.R., Assn. Supervision Curriculum Devel., Assn. for Childhood Edn., Assn. Childhood Edn. Internat. (adviser Pfeiffer Coll. chpt. 1972-73), N.C. Assn. Supervisory Educators. Mitchell Bus. and Profl. Women Club, Albemarle Bus. and Profl. Women (pres. 1972-73), Phi Kappa Phi (pres. 1964-66), Delta Kappa Gamma (pres. 1964-66), Pi Gamma Mu. Methodist. Mem. Order Eastern Star. Home: 136 College St Winchester KY 40391 Office: Pfeiffer Coll Misenheimer NC 28109

ADAMS, HELLEN ANNE HUTCHINSON, educator; b. Hamilton, Miss., Aug. 25, 1935; d. James Perry and Lois (Wright) Hutchinson; student Miss. State U., 1953-54; B.S., Miss. State Coll. Women, 1956; M.Ed., Duke, 1957; Ed.D., U. Miss., 1966; postgrad. U. Ga., 1966-67; m. Charles Floyd Adams, June 27, 1959 (div.); 1 son, Charles Floyd. Elementary tchr., Atlanta, 1957-59, Tampa, Fla., 1959-60, Hattiesburg, Miss., 1960-61, Oxford, Miss., 1961-64; dir. elementary edn., Columbus, Ga., 1965-67; dir. edn. LeFlore County Sch. Dist., Greenwood, Miss., 1967-69; asso. dir. staff tng. Exemplary Early Edn. Centers, U. Tex.; mem. faculty U. Miss., 1964, U. Ga., 1966; asst. prof. spl. edn. U. Tex., Austin; asso. prof. Duke, Durham, N.C., 1971-73, prof., 1973—, dir. Univ. Reading Clinic, 1972—. Mem. nat. adv. bd. J. B. Lippincott Co., 1966—, Internat. Textbook Co., Inc., 1968—, Miss. Authority for Educational Television, 1969—; reading cons.; dir. Diagnostic and Remedial Reading Center, Columbus, 1967—. Named Outstanding Young Woman of Am., Miss. State Coll. Women, 1967; recipient Outstanding profl. award Duke, 1971-72. Mem. N.C. Assn. Univ. Profs. of Reading (pres. 1972—), Internat. Platform Assn., Phi Delta Epsilon, Alpha Delta Kappa, Pi Gamma Mu, Delta Kappa Gamma, Chi Omega. Author: The Clock Struck One; The Reading Clinic; co-author Random House Reading Program; sr. author Learning Abilities for Children with Handicaps, Sounds for Me, Plan Readiness Experiences Program; cons. Webster's New World Dict. Contbr. numerous articles to profl. jours. Home: 2727 Spencer St Durham NC 27705

ADAMS, JACQUELINE, artist; b. Ennis, Tex., Sept. 24, 1935; d. Woodson Bryan and Sarah Elizabeth (Hickox) Adams; B.A., Tex. State Coll. Women, 1956; postgrad. Tex. Women's U., 1956-58. Dir. occupational therapy Children's Service, Neb. Psychiat. Inst., Omaha, 1958-60; occupational therapist St. Joseph's Hosp., Omaha, 1960-62; tchr. art, Bryant, Ark., 1962—; designer, dir. Jacqueline's Originals, Bryant, 1971—; one-man shows Ark. State Capital, 1970, El Dorado (Ark.) Fine Arts Center, 1970, Seabrooks Gallery, Memphis, 1971, A & B Originals Gallery, Dallas, 1971; exhibited in group shows Bryant Art Galleries, Harrison, Ark., 1970-74, Art Fair Art Gallery, Little Rock, 1970-74, Sketch Box Art Gallery, Little Rock, 1969, S.E. Ark. Art Gallery, Pine Bluff, 1972, Internat. Galleries, Houston, 1973, others; represented in permanent collections various cities. Mem. Ark. Art Center, Am. Therapy Assn. Clubs: Arkansas Kennel (Little Rock); Southeast Arkansas Kennel (Pine Bluff). Home: Box 86 Bryant AR 72022

ADAMS, JEAN, columnist, author; b. Dallas, Nov. 19, 1932; d. Willmer M. and Susan Elizabeth (Foreman) Mason; B.B.A., U. Tex., 1954; M.A., U. Colo., 1958, now postgrad.; m. Martin R. Adams, Jan. 29, 1955; children—LeSue, Mason. Syndicated columnist United Features, 1968—; contbr. Family Weekly mag.; lectr., chmn. bd. Contemporary Programs, Inc., Houston. Trustee All-Am. Family Inst. Author: The Emerging Couple, 1973. Address: care Richard Fulton Inc 200 W 57th St New York City NY 10019

ADAMS, JEAN ELIZABETH, librarian; b. Rochester, N.Y., Apr. 23, 1924; d. Edward Leland and Sarah Robison (Fries) Adams; B.S. in Library Edn., State Tech. Coll., Geneseo, N.Y., 1950; teaching certificate Syracuse U., 1960. With Clifton Springs (N.Y.) San. and Clinic, 1950-53, Ontario County Lab., Canandaigua, N.Y., 1954-55; substitute sch. librarian, Niagara Falls, N.Y., 1955; high sch. librarian, Port Byron, N.Y., 1955-62; elementary librarian Phelps (N.Y.) Central Sch., 1962—. Served with USNR, 1944-45. Mem. N.Y. State United Tchrs., Am. Fedn. Tchrs., N.E.A., Phelps-Clifton Springs Faculty Assn., Am. Assn. U. Women (chpt. membership chmn. 1970—), D.A.R., Delta Kappa Gamma (chpt. necrology chmn. 1970-72, Pi state research com. 1971-72, chpt. chmn. profl. growth and services 1974-75). Republican. Baptist (lit. chmn.). Mem. Order Eastern Star. Address: 29 Teft Av Clifton Springs NY 14432

ADAMS, JUDITH MARIE, cons. TV prodn.; b. South Bend, Ind., Apr. 29, 1940; d. Peter Xavier and Marie A. (Buczkowski) Kowalski; B.A., St. Mary's Coll., 1963; M. Radio and Television, Ind. U., 1967; M.A. in Teaching, Notre Dame U., 1968; student Marquette U., 1958-60. Dir. drama dept. St. Joseph High Sch., South Bend, 1963-66; dir. TV news dept. Elkhart (Ind.) High Sch., 1967-68; dir. radio and TV, Sam Houston U., Huntsville, Tex., 1968-71; tech. dir. South Bend Civic Ballet and Dance Co., 1962-68, 71-73; continuity dir. WUHQ-TV, Battle Creek, Mich., 1971; tech. theatre cons. South Bend Civic Ballet and Dance Co., 1962—. Mem. Nat. Assn. Ednl. Broadcasters, Am. Theatre Assn., Women Polit. Caucus. Club: Altrusa. Home: 519 Woodcliff South Bend IN 46615 Office: Suite 506 120 W LaSalle St South Bend IN 46601

ADAMS, KELA OSBOURN (MRS. C. DONOVAN ADAMS), univ. adminstr.; b. Louisville, June 2, 1939; d. Jefferson E. and Ava L. (Carter) Adams; student Ursuline Coll., 1957-59; B.S., U. Louisville, 1961; M.A., Ind. U., 1965, Ph.D., 1970; m. C. Donovan Adams, Dec. 26, 1963; 1 son, Thaddeus Andrew. Tchr., New Albany (Ind.) Schs., 1961-64; tchr., adminstr. U. Louisville, 1965-68, tchr., mem. student affairs adminstrn. Ind. U. S.E., New Albany, 1971—. Mem. Am. Assn. Higher Edn., Nat. Assn. Women Deans, Counsellors, Admintrs., Assn. Coll. Unions-Internat., A.A.H.P.E.R., Kappa Delta Pi, Pi Lambda Theta. Home: 1427 Slate Run Rd New Albany IN 47150 Office: Ind U Southeast New Albany IN 47150

ADAMS, LUCILLE JOAN, child psychotherapist; b. Hartford, Conn., Apr. 2, 1933; d. Charles William and Catherine Therese (Messmer) Adams; Asso. Sci., Hartford Coll. for Women, 1958; B.A., Wheaton Coll., Norton, Mass., 1960; M.S.W., Smith Coll., 1962; certificate in child psychotherapy Inst. Psychoanalysis, Chgo., 1972. Caseworker I and II, Family Service Milw., 1962-66; child therapist Lakeside Children's Center, Milw., 1966-69; child therapist Jewish Children's Bur., Chgo., 1969—; field instr. U. Chgo., Sch. Social Service Adminstrn., 1970—. Community cons. Active Chgo. Symphony Soc., 1970—; mem. com. for establishment of clinic for treatment emotionally disturbed children Chgo. area, 1968-70; class sec. Smith Coll. Sch. Social Work, 1974—. Mem. Nat. Assn. Social Workers (sec. N.E. Wis. family and children's Service council 1965-66), Acad. Certified Social Workers, Am. Orthopsychiatric Assn., Assn. Child Psychotherapists (sec. 1972-73). Author article in field. Home: 1455 N Sandburg Terrace 1104 Chicago IL 60610 Office: 1 S Franklin St Chicago IL 60606

ADAMS, MARY BUDDIN, city council; b. Balt., Sept. 23, 1923; d. Mallard H. and Geneva (Kennedy) Buddin; B.A., Morgan State Coll., 1950; M.A., N.Y.U., 1954; m. Donald Adams (div.) Tchr., art specialist Balt. Pub. Schs., 1960-68; asso. prof. art Coppin State Coll., 1962-63, dir. Early Childhood Research Center, 1969-70, dir. spl. services for students in higher edn., 1970—; dir. Vol. Service Corps, Balt. Anti-Poverty Project, 1965-66; asst. pub. information dir. Dept.

Pub. Works, Balt., 1968-69; councilwoman Balt. City Council, 1971—. Pres., Greenlawn Neighborhood Orgn., 1956, Community Action to Improve Neighborhoods, 1968—; mem. Gov.'s Commn. on Status of Women in Md., 1966-68; dir. WBAL-TV City Hall Action Van, 1968; hostess Neighborhood Clinic, Radio Sta. WITH 1970—. Dir. 4th Dist. Democratic Orgn.'s Town Hall Forum, 1968-72. Bd. dirs. Vol. Tutorial Agy. Council Met. Balt., Johns Hopkins, Univ. Tutorial Services, YWCA. Recipient Distinguished Community Service awards Alpha Kappa Alpha, 1965, Balt. chpt. Bus. and Profl. Women, 1965, N.A.A.C.P., 1965. Baptist. Home: 2414 W Lafayette Av Baltimore MD 21216 Office: City Hall Baltimore MD 21202

ADAMS, MARY ELIZABETH (MRS. HAROLD S. ADAMS), social worker; b. Sioux City, Ia., Oct. 17, 1928; d. Aaron James and Mary (Street) Cabbell; A.B., Morningside Coll., 1950; M.S.W., U. Kan., 1965; m. Harold S. Adams, Sept. 14, 1950. Caseworker neurology service Kan. Neurol. Inst., Topeka, 1965-66, tng. supr., 1967-68, worked on spl. projects with social work students, 1966-68, acting chief social worker, 1968, profl. social work supr. on 3 services, instr. psychiat. in-service tng., 1969-70, treatment team leader adolescent service, 1970-71, treatment team leader acad. pre-vocational service, 1971-72, asst. dir. community services, 1972-74; with children's service, intake out-patient evaluations, supr. social workers Topeka State Hosp., 1968-69, mental retardation service program coordinator Biddle Hosp., Topeka, 1974—. Field instr. Kan. U., 1968-69, Washburn U., 1968, Sch. Social Welfare U. Kan., 1968-69, 72-74. Mem. Am. Assn. Mental Deficiency, Nat. Assn. Social Workers (chpt. treas. 1968-70, mem. adminstrn. bd. 1970), Kan., Topeka assns. retarded children, Kan. Conf. Social Welfare, Kan. U. Social Work Alumni, Council Family and Childrens Services. Mem. Order Eastern Star. Club: Quota (bd. mem. local chpt. 1971-72, 72-73. Office: Topeka State Hosp 2700 W 6th St Topeka KS 66606

ADAMS, MILDRED GRIZZARD, oil and securities investor; b. Naples, Tex., Feb. 28, 1903; d. Harry McNeill and Lucy (Brown) Grizzard; student Tex. Christian U., 1920-23; m. Homer Hastings Adams, Aug. 9, 1930 (dec. Aug. 1947); children—Martha Lucy (Mrs. Robert Samuel Rubin), Jane McNeill (Mrs. Jane Adams Breed). Mgr. H.H. Adams Estate, Abilene Tex., 1947—. Bd. dirs. A.R.C., Abilene Fine Arts Mus. Mem. West Central Tex. Oil and Gas Assn. Republican. Episcopalian. Home: 825 Amarillo St Abilene TX 79602 Office: First Nat Bank Bldg Abilene TX 79601

ADAMS, PAT, artist; b. Stockton, Cal., July 8, 1928; d. Roy Alanson and Minerva Matilda (Smith) Adams; B.A., U. Cal. at Berkeley, 1949; student Bklyn. Mus. Art Sch., 1950; m. Vincent Longo, 1951 (div. 1968); children—Matthew Adams Longo, Jason Rice Longo; m. 2d, R. Arnold Ricks, 1972. One-man shows at Zabriskie Gallery, 1954, 56, 60, 62, 65, 67, 70, 72, 74, Kanegis Gallery, Boston, 1959, Windham Coll., Vt., 1967, Williams Coll., 1972; exhibited in group shows: 41 Aquarellistes, Americains d'Aujourd'hui, Mus. Modern Art Traveling Exhbns., 1956, Stable Gallery, 1956, The Private Myth, Tanager Gallery, 1957, Experiences in Art, Hirschl-Adler Galleries, 1959, Am. Fedn. Arts Exhbns., U. Tex. at Austin, 1972; represented pub. collections Whitney Mus. Am. Art, Joseph Hirschorn Collection, U. Mich., U. Cal., U. N.C., at Greenfield, others. Mem. art faculty Bennington Coll., Bennington, Vt., 1964—; vis. critic painting Yale U. Grad. Sch. Art and Architecture, 1971-72; vis. lectr. Grad. Sch. Fine Arts, Queens Coll., 1972. Summer Yaddo fellow, 1954, 64, 69, 70; MacDowell Colony fellow, 1968, 72; Fulbright scholar to France for painting, 1956; Nat. Council Arts cash prize award in painting, 1969. Mem. Phi Beta Kappa. Home: Bennington Coll Bennington VT 05201

ADAMS, PAULINE AUSTIN, psychologist; b. N.Y.C., Aug. 14, 1931; d. Harry Gregory and Pauline (Moore) Austin; A.B., Bryn Mawr Coll., 1952; Ph.D., U. Cal. at Berkeley, 1956; children by previous marriage—Kennedy, Naidine. Postdoctoral research fellow and research asso. dept. psychology Stanford, 1956-58; research asst., 1961-62, psychologist Children's Hosp. Stanford, 1964—; research asso. VA Hosp., Palo Alto, Cal., 1961; postdoctoral trainee, 1963-64; pvt. practice psychol. testing, 1966—. Mem. adv. council Charles Armstrong Sch., Menlo Park, Cal., 1968—. Nat. Inst. Mental Health grantee, 1956-58, 58-59; Nat. Inst. Child Health and Devel. grantee, 1965-68. Mem. Soc. for Research in Child Devel., Am. Psychol. Assn., Psychonomic Soc., Cal. State Psychol. Assn., Orton Soc., Phi Beta Kappa, Sigma Xi. Home: 1020 San Mateo Dr Menlo Park CA 94025 Office: 520 Willow Rd Palo Alto CA 94304

ADAMS, RAMONA SHEPHERD (MRS. WENDELL ELLISON ADAMS), univ. dean; b. Paris, Ida., Dec. 17, 1921; d. Earl Budge and Jhoun (Chugg) Shepherd; B.A., U. Cal. at Berkeley, 1943; M.S.W., U. Utah, 1964, Ph.D., 1969; m. Wendell Ellison Adams, Dec. 26, 1941; children—Graig (dec.), Stanley Shepherd, John Shepherd, Ann Shepherd (Mrs. H. Brent Whitney), Douglas Shepherd, Richard Shepherd, Wendy Shepherd, Kathryn Shepherd. Asst. dir. pub. relations Henry J. Kaiser Co., Richmond, Cal., 1943-45; mem. social work staff Salt Lake City Bd. Edn., 1964-65; sr. staff, counseling center U. Utah, Salt Lake City, 1965-69, counseling psychologist, marriage and family counseling bur., 1969-70, asso. prof. Grad. Sch. Social Work, 1970, mem. staff Sch. on Alcoholism and Other Drug Dependencies, 1969—, asso. dean of students, 1970-73, dean student programming, 1973—. Lectr.; cons.; pvt. practice marriage and family counseling. Mem. adv. bd. Community Mental Health, Salt Lake City, 1970-72, UN, State of Utah, 1960-64. Recipient Mary E. Jarrett award Grad. Sch. Social Work, 1964. Mem. Nat. Assn. Social Workers, Acad. Certified Social Workers, Am. Assn. Marriage and Family Counselors, Nat. Assn. Women Deans, Adminstrs. and Counselors, Am., Utah personnel and guidance assns., Am. Psychol. Assn., Mortar Bd., Phi Beta Kappa, Alpha Gamma Sigma, Phi Kappa Phi, Delta Kappa Gamma. Home: 1727 Countryside Dr Salt Lake City UT 84106

ADAMSON, GRACE ELOISE, economist; b. Hampstead, N.B., Can., Sept. 30, 1912; d. Donald Allen and Lena Helen (Beckett) Adamson; B.S. in Commerce, Sir George Williams U., 1948; M.B.A., Boston U., 1953. Came to U.S., 1947, naturalized 1953. With Forest Service Govt. of N.B., Fredericton, 1931-41; asst. statistician Van Alstyne, Noel Investment Corp., N.Y.C., 1948-49; pvt. sec., statistician Burnham Corp., Irvington, N.Y., 1953-62; indsl. economist Dept. Labor, N.Y.C., 1963-66, Fed. Power Commn., 1966—. Mem. Am. Statis. Assn., Am. Econ. Assn., Am. Acad. Polit. and Social Sci., League Women Voters (unit chmn. 1967-69), Appalachian Mountain Club, Potomac Appalachian Trail Club, Canoe Cruisers Assn. Home: 950 25th St NW Washington DC 20037 Office: Union Center Plaza Bldg 825 N Capitol St NE Washington DC 20426

ADAMSON, JOY, conservationist, author, painter, illustrator; b. Troppau, Silesia, Jan. 20, 1910; d. Victor and Traute Gessner; ed. music, art, medicine Vienna, Austria, 1933-35; m. Victor von Klarwill, 1935; m. 2d, Peter Bally, 1938; m. 3d, George Adamson, 1943. Painter, illustrator, 1938—; researcher wild animals, 1956—; works exhibited Nat. Museum, Nairobi, Kenya, Tryon Gallery, Nairobi. author, 1958—. Head Elsa Wild Animal appeal, U.K., 1961, U.S., 1969, Can., 1971. Recipient Gold Grenfall medal Royal Hort. Soc., 1947; award merit (Czechoslovakia); Joseph Wood Krutch medal Humane Soc. U.S., 1971. Clubs: Nanyuki, Nairobi (Kenya). Author: Born Free: a lioness of two worlds, 1960 (film 1966); Elsa, The True Story of a Lioness, 1961; Living Free, 1961, 64 (film 1971); Forever Free, 1962, 66 (film 1971); Elsa and her Cubs, 1965; The Story of Elsa 1966; (also illustrator) The Peoples of Kenya, 1967; The Spotted Sphinx, 1969 (film 1970); Pippa's Challenge, 1972; Joy Adamson's Africa, 1972. Illustrator 7 bot. books. Contbr. articles to mags. Home: PO Box 254 Niavasha Kenya

ADAMSON, JUNE NEILSON (MRS. GEORGE M. ADAMSON, JR.), educator, journalist; b. Salt Lake City, June 30, 1922; d. Perry Neilson and Annie Lillias (Livingston) Neilson; student Brigham Young U., 1940-42; B.S., U. Tenn., 1969, M.S., 1971; m. George M. Adamson, Jr., July 18, 1942; children—Stanley D. (dec.), Neil Douglas. Free-lance publicist City of Oak Ridge, 1955-59; gen. assignment reporter The Oak Ridge (Tenn.) Newspaper, 1959-68; instr. Sch. Journalism, Coll. Communications, U. Tenn., Knoxville, 1970-73, asst. prof., 1973—. Mem., publicity dir. Oak Ridge Symphony, 1950-56, Oak Ridge Civic Music Assn., 1950-56. Mem. Tenn. Press Assn. (mem. com. 1972—), Phi Kappa Phi, Kappa Tau Alpha, Sigma Delta Chi, (adviser student chpt. U. Tenn. 1973—). Editor, pub. periodicals. Contbr. articles Christian Century, Christian Sci. Monitor. Home: 382 East Dr Oak Ridge TN 37830 Office: Sch Journalism Coll Communications U Tenn Knoxville TN 37916

ADAMSON, THELMA ELAINE, health services adminstr.; b. Flushing, N.Y., Dec. 3, 1935; d. Dudley Carlyle and Muriel Elaine (Farmer) Adamson; student Clark U., Worcester, Mass., 1954-55; B.S., Bucknell U., Lewisburg, Pa., 1957; M.P.H., U. Cal., Berkeley, 1970. Research chemist Cancer Research Lab., U. Va. Med. Sch., 1957-59; asst. benevole U. Geneva, Switzerland, 1959-60; asso. scientist Gen. Dynamics/Electric Boat, Groton, Conn., 1961-64; scientist Lockheed Missile & Space Co., Sunnyvale, Cal., 1964-68; asst. coordinator health services research unit, asso. specialist, evaluator nurse practitioner tng. program, lectr. community and ambulatory medicine U. Cal. at San Francisco, 1970—. Trustee, World Affairs Council No. Cal., 1969-71. Mem. A.A.A.S., Am. Pub. Health Assn. Democrat. Contbr. articles profl. jours. Home: 806 Dolores St San Francisco CA 94110 Office: U Cal 1319 3d Av San Francisco CA 94143

ADDISON, ANNE SIMONE POMEX (MRS. JOHN ADDISON), television exec.; b. Antwerp, Belgium, Dec. 2, 1927; d. Eli and Mary Deborah (Rubinstein) Cleeman; B.A., Barnard Coll., 1947; M.A., Columbia, 1952; m. Joseph B. Pomex, Mar. 6, 1947 (div. Apr. 1954); 1 son, Steven M. Pomex; m. 2d, John Addison, Sept. 1, 1966. Instr., Columbia, 1947-48; circulation dir. Ford Found., N.Y.C., 1952-58; asso. dir. Broadcasting Found. Am., radio, N.Y.C., 1958-60; dir. NET (WNET-13) TV internat. dir., 1960—. Cons. cultural dept. Dept. State, Washington, 1961. Bd. dirs. Coll. Skills, Inc., N.Y.C. Recipient awards, medals for fostering understanding and cultural cooperation, Austria, Belgium, Holland, Israel, Italy, Brazil. Mem. Am. Women Radio and TV (1st v.p. 1972—), Advt. Club Am., Am. Women in Communications. Contbr. articles to profl. jours. Home: 1035 Fifth Av New York City NY 10028 Office: 10 Columbus Circle New York City NY 10019

ADDISON, ELIZABETH RUTH HEYECK (MRS. LEWIS ERNEST ADDISON), librarian; b. Irvington, N.J., Feb. 11, 1929; d. Anthony John and Ruth Minnie (Van Ness) Heyeck; B.S., Trenton State Coll., 1952; M.L.S., Rutgers, 1959; postgrad. Rutgers, 1970-72, Montclair State Coll., 1970-71; m. Lewis Ernest Addison, Oct. 25, 1952. Childrens librarian Union (N.J.) Pub. Library, 1953-57; librarian Newark Bd. Edn., 1959-62, New Providence (N.J.), 1962—. Mem. N.E.A., N.J. Ednl. Assn., N.J. Sch. Media Assn., Union County Sch. Librarians Assn. (sec., treas. 1965-66). Presbyn. (chmn. com. 1959-60, elder 1974). Home: 25 Woodland Rd N Millington NJ 07946 Office: Hillview Sch 340 Central Av New Providence NJ 07974

ADDISON, PATRICIA CHARMIENNE YARWOOD, clergywoman, engrng. co. exec.; b. Newport, Ky., May 15, 1926; d. Clare George and Hannah Irene (Sargeant) Yarwood; A.B. in French, Wellesley Coll., 1947; grad. Program in Bus. Adminstrn., Harvard-Radcliffe, 1952; m. John Hastings Hughes, June 28, 1952 (div. July 1964); children—Charmienne Sargeant, John Forbes; m. 2d, Howard Willis Addison, Mar. 19, 1971. Mgr., Raffi Export-Import House, Cambridge, Mass., 1952-53; lighting designer, summer and winter stock theaters North Shore Music Circus, Beverley, Mass., Charles Playhouse, Boston, Poet's Theatre, Cambridge, Cambridge Drama Festival, 1957-64; resident lighting designer Bradford Dinner Theatre, Boston, also Tappan Zee Playhouse, Nyack, N.Y., 1960-62; resident lighting designer, actress Upstage Theatre, Miami, Fla., 1964—; profl. astrologer, 1960—; ordained to ministry Internat. Gen. Assembly Spiritualists, 1970; asst. pastor St. Peter's Ch., Opa-Locka, Fla., 1970—; v.p. Addison Engring. & Devel., Inc., Miami, 1973—. Mem. ministerial bd. Roosevelt Meml. Spiritual Benevolent Assn. Mem. Am. Fedn. Astrologers. Contbr. articles to Fla. Visitor Mag. Address: 210 Bal Cross Dr Bal Harbour FL 33154

ADELBERG, HELEN MIRIAM KOHN (MRS. MARVIN ADELBERG), physician; b. Bronx, N.Y., May 5, 1937; d. Nathan and Lillian (Pisnoy) Kohn; student Coll. City N.Y., 1959, U. Cal. at Los Angeles, 1959-60; M.D., U. S.C., 1964; m. Marvin Adelberg, Aug. 30, 1959; children—Diane, Kenneth. Intern, Los Angeles County-U. So. Cal. Med. Center, Los Angeles, 1964-65, now staff mem.; resident Cedars-Sinai Med. Center, Los Angeles, 1965-68; fellow in endocrinology U. So. Cal., 1968-69, now asst. in medicine; practice medicine specializing in internal medicine and endocrinology, Los Angeles, 1970—; mem. staffs Cedars of Lebanon, Mt. Sinai, Temple, Midway, Hollywood Presbyn hosps. (all Los Angeles), Sherman Oaks (Cal.) Community Hosp. Vice pres. Adelberg Research and Devel. Labs., Sherman Oaks; cons. on med.-hosp. devices and procedures to industry. Mem. A.M.A., Cal. Med. Assn., Los Angeles Soc. Internal Medicine, Diabetes Assn. So. Cal., Phi Delta Epsilon. Contbr. articles to med. jours. Home: 4043 Cody Rd Sherman Oaks CA 91403 Office: 321 N Larchmont Blvd Los Angeles CA 90004

ADELMAN, MARIA MILNER (MRS. JULIAN ADELMAN), physician; b. Gorki, U.S.S.R., Apr. 23, 1919; d. Joseph and Esther (Rummel) Milner; physician State Med. Inst., USSR, 1941; m. Julian Adelman, Apr. 30, 1947; children—Alexander, Joseph, Roma. Intern, Rybinsk, USSR, 1941; practice medicine specializing in pediatrics, 1947—, USSR, 1959, Wroclaw, Poland, 1959-61; with Wadley Research Inst., Dallas, 1962-68; resident pathology Meth. Hosp., Dallas, 1968-73. Served with USSR Army, 1941-46. Home: 7130 Aberdeen St Dallas TX 75230

ADEN, ESTELLE (MRS. PAUL ADEN), lectr.; b. Bklyn., Aug. 12, 1925; d. Victor and Anna (Gorenberg) Steinberg; B.A., Bklyn. Coll., 1947; M.A., Adelphi U., 1970; m. Paul Aden, Mar. 25, 1945; children—Vicki, Amy Judith. Lectr. drama dept. Hofstra U., 1970—; profl. performances of one-woman show storytelling at libraries, schs., 1964—; touring Eastern U.S. with lectures, readings poetry, theatre, 1964-69; tchr. dramatic, contemporary lit. Temple Beth-El, Great Neck, N.Y., 1969. Chmn. environmental studies Town Hempstead South (N.Y.) League Women Voters, 1958-60, bd. mem. 1960-69. Mem. Am. Theatre Assn., Speech Communication Assn. Mem. B'nai B'rith. Home: 980 Stanton Av Baldwin NY 11510 Office: Hofstra Playhouse Hempstead NY 11550

ADES, JANET, govt. ofcl.; b. Washington, July 26, 1938; d. Bernard and Mary Ethel (Hechler) Ades; B.A. (with honors) in English, City Coll. N.Y., 1959; M.S.W. (Nat. Inst. Mental Health fellow, 1962—, 63), N.Y. U., 1964. Dist. dir. for Upstate N.Y. Community Action Program Office Econ. Opportunity region I, N.Y.C., 1966-68; asst. prof. social work W.Va. U., Morgantown, 1969-71; dir. profl. services Planned Parenthood Assn., Chgo., 1971; asso. regional commr. Youth Devel. and Delinquency Prevention Services Dept. Health, Edn. and Welfare-Social and Rehab. Services region V, Chgo., 1971, regional program dir. Office Youth Devel., 1971—. Bd. mem. Monongalia County Comprehensive Health Planning Council. Mem. Am. Civil Liberties Union. Home: 536 W Deming Pl Chicago IL 60614 Office: 300 S Wacker Dr Chicago IL 60606

ADIX, SHAUNA MCLATCHY, educator; b. Salt Lake City, June 13, 1932; d. Frank B. and Charlotte (Ulke) McLatchy; B.A., U. Utah, 1953; M.A., Ohio U., Athens, 1958; m. Vern Adix, Mar. 1, 1957; children—David Matthew, Allison. Student activities adviser U. Utah, 1956-58; dir. Brighton (Utah) Camp, 1958-64; coordinator project on aging Community Services Council, Salt Lake City, 1966-68; with U. Utah, 1968—, dir. Women's Resource Center, 1971—, asst. prof. Grad. Sch. Social Work, 1972—. Dir. Behavioral Sci. Cons., Inc., 1972—. Mem. Nat. Assn. Women Deans, Adminstrs. and Counselors (regional adv. com.), Am. Assn. U. Women (corporate del.), Am. Assn. U. Profs. (chpt. dir.), U. Utah Alumni Assn. (v.p. 1967-69), Jr. League Salt Lake City, Mortar Bd. (nat. pres. 1970-73). Author children's plays. Home: 1532 Michigan Av Salt Lake City UT 84105

ADKINS, CATHERINE RUTH (MRS. JOHN FERGUSON ADKINS), realtor; b. Cambridge Springs, Pa., Dec. 18, 1907; d. Claude Taylor and Mary Emeline (Dyne) Reynolds; certificate U. Cal. at Los Angeles, 1964; m. John Ferguson Adkins, Aug. 24, 1933; children—Sharon Irene (Mrs. Anthony Magusin), Joyce Patricia (Mrs. Thomas Hernandez), Denis Hugh. Pres., mgr. Pickering Land Co., Inc., real estate tract sales and comml. devel., El Monte, Cal., 1964-68; sec. Pickering Enterprise, land developing and bldg., El Monte, 1961-66; owner San Gabriel Valley Escrow, Inc., El Monte, 1963—; owner, broker Adkins Realty, El Monte, 1961—. Active Boy Scouts Am., P.T.A. Mem. San Gabriel Valley Bd. Realtors (pres. woman's div. 1961, dir. 1969). Home: PO Box 141 El Monte CA 91734 Office: 2612 Mt View Rd El Monte CA 91734

ADKINS, ELIZABETH FRANCES, librarian; b. Richmond, Va., July 29, 1910; d. Thomas Eaton and Martha Elizabeth (Giesendoffer) Adkins; student Hollins Coll., 1928-30; B.S., U. Va., 1932; A.B. in L.S., U. N.C., 1938, postgrad., 1945-46. Cataloger, U. Va. Alderman Library, Charlottesville, 1938-41; librarian in charge Latin Am. materials U. N.C., Chapel Hill, 1942-46, cataloger, 1962-63, head tech. processes Med. Sch., Durham, 1962-63; librarian Army Ground Forces Hdqrs. Library, Ft. Monroe, Va., 1946-47; med. librarian U. Va. Med. Sch. Library, Charlottesville, 1947-62; librarian Scott & White Clinic, Temple, Tex., 1963—. Contbr. articles to profl. jours. Home: 818 S 27th St Apt 3 Temple TX 76501 Office: Scott and White Hosp Temple TX 76501

ADKISON, SHIRLEY FORESMAN (MRS. AUGUSTUS M. ADKISON), coll. adminstr.; b. Appleton, Wis., Nov. 26, 1924; d. Carl Earl and Meta (Lutgen) Foresman; B.A., Lawrence U., 1946; M.A., Mich. State U., 1947; postgrad. Montclaire State U., 1955-59, Rutgers U., 1957, N.Y. U., 1957-58, Boston U., 1968, Cal. State U., 1970; m. Augustus M. Adkison, Mar. 24, 1961; children—Augustus Scott, Lee Carl. Dir. drama Whitewater (Wis.) State U., 1947-48, Hockaday (Tex.) Jr. Coll., 1948-49; instr. English and drama Clifford Scott High Sch., East Orange, N.J., 1950-57; counselor Glen Rock (N.J.) High Sch., 1957-64; counselor Chipola Jr. Coll., Marianna, Fla., 1964-73, dir. student personal service, 1967-73, dir. counseling, 1973—. Residental chmn. Am. Cancer Crusade, Marianna, Fla., 1968-74; sec. Chipola Services Assn., 1971-72; pres. Golson Elementary Sch. P.T.A., 1973-74. Mem. steering com., council student affairs Fla. Jr. Colls., 1972-73, council deans students, 1967-73. Mem. Nat. Def. Edn. Act Inst., Boston U., 1959; Ednl. Profl. Devel. Act Inst., Cal. Tech. Los Angeles, 1970. Mem. Fla. Assn. Community Colls., Fla. Personnel and Guidance Assn., Chipola Services Assn. (sec. 1971-72), Pi Beta Phi. Episcopalian. Republican. Clubs: Pilot of Marianna (pres. 1971); Pilot International (mem. internat. compass club com. 1972). Home: 1703 College St Marianna FL 32446

ADLER, ALICE JOAN SALZMAN (MRS. DAVID ADLER), biochemist; b. Jersey City, Dec. 8, 1935; d. Harmon Theodore and Ruth (Spector) Salzman; B.A., Barnard Coll., 1956; Ph.D. (NSF pre-doctoral fellow), Harvard, 1961; m. David Adler, June 8, 1958; children—Kyle, Andrew, Carrie. NIH postdoctoral fellow Children's Cancer Research Found., Boston, 1961-62, Mass. Inst. Tech., Cambridge, 1962-64; research asso. Oxford U., 1965; sr. research asso. Brandeis U., Waltham, Mass., 1966—. Mem. Am. Chem. Soc., Biophys. Soc., A.A.A.S. Contbr. articles in field to chem. jours. Research on phys. properties of biol. macromolecules. Home: 8 Welch Rd Lexington MA 02173 Office: Biochem Dept Brandeis U Waltham MA 02154

ADLER, ELIZABETH THOMPSON (MRS. MILTON P. ADLER), civic worker; b. South Bend, Ind., Sept. 16, 1914; d. David Headley and Emma (Crawford) Thompson; B.S. in Phys. Edn. and Psychology, U. Wis., 1937; postgrad. Purdue U., 1934-35; m. Milton Pokorny Adler, Dec. 28, 1938; children—Ruth Louise (Mrs. Phillip Ruder), Coleman E. II. Instr. phys. edn. Sophie Newcomb Coll., New Orleans, 1937-38, McMain High Sch., New Orleans, 1938-39; supr. Dr. Alton Ochsner Cancer Clinic, Charity Hosp., New Orleans, 1946-49; mem. Touro Infirmary Bd. Aux., 1947-48; mem. citizenship awards com. Orleans Parish Sch. Bd., 1947-57, chmn., 1950-56; mem. vol. administrv. bd. Charity Hosp., 1947-50; life mem. Sara Mayo Hosp. Guild, 1953—, bd. dirs., 1961-62; exec. com. Nat. Conf. Christians and Jews, 1950, bd. dirs., 1951-61; mem. House of Detention Bd., City of New Orleans, 1951-54; mem. health edn. com. New Orleans YWCA, 1939-41, bd. dirs., 1939-52, v.p., 1948 pres., 1949-52, chmn. reconstrn. fund dr., 1947, del. regional conf., Atlanta, 1948, chmn. Y-Teens com., 1947-48, del. nat. conv., San Francisco, 1949, mem. resolutions com., 1949, del. regional conf., Houston, 1950, mem. nat. conv. com., discussion leader, 1950, del. nat. conv., Chgo., 1952, mem. centennial planning com., 1952-55, del. Y-Teen planning conf., Jackson, Miss., 1950, dean discussion leadership tng. conf. Gulf Park (Miss.) Coll., 1951-53, mem. nat. support com., 1948-53, rep. from La. to nat. bd. for centennial, 1952-55; chmn. New Orleans Com. Race Relations, 1952-53; mem. Tulane-Lyceum Assn. Bd., 1951-61, financial sec., 1954-59, treas., 1960-61; chmn. speakers bur. Mother's March on Polio, 1952; vice chmn. campaign United Fund, 1954; chmn. citizens com. services to children Dept. Pub. Welfare, 1954-61; mem. La. com. White House Conf. Children and Youth, 1959-60, La. del., 1960, exec. com., 1960; bd. dirs. Urban League, 1955-61; chmn. Eisenhower Birthday Dinner Celebration, 1956; chmn. women's div. pub. and pvt. schs. U.S. Treasury Bond Drive, 1957-58; hospitality chmn. Brandeis U. Area Conf., 1957; bd. dirs. inst. com. Community Vol. Service, 1952; hospitality chmn. Nat.

and La. Conf. Social Work conv., New Orleans, 1953; v.p. bd. lay regents Xavier U., 1959, pres. 1960-61; bd. dirs. DePaul Hosp. Guild, 1961-69; mem. New Coll. Library Com., Sarasota, Fla.; mem. bd. Fed. Housing Authority, Ft. Myers, 1966-69, Girl Scouts U.S.A., 1965-67; pres. Blue Water Forest Assn., 1971-72; mem. Central Fla. Regional Library Bd., 1971-73; chmn. bd. trustees Context Industries Library Scholarship Fund, 1973—. Free lance writer-photographer, 1973—. Recipient Merit certificate for distinguished service to City of New Orleans, from mayor of New Orleans. Mem. D.A.R., Needlework Guild Am., League Women Voters, Women's Auxiliary New Orleans C. of C. Presbyn. Contbr. poetry to Caravan of Verse, An Anthology, 1949. Club: Sanibel-Captiva Shell Club (v.p. 1965-66). Home: Blue Waters Box 515 Homosassa Springs FL 32647

ADLER, EVA, child psychiatrist; b. Cluj, Romania, Sept. 3, 1926; d. Sigismund and Rosalia (Jakober) Adler; M.D., U. Rome (Italy), 1952. Came to U.S., 1955, naturalized, 1961. Intern, N.Y. Infirmary, N.Y.C., 1956; resident Grasslands Hosp., Valhalla, N.Y., 1957-59; fellow child psychiatry Mt. Sinai Hosp., N.Y.C., 1959-60; staff psychiatrist Union County Psychiat. Clinic, Elizabeth, N.J., 1960-62; staff, children's unit Creedmoor State Hosp., Queens Village, N.Y., 1964-71; staff Rockland Children's Psychiat. Hosp., Orangeburg, N.Y., 1971-72, Rockland State Hosp., 1972—; child psychiatry cons. Greystone Park Psychiat. Hosp., Morris Plains, N.J., 1966—; practice child psychiatry, Haworth, N.J., 1971—. Mem. Am. Psychiat. Assn. Address: 107 Maple St Haworth NJ 07641

ADLER, LETA MCKINNEY, sociologist, educator; b. Lincoln, Neb., Mar. 17, 1920; d. James G. and Leta (Linn) McKinney; B.A., U. Cal. at Los Angeles, 1942; M.A. State Coll. Wash., 1946; Ph.D., U. Wis., 1958; m. Franz Adler, May 9, 1943 (div. 1964); children—James, Debora Linn. Tchr., analyst, various colls. and War Dept., 1942-47, 49-52; recipient pre-doctoral fellowship Nat. Inst. Mental Health, USPHS, 1956; instr. U. Cal. Med. Center Sch. of Nursing, Los Angeles, 1958-59; asso. social research technician Statis. Research Bur., State Dept. Mental Hygiene, 1959-60; asst. research educationist dept. edn. U. Cal. at Los Angeles, 1960-61; research asso. to asso. prof. psychiatry (sociology) Sch. Medicine, U. So. Cal., 1961-69; research coordinator Los Angeles County Dept. Hosps., 1969-70; prof. sociology Cal. State Coll., San Bernardino, 1970-72; prof. med. edn. So. Ill. U. Sch. Medicine, Springfield, 1972—. Fellow Am. Sociol. Assn.; mem. Assn. Am. Med. Colls., Phi Beta Kappa, Pi Gamma Mu, Alpha Kappa Delta. Author: Help the Patient Tell His Story, 1971; also articles in field; contbr. to Mental Health and Mental Disorder, 1955, Effective Psychotherapy, 1965, Interviewing and Patient Care, 1972. Office: Sch Medicine Southern Ill U PO Box 3926 Springfield IL 62708

ADLER, MYRIL (MRS. JACK ADLER), artist, art tchr., printmaker; b. Vitebsk, Russia, Sept. 22, 1920; came to U.S., 1923, naturalized, 1943; d. Sam and Sarah (Pakul) Stangen; student Art Students League, N.Y.C., 1937-38, Theatre Arts Workshop, N.Y.C., 1938-39, Atelier Moi Solotaroff, 1939-44, Pratt Graphics Center, N.Y.C., 1960-64; m. Jack Adler, Oct. 18, 1941; children—David, Sharon. Exhibited in one-man shows at Gallerie Bernheim Jeune, Paris, 1950, Casa Municipale, Merano, Italy, 1952, Royal Athena II Gallery, N.Y.C., 1964, Hudson River Mus., Yonkers, N.Y., 1972, Westbroadway Gallery, N.Y.C., 1973; exhibited in group shows at Salon de Mai, Salon des Femmes Peintres, Paris, 1950, USIS traveling exhbn., France, Germany, N. Africa, 1950, 51, Pan Am. Bldg., N.Y.C., Salute to 1965, Internat. Miniature Print Show, Audubon Artists, N.Y.C., 1970, 71; represented in permanent collections at Mus. Modern Art, Caracas, Venezuela, U. Cal. at Berkeley, U. R.I., Hudson River Mus. Organizer, dir. art program Hawthorne (N.Y.) Cedar Knolls Sch., 1953-56; tchr. art for children and adults, Briarcliff Manor, N.Y., 1956—; organizer monthly exhibits internat. graphic artists Briarcliff Pub. Library, 1963-67; chmn. local com. Rescue Italian Art, 1967; chmn. Citizens Com. Recreation, Briarcliff Manor, 1960; adv. com. Pratt Graphic Center, 1967. Recipient 1st prize graphics and sculpture Artists No. Westchester Juried Ann., 1968, 1st prize, 1969; Claude Gallery award, purchase award Yonkers Art Assn., 1970, Camhi Graphics award, 1971. Mem. Westchester Art Soc. (bd. dirs. 1969-71), Yonkers Art Assn., Nat. Assn. Women Artists. Home: 266 Dalmeny Rd Briarcliff Manor NY 10510

ADLERBLUM, NIMA H., author; b. Jerusalem, Palestine, Aug. 4, 1886; d. Hayyim and Eva (Hakohen) Hirschensohn; brought to U.S., 1904; student Barnard Coll., also Paris, France; Ph.D., Columbia, 1926; m. Israel S. Adlerblum, Apr. 9, 1914; 1 dau., Ivria (Mrs. Alexander H. Sackton). Founder, mem. Am. Com. Translation and Dissemination John Dewey's and Am. Philosophy in Latin Am., chmn. internat. com. to celebrate John Dewey's birthday, 1949; also translation and dissemination Am. works in philosophy of edn.; founder Hadassah Nat. Cultural work (chmn. nat. com., mem. nat. bd. 1920-33); founder Exchange of Thought Movement, Am. and European scholars, 1920; research work throughout Europe, Near East for studying problems of minority nationalities, Latin Am. for intercultural relationship and immigration of refugees. Fellow Internat. Inst. Arts and Letters (life); mem. Am. Philos. Assn., Inter-Am. Congress Philosophy (elected editor of contemplated edit. of Contemporary Philos. Tendencies throughout the World), Internat. Congress of Philosophy, Hadassah, many other orgns. Author: A Study of Gersonides in his Proper Perspective, 1926; A Perspective of Jewish Life through its Festivals, 1930 (transcribed into Braille); Memoirs of Childhood in Guardians of Our Heritage, 1958; also biographies. Contbr. chpt. to Men of the Spirit; other chpts. in various publs., articles in philos. jours. Home: Sharon Hotel Hezila Israel

ADREON, BEATRICE MARIE RICE (MRS. HARRY BARNES ADREON, JR.), pharmacist; b. Huntington, W.Va., July 23, 1929; d. Lloyd Emerson and Beatrice (Odell) Rice; student Mary Washington Coll., 1947-49; B.S. in Pharmacy, Med. Coll. Va., 1952; postgrad. George Washington U., 1958-59, 73—; m. Harry Barnes Adreon, Jr., Dec. 27, 1952. Summer vol. worker pharmacies De Paul Hosp., Norfolk, Va., 1949, U.S. Marine Hosp., Norfolk, 1950; pharmacist Washington Clinic, 1954-69; cons. medicine control, traffic patterns nursing home designs Cross & Adreon, Washington, 1962—; asst. treas., dir. Auto World, Inc., New Bern, N.C. Instr. advanced first aid A.R.C., 1952—, civil def. instr., 1952—; vol. Spanish Edn. Devel. Center, Washington, 1972. Mem. Acad. Gen. Practice Pharmacy, Am. Pharm. Assn., A.A.A.S., Panhellenic Assn., Kappa Epsilon. Republican. Episcopalian (mem. bishop's com. neighborhood services 1967-69, chmn. services for aged div. 1967-69). Home: 4524 N 19th Rd Arlington VA 22207

ADRIAN, BARBARA (MRS. FRANKLIN C. TRAMUTOLA), artist; b. N.Y.C., July 25, 1931; d. Allen Issac and Mildred (Brown) Adrian; student Art Students League, 1947-54, Hunter Coll., 1951, Columbia Sch. Gen. Study, 1952-54; m. Franklin C. Tramutola, July 26, 1972. Art cons. Doyle-Dane-Bernbach, advt. agy., 1960, A. H. Macy, N.Y.C., 1960-61, Saks Fifth Avenue, 1960, Black, Starr & Gorham, 1960; instr. art workshop, Jamaica, N.Y., 1958-59; pvt. tchr. art, 1960—; instr. Art Students League N.Y., 1968—. One-man shows Gallery, 1957, San Juan P.R., 1951, Grippi Gallery, N.Y.C., 1963, Banfer Gallery, N.Y.C., 1966; exhibited in group shows G Gallery, 1955-59, City Center Gallery, N.Y.C., 1954, N.Y.C. Festival, 1957, Portland (Me.) Mus., 1958, Worshop Gallery, N.Y.C., 1959, Grippi Gallery, 1960-63, Lane Gallery, Cal., 1962-63, Mus. Gallery, Lubbock, Tex., 1962-63, The Gallery, Norwalk, O., 1962, Gallery 777, Plainview, L.I., N.Y., 1963, N.A.D., 1963, Butler Inst., Youngstown, O., 1963, U. Miami, 1968, Orr's Gallery, San Diego, 1968, Child Hassam Fund Purchase Exhbn., 1968, Gallery of Modern Art, N.Y.C., 1969, Eileen Kulicke Gallery, N.Y.C., 1973; represented in permanent collections Grippi Gallery, Summer Found., Butler Inst., McMay Mus., San Antonio, Corcoran Gallery, Washington; also pvt. collections in U.S., P.R., Mexico; represented by Kenmore Galleries, Phila., Capricorn Gallery, Washington, Eileen Kulick Gallery, N.Y.C. Recipient Benjamin Altman Figure prize N.A.D., 1968. Mem. Artists Equity of N.Y., Pen and Brush. Address: 420 E 64th St New York City NY 10021

ADRIAN, MARY (MRS. HENRY JORGENSEN), author; b. Sewickley, Pa.; d. George Charles and Claire (Adrian) Venn; student N.Y.U., 1935-36; m. Henry G. Jorgensen, Nov. 10, 1957. Author: Refugee Hero, 1957; Garden Spider, 1951; Honeybee, 1952; Fiddler Crab, 1953; Gray Squirrel, 1955; American Eagle, 1963; American Alligator, 1967; American Prairie Chicken, 1968; A Day and a Night in a Forest, 1967; A Day and a Night in the Arctic, 1970; American Mustang, 1964; North American Wolf, 1965; North American Bighorn Sheep, 1966; Ghost Town Mystery, 1971; Secret Neighbors, 1972; A Day and a Night in a Tide Pool, 1972; numerous others. Mem. Am. Ornithologists Union, Nat. Audubon Soc., Nat. Wildlife Fedn., Am. Nat. Womens Book Assn. Home: 1000 SW Vista Av Portland OR 97205

ADWON, SAIDIE, TV sta. exec.; b. Wilson, Okla.; d. Addy Nicholas and Rosa (Mettry) Adwon; student Oklahoma City U., 1936-38. Publicity dir., box office mgr. Okla. State Symphony Soc., 1939-45; account exec. KTUL radio, 1948-54, KTUL-TV, Tulsa, 1954—. Chmn. nursing edn. com. Hillcrest Hosp., 1966-68. Named Advertising Man of Year, 1968. Mem. Tulsa C. of C. (charter awareness com. 1973, communications council 1974), Am. Women in Radio and TV (pres. Okla. chpt. 1956-58, nat. v.p. 1962-64, Woman of Year, Southwestern area 1964), Advt. Club Tulsa (pres. 1972-73), Am. Advt. Fedn. (dir. 10th dist. 1972—). Unitarian (finance com.). Club: Quota of Tulsa (past pres.). Home: 6828 E 57th Pl Tulsa OK 74145 Office: PO Box 8 Tulsa OK 74101

AFF-DRUM, HELEN MARGARET, physician; b. St. Louis, 1908; M.D., Washington U., St. Louis, 1934. Intern St. Louis Children's Hosp., 1934-35, Harriet Lane Home for Invalid Children, Johns Hopkins Hosp., 1935-36; asst. chief resident physician Children's Hosp., Phila., 1936-37, asst. chief resident physician in charge outpatient dept., 1937-38; asst. prof. clin. pediatrics Washington U.; mem. pediatric staff St. Louis Children's Hosp., St. Louis Maternity Hosp.; cons. staff St. Louis County Children's Chest Clinic; sch. physician, Clayton, Mo.; pres. Listen Inn Counseling Service, 1973—; instr. pediatrics U. Pa., 1936-38. Mem. St. Louis County Narcotics Commn., 1968-73, St. Louis County Adv. Com. Drug Abuse, 1974—. Bd. dirs. TB and Respiratory Disease Soc., 1967—. Diplomate Am. Bd. Pediatrics. Mem. Am. Acad. Pediatrics, Am. Thoracic Soc., Mo., St. Louis County med. socs., St. Louis Pediatric Soc., Valley Park, Warrenton child health confs., Alpha Omega Alpha. Office: 1412 Spoede Rd St Louis MO 63131

AFRICK, LENORE JEAN PETCHAFT (MRS. HYMAN AFRICK), librarian; b. Oak Park, Ill., Aug. 17, 1922; d. Bernard and Rae (Barnett) Petchaft; B.S. magna cum laude, Beloit Coll., 1943; m. Hyman Africk, Aug. 1, 1954. Chem. research librarian Armour Auxs., Chgo., 1943-60, Armour Indsl. Chem. Co., McCook, 1961-70, Armak Co., McCook, 1971—. Mem. Am. Soc. Information Sci., Am. Chem. Soc., Spl. Libraries Assn. (Ill. pres. 1953-54), Phi Beta Kappa, Phi Sigma Iota. Mem. B'nai B'rith. Editor Soap and Detergent Abstracts, Jour. Am. Oil Chemists Soc., 1944-60. Home: 11024 Nelson St Westchester IL 60153 Office: 8401 W 47th St McCook IL 60525

AGER, ALMA CHAMBERS, educator, psychologist; b. Birmingham, Ala., Jan. 9; d. James Richard and E. Clyde (Garrett) Chambers; A.B., Columbia Union Coll., 1944; A.M., U. Redlands, 1960; Ph.D., U. So. Cal., 1967. Tchr. sci. Garden State Acad., 1945-56; asst. dept. pharmacology Sch. Medicine, Loma Linda (Cal.) U., 1956-64; research asso. U. So. Cal., Los Angeles, 1965; chmn. dept. behavioral scis. So. Missionary Coll., Collegedale, Tenn., 1965-72; psychologist intern VA Hosp., Brockton, Mass., 1972-73; psychologist VA Center, Hot Springs, S.D., 1973—. Mem. Am., S.D. psychol. assns., Assn. Advancement Behavior Therapy, Psi Chi, Pi Lambda Theta. Home: PO Box 293 Belle Fourche SD 57717

AGER, PHYLLIS JOYCE, physician; b. Bklyn., Dec. 14, 1943; d. Joseph S. and Esther (Weinman) Ager; B.S., U. Miami, 1963, M.D., 1967. Intern L.I. Coll. Hosp., Bklyn., 1967-68; resident in diagnostic radiology Roosevelt Hosp., N.Y.C., 1968-69; resident in diagnostic and therapeutic radiology Einstein-Jacobi Hosp., N.Y.C., 1969-72; attending radiologist Meml. Hosp., N.Y.C., 1973—; mem. faculty Cornell Med. Sch. Diplomate Am. Bd. Radiology. Mem. Radiol. Soc. N.Am., Am. Coll. Radiology, Am. Soc. Therapeutic Radiology, N.Y. Roentgen Soc., Am. Soc. Clin. Oncology. Home: 165 West End Av New York City NY 10023 Office: Meml Hosp 1275 York Av New York City NY 10021

AGGER, CAROLYN E. (MRS. ABE FORTAS), lawyer; b. N.Y.C., May 27, 1909; d. Eugene Ewald and May (Hessler) Agger; B.A., Barnard Coll., 1931; M.A., U. Wis., 1932; LL.B., Yale, 1938; m. Abe Fortas, July 9, 1935. Admitted to D.C. bar, 1938; atty. U.S. Dept. Justice, 1934-43; asso. firm Lord, Day & Lord, 1943-46; asso. and partner Stevenson, Paul, Rifkind, Wharton & Garrison, 1946-60; partner Arnold & Porter, Washington, 1960—. Dir. Madison Nat. Bank. Trustee Found. for Preservation of Historic Georgetown; trustee, treas. Soc. for a More Beautiful Capitol. Mem. Fed., Am. bar assns, D.C. Bar Assn., Order of Coif. Home: 3210 R St NW Washington DC 20007 Office: Arnold & Porter 1229 19th St NW Washington DC 20036

AGLER, BETTY HEUSCH, fraternity exec., civic leader; b. Chgo.; d. Elbert L. and Lilie (Goebel) Heusch; B.S., U. Cin.; postgrad. U. Ill. at Champaign, 1934-35; children—McClellan H., Linda Anne. Mem. emergency relief staff Franklin County (O.) Welfare, 1935; mem. disaster staff Nat. A.R.C., 1936-40; supr. office Franklin County Ct. House, 1940-42; demonstrator Frigidaire Co., 1953-60; exec. dir. U.S.O. Council, Columbus, O., 1965-69. Pres. Mifflin Schs. P.T.A., 1952-56; mem. Mifflin Twp. Bd. Edn., 1958-62, v.p., 1960-62; active Ohio council Girl Scouts U.S.A.; mem. Armed Forces Community Council. Bd. dirs. Hearing and Speech Center, Columbus. Mem. Delta Zeta (nat. dir. philanthropies, 1958-60, nat. v.p., 1960-66, nat. pres., 1966-70, exec. sec. 1969—). Home: 895 Manor Lane Columbus OH 43221 Office: 21 E State St Columbus OH 43215

AGNES, CAROL JOAN, coll. adminstr.; b. Anneston, Ala., Jan. 12, 1945; d. John Everett and Geneva Mary (Gass) A.; B.S., Coll. St. Catherine, St. Paul, 1967; M.S., St. Cloud (Minn.) State Coll., 1973—. Girls phys. edn. instr. Hazel Park Jr. High Sch., St. Paul Pub. Schs., 1967-72; recreation and student activities coordinator, phys. edn. instr., head coach volleyball and basketball, Coll. St. Benedict, St. Joseph, Minn., 1972—. Girl Scout camp staff, camp dir. Sioux Trails council, Sioux City, Ia., 1963-64, St. Croix Valley, St. Paul, 1965-67, Bangor, Me., 1968, Boise, Ida., 1969-72, council leader St. Croix Valley, 1967-68, campus scout adviser, 1967-72, scout leader trainer, 1970-72; outdoor edn. field summer supr. San Francisco State U., 1972. Mem. A.A.H.P.E.R. (outdoor edn. and camping council 1973), N.E.A., Minn. Edn. Assn., Am. Camping Assn., Coll. St. Catherine Alumni Assn. Roman Catholic. Club: Seratoma (Service award Sioux City 1963). Home: 109 12th St Sioux City IA 51103 Office: Coll St Benedict St Joseph MN 56374

AGNEW, JEANNE LECAINE (MRS. THEODORE AGNEW, JR.), educator; b. Port Arthur, Ont., Can., May 3, 1917; d. Hubert Clarence and Susie Elma (Smith) LeCaine; B.A., Queen's U., Kingston, Ont., 1937, M.A. (Marty Meml. fellow), 1938; Ph.D., Radcliffe Coll., 1941; m. Theodore L. Agnew, Jr., Dec. 25, 1942; children—Theodore Agnew III, Susan Elizabeth (Mrs. Edward L. Dollmeyer), Hugh LeCaine, Peter Wallace, Marion Jeanne. Traveling fellow Canadian Fedn. U. Women, 1939; instr. Smith Coll., 1941-42; jr. research physicist NRC Can., 1942-46; asst. prof. math. Okla. State U., Stillwater, 1956-62, asso. prof., 1962-69, prof., 1969—. Vis. asso. prof. Ga. State Coll., 1966-67. Named Outstanding Tchr., Okla. State U. Alumni Assn., Blue Key, 1964. Mem. Math. Assn. Am., Am. Math. Soc., Phi Beta Kappa, Sigma Xi, Pi Mu Epsilon. Methodist. Author: Explorations in Number Theory, 1972. Contbr. articles to profl. jours. Home: 1216 N Lincoln St Stillwater OK 74074

AGRESS, ELLEN SHAW (MRS. HARRY AGRESS JR.), lawyer; b. N.Y.C., May 20, 1947; d. David Samuel and Vivian Rosalind (Rosenthal) Shaw; student Coll. City N.Y., 1964-65; B.A. with honors, U. Mich., 1968; J.D., Harvard, 1971; m. Harry Agress Jr., Nov. 12, 1972. Admitted to Mass. bar, 1971, N.Y., D.C. bars, 1973; asso. Hale & Dorr, Boston, 1971-72, Paul, Weiss, Rifkind, Wharton & Garrison, N.Y.C., 1972-73; atty. Citizens Communications Center, Washington, 1973—. Mem. Phi Beta Kappa. Home: 12513 Winexburg Manor Dr Silver Spring MD 20906 Office: 1914 Sunderland Place NW Washington DC 20036

AGUILERA, DONNA CONANT (MRS. GEORGE LIMON AGUILERA), nurse educator; b. Kinmundy, Ill.; d. Charles E. and Daisy L. (Frost) Conant; R.N., Gordon Keller Sch. Nursing, 1947; A.A., Los Angeles Valley Coll., 1960; B.S., U. Cal. at Los Angeles, 1963, M.S., 1965; Ph.D., U. So. Cal., 1974; m. George Limon Aguilera, Feb. 17, 1948; children—Bruce Allen, Craig Steven. Teaching asst. U. Cal. at Los Angeles, 1965, grad. research asst., 1965-66; asso. prof. nursing edn. Cal. State U., Los Angeles, 1966—. Nurse-cons. crisis intervention Benjamin Rush Center, Venice, Cal., 1967—; NIH fellow U. So. Cal., 1972—; originator, project dir. Project Link, Lab. for Ind. Nursing Knowledge, Cal. State U. Mem. Am. Nurses' Assn., Nat. League Nursing, Faculty Women's Assn., Am. Assn. U. Profs., Alpha Tau Delta. Career tchr. appointee Nat. Inst. Mental Health, 1965-66. Author: Crisis Intervention: Theory and Methodology, 1970. Contbr. articles profl. publs. Home: 3924 Dixie Canyon Av Sherman Oaks CA 91403 Office: Cal State U 5151 State University Dr Los Angeles CA 90032

AHERN, ARLEEN FLEMING (MRS. GEORGE IRVING AHERN), librarian; b. Mt. Harris, Colo., Oct. 15, 1922; d. John R. and Josephine (Vidmar) Fleming; B.A., U. Utah, 1943; M.A., U. Denver, 1962; postgrad. U. Colo., 1967; m. George Irving Ahern, June 14, 1944; 1 son, George Irving. Library asst. Army Air Force Library, Salt Lake City, 1943-44; library asst. Colo. Woman's Coll. Library, Denver, 1952-60, acquisitions librarian, 1960—, rep. Adult Edn. Council Denver, 1960—. Committeewoman, Republican Com., Denver, 1958-59. Mem. Am., Mountain Plains, Colo. (1st v.p., pres. 1969-70, dir. 1971—) library assns., Altrusa Club of Denver (2d v.p. 1968-69, dir. 1971-74), Soc. Am. Archivists, Mountain Plains Adult Edn. Assn., Am. Assn. U. Profs. Home: 746 Monaco Pkwy Denver CO 80220 Office: 7055 E 18th Av Denver CO 80220

AHL, FRANCES NORENE, author; b. Santa Rosa, Cal.; d. Jacob and Minnie (Huff) Ahl; A.B., U. Cal. at Berkeley, M.A.; postgrad. U. So. Cal., 1935-36, 48-49. Author: Andrew Jackson and the Constitution, 1939, Wings over South America, 1939, Let's Fly, 1940, Two Thousand Miles Up the Amazon, 1941, Audio-Visual Materials in the High School, 1946, New Zealand Through American Eyes, 1948, Wings over the Congo, 1956. Mem. Republican State Central Com. Cal.; chmn. study hour Rep. Women's Study Club, 1962-73, also hon. life mem.; chmn. constn. and govt. com. Cal. Fedn. Rep. Women. Recipient Freedoms Found. medal, 1955, 57, 59, 62, Mem. Am. Assn. U. Women, So. Cal. Social Sci. Assn. (pres. 1957-59), Women's Civic League (coordinator study group 1961-62, pres. 1963-64, named Woman of Year 1963), Internat. Platform Assn., Americanism Edn. League (speakers bur.), Kappa Delta (nat. editor 1951-53), Pi Gamma Mu, Delta Kappa Gamma. Conglist. Writer numerous mag. articles; lectr. Home: 1631 Ramona Av Glendale CA 91208

AHLANDER, LESLIE JUDD, mus. curator; b. N.Y.C., May 13, 1915; d. Arthur Curtis and Edith M. (Henley) Judd; B.F.A., Pa. Acad., 1939; m. Robert Portner, Nov. 1946 (div. Aug. 1956); m. 2d, Björn Ahlander, Jan. 31, 1958 (div. Nov. 1968); children—Henley (Mrs. William Snyder), Robert Portner. Asst. to dir. Mus. of Modern Art, N.Y.C., 1940-43; exhibits specialist U.S. Office of Edn., Washington, 1944; art dir. Pan-Am. Union, Washington, 1945; art critic Washngton Post, 1948-61; curator edn. Corcoran Gallery, Washington, 1968-69; dir. edn. Ringling Mus., Sarasota, Fla., 1970-73, curator, 1973—. Mem. Coll. Art Assn. (critics awards 1952, 53). Home: 810 Plymouth St Sarasota FL 33581 Office: Ringling Museum of Art Sarasota FL 33578

AHLGREN, MILDRED CARLSON (MRS. OSCAR ALEXANDER AHLGREN), club woman, lectr., writer, pub. relations cons.; b. Chgo.; d. August John and Hilda Sophia (Peterson) Carlson; student Columbia Coll., U. Chgo.; m. Oscar Alexander Ahlgren, June 6, 1923; 1 dau., Adrienne (Mrs. Charles Haeuser). Spl. corr. Hammond (Ind.) Times 1935-52. Pres. Ind. Fedn. Women's Club, 1941-44; dean of dirs., mem. exec. com. Gen. Fedn. Women's Clubs, 1943-44, rec. sec., 1944-47, 2d v.p., 1947-50, 1st v.p., 1950-52, pres., 1952-54; nat. sponsoring com. Allied Youth; nat. adv. com., pub. relations panel Savs. Bonds, U.S. Treasury; mem. Planning Commn. Indiana State, 1941-43. Personnel Bd., 1943-46; chmn. women's div. Ind. War Finance Com., 1940-46; chmn. women's com. Ind. War History Commn., 1945-48; mem. Ind. com. George Foster Peabody radio awards; mem. Govs. Com. of Children and Youth. Chmn. Women's Nat. Com. Savings Bonds; mem. nat. planning com. White House Conf. on Edn., 1953-54; asst. to dir. U.S. Savs. Bonds Div., Treas. Dept., 1955-57; pub. relations cons.; observer food gift program FOA Austria, 1953; ruling elder Nat. Presbyn. Ch. Trustee Ind. State Employes Retirement Fund, 1949-52, Ind. State Tchrs. Colls., 1952-58; bd. Ind. Inst. Psychiat. Research: trustee Radio Liberty Com.; v.p. All Am. Conf. Nat. co-chmn. Women for Nixon and Lodge, 1960. Recipient Royal Order of Vasa (Sweden), 1954, George Washington medal Freedoms Found., 1954, 70, Hoosier Halo, Hammond Newspaper Guild, 1953; numerous other honors and awards; named Ind. woman of year Theta Sigma Phi, 1952. Mem. Nat. Fedn. Press Women, Nat. League Am. Penwomen, Bus. and Profl. Women's Am. Legion Aux., Am. Women in Radio and Television, Women in Communications, Scandinavian Found. (hon.), League

Women Voters, P.E.O., Alpha Delta Pi, Phi Beta, Beta Gamma Epsilon. Republican. Presbyn. Clubs: San Antonio Breakfast: Chautauqua (N.Y.) Woman's: Ind. Harbor (Ind.) Women's (hon.); Ind. Women's Press; Whiting (Ind.) Woman's (hon. life, dir.); Nat. Press (Washington); Lake Hills Country; Am. Newspaper Women's (Washington); Washington. Research on status of women, S.Am., 1950, W.I. and Alaska, 1953, Russia, 1956, 71. Home: Dupont East 1545 18th St NW Washington DC 20036 Office: 1734 N St NW Washington DC 20036

AHLSTROM, FAE TERRY, dentist; b. Rockville, Utah, Jan. 1, 1917; d. Marvin David and Lamar (Timothy) Terry; Asso. Sci., Dixie Jr. Coll., St. George, Utah, 1936; D.D.S., U. So. Cal., 1941; m. Jack Evans Ahlstrom, July 3, 1941 (dec. 1969); children—Daniel, Robert, Jacqueline; m. 2d, Victor Henacaro, Dec. 25, 1973. Practice pediatric dentistry, Las Vegas, Nev., 1946—. Councilor Pacific Coast Dental Conf., 1960-63; mem. Nev. Bd. Dental Examiners, 1971—. Chmn. Clark County Dist. Bd. Health, Nev., 1969-70, 70-71; bd. dirs. Nev. Heart Assn., 1963-70. Diplomate Am. Bd. Pedodontists. Fellow Internat., Am. colls. dentists; mem. Clark County Dental Soc. (pres. 1960-61), Nev. Dental Assn. (pres. 1962-63), Am. Acad. Pedodontists, Assn. Pedodontic Diplomates (pres. 1969-70), Acad. Dentistry Handicapped, Am. Soc. Dentistry for Children (mem. exec. council 1967-72), Assn. Am. Women Dentists (pres. 1969-70), Fedn. Dentaire Internat., Upsilon Alpha, Omicron Kappa Upsilon, Phi Kappa Phi. Home: 2694 Heritage Circle Las Vegas NV 89005 Office: 2950 S Maryland Pkwy Las Vegas NV 89109

AHRENS, RUTH HIGGINS, sch. psychologist; b. Jersey City, Apr. 16, 1942; d. Emery Richard and Ellen Harriet (Allen) Higgins; B.A., Jersey City State Coll., 1964, M.A., 1969, profl. diploma in sch. psychology, 1971; postgrad. Rutgers U., 1970—; m. Robert C. Ahrens, May 29, 1969. Tchr., Toms River (N.J.) Pub. Schs., 1963-67; psychology intern Union County Psychiat. Clinic, 1970-71; sch. psychologist Bernardsville (N.J.) Pub. Schs., 1971—. Mem. Am., N.J. psychol. assns., N.J. Assn. Sch. Psychologists. Home: RD 3 Box 45 Flemington NJ 08822 Office: 25 Olcott Av Bernardsville NJ 07924

AIKINS, MARY (MRS. DELBERT AIKINS), state ofcl.; b. Osgood, Ind.; student Ky. Bapt. Hosp. Sch. Nursing; m. Delbert Aikins; children—Peggy (Mrs. Eugene Brown), William R., Sue (Mrs. Gary Wolf). Mgr. Aikins Motor Express Co., over 30 yrs.; now state auditor Ind. Active Ind. Mental Health Assn. Vice committeeman Democratic precinct com., 20 yrs.; vice chmn. Dem. 9th dist. com.; pres. Ripley County Council, 1958-61; chmn. Ripley County com., 1962-70. Mem. Ind. Fedn. Women's Clubs, Ind. C. of C., Bus. and Profl. Women (past pres. Osgood-Versailles chpt., now legislative chmn.). Methodist. Mem. Order Eastern Star. Club: Altrusa. Office: State Capitol Bldg Indianapolis IN 46204*

AIKMAN, BONNIE ELLEN, editor; b. Omaha, Oct. 20, 1933; d. Cornelius Howard and Honora Ellen (Towey) Aikman; B.A. in English, Am. U., 1955, postgrad. TV play writing, 1956-57; student various spl. courses. Entertainment writer, columnist Washington Star-News, 1960-69; staff writer Nat. Observer, 1969-70; news editor pub. relations dept. Am. Automobile Assn., Falls Church, Va., 1970—. Mem. adv. council Keep Am. Beautiful, 1970—. Recipient Spl. Merit award outstanding service in publs. Am. U., 1955. Mem. Pub. Relations Soc. Am., Am. Assn. U. Women. Home: 2400 Virginia Av NW Washington DC 20037 Office: 8111 Gatehouse Rd Falls Church VA 22042

AILLET, GENEVIEVE FUSELIER (MRS. CLARENCE JOHAHNI AILLET), librarian; b. St. Martinville, La., Aug. 27, 1922; d. Ernest Frank and Madeliene Sophie (Barras) Fuselier; B.A., U. Southwestern La., 1942; M.S., La. State U., 1957; m. Clarence Johahni Aillet, Sept. 2, 1942; children—Elizabeth (Mrs. William T. Johnson), Janice (Mrs. Charles Crochet), Robert, Rebecca, Debra. Lab. technician Humble Oil Co., Baton Rouge, 1945-46; tchr., librarian Hahnville (La.) High Sch., 1941; librarian Zachary (La.) High Sch., 1951-59, Istrouma (La.) Jr. High Sch., 1960-62, Baton Rouge High Sch., 1965-74, Broadmoor Sr. High Sch., 1974—. Instr. La. State U. Library Sch. Extension, Baton Rouge, 1967-69. Mem. La. Assn. Sch. Librarians, La. Library Assn., Baton Rouge Library Club (sec. 1970), Am. Contract Bridge League, Phi Kappa Phi, Beta Phi Mu, Kappa Delta Pi. Home: 9548 Meredith Dr Baton Rouge LA 70815 Office: 10100 Goodwood Blvd Baton Rouge LA 70815

AINSWORTH, MARY DINSMORE SALTER (MRS. MARY D. AINSWORTH), psychologist; b. Glendale O., Dec. 1, 1913; d. Charles Morgan and Mary (Hoover) Salter; B.A., U. Toronto, 1935, M.A., 1936, Ph.D., 1939; m. Leonard H. Ainsworth, June 10, 1950 (div. Aug. 1960). With U. Toronto, 1935-42; cons. to dir. personnel selection Canadian Women's Army Corps., 1942-45; supt. women's rehab. Dept. Vets. Affairs, Can., 1945-46; asst. prof. dept. psychology U. Toronto, 1946-50; sr. research psychologist Tavistock Clinic, London, 1950-54; sr. research fellow East African Inst. Social Research, Kampala, Uganda, 1954-55; asso. prof. psychology Johns Hopkins, Balt., 1956-63, prof. of psychology 1963—. Clin. psychologist Sheppard and Enoch Pratt Hosp., 1956-61. Fellow Center Advanced Study in Behavioral Scis., 1967-68. Diplomate Am. Bd. Examiners Profl. Psychology. Fellow Am. Psychol. Assn.; mem. Soc. for Research Child Devel. Brit. Psychol. Soc. Author: (with A. W. Ham) Doctor in the Making, 1942; (with B. Klopfer, W. Klopfer, R. R. Holt) Developments in the Rorschach Technique, 1954; (with L. H. Ainsworth) Measuring Security in Personal Adjustment, 1958; Infancy in Uganda, 1967. Home: 7511 Club Rd Ruxton MD 21204

AINSWORTH, NORMA PAUL RUEDI (MRS. FREEDOM H. AINSWORTH), editor; b. Clinton, Mo.; d. Paul J. and Minnie Lee (Morris) Ruedi; A.B., Lindenwood Coll.; M.A., So. Methodist U.; postgrad. U. Mo.; m. Freedom H. Ainsworth, July 31, 1954. Asst. editor Colo. A. and M. Coll., 1943-44; chief editorial sect. mag., radio asst. and administrv. officer Bur. Reclamation, 1944-49; dir. publicity Bur. Land Mgmt., Dept. Interior, Washington, 1949-54; free-lance publicity and advt. work, 1954-60; mng. editor MacFadden Publs., N.Y.C., 1960-61; fiction editor Practical English, also Co-ed, Scholastic Mags., Inc., 1961-62; fiction editor Scholastic Mags. and Book Services, Inc., N.Y.C., 1962-67, editor manuscript dept., 1967—. Editor juvenile anthologies pub. Scholastic Mags., Inc. Mem. staff, panelist Writer's Workshops, Mich., Wash., Tex. Mem. Mystery Writers Am., (chmn. Juvenile Judges Edgar awards 1963-64, dir. 1973—), Authors Guild Inc., Chi Omega, Alpha Sigma Tau, Sigma Tau Delta, Deta Pi Theta, Pi Alpha Delta. Contbr. articles, short stories and poetry to nat. mags. Home: 27 W 10th St New York City NY 10011 Office: 50 W 44th St New York City NY 10036

AITCHISON, BEATRICE, transp. economist; b. Portland, Ore., July 18, 1908; d. Clyde Bruce and Bertha (Williams) Aitchison; A.B., Goucher Coll., 1928; A.M., Johns Hopkins, 1931; Ph.D. in Math., 1933; M.A. with honors in Econs., U. Ore., 1937. Asso. prof. math. U. Richmond, 1933-34; lectr. statistics Am. U., 1934-44; instr. econs. U. Ore., 1939-41; jr. statistician advancing to sr. statistician ICC, 1938-48, prin. transport economist, 1948-51; dir. transport econs. div. Office Transp., Dept. Commerce, 1951-53; dir. transp. research Post Office Dept., Washington, 1953-58, dir. transp. research and statistics, 1958-67, dir. transp. rates and econs., 1967-71; transp. cons., 1971—. Cons. Traffic Analysis and Forecasting Office Def. Transp., 1942-45; cons. mil. traffic. service U.S. Dept. Def., 1950-53. Recipient Alumnae Achievement citation Goucher Coll., 1954; First Ann. Fed. Woman's award, 1961, Career Service award Nat. Civil Service League, 1970. Fellow Am. Statis. Assn., A.A.A.S.; mem. Am. Econ. Assn., Am. Soc. Traffic and Transp., Transp. Research Forum, Phi Beta Kappa, Sigma Xi, Pi Lambda Theta, Phi Delta Gamma. Episcopalian. Contbr. to numerous govt. publs. Home and office: 1929 S St NW Washington DC 20009

AITKEN, MARLENE JOAN MCVAY (MRS. DAVID RODGER AITKEN, III), occupational therapist; b. Hudson, S.D., Sept. 2, 1936; d. James Fennimore and Myrtle Minnie (Jordal) McVay; B.A., State U. Ia., 1959; m. David Rodger Aitken, III, Dec. 5, 1962; children—David Rodger IV, James Robert, Mary MacLean. Staff therapist VA Hosp., Knoxville, Ia., 1959-60; asst. dir. occupational therapy Fla. State Hosp., Chattahoochee, 1960; dir. occupational therapy W.T. Edwards Hosp., Tallahassee, 1960-65; staff therapist Ga. Mental Health Inst., Atlanta, 1966-67; supr. occupational therapy Marianjoy Rehab. Hosp., Wheaton, Ill., 1972—. Mem. Am., Ill. occupational therapy assns., Zeta Tau Alpha, Beta Sigma Phi. Home: 1515 E Harrison St Wheaton IL 60187 Office: Marianjoy Rehab Hosp PO Box 795 Wheaton IL 60187

AJEMIAN, INA ETHEL (MRS. GEORGE AJEMIAN), physician; b. Sawyerville, Que., Can., Mar. 31, 1939; d. Ernest Stanley and Kathleen Shorten (Laberee) Cummings; B.Sc. with honors, Bishops's U., 1960, M.D., C.M., Mc Gill U., 1964; m. George Ajemian, May 30, 1964; children—Krikor, Stanley. Intern, Montreal Gen. Hosp., 1964-65, resident, 1966-67; practice medicine specializing in family practice, Beaconsfield, Que., 1967-70, Pointe Claire, Que., 1970—; mem. staff Lakeshore Gen. Hosp., Pointe Claire. Mem. Canadian Med. Assn., College Family Practice. Presbyn. Home: 248 Sherbrooke St Beaconsfield PQ H9W 1P7 Canada Office: 108 Oakridge Pointe Claire PQ H9R 3C1 Canada

AJZENBERG-SELOVE, FAY, educator, physicist; b. Berlin, Germany, Feb. 13, 1926 (came to U.S. 1940, naturalized 1946); d. Mojzesz A. and Olga (Naiditch) Ajzenberg; B.S. in Engring., U. Mich., 1946; M.S., U. Wis., 1949, Ph.D., 1952; m. Walter Selove, Dec. 18, 1955. Research fellow Cal. Inst. Tech., 1952, 54; lectr. Smith Coll., 1952-53; cons., fellow Mass. Inst. Tech., 1952-53; asst. prof., hon. asso. prof. Boston U., 1953-57; mem. faculty Haverford Coll., 1957-70, prof. physics, 1962-70, acting chmn. dept. physics, 1967-69; research prof. physics U. Pa., Phila., 1970-73, prof. physics, 1973—. Vis. asst. prof. Columbia, summer 1955, Nat. U. Mexico, summer 1955; lectr. U. Pa., 1957; cons. in field, 1962-63; exec. sec. com. physics faculties in colls. Am. Inst. Physics, 1962-65, mem. adv. com. manpower, 1963-67; adv. com. vis. scientists program, 1963-67; mem. U.S. delegation low energy nuclear physics to USSR, AEC, 1966; commr. Commn. on Coll. Physics, 1968-72; mem. data panel, physics survey com. Nat. Acad. Scis., 1970-72; vis. asso. Cal. Inst. Tech., 1973-74; vis. staff mem. Los Alamos Sci. Lab., 1971—. Smith-Mundt fellow, 1955; Guggenheim fellow, 1965-66. Fellow Am. Phys. Soc. (exec. com. div. nuclear physics 1970-72, vice chmn. 1972-73, chmn. 1973-74); mem. Am. Assn. U. Profs., A.A.A.S. (governing council), Internat. Union Pure and Applied Physics (nuclear physics com.), Phi Beta Kappa, Sigma Xi. Editor: Nuclear Spectroscopy, Vol. A and B, 1960. Home: 118 Cherry Lane Wynnewood PA 19096 Office: U Pa Philadelphia PA 19104

AKAU, TRUDE MICHELSON, educator; b. Boston, Nov. 24, 1917; d. Maurice and Sophia Michelson; M.Ed., U. Hawaii, 1951; children—Nadya, Ilsa, George, Adrian, Sheila, Marsha. Tchr. lang. arts Kalihi Elementary Sch., Honolulu, 1951—. Contbg. author Constn. State Hawaii. Hawaii Congress Parents and Tchrs. grantee, 1947—, Nat. Def. Edn. Act grantee, 1962-65, Office Econ. Edn. grantee, 1966-68. Mem. Pacific Speech Assn. (v.p., exec. bd. 1967-71), Hawaii Council English Tchrs. (exec. bd. 1967-71), Hawaii Fedn. Tchrs. (exec. bd. 1960-63). Contbr. articles to newspapers. Home: 2622 B Waolani Av Honolulu HI 96817 Office: Kalihi Elementary Sch Honolulu HI 96819

AKHURST, ENID SHEILA STOKES (MRS. DENYS O. AKHURST), mus. ofcl.; b. Nottingham, Eng., Feb. 26, 1931; d. Bernard and Gladys Danvers (Gretton) Stokes; B.Sc., U. Nottingham, 1951, Diploma in Edn., 1952; M.S., U. Ark., 1966, Ph.D., 1970; m. Denys O. Akhurst, Aug. 11, 1952; children—Thomas Henry Wyatt, James Michael Willoughby. Came to U.S., 1955, naturalized, 1963. Editor dept. food tech. Mass. Inst. Tech., 1955-59; research asst. U. Miami Med. Sch., 1959-62; lectr. botany and biology U. Ark.,Fayetteville, 1962-69, research asso. agronomy dept., 1969-70; tchr. Broward County Bd. Pub. Instrn., Pompano, Fla., 1970-71; dir. Sci. Mus. and Planetarium Palm Beach County, Inc., West Palm Beach, Fla., 1971—. Adj. prof. dept. biology Fla. Atlantic U., Boca Raton, 1971—; cons. Smithsonian Instn., 1973—. Chmn. polit. and legislative action com. Fla. Assn. for Gifted, 1974—. Mem. Soc. Internat. Taxonomists, Sigma Xi, Phi Beta Kappa. Home: 263 Valencia St West Palm Beach FL 33402 Office: 1141 W Lakewood St West Palm Beach FL 33405

ALAUPOVIC, ALEXANDRA VRBANIC, educator; b. Slatina, Yugoslavia, Dec. 21, 1921; d. Joseph and Elizabeta (Papp) Vrbanic; student Bus. Sch., Zagreb, Yugoslavia, 1940-41, Acad. Visual Arts, Zagreb, Yugoslavia, 1944-48; postgrad. Acad. Visual Arts, Prague, Czechoslovakia, 1949, Art Sch., U. Ill., 1959-60; M.F.A., U. Okla., 1966; m. Peter Alaupovic, Mar. 22, 1947; children—Betsy, H. Clark Hyde. Came to U.S., 1958, naturalized, 1964. Secr. Arko Liquer & Yeast Factory and Distillery, Zagreb, Yugoslavia, 1941-44; instr. U. Okla., Norman, 1964-66; instr. three dimensional design sculpture Oklahoma City U., 1969—, Okla. Sci. Found., Oklahoma City, 1969—. One-woman shows at Okla. Art Center, Oklahoma City; exhibited art in group shows Springfield (Mo.) Art Mus., Okla. U. Mus., Norman, 7th Ann. Temple Emanuel Brotherhood Arts Festival; represented in permanent collections at Okla. U. Art Mus., Okla. State Art Collection, Mercy Health Center. Recipient Jacobson award U. Okla., 1964; Hon. Mention in sculpture Philbrook Art Center, Tulsa, 1967; First sculpture award Philbrook Art Center, Tulsa, 1970. Club: MacDowell of Allied Arts (Oklahoma City). Home: 11008 N Bryant St Oklahoma City OK 73111 Office: Route 1 Box 167 A Oklahoma City OK 73111

ALBECK, DORIS LILLIAN HANSON, librarian; b. Helena, Mont., May 26, 1934; d. Richard E. and Lillie Paula (Kjos) Hanson; B.S. in Elementary Edn., Western Mont. Coll. Edn., 1958; M.L.S., U. Wash., 1961; postgrad. Inst. Sch. Library Supervision and Centralized Tech. Services, La. State U., 1967; m. Arlie W. Albeck, Dec. 26, 1955 (div. Apr. 1962). Tchr. pub. schs., Mont., Wash., 1958-61; librarian Seattle Pub. Schs., 1961-65, Air Force Dependent Schs., France, Germany, Japan, 1965-68, Long Beach, Cal., 1968-70; br. librarian Long Beach Pub. Library, 1970—. Tchr. English to Japanese, Tokyo, 1968-69. Mem. Am., Cal. library assns., Beta Phi Mu. Home: 32 5th Pl Long Beach CA 90802 Office: 2900 Studebaker Rd Long Beach CA 90802

ALBEE, GRACE ARNOLD, artist; b. Scituate, R.I., July 28, 1890; m. Percy F. Albee, May 10, 1913; children—Edward F. II, John F., Nathaniel E., William C., P. Frederick, Jr. Painter, engraver. Rep. Bklyn. Mus. by purchase award, 1947; rep. mus. of R.I. Sch. Design; Library of Congress, Met. Mus., N.Y.C., Nat. Gallery Art, Washington, Carnegie Inst. Mus., Pitts., Okla. A. and M. Coll., Stillwater, Nat. Mus. Art, Stockholm, Sweden, Cleve. Mus. Art; Kansas City Mus., Bklyn. Mus., John Herron Art Mus., N.Y.C., Boston Pub. Library, Melrose (Mass.) Pub. Library, Newark Pub. Library, Bethlehem (Pa.) Pub. Library, Peacham (Vt.) Pub. Library, Lynchburg (Va.) Pub. Library, Phila. Mus., Nat. Gallery, Washington; collection of King Victor Emmanuel of Italy (1940); Nat. Bezaled Mus., Jerusalem, Israel; Culver Mil. Acad.; Cayuga Mus. History and Art, Auburn, N.Y.; Albany (N.Y.) Print Club, Norton Mus. West Palm Beach, Fla., Portland (Me.) Mus. Art, Woodmere Art Gallery, Chestnut Hill, Pa., U. Notre Dame; others; various pvt. collections; USIA overseas exhbn., North Africa, Far East, S.Am., 1962-64. N.A., 1946. Chmn. Jury of Awards Graphic Art, N.A.D., 1965, 68; chmn. com. on prints, chmn. jury selection and awards Am. Artists Profl. League, 1972; Recipient Eugenia F. Atwood Purchase prize at Phila. Print Club, 1949; print prizes N.A.D., Conn. Acad. Hunterdon County Art Center, 1959; purchase prize Albany Print Club, 1959; gold medal Am. Artists Profl. League, 1961; 3d purchase prize Conn. Acad. Fine Arts, 1961; Samuel Finley Breese Morse medal Nat. Acad. Design, 1962-72; hon. mention Acad. Artists Assn. Springfield, 1963, 67, Helen Gould Kennedy award, 1968; Florence Kane award 1964; Oakes-on-the-Hill award 1964; John Taylor Arms meml. prize, 1964; prize Am. Artists Profl. League, 1965, 1st prize in graphics, 1973; John Lucas Bowen purchase prize Albany Print-Club, 1967; hon. mention Kent Art Assn., 1969, 1st prize for graphics, 1970, award for outstanding work in any medium, 1970; purchase prize Print Club Albany, 1969, Alan Crane Meml. Purchase prize, 1971; others. Fellow Providence Water Color Club (life); mem. Springfield Art League, Met. Opera Guild, N.A.D. (awards jury 1974), Conn. Acad., Phila. Water Color Club, Hunterdon County Art Center, Audubon Artists, Providence Art Club, Boston Printmakers, Academic Artists' Assn., Soc. Am. Graphic Artists, Smithsonian Instn., Nat. Trust for Historic Preservation, Albany Print Club, Am. Artists Profl. League (chmn. com. on prints 1968-73, chmn. jury selection and award 1967-73, prize 1973). Reproduction in numerous publs. Fellow Met. Mus. (life). Address: 84-43 123d St Kew Gardens NY 11415

ALBERS, ROBERTA ANNE, profl. golfer; b. Tampa, Fla., Dec. 22, 1946; d. Thomas Joseph and Giulia Carmen (Bottari) Albers; B.B.A., U. Miami, 1968; M.S. (NSF fellow), Ariz. State U., 1969. Research analyst Mckinsey & Co., mgmt. cons., Los Angeles, 1969-70; dir. marketing Leisure Group, Inc., Los Angeles, 1970-72; profl. golfer, 1973—. Mem. Ladies Profl. Golf Assn., Zeta Tau Alpha. Roman Catholic. Home: 7932 Biltmore Blvd Miramar FL 33023

ALBERT, ETHEL MARY, educator; b. New Britain, Conn., Mar. 28, 1918; d. Zundel and Dorothy (Eisenstadt) Sokolsky; B.A., Bklyn. Coll., 1942; M.A., Columbia, 1947; Ph.D., U. Wis., 1949. Instr. philosophy Bklyn. Coll., 1946-47; instr. philosophy U. Wis., 1947-49; instr. philosophy Syracuse U., 1949-52; prof. speech U. Cal. at Berkeley, 1958-66; prof. anthropology Northwestern U. 1966—, chmn. dept., 1972-73. Research asso. Harvard U. Lab. Social Relations, 1953-55; Ford Found. Overseas fellow, Africa, 1955-57; asst. dir. NSF Project on anthropology, 1961; Social Sci. Research Council faculty research fellow, 1962; NSF Sr. postdoctoral fellow, 1965-66. Fellow Am. Anthrop. Assn.; mem. A.A.A.S., Am. Philos. Assn., Philosophy of Sci. Assn., African Studies Assn. Author: (With Peterfreund and Denise) Great Traditions in Ethics, rev. edit., 1969; (with Kluckhohn) A Selected Bibliography on Values, Ethics and Esthetics, 1959; (with Mandelbaum and Lasker) Teaching of Anthropology, 1963; (with Vogt) The People of Rimrock, 1966. Contb. articles profl. jours. Home: 612 Mulford St Evanston IL 60202

ALBERTI, AURORA FRANCES (MRS. PETER FRANK GORDON), physician; b. Bklyn., Sept. 19, 1915; d. John and Ida (Brodvin) Alberti; B.A., Smith Coll., 1937; M.D., U. Md., 1941; m. Peter Frank Gordon, Feb. 1, 1945 (dec. June 1967); children—Paul Vincent, Daniel Peter, Susan. Intern, Jersey City Med. Center, 1941-42; resident Children's Hosp., Washington, 1942-43, asso. jr. staff, 1956-60, attending staff, 1960—; resident Kings County Hosp., Bklyn., 1943-44; chief Well-baby Clinics, King County Health Dept., Seattle, 1945-46; asst. in child clinics St. Johns Hosp., Bklyn., 1946-48; clin. instr. Georgetown U. Med. Sch., 1954-55; sch. med. adviser Montgomery County (Md.) Health Dept., 1958-64; practice medicine, specializing in pediatric allergy, Bethesda, Md., 1961-69; chief div. child health services Prince George's County Health Dept., 1969-73; chief Allergy Clinic, Ft. Myer, Va., 1973—. Fellow Am. Acad. Pediatrics, Am. Coll. Allergists; mem. Am. Acad. Allergy, Montgomery County (asso.), Montgomery County Pediatric Soc. (sec. 1961-62), Women's Med. Soc. Washington (pres. 1965-66), Allergy Soc. Washington, Phi Beta Kappa, Sigma XI. Democrat. Roman Catholic. Home: 3810 47th St NW Washington DC 20016

ALBERTI, JEAN MAE CLAIRE, ednl. psychologist, med. educator; b. Buffalo, N.Y., Sept. 3, 1935; d. Anthony Aloysius and Mary Grace Agnes (Gervase) Alberti; B.S., D'Youville Coll., 1957; Ed.M., U. Buffalo, 1962, Ph.D., State U. N.Y. at Buffalo, 1970. Elementary tchr. Maryvale Sch. System, Cheektowaga, N.Y., 1957-62, Sweet Home Central Sch., Amherst, N.Y., 1962-65; grad. research asst. State U. N.Y. at Buffalo, 1965-68, dir. U. Research, 1968-72; asso. prof. Genesee Community Coll., Batavia, N.Y., 1970-71, research cons., 1971-72; asst. prof. med. edn. Center for Ednl. Devel., U. Ill. Coll. Medicine, Chgo., 1972—. Mem. Nat. Orgn. for Women (chpt. co-pres. 1971-72), Am. Ednl. Research Assn., A.A.A.S., Nat. Council on Measurement in Edn., Am. Civil Liberties Union, Pi Lambda Theta (Nat. v.p. 1969-73). Editor: Biography of a Class, 1965-72. Office: U Ill Coll Medicine Center for Ednl Devel 835 S Wolcott Av Chicago IL 60612

ALBERTS, CHARLENE EDITH, lawyer; b. Bellevue, O., Mar. 28, 1944; d. Charles Tinker and Mildred Edith (German) Alberts; B.S. in Edn., Bowling Green State U., 1965; J.D., Ohio No. U., 1969; m. Jesse William Brogan. High sch. English tchr., Napoleon, O., 1966-67; admitted to Fla. bar, 1970, since practiced in Clearwater. Mem. Nat., Fla. assns. women lawyers, Am., Fla., Clearwater bar assns., Nat. Orgn. Women, Bus. and Profl. Women, Kappa Beta Pi. Lutheran. Home: PO Box 4988 Clearwater FL 33518 Office: 1215 Drew St B-6 Clearwater FL 33515

ALBERTS, LILY SUSAN (PEN NAME LILY S. KRUG-ALBERTS), artist, author; b. Hamburg, Germany, Nov. 19, 1890; d. Simon and Sophie (Lipman) Hirsche; student U. Hamburg, 1908-10; m. Werner Krug, 1922 (dec.); m. 2d, Alfred Alberts, 1951 (dec.). Lab. technician, Germany, Japan, China; newspaper work in numerous countries; exhibited paintings; author: Married to Life; Don't Count the Wrinkles; Leisure is Treasure; Impressions-Expressions. Home: 531 Kenyon Av Berkeley CA 94708

ALBRECHT, LOIS KINDELBERGER, librarian; b. Wheeling, W.Va., Oct. 3, 1930; d. Harry Monroe and Vonda Elmira (Defibaugh) Kindelberger; B.S. in Edn., Clarion (Pa.) State Coll., 1952; M.L.S., U. Pitts., 1963; postgrad. U. Md., 1969-71; m. Charles Otto Albrecht,

June 29, 1963. Librarian Richland Twp. Schs., Johnstown, Pa., 1952-62; head tech. services Washington County (Md.) Free Library, Hagerstown, 1963-68; system librarian Washington County Bd. Edn., Hagerstown, 1968-71; library devel. adviser Pa. State Library, Harrisburg, 1972—. Sec. bd. trustees Highland Community Library, Johnstown, 1961-62. Mem. A.L.A. (rep. N.Y. World's Fair 1965), Pa., Cumberland Valley (pres. 1967-68) library assns., Beta Phi Mu. Mem. Order Eastern Star. Author: Library Service, Southern Style, 1966. Home: 502 Ellen Rd Camp Hill PA 17011 Office: Box 1601 Harrisburg PA 17126

ALBRECHT, RUTH, educator; b. Wittenberg, Mo.; d. Frank and Johanna (Bregas) Albrecht; B.S., Washington U., St. Louis, 1934; M.A., U. Chgo., 1946, Ph.D., 1951. Lectr. psychology Ind. U., 1947; lectr. child psychology U. Kan., 1947; research asst. U. Chgo., 1947-48; research asso., 1948-50; research prof. Auburn Research Found. and Sch. Home Econs., Ala. Poly. Inst. (now Auburn U.), 1951-57; prof., head dept. family life Coll. Arts and Sci., U. Fla., Gainesville, 1957-60; prof. sociology, 1960—. Human devel. cons. Inter-U. Sch. Study, 1949. Trustee Fla. Council Aging, v.p., 1962-64; bd. dirs. Nat. Council Family Relations, 1963-66. Fellow Am. Gerontological Soc. (sec. psychol. and social scis. sect. 1960-63, chmn. 1963-65), A.A.A.S., Am. Sociol. Assn. (sec. family sect. 1967-70), Am. Acad. Polit. and Social Sci.; mem. Am., So. (chmn. problems of aging sect. 1965-66, mem. exec. bd. 1969-72, 1st v.p., 1973-74) sociol. socs., World Fedn. for Mental Health, Southeastern Council on Family Relations (editor newsletter, 1959-61), Pi Lambda Theta, Alpha Kappa Delta. Club: University Women's. Author: (with R. J. Havighurst) Older People, 1953; Aging in a Changing Society, 1962; (with E.W. Bock) Encounter: Love, Marriage and Family, 1972; also articles in sci. jours. Home: 1218 N W 6th St Gainesville FL 32601 Office: Peabody Hall U Fla Gainesville FL 32601

ALBRECHT-CARRIE, KIRSTEN SHARKE, occupational therapist; b. Pittsfield, Mass., July 12, 1948; d. Karl G.E. and Ann (Swensson) Sharke; B.S. in Occupational Therapy, Tufts U., 1970; m. Pierre A. Albrecht-Carrie, May 5, 1973. Occupational therapist Eastern Pa. Psy. Inst., Phila., 1970-73; head occupational therapist Waltham (Mass.) Hosp., 1973-74; clin. trainee supr. occupational therapy VA Hosp., Bedford, Mass., 1974—. Regional v.p. Pa. Social Services Union, 1972-73. Mem. Am. Occupational Therapy Assn. Home: 100 Crescent St Auburndale MA 02166 Office: VA Hosp Bedford MA 01730

ALBRITTON, THELMA PAULINE, educator; b. Snow Hill, N.C., Apr. 24, 1933; d. Floyd E. and Pauline (Eason) Albritton; A.B., Greensboro Coll., 1956; M.Ed., U. Ore., 1961; postgrad. U. Mich., 1968. Speech pathologist, Greensboro, N.C., 1956, Austin, Tex., 1956-57, Corvallis, Ore., 1957-60; now asst. prof. spl. edn. Eastern Mich. U., Ypsilanti; exec. staff Am. Speech & Hearing Assn., Washington, 1969-70, v.p. for planning, 1972—. Speech therapist Soc. Crippled Children, summers 1955-56; camp dir. Girl Scouts USA., summers 1957-61. Named Distinguished Alumna Greensboro, Coll., 1972. Fellow Am. Speech and Hearing Assn. (v.p. planning 1972—); mem. Mich. Speech and Hearing Assn. (pres. 1969), Delta Kappa Gamma (2d v.p. 1965-67). Democrat. Methodist. Home: 1710 Gregory St Ypsilanti MI 48197

ALCARAZ, GERTRUDE ELIZABETH TAMMANY (MRS. ERNEST P. ALCARAZ), civic worker; b. San Francisco, June 2, 1907; d. Harvey William and Elizabeth (Bucholz) Tammany; student San Diego State Coll., 1958-65; m. Ernest P. Alcaraz, June 14, 1930; children—Ernest Charles, Frances E. Dir., AFL-CIO womens activity div. San Diego County Labor Council, 1956—; bd. mem., leader Campfire Girls, 1944-50; mem. San Diego County Welfare Bd., 1960—, chmn., 1974—; mem. Library Bd., Community Welfare Council, 1966-67; mem. bd. Comprehensive Health Assn., 1972—; mem. subcom. on legislation Com. Cal. Atty. Gen. on Crime, 1972—. Bd. dirs. A.R.C., Homemakers. Recipient Community Service award, 1963, A.R.C. award, 1964. Mem. Phi Sigma Alpha (named Woman of Yr. 1972, chmn. Beta Phi Chpt., vice chmn. Cabrillo Assembly). Mem. Unity Ch. Home: 3280 Altadena Av San Diego CA 92105 Office: 2232 El Cajon Blvd San Diego CA 92104

ALCARESE, ANDREA M., lawyer; b. Balt., May 15, 1921; d. Antonio and Helen Marie (Ziegler) M.; B.S., Loyola U., 1952; LL.B., U. Md., 1955; m. I.M. Alcarese, May 22, 1947; children—Anthony, Gregory, Kathleen, Terry, Steven, Gary. Admitted to Md. bar, 1955; mem. Legal Aid Bur., Inc., Westminster, Md., 1957—. Treas. P.T.A., 1972-73. Mem. Carroll County Bar Assn.

ALCORN, ESTHER EASTVOLD (MRS. STANLEY M. ALCORN), physician; b. Minot, N.D., July 27, 1926; d. Joseph and Tena Olene (Tjon) Eastvold; A.B. summa cum laude, U. Cal. at Berkeley, 1948; M.D., U. Cal. at San Francisco, 1955; m. Stanley M. Alcorn, June 18, 1949; children—Steven R., Joseph M., Eric E., Mark B. Intern, Tucson Med. Center, 1957-58; gen. practice medicine, Tucson, 1960-65; planned parenthood physician, Tucson, 1960—; physician Yaqui Indian Village, Tucson, 1962-72; mem. staffs Pima County Hosp. Med. Clinics, 1961—, Pima County Health Dept. Well Child Clinics, 1961-72; cons. vocational rehab. State of Ariz., 1960—; cons. Pima County Welfare Dept., 1974—. Recipient Physicians' Recognition certificate for continuing edn., 1973. Mem. A.M.A., Ariz., Pima County med. assns., Assn. Planned Parenthood Physicians, Am. Med. Womens Assn. Methodist. Home: 3430 N Calle de Beso Tucson AZ 85715

ALCORN, MARCIA POWELL (MRS. H. MEADE ALCORN), state ofcl. Panelist weekly TV show What in the World; chmn. Conn. Commn. on Arts; founding mem. bd. dirs. Hartford Stage Co.; bd. dirs., actress Suffield Players; chmn. Conn. Found. for Arts; mem. New Eng. Regional Arts Programming Study Group. Address: Conn Commn on Arts 340 Capitol Av Hartford CT 06106

ALCOTT, AMY STRUM, golfer; b. Kansas City, Mo., Feb. 22, 1956; d. Eugene Yale and Lea (Strum) Alcott; grad. high sch. Pres. Cal. Jr. Girls Golf Assn., 1971-72. Recipient Outstanding Record in Golf award Beverly Hills B'nai B'rith, 1971; Charles Curtis Memory trophy Los Angeles Times, 1973; named winner Jr. World Champion, San Diego, 1970, runnerup, 1972; Los Angeles City Jr. Champion, 1971, 72, 73; Los Angeles City Womens Champion, 1973; U.S. Jr. Girls Champion, 1973; U.S. Jr. Girls Runnerup, 1971; Cal. State Women's Amateur Champion, 1973; recipient Ray Feliz Memory award Los Angeles Dept. Recreation and Parks, 1973. Mem. Cal. Scholastic Fedn. Address: 504 S Avondale Av Los Angeles CA 90049

ALDEBORGH, SIGNE HENRIETTE JOHNSON (MRS. ERIK ALDEBORGH), gage co. exec.; b. Broby, Sweden, June 24, 1898; d. Nils and Nilla Tessing (Person) Johnson; student Osby Jr. Coll., 1911-16, Bendz Inst., 1916-17; m. Erik Aldeborgh, May 4, 1919; children—John Erik, David Henry. Came to U.S., 1919, naturalized, 1930. Vice-pres., sec. Standard Gage Co., Inc., Poughkeepsie, N.Y., 1925—. Bd. mgr. Children's Home, Poughkeepsie, Mem. Jr. League. Republican. Mem. Ref. Ch. Clubs: Poughkeepsie Tennis, Poughkeepsie Garden (v.p. 1959-61), Dutchess Golf and Country (Poughkeepsie), Everglades (Palm Beach, Fla.); Garden of Orange and Dutchess Counties. Home: 28 Yates Blvd Poughkeepsie NY 12601

ALDERFER, ARLETA ANNA ANDERSON (MRS. ELMER J. ALDERFER), librarian; b. Denver, June 9, 1911; d. Ben and Esther Elizabeth (Ranster) Anderson; B.A., U. Denver, 1932; m. Elmer J. Alderfer, Oct. 11, 1935; children—Edward, Charlotte (Mrs. W.M. Schultz), Henry. Librarian, Colo. Sch. Mines Library, Golden, 1932-33; Rocky Mountain News Library, Denver, 1933-35; with Cattle & Fox Ranch, Evergreen, Colo., 1938-56; librarian Evergreen (Colo.) Sr. High Library, 1956—, Leader, Camp Fire Girls, Evergreen, 1949-55; mem. Denver Bd. Camp Fire Girls, 1950-55. Recipient Leaders award Camp Fire Girls, 1953. Mem. Sigma Kappa. Episcopalian (pres. 1949-51, treas. 1951-61). Home: Rural Route 4 Box 522 Evergreen CO 80439

ALDERMAN, ALICE MAE (MRS. DONALD C. ALDERMAN), librarian; b. Westby, Wis.; d. Hjalmar Otto and Agatha Hilda (Mortenson) Rudrud; A.A., North Park Coll., 1945; B.S. magna cum laude, U. Wis., 1965, M.S., 1966, postgrad., 1966—; m. Donald C. Alderman, Dec. 12, 1946; children—Deborah (Mrs. Cecil Rolfe), Andrew, Brent, Marsha. Lab. technician Leaf Brands, Chgo., 1945-46; teaching asst. U. Wis., Madison, 1965-66; with Wis. State Hist. Soc., Madison, 1966—, cataloger documents, 1967—. Mem. library mgmt. com. Madison City Sch., 1973. Mem. A.L.A. (mem. state documents task force classification com., documents on documents com. 1973—), Kappa Delta Phi, Beta Phi Mu. Mem. Modern Woodmen of Am. Author: Organizing Wisconsin Public Documents, 1974. Home: 1715 Laurel Crest Madison WI 53705 Office: 816 State St Madison WI 53707

ALDERMAN, MINNIS AMELIA, psychologist; b. Douglas, Ga., Oct. 14, 1928; d. Louis Cleveland and Minnis (Wooten) Alderman; A.B., Ga. Coll. at Milledgeville, 1949; M.A., Murray State U., 1960. Camp counselor Camp Sloan, Conn., summer 1949; music dir. Umatilla (Fla.) pub. sch., 1949-50, Campbell High Sch., Fairburn, Ga., 1950-54; music and drama dir., tchr. English and speech Wells (Nev.) High Sch., 1954-59; tchr. English and history Sinking Fork Sch., Hopkinsville, Ky., 1960; counselor White Pine High Sch., Ely, Nev., 1960-68; instr. psychology, guidance and counseling Murray State U., summers 1961, 62; instr. guidance and counseling U. Nev. Extension, 1963-68; psychologist Ely Mental Health Center, 1969—. Owner, Minisizer Exercising Salon, 1969-71, Minimimeo Mimeographing, 1969—; owner Knit Knook, 1969—, City Service Sta.; sec.-treas. Great Basin Enterprises Corp., 1969-71. Test supt. Coll. Entrance Examination Bd. and Am. Coll. Testing, 1960-68. Pres. White Pine County Mental Health Assn., 1960-63; mem. Mental Health State Commn., 1963-65; bd. dirs. White Pine County Sch. Employees Fed. Credit Union, 1961-68, pres., 1963-68; 2d v.p. White Pine Community Concert Assn., 1965-67, pres., 1967-68; mem. Gov.'s Commn. on Status Women, 1968—; sec.-treas. White Pine Rehab. Tng. Center for Retarded Persons, 1973—; dir. Ret. Sr. Vol. Program, 1973; vice chmn. Great Basin Health Council, 1973—; sec.-treas. Great Basin chpt. Nev. Employees Assn. Precinct reporter ABC News, 1966. Mem. N.E.A. (life), Nev. Edn. Assn., Am. Assn. U. Women (pres. 1964-65, state area rep. in edn. 1965-67; state implementation chmn. edn. 1967-69, state area adviser 1969—), Bus. and Profl. Women's Club (1st v.p. 1965-66, pres. 1966-68, asst. dist. dir. 1967-68, state civic participation chmn. 1967-68, dist. dir. 1968-70, state 2d v.p. 1969-70, state rec. sec. 1968-69, state 1st v.p. 1970-71, state pres.-elect 1971-72, state pres. 1972-73), D.A.R., Internat. Platform Assn., Mensa (test adminstr. 1966—), Am. Personnel and Guidance Assn. (state memberships chmn. 1962-65), Am. Sch. Counselors Assn., Nat. Vocational Counselors Assn., Nat. Fedn. Ind. Bus. (dist. chmn. 1971—), Nat. Assn. Women Deans and Counselors, Nat. Assn. Female Execs., Nat. Orgn. for Women, Delta Kappa Gamma (2d v.p. 1964-66, state program chmn. 1965-69, 1st v.p. 1966-68, state 1st v.p. 1967-69, chpt. pres. 1968—, state pres. 1969-71), Gen. Fedn. Womens Clubs (dist. pres. 1970—), Beta Sigma Phi (chpt. sponsor 1970-72). Clubs: White Pine Knife and Fork (2d v.p. 1968-69, 1st v.p. 1969-70, pres. 1970-71), Ely Woman's (pres. 1969-70). Methodist (lay speaker 1967—, choir dir. 1960—). Author: Handbook for Counselors; Guidance Handbook for Teachers; Guidance Handbook for Administrators; Discipline Handbook, also articles. Home: 945 Av H PO Box 457 East Ely NV 89315 Office: Campton St PO Box 187 Ely NV 89301

ALDERMAN, ROALDA JENSEN (MRS. WILLIAM WALTER ALDERMAN), hosp. adminstr.; b. Rochester, Minn., Apr. 23, 1930; d. Lloyd Bryan and Marvel Dora (Johannesen) Jensen; B.A., U. Chgo., 1949, M.A., 1967; postgrad. Ill. Tchrs. Coll., 1963; m. William Walter Alderman, Nov. 19, 1968; children—Bruce Donald, Karen Laurie. Dietary supr. Billings Hosp., U. Chgo., 1951-53, psychometrist Office Vocation Guidance Counsel, U. Chgo., 1950-51, 53-54; project research specialist div. hosp. and scientific orgn., asst. dir. project new fields sci. inquiry, exobiology Indsl. Relations Center, U. Chgo., 1965-68; dir. tng. Cook County Hosp., Chgo., 1968-69, dir. personnel, 1969-71, asso. hosp. dir. personal services, 1969-70; exec. adminstr. Ill. Dept. Pub. Health Hosp. and Clinics, Chgo., 1971—; Chgo. region asst. to dep. dir. Ill. Dept. Pub. Health, 1971-73. Co-founder Chel-win South Improvement Assn., 1965, sec., 1966, dir., 1965-67. Recipient State Ill. Gov.'s awards, Superior Achievement certificate, 1972. Mem. Chgo. Hosp. Personnel Mgmt. Assn., Ill. Pub. Health Assn. (mem. membership com. 1971). Home: 333 S East Av Oak Park IL 60302 Office: 1919 W Taylor St Chicago IL 60612

ALDERSON, JOANNE BARTELS (MRS. JAMES M. ALDERSON), author; b. Janesville, Wis., Sept. 21, 1930; d. Frederick Carl and Rose (Griesbach) Bartels; B.A. cum laude, Milton (Wis.) Coll., 1952; postgrad. U. Wis., 1952, 59-60; m. James M. Alderson, June 21, 1952; children—James Michael, Kaye Joanne, Jaye Marie, Ann Julia, Erica Jane. Editor high sch. ann., coll. paper, 1948-52; reporter Janesville Daily Gazette, 1949-52; free-lance writer, 1952—; proofreader, writer The Paper for Central Wis., 1968-70; tchr., dir. dramatic prodns. for Oshkosh High Sch., Oshkosh Recreation Dept.; dir. Oshkosh Community Players, Oshkosh Jr. Theatre, Mask and Wig Childrens Theatre; co-founder Greenroom Exptl. Drama Group Oshkosh Community Players; now writer, drama critic The Spirit, Cath. newspaper N.E. Wis. Block, area chmn. various health drives, 1964—; mem. study group Wis. Arts Council, 1966-67; tchr. poetry sect. Wis. Regional Writers Student Writers Workshop Ripon Coll., 1969-70. Authored and appeared in (dramas) A Dialogue With the Brownings, Interview with Emily. Co-chmn. publicity Oshkosh Heart Fund, 1970. Pres., bd. dirs. Grand Opera House Com., Wis. Fellowship Poets. Mem. Council Wis. Writers, Wis. Press Women, Sigma Phi Zeta. Co-editor: Poems Out of Wisconsin III, 1967. Contbr. poems to mags., articles to newspapers and gen. and trade mags. Address: 1950 Georgia St Oshkosh WI 54901

ALDIS, PAMELA WANDA (MRS. JOHN HOWARD DICKINSON), physician; b. Johore, Barhu-Malaya, Nov. 14, 1939; d. Alison Stoughton and Phyllis Nancy Napier (Andrews) Aldis; student Norwich Tech. Coll., 1956-58; student London U., 1958-63; M.B.B.S., St. Bartholomews Hosp. Med. Sch., 1963; m. John Howard Dickinson, Apr. 8, 1968; children—Louisa Anne, Lara Dea. Houseman ear, nose and throat St. Bartholomew's Hosp., 1963; med. houseman Royal Devon and Exeter Hosp., 1964; rotating intern Vancouver Gen. Hosp., 1964-65; gen. practice medicine Seymour Clinic, Vancouver, B.C., Can., 1965-67; individual practice, Vancouver, 1967-74, Royston, B.C., 1974—. Mem. attending staff dept. family practice Vancouver Gen. Hosp. Mem. Vancouver Med. Assn., Canadian Med. Assn., Coll. Family Practice Can., Vancouver Woman's Med. Assn., Med. Asso. Whistler Mountain. Club: Kiawassa (Vancouver, B.C., Can.). Home: Trentower Gardens Royston BC Canada

ALDRICH, GERTRUDE VESSIE MORRIS (MRS. JAMES CLEMENT ALDRICH), ednl. adminstr.; b. nr. Charlottesville, Va., Sept. 17, 1917; d. Edward Sewell and Duane (Knight) Morris; student Strayer Bus. Coll., 1934-35; B.A. magna cum laude, Lee Coll., 1968; M.Ed., Xavier U., 1973; m. James Clement Aldrich, June 7, 1941 (dec. 1964); children—James Edward, Miriam (Mrs. Raymond Wayne Cross), Carolyn (Mrs. Robert C. Abbott), Larry Morris. Sec., Dairy Industries Supply Assn., Washington, 1949-52; stenographer, statis. clk. U.S. Army, Arlington, Va., 1962-65; dean women Lee Coll., Cleveland, Tenn., 1968—, dir. dormitory, 1966-68. Sec., Hiwassee Student Services Assn., 1973-74. Mem. So. Coll. Personnel Assn., Nat. Assn. Women Deans, Adminstrs. and Counselors, Christian Assn. Deans Women, Phi Delta Omicron. Home: 1655 Ocoee St Cleveland TN 37311

ALDRICH, WILLIE L. B. (MRS. THOMAS N. ALDRICH), librarian; b. Cleve., Sept. 9, 1924; d. Alfred and Hattie Ross (Batts) Banks; B.S., Coll. of Livingstone, Salisbury, N.C., 1945, C.R.E., 1949; M.S. in L.S., Atlanta U., 1964; m. Thomas N. Aldrich, Feb. 11, 1947. Tchr. Bible pub. schs., Salisbury, 1953-54; asst. librarian Rowan County Br. Library, 1955-58; tchr., librarian Cleveland High Sch., Shelby, N.C., 1957-58; librarian Dunbar High Sch., East Spencer, N.C., 1958-60; asst. librarian Carnegie Library, Livingstone Coll., 1960-62, hood seminarian librarian W.J. Walls Center, Livingstone Coll., 1962—. Sec. edn. sect. Salisbury Mayor's Commn. on Status of Women, 1970—; mem. Rowan Citizens for Better Libraries. Bd. dirs. N.C. Easter Seals, Bishop J.W. Walls Found. Mem. A.L.A., Salisbury. Rowan Library Assn., Ch. Women United, Delta Sigma Theta. Home: 405 Milford Hills Rd Salisbury NC 28144

ALDRIDGE, HARRIETT JULIA, editor; b. Plum Island, N.Y., Aug. 31, 1923; d. Harry Vincent and Erna (Loudon) Kennedy; B.S., Tex. State Coll. for Women, 1945; m. Herbert J. Aldridge, Mar. 28, 1947; (dec. Mar. 30, 1960); children—Michael Edwin, Frederick James. Tchr. home econs. Mission (Tex.) High Sch., 1946-47; asst. food and home editor Ark. Gazette, Little Rock, 1961-65, food and home editor, 1965—. Mem. Am. Home Econs. Assn., Assn. Newspaper Food Editors and Writers, Sigma Delta Chi, Phi Upsilon Omicron. Home: 5143 Glenmore Rd North Little Rock AR 72116 Office: Box 1821 Little Rock AR 72203

ALEANDRI, EMELISE FRANCES, educator; b. Riva del Garda, Italy, Jan. 23, 1943; d. John Baptist and Elodia Vladimira (Lutterotti) Aleandri; A.B. (N.Y. State Regents scholar, Coll. library scholar), Coll. New Rochelle, 1965; postgrad. Lehman Coll., 1965-66, Hunter Coll., 1966, 68-70, City U. N.Y., 1970—. Caseworker, ct. rep. N.Y.C. Dept. Social Services, 1965-69, social services rep., med. social worker, 1969-71; adj. lectr. Hunter Coll., N.Y.C., 1971-72; editorial asst. First Casualty Press, Bklyn., 1972; asst. dir. N.Y. Shakespeare Festival Pub. Theatre, 1972; adj. lectr. Borough of Manhattan Community Coll., 1972; research and editorial asst. Council on Founds., Inc., N.Y.C., 1973; instr. verbal expression N.Y. City Community Coll., 1973—. Am. Inst. for Devel. Am. Repertory Theatre research grantee for ethnic theatre research, 1970. Mem. Am. Assn. U. Women, Am. Inst. for Devel. Am. Repertory Theater, Am. Theatre Assn. (recorder 1970), Italian Hist. Soc. Am. Democrat. Theatre editor TV Facts mag., 1973—. Home: 73 Bedford Mews New York City NY 10014

ALENIEWSKI, MONICA IRENE (MRS. IRWIN J. FRIEDFELD), physician; b. Harrison, N.J., Sept. 29, 1928; d. George D. and Wladyslawa (Jacunski) Aleniewski; B.S., Douglass Coll., 1949; M.D., Hahnemann Med. Coll., 1953; m. Irwin J. Friedfeld, June 2, 1957; children—Lauren Suzanne, John Eric, Stefanie Ann, Robert Bonheur, Eric George. Intern, St. Michaels Hosp., Newark, 1953-54; resident Columbia Presbyn. Med. Center, N.Y.C., 1955-57; practice medicine, specializing in anesthesiology, East Orange, N.J., 1957—; chief anesthesiology VA Hosp., East Orange, 1959—; asst. clin. prof. surgery N.J. Coll. Medicine and Dentistry, 1964-67, asso. clin. prof. surgery, 1967—; asso. prof. anesthesiology, 1970—. Diplomate Am. Bd. Anesthesiology. Mem. A.M.A., Am. Soc. Anesthesiologists, N.J. Soc. Anesthesiologists, Internat. Anesthesia Research Soc., Am. Med. Women's Assn., Hahnemann Med. Coll. Alumni Assn. Roman Catholic. Home: 44 S Kingman Rd South Orange NJ 07079 Office: Tremont Av East Orange NJ 07019

ALEXANDER, ALICE A. (MRS. HOWARD C. ALEXANDER), furniture mfg. exec.; b. Decatur, Ill., Oct. 17, 1925; d. Lawrence Louis and Mary (Finn) Lynch; spl. courses Western Mich. Coll., 1946, N.Y.U., 1952-53; m. Howard C. Alexander, Jan. 25, 1947. Women's feature writer Kalamazoo (Mich.) Gazette, 1947, Detroit News, 1949-50, United Press, 1951, N.Y. Times, 1952-55, Chgo. Sun-Times, 1955-56; pub. relations account supr. Pub. Relations Bd., 1959-62; pub. relations dir. Kroehler Mfg. Co., 1962-73, v.p. pub. relations, 1973-74, v.p. corp. communications and consumer affairs, 1974—. Mem. Nat. Home Fashions League (pres. Ill. chpt. 1968-70, sec. 1970-71, exec. v.p. 1971-72; nat. v.p., 1971-72, nat. pres. 1972-73). Home: 1811 Sedgwick Chicago IL 60614 Office: 222 E 5th Av Naperville IL 60540

ALEXANDER, ANNETTE COMPTON, civic worker; b. Alexandria, La., Sept. 11, 1909; d. Sanford E. and Mary E. (Compton) Compton; student pub. schs.; m. Clyde Wayne Alexander, Oct. 5, 1935; children—Clyde Wayne, Charles Compton, Jane Antoinette, Janet Ann. Mem. exec. bd., membership chmn. Jackson Council on Alcoholism, 1961-63; del. to Community Services Council; social chmn. Hinds County Planning Alcohol Edn. Group; vol. Miss. State Hosp., Miss. Bapt. Hosp., St. Dominic's Meml. Hosp. Recipient service award for vol. work Miss. State Mental Hosp., 1960. Mem. Miss. Assn. Schs. Alcohol Studies, Jackson Opera Guild, Jackson Symphony Assn., Jackson Little Theatre, Miss. Art Assn. Episcopalian (past mem. bd., Christian social chmn.). Clubs: Jackson Country, Jackson. Home: Apt C-5 Chateau Royale 5155 Wayneland Dr Jackson MS 39211

ALEXANDER, CAROL MARIE GREENE (MRS. KENNETH ALEXANDER), librarian; b. Washington, Oct. 13, 1933; d. Lawrence William and Inez Ages (Browne) Greene; student Ohio Wesleyan U., 1950-51; A.B., Brown U., 1954; M.S., Case Western Res. U., 1957; m. Kenneth Alexander, Oct. 14, 1968; 1 dau., Donna. Reference librarian, sci. div. N.Y. Pub. Library, 1957-58; sci. reference librarian Library of Congress, Washington, 1959-66; adminstrv. librarian AEC, Germantown, Md., 1966-70, Nat. Agrl. Library, Beltsville, Md., 1970-72; librarian John Jay Coll. Criminal Justice, City U. N.Y., 1972—. Mem. Am. Soc. Information Sci., N.Y. Library Assn., Alumni Assn. Brown U. (dir. 1973-74), Common Cause. Democrat. Home: 20

W 64th St New York City NY 10023 Office: 455 W 59th St New York City NY 10019

ALEXANDER, CATHERINE SVOBODA (MRS. ANDREW E. ALEXANDER), physician; b. Kingfisher, Okla., July 21, 1923; d. Karel and Hannah Esther (Newer) Svoboda; M.D., Okla. U., 1953; m. John R. Spink, Oct. 29, 1957 (dec.); children—Miriam, Russell, Carol, Paul; m. 2d, Andrew E. Alexander, Dec. 9, 1972. Intern, Presbyn. Hosp., Oklahoma City; staff physician Western Okla. Tb Sanatorium, Clinton, 1954-57, Central State Hosp., Norman, Okla., 1958—. Mem. Am. Coll. Chest Physicians (asso.), Nat., Okla. thoracic socs. Roman Catholic. Home: 2103 W Briggs St Norman OK 73069 Office: Box 151 Norman OK 73069

ALEXANDER, CYNTHIA LYNN, educator; b. Muncie, Ind., Dec. 4, 1948; d. Francis Hauens and Helen Ruth (Newbold) Hubbard; B.S. magna cum laude, Ball State U., 1970, M.A. summa cum laude, 1973; m. Louis B. Alexander II, July 11, 1970. Import mgr. L.S. Ayres & Co., Indpls., 1970-72; grad. asst. Ball State U., Muncie, Ind., 1972-73; asst. prof. San Diego State U., 1973—, also financial aid and scholarship adviser, 1974—. Cons., Phoenix Center Psychology, San Diego, 1974—; lectr. U. Cal. at San Diego, 1974—; cons. in field. Mem. Nat. Assn. Women Deans and Counselors, Am. Personnel and Guidance Assn., Am. Coll. Personnel Assn., Pi Beta Phi. Episcopalian. Author: (with Dr. Frank H. Krause) Prostitution: For Love or Money, 1974. Home: 5633 Scripps St San Diego CA 92122 Office: 3760 3d Av San Diego CA 92100

ALEXANDER, ELIZABETH JONES (MRS. CHARLES FRANCIS ALEXANDER), social worker; b. Hinsdale, Ill., July 22, 1913; d. Burgoyne and Lilian (Davis) Jones; student Goucher Coll., 1931-32; B.A., U. Cin., 1935, certificate social work, 1937; m. Charles Francis Alexander, Apr. 25, 1942 (dec. Dec. 1953); 1 dau., Anne Davis. Caseworker, Travelers Aid Soc., Washington, 1937-40, exec. dir., 1940-48; exec. dir. Washington Home for Foundlings, 1956-60; license officer D.C. Dept. Human Resources, Washington, 1960-65, spl. asst. to dir. pub. welfare, 1965-70, acting chief social services br. licensing and standards div., 1970—. Mem. Nat. Assn. Social Workers, Acad. Certified Social Workers. Club: Woman's (Kensington, Md.). Home: 5443 41st Pl NW Washington DC 20015 Office: 122 C St NW Washington DC 20001

ALEXANDER, FRANCES LAURA, author; b. Blanco, Tex., Feb. 12, 1888; d. Thomas Jefferson and Ella Jo (Carson) Alexander; A.B., Baylor U., 1911; M.A., Columbia U., 1923. Tchr. math. San Marcos (Tex.) High Sch., 1911-14, Port Arthur (Tex.) High Sch., 1914-18; tchr. English, Tex. Coll. Arts and Industries, Kingsville, 1925-45, U. Tex. at Austin, 1946-48. Recipient Poetry award Inst. Letters, 1938, Juvenile award, 1969. Mem. Tex. Inst. Letters, Tex. Poetry Soc., Poetry Soc. Am. Author: Seven White Birds, 1938; Mother Goose on the Rio Grande, 1944; Time at the Window, 1948; Conversation with A Lamb, 1955; Pebbles from a Broken Jar, 1963; Mary Charlotte Alexander, 1968; Choc, The Chachalaca, 1969; The Diamond Tree, 1970; Orphans on the Guadalupe, 1971; Hospitality of Earth, 1973; (with Mary C. Alexander) Handbook On Chinese Art Symbols, 1958. Home: 2708 Enfield Rd Austin TX 78703

ALEXANDER, GAIL SUSAN (MRS. MARTIN ALEXANDER), physician; b. N.Y.C., Feb. 15, 1940; d. Herman and Bertha (Bashist) Felsher; Vassar Coll., 1957-60; M.D., N.Y. U., 1966; m. Martin Alexander, Aug. 15, 1965; children—Dierdre, Peter, Margo. Intern, Greenwich (Conn.) Hosp., 1966-67, resident, 1967-68; physician Dept. Health, Greenwich, 1970—. Home: 157 Stanwich Rd Greenwich CT 06830

ALEXANDER, MRS. JAMES ATWELL (PAULINE HILL ALEXANDER), educator, clubwoman; b. Stony Point, N.C., Apr. 7, 1916; d. James Lolo and Eva (Shuford) Hill; student Mitchell Coll., 1932-34, Lenoir Rhyne Coll., 1935-36, Western Carolina Tchrs. Coll., 1937, U. Houston, 1939; m. James Atwell Alexander, Dec. 23, 1938; children—Mary Anna, Eva Pauline. Tchr. Central High Sch., Statesville, N.C., 1934-45, dramatics coach, 1939-41. Leader Stony Point Council Girl Scouts U.S.A., 1951-60; adult leader 4-H Clubs, Alexander County, N.C., 1958-61; area chmn. Mitchell Coll. Endowment, 1956. Recipient oratorical and essay awards Am. Legion, 1931, W.C.T.U., 1933; Woman of Year, Alexander County, 1959. Mem. D.A.R. (dir., chpt. conservation chmn., chpt. regent 1965—, nat. def. chmn. 1967—), Colonial Daus. 17th Century, Mitchell Coll. Alumni Assn. (pres. 1963-64). Democrat. Presbyn. (choir dir. 1958—, ch. organist 1958—). Club: Stony Point Woman's (pres. 1953-54). Home: Stony Point NC 28678

ALEXANDER, JANE, actress; b. Boston, Oct. 28, 1939; d. Thomas Bartlett and Ruth (Pearson) Quigley; student Sarah Lawrence Coll., 1957-59, U. Edinburgh, 1959-60; m. Robert Alexander, July 23, 1962 (div. 1969); 1 son, Jason. Appeared prodns. Charles Playhouse, Boston, 1964-65, Arena Stage, Washington, 1965-68; Broadway prodns. Great White Hope, 1968-69, 6 Rms Riv Vu, 1973, Find Your Way Home, 1974; films Great White Hope, 1969, A Gunfight, 1970, Welcome Home, Johnny Bristol, 1971, The New Centurions, 1972, A Miracle on 34th St., 1973; appeared Am. Shakespeare Festival, 1971-72. Recipient Antoinette Perry award, 1969; Theatre World award; Drama Desk award.

ALEXANDER, JANNETTE WAGNER (MRS. HOWARD ALEXANDER), psychotherapist; b. N.Y.C., Sept. 11; d. Sigmund and Lilly (Newman) Wagner; student Fresno State Coll., 1934-36; B.A., U. Cal. at Berkeley, 1937; postgrad. U. Chgo., 1938; M.S.W., N.Y. Sch. Social Work, 1940; m. Howard Alexander, Apr. 15, 1945; children—Marc, Lori. Caseworker, Jewish Family and Children's Bur., Balt., 1940-42; psychiat. caseworker Mt. Zion Hosp. Psychiat. Clinic, San Francisco, 1942-43; psychiat. casework supr. A.R.C. Hosp. Service, 1943-45; psychiat. caseworker Reiss-Davis Child Study Center, Los Angeles, 1953-62; adminstrv. supr. So. Cal. Permanente Med. Group, dept. psychiatry, 1962-66; adminstrv. supr. Retail Clks. Mental Health Center, Los Angeles, 1966-70; pvt. practice as clin. social work psychotherapist, Los Angeles, 1970—. Field work tchr. U. Cal. at Los Angeles Sch. Social Work, 1961-70, staff supr. dept. psychology clinic, 1970-72; cons. Westland Sch., Los Angeles, 1971—; field dir. research Child Mental Health in Alternative Family Styles, U. Cal. at Los Angeles Neuropsychiat. Inst., 1972—. Adv. bd. Lawrence Sch., Los Angeles, 1965-70; mem. com. on community mental health services Los Angeles Council Social Welfare, 1966; examiner clin. social work Cal. State Bd. Behavioral Scis., 1972. Fellow Soc. Clin. Social Work (chairperson 2d biennial sci. conf. 1973), Am. Orthopsychiat. Assn., Nat. Assn. Social Workers, Acad. Certified Social Workers. Home: 1116 Chantilly Rd Los Angeles CA 90024 Office: 924 Westwood Blvd Los Angeles CA 90024

ALEXANDER, MADELINE J., mathematician; b. San Francisco, May 13, 1921; A.B., Stanford, 1943, M.A., 1943, Ph.D., 1946; m. 1951; 3 children. Instr. math. Purdue U., 1946-52; lectr. U. Del., 1955-57; mem. tech. staff Rocketdyne div. N.Am. Rockwell Co., 1962-70; sr. math. specialist Aerojet Electrosystems Co., Azusa, Cal., 1970-72; sect. head TRW, Inc., Redondo Beach, Cal., 1972—. Mem. Am. Math. Soc., Am. Statis. Assn. Address: 19380 Halsted St Northridge CA 91324

ALEXANDER, MARGARET LOUISE PITCAIRN STRACHAN (MRS. JACK M. ALEXANDER), author; b. Phila., Nov. 13, 1908; d. Frank Russel and Margaret (Marcus) Pitcairn; student U. Pa., 1929-31, U. Wash., 1946-48; m. John E. Strachan, Jr., Dec. 15, 1928 (dec. Oct. 1958); children—Jacqueline (Mrs. Jack T. McCarthy), Bruce Pitcairn, John; m. 2d, Jack M. Alexander, Feb. 9, 1963. Staff feature writer Seattle Times, 1945-51, asst. to Dorothy Neighbors, 1961-64; staff feature writer Long Beach (Cal.) Press Telegram, 1952; dir. publicity Sheraton-Gibson Hotel, World Affairs Inst., Better Housing League, 1954-59; dir. publicity Ford Found. workshops Berea (Ky.) Coll., 1959; instr. creative writing Northshore Sch. Dist., Bothell, Wash., 1966. Moderator juvenile writing panel Pacific N.W. Writers Conf., 1966—, pres., 1970. Recipient 3d pl. award for juvenile books Nat. Press Women, 1972. Mem. Wash. State Press Women (award 1967), Nat. League Am. Pen Women (award 1965), Women in Communications. Author (under name Margaret Pitcairn Strachan) numerous childrens and young adult novels, novels including: Class President, 1959; Mennonite Martha, 1961; Dolores and the Gypsies, Patience and the Mulberry Leaf, 1962; Summer in El Castillo, A Batch of Trouble, 1963; Cabins with Window Boxes, 1964; The Hop Ranch Mystery, 1965; Maria Takes a Fancy, 1966; Trouble at Torrent Creek, 1967; Chinese Scroll Mystery, 1967; Winds of Fate, 1968; Two Families Make One, 1969; Mystery of Blue Barn Stables, 1970; Volunteering: A Practical Guide for Teenagers, 1971. Address: 1936 S Pinecrest Av Coupeville WA 98239

ALEXANDER, MARY LOUISE, educator; b. Ennis, Tex., Jan. 15, 1926; d. Emmett F. and Florence (Hill) Alexander; B.A., U. Tex., 1947, M.A., 1949, Ph.D., 1951. Instr., research asst. Genetics Found., U. Tex., 1944-51; postdoctoral fellow biology div. AEC, Oak Ridge, 1951-52; postdoctoral research fellow U. Tex., 1952-55; research asso. U. Tex.-M.D. Anderson Hosp. and Tumor Inst., Houston, 1956-58, asst. biologist, 1959-62; research scientist Genetics Found. U. Tex., Austin, 1962-67; research cons. Brookhaven Nat. Lab., Upton, N.Y., 1955; research participant Oak Ridge Inst. Nuclear Studies, 1951—; asso. prof. biology S.W. Tex. State U., San Marcos, 1966-69, prof., 1969—. Nat. Cancer Inst. fellow Inst. Animal Genetics, Edinburgh, Scotland, 1960-61. Mem. Genetics Soc. Am., Radiation Research Soc., Am. Soc. Human Genetics, Sigma Xi, Gamma Phi Beta, Phi Sigma, Alpha Epsilon Delta. Home: Hunter's Glen Route 2 Box 119 San Marcos TX 78666

ALEXANDER, MILLIE VIRGINIA CLEVELAND, variety store exec.; b. Seneca, S.C., July 6, 1923; d. Harrison Earle and Hattie Lou (Gilstrap) C.; grad. Draughan's Bus. Coll., 1941; m. Claude Neal Alexander, Sr., Nov. 3, 1946; children—Claude Neal, Jr., Anne (Mrs. Ernest Cannon, Jr.), Susan (Mrs. Douglas Hoolifield), Thomas Cleveland, William Keith. Sec. Anderson Prodn. Credit Assn., Walhalla, S.C., 1941-42, Pendleton Mfg. Co., LaFrance, S.C., 1942-43; with Harpers Stores, Seneca, S.C., 1943—, office mgr., 1945—, exec. sec., treas., 1949—. Pres. Walhalla (S.C.) Pilot Club, 1972, gov. dist. 5, 1974—; sec. Walhalla Band Parents Club, 1969-70. Presbyn. (treas. Women of Ch. 1964-70). Club: Ladies Auxiliary Shrine (Seneca). Home: 207 N Pine St Walhalla SC 29691 Office: PO Box 977 Seneca SC 29678

ALEXANDER, NANCY JEANNE (MRS. DAVID FREDERICK STAAT), physiologist; b. Cleve., Dec. 1, 1939; d. Ralph Stanley and Dorotha Mae (Hunt) Hilditch; B.S., Miami U., Oxford, O., 1960; M.A., 1961; Ph.D., U. Wis., 1965; m. David Frederick Staat, Nov. 28, 1970; children by previous marriage—Benjamin Russell, Wendy Jeanne. Asst. prof. zoology Miami U., Oxford, O., 1966-67; research fellow Ore. Regional Primate Research Center, Beaverton, 1967-69, asst. scientist, 1969-72, asso. scientist, 1973—. Adv. bd. research com. Ore. Zool. Research Center, Portland; mem. animal resources adv. com. NIH. NIH grantee, 1970-73. Mem. A.A.A.S., Am. Soc. Cell Biologists, Soc. for Study Reprodn., Am. Fertility Soc. Author: (with P. F. Parakkal) Keratinization: A Survey of Vertebrate Epithelia, 1972; also articles. Home: 3450 NW 178th St Portland OR 97229 Office: 505 NW 185th St Beaverton OR 97005

ALEXANDER, RAYMONDE ALWYN, journalist; b. Oglethorpe, Ga., June 6, 1921; d. William Linton and Dade (Partee) Alexander; student Central Mo. State Coll., 1939-40; A.B. in Journalism, U. Ga., 1943. Fashion copywriter Davison-Paxon Co., Atlanta, 1943-48; free lance copywriter, Atlanta, 1948-54; menswear copywriter Rich's, Inc., Atlanta, 1955-57; fashion editor Atlanta Constn., 1957—. Mem. Atlanta Ballet, Inc., High Mus. Art. Mem. Atlanta Fashion Group (past dir.), Women in Communications, Sigma Sigma Sigma. Democrat. Methodist. Clubs: Atlanta Press, Atlanta Music, Ansley Golf. Home: 3083 Andrews Dr NW Atlanta GA 30305 Office: 72 Marietta St NW Atlanta GA 30303

ALEXANDER, SADIE TANNER MOSSELL, lawyer; b. Phila.; B.S. in Edn. (with honors), M.A. in Econs. (Frances Sarjeant Pepper fellow) Ph.D. in Econs., LL.B., U. Pa.; m. Raymond Pace Alexander, 1923; children—Mary Elizabeth, Rae Pace. Admitted to Pa. bar, 1927; practiced in Phila., 1927—; asst. city solicitor, Phila., 1928-30, 34-38. Lectr. univs. Norway, Sweden, Finland, 1963, also in Europe, Russia, Asia, S.Am., W.I., Hawaii, Philippines. Sec., Nat. Urban League, N.Y., 25 years, now hon. mem. bd.; mem. Pres. Truman's Commn. on Civil Rights; mem. Phila. Commn. on Human Relations, 1952—, now chmn.; mem. Am. delegation Internat. Conf. on Social Work, Madras, India, 1957, sect. leader, Tokyo, Japan, 1959; mem. Citizens Adv. Com. to Supt. Bd. Edn. on Integration and Intergroup Edn.; mem. Lawyers' Com. on Civil Rights; mem. Phila. Housing Devel. Corp.; mem. Phila. Council for Community Advancement; mem. Manpower Utlzn. Commn. Mem. nat. com. bd. dirs. Greater Phila. br. Am. Civil Liberties Union. Mem. Am., Pa., Phila. (chmn. sub-com. on human rights) bar assns., Lawyers' Club Phila., Am. Judicature Soc. Address: 700 Westview St Mt Airy Philadelphia PA 19119

ALEXANDER, SHANA, editor; b. N.Y.C., Oct. 6, 1925; d. Milton and Cecelia (Rubenstein) Ager; student Vassar Coll., 1942-45; m. Stephen Alexander, 1951 (div.); 1 dau., Katherine. Feature writer PM newspaper, N.Y.C., 1944-46; with Harper's Bazaar, N.Y.C., 1946-47; entertainment editor Flair, N.Y.C., 1950; reporter Life mag., N.Y.C., 1951-61, staff writer, 1961-64, writer twice monthly column The Feminine Eye, 1964-69; editor McCall's Mag., N.Y.C., 1969-71; v.p. Norton Simon Communications, Inc., 1971-72; radio and TV commentator Spectrum, CBS News, 1971-72; columnist, contbg. editor Newsweek, 1972—. Recipient Journalism award Sigma Delta Chi and U. So. Cal. Nat., 1965, Golden Pen award Am. Newspaper Women's Club, 1969; named Woman of Year, Los Angeles Times, 1967. Author: The Feminine Eye, 1970. Office: 444 Madison Av New York City NY 10022

ALEXANDER, SHARON ANN HAMPTON, psychologist; b. Lawrence, Kan., June 3, 1936; d. Billy Vincent and Alma Isabel (Orendorff) Hampton; student U. Kan., 1953-54; diploma Northwest Inst. Med. Tech., 1955; student Washburn U., 1961-62, Friends U., 1965-66; B.A. in Psychology, U. Mo., 1969, M.A. in Psychology, 1971; m. Donald Herman Alexander Buitenhuis, Nov. 10, 1962; children—Karen Ann, Matthew Vincent. Bacteriologist Guam Meml. Hosp., Guam, Marianas Islands, 1957; mgr. Operation Discovery Presch., Kansas City, Mo., 1970-71; research asso. United Community Services, Kansas City, Mo., 1971-74, asso. dir. research and devel., 1974—; research dir. Drug Intervention Group, Olathe, Kan., 1971-72. Cons. Villa Manor Nursing Home, Pratt, Kan.; sec. Behavior Devel. Research Corp., Kansas City, Mo., 1970-71; group co-leader Midwest Christian Counseling Center, Kansas City, Mo., 1971-72. Bd. dirs. Zero Population Growth, Kansas City, Mo., 1971—; sec. adv. council Johnson County Mental Health Center, Mission, Kan., 1972-74, chairperson, 1974—. Mem. Nat. Orgn. for Women (chmn. task force on credit discrimination 1973—), Am. Psychol. Assn., Am. Personnel and Guidance Assn., Mo. Assn. for Social Welfare, A.A.A.S., Nat. Rehab. Assn., Am. Med. Technologists, Am. Bridge Tchr. Assn., Psi Chi. Unitarian. Club: Metropolitan Investment (Kansas City, Mo.). Home: 8747 Rosewood Dr Prairie Village KS 66207 Office: 320 E 10th St Kansas City MO 64106

ALEXANDER, SHIRLEY JOANNE SWINFORD, educator; b. Shelbyville, Ind., Jan. 27, 1938; d. Charles Herschel and Lucille Ione (Weinantz) Swinford; B.S. in Phys. Edn. and Health, Milligan Coll., 1960; M.S. in Phys. Edn., Ind. U., 1966, M.S. in Edn., 1968; m. Scott Allen Alexander, Nov. 27, 1960; children—Lesley, Mark. Tchr., coach Franklin (Ind.) Jr. High Sch., 1960-67; guidance counselor, tchr. phys. edn. and health Southwestern High Sch., Shelbyville, Ind., 1967-69; asst. prof. phys. edn. Ind. Central Coll., Indpls., 1969—. Mem. A.A.H.P.E.R., Ind., Midwest assns. for health, phys. edn. and recreation, Midwest Assn. Phys. Edn. for Coll. Women. Mem. Christian Ch. Home: 1415 E Epler St Indianapolis IN 46227

ALEXANDER, VERA, educator; b. Budapest, Hungary, Oct. 26, 1932; came to U.S., 1950; d. Paul and Irene (Constantin) Alexander; B.A. in Zoology, U. Wis., Madison, 1955, M.S. in Zoology, 1962; Ph.D. in Marine Sci., U. Alaska, 1965; children (by previous marriage)—Graham, Elizabeth. Research asst. U. Ky., Lexington, 1957-58; grad. research asst. U. Pitts., 1958-62; research asst. U. Alaska, Fairbanks, 1962-65, asst. prof., 1965-69, asso. prof. marine sci., 1969—, head program in oceanography and ocean engring., 1973—. Bd. dirs. Fairbanks Light Opera Theatre, 1969-71, pres., 1971-72. Research grantee Environmental Protection Agy., NSF, Nat. Oceanographic and Atmospheric Adminstrn. Sea grantee, others. Mem. A.A.A.S., Am. Soc. Limnology and Oceanography, Internat. Oceanographic Found., Brit. Freshwater Biol. Assn., Am. Assn. U. Women (v.p. Fairbanks br. 1964-66; dir. Alaska div. 1966-68). Contbr. articles to profl. jours. Home: Box I College AK 99701 Office: Inst Marine Sci University Alaska Fairbanks AK 99701

ALFIN-SLATER, ROSLYN BERNIECE, educator; b. Bklyn., July 28, 1916; d. Sam and Lillian (Rubinsky) Alfin; B.A., Bklyn. Coll., 1936; A.M., Columbia, 1942, Ph.D., 1946; m. Grant G. Slater, July 30, 1948. Asst. in charge lecture div. chemistry dept. Bklyn. Coll. 1938-43, tutor gen. inorganic chemistry, 1943, asst. instr. inorganic chemistry, qualitative analysis, evenings 1946-48; asst. instr. inorganic chemistry, exptl. phys. chemistry, food analysis Columbia, 1943-45, research fellow Corn Industries Research Found., 1945-46; instr. biochemistry Coll. Dentistry, N.Y.U., 1945-46; research chemist indsl. enzymes Takamine Labs., Clifton, N.J. 1946-47; research fellow Sloan Kettering Inst. Cancer Research, 1947-48; research asso. dept. biochemistry and nutrition Sch. Medicine, U. So. Cal., 1948-52, vis. asst. prof., 1952-56, vis. asso. prof., 1956-59; asso. prof. nutrition U. Cal. at Los Angeles, 1959-65, prof., 1965—, prof. biol. chemistry Sch. Medicine, 1972—. Mem. nutrution study section NIH, 1968-72, mem. gastroenterology and nutrition tng. grants com., 1972—; mem. com. on dietary allowances Food & Nutrition Bd. NRC. Recipient Osborne-Mendel award Am. Inst. Nutrition, 1970, Distinguished Alumna award Bklyn. Coll., 1972, Woman of Sci. award Women's Med. Aux. U. Cal. Los Angeles, 1973. Fellow A.A.A.S., Am. Pub. Health Assn.; mem. N.Y. Acad. Scis., Am. Soc. Biol. Chemists, Am. Inst. Nutrition (Osborne-Mendel award 1970), Soc. Exptl. Biology and Medicine, Am. Oil Chemists Soc. Am. Heart Assn. (fellow council on arteriosclerosis), Internat. Soc. Cardiology, Sigma Xi, Phi Sigma, Iota Sigma Pi, Delta Omega. Author: (with Lilla Aftergood) Nutrition for Today, 1973. Mem. editorial bd. jour. Nutrition, 1966-70, Advances in Lipid Research. Contbr. pages sci. books and jours. Home: 986 Somera Rd Los Angeles CA 90024

ALFONSI, SANDRA RESNICK (MRS. FERDINANDO PETER ALFONSI), educator; b. Washington, Mar. 1, 1943; d. Abraham Jacob and Bertha (Berman) Resnick; B.A., George Washington U., 1964; Ph.D. in French (Nat. Def. Edn. Act fellow), Cath. U. Am., 1970; m. Ferdinando Peter Alfonsi, June 25, 1971. Instr., George Washington U., Washington, 1964-66, Cath. U. Am., 1969-70; acting asst. prof. French, Lynchburg (Va.) Coll., 1972—. Recipient Edward Carrington Goddard award George Washington U., 1964. Mem. Modern Lang. Assn., Am. Assn. Tchrs. French, Mediaeval Acad., Societe Rencesvals. Contbr. articles to profl. jours. Home: 61-25 97th St Rego Park NY 11374

ALFONSO, LINDA GROSSMAN (MRS. LOUIS J. ALFONSO), lawyer; b. N.Y.C., June 15, 1943; d. Fred and Sara (Wallman) Grossman; A.B., Douglass Coll., 1964; LL.B., Rutgers U., 1967; m. Louis J. Alfonso, June 7, 1964; children—Jennifer Nanci, Stefanie Rachel. Admitted to N.J. bar, 1967, practiced in East Orange, 1967-68, Old Bridge, 1969—; mem. firm Alfonso, Grossman & Alfonso. Legal adviser League for Parent Edn., 1971, 73, pres., 1972. Democratic county committeewoman, 1968—; v.p. Reform Dems., 1972. Trustee Madison Twp. Pub. Library, 1973—. Mem. N.J., Middlesex County bar assns., Women's Polit. Caucus (Madison Twp. chpt.), League Women Voters. Home: 24 Sycamore Dr Old Bridge NJ 08857 Office: 325 Hwy 516 Old Bridge NJ 08857

ALFRIEND, SUE LANDON, banker, marketing exec.; b. North Wilkesboro, N.C.; d. Henry Clayton and Sue (Ennis) Landon; student Salem Coll., 1944-46; A.B., Randolph-Macon Woman's Coll., 1948; M.S., U. N.C., 1951; postgrad. Northwestern U., 1962; m. Richard Jeffrey Alfriend III, Jan. 12, 1952 (div. July 1958); 1 dau., Sue Landon. Tchr., Norfolk (Va.) City Schs., 1953-55, elementary sch., Princess Anne County, Va., 1955-56, advt. mgr. Northwestern Bank, North Wilkesboro, N.C., 1958-61, asst. treas., 1961-62, asst. v.p. charge advt. dept., 1962-69, v.p. charge marketing div., 1969—. Chmn. publicity Wilkes United Fund, 1962-63, mem. publicity com. 1965; mem. exec. bd. Pilot area council Girl Scouts U.S.A., 1968-69, Tarheel Triad council, 1969-72. Mem. Bank Marketing Assn., N.C. Bankers Assn., Wilkes C. of C. (dir. 1968-69), Delta Delta Delta. Presbyn. Home: 611 8th St North Wilkesboro NC 28659 Office: 924 B St North Wilkesboro NC 28659

ALGER, NELDA ELIZABETH, immunoparasitologist; b. Ithaca, N.Y., Dec. 14, 1923; d. Harry B. and Edna Alice (Underwood) Alger; B.S., U. Mich., 1945, M.S., 1947; Ph.D., N.Y. U., 1962. Instr. Highland Park (Mich.) Jr. Coll., 1942-48, Hunter Coll., N.Y.C., 1949-50, Columbia U., N.Y.C., 1949-51; asst. prof. N.Y. U., N.Y.C., 1951-64; asso. prof. dept. zoology U. Ill., Urbana, 1964—. Co-dir. AID Malaria research contract, 1970-72, dir. research in biol. control of mosquitoes, 1972—. Mem. Am. Soc. Protozoologists, Am. Soc.

Parasitologists, Am. Soc. Tropical Medicine and Hygiene. Home: 2206 Southmoor St Champaign IL 61820

ALGIER, AUDREY JANE MONTGOMERY (MRS. JERRY PETER ALGIER), ednl. adminstr.; b. Rochester, N.Y., Apr. 3, 1931; d. Samuel Collins and Lucille Irene (Nolte) Montgomery; B.S., State U. Coll., Geneseo, N.Y., 1954, M.S., 1959; m. Jerry Peter Algier, Oct. 18, 1951; children—Jerry, Daniel, Robert. Instn. tchr. Craig State Sch., Sonyea, N.Y., 1954-58; spl. edn. tchr. Mt. Morris (N.Y.) Central Sch., 1958-63; sr. instn. tchr. Craig State Sch., Sonyea, 1963-69, edn. supr., 1969-74, staff devel. specialist IV, 1974—. Mem. Am. Assn. Mental Deficiency, Mental Hygiene Educators Assn., N.Y. State Assn. Tchrs. Mentally Handicapped, Livingston-Wyo. Assn. Retarded Children (dir. 1970-73). Home: 4194 Reservoir Rd Geneseo NY 14454 Office: Craig State Sch Sonyea NY 14556

ALGMINAS, DIANA ANNA, sch. psychologist; b. Kaunas, Lithuania, Mar. 4, 1939; d. Valerian Felix and Ella Lydia (Heinrich) Radys; came to U.S., 1949, naturalized, 1956; B.S., U. Ill., 1962; M.A., DePaul U., Chgo., 1965; m. Arvydas Algminas, July 4, 1964. Psychologist intern Ill. State Tng. Sch. for Girls, Geneva, 1963-64, Bur. Child Study, Chgo., 1965-66; psychologist, supr. psychology interns Proviso Twp. Area Dept. Edn. for Exceptional Children, Maywood, Ill., 1966—, tchr. in-service tng., 1969—. Tchr. adult edn. Wright Jr. Coll.; organizer, condr. Proviso Twp. Parent Evening Seminar and Discussion Group, 1972; cons., group therapist G.R. Lewis Found., Oak Brook, Ill., 1967—. Mem. Nat. Assn. Sch. Psychologists (charter), Am. (asso.), Ill. psychol. assns., Chgo. Transactional Analysis Inst., West Suburban Sch. Psychologists Assn. (treas. 1973-74). Office: 1000 Van Buren St Maywood IL 60153

ALI, RACHAEL MARILYN, educator; b. Passaic, N.J.; d. Sam Sheh and Louise (Geswaldo) A.; B.A., Marquette U.; postgrad. Cath. U., 1967, 68, 69, San Jose State U., 1970; M.A., U. Del., 1972. Tchr. 4th grade Our Lady of Sorrows Elementary Sch., Garfield, N.J.; tchr. speech-Latin, Queen of Peace Girls High Sch., North Arlington, N.J.; tchr. guidance, Latin, social sci., speech Sacred Heart High Sch., Vineland, N.J.; tchr. speech and dramatic arts, chmn. dept. St. Mark's High Sch., Wilmington, Del., 1969—. Mem. cultural com. Cath. Youth Orgn. cultural com. chmn. Parent-Tchr.-Student Orgn., 1972-73. Mem. Am. Theatre Assn. (del. conv. 1970-74), Sceptre and Sword, Phi Eta Chi, Eta Sigma Phi. Home: 66 Garden Quarter 6B Newark DE 19711 Office: Henderson Rd Wilmington DE 19808

ALIHAN, MILLA, psychologist, sociologist, mgmt. counsel; b. Vladikavkas, Russia; d. Alexander and Maria Sidamon (Tolpar) Alihan; M.A., Smith Coll.; Ph.D., Columbia; m. Bertram Cecil Eskell, July 16, 1938 (dec.). Former lectr. sociology Smith Coll., Barnard Coll., Columbia; editorial advisor Can. Forum publ.; editorial writer Good Housekeeping mag.; pub. relations exec. transp., housing and welfare sects. N.Y. World's Fair; publicity dir. Beekman Downtown Hosp., Bldg. and Maintenance Fund; asso., research and preparation of U.S. Civil Def. program submitted to Sec. of War; simultaneous interpreter Nurenberg trials, U.S. War Dept.; pres. Milla Alihan Assos.; with Kollsman Instrument Corp., Paul Kollsman Labs., Bolsey Corp. of Am.; now with Walter Kidde & Co., Inc.; formerly with Walter Kidde Constructors, Inc.; now with Colvin Labs., Avien, Inc., Instruments for Industry, McKinsey and Co., Genesco, Inc., Seaboard and Eastern; also performs intermittent services other indsl. firms; trustee, supervisory psychology staff Morton Prince Hypnotherapy Clinic, N.Y.C.; faculty Internat. Grad. U., Am. Coll. Switzerland; pvt. clin. practice. Licensed psychologist, State N.Y. Fellow Am. Sociol. Soc.; mem. Nat. Planning Assn. (nat. council), Am. Psychol. Assn., Aviation Writers Assn., Am. Mgmt. Assn., Caucasian Soc. Allaverdy, Am. Acad. Psychotherapists, Mensa. Club: Smith College. Author synchronized Eng. script: Wait for Me, 1944. Author: Social Ecology, 1938, 64; Corporate Etiquette, 1970 (German edit. 1970, Portuguese edit. 1971). Editor-in-chief: America, 1944; editor: Illustrated America, 1944; editor-in-chief Newsletter Soc. for Clin. and Exptl. Hypnosis; also articles, brochures in field. Home: 10 New St Port Washington NY 11050 Office: 25 E 83d St New York City NY 10028

ALKON, ELLEN SKILLEN BOGEN (MRS. PAUL K. ALKON), pediatrician; b. Los Angeles, Apr. 10, 1936; d. Emil and Jane (Skillen) Bogen; B.A., Stanford, 1955; M.D., U. Chgo., 1961; M.P.H., U. Cal. at Berkeley, 1968; m. Paul Kent Alkon, Aug. 31, 1957; children—Katherine Ellen, Cynthia Jane, Margaret Elaine. Intern U. Chgo Hosps., 1961-62; resident in pediatrics Children's Hosp., San Francisco, 1962-64; pediatrician Highland Alameda County Hosp., Oakland, 1964-66, No. Cal. Regional Child Devel. Center, Oakland, 1968-70; chief sch. health Anne Arundel (Md.) County Health Dept., 1970-71; pediatrician Mpls. Health Dept., 1971-73, dir. Bur. Maternal and Child Health, 1973—; adj. asst. prof. pub. health U. Minn., 1971—. Mem. Am. Acad. Pediatrics, Hennepin County Med. Soc., Am. Pub. Health Assn., Am. Sch. Health Assn., Delta Omega. Home: 4733 Girard Av S Minneapolis MN 55409 Office: Mpls Health Dept 250 S 4th St Minneapolis MN 55415

ALLABACH, DAISY MARIE DUVALL (MRS. GRAYDON DUNCAN ALLABACH), educator; b. Monroe, Mich., Aug. 24, 1932; d. Marceillus Francis and Grace Daisy (McCrow) DuVall; A.A., Glen Oaks Coll., 1968; B.A., Western Mich. U., 1970, M.A., 1971; m. Graydon Duncan Allabach, Mar. 18, 1950; children—Ken, Denise (Mrs. Keith McCoy), Crystal, Scot. Instr., Arch, sheltered workshop, Sturgis, Mich., 1968; student tchr. Coldwater (Mich.) State Tng. Sch., 1970; tchr. spl. edn. White Pigeon (Mich.) Community Sch., tchr. 4th grade, 1973—; tchr. exceptional children course Glen Oaks (Mich.) Community Coll., 1973. Mem. Am. Assn. Mental Deficiency, Council Exceptional Children, Nat. Educators Fellowship, N.E.A., Mich. Edn. Assn., Royal Soc. for Promotion Health London (Eng.). Home: RFD 3 Sturgis MI 49091 Office: Featherstone at Balk Sturgis MI

ALLAN, MARGARET BURRELL (MRS. HARRY W. ALLAN), librarian; b. Hamilton, O., Nov. 2, 1915; d. William Eubert and Lucie Ruth (Armstrong) Burrell; B.A., Pomona Coll., 1935; postgrad. U. Cal., 1937; m. Harry W. Allan, Oct. 9, 1961. Asst. librarian Kern County Free Library System, Bakersfield, Cal., 1937-40; librarian Aircraft div. Hughes Tool Co., Culver City, Cal., 1940-59; base librarian Eielson AFB, Alaska, 1959-65; asst. librarian Elmendorf AFB, Alaska, 1965-69, med. librarian, 1969—. Mem. Am., Alaska, Med. library assns., D.A.R., Am. Philatelic Soc. Republican. Home: 6801 Cherokee St Anchorage AK 99504 Office: Med Library USAF Hosp Elmendorf AFB APO Seattle WA 98742

ALLAN, NANCY ELLEN VANDE WIELE (MRS. PATRICK L. ALLAN), editor; b. Antigo, Wis., Apr. 13, 1928; d. William E. and Edith Sarah (McCarthy) Vande Wiele; grad. high sch.; m. Patrick L. Allan, Dec. 10, 1946; children—Terrance, Kathleen, Michael, Brian. Reporter, Greenfield (Wis.) Observer Newspaper, 1962-64, news editor, 1964—. Active P.T.A., Greenfield Little Theater. Recipient Am. Press award Jr. C. of C., 1973. Home: 3630 S 47th St Greenfield WI 53220 Office: 640 E Ryan Rd Oak Creek WI 53154

ALLAN, VIRGINIA RACHEL, govt. ofcl.; b. Wyandotte, Mich., Oct. 21, 1916; d. Clare Floyd and Leta (Benedict) Allan; student Olivet Coll., 1935-36; A.B., U. Mich., 1939, M.A. (fellow), 1945. With Detroit Bd. Edn., 1939-55; pres., co-owner Cahalan Drug Stores, Wyandotte, Mich., 1955-72; dep. asst. sec. state for pub. affairs, Washington, 1972—. Pub. mem. fgn. service officer selection bd. State Dept., 1971; prin. observer U.S., UN Seminar on Participation of Women in Econ. Life, Gabon, Africa, 1971; del., UN Seminar on Women, Moscow, 1970; chmn. Pres. Nixon's Task Force Women's Rights and Responsibilities, 1969. Regent, Eastern Mich. U., Ypsilanti, 1964—. Recipient Outstanding Achievement award U. Mich., 1964, Athena award Intercollegiate Assn. Women Students, 1971, Diamond award City Wyandotte, 1963; named one of Top Ten Working Women in Met. Detroit, 1963. Mem. Nat. Fedn. Bus. and Profl. Women's Clubs (nat. pres. 1963-64), Mortar Bd., Phi Beta Kappa, Phi Kappa Phi, Delta Kappa Gamma. Home: 3504 Stoney Brae Rd Falls Church VA 22044 Office: State Dept 2201 C St NW Washington DC 20520

ALLARD, MARY MARGARET KERR (MRS. WILLARD R. ALLARD), librarian; b. Horton, Kan., Aug. 10, 1915; d. John M. and Clare (Scriven) Kerr; student Kan. Tchrs. Coll., 1953; m. Willard R. Allard, Sept. 13, 1934. Substitute librarian Beck Bookman Library, Holton, 1944-48, head librarian, 1948—. Active Girl Scouts U.S.A., 1941—, mem. com. for spl. awards Kaw Valley council, 1960-65, patch resource person 60th anniversary, 1972; book cart chmn. Holton Hosp. Mem. Republican Womens Club, 1950—. Mem. D.A.R., Kan. Library Assn. Republican. Presbyn. Mem. Rebekah Lodge. Clubs: Business Womens, Bookman. Author: Holton, Kansas 1856-1970. Home: 617 Iowa Av Holton KS 66436 Office: 420 W 4th St Holton KS 66436

ALLARD, META KAY, librarian; b. Bklyn., Jan. 2, 1916; d. Charles and Muriel (Wahrer) Kay; B.A. in Biology, Rice U., 1937; certificate med. tech. Harris County (Tex.) Hosp., 1938; M.L.S., State U. N.Y. at Geneseo, 1962; m. Albert Henry Allard, Dec. 7, 1941; children—Barbara (Mrs. Archie O. Wayman), David. Med. technician Henderson (Tex.) Hosp., 1938-39, Gorgas Hosp., Panama C.Z., 1939-42; research technologist U. Chgo., 1943-44; asso. prof. library Rochester (N.Y.) Inst. Tech., 1962-68, librarian Grad. Chemistry Research Library, 1968-70; cons., div. library extension service projects Ariz. Dept. Library and Archives, Phoenix, 1970-71; dir. library services Lincoln First Banks, Inc., Rochester, 1972—. Coordinator seminar in use of chem. abstracts Rochester Regional Library Council, 1971. Mem. Spl. Libraries Assn., Monroe County Library Club (pres. 1974—). Editor Upstate N.Y. Spl. Libraries Bull., 1974—. Home: 50 Bright Oaks Dr Rochester NY 14624 Office: Lincoln First Banks Inc 1 Lincoln First Sq Rochester NY 14643

ALLEN, AGNES, portrait painter; b. Phila., June 22, 1897; d. Perry S. and Virginia (Oliver) Allen; B.F.A., U. Pa., 1942. Portrait painter, 1927—; exhibited Pa. acad. Fine Arts, Nat. Mus., Harcum Jr. Coll., Bryn Mawr, Woodmere Gallery, and elsewhere; work in permanent collection State in Schuylkill, Andalusia, Pa., Am. Oncologic Hosp., Drexel Inst., U. Pa., Ins. Co. of N.A., Phila. City Hall, Yale Law Sch., Campbell Soup Co., Rittenhouse Club, Atheneaum, Phila., Acad. of Music, Phila., others. Dir. women's com. Phila. Orch. Recipient Mary Smith prize, Pa. Acad. Fine Arts, 1947; profl. achievement award in art Nat. League Am. Pen Women, 1948; prizes North Atlantic States Regional Exhbn., Nat. League Am. Pen Women, 1953, 55, 58; Alumnae award for outstanding achievement in arts Agnes Irwin Sch., 1971; Phila. Com. hon. award for distinguished service Nat. Jewish Hosp. and Research Center, 1969. Mem. Artists Equity, Phila. Art Alliance (life), Nat. Soc. Colonial Dames, Pa. Acad. Fine Arts, Nat. League Am. Pen Women (3d nat. v.p. 1962-64, pres. Pa. 1964-66, pres. Phila. br.), Rittenhouse Sq. Flower Market Assn. (dir.). Republican. Presbyn. Clubs: Altrusa (Phila.), Peale. Home: 1714 Walnut St Philadelphia PA 19103

ALLEN, ALICE S(TANDISH), govt. ofcl., geologist; b. Boston, Nov. 23, 1907; A.B., Mt. Holyoke Coll., 1929; A.M., U. Wis., 1931; postgrad. Northwestern U., 1931-36. Sec. com. geol. names U.S. Geol. Survey, 1936-41, mem. mil. geol. unit, 1942-45, asst. to chief engr. geology br., 1946-60, staff geologist, 1960-65; geologist extraterrestrial research sect. C.E., 1965-71; geologist div. environment U.S. Bur. Mines, Washington, 1971—. Fellow Geol. Soc. Am.; mem. Assn. Engrs. Geology. Address: 4531 Warren St NW Washington DC 20016

ALLEN, ANNE MARIE ROUST, ednl. work; b. Boston, Apr. 15, 1932; d. Arthur Joseph and Helen Margaret (McCarten) Roust; grad. high sch.; m. William A. Allen, Sept. 15, 1956; children—Mark, Billy, Maribeth, Paul. Nurses aide Carney Hosp., 1946-50; with John Hancock Ins. Co., 1950-51; operator Bell Telephone, 1951-52; para-profl., Oxford (Pa.) Intermediate Sch., 1966—. Vol., Community Meml. Hosp., Jennersville, Pa., 1967-71. Served with USNR, 1952-54. Roman Catholic. Mem. Aux. K.C. Home: RD 3 Box 38 Oxford PA 19363

ALLEN, ARDATH BLANCHE, mus. ofcl.; b. Grand Ledge, Mich., Nov. 16, 1916; d. Elmer Sherwood and Frances Blanche (Rosevear) Allen; Asso. Sci., Grand Rapids Jr. coll., 1937; A.B., Calvin Coll., 1939; postgrad. Mich. State U., 1939-40; M.S., Columbia Tchrs. Coll., 1950; postgrad. U. Mich., 1959, 61. Tchr. anatomy and physiology to nurses Grand Rapids (Mich.) Jr. Coll., 1946-49; ednl. asst. Grand Rapids Pub. Mus., 1952-61, curator of exhibits, 1962—. Mem. Mich., Midwest museums assns., Grand Rapids Municipal Employees Assn. Home: 1891 Laraway Lake Dr SE Grand Rapids MI 49506 Office: 54 Jefferson Av Grand Rapids MI 49502

ALLEN, BESSIE MENDENHALL (MRS. JAMES STEWART ALLEN), artist civic worker; b. Blue Ball, Md., Nov. 10, 1910; d. Abraham Hamer and Nora Bell (Yerkes) Mendenhall; student art Tchrs. Coll., Md., 1928-29, Md. Art Sch., 1930-31; tchrs. certificate U. Del., 1933; m. John Graver Berret, Apr. 27, 1937 (div. Jan. 1942); 1 son, Bruce Hamer; m. 2d, James Stewart Allen, Oct. 9, 1953; 1 dau., Gay Olivia. Occupational therapist Del. State Hosp., Wilmington, 1933-36, N.Y. Creedmore Hosp., L.I., 1936, Pa. Schuykill Hosp., Schuykill Haven, 1937, 38, Tex. State Hosp., Austin, 1941, Shepard Pratt Hosp., Balt., 1942-43; with Dept. Navy, Washington, 1943-45; dir. occupational therapy Navy Tng. Center, Bainbridge, Md., 1946-47; with Glendale (Md.) Civil Service, 1947-53; owner, operator gift shop, Newark, Del., 1933-34, Rehoboth, Del., 1945, Wilmington, 1953—. Exhibitor paintings numerous art shows. Active various communi orgns. Mem. Am. Occupational Therapists Assn. Club: Professional Women's (Wilmington). Address: 2108 Covington Rd Carrcroft DE 19803

ALLEN, BETTY LOU (MRS. RITTEN EDWARD LEE, III), mezzo-soprano; b. Campbell, O.; d. James Corr and Dora Catherine (Mitchell) A.; student Wilberforce U., 1944-46; certificate Hartford Sch. Music, 1952; pupil voice Sarah Peck More, Paul Ulanowsky, Carolina Segrera Holden, now studying with Madame Zinka Milanov.; L.H.D., Wittenberg U., 1971; m. Ritten Edward Lee, III, Oct. 17, 1953; children—Anthony Edward, Juliana Catherine. Appeared as soloist Leonard Bernstein's Jeremiah Symphony, 1951, Virgil Thomson's Four Saints in Three Acts, 1952, N.Y.C. Opera Co., 1953; recitalist, also soloist with major symphonies on tours including ANTA-State Dept. tours, Europe, North Africa, Caribbean, Can., U.S., S.Am., Far East, 1954—; S.Am. tour, 1970, Bellas Artes Opera, Mexico City, 1970; recital debut Town Hall, N.Y.C., 1958; ofcl. debuts London, Eng., The Hague, Netherlands, Oslo, Norway, Berlin, Germany, 1958; formal opera debut, Teatro Colon, Buenos Aires, Argentina, 1964; opened new civic theaters in San Jose, Cal., Regina, Sask., Can.; opened concert hall Lyndon Baines Johnson Library, Austin, Tex., 1971; faculty Phila. Mus. Acad., Manhattan Sch. Music; appeared with Caramoor Music Festival, summer 1971, Cin. May Festival, 1972, Santa Fe Opera, 1972, Canadian Opera Co., Winnipeg, Man., 1972, Washington Opera Co., 1971; numerous radio-TV performances, U.S., Can., Eng., Germany, Scandinavia; rec. artist Boston, Vox, Capitol, Odeon-Pathe, Decca records. Represented U.S.A. in Cultural Olympics, Mexico City; mem. adv. bd. music panel Amherst Coll.; mem. music panel Office Cultural Presentations, Dept. State. Bd. dirs. Karl Weige Found. Recipient Marian Anderson award, 1953-54, Nat. Music League Mgmt. award, 1953; named Best Singer of Season, Critics' Circle, Argentina and Chile, 1959, Uruguay, 1961. Martha Baird Rockefeller Aid to Music grantee, 1953, 58; John Hay Whitney fellow, 1953-54; Ford Found. concert soloist grantee, 1963-64. Mem. N.A.A.C.P., Urban League, Nat. Music League (bd.), Hartford Mus. Club, Am. Guild Music, Artists Equity, A.F.T.R.A., Silvermine Guild Artists, Jeunesses Musicales, Gioventu Musicale, Student Sangverein Trondheim, Unitarian-Universalist Women's Fedn., Nat. Negro Musicians Assn. (life), Met. Opera Guild, Amherst Glee Club (hon. life), Am. Mus. Natural History, Sigma Alpha Iota (hon.), Unitarian-Universalist. Club: Cosmopolitan. Office: Columbia Artists Management Inc Ries Div 165 W 57th St New York City NY 10019

ALLEN, BOBBIE JO (MRS. HAROLD MILTON ALLEN), city ofcl.; b. Lufkin, Tex., Nov. 22, 1931; d. Kimble Thomas and Bobbie Marze (Atkinson) Hutson; student Am. Inst. Banking, 1967; certificate accounting U. Tex., 1970; certificate N. Tex. State U., 1973; m. Harold Milton Allen, Nov. 16, 1951; children—Sharon Lee, Harold Ray. With Walgreen Drug Store, Galveston, Tex., 1949-51; with Cotton Concentration Co., Galveston, 1949-52; bookkeeper Lufkin (Tex.) Foundry & Machine Co., 1952-55, 1958-59; legal sec., Lufkin, 1962-63; sec., treas. El Campo (Tex.) Ornamental Iron Works, 1963-65; with Accounting Dept., May Aluminum, El Campo, 1965-66; sec. to v.p. and comptroller Victoria (Tex.) Bank & Trust Co., 1966-67; city sec. City of San Benito (Tex.), 1967—. Sec. Dr. Cash Elementary P.T.A., 1968-70; mem. San Benito Retirement Com. Sec.-treas. Vol. Firemen's Pension Bd., 1967—. Mem. Tex. Assn. City Clks. and Secs., Rio Grande Valley City Clks. and Secs. Assn. (v.p. 1970-71), Lower Rio Grande Valley City Ofcls. Assn. (sec. treas. 1971), Tex. Public Health Assn., Internat. Inst. Municipal Clks. Baptist (Sunday sch. tchr. 1969-72, budget and finance com. 1970-71). Mem. Order Eastern Star. Home: 721 E Pierce St Harlingen TX 78550 Office: 485 N Sam Houston St San Benito TX 78586

ALLEN, CASSIE JEAN PATRICK, lawyer; b. Salyersville, Ky., Oct. 13, 1922; d. Kern and Willie (Bailey) Patrick; student U. Ky., 1946; J.D., U. Miami, 1953; m. Jarvis Allen, Aug. 17, 1946 (div. Dec. 1957); children—David Patrick, Patricia (Mrs. Marvin Bolivier Meade). Admitted to Fla. bar, 1953, Ky. bar, 1957; pvt. practice law, Prestonsburg, Ky., 1957—. Served to sgt. USMC Women's Res., 1943-45. Mem. Am. Judicature Soc., Fla. Bar, Ky. State Bar, Fed. Bar Assn., Kappa Beta Pi. Home: Box 22-B East Point KY 41216 Office: One S Lake Dr Prestonsburg KY 41653

ALLEN, DORIS TWITCHELL (MRS. ERASTUS SMITH ALLEN), psychologist; b. Old Town, Me., Oct. 8, 1901; d. Asa Howard and Cora (Snow) Twitchell; A.B. in Chemistry, U. Me., 1923, M.A. in Biology, 1926, Sc.D., 1965; Ph.D. in Psychology, U. Mich., 1930; postgrad. U. Berlin, 1931-32, U. Munich, 1931; D.Human Reconstrn., Wilmington Coll., 1971; LL.D., Xavier U., 1972; m. Erastus Smith Allen, Oct. 26, 1935 (dec. 1963); 1 son, Erastus Twitchell. Tchr., Orono (Me.) High Sch., 1923-24; instr. U. Me., 1923-25, prof. psychology summers, 1962—; research asst. Bur. Ednl. Research, U. Mich., 1926-31; dir. field lab. Child Edn. Found., N.Y.C., 1932-35; founder, dir. Out-of-Door Sch., Bar Harbor, Me., summers 1934, 35; psychologist Children's Hosp., Children's Convalescent Home, Cin., 1936-47; chief psychologist Longview State Hosp., Cin., 1944-57; asso. prof. clin. psychology, U. Cin., 1949-62, adj. prof., 1962-72, prof. emerita, 1972—. Founder, internat. pres., internat. bd. dirs. Children's Internat. Summer Villages, 1951-65, hon. counselor to internat. bd. dirs., 1965—, chmn. internat. com. on research, 1951-67, mem. com., 1967—; pres. U.S. Assn. Children's Internat. Summer Villages, 1956-65, life trustee; founder, internat. bd. dirs. internat. Sch.-to-Sch. Experience, 1972—. Mem. Pres.'s White House Conf. of 100 for People-to-People Program, Washington, 1956; chmn. Hamilton County (O.) Com. on Civilian Morale, 1941-44. Recipient Gold medal City Stockholm, 1953; award French govt., 1961; named Woman of Year, Cin. Enquirer, 1970. Diplomate Am. Bd. Examiners in Profl. Psychology. Fellow A.A.A.S., Am., Ohio (hon. life, bd. govs. 1943-46) psychol. assns., Internat. Soc. Applied Psychology, Internat. Council Psychologists (pres. 1969-71, award 1962), Interam. Soc. Psychology, Am. Soc. Group Psychotherapy and Psychodrama (v.p. 1967-71), Psychologists Interested in Advancement Psychotherapy (exec. bd. 1961-63), Soc. Projective Techniques; mem. Glendale (O.) Lit. Club, Glendale Lyceum, Sigma Xi, Phi Beta Kappa, Delta Delta Delta, Phi Kappa Phi, Sigma Phi, Delta Kappa Gamma. Author: (with W.P. Matthews, Jr.) A Handbook for Procedure for Children's International Summer Villages, 1961; Summary of Research, 1969; Twitchell-Allen Three Dimensional Personality Test. Contbr. articles to profl. jours. Address: RFD 1 Box 147A Ellsworth ME 04605

ALLEN, DOROTHEA CAROTHERS (DEDE) (MRS. STEPHEN FLEISCHMAN), film editor; b. 1924; m. Stephen Fleischman, 1946; 2 children. With Columbia Pictures, Hollywood, 1943-50; film editor motion pictures including Woman from The Year 2000, Odds Against Tomorrow, The Hustler, America, America, Bonnie and Clyde, Alice's Restaurant, Little Big Man, Rachel, Rachel, Slaughterhouse Five, Serpico, others. Address: 33 W 93d St New York City NY 10025

ALLEN, DOROTHY BURGE, library cons.; b. El Reno, Okla., May 8, 1914; d. James Homer and Allinette (Flournoy) Burge; A.B., U. Okla., 1934; M.S., Columbia, 1949; postgrad. U. Valencia (Spain), 1956; m. Richard K. Allen, Apr. 3, 1958. Librarian, Ponca City (Okla.) Jr. High Sch., 1936-39; sch., reference asst. N.Y. Pub. Library, N.Y.C., 1940-41; indsl. analyst WPB, Washington, 1942-45; asst. librarian Antilles Command, San Juan, P.R., 1945-46; librarian Am. Inst. Fgn. Trade, Phoenix, 1949-56; librarian West Islip (N.Y.) High Sch., 1957-58; librarian Montpelier (Vt.) High Sch., 1959-65; spl. services cons. Vt. State Library, 1968—. Mem. A.L.A. (life), N.E.A. (life), Am. Assn. Univ. Women (state bd. 1973—), League Women Voters (state bd. 1968-70), Nat. Orgn. Women, Vt. Acad. Arts and Scis., Vt. Library Assn., Women's Polit. Caucus. Unitarian. Contbr. articles to profl. jours. Home: 4 Meadow Lane Montpelier VT 05602 Office: 111 State St Montpelier VT 05602

ALLEN, DOROTHY E., social worker; b. Glen Easton, W. Va., May 16, 1922; d. Anderson Andrew and Blanche (McCosh) A.; A.B. in Secondary Edn., West Liberty State Coll.; M.S. in Social Work, Western Res. U. With W. Va. Div. Child Welfare (now Div. Social Services), 1944—, now dir. Mem. Nat. Assn. Social Workers, Am.

Pub. Welfare Assn., Council Social Work Edn. and Personnel. Home: 1800 Roundhill Rd Charleston WV 25314 Office: 1900 Washington St E Charleston WV 25305

ALLEN, EDITH, hosp. adminstr.; b. Scammon, Kan., Nov. 24, 1912; d. Ebenezer and Annie (Longstaff) Allen; certificate Kan. State Tchrs. Coll., Pittsburg, summers 1931-35; Tchr. elementary schs., Cherokee County, Kan., 1931-35; sec. Joplin Bus. Coll., Mo., 1936; auditors office State Hwy. Dept., Topeka, Kan., 1937-38; stenographer-clk. County Clk.'s Office, Columbus, Kan., 1938-42; asst. Office Judge Probate Ct., Columbus, 1942-47; dr.'s asst., Columbus, 1947-70; hosp. adminstr. Maude Norton Meml. City Hosp., Columbus, Kan., 1970—. Mem. Bus. and Profl. Women's Club (pres. 1940-43), S.E. Kan. Med. Assistants, Kan. Med. Assts. Soc., Am. Assn. Med. Assts. Home: Rural Route 1 Scammon KS 66773 Office: 220 N Pennsylvania St Columbus KS 66725

ALLEN, EDITH BEAVERS (MRS. VIVIAN CLYDE ALLEN), automotive rustproofing co. exec.; b. Berwind, W.Va., Feb. 15, 1920; d. Charles Thomas and Bertha Bell (Belcher-Beavers) Beavers; student Menke Real Estate Sch., Clearwater, Fla., 1955-56; m. Vivian Clyde Allen, July 18, 1935; children—Fred Kent, Dwight Mason. Owner, operator Allen's Gift Shop and Restaurant, Tazewell, Va., 1945-50; mgr. Allen's Gift Shop, Clearwater, Fla., 1950-55; real estate broker, Clearwater, 1956-71; sec., co-mgr. Ziebart, auto-truce rustproofing, Tampa, Fla., 1971—. Writer, 1971—. Mem. Fla. Assn. Realtors, Epsilon Sigma Alpha (chpt. pres. 1956). Baptist (Sunday sch. tchr.). Author: New Testament Bible Games, 1964; 100 Bible Games, 1966; Bridal Showers, 1969; Better Bible Games, 1969; Get in the Game, 1971; Let's Plan a Bridal Shower, 1974. Home: 904 Sevard Av Clearwater FL 33516 Office: 2208 N Florida Av Tampa FL 33602

ALLEN, ETHEL K(ULLMANN), bacteriologist; b. Milw., July 13, 1906; A.B., U. Wis., 1928, M.S. (Herman Frasch fellow 1928-30), 1930; m. 1930. Collaborator bacteriology expt. sta. U. Hawaii, 1932-39, researcher, 1939-44; analyst water testing sta. U.S. Engring. Dept., 1942-43; bacteriologist Honolulu Blood Bank, 1943-44; tchr. sci. Punahou Acad., 1944-45; now individual research U. Wis. at Madison. Asso. mem. Internat. Congress Soil Sci., Netherlands, 1950, Wis., 1960, Internat. Bot. Congress, Sweden, 1950, Scotland, 1964, Internat. Congress Microbiology, Italy, 1953, Internat. Soil Conf., New Zealand, 1962; mem. N.W. European Microbiology Group, Stockholm, Sweden, 1969, 10th Internat. Congress Microbiology, Mexico, 1970, tech. meeting Internat. Biol. Program, Netherlands, 1970, Scotland, 1973. Mem. Sigma Xi, Sigma Delta Epsilon. Author sci. papers and revs. Home: 4142 Hiawatha Dr Madison WI 53711 Office: 336 Steenbock Memorial Library U Wisconsin Madison WI 53706

ALLEN, FRANCES MARION, social worker; b. Dallas, July 20, 1908; d. James Walter and Daisy (Emery) Allen; student Tex. Christian U., 1924-26; B.A., U. Tex., 1929; M.S.W., Tulane U., 1948; advanced certificate social work Smith Coll., 1952. Case worker Ill. Emergency Relief Commn., 1931-34, case supr., 1934-35; social worker Family Service Assn., Dallas, 1935-38; regional supr. Tex. Old Age Assistance Commn., 1938-42; supr. A.R.C., Ft. Worth, 1943-47; psychiat. social worker Child Guidance Clin., Fort Worth, 1948-58, chief social worker, asso. dir. clinic, 1958-67; individual practice social work, Ft. Worth, 1967-70. Prof., mem. adv. com. U. Tex. Sch. Social Work, 1950-58. Fellow Am. Orthopsychat. Assn., Acad. Certified Social Workers; mem. Nat. Assn. Social Workers, Nat. Conf. Social Welfare, Tex. Mental Health Assn., Nat. League Women Voters. Address: 2256 5th Av Fort Worth TX 76110

ALLEN, HELEN PASTERNAK (MRS. LAWSON I. ALLEN), coll. ofcl.; b. Passaic, N.J., Dec. 13, 1929; d. Thomas and Mary (Mikolajczyk) Pasternak; B.S., N.Y. U., 1955; m. Lawson I. Allen, May 31, 1968. Reporter, Paterson (N.J.) Morning Call, 1955-59, Tucson Daily Citizen, 1959-69; writer-information specialist Pima Community Coll., Tucson, 1970—. Recipient award of excellence Tucson Communigraphics, 1971, 4 awards of excellence Tucson Communigraphics exhbn., 1972; certificate of excellence Chgo. Communicating Arts Exhbn., 1973. Mem. Ariz. Press Women, Nat. Fedn. Press Women. Presbyn. (deacon 1967-68). Home: 2640 S Cottonwood Lane Tucson AZ 85713

ALLEN, HELENE THERESE DOBRICK (MRS. JAMES W. ALLEN, SR.), nurse, civic worker; b. Johnstown, Pa.; d. Joseph and Mary (Piron) Dobrick; R.N., Lebanon Hosp. Sch. Nursing, 1936; student Elmira Coll., 1962-63; m. James W. Allen, Oct. 18, 1942; children—Barbara, James W., Joseph. Pvt. duty nurse N.Y.C., 1937; airline nurse-hostess United Air Lines, 1937-42. Dir. Finger Lakes Assn., 1967-69, 72—. Lectr. on travel local clubs. Pres., P.T.A., Odessa, N.Y., 1960-62; Schuyler County chmn. fund drive So. Tier Heart Assn., 1969; Red Cross nurse; chmn. ways and means fund raising Schuyler Hosp. Assn., 1967; mem. bldg. fund Jane Delano Hosp., 1968; legislative chmn. P.T.A., Finger Lakes Dist., 1962-68, N.Y. state cultural arts chmn., 1968-70; chmn. plan and zoning Town of Catherine, N.Y., 1964-67; mem. citizens adv. com. Bldg. Odessa Sch., 1963; life mem. Eisenhower Med. Center Aux. Bd. dirs., 1st treas. Schuyler County Council on Arts, 1964. Recipient Scholarship award Am. Legion, 1929, Gold medal Nat. Honor Soc., 1942, G.E. Halperin Legion, 1929, Gold medal Nat. Honor Soc., 1942, G.E. Halperin Gold medal for most efficient nurse Lebanon Hosp., 1936, Gold Watch S.Am. Admiral, 1942. Mem. St. Benedict Soc. (treas. 1965—, mem. com. to build chapel 1955), Internat. Platform Assn., Clipped Wings, United Air Lines Alumna, League Women Voters, Elmira Coll. Club Schuyler County, N.Y. State P.T.A. (life), Desert Mus., Palm Springs, Cal. Clubs: Zonta, Ithaca Garden. Home: RD 1 Alpine NY 14805

ALLEN, IRENE KARST (MRS. BALDWIN JAMES ALLEN), civic worker; b. New Orleans, July 24, 1911; d. Michael Joseph and Irene M. (Fitzgerald) Karst; grad. Gulfpark Coll.; B.A., La. State U., 1932; m. T. Edward Ernst, Sept. 15, 1934 (dec. Oct. 1964); children—Irene Mary (Mrs. Donald Irwin Mackenroth), Thomas E., Gerald Edward; m. 2d, Baldwin James Allen, Sept. 27, 1968. Clk. classified project U.S. Weather Bur., 1943-45; v.p. T. Edward Ernst, Inc., cons. engrs., New Orleans, 1960-66, pres., 1966—; Capt., United Fund Campaign; active worker Muscular Dystrophy and Cerebral Palsy campaigns. Bd. mem. Workers Magnolia Sch. Retarded Children. Mem. Le Petite Theatre Guild, Loyola U. Music Salon, St. Rita's Altar Soc., Art. Assn. Guild (life bd. mem.), Res. Officers Assn. Ladies (pres. New Orleans chpt. 1949-50, pres. La. 1960), Women's Aux. Eye, Ear, Nose and Throat Hosp. (1st v.p. 1960-63, chmn. fund raising 1961-67, pres. 1967-69, chmn. fund raising 1969-73), La. State U. Found., Am. Assn. U. Women (life, S.E. hospitality chmn.), Womens Aux. New Orleans Sara Mayo Hosp. (rec. sec. 1960-63, dir.), Women's Guild New Orleans Opera House Assn. (rec. sec. 1961-63, dir. 1964-67, 70-73), Womens Aux. Goodwill Industries, Inc. of New Orleans (pres. 1962-64, dir. 1964-73, co-chmn. fund raising), Metairie Lit. Guild (pres. 1960-61), Sara Mayo Hosp. Guild (dir., pres.-elect 1972-73, pres. 1973—), Art Assn. Guild New Orleans (2d v.p. New Orleans, 1961, Fund raising chmn. 1956-62, hon. life, 1st v.p. 1962-64), DePaul Hosp. Guild Aux. (bd. mem.), New Orleans Garden Soc., Inst. Oriental Relations (mem. bd.), Fgn. Relations Assn. New Orleans, English Speaking Union, Womens Aux. La. Engring. Soc., Delta Zeta, Delta Sigma Chi. Roman Catholic. Club: New Orleans County. Home: 503 Hillary St New Orleans LA 70118

ALLEN, JANE ALLEN (MRS. HOMER RICHARD ALLEN), educator; b. Phila., May 17, 1920; d. Robert Louis and Lois (McKinney) Allen; student Grove City Coll., 1938; B.B.A., Westminster Coll., 1965; M.A., Case Western Res. U., 1967, Ph.D., 1973; m. Homer Richard Allen, Apr. 19, 1941 (dec. Apr. 1963); children—Robert McKinney, Homer Gerald, Emily Jane (Mrs. Joseph Berg). Psychologist, Bd. Edn. Cleve., 1968-70, Spl. Edn. Dist. Lake County, Ill., 1970-73; instr., Roosevelt U., Chgo., Loyola U., Chgo., 1973—; treas. Chgo. Area Spl. Edn. Services, Ltd., 1973—; project dir. NSCC Consortium, ESEA, 1974, Psychol. Coop. Edn. Service Agy.-18, Burlington, Wis., 1974-75. Founder, New Group for Adult Singles, Evanston, Ill., 1970. Mem. Am. Psychol. Assn., Assn. for Humanistic Psychology, Am. Assn. Mental Deficiency, Council for Exceptional Children. Unitarian (trustee). Home: 731 Michigan Av Evanston IL 60202

ALLEN, JOAN DE RIS, architect; b. Ridgewood, N.J. Jan. 20, 1931; B.Arch., Columbia, 1956. Prin., Joan deRis, architect, South Egremont, Mass., 1961—. Registered architect, Mass., N.J., N.Y., Pa. Mem. A.I.A. Prin. works include Abt Residence, Richmond, Mass., 1964; residential units 4-9, Camphill Village, Copake, N.Y., 1965-68; residential units 1-3, Camphill Spl. Schs., Glenmore, Pa., 1967, Community Hall, 1968, Waldmann Residence, Canaan, N.Y., 1968. Home: PO Box 275 South Egremont MA 02158

ALLEN, JOANN HARTMAN, retail store exec.; b. Barnard, Mo., Apr. 18, 1943; d. Willard Miles and Frances Powell (Thompson) Hartman; B.S. in Edn., Central Mo. State Coll., Warrensburg, 1967; student U. Mo.-Columbia, 1968, 70. Extension home economist in Lincoln County, U. Mo. Extension Center, Troy, 1967-68, continuing edn. coordinator Booneslick area, 1969, extension home economist in St. Louis County, Clayton, 1970-73; asst. buyer china and glassware Stix, Baer & Fuller Dept. Store, St. Louis, 1974—. Mem. consumer adv. council Better Bus. Bur. Greater St. Louis, 1970—; mem. ednl. adv. com. for St. Louis, J.C. Penney Co. Ednl. Conf., 1970-73. Mem. Friends of St. Louis City Art Mus., also mem. Decorative Arts Soc. of mus. Mem. Am., Mo. (legislative chmn. 1970-73) home econs. assns., Nat. Assn. Extension Home Economists, U. Mo. Extension Assn. (chmn. home econs. category recruitment), Am. Assn. U. Women, Kappa Omicron Phi. Methodist. Club: Zonta (St. Louis). Home: 4400 Lindell Blvd St Louis MO 63108 Office: Stix Baer & Fuller 6th and Washington Sts St Louis MO 63101

ALLEN, JODIE T. (MRS. GEORGE VENABLE ALLEN, JR.), polit. scientist; b. N.Y.C., Sept. 1, 1938; d. Theodore A. and Hilda (Liccione) Tetreault; B.A. with highest honors, Vassar Coll., 1959; m. George Venable Allen, Jr., June 15, 1960; 1 son, Theodore Tetreault. Asst. internat. economist Exec. Office Pres., Washington, 1959-60; computer analyst U.S. Army Corps Engrs., 1960-62, Nat. Planning Assn., Washington, 1962-64; mem. tech. staff Research Analysis Corp., McLean, Va., 1964-66, cons., 1966-68; research asso. Brookings Instn., 1966; with office sec. Dept. Health, Edn. and Welfare, Washington, 1966-70, dir. income maintenance experimentation, 1969-70, chief Office Research and Policy Coordination, Family Assistance Planning Agy., 1970; sr. research staff Urban Inst., Washington, 1970-73, asst. v.p. research, 1973—; v.p., dir. Policy Studies group Mathematica, Inc., 1974—. Cons. Planning Research Corp., 1966-68, Nat. Planning Assn., 1966-67. Mem. community resource com. Jr. League Washington, 1969-70; vol. Planned Parenthood D.C., 1965-70. Mem. Phi Beta Kappa. Clubs: Sulgrave Vassar (prospective students com. 1964-69) (Washington); Chevy Chase (Md.). Author: A Funny Thing Happened on the Way to Welfare Reform, 1972; Perspectives on Income Maintenance: Where Do We Go from Here and How Far, 1972; also chpts. in Blue Collar Workers, 1971, Setting National Priorities: The 1972 Budget, 1971. Home: 3100 Foxhall Rd NW Washington DC 20016

ALLEN, JUDITH, ednl. adminstr.; b. Norwood, Mass., Dec. 13, 1938; d. Roland L. and Helen Studley; B. Liberal Studies cum laude, Boston U., 1970; postgrad. Salem State Coll., 1971—. Asst. personnel dir. Grass Instrument Co., Quincy, Mass., 1963-64; personnel rep. Boston U., 1960-62, 64-66, asst. to dir. financial aid, 1967-70; dir. financial aid Regis Coll., Weston, Mass., 1970—. Cons. Bd. Higher Edn. Mass., 1972—; mem. Mass. State Scholarship adv. com. Mem. Nat., Mass. (pres. 1973—), Eastern (mem. exec. council 1972—) assns. of student financial aid adminstrs., Am. Assn. Higher Edn., Am. Personnel and Guidance Assn., Coll. Entrance Examination and Coll. Scholarship Service. Home: 88 Pierce Rd Watertown MA 02172 Office: Regis College Wellesley St Weston MA 02193

ALLEN, KATHERINE, editor-writer; b. Williamstown, Mass.; d. George E. and Katherine (Wallace) Allen; student N.Y.U.; A.B. cum laude, Bklyn. Coll., 1961. Editor-writer U.S. Mission to UN, N.Y.C., 1948—. Recipient Meritorious Honor award Dept. State, 1970. Office: 799 UN Plaza New York City NY 10017

ALLEN, LOMA MOYER (MRS. DELESLIE ALLEN), ednl. adminstr.; b. Niagara Falls, N.Y., May 16, 1913; d. Arnold R. and Edyth (Hawkins) Moyer; student Wheelock Coll., 1930-31; m. DeLeslie Allen, Feb. 24, 1934 (dec. Nov. 1973); children—Loma Joy (Mrs. Rush Clarke III), Leslie Cornelia (Mrs. Henry Hays, Jr.). Dir. Assn. Jr. Leagues of Am., 1948-50, sec., 1950-52, pres., 1952-54; sec., mem. exec. com. Nat. Social Welfare Assembly, 1954-68; dir. Am. Social Health Assn., 1955-67, exec. bd., 1956-67; past dir., past mem. adv. council Am. br. Internat. Social Service; formerly dir. community relations Rochester Inst. Tech., asst. to pres., 1974—; vice chmn. social welfare com. Nat. Council of Chs., 1960-66; incorporator Family Life Found., 1957-60; v.p. Nat. Family Life Found.; bd. dirs. Rochester Area Council Chs., 1962-65; v.p. Nat. Fedn. Settlements and Neighborhood Centers, 1962-66, pres., 1966-68; past mem. Rochester Housing Authority; past mem. Rochester and Monroe County Youth Bd., past chmn. adv. com. Rochester Careers in Social Work; mem. Nat. Assembly for Social Policy and Devel., 1968-73; mem. Rochester Met. Housing Study Com., 1967-70; mem. adv. com. 1970 White House Conf. on Children and Youth. Bd. dirs. Rochester Family Service Assn., 1955-60; bd. dirs. Baden St. Settlement, Rochester, 1954-72, hon. bd. dirs., 1972—, sec. 1956-57, pres., 1964-66; mem. adv. council welfare services Dept. Health, Edn. and Welfare, 1964-66; formerly trustee The Harley Sch. Recipient Ethel H. Wise Spl. Merit award Columbia U. Sch. Social Work, 1967; Distinguished Service award Nat. Conf. on Social Welfare; Forman Flair award for outstanding community service, 1971. Mem. Buffalo and Erie County Council of Social Agys. (dir. 1947-53), Buffalo YWCA (dir. 1948-50), Buffalo City Planning Assn. (dir. 1947-50), Planned Parenthood League (sec. 1960), Jr. League of Buffalo, Inc. (hon.), Am. Social Health Assn. (v.p. 1962-67), Urban League of Rochester (v.p. 1965-70). Home: 22 Barrington Park Rochester NY 14607

ALLEN, LORETTA BELLE BROOME (MRS. CLARENCE CANNING ALLEN), artist, journalist; b. Caney, Kan., June 22, 1916; d. Floyd Leroy and Lillie Elizabeth (Trumbly) Broome; student Anatomy Studios, 1933-34, Fed. Art Schs., 1934-36, Famour Writers Sch., 1959-61; m. Marcellus Davis Douglas, Dec. 20, 1934; 1 son, Jesse Davis; m. 2d, Clarence Canning Allen, Feb. 4, 1957. Costume designer Pat Rooney Studios, Oklahoma City, 1934-35; illustrator Dona Dress & Robe Co., Oklahoma City, 1933-36; designer Dona Dress & Robe Mfg. Co., Oklahoma City, 1968-71; columnist Southside Times, Tulsa, 1971—, Bixby (Okla.) Jour., 1973—; exhibited art in one-woman shows at Tulsa Studio Club Gallery, Fourth Nat. Gallery, Tulsa Little Theatre Gallery; exhibited art in group shows at Oklahoma City Art Center, Allen Art Group, Fourth Nat. Gallery, Tulsa; represented art in permanent collections at Osage County Mus., Pawhuska, Okla. Tchr. drawing adult class Allen Art Studio, Tulsa, 1959-61. Mem. Tulsa Press Club (v.p. 1960-62), Assn. Am. Editorial Cartoonists (v.p. aux. 1967-68), Am. Artists Profl. League. Democrat. Address: 1645 E 17th Pl Tulsa OK 74120

ALLEN, MADELINE MAY, ednl. adminstr.; b. Troy, N.C., July 18, 1935; d. James Bruton and Madeline (May) Allen; B.Mus., Salem Coll., 1957; Mus.M., U. Miss., 1959; Ph.D., Fla. State U., 1957. Instr. music Samford U., Birmingham, Ala., 1959-61; asst. to dir. admissions Salem Coll., Winston-Salem, N.C., 1961-69; asso. dean students, asst. prof. edn. Clinch Valley Coll., U. Va., Wise, 1971—. Sec., treas. Wise and Lee Counties Humanities Council, 1972—; mem. Drug Awareness Council, Wise, 1973—. Mem. Nat. Assn. Women Deans, Adminstrs. and Counselors, Am. Assn. for Higher Edn., So. Coll. Personnel Assn. Office: Clinch Valley Coll Wise VA 24293

ALLEN, MARGARET PROSSER, painter, educator; b. Vancouver, B.C., Can., Jan. 26, 1913; B.A., M.F.A., U. Wash.; student Alexander Archipenko, Amedee Ozenfant. Exhibited in shows at Wilmington Soc. Fine Art, 1942-45, 47-49, 51, 53-64, U. Del., 1946, N.W. Ann. Exhbn., 1938, 41, 43, 45, 47, 48, Weyhe Gallery, 1947, Rehoboth Art Gallery, 1952, numerous group shows in Del. area; exhibited one-man photog. show Smithsonian Traveling Exhbn., 1968-72; instr. art U. Del., Newark, 1942-48, asst. prof., 1949-72, asso. prof., 1972—. Address: 119 Briar Lane Newark DE 19711

ALLEN, MARGO (NEWTON) (MRS. HARRY HUTCHISON SHAW), artist; b. Lincoln, Mass.; d. George Frederick and Alice (Jewett) Newton; student Boston Mus. Sch. Fine Arts, 1917-19, Naum Los Sch. of Anatomy, Rome, 1927; Brit. Acad., Rome, 1927; m. Thomas Lamb Allen, June 7, 1917 (d. 1932); children—Margot (Mrs. Howard S. Giberson), William Henry, Hope (Mrs. Harold F. Cross); m. 2d, Harry Hutchison Shaw, June 24, 1942. One man shows Palace of Fine Arts, Mexico City, Mexico, 1938, Marie Sterner Galleries, N.Y.C., 1939, Fogg Art Mus., Cambridge, Mass., 1939, Currier Art Galleries, Manchester, N.H., 1939, Houston Art Mus., 1940, Dallas Mus. Fine Arts, 1940, Taylor Mus., Colorado Springs, Colo., 1940, Seattle Art Mus., 1940, Fine Arts Gallery, San Diego, 1940, Joslyn Art Mus., Omaha, 1940, Mus. N.M., 1940, Clearwater (Tex.) Art Mus., 1941, M. H. DeYoung Meml. Mus., San Francisco, 1948, Isaac Delgado Mus. Art, New Orleans, 1950, Am. Assn. U. Women, Lafayette, La., 1954, Gallery Contemporary Art, Lafayette, 1954, U. S.W. La., Lafayette, 1954, Beaumont (Tex.) Art Mus., 1958, Inst. Mexican-N.Am. Cultural Relations, Mexico City, 1959, Galerie Arlette Chabaud, Paris, France, 1961, Heffer Galleries, Cambridge, Eng., 1962, Longboat Key Art Center, Center Gallery, Hilton Leech Gallery, Sarasota, Fla., Andre Smith Meml., Maitland, Fla., Beaumont Art Mus., Tex., Columbia Mus. Art, Columbia, S.C., 1965-69; exhibited in group show S.N.A.D., N.Y.C., Nat. Sculpture Soc., Pa. Acad. Design, Phila., Phila. Art Alliance, Addison Gallery Am. Art, Andover, Mass.; Boston Mus. Fine Arts, 1929, Butler Art Inst., Youngstown, O., Isaac Delgado Mus. Fine Arts, 1954-55, Dallas Mus. Fine Arts; Palace of Legion of Honor, San Francisco; 1929; Beaumont Art Mus., 1957; represented in permanent collections Palace Legion Honor, San Francisco, Dallas Mus. Fine Arts, Mus. N.M., Beaumont (Tex.) Art Mus., Butler Mus. Am. Art (O.), Nat. Mus. Mexico, Mus. Modern Art Mexico, Columbia (S.C.) Mus. Fine Arts. Recipient two first prizes Isaac Delgado Mus. of Art, New Orleans, 1951. Mem. Nat. Sculpture Soc., Ringling Mus., Art League of Manatee County, Sarasota Art Assn., New Eng. Assn. Contemporary Sculpture, Nat. League Am. Pen Women, Alpha Omicron Pi. Research on indigenous people of Mexico and S.W. Address: 501 Sloop Lane Sarasota FL 33577

ALLEN, MARY CATHERINE MITCHELL (MRS. WALTON ALBERT ALLEN), educator; b. Iva, S.C.; d. George Francis and Cinderella (Harris) Mitchell; A.A., Anderson Jr. Coll., 1946; B.S. in Edn., Central State Coll., Edmond, Okla., 1962; M.Ed., U. Ga., 1968; m. Walton Albert Allen, Apr. 15, 1949; children—Susan Marie, Joel Walton, Barbara Ann. Tchr., prin. Anderson County (S.C.) Schs., 1946-52; tchr. West Clayton Sch., College Park, Ga., 1964-66, guidance counselor, 1966—. Active Girl Scouts U.S.A., 1946-68. Mem. N.E.A., Ga., Clayton County (pub. relations com. 1967-68) edn. assns., Am. Assn. U. Women, Am. (state coordinator elementary counselors), Ga. personnel and guidance assns., Ga. Assn. Sch. Counselors, Alpha Delta Kappa (chpt. treas. 1970-72, dist. chaplain 1972—), Kappa Delta Pi. Home: 2765 Jerome Rd College Park GA 30337 Office: 5580 Riverdale Rd College Park GA 30337

ALLEN, MARY-MAURICE BELT, geneticist; b. Beaumont, Tex., Aug. 16, 1915; B.A., Rice U., 1937; M.S., U. Houston, 1957; Ph.D. in Biochemistry and Genetics, U. Tex., 1962; m. 1941. Tchr. pub. schs., Tex., 1937-52; instr. zoology U. Houston, 1955-57; technician genetics M.D. Anderson Hosp. and Tumor Inst. U. Tex., 1957-58, fellow, 1959-62, project investigator trace metals, 1962-63, univ. research scientist genetics, 1958-59; research asso. Rice U., 1963-64; research chemist Baylor Coll. Medicine, 1964—; instr. South Tex. Coll., 1956; lectr. San San Jacinto Jr. Coll., 1962-63. Asst. dir. metabolic research Hermann Hosp., U. Tex. system. Mem. Genetics Soc. Am. Address: 10944 Jo Edna St Houston TX 77034

ALLEN, MARYON PITTMAN (MRS. JAMES BROWNING ALLEN), journalist, interior decorator; b. Meridian, Miss., Nov. 30, 1925; d. John D. and Tellie (Chism) Pittman; student U. Ala., 1944-47, Internat. Inst. Interior Design, 1970; m. Joshua Sanford Mullins, Jr., Oct. 17, 1946 (div. Jan. 1959); children—Joshua Sanford III, John Pittman, Maryon Foster; m. 2d, Senator James Browning Allen, Aug. 7, 1964; 1 stepson, James Browning Allen. Office mgr. Dr. Alston Callahan, Birmingham, Ala., 1959-60; bus. mgr. psychiat. clinic U. Ala. med. Center, Birmingham, 1960-61; agt. Protective Life Ins. Co., Birmingham, 1961-62; women's editor Sun Newspapers, Birmingham, Ala., 1962-64; columnist The Birmingham News, 1964—; writer weekly column Reflections of a News Hen; v.p. Emerald Valley Corp., partner J.D. Pittman Partnership Co. Mem. com. to choose artist of year Birmingham Festival Arts, 1967—. Vice pres. Ladies Senate Red Cross, Ala. Arts Commn.; mem. Blair House Fine Arts Commn. Democratic presdl. elector, 1968. Trustee Children's Fresh Air Farm, Birmingham, 1947—. Recipient Ala. Press Assn. 1st place award, 1962, 63; other state and nat. press awards for typography, fashion writing, food pages. Mem. Birmingham Com. 100 for Women (charter), Ala. Art League, Nat. League Am. Pen Women, Arlington Hist. Assn. (dir. 1968—), Ala. Hist. Commn. (mem. at large), Ala. Writers Conclave, Antiquarian Soc. Gadsden, Gadsden Art Assn., U.S. Capitol Hist. Soc., Nat. Trust Historic Preservation. Presbyn. Clubs: Music Study, Gadsden Country, Music (Gadsden); Mountain Laurel Garden; Am. Newspaper Women's (membership com.), 91st Congress, Congressional, 1925 F Street (Washington).

Home: 7405 Hallcrest Dr McLean VA 22101 also 1321 Bellevue Dr Gadsen AL 35901

ALLEN, MELBA TILL (MRS. MARVIN E. ALLEN), state ofcl.; b. Butler County, Ala., Mar. 3, 1933; d. Samuel Ben and Gertrude (Johnson) Till; grad. high sch.; m. Marvin E. Allen, Dec. 24, 1950; children—Judy Kathryn, Randy Earl. With Haas-Davis Packing Co., Mobile, Ala., 1951-52, W. T. Smith Lumber Co., Chapman, Ala., 1953-54, Cooper Stevedoring Co., Mobile, 1956-63, Algernon Blair Inc., Montgomery, Ala., 1963-66; now auditor State of Ala., Montgomery. Mem. Bus. Women's Assn. Democrat. Baptist. Mem. Order Eastern Star. Home: Box 3 Route 1 Grady AL 36036 Office: State Capitol Bldg Montgomery AL 36104

ALLEN, MONIQUE SORBIER (MRS. JON LEWIS ALLEN), retail store exec.; b. Strasbourg, France, May 30, 1936; d. Jacques and Mariette Rose (Dreyfus) Schumacher; came to U.S., 1942, naturalized, 1952; B.A., Smith Coll., 1958; postgrad., N.Y. U., 1960-61; m. Jon Lewis Allen, Sept. 29, 1961; children—Christopher Jacques Lewis, Victoria Cecile. Asst. buyer Bloomingdale's Inc., N.Y.C., 1959-61; nat. buyer Frederick Atkins, Inc., N.Y.C., 1961-63; with Sears Roebuck & Co., N.Y.C., 1964—, nat. buyer, 1965—. Mem. Smith Coll. Alumni Assn. (fund agt.), N.Y. Fashion Group. Club: Smith (N.Y.C.). Home: 1633 Broadway New York City NY 10019 Office: 360 W 31st St New York City NY 10001

ALLEN, NELL R(UTH), speech pathologist, audiologist; b. Winnfield, La.; d. Columbus Willma and Caroline (Long) Allen; B.A., Northwestern State Coll., 1950; M.Ed., Wayne U., 1957; postgrad. State U. N.Y. at Buffalo, summer 1951, Tulane U., 1957, La. State U. Med. Sch., 1963-64, 66. Dept. head, speech therapist La. Spastic Sch., Alexandria, 1950-51, Detroit Cerebral Palsy Center, 1951-54, N.E. Cerebral Palsy Sch., Monroe, La., 1954-55, Rapides Parish Rehab. Center, Alexandria, 1955-57; dept. head, dir. speech and hearing clinic Crippled Children's Hosp., New Orleans, 1959—; spl. lectr. speech La. State U., 1963; instr. speech pathology and audiology Tulane U., 1966—; supr. speech therapy majors St. Mary's Dominican Coll., New Orleans, Northwestern State Coll., Natchitoches, La., Tulane U., 1960—. Lectr. civic orgns. United Cerebral Palsy Assn. La. scholar, 1954; Office Vocational Rehab. scholar, 1957; awarded clin. competence in speech pathology, audiology Am. Speech and Hearing Assn., 1965, 67. Mem. Am., La. (pres. 1969-70) speech and hearing assns., Internat. Platform Assn. Research pertaining to hearing acuity of muscular dystrophic individuals. Home: 6755 River Rd New Orleans LA 70123 Office: 200 Henry Clay Av New Orleans LA 70118

ALLEN, NEPPIE JANE, educator; b. Corpus Christi, Tex., Mar. 7, 1931; d. John Raymond and Penelope Jane (Storm) Allen; B.S., S.W. Tex. State U., 1950; M.A., Tex. Woman's U., 1953; Ph.D., U. Tex., 1972. Tchr., Donna (Tex.) Ind. Sch. Dist., 1950-53, Houston Ind. Sch. Dist., 1953-54; asst. dir. co-recreation U. Tex., Austin, 1957-59, acad. asst. depts. ednl. adminstrn., ednl. psychology and spl. edn., 1968-69, acad. asst. dept. spl. edn. 1970-71; tchr. Hutto (Tex.), Ind. Sch. Dist., 1963-65, Del Valley (Tex.) Ind. Sch. Dist., 1965-67; project dir. Stonewall Jackson Learning Disabilities Center, Va. Commonwealth U., Richmond, 1969; asst. project dir. lang. devel. program Austin State Sch. Mentally Retarded, U.S. Office Edn. Grant, 1971-72; unit dir. Gen. Contract Services div. State Dept. Pub. Welfare, Austin, 1972-73; asst. prof. edn. Sam Houston State U., Huntsville, Tex., 1973—. Cons. Edn. Service Center, Region XIII, Austin, 1968-71. U.S. Office Edn. fellow, 1969-71. Mem. Council Exceptional Children, Am. Assn. Mental Deficiency Assn. Children with Learning Disabilities, Nat. Soc. Study Edn. Home: 2711 Pine Shadows Huntsville TX 77340

ALLEN, PATRICIA BURR (MRS. GEORGE BOTT), artist; b. Old Lyme, Conn.; d. George B. and Lucretia Allen (Phinney) Burr; student Rollins Coll., 1948-50, Art Students League, 1951; studied with George B. Burr, Malcolm Fraser, Ivan Olinsky, Harry Sternberg; m. George Bott, Sept. 17, 1945. One-man shows at Fla. Fedn. Art, Orlando, 1948, Burr Gallery, N.Y.C., 1955, New Stanley Art Gallery, Nairobi, Kenya, 1970, New Hilton Art Gallery, Nairobi, 1970, East African Wildlife Gallery, Nairobi, 1971; exhibited in group shows at Fla. Fedn. Arts, 1934, Artists Equity, Riverside Mus., 1954, Yonkers (N.Y.) Mus., 1953, Nat. Acad., 1950, Brygider Gallery, La. State Graphic Exhbn., Yorktown Heights, N.Y., 1960, High Plains Gallery, Amarillo Tex., 1960, Collectors Corner Gallery, Washington, 1965, Massillon (O.) Mus. Art, 1965, Farnsworth Mus., 1965, Greenville (S.C.) Mus. Art, 1966, Hickory (N.C.) Mus. Art, 1966, N.Y. Soc. Animal Artists, 1970, N.Y. World's Fair, 1965, Grand Central Art Galleries, N.Y.C., 1970, Thomson Galleries, N.Y.C., 1966, Boston Mus. Sci., 1969, Maryhill Mus., Washington, 1970, others; represented in permanent collections at Riveredge Found., Calgary, Ont., Can., Bronx Zoo Galleries, Greenville Mus. Art, Hickory Mus. Art, Grand Central Art Galleries; dir. Burr Gallery, N.Y.C., 1955—; in charge sales Grand Central Art Galleries, 1965—. Recipient medal Fla. Fedn. Arts, 1944, 1st prize Gotham Painters, 1969, 2d prize, 1970. Mem. Soc. Animal Artists (founder, sec.), Nat. Arts Club N.Y.C., Nat. League Am. Pen Women, Bronx Zool. Soc. Home: 151 Carroll St City Island Bronx NY 10464 Office: Grand Central Art Galleries 40 Vanderbilt Av New York City NY 10017

ALLEN, PHYLLIS ADELLE GRISHAM (MRS. MCCURDY ALLEN), charitable assn. exec.; b. Stockton, Cal., Aug. 11, 1927; d. Clarence William and Norma Grace (Collins) Grisham; student Long Beach City Coll., 1945-46, U. Ore., 1957, Portland State U., 1967; m. Robert McCurdy Allen, Sept.1968; children—Carole Freeland, Susan, Stephen, Thomas, Patricia. Women's dir., broadcaster KMED Radio and TV, Medford, Ore., 1957-65; copywriter, account exec. Parma Advt., Portland, Ore., 1965-66; sec.-treas., account exec. Williams Advt. and Pub. Relations, Portland, 1966-68; pub. relations dir. United Fund, Akron, O., 1969-70; asso. pub. relations dir. Akron Gen. Med. Center, 1972-73; exec. dir. Akron Gen. Devel. Found., 1973—. Pres., Support, Inc., 1973—; mem. community relations com. Akron YMCA, 1972-73. Recipient 1st Pl. Pillsbury invitational recipe contest Food Editors, 1964. Mem. Pub. Relations Soc. Am. (sec. Akron chpt. 1973-74), Nat. Assn. Hosp. Devel., Ohio Hosp. Devel. Assn., Akron Press Club, Family and Children's Service Soc. Akron, Women in Communications (sec. 1973-74). Home: 5740 West Blvd Canton OH 44718 Office: 400 Wabash Av Akron OH 44307

ALLEN, RUTH, orthodontist; b. Tampico, Ill.; d. Richard S. and Nora (Antisdel) Allen; A.A., Pasadena Jr. Coll., 1937; D.D.S., U. So. Cal., 1950, certificate orthodontics, 1951, M.Dental Surgery in orthodontics, 1953. Pres. Pasadena Dental Assts., 1941-42, So. Cal. Dental Assts., 1945; asso. Dr. Spencer R. Atkinson in pvt. practice and orthodontic research, 1950-67; now practice orthodontics, Pasadena, Cal.; guest lectr. Los Angeles City Coll., 1950-58; asst. prof. grad. orthodontics U. So. Cal., 1954-57. Mem. Am., So. Cal. dental assns., Am. Assn. Orthodontists, Pacific Coast Orthodontic Soc., Assn. Am. Women Dentists, Upsilon Alpha, Beta Sigma Phi. Club: Altrusa (pres. Pasadena 1956-57). Home: 2081 Garfias Dr Pasadena CA 91104 Office: 65 N Madison Av Pasadena CA 91101

ALLEN, RUTH MARGARET KABELE (MRS. HARRY R. ALLEN), civic worker; b. Chgo., Oct. 20, 1902; d. George Philip and Rosina (Welgel) Kabele; A.B., Carthage Coll., 1923; postgrad. Kan. State Tchrs. Coll., summers 1924-25; m. Harry R. Allen, June 17, 1926; children—John E., David G., Margaret (Mrs. William F. Benson). Tchr. pub. schs., Pearl City, Ill., 1923-24, Yorkville, Ill., 1924-25, Hays, Kan., 1925-26; Chgo. area admissions counselor Carthage Coll., 1947-51. Mem. exec. bd. Pacific Synod, Women's Missionary Soc. of United Luth. Ch. in Am., 1934-40; ofcl. del. organizing conv. Luth. Ch. Women of Central States Synod, 1962; mem. bd. S.E. Conf. United Luth. Ch. Women Synod of Central States, 1956; mem. Aux. Trinity Luth. Hosp., Kansas City, Mo. Hon. trustee Kansas City (Mo.) Art Inst. Mem. English Speaking Union, Friends Art Nelson Gallery Art, Jackson County (Mo.) Hist. Soc., U. Mo. Assos. Am. Assn. U. Women, Planned Parenthood Kansas City, Kansas City (Mo.) Philharmonic Assn. Club: Leawood (Kan.) Women's. Contbr. articles to ch. papers. Home: 8033 Ensley Lane Leawood KS 66206

ALLEN, SALLY VANCE (MRS. JAMES W. ALLEN), ednl. adminstr.; b. Boston, Feb. 3, 1940; d. Henry Thomas and Laurie Helena (Burnaby) Vance; B.A. in History, Smith Coll., 1962; M.A. in History, U. Cal. at Los Angeles, 1963; m. James Wentworth Allen, May 30, 1964; children—James Vance, Craig Wentworth. Research asst. Gov. Nelson Rockefeller's Fgn. Affairs Staff, N.Y.C., 1963-64; research asso. Edn. and World Affairs, N.Y.C., 1964-66; spl. asst. to Mayor Lindsay, N.Y.C., 1966; editor COMPACT mag. Edn. Commn. States, Denver, 1967-71, project dir. early childhood task force, 1971—. Sec.-treas., dir. Alter, Akerman & Assos., cons., Denver, 1970—. Mem. Colo. Gov.'s Commn. on Children and Youth, 1971—. Mem. bd. Denver Head Start, 1972-73, Graland Country Day Sch., Denver, 1972—. Woodrow Wilson Found. fellow. Mem. Phi Beta Kappa. Clubs: Denver; Smith College Colo. Editor: Met. Opportunities for Women, 1971. Home: 4600 E 3d Denver CO 80220 Office: Education Commn of the States 1860 Lincoln St Denver CO 80203

ALLEN, SYLVIA DUNNAVANT (MRS. HUNTER MAPHIS ALLEN), ednl. adminstr.; b. Buckingham, Va.; d. Samuel Edward and Jennie (Springer) Dunnavant; B.S., Longwood Coll., Farmville, Va., 1940; M.A., George Washington U., 1948, Ed.D., 1970; m. Hunter Maphis Allen, July 30, 1944. Tchr., 1936-40, in Fairfax County, Va., 1940-43; prin. Floris Sch., Fairfax County, 1943-44, Woodlawn Sch., 1944-55, Bucknell Sch., 1955-62; supr. curriculum and research Prince William County, Va., 1962-63; coordinator elementary edn. Prince William County, Va., 1963-69, supr. elementary edn., 1969—. Bd. dirs. No. Va. Community Coll., 1973—. Life mem. Nat. Congress Parents and Tchrs. Mem. Nat., Va., Prince William edn. assns., No. Va. Suprs. Assn. (sec.-treas. 1972-74), Fairfax County Prins. Assn. (past pres.), Nat. Assn. Curriculum Devel., Columbian Women, Pi Lambda Theta, Phi Delta Gamma (pres. 1972-73), Alpha Phi Sigma, Kappa Delta Pi, Delta Kappa Gamma (past pres.). Mem. Order Eastern Star. Contbr. articles to profl. jours. Home: 1209 Davis St Woodbridge VA 22191

ALLENBY, KATHLEEN KEER (MRS. HAROLD F. ALLENBY), artist; b. Newark, Mar. 8, 1918; d. Theodore F. and Florence (MacRae) Keer; B.A., Smith Coll., 1940; postgrad. Columbia, 1943, N.J. Tchrs. Coll., 1946-49; m. B.C. Breeden, June 29, 1940 (div. 1943); 1 dau., Kathy; m. Harold F. Allenby, July 28, 1949; 1 stepdau., Hope (Mrs. Bert Personius). Kindergarten tchr. Kimberly Sch., Montclair, N.J., 1946-49; tchr. art to handicapped Kessler Inst. Rehab., West Orange, N.J., 1961—. Exhibited one-man shows, Woman's Club Montclair, 1st Savs. & Loan Bank, Cedar Grove, N.J., Music Sch., Cedar Grove, Piggins Art Gallery, Montclair, N.J., all 1972; exhibited in group shows N.J. State Fedn. Women's Clubs, Art Center of Oranges. Leader, Girl Scouts U.S.A., Little Falls, N.J., 1955-56; social dir. P.T.A., Great Notch, N.J., 1955-56. Recipient art awards Upper Montclair Women's Club; certificate of merit in art N.J. Fedn. Women's Clubs, 1st pl. essay award, 1973. Mem. Art Center Oranges, West Essex Art Assn., N.J. State Fedn. Women's Clubs (7th dist. art chmn. 1973-74). Clubs: Glen Ridge Country (N.J., handicap chmn. 1970, publicity chmn. women's golf group 1973—); Upper Montclair Women's (dir. art dept. 1971-72); Little Falls Women's (treas. 1959-61). Home: 55 Jacobus Av Great Notch Little Falls NJ 07424 also Cape Cod Circle Lake Worth FL 33460

ALLENDE-KENDRICK, CARMEN HILDA, health adminstr.; b. Santurce, P.R., Aug. 29, 1936; d. Antonio Allende and Angelina Calderon (Correa) Velazquez; B.S., in Occupational Therapy, U. P.R., 1960; M.S., Cal. State U. at San Jose, 1968; M.P.H., Columbia, 1973; postgrad. N.Y. U.; m. Donald G. Kendrick, Apr. 6, 1963; children—Naida Lourdes, Aixa Ellina, Donald Gatutsi. Asst. Supr. P.R. State Ins. Fund Rehab. Clinic, Santurce, 1958-62; staff phys. therapist, then dir. occupational therapy dept. Santa Clara Med. Center, San Jose, 1963-70; dir. health planning Yonkers (N.Y.) Community Action Program, 1972—; cons. in field. Mem. Yonkers P.R. Council, Fund Urban Neighborhood Devel. P.R. State Ins. Fund scholar, 1955-58; trainee Vocational Rehab. Adminstr. Cal. State U., 1962-63; USPHS grantee, 1972-73. Recipient commendation Santa Clara Med. Center, 1968. Mem. Am. Occupational Therapy Assn., Am. Pub. Health Assn., World Fedn. Occupational Therapists, Fedn. Am. Scientists, Nat. Assn. Health Service Execs., Physicians Forum, League Women Voters, Orgn. Am. States. Democrat. Methodist. Home: 357-31 N Broadway Yonkers NY 10701 Office: 866 UN Plaza New York City NY 10017

ALLENSWORTH, ELOISE BALL (MRS. ANDREW JACKSON ALLENSWORTH), charitable assn. exec.; b. Grinnell, Ia., June 20, 1909; d. Charles Clyde and Roslyn Marie (Steinke) Ball; B.S. with honors, Tex. Women's U., 1930; postgrad. U. Minn., 1934-36; m. Andrew Jackson Allensworth, June 14, 1940; children—Roslyn Anne, Margaret Eloise (Mrs. James Franklin). Resident worker N.E. Neighborhood House, Mpls., 1931-34; tchr. design and crafts Miller Vocational High Sch., Mpls., 1932-40; tchr. shop Emerson Jr. High Sch., San Antonio, 1941-42; tchr. art St. Mary's Hall, San Antonio, 1943-44; exec. dir. San Antonio Assn. Retarded Children, 1957—, pres., 1952-57. Mem. Adv. Com. City Health, 1957-63; pres. Good Samaritan Center, 1944; mem. City Welfare Adv. Com., 1968; mem. Gov.'s Adv. Council Mental Retardation Planning, 1964—; mem. Devel. Disabilities Council, 1971-73. Bd. dirs. Community Welfare Council, 1956-62. Recipient Distinguished Service award Tex. Assn. Retarded Children, 1963, Outstanding Contbn. award YWCA and Council Jewish Women, 1962. Mem. League Women Voters (v.p. 1947-51), Council Exceptional Children, Am. Assn. Mental Deficiency, Community Welfare Council, Nat. Assn. Retarded Children, Conf. Execs., Tex. Social Welfare, Tex. P.E.O. Home: 112 Ridgemont St San Antonio TX 78209

ALLER, MARGO FRIEDEL (MRS. HUGH ALLER), scientist; A.B., Vassar Coll., 1960; spl. student astronomy Harvard, 1961-62; M.S., U. Mich., 1964, Ph.D., 1969; m. Hugh Aller. Mathematician programmer Smithsonian Astrophys. Obs., 1960-62; research asst. Nat. Radio Astronomy Obs., summer 1964; research asst. to D. Wentzel U. Mich., summers 1963, 65, to G. Elste, 1966-68, research asso., 1969—. Mem. Am. Astron. Soc., Internat. Astron. Union, Sigma Xi. Contbr. articles to profl. jours. Address: 1103 Shady Oaks Ct Ann Arbor MI 48103

ALLILUYEVA, SVETLANA (MRS. WILLIAM WESLEY PETERS), author; b. USSR, 1926; d. Joseph Stalin and Nadezhda Alliluyeva; m. William Wesley Peters; 1 dau., Olga; children by previous marriages—Katherine, Joseph. Author: Twenty Letters to a Friend; Only One Year. Address: 50 Wilson Rd Princeton NJ 08540

ALLINSMITH, BEVERLY BALCH, clubwoman; b. Orange, N.J., Jan. 13, 1924; d. Everett Purdy and Hazel (Phillips) Balch; B.A., Smith Coll., 1946; M.A., U. Mich., 1949, Ph.D., 1954; m. Wesley Allinsmith, June 30, 1947; children—Bryan, Wendy, Craig. Instr. psychology U. Mich. at Ann Arbor, 1953-54; psychologist Univ. Elementary Sch., Ann Arbor, 1954-55; supr. Walk-in-Clinic, U. Cin., 1973. Pres. Concord Family Service Soc., 1960-61, bd. dirs., 1958-61; pres. Woman's City Club, Cin., 1973—, bd. dirs., 1966-69, 73—. Mem. Am., Ohio psychol. assns., A.A.A.S., Soc. Research in Child Devel., Council Anthropology and Edn., Sigma Xi. Home: 3850 Clifton Av Cincinnati OH 45220

ALLINSON, SARAH CHASNOFF (MRS. CARL ALLINSON), psychologist; b. Beacon Falls, Conn., July 5, 1916; d. Abraham and Rebecca (Serow) Chasnoff; B.S., So. Conn. Coll., 1960; M.S., So. Ill. U., 1963, Edn. Specialist, 1965; m. Carl Allinson, July 1, 1960; children—Nancy Livingston, John Livingston. Sch. psychologist Franklin-Jefferson County Spl. Edn. Dist., Frankfort, Ill., 1965; sch. psychologist The Exceptional Child, Benton, Ill. Mem. Assn. of Mentally Retarded, Kappa Delta Pi, Phi Kappa Phi, Pi Lambda Theta. Home: 511 W 6th St Benton IL 62812 Office: Casey and 8th St Mount Vernon IL 62864

ALLISON, ADA ADELINE SANDIN (MRS. GEORGE BOGGS ALLISON), civic worker; b. Marquette, Neb.; d. Gustaf Wilhelm and Edna (Cowling) Sandin; student U. Neb., Lincoln Sch. Commerce; m. George Boggs Allison, Sept. 6, 1936; 1 son, George Richard. Admitted to Neb. bar, 1924; practiced in Aurora, Neb., 1924-30; mem. firm Hainer, Craft, Edgerton & Fraizer, Aurora, 1924-30. Pres., Women's Com. So. Cal. Symphony-Hollywood Bowl Assn., 1970-71, del. Women's Assn. for Symphony Orchs., 1967; treas. Assistance League So. Cal., 1959-63; dir. U. Religious Conf., U. Cal. at Los Angeles, 1961-70; dir. So. Cal. Choral Music Assn., 1968—, v.p., 1973—; pres. P.T.A., Louis Pasteur Jr. High Sch., Los Angeles, 1951-52. Bd. dirs. Internat. Christian Scholarship Found. (pres. 1966-70), Vis. Nurse Assn. Los Angeles (pres. 1966-67), Child Guidance Clinic, Los Angeles, Cal. Mus. Sci. and Industry. Recipient award for distinguished service Meml. Activities Center campaign U. Cal. Alumni Assn., Los Angeles, 1964. Mem. U. Affiliates of U. Cal. at Los Angeles (pres. 1965-66), Muses, Cal. Mus. Sci. and Industry (chmn. 1973—). Methodist (pres. Woman's Soc. of Christian Service 1955-56). Club: Ebell (Los Angeles). Home: 2227 Guthrie Dr Los Angeles CA 90034

ALLISON, CAROL DAILY WAGNER (MRS. RICHARD CASE ALLISON), museum curator; b. Fairbanks, Alaska, Jan. 15, 1932; d. Arthur Ford and Helen Elizabeth (Romig) Daily; B.A., U. Cal. at Berkeley, 1953, M.A., 1963, Ph.D., 1970; m. Richard Case Allison, Oct. 20, 1967; children—Ruth Elizabeth, Paul Barnaby. Micropaleontologist, Shell Oil Co., Bakersfield, Cal., 1953-54; research asst. U. Cal. at Berkeley, 1963-67; curator Museum of U. Alaska, Fairbanks, 1970—. Sec., Pioneer Meml. Park Bd., Fairbanks, 1973—. Mem. Geol. Soc. Am., Paleontol. Soc., Paleontol. Research Inst., Alaska Geol. Soc., A.A.A.S., Tanana-Yukon Hist. Soc. (v.p. 1970-73). Home: 1055 Kodiak St Fairbanks AK 99701 Office: Museum U Alaska Fairbanks AK 99701

ALLISON, DEE, county ofcl.; b. Portland, Ore., Dec. 23, 1938; d. Henry E. and Margaret (Brandenberg); student Portland State Coll., 1955-57, Ore. State Coll., 1957-59. Spl. editions editor Am. Motorist Mag., Am. Automobile Assn., Washington, 1964-68; pub. information dir. Washington Suburban Transit Commn., Silver Spring, Md., 1968-73; transit adminstr. Dept. Pub. Works and Transp., Prince George's County, Forestville, Md., 1973—. Nat. committeewoman Md. Young Democrats, 1969-70. Mem. Pub. Relations Soc. Am., Montgomery County Press Assn., Prince George's Pub. Relations Assn. Home: 8150 Lakecrest Dr Greenbelt MD 20770 Office: 8400 D'Arcy Rd Forestville MD 20028

ALLISON, MARION LESLIE (MRS. DONALD P. MEARIN), interior designer; b. Washington; d. William L. and Hazel B. (Cook) Allison; B.S., Panzer Coll., Montclair State Tchrs., Coll., 1942; postgrad. N.Y. Sch. Interior Design, 1954; m. Donald P. Mearin, July 7, 1962. Tchr. phys. edn. and health elementary schs., Elizabeth, N.J., 1942-43; jr. price engr. Western Electric Co., Kearny, N.J., 1943-45; tchr. phys. edn., health and biology North Plainfield (N.J.) High Sch., 1945-47; fashion and photog. model John Robert Powers and Harry Conover and profl. ballet dancer in concerts and TV, N.Y.C., 1947-53; cons. decorating and publicity Congoleum-Nairn, Inc., N.Y.C. and Kearny, 1953-58; asst. dir. design div. Am. Biltrite Rubber Co., Inc., Trenton, N.J., 1958-69; mgr. floor covering fabric devel. fibers div. Am. Cyanamid Co., N.Y.C., 1970-73, mgr. yarn and fabric devel., 1973—; design and color cons. Wood-Mode Kitchens div. Wood-Metal Industries, Kreamer, Pa. Mem. Nat. Home Fashions League, Am. Inst. Interior Designers, Nat. Soc. Interior Designers (dir., past chmn. bd.). Contbr. articles profl. jours. Home: Cedar Ridge Rd Lebanon NJ 08833 Office: Am Cyanamid Co 630 Fifth Av New York City NY 10022

ALLISON, MARTHA JEANE, occupational therapist; b. Charleston, Ill., June 19, 1927; d. Samuel Parker and Lucille (Work) Allison; B.S. in Recreational Leadership, U. Mass., 1949; certificate occupational therapy Boston Sch. Occupational Therapy, 1957. Tchr., counsellor Long Beach (Cal.) Pub. Sch. Camp, 1949; dir. recreation City of Springfield (Vt.), 1950-53; dir. Service Club Craft Shop, U.S. Army Spl. Services, Camp Fuji, Japan, 1954-56; dir. occupational and recreational therapy Charles S. Wilson Meml. Hosp., Johnson City, N.Y., 1958—. Mem. home care adv. and utilization com. Broome County (N.Y.) Health Dept., 1970—. Bd. dirs. Broome County unit Am. Cancer Soc. Mem. Am., N.Y. State (pres. 1960-61) occupational therapy assns., World Fedn. Occupational Therapy, Nat. Park and Recreation Assn., N.Y. State Park and Recreation Assn. Home: 312 Orchard St Vestal NY 13850 Office: CS Wilson Meml Hosp Johnson City NY 13790

ALLISON, PATRICIA LEE, plant pathologist; b. Washington, May 8, 1923; d. Lisle Reed and Marcella (Sterling) Van Burgh; B.A., U. Houston, 1946, B.S., 1946; M.S., Ohio State U., 1948, Ph.D., 1950; postgrad. U. Minn., 1949; m. Clyde Clarence Allison, Dec. 1950 (div. Feb. 1956). Lab. asst., fellow biology U. Houston, 1943-46; asst. botanist and plant pathologist Ohio State U., 1946-48, 49-50, research asst. plant pathology, 1950, research asso., 1951-55; research asst. U. Minn., 1949, asst. prof., 1957; asso. pathologist Morris Aboretum U. Pa., 1957-63, pathologist, 1963—; prof. U. Guayaquil (Ecuador), summer 1963; cons. poisonous plants and animals Phila. Dept. Health; lectr. in field. Mem. Cinnaminson Twp. (N.J.) Conservation com., 1963-65. Recipient citation Consejo Directivo U. Guayaquil, 1963, Bronze award Neographics, 1972. Mem. Am. Phytopath. Soc., Mycol. Soc. Am., Bot. Soc. Am., A.A.A.S., Sigma Xi, Gamma Sigma Delta, Phi Epsilon Phi. Editor: Morris Arboretum Bull., 1968-73. Contbr. articles to profl. jours. Home: 908 Hunters Lane Oreland PA 19075

Office: Morris Arboretum 9414 Meadowbrook Philadelphia PA 19118

ALLIVATO, BARBARA ROSE, banker; b. Mpls., Mar. 11, 1938; d. William Joseph and Marjorie Rose (Jonas) Allivato; student U. Minn., 1956-59; certificate Am. Inst. Banking, 1972. Cashier, Clancy Drugs, Inc., Mpls., 1956—; mortgage banker First Nat. Bank Mpls., 1959—. Mem. Capital Long Range Improvements Commn., City of Mpls. Senate dist. chairperson Minn. Democratic Farmer Labor Party. Mem. Citizens League Mpls., Am. Inst. Banking (bd. govs. Mpls. chpt. 1973—, vice chairperson nat. conv. 1975). Home: 5007 France St Minneapolis MN 55410 Office: 120 S 6th St Minneapolis MN 55402

ALLMAN, ELAINE GIBBARD (MRS. MAURICE R. ALLMAN), lawyer; b. Sulphur, Okla., Mar. 14, 1945; d. Frank and Veva Jean (Rogers) Gibbard; student Swarthmore Coll., 1962-64; B.A., Okla. U., 1966, J.D., 1969; m. Maurice R. Allman, Nov. 25, 1967. Admitted to Okla. bar, 1969; mem. firm Gibbard, Allman & Allman, Sulphur, Okla., 1969—; U.S. Magistrate, Eastern Dist. of Okla., 1971—. Pres. Murray County Women's Democratic Club, 1972—; 1st alt. del. to Dem. Nat. Conv., 1972; co-chmn. Murray County Dem. Central Com., 1973—. Mem. Order of the Coif, Am. Bar Assn., Okla. Bar. Assn. (civil rights com. 1971), Okla. Trial Lawyers Assn., Phi Alpha Delta. Club: Sorosis (Sulphur). Home: PO Box 624 Sulphur OK 73086 Office: PO Box 436 Sulphur OK 73086

ALLMAN, REVA WHITE (MRS. WILLIAM C. ALLMAN), educator; b. Birmingham, Ala.; d. John Edward and Isabel (Glasscoe) White; A.B., Miles Coll., 1935; M.A., Fisk U., 1940; Ph.D., U. Mich., 1951; m. William C. Allman, May 9, 1942; 1 dau., Marian Isabel. Tchr., Birmingham (Ala.) Pub. Schs., 1934-37; prin. Lab. Sch., A. and M. Coll., Normal, Ala., 1937-39, chmn. dept. edn., 1940-48; chmn. dept. edn. Miles Coll., 1949-50, prof. edn., 1951-62, dean Grad. Sch., summer 1963, chmn. dept. secondary edn. and psychology, 1965—, also chairperson dept. ednl. founds. and media. First v.p. City Fedn. of Montgomery, 1961-62; bd. dirs. Montgomery Urban League. Recipient Service plaques Ala. chpt. youth group N.A.A.C.P., 1973. Mem. Gen. Alumni Assn. Fisk U. (parliamentarian), Alpha Kappa Alpha (dir. Southeastern region 1962-66), Kappa Delta Pi. Baptist (gen. supr. Sunday Sch., editor ch. bull.). Clubs: Tens Civic and Federated (pres. 1961-64), Montgomery Fisk Alumni (pres.), Agnes J. Lewis Federated. Home: 166 Pinetree Dr Montgomery AL 36109

ALLMAND, LINDA F., librarian; b. Port Arthur, Tex., Jan. 31, 1937; d. Clifton James and Jewel Etoile (Smith) Allmand; B.A. cum laude (Pilot Club scholar), North Tex. State U., Denton, 1958; M.A. in Librarianship, U. Denver, 1962. Library asst. Gates Meml. Library, Port Arthur, 1953-55; mem. staff Houston Pub. Library, 1955-58; 1st asst., children's librarian Univ. Hills br. Denver Pub. Library, 1960-63; coordinator children's services Anaheim (Cal.) Pub. Library, 1963-64; mem. staff Dallas Pub. Library, 1965—, chief br. services, 1971—. Instr., North Tex. State U., 1967-71. Mem. continuing edn. com. Goals for Dallas, 1968-69. Library Binding Inst. scholar, 1958. Mem. Am. (chmn. local arrangements Dallas childrens services div. 1971, task force on children's services, 1972-73, standards com. 1973—), Tex. (chmn. for pub. libraries Nat. Library Week 1968-69, sec.-treas. pub. library div. 1973-74), Southwestern (membership chmn. 1973-74), Dallas County (pres. 1968-69) library assns., Bus. and Profl. Women's Assn., Beta Phi Mu. Home: 2930 Woodmere St Dallas TX 75233 Office: 1954 Commerce St Dallas TX 75201

ALLRED, ELIZABETH SCHRILLO (MRS. ROBERT E. ALLRED), diversified mfg. co. exec.; b. Hoboken, N.J., June 8, 1915; d. Anthony T. and Teresa (Herger) Schrillo; grad. normal tng. Loma Linda U., 1934; postgrad. Pacific Union Coll., 1938-39; m. Robert E. Allred, Sept. 14, 1944. Tchr. elementary sch., Cal., 1934-37; office mgr. Schrillo Aero Tool Engring. Co., West Hollywood, Cal., 1939-55; sec.-treas. Schrillo Co., Sepulveda, Cal., 1955—, exec. v.p., 1968—; sec.-treas. Aero Components, Los Angeles. Home: 17400 Halsted St Northridge CA 91324

ALLRED, ELSIE WILHELMINA HAWKINS (MRS. CHARLES ORVILLE ALLRED, JR.), hosp. adminstr.; b. Belton, S.C., July 14, 1925; d. Julian Folger and Daisy Estelle (Bell) Hawkins; grad. nursing Spartanburg (S.C.) Gen. Hosp., 1945; m. Charles Orville Allred, Jr., Nov. 2, 1946; children—Susan (Mrs. Wayne Scruggs), Charles Orville III, Elizabeth (Mrs. Woodrow McIntyre), Julian Park. Dir. Montgomery County Red Cross Nursing Services, 1958-64; dir. nursing services Mizell Meml. Hosp., Opp, Ala., 1964-68; hosp. adminstr. Grove Hill (Ala.) Hosp., 1968—. Instr. A.R.C., 1958-64; active Am., Ala. heart assns., Am., Ala. rehab. assns. Mem. Ala. Assn. Hosp. Execs., Ala. Hosp. Assn., S. Ala. Hosp. Council. Lady Card Holder Mason (32 deg., Shriner). Home: PO Box 355 Grove Hill AL 36451 Office: PO Box 577 Grove Hill AL 36451

ALLSHOUSE, CAROLE ANN, ednl. adminstr.; b. Akron, O., Mar. 18, 1946; d. Paul Emerson and Ethel Harriet (Brigge) Allshouse; B.S., Ohio State U., 1969; M.S., Ind. U., 1974. Occupational therapist Cerebral Palsy Clinic, Ind. Med. Center, Indpls., 1969-71; dir., tchr., therapist Monroe County Presch. for Handicapped Children, Bloomington, Ind., 1971—. Clin. lectr. Ind. U. Med. Center, 1969-71. Adviser, planning com. mem. Community Child Care Council, Bloomington, 1973. Recipient fellowship in mental retardation Dept. Spl. Edn., Ind. U., 1969-71. Mem. World Fedn. Occupational Therapists, Council Early Childhood Edn., Council Exceptional Children, Assn. Retarded Children, Am. Assn. Mental Deficiency, Am., Ind. (recruitment-information chmn. 1970) occupational therapy assns., Pi Lambda Theta. Home: 2604F Eastgate Lane Bloomington IN 47401 Office: 221 E 6th St Bloomington IN 47401

ALMORE, MARY GRACE, educator; b. Pitts., Sept. 23, 1932; d. George Peter and Virginia Blanche (Thompson) Almore; B.S. cum laude, Fla. State U., 1955, M.S. in Criminology, 1956, M.S. in Psychology, 1958; Ph.D. in Psychology, Tex. Christian U., 1971. Instr. Jacksonville (Fla.) U., 1957-59; probation officer Dallas County Juvenile Dept., 1960-63; vis. tchr. Dallas Ind. Sch. Dist., 1963-65; prof. Tex. Wesleyan Coll., Ft. Worth, 1965-73; prof. Inst. Urban Studies, U. Tex., Arlington, 1973—. Cons. Human Relations Commn., Ft. Worth, 1971-74. Sec. exec. com. Case Coordinators' Com., Dallas Inter-Agy. Project, 1963-65; mem. com. income and econ. opportunity United Way Met. Tarrant County, 1973. Served with USMC, 1950-52. Mem. Am., Western psychol. assns., Am. Soc. Criminology, Nat. Council Crime and Delinquency, Soc. for Psychol. Study Social Issues, Phi Kappa Phi, Psi Chi. Contbg. author: The Organization and Administration of Criminal Justice in Texas, 1973. Editor: The State of the City of Fort Worth, 1974. Office: Inst Urban Studies U Tex Arlington TX 76019

ALMQUIST, JUNE ANDERSON (MRS. OSCAR LEONARD ALMQUIST, JR.), journalist; b. Yakima, Wash., Jan. 2, 1925; d. Axel Wilhelm and Hilma Victoria (Sundin) Anderson; B.A. in Journalism, U. Wash., 1946; M.A. in Journalism, Stanford, 1951; m. Oscar Leonard Almquist, Jr., Nov. 10, 1951. Reporter, Seattle Post-Intelligencer, summers 1945, 50, Tacoma News-Tribune, 1946; with William C. Speidel, Jr., pub. relations agy., 1946-49; with Seattle Times, 1951—, women's editor, 1968—. Tchr. newswriting course U. Wash. Mem. Nat. Fedn. Press Women (awards), Wash. State Press Women (past treas., awards), Sigma Delta Chi (Wash. State Press awards), Theta Sigma Phi (past pres. Seattle profl. chpt.). Club: Washington Press. Home: 5145 NE 41st St Seattle WA 98105 Office: PO Box 70 Seattle WA 98111

ALONSO, LOU JOHNSON, educator; b. Mason, Mich., Feb. 2, 1925; d. James Reginald and Mabel Elizabeth (Reid) Johnson; B.A., Mich. State U., 1947, M.A., 1950, postgrad., 1951-54; m. Noah Alonso, Dec. 17, 1948; 1 son, Jose Gregory II (dec.). Speech pathologist Flint (Mich.) Pub. Schs., 1947-48; tchr., then asst. prin. Mich. Sch. for Blind, Lansing, 1949-56; prof. spl. edn., coordinator programs preparing personnel for visually handicapped and deaf-blind pupils, dir. Gt. Lakes Region Spl. Edn. Instl. Materials Center, Mich. State U., East Lansing, 1959—. Cons., U.S. Office Edn.; adv. bd. numerous agys. Mem. Council for Exceptional Children, Assn. Ednl. Communication and Tech., Assn. Educators Visually Handicapped, Delta Zeta. Author books, research reports, numerous articles, brochures and instrnl. media. Home: 1031 Larkspur Dr East Lansing MI 48823

ALPERIN, GOLDIE GREEN, cons. librarian, lawyer; b. Des Moines, Aug. 16, 1905; d. Morris and Bessie (Miliwer) Green; LL.B., Drake U., 1927; m. Moses Alperin, Dec. 25, 1930 (dec. 1950); children—Herschel Burton, Judith Miriam. Admitted to Ia. bar, 1927; practice in Des Moines, 1927-30; law librarian Chgo. Bar. Assn., 1951-63; dir. Def. Information Office, Chgo., 1963-65; librarian book selections Northwestern U. Law Sch. Library, 1966-72; ret., 1972. Named one of 20 rep. U.S. women lawyers of various phases practice Women's Adjustment Bd., London, Eng., 1957. Certified religious sch. tchr. Bd. Jewish Edn., Chgo., 1951. Mem. Am. (sec. 1960-65), Chgo. (past exec. bd., editor 1958-59) assns. law libraries, Nat. Assn. Women Lawyers (regional) dir. 1960-64), Decalogue Soc. Lawyers Womens Bar Assn. Ill., Internat. Assn. Law Libraries, Internat. Platform Assn. Jewish religion. Asst. editor Women Lawyers Jour., 1961-67, exec. bd., 1961-67. Home: 316 Barry Av Chicago IL 60657

ALPERSTEIN, PEARL (MRS. ARNOLD ALPERSTEIN), city ofcl.; b. Kansas City, Mo., Jan. 26, 1927; d. Alex Greenblot and Tillie (Kaplan) Greenblot; B.Jour., U. Mo., 1947; postgrad. U. Colo., 1967; m. Arnold Alperstein, Mar. 25, 1948; children—Donald, Ellen. With counseling dept. Stephens Coll., 1948-50; exec. dir. Colo. chpt. Am. Jewish Com., 1967-70; mem. Lakewood (Colo.) City Council, 1973—. Co-chmn. Lakewood Housing Com., 1971-72; mem. Denver Regional Council Govt. Housing Task Force, 1972-73; chmn. Lakewood Housing Authority, 1974—; mem. bd. Colo. Mental Health Assn., 1969; sec. Centro Cultural, Denver, 1967. Precinct committeewoman Democratic Party, 1955-61, dist. capt., 1961-66; mem. State Dem. Central Com., 1966-70; co-chmn. State Finance Dr., 1965; del. Dem. Nat. Conv., 1972. Author: Ring Around the World, 1953. Editor: House Organ, 1950-51. Home: 12125 W 20th Av Lakewood CO 80215 Office: City Hall 1580 Yarrow Lakewood CO 80215

ALPERT, DELIA ELIZABETH, govt. ofcl.; b. Dannemora, N.Y.; d. Louis and Celia (Greenburg) Alpert; B.S., Plattsburg State Tchrs. Coll., 1947; M.S., State U. of N.Y., 1955; postgrad. Mich. State U., 1969. Tchr. pub. schs., N.Y. State, 1939-49; tchr. Overseas Dependents Schs., Dept. Def., Japan, Germany, Morocco, France, Eng., 1949-53, prin. 1953-65, dep. supt., 1965-70; edn. program specialist Office Edn., Office Equal Ednl. Opportunity, Washington, 1970—. Home: 1600 S Eads St Arlington VA 22202 Office: Equal Ednl Opportunity Room 2033 400 Maryland Av Washington DC 20202

ALPERT, ESTHER SHIRLEY OFFERMAN (MRS. BARNETT ALPERT), civic worker; b. N.Y.C.; d. Samuel and Sadie (Meyers) Offerman; B.A., Hunter Coll., 1930, postgrad., 1933-36; m. Barnett Alpert, June 17, 1932; children—Michael Allen, Judith Ruth. Substitute tchr. N.Y.C. Sch. System, 1940-45; caseworker Dept. Welfare, N.Y.C., 1933-38. Vice pres. Mental Health Assn. Broward County, Fla., 1961, pres., 1962-65; coordinator vol. services South Fla. State Hosp., 1963-65; mem. Community Mental Health Planning Com., 1964-70, 73—; chmn. South br. Broward County Med. Aux., 1965-66; state chmn. mental health Fla. Med. Aux., 1966-68; v.p. Henderson Clinic Broward County, 1965-66, pres., 1966-67, corr. sec., 1967-68, 72-73, rec. sec., 1973—, bd. dirs., 1971—; mem. exec. com. N.Y. Philanthropic League, N.Y.C., 1952-56; vice-chmn. Fla. Adv. Council on Mental Health, 1969-71; mem. Com. on Aging, 1964-65; founder, adviser Mental Health Forum, Broward County, 1961-70; mem. Broward County Community Mental Health Bd. Recipient Bronze plaque for services rendered to mentally ill Mental Health Assn. Fla., 1965. Mem. Nat. Council Jewish Women (exec. com. 1958-60), Hadassah (pres. United Order True Sisters 1950-51), Hunter Coll. Alumni Assn., Am. Jewish Congress. Jewish religion. Home: 1135 N North Lake Dr Hollywood FL 33020

ALPERT, GRACE KENNISON, psychologist; b. Providence, Sept. 18, 1929; d. Samuel Isaacson and Bertha (Sherman) Kennison; A.B. cum laude, Brown U., 1951; Ed.M., Boston U., 1959; m. Wesley Simon Alpert, May 10, 1968. Psychol. staff R.I. Mental Hygiene Services, Providence, 1955-58, 59-72, psychometrist, 1955-58, 59-60, clin. psychologist, 1960-72, cons. R.I. Tng. Sch. for Girls, 1967-68, supr., 1968-72; pvt. practice clin. psychology, Providence, 1970—; clin. psychologist-cons. Project Grow, Providence Sch. Dept., 1973-74. Bd. dirs., corr. sec. Providence chpt. Brandeis U. Nat. Women's Com., 1972—; bd. dirs. dist. 1, Nat. Fedn. Temple Sisterhoods, 1973—. Chmn., Mid-Atlantic region Central Scholarship Com., Pembroke Coll., Brown U., 1970-72. Mem. Am., Eastern, New Eng., R.I. (subcom. on ednl. system 1971—) psychol. assns., Pi Lambda Theta. Jewish religion (Uniongram-YES fund chmn. temple sisterhood). Clubs: Pembroke Coll., Brown U., Ledgemont Country. Home: 53 Wingate Rd Providence RI 02906

ALSCHER, RUTH PAULA, educator; b. N.Y.C., Sept. 11, 1921; B.A., Coll. New Rochelle, 1943; M.S., Fordham U., 1946, Ph.D. in Physiology, 1951. Research asst. dept. nutrition Fleischmann Labs, Standard Brands, Inc., N.Y.C., 1943-45; asst. gen. physiology, grad. sch. and gen. sci sch. edn. Fordham U., 1945-46, dept. biology and genetics, 1950-51; successively instr., prof. biology, chmn. dept. biology Manhattanville Coll., 1946—; mem. corp Marine Biology Lab., Woods Hole, Mass., 1952. Fellow A.A.A.S., Am. Microscopic Soc., Am. Soc. Zoologists, Am. Forestry Assn., Internat. Oceanographic Found., Bus. and Profl. Women's Club, Zonta Internat., Sigma Xi, Delta Kappa Gamma, Kappa Gamma Phi. Sci. Address: Dept of Biology Manhattanville College Purchase NY 10577

ALSPAUGH, JANE BRADNER (MRS. ROBERT ODO ALSPAUGH), civic worker; b. Cleve., Mar. 13, 1920; d. Hosea Townsend and Jessie (Morison) Bradner; student Smith Coll., 1941; m. Robert Odo Alspaugh, Dec. 6, 1941; 1 dau., Janet Bradner. Dir. Am. Commerce Corp., Cleve., Alspaugh & Co., Cleve. Chmn. garden club Cleve. Jr. League, 1954; chmn. jr. council Cleve. Mus. Art, 1957-59, mem. adv. bd., 1958-59; mem. Adult Edn. Council Greater Cleve.; mem. jr. bd. St. Luke's Hosp., Cleve.; mem. bd. of women's com. Cleve. Orch., 1963-66, membership chmn., 1965-66; bd. of women's com. Inst. Music Cleve., 1963-67; mem. women's Play House; mem. careers in social work Scholarship com. Welfare Fedn.; exec. com. women's com. Natural Sci. Mus.; sec. women's com. Natural History Mus., 1972—; mem. women's adv. council Western Res. Hist. Soc., 1973—. Corr. sec. Western Res. Women's Republican Club, 1955-57. Mem. Alumnae Assn. Laurel Sch. Alumnae Assn. Smith Coll. Trustee; mem. exec. com. Garden Center Greater Cleve., 1957-61; bd. women's com. Cleve. Inst. Art, chmn. membership com., 1962-64; bd. mem. Cleve. Orch., chmn. edn. com., 1964-65. Episcopalian. Clubs: Town and Country Garden (v.p. 1966-68, pres. 1968-69), Smith College of Cleveland (pres. 1960-62, women's com. Cleve., scholarship chmn., 1965-67, nominating chmn. 1967-68). Home: 2952 Fairmount Blvd Cleveland Heights OH 44124

ALSPAUGH, LILYAN MAE (MRS. RALPH B. ALSPAUGH), lectr., writer, educator; b. Chgo.; d. Frank R. and Sarah E. (Sanders) Haas; Ph.B., U. Chgo., 1927, grad. fellow, 1927-28; M.A., Ohio State U., 1932; Ph.D., Coll. Communication Arts, Mich. State U., 1969; m. Ralph B. Alspaugh, Nov. 28, 1928. Asst. to pres. Blackett-Sample-Hummert, Inc., Advt. Agy., 5 years, dir. community relations WKRC radio-TV, Cin., 5 years; now profl. lectr. throughout U.S.; v.p., dir. pub. relations Albros Engring., Inc.; now prof. Sch. Bus. Adminstrn., Central Mich. U., Mt. Pleasant. Named honored alumna Ohio State U.; recipient Centennial achievement award Phi Mu; citation award U. Chgo.; named to Exec. and Profl. Hall Fame, Outstanding Educators Am. Mem. Am. Assn. U. Women (pres. Cin. 1944-46, Ohio pres. 1947-49, nat. v.p. 1949-53, fellowship awards com. 1963-67, dir. Mich. div. 1974—), Speech Communication Assn. Am., Internat. Platform Assn., Pub. Relations Soc. Am., Am. Bus. Communication Assn., Am. Women in Radio and TV, Am. Mgmt. Assn., Am. Acad. Advt., Am. Marketing Assn., Phi Beta Kappa, Delta Kappa Gamma (hon. life), Phi Mu. Clubs: Peninsular (Grand Rapids, Mich.); College (Cin.). Contbr. articles to ednl. jours. Home: 810 Pleasant Av Mount Pleasant MI 48858

ALSTADT, LAURA MAY KUIKOLONO (MRS. WILLIAM R. ALSTADT), civic worker; b. Maui, Hawaii, Sept. 21, 1928; d. Reuben and Fannie Kahula (Apo) Goodness; B.S., Brigham Young U., 1950; postgrad. U. Hawaii, 1951-53; m. William R. Alstadt, Aug. 31, 1962; stepchildren—Richard L., Mary Lynn (Mrs. Roger Walker), Thomas H. Tchr. elementary sch., Maui, 1950-54, Honolulu, 1954-62. Mem. adv. bd. Salvation Army, Little Rock, Ark., 1968—, pres. Women's Aux., 1971-72; mem. Gov.'s Citizens Adv. Com., 1967-68; chmn. dental health edn. Ark. Dental Aux., 1966-68, treas., 1968-69, pres.-elect, 1973-74; treas. Ark. Womens Com. Pub. Affairs, 1971—; pres. Central Dist. Dental Aux., 1969-70; mem. dental health edn. com. Women's Aux. Am. Dental Assn., 1966-70, chmn., 1969-70, program and nomination chmn., 1967-68; mem. Ark. Arts Center; mem. Citizens Adv. Com. to Gov. Ark. Methodist. Democrat. Home: 11 Edgehill St Little Rock AR 72207

ALSTON, MARYELLA TRANSMORE (MRS. ANTHONY BUCKNER ALSTON), coll. dean; b. Beckley, W. Va., Mar. 6, 1928; d. Herbert Ferguson and Helen Ruth (Freeman) Wright; student Bluefield State Coll., 1946-49; B.A., W. Va. State Coll., 1971; m. Anthony Buckner Alston, May 21, 1963. Vista coordinator for mental health Lakin (W.Va.) State Hosp., 1954-59, coordinator for emotionally disturbed children, 1959-64, coordinator for psychiat. aides for Dept. Mental Health, 1964-68; counselor residence halls W. Va. State Coll., Institute, 1968-70, asso. dean student affairs, 1970—. Mem. N.A.A.C.P., Nat. Assn. Women Deans and Counselors, So. Coll. Personnel Assn., W. Va. Assn. of Colls. and Univs. (pres. elect 1974-75). Home: 201 1/2 Hillside Dr Nitro WV 25143 Office: Office Student Affairs West Virginia State College Institute WV 25112

ALSTROM, MARGUERITE LURENE GRIFFITH (MRS. JOHN THOMAS ALSTROM), univ. adminstr.; b. Coffeyville, Kan., Feb. 14, 1915; d. Clyde Earl and Mary Lurene (Spear) Griffith; A.B., U. So. Cal., 1946; postgrad., 1957; M.A., Occidental Coll., 1948; m. John Thomas Alstrom, Feb. 23, 1952. Job analyst War Manpower Commn., Los Angeles, 1942-44; asst. dir. Vocational Planning Service, Los Angeles, 1945-46; vocational and mgmt. cons., 1946-66; instr. psychology Occidental Coll., Los Angeles, 1946-47, dir. vocational guidance, 1947-51; lectr. pub. adminstrn. U. So. Cal., 1955-58; city clk. Monterey Park, Cal., 1956-65; vocational cons. U.S. Dept. Health, Edn. and Welfare, Los Angeles, 1962-66, Agana, Guam, 1966-73, Sun City, Ariz., 1973—; asst. to pres. U. Guam, 1966-69, asst. v.p. acad. affairs, 1969-70, chmn. dept. pub. adminstrn., 1970-73. Served as capt. USAF, 1951-53. Mem. Am. Psychol. Assn., Nat. Vocational Guidance Assn., Phi Kappa Phi, Pi Sigma Alpha, Psi Chi, Chi Omicron Gamma. Presbyn. Author: Administrative Analysis Techniques, 1968. Contbr. articles to profl. jours. Home: 10914 Topaz Dr Sun City AZ 85351

ALTABE, JOAN BERG (MRS. DAVID ALTABE), pub. co. exec.; b. N.Y.C., Apr. 27, 1935; d. Harold and Evelyn (Cooperman) B.; B.A., Hunter Coll., 1956, postgrad., 1957; m. David Altabe, Sept. 28, 1958; children—Richard Jonathan, Madeline Nissa. Sculpture instr. N.Y. Lighthouse for Blind, 1949-55; art coordinator Croton-on-Hudson Sch. System, 1957; tech. drafting tchr. Haaren High Sch., N.Y.C., 1958-59; art tchr. jr. high schs., N.Y.C., 1959-72; art dir., partner Regina Pub. Co., 1973—. Tchr. art appreciation Valley Stream, Long Beach (N.Y.) Adult Edn., 1962-64; prodn. mgr. trade mag. Am. Hairdresser, 1956-57. Mem. council com. Democratic party N.Y., 1957-58. Gen. bd. dirs. Hebrew Acad. Long Beach, N.Y. Recipient certificate of Merit, N.Y. Internat. Art Show, 1970. Mem. Nat. Soc. Mural Painters, Artists Equity Assn., League Women Voters. Home: 421 W Olive St Long Beach FL 11561 Office: Regina Pub House Box 301 Long Beach NY 11561

ALTENHAUS, CORRINNE BATLIN (MRS. JULIAN ALTENHAUS), psychologist; b. N.Y.C., July 27, 1926; d. Louis and Rose (Cuttler) Batlin; B.S., Purdue U., 1946; M.Ed., Rutgers U., 1955, Ed.D., 1964; postdoctorate certificate in child psychiatry and child guidance (postdoctorate fellow), Postgrad. Center Mental Health, N.Y.C., 1971; m. Julian Altenhaus, Nov. 27, 1947; 1 dau., Amy Louise. Sch. psychologist Orange (N.J.) Bd. Edn., 1951-64, Millburn (N.J.) Bd. Edn., 1964-67; pvt. practice as psychologist, Millburn, 1967—. Coadj. staff Rutgers U., 1964-65, Newark State Coll., 1965-68, Seton Hall U., 1969-70; psychologist Stevens Inst. Tech. Psychol. Lab., 1965-68; faculty Postgrad. Center Mental Health, N.Y.C., 1972—. Mem. profl. adv. bd. Children's Inst., 1973. Trustee Child Guidance Clinic Oranges and Maplewood, N.J., 1961-69. Diplomate Am. Bd. Psychol. Examiners in Sch. Psychology. Fellow Am. Orth-Psychiat. Assn.; mem. Am., N.J., Essex County (trustee) psychol. assns., Kappa Delta Pi, Phi Delta Kappa. Home: 49 Claremont Dr Maplewood NJ 07040 Office: 120 Millburn Av Millburn NJ 07041

ALTER, PATRICIA ULRICH (MRS. DAVID B. ALTER III), TV broadcasting exec.; b. Cin., May 6, 1936; d. Emil Joseph and Ruth (Wuelzer) Ulrich; B.B.A., U. Miami, 1960; m. David B. Alter III, Aug. 20, 1955; children—David B. IV, Amie Patricia, Jennifer Leigh. Dir. pub. relations/advt. WLBW-TV/WPLG-TV Channel 10, Miami, 1960-71; adminstrv. mgr. Americable, Inc., Cable TV, Homestead, Fla., 1971—. Owner, Multi-Media, Inc., 1970—. Mem. Am. Women in Radio-TV, Women in Communications, Homestead/South Dade C. of C. (mem. task force com. 1973-74), Kappa Kappa Gamma.

Home: 8721 SW 192 Terrace Miami FL 33157 Office: 102 SW 6th Av Homestead FL 33030

ALTHAUSER, ELISABETH KNIGHT, banker; b. Cass City, Mich., Apr. 10, 1915; d. Robert J. and Grace (Karr) Knight; B.S., Mich. State U., 1937; m. William Edward Althauser, June 27, 1958; 1 stepson, William Edward. Office mgr. S.C. Champion Advt. Co., Cass City, 1938-40; asst. to gen. mgr. Tuttle & Clark, Detroit, 1940-42; personnel research Fisher Body div. Gen. Motors Corp., 1942-43; asst. v.p., personnel officer Nat. Bank Commerce, Memphis, 1947-73, v.p. personnel, 1973—. Mem. Nat. Assn. Bank Women (mem. nat. exec. com. 1970-71, dir.), Am. Inst. Banking, Am. Soc. Personnel Adminstrn. Presbyn. Adviser staff Women Banker, 1958—. Office: One Commerce Sq Memphis TN 38150

ALTHOUSE, LAVONNE, editor; b. Ephrata, Pa., Mar. 30, 1932; d. Harvey Shimp and Arletta May (Fry) A.; B.A. in Journalism, Pa. State U., 1953; M.Div., Union Theol. Sem., N.Y.C., 1959; postgrad. New Sch. Social Research, N.Y. U. Writer Office Edn. and Publicity, Presbyn. Ch. U.S.A. Bd. Nat. Missions, 1953-56; mem. staff Quadrennial Conf. Ch. World Mission, Athens, O., 1959-60; staff writer Bd. Higher Edn., United Luth. Ch. Am., 1960-62; editor Luth. Women, Luth. Ch. Women, Phila., 1962-74; ordained to ministry Luth. Ch., 1974; pastor Salem Luth. Ch., Phila., 1974—. Vice chmn. dept. specialized ministries div. overseas ministries Nat. Council Chs. of Christ U.S.A., 1969-71; mem. dept. edn. for mission Nat. Council Chs. of Christ U.S.A., 1962—, chmn. commn. adults, 1967-70. Mem. League Women Voters, Phila., 1963—, Urban League, 1967—. Mem. Asso. Ch. Press (bd. dirs. 1966-71, 1st v.p. 1971-73, pres. 1973—), Internat. Assn. Women Ministers (editor The Women's Pulpit 1972—), N.W. Interfaith Movement (bd. dirs. Phila. 1970-71), Am. Civil Liberties Union, Mensa, Women in Communications (pres. Phila. chpt. 1968-70). Pi Gamma Mu. Author: When Jew and Christian Meet, 1966. Home: 2809 Queen Lane Philadelphia PA 19129 Office: Lutheran Women 2900 Queen Lane Philadelphia PA 19129

ALTLAND-TENG, NANCY RAE, occupational therapist; b. Harrisburg, Pa., Oct. 20, 1937; d. Raymond Bair and Mary Elizabeth (Winters) Altland; student (Bogar scholar) Susquehanna U., 1955-57; B.S., Richmond Profl. Inst. Coll. William and Mary, 1959; M.A., N.Y. U., 1966; m. Chao-Son Teng, June 24, 1972. Occupational therapist Shriner's Crippled Children's Hosp., Phila., 1960-61; occupational therapist Children's Rehab. Inst., Reisterstown, Md., 1961-63; sr. occupational therapist Inst. Rehab. Medicine, N.Y. U., 1963-66; chief occupational therapy Health Sci. Center Temple U., 1966-69; coordinator research Temple U., 1969-72; coordinator research, vis. asso. prof. occupational therapy Nat. Taiwan U., 1972—; cons. in field. Mem. adv. com. Diabetes and Arthritis Control Dept. Health Edn., Welfare, 1966-69; program chmn. Allied Health Professions sect. Arthritis Found., 1966-69; profl. cons. Cheng Hsin Rehab. Center, Taiwan, 1974—. Prosthetics fellow Dept. Health, Edn. and Welfare, 1966. Mem. Alpha Delta Pi. Contbr. articles to profl. jours. Home: 4 Alley 8 Lane 35 Ho-Pin East Rd Sec II Taipei 106 Taiwan Republic of China Office: 1 Chang te Taipei 106 Taiwan Republic of China

ALTMAN, FLORENCE SKELLY (MRS. EUGENE ALTMAN), market social researcher; b. N.Y.C., Oct. 18, 1924; d. Edward and Ray Dora (Graubard) Rosen; A.B. cum laude, Hunter Coll., 1944; postgrad. Columbia, 1945-48; m. Eugene Altman, Feb. 2, 1952; children—Alexandra, Jonathan. With Stewart Doucall & Assos., N.Y.C., 1945-61, U.S. Census, Washington, 1950-52; exec. v.p. Daniel Yankelovich, Inc., N.Y.C., 1961—. Home: 239 Central Park W New York NY 10024 Office: 575 Madison Av New York NY 10022

ALTSHILLER, GLORIA SILVERN (MRS. ARTHUR L. ALTSHILLER), computer co. exec.; b. N.Y.C., Aug. 1, 1925; d. Charles and Rose (Bursh) Marantz; B.A., Bklyn. Coll., 1945; M.A., Columbia, 1946, Ed.D., 1952; m. Leonard C. Silvern, June 30, 1948 (div. Jan. 1968); 1 son, Ronald Paul; m. 2d, Arthur L. Altshiller, Nov. 25, 1970. Tchr. math. N.Y.C. Bd. Edn., Bklyn., 1945-49, Meml. High Sch., Pelham, N.Y., 1955-56; instr. cryptanalysis adult edn., Albany, N.Y., 1951; research analyst Sterling-Winthrop Research Inst., Rensselaer, N.Y., 1952-55; sr. mathematician, head Customer Computer Programmer Tng., Bendix Computer div. Bendix Corp., Los Angeles, 1956-59; sr. engr., head diagnostic programming group Litton Systems, Inc., Woodland Hills, Cal., 1959-62; with space and information systems div. N.Am. Aviation, Inc., Downey, Cal., 1962-66, research specialist, 1962-64, sr. tech. specialist, dir. programmer tng., 1964-66; v.p. Edn. and Tng. Cons., Los Angeles, 1966-67; cons., pres. Computer-Assisted Instrn. Systems, Los Angeles, 1967—; engring. specialist data systems div. Litton Industries, Culver City, Cal., 1973—. Lectr. cryptography, cryptanalysis, N.Y.C., 1945-49, Albany, 1951-56, Los Angeles, 1959-66; substitute tchr. Albany Pub. Schs., 1950-52; cons. Edn. & Tng. Cons., Albany, 1952-55, dir. programming, Los Angeles, 1959-66; teaching staff U. Cal. Extension, Los Angeles, 1966-68. Recipient Automation Educator Year award Bus. Automation Mag., 1967. Mem. Assn. Computing Machinery (chmn. tech. sessions Nat. Conf. 1961-64, chmn. spl. interest com. on digital computer programmer tng. 1960-67, chmn. spl. interest com. computer-assisted instrn., 1967-69, Outstanding Mem. award 1966), Am. Cryptogram Assn. (pres. 1963-65), Los Angeles Soc. for Cryptanalysis (pres. 1960-64), Am. Soc. Tng. Dirs. (pres. Pacific Riviera chpt. 1963), Nat. Council Tchrs. Math. Contbr. articles to profl. jours. Address: 979 Teakwood Rd Los Angeles CA 90049

ALTUS, GRACE MERRIMAN THOMPSON, psychologist; b. Santa Barbara, Cal., Jan. 6, 1924; d. James Roderick and Mary Augusta (Merriman) Thompson; B.A., Santa Barbara Coll., 1944; M.A. (Allan D. Wilson Jr. Meml. scholar 1947-48), U. Cal. at Berkeley, 1947, Ph.D., 1949; m. William David Altus, Dec. 24, 1951; children—Martha Helen, Elizabeth Diane, Deborah Elaine. Tchr. Redlands (Cal.) Jr. High Sch., 1944-46; psychologist Santa Barbara (Cal.) County schs., 1949-53, dir. guidance, 1953-56; psychologist Goleta (Cal.) Union Sch. dist., 1966—. Fellow A.A.A.S., Am. Psychol. Assn.; mem. Cal. Tchrs. Assn., N.E.A., Goleta Edn. Assn., U. Cal. at Santa Barbara Faculty Women (pres. 1958), Sierra Club. Club: Channel City Women's Forum (Santa Barbara). Contbr. articles to profl. jours. Home: 767 Las Palmas Dr Santa Barbara CA 93110 Office: 5689 Hollister Av Goleta CA 93017

ALTVATER, CATHY COMFORT THARP (MRS. FRED L. ALTVATER), artist; b. Little Rock, Ark.; d. William Joseph and Catherine (Collins) Tharp; student Grand Central Sch. Contemporary Arts and Crafts, 1930, Art League L.I., 1946-49, Nat. Acad. Fine Arts, 1950-53; m. W. F. Scott, Jr., July 18, 1924 (div. Aug. 1927); 1 son, Wellington F. III; m. 2d, Fred L. Altvater, May 30, 1930. Featured artist Lord & Taylor, N.Y.C., 1965-74; tchr. Linden Beach Club, Flushing, N.Y., Casino Community Club, Garden City, N.Y.; tchr., demonstrator Ark. Arts Center, Little Rock, Eldorado (Ark.) Arts Center, Wichita (Kan.) Arts Center, 1970-71; one-man shows at Art League L.I., Reading (Pa.) Mus., Little Gallery, N.Y.C., Shreveport, La., Dallas, Atlanta, Falls Church, Va., others; exhibited in group shows at Royal Soc. Watercolor Painters, Mexico City Mus., Met. Mus., museums and art galleries London, Paris, Monaco, Canada, N.Y.C.; represented in internat. and nat. permanent collections. Recipient numerous awards and prizes. Mem. Art League L.I. (pres. 1953-58), Hudson Valley Art Assn. (sec. 1950-68), Am. Artist Profl. League (treas. 1964-65), Am. Watercolor Soc. (treas. 1959-67, sec. 1968-69, asst. sec. 1969—), So. (founding mem.), Midsouthern Watercolorists, Catherine Loriallard Wolfe Art Club, Nat. Arts Club, Nat. Art League, Allied Artists Am. Home: Route 2 Box 44 Scott AR 72142 also 43 Rocky Neck Av East Gloucester MA 01930

ALTWERGER, LIBBY, painter; b. Toronto, Ont., Can., July 13, 1921; ed. Ont. Coll. Art; married. One man shows Pascall Gallery, Toronto, 1964, Sonneck Gallery, Kitcehenr, Ont., 1968; instr. drawing Ryerson Poly. Sch.; represented in many pvt. collections. Recipient Lt. Gov. Gen.'s medal, 1959, Grand Prix Gold medal Internat. Feminine Culturelle, Vichy, France, 1963, Sterling Trust award, 1965. O'Keefe scholar, 1956; hon. mention watercolors, 1967. Mary Dingham scholar, 1958. Address: 526 Dovercourt Rd Toronto ON M6H 2W4 Canada

ALUMBAUGH, ELNORA GARNETT VANALSTINE (MRS. DARREL CHANNING ALUMBAUGH), coll. adminstr.; b. Lincoln, Kan., July 20, 1922; d. Alfred Carl and Elsie Daisy (Kanzius) Vanalstine; grad. Salt City Bus. Coll., 1942; m. Darrel Channing Alumbaugh, July 5, 1944; children—Ronald Wayne, Sandra Sue, Michael LaVerne, Janet Lynn, Keith Edward. Bookkeeper accounts receivable dept. Wiley's, Inc., Hutchinson, Kan., 1942-43; bookkeeper Goodpaster's Ins., Hutchinson, Kan., 1943, Roberts Printing and Stationery, Hutchinson, Kan., 1943-44; sales clerk Sears Roebuck & Co., Hutchinson, Kan., 1944-46; accountant, Ultra, Inc., Hutchinson, Kan., 1966; Nat. Defense Edn. Act financial aid officer Sterling (Kan.) Coll., 1966-69; coordinator student financial aid Mid-Am. Nazarene Coll., Olathe, Kan., 1969-73, exec. sec. Office Financial Aid, 1973—. Active P.T.A., Boy Scouts Am. Recipient Certificate Profl. Proficiency, Kan. Assn. Student Financial Aid Adminstrs., 1972. Mem. Ch. Nazarene. Author: Happiness . . . Dollars and Cents, 1974. Home: 805 Sheridan Circle Olathe KS 66061

ALVAREZ, THELMA LUCIA, librarian; b. Tampa, Fla., July 30, 1923; d. Benigno and Antonia (Carnus) Alvarez; A.B., Fla. State U., 1945, postgrad., 1961-62. Owner Carousel, children's shop, Sarasota, Fla., 1949-51; tchr. art Manatee county, Fla., 1954—; with Fla. Div. Family Services, Sarasota, 1955—, case worker, 1955-60, supr., 1960-70, librarian, region orientation supr., art dir., 1970—. Bd. dirs. Sarasota United Need, 1967-68, Migrant Edn. Orgn., 1965—, Planned Parenthood Assns., 1968-69. Mem. Beta Sigma Phi. Club: Altrusa (pres. 1971-72). Home: PO Box 901 Sarasota FL 33578 Office: 2828 N Trail St Sarasota FL 33570

ALVORD, JUNE, home economist, govt. ofcl.; b. Noble, Ill., June 11, 1922; d. John Rawlings and Mary Irene (Eck) Alvord; B.A., Ind. Central Coll., 1944. Insp., Curtiss Wright Corp., Indpls., 1944-45; instr. English, Olney Twp. (Ill.) High Sch., 1945-46; saleswoman, cashier Sears Roebuck & Co., Indpls., 1946-48; sch. program adviser home service Indpls. Power & Light Co., 1948-55; group leader home econs. sect. Midwest Research Inst., Kansas City, Mo., 1955-57; sr. home economist Niven-Russell Research, Inc., Kansas City, 1957-65, asst. dir. home econs., 1965-69; home econs. writing cons. Dairy Council of Greater Kansas City, 1969-70; consumer protection specialist FTC, 1970—. Dir., coordinator consumer panel Kansas City Met. area, 1959-63. Home: Santa Fe Village 8519 Holmes Apt 213 Kansas City MO 64131 Office: 911 Walnut St Kansas City MO 64106

AMARA, LUCINE, soprano, opera and concert singer; b. Hartford, Conn., March 1, 1927; d. George and Adrine (Kazanjian) Armaganian; student Music Acad. of West, 1947, U. So. Cal., 1949-50; m. Gil H. Rudy, Jan. 7, 1961 (div. 1964). Appeared in Hollywood Bowl, 1948; soloist San Francisco Symphony, 1949-50; with Met. Opera, 1950—; recorded Pagliacci, 1951; singer with Hartford, Pitts., Central City, New Orleans operas, 1952-54; appeared Glyndebourne Opera, also Edinburgh Festival, 1954; singer Aida, Terme Di Caracalla, Rome, 1954, also Stockholm Opera, N.Y. Philharmonic, St. Louis Civic Light Opera, 1955-56; tour of Israel, 1960; leading roles La Boheme and Pagliacci, Vienna Staatsopera, 1960, La Boheme and Aida, Stuttgart Staatsopera, 1961; grand opening night performance Lincoln Center for Performing Arts, N.Y.C., 1962. Toured Russia, Dec. 1965. Rec. artist Angel Records, Columbia, RCA Victor, Met. Opera Record Club. Recipient 1st prize Atwater-Kent Radio auditions, 1948. Mem. Sigma Alpha Iota. Home: 260 West End Av New York City NY 10023 Office: Metropolitan Opera New York City NY

AMATNIEK, SARA BERLIN, artist; b. N.Y.C.; d. Alexander and Martha (Aranow) Berlin; B.A., Bklyn. Coll., 1942; M.A., Tchrs. Coll., Columbia, 1952; m. Ernest Amatniek, Apr. 1, 1949; children—Kathie, Joan Cindy. Tchr. art Sch. Music and Art, N.Y.C., 1951-54, Port Chester (N.Y.) High Sch., 1954-58; v.p. Bioelectric Instruments, Hastings-on-Hudson, N.Y., 1960-70; artist, printmaker, 1970—; one-woman show at Huntington Library, 1974; exhibited art in group shows at Nat. Acad., N.Y.C., Hecksher Mus., Huntington, Firehouse Gallery, Garden City, N.Y., Brookwood East Gallery, Islip, N.Y., C.W. Post Coll. Recipient Graphics award 14th Ann. L.I. Art Exhibit, 1973, Huntington Twp. Art League Members Show, 1973, 1st prize Malverne Artists, 1974, Islip Art and Cultural Festival, 1974. Address: 154 Bay Rd Huntington NY 11743

AMBROSE, VIRGINIA DICKEY (MRS. PETER J. AMBROSE), ednl. counselor; b. Binghamton, N.Y., May 19, 1945; d. Nelson Daniel and Frances Phoebe (Ryder) Dickey; B.A., Keuka Coll., 1968; M.S., State U. N.Y. at Albany, 1969, postgrad., 1971—; m. Peter J. Ambrose, Aug. 28, 1971. Dir. counseling services Columbia-Greene Community Coll., Athens, N.Y., 1969-72; counselor jr. high sch. with Cairo (N.Y.) Central Sch., 1973—. Sales rep. Schneider Realty, Claverack, N.Y., 1972—. Sec. Town of Claverack (N.Y.) Planning Bd., 1972—; sec. Town of Claverack (N.Y.) Bd. of Appeals, 1972—. Bd. dirs. Columbia County Assn. for the Blind, 1970-72, 74—. Mem. N.Y. State Personnel and Guidance Assn., N.Y. Counselors Assn., Greene County Guidance Assn., Alpha Psi Omega. Author: (with Frances Smith) Quality Engineering, 1966; A Question of Honor (3-act play), 1966. Home: Box 54 Hollowville NY 12530 Office: Cairo Central School Main St Cairo NY 12514

AMBROSE, ZELDA MARIE STEVENS (MRS. JOSEPH JAMES AMBROSE), educator; b. Pitts., Jan. 30, 1932; d. Rudy S. and Ida May (Read) Stevens; B.S., N.Y. State U. at Geneseo, 1955; postgrad. Tchrs. Coll., Columbia, N.Y. U., State U. N.Y. at New Paltz; m. Joseph James Ambrose, July 2, 1955; children—Cassendra Stevens, Beth Ann. Tchr., Bd. Coop. Ednl. Services, No. Westchester, Chappaqua and Yorktown Centers, 1955-61; tchr. White Plains (N.Y.) Pub. Schs. System, 1963—, Battle Hill Elementary Sch., 1963—. Mem. Am. Assn. Mental Deficiency, Assn. Children with Learning Disabilities, N.Y. State United Tchrs., N.Y. Zool. Soc. Presbyn.

AMBRUS, CLARA MARIA (MRS. JULIAN L. AMBRUS), physician; b. Rome, Italy, Dec. 24, 1924; d. Anthony and Charlotte (Schneider) Bayer; student U. Budapest, 1943-47; M.D., U. Zurich, 1949; postgrad. U. Paris, 1949; Ph.D., Jefferson Med. Coll., 1955; m. Julian Lawrence Ambrus, Feb. 17, 1945; children—Madeline, Peter, Julian, Linda, Steven, Katherine, Charles. Came to U.S. 1949, naturalized 1955. Research asst. Inst. Histology, Embryology and Biology, U. Budapest, 1943-45; demonstrator in pharmacology U. Budapest Med. Sch., 1946-47; asst. dept. pharmacology U. Zurich Med. Sch., 1947-49; asst. dept. therapeutic chemistry and virology Inst. Pasteur, Paris, France, 1949; asst. prof., asso. prof. pharmacology Grad. Sch., Phila. Coll. Pharmacy and Sci., 1950-55; research asso. Roswell Park Meml. Inst., Buffalo, 1955-58, sr. cancer research scientist, 1958-64, asso. scientist, 1964-69, prin. cancer research scientist, 1969—; prof. pharmacology, asso. research prof. pediatrics State U. N.Y. Buffalo Med. and Grad. Schools. Diplomate Am. Bd. Clin. Chemists. Fellow Am. Coll. Clin. Pharmacology, Am. Coll. Angiology, Internat. Soc. Hematology, Royal Soc. Medicine (London); mem. Am. Soc. Pharmacology and Exptl. Therapeutics, Am. Soc. for Cancer Research, Soc. for Exptl. Biology and Medicine, Am. Fedn. Clin. Research, Am. Physiol. Soc., Am. Soc. Hematology, Am. Assn. U. Women, Am. Med. Women's Assn., A.M.A., Sigma Xi, Rho Chi. Clubs: Women's Faculty (U. Buffalo); Women's (Phila.); Clarksburg Country, Saturn. Contbr. numerous articles to med. and sci. periodicals. Home: 143 Windsor Av Buffalo NY 14209 also West Hill Farms Boston NY 14025 Office: 666 Elm St Buffalo NY 14203

AMBURGEY, ROSE NELL, govt. ofcl.; b. nr. Charleston, W.Va., Nov. 22, 1919; d. William E. and Lucy (Foster) Amburgey; Ph.D. (hon.), Colo. State Christian Coll., 1973. With U.S. Dist. Atty., Lexington, 1953—, now adminstrv. asst. Pres., Lex-Kay Fed. Credit Union, Lexington, 1957-58, 68-69, 70. Served with USMCR, 1944-46. Mem. Christian Ch. Mem. Blue Grass Bus. and Profl. Women's Club. Home: 2139 St Mathilda Dr Lexington KY 40502 Office: Fed Bldg Lexington KY 40501

AMDUR, MARY O(CHSENHIRT), educator; b. Pitts., Feb. 18, 1921; B.S., U. Pitts., 1943; Ph.D. in Biochemistry, Cornell U., 1946; m. 1944. Asst. ophthal. research Howe Lab. Harvard Med. Sch., 1947-48; research biochemistry VA Hosp., 1948-49; research asso. Harvard Sch. Pub. Health, 1949-57, asst. prof. physiology, 1957-63, asso. prof. toxicology, 1963—. Mem. A.A.A.S., Am. Chem. Soc., Am. Indsl. Hygiene Assn., N.Y. Acad. Sci., Am. Acad. Indsl. Hygiene, Soc. Toxicology. Address: Sch Pub Health Harvard Boston MA 02115

AMEMIYA, FRANCES (LOUISE) CAMPBELL, educator; b. Riverside, Cal., June 16, 1915; A.B., U. Cal. at Los Angeles, 1935, M.A., 1936; Ph.D. in Math., U. Mich., 1945; m. 1952; 2 children. Teaching fellow math. U. Cal. at Los Angeles, 1935-37; prof. George Pepperdine Coll., 1937-58; asso. prof. Cal. Western U., 1958-62, Parsons Coll., 1962-64; mem. faculty Cal. State U. at Hayward, 1964—, prof., 1971—. Bd. dirs. Fremont (Cal.) chpt. Japanese Am. Citizens League, 1969-73; bd. dirs. Philharmonic Soc. Fremont-Newark, 1969—, sec., 1973—. Vis. prof. Ibaraki Christian Coll., Japan, 1949-50. Recipient Faculty award Cal. Western U., 1962. Mem. Math. Assn. Am., Inst. Math. Statistics, Nat. Council Tchrs. Math., Am. Assn. U. Women, Sigma Xi, Delta Kappa Gamma. Address: Dept Math Cal State U at Hayward Hayward CA 94542

AMEN, JO ANN ROSALIE, state ofcl.; b. Cheyenne, Wyo., May 7, 1938; d. Adolph and Amelia (Sitzman) Amen; student Cascade Coll., 1958; student U. No. Colo., 1959-61, B.A., 1965; student Wake Forest U., 1965. Dep. state registrar, vital records services, div. health and med. services Wyo. Dept. Health and Social Services, Cheyenne, 1968—. Mem. Am. Assn. Vital Records and Pub. Health Atatistics (mem. governing council 1968—), Population Assn. Am., Wyo. State Employees Assn., Wyo. Human Resources Confedn., Am. Pub. Health Assn., Smithsonian Assos. Republican. Baptist. Home: 3430 Concord Rd Cheyenne WY 82001 Office: State Office Bldg West Cheyenne WY 82002

AMERSHEK, KATHLEEN, educator; b. Johnstown, Pa., Dec. 1, 1929; d. Rudie J. and Helen (McKernan) Amershek; B.S., Western Pa. State Coll., 1951; M.Ed., Pa. State U., 1957; Ph.D., U. Minn., 1966; m. E.P. McLoone, 1973. Tchr. Westmont-Upper Yoder Sch. Dist., Johnstown, 1951-56; grad. asst. Pa. State U., 1956-57; supr. State U. N.Y. at Brockport, 1957-60; instr. U. Minn., 1960-63; asso. prof. State U. N.Y. at Buffalo, 1963-66; asso. prof. early childhood and elementary edn. U. Md., College Park, 1966—. Cons. Student Vol. Programs of Catholic Student Center, Pa. Dept. Pub. Health. Mem. Md. Com. Early Childhood Edn. 1969—, Mem. Tri-state Assn. Student Teaching (past rec. sec. Minn.), Md. Tchrs. Assn. (pres. higher edn. council 1973-75), Am. Ednl. Research Assn., Assn. Student Teaching, Pi Lambda Theta. Contbr. to Ency. Research in Edn. Home: 4602 Clemson Rd College Park MD 20740 Office: College of Education University of Maryland College Park MD 20740

AMES, BARBARA BOWER (MRS. VICTOR ARNOLD AMES), ednl. adminstr.; b. Ottawa, Kan., Mar. 5, 1916; d. Kenneth Dewitt and Charlotte (Smart) Bower; B.S., Syracuse U., 1936; m. Victor Arnold Ames, Jan. 3, 1938 (dec. Nov. 1960); children—Judy (Mrs. Thomas H. Walters, Jr.), Robert Arnold. Editor, Trethway Pub. Co., Wilkes-Barre, Pa., 1936-37; prodn. mgr. Flack Advt. Agy., Syracuse, N.Y., 1937-38; promotion mgr. Syracuse U. Press, 1956-58; bull. editor Syracuse U., 1958-61; asso. dir. pub. relations (publs.) U. Rochester (N.Y.), 1961—. Cons. publs. Acad. Assos., Rochester, 1972—. Mem. Am. Coll. Pub. Relations Assn., Central N.Y. Coll. Pub. Relations Council (pres. 1971-73), Women in Communications (chpt. treas. 1971-73), P.E.O., Kappa Kappa Gamma, Methodist. Home: 62A Manor Pkwy Rochester NY 14620 Office: 1351 Mount Hope Av Rochester NY 14620

AMES, BERNICE OLDS (MRS. ELI BARLOW AMES), poet; b. Corry, Pa.; d. Murray Raymond and Bernice (Edwards) Olds; A.B., Wilson Coll., 1936; m. Eli Barlow Ames, Aug. 28, 1937; children—Lauren Barlow, Murray Newton, Carolyn, Roger Scott. Wroxton fellow, summer 1967. Mem. Poetry Soc. Am. (James Joyce award 1967, Cecil Hemley award 1971), Nat. League Am. Pen Women, P.E.N., Cal. Writer's Guild, Santa Monica Writer's Club (pres. 1962-64). Author poetry books: Where the Light Bends, 1955, In Syllables, of Stars, 1958, Antelope Bread, 1966. Home: 12223 Dunoon Lane Los Angeles CA 90049

AMES, ELINOR (MRS. WALTER RANZINI), newspaper editor; b. Ticonderoga, N.Y.; student Hunter Coll., 1929-32, New Sch., 1933, Columbia, 1933-34; m. Walter Ranzini, Oct. 15, 1938; 1 dau., Rosemary (Mrs. Edward Lee Werner). Asst. child tng. editor The News, N.Y.C., 1932-34, etiquette editor, 1934, Chgo. Tribune news syndicate, 1934—. Tchr. Social usage Pratt Inst., Bklyn., 1939-49; spl. lectr. Coll. City N.Y., 1946, Fordham U., N.Y.C., 1949; asso. prof. St. Joseph's Sem., N.Y.C., 1963-68; moderator Teen TV Show, WPIX, N.Y.C., 1952-53; Talked on Etiquette Home Show, NBC-TV, 1954. Mem. Arista, English Speaking Union, Chi Omega. Author: Modern Etiquette, 1935; Children's Table Manners, 1940; Guide for the Executive's Wife, 1965. Office: The NY News 220 E 42d St New York City NY 10017

AMES, JEAN GOODWIN (MRS. ARTHUR F. AMES), artist; b. Santa Ana, Cal.; d. Joseph R. and Margaret (Grant) Goodwin; student Pomona Coll., 1921-23, Art Inst. Chgo., 1923-26; B.E., U. Cal. at Los Angeles, 1931; M.F.A., U. So. Cal., 1937; m. Arthur F. Ames, Sept. 5, 1940. Prof. art Scripps Coll., Claremont, Cal., 1940-69, Claremont Grad. Sch., 1940-69; one-man show at Scripps Coll. Lang Gallery, 1969, Riverside Art Center (Cal.), 1970; exhibited enameling in shows at Syracuse (N.Y.) Mus. Fine Art, 1969, Mus. Contemporary Crafts, N.Y.C., 1967; executed murals at Rose Hills Meml. Park, Whittier, Cal., 1957, Fresno (Cal.) Guarantee Savs. & Loan Assn., 1958, Cal. Fed. Plaza Bldg., Los Angeles, 1965, Garrison Theater, Claremont, 1965, others. Recipient award for distinguished archtl. decoration A.I.A., 1956, 58; named Woman of Year in art Los Angeles Times, 1958. Mem. Am. Craftsmen's Council. Home: 4094 Olive Hill Dr Claremont CA 91711

AMES, LE VERLE MOORE, city ofcl.; b. Cross Plains, Tex., Aug. 23, 1921; d. George Anderson and Cora Lorena (Westerman) Moore; B.A., Kilgore Jr. Coll., 1942; grad. Masseys Bus. Sch., Houston, 1955; m. William W. Ames, Jr., Apr. 23, 1943 (div. June 1956); 1 son, George Anderson. Office sec. Union Carbide Corp., Houston, 1951-56, Grissom Russell Engring Co., Houston, 1957-67, Monsanto Chem. Co., Houston, 1960-61; city sec. City of Ranger (Tex.), 1968-74, mcpl. judge, 1974—. Mem. Tex. Municipal League, Tex. Secs. and Clks. Home: 616 Young St Ranger TX 76470 Office: 314 W Main St Ranger TX 76470

AMES, LOUISE BATES, child psychologist; b. Portland, Me., Oct. 29, 1908; d. Samuel Lewis and Annie Earle (Leach) Bates; A.B., U. Me., 1930, M.A., 1933, Sc.D., 1957; Ph.D., Yale, 1936; Sc.D., Wheaton, 1967; m. Smith Ames, May 22, 1930 (div. 1937); 1 dau., Joan (Mrs. Robert Clifford Chase). Research sec., personal asst. to Dr. Gesell, Yale Clinic Child Devel., Yale Med. Sch., 1933-36, instr., 1940-44, asst. prof., 1944-50; curator Yale Films of Child Devel., 1944-50; co-founder Gesell Inst. Child Devel., New Haven, dir. research, sec.-treas., 1950-67, asso. dir., chief psychologist, 1967-72, co-dir., 1970—; daily syndicated newspaper column Child Behavior, 1951—; weekly TV broadcast on child behavior WBZ, Boston, 1952-55, WEWS, Cleve., 1960-61. Sec., Life Enrichment Program, 1968—; mem. White House Conf. on Children, 1970. Certified psychologist, Conn. Mem. Conn. Psychol. Soc., Am. Psychol. Assn., Soc. Research Child Devel. Internat. Council Psychologists (dir. 1945-47), Soc. Projective Techniques, Rorschach Inst. (sec. 1964-66, pres. 1969-70), Author's Guild, Sigma Xi. Author: (with Arnold Gesell and others) First Five Years of Life, Infant and Child, Child from Five to Ten, Years Ten to Sixteen, Child Behavior, Child Rorschach Responses, Rorschach Responses in Old Age, Adolescent Rorschach Responses, Parents Ask, Mosaic Patterns of American Children, The Guidance Nursery, School Readiness; Is Your Child in the Wrong Grade?; Child Care and Development, 1970; Stop School Failure, 1972. Mem. editorial bd. Jour. Learning Disabilities, Jour. Genetic Psychology, Edn. Digest, Internat. Jour. Child Psychotherapy, Family Circle. Home: 283 Edwards St New Haven CT 06511 Office: 310 Prospect St New Haven CT 06511

AMES, MARION PATTERSON (MRS. GEORGE J. AMES), lawyer, Civic worker; b. N.Y.C., Oct. 18, 1917; d. William and Mary (Gavigan) Patterson; A.B., Barnard Coll., 1937; J.D., Fordham U., 1942; m. George J. Ames, July 19, 1941; children—Ruth (Mrs. John E. Solie), Joan (Mrs. Asa J. Berkowitz), Margery, Dorothy. Admitted to N.Y. State bar, 1942; asso. firm Spence, Windels, Walser, Hotchkiss & Angell, N.Y.C., 1942-46; editorial asst. Uniform Comml. Code Project of Am. Law Inst., 1946-48. Pres. Westchester Council of Social Agys., 1971—; mem. exec. com. State Communities Aid Assn., 1966—; pres. N.Y. State Assn. for Community Services, 1971-73, Found. for Citizen Edn., 1971—; mem. Nat. Council on Crime and Delinquency, 1960—, Com. for Modern Cts., 1957—, Adv. Council on Mental Retardation Facilities, 1966-71, Commn. on Compensation of Auto Accident Victims, 1968-69, Westchester Coalition, 1972—, N.Y. State Jud. Screening Com.; pres. League Women Voters N.Y. State, 1967-71. Trustee, Coll. of New Rochelle. Home: Seville Av Rye NY 10580 Office: 817 Broadway New York City NY 10003

AMES, (POLLY) SCRIBNER, artist; b. Chgo., Feb. 16, 1908; d. Edward Scribner and Mabel (Van Meter) Ames; Ph.B., U. Chgo., 1928; student Art Inst. Chgo., 1929, student Hans Schwegerle, Munich, Germany, 1932, Jose de Creeft, N.Y.C., 1933, Hans Hofmann, N.Y.C., 1934-36. Tchr., City and Country Sch., N.Y.C., 1939-41; exhibited paintings Cercle Universitaire, Aix-en-Provence, France, 1950, Esher-Surry Gallery, The Hague, Netherlands, 1949, Chardin Gallery, Paris, France, 1950, in maj. U.S. cities; costumier Met. Opera, N.Y.C. Active Recs. for Blind, Chgo., 1958—. Recipient Purchase award State Mus. Springfield, Ill., 1963. Mem. Arts Club of Chgo. (dir.), Archaeol. Inst. Paintings include Impression of Geraldine Page in Sweet Bird of Youth; portraits of Povla Frijsh, Town Hall, N.Y.C., Bernadotte E. Schmitt, Marion Morehouse (Mrs. E. E. Cummings), Maureen Ting-Klein, Mrs. Alan Rothnie (wife Brit. ambassador to Saudi Arabia). Author, illustrator: Marsden Hartley in Maine, 1972. Home: 5843 S Stony Island Av Chicago IL 60637

AMES, VELDA TITTLE CLIPPINGER, newspaper publisher; b. nr. McLeansboro, Ill., Mar. 19, 1911; d. Joseph Marshall and Ethel (Lasater) Tittle; diploma Eastern Ill. U., 1931; m. Roy Clippinger, Apr. 7, 1949 (dec. 1962); m. 2d, Douglas J. Ames, July 31, 1963. Former tchr. rural schs.; pub. Carmi (Ill.) Times, Norris City (Ill.) News, 1962—; pres., editor, gen. mgr. Carmi Times Pub. Co., 1962—; dir. Carmi Broadcasting Co., radio sta. WROY, 1963—. Publicity chmn. White County chpt. A.R.C., 1963-70. Named One of Top Editors Year, Ill. Press Assn., 1965; Citizen of Month, Citizen of Year in So. Ill., 1972. Mem. Carmi Bus. and Profl. Women's Club (pres. 1938-39, dist. pres. 1939-40), Home Culture Circle, V.F.W. Aux., Am. Legion Aux., Carmi C. of C., Ill., Inland Daily, So. Ill. press assns., Nat., Am. newspaper assns. Democrat. Methodist. Mem. Order Eastern Star. Home: 205 W Cherry St Carmi IL 62821 Office: 323-325 E Main St Carmi IL 62821

AMICARELLA, EFFIE MAE MELCHING (MRS. CLAUDE L. AMICARELLA), librarian; b. Denver, Oct. 31, 1915; d. William C. and Augusta P. (Seipp) Melching; A.A., Colo. Woman's Coll., 1936; m. Claude L. Amicarella, Nov. 5, 1944; children—Claudia Louise (Mrs. Thomas G. Simmons), Linda (Mrs. Terrance Lester). Med. technician St. Luke's Hosp., 1936-40, Edward E. Taylor, M.D., 1940-44; dir. Lafayette (O.) Pub. Library, 1959—. Recipient Wakan award Camp Fire Council, 1963. Mem. Colo. Library Assn., Wednesday Study Club. Home: 107 W Geneseo St Lafayette CO 80026 Office: 300 E Simpson St Lafayette CO 80026

AMICK, CAROL CAMPBELL, editor; b. Cleve., June 17, 1945; d. Charles Lorayne and Janet Robertson Gilchrist (Campbell) Amick; B.S., Ia. State U., 1968. Reporter radio-TV news WOI-AM-FM-TV, Ames, Ia., 1967-68; asst. editor Belmont (Mass.) Citizen, 1968-69; reporter-announcer WCAS Radio, Cambridge, Mass., 1968-69; editor Minute-Man, Bedford, Mass., 1969-74. Journalism instr. night sch. Middlesex Community Coll., 1972, adviser student newspaper, 1973; project coordinator photography class Concord (Mass.) Prison, 1972-73; journalism lectr. Bedford (Mass.) Pub. Schs., 1969—. Mem. Charter Commn., Bedford, Mass., 1973-74; mem. Opportunities Industrialization Center, Inc., 1972, Friends of Bedford Library, 1973—; inspector wood, bark, and manure Town of Bedford, Mass., 1972—, mem. publs. com., 1973—; community cabinet dir. United Way, 1973. Mem. Bedford (Mass.) Democratic Town Com., 1972—; candidate Mass. Ho. of Reps., 1974. Recipient Reporting award New Eng. Press Assn., 1970. Mem. Women in Communications, Nat. Newspaper Assn., New Eng., Mass. press assns., Alpha Lambda Delta, Sigma Kappa. Mem. Ch. of Christ. Club: Woman's Community (Bedford). Home: 277 The Great Rd Bedford MA 01730 Office: 9 Meriam St Lexington MA 02173

AMICO, FRANCES EDITH PELLITERI (MRS. VINCENT J. AMICO), excavating co. exec., polit. worker; b. Sicily, Italy, June 12, 1920; d. Gaetano and Giovanna (Russo) Pelliteri; brought to U.S., 1921, naturalized, 1926; grad. high sch.; m. Vincent James Amico, Oct. 19, 1946; children—Joseph Thomas, Thomas James. Owner, designer Pel's Fashion Designs, Rochester, N.Y., 1942-44; treas. Amico Bros., Inc. (Now Jim Amico and Sons, Inc.), Rochester, 1960—, also partner, treas., sec. Auditor Women's Republican Club of Gates, Rochester, 1954-58, pres., 1971-72, chmn. exec. bd., 1972-73; treas. Gates Rep. Town and County Com., 1974—. Club: Gates Amita (dir. 1966-67) (Rochester). Address: 3570 Lyell Road Rochester NY 14606

AMIDON, DEBRA MAE, educator; b. Boston, Oct. 20, 1946; d. Frederick Elias and Mildred Therese (MacDonald) Amidon; B.S. in Elementary Edn., Boston U., 1968; M.A. in Student Personnel Services, Columbia Tchrs. Coll., 1973. Tchr. perceptually handicapped Marshfield (Mass.) pub. schs., 1968-69; 2d grade tchr. Natick (Mass.) pub. schs., 1969-70; asst. dean women Rider Coll., Trenton, N.J., 1971-73; asso. dean student activities and residential life, Babson Coll., Babson Park, Mass., 1973—. Mem. N.J. Task Force on Consortium of Community Colls., 1972-73. Mem. Women's Resource Center, Natick. Mem. Boston Assn. Coll. Housing Adminstrs. (steering com., workshop chmn.), Nat. Assn. Women Deans and Counselors (com. on concern for students), Nat. Assn. Student Personnel Adminstrs. (regional exec. com., profl. standards and devel. com., regional conf. chmn. 1975), Nat. Entertainment Conf. (regional conf. chmn. 1974), Assn. Coll. Unions, Internat. Sports Car Club Am., Boston U. Women Grads. Club (pres.), Greater Wellesley Profl. Bus. Women's Assn. (charter), Cardinal Key (hon.), Sigma Kappa, Pi Lambda Theta (scholarship 1967). Home: Woodland Hill Babson Coll Babson Park MA 02157

AMMANN, MARGOT (MRS. GUSTAV T. DURRER), physician; b. Morristown, N.J., May 31, 1922; d. Othmar Hermann and Lily (Wehrli) Ammann; B.A., Vassar Coll., 1944; M.D., N.Y. Med. Coll., 1949; m. Gustav T. Durrer, July 9, 1960. Intern, Bellevue Hosp., N.Y.C., 1949-50, Mountainside Hosp., Montclair, N.J., 1950-51; resident Hague Maternity Hosp., Jersey City, N.J., 1955-57, Woman's Hosp., N.Y.C., 1957-58, Roosevelt Hosp., N.Y.C., 1958-59; pvt. practice medicine, specializing in obstetrics and gynecology, N.Y.C., 1959—; asso. attending obstetrics-gynecology Roosevelt Hosp. Bd. dirs. Swiss Benevolent Soc., 1964—. Home: 215 E 68th St New York City NY 10021 Office: 930 Park Av New York City NY 10028

AMMERMAN, CAROL APPLE, ednl. adminstr.; b. Plymouth, Ind., Sept. 2, 1935; d. Herschell Otto and Shirley Marie (Coar) Apple; B.S. in Home Econs., Purdue U., 1960; M.A. in Guidance and Counseling, Ball State U., 1965; postgrad. Ariz. State U., 1973; children by previous marriage—Connie Lynn, Scott Paul, Brett Alan, Curtt Nelson. Tchr. high sch. Ind., 1960-65; counselor Laramie (Wyo.) Jr. High Sch., 1965-69; founding faculty counselor Yavapai Coll., Prescott, Ariz., 1969-72, dir. student activities, 1972—. Bd. dirs. Girl's Ranch Inc., Phoenix, 1973—, Yavapai County Planned Parenthood, 1971—. Recipient Outstanding Service award to faculty mem. Yavapai Coll., 1973. Mem. Am. Personnel and Guidance Assn., Am. Coll. Personnel Assn., Nat. (adv. council 1973—), Ariz. (sec. 1973) assns. women deans, adminstrs. and counselors D.A.R., Soroptimist (1st v.p. Prescott 1973-74, pres. 1974-75), Toastmistress (treas. 1971-72, v.p. 1972-73, pres. 1973-74, rep. 1974-75), Zeta Tau Alpha (v.p. 1956-57, chmn. state recommendations 1972-74). Office: 1100 E Sheldon St Prescott AZ 86301

AMMERMAN, LEILA TREMAINE (MRS. ROY EARLE AMMERMAN), writer; b. Buffalo, Feb. 3, 1912; d. DeWitt Charles and Alice Nelson (Bowd) Tremaine; grad. high sch.; m. Roy Earle Ammerman, July 14, 1934; children—Earle, Dorothy, Alice, Garnette. Exec. dir. Girl's Club, Portsmouth, Va., 1963-65; exec. dir. The Little Library, St. Petersburg, Fla., 1965-73; service clk. Webb's City, Inc., St. Petersburg, 1973—; sec. Colonial Chapel, Gulfport, Fla., 1974—. Mem. curriculum and program planning council Nat. Bd. Christian Chs., Portsmouth, 1959-61. Democrat. Mem. Christian Ch. Author: Of Such is the Kingdom, 1954; Abingdon Promotion Rally Day Book, 1960; Abingdon Easter Programs, 1960; Abingdon Mother's Day Programs, 1960; Christmas Programs # 2, 1960; Inspiring Devotional Programs, 1960; Programs for Special Days, 1961; Golden Ladder of Stewardship, 1962. Home: 200 57th Av S St Petersburg FL 33705 Office: 1099 49th St South Gulfport FL 33707

AMMERMAN, LENELL Y. GOODMAN (MRS. HARVEY HIRSCH AMMERMAN), civic worker; b. Fond du Lac, Wis., May 11, 1918; d. Samuel Nathan and Ida (Swerdel) Goodman; B.A., U. Wis., 1940; m. Harvey Hirsch Ammerman, Feb. 28, 1943; children—Elaine, Bruce, Joy Rumizen, Seth. Economist, WPB, War Labor Bd., Nat. Wage Stblzn. Bd., Washington, 1941-53. Pres., Temple Sinai, Washington, 1965-67. Chmn. hospitality cart vol. service Sibley Meml. Hosp., Washington, 1961-64. Mem. Israel com. Union Am. Hebrew Congregations, 1967-72, chmn. Israel Com. Mid-Atlantic region, 1971—; mem. Joint Commn. on Israel (rep. Union Am. Hebrew Congregations and Central Conf. Am. Rabbis), 1972—; gen. coordinator Area Reform Congregations Yom Ha-Atzmauf Observance, 1971-74. Recipient Woman of Valor award Israel Bonds, 1971. Jewish religion. Home: 5511 Uppingham St Chevy Chase MD 20015

AMMONS, ROSE MARY, psychologist, ednl. adminstr.; b. Brunswick, Ga., May 30, 1933; d. K. Eugene and Frances Annette (Brady) Ammons; B.S. in Edn., Ga. Tchrs. Coll., 1954; M.A., George Peabody Coll., 1957; Ed.D., U. Fla., 1972. Tchr. sci. Statesboro (Ga.) High Sch., 1954-55, Glynn Acad., Brunswick, 1955-56; sci. tchr., asst. dean of girls H.B. Plant High Sch., Tampa, Fla., 1956-58, guidance dir., 1958-61; dir. testing services St. Petersburg (Fla.) Jr. Coll., 1961—. Cons. ednl. measurement, research. Bd. dirs. Adult Mental Health Clinic of Pinellas County, Fla., pres., 1972, sec., 1974. Mem. Am., Fla. psychol. assns., Am., Fla. ednl. research assns., Mental Health Assn. Pinellas County (pres. 1967), Pinellas Assn. for Specific Learning Disabilities (dir., v.p. 1972-74), Delta Kappa Gamma. Home: PO Box 3166 Seminole FL 33542 Office: PO Box 13489 St Petersburg FL 33733

AMODIO, BARBARA ANN, educator, philosopher; b. Middletown, N.Y., Feb. 14, 1948; d. Arthur West and Dorothy Elizabeth (Curran) Amodio; degré superieur U. d'Aix Marseille, Aix-en-Provence, France, 1968; B.A. in Philosophy and French Lit., Fordham U., 1970, M.A. in Philosophy, 1972, Ph.D., 1974; French drill instr. dept. Romance langs. Fordham U., 1968-70, tchr. philosophy, 1971-73, mem. gov. bd. dept., 1970-73. Guest of French Govt., 1972. Mem. Am. Assn. U. Profs., Middle East Studies Assn., N.Y. State Archeol. Assn., Am. Philos. Assn., Phi Alpha Mu Gamma (French medal 1970). Home: 122 Cantrell Av Middletown NY 10940

AMORANTO, ERLINDA VICTORINO, dietitian; b. Manila, Philippines, July 19, 1942; d. Carlos Solatre and Leonila Landicho (Jugo) Victorino; B.S. in Foods and Nutrition, U. Santo Tomas, 1962; Certificate in Health Care Mgmt., B.C. Inst. Tech., 1973; m. Jorge U. Amoranto, May 8, 1965; 1 son, Carlos Jose. Therapeutic dietitian Edgewater Hosp., Chgo., 1963, Ravenswood Hosp., Chgo., 1963; supr. food services Sulo Restaurant, Inc., Phila., 1964; dietitian, dept. head G.F. Strong Rehab. Center, Vancouver, B.C., Can., 1966—; instr. adult edn. programs Vancouver Sch. Bd., 1967-71. Mem. Canadian, B.C. (com. 1973—) dietetic assns., Vancouver Soc. for Asian Arts, Minerva Assn., Filipino Assn. B.C. Roman Catholic. Home: 5949 Oak St Vancouver BC Canada Office: 4255 Laurel St Vancouver BC Canada

AMORE, THERESA RITA MANZI (MRS. MICHAEL J. AMORE), hearing cons.; b. Lawrence, Mass.; d. Edward and Mona (Santinello) Manzi; student Boston U., 1945-47; certificate Emerson Coll., 1960; m. Michael J. Amore, Aug. 26, 1951 (dec. Oct. 1966); children—Francine Michele. Mgr., Sonotone of Lawrence (Mass.), 1954—, owner, 1970—; mgr. Sonotone of Haverhill (Mass.), 1962—, owner, 1970—. Gen. chmn. Heart Fund, Andover, Mass., 1970; neighborhood chmn. Epilepsy Found. Am., 1969. Area chmn. Woman's Democratic Club Merrimack Valley, Andover, 1965-66. Bd. dirs., mem. exec. com. Heart Assn., 1972—, mem. adv. com., 1970-72. Recipient awards for outstanding performance Sonotone Corp., Elmsford, N.Y., 1957-69; award for services to children at sch. St. Augustine Sch., Andover, 1958. Mem. Mass. Hearing Aid Soc. (sec. 1964—), Sales and Marketing Execs. Merrimack Valley (sec. 1965—), Nat. Hearing Aid Soc., C. of C. Clubs: Emblem (sec. Lawrence 1960, 69), Jefferson-Jackson Political (Lawrence). Home: 53 Wildrose Dr Andover MA 01810 Office: 301 Essex St Lawrence MA 01840 also 3 Washington Sq Haverhill MA 01830

AMOS, IRIS ELIZABETH, psychologist; b. Seat Pleasant, Md., Dec. 31, 1929; d. Aubrey Earl and Fannie Iris (Thompson) Amos; B.A., Western Md. Coll., 1949; M.A., George Washington U., 1955; Ph.D., La. State U., 1959. With Child Guidance Clinic, Child Study Center, Fort Worth, 1959-72, chief psychologist, 1968-72, acting dir., 1969-71; pvt. practice child psychology, Ft. Worth, 1971—. Cons. Child Study Center, 1971—; adj. prof. N. Tex. State U., Denton, 1971—. Mem. Am., Tex., Tarrant County (mem. com. 1970—) psychol. assns., Soc. Pediatric Psychology. Office: 927 8th Av Fort Worth TX 76104

AMOS, MABEL SANDERS, state ofcl.; b. Brooklyn, Ala.; d. James and Hattie Bethea Sanders; ed. Ala. Coll. at Montavallo, State Tchrs. Coll. at Troy, Peabody Coll. Formerly tchr. pub. schs.; stenographer Ala. Tax Commn., 1931; rec. sec. to gov. of Ala., 1939-66; sec. of state State of Ala., 1967—. Mem. Zonta. Democrat. Baptist. Club: Business and Professional Women's (exec. sec., com. on status of women). Address: State Capitol Bldg Birmingham AL 35202*

AMOSS, BERTHE MARKS (MRS. WALTER JAMES AMOSS, JR.), author; b. New Orleans, Sept. 26, 1925; d. Sumter Davis and Berthe Martin (Lathrop) Marks; B.A., Newcomb Coll., 1946; m. Walter James Amoss, Jr., Dec. 21, 1946; children—James, Robert, William, Mark, Thomas, John. Writer, illustrator children's books, New Orleans. Mem. New Orleans Jr. League, Kappa Kappa Gamma. Author books including: It's Not Your Birthday, 1966; Tom in the Middle, 1968; By the Sea, 1969; The Marvelous Catch of Old Hannibal, 1970; Old Hasdrubal and the Pirates, 1971; The Very Worst Thing, 1972; The Big Cry, 1972. Address: 3723 Carondelet St New Orleans LA 70115

AMOURY, GLORIA ANNE, writer, assn. exec.; b. Bklyn.; d. E.J. and Hanna (Balish) Amoury; B.A., Notre Dame Coll.; M.S., Columbia. Writer short stories for various mags., including Saturday Evening Post, Redbook, Argosy; contbr. to anthologies; story dramatized on TV as Come Into My Parlor, 1973; exec. sec. Mystery Writers Am., N.Y.C., 1965—, also dir. Home: 57 Palmer Av Staten Island NY 10302 Office: 105 E 19th St New York City NY 10003

AMPOLA, MARY GIAMBATTISTA (MRS. VINCENT AMPOLA), pediatrician; b. Syracuse, N.Y., Nov. 2, 1934; d. Mariangelo and Filomena (Albanese) Giambattista; B.A., Syracuse U., 1956; M.D., State U. N.Y. at Syracuse, 1960; m. Vincent George Ampola, Aug. 7, 1966; children—Leanna Marie, David Vincent. Intern George Washington U. Hosp., Washington, 1960-61; resident Children's Hosp. Washington, 1961-63, chief resident, 1963-64; genetics fellow Children's Hosp. Med. Center, Boston, 1964-66; Amino acid research fellow Mass. Gen. Hosp., 1966-67; asst. prof. pediatrics Tufts-New Eng. Med. Center, Boston, 1967—, staff pediatrician, 1967—. Mem. Phi Beta Kappa, Phi Kappa Phi. Home: 8 Willowdale Dr Lynnfield MA 01940 Office: Tufts-New England Medical Center 171 Harrison Av Boston MA 02111

AMSTER, BETTY LOU (MRS. CLARENCE H. AMSTER), editor; b. Cleve., Nov. 9, 1924; d. Louis S. and Marie Belle (Stoner) Lawson; Little Nieman fellow U. Louisville, 1949-50; student Ind. U.; m. Clarence H. Amster, June 18, 1941. Reporter, New Albany (Ind.) Tribune, 1943-44, Courier Jour. and Louisville Times, 1944-52; pub. relations dir. Roosevelt U., Chgo., 1952-55; founder, mgr. Amster & Assos., Louisville, 1963-70; editor Louisville Mag., 1971—. Bd. dirs. Ind. United Appeal, New Albany, 1957-60. Mem. Pub. Relations Soc. Am., League Women Voters. Author: New Albany on the Ohio, 1963. Home: 425 W Ormsby Louisville KY 40203 Office: 300 W Liberty Louisville KY 40202

AMSTUTZ, LEORA EDWARDS (MRS. MELVIN E. AMSTUTZ), former ch. assn. exec.; b. Marion, Ind., Sept. 12, 1909; d. Charles W. and Josephine (Bouvier) Edwards; student Sherwood Coll. Music and Dramatic Art, 1926-28; also pvt. study; m. Melvin E. Amstutz, Nov. 21, 1931 (dec. Jan. 1970); children—Carol Dawn (Mrs. Ernest J. Kozma), Joy Diane (Mrs. Robert H. Caldwell). Exec. sec. Waukegan Area Council Chs., 1952-69; has own radio program Religion in the News, sta. WKRS, 1958—, also chmn. Radio Ministry sta. WKRS; sec. bd. mgmt. Lake County Mental Health Clinic, 1959-69; profl. dramatic reader, soloist, dir. plays, actress in amateur plays, 1923—. Council mem. Girl Scouts U.S.A., 1937-45, pres., 1940-43, v.p., 1939, treas., 1943-45; bd. dirs. YWCA, 1945-52; sec. bd. dirs. North Lake County Mental Health Soc., 1953-70; bd. dirs. Lake County Welfare Council, Community Chest, U.S.O.; v.p. orgn. bd. 1st v.p. Civic Music Assn.; sec. orgn. bd. Lake County Council on Alcoholism; organizer 1st Interfaith Women's Council, 1964—; co-founder, mem. exec. bd. Waukegan Area Interfaith Conf. Religion and Race, 1963—; treas. Lake County Welfare Council, 1961-67; bd. dirs. Lake County Music Center; mem. Am. Field Service Exchange Student Orgn.; charter bd. mem. OEO Vol. Adv. Council; bd. mem. Chgo. Home Missionary Soc.; mem. edn. com. Am. Cancer Soc.; mem. adv. council Lake County Health Dept.; mem. Lake County Urban League European Tour, 1966; bd. dirs., charter mem. Christian Ch. Supplies, Inc.; bd. dirs. Victory Hosp. Aux., mem. Victory Hosp.

Assn.; mem. Community Concert Assn., Waukegan Symphony Assn., League Women Voters (radio chmn.), Family Service Agy., Nat. Assn. Council Secs. (nat. exec. bd. 1965-68), Planned Parenthood Aux. of Lake County, WCTU, Woman's Soc. of Christian Service (past pres.); home service com. A.R.C.; adv. com. Practical Nurse Program, 1955-70. Selected Community Woman of Achievement, 1956; Brotherhood award N.A.A.C.P., 1957; Brotherhood award B'nai B'rith, 1959; Ann. Lake County Mental Health award 1969, Appreciation award Happy Day Sch., 1967, Community Service award Met. Council N.A.A.C.P., 1968. Mem. Internat. Platform Assn., League Women Voters, Republican. Methodist (numerous offices and com. memberships in ch. orgns.). Clubs: Altrusa (dir.), Woman's. Home: 2200 Hyde Park Av Waukegan IL 60085

AMUNDSON, NANCY ELLEN ANDERSON (MRS. LOREN AMUNDSON), gift and antiques shop prop.; b. Monroe, Wis., Oct. 10, 1936; d. Wallace Lowell and Martha Elizabeth (Burmaster) Anderson; student Kalamazoo Coll., 1954-55; B.S., U. Minn., 1958, postgrad., 1973—; m. Elmo Erickson, May 12, 1957 (div. Dec. 1969); children—Jeffrey Alan, Darcy Lynn. Therapist out-patient rehab. Mpls. Curative Workshop, 1960, outpatient therapy supr., 1961-62, 67-69; cons. Mpls. Nursing Homes, 1965-66; therapist Met. Med. Center, Mpls., 1970; cons. retarded children Didlake Sch., Manassas, Va., 1970-71; prop. Hand Some Things, Mpls., 1974—. Vol. learning disabilities Mpls. Sch. System, 1972—; vol. Vols. Am., 1972-73; leader 4-H, 1973-74; active Boy Scouts Am. Mem. Am., Minn. occupational therapy assns., Minn. Civil Liberties Union, Children's Home Soc. Minn., Delta Zeta. Democrat. Presbyn. Home: 3420 32d Av S Minneapolis MN 55406

AMYOT-LEGAULT, ARLETTE MARIE (MRS. ROBERT LEGAULT), obstetrician, gynecologist; b. Montreal, Que., Can., Dec. 15, 1940; d. Horace and Armandine (Raymond) Amyot; B.A., Coll. Basile-Moreau, 1959; M.D., U. Montreal, 1964, certificate obstetrics-gynecology, 1969; m. Robert Legault, Apr. 23, 1962; children—Marie-Claude, Christine, Annie. Rotating intern hosps. Saint-Luc, Sainte-Justine pour Engants, Notre-Dame (all Montreal), 1963-64; med. resident Hosp. Notre Dame, 1967-69, Hosp. Saint-Luc, 1965-66, Royal Victoria Hosp., Montreal, 1966-67; practice medicine specializing in obstetrics and gynecology, Montreal, 1969—; mem. staff Santa Cabrini's Hosp., Montreal; cons. Family Planning Centre Montreal, 1968-70; clin. tchr. U. Montreal, 1969—. Mem. Assn. des medecins de langue française du Can. Home: 5605 Maurice-Duplessis Montrealnord PQ Canada Office: 5601 est Belanger Montreal Quebec Canada

AMYX, KATHERINE MCCLURE (MRS. ORA BOYD AMYX), poet; b. Yocum, Ky., Oct. 29, 1902; d. Matthew B. and Margaret Jociphine (Kilgore) McClure; student Morehead State U., 1925; m. Ova Boyd Amyx, Jan. 18, 1929; 1 son by previous marriage, Frank Ferguson. Postmistress, Grassy Creek, Ky., 1946-63; tchr., Grassy Creek, Ky., 1926-29, West Liberty, Ky., 1930. Mem. Nat. League Pen Women (state pres. 1963), D.A.R. (regent 1954), Ky. State Poetry Soc. (dir.). Mem. Order Eastern Star (worthy matron 1959, 61). Author: The Changing Hills (poetry), 1959; Eastward in Eden (poetry), 1972; Wedding of the Waters (poetry), 1973. Contbr. numerous poems. to anthologies, mags., newspapers. Home: Grassy Creek KY 41435 also Caloosa Park North Fort Myers FL 33903

ANABLE, ANNE CURRIER STEINERT (MRS. ROBERT HENRIQUES), journalist; b. Boston, Feb. 18; d. Robert Shuman and Lucy Pettingill (Currier) Steinert; grad. West Hill Jr. Coll., Boston, 1951; m. Robert Henriques, Feb. 3, 1973. Reporter women's pages N.Y. Jour. Am., N.Y.C., 1961-66, World Jour. Tribune, N.Y.C., 1966-67; fashion editor Cleve. Plain Dealer, 1967-73; fashion and beauty editor New Woman Mag., Ft. Lauderdale, Fla., 1973—. Recipient Fashion Reporting award N.Y., 1970. Mem. Fashion Group. Home: 285 Noroton Av Darien CT 06820

ANAGNOST, CATHERINE COOK, lawyer; b. Tegea, Greece, Feb. 10, 1919; d. Peter and Athena (Reppas) C.; diploma Northwestern U., 1942; C.P.A., 1943; m. Themis Anagnost, Aug. 15, 1942; children—Maria, Alexander, James. Accountant, 1942-48; admitted to Ill. bar, 1948, U.S. Supreme Ct. bar, 1960, since practiced law in Chgo.; mem. Anagnost & Anagnost. Former dir. Chgo. chpt. Girl Scouts U.S.A. Dir. Women's Adv. Council N.Y. World's Fair, 1964-65; v.p., dir. Beverly Farm Found.; chmn. 1966 Founders Day Program, Northwestern U. Mem. United Rep. Fund Ill.; mem. finance com. for re-election Pres. Nixon; Rep. candidate for judge Municipal Ct., Chgo., 1960, 62, for judge Circuit Ct. Cook County, 1964, 74; alternate del. to Rep. Nat. Conv., 1964. Recipient Merit award Northwestern U., 1964. Mem. Nat., Ill. fedns. bus. and profl. women's clubs, Nat., Ill., N.W. fedns Republican women, Am. (ho. of dels. 1965-67), Ill., Chgo., West Suburban (past pres.), Hellenic (past pres.) bar assns., Women's Bar Assn. Ill. (past dir.), Hellenic Profl. Soc. Ill., Nat. Assn. Women Lawyers (pres. 1963-64), Ill. Trial Lawyers Assn., Internat. Fedn. Women Lawyers, Am. Judicature Soc., Am. Assn. Attys.-C.P.A.'s, Internat. House Assn. (past treas. Chgo.), Northwestern U. Alumni Assn. Republican. Mem. Order Eastern Star, White Shrine. Clubs: Greek Women's University; 1200 of Ill. Home: 2345 N Oak Park Av Chicago IL 60635 Office: 11 S LaSalle St Chicago IL 60603

ANASTASI, LORENE MARY (MRS. HING CHANG JR.), ophthalmologist; b. Harlan, Ia., Sept. 26, 1936; d. Gerald Carl and Angeline Theresa (Arkfeld) Anastasi; B.S. summa cum laude, Creighton U., 1958, M.D., 1963; M.S. in Ophthalmology, Mayo Clinic and U. Minn. Grad. Sch. Medicine, 1967; m. Hing Chang, Jr., Sept. 9, 1967; children—Steven, Alan, Julie. Intern, Meml. Hosp., Long Beach, Cal., 1963-64; resident Mayo Clinic, Rochester, Minn., 1964-67; practice medicine specializing in ophthalmology, Honolulu, 1968—; mem. staff Queen's Med. Center, St. Francis, Kapiolani, Children's hosps. Diplomate Am. Bd. Ophthalmology. Mem. A.C.S., Am., Hawaii med. assns., Am. Acad. Ophthalmology and Otolaryngology, Honolulu County Med. Soc., Hawaii Eye, Ear, Nose and Throat Soc. Home: 2305 Round Top Dr Honolulu HI 96822 Office: 839 S Beretania St Honolulu HI 96813

ANDELMAN, EVELYN BERMAN (MRS. JACOB ANDELMAN), lawyer; b. Boston, Aug. 13, 1909; d. Abraham and Minnie (Goodman) Berman; LL.B. cum laude, Portia Law Sch., 1930; m. Jacob Andelman, June 9, 1935; children—Frederick, Sherman. Admitted to Mass. bar, 1931, Fed. Ct., 1932, U.S. Supreme Ct., 1934; individual practice, Boston, 1931-41; mem. firm Klainer & Kappel, Boston, 1956-68; asst. probate specialist trust dept. Nat. Shawmut Bank, Boston, 1968-71; legal counsel Sr. Citizens, Brookline, Mass., 1973—. Mem. Am. Jewish Com. Mem. Mass. Assn. Women Lawyers, League Women Voters. Jewish religion. Club: Jewish Women's College. Office: Multi-Service Senior Center 61 Park St Brookline MA 02146

ANDERS, EVELYN OLGA, office sec., author; b. Newark, Feb. 28, 1916; d. Emil and Marie (Kalberer) Anders; A.B., Rutgers U., 1963. Sec. to v.p., sales mgr. H.C. Brill Co., Newark, 1935-40; sec. to asst. dir. Tng.-Within-Industry, War Manpower Commn., Newark, 1940-45; head stenographic dept. M & M Ltd., Newark, 1945-49; sec. to v.p.-gen. counsel Colgate-Palmolive Co., N.Y.C., 1949—. Author: (with Esther Becker) The Successful Secretary's Handbook, 1971. Home: 101 Stuyvesant Av Newark NJ 07106 Office: 300 Park Av New York City NY 10022

ANDERS, SARAH FRANCES, educator; b. Monroe, La.; d. Edward Eugene and Malda M. (Elliott) Anders; A.B., La. Poly. Inst., 1945; M.R.E., So. Baptist Theol. Sem., 1948; M.A., Fla. State U., 1952, Ph.D., 1955; postdoctoral Renselaer Poly Inst., 1965, U. N.H., 1968. Ednl. dir. 1st Bapt. chs., Quincy, Fla., 1948-52, Gadsden, Ala., 1952-53; asst. dir. research lab. Fla. State U., Tallahassee, 1953-55; faculty, chmn. sociology dept. Mary Hardin Baylor Coll., Belton, Tex., 1955-62; prof. sociology, head dept. La. Coll., Pineville, 1962—, dean, 1972-73. Vis. prof. So. Methodist U., summer 1961. Mem. Tex. Gov.'s Com. on Children and Youth, 1959; treas. La. Council Family Relations. Bd. dirs. Rapides YWCA; pres. bd. dirs. Cenla Community Action, 1965-68; mem. bd. Family Service Agy., Child Guidance Center, Children's Receiving Center. Named Piper prof., State of Tex., 1959; NSF fellow, 1965, 1968. Mem. Am. Assn. U. Women (del.-at-large), Southwestern Religious Research Assn. (past pres.), Nat., Tex. (past pres.), La. (treas.) councils on family relations, Southwestern Social Sci. Assn., Am. Sociol. Assn. Author book. Contbr. numerous articles to profl. jours. Home: 111 Mary St Pineville LA 71360

ANDERSEN, ALICE EVELYN KLOPSTAD (MRS. DANIEL JOHANNES ANDERSEN), govt. ofcl.; b. nr. Elk Point, S.D., Apr. 12, 1912; d. Samuel Andreas and Anna Marie (Larson) Klopstad; A.B., George Washington U., 1941; m. Daniel Johannes Andersen, June 28, 1937; children—Dianne Marie (Mrs. Paul L. Tecklenberg). With Prudential Life Ins. Co. Am., Sioux Falls, S.D., 1930-31, Wilson Transp. Co., Sioux Falls, 1931-33, Home Owner's Loan Corp., Sioux Falls, 1933-34; sec. to U.S. Senator William J. Bulow, S.D., clk. to Senate Civil Service Com., 1934-43; exec. sec. Religious Heritage Am., Washington, 1961-64; govt. adminstrn. asst. U.S. Ho. Reps., Washington, 1966—. Co-chmn. Am. Cancer Crusade, 1958-59; pres. Wesley Heights circle Florence Crittenton Home & Hosp., 1954-58, v.p., mem. bd. mgrs., Washington, 1958-60, pres., 1960-62; mem. women's bd. George Washington U. Hosp., 1962—, vol. gift shop, 1962-63, v.p. bd. mgrs., 1963-64. Mem. George Washington U. Gen. Alumni Assn. (service award 1963, gov. bd. 1964-71), Kappa Kappa Gamma. Lutheran. Clubs: American Newspaper Women's (Washington), Friday Morning Music (Washington), Chevy Chase. Home: 4441 Lowell St NW Washington DC 20016 Office: Longworth Bldg Washington DC 20515

ANDERSEN, BARBARA BOROWICK (MRS. CHARLES ANDERSEN), equipment co. exec.; b. Perth Amboy, N.J., June 3, 1938; d. Bernard and Anna (Wisniewski) Borowick; grad. pub. high sch., 1956; m. Charles Andersen, Sept. 15, 1956. Treas. Gusmer Corp., Old Bridge, N.J., 1962-65, sec.-treas., 1965—, dir., 1962—. Home: 58 Bennington Rd Freehold NJ 07728 Office: 414 Route 18 Old Bridge NJ 08857

ANDERSEN, INGEBORG (MRS. HELGE A. ANDERSEN), physician; b. Berlin, Germany, Feb. 24, 1924; d. Fred Otto and Erna Lucy (Silberberg) Anderson; M.D., U. Berlin, 1951; m. Helge A. Andersen, Apr. 5, 1947; children—Miriam (Mrs. Bruce Petty), Flori B., Renee M. Came to U.S., 1953, naturalized, 1958. Intern, Ia. Meth. Hosp., Des Moines, 1953-55, resident, 1955; practice medicine, specializing in anesthesiology, Des Moines, 1955-72; sch. physician Des Moines Pub. Schs., 1973—. Mem. A.M.A., Am. Soc. Anesthesiologists, Ia., Polk County med. socs. Home and office: 5803 Walnut Hill Dr Des Moines IA 50312

ANDERSEN, JOANNE ELAINE BURGES (MRS. LAWRENCE P. ANDERSEN), newspaper editor; b. Milbank, S.D., June 25, 1933; d. Charles C. and Mary Lucille (Whittom) Burges; B.A., U. S.D., 1958; m. Lawrence P. Andersen, Jan. 17, 1953; children—Charles Peter, Mary Jo. Editor, Milbank Herald Advance, 1963—. Mem. Gov.'s Adv. Council on Mental Health and Retardation Facilities, 1967-73. Mem. Grant County Republican Com., 1959-74. Mem. Phi Beta Kappa, Alpha Phi. Conglist. Mem. Order Eastern Star (matron 1967, 69). Club: Makocha Study. Home: 501 S 6th St Milbank SD 57252 Office: Box 630 Milbank SD 57252

ANDERSEN, JUDITH COOPER (MRS. DANA KIMBALL ANDERSEN), physician; b. Phila., May 24, 1944; d. Ernest Arthur and Frances Grace (Murphy) Cooper; A.B., Wellesley Coll., 1965; M.D., Jefferson Med. Coll. Phila., 1969; m. Dana Kimball Andersen, Dec. 27, 1970. Intern internal medicine Duke Med. Center, Durham, N.C., 1969-70, resident internal medicine, 1970-71; fellow cardiology, research asso., biochemistry, instr. phys. diagnosis and medicine, physician's asso. program, 1971—. Recipient Erf award Jefferson Med. Coll., 1969, Strickler award Am. Cancer Soc., 1969; USPHS fellow, 1967, 68, 69; Shackford Hon. Med. scholar Wellesley Coll., 1968-69; Nat. Hemophilia Found. fellow, 1972-74. Mem. Hare Med. Soc. (sec. 1968-69), League Women Voters, Sigma Xi, Alpha Omega Alpha. Democrat. Office: Clin Center NIH Bethesda MD 20014

ANDERSEN, LOUISE STEVENSON (MRS. HENRY TESTMAN ANDERSEN), assn. exec.; b. Glastonbury, Conn., Apr. 1, 1919; d. Lewis William and Mabel Jane (Bidwell) Stevenson; B.A., Conn. Coll., 1941; M.Ed., U. Md., 1968; m. Henry Testman Andersen, July 5, 1941; children—Marcia (Mrs. David Wilder Welles), Susan (Mrs. Anthony Alexander Kossiakoff). Asst. social worker State of Conn., 1941-43; tchr. Lafayette Sch., Havana, Cuba, 1951-53; dir. Karachi (Pakistan) Am. High Sch., 1955-57; tchr. social studies Richard Montgomery High Sch., Rockville Md., 1961-71; exec. dir. Conn. Coll. Alumni Assn., New London, 1971—. Mem. Soroptomist Club of S.E. Conn. Home: 15 Church St Noank CT 06340 Office: Conn Coll Mohegan Av New London CT 06320

ANDERSLAND, LOUISE SOPHIE, occupational therapist; b. Detroit Lakes, Minn., Mar. 5, 1913; d. Ole Lars and Brita (Okland) Andersland; B.S., U. Minn., 1943; certificate occupational therapy, U. Ill., 1946; M.S., San Jose State U., 1965. Tchr. home econs. Sanborn (Minn.) Sch., 1943-44; commd. maj. U.S. Army Med. Specialist Corps, 1946, retired 1963; rehab. counselor Goodwill Industries, San Jose, Cal., 1966; occupational therapy in mental health Bradley Center, Columbus, Ga., 1968-70; occupational therapist mental health unit La Habra (Cal.) Community Hosp., 1971—. Mem. Am., So. Cal. occupational therapy assns., Retired Mil. Officers Assn. Home: 16040 Leffingwell Rd 76 Whittier CA 90603 Office: 1251 W Lambert Rd La Habra CA 90631

ANDERSON, AGNES M., travel service sales rep., banker; b. Beloit, Wis., May 2, 1900; d. Albert C. and Rose E. (Welter) Anderson; student Am. Inst. Banking, 1920-50, also various coll. and night sch. courses. With Beloit State Bank, 1918-28; with 1st Wis. Nat. Bank of Milw., 1928-65, secretarial asst., 1928-48, mgr. women's dept., 1949-65, asst. cashier, 1951-65; sales rep. Voyager Travel Service, Inc., Milw., 1966-71; travel counsellor Bay Travel Mart, Inc., Milw., 1971-73; asso. v.p. customer service Univ. Nat. Bank, Milw., 1971-73. Wis. women's chmn. U.S. Savs. Bonds Program, 1953—. Sec. to bd. dirs. Bishop Haas Social Service Fund, 1958-69. Bd. dirs. Cerebral Palsy of Greater Milw.; sec. bd. dirs. Eisenhower Meml. Cerebral Palsy Work Tng. Center, Milw. Recipient Eisenhower award U.S. Savs. Bonds Com., 1956, Cerebral Palsy award, 1963. Mem. Am. Inst. Banking (nat. women's com. 1949), Nat. Assn. Bank Women (chmn. Milw. group 1956, chmn. Wis. membership com. 1958), Lalumiere League (publicity chmn. Milw. 1970-72). Roman Catholic (past pres. Altar Soc.). Clubs: Woman's of Wis., Milw. Tiffany (v.p., mem. bd. 1959-73). Co-author: Stretching the Dollar, Budget Book, 1951, rev., 1961. Home: 4001 N Prospect Av Milwaukee WI 53211 Office: Bay Travel Mart Inc 517 E Silver Spring Dr Milwaukee WI 53217

ANDERSON, ALISON MARGARET GREY, lawyer, educator; b. San Francisco, Sept. 15, 1943; d. George Cunningham and Aileen Margaret (O'Connor) Grey; B.A., Radcliffe Coll., 1965; J.D., U. Cal. at Berkeley, 1968; m. C. David Anderson, 1972. Admitted to Cal., D.C. bars; law clk. to judge U.S. Ct. Appeals, 1968-69; asso. firm Covington & Burling, Washington, 1969-72; acting prof. law U. Cal. at Los Angeles Law Sch., 1972—. Article editor Cal. Law Rev., 1967-68. Office: U Cal Law School 405 Hilgard Av Los Angeles CA 90024

ANDERSON, ANITA SUNDBY (MRS. GLENN E. ANDERSON), librarian; b. Harmony, Minn., May 10, 1918; d. August K. and Alma T. (Fradd) Sundby; B.S., Winona State Coll., 1940; postgrad. U. Minn., 1951-52; m. Glenn E. Anderson, June 23, 1953. Tchr. pub. sch., Big Fork, Minn., 1940-41, Spring Grove (Minn.) High Sch., 1941-44, Rushford (Minn.) High Sch., 1944-46, Chosen Valley Sch., Chatfield, Minn., 1946-48, Ind. Sch. Dist., Canby, Minn., 1948-52; librarian Canby (Minn.) Sch. System, 1953—. Mem. Canby Devel. Com., 1973. Bd. dirs. Canby Community Chest, 1952; trustee Canby Pub. Library Bd., 1958—. Mem. Yellow Medicine County Hist. Soc. (sec. Canby chpt. 1968—), N.E.A., Minn. Ednl. Assn., Minn. Assn. Sch. Librarians, Metric Assn. Lutheran. Mem. Order Eastern Star. Clubs: Federated Women's (pres. 1955-56), Canby Women's. Home: 1101 St Olaf Canby MN 56220 Office: Canby Elementary School Canby MN 56220

ANDERSON, ANN LOUISE (MRS. LEONARD ANDERSON), ednl. adminstr.; b. Columbia City, Ind., Nov. 4, 1920; d. James A. and Lela Maud (Knisely) Miner; student Bowling Green State U., 1939-40, Toledo U., 1940-42; m. Leonard Anderson, Feb. 5, 1942; children—Judith (Mrs. Edward McCalla), Joyce (Mrs. Noah Yoder), Janet, James. Accountant, Johns Manville, Defiance, O., 1959-63; purchasing agt., office mgr. Nat. Ideal Co., Hicksville, O., 1963-67; counselor Tower Personnel, Ft. Wayne, Ind., 1967-71; placement dir. Internat. Jr. Coll., Ft. Wayne, 1971—. Mem. Nat. Accountants Assn. (asso. dir. edn. 1973—), Adminstrv. Mgmt. Assn., Data Processing Mgmt. Assn., Nat. Personnel Assn., Am. Soc. Personnel Adminstrn. Home: 104 Greenlawn Hicksville OH 43526 Office: 120 W Jefferson St Fort Wayne IN 46802

ANDERSON, ANNABELLE (LEE), librarian; b. Naylor, Mo., May 26, 1934; d. George Albert and Veda Pauline (Atwood) Lee; B.S. in Edn., S.E. Mo. State Coll., 1957; M. Ed., Stephen F. Austin State Coll., 1962; M.S. in L.S., East Tex. State U., 1965; m. Campbell Barnwell Anderson III, Oct. 2, 1955. Tchr. pub. schs., Naylor, 1955-57; acting librarian Jacksonville (Tex.) Coll., 1959-62, librarian, 1962—. Del. County Democratic Conv., 1962—, del. state conv., 1966—. Named Woman of Year Jacksonville Bus. and Profl. Women, 1973. Mem. Tex. Library Assn., Kappa Delta Pi. Baptist. Home: 525 W Pine St Jacksonville TX 75766

ANDERSON, ANNE LEE TOWERS (MRS. SAMUEL C. ANDERSON), newspaper editor; b. Churdan, Ia., Sept. 18, 1925; d. Joe A. and Doris Lorena (Rogers) Towers; grad. high sch.; m. Samuel C. Anderson, Mar. 20, 1948; children—Michael, Richard, James. Supr. teletype communications Wright Patterson AFB, Dayton, O., 1943-49; with Bowling-Moorman Publs., Inc., West Milton, O., 1965-66, 68—, asst. editor West Milton Record, 1966-68, editor, 1968—. Mem. Nellie Lowry Will Adv. Com., 1972—. Mem. West Milton Comprehensive Planning Com., 1972-73. Mem. Am. Legion Aux. Home: 44 Wagner Rd West Milton OH 45383 Office: 2 South Miami West Milton OH 45383

ANDERSON, ARLENE MAY, ednl. adminstr.; b. Harlan, Kan., Feb. 10, 1921; d. James St. Clair and Iva Leona (Cook) Anderson; certificate Hays Kan. State Tchrs. Coll., 1940; B.S., Eastern Ore. Coll., 1949; Ed.M., U. Ore., 1959. Tchr. country schs., Kan., 1939-43; tchr. pub. schs., Ore., 1943-53; tchr. educable mentally retarded, Ore., 1953-62; supr. Exceptional Child Services, Portland, Ore., 1962—. Bd. dirs. Epilepsy League of Ore. Mem. Nat. Assn. Women Adminstrs. in Edn., Council for Exceptional Children (state pres. 1964-66), Ore. Assn. Children with Learning Disabilities (library com. 1973—), Multnomah Assn. for Retarded Children (sec. 1953-73), Delta Kappa Gamma. Home: 603 SE 153rd Av Portland OR 97233 Office: 2900 SE 122d Av Portland OR 97236

ANDERSON, BERYL LAPHAM, librarian; b. Canso, N.S., Can., Apr. 15, 1925; d. George Henry Percy and Hazel Annie (Fader) Anderson; B.A., Dalhousie U., 1946, M.A., 1949; B.L.S., McGill U., 1956. Tchr. schs., N.S. and Que., 1946-48, 49-50; lectr. classics Dalhousie U., Halifax, N.S., 1951-55; lectr./librarian McGill U. Grad. Sch. Library Sci., 1956-62, asst. prof., 1962-68, asso. prof., 1968-71; chief Library Documentation Centre, Nat. Library Can., Ottawa, Ont., 1973—. Recipient Profl. fellowship Canadian Fedn. U. Women, 1955, Howard V. Phalin-World Book grad. scholarship, 1971. Mem. Canadian (chmn. cataloging sect. 1963-64), Am. library assns., Canadian Assn. Spl. Libraries and Information Services (pres. 1970-71), Spl. Libraries Assn., Am. Soc. Information Sci., Canadian Assn. Information Sci., Archaeol. Inst. Am. Editor: (with J. Morris) Selected Bibliography on Algae, 1960; Union List of Serials in Libraries of Montreal and Vicinity, 1965; Basic Cataloguing Tools for Use in Canadian Libraries, 1968; Special Libraries in Canada: An Analysis and Commentary, 1969; Special Libraries and Information Centres in Canada, A Directory, 1970, Supplement, 1972. Home: 175 Bronson Av Ottawa ON K1R 6H2 Canada Office: 395 Wellington St Ottawa ON K1A 0N4 Canada

ANDERSON, BETTY JANE REYNOLDS (MRS. ANDREW KENT ANDERSON), state ofcl.; b. Houston, Jan. 27, 1927; d. Clarence and Ruth Catherine (Milligan) R.; student Tex. State Coll. Women, 1944-46, U. Houston, 1946-47; m. Douglas Warren Ratcliff, Dec. 20, 1946, (div. Mar. 1957); children—James Marion II, Douglas C.; m. 2d, Andrew Kent Anderson, Feb. 8, 1958; 1 dau., Sharon K. Sec. to pres., v.p., treas. Moncrief-Lenoir Mfg. Co., Houston, 1947-48; travel counselor Am. Automobile Assn., Austin, Tex., 1952-53; chief clk. Tex. Bd. Examiners in Basic Scis., Austin, 1953-55, exec. sec., 1963—; office mgr., sec. to mgr., co-owner Littlefield Bldg., Austin, 1962-63. Mem. Austin State Ofcls. Ladies Club, Tex. State Agys. Bus. Adminstrs. Assn., Austin Soc. Pub. Adminstrn., Alpha Lambda Delta. Home: 2507 Lansbury Dr Austin TX 78723 Office: Sam Houston State Office Bldg 201 E 14th St Austin TX 78701

ANDERSON, BETTY MARIE, realtor; b. Cedar Rapids, Ia., Oct. 6, 1925; d. Leonard Clifford and Marie Elizabeth (Lorenz) Anderson; B.S.C., U. Ia., 1949; student Minn. Realtors Inst., Mpls., 1967-69. Retail buyer Killian Co., Cedar Rapids, 1943-52; store mgr. Grayson-Robinson, Inc., 1954-61; salesman Don Fishel realtor, Cedar Rapids, 1961-64; sec. Century Bldgs. & Supply, Inc.; pres. Hawkeye

Realty, Inc., Cedar Rapids, 1964-72; asst. treas. John Zachar, Jr. & Co., Cedar Rapids, 1972—. Mem. Nat. Assn. Real Estate Bds., Ia. Assn. Realtors, Cedar Rapids Bd. Realtors, League Women Voters (dir. 1962-64, 66-71, pres. 1971-73). Presbyn. (elder). Home: 3104 C Av NE Cedar Rapids IA 52402 Office: 3700 1st Av NE Cedar Rapids IA 52402

ANDERSON, CAMILLA MAY (MRS. LEONARD FRIENDLY), psychiatrist; b. Sidney, Mont., June 21, 1904; d. Peter and Bertha Christina Dorothy (Josephsen) Anderson; B.A., U. Ore., 1925, M.D., 1929; m. Leonard Friendly, July 5, 1941; 1 dau., Janet Carol. Rotating intern U. Ore. Med. Sch., Hosps., Portland, 1929-30; resident psychiatry Binghamton (N.Y.) State Hosp., 1931-32, Allegheny County Hosp., Pitts., 1934-36; practice medicine specializing in psychiatry, Pitts., 1934-36, Phila., 1936-41, Washington, 1941-48, Salt Lake City, 1948-57, Seattle, 1957-58, Salem, Ore., 1958-64, Frontera, Cal., 1964-69, Sidney, Mont., 1971—; faculty Duquesne U., Pitts., 1935-38, U. Pa., Phila., 1937-42, Temple U. Med. Sch., Phila., 1939-41, U. Utah, Salt Lake City, 1948-57, Williamette U., Salem, Ore., 1962-64, Portland U., 1958-61, U. Ore. Extension, Salem, 1959-60, Chaffey Coll., Alta Loma, Cal., 1968. Cons. psychiatry Western Interstate Commn. on Higher Edn., 1954, Ore. Gov's. Commn. on Childhood and Youth, 1961-64. Bd. dir. Region V (Mont.) Adv. Council and Facilities for the Developmentally Disabled, 1971—, Meals on Wheels, 1972—. Fellow Am. Psychiat. Assn.; mem. Am. Med. Women's Assn., San Diego Psychiat. Assn., Acad. Religion and Mental Health, Delta Kappa Gamma. Author: Emotional Hygiene, 1937; Saints, Sinners and Psychiatry, 1950; Beyond Freud, 1957; Jan, My Brain Damaged Daughter, 1963; Society Pays, 1972. Home and office: 405 W Main St Sidney MT 59270

ANDERSON, CAROLINE BUCKLEY (MRS. ARTHUR J. ANDERSON), home economist; b. Prentiss, Miss., May 5, 1935; d. Hezekiah and Swrintha (Brinson) Buckley; B.S., Jackson (Miss.) State Coll., 1956; m. Arthur J. Anderson, Feb. 2, 1957; children—Arthur J., Carlisa. Tchr. home econs. Amite County (Miss.) Bd. Edn., 1956-58; elementary sch. tchr. Wilkinson County (Miss.) Bd. Edn., 1959-60; home economist Miss. Coop. Extension Service, Brookhaven, 1960—. Mem. Miss. Home Econs. Assn., Miss. Assn. Extension Home Economists, Sigma Gamma Rho, Epsilon Sigma Phi. Baptist. Home: 508 Moak St Brookhaven MS 39601 Office: PO Box 885 Brookhaven MS 39601

ANDERSON, CARRIE VIRGINIA, former librarian; b. Danville, Va., Mar. 2, 1907; d. Ellis George and Mary Shepherd (Shelton) Anderson; A.B., William and Mary Coll., 1943; B.S. in L.S., U. N.C., 1944. Asst. librarian Hagerstown (Md.) Pub. Library, 1944-45; organizer, chief art and music dept. Richmond (Va.) Pub. Library, 1945-73. Pres. Richmond Mus. Theater, 1956-60; mem. Richmond Symphony Bd., 1957—. Mem. Va. Library Assn., Chamber Music Soc. (pres. 1961—), Musician's Club Richmond (pres. 1956-62). Home: 1400 Oakhurst Lane Apt 1 Richmond VA 23225

ANDERSON, CATHERINE TILLERY, nursing home adminstr.; b. Knoxville, Tenn., Mar. 22, 1911; d. Joseph Franklin and Mary Elizabeth (Davies) Tillery; student pub. schs.; children—Joseph F., E. Riley. Dir. occupational and recreational therapy Eastern State Hosp., Knoxville, 1932-51; office worker St. Mary's Meml. Hosp., Knoxville, 1951-54; owner, adminstr. Anderson Nursing Home, Knoxville, 1954-71; adminstr. Fountain View Nursing Center, Knoxville, 1963-66. Cons. on nursing home constrn. Mem. Tenn. Council on Aging, 1958-64; mem. Gov.'s Com. on Aging, 1959-63; del. White House Conf. on Aging; mem. gen. and profl. bd. Tenn. Home Health Care. Bd. dirs. Multiple Sclerosis Found., Knox County Rheumatoid and Arthritic Found. Recipient Meritorious Service award Tenn. Nursing Home Assn., 1972. Fellow Am. Coll. Nursing Home Adminstrs. (founding pres. Tenn. chpt.); mem. Tenn. Nursing Home Assn. (pres. 1959-61, sec. 1957-59, treas. 1961-63, pres. Knoxville dist. 1956-59, 60-64, v.p. dist. 1966-67, 68, 71-72, mem. state exec. bd. 1954-68, pub. relations chmn.), Am. Nursing Home Assn. (regional dir. 1959, regional v.p. 1963), Mental Health Assn., Internat. Platform Assn. Presbyn. Club: Social Service. Home: 206 W Tennessee Av Oak Ridge TN 37830

ANDERSON, CHARLOTTE LOUISE (MRS. DALE G. ANDERSON), mfg. co. exec.; b. Kellerton, Ia., Jan. 20, 1921; d. Arthur Leroy and Atha Ina (Kuder) Lawhorn; student Augustana Coll., 1937-38, 50-52, U. Rochester, 1943-44, Marycrest Coll., 1956-58; m. Dale G. Anderson, Aug. 29, 1947; 1 dau., Christine D. Petty. Exec. sec. Deere & Co., Moline, Ill., 1944-58, mgr. library services, 1958-73, corporate historian, 1973—, mgmt. devel. lectr., 1971-73. Lectr., Am. Mgmt. Assn., 1966, 70. Mem. steering com. Nat. Com. Concerned with Lit. of Hwy. Safety, 1971-72; mem. planning com. Quad-City Library Council, 1970-71; adv. council U. Ill. Grad. Sch. Library Sci., Ill. State Library, 1967-70; participant Fed. Information Resources Council, 1971. Pres., Augustana Coll. Parents Assn., 1972. Mem. Spl. Libraries Assn. (chmn. bus. and finance div. 1970-71), Soc. Am. Archivists, Am. Soc. State and Local History, Rock Island County Hist. Soc. Republican. Presbyn. (life elder). Home: 1402 1st St Moline IL 61265 Office: Deere & Co John Deere Rd Moline IL 61265

ANDERSON, DELIA MAY CASH (MRS. MACK HARVIE ANDERSON), ret. librarian; b. Collins, Ark.; d. Hogan Allen and Carrie (Oliver) Cash; A.B., Ark. A. and M. Coll., 1938; M.S., U. Ark., 1952; M.S. in L.S., La. State U., 1955; m. Mack Harvie Anderson, June 20, 1925; children—Mack Hogan, Alice Carolyn (Mrs. Earl Craig Beard). Tchr., Descha County Ark. Schs., 1923-54; librarian Delhi (La.) High Sch., from 1954; then librarian Dermott (Ark.) Pub. Schs.; vis. librarian Ark. State Coll. (now Ark State U.), summer 1964; vis. instr. N.E. La. State U., summers 1965-68. Mem. N.E.A., Ark. Edn. Assn., Ark. Classroom Tchrs., Ark. Library Assn., Ark. Sch. Librarians Assn., Bus. and Profl. Women's Club (pres. 1948-49), Am. Assn. U. Women, Kappa Delta Pi, Delta Kappa Gamma. Baptist. Mem. Order Eastern Star. Home: Route 1 Box 61 McGehee AK 71654

ANDERSON, DORIS ELAINE, lawyer; b. Elkhart, Ind., Nov. 6, 1934; d. Frederick John and Hazel Elizabeth (Bergman) Anderson; Mus. B., U. Mich., 1956; postgrad. Northwestern U., summer 1958; J.D., U. Cal. at Berkeley, 1964. Tchr. music Niles (Mich.) Jr. High Sch., 1956-59; admitted to Cal. bar, 1968; atty., asst. to corp. sec. Fibreboard Corp., San Francisco, 1965—. Mem. Am. Bar Assn., State Bar Cal. Club: Queen's Bench (San Francisco). Home: 1079 Cragmont Av Berkeley CA 94708 Office: 55 Francisco St San Francisco CA 94133

ANDERSON, DORIS HILDA MCCUBBIN (MRS. DAVID ALLISON ANDERSON), editor; b. Calgary, Alta., Can., Nov. 10, 1925; d. Thomas and Rebecca (Laycock) McCubbin; B.A., U. Alta., 1945, LL.D., 1973; m. David Allison Anderson, May 24, 1957; children—Peter David, Stephen Robert, Mitchell Richard. Copywriter, T. Eaton Co. Ltd., 1948-51; asst. editor Maclean-Hunter Pub. Co., Ltd., Toronto, Ont., Can., 1951-52, asso. editor, 1952-55, mng. editor, 1955-57, editor, 1958—; dir. Maclean-Hunter Pub. Co., Macmillan Pub. Co. Can., Canadian Film Devel. Corp. Mem. nat. planning com. Nat. Centennial Confedn., 1965-67; mem. Tri-Lateral Planning Commn. N.Am., 1973. Bd. dirs. Met. Children's Aid Toronto, 1966-69, York U., 1971—, Inst. Policy Planning, 1973—. Recipient Centennial medal Govt. of Can., 1967. Home: 95 South Dr Toronto ON Canada Office: 481 University Av Toronto ON Canada

ANDERSON, DORIS JONES (MRS. C. MACK ANDERSON), banker; b. Sanford, Fla., Nov. 7, 1935; d. William Leon and Emma Lenora (Lee) Jones; grad. Fla. Bankers Assn. Trust Sch.-U. Fla., 1969; postgrad. Nat. Grad. Trust Sch.-Northwestern U., 1971-73; m. Carlos Mack Anderson, Mar. 3, 1969. Sec., Sanford Atlantic Nat. Bank (Fla.), 1954-55, Citizens & So. Nat. Bank, Savannah, Ga., 1956-58; sec. Atlantic Nat. Bank Jacksonville (Fla.), 1958-67, adminstrv. asst., 1968-69, asst. trust officer, 1970, trust officer, 1971—, v.p., 1974—. Mem. Nat. Assn. Bank Women, Am. Inst. Banking, Jacksonville Area C. of C., Altrusa Club. Republican. Baptist. Home: 4455 Confederate Point Rd 24-G Jacksonville FL 32210 Office: Atlantic Nat Bank Jacksonville West Bay Sta Jacksonville FL 32203

ANDERSON, DOROTHEDA PATRICIA AVERY (MRS. GEORGE FRANCIS ANDERSON), journalist; b. Edgar, Neb.; d. George Hoffman and Grace (Saxton) Avery; student U. So. Cal., 1924-25; grad. Va. Jr. Coll., 1926; Mus.B., U. Wash., 1928; M.A., Azusa-Pacific Coll., 1974; Ph.D. (hon.), 1973; m. George Francis Anderson, Jan. 17, 1931; children—Dorotheda Revay, George Avery. Supr. music and art Enumclaw (Wash.) Sch. System, 1928-31; free lance writer, 1930—; columnist Desert Sun, Palm Springs, Cal., 1958-62; womans editor Daily News, Indio, Cal., 1962-69; home agy. specialist Coachella Valley Title VI Project, 1969-70; women's editor Desert Sun, Palm Springs, Cal., 1970-73; instr. writing for publ. Coll. of Desert, Palm Desert, Cal., 1971—, community coordinator Center Performing Arts, 1973—. Appeared in Gilbert and Sullivan prodns. on univ. series, 1937-41; pvt. tchr., Los Angeles, 1940-45. Service worker transp. and communications A.R.C., San Francisco, 1940-57; womans aux. and vol. Youth Guidance Center, San Francisco, 1944-57; mem. Palm Springs Opera Co., Coachella Valley Colleagues; mem. woman's com. Desert Mus.; vol. coordinator Helping Handers. Chmn. Republican Dist. Com., Berkeley, Cal., 1936-40. Bd. dirs. Mentally Retarded Children of the Desert Found., Inc. Mem. Nat. League Am. Pen Women, Palm Springs Civic Art Assn., WAIF, Nat. Charity League, Pathfinders, Eisenhower Meml. Hosp. Aux., Alpha Chi Omega, Theta Sigma Phi. Home: Sun Lane Silver Spur Ranch Box 276 Palm Desert CA 92260 Office: 611 S Palm Canyon Dr Palm Springs CA 92262

ANDERSON, DOROTHY ESTHER, nurse; b. Chgo., Aug. 21, 1918; d. George E. and Lillian (Petrie) Anderson; R.N., Johns Hopkins Hosp. Sch. Nursing, 1941; B.S., Western Mich. Coll., 1942; M.P.H., U. Mich., 1945. Staff pub. health nurse Washtenaw County Health Dept., Ann Arbor, Mich., 1943-45, San Joaquin County Health Dept., Stockton, Cal., 1945-46; supr. Women's Clinic, Stanford U. Hosp., San Francisco, 1946-48; dir. pub. health nursing La Crosse (Wis.) City Health Dept., 1948-50, Rochester-Olmsted County Pub. Health Unit, Rochester, 1950-56; dir. nursing services Chgo. chpt., A.R.C., 1956-64, Western area, San Francisco, 1964; nursing cons. Cal. Dept. Pub. Health, Los Angeles and Orange Counties, 1964-68; asst. coordinator, nurse regional med. programs U. Cal. at Irvine Med. Sch., 1968-69; asst. coordinator Area V regional med. programs U. So. Cal. Sch. Medicine, 1969-73, asso. prof., 1973—, nursing cons. outpatient dept. Los Angeles County-U. So. Cal. Med. Center, 1973—. established 1st Am. Indian Free Clinic, Compton, Cal., 1970. Mem. nat. rev. com. Regional Med. Programs Service, 1971-73. Bd. dirs., chmn. scholarship com. Chgo. Council on Community Nursing, 1956-64; mem. nursing adv. com. Los Angeles Cancer Soc., Cal. div. Am. Cancer Soc., Los Angeles Tb Assn.; vol. Southwestern dist. A.R.C. Fellow Am. Pub. Health Assn. (vice chmn. pub. health nursing sect. 1966-70, membership chmn. Western area 1970—); mem. So. Cal. Pub. Health Assn. (dir.), Am., Minn. (dir.), 1st Dist. (1st v.p., dir.), Ill. nurses assns., Nat. League Nursing, 99's Women Flyers (Minn. and Ill. sec. 1951-54), Johns Hopkins Alumni Assn. (dir. Ill. 1956-64, sec. So. Cal. 1966-71), Women's Symphony-Hollywood Bowl Assn., Pi Lambda Theta. Club: Zonta. Home: Apt 27 410 E Live Oak St San Gabriel CA 91776 Office: 1200 N State St Los Angeles CA 90033

ANDERSON, DOROTHY MAE, univ. dean; b. Phila., Dec. 30, 1939; d. Raymond Francis and Georgene Vivian (Roesch) Anderson; B.A., Susquehanna U., 1962; M.A., Syracuse U., 1964. Dir. Shaw Hall, Syracuse U., 1964-66, program coordinator Shaw and Haven halls, 1966-67; asst. dean of women Susquehanna U., Selinsgrove, Pa., 1967-70, dean freshmen, asst. dean women, 1970-73, dean freshmen, asst. dean students, 1973—. Bd. dirs. Snyder County Day Care Center. Mem. Nat., Pa. (pres. 1973-75) assns. women deans, adminstrs. and counselors Nat. Assn. Fgn. Student Affairs, Nat. Orientation Dirs. Conf., Am. Assn. U. Women, Pi Gamma Mu, Kappa Delta. Home: RD 3 Box 74 Selinsgrove PA 17870

ANDERSON, DORRINE ANN PETERSEN (MRS. HAROLD EDWARD ANDERSON), librarian; b. Ishpeming, Mich., Feb. 24, 1923; d. Herbert Nathaniel and Dorothy (Eman) Petersen; B.S. with distinction, No. Mich. U., 1944; postgrad. Northwestern U., summer 1945, U. Wash., summer 1967, U. Mich. Extension, 1958-65; M.S. in L.S., Western Mich. U., 1970; m. Harold Edward Anderson, Aug. 23, 1947; children—Brian Peter, Kent Harold, Bruce Herbert, Timothy Jon. Tchr. English jr. high sch., Eaton Rapids, Mich., 1944-45; tchr. English, speech Arlington Heights (Ill.) High Sch., 1945-48; tchr. English high sch., Nahma, Mich., 1948-49, 54-61, Gladstone, Mich., 1961-62; librarian Gladstone Sch. and Pub. Library, 1962-70; dir. library services Gladstone Area Pub. Schs., 1971—. Acting dir. Mid-Peninsula Library Fedn., 1965-66; chmn. Region II Media Adv. Council, 1972—. Pres., Delta County League Woman Voters, 1970-72; mem. human resources subcom. Upper Peninsula Com. for Area Progress, 1964—; mem. com. for library devel. Upper Peninsula, chmn. Delta County Library Bd., 1967—; mem. region 17, Polit. Action Team, 1968-70. County del. Delta County Democratic Com., 1968—. Named Tchr. of Year, Region 17 (Mich.), 1969. Mem. N.E.A., Mich. Edn. Assn. (pres. region 17 council 1967-68, chmn. upper Peninsula dels. to rep. assembly 1966-68), Am. Mich. library assns., Mich. Assn. Media in Edn. (state Library Week chmn. 1971-74), Mich. Assn. Sch. Library Suprs., Am. Assn. U. Women, Assn. Ednl. Communications and Tech., Kappa Delta Pi, Phi Epsilon, Beta Phi Mu, Delta Kappa Gamma. Home: 1325 Wisconsin St Gladstone MI 49837 Office: Gladstone Sch and Pub Library Gladstone MI 49837

ANDERSON, DRUCILLA ALENE (MRS. ROBERT NEIL ANDERSON), journalist; b. Newport, Minn., Oct. 4, 1942; d. Richard William and Mary Elizabeth (Goshaw) Challberg; student Winona State Coll., 1959-60; B.A., San Jose State Coll., 1963; M.S., Cal. State U. at San Jose, 1970; m. Robert Neil Anderson, Feb. 20, 1965; 1 son, Todd Robert. Reporter, photographer Los Gatos (Cal.) Times Observer, 1962-63; asst. tech. editor U.S. Navy Radiol. Def. Lab., San Francisco, 1963; reporter, teen Page editor Sacramento Bee, 1963-65; reporter Redwood City (Cal.) Tribune, 1965-69; head, pub. relations Canada Coll., Redwood City, 1969-71; ednl. research writer San Mateo (Cal.) Jr. Coll. Dist., 1971-72; instr. journalism Cal. State U. at Hayward, 1972. Mem. Women In Communications, Sigma Delta Chi. Home: 3084 Stelling Dr Palo Alto CA 94303

ANDERSON, EDITH, univ. dean; b. Elizabeth, N.J., June 3, 1927; B.S., Manhattanville Coll., 1951; M.A., N.Y. U., 1958, Ph.D., 1963. Staff nurse Halloran VA Hosp., S.I., N.Y., 1948-49; pub. health nurse Vis. Nurse Assn. of N.J., 1950-54, Community Service Soc., 1954-56; instr. practical nursing program Bd. Edn., Elizabeth, 1956-58; teaching fellow grad. program parent-child nursing Nursing div. N.Y. U., 1958-60, asst. prof., dir. grad. program, 1960-64; acting chief nursing sect. children's bur. Social and Rehab. Service, Dept. Health, Edn. and Welfare, 1967-68, cons. nursing edn. nursing sect., 1964-69; prof. nursing, dean Sch. Nursing, U. Hawaii, 1969—; cons. P.R. Dept. Health, U. P.R., 1963, V.I. Dept. Health, 1964, Inst. Tech. Interchange, East-West Center, U. Hawaii-Provincial Health Dept. Republic of China, tchr., trainer for field tng. program, Taiwan, 1969. Mem. Am. Assn. U. Profs., Am. Nurses Assn. (chmn. state edn., adminstrv., cons. and tchrs. sect. 1960-62), Hawaii League Nursing (1st v.p. 1973), Nat. League Nursing (chmn. dist. maternal child nursing sect. 1962-63), Hawaii Nurses Assn. (editor Pipeline mag. 1973—, chmn. publicity com. 1973—), Hawaii Pub. Health Assn., Am. Assn. Colls. Nursing, Sigma Theta Tau (sec., chmn. Upsilon chpt., mem. publicity com., editor newsletter 1963-64, area rep. Image 1966—), Pi Lambda Theta. Co-editor: Current Concepts in Clinical Nursing, Vols. I, II, III, IV, 1967, 69, 71, 73; Maternity Care in the United States: Gains and Gaps, 1966. Contbr. articles to profl. jours. Address: Sch Nursing 2528 The Mall U Hawaii Honolulu HI 96822

ANDERSON, ELISABETH MADGE KEHRER (MRS. PAGE MORRIS ANDERSON), physician; b. Aberdeen, S.D.; d. Robert Ewald and Oriole (Johnston) Kehrer; B.A., U. Louisville, 1946, M.D., 1949; M.P.H., U. Hawaii, 1971; m. Page Morris Anderson, Jan. 6, 1951; children—Bruce Statham, Catherine Mercer, Mary Elisabeth. Intern, resident Queen's Hosp., Honolulu, 1949-51; physician, dir. research Pacific Inst. Rehab. Medicine, 1960-69; asst. to pres. Hawaii Med. Assn., 1972—; cons. staff Queen's Hosp., St. Francis Hosp., Kuakini Hosp. Sec. bd. trustees Hawaii Loa Coll., 1962—; exec. bd. Community Scholarship program, 1966-71; vice chmn., trustee Multiple Sclerosis Found. Hawaii; exec. bd. Health and Community Service Council; mem. Planning, improvement and evaluation bd. Hawaii Regional Med. Program. Mem. exec. com. Women's Assn. Am. Bar Assn. Conv., 1966-67. Mem. A.M.A., Am. Coll. Preventive Medicine, Hawaii Med. Assn., Honolulu County Med. Soc., Sierra Club, Honolulu Acad. Arts, Outdoor Circle. Episcopalian. Clubs: Kaneohe Yacht, Punahou Tennis. Contbr. articles to profl. jours. Home: 1503 Ualakaa Pl Honolulu HI 96822

ANDERSON, ELSIE (MRS. ROBERT HILTON), author; b. N.Y.C., Jan. 15, 1918; d. Albert Marshall and Elsie (Hunt) Brink; grad. high sch., 1935; m. Robert Hilton, Feb. 7, 1948. Free lance writer, 1965—. Recipient certificates of merit, Ariz. State U., 1970, Studio DaVinci, Italy, 1972, 73. Author: Rambling Thoughts, 1970; Vagabond Thoughts, 1971; Vagrant Thoughts, 1973. Contbr. numerous poems to newspapers, mags., anthologies. Address: 1803 Maryland St Los Angeles CA 90057

ANDERSON, ERNA G(OETTSCH) (MRS. DONALD GRIGG ANDERSON), physician; b. Cin., Dec. 13, 1913; d. Henry Max and Caroline (Dietz) Goettsch; B.A., U. Cin., 1935; M.D., Columbia, 1939; m. Donald Grigg Anderson, June 25, 1938; children—Patricia (Mrs. Wesley J. Metzger), Roberta (Mrs. Garrett D. Pagon), James Henry. Intern Strong Meml. Hosp., Rochester, N.Y., 1939-40; resident New Eng. Hosp. for Women and Children, Boston, 1940, Babies Hosp., N.Y.C., 1941-42, Mass. Gen. Hosp., Boston, 1942-43; practice medicine specializing in pediatrics, Boston, 1943-46; dir. health Simmons Coll., Boston, 1946-47; staff physician Eastman Kodak Co., Rochester, N.Y., 1956—; clin. instr. dept. preventive health U. Rochester Sch. Medicine, 1966—. Mem. bd. Rochester Community Players, 1970-73, v.p., 1971-73. Mem. Indsl. Med. Assn., Mortar Board, Genesee Ornithol. Soc. (librarian 1970—), Phi Beta Kappa, Alpha Omega Alpha. Club: University of Rochester Women's (pres. 1967-69). Home: 151 Panorama Trail Rochester NY 14625 Office: 1669 Lake Av Rochester NY 14650

ANDERSON, ETHEL COWLEY (MRS. MOYLE W. ANDERSON), educator; b. Malad City, Ida., Jan. 10, 1921; d. Alexander H. and Cathryn R. (Hill) Cowley; B.S., Utah State U., 1960; M.Ed. (Nat. Def. Edn. Act fellow), U. Wyo., 1965, Ed.D., 1966; m. Moyle W. Anderson, Jan. 1, 1940; children—John, Barry, Karen, Scott, Jeffrey, Gregory. Tchr., Inkom, Ida., 1947-49, Evanston, Wyo., 1949-52, Superior, Wyo., 1957-61; prin., Superior, 1961; tchr., Powell, Wyo., 1962; counseling psychologist, asso. prof. Ariz. State U., Tempe, 1966—; pvt. practice counseling psychologist. Asst. prof. U. Wyo., summer 1966; guest prof. Fla. State U., summer 1967, 69, 70, U. Wyo., summer 1968, Cornell U., summers 1971-73; project coordinator drug abuse program Tempe Elementary Sch. Dist. 3, 1973. Mem. Am., Ariz. psychol. assns., Am., Wyo. (author handbook 1966), Ariz. personnel and guidance assns., Assn. Counselors, Edn. and Supervision, Am. Sch. Counselor Assn., Central Ariz. Guidance Assn., Psi Chi. Author: From Here to There, elementary curriculum, 1974, also articles. Home: 1024 E Palmcroft Tempe AZ 85282

ANDERSON, SISTER EVANGELINE, coll. pres.; b. Blunt, S.D., June 17, 1924; d. William John and Catherine Elizabeth (Sullivan) Anderson; B.A., Mt. Saint Scholastica Coll., 1949; M.A., Catholic U., 1951, Ph.D., 1953. Tchr., St. Mary's Elementary Sch., Aberdeen, S.D., 1944-47, Mt. Marty High Sch., Yankton, S.D., 1949-50; prof. philosophy Mt. Marty Coll., 1953—, dean students, 1954-57, pres. 1957-74). Bd. dirs., sec. Sacred Heart Hosp., Yankton, 1970-75. Mem. S.D. Assn. Pvt. Colls. (dir.), S.D. Found. Pvt. Colls. (pres. 1970-73), Am. Benedictine Acad., N.E.A., Nat. Catholic Edn. Assn., Yankton C. of C. (dir. 1970-73). Home: 1101 W 5th St Yankton SD 57078

ANDERSON, EVELYN MAE (MRS. ANDREW LEWIS CARNEY), physician; b. Chgo., Jan. 14, 1932; d. Gunnar Louis and Esther Amelia (Liljequist) Anderson; B.S., Roosevelt U., 1956; M.D., U. Ill., 1960; m. Andrew Lewis Carney, June 23, 1963; 1 son, Alexander Peter. Intern Cook County Hosp., Chgo., 1960-61; resident in pediatrics Research and Edn. Hosps., 1961-63; practice medicine specializing in electroencephalography, Chgo., 1963—; practice medicine, specializing in electroencephalography, also pediatric neurology and epiletology, Oak Park, Ill., 1968—; cons. staffs Luth. Gen. Hosp., Forest Hosp., both DesPlaines, Ill., Rockford (Ill.) Meml. Hosp., Swedish Hosp., Rockford, St. Mary's Hosp., Green Bay, Wis., Meml. Hosp., Springfield, Ill., St. Joseph's Hosp., Chgo., St. Mary's Hosp., Chgo., Hinsdale (Ill.) Hosp., St. Luke's Hosp., Davenport, Ia., St. Catherine's Hosp., East Chicago, Ind., others; asst. prof. neurology and neurosurgery U. Ill. Med. Sch., 1966—. Mem. Am. Med. Electroencephalographers Assn., Am. Epilepsy Soc., Am. Med. Women's Assn. (br. pres. 1968). Home: 222 Forest St Oak Park IL 60302 Office: 720 N Michigan Av Chicago IL 60611

ANDERSON, FLORENCE ROSAMOND, aerospace co. exec.; b. San Francisco; d. Gustave Emil and Nellie Elizabeth (Bengtson) Anderson; A.B., U. Cal. at Los Angeles, 1933, M.A., 1938; postgrad. 1957-58, U. So. Cal., 1949-57. Instr. aircraft navigation for U.S. Navy, Cal. Poly. Coll., San Luis Obispo, 1943-46; lectr. math. U. So. Cal.,

Los Angeles, 1946-50; group leader numerical analysis Northrop Aircraft, Hawthorne, Cal., 1950-52; instr. El Camino (Cal.) Coll., 1952-53; mem. tech. staff dir. computer programming edn., cons. in numerical analysis Rockwell Internat., Los Angeles, 1953—. Mem. Am. Math. Soc., Math. Assn. Am., Assn. for Computing Machinery (spl. interest group in numerical analysis, treas. 1964-68, sec. 1970—), Am. Assn. U. Women (br. sec. 1964-65, br. treas. 1965-66), Pi Mu Epsilon. Presbyn. Home: 5225 Onaknoll Av Los Angeles CA 90043 Office: Rockwell Internat International Airport Los Angeles CA 90009

ANDERSON, FRANCES JEAN MILLER (MRS. WILLARD EUGENE ANDERSON), physicist; b. Watertown, S.D., Apr. 23, 1937; d. Francis John and Ethel (Anderson) Miller; B.S. with highest honor, S.D. State U., 1959; M.S., U. Minn., 1964, Ph.D., 1968; m. Willard Eugene Anderson, Aug. 25, 1959. Student instr. math. S.D. State U., Brookings, 1957-58; teaching asst. U. Minn., Mpls., 1959-61, research asst., 1962-68, research asso., 1968—; instr. Northwestern Hosp. Sch. Anesthesia, 1974—. Cons., Lighting and Transients Research Inst., St. Paul, 1967—. Asst. leader Girl Scout U.S.A., Mpls., 1960-61. Mem. Am. Geophys. Union, Am. Phys. Soc., Am. Assn. Physics Tchrs., Aircraft Owners and Pilots Assn., Am. Meteorol. Soc., Sigma Xi, Sigma Pi Sigma, Phi Kappa Phi. Club: Lauderdale Civic (Minn.). Author: (with G.D. Freier) A Demonstration Handbook for Physics, 1972. Contbr. articles to profl. jours. Home: 2418 Ione St Lauderdale St Paul MN 55113 Office: Sch Physics U Minn Minneapolis MN 55455

ANDERSON, FRANCES SWEM (MRS. CLARENCE A.F. ANDERSON), nuclear med. technologist; b. Grand Rapids, Mich., Nov. 27, 1913; d. Frank Oscar and Carrie (Strang) Swem; student Muskegon Sch. Bus., 1959-60; certificate Muskegon Community Coll., 1964; m. Clarence A.F. Anderson, Apr. 9, 1934; children—Robert Curtis, Clarelyn Christine (Mrs. Roger L. Schmelling), Stanley Herbert. X-ray file clk., film librarian Hackley Hosp., Muskegon, Mich., 1957-59; student refresher course in nuclear med. tech. Chgo. Soc. Nuclear Med. Techs., 1966; radioisotope technologist and sec. Hackley Hosp., 1959-65; nuclear med. technologist Butler Meml. Hosp., Muskegon Heights, Mich., 1966-70, Mercy Hosp., Muskegon, 1970—. Mem. Muskegon Civic A Capella choir, 1932-39; mem. Mother-Tch. Singers, P.T.A., Muskegon, 1941-48, treas. 1944-48; with Muskegon Civic Opera Assn., 1950-51. Mem. Am. Soc. Radiologic Techs., Soc. Nuclear Medicine (charter mem. technologists sect.), Am. Registry Radiologic Technologists, Internat. Platform Assn. Mem. Evang. Covenant Ch. (mem. choir 1953—, choir sec. 1963-69, Sunday sch. tchr. 1954—). Home: 5757 E Sternberg Rd Fruitport MI 49415 Office: 1500 E Sherman Blvd Muskegon MI 49443

ANDERSON, GLORIA FAY (BROWN), editor; b. Lubbock, Tex., Dec. 26, 1944; d. Harvey Patrick and Linnie Linue (Papasan) Brown; B.J., U. Tex., 1967; M.A., U. Wis., 1969; m. Jerry Lee Anderson, Jan. 28, 1967. Legislative reporter A.P., Madison, Wis. and Pierre, S.D., 1968-69; mag. writer Cin. Enquirer, 1970, mag. editor, 1971—; lectr. U. Cin. Nat. Fedn. Women Press scholar, 1967. Mem. Women in Communications, Kappa Tau Alpha, Sigma Delta Chi. Home: PO Box 2055 Cincinnati OH 45201 Office: 617 Vine St Cincinnati OH 45201

ANDERSON, GLORIA LONG, educator; b. Altheimer, Ark., Nov. 5, 1938; d. Charley and Elsie Lee (Foggie) Long; B.S., Ark. A. and M. Coll., 1958; M.S., Atlanta U., 1961; Ph.D., U. Chgo., 1968; m. Leonard Sinclair Anderson, June 4, 1960; 1 son, Gerald L. Instr. chemistry S.C. State Coll., Orangeburg, 1961-62; instr. Morehouse Coll., Atlanta, 1962-64; asso. prof., chmn. dept. Morris Brown Coll., Atlanta, 1968-72, prof., chmn., 1972—. Bd. dirs. Corp. Pub. Broadcasting. Mem. Am. Chem. Soc., N.Y., Ga. acad. sci., A.A.A.S., Nat. Sci. Tchrs. Assn., Am. Assn. Univ. Profs., Alpha Kappa Mu, Beta Kappa Chi, Delta Sigma Theta. Home: 560 Lynn Valley Rd SW Atlanta GA 30311

ANDERSON, GRACE WAN, advt. agy. exec.; b. Hangchow, China, June 10, 1934 (derivative citizenship); d. Charles and Corinne (Hee) Wan; student North Tex. State U., 1950-51, Art Center Sch., Los Angeles, 1959-60; m. Arthur J. Hendrickson, Feb. 14, 1960 (div.); m. 2d, John C. Anderson, Feb. 3, 1974. Prodn. mgr. Smith-Klitten, Inc., Los Angeles, 1959-62, Baus & Ross Co., Los Angeles, 1962-63, Davis, Johnson, Mogul & Colombatto, Inc., Los Angeles, 1963-65, Erwin Wasey Inc., Los Angeles, 1965, Carson Roberts, Inc., Los Angeles, 1965-72, Sanders White & Assos., Los Angeles, 1972-73, Benton & Bowles, Inc., 1973—. Mem. Advt. Prodn. Mgrs. Club Los Angeles (sec. 1964-65, membership chmn. 1967—), Am. Maltese Assn. Club: Cal. Maltese (pub. newsletter 1967—). Home: 336 S Occidental Blvd Los Angeles CA 90057 Office: 1800 N Highland Av Hollywood CA 90028

ANDERSON, GWENDOLYN RUTH ORSINGER (MRS. JOHN G. ANDERSON) (PROFL. NAME ORSINI), artist-craftsman; b. Chgo., May 31, 1912; d. Lee and Hazel (Fader) Orsinger; student U. Cal. at Los Angeles, 1934-35; B.S., U. Ill., 1937, postgrad., 1937-38; postgrad. U. Va., 1955-56; m. John G. Anderson, June 25, 1938; children—Warren Earl, Lynne Jeanette. Tchr., Pekin (Ill.) High Sch., 1937-38; partner, dir. Artists' Mart Georgetown, Washington, 1954-73; tchr. enamel work-shop Thousand Islands Mus. Craft Sch., Clayton, N.Y., 1966-67, Am. Artists Assn., Washington, 1967—, Cross Creek Ceramics, Pitts., 1972, Lake Worth (Fla.) Art League, 1974—; enamel art tchrs. workshop for Fairfax county, 1972; enameling cons. for Fairfax County Secondary Sch. System; one man shows Artists' Mart, Washington, Va. Handcrafts, Lynchburg, Galleries Greif, Balt., U. Va., Charlottesville, Handwork Shop, Richmond, Va., Duke U., Artists Mart, Gallery Modern Art, Fredericksburg, Va.; exhibited in group shows Smithsonian Mus., Corcoran Gallery Art, Art Inst. Chgo., Balt. Mus. Art, Denver Mus., Norfolk Mus., Richmond Mus., World Craft Exhbn., Lima, Peru, Norton Gallery of Art, 31st Nat. Conf. on Religious Architecture, Rochester Festival Religious Art, 1972, Galaire Santiago, San Juan, P.R., 1972, many others represented in permanent collections Thomas C. Thompson and Co. Contemporary Am. Enamel collection, Highland Park, Ill., William Perkins Art Collection, Lynchburg, Va., Samuel Pendelton Art Collection, Charlottesville, Va., Bushart Collection World Enamels. Recipient 1st prize Fifth Creative Craft Biennial, 1962, 66, Va. State Art Exhibit, 1963, 65, 67, 69, Craft Ann., 1967; Enameling award 9th Internat. Ceramic Exhbn., 1963; Purchase prize 22d Biennial Art Nat., 1964, 1st prize in enamels Nat. League Am. Pen Women Biennial, Washington, 1964, 68, Salt Lake City, 1970. Mem. P.E.O. (chpt. v.p. 1966-67, pres. 1968-69), Nat. League Am. Pen Women (br. pres. 1958-60), McLean Art Group, Palm Beach Art League, Am., Va., Md., Fla. craftsmans councils, World Craft Council, Enamelists' Guild Washington (pres. 1973-74). Club: Kiln (Washington). Home: 6520 Ivy Hill Dr McLean VA 22101

ANDERSON, HELEN HEBER (MRS. AXEL E. ANDERSON), meat packing co. employee; m. Big Island, Ill., Apr. 4, 1921; d. George Otto and Julia (Seefeldt) Heber; student Rock Island (Ill.) Bus. Coll., 1938-39; m. Axel E. Anderson, Apr. 4, 1958; 1 son, Gary Gene. Office employee Marcus S. Brough Ins., Rock Island, 1939-44, J.I. Case Co., Rock Island, 1944-46; with Davenport Packing Co., Inc., Milan, Ill., 1952-54, 56-67, 68—, office mgr., 1956-67, 68—; sec. Rock Island Bd. Edn., 1954-56; bookkeeper Phillips Plumbing and Heating, Davenport, Ia., 1967-68. Pres., P.T.A., 1953-54. Presbyn. (Sunday sch. supt. 1963-67, elder 1968-73). Mem. Order of Vasa. Club: Ostegota. Home: 2013 34th Av Rock Island IL 61201 Office: 1st Av and 8th St Milan IL 61264

ANDERSON, JANE ETHELYN, clin. psychologist; b. Youngstown, O., Aug. 22, 1936; d. Richard Harris and Helen Rachel (Hick) Middleton; A.B., De Pauw U., 1958; M.S., Purdue U., 1961, Ph.D., 1963; m. Charles Van Horn Anderson, Aug. 20, 1966; 1 dau., Mary Elisabeth. Staff Psychologist Judge Baker Guidance Center, Boston, 1965-66; asst. prof. pediatrics U. Ia., 1966-69, asst. prof. pediatrics and psychology, 1969-70, clin. asst. prof., 1970-72, staff Research and Tng. Clinic, 1972—. Psychol. cons. Civil Service Commn., 1973. Chmn. steering com. dist. Common Cause, 1972—. Nat. Inst. Mental Health fellow, 1958-59. Diplomate Am. Bd. Profl. Psychology. Mem. Am., Ia. psychol. assns., Soc. Research Child Devel., Am. Orthopsychiat. Assn., Sigma Xi (asso.), Phi Beta Kappa, Kappa Alpha Theta, Alpha Lambda Delta. Home: 600 Manor Dr Iowa City IA 52240

ANDERSON, JANE VIRGINIA, psychiatrist; b. Boston, Oct. 1, 1931; d. Robert Emery and Virginia (McLean) Anderson; B.A., Smith Coll., 1955; M.D. cum laude, Boston U., 1960; m. Paul Libbey Russell, Oct. 7, 1961 (div. 1973). Intern, Bellevue Hosp., N.Y.C., 1960-61; resident, Mass. Mental Health Center, Boston, 1961-62, 64-66, Beth Israel Hosp., Boston, 1966-68; teaching fellow psychiatry Harvard Med. Sch., 1961-62, 64-66, research fellow psychiatry 1966-68, asst. in psychiatry, 1968-70, clin. instr. psychiatry, 1970—; practice medicine specializing in psychiatry Brookline, Mass., 1968—; mem. staff Beth Israel Hosp., Boston. Assn. for Study Abortion grantee, N.Y.C., 1970-71; Pathfinder Fund grantee, 1972. Diplomate Am. Bd. Psychiatry and Neurology. Mem. Am. Psychiat. Assn., Am. Med. Women's Assn., Phi Beta Kappa, Alpha Omega Alpha. Office: 1419 Beacon St Brookline MA 02146

ANDERSON, JANET LYNNE (MRS. CHARLES V. ANDERSON), sch. psychologist; b. Cin., Feb. 14, 1943; d. John Michael and Jeanette May (Jehhy) Tucker; B.S. summa cum laude, Ohio State U., 1965, M.A., 1967; m. Charles V. Anderson, Aug. 19, 1967; 1 dau., Dana Lynne. Sch. psychologist Muskingum County Bd. Edn., Zanesville, O., 1967-68, Darke County Bd. Edn., Greenville, O., 1968-72, Ross County Bd. Edn., Chillicothe, O., 1972—. Mem. Am. Assn. U. Women, Nat. Assn. Sch. Psychologi sts, Ohio Sch. Psychologists Assn., Council Exceptional Child ren, Psi Chi. Home: 712 South St Greenfield OH 45213 Office: Rural Route 1 Bainbridge OH 45612

ANDERSON, JAYNE WADE, ednl. adminstr.; b. Plainview, Neb., Jan. 11, 1930; d. J.C. and Clara (Garling) Wade; A.B., U. Neb., 1952, M.Ed., 1966; m. Bill Gene, June 8, 1953 (dec.); 1 dau., Laurie Wade. Instr. Spanish and English, high sch., Auburn, Neb., 1952-53; with United Air Lines, San Diego, Cal., 1953-56; instr. Jr. High Sch., Waynesville, Ill., 1956-57; faculty U. Neb. (Lincoln), 1966—, adminstr. student affairs, 1964-72, coordinator sororities, frats., coops., 1972—, chairperson chancellor's commn. status of women, 1973-74. Nat. dir. of finance Mortar Bd., Inc., 1970—. Mem. Lancaster County Child Guidance Bd., 1968-73. Mem. Neb. (pres. 1968-69, Nat. assns. women deans, adminstrs. and counselors, Nat. Panhellenic Conf. liasion com. 1972-74), P.E.O. Alpha Xi Delta. Republican. Conglist. (bd. christian religion 1966-67). Mem. Order Eastern Star. Home: 5344 Fairdale Rd Lincoln NE 68510

ANDERSON, JEAN, author; b. Raleigh, N.C., Oct. 12, 1931; d. Donald Benton and Marian March (Johnson) Anderson; B.S., Cornell U., 1951; M.S. (Pulitzer Traveling scholar), Columbia, 1957. Women's editor N.C. Agrl. Extension Service, 1951-54, Raleigh Times, 1954-56; asst. editor Ladies' Home Jour., N.Y.C., 1957-59, editorial asso., 1959-62, mng. editor, 1963; sr. editor Venture Mag., 1964-71. Recipient So. Women's Achievement award Reed & Barton, 1963, George Hedman Meml. award, 1971. Mem. Am. Home Econs. Assn., Home Economists in Bus., N.Y. Travel Writers, Gamma Phi Beta, Phi Kappa Phi, Omicron Nu. Author: The Art of American Indian Cooking, 1965; Food Is More Than Cooking, 1968; Henry the Navigator, Prince of Portugal, 1969; The Family Circle 16-Volume Illustrated Library of Cooking, 1972; The Haunting of America, 1973; The Family Circle Cookbook, 1974. Home: care McIntosh and Otis 18 E 41st New York City NY 10017

ANDERSON, JEAN RILEY (MRS. LEWIS B. ANDERSON, JR.), assn. exec.; b. Orange, N.J., Jan. 10, 1925; s. Harold Albinson and Grace (Bryant) Riley; B.A., Smith Coll., 1946; M.A., U. Rochester, 1972; m. Lewis Bruce Anderson, Jr., June 14, 1947; children—Jeffrey, Cynthia, Kitty, David, Julie. Pres., League Women Voters, Billings, Mont., 1965-67, pres. Mont. 1970-73. Mem. Sigma Xi. Unitarian. Home: 3220 Country Club Circle Billings MT 59102

ANDERSON, JEANNE ANNE, psychologist; b. Kansas City, Mo., Oct. 4, 1938; d Ernest W. and Irene (Davidson) Anderson; B.S., Butler U., 1960; M.S., Purdue U., 1964, Ph.D., 1968; m. Steven Goldstein, Aug. 18, 1963 (div.); children—Rebecca Anne, Douglas Allen. Staff psychologist LaRue Carter Hosp., Indpls., 1967-68; psychologist Dammasch Hosp., Wilsonville, Ore., 1968-69; staff psychologist Community Child Guidance Clinic, Portland, Ore., 1969-70; mem. clin. staff U. Ore. Med. Sch., 1968-70; adj. asst. prof. U. Vt., Burlington, 1970—; pvt. practice psychology, Shelburne, Vt., 1971—. Mem. Am. Psychol. Assn., A.A.A.S., Sigma Xi, Kappa Mu Epsilon. Home: 360 Colchester Pl Colchester VT 05404 Office: PO Box 372 Shelburne VT 05482

ANDERSON, SISTER JOSEPH MARIE, librarian; b. New Orleans, Sept. 30, 1929; d. Edgar Kerr and Josephine (Eason) Anderson; student Notre Dame Jr. Coll., 1946-49; B.A. in Secondary Edn., Loyola U. South, 1955; M.A. in L.S., Immaculate Heart Coll., 1961. Joined Order Sch. Sisters Notre Dame, 1946; tchr. elementary sch., New Orleans and Tulare, Cal., 1949-60; periodicals librarian Notre Dame Coll., St. Louis, 1961-66; periodicals librarian U. Dallas, Irving, Tex., 1966-67, head librarian, 1967—. Mem. Am., Tex., Southwest, Dallas County (sec.) library assns. Home: Route 2 Box 4 Irving TX 75062 Office: U Dallas Sta Irving TX 75061

ANDERSON, JOY ANN, sch. psychologist; b. Ft. Worth, Apr. 2, 1934; d. Robert Freelin and Zara Ann (Hardin) Anderson; B.S. in Edn., Baylor U., 1955; M.Ed., N. Tex. State U., 1960; M.A., Tex. Woman's U., 1971, postgrad., 1971—. Classroom tchr. Dallas Ind. Sch. Dist., 1955-62; asst. dean girls Mid-Pacific High Sch., Honolulu, 1962-65; sch. psychologist Plano (Tex.) Ind. Sch. Dist., 1965—. Mem. adv. bd. Nat. Council Jewish Women Child Protection Center, 1974—. Bd. dirs. Plano Coop. Pre-Sch. for Spanish-Speaking Children, 1971-74, Plano Child Guidance Clinic, 1972—. Mem. Am., Tex. (sec. div. psychol. assos. 1972, dir. 1973, mem. state legislation com. 1974) psychol. assns., Dallas Assn. for Mentally Retarded Children, Council for Exceptional Children, Dallas Mental Health Assn., Tex. Assn. for Children with Learning Disabilities, Tex. Tchrs. Assn., Dallas Assn. Vocational Rehab., Nat. Fedn. Bus. and Profl. Women. Home: 3301 Crestforest Circle Plano TX 75074 Office: 1517 Av H Plano TX 75074

ANDERSON, JUDITH CAROLYN HARVEY (MRS. C. L. ANDERSON), physician; b. Little Rock, Jan. 16, 1940; d. V.T. and Pearle E. (Eden) Harvey; B.A., Hendrix Coll., 1961; M.D., U. Ark., 1965; m. C.L. Anderson, July 26, 1969; children—Catherine E., Carl James. Intern, U. Tex. Med. Br., Galveston, 1965-66; resident U. Ark. Med. Center, Little Rock, 1966-68, chief resident, instr. pediatrics, 1968-69; infectious disease fellow Children's Hosp., Pitts., 1969-72. Fellow Am. Acad. Pediatrics. Contbr. to publs. in field. Home: 114 Woodshire Dr Pittsburgh PA 15215 Office: 3600 Forbes Av Pittsburgh PA 15213

ANDERSON, JUNE S., educator; b. Covington, Tenn., Feb. 11, 1926; B.S., Peabody Coll., 1947, M.A., 1948; postgrad. (Gen. Electric summer fellow) Case Western Res. U., 1954, (NSF fellow) Converse Coll., 1958; Ph.D., Fla. State U., 1964. Tchr. sci. pub. schs., Davidson County, Tenn., 1947-48; head dept. sci. Nashville City Schs., 1948-58; seed analyst Davidson County Coop., 1955-56; asso. prof. chemistry Middle Tenn. State U., Murfreesboro, 1958-69, prof., 1969—; tchr. Peabody Demonstration Sch., summers 1955-57; cons. in field. Recipient Tenn. Distinguished Tchr. award, 1957. Mem. Am. Chem. Soc. (mem. brief qualitative analysis subcom. on chem. end.). Address: Dept Chemistry Middle Tenn State U Murfreesboro TN 37130

ANDERSON, KATHARINE POPE, lawyer; b. Ventura, Cal., May 11, 1932; d. James Edward and Margaret Jean (Hammons) Pope; B.A., Humboldt State U., 1956; J.D., Loyola U., Los Angeles, 1969; m. Robert R. Anderson, July 8, 1968; children from previous marriage—James E. Millar, Hal G. Millar, Paul S. Millar. Tchr. elementary sch., Arcata, Cal., 1956-60, Ventura, Cal., 1960-65; admitted to Cal. bar, 1970; practice in Ventura, 1970-71, Santa Paula, Cal., 1971—; mgr. Pope Ranches, Santa Paula, 1968—; dir. Citrus Mut. Water Co., Santa Paula. Mem. Cal. State Bar, Ventura County Bar Assn., Santa Paula C. of C., Phi Alpha Delta. Soroptimist. Home: 20419 Telegraph Rd Santa Paula CA 93060 Office: 621 E Main St Santa Paula CA 93060

ANDERSON, LAVERE FRANCIS SHOENFELT (MRS. FRENCH ANDERSON), author, editor; b. Muskogee, Okla., Apr. 15, 1907; d. George Burket and Jessie Jonesia (Jordan) Shoenfelt; B.A., U. Tulsa, 1928; postgrad. Columbia, 1928, U. Okla., 1951; m. French Anderson, June 16, 1928; children—Jessica (Mrs. J.M. Parker), Audrey (Mrs. Thomas C. Thixton), W. French. Reporter, Tulsa Daily World, 1930-42, book editor, 1942-50, 52—; also free-lance writer. Instr. creative writing U. Tulsa, 1942-50, 52-68, Philbrook Art Center, 1953-61; lectr., panel mem. Regional Writers' Conf., Drury Coll., Springfield, Mo. Active Girl Scouts U.S., YWCA. Mem. Nat. League Am. Pen Women, Am. Assn. U. Women, D.A.R., Theta Sigma Phi, Delta Delta Delta. Presbyn. Clubs: Tulsa Press, University. Author children's books: A Story a Day to Read Aloud, 1962; Stories About America, 1963; Animal Stories, 1964; Abraham Lincoln, 1965; Robert Todd Lincoln, 1967; Sitting Bull, 1970; Quanah Parker, 1970; Abe and the River Robbers, 1971; Frederic Remington, 1971; Tad Lincoln, 1971; Allan Pinkerton, 1972; Black Hawk, 1972; Martha Washington, 1973; Johnny Appleseed, 1974; Saddles and Sabers, 1975; Contbr. stories to mags., book chpts. to anthologies, paperback reprints, syndication, fgn. edits., broadcasting, Braille, audiovisual edn. Home: 232 E 27th Pl Tulsa OK 74114 Office: Tulsa Daily World PO Box 1770 Tulsa OK 74102

ANDERSON, LEE BERGER (MRS. WILLIAM HOOKER RYLAND), lawyer; b. Holden, W.Va., Feb. 22, 1912; d. Arthur F. Berger; J.D. with highest honors, George Washington U., 1939, LL.M., 1941; m. Donald Anderson (dec.); m. 2d, William Hooker Ryland. Admitted to D.C. bar, 1939, Ida. bar, 1949, Md. bar, 1973; practiced in Caldwell, Ida., 1948-53; trial atty. U.S. Dept. Justice, Washington, 1965-71; arbitrator arbitration panel Office Consumer Affairs, Montgomery County (Md.), 1973. Chmn. legal sub-com. D.C. Commn. Status Women, 1967-69; mem. judicial conf. U.S. Ct. Appeals, D.C. Circuit. Mem. Am., D.C. Internat., Fed., Md. State, Montgomery County Bar assns., Women's Bar Assn. D.C. (pres. 1969-70), Nat. Assn. Women Lawyers (sec., chmn. com. women in pub. service 1969-72, editor jour. 1973, v.p. 1974-75, pres. elect 1975-76), D.C. Fedn. Bus. and Profl. Women (sec. state chpt., chmn. state legislation com. 1969-71), Potomac Toastmistress Club (pres.), D.C. Quota Club (dir.), Phi Delta Delta (pres. alumnae chpt. 1964, 71). Republican. Home: 3809 Montrose Driveway North Chevy Chase MD 20015

ANDERSON, LINDA COOK (MRS. JOHN GLEN ANDERSON), advt. co. ofcl.; b. Iredell County, N.C., Dec. 23, 1943; d. Esther William and Virginia Lee (Lippard) Cook; student, Mitchell Coll., 1962-63; m. John Glen Anderson, Nov. 6, 1966; 1 son, John Glen. Prodn. mgr. Aim, Inc., Statesville, N.C., 1969-70; with Miniboards, Inc., Statesville, N.C., 1970-73, tng. dir., 1972-73; tng. dir. Better Marketing Concepts, Statesville, 1973—; sec. Carolina Miniboards, Statesville, 1971-72. Mem. Statesville Little Theater, 1968-74; mem. Statesville Safety Council, 1973—; mem. Statesville Recreation Commn., 1973—; correctional sch. commn. N.C. Fedn. of Women's Club, 1969-72, dist. pres. 1971-74; sec. Iredell County (N.C.) Cancer Soc., 1974-75; adv. bd. N.C. Fedn. Sub-Jrs. Vice-chmn. Young Rep. Club, 1973-74. Mem. Statesville Jr. Service League (Woman of Year award 1971). Home: 650 Holland Dr Statesville NC 28677 Office: Old Mountain Rd Statesville NC 28677

ANDERSON, LOIS MCCLELLAN (MRS. WILLIAM H. ANDERSON), photographer; b. Memphis, July 10, 1911; d. James William and Emma (Harrell) McClellan; A.B., William Woods Coll., 1931; B.A., U. Miss., 1936; m. William H. Anderson, Feb. 13, 1938; children—Carolyn (Mrs. John Hopkins), Jane (Mrs. Ray McClain). Editor, So. Sentinel, Ripley, Miss., 1938-72; owner Custom Photography, Ripley, 1972—. Pres., Jr. League, Ripley, 1947-48. Mem. Nat. Fedn. Press Women (sec. 1954-55), Miss. Press Women (pres. 1951-52), Am. Assn. U. Women, Order Eastern Star. Democrat. Baptist. Club: Garden (Ripley). Author: Cookin via Party Line, Vol. I, 1941, Vol. II, 1950, Vol. III, 1959. Home: 207 E 3rd St Ripley MS 38663 Office: 112 N Commerce St Ripley MS 38663

ANDERSON, LOUISE ELEANOR, biochemist, educator; b. Cleve., May 18, 1934; d. Bertil Gottfrid and Lorraine Dorothy (Ossian) Anderson; A.B., Augustana Coll., 1956; Ph.D., Cornell U., 1961. Research asso. Washington U., St. Louis, 1960-62, Dartmouth Med. Sch., Hanover, N.H., 1962-64, 66-67; research fellow U. Sydney (Australia), 1964-65; research asst. prof. Grad. Sch., U. Tenn. at Oak Ridge, 1967-68; asst. prof. U. Ill. Chgo. Circle, 1968-70, asso. prof., 1970—. Kettering Found. Internat. fellow, 1964-65; NSF grantee, 1971—; U. Ill. Research Bd. grantee, 1969-73. Mem. Am. Chem Soc., Am. Soc. Plant Physiology, Am. Soc. Microbiology, Am. Assn. U. Profs., A.A.A.S., Sigma Xi, Phi Kappa Phi. Lutheran. Research in metabolic regulation in plants and photosynthetic bacteria. Home: Apt 1309 1130 S Michigan Av Chicago IL 60605

ANDERSON, LUCIA LEWIS (MRS. ALLAN G. ANDERSON), microbiologist, educator; b. Pitts., Aug. 9, 1922; d. Constanty and Maryanna (Kulwicki) Zylak; B.S., U. Pitts., 1943, M.S., 1944, Ph.D., 1946; m. Allan G. Anderson, Apr. 30, 1955; children—Geoffrey J., Kristina (by previous marriage), Patricia Lynn. Instr., asst. prof. U.

Pitts., 1949-53; asst. prof. Duquesne U., 1953-55; research asso. U. Pitts. Med. Sch., 1956-57; asso. prof. microbiology Western Ky. State Coll., Bowling Green, 1958-63, prof., 1963-65; sr. information research scientist E. R. Squibb & Co., New Brunswick, N.J., 1965-66; asso. prof. Parsons Coll., Fairfield, Ia., 1966-68; prof. biology Queensborough Community Coll. of City U. N.Y., Bayside, 1968—. NSF guest lectr. high schs., 1963-65. Mem. Ky. Acad. Sci., Am. Soc. for Microbiology (exec. com. bd. edn. and tng., chmn. com. on elementary and secondary edn.), Am. Assn. U. Women. Episcopalian. Author: Laboratory Manual for Microbiology, 1953; First Book of Microbes, 1955, rev., 1972. Author: Microbiology for Nursing Students, 1974. Mem. editorial com., contbr. spl. edition on microbiology Am. Biology Tchr., 1968. Home: 41 Bourndale Rd N Manhasset NY 11030

ANDERSON, LULEEN SANDEFUR, psychologist; b. Roberta, Ga., Dec. 13, 1933; d. Rufus Wesley and Mary Julia (Kinney) Sandefur; B.A. cum laude, Wesleyan Coll., 1958; M.A. in Psychology, Emory U., 1961; Ph.D. in Clin. Psychology, Boston U., 1965; m. Carl Alan Anderson, Aug. 16, 1963; 1 son, Eric Alan. Staff psychologist Judge Baker Guidance Center, Boston, 1964-69; cons. psychologist Boston U. Med. Center, Boston, 1965-68; sr. staff psychologist South Shore Mental Health Center, Quincy, Mass., 1969-72; dir. Quincy Child Diagnostic Team, South Shore Mental Health Center, 1972—; chief cons. Quincy Pub. Schs. Dept. Pupil Personnel, 1972—. Pres. Women's Assn., Curry Coll., 1968-70. Recipient Award for Distinguished Achievement Wesleyan Coll., 1973. Mem. League Women Voters Quincy (pres. 1971-73; dir. 1970—), Am., Mass., Eastern psychol. assns. Contbr. articles to profl. jours. Home: 39 Knollwood Rd Quincy MA 02171 Office: 77 Parkingway St Quincy MA 02169

ANDERSON, LYDIA LOUISE, ret. educator; b. Boone, Ia., Oct. 1, 1900; d. Joseph Alfred and Ellen (Carlson) Anderson; A.B., Augustana Coll., Rock Island, Ill., 1923; M.A., U. Wash. 1928; postgrad. U. Ore., Reed Coll., U. So. Cal. Tchr. English, creative writing, coll. coordinator Portland (Ore.) Pub. Schs., 1929-66, originator lit. mag. and students handbook Portland Pub. Schs.; writer Fed. Project English, U. Ore., 1963-64; vis. prof., asst. dir. Nat. Def. Edn. Act Inst. Applied Linguistics, Marylhurst Coll., summer 1966; asst. prof. English edn. Ore. Coll. Edn., Monmouth, 1966-67; asst. prof. English edn. Ore. State U., 1967-68, Ore. State System Higher Edn., div. continuing edn., 1967-70; tchr. English as 2d lang. under Soviet Govt. Purchasing Commn. in U.S., 1945; workshop tchr. U. Ore., summer 1956; tchr. Laubach literacy, English as 2d lang., 1970—. Cons., Advanced Placement Program in English, 1963-66; chmn. Com. for Writing Lang. Arts Norms for certification of English tchrs. State of Ore., 1959-60. Local chmn. informative and protective services Retirement and Nursing Homes, 1972—; chmn. N.W. Center Loaves and Fishes, Inc., Portland, 1972—; mem. Task Force Project A Better Life for Elderly. Mem. English Speaking Union, Am-Scandinavian Found., Nat. Ret. Tchrs. Assn., Ore. Council Tchrs. of English (1st sec.-treas. 1954-55, pres. 1959-60), Nat. Council Tchrs. English, Am. Assn. U. Women, Conf. on English Edn., Ore. Ret. Educators Assn. (chmn. informative and protective services), Portland Fedn. Women's Orgns., Portland Women's Forum, Ret. Profl. Assos. Portland State U. Republican. Lutheran. Contbr. writings in fields of methods in English, linguistics, rhetoric for tchrs. to books on curriculum, teaching units, mags. Home: 2336 SW Osage St Portland OR 97205

ANDERSON, MABLE BELL, educator; b. Birmingham, Ala., Sept. 7, 1930; d. I.C. and Beatrice (Craddock) Bell; B.S. (inst. scholar), Tuskegee Inst., 1950; M.A. (univ. scholar), Mich. State U., 1952; Ed.D., Pa. State U., 1965; postgrad. Grambling Coll., summer 1960, Bank St. Coll. Edn., summer 1967, Yeshiva U., summer 1967; m. Furman C. Anderson, June 9, 1958 (div. May, 1965). Instr. home econs. and health Fayette Co. Tng. Sch., Fayette, Ala., 1950-51; tchr.-trainer in home econs. edn. and child devel. Grambling Coll., 1952-54; mem. faculty child devel. and family relationships Miles Coll., Birmingham, 1954-60; presch. asst. tchr. Pa. State U., 1961-62; dir. Migrant Day Care Center, Dept. Child and Family Welfare, Harrisburg, Pa., summer 1961, social caseworker, summer 1962; prof. child devel., chmn. grad. studies in home econs. Tenn. A. and I. State U., 1963-66; prof. elementary edn. Western Ky. U., Bowling Green, 1966-69, supr. student tchrs. elementary edn., 1966; prof. early childhood edn. Center Early Childhood Personnel Devel., State Coll. Ark., Conway, 1969-70; prof. edn., coordinator early childhood edn. Albany (Ga.) State Coll., 1970—. Instr., guest lectr. Head Start Tchr. Tng. programs George Peabody Coll., Pa. State U., 1965; workshop leader TACUS tchrs., Chattanooga and Knoxville, Tenn., 1966, 67; rep. Ky. Com. on Early Childhood Edn., 1966—; adviser, cons. kindergartens, day care centers, Bowling Green; adviser undergrad. chpt. Alpha Kappa Alpha, 1967-69; cons. Warren Co.-Bowling Green Assn. Mental Retardation, 1966—; bd. dirs., tech. adv. So. Ky. Econ. Opportunity Council, 1967—; cons. S.W. Edn. Devel. Lab. Pilot Project, 1969—; chmn. Task Force on Early Childhood Edn. for Albany-Dougherty County, 1972—; mem. state com. Ga. Comprehensive Early Childhood Edn. Programs; mem. Ga. Accrediting Commn., 1972—; mem. com. So. Regional Edn. Bd.; cons. Nat. Day Care Council Am., Heritage Found. Mem. Soc. Research in Child Devel., Assn. Childhood Edn. Internat. (dir.), Nat. Assn. Edn. Young Children, Nat. Council Family Relations (dir. 1969—), N.E.A., Ky. Edn. Assn., Am. Home Econs. Assn., Am. Assn. U. Women, Am. Assn. U. Profs., Child Devel. Assn. Consortium (dir. 1972—). Address: PO Box 876 Albany GA 31702

ANDERSON, MARGARET BALL (MRS. ROBBIN C. ANDERSON), club women; b. Lansing, Mich., Nov. 16, 1921; d. Charles Dodson and Elizabeth Olds (Foster) Ball; B.A., Oberlin Coll., 1943; M.A., Mt. Holyoke Coll., 1945; m. Robbin Colyer Anderson, July 20, 1946; children—Charles Ward, Robbin Bruce, Richard Ball. Asst. to dean women U. Tex., Austin, 1945-46. Mem. Gov.'s Adv. Com. on Land Resource Mgmt., 1973—. Pres., League Women Voters of Ark., 1973—; mem. Am. Assn. U. Women. Home: 1599 Halsell Rd Fayetteville AR 72701

ANDERSON, MARGARET EVELYN (MRS. FORREST H. ANDERSON), wife gov. Mont.; b. Lewistown, Mont., Aug. 27, 1914; d. Walter G. and Margaret J. (Newell) Samson; student U. Mont., 1933, Madame Charette's Sch. Design, 1935; m. Forrest H. Anderson, Jan. 30, 1941; children—Margaret (Mrs. Gary Templin), Arlee J., Newell B. Designer Woodward Blouse and Sportswear, Los Angeles, 1936-39; buyer Fisher's Dress Shop, Helena, Mont., 1939-40. Hon. chmn. Mental Health Assn. Mont. 1970-72, Cystic Fibrosis Found., Helena, 1971—. Bd. dirs. YWCA, Helena, St. Peter's Hosp., Helena, St. John's Hosp., Helena, Green Thumb, Mont. Mem. Rainbow Girls, Daus. of the Nile, Scandinavian Lodge. Democrat. Mem. Order Eastern Star. Home: 1712 Jerome Pl Helena MT 59601

ANDERSON, MARIAN, contralto; b. Phila.; student pub. schs., Phila.; mus. edn. pvt. study in Phila., N.Y., and abroad; hon. degrees 35 Am. ednl. instns., 1 Korean; m. Orpheus H. Fisher, July 24, 1943. As child sang in Union Bapt. Ch. choir, Phila.; a fund raised through a church concert enabled her to take singing lessons under an Italian instr.; won 1st prize in competition with 300 others at New York Lewisohn Stadium, 1925; began singing career, 1924; has made many concert tours of the U.S. and Europe; one of the leading contraltos of the world, appearances in all famous concert halls, stadia; at Met. Opera, N.Y.C.; ret., 1965. U.S. del. 13th Gen. Assembly, UN. Mem. Nat. Council on the Arts, Conn. Council Arts. Recipient Bok award, 1940; Finnish decoration probenignitate humana, 1940; decorations from Sweden, Phillippines, Haiti, Liberia, France, numerous states and cities in U.S.; Yokus Lo medal (Japan). Named to Nat. Arts Hall Fame (1 of 1st), 1972. Mem. Alpha Kappa Alpha. Author: (autobiography) My Lord, What A Morning, 1956. Home: Danbury CT 06810

ANDERSON, MARIE, univ. dean; b. Pensacola, Fla., May 15, 1916; d. Robert H. and Marie (Willard) Anderson; A.B., Duke, 1937; postgrad. Katharine Gibbs, 1939. Researcher Batten, Barton, Durstine & Osborne, N.Y.C., 1946; reporter, copy reader women's dept. Miami (Fla.) News, 1946-50; sub-editor Miami Herald, 1950-55, asst. women's editor, 1955-59, women's editor, 1959-71; dean univ. relations and devel. Fla. Internat. U., 1973—. Recipient Fla. Women's Press Club award, J.C. Penney U. Mo. award. Mem. Jr. League, C. of C., Phi Beta Kappa, Soc. Profl. Journalists, Women in Communications, Delta Delta Delta, Theta Alpha Phi, Delta Kappa Gamma. Democrat. Episcopalian. Home: 2840 SW 28 Terrace Miami FL 33133 Office: Fla Internat U Tamiami Trail Miami FL 33144

ANDERSON, MARJORIE ANN VALLEY (MRS. A. REINOLD ANDERSON), journalist; b. Shelton, Wash., Aug. 6, 1928; d. William Stephen and Marjorie Anita (Swan) Valley; B.A., Wash. State U., 1950; m. A. Reinold Anderson, Nov. 24, 1950; children—Robert Louis, John William. With Ore. Jour., Portland, 1964—, asst. food and fashion editor, 1966-67, fashion and beauty editor, 1967—, food editor, 1967-73, asst. food editor, 1973—. Alumni woman at large Alumni Bd. Wash. State U., 1970—. Named Queen Mother, Wash. State U., 1970. Mem. Ore. Press Women, Nat. Fedn. Press Women, Elec. Women's Roundtable, Fashion Group, Sigma Delta Chi, Chi Omega. Republican. Lutheran. Home: 1806 Laurel Dr Newberg OR 97132 Office: 1320 SW Broadway Portland OR 97201

ANDERSON, MARY CHRISTINE MCKEE (MRS. WENDELL R. ANDERSON), wife of Minn. gov.; b. Bemidji, Minn., Nov. 10, 1939; d. John Henry and Norma Lee (Babcock) McKee; m. Wendell R. Anderson, Aug. 11, 1963; children—Amy Christine, Elizabeth Ann, Brett John. Draftsman, Nat. Park Service, 1960; asst. to architect, Copenhagen, Denmark, 1961; tchr. elementary sch., 1963-66. Address: 1006 Summit Av St Paul MN 55105

ANDERSON, MARY CROW (MRS. JAMES ROBERT DICKIE ANDERSON), educator; b. Sumter, S.C., July 21, 1922; d. Orin Faison and Innis (Cuttino) Crow; student Winthrop Coll., 1938-39; A.B. magna cum laude, U. S.C., 1942, M.Ed., 1952, Ph.D., 1966; postdoctoral study Exeter Coll., Oxford U., 1971; m. James Robert Dickie Anderson, July 5, 1942; children—James Orin, Barbara Innis, Richard Cothonneau. Tchr. high sch., Bamberg, S.C., 1942, Dentsville, S.C., 1950-51, Columbia, S.C., 1951-56, 60-71; prin. Heathwood Hall Episcopal Sch., Columbia, 1956-60; tchr. English and humanities Dreher High Sch., Columbia, 1960-71, chmn. English dept., 1967-69; asst. prof. U. S.C., 1971—. Mem. creative writing, sch. participation coms. S.C. Tricentennial Commn. Mem. Internat. Soc. Gen. Semantics, Nat., S.C. (pres. 1967-68) councils tchrs. English, Modern Lang. Assn., South Atlantic Modern Lang. Assn., D.A.R. (chpt. 1st vice regent 1960-62), Daus. Holy Cross (chmn. chpt. 1953, co-chmn. chpt. 1967-68), Huguenot Soc., Columbia Music Festival Assn., Columbia Stage Soc., Columbia Historic Found., Columbia Art Assn., English-Speaking Union (bd. dirs. Columbia br. 1971-73), Phi Beta Kappa, Delta Kappa Gamma, Alpha Psi Omega, Chi Omega. Episcopalian. Author: The Huguenot in the South Carolina Novel. Home: 727 Abelia Rd Columbia SC 29205 Office: Univ South Carolina Columbia SC 29208

ANDERSON, MARY ELIZABETH KERWIN (MRS. RICHARD MARTIN KERWIN), anesthesiologist; b. Lincoln, Neb., Nov. 30, 1923; d. Arthur and Gretchen Elizabeth (Haslam) Anderson; A.A., Stephens Coll., 1942; B.A., U. Neb., 1944, M.D., 1947; m. Richard Martin Kerwin, Apr. 6, 1957; children—Allison, Charles, Sean. Intern, Phila. Gen. Hosp., 1947-49, resident, 1949-50; resident Presbyn. Hosp., 1950-51, mem. staff, 1951-53; chief anesthesiology Chester County Hosp., West Chester, Pa., 1953-74; now staff Cheshire Meml. Hosp., Keene, N.H., Monadnokh Community Hosp., Peterborough, N.H., Brattleboro (Vt.) Meml. Hosp. Home: Box 17 Old Harrisville Rd Hancock NH 03449

ANDERSON, MARY JANE, cons.; b. Richmond, Va., May 27, 1930; d. Francis Wilbur and Margaret Genevieve (Esbrook) Anderson; B.A., Wayne U., 1953. With Fairchild Publs., Detroit and Chgo., 1954-67; food service editor Vend mag., Chgo. and N.Y.C., 1967-72; free lance cons. in food service industry, 1972—. Mem. Instl. Food Editorial Council (past v.p.), Women In Communications. Republican. Christian Scientist. Address: 175-20 Wexford Terrace Jamaica Queens NY 11431

ANDERSON, MARY JANE MCPHERSON, assn. exec.; b. Des Moines, Jan. 23, 1935; d. William Kenneth and Margaret Louise (Snider) McPherson; B.A., U. Fla., 1957; M.S. in Library Sci., Fla. State U., 1963; m. Charles Robert Anderson, Oct. 21, 1965; 1 dau., Mary Margaret. Librarian, Oak Grove Elementary Sch., Miami, 1957-61; children's and young adult librarian Santa Fe Regional Library, Gainesville, Fla., 1961-63; br. librarian Jacksonville (Fla.) Pub. Library, 1963-64, chief children's services, 1964-67; pub. library cons. Fla. State Library, Tallahassee, 1967-70; cataloger St. Mary's Coll. Md., St. Mary's City, 1970-72; coordinator children's services Baltimore County Pub. Library, Towson, Md., 1972-73; exec. sec. children's and young adult services div. Am. Library Assn., Chgo., 1973—. Mem. Am., Md. (2d v.p. 1973) library assns., Beta Phi Mu. Editor Fla. State Library Newsletter, 1967-70, Top of the News, 1971-73. Home: 1702 Colonial Lane Northfield IL 60093 Office: 50 E Huron St Chicago IL 60611

ANDERSON, MARY JILL, graphic designer; b. Madison, Wis., Dec. 28, 1943; d. Frank Reed and Kathryn Grace (Murrie) Anderson; B.S. in Art, U. Wis., 1967. Designer Hallmark Card Co., Kansas City, Mo., 1962-63; set designer Hiram Ash Inc., N.Y.C., 1967-68; jr. designer with Eisenman & Enock, N.Y.C., 1969-70; designer Stephan & Brady, Inc., Madison, 1970—. Tchr. graphic design Madison area Tech. Coll., 1972-73. Mem. Strollers Theater, Madison. Vol. Madison Community Rap Center. Recipient Bravo 68 Graphics award Graphic U.S.A./Graphics, N.Y.C., 1968; awards Milw. Soc. Communicating Arts, 1970, 73. Mem. Delta Gamma. Home: 4934 Whitcomb Sq Madison WI 53711 Office: 1850 Hoffman St Madison WI 53701

ANDERSON, MARY RUTH (MRS. BRUCE ALLEN ANDERSON), educator; b. Bellingham, Wash., Feb. 3, 1939; d. Ralph A. and Minnie J. (Troost) Van Dyk; B.A. summa cum laude, Hope Coll., 1961; M.S. (Nat. Def. Edn. Act fellow), U. Ia., 1963, Ph.D., 1966; m. Bruce Allen Anderson, Aug. 24, 1963; children—Taldon Mark Allen, Trevon Dean VanDyk. Teaching asst. U. Ia., Iowa City, 1964-66; lectr. math. statistics Ariz. State U., Tempe, 1966-72, asst. to dean Coll. Liberal Arts, 1972-74, asst. prof. indsl. engring., 1974—. Mem. Alpha Gamma Phi. Club: Tempe Tee-Birds. Home: 1235 E Pebble Beach Dr Tempe AZ 85282

ANDERSON, MARY SEXTON GRAYSON (MRS. FRANCIS SIDNEY ANDERSON JR.), sch. adminstr.; b. Saltville, Va., Apr. 17, 1921; d. John Tate and Nannie Lou (Altice) Grayson; A.B., Radford Coll., 1942; M. Ed., Ga. State U., 1970, Specialist in Edn. degree, 1972; m. Francis Sidney Anderson, Jr., July 12, 1944; children—Patsy (Mrs. Robert Christy McFarland), Ellen, Mary Sidney. Tchr. Bristol (Va.) High Sch., 1942-44; tchr. N. Av. Presbyn. Sch., Atlanta, 1944-45, Lavras, Minas, Gerais, Brazil, Presbyn. Ch., U.S., 1945-47, Porterdale (Ga.) Sch., 1950-52, 56-57, Westminster Schs., Atlanta, 1960-68, counselor, 1968—, dir. admissions Westminster Girls Sch., 1971—; mem. working com. and charter mem. bd. dirs. Secondary Sch. Research Program, Inc., Boston, 1971—. Mem. Nat. Assn. of Ind. Schs. (chmn. counseling sect. meeting with Mid-South Assn. of Ind. Schs. 1971), Columbia Scholastic Press Assn. (bd. judges 1969—, gold key 1973), Kappa Delta Pi, Tau Kappa Alpha, Alpha Psi Omega. Presbyn. Home: 1384 Altmont Dr Decatur GA 30033

ANDERSON, MAY KATHERINE ARMSTRONG, librarian; b. Greenville, Tex., Nov. 1, 1917; d. John Powers and Hattie Mabel (Goodrich) Armstrong; B.A., Tex. State Coll. Women, 1938; M.L.S., Tex. Woman's U., 1958; m. Ralph White Anderson, Dec. 25, 1942 (div. Aug. 1966); children—James Edwin, Robert Lee. High sch. English tchr., librarian, Honey Grove, Tex., 1938-39; high sch. librarian, Odessa, Tex., 1939-42; pub. librarian, Odessa, Tex., 1942, Abilene, Tex., 1943; high sch. librarian Midland (Tex.) High Sch., 1952-55; library supr. Midland Pub. Schs., 1955-61; librarian Robert E. Lee High Sch., Midland, 1961—. Mem. D.A.R., Tex. Library Assn. (pres. local library sect. 1952-54), Tex. State Tchrs. Assn., Kappa Kappa Iota. Mem. Order Eastern Star. Home: 4311 W Dengar St Midland TX 79701 Office: 3500 Neely St Midland TX 79701

ANDERSON, MERLE (MRS. H.R. ANDERSON), former assn. exec.; b. Smith Center, Kan., July 26, 1888; d. Charles Broderick and Laura (McNulty) Egan; grad. high sch.; m. H.R. Anderson, June 17, 1919; 1 son, Robert Ray. With, Colo. Telephone Co., 1906-09; tchr. schs., Sheridan, Wyo., 1909-10; with Mountain States Bell Telephone of Mont., 1910-18, acting No. div. traffic supt. 1915; chief operator Am. Peace Commn., Paris, France, 1918-19. Mem. Women's Overseas Service League (nat. legislation chmn. 1950-51). Active in attempting to obtain recognition of World War I Women's Signal Corps Operators as vets. Home: 23600 Marine View Dr Zenith WA 98188

ANDERSON, MOSELLE WILCOX (MRS. JOSEPH S. ANDERSON), extension home economist; b. Preston, Ida., Apr. 17, 1917; d. William Harvey and Mabel (Mickelson) Wilcox; student Utah State Agrl. Coll., 1934-37; B.S. in Home Econs., Ida. State U., 1966; m. Joseph S. Anderson, Mar. 17, 1941; children—Zee Ray W., Jo Zelle (Mrs. Vernon Buffaloe), Tyron W. Saleslady Fargo's Dept. Store, Pocatello, Ida., 1961-66; extension home economist U. Ida., Fort Hall Indian Reservation, Fort Hall, Ida., 1967—, asso. extension prof., 1972—. Rep. S.E. Ida. to Gov.'s Housing Coalition for Ida., 1971—, also mem. steering com. for S.E. Ida., 1971—; mem. Legis. Steering Com. Housing, 1971—; chmn. Ida. State Housing Coalition. Recipient Superior Service award U.S. Dept. Agr., 1973. Mem. Ida. (dist. chmn.), Am. home econ. assns., Ida., Nat. (mem. hospitality com. 1972) assns. extension home economists, Aux. to Brotherhood R.R. Train Men (past pres.), Epsilon Sigma Phi, Alpha Sigma Phi. Mem. Ch. Latter-Day St. Club: Union Pacific Junior Old Timers Club 10. Address: PO Box 24 Fort Hall ID 83203

ANDERSON, MYRNA OLSON, book store operator; b. Dubuque, Ia., July 15, 1935; d. Ernest Theodore and Ardis Alvina (Thompson) Olson; student U. Neb., 1953-56, Ill. Inst. Tech., 1956-57; m. Courtney William Anderson, June 9, 1956; children—Alison, Ardis, Clayton, Courtney. Owner, bookkeeper Courtney's Books & Things, Sioux Falls, S.D., 1967—, Courtney's Books & Things, Brookings, S.D., 1967—, Courtney's Index Stationers, Vermillion, S.D., 1972—; owner Courtney's Books & Things, Aberdeen, S.D., 1969—; mgr. The Book Store, Sioux Falls, 1970—; dir. Courtney's Books & Things, Inc. Pres. S.D. Women's TV Council, 1968; v.p. Lutheran Ch. Women, 1970-73. Bd. dirs. S.D. Polit. Action Com., 1968-72. Mem. Seventh Dist. Med. Aux. (pres. 1966-67), S.D. Med. Aux. (pres. 1969-70), Phi Beta Phi. Lutheran (ch. sch. supt. 1971-73). Club: LaSertoma (Sioux Falls). Illus. med. booklets, also cookbook; designer mosiac wall mural for office bldg. Home: Fair Oaks Route 2 Sioux Falls SD 57101 Office: 2127 S Minnesota Av Sioux Falls SD 57105

ANDERSON, NANCY SAGRID, educator; b. Akron, O., Aug. 15, 1930; d. Edmond Ralph and Sagrid (Pihlblad) Anderson; B.A., U. Colo., 1952; M.A., Ohio State U., 1953, Ph.D., 1956. Psychologist IBM, Yorktown Heights, N.Y., 1956-59; mem. faculty U. Md., College Park, 1959—, prof. psychology, 1966—. NSF Sr. Postdoctoral fellow, NSF, 1964. Fellow Am. Psychol. Assn., A.A.A.S.; mem. Psychonomic Soc., Psychometric Soc. Contbr. articles to sci. jours. Home: 5057 Berwyn Rd College Park MD 20740

ANDERSON, NORMAJEAN ILEAN, educator; b. Imlay City, Mich., Apr. 19, 1914; d. Thomas Rennie and Clarissa Belle (Fritch) Anderson; B.S., Mich. State Normal Coll., 1935; B. Comml. Sci., Cleary Coll., 1935; M.A., U. Mich., 1944. Tchr., head comml. dept. Ionia (Mich.) High Sch., 1935-38; tchr. Mt. Clemens (Mich.) High Sch., 1938-44; clerical trainer, tng. sect., personnel div. Oakland (Cal.) Army Base, 1944-45; tchr. Roosevelt High Sch., Wyandotte, Mich., 1945-47; tchr., dean of women Lansing (Mich.) Secretarial Sch., 1947-48; faculty bus. edn. dept. Coll. Bus., Eastern Mich. U., Ypsilanti, 1948—, asso. prof. 1964—. Recipient Outstanding Woman Faculty award Adahi Sr. Women Leaders, 1971. Mem. Pi Omega Pi (adviser 1951—; mem. nat. council), Delta Pi Epsilon (Kappa chpt.). Presbyn. (chmn. Christian ednl. com. 1968-70, elder 1968-71). Editor Here and There, 1966-68. Home: 405 N Harris Rd Ypsilanti MI 48197 Office: Bus Edn Dept Eastern Mich U Ypsilanti MI 48197

ANDERSON, OLGA, librarian; b. Hafford, Sask., Can., June 20, 1931; d. Elias and Xenia (Cherney) Shklanka; B.A., U. Sask., 1950; B. Ed., U. Atla. (Can.), 1955; M. L.S., U. Wash., 1956; m. Peter George Anderson, July 11, 1964 (div. 1970); 1 son, David George. Tchr. high sch., Alta. and Sask., 1951-55; sch. librarian Mercer Island (Wash.), 1955-60; supr. sch. libraries, Red Deer, Alta., 1964-65; head library reference dept. U. Alta., Edmonton, 1968-73; asst. univ. librarian Sir George Williams U., Montreal, Que., Can., 1973—; lectr. in field. Recipient Ruth Worden medal outstanding achievement U. Wash., 1956. Editor. Alta. Sch. Library Jour., 1963-66, Moccassin Telegraph, 1963-65. Home: 1749 Sunnybrooke Dr Dollard Des Ormeause PQ Canada Office: Sir George Williams U 1435 Drummon St Montreal PQ Canada

ANDERSON, PENELOPE PENCE (MRS. DAVID JOHN ANDERSON), journalist; b. Salt Lake City, Jan. 23, 1943; d. Joseph Thomas and Carol Gretchen (Hofmann) Pence; B.A., U. Wash., 1963; m. David John Anderson, Sept. 28, 1969. Asst. media buyer J. Walter Thompson Advt., Los Angeles, 1963-64; pub. relations dir. John Lithen Corp., Beverly Hills, Cal., 1964-65; pub. service dir.

Metromedia KTTV, Los Angeles, 1965-66; asso. producer Winchell-Mahoney Show, Metromedia KTTV, Los Angeles, 1966-67; with Sterling Publs., Tarzana, Cal., 1967—; spl. features corr. N.Y. Times, 1972—. Mem. Women In Communications. Club: Hollywood (Cal.) Women's Press. Home: 21520 Marchena St Woodland Hills CA 91364 Office: 19653 Wells Dr Tarzana CA 91356

ANDERSON, R. DONELDA CAMPBELL, psychologist; b. Anadarko, Okla., Mar. 16, 1932; d. John Melt and Ruby Viola (Harris) Campbell; A.A. (Roger's Merit scholar, Delta Kappa Gamma scholar), San Bernardino Valley Coll., 1964; B.A. (Panhellenic scholar), Cal. State U., 1966; M.A., 1967, postgrad., 1968; postgrad Pepperdine U., 1970-71, U. Cal. at Riverside, 1971; children by previous marriage—Larry Robert Pietsch, Cynthia Lynn Pietsch. Profl. intern Fairview State Hosp., Costa Mesa, Cal., 1966; asso. prof. psychology and sociology Mt. San Antonio Coll., Walnut, Cal., 1967-69; lectr. psychology Cal. State Coll. at San Bernardino, 1969; asso. prof. psychology and sociology San Bernardino Valley (Cal.) Coll., 1969-70; staff psychologist San Bernardino (Cal.) County Probation Dept., 1970-72; clin. psychologist Riverside (Cal.) Dept. Pub. Health, 1972—. Mem. Am., Cal. State psychol. assns., Cal. Probation, Parole and Correctional Officers Assn., Psi Chi. Home: 3700 Mountain Av San Bernardino CA 92404 Office: Court House 11th St and Orange Av Riverside CA 92502

ANDERSON, RUTH IRENE, educator; b. Millerton, Pa., Apr. 17, 1919; d. Ralph W. and Pearle (Blakeslee) Anderson; B.S., Grove City Coll., 1941; M.C.S., Ind. U., 1943, Ed.D., 1946. Tchr. bus. Cranberry Twp. High Sch., Seneca, Pa., 1941-42; teaching fellow Ind. U., Bloomington, 1942-43, 44-46; instr. U.S. Naval Tng. Sch., Bloomington, 1943-44; chmn. dept. bus. edn. and secretarial adminstrn. Tex. Christian U., Ft. Worth, 1946-53; prof. bus. adminstrn. N. Tex. State U., Denton, 1953—. Cons. San Angelo (Tex.) Schs., 1961-62, Arlington, (Tex.) High Sch., 1964-65. Mem. Fine Arts Council Denton, 1968-70, Denton Community Chorus, 1968-73, Bd. Adjustment City of Denton, 1967—; mem. adv. bd. Bishop Coll., Dallas, 1968-69. Mem. Tex. Educators for Tower, 1972-73. Recipient Bus. Woman of Year award Bus. and Profl. Women's Club Denton, 1965; Distinguished Alumni award Grove City Coll., 1970; John Robert Gregg award Gregg Co., 1971; Bus. Tchr. of Year award State of Tex., 1972; Distinguished Teaching award N. Tex. Alumni Assn., 1972; Piper Profl. of Tex. award Piper Found., 1973. Mem. Nat. (Mountain-Plains Leadership award 1970, nat. bd. 1970-73), Tex., Mountain Plains bus. edn. assns., Nat. Bus. Tchr. Edn. Assn., Tex. Bus. Tchrs. Edn. Council, Pi Omega Pi, Pi Kappa Delta, Pi Gamma Mu, Delta Pi Epsilon (nat. pres. 1963-65). Presbyn. (deacon, elder). Author: (with Lloyd Douglas, James Blanford) Teaching Business Subjects, 3d edit., 1972; (with Esta R. Stuart, Vernon V. Payne) Complete College Typewriting, 1958; Secretarial Careers, 1963; (with Leonard Porter) 120 Basic Typing Jobs, 2d edit., 1964; (with Dana Gibson, Lura L. Straub) Word Finder, 4th edit., 1974; (with others) Administrative Secretary: Source Book and Practicum, 1970. Home: 810 Stanley St Denton TX 76201

ANDERSON, RUTH MESSER (MRS. FRED ANDREW ANDERSON), anesthesiologist; b. Boston, Apr. 25, 1915; d. John Hoag and Evelyn Sanford (Grover) Messer; B.S., Boston U., 1937; M.D. cum laude, Boston U., 1940; m. Fred Andrew Anderson, June 1, 1940; children—Fred Andrew, Martin R., John G., Frank L. Intern, New Eng. Hosp. for Women and Children, Boston, 1940-41; resident anesthesia Hartford (Conn.) Hosp., 1942-44; staff anesthesia Faulkner Hosp., Boston, 1944-47; chief sect. anesthesia Cushing VA Hosp., Framingham, Mass., 1947-50; staff anesthesia W.W. Backus Hosp., Norwich, Conn., 1950-70, chief dept. anesthesia, 1970—; cons. anesthesia Day Kimball Hosp., Putnam, 1971—. Corporator Norwich Savs. Soc. . (Conn.). Diplomate Am. Bd. Anesthesiology. Mem. Am. Soc. Anesthesiologists, New Eng., Conn. socs. anesthesiology, A.M.A., Conn., New London County med. socs., Delta Delta Delta. Mem. United Ch. of Christ. Home: 15 Butternut Dr Norwich CT 06360 Office: WW Backus Hosp Norwich CT 06360

ANDERSON, SARAH JONEANE, ednl. adminstr.; b. Grand Rapids, Mich., Dec. 29, 1935; d. Joseph Damon and Sara Priscilla (Brown) Anderson; B.S., Wayne State U., 1959, M.Ed., 1966. Elementary tchr. Detroit Bd. Edn., 1959-65; employment counselor Mich. Employment Security Commn. Youth Opportunity Center, Detroit, 1965-66; sch. community agt. Detroit Bd. Edn., 1966-67; counselor Oakland Community Coll., Farmington, Mich., 1967-74; dir. Youth Home, Washington, 1974—. Mem. exec. bd. Center for Edn. of Returning Vets., 1970-73. Mem. Nat., Mich. edn. assns., Am., Mich. personnel and guidance assns., Nat. Assn. Women Deans, Adminstrs. and Counselors. Home: 421 34th St NE Washington DC 20019

ANDERSON, SHIRLEY PATRICIA, recreation specialist, musician; b. Aberdeen, Wash., Oct. 10, 1933; d. Donald Chester and Lylas (Broom) Anderson; A.A., Colo. Woman's Coll., 1954; Mus.B., Phila. Musical Acad., 1959; Mus.M., Combs Coll. Music, 1961, Mus.D., 1963. Mem. aquatics staff, day camp counselor Phila. YWCA, 1963-64, supr. recreational aquatics, 1968—; recreation specialist Carousel House, Dept. Recreation, City of Phila., 1972—; instr. English, fine arts Rider Coll., Trenton, 1964-66; asso. dir. U.S.O., Hoover Park, Guam, 1966-68; social worker A.R.C., Phila., 1968-73. Active Girl Scouts of Am., 1942—. Bd. dirs. Alumni Assn. Youth Orch. of Greater Phila., 1973—. Mem. Phila. Musical Soc., Percussive Arts Soc., Am. Musicol. Soc., Am. Recorder Soc. Club: Phila. Sea Horses. Home: 2101 Chestnut St Philadelphia PA 19103 Office: Carousel House Dept Recreation City of Phila Philadelphia PA 19103

ANDERSON, SYLVIA (MRS. MATTHIAS KUNTZSCH), mezzo-soprano; b. Denver, Mar. 26, 1937; d. S.T. and Florence (Schack) Anderson; B.A. cum laude, MacMurray Coll., Jacksonville, Ill., 1959; Mus.M. and Performer's certificate in Voice and Opera, Eastman Sch. Music, 1961; pupil Anna Kaskas; m. Matthias Kuntzsch, Aug. 12, 1966. Concert soloist Eastman Philharmonia Orch., Rochester, N.Y. Rochester Civic Orch., Rochester Oratorio Soc. and Bach Festival, 1960-61; concert soloist in Berlin, Cologne, Bremen (Germany), Basel, Geneva (Switzerland), Brussels (Belgium), 1961-66; opera debut Boris Godonov, Cologne (Germany) Opera House, 1962, Nabucco, Vienna (Austria) Volksoper, 1963, lead roles in Carmen, Der Rosenkavalier, Barber of Seville, Die Fledermaus, La Forza del Destino, Mannheim (Germany) Nat. Theater, 1963-66, Cosi Fan Tutte, Germany, Belgium, Netherlands, La Cenerentola, Hansel and Gretel, Prince Igor, Frankfurt (Germany) Opera, 1965—; Cosi Fan Tutte, Brussels and Amsterdam royal operas, 1967, Der Rosenkavalier, Dortmund, Germany, 1966, 2d San Francisco, 1967, Santa Fe (N.M.) Opera Summer Festival, 1968, Hamlet, Marriage of Figaro, Hamburg (Germany) State Opera, 1968, Carmen, Essen, Germany, 1967, 68, Antigone, Festival Greek Tragedy, Athens, 1967 and Festival Carl Orff, Stuttgart, Germany, 1968, Albert Herring, Schwetzingen (Germany) Festival, 1967; recorded for radio Germany, Belgium, Switzerland. Prize winner Internat. Singing Competition, Brussels, 1962; named winner Internat. Competition Mus. Performers, Geneva, 1962. Fulbright scholar, 1961. Address: care San Francisco Opera San Francisco CA 94108

ANDERSON, TIRZAH WAITE (MRS. F. KENDALL ANDERSON), retired assn. exec.; b. Rockland, Me.; d. David Standish and Sarah (Perkins) Waite; student Mt. Holyoke Coll., 1926; B.A., U. Ia., 1939; M.A., Columbia, 1940; postgrad., 1940-44; m. Forrest Kendall Anderson, Sept. 24, 1932 (dec. Feb. 1937). Social worker Girls Service League, 1928; dir. parole Letchworth Village, 1930-34; vocational counselor, asst. dir. employment YWCA, N.Y.C., 1940-42, mem. field staff, 1942-44, nat. bd. 1944-48, dir. Syracuse, 1950-67; exec. dir. YWCA Syracuse and Onondaga County, 1967-70; asst. prof. U. N.C., 1944. Mem. planning com. for women's program Onondaga Community Coll.; pres. Silverman Pub. Health Hosp., 1971-74; sec. bd. mgrs. Syracuse Home Assn., 1972—. Mem. Nat. Assn. Social Workers, Am. Camping Assn. (mem. bd. for central N.Y., sec. bd. 1968-69), Acad. Certified Social Workers, UN Assn. Am. (v.p. Central N.Y. chpt.), Soc. Mayflower Descendants, Pi Lambda Theta, Kappa Delta Pi, Assn. Universalist Women. Clubs: Zonta (dir. 1959-61, 66-68, v.p. 1960-61, 67-68), Corinthian, Syracuse Antiques (Syracuse); Mt. Holyoke College. Author articles and pamphlets in field. Home: 145 Durston Av Syracuse NY 13203

ANDERSON, URSULA MARY, physician; b. Cheshire, Eng., 1929; d. Francis David and Beatrice Mary Anderson; came to U.S., 1958; ed. Loreto Coll., Llandudno, North Wales, U. Liverpool (Eng.), U. London (Eng.), Yale; m. Lino H. Dominguez, May 10, 1969. Formerly sr. asst. med. officer of health, Reading, Eng.; pediatric cons. N.C. State Bd. Health, 1960-62; dir. maternal and child health Erie County (N.Y.) Health Dept., 1962-69; asso. clin. prof. pediatrics N.Y. State U. at Buffalo, 1962-69; asso. attending pediatrician Buffalo Childrens Hosp., 1962-69; chief div. community health Hosp. for Sick Children, Toronto, Ont., Can., 1969-72; asso. prof. pediatrics U. Toronto, 1969-73. Cons., Head Start, 1965-69, WHO, 1970-71; chmn. N.Y. State Task Force on Health Manpower, 1968-69. Fellow Am. Acad. Pediatrics, Am. Pub. Health Assn.; mem. World, Brit., Canadian med. assns., Pan Am. Med. Fedn. Author articles in field. Address: Box 88 East Otto NY 14729

ANDERSON, VIVA LEONE, lawyer, educator; b. Northport, Wash.; d. Christopher and Nena (Huson) Anderson; student Portland State Coll.; LL.B., Northwestern Coll. Law, 1943. Employed Portland pub. schs., 1939-43; admitted to Ore. bar, 1943, Supreme Ct. of Korea, 1948; counselor Ore. Shipbldg. Corp., 1943-45; adminstrv. officer UNRRA, Greece, 1945-47; edn. dir. Civil Service, Osan AFB, Korea, 1947-59; adjudicator VA, Washington, 1960, authorization officer, 1960-64; sr. claims examiner U.S. VA, Manila, Phillippines, 1964-65, rating specialist, 1965-68; rating specialist Vets. Benefits Office, Washington, 1968—. Recipient Civil Service Sustained Superior Performance awards, citation for work done in behalf of Korean people, Republic Korea, 1958. Mem. Women's Overseas Service League, Sons and Daus. Ore. Pioneers, Fed. Bar Assn., Kappa Beta Pi. Mem. Order of Eastern Star, Rebekahs. Author numerous articles on Europe, Far East, also govt. pamphlets. Home: 1110 Dryden St Silver Spring MD 20901 Office: Veterans Benefits Office 2033 M St NW Washington DC 20036

ANDERSON, VIVIENNE (MRS. PRESCO ANDERSON), state ofcl.; b. Phila., July 28, 1916; B.S., Temple U., 1936, Ed.M., 1939; Ed.D., Columbia U., 1955; m. Presco Anderson, Dec. 27, 1947; 1 son, James. Tchr., Phila. Pub. Schs., 1936-47; adminstrv. asst. to asso. supt., 1947-50; with N.Y. State Edn. Dept., Albany, 1950—, chief bur. continuing edn. curriculum devel., dir. div. humanities and arts 1965-74, asst. commr. for gen. edn., 1974—. Adj. prof., coordinator paperback books in edn. project Tchrs. Coll., Columbia, 1960-66; adj. prof. doctoral program State U. N.Y., Albany, 1963-66; writing, planning and/or pub. relations cons. to Kellogg Found., CBS, Gestetner Corp., Kelly & Grutzen, Am. Jr. Red Cross and Tchrs. Coll., Columbia; adviser on edn. Lincoln Center for Performing Arts, Saratoga Performing Arts Center, 1964—; pres. Albany League of Arts, 1968-70; v.p. N.Y. State Citizens Com., 1973—; N.Y. state chmn. Nat. Alliance for Arts in Edn., 1973—. Recipient award Freedoms Found., 1960; Distinguished Civic Leadership award Citizens Planning Com. for Greater Albany, 1965; Distinguished Leadership award Nat. Humanities Assn., 1973. Writing fellow Yaddo, Saratoga Springs, N.Y., 1957. Mem. Council Sch. Dist. Adminstrs., Sch. Adminstrs. N.Y. State, Assn. for Supervision and Curriculum Devel. Author: Patterns of Educational Leadership, 1956; The School Administrator and the Press, 1956; The School Adminstrator and his Publications, 1957; Your America, 1965, rev. edit., 1968; Paperbacks in Education, 1966. Contbr. articles to profl. jours. and newspapers. Office: Division of Humanities and Arts New York State Education Dept Albany NY 12224

ANDERSON, ZOE ESTELLE, educator; b. Glenview, Ill., Jan. 20, 1913; d. Frederick Reade and Mary Judith (Reed) Anderson; B.S. in Arts and Sci., Ill. Inst. Tech., 1939; M.S. in Nutrition, U. Ill., 1947, Ph.D., 1950. Mgr. plant cafeteria Hydrox Ice Cream Co. (now Sealtest Foods div. Nat. Dairy Products Corp.), Chgo., 1935-39; tchr. cafeteria mgmt., home econ. West Frankfort (Ill.) Community High Sch., 1939-42; dietitian Sterling Morton High Sch, Cicero, Ill., 1942-43; dir. nutrition research Nat. Dairy Council, Chgo., 1949-60; prof. home econ. Wayne (Mich.) State U., 1960-62; asso. prof. nutrition dept. internal medicine State U. Ia., 1962-64, asso. prof. home. econs. San Diego State U., 1965—. Teaching intern Hull House, also Chgo. Commons, 1935-36; program planner, moderator, radio, TV stas. Wayne State U., 1961-62; guest lectr. numerous local, state nat. and internat. groups; research cons. dairy industry, Chgo., 1949-60; developer instl. advt. program profl. jours and dairy industry publs., 1949-60; participant White House Conf. on Food, Nutrition and Health, 1969. Served with waves, USNR, 1943-45. Mem. Am. Inst. Nutrition, Am. Home Econs. Assn., Am. Dietetics Assn., Am. Assn. U. Profs., Sigma Xi, Sigma Delta Epsilon. Editor, Dairy Council Digests, 1949-60. Contbr. articles to profl. jours., chpts. to textbooks. Home: 5065 54th St San Diego CA 92115

ANDERTON, LAURA GADDES, educator; b. Providence, Sept. 6, 1918; B.A., Wellesley Coll., 1940; M.S., Brown U., 1948; postgrad. (Fulbright scholar), U. London, 1952-53; postgrad. (Danforth fellow), U. N.C., 1955-56, research grantee, 1958-59, Ph.D., 1959. Instr. biology, chemistry Howard Sem., 1941-43; instr. biology, counselor U. N.C. at Greensboro, 1948-55, instr. biology, 1956-58; asso. prof. biology, 1959-68, prof., 1968—, dir. cytogenetics lab., 1965—. NIH grantee, 1968-71. Cons. Moses H. Cone Meml. Hosp., 1969—. Served as lt. WAVES, 1943-46. Mem. Am. Inst. Biology Sci., Am. Soc. Human Genetics, Am. Soc. Zoology, Internat. Union Against Cancer. Office: Dept Biology Cytogenetics Lab U N C Greensboro NC 27412*

ANDES, MARY LOU, educator; b. Dayton, O., Sept. 21, 1933; d. Stuard S. and Ivolue (Freeders) Andes; student U. Wis., 1951-53; B.A. in Journalism, Ohio State U., 1956; M.A. in Edn., U. Dayton, 1971. With media dept. Monroe F. Dreher, Inc., N.Y.C., 1957; mem. jr. staff, newsroom Christian Sci. Monitor, Boston, 1958; instr. English Fairborn (O.) City Sch. Dist., 1960—. Mem. Greene County (O.) Hist. Soc., 1974. Mem. Women in Communications (pres. Dayton chpt. 1966-68), Nat. Council Tchrs. of English, English Assn. Ohio, Ohio, Western Ohio (chmn. human relations com. 1968-69, exec. com. 1974—), Fairborn edn. assns., Ohio Assn. Classroom Tchrs., Fairborn Bus. and Profl. Women's Club, Delta Kappa Gamma. Home: 1447 Mill Race Dr Fairborn OH 45324 Office: 221 N Central Av Fairborn OH 45324

ANDING, BETTYE ANN TUCKER (MRS. ROBERT DAVIDSON ANDING), editor; b. Shreveport, La., July 7, 1935; d. Robert Kuroki and Martha Geneva (Hill) Tucker; B.S., U. So. Miss., 1957; m. Robert Davidson Anding, Mar. 15, 1959; children—William Mark, Jill Tucker. Reporter, Hattiesburg (Miss.) Am., 1953-57, Jackson (Miss.) Daily News, 1957-59; reporter New Orleans States Item, 1959—, women's editor, 1971—, food editor, 1967-71. Mem. Women in Communications, Sigma Sigma Sigma. Presbyn. Club: New Orleans Press. Home: 2112 Harvard Lane Gretna LA 70053 Office: 3800 Howard Av New Orleans LA 70140

ANDRADE, CAROLYN MARIE, govt. ofcl.; b. Rochester, N.Y., Dec. 29, 1922; d. John Francis and Catherine Anna Andrade; student U. Conn., 1942-43, George Washington U., 1959-61, Catholic U., 1965-66. Cryptographic clk. Arlington Hall Sta., 1943; sec. Signal Corps., 1944, sec. Foster Gift Shop 1944-47; night mgr. Shoreham Coffee Shop, 1945-49; sec. A.B. Wigley & Asso., 1947-49; sec. Jack Darling, mfg. rep., 1948-52; asst. office mgr. Henry Kaiser Co., 1952-53; office mgr., partner Walter Huenemoerder Asso., constrn., 1953-58; sec. Rep. Gray, 1958; adminstrv. asst. Rep. Levering, 1959; staff asst. Senator Stephen Young, 1960-63; exec. sec. Rep. Seymour Halpern, 1963, 69-70, Rep. Pepper, 1963-64; exec. sec. Congressman Clair A. Callan of Neb., Washington, 1965-66; asso. Internat. Devel. Assn., 1966-68; pub. relations cons., 1966-68; with P.O. and Civil Service Com. U.S. Senate, 1968-69; exec. asst. to chmn. Price Commn., 1971-73; adminstrv. asst. U.S. Senate Select Com. on Presdl. Campaign Activities, 1973—. Mem. Georgetown Citizens Assn., Nat. Etching Soc. (sec.). Home: 1334 31st St NW Washington DC 20007 Office: 2000 M St NW Washington DC 20036

ANDRADE, EDNA, artist; b. Portsmouth, Va.; d. Thomas Judson and Ruth (Porter) Wright; B.F.A., Pa. Acad. Fine Arts U. Pa., 1937; m. C. Preston Andrade Jr., July 12, 1941 (div. 1960). Supr. art elementary schs., Norfolk, Va., 1938-39; instr. drawing and painting Newcomb Art Sch. Tulane U., 1939-41; artist, designer OSS, 1942-44; free-lance designer, Washington, 1944-46; free-lance painter, designer, muralist, Phila. and N.Y.C., 1946—; artist-in-residence Hartford Sch. Art and Tamarind Inst., 1971; lectr. U. N.M., 1971; prof. Phila. Coll. Art, 1959-72, 73—; prof. art Temple U., 1972-73; one-man shows East Hampton Gallery, N.Y.C., Peale Galleries Pa. Acad., Rutgers U., Marian Locks Gallery, Phila.; group shows include Am. Acad. Arts and Letters, Pa. Acad. Fine Arts, Phila. Mus. Art, Bklyn. Mus., Ft. Worth Art Center, Des Moines Art Center, Fordham U., Dartmouth and Southampton Colls., Ohio State U., Meml. Art Gallery, Rochester, N.Y., Philbrook Art Center, Tulsa, Am. Color Print Soc., Skidmore Coll., and others; represented permanent collections Phila. Mus. Art, Pa. Acad. Fine Arts, Print Club Permanent Collection, U. Cal. at Berkeley, U. Mass., Phila., Chrysler Mus., Balt. Mus. Art, Addison Gallery Am. Art, McNay Art Inst., San Antonio, Montclair (N.J.) Art Mus., Nat. Collection Fine Arts, Library of Congress, USIA, Bklyn. Coll., Albright-Knox Art Gallery, Buffalo, Colonial Penn Group, First Pa. Banking & Trust Co., Phila., Tamarind Collection, U. N.M. Mus., Yale Art Gallery, Dickinson Coll., Prudential Life Ins. Co., Westinghouse Corp., others. Recipient 1st and 2d Cresson European traveling scholarships, 1936, 37, prizes Pa. Acad., 1964, 68, Eyre Medal Phila. Water Color Club, 1968, Childe Hassam Meml. purchases Am. Acad. Arts and Letters, 1967, 68, Sloan Meml. Print Prize Cheltenham (Pa.) Art Center, 1970; Merit award Pennsylvania '71; ann. Katzman prize Print Club, 1972; Klein prize Am. Color Print Soc. Mem. Pa. Acad. Fine Arts, Phila. Art Alliance, Artists Equity Assn., Am. Color Print Soc. Address: 415 S Carlisle St Philadelphia PA 19146

ANDRADE, ETHEL KAANOHILANI CHONG, rancher; b. Hamakua, Hawaii, Dec. 3, 1926; d. Henry Kaihi and Christina Kilikina (Mahi) Chong; grad. Honolulu Bus. Coll., 1946; m. Sept. 3, 1949; 1 dau., Jadelyn Hoonanea (Mrs. David Bruce Ramos). Pvt. sec. Honokaa Sugar Co., Haina, Hawaii, 1946-61; exec. sec., pub. relations ofcl. Hawaii Pavilion, N.Y. World's Fair, 1964-65; rancher, nr. Kamuela, Hawaii. Sesquicentennial coordinator, Hawaii, 1969-70; mem. South Kohala Traffic and Safety Com., 1970; pres. Kamuela-Kohala U. Extension Council, 1972—; chmn. Hawaii Extension Homemakers, 1972—, v.p. council, 1974-75. Chmn. Republican State Conv., Kauai, 1969; del. Hawaii Constl. Conv., 1968. Mem. Am. Nat. Cowbelles, Kaahumanu Soc., Hale O Na Alii Soc. Address: PO Box 104 Kamuela HI 96743

ANDRADE MATTHEWS, ANNE MCILHENNEY (MRS. MICHAEL R. ANDRADE), newspaper woman; b. Phila.; d. William and Clara (McCollum) McIlhenney; student U. Buffalo, 1950-54, Ecole des Beaux Arts, Paris, France; D.Litt., Rosary Hill Coll.; m. Burrows Matthews, Oct. 7, 1947 (dec. 1954); m. 2d, Michael R. Andrade, Apr. 1972. Reporter Buffalo Courier Express, 1924-47, aviation editor, 1935-47, also drama critic, motion picture columnist, feature writer, gen. news reporter, 1935-47, art critic and promotions editor, 1959-63, dir. radio promotions, 1963-64, by-line feature columnist, 1964—; speech writer, pub. relations Supreme Command, Far East, Tokyo, Japan, also NATO, 1952-53; swimming instr. Buffalo Athletic Club, 1927-38, Kensington High Sch., Buffalo, 1938-42. Bd. dirs. Soc. Prevention Cruelty to Animals; trustee Buffalo and County Pub. Library; mem. council Niagara U. Served as maj. WAC, 1942-47. Decorated Purple Heart, Bronze Star. Recipient Someone Cares award Bros. of Mercy, 1972, Liberty Bell award Erie County Bar Assn., 1972, Community Service award 6th dist. V.F.W., 1972, Americanism award Am. Legion, 1972; also over 30 awards for journalism. Mem. Buffalo Chapitre de la Chaine des Rotisseurs, Eden Citizen's Assn. (dir.). Clubs: Frontier Press (dir.); Saturn; Overseas Press (N.Y.C.) 1st woman named pub. relations officer in charge U.S Army; 1st woman dir. Buffalo unit Assn. U.S. Army. Home: 9293 Sission Hwy Eden NY 14057 Office: Buffalo Couriër-Express Buffalo NY 14240

ANDRÉ, FLORENCE DE FROSCIA (MRS. THOMAS JAMES ANDRE JR.), coll. dean; b. Coatesville, Pa., Dec. 18, 1944; d. William Francis and Reba Juliet (Whisler) De Froscia; B.A., Sophie Newcomb Coll., 1966; Ed.M., Tulane U., 1973; m. Thomas James Andre Jr., July 11, 1970. Customer rep. Xerox Corp., New Orleans, 1966-67, customer rep., regional coordinator, Dallas, 1967-68; asst. to dir. Univ. Alumni Assn., Tulane U., New Orleans, 1969, counselor to women, Newcomb Coll., 1969—. Bd. dirs. S.E. La. council Girl Scouts U.S.A. Mem. Nat. Assn. Women Deans and Counselors, Am. Assn. Coll. and U. Housing Officers, Am. Assn. U. Women, Mortar Bd., Kappa Kappa Gamma, Alpha Lambda Delta. Home: 7039 Freret St New Orleans LA 70118

ANDRESS, CHARLOTTE FRANCES, social work exec.; b. Birmingham, Ala., Apr. 22, 1910; d. Francis Samuel and Tommie (Daniel) Andress; B.S., Birmingham-So. Coll., 1932; A.M. in Social Service Adminstrn., U. Chgo., 1943. Asst. dir. Girl Scouts Am., Birmingham, 1932-35; exec. dir., Nashville, 1935-41; instr. Loyola U., Chgo., 1942-45; dir. U.S.O., Augusta, Ga., 1945-48; asst. dir. YWCA, Chgo., 1948-50, exec. dir., St. Louis, 1950-53; dir. group work, youth service Fedn. Protestant Welfare Agys., N.Y.C., 1953-59; exec. dir. Inwood House, N.Y.C., 1959—. Chmn. adv. bd. Jefferson Park

Center, 1959-65; nat. camp com. Camp Fire Girls, 1959-68; bd. Social Work Vocational Bur., 1961-66; dir. Vols. Am. Auxiliary, Trail Blazer Camps, 1957—; mem. Camp Sharparoon com. N.Y.C. Mission Soc., 1960—, mem. personnel com., 1962-66; adv. bd. social welfare Meth. Ch. 1958-63; mem. United Meth. Bd. Missions, 1964-72; bd. Bethel Meth. Home, 1965-72, sec. bd., 1966-72; Women's com. Japan Internat. Christian U. Found., 1969—; adv. bd. Isabella Thoburn Coll., 1967—; chmn. nat. com. Wesleyan Service Guild, 1970-72. Mem. Nat. Assn. Social Workers (sec. bd. N.Y.C. chpt. 1958-60, chmn. personnel standards and practices 1960-69, 73—), Acad. Certified Social Workers, Nat. Conf. on Social Welfare, Bethany Deaconess Soc., Am. Found. Religion and Psychiatry, International Conf. Social Welfare, N.Y. Deaconess Assn. (bd. 1969—), Gamma Phi Beta. Democrat. Methodist. Home: 102 E 22d St New York City NY 10010 Office: 320 E 82d St New York City NY 10028

ANDRESS, RUTH ANN (MRS. GENE BISHOP ANDRESS, SR.), educator; b. Palacios, Tex., Aug. 23, 1933; d. James Roy and Rubie Lee (Ramsey) Williams; B.B.A., Tex. Tech. U., 1965, M.B.A., 1966; m. Gene Bishop Andress, Sr., Sept. 24, 1951; 1 son, Gene Bishop. Grad. asst. Tex. Tech. U., Lubbock, 1965-66; grad. asst. San Diego State Coll., 1966; instr. bus. adminstrn. Mesa Coll., San Diego, 1966-68; asst. prof. econs. Baptist Coll. at Charleston (S.C.), 1968-72; asst. prof. econs. and marketing U. S.C., Columbia, 1972—. Mem. S.C. Mental Health Assn., Am., So. econs. assns., Am., So. marketing assns., Am. Acad. Polit. and Social Scis., Am. Assn. U. Profs., Tex. Tech. Alumni Assn. (sec. San Diego chpt. 1966-68), Women's Equity Action League, Omicron Delta Epsilon, Beta Gamma Sigma, Pi Gamma Mu, Phi Gamma Nu. Address: Box 1884 Columbia SC 29202

ANDREW, SISTER MARY, educator; b. N.Y.C.; d. P.J. and Margaret (Newell) Mulcahy; student (John White Alexander Scholar) Parsons Sch. Fine and Applied Art, 1915; B.A., Coll. of Mt. St. Vincent, 1927, M.A., 1929; postgrad. Catholic U. Am., 1921, Fordham U., 1922-29, N.Y. Sch. Interior Decoration, 1925, N.Y. Sch. Allied Arts, 1934, 35, Columbia, 1933, Inst. Pius XII, Florence, Italy, 1949-50. Professed Sister of Charity of N.Y.; art tchr. Acad. of Mt. St. Vincent, 1918-27, prof. fine art of Coll., 1927-61, chmn. art dept., 1930-61; fine arts dir., editor, cons., contbr. Cath. Ency. for Home and Sch., 1959-65; prof. painting, adult edn. div. Elizabeth Seton Coll.; prof. fine arts Fordham U., 1952-53, prof. fine arts Coll. Holy Cross, Worcester, Mass., summer 1959, Aquinas Coll., Grand Rapids, summer, 1960; fine arts prof., continuing edn. dept., sisters div. Coll. Mt. St. Vincent, N.Y.; archivist printed events, photos, publicity souvenirs, Cardinal Spellman, 1941-67, Cardinal Cooke, 1967—, curator Cardinal Spellman Numis. Collection, 1959-69, Cardinal Cooke Numis. Collection, 1969; lectr. on travel, religion, art topics. Medieval manuscript illuminator, works for Pope Pius XI, Pope Pius XII, Cardinal Spellman, Cardinal Mercier, Cardinal Hayes, Hon. Myron Taylor, others; research on illuminated manuscripts in the Laurenciana and S. Marco Libraries, Florence; Piccolomini Library, Siena; Ambrosiana, Milan; Marciana, Venice; Vatican Library, Rome; Bodleian, Oxford; Trinity Library, Dublin; Morgan and Lenox Libraries, N.Y. Exhibits Met. Mus. Art, Stamp Shows in N.Y., Phila., Boston, others. Mem. N.Y. Archdiocesan planning com. for visit of Pope Paul VI to UN, 1965. Mem. Met. Mus. Art. Recipient Myron Taylor scholarship to Inst. Pius XII, Florence, Italy, publicity in N.Y. Sun and Herald Tribune, N.Y. Times, N.Y. Daily News, Canadian, U.S. mags., papers; Pro Ecclesia et Pontifice medal Pope Paul VI, 1966. Mem. Coll. Art Assn. N.Y., Cath. Fine Arts Soc. (founder pres.), Nat. Assn. Philatelists, Met. Mus. Art. Author: Modern Methods of Manuscript Illumination, 1947; Illuminated Initials for Way of the Cross, Novena Book, Word of God, 1955, 56, 57. Collaborator: Masterpiece and Rembrandt edits. Cath. Bible. Contbr. articles to Cath. Ency. for Home and Sch., also Coin World, Numis. Scrapbook and Philately and Numismatics. Home: 1175 3d Av New York City NY 10021

ANDREWS, BARBARA LOUISE, clergywoman; b. Mpls., May 11, 1935; d. Lee W. and Louise C (Christ) A.; B.A., Gustavus Adolphus Coll., 1958; B.D. (Danforth fellow), 1969; postgrad. 1969-71. Ordained to ministry Am. Lutheran Ch., 1970; counselor to students Lutheran Campus Ministry U. Minn., Mpls., 1962-68; student chaplain Metro. Hosps., Mpls., 1969-71; parish pastor Edina Community Lutheran Ch., Mpls., 1971—. Adv. dist. youth com. Am. Lutheran Ch., since 1971; chaplain Samaritan Hosp. St. Paul, 1972—. Bd. dirs. Minn. Soc. for Crippled Children and Adults. Mem. Greater Mpls. Council of Chs. (dir. 1971—). Home: 2300 Franklin Av E Minneapolis MN 55406 Office: 4113 W 54th St Edina MN 55424

ANDREWS, BETTY SUE, assn. exec.; b. Cedartown, Ga., Jan. 22, 1933; d. Clifford Ray and Verna Jane (Lanham) Rainey; student W. Ga. Coll., 1950; diploma St. Joseph's Infirmary Sch. Nursing, 1953; student Shorter Coll., 1957; m. Russell Edgar Andrews III, Sept. 10, 1961; children—Russell Edgar IV, Christopher Ray, Betty Rana. Nurse, Bremen (Ga.) Gen. Hosp., 1954-56; night supr. Folk Gen. Hosp., Cedartown, 1956-57; evening supr. Floyd Hosp., Rome, Ga., 1957-62; clin. instr., 1964-65; chmn. elementary schs. cancer edn. program, Rome, 1969-70; chmn. mental health Ga. Med. Aux., 1969-71; chmn. Ga. sect. A.M.A. Ednl. and Research Found., 1972-74; 3d v.p. women's aux. Med. Assn. Ga., 1974-75. Pres., Floyd-Polk-Chattanooga Med. Aux., 1968, 72; chmn. spl. gifts div. Ga. Heart Fund, 1974. Recipient award radio sta. WROM, 1972. Mem. So. Med. Soc. Episcopalian. Home: 1409 Route 8 Kingston Rd Rome GA 30161

ANDREWS, BYTHELLA BRYANT (MRS. OBEDIAH ANDREWS, SR.), home economist; b. Ebony, Ark., Dec. 31, 1929; d. James and Jessie (McClain) Bryant; B.S., Alcorn A. and M. Coll., 1952; m. Obediah Andrews, Sr., Aug. 26, 1951; children—Obediah, Gerald, Kasper, Terrance. Tchr. homemaking Liberty (Miss.) High Sch., 1952-59; tchr. sci. and homemaking Eva Gordon Sch., Magnolia, Miss., 1960-69; extension home economist, food and nutrition Coop. Extension Service, Pike County, Magnolia, 1969—. Sec. Coordinating council, 1970-71; active Council for Aging, Cancer Fund. Mem. Miss. Extension Home Economist Assn., Miss. Federated Womens Club. Baptist. Home: 234 Robb St Magnolia MS 39652 Office: PO Box 469 Magnolia MS 39652

ANDREWS, EDNA MAE STONE (MRS. JOHN HAITON ANDREWS), educator; b. Kansas City, Mo., Dec. 12, 1918; d. William Barley and Anna (Rodabaugh) Stone; B.S., Cal. State Coll. at Long Beach, 1960, M.B.A., 1967; Ph.D. (hon.), Colo. State Christian Coll., 1973; m. Harry E. Wiles, 1936 (div. 1942); m. 2d, John Haiton Andrews, Aug. 15, 1946; children—Harry Edward, John Gene. Supr., Sears, Roebuck & Co., Kansas City, Mo., 1935-39, Naval Supply Depot, San Diego, 1940-44; owner Fallon & Hawthorne, restaurant and club, Nev., 1946-50; accountant J. C. Gentry, C.P.A., Long Beach, 1958-61, 62-64, Windes, McClaughry & Co., C.P.A.'s, Long Beach, 1961-62; practice accounting, Long Beach, Cal., 1963—; prof. accounting Cal. State Coll., Long Beach, 1964—, also asst. chmn. dept. accounting. C.P.A., Cal. Mem. Am. Assn. U. Profs., Am. Accounting Assn., Am. Inst. C.P.A.'s, Cal. Soc. C.P.A.'s, Accounting Soc. Cal. State Coll. at Long Beach (pres. 1960), Beta Alpha Psi, Phi Kappa Phi (exec. bd. 1969—, treas. 1970-72, corr. sec. 1972-73, v.p. 1973-74, pres. 1974—), Phi Delta Gamma (treas. 1968-69, pres. 1969-71, faculty adviser 1971-72, nat. council rep. 1972—, nat. dir. finance 1972—), Beta Gamma Sigma. Home: 4600 E 7th St Long Beach CA 90804 Office: 6101 E 7th St Long Beach CA 90801

ANDREWS, ELIZABETH KATHERINE BAUMGARTNER (MRS. LLOYD E. ANDREWS), educator; b. Chgo., July 22, 1903; d. Charles Brentford and Alta M. (Jones) Baumgartner; student Cornell Coll., 1919, Drake U., 1920-21, Northwestern U., 1921-23; degree in speech Chgo. Musical Coll., 1924; postgrad. Inst. Juvenile Research; m. Lloyd Edward Andrews, June 17, 1925; children—Charles B., Dianne Elizabeth. Pvt. tchr. dramatics and speech, dir. dramatics and reading program Manchester (Ia.) Pub. Schs., also reviewer dramatics and reading program; editor features Community Newspapers, Inc., Chgo., 1924-25; dir. remedial programs and dramatics Arlington Heights (Ill.) Pub. Schs., 1938-43; dir. children's dramatics Am. Conservatory Music, Chgo., 1943-46; founder, dir. Day Sch., Chgo., 1944—; founder, dir. Camp-4-Fun for Emotionally Disturbed Children, Chgo., 1950—. Mem. Ind. Schs. Assn. (past pres.), Assn. Edn. Exceptional Children (chpt. pres.), Council Children with Behavioral Disorders, Ikebana Internat., Smithsonian Inst., Art Inst. Chgo., Delta Zeta. Clubs: Zonta, Cordon, Woman's City (Chgo.); Naples Women's, Country of Naples (Fla.). Author: Teaching Manual for Special Education, 1954, rev., 1958, 63; also childrens books, plays, operettas, teaching games. Home: 525 Turtle Hatch Rd Naples FL 33940 Office: 800 Buena Av Chicago IL 60613

ANDREWS, FRED, lawyer; b. Cecil, Ark., Jan. 14, 1895; d. John Franklin and Katie Elizabeth (Stockton) Andrews. Admitted to Okla. bar, 1934, since practiced in Ada; judge Pontotoc County and Juvenile Ct., Ada, 1955-69. Crusade chmn. Am. Cancer Soc., 1955-59, Ada Community Chest, 1961. Adv. bd. Valley View Hosp., Ada. Mem. Bus. and Profl. Women's Club (past pres., honor award 1958), Order Eastern Star. Home: 1213 S Cherry St Ada OK Office: Box 336 Ada OK

ANDREWS, JEAN, author, artist, educator; b. Kingsville, Tex., Dec. 23, 1923; d. Herbert and Katharine (Smith) Andrews; B.S., U. Tex., 1944; postgrad. So. Meth. U., 1957-58, U. Corpus Christi, 1960-61; M.S., A. and I. U., 1966; postgrad. Tex. A. and M. U., 1970-71, N. Tex. State U., 1973—; m. Robert F. Wasson, May 5, 1944 (div. May 1969); children—Robert F., Jean A. (dec.). Exhibited one man shows Witte Mus., San Antonio, 1965, Bright Shawl Gallery, San Antonio, 1966, Little Theater, Midland, Tex., 1963, McNamarra-O'Connor Mus., Victoria, Tex., 1967, A. and I. U., Kingsville, Tex., 1966; represented by Nye Gallery, Dallas; tchr. art W.B. Ray High Sch., Corpus Christi, Tex., 1967-73. Master judge Nat. Council State Garden Clubs. Mem. Friends of Corpus Christi Mus., Corpus Christi Art Found.; bd. dirs. Art Mus. of S. Tex., Corpus Christi, 1960-63. Alice G.K. Kleberg grantee, 1969. Mem. Am. Malacol. Union, Tex. Tchrs. Assn., D.A.R., Colonial Dames VII Century, Coastal Bend Shell Club (hon. life), Paisano Garden Club, Lantana Garden Club, Tex. Watercolor Soc., Collectors Inst. Tex., Big Thicket Assn., Zeta Tau Alpha. Episcopalian. Author: Sea Shells of the Texas Coast, 1971. Home: 241 Melrose St Corpus Christi TX 78404

ANDREWS, LUCY GORDON (MRS. CHARLES LAWRENCE ANDREWS), educator; b. Washington, Mar. 27, 1941; d. James Harrison and Gertrude Leona (Yocum) Gordon; B.A., Agnes Scott Coll., 1963; Ph.D. (Nat. Def. Edn. Act fellow), U. Ga., 1967; m. Charles Lawrence Andrews, Aug. 28, 1965; children—Charles Lawrence, Robert Gordon. NSF research asst. U. Ga. Athens, summer 1963, lab. instr., 1965, research asst., 1966-67; prof. biology Brenau Coll., Gainesville, Ga., 1967—; genetic counselor, dept. psychiatry Emory U. Sch. Medicine, Atlanta, 1973—. Mem. Hastings Center Inst. of Soc., Ethics and Life Scis. Vice pres. Hall County unit Am. Cancer Soc., 1973. Nat. Endowment for Humanities grantee, 1973-74. Mem. Nat. Acad. Scis., Canadian Soc. Plant Physiologists, A.A.A.S., Bot. Soc. Am., Assn. Southeastern Biologists, Am. Inst. Biol. Scis., Am. Soc. Human Genetics, Am. Assn. U. Women. Presbyn. Home: 621 Crestview Terrace Gainesville GA 30501

ANDREWS, LYDIA CLEMENTINE WADE SWANSON, ednl. adminstr.; b. Hanson, Mass., Sept. 2, 1901; d. Arthur Clifford and Clementine Guigon Brooks (Ellis) Wade; grad. Tchrs. Coll., Salem, Mass., 1922, grad. Lyndon State Tchrs. Coll., Vt., 1936, B.Ed., 1943; postgrad. (scholar) Oxford (Eng.) U., 1951; m. Charles Axel Swanson, Oct. 24, 1925; 1 son, Levi William; m. 2d, Norman John Andrews, June 30, 1962. Asst. prin. elementary sch., Lynn, Mass., 1922-23; rural tchr., Harrisville, N.Y., 1927; tchr., prin. elementary schs. Northeastern Vt., 1924-62; prin. Ginette Roy Sch., Dixville, Que., Can., 1962-74; librarian Dixville Home, also staff tchr. edn. anatomy, 1962-74. Selectman, auditor, mem. sch. bd., moderator town meeting, justice of peace, Norton, Vt. Mem. Nat., Vt. ret. tchrs. assns., D.A.R., Anglican Ch. Women. Mem. Order Eastern Star. Home: Swanson Oldfarm Norton VT 05907

ANDREWS, MARGARET E., educator; b. Mpls.; d. James and Eugenia (Goff) Andrews; B.S., M.A., U. Minn.; Ed.D., U. Colo., 1954; fellowship Stanford U., 1940-41, U. Colo., 1953-54; postgrad. N.Y.U., 1949. Tchr. high sch., Buffalo, Minn., 1931-34; exec. sec. to v.p. Northwestern Nat. Bank, Mpls., 1934-36; instr. terminal bus. Virginia (Minn.) Jr. Coll., 1936-37; tchr. high sch., Mpls., 1937-40; coordinator Mpls. Vocational High Sch., 1941-42; social worker Mpls. Pub. Schs., 1942-43; cons. bus. edn. and placement, 1943-69; prof. edn. Coll. St. Catherine, St. Paul, 1969—; prof. U. N.D., summer 1965, U. Ill., summer 1955. Specialist U.S. Office of Edn., Washington, 1958. Mem. Gov.'s Commns. on Status of Women, Youth and Juvenile Delinquency, Mayor's Com. on Fair Employment Practices in Mpls., Pres.'s Com on Young Workers. Bd. dirs. Hennepin County div. Am. Cancer Soc., 1967-69, St. Croix Valley Council Girl Scouts U.S., 1974—. Mem. Nat. Secs. Assn. (hon.), Adminstrv. Mgmt. Soc. (hon.), Am. Assn. U. Women (past dir. Mpls. br.), Am. Personnel and Guidance Assn. (emeritus), Nat. Vocational Guidance Assn. (past. sec.), Am. Sch. Counselors Assn., Am. Vocational Assn. (v.p. 1957-58), Nat. Assn. Suprs. Bus. Edn. (hon.; past sec.-treas.), North Central Bus. Edn. Assn. (past v.p.), Minn. Edn. Assn., Minn. Bus. Edn. Assn., Minn. Coordinators Assn., Minn. Vocational Assn., Minn. Psychol. Assn., Twin City Vocational Guidance Assn. (pres. 1945-46, dir. 1943-65), Delta Pi Epsilon, Pi Lambda Theta. Club: Zonta. Author: Opportunity Knocks Series, 1968; (with D. Mulkerne) Civil Service Tests for Typists, 1969. Cons. editor Office Job Tng. Program, McGraw Hill Book Co., 1972; past mem. editorial bd. Vocational Guidance Quar., Am. Vocational Jour. Home: 7220 Monardo Lane Minneapolis MN 55435 Office: Coll of St Catherine St Paul MN 55116

ANDREWS, MARGARET SUSANNA, lawyer, state librarian; b. Pine Island, Minn., Apr. 28, 1901; d. Jacob A. and Mary Alice (Finn) Bringgold; LL.B., U. Minn., 1926; m. Raymond C. Andrews, June 30, 1927; children—Mary Ellen (Mrs. Robert Anderson), Susan Margaret, Charles Bringgold. Admitted to Minn. bar, 1926; asst. clk. judiciary com. Minn. Ho. of Reps., 1927; office mgr. Chgo. Country Coop. Assn., Lindstrom, Minn., 1938-52; gov.'s legislative clk., 1953; law librarian State of Minn., 1953—. Sec. Minn. Rep. Com., 1946-53, dir. speaker's bur. state and nat. campaigns, 1952. Parliamentarian Minn. Hosp. Aux., 6 yrs., Mpls.-St. Paul Archdiocesan Council Cath. Women. Mem. St. Paul Bus. and Profl. Woman's Club, Minn. Congress Parents and Tchrs. (state parliamentarian 8 yrs., chmn. state office procedure), Am. Assn. Law Libraries, Am. Legion Aux. (state conv. parliamentarian 10 yrs.). Home: Lindstrom MN 55045 Office: State Capitol St Paul MN 55101

ANDREWS, MARION, artist; b. Norton, Mass.; d. George Emory and Ora (Greene) Andrews; grad. Worcester Art Mus. Sch., 1933; B.S., Mass. Coll. Art, 1935; student Yale, summer 1952; m. Herman Lopez, Sept. 16, 1942 (annullment 1954). With art dept. L.G. Balfour Co., Attleboro, Mass., 1936-42; one man show Pen and Brush Club; exhibited in group shows Nat. Acad. Galleries, Lever House Gallery, Salmagundi Club Gallery, Attleboro Art Mus., travel exhbns. fgn., U.S.; represented in permanent collections USN Combat Art Collection, Washington Navy Yard; freelance calligraphy, 1942—; sec., dir. Ora A. Andrews Ins. Agy., Inc., Norton, Mass., 1966-70. Bd. dirs. All Woman Transcontinental Air Race, Inc., 1964—. Mem. Ninety-Nines (sect. gov. 1960-62), Nat. Assn. Women Artists, Am. Artists Profl. League, Art League L.I., NACAL, Aircraft Owners and Pilots Assn., Nat. Pilots Assn., Knickerbocker Artists. Clubs: Pen and Brush, National Arts, Salmagundi, Jackson Heights Art (v.p. 1970—). Home: 162-11 9th Av Whitestone NY 11357

ANDREWS, MARY LUCILLE (MRS. JAMES MURREL ANDREWS), educator; b. Cleve., Oct. 4, 1927; d. John Robert Louis and Margaret Louise (Busser) Colberg; A.B. magna cum laude, Western Coll., 1949; M.S., Mich. State U., 1950, postgrad., 1949-51; m. James Murrel Andrews, July 31, 1954; children—Paul Thomas, Margaret Patricia. Grad. asst. Mich. State U., 1949-51; research asst. Willow Run Research Center, U. Mich., Ypsilanti, 1951-52; instr. Ohio U., Athens, 1952-54; substitute tchr. Chatham Coll., Pitts., 1954; lectr. math. Cleve. State U. (formerly Fenn Coll.), 1957—. Pres. Euclid (O.) Citizens for Basic Edn., 1962; mem. Euclid Sch. Bd. com., 1962, also active sch. bd. campaigns; mem. Euclid Drug Com., 1971. Bd. mgrs. Euclid YWCA, mem. pub. affairs com., 1969-73, vol. swimming instr. for retarded, 1970-72. Mem. Am. Math. Assn., Sigma Xi, Pi Mu Epsilon. Republican. Roman Catholic. Club: Holy Cross Married Couples (Euclid). Home: 20171 Ardwell Dr Euclid OH 44123 Office: Cleveland State University Cleveland OH 44115

ANDREWS, MINNA FEINBERG (MRS. NATHAN ANDREWS), artist; b. N.Y.C.; d. Joseph and Bessie (Atkin) Feinberg; student Parson's Sch. Design; grad. Pratt Inst. Fine Arts, 1920; studied with George Elmer Brown, Joseph Newman, Alex Redein, Umberto Romano; m. Nathan Andrews, July 3, 1952. Partner, Twins Advt. Art Service, N.Y.C., 1923—; one-man shows Town House Gallery, Woodstock, N.Y., 1952, Charles Barzansky Galleries, N.Y.C., 1957; exhibited in group shows Ward Eggeleston Galleries, 1953, 54, 55, Nat. Acad. Design, N.Y.C., 1957—, Tokyo (Japan) Municipal Art Mus., 1960, Riverside Mus., N.Y.C., 1960, Royal Acad. Galleries, Edinburgh, Scotland, 1963, Royal Soc. Birmingham Eng. Galleries, 1964, Nat. Acad. Design Annual, 1963, Allied Artists Annuals, 1961-63, Palazzo Vecchio, Naples at the Salvator Rosa in the Pub. Gardens, 1972, Norfolk (Va.) Mus. Arts and Scis., Lever House, N.Y.C., 1965, 67, 68, 72; represented in permanent collections at Rose Art Mus., Brandeis U., Waltham, Mass., Yeshiva U., N.Y.C., Norfolk Mus. Arts and Scis. (Va.). Mem. Nat. Assn. Women Artists, Artists Equity, Assn. N.Y., Woodstbck Artists Assn. Home: 239 E 79th St New York City NY 10021

ANDREWS, NANCY CURRIER, actress; b. Mpls.; d. James Currier and Grace (Gerrish) Andrews; student Pasadena Playhouse; m. Parke N. Bossart, Nov. 5, 1945 (div. Aug. 1952); 1 dau., Cynthia. Appearances in Broadway musicals, including Touch and Go., 1949, Hazel Flagg, 1954, Plain & Fancy, 1955, Pipe Dream, 1956, Juno, 1959, Christine, 1960, Little Me, 1962-64, Funny Girl, 1966, 70 Girls, 70, Two By Two, 1971; appearance in off-broadway prodns., including Three-penny Opera, 1959-61, Madame Aphrodite, 1961, The Cradle Will Rock, 1964, Say Nothing, 1965; performances in Manhattan at Bon Soir, Blue Angel, London at Embassy Club, Colony, 1954-56, Dublin Internat. Theatre Festival in In the Summer House, 1969; How Much, How Much?, 1970; appeared in TV series Bewitched, As the World Turns; films Summer Wishes, Winter Dreams, 1972, W.W. and The Dixie Dance Kings, 1974; recs. include (albums) Jerome Kern Revisited, 1967, Noel Coward Revisited, 1969, Harold Arlen Revisited, 1971. Apt. house chmn. UNICEF. Bd. dirs. Vets. Hosp. Radio and TV Guild. Recipient Theatre World award for performance in Touch and Go, 1949, Israel Bond award, 1963. Mem. Nat. Acad. Television Arts and Scis. (events com.), A.F.T.R.A. (membership com.). Home: 302 W 12th St New York City NY 10014

ANDREWS, NAOMI FINE, broadcasting co. exec.; b. N.Y.C., Mar. 31, 1925; d. Charles and Mary B. (Frankfort) Fine; A.B., Hunter Coll., 1945; postgrad. Columbia Sch. Spl. Studies. With CBS, N.Y.C., 1948—, successively sec., copywriter, copy chief, now dir. advt. operations. Advt. coordinator various polit. campaigns. Recipient award of excellence Communications Arts Mag., 1970; certificate of honor Copy Club N.Y. Mem. N.A.D. Democrat. Jewish religion. Editorial contbr. Madison Av. Mag., 1967. Home: 6 E 65th St New York City NY 10021 Office: 51 W 52d St New York City NY 10019

ANDREWS, SYBIL (MORGAN), painter; b. Bury St. Edmund's, Eng., Apr. 19, 1898; ed. Heatherley Sch. Fine Arts, London, Eng.; pupil Boris Heroys. Works exhibited 200 Years Brit. Graphic Art, Prague, Bucharest and Vienna, 1936, Buenos Aires, 1954, also in U.S., Can., South Africa, Australia, China; represented collections Victoria and Albert Museum, London, Leeds (Eng.) Mus., Dublin (Ireland) Mus., Los Angeles Mus. Art, Mass. Soc. Art, Nat. Gallery, South Australia. Mem. Canadian Soc. Painter-Etchers and Engravers. Address: 2131 South Island Hwy Willow Point Campbell River BC Canada

ANDREWS, THEODORA ANNE, educator; b. Carroll County, Ind., Oct. 14, 1921; d. Harry Floyd and Margaret Grace (Walter) Ulrey; B.S. with distinction, Purdue U., 1953; M.S. (Univ. fellow), U. Ill., 1955, certificate as medical librarian, 1958; m. Robert William Andrews, July 18, 1940 (div. May 1946); 1 son, Martin Harry. Asst. reference librarian Purdue U., W. Lafayette, Ind., 1955-56, instr., pharmacy librarian, 1956-60, asst. prof., pharmacy librarian, 1960-65, pharmacy librarian, asso. prof. library sci., 1965-71, prof., pharmacy librarian, 1971—. Vis. lectr. Syracuse (N.Y.) U., 1958, 59, 61, 63, 65, U. Ill., 1960, 62, 71, Ind. State U., 1967-69. Bd. dirs. Purdue Womens Caucus, 1973—. Recipient John H. Moriarty award for distinguished librarianship Ind. chpt. Spl. Libraries Assn., 1972. Mem. Med. Library Assn. (chmn. pharmacy group 1960-61), Am. Assn. U. Profs., Am. Assn. Colls. of Pharmacy, Spl. Libraries Assn. (dir. 1966-69, pres. Ind. chpt. 1962-63), Delta Rho Kappa, Kappa Delta Pi. Baptist. Author: World List of Pharmacy Periodicals, 1963. Editor: Ind. Slant, 1969—. Home: 2209 Indian Trails Dr West Lafayette IN 47906

ANDRIASCHUK, SOPHIE MARY, anesthesiologist; b. Vegreville, Alta., Can., May 7, 1940; d. Korneli and Mary (Mudrak) Andriaschuk; B.S., U. Alta, 1961, M.D., 1965. Intern, St. Michaels Hosp., Toronto, Ont., Can., 1965-66; resident Toronto Gen. Hosp., 1966-70; practice medicine specializing in anesthesiology, Vancouver, B.C., Can., 1970—; mem. staff Royal Columbian Hosp., New Westminster, B.C., 1971—; tchr. Royal Columbian Hosp., New Westminster, B.C., 1971—. Fellow Royal Coll. Physicians and

Surgeons Can.; mem. Acad. Medicine Toronto. Club: Vancouver Lawn Tennis and Badminton. Home: No 1104 2370 W 2d Av Vancouver BC Canada Office: 6325 Fraser St Vancouver BC Canada

ANDRIOLA, MARY TERESA (MRS. MICHAEL JOHN ANDRIOLA), physician; b. N.Y.C., Sept. 13, 1942; d. Anthony Frances and Florence Elizabeth (Elliott) Repole; A.B., Johns Hopkins, 1962; M.D., Duke, 1965; m. Michael John Andriola, July 21, 1962; children—Margaret Mary, Joseph Anthony, James Michael. Intern pediatrics Duke Hosp., 1965-66; resident pediatrics U. Fla. Hosp., 1966-67, resident neurology, 1967-70; practice medicine specializing in pediatric neurology; asst. prof. neurology and pediatrics La. State U. Sch. Medicine, 1970-72; clin. asst. prof. pediatrics U. South Fla., Tampa; clin. instr. medicine in neurology U. Fla., Gainesville. Mem. Am. Women's Med. Assn., Am. Acad. Neurology, Am. Acad. Pediatrics, Am. Epilepsy Soc., So. EEG Soc., Fla. Pediatrics Soc., Fla. Med. Assn., Pinellas County Med. Soc. Home: 1320 Indian Rocks Rd Clearwater FL 33516 Office: 1011 Jeffords Clearwater FL 33516

ANDRULIS, MARILYN WANG, physicist, research co. exec.; b. Fort Monmouth, N.J., Sept. 6, 1940; d. Theodore Joseph and Rebecca (Snyder) Wang; B.S. in Theoretical Math., U. Mich., 1962; M.S., U. Ill., 1964; Ph.D. in Mech. Engring., U. Tex. at Austin, 1968; m. Peter Joseph Andrulis, Jr., Jan. 25, 1964; children—Peter J. III, Erik David. Sr. cons. B-K Dynamics, Inc., Rockville, Md., 1969-71; staff cons. Tracor, Rockville, 1971-72; exec. v.p. Andrulis Research Corp., Bethesda, Md., 1971—; dir. Mid-Atlantic Research Inst., Bethesda, 1973—. Research asso. Cath. U. Am., 1972-73. R.C. Baker fellow U. Tex. Mem. Acoustical Soc. Am., Inst. Noise Control and Engring. (asso.), Mortar Board, Delta Gamma. Editor: (with others) Topics in Ocean Acoustics. Office: 7315 Wisconsin Av Bethesda MD 20014

ANDRUS, VERA, painter, lithographer, writer; b. Plymouth, Wis.; ed. U. Minn., Mpls. Inst. Art; student Boardman Robinson, George Grosz. Exhibited one-man shows at Smithsonian Instn., Concord (Mass.) Art Mus., U. Me., Am. Mus. Nat. History, Rockport (Mass.) Art Assn., Gulf Coast Art Center, Clearwater, Fla., Carlisle Gallery; exhibited in group shows at Carnegie Inst., Boston Art Festival, 1959, Art Inst. Chgo., N.Y. World's Fair, Am. Fortnight, Hong Kong, others; represented in permanent collections Met. Mus. Art, N.Y.C., Library of Congress, Washington, Mpls. Inst. Art, Smithsonian Instn., Boston Mus. Fine Art, Boston Pub. Library, U. Minn., U. Me. Recipient prize Mpls. Inst. Art, 1928, Albert H. Wiggins Meml. prize, Boston Printmakers prizes Hudson Valley Art Assn., 1941, 43, 44, Honor medal Nat. Assn. Women Artists, 1941, numerous others. Mem. Nat. League Am. Pen Women, Rockport Art Assn. Author, illustrator: Sea-Bird Island, 1939; Sea Dust, 1955; Black River: a Wisconsin Story, 1967. Address: 6 Pleasant St Rockport MA 01966

ANGELO, PRISCILLA JENNIFER, educator; b. Schenectady, Apr. 29, 1943; d. Anthony D. and Filamena M. (Napolitana) Angelo; student U. Vienna (Austria), 1964; B.S. cum laude, State U. N.Y. at Oswego, 1965; postgrad. U. Rochester, 1966; M.S., Ind. U., 1968. Tchr. high sch., Schenectady, 1965-67; asst. dean of student St. Lawrence U., Canton, N.Y., 1968-71, acting dean of students, summer 1971, asso. dir. student services, 1971—; instr. geography Mater Dei Coll., Ogdensburg, N.Y., 1969—; vis. dir. student services Chapman Coll., World Campus Afloat, 1974. Mem. Commn. on Higher Edn. Middle States Accreditation Team, 1973; mem. Coop. Edn. Inst., Tampa, Fla., 1973; participant Challenge: Women in Higher Edn. Workshop, U. Tenn., 1972. Mem. Am. Assn. U. Women, Am. Coll. Personnel Assn., Am. Personnel and Guidance Assn., Nat. Assn. Women Deans and Counselors, Sex Information and Edn. Council U.S., Nat. Assn. Student Personnel Adminstrs., Nat. Center for Innovative Higher Edn., Nat. Orgn. Women, St. Lawrence U. County Hist. Assn. (mem. adv. bd. 1973—, chmn. county citizens fund raising for historic house museum 1973-74), Mortar Bd., Kappa Delta Pi, Pi Gamma Nu, Pi Lambda Theta. Home: RD 4 Pierrepont Rd Canton NY 13617

ANGRIST, SHIRLEY SARAH (MRS. STANLEY W. ANGRIST), educator; b. Montreal, Ont., Can., Dec. 15, 1933; d. William and Pauline (Zlatis) Bloomstone; B.A., McGill U., 1954, M.A., 1955; Ph.D., Ohio State U., 1960; m. Stanley Wolff Angrist, Feb. 6, 1955; children—Joshua, Misha, Ezra. Came to U.S., 1955, naturalized, 1965. Instr. dept. psychiatry Ohio State U., Columbus, 1960-61; asst. prof. psychiatric nursing U. Pitts., 1962-64; asst. prof. bus. and resource mgmt. Carnegie-Mellon U., Pitts., 1964-68; asso. prof. sociology Sch. Urban and Pub. Affairs Carnegie-Mellon U., 1969—. Research affiliate Radcliffe Inst., Cambridge, Mass., 1968-69. Mem. Am. Sociol. Assn., North Central Sociol. Assn., Nat. Council Family Relations. Author (with S. Dinitz, M. Lefton, B. Pasamanick) Women After Treatment, 1968. Author numerous articles in field.

ANGUS, MARGARET SHARP (MRS. WILLIAM ANGUS), author; b. Chinook, Mont., May 23, 1908; d. Ulysses S. Grant and Cora Alodie (Krauss) Sharp; B.A., U. Mont., 1930; LL.D., Queen's U., 1973; m. William Angus, Aug. 28, 1929; children—Barbara (Mrs. Owen B. Morgan), James Grant. Asst. drama Queen's U., Kingston, Ont., Can., 1938-57, dir. radio, 1957-68. Chmn. Civic Centennial Com., 1967; chmn. Civic Com. Archtl. Review, 1970-72; dir. Ont. Hist. Studies Series, 1970—; vice chmn. Ont. Geographic Names Bd., 1971-74. Bd. govs. Kingston (Ont., Can.) Gen. Hosp.; bd. dirs., pres. Frontenac Historic Found. Recipient Alumni award Queen's U., 1968, Heritage Can. travelling award, 1974; named Citizen of Year, Jr. C. of C., 1967. Mem. Canadian Hist. Assn., Archtl. Conservancy Ont., Ont. (pres. 1969-72, Cruikshank Gold Medal), Kingston (pres. 1972-74) hist. socs. Author: The Old Stones of Kingston, 1966, rev. edit., 1970; Kingston General Hospital, 1973; Bellevue House, 1967; Oliver Mowat's Ontario, 1972. Home: 20 Beverley St Kingston ON K7L 3Y4 Canada

ANNAN, GERTRUDE LOUISE, librarian; b. Providence, Dec. 19, 1904; d. Arthur H. and Ada (Allen) Annan; B.A., Brown U., 1925. Cataloger John Carter Brown Library, Providence, 1927-29; head rare book dept. N.Y. Acad. Medicine Library, 1931-52, asso. librarian, 1953-55, librarian, 1956-70, retired. Mem. Med. Library Assn. (pres. 1961-62), Bibliog. Soc. Am., Am. Assn. for State and Local History, N.Y. Hist. Soc., English-Speaking Union, Am. Assn. UN. Author chpt. in Handbook of Library Practice, 1943, 56, editor 3d edit. 1970. Contbr. articles profl. jours. Home: 118 E 91st St New York City NY 10028

ANNESS, KAY KEIGHTLEY (MRS. KEITH WOODSON ANNESS), assn. exec.; b. Harrodsburg, Ky., Nov. 16, 1946; d. William Glenn and Mary Vivian (Martin) Keightley; student U. Ky., 1964-65; m. Keith Woodson Anness, Sept. 18, 1965; 1 son, Adam Kent. Office mgr. Mercer C. of C., Harrodsburg, Ky., 1969—. Mem. Christian Ch. Home: 358 Midland Ct Harrodsburg KY 40330 Office: 208 W Lexington St Harrodsburg KY 40330

ANNICH, VIRGINIA LONG (MRS. RUSSELL W. ANNICH, JR.), lawyer; b. Elizabeth, N.J., Mar. 1, 1942; d. John Vincent and Eleanor Constance (Triana) Long; B.A., Dunbarton Coll., 1963; LL.B., Rutgers U., 1966; postgrad. N.Y. U., 1968-69; m. Russell W. Annich, Jr., May 6, 1967. Law asst. Office Atty. Gen., 1966-67, dep. atty. gen., 1967-72, sect. chief, 1970-72; dep. asst. atty. gen.-appeals, Trenton, N.J., 1972-73; asso. firm Pitney, Hardin & Kipp, Newark, 1973—. Chmn. subcom on evening law schs. Master Plan Com. on Legal Edn., 1973. Mem. Rutgers Law Sch. Alumnae Council, 1971-73. Named Outstanding Young Careerwoman, Bus. and Profl. Woman's Club, 1969. Mem. Am., N.J. (gen. council 1972, trustee young lawyers sect. 1970—), Mercer County (trustee) Essex County bar assns., Dunbarton Coll., Rutgers Law Sch. alumni assns. Home: 152 E Delaware Av Pennington NJ 08524 Office: 570 Broad St Newark NJ 07102

ANNIXTER, JANE (MRS. PAUL ANNIXTER), author; b. Detroit, June 22, 1903; d. Will Levington and Ada Althea (Duffy) Comfort; student pub. schs.; m. Paul Annixter, Feb. 18, 1920. Author: From These Beginnings, 1937; Time Out for Eternity, 1938; The Runner, 1956; Buffalo Chief, 1958; Horns of Plenty, 1960; Peace Comes to Castle Oak, 1961; The Phantom Stallion, 1961; Trouble at Paintrock, 1962; The Great White, 1966; Wagon Scout, 1965; Vikan the Mighty, 1969; Ahmeek, 1970; White Shell Horse, 1971; Sea Otter, 1972; Trumpeter, 1973. Home and office: 2581 Bonita Way Laguna Beach CA 92651

ANSINGH, MARIE, psychiat. social worker, artist; b. Didsbury, Eng.; d. Herman Kimball and Celena (Johnson) Ansingh; B.A., U. Toronto, 1936, B.S.W., 1954; M.S.W., Fla. State U., 1960; postgrad. McGill U., 1953; m. J. Grosheintz-Laval, May 15, 1946 (div. Mar. 1954). Sr. radiotherapist Toronto Gen. Hosp., 1941-46; child welfare worker Fla. Dept. Pub. Welfare, St. Petersburg and Tampa, 1955-59; psychiat. social worker Sunland Tng. Center, Fort Myers, Fla., 1960-67; with Hosp. and Welfare Bd., Tampa, 1962—; chief supr. social service dept. Tampa (Fla.) Gen. Hosp., 1962, psychiat. social work supr., 1962, dir. social service, 1963; lectr. psychiat. social work Gordon Keller Sch. Nursing, 1962—; supr. Specialized Casework Services, 1964—; dir. social service A.G. Holley State Hosp., Lantana, Fla., 1969—; med. social cons. Fla. Crippled Children's Commn., 1967—. Staffed, set up policies and procedures for Halfway House in Alcoholic Rehab., Tampa, Fla.; devised and designed application for fed. funds, Operation Ade, under Office Econ. Opportunity, 1965, project dir. Operation Ade, 1965-66. Exhibited one-man show in mosaics Charles Henry Gallery, St. Petersburg Beach, Fla. Mem. Nat. Assn. Social Workers, Acad. Certified Social Workers, St. Petersburg Mus. Fine Arts, Internat. Platform Assn. Democrat. Anglican. Home: 119 N Palmway Lake Worth FL 33460 Office: AG Holley State Hosp Palm Beach County FL 33460

ANSON, RUTH LESLIE (MRS. RICHARD LAMONT SOWBY), broadcasting exec.; b. Chgo., Oct. 11, 1944; d. Bill Paul and Geraldine Constance (Manus) Anson; B.A., U. Cal. at Los Angeles, 1966; m. Richard Lamont Sowby, Oct. 31, 1970. Staff newscaster, reporter KTTV, 1968, KNJ-TV, 1967; staff reporter KABC-TV, 1964-67, moderator, producer 1964-67, panelist, 1965-67; moderator interview programs Los Angeles County Heart Assn., KCET-TV, KCOP-TV, KTTV-TV, KTLA-TV, 1967; narrator, writer, producer The Singles Industry, KCOP-TV, KABC-TV, Los Angeles, 1967; West Coast corr.-reporter Voice Am. radio broadcasts, U.S.I.A., 1965-68, ABC Radio News, Am. Contemporary Network, 1968; U.S. hostess-writer Nippon-TV Network Corp., Tokyo, Japan, 1969-71; broadcast supr., account exec. Daniel J. Edelman, Inc., 1970-71. Named Cal. Career Girl, Cal. Fedn. Bus. and Profl. Women, 1966. Mem. Am. Women in Radio and Television, Radio and Television News Assn. So. Cal., Nat. Acad. Television Arts and Scis. Home: 1443 Campbell St Glendale CA 91207

ANSTEY, JULIA LAMY (MRS. GEORGE STEPHEN ANSTEY), occupational therapist; b. St. Louis, Apr. 9, 1937; d. Charles Sheehan and Julia (Walsh) Lamy; B.A., Newton Coll., 1959; certificate occupational therapy Washington U., St. Louis, 1962; M.A., St. Louis U., 1972; m. George Stephen Anstey, Dec. 30, 1972. Occupational therapist Bellevue Hosp., N.Y.C., 1962-63, St. John's Mercy Hosp., St. Louis, 1963-65; chief occupational therapist Mo. Bapt. Hosp., St. Louis, 1966-69, Cardinal Glennon Hosp., St. Louis, 1969—. Clin. instr. occupational therapy Washington U., St. Louis, bd. mem. Jr. League of St. Louis, 1967-68, vice chmn. league admissions com., 1975. Mem. Am. (council edn. standards and practice 1969—), Mo. (treas. 1967) occupational therapy assns. Home: 125 N Hanley St St Louis MO 63105 Office: 1465 N Grand Av St Louis MO 63104

ANSTEY, MIRIAM ELIZABETH, coll. adminstr.; b. Cumberland, Ia., July 27, 1927; d. Archibald William and Annice Faye (McGrew) Anstey; B.A., Marycrest Coll., 1954; Mus.M., U. Notre Dame, 1958; M.A., St. Louis U., 1971; Ph.D. (fellow), So. Ill. U., 1974. Music tchr. Davenport, Ia., 1955-58, Mpls., 1959-60, Des Moines, 1961, LeMars (Ia.) High Sch., 1962; tchr. music, counselor, asst. prin. Fort Madison (Ia.) High Sch. 1963-68; tchr. music, counselor Marycrest Coll., Carbondale, Ill., 1969—, v.p., 1970—. Cons. La. Bd. Edn. Mem. Cath. Music Educators Assn. (state treas. 1960-65). Roman Catholic. Home: 1620 W 12th St Davenport IA 52804

ANSTINE, LUCILLE ALBERTA (MRS. CHARLES B. CURRIER), physician; b. Washington, July 6, 1934; d. Clarence LeRoy and Annabelle (Miller) Anstine; B.S. in Chemistry, George Washington U., 1956, M.D., 1960; m. Charles Betram Currier, Apr. 15, 1967; children—Charles Bertram, Anna Lucille, Elizabeth Alberta. Intern Balt. City Hosps., 1960-61; resident in neurology D.C. Gen. Hosp., Washington, 1961-62, VA Hosp., Boston, 1962-64; fellow in rehab. medicine Tufts New Eng. Center, 1965, Boston U., 1966; practice medicine specializing in rehab. medicine, Richmond, Va., 1972—. Mem. New Eng. Soc. Phys. Medicine, Mass. Med. Soc., Am. Acad. Neurology, Mortar Bd., Kappa Delta, Alpha Lambda Delta. 3751 Northampton St NW Washington DC 20015

ANTARAMIAN, ANNA ARLENE, actress, director; b. Kenosha, Wis., Aug. 19, 1947; d. Martin Bedros and Noreen (Semerdjian) Antaramian; B.S., U. Wis., 1969; postgrad. U. Tenn., 1974, N.Y. U., 1974-75. Dir., New Theatre Prodns., Kenosha, also Racine, Wis., 1970-72; choreographer U. Wis., Parkside, also Kenosha, 1970-71; establisher theatre workshop, Kenosha, 1971; actress, Everyman Players, toured U.S. and Germany, 1972-73; female voices Pupples pilot Hare Hollow, 1973. Tchr., Racine, 1969-70, Kenosha, 1971. Recipient Bernard Tallent Forensic award U. Wis., 1967. Mem. Am. Theatre Assn. Armenian Apostolic. Home: 6565 Pershing Blvd Kenosha WI 53140 Office: 65 2d Av Apt 4A New York City NY 10003

ANTE, GLORIA LICUP (MRS. JOSE P. ANTE), physician; b. Manila, P.I.; d. Jose Santos and Sotera (Guevara) Licup; A.A., U. Santo Tomas, 1949, M.D., 1954; m. Jose P. Ante, Nov. 29, 1954; children—Mary Ann, Alexander, Mary Jane, Mary Lynn, William. Intern, Orange (N.J.) Meml. Hosp., 1955, resident, 1956-57; resident Med. Center, Jersey City, 1957-58; house anesthesiologist Margaret Hague Maternity Hosp., Jersey City, 1959-61; asst. prof. anesthesiology Seton Hall Coll. Medicine and Dentistry, Jersey City, 1959-61; anesthesiologist Sta. Teresita Hosp., Legaspi City, P.I., 1961-68; mem. med. staff Dayton (O.) State Hosp., 1969, Western State Hosp., Staunton, Va., 1970-71, Peoria (Ill.) State Hosp., 1972-73, Hazelwood Hosp., Louisville, 1973—, Rollman Psychiat. Inst. (O.), 1974. Home: 4220 Wheeler St Louisville KY 40215

ANTELL, JOAN BARKON (MRS. HERBERT D. ANTELL), editor; b. Bridgeport, Conn., Apr. 15, 1934; d. Paul and Beatrice G. (Gordon) Barkon; B.A., Conn. Coll., 1955; postgrad. Fairfield U., 1971-74; m. Herbert D. Antell, Aug. 13, 1961; children—Andrew Gordon, Pamela Emily, Matthew Eric. Editorial asst. Current History, Phila., 1956-58, asst. editor, 1958—. Club: Connecticut College (chmn. scholarship benefit Fairfield County 1972-73) Editor: (with Carol Thompson, others) Current History Review of 1959, 1960; (with C. Thompson, others) Current History Annual, 1970-72. Home: 12 Greenwood Lane Westport CT 06880 Office: 4225 Main St Philadelphia PA 19127

ANTES, EDNA DWINELL (MRS. CHARLES ANTES), newspaperwoman; b. Hamilton, O., Oct. 17, 1919; d. Harry Gould and Georgianna (Duncil) Dwinell; grad. Butler Bus. Coll., 1938; student Miami U., Oxford, O., 1969-71; m. Charles A. Antes, July 16, 1938; children—Suzanne (Mrs. William Merkle), Ernest. Various secretarial positions, 1945-56; editor Fairfield (O.) Echo, weekly newspaper, 1960-72, news editor, 1972—; corr. Cin. Post and Times-Star, 1964—, also Cin. Enquirer, 1964-74. Chmn. dedication Fairfield City Bldg., 1965, Fairfield Library, 1966; pres. Fairfield Residents Assn., 1968-69; exec. sec. Fairfield Safety Council, 1960-74, pres., 1974—; mem. Fairfield Hosp. Devel. Com., 1974—. Clk., Fairfield Planning Commn., 1966—, Fairfield Park and Recreation Commn., 1973—. Bd. dirs. Butler County unit Am. Cancer Soc., 1965—. Mem. Women in Communications, Ohio Newspaper Women, Order Eastern Star. Author: Today in Michigan History, 1960; Day by Day in Illinois, 1961; composer Fair Fairfield, adopted as city ofcl. song, 1966. Home: 270 Cole Dr Fairfield OH 45014 Office: 564 Riegert Sq Fairfield OH 45014

ANTHIS, PATRICIA WEAVER (MRS. BILL CLINTON ANTHIS), psychologist; b. Rockville, Ind., Dec. 22, 1930; d. Paul Commons and Ruth Mayme (Goddard) Weaver; R.N., Ind. State U., 1952, B.S., 1965; M.S., St. Francis Coll., 1966; m. Bill Clinton Anthis, May 23, 1952; 1 son, Clinton Weaver. Nurse, R.N. Gibson Gen. Hosp., Princeton, Ind., 1952-58; instr. St. Joseph's Hosp. Sch. Nursing, Ft. Wayne, Ind., 1959-66; sch. psychometrist Ft. Wayne Community Schs., 1966—; pvt. practice psychology, Ft. Wayne, 1966—. Instr. St. Francis (Ind.) Coll., part-time 1966-72. Bd. dirs. League for Blind, Ft. Wayne, 1959-65, sec., 1964-65. Mem. Laubach Soc., Assn. for Childhood Edn., Ft. Wayne Adminstrv. Assn., Internat. Reading Assn., N.E.A., Nat. Assn. Sch. Psychologists, Ft. Wayne Psychologists Assn., Tri Kappa (sec. 1957-58), Delta Kappa Gamma (sec. 1972-73). Mem. Order Eastern Star. Home: 3939 Evergreen Lane Fort Wayne IN 46805 Office: 1230 S Clinton St Fort Wayne IN 46802

ANTHONY, CATHERINE WILSON (MRS. EUGENE H. ANTHONY), physician; b. Grenada, Miss., Nov. 11, 1921; d. Joseph L. and Margaret (Good) Wilson; B.A., Colo. Coll., 1943, postgrad. 1945-46; M.D., U. Colo., 1950; m. Eugene H. Anthony, Nov. 28, 1947; children—Paul B., Margaret K. Intern, Presbyn. Hosp., Denver, 1950-51, resident in pathology, 1951-53, staff pathologist 1955-61; resident St. Lukes Hosp., 1953-54, Childrens Hosp., 1954-55; chief lab. service VA Hosp., Denver, 1961—, chmn. infection control com., 1964-72; asst. prof. pathology U. Colo. Med. Sch., 1961—. Mem. Mayor's Citizen Budget Com., Denver, mem. Denver Pres.'s Council of Women's, Service Orgn., 1964—, treas., 1969-70. Mem. bd. Kidney Found Aux. Rocky Mountain Region, 1967—, sec., 1969, 2d v.p., 1970, 1st v.p., 1971, pres., 1972-73, mem. exec. bd., 1971—. Fellow Coll. Am. Pathologists, Am. Soc. Clin. Pathologists; mem. A.M.A., Am. Med. Women's Assn. (dir. jr. membership 1966-69, councilor research, edn. and tng. 1970-72, 2d v.p., 1972, 1st v.p. 1973—, pres. Colo. br. 1965, dir. 1952—), Am. Soc. Cytology, Colo., Denver med. socs., Colo. Soc. Clin. Pathologists, Electron Microscopy Soc. Am., Soroptimist Internat. Assn. (chmn. regional com. 1964-66, pres. Denver 1964-65, dir. Rocky Mountain region 1970-72, sec. 1972—; fellowship award 1968-70, 74), Colo. State Soc. Med. Technologists (hon.), Med. Women's Internat. Assn., Assn. Fed. Profl. and Adminstrv. Women (vice coordinator fed. women's program 1973-74), Federally Employed Women. Club: Les Femmes Sonar Toast-Mistress (charter pres.). Contbr. articles to tech. jours. Home: 3040 S High St Denver CO 80210 Office: VA Hosp 1055 Clermont St Denver CO 80220

ANTHONY, MARGERY STUART, educator; b. N.Y.C., Feb. 23, 1924; d. Harold Elmer and Margaret (Feldt) Anthony; B.A., U. Mich., 1945, M.A., 1946, Ph.D., 1949. Mem. faculty Cal. State U. at Chico, 1949—, asst. prof., 1949-56, asso. prof., 1956-62, prof. biology, 1962—; vis. lectr. NSF-AEC Summer Inst. in Radiol. Biology U. Wyo., 1958-62. Harvard NSF-AEC Summer Inst. in Radiol. Biology fellow, 1957; Oak Ridge NSF-AEC Summer Inst. in Radiol. Biology fellow, 1964. Fellow A.A.A.S.; mem. Ecol. Soc. Am., Health Physics Soc., Am. Inst. Biol. Sci. Home: 5200 Country Club Dr Paradise CA 95969

ANTOINE, SISTER MARY JOSEPH, hosp. adminstr.; b. Mallow, Ireland, Oct. 27, 1917; d. Stephen and Elizabeth (O'Callaghan) Moylan; came to U.S., 1935, naturalized, 1943; R.N., St. Joseph's Hosp. Sch. Nursing, 1940; B.S., Cath. U. Am., 1946. Adminstr., Our Lady of Hosp., Pensacola, Fla., 1958-62, Mt. Alvernia Hosp., Mallow, Irish Republic, 1962-70, St. Anthony Hosp., Pendleton, Ore., 1970—, also trustee. Bd. dirs. Umatilla br. A.R.C. Mem. Ore. Hosp. Assn. (edni. com. 1972), Cath. Hosp. Assn. Ore. (pres. 1973). Address: 1606 SE Court Pl Pendleton OR 97801

ANTON, ANASTASIA (MRS. GEORGE T. ANTON), librarian; b. Ft. Dodge, Ia., Apr. 20, 1928; d. Gust N. and Maria (Brotsos) Pappas; B.A., State U. Ia., 1950; M.A., U. Minn., 1957; m. George T. Anton, Sept. 16, 1961; children—Tom G., Blair. With Ft. Dodge (Ia.) Library, 1951-57; adminstr. library Robbinsdale (Minn.) High Sch., 1957-61; reference librarian Evanston (Ill.) Pub. Library, 1962; with Winnetka (Ill.) Pub. Library, 1969—, reference and acquisitions librarian, 1974—. Mem. Ill. Library Assn. Club: Winnetka (Ill.) Women's (mem. finance bd. 1971-74). Reviewer, Babbling Bookworm Newsletter, 1972—. Home: 290 Poplar St Winnetka IL 60093 Office: Winnetka Public Library Winnetka IL 60093

ANTON, BARBARA MILLER (MRS. ALBERT ANTON), jewelry designer; b. Pocona Pines, Pa.; d. Walter B. and Emma (Hess) Miller; grad. Gemological Inst. Am., 1964; student various artists; m. Albert Anton, June 23, 1949. Jewelry exhibited in Amsterdam, Holland, Phila. Mus. Art, Boston Mus. Fine Arts; designer jewelry collection Pakistan Pavillion, N.Y. World's Fair, 1964; lectr., 1964—; pres., chmn. bd. Barbara Anton, Inc., Godart, Inc.; pres. Godsong, Ideas Untld. Recipient Diamonds Internat. award, 1963; 3 awards Cultured Pearl Assn. Am. and Japan Ann. Design Competition, 1966, 2 awards, 1967, highest award, 1968, 4 awards, 1967, 1 award, 1970, 71, 72; awards Retail Jewelers Assn., 1970. Mem. A.S.C.A.P. Contbr. articles on gems and jewelry to various publs. Compiler anniversary gemstone list; founder Give Your Girl a Pearl Day, 1967. Home: Box 533 Alpine NJ 07620 Office: 10 Engle St Englewood NJ 07631

ANTONSON, F(LORENCE) GENEVIEVE, educator; b. Port Allegany, Pa., Mar. 22, 1921; d. Oscar L. and Jennie M. (Peterson) Antonson; B.S., Mansfield State Coll., 1942; certificate program in occupational therapy (United Cerebral Palsy scholar) Va. Commonwealth U., 1955; M.S., Fla. State U., 1966, Ph.D., 1969. Supr. occupational therapy Happiness House, Sarasota, Fla., 1958-62; dir. occupational therapy Meml. Hosp., Sarasota, 1963-65; asst. prof.

Tex. Woman's U., Dallas, 1970-72; chmn. occupational therapy dept. Fla. Internat. U., Miami, 1972—. Cons. developmental retardation, 1966—. Recipient Vocational Rehab. traineeship Am. Occupational Therapy Assn., 1965. Mem. Am. Fla. occupational therapy assns., Am., Personnel and Guidance Assn., Nat. Vocational Guidance Assn., Dade County Assn. Retarded Children.

ANTOUN, ANNETTE AGNES, newspaper editor-publisher; b. Franklin, Pa., Mar. 7, 1927; d. Adrien Uriel and Charlotte Mary (McMullen) Adelman; student Allegheny Coll., Meadville, Pa., 1946-47; m. Frederic George Antoun, July 19, 1947; children—Frederic G., Gregory S., Lawrence J., Mark J. (dec.), Laureace A., Scott J., Jonathan M., Lisa A. Founder, 1960, since editor-pub. Paxton Herald, Harrisburg, Pa.; founder, 1973, since owner Graphic Services, advt. and graphics, Harrisburg; co-editor French Creek Patriot, community newspaper, Cochranton, Pa., 1972. Bd. dirs. Tb and Health Soc., 1967—, exec. bd., 1967—, sec., 1972—; mem. communications com. Tri-County United Fund, 1973; rep. dir. Pa. Lung Assn., 1973; exec. bd. Lower Paxton Coalition Community Groups, 1973—; mem. communications bd. Catholic Diocese Harrisburg, 1971—. Bd. dirs. Catholic Social Services, 1971—. Recipient Advocate award Paxton Area Jaycees, 1968, 73; citation Am. Legion Pa., 1971, Civil Air Patrol, 1972, medallion Am. Legion Pa., 1972; also numerous pub. service awards. Club: Pleasant Hills Community. Home: 4910 Earl Dr Harrisburg PA 17112 Office: 101 Lincoln St Harrisburg PA 17112

ANTOUN, SISTER M. LAWREACE, coll. pres.; b. Meadville, Pa., Dec. 30, 1927; d. George K. and Freda (Habib) Antoun; B.S. Villa Maria Coll., 1954; M.S., Notre Dame U., 1959, Ph.D., 1965. Instr. chemistry Villa Maria Coll., Erie, Pa., 1955-61, asst. prof. chemistry, 1965-66, pres. 1966—. Mem. Erie County Higher Edn. Com., 1968—, Erie Council on Alcoholism, 1969—, Home Rule Charter Com., Erie Conf. on Community Devel., United Community Services. Bd. incorporators St. Vincent Hosp. Mem. Am. Chem. Soc., Am. Assn. Ind. Coll. and U. Pres., Pa. Assn. Coll. and U., Nat. Cath. Edn. Assn., Sigma Xi. Home: 2551 W Lake Rd Erie PA 16505

ANZINGER, MARGARET ELIZABETH FRAZIER, pub. relations exec.; b. Selma, Ala., July 10, 1923; d. Irl Waitman and Ethel May (Brown) Frazier; B.A., U. Ala., 1945; postgrad. Wayne State U., 1964-65; m. Richard L. Anzinger, May 24, 1952 (div. Jan. 1966); children—Katheryn Ellen, Richard Louis. Soc. editor Martinsville (Va.) Daily Bull., 1945-46; soc. editor Springfield (O.) News-Sun, 1946-49; soc. supr. Toledo Blade, 1949-51; women's copy chief Detroit News, 1951-52; pub. relations dir. United Community Services Met. Detroit, 1953-55; dir. press relations United Found., Detroit, 1966-72; dir. pub. relations Detroit Med. Center, 1972—. Bd. dirs. Big Bros.-Big Sisters Wayne County, 1972-73. Mem. Women in Communications (v.p. Detroit profl. chpt. 1972-73), Pub. Relations Soc. Am., Mich. Heart Assn. (pub. relations com. 1974—), Econ. Club Detroit, Alpha Xi Delta. Republican. Episcopalian. Club: Detroit Press. Home: 588 Rivard Blvd Grosse Pointe MI 48230 Office: Suite 604 3800 Woodward St Detroit MI 48201

APGAR, B. JEAN FRANCIS, research chemist. Research chemist U.S. Plant, Soil and Nutrition Lab., Ithaca, N.Y. Recipient Fed. Woman's award, 1970. Address: US Plant Soil and Nutrition Lav Ithaca NY 14850

APGAR, DOROTHEA TIPPER, journalist; b. N.Y.C.; d. Harry and Grace D. (Mattison) Tipper; student Academie des Arts, Paris, France, Art Students League, Fashion Inst. Tech., Bergen Jr. Coll.; m. Mahlon Apgar (div.); 1 son, Mahlon IV. Mdse. trainee B. Altman & Co., N.Y.C., 1953-54; asst. women's editor, feature writer Ridgewood (N.J.) Herald News, 1954-59; women's editor Evening Jour., fashion editor News-Jour., Wilmington, Del., 1960-65; fashion editor, feature writer Indpls. News, 1965-68; women's editor News Am. (Hearst), Balt., 1968-72, fashion editor, columnist, 1972—; spl. writer Hearst Headline Service, 1972—. Mem. jr. bd. Spence-Chapin Adoption Agy., N.Y.C. Recipient award for women's page feature writing Md.-Del. Press Assn.; 2d pl. award for fashion and news feature story Ind. Press Women. Mem. Women's Nat. Press Club, Nat. Press Women, Washington Press Club, Women in Communications, Sigma Delta Chi. Home: 920 W University Pkwy Baltimore MD 21210 Office: Lombard and South Sts Baltimore MD 21203

APGAR, PEGGY ANN, rehab. counselor; b. Nurenberg, Germany, July 14, 1948; d. Charles Fredrick and Mary Elizabeth (Camp) Apgar; came to U.S., naturalized, 1966; M.A., U. South Fla., Tampa, 1974; m. Ray H. Doyle, Jr., July 14, 1974; children by previous marriage—Michele Elizabeth, Mathew Kim. Paraprofl. counselor and trainer for women U. South Fla., 1972-74, adj. instr. women's studies dept., 1974—; individual practice rehab. counseling, Tampa, 1973—; mem. faculty Fla. Mental Health Inst., Tampa, 1973—; cons. in field. Mem. Nat. Rehab. Assn., Nat. Rehab. Counseling Assn., Nat. Assn. Women Deans, Adminstrs. and Counselors, Omicron Delta Kappa. Research psychology rape and rape rehab. Office: 13301 N 30th St Tampa FL 33612

APGAR, VIRGINIA, physician; b. Westfield, N.J., June 7, 1909; d. Charles Emory and Helen (Clarke) Apgar; A.B., Mt. Holyoke Coll., 1929, Sc.D., 1965; M.D., Columbia, 1933; M.P.H., Johns Hopkins, 1959; Med. Sc.D. (hon.), Woman's Med. Coll., 1964; Sc.D. (hon.), N.J. Coll. Med. and Dentistry, 1967, Boston U., 1969; D.H.L., Russell Sage Coll., 1973. Intern surgery Presbyn. Hosp., N.Y.C., 1933-35; resident anesthesiology U. Wis. and Bellevue Hosp., N.Y.C., 1937; clin. dir. dept. anesthesiology Columbia-Presbyn. Med. Center, 1938-59; prof. anesthesiology Columbia, 1949-59; med. staff The Nat. Found., 1959—, dir. basic research, 1967-68, v.p. for med. affairs, 1968-73, sr. v.p. med. affairs, 1973—; lectr. pediatrics (teratology) Cornell U. Med. Coll., 1965-72, clin. prof. pediatrics (teratology), 1972—; lectr. medicine Johns Hopkins, 1973—. Mem.-at-large Meth. Bd. Health and Welfare, 1964-72; alumnae trustee Mt. Holyoke Coll., 1966-71; mem. spl. com. Institut de la Vie. Recipient Mt. Holyoke Coll. Alumnae award in 1954; Elizabeth Blackwell award, 1960; distinguished service award Am. Soc. Anesthesiology, 1959; Variety Great Heart award, 1967; Westchester Federated Woman's Club award, 1967, Silver Medal award Columbia, 1968; Outstanding Women award Camp Fire Girls, 1971; Children's award Javer Med. Research Fund, 1973; Nelson Rosenthal award, 1973; Ralph M. Waters award anesthesiology, 1973, City of Hope award, 1973. Fellow Am. Coll. Anesthesiology (chmn. bd. govs. 1950-52), N.Y. Acad. Medicine, Am. Coll. of Obstetrics and Gynecology (asso.), Am. Acad. Pediatrics (hon. asso.), N.Y. Acad. Scis., Am. Public Health Assn.; mem. Am. Soc. Human Genetics, The Teratology Soc., Am. Soc. Anesthesiology (treas. 1939-45), Wash. State Soc. Obstetrics and Gynecology (hon.), Alaska Med. Soc. (hon.), Genetic Soc. Am., Pan Am. Med. Assn., Am. Assn. U. Women, Am. Philatelic Soc., Am. Chamber Music Players, Harvey Soc. Catgut Acoustical Soc. (v.p.), A. O. Whipple Surg. Soc., Perinatal Research Soc., Congenital Anomalies Research Soc. Japan, Soc. Alumni Sloane Hosp. for Women, A.A.A.S., Environmental Mutagen Soc., Soc. Study Social Biology, Pediatric Soc. Dominican Republic (hon.), Anesthesiology Colombia, Colombian Soc. Pediatrics (hon.), Diaper Service Accreditation Council, Irish-Am. Pediatric Soc., Research Soc. Japan, Ubiquiteers (treas. 1959), Sigma Delta Epsilon (hon.), Alpha Omega Alpha. Club: 25 Year of Presbyterian Hospital (N.Y.C.); Cosmopolitan. Home: 30 Engle St Tenafly NJ 07670 Office: 1275 Mamaroneck Av White Plains NY 10606

APOSTOL, ALMA ALINGOD (MRS. EMILIO BANIGUED APOSTOL), psychiatrist; b. Manila, Philippines, Aug. 27, 1938; d. Lucio Quinto Alingod and Bella Balabbo Aviles; M.D., U. Santo Tomas, 1961; m. Emilio Banigued Apostol, Jan. 2, 1966; children—Joseph Vincent, Christopher Lucio. Came to U.S., 1966. Jr. resident physician, Isabela, Philippines, 1962-66; intern, Santa Rosa Med. Center, San Antonio, 1967-68; psychiat. resident, 1968-71; practice medicine specializing in psychiatry, St. Louis, 1972, San Antonio, 1972; mem. staff Santa Rosa Med. Center, San Antonio, Malcolm Bliss Mental Health Center, St. Louis. Mem. Hon. Nat. Scholars Philippines, Alamo Womens Med. Assn., Isabella, Philippine med. assn. Home: 12 Chartres Ct Lake St Louis MO 63367 Office: Malcolm Bliss Mental Health Center 1420 Grattan St St Louis MO 63104

APP, MARY PATRICIA, life ins. co. exec.; b. Denver, June 21, 1927; d. Francis Howard and Sarah Patricia (Kelleher) App; student Mt. St. Scholastica Coll., 1945-46; B.A., U. Denver, 1949. Salesman, Daniels & Fisher Stores, 1949-51, fashion coordinator, 1951-54, copywriter, 1951-58, asst. to dir. advt., 1953-58; advt. dir. Robert Wilson & Co., 1958-62; copywriter Capitol Life Ins. Co., Denver, 1962-66, asst. to dir. advt. and pub. relations, 1966—, mgr. publicity and publs., 1966—. Recipient Ad Woman of Year award Advt. Club Denver, 1969; citation Nat. Assn. Newspaper Editors, 1960; 1st pl. award Advt. Fedn. Am., Advt. Assn. West, 1964. Mem. Advt. Club Denver (dir. 1965-68). Club: Denver Women's Press. Roman Catholic. Home: 1250 S University Blvd Denver CO 80210 Office: 1600 Sherman St Denver CO 80201

APPEL, ANTOINETTE RUTH, neuropsychologist, educator; b. N.Y.C., Mar. 31, 1943; d. Leon Solomon and Augusta (Marienberg) Appel; B.A., (NSF grantee), U. Vt., 1964; M.A., Mt. Holyoke Coll., 1965; postgrad. Yeshira U., 1965-66, Hofstra U., 1966; Ph.D. (USPHS fellow, Nat. Inst. Mental Health fellow, univ. fellow), City U. N.Y., 1972. Instr. psychology C.W. Post Coll., Greenvale, N.Y., 1968-69; instr. psychology Queens Coll., Flushing, N.Y., 1970, 71, lectr., 1970-71; fellow neurology Mt. Sinai Sch. Medicine, N.Y.C., 1971-72; instr. ophthalmology, 1972-74; asst. prof. So. Ill. U. Sch. Medicine at Carbondale, 1974—. Corr. sec. FDR Democratic Club, Elmont, N.Y., 1970-71. Mem. internat. exec. com. and bd. dirs. B'nai B'rith Girls, 1960-61; chmn. Governing Bd. University Center, U. Vt., 1963-64. Mem. Am. Women in Sci., Am. Women in Psychology, A.A.A.S., Am., Eastern, Midwestern psychol. assns., N.Y. Acad. Scis. (mem. adv. com. psychology sect. 1973-74), Sigma Xi, Psi Chi. Contbr. articles to profl. jours. Home: Bldg C Park Town Apts Carbondale IL 62901

APPEL, MARGRET ANNEMARIE, psychologist; b. Eschenstruth, West Germany, Apr. 25, 1946; d. Karl Andreas and Elfriede (Ost) Appel; B.A., Dalhousie U., 1967; M.A., U. Denver, 1969, Ph.D., 1971. Asst. prof. dept. psychology Ohio U., Athens, 1971—. Nat. Inst. Mental Health fellow, 1969-71. Mem. Am. Psychol. Assn., Soc. for Research in Child Devel., Soc. for Psyphysiol. Research, Midwestern Psychol. Assn., Psi Chi. Research on infant behavior, psychophysiology, perception. Home: 31-B Lorene Av Athens OH 45701

APPEL, PHYLLIS ACKERMAN (MRS. LEONARD APPEL), psychiatrist; b. N.Y.C., Nov. 7, 1938; d. Jack Harold and Mary (Hyman) Ackerman; B.A., Barnard Coll., 1959; M.D., N.Y. Med. Coll., 1963; m. Leonard Appel, July 18, 1959; children—Amy, Sharon, Nancy, David. Intern, Monmouth Med. Center, 1963-64; clinic physician Lincoln Hosp., N.Y.C., 1964-65; resident psychiatry St. Elizabeths Hosp., Washington, 1965-68; staff cons. psychiatrist Montgomery County Mental Health Dept., 1968-70; practice medicine specializing in psychiatry, Bowie, Md., 1968—. Guest lectr. Prince Georges Community Coll., Largo, Md., 1970—. Grantee Nat. Inst. Mental Health, 1968. Mem. Am. Med. Women's Assn., Am. Psychiat. Assn., Washington Psychiat. Soc., Md. State, Prince Georges County, Belair med. socs., Bus. and Profl. Women's Assn. Home: 12421 Sandal Lane Bowie MD 20715 Office: 3233 Superior Lane Bowie MD 20715

APPELDOORN, HELEN WINIFRED, ret. educator, psychologist; b. Kalamazoo; d. Fred A. and Julia (Hoebeka) Appeldoorn; A.B., Kalamazoo Coll., 1929; M.A., Columbia, 1930; postgrad. Columbia, summer 1940, Wayne U., 1942-46, Ohio State U., summer 1945. Tchr., Kalamazoo and Highland Park, Mich., 1931-42; sch. psychologist, Highland Park, Mich., 1942-46; asst. prof. psychology Ohio State U., 1946-49; dir. spl. edn. Springfield (Ill.) pub. schs., 1949-59; research asso. Inst. for Research on Exceptional Children, U. Ill., 1959-60; exec. dir. South Suburban Pub. Sch. Coop. Assn. Cook County, Ill., 1960-62; dir. spl. edn. N.W. Surburban Spl. Edn. Orgn., Arlington Heights, Illinois, 1962-68, Suburban Low Incidence Devel. Exemplary Services, Park Ridge, Ill., 1968-73. Bd. dirs. Sangamon County Heart Assn.; mem. United Community Services coms., 1953-59. Mem. Internat. Council Exceptional Children (pres. Springfield chpt. 1951-52), Am. Assn. on Mental Deficiency, Ill. Adminstrs. of Spl. Edn. (chmn. 1962-63), Am., Ill. psychol. assns. Club: Soroptomist. Home: 205 S Dryden St Arlington Heights IL 60004 Office: 400 S Western Av Park Ridge IL 60068

APPELL, LOUISE SOPHIA (MRS. MELVILLE J. APPELL), educator; b. Northampton, Mass., Sept. 22, 1930; d. Romeo Edward and Phyllis Theresa (Szynal) Fortier; B.A., Smith Coll., 1951; postgrad. Columbia, 1953-54, U. Akron, 1954-57, U. Louisville, 1965; M.A., U. Ky., 1966, Ph.D., 1972; m. Melville J. Appell, July 26, 1953; children—Melissande, David. Tchr. multiply-handicapped Woods Sch., Langhorne, Pa., 1952; tchr. Nutley (N.J.) Pub. Schs., 1953-54; remedial reading tutor Child Welfare, Akron, O., 1954-59; tchr. homebound handicapped Akron Pub. Schs., 1959; tchr. Bd. Cooperative Ednl. Services, Monroe County, N.Y., 1963-64; instructional materials specialist Spl. Edn. Instructional Materials Center, U. Ky., Lexington, 1967-69; asst. prof. spl. edn., dir. grad. Cath. U. Am. Sch. Edn., Washington, 1969—. Cons. to various pub. sch. workshops, pvt. schs. for handicapped, N.Y. State Research and Rehab. Hosp. Mem. Am. Assn. on Mental Deficiency, Council for Exceptional Children, Kappa Delta Pi. Office: Sch Edn Cath U Am Washington DC 20017

APPERSON, MARJORIE MAY (MRS. ORBELL O. APPERSON JR.), newspaper exec.; b. San Francisco, Apr. 22, 1929; d. John Philip and Jessie Lucille (Earl) Sampson; B.A., Stanford, 1950; m. Orbell O. Apperson Jr., Dec. 24, 1949; children—Virginia, April, John. Co-owner, editor Mount Shasta Herald (Cal.), 1950—, Weed (Cal.) Press, 1970—. Mem. Mount Shasta Planning Commn., 1966-70, chmn. 1969; mem. Overall Econ. Devel. Planning Com. Siskiyou County (Cal.), 1970. Mem. Am. Assn. U. Women. Home: 310 Adams Dr Mount Shasta CA 96067 Office: PO Box 127 Mount Shasta CA 96067

APPERSON, MRS. POLLY MERRILL, phys. therapist, club woman; b. Norwalk, Conn., Apr. 29, 1910; d. Frank Herbert and Clara (Ryder) Merrill; B.S. in Phys. Edn., Arnold Coll., 1930, B.S. in Phys. Therapy, N.Y.U., 1954; m. Van Doren Apperson, June 25, 1938 (dec.). Tchr. phys. edn. Norwalk Jr. High Sch., 1930-38, Norwalk High Sch., 1938-62, 63-64. Phys. therapist N.Y. Hosp.-Cornell Med. Coll., N.Y.C., 1954—, Inst. Phys. Medicine and Rehab., 1962-63, 64-65; phys. therapist Inst. Rehab. Medicine, N.Y.C., summer 1967; child care, instr. in English, An-Lac Orphanage, Saigon, Vietnam, 1967; staff Sivananda Yoga Vedanta Ashram, Paradise Island, Nassau, The Bahamas, 1969, Inst. Rehab. Medicine, N.Y. U. Bellevue Med. Center, N.Y.C., 1970, Silver Hill Found., New Canaan, Ct., 1971; Yoga instr. Broad River Community Club, 1971; therapist out-patient dept. VA, 1972-73. Asst. troop leader Girl Scouts U.S.A., 1926-27, troop capt., 1944-45; life saving examiner A.R.C., Norwalk, 1930-33, active fund drives, 1941-46, first aid instr., 1941-44, 54-57, tchr. sponsor Jr. Red Cross at Norwalk High Sch., 1961-62, also sponsor exchange visit with St. John, N.B., Can. Jr. Red Cross, 1961-62; active fund drive Community Chest, Norwalk, 1932; mem. Norwalk Recreation Commn., 1939-41; mem. adv. com. Norwalk Park Commn., 1941-43; air raid warden Silvermine Sector 1, Norwalk, 1941-45; active fund raising drive Silvermine Vol. Fire Co. 1, 1942-43; bd. dirs., 1943-50; mem. common interest group Preservation Mathews Mansion, 1961-62; mem. subcom. edn. Mid-Fairfield County Com. Alcoholism, 1958-59; mem. New Horizons Club. Recipient certificate for 500 hours service Civil Def., 1945. Mem. Nat., Conn. edn. assns., Norwalk Tchrs. Assn. (chmn. social com. 1951-52), Am., Conn. assns. health, phys. edn. and recreation, Am. Phys. Therapist Assn., Silvermine Community Assn., True World Order, Divine Life Soc., Sivanda Yoga Vedanta Center, N.Y.C., N.Y.U. Alumni Assn., Am. Soc. Dowsers, Nat. Trust for Historic Preservation, Spiritual Frontiers Fellowship, Sivananda Yoga Vedanta Center, Silvermine River Conservation, Am. Soc. for Psychical Research, Nat. Ret. Tchrs. Assn. Baptist (Sunday Sch. tchr. 1930-33, social chmn. Young Peoples United Ch. League, 1931-32). Clubs: N.Y. University Alumni (N.Y.C.); Adventurers (Windsor, Conn.). Home: PO Box 539 New York City NY 10016

APPLBAUM, HELEN (MRS. KARL APPLBAUM), educator, cons; b. N.Y.C., Feb. 14, 1910; d. Nathan and Fanny (Libitz) Siegel; tchrs. certificate Nat. Hebrew Sch., 1930; B.A., Bklyn. Coll., 1938; m. Karl Applbaum, June 9, 1934; children—Elaine Claire (Mrs. David Feldman), Florence Rene (Mrs. Ephraim Laifer), Joseph S. Tchr. various Hebrew instns., 1940-56; mem. staff Queens County Dist. Atty., Flushing, N.Y., 1956—; pres. Goldflo Realty Corp., N.Y.C., 1944-45. Sec., Av. M Jewish Center, Bklyn., 1938-70. Mem. Planning Bd. 8, Queens County, 1970—. Mem. Queens Ladies Club (pres. res. officers assn. 1973-74), Mizrachi Women of Am. (chpt. pres. 1965-68), Assn. of U.S. Army, Womens League, Young Israel of Kew Gardens Hills (v.p. 1968-70), Odd Fellow Ladies Club. Home: 136-80 71st Rd Flushing NY 11367 Office: 125-01 Queens Blvd Kew Gardens NY 11414

APPLEBAUM, SADA ROTHMAN (MRS. SAMUEL APPLEBAUM), writer; b. Lubar, Russia, Jan. 14, 1905; d. Joseph and Rebecca (Ryvitch) Rothman; came to U.S., 1906, naturalized, 1919; m. Samuel Applebaum, Aug. 14, 1927; children—Michael Tree, Lois May (Mrs. Sheldon Leibow). Asst. Am. editor Strad mag., London, Eng., 1937—; free-lance writer, 1937—. Mem. Am. String Tchrs. Assn., Nat. Council Jewish Women, Friends Manhattan Sch. Music, Hadassah (life), Orgn. Rehab. through Tng. Author: (with Samuel Applebaum) With the Artists, 1955; (with Alan Grey Branigan) The Way They Play series, 1973; Poems, 1965. Address: 23 North Terrace Maplewood NJ 07040

APPLEBY, DORIS CHAMBERS (MRS. L. THOMAS APPLEBY), educator, contralto; b. Mpls., July 10, 1930; d. Harry Ivor and Edle Sofia Amalia (Davidson) Chambers; fellow U. Minn., 1949; B.S. (honors grad.), So. Conn. State Coll., 1964; fellow Yale, 1964; M.A. (Danforth fellow for women), U. Md., 1969; Ph.D. candidate, Columbia, 1972—; m. L. Thomas Appleby, June 10, 1950; children—Paul H., Ruth Donna, Karen Chambers. Physics aide U.S. Naval Research Lab., Washington, 1951-52; tchr. math. Troupe Jr. High Sch., New Haven, 1964-65, Hendrick Hudson High Sch., Montrose, N.Y., 1970-72; asst. statistics course Tchrs. Coll., Columbia, 1973—. Contralto Baroque Ensemble, 1972—, Musica Reservata, 1972—. Bd. dirs. Women's Council Interracial Coop., Norfolk, Va., 1953-56, League Women Voters, Hamden, Conn., 1957-61, Neighborhood Music Sch., New Haven, 1958-60. Mem. Assn. for Symbolic Logic, Am. Math. Assn., Nat. Council Tchrs. Math., N.Y. Assn. Math. Tchrs., Am. Ednl. Research Assn., N.E.A., Spl. Interest Group/Research in Math. Edn.. Home: Beach Rd Ossining NY 10562

APPLEGARTH, ANNA REX (MRS. A. RUFUS APPLEGARTH), mfg. co. exec.; b. Norristown, Pa., June 9, 1918; d. John Harvey and Anna Virginia (Schall) Rex; ed. pub. schs., Pierce Bus. Coll.; m. A. Rufus Applegarth, Feb. 23, 1974. Sec. Charles P. Cochrane Co., Phila., 1936-37, The Dill Co., Norristown, 1937-42; sec. to exec. v.p. G. and W.H. Corson, Inc., Plymouth Meeting, Pa., 1942-73, office mgr., 1960-73, asst. sec., 1967-69, sec. of corp., 1969-72; pres. Rexwyn Enterprises, 1973—; sec. Poz-O-Pac Co. of Am., Cordol Corp., Corson Concrete Co., Home-Crete Corp., John Boyd Concrete Service, Inc., 1967-73. Dir. Children's Aid Soc. Montgomery County; active Phila. Mus. Art, Nat. Audubon Soc. Sec. The Corson Found. Mem. Nat. Soc. Colonial Dames of Am., Huguenot Soc., D.A.R., Kappa Sigma Delta. Republican. Lutheran. Clubs: Philadelphia Cricket, Philadelphia Aviation Country; Plymouth Country. Home: La Casita 202 Montgomery Av Coleston PA 19401 Office: G and WH Corson Inc Plymouth Meeting PA 19462

APPLEGATE, JOAN PATRICIA, journalist; b. Bremerton, Wash., Mar. 30, 1947; d. Tracy W. and Patricia E. (Eckroat) Applegate; B.A. in Journalism, U. Wash., 1970. Reporter Spokesman-Rev., Spokane, Wash., 1970—. Mem. Women in Communications, Spokane Editorial Soc., Spokane Press Club, Poor Press Club, Forest Ridge Alumnae. Home: 704 S Adams Spokane WA 99204 Office: 927 W Riverside Spokane WA 99204

APPLEGATE, MARY KEHOE (MRS. GEORGE M. APPLEGATE), research co. exec.; b. Lynn, Mass., Jan. 4, 1918; d. Matthew and Elizabeth (McGovern) Kehoe; certificate bus. adminstrn. Temple U., 1952; m. George M. Applegate, Oct. 2, 1944. Supr. supply cataloging U.S. Marine Corps, Phila., 1951-57; adminstrv. asst. to pres. Aero. Research Asso., Princeton (N.J.), 1958-59, sec.-treas., 1959—, also dir. Mem. Bus. and Profl. Womens Club (treas. 1968-70), Nat. Assn. Accountants (asso. dir. 1970-71). Soroptomist (pres. 1973-74). Home: 347 Dodds Lane Princeton NJ 08540 Office: 50 Washington Rd Princeton NJ 08540

APPLETON, VIOLET ELLEN (MRS. THOMAS EDWARD APPLETON), editor; b. London, Eng., June, 1, 1912; d. Joseph and Ellen (Newman) Cousins; student Pitman's Central Coll., London, 1927-30; m. Thomas Edward Appleton, Sept. 26, 1940; children—Janet (Mrs. W.D. Seabrook), Thomas, Andrew, Peter. Confidential sec. Mut. Finance, London, 1930-35; sec. to mng. dir. Barclay Corsets, London, 1935-37; with Canadian Psychiat. Assn., Ottawa, Ont., Can., 1954—, mng. editor Assn. Jour., 1957—. Mem. Council Biology Editors. Club: Britannia Yacht (Ottawa). Home: 2789 Jamieson St Ottawa ON K2B 6P3 Canada Office: 225 Lisgar St Ottawa ON Canada

APPLEWHITE, MARY ELIZABETH (MRS. JOE CRAWFORD APPLEWHITE), piano tchr.; b. El Paso, Tex., June 28, 1928; d. Robert Emmett and Pearl Hazel (Blackburn) McFadden; student Columbia (Mo.) Coll., 1945-47; Mus.B., Northwestern U., 1949; postgrad. Miss. State U., 1966-67; m. Joe Crawford Applewhite, Sept. 27, 1952; children—Walter Robert, Joe Crawford, James Byron. Tchr.

piano, choral dir. Radford Sch., El Paso, 1949-52; pvt. tchr. piano, Starkville, Miss., 1960-70, Plano, Tex., 1970—. Judge, Nat. Guild Piano Tchrs.; mem. Plano Fine Arts League, 1970—. Del., Republican Nat. Conv., 1968, mem. conv. rules com. 1968; del. Tex. State Rep. Conv., 1972; vice chmn. Collin County Rep. party, 1970. Trustee Plano Ind. Sch. Dist. Mem. Am. Legion Aux., Plano Music Tchrs. Assn., Phi Beta. Baptist. Clubs: Public Affairs Luncheon, Dallas (legislative co-chmn. pub. affairs 1973—); Plano Federated Music (parliamentarian-historian 1973—). Home: Rural Route 2 Box 108E Plano TX 75074

APPLEWHITE, SUE S. SMITH (MRS. JAMES AUBREY APPLEWHITE, JR.), social worker; b. Benson, N.C., Nov. 25, 1925; d. Robert F. and Myrtle (Weeks) Smith; B.A., U. N.C. Woman's Coll., 1946; M.S.W., U. N.C., 1962; m. James Aubrey Applewhite, Jr., Aug. 14, 1948; 1 dau., Jennifer Sue. Case work aide Johnston County (N.C.) Dept. Pub. Welfare, Smithfield, summer 1945, child welfare worker, 1947-48; child welfare worker New Hanover Dept. Pub. Welfare, Wilmington, N.C., 1948-50; child welfare worker Onslow County (N.C.) Dept. Pub. Welfare, Jacksonville, 1950-52, 56-58, social work supt., 1958—. Sec., Onslow County Planning Council on Mental Retardation, 1967—, bd. dirs., 1966—; bd. dirs. N.C. Conf. for Social Service, 1962-68, Onslow County Mental Health Assn., 1966—, Carobell, 1969—; mem. adv. bd, Onslow County Mental Health Dept., 1967—. Recipient N.C. Social Service Employee of Year award, 1973. Mem. N.C. Caseworkers Assn. (pres. 1958-60), Nat. Assn. Social Workers (chpt. sec. 1968-70), Acad. Certified Social Workers, Am. Pub. Welfare Assn., Jacksonville-Camp Lejeune Assn. for Retarded Children, N.C. Social Services Assn. (exec. bd. 1968, pres. 1971). Baptist. Clubs: Jacksonville Country, Onslow County Cotillion. Home: 901 Daniel Dr Jacksonville NC 28540 Office: PO Box 910 Jacksonville NC 28540

APTER, JULIA TUTELMAN (MRS. NATHANIEL S. APTER), physician, educator; b. Phila., Apr. 7, 1918; d. Carl and Anna (Aaronson) Tutelman; B.A., U. Pa., 1939; M.D., Johns Hopkins, 1943; M.S. in Physiology, Northwestern U., 1959; Ph.D. in Math. Biology, U. Chgo., 1964; m. Nathaniel S. Apter, Dec. 13, 1941; children—Marion Hope, Terry Eve. Intern, Balt. City Hosp., 1943; resident U. Chgo. Clinics, 1949-51; instr. ophthalmology Johns Hopkins Med. Sch., 1943-46; dir. neurophysiology research Manteno State Hosp., 1951-57; asst., instr., asso. in ophthalmology Northwestern Med. Sch., 1951-59; trainee math. biology U. Chgo., 1961-64, spl. fellow Nat. Heart Inst., 1965, research asso. math. biology, 1964-66, asso. prof. surgery, 1966; asso. prof. surgery U. Ill., 1966-68, prof. surgery, 1968-71, also dir. math. biology; prof. surgery Rush Med. Coll., 1971—; attending surgeon Presbyn. St. Luke's Hosp., Chgo., 1966—. Chmn. Gordon Research Conf. on Biomath., 1969. Recipient Bothman award for best research Chgo. Ophthalmology Soc., 1952; named hon. citizen Commune Libre de l'Ilot Sacre' Brussels, 1968. Diplomate Am. Bd. Ophthalmology. Fellow Acad. Ophthalmology and Otolaryngology; mem. Am. Med. Women's Assn. (v.p. 1956), Biophys. Soc. (dir. placement service 1970—), Am. Physiol. Soc., A.A.A.S. (nominating com. med. scis.), Soc. Exptl. Biology and Medicine, Soc. for Rheology, Am. Inst. Physics, I.E.E.E. (sr. mem.; chmn. regional council 1971; cons. ednl. activities bd. 1971—, mem. U.S. activities com., chmn. com. on profl. opportunities for women 1971—, chmn. com. on med. engrng. tng. 1971—, mem. pre-coll. guidance com. 1971—; com. environmental quality 1970—; mem. nat. adminstrv. com. of group on engrng. in medicine and biology 1971—, Acad. Mechanics (founding mem. 1970—), Soc. for Engrng. Sci., Soc. for Advanced Med. Systems, Assn. for Advancement Med. Instrumentation, N.Y. Acad. Scis., Ill. Soc. for Prevention Blindness, Chgo. Inst. Medicine, Chgo. Ophthal. Soc., Fedn. for Clin. Research, Phi Beta Kappa, Sigma Xi. Asso. editor Computers in Biology and Medicine. Home: 7316 S Paxton Av Chicago IL 60649 Office: 1753 W Congress Pkwy Chicago IL 60612

ARAI, M(ARY) N(EEDLER), educator; b. Summerside, P.E.I., Can., Sept. 18, 1932; B.Sc., U. N.B., 1952; M.A., (NRC Can. bursary 1952-53; Research Council Ont. scholar 1953-54), U. Toronto, 1956; postgrad. U. London (Eng.), 1954-55; Ph.D. (USPHS trainee), U. Cal. at Los Angeles, 1962. Instr. human physiology Mt. Holyoke Coll, 1956-57; lectr. zoology U. B.C., 1960-61; asst. prof. Ill. State Coll., 1961-62, research asso., 1962-63; sessional instr. U. Calgary (Alta.), 1963-64, spl. instr., research asso., 1964-68, asst. prof., 1969-73, asso. prof., 1973—; vis. instr. U. Ill., 1962, research asso., 1963; vis. asst. prof. Rice U., 1968-69. NRC Can. grantee, 1964—. Mem. A.A.A.S., Am. Soc. Zoology, Canadian Soc. Zoology, Marine Biology Assn. U.K. Address: Dept Biology U Calgary Calgary AB Canada

ARANOW, RUTH LEE HORWITZ (MRS. GEORGE ARANOW, JR.), scientist; b. Bklyn., Aug. 25, 1929; d. David and Tillie Ethel (Wolf) Horwitz; B.A. in Chemistry, Bklyn. Coll., 1951; M.A. in Chemistry Johns Hopkins, 1952, Ph.D. in Chemistry, 1957; m. George Aranow, Jr., June 25, 1950; children—David, Eric, Jeanne. Teaching fellow Johns Hopkins, Balt., 1954-57, research scientist chemistry dept., 1969-72, research scientist dept. geography and environmental engrng., 1972—; staff scientist Research Inst. for Advanced Study Div. Martin-Marietta, Balt., 1957-69. Recipient Martin-Marietta Recognition award, 1964. Gesellschaft Fur Physikalische Biologie grantee, 1965; NIH grantee, 1969-71. Mem. Am. Phys. Soc., Orton Soc., A.A.A.S., Phi Beta Kappa, Sigma Xi. Contbr. articles to sci. jours.

ARATA, DOROTHY ANN, educator; b. N.Y.C., Mar. 8, 1928; d. Charles Anthony and Anna (Mancini) Arata; B.S., Pratt Inst., 1948; M.S., Cornell, 1950; Ph.D., U. Wis., 1956. Research technician Med. Coll., Cornell, 1950-52, postdoctoral researcher dept. biochemistry, 1956-57; asst. prof. nutrition Mich. State U., 1957-60, asso. prof., 1960-65, prof., 1965-69, prof. human devel., 1969—, asso. dir. honors Coll., 1969-71, asst. provost, 1971—; acad. adminstrv. fellow Am. Council Edn., 1968-69, Inst. for Deans, 1973. Mem. adv. com. Am. Council on Edn., 1972—, mem. Commn. ednl. credit, 1974—. Mich. Dept. Labor, 1972—. Mem. Am. Chem. Soc., Mich. Soc. Sci. Arts, and Letters, A.A.A.S., Am. Inst. Nutrition, Am. Assn. Higher Edn., N.Y. Acad. Sci., Am. Inst. Chemists, Sigma Xi, Phi Kappa Phi, Sigma Delta Epsilon. Author articles sci. jours. Research in field chem. aspects nutrition. Home: 2222 Haslett Rd East Lansing MI 48823

ARBAUGH, EVELYN RUTH DAVIDSON (MRS. HENRY W. ARBAUGH), artist; b. Columbus, O., Mar. 28, 1910; d. Charles Clinton and Kathryn (Heath) Davidson; student Columbus Coll. Art and Design, part-time 1938-60; m. Henry Webster Arbaugh, Dec. 25, 1930 (dec.); 1 son, Henry Webster; m. 2d, Theodore Joseph Eisenman. Exhibited group shows at Columbus Gallery Fine Arts, 1953-66, Cin. Art Mus., 1967, Butler Art Inst. Am. Art, 1964, Ohio U., 1959, Smithsonian Inst., 1960, 62, 64, Battelle Meml. Inst., 1967, Dayton Art Mus., Capital U.; traveling show Nat. League Am. Pen Women, 1965, Eastern U.S., 1965. Recipient numerous awards. Mem. Nat. League Am. Pen Women (br. art chmn. 1960, Ohio art chmn. 1961-62), Columbus Art League (art chmn. union exhibit, 1960), Columbus Gallery Fine Arts, Central Ohio Watercolor Soc. Club: Players (art chmn. 1955, 56). Address: 3820 Overdale Dr Columbus OH 43220

ARBUCKLE, DOROTHY FRY (MRS. LLOYD ARBUCKLE), bus. exec., librarian; b. Eldred, Ill., Jan. 23, 1910; d. William George and Sylvia (Mitchell) Fry; student Northwestern U., 1927-28, U. Ill., 1928-30; m. Lloyd Arbuckle, May 13, 1933 (dec. May 1960); children—Kathryn Diane, William Franklin. Free-lance reporter, Ind., Ill., 1931; librarian Lake Village, Ind. Meml. Twp. Library, 1946—; petroleum jobber, distbr. Lake Village Shell Oil Co., 1960—, pres. Arbuckle Oil Co., Inc. Pres., Lake Village Sch. Corp., 1962—; twp. chmn. Multiple Sclerosis, Newton County, Ind., 1962-65, Cancer Soc., 1971—; mem. Heart Assn. Northwest Ind., George Ade Meml. Hosp. Aux., 1968—; nat. oil industry chmn. Laymen's Nat. Bible Com., 1970, asso. chmn. Com., 1971-72; dir. exec. bd. N.W. Ind. Planning Commn. Area Library Services Authority; mem. exec. bd. Newton County Health Planning Commn., 1973—. Bd. dirs. Newton County Hist. Soc. Corp. Mem. Ind., Small library assns., Ill. Woman's Press Assn., Nat. Fedn. Press Women, Midland Authors, Children's Reading Roundtable, D.A.R., A.S.C.A.P., Ind., Ill., Newton County (vice pres., program chmn. 1966—) hist. socs., Grange, Internat. Platform Assn. Presbyn. (elder). Author: The After-Harvest Festival, 1955; Andy's Dan'l Boone Rifle, 1965; anthem: words and music The Church Wherein I Worship, 1955; The Hour Will Come, 1962; ballads: I Never Knew, 1960, By the Kankakee River, 1973. Address: Lake Village IN 46349

ARCARO, ANN GIGANTE (MRS. G.C. ARCARO), social worker; b. N.Y.C.; d. Charles and Tessie (Cristiano) Gigante; B.A., Bklyn. Coll.; postgrad. Hunter Coll., N.Y. U., 1942, St. John's U., 1943; M.S.W., Columbia, 1944; postgrad. Smith Coll. Social Work, 1963; m. G.C. Arcaro, July 1, 1940 (dec. Aug. 1961); 1 son, Gregory David Roger. Various positions in social work, 1940-46; med. and psychiat. social worker Mt. Sinai Hosp., 1960-62; child welfare tng. cons. N.Y. State Dept. Social Service, Albany, 1962-68; adminstrv. supr. Children's Aid Soc., N.Y.C., 1968-69; tng. dir. Rockland County Dept. Social Services, N.Y.C., 1969; instr. Postgrad. Center for Mental Health, N.Y.C., 1969-70, Coll. New Rochelle (N.Y.), 1971-72; asso. prof. Fordham U. Grad. Sch. Social Work, 1970—. Mem. planning bd. Patterson Center, Bronx, N.Y., 1951-55; mem. women's com. Harlem House, N.Y.C., 1952-53. Mem. personnel com. Borough YWCA, 1951-55. Mem. Nat. Assn. Social Workers, Acad. Certified Social Workers, Am. Soc. Tng. Dirs. (com. on community leadership tng. project 1963-68), Am. Pub. Welfare Assn. Author: Six Ethnic Case Studies; Selected Readings for Casework Supervisors in Public Agencies; co-author: An Educational Program for Supervision in Public Welfare. Contbr. papers to profl. jours. Home: 62 Stoneleigh Rd Scarsdale NY 10583 Office: Fordham U Grad Sch Social Work Lincoln Plaza New York City NY

ARCHER, CANDACE ROBERTA (MRS. LANCE HOWARD ARCHER), publs. writer; b. Duluth, Minn., Jan. 4, 1947; d. Leonard Harold and Lillian Ida (Lakela) Olson; B.A. in Communications, Wash. State U., 1969; m. Lance Howard Archer, Aug. 15, 1970. Traffic mgr. sta. KGSC-TV, San Jose, Cal., 1969-70; pub. relations dir. Officers Club, Ft. Riley, Kan., 1970-71; edn. and pub. relations writer Clover Park Sch. Dist., Tacoma, Wash., 1971-72; advt. copywriter Nordstrom, Seattle, 1972-73; pub. relations staff Seattle Opera, 1973-74; publs. writer Am. Plywood Assn., Tacoma, Wash., 1974—. Free lance pub. relations, 1972—; cons. Western Community Bank, Tacoma, 1972. Mem. Nat. Assn. Press Women, Wash. Press Women, Women in Communications (co-chmn. com. 1971-72, co-chmn. new profls. 1973-74), Alpha Omicron Pi. Home: 4545 88th Av SE Mercer Island WA 98040 Office: 1119 A St Tacoma WA 98401

ARCHER, DOLORES ANN (MRS. DONALD EDWARD ARCHER), real estate broker; b. Taft, Cal., Mar. 20, 1929; d. Walter Sherman and Esther Olga (Kolbe) McWhorter; student Santa Monica City Coll.; m. Donald Edward Archer, July 14, 1968; children by previous marriage—Karen (Mrs. Kennith Holliday), Patricia. Profl. fashion model, 1948-54; real estate salesman, 1959-61; broker DK Realty, 1961-68; co-owner Exec. Realtors, Encino, Cal., 1968—; v.p. Exec. Homes, Inc., Encino, 1968—. Home: 4327 Grimes Pl Encino CA 91316 Office: 17043 Ventura Blvd Encino CA 91316

ARCHER, MARGUERITE PAUL (MRS. FRED COLEMAN ARCHER), educator; b. W. Chester, Pa., Jan. 10, 1917; d. Jacques Rene Alexandre and Elinor (Worthington) Hagemans; B.S., W. Chester State Coll., 1938; B.S., St. Cloud State Coll., 1951, M.S., 1956; postgrad. Columbia U., 1957-60; postgrad. N.Y. U., 1958-71; M.L.S., Queens Coll., City U. N.Y., 1967; m. Fred Coleman Archer, Feb. 7, 1943; 1 son, Eric Hagemans. Instr. St. Cloud (Minn.) State Coll., 1953-54; tchr. Prospect Hill Sch., Pelham, N.Y., 1957-58; reading cons., 1958-63; librarian Mamaroneck (N.Y.) Av. Sch., 1963-70; instr. children's services U. Pitts. at Harrisburg Pub. Library, 1971; reading tchr. Central Jr. High Sch., Chambersburg, Pa., 1971-72; asst. prof. library sci. Shippensburg (Pa.) State Coll., 1972—. Cons., Sch. Library Jour., 1964-66; com. mem. Childrens Book Council, 1967-70. Mem. Bd. Health, St. Cloud, 1954-56; sec. Chester County (Pa.) Art Assn., 1939-41; rec. sec. Cumberland Valley (Pa.) Arts Council, 1972—; v.p. N.Y. English Council, 1963-64. Bd. dirs. Minn. Civil Liberties Union, 1953-56, New Rochelle (N.Y.) Art Assn., 1957-60; bd. dirs., publicity chmn. Chambersburg Community Concerts Assn., 1972—. Mem. Nat. Council of Tchrs. of English (dir. 1958-67, pres. adolescent lit. assembly 1973-74), A.L.A., N.E.A., Pa. Library Assn. (vice chmn. S. Central chpt. 1973-74, chmn. 1974-75), Am. Assn. U. Women, Pa. Council Tchrs. English, N.Y. State Congress Parents-Tchrs. (hon.), Nat. Soc. Study Edn., Assn. Ednl. Communications and Tech., Internat. Reading Assn., Council on Elementary Sci. Internat., Assn. Study Afro-Am. Life and History, Cumberland Valley Reading Council, Modern Lang. Assn., Popular Culture Assn., Freedom to Read Found., Am. Assn. U. Profs., Kittochtinny Hist. Soc., Franklin County Heritage Soc., Beta Phi Mu, Delta Kappa Gamma. Episcopalian. Contbr. articles in field to profl. jours. Home: 330 Overhill Dr Chambersburg PA 17201 Office: Box 301 Shippensburg State College Shippensburg PA 17257

ARCHER, MARION FULLER (MRS. LEONARD BENJAMIN ARCHER, JR.), author, librarian; b. Eugene, Ore., Feb. 9, 1917; d. Oscar LeRoy and Erma Grace (Padden) Fuller; B.A. with honors, U. Ore., 1938, postgrad., 1938-39; B.A. in Library Sci., Columbia, 1941; m. Leonard Benjamin Archer, Jr., Feb. 14, 1945; children—Marian (Mrs. Ben Timms), Ruth (Mrs. James Helke), Jane, Benjamin. Catalog librarian Forrest R. Polk Library U. Wis., Oshkosh, 1963-72, asst. dir. Ednl. Materials Center, 1972—; asst. prof. library sci. dept., U. Wis., 1965-73, tchr. writing for children U. Wis. Extension Rhinelander Sch. Arts, 1971—. Author children's books Albert Whitman Co., Chgo., 1963—. Recipient award of Merit, State Hist. Soc. Wis., 1969. Mem. Council for Wis. Writers (award for outstanding juvenile book of year 1968, 72), Nat. Fedn. Am. Press Women (award 1973), Wis. Regional Writers Assn. (dir. 1971-74), Nat. League Am. Pen Women, Wis. Library Assn., Phi Beta Kappa. Author: There is a Happy Land, 1963; Keys for Signe, 1965; Nine Lives of Moses on the Oregon Trail, 1968; Sarah Jane, 1972. Home: 520 Mount Vernon St Oshkosh WI 54901 Office: 800 Algoma Blvd Polk Library Univ Wis Oshkosh WI 54901

ARCHER, MARTHA JANE HELLER (MRS. ROBERT DALE ARCHER), psychologist; b. Cambridge, O., Nov. 30, 1933; d. Ralph Herbert and Edith Sarah (Lemmon) Heller; student Muskingum Coll., 1951-53; B.A., Kent State U., 1968, M.Ed., 1969; m. Robert Dale Archer, Sept. 26, 1953; children—Robert, Gregory, Richard. Psychologist, coordinator in-patient adolescent program Fallsview Mental Health Center, Cuyahoga Falls, O., 1970-72; counselor Hawthornden State Hosp., Northfield, O., 1972; counselor-coordinator YWCA Residential Intervention Center, Akron, O., 1973—. Mem. Am., Ohio psychol. assns., Alpha Epsilon Delta, Psi Chi. Home: 1102 Ledgeview Rd Macedonia OH 44056 Office: 146 S High St Akron OH 44308

ARCHER, SARA KATHERINE LAYTON, univ. dean; b. Goldsboro, N.C., July 17, 1918; d. Charles R. and Milly S. (Swinson) Layton; R.N., Washington Sanatorium and Hosp., 1940; B.S. (Fla. State Nursing scholar), U. Miami, 1962; M.S., Boston U., 1966, certificate advanced gerontological study, 1967, Ed.D., 1970; children from previous marriage—Benjamin J., Charles R. Layton III, Zelda L., Stephen J. Layton. Pvt. duty nurse, Washington, 1940-46; staff nurse, supr. Vis. Nurse Assn., Dade County, Fla., 1959-64; asst. prof. Boston U., 1966-68, asso. prof., 1968-69, dir. gerontology program for pub. health nurses, 1967-69; dir. grad. program in med.-surg. nursing Vanderbilt U. Sch. Nursing, Nashville, 1969-71, prof., asso. dean Sch. Nursing, 1971-72, dean, 1972—. Mem. consultative nat. dean's com. on nursing VA, 1972—; cons. Rush Presbyn.-St. Luke's Med. Center, Medicus System, 1972; gerontological cons. VA Hosp., Murfreesboro, Tenn., 1972—. Mem. Tenn. Medicaid Med. Adv. Com., 1971—; mem. nursing adv. com. Tenn. Higher Edn. Commn., 1972—; mem. Ad Hoc Com. to Study Collaboration Between Nursing and Med. Educators in So. Regional Edn. Bd., Atlanta, 1971—; mem. Tenn. White House Conf. on Aging, 1971; mem. ad hoc com. on grad. edn. in nursing So. Regional Edn. Bd., Atlanta, 1969—, mem. council on collegiate edn. for nursing, 1972—. Recipient Outstanding Nursing Alumnae award U. Miami, 1972. Mem. Am. Nurses Assn. (adv. com. for clin. sessions 1968, 70), Tenn. Nurses Assn. (v.p. gerontology sect., dist. 3 1972-73, cons. to com. on practice of council on practice 1970—), Gerontological Soc. (mem. nurse visibility com. 1969-70), Tenn. Pub. Health Assn. Home: 4704 Villa Green Dr Nashville TN 37215

ARCHER, VIOLET BALESTRERI, educator, composer, pianist; b. Montreal, Que., Can., Apr. 24, 1913; d. Cesar B. and Beatrice (Azzi) Archer; licentiate in piano, McGill U., 1934, B.Mus., 1936, Mus.D. (hon.), 1971; Asso., Canadian Coll. Organists, 1939; B.Mus., Yale, 1948, M.Mus., 1949. Instr. music McGill U., 1944-47; concert season, England, 1950; resident composer North Tex. State Coll., Denton, 1950-53; asst. prof. music U. Okla., 1953-61; asso. prof. U. Alta., Edmonton, 1962-70, prof. music, 1970—, also chmn. div. music theory and composition; cons. in music theory Western Bd. Music Alta.; mem. theory com. Canadian Assn. U. Schs. Music. Mem. panel judges for McMaster prize in chamber music composition, 1970-71. Composer numerous works including Divertimento for Brass Quintet, Sing, The Muse, Prelude-Incantation; compositions performed extensively in Can., U.S., Europe. Recipient citation Yale Sch. Music Alumni Assn., 1968, Merit award for contbn. to music Govt. of Alta., 1970, Performing and Creative award City of Edmonton, 1972. Fellow MacDowell Colony, 1956; Can. Council sr. fellow, 1958-59. Mem. Am., Canadian music centres, BMI Can. Ltd., Am. Fedn. of Musicians, Canadian League Composers, Canadian Assn. U. Profs., Alta. Registered Music Tchrs. Assn., Music Tchrs. Nat. Assn. U.S., Canadian Fedn. Music Tchrs., Internat. Folk Music Council, Canadian Folk Music Soc., Canadian Music Educators Assn., Music Educators Nat. Conf., Sigma Alpha Iota, Pi Kappa Lambda. Composer works including Three Sketches, Divertimento for Orch., Sonatina for Piano, Sonatina for Organ, opera Sganarelle, anthems for mixed chorus and organ. Club: Women's Musical (Edmonton). Home: 10805 85 Av Edmonton AB T6E 2L2 Canada

ARCHIBALD, MARGARET NEOMA, lawyer; b. Chatham, Ont., Can., Aug. 10, 1927; d. Harry Ross and Isabella Jane (MacHardy) Archibald; B.A., U. Western Ont., 1948; Barrister-at-Law, Osgoode Hall Sch. Law, Toronto, 1957. With Imperial Oil Ltd., Sarnia and Toronto, Ont., 1948-53, Chevron Oil Co., Calgary, Alta., Can., 1957-60; practice law, Chatham and Dresden, Ont., 1960—. Mem. Ont. Status of Women Council. Former pres. Chatham Progressive Conservative Women. Mem. Canadian Bar Assn., Zonta Internat. (past pres. Chatham chpt., co-chmn. legal adv. com.), Kappa Alpha Theta. Mem. United Ch. Can. (chmn. bd. local ch.). Office: Box 214 Chatham ON N7M 5K3 Canada

ARCHIBALD, PATRICIA ANN, botanist, phycologist; b. Olney, Ill., July 18, 1934; d. Stanley Ray and Mable Ellen (Seed) Archibald; B.S., M.A., Ball State U., 1961; Ph.D. in Botany, U. Tex. at Austin, 1969. Tchr. Elkhart (Ind.) Sr. High Sch., 1959-63; instr. Palm Beach Jr. Coll., Lake Worth, Fla., 1963-65; asso. prof. biology Slippery Rock (Pa.) State Coll., 1969—. Fulbright Exchange tchr., Eng., 1962-63. NSF Coll. Sci. Faculty fellow, U. Tex. at Austin, summer 1966, Marine Biol. Lab., Woods Hole, summer 1967, U. Tex. at Austin, 1967-69. Mem. Am. Bot. Soc., Phycol. Soc. Am., Brit. Phycol. Soc., Internat. Phycol. Soc., Bus. and Profl. Womens Club, Am. Bus. Womens Assn., Sigma Xi. Home: 119 N 5th St Box 11 Spiceland IN 47385 Office: Slippery Rock State Coll Slippery Rock PA 16057

ARD, CONSTANCE CALLAHAN (MRS. BEN N. ARD, JR.), marriage, family and child counselor; b. Watseka, Ill., Mar. 4, 1941; d. Donald Everett and Winona Alice (Wilson) Callahan; B.A., Eastern Ill. U., 1963; M.A., San Francisco State U., 1967; m. Ben N. Ard, Jr., June 11, 1967. Lectr. counseling dept. San Francisco State U., 1966, grad. asst., 1966-67; pvt. practice marriage counselor, San Francisco, 1967—. Cons. Bur. Indian Affairs, Alameda, Cal., 1967-68. Camp counselor, Honesdale, Pa., 1964-65, Phelps, Wis., 1960. Mem. Nat. Council on Family Relations, Am. Assn. Marriage and Family Counselors. Editor: (with Ben Ard) Handbook of Marriage Counseling, 1969. Contbr. articles in field to profl. jours. Home: 131 Rollingwood Dr San Rafael CA 94901 Office: 4200 California St Suite 206 San Francisco CA 94118

ARDEN, JUNE LOUISE (MRS. SIDNEY H. ARDEN), lawyer; b. Los Angeles, May 26, 1930; d. Bertram H. and Eleanor (Hartmann) Erlanger; LL.B. magna cum laude, U. San Fernando, 1964-68; m. Sidney H. Arden, Mar. 22, 1956; children—Jim, Nancy, Dennis. Admitted to Cal. bar, 1969, U.S. Court Appeals, 1969; ins. solicitor, industrial real estate salesman Jules B. Altemus Co., Beverly Hills, Cal., 1953-56; law clk. Plotkin, Schreiber & Schiff, Westwood, Cal., 1968-69; atty., 1969; atty. Max A. Keller, Beverly Hills, Cal., 1969-73; mem. firm Arden & Arden, Beverly Hills Cal., 1973—. Mem. Los Angeles panel of selective service attys., mil. and selective service counseling Valley Peace Center and Legal Counsel Community Union, Pasadena, 1969—. Mem. State Bar Cal., Nat. Assn. Women Lawyers, Los Angeles County Bar Assn., Screen Smart Set, Hadassah, ORT. Republican. Jewish religion. Clubs: Soroptimist (v.p. program 1972-73) (Beverly Hills, Cal.); Los Angeles Lawyers (past chmn. speakers bur.). Home: 23721 Mariano St Woodland Hills CA 91364 Office: 9570 Wilshire Blvd Beverly Hills CA 90212

ARDES, MAE SARIG (MRS. STEPHEN J. ARDES), lawyer; b. Temple, Pa., June 24, 1908; d. Wilson George and Jennie (Gundy) Sarig; tchr.'s certificate Kutztown State Coll., 1925; B.A., Albright Coll., 1927; LL.B., Temple U., 1953; m. Stephen J. Ardes, Aug. 19,

1955. Tchr. jr. high sch. English, Muhlenberg Twp. High Sch., Laureldale, Pa., 1927-29; supr. handwriting, Grafton, W.Va., 1929-31; sec. to speaker Pa. Ho. of Reps., Harrisburg, 1935-39; sec. to state treas., auditor gen., then judge of Superior Ct. of Pa., 1939-55; admitted to Pa. bar, 1955; individual practice, Reading, Pa., 1955-58, Pottstown, 19——. Vice pres. Young Democrats of Pa., 1936-38. Mem. United Ch. of Christ. Club: Pottstown Garden. Adress: Lightcap Rd RD 3 Pottstown PA 19464

ARDMORE, JANE KESNER (MRS. ALBERT ARDMORE), writer; b. Chgo., Sept. 12, 1915; d. David Leon and Florence (Behrend) Kesner; Ph.D., U. Chgo., 1932; m. Albert Ardmore, Nov. 10, 1951; 1 dau., Ellen. Editor, Woodlawn Booster, Chgo., 1932-33; advt. copywriter U. Chgo. Press, 1933-34; contbr. non-fiction to maj. mags. throughout U.S. including Ladies Home Jour., McCall's, Playgirl, Photoplay, 1950—. Lectr. writing techniques VA Hosp., Brentwood, 1963—; lectr. numerous profl. groups, and confs. Recipient fiction prize Ind. U. Writer's Conf., 1942; Nat. Fiction prize Nat. Fedn. Press Women, 1962; Nat. Headliner award Theta Sigma Phi, 1968. Mem. Women in Communications, Hollywood Women's Press Club. Club: La Costa Country (Carlsbad, Cal.). Author: Women Inc. (Ind. Writers Conf. award), 1946; Julie, 1952; Take My Life, 1957; The Dress Doctor, 1959; The Self Enchanted, 1960; A Portrait of Joan, 1962; To Love is to Listen, 1967. Home: 10469 Dunleer Dr Los Angeles CA 90064

AREEN, JUDITH CAROL, educator; b. Chgo., Aug. 2, 1944; d. Gordon Eric and Pauline Jeanette (Payberg) Areen; A.B., Cornell U., 1966; LL.B., Yale, 1969. Admitted to Mass. bar, 1971, D.C. bar, 1972; program planner for higher edn. Office of the Mayor of City of N.Y., 1969-70; dir. edn. voucher study Center for the Study of Pub. Policy, Cambridge, Mass., 1970-72; adj. prof. law Georgetown U. Law Center, Washington, 1971-72, asso. prof. law, 1972—. Mem. Am., D.C. bar assns., Nat. Legal Aid and Defender Assn., Nat. Orgn. for Women, Pi Beta Phi. Author: (with Christopher Jencks) Education Vouchers: A Report on Financing Elementary Education by Grants to Parents, 1970. Home: 1621 34th St NW Washington DC 20007 Office: 600 New Jersey Av Georgetown University Law Center Washington DC 20001

ARELLANES, AUDREY SPENCER, personnel exec.; b. Lance Creek, Wyo., Feb. 23, 1920; d. William Sidney and Edith Catherine (Hall) Spencer; student U. Cal. at Los Angeles, 1944; m. Lester Glenn Arellanes, Sept. 28, 1946; 1 dau., Denetia Ynez. Sec. to claims mgr. Cal. Physicians Ser., Los Angeles, 1946-54; asst. editor house organ, sec. to v.p. Calcor, Whittier, Cal., 1954-58; research asst. biokinetics lab. Cal. Coll. Medicine, Los Angeles, 1958-62; mem. staff benefits program and employee relations Avery Products Corp., San Marino, Cal., 1963—; propr. Bookworm Press, Pasadena, Cal., 1965—. Dir., Am. Soc. Bookplate Collectors and Designers, 1970—, editor Bookplates in the News, quar. newsletter, 1970—, Year Book, 1970—; registered reader Henry E. Huntington Library, 1863—. Mem. Manuscript Soc. Am. (nat. dir., v.p., treas. So. Cal. chpt.), Soc. Cal. Archivists (charter). Author: Bookplates: A Selected Annotated Bibliography of the Periodical Literature, 1971. Publisher: (handset printed and bound) Beauregard, 1965; Elephant Cutlet, 1966; Fireflies, 1968, Thomas Bird Mosher, 1972. Home: 429 N Daisy Av Pasadena CA 91107 Office: 415 Huntington Dr San Marino CA 91108

ARENAL, JULIE (MRS. BARRY PRIMUS), choreographer. Dancer with companies of Anna Sokolow, Sophie Maslow, John Butler, Jack Cole, Jose Limon; tchr. Herbert Berghof Studio; choreographer Marat/Sade for Theatre Co. of Boston; asst. on tng. program Lincoln Center Repertory Theatre; choreographer at Loeb Theatre at Harvard, A Municipal Theatre, Atlanta; choreographer Hair on Broadway (Most Original Choreographer of Yr. award Sat. Rev. 1968), also London; dir., choreographer Hair, Stockholm, Sweden (Best Dir.-Choreographer of Year award 1969); choreographer Indians, on Broadway; choregrapher, dir. Isabel's a Jezebel; choreographer Fiesta for Ballet Hispanico, 1972, 20008 1/2. Nat. Endowment grantee for A Puerto Rican Soap Opera, Ballet Hispanico, 1973. Address: 205 E 10th St New York City NY 10003

ARENDALE, MARIROSE, educator; b. Chattanooga, Jan. 24, 1930; d. William Carl and Ora Bird (Brewer) Arendale; B.A., U. Chattanooga, 1952; M.A., U. Tenn., 1965; postgrad. Oxford (Eng.) U. With TVA, 1952-55, Hamilton County Sch. System, 1955-64; asso. prof. social studies Chattanooga State Tech. Community Coll., 1967—. Mem. adv. bd. area consumer edn. project; arbitration panel Better Bus. Bur.; active Ct. Watchers, Adult Edn. Council. Mem. Nat. Assn. Mgmt. Educators, So. Econs. Assn., Am. Assn. U. Women, Quota, Delta Kappa Gamma. Creator, writer Money Matters, consumer econs. TV series; film documentaries. Author articles. Home: 133 Flora Circle Chattanooga TN 37415

ARENDT, HANNAH, author, polit. scientist, educator; b. Hanover, Germany, Oct. 14, 1906; d. Paul and Martha (Cohn) Arendt; B.A., Konigsberg Pr., 1924; student univs. Marburg, Freiburg; Ph.D., Heidelberg U., 1928; H.L.D., Bard Coll., 1959, Goucher Coll., 1960, Smith Coll., 1966, York U., 1968, Loyola U., Chgo., 1970, Yale, 1971, U. Notre Dame, 1972, Fordham U., 1972, Princeton U., 1972, Dartmouth, 1972; m. Heinrich Bluecher, 1940 (dec. 1970). Came to U.S., 1941, naturalized, 1951. Social worker, Paris, France, 1933-40; research dir. Conf. on Jewish Relations, 1944-46; chief editor Schocken Books, Inc., 1946-48; exec. dir. Jewish Cultural Reconstrn., N.Y.C., 1949-52; prof. U. Chgo., 1963-67, vis. professional lectr., 1968—; prof. grad. faculty New Sch. Social Research, 1967—. Vis. prof. U. Cal. at Berkeley, 1955, Princeton, 1959, Columbia, 1960; fellow Center for Advanced Studies, Wesleyan U., 1961. Guggenheim fellow, 1952-53; recipient award Nat. Inst. Arts and Letters, 1954, Sigmund Freud prize, 1967, Emerson Thoreau medal, 1969. Rockefeller fellow, 1959-60, 1969-70; M. Carey Thomas prize Bryn Mawr Coll., 1971. Mem. Am. Acad. Polit. Sci., Am. Acad. Arts and Scis., Am. Polit. Sci. Assn., Am. Soc. Polit. and Legal Philosophy, Deutsche Akademie für Sprache and Dichtung (corr. mem.), Nat. Inst. Arts and Letters, Inst. Internat. de Philosphie Politique, Nat. League Am. P.E.N., Author: The Origins of Totalitarianism, 1951, new edit., 1968; Rahel Varnhagen, 1957; The Human Condition, 1958; Between Past and Future, 1961, enlarged edit., 1968; On Revolution, 1963; Eichmann in Jerusalem, 1963, 2d edit., 1964; Men in Dark Times, 1968; On Violence, 1970; Crises of the Republic, 1972. others. Editor: The Great Philosophers (Karl Jasper), 2 vols., 1970; editor, author introduction: Walter: Banjamin Illuminations, 1968. Address: Grad Faculty New Sch Social Research 66 W 12th St New York City NY 10011

ARESTY, ESTHER BRADFORD, writer; b. Syracuse, N.Y.; d. Jacob and Bertha (Levin) Bradford; student De Paul U.; m. Jules Aresty, June 20, 1936; children—Robert Joseph, Jane. Radio commentator, sta. WJJD, Chgo., 1931-35; advt. mgr. Mandel Bros., Chgo., 1934-36; free lance writer, radio and TV scriptwriter, 1936—, also stories children mags. Mem. bd. Trenton Community Found. (pres. 1962-64), Florence Crittenton Home, Child Guidance Center, Union Indsl. Home. Member Women's Nat. Book Assn., Authors League Am. Author: The Grand Venture, 1963; The Delectable Past (Cookbook Guild selection), 1964; The Best Behavior, 1970. Home: 32 Hilvista Blvd Trenton NJ 08618

ARGANO, BEATRICE JOLANDA CASAVECCHIA, physician; b. Milano, Italy, Nov. 19, 1934; d. Spartaco and Joyce (Templeton) Casavecchia; B.Sc., Liceo Carducci, 1951; M.D., Milan U., 1958; diploma as specialist in cardiology Turin U., 1961. Came to U.S., 1963. Assistente incaricata Fatebenefratell;, Milan, 1959-61; practice medicine, specializing in internal medicine, Italy, 1961-63; fellow in cardiology, asso. in medicine Chgo. Med. Sch., 1968-70; dir. phonocardiography and graphic tracings lab. Mt. Sinai Hosp., Chgo., 1970-71; asst. prof. medicine Chgo. Med. Sch., 1970-71, clin. asst. prof. medicine, 1971—; asst. med. dir. CNA Corp., Chgo., 1971—. NIH fellow, 1966-68. Mem. Sigma Xi. Home: 1700 E 56th St Chicago IL 60637 Office: CNA Plaza Chicago IL 60685

ARGENTO, ANNE MARIE, educator; b. Bklyn., Oct. 24, 1947; d. Edward Salvatore and Mary (Scarpa) Argento; B.A., City U. N.Y., 1969; M.S. in Edn., Queens Coll., 1973; m. Anthony Nicholas Fresco, July 27, 1974. Tchr. speech and drama Washington Irving High Sch., N.Y.C., 1969-70; tchr. pub. speaking, drama, speech therapy William C. Bryant High Sch., Queens, N.Y., 1970—, dramatics coach, dir., 1971-72. Mem. Communication Assn. Am., N.Y. State United Tchrs., Inc., N.Y.C. Speech Tchrs. Assn., Queens Coll. Alumni Assn., Kappa Delta Pi. Home: 83-47 116th St Kew Gardens NY 11418 Office: 48-10 31st Av Long Island City NY 11103

ARGO, DOROTHY PECK (MRS. HARALSON BUTLER ARGO), chems. co. exec.; b. Cunningham, Ky.; d. Clifton Bolen and Dean (Brooks) Peck; student Union U., 1922-23, Memphis Acad. Arts, 1936-37, 44-45; m. Haralson Butler Argo, Apr. 28, 1937; 1 dau., Anne Evans (Mrs. Edward Lorraine Sanders). Dress designer, mfr., Memphis, 1935-37; inventor, pres. Argosheen Products Corp., Argo & Co., Inc., Memphis, Spartanburg, S.C., 1942—. Div. chmn. A.R.C., 1957; capt. United Fund, 1967; patron Music Found. Spartansburg, Little Theatre, Ballet Guild. Mem. Hotel Sales Mgmt. Assn., Am., Fla., S.C. hotel-motel assns., Internat. Sani. Supply Assn. Episcopalian. Clubs: Piedmont, Country of Spartanburg. Contbr. articles to profl. jours., consumer publs. Home: 705 DuPre Dr Spartanburg SC 29302 Office: 182-190 Ezell St Spartanburg SC 29302

ARGO, REBECCA MARIE WHITE (MRS. MAX ARGO), physician; b. Covington, Ky., Dec. 7, 1940; d. Robert G. and Ivy (Miranda) White; B.A., U. Cal. at Los Angeles, 1963; M.D., U. Cal. at Irvine, 1968; m. Max Argo, Apr. 8, 1971. Social worker Los Angeles County Dept. Pub. Social Services, 1963-64; intern Fresno Gen. Hosp., 1968-69; resident psychiatry Camarillo (Cal.) State Hosp., 1969-72; emergency room physician, staff mem. St. John's Hosp., Oxnard, Cal., 1969—; psychiat. cons. Camarillo State Hosp., 1972—; pvt. practice medicine, specializing in psychiatry, 1973—. Cons. psychiatry Ventura Coll. Counselling Center, Ventura Sch. Youth Authority, Port Hueneme Sch. Dist. Mem. Student Am. Med. Assn., Am. Psychiat. Assn., So. Cal. Psychiat. Soc., Ventura County Med. Soc., Am., Cal. med. assns., Christian Med. Soc., Christian Bus. and Profl. Women's Council. Mem. Ch. of Nazarene. Office: PO Box 994 266 N Mobil Av Camarillo CA 93010

ARGYROS, DIANA COHEN, physician; b. N.Y.C., Oct. 31, 1936; d. Isidor M. and Mary Frances (Eskew) Cohen; A.B., Washington Sq. Coll., 1959; M.D., N.Y. U., 1962; m. Thomas Argyros, May 26, 1956 (div. Aug. 1965); 1 dau., Shersten Killip. Intern, Lenox Hills Hosp., N.Y.C., 1962-63; resident medicine N.Y. U.-Bellevue Hosp., N.Y.C., 1963-66; fellow cardiology Cornell U. Med. Coll., N.Y.C., 1968-70, asst. prof. medicine, 1970-73, clin. research in cardiology, 1970-73, clin. asst. prof. medicine, 1973—; mem. staff N.Y. Hosp., N.Y.C.; attending physician Gen. Electric Co., 1973—. Mem. Phi Beta Kappa. Address: 2300 Lincolnwood Dr Evanston IL 60201

ARIAS, DAME MARGOT FONT EYN DE see Font eyn, Margot

ARIAS, DORALYS ELIZABETH, physician; b. Tampa, Fla., Oct. 11, 1930; d. Joseph and Carmen (Castro) Arias; A.A., Stephens Coll., 1950; A.B., U. Miami, Coral Gables 1952, M.A., 1955, B.S., 1958, M.D., 1962. Rotating intern Jackson Meml. Hosp., Miami, Fla., 1962-63, pediatric resident, 1963-65, chief resident pediatrics, 1965-66; began as co-director, then director of the Newborn Nursery and Premature Center, 1967—; practice medicine specializing in pediatrics, Miami, 1966-67; faculty U. Miami Sch. Medicine, Coral Gables, Fla., 1967—, asst. dir. Birth Defects Center, 1967—; pediatric cons. to maternal and infant care project 515, Dade County, Fla., 1967—, asst. chief Office Consumer Care, pediatricians-in-chief Dade County Dept. Pub. Health, 1970-71, coordinator Children and Youth Project 636, 1970-71; chief pediatrician Orange County Health Dept., Orlando, 1971—. Fulbright scholar, Italy, 1952-53. Diplomate Fla. Bd. Med. Examiners, Cal., Nat. bds. med. examiners, Am. Bd. Pediatrics. Fellow Am. Acad. Pediatrics; mem. Fla. Med. Assn., Orange County Med. Soc., So. Soc. Pediatric Research, Fla., Soc. med. socs., Fla. Pediatric Soc., Am. Acad. Pediatrics, Chi Omega. Home: 916 Hillary Ct Orlando FL 32804 Office: 832 W Central Blvd Orlando FL 32802

ARKEMA, KATHERINE KEMP (MRS. EDWARD L.S. ARKEMA, JR.), radiologist; b. Birmingham, Ala., Dec. 8, 1940; d. Karlton Hubert and Flora Mildred (Steel) Kemp; B.A., Vanderbilt U., 1962; M.D., Baylor U., 1966; m. Edward L.S. Arkema, Jr., Aug. 21, 1971; children—Dawn Elizabeth, Kirsten Katherine. Intern, Chgo. Wesley Meml. Hosp., 1966-67; resident Presbyn.-St. Luke's Hosp., Chgo., 1967-70, adj. in radiology, 1970-71; adj. in radiology Oak Park (Ill.) Hosp., 1971-72; attending radiologist Northwestern Meml. Hosp., Chgo., 1972—; asso. in radiology Northwestern U. Med. Sch., Chgo., 1972—. Diplomate Am. Bd. Radiology. Mem. A.M.A., Am. Coll. Radiology, Radiology Soc. N.Am., Gamma Phi Beta. Home: 2121 Hudson St Chicago IL 60614 Office: Northwestern Meml Hosp Chicago IL 60611

ARKIN, FRANCES SADIE, psychiatrist; b. Boston, Apr. 8, 1904; d. Max and Fannie (Field) Arkin; M.D., Tufts Med. Coll., 1929. Intern, New Eng. Hosp. for Women, Boston, 1929-30; resident N.Y. State Psychiat. Inst., 1930-31. Neurol. Inst.-Columbia Presbyn. Hosp., 1931-32; Rockefeller Inst. fellow, Inst. Juvenile Research, Chgo., 1932-33; practice medicine specializing in psychiatry, psychoanalysis, N.Y.C., 1933-68; asso. clin. prof. psychiatry N.Y. Med. Coll., 1945-68, founder, tng. analyst comprehensive course in psychoanalysis, 1945-68; cons. psychiatrist Miami (Fla.) VA Hosp., 1970—. Diplomate Am. Bd. Psychiatry. Fellow Am. Psychiat. Assn. (life), Am. Orthopsychiat. Assn. (life), Am. Acad. Psychoanalysis (charter pres. 1960-61, N.Y. Soc. for Med. Psychoanalysts (hon.). Contbr. articles to profl. jours. Home: 11 Island Av Miami Beach FL 33139

ARLANDSON, ELLA LEONE RYLAND, editor; b. Baker, Ore., Oct. 30, 1917; d. Frank Rucker and Ella Washington (Wilbourn) Ryland; student Lake Merritt Bus. Coll., 1937-39; m. Robert Andrew Arlandson, Dec. 25, 1953; children—Carolyn (Mrs. Earl Harris), David, John, Janis and Jim (twins). Interviewer personnel/pub. relations Ore. State Welfare Commn., 1938; timekeeper Pictsweet Frozen Foods, 1950; editor RCL Pubs., Medford, Ore., 1971—. Recipient Lit. award Pacific N.W. Writers Conf., 1972. Mem. Rogue Valley Authors Guild. Clubs: Cal.-Ore. Appaloosa Horse (show sec., publicity dir. 1966-70) (Medford); Appaloosa Horse (Moscow, Ida.). Author: Mr. Puffer-Bill, 1965; Gordon and the Glockenspiel, 1966; The Whistle-Bell Train, 1967; Know the Appaloosa Horse, 1973. Contbr. numerous articles to mags. specializing in horses and western Americana. Home: 2170 Milford Dr Medford OR 97501

ARLEN, MARY MICHAEL TOSCANO (MRS. HAROLD WILLIAM ARLEN), civic worker, artist; b. Syracuse, N.Y., May 8, 1929; d. Anthony John and Emily (Garafalo) Toscano; B.A., Syracuse U., 1950; m. Harold William Arlen, Aug. 18, 1951; children—Michael William, Elizabeth Faye. Record librarian, gen. office work City Health Dept., Syracuse, 1950-53; sec. office pub. relations Santa Monica (Cal.) Hosp., 1953. Chmn. ways and means com. Winter Wives Assn., Winter VA Hosp., Topeka, 1957; library chmn. Canyon Elementary Sch. P.T.A., 1961, pres., 1962, parliamentarian, 1963, publicity chmn., 1964; 1st v.p. Ocean View Council Parents and Tchrs., 1962, pres., 1963, parliamentarian, 1964; 2d v.p. Westside Med. Wives, 1963, pres., 1964; 2d v.p. Santa Monica Hosp. Aux., 1964, 1st v.p., 1965, pres., 1966-67, art chmn., 1965-68, 70-72; N.W. area counselor 10th dist. Cal. Congress Parents and Tchrs., 1965-66; treas. Fashionettes, Inc., Hollywood Presbyn. Hosp., 1966, pres., 1967, membership chmn., 1972; pres. Paul Revere Jr. High Sch. P.T.A., 1967; 1st v.p. Pacific Palisades Art Assn., 1968, pres., 1973; P.T.A. del. to community coordinating council, 1963; ofcl. rep. to civic league and community coordinating council Pacific Palisades Jr. Women's Club, 1962-63, 2d v.p., 1962; active various community drives. Bd. dirs. Santa Monica Hosp. Recipient State of Cal. Civil Def. award Fedn. Women's Clubs Marina Dist., 1960-61, Citizen of the Year awards Marina dist. Fedn. Women's Clubs, 1963, Cal. Fedn., 1963. Mem. Pacific Palisades Art Assn., Los Angeles County Mus. Art, Beverly Hills Art League, Los Angeles County Physicians Art Soc., Westwood Art Assn., Human Relations Council, Santa Monica Hosp., Los Angeles County med. auxs., Med. Faculty Wives U. So. Cal., A.M.A. Woman's Aux. Home: 1265 N Amalfi Dr Pacific Palisades CA 90272

ARLITT, ADA HART, educator; b. New Orleans, July 27, 1890; d. John Hamilton Brower and Ada Hullen Spencer (Mott) Hart; B.A., Sophie Newcomb Coll. of Tulane U., 1913; Ph.D., U. Chgo., 1917; m. J. L. Arlitt, Feb. 7, 1909. Fellow in zoology Tulane, 1913-14, in psychology U. Chgo., 1914-16, Otto S. A. Sprague Inst. for Med. Research, 1916-17; asso. in psychology Bryn Mawr (Pa.) Coll., 1917-23; chief psychologist Mental Hygiene Clinic, Cin., 1923-25; prof., head dept. child care and tng., grad. sch. arts and scis. U. Cin., 1925-51, prof. psychology, 1947-51, prof. emeritus, 1951—. Adv. mem. Com. on Parent Edn. and cons. to staff White House Conf. on Child Health and Protection, 1930-31; mem. governing bd. Nat. Council Parent Edn., 1926-31, 36-38; nat. chmn. parent edn. Nat. Congress Parents and Teachers, 1927-43. Fellow A.A.A.S., Soc. for Research in Child Development, Am. Psychol. Assn.; mem. Phi Beta Kappa, Pi Gamma Mu, Sigma Xi, Kappa Delta Pi, Delta Kappa Gamma, Omicron Nu. Episcopalian. Clubs: Woman's Town, College (Cin.). Author: Psychology of Infancy and Early Childhood, 1928, 46; The Child from One to Twelve, 1931; Adolescent Psychology, 1933; The Adolescent, 1938; Family Relationship, 1942. Editor: Parent Edn. Yearbook, 1930-34; asso. editor Childhood Education, 1925-27, Nat. Parent Teacher, 1927—. Contbr. physchol. publs. Home: 3420 Manor Hill Dr Cincinnati OH 45220

ARMAN, ELVIRA JEANNE, owner automobile agy.; b. Italy, Jan. 11, 1921; came to the U.S., 1927, naturalized, 1927; d. Louis Victor and Palmira (Machiovecchio) Cacio; grad. high sch.; m. Dallas R. Arman, Sept. 17, 1940 (dec.); children—Donna, Barbara; m. 2d, Clarence C. Reed, Dec. 21, 1973. With Lamerdin Pontiac (name changed to Arman Pontiac Inc. 1969), Compton, Cal., 1949—, gen. mgr., 1950-67, owner, 1967—; owner Compton Toyota (Cal.), 1970—. Pres. YMCA, 1970-72. Chairwoman Los Angeles Internat. Automobile Show, 1972. Mem. Compton C. of C. (v.p. 1969-74), Nat. (council 1972-73), Los Angeles, Orange County Pontiac dealers assns. (pres. 1970), Motor Car Dealers Assn. So. Cal. (treas., dir. 1973—). Club: Friday Morning (Los Angeles). Home: 30114 Via De Calma Palos Verdes Peninsula CA 90274 Office: 302 N Long Beach Blvd Compton CA 90224

ARMBRUSTER, NADINE NEWELL (MRS. ROBERT FREDERICK ARMBRUSTER), educator; b. Eddyville, Ia., Feb. 19, 1940; d. Albert Emerson and Alice Ealen (Murphy) Newell; B.S. in Edn., Northeast Mo. State Tchrs. Coll., 1961, M.A., 1964; m. Robert Frederick Armbruster, Aug. 16, 1964. Tchr. pub. sch., Chariton, Ia., 1961-63; instr. phys. edn. Carthage Coll., Kenosha, Wis., 1963-65; prof. phys. edn. William Penn Coll., Oskaloosa, Ia., 1965—. Instr. first aid A.R.C., 1964—. Committeewoman Columbia Twp. Ia., 1962-64. Mem. Am. Legion, Chariton Edn. Assn. (pres. 1963), Ladies of Elks, Beta Sigma Phi, Sigma Kappa. Democrat. Methodist. Home: Rural Route 1 Keomah Village Oskaloosa IA 52577

ARMENTROUT, MARY BETH KITSCH, librarian; b. Devils Lake, N.D., May 10, 1925; d. John and Mary Agnes (Connor) Kitsch; student Valley City State Tchrs. Coll., 1957-59; B.A. cum laude, U. N.D., 1963; postgrad. U. Mont., 1967-74; m. Darrel Charles Armentrout, May 11, 1950; children—John Patrick, Michael Darrel. Tchr., Fairdale, N.D., 1959-62, Glasgow, Mont., 1963-64, Browning, Mont., 1964—; elementary library coordinator Sch. Dist. No. 9, Browning, 1973—. Mem. Confrat. Christian Doctrine (dir. 1964-67), Kappa Delta Pi, Pi Lambda Theta. Toastmistress (pres. 1973-74). Club: Garden (Browning). Home: Box 399 Browning MT 59417 Office: Browning Pub Schs Sch Dist # 9 Browning MT 59417

ARMER, ALBERTA MARY (MRS. AUSTIN ARMER), author; b. Huntingburg, Ind., Feb. 11, 1904; d. Henry Bernard and Mary Christina (Katterhenry) Roller; B.A. summa cum laude, U. Cal. at Berkeley, 1926; m. Austin Armer, Dec. 25, 1928; children—Elinor, Beret (Mrs. Dwight Worsham), Rollin. Editor agrl. publs. U. Cal., Davis, 1953-57, asst. prof. English, 1958-59. Cons. to creative writing classes, elementary, high sch. and adult groups. Vol. worker children's dept. Cal. State Hosp., Napa, 1967-68. Mem. Women's Internat. League for Peace and Freedom, Phi Beta Kappa. Democrat. Unitarian. Author: Cherry House, 1958; Hark the Herald Angel, 1959; The 2 Worlds of Molly O', 1962; Screwball, 1963; Steve and the Guide Dogs, 1965; Troublemaker, 1966; The View from Stevenson House, 1967; Runaway Girl, 1969. Contbr. weekly column to Woodland Daily Democrat, 1973-74. Address: 725 Oak Av Davis CA 95616

ARMIGER, SISTER BERNADETTE, dean univ.; b. Balt., Apr. 7, 1915; d. Joseph Griffith and Sallie (Harcourt) Armiger; B.S., Cath. U. Am., 1944, M.S., 1947; Ph.D., St. John's U., 1968. Joined Order of Daus. Charity St. Vincent de Paul, 1933; asst. med. and surg. nursing Cath. U. Am., Washington, 1944-47; dir. nursing edn. and nursing service De Paul Hosp., Norfolk, Va., 1947-49; asst. prof. nursing, dir. undergrad. div. Cath. U. Am. Sch. Nursing, 1949-50; supr. med. and surg. nursing Our Lady Lourdes Hosp., Binghamton, N.Y., 1950-51; co-ordinator med. and surg. nursing Catherine Laboure Sch. Nursing, Boston, 1951-55; asst. prof. nursing St. Joseph Coll., Emmitsburg, Md., 1955-63; cons. dept. nursing edn. St. John's U., N.Y., 1963-64, asso. prof. nursing, chmn. dept. nursing edn., 1964-67, asst. to dean Sch. Edn., 1967-68; dean, prof. nursing Niagara U., Sch. Coll. Nursing N.Y., 1968—. Speaker various confs., convs., workshops, seminars, 1946-68; mem. NIH Research in Nursing in Patient Care Rev. Com., 1969-71, Nursing Research and Edn. Adv. Com., 1971-73. Bd. dirs. Niagara County A.R.C., Am. Camcer Soc., N.Y. Cancer Soc., Lakes Area Regional Med. Program, Health Assn. Niagara County. Recipient Alumni Achievement award, Cath. U. Am., 1968. Mem. Am. Nurses Assn., Nat. League for Nursing, Am. Assn. Colls. Nursing (pres. 1972-74), Am. Psychol. Assn., Am. Assn. U. Profs., Am. Assn. U. Women, Am. Assn. Higher Edn., Delta Epsilon Sigma, Sigma Theta Tau, Psi. Chi. Editorial bd. Health Care Dimensions. Contbr. numerous articles to profl. jours. Home: 625 Center St Lewiston NY 14092

ARMITAGE, CONSTANCE DEAN (MRS. NORMAN CUDWORTH ARMITAGE), linguist, polit. worker, educator; b. San Francisco, May 13, 1920; d. Robert A. and Constance (Lawrence) Dean; A.B., U. Cal., 1939; M.A., U. Ga., 1961; student U. Florence (Italy), 1938-39, U. Perugia (Italy), 1938; m. Norman Cudworth Armitage, Sept. 20, 1941; children—Leslie (Mrs. Carles Enric Vallhonrat), Robert Dean. Prof. art history Wofford Coll., Spartanburg, S.C., 1964—. Mem. Pres.'s Adv. Council on European Affairs, 1971-73; mem. S.C. State Art Purchasing Com., Nat. Endowment for Arts, 1967-72. Vice chmn. Pres.'s Commn. Observance World Population Year, 1974—. Second v.p. Nat. Fedn. Republican Women, 1962-67, 1st v.p., 1967-71, pres., 1972-73, 74—; vice chmn. S.C. Rep. Com., 1960-61, mem. S.C. Rep. Com., 1970-72; pres. S.C. Fedn. Rep. Women, 1962-64; alternate-at-large Rep. Nat. Conv., 1960, del.-at-large, 1964, 68, 72, mem. nat. platform com., 1964, 68, 72. Named Woman of Year Women's Nat. Republican Club, Inc. Recipient scholarships Am. Council Learned Socs. for study of Arabic, 1942-43, Chinese, 1945-46. Fellow Am. Council Learned Socs. Episcopalian. Editorial work on Polylingual Bibliog. Ency. of Chinese Works, Am. Council of Learned Socs., 1945-46. Home: 800 S Lee St Alexandria VA 22314 also 268 Connecticut Av Spartansburg SC 29302

ARMS, KATHARINE HELENA (MRS. JOSEPH EDWARD ARMS), banker; b. Brockton, Mass., July 30, 1922; d. Louis John and Anne Isabel (Murphy) Daniels; student Burdett Coll., 1940-41; m. Robert Sheppard, Mar. 10, 1942 (dec. Nov. 1962); m. Joseph Edward Arms, Feb. 12, 1967; children—Phillip A. Sheppard, Anne T. Sheppard (Mrs. Bernard M. LaBelle), Stephen D. Sheppard, Edward W. Arms. Payroll clk. Dartmouth Shoe Co., Brockton, 1950-52; with Nat. Bank of Plymouth County (name later changed to First County Nat. Bank), Brockton, 1961—, asst. supr. bookkeeping dept., 1962-63, br. mgr., 1964—. Notary Pub., 1965—. Club: Quota (Brockton). Home: 38 Hall St Brockton MA 02402 Office: 712 Crescent St Brockton MA 02402

ARMSTRONG, ALICE CATT, author, publisher; b. Ft. Scott, Kan.; d. Charles H. and Florence (Pakenham) Catt; ed. jr. coll., also specialized courses; Litt.D (hon.), St. Andrews U., London, 1969; D.Lit., St. Paul's Coll., Rome, Italy, 1970; L.H.D., St. Olav's Acad., Sweden, 1969; Dr. Cultural Letters, Bodkin Bible Inst., W. Va., 1973; D.D. (hon.), Cal. Christian Inst., 1970; Ph.D., Colo. State Christian Coll., 1972. Actress Little Theatre groups Pasadena Playhouse, 1942-48; tchr. dramatic arts, Hollywood, Cal., 1946-48; editor, pub. Cal. History and Biography Research Publs., Los Angeles, 1949—. Co-chmn. Cal. com. Freedom Found., Valley Forge, Pa., 1956; founder, organizing dir., v.p. Execs. Dinner Club of Beverly Hills and Bel-Air, Cal., 1958; mem. Opera Guild So. Cal.; mem. blue ribbon com. Music Center Los Angeles, 1962; Internat. Student Center, Inc., U. Cal. Los Angeles, 1963-65; Cal. State Travel and Recreation Com. Cal. C. of C., 1956-68; internat. chmn. Sibelius Centennial celebrations U.S., 1965; chmn. Hollywood Bowl Concert, 1965; mem. nat. com. Nat. Bible Week, 1968; nat. adv. council Addictive Drugs Ednl. Found., 1969—. Adviser U.S. Security Council. Hon. dir. Royal Blue Book, London, 1968—. Recipient Woman of Achievement award Cal. Women Golden West, 1951; Nat. Travel Guide award Nat. Writers Club, Denver, 1958, Wisdom award of Honor, Wisdom Mag., 1965, Outstanding Citizen of Month Cal.-Ariz.-Hawaii Sr. Citizens, 1966, Am. Edn. League award, 1967; Journalism award, London, Eng., 1967; dame grand cross Sovereign and Royal Order Plost, Hospitalier Order St. John Jerusalem Sovereign and Royal Order Imperial Crown Byelorussia, Sovereign and Royal Order St. Laurent, numerous others. Mem. Los Angeles World Affairs Council, Nat. Writers Club, Historic Los Angeles Assn., Save-the-Redwoods League, Art Patrons Assn. Am. (patron), So. Cal. Choral Music Assn., Internat. Platform Assn. (publicity dir. West Coast div.), Town Hall Cal., Soc. Descs. Knights Garter, Nat. Soc. Magna Charta Dames; UN Assn., Friends FBI, Smithsonian Inst. (asso.). Mem. Order Eastern Star. Author: California Biographical and Historical Series, 1950—; Dining and Lodging on the North American Continent, 1958; And They Called It Society, 1961-62; also research and history books, radio skits, travel guides, children's stores. Address: Cordell Views 1331 Cordell Pl Los Angeles CA 90069

ARMSTRONG, BETTY WINSTEAD (MRS. WILLIAM MARION ARMSTRONG), coll. dean; b. Covington, Ky., Feb. 25, 1927; d. Thomas Manly and Isabelle Sara (Corwin) Winstead; B.S., U. Cin., 1961, Ph.D., 1968; M.S., U. Ky., 1963; m. William Marion Armstrong, Mar. 8, 1948; 1 son, Thomas Neuman. Tchr., Kenton Elementary Sch., Independence, Ky., 1960-64; instrnl. supr. Kenton County Bd. Edn., 1964-66; instr. elementary edn. U. Cin., 1967-68, asst. prof. 1967-72; asst. dean, 1970-72; asso. prof., asso. dean Coll. Edn., 1972—. Cons. local sch. dists., 1967—; instnl. rep. Am. Assn. Colls. Tchr. Edn., 1970—. Mem. Assn. Tchr. Educators (co-chmn. nat. meeting 1972), Delta Kappa Gamma, Kappa Delta Pi. Home: 37 Rock Hill Lane Fort Thomas KY 41075 Office: University of Cincinnati College of Education Cincinnati OH 45221

ARMSTRONG, CLARA JULIA EVERSHED (MRS. ROLLIN S. ARMSTRONG), coll. adminstr.; b. Murray, Utah, Aug. 25, 1911; d. Elmer B. and Lenora K. (Tripp) Evershed; student Henager Bus. Coll., 1936-37; m. Rollin S. Armstrong, Sept. 29, 1956; foster children—Maxwell Rollin, Ruth Elizabeth, Robert Neil, Philip Samuel. Office mgr., credit mgr. D.N. & E. Walter & Co., Salt Lake City, 1937-48; with Latter Day Saints Bus. Coll., Salt Lake City, 1948—, sec., 948-52, fgn. student adviser, 1952-55, vet. coordinator, 1952-55, rehab. counselor, 1952-55, registrar, 1955-62, sec.-treas., 1962—. Mem. Ch. of Jesus Christ of Latter-day Saints (pres. Ward Mut. Improvement Assn. 1941-45). Home: 35 F St Salt Lake City UT 84103 Office: 411 E South Temple Salt Lake City UT 84111

ARMSTRONG, CLARA KATHERINE, govt. research asst.; b. Stafford County, Va.; d. Enoch T. and Mary B. (Armstrong) Armstrong; B.A., Am. U., 1965, postgrad., 1967-68. Legal sec. Roberts & McInnis, Washington, 1947-56; mem. minority staff, Com. on Govt. Operations, Ho. of Reps., Washington, 1956-68, minority research asst., 1969—. Baptist. Clubs: Potomac Toastmistress (corr. sec. 1969, rec. sec. 1969, v.p. 1970, pres. 1971), Senate Toastmasters (v.p. 1974). Home: 2525 N 10th Arlington VA 22201 Office: Rayburn Bldg Washington DC 20515

ARMSTRONG, EDITH ELAINE, telephone co. exec.; b. East Walpole, Mass., Oct. 6, 1935; d. Richard G. and Jessie Irene (Hutchins) Sprague; grad. high sch.; m. Howard J. Armstrong, May 17, 1957 (div. Dec. 15, 1965; 1 dau., Pamela. With New Eng. div. Continental Telephone Co. System, Concord, 1966—, adminstr. personnel policies and benefits since 1973—. Conglist. Home: 203 Loudon Rd Webster House Concord NH 03301 Office: 163 Loudon Rd Concord NH 03301

ARMSTRONG, ELEANOR SINCLAIR (MRS. DONALD BUDD ARMSTRONG, JR.), painter; b. Union City, N.J., Apr. 21, 1922; d. William Wiland and Josephine Virginia (Canal) Dippel; grad. Lincoln High Sch., 1939; student Art Students League, N.Y.C., 1959-64; m. Donald Budd Armstrong, Jr., Jan. 24, 1955. Exec. sec. Foote, Cone & Belding, N.Y.C., 1947-50, McCann-Erickson, N.Y.C., 1951-54; exhibit one-woman shows Ruth White Gallery, N.Y.C., 1967, Scarborough (N.Y.) Art Gallery, Scarborough, 1971; exhibited in group shows Am. Acad. Arts and Letters, 1967-68, N.Y. Exhbn. Painters and Sculptors, Avanti Galleries, N.Y.C., 1969, Nat. Acad. Arts, 1969-71, N.J. Painters-Sculptors Soc., 1970-71, Casino Municipal, Cannes, France, 1969, Chateau de la Napoule, Cannes, 1969, London (Ont., Can.) Art Mus., 1969; represented in museums and private collections. Mem. Nat. Assn. Women Artists, Artists Equity, Painters and Sculptors Soc. N.J. (award in oils 1971). Club: Sleepy Hollow Country. Home: 151 Revolutionary Rd Scarborough NJ 10510

ARMSTRONG, ELIZABETH LOUISE (MRS. BOB JUNIUS ARMSTRONG), lawyer; b. Houston, Dec. 19, 1929; d. Bruno Julius and Margaret Louise (Kehr) Reich; B.A., U. Houston, 1952; m. Bob Junius Armstrong, June 28, 1952; children—Pamela Beth, Robert Paul and Cynthia Ann (twins). Admitted to Tex. bar, 1956, U.S. Dist. Court, U.S. Court of Appeals, U.S. Supreme Ct.; practice law, Lake Jackson, Tex. Mem. City of Lake Jackson Tax Equalization Bd., 1970, chmn. 1971; mem. budget and admissions com. Brazoria County United Fund, 1970; pres. Elisabet New Elementary Sch. P.T.A., 1964-66, Lake Jackson Intemediate P.T.A., 1971-72; mem. Brazoria County Family Counseling Service Bd., Lake Jackson, Tex., 1967—. Trustee, Brazoria County Sch. Bd., 1972—. Mem. Am. Judicature Soc., State Bar Tex. (mem. pub. affairs com. 1971—), Brazoria County Bar Assn. (dir. 1966-68, sec., treas. 1971-72), Nat. Assn. Women Lawyers, Delta Kappa Gamma, Kappa Beta Pi. Club: Brazosport Yacht. Home: 114 Sleepy Hollow Dr Lake Jackson TX 77566 Office: 628 Dixie Dr PO Box 124 Lake Jackson TX 77566

ARMSTRONG, ELIZABETH PHYLLIS, librarian; b. Ridgefield, Conn., May 2, 1926; d. Nobel and Phyllis (Beck) Armstrong; B.A. magna cum laude, Tufts U., 1951; M.L.S., Rutgers U., 1960. Asst. command dir. recreation Spl. Services, Europe, 1952-56; post entertainment dir. Spl. Service, Ft. Knox, Ky., 1956-59; loan librarian U. Ida., 1960-62; reference librarian Long Beach (Cal.) Pub. Library, 1962-63; head pub. services U.S. Internat. U., San Diego, 1963-65, chief librarian, 1965-68; chief librarian Cal. Inst. Arts, 1968—. Vice pres. Film and TV Study Center. Mem. Am., Theatre, Ida. (chmn. conf. 1962) library assns., Spl. Libraries Assn. (v.p. San Diego chpt. 1967-68), Am. Soc. Information Scis. Home: 808 4th St Apt 107 Santa Monica CA 90403 Office: 24700 McBean Pky Valencia CA 91355

ARMSTRONG, ELLEN CHILDS, educator; b. Princeton, N.J., Mar. 24, 1949; d. Richard Stoll and Margaret Frances (Childs) Armstrong; B.A. with honors, Wellesley Coll., 1970; postgrad. U. Mich., 1973—. Registrar, Westminster Choir Coll., Princeton, 1970-72, dean, 1972-73; asst. to dir. Inst. Adminstrv. Advancement, U. Mich. at Ann Arbor, 1973—. Producer Princeton Gilbert and Sullivan Assn., 1973. Mem. Am. Assn. Higher Edn., Middle States Assn. Collegiate Registrars and Officers of Admission, Mensa. Home: 502 Burson Pl Ann Arbor MI 48104

ARMSTRONG, JANE BOTSFORD (MRS. ROBERT T. ARMSTRONG), sculptress; b. Buffalo; d. Samuel Booth and Edith (Pursel) Botsford; student Middlebury Coll., 1939-40, Pratt Inst., 1940-41, Art Students' League, 1962-64; m. Robert Thexton Armstrong, July 3, 1960. Exhibited one-man shows Frank Rehn Gallery, 1971, Columbus (O.) Gallery Fine Arts, 1972, Aqra Gallery Washington, 1972, 73, Aqra Gallery Palm Beach (Fla.), 1972, Phila. Mus. Art, 1972, Johnson Gallery, Middlebury, Vt., 1973, Mary Duke Biddle Gallery for Blind N.C. Mus. Art, 1974, Arnot Art Mus., Elmira, N.Y.; represented in exhbn. Sculpture Center, N.Y.C., Nat. Collection Fine Arts Jr. Mus., 1971, 72; also represented in numerous pvt. collections. Recipient Pauline Law Prize Allied Artists Am., 1969, 70; certificate merit N.A.D., 1973; Council Am. Artists' Socs. prize Nat. Sculpture Soc., 1973; Charles N. Whinston Meml. prize Nat. Assn. Women Artists, 1973. Mem. Nat. Arts Club (gold medal for sculpture 1968, 69, 71, best in show 1973), Soc. Animal Artists, Audubon Artists (medal of honor 1972), Knickerbocker Artists (Alice Standish Buell Meml. prize 1972). Home: High Meadows Manchester Center VT 05255

ARMSTRONG, LILLIAN JEANNETTE (MRS. RICHARD SIDNEY ARMSTRONG), real estate broker; b. Los Angeles, Dec. 11, 1929; d. Lee and Lillian Alma (Ensign) Wilson; grad. Realtors Inst., 1971; student, Cal. State U., 1973; certificate Community Coll., 1973; m. Richard Sidney Armstrong, Mar. 7, 1948; children—Roxanne (Mrs. James John Vertiglia), R. Lance. Sec., Barnard Quinn Photo Engraving, Los Angeles, 1947-48; operator Pacific Telephone Co., San Luis Obispo, Cal., 1948-51; partner, sales-office mgr. Garden Dairy, Santa Maria, Cal., 1956-68; sales rep. Town & Country Realty, Santa Maria, 1966-68, broker, sales mgr., 1968-69; sales mgr. Crest Realty Santa Maria, 1969-72; v.p., sales office mgr. Weber & Armstrong, Inc., Santa Maria, 1972—. Lectr. Allan Hancock Community Coll., Santa Maria, 1970-72; real estate instr. Cal. Community Coll., Santa Maria, 1973—. Leader, Girl Scouts Am., Santa Maria, 1958-64; pres. Lakeview P.T.A., Santa Maria, 1964-65. Bd. dir. Tres Condados Girl Scout Council, 1963-64; United Way of Santa Maria Valley, Cal., 1973. Mem. Nat. Assn. Realtors, Nat. Inst. Farm and Land Brokers, Nat. Inst. Real Estate Brokers, Santa Maria Bd. Realtors (pres. 1972, dir. 1971—), Cal. Real Estate Assn. (dir. 1971-72, vice chmn. membership com. 1973—), Central Coast Exchangers (sec. 1972), Santa Maria Valley Developers. Club: Soroptomist (pres. 1965—) (Santa Maria). Home: 715 S Bradley Rd Apt 10 Santa Maria CA 93454 Office: 612 S Broadway PO Box 999 Santa Maria CA 93454

ARMSTRONG, MARGARET BLAIR MORTON (MRS. JOHN SAMUEL ARMSTRONG III), art coordinator; b. Tulsa, Sept. 9; d. Franklin Craig and Margaret (Moberly) Morton; student Am. Acad. Dramatic Arts, 1943-44, Md. Inst. Art, 1949-50; m. John Samuel Armstrong III, Mar. 20, 1951; children—Sally Margaret (Mrs. Stephen Wayne Lewis), Leila Louise Moberly, John Samuel IV, Roxanna Maude. One man show Craftsman's Restaurant Scottsdale, Ariz., 1953; producer Nat. Art Observance, Scottsdale, 1954, Correlation Art and Fashion to benefit Am. Cancer Soc. Ariz., 1960, 61, Correlation Art of Ariz. with Phoenix Symphony, 1965-66; cons. film Composition; founder, producer traveling religious exhibit, 1966, Religious Art and Music Festival, 1968; owner Mnemosyne Films, 1969—. Founder, 1st curator Episcopal Diocese Ariz. Art Collection, 1970—. Recipient 1st, 3d prizes Womans Nat. Republican Club N.Y., 1964; nat. citation Am. Artists Profl. League for producing Nat. Art Week Scottsdale; plaque for distinguished leadership Am. Cancer Soc.; 1st prize ann. poetry competition Phoenix Writers Club, 1973. Mem. Nat. Soc. Arts and Letters (founding v.p. Ariz. chpt., 2d v.p. 1969-70), English Speaking Union (founding chmn. poets' group 1969-70, editor newsletter and poetry page 1969-72, founding mem. Phoenix 1969-70). Author, compiler, illustrator An Anglophile's Cookery Book, 1972. Home: 6246 Joshua Tree Lane Scottsdale AZ 85253

ARMSTRONG, MARIAN LOUISE, educator; b. Bedford, Ind., June 24, 1929; d. John Frank and Maude Corinne (Pafford) Armstrong; B.S., Ind. U., 1952, M.A., 1958. Librarian, Edison Sch., Gary, Ind., 1952-56, Paris (France) Am. Sch., 1956-57; librarian, instr. library sci. Ind. U., Bloomington, 1958-68, asst. prof. Grad. Library Sch., 1968—. Pres. bd. dirs. Monroe County Pub. Library Founds., 1973—. Mem. Am., Ind. library assns., Am., Ind. sch. librarians assns., Am. Assn. Library Schs., Ind. U. Alumni Assn. (sec., treas. grad. library sch. 1968—), Pi Lambda Theta, Beta Phi Mu, Delta Kappa Gamma. Editor: Grad. Library Sch. Newsletter, 1969. Home: 2030 E Third St Bloomington IN 47401 Office: Graduate Library School Indiana University Bloomington IN 47401

ARMSTRONG, MYRTLE W. COOPER (MRS. ARNOLD ARMSTRONG), state ofcl.; b. Aurora, Ill., Mar. 9, 1925; d. Paul Francis and Myrtle (Vass) Cooper; student Aurora Coll., 1964-72; m. Arnold Armstrong, Dec. 23, 1945; children—Arnold, Jr., Keith Bradford. Stenographer Ill. State Employment Service, Aurora, 1950-56, employment interviewer, 1956-70, mgr., 1970—. Bd. dirs. Office Econ. Opportunity, 1971—, A.R.C., 1971—, United Way, 1972—; chmn. Aurora Scholarship Found., 1972—. Mem. Am. Bus. Womens Assn. (chmn. edn. 1972—), Local Office Mgrs. Assn., Valley Personnel Assn., Aurora C. of C. (mem. com. 1973—), Altrusa Internat. Home: Route 1 Box 113 Sugar Grove IL 60554 Office: 221 Spruce St Aurora IL 60506

ARMSTRONG, PATRICIA KAY (MRS. CHARLES W. ARMSTRONG), educator, ecologist; b. Highland Park, Mich., Dec. 18, 1936; d. El M. and Vivian (Thompson) Stoddard; B.A. cum laude, North Central Coll., Ill., 1958; M.S. (Robert Ridgeway fellow), U. Chgo., 1968; m. Charles W. Armstrong, Jan. 27, 1955; children—Jacqueline Joy, Rebecca Raye. Sci. tchr. Washington Jr. High Sch., Naperville, Ill., 1960-69, head sci. dept., 1963-67; asst. research specialist Morton Arboretum, Lisle, Ill., 1969—, staff Inst. Glaciological and Arctic Scis., 1968; study botany, Juneau Ice Field, Alaska, 1966, 68; tchr. rock climbing, mountaineering, leader expdns., 1964—. Mem. Ill. Edn. Assn., Nat. Sci. Tchrs. Assn., Ecol. Soc. Am., Am. Mus. Nat. History, Arctic Inst. Am., Brit. Lichen Soc., Am. Bryological Soc., Sigma Xi, Tri Beta. Baptist. Clubs: Ia. Mountaineering; Chicago Mountaineering, Sierra (Chgo.). Author: Trilobites of the Chicago Region, 1962. Contbr. articles, poems and photographs to nat. mags. Solo climber four highest mountains Mexico. Home: 535 S Washington St Naperville IL 60540 Office: Morton Arboretum Lisle IL 60532

ARMSTRONG, RUTH ELEANOR, pub. relations exec., govt. ofcl.; b. McCook, Neb., Apr. 4, 1937; d. Robert Burns and Bess (Furman) Armstrong; B.A. in Communications, Am. U., 1959, M.A., 1969. Editor Joint Publs. Research Service, Washington, 1963-68; press asst. Dallas Times Herald, Washington, 1968-69; writer, editor Social Security Bull., Washington, 1969-70; programs coordinator Nat. Library Medicine, Bethesda, Md., 1970-73; writer Fed. Energy Adminstrn., 1974—. Mem. Soc. for Tech. Communication, Alpha Psi Omega, Theta Sigma Phi, Zeta Phi Eta. Home: 10500 Weymouth St Bethesda MD 20014 Office: Ben Franklin Sta Washington DC

ARMSTRONG, VALERIE, city ofcl.; b. Hamilton, Ont., Can., Sept. 21, 1919 (came to U.S. 1941, naturalized 1948); d. Westropp and Winifred (Colquhoun) Armstrong; student Purdue U., 1937-39, Northwestern U., 1940, U. Chgo., 1942-43, U. Pa., 1956, 57, 61. Campus shopper promotion Mandel Bros., Chgo., 1939; supr. tng. Sears, Roebuck & Co., 1940, methods and time study engr., 1941-44, Phila., 1946-47; asst. mgr. Leave Center for Service Women, Ottawa, Ont., 1944-45; home lighting adviser Phila. Electric Co., 1948; legal recorder Seaboard Finance Co., 1949-51; statis. analyst RCA Quality Control Lab., 1952-53, Franklin Inst., 1954; records mgmt. analyst City of Phila., 1955-57, adminstrv. analyst, 1957—. Mem. watershed mgmt. com. Water Resources Assn. of the Delaware River. Mem. Am. Soc. Pub. Adminstrn., Pan Am. Assn., Phila. Mus. Art, Univ. Mus., Delaware Valley Protective Assn., Am. Acad. Polit. and Social Sci., World Affairs Council Phila., Hist. Soc. Pa., Geneal. Soc. Pa. Episcopalian. Clubs: Plays and Players, Charlotte Cushman, Purdue (sec. 1952-53, dir. 1954-58). Home: The Dorchester 226 W Rittenhouse Sq Philadelphia PA 19103 Office: Water Dept Philadelphia PA 19107

ARNAUD, SARA HAYES (MRS. EDOUARD X. ARNAUD), psychologist; b. Woonsocket, R.I., Dec. 26, 1921; d. Alfred and Elmina (Bleakney) Hayes; B.S., Simmons Coll., 1943; M.A., Boston U., 1949, Ph.D., 1957; m. Edouard X. Arnaud, Aug. 20, 1950. Faculty dept. psychiatry U. Pitts., 1957—, clin. asso. prof. psychology, 1969—, asso. prof. psychology dept. child devel. and child care, 1969—; dir. Arsenal Family and Children's Center, 1971—; dir. tng. grant U.S. Office Edn., 1970—; play filming grant, 1971—. Diplomate in clin. psychology Am. Bd. Profl. Psychology. Fellow Am. Orthopsychiat. Assn.; mem. Am. Psychol. Assn., Soc. Personality Assessment, Am. Assn. U. Profs., A.A.A.S. Producer series of films on children's play, 1973—. Home: 236 Chatham Park Dr Pittsburgh PA 15220 Office: Arsenal Family and Children's Center 3939 Penn Av Pittsburgh PA 15224

ARNDT, ELIZABETH DELANO MOORE (MRS. JOSEPH MANNING ARNDT, JR.), civic worker; b. Newburyport, Mass., Aug. 25, 1920; d. Frederick Arnold and Miriam Chelis (Delano) Moore; Registered Nurse, Boston City Hosp. Sch. Nursing, 1941; m. Joseph Manning Arndt, Jr., May 11, 1946; children—Margaret Anne (Mrs. Jerry Shinn), Martha Howard, Joseph Manning III, Marilyn Delano. Asst. head nurse outpatient dept. Boston City Hosp., 1941-42. Pres., Heart of Mo. council Girl Scouts U.S.A., 1967-71, council communicator region V, 1973, day camp dir., 1966-72; chmn. Centralia (Mo.) United Fund, 1967; sec. E. Central Mo. Mental Health Council, 1971-72; co-organizer Centralia Mental Health Council, 1972—. Pres., Centralia Federated Republican Women's Club, 1960-62; treas. 8th Dist. Republican Woman's Club, 1962; pres. Mo. Federated Rep. Woman's Club, 1969-71; del. Rep. Nat. Conv., 1964; committeeman Rep. party, Centralia, 1966—; chmn. youth involvement Nat. Federated Rep. Women, 1972-73; mem. Mo. State Rep. Com., 1970—. Served with Nurses Corps, AUS, 1942-46; ETO. Mem. Am. Legion. Mem. Christian Ch. (deaconess 1963-66). Club: Sorosis Federated Women's (pres. 1954-56), Bridge (Centralia). Home: 5 Sunrise Circle Centralia MO 65240

ARNDT, HILDA CHRISTINE MARGARET, educator; b. New Orleans, Aug. 7, 1912; d. William and Augusta Christine (Scherer) Arndt; B.A., Newcomb Coll., 1932; M.S., Washington U., St. Louis, 1934; Ph.D., U. Chgo., 1965. Caseworker, St. Louis Children's Aid Soc., 1934-38; caseworker, supr. Family Service Soc., New Orleans,

1938-43; dist. supr. Family Service Assn., Cleve., 1943-47; asst. prof. Sch. Social Welfare, La. State U., Baton Rouge, 1947-50, asso. prof., 1950-58, prof., dir. field practice, 1958—. Summer faculty U. Chgo., 1961-64; cons. social work staffs VA Hosp., Gulfport, Miss., 1969—, Alexandria, La., 1970—; cons. and workshop leader for various agys. and profl. orgns.; social work cons. Manpower and Tng. div. Nat. Inst. Mental Health, Dept. Health, Edn. and Welfare, 1962-66, cons. tng. com. Children's Bur., Social Rehab. Service, 1968-71. Recipient Outstanding Community Service award Washington U. Alumni, 1961. Mem. Am. Assn. U. Profs., Council on Social Work Edn. (commn. on accreditation 1961-64, com. on internat. social work 1957-60, mem. accreditation teams 1964—), La. Vis. Tchrs. Assn. (hon.), Nat. Assn. Social Workers, Family Service Assn. Am. Contbr. articles to profl. jours. Home: 2740 Morning Glory St Baton Rouge LA 70808

ARNELL, PAULA ANN YOUNGBERG (MRS. RICHARD ANTHONY ARNELL), pathologist; b. Moline, Ill., Nov. 25, 1938; d. Paul Phillip and Mabel Eleanor (Arnell) Youngberg; B.A. summa cum laude, Augustana Coll., 1960; M.D., U. Ia., 1964; m. Richard Anthony Arnell, June 28, 1964; children—Carla Ann, Paula Marie. Intern, St. Lukes-Mercy Hosp., Cedar Rapids, Ia., 1964-65; resident pathology U. Ia., Iowa City, 1965-68; chief resident State U. Ia. Hosp., Iowa City, 1968-69; pathologist, dir. labs. Luth. Hosp., Moline, Ill., 1969—; mem. staffs Moline Pub. Hosp., Franciscan Hosp., Rock Island, Ill. Sec., Rock Island County Blood Bank, 1972-73, v.p., 1973-74; cons. Rock Island Tb Center, 1970-72; profl. del. Am. Cancer Soc., 1971-73; tchr. Luth. Hosp. Sch. Inhalation Therapy, Sch. Nursing, 1970—. Mem. alumni bd. Augustana Coll., Rock Island, 1972—. Fellow Am. Coll. Pathologists, Am. Soc. Clin. Pathologists; mem. Internat. Acad. Pathologists, Am. Assn. Cytologists, Am. Assn. Blood Banks, Am. Assn. Clin. Scientists, Am. Womans Med. Assn., A.M.A., Ia. Ill. Med. Soc., Phi Beta Kappa, Beta Beta Beta. Home: 3904 7th Av Rock Island IL 61201 Office: Luth Hosp 501 10th Av Moline IL 61265

ARNETT, MAXINE HILDNER, lawyer; b. Bronx County, N.Y., Sept. 20, 1030; d. Egmont Goetz and Miriam (Levin) Hildner; A.B., Hunter Coll., 1956; LL.B., N.Y. Law Sch., 1962; m. George Richard Arnett, July 30, 1959; children—Renee Christine, Suzanne Melina, Scott Richard. Admitted to Ind. bar, 1963, practice in Greenfield; dep. atty. gen. State Ind., 1965-69; asst. majority atty. Ind. Senate, 1965. Candidate pros. Hancock County (Ind.), 1970. Bd. dirs. Easter Seal Com., Hancock County, 1966-72. Mem. Ind. (chmn. subcom. on alcoholism com. rehab. offenders and corrections criminal justice sect.), Indpls., Hancock county bar assns., Greater Indpls. Women's Polit. Caucus. Presbyn. Home: Rural Route 1 Box 144 Charlottesville IN 46117 Office: 22 N State St Greenfield IN 46140

ARNEY, DORA ADELIA QUINN, educator; b. Springfield, Mo., Jan. 15, 1929; d. George Edwin and Lida Louise (Whitlock) Quinn; B.S. in Edn., Southwest Mo. State U., 1950; M.Ed., U. Ark., 1970; postgrad. S.W. Mo. State U., U. Ark.; m. Nelson D. Arney, Sept. 3, 1950 (dec. 1963); children—David Rex, Rex Allen. Instr. health and phys. edn. Lindenwood Coll., St. Charles, Mo., 1951-52, S.W. Mo. State U., 1953-54, U. Kansas City, 1958-62, S.W. Mo. State Tng. Sch., Springfield, Mo., 1965-74; mem. faculty Sch. Ozarks, Point Lookout, Mo., 1950—, asso. prof. phys. edn., 1965—. Coach, staff Kawanis Twin Lakes Camp, Plymouth, Ind., 1950-51, Bemedji Camp, Thunderbird, Minn., 1951-52; counselor arts and crafts Springfield (Mo.) Red Cross, 1950-74; instr. first aid Am. Nat. Red Cross, Point Lookout, Mo., 1960-74. Mem. A.A.H.P.E.R., Mo. Assn. Intercollegiate Athletics Women, Delta Psi Kappa. Home: Box 277 Point Lookout MO 67626 Office: Sch of Ozarks Point Lookout MO 65726

ARNHEIM, JULIETTE O'NEIL, librarian; b. Knoxville, Tenn., Nov. 23, 1939; d. William Patrick and Lelia Louise (Boyd) O'Neil; A.B., Sweet Briar Coll., 1961; student U. Paris (France), 1959-60; M.L.S., Rutgers U., 1972; m. William Maurice Arnheim III, May 25, 1963; 1 dau., Lelia Boyd. Asst. librarian Inmont Corp., N.Y.C., 1961-63; tech. editor Esso Research & Engring. Co., Linden, N.J., 1963-66, research librarian, 1966-69; state tech. services librarian Rutgers U., New Brunswick, N.J., 1969-72, phys. scis. and engring. resources librarian, 1972—. Mem. Spl. Libraries Assn. (treas. N.J. chpt. 1970-72, dir. 1973-75), Research Soc. Am., Beta Phi Mu. Home: 751 St Mark's Av Westfield NJ 07090 Office: Library Sci and Medicine Rutgers U New Brunswick NJ 08903

ARNHOLTER, ETHELWYNE GRETHEL NALLEY (MRS. HAROLD H. ARNHOLTER), psychologist; b. Lafayette, Ind., Dec. 4, 1904; d. Albert and Lola (Swaynje) Nalley; A.B., Butler U., 1949; M.A., Ind. U., 1951; Ph.D., Purdue U., 1953; m. Harold H. Arnholter, Aug. 1, 1923; children—Richard, Albert, Carol Simmons. Chief psychologist Central State Mental Hosp., 1953-56, Ind. Women's Prison and Ind. Girls Sch., 1956-59; research psychologist Goodwill Industries, 1959-61; chief psychologist Atterbury Job Corps, 1959-62; chief psychologist Crossroads Rehab. Center, 1963-65, Community Services Council, 1965-67; psychologist Adult Mental Health Clinic Pinellas County, 1969-71; practicing psychologist, St. Petersburg, Fla., 1972—. Cons. Noble Sch. Retarded Children, 1958-59, Met. Schs. Lawrence Twp., 1963-64, Indpls. Pub. Schs., United Christian Missionary Soc., 1955-56, Standard Life Ins. Co., 1956-57, Eli Lilly Co., 1959-61. Diplomate Am. Bd. Examiners Profl. Psychology. Address: 4109 Alberca Way S St Petersburg FL 33712

ARNOLD, ALISON (MRS. W. RICHMOND ARNOLD), editor; b. Boston; d. George and Gertrude (Pratt) Alison; student Mass. Coll. Art, 1917-21; m. W. Richmond Arnold, June 16, 1924 (dec. July 1957); children—Mary Katharine (Mrs. Percival Gilbert, Jr.), John Arnold. Soc. editor Boston Herald Traveler, 1938-72; soc. editor Boston Globe, 1972—. Home: 4 Surplus St Duxbury MA 02332 Office: 135 Morrissey Blvd Boston MA 02107

ARNOLD, BERNIE WYCKOFF (MRS. HENRY O. ARNOLD JR.), journalist; b. Cambridge, O., Jan. 22, 1927; d. Walter Wayne and Golda Larie (Pryor) Wyckoff; B.A., David Lipscomb Coll., 1948; postgrad. George Peabody Coll., 1948-49; m. Henry O. Arnold Jr., Sept. 2, 1948; children—Chip, Nan, Cris, Tim. Food editor Nashville Tennesseean Newspaper, 1965-73; home editor Nashville Mag., 1973—. Instr. U. Tenn., Nashville, 1973—, YWCA, 1974—. Mem. Ch. of Christ. Home: 1110 Belvidere Dr Nashville TN 37204 Office: 5519 Charlotte Av Nashville TN 37209

ARNOLD, CARRIE KAREN, artist, art dir.; b. Greeley, Colo., May 25, 1944; d. James P. and Dorothy Adeline (Sweet) Forman; student Colo. State Coll. at Greeley, 1961-62; m. Samuel P. Arnold, 1971. Mgr. ABC Copy Service, Denver, 1962-65; draftswoman Iraola Drafting Service, Denver, 1965-67; owner Carrie's Copy & Color Service, Denver, 1967-71; owner The Fort Restaurant, Morrison, Colo., 1971—, Arnold & Co., Denver, 1971—. Commd. New Year's card Sri Lanka, 1974; pub. relations cons. Colo. Open Space Council, 1973. Program chmn. Opera on Tuesday, Denver Lyric Opera Guild, Jr. Symphony Guild. Republican. Conglist. Address: 2221 S Fillmore St Denver CO 80210

ARNOLD, ELIZABETH MULLEN (MRS. WILLIAM H. ARNOLD), civic worker; b. St. Louis, June 19, 1905; d. Joseph and Elizabeth (Welsh) Mullen; student les Fougeres (Switzerland), 1922-23, Washington U., 1923-26; m. William H. Arnold, Feb. 16, 1926; children—Elizabeth (Mrs. James H. Dallman), Emily (Mrs. Parkman H. Clancy) (dec.), William H., Joseph C. Mem. bd. dirs. Lake County (Ill.) chpt. A.R.C., 1956-58; bd. mem. Nat. Symphony, Washington, 1948-50; 1st chmn., co-organizer Army, Navy, Air Force Jr. Cotillion; active in Cath. charities Salzburg, Austria, 1953-55, also active other Austrian charities including Altenheim Old Peoples Home, Hellbrunn Old Peoples Home, Felbertal Sch., World Mission for Children, Grodig Kindergarten, Displaced Persons Camps; mem. bd. Ill. Children's Home and Aid Soc.; hon. chmn. USO Women's Bd.; charter mem. Loyola and Field Mus. Women's Bd. Recipient Pro Ecclesia et Pontifice, 1953, Lady of the Grand Cross, Equestrian Order of the Knights of the Holy Sepulchre (both Vatican), 1955; Chevaliere of the Conference du Tastevin (French), 1954. Mem. Armed Forces Hostess Assn. (pres. 1950), Women's Army and Navy and Air Force League (pres. 1946-48), Turkish-Am. Women's Cultural Soc. (v.p. 1951-53), Cath. Ladies Sodality (organizer, 1st pres. Salzburg, Austria 1953-55), Nat. Soc. Colonial Dames in State of Va., Kappa Kappa Gamma. Roman Catholic. Clubs: Fifth U.S. Army Women's (hon. pres. 1955-61), Fort Sheridan's Women's (bd. advisors 1955-61), JAMMAT Womens (organizer, 1st pres. Ankara, Turkey, 1950-53), USFA Women's (hon. pres. Salzurg, Austria 1953-55), Women's Athletic (Chgo.). Home: 261 South Bluff's Edge Dr Lake Forest IL 60045

ARNOLD, FLORENCE MILLNER, artist; b. Prescott, Ariz., Sept. 16, 1900; d. George Thomas and Cora Grace (Paxton) Millner; diploma Mills Coll., 1923; B.S. in Edn., U. So. Cal., 1937; postgrad. Claremont Coll., 1938-40; m. Archibald Adrian Arnold, Aug. 14, 1925; 1 dau., Adrienne (Mrs. Jonathon Chakerian). Supr. music Placentia (Cal.) schs., 1924-41; tchr. music Fullerton (Cal.) High Sch., 1941-48, Buena Park (Cal.) schs., 1948-66; one-woman shows Long Beach Mus. Art, 1961, 69, 70, Cal. State U. at Fullerton, 1967; retrospective Fullerton Arts Commn., 1974; numerous group shows including Esther Robles Gallery, Los Angeles, 1965, Laguna Beach Mus. Art, 1966-68, Women U.S.A., 1973; represented in permanent collections at Long Beach Mus. Art, Laguna Beach Mus. Art, Fullerton Coll., Mills Coll. Art, Cal. State U. at Fullerton. Cons. program for gifted children Buena Park Schs., 1973-74. Mem. goals com. City Fullerton, Cal., 1970. Bd. dirs. Muckenthaler Cultural Center, 1964-72, Art Alliance Cal. State U., Fullerton, 1969-74; bd. trustees Fullerton Sci. Mus., 1971-74. Named Woman of Year Fullerton C. of C., 1973. Mem. Los Angeles County Mus. Art, Laguna Beach Mus. Art (dir. 1967-69), Orange County Art Assn. (pres. 1960-62, 1968-69), Delta Kappa Gamma. Address: 1136 Valencia Mesa Dr Fullerton CA 92633

ARNOLD, GALE HUSSMAN, newspaperwoman; b. Texarkana, Ark., July 17, 1935; d. Walter Edward and Betty M. (Palmer) Hussman; B.A., Washington U., St. Louis, 1958; M.A., George Washington U., 1970; m. Richard Sheppard Arnold, June 14, 1958; children—Janet Sheppard, Lydia Palmer. Reporter Hot Springs (Ark.) Sentinel-Record, 1953-54; sec. Moonwatch project Smithsonian Astrophys. Obs., Cambridge, Mass., 1958-59; sec. to Prof. Paul A. Freund, Harvard Law Sch., 1959-60; clk. staff Senator J.W. Fulbright, 1960-61; asst. to law librarian, law library Dept. Health, Edn. and Welfare, Washington, 1961-62; book rev. editor Texarkana Gazette, 1972-74; Washington corr. Ark. Democrat, Little Rock, 1975—. Sec. sta. KCMC-TV, Texarkana, 1969—. Mem. budget com. United Way Crusade, 1971. Sec. bd. trustees Palmer Found., 1967—; bd. dirs. Sheltered Workshop, 1972—; trustee St. James Day Sch., 1965-71. Mem. D.A.R. (constn. week chmn. 1958-65, regent 1969-71), Children of Am. Revolution (pres. Sr. Soc. 1961; Endowment pin 1967), Sue Sanderson Garden Club (nat. bd. mgmt. 1965-68, pres. 1972), Jr. Leagues Texarkana (community research chmn. 1971-72, publns. chmn. 1972-73, edn. chmn. 1973-74), Washington. Democrat. Episcopalian. Club: Nat. Press. Address: 3540 Springland Lane NW Washington DC 20008

ARNOLD, HELEN T. (MRS. M. E. ARNOLD, JR.), assn. exec.; b. Marysville, Kan.; B.S. in History and Govt., Kan. State U.; postgrad. Tex. Tech. Inst., U. Wyo., U. Colo. Former tchr. Dir. Tex. League of Women Voters, 1957, pres. Tulsa, 1965-69, 2d v.p. Okla., 1969-71, pres., 1971—; 1st v.p. Tulsa Adult Edn. Council, 1967-70; gov. appointee Okla. Constl. Revision Com., 1969-70; active Goals for Tulsa Task Force on Pollution, Scenic Rivers Assn. Mem. UN Assn. (dir. 1970), Tulsa Geol. Geophys. Aux. (parliamentarian 1973-74), Alpha Delta Kappa (2d v.p. 1970-72). Unitarian (Unitarian-Universalists Womens Alliance). Office: League of Women Voters of Oklahoma 808 S Peoria St Tulsa OK 74120*

ARNOLD, HENRIETTA DOWS, corporate exec.; b. Cedar Rapids, Ia., Oct. 19, 1921; d. Sutherland C. and Frances Daisy (Mills) Dows; student The Masters Sch., Dobbs Ferry, N.Y., 1936-37; student Greenwood Sch., Ruxton, Md., 1938-39, Coe Coll., 1939-41, Chgo. Art Inst., 1945-46; m. Duane Arnold, Apr. 27, 1946; children—Margaret, Helen, Duane, Elizabeth (Mrs. Michael Barnett), Mary. Sec. Ta. Electric Light & Power, Cedar Rapids, 1942-43; with advt. dept. Sunkist Fruit Growers, Los Angeles, 1943-45; v.p., dir. Central Ia. Telephone Co., Cedar Rapids, 1960-66; v.p., corporate dir. Dows Real Estate Co., Cedar Rapids, 1969—; v.p., dir. Dows Maniti Dairy Farm, Inc., Cedar Rapids, 1969—; v.p., dir. Dows Farms, Inc., Cedar Rapids, 1969—; dir. Sutherland Sq., Cedar Rapids. Bd. dirs. YWCA, Cedar Rapids Art Assn., Pub. Health Nursing Assn.; trustee, mem. exec. com., bldg. com. Coe Coll.; trustee, mem. acad. com., bldg. com. Cornell Coll., Mt. Vernon, Ia.; trustee Menninger Found., Topeka. Mem. Jr. League, Cedar Rapids Hist. Assn. Republican. Presbyn (mem. religious edn. com., instr., trustee). Home: 321 Crescent St Cedar Rapids IA 52403 Office: 212 Dows Bldg PO Box 409 Cedar Rapids IA 52406

ARNOLD, JOANNE EASLEY (MRS. SANDERS GIBSON ARNOLD), ednl. adminstr.; b. Hutchinson, Kan., June 18, 1930; d. Orland Royce and Bernice Anna (Daugherty) Easley; B.A., U. Colo., 1952, M.A., 1965, Ph.D., 1971; m. Sanders Gibson Arnold, June 7, 1952; 1 son, Sanders Gibson. Reporter, mem. editorial staff Boulder (Colo.) Daily Camera, 1955-56; tchr. journalism, speech and English, Boulder (Colo.) High Sch., 1956-71, dir. publs., 1958-69, chmn. dept. English, 1967-69; asst. dir. Nat. Center for Higher Edn. Mgmt. Systems, Western Interstate Commn. for Higher Edn., Boulder, Colo., 1971—. Adviser, Elementary and Secondary Edn. Act, Title III, Colo., 1972—; cons. Bur. Communications, U. Colo., 1970-71; cons. elementary and secondary edn., organizational communication, lectr.; Commr., vice chmn. Boulder (Colo.) Pub. Libraries, 1973—; mem. com. on fiscal policy City of Boulder, 1972-73. Mem. Womens Rep. Club, Boulder, Colo., 1968—. Recipient Newspaper Fund fellowship Wall Street Jour., 1961. Mem. Nat. Soc. for the Study of Communication, Speech Assn. Am., Colo. Edn. Assn., Theta Sigma Phi, Alpha Delta Kappa, Pi Beta Phi. Club: U. Colo. Alumni (dir. 1954) (Boulder). Editor: Higher Edn. Mgmt., 1971—. Contbr. articles in field to profl. jours. Home: 815 Park Lane Boulder CO 80302 Office: PO Drawer P Boulder CO 80302

ARNOLD, MARGARET JANE, librarian; b. N.Y.C., Aug. 15, 1920; d. Glenn and Viola (Schimpf) Arnold; B.A., Syracuse U., 1942; B.S., Simmons Coll., 1943. Gen. asst. Detroit Pub. Library, 1943-45, Simmons Coll. Sch. Library Sci., 1947-48; asst. librarian Wellesley (Mass.) Free Library, 1946-47, librarian, 1950—. Mem. exec. bd. Eastern Regional Library Adv. Council, 1965—. Mem. Town Meeting, Wellesley, 1952-62. Trustee Isabel Babson Meml. Library, League Women Voters, Human Relations Service Wellesley, 1956-60. Mem. Mem. New Eng., Mass. library assns., Greater Boston Pub. Library Adminstrs. (pres. 1960—), Charles River Library Club (pres. 1952-53). Club: Quota (Wellesley). Home: 20 Abbott St Wellesley MA 02181 Office: 530 Washington St Wellesley MA 02181

ARNOLD, MARY BERTUCIO, pediatric endocrinologist; b. Fitchburg, Mass., Sept. 29, 1924; d. George E. and Louise Mary (Byrolly) Bertucio; A.B., Vassar Coll., 1945; M.D. cum laude, U. Vt., 1950; M.A., Brown U., 1974; m. John Hampton Arnold, July 28, 1956 (dec. Apr. 14, 1972); children—John Hampton, Mark, Matthew. Rotating intern Hartford Hosp., 1950-52; asst. resident in pediatrics Babies' Hosp., Columbia-Presbyn. Med. Center, N.Y.C., 1952-54; research fellow in pediatric endocrinology Mass. Gen. Hosp., Boston, 1954-57; asst. in pediatrics Harvard U. Sch. Medicine, 1955-57; instr. in pediatrics U. N.C., Chapel Hill, 1957-59, asst. prof. pediatrics, 1959-65; lectr. in bio-med. scis. Brown U., Providence, 1966-71, asso. prof. pediatrics (clin.) program in medicine, 1971—, dir. pediatric-endocrine div., Providence, 1966, cons. in biochemistry, 1966-68, acting chmn. dept. pediatrics, 1971—; asst. physician dept. pediatrics R.I. Hosp., 1970—; attending pediatrician Roger Williams Gen. Hosp.; cons. pediatric endocrinology Providence Lying-In Hosp., 1966. Diplomate Am. Bd. Pediatrics. Mem. Am. Fedn. for Clin. Research, Endocrine Soc., A.A.A.S., Am. Acad. Pediatrics, Pan Am. Med. Assn. (council sect. on pediatrics), Am. Assn. U. Profs., So. Soc. Pediatric Research, R.I. Clin. Diabetes Assn., New Eng. Pediatric Soc., A.M.A., R.I. Med. Soc., Providence Med. Assn., New Eng. Diabetes Assn., Lawson Wilkins Pediatric Endocrine Soc. (founder mem.), N.Y. Acad. Scis., Sigma Xi. Contbr. numerous articles in field to med. jours. Home: 21 Lee Rd Barrington RI 02806 Office: 825 Chalkstone Av Providence RI 02908

ARNOLD, SISTER MARY FREDERICK, educator; b. San Diego, June 11, 1930; d. Frederick Grey and Nonie Bernadine (Finn) Arnold; B.A., Mt. St. Mary's Coll., 1956; M.A., Loyola U., 1965, Ph.D., 1966; Gen. Electric Math. fellow, Stanford U., 1959; postgrad. U. Portland, 1961. Tchr. elementary sch., Encino, Cal., 1951-54, Los Angeles, 1954-56; tchr. Bishop Conaty High Sch., Los Angeles, 1956-61; mem. faculty Mt. St. Mary's Coll., Los Angeles, 1966—, asso. prof. psychology, 1972—, chmn. dept. psychology, 1966—, counselor, 1966—, dir. short term programs, 1973—, cons. psychol. testing, 1959. Nat. Inst. Mental Health grantee for clin. internship Northwestern U., 1963-64. Mem. Am., Western psychol. assns., Sisters of St. Joseph Caron. Address: 12001 Chalon Rd Los Angeles CA 90049

ARNOLD, MILDRED M., govt. ofcl.; b. South Bend, Ind.; d. John Wesley and Vanneska (Mohney) Arnold; B.S., U. Chgo., 1924; student U. Chgo., 1924-25, 27-28. Agt., Dependent Children, Madison County, N.Y., 1925-27; child welfare dir. Council Social Agys., Chgo., 1927-29; exec. sec. Childrens Service League of Sangamon County, Springfield, Ill., 1929-36; dir. children's div. State Dept. Pub. Welfare, Indpls., 1936-42; dir. div. social services Children's Bur., Dept. Health, Edn. and Welfare, Washington, 1942-69, asst. commr. Community Services Adminstrn., 1969—. Mem. Am. Pub. Welfare Assn., Nat. Conf. Social Welfare, Internat. Council on Social Welfare, Nat. Assn. Social Workers. Home: 2601 Woodley Pl NW Washington DC 20008 Office: 330 C St SW Washington DC 20201

ARNOLD, SANDRA PETERSON (MRS. LAWRENCE JOHN ARNOLD), data processing exec.; b. Los Angeles, Apr. 18, 1936; d. Kenneth Talbot and Yolanda Helena (Chiapetta) Peterson; B.A. cum laude, Immaculate Heart Coll., 1958; m. Lawrence John Arnold, Jan. 4, 1964; children—Erica Lynn, Lauren Anne. Research asst. Johns Hopkins, Bethesda, Md., 1959-60; programming instr. System Devel. Corp., Santa Monica, Cal., 1960-65; documentation mgr. Digitek Corp., Los Angeles, 1965-69; mgr. network support Computer Scis. Corp., El Segundo, Cal., 1969—. Active Girl Scouts U.S.A., 1972—; mem. Community Adv. Council Elementary Sch., Hollywood, Cal., 1972—. Mem. Club: Sierra. Home: 2907 Nichols Canyon Rd Hollywood CA 90046 Office: 650 N Sepulveda El Segundo CA 90245

ARNOT, JANE EMILIE, socio-econ. cons.; b. Flint, Mich., Nov. 14, 1920; d. Eli Jacob and Eda (Jacob) Arnot; B.A., U. Toledo, 1943; M.B.A., Ohio State U., 1951; postgrad. Marquette U., 1963-64. Market research analyst Gen. Tire & Rubber Co., Textileather div., 1954-62, Cutler Hammer, Inc., Milw., 1962-64, Eagle Picher Inc., Ohio Rubber Div., Willoughby, O., 1964-66; project mgr. Nat. Family Opinion, Inc., Toledo, 1966-68; socio-econ. planner Toledo-Lucas County Plan Commns., 1968-71; chief research analyst, social programming group Samborn, Steketee, Otis & Evans, Toledo, 1971-73; cons. socio-econs., marketing research, urban and environmental planning, 1974—. Mem. Am. Marketing Assn. (nat. dir. 1966-68), Internat. Platform Assn., Urban and Regional Information Systems Assn., Am. Assn. U. Women, Ohio Planning Conf., Common Cause, Am. Acad. Soc. and Polit. Sci., Am. Soc. Planning Ofcls., Am. Inst. Planners, Urisa, Pi Gamma Mu. Clubs: Quota of Lake County (past pres.), Quota of Toledo. Home: 2258 Whitney Av Toledo OH 43606

ARNOTT, ALICE ANN, editor; b. Blue Rapids, Kan., Feb. 14, 1943; d. Chester Marshall and Alice (Britschge) Arnott; student Kan. State Tchrs. Coll., 1960-62; B.S. cum laude, Kan. State U., 1964. Staff home economist Maytag Co., Newton, Ia., 1964-66, sr. staff home economist, 1966-67; home equipment editor Redbook mag., N.Y.C., 1967—. Recipient ALMA award Assn. Home Appliance Mfrs., 1969, 70, 71, 73. Mem. Am. Home Econs. Assn. (mem. nat. com. 1969-70), Home Economists in Bus. (mem. nat. com. 1969-71, membership chmn. nat. exec. bd. 1971-73, officer local group 1972-74), Elec. Women's Round Table (mem. nat. com. 1969-71, chpt. officer 1971-73), Women in Communications, Omicron Nu, Phi Upsilon Omicron, Phi Kappa Phi, Kappa Alpha Theta. Office: 230 Park Av New York City NY 10017

ARNOTT, MARGARET L., educator; b. St. Louis; d. David Shiress and Louise (Baird) Arnott; B.A., Harris Tchrs. Coll., 1931; M.A., Hartford Sem. Found., 1953; diploma U. Athens, 1954; certificate Oxford (Eng.) U., 1948, U. Florence, 1972; student St. Augustine's Coll., summer 1966. Tchr., Kemper Hall, Kenosha, Wis., 1933-43, 49-51; mem. staff Internat. Grenfell Assn., St. Anthony, Nfld., Can., 1943-45; tchr. Anatolia Coll., Thessaloniki, Greece, 1946-49, Am.-Hellenic Inst., Athens, Greece, 1954-57, USIS, Greece, 1956-57; researcher Harvard U., Cambridge, Mass., 1957-58; tchr. N.Y.U., N.Y.C., 1958-59; lectr. English dept. U. Pa., Phila., 1959-67, research asso. dept. environmental studies, 1967-71; lectr. Phila. Coll. Textiles and Sci., 1967—, Phila. Coll. Pharmacy and Sci., 1971—. Fellow Am. Anthrop. Assn.; mem. Am. Ethnol. Soc., Am. Folklore Soc. (councillor 1959-60), English Speaking Union (mem. scholarship com. 1966—), Am.-Hellenic League (chmn. membership com. 1967),

Nat. Assn. Fgn. Student Affairs (dist. rep. 1963-66), Current Anthropology (asso.), Internat. Com. Anthropology of Food and Food Habits (pres. 1968—). Episcopalian. Contbr. articles in field to profl. jours. Home: 324 S 21st St Philadelphia PA 19103

ARNOW, JENNIE MARTIN (MRS. LESLIE EARLE ARNOW), club woman; b. Meridian, Miss., May 24, 1913; d. Edwin McLemore and Sarah (Woodruff) Martin; m. Leslie Earle Arnow, July 17, 1933; 1 son, Peter Leslie. Mem. Phila. Art Alliance. Clubs: Women's of Morristown (N.J.), Morris County Art Assn., Morris County Golf Club. Home: 14 Fairfield Dr Convent Station NJ 07961

AROESTE, JEAN LISETTE, librarian; b. Richmond, Va., Oct. 2, 1932; d. Charles Alfred and Katherine Joyce (Graham) Buck; B.A., U. Wis., 1954; M.L.S. Simmons Coll., 1962; M.A. in English, U. Cal. at Los Angeles, 1967; m. Henry Aroeste, Sept. 16, 1967. Asst. acquisitions dept. Harvard Coll. Library, Cambridge, Mass., 1954-62; reference librarian U. Cal. at Los Angeles, 1962-73, asst. head reference dept., 1973—. Mem. staff Library/U.S.A., N.Y. World's Fair, summer 1965. Mem. Writer's Guild Am. West. Writer teleplays for Star Trek TV series, 1968-69. Editor: New Reference Books at UCLA, 1967—, Ann. Register of Grant Support, 1970, 71, 72; co-editor: Directory of Scholarly and Research Publishing Opportunities. Contbr. articles to profl. jours. Office: Reference Dept U Research Library U Cal at Los Angeles Los Angeles CA 90024

ARON, ADRIENNE (MRS. MARTIN J. ARON), real estate exec.; b. Fitchberg, Mass., Oct. 24, 1934; d. Samuel and Bessie (Bermack) Lewis; grad. high sch.; m. Martin J. Aron, Sept. 10, 1950; children—Frederic Bruce, Mark Steven. Mgr. real estate sales Schiller Real Estate, North Miami Beach, Fla., 1961-65, Southland Real Estate Co., North Miami Beach, 1965-66, Win Realty, Inc., 1967-69; pres. Adrienne Realty, Inc., 1969—. Compiler, reporter all real estate news TV sta. WCIX-TV, 1970. Mem. Fla. Assn. Realtors, Nat. Assn. Real Estate Bds., Miami Bd. Realtors (sec. roundtable 1969), Miami Beach Bd. Realtors, North Miami Beach C. of C. Home: North Miami Beach FL 33162 Office: 2020 NE 163d St North Miami Beach FL 33162

ARONFREED, EVA, educator; b. Phila., July 15, 1911; d. Joseph and Johanna (Scheindling) Aronfreed; B.F.A., U. Pa., 1933, A.M., 1947, Ph.D., 1958. Cons. pub. relations, Phila., 1933-42; asso. editor Pub. Health Nurses, N.Y.C., 1945-46; publs. editor Phila. City Planning Commn., 1947-56; cons. municipal pub. relations, Phila., 1956-61; asst. prof. Monmouth Coll., 1961-62; prof. polit. sci., chairperson polit. sci., econs. dept. Glassboro (N.J.) State Coll., 1962—. Served with WAC, 1942-45. Recipient Certificate of Merit, Internat. Union Local Authorities, 1961. Fels Inst. grantee, 1950-57. Mem. Internat. Union Local Authorities, Internat. Polit. Sci. Assn., Internat. Inst. Adminstrn. Studies, Am. Polit. Sci. Assn., Acad. Polit. Scis., Am. Acad. Polit. and Social Scis., Am. Soc. Pub. Adminstrn., League Women Voters, Am. Civil Liberties Union. Contbr. articles to profl. jours. Home: 403 S Cummings St Glassboro NJ 08028

ARONSON, FRANCES ANNE ROUSE, art dealer, artist; b. Lucedale, Miss., Nov. 30, 1933; d. Robert Lee and LaVonne Sumrall (Denson) Rouse; A.A., Jones Jr. Coll., 1952; postgrad. U. So. Miss., 1953-54; B.F.A., Atlanta Coll. Art, 1966; m. Leonard Aronson, Jan. 18, 1958; children—Amy Lee, Laura Jane. Art dealer Aronson Gallery, Atlanta, 1970—; one-woman shows Partheon Mus., Nashville, Monterey Gallery Savannah (Ga.) Art Assn., Jens Risom Gallery, Atlanta, Midtown Gallery, Atlanta; exhibited art in group shows at High Mus., Atlanta, Atlanta Arts Festival, 1960-70, Art to Embassies, 1965; represented in permanent collections at High Mus., numerous pvt. collections. Bd. dirs. Met. Atlanta Council Alcohol and Drugs, 1973-74, Atlanta Civic Design Commn., 1973-74. Recipient First prizes Atlanta Water Colour Club, 1967, 68, 69. Mem. Grand Jurors Assn. Fulton County. Home: 3136 Habersham Rd Atlanta GA 30305 Office: PO Box 11771 Atlanta GA 30305

ARP, HILDA DORA PAPE (MRS. RUDOLPH ARP), artist; b. Harburg, Germany; d. Peter Johann and Minna (Warnecke) Pape; student New Sch. Social Research, 1955, Bklyn. Mus., 1956, Art Student League, 1961, Pratt Graphic Center, 1966; m. Rudolph Arp, Oct. 5, 1937; children—Rolf, Rudolf, Peter. Exhibited in group shows throughout U.S., Europe, including Bklyn. Mus., Everhardt Mus., Scranton, Danbury Scott-Fanton Mus., Cayuga Mus. History, Brick Store Mus., Wutsum Mus. Fgn. Arts, Mary Buie Mus., Lubbock Mus., Ft. Worth Art Mus., one-man shows A. Artzt Gallery, N.Y.C., 1962, N.Y. Worlds Fair, 1964, 65, Artzt Gallery, N.Y.C., 1965; represented in permanent collections Norfolk (Va.) Mus., Wagner Coll., S.I., N.Y., Union Ch., Bayridge, Bklyn.; gallery artist Gallery Internationale, N.Y.C. Dir. art adv. bd. John F. Kennedy Library. Recipient Am. Heritage award John F. Kennedy Library, 1972. Mem. Nat. Assn. Women Artists, Am. Fed. Arts, Mus. Modern Art, Bklyn. Mus., Artist Equity Assn. N.Y., Arcanum Artists, N.Y. Internat. Platform Assn., Soc. Arts and Letters, Met. Painters and Sculptors N.Y.C. Address: 4516-7 Av Brooklyn NY 11220

ARRASMITH, JEAN LEONORE, educator; b. Ames, Ia., Apr. 22, 1923; d. Lyman C. and Emma (Gildersleeve) Arrasmith; B.A., Ia. State Tchrs. Coll., 1945; M.A., U. Minn., 1952; Ph.D., U. Ore., 1967. Jr. supr. phys. edn. Campus Sch., Ia. State Tchrs. Coll., Cedar Falls, Ia., 1944-45; tchr. phys. edn. Pub. Schs., Decorah, Ia., 1945-47; instr. phys. edn. for women Macalester Coll., St. Paul, 1947-52; tchr., supr. phys. edn. Pub. Schs., Ames, 1953; instr. phys. edn. for women Ia. State Coll., 1952, 53-54; instr., asst. prof. phys. edn. for women, head swimming Purdue U., Lafayette, 1954-64; asso. prof., dir. phys. edn. for women U. Denver, 1964-69; asso. prof., coordinator undergrad. profl. programs health, phys. edn. and recreation, 1969-73; prof., head women's phys. edn. dept. Ball State U., Muncie, Ind., 1973—. Conf. dir. First Nat. Aquatics Conf. on Profl. Standards, 1970. Water safety instr. A.R.C., 1941—; instr.-trainer, 1954—. Mem. A.A.H.P.E.R. (v.p. gen. div. 1972-73, Honor award Aquatics Council 1971), Am. Camping Assn., Nat. Assn. Phys. Edn. for Coll. Women, Am. Assn. U. Women, Am. Assn. U. Profs., Colo. (Honor award 1973), Ind. assns. for health, phys. edn. and recreation, Women's Nat. Aquatic Forum (research chmn., 1963-69). Contbr. articles to profl. jours. Home: 205 Hunter Rd Yorktown IN 47396 Office: Ball State Univ Muncie IN 47306

ARRIGHI, FRANCES ELLEN, biologist; b. Topeka, July 24, 1924; B.S., Marymount Coll., 1947; M.S., La. State U., 1961; Ph.D. in Zoology (NIH fellow 1962-65), U. Tex., 1965. Med. technologist Charity Hosp., New Orleans, 1947-54; with Meml. Hosp., Greenwood, S.C., 1954, La. State U. Sch. Medicine, 1954-58; asst. biologist M.D. Anderson Hosp. U. Tex., Houston, 1965-72, asso. biologist, asso. prof. biology, 1972—. Mem. Genetics Soc. Am., Am. Soc. Mammals, Tissue Culture Assn. Address: Dept Biology M D Anderson Hosp Houston TX 77025

ARRINGTON, MARIE KOONTZ, social worker; b. nr. Lacey Springs, Va., Sept. 1, 1917; d. Compton H. and Sallie (Shipp) Koontz; B.S., Madison Coll., 1938; postgrad. Richmond Profl. Inst., Va.; M.S. in Social Work, Va. Commonwealth U., 1967; m. James Noel Arrington, Nov. 30, 1939; 1 son, Andrew Koontz. Tchr. county schs., Amelia County, Va., 1938-40, 42-44; case worker Amelia County Welfare Bd., 1940-42; supt. Bd. Pub. Welfare, Harrisonburg, Va., 1946-69, dir. social services, 1969—. Instr. part time Bridgewater Coll., 1969-71, Madison Coll., 1970-72, Eastern Mennonite Coll.; 1971-72; Va. del. White House Conf. on Children, 1970. Chmn. bd. dirs. Community Services Council for Harrisburg and Rockingham County; treas., mem. exec. bd. Massanutten Mental Health Center. Mem. Am. Pub. Welfare Assn. (membership chmn. State Va. 1964-66), Va. Conf. Social Work (chmn. dist. 9 1951-53, state dir.-at-large 1953-54), Va. League Local Welfare Execs., Va. Council Social Welfare, Am. Assn. U. Women. Mem. Evang. United Brethren Ch. Club: Quota. Author: A White Church on a High Hill, 1970. Home: Broadway VA 22815 Office: Municipal Bldg Harrisonburg VA 22801

ARROYO, MARTINA, soprano; m. Emilio Poggioni. Leading soprano with Met. Opera, N.Y.C., in roles including Aida, Il Trovatore, Madam Butterfly, Un Ballo in Maschera, Cavalleria Rusticana, La Forza del Destino, Don Giovanni; sang opening night performances Met. seasons 1970-71, 71-72; participant Met. tour, June Festival; performances Vienna State Opera, Covent Garden, La Scala, Milan, Italy, Teatro Colon, Buenos Aires, San Francisco, other maj. opera houses; soloist with N.Y., Vienna, Berlin, Royal philharmonics, San Francisco, Pitts. symphonies, Concertgebrouw, other major orchs. frequent performer at Saratogo, Ravinia, Tanglewood festivals, also festivals Vienna, Berlin, Helsinki; oratorios include Verdi and Dvorak Requiems, Beethoven Missa Solemnis and Choral Fantasy. Honored as outstanding alumna Hunter Coll. Recs. for Columbia, Angel, DGG. Address: care Maurice Feldman 745 Fifth Av Suite 1404 New York City NY 10022

ARSENAULT, JOAN EMERSON NORMENT (MRS. JOSEPH FRANCIS ARSENAULT), mag. editor; b. Hagerstown, Md., Apr. 19, 1928; d. Richard Baxter and Vola (Caltrider) Norment; A.B., Washington U., St. Louis, 1949; m. Joseph Francis Arsenault, May 26, 1951— children—Ellen Belleveau, Amy Emerson, James Baxter, Robert Norment. Publs. editor med. jours. C.V. Mosby Co., St. Louis, 1949-51; asst. editor Florrissant Valley Reporter, 1963-65; asst. editor Optimist Mag., St. Louis, 1965-66, asso. editor, 1966—. North County rep. to Mo. Extension Council, U. Mo., 1969-71. Bd. dirs. St. Louis-St. Louis County White House Conf. on Edn., 1961-64, Ferguson Citizens' Com., 1967-70. Mem. Nat. Fedn. Press Women (awards, nat. placement dir. 1969-71, nat. contest chmn. 1971-72, nat. v.p. 1973-75), Mo. Press Women (awards state contest chmn. 1969), Indsl. Editors Greater St. Louis, Women in Communications. Home: 15 Buckeye Dr Ferguson MO 63135 Office: 4494 Lindell Blvd St Louis MO 63108

ARSHAWSKY, PEARL ROSE (MRS. GEOFFREY H. ISAAC), physician; b. Melville, Sask., Can., Feb. 20, 1929; d. Jack and Rebecca (Sternberg) Arshawsky; B.Sc. with honors, McGill U., 1951, M.D.C.M., 1955; m. Geoffrey H. Isaac, June 21, 1956; children—Beverley Miriam, Sandra Lynn. Intern, New Mt. Sinai Hosp., Toronto, Ont., Can., 1955-56; practice family medicine, Scarborough, Ont., 1956—; mem. staff Scarborough Gen. Hosp. Home: 8 Balding Ct Willowdale ON M2P 1Y7 Canada Office: 2901 Lawrence E Scarborough ON Canada

ARSHT, ROXANA CANNON (MRS. S. SAMUEL ARSHT), judge; b. Wilmington, Del., July 18, 1915; d. Samuel and Matilda (Stat) Cannon; B.A., Goucher Coll., 1935; LL.B., U. Pa., 1939; m. S. Samuel Arsht, May 9, 1940; children—Adrienne, Alison (dec.). Admitted to Del. bar, 1941; master Del. Family Ct., 1962-71, judge, 1971—. Mem. Del. Commn. Pub. Schs. Systems, 1965-67. Trustee Wilmington Med. Center, 1968—; bd. mgrs. Vis. Nurse Assn., Wilmington, 1948-69, pres., 1952-54; bd. dirs. Del. League Planned Parenthood, 1956-67, pres., 1958-59, chmn. bd., 1959-60, mem. adv. bd., 1967—; bd. dirs. Girls Club Wilmington, 1954-59, v.p., 1955-57; bd. dirs. United Fund and Council Del., 1966—. Mem. Del. Bar Assn. Home: 415 Old Kennett Rd Wilmington DE 19807 Office: Family Ct Bldg PO Box 1327 Wilmington DE 19899

ARTASERSE, BONNIE, educator; b. Jersey City; d. Ambrose and Rosina (De Rosa) Artaserse; B.S., Columbia, 1944; pvt. studies with various artists. Tchr. elementary sch., Jersey City, 1919-24; tchr. art Henry Snyder Jr. High Sch., Jersey City, 1924-29, William L. Dickinson High Sch., Jersey City, 1929-40; supr. art, Jersey City, 1940-70; cons. art programs, Jersey City, 1970—; exhibited in group shows at Newark Mus., Montclair Mus., Jersey City Mus. Tchr. design, painting, Jersey City, 1960—. Mem. adv. com. Jersey City Adult Edn. Sch. Mem. exec. com. Jersey City Tercentenary, 1960; active various community fund drives. Recipient First award for oil painting N.J. State Fedn. Women's Clubs, 1960; 1970 Jersey City Pub. Sch. Children's Art Show dedicated in her honor by Jersey City Parents Council. Mem. Bus. Profl. Woman's Club (charter), Am. Assn. U. Women, Allied Artists N.Y., Jersey City Mus. Assn. (trustee), Hudson Artists, Nat., N.J. art edn. assns., Assn. Arts N.J. State Mus. Club: Jersey City Woman's. Home: 2016 Kennedy Blvd Jersey City NJ 07305

ARTECHE, BERTHA ITURRIOZ (MRS. JOSE RUBEN ARTECHE), pharm. co. exec.; b. Havana, Cuba, Oct. 8, 1923; d. Gonzalo Jose and Maria Magdalena (Plasencia) Iturrioz; Dr. Pharmacy, U. Havanna, 1944; B.S. summa cum laude, So. Sch. Pharmacy of Mercer U., 1967; m. Jose Ruben Arteche, Dec. 16, 1944; 1 son, Miguel. Came to U.S., 1960, naturalized, 1969. Tech. dir. Labs. Iturrioz, Havana, Cuba, 1943-51; owner, pres. Labs. Dr. Bertha Iturrioz, Havana, 1952-60; founder, tech. dir. Pharm. Enterprises, Hialeah, Fla., 1960-63; v.p. sci. affairs Reid Provident Labs., Inc., Atlanta, 1964—, tech. dir. Internat. Labs, Inc., fgn. subsidiary, 1971—, tech. dir. research and devel., 1971—. Mem. Am. Pharm. Assn., Acad. Pharm. Scis., Am. Soc. Cosmetic Chemists. Roman Catholic. Contbr. articles to profl. pubs. Office: 25 5th St NW Atlanta GA 30308

ARTHUR, BEATRICE, actress; b. N.Y.C.; d. Philip and Rebecca Frankel; student Blackstone Coll., also Franklin Inst. Sci. and Arts; student actor with Erwin Piscator, Dramatic Workshop, New Sch. Social Research; m. Gene Saks, May 28, 1950; 2 sons. Theatrical appearances include Lysistrata, 1947, Dog Beneath the Skin, 1947, Gas, 1947, Yerma, 1947, No Exit, 1948, The Taming of the Shrew, 1948, Six Characters in Search of An Author, 1948, The Owl and the Pussycat, 1948, Le Bourgeois Gentil Homme, 1949, Yes is For a Very Young Man, 1949, Creditors, 1949, Heartbreak House, 1949, Three Penny Opera, 1954, 55, Shoestring Revue, 1955, Seventh Heaven, 1955, The Ziegfeld Follies, 1956. What's The Rush?, summer, 1956, Mistress of the Inn, 1957, Nature's Way, 1957, Ulysses in Nighttown, 1958, Chic, 1959, Gay Divorcee, 1960, A Matter of Position, 1962, Mame (Tony award best supporting mus. actress), 1966; stock appearances with Circle Theatre, Atlantic City, summer 1951, State Fair Music Hall, Dallas, 1953, Music Circus, Lambertville, N.J., 1953; resident commedienne Tamiment (Pa.) Theatre, 1953; numerous TV and nightclub appearances, 1948—, including Maude, 1973—; motion picture appearance in That Kind of Woman, 1959, Mame, 1974. Mem. Artists Equity Assn., Screen Actors Guild, A.F.T.R.A. Address: Buckburg Rd Tomkins Cove NY 10986*

ARTHUR, HOPE RISSMAN (MRS. ARTHUR B. FROMMER), actress, dir., writer; b. Chgo.; d. Henry Aaron and Pauline (Strassman) Rissman; B.S., Northwestern U., 1953; student Royal Acad. Dramatic Art, London, Eng., 1953-54; m. Arthur B. Frommer, Nov. 26, 1958; 1 dau., Pauline Hadley Frommer. Made debut on Broadway appearing as Maria in The Best House in Naples, 1957; drama supr. the Lighthouse, 1957-59; leading roles in off Broadway plays, 1960—, including: Song For a Certain Midnight, The Learned Ladies, Blood Wedding, The Lady From the Sea, Twice Over Nightly, Electra; with Boston Herald Repertory Co., 1965-66, playing Gertrude in Hamlet, Kate in Taming of the Shrew, Calpurnia in Julius Caesar; appeared as Ellen in Luv at Green Hills Playhouse, Reading, Pa., Summer 1967, as Rita Hush in Ergo, N.Y. Pub. Theater, 1968, as Miss X in The Stronger, The Actor's Place, 1970; female leads Looking for Billy, 1971-72; dir. Coping, Cherry Lane Theatre, 1972, Snowangel, Circle Theater, 1973, A Head's A Head, Take a Swim Charlie, Stage lights Theatre Club, 1974; chmn. bd. dirs. Arthur Frommer, Inc., $5 A Day Tours, Inc., Frommer/Pasmentier Pub. Corp. Mem. Actors Equity Assn., A.F.T.R.A., Screen Actors Guild, ANTA, Nat. Orgn. Women, Northwestern U. Alumni Assn., Citizens for Clean Air, Wilderness Soc., World Federalists, Common Cause, Another Mother for Peace, Smithsonian Assos., N.A.A.C.P., Nat. Acad. TV Arts and Scis. Co-author: Europe on $5 A Day. Contbr. articles to periodicals. Home: 50 Central Park W New York City NY 10023 Office: 70 Fifth Av New York City NY 10011

ARTHUR, JEANNE LENORE, lawyer; b. Los Angeles, Apr. 21, 1939; d. James Leland and Lenora (Barba) Arthur; B.A., Stanford U., 1964; J.D., U. Santa Clara, 1967. Admitted to Cal. bar, 1967; asso. Morton P. MacLeod, Los Altos, Cal., 1968-70; Skornia, Rosenblum & Gyemant, Palo Alto, Cal., 1970-72; pvt. practice of law, Palo Alto, Cal., 1972—. Mem. State Bar Cal., Santa Clara, Palo Alto bar assns., Peninsula Estate Planning Council, Palo Alto Financial Planning Forum, Santa Clara Estate Planning Council. Club: Commonwealth of Cal. Asso. editor: U. Santa Clara Law Rev., 1966-67. Office: 459 Hamilton Av Palo Alto CA 94301

ARUNDELL, FAYE DAWN (MRS. KENNETH BURDICK), dermatologist; b. Timmins, Ont., Can., Sept. 8, 1931; d. William Frederick and Robena Susan (Sopha) Arundell; B.A., U. Western Ont., London, 1955, M.D., 1956; m. Kenneth Hugh Burdick, Sept. 3, 1965. Came to U.S., 1962. Intern, Victoria Hosp., London, Ont., 1956-57; resident Westminster Hosp., London, Ont., 1957-58; fellow in dermatology Cleve. Clinic Found., 1958-61, staff dept. dermatology, 1963-65; registrar in dermatology St. Thomas' Hosp., London, Eng., 1961-62; Osborne fellow in dermatopathology Armed Forces Inst. Pathology, Washington, 1962-63; asst. prof. dermatology Stanford U. Sch. Medicine, 1966-69, clin. asst. prof. dermatology, 1969—; practice medicine, specializing in dermatology, Menlo Park, Cal., 1969—. Med. cons. Syntex Labs., Palo Alto, Cal., 1971—. Diplomate Am. Bd. Dermatology. Fellow Royal Coll. Physicians; mem. San Mateo County Med. Soc., Am., Cal. med. assns., San Francisco, Pacific dermatology socs., Am. Acad. Dermatology, Soc. Investigative Dermatology, Soc. Dermatopathology. Contbr. numerous articles to profl. jours. Office: 934 Santa Cruz Av Menlo Park CA 94025

ARVEY, VERNA (MRS. WILLIAM GRANT STILL), journalist, pianist, librettist; b. Los Angeles, Feb. 16, 1910; d. David and Bessie (Tark) Arvey; student pub. schs. pvt. study Marguerite d'Aleria, Rose Cooper Vinetz, Alexander Kosloff, Ann Eachus; m. William Grant Still, Feb. 8, 1939; children—Duncan Allan, Judith Anne. Concertized U.S., Latin Am.; soloist Raymond Paige's orch., CBS; with Los Angeles Philharmonic Orch., in Still's Kaintuck, 1939; librettist Still's opera, Hwy. 1, U.S.A. Author: Choreographic Music, 1941; numerous articles in profl. mus. mags. Authors of texts for numerous compositions of William Grant Still, including: Little Song, Rhapsody, Miss Sally's Party, Mississippi, Song for the Valiant, Song for the Lonely, Up There, Lament, Wailing Woman, Those Who Wait, A Bayou Legend, A Psalm for the Living, Costaso, Mota, Lenox Avenue, Minnette Fontaine; (with William Grant Still) Las Pascuas; co-author: William Grant Still and the Fusion of Cultures in America, 1972. Mem. A.S.C.A.P. Home: 1262 Victoria Av Los Angeles CA 90019 Office: care ASCAP 575 Madison Av New York City NY 10022

ARVIN, KAY KREHBIEL (MRS. LESTER C. ARVIN), lawyer; b. Cullison, Kan., June 7, 1922; d. Arthur and J. Rozella (Richardson) Krehbiel; A.B., Ottawa U., 1943; J.D., Washburn U., 1950; m. Lester C. Arvin, May 13, 1945; children—Scott Brentwood, Reed Richardson. Admitted to Kan. bar, 1951; mem. firm Arvin, Arvin, Busey & Thomas and predecessor firms, Wichita Falls, Kan., 1951—. Bd. dirs. Kan. Found. Blind, Monica House. Recipient spl. commendation Women in Communications, 1971. Fellow Am. Acad. Matrimonial Lawyers; mem. Nat. Counsel Juvenile Judges (asso.), Am., Kan. (family law com.) Wichita (life) bar assns., Nat. Homemaker's Assn. (life) Author: 1 plus 1 equals 1, 1969. Home: 8 Cypress Dr Wichita KS 67206 Office: 814 Century Plaza Wichita KS 67202

ASBJORNSON, HELEN E. (LONGSTRETH), lawyer; b. N.Y.C., Dec. 8, 1935; d. Dr. Clyde Marion and Elizabeth (Rudolph) Longstreth; B.A., State U. Ia., 1957, J.D., 1959, postgrad., 1960; M.Ed., Mont. State Coll., 1961; postgrad. U. Minn., 1961-62; m. Norman H. Asbjornson, March 1963; children—Elizabeth Erica, Scott Marion. Mem. bus. adminstrn. staff Northwestern Bell Telephone Co., Omaha, 1959-60; bus. adminstrn. mgr. Diversified Equities, Mpls., 1961—. Vol. worker Children's Hosp.; active Omaha Symphony Guild, Women's Assn. of Joslyn Art Mus., Omaha Civic Music Assn. Mem. Am. Council Christian Ch., Amvets Aux., C. of C., Am. Legion Aux., State U. Ia. Alumni Assn., Am. Assn. U. Women, Soc. Liberal Arts, Nat. Vocational Guidance Assn., Inc., Am. Personnel and Guidance Assn., Inc., Nat. socs. profl. engrs. auxs., Omaha Montessori Soc., Neb. Hist. Soc., Airplane Owners' and Pilots' Assns., Am. Citizens' Forum, Psi Chi, Kappa Beta Pi (pres. chpt. 1957-58, del. Province conv. 1958). Republican. Baptist. Home: High St Carson IA 51525 Office: Diversified Equities Soo Line Bldg Minneapolis MN 55402

ASBURY, EMILY WEST (MRS. JOHN H. WOLF), newspaper editor; b. Carlisle, Ky., June 13, 1926; d. Hicel F. and Lorraine (West) Asbury; student Ward-Bellmont Coll., 1945, U. Ky., 1945-48; m. John H. Wolf. Assoc. Editor Carlisle (Ky.) Mercury, 1948-51; editor Nicholas County Star, 1951-55; news editor U.S. Government Advertiser, Washington, 1955; editor Jefferson Reporter, Louisville, 1955-66; exec. editor, asst. to pub. Cin. Suburban Newspapers Inc., 1966—. Cordinator of information White House Study Conf. on Recreation, 1959-60; founder, sec. Carlisle-Nicholas County Recreation Com., 1949—; publicity com. local drive A.R.C., 1958; dir. Carlisle Youth Center and Playground, 1949-52; Girls Scout leader, 1949-55. Recipient Flying Dutchman award for work with young people; Best Weekly Newspaper award Ky. Press Assn., 1966-67. Mem. Carlisle-Nicholas County C. of C. (dir. 1954-55). Democrat. Methodist. Club: Carlisle Younger Woman's. Home: 3506 Arnold Av Cincinnati OH 45226 Office: 4415 Montgomery Rd Cincinnati OH 45212

ASCHER, MARY (GOLDMAN), artist, author; b. Leeds, Eng.; d. Jacob and Naomi (Goldsand) Goldman; B.B.A., Coll. City N.Y., 1923; M.A., N.Y.U., 1934; postgrad. Columbia U. Tchrs. Coll.; art studies pvt. instrs., also Grand Central Sch. Art, Art Students League, Famous Artists Sch., N.Y. Sch. Applied Design for Women. Tchr. in secondary schs., 1925-39, chmn. dept., 1939-46; dean, guidance dir., adminstrv. asst. William Howard Taft High Sch., 1946-53; lectures and limited folio edits. of lithographs on Women of Old Testament and Apocrypha (exhibited in 50 traveling one-man shows throughout U.S. 1965-70), designed, executed stained glass window of Lot's wife. Paintings exhibited N.Y. galleries, Argentina, Japan, Scotland, France, Eng., Italy, Israel, Mexico, also Provincetown, Art USA 58, Coliseum-Art USA 59; one-man shows Charles Barzansky Galleries, N.Y.C., 1959, Interch. Center, N.Y.C., 1965, Advt. Club N.Y., 1968, Fordham U., 1968, 30-Yr. Retrospective Exhbn., Nat. Arts Club, 1973; paintings and lithographs in permanent collections Alfred Khouri Meml. collection, Norfolk (Va.) Mus., U.S. Nat. Mus. Sports, Fordham U. (both N.Y.C.), Nat. Collection Fine Arts, Smithsonian Instn., Washington, Bat Yam and Ein Harod, Israel, pvt. collections. Recipient gold medal of honor Painters and Sculptors Soc. N.J. Nat. Ann., 1958; winner group show Prix de Paris, 1959; Marcia Brady Tucker award Nat. Assn. Women Artists, 1960; Huntington Hartford Found. fellow, 1961; 1st prize modern watercolor and print N.Y. State and Nat. Biennial, Nat. League Am. Pen Women, Washington, 1962; Burndy Corp. award 17th Ann. New Eng. States, 1967; Achievement medallion in arts Baruch Alumni Soc., 1968; Heydenryk award A.S.C.A., 1971; Distinguished Career medal Pres. of City Coll. N.Y., 1973. Fellow Royal Soc. Arts London; mem. Nat. League Am. Pen Women (1st prize for poetry Lady Graham competition 1968, 70, 1st prize poetry N.Y.C. br.; v.p. N.Y.C. br. 1970), Nat. Assn. Women Artists (Seligson Meml. award 1970; Hydenryk award 1971, Putnam award 1972; mem. adv. bd. 1973), Artist Equity Assn., Am. Fedn. Artists, Met. Mus. Art, Mus. Modern Art, Am. Assn. U. Woman, Internat. Platform Assn., Nat. Soc. Arts and Letters (chaplain Empire State br.) Am. Soc. Contemporary Artists (pres. 1973, dir.). Author: Poetry-Painting, 1958. Home: 116 Central Park S New York City NY 10019

ASCHKENASY, LINDA SCHULDER (MRS. JACOB ASCHKENASY), librarian; b. Bklyn., Apr. 8, 1942; d. Louis and Shirley (Harris) Schulder; B.A. (N.Y. State Regents scholar), Bklyn. Coll., 1963; M.L.S., Pratt Inst., 1964; m. Jacob Aschkenasy, Dec. 10, 1967. Librarian Joel Braverman High Sch., Bklyn., 1964-67; librarian, head acquisitions Jewish Theol. Sem., N.Y.C., 1973—. Bklyn. Coll. '34 fellow, 1963-64. Mem. A.L.A., Phi Beta Kappa, Beta Phi Mu. Home: 451 West End Av New York City NY 10024 Office: 3080 Broadway New York City NY 10027

ASCHKINASI, SONJA HENRIETTA, physician; b. Koenigsberg, Germany; d. Joseph and Malvina (Finkelstein) Ashkenazy; Asst. Med. Officer and midwife Med. Technicum (Yakutsk, USSR), 1944; M.D., U. Munich (Germany), 1955. Came to U.S., 1961, naturalized, 1967. Asst. med. officer Yakutsk Policlinic, 1944-45; asst. psychiatrist Univ. Hosp. Psychiatry and Neurology, Munich, Germany, 1955-56; asst. dept. dermatology Municipal Hosp., Munich-Schwabing, Germany, 1956; asst. gen. pathology Pathology Inst. U. Munich, 1956-57; asst. in neuropathology dept. brain pathology German Research Inst., Max-Plank Inst., 1957-58; resident Montreal (Que., Can.) Childrens Hosp., 1959-60, Allan Meml. Inst., Royal Victoria Hosp., Montreal, 1960-61, dept. psychiatry St. Lukes Hosp., N.Y.C., 1961-62; rotating intern Grand Central Hosp., N.Y.C., 1962, Knickerbocker Hosp., N.Y.C., 1962-63; fellow Mount Sinai Hosp., N.Y.C., 1963-64, N.Y. Med. Coll., 1964-65; staff psychiatrist, child psychiatry clinic and adolescent psychiatry clinic Queens Hosp. Center, N.Y.C., 1965-67; practice medicine, specializing in psychiatry adults, children, family therapy, N.Y.C., 1964—; attending clin. asso. child psychiatrist Mt. Sinai Hosp. and Med. Sch., N.Y.C., 1971—. Diplomate Am. Bd. Psychiatry and Neurology. Address: 315 E 86th St New York City NY 10028

ASCUE, NANCY KATHERINE HORNE (MRS. WILMER GEORGE ASCUE), home economist; b. Marion, Va., Dec. 22, 1939; d. Enoch and Mary Virginia (Branscum) Horne; B.S., Va. Poly. Inst. and State U., 1962; m. Wilmer George Ascue, Aug. 27, 1966. Asst. home demonstration agt., Tazewell County, Va., 1961-66; extension agt., Russell County, Va., Lebanon, 1966—. Mem. Nat. (pres. elect 1974), Va. (pres. 1970-71) assns. extension 4-H agts., Nat., Va. assns. extension home economists, S.W. Va.-East Tenn. Home Econs. Assn., Va. Extension Service Assn. (pres. 1973—). Methodist. 4-H All Star. Home: Route 2 Box 89 Cedar Bluff VA 24609 Office: Box 697 Lebanon VA 24266

ASEL, JUDITH ANN, pub. relations exec.; b. Little Rock, Nov. 9, 1941; d. Richard Burt and Mary Frances (Jewett) Asel; student U. Kan., 1959-61; B.J., U. Tex., 1967. Copywriter, publicist Jim Battersby Pub. Relations Firm, San Antonio, 1964-65; acting dir. pub. relations Tex. Pavilion, N.Y. World's Fair, N.Y.C., 1964; pub. relations dir., account exec. Claude Aniol Advt., San Antonio, 1965-68; owner, J.A. Asel Advt./Pub. Relations, San Antonio, 1968-69; radio/TV newswriter, entertainment publicity coordinator Hemis Fair, 1968, San Antonio, 1968; editor, pub. relations asst., pub. relations dir. Tracor, Inc., Austin, Tex., 1969—. Mem. Pub. Relations Soc. Am., Internat. Assn. Bus. Communicators (dir., 1st pl. award excellence 1969, 73), Am. Women in Radio/TV, Women in Communications (dir.), Nat. Women in Communications (S.W. region chmn. pub. relations adv. bd. 1973-75), Tex. Pub. Relations Assn. (dir.), P.E.O., Alpha Phi, Phi Sigma Chi, Gamma Alpha Chi. Contbr. articles to profl. jours. Home: 8042 Purnell St Austin TX 78753 Office: 6500 Tracor Lane Austin TX 78721

ASH, AGNES MCCARTY (MRS. CLARKE BENEDICT ASH), pub. exec.; b. N.Y.C., Nov. 14, 1924; d. Mathew Paul and Olga (Zacharias) McCarty; student Sinclair Coll., 1949-51; m. Clarke Benedict Ash, Feb. 2, 1957; children—David, Eric, James, Jennifer. City desk clk., feature writer Dayton (O.) Daily News, 1948-51; reporter Washington Times Herald, 1951; woman's editor Atlanta Constitution, 1952-54; reporter New York Times Women's News, 1954-59; bus. editor Miami News, 1959-67; Miami Bur. chief Fairchild Publs., 1967—. Recipient First prize Fla. Newspaper Women's Club, 1961; First prize N.Y. Newspaper Women's Club, 1958; First prize Ohio Newspaper Women's Club, 1950. Mem. N.Y. Newspaper Women's Club. Roman Catholic. Home: 576 NE 97th St Miami FL 33138 Office: 11055 NE 6th Av Miami FL 33131

ASH, MARY ELLEN (MRS. JAMES THEODORE ASH), lawyer; b. Wichita, Kan., Oct. 3, 1908; d. Loyd Inman and Nora (Martin) Aldrich; Brown's Bus. Coll., 1925, Western Ill. U., 1926-27; LL.B., Columbus U., 1940; m. James Theodore Ash, Oct. 4, 1941 (dec. June 1969); 1 dau., Mary Jo (Mrs. Orris Edward Farley). Admitted to U.S. Dist. Court, 1941, Ill. bar, 1949; adjudicator Social Security Bd., Washington, 1940-41, Chgo., 1942-43; pvt. law practice, Mendota, Ill., 1956—. Mem. Ill. Bar Assn., Sigma Delta Kappa. Club: Mendota Woman's. Home: 1311 Monroe Mendota IL 61342 Office: 1311 1/2 Monroe Mendota IL 61342

ASH, MARY KAY WAGNER (MRS. MELVILLE JEROME ASH), cosmetic co. exec.; b. Hot Wells, Tex.; d. Edward Alexander and Lula Vember (Hastings) Wagner; student U. Houston, 1942-43; m. Melville Jerome Ash., Jan. 6, 1966; children—Marylyn (Mrs. Gene Reed), Ben Rogers, Richard Rogers. Mgr., Stanley Home Products, Houston, 1939-52; nat. tng. dir. World Gift Co., Dallas, 1952-63; founder, pres., chmn. Mary Kay Cosmetics, Inc., Dallas, 1963—. Bd. dirs. YWCA. Mem. Bus. and Profl. Women's Club. Club: Zonta. Home: 7246 Lupton Circle Dallas TX 75225 Office: 8900 Carpenter St Dallas TX 75247

ASHCROFT, EDITH MARGARET EMILY, actress; b. Dec. 22, 1907; d. William Worsley and Violet Maud (Bernheim) Ashcroft; ed. Woodford Sch., Croydon, Eng., Central Sch. Dramatic Art; D.Litt (hon.), Oxford (Eng.) U., 1961, Leicester (Eng.) U., 1963; m. Rupert Hart Davis, 1929 (marriage dissolved); m. 2d, Theodore Komisarjevsky, 1934 (marriage dissolved); m. 3d, Jeremy Hutchinson, 1940 (marriage dissolved 1966); 2 children. Performed various Shakespearean lead roles, other lead roles Birmingham (Eng.) Repertory Theatre, 1926-32; joined Old Vic Co. (Eng.), 1932; also with Royal Shakespeare Theatre Co. (formerly Shakespeare Meml. Theatre Co.) Eng.; starring roles (with both cos.) in Cymbeline, As You Like It, Romeo and Juliet, Merchant of Venice, Midsummer Night's Dream, King Lear, Twelfth Night, Antony and Cleopatra, other Shakespearean plays; other starring roles in Caesar and Cleopatra, Three Sisters, Importance of Being Earnest, Edward My Son, Hedda Gabler, Duchess of Malfi, Seagull, Cherry Orchard, others; film appearances in Wandering Jew, 39 Steps, Rohdes, Quiet Wedding, Nun's Story, Channel Incident, We Serve, numerous touring vehicles; TV, radio appearances BBC. Councilor, English Stage Co., 1957—. Created comdr. Brit. Empire, 1951, dame Brit. Empire, 1956. Recipient Ellen Terry Theatre award, 1947, King of Norway medal, 1955, Evening Standard (Eng.) Drama award, 1956, Paris Theatre Festival award, 1962; hon. fellow St. Hugh's Coll. Oxford U., 1964. Mem. Brit. Actors Equity Assn., English Arts Council, Wordester's Soc. Advancement of Music and Arts; founder Apollo Soc., 1943. Address: Manor Lodge Frognal Lane Hampstead London NW 3 England*

ASHDOWN, MARIE MATRANGA (MRS. CECIL SPANTON ASHDOWN, JR.), writer, lectr.; b. Mobile, Ala.; d. Dominick and Ava (Mallon) Matranga; student Maryville Coll. Sacred Heart, 1945-46, Springhill Coll., 1946-47; m. Cecil Spanton Ashdown, Jr., Feb. 7, 1958; children—John Stephen Gartman, Vivian Marie Gartman, Cecil Spanton 111, Charles Coster. Feature star daily program Sta. WALA, also WALA-TV, Mobile, 1953-58; photographer, model for Louise Sheridan, Mobile, 1955-58; feature columnist Isle Dauphine News, Mobile, 1957. Lectr. women's clubs, other orgns., 1953-58. Mem. Am. Women in Radio and TV, 1956-57, Am. Businesswomen's Assn., Mobile, 1955-58. Bd. dirs. Met. Opera Guild, Soc. 3d St. Mus. Sch. Settlement. Recipient certificate merit for extraordinary service March of Dimes, 1958. Mem. Nat. Inst. Social Scis. Home: 25 Sutton Pl S New York City NY 10022

ASHDOWN, MARION ELIZABETH VON WILMEROTH (LADY CECIL S. ASHDOWN), civic worker; b. San Francisco, Aug. 21, 1891; d. Charles William and Alicia (De La Guerra) Von Wilmeroth; grad. Mt. Vernon Sem., 1909; LL.D., Andahar U., 1948; Ph.D., U. So. Cal., 1950; m. John Barrett, June 20, 1910 (dec.); 1 son, Juan De La Guerra; m. 2d, Sir Cecil S. Ashdown, June 1, 1958 (dec.). Pres., Wilmeroth Estate, San Francisco, 1941—, Twin River Ranch Co., San Francisco, 1943—; v.p. New's and View's Inc., Los Angeles, 1941—; dir. Colo. Pub. Co., Denver. Mem. women's bd. Golden Gate Expn., 1937-39; mem. Pres.'s Commn. Hosps., 1942-46; chmn. vol. and trustee sect. Am. Hosp. Assn., 1944-47; v.p., life mem. bd. women councilors U. So. Cal., 1929—. Vice chmn. Republican Campaign Com., 1951-68; mem. exec. bd. Lincoln Rep. Club, 1950—. Bd. mgrs. Children's Hosp., 1932—; bd. dirs. Meml. Cancer Hosp., 1940—; bd. regents Mt. Vernon Sem., 1940—. Named Woman of Yr., City of Los Angeles, 1948; recipient Gold medal Am. Hosp. Assn., 1951. Roman Catholic. Clubs: Ebell (v.p. 1958-62) (Los Angeles); Town and Gown (San Francisco); Women's Athletic (San Francisco and Los Angeles); Congressional (Washington); Green Valley Country (Carmel, Cal.). Home: Casa De La Guerra Box 6638 Carmel CA 93421

ASHE, AMELIA H. (MRS. DAVID I. ASHE), educator; b. Bklyn., Oct. 16, 1916; d. Isadore M. and Sophie (Yancovici) Haimowitz; B.A., Hunter Coll., 1938; M.A. in English, Bklyn. Coll., 1945; M.A. in Guidance and Counseling, 1955; Ph.D. in Guidance and Personnel, N.Y.U., 1966; m. Murray Wexler, June 20, 1937 (dec. 1961); children—Richard Mark, Susan Ellen (Mrs. Stuart Lahn); m. 2d, David I. Ashe, Dec. 26, 1962. Tchr. English, Far Rockaway High Sch., N.Y.C., 1948-59; guidance counselor Plainview (L.I.) High Sch., N.Y., 1959-63; supr. NDEA Inst. Counseling, Bklyn. Coll., summer 1963; instr. guidance and personnel dept. Sch. Edn., N.Y. U., 1963-67, supr. NDEA Inst., 1963-64; asst. prof., coordinator grad. program in guidance and counseling Richmond Coll., City U. N.Y., 1967-69, asso. prof., 1970—; chmn. com. coordinators grad. programs in guidance and counseling City U. N.Y., 1971—; cons. Center Urban Edn., N.Y. State Dept. Edn.; dir. Consortium for Bilingual Counselor Edn., 1972-73, 74—. Mem. N.Y.C. Bd. Edn., 1974—. Mem. Am., N.Y. State, N.Y. City (pres. 1971-72) personnel and guidance assns., Nat. Vocational Guidance Assn., Am. Coll. Personnel Assn., Am. Counselor Educators and Suprs., Am. Ednl. Research Assn., Nat. Council Measurements Used in Edn., Am. Assn. U. Profs., Kappa Delta Pi, Alpha Epsilon Phi. Home: 201 E 79th St New York City NY 10021

ASHE, MARGARET RUTH BERRY, educator; b. Denton, Tex., Mar. 29, 1905; d. Thomas Eugene and Viola Eugenia (Riley) Berry; B.S., Tex. State Coll. for Women, 1950, M.A., 1951; Ph.D. (Nat. Def. Ednl. Act. scholar 1961), U. Tex., 1964; m. Claude Harmon Ashe, Sept. 21, 1922; children—Claude Harmon, Jr., James Henderson III, Margaret Ruth (Mrs. Harry Arnold Davidson), John Berry. Tchr. White Deer (Tex.) Ind. Sch. Dist., 1950-51; counselor Angleton (Tex.) Ind. Sch. Dist., 1951-53, Houston schs., 1953-64; mem. faculty San Jacinto Coll., Pasadena, Tex., 1964—, chmn. psychology dept., 1969—. Mem. Am., Southwestern, Tex., Houston psychol. assns., D.A.R., Tex. Jr. Coll. Tchrs. Assn., Am. Legion, Tex. Ex Students Assn., Delta Kappa Gamma, Alpha Chi, Sigma Tau Delta. Democrat. Mem. Order Eastern Star. Clubs: San Jacinto College Faculty Women's Club. Home: 8734 Collingdale LaPorte TX 77571 Office: 8060 Spencer Hwy Pasadena TX 77505

ASHER, JANE FITZGERALD (MRS. JACK O'HAIR ASHER), lawyer; b. Little Rock, Dec. 3, 1929; d. Sam L. and Georgia Duffey (Hubbert) Fitzgerald; A.A., Los Angeles City Coll., 1951; student U. Cal. at Los Angeles, 1951-52; J.D., Tulane U., 1957; m. Jack O'Hair Asher, Aug. 22, 1957; children—Duffey Ann, William Michael Fitzgerald, John Russell II (dec.). Admitted to La. bar, 1957, Alaska bar, 1959, U.S. Ct. of Appeals bar, 1960, Dist. Ct. bar, 1960, Ill. bar, 1968; law clk. U.S. Dist. Ct. of Alaska, Juneau, 1957-58; atty. Vets. Affairs Commn., Juneau, 1958-59; asst. atty. gen. State of Alaska, Juneau, 1959-60, reviser of statutes, 1960-67; counsel judiciary coms. Alaska Senate, 1963-66, Alaska House, 1965-66; with Dillavou, Overaker, Asher and Bonaldi Esqrs. Chmn. Alaska Am. Cancer Soc. Crusade, 1959; sec. Juneau-Douglas Concert Assn., 1961-62, treas., 1962-66; dir. Gold Creek Summer Theatre, 1964-66; v.p., mgr. Edgar County Concert Assn., 1969—. Bd. dirs. Juneau-Douglas Little Theatre, 1961-62, 64-65, YMCA, Paris, Ill., 1969-71; Edgar County Childrens Home, 1968—, Hangar, Inc., teen-age center, 1972—; pres. bd. dirs. Paris Tiger Tots Nursery, 1969-73. Mem. Alaska, Am., La., Ill. bar assns., Nat. Women Lawyers (state del. 1959-67), Nat. League Women Voters, Am. Assn. U. Women, Phi Delta Delta. Club: Quota (treas. Juneau chpt. 1961-62, dir. 1962-64). Home: Box 501 Chicago Rd Paris IL 61944 Office: 236 W Court St Paris IL 61944

ASHER, LILA OLIVER, artist; b. Phila., Nov. 15, 1921; d. Benjamin O. and Molly (Finkelstein) Oliver; grad. Phila. High Sch. for Girls; certificate, Phila. Coll. Art (bd. edn. scholarship), 1943; student Phila. Sketch Club; m. Sydney S. Asher, Jr., May 5, 1946; children—Barbara Sydney, Warren Oliver. Faculty, Wilson Tchrs. Coll., Washington, 1953-54; instr. art dept. Howard U., 1947-51, lectr., 1961-64, asst. prof., 1964-66, asso. prof., 1966-71, prof,, 1971—. Artist in sculpture, graphics, watercolor, oil including murals; one-person shows Barnett-Aden Gallery, 1951, William C. Blood Gallery, 1955, Arts Club, Washington, 1957, Collectors Gallery, 1959, Garrett Park Pub. Library (Md.), 1960, Art Shop, Silver Spring, Md., 1961, Potters' House, Washington, 1963, Burr Galleries, N.Y.C., 1963, Gallery 222, El Paso, Tex., 1965, Thomson Gallery, N.Y.C., 1968, B'nai B'rith Nat. Hdqrs. Gallery, 1969, Cedar Lane Unitarian Ch., Bethesda, Md., 1969, U. Va., Charlottesville, 1970, Green-Field Gallery, El Paso, Tex., 1972, Northwestern Mich., Coll., 1972, Am. Club, Tokyo, Japan, 1973, Govt. Coll. Arts and Crafts, Madras, India, 1974; in group shows World's Fair, N.Y.C., 1965, Pa. Acad. Fine Arts, Smithsonian Instn., Washington, 1950, 54-58, 60-63, Library of Congress, Washington, 1954, Corcoran Gallery Art, Washington, 1949, 51, 52, 55, 57-59, Howard U., 1952, 61-63, 65, 67, George Washington U., 1968, Pan-Am Union, Woodmere Gallery, 1949-50, Phila. Print Club, Washington Water Color Soc., Washington Printmakers Soc., Balt. Mus. Art, 1959, Hood Coll., U. Va., Charlottesville, 1964, 66-68, 70, 71, Me., 1959, Riverside Mus., N.Y.C., 1959, Rochester (N.Y.) Meml. Art Gallery, 1954, Franz Bader Gallery, Washington, 1955, 71, Graphic Soc. (N.Y.C.), Va. Intermont Coll., Nat. Collection Fine Arts, Washington Watercolor Assn., Arts Club Washington, Soc. Washington Artists Ann., 1971, 72, Soc. Washington Printmakers, Dimock Gallery, George Washington U., numerous others; retrospective show Frahz Bader Gallery, Washington, 1972; represented in collections Nat. Collection Fine Arts, Washington, Howard U., Barnett Aden Gallery, Corcoran Gallery, U. Va., Sweetbriar (Va.) Coll., Superior Ct. D.C., B'nai B'rith, Washington, City of Wolfsburg (Germany), Down East Gallery, Washington, U. Tex., U.S. Mediation and Conciliation Service, Bur. Nat. Affairs, Center for Research in Edn. Disadvantaged, Jerusalem, Israel, Am. embassy, Tel Aviv, Israel, also pvt. collections. Guest artist U. Tex. print program, 1972. Recipient 3d prize Washington Arts Club, 1955, 1st prize, 1959; 1st prize Chevy Chase Center, 1955, 59; 3d prize Woodward and Lothrop, 1956; prize for print Corcoran Gallery Art 10th Area Exhbn., 1956; 3d prize Va. Intermont Coll.; 1st prize prints Chevy Chase Center, 1960, Harrigan's of D.C., 1961, Old Market Gallery Art Show, 1961, Grumbacher award, Harpers Ferry, W.Va., 1963, U. Va., 1963, 70; guest artist City of Wolfsburg (Germany), 1968, 71. Mem. Soc. Washington Artists (past pres.), Soc. Washington Printmakers (rec. sec.), Washington Water Color Club, Artists Equity (treas.). Home and studio: 4100 Thornapple St Chevy Chase MD 20015

ASHER, MARTHA ELIZABETH (MRS. ANIL P. ASHER), art inst. exec.; b. Pittsfield, Mass., July 12, 1934; d. Ralph Philip and Mary Elizabeth (Johnson) Winch; student Bates Coll., 1952-53, Williams Coll., 1953-55; m. Anil P. Asher, July 3, 1957. Sec. to the librarian Williams Coll. Library, Williamstown, Mass., 1953-55; exec. sec. Harter Chair Corp., N.Y.C., 1955-57; office mgr. D.R. Das & Co., Calcutta, Inda, 1962-69; with Sterling and Francine Clark Art Inst., Williamstown, Mass., 1970—, registrar 1971—; owner Martha Asher Import-Export Bus., Williamstown, 1969—. Home: Box 3 Williamstown MA 01267 Office: Sterling and Francine Clark Art Institute Williamstown MA 01267

ASHFORD, FREDDYE GEORGE (MRS. JESSE ASHFORD), librarian; b. Paducah, Ky., Mar. 21, 1914; d. Fred and Martha Ann (Brown) George; A.B., Ky. State U., 1937; B.L.S., Atlanta U., 1948; M.Ed., U. Mo., 1958; m. Jesse Ashford, July 3, 1957. Tchr. pub. schs., Lynch, Ky., 1934-36, Caruthersville, Mo., 1937-50; asst. librarian Lincoln U., Jefferson City, Mo., 1950-69, acting univ. librarian, 1969-72, univ. librarian, 1972—, reading cons., 1952—. Mem. Lincoln Univ. Fed. Credit Union. Recipient Twelve Pearl award Phi Beta Sigma, 1972. Mem. Am., Mo. library assns., Am. Assn. Univ. Women, Assn. Co-op Library Orgn., Alpha Kappa Alpha. Methodist. Home: 825 Clark St Jefferson City MO 65101 Office: Page Library Lincoln Univ Jefferson City MO

ASHHURST, ANNA WAYNE, educator; b. Phila., Jan. 5, 1933; d. Astley Paston Cooper and Anne Pauline (Campbell) Ashhurst; A.B., Vassar Coll., 1954; M.A., Middlebury Coll., 1956; Ph.D., U. Pitts., 1967. English tchr. Internat. Inst. Spain, Madrid, 1954-56; asst. prof. Juniata Coll., Huntingdon, Pa., 1961-63; asst. prof. Spanish dept. Franklin and Marshall Coll., Lancaster, Pa., 1968-74, acting chmn. Spanish dept., 1972, convenor, fgn. lang. council, 1972-74; asso. prof. dept. modern fgn. langs. U. Mo., St. Louis, 1974—. Mem. Welcome Wagon W. of Lancaster, Pa., 1968-70, 71-74. Fulbright-Hays grantee, Colombia, S.Am., summer 1963; Ford Humanities fellow, summer 1970; Mellon fellow, 1970-71. Mem. Internat. Inst. in Spain, Instituto Internacional de Literatura Iberoamericana, Am. Assn. U. Profs., Modern Lang. Assn., Pa. State Modern Lang. Assn., Am. Assn. Tchrs. Spanish and Portuguese. Home: 328 Chez Paree Hazelwood MO 63042

ASHLEY, MRS. JERRY (THELMA TOWNSEND ASHLEY), club woman; b. Frederick, Okla., Nov. 10, 1904; d. Jay E. and Anna (McGuire) Townsend; B.S., U. Okla., 1927, postgrad. U. Colo., summer 1928; m. Jerry S. Ashley, June 25, 1932. Tchr. home econs. high schs., Temple, Walters and Lawton, Okla., 1923-24, 28-32; mgr. Jerry Ashley Chevrolet Inc., Crowley, La., 1941-47, now v.p. Crowley Little Theater, 1949; vice pres. Community Concert, 1950; asso. dir. La. Girls State, 1972, also mem. bd. dirs. Mem. Am. Legion Aux. (state pres. 1954, nat. exec. committeewoman 1955, nat. v.p. 1957, nat. vice chmn. nat. security 1959-61, nat. chmn. edn. scholarships 1962, state historian 1951, 1st v.p. 1952, 2d v.p. 1953, regional chmn. legislation 1958, state finance chmn., nat.-regional civil def. chmn., mem. state finance com. 1960—), Crowley Bus. and Profl. Women (pres. 1958), Delta Zeta (province dir. 1951, 52). Democrat. Mem. Christian Ch. Home: 1601 N Parkerson Av Crowley LA 70526

ASHLEY, NOVA TRIMBLE (MRS. JAMES ERCLE ASHLEY), author; b. Selden, Kan., July 10, 1911; d. Rufus William and Margaret Gilliland (Lipton) Trimble; continuing edn. student Wichita State U., part-time 1967-71; m. James Ercle Ashley, Aug. 20, 1929; children—Keith, Kenneth, James (dec.), Joyce (Mrs. Donald C. Olson). Ins. supr. Wesley Med. Center, Wichita, Kan., 1952-70; creative writing tchr. Twentieth Century Club, Wichita, 1966-70; condr. numerous workshops. Named Kan. Poet of Year, Chaparral Poets, 1969, 71, 73. Mem. Internat. Platform Assn., Nat. Fed. Press Women, Nat. League Am. Pen Women (pres. Wichita br. 1973—),

Kan., Wichita press women, Kan. Authors Club, Wichita Line Women, Midwest Chaparrals (bd. mem. Kan. chpt.). Author: Through Ocean of Gold, 1963; Coffee with Nova, 1966; Loquacious Mood, 1970; Haps and Mishaps, 1973. Contbr. articles to profl. jours. Home: 2101 S Glendale St Wichita KS 67218

ASHODIAN, MILA JEANETTE (MRS. HOWARD WILLIAM PAYNE), ophthalmologist; b. Providence, Aug. 21, 1925; d. Vahan and Sona (Bahchegulian) Ashodian; A.B., Bryn Mawr Coll., 1945; M.D., Temple U., 1950; m. Howard William Payne; 1 dau., Barbara. Resident, Wills Eye Hosp., Phila., 1952-54, sr. asst. surgeon, 1971—; asso. ophthalmologist Lankenau Hosp., Phila., 1954—; clin. instr. U. Pa. Grad. Sch. Medicine, 1956-60; asso. clin. prof. Pa. Med. Coll., 1964-72, Thomas Jefferson U., 1974. Fellow Am. Acad. Ophthalmology and Otolaryngology, A.C.S.; mem. Am. Med. Womens Assn. (treas. 1972), Phila. Club Med. Women (treas.). Club: Phila. Skating. Home: 1014 Centennial Rd Narbeth PA 19072 Office: Lankenau Med Bldg Philadelphia PA 19151

ASHUR, GERTRUDE, ednl. adminstr.; b. Bridgeport, Conn., Apr. 18, 1916; d. Jacob and Miriam (Koenig) Raport; B.A., Hunter Coll.; M.A., Coll. City N.Y., 1951; Ph.D., N.Y. U., 1958; certificate in child therapy Postgrad. Center for Psychotherapy, N.Y.C.; m. Milton Ashur, Nov. 26, 1970; children by previous marriage—Beth (Mrs. Peter Rosenthal), Leslie (Mrs. Marvin Kreithen). Social investigator Bridgeport Dept. Welfare, 1938-40; substitute tchr., N.Y.C., 1946-48; psychologist intern Mt. Sinai Hosp., N.Y.C., 1951-52; psychologist intern Postgrad. Center for Psychotherapy, 1952-53, clin. psychologist, 1953-55; sch. psychologist Bur. Child Guidance, N.Y.C. Bd. Edn., 1955-60, supr. sch. psychologists, 1960—. Diplomate Am. Psychol. Assn. Vis. prof. Lehman Coll., Queens Coll., 1967-69; psychotherapist specializing in family therapy, 1967—. Mem. Am. Acad. Psychotherapy, N.Y. Soc. Clin. Psychology, N.Y. State Psychol. Assn. Developed curriculum in sch. psychology for proposed profl. sch. Home: 681 Bergen Av Jersey City NJ 07304 Office: Bureau Child Guidance W 195th St and Reservoir Av New York City NY 10468

ASHWORTH, EDITH ALIZABETH, educator; b. Danville, Va., June 9, 1920; d. Guy Rupert and Elizabeth Ware (Blair) Ashworth; diploma Averett Coll., 1938; B.S. in L.S., Madison Coll., 1942; M. Ed., U. Va., 1952; postgrad. U. Mexico, 1953, U. Va., 1968, 71. Sch. librarian Brosville High Sch., Danville, 1942-53; librarian Va. Hills Elementary Sch., Fairfax County, Va., 1953-67; project dir. Title II State Demonstration Library Brookefield Elementary Sch., Chantilly, Va., 1968-69; media specialist supr. Area I, Fairfax County, 1969—. Mem. A.L.A., Va. Library Assn. (steering com. 1963-65), Va. Edn. Assn. (sec.-treas. dist. 1963-65, sec. sch. librarians sect. 1966-68, pres. 1971-73), Asso. Sch. Librarians Fairfax County (pres. 1961-63), Delta Kappa Gamma. Home: 7521 McWhorter Pl Annandale VA 22003 Office: 3011 Memorial St Alexandria VA 22306

ASK, ANN MARIE (MRS. MERRILL G. ASK), newspaper editor; b. Boone County, Ia., Jan. 5, 1935; d. Gerald S. and Velda M. (Stuart) Tripp; grad. high sch.; m. Merrill G. Ask, Apr. 28, 1960; 1 son, Andrew Sanford. With layout and design Am. Yearbook Co., Topeka, 1961-64; personal sec. Crane Investment & Reality Co., Ames, Ia., 1964-65; bookkeeper Hallinan Bakery Co., Carroll, Ia., 1965-69; editor, pub. Hale (Mo.) Leader, 1969—. City collector Hale, Mo., 1971—. Mem. Nat. Newspaper Assn., Mo. Press Assn., Democrat Editors of Mo. Democrat. Methodist. Address: Box 128 Hale MO 64643

ASKEW, DONNA LOU HARPER (MRS. REUBIN O'DONOVAN ASKEW), wife of gov. Fla.; b. Tampa, Fla., Feb. 11, 1934; d. Donald Lazarre and Ercel Agness (Smethurst) Harper; student Pensacola Jr. Coll., Stetson U., summer 1953; B.S. in Elementary Edn., Fla. State U., 1955; m. Reubin O'Donovan Askew, Aug. 11, 1956; children—Angela Adair, Kevin O'Donovan. Tchr. elementary schs., Miami, Fla., 1955-56, Pensacola, Fla., 1956-57, Brownsville Jr. High Sch., Pensacola, 1958-60. Active Pensacola Jr. Woman's Club, 1961-63; pres. Pensacola Panhellenic, 1958-59. Mem. League Women Voters, Fla. State U. Alumnae Assn., Kappa Delta Gamma (hon.), Kappa Alpha Theta (alumnae pres. 1968-69). Democrat. Presbyn. Mem. Daus. of Nile. Home: 700 N Adams St Tallahassee FL 32303

ASKEW, ELIZABETH ENGLE, librarian; b. Richmond, Va., June 22, 1943; d. James Brasington and Minnie Webb (Engle) Askew; B.A., Westhampton Coll., 1964; M.L.S., Rutgers U., 1965. Reference asst. Richmond Pub. Library, 1965-68; asso. librarian Fed. Reserve Bank, Richmond, 1968-72; head dept. bus. sci. and tech. dept. Richmond Pub. Library, 1972—. Mem. Am., Va. (chpt. sec. 1969-71) library assns., Spl. Libraries Assn. Episcopalian. Home: 4809 Rodney Rd Richmond VA 23230 Office: 101 E Franklin St Richmond VA 23219

ASKEW, MARY EUGENIA, coll. dean; b. Houston, Nov. 12, 1941; d. Hubert Carl and Mary Eugenia (Philp) Askew; B.S., Sam Houston State U., 1965; postgrad. Lamar State U., 1967-69; M.Ed., U. Okla., 1971; postgrad. Columbia, 1973. Tchr., Vidor (Tex.) Ind. Sch. Dist., 1966-69; art, English, drama, speech tchr. Keyes (Okla.) Ind. Sch. Dist., 1969-71; asst. prof., head tennis coach, dean women Baker U., Baldwin City, Kan., 1971—, head women's phys. edn., 1973-74, dir. women's phys. edn., 1974—. Kansas City Region of Higher Edn. grantee, 1973—. Mem. Am. Assn. U. Women, A.A.H.P.E.R., Central Assn. Phys. Edn. for Coll. Women. Methodist (sr. youth fellowship dir. 1972—). Mem. Order Eastern Star. Home: Box 516 Baldwin City KS 66006

ASKEW, PAMELA, educator; b. Poughkeepsie, N.Y., Feb. 2, 1925; A.B. Vassar Coll., 1946; M.A., Inst. Fine Arts, N.Y.U., 1951; Ph.D., U. London (Eng.), 1954. Instr. art Vassar Coll., Poughkeepsie, 1950-51, 54-55, now prof. art. Address: Vassar College Poughkeepsie NY 12601

ASKEY, BERNICE HELEN, ednl. adminstr.; b. Grinnell, Ia., Oct. 27, 1920; d. Hugh James and Beulah T. (Larsen) Askey; B.S., U. Neb., 1943; postgrad. U. So. Cal., San Diego State Coll. Asso. health edn. dir. San Diego YWCA, 1943-49; phys. edn. tchr. Chula Vista (Cal.) Jr. High Sch., 1951-55; tchr., counselor Castle Park Jr. High Sch., Chula Vista, 1955-59, asst. prin., 1959—. Mem. adv. bd. Rainbow Girls Myrtle Assembly. Mem. Nat. Assn. Women Deans and Counselors, Cal. Assn. Women Adminstrs. and Counselors (So. region jr. high chmn. 1964-66, state treas. 1967-69, state pres. 1973—), Am. Bus. Women's Assn., Alpha Xi Delta (Brinkmann Alumnae award 1963, nat. pledge counselor 1965—). Mem. Order Eastern Star (worthy matron 1974—). Episcopalian. Home: 4038 Alicia Dr San Diego CA 92107 Office: 160 Quintard St Chula Vista CA 92011

ASKINS, PEGGY JOYCE CORLEY (MRS. DONALD W. ASKINS), educator; b. Fame, Okla., Aug. 1, 1935; d. Carlon Clifford and Evadew (Bruce) Corley; B.S., Okla. Bapt. U., 1957; m. Donald W. Askins, Aug. 24, 1957; children—Michael David, Anna Kathleen. Asst. in peronnel Okla. Bapt. U., Shawnee, 1960-63, asst. in art, 1961—, registrar, 1963—, also sponsor Mortar Bd. chpt. Mem. Okla. Assn. Collegiate Registrars and Admissions Officers (past v.p., past pres.), Am. Assn. Collegiate Registrars and Admission Officers, U. Alliance, Nat., Okla. edn. assns., Kappa Pi, Theta Alpha Phi, Zeta Chi, Delta Kappa Gamma. Democrat. Baptist. Home: 3907 Pine Ridge Rd Shawnee OK 74801

ASMAR, ALICE, artist; b. Flint, Mich., Mar. 31, 1929; d. John George and Helen (Touma) Asmar; B.A. magna cum laude, Lewis and Clark Coll., 1949; M.F.A., U. Wash., 1951; student Ecole Nationale Superieure Des Beaux-Arts (Paris, France), 1958-59. Engraver, metal muralist, book illustrator, painter, graphics; one man shows at Los Angeles Municipal Art Gallery 1968, Roswell Mus., 1968, Jamison Gallery, 1968, Mpls. Inst. Fine Arts, Jamison Gallery, Burbank Library, Pasadena Art Mus., Salem Art Mus., Downey Mus. Art, Adele Bednarz Gallery, Bullock's Wilshire, Los Angeles, Bullock's Wilshire, Palm Springs, Mary Livingston's Little Gallery, Santa Ana, Cal., 1969, 70, 72, Mary Livingston's Gallery 2, 1971, 72, Downey Mus. Art, 1972, Southwest Mus. Los Angeles, 1973, Frame House Gallery, Lewisville, 1973, Toledo Edison Exhibits, 1973, San Marino and Burbank (Cal.) pub. libraries, 1973—, Scottsdale (Ariz.) Civic Center, 1974, many others, exhibited in group shows at Madison Gallery, Scripps Coll., Reed Coll., Lyman Alleyn Mus., Los Angeles County Art Mus., Oakland Art Mus., Nambe Mills of Santa Fe, Feingarten Gallery, Minn. Mus. Art, Dominican Edn. Center, Sinsinawa, Wis., Western Assn. Art Museums Ann. Circuit Show, Laguna Gloria Arts Mus., Tex., Am. embassies, Brussels, Belgium, and Paris, France, Springville (Utah) Mus. Art, Museo de Arte, Ibiza, Spain, many others; traveling exhibits Minn. Mus. Art-Drawings U.S.A. Travelshow, 1971—, Tex. Fine Arts Assn. Traveling Show, 1972-73; represented in permanent collections at Security Pacific Nat. Bank Airport Br., Los Angeles, Joseph Magnin Store, Santa Barbara, Cal., Savs. & Loan Assn., Pasadena, Cal., Standard Oil, Louisville, Roswell (N.M.) Mus. and Art Center, Huntington Hartford Mus., N.Y., also pvt. collections; faculty Lewis and Clark Coll., 1955-58, St. Helen's Hall, 1949-50; tchr. adult edn., Lennox, Hawthorne, West Los Angeles, Santa Monica, 1963-66; pvt. tchr., 1945-65; executed Cal. Triptych, Security Pacific Internat. Bank, N.Y.C., 1970. MacDowell Colony fellow, 1960; Festival of Two Worlds fellow, 1959; Harriet Hale Woolley scholar, 1958; decorated Biennale Delle Regione, Ancona, Italy, 1968-69. Mem. Centro Studi E Scambi Internazionali (Rome, Italy), Smithsonian, Am. Fedn. Arts, Desert Art Center, S.W., Los Angeles County art museums, Artists Equity, Sierra Club, Mu Phi Epsilon. Republican. Office: PO Box 1965 Hollywood CA 90028 Mailing Address: 1125 N Screenland Dr Burbank CA 91505

ASPREY, WINIFRED ALICE, educator; b. Sioux City, Ia., Apr. 8, 1917; d. Peter and Gladys (Brown) Asprey; A.B., Vassar Coll., 1938; M.S., State U. Ia., 1943, Ph.D., 1945. Student tchr. Brearley Sch., N.Y.C., 1938-40; tchr. Girl's Latin Sch., Chgo., 1940-42; asst. instr. State U. Ia., 1942-45; instr. Vassar Coll., 1945-46, asst. prof., 1946-51, asso. prof., 1951-57, chmn. math. dept., 1956-62, prof. math., 1957—, Elizabeth Stillman Williams prof. math, 1961—, dir. Computer Center, 1966—. Dir. Computer Inst;, 1964-67; IBM exchange prof. IBM, Poughkeepsie, 1969-70; mem. vis. staff, cons. Los Alamos Sci. Lab., U. Cal., summer 1971, 72—. NSF grantee summer inst., Eugene, Ore., 1954, Los Angeles, 1962, faculty fellow, 1964-65; IBM postdoctoral indsl. research fellowship, 1957-58; Fellow A.A.A.S., Ia. Acad. Sci.; mem. Am. Math. Soc., Math. Assn. Am., Am. Assn. U. Profs., Ia. Acad. Sci., Am. Statis. Assn., Assn. for Computing Machinery (nat. lectr. 1970-71), Nat. Council Tchrs. Math., Soc. Indsl. and Applied Math., Phi Beta Kappa, Sigma Xi. Address: Vassar Coll Poughkeepsie NY 12601

ASSATOURIAN, ALICE HUSISIAN (MRS. HAIG GOURJI-KHAN ASSATOURIAN), editing co. exec.; b. Batoum, Russia, Oct. 15, 1920; d. Leon Nishan and Araxi (Zorian) Husisian; came to U.S., 1923; naturalized, 1944; diploma in Gen. Edn. and Sec. Sci., Boston U., 1940; student Clark U., 1943-45; B.S. in English, Columbia, 1964; M.A., N.Y. U., 1966; m. Haig Gourji-Khan Assatourian, Oct. 26, 1946; children—Seta, Sona, Lora. 1st violinist, v.p. Worcester (Mass.) Philharmonic Orch., 1936-43; exec. asst. to pres. Clark U., research asst. to pres. RKO Films Corp., Worcester, Mass., 1943-46; mem. conf. services dept. UN, N.Y.C., 1955-57; owner Profl. Editing & Typing Services, N.Y.C., 1960—. Lectr. on writing and manuscript preparation, 1957—. Dist. commr. Girl Scouts U.S.A., 1962-64, recipient Spl. award Greater N.Y. council, 1967. Mem. Nat. Assn. Armenian Studies and Research, Internat. House, Modern Lang. Assn. Am., Constantinople (patron debutante ball 1972-74), Armenian (chmn. cotillion 1970-72) relief socs., Armenian Gen. Benevolent Union, U.S. Paddle Tennis Assn. Mem. Daus. of Vartan (grand recorder grand council 1971-73, gen. chairwoman 34 ann. convocation 1974, matron Ani chpt. 1974-75). Home: 410 E 20th St New York City NY 10009

ASSUMPTA, SISTER VIRGINIA MCNABB, ednl. adminstr.; b. Allentown, Pa., Oct. 28, 1932; d. Harry and Helen V. (Chesney) McNabb; B.S., Immaculata Coll., 1957; M.A., Cath. U. Am., 1971. Instr. bus. edn. Immaculata (Pa.) Coll., 1955-58; tchr. Cath. High Sch., Mt. Carmel, Pa., 1958-60, Notre Dame Acad., Miami, Fla., 1960-68; financial aid officer Immaculata (Pa.) Coll., 1968-73, treas., 1973—, asst. prof. econs. and bus. adminstrn., 1968—. Mem. Eastern Assn. Coll. and Univ. Bus. Officers. Address: Immaculata Coll Immaculata PA 19345

ASTBURY, EFFIE CONSTANCE, educator; b. Montreal, Que., Can., Dec. 9, 1916; d. John Simpson and Effie (Patterson) Astbury; B.A. magna cum laude, McGill U., 1938, B.L.S., 1939; M.L.S., U. Toronto, 1956. Asst. order librarian McGill Med. Library, Montreal, 1939-40, head circulation and reference, 1940-49; faculty McGill U. Grad. Sch. Library Sci., 1949-69, prof. library sci., 1969—, dir., 1972—; also mem. senate. Mem. Canadian (council 1958-61), Que. (council 1957-59) library assns., Canadian Assn. Coll. and Univ. Libraries (council 1967-69). Home: 3450 Drummond St Apt 1414 Montreal PQ H3G 1Y2 Canada Office: 3459 McTavish St Montreal PQ H3A 1Y1 Canada

ASTOR, ESTA JUNE VENNER (MRS. DAVID ASTOR), librarian; b. Portland, Me., June 26, 1922; d. Abraham Louis and Marian (Rapoport) Venner; student U. Me., 1969; m. David Astor, Jan. 16, 1943; children—Kenneth Alan, Martha Jane (Mrs. William Henry Foster III). Library asst. Portland (Me.) High Sch., 1965-69; reference librarian Me. Hist. Soc., Portland, 1970—. Mem. Women's Exchange, New Eng. Assn. Museums and Hist. Socs., Soc. Preservation New Eng. Antiquities, Me. Assn. Tchr. Aides and Assts. (pres. 1967), Me. Library Assn., Me. Acad. Librarians Assn., Me. Hist. Soc., Greater Portland Landmarks. Home: 119 Pitt St Portland ME 04103 Office: 485 Congress St Portland ME 04111

ATHANASAKOS, ELIZABETH, judge; b. Bklyn.,; d. Clement and Irene (Vrettakos) Athanasakos; B.A., St. John's U., 1948, LL.B., 1956. Marketing research work Psychol. Corp., A.C. Nielsen Co., N.Y.C., 1948-56; claims adjuster Allstate Ins. Co., Bklyn., 1956-57; admitted to N.Y. bar, 1956, Fla. bar, 1957; partner Alexas & Athanasakos, Fort Lauderdale, Fla., 1958-61; gen. practice, Fort Lauderdale, 1961—; municipal judge City of Wilton Manors, Fla., 1964; asso. municipal judge City of Oakland Park, Fla., 1968—. Dir. United Way Broward County (Fla.). Mem. Pres.' Task Force on Women's Rights and Responsibilities, 1969; chairperson adv. com. on women's rights and responsibilities Dept. Health, Edn. and Welfare, 1972—; pres. Womens Republican Club Broward County, 1967-69, 73—; bd. dirs. Nat. Fedn. Rep. Women, 1968-71, vice chmn. nationalities com., chmn. women's rights and responsibilities; mem. nat. adv. com. Women for Nixon-Agnew, 1968; mem. nat. adv. com. for re-election Pres., 1972. Bd. advisers Prospect Hall Coll. Mem. Am., Fla., Broward County bar assns., Fla. Assn. Women Lawyers, Broward County County Municipal Judges, N.Am. Judges Assn., Nat. Assn. Women Lawyers, League Women Voters, Bus. and Profl. Women (woman of achievement dist. 10, 1969-70, 73, dir. dist. 10, 1973-74, pres. Ft. Lauderdale 1970-72), Am. Assn. U. Women (legislative chmn. Ft. Lauderdale br. 1971-73), Fla. Women's Polit. Caucus Council Phi Delta Delta. Republican. Mem. Greek Orthodox Ch. Mem. Order Eastern Star (past matron), Daus. of Penelope (grand pres. 1965-66). Clubs: Ft. Lauderdale Womens; Women's Civic; Broward Women's Breakfast (past pres.); Zonta (corr. sec. 1971-73; chmn. dist. XI Status Women Com. 1972—; mem. internat. by-laws com. 1972—). Home: 2113 NE 16th Av Fort Lauderdale FL 33305 Office: 2633 N Federal Hwy Fort Lauderdale FL 33306

ATHANASIOU, BETTYE JO RAIDEN, pub. relations exec.; b. Dallas, June 15, 1923; d. J.L. and Edythe (Stewart) Raiden; student Massey Bus. Sch., 1947; children—Rolanette MacKie, Susan Saul. Pvt. sec. to sec.-treas. Mission Mfg. Co., Houston, 1947-49; pvt. sec. to pres. Marine Exploration Co., Houston, 1949-52; personnel sec., seismic sec., editor co. mag. Robert H. Ray Co., Houston, 1952-56; mgr. pub. relations, editor co. mag. Geo Space Corp., Houston, 1963-73, Walker-Hall-Sears, Inc., Houston, 1973—. Pres., dir. Hedgecroft Hosp. Aux., 1958-69; chmn. Gov. Bill Daniel's Ann. Crippled Children's Party, 1956-59; capt. Pin Oaks Charity Horse Show, Tex. Children's Hosp., 1959-64; mem. bd. Tex. Hosp. Aux., 1958-59; pres. Pres.' Council of Houston Hosp. Aux., 1958-59. Recipient service award Geophys. Soc. Houston, 1968. Mem. Internat. Assn. Bus. Communicators, Soc. Exploration Geophysioists (co-chmn. Publicity 36th, 40th ann. meetings), Am. Bus. Women's Assn. (pres. 1952-54), Geophys. Soc. Houston, (publicity chmn. 1971—), Offshore Tech. Conf. (tech. com. 5th-6th ann. meetings), European Assn. Exploration Geophysicists, Asociacion Mexicana de Geofisicos de Exploracion, Am. Soc. for Oceanography, Houston C. of C. (communications/information com. 1972-73), Marine Tech. Soc. Home: 3102 Suffolk St Houston TX 77027 Office: 8400 Westpark Dr Houston TX 77042

ATHERTON, AUDREY L., educator; b. Portsmouth, N.H., Sept. 20, 1920; d. Fred William and Ola (Miller) Atherton; A.B., Fla. State Coll. for Women, 1942; M.A., Fla. State U., 1950, Ed.D., 1953; postgrad. U. Cal. at Los Angeles, 1957. Dir. undergrad. counseling Fla. State U., Tallahassee, 1951-53; dir. guidance and counseling Dade County schs., Miami, Fla., 1953-56; adminstrv. asst. Los Angeles County Schs., Azusa, 1956-64; dir. guidance and counseling Orange County Schs., Garden Grove, Cal., 1964-71; prof. psychology and human relations Pensacola (Fla.) Jr. Coll., 1971—. Dir., cons. Nat. Defense Edn. Act., 1965-68. Bd. dirs. Orange County Mental Health Assn., Santa Ana, Cal., 1967-69. Served as lt. USNR, 1943-46. Mem. Am. Personnel and Guidance Assn., Am. Sch. Counselor Assn., Cal. Counseling and Guidance Assn., Cal. Assn. Secondary Sch. Adminstrs., Nat. Assn. Guidance Suprs., Kappa Delta Pi, Delta Delta Delta. Soroptomist (pres.). Home: 1801 E Scott St Pensacola FL 32503

ATHERTON, JEANNE DAVIS (MRS. LAWRENCE ATHERTON), coll. ofcl.; b. N.Y.C., May 19, 1936; d. John J. and Mabel (Reed) Davis; B.S., State U. N.Y. at New Paltz, 1957; M.A., N.Y. U., 1963; postgrad. U. Colo., summer 1966; m. Lawrence Atherton. Tchr. elementary schs., Garrison, N.Y., 1957-60, Yorktown, N.Y., 1960-63; Fulbright exchange tchr., Cottingham, Eng., 1964-65; dir. ednl. communications Yorktown Schs., 1965-67; asso. in ednl. tv N.Y. State Edn. Dept., Albany, 1967-68; mgr. audio-visual dept. N.Y. Times, N.Y.C., 1968-71; sr. program specialist Nat. Center for Ednl. Tech., U.S. Office of Edn., Washington, 1971-72; tech. cons., 1972-73; dir. Ind. Learning Center, San Diego Mesa Coll., 1973—. Cons. ednl. tv and information retrieval systems; staff lectr. Briarcliff Coll., 1968-70, San Diego State U., 1973-74. Mem. Nat. Assn. Ednl. Broadcasters, N.E.A., N.Y. State Ednl. Radio and TV Assn., N.Y. State Audio-Visual Assn., English Speaking Union, State U. N.Y. Tchrs. Coll. Alumni Assn., Mu Sigma Epsilon, Delta Kappa Gamma. Developed prototype materials for information retrieval systems, multi-media curriculum. Home: 8458 Jackie Dr San Diego CA 92119

ATHEY, MARY FRANCES WILSON (MRS. RODERICK ELWYN ATHEY), journalist; b. Kansas City, Mo., Oct. 21, 1944; d. Albert Francis and Ilah May (Wallace) Wilson; B.A., Kan. State U., 1965; M.A., U. Colo., 1967; m. Roderick Elwyn Athey, Aug. 21, 1965; 1 son, Joel Michael. Reporter, Arapahoe Herald, Littleton, Colo., 1965; copywriter, Dacey, Wolff & Weir Advt. Agy., Boulder, Colo., 1966; editor, Geol. Soc. Am., Boulder, Colo., 1967-68; newswriter, journalism instr., pub. relations for chancellor U. Kan., Lawrence, 1968-71; writer, St. Luke's Hosp., Kansas City, Mo., 1971—. Mem. Women in Communications (v.p. Kansas City chpt. 1973-74), Sunflower Girls State Kan. (alumna pres. 1969-70). Home: 8507 Glenwood St Overland Park KS 66212 Office: 44th and Wornall Rd Kansas City MO 66414

ATKIN, FLORA BLUMENTHAL (MRS. MAURICE DAVID ATKIN), theater dir., playwright; b. Balt., May 15, 1919; d. Joseph and Anna (Levy) Blumenthal; student George Washington U., 1935-38; A.B., Syracuse U., 1940; postgrad. Bennington Coll., 1941, Cath. U., 1959-61; m. Maurice David Atkin, Dec. 25, 1941; children—Joseph, Barrie, Jonathan. Dir. recreational arts dept., founder dir. Day Camp, Jewish Community Center, Washington, 1940-44; dir., choreographer community theatres, instr. creative dance, drama and music pvt. schs. and colls., 1940-68; founding dir., playwright In-Sch. Players Adventure Theatre, Glen Echo Park, Md., 1969—. Theatre arts cons. D.C. Recreation Dept., 1968; mem. TV com. Jewish Community Council, Washington, 1968—; guest lectr. Hebrew U., Jerusalem, 1970, U. Md., 1972; instr. creative edn. Nat. Park Service, Glen Echo, Md., 1973-74; instr. Coast Guard Aux., 1967-73. Recipient Pauline Eaton Oak award 42d ann. D.C. One-Act Play Tournament, 1970, Sybil Baker award 43d and 45th ann. tournament, 1971, 73; Best Dir. award Eastern States Theatre Assn. Festival, 1971, Best Prodn. award, 1973. Mem. Am., Children's Theatre assns., D.C. Fedn. Music Clubs (state jr. counselor 1944), Washington Music Tchrs. Assn. (sec. 1945), Washington Modern Dance Soc., Phi Sigma Sigma. Democrat. Jewish religion. Author: (plays) Tarradiddle Tales, 1970; Tarradiddle Travels, 1971; Golliwhoppers!, 1973. Home: 5507 Uppingham St Chevy Chase MD 20015

ATKINS, CAROLYN PELUSO, educator; b. Morgantown, W.Va., Nov. 2, 1947; d. John and Mildred (Tiano) Peluso; A.B. (Benedum scholar), W.Va. U., 1969, M.A., 1970, postgrad. 1970—; m. Billy Bruce Atkins, Aug. 23, 1969. Grad. asst. dept. speech W.Va. U., Morgantown, 1969-70, instr. speech, 1970-73, instr. English, 1974—, chmn. voice and diction, 1972-73. Speech clinician Marion County (W.Va.) Speech and Lang. Services, Fairmont, 1972-73. Mem. Internat. Communication Assn., Am. Assn. U. Profs., Am. Assn. U. Women, Morgantown Jr. Women's Club, Mortar Bd., Kappa Delta,

Zeta Phi Eta. Democrat. Club: Pines Country. Author: (with Enid J. Portnoy) Phonetically Speaking, 1971. Home: 880 Vandalia Rd Morgantown WV 26505

ATKINS, DOROTHY DUBOIS (MRS. BEN SLOAN ATKINS), lawyer; b. Charleston, S.C., Nov. 3, 1922; d. Clifton B. and Ronella K. (Knight) DuBois; grad. Perry Bus. Sch., 1941; LL.B., Atlanta Law Sch., 1948, LL.M., 1949; m. Ben Sloan Atkins, Dec. 24, 1942. Sec., personnel dir. U.S.C.E., Walterboro, S.C., 1941-43; sec., U.S. Retirement Bd., Atlanta, 1945-47; adminstrv. asst. Internal Revenue Service, Atlanta, 1947-59; admitted to Ga. bar, 1949; practiced in Atlanta, 1959—; mem. firm Atkins & Atkins, Atlanta, 1959—. Pres., Wesleyan Service Guild, 1962-64. Mem. Ga. Bar Assn. Clubs: Equity (pres. 1965), Am. Contract Bridge League (Atlanta). Home: 4069 Statewood Rd NE Atlanta GA 30342 Office: 1221 First Nat Bank Tower Atlanta GA 30303

ATKINS, HANNAH DIGGS, state legislator; b. Winston-Salem, N.C., Nov. 1, 1923; d. James Thackeray and Mabel (Kennedy) Diggs; B.S., St. Augustine's Coll., 1943; B.L.S., U. Chgo., 1949; postgrad. Oklahoma City Sch. Law, 1963-64, U. Okla., 1968; m. Charles N. Atkins, May 24, 1943; children—Edmund, Charles N. II, Valerie. Reporter, Winston-Salem Jour. and Sentinel, 1945-48; tchr. French Atkins (N.C.) High Sch., 1945-48; research asst. biochemistry Meharry Med. Coll., 1948-49; reference librarian Fisk U., 1949-50; sch. librarian Kimberly Park Elementary Sch., Winston-Salem, 1950-51; br. librarian Oklahoma City Pub. Libraries, 1953-56, reference librarian, 1962-63; acting law librarian Okla. State Library, 1962-68; instr. law Oklahoma City U.; instr. library sci. U. Okla.; mem. Okla. Ho. of Reps. from 90th Dist., 1968—, chmn. mental health and retardation com., 1972—. Mem. Okla. Commn. Edn., Gov. Okla. Commn. Reorgn. Exec. Br.; task force early childhood edn. Edn. Commn. States; nat., state bds. Family Service Assn. Am. Pres. Vis. Nurse Assn. Oklahoma City. Mem. policy council, nat. assembly Nat. Black Polit. Conv. Bd. dirs. Sunbeam House. Recipient Distinguished Service award local Masonic lodge, 1973; Outstanding Legislator award Rutgers Inst., 1972; Finer Womanhood award Zeta Phi Beta, 1969. Mem. Am. Assn. Law Libraries (past chpt. pres.), Jack and Jill Am. (past regional dir.), N.A.A.C.P., Urban League, Nat. Links (Distinguished Service award 1972), Alpha Kappa Alpha (Nat. Founders Service award 1970). Democrat. Home: Route 4 Box 799 Oklahoma City OK 73111 Office: Room 334 State Capitol Oklahoma City OK 73105

ATKINS, JANINA KANIEWSKI (MRS. THOMAS V. ATKINS), librarian; b. Warsaw, Poland, Jan. 18, 1933; d. Ignacy and Stella (Gordon) Kaniewski; came to U.S., 1964, naturalized, 1970; M.A., Warsaw U., 1955; M.L.S., Columbia, 1968; m. Thomas V. Atkins, June 17, 1965. Editor Polish Press Agy., Warsaw, 1955-64; librarian Law Sch., N.Y. U., N.Y.C., 1968-69, Lehman Coll., City U. N.Y., 1969—. Author: (with Thomas V. Atkins) Cross Reference Index, 1974. Home: 120 34th St New York City NY 10016 Office: Bedford Park Blvd W New York City NY 10468

ATKINS, MATILDA PERGE, educator; b. Akron, O., Oct. 9, 1924; d. Alexander and Matilda (Cseh) Perge; B.S., Kent State U., 1959, B.S. in Edn., 1964, M.A., 1969, postgrad., 1972; m. George Phillip Atkins, July 26, 1942; children—Hope (Mrs. Robert Phillip Kropac), George Phillip, Cheryl (Mrs. Steven Urszeni), Alan Paul, Alexander Charles. Copy writer Clayton & Assos. Advt. Agy., Akron, 1959; substitute tchr., Summit and Portage County, O., 1959-60; tchr., Crestwood High Sch., Mantua, O., 1960-61, Ellet High Sch., Akron, 1961—. Capt., Muscular Dystrophy Drive. Mem. Women in Communications, (rec. sec. 1972-73), Ohio, Akron edn. assns., English Assn. Ohio, Northeastern Ohio Tchrs. Assn., Greater Akron Tchrs. English, Akron Area Journalism Assn. (pres. 1970—), Nat. Council Tchrs. English, Northeastern Ohio Scholastic Press Assn. (chmn. bd. 1974-75), Kent State U. Journalism Alumni Assn. Home: 4470 Fishcreek Rd Stow OH 44224 Office: 309 Woolf Av Akron OH 44312

ATKINS, MERRILEE R., social worker; b. Amherst, Mass., Apr. 18, 1940; d. Howard William and Ruth (Wheeler) Atkins; B.A. summa cum laude, U. Mass., 1962; M.S.W., Smith Coll. Sch. for Social Work, 1964. Social worker Family Service Greater Cin., 1964-71, asst. dir. alcoholism research, 1969-71; field instr. Smith Coll. Sch. Social Work, 1969-71; supr. Central Psychiat. Clinic, 1971—; asst. prof. social work U. Cin., 1971—. Trustee Mt. Auburn Community Council, 1965-67; chmn. benefit lecture Cin. Smith Sch. Social Work Alumni, 1967, 68. Bd. dirs. Mt. Auburn Good Housing Found., chmn. family com., 1967-70. Mem. Nat. Assn. Social Workers, Acad. Certified Social Workers, Am. Group Psychotherapy Assn., Smith Coll. Sch. for Social Work Alumni. Sigma Xi, Phi Beta Kappa, Alpha Lamda Delta, Lambda Delta Phi, Phi Kappa Phi, Mortar Bd. Office: Logan Hall Gen Hosp Burnet & Elland Sts Cincinnati OH 45229

ATKINSON, BEVERLY MOON (MRS. CHARLES FRED ATKINSON), polit. worker; b. Warren, O., Apr. 25, 1924; d. Henry Albert and Frances Emma (Lehman) Moon; student Am. Inst. Banking, Youngstown, O., 1942-44; m. Charles Fred Atkinson, May 13, 1944; children—Thomas Temple, Amy Allen. An organizer Playladies program, pediatric ward Trumbull Meml. Hosp., Warren, 1957; chmn. women's com. capital fund campaign YMCA, 1974. Mem. Trumbull County Rep. Central and Exec. Com., 1960-72, Ohio Central and Exec. Rep. Com., 1966—; del. Ohio Rep. Conv., 1966, 68, 70, 72; alternate del. Rep. Nat. Conv., 1968, del., 1972; chmn. 19th Congl. Dist. Women for Nixon-Agnew, 1968; Trumbull County chmn. Roger Cloud for Gov., 1970; Trumbull County chmn. Nixon Phone Center, 1972; bd. mgmt. Ohio Fedn. Rep. Women, 1966—. Mem. Trumbull County Bar Assn. Aux. (pres. 1955-56), Martha Kinney Cooper Ohioana Library Assn. (local co-chmn. 1965-71), Am. Legion Aux. Baptist (deaconess 1965-68). Home: 530 Oak Knoll NE Warren OH 44483

ATKINSON, LENETTE ROGERS (MRS. GEOFFROY ATKINSON), educator; b. South Carver, Mass., Mar. 30, 1899; d. Lawrence Monroe and Mary Briggs (Crowell) Rogers; grad. Lasell Sem., 1917; B.A., Mt. Holyoke Coll., 1921; M.A., U. Wis., 1922, Ph.D., 1925; m. Geoffroy Atkinson, June 19, 1928; children—Beryl (Mrs. Joseph Rhea), Joan (Mrs. J.A. Newman). Asst. botany U. Wis., 1921-25; fellow Commn. Relief in Belgium Ednl. Found., 1925-27; acting asst. prof. Mt. Holyoke Coll., 1928; research asso. Amherst (Mass.) Coll., 1947—. Mem. Am. Fern Soc. (sec. 1963-68), Bot. Soc. Am., Am. Soc. Plant Taxonomists, Internat. Assn. Plant Taxonomy, Internat. Soc. Plant Morphologists, Linnean Soc. London, Sigma Xi, Sigma Delta Epsilon. Contbr. articles to profl. jours. Home: 415 S Pleasant St Amherst MA 01002

ATKINSON, MADELYN RUCKS (MRS. ROBERT CHARLES ATKINSON), county ofcl.; b. Camden, Ark., Dec. 13, 1930; d. Edmond D. and Mamie Ruth (Hodnett) Rucks; grad. high sch.; m. Robert Charles Atkinson, Jan. 1, 1965; 1 son, Charles Randall. With Security Abstract Co., El Dorado, Ark., 1948-51; dep. county clk. Union County, El Dorado, 1951-62, 65-66, county and probate clk., 1967—; sec. Urbana Lumber Co. (Ark.), 1962-65. Sec. Union County Democratic Central Com., 1958—. Mem. Bus. and Profl. Women's Club (pres. 1963-64). Home: Rural Route 1 Box 219 El Dorado AR 71730 Office: Courthouse El Dorado AR 71730

ATKINSON, VIRGINIA SUMMEY, guidance counselor; b. Pickens, S.C., Sept. 18, 1934; d. Shala Wells and Cecile (Field) Summey; B.A., Furman U., Greenville, S.C., 1955, M.Ed., 1958; postgrad. Clemson U., 1971-73; m. Jack Lloyd Atkinson, June 25, 1955; 1 son, Jack Lorick. Tchr. Parker High Sch., Greenville, S.C., 1955-66, guidance counselor, 1966—; tchr. evening div. Greenville Tech. Edn. Center, 1966-67; employment counselor S.C. Employment Security Commn., summer 1964. Adv. admission com. Greenville Tech. Edn. Center, 1972-73; state adviser Future Bus. Leaders Am., 1959, Parker Sch. adviser, 1956-73, dist. adviser, mem. state exec. com., 1956-75. Mem. Greenville Civic Chorale, 1965-75; edn. chmn. Sans Souci Study Club, 1973. Mem. S.C. Bus. Edn. Assn. (pres. 1961-62), Pupil Personnel and Guidance Assn. (treas. 1969-71, membership chmn. Upper S.C. chpt. 1972), S.C. Assn. Women Deans and Counselors (high sch. sec. 1967-68, 71-72), Greenville County Counselors Assn. (chmn. 1972-75), Adminstrv. Mgmt. Soc., D.A.R., Delta Kamma Gamma. Baptist (pianist, Sunday sch. Tchr. 1960—). Home: 500 Trinity Way Greenville SC 29609 Office: Parker Sch Woodside Av Greenville SC 29611

ATKINSON, YVONNE WHITNEY YOUNG, civic worker; b. Detroit, Nov. 25, 1921; d. William Russel and Ardis (Shaw) Young; student Wayne State U., 1942-44; m. James Wright Atkinson, Sept. 12, 1959. Active League Women Voters, Mich., 1960—, mem. bd., Birmingham-Bloomfield, 1960-64, mem. state bd., 1965-71, chmn. state study Mich. cts., 1967-69, pres., 1969-71, state tax position chmn. 1973—; mem. subcom. on delinquency to adv. com. on services to children and youth Mich. Dept. Social Services, 1968-69; mem. legislative commn. to revise jud. article of Mich. constn., 1971-72; mem. Nat. Task Force to Montor Revenue Sharing, 1973—. Mem. Friends of Bloomfield Twp. Library, 1968—, sec., 1968-69. Editor Village Woman's Club Paper, Bloomfield Hills, Mich., 1967-68. Address: 3948 Mt Vernon Dr Birmingham MI 48010

ATKOCUNIS, MARY VAN DEMARK (MRS. CHARLES PETER ATKOCUNIS), occupational therapist, ednl. adminstr.; b. Oak Park, Ill., Apr. 4, 1929; d. H. Leo and Julia Agnes (O'Reilly) Van Demark; B.S., Western Mich. U., 1951; m. Charles Peter Atkocunis, Aug. 13, 1955. Occupational therapist Ypsilanti (Mich.) State Hosp., 1951-55; program supr. Coldwater (Mich.) State Home and Tng. Sch., 1955—. Mem. World Fedn. Occupational Therapists, Am., Mich. occupational therapy assns., Am. Assn. on Mental Deficiency, Am. Assn. U. Women, Rosary Soc. Roman Catholic. Club: Bronson Women's. Home: 222 Lincoln Bronson MI 49028 Office: Box 148 Coldwater MI 49036

ATLAS, DALIA, condr.; b. Haifa, Israel; ed. Haifa Coll., Haifa Conservatory, Israel Acad. Music, Tel Aviv, Rubin Acad. Music; pupil M.S. Celibidache, F. Ferrara, Italy, H. Swarowsky, Vienna, Austria, Pier Boulez, Bazel; m. Joseph Atlasowitz; 3 children. Permanent condr., dir. Israel Promusica. Orch., 1963—, Israel Technion Symphony Orch. and Choir, 1963—; guest condr. Royal Liverpool (Eng.) Philharmonic Orch., 1964-65, BBC No. Orch., 1964—; fellowship condr. Tanglewood Symphony Orch., Berkshire, Mass.; guest appearances Israel Philharmonic Orch., Kol Israel Broadcast Service, Haifa Symphony Orch., Ramat Gan Chamber Orch.; concert tour Eng., Italy, Scandinavia, 1968, 70, with orch., Italy, 1969. Recipient Silver medal and spl. citation' Dimitri Mitropoulas Music Competition, N.Y.C., 1964, 4th prize Third Internat. Condrs. Competition Royal Liverpool Philharmonic Soc., 1964, Finalists' medal Guide Cantello Competition, Novara, Italy, 1963. Address: PO Box 7191 Haifa Israel

ATLAS, HELEN VINCENT (MRS. SHELDON M. ATLAS), editor; b. N.Y.C., June 28, 1931; d. Louis A. and Irene (Papkevich) Vincent; grad. Riverdale Country Sch. Girls, Riverdale-on-Hudson, N.Y., 1945-49; B.A., Mt. Holyoke Coll., 1953; m. Kenyon Gillespie, Apr. 2, 1954 (div. 1958); m. 2d, Sheldon M. Atlas, June 2, 1967. Adminstrv. asst. Russian Inst. Columbia, 1956-61; interpreter trainee French and Russian into English, UN, 1961-62; interpreter Russian and French, also Soviet and Fr. cons. Hurok Mgmt., 1963-68; pub., editor Dance News, N.Y.C., 1969—. Recipient award distinguished service for outstanding assistance to USIA, Am. Exhbn. Moscow, USSR, 1959. Translator: Un Pieton de l'Air (Ionesco), La Vie Parisienne (Meilhac and Helevy), Salut a Moliere, Un Fil a La Patte (Georges Feydeau), La Reine Morte (Henry de Montherlant), La Troupe du Roi. Home: 211 Central Park W New York City NY 10024 Office: 119 W 57th St New York City NY 10019

ATLAS, LIANE ROSALIND WIENER (MRS. MARTIN ATLAS), economist, govt. ofcl.; b. N.Y.C.; d. Louis and Frances (Ferne) Wiener; B.A., Vassar Coll., 1943; postgrad. Johns Hopkins, 1954-56; m. Martin Atlas, Mar. 5, 1944; children—Stephen Terry, Jeffrey Lewis. Research asst., policy reports officer, internat. economist Dept. State, Washington, 1948-53, internat. relations officer ICA, 1957-62; fgn. affairs officer Bur. Internat. Orgn. Affairs, Dept. State, Washington, 1962-67; cons., dir. research for agr. bus. Bur. Internat. Commerce, Dept. Commerce, Washington, 1967-71, sr. economist Office Export Devel., 1971—. Mem. U.S. delegation to UN Econ. Commn. to Europe, 1963, 64. Mem. Am. Econ. Assn. Clubs: Washington Print (dir. 1966—, pres. 1972—), Vassar of Washington (chmn. scholarship com. 1965-70, book sale treas. 1970-72), Home: 2254 48th St NW Washington DC 20007 Office: Dept Commerce 14th St NW Washington DC 20025

ATLEE, ISABEL HALL (MRS. RICHARD YORKE ATLEE), lawyer; b. Galveston, Tex., Dec. 22, 1944; d. Lewis Harvey and Exa Isabel (Thomas) Hall; B.S., U. S.C., 1966; LL.B., U. Richmond, 1969; m. Richard Yorke AtLee, June 10, 1969; children—Richard Yorke, Michael Lewis. Admitted to Va. bar, 1969; partner firm Hall, Fox & AtLee, Newport News, Va., 1973—. Bd. dirs. Soc. Prevention Cruelty to Animals, 1972—. Mem. Am., Va., Newport News bar assns., Am., Va. trial lawyers assns., Am. Assn. Women Lawyers, Peninsula Estate Planning Council, P.E.O., D.A.R., Bus. and Profl. Women's Club. Soroptimist. Home: 102 James Landing Rd Newport News VA 23606 Office: PO Box 23 Newport News VA 23607

ATTEA, MARY, educator; b. Buffalo, July 16, 1929; d. George H. and Madeline Barbara (Bitar) Attea; student Nazareth Coll. at Kalamazoo, 1947; A.B., Nazareth Coll. at Rochester, N.Y., 1950; Ed.M., State U. N.Y. at Buffalo, 1952, Ed.D., 1966. Tchr. Clarence (N.Y.) Central Schs., 1951-65; reading tchr. Sweet Home Central Schs., Amherst, N.Y., 1965-68; asso. prof. elementary edn. D'Youville Coll., Buffalo, 1968-70, State U. N.Y. Coll. at Buffalo, 1970—; coordinator Sweet Home secondary sch. summer reading program, 1968-70; cons. to Niagara Wheatfield, Clarence Central, Sweet Home schs. Mem. N.E.A., Internat. (pres. 1968 Niagara Frontier council), N.Y. (sec. 1970) reading assns., Am. Ednl. Research Assn., Am. Assn. U. Profs., Nat. Council Tchrs. English, League Women Voters. Author: Turning Children On Through Creative Writing, 1973; Weep Willow Weep, 1974. Contbr. articles to profl. jours. Home: 4080 Clardon Dr Williamsville NY 14221 Office: 1300 Elmwood Av Buffalo NY 14222

ATTEBERRY, EVELYN JULIAN, mfg. co. exec.; b. Attica, Ind., Oct. 22, 1912; d. Oliver Enzly and Cora May (Stover) Julian; student Utterback Bus. Coll., 1951; m. Raymond Ralph Kelsheimer, Oct. 29, 1933 (dec. July 1943); children—Thomas R., Sandra S. (Mrs. Herley D. Redenbaugh); m. 2d, David M. Atteberry, Sept. 16, 1950 (div. Feb. 1973). With Ill. Fireworks Co., Danville, 1945—, office mgr., corporate asst. sec., 1950—. Instr. courses for certified profl. sec. rating, Danville, 1971-73; notary pub. Mem. adv. com. Danville (Ill.) Jr. Coll., 1968-70; mem. lay adv. com. VoTec, 1972—; adviser future Secs. Assn. Danville, Scholarman High Sch., 1962-63, 70-73. Mem. Nat. Secs. Assn. (pres. 1961-64, coordinator Ill. sect. meeting 1966), Methodist. Club: Toastmistress (1st v.p. Danville 1973-74). Mem. Order of Eastern Star. Home: 307 Brentwood Av Danville IL 61832 Office: 1706 King St Danville IL 61832

ATTERBURY, ANNABEL LEE (MRS. HAROLD B. ATTERBURY), editor; b. West Hoboken, N.J., May 1, 1910; d. George MacDonald and Rose (Blau) Lee; student N.J. Coll. Women, 1927-28; certificate Columbia Library Sch., 1935; m. Harold B. Atterbury, Aug. 16, 1947; children—Lee, Bruce. Library asst. Free Pub. Library, Newark, 1928-30; reference librarian N.J. State Tchrs. Coll., Newark, 1930-43; librarian postwar policy div. Am. Type Founders, Elizabeth, N.J., 1943-45; librarian Fed. Reserve Bank, N.Y.C., 1945-48; editor, columnist Dodge County Ind.-News, Juneau, Wis., 1958—, sec.-treas., 1962—. Pres., Dodge County Library System Bd., 1962—; chmn. County Library Planning Commn., Juneau, 1972—. Recipient Columnist award Nat. Fedn. Press Women, 1972. Mem. Nat. Fedn. Press Women, Wis. Press Women, Wis. Press Assn., Wis. Library Assn. Home: 253 Oakwood Blvd Hustisford WI 53034 Office: 350 E Oak St Juneau WI 53039

ATWATER, ELIZABETH AMANDA, educator; b. McKeesport, Pa., Sept. 6, 1912; d. Asaph Sherwood and Margaret M. (McGettigan) Atwater; A.B., Duquesne U., 1935; M.A., U. Pitts., 1936, Ph.D., 1938; postgrad. Cornell U., 1941. Grad. asst. classics dept. U. Pitts., 1936-38; instr. St. Mary-of-the-Woods Coll., Terre Haute, Ind., 1938-39; prof. journalism and speech, also head dept. Potomac State Coll. of W.Va. U., Keyser, 1939—, dir. pub. relations, 1939-72. Mem. W.Va. Arts and Humanities Council, 1967—; active A.R.C. Recipient W.Va.'s Advt. Person of Yr. award W.Va. U. chpt. Alpha Delta Sigma, 1972. Mem. Nat., W.Va. edn. assns., W.Va. Intercollegiate Press Assn. (faculty adviser 1939-40), W.Va. Assn. High Edn., Duquesne U. Alumni Fedn. (life), Speech Assn. Am., Nat. Jr. Coll. Journalism Assn., Delta Kappa Gamma. Republican. Roman Catholic.

ATWOOD, MARGARET ELEANOR, author; b. Ottawa, Ont., Can., Nov. 18, 1939; d. Carl Edmund and Margaret Dorothy (Killam) Atwood; B.A., U. Toronto, 1961; A.M., Radcliffe Coll., 1962. Lectr., U. B.C., 1964-65, Sir George Williams U., 1967-68; asst. prof. U. Alta., 1969-70, York U., 1971-72; free lance writer, 1972—; writer in residence U. Toronto, 1972-73. Recipient E.J. Pratt medal, 1961; Pres.'s medal U. Western Ont., 1965; Gov. Gen.'s award, 1966; Centennial Commn. Poetry Competition first, 1967; Union Poetry prize Poetry mag., 1969. Author: The Circle Game, 1966; The Animals in That Country, 1968; The Journals of Susanna Moodie, 1970; Procedures for Underground, 1970; Power Politics, 1971; The Edible Woman, 1969; Surfacing, 1972; Survival-A Thematic Guide to Canadian Literature, 1972. Contbr. short stories, poetry to various mags. including Atlantic Monthly, Quarry, Prism, New Yorker, Harper's, Tamarack Rev. Address: Box 1401 Alliston ON Canada

ATWOOD, PATRICIA KAY, banker, village ofcl.; b. Terre Haute, Ind., Mar. 15, 1939; d. Chambers Lee and Opal Garnet (Akeman) Cox; grad. Buick Motor Div. Tng. Sch., 1968; m. Ronald B. Atwood, Oct. 15, 1960 (div. Apr. 1962); 1 dau., Rhonda Kay. With Farmers & Merchants Bank, Hutsonville, Ill., 1958—, asst. cashier, 1968—; bookkeeper Woolverton's Auto Sales, Robinson, Ill., 1963-70; treas. Village of Hutsonville, 1971—. Mem. Hutsonville High Sch. Alumni Assn. (treas. 1968—). Home: Box 62 301 Cherry St Hutsonville IL 62433 Office: Farmers & Merchants Bank Box 277 Hutsonville IL 62433

ATWOOD, SARA ELAINE, newspaper co. exec.; b. Los Angeles; d. Robert B. and Evangeline (Rasmuson) Atwood; B.A., Mills Coll.; postgrad. U. Geneva, Switzerland, Am. U. Past dir. information center Boston World Affairs Council; with Anchorage (Alaska) Daily Times, 1964—, asst. to pub., 1973—. Chmn. Mayor's Park Com., Anchorage, 1969. Bd. dirs. Alaska World Affairs Council, 1965—, pres., 1972-73; bd. dirs. Alaska Heart Assn., 1965—, Alaska Hist. Soc., Anchorage Hist. and Fine Arts Mus. Recipient writing awards Alaska Press Club, 1966-67. Mem. Nat. Fedn. Press Women, Alaska Fedn. Press Women. Club: Alaska Press (state v.p. bd. dirs. chpt. chmn. bd. dirs.). Home: 2300 Forest Park Dr Anchorage AK 99503 Office: Box 40 Anchorage AK 99510

AUBERT, RUTH ELIZABETH, city ofcl.; b. Lowell, Mass.,Nov. 20, 1925; d. James Patrick and Alice Mary (Burton) Kiernan; grad. high sch.; m. Roland R. Aubert, June 20, 1954; children—Steven Paul, Celine. Various secretarial positions with various cos., 1943-61; exec. sec. Dracut (Mass.) Bd. Selectmen, 1961-69, City of Tewksbury (Mass.) Bd. Selectmen, 1969—. Chmn., Dracut United Fund drive, 1967; sec. March of Dimes, Dracut, 1967-68. Mem. Mass. Municipal Mgrs. Assn. Home: 291 OlO Marsh Hill Rd Dracut MA 01826 Office: Town Hall Tewksbury MA 01876

AUBIN, BARBARA, artist, educator; d.; Philip Theodore and Dorothy (Chapman) Aubin; B.A., Carleton Coll., 1949; B.A.E., Sch. Art Inst. Chgo., 1954, M.A.E., 1955. Instr. painting and drawing Centre d'Art, Port-au-Prince, Haiti, 1959-60; instr. figure drawing, water color, basic drawing Wayne State U., Detroit, 1964-65; instr. figure drawing Chgo. Acad. Fine Arts, 1965-66; asst. prof. Sch. Art Inst. Chgo., 1960-68; gallery dir., asst. prof. fine arts dept. Loyola U.-Lewis Towers, Chgo., 1968-72; asst. prof. art Chgo. State U., also lectr. St. Jospeh's Calumet Coll., East Chicago, Ind., 1971—; exhibited in one-woman shows at Chgo. Pub. Library, 1960, Fairweather Hardin Gallery, Chgo., 1963, Blackhawk Gallery, Chgo., 1964, Ox-Bow Summer Sch. of Painting, Saugatuck, Mich., 1966, La Grange Art League, 1968, Elmhurst Coll., 1970, others; exhibited in group shows at Am. Water Color Soc. Ann., N.Y.C., 1957, Ball State Tchrs. Ann. Drawing and Small Sculpture Show, 1961 62, 64, Fine Arts Festival, U.S.D., 1966, Art Assn. of Newport (R.I.), 1967, Art Dirs. Ann. Drawing and Print Show, Chgo., 1970, New Horizons in Painting and Sculpture, 1970, 73, Ill. Bell Telephone Competition, 1970, Chgo. Pub. Library Ten Years Later, 1970, Women '71, No. Ill. U., 1971, Exhbn. Women Artists, Barat Coll., 1972, 2d Biennial of Arts U. Minn., 1972, Stitchery '73, Union League Club, Chgo., 1973, numerous others; represented in permanent collections Art Inst. Chgo., Centre d'Art, Haiti, Ball State U. Chmn. Shimer Coll. Assn. Recipient Eugenie Mayer Bolz award Wis. Salon of Art, Madison, 1957, Purchase award Ball State Tchrs. Coll., 1962, honorable mention Art Gallery Cover Competition, 1962, award Mich. Water Color Soc., 1965, 70, 1st prize New Horizons in Painting, Chgo., 1968, numerous others; Huntington Hartford grantee for painting, 1963; George D. Brown fellow Sch. Art Inst. Chgo., Buenos Aires Conv. Act grantee, Haiti, 1958, 59. Mem. Am. Assn. Museums, Am. Assn. U. Profs., Coll. Art Assn. Am., Mich. Water Color Soc., Am. Crafts Council, Handweavers Guild Am. Home: 1925 N Hudson St

Chicago IL 60614 Office: Chicago State U 95th and Martin Luther King Dr Chicago IL 60628

AUBREY, MARJORIE ELDORA, brewing co. exec.; b. Fort Wayne, Ind., Mar. 7, 1919; d. Frank J. and Jessie A. (Hermann) Aubrey; grad. high sch. Asst. office mgr. Interstate Stores Buying Corp., N.Y.C., 1937-43; statis. clk. Centlivre Brewing Corp., Fort Wayne, Ind., 1943-44, pvt. sec. to pres. chmn. bd., 1944-52, asst. to pres., 1952-61; corporate asst. sec., asst. to pres. Old Crown Brewing Corp., Fort Wayne, 1961-65, corporate sec. dir., asst. gen. mgr., 1965-71, corporate sec. dir., gen. mgr., 1971—. Ky. col. Mem. Brewers Assn. Am. (dir.), Fort Wayne C. of C., Am. Turners. Roman Catholic. Home: 2416 Dellwood Dr Fort Wayne IN 46803 Office: 2501 Spy Run Av Fort Wayne IN 46805

AUCHTER, NORMA HOLMES (MRS. ERVIN FRANK AUCHTER), educator, concert pianist; b. Rochester, N.Y., Jan. 3, 1922; d. Robert Edgar and Rubena Monroe (Lyon) Holmes; Mus.B., Eastman Sch. Music, 1942, Mus.M., 1944, Artists diploma, 1950, postgrad., 1971, 74—; m. Ervin Frank Auchter, June 4, 1955; children—Robert, Ceci Ann, Allan. Grad. asst. Eastman Sch. Music, Rochester, 1942-43, tchr. piano, 1946-50; faculty U. Conn., Storrs, 1943-45, U. Tex., Austin, 1945-46, Middlebury Coll., Middlebury, Vt., 1956-60, U. Vt., Burlington, 1960-72, St. Michaels Coll., Winooski, Vt., 1968-72; asso. prof. piano Tex. Tech. U., Lubbock, 1972—; concert pianist, throughout U.S. and Can., 1948—. Mem. Music Tchrs. Nat. Assn. (div. sec. 1964-66), Mu Phi Epsilon. Home: 3209 68th St Lubbock TX 79413

AUCLAIR, LOIS GREGG (MRS. JEAN LOUIS AUCLAIR), univ. dean, artist; b. Wetonka, S.D.; d. Edward Lloyd and Mary (Robinson) Hamilton; B.A., U. Cal. at Los Angeles, 1932; M.A., Pacific Sch. Religion, 1935; M.A. in Counseling and Personnel Adminstrn., Stanford, 1964; postgrad. art Fresno State Coll., 1953-59; m. John Hinton Gregg, June 25, 1933 (dec. July 1960); children—Carol Gregg (Mrs. Thomas Arthur Emery), Douglas Hamilton; m. 2d, Jean Louis Auclair, May 29, 1974. Dir. religious edn. 1st Congl. Ch., Fresno, Cal., 1945-53; mem. personnel adminstrn. staff Stanford, 1961-65; asso. dean student affairs State U. N.Y., Albany, 1965—. Exhibited in group shows at Fresno Art Center, Fresno Artists Assn.; one-man shows, Fresno, 1958, Stanford, 1964, State U. N.Y., Albany, 1968; represented in pvt. collections. Recipient awards Fresno Artists Assn., San Joaquin Valley Artists, 1957, 58. Mem. Am. Assn. U. Women, UN Assn., Am. Personnel and Guidance Assn., Nat. Assn. Women Deans and Counselors, Nat. Assn. Student Personnel Adminstrs., N.Y. State Personnel and Guidance Assn., N.E.A. Conglist. Home: 10-5 Woodlake Rd S Albany NY 12203

AUDIBERT, SISTER CECILE HILDA, hosp. adminstr.; b. Fort Kent, Me., May 4, 1915; d. Joseph Henry and Esther (Michaud) Audibert; R.N., Hotel Dieu of St. Joseph Sch. Nursing, Edmunston, N.B., Can., 1946. Nurse, Hotel Dieu St. Joseph, Van Buren, Me., 1946-48, Hotel-Dieu, Sorel, Que., Can., 1948-55, Hotel-Dieu, Bathurst, N.B., 1955-58, St. Joseph Sanatorum, 1958-59, Hotel Dieu St Joseph, Cornwall, Ont., 1960-61, Hotel-Dieu St. Joseph, Campbellton, N.B., 1961-66; dir. nursing Hotel-Dieu, Tracadie, N.B., 1966-69, Villa St. Joseph, Yarmouth, N.S., 1969-70; adminstr. St. Joseph Hosp., Polson, Mont., 1971-74; adminstr. St. Joseph Residence, New London, Wis., 1974—. Mem. Am. Coll. Hosp. Adminstrs. Home and office: St Joseph Residence Inc 1925 S Division St New London CT 54961

AUER, RUTH THOMPSON (MRS. RICHARD BASIL AUER), sch. adminstr.; b. Buffalo, Aug. 9, 1928; d. George Harold and Helen Victoria (Peters) Thompson; A.A., Albright Art Sch., 1948; B.S., Buffalo State Tchrs. Coll., 1949; Ed.M., U. Buffalo, 1952, Specialist in Edn. Adminstrn., 1970; Ed.D., Laurence U., 1972; m. Richard Basil Auer, June 28, 1952. Art tchr. Buffalo Pub. Schs., 1949-58; asst. prin. P.S. 19, Buffalo, 1958-65; prin. P.S. 42, Buffalo, 1965-67, Allendale Sch., West Seneca, N.Y., 1967—. Sec., West Seneca Teen Center, 1955-59. Mem. Nat. Assn. Elementary Sch. Prins., Am. Assn. Sch. Adminstrs., Soc. Ednl. Adminstrs., Ten Towns Prins. Assn. (chmn. 1969-70), West Seneca Adminstrv. Assn. (chmn. 1970-71), Sch. Adminstrn. Assn. N.Y. State (exec. council 1973-74, regional dir. 1971—), League Women Voters (treas. 1957-62), West Seneca C. of C. (edn. com. 1954-55). Roman Catholic (treas. Altar and Rosary Soc. 1972—). Home: 5675 Brown Hill Rd Springville NY 14141 Office: 1399 Orchard Park Rd West Seneca NY 14224

AUERBACH, KAY JOAN, economist; b. Bismarck, N.D., July 13, 1936; d. Wallace Joseph and Betty (Newton) Maddock; student St. Mary's Coll., Notre Dame, Ind., 1954-55; B.A. in Fgn. Affairs with honors, George Washington U., 1958, M.A. in Econs. with honors, 1963; m. Ernest S. Auerbach, June 11, 1960 (div. 1965); children—Hans Kevin, Kelley Michelle. Economist bd. govs. Fed. Res. System, Washington, 1959-63; lectr. econs. U. Md. at Heidelberg, Germany, 1963-65, U. Md. at Seoul, Korea, 1965; internat. economist AID, Seoul, South Korea, 1965-68; economist Fed. Res. Bank Mpls., 1969-71; economist OECD, Paris, France, 1971-73; economist Fed. Res. Bank, Mpls., 1973—. Recipient certificate of appreciation Dep. Prime Minister, Republic South Korea, 1968. Mem. Am. Econ. Assn., Am. Contract Bridge Assn., Phi Beta Kappa. Club: Minnesota Economists. Author: A Survey of Regional Economic Policy in the U.S., U.K. and France, 1971; Korean Import and Export Projections for the Second Five-Year Plan, 1968. Home: 3011 Decatur Av South Minneapolis MN Office: Fed Res Bank Mpls Minneapolis MN 55480

AUERBACH, STEVANNE STOCKHEIM (MRS. DONALD FINK), ednl. adminstr., cons.; b. N.Y.C., Sept. 22, 1938; d. Nathan and Jeane Sydney (Rosen) Stockheim; B.A., Queens Coll., 1960; postgrad. U. Md., 1961-65; M.A. (fellow), George Washington U., 1965; Ph.D. in Child Devel., Union Grad. Sch., 1973; m. Arthur Auerbach, Nov. 24, 1961 (div. Dec. 1968); 1 dau., Amy Beth; m. 2d, Donald Fink, Feb. 4, 1972; 1 dau., 2 sons. Tchr. recreation and swimming N.Y. Bd. Edn., 1958-60; tchr. 6th grade, N.Y.C., 1959-60; tchr. 4th grade Glen Haven Elementary sch., Silver Spring, Md., 1960-61; profl. asst. Am. Personnel and Guidance Assn., Washington, 1961-63; editorial and profl. asst. B'nai B'rith Vocational Service, Washington, 1963-64; tchr., phys. edn. coordinator mentally retarded children, St. John's Devel. Service for Children, Washington, 1965-66; research asso. analytic study of state legislation for handicapped children Council for Exceptional Children, Washington, 1966-67; operations coordinator Mid-Atlantic Region Spl. Edn. Instructional Materials Center, George Washington U., Washington, 1967; tchr. Anthony Bowen Elementary Sch., Washington, 1968; cons. Theatre Arts in Edn. Program, Central Atlantic Regional Ednl. Lab. and Arena Stage, Washington, 1968-69; edn. program specialist evaluation sect., div. compensatory edn. officer of commr. U.S. Office Edn., Washington, 1968-69, child care research and program devel. br. Office Econ. Opportunity, 1970-71; intern in child devel. Far West Lab., Berkeley, Cal., 1971—. Mem. U.S. Nat. Com. Early Childhood Edn. Mem. Council for Exceptional Children (pres. student chpt. Nat. Capital area 1965-66), Am. Personnel and Guidance Assn. (life), Nat. Vocational Guidance Assn., N.E.A. (pres. student chpt. Queens Coll. 1958-59), Nat. Assn. for Edn. Young Children, Assn. Childhood Edn. Internat., Am. Assn. U. Women. Editor: Child Care Handbook, 1974. Contbr. articles to profl. jours., chpts. in books. Home: 190 Amber Dr San Francisco CA 94131 Office: Far West Lab for Educational Research 1855 Folsom St San Francisco CA 94103

AUERSPERG, NELLY, educator, physician; b. Vienna, Austria, Dec. 13, 1928; M.D., U. Wash., 1955; Ph.D. in Zoology (Nat. Cancer Inst. Can. fellow, U. B.C., 1968; m. 1955; 2 children. Intern Vancouver (B.C.) Gen. Hosp., 1955-56, research asst. tissue culture, 1959-60; cytologist Cytology Lab., Vancouver, 1960-65; asso. prof. cancer research and cell biology U. B.C., 1968—. Mem. Tissue Culture Assn., Am. Assn. Cancer Research. Address: Dept Zoology U B C Vancouver BC V6T 1W5 Canada

AUFDENKAMP, JO ANN, librarian; b. Springfield, Ill, Mar. 22, 1926; d. Erwin C. and Johanna (Ostermeier) Aufdenkamp; B.A., MacMurray Coll. for Women, 1945; B.L.S., U. Ill., 1946; postgrad. U. Chgo., 1964-66, John Marshall Law Sch., 1970—. Asst. librarian Commerce Library U. Ill., 1946-48; librarian Fed. Res. Bank of Chgo., 1948—; Office Nat. Planning, Liberia, 1963. Mem. Spl. Libraries Assn. (chmn. financial div. 1951-52, pres. Ill. 1954-55). Republican. Lutheran. Office: 230 S La Salle Chicago IL 60690

AUGENSTEIN, HELEN MARGARET LIVINGSTON (MRS. HAROLD DONITHEN AUGENSTEIN), museum curator; b. Etowah, Tenn., Aug. 31, 1912; d. Joseph Owen and Bessie Belle (McBride) Livingston; student pub. schs.; m. Harold Donithen Augenstein, Sept. 20, 1930; children—Virginia (Mrs. Edwin Earl Kirder), Ruth (Mrs. Kermit Eugene Converse), Helen. Caretaker, Harding Home, Harding Meml. Assn., Marion, O., 1948-64, curator Harding Home and Museum, 1965—. Mem. Harding Meml. Assn. Lutheran. Club: Three Arts Federated. Home: 1223 E Church St Marion OH 43302 Office: 380 Mount Vernon Av Marion OH 43302

AUGER, DIANA JEANNETTE, lawyer; b. Lynn, Mass., Feb. 2, 1916; d. Oscar Aloysius and Diana Helena (Dion) Auger; student Boston U., 1933-35; J.D., Northeastern U., 1939; A.B., Avon U., 1964. Admitted to Mass. bar, 1941, U.S. Supreme Ct. bar 1952, N.Y. State bar, 1966, mem. firm Gallup and Hadley, Boston, 1942-44, Roberts, Cushman and Grover, Boston, 1944-56, Arthur D. Thomson, Boston, 1956-65; mem. firm Kane, Dalsimer, Kane, Sullivan and Kurucz, N.Y.C., 1965—, partner, 1966—. Pres., treas., dir. Mec-Elec Engring. Co., Boston, 1946-61; dir. Graham Mfg. Corp., Detroit, 1947-59, sec., treas. 1956-59; v.p., dir. AGM Industries, Inc., Canton, Mass., 1963—. Trustee, mem. corp. Northeastern U., also mem. nat. council. Recognized as Ark. Traveler, State of Ark., 1955; toured German Courts as guest Fed. German Republic, 1956. Mem. Am. Bar Assn. (ho. dels. 1956-57), Nat. Assn. Women Lawyers (pres. 1954-55), Inter-Am. Bar Assn., Internat. Fedn. Women Lawyers, N.Y. Patent Law Assn., Phi Kapps Phi. Club: Waltz (N.Y.C.). Home: 60 Sutton Place S New York City NY 10022 Office: Kane Dalsimer Kane Sullivan and Kurucz 420 Lexington Av New York City NY 10017

AUGHINBAUGH, LORINE ANDERSON (MRS. GEORGE AUGHINBAUGH, JR.), jr. coll. ofcl.; b. Ventura, Cal., May 29, 1913; d. Hervey James and Ethel E. (Peugh) Anderson; A.B., Stanford, 1934, M.A., 1954; m. George Franklin Aughinbaugh, Jr., Sept. 11, 1943; children—Susan, Nancy, Karen, Robin, Debra. Tchr., Taft (Cal.) Elementary Sch., 1936-37; tchr., counselor Taft Union High Sch., 1937-40; psychologist Seattle Pub. Sch., 1940-41; dean of girls San Luis Obispo (Cal.) Jr. High Sch., 1941-42; dir. testing and orientation McClellan Field, Sacramento, 1942-44; dir. Travelers Aid USO Lounges, 1944-46; psychologist Arden Carmichael Sch. Dist., 1954-56; instr. psychology Sacramento State Coll., summer 1956; counselor, instr. psychology American River Jr. Coll., 1956-61, div. chmn. guidance and psychology, 1961-64, coordinator of counseling admissions, 1964-68, asst. dean of research, 1968—; practice psychology, Sacramento, 1954—. Mem. troop com. Gold Trail council Girl Scouts of U.S., 1952-66; mem. com. Community Welfare Council, 1956-60. Bd. dirs. Family Service Agy., 1954-60, treas., 1956; bd. dirs. YWCA, 1957-59. Mem. Am., Cal. (sec. 1959, treas. 1960, dir. 1959-61), Sacramento Area (pres. 1957) personnel and guidance assns., Cal. (dir. 1961-63, 73-74, mem. standing com. research and devel. 1969—, chmn. 1973-74), No. Cal. (treas. 1960-61, pres. 1961-62) jr. coll. assns., American River Jr. Coll. Faculty Assn. (pres. 1958-59), Cal. Counseling and Guidance Assn. (dir. 1962-65), Cal. Tchrs. Assn., N.E.A., Cal. Psychol. Assn., Sacramento Area Psychologists, Cal. Jr. Coll. Student Personnel Services Assn., Sacramento Mental Health Assn., Chi Omega, Pi Lambda Theta. Republican. Presbyn. (elder). Home: 5098 Keane Dr Carmichael CA 95608 Office: 4700 College Oak Dr Sacramento CA 95841

AUGST, BONITA ANN, home economist; b. Montgomery, Minn., Feb. 9, 1943; d. Arthur and Susan (Deckert) Augst; B.A. in Home Econs., Augsburg Coll., Mpls., 1965. Extension home economist Dodge County (Minn.) Extension Service, 1965-67, Olmsted County (Minn.) Extension Service, 1967-73, Hennepin County (Minn.) Extension Service, 1973—; organizer Expanded Food and Nutrition Program, Olmsted County, 1970, 4-H Clubs for Retarded, 1969. Recipient Alumni award 4-H Club, 1971. Mem. Minn. Home Econs. Assn., Minn. Assn. Extension Home Economists (Distinguished Service award 1971). Home: 7330 Gallagher Dr Edina MN 55435 Office: 110 S 4th St Minneapolis MN 55401

AUGUSTUS, ALICE ADAMS, art historian; b. Blackstone, Mass., Oct. 2, 1926; d. Ralph and Myla Randall (Adams) Cavedon; student Regis Coll., 1943-44, Wellesley Coll., 1945-46, Katherine Gibbs Sch., 1946-47, N.Y. Sch. Interior Design, 1952-53; N.Y. Inst. Finance, 1968-69; m. Charles Augustus, June 5, 1947 (div. Mar. 1968); 1 dau., Barbara A. With Soverign Am. Arts Corp., N.Y.C., London, 1972—; with Anglo-Am. Stamp Co., Ltd., N.Y.C., London 1971—. Mem. Nat. Soc. New Eng. Women, Nat. Bibliog. and Geneal. Soc., Nat. Steeplechase and Hunt, Am.-Italian Soc., D.A.R., English Speaking Union, Adams Soc., Quincy Hist. Soc., Curzon House (London), Internat. Underwater Explorers Soc. Clubs: York (N.Y.C.); Palm Beach Casino, Internat. Sporting, Claremont (London). Address: 1010 Fifth Av New York City NY 10028

AULICK, JUNE LETITIA, journalist; b. N.Y.C., June 19, 1906; d. Will Wroth and Letitia (Fraser) Aulick; student Syracuse U., 1924-25; m. James M. Kieran, Jr., July 7, 1925 (div. 1931). Soc. corr. N.Y. World Telegram, 1930-33; with publicity dept. CBS, N.Y.C., 1933-45; columnist N.Y. Daily Mirror, 1971-72, El Tiempo, 1973—. Free-lance mag. writer, 1945—; asso. editor World Trade Acad. Press, 1969—. Mem. br. council YMCA, McBurney, 1969—, founder Teenage Career Contest, 1969; mem. Chelsea Com. for Neighborhood Devel. Recipient Community Service award McBurney YMCA, 1968. Republican. Club: Woman's Press (dir. N.Y.C. 1970—). Author: What's News, 1964; (with Wilbur Cross) Careers in the Age of Automation, 1969. Home: 234 W 21st St New York City NY 10011

AULL, FELICE BRIGITTE (MRS. MARTIN S. NACHBAR), physiologist; b. Vienna, Austria, Aug. 12, 1938; brought to U.S., 1940, naturalized, 1946; d. Henry B. and Gertrud Joan (Aull) Aull; A.B., Barnard Coll., 1960; Ph.D. (USPHS predoctoral fellow), Cornell U., 1964; m. Martin S. Nachbar, June 15, 1962; 1 dau., Nancy Ellen. Physiologist Bur. Comml. Fisheries, N.C., 1964-65; USPHS postdoctoral fellow, 1965-66; instr. in physiology N.Y. U. Sch. Medicine, N.Y.C., 1966-69, asst. prof. physiology, 1969-72, asso. Prof., 1972—, grad. adviser in physiology, 1971—. USPHS research grantee, 1968-71, 71—. Mem. Soc. Gen. Physiologists, A.A.A.S., Am. Physiol. Soc., Harvey Soc. Home: 245 E 19th St New York City NY 10003

AULSEBROOK, LUCILLE HAGAN, anatomist; b. Houston, Dec. 31, 1925; d. William Fredrick and Emily Eliza (Ross) Hagan; B.A., U. Tex., 1946, M.A., 1947; postgrad. U. Wis., 1950-53; Ph.D., U. Ark. Med. Sch., 1966; m. Kenneth Alfred Aulsebrook, May 10, 1952 (div. 1974); children—Elizabeth Ann, Jan Emily, Robert William, Patrice. Instr. U. Tex. at Austin, 1948; research asso. M.D. Anderson Cancer Research, Houston, 1949-50; instr. Little Rock U., 1957-60; postdoctoral fellow Vanderbilt U., Nashville, 1966-69, instr., 1969-70, asst. prof. anatomy Sch. Medicine, 1969-74, asso. Prof., 1974—. Mem. Soc. for Neuroscis., Am. Assn. Anatomists, So. Soc. Anatomists, Sigma Xi. Home: 203 Cherokee Rd Nashville TN 37205

AUNIO, IRENE MARIA (MRS. ERNEST SAASTO), artist; b. Iso Kyro, Finland; d. Walter and Hilda (Latvala) Aunio; came to U.S., naturalized, 1923; student Bklyn. Mus. Fine Arts, 1949-52, Art Students League N.Y., 1948-52; m. Ernest Saasto, Dec. 9. 1942; children—Laurel (Mrs. Justin Cappiello), Ernest and Robert (twins). One-man shows at Pen and Brush Club N.Y., Studio Gallery, N.Y. Bklyn. Mus. Art Sch. Gallery, Panoras Gallery; exhibited in group shows Bklyn. Mus., Nat. Acad. Galleries; represented in permanent collections Art Students League N.Y., Evansville (Ind.) Mus. Fine Arts, Seton Hall U., Reading (Pa.) Mus. Fine Art, Norfolk (Va.) Mus. Fine Art. Recipient Henry Ranger Fund Purchase prize Nat. Acad. Design, 1953; Michael Engel award Seton Hall U., 1958; Windor Newton prize, 1958; 1st prize for watercolor, New Rochelle, 1962; 1st award 3d Ann. Jamaica Art Festival, 1969; 1st prize North Bellmore Arts Council, 1969, Marshall-Vogeney Exhibit, 1970; others. Mem. Am. Water Color Soc., Allied Artists Am., Nat. Assn. Women Artists (Goldie Paley prize 1952, Grumbacker award 1958, Leonebel Jacobs prize 1967); Am. Soc. Contemporary Artists, Art Students League, Catherine Lorrillard Wolfe Art Club (1st water color award 1955, gold medal for landscape 1962). Home: 1032 78th St Brooklyn NY 11228

AURAND, ELOISE CLARA, hosp. editor; b. Harrisburg, Pa., May 31, 1942; d. Orris H. and Edna Shaver (Woolbert) Aurand; B.A., Pa. State U., 1964, postgrad., 1967-70. Writer, Lancaster (Pa.) New Era Newspaper, 1964-65, copy editor, 1965-67; dir. pub. information, instr. English, Elizabethtown (Pa.) Coll., 1967-69; editor of news releases and publs. Hershey Med. Center, Pa. State U., 1969—. Mem. pub. relations adv. com. Am. Heart Assn., Harrisburg, 1972—; dir. publicity Channel 33 TV Auction, Hershey, 1973; sec. Lancaster (Pa.) Opera Workshop, 1967-68. Mem. Hosp. Assn. Pa., Pub. Relations Soc., Assn. of Am. Med. Colls. Pub. Relations Soc., Theta Sigma Phi, Kappa Tau Alpha. Methodist. Home: 530 Ridge Rd Elizabethtown PA 17022 Office: Hershey Medical Center Pennsylvania State University Hershey PA 17033

AURELL, MARY LOU ELIZABETH, editor; b. Grand Rapids, Minn., July 28, 1938; d. David and Hildegarde Pauline (Hoppe) Aurell; Charles T. Miller scholar, Macalester Coll., 1956-58; B.J., U. Minn., 1962. Exec. prodn. editor Leland Pubs., St. Paul, 1962-68; editor, Minn. Alumni Assn., St. Paul, 1968-72, asst. dir., editor, 1972—. Spl. publicist Am. Hoist & Derrick, St. Paul, 1973—. Mem. Women in Communications (sec. Mpls. chpt. 1971-72). Democrat. Mem. Order Eastern Star. Home: 4114 30th Av S Minneapolis MN 55406 Office: 2610 University Av St Paul MN 55114

AUSTER, NANCY EILEEN ROSS (MRS. DONALD AUSTER), educator; b. N.Y.C., Aug. 19, 1926; d. Norman Lask and Edith Cornelia (Jacobson) Ross; A.B., Barnard Coll., 1948; M.B.A., Ind. U., 1954; postgrad. St. Lawrence U., 1960-62, 71, State U. N.Y. Coll., Potsdam, 1968, 70; m. Donald Auster, Aug. 18, 1946; children—Carol Jean, Ellen Ruth. Research asso. The Conf. Bd., N.Y.C., 1948-51; research asst. Sch. Bus., Ind. U., Bloomington, 1952-54, editor publs. Bur. Bus. Research, 1954-56; lectr. St. Lawrence U., Canton, N.Y., 1962-66; asst. prof. econs. State U. N.Y. Agrl. and Tech. Coll., Canton, 1966-70, asso. prof., 1970-73, prof., 1973—; Canton faculty senator to State U. N.Y. Faculty Senate, 1969-73, mem. exec. com., 1970-71, pres., 1973—; statistician for USPHS grant, 1966-70. Mem. adv. council select com. higher edn. N.Y. State Legislature, 1973—. Sec. Thousand Islands Girl Scout council camp com., 1967-69. Mem. Am., N.Y. State (sec., treas. 1970-71) econ. assns., Am. Statis. Assn., N.Y. State Assn. Jr. Colls., League Women Voters (mem. exec. bd. Canton-Potsdam 1960-62). Unitarian-Universalist. Author: (with Donald Auster) Men Who Enter Nursing: A Sociological Analysis, 1970. Contbr. articles to profl. jours. Home: 21 Craig Dr Canton NY 13617

AUSTIN, ARLITA KAY WARRICK (MRS. JULIAN MORGAN AUSTIN), librarian; b. Peoria, Ill., June 28, 1944; d. Jesse Edward and Hazel Winifred (McClister) Warrick; B.S., Ill. State U., 1965; M.S., U. Ill., 1968; m. Julian Morgan Austin, June 28, 1964. Clk., Withers Pub. Library, Bloomington, Ill., 1962-64; dir. Normal (Ill.) Pub. Library, 1965-67; dir. Fondulac Dist. Library, East Peoria, Ill., 1967-74; field rep. Ill. Bicentennial Commn., 1974—. Instr. Ill. Central Coll., 1970—. Chmn. ecology weeks, East Peoria, Ill., 1970-71; v.p. Environmental Forum, 1972—; mem. Riverfront Devel. and Beautification Commn., 1971-72; mem. East Peoria Citizen's Adv. Council, 1968-70; mem. women's adv. bd. Peoria Jour. Star, 1970-73; exec. dir. Nat. Library Week in Ill., 1973; mem. East Peoria Youth Guidance Council, 1974; mem. Open Space and Recreation Adv. Com., 1971; mem. Tazewell County Am. Bicentennial Commn., 1974—. Mem. Am. Bus. Woman's Assn. (v.p. 1971-72, Woman of Year 1974), East Peoria C. of C. (sec. 1971-72, v.p. 1972-73, pres. 1974), Am., Illinois Valley (pres. 1971), Ill. (sec. 1972-73, chmn. pub. library sect. 1974-75) library assns., Pere Marquette Librarians Assn. (pres. 1968-69), Alpha Beta Alpha (nat. treas. 1963-64), Sigma Tau Delta, Phi Beta Mu. Republican. Methodist. Home: Box 2413 101 Patricia St East Peoria IL 61611 Office: Ill Bicentennial Commn Box 2200 East Peoria IL 61611

AUSTIN, BARBARA ELIZABETH, pub. relations exec.; b. Jackson, Miss., Aug. 18, 1941; d. William Thomas and Ella Bess (Hutchison) Austin; B.A. magna cum laude, Miss. State Coll. for Women, 1963; exchange student, Ireland, No. Ireland, 1963. Asst. dir. pub. relations Belhaven Coll., Jackson, 1964-67; asst. to dir. pub. information U. Miss. Med. Center, 1967-69, asst. dir. pub. information, 1969-73, asst. dir. spl. services, head information services, 1973—. Editor, Libretto, Newsletter Miss. Opera Assn., 1970—; v.p. Jackson Opera Guild, 1970-71, 1973-74. Mem. exec. bd. Miss. Young Republican Fedn., 1964-73, vice chmn., 1964-73; exec. com. Hinds County Rep. Party, 1972—. Bd. dirs. Hinds County Kidney Found., 1973—; mem. adv. bd. Miss. chpt. Nat. Found., 1972—; vol. dir. pub. relations Jackson Symphony Orch., 1964—, bd. govs., 1974—. Mem. Women in Communications (v.p. Jackson chpt. 1972-73), Nat. Fedn. Press Women, Miss. Press Women (v.p. 1970-72, pres. 1972-74), Miss. State Coll. for Women Alumnae (pres. Hinds chpt. 1972-74), Assn. Am. Med. Colls., Pub. Relations Group. Home: 1069 Poplar Jackson MS 39202 Office: Univ Mississippi Medical Center Jackson MS 39216

AUSTIN, JO-ANNE JORDAN, artist; b. Springfield, O., Nov. 15, 1925; d. William Conrad and Pauline Nell (McAdams) Jordan; B.A. cum laude, Western Reserve U., 1947; postgrad. Chgo. Acad. Fine Arts, 1947-48; M.F.A., San Diego State Coll., 1956; children—William, Robert, Kathleen (Mrs. Alan R. Brown), Jill, Audrey. Pub. information officer San Diego Fine Arts Gallery, 1956-57, tchr., 1954-57; tchr. Santa Barbara (Cal.) schs., 1957-60; owner, operator Austin Gallery, Santa Barbara, 1966—; one-woman shows Park's Art Gallery, San Jose, Cal., Lucile Fickett Gallery, Los Angeles; exhibited in group shows at Santa Clara U., San Diego State Coll., Fine Arts Gallery; represented in pub. and pvt. galleries. Tchr. San Diego Art Inst., Fine Arts Gallery San Diego, Santa Barbara schs. Recipient various art awards, San Diego, 1952-56. Mem. Santa Barbara Mus. Art, Art Assn. San Diego, Phi Beta Kappa. Republican. Presbyn. Home: 1491 Monte Vista Rd Santa Barbara CA 93108 Office: 539 San Ysidro Rd Santa Barbara CA 93108

AUSTIN, LOUISE THAYER FAVILLE, performing artist; b. Menomonee, Wis., Aug. 22, 1930; d. John and Esther Aline (Rosenblatt) Faville; student Beloit Coll., 1948-50, Stone-Camryn Sch. Ballet, 1960—; m. Donald E. Austin, Sept. 23, 1963; children—Dale, Lynn, Jill, Gregory. Dancer, singer, announcer, pantomimist Hormel Girls ABC-CBS Radio and Variety Show, 1950-52; pvt. tchr. flute and recorder, Oak Park, Ill., 1968—; tchr. flutes and recorder to various groups, workshops and colls., 1970—; tchr. renaissance dance Milton and Madison, Wis., Chgo., Oak Park, 1963—; dir. Oak Park Recorder Consort, 1970—; performer Chgo. Baroque Ensemble, 1972—, Camarata Trio, 1971-73, Cole Pipers, 1971—; solo performer, 1969—. Choreographer, performer Oak Park Mus. Theatre, 1969—. Mem. Am. Recorder Soc. (chpt. pres. 1971; bd. dirs. 1973—, dir. workshop 1974). Review editor Am. Recorder Mag., 1972—. Home: 112 Clinton St Oak Park IL 60302

AUSTIN, MARY CARRINGTON (MRS. GEORGE H. AUSTIN), educator; author; b. Sherrill, N.Y.; d. Curtis and Anna (Lynch) Carrington; student Oswego State, 1932-35; B.S., Syracuse U., 1944, M.S., 1945, Ed.D., 1949; m. George H. Austin, July 30, 1939. Tchr., Phoenix (N.Y.) High Sch., 1935-44; grad. asst., instr. edn. Syracuse U., 1945-48; asst. prof. edn. Western Res. U., Cleve., 1948-51, asso. prof. edn. dir. Reading Improvement Service, 1951-55, prof. edn., 1963-69; prof. edn. U. Hawaii, 1969—; lectr. edn. Harvard Grad. Sch. Edn., 1955-63, dir. Harvard-Carnegie Reading Studies, 1959-63; ednl. cons. Garrard Pub. Co., Scholastic Mags. Mem. Internat. Reading Assn. (past pres.), Nat. Conf. Research English (past pres.), Am. Ednl. Research Assn., Am. Childhood Edn. Assn., Nat. Council Tchrs. English, Am. Psychol. Assn. Author: (with C. Morrison) The Torch Lighters; Tomorrow's Teachers of Reading, 1961; (with C. Morrison) The First R: The Harvard Report of Elementary School Reading, 1963; (with C. Bush, M. Huebner) Reading Evaluation, 1961; (with Q.B. Mills) Sound of Poetry, 1963. Home: Monte Vista Dublin NH 03444 also 3065 Kalakaua Av Honolulu HI 96815

AUSTIN, PATRICIA, advt. exec.; b. Fort Worth, Tex.; B.A., So. Meth. U. Art dir., account exec. Read-Poland Agy., Fort Worth, 1955-63; account exec. Bloom Agy., Dallas, 1963-66, acct. supr., v.p., 1968-73, mgmt. supr., v.p., 1973—; sales promotion dir., advt. dir. Sakowitz Dept. Store, 1966-68. Office: Bloom Advertising Agency Inc 3000 Diamond Park Dr PO Box 5975 Dallas TX 75222

AUSTIN, PAULINE MORROW (MRS. JAMES M. AUSTIN), meteorologist; b. Kingsville, Tex., Dec. 18, 1916; d. Rufus Clegg and Medora Reeves (Askew) Morrow; B.A., Wilson Coll., 1938, Sc.D. (hon.), 1964; M.A., Smith Coll., 1939; Ph.D., Mass. Inst. Tech., 1942; m. James Murdoch Austin, June 14, 1941; children—Doris Anne (Mrs. Anthony B. Hull), Carol (Mrs. Lester D. Taylor). Research staff mem. radiation lab. Mass. Inst. Tech., Cambridge, 1942-45, research staff mem. dept. meteorology, 1945-53, sr. research asso. dept. meteorology, 1955—; lectr. in physics Wellesley (Mass.) Coll., 1953-55. Internat. Union Radio Scientists. Trustee Wilson Coll. Mem. Am. Meteorol. Soc. (profl. mem.; chmn. com. radar meteorology 1956-62, councilor 1974—). Asso. editor Jour. Applied Meteorology, 1971—. Home: 36 Wood St Concord MA 01742 Office: Mass Inst Tech 77 Massachusetts Av Cambridge MA 02139

AUSTIN, ROXANNA, educator; b. Kenwood, Ga., June 5, 1919; d. Charles and Leone (McVicker) Austin; A.B., Ga. State Coll. for Women, 1939; B.S. in L.S., U. N.C., 1945; Advanced M. L.S., Fla. State U., 1969. Tchr., librarian Pike County High Sch., Zebulon, Ga., 1939-41; tchr. R.L. Hope Sch., Atlanta, 1941-42; asst. librarian N. Fulton High Sch., Atlanta, 1942-45; asst. to sch. library cons. Ga. Dept. Edn., Atlanta, 1945-47; dir. Town-Union Regional Library, Young Harris, Ga., also supr. sch. and county libraries in several N. Ga. counties, 1948-51; library cons. Pub. Library Service, Ga. Dept. Edn., Atlanta, 1951-69; asso. prof. library sci. Sch. Library Sci., Fla. State U., Tallahassee, 1969—. Mem. Am. (chmn. awards com. 1964, 65), Southeastern (treas. 1964-66), Ga., Fla. library assns., League Women Voters, Delta Kappa Gamma, Beta Phi Mu. Democrat. Baptist. Club: Pilot (Tallahassee). Home: 1951 N Meridian Rd Tallahassee FL 32303

AUSTRIAN, FLORENCE HOCHSCHILD (MRS. CHARLES R. AUSTRIAN), artist; b. Balt., Sept. 8, 1889; d. Max and Lina (Hamburger) Hochschild; A.B., Goucher Coll., 1906-10; student Md. Inst. Art, 1926-31, D.F.A., 1974; m. Charles R. Austrian, Dec. 9, 1914 (dec.); children—Robert, Janet (Mrs. Burton R. Fisher). Exhibited one man shows Balt. Mus. Art, Delphic Studios, N.Y.C., Friends of Art, Md. Inst.; exhibited group shows Balt. Mus. Art, Pa. Acad. Art, Peale Mus., Phillips Gallery, Washington, Corcoran Art Gallery, Washington; represented in permanent collections Peale Mus., Womans Club Roland Park, Balt., Johns Hopkins Hosp. Tchr. art Coll. Club, Balt., 1955—. Trustee emeritus Peabody Inst., Balt., Happy Hills Hosp., Balt. Recipient Purchase prize Peale Mus., 1945; Bronze medal Md. Inst. Art, 1931; Citation for civic interest Mt. Royal Improvement Assn., 1972. Mem. Nat. Assn. Women Artists, Artists Equity, Am. Fedn. Arts, Municipal Art Soc. Boston, Water Color Soc. Balt. Clubs: College, Mt. Royal Garden, Johns Hopkins (Balt.). Home: 1417 Eutaw Place Baltimore MD 21217

AUTEN, VERA, librarian; b. Rawson, O., Sept. 30, 1910; d. Elbert Bryant and Rachel (Buckwalter) Auten; A.B., Ohio No. U., 1931; A.B. in Library Sci., U. Mich., 1933. Tchr., librarian Ohio Pub. Schs., 1938-50; first asst. librarian Toledo Pub. Library, 1950-56; med. librarian VA Hosp., Sunmount, N.Y., 1956-58; nursing sch. librarian Geisinger Med. Center, Danville, Pa., 1958-59; with Thomas Library, Wittenberg U., Springfield, O., 1959—, asst. reference librarian, 1973—. Mem. Nat. Ret. Tchrs. Assn., Ohio Library Assn. (sec. audio visual roundtable 1970). Methodist. Home: 477 Woodlawn Apt D Springfield OH 45504

AUTOR, SHERRY BLUMENTHAL, psychologist; b. N.Y.C., May 1, 1935; d. Herman and Clara Florence (Michaels) Blumenthal; B.A., Barnard Coll., 1956; M.A., Columbia, 1958; Ph.D., Harvard, 1961; m. Sanford Manuel Autor, June 8, 1958; children—Robert Stuart, David Harold, Deborah Merril. Clin. psychologist dept. psychiatry Mass. Gen. Hosp., Boston, 1964—, dir. psychology tng., head psychology lab., 1968—; clin. instr. psychiatry Harvard Med. Sch., 1967—; instr. Boston U. Grad. Sch. Edn., 1972-73; pvt. practice clin. psychology. Cons., Mass. Gen. Hosp. Sch. Nursing, 1966-73. Thomas Dana fellow, 1957-58; USPHS fellow, 1958-60. Fellow Mass. Psychol. Assn. (sec. 1973—); mem. Am. Psychol. Assn., Sigma Xi. Home: 91 Bishopsgate Rd Newton Centre MA 02159 Office: Dept Psychiatry Mass Gen Hosp Fruit St Boston MA 02114

AUTRY, BERTA ANN (MRS. THOMAS GORDAN AUTRY), accountant; b. Savannah, Ga., Nov. 10, 1938; d. James Ramsey and Mary Emily (Williams) Sims; ed. pub. and vocational schs.; m. Thomas Gordan Autry, July 28, 1968; 1 dau., Tammy Suzanne. With Interstate Securities Co., Kansas City, Mo., 1959-68; accountant Milton F. Eisenberg & Co., Inc., Savannah, 1968—, office mgr., 1969—, now also sec. Notary pub., Chatham County, Ga., 1960—. Mem. Savannah Outboard Racing Assn. Baptist. Home: 2220 Louisiana Av Savannah GA 31404 Office: PO Box 8063 Savannah GA 31402

AUYER, ZADEAN (MRS. WARREN GERALD AUYER), newspaper co. exec.; b. Colorado Springs, Colo., July 22, 1935; d. Opal Dean and Ruth Eugenia (Albright) Pearson; B.S., Colo. State U., 1957; m. Warren Gerald Auyer, Oct. 11, 1958. Home economist Ariz. Pub. Service Co., Flagstaff, 1957-62; county extension agt. Wasco County, Ore. State U., The Dalles, 1963-66; co-owner Malheur Enterprise, Vale, Ore., 1966—. Mem. adv. com. for the graphic arts program Treasure Valley Community Coll., Vale, 1967—; mem. career edn. adv. com. Sch. Dist. 15, Vale, 1973—. Named Bus. Woman of the Year, Flagstaff Bus. and Profl. Women, 1961. Mem. Am. Assn. U. Women (treas. 1969-71), Am., Ore. home econs. assns., Treasure Valley Home Economists in Homemaking (pres. 1973-74), Bus. and Profl. Womens Club (pres. 1960-61), Ore. Newspaper Publishers Assn., P.E.O. (treas. 1973-74), C. of C. (v.p. 1974-75). Home and office: PO Box 310 Vale OR 97918

AVENT, JACQUELINE, museum ofcl.; b. Peiping, China, July 22, 1930; d. James Manroe and Jeanette Ester (Nelson) Avent; A.A., Gulf Park Coll., 1951; B.F.A. in Drawing and Painting, U. Ga., 1953; postgrad. in elementary edn., George Peabody Coll. Tchrs., 1954. Tchr. pub. schs., El Cajon, Cal., 1955-56, Bell Gardens, Cal., 1956; curator The Children's Museum, Nashville, 1958—. Sec.-treas. Museum Council Nashville, 1954-62. Mem. Nashville Astron. Soc. (sec.-treas.), Inter Mus. Council Nashville, So. Mus. Conf., Southeastern Planetarium Assn., Internat. Soc. Planetarium Educators, Alpha Omicron Pi. Episcopalian. Club: Les Amis du Vin. Home: 3620 Brighton Rd Nashville TN 37205 Office: Children's Museum PO Box 7067 Nashville TN 37210

AVERILL, ESTHER, author, illustrator; b. Bridgeport, Conn., July 24, 1902; d. Charles Ketchum and Helen (Holden) Averill; grad. Vassar Coll., 1923. Author, illustrator: The Cat Club, 1944; The Adventures of Jack Ninepins, 1944; The School for Cats, 1947; Jenny's First Party, 1948; Jenny's Moonlight Adventure, 1949; King Philip: the Indian Chief, 1950; When Jenny Lost Her Scarf, 1951; Jenny's Adopted Brothers, 1952; How the Brothers Joined the Cat Club, 1953; Jenny's Birthday Book, 1954; Jenny Goes to Sea, 1957; Jenny's Bedside Book, 1959; The Fire Cat, 1960; The Hotel Cat, 1969; Captains of the City Streets, 1972, and others. Home: 30 Joralemon St Brooklyn NY 11201

AVERILL, VERDA MAE (MRS. DAVID LAWRENCE AVERILL), editor; b. Portland, Ore., Aug. 6, 1928; d. Walter Henry and Rosa Esther (Reeck) Griesinger; B.A. with great distinction, Stanford, 1949; m. David Lawrence Averill, Aug. 19, 1949; children—Charles, John, Susan, Robert. Reporter Kitsap County Herald, Poulsbo, Wash., 1959-60, women's editor, 1960-69, editor, 1970—. Mem. adv. com. Sch. Communications, U. Wash. Mem. League Women Voters, Wash. Newspaper Pubs. Assn., Phi Beta Kappa. Mem. Unitarian Ch. Home: Route 8 Box Mb23 Bainbridge Island WA 98110 Office: PO Box 278 Poulsbo WA 98370

AVERS, CHARLOTTE J(O), educator; b. Bklyn., Apr. 4, 1926; B.S., Cornell U., 1948; Ph.D. in Botany, Ind. U., 1953. Instr., research asso. botany Conn. Coll., 1953-56; asst. prof. U. Miami, 1956-59; mem. faculty Douglass Coll., Rutgers U., 1959—, now prof. Mem. A.A.A.S., Soc. Devel. Biology, Bot. Soc. Am., Genetics Soc. Am., Am. Soc. Cell Biology. Address: Dept Biological Sciences Douglass Coll Rutgers The State U New Brunswick NJ 08903

AVERY, CONSTANCE DORIS ROSEN, psychologist; b. Boston, June 3, 1929; d. Henry and Annie Lena (Miller) Rosen; B.A., Boston U., 1950; M.Ed., U. Hartford, 1963; Ph.D., Fordham U., 1975; children—Marsha, Shelley, Jeffrey Lasker. Clin. psychologist Mass. Gen. Hosp., Boston, 1951-52; research psychologist Inst. of Living, Hartford, Conn., 1963-66; psychologist Conn. Inst. for Blind, Hartford, 1965-68, Mt. Vernon Bd. Edn., Mt. Vernon, N.Y., 1968—; clin. dir. New Rochelle (N.Y.) Center for Psychol. Services and Edn., 1973—; therapist, New Rochelle, 1974—. Clin. psychologist for Dr. Edwin Cole, Mass. Gen. Hosp., Boston, part-time, 1955-58; clin. psychologist Diagnostic Clinic for Mentally Retarded, Hartford (Conn.) Health Dept., 1963; adj. instr. child psychology U. Hartford, 1967; cons. Am. Found. for Blind, N.Y.C., 1970. Mem. Am., N.Y., Westchester psychol. assns. Contbr. articles to various publs. Home: 753 Webster Av New Rochelle NY 10804 Office: Mt Vernon Bd Edn 165 N Columbus Av Mt Vernon NY 10550

AVERY, EDWINA AUSTIN, lawyer; b. Silver Creek, N.Y., Oct. 11, 1896; d. Llewellyn Philip and Harriet (Robinson) Austin; J.D., M.P.L., Nat. U. Law, 1927; student George Washington U., 1928-30, Dept. Agr. Grad. Sch., 1928-31, 41-42; m. Hastings Palmer Avery, June 11, 1924 (dec. June 13, 1973); children—Cecilia Ann (dec.), Barbara Ann (Mrs. Homer Dean Huffman). Admitted to D.C. bar, 1926, U.S. Supreme Ct. bar, 1938, with U.S. Govt., 1918-58, clk. with Office Adj. Gen., 1918-22, Dept. Interior, 1922-24, successively clk., asst. editor, asso. editor Bur. Plant Industry, Dept. Agr., 1924-43, editor, later naturalization examiner Immigration and Naturalization Service, Dept. Justice, 1943-58; practice law, 1958—; also cons. in immigration and nationality law. Chmn. Govt. Workers Council, 1929-37; only woman mem. Blue Ribbon Zoning Com.; only woman pres. Diston Heights Civic Assn., 1966-67. Trustee O. E. How Home for Unfortunate Girls, 1954—. Recipient citation D.C. State Fedn. Bus. and Profl. Women's Clubs. Mem. Am., D.C., Fed., Women's (pres. 1933-35) bar assns., Nat. Assn. Women Lawyers, League Women Voters, D.A.R., Bus. and Profl. Women's Club, West Coast (Fla.) George Washington U. Alumni Assn. (pres. 1973—), Kappa Beta Pi (grand dean 1943-47). Christian Scientist. Author: A Welcome to U.S.A. Citizenship (Freedoms Found. award), 1951; (motion picture script) Twentieth Century Pilgrim (Freedom Found. award); It Did Happen Here; also TV scripts, articles. Editor and compiler: Laws and Regulations, Immigration and Naturalization Service, 1944; Laws Applicable to Immigration and Nationality, 1952. Address: 1991 42d St N St Petersburg FL 33713

AVERY, MARY ELIZABETH (MRS. WILFRED M. AVERY), agrl. exec., frat. exec.; b. Oklahoma City, Nov. 12, 1920; d. Edwin W.H. and Susie Mae (Koch Loring) Falter; student Lindenwood Coll., 1938-39; B.S., U. Okla., 1942; m. Wilfred M. Avery, Dec. 3, 1943; 1 son, Robert D. Accountant E.W.H. Falter Co., Oklahoma City, 1942-52; v.p. Falter Plantation, Inc., Eudora, Ark., 1968—; sec. Oklahoma City alumnae chpt. Delta Gamma, 1947, pres., 1961-63; treas. Alpha Iota of Delta House Corp., 1954-57, financial adviser, 1957-65; nat. chmn. Delta Gamma, 1967-70, nat. sec.-treas., 1970—, mem. nat. nominating com., 1970. Organizer pre-sch. vision testing program Oklahoma City, 1953-54, New Eyes for the Needy, 1957; mem. Okla. Art and Arts and Sci. Rep. gov.'s com. for employment of handicapped, 1965; treas. Oklahoma City Republican Women's Club, 1965-66; dir. Oklahoma City Rep. presdl. campaign, 1960. Sec.-treas. Delta Gamma Found., 1970—. Named Outstanding Greek Alumna U. Okla., 1972. Mem. Oklahoma City Panhellenic Assn. (pres. 1968-69), Okla. Soc. Prevention Blindness (dir. 1958—), U. Okla. Alumni Assn. (mem. adv. council 1969—), Okla. Heritage Assn., Okla. Symphony Soc., Town Hall. Conglist. Home: 5609 NW 36th St Oklahoma City OK 73122

AVERY, PATRICIA ANN, editor; b. New Haven, July 9, 1934; d. John Edwin and Veronica Louise (Gallagher) Avery; B.A., Manhattanville, Coll., 1957. Copy reader Town and Country mag., 1957-58; editorial asst. U.S. News and World Report mag., Washington, 1959-69, news desk editor, 1969-72, spl. editor, 1972—. Mem. White House Corrs. Assn., Washington Press Club, Brownson Honor Soc. Home: 2500 Q St NW Washington DC 20007 Office: 2300 N St NW Washington DC 20037

AVERY, SUSAN HOPPOCK (MRS. JOHN HOWARD AVERY), physician; b. Orange, N.J., Mar. 13, 1942; d. David Willard and Cora Ruth (Farr) Hoppock; B.A., Mt. Holyoke Coll., 1964; M.D., Ind. U., 1968; m. John Howard Avery, Dec. 30, 1966; children—Anne Katharine, Rachel Susan. Intern medicine Ind. U. Sch. Medicine, Indpls., 1968-69, research fellow, 1969-71; emergency room staff physician Meth. Hosp., Indpls., 1971-73; staff Gen. Med. Clinic, Munson Army Hosp., Ft. Leavenworth, Kan., 1973—. USPHS tng. grantee, 1969-71. Mem. A.M.A. (Physician's Recognition award 1972), Am. Acad. Family Physicians, Alpha Omega Alpha. Address: 60 5th Artillery Rd Fort Leavenworth KS 66027

AVERY, SUSAN IRENE, newspaperwoman; b. San Francisco, Sept. 18, 1938; d. Wallace Elroy and Viola Laura (Rohrs) Avery; A.B., Stanford, 1960. With A.P., San Francisco, 1961-64; writer Los Angeles Times, 1964—. Bd. dirs. Girls Club Pasadena (Cal.), 19—. Mem. Jr. League Pasadena, Stanford Alumni Assn. Home: 411 Magnolia St South Pasadena CA 91030 Office: 9159 E La Rosa St Temple City CA 91780

AVIEL, JOANN B. FAGOT (MRS. SHIMON DAVID AVIEL), educator; b. Mpls., May 15, 1942; d. Joseph Burdell and Joyce (Cawley) Fagot; B.A., San Francisco Coll. for Women, 1964; M.A., Tufts U., 1965, M.A. in Law and Diplomacy, 1966, Ph.D., Fletcher Sch. Law and Diplomacy, 1971; student U. Minn., summer 1962, U. Paris, 1963, Georgetown U., summer 1965.; m. Shimon David Aviel, Aug. 1970. Edn. and program specialist U.S. Office of Edn., Washington, summer 1965; teaching asst. history Tufts U., Medford, Mass., 1965-66; asst. supr. social studies ministry of edn., asst. prof. social studies U. Costa Rica, 1966-68; asst. prof. polit. sci. Humboldt State Coll., Arcata, Cal., 1968-70; asst. prof. internat. relations dept. Cal. State U., San Francisco, 1970-74, asso. prof., 1974—. Mem. Am., No. Cal., Western polit. sci. assns., Pacific Coast Council Latin Am. Studies (president's adv. com. Pacific Coast 1972, bd. govs.), Internat. Studies Assn., Latin Am. Studies Assn., World Affairs Council, Women's Caucus for Polit. Sci. (pres.), Faculty and Alumni Assn. of Model UN of Far West (dir.). Contbr. articles to profl. jours., chpts. to books. Home: 724 Ada St San Mateo CA 94401

AVIL, E. MAY, city ofcl; b. Phila., May 3, 1900; d. David Duncan and Nona (Kearney) Avil; ed. Trenton (N.J.) Normal Sch., 1917, So. Bus. Coll., 1932. Tchr. pub. schs. Oaklyn, N.J., 1917-24; bookkeeper Singer Sewing Machine Co., Miami, Fla., 1926-32, clk., typist City of North Miami (Fla.), 1932, city clk., treas., 1933—, acting city mgr., 1960, 64, 71. Sec. North Miami Youth Found., 1945-50; chmn. bd. City Library, 1940—, treas., 1952—; bd. mgmt. local br. YMCA, 1961-64, sec. bd., 1962-64. Mem. C. of C., Municipal Finance Officers Assn., Nat. Inst. Municipal Clerks, Fla. Library Assn., Peoples Credit Union (dir.), Bus. and Profl. Women's Club. Club: Soroptimist. E. May Avil-North Miami Pub. Library named in honor, 1970. Died Apr. 24, 1974. Home: 14610 NE 6th Av North Miami FL 33161

AVIS, EILEEN FAITH HUTCHISON, pub. relations exec.; b. Spalding, Sask., Can., Nov. 8, 1924; d. Joseph William and Edith (Stevens) Hutchison; B.A., U. Sask., 1945; B.J., Carleton U., 1946; m. Walter Spencer, Sept. 30, 1946; children—James, Peter, John. Book reviewer Kingston Whig-Standard, 1946-50; exec. sec. Kingston (Ont., Can.) Social Welfare Council, 1947-50; pub. relations cons. Angada Children's Hosp., Kingston, Ont., Can., 1952—; dir. pub. relations Kingston Gen. Hosp., 1962—. Sec., Sunnyside Children's Home, 1958-59. Mem. Am. Soc. Hosp. Pub. Relations Dirs., Ont. Hosp. Assn. (mem. pub. relations com. 1966-71), E. Fry Soc. (pres. 1960-62). Club: Curling (pres. ladies sect. 1970) (Kingston, Ont., Can.). Home: 69 Cartwright's Point Kingston ON Canada Office: Kingston Gen Hosp Stuart St Kingston ON Canada

AVIZONIS, ANGELE (MRS. KONSTANTINAS AVIZONIS), educator; b. Alvitas, Lithuania; d. Tomas and Magdalena (Matulaitis) Asevicius; M.A., U. Lithuania, 1929, advanced studies U. Berlin, Munich and Vienna, 1932-35; B.S. in L.S., U. N.C., 1953; m. Konstantinas Avizonis, Dec. 19, 1942. Prof. German lang. and lit. State Gymnasiums in Kaunas and Vilnius, Lithuania, 1927-44; pvt. tchr. German and Russian langs., Germany and U.S., 1945-52; asst. cataloger, library U. N.C. at Chapel Hill, 1953-59, sr. cataloger, library, 1960-68; asst. prof. German, Elon (N.C.) Coll., 1968—. Mem. Am., Southeastern, N.C. library assns., Am. Assn. U. Women, So. Conf. Slavic Studies, Am. Assn. Tchrs. German. Translator into Lithuanian, editor: Der moralische Schwachsinn, 1930, German Short Stories, 1930-32. Contbr. articles to profl. jours. Home: 420 Smith Av Chapel Hill NC 27514

AVLON-DAPHNIS, HELEN, painter, educator; b. N.Y.C., June 18, 1932; B.F.A., M.A., Hunter Coll. One-man shows at Bertha Schaefer Gallery, N.Y.C., Phoenix Gallery, N.Y.C., 1960, Gallery East, N.Y.C., 1964-65, United Fedn. Tchrs. Art Gallery, 1968-69, Westbeth Galleries, 1972-74, exhibited in group shows at Colorado Springs Fine Art Center, 1953, N.Y. City Center, 1952, Rochester Meml. Art Gallery, Ohio U., Athens, 1958, No. Ill. State Tchrs. Coll., Saginaw Mus. Art, New Gallery, Provincetown, Mass., 1960, Bertha Schaefer Gallery, N.Y.C., 1963, Thomas Gallery, Provincetown, 1964, Core-Graham Gallery, 1965, Hudson Guild-Chelsea Art Exhibit, 1968, 69, Mass. Women Interart Center Show, 1973, numerous others; tchr. painting and drawing Washington Irving Adult Art Edn.; tchr. music and art Bklyn. Coll., Walt Whitman Jr. High Sch., N.Y.C.; dir. Paint In, Chelsea Park, 1968, founder New Gallery, 411 Gallery, Provincetown, Mass., Avlons Coop. Gallery, Provincetown. Mem. Westbeth Graphic Artists Workshop Group, 1970-73; chmn. multi-media Westbeth, N.Y.C. Bd. dirs. Merce Cunningham Video Exchance Film, Stephen Dance Co., Save N.Y. Piers, Westbeth Art Center. Recipient Hunter Coll. Achievement award, 1963. Mem. Provincetown Art Assn., Womans Interant. Photos. Address: 463 West St Apt 632 B New York City NY 10011 also 463 West St Westbeth New York City NY 10014 also 11 Bangs St Provincetown MA 02657

AWSUMB, GWENDOLYN ROBINSON (MRS. WELLS AWSUMB), city ofcl.; b. Marshall, Mich., Sept. 25, 1915; d. Carl Arnold and Catherine Varina (Pritchartt) Robinson; student Memphis State U., 1933-34; B.S., Southwestern U., 1937; m. Wells Awsumb, Dec. 22, 1937; children—George Wells, Carl David, Helen Catherine. Tchr., St. Mary's Sch., Sewanee, Tenn., 1937-38; editor Forward in Tenn. newspaper, Memphis, 1950-60; financial sec. Episcopal Diocese of Tenn., Memphis, 1957-67; city councilwoman City of Memphis, 1968—, chmn. 1970. Mem. nat. adv. council on equal ednl. opportunity Dept. Health, Edn. and Welfare, 1973—. Sec., Program of Progress Com., Memphis, 1965-66. Mem. Tenn. Republican Exec. Com., 1966—; W. Tenn. campaign mgr. Senator Howard Baker, 1972; alternate del. Rep. party conv., 1972. Bd. dirs. Memphis Little Theatre, 1970—, Jr. Achievement, 1970—. Mem. Delta Kappa Gamma, Kappa Delta. Club: Zonta Internat. (Memphis). Home: 4411 Walnut Grove Rd Memphis TN 38117 Office: 125 N Main St Memphis TN 38103

AWTRY, NELL CATHERINE (MRS. JOHN HIX AWTRY), former real estate exec.; b. Dallas, Sept. 29, 1900; d. Henry Hibbler and Laura Jane (Harris) Jacoby; B.A., So. Meth. U., 1935; postgrad. Columbia, 1941-42; m. John Hix Awtry, Apr. 24, 1922; 1 dau., Nell Catherine (Mrs. William W. Gilchrist) (dec.). Real estate saleswoman Prince & Ripley, Scarsdale, N.Y., 1948, Midgeley Parks, Scarsdale, 1949, Cleveland E. Van Wert Inc., Scarsdale, 1954-60, Julia B. Fee, Inc., Scarsdale, 1960—. Mem. Scarsdale Realty Bd., Westchester Realty Bd., Zeta Tau Alpha. Republican. Baptist. Mem. Order Eastern Star (worthy matron 1961, 67). Author poems and lyrics. Clubs: Scarsdale (N.Y.) Golf; Dallas Athletic, Dallas Athletic Country. Home: 3228 B Via Carrizo Rossmoor Leisure World Laguna Hills CA 92653

AX, TONI SUE, lawyer; b. Evansville, Ind., Oct. 1, 1940; d. John R. and Kathryn (Steinkamp) Ax; A.B., cum laude Butler U., 1962, Ed.S., 1966; M.A.T., Harvard, 1963; J.D. magna cum laude, Ind. U., Indpls., 1970; postgrad. U. Americas, Mexico City, U. Fla., U. N.M. and Universidad Central del Ecuador. Tchr., Spanish and English, Manual High Sch., Indpls., 1963-64, Eastwood Jr. High Sch., Indpls., 1964-65; lectr. Spanish evening div. Butler U., Indpls., 1964-65; English cons. Ind. Dept. Pub. Instr., Indpls., 1965-67; contracts adminstr. U.S. Naval Avionics Facility, Indpls., 1967-70; cons. D.c. Heath & Co., 1967-68; asso. firm Barnes, Hickam, Pantzer & Boyd, Indpls., 1970—. Rep. scholarship found. bd. Meridian Mut., 1966; group chmn. Butler U. Alumni Fund drive, 1965. Recipient citation for outstanding contbns. in field English edn. Ind. Council Tchrs. English, 1967; nat. leadership award Delta Delta Delta, 1962; Indpls. Bar Assn. award, 1969; Lawyers Coop. Pub. Co. award, 1969; West Pub. Co. award, 1969, 70, Prentice Hall Tax award, 1970. Mem. Am., Ind., Indpls. 7th Circuit bar assns., Ind. U. Indpls. Law Sch. Alumni Assn. (dir., treas.). Home: 3705 Cheviot Pl Indianapolis IN 46205 Office: 1313 Merchants Bank Bldg Indianapolis IN 46204

AXELSEN, DIANA ELNA, educator; b. Nampa, Ida., June 17, 1941; d. Milo Clifton and Peggy Mae (Lewis) Axelsen; A.B. in Philosophy, Stanford, 1962, Ph.D., 1968. Woodrow Wilson fellow Harvard, 1962-63; research asst. Stanford Inst. Math. Studies in Soçial Scis., 1964-69; asst. prof. philosophy half-time San Jose (Cal.) State Coll., 1967-68; asst. prof. philosophy Spelman Coll., Atlanta U. Center, 1969—; cons. philosophy Inst. for Services to Edn., 1973—, So. Assn. Colls. and Univs., 1974. Nat. Merit scholar, 1958-62; Stanford fellow, 1963-64. Mem. Am. Assn. U. Profs., Am. Philos. Assn., Soc. Philosophy and Pub. Affairs, Am. Civil Liberties Union, Sierra Club, Soc. for Women in Philosophy, Wilderness Soc., Save-The-Redwoods League, Phi Beta Kappa. Home: 825 Courtenay Dr NE Atlanta GA 30306

AXFORD, LAVONNE ANNA (MRS. HIRAM WILLIAM AXFORD), author; b. Ft. Collins, Colo., June 30, 1928; d. Cornelius Joseph and Alice Anna (Dondelinger) Brady; B.A., U. Colo., 1952; M.A., U. Denver, 1956; postgrad., Fla. State U., 1969-70; m. Hiram William Axford, Nov. 11, 1956. Head of library St. Thomas Sem., Denver, 1958-64; dir. Jefferson County Pub. Library System, Golden, Colo., 1964-65; head of library Arapahoe Jr. Coll., Littleton, Colo., 1965-67; head of library and media centre Fla. U. System, Miami Beach, 1968-69; dir. library services Scottsdale (Ariz.) Community Coll., 1970-73; vis. prof. U. Ore., 1974—. Cons. Seminary Libraries, Seoul, Korea and Rangoon, Burma, 1960-64; lectr. U. of the Punjab, Lahore, Pakistan, 1962-63; information center cons. Bendix Avionix Corp., Ft. Lauderdale, Fla., 1969; cons. migrant edn. program grant Fla. Atlantic U., Boca Raton, 1969-70; N. central accreditation adv. com. cons. Coll. Del Rey, Phoenix, 1971-72. Internat. Found. for Gifted Children grantee, 1969. Mem. Am., Ore. library assns., Handweaver's Guild Am. Author: Educational Programs for the Gifted Child, 1970; An Index to the Poems of Ogden Nash, 1972; An Annotated Guide to Books on Weaving, Spinning and Dyeing, 1974; Cookbooks in the English Language, 1974. Home and office: 3182 Beech St Eugene OR 94705

AXLER, MARJORIE FRIEDMAN, physicist; b. N.Y.C.; B.S., Queens Coll., 1942; M.S., N.Y. U., 1961. Mem. sci. staff Columbia Radiation Lab., 1943-46; asst. engr. electron tube div. Sperry Gyroscope Co., 1952-54; microwave tube engr. Amperex Electronic Co., 1954-56; physicist electronics div. U.S. Naval Materiel Lab., 1956-60; sr. engr. PRD Electronic Co., 1960-61; research engr. Gen. Telephone and Electronics Labs., Inc., 1961-66; sr. engr. aerospace div. Westinghouse Electric Co., 1966-68; instr. physics N.U. Inst. Tech., 1968-69; tech. staff physicist Hughes Aircraft Co., Fullerton, Cal., 1969—. Asso. mem. adv. group electron devices U.S. Dept. Def., 1957-60. Mem. A.A.A.S., Am. Phys. Soc., I.E.E.E. Research microwave device devel. Address: Electronics Lab Ground Systems Group Hughes Aircraft Co Fullerton CA 92634

AXTON, FLORENCE GOTTHELF, civic worker, club woman; b. Saguache, Colo., Mar. 6, 1915; d. Earl G. and Agnes (Noland) Gotthelf; degree in fine arts and drama, Finch Coll., 1936; m. Tracy Axton, Jr., Jan. 7, 1939 (div. 1954); 1 son, Gordon. Asst. drama dir. Finch Coll., 1937, alumnae class sec., 1934. Mem. Historic Denver; mem. Colo. Citizens for Central City, historian Central City Opera House Assn. Festival, summer 1973; trustee, vol. spl. projects Denver Art Mus.; bd. dirs. Internat. House; vol. spl. projects Cystic Fibrosis Assn., publicity chmn., bd. dirs., exec. com. Colo. chpt. Women's Aux. Cystic Fibrosis Assn.; mem. Denver Civic Theatre, Denver Press Council; membership com., Palo Club Worker, fund drive Denver Symphony; co-chmn. internat. relations Denver Women's Club; mem. Denver Civic Ballet, Seward House Rehab. Center Guild, Friends of Library; social dir. Denver Opera Aux.; co-chmn. patron com. Met. Opera Nat. Council Rocky Mountain Regional Auditions, Denver U. Theatre; mem. membership com. Bonfils Theatre; patron mem. Central City Opera House Assn.; chmn. Nat. Library Week, 1966; active coms. Denver Lyric Opera Guild, active numerous other orgns. Dist. 23 committeewoman Colo. Republican Com.; mem. Rep. 1200 Colo. Club. Trustee Randell-Moore Sch., Denver; bd. dirs. Internat. House Denver, People to People; mem. new mem. promotion-social com. mem. bd., publicity chmn. aux. Denver Symphony Guild; publicity com., bd. dirs. Rocky Mountain region Kidney Found. and Aux. Recipient awards Central City Opera, 1963, Internat. House, 1964, Cancer Fund Drive, 1965, Care, Inc., 1966, others. Mem. Denver Press Council (2d prize poetry), Internat. Platform Assn., Alliance Francaise (trustee), Japanese Soc. Colo., English Speaking Union (bd. govs. scholarship fund). Mem. Central Christian Ch. Clubs: Brown Palace, Woman's (spl. reporter internat. affairs com.) (Denver). Address: 3131 E Alameda Denver CO 80209

AYDELOTTE, MYRTLE E. KITCHELL, nurse educator; b. Van Meter, Ia., May 31, 1917; d. John and Lavara Josephine (Gutshall) Kitchell; B.S., U. Minn., 1939, M.A., 1947, Ph.D., 1955; m. William Osgood Aydelotte, June 22, 1955; children—Marie Elizabeth, Jeannette Farley. Head nurse The Charles T. Miller Hosp., St. Paul, 1939-41; surg. teaching supr. St. Mary's Hosp. Sch. Nursing, 1941-42; instr. U. Minn., 1945-49; dir., dean-elect State U. Ia., 1949, prof., dean, 1949-57, prof., acting chmn. psychiat. nursing dept., 1957-58; prof. Coll. Nursing, U. Ia., 1949-62, 65—, dir. dept. nursing U. Ia. Hosps. and Clinics, 1968—; asso. chief nurse VA Hosp., Iowa City, Ia., 1963-64, chief of nursing research, 1964-65. Mem. nursing adv. council VA; adv. com. div. nursing W. K. Kellogg Found. Served as capt. U. S. Army Nurse Corps, 1942-46; asst. chief nurse 26th Gen. Hosp., Eng., Africa, Italy, 1942-45; chief nurse 52d Sta. Hosp., Italy, 1945. Recipient Outstanding Achievement award U. Minn., 1959, Distinguished Service award U. Ia. Mem. Am. Nurses Assn., Nat. League for Nursing (pres. Ia. league 1962-66), Psi Chi, Pi Lambda Theta, Sigma Theta Tau (nat. pres. 1955-57). Author numerous articles in field. Mem. editorial bd. Nursing Research Mag. Home: 330 S Summit St Iowa City IA 52240 also 149 Oswegatchie Rd Waterford CT 06385

AYDLETT, LOUISE CLATE, educator; b. Elizabeth City, N.C., Aug. 4, 1941; d. Julian Edwin and Dorothy (Brock) Aydlett; B.A., Duke, 1962; M.A., East Carolina U., 1966. Tchr. math. Virginia Beach (Va.) City Schs., 1962-64; prof. math. Coll. of Albermarle, Elizabeth City, 1964—. Mem. Math. Assn. Am. Methodist. Home: 510 W Main St Elizabeth City NC 27909

AYER, M. JANE, educator; b. Goodman, Wis., May 5, 1930; d. Owen Lee and Alice Nina (Miller) Ayer; R.N., Bethesda Hosp., St. Paul, 1951; B.S., U. Wis.-Madison, 1959, M.S., 1964, Ph.D., 1966. Nurse Ancker Hosp., St. Paul, 1951-52, Univ. Hosps., Madison, 1952-57; pub. health field worker City Health Dept., Madison, 1959-63; asst. prof. counseling U. Ia., 1966; asso. prof. rehab. psychology Wis.-Madison, 1967-74, prof., 1974—; cons. Affirmative Action office U. Wis. System, 1973; cons. in field. Dept. Health, Edn. and Welfare grantee counseling process with retarded, 1968-69, problem solving abilities of the retarded, 1969-72. Mem. Am. Rehab. Counseling Assn. (publs. com. 1967—), Nat. Rehab. Assn. (research com. 1967-68), Am. Psychol. Assn. Editor Rehab. Counseling Bull., 1970—, Joint Nat. Rehab. Assn. Am. Rehab. Counseling Assn. publs., 1972—. Office: University of Wisconsin 2605 Marsh Lane Madison WI 53704

AYERS, CYNTHIA GERTRUDE (MRS. ROBERT SPENCER AYERS), physician; b. Phila., Sept. 10, 1942; d. Julius and Zenobia (Faulk) Keller; B.S., Howard U., 1964, M.D., 1968; m. Robert Spencer Ayers, Nov. 16, 1968; 1 dau., Kimberly. Intern Hosp. of U. Pa., Phila., 1968-69; resident internal medicine Albert Einstein Med. Center, Phila., 1969-70; resident medicine Mercy Hosp., Pitts., 1970-71, sr. active staff, co-dir. med. clinic, 1971—. Diplomate Nat. Bd. Med. Examiners, Am. Bd. Internal Medicine. Mem. Sickle Cell Soc. (trustee), A.M.A., Allegheny County Med. Soc., Alpha Kappa Alpha. Home: 7000 Thomas Blvd Pittsburgh PA 15208 Office: Mercy Hosp Health Center Pride and Locust Sts Pittsburgh PA 15219

AYERS, HARRIET WILSON, civic worker; b. Akron, O., Mar. 19, 1890; d. Mont. R. and Mary (Stanley) Beckwith; grad. Perkins Normal Sch., 1909; student U. Akron, 1928-33; m. Ralph B. Wilson, June 23, 1911; children—Robert B., Ralph B., Nancy Irene (dec.); m. 2d, Allan F. Ayers, July 29, 1954 (dec. March 1963). Sec., treas. Portage Lumber & Bldg. Co., 1932-48; ins. broker Chas. Slusser Agy., 1949-55. Founder Bus. Women's Current Event Club, 1940, hon. pres., 1944—; founder Coach House Theater, 1927, hon. pres., 1933—; dir. Womans City Club, Stan Hywet Hall Found., Children's Symphony Orch., Akron Art Inst.; lectr. on religious subjects. Chmn. Republican Women's Orgn., 1939-40. Named Outstanding Woman of Yr. in Akron, Inter Club Council of Women, 1957. Mem. Platform Speakers Am. Club: Zonta (dir.) Home: 1368 W Exchange St Akron OH 44313

AYERS, HELEN ZIPS FRY (MRS. A. RICHARD AYERS), educator; b. Johnstown, Pa., Oct. 15, 1922; d. Frank J. and Josephine (Partsch) Zips; B.S., U. Pitts., 1943; postgrad. U. Ill., 1962; m. Thomas A. Fry, Sept. 13, 1944 (dec. July 1966); children—James, Stephen, William, Robert, Betty; m. 2d, A. Richard Ayers, Sept. 29, 1973. Tchr. Verona (Pa.) High Sch., 1943-46; audit reviewer Main & Co., Pitts., 1948-50; exec. sec. J.C. Kepple Co., Pitts., 1954-60; instr. agrl. communications U. Ill., Urbana, 1964-68, asst. prof., 1968—. Communications cons. Applied Behavioral Sci., Inc., Chgo., 1972—. Mem. Am. Assn. Agrl. Coll. Editors (editor newsletter 1963-65, asst. mag. editor 1964-65), Am. Home Econs. Assn., Am. Assn. U. Women, Women in Communications, Kappa Alpha Theta. Author: (with Hadley Read) Partners with India: Building Agricultural Universities. Editor: Communications Handbook, 1967. Home: 448 N Piatt St Bement IL 61813 Office: Dept Agrl Communications College of Agr U Ill Urbana IL 61801

AYERS, JANE BALDWIN AVERY (MRS. SAMUEL HAINES AYERS), assn. exec.; b. Aurora, N.Y., Jan. 31, 1916; d. James and Pearl Woodworth (Barnes) Avery; B.A., Wells Coll., 1936; m. Samuel Haines Ayers, Sept. 3, 1940; children—Augustine Ridenour, Lucinda (Mrs. James Ansley Carnahan), Timothy Haines, Avery Tarleton. Co-dir. file dept. Lawyers Title Ins. Corp., Richmond, Va., 1938-40; exec. sec. Wells Coll. Alumnae Assn., Aurora, N.Y., 1963—. Mem. Red Cross Motor Corps, Media, Pa., 1941-44; sec. Aurora (N.Y.) Sch. Assn., 1958-60; pres. Aurora Community Players, 1952-54; librarian Aurora Pub. Library, 1950-52. Mem. Ledyard (N.Y.) Republican Com., 1960. Mem. Am. Alumni Council, Am. Coll. Pub. Relations Assn. Presbyn. (elder 1964—). Club: Thursday (pres. 1973) (Aurora, N.Y.). Home: Main St Aurora NY 13026 Office: Wells Coll Aurora NY 13026

AYMAR, CATHERINE BEATRICE (MRS. CLARENCE PHILLIP AYMAR), real estate broker; b. Ferndale, Wash., Nov. 28, 1922; d. Morley Victor and Jessie Edna (Fredenberg) Pomeroy; student Santa Rosa Jr. Coll., 1963, DeAnza Jr. Coll., 1967—, U. Cal. at Berkeley, 1967, U. San Francisco, 1972; m. Clarence Phillip Aymar, July 27, 1955; 1 son, Patrick Mercer. Real estate salesman Miranoma Realty, Petaluma, Cal., 1963-66, Vivian Krodel, Sunnyvale, Cal., 1967-68; real estate salesman Rylander & House, Sunnyvale, 1968-69, real estate salesmam, real estate broker, 1969-71; real estate broker Aymar Properties, Cupertino, Cal., 1971—. Mem. Ming Quong Children's Guild, Los Gatos, Cal., 1968-72. Mem. Nat. Assn. Realtors, Grad. Realtors Inst., Assn. Profl. Mortgage Women, Nat. Notary Assn., Sunnyvale Bd. Realtors, Women's Council Realtors (corr. sec. San Jose chpt. 1974), Am. Mgmt. Assn., San Jose Real Estate Bd. (mem. multiple listing com. 1972-73, equal rights com. 1974). Republican. Mem. United Ch. of Christ. Club: Santa Clara (Cal.) Toastmistress (pres. 1972). Home: 917 Kennard Way Sunnyvale CA 94087 Office: 20430 Town Center Lane Cupertino CA 95014

AYOUB, CHRISTINE WILLIAMS (MRS. RAYMOND G. D. AYOUB), educator; b. Cin., Feb. 7, 1922; d. W. Lloyd G. and Anne (Sykes) Williams; A.B., Bryn Mawr Coll., 1942; A.M., Radcliffe Coll., 1943; M.A., McGill U., 1944; Ph.D., Yale, 1947; m. Raymond G. D. Ayoub, July 1, 1950; children—Cynthia, Daphne. Mem. Inst. for Advanced Study, 1947-48; instr. Cornell U., 1948-51; research fellow Radcliffe Coll., 1951-52; faculty Pa. State U., University Park, 1953—, prof. math., 1968—. Vis. prof. U. Frankfort (Germany), 1966-67. Home: 120 Ridge Ave State College PA 16801 Office: Pa State University McAllister Bldg University Park PA 16802

AYRAULT, MARGARET WEBSTER, educator; b. Tonawanda, N.Y., Sept. 8, 1911; d. Miles and (Maud) Eleanor (Webster) Ayrault; A.B., Oberlin Coll., 1933; B.S. in L.S., Drexel Inst. Tech., 1934; M.S. in L.S., Columbia U., 1940. Gen. asst. Drexel Inst. Tech. Library, Phila., 1934; cataloger, Pratt Free Library, Balt., 1934-38; asst., reference dept. Library Columbia, 1939-40; head cataloger Carnegie Endowment for Internat. Peace Library, Washington, 1941-43; chief, processing sect. Library Agr. Dept., Washington, 1943-50; chief bibliog. control sect. Tech. Library Naval Ordnance Test Sta., Inyokern, Cal., 1950-51; asst. librarian Bur. Budget, Washington, 1952-54; head cataloging dept. library U. Mich. at Ann Arbor, 1954-65; prof. Grad. Sch. Library Studies U. Hawaii, Honolulu, 1965—. Mem. A.L.A. (past counselor; exec. bd. resources and tech. Services div. 1958-62, orgn. com. 1968-70), Hawaii Library Assn. (pres. 1974—), Am. Assn. U. Profs., Hawaii Assn. Sch. Librarians, Phi Beta Kappa, Beta Phi Mu. Contbr. articles to profl. jours. Home: 2415 Ala Wai Blvd # 1906 Honolulu HI 96815

AYRES, EL DANA STEWART (MRS. JAMES R. AYRES), banker; b. Eskridge, Kan., Nov. 25, 1909; d. Franklin Charles and Sylvia Alice (Tufts) Stewart; student Kan. State U., 1927-29; m. James R. Ayres, Sept. 18, 1937; 1 dau., Susanne (Mrs. Dale A. Bradley). With Citizens State Bank, Miltonvale, Kan., 1946—, v.p., 1966—, dir., 1956—. Mem. P.E.O., Am. Legion Aux., Kappa Delta. Republican. Methodist. Mem. Order Eastern Star. Home: Miltonvale KS 67466 Office: Box 413 Miltonvale KS 67466

AYRES, JANICE RUTH, assn. exec.; b. Idaho Falls, Ida., Jan. 23, 1921; d. Lowell Ray and Frances Mae (Salem) Mason; B.A., U. So. Cal., 1945, postgrad., 1946-47; m. Thomas W. Ayres, Sr., Nov. 27, 1943; 1 son, Thomas W. Adminstrv. asst., dir. personnel Disneyland, Inc., Anaheim, Cal., 1954-59; program and pub. relations dir. Am. Heart Assn., Santa Ana, Cal., 1966-69; exec. dir. Nev. Mental Health Assn., Las Vegas, 1969-71; adminstr. Easter Seal Soc., Las Vegas, 1971-73; pub. edn. and devel. officer So. Nev. Drug Abuse Council, Las Vegas, 1973-74; state exec. dir. Nev. Assn. Retarded Citizens, 1974—. Guest lectr. pub. relations Santa Ana (Cal.) Jr. Coll., 1966-69, San Jose State Coll., 1966-69, Fullerton State Coll., 1966-69; mem. Gov. Nev. Adv. Bd. Mental Hygiene and Mental Retardation, 1971-74. Bd. dirs. Clark Council Council Social Agys., 1969-74; adv. bd. State P.T.A., 1969-74; mem. curriculum bd., social services dept. U. Nev., Las Vegas, 1969-74; bd. dirs., children behavioral scis. County Dept. Mental Health, 1973-74. Mem. Am. Assn. U. Women, Pub. Relations Soc. Am. (county sec. 1969-74), Am. Found. for Religion and Psychiatry (dir. 1969-74), Mental Health Council of Profl. Staff, Greater Las Vegas Press Club. Contbr. articles to profl. jours. Office: 1115 S Casino Center Blvd North Las Vegas NV 89101

AYRES, MARY ANDREWS (MRS. CHARLES AYRES), advt. agy. exec.; m. Charles Ayres. Account exec. Sullivan Stauffer Colwell & Bayles, N.Y.C., 1948-50, account supr., v.p., 1950-59, mgmt. supr., sr. v.p., 1958-68, exec. v.p., 1968—, also dir. Bd. dirs. Am. Assn. Advt. Agys., 1970, Inwood House. Recipient Headliner of Yr. award Women in Communications, 1973. Mem. Fashion Group (chmn. membership com.). Home: 45 Sutton Pl S New York City NY 10022 Office: Sullivan Stauffer Colwell & Bayles 1 Dag Hammarskjold Plaza New York City NY 10022*

AZAROWICZ, MARJORY FRANCES BROWN, educator; b. Calgary, Alta., Can., Nov. 10, 1922; d. Charles and Isobella Margaret (Glenday) Brown; B.A., U. B.C., 1950; B.Ed., U. Alta., 1953, Asso. in Music, 1954; asso. Royal Conservatory Music, U. Toronto, 1953; M.A., U. Wash., 1956, Ph.D., 1961; children—Edward, Diane, Calvin. Came to U.S., 1956, naturalized, 1967. Tchr. Wheatland (Alta.) Sch. Dist., 1941-43, Turner Valley, 1943, Calgary, 1944-56; asso. prof. State U. N.Y. at Buffalo, 1960-66; tchr. reading elementary and secondary schs., Fairfax County, Va., 1967-68; prof. elementary and secondary edn. George Mason U., Fairfax, Va., 1968—. Cons. reading and math. to local sch. dists., 1941—. Recipient many musical festival awards in Can. Mem. Va. Edn. Assn. (chpt. pres. 1972), Pi Lambda Theta. Author: Handbook of Creative Choral Speaking, 1970. Editor: Quar. Mag. George Mason U., 1970-73. Home: 4406 Middle Ridge Dr Fairfax VA 22030

AZENARA, MARY LOUISE, real estate broker; b. Bennettsville, S.C., Sept. 8, 1924; d. William Hope and Mary Howell (Sullivan) Bounds; student U. Miami, 1943-45, Pembroke State Coll., 1954-56, San Bernardino Valley Coll., 1968-70; m. George Samuel Azenara, Mar. 15, 1945 (div. June 1970); 1 son, George Samuel. Draftsman, Blueprint Co., Burbank, Cal., 1953; self employed in advt. layouts for newspapers, 1954-59; salesman On Your Lot Homes, Colton, Cal., 1960; real estate salesman Frank Scott Realty, Yucaipa, Cal., Aladdin Realty, Rialto, Cal., 1962-69; partner, real estate broker Red Carpet Real Estate, Rialto, 1973—. Cons. Pioneer Mgmt. Corp., Upland, Cal., 1973—. Fund dr. chmn. San Bernardino (Cal.) Underprivileged Children, 1969-72. Mem. Nat. Assn. Real Estate Brokers, San Bernardino Bd. Realtors, San Bernardino Red Carpet Council. Office: 517 W Foothill Blvd Rialto CA 92376

BAA, ENID M., ret. librarian; Chief librarian, dir. Libraries and Museums, Dept. Edn. V.I. of U.S., St. Thomas; dir. libraries and museums Virgin Islands Dept. of Conservation and Cultural Affairs, until 1974; ret., 1974—. John Hay Whitney Found. fellow, 1955. Mem. Assn. Coll. and Research Libraries (resources and tech. services div.), A.L.A., Caribbean (treas. 1967—), Am., Jewish hist. assns., Friends of Denmark, St. Thomas Historic Trust, Internat. Platform Assn., Community Music Assn., P.R. Library Assn., V.I. Conservation Soc. Author: Bibliography of Doctoral Dissertations and Selected theses on Caribbean Topics, 1788-1968, 1969. Home: PO Box 822 Charlotte Amalie St Thomas VI 00801

BAACK, BARBARA MARIE, writer, editor, printing co. exec.; b. Berkeley, Cal., June 7, 1937; d. Ernest Charles and Frieda (Baggley) Baack; B.A. in Journalism, U. Cal. at Berkeley, 1959. Women's editor Watsonville (Cal.) Register-Pajaronian, 1959-61; pub. information specialist Naval Air Sta., Alameda, Cal., 1966-72, writer-editor Naval Air Work Facility, Alameda, 1961-66, 72—; owner Acme Printing Co., Berkeley, 1972—. Mem. Federally Employed Women (pres. chpt. 1973-74), Berkeley Bus. and Profl. Women's Club, Women in Communications, Am. Humane Soc. Democrat. Home: 16148 Via

Sonora San Lorenzo CA 94580 Office: 1301 University Av Berkeley CA 94702

BAAK, ODELLA SOLHEIM (MRS. LEONARD E. BAAK), librarian; b. Valley City, N.D., Sept. 26, 1913; d. Elling Severin and Helene G. (Sogaarden) Solheim; B.A. cum laude, St. Olaf Coll., 1936; postgrad. U. Minn., summers 1939, 41; M.A. in Library Sci., Kan. State Coll. of Emporia, 1956; m. Leonhard E. Baak, Aug. 8, 1953. Tchr. high sch. English and music, Westhope, N.D., 1936-39, Faulkton, S.D., 1939-42, Alexandria, Minn., 1942-45; res. books librarian St. Olaf Coll., 1946-53; asst. librarian Coll. of Emporia, 1953-60; vis. lectr. library sci. Kan. State Coll. of Emporia, 1959-60; asst. prof. library sci., asst. librarian Morningside Coll., Sioux City, Ia., 1960-70, asso. prof., 1970—, chmn. library sci. dept., 1970—. Library cons. tri-county insts. for pub. schs. N.W. Ia., 1966. Mem. Am., Ia. library Assns., Am. Assn. U. Women, Lutheran Acad. for Scholarship, Beta Phi Mu, Alpha Lambda Delta, (faculty adviser), Faculty Women's Club. Lutheran (chmn. library com.). Home: 4227 Morningside Av Sioux City IA 51106

BAAL, IONE THOMPSON, educator; b. Mount Ayr, Ia., Apr. 10, 1923; d. Osmer R. and Jessie (Butler) Thompson; B.S., N.W. Mo. State Coll., 1944; postgrad Ia. State Coll., 1950, U. Pa., 1953-55, Ohio U., 1959; M.Ed., Drake U., 1962; m. John Lowell Baal, 1946 (div.); 1 son, Terry Thompson. Vocational homemaking tchr. Modale (Ia.) Consol. High Sch., 1944-45, Villisca (Ia.) High Sch., 1945-46; homemaking tchr. East High Sch., Des Moines, 1947-59, counselor, 1959-60, girls' adviser, 1960-63; supr. guidance counseling Des Moines Bd. Edn., 1963-71, supr. guidance counseling and testing, 1972—. Mem. adv. bd. Midwest region Seventeen mag.; lectr. family financial security workshop U. Pa. Active P.T.A., YWCA. Mem. Ia. Vocational Assn. (pres. 1956), Ia. Vocational Homemaking Tchrs. Assn. (treas. 1954, pres. 1955), Des Moines Home Econs. Club (pres. 1953), N.E.A. (del. nat. conv.), Des Moines Edn. Assn., Am., Ia. (mem. exec. bd. 1971-72), Des Moines personnel and guidance assns., Des Moines Symphony Orch., Des Moines Community Playhouse, Des Moines C. of C. (mem. mil. affairs com. 1970-72), Ia. Assn. Coll. Admission Counselors (mem. exec. bd. 1968-71), Ia. Assn. Counselor Edn. and Supervision (sec.-treas. 1971-72), Delta Kappa Gamma sec. 1966-68, pres. 1970-72), Kappa Omicron Phi. Club: Altrusa. Author (with Dorothy Jones, Rex Withers): Mcderns Make Money Behave, 1952; (with Dr. Hazel Anthony) Learning Experiences in Personal and Family Finance, 1955. Contbr. articles to profl. jours. Home: 1409 Lewis St Des Moines IA 50315 Office: 1800 Grand Av Des Moines IA 50307

BAALMAN, WILMA ALICE JONES (MRS. CLARENCE G. BAALMAN), occupational therapist; b. Hill City, Kan., June 27, 1914; d. William Thomas and Elsie Elvira (Knox) Jones; grad. high sch.; m. Clarence G. Baalman, June 3, 1931; children—Betty Joan (Mrs. William E. Farber), Peggy Louise (Mrs. William H. Weber). Asst. to doctor, Hoxie, Kan., 1948-53; lab. asst. Sheridan County Hosp., Hoxie, 1968-71, occupational therapist, 1971—. Chmn. Sheridan County Democratic Com., 1968—. Roman Catholic (mem. bldg. com. 1968—). Home: 1501 Royal Av Hoxie KS 67740 Office: Sheridan County Hosp 826 18th St Hoxie KS 67740

BAAR, LILLIAN MARY (MRS. WILLIAM D. BAAR), business exec.; b. Chgo.; d. James and Frances (Stanek) Shuss; student evening sch. J. Sterling Morton Jr. Coll., 1934-36; m. William D. Baar, July 25, 1942; 1 dau., Judith Barbara (Mrs. Joseph Topinka). Sec. to pres. Thordarson Mgr. Co., Chgo., 1935-37; sec. to ofcls. of Sears, Roebuck & Co., Chgo., 1937-43; real estate sales, Berwyn, Ill., 1943-44; broker, owner The Baar Realty Co., Berwyn, 1944-69; real estate cons. Baar Realty, Inc. (now Baar Harps Realty, Inc.), 1969—; ins. broker Lillian Baar Ins. Agy. Active A.R.C., Am. Heart Fund; v.p. Berwyn Community Chest, 1968-70, chmn., 1971-72, dir., 1973; mem. Berwyn-Cicero Gov.'s Council Employment Handicapped, 1965-73; co-chmn. Berwyn Heart Fund, 1968-72. Bd. dirs. Dialogue, 1st v.p., 1971-72, pres. (1st woman), 1972-73. Recipient Meritorious Service award Dialogue, 1971; Town of Cicero Resolution as outstanding bus. and civic leader, 1972. Mem. Cermak Rd. Bus. Assn. (pres. 1961-64, dir. 1965-72), West Towns Bd. Realtors (pres. 1965-66), Nat. (mem. women's council), Ill. assns. real estate bds., Nat. Inst. Real Estate Brokers, Ill. C. of C., Berwyn Bus. and Profl. Women's Club (pres. 1973-74). Clubs: Mothers of Alpha Gamma Delta, Ladies Aux. The Bohemian of Ceska Beseda. Home: Riverside IL 60546 Office: 6335 W Cermak Rd Berwyn IL 60402

BABB, BARBARA CAROLINE, lawyer; b. Fountain Inn, S.C., Dec. 16, 1933; d. Victor Morgan and Ida Kate (Morrison) Babb; student Sweet Briar Coll., 1951-53; B.A., U. N.C., Chapel Hill, 1959, postgrad., 1963; J.D., U. S.C., 1968. Sec. Woodside div. Dan River Mills, Greenville, S.C., 1954-58, 60-65, indsl. relations artist, Woodside, 1954-72; admitted to S.C. bar, 1968; exec. dir. S.C. Bar Assn., 1970-71; exec. sec.-treas. S.C. State Bar, 1970—; pvt. practice, Fountain Inn, 1972—; spl. instr. prospective legal secs. Greenville Tech. Inst., 1969-70; spl. cons. Appalachian Regional Commn., Greenville, 1970. Mem. Chief Justice S.C. Ct. Reform Com., 1970—. Mem. Am., S.C. bar assns., S.C. State Bar, Am. Judicature Soc., Nat. Assn. Bar Execs., Am. Hort. Soc., Met. Opera Guild, Smithsonian Instn. Presbyn. Home: 407 S Main St Fountain Inn SC 29644 Office: PO Box 11297 Capitol Station Columbia SC 29644

BABBAGE, JOAN DOROTHY, journalist; b. Montclair, N.J., Jan. 10, 1926; d. Laurence Washburn and Dorothy A. (Davenport) Babbage; B.A. in English, Mt. Holyoke Coll., 1948; postgrad. Art Students League, New Sch. for Social Research; m. Vernon H. Ellsworth, Mar. 6, 1971. Publicist, Paramount Internat. Films, N.Y.C., 1952-58; reporter Newark News, 1960-67, food editor, 1967-72; feature writer Star-Ledger, Newark, 1972—. Vice pres. jr. group Women's Nat. Republican Club, N.Y.C., 1955. Contbr. restaurant revs., bus. articles N.J. Bus. Mag. Home: 412 Washington Av Montclair NJ 07042 Office: Star-Ledger Court St Newark NJ 07101

BABCOCK, HELEN ZOE (MRS. EMMETT HENRY BABCOCK), real estate co. exec.; b. Chgo., Mar. 6, 1916; d. Oscar Christian and Harriet Marie (Flemal) Andersen; diploma Bryant and Stratton Bus. Coll., 1934; student Mt. San Antonio Jr. Coll., 1962-64; m. Emmett Henry Babcock, Aug. 21, 1937; children—Jeanne Marie (Mrs. Landon Carter), Carol Ann (Mrs. Gerald W. Evans). Salesman, Ward M. Turney Co., Pomona, Cal., 1965-67; real estate salesman and asso. Wheeler Steffen Co., Claremont, Cal., 1967-69; owner Babcock Realty Co., 1969—. Mem. Pomona Beautification Com., 1958-60; active Blue Birds Am., 1955-58. Mem. Musician's Club, Claremont C. of C., Pomona Valley Bd. Realtors, Cal. Real Estate Assn., Nat. Assn. Realtors. Mem. Ch. Jesus Christ of Latter-day Saints. Club: Ebell. Home: 4750 Live Oak Canyon Rd La Verne CA 91750 Office: 111 Harvard Av Claremont CA 91711

BABCOCK, MICHAEL JANE ALLEN (MRS. JAMES D. BABCOCK), computer co. exec.; b. Wichita, Kan., Sept. 17, 1926; d. Harry R. and Alma (Garrison) Allen; B.A., Roosevelt U., 1948; postgrad. U. Tex., 1948-49, U. Cal. at Los Angeles, 1960-62; m. James D. Babcock, Aug. 27, 1949 (div. Apr. 1969); 1 dau., Carla Anne. Sec.-treas. Allen-Babcock Computing, Inc., Los Angeles, 1965-67, exec. v.p., 1967-69, pres., 1969—, also dir.; Pres. Midro Computer Corp., Los Angeles, 1973—. Bd. dirs. Century City Civic Council. Bd. dirs., exec. v.p. Know Found. Mem. Delta Phi Upsilon. Home: 805 San Vicente St Santa Monica CA 90402 Office: 1800 Av of the Stars Los Angeles CA 90067

BABCOCK, ROWENA BERYL PETERSON (MRS. ALFRED JAMES F. BABCOCK), librarian; b. Watertown, N.Y., Apr. 26, 1916; d. Arthur John and Inez Pearl (Dolin) Peterson; A.B., Houghton Coll., 1938; B.S. in L.S., State U. N.Y., Geneseo, 1941; A.M., Cornell U., 1946; m. Alfred James F. Babcock, Feb. 14, 1970. Research analyst N.Y. Air Brake Co., Watertown, 1947-48; adviser work with children and young people in libraries of St. Lawrence, Jefferson and Lewis Counties, N.Y. State Dept. Edn., 1953-56; tchr., library media specialist Gen. Brown Sch., 1938-47, Holland Patent (N.Y.) Sch., 1948-52, Sandy Creek, N.Y., 1965-68, Wayne Central Sch., Ontario Center, N.Y., 1969-74. Tchr. creative writing Watertown High Sch., 1962, 63, 64; instr. English, Missionaries of Sacred Heart Sem., Watertown, 1964; v.p. multimedia orgn. Resources, 1972-74. Mem. N.E.A., N.Y. State United Teachers, N.Y. State Ednl. Communications Assn., N.Y. Library Assn., N.Y. Folklore Soc., Internat. Platform Assn. Methodist. Contbr. articles to profl. jours. Home: 130 Stuart St Watertown NY 13601

BABER, ALICE, painter; b. Charleston, Ill., Aug. 22, 1928; B.A., Ind. U.; postgrad. Fontainebleau Sch. Art (France). Exhibited in one-man shows at Galerie de la Librairie Anglaise, Paris, France, 1963, New Vision Art Centre, London, Eng., 1963, A.M. Sachs Gallery, N.Y.C., 1965, 66, 69, 71, 73, Cologne (Germany) Mus., 1966, Bernard M. Baruch Coll., N.Y.C., 1968; exhibited in group shows at Stable Gallery, N.Y.C., 1957, Deuxieme Biennale de Paris, 1961, Am. Embassy, London, 1961, Mulvane Art Center and Washburn Gallery, Topeka, 1965, Le Havre Internat. Exhbn., 1966-67, Am. Embassy, Paris, France, 1966, Kent State U., 1968; represented in permanent collections at Fordham U., Peter Stuyvesant Coll., Amsterdam, Netherlands, U. Cal. at Berkeley, U. Notre Dame, Brandeis U., Waltham, Mass., Cornell U., Ithaca, N.Y., Nat. Mus. Israel, White House Loan Collection, U.S. Embassy, Madrid, Spain, New Delhi, India, numerous others. Address: 73 Bedford St New York City NY 10014

BABEY-BROOKE, ANNA M. (MRS. PAUL P. BROOKE), educator; b. Bklyn., July 16, 1911; d. John J. and Mary (Petrocy) Babey; B.A., cum laude, Hunter Coll., 1931; M.A., Columbia U., 1932, Ph.D., 1938; D.A., Tai Pei, Formosa 1964; m. Paul P. Brooke, Mar. 31, 1945 (div. Aug. 1951); 1 son, Paul A. Lectr. New Coll. Tchrs. Coll., Columbia U., 1932-36, instructional asst. to lectr., 1936-38; tutor to asso. prof. Bklyn. Coll., U. City of N.Y.; chmn., grad. studies as sr. Fulbright grantee Lady Doak Coll., Madurai, South India, 1963-64; guest lectr. Internat. Congress of Acupuncture, Tokyo, Japan, 1965, Paris, France, 1969, Seoul, Korea, 1973. Mem. Chinese Acupuncture Soc. (first Am. woman), Am. Assn. U. Profs., Am. Assn. U. Women, Am. Acupuncture and Moxibustion Soc. (sec.), Nat. Orgn. Women (pres. Queens chpt. 1972—). Author: Americans in Russia, 1776-1917, 1938; The Pulse in Occident and Orient: Its Philosophy and Practice in India, China, Iran and the West, 1966. Contbr. articles in field to profl. jours. Home: 6922 Dartmouth St Forest Hills NY 11375

BABLADELIS, GEORGIA, educator; b. Manistique, Mich., Jan. 30, 1931; d. Alex and Bertha (Prokas) Babladelis; B.A., U. Mich., 1953; M.A., U. Cal. at Berkeley, 1957; Ph.D., U. Colo., 1960. Psychol. intern VA Hosp., Palo Alto, Cal., 1954-55; clin. psychologist Alameda County Probation Dept. Guidance Clinic, 1955-57, sr. clin. psychologist, 1960-63; instr. Oakland City Coll., 1960-62, Coll. San Mateo, 1964-66; asst. prof. psychology Cal. State U., Hayward, 1963-65, 1966-67, asso. prof. psychology, 1967-72, prof., 1972—. Research cons. State Cal. Correctional Inst., 1961. USPHS Nat. Inst. Mental Health Tng. grantee, 1960-63, Research grantee, 1969; Social Sci. Research Council-NSF tng. grantee, 1971; A.A.A.S.-N.S.F. tng. grantee, 1972-73. Mem. Am. Psychol. Assn., Am. Civil Liberties Union, various wildlife and humane socs. Author: (with Suzanne Adams) The Shaping of Personality, 1967. Contbr. research articles to profl. jours. Home: 1064 Sterling Av Berkeley CA 94708 Office: Dept Psychology Cal State U Hayward CA 94745

BABLANIAN, LILLIAN MURAD (MRS. ROSTOM H. BABLANIAN), textile co. exec.; b. Tiflis, USSR, May 29, 1917; d. Levon Murat and Veronica (Arvanian) Gondaktchian; diploma Conservatory Music, Nice, France, 1933; B.S. in Chem. Engring., Pratt Inst., 1947; postgrad. N.Y. U., 1958-60, Hofstra U., 1968-72; m. Rostom H. Bablanian, Oct. 29, 1955; children—Gregory Armen, Gayne Maria. Tracer, textile designer Rex Studios, N.Y.C., 1941-42; asst. to mgr. Pacific Food Products, Inc., Bklyn., 1947-48; with Murad Textile Print Works, Bklyn., 1948—, v.p., mgr., 1954-56, v.p., cons., 1956—; owner, mgr. Muratex Chems., Inc., N.Y.C., 1949-54; tchr. chemistry Central Sch. Dist. #6, Oyster Bay, N.Y., 1958—; lectr., demonstrator Armenian dance, Library Performing Arts, N.Y.C., Boston, Detroit, Washington. Recipient Adm. Richard L. Conolly Outstanding Tchrs. award C.W. Post Coll., 1968, Chem. Engring. Alumni award Pratt Inst., 1948. Mem. Soc. Women Engrs. (pres. 1952-53, trustee, 1960-62), Nat. Sci. Tchrs. Assn. (life), N.Y. State Tchrs. Assn., Tau Beta Pi. Patentee water-base pigment binders. Home: 147 Anstice St Oyster Bay NY 11771 Office: 98 West St Brooklyn NY 11222

BACALL, LAUREN, actress; b. N.Y.C., Sept. 16, 1924; d. Natalie Bacall; student of pub. schs.; m. Humphrey Bogart, May 21, 1945 (dec. 1957); children—Stephen H., Leslie. Actress Broadway plays, Johnny 2x4, Franklin Street, 1942, Goodbye Charlie, 1960, (Broadway musical) Applause, 1970 (Tony award 1970); also motion picture actress, 1942—, pictures include: To Have and Have Not, The Big Sleep, 1944, Confidential Agent, 1945; Dark Passage, 1947; Key Largo, 1948, Young Man With a Horn, 1949, Bright Leaf, 1950, How to Marry a Millionaire, 1953, Woman's World, 1954, The Cobweb, Blood Alley, 1955, Written on the Wind, Designing Woman, Gift of Love, Flame Over India, 1959, Shock Treatment, 1962, Sex and the Single Girl, 1963, Harper, 1965; Broadway play Cactus Flower, 1965-67; Broadway play Applause, 1969-71, nat. co., 1971-72. Office: 6363 Wilshire Blvd Los Angeles CA 90048

BACH, MURIEL DUNKLEMAN (MRS. IRA J. BACH), author, actress; b. Chgo., May 14, 1918; d. Gabriel and Deborah (Warshauer) Dunkleman; student Carleton Coll., 1935-37; B.S. in the Arts, Northwestern U., 1939; m. Joseph Wolfson, June 16, 1940 (div. Apr. 1962); 1 dau., Susan; m. 2d, Ira J. Bach, Apr. 14, 1963; stepchildren—Caroline (Mrs. Dennis Paul Marandos), John Lawrence. Researcher original manuscripts for One-Woman Theatre, also costume designer, writer, set designer; actress TV commls., indsl. films, radio commls.; photographic model. Active sr. citizens groups, youth groups. Recipient Career Achievement award Chgo. Area Profl. Pan Hellenic Assn., 1971. Distinguished Woman Visitor, Carleton College, 1974. Mem. Screen Actors Guild, A.F.T.R.A., Zeta Phi Eta. Clubs: Arts, Tavern (Chgo.). Author: (plays) Two Lives, 1958; Mothers of the Great, 1963; Madame, Your Influence is Showing!, 1969; Ms... Haven't We Met Before?, 1972; also author vignettes for theater. Address: 748 Buena Av Chicago IL 60613

BACHARACH, FRANCES FANNY, editor; b. Phila., Nov. 7, 1914; d. Newton and Frieda (Abrahams) Bacharach; student Temple U., 1936-53. Tchr., Phila. pub. and pvt. schs., 1948-51, editorial asst. Haddon Press, 1941-42; time and motion engr. RCA, 1942-44; asst. chief indsl. engr. Super-Electric Co., 1944-45; self-employed as indsl. engr., 1945-48; indsl. specialist Naval Aviation Depot, 1951-53; adminstrv. analyst, supr. forms and analysis City of Phila., 1958-64; editor, George Shumway Pub., York, Pa., 1965—. Tchr. methods engring. Rutgers U., 1945. Recipient Plaque, Poor Richard Club, 1941, awards for photographs. Mem. Am. Inst. Indsl. Engrs. Author: Pocketknife Panorama, 1974. Address: 6232 N 13th St Philadelphia PA 19141

BACHAUER, GINA, concert pianist; b. Athens, Greece, May 21, 1913; grad. Athens Conservatory; studied with Cortot, Rachmaninoff; H.H.D., U. Utah, 1971; m. Alec Sherman. Made debut with Athens Orch., 1935, European tour 1937-39; London debut as soloist with New London Orch., 1946, N.Y.C. debut at Carnegie Hall with N.Y. Philharmonic Orch., 1950; founding artist Kennedy Center for Performing Arts, Washington, 1971; ann. tours U.S., also others throughout world. Decorated Order Golden Phoenix, Order of Welfare (Greece). Club: Cosmopolitan (N.Y.C.). Address: 6 Cumberland Terrace Regent's Park London NW 1 England also care Hurok Concerts Inc 730 Fifth Av New York City NY 10019

BACHELIS, FAITH G(INSBURG) (MRS. LEONARD A. BACHELIS), med. assn. exec., therapist; b. Palmer, Mass.; d. David and Frieda Ginsburg; B.S., Lesley Coll., 1957; M.A., Columbia, 1958; Ph.D., Yeshiva U., 1966; m. Leonard A. Bachelis, Aug. 5, 1962; 1 son, Douglas. Tchr. pub. schs., N.Y.C., 1958-59; psychology intern Kings County Hosp., Bklyn., 1960-61; psychologist child guidance bur. bd. of edn., N.Y.C., 1961-67; adminstr., behavior therapist Behavior Therapy Center of N.Y., N.Y.C., 1969—. Mem. Am. Psychol. Assn., Assn. Advancement Behavior Therapy, Biofeedback Research Soc. Address: 111 E 85th St New York City NY 10028

BACHER, ROSALIE WRIDE, counselor; b. Los Angeles, May 25, 1925; d. Homer M. and Irene (Rogers) Wride; A.B., Occidental Coll., 1947, M.A., 1949; m. Archie O. Bacher, Jr., Mar. 30, 1963. Tchr., English, Latin, history David Starr Jordan High Sch., Long Beach, Cal., 1949-55, counselor, 1965; counselor Poly. High Sch., 1966; vocational counselor Office Occupational Preparation, 1967-68; v.p. Washington Jr. High Sch., 1968-70; counselor Lakewood Sr. High Sch., Cal., 1965-66, asst. prin., 1970; vice prin. Jefferson Jr. High Sch., Long Beach, Cal., 1970—. Chmn. vocational guidance steering com Long Beach Unified Sch., Dist., 1963-68; mem. youth adv. com. Long Beach chpt. A.R.C. Mem. Am. Assn. U. Women, Long Beach Personnel and Guidance Assn. (dir. 1958-60), Long Beach C. of C., Long Beach Sch. Counselors Assn. (sec. high sch. segment 1963-64), Phi Beta Kappa, Delta Kappa Gamma (chpt. pres. 1964-66, area dir. Cal., 1969-71, mem. state exec. bd. profl. affairs com. 1971-72, chmn. state profl. affairs com. 1972—), Phi Delta Gamma, Pi Lambda Theta. Home: 17721 Misty Lane Huntington Beach CA 92649 Office: 750 Euclid Long Beach CA 90804

BACHERT, HILDEGARD GINA, art gallery exec.; b. Mannheim, Germany, Apr. 3, 1921; d. Gustav and Frieda (Reis) Bachert; B.A. summa cum laude, Hunter Coll., 1954. Sec., Nierendorf Gallery, N.Y.C., 1939-40; corporate sec. Galerie St. Etienne, Inc., N.Y.C., 1940—, Grandma Moses Properties, Inc., N.Y.C., 1950—. Sec., Friends of SOS Children's Villages, Inc., N.Y.C. Mem. Phi Beta Kappa. Collaborator: (with Otto Kallir) Egon Schiele, Oeuvre Catalogue of the Paintings, 1966, Econ Schiele: The Graphic Work, 1970, Grandma Moses, 1973. Home: 290 West End Av New York City NY 10023 Office: Galerie St Eitenne 24 W 57th St New York City NY 10019

BACHMAN, ILSE (MRS. HENRY BACHMAN), polit. worker; b. Nurnberg, Germany, May 9, 1924; d. Fred and Steffi Rosenfeld; came to U.S., 1939, naturalized, 1944; student U. Chgo., 1958-59; m. Henry Bachman, Oct. 11, 1942; children—David S., Thomas Michael, Barbara (Mrs. Neal Bronson), James J. Mem. Ohio Dem. Central Com., 1962-66, Ohio Dem. Exec. Com., 1968-70; treas. 10th Dist. Dem. Action Club, 1969-72; del. Dem. Nat. Conv., 1964, alternate del., 1968; v.p. Morgan County Dem. Exec. Com., 1970—. Trustee Kate Love Simpson Library, McConnelsville, O., 1962-73, sec., 1968-72. Club: Zanesville (O.) Country. Home: 426 E Union Av McConnelsville OH 43756

BACHMAN, LILLIAN H., pedodontist; b. Jackson Heights, N.Y., July 12, 1938; d. Curt and Lillian (Koch) Bachman; D.D.S., Columbia, 1963, certificate in pedodontics, 1966, M.A., 1967. With St. Johns Guild Floating Hosp., N.Y.C., 1963, 65; asst. in dentistry Columbia Sch. Dental and Oral Surgery, N.Y.C., 1963-64, asst. prof., 1970—; practice dentistry specializing in pedodontics, N.Y.C., 1967—; attending dentistry, dir. children's dentistry Roosevelt Hosp., N.Y.C. Fellow Am. Coll. Dentists; mem. Am., N.Y. State dental assns., 1st Dist. Dental Soc., Am. Acad. Pedodontists, Am. Soc. Dentistry for Children, Assn. Am. Women Dentists, Assn. Women Dentists of N.Y., Assn. Dental Alumni of Columbia U. (sec. 1967-68, exec. bd. 1964—, pres. 1969-70), Queens Coll. Alumni Assn., Bus. and Profl. Womens Club (1st v.p. 1964-65). Home: 33-34 60th St Woodside NY 11377 Office: 30 E 60th St New York City NY 10022

BACHMAN, PATRICIA BENSON, sch. psychologist; b. Niles, Mich., July 28, 1915; d. G. Dwight and Jeanne C. (Smith) Benson; B.S., Western Mich. U., 1938, B.A., M.A., 1955; postgrad. LaSalle Law Sch., 1972—. Tchr. pub. schs. Mich.; psychologist Coldwater State Home and Tng. Sch.; speech and hearing pathologist Lapeer State Home and Tng. Sch.; now sch. psychologist Genesee County, Mich. Author: Carey Mission, Home of The Brave, 1972.

BACHMANN, BARBARA JOYCE, microbiologist; b. Ft. Scott, Kan., May 16, 1924; A.B., Baker U., 1945; M.S., U. Ky., 1947; Ph.D. in Microbiology (AEC fellow, NSF fellow), Stanford, 1954. Asso. bacteriologist U. Cal., 1953-56, asst. prof. bacteriology, summers 1958, 59; research asso. in biochemistry Columbia, 1957-58; lectr., also research asso. Yale Sch. Medicine, New Haven, 1958-64, 68—, curator Coli Genetic Stock Center, 1970—; asst. prof. N.Y.U. Sch. Medicine, N.Y.C., 1964-68. Research asst. Oak Ridge Nat. Lab., 1947-48. Mem. A.A.A.S., Am. Soc. Microbiology, Genetics Soc. Am. Editor: Neurospora Newsletter, 1961—. Research in microbiol. genetics. Office: Dept of Human Genetics Yale University School Medicine 310 Cedar St New Haven CT 06510

BACHNER, ANNETTE, film dir.; b. N.Y.C., Sept. 25, 1928; d. Lewis and Sophia (Graydon) Bachner; student Mary's Coll., 1948. Stage mgr., dir. NBC-TV, N.Y.C., 1950-54; producer, dir. N.W. Ayer & Son, Inc., advt. agy., N.Y.C., 1954-59; producer Benton & Bowles, advt. agy., N.Y.C., 1959-66; producer, dir. TVA Group, Inc., N.Y.C., 1966-69; producer, dir. commls., indsls., documentaries Bachner Prodns., Inc., N.Y.C., 1969—. Recipient award Cannes Film Festival, 1969, Am. Comml. Film Festival, 1961, 64, 65, 67, 69, Ann Retailing Comml. award, 1971. Mem. Dirs. Guild Am., Am. Women in Radio and TV, Nat. Acad. TV Arts and Scis. Home: 360 1st Av New York City NY 10010 Office: Bachner Productions Inc 501 Madison Av New York City NY 10022

BACHRACH, GLADYS BARUCH WERTHEIM, artist; b. N.Y.C., June 10, 1909; d. Solomon and Jennette (Schlesinger) Wertheim; student Columbia, 1926-27; studied in Europe, 1928-30; m. Leo Bachrach, Mar. 31, 1938. Profl. artist, oils and drawings, 1941—; working as artist in Spain and Greece, 1962-64; one man exhbns. Galerie St. Etienne, N.Y.C., 1949, Loring Art Gallery, Wickford, R.I., 1952, Cayuga Mus. History and Art, Auburn, N.Y., 1952, A.F.I. Gallery, N.Y.C., 1952, Neville Pub. Mus., Green Bay, Wis., 1953, Fine Arts Gallery Ohio Wesleyan U., 1953, Massillon Mus., 1953, South Bend (Ind.) Art Assn., 1953, Mint Mus. Art, Charlotte, N.C., 1953, Fine Arts Gallery, U. Ky., 1953, Condon Riley Gallery, N.Y.C., 1958, 59, others; group exhibits including 10th Anniversary Gallerie St. Etienne, 10th Am. Drawing Ann., Norfolk (Va.) Mus. Arts and Scis., 1951, Grand Central Art Galleries, 1952, Berkshire Art Center, Canaan, N.Y., 1951-53, Roosevelt Art Center, Garden City, N.Y., 1958, Boston Mus. Fine Arts, Fla., Internat. Art Exhbn., 1952, Condon Riley Gallery, 1958 others; represented pvt. collections, U.S. and Europe. Chmn. jury Berkshire Art Center, Canaan, N.Y., 1953. Mem. Artists Equity Assn., Met. Mus. Art. Home: Millbrook NY 12545 Studio: 305 E 72d St New York City NY 10021

BACHTOLD, LOUISE MARIE, psychologist, educator; b. San Francisco, June 10, 1918; d. Earl Walker and Marie Dellina (Fallini) Hollingsworth; A.B., U. Cal. at Berkeley, 1940; M.A., Sacramento State U., 1956; Ed.D., U. Pacific, 1963; m. Harold Ernest Bachtold, May 16, 1939; children—Barbara (Mrs. Robert Zinky), Patricia (Mrs. Dennis Criddle), Christine (Mrs. Anthony De Maria). Tchr. elementary sch., 1951-57; guidance counselor, 1957-61; edn. research project cons., 1963-66; sch. psychologist, 1966-67; asst. prof. psychology U. Cal. at Davis, 1967-73, asso. prof., 1973—. Mem. Am., Western, Cal. psychol. assns. Contbr. articles to profl. jours. Home: 2941 Garden Ct El Macero CA 95618 Office: Applied Behavioral Sciences U Cal Davis CA 95616

BACKER, DOROTHY ANNE LIOT (MRS. ERIC F.L. BACKER), educator; b. West New York, N.J., Jan. 16, 1925; d. William T. and Anna M. (Schwarz) McShea; student Queens Coll., 1943-46; B.A. with honors, U. London, 1960, M.A., 1962, Ph.D., 1968; m. Eric F.L. Backer, Sept. 17, 1953; 1 dau., Anne-Marie. Tchr., St. Marys Coll., U. London, Twickinham, Eng., 1963-65, Birkbeck and Westfield Colls., U. London, 1965-69; faculty St. Johns U., N.Y.C., 1969-73; prof. French, Dickinson Coll., Carlisle, Pa., 1973—. Mem. Modern Lang. Assn., French Inst., Am. Assn. Tchrs. French. Author: Precious Women, 1974. Contbr. articles profl. jours. Home: 372 Central Park W New York City NY 10025 Office: Dickinson Coll Carlisle PA 17013

BACKER, MARY BARBARA (MRS. GEORGE P. BACKER), physician; b. Richland, Ind., Oct. 15, 1931; d. Carl Wilhelm and Emma Virginia (Hayford) Yeager; A.B., Ind. U., 1952, M.D., 1955; m. George P. Backer, June 19, 1954; children—Linda, Mark, Tim, David, Laura. Intern, Indpls. Gen. Hosp., 1955-56; resident Ind. U. Men. Center, Indpls., 1956-57, Rush-Presbyn.-St. Luke's Hosp., Chgo., 1957-60; mem. med. staff LaPorte (Ind.) Hosp., 1960—, dir. med. edn., 1971—; mem. med. staff Rush-Presbyn.-St. Luke's Med. Center, Chgo., 1960—. Mem. LaPorte County Emergency Med. Services Council, 1973—, LaPorte County Comprehensive Mental Health Council, LaPorte County Bd. Health. Bd. govs. LaPorte Hosp. Vis. Nurse Assn. LaPorte County; Diplomate Am. Bd. Internal Medicine. Mem. A.C.P. Home: 1533 Michigan St LaPorte IN 46350 Office: LaPorte Hosp 1007 Lincolnway LaPorte IN 46350

BACKMAN, MARGARET ESTHER, psychologist; b. Johnstown, Pa.; d. Peter Louis and Helen (McNulty) Backman; student Pa. State U., 1956-58; A.B., Barnard Coll., 1960; M.A., Columbia Tchrs. Coll., 1961, Ph.D., 1970. Student counselor Rutgers U. Coll. of Nursing, New Brunswick, N.J., 1961-62, asst. prof. edn., 1970-73; information specialist Inst. Internat. Edn., N.Y.C., 1962-65; counselor, social dir. Mt. Sinai Hosp., N.Y.C., 1965-66; ednl. research trainee Columbia Tchrs. Coll., N.Y.C., 1966-69; supr. research ICD Rehab. & Research Center, N.Y.C., 1973—; testing cons. New Lincoln Sch., N.Y.C., 1968-69. Vol. tchr. Am. Council Emigres in Professions. Mem. Am., Eastern psychol. assns., Am. Ednl. Research Assn., Nat. Rehab. Assn., Nat. Council on Measurement in Edn., Psi Chi, Kappa Delta Pi. Contbr. articles to profl. publs. Office: 340 E 24th St New York City NY 10010

BACKMAN, ROSA SACK (MRS. SAMUEL P. BACKMAN), lawyer; b. Russia, May 15, 1900; d. Max and Katie (Waldman) Sack; came to U.S., 1906, naturalized, 1924; LL.B., Portia Law Sch., 1926, LL.M. magna cum laude, 1946; m. Samuel P. Backman, July 10, 1921; 1 son, Bradlee M. Admitted to Mass. bar, 1926; since practiced Lynn. Sec. Bd. Appeals, Lynn, Mass., 1960—; bd. dirs. New Engl. Law Sch., Boston, 1973—, Jr. Achievement, 1958, Mental Health Assn., North Shore Jewish Community Center, Marblehead Mass., 1968—; trustee numerous real estate trusts. Mem. Lynn Bar, Mass. Bar Assn., Mass. Trial Lawyers, Bus. and Profl. Club (organizer 1935; hon. pres. 1938—). Home: 317 Lynn Shore Dr Lynn MA 01902 Office: 31 Exchange St Lynn MA 01901

BACKSTROM, FLORENCE MARTHA MATTHEWS (MRS. KENNETH F. BACKSTROM), employment counselor; b. Pitts., July 15, 1920; d. Luke C. and Florence D. (Weaver) Matthews; grad. high sch.; m. Kenneth F. Backstrom, July 30, 1939; 1 dau. Leah Louise (Mrs. Otha H. Williams). Sales mgr. L.C. Matthews & Sons, DuBois, Pa., 1939-52; dist. sales mgr. Avon Products Inc., Newark, Del., 1954-61; employment counselor Snelling & Snelling, Trenton, N.J., 1964-70; mgr. tech. div. Swift & Swift, Trenton, 1970-73; owner Martha's Antiques, Lambertville, N.J., 1973—. Neighborhood chmn. Bucks County council Girl Scouts, 1953-58. Named Counselor of Year, Snelling & Snelling, 1969. Home: 10 Winding Way W Morrisville PA 19067 Office: Martha's Antiques Route 29 Lambertville NJ 08530

BACKSTROM, MARTHA CAROLYN MURPHREE (MRS. JAMES WALTON BACKSTROM), educator; b. Pittsboro, Miss., Aug. 20, 1916; d. Stanley Thomas and June Elizabeth (Byars) Murphree; B.A. cum laude, Miss. State Coll. for Women, 1937; m. James Walton Backstrom, May 22, 1938; 1 son, James Walton. Tchr. pub. schs., Greene County, Miss., 1937-64; coordinator Elementary and Secondary Edn. Act Program, Greene County Sch. Dist., Leakesville, 1966—. Sec., Backstrom Timber Co. Mem. fund raising coms. Nat. Found., Cancer Fund, A.R.C., Tb. Soc.; mem. Leakesville Beautification Com., 1966. Mem. D.A.R. (chpt. chmn. 1963—, state chmn. 1965-68, sec. 1966-69, vice regent chpt. 1969-71, chpt. regent 1971-74), Miss. State Coll. for Women Alumnae Assn. (dir. 1967-69), Murphree Geneal. Soc., Miss., Nat. edn. assns., Miss., Calhoun County (charter) hist. socs., Pi Gamma Mu. Methodist; also active Baptist Ch. Clubs.: Three Arts (v.p. 1940-41, pres. 1941-42, 65-66) (Leakesville). Home: PO Box 108 Leakesville MS 39451 Office: Dept Edn Greene County Sch Dist Leakesville MS 39451

BACKUS, JEAN LOUISE, author; b. Pasadena, Cal., Feb. 24, 1914; d. Charles Shepherd and Cora Montross (Pope) Backus; B.A., U. Cal. at Berkeley, 1937. Mem. Mystery Writers Am. (chpt. v.p. 1974—). Republican. Episcopalian. Author: (pseudonym David Montross) Traitor's Wife, 1962, Troika, 1963, Fellow-Traveller, 1965; Dusha, 1971. Address: 265 Purdue Av Kensington CA 94708

BACON, CHARLOTTE ALZERA MEADE (MRS. EDWARD D. BACON, JR.), educator; b. Alberta, Va.; d. Ollie and Pinkie Ann (Manson) Meade; B.S., Hampton Inst., 1946; M.Ed., U. Pitts., 1952; m. Edward D. Bacon, Jr., Aug. 11, 1962; children—Judith, Edward, Susan. Tchr. Downingtown (Pa.) Indsl. Sch., 1946-50; tchr. Aliquippa (Pa.) pub. schs., 1950—. Mem. program com. YMCA, Aliquippa, 1955-65; vice chmn. Mayor's Commn. on Human Rights, 1972—. Recipient Woman of Yr. award Aliquippa Negro Bus. and Profl. Women's Club, 1970, Community Involvement award Delta Sigma Theta, 1972. Mem. Am. Assn. U. Women (Aliquippa corr. sec. 1971-73), Pa. Fedn. Negro Women's Clubs (pres. 1969-73), Aliquippa Edn. Assn. (rec. sec. 1969-72), Negro Bus. and Profl. Women's Club (pres. 1960-62, 63), N.A.A.C.P. Baptist. Home: 201 Spaulding St Aliquippa PA 15001 Office: New Sheffield Sch 21st St Aliquippa PA 15001

BACON, DAISY SARAH, editor, writer; b. Pa.; d. E. Ellsworth and Jessie M. (Holbrook) Bacon; student pvt. tutors. Editor: Love Story mag., 1928—, Ainslee's Mag., 1934-38, Smart Love Stories, 1937-39, Pocket Love mag., 1937, Detective Story and Romantic Range mags., 1940—; publisher paperbound books, 1962—; spl. overseas edit. Detective Story mag. for armed forces distbn. by Spl. Services div. A.S.F., U.S. Army, 1942-46; Spur awards judge Western Writers Am., 1967-68. Mem. D.A.R. Republican. Episcopalian. Compiler of four prize-story anthologies annually: Detective Story Annual, All Fiction Detective Stories, All Fiction Stories, Love Story Annual, Playing mag., 1974. Author: Love Story Writers, 1953, 3d edit., 1959; Love Story Editor, 1964; also author mag. articles. Desc. Gov. William Bradford of Plymouth Colony and Capt. John Holbrook of Weymouth. Home: 7 Hillside Av Port Washington NY 11050 Office: 520 Fifth Av New York City NY 10036

BACON, GERTRUDE MARDEN (MRS. LOU BACON), judge; b. N.Y.C.; d. Ben and Eva (Spevak) Marden; B.S., Fordham U., 1939, LL.D. (only woman to receive sch. prize for highest grades), 1942; m. Lou Bacon, Jan. 21, 1943; children—Joy, Joel, James. Admitted to N.Y. bar, 1943. Vol. atty. Legal Aid Soc., 1954—; pres. Joshua Orphan Aid, 1947-49; active Assn. for Mentally Retarded Children. Pres. bd. trustees Calhoun Sch., 1959-68; judge Family Ct., N.Y.C., 1968-72; pres., founder Parents Anonymous, N.Y.C., 1972—; mem. adv. bd. Filium, Internat. Orgn. to Re-evaluate our Treatment of Youth. Fellow Am. Acad. Matrimonial Lawyers, mem. Assn. Bar City N.Y. (mem. domestic relations ct. com.), N.Y. County Lawyers' Assn. (family ct. com.), Am. Bar Assn. Home: 7 W 81st St New York City NY 10024 Office: Parents Anonymous 250 W 57th St New York City NY 10019

BACON, HELEN HAZARD, educator; b. Berkeley, Cal., Mar. 9, 1919; d. Leonard and Martha (Stringham) Bacon; B.A., Bryn Mawr Coll., 1940, Ph.D., 1955; postgrad. U. Cal. at Berkeley, 1940-41, Radcliffe Coll., 1941-42; Litt.D., Middlebury Coll., 1970. With communications div. U.S. Navy Dept., 1942; instr. Greek and freshman English, Bryn Mawr Coll., 1946-49; instr. Latin, N.C. Women's Coll., Greensboro, 1951-52; from instr. to asso. prof. Classics, Smith Coll., 1953-61; mem. faculty Barnard Coll., 1961—, prof. Greek and Latin, 1965—, chmn. dept., 1962—; mem. faculty Bread Loaf Sch. English, summer 1966, 68; scholar-in-residence Am. Acad., Rome, 1968-69. Served to lt. WAVES, USNR, 1942-46. Fulbright fellow Am. Sch. Classical Studies, Athens, Greece, 1952-53; Founders fellow Am. Assn. U. Women, 1963-64. Mem. Am. Philol. Assn., Archaeol. Inst. Am., Classical Assn. Empire State, Classical Assn. Atlantic States, N.Y. Classical Club (v.p. 1965-67), Am. Civil Liberties Union (dir. Hampshire-Hampden chpt. 1959-60), Phi Beta Kappa (hon.). Author: Barbarians in Greek Tragedy, 1961; (with Anthony Hecht) transl. Seven Against Thebes (Aeschylus). Contbr. articles, revs. to profl. jours. Home: 464 Riverside Dr New York City NY 10027

BACON, HELEN MABEL (MRS. FAUGHT D. BACON), real estate salesman, artist; b. Saskatoon, Sask., Can., May 3, 1906; d. James Joseph and Ellen Mary (Lefaivre) Costello; 1st Class Teaching certificate Calgary Normal Sch., 1924; student Grace Hosp. Tng. Sch. for Nurses, Detroit, 1925-28; m. Faught D. Bacon, May 28, 1932. Came to U.S., 1925, naturalized, 1930. Tchr. schs., Alta., Can., 1924-25; pvt. duty nurse Grace Hosp., 1928-35; with husband built 2 homes, fruit farmer, 1937-48; raised chincillas Allied Fur Industries, Gardena, Cal., 1948-56; salesman Salem Real Estate, Plymouth, Mich., 1960—; free lance artist, exhibiting in Ann Arbor and Detroit galleries and metaphys. groups, 1957—; exhibited in one man show Concordia Lutheran Coll., Ann Arbor, 1972. Recipient 1st Pl. award State Fair Invitational Winners Show, Detroit, 1959. Mem. Spiritual Frontiers Fellowship, Mich. Metaphys. Soc., Silva Mind Control, Laredo, Tex. and Detroit, Plymouth Study Group, Ann Arbor Women Painters. Home: 40444 Newport St Plymouth MI 48170 Office: 747 S Main St Plymouth MI 48170

BACON, LORRAINE GRAHAM (MRS. EDWARD A. BACON), civic worker; b. Phila., May 15, 1898; d. Edwin Eldon and Lorraine (Goodrich) Graham; grad. Agnes Irwin Sch., Phila., 1915; m. Edward A. Bacon, Feb. 17, 1920; children—Edward A., Lorraine (Mrs. David Bethune Holdsworth), Ellen (Mrs. Richard S. McKinley III). Former mem. casework com. Council Social Agys., Milw., Jr. League Milw.; budget com. Community Fund, Milw.; former mem. Internat. Student House Com., Washington; mem. bd., chmn. library com. fgn. service sect. Am. Friends Service Com., 1954-60, bd. dirs., 1958-60; former mem. bd. Friends House, chmn. library com. and librarian Children's Library, 1954; past chmn. library com. Chibmark (Mass.) Pub. Library, past. chmn. Campaign Com. to raise funds for addition to library; vol. tutor pub. elementary schs. Mem. Soc. of Friends, Miami Friends Meeting (treas., librarian). Clubs: Acorn (Phila.); Coral Reef Yacht (Miami, Fla.); Sulgave (Washington). Home: 6904 Corsica St Coral Gables FL 33146

BACON, LYNN FLORA, civic worker; b. Mpls., Oct. 14, 1918; d. Guy Wilbur and Edna Etta (Nichols) Bacon; student Compton (Cal.) Jr. Coll., 1936, Met. Bus. Sch., Los Angeles, 1938; m. Charles Albert Elwell, July 30, 1942. Trust and found. sec. Bishop Trust Co., Honolulu, 1953-66; asst. adminstr. Oceanic Found., 1967; sec. to dir. 5th East-West Philosophers Conf., 1968-69; pub. health adminstrv. officer Hawaii Dept. Health, 1970; arts program specialist Hawaii Found. on Culture and the Arts, 1971-72; fund drive coordinator Kapiolani Maternity Hosp., Honolulu, 1973—. Ofcl. del. White House Conf. on Children and Youth, Washington, 1960; mem. steering com. Hawaii Conf. on Children and Youth, 1960; vice chmn., sec., mem. exec. com. Oahu Commn. on Children and Youth, 1966-69. Bd. dirs. Child and Family Service, Honolulu Council Social Agys., Hawaii Tb. Assn., Mental Health Assn., Palama Settlement, Salvation Army Childrens Facilities; hon. mem. 4-H Club, Salvation Army. Mem. Honolulu Acad. Arts, Friends of East-West Center, Friends of Library of Hawaii. Home: 1505 Kewalo St Apt 303-A Honolulu HI 96822 Office: 1319 Punahou St Honolulu HI 96822

BACON, SYLVIA, judge; b. Watertown, S.D., July 9, 1931; d. Julius Franklin and Anne Rae (Hyde) Bacon; A.B., Vassar Coll., 1953; certificate London Sch. Econs., 1953; LL.B., Harvard, 1956; LL.M., Georgetown U., 1958. Admitted to D.C. bar, 1956; asst. U.S. atty D.C., 1957-65; asso. dir. D.C. Crime Commn., 1965-67; trial atty. Justice Dept., 1967-69; exec. asst. to U.S. atty., Washington, 1969-70; asso. judge D.C. Superior Ct., 1970—. Mem. Am., D.C. bar assns., Am. Judicature Soc., Bus. and Profl. Women's Club. Office: 613 G St Washington DC 20001 Home: 2500 Que St NW Washington DC 20007

BADE, MARIA LEIPELT, biochemist, educator; b. Hamburg, Germany, Dec. 13, 1925; B.S., U. Neb., 1951, M.S., 1954; postgrad. Cornell U., 1954-56; Ph.D. in Biochemistry (USPHS fellow), Yale, 1960; m.; 1 child. Came to U.S., naturalized. Fellow in biochemistry Harvard, 1960-62, Sch. Medicine, 1963-64; USPHS fellow Mass. Inst. Tech., Cambridge, 1964-65, research asso., 1965-67; asst. prof. biology Boston Coll., Chestnut Hill, Mass., 1967-72, asso. prof., 1972—. Mem. A.A.A.S., Am. Chem. Soc., Am. Soc. Zoologists, N.Y. Acad. Scis., Am. Physiol. Soc., Am. Soc. Biol. Chemistry. Research on biochemistry and structure of arthropod cuticle and water quality. Office: Dept of Biology Boston College Chestnut Hill MA 02167

BADEN, JO ANN FELTS (MRS. KENNETH BADEN), polit. party ofcl.; b. Wickes, Ark., Sept. 20, 1930; d. Butler James and Florence Gretchen (Smith) Felts; student Kan. State Coll., 1949-50, Ind. Community Jr. Coll., 1960, 71; m. Kenneth Baden, Feb. 11, 1951; children—Steve, Stan. Sec.-treas. Manor Nursing Home Aux., 1968; gov. appointee S.E. Kan. Library System, 1970. Vice pres. Montgomery Young Democrats, 1965; Dem. precinct committeewoman, 1966; vice chmn. Montgomery County Dem. Central Com., 1966-70, chmn., 1970—; chmn. Dem. Hdqrs., 1966-70; mem. Gov.'s. Inaugural Com., 1967; mem. Humphrey-Muskie Com., 1968. Mem. Epsilon Sigma Alpha. Lutheran. Home: Rural Route 1 Box 55A Independence KS 67301 Office: Montgomery County Central Com Rural Route 1 Box 55A Independence KS 67301

BADER, ANNE SHANE, assn. exec.; b. Bklyn., Apr. 2, 1923; d. Bevier and Anna E. (Shane) Schoonmaker; m. Donald L. Shane, Sept. 25, 1945 (dec. 1971); children—Tracy (Mrs. James H. Kramer), Donald L.; m. 2d John Merwin Bader, Jan. 15, 1973. Asst. to adj. Base Hosp., New Castle AFB, Del., 1953-58; exec. dir. Del. Acad. Family Physicians, 1966—, Del. Med. Soc., 1965—; bus. mgr. Del. Med. Jour., 1965—. Bd. dirs. Del. chpt. A.R.C., New Castle County Med. Soc. Mem. A.M.A. (asso.), Am. Assn. Med. Soc. Execs., Del. Acad. Medicine, Advt. Club Wilmington. Club: Brandywine Century. Home: 1107 Nottingham Rd Wilmington DE 19805 Office: 1925 Levering Av Wilmington DE 19806

BADER, ELIZABETH JEAN (MRS. JOHN JULIUS BADER), newspaper editor; b. Detroit, Apr. 21, 1919; d. Karl Edward and Dorothy Mary Hebrank (LaTulip) Scheide Mantel; student pub. schs.; m. John Julius Bader, Mar. 25, 1940; children—Kathryn, John, Fredric, Dorothy, Thomas and Jeanne and Robert (triplets). With News-Review, Petoskey, Mich., 1966—, woman's editor 1974—. Active Girl Scouts, Petoskey. Rep. del. for city ward, Petoskey, Mich., 1972-74. Mem. Nat. Press Women, Bus. and Profl. Women's Club. Club: Zonta (Petoskey). Home: 1131 Emmet St Petoskey MI 49770 Office: News-Review Petoskey MI 49770

BADGER, VIRGINIA MAE, physician; b. Chgo., Dec. 6, 1925; d. Harry Ralph and Dorothea I. (Cairns) Badger; certificate in Phys. Therapy, U. Cal. at Los Angeles, 1948; B.A., Occidental Coll., 1950; M.S., U. So. Cal., 1957; M.D., Woman's Med. Coll. Pa., Phila., 1961. Phys. therapist Orthopedic Hosp., Los Angeles, 1948-56; head phys. therapist Rancho Los Amigos Hosp., Downey, Cal., 1956-57; intern Cook County Hosp., Chgo., 1961-62; resident orthopedic surgery U. Ill. Research Edn. Hosps., Chgo., 1962-66; practice medicine specializing in orthopedic surgery, St. Louis, 1966—; attending surgeon Barnes and Allied Hosps., St. Louis Shriners Hosp. for Crippled Children; clin. instr. Phys. Therapy Sch., U. So. Cal., 1950-57, instr. phys. therapy prosthetics edn., 1955-57; asst. in orthopedic surgery U. Ill., 1962-64, instr., 1964-66; instr. orthopedic surgery Washington U., St. Louis, 1966-69, asst. prof. orthopedic surgery, 1969—. Diplomate Am. Bd. Orthopedic Surgery. Fellow A.C.S., Am. Acad. Orthopedic Surgeons, Scoliosis Research Soc.; mem. A.M.A., Ill. Med. Assn., Chgo., St. Louis med. socs., A.A.A.S., Western Soc. Naturalists, Am. Med. Womens Assn., St. Louis Orthopedic Soc., Am. Acad. Cerebral Palsy, Mo. Orthopaedic Assn. Home: 113 Stoneyside Lane St Louis MO 63132 Office: 4960 Audubon Av St Louis MO 63110

BADOLLET, BERTHA EVA (MRS. WAYNE JORDAN BADOLLET), county ofcl.; b. Hinton, W.Va., June 2, 1910; d. Luther McDonald and Amanda Dane (Lowery) Foster; spl. student courses St. Mary's Coll., Ind. U.; m. Wayne Jordan Badollet, Nov. 30, 1928. Dir. vol. services Council for Retarded, South Bend, Ind., 1964-67; dir. community relations St. Mary's Coll., South Bend, 1967-69; mem. St. Joseph County Council, 1958—, pres., 1971—. A founder Continuing Edn. Series for Women, South Bend, 1953-57; Protestant founder Women's Council for Human Relations, South Bend, 1949. Mem. St. Joseph County Dem. Women, 1960—. Bd. dirs. Roger Williams Found. of Purdue U., Crippled Children's Soc. Mem. C. of C. (tourist and conv. bur.). Clubs: South Bend Press, Progress (dir. 1971-72) (South Bend). Home: 1814 E Donald St South Bend IN 46613 Office: County City Bldg South Bend IN 46601

BAER, DORICE BENTLEY (MRS. CHARLES ANDREW BAER), mus. curator; b. Huntington, Ore., Sept. 20, 1892; d. John Edward and Mary Elizabeth (Bentley) Kurtz; student Walla Walla Coll., Wash., 1907-08; m. Charles Andrew Baer, May 13, 1912; children—Samuel Edward, Charles William, Patricia Wylie, Mary E. Bookkeeper Dalles Box & Lumber Co., The Dalles, Ore., 1909-11; curator Coos-Curry Mus., Simpson Park, North Bend, Ore., 1964—. Clk., Election Bd., Coos Bay, Ore., 1940-64. Mem. D.A.R. (chpt. regent 1946-48), Coos-Curry Pioneer and Hist. Assn.

BAER, EVELYN, educator; b. Cleve., Jan. 18, 1915; d. Joseph A. and Sarah (London) B.; student Westminster Coll., 1932-34; B.A., U. Chgo., 1936; M.A., U. Akron, 1948; postgrad. Western Res. U., 1952-56. Tchr., West High Sch., Akron, O., 1936-45; rehab. dir. Stark County Tb and Health Assn., Canton, O., 1945-47; vis. tchr. child study dept. Akron Pub. schs., 1947-57; coordinator Akron Child Devel. Center, 1956-60; tchr. South High Sch., Akron, 1957-66; dir. summer speech and hearing clinic U. Akron, 1957-66, coordinator clin. services, asst. prof. speech, 1966-70, asso. prof., 1970-74, emeritus, 1974—, asso. dir. speech and hearing center, 1969-74; adoption investigator Summit County Probate Ct., 1965-69. Dir., Comprehensive Services for Deaf. Mem. Acad. Certified Social Workers, Nat. Assn. Social Workers, Am. Speech and Hearing Assn., Nat. Assn. of Speech and Hearing, Council for Exceptional Children, Nat., Summit County councils tchrs. English, Nat. Rehab. Assn. Home: 874 Westgrove Rd Akron OH 44303 Office: Speech and Hearing Center U Akron 162 E Center St Akron OH 44325

BAER, JEAN HITCHCOCK, educator; b. Peking, China, Nov. 15, 1918 (parents Am. citizens); d. Allison Harvey and Lillian Elizabeth (Cozier) Baer; B.A., U. Ida., 1939; postgrad. Stanford, 1939-41; (scholar) Harvard, 1955; certificate U. Colo., 1944; M.A., Columbia U., 1947; Ph.D. (fellow), U. Ia., 1958. Asst. instr. Stanford, 1939-41; lang. tchr. Kellogg (Ida.) High Sch., 1941-43, Nampa (Ida.) High Sch., 1941-43; counselor Stephens Coll., Columbia, Mo., 1947-49; counselor and instr. U. Ia., Iowa City, 1949-51, asst. prof., 1951-53, adminstrv. asst., asso. prof., 1953-56, research asso. Office of Admissions, 1956-58; mem. faculty U. Ill. at Chgo. Circle, 1958—, counselor, 1958-60, adminstrv. asst., 1960-71, asso. dir. counseling service, 1971—, asso. prof. edn., 1963-68, prof. edn., 1968—; vis. prof. U. Ill. at Urbana, summer 1959, 60; Ill. State U. at Normal, summer, 1966, 67; vocational cons. Social Security Disability Program, U.S. Dept. Health, Edn. and Welfare, 1962—. Served to lt. (j.g.) USNR, 1944-46. Mem. Ill. Vocational Guidance Assn. (charter, pres. 1971-72), Ill. Psychol. Assn. (chmn. acad. sect. 1972-73), Chgo. Guidance and Personnel Assn. (sec. 1963-64, dir. 1969-72, 73-74), Nat. Vocational Guidance Assn. (program chmn. 1972, nat. sec. 1973-75), Am. Psychol. Assn., Am. Coll. Personnel Assn. (commn. chmn. 1967-69), Am. Assn. U. Profs., Am. Assn. U. Women (chpt. sec. 1962-63, chpt. v.p. 1953-55), Phi Beta Kappa (v.p. chpt. 1955-57), Pi Lambda Theta, Alpha Lambda Delta, Delta Gamma (chpt. pres. 1954-56, 62-64). Editorial bd. The Vocational Guidance Quar., 1972—. Contbr. articles to profl. jours. Home: 14 Cour Madeleine Palos Hills IL 60465 Office: University Illinois at Chicago Circle Chicago IL 60680

BAER, JEAN LOUISE (MRS. HERBERT FENSTERHEIM), editor, author; b. Chgo., May 17, 1926; d. Fred E. and Helen (Roth) Baer; B.A., Cornell U., 1945; m. Herbert Fensterheim, June 20, 1968. Writer, press dept. MBC, N.Y.C., 1945-46; publicist Air Features, Inc., N.Y.C., 1946-49, Coll & Freedman Pub. Relations, N.Y.C., 1949-51; program information editor Voice of Am., N.Y.C. and overseas, 1953; publicity dir. Seventeen mag., N.Y.C., 1953-68, spl. projects dir., 1968-74. Mem. Am. Women in Radio and TV, Overseas Press Club Am., Newswomen's Club N.Y. Club: Woman Pays (N.Y.C.). Author: Follow Me!, 1965; The Single Girl Goes to Town, 1965; The Second Wife, 1972; Don't Say Yes When You Want to Say No, 1975. Home: 151 E 37th St New York City NY 10016

BAEZ, JOAN, folk singer; b. S.I., N.Y., Jan. 9, 1941; d. Albert V. and Joan (Bridge) Baez; student Fine Arts Sch. Drama, Boston U. 1958; m. David Victor Harris, Mar. 26, 1968; 1 son, Gabriel Earl Harris. Appeared in coffee houses, Ballad Room, Club 47, 1958-60, Gate of Horn, Chgo., 1958, Newport (R.I.) Folk Festival, 1959, 60; extended tour to colls. and concert halls, 1961—, European tours, 1970, 71, 73, U.S. tours, 1970, 71, 72; appeared at Carnegie Hall, N.Y.C., 1962, 68, 71. Rec. artist A & M Records, Los Angeles. Founder, v.p. Inst. for Study of Nonviolence, Palo Alto, Cal. Author: Daybreak, 1968. Home: PO Box 1001 Palo Alto CA 94302 Office: care Folklore Productions 1671 Appian Way Santa Monica CA 90401

BAGBY, LOUISE WALKER HALL (MRS. GEORGE WILSON BAGBY), civic worker, genealogist; b. Marshall, Mo., May 7, 1905; d. John Monroe and Anne May (Clark) Walker; m. John Randolph Hall, Jr., July 3, 1929 (dec. July, 1968); 1 dau., Ann Hall (Mrs. Lanny Ray Patten); m. George Wilson Bagby, July 17, 1971. Pres., Friends of Arrow Rock (Mo.), 1969—; mem. Saline County Com., Lewis and Clark Trails Com. Mem. D.A.R. (regent Marshall chpt. 1962-64), Sons and Daus. Pilgrims (Mo. treas. 1962-66), Colonial Dames XVII Century (historian Mo. com. 1964-68, insignia chmn. 1968-72, v.p. Mary Chilton chpt. 1973—), Daus. Colonists, Fitzgibbon Meml. Hosp. Aux., Mo. Hist. Soc., Saline County Hist. Soc., P.E.O. Club: Monday (Marshall Mo.). Home: 526 E Arrow St Marshall MO 65340 Office: Main St Arrow Rock MO 65340

BAGBY, MARTHA L. GREEN (MRS. JOSEPH R. BAGBY), writer, investment banker; b. West Palm Beach, Fla., June 17, 1937; d. Hampton and Louise (Lambert) Green; A.A., Palm Beach Jr. Coll., 1957; A.B., U. Miami, 1959; M.A., Pa. State U., 1964; postgrad. Columbia, 1962; m. Joseph R. Bagby, 1966; 1 dau., Meredith Elaine. Tchr. English, journalism Palm Beach County, Fla., 1959-62; instr. journalism Pa. State U., 1962-63; city editor, writer Palm Beach Daily News, also writer, editor Palm Beach Life, 1963-64; editor Alfred Hitchcock Mag., Riviera Beach, Fla., 1964; editor employee newspaper, supr. editorial service, pub. relations Nat. Airlines, Miami, Fla., 1965-73; corporate sec., mortgage broker Property Resources Co., Coral Gables; instr. Barry Coll., 1969-72. Founder, Joseph R. Bagby Lit. Found. Recipient Editorial award Freedoms Found. Mem. Fla. Pub. Relations Assn., South Fla. Indsl. Editors, Internat. Council Indsl. Editors, Airline Editors Conf. (chmn.), Air Transport Assn. Am. (chmn.; awards for publs.), Women in Communications (chpt. pres.), Kappa Tau Alpha. Home: 2506 N Greenway Coral Gables FL 33134 also 172 N County Rd Palm Beach FL Office: 2355 Salzedo Coral Gables FL 33134

BAGGETT, AGNES, state ofcl.; b. Columbus, Ga.; d. John R. and Leila (Thomason) Beahn; student pub. schs., Columbus; m. George Lamar Baggett, Oct. 14, 1926 (dec. 1949). With L. & N. R.R., 1925-27; various positions sec. state's office State of Ala., Montgomery, 1927-46, sec. state, 1951-55, 63-66, auditor, 1955-58, state treas., 1959-63, 67-70, 71—; asst. clk. Supreme Ct. of Ala. 1946-50. Mem. Am. Legion Aux. (state legislative chmn.; chmn. Girls State, Ala.). Bus. and Profl. Women's Club (state pres.). Mem. Order Eastern Star. Club: Altrusa (past pres.). Home: 3202 Montezuma Rd Montgomery AL 36106 Office: State Capitol Montgomery AL 36104

BAGGS, LEAH L. BATES (MRS. LINTON DANIEL BAGGS, JR.), social leader; b. Franklinville, N.Y.; d. William Henry and Arlie Mae (Bozworth) Bates; A.B., Barnard Coll., 1922; student spl. courses various univs.; m. Linton Daniel Baggs, Jr., Oct. 1, 1926; children—Joan Bates (Mrs. Herbert A. McKenzie, Jr.), Linton Daniel III. Hon. bd. dirs. Macon Community Concert Assn., 1968—, pres., 1959-64; bd. dirs. Middle Ga. Camellia Soc.; v.p. Macon Grand Opera Assn., 1954—; vice regent Magna Charta Dames, 1968-70, regent Ga. div., 1970-72; hon state regent Daus. Am. Colonists, 1962, nat. chmn. colonial heritage com., 1962-64; com. chmn. Ga. br. Sons and Daus. of Pilgrims Soc., 1954-55. Mem. Am. Assn. U. Women, Ga. Soc. Mayflower Descs. (corr. sec. 1960-62), Pilgrim John Howland Soc., D.A.R., Middle Ga. Hist. Soc. (charter mem.). Am., Ga., S.C., Middle Ga. (dir.) camellia socs., Nat. Trust for Historic Preservation, Sigma Alpha Iota. Presbyn. Clubs: Barnard College (Atlanta, v.p. 1967-72), Morning Music (pres. 1951-53), Atlanta Music, Capitol City Atlanta, Idle Hour Country (Macon, Ga.). Home: 1137 N Jackson Springs Rd Macon GA 31201

BAGLEY, CAROL LENORE HESS, educator; b. Cleve., May 12, 1919; d. Harry Leon and Mildred (Van Voorhees) Hess; B.A., with honors, Wash. State U., 1960, M.A., 1963, Ph.D., 1966; m. Leon Richard Bagley, Nov. 16, 1946 (dec. Jan. 1956); 1 dau., Kathleen Elaine. Instr. ground sch. Miss. Inst. Aeros., Jackson, 1943; teaching asst. Wash. State U., Pullman, 1960-64, teaching asso. dept. extension services, 1964-65; instr. English, Ida. State U., Pocatello, 1965-66, asst. prof., 1966-67, 68-70, asso. prof., dir. Am. studies, 1970—, acting chmn. dept., 1967; on leave as fellow Center for History of Am. Indian, Newberry Library, Chgo., 1973-74. Mem. Modern Lang. Assn., Am. Studies Assn. (pres. Rocky Mountain chpt. 1968-69), Am. Assn. U. Profs., Rocky Mountain Modern Lang. Assn., Melville Soc., Western Lit. Assn., Popular Culture Assn. (v.p. 1972-73), Phi Beta Kappa, Phi Kappa Phi, Psi Chi. Author: Young Man River: A Selected Bibliographical Guide for History-English Oriented American Studies Ph.D. Programs, 1964; also articles, revs. Home: 718 Cypress St Pocatello ID 83201

BAGWELL, BETTY RAE, hosp. adminstr.; b. Akron, O., Mar. 29, 1929; d. Zebulon Vance and Birdie Blaine (Moss) Bagwell; grad. Ohio State U., 1972. With Green Cross Gen. Hosp., Cuyahoga Falls, O., 1947—, asso. dir., 1965-68, exec. dir., 1969—. Mem. Mayor's Com. Health Care, Cuyahoga Falls, 1972; chmn. com. Capital Fund drive United Appeal, 1969-71; chmn. A.R.C. Blood Programs, 1963-70; mem. adv. bd. Cuyahoga Falls Sch. Practical Nursing, 1971—, Mobile Meals, Akron, 1973—. Mem. Vis. Nurse Assn. (trustee), Am. Coll. Osteo. Hosp. Adminstrs., Ohio Osteo. Hosp. Assn. (pres. 1973-74), Akron Bus. and Profl. Women's Club, Ohio Hosp. Assn. Home: 338 Beaumont Dr Akron OH 44313 Office: 1900 23d St Cuyahoga Falls OH 44323

BAHN, CATHERINE ROWELL INMAN (MRS. THEODORE HERMAN BAHN), librarian; b. Beaver Dam, Wis., Feb. 23, 1908; d. Ralph Caleb and Edla Ingram (Rowell) Inman; student Hood Coll., 1925-26; B.S., Millersville State Coll., 1929; postgrad. U. Chgo., 1933, 34; M.A., Columbia, 1938; m. Theodore Herman Bahn, Oct. 5, 1935; 1 son, Theodore Inman. Tchr., Edward Hand Jr. High Sch., Lancaster, Pa., 1928-36; accountant Panama Canal Co., Balboa, C.Z., 1941-50; cartographer, USAF Aero. Chart and Information Center, Washington, 1950-57; head acquisitions sect. Geography and Map div., prin. recommending officer Sci. and Tech. div., Library of Congress, Washington, 1957—; instr. U.S. Dept. Agr. Grad. Sch., Washington, 1952—. Treas.-sec. Lyon Village Citizens Assn., Arlington, Va., 1957-70. Mem. Assn. Am. Geographers (mem. placement com. 1965-72), Spl. Libraries Assn. (pres. geography and map group 1957, sci. and tech. group 1971). Carto Philatelists (regional v.p. 1959—), Arlington Hist. Soc. Editor Arlington Hist. Mag., 1967-74, Jobs in Geography Bull., 1965-71. Contbr. articles to profl. jours. Home: 2613 Key Blvd Arlington VA 22201 Office: Library of Congress 1st SE and Independence Av Washington DC 20540

BAHN, LORENE A., educator; b. St. Louis, July 12, 1909; d. Adolph H. and Mamie (Moellering) Bahn; A.B., Harris Coll., 1929; M.A., Washington U., St. Louis, 1946, Ed.D., 1963; student U. Chgo., summers 1937, 38, 39. Instr. physics Harris Coll., St. Louis, 1929; tchr. pub. schs., St. Louis, 1930-48; asst. prof. elementary edn. Washington U., 1949-63, dir. Univ. Nursery Sch., 1961-63; prof. elementary edn. Drury Coll., Springfield, Mo., 1964—. Mem. Am. Assn. U. Profs., Comparative Edn. Assn., John Dewey Soc., Nat. Soc. for Study of Edn., Mo. State Tchrs. Assn., Assn. Supervision and Curriculum Devel., Kappa Delta Pi, Delta Kappa Gamma. Home: 2843 Lomita Circle Springfield MO 65804 Office: Drury Coll Springfield MO 65802

BAHNSEN, JANE CUTLER (MRS. MONROE JOHN BAHNSEN), librarian; b. Evansville, Ind., Nov. 13, 1910; d. James Tipton and Estelle (Corlew) Cutler; A.B., Western Res. U., 1931; B.S. in Library Sci., Sch. Library Sci., U. N.C., 1954; m. Monroe John Bahnsen, Dec. 23, 1933; children—Ann (Mrs. Leslie A. Irish), Mary (Mrs. Leslie P. Mullen), Sally (Mrs. Daniel P. Connerton). Asst. librarian N.C. collection U. N.C. at Chapel Hill, 1954—, acting curator, 1973-74, asst. librarian, 1974—. Mem. N.C. Library Assn., Beta Phi Mu. Democrat. Episcopalian. Home: 6 Cobb Terrace Chapel Hill NC 27514 Office: North Carolina Collection Univ of North Carolina Chapel Hill NC 27514

BAHR, SISTER ROSE THERESE, educator; b. Great Bend, Kan., Mar. 1, 1930; d. Frank W. and Mary (Schneider) Bahr; B.S. in Nursing, Cath. U. Am., 1960, M.S. in Nursing, 1962; Ph.D., St. Louis U., 1967. Nursing supr. St. Francis Hosp., Carlsbad, N.M., 1954-58; dir. nursing St. Mary's Hosp., Enid, Okla., 1962-63; mem. faculty Sacred Heart Coll., Wichita, Kan., 1967-70, asst. prof. psychology, 1967-70, dean acad. affairs, 1967-69, chmn. dept. nursing, 1969-70; asst. prof. nursing, asst. chmn. grad. program in nursing, dept. nursing edn. U. Kan., 1970—. Nursing edn. cons., 1963-68, 70—; mem. Kan. Master Plan Commn. Nursing and Nursing Edn., 1972—. Mem. exec. com. Upward Bound Program, Wichita, 1967-70; active A.R.C., 1967—; mem. Comprehensive Health Planning Council, 1969-70. Mem. Am., Kan. (dist. 2d v.p. 1968, sect. vice chmn. 1968, chmn. resolutions com. 1974) nurses assns., Nat. (sec. Heartland regional assembly 1973—), Kan. (pres. 1973-75) leagues for nursing, Kan. Bd. Nursing, Am. Pub. Health Assn., Am. Assn. Higher Edn., Panel Am. Women, League Women Voters. Democrat. Roman Catholic. Home: 1420 N 78th St Kansas City KS 66112

BAICH, ANNETTE, biochemist, educator; b. Chgo., Mar. 2, 1930; B.S., Roosevelt U., 1951; M.S., U. Ore., 1954, Ph.D. in Chemistry, 1960; m. 1950. Asst. chemist U. Ore., 1951-54; lab. technician Agrl. Expt. Sta., U. Cal., 1954-55; fellow in biochemistry Ore. State U., 1960-61, asst. prof., 1963-69; microbiologist Rutgers U., 1961-62; asso. prof. biology So. Ill. U. at Edwardsville, 1969-74, prof., 1974—. NIH career devel. award, 1965-69. Mem. A.A.A.S., Am. Chem. Soc., Am. Soc. Microbiologists. Research on relation and response of organism to its environment and explaining it in chem. terms. Office: Dept of Biological Sciences Southern Ill University Edwardsville IL 62025*

BAIER, GEORGIA LOUISE BRITTAIN (MRS. HARRISON WILLIAM BAIER), museum ofcl.; b. Spickard, Mo., Mar. 7, 1922; d. Melvin Orlando and Nellie Ann (Miller) Brittain; licensed Lamar U. Vocational Sch., 1968; m. Harrison William Baier, May 23, 1940; children—Roger Ray, Robert William, Richard George. Bus. mgr. Beaumont (Tex.) Symphony Orch., 1962-69; asst. to profl. fund raiser Schlesinger Geriatric Center, Beaumont, 1969-70; interim dir. Beaumont Art Museum, 1970, asst. for adminstr., 1970—. Pres. P.T.A., Averill Sch., Beaumont, 1953-54, Austin Jr. High Sch., Beaumont, 1969, Beaumont High Sch., 1959-60, 70. Bd. dir. YWCA, Beaumont, Beaumont Community Council, Beaumont Symphony Orch.; bd. advisers Neches River Festival, Inc. Mem. D.A.R. (chpt. treas. 1972-74), P.E.O. (pres. 1968). Methodist. Club: Beaumont Country. Home: 1210 Longfellow St Beaumont TX 77706 Office: 1111 9th St Beaumont TX 77702

BAIL, GRACE SHATTUCK, composer-poet, author, music tchr.; b. Cherry Creek, N.Y., Jan. 17, 1898; d. Frederick John and Clarissa (Richmond) Shattuck; spl. student Meadville Coll. Music, 1911-12; grad. Dana Music Sch. of Youngstown U., 1919; foster children—Richard, Roland Hornby. Tchr. piano, organ, violin, theory, Beaumont, Cal.; tchr. violin United Brethren Pvt. sch., Cherry Valley. Composer numerous selections including Sleepy Song, Autumn Love, Dreams, Minuet for Two Violins, 23d and 24th Psalms of David, Evening Reverie, A Bird Sings, 465 bible songs, and numerous others. Recipient Poem of Month award, Desert mag., 1961, 62; Edwin Markham Silver Medal, 1961; couplet award, sonnet award Am. Bard, 1967; bronze medal Centro E Scambi; also Internat. Poetry's Shrine Gold medal 1969; 1st prize Cal. Fedn. Chaparral Poets, 1972; award Friendly Way mag., 1972; Sweepstakes prize poems Mich. Poetry Soc., 1972, also certificates merit. Mem. Nat. League Am. Penwomen (Biennial awards, Nat. Biennial award 1970), Composers, Authors, Artists Am. (nat. dir., award violin solo 1965, 68), Am. Poetry League, Poetry Soc. Mich., Mary Carr Moore Manuscript Club (prize winners chpt. Cal. Chaparral Poets). Republican. Methodist. Author books including: Arethusa, 1945; Singing Heart, 1948; Daily Bread, 1952; Phantasy, 1954; Whispering Leaves, 1957; For the Dreamer, 1965; Heartstrings, 1968; Golden Days, 1970; Cantabile, 1974. Editor weekly poetry column Daily Record-Gazette, Banning-Beaumont, Cal. Home: 873 1/2 Beaumont Av Beaumont CA 92223

BAILEY, ALICE COOPER (MRS. GEORGE W. BAILEY), author, lectr.; b. San Diego, Dec. 9, 1890; d. Henry Ernest and Mary (Porter) Cooper; resident, Honolulu, 1891-1913; grad. Oahu Coll., 1907; student U. Hawaii, 1908, teaching diploma, 1911; m. George W. Bailey, June 16, 1913; children—Mary Alice (Mrs. Luke Hamilton Montgomery II), George William II, Richard Briggs. Lectr. Life mem. Weston Community League. Mem. Women's Nat. Book Assn., Nat. League Am. Pen Women (past br. pres., state pres.), Hawaiian Hist. Soc., Friends of Iolani Palace, Internat. Platform Assn., Concord Antiquarian Soc. Clubs: Boston Authors (past pres., past dir.); Concord (Mass.) Women's. Author: juvenile books including: The Flying Umbrella; Footprints in the Dust; The Hawaiian Box Mystery; To Remember Robert Louis Stevenson, 1966; Rainbow over Manoa, biography of Henry E. Cooper. and others. Contbr. short stories to mags. Home: 255 Lexington Rd Concord MA 01742

BAILEY, AUDREY JOYCE, hosp. adminstr.; b. Toronto, Ont., Can., Feb. 4, 1935; d. Irvin Wallace and Galdys Mae (Rowan) Bailey; diploma Wellesley Sch. Nursing, 1956; B.Sc. in Nursing, U. Toronto Sch. Nursing, 1964; M.Sc. in Nursing, Case Western Res. U., 1968. Staff nurse Wellesley Hosp., Toronto, 1956-57, asst. head nurse, 1957-60, head nurse, 1960-62, asst. dir. nursing, 1966-67, dir. nursing services, 1967—. Instr. U. Toronto Sch. Nursing, 1963; surveyor Can. Council on Hosp. Accreditation, 1969—. Can. Nurses' Found. scholar, 1966. Mem. Registered Nurses Assn. Ont., Canadian Nurses Assn., Alumnae assns. U. Toronto, Case Western Res. U., Dirs. Nursing Met. Toronto (chmn. 1973-74), Canadian Hosp. Assn. Home: 400 Walmer Rd Toronto ON M5P 2X7 Canada Office: 160 Wellesley St E Toronto M4Y 1J3 ON Canada

BAILEY, BERNADINE FREEMAN, author; b. Mattoon, Ill.; d. Thomas Oscar and Nellie (Voigt) Freeman; B.A., Wellesley Coll.; M.A., U. Chgo.; m. John Hays Bailey (div.). Former editor Laidlaw Bros., Quarrie Corp.; freelance writer. Bd. dirs. Ivy Cancer Research Found. Mem. Ill. Womans Press Assn. (past pres.), Soc. Midland Authors, English Speaking Union. Clubs: Arts, Lake Shore, Chicago Press (Chgo.); London Press. Author: Austria and Switzerland, 1969; The Captive Nations, 1969; Greenland, 1973; Malawi, 1973, others. Contbr. numerous articles to various mags. including Reader's Digest, Coronet, N.Y. Times, Christian Sci. Monitor, Ford Times, others. Home: 6 Lee Terrace Blackheath London SE 3 9TZ England

BAILEY, BERTHA FRANCETA GREEN, librarian; b. Clarinda, Ia., Sept. 5, 1913; d. John and Maude May (Fickel) Green; student Clarinda Jr. Coll., 1956-58, U. Wash., 1960, Ida. State U., 1957; B.S. in Edn., N.W. Mo. State Coll., Maryville, 1959; M.A. in Library Sci., U. Denver, 1965; postgrad. Appalachian State U., Boone, N.C., 1970; m. Harold Dean Bailey, June 1, 1946; 1 dau., Marilyn Joy (Mrs. Max Fiandt). Children's librarian Clarinda Pub. Library, 1933-40; med. librarian, Clarinda, 1940-43; ins. agt., 1943-46; high sch. and jr. coll. librarian, coordinator libraries, Clarinda, 1959-63; head librarian Ia. Western Community Coll., Clarinda, 1963—. Library cons. elementary through jr. coll. libraries. Mem. Nat., Ia. edn. assns., Am., Ia. Jr. Coll. (past pres., dir., dist. officer) library assns., Ia. Higher Edn. Assn., Ia. Ednl. Med. Assn., Nat. Platform Assn., Delta Kappa Gamma. Home: 611 W State St Clarinda IA 51632

BAILEY, B(EVERLY) JOYCE, educator; b. Jefferson City, Mo., Jan. 7, 1940; d. Ray O. and Lillie J. (Clardy) Bailey; B.S.E., Central Mo. State Coll., 1962, M.S.E., 1963; Ph.D., U. Ia., 1968. Instr. phys. edn. Central Mo. State Coll., Warrensburg, 1963-67, asst. prof. phys. edn., 1967-71, asso prof., 1971—; research asst. U. Ia., 1967-68. Dir. Red Cross Swimming Program, Jefferson City, 1969—; mem. exec. bd., chmn. water safety Johnson County chpt. A.R.C. Recipient Red Cross Service award, 1969. Mem. A.A.H.P.E.R., Central Assn. Phys. Edn. for Coll. Women (v.p. 1971-72), Mo. Assn. for Health, Phys. Edn. and Recreation (research chmn. 1971, conv. mgr. 1972, pres. 1973-74), Am. Assn. U. Profs., N.E.A., Mo. State Tchrs. Assn., Sigma Sigma Sigma, Phi Kappa Phi. Home: 306 Franklin St Warrensburg MO 64093

BAILEY, CATHERINE HAYES, pomologist, educator; b. New Brunswick, N.J., May 9, 1921; B.A., Rutgers U., 1942, Ph.D. in Fruit Breeding, 1957. Tech. asst. in pomology Agrl. Expt. Sta., Rutgers U., New Brunswick, 1948-54, research asso., 1954-57, asst. prof., 1957-66, asso. research prof., 1966-72, research prof., 1972—. Exchange scientist Canadian Dept. Agr. Research Sta., B.C., 1965-66. Recipient ann. recognition award Nat. Peach Council, 1969. Mem. Am. Inst. Biol. Scis., Am. Pomol. Soc., Bot. Soc. Am., Internat., Am. socs. hort. sci., Torrey Bot. Club. Research on fruit breeding, disease resistance breeding in pears, peaches and apples. Office: Dept of Horticulture and Forestry Rutgers University New Brunswick NJ 08903

BAILEY, SISTER DOLORES, ednl. adminstr.; b. Pitts., July 10, 1936; d. Francis Regis and Cora Margaret (Loper) Bailey; B.A., Seton Hill Coll., 1965; postgrad., U. London, 1972. Sec., Joseph Novak, M.D., Pitts., 1954-55; exec. sec. Sisters of Charity, Seton Hill Coll., Greensburg, Pa., 1956-69, mission procurator, 1967-72, dir. career counseling and placement, 1969—. Mem. Am., Pa. personnel and guidance assn., Pitts. Personnel Assn., Cath. Bus. Edn. Assn. (pres.), Nat. Cath. Devel. Conf., Assn. for Sch., Coll. and Univ. Staffing, Coll. Placement Council. Address: Seton Hill College Greensburg PA 15601

BAILEY, GANO RUTH HOOVER, assn. exec.; b. Ambridge, Pa.; d. Ralph Emerson and Marie Gano (Heberline) Hoover; student N.Y. U., 1961-62; m. Louis H. Bailey; children—Anne Gano (Mrs. Robert R. Grew), Louis M., Gretel Marie (Mrs. Donald Stubbs). Adminstrv. asst. chief engr. Seelye Stevenson, Value & Knecht, N.Y.C., 1957-58; adminstrv. asst. dir. pub. relations Broadcast Music, Inc., N.Y.C., 1959; adminstrv. asst. project mgr. Grad, Urbahn & Seelye, N.Y.C., 1960; adminstrv. asst. partner Wall & Smoot, N.Y.C., 1961; adminstrv. asst. William S. Smoot, cons. engr., N.Y.C., 1961-62; exec. dir. Holland Soc. N.Y., N.Y.C., 1963-71; exec. Sec. St. Nicholas Soc., N.Y.C., 1971—. Cons. Symposium on New Netherland, 1971, 72. Bd. dirs. Louis Beach Vreeland Found. Inst. on Man and Sci. Mem. Writers Roundtable, Municipal Art Soc. Republican. Methodist. Adviser, mem. pub. com.: New York Historical Manuscripts: Dutch; N.Y. Marriage Bonds, 1753-1783. Contbr. articles, fiction to mags. Home: 525 E 84th St New York City NY 10028 Office: 122 E 58th St New York City NY 10022

BAILEY, HELEN MILLER, educator; b. Modesto, Cal., Mar. 13, 1909; d. Guy H. and Maud P. (Piggott) Miller; A.B., U. Cal. at Berkeley, 1929; M.A., 1930; Ph.D., U. So. Cal., 1934; m. Henry Morle Bailey, June 19, 1932; adopted children—Bruce M., Theodore R., Donald Lee. Tchr. high sch., Los Angeles, 1931-46; chmn. social sci. dept. East Los Angeles Coll., 1956—. Trustee Eastern area welfare planning council Los Angeles Community Chest, 1956-65, East Los Angeles-Belvedere Area Coordinating Council, 1948—, Eastside Boys' Club, 1952-57, Cleland House of Neighborly Service, 1955-57. Chmn. Brotherhood Observance East Los Angeles Area, 1959-65; treas. Scholarship Fund for Students of Mexican Ancestry, Los Angeles County, 1958—; Los Angeles community cons. Cal. Gov.'s Com. Youth, 1961-62, Cal. rep. jr. colls., 1962-63; rep. Los Angeles jr. colls. Youth Opportunities Bd., 1962-63. Fulbright seminar Brazil summer, 1964. Recipient Pub. Service award Los Angeles County Conf. on Human Relations, 1956; Human Relations award Jewish War Vets, 1963; Spl. Service award Los Angeles Council Mexican-Am. Affairs, 1964. Mem. Phi Beta Kappa, Phi Alpha Theta. Author: (with Eugene Lazare) Your American Government, 1956; (with Harriet Brown) Our Latin American Neighbors, 1950; Santa Cruz of the Etla Hills, 1958; (with Abraham Nasatir) Latin American, The Development of Its Civilization, 1960, 3d rev. edit., 1973; Forty American Biographies, 1964; (with Maria Grijalva) Fifteen Famous Latin Americans, 1970; (with Frank Cruz) Latin Americans, Past and Present, 1972. Contbr. to Ency. Americana. Prepared ednl. films for jr. colls. Home: 1026 Bradshawe Av Monterey Park CA 91754 Office: East Los Angeles Coll 5357 Brooklyn Av Los Angeles CA 90022

BAILEY, JANE TERRY ELLIS (MRS. WILLIS BUCKINGHAM BAILEY), art educator; b. Louisville, May 30, 1919; d. Guy Tempest and Ella Mary (Tilford) Ellis; B.A., Wellesley Coll., 1941, M.A., 1946; m. Willis Buckingham Bailey, Feb. 15, 1947; children—Claudia (Mrs. William Paul Heilman), Eleanor Buckingham (Mrs. John Arthur Martin). Dir. Zanesville (O.) Art Inst., 1946-47; vis. lectr. Asian art Denison U., Granville, O., 1963—, curator Burmese collection, 1968—, univ. research grantee, 1971. Bd. dirs. Zanesville Art Center, 1964-70, 72—, hon. curator oriental art. Served with WAC, 1943-45. Gt. Lakes Coll. Assn. grantee, 1966; Dept. Health, Edn. and Welfare grantee, 1967; Kress grantee, 1968, Ford grantee, 1970. Home: 2738 Dresden Rd Zanesville OH 43701 Office: Burke Hall Denison U Granville OH 43023

BAILEY, JANET DEE, editor; b. Newark, Aug. 23, 1946; d. Richard and Mary Louise (Dee) Shapiro; B.A. in English, U. Del., 1968; postgrad. in pub. N.Y. U., 1968-70; m. John Bailey, May 9, 1971. Prodn. editor bus. and profl. books dept. Prentice-Hall, Inc., Englewood Cliffs, N.J., 1968-70; editor Spl. Libraries jour., mgr. publs. dept. Spl. Libraries Assn., N.Y.C., 1971—. Mem. Smithsonian Instn., Early Am. Soc. Home: 414 Benedict Av Tarrytown NY 10591 Office: 235 Park Av S New York City NY 10003

BAILEY, JOAN DARLENE DOUTRE, stock broker; b. Beloit, Wis., Jan. 4, 1935; d. Raymond Joseph and Ruth Laura (Gwin) Doutre; student Miss. Coll., 1952-55; m. Robert Vernon Bailey, Aug. 17, 1956 (div. 1973); children—Diane Elaine, Steven Robert. Dist. mgr. B. J. Leonard & Co., Casper, Wyo., 1969—. Home: 1901 W 38th St Casper WY 82601 Office: 145 E 8th St Casper WY 82601

BAILEY, LOIS LOREEN, clin. psychologist; b. Indpls., Jan. 21, 1926; d. Perry Wilson and Bessie (Hoff) Bailey; B.A., Pomona Coll., 1947; M.A., U. Ariz., 1952. Statistician, U.S. Navy Personnel Research Field Activity, 1953-58; now clin. psychologist, San Diego City Schs. Presbyn. (deacon). Home: 3903 Wildwood Rd San Diego CA 92107 Office: 4100 Normal St San Diego CA 92103

BAILEY, NANCY DUFF (MRS. RONALD JOHN BAILEY), statistician; b. Alton, Ill., Nov. 15, 1939; d. Richard Dwight and Marguerite Beulah (Smith) Duff; B.A., Northwestern U., 1961; M.S., U. Chgo., 1963; m. Ronald John Bailey, Mar. 28, 1961; children—John Duff, Steven Christopher. Research asst. Nat. Merit Scholarship Corp., Evanston, Ill., 1960-62; jr. analyst Caywood-Schiller Assos., Chgo., 1963-68, sr. analyst, 1968-70; sr. operations analyst A.T. Kearney, Inc., Chgo., 1970—. Mem. Am. Statis. Assn., Mil. Operations Research Soc. Home: 347 Oak Circle Wilmette IL 60091 Office: 100 S Wacker Dr Chicago IL 60606

BAILEY, PEARL (MAE), singer; b. Newport News, Va., Mar. 29, 1918; d. Joseph James Bailey; student pub. schs., Phila.; m. John Randolph Pinkett, Jr., Aug. 31, 1948 (div. Mar. 1952); m. 2d, Louis Bellson, Jr., Nov. 19, 1952. Singer, 1933—; vocalist various popular bands; stage debut St. Louis Woman, N.Y.C., 1946; role Broadway musical House of Flowers; motion pictures include Variety Girl, Carmen Jones; contract artist Coral Records, Columbia Records, Decca; night club engagements, N.Y.C., Boston, Hollywood, Las Vegas, Chgo., also London, 1950—; guest artist various TV programs. Recipient Donaldson award, 1956. Home: 109 Bank St New York City NY 10014 Office: care William Morris Agy 1740 Broadway New York City NY 10019

BAILEY, SALLY (MRS. ROBERT W. JASPERSON), ballet dancer; b. Oakland, Cal., Aug. 16, 1932; d. William Attebury and Sidney (Cheyney) Bailey; student San Francisco Ballet Sch.; m. John Griggs Flynn, June 22, 1957 (div. Dec. 1961); m. 2d, Robert W. Jasperson, July 29, 1972. Ballerina San Francisco Ballet Co., 1948-67, asst. ballet mistress, 1966-67; guest soloist N.Y.C. Ballet Co., 1953; State Dept. tours under ANTA, Far East, 1957, Latin Am., 1958, Middle East, 1959; acting mgr. Ballet '64, Ballet '65, tours under Columbia Artists Mgmt., Inc.; guest tchr. U. Utah, 1952; tchr. San Francisco Ballet Sch., 1954-66; co-ordinator for San Francisco Ballet Guild fund raising activities, 1967-70; tchr. seminar in contemporary ballet San Francisco State U., summers 1971, 72. Recipient Gold medal Emperor Haile Selassi, Ethiopia, 1959. Mem. Am. Guild Mus. Artists. Republican. Episcopalian. Contbr. articles to various publs. Home: 550 Battery St Apt 517 San Francisco CA 94111

BAILEY, SARAH ANN, lawyer; b. Tucson, Nov. 14, 1931; d. Weldon Murry and Josephine (Cotter) Bailey; B.A. in Govt., U. Ariz., 1961; J.D., Cumberland Coll. Law, 1965; div.; children—Thomas Earley, Anne Josephine Earley. Admitted to Ala. bar, 1965, Ariz. bar, 1965; law clk., Phoenix, 1965; asst. pub. defender Maricopa County, 1966, dep. county atty., 1967-68, chief dep. juvenile div., 1968; dep. county atty. Santa Cruz County, 1968-72; asst. U.S. dist. atty. for Ariz., Tucson, 1972—. Mem. Gov.'s Adv. Com., 1971. Pres. Tubac Sch. Bd., 1972. Mem. State Bar Ariz. (mem. com. on unauthorized practice law 1970—), Santa Cruz County Realtors (mem. by-laws com. 1973). Club: Zonta Internat. (chmn. women's rights com. 1970-73) (Nogales, Ariz.). Home: Box 176 Tumacacori AZ 85640 Office: Box 2261 Tucson AZ 85702

BAILEY, SHIRLEY ELSIE DADDOW, control corp. exec.; b. Butler, N.J., Jan. 26, 1930; d. Richard and Eva M. (Kitchell) Daddow; grad. high sch.; m. Russell A. Bailey, Oct. 1, 1950 (div. Oct. 1967). Asst. corporate sec. Hydrospace Tech., West Caldwell, N.J., 1960-62; sec. to pres. R.J. Dick Co., Totowa, N.J., 1962-63, Microlab, Livingston, N.J., 1963; asst. corporate sec. Astrosystems Internat., West Caldwell, N.J., 1963-65; corporate sec. Internat. Controls Corp., Fairfield, N.J., 1965-73. Home: 41-1A Mt Pleasant Village Route 10 Morris Plains NJ 07950

BAILEY, STELLA WINN BROWN (MRS. SAMUEL B. BAILEY), ret. educator; b. Elsberry, Mo., Mar. 12, 1902; d. Joseph Walker and Mary Elizabeth (Davis) Brown; A.A., Coll. of Sequoias, 1948; A.B. magna cum laude, Fresno State Coll., 1951, M.A., 1962; m. Samuel B. Bailey, Aug. 7, 1921 (dec. Mar. 1965); children—Samuella Sue (Mrs. Joseph P. Kutger), William B., Julia Leewinn. Tchr. rural schs., Mo., 1920-21; dep. commr. Girl Scouts U.S.A., St. Joseph, Mo., 1934-35; tchr. Earlimart (Cal.) Sch., 1944-45; prin., tchr. Linder Sch., Tulare County, Cal., 1945-46, Oakland Colony Sch., 1946-47, Pixley (Cal.) Union Sch., 1948-57, Tulare City Sch., 1957-67; instr. mentally retarded State Mental Health Center, Camarillo, Cal., 1968-71. Hon. life mem. P.T.A. Mem. State Cal. Tchrs. Assn. (life), Assn. Childhood Edn. (chpt. v.p. 1950-51), Nat. Ret. Tchrs. Assn., Sequoia Geneal. Soc. (charter), Am. Assn. Ret. Persons, D.A.R. (regent Alta Mira chpt.), Cal. State Employees Assn., N.E.A. (life), Tulare County Mineral. and Gem Soc. (charter), Mo. Hist. Soc., Kappa Delta Pi. Author: History of Education in Tulare County, California, 1962; Teachers Associations in American Education, 1966. Contbr. articles to profl. jours. Home: 474 Cherry St Tulare CA 93274

BAILEY, SYLVIA MAE, phys. chemist, govt. ofcl.; b. Lee's Summit, Mo., May 14, 1929; d. Chester Irwin and Hazel Anna (Underwood B.; A.A., Stephens Coll., 1949; B.S., U. Mo., 1951; Ph.D. in Chemistry, U. Cal. at Berkeley, 1959. Phys. chemist polymer div. Nat. Bur. Standards, 1960-64, thermochem. sect. phys. chemistry div., 1964-69; chemist materials div. Office of Research, Fed. Hwy. Adminstrn., Washington, 1969-72, environmental design and control div., 1972—. Bd. dirs. Citizens Orgn. for Sane World. Mem. Women Strike for Peace, Women's Internat. League for Peace and Freedom, Am. Chem. Soc. Presbyn. Home: 6908 Strathmore St Chevy Chase MD 20015 Office: Fed Hwy Adminstrn Office of Research 400 7th St SW Washington DC 20590*

BAILEY, V. MAXINE SHELDON (MRS. RAY V. BAILEY), civic worker; b. Rowan, Ia., Feb. 20, 1915; d. Guy R. and Edna (Schroeder) Sheldon; B.A., State U. Ia., 1937; m. Ray V. Bailey, June 18, 1938; children—Theron Sheldon, G. Bryan. Tchr. high schs., Thor, Ia., 1937-38, Moline, Ill., 1944-45. Participant Arms Control and Disarmament Conf., State U. Ia. Campus, 1962, Regional Fgn. Policy Conf., U.S. Dept. State, Milw., 1964; guest Japan govt. fact finding missions, 1972. Mem. Clarion (Ia.) Planning and Zoning Comm., 1961—. Mem. Nat. Com. for Support Pub. Schs.; mem. gen. operations and policy com. Ia. State Ednl. TV. Mem. Am. Assn. U. Women (pres. Clarion br. 1945-55, mass media chmn. Ia. div. 1958-62, 1st v.p., program chmn. 1962-64, div. pres. 1964-66, v.p. N.W. Central region 1971—, nat. dir. 1971—, nat. dir. ednl. found. 1971—), Ia. Legislative Ladies League, U. Ia. Alumni Council. Democrat. Methodist (past chmn. edn. commn.). Home: Millers Bay Lake Okoboji Milford IA 51351

BAILLARGEON, ELAINE MARIE LADIEU (MRS. ROBERT J. BAILLARGEON), newspaper editor; b. Laconia, N.H., Oct. 24, 1948; d. Ray Francis and Lillian Rose (Dickson) Ladieu; B.S. in Journalism and Internat. Relations, Syracuse U., 1971; m. Robert J. Baillargeon, June 26, 1971. Asst. Rumford Press, Concord, N.H., 1971-72; asst. city editor Concord (N.H.) Monitor, 1972—. Mem. Women In Communications. Home: Putney Rd RFD 3 Concord NH 03301 Office: 3 N State St Concord NH 03301

BAIN, BARBARA, hematologist, educator; b. Montreal, Que., Can., May 8, 1932; B.Sc., McGill U., 1953, M.Sc., 1957, Ph.D. in Exptl. Medicine (J.B. Collip fellow), 1964. Demonstrator in exptl. medicine McGill U., Montreal, 1965-67, lectr., 1967-68, asst. prof., 1968—; research asst. in hematology Royal Victoria Hosp., Montreal, 1965-68, asso. scientist, 1968—. Med. Research Council of Can. scholar, 1966-71, grantee, 1970—. Mem. Tissue Culture Assn., Reticuloendothelial Soc., Transplantation Soc., Canadian Soc. Immunology, Am., Canadian socs. cell biology, Sigma Xi (sec.-treas. chpt. 1971-72). Research on lymphocyte transformation to blast cells in vitro, mechanisms of blast cell transformation, application of mixed leukocyte reaction to histocompabilility testing. Office: Hematology Div Royal Victoria Hospital Montreal PQ H3A 1A1 Canada Home: 100 Francois St Montreal PQ H3E 1G2 Canada

BAIN, ELIZABETH ELLEN, TV exec.; b. Dubuque, Ia., Oct. 8, 1913; d. George Edward and Elizabeth Adelaide (Behnke) Bain; B.A. summa cum laude, Clarke Coll., 1935; postgrad. Juilliard Coll., 1938, U. Dubuque, 1940. Exec. dir. participating agreements United Artists Assn., N.Y.C., 1959-60; asst. v.p. program Columbia TV stas. CBS, Inc., N.Y.C., 1960-68; asso. dir. audience devel. Katz TV, N.Y.C., 1968—. Chmn. Luth. Found. Religious Drama, 1966-73, vice-chmn., 1973—. Mem. Internat. Radio/TV Execs. (dir. 1971), Am. Women Radio/TV (chmn. found. 1962-64, nat. pres. 1964-65). Lutheran (mem. council 1971-74). Home: 5 Cat Rock Rd Cos Cob CT 06807 Office: 245 Park Av New York City NY 10017

BAIN, ELIZABETH JEAN KNIGHT, state legislator; b. Denver, Sept. 27, 1909; d. Roger Davis and Nelle (Hoop) Knight; A.B., U. Colo., 1931; m. Francis M. Bain, June 12, 1933; children—Donald Knight, Lawrence Joseph, Liliana. Mem. Colo. Gen. Assembly, 1960-72. Dir. Mr. Steak, Inc. Mem. Def. Adv. Com. on Women in Services, 1960-63; mem. citizens adv. com. Ft. Logan Mental Health Center, 1964—; mem. Commn. on Community Relations City and County Denver, 1958-69; treas. League of Women Voters of Denver, 1950-52, Colo., 1952-54; active P.T.A.; sec. Denver Mental Health Clinic, 1963—; sec. Met. Mental Health Assn., 1964-70; treas. Denver Symphony Guild, 1955-56; chmn. Rearing Children of Good Will com. Nat. Conf. Christians and Jews, 1963-71; v.p. Better Bus. Bur. Met. Denver, 1974; mem. Colo. Commn. Status Women, Colo. Commn. Higher Edn. Adv. Bd., Colo. Centennial Bi-centennial Com.; residential chmn. United Way. Trustee Voice of Youth, Doane Coll., U. No. Colo.; bd. dirs. Met. Denver YMCA, Colo., program chmn., 1972—; bd. dirs. Friends of Denver Pub. Library, Colo. Housing, Inc., Colo. Women's Polit. Caucus, Girls Club Denver. Mental Health Assn. Mem. Am. Assn. U. Women (treas. Denver br. 1948-50), Community Homemaker Service Inc. (dir.), Am. Recorder Soc. (treas. Denver chpt. 1965-67), Nat. Order Women Legislators, Latin-Am. Ednl. Found., Republican Roundtable, Rep. Asso., Colo. Fedn. Rep. Women, Altrusa Internat., Nat. Orgn. Women, Kappa Kappa Gamma, Delta Kappa Gamma. Mem. United Ch. Christ (exec. council 1973—). Home: 755 Gaylord St Denver CO 80206

BAIN, HELEN PATE, educator, assn. exec.; b. Nashville, May 9, 1924; B.A., George Peabody Coll., 1945; M.A., U. Mich., 1949; Ed.D., U. Tenn.; m. 1946; 2 children. Tchr. English and speech Cohn High Sch., Nashville, from 1946; now coordinator vol. services Met. Schs., Nashville. Del. conf. World Confedn. Orgn. Teaching Profession, Ivory Coast, 1969; mem. Pres.'s Adv. Com. Title III Edn. Act; past pres. Edn. Council Nashville. Mem., organizer Nashville Citizens and Politics; past chmn. Women's Caucus. Bd. dirs. Davidson County (Tenn.) Tng. and Rehab. Center, Wis. Research and Devel. Center; chmn. housing com. Nashville Sr. Citizens. Mem. N.E.A. (mem. exec. com., dir., past nat. pres., mem. task force human rights, chmn. regional faculty desegregation conf., participant polit. clinics), Nat. Council Urban Edn. (pres., founder). Address: 4427 Lealand Lane Nashville TN 37204

BAIN, MILDRED JOSEFINE LUNAAS (MRS. JEROME BAIN), ednl. adminstr.; b. Stamford, Conn., Aug. 21, 1929; d. Magne and Aslaug Hjordis (Langmyhr) Lunaas; B.A. cum laude, U. Miami, 1951; M.Ed., U. Fla., 1956, Ed.D. (Grad. fellow), 1963; m. Jerome Bain, July 1, 1967. Tchr. Ponce de Leon Jr. High Sch., Coral Gables, Fla., 1951-54, asst. prin. for curriculum, 1955-56; tchr. P.K. Yonge Lab. Sch., U. Fla., Gainesville, 1956-57; asst. prin. curriculum Rivier Jr. High Sch., Miami, Fla., 1963-64, Miami Springs (Fla.) Sr. High Sch., 1964-66; vis. asso. prof. U. Miami, Coral Gables, 1966-67; mem. faculty Miami-Dade Community Coll., Miami, 1967—, staff asst. acad. affairs office, 1967-68, dir. learning resources div., 1968-70, dir. humanities div., 1970, dean acad. affairs, 1970—. Cons. program for developing instns. Am. Assn. Community and Jr. Colls., 1968-69; speaker, participant numerous orgns. and coms., 1968—. Mem. Am. Ednl. Research Assn., Mortar Bd., Am. Assn. Higher Edn., Fla. Assn. Community Colls. (chmn. exec. com. 1971-72), Am. Assn. U. Women, Phi Alpha Theta, Phi Lambda Theta, Kappa Delta Pi, Delta Kappa Gamma, Kappa Kappa Gamma. Home: 441 Bianca Av Coral Gables FL 33146 Office: 11011 SW 104th St Miami FL 33156

BAIN, WANDA LEE, assn. exec.; b. Jefferson County, Ky., Oct. 28, 1937; d. Claude Lawrence and Olis Erchal (Hudson) Gregory; student Jacksonville (Fla.) U., 1963-64; children—Mark, Eric, Crystal. Gen. sec. Fla. Med. Assn., 1960-61, asst. dir. adminstrv. dept., 1961-65, adminstrv. asst. to exec. v.p., 1965-70, dir. adminstrv. services dept., 1970—; exec. sec. Women's Aux. Fla. Med. Assn., 1972—. Adv. bd. Order of Rainbow, 1973—. Mem. Order Eastern Star. Home: 1441 Manotak Av Apt 802 Jacksonville FL 32210 Office: PO Box 2411 Jacksonville FL 32203

BAINTON, DOROTHY FORD, physician, educator; b. Magnolia, Miss., June 18, 1933; B.S., Millsaps Coll., 1955; M.D., Tulane U., 1958; M.S., U. Cal. at San Francisco, 1966; m. 1959; 3 children. Intern in medicine Strong Meml. Hosp., U. Rochester (N.Y.), 1958-59, resident in internal medicine, 1959-60; resident in hematology U. Wash. Sch. Medicine, Seattle, 1960-62; fellow in pathology U. Cal. Sch. Medicine, San Francisco, 1963-66, asst. prof., 1966—. Mem. Am. Soc. Cell. Biology. Research on hematology and cell biology, histochemistry and cell fractionation procedures, leukocyte maturation and function with light and electron microscopes. Office: Dept of Pathology University of Cal San Francisco CA 94143

BAIR, JEANETTE MARINO (MRS. DONALD RICHARD BAIR), occupational therapist; b. N.Y.C., June 7, 1942; d. George Alfred and Dorothy (Giannattasio) Marino; B.S. in Occupational Therapy (Nat. Health Found. scholar), U. N.H., 1964; m. Donald Richard Bair, Jan. 3, 1970. Staff therapist Bronx Municipal Hosp. Center, 1965-66; dir. occupational therapy Berkshire Rehab. Center, Pittsfield, Mass., 1966—; clin. asso. in occupational therapy Sargent Coll. Allied Health Professions, Boston U. Cons. nursing home programs, 1969. Mem. Am., Mass. occupational therapy assns., Jr. League of Berkshire County.

BAIRD, ANNA JANE OLSON (MRS. LEONARD H. BAIRD), home economist; b. Pitts., Apr. 19, 1920; d. Oscar R. and Elizabeth (Miller) Olson; B.S., Pa. State U., 1941, postgrad., 1962; student Westminster Coll., 1962; m. Leonard H. Baird, Feb. 26, 1942; children—Elizabeth Ann (Mrs. Wilmont Schwind, Jr.), Jane (Mrs. Jerry M. Homer), Nancy. Mgr., Olson's Dining Room, Butler, Pa., 1941-43; realtor Petrini Realty & Ins. Co., Sharon, Pa., 1955-62; home service rep. Pa. Power Co., Clark, 1962-65; home economist Kan. Wheat Commn., Hutchinson, 1966—. Named Wheat Woman of Year, Kan. Wheathearts, 1971. Mem. Am. Home Econs. Assn., Electric Womans Rountable Pitts., Home Economists in Bus. (chmn. elect 1969, chmn. 1970), Zonta Internat. (charter), Chi Omega Alumnae (past pres.). Presbyn. Mem. Order Eastern Star. Home: 305 E 15th St Hutchinson KS 67501 Office: 1021 N Main St Hutchinson KS 67501

BAIRD, KITTY ROGERS, educator; b. Henry County, Va., Nov. 27, 1932; d. Charlie Daniel and Emma Byrd (Hankins) Rogers; B.S. in Edn., Radford Coll., 1954; M.S. in Phys. Edn., U. N.C., 1960; m. Ernest Columbus Baird, Apr. 21, 1962; 1 dau., Kathryn Ann. Tchr., Radford (Va.) City Schs., 1954-58; faculty Centre Coll., Danville, Ky., 1959—, women's tennis coach, 1962—. First aid instr. A.R.C., 1953—, water safety instr., 1960-70; club leader 4-H Clubs, 1954-61, 73—; leader Girl Scouts, 1972-73. Mem. Am. (chmn. girls and women's sports So. dist.), Ky. (v.p., pres., mem. jour. editorial bd., distinguished service award) assns. for health, phys. edn. and recreation, Ky. Women's Intercollegiate Conf. (pres. 1973—), Delta Kappa Gamma (chpt. rec. sec. 1972-74), Chi Beta Phi (Key award). Baptist (youth leader 1952-64). Home: 353 Swope Dr Danville KY 40422

BAIRD, MARIE LOUISE (MRS. HUGH ALEXANDER BAIRD), librarian; b. St. Paul, Feb. 28, 1910; d. Adolph and Etta Eunice (Kannary) Larson; B.A., Carleton Coll., 1932; M.A., Columbia, 1937; postgrad. Mankato State Coll., summers 1958-60; m. Hugh Alexander Baird, June 19, 1937; children—Gwen, Helen (Mrs. James Philip Sundquist), Macaran. Tchr. pub. sch., Ellendale, Minn., 1932-34; tchr. English, librarian, drama coach, Dodge Center (Minn.) Pub. Sch., 1934-36, 56-68, librarian, drama coach, 1968—. Organizer Dodge County Mental Health Assn., 1955. Mem. A.L.A., Phi Beta Kappa. Republican. Conglist. Home: 303 Central Av N Dodge Center MN 55927 Office: Public School Dodge Center MN 55927

BAIRD, MAURA LOUISE, author; b. Los Angeles, July 23, 1921; d. Francis E. and Louisa Eugenia (Wilson) Fensch; B.A., U. Cal. at Berkeley, 1972; m. Thomas L. Baird, Sept. 8, 1955; 1 dau., Lisa Lorena. Founding pres. Humane Soc. Napa County (Cal.) Inc., 1972-73. Mem. Children of Am. Revolution, Phi Beta Kappa. Author poems in mags., also newspaper column on travel. Address: Gen Delivery Carmel-by-the Sea CA 93921

BAIRSTOW, FRANCES KANEVSKY (MRS. DAVID STEELE BAIRSTOW), educator, labor relations cons.; b. Racine, Wis., Feb. 19, 1920; d. William and Minnie (DuBow) Kanevsky; student U. Wis., 1937-42; B.S., U. Louisville, 1949; student Oxford U. (Eng.), 1953-54; postgrad. McGill U., Montreal, Que., 1958-59; m. Irving P. Kaufman, Nov. 14, 1942 (div. 1949); m. 2d, David Steele Bairstow, Dec. 17, 1954; children—Dale Owen, David Anthony. Research economist U.S. Senate Labor-Mgmt. Subcom., Washington, 1950-51; labor edn. specialist U. P.R., San Juan, 1951-52; chief wage data unit WSB, Washington, 1952-53; labor research economist Canadian Pacific Ry. Co., Montreal, 1956-58; asst. dir. indsl. relations centre McGill U., 1960-66, asso. dir., 1966-71, dir., 1971—, lectr., indsl. relations dept. econs., 1960-72, asst. prof. faculty mgmt., 1972—. Cons., Nat. Film Bd. of Can., 1965-69; arbitrator Que. Superior Labour Council Panel of Arbitrators, 1968—, Canadian Dept. Labour, 1971—; mediator Canadian Pub. Service Staff Relations Bd., 1973—; contbg. columnist Montreal Star, 1971—. Fulbright fellow, 1953-54. Mem. Canadian Indsl. Relations Research Inst. (exec. bd. 1965-68), Indsl. Relations Research Assn. Am. (mem. exec. bd. 1965-68), Nat. Acad. Arbitrators, Soc. Profls. in Dispute Resolution (adv. council). Home:

593 Lakeshore Rd Beaconsfield PQ Canada Office: 1001 Sherbrooke St West Montreal PQ 110 Canada

BAK, HEDI (HEDWIG) ELISABETH MUELLER (MRS. BRONISLAW M. BAK), artist, author; b. Pirmasens, Germany, Nov. 22, 1924; d. Fritz and Hedwig (Herbst) Mueller; M.F.A., Schule fur Kunsthandwerk, Kaiserslautern, Germany, 1943; postgrad. Freie Akademie der Bildenden Kunste, Mannheim, Germany, 1946-50; m. Bronislaw M. Bak, Feb. 15, 1949; children—Matthew Thomas, Clemens Richard, Pieter Jan. Came to U.S., 1952. Began career as archtl. draftsman, designer Office Eric Herrmanns, and Siemens and Halske, Germany; exhibited in shows in U.S. and Europe; represented in permanent collections at Mus. of Kaiserslautern, Gutenberg Mus., Mainz, Germany, Art Inst. Chgo., Newberry Library, Chgo., others; writer, illustrator series childrens books for Fides Pubs., Notre Dame, Ind. Mgr. Mid-North Gallery, 1965-67.; co-founder Studio 22, printmakers workshop, Chgo. Author: Trumpet Books, 1963; Song of Songs. Home: 2238 N Lincoln Av Chicago IL 60608 Office: 63 W Ontario St Chicago IL 60611

BAKEMAN, CAROL ANN (MRS. DELBERT CLIFTON BAKEMAN), librarian, singer; b. San Francisco, Oct. 27, 1934; d. Lars Hartvig and Gwendolyne Beatrice (Zimmer) Bergh; student U. Cal. at Los Angeles, 1954-62; m. Delbert Clifton Bakeman, May 16, 1959; children—Laurie Ann, Deborah Ann. Singer, Roger Wagner Chorale, 1954—, Los Angeles Master Chorale, 1964—; librarian Hughes Aircraft Co., Culver City, Cal., 1954-61; head econs. library Planning Research Corp., Los Angeles, 1961-63; corporate librarian Econ. Cons., Inc., Los Angeles, 1963-68; head econs. library Daniel, Mann, Johnson & Mendenhall, architects and engrs., Los Angeles, 1969-71, corporate librarian, 1971—. Pres., Creative Library Systems, Los Angeles, 1974—; library cons. ArchiSystems, div. SUMMA Corp., Los Angeles, 1972—, Property Rehab. Corp., Bell Gardens, Cal., 1974—, VTN Corp., Irvine, Cal., 1974—. Mem. Assistance League, So. Cal., 1956—, mem. nat. auxiliaries com. 1968-72, mem. nat. by laws com. 1970—, mem. asso. bd. dirs., 1966—. Mem. Am. Guild Musical Artists, Am. Fedn. TV and Radio Artists, Spl. Libraries Assn. (mem. So. Cal. adv. council 1960-73), Council of Planning Librarians, So. Cal. Choral Music Assn. Office: 3250 Wilshire Blvd Los Angeles CA 90010

BAKER, AUGUSTA (MRS. GORDON ALEXANDER), ret. librarian; b. Balt., Apr. 1, 1911; d. Winfort J. B. and Mabel (Gough) Braxston; A.B., N.Y. State Coll., 1933, B.S. in Library Sci., 1934; m. Gordon Alexander, Nov. 23, 1944; 1 son, James H. Children's librarian N.Y. Pub. Library, 1937-53, asst. co-ordinator children's service and story telling specialist, 1953-61, coordinator children's services, 1961-74. Recipient Dutton-Macroe award, 1953; Parents Mag. award, 1966; Grolier award, 1968; Constance Lindsay Skinner award, 1971; Distinguished Alumni award State U. N.Y. at Albany, 1974. Mem. Am. (Clarence Day award 1974), N.Y. library assns., Women's Nat. Book Assn., Delta Sigma Theta. Episcopalian. Author: The Talking Tree, 1955; Golden Lynx, 1960; also pamphlet. Editor-in-chief: Young Years, 1960. Home: 115-33 174th St St Albans NY 11412 Office: 8 E 40th St New York City NY 10016

BAKER, BETTY, author; b. Bloomsburg, Pa., June 20, 1928; d. Robert Weidler and Mary (Wentling) Baker; student pub. schs., Orange, N.J.; m. Robert George Venturo, May 18, 1949 (div. 1964); 1 son, Christopher Patrick. Author: The Sun's Promise, 1962; Little Runner of the Longhouse, 1962; The Shaman's Last Raid, 1963; Killer-or-Death, 1963 (Western Heritage award 1963); The Treasure of the Padres, 1964; Walk the World's Rim, 1965; Blood of the Brave, 1966; Dunderhead War (Golden Spur award), 1967; Do Not Annoy the Indians, 1968; Arizona, 1969; The Pig War, 1969; And One Was a Wooden Indian (Western Heritage award), 1970; The Big Push, 1972; A Stranger and Afraid, 1972; At the Center of the World, 1973; The Spirit is Willing, 1974. Mem. P.E.N., Western Writers Am. Home: 3232 E First Tucson AZ 85716

BAKER, CAROLINE FRANCES, librarian; b. Muskegon, Mich., May 4, 1922; d. Frank Anthony and Cora Caroline (Kramer) Schnitzler; A.B., Aquinas Coll., 1962; A.M., U. Mich., 1965; postgrad. Central Mich. U., 1970; m. Joseph Gerard Baker, Aug. 31, 1940 (dec. 1957); children—Thomas Raymond, Joseph Francis, Mary Theresa. Instr. English, Davenport Coll., Grand Rapids, Mich., 1962-64; asst. librarian Aquinas Coll., Grand Rapids, 1964-67; documents librarian, instr. library sci. Central Mich. U., Mt. Pleasant, 1967—. Mem. Am. Assn. U. Profs., Nat. Geog. Soc., Spl. Libraries Assn., Mich. Library Assn., Library Dirs.' Adv. Council, Altar Soc., Phi Alpha Theta, Beta Phi Mu. Roman Catholic. Club: Faculty Women's (Mt. Pleasant). Asst. editor: Dag Hammarskjold Collection on Developing Nations, 1968, 70. Home: 403 E Grand Av Mount Pleasant MI 48858

BAKER, DOROTHEA ANNA, judge; b. Gilbertville, Mass., Feb. 11, 1927; d. Andrew and Ella (Gibbs) Baker; student Clark U., 1944-47; A.B., George Washington U., 1947, LL.B., 1948, LL.M., 1959; postgrad. Georgetown U., 1952-53. Admitted to D.C. bar, 1948; atty. Dept. of Def., 1948-51; practice law, 1951—, also adminstrv. law judge Dept. Agr. Treas. Fed. Adminstrv. Law Judges Conf. Mem. Met. Bd. Trade. Recipient D.A.R. award as outstanding youthful citizen, 1937. Mem. D.C., Women's bar assns., Mass. State Soc., Women's Republican Fedn. D.C., YWCA, Nat. Trust for Historic Preservation, Order of Coif, Phi Delta Delta, Zeta Tau Alpha. Club: Congressional Country, Nat. Lawyers Contbr. articles to profl. jours. Home: 5606 Harwick Rd Wood Acres Washington DC 20016 Office: Dept of Agriculture Washington DC 20250

BAKER, DOROTHY ELIZABETH, child psychiatrist; b. Kingston, N.Y., Aug. 9, 1925; d. Orlando L. and Anna (Parslow) Baker; B.A., Barnard Coll., 1949; M.D., Woman's Med. Coll. Phila., 1954; m. Arthur H. Auerbach, June 6, 1956 (div. 1963). Intern Phila. Gen. Hosp., 1954-55; resident in psychiatry Fairfield State Hosp., Newtown, Conn., 1955-56, Phila. Psychiat. Hosp., 1956-57; fellow in child psychiatry Child Study Center, Phila., 1957-59, staff psychiatrist, 1959-60; staff psychiatrist Phila. Gen. Hosp., 1959-60, Jefferson Med. Coll. Hosp., 1961-62, Vineland (N.J.) Tng. Sch., 1960-68, Montgomery County Pub. Schs., Lansdale, Pa., 1960—; dir. Eastern Diagnostic and Evaluation Center, Phila., 1962-70; staff psychiatrist Devereux Schs., Devon, 1968-70; dep. dir. West Seneca Children's Psychiat. Hosp., 1970-72; child psychiat. cons. children's unit Allentown State Hosp., 1960-65; cons. Eleanor Roosevelt Developmental Services, Troy, N.Y., 1972; dep. dir. Newark (N.Y.) State Sch., 1972—. Named Barnard Coll. Prominent alumnae Phila. area, 1964. Diplomate in psychiatry and child psychiatry Am. Bd. Psychiatry and Neurology. Mem. Am. Psychiat. Assn., Am. Acad. Child Psychiatry. Home: 703 E Maple Av Newark NY 14513 Office: Newark State Sch Newark NY 14513

BAKER, DOROTHY GILLAM, educator; b. Saratoga, N.Y., June 9, 1906; d. Albert Burns and Mae (Fowler) Gillam; B.A., Hunter Coll., 1929; M.A., U. Cal. at Los Angeles, 1954; Ph.D., N.Y. U., N.Y.C., 1962; m. Melville Pratt Baker, May 17, 1946 (dec. Apr. 1958). Profl. actress, 1930-39; promotion dir. Fed. Theatre, New Orleans, 1938-39; produced all-star benefits and field organizer United China and related war relief agencies, 1940-42; adminstrv. asst. Office Civil Def., 1943; tchr. drama and speech grad.-div. Hunter Coll., 1953-60; tchr. Bronx Community Coll., 1962-63, Coll. City N.Y., 1956-57; adj. asst. prof. edn. L.I. U., 1963-64. Mem. Found. Intergrative Edn. Served from lt. (j.g.) to lt. USCG, 1943-45; producer Tars and Spars (revue), 1944. Mem. Alumni Assn. Hunter Coll., Soc. Social Responsibility in Sci. (asso.). Home: 140 West End Av New York City NY 10023

BAKER, EMILY ROSE, real estate broker, ins. agt.; b. East Mauch Chunk, Pa., May 5, 1919; d. John and Josephine (Perrone) Sully; grad. courses Henry's Sch. Cosmotology, 1937, Anthony's Sch. Real Estate, 1951, 54, Anthony's Sch. for Ins., 1953; m. Dennis Baker, Jan. 20, 1939 (div. Apr. 1944); 1 son, Nicholas J. Salesman, Pengilly Real Estate, Los Angeles, 1951-54; ins. agt., Los Angeles, then Montebello, Cal., 1953—; Emily R. Baker Realty, Los Angeles, 1954-65, Baker Realty, Montebello, 1965—. Chmn. East Los Angeles, Montebello Multiple Listing Service, 1965-66, 67-68, 70-71, 71-72. Named Realtor of Year, Montebello, 1973. Mem. Cal. Real Estate Assn. (dir. 1973-74), Make Am. Better Assn. (pres. bd. 1972, dir. 1969, mem. profl. panel 1968—), Montebello Dist. Bd. Realtors (sec. 1968-69, pres. 1972), Nat. Realtors Assn., Montebello C. of C. Roman Catholic. Mem. Am. Lodge. Home: 200 Casa Grande Av Montebello CA 90640 Office: 2513 W Whittier Blvd Montebello CA 90640

BAKER, EMILY VAUGHN, lawyer; b. New Orleans, Aug. 16, 1930; d. Robert Lee and Laura Fay (Tillman) Vaughn; student Sophie Newcomb Coll., 1946-48; LL.B. cum laude, Jackson Sch. Law, 1969; postgrad. U. So. Miss., 1968-70; children—Carryl (Mrs. T.C. Simpson), William, Robert, Charles. Admitted to Miss. Bar., 1969; with South Central Bell Telephone Co., Jackson, ret., 1971; practice law, Pascagoula, Miss., 1971—; partner firm McRae & Baker, Pascagoula, 1971—. Instr. Miss. Bar Rev., 1973—. Mem. Com. for Ratification Equal Rights Amendment, 1972, vice chmn., 1973; pres. P.T.A., Pascagoula, 1972, del. City Council, 1972; active Boy Scouts Am. Bd. dirs., chmn. Jackson County Health Edn. Miss. Lung Assn., 1971-73. Mem. Am. (mem. consumer class action com. gen. practice sect.), Miss., Jackson County bar assns., Nat. Assn. Women Lawyers, Miss. Trial Lawyers Assn., Am. Judicature Soc., Nat. Orgn. for Women, Bus. and Profl. Women's Clubs (3d v.p. Miss. Fedn. chpt. 1971, pres. Pascagoula chpt. 1973, Woman of Achievement award). Episcopalian. Home: 2316 Glendale Pascagoula MS 39567 Office: 712 Watts St PO Box 1692 Pascagoula MS 39567

BAKER, ETHEL BOWDEN (MRS. VICTOR M. BAKER), state legislator; b. Orrington, Me., May 21, 1906; d. Ferd D. and Ellen (Lewis) B.; student Gilman Comml. Sch.; m. Victor M. Baker, June 18, 1927; children—Alan L., Gladyce (Mrs. Stais). Clk., Town of Orrington, 1931-53; sch. lunch supt., Bucksport, Me., 1947-58, Orrington, 1947-61; mem. Me. Ho. of Reps., 1959-60, 61-62, 65-66, 67—, mem. legislative research com., 1967-72. Bd. dirs. Garden Club Fedn. Me. Mem. Me. Town and City Clks. Assn. (past pres.). Mem. Order Eastern Star. Club: Orrington Garden. Address: Center Dr Orrington ME 04474

BAKER, EVELYN M., retail store exec.; b. Garrett, Ind., Apr. 4, 1909; d. Martin L. and Cleatus Gertrude (Beber) Miller; grad. high sch.; m. Charles Barry Baker, Nov. 9, 1931; 1 dau., Judy Ann (Mrs. Gary P. Snider). With Haffner's 5 cents to $1.00 Stores, Garrett, 1934—, office mgr., 1951—, accountant, 1955—, asst. sec.-treas., 1958—, dir., 1968—. Home: 524 S Randolph St Garrett IN 46738 Office: 214 S Randolph St Garrett IN 46738

BAKER, GERALDINE HELEN (MRS. JAMES BERNARD BAKER), ednl. adminstr.; b. Springfield, Mass., Feb. 6, 1923; d. William A. and Helen (Scully) Hervieux; B.A. in Edn., U. Mass., 1964, M.Ed., 1970; m. James Bernard Baker, Aug. 25, 1942; children—Penelope (Mrs. David O'Connor), James Bernard, William W. Tchr. spl. class Belchertown (Mass.) State Sch. for Mentally Retarded, 1959-66, supr. spl. edn., 1966-68, dir. spl. edn., 1968—, project dir. innovative programs, 1968—. Instr., Am. Internat. Coll., Springfield, 1972-73; cons. in spl. edn. for mentally retarded, 1968—. Vice. pres. Democratic Town Com., Belchertown, 1970—. Bd. dirs. Work Opportunity Center, West Springfield, Mass., 1969—. Mem. Am. Assn. Mental Deficiency, Mass. Tchr's. Assn., Catholic Women's Club. Roman Catholic. Home: Springfield Rd Belchertown MA 01007 Office: Box 486 Belchertown MA 01007

BAKER, IRENE VICKERS (MRS. MARSHALL HENRY BAKER), theatrical adminstr.; b. Lowell, Kan., Feb. 17, 1895; d. William Howard and Belle Catherine (Foster) Vickers; grad. San Diego State Tchrs. Coll., 1917, Leland Powers Sch. of the Theatre, 1922; B.S., Boston U., 1936; postgrad. Boston U., England, 1939; P. Pub. Service (hon.), Friends U., 1972; m. Marshall Henry Baker, Apr. 4, 1923. Head speech and drama dept. Friends U., Wichita, Kan., 1931-44; founder, mng. dir. Wichita Childrens Theatre, 1946—. Organized C. Theatre Troupers, 1961—. Dist. comdr. Am. Cancer Soc. Field Army, 1945-46. Bd. dirs. Wichita Art Assn., Friends U. Mus. Recipient Meritorious Service award Soroptimist Club, Wichita, Kan., 1944; Distinguished Service award U.S.O., 1945; Medal of Honor award Wichita Art Assn., 1965; named Woman of the Year, Theta Sigma Phi, 1966; recipient Recognition award Wichita Fine Arts Council, 1971; theatre named Irene Vickers Baker Theatre by Art Assn. Trustees, 1971; Spl. Recognition citation Am. Theatre Assn., 1972. Mem. Theta Sigma Phi. Club: Kansas Author's. Address: 1422 University Av Wichita KS 67213

BAKER, MRS. IVAN (LUCILE ATKINSON BAKER), bus. archives cons.; b. Carroll, Ia., July 27, 1892; d. Walter Edward and Dessa (Waterman) Atkinson; student in drama, Drake U., 1908; student Morningside Coll., 1909-10, Chatham Coll., 1910-12; m. Ivan F. Baker, Oct. 19, 1911; 1 dau., Helen Merle (Mrs. Robert Cushman). Tchr. piano Japan, 1920-27; mem. Motor Corps, A.R.C., 1942-46; cons. Internat. Trade Fair, Tokyo, Japan, 1955, Jakarta, 1955; mem. nat. women's planning com. Japan Internat. Christian U., Tokyo, 1953—. Mem. P.E.O., ZET. Soc. Home: 266 E Dudley Av Westfield NJ 07090

BAKER, JOSEPHINE L. REDENIUS (MRS. MILTON G. BAKER), pub. relations dir.; b. Oceanville, N.J., Aug. 31, 1920; d. Jacob and Josephone (Palmer) Redenius; student Columbia, 1948-49, L.I. U., 1957-58, George Washington U., 1947-48; M.A. in Journalism, Am. U., 1953; L.H.D., Temple U., 1964; m. Milton G. Baker. Enlisted as pvt. WAAC, 1943, advanced through grades to lt. col. U.S. Army, 1963; intelligence officer atomic installations throughout U.S. and Can., 1943-53; asst. in Office Chief of Staff, Army Forces Far East, Japan, 1954-56; pub. information officer Office Chief of Information, Washington, 1958-61; chief Women's Army Corps Recruiting, U.S. Army, 1962-66; information liaison officer U.S. Army, 1966-67, ret., 1967; dir. pub. relations and devel. Valley Forge Mil. Acad. and Jr. Coll., Wayne, Pa., 1967-70, dir. found., 1970—. Dir. Republican Women of Pa. Bd. dirs. Freedom Valley Council Girl Scouts U.S.A., 1970—, Opera Guild Miami (Fla.). Decorated Legion of Merit, U.S. Army Commendation Medal with 1st oak leaf; recipient Pa. Meritorious Service medal; Distinguished Alumnus, Am. U., 1969. Mem. Pub. Relations Soc. Am., Am. Personnel and Guidance Assn., Am. Coll. Personnel Assn., Nat. Vocational Guidance Assn., Am. Sch. Counselors Assn., Am. Legion Aux., Ret. Officers Assn., Assn. U.S. Army (Anthony J. Drexel Biddle medal 1968), Army-Navy Union, Soroptomist Club, Assn. Measurement and Evaluation in Guidance, Emergency Aid of Pa., Am. Legion, La Boutique des Huit Chapeaux et Quarante Femmes, Women in Communication, Inc. Presbyn. Address: Crossed Sabres Wayne PA 19087 also Surf Club Apts 9133 Collins Av Surfside FL 33154

BAKER, KATHERINE FRANCES GEHRES (MRS. RAYMOND EARL BAKER), owner advt. agy.; b. Phila., Nov. 17, 1919; d. Blaine Jacob and Louise Margaret (Smith) Gehres; student Spring Garden Inst., 1939-41, Pa. State U., 1963-64, Temple U., 1970-71; m. Raymond Earl Baker, Mar. 14, 1942; children—Raymond Earl, Gordon, Donna Jean, Kenneth. Owner, Kitty Baker Dress Design Co., Alexandria, La., 1942-44; designer Bergdorf Goodman, N.Y.C., 1945-47; owner Baker Advt., Hatboro and Jenkintown, Pa., 1961—. Artist with works in numerous shows, pvt. collections. Chmn. Old York Rd. Council for UN, 1953-55; chmn. Jenkintown Festival of Arts, 1973. Chmn. bd. dirs. Upper Moreland Adult Evening Sch., 1963-65. Mem. Women's Internat. League for Peace and Freedom (publicity sec. 1963-66), Nat. Orgn. for Women, Citizens Orgn. for Sane World, Old York Rd. Art Guild. Contbr. articles to newspapers and bus. mags. Home: 638 S York Rd Hatboro PA 19040 Office: 815 Greenwood Av Jenkintown PA 19046

BAKER, KATHRYN LOU, educator; b. Norborne, Mo., Apr. 14, 1928; d. Ralph Charles and Gertrude (Bales) Baker; B.S. in Edn., B.S. in Bus. Adminstrn., Central Mo. State U., 1951; M.S., Ind. U., 1961, postgrad., 1967-68, now doctoral candidate; postgrad. U. Ia., summer 1967. Tchr. Blue Mound Sch., nr. Dawn, Mo., 1946-48, Sr. High Sch., Roswell, N.M., 1951-62; instr. Roswell Community Coll., evenings 1958-62; asst. prof. bus. Central Mo. State Univ., Warrensburg, 1962—, on leave as teaching asso. Ind. U., Bloomington, 1967-68; sec. various bus., govt. A.F. instr., summers 1951-57. Active Cancer Crusade Campaign, Roswell, 1958-62; mem. cast variety shows Roswell Assistance League, 1957, 61; vol. worker Community Concert Campaign, Warrensburg, 1965-68; state sponsor N.M. High Sch. Cheerleaders Assn., 1954-55. Birdie Adams scholar Delta Kappa Gamma, 1960; Ford Found. fellow Ind. U., summer 1965; Berneta Minkwitz Internat. scholar Delta Kappa Gamma, 1971-72; recipient Centennial Medallion award Central Mo. State U., 1971. Mem. Community Tchrs. Assn. Central Mo. State U. (sec.-treas. 1964-65), Am. Assn. U. Women (v.p., program chmn. Roswell 1956-57), Am. Bus. Women's Assn. (sec. Roswell 1956-57, v.p., program chmn. 1955-56), Am. Assn. U. Profs., N.E.A., Mo. State Tchrs. Assn., Nat., Mo. (sec.-treas. 1970-72; sec.-treas. central dist. 1970-72, v.p. central dist. 1972-74, pres. central dist. 1974-75) bus. edn. assns., Midwest Bus. Adminstrn. Assn., Mo. Vocational Assn., Adminstrn. Mgmt. Soc., Am. Vocational Assn., Am. Bus. Communication Assn., Ind. U., Central Mo. State U. alumni assns., Internat. Platform Assn., Delta Zeta (dir. Epsilon Gamma chpt. 1964-67, province treas. 1970-72, v.p. Warrensburg alumnae chpt. 1970-71), Beta Sigma Phi, Delta Pi Epsilon, Pi Lambda Theta, Delta Kappa Gamma (corr. sec. N.M. chpt. 1957-59; chmn. budget com. Warrensburg chpt. 1963-68, chmn. scholarship com. 1972-74), Phi Beta Lambda, Kappa Delta Pi, Kappa Kappa Iota. Methodist. Club: Business and Professional Women (chmn. audit com. 1964-65; legislative com. 1965-67, personal devel. com. 1968-69; chmn. world affairs com. 1969-70; finance com. 1972-74). Asso. editor: CMSC Business Keynotes, 1969. Home: 1905 Webster St Chillicothe MO 64601 Office: Sch Bus and Econs Central Mo State Univ Warrensburg MO 64093

BAKER, LETHA ELIZABETH (MITTS), author; b. Capron, Okla., June 26, 1913; d. Olie Elmer and Bessie Belle (Roberson) Mitts; B.A. in Spanish and English, Northwestern Okla. State U., 1933; M.A. in Spanish and English, Okla. State U., 1937; postgrad. in French Ore. State U., 1939-41; m. Elton M. Baker, May 19, 1935; children—Ronald Murray, David Scott. Tchr. pub. high schs., Forgan, Okla., 1933-35, Gage, Okla., 1936-38; tchr. Spanish and English, Southwestern Okla. State U., Weatherford, 1938-39; tchr. Spanish, Ore. State U., Corvallis, 1941-42, Fresno (Cal.) State U., 1946-47; prin. Am. Sch., Colomba, Ceylon (now Sri Lanka), 1958-59; cons. writer Cinecrest, Inc., Seattle, 1970—, Screen Enterprises, Seattle, 1971—. Bd. dirs. Warren Reading Found., 1966-71. Mem. Nat. Writers Club, Okla. Hist. Soc., Cherokee Nat. Hist. Soc. Club: Indianola Community, Phi Kappa Phi. Author: Time is Not Enough, 1964; Cherokee Country, 1968. Contbr. articles on travel to mags. and newspapers. Address: PO Box 149 Indianola WA 98342

BAKER, LOUISE, bacteriologist; b. South Boston, Mass.; d. Joseph Willard and Lillie Carolyn (Cranston) Baker; B.S., U. R.I., 1920; M.A. in Pure Sci., Columbia, 1922; med. student Yale, 1926. Head technician Sayles Hosp., Pawtucket, R.I., 1919-21, Anna Jaques Hosp., Newburyport, Mass., 1924-26; county bacteriologist Warren County, N.Y., 1926-29; head technician Frank Fulton Med. Clinic, Providence, 1929-40; technician, head technician Lockport City Hosp. (N.Y.), 1940-43; county bacteriologist Livingston County Lab., Dansville, N.Y., 1943-45; head bacteriologist Arnot-Ogden Hosp., Elmira, N.Y., 1945-57, Arlington Hosp. (Va.), 1957-58; head bacteriologist and mycologist Clifton Springs Hosp. and Clinic (N.Y.), 1958-69; tchr. bacteriology student nurses Anna Jaques Hosp., 1925, Arnot-Ogden Hosp., 1945, 46, to lab. technicians preparing for registry, 1955. Violin player in 2 amateur mus. clubs, Elmira, N.Y., 1956, 57, 48-57; sec.-treas. Hosp. Technicians Soc. Providence-Pawtucket, 1936-37; mem. diaconate bd. First Baptist Ch., Elmira, 1952-57, 1st vice chmn. bd., 1956, 57, Sunday Sch. tchr. jrs., 1952-57, tchr. jr. high age Clifton Springs Bapt. Ch., 1963-66, 1st v.p., devotional leader, 1963, 64, v.p. missions Women's Missionary Soc., 1964, v.p. missions, 1964—. Named to Exec. and Profl. Hall of Fame, 1966. Fellow Royal Soc. Health; mem. Am. Soc. Med. Technologists, Am., N.Y. State pub. health assns., Blackstone Valley Hist. Soc., Yale Assn. R.I., R.I. Soc. Med. Technologists, Grad. Faculties Alumni Columbia, Internat. Platform Assn., Chi Omega. Baptist (deaconess). Mem. Order Eastern Star. Home: 37 Allen Av Pawtucket RI 02860

BAKER, LUCINDA (MRS. WILLARD ALAN GREINER), writer; b. Atlanta, Ill., July 10, 1916; d. Hazle Howard and Adah Rebecca (Mason) Baker; student Ariz. State Coll., 1934-37, 39-40; m. Willard Alan Greiner, June 27, 1946. Writer fiction for mags., including Redbook, Ladies Home Jour., Family Circle, Ingenue, also pub. in Eng., Australia, Denmark, other fgn. countries, 1936—. Recipient 1st prize Nat. Panhellenic Essay Contest, 1937. Mem. Authors Guild Am., Cal. Writers, Cal. Geneal. Soc. Home: 2415 Massachusetts Av Redwood City CA 94061

BAKER, MARIAN GRAY CHAMBERS, occupational therapist; b. Youngstown, O., Feb. 5, 1931; d. James Edward and Josie Bell (Alston) Chambers; B.S., Washington U., St. Louis, 1958; postgrad. Wayne State U.; m. James Baker, Aug. 2, 1958. Staff therapist Deaconess Hosp., St. Louis, 1958-63; dir. occupational therapy Kenny-Mich. Rehab. Found., Pontiac (Mich.) Gen. Hosp., 1963—. Cons. occupational therapy Grovecrest Convalescent Center, Pontiac, 1970—. Vol. case aide worker Oakland County Juvenile Ct., 1969—. Mem. World Fedn. Occupational Therapists, Am., Mich. occupational therapy assns., Negro Bus. and Profl. Women. Elk. Home: 163 Green St Pontiac MI 48503 Office: Pontiac Gen Hosp Seminole at W Huron Pontiac MI 48053

BAKER, MARY ANN, neurophysiologist, educator; b. Los Angeles, Oct. 11, 1940; B.A., U. Redlands, 1961; M.A., U. Cal. at Santa Barbara, 1964; Ph.D. in Anatomy, U. Cal. at Los Angeles, 1968; m. 1970. NIH trainee U. Cal at Los Angeles, 1964-68; Bank Am.-Giannini Found. research fellow, 1968-69; research fellow in neurosci. Mass. Inst. Tech., Boulder, Colo., summer 1969; NIH trainee in physiology and biophysics U. Wash., Seattle, 1969-70; asst. prof. physiology U. So. Cal. Sch. Medicine, Los Angeles, 1970-73, asso. prof., 1973—. Mem. A.A.A.S., Am. Physiol. Soc., Am. Assn. Anatomists, Soc. Neurosci. Research on mammalian thermoregulation, neurophysiology of temperature sensation and control in mammals. Office: Dept of Physiology University of Southern Cal School of Medicine 2025 Zonal St Los Angeles CA 90033

BAKER, MEREDITH LEE DEAN, educator; b. Bryn Mawr, Pa., Oct. 14, 1942; d. W. Kenneth and Virginia Lee (Phillips) Dean; B.S., East Stroudsburg State Coll., 1964; postgrad. U. Wis., 1965-66; M.Ed., Temple U., 1969; m. E. Willson Baker. Tchr. phys. edn. Abington (Pa.) High Sch., 1964-65; instr. phys. edn. St. Lawrence U., Canton, N.Y., 1965-67, Am. Kiz Koleji, Istanbul, Turkey, 1967-68; dir. womens phys. edn. Franklin and Marshall Coll., Lancaster, Pa., 1969-70; asso. athletic dir., dir. phys. edn. Princeton, 1970—. Mem. Princeton (N.J.) Community Joint Bd. Recreation, 1972—. Mem. A.A.H.P.E.R., U.S. Gymnastics Fedn. (nat. edn. chmn. 1973—), Eastern Assn. Intercollege Athletics for Women (dir. 1973—), Womens Coll. Athletic Adminstrn. of N.J. (pres. 1973—), New Atlantic All Coll. Field Hockey Assn. (v.p. 1971-73). Home: 100 W Broad St Hopewell NJ 08525 Office: Princeton University Box 72 Princeton NJ 08540

BAKER, MILDRED (MRS. JACOB BAKER), mus. exec.; b. Bklyn., Aug. 14, 1905; ed. U. Rochester; m. Jacob Baker. Asst. to exec. dir. C.A.A., 1929-32; asst. to dir., then asst. dir. Fed. Art Project, 1935-43; asst. to dir. Newark Mus., 1944-49, asst. dir., 1949-53, asso. dir., 1953-70. Vice chmn. N.J. Gov.'s Commn. for Study of Arts in N.J.; mem. N.J. State Council on the Arts, 1966—. Trustee Newark Mus., mem. acquistion, membership and nominating coms. Mem. Am. Mus. Assn., Am. Fedn. Arts, N.J. Hist. Soc. (museum com.), Archives Am. Art. Clubs: Women's City of N.Y., Cosmopolitan of N.Y., Woman Pays. Home: 569 Mt Prospect Av Newark NJ 07104

BAKER, MYRTLE ELEANOR PITZER (MRS. MICHAEL BAKER, JR.), business exec., civic worker; b. West Shenango, Pa., May 26, 1912; d. George F. and Nettie (Miller) Pitzer; student pub. schs. Pa.; L.H.D., Coll. Steubenville, 1970; m. Michael Baker, Jr., Mar. 23, 1932; children—Michael III, Carl Gene, Keith Joel (dec.). Asst. sec. Euthenics Systems Corp., Michael Baker, Jr., Inc., 1959—; dir., sec. Hub Devel. Corp., 1962—. Chmn. Myrtle E. Baker Scholarship Fund. Home: 130 Evergreen Circle Beaver PA 15009 Office: 4301 Dutch Ridge Rd PO Box 280 Beaver PA 15009

BAKER, NANCY ANN, librarian; b. Charleston, W.Va., Oct. 6, 1921; d. Donald James and Genevieve P. (Gaskill) Baker; B.S. in Edn., U. Pa., 1943; M.L.S., U. Pitts., 1965. Classroom tchr., Spring City, Pa., 1943-44, Upper Darby, Pa., 1944-48; tchr. Mt. Lebanon Sch. Dist., Pitts., 1948-65, librarian, 1965—. Mem. Am., Pa., Pitts., Suburban library assns., Nat., Pa., Mt. Lebanon (sec.-treas. 1962-63) edn. assns. Home: 19 Ralston Pl Pittsburgh PA 15216

BAKER, NANCY CAROLYN MOLL (MRS. JAMES ROSS BAKER), coll. adminstr.; b. Milw., Dec. 9, 1944; d. Alvin Donald and Wilma Carolyn (Robertson) Moll; B.A., U. Minn., 1965, M.A., 1974; m. James Ross Baker, Aug. 28, 1965; 1 son, Bradley. Reporter, St. Paul Dispatch, 1965-66; editor, writer pub. relations U. Minn., Mpls., 1966-67, Northwest Airlines, Mpls., 1967-69; freelance writer, Mpls., 1969-71; TV scriptwriter Control Data Corp., Mpls., 1971-73; dir. news and publs. Minn. Metro State Coll., St. Paul, 1973—. Mem. Chi Omega, Kappa Tau Alpha. Home: 104 Davern St Paul MN 55116 Office: Metro Sq 7th and Robert St Paul MN 55101

BAKER, ORPHA MAE PHILLIPS, mus. curator; b. Dinuba, Cal., Apr. 13, 1922; d. Philip E. and Beulah Vesta (Bartholomew) Phillips; student Coll. Sequoias, 1955, 58-59, Fresno State Coll., 1957; m. Raymond A. Morris, Jan. 26, 1941; children—Philip R., Carol (Mrs. Richard Obegi), Laura (Mrs. Robert Williams), Margaret Morris; m. 2d, Jerry D. Baker, Feb. 16, 1960 (div. Dec. 1973). Bookkeeper Morris Roofing Co., 1947-53, various other positions, 1960-67; curator, dir., Desert Caballeros Western Mus., Maricopa County Hist. Soc., Wickenburg, Ariz., 1967—, also mus. rep. to soc., bd. dirs. soc. Recipient Outstanding Citizen Achievement award Desert Caballeros Orgn., 1970; named Citizen of Year, Wickenburg C. of C., 1971. Mem. Wickenburg Bus. and Profl. Women's Club (pres. 1971-72, Woman of Year 1973), Ariz. Fedn. Bus. and Profl. Women's Clubs (dir. dist. 7 1973-74). Designed and executed mus. displays including dioramas with sculptured figurines. Home: Rincon Rd PO Box 863 Wickenburg AZ 85358 Office: 20 N Frontier St Wickenburg AZ 85358

BAKER, PATRICIA COOPER, biologist, educator; b. Greenville, Tex., Dec. 9, 1936; B.A., U. Hawaii, 1960; Ph.D. in Zoology, U. Cal., 1964; 1 child. USPHS fellow in developmental biology U. Ore. Sch. Medicine, 1964-67, asst. prof. pathology, 1967-69; faculty dept. zoology U. Cal. at Berkeley, 1969—. Mem. Am. Soc. Zoologists, Am. Soc. Cell Biology, Soc. Developmental Biology. Research on mechanics of morphogenetic movement, cell movement and membranes. Office: Dept of Zoology University of Cal Berkeley CA 94720

BAKER, POLLY D., advt. agy. exec.; b. Ohio; ed. Coll. Wooster, Kent State U., Boston U.; B.A., Western Res. U. Womens news editor, commentator WHK-CBS, Akron, O., 1930-34, WTAM-NBC, Cleve., 1934-35, dir. womens programs WTAM, 1934-50; feature writer Escondido Times-Advocate, 1951-53; editor, columnist, society editor, advt. mgr. Borrego Sun newspaper Copley Press, 1954-69; now pres. Baker, Rhodes & Letson, Inc., exec. dir. PRS Agy., San Diego. Wrote, produced and directed (under names Paula Dale and Jane Weaver) radio programs for 15 years; originator Quiz Kids, W6N, Chgo.; writer, producer, narrator Matinee Memories, NBC; produced poetry show Cobwebs and Cadenzas with Cleve. Symphony Ensemble for NBC; dir.-instr. First Aid on the Air; wrote You Can If You Care, original dramas, NBC (later edited and pub. in book Victorious); commentator (with Graham McNamee) Nat. Air Races; speaker RKO-Keith Lecture Bur. Mem. Navy League (mem. San Diego women's council, pres.), S.F.A. (dist. dir. Pacific region), S.Y.C.A. (regional chmn.), F.F.V.F. (charter, former editor Forge), Theta Sigma Phi. Home: 12911 Caminito En Flor Del Mar CA 92014 Office: PRS Agency 4040 30th St San Diego CA 92104

BAKER, RETA NEIL (MRS. WEBSTER B. BAKER, SR.), banker; b. Tampa, Fla., Oct. 15, 1929; d. Matthew and Edna (Seivers) Neil; grad. high sch.; m. Webster Bedorial Baker, Sr., Oct. 3, 1946; children—Webster Bedorial, W. Everett, Bernice A., Brenda Sue. Clk.-typist Thurow Electronics, Lakeland, Fla., 1958; bookkeeper, teller First State Bank of Lakeland, 1959-61; bookkeeper, teller First Nat. Bank of Lakeland, 1963-66, head bookkeeper, 1966-67, asst. cashier, 1967-71, asst. v.p., 1971-73, v.p., 1973—. Mem. Am. Inst. Banking (dir. Polk County chpt. 1973-74), Nat. Assn. Bank Women Officers (chmn. central group 1972), Credit Women Internat. (3d v.p. Lakeland chpt. 1969). Home: 1831 Roanoke Av Lakeland FL 33803 Office: 2211 S Florida Av Lakeland FL 33803

BAKER, SARA LANDERS (MRS. WILLIAM BRADLEY BAKER), editor; b. Huntsville, Ala., July 14, 1918; d. Elroy Cooper and Henrietta (Delp) Landers; student U. Montevallo, 1937-39; m. William Bradley Baker, Feb. 7, 1943. Soc. editor, women's editor Huntsville (Ala.) Times, 1948-59, 62—. Mem. Huntsville Symphony Orch. Guild, 1964—. Mem. Ala. Women's Press Assn. (sec. 1970). Home: 1213 Hermitage St Huntsville AL 35801 Office: Memorial Pkwy Huntsville AL 35807

BAKER, SUSAN PARDEE (MRS. TIMOTHY DANFORTH BAKER), epidemiologist; b. Atlanta, May 31, 1930; d. Charles Laban and Susan (Lowell) Pardee; B.A., Cornell U., 1951; M.P.H., Johns Hopkins, 1968; m. Timothy Danforth Baker, June 23, 1951; children—Timothy D., David C., Susan L. Research asst. Psychobiology Lab., Johns Hopkins, 1951-53, data analyst, dept. chronic diseases, 1962-66, instr. epidemiology and biostatistics, 1966-67, research asso., div. forensic pathology, 1968-71, asst. prof., 1971—; research asso. Office Chief Med. Examiner, 1968—. Chmn. United Appeal, Balt., 1962. Bd. dirs. Balt. Safety Council. Mem. Am. Assn. Automotive Medicine (dir., pres. elect), Am. Trauma Soc. (founding mem.), Mortar Board, Phi Beta Kappa, Kappa Alpha Theta. Episcopalian. Home: 4705 Keswick Rd Baltimore MD 21210 Office: Johns Hopkins U Sch Hygiene Baltimore MD 21205

BAKER, VERNA TOMLINSON (MRS. EARL M. BAKER), librarian; b. Phila., Apr. 14, 1915; d. Joseph Ullman and Mabel (Dolton) Tomlinson; student (scholar) Temple U., 1937-39, Phila. Coll. Bible, 1959-62; B.S., Bryan Coll., 1963; M.A., George Peabody Coll., 1964; M.A., Chgo. Grad. Sch. Theology, 1970; m. Earl M. Baker, Dec. 31, 1938 (dec. Nov. 1958); children—Earl M. III, B. Kimball. Asst. to expediter Brit. Admiralty Delegation, Naval Aviation Supply Depot, Phila., 1944-45; sec., manuscript reader Westminster Press, Phila., 1947-53; librarian Ben Lippen Sch., Asheville, N.C., 1953-58; gen. library work Nashville Pub. Library, 1963-64; with King's Coll., Briarcliff Manor, N.Y., 1964—, reader services librarian, 1967—. Mem. N.Y., Westchester library assns. Christian Librarians fellow, 1965—. Author: Here in the Spring, 1968. Contbr. poems to anthologies, various mags. Office: King's Coll Briarcliff Manor NY 10510

BAKER, VIOLET EVA SIMMONS, chemist; b. Phila., Nov. 18, 1932; A.B., U. Pa., 1953; Ph.D. in Inorganic Chemistry (Univ. fellow, NSF fellow), Boston U., 1963; m. 1964; 2 children. Instr. chemistry Wellesley Coll., 1958-59; Ramsay Meml. fellow, also NATO fellow in sci. Oxford (Eng.) U., 1963-64; adminstrv. asst. to chmn. dept. chemistry Georgetown U., Washington, 1964-65, 69—, lectr. chemistry, 1967-68. Mem. Am., Brit. chem. socs. Research on structures, properties and bonding in heteropoly electrolytes, coordination complexes, magnetic interaction theory. Office: Dept of Chemistry Georgetown University Washington DC 20007

BAKER, VIRGINIA HARRIET, research exec.; b. Scranton, Pa., Dec. 8, 1938; d. Samuel and May (Naidorff) Baker; B.S., Pa. State U., 1960; M.D., Woman's Med. Coll. Pa., 1964; M.P.H., Columbia, 1968. Intern Mt. Zion Hosp. and Med. Center, San Francisco, 1964-65; resident obstetrics and gynecology Women's Med. Coll., Phila., 1965-66, pub. health resident N.Y.C. Health Dept., 1966-69, dist. health officer, 1969-73, mgr. health service, 1972-73; asst. dir. clin. research Schering Corp., Bloomfield, N.J., 1973—. Mem. Am., N.Y.C. pub. health assns., Am. Med. Women's Assn., A.M.A., Kings County, N.Y. State med. socs., Profl. Women's Caucus, Royal Soc. Health. Home: 172 Washington St Bloomfield NJ 07003 Office: Schering Corp 60 Orange St Bloomfield NJ 07003

BAKER, VIVIAN HORNSBY MCLAIN, architect; b. Tallassee, Ala., Oct. 23, 1924; d. John Hamilton and Vivian Iione (Hornsby) McLain; student in archtl. design Auburn U., 1946-50; 1 son, Jonathan. Designer, Reed Engring. Co., Carthage, Mo., 1951-52; architect Allgeir-Martin & Assos., architects, 1952-66; self-employed as architect, Joplin, Mo., 1966—. Bd. dirs. Am. Cancer Soc. Served with WAC, 1944-46. Prin. archtl. works include Residential Housing for the Sisters of Mercy, Omaha Province, Joplin, Mo. Home: 3407 Oak Ridge Dr Joplin MO 64801 Office: 512 E 32d St Joplin MO 64801

BALARDO, MARILYNN JEAN, adminstrv. judge; b. Kent County, Mich., Apr. 3, 1924; d. Lyle J. and Marion Elizabeth (Watson) Thompson; A.A., Grand Rapids Jr. Coll., 1957; B.A. with high distinction, U. Mich., 1959, J.D., 1962; 1 dau., Cynthia Cheryll. Admitted to Mich. bar, 1962; atty. N.Y. Central R.R., Detroit, 1962-63, Mich. Legislative Service Bur., Lansing, 1963; practice law, Detroit, 1964-73; hearing officer Mich. Dept. Licensing and Regulation, Lansing, 1973—. Mem. State Central Com., 1968-72; co-chmn. credentials com. State Conv., 1972. Mem. State Bar Mich., Detroit Bar Assn. (mem. recorders ct. com., speaker for speakers bur.), Women Lawyers of Mich., Mich. Inter-Profl. Assn., Urban League, Phi Beta Kappa, Delta Pi Alpha. Club: Buenos Vecinos (Grosse Pointe, Mich.). Home: 11800 Duchess St Detroit MI 48224 Office: 1008 S Washington St Lansing MI 48926

BALCHEN, BESS INGER ENGELBRETHSEN, editor; b. Oslo, Norway; d. Ingvald A. and Hildegard (Jaeger) Engelbrethsen; came to U.S., 1948, naturalized, 1952; grad. Sch. Journalism, Comml. Coll., Norway; student Nat. Sch. Dress Design, Chgo., 1954-55; m. Bernt Balchen, Feb. 26, 1948 (div. Oct. 1966); 1 son, Laurtiz. Mem. editorial rev. staff Jacob Dybwad Pub. Co., Oslo, Norway, 1939-45; corr. in U.S. for Morgenbladet, Oslo, 1945-46; free lance writer, researcher, corr., 1946-66; asst. editor Fordham publ., Fordham U., 1966-67; mng. editor A.I.A. Jour., Washington, 1967-74; editor Traffic Engring., 1974—. Mem. Soc. Woman Geographers. Author: Summer Holidays in Alaska, 1951; (cookbook) Food in a Flying Hurry, 1951. Home: 1307 Forestwood Dr McLean VA 22101 Office: AIA 1735 New York Av Washington DC 20006

BALCOM, MARGARET PLUMB (MRS. STEPHEN VAUGHN BALCOM), journalist; b. San Diego, Sept. 21, 1946; d. Robert Thompson and Elsie Jane (Burkett) Plumb; student U. So. Cal., 1964-65, U. Ore., 1965-66; m. Stephen Vaughn Balcom, Nov. 26, 1966; 1 son, Stephen Vaughn. Pub. information and communications specialist, writer News Bur., U. N.C., Chapel Hill., 1970—. Active P.T.A. Mem. Women in Communications (v.p. 1971-72, pres. 1972-73), Chapel Hill Art Guild, Internat. Order Job's Daus., Chi Omega. Methodist. Home: 400 Knob Court Chapel Hill NC 27514 Office: 306 Bynum Hall Univ North Carolina Chapel Hill NC 27514

BALD, MARGARET, librarian; b. Pitts., Sept. 3, 1913; d. Edmund James and Margaret Louise (Siemon) Bald; B.A., Asbury Coll., 1934; B.S. in L.S., Carnegie Inst. Tech., 1935. Library asst. Carnegie Library, Pitts., 1935-37; asst. librarian Carnegie-Ill. Steel Corp., Pitts., 1937-40; library asst. Pasadena (Cal.) Pub. Library, 1940-44; various positions Bur. Naval Personnel, Washington and Norfolk, Va., 1944-48; head librarian Bob Jones U., Greenville, S.C., 1948—, prof. library sci., 1958—. Mem. Southeastern, S.C. library assns., Univ. Opera Assn. Contbg. author: Careers for Christian Youth, 1956; How I Found God's Will for My Life, 1960. Address: Bob Jones U Greenville SC 29614

BALDASSANO, CORINNE LESLIE, broadcasting exec.; b. N.Y.C., May 16, 1950; d. Nicholas and Olga (Phillips) Baldassano; B.A. cum laude, Queens Coll., 1970; postgrad. Hunter Coll., 1970—. Asst. to Dean Lewis, news commentator, WHN radio, N.Y.C., 1970-72, asso. producer These Are Your Schs., 1971-72, producer Dean Lewis Interviews, 1972; music dir. WHN Radio, 1972-73, WPLJ-FM Radio, N.Y.C., 1973—. Mem. A.F.T.R.A., Am. Theatre Assn., Internat. Radio and TV Soc., Am. Mensa Soc. Roman Catholic. Club: Manhattan Theatre (N.Y.C.). Home: 12-25 31st Av Astoria NY 11106 Office: 1330 Av Americas New York City NY 10019

BALDERSTON, JEAN MERRILL (MRS. DAVID CHASE BALDERSTON), psychotherapist; b. Providence, Aug. 29, 1936; d. Frederick Augustus and Helen May (Cleveland) Merrill; B.A., U. Conn., 1957; M.A., Columbia, 1965, Ed.D., 1968; m. David Chase Balderston, June 1, 1957. Mem. faculty Douglass Coll. for Women, also Rutgers U., New Brunswick, N.J., 1965-68, Queens Coll., N.Y.C., 1966-69, Hunter Coll., N.Y.C., 1968-71, Montclair (N.J.) State Coll., 1966-68; pvt. practice as psychotherapist, N.Y.C., 1968—. Vis. prof. Tchrs. Coll., Columbia N.Y.C., summers 1968-70, Mt. St. Vincent U., Halifax, N.S., Can., summer, 1970; asso. Gould Farm, residental mental health treatment center, Monterey, Mass., 1971—; cons. asso. Homosexual Community Counseling Center, N.Y. U., 1971—. Active poetry workshops, N.Y.C.; poetry readings. Mem. Am. Psychol. Assn., Nat. Council on Family Relations, Am. Assn. Marriage and Family Counselors, Nat. Orgn. for Women, N.Y. Assn. Marriage and Family Counselors. Editorial staff N.Y. Quar., N.Y.C., 1971—; editorial bd. Homosexual Counseling jour., N.Y.C., 1973—. Address: 1225 Park Av New York City NY 10028

BALDRIDGE, EMILY MAE GAHR (MRS. JOE BRASFIELD BALDRIDGE), educator; b. Miami, Fla., Nov. 18, 1928; d. Douglas Hutchins and Hazel (Harryman) Gahr; A.B., Fla. State U., 1950; M.S., Ind. U., 1952; postgrad. Stetson U., 1959, U. S. Fla., 1964; m. Joe Brasfield Baldridge, Aug. 24, 1955; children—Suzanne Gahr, James Douglas. Asst. dean women Vanderbilt U., Nashville, 1951; head counselor Okla. State U., Stillwater, 1952-55; tchr. Shelby County Sch., Memphis, 1955-57, Edgewater High Sch., Orlando, Fla., 1957-59; guidance coordinator Mid-Fla. Tech. Inst., Orlando, 1966-74; guidance dir. Edgewater High Sch., Orlando, 1974—. Active Orlando Day Nursery Assn., 1965—. Mem. N.E.A., Fla. Edn. Assn., Classroom Tchrs. Assn., Orange County Guidance Assn., Fla. State Pharmacy Aux., Pi Lambda Theta. Presbyn. (Sunday sch. tchr. 1964—). Republican. Home: 1055 Lancaster Dr Orlando FL 32806

BALDWIN, ANNE NORRIS (MRS. ROBERT L. BALDWIN), author; b. Phila., Mar. 25, 1938; d. Robert Fogg and Mary Morris (Scattergood) Norris; B.A. summa cum laude, Smith Coll., 1959; Ph.D., Harvard, 1963; m. Robert Lesh Baldwin, Aug. 28, 1965; children—David Norris, Eric Lawrence. NIH postdoctoal fellow biochemistry, Stanford, 1963-65; ind. research under NSF grant, 1965-66; author children's fiction The Sometimes Island, 1969; Sunflowers for Tina, 1970; Sunlight Valley, 1971; A Friend in the Park, 1973; Jenny's Revenge, 1974. Home: 1243 Los Trancos Rd Portola Valley CA 94025

BALDWIN, E. JOAN BOLLING (MRS. DONALD WINSTON BALDWIN), govt. ofcl.; b. Norton, Va., Aug. 31, 1930; d. Henry Cecil and Nelle (Mann) Bolling; A.B., Hollins Coll., 1953; M.A., U. Va., 1955; m. Donald Winston Baldwin, Nov. 16, 1957; children—Winston Monroe, Elizabeth Bolling, Alan Henry. Adminstrv. sec. to asst. register of copyrights Library of Congress, 1955-59; profl. staff mem. U.S. Senate Republican Policy Com., 1959-62; press and research asst. to U.S. Senator Len B. Jordan, 1962-64; polit. analyst, researcher Rep. Nat. Com., 1964; polit. researcher James N. Juliana & Assos., Washington, 1964-69; legislative asst. to U.S. Senator James B. Pearson, Washington, 1969-71; spl. asst. to asst. sec. for community and field services Dept. Health, Edn. and Welfare, Washington, 1971-73; mem. profl. staff for legislation U.S. Senate Rep. Policy Com., 1973—. Treas. Twig, Alexandria, Va., 1968. Pres. Alexandria Rep. Women's Club, 1965-66. Mem. D.A.R. (chpt. provisional mem.), Chi Omega Alumnae No. Va., Hollins Coll. Alumnae No. Va. Episcopalian. Clubs: Belle Haven Country (Alexandria), Capitol Hill (Washington). Home: 1309 Trinity Dr Alexandria VA 22314 Office: 333 Russell Senate Office Bldg Washington DC 20510

BALDWIN, ELISABETH GRACE, occupational therapist; b. Brookings, S.D., Dec. 20, 1919; d. Thomas Whitfield and Regina Elisabeth (Petrich) Baldwin; grad. Phila. Sch. Occupational Therapy, 1943; B.F.A. with high honors, U. Ill., 1945. Occupational therapist Danville (Pa.) State Hosp., 1943-45; tchr. Wood's Sch., Pa., 1946-47; mem. staff Liverpool (Eng.) Sch. Occupational Therapy, 1947-49; head occupational therapy Walton Hosp., Liverpool, 1949—. Painter, works exhibited throughout so. U.S. Mem. Am., English occupational therapy assns. Home: 807 Schwartz St Carbondale IL 62901 Office: Walton Hosp Liverpool 9 England

BALDWIN, ELLEN JANE (MRS. HAL WEST), real estate co. exec.; b. N.Y.C.; d. Whitney and Edna Estelle (Bolles) Eckert; student N.Y. Sch. Design, 1956-58, New Sch. Coll. City N.Y., 1958-60; Lic. Broker, Anthony Sch. Real Estate, 1969; m. Hal West, Oct. 18, 1968; children (by previous marriage)—Richard A., Suzanne E. Real estate salesman, 1963-71; owner Baldwin West and Assos., San Rafael, 1971—. Sec., Marin County (Cal.) Cerebral Palsy, 1962-64. Mem. Santa Margarita Valley Homeowners Assn. (dir. 1972—, v.p. 1972—), Nat. Assn. Real Estate Brokers, Million Dollar Club. Home: 16 Galleon Way San Rafael CA 94903 Office: 200 Northgate One San Rafael CA 94903

BALDWIN, ESTHER EBERSTADT (MRS. ROBERT HOWE BALDWIN), personnel and ins. co. exec.; b. East Orange, N.J.; d. Edward Frederick and Elenita Contreras (Lembcke) Eberstadt; B.A., Notre Dame Coll. Md., 1919, M.A. (hon.), 1941, LL.D., 1958; Mus.B., Am. Inst. Applied Music, 1921; m. Robert Howe Baldwin, June 7, 1933. Pres., Mrs. E.E. Brooke, Inc., Personnel Cons., N.Y.C., 1923—, Robert H. Baldwin, Inc., Ins. Brokers, N.Y.C., 1955—; v.p. Davis, Dorland & Co., N.Y.C., 1955—. Lectr. to colls., bus. and profl. groups. Mem. nat. council U.S. Com. for Refugees, 1963-64; mem. White House Conf. For World Refugee, 1963; mem. nat. council Am. Friends of Middle East, 1956-63, Pakistan-Am. Students Assn., 1957-62; mem. Greater N.Y. council Boy Scouts Am., 1956-58; Greater N.Y. chpt. ANTA. Pres. Robert H. Baldwin Found., 1956—. Mem. bd., exec. Com. Women's Nat. Republican Club, 1956-60, now life member. Bd. dirs., chmn., pres. Am. Com. to Befriend Arab Refugees, 1958—; bd. dirs. Council on Islamic Affairs, 1957-65, vice-chmn., 1958-63; bd. dirs. Near East Found., Notre Dame Coll. Md., Camp Fire Girls, Inc., Internat. Ednl. Devel.; mem. nat. council Met. Opera, 1967—; mem. Pres.'s Council Columbia. Decorated Order Chevalier Ct. by Shah of Iran; recipient Pres.'s Medal Coll. Notre Dame. Fellow Archeol. Inst. Am., Am. Geog. Soc.; founding mem. Jr. League of Oranges (Orange, N.J.); life mem. Acad. Polit.

Sci., Am. Mus. Natural History, Assistance League So. Cal. Met. Mus. Art, N.Y. Zool. Soc.; mem. Nat. Inst. Social Scis., Pakistan-Am. C. of C., Soc. Women Geographers, Am. Assn. U. Women, English Speaking Union, Columbia Assos., Soc. of Jesus (hon.), Delta Epsilon Sigma. Author: The Girl and Her Job, 1933; Career Clinic, 1940; The Right Job For You and How To Get It, 1944; Career Guide, 1943; Guide to Career Success, 1947; You and Your Personality, 1949. Contbr. articles to Cosmopolitan, Good Housekeeping, Mademoiselle, others. Home: 4 Pleasant St Woodstock VT 05091 Office: Hotel Imperial Vienna I Austria

BALDWIN, ESTHER LILLIAN, pianist, composer; b. Chgo.; d. George and Minnie Neidigh; pvt. study Dr. Francis Hemington Chgo.; B.Mus., Columbia Sch. Music and Art, 1946, Mus.D., 1951. Tchr., dir. Baldwin Music Studios, Columbia, S.C., 1927—, concert pianist, 1946—; composer Sonata in C Major; Sonata in D Major. Adjudicator Nat. Guild Piano Tchrs. Fellow Internat. Inst. Arts and Letters; mem. Exec. and Profl. Hall of Fame (bd. govs.), Internat. Platform Assn., Internat. Pianist's Guild, Piano Guild Hall of Fame, Musicians Club Am., Am. Coll. Musicians, Nat. Guild Piano Tchrs. (chmn. Columbia Mus. Sch. chpt.). Home: Davis Hotel Box 114 Columbia SC 29202

BALDWIN, FAITH, writer; b. New Rochelle, N.Y., Oct. 1, 1893; d. Stephen Charles and Edith Hervey (Finch) Baldwin; ed. Briarcliff, Mrs. Dow's Sch., Briarcliff Manor, N.Y.; m. Hugh H. Cuthrell, Nov. 6, 1920 (dec. Aug. 1953); children—Hugh (dec.), Hervey, Stephen, Ann. Nat. sponsor, dir. Conn., Save the Children Fedn. Bd. dirs. Silver Hill Found. Mem. Women's Nat. Book Assn. Author: Mavis of Green Hill, 1921; Laurel of Stony Stream, 1923; Magic and Mary Rose, 1924; Signposts (verse), 1924; Thresholds, 1925; Those Difficult Years, 1925; Three Women, 1926; Departing Wings, 1927; Alimony, 1928; Garden Oats, 1929; The Incredible Year, 1929; Broadway Interlude (with Achmed Abdullah), 1929; Office Wife, 1930; Make Believe, 1930; Judy (juvenile), 1931; Skyscraper, 1931; Babs and Mary Lou (juveniles), 1931; Myra (juvenile), 1932; Week-End Marriage, 1932; District Nurse, 1932; Self-Made Woman, 1932; Girl-on-the-Make (with Achmed Abdullah), 1932; Beauty, 1933; White Collar Girl, 1933; Love's a Puzzle, 1933; InnocentBystander, 1934; Honor Bound, 1934; Within a Year, 1934; American Family, 1935; The Puritan Strain, 1935; The Moon's Our Home, 1935; This Man is Mine, 1936; Men Are Such Fools, 1936; The Heart Has Wings, 1937; Twenty-Four Hours a Day, 1937; Manhattan Nights, 1937; Enchanted Oasis, 1938; Rich Girl, Poor Girl, 1938; Hotel Hostess, 1938; The High Road, 1939; Career By Proxy, 1939; White Magic, 1939; Station Wagon, 1939; Rehearsed for Love, 1939; Something Special, 1939; Letty and the Law, 1940; Medical Centre, 1940; And New Stars Burn, 1941; Temporary Address: Reno, 1941; The Heart Remembers, 1941; Blue Horizons, 1942; Breath of Life, 1942; Five Women in Three Novels, 1942; Rest of My Life with You, 1942; Washington, U.S.A., 1943; You Can't Escape, 1943; He Married a Doctor, 1943; Change of Heart, 1944; Arizona Star, 1945; A Job for Jenny, 1945; No Private Heaven, 1946; Woman on Her Way, 1946; Sleeping Beauty, 1947; Give Love the Air, 1947; Marry for Money, 1948; They Who Love, 1948; Golden Shoestring, 1949; Lookout for Liza, 1950; The Whole Armor (book), 1956; (poems) Widow's Walk, 1954; Three Faces of Love, 1957; Many Windows, 1958; Blaze of Sunlight, 1958; Testament of Trust, 1960; The West Wind, 1962; Harvest of Hope, 1962; The Lonely Man, 1964; Living by Faith, 1964; also serials, short stories and verse. Contbr. to Woman's Day mag., 1958—. Radio and motion pictures from books and stories: Apartment for Peggy, 1948; Second Chance, 1950; The Juniper Tree, 1952. Republican. Home: Route 2 Weed Av Norwalk CT 06850

BALDWIN, LOIS KAHL (MRS. WILLIAM S. BALDWIN), civic worker; b. Balt., Apr. 9, 1928; d. Christian Henry and Marion Sayford (Meese) Kahl; student N.J. Coll. for Women, 1945-47; B.A., Goucher Coll., 1949; postgrad. Johns Hopkins, 1949-50, Innsbruck U., 1951-53; m. William Smith Baldwin, Aug. 5, 1960; children—William Streett, Nancy Lois. Tchr. Balt. City Pub. Schs., 1949-50; agt. Christian H. Kahl & Co., Inc., Towson, Md., 1953-55, 57-59; tchr. Baltimore County pub. schs., 1956-57; mem. staff Un-Am. Activities Com., Washington, 1959-60; jud. sec. Baltimore County Circuit Ct., 1960-63; tchr. English to German-speaking adults USIS, Innsbruck, Austria, 1951-52. Mem. Baltimore County Commn. on Aging, 1968—, chmn., 1970—; del. White House Conf. on Aging, 1971; mem. Baltimore County Bi-Centennial Steering Com., 1973—. Vice pres. Baltimore County Young Democrats, 1954-55; exec. sec. Young Democratic Clubs Md., 1955-56, nat. committeewoman, 1956-57, spl. asst. to pres., 1957-58. Bd. dirs. Baltimore County Sr. Centers, 1962—. Home: 406 Campbell Lane Towson MD 21204 Office: 121 W Susquehanna Av Towson MD 21204

BALDWIN, MARCIA, mezzo soprano; b. Milford, Neb., Nov. 5, 1936; d. George W. and Edna (Carlson) Baldwin; student Music Sch., Northwestern U. Debut in recital Carnegie Hall, N.Y.C., 1959; apprentice Santa Fe Opera Co., 1960-61, Balt. Symphony Orch., 1961; W. coast tour of Rigoletto with Goldovsky Opera Theatre, 1962; appearances with San Francisco Spring Opera, 1962, Cin. Zoo Opera, 1963, Met. Opera Co., 1963—, Phila. Lyric Opera, 1964, 65, Central City Opera Festival, Central City, Colo., 1964, 66, Am. Opera Soc., 1966. Ford Found. fellow, 1962; recipient award Internat. Music Competition, Munich, Germany, 1962. Mem. Alpna Phi. Home: 155 W 68th St New York City NY 10023 Office: Metropolitan Opera Co Lincoln Center Plaza New York City NY 10023

BALDWIN, RUBYE MAE MCCANDLESS (MRS. DANIEL BALDWIN), banker; b. Chulahoma, Miss.; d. C. P. and Luvie (Palmer) McCandless; student extension accounting course U. Miss., 1950, Northwestern U. Trust Sch., 1969; m. Daniel Baldwin, Oct. 17, 1962. With Coahoma Nat. Bank, Clarksdale, Miss., 1940—, trust officer, 1966—, v.p., 1968—. Dir. Hirsh Delta Electronics, Inc., Memphis; co-owner, operator RuDan Bowling Lanes, Clarksdale, Miss., 1966—; past mem. Miss. adv. council Small Bus. Adminstrn. Mem. Hwy. Improvement Com. Bd. dirs. Clarksdale Community Concerts Assn., North Miss. Recreation Devel. Commn. sec.-treas. Clarksdale Speech and Hearing Center, 1960—. Mem. Nat. Assn. Bank Women (regional v.p. 1966, pres. Miss. group, transp. chmn. regional conf. and chmn. nomination com. North Miss. group 1969-70, nat. rec. sec. 1970-71, mem. pub. relations com. 1973-74), Clarksdale Bus. and Profl. Women's Club (pres. 1951-52, Woman of Achievement 1971), Delta Council and Coahoma County C. of C. (chmn. recreation and tourism com. 1973-74), Am. Bankers Assn. (chmn. dist. 2 savs. bond program 1972—), Bank Adminstrn. Inst. (dir. Delta chpt., sec. 1974—), Beta Sigma Phi. Baptist. Club: Zonta (Clarksdale, pres. 1959-60). Home: 745 W Pecan St Clarksdale MS 38614 Office: Coahoma Nat Bank Delta and 3d Sts Clarksdale MS 38614

BALDWIN, RUTH WORKMAN, pediatrician; b. Chgo., Nov. 3, 1915; d. John J. and Lucille (Hayes) Workman; student Lewis Inst., 1936-38; B.S., U. Md., 1942 M.D., 1943; m. Gary Martin Baldwin, Sept. 2, 1939; children—John Workman, Gary Martin, Thomas Michael, Robert Hayes. Intern, asst. resident, then resident medicine West Balt. Gen. Hosp., 1944-46; asst. resident, fellow pediatrics U. Hosp., 1948-50; pvt. practice Catonsville, Md., 1946-48, 50-52; asst. prof. pediatrics, dir. seizure unit U. Md. Sch. Medicine, 1950-64, asso. prof. pediatrics, 1964—, asst. electroencephalographer, 1952; dir. clinic for the exceptional child; cons. Rosewood State Tng. Sch., Md. State Dept. Health. Mem. Md. Council Developmental Disabilities; mem. adv. bd. Assn. for Mentally Handicapped Children in Md., Md. Eastern Shore Epilepsy Assn. Chesapeake Assn. Epilepsy, Assn. Children with Specific Learning Disabilities, others; chmn. med. adv. bd. Dept. Motor Vehicles, Md. Diplomate Am. Bd. Pediatrics. Fellow Am. Acad. Pediatrics: mem. Med. and Chirurg. Faculty of Md., Am. Acad. Neurology (asso.), Eastern Assn. Electroencephalographers. Republican. Presbyn. (elder). Club: Soroptimist (Catonsville, Md.). Home: 324 Gun Rd Relay MD 21227 Office: U Hosp Baltimore MD 21201

BALDWIN, VELMA NEVILLE WILSON (MRS. CLAUDE DAVID BALDWIN), govt. ofcl.; b. Meade, Kan., Aug. 31, 1918; d. Charles Chester and Anna Velma (Neville) Wilson; A.B., U. Kan., 1940; m. Claude David Baldwin, Jan. 31, 1942. Placement working students U. Kan., 1940-41; personnel War Dept., Washington, 1942-45; research asst. Dr. A.C. Kinsey, Ind. U., 1946; with Carter Oil Co., Denver, 1948-50; personnel Bur. of Budget, Washington, 1951-55; asst. to dir. personnel Treasury Dept., 1955-59; personnel officer, dir. adminstrn. Office Mgmt. and Budget, 1959—. Mem. Am. Soc. Pub. Adminstrn. (past exec. bd.), Soc. for Personnel Adminstrn. (exec. bd.). Home: 2234 49th St NW Washington DC 20007 Office: Office of Mgmt and Budget Washington DC 20503

BALE, HELEN TIERNEY (MRS. HUGH NEWTON BALE), editor; b. West Paterson, N.J., Dec. 25, 1920; d. James J. and Catherine (Troast) Tierney; m. Hugh Newton Bale, Sept. 9, 1950; children—Lila E. (Mrs. Jay Levinson), Michelle Y. (Mrs. John Dubois), James A. Reporter, Evening News, Paterson, N.J., 1937-45; stringer Asso. Press, Newark, 1945; reporter, feature writer Telegraph-Herald, Dubuque, Ia., 1947-48; reporter, photographer Rock Island (Ill.) Argus, 1948-51; editor-pub. Chronicle, Odebolt, Ia., 1952; head woman's dept. Star & Register Republic, Rockford, Ill., 1952-54, dir. woman's programs WREX-TV, 1954-55; newscaster-producer radio and tv news KCRA Inc., Sacramento, 1955-58; newscaster, Producer KOVR-TV, Sacramento, 1958-66; asso. editor Auburn (Cal.) Jour., 1966-72, editor, 1972—; editor subsidiary newspaper Placer Herald, Rocklin, Cal., 1966—. Active A.R.C., 1947-52. Trustee Placer (Cal.) Joint Union High Sch., 1967-73, chmn. bd. 1970-73. Mem. Mental Hygiene Soc., Cal. Sch. Bd. Assn. (del. assembly 1971). Home: Newcastle CA Office: 1031 High St Auburn CA 95603

BALES, GERTRUDE ARCHER (MRS. HAROLD W. BALES), otolaryngologist; b. Greensboro, N.C., Feb. 16, 1926; d. David Ross and Jennie Lee (Hunter) Archer; A.B. cum laude, U. N.C., 1948, postgrad., 1948-50; M.D., U. Rochester (N.Y.), 1952; m. Harold W. Bales, Aug. 15, 1953; children—Laura Lee, Susan Locke. Intern Strong Meml. Hosp., Rochester, 1952-53, resident otolaryngology, 1953-55; staff physician VA Hosp., Batavia, N.Y., 1956; practice medicine specializing in otolaryngology, Rochester, 1956—; mem. staff Strong Meml. Hosp., Rochester, Highland Hosp., Rochester; cons. VA hosps., Batavia and Canandaigua, N.Y.; sr. instr. otolaryngology U. Rochester, 1955-61, asst. prof., 1963-68, clin. asso. prof., 1968—. Diplomate Am. Bd. Otolaryngology. Fellow A.C.S.; mem. Am. Acad. Ophthalmology and Otolaryngology, Am. Council Otolaryngology, Central N.Y., Rochester ear, nose and throat socs., Rochester Pathol. Soc., N.Y. State, Monroe County med. socs., Rochester Acad. Medicine, Centurion Deafness Research Club, Phi Beta Kappa. Home: 1924 Clark Rd Rochester NY 14625 Office: 335 Mt Vernon Av Rochester NY 14620

BALF, MARY BURCH (MRS. CHARLES L. BALF), mus. curator; b. Lowestoft, Eng., Aug. 13, 1920; d. James Cyril and Marhery England (Morriss) Burch; B.A. with honors (state scholar), Oxford U., Eng., 1942, B.M., B.Ch., 1945; m. C.L. Balf, Aug. 4, 1943 (dec. Oct. 1960); children—Richard John, Margaret Ann (Mrs. John Lyon), Ruth Elizabeth. Curator, Kamloops (B.C., Can.) Mus., 1966—, lectr., 1967—. Dir., Pollution Probe, Kamloops, 1970. Mem. B.C. Mus's. Assn., (pres. 1973), Kamloops U. Women (pres. 1959), Mika Nika Club (dir. 1962), B.C. Archivists Assn. Author: Kamloops History, 1969; hist. booklets. Contbr. hist. articles to local newspapers. Office: 207 Seymour St Kamloops BC Canada

BALFANZ, ROBERTA FARRAR, clothing shop owner; b. Axtell, Kan., Feb. 19, 1914; d. Henry Horatio and Ivy W. (Riley) Farrar; A.B., Baker U., 1934; m. William R. Balfanz, Oct. 25, 1936 (div. 1949); 1 son, William Farrar. Tchr. high sch., Parkerville, Kan., 1934-35; saleslady various shops, 1935-36; corset dept. buyer Wolke & Kotler, Chgo., 1937-39, The Fair, 1939-41; with transp. dept. Green River Ordnance Plant, Amboy, Ill., 1941-43; mgr. Farrar's, Kansas City, Mo., 1943-44; buyer Marshall Field & Co., Chgo., 1944-46; owner, operator of Roberta Balfanz Maternity Wardrobes, Evanston, Ill., 1946-71, Hawaiian Shop, 1964—. Budget bd. Evanston United Fund, 1950-59; dir. Evanston Family Service, 1950-54; mem. Evanston Welfare Council, 1959-63. Bd. dirs. Kendall Coll. Mem. Bus. and Profl. Womens Club (pres. Evanston, 1954-56), C. of C. (dir. 1952-57, chmn. mchts. council 1957-58, v.p. 1959-60), Am. Assn. U. Women, Alpha Chi Omega. Republican. Presbyn. Clubs: University (Evanston); Zonta (treas. 1952-54). Home: 1411 Mulford St Evanston IL 60202 Office: 1630 Orrington Av Evanston IL 60201

BALFOUR, BERNICE ELAINE BRILE (MRS. LEO BALFOUR), copyeditor, writer; b. N.Y.C., Nov. 7, 1922; d. Lawrence Miller and Fanny Molly (Rosenthal) Brile; B.A., Wooster Coll., 1944; m. Leo Balfour, Aug. 21, 1955; 1 dau., Laura. Textbook copyeditor Harcourt Brace Jovanovich, Inc., N.Y.C., 1956-60; freelance copyeditor, writer, Anaheim, Cal., 1960—. Recipient various awards. Mem. Writers Club Whittier, Inc., Nat. Orgn. Women. Editor: Radical Sophistication (Max F. Schulz), 1969; Forgotten Children (Richard Greene Leswing), 1972. Address: 1219 Ralston St Anaheim CA 92801

BALICK, HELEN SHAFFER (MRS. BERNARD BALICK), judge; b. Bloomsburg, Pa., Oct. 2, 1935; d. Walter W. and Clarissa K. (Bennett) Shaffer; J.D., Dickinson Sch. Law, 1966; m. Bernard Balick, June 29, 1967. Admitted to Pa. bar, 1967, Del. bar, 1969; probate adminstr. Girard Trust Bank, Phila., 1966-68; staff atty. Legal Aid Soc. Del., Wilmington, 1968-71; master Family Ct. of the State Del., Wilmington, 1971-74; now bankruptcy judge, fed. magistrate. Mem., Citizens Adv. Com., Wilmington, 1973-74. Pres. bd. trustees Community Legal Aid Soc., 1972-74, Wilmington Bd. Edn., 1974—. Mem. Pa., Del. Bar assns., Del. Council on Crime and Justice, Phi Alpha Delta. Home: 2319 W 17th St Wilmington DE 19806 Office: 844 King St Wilmington DE 19801

BALK, JUDITH ANN MECUM (MRS. MELVIN W. BALK), educator; b. Bloomington, Ill., Sept. 5, 1944; d. Glenn Weston and Ernestine (Yanney) Mecum; B.S., Ill. State U., 1966; M.Ed., U. Ill., 1967; m. Melvin W. Balk, June 8, 1969. Grad. asst. Office Dean Women, U. Ill. at Urbana, 1966-67, head resident, 1967-69; tchr., counselor St. Andrews Sch., Bethesda, Md., 1969-70; tchr. Montgomery County Schs., Bethesda, 1970-73; tchr. Hershey (Pa.) Elementary Sch., 1973—. Mem. Nat. Assn. Women Deans and Counselors, Ill. Guidance and Personnel Assn., N.E.A., Pa. Edn. Assn., Army Surgeon Gen. Wives, Am. Vet. Wives' Assn., Faculty Wives Orgn. Milton S. Hershey Med. Center Pa. State U., Hui O Wahine, Tripler Officers Wives' Club. Home: 6829 N Ottawa Chicago IL 60631 Office: 47-761-2 Hui Kelu Kaneohe HI 96744

BALKUS, THELMA LOUISE (MRS. JOSEPH F. BALKUS), city ofcl.; b. Denver, Jan. 26, 1915; d. C. Guy and Mary (Ganschow) Boatwright; student extension courses U. Cal. at Los Angeles, 1938-39; m. Joseph F. Balkus, Feb. 17, 1941; children-Jo Ann (Mrs. Charles B. Tanner), Joseph C. With travel bur. Continental Oil Co., Denver, 1936-37; secretarial position, artist Burroughs, Inc., dir. mail advt., Los Angeles, 1937-42; secretarial position Wianko Engring., Pasadena and Davidson Optronics, West Covina, Cal., intermittently, 1957-58; city clk. City of Baldwin Park, Cal., 1958—, acting city mgr., 1962-63, 71; adminstrv. aide Baldwin Park City Council, 1959—; sec. Baldwin Park Personnel Bd., 1965—, Charter Commn., 1970-71. Sec. Edgewood Family Counselling Agy., Covina, 1963-64. Mem. Democratic State Central Com., 1969—. Mem. Internat. City Clks. Assn., League Cal. Cities City Clks. Assn., League Women Voters, Baldwin PArk C. of C., Baldwin Park Hist. Soc. (pres. 1970—), Bus. and Profl. Women's Club. Roman Catholic. Clubs: Altrusa (Covina-West Covina); Women's (judge Bank Am. scholarship awards). Home: 4625 N Harlan Av Baldwin Park CA 91706 Office: 14403 E Pacific Av Baldwin Park CA 91706

BALL, BARBARA RUTH, psychologist; b. Chester, Pa., Jan. 27, 1934; d. Herman William and Isabel Victoria (Matthews) Hess; B.S., Bob Jones U., 1955; M.S., Portland State U., 1967; postgrad. U. Ore., 1971; m. Robert W. Ball, Jr., Aug. 18, 1955; children—Margaret, Carolyn, David. Tchr., Henley High Sch., Klamath Falls, Ore., 1955, Kings Garden High Sch., Seattle, 1960, Milwaukee (Ore.) Jr. High Sch., 1964; sch. psychologist Portland (Ore.) Pub. Schs., 1968—. Condr. womens program Your Preschooler, Radio Sta. KGDN, Seattle; moderator parent discussion group Portland Schs.; v.p. Hector Campbell Elementary P.T.A.; diagnostic cons. pvt. facility for trainable children. Mem. Nat. (charter), Ore. (membership com. 1972) assns. sch. psychologists, Portland Psychol. Assn., Council for Exceptional Children. Baptist (Sunday sch. tchr., bd. Christian edn.). Author: Developmental Readiness Scale for Kindergarten Screening, 1972; cons. book Preventing Academic Failure, 1973. Research on preschoolers performance on Wide Range Achievement Test. Home: 1601 SW Country Club Rd Lake Oswego OR 97034 Office: 6318 SW Corbett St Portland OR 97201

BALL, GENEVRA LOUISE, librarian; b. Mayville, N.Y., July 22, 1934; d. Herbert Oscar and Genevra (Green) Ball; B.S., Stetson U., DeLand, Fla., 1956; M.S. in L.S., Syracuse U., 1967. Tchr. grammar sch., Sanford, Fla., 1956-57, elementary sch., Longwood, Fla., 1957-58; tchr., librarian Enterprise (Fla.) Sch., 1958-63; librarian, media specialist Boston Av. Sch., DeLand, Fla., 1963—; area dir. for Volusia County, Fla. Edn. Assn., 1963-65. Charter mem. W. Valusia Meml. Hosp. aux., DeLand, 1962-73; Girl Scout leader, 1955-56. Bd. dirs. Alhambra Villas Home Owners Assn., 1972-73. Mem. Am. Assn. U. Women (2d v.p. chpt. 1965-67, rec. sec. 1961-65), Assn. Childhood Edn. (1st v.p. 1965-66, corr. sec. 1963-65), D.A.R. (chpt. registrar 1969-73; asst. chief page Continental Congress, Washington 1962-65), Bus. and Profl. Women's Club (corr. sec. DeLand 1968-71, 2d v.p. 1969-70), Stetson U. Alumni Assn. (class chmn. for ann. fund drive 1968—), Delta Kappa Gamma. Democrat. Episcopalian. An author Volusia County manual Instructing the Library Assistant, 1965. Home: PO Box 241 DeLand FL 32720 Office: 340 N Boston Av DeLand FL 32720

BALL, HELEN ELIZABETH VOELLMIG (MRS. ROBERT TYLER BALL), office supply co. exec.; b. Detroit; d. William and Ida (Slinger) Voellmig; A.B., Wayne State U., 1929, M.A., 1936, also tchrs. life certificate; studied voice and piano at Detroit Inst. Mus. Art; m. Robert Tyler Ball, June 20, 1936. Tchr. English, Western High Sch., Detroit, 1936-41; sec., buyer Ball Office Supply, Inc., Ann Arbor, Mich., 1953—. Mem. Am. Assn. U. Women, Alpha Gamma Delta. Clubs: Zonta, Ann Arbor Garden, Women's City (charter mem.) (Ann Arbor). Home: 1310 Iroquois Dr Ann Arbor MI 48104 Office: 116 S Main St Ann Arbor MI 48108

BALL, JEAN GAIL LYONS (MRS. EDWIN LEE BALL), realtor; b. Elizabeth City, N.C., Jan. 17, 1927; d. George Cluster and Dorothy Louise (Tillett) Lyons; student Temple U., 1945; diploma Moore Inst. Design, 1945, Kesley Jenney Coll., 1959, Anthony Schs. Real Estate, 1970; m. Edwin Lee Ball, June 28, 1946; 1 dau., Dianna Lee. Profl. fashion model, singer with various agys. including Neufelt, Phila., Walters, Balt., Powers, San Diego, N.Y.C., Fashionality, San Diego, intermittently, 1942-58; owner, broker Ball Realty, El Cajon, Cal., 1970—; pres. Ball/McKinnon, Inc.; owner Dyana's Beauty Salons, El Cajon, 1973—. Exhibited art in shows at Tivoli Hotel Little Gallery, C.Z. various commns. Mem. Nat. League Am. Pen Women, Inc., El Cajon Valley Bd. Realtors, Cal. Real Estate Assn., Nat. Assn. Real Estate Bds. Home: 1787 Hillsdale Rd El Cajon CA 92020 Office: 790 E Washington Av El Cajon CA 92020

BALL, JOYCE (MRS. ROBERT S. BALL), librarian; b. East Paterson, N.J., Oct. 31, 1932; d. Frank Geza and Elizabeth Martha (Hopper) Csaposs; A.B., Douglass Coll., Rutgers U., 1954; M.A., Ind. U., 1959; m. Robert S. Ball, Sept. 10, 1955; children—Stephanie, Valerie, Steven. Asst. chief govt. documents div. Stanford Libraries, 1961-66; head reference/govt. publs. librarian U. Nev., Reno, 1966—. Mem. editorial adv. bd. Congl. Information Service, Washington, 1969—. Mem. Am. (chmn. interdivisional com. on pub. documents 1971-73, Mudge citation com. 1973), Nev. (mem. state library devel. com. 1969—, mem. legislative action com. 1970—, treas. 1973-75, Cal. library assns., Am. Assn. U. Profs., Nat. Soc. Profs., Sigma Delta Pi, Alpha Kappa Delta. Home: 1765 Carlin St Reno NV 89503 Office: U Nev Libraries Reno NV 89507

BALL, MARTHA COLE, city ofcl.; b. Newnan, Ga., Jan. 13, 1922; d. Ed and Mary Elizabeth (Hubbard) Ball; grad. high sch. Stenographer, clk. City of Newnan, 1940-42, asst. city clk., 1942-49, asst. clk., 1955-70, city clk., 1970—; payroll clk. Gaines Constrn. Co., Miami, Fla., 1949-51. Charter mem., dir. City of Newnan Employees Fed. Credit Union, treas., mgr., 1971—; mngr. Coweta County Employees Fed. Credit Union, 1973—. Mem. Ga. Municipal Clks. and Finance Officers Assn. (dir. 1972-73). Club: Pilot (corr. sec. 1971-73, treas. 1974—) (Newnan). Home: 18 Jackson St Newnan GA 30263 Office: PO Box 1193 Newnan GA 30263

BALLANTINE, MORLEY COWLES, newspaper publisher; b. Des Moines, May 21, 1925; d. John and Elizabeth (Bates) Cowles; student Smith Coll., 1943-44, Stanford, 1944-45, U. Minn., 1948-49; m. Arthur Ballantine, July 26, 1947; children—Richard, Elizabeth, William, Helen. Pub. (with husband) Durango (Colo.) Herald, 1952—, Cortez (Colo.) Sentinel, 1958-60. Mem. Colo. Anti-Discrimination Commn., 1959-61; mem. Colo. Com. on Ednl. Endeavor, 1959-63; mem. Colo. bd. League Women Voters, 1954-57, mem. Durango bd., 1953-59; mem. Jud. Dist. Selection Com., 1967-72; pres. S.W. Colo. Mental Health Center, 1964-65; mem. State Welfare Adv. Com., 1967-71, Colo. Population Adv. Council, 1972—; mem. Colo. Commn. Status Women, 1972—. Recipient 1st place award for editorial writing Nat. Fedn. Press Women, 1955, (with husband)

Outstanding Journalist award U. Colo., 1967, Outstanding Alumna award Rosemary Hall, Wallingford, Conn., 1969, (with husband) Distinguished Service award Ft. Lewis Coll., 1970. Clubs: Federated Woman's (Durango); Mill Reef (Antiqua, W.I.); Colo. Press; River (N.Y.C.); Washington Press. Episcopalian. Home: 175 W Park Av Durango CO 81301 Office: care Herald Durango CO 81301

BALLARD, ERNESTA DRINKER, horticulturist; b. Wynnewood, Pa., May 13, 1920; d. Henry S. and Sophie (Hutchinson) Drinker; grad. Pa. Sch. Horticulture for Women, 1954; m. Frederic L. Ballard, Dec. 22, 1939. Pres. Pa. Hort. Soc.; lectr., writer horticulture. Vice pres. Greater Phila. Cultural Alliance. Bd. dirs. Am. Hort. Soc., Am. Bonsai Soc., Pa. Roadside Council, Pa. Program for Women and Girl Offenders, Pa. Environmental Council. Recipient Charles Day Meml. medal Pa. Sch. Horticulture for Women, 1958, certificate of merit Pa. Hort. Soc., 1959, Distinguished Service medal Garden Club Am., 1969; named Distinguished Alumna, Temple U., 1964, Distinguished Daus. Pa., 1968. Author: Garden in Your House, 1958, rev. edit., 1971; The Art of Training Plants, 1962. Editor: Directory Am. Hort. jour, 1971. Home: 9120 Crefeld St Philadelphia PA 19118 Office: 325 Walnut St Philadelphia PA 19106

BALLARD, JEANNETTE EVANS (MRS. GEORGE T. BALLARD), librarian; b. Camden, N.J., Feb. 8, 1917; d. Clinton I. and Bessie J. (Coveney) Evans; B.A., Bucknell U., 1937; M.S. in L.S., Drexel U., 1969; m. George T. Ballard, Nov. 16, 1940; 1 son, James Wray. Library asst. Ins. Co. North Am. Library, Phila., 1966-68, asst. librarian, 1970-72, head librarian, 1972—; asst. circulation librarian U. Pa., Phila., 1969-70. Mem. Spl. Libraries Assn., Am. Soc. Information Sci., Beta Phi Mu. Home: 88 Chelsea Circle Clementon NJ 08021 Office: Ins Co North Am Library 1600 Arch St Philadelphia PA 19101

BALLARD, JULIET LYLE BROOKE BOND, poet, editor; b. Madison, Wis., Feb. 6, 1913; d. Francis Marvin and Juliet Lyle (Chermside) Bond; B.A. in Sociology and Econs. with honors, Randolph-Macon Women's Coll., Lynchburg, Va., 1934; certificate social case work, Coll. William and Mary, 1938; m. Lyttleton Waters Ballard, Sept. 3, 1937; children—Thomas Brooke, Juliet Lyle (Mrs. John H. Lutz). Author poetry pub. in periodicals and anthologies, 1932—; asso. editor A.R.E. Jour., 1966-70, A.R.E. Children's mag., 1970; editor Treasure Trove, 1971-73. Mem. Assn. Research and Enlightment, Am. Poetry League, Composers, Authors and Artists Am., Phi Beta Kappa, Pi Gamma Mu. Author: Under a Tropic Sun, 1945; Winter Has Come, 1945; The Ballad of the Widow's Flag (ofcl. poem Star-Spangled Banner Flag House Assn., Balt.), 1956. Included in Syracuse U. Library MS Collection, 1964. Address: 2217 Wake Forest St Virginia Beach VA 23451

BALLARD, KAYE, actress; b. Cleve, Nov., 1926; d. Vincent and Lena (Nararata) Balotta. Broadway appearances include Touch and Go, Golden Apple, Ziegfield Follies, Carnival; TV appearances include Jack Paar, Johnny Carson and Perry Como shows, The Mothers-in-Law, Hollywood Squares, The Jerry Lewis Show, The Steve Allen Show; nightclub appearances include Plaza Hotel and Bon Soir, N.Y.C., Palmer House, Chgo., Recipient Italian-Am. award. Mem. Actors Equity Assn., A.F.T.R.A., Screen Actors Guild, Am. Guild Variety Artists. Home: 7250 Franklin Av Los Angeles CA 90046

BALLARD, MARGUERITE CANDLER, physician; b. Atlanta, June 14, 1920; d. Asa Warren and Hattie Lee (West) Candler; B.A., Vassar Coll., 1942; M.S., Emory U., 1943, M.D., 1948; m. George Speights Ballard, Feb. 3, 1973. Rotating intern Md. Gen. Hosp., Balt., 1948-49, asst. resident in medicine, 1949-50, resident in medicine, 1950-51; examining physician Lockheed Aircraft Corp., Marietta, Ga., 1951-52; clin. fellowship in hematology Emory U. Clinic, Atlanta, 1952-54; commd. sr. asst. surgeon USPHS, 1955, advanced through grades to med. dir., 1963; hematology tng. and consultation officer, tng. and consultation br., lab. div., Center for Disease Control, U.S. Dept. Health, Edn. and Welfare, Atlanta, 1954—; mem. staff dept. medicine Grady Meml. Hosp., Atlanta, 1952—. Mem. med. adv. council Ga. chpt. Nat. Hemophilic Found., 1963—; clin. asso. dept. medicine Emory U. Sch. Medicine, 1957—. Mem. Met. Christian Council, Met. Atlanta Commn. Alcohol and Drugs. Fellow Internat. Soc. Hematology; mem. Research Soc. Am., A.A.A.S. (life), N.Y. Acad. Sci., Ga. Assn. for Advancement Sci., Ga., Am. pub. health assns., Comd. Officers Assn. Pub. Health Service, Med. Assn. Ga., Med. Assn. Atlanta, Am., So. (life) med. assns., Am. Med. Women's Assn. (del. 1962, 63, councillor, exec. bd. 1965-66), Med. Women's Internat. Assn., Am. Soc. Hematology, Ga., Am. heart assns., Atlanta Music Club, Am. Camillia Soc., Atlanta Arts Alliance, Atlanta Symphony Women's Assn., High Mus. Art, Am. Contract Bridge Assn., YWCA, Internat. Platform Assn., Daus. of Kings. Episcopalian (mem. cathedral worship com.). Club: Zonta (trustee Atlanta 1970-72; del. internat. conv. 1970, 72). Contbr. numerous articles on hematology and pub. health to sci. jours. Home: 3092 Argonne Dr NW Atlanta GA 30305 Office: 1600 Clifton Rd NE Atlanta GA 30333

BALLIETTE, ANDREA CAFIERO, lawyer; b. Phila., Jan. 15, 1938; d. Anthony James and Hazel (Koenig) Cafiero; B.A., Rosemont Coll., 1959; LL.B., U. Pa., 1962; m. William Markes Balliette, Jr., May 19, 1962; children—Lynne, Lauren, William III, Nicole, Anthony James. Admitted to N.J. bar, 1962; clk. firm Toner, Crowley, Woelper & Vanderbilt, Newark, 1962-63; jud. clk. Superior Ct., 1966-67; mem. firm Cafiero & Balliette, Wildwood, N.J., 1968—. Mem. Middle Twp. Bd. Edn., 1970—. Mem. Am. Assn. U. Women. Republican. Roman Catholic. Home: Dennisville Rd 76B Cape May Courthouse NJ 08210 Office: 3303 New Jersey Av Wildwood NJ 08260

BALLOU, ELLEN BARTLETT (MRS. NORMAN V. BALLOU), author; b. Pitts., Sept. 24, 1905; d. Dwight Kellogg and Maud (Orr) Bartlett; A.B., Wellesley Coll., 1927; M.A., Northwestern U., 1929; m. Norman V. Ballou, June 29, 1932. Actress, New Playwrights Theatre, 1927; dir. of drama Wheaton Coll., 1929-41; with outpost desk OSS, 1945-46; dean Katharine Gibbs Sch., 1948-55; asst. English dept. Brown U., 1955-62. Mem. R.I. Hist. Soc., Peterborough Hist. Soc., Friends of Houghton Library (Harvard), Boston Athenaeum, Providence Athenaeum, Soc. for Protection N.H. Forests. Clubs: Agawam Hunt (Providence); Boston Authors; Dublin Lake, Garden of Dublin; Garden of America. Author: The Centennial (plays), 1935; The Building of the House, Houghton Mifflin's Formative Years, 1970. Address: Blueberry Hill Box 271 Dublin NH 03444

BALLOU, ESTHER WILLIAMSON, composer, educator; b. Elmira, N.Y., July 17, 1915; d. E. Duff and Marbury (Clark) Williamson; B.A., Bennington Coll., 1937; M.A. in Composition, Mills Coll., 1938; grad. degree in composition Juilliard Grad. Sch., 1943; received honorary degree, Hood College, 1964; m. Harold Ballou, Aug. 10, 1950. Mem. faculty Juilliard Sch. Music, N.Y.C., 1943-50; lectr. Catholic U. Am., 1951-54; asst. prof. theory Am. U., Washington, 1957-70, asso. prof., 1970—; mem. staff Composer's Conf. Middlebury, Bennington, Vt., 1949-53, MacDowell Colony 1944-45, 54-55. Composer: Senatina for Piano, 1941; Sonata for Two Pianos, 1942; Intermezzo for Orchestra, 1943; Prelude and Allegre, 1949; Beguine, 1950; Sonata for Piano, 1954; Oboe Concertino, 1953; Trio, 1955; Suite for Winds, 1957; Divertiment for String Quartet, 1958; Sonata for Two Pianos No. 2, 1958; Capriccio (violin and piano, premiered White House), 1963; 5-4-3, harp, viola and voice, 1966; American Portrait, voice and orch., 1965; Hear Us!, chorus, brass and percussion, 1967; Piano Concerto, 1965; Konzertstuck for viola and orch., 1969; Prism, 1969; numerous works for modern dance. Mem. Am. Composers Alliance, MacDowell Assn., Nat. Assn. Am. Composers and Condrs., Nat. Fedn. Music Clubs, Music Tchrs. Nat. Assn., Md. Music Tchrs. Assn. Clubs: Friday Morning Music, Federated Music (Washington). Contbr. articles, book revs. to profl. jours. Home: 8909 Connecticut Av Chevy Chase MD 20015

BALLOU, MARY ELLEN (MRS. ROBERT A. BALLOU), librarian; b. Mineola, N.Y., Mar. 21, 1928; d. Daniel G. and Agnes (Cody) Lee; A.B., Trinity Coll., 1950; M.L.S., Columbia, 1951; m. Robert A. Ballou, Aug. 20, 1955; children—Robert, Mary Lee, Anne Marie, Kate. Researcher, Batten Barton Durstine & Osborne, N.Y.C., 1951-53, copywriter, 1953-55; librarian Antrim Sch., Point Pleasant, N.J., 1966—. Mem. Nat., N.J. edn. assns., A.L.A. Home: 404 Boston Blvd Sea Girt NJ 08750 Office: Antrim Sch Point Pleasant NJ 08742

BALLOU, MILDRED ORALEE TESDAHL (MRS. PHILIP E. BALLOU), educator; b. Clarion, Ia.; d. Henry and Anna (Larson) Tesdahl; B.S. with honors, Drake U., 1949, M.S. in Edn. with honors, 1955; Ed.D. (Ia. Congress Parents and Tchrs. scholar), Colo. State Coll., 1960; m. Philip E. Ballou, Apr. 27, 1946; 1 son, Stephen Philip. Tchr. pub. schs., Winterset, Ia., 1949; operator Ballou Nursery Sch., Winterset, 1950-52; tchr. sci. sta. KDPS-TV, Des Moines Pub. Schs., 1952-60; lectr. Drake U. Community Coll., Des Moines, 1955-60; mem. faculty Ball State U., Muncie, 1960—, prof. edn., dept. head, 1970—. Elementary tchr. Drake U. Lab. Sch., summers, 1951-54; coordinator Airborne TV project Purdue U., 1962; speaker, 1955—; cons. elementary sci., 1958—. Bd. dirs. Muncie Symphony Women's League, 1970—. Mem. Nat. Sci. Tchrs. Assn. (sec. 1960-62), Assn. for Childhood Edn. Internat., A.A.A.S., N.E.A., Assn. Supervision and Curriculum Devel., Am. Assn. U. Profs., Ind. Psychol. Assn., Ind. Assn. for Edn. Young Children (pres.), Council for Elementary Sci. Internat. (pres. 1968-69), Delta Kappa Gamma, Pi Lambda Theta, Delta Zeta (adviser), Kappa Delta Pi. Republican. Clubs: Delaware Country (social chmn.), Delaware County Woman's (Muncie). Co-author: Science Through Discovery, series, 1967-68. Contbr. articles and chpts. to profl. publs. Home: 601 Brentwood Lane Muncie IN 47304

BALMACEDA, MARGARITA MERCEDES (MRS. EUDORO BALMACEDA), mus. ofcl.; b. Ponce, P.R., Dec. 30, 1933; d. Miguel A. and Margarita M. (Wirshing) Sastre; B.F.A., Manhattanville Coll., 1954; postgrad., Immaculate Heart Coll., 1954-55, Cath. U. of P.R., 1970—; m. Eudoro Balmaceda, Feb. 22, 1958; children—Casilda, Eudora, Margarita. Art, English tchr. Van Nuys (Cal.) Jr. High Sch., 1955-58; tchr. Spanish, art Am. Community Sch., Buenos Aires, Argentina, 1959-66; with Ponce (P.R.) Art Mus., 1966—, asst. dir., 1968—. Instr. Cath. U. of P.R., 1967—. Mem. Asociacion Puerto Riquena Dela Unesco, Kappa Gamma Pi, Phi Alpha Theta. Author: Tierra Y Alma (poems), 1968. Home: 94 Salvo Ponce PR 00731 Office: Las Americas Av Ponce PR 00731

BALMER, HELEN HOWICK (MRS. JAMES G. BALMER), pub. relations exec.; b. Louisville, June 19, 1926; d. Oscar J. and Elizabeth Mary (Durning) Howick; student Highland Park Jr. Coll., 1943-48, Wayne State U., 1944-45; m. James G. Balmer, Aug. 12, 1950; children—Janet Durning (Mrs. John Quiring), James G. III, Lindsay Dianne. Buyer, tng. program J.L. Hudson Co., Detroit, 1945-46; personnel counsellor Aames Employment Bur., Detroit, 1946-50; pub. relations dir. The Community House, Birmingham, Mich., 1962-74. Cons. pub. relations Republican party, 1966-68. Mem. Village Players (v.p. 1964-74), Village Women's Club, Women in Communications, Project Hope, Starr Commonwealth, Arts Council Triangle. Republican. Home: 3670 Forest Hill Dr Bloomfield Hills MI 48013 Office: 380 S Bates St Birmingham MI 48009

BALSAM, GOLDALIE FRANK (MRS. SOLOMON BALSAM), advt. agy. exec.; b. Jacksonville, Tex., Aug. 8, 1908; d. Louis and Tillie (Mandelstam) Frank; student Dallas Art Inst.; m. Solomon Balsam, Nov. 22, 1945. Comml. artist, 1930-32; asst. advt. mgr. Goldrings, N.Y.C., 1931-37; v.p. Cramer-Tobias-Meyer Advt. Agy., N.Y.C., 1937-46; pres. Contempo Advt. Agy., Inc., N.Y.C., 1946-73; v.p. Tex. Creative Arts, Inc., Jacksonville, Tex., 1965—. Bd. dirs. Hosp. Ednl. and Research Found., Jacksonville. Mem. C. of C. Jacksonville (Woman of Year 1972, chmn. civic com. 1973). Author: Mother, I'd Rather Buy It Myself, 1964. Home: 914 Crestwood Dr Jacksonville TX 75766 Office: 1220 S Bolton St Jacksonville TX 75766

BALSEN, KATHERINE LARSEN (MRS. RAYMOND E. BALSEN), med. researcher; b. Grand Forks, N.D., Oct. 21, 1937; d. Charles Christian and Agnes (Johnson) Larsen; student U. N.D., 1956-58; m. Raymond E. Balsen. Histology trainee and technician U. N.D., 1955-58; research technician, electron microscopy trainee U. Chgo., 1958-63; electron microscopist in charge electron microscopy lab. Hektoen Inst. for Med. Research, Chgo., 1963—. Recipient (with others) Hektoen Gold medal A.M.A., 1965, (with others) Silver award for original exhibit Am. Soc. Clin. Pathologists, Coll. Am. Pathologists, 1967, Gold award, 1973. Mem. Midwest Soc. Electron Microscopists, Am. Soc. for Cell Biology, Art Inst. Chgo. Presbyn. Research and publs. in field. Home: Apt 3010 400 E Randolph St Chicago IL 60601 Office: 627 S Wood St Chicago IL 60612

BALSLEY, EUGENIA LOUISE, supr. publs.; b. Connellsville, Pa., Dec. 4, 1917; d. James I. and Nelle (Newcomer) Balsley; B.S., Slippery Rock State Tchrs. Coll., 1939; M.A., U. Pitts., 1948. Tchr. high schs. Somerset and Brentwood, Pa., 1945-50; tchr. schs. Prince George's County (Md.), 1950-57, supr. publs., 1957—. Mem. N.E.A., D.A.R. (historian), Delta Kappa Gamma. Methodist. Mem. Order of Eastern Star. Reporter sch. news to local and met. newspapers, 1957—. Co-editor: The Curriculum in the Prince George's County Pub. Schs., 1960. Editor: P.G. Pointers, tchrs. mag., 1957—; The Focal Point, tchrs. assn. newsletter, 1958-60; monthly bulls. to parents of pupils. Office: Prince George's County Bd Edn Upper Marlboro MD 20870

BALSLEY, IROL WHITMORE (MRS. HOWARD L. BALSLEY), educator; b. Venus, Neb., Aug. 22, 1912; d. Sylvanus Bertrand and Nanna (Carson) Whitmore; B.A., Neb. State Tchrs. Coll., Wayne, 1933; M.S., U. Tenn., 1940; Ed.D., Ind. U., 1952; m. Howard Lloyd Balsley, Aug. 24, 1947. Tchr. high schs., Osmond and Walthill, Neb., 1934-37, Van Sant Sch. Bus., Omaha, 1938; asst. prof. Ind. U., 1942-49; lectr. U. Utah, 1949-50, Russell Sage Coll., 1951-52; prof. office adminstrn. La. Tech. U., 1954-65, head dept., 1963-65; prof. bus. edn. and secretarial adminstrn. Tex. Tech U., Lubbock, 1965-72, prof. edn., chmn. bus. tchr. edn. program, 1972—; coordinator of USAF clk.-typist tng. program Pa. State, 1951, inst., head office tng. sect. TVA, 1941-42; editorial asst. Southwestern Pub. Co., 1940-41. Mem. Nat. (past pres. research Found.), Mountain-Plains bus. edn. assns., Nat. Assn. Bus. Tchrs. Edn., Nat. Collegiate Assn. for Secs. (co-founder, past nat. pres.), Pi Lambda Theta, Delta Pi Epsilon, Beta Gamma Sigma, Pi Omega Pi, Sigma Tau Delta, Alpha Psi Omega. Author: (with Wanous) Shorthand Transcription Studies, 1968; (with Robinson) Integrated Secretarial Studies, 1963; (with Wood and Whitmore) Homestyle Baking, 1973. Home: 2609 Ridge Rd Lubbock TX 79403

BALTER, FRANCES SUNSTEIN (MRS. JAMES STONE BALTER), civic worker; b. Pitts.; d. Elias and Gertrude (Kingsbacher) Sunstein; student Sarah Lawrence Coll., 1939-41, New Sch. Social Research, 1941-43, Bennington Coll., summers 1941, 42; certificate Harvard Inst. Arts Adminstrn., 1973; m. James Stone Balter May 15, 1948; children—Katherine, Julia Frances, Constance, Daniel Elias. Adminstrv. asst., asso. producer Ednl. Television WQED-TV, Pitts., 1963-67; producer, mng. dir. Freedom Readers, 1964-67; a founder, incorporator, sec. bd. dirs. Pitts. Council for Arts, 1967-70; cultural cons. Mayor's Office, Dir. of Office of Cultural Affairs, Pitts., 1968; a founder Three Rivers Arts Festival 1960; co-dir. Ohio and Miss. River Valley Art Festival, 1961-62; mem. Pa. Council on Arts, 1972—; co-founder Pioneer Crafts Council Mill Run Pa., 1972; mem. cultural com. Am. Revolution Bicentennial. Recipient Woman of Year award in art Post Gazette, 1969. Mem. Asso. Councils on Arts. Clubs: Westmoreland Country, Concordia. Home: 5307 Pembroke Pl Pittsburgh PA 15232

BALTIMORE, GERTRUDE LIPSHITZ (MRS. RICHARD BALTIMORE), psychologist; b. N.Y.C., Sept. 1, 1909; d. David and Dora (Soloway) Lipshitz; B.A., Washington Sq. Coll., N.Y. U., 1929; M.A., New Sch. for Social Research, 1954; m. Richard Baltimore, May 15, 1930; children—David, Robert. Instr. New Sch. for Social Research, N.Y.C., 1952-66; prof. psychology Sarah Lawrence Coll., Bronxville, N.Y., 1965-73, dean Grad. Studies, dean Center Continuing Edn., 1973—. Mem. Am. Psychol. Assn. Home: 6 W 77th St New York City NY 10024 Office: Sarah Lawrence Coll Bronxville NY 10708

BALTZAN, NANCY ALICE (MRS. RICHARD B. BALTZAN), assn. exec.; b. Calgary, Alta., Can., Mar. 14, 1942; d. Arthur Dwight and Marguerite (Wynn) Ross; student U. B.C., 1958-59; R.N., Royal Victoria Hosp. Sch. Nursing, 1963; m. Richard B. Baltzan, May 28, 1965; children—Pamela Marguerite, Stephanie Susan. Nurse, Royal Victoria Hosp., Montreal, Que., Can., 1963-64, Canadian Forces Base, 3 Wing Germany, 1964, intensive care unit Univ. Hosp., Saskatoon, Sask., Can., 1965. Jr. leader Marina Creations, Saskatoon, 1966-67; pres. St. Paul's Hosp. Women's Aux., Saskatoon, 1972—. Mem. Fed. Conservative party Can., 1968—, Provincial Conservative party Sask., 1973. Clubs: Saskatoon Tennis; Riverside Golf and Country (Saskatoon). Home: 312 Saskatchewan Crescent W Saskatoon SK Canada

BAMBERGER, GAY GABRIELLE, pub. relations exec.; b. Berlin, Germany, June 8, 1938; d. Fritz and Kate (Schwabe) Bamberger; came to U.S., 1939, naturalized, 1944; B.A., Oberlin Coll., 1960. With Philip Lesly Co., N.Y.C., 1961-68, account exec., 1963-68; owner Gay Bamberger Pub. Relations Firm, N.Y.C., 1968—. Mem. Am. Women in Radio and TV, Elec. Women's Round Table (chmn. N.Y. chpt. 1972-73). Home: 414 E 65th St New York City NY 10021 Office: 663 Fifth Av New York City NY 10022

BAMFORTH, BETTY J., physician; b. New Britain, Conn., Jan. 20, 1923; d. Harry Stacy and Marion (Collyer) Bamforth; B.S., Bates Coll., 1944; M.D., Boston U., 1947. Intern Mount Auburn Hosp., Cambridge, Mass., 1947-48; resident Wis. Gen. Hosp., Madison, 1948-51; asst. prof. U. Okla. Med. Sch., Oklahoma City, 1951-54; asso. prof. U. Wis. Med. Sch., Madison, 1954-64, prof. anesthesiology, 1964—, now asst. dean ednl. adminstrn. Unitarian. Club: Altrusa (pres. 1969-70). Home: 3519 Sunset Dr Madison WI 53705 Office: 1300 University Av Madison WI 53706

BANAS, NORMA EDYTHE ELISCU, ednl. services co. exec.; b. N.Y.C., July 28, 1933; d. Frank and Mildred (Norman) Eliscu; student U. Fla., 1951-52; B.Ed., U. Miami (Fla.), 1957, M.Ed., 1965; divorced; children—Suzanne, Joanne. Tchr., Miami, Fla., 1951-52; instr. reading clinic U. Miami, 1960-62; curriculum dir. McGlannan Clin. Sch., Miami, Fla., 1963-67; pres., also curriculum dir. Ednl. Guidance Services, Inc., Miami, 1967—. Cons. pub., pvt. schs.; lectr. state, nat. profl. orgns. Bd. dirs. Dade County (Fla.) Youth Fair Assn., 1972—. Mem. Assn. Children with Learning Disabilities, So. Assn. Children under Six, Dade Reading Found., Greater Miami Dog Club (advt. chmn., lectr., exhibitor 1958—). Author: (with others) Success Begins with Understanding, 1972. Contbg. editor Academic Therapy Publs. Contbr. articles to ednl. jours. Home: 9360 SW 66th St Miami FL 33173 Office: 7200 SW 39th Terr Miami FL 33155

BANAY-SCHWARTZ, MIRIAM, chemist, educator; b. Sibiu, Rumania, Oct. 9, 1929; M.Sc., Hebrew U., Jerusalem, 1954, Ph.D. in Biochemistry, 1961; m. 1951; 2 children. Came to U.S., naturalized. Instr. biochemistry Albert Einstein Coll. Medicine, Bronx, N.Y., 1962-68, asst. prof., 1968—; sr. research scientist N.Y. State Research Inst. Neurochemistry and Drug Addiction, N.Y.C., 1968—. Mem. Am. Inst. Chemists, Am. Soc. Neurochemistry, N.Y. Acad. Scis. Research on intermediate metabolism, electron transport. Office: NY State Research Institute for Neurochemistry and Drug Addiction Ward's Island New York City NY 10035

BANCROFT, ALICE WILLIAMS, advt. exec.; b. Chgo., Oct. 23, 1906; d. William R. and Esther (Williams) Williams; student Laird Extension Inst., 1931-33, Minn. Sch. Music and Dramatic Art, 1943; m. Arthur G. Buchanan, Jan. 7, 1925 (dec.); children—Roger L., Jacqueline (Mrs. Esmond C. Appleyard, Jr.), William G.; m. 2d, Lyle H. Bancroft, Aug. 26, 1950 (dec. 1973). Columnist, Lime Springs (Ia.) Herald, 1931—; writer, broadcaster sta. WMIN, St. Paul, 1943-44; continuity dir. sta. KSO, Des Moines, 1945-49; writer sta. WJIM, Lansing, Mich., 1949-53; writer, promotion mgr. sta. WJIM-TV, 1956-57; asst. editor bulls. Mich. State U., 1959; publicist Mich. State Employees Assn., 1959-62; gen. mgr. Alison-Biart Enterprises, Lansing, 1962—. Mem. Mayor's Com. Refugee Relief, Lansing, 1963-64. Mem. Am. Women in Radio and TV, Pub. Relations Assn. Mich., Zonta Club (charter mem., v.p. Des Moines 1948). Republican. Presbyn. Mem. Order Eastern Star. Author: (album) Characters I Have Known, 1962. Home: 13420 Bancroft Dr Grand Ledge MI 48837 Office: PO Box 337 Lansing MI 48902

BANCROFT, ANNE, actress; b. N.Y.C., Sept. 17, 1931; d. Michael and Mildred (DiNapoli) Italiano; grad. Christopher Columbus High Sch., N.Y.C.; m. Mel Brooks. Broadway debut in Two for the Seesaw, 1958; starred as Anne Sullivan in The Miracle Worker, Broadway, 1959-60, The Devils, a broadway prodn.; motion pictures include Don't Bother to Knock, Tonight We Sing, Demetrius and the Gladiators, The Pumpkin Eater, The Silver Thread, 7 Women, The Graduate, Young Winston, 1971; television appearances include The Goldbergs, Danger, Suspense, Philco-Goodyear Playhouse; guest on Perry Como show, Bob Hope-Chrysler show; TV spl. Annie-The Woman in the Life of a Man, Tom Jones Show. Recipient Oscar award best actress of Yr. for movie recreation of role in Miracle Worker, also Tony award for stage version, 1963, Emmy award for tv spl., 1970. Address: care David Cogan 350 Fifth Av New York City NY 10001

BANCROFT, EDITH DOROTHY, physician; b. Morristown, N.J., Aug. 14, 1906; d. Walter H. and Almira (Beach) Bancroft; student Bryn Athyn Acad., 1924-26; M.D., Womans Med. Coll. Pa., 1932; children—Peter A., Jane (Mrs. John E. Kearns), Nan (Mrs. George U. Naill). Intern Woman's Hosp., Phila., 1931-32, resident, 1932-34; physician Babies Hosp., Phila., 1934-36; practice medicine specializing in obstetrics, Lewistown, Pa., 1936-62; resident psychiatry Norristown (Pa.) State Hosp., 1962-65, staff psychiatrist, 1965-67, dir. woman's continued treatment div., 1967-69, dir. outpatient services, 1969—. Mem. A.M.A., Pa., Montgomery County med. assns., Am., Pa. psychiat. assns. Home: 2696 Huntingdon Pike Bryn Athyn PA 19009 Office: Norristown State Hosp Norristown PA 19401

BAND, HENRETTA TRENT, geneticist; b. Danville, Va., June 28, 1932; d. Oscar Everett and Lucille Hughs (Allen) Trent; B.S., Coll. William and Mary, 1954; exchange scholar U. Exeter (Eng.), 1952-53; Ph.D. in Genetics (USPHS fellow), U. Cal. at Berkeley, 1959; postgrad. (USPHS fellow) Amherst Coll., 1958-59, (USPHS spl. fellow) U. Cambridge (Eng.), 1965-66; m. Rudolph Neal Band, July 16, 1955; 1 dau., Elizabeth Lee. Lectr. zoology U. B.C., 1959-60, 61-62; NRC Can. research grantee, 1959-63, research asso., 1960-63; research asso. Mich. State U., East Lansing, 1963-65, asst. prof. zoology; 1965, asst. prof. natural scis., 1967-68; research fellow genetics U. Cal. at Davis, 1972-73. Mem. symposium genetic load Internat. Congress Genetics, Tokyo, 1968. NSF research grantee, 1960-64. Mem. Genetics Soc. Am., A.A.A.S., Soc. for Study Evolution, Am. Soc. Naturalists, Internat. Platform Assn., Genetics Soc. Can., Phi Beta Kappa, Sigma Xi. Delta Delta Delta. Research on population and ecol. genetics, genetics of Drosophlia. Home: 5854 Smithfield Av East Lansing MI 48823

BANKER, MARGARET JENNINGS, community services dir.; b. Clinton, Ind., Feb. 1, 1922; d. Claude Edgar and Margie (Griffiths) Jennings; grad. high sch.; m. Ralph Banker, Feb. 6, 1944 (div. June 1951); children—Harry, Steven, Timothy. With Gen. Telephone Co., 1946-74; editor Terre Haute (Ind.) Adv., 1969-71; rec. sec. Wabash Valley Central Labor Council, Terre Haute, Ind., 1968-73, edn. chmn., 1970-73, now community services dir. Labor liaison United Way of Wabash Valley, 1973—. Chmn. Com. On Polit. Edn., Terre Haute, 1968-70; co-chmn. Vigo County Humphrey-for-Pres. Com., 1968; co-chmn. 7th Dist Labor for McGovern Com., 1971; del. Democratic State Conv., 1972. Bd. dirs. Eugene V. Debs Found., 1969-73, treas. 1971-72; bd. dirs. Vigo County Community Action Program, 1968—, chmn. 1969-70. Recipient Wabash Valley Central Labor Council Community Services award, 1971. Mem. Internat. Labor Press, Communications Workers Am. Home: 512 S 6th St Terre Haute IN 47807 Office: 20 Chestnut St Terre Haute IN 47808

BANKS, ANNE PALMER JOHNSON, educator; b. New London, Conn., Aug. 10, 1924; d. James Reid and Neva Fenno (Palmer) Johnson; B.A. in Chemistry, Wellesley Coll., 1946; postgrad. Honolulu Sch. Art, 1948-50; M.F.A., George Washington U., 1968; m. William Ross Banks, Sept. 13, 1947; children—Ellison (Mrs. Robert Craig Findly), William Ross, Jr., Anne. Chemist Pub. Health Research Inst., N.Y.C., 1946-47; teaching asst., art lectr. George Washington U., Washington, 1967-68; instr. art George Mason U., Fairfax, Va., 1968-69, Bapt. Coll., Charleston, S.C., 1970; mem. faculty No. Va. Community Coll., Alexandria, 1971—, instr. art, 1973—, asst. div. chmn. art, 1973—; one-man shows Lyman Allyn Mus., New London, Conn., Art League, Alexandria, Va.; exhibited art in group shows at Va. Mus., Richmond, Norfolk Mus., Madison Gallery, N.Y.C., Soc. Washington Artists; represented in permanent collections at Lyman Allyn Mus., George Washington U., Madison Gallery, N.Y.C. Recipient Hon. Mention Fairfax County Area show, 1971; Merit award No. Va. Fine Arts Assn., 1971, others. Mem. Art League (chmn. com. 1973-74), Fairfax County Council of Arts. Club: Washington Wellesley (Washington). Home: 1104 Croton St Alexandria VA 22308

BANKS, DORIS NININGER (MRS. JOHN C. BANKS), Democratic nat. committeewoman; b. McPherson, Kan., Oct. 3, 1921; d. Harvey Harlow and Addie (Delp) Nininger; B.A. with honors, Grinnell Coll., 1943; m. John C. Banks, Mar. 17, 1954; children—Nancy, James; stepchildren—John Robert, Carolyn (Mrs. Gary Ivey). Reporter Denver Post, 1945-49; information writer, City and County of Denver, 1952-54; Denver Democratic vice chmn., 1965-68; Dem. nat. committeewoman from Colo., 1968—; Denver election commr., 1966; mem. Denver Commn. on Community Relations, 1967-71, chmn., 1969; mem. Dem. Charter Commn., 1972—. Mem. Phi Beta Kappa. Home: 1220 Olive St Denver CO 80220

BANKS, GERTRUDE MARY, mfg. co. exec.; b. Newark, May 14, 1920; d. Thomas P. and Helen G. (Cosgrove) Mullins; grad. high sch.; m. William Kenneth Banks, May 24, 1941 (dec. Jan. 1972); 1 dau., Barbara A. With A.B. Murray Co., Elizabeth, N.J., 1948-56, Thomas A. Edison Industries, Neptune, 1956-60, with D & D Tool Co., Inc., Eatontown, 1960—, sec.-treas., 1966—. Chmn. A.R.C., Berkley Heights, 1955. Recipient citation Deborah Hosp., Browns Mills, N.J., 1969, Nat. Jewish Hosp., Denver, 1969, hon. achievement plaque C. of C., 1969. Mem. C. of C. Eatontown (dir. 1971-72), Am. Legion Aux. (pres. Union County 1960—), 8 and 40 (N.J. pres. 1969). Home: 43 Parmly Rd New Shrewsbury NJ 07724 Office: D & D Tool Co Inc Lewis St and Maple Av Eatontown NJ 07724

BANKS, VIRGINIA, artist; b. Norwood, Mass., Jan. 12, 1920; d. Henry Lewis and Ottilie (Rietzel) Banks; A.B., Smith Coll., 1941; M.A., State U. Ia., 1944; m. Arthur W. Freidinger, Jan. 1, 1946. One man shows include Grand Central Moderns, N.Y.C., 1950, 52, 56, 59, 65, Dusanne Gallery, Seattle, 1952, 58, Collectors Gallery, Bellevue, Wash., 1965; exhibited in nat. and internat. shows, 1946—; rep. permanent collections U. Ill., Seattle Art Mus., IBM Coll., U. Ore., San Francisco Mus. Art, Springfield (Mo.) Art Mus., Davenport (Ia.) Municipal Art Gallery, Plattsburg (N.Y.) State Tchrs. Coll., State U. Ia., U. Notre Dame, Cornell U., Nat. Acad. Scis., Washington; instr. art State U. Ia., 1942-47, Albright Art Sch., 1947-48, U. Buffalo, 1947-48, N.Y. State Tchrs. Coll., 1947-48, U. Wash., 1949, Cornish Art Sch., Seattle, 1951-52. Area chmn. Wash. State and Brit. Columbia for Smith Coll. capital campaign, 1968-70. Recipient award Pepsi-Cola Competition, 1948, Hallmark Internat. Art award, 1949. Mem. Alpha Phi Kappa Psi, Pi Lambda Theta. Clubs: Smith College (pres. 1960-61, hon. bd. mem. 1967-68) (Seattle). Home: 3879 51st Av NE Seattle WA 98105 Office: 214 214 1305 NE 45th St Seattle WA 98105

BANKS, VIRGINIA ANNE, assn. exec.; b. Dallas, Mar. 19, 1949; d. James Houston and Mary Virginia (Bussey) Banks; B.J., U. Tex., 1971. Reporter, Austin (Tex.) Am.-Statesman, 1969; pub. relations asst. to lt. gov. State of Tex., Austin, 1970; traveling cons. Alpha Omicron Pi sorority, Indpls., 1971-73, adminstrv. asst., 1973—. Bd. dirs. Lone Star council Girl Scouts U.S.A., 1970-71, 73—, troop leader, 1970-71, mem. troop camp com., 1968-70, chmn. pub. relations com., 1973—. Mem. Women in Communications, Alpha Omicron Pi. Methodist. Contbr. articles to various mags. Home: 6113 Rickey Dr Austin TX 78731 Office: 3000 Meadows Pkwy Indianapolis IN 46205

BANNING, ELIZABETH (MRS. CHARLES PERRY DAVIES), color cons.; b. Waterloo, Ia., Sept. 11, 1908; d. Evert Alonzo and Odessa Rebecca (Fogleman) Hollenbeck; student Art Inst. Chgo., 1928-29, Northwestern U., 1930; research in color in Germany, 1932-35; m. William Clyde Morehead, Aug. 15, 1942; m. 2d, Charles Perry Davies, July 17, 1956. As color technician and archtl. color cons. established office and lab. under name of Elizabeth Banning, San Francisco, 1936, since retained as color cons. for many orgns., including A.T. & S.F. R.R., W. P. Fuller & Co., Mannings, Inc., Petroleum Exhibitors, Spreckles Sugar Co., Standard Oil (Cal.), Fred Harvey, and architects for Ford Motor Co. Bd. dirs. Marin Symphony; mem. Park Commn. of Marin County. Republican. Collector Modern French and Am. fine art including Rubin, Gladys Rockmore Davis, Dan Lutz, Gluckman, Feininger, Henry Moore, Chana Orloff, Matisse, Marie Laurencin. Mem. Am. Inst. Interior Decorators. Home: Indian Valley Ranch Novato CA 94947 Office: 1709 Indian Valley Rd Novato CA 94947 also Star Route Box 60 Captain Cook HI 96704

BANNING, MARGARET CULKIN, author; b. Buffalo, Minn., Mar. 18, 1891; d. William Edgar and Hannah Alice (Young) Culkin; A.B., Vassar Coll., 1912; certificate Chgo. Sch. of Civics and Philanthropy, 1913; m. Archibald Tanner Banning, Oct. 23, 1914; children—Mary Margaret, Archibald Tanner, William Culkin (dec.), Margaret Brigid (dec.); m. 2d, LeRoy Salsich, Nov. 15, 1944. Russell Sage Found. research fellow, 1913. Chmn. commn. edn. women, mem. nat. conf. continuing edn. women Am. Council Edn. Trustee Duluth Pub. Library, 1930—, Vassar Coll., 1937-45, Alworth Meml. Scholarship Fund. Hon. mem. Jr. League (Duluth); mem. Am. Assn. U. Women (past pres. Duluth), League Women Voters, Authors League Am. (council 1948-50), League Am. Penwomen, Bus. and Profl. Women's Club, P.E.N., Phi Beta Kappa. Republican. Catholic. Clubs: The Arts, The Cordon (Chgo.); Northland Country (Duluth); Tryon (N.C.) Country, Tryon Riding and Hunt, Pen and Brush, Cosmopolitan (N.Y.C.). Author: This Marrying, 1920; Half Loves, 1921; Spellbinders, 1922; Country Club People, 1923; A Handmaid of the Lord, 1924; The Women of the Family, 1926; Pressure, 1927; Money of Her Own, 1928; Prelude to Love, 1929; Mixed Marriage, 1930; The Town's Too Small, 1931; Path of True Love, 1932; The Third Son, 1933; The First Woman, 1934; The Iron Will, 1935; Letters to Susan, 1936; The Case for Chastity, 1937; Too Young to Marry, 1938; Enough to Live On, 1939; Out in Society, 1940; Salud: A South American Journal, 1941; Letters from England, 1942; Conduct Yourself Accordingly, 1944; The Clever Sister, 1947; Give Us Our Years, 1949; Fallen Away, 1951; The Dowry, 1955; The Convert, 1957; Echo Answers, 1960; The Quality of Mercy, 1963; The Vine and the Olive, 1964; I Took My Love to the Country, 1966: Mesabi, 1969; Life Boat Number Two, 1971; The Will of Magda Townsend, 1974. Contbr. short stories to mags.; writer of essays on phases of Am. life and activities. Home: Tryon NC 28782

BANNISTER, MARGARET ALICE TRIMBLE, pub. relations ofcl.; b. Oklahoma City, Okla., Dec. 15, 1924; d. Clyde Waldrop and Mary Melissa (Murray) Trimble; B.A. in Journalism, U. Okla., 1945; teaching certificate U. Mo., St. Louis, 1969, postgrad. extension, 1970-71; postgrad. U. Wash., 1973; m. Lawrence R. Bannister, Jan. 18, 1947 (div. 1968); children—Karen, Barbara Jean, Sally Ann. Reporter, Alva (Okla.) Review-Courier, 1945-46, Clinton (Okla.) Daily News, 1946-47; pub. relations asst. U. Okla., Norman, 1947-51; editorial asst. Consol.-Vultee Aircraft Corp., Ft. Worth, 1951-53; coordinator community relations Berkeley (Mo.) Sch. Dist., 1968-72, dir. community relations, 1973—. Mem. Women in Communication, St. Louis Press Club, Nat. Sch. Pub. Relations Assn. (officer Greater St. Louis chpt. 1969-71, 73-74), Berkeley C. of C., Soroptimists Internat. (charter mem. N. St. Louis County chpt.). Methodist (past mem. bd. stewards, youth council). Home: 2040 Argo Dr Florissant MO 63031 Office: 6001 Berkeley Dr Berkeley MO 63134

BANNISTER, VIVIAN ODESSA, public relations exec.; b. Habor Beach, Mich., 1906; d. Burton Fulmer and Grace Greenwood (Winches) Browne; grad. Chgo. Acad. Fine Arts, 1927, Chgo. Art Inst., 1928, U. Mich., 1929; pupil of Gaston Balande, 1930; m. Thomas J. Bannister, May 3, 1974. Instr. art Chgo. Acad. Fine Arts, 1931-33; founder, dir. Chgo. Profl. Sch. Art, 1938-45; cultural attache Am. embassy, French Indo-China, 1951-53; dir. pub. relations Tb Inst. Chgo. and Cook County, 1945-51, Ill. Soc. Prevention Blindness, 1966-72, Gaslight Clubs, Inc., Chgo., 1954-65; painter hist. murals Century of Progress Expn., Chgo., 1933, Palais du Justice, Lyons, France, 1935, Mich. State Capitol Bldg., Lansing, 1934. Mem. Pub. Relations Soc. Am., Chgo. Publicity Club, Welfare Pub. Relations Soc., Delta Phi Delta. Address: 860 DeWitt Pl Chicago IL 60611

BANNON, BARBARA ANNE, pub. co. exec., editor; b. Auburn, N.Y., Aug. 27, 1929; d. Thomas Joseph and Rose Catherine (McCauley) B.; grad. with honors, Manhattanville Coll., 1949—. With Pub.'s Weekly, N.Y.C., 1949—, sr. editor, 1971—. Editorial cons. White House library Am. Booksellers Assn., 1960—; mem. awards policy com. Nat. Book awards, 1960-71; mem. book selections com. Books Across the Sea program English Speaking Union, 1965—. Mem. Pubs. Publicity Assn. (founder, dir.), Women's Nat. Book Assn. (v.p. 1973). Home: 7 E 14th St New York City NY 10003 Office: RR Bowker Co 1180 Av of the Americas New York City NY 10036

BANNON, SISTER MARY EILEEN, educator; b. Joliet, Ill., July 15, 1921; d. Robert Joseph and Henrietta Marie (Braun) Bannon; A.B., Coll. St. Francis, 1943; M.A., St. Louis U., 1959; postgrad., U. Ill., 1968, Am. Conservatory Theatre, 1970, Trinity Coll., Dublin, Ireland, 1971, Northwestern U., 1973. Joined Sisters of St. Francis of Mary Immaculate, 1942; tchr. St. Francis DeSales High Sch., Chgo., 1943-46, St. Mary's High Sch., Columbus, O., 1946-52, Sts. Peter and Paul High Sch., Chgo., 1952-58, St. Francis Acad., Joliet, 1958-63, St. Peter's High Sch., Mansfield, O., 1963-68; asst. prof. Coll. St. Francis, Joliet, 1968—. Bd. dirs. Children's Theatre Tangerine Tent, Lockport, Ill., summer, 1969, Touring Children's Theatre Coll. St. Francis, Joliet, 1972. Mem. Am. Assn. U. Profs., Am. Ednl. Theatre Assn., Ill. Theatre Assn., Ill. Speech and Theatre Assn., Alpha Mu Omega. Club: Gaelic-Am. Home: 421 Whitney St Joliet IL 60435 Office: 500 Wilcox St Joliet IL 60435

BANOCZI, JEANNETTE BERNADETTE BOULAY (MRS. JOHN R. BANOCZI), broadcasting co. exec.; b. Dracut, Mass., Jan. 21, 1922; d. Albert Anthanas and Rhea Marie (Venne) Boulay; student pub. schs.; m. Humbert R. Pennino, Dec. 14, 1946 (dec. Mar. 1955); children—Jeannette Claire (Mrs. Dean Charles Rathbun), Madelaine Lynn, Naomi Gloria; m. 2d, John R. Banoczi, July 16, 1960. First trumpeter Phil Spitalny Hour of Charm, All Girl Orch., N.Y.C., 1940-42; free lance trumpeter NBC, N.Y.C., 1942-46; tchr. trumpet, N.Y.C., 1941-46; pres. Pennino Music Co., Inc., Los Angeles, 1946—, Radio Sta. KGGK, Garden Grove, Cal., 1961-66, Radio Sta. KNOB, Anaheim, Cal., 1966—, Radio Station KCNA, Henderson, Nev., 1970—. Mem. Sales and Marketing Execs. of Orange County (dir. 1967—), Orange County C. of C. (life), Better Bus. Bur. (exec. bd. 1965—). Roman Catholic. Club: Soroptimist (pres. 1963-65) (Garden Grove). Home: 4955 Los Feliz Blvd Hollywood CA 90027 Office: 1700 S Harbor Blvd Anaheim CA 92802 also 5670 Wilshire Blvd Los Angeles CA 90036

BANOV, JOAN HEINEMANN (MRS. ABEL BANOV), artist; b. Mainz, Germany, May 17, 1921; d. Richard and Aenne (Berney) Heinemann; student Bazirkschule, Mainz, 1936-37; pvt. art instrn. with Herman Lissman of Bauhaus, 1937-38; student Ringling Art Sch., Sarasota, Fla., 1944-45, Pa. Acad. Fine Arts, 1946; m. Abel Banov, Apr. 3, 1941; 1 dau., Beverly. One-man shows Bryant Library Gallery, Roslyn, N.Y., 1963, 68, 69, 73, Contemporary Arts, Inc., N.Y.C., 1963, Shelter Rock Library, 1973; exhibited in group shows Ringling Art Assn., Phila. Art Alliance, Nat. Arts Club, N.Y.C., Heckscher, Suffolk museums, Argent Gallery, Nat. Acad. Fine Arts, N.Y.C., Lever House, N.Y.C., Carolina Art Assn., Charleston, S.C., Contemporary Arts, Inc., N.Y.C., Artium Gallery, Port Washington Gallery, Village Gallery, Sea Cliff, L.I., N.Y., Donnell Art Library, N.Y.C., North Shore Portfolio, others; represented in permanent collections Honolulu, Phila., N.Y.C., Swarthmore, Pa., U.S. Embassy, Tokyo, Japan, others; traveling exhbns. Nat. Assn. Women Artists, S. Am., 1963-65, France, 1965, also univs. and museums U.S.; traveling show of graphics maj. colls. L.I. Tchr. art adult edn., Roslyn, N.Y. Recipient 1st prize watercolors Ringling Art Assn., 1945; prizes Carolina Art Assn., Manhasset Art Assn.; 2d prize in oil, Manhasset Art Assn., 1965. Mem. Profl. Artists Guild, Nat. Assn. Women Artists (recipient Elizabeth Morse Genius Meml. prize 1966), Manhasset Art Assn., Collectors Am. Art. Home: 110 Overlook Terrace Roslyn Heights NY 11577 Office: 156 Fifth Av New York City NY 10010

BANSAVAGE, JUDITH CHASIN, psychologist; b. N.Y.C., Feb. 24, 1921; d. Benjamin A. and Evelyn Chasin; B.A., U. Miami, 1947, M.S., 1949; Ph.D., U. Pitts., 1967; m. Joseph W. Bansavage, Aug. 1, 1951; children—Elizabeth A., David E. Practice clin. psychology, 1968—; instr. Pa. State U., 1960-64; asst. prof. Point Park Coll., 1966-68. Mem. personnel com. YWCA, 1958-62; treas. Pitts. Drama League, 1972; bd. dirs. Planned Parenthood, Pitts., 1972—. Served to 1st lt. WAC, 1943-46. Vocational Rehab. fellow Dept. Health, Edn. and Welfare, 1961-64. Mem. Am. Psychol. Assn. Home: 4243 Parkman Av Pittsburgh PA 15213

BANUELOS, ROMANA ACOSTA (MRS. ALEJANDRO BANUELOS), former treas. U.S.; b. Miami, Ariz., Mar. 20, 1925; d. Juan Francisco and Teresa (Lugo) Acosta; ed. elementary sch., Mexico; m. Alejandro Banuelos, Dec. 31, 1949; children—Martin Torres, Carlos Torres, Ramona. Founder, Ramona's Mexican Food Products, Inc., Los Angeles, 1949; founding dir. Pan Am. Nat. Bank, East Los Angeles, Cal., 1964, chmn. bd. dirs., 1969—; treas. U.S., Washington, 1971-74. Founder, Romona's Mexican Food Products Scholarship Found., Inc., 1970. Named Outstanding Businesswoman of Year Mayor of Los Angeles, 1969; recipient Commendation award Bd. Suprs. County Los Angeles, certificate of merit Mexican-Am. agy. Met. Los Angeles, 1971. Home: 5079 Loz Feliz Blvd Los Angeles CA 90027

BARAN, ELIZABETH TCREZA, editor; b. Homer City, Pa., Sept. 13, 1929; d. Michael and Anna (Barron) Baran; student Pa. State U., 1960-61, Indiana U. of Pa., 1966-67. Exec. sec. FMC Corp., Homer City, 1959-65, asst. advt. mgr., 1965-73, editor employee relations, 1973—. Pub. relations chmn. United Way of Indiana County (Pa.), 1970—; sec. bd. dirs. Indiana County YMCA, 1970—; adv. Bd. Western Pa. Comprehensive Health Planning Commn., 1972—. Mem. Internat. Mgmt. Council (pub. relations chmn. 1972—, past pres. Indiana County chpt.), Western Pa. Mgmt. Conf. (bd. govs.). Home: 54 Center St Homer City PA 15748 Office: FMC Corp Homer City PA 15748

BARAS, CAROL ROSE FORMOST (MRS. WILLIAM T. BARAS), pub. relations exec.; b. Chgo., Oct. 1, 1930; d. August and Celestina (Ristucce) Formost; student San Diego State Coll., 1947-49, U. Cal. at La Jolla, 1967, 70-71, U. London, 1971; m. William T. Baras; children—Gary Rose, Frank Rose, Linda Rose. Disc jockey Carol's Frolics, radio sta. KSDO, San Diego, 1947, exec. sec. programming, copywriting, 1951-52; clk. record mgmt., receptionist, 1948-49; pub. relations staff Circus Foods, 1948-51; bookkeeper Sunset Engraving, 1948-49; copy writer program scheduling radio sta. KGB, 1950-51; mgr. Formost Rental Agy., 1952-54; instr., mgr., cons. Roman Health Spa, 1967-68; owner, dir. Hypnos Morpheus Center, San Diego, 1968—; partner, pub. relations exec. Formost Advt., San Diego, 1969—; treas., Universal Jet, Inc., San Diego, 1971—, Santa Clara Mobile Homes, 1973—; partner, decorator Formost Furniture, 1973—; partner SEB Enterprises, Escondido, Cal., 1973—. Active Salvation Army Assn., Zool. Soc. San Diego, San Diego County Assn. Retarded Children. Mem. Am. Parapsychol. Research Found. Assn. to Advance Ethical Hypnosis, Cal. Profl. Hypnotists Assn., Cal. Assn. Ethical Hypnosis, Cal. State Hypnosis Assn., San Diego C. of C., Advt. and Sales Club, Media Club, Nat. Acad. TV Arts and Scis., Alpha Phi. Office: 2423 Camino del Rio S Suite 208 San Diego CA 92108

BARASH, MARIAN UNGAR (MRS. SY BARASH), mag. pub. co. exec.; b. Wilkes-Barre, Pa., June 11, 1933; d. Max H. and Tillie (Landau) Ungar; B.A., Pa. State U., 1953; m. Sy Barash, Jan. 31, 1954; children—Carol Lynn, Nan Ruth. Tech. writer Kling Studios, Chgo., 1951; editorial dir. Daily Collegian, State College, Pa., 1953; grad. asst. dept. speech Pa. State U., State Coll., 1953-55; writer, salesman Friedman & Barash, State College, 1956-59; v.p. State College Town-Gown, 1959—. Cons. marketing and pub. relations to various financial instns.; instr. marketing Pa. State U., University Park, 1973—. Chmn. Art Alliance Fund Campaign, 1971; mem. pub. relations com. Central Pa. Heart Assn., 1973; chmn. Cancer Crusade, State College, 1973—. Pres. Nittany Council of Republican Women, 1960-61. Bd. dirs. United Fund, 1965-70, asst. chmn., 1969. Mem. Nat. (pub. relations com. 1972-73), Pa. (pub. relations counsel 1967—) cable television assns., Women in Communications, C. of C. (dir. 1973—, pres. 1974), Phi Sigma Sigma. Mem. B'nai B'rith (pres. 1956). Contbr. articles to profl. jours. Home: 325 Homan Av State College PA 16801 Office: 403 S Allen St State College PA 16801

BARB, MARIAN LESTER SHAFER, assn. exec.; b. Los Angeles, June 13, 1925; d. Lester and Marian (Chace) Shafer; B.A., Am. U., 1958, certificate in pub. relations, 1969; m. John Charles Barb, Sept. 1944 (div.); 1 dau., Jeannette (Mrs. Robert Edward Hurley). Partner Jeanne Viner Assos. pub. relations, Washington, 1959-62; asso. dir. pub. relations United Givers Fund, Washington, 1962-66; dir. alumni relations Am. U., Washington, 1966-71, dir. ann. fund, 1971-72, instr. pub. relations, 1970-72; press. sec. U.S. Rep. Lawrence J. Hogan, 1972-74; dir. devel. Nat. Capital area YWCA, 1974—. Cons. pub. relations YWCA Montgomery County, Md., 1968-73, bd. dirs., 1967-71. Mem. pub. relations com. Family and Child Services, Washington, 1971—; vol. services com. Health and Welfare Council Nat. Capital Area, 1969—. Mem. Pub. Relations Soc. Am. (chmn. awards com. Washington chpt. 1971; dir. 1969), Am. Women in Radio and TV, Phi Delta Gamma (pres. Alpha chpt. 1972-73), Women in Communications, Inc. Home: 4707 Connecticut Av NW Washington DC 20008

BARBEE, MARY KEENUM, civic worker; b. North Kansas City, Mo., June 15, 1935; d. John C. and Virginia Elizabeth (Garton) Keenum; B.A., U. No. Colo., 1959; m. David Edwin Barbee, Aug. 30, 1956; children—Mark Edwin, Michael David, Mary Elizabeth, John Eric. Tchr., 1956, 61, 62; owner bus. The Peppermint Tree, Aspen,

Colo., 1961-67. Chmn., Aspen Homes and Gardens Tour, 1962-67. Trustee Pitkin County Library, 1971—. Bd. dirs. Aspen Hist. Soc., 1971—. Mem. Sigma Sigma Sigma (nat. membership comn. 1965-68, nat. collegiate chmn. 1968-70, spl. services and rush counselor 1969-72, nat. panhellenic del. 1972—, exec. council 1972—). Home: Box 788 Aspen CO 81611

BARBEE, WILLARD LOUISE (MRS. L.B. BARBEE), educator; b. Watertown, Tenn., Oct. 4, 1921; d. James Eli and Laura Belle (Stallings) Allen; B.A., Eastern Mich. U., 1959; M.A., U. Mich., 1961, Ph.D., (teaching fellow), 1968; m. L.B. Barbee, Aug. 30, 1943; 1 son, Christopher Barbee. Instr. mathematics Eastern Mich. U., Ypsilanti, 1965-66, asst. prof. math., 1967-72. Mem. Am. Math. Soc., Math. Assn. Am., Sch. Sci. and Math., A.A.A.S., Am. Assn. U. Women (treas. Ypsilanti 1968-72. Address: 370 Oxford Av Palo Alto CA 94306

BARBER, JANICE ANN, journalist; b. Buffalo, May 30, 1947; d. Warren Richard and Betty Agnes (Stabler) Barber; B.A. summa cum laude, U. Ky., 1969. Reporter The Courier-Express, Buffalo, 1968; reporter The Times-Union, Rochester, N.Y., 1969—. Mem. Newspaper Guild Rochester, Women in Communications (sec. Rochester chpt. 1971—, mem. exec. bd. 1971-72, del. to nat. conv. 1972), Phi Beta Kappa, Sigma Delta Chi, Alpha Lambda Delta. Home: 19 Rowley St Rochester NY 14607 Office: 55 Exchange St Rochester NY 14614

BARBER, JEAN ELAINE, advt. exec.; b. Hackensack, N.J., Sept. 16, 1936; d. George Edward and Edna Adelaide (Ahrendt) Barber; student Knox Coll., 1955-57. Asst. editor Locksmith Ledger, Inc./Sales Aids Pub. Co., Little Falls, N.J., 1960, bus. mgr., 1961-68, editor, 1968-70; asst. exec. dir. Asso. Locksmiths Am., Kingston, N.Y., 1970, editor, 1971; asst. gen. mgr., dir. advt. Baxter Systems, Inc., El Cajon, Cal., 1972—, also editor tech. books. Mem. Phi Mu. Home: 1244-C E Madison Av El Cajon CA 92021 Office: Baxter Systems Inc 419 S Marshall St El Cajon CA 92020

BARBER, JEAN MCEVOY (MRS. TIMOTHY L. BARBER, III), journalist; b. Chgo., July 29, 1915; d. Harry Kirby and Louise (Cavey) McEvoy; student U. Ill., 1934-37; m. Timothy L. Barber, III, Apr. 19, 1941; children—James, Daniel, Elizabeth, Andrew. Mgr. community service and advt. Wood County Bank, Parkersburg, W.Va., 1961-63; women's editor Cocoa (Fla.) Evening Tribune, 1963-69; spl. writer Today, Cocoa, Fla., 1969-70; feature writer, corr. Brevard Sentinel Star, Cocoa, 1970—. Dir. Brevard County Mus., Cocoa, 1971-74, Am. Lung Assn., Daytona Beach, Fla., 1972—. Mem. Delta Gamma. Home: 1610 Seashell Dr Merritt Island FL 32952 Office: Brevard Sentinel Star 26 Forrest Av Cocoa FL 32922

BARBER, MARY LEE, educator, biologist; b. Ft. Wayne, Ind., May 20, 1934; s. George Hewson and Velmah Evelyn (McClain) Sparling; B.S., U. Miami (Fla.), 1955; M.A., Duke, 1958; Ph.D., U. Cal. at Los Angeles, 1962; m. Albert Alcide Barber, Sept. 1, 1956; children—Sally Frances (dec.), Bonnie Lee, Bradley Paul. Teaching asst. Duke, 1955-58; cons. Union Carbide Nuclear Corp., Oak Ridge, 1959-69; lab. technician physiology U. Cal. at Los Angeles Med. Sch., 1958-59, lectr. zoology, 1962-63; prof. biology Cal. State U., Northridge, 1966—. Mem. scholarship trust Bonner Sch., Los Angeles. Summer fellow NSF, 1955, 56, predoctoral fellow, 1959-61; AEC fellow Assn. Western Univs., summer 1973; trainee Woods Hole (Mass.) Biol. Lab., summer 1974. Mem. Soc. Devel. Biology, Am. Soc. Zoologists, Soc. Bell Biology, Nat. Charity League, Sigma Xi. Contbr. articles to profl. jours. Home: 2100 Eric Dr Los Angeles CA 90049 Office: Biology Dept State Univ Cal Northridge CA 91324

BARBER, MELANIE WILMER BYRON, writer, artist; b. Anniston, Ala., Dec. 28, 1896; d. Frederick Elliott and Fanny Barclay (Hammond) Gordon; grad. Columbia; studied U. N.M., also in Europe; m. William Alexander Barber; 1 son Gordon (dec.). Began career in Theatre Guild prodns. of Euripides' Medea, others, N.Y.C.; stage appearances include role with Minnie Maldern Fiske, New Orleans, also in An Innocent Idea, N.Y.C.; author Peace, An Ode for the Morning of Christ's Nativity; The Third Anniversary—Tom Dooley's Vietnam and Laos; contbr. to periodicals and anthologies. Mem. ofcl. exec. bd. women's nat. com. N.Y. World's Fair, 1939; hospitality chmn. Office Inter Am. Affairs, also cultural relations div. U.S. State Dept., World War II. Former bd dirs. Girl Scout Council Greater N.Y.; bd. dirs. Tom Dooley Heritage, Inc.; adv. bd. An Lac Orphanage, Saigon, Viet Nam. Mem. Art Students League (life), N.Y. Altar Guild (life), Poetry Soc. Am., Craftsman Group Poets, Friends of Columbia Libraries, D.A.R., Nat. Soc. Colonial Dames. Clubs: Three Arts (past v.p.), Colony, Metropolitan (hon. life guest) (N.Y.C.). Home: Taconic CT 06079

BARBER, SHIRLEY PATRICIA (MRS. DELOS PAUL BARBER), home economist; b. Aitkin, Minn., Mar. 17, 1939; d. Andrew William and Aili Marian (Niemi) Lake; B.S., U. Minn., 1961; m. Delos Paul Barber, May 29, 1965; 1 dau., Linda Halie. Extension home economist Wadena County, Wadena, Minn., 1961-65; tchr. Community Sch. Dist. 300, Carpentersville, Ill., 1966-68; extension home economist Ramsey County Extension Service, St. Paul, 1968—; asst. prof. extension edn. U. Minn., St. Paul, 1970—. Mem. Nat., Minn. (state sec. 1964; state treas. 1969-71) assns. extension home economists, Am., Minn. home econs. assns., Minn. Nutrition Council, Epsilon Sigma Phi. Home: Route 1 Jordan MN 55352 Office: 2020 White Bear Av St Paul MN 55109

BARBERII, NANCY JANE KENDALL (MRS. EFRAIN EMETERIO BARBERII), architect; b. Oklahoma City, June 8, 1922; d. Reginald W. and Effie (Tucker) Kendall; B.A. in Arts and Sci., U. Okla., 1943, B.S. in Archtl. Engring., 1945; postgrad. U. Ariz., 1971-73; m. Efrain Emeterio Barberii, July 26, 1944; children—Nancy K. (Mrs. Bruce Silberman), John K. Draftsman U. Okla., Norman, 1945-46, Welch Constrn. Co., Tulsa, 1949-51; archtl. cons. Okla. Natural Gas, Tulsa, 1950-51; architect U. Zulia, Maracaibo, Venezuela, 1955-58; tech. asst. to exec. dir. Nat. Council Archtl. Registration Bds., Oklahoma City, 1961-63; research engr. U. Ariz., Tucson, 1968-70, dir. Office Civil Def. Adv. Center, 1970-73, part-time lectr. structures for archtl. students dept. civil engring., 1971-72; architect Western Div. Naval Facilities Engring. Command, San Diego, 1973—. Tchr. Spanish KETA-TV U. Okla., 1960-61; cons. to Dr. R. Spicher, San Jose, Cal., 1972—; adviser Beta Rho Delta, 1968-71. Mem. Soc. Women Engrs. (chmn. S.W. sect.), Gamma Phi Beta. Home: 440 S Country Club Tucson AZ 85713 Office: Western Div Naval Facilities Engring Command 1220 Pacific Hwy San Diego CA 92135

BARBEROUSSE, ELEANOR VIRGINIA HARRELL (MRS. EUELL ROBERT BARBEROUSSE), educator; b. Truxno, La.; d. Virgil Monroe and Virginia Ione (Read) Harrell; B.S., La. Poly. Inst., 1940; M.S., La. State U., 1953; Ed.S., Auburn U., 1962, Ed.D., 1965; m. Euell Robert Barberousse, Aug. 10, 1941; 1 dau., Virginia Louise (Mrs. Andrew Everett Colclough). Tchr. high sch., Webster, Union, Morehouse parishes, La., 1940-49; tchr. Bastrop (La.) Jr. High Sch., 1949-60, counselor, 1958-61; parish guidance counselor, coordinator Morehouse Parish Testing Program, Bastrop, 1961-63; counselor, coordinator counseling, asst. prof. counselor edn. Auburn (Ala.) U., 1964-67; counselor Walt Whitman High Sch., Bethesda, Md., 1967—; asst. prof. counselor edn. George Washington U., Washington, 1968-69. Cons. counseling psychologist VA Hosp., Tuskeegee, Ala., 1965-67. Mem. C.G. Jung Found. Analytical Psychology, N.Y.C., also Friends of the C.G. Jung Found. Analytical Psychology, Los Angeles. Mem. Am., Md. (editor Compass Points 1968-70), Montgomery County personnel and guidance assns., Am. Coll. Personnel Assn., Assn. Measurement Edn. Guidance, Am. Sch. Counselors Assn., Am., Md. psychol. assns., N.E.A., Montgomery County Edn. Assn., Md. State Tchrs. Assn., Am. Assn. Humanistic Psychologists, Delta Kappa Gamma, Psi Chi, Alpha Chi Omega. Home: 17500 McDade Ct Rockville MD 20855 Office: Whittier Blvd Bethesda MD 20034

BARBOUR, SISTER JANE MARIE, educator; b. Owensboro, Ky., Feb. 13, 1905; d. Charles Hall and Jane Marie (Edelen) Barbour; B.A., Our Lady of Lake Coll., San Antonio, 1936, B.S. in L.S., 1944; M.A., Cath. U. Am., 1941; M.S. in L.S., Columbia, 1957, postgrad., 1964-65. Joined Sisters of Divine Providence, 1923; tchr. secondary sch., Tex., Okla., La., 1925-44; mem. faculty Our Lady of Lake Coll., 1944-70, prof. library sci., dir. grad. dept., 1966-70; prof. library sci. Grad. Sch., Rosary Coll., River Forest, Ill., 1970-71; cons. F.E. Compton Co., Chgo., 1970—. Recipient Matrix award Theta Sigma Phi; govt. grantee to participate in workshop Internationalism in Library Edn., 1969. Mem. Am. (Letter Librarian award 1956), Catholic (exec. bd. 1970—), Tex. (pres. 1963-64) library assns., Am. Assn. U. Profs., Zonta Internat. Democrat. Home: 411 SW 24th St San Antonio TX 78285

BARCK, JEANNE COLLINS, ednl. adminstr.; b. Cedartown, Ga., May 23, 1936; d. William Goodall and Emily Cater (Sanders) Collins; B.A., Duke, 1958, M.A. in Teaching, 1959; m. P.H. Barck, Feb. 24, 1973. Tchr. New Mexico Girls Sch., Albuquerque, 1962-65, prin., 1965-67; dir. edn. Los Lunas (N.M.) Hosp., and Tng. Sch., 1968-71; asst. dir. N.M. Dept. Edn., Santa Fe, 1971-73; curriculum cons. Farmington (N.M.) Municipal Schs., 1973—. Lectr. ednl. programs for children, also cons. Mem. Am. Assn. on Mental Deficiency. Home: 1725 Mesa Dr Aztec NM 87401 Office: 208 North Wall St Farmington NM 87410

BARCLAY, JEAN CARLETON HATFIELD (MRS. WENDELL FRANCIS BARCLAY), advt. exec., civic leader; b. Chgo., Jan. 3, 1915; d. W. Wilbur and Grace (Chamberlain) Hatfield; A.B., U. Mich., 1937; M.S., Northwestern U., 1940; m. Wendell Francis Barclay, Aug. 3, 1940; 1 son, David Kent. Pub. relations dir. Cleary Coll., Ypsilanti, Mich., 1937-38; with advt. dept. A. J. Nystrom & Co., Chgo., 1939-40; advt., pub. relations Bank for Savs. and Loan Assns., Chgo., 1967-68. Chmn. spl. gifts appeal Beverly Hills-Morgan Park div. women's div. Chgo. Heart Assn., 1966, city co-chmn., 1967-70, campaign chmn., 1971-72, co-chmn., 1973, chmn. fund raising com., 1973—; pres. Kellogg Elementary Sch. P.T.A., Chgo., 1957-59, active Morgan Park High Sch. P.T.A.; organizer women's aux. Goodwill Industries Chgo., pres., 1961-65, 4th v.p., 1965-69, sec., 1969-70, hon. life mem., 1972—; pres. sr. aux. Beverly Hills, Mary Bartelme Home Girls Met. Chgo., 1968-69, bd. mgrs. Chgo., 1968-69; sec. Beverly Hills aux. Ill. Children's Home and Aid Soc., 1958; active Infant Welfare Soc., Chgo.; chmn. door-to-door campaign Beverly Hills-Morgan Park Community Fund 1954; co-chmn. Women's div. Chgo. Community Fund, 1955-57; pres. Ridge Service Guild, Chgo., 1965-67; bd. dirs. Drama League, 1969—, Beverly Hills Community Concerts, 1973—; program dir. Beverly Art Center, 1969—, bd. dirs., 1970—, mem. exec. com., 1971—, bd. asso. dirs., 1972—, chmn. programming com., 1972—. Vol. Citizens for Merriam for mayor campaign, Chgo., 1955. Mem. Pike County (Ill.) Farm Bur., D.A.R. (chmn. various coms.), League Women Voters Ill., Ridge Hist. Soc. (program dir. 1971-73, dir. 1971—), Internat. Platform Assn., Drama League, Crerar Library Assos. (mem. council 1968—), Women in Communications, Delta Gamma. Conglist. Clubs: Sewing, Cotillion, Beverly Country, Thursday Book (pres. 1962, 71-72, Wednesday Book (Chgo.); Woodmar Country (Hammond, Ind.). Address: 9326 S Pleasant Av Chicago IL 60620

BARCLAY, LILLIAN E., social worker; b. Boston; d. Alexander Hugh and Jane (Leslie) Barclay; A.B., Radcliffe Coll.; M.A., Boston U.; M.S.W., Simmons Sch. Social Work. Social worker Grace New Haven Hosp.; sch. social worker Guidance Dept., Hartford; supr. for social work Meth. Hosp., Bklyn.; dir. med. services Childrens Aid Soc., N.Y.C.; spl. projects supr. Protestant Big Sisters of N.Y.; caseworker Family Service Assn., Boston, later group leader; now supr. Manhattan office Protestant Big Sisters, N.Y.C. Mem. League Women Voters, Nat. Assn. Social Workers, Citizens for Boston Schs. Conglist. Club: Womens City. Home: 266 Newbury St Boston MA 02116 Office: 135 E 22d St New York City NY 10010

BARD, LEONA BRENDA, clin. psychologist; b. N.Y.C., Dec. 12, 1941; d. Samuel Kalman and Yetta (Rubenstein) Fliegner; B.A., Coll. City N.Y., 1962; M.A., George Washington U., 1966; postgrad. U. Md., 1966-67, Mich. State U., 1968-69; m. Michael Bard, Aug. 27, 1961; 1 son, Erik Clive. Research asst. Nat. Inst. Mental Health, Bethesda, Md., 1962-63; psychologist Naval Med. Hosp., Bethesda, 1963-66; clin. psychologist Anne Arundel County Mental Health Center, Annapolis, Md., 1966-67; psychologist Area Learning Center, Grand Rapids, Mich., also Kent County Mental Health Center, Ionia (Mich.) Mental Health Center, 1967-69; psychologist Children's Friend Soc., Salem, Mass., 1969-71; sch. adjustment counselor Masconomet Regional High Sch., Boxford, Mass., 1971—. Cons., Kent County Schs., Ionia County Schs., Ionia Ct. System, Ionia Welfare Dept., Lynn (Mass.) Schs. Neighborhood chmn. March of Dimes. Asst. treas. ind. state senatorial campaign Md., 1966; neighborhood chmn. presdl. campaign, 1968. Mem. Am., Mass. psychol. assns., Mass. Tchrs. Assn., Psi Chi. Home: 61 Alderbrook Dr Topsfield MA 01983 Office: Masconomet Regional High School Boxford MA 01983

BARD, PATRICIA HAIRE (MRS. ROGER H. BARD), author; b. Binghamton, N.Y., May 3, 1935; d. Oliver Wilbur and Jane (Purple) Haire; B.A., Keuka Coll., 1957; postgrad. U. Laval, Quebec, summers 1969-70, New Sch. for Social Research, 1969-71, Instituto Allende, San Miguel, Mexico, 1973; m. Roger H. Bard, Nov. 21, 1959; children—Amy-Carol, Jane-Lynnette. Field dir. MidFairfield council Camp Fire Girls, Danbury, Conn., 1957—; free lance writer, contbr. articles to various mags., newspapers, including Eternity, Guideposts, Newsday. Leader, mem. exec. com. Tioga council Girl Scouts, 1959-62; participant Rural Social-Help Projects, Tioga Center, N.Y., 1959-62; neighborhood worker Full Circle, Inc., Inner-City Neighborhood Projects, N.Y.C., 1969-70; vol. tchr. creative writing with children Bay Community Sch., Brookhaven, N.Y., 1970-71; pub. relations worker Family Coop., Riverhead, N.Y., 1970-72; participant in exptl. sch. community, 1970—; active womens' Study and Action Group, Southampton, N.Y. Recipient award for valued service East Quogue Sch., 1972. Mem. Pi Delta Epsilon, Chi Beta Phi, Alpha Psi Omega, Pi Gamma Mu. Author: Games Christians Play, 1967; The Fragmented, 1969; Little White Book on Race, 1970; At the Risk of Being A Wife, 1971. Home: PO Box 736 East Quogue NY 11942

BARDEEN, ANN (MRS. ERNEST O. HENSCHEL), physician; b. Milw., Sept. 17, 1921; d. Charles Russell and Ruth (Hames) Bardeen; B.S., U. Wis., 1942, M.D., 1945; m. Ernest O. Henschel, June 17, 1953; children—Kira, Ingrid, Rhonda (dec.). Intern Jersey City Med. Center, 1945-46, resident in internal medicine, 1946-47, resident in anesthesiology U. Wis. Hosp., Madison, 1947-50; Am. Assn. U. Women fellow, Wales, Gt. Britain, 1950-51; European locum tenens anesthesiology, jr. instr. WHO, Copenhagen, 1951-52; instr., asst. prof. anesthesiology U. Wis., 1952-53; clin. instr. U. Sask. (Can.), 1954-56; practice medicine specializing in anesthesiology, Milw. and Sask., 1956-65; asst. prof. anesthesiology Med. Coll. Wis. (formerly Marquette Sch. Medicine), Milw., 1965-68, asso. prof., 1968—; mem. staffs Milwaukee County Gen. Hosp., Milw. Children's Hosp., VA Center, Deaconess Hosp., Oconomowoc Meml. Hosp. Diplomate Am. Bd. Anesthesiologists, Royal Coll. Physicians and Surgeons Can. Fellow Am. Coll. Anesthesiologists, Faculty Anaesthetists Royal Coll. Surgeons London, Royal Coll. Physicians and Surgeons Can., mem. Royal Soc. Medicine, Am., Wis., Milw. socs. anesthesiology, Am. Soc. Neuroanesthesiology, A.M.A., Canadian Anaesthesiol. Soc., Assn. Anaesthetists of Gt. Britain and Ireland, Am. Assn. U. Women, Am. Med. Women's Assn., also conservation and wildlife socs. Home: 412 N Lake Rd Oconomowoc WI 53066 Office: Milwaukee County Gen Hosp 8700 W Wisconsin Av Milwaukee WI 53226

BARDELL, EUNICE RUTH (MRS. ROSS H. BARDELL), educator; b. Milw., Feb. 8, 1915; d. Eric A. and Alma Helen (Stark) Bonow; B.S., U. Wis., 1938, M.S., 1949, Ph.D., 1952; m. Ross H. Bardell, Nov. 23, 1972. Intern Rennebohm Drug Co., Madison, Wis., 1938-40; pharmacist Ed Schuster & Co., Milw., 1940-42, Kremers Urban Co., Milw., 1942-44; teaching asst. Sch. Pharmacy, U. Wis.-Madison, 1944-48; instr. U. Wis.-Milw., 1948-52, asst. prof. pharmacy, 1952-60, asso. prof., 1960-72, prof. pharmacy and health services, 1972-73, prof. emeritus, 1973—. Fellow Am. Found. for Pharm. Edn., Royal Soc. for Promotion Health (U.K.); mem. Am., Wis. pharm. assns., Pharmacists Soc. Milw. County, Am. Inst. History Pharmacy, Am. Bd. Diplomats in Pharmacy, N.Y. Acad. Scis., Am. Soc. Microbiology, Sigma Xi, Kappa Epsilon (Key of Excellence), Rho Chi, Sigma Delta Epsilon, Phi Sigma, Delta Kappa Gamma. Author: She Is A Pharmacist, 1958. Home: 1539 N 51st St Milwaukee WI 53208

BARDES, JUDITH LEOPOLD (MRS. CHARLES ROBERT BARDES), civic worker; b. Phila., Aug. 17, 1931; d. Charles Stein and Marian Rose (Bettman) Leopold; B.A. cum laude, Bryn Mawr Coll., 1953; m. Charles Robert Bardes, June 20, 1953; children—Charles Leopold, Peggy Anne, Diane Lisa. Librarian, William Jeanes Meml. Library, Plymouth Meeting, Pa., 1961-68; exec. sec. Alfred and Mary Douty Found., Plymouth Meeting, 1969—; agt. Sun Life Assurance Co. Can., Phila., 1970—; security salesperson Suncan Equity Services Co., Boston, 1971—. Co-chmn. Com. for A New Library, Lafayette Hill, Pa., 1968; adv. com. William Jeanes Meml. Library Bldg. Fund, Plymouth Meeting, 1970-71; mem. Citizens' Council Whitemarsh Twp. Candidate Whitemarsh Twp. Sch. Bd., 1963. Trustee Alfred and Mary Douty Found., 1969—; trustee William Jeanes Meml. Library, Lafayette Hill, 1968—, v.p., 1969-73, pres., 1973—; bd. dirs. Friends of William Jeanes Meml. Library, Plymouth Meeting, 1963—, pres., 1964-68; information chmn. Dist. III Bryn Mawr Coll., 1973—. Mem. Pa. Library Assn., League Women Voters, Council for Internat. Visitors, Phila., Plymouth Meeting Hist. Soc. Club: Bryn Mawr (v.p. 1973—) (Phila.). Home: 5070 Militia Hill Rd Plymouth Meeting PA 19462 Office: 1339 Chestnut St Philadelphia PA 19107

BARDO, PAMELA PIERREPONT, museum curator; b. Albany, N.Y., Feb. 4, 1947; d. August John and Beatrice (Varney) Bardo; B.A., Briarcliff Coll., 1969; M.A., U. Pitts., 1971. Teaching asst. U. Pitts., 1969-70; dir. Univ. Art Gallery U. Pitts., 1972-73; curator collections New Orleans Mus. Art, 1973—. Mem., sec. Save Venice, Inc., 1974—. Mem. Western Pa. Episcopal Bishop's Commn. Higher Edn., 1972-73. Bd. dirs., sec. Italian Art and Landscape Found., Pitts., 1972-73. Mem. Coll. Art Assn. Am., Am. Assn. Museums, Am. Assn. U. Profs., Brit. Nat. Trust. Democrat. Episcopalian. Home: 508 Frenchmen St PO Box 19708 New Orleans LA 70179 Office: New Orleans Museum Art City Park New Orleans LA 70119

BARE, GERTRUDE BLUM JUNGCK (MRS. WALTER RAY BARE), clubwoman; b. Rushville, Neb., June 23, 1902; d. Louis John and Pauline (Blum) Jungck; grad. high sch.; m. Walter Ray Bare, Nov. 6, 1923; 1 son, Teddy Lewayne. Telephone operator Northwestern Bell, Wyo., Neb., 1917-19, 22-23; rural sch. tchr., Rushville, 1920-21; Star Route mail carrier, Rushville, 1938-42; postal clk., Rushville, 1943-67. Recipient Declaration of Chivalry, Rebekah Lodge, 1967. Mem. Royal Neighbor Am. (recorder 1943-74), Sheridan County Hist. Soc. (sec. 1963—, asst. curator 1974—). Lutheran. Rebekah. Club: Extension (Rushville). Home: 111 Sprague St Rushville NE 69360

BAREIS, MILDRED CAROLYN, paper products co. exec.; b. Montara, Cal., May 25, 1918; d. Karl and Johanna (Peppert) Bareis; B.A., U. Cal. at Berkeley, 1938; M.A., U. Cal. at Berkeley, 1939. Econ. asst. Am. Bankers Assn., N.Y.C., 1940-41; econ. analyst Fed. Res. Bank of San Francisco, 1941-45; asst. to economist Henry J. Kaiser Co., Oakland, Cal., 1945-47; sr. marketing research analyst Crown Zellerbach Corp., San Francisco, 1947—. Mem. Am. Statis. Assn. (pres. San Francisco chpt. 1972-73), Nat. Assn. Bus. Economists, Am. Marketing Assn. Home: 1935 Funston St San Francisco CA 94116 Office: 1 Bush St San Francisco CA 94119

BARFIELD, MARGUERITE IRL, psychologist; b. Houston, June 20, 1938; d. John Irl and Arline (Leeth) Durham; B.A. in English, Rice U., 1960; M.A. in Psychology, U. Houston, 1968, Ph.D., 1971. Tchr., Spring Branch Ind. Sch. Dist., Tex., 1960-65; psychol. asso. Almeda Clinic, Houston, 1971-73, clin. psychologist, 1973—. Tchr. marriage, family and sex edn. U. Houston, 1973—. Mem. Am., Southwestern, Tex., Houston psychol. assns., Phi Kappa Phi. Research on sex edn. Home: 12752 Huntingwick St Houston TX 77024 Office: St Joseph Profl Bldg Houston TX 77002

BARHAM, PATRICIA ANN, author, columnist; b. Los Angeles; d. Frank and Jessica (Gorham) Barham; student U. So. Cal., U. Ariz.; Litt.D., Trinity So. Bible Coll. Columnist, Los Angeles Herald Express; spl. features Hearst Predate-Ky. Features Synod.; syndicated fashion columnist small town newspapers, Hollywood; Westcoast editor Spotlight mag.; asso. editor Leisure Living mag.; feature writer, syndicated columnist chain small-town newspapers; society editor Millionaire mag.; nationally syndicated entertainment-society columnist, feature writer. Mem. U.S. Olympic Com.; life mem. Amateur-Athletic Union U.S., now v.p. pub. relations com. Mem. Nat. League Am. Pen Women, Nat. Soc. Letters, Arts and Scis., Greater Los Angeles Press Club, Hollywood Women's Press Club, Tokyo Corrs., Pan Am. Cultural Soc., Am. Nat. Theatre Assn. and Acad., Mus. Alliance, Opera Guild So. Cal., Costume Council Los Angeles County Mus., Aviation Space Writers Assn., English Speaking Union, D.A.R., St. Anne's Hosp. Guild, Navy Belles, Social Service Aux., Internat. Com. So. Cal. Philharmonic, Delta Gamma, Theta Sigma Phi. Clubs: Beverly Hills, Outrigger Canoe (Hawaii), Ebell (Los Angeles). Author: Pin up Poems; Operation Nightmare. Address: 100 Fremont Pl Los Angeles CA 90005

BARHYDT, EMILY TARBELL (MRS. RAYMOND BARHYDT), educator; b. Milford, N.H., May 13, 1896; d. George and Elizabeth (Bennett) Tarbell; A.B., Syracuse U., 1916; B. Oral English, 1924, M.A., 1954; postgrad. student U. Havana, 1953; m. Raymond S. Barhydt, July 29, 1949. Tchr. Odessa (N.Y.) High Sch., 1916-18, Syracuse (N.Y.) Vocational High Sch., 1918-1960, adult evening sch., 1960-71. Mem. Syracuse Everson Mus.; chmn. film festival N.Y. State Fair, 1955. Trustee Robert R. Decormier Meml. Fund. Recipient Gov. Averell Harriman tchr. award, 1956; named N.Y. State Ret. Tchr. of Yr., 1972. Mem. N.E.A. (mem. exec. com. 1942-46, pres. dept. classroom tchrs. 1937-38, eastern regional dir. 1934-37, editor News-Bull. 1938-39, mem. ednl. policies commn. 1939-44), Am. Assn. U. women (Central N.Y. pres. 1934-36), Nat. League Tchrs. Assns. (v.p. Eastern region 1953-56), N.Y. State (dir. 1948-56), Syracuse (editor bull. 1932-53) tchrs. assns., N.Y. State Speech Assn., Tchrs. Welfare League of N.Y. State (pres. 1929-33), Nat. Parliamentarians Assn., N.Y. State Ret. Tchrs. Assn. (2d v.p. 1969-73), Onondaga County and Syracuse Council of State Commn. for Human Rights, Am. Acad. Polit. and Social Sci., Nat. Ret. Tchrs. Assn., Am. Assn. Ret. Persons (nat. legislative council 1965-71), Onondaga Hist. Assn., Syracuse Profl. Woman's League, Inc. (pres. 1928-30), League Women Voters, Alpha Omicron Pi (Nat. Achievement award 1971), Pi Lambda Theta. Author: (with others) Teacher and Public, 1934. Contbr. to profl. publs. Home: Regency House 33 W Adams St Jacksonville FL 32202

BARIANI, GERALDINE DONNA, librarian; b. Denver, May 14, 1915; d. Joseph B. and Eura LeMieux (McClintick) Bariani; B.S. in Bus., U. Denver, 1936, B.S. in Library Sci., 1937; M.S. in Bus., Ind. U., 1941. Asst. reference and circulation dept. Northwestern U., 1937-38; librarian Sch. Bus., Ind. U., 1938-62; supr. deptl. libraries, 1939-41; reference librarian Colo. Sch. Mines, Golden, 1962—. Mem. Spl. Libraries Assn. (chmn. bus. div. 1950), Phi Chi Theta. Author: Arthur Lakes Library Serials Holding List, 1972. Home: 8 Mines Park Golden CO 80401

BARKAN, BEBE ROSENFELD, art editor; b. Bklyn., Mar. 8, 1943; d. Jerry and Gertrude (Margolin) Rosenfeld; B.A., Hunter Coll., 1964, M.A. in Art, 1969; student Instituto Allende, 1967; m. Stanley H. Barkan, June 21, 1964; children—Jacqueline Mia, Joseph Scott. Tchr. art N.Y.C. Bd. Edn., 1964-69; art editor Bitterroot, Bklyn., 1972—, Cross-Cultural Communications, Merrick, N.Y., 1972—; commn., sculptor sterling silver jewelry Brentano's, Manhasset, N.Y., 1968; exhibited art in group shows at Ninth Ann. Exhbn. Graphics, Mercyhurst Coll., Erie, Pa.; 16th Ann. Exhbn., Community Arts Council, South Shore, Hempstead, N.Y.; Invitational Show Nat. Council Jewish Women, Ann. Open Exhbn., Long Beach Art Assn., 1970. Dir. Bebe Originals, Merrick, N.Y. Recipient 2d prize in graphics Merrick Art League, 1969. Mem. Internat. Platform Assn. (2d prize 1973), Merrick Art League, Long Beach Art Assn. Author: (with Stanley H. Barkan) The American Hototogisu, 1969. Illustrator Shantih, 1972; Child of An Oak, 1972, The Washington Square Jour., 1969. Home: 239 Wynsum Av Merrick NY 11566 Office: Cross-Cultural Communications PO Box 383 Merrick NY 11566

BARKER, ELIZABETH JANE BELL (MRS. OTELLO DALE SMITH), psychiatrist; b. Knoxville, Tenn., Mar. 17, 1930; d. Robert Monroe and Myrtle (Dekle) Bell; B.A., Johnson Bible Coll., 1950; B.A., U. Tenn., 1952, M.D., 1955; m. Otello Dale Smith, Feb. 26, 1971; children (by previous marriage)—Jennifer Lee, Susan Lynn. Intern, John Gaston Hosp., Memphis, 1956; resident, Gailor Meml. Hosp., Memphis, 1957-60; practice medicine specializing in psychiatry, Tripoli, Libya, 1961-63, Memphis, 1964-65, Prairie Village, Kan., 1965—; mem. staff Menorah Med. Center, Kansas City, Kan. Cons. Johnson County Mental Health Center, 1966-67, Jackson County Juvenile Ct., 1965-69, Shawnee Mission Sch. Dist., 1972—. Mem. Am. Psychiat. Assn., Johnson County Med. Soc., Internat. Transactional Analysis Assn. (clin. mem.). Home: 5400 W 83d St Prairie Village KS 66208 Office: 4121 W 83d St Prairie Village KS 66208

BARKER, EVELYN ANN MASI, educator; b. Franklin, Mass., Feb. 16, 1927; d. Aniello and Mary (Verna) Masi; A.B. summa cum laude, Wheaton (Mass.) Coll., 1948; M.A., Vassar Coll., 1949; Ph.D., Radcliffe Coll., 1956; m. Stephen F. Barker, Aug. 28, 1961; children—Charles, George. Instr. philosophy Wells Coll., 1950-51; lectr., asst. prof. philosophy Mt. Holyoke Coll., 1956-61; vis. prof. Ohio Wesleyan U., 1962-63; asso. prof. Univ. Coll. of U. Md., 1964-66; asso. prof. evening and summer sessions Johns Hopkins, 1964-65; asso. prof. philosophy U. Md., 1966—. Mem. Am. Philos. Assn., Am. Assn. U. Profs., Phi Beta Kappa. Democrat. Roman Catholic. Contbr. to profl. jours. Editor: The Humanity of Man (R.B. Berry), 1956. Home: 4003 Keswick Rd Baltimore MD 21211

BARKER, JOYCE (MRS. HAROLD ELWYN DYER), opera singer; b. Durban, South Africa, June 6; d. Edward Chase and Henrietta May (McBean) B; ed. pvt. schs., S. Africa, Natal U., Royal Acad. Mus.; m. Harold Elwyn Dyer, June 27, 1959; children—Sandra, Deborah. Performed in concert, oratorio opera, broadcasting engagements, Eng., S. Africa; appeared N.Y.C., Santa Fe, Seattle operas, 1970-72; appeared Covent Garden, Slyndbourne, Royal Albert Hall (royal command performance), 1972. Recipient 1st Kathleen Ferrier scholarship; Gold medal Internat. Coucour de Chant. Recording of Mahler's Symphony of a Thousand (8th). Address: 122A Buckingham Av Craighall Park Johannesburg South Africa

BARKER, LOUISE SHEDD (MRS. ROGER G. BARKER), social scientist; b. Reziah, Iran, Sept. 10, 1906 (parents Am. citizens); d. William Ambrose and Louise (Wilbur) Shedd; A.B., Stanford U., 1928, M.A., 1930; m. Roger Garlock Barker, June 17, 1930; children—Celia Louise (Mrs. Stephen S. Lottridge), Jonathan, Lucy Garlock. Tchr. pub. schs. Redwood City, Cal., 1930-35, counsellor, 1942-45, Central Y.M.C.A. Coll., Chgo., 1941-42; mem. research staff Midwest Psychol. Field Sta., U. Kan., Oskaloosa, 1948—, field work dir., editorial asst., research asso. Chmn. N.E. Kan. Library Grant Area, Kan. State Library, 1965-68; mem. State Library Systems Council, 1969—. Bd. dirs. Oskaloosa Pub. Library, 1962-69; pres. bd. dirs. N.E. Kan. Library System; bd. dirs. Jefferson County Meml. Hosp., Winchester, Kan. Mem. Kan. Library Assn. (recipient trustee award 1966), Phi Beta Kappa. Presbyn. (deacon, elder). Author: (with others) Specimen Records of American and English Children, 1961. Home: 522 Atchison Box 98 Oskaloosa KS 66066

BARKER, MARJORIE WHEELER, librarian; b. Goffstown, N.H., Sept. 14, 1914; d. Mark Cleveland and Florence Winona (Kelley) Wheeler; B.A., Goucher Coll., 1936; M.L.S., U. Md., 1966; m. John Paul Barker, Nov. 25, 1939 (div. Dec. 1969); children—John, Mark, Mary Helen, Charles. Asst. children's dept. Enoch Pratt Free Library, Balt., 1936-39; asst. tech. service dept., cataloguer br. librarian George County Meml. Library, Hyattsville, Md., 1963-70; with Nashua (N.H.) Pub. Library, 1970—, supr. children's dept., 1971—. Cons. Merrimack Br. U. N.H. Sch. Library Sci., Manchester, 1973—, great books leader 1973—. Mem. Am., N.H., New Eng. library assns., Alpha Gamma Delta. Republican. Episcopalian. Home: 76 Beauview Nashua NH 03060 Office: 2 Court St Nashua NH 03060

BARKER, MARY LOU WYLIE (MRS. ROBERT L. BARKER), advt. exec.; b. Stamford, Tex., Mar. 3, 1931; d. David C. and Blanche (Thomason) Wylie; student U. Tex., 1948-52; m. Robert L. Barker, Apr. 22, 1963; children—William Lopaka, David Keaka. With KVKM Radio, Monahans, Tex., 1950-51; tv traffic mgr. KTBC-TV, Austin, 1952-54; tv prodn. mgr., sr. dir. KLTV, Tyler, Tex., 1954-56; sr. dir. KTUL-TV, Tulsa, 1956-59; staff dir. KHVH-TV, Honolulu, 1960-61, KGMB-TV, Honolulu, 1961-63; spl. projects supr., dir. radio and tv Patt Patterson & Assos., Inc., Honolulu, 1965-71, v.p. operations, 1971—. Home: 745 Kapulena Loop Honolulu HI 96825 Office: 333 Queen St Honolulu HI 96813

BARKER, PAULA STAPLETON, editor; b. Chgo., Dec. 5, 1945; d. George William and Phyllis Margaret (Stapleton) Barker; B.A., Smith Coll., 1967; student Inst. des Scis. Politiques, Paris, 1965-66. Program coordinator African Studies Program Northwestern U., Evanston, Ill., 1967-69; editor, adminstrv. dir. African Studies Assn., Brandeis U., Waltham, Mass., 1970—. Editor: African Studies Newsletter, 1970—; Issue: A Quar. Jour. Africanist Opinion, 1971—. Home: 119 Pembroke St Boston MA 02154 Office: 218 Shiffman Center Brandeis Univ Waltham MA 02154

BARKHORN, JEAN COOK (MRS. HENRY C. BARKHORN), mag. editor; b. N.Y.C., Apr. 3, 1931; d. Francis Howell and Janet (McCord) Cook; B.A., Vassar Coll., 1953; m. Henry C. Barkhorn, May 14, 1971. Asst. to decorating editor Town and Country mag., N.Y.C., 1956-63, exec. editor, 1963-68, mng. editor, 1968—. Home: 36 E 72d St New York City NY 10021 Office: 717 Fifth Av New York City NY 10022

BARKIN, ELAINE, composer, educator; b. N.Y.C., Dec. 15, 1932; d. Victor and Edith (Shukman) Radoff; B.A., Queens Coll., 1954; M.F.A., Brandeis U., 1956, Ph.D., 1970; certificate in composition and piano Berlin Hochschule fur Musik, 1957; m. George Jean Barkin, Nov. 28, 1957; children—Victor, Jesse, Gabriel. Lectr., Queens Coll., 1964-69; instr. Sarah Lawrence Coll., 1969; asst. prof. music theory U. Mich. Sch. Music, Ann Arbor, 1970—; vis. lectr. Princeton, 1974. Teaching fellow Brandeis U., 1954-56. Recipient N.Y. State Council on Arts-Internat. Soc. for Contemporary Music commn., 1974, Nat. Endowment for Arts award, 1974. Tanglewood fellowship, 1955; Fulbright award Berlin, 1957; Brandeis U. scholarship, 1967-68; U. Mich. Faculty Research grantee, 1972; Princeton U. Council Humanities jr. fellow, 1974. Mem. Am. Soc. U. Composers (mem. exec. com. 1967-69), League Composers, Internat. Soc. for Contemporary Music (exec. sec. 1968-69), Coll. Music Soc., Am. Composers Alliance, Phi Beta Kappa. Composer: Woodwind Quartet, 1956; Essay for Orchestra, 1957; String Trio, 1957; Refrains for 6 Players, 1967; 6 Pieces for Piano, 1968; String Quartet, 1969; Plus ca change (for strings and percussion), 1972; Prim Cycles (for 4 players), 1973; Sound Play (violin solo), 1974. Co-editor Perspectives of New Music, 1963—. Contbr. articles to music jours. Home: 1208 Ferdon Rd Ann Arbor MI 48104

BARKLEY, CAROLYN ESTHER, charity exec.; b. Austin, Tex., Nov. 21, 1944; d. Edward M. and Hermine Winifred (Pearce) Barkley; B. in Journalism, U. Tex. at Austin, 1967. Pub. information specialist City Austin (Tex.) Parks and Recreation Dept., 1967-69; community information coordinator City Austin City Mgr's Office, 1969-70, City Austin Pub. Information Dept., 1970; dedication office staff mem. L.B. Johnson Library Dedication Office, U. Tex. at Austin, 1971; spl. asst. to campaign dirs. Dolph Briscoe for Gov. State Headquarters, Austin, 1972; dir. pub. relations United Way Capital Area, Austin, 1973—. Del. Travis County Dem. Conv., 1968, 72. Named Miss Austin Aqua Beauty, Austin Aqua Festival, 1970. Mem. Internat. Assn. Bus. Communicators. Democrat. Home: 2501 E St Elmo Rd Austin TX 78744 also 500 S Congress St #111 Austin TX 78740 Office: 610 Guadalupe PO Box 1925 Austin TX 78767

BARKLEY, KATHERINE TRAVER (MRS. ROBERT BARKLEY), librarian; b. Center Brunswick, N.Y., Sept. 25, 1914; d. Amos John and Florence Adeline (Fake) Traver; B.A., Hood Coll., 1935; postgrad. Western Res. U., 1958-64, postgrad. Miami U., Dayton, O., 1960, U. Cin., 1971-72; m. Robert Barkley, June 4, 1935; children—Robert, Bruce Traver, Betty Louise (Mrs. Leo Rota). Asst. to librarian John Hay High Sch. Library, Cleve., 1954-58; asst. to librarian Northtown-Shiloh br. Dayton and Montgomery County Pub. Library, Dayton, 1958-60, librarian Vandalia br., 1960-64; med. librarian Jewish Hosp. Med. Library, Cin., 1965—. Recipient Murray Gottlieb prize, 1969. Mem. Am., Ohio, Med., Ohioana library assns., Midwest Regional Med. Library Assn. (dir. 1970-71, sec., treas. 1972-73), Am. Assn. History of Medicine, Spl. Libraries Assn. (pres. Cin. chpt. 1969-70), Ohio Acad. History of Medicine, Ohio Hist. Soc. Contbr. articles to med. jours. Home: 6713 Red Bird Rd Loveland OH 45140 Office: Jewish Hospital Medical Library Cincinnati OH 45229

BARKLEY, SARA JOYCE LOWEN, editor; b. Delmeny, Sask., Can., Nov. 8, 1913; d. George I. and Marie (Laubenstein) Lowen; came to U.S., 1920, naturalized, 1944; student U. Ore., 1933-37, U. Cal. at Berkeley, 1939, Lewiston Normal Sch., 1940-41, Butte Coll., 1973; m. Edgar Eric Barkley, Feb. 11, 1933 (div. 1956); children—Edgar Eric, Michael Bruce, Karen Marie (Mrs. Thomas Joseph Ward). Reporter, photographer Santa Rosa (Cal.) Democrat, 1950-54; editor Montgomery Village News, Santa Rosa, 1954; women's editor Ukiah (Cal.) Daily Jour., 1954-56, Chico (Cal.) Enterprise-Record, 1956—. Leader, Camp Fire Girls, Woodland, Wash., 1936-37; pres. Ft. Bragg, (Cal.) P.T.A., 1948-49; dist. 2d v.p. Cal. P.T.A., 1950-52; vol. worker A.R.C., 1942-54; mem. Am. Mus. Natural History, N.Y.C. Recipient nat. 1st award in spl. edit. Am. Laundry Mfrs. Assn., 1961; award for photography Silver Dollar Fair, Chico, 1966, 69, 70-73. Mem. Nat. Geog. Soc., Cal. Press Photographers Assn., Bus. and Profl. Women's Luncheon Club, Golden Empire Mineral Soc. (dir.). Republican. Rebekah. Club: Chico Women's (hon.). Home: 1538 Sunset Av Chico CA 95926 Office: PO Box 9 700 Broadway Chico CA 95926

BARKS, ELSIE DICKSON (MRS. HORACE BUSHNELL BARKS), editor; b. Masterton, O., Nov. 26, 1923; d. Harry Ellis and Ula Faye (Pryor) Dickson; student Marietta Coll., 1941-43; B.J., U. Mo., 1945; m. Horace Bushnell Barks, June 14, 1947; children—Elizabeth, Jean, Joseph, Barbara, William. Staff corr. U.P., Charleston, W.Va., 1945-46; instr. journalism U. Mo., Columbia, 1946-47; writer Ridings & Ferris, Inc., Chgo., 1947-49; editor, asso. pub. Barks Publs., Inc., St. Louis, 1951-66, editorial dir., asso. pub. 1971—. Mem. Women in Communications, Am. Soc. Bus. Press Editors, Kappa Tau Alpha, Pi Beta Phi. Episcopalian (pub. relations coordinator diocese of Mo. 1964-66, dir. communications 1966-67). Home: 247 E Chestnut St Chicago IL 60611 Office: 400 N Michigan Av Chicago IL 60611

BARKSDALE, ETHEL BIRDIA COX (MRS. EDWARD W. BARKSDALE), foundry exec.; b. Centreville, Ala., Dec. 19, 1910; d. Merton W. and Mary Jane (Stamps) Cox; grad. high sch.; m. Edward W. Barksdale, Sept. 30, 1928; children—Edward Ward, Robbie Eioise (Mrs. Nicholas Alfard Walsh). Formerly in cosmetics industry; owner beauty shop, Los Angeles; with Buddy Bar Casting Corp., South Gate, Cal., 1953—, now co-owner, treas. Club: Soroptimist (pres. 1971-72) (South Gate-Lynwood, Cal.). Home: 9068 Gallatin Rd Downey CA 90240 Office: 10801 Sessler St South Gate CA 90280

BARLOW, ANNE LOUISE (MRS. ALASTAIR GEORGE RAMSAY), physician, pharm. mfg. co. exec.; b. Skipton, Yorkshire, Eng., Jan. 28, 1925 (came to U.S. 1951, naturalized 1954); d. John and Louise Baker (Pollok) Barlow; M.B., B.S., London U., 1948; D.C.H., Royal Colls., 1950; M.P.H., Yale, 1952; m. Howard Paine Cadwell, May 19, 1951 (div. Feb. 1969); children—Barbara Anne, John James Stewart; m. 2d, Alastair George Ramsay, Dec. 19, 1969. Research asso. Yale, 1951-52, U. Pitts., 1957-61, U. Ill., 1962; intern, North Lonsdale Hosp., Barrow-in-Furness, Eng., 1948, Royal Infirmary, Glasgow, 1948; resident, Royal Hosp. Sick Children, Glasgow, 1949, Anniesland Infectious Diseases Hosp., Glasgow, 1950; practice medicine specializing in pediatrics, Pitts., 1958-63; mem. staff St. Margaret's Meml. Hosp., Pitts.; med. writer Abbott Labs., North Chicago, Ill., 1963-66, antibiotic specialist, 1966-68, mgr. clin. devel., 1968-71, asst. med. dir. Pharm. Products div., 1971-73, med. dir., Hosp. Products div., 1973—. Cons. in child health Lake County Health (Ill.) Dept., 1963—. Mem. Grant Community High Sch. Bd. Edn. Dist. 124; adviser Lake County Head Start Program, 1971—. Rotary Internat. Found. fellow, 1950-51. Mem. Am. Med. Women's Assn., Drug Information Assn. (dir. 1966-68). Home: 1114 Lake Shore Dr Ingleside IL 60041 Office: Abbott Labs 14th and Sheridan Rd North Chicago IL 60064

BARLOW, JOYCE KRUTICK (MRS. ROBERT S. BARLOW), lawyer; b. Bklyn., Mar. 26, 1946; d. Sidney and Esther (Stone) Krutick; B.A., L.I. U., 1966; J.D., Bklyn. Law Sch., 1969; m. Robert S. Barlow, May 25, 1971. Admitted to N.Y. bar, 1969, since practiced in N.Y.C.; asso. firm Sabbatino & Todarelli, 1969-70; asso. atty. criminal def. div. Legal Aid Soc., 1970-73; pvt. practice, N.Y.C., 1973—. Alternate del. to jud. conf. state N.Y., 1970-71. Recipient Pres.'s award for distinguished service Bklyn. Law Sch., 1968-69. Mem. Am., Bklyn. bar assn., N.Y. County Lawyers Assn., Iota Alpha Pi. Home: 230 Jay St Brooklyn NY 11201 Office: 233 Broadway New York City NY 11201

BARLOW, RITA HOUSTON (MRS. EARLE BERKELEY BARLOW), author, editor; b. Juiz De Fora, Minas Geraias, Brazil, Feb. 11, 1922 (parents Am. citizens); d. Benjamin Herriot and Laura Clifton (Crump) Houston; student Greensboro Coll., 1938-41, U. West Indies, 1960; B.S. with honors, U. Fla., 1967; m. Earle Berkeley Barlow, June 15, 1946; children—Amy, Scott, Lisa. Free-lance editor, writer Gainesville, Fla., 1962; prin. R.H. Barlow, Editor, Gainesville, 1962—. Cons. in publs. to P.K. Yonge Sch., Gainesville, 1972—, Santa Fe Community Coll., Gainesville, 1971-72. Bd. dirs. Alachua County Meml. Soc., 1970-72. Mem. Women in Communications, Phi Kappa Phi, Kappa Tau Alpha. Author: Friends in Jamaica, 1960. Co-author biog. articles McGraw-Hill Ency. World Biography. Contbr. sci. articles to profl. jours. and popular publs. Home: 404 NW 19th St Gainesville FL 32603

BARMAN, ALICEROSE SCHNADIG (MRS. MATTHEW J. BARMAN), educator; b. Chgo., May 14, 1919; d. Edgar L. and Nell (Fackson) Schnadig; student U. Ill., 1936-37; B.Ed., Pestalozzi Froebel Tchrs. Coll., 1939; M.A., U. Chgo., 1944; m. Matthew J. Barman, Dec. 17, 1939; children—Thomas, Charles. Tchr. elementary and nursery sch., Chgo., 1940-43; race relations worker Julius Rosenwald Fund, Chgo., 1943-45; asst. to dean, dept. edn., U. Chgo., 1940-43; group worker parent edn. Assn. for Family Living, Chgo., 1948-55; guidance counselor North Chicago (Ill.) Community High Sch., 1957-59, Glenbrook High Sch., Northbrook, Ill., 1959-60; asso. dir. in charge edn. North Shore Mental Health Assn. and Irene Josselyn Clinic, Northfield, Ill., 1960-72; cons. in-service edn., nursery sch. cons. Sch. Dist. 108, Highland Park, Ill., 1972—; nursery sch. cons., 1971—. Instr. child devel. Loop Coll., Chgo., 1968, 69, Pestalozzi Froebel Tchrs. Coll., 1949-51; faculty Northeastern Ill. State U., 1970—. Mem. Sch. Bd. No. 28, Northbrook, Ill., 1960-66. Past dir. Jewish Vocational Service, Fund for Perceptually Handicapped, Ill. Assn. Mental Health Center Adminstrs. (hon.). Fellow Am. Orthopsychiat. Assn.; mem. Assn. for Early Childhood Edn., Sigma Delta Tau. Jewish religion. Author: Mental Health in Classroom and Corridor, 1968; (with Lisa Cohen) Help for Your Troubled Child, 1970; Your First Months with Your New Baby, 1972. also pamphlets, articles pub. in profl. jours. and mags., radio show on family living. Home: 730 Lexington Ct Northbrook IL 60062

BARNARD, JEAN SYMMES (MRS. JOHN REEVE BARNARD), city ofcl.; b. Mt. Vernon, N.Y., Oct. 30, 1918; d. Laurence Metcalf and Dorothy May (Boericke) Symmes; A.B., Vassar Coll., 1940; postgrad. (fellow) U. Cal. at Berkeley, 1940-42; m. John Reeve Barnard, Sept. 15, 1940; children—Ralston White, Geoffrey Symmes. Piano tchr., Mill Valley, Cal., 1947-70; journalist Ross Valley Reporter, San Anselmo, Cal., 1968-72. Councilman, City of Mill Valley, 1970—, pres., 1972-74. Mem. Am. Assn. U. Women, League of Women Voters (dir. 1960-61), Sierra Club, Phi Beta Kappa. Democrat. Conglist. Clubs: Vassar (San Francisco); Outdoor Art (dir. 1968-70) (Mill Valley). Home: 1 El Capitan Mill Valley CA 94941

BARNARD, KATHLEEN RAINWATER, educator; b. Wayne City, Ill., Dec. 28, 1927; d. Roy and Nina (Edmison) Rainwater; B.S., So. Ill. U., 1949, M.S., 1953; postgrad. Ind. U., 1953; Ph.D., U. Tex., 1959; m. Donald L. Barnard, Aug. 17, 1947 (div. Mar. 1973); children—Kimberly, Jill. Tchr. pub. high sch. Wayne City, 1946-51; faculty asst. and lectr. Vocational Tech. Inst., So. Ill. U., Carbondale, 1951-53; lectr. bus. edn. Northwestern U., Chgo., 1953-55; chmn. dept. bus. edn. San Antonio Coll., 1955-60; chmn. dept. tchr. edn. DePaul U., Chgo., 1960-62; chmn. dept. bus. adminstrn. Chgo. City Coll., 1962-67, prof., 1968—. Cons. edn. and tng. div. Continental Ill. Nat. Bank & Trust Co., Chgo., 1967, Victor Corp., 1965—, First Nat. Bank Chgo., 1974; ednl. cons. Oak Park Public Schs., 1969-70. Mem. Chgo. Assn. Commerce and Industry (edn., mgmt. coms.), Adminstrv. Mgmt. Soc. (edn., mgmt. coms.), Small Bus. Opportunities Corp. (mgmt. devel. com.), Nat., North Central bus. edn. assns., Cosmopolitan C. of C. (past dir.), Delta Kappa Gamma, Phi Lambda Theta, Pi Omega Pi, Alpha Delta Pi (sponsor), Sigma Phi (sponsor, pres. Alpha Theta chpt. 1958), Delta Pi Epsilon. Contbg. author: College Typewriting, 1960; Business Correspondence, 1962. Collaborator Ency. Brit., 1969—. Home: 920 Courtland Av Park Ridge IL 60068 Office: 64 E Lake St Chicago IL 60601

BARNARD, MARY ELIZABETH, real estate broker; b. Twin Falls, Ida., May 4, 1921; d. Zene Howard and Esther Merle (Fullington) Bucy; grad. with honors Life Bible Sch., 1941; m. Austin L. Barnard, June 7, 1942 (dec. Feb. 1969); children—Kenneth A., Susan Darlene (Mrs. Charles E. Garber), Ronald Lynn. Realtor, 1959—. Mem. Whittier Dist. Bd. Realtors, chmn. attendance and hospitality, 1969-73, dir., 1973-75. Mem. USAF Mothers, 1961-73, chaplain 1962-65, historian 1966-69, v.p., 1970-74; vol. Meals on Wheels. Mem. Ch. of The Foursquare Gospel. Home: 9613 Greening Av Whittier CA 90605 Office: 12822 East Whittier Blvd Whittier CA 90602

BARNES, BARBARA BOYD (MRS. LAWRENCE C. MURDOCH), journalist; b. Wayne, Pa., July 13, 1898; d. David Knickerbacker and Elizabeth (Mifflin) Boyd; grad. Pa. Acad. Fine

Arts, 1919; m. Lawrence C. Murdoch, Apr. 10, 1923; children—Lawrence C., Samuel Mifflin. Owner Sydenham Studio, Phila., 1920-30; buyer John Wanamcker, Phila., 1930-35; womens dir. WPA, Eastern, Pa., 1935-37; commentator sta. WCAU, Phila., 1938-40; columnist Phila. Bull., 1941-49, war corr., ETO, 1945, feature writer, 1949—, home editor, 1949-72; free-lance writer; syndicated columnist on homes, 1967—; writer Am. Friends Service Com., 1971—. Bd. dirs. Phila. Com. UNICEF, 1961—; mem. antiques show bd. U. Pa. Hosp., 1971—. Recipient Dorothy Dawe award for distinguished achievement in home furnishing journalism, 1958, 63, 67; nat. award for best sect. in newspaper on home appliances Am. Home Laundry Mfrs. Assn., 1963, 65; nat. award for story on architecture A.I.A., 1959; Catherine O'Brien award for best stories on women's interests, 1965, 71; Keystone State award for series stories on drug users, 1971. Mem. Am. Inst. Interior Designers (Eastern Pa. chpt. award 1961), Nat. Soc. Interior Designers (Eastern Pa. chpt. award 1966), Nat. Home Fashions League. Home: 7818 Lincoln Dr Philadelphia PA 19118

BARNES, BETTY JO FOLKES, coll. adminstr.; b. Kaufman, Tex., Feb. 23, 1931; d. James Otis and Lola Beta (Ray) Folkes; B.A., Mary Hardin-Baylor Coll., 1951; postgrad. Southwestern Bapt. Sem., 1952-54; m. Roy Gerald Barnes, Dec. 17, 1954; 1 dau., Gina Raeanne. Publicity asst. Southwestern Sem., Fort Worth, 1952-54; asso. pub. relations First Nat. Bank, Ft. Worth, 1954; employee relations asst., rocket fuels research and devel. Phillips Petroleum Co., McGregor, Tex., 1954-57; elementary tchr., music asst. Long Point Bapt. Ch. and Sch., Houston, 1959-61, 67-72; personnel asst. H.E. Butt Grocery Co., Corpus Christi, Tex., 1961-62; tchr. Tudor Hall Sch. and Heritage Christian Sch., Indpls., 1963-66; dir. alumni, ex-student affairs Mary Hardin-Baylor Coll., Belton, Tex., 1972—. Mem. Am. Assn. U. Women, Am. Alumni Council, Tex. Bapt. Day Sch. Assn. Democrat. Baptist. Club: Bell County Media (Belton). Home: 3320 Thornton Lane Temple TX 76501

BARNES, BETTY LUCILLE (MRS. ROBERT EUGENE BARNES, SR.), real estate broker; b. Brownell, Kan., June 29, 1929; d. Oscar Guy and Charlotte Martha (Fuller) Barnes; student real estate sch., 1969; m. Robert Eugene Barnes, Sr., Sept. 7, 1947; children—Robert Eugene, Dennis Wayne. Sec., bookkeeper Tri-B Industries, Inc., Monroe City, Mo., 1966—; owner, broker Barnes Realty, Monroe City, 1969—. Treas. Monroe City service unit Salvation Army; chmn. Monroe City Cancer Meml. Fund. Republican committeewoman, 1951—, vice chmn. Monroe County Rep. Com., 1962—. Named Woman of Year, Bus. and Profl. Women's Club, Monroe City, 1969. Mem. Nat. Assn. Real Estate Bds., Bus. and Profl. Women's Club (pres. 1967—). Baptist (chmn. women's group 1967-68). Home: 511 N Chestnut Monroe City MO 63456 Office: 109 Winter St Monroe City MO 63456 also 1st and E Border St Monroe City MO 63456

BARNES, CARLA LEDDY (MRS. PATRICK DWYER BARNES), social worker, educator; b. Zanesville, O., Dec. 9, 1938; d. William Frederick and Mary (Kopshak) Leddy; B.A. (Goodrich scholar), Hanover Coll., 1960; M.A. in Social Service (Nat. Inst. Mental Health grantee), Ind. U., 1962; postgrad. Columbia, 1964, Wayne State U., 1968; m. Patrick Dwyer Barnes, July 8, 1967; children—Michael Leddy, Jennifer Dwyer. Social worker Children's Service, LaRue Carter Hosp., Indpls., 1962-64, chief psychiat. social worker, 1964-66; supr. outpatient dept. Lafayette Clinic, Detroit, 1966-68; supr. St. Lawrence Community Mental Health Center, Lansing, Mich., 1969-71; asst. prof. and practicum instr. Mich. State U., East Lansing, 1971—. Field instr. Ind. U., Indpls. 1964-65, Smith Coll., Northampton, Mass., 1967-68, Wayne State U., 1967-68, Mich. State U., 1969-71; pvt. practice social work, Indpls., 1964-66, Grosse Pointe, Mich., 1967-68. Mem. Fine Arts Council Com., Lansing, Mich., 1970. Democratic precinct del., East Lansing, 1972—, precinct chmn., 1972—. Fellow, Am. Orthopsychiat. Assn., Nat. Assn. Social Workers (pub. chmn. Indpls. 1963-65, mem. memberships com. Indpls. 1963-65), Acad. Certified Social Workers, Council on Social Work Edn., Alpha Omicron Pi (mem. pub. relations com. 1957-58, v.p. 1959-60), Roman Catholic. Home: 3301 Melody Lane Lansing MI 48912 Office: 214 Baker Hall Mich State U East Lansing MI 48824

BARNES, CONSTANCE INGALLS (MRS. RUSSELL C. BARNES), librarian; b. Atchison, Kan., July 30, 1903; d. Sheffield and Lucy (Van Hoesen) Ingalls; B.A., U. Kan., 1925; M.A., U. Mich., 1950, M.A. in L.S., 1955; postgrad. Ecole du Louvre, France, 1960, Vergilian Soc., Cumae, Italy, summer 1963; m. Russell C. Barnes, Oct. 1, 1927; children—Lucie-Jeanne (Mrs. Todd Seymour), John J.I. Libarian, Cranbrook Acad. Art, Bloomfield Hills, Mich., 1955—. Mem. Spl. Libraries Assn., A.L.A., League Women Voters, Alliance Francaise, Founders Soc. Detroit Inst. Arts, Kappa Alpha Theta. Club: Village Woman's (Bloomfield Hills). Home: 788 Randall Ct Birmingham MI 48009 Office: 500 Lone Pine Rd Bloomfield Hills MI 48013

BARNES, ELINOR J., indsl. psychologist; b. Newark, O., Feb. 25, 1902; d. Albert S. and Martha (Armstrong) Barnes; B.S., Ohio State U., 1922, M.A., 1929, Ph.D., 1931. Tchr. Latin, high schs., O., 1922-28; head dept. psychology Beaver Coll., 1931-43; asst. dir. marketing, social research div. Psychol. Corp., N.Y.C., 1943-61; pvt. practice indsl. psychology, Tucson, 1961—; research specialist Div. Econ. and Bus. Research, Coll. Bus. and Pub. Adminstrn., U. Ariz., Tucson, 1961-72, chmn. grad. com. gerontology, 1966-72, dir. grad. program adminstrs. retirement housing, 1968-72; pres. Ariz. Research Assos., 1961—. Mem. Ariz. Gov.'s Adv. Council for Aging; mem. Ariz. steering com. White House Conf. on Aging, tech. com. on tng. White House Conf. on Aging, 1970-72; mem. tech. adv. com. aging research Dept. Health, Edn. and Research, 1972—. Vice pres. bd. dirs. Marshall Home for Men. Diplomate Am. Bd. Examiners Profl. Psychology. Fellow Am. Psychol. Assn., Gerontological Soc., N.Y. State Psychol. Assn. (sec. 1952-56); mem. Advt. Women N.Y. (dir. 1958-60, corr. sec. 1960-61), Am. Marketing Assn., Pi Lambda Theta (nat. treas. 1931-35), Phi Delta Gamma (nat. pres. 1932-36), Delta Zeta, Chi Delta Phi, Theta Alpha Phi, Gamma Psi Kappa. Republican. Unitarian. Club: Altrusa (gov. 1st dist. 1944-46). Home: 1694 W Glendale Av Apt 354 Phoenix AZ 85021

BARNES, ELIZABETH VIRDIN (MRS. WILEY L. FORMAN), physician; b. Charlottesville, Va.; d. John Lumsden and Minnie (Perry) Barnes; student Holins Coll., Roanoke, Va., 1929-30; M.D., U. Va., 1938; m. Wiley Lewis Forman, Sept. 20, 1941; children—Susan (Mrs. James Quisenberry), John F., Robert. Intern, Cleve. City Hosp., 1938-39, asst. resident pediatrics, 1939-40; resident pediatrics Union Meml. Hosp., Balt., 1940-41; clin. instr. pediatrics Ohio State U. Med. Sch., 1942-72; pediatrician Columbus Health Dept., Well Child Clinics, 1942-68; pediatrician Garfield House, Children and Youth Health Clinic, 1968—; pediatric cons. Ohio State Health Dept., Pediatric Otological Diagnostic clinics, 1955-67; mem. staff Ohio State U. Hosp., Children's Hosp. of Columbus. Mem. Columbus Acad. Medicine, Central Ohio Pediatric Soc., Women's Aux. to Columbus Acad. Medicine, Chi Omega. Presbyn. Address: 387 S Parkview Av Columbus OH 43209

BARNES, EVA LOUISE BLUM (MRS. MALCOLM LYNN BARNES), civic worker; b. Ellsworth, Kan.; d. Samuel and Emma Lena (Kunz) Blum; M.A., U. Cal. at Berkeley, 1939; m. Malcolm Barnes, June 10, 1946; children—Marsha Evangeline, Malcolm Samuel John. Counselor, Oakland (Cal.) Pub. Sr. High Sch., 1939-42; club dir. A.R.C., Eng. and France, 1942-46; civilian club dir., Germany, 1946. Publicity chmn. lit. events Golden Gate Expn., 1940-41; publicity chmn. Writers Conf. of West, 1941; mem. Louisville com. Nat. Conf. Christians and Jews, 1960—; mem. com. for passing new Ky. Contn., League of Women Voters, 1966. Bd. dirs. Library Assos. Louisville, 1963—. Life mem. Filson Club, Speed Mus., Women's Aux. of Orch. Assn., Louisville, U. Cal. Alumni Assn. (br. pres. Santa Barbara Bay area 1938-40); mem. Women's Aux. Jefferson County Med. Soc. (publicity chmn. 1950-51), Women's Aux. Ky. Med. Soc. (chmn. aux. conv. 1953, chmn. cancer sta. wagon drive 1953-54), Aux. U. Louisville (v.p. program chmn. 1951-52), Assn. Sch. Adminstrs. (asso.), Internat. Platform Assn. Cleve., Chgo. Council on Fgn. Relations, English Speaking Union, Phi Lambda Theta, Lambda Kappa Sigma, Delta Chi Delta. Clubs: Louisville Boat, Pendennis (Louisville), California Writers (dir.), University Women's (life mem.) (Washington). Art work exhibited in many galleries in Cal. Home: 425 Country Lane Louisville KY 40207

BARNES, FANNIE BURRELL (MRS. RICHARD ALEXANDER BARNES), librarian; b. New Orleans, Apr. 6, 1923; d. Alexander and Lorenza (Nicholas) Burrell; B.A. in English, Dillard U., 1945; M.S. in Library Sci., Atlanta U., 1950; m. Richard Alexander Barnes, May 29, 1968; children—Erica (Mrs. Steve Lewis Jones), Maria. Tchr. English Gilbert Acad., New Orleans, 1945-49; asst. librarian Sch. Library Service, Atlanta, 1950; head librarian Claflin Coll., Orangeburg, S.C., 1950-54; children's librarian Atlanta Pub. Library, 1961; head librarian M.L. Harris Library Clark Coll., Atlanta, 1954—, asst. prof. children's lit., 1956-69. Pres. P.T.A., Atlanta, 1969-70, C.L. Harper High Sch., Atlanta, 1967-70, M. Agnes Jones Elementary Sch., Atlanta, 1969-72. Mem. Am., Ga., South Eastern library assns., N.A.A.C.P., Alpha Kappa Alpha. Baptist. Club: Presidents (pres. 1968-71) (Atlanta). Home: 1981 Valley Ridge Dr SW Atlanta GA 30331 Office: ML Harris Library 240 Chestnut St SW Atlanta GA 30314

BARNES, GEORGENE GRACE NOLTE (MRS. THOMAS BRADLEY BARNES), lawyer; b. St. Louis, May 30, 1943; d. George Albert Oscar and Francies Julia (Risley) Nolte; A.B., Vassar Coll., 1965; postgrad. George Washington U. Law Sch., 1966-68; J.D., U. Tex. Law Sch., 1970; m. Thomas Bradley Barnes, Dec. 30, 1972. Adminstrv. asst. U.S. Dept. Agr., Washington, 1965-68; admitted to Mo. bar, 1970, Fed. Ct. bar, 1973; research asst. to Tex. Rep. Tom Bass, Austin, 1969; gen. practice law, Clayton, Mo., 1970—; asst. staff counsel Am. Optometric Assn., St. Louis, 1971-72; atty. Vision Inst. Am., St. Louis, 1973—. Pres. Rock Twp. Republican Club, Jefferson County, Mo., 1971; chmn. govs. reception Arnold Celebration Com., Arnold, Mo., 1973. Mem. Mo. (juvenile law com. 1973-74), St. Louis, Jefferson County bar assns. Methodist. Address: 1544 Jeffco Blvd Arnold MO 63010

BARNES, GEORGENE O'DONNELL, advt. exec.; b. Chgo., July 2; d. James George and Betty Frances (Schlundt) O'Donnell; student Northwestern U., 1947-49, U. Chgo., 1949-50; m. W. Wade Barnes, July 13, 1957. TV comml. supr. Benton & Bowles, Chgo., 1951-54; asso. producer films series, writer Laufman Prodns., Chgo., 1954-57; TV producer WNBC-TV, N.Y.C., 1957-63; TV writer Goodson-Todman, game show producers, N.Y.C., 1963-65; v.p. radio and TV spl. events MSEI, N.Y.C., 1965-70; pres. Barnes Assos., diversified pub. relations and advt. marketing, N.Y.C., 1970—; dir. Emerson Travel. Pub. relations dir. City Center Music and Drama Young People's Theater, 1970-73. Recipient award for Children's Center program WNYC-AM and FM, 1973. Mem. Am. Women in Radio and TV (dir., pres. elect 1968-69), Nat. Assn. TV Arts and Scis. (gov. N.Y. 1973—), N.Y.C. Ballet Guild, N.Y.C. Opera Guild, Broadcast Industry Forums (nat. chmn. 1962-70). Author: Miniaturia, 1951. Home: 20 Beekman Pl New York City NY 10022 Office: 1271 Av of Americas New York City NY 10020

BARNES, JEANNE JEFFERIES, editor; b. Clarendon, Tex., Apr. 15, 1920; d. William Charles and Hazel (Jefferies) McDonald; grad. Clarendon Jr. Coll., 1939; B.A. in Journalism, Tex. Tech. U., 1941; m. Edwin J. Barnes, July 17, 1943 (div. June 1948). Asst. women's editor Ft. Worth Press, 1945-48; home editor, women's editor The Houston Chronicle, 1948-52; home and fashion editor San Antonio Express, 1952-56; home editor San Antonio Light, 1956-57; home editor The Dallas Morning News, 1958—. Mem. Nat. Soc. Interior Designers, Nat. Home Fashions League, Am. Inst. Interior Designers, Women in Communication, Press Club of Dallas. Home: 3002 B Mahanna Springs Dallas TX 75235 Office: Communications Center Dallas TX 75222

BARNES, MADELINE ADELE, educator; b. San Antonio, May 6, 1919; d. William L. and Lydia (O'Bannon) Barnes; B.S., B.A., Tex. Women's U., 1941; M.A., N. Tex. State U., 1944; postgrad. U. Mich., U. Colo., U. Oslo (Norway), Rocky Mt. Biol. Lab. Tchr., trainer W. Tex. U., Canyon, 1942-46; tchr. Tex. Wesleyan Coll., summer 1955; prof. biology, chmn. dept. biol. scis. Amarillo (Tex.) Coll., 1946—. Mem. Nat., Tex. Panhandle (past pres.) Audubon socs., Tex. State, Tex. Jr. Coll. (Tchr. of Year award 1966) tchrs. assns., A.A.A.S., Am. Assn. U. Profs., Am. Assn. U. Women, Am. Inst. Biol. Scis., Nat. Assn. Biol. Tchrs., Tex. Acad. Sci., Southwestern Assn. Naturalists, Delta Kappa Gamma (Alpha (Tex.) chpt. Achievement award 1972). Home: 3625 Doris Dr Amarillo TX 79109

BARNES, MAGGIE LUE SHIFFLETT (MRS. LAWRENCE BARNES), nurse; b. nr. Spur, Tex., Mar. 29, 1931; d. Howard Eldridge and Sadie Adilene (Dunlap) Shifflett; student Cogdell Sch. Nursing, 1959-60, Western Tex. Coll., 1972-74, Meth. Hosp. Sch. Nursing, Lubbock Tex.; m. T.C. Fagan, Jan. 1950 (dec. Feb. 1952); 1 son, Lawayne L.; m. 2d, Lawrence Barnes, Sept. 2, 1960. Floor nurse D.M. Cogdell Meml. Hosp., Snyder, Tex., 1960-64, medication nurse, 1964-73, charge nurse, 1973—. Den mother Cub Scouts Am., Holliday, Tex., 1960-61; mem. P.T.A., Snyder, Tex., 1960-69. Mem. Vocational Nurses Assn. Tex. (mem. bd. 1963-65, div. pres. 1967-69). Apostolic Faith Ch. (sec., treas. 1956-58). Home: Route 1 Box 9B Hermleigh TX 79526 Office: Med Arts Center DM Cogdell Meml Hosp Snyder TX 79549

BARNES, MARTHA COGHILL (MRS. EMORY J. BARNES), lawyer; b. Bklyn., Aug. 11, 1909; d. Walter LeRoy and Camilla (Nelms) Coghill; B.A., Vassar Coll., 1931; postgrad. N.Y. Sch. Social Work, 1935-37; LL.B., Columbia, 1960; m. Emory Jennings Barnes, July 10, 1937; 1 son, Gordon Coghill. Pres., Martha Coghill Barnes Assos., Health and Welfare Interpretation, N.Y.C., 1945-49; admitted to N.Y., Conn. bars, 1961; asso. ct. reporter Supreme Ct. Conn., Hartford, 1962-63; atty. Maguire, Cole, Bentley & Babson, Stamford, Conn., 1963-69, partner, 1970—. Mem. Women's City Club N.Y., 1943-52, pres., 1947-49; chmn. legislative com. Health Council Greater N.Y., 1949-50; pres. Darien (Conn.) Community Council, 1951-53. Mem. Republican Town Com., Darien, 1956-57. Bd. dirs. Darien Community Fund, Darien Family Counselling Service. Mem. Am., Conn., Stamford bar assns., Assn. Bar City N.Y. Episcopalian. Club: Cosmopolitan. Home: 25 Inwood Rd Darien CT 06820 Office: 1 Atlantic St Stamford CT 06901

BARNES, MARY DILWORTH (MRS. RICHARD L. BARNES), govt. ofcl.; b. Pitts.; d. John Crossan and Helen (Thompson) Dilworth; A.B., Vassar Coll., 1936; LL.B., U. Pitts., 1939, postgrad. in pub. adminstrn., 1958-59; m. Richard L. Barnes, June 24, 1938 (dec.); children—Richard D., John C., Mary (Mrs. David Blair), Helen L. (Mrs. Peter Vantine). Admitted to Pa. bar, 1940; pvt. practice law, Pitts., 1950—; mem. Fed. Women's Prison Bd., Washington, 1953-60; staff office Pa. senator, Pitts., 1959; with Bur. Census, U.S. Dept. Commerce, Pitts., 1960; mem. Pa. Civil Service Commn., 1963-72. Mem. spl. adv. com. for pub. opinion Dept. State, 1970-72; mem. White House Conf. on Aging; mem. council Nat. Inst. Child and Human Devel., Bethesda, Md., 1972—. Exec. dir. Allegheny County (Pa.) Citizens for Eisenhower, 1952, vice-chmn., 1956; vice-chmn. Allegheny County Citizens for Scott, 1958; vice-chmn. Western Pa. Citizens for Scranton, 1962. Mem. Allegheny County Bar Assn. Republican. Home: 142 Shady Lane Pittsburgh PA 15215

BARNES, MILDRED JANE, educator; b. Albany, N.Y.; d. Paul S. and Elsie (Dougherty) Barnes; B.S., Sargent Coll., 1951; Ed.M., Boston U., 1956, Ed.D., 1961. Tchr. Westfield (Mass.) High Sch., 1951-53, Winchester (Mass.) High Sch., 1953-61; asst. prof. U. Ia., 1961-64, asso. prof., 1965-69; asso. prof. Central Mo. State U., 1969-73, prof., 1973—; vis. instr. Pine Manor Jr. Coll., spring 1961, Sargent Coll., 1952, 63, Cortland Coll., 1965, cons. Athletic Inst. slide film, Basketball for Girls, 1964, Soccer for Girls, 1966; NCAA rep. to U.S. Olympic Games Basketball Com., 1965—; mem. basketball com. U.S. Collegiate Sports Council, 1971—. Bd. dirs. Ia. Girls High Sch. Athletic Union. Mem. Am., Mo. assns. for health, phys. edn. and recreation, Nat., Central assns. for phys. edn. for coll. women, Internat. Assn. for Phys. Edn. and Sports for Girls and Women, Nat. Assn. for Girls and Women in Sports (pres. 1974—), Pi Lambda Theta. Mem. U.S. women's lacrosse team, 1950-61, touring team to Brit. Isles, 1957. Author: Program in Self Instruction for DGWS Volleyball Rules and Techniques of Officiating; Sports Activities for Girls; Field Hockey for Coach and Player, 1969; Women's Basketball, 1972. Contbr. articles to profl. jours. Home: Green Acres Route 5 Warrensburg MO 64093

BARNES, MYRTLE SUE SNYDER (MRS. SHELTON WINBORNE BARNES), editor; b. Farmville, Va., July 14, 1933; d. George McClure and Alma White (Hillsman) S.; B.S.J. with highest distinction, Northwestern U., 1955; m. Shelton Winborne Barnes, Dec. 23, 1954; children—Donna Leigh, David Brian. Reporter, Times-Herald, Newport News, Va., 1956-60, edn. reporter, 1967-70, asst. city editor, 1970-72, city editor, 1972—; editor Teen Herald, 1962-67. Pres. Newport News Fedn. Parents and Tchrs., 1970-71. Bd. dirs. Soc. for Prevention Cruelty to Animals, 1960-64, Peninsula Jr. Arts Series, 1967-70. Mem. Nat. (life), Va. (life) congresses parents and tchrs., Nat. Fedn. Press Women (mem. bd. 1970-72), Va. Press Women (pres. 1970-72, named Press Woman of Year 1973), Peninsula Ind. Editorial Workers Assn. (pres. 1960), Va. Press Assn. (news com. 1971), Sigma Delta Chi, Kappa Alpha Theta. Baptist. Home: 15 Sinton Rd Newport News VA 23601 Office: PO Box 746 Newport News VA 23607

BARNES, PHOEBE WASHBURN (MRS. CHARLES BENJAMIN BARNES), author; b. Worcester, Mass., May 10, 1908; d. Reginald and Dorcas (Bradford) Washburn; ed. Radcliffe Coll., 1931; m. Charles Benjamin Barnes, June 15, 1929; children—Phoebe (Mrs. John E.Z. Caner), J. Lea (Mrs. John Jay Iselin), Charles Benjamin, Cornelia B. Chmn. benefit art tour com. Peter Bent Brigham Hosp., 1946, 65, 66, 67, 68, 70; v.p. Parents League, 1947; mem. exec. com. friends New Eng. Conservatory Music, 1966-68; mem. ladies com. Mus. Fine Arts, 1969, now asso. ladies com.; vol. tchr. Council Pub. Schs. Boston, 1969-72; mem. library com. Harvard Divinity Sch., 1971-72; artist MacDowell Colony, 1972. MacDowell Colony fellow. Club: Parliamentary Law (Boston). Author: Through Prisms, 1961; Soundings and Bearings, 1967. Contbr. articles to profl. jours., mags. Home: 267 Fox Hill St Westwood MA 02090

BARNES, PRISCILLA ANTONIA (MRS. JOHN BARNES), therapeutic radiologist; b. Bristol, Eng., Oct. 7, 1929; d. James Henry and Antonia Florence (James) Ridge; student Howells' Sch., Eng., 1939-43, Tiffin Girls' Sch., Eng., 1943-47; m. John Barnes, Sept. 29, 1969; 1 dau., Elizabeth Antonia. With Royal Free Hosp. Med. Sch., London, Eng., 1948-53; intern, resident, London, 1953-62; sr. radiologist Cancer Clinic, Calgary, Alta., Can., 1961—. Mem. Royal Soc. Medicine, British-Can. Med. Assn., Faculty Radiologists. Author: Basic Textbook of Radiology, 1971. Home: Box 116 Bragg Creek AB T0L 0K0 Canada Office: Cancer Clinic 2104 2nd St SW Calgary AB Canada

BARNES, ROBERTA J., educator; b. San Francisco, Jan. 1, 1933; d. Frederick Henry and Mabel (Carter) Barnes; B.S., U. Cal. at Berkeley, 1955; M.A., U. N.M., 1958; student George Washington U., summer 1965, U. Wash., summer 1966, U. Cal. at Berkeley, 1967-68, summer 1969. Dean of girls, tchr. phys. edn. Willits (Cal.) Union High Sch., 1958-59; womens counselor U. Nev., Reno, 1959-61, asst. dean of women, 1961-67, dean of women, 1968-71, dean of students, 1971—. Mem. Def. Adv. Com. on Women in Services, 1971—. Mem. Am. Assn. U. Women, Nat. Assn. Women Deans and Counselors, Cal. Assn. Women Adminstrs. and Counselors (regional treas. 1966-68), Am. Personnel and Guidance Assn., Am. Coll. Personnel Assn., Phi Kappa Phi, Pi Lambda Theta, Phi Chi Theta. Home: 1701 Wesley Dr Reno NV 89503

BARNES, VIOLA FLORENCE, former educator, historian; b. Albion, Neb., Aug. 28, 1885; d. Cass Grove and Isabella (Smith) Barnes; B.Mus., Univ. Sch. Music, Lincoln, Neb., 1906; B.A., U. Neb., 1909, M.A., 1910, LL.D., 1941; postgrad. Harvard, summer 1914, U. Wis., 1915; Ph.D. (Currier fellow 1916-17, Susan Rhodess Cutler fellow, 1917-19), Yale, 1919. Teaching fellow in history, U. Neb., Lincoln, 1910-13, instr., 1913-16; instr. history Mount Holyoke Coll., South Hadley, Mass., 1919-20, asst. prof., 1920-24, asso. prof., 1924-33, prof., 1933-52, prof. emeritus, 1952—, chmn. dept., 1939-42; asso. prof. history Smith Coll., 1933; research historian, 1952—. Cited 1 of 100 Career Women in U.S., Women's Centennial Congress, 1940. Am. Assn. U. Women Palmer Meml. fellow, 1926-27; Guggenheim fellow, 1930-31; Am. Council Learned Socs. grantee, 1929; Social Sci. Research Council grantee, 1933, 49, 55. Mem. Am. Hist. Assn., Berkshire Hist. Conf., Brit. Studies Conf., Phi Beta Kappa, Kappa Kappa Gamma. Democrat. Club: Mount Holyoke Faculty (South Hadley). Author: Dominion of New England, 1923, 1960. Editor: (with L.W. Labaree and S.M. Pargellis) Essays in Colonial History, 1931. Contbr. chpts. to books, essays, articles to dictionaries and encys., articles to mags. and jours. Home: 16 North Sycamore South Hadley MA 01075

BARNETT, ELEANOR MAE, educator; b. Colorado Springs, Colo.; d. John C. and Cora (Ingram) Barnett; B.A., U. Denver, 1937; M.A., U. Minn., 1947. Field dir. service to mil. hosps. A.R.C., 1942-49; dir. and casework supr. dept. social work Denver (Colo.) Gen. Hosp., 1949-55; mem. faculty Grad. Sch. Social Work, U. Denver, 1955—, prof. social work, 1962—. Cons. heart disease and stroke control program div. chronic disease programs USPHS, U.S. Dept. Health, Edn. and Welfare, Washington, 1964-69, mem. social work adv. com., rehab. services adminstrn., social and rehab. services, 1969-70, mem. nat. adv. council pub. health tng. USPHS, 1966-69. Mem. Pres.'s Council of Denver, 1967—, pres., 1968-69, treas., 1972-73. Mem. Nat. Assn. Social Workers, Am. Pub. Health Assn., Nat. Rehab. Assn., Am. Soc. Hosp. Social Work Dirs., Alpha Gamma Delta. Club: Altrusa (pres. 1967-68). Office: Grad School Social Work U Denver Denver CO 80210

BARNETT, JONI EVANS (MRS. JERROLD HYATT BARNETT), educator; b. Chgo., Feb. 24, 1931; d. James Morgan and Nona M. (Murphy) Evans; A.A. cum laude, Wright Jr. Coll., 1948-50; B.Ed., Chgo. Tchrs. Coll., 1953; M.S., U. Ill., 1957; m. Jerrold Hyatt Barnett, Nov. 15, 1963; children—James R., Frank Evans. Tchr. girls phys. edn. Chgo. Pub. Schs., 1953-55; tchr. health, phys. edn. Franklin Jr. High Sch., Champaign, Ill., 1955-57; instr. women's phys. edn. So. Conn. State Coll., New Haven, 1959-61, 70-72, women's recreation assn., 1970-72; tchr. health, phys. edn. Amity Regional Sch. Dist., Bethany, Conn., 1963-66; aquatics instr. women's phys. edn. Yale, 1969-71, dir. women's phys. edn., 1971-72, dir. phys. edn., dept. athletics, phys. edn. and recreation, 1973—. Chmn., Park and Recreation Commn. Bethany, 1959-66. Mem. Bd. Edn. Bethany, 1965-73. Mem. Eastern Assn. Phys. Edn. for Coll. Women. Republican. Conglist. Clubs: Yale Faculty (New Haven); Woodbridge (Conn.). Home: Downs Rd Bethany CT 06525 Office: Payne Whitney Gym Tower Pkwy Yale New Haven CT 06520

BARNETT, JOSEPHINE (MRS. DAVID BARNETT), actress; b. N.Y.C., July 20, 1909; d. Marks A. and Jennie (Weise) Wolfe; B.S., Tchrs. Coll. of N.Y., 1928; student Cornell U., 1929-30; postgrad. Columbia 1930-31, 35-36; m. David Barnett, Dec. 31, 1929; 1 son, Jonathan. Tchr. N.Y.C. Pub. Schs., 1929-35; tchr. drama Master Inst., 1931-32; profl. staff Westport Country Playhouse, 1946-50; dir. drama N.E. Conservatory of Music, 1950-59; spl. lectr. Emerson Coll., Boston, 1957-58; tchr. Leland Powers Sch. Theater, 1962-65, Thomas Sch., Rowayton, Conn., 1965-67; active actress Westport Country Playhouse, 1946-49. Exec. bd. Friends of Wellesley Library, Darien Community Assn., Alliance Unitarian Soc. Wesport; exec. bd. Westport Friends of Music. Mem. Nat. League Am. Pen Women (past pres.), League Women Voters (v.p.), Weston-Westport Arts Council (charter mem., exec. bd.), Sigma Alpha Iota. Unitarian. Club: Southeastern Conn. Wellesley (asso.). Address: Ledgebrook Ct Weston CT 06880

BARNETT, JUNE W. WOLFE (MRS. E. HARVEY BARNETT), author, educator; b. Neenah, Wis., June 12, 1920; d. Andrew H. and Bertha (Addicks) Wolfe; B.A., U. So. Cal., 1947; m. E. Harvey Barnett, Apr. 8, 1949; children—Ewin Harvey III, Andrew Holden. Buyer, Scruggs, Vandervoort & Barney, St. Louis, 1947-49; instr. adult edn. courses, Kirkwood, Mo., University City, Mo., 1960-66, 171 Cedar Art Council., Corning; served with WAVES, 1942-45; own program Radio Sta. WIQT, Horseheads, N.Y., 1966-67; instr. Corning (N.Y.) Community Coll., 1967-72; lectr. numerous orgns., schs., others. Past pres. St. Louis Weavers Guild. Mem. N.Y. Assn. Continuing Edn., Nat. Assn. Pub. Sch. Adult Edn., Adult Edn. Assn. U.S.A. Author: Your Fashion Fortune in Line and Color; Are You Yin or Yang?, 1968, Kitchen Kosmetics. Office: 761 Brookside Circle RD 1 Elmira NY 14903

BARNETT, LUCILE CATHERINE FECHTER, psychologist; b. East Peoria, Ill., Nov. 18, 1923; d. Frederick William and Mary (Hatfield) Fechter; student Ill. State U., 1941-44; B.A., U. Mo., 1950, M.A., 1958, M.A. in Clin. Psychology, 1965, Ph.D., 1971; m. William Richard Barnett, Aug. 17, 1945 (div. June 1946); 1 son, Gary J. Tchr. elementary schs., Kansas City, Mo., 1953-63; asst. sch. psychologist Kansas City (Mo.) Sch. Dist., 1963-67; instr. psychology Met. Jr. Coll., Kansas City, Mo., 1968-69, Johnson County Community Coll., Overland Park, Kan., 1971, Haskell Indian Jr. Coll., Lawrence, Kan., 1971-72; instr., counselor edn. U. Mo. at Kansas City, 1969-70, Ill. State U., Normal, 1971; cons. mental health research A. MacFarland Zone Center, Springfield, Ill., 1972; counseling psychologist VA, Louisville, 1973—. Vol. Human Rescue, Inc., Kansas City, Mo., 1970-72. Mem. Am., Ky. psychol. assns. Office: 600 Federal Pl Louisville KY 40202

BARNETT, MITZI MUSICK (MRS. WILLIAM TRAVIS BARNETT), pub.; b. Abilene, Tex., June 29, 1930; d. James Austin and Gladys Marie (Hailey) Musick; student Hardin Simmons U., 1946, U. Tex., 1946-48; m. William Travis Barnett, May 29, 1949; children—James Rex, Mitra Leah, William Andrew. Tchr. elementary sch. Denton Valley Pub. Sch., Clyde, Tex. 1948-49, Amherst (Tex.) Pub. Sch., 1949-50; owner, co-pub. Copperas Cove (Tex.) Courier, 1952-57; publs. coordinator Am. Reference Pubs., Inc., Ft. Worth, 1968-69, pres. (name changed to Miran Pubs.), 1970—. Active Girl Scouts Am., since 1967; Cub Scout den mother, 1961-65. Mem. Tex. Geneal. Soc., Central Tex. Geneal Soc., Bus. and Profl. Women (sec. 1956). Methodist (Sunday sch. tchr. 1956-70). Mem. Order Eastern Star. Author: How to Publish, rev. edition, 1973. Editor: West Virginia Estate Settlements, 1970; Aztec, 1972. Home: 4241 Whitfield Av Fort Worth TX 76109 Office: 3327 Winthrop Fort Worth TX 76116

BARNETT, NANCY JANE, editor; b. Los Angeles, Aug. 22, 1948; d. Harold Jack and Lala Muriel (Reeside) Barnett; B.A., U. N.M., 1970. Radio operator N.M. Dept. of Fish & Game, Albuquerque, 1970-71, asst. project leader for Hunter Safety Program, 1971-72, asst. editor N.M. Wildlife Mag., 1972-73, editor, 1973—. Mem. Women In Communications. Home: 374 Antelope Circle SE Albuquerque NM 87123 Office: Dept Game and Fish State Capitol Bldg Santa Fe NM 87501

BARNETT, PATRICIA RUTH, educator; b. Sioux Falls, S.D., Feb. 26, 1927; d. George Richard and Ruth Theresa (Bauch) Barnett; B.A. (Nat. Pepsi-Cola scholar), Coll. St. Catherine, 1949; M.A., Catholic U. Am., 1952; Ph.D., U. Denver, 1967. Mem. profl. touring co., Players, Inc., Washington, 1951-54, 55-56; prodn. asst. and script girl NBC, Chgo., 1954-55; actress, prodn. asst. CBS, ABC, N.Y.C., 1956-58; exec. asst. Writers Guild Am., N.Y.C., 1958-60; asst. prof. St. Louis U., 1960-64; teaching fellow drama U. Denver, 1964-67; asst. prof. drama, then asso. prof. U. N.C. at Chapel Hill, 1967—. Dir., community theatre, Durham, N.C., 1968; pvt. drama coaching, 1960—. Bd. dirs. Durham Theatre Guild, 1973—. Served with Spl. Service, 1952-53. Decorated Silver medals. Mem. Am. Assn. U. Profs., Am. Theatre Assn., Children's Theatre Conf., Southeastern Theatre Conf., U. N.C. Faculty Assn., Phi Beta Kappa, Pi Kappa Delta, Pi Epsilon Delta, Delta Phi Lambda. Republican. Roman Catholic. Office: U NC Chapel Hill NC 27514

BARNETT, ROSALIND CHAIT, psychologist; b. N.Y.C., July 10, 1937; d. Reuben and Dorothy (Klein) Chait; B.A., Queens Coll., 1959; Ph.D., Harvard, 1964; m. Norman Lawrence Barnett, Oct. 20, 1963; children—Jonathan David, Army Elizabeth. Research fellow Harvard Bus. Sch., Boston, 1965-73; research affiliate Radcliffe Inst., 1973—; individual practice psychotherapy, Newton and Weston, Mass., 1965—; vis. lectr. Mass. Gen. Hosp. Sch. Nursing, 1965—; cons.-therapist Boston Area Assos. Learning Therapies, 1972—. Bd. dirs. Red Barn Nursery Sch., Weston, 1970-72. Fellow Community Mental Health, Mass. Gen. Hosp., 1964-65. Fellow Mass. Psychol. Assn.; mem. Am., Eastern, Psychol. assns., Am. Personnel and Guidance Assn. (award outstanding research 1972), Phi Beta Kappa. Home: 21 Partridge Hill Rd Weston MA 02193 Office: 3 James St Cambridge MA 02138

BARNETT, WILMA MAYBELLE, educator; b. Clarksburg, W.Va., May 9, 1911; d. Clarence Worothy and Mabel (Skipton) Barnett; B.S., Muskingum Coll., 1941; M.A., Columbia, 1951, postgrad., spring 1973; student London U., 1962-63. Tchr., Wolf Creed Bd. of Edn., Waterford, O., 1930-37, Beverly (O.) Village Bd. of Edn., 1937-53; asst. prof. edn. Muskingum Coll., New Concord, O., 1953-56, asso. prof. 1956—. Ednl. cons., workshop dir. pub. schs. Mem. Am. Assn. U. Women, Ohio Assn. Student Teaching, Am. Assn. Higher Edn., N.E.A., Ohio Edn. Assn., Ohio Coll. Assn., Internat. Reading Assn., Delta Kappa Gamma. Republican. Presbyn. Home: 154 W High St New Concord OH 43762

BARNETTE, EMMA CHRISTINE HANSEN (MRS. FOSTER I. BARNETTE), bottling co. exec.; b. Omaha; d. Jens Nielsen and Luarentine (Larsen) Hansen; student pub. schs.; m. Foster I. Barnette, Aug. 23, 1930. Dress designer M.E. Smith Co., Omaha, 1917-20, Ely Walker Dry Goods, St. Louis, 1920-33, Carson Pirie Scott & Co., Chgo., 1933-35, Lee Garment Co., Chgo., 1935-40; v.p., treas. Pepsi-Cola Bottling Co., Rockford, Ill., 1945—. Club: Quota. Home: 23 Country Club Beach Rockford IL 61103 Office: 3831 Auburn St Rockford IL 61103

BARNETTE, HARRIETTE LOUISE AMOS (MRS. LEWIS FREDERICK BARNETTE), bookseller; b. Chgo., July 20, 1912; d. Gilbert Bitters and Harriette Louise (Medicus) Amos; student Western Mich. U., 1930-32; m. Lewis Frederick Barnette, Aug. 10, 1942; 1 son, William Amos (dec.). Owner Barnette's Books, specializing in antiquarian Americana, South Bend, Ind., 1962—. Mem. Ind. Hist. Soc., Antiquarian Booksellers' Assn. Am., Internat. League Antiquarian Booksellers. Address: 22727 Adams Rd South Bend IN 46628

BARNEY, ANNA SUE, educator; b. El Reno, Okla., Apr. 14, 1934; d. Marion Francis and Emilyn (McGuire) Barney; grad. Cottey Coll. for Women, 1954; B.S., U. Okla., 1956, M.Ed., 1960, Ph.D., 1972. Tchr. pub. schs., Oklahoma City, Broward County, Fla., 1956-59; grad. counselor U. Okla., Norman, 1959-60; resident hall dir. Ball State U., Muncie, Ind., 1960-65; asso. dean students, dean of women, dir. housing, fgn. student advisor Ore. Tech. Inst., Klamath Falls, 1965-69; grad. asst. U. Okla., 1969-70, dir. career exploration office, 1970-71; adminstrv. asst. coll. exec. council William Woods Coll., Fulton, Mo., 1972-73; ednl. cons., 1973—. Mem. Am. Assn. U. Women, Am., Okla. personnel and guidance assns., Nat., Ore. assns. women deans, adminstrs., and counselors, Am., So. coll. personnel assns., Am. Assn. Higher Edn., Alpha Gamma Delta, Kappa Delta Pi, P.E.O. Club: Quota. Home: 3721 N College St Bethany OK 73008

BARNHART, CHARLOTTE KENNEDY (MRS. HOWARD KENNETH BARNHART), research co. exec.; b. Chambersburg, Pa., Jan. 29, 1919; d. John Harry and Marguerite (Hafer) Kennedy; grad. high sch., Chambersburg; m. Howard Kenneth Barnhart, June 22, 1939;children—Joy Ann (Mrs. James K. Knox), Virginia Kay, Pamela Ellen. Propr. Park Av. Style Shop, Chambersburg, 1950-53; sec., dir. Facts, Inc., Chambersburg, 1960—. Mem. Kittochtinny Hist. Soc., Internat. Platform Assn., Sr. Hosp. Aux. Methodist. Mem. Order Eastern Star. Clubs: Republican, Chambersburg Women's (pres. 1967-68). Artist and art collector. Home: 280 Park Av Chambersburg PA 17201 Office: Trust Co Bldg Chambersburg PA 17201

BARNHOUSE, GLORIA KAY, city ofcl.; b. Marietta, O., Sept. 5, 1936; d. T. Dye and Florence Mabel (King) Barnhouse; B.A. in Journalism, So. Meth. U., 1958. Editor, Transp. Research, Washington, 1958-59; information writer Ohio Dept. Indsl. and Econ. Devel., 1959-61; sec., editor Ohio Pharm. Assn., 1963-67; recreation leader, dir. Columbus (O.) Recreation and Parks Dept., 1967—. Mem. Women in Communications, Ohio Parks and Recreation Assn., A.A.H.P.E.R., German Village Soc., Ohio Geneal. Soc. Office: 1100 E Broad St Columbus OH 43205

BARNHOUSE, RUTH TIFFANY, physician; b. La Mur, Isere, France, Oct. 23, 1923 (parents Am. citizens); d. Donald Grey and Ruth (Tiffany) Barnhouse; came to U.S., 1925; student Vassar Coll., 1940-41; B.A., Barnard Coll., 1945; M.D., Columbia, 1950; Th.M., Weston Coll. Sch. Theology, 1974; m. Francis C. Edmonds, Jr., Aug. 11, 1941 (div. July 1947); children—Francis C. III, Ruth T.; m. 2d, Dr. William F. Beuscher, Apr. 6, 1950 (div. 1968); children—Robert Conrad, William David, Christopher Grey, Thomas Frederick, John Franklin. Intern, Monmouth Meml. Hosp., Long Branch, N.J., 1950-51; resident McLean Hosp., Waverly, Mass., 1953-55; USPHS fellow in psychiatry Mass. Gen. Hosp., Boston, 1955-56; practice medicine, specializing in psychiatry, 1955—; staff McLean Hosp., 1958—; asst. in psychiatry Harvard, 1959—; dir. clin. psychiatry Children's Unit Met. State Hosp., Waltham, Mass., 1956-58; staff psychiatrist Mass. Mental Health Center, Boston, 1958-59; lectr., supr. Weston Coll. Sch. Theology, Cambridge, Mass., 1971—. Participant, Conf. on Catholics and Divorce, Paulist Center, Boston, 1972; mem. planning com., speaker, workshop leader Symposium for Laity and Clergy on Women and Priesthood, 1973. Diplomate in psychiatry Am. Bd. Psychiatry and Neurology. Mem. A.A.A.S., Mass., Eastern Middlesex Dist. med. socs., Am. Psychiat. Assn., Am. Med. Women's Assn., Fedn. Am. Scientists, Common Cause. Episcopalian. Address: 159 Chestnut St Cambridge MA 02139

BARNING, ELSIE CHRISTENE SEILER, state legislator; b. Evansville, Ind., Mar. 24, 1905; d. Christian Martin and Carrie Emma (Seifert) Seiler; m. Carl Phillip Barning (dec.); children—Carl Phillip, David Lee, Jerry Ralph. Mem. Ind. Ho. of Reps., 1949-50, 55-56, 61-64, 67-68, 71-72; staff mem. twp. dep. assessor's office, 1950-55, twp. chief dep. trustee's office, 1957-66. Mem. Nat. Order Women Legislators, Gen. Assembly Club, Ind. Fedn. Democratic Women, Ind. Fedn. (legislative chmn. 1964-66), Evansville (chmn. legislative com.) bus. and profl. women's clubs, Ind. Congress Parents and Tchrs. Democrat. Mem. Ch. of Christ Ch. Home: 1703 S Helfrich Av Evansville IN 47712 also 13 Apache St Lehigh Acres FL 33936

BARNS, CAROLE SUSAN (MRS. LEE MILLER BARNS), telephone co. exec.; b. Nome, Alaska, Nov. 21, 1944; d. Anton Raymond and Dorothy Virginia (Nelson) Johansen; B.A. in Advt.-Journalism, U. Wash., 1967; m. Lee Miller Barns, July 11, 1970. Mgr. internal communications Gen. Tel. Co. of N.W., Everett, Wash., 1967-70, mgr. pub. affairs, 1973—; newswoman A.P., Spokane, Wash., 1970-73. Publs. editor Wash. Community Coll. Dist. 17, 1970-71. Mem. Spokane Humane Soc. Trustee Susan Hutchison Bosch Meml. award. Mem. Women in Communications, Wash. Press Women. Club: Spokane Racquet. Home: W 443 28th St Spokane WA 99203 Office: PO Box 1179 Coeur d'Alene ID 83814

BARNSHAW, HILDA CORINNE HENNEMUTH (MRS. DANIEL LESTER BARNSHAW), occupational therapist; b. Allentown, Pa., Oct. 3, 1932; d. John Henry and Melba Winifred (Krammes) Hennemuth; B.A. in Music, U. N.D., 1954; certificate occupational therapy U. Pa., 1965; m. Daniel Lester Barnshaw, Jan. 30, 1965 (div. 1967); 1 son, Daniel John. Unit leader Emma Pendleton Bradley Home, Riverside, R.I., 1954-55; dir. Lehigh County chpt. Retarded Children, Allentown, Pa., 1955-57; activity worker Allentown (Pa.) State Hosp., 1958-65; therapist R.I. Arthritis Found., Providence, 1966-69; chief therapist Our Lady Fatima Hosp., North Providence, 1969—. Cons. to nursing homes, 1973—. Mem. Am., R.I. occupational therapy assns. Home: 6 General Hawkins Dr Warwick RI 02888 Office: Our Lady of Fatima Hosp 200 High Service Av North Providence RI 02908

BARNWELL, ADRIENNE KAY KNOX (MRS. FRANKLIN BARNWELL), educator; b. Elkhart, Ind., Jan. 31, 1938; d. Everett K. and Arlyne (Miller) Knox; B.S., Northwestern U., 1959, M.A., 1962, Ph.D., 1965; m. Franklin Barnwell, June 13, 1959; 1 dau., Elizabeth Brooks. Regional examiner Dept. of Mental Health, State of Ill., 1964-66; staff psychologist Alcoholic Rehab. Center, Avon Park, Fla., 1966; asst. prof. psychology Northwestern U., Evanston, Ill., 1967-70; sr. psychologist, pediatrics dept. Ramsey Hosp., St. Paul, 1971—; lectr. Hamline U., 1972-73; asst. prof. U. Minn. Med. Sch., 1972—. Cons. pre-sch. edn. Episcopal Ch. Costa Rica, C.Am., 1966; diagnostic cons. Inst. for Juvenile Research, Chgo., 1967. Mem. Am., Midwestern, Minn. psychology assns., N.Y. Acad. Sci., Pi Lambda Theta. Home: 2015 Kenwood Pkwy Minneapolis MN 55405 Office: Dept of Pediatrics St Paul-Ramsey Hospital St Paul MN 55101

BARON, CLAIRE LIBRESCOT, librarian; b. Phila., Oct. 3, 1912; d. Solon and Hannah (Margles) Librescot; B.A., Hunter Coll., 1931; M.A., Columbia, 1932, M.L.S., 1934; m. Murray Baron, Oct. 11, 1934; children—Lynn Mary (Mrs. Eric Beard Henson), Alice L. Personal librarian to Gov. N.Y., 1934-36; librarian Walton High Sch., N.Y.C., 1938-42, Milton Sch., Rye, N.Y., 1957—. Served in Library/USA, N.Y. World's Fair, 1965. Mem. Am., N.Y. State Westchester library assns., Rye Hist. Soc. Contbr. articles to newspapers and other publs. Home: Milton Harbor House Rye NY 10580

BARON, GAIL CUMINS, lawyer; b. N.Y.C., June 6, 1939; d. Sigmund Joseph and Ada Miriam (Schochat) Cumins; A.B. cum laude, U. Mich., 1960; J.D., Harvard, 1963; certificate Inst. de Hautes-Etudes Internationales, U. Geneva (Switzerland), 1959; m. Joel R. Baron, May 22, 1966; children—Allison Meredith, Samantha Jeanne. Admitted to N.Y. bar, 1963, since practiced in N.Y.C.; asso. firm Sharretts, Paley, Carter & Blauvelt, 1964-68, partner, 1969—. Mem. Customs Bar Assn. (membership com. 1966—, com. practice, procedure and legislation 1972-73), Am. Importers Assn. (mem. spl. dumping com. 1971—), Internat. Apparel Importers Assn. (sec.-treas.), Phi Sigma Alpha. Home: 1050 Fifth Av New York City NY 10028 Office: 80 Broad St New York City NY 10004

BARON, HANNELORE (MRS. HERMAN T. BARON), artist; b. Dillingen, Germany, June 8, 1926; d. Julius and Frida (Lichtenstein) Alexander; self taught; m. Herman T. Baron, Apr. 16, 1950; children—Julie (Mrs. Martin Shenkman), Mark. came to U.S., 1941, naturalized, 1947. Exhbns. of water colors and collages at Nat. Acad. Design, Nat. Arts Club, Riverside Mus., Herbert E. Feist Gallery, Lever House, A.M. Sachs Gallery (all N.Y.C.), Hudson River Mus., Yonkers, N.Y., Katonah (N.Y. Gallery, Ulster County Community Coll., Stone Ridge, N.Y. Marlboro (Vt.) Art Gallery; rep. instl. and pvt. collections. Recipient 1st prize Audubon Artists, 1971, 73, Nat. Assn. Women Artists, 1967, Yonkers Art Assn., 1962, 63, 65, 72. Mem. Artists Equity, Audubon Artists, Nat. Assn. Women Artists, Yonkers Art Assn. Address: 5621 Delafield Av Riverdale Bronx NY 10471

BARON, SELMA ARLEEN (MRS. STANLEY M. BARON), advt. co. exec.; b. Ft. Worth, July 31, 1926; d. Harry and Libby (Simon) Ginsburg; B.S., Northwestern U., 1947; m. Stanley M. Baron, June 20, 1947; children—Sandra Sue, Michael David. With NBC network, Chgo., 1943-47; TV dir. Amundson Bolstein Co., Sioux City, Ia., 1953-58; group v.p. Nelson Stern & Assos., Cleve., 1959-73; pres. Baron Advt., Inc., Cleve., 1973—. Trustee Council on Human Relations, 1970—. Mem. Indsl. Marketers of Cleve. (bd. govs. 1973—), Cleve. Advt. Club (trustee 1973—), Alpha Lambda Delta. Club: Shi Ai. Office: 840 Hanna Bldg Cleveland OH 44115

BARONE, ROSE MARIE PACE (MRS. JOHN BARONE), educator, assn. exec.; b. Buffalo, Apr. 26, 1920; d. Dominic and Jennie (Zagara) Pace; B.A., U. Buffalo, 1943; M.S., U. So. Cal., 1950; certificate advanced study Fairfield (Conn.) U., 1963; m. John Barone, Aug. 23, 1947. Tchr., Angola (N.Y.) High Sch., 1943-46, Puenta (Cal.) High Sch., 1946-47, Jefferson High Sch., Lafayette, Ind., 1947-50; dir. Warren Inst., Bridgeport, Conn., 1951-53; instr. U. Bridgeport, 1953-54; tchr. business subjects Bassick High Sch., Bridgeport, 1954—. Instr. Fairfield U., 1969. Recipient Playwriting prize Conn. Federated Women's Clubs, 1955, Auerbach Found. scholarship, 1956. Mem. N.E.A., Am. Assn. U. Women (treas. 1957-58), Nat. League Am. Pen Women (Bridgeport historian, 1966—), UN Assn. U.S.A. (pres. Bridgeport, 1964-66, 68-70, chmn. area UN Days, 1960—, pres. Conn. 1971—), Conn. Bus. Tchrs., Bridgeport Edn. Assn. (sec. 1966-68), Internat. Platform Assn., Fairfield Philatelic Soc. (sec. 1971—), Pi Omega Pi. Clubs: Fairfield University Women's (founder, pres. 1950, v.p. 1973—) Southport Woman's (Fairfield). Home: 1283 Round Hill Rd Fairfield CT 06430 Office: Bassick High School Bridgeport CT 06605

BARONS, VIRGINIA MACON (MRS. KENNETH JAMES BARONS), museum ofcl., historian; b. Rochester, N.Y., Mar. 25, 1914; d. Thomas Woodward and Kathryn (Limback) Macon; student in home econs. State U. N.Y., Cobleskill, 1933-35; m. Kenneth James Barons, Aug. 26, 1939; children—Kenneth James, Micheal W., Richard I., Christopher M., James N. Town historian Town of Bergen (N.Y.), 1962—; dir., curator Bergen Museum of Local History, Bergen Hist. Soc., 1966—; asst. librarian Nioga Library System, Bergen Reading Room, 1968-70; county history Genesee County, Batavia, 1970—. Coordinator Genesee County 1976 Bi-Centennial of Revolutionary War Celebration, 1973—. Mem. Nat. Trust for Historic Preservation, Am. Assn. for State and Local History, Western N.Y. Landmark Soc., Genesee County Landmark Soc., Leroy Hist. Soc., Byron Hist. Soc., Genesee County Officially Apptd. Historians, Amateur Fencers League Am. (dir. Western N.Y. 1964-66, 72-74), Bergen Hist. Soc. (pres. 1963—), Eighth Dist. Municipal Historians of N.Y. State (pres. 1972-74), N.Y. State Assn. County Historians (pres. 1973-74). Club: Rochester (N.Y.) Fencers. Home: 24 Clinton Av Bergen NY 14416 Office: 131 W Main St Batavia NY 14020

BARR, ARLENE NORMA (MRS. H.J. BARR), neurologist, educator; b. N.Y.C., Nov. 14, 1938; d. Melvin and Hattie (Strauss) Bach; A.B., Barnard Coll., 1960; M.D., Case Western Res. U., 1966; m. H.J. Barr, Jan. 26, 1961; 1 son, Michael Andrew. Intern U. Wis., Madison, 1966-67, resident in neurology, 1967-70, exec. resident, 1969-70; asst. prof. dept. neurology U. Wis., 1970-72, U. Ill., Chgo., 1972—. Cons. in neurology West Side VA Hosp., Chgo., 1973—. NIH fellow, 1967-70. Mem. Am. Acad. Neurology. Home: 1201 N East Av Oak Park IL 60302 Office: 912 S Wood St Chicago IL

BARR, BONNIE EILEEN, editor; b. Indpls., Apr. 17, 1935; d. Albert Victor and Helen Juanita (Kirkpatrick) Barr; A.B., Butler U., 1957; M.A., Ball State U., 1970. Copy editor Bobbs-Merrill Pub. Co., Inc., Indpls., 1959—. Leader Camp Fire Girls, Indpls., 1957-61; mem. Westview Hosp. Guild, 1969—. Mem. Women in Communications, Trianon Sorority (pres. 1965-66, nat. coordinator 1966-68). Republican. Mem. Christian Ch. (editor ch. paper 1962-70, tchr. 1969—, circle v.p. 1969-71). Home: 2126 Webb St Indianapolis IN 46225 Office: 4300 W 62nd St Indianapolis IN 46228

BARR, DORIS WILSON (MRS. JOHN HUGH BARR), educator; b. Vincennes, Ind., July 31, 1923; d. Guy H. and Mary E. (Ecker) Wilson; A.B., Ind. U., 1945; M.S., Northwestern U., 1949; M.A., U. Ill., 1956, Ph.D., 1958; m. John Hugh Barr, Jan. 9, 1950; children—David W., John V. Reporter, Chgo. Jour. of Commerce, 1947; asst. dir. pub. relations State St. Council, Chgo., 1948-50; with U. Ill. Survey Research Lab., Urbana, 1965-67; instr. English, Parkland Coll., Champaign, Ill., 1967—. Mem. bd. edn. St. Matthew Sch., Champaign, Ill., 1970-73. Author: Effective English for the Career Student, 1971; Writing, Listening, Speaking for Business and Professional Students, 1973. Home: 1209 Waverly Champaign IL 61820 Office: C 124 2400 W Bradley Champaign IL 61820

BARR, GLADYS HUTCHISON (MRS. THOMAS C. BARR), author; b. Butte, Mont., Dec. 19, 1904; d. David and Laura (Mooney) Hutchison; student U. State N.Y., 1924-25; LL.B., Albany Law Sch., 1926; m. Thomas C. Barr, Oct. 27, 1928; children—Thomas C., Ann (Mrs. Donald A. Weems), Jane, William Hume. Admitted to N.Y. State bar, 1927; practiced in N.Y.C., 1926-29. Lectr. schs., colls., womens clubs, others. Vice chmn. bd. Pub. Libraries of Met. Govt. of Nashville and Davidson County (Tenn.), 1959—. Mem. Am., Tenn., Southeastern library assns., Women's Nat. Book Assn., Authors Guild, Authors League of Am. Democrat. Presbyn. Club: Centennial. Author: Monk in Armour, 1950; Cross, Sword and Arrow, 1955; Master of Geneva and the Tinker's Armor, 1961; The Pilgrim Prince, 1963; Famous Witches and Ghost Series, 1969; The Bell Witch at Adams, 1969; The Ghost at Epworth Rectory, 1970; various stories and articles. Home: B 110 Jefferson Square 5039 Hillsboro Rd Nashville TN 37215 Office: Box 706 Nashville TN 37215

BARR, JENE, author; b. Kobrin, Russia, July 28, 1900; d. Joseph and Goldie (Barr) Cohen; came to U.S., 1904, naturalized, 1925; grad. Chgo. Normal Sch. Phys. Edn., 1920; student U. Chgo., 1928-29, Northwestern U., 1935-37, Chgo. Tchrs. Coll., 1931, 33, 49-50, Art Inst. Chgo., 1932. Phys. Instr. phys. Chgo. Bd. Edn. 1925-35, tchr., 1935-50, tchr.-librarian, 1950-64; now cons. social studies Albert Whitman and Co. Tchr. creative writing Downtown YWCA, Chgo., 1953-56; editor children's column Back of Yards Jour., 1946-48, editor women's column, 1947-48, 52. Mem. Ill. Library Assn., Soc. Midland Authors, Children's Reading Round Table (pres. 1965-66, Midwest award 1959), Nat. Fedn. Press Women (awards 1950, 51, 55), Ill. Woman's Press Assn. (Mate Palmer award for books 1950, 51, 55, 59; Helen Miller Malloch Meml. award 1966). Club: Chicago Teacher-Librarians. Author: Conrad the Clock, 1944; Little Prairie Dog, 1949; Little Circus Dog, 1949; Surprise for Nancy, 1950; Texas Pete, Little Cowboy, 1950, Policeman Paul, 1952; Fireman Fred, 1952, Mike, the Milkman, 1953; Baker Bill, 1953; Mr. Mailman, 1954; Big Wheels! Little Wheels!, 1955; Ben's Busy Service Station, 1956; Fast Trains! Busy Trains!, 1956; Good Morning, Teacher, 1957; Dan the Weatherman, 1958; This is My Country, 1959; Miss Terry at the Library, 1962; (with Robert J. Antonacci) Baseball for Young Champions, 1956, Football for Young Champions, 1958, Basketball for Young Champions, 1960, Physical Fitness for Young Champions, 1962; (with Catherine Bowers) Here Is Chicago, 1958, rev. 1965; (with others) How Americans Produce and Obtain Goods and Services, 1962; Mr. Zip and the U.S. Mail, 1964; Fire Snorkel Number 7, 1965; (with Cynthia Chapin) What Will the Weather Be?, 1965; (with Cynthia Chapin) Squad Car 55, 1966; What Can Money Do?, 1967. Address: 5910 N Sheridan Rd Chicago IL 60690

BARR, LOUISE MAXWELL (MRS. ROBERT SPENCER BARR), lawyer, state ofcl.; b. Beckley, W.Va., Jan. 4, 1913; d. James William and Lieutetia (Pierson) Maxwell; student Wesleyan Coll., Macon, Ga., 1930-32; LL.B., Duke, 1936; m. Robert Spencer Barr, Nov. 1, 1947; 1 son, William Robert. Admitted to W.Va. bar., 1936; asso. firm Maxwell & Maxwell, Beckley, 1936-40; practiced in Beckley; with W.Va. Pub. Service Commn., Charleston, 1942-47; law clk., sec. W.Va. Workmens Compensation, Charleston, 1947-51; atty. tax dept. State of W.Va., Charleston, 1962-63; asst. atty. gen. State Tax Dept., 1963-72; law clk. W.Va. Supreme Ct. Appeals, 1972-73; asst. atty. gen. W.Va. Bd. Regents, Charleston, 1973—. Mem. W.Va. State Bar, Am., W.Va. bar assns., Kappa Delta. Republican. Baptist. Home: 5 Staehlin Rd Charleston WV 25314 Office: W Va Bd of Regents 1316 Charleston Nat Plaza Charleston WV 25301

BARR, MARY ELIZABETH YOUNG (MRS. JENNINGS BRYAN BARR), librarian; b. West Sunbury, Pa., Mar. 21, 1919; d. Earl Wayne and Gladys Evelyn (Dann) Young; B.A., Capital U., 1940; M.S. in L.S., Western Res. U., 1950; postgrad., U. Wis., 1946, U. Pitts., intermittently, 1945-63; m. Jennings Bryan Barr, Nov. 27, 1957; children—Jennifer Evelyn, Jennings Bryan II, Carl Thomas. Tchr., New Vienna (O.) Jr.-Sr. High Sch., 1940-42, Westerville (O.) High Sch., 1942-43, Butler (Pa.) Jr. High Sch., 1943-46, librarian, 1946-52; librarian Butler Sr. High Sch., 1952-57; asst. librarian Slippery Rock (Pa.) State Coll., 1957-64, asst. prof. library sci., 1964-66; head librarian Butler (Pa.) County Community Coll., 1969—. Bd. dirs. Butler Pub. Library, 1958-63. Mem. Pa. Library Assn. (com. 1971-72), Pitts. Suburban Council Sch. Librarians (pres. 1956), Nat., Pa., Midwestern Dist. Pa. (sect. chmn. 1951) edn. assns., Tri-State Assn. Coll. and Research Libraries, Am. Assn. U. Women, Delta Kappa Gamma (chpt. corr. sec. 1962-64, chmn. com. 1970-72), Phi Beta, Beta Sigma Phi (pres. 1956-57, sec. 1970-71). Mem. Order Eastern Star. Home: 805 N Main St Butler PA 16001 Office: College Dr Oak Hills Butler PA 16001

BARR, MARY KING, pub. relations exec.; b. Milw., Jan. 15, 1936; d. Frank Thomas and Lyle Mayburn (Fliege) King; tchrs. certificate Wis. Coll. Music, 1952; certificate Albany Bus. Coll., 1964; B.A., Loretto Heights Coll., 1973; m. Daniel F. Barr, Mar. 6, 1956 (div. Dec. 1965); 1 dau., Kristin Anne. With Mullins Broadcasting Co., Denver, 1964-70; pres. Mary K. Barr, pub. relations, Denver, 1970-71; nat. dir. pub. relations Navajo Freight Lines, Denver, 1971-72; regional pub. information officer Small Bus. Adminstrn., Denver, 1973—. Lectr. pub. relations U. Colo., 1970—, Loretto Heights Coll., 1969—, Colo. Womens Coll., 1972—, Colo. Mountain Coll., 1973—. Bd. dirs. Cherry Creek Townhouse Corp., 1967-68. Named Young Artist of Year, Colony Club, N.Y.C., 1952; Philharmonic Soc. N.Y. award, 1952. Mem. Am. Women in Radio and TV (chpt. pres. 1969-70), Women In Communications. Club: Advt. (dir. 1967-69) (Denver). Home: 5621 Blue Sage Dr Littleton CO 80123 Office: Room 446 721-19th St Denver CO 80202

BARR, SUSAN MCADOO, corp. exec., civic worker; b. Detroit, May 2, 1935; d. Joseph Stanly and Jessie E. (Colquhoun) McAdoo; B.S., La. State U., 1957; m. Gavin Chaundy Barr, June 21, 1958; children—Susan, Jessie Jo, Gavin Chaundy, Bryce C. Social welfare worker N.J. Bd. Child Welfare, Camden, 1957-60; with G.C. Barr, M.D., Bethlehem, Pa., 1971—, v.p., 1972—. Pres. Soc. of Arts of Allentown (Pa.) Art Museum, 1972-74. Bd. dirs. Young Reps. Lehigh County, 1963-66, Council Rep. Women, 1964-68. Bd. dirs. Lehigh County unit Am. Cancer Soc., 1966—; trustee Allentown Art Mus., 1972—; trustee Lehigh Valley Center Performing Arts. Kate Duncan Smith Sch. grantee, Ala., 1971—. Named Pa.'s outstanding jr. mem. D.A.R., 1971, nat. outstanding jr. mem., 1971. Mem. D.A.R. (chpt. vice regent 1968-74, nat. vice chmn. jr. membership in charge sales 1971-74), Woman's Aux. Northampton County Med. Assn. (pres.-elect 1974), Lehigh County Aux. Med. Soc. Clubs: Altrusa, Alpha Omicron Pi Alumni, Lehigh Country (Allentown, Pa.); Saucon Valley Country (Bethlehem). Home: RD 5 Whiteacre Dr N Bethlehem PA 18015

BARRAGA, NATALIE CARTER, educator; b. Troy, Tex., Oct. 10, 1915; d. Bascom Debo and Grovie (Harrison) Carter; B.S., N. Tex. U., 1938; M.Ed., U. Tex. at Austin, 1957; Ed.D., Peabody Coll. Tchrs., 1963; m. John Thomas Barraga, Aug. 9, 1943; 1 dau., Karen Jeanne. Tchr. pub. schs., Liberty, Tex., 1939-42; teaching asst. N. Tex. U., Denton, 1942-43; tchr. N.Y. Inst. for Blind, N.Y.C., 1948-51, Tex. Sch. Blind, 1952-61; instr. spl. edn. U. Tex. Inst., Austin, 1952-61, Peabody Coll. Inst., Nashville, 1961-62; asst. prof. spl. edn. U. Tex. at Austin, 1963-66, asso. prof., 1966-71, prof., 1971—; cons. edn. to 17 states. Bd. dirs. Austin Cerebral Palsy Center, also sec., 1963-67. Recipient citation Tex. Mental Health Assn., 1966; Teaching Excellence award Student Assn. U. Tex., 1966; U.S. Office Edn. grantee, 1965-70. Fellow Am. Acad. Optometry; mem. Assn. Edn. Visually Handicapped (editor jour. 1968-72), Internat. Council for Edn. Visually Handicapped, Council for Exeptional Children, Pi Lambda Theta, Delta Kappa Gamma, Kappa Delta Pi. Mem. Christian Ch. (elder, mem. ofcl. bd.). Author: Increased Visual Behavior in Low Vision Children, 1964. Editor: Education of Visually Handicapped, 1968; Teaching Aids for Blind Children, 1968; Development of Visual Learning Abilities and Utilization of Low Vision, 1970; Utilization of Sensory-Perceptual Factors, 1973; (with B. Dorward, P. Ford) Basic Concept Teaching Aids for Multi-impaired Visually Handicapped Children, 1973. Home: 1215 Larkwood Dr Austin TX 78723 Office: Sutton 213 U Tex Austin TX 78712

BARRANGER, MILLY HILLIARD SLATER (MRS. GARIC KENNETH BARRANGER), educator; b. Birmingham, Ala., Feb. 12, 1937; d. C.C. and Mildred C. (Hilliard) Slater; B.A., U. Montevallo, 1958; M.A., Tulane U., 1959, Ph.D., 1964; m. Garic Kenneth Barranger, Aug. 26, 1961; 1 dau., Heather Dalton. Spl. lectr. English, La. State U., New Orleans, 1964-69; asst. prof. theatre Tulane U., New Orleans, 1969-73, asso. prof., 1973—, acting chmn. dept. theatre and speech, 1971, chmn. 1971—. Mng. dir. Tulane Center Stage Summer Theatre, New Orleans, 1973—; mem. community liaison com. New Orleans Pub. Schs. Creative Art Center, 1973—. Mem. Am. Theatre Assn. (chmn. program for chief adminstrs. 1973, chmn. conv. program com. 1975), Speech Communications Assn., S.W. Theatre Conf., Theatres of La., Inc. Author: Henrik Ibsen: Peer Gynt A Doll's House, Enemy of the People, 1969; Henrik Ibsen: Ghosts The Wild Duck, 1969. Co-editor: Generations: An Introduction to Drama, 1971. Home: 1414 Jahncke Av Covington LA 70433 Office: Dept Theatre and Speech Tulane University New Orleans LA 70118

BARRANGER, MIRIAM RUTH GARIC (MRS. DALTON JOSEPH BARRANGER), artist, craftsman; b. New Orleans; d. Henry Lawson and Lilly (Guedry) Garic; student Tulane U., 1927-28, 62-63; m. Dalton Joseph Barranger, Sept. 12, 1928; 1 son, Garic Kenneth. Exhibited one-man shows Isaac Delgado Mus. Art, New Orleans, 1951, Carl Barnetts, Inc., Dallas, 1952, La. Art. Commn. Gallery, 1952, Mus. Art, Columbia, S.C., 1953, 331 Gallery, New Orleans, 1959, St. Tammany Art Assn., Covington, La., 1964, Foster Art Gallery, Baton Rouge, 1965; exhibited in numerous group shows including, La. Commn. Galleries, Baton Rouge, 1953, 63, 65, 66, Isaac Delgado Mus., 1950-53, 58, New Orleans Downtown Gallery, 1961-63, Mint Mus. Art, Charlotte, N.C., 1966, 67 (hon. mention 1966), Mus. Contemporary Crafts, N.Y.C., 1963, N.C. Mus. Art, Raleigh, 1963, 66, Brooks Meml. Art Gallery, Memphis, 1965, La. Craft Council Gallery, New Orleans, 1965, Cabild. Presbytere, New Orleans, 1966. Chmn., St. Tammany Parish Welfare Bd., 1943-48; mem. adv. bd. La. Mental Health, 1959-61; chmn. home nursing, supr. surg. dressings groups A.R.C., 1942-45; vol. occupational therapist S.E. La. Hosp., Mandeville, La., 1962-63; membership chmn., editor Newsletter, La. Assos. Acad. Religion and Mental Health, 1962-65; chmn. St. Tammany Parish (La.) Tb Assn., 1942-48; mem. nat. adv. com. Am. Crafts Council, 1970. Bd. dirs. New Orleans Tourist and Conv. Commn., 1971-73. Recipient 1st prize in crafts New Orleans Art Assn., 1951; 1st prize Hodges Gardens Art Festival, 1971. Dir., v.p. Playmaker's, Inc., Covington, 1966-67. Mem. St. Tammany Art Assn. (founder, hon. dir., past pres., 1st prize crafts 1971), Am. Craftsmen's Council (La. rep. S.E. region 1968-70), Am. Crafts Council (adv. com. internat. sect. 1973—), La. Craft Council (bd. mem., chmn. pub. relations 1966-70, hon. dir. 1970—, 1st prize in jewelry 1971, 72), Theosophical Soc. (past pres. Covington lodge). Designed, executed murals Comml. Bank and Trust Co., Covington, La., 1962, glass doors Barranger Bldg., Covington, 1969. Address: Box 1268 Covington LA 70433

BARREN, JEAN VAN AKEN (MRS. HENRY ALEXANDER BARREN, JR.), coll. dean; b. Cleve., July 2, 1917; d. William John and Florence Emily (Swallow) Van Aken; student U. Wis., 1935-37; B.S., Case Western Res. U., 1939; m. Henry Alexander Barren, Jr., Mar. 30, 1940 (dec. Oct. 1970); children—Henry Alexander III, William John, Martha (Mrs. Robert Bruce Besuden), Roger Scott. Asst. to dean of student affairs Coll. of Steubenville (O.), 1971, dean of women, 1972—. Pres. Harding P.T.A., Steubenville, 1958, Steubenville County P.T.A., 1960-62. Chmn., Vols. for Eisenhower, 1952, 56, Vols. for Nixon, 1960; mem. Precinct Republican Com., Steubenville, 1956-73; chmn. Jefferson County Rep. Exec. and Central Com., 1964-72, Jefferson County Rep. Party, 1973—; del. Rep. Nat. Conv., 1972; mem. Bd. Elections Jefferson County, 1966—; mem. Steubenville Met. Planning and Devel. Commn., 1957-72, chmn., 1966-70; mem. Jefferson County Regional Planning Commn., 1966-68. Bd. dirs. YWCA, Steubenville, 1960-64, Am. Cancer Soc., Jefferson County, 1960; adv. bd. Salvation Army, Jefferson County, 1966-70; bd. advisers Coll. of Steubenville, 1970—. Mem. Ohio Assn. Women Deans and Counselors, Ohio Assn. Election Ofcls. (trustee 1972—). Presbyn. (elder 1972—). Club: Steubenville Country. Home: 1948 McCausley Manor Steubenville OH 43952

BARRER, MYRA EDITH (MRS. LESTER A. BARRER), pub. co. exec.; b. N.Y.C., Oct. 21, 1927; d. George and Estelle (Lifschitz) Puchkoff; B.A., Hunter Coll., 1947; M.A., Columbia, 1951; m. Lester A. Barrer, July 3, 1949; children—Susan, Amy. Field investigator N.J. Dept. Health, Trenton, 1958-61; tchr. N.Y.C. Bd. Edn., 1948-50, 51-58, Raleigh (N.C.) Bd. Edn., 1950-51, Montgomery County (Md.) Bd. Edn., 1964-65; owner, dir. Barrer & Asso., Inc., Washington, 1967-68, subsidiary Pa. Research Assos., Inc., sec.-treas., dir., 1969-70, mgr. bus. operations, 1969-70; v.p., owner, dir. Systems Evaluation Co., Washington, 1970—, Today Publs. & News Service, Inc., 1970—; pres., owner Alpha Composition & Arts, Inc., Washington, 1973-74. Mem. Montgomery County (Md.) Ad Hoc Commn. on Status Women, 1971-72; field worker Suburban Md. Fair Housing Assn., 1960-62. Mem. Women in Communications, Md., Montgomery County women's polit. caucuses, Alumni Assn. Hunter Coll. (pres. D.C. chpt. 1973-75), Phi Beta Kappa. Editor: Women's Organizations and Leaders-1973 Directory. Home: 12605 Eldrid Ct Silver Spring MD 20904 Office: Nat Press Bldg Washington DC 20004

BARRETT, AGNES PATRICIA BROWN (MRS. CLARK J. BARRETT), lawyer, educator; b. Indpls., Nov. 11, 1920; d. Clarence A. and Jane L. (Egan) Brown; B.S., Ind. U., 1942, J.D., 1964; m. Clark J. Barrett, July 21, 1973. Admitted to Ind. bar, 1964; with Am. States Ins. Cos., Indpls., 1953-72, asst. sec., 1962-72; asso. prof. law Ind. U., Indpls., 1972—. Mem. Indpls. Police Merit Bd., 1974—. Mem. Indpls. Mus. Art, Ind. Symphony Soc., Indpls., 1966—. Bd. dirs. Lucille Raines Residence Hall, 1970—. Mem. Am. Assn. U. Women (regional v.p. 1973—), Am., Ind. bar assns., St. Thomas More Soc. of Indpls. (pres. 1972-73), Ind. U. Alumni Assn. (dir., sec. 1967-73), D.A.R., Order of Coif, Pi Beta Phi. Rotarian (pres. 1967-69). Club: Propylaeum (pres. 1971-72). Home: 4815 Cavendish Rd Indianapolis IN 46220 Office: 735 W New York St Indianapolis IN 46202

BARRETT, CHRISTINE MARGARET ROLLMAN (MRS. WILLIAM EDMUND BARRETT), writer; b. Denison, Tex.; d. Louis Stephen and Dora (O'Neal) Rollman; student Coll. Mt. St. Joseph on the Ohio, 1922-25; m. William Edmund Barrett, Feb. 15, 1925; children—Marjorie Christine, William Edmund. Corr. Diplomat Mag., 1956-63; writer articles mags. including Red Book, D.A.R., articles newspapers, 1937—. Active various community drives. Mem. Temple Buell Coll. Library Assos., Friends of Denver Pub. Library, Mount St. Joseph's Alumnae Assn. Republican. Roman Catholic. Clubs: Denver Woman's Press, Denver Athletic. Home: 1282 Detroit St Denver CO 80206 also 1868 Columbia Rd NW Washington DC 20009

BARRETT, CLAIRE MIRIAM RONDEAU (MRS. CLIFFORD J. BARRETT), educator; b. Malden, Mass.; d. Charles E. and Gelia A. (Tessier) Rondeau; B.S., Tchrs. Coll. Providence, 1956; M.S., Fordham U., 1960, Ph.D., 1964; m. Clifford J. Barrett, Aug. 29, 1970. Guidance counselor Stella Viae Internat. Coll., Rome, Italy, 1964-65; asst. prof. Sch. Edn. Catholic U., Washington, 1966-68; prof. psychology Holy Trinity Mission Sem., Silver Spring, Md., 1965-69; asso. prof. Seton Hall U., Sch. Edn., South Orange, N.J., 1969—, chmn. dept. gen. profl. edn., 1972—; guidance dir. Regina High Sch., Hyattsville, Md., 1965-69; coll. supr. student teaching N.J. Pub. Schs., 1969—. Mem. N.J. Right to Life Com.; mem. N.J. Council for Ednl. Founds., 1970-72, Pro Ecclesia Com. Catholic Laymen, N.Y.C., 1971—. Mem. Am. Acad. Religion, Mem. Am. Assn. U. Profs. Roman Catholic. Home: 595 Northfield Av West Orange NJ 07052 Office: Seton Hall U South Orange NJ 07079

BARRETT, JOANN ELAINE, educator; b. Reno, Aug. 16, 1932; d. Roy Henry and Ethel Viola (Wyatt) Barrett; B.A., U. Redlands, 1954; M. Criminology, U. Cal. at Berkeley, 1959; 1 dau., Diana J. Probation officer, Alameda County Adult Probation Office, Oakland, Cal., 1954-56; social worker Sacramento County Welfare Dept., 1956-57; statistician Cal. Youth Authority, Sacramento, 1957-65; researcher Job Corps program, Pleasanton, Cal., New Bedford, Mass., Washington, 1965-68; mem. liaison staff Model Cities program. Lt. Gov. Cal., 1969-72; prof. criminal justice Cal. State U. at Sacramento, 1972—. Mem. Am., Sacramento (past pres.) statis. assns., Cal. Probation, Parole and Corrections Assn., Sacramento Women's Justice Forum, Am. Soc. Criminology, Assn. Criminal Justice Research. Home: 242 Rice Lane Davis CA 95616 Office: 6000 J St Sacramento CA 95819

BARRETT, RUTH MENDENHALL, pathologist; b. Kokomo, Ind., Dec. 27, 1922; d. Owen F. and Maude (Weaver) Mendenhall; A.B. (Laura Kindig scholar 1941-44), Goshen Coll., 1944; M.B., Northwestern U., 1948, M.D., 1949; m. Edward A. Barrett, Mar. 20, 1949; children—M. Scott, Edward M., William W., Elizabeth. Intern, Michael Reese Hosp. Chgo. 1948-49; gen. practice medicine, Mt. Ayr, Ia., 1950-51; resident pathologist Highland Alameda County Hosp., Oakland, Cal., 1951-52, Meadowbrook Hosp., Hempstead, N.Y., 1952-53, Grassland Hosp., Valhalla, N.Y., 1953-54; asst. med. examiner Westchester County, N.Y., 1954-57, 62-64; dir. labs. Beth David Hosp., N.Y.C., 1957-58; pathologist Arnold Gregory Meml. Hosp., Albion, N.Y.; cons. pathologist VA Hosp., Montrose, N.Y., 1958-68, VA Hosp., Batavia, N.Y., Genesee Meml. Hosp., Batavia. Coroner, Orleans County, 1967—. Mem. Orleans County Bd. Health. Violinist, Brockport Coll.-Community Orch. Mem. Orleans Housing Co., Inc. Diplomate in path. anatomy and clin. pathology Am. Bd. Pathology. Mem. Coll. Am. Pathologists, Am. Soc. Clinc. Pathology, A.M.A., N.Y. State Soc. Medicine, Orleans County Med. Soc. (pres.), Am. Assn. U. Women, D.A.R., Nu Sigma Phi. Methodist. Home: Albion NY 14411 Office: Arnold Gregory Hosp Albion NY 14411

BARRETTE, ELISE DRAPER (MRS. PAUL A. BARRETTE), educator; b. Gainesboro, Tenn., July 21, 1912; d. Eldon Pate and Zora (Cherry) Draper; B.S., Tenn. Tech. U., 1931; B.S. in L.S., George Peabody Coll., 1937, M.A., 1945; postgrad. U. Chgo. Grad. Library Sch., 1948; m. Paul A. Barrette, Aug. 23, 1952. Tchr., Jackson County High Sch., Gainesboro, 1931-37; librarian David Lipscomb Coll., Nashville, 1937-44, Shorter Coll., Rome, Ga., 1944-48; prof. library sci., dir. dept. library edn. E. Tenn. State U., Johnson City, 1948—. Mem. Am., Southeastern Tenn. library assns., Am. Assn. U. Women, Phi Gamma Mu, Kappa Delta Pi. Mem. Ch. of Christ. Contbr. profl. jours. Home: 1203 College Heights Dr Johnson City TN 37601

BARRIGA, BERTHA, pedodontist; b. La Paz, Bolivia, Feb. 28, 1936; d. Victor and Sylvia (Mena) Barriga; Dental-Surgen, University Mayor de San Andres, La Paz, 1959; D.M.D., U. Ore., 1966; M.S.D., U. Wash., 1971. Came to U.S., 1959, naturalized, 1966. Pvt. practice children's dentistry, Seattle, 1966—. part time clin. asst. pediatric dentistry U. Wash., 1966—; mem. staff Children's Orthopedic Hosp., Seattle. Mem. Am., Wash., Seattle-King County dental socs., Am. Acad. Pedodontics, Am. Soc. Dentistry for Children, Am. Assn. Women Dentists, Soroptimist Club, Metropolitan University Toastmistress Club. Home: 6533 38th St NE Seattle WA 98115 Office: 1563 Medical-Dental Bldg Seattle WA 98101

BARRINGTON, CAROL JOANNE BISBEE (MRS. EUGENE ARNOLD BARRINGTON), editor; b. Covina, Cal., Aug. 18, 1935; d. David Peter and Josephine Christine (Colville) Bisbee; B.A. with distinction, San Jose State Coll., 1956; m. Eugene Arnold Barrington, Aug. 5, 1956; children—Mark Patrick, Jay Ashley, Julia Elizabeth. Reporter Mountain View (Cal.) Register Leader, 1955-57; clk. U. Cal. at Berkeley Press., 1957; office mgr. dept. psychology, U. Cal. at Berkeley, 1958-59; pub. relations dir. Florissant Valley Community Coll., St. Louis, 1967-68; free lance writer, editor James T. White Co., pubs., Clifton, N.J., 1969—. Chmn. youth activities Huntwick Civic Assn., Houston, 1973-74; active P.T.A. Mem. Women in Communications, Sigma Kappa, Kappa Tau Alpha. Address: 5323 Lookout Mountain Dr Houston TX 77069

BARRITT, EVELYN RUTH BERRYMAN (MRS. WARD LEROY BARRITT), nurse, educator; b. Detroit, Sept. 4, 1929; d. George C. and Ruby (Mathews) Berryman; A.A., Graceland Coll., 1949;

diploma Independence (Mo.) Sanitarium and Hosp. Sch. Nursing, 1952; B.S., Ohio State U., 1956, M.A., 1962, Ph.D., 1971; m. Ward LeRoy Barritt, Oct. 28, 1951; 1 dau., Kelli Jo. Asst. instr. nursing Atlantic City City Hosp., 1952-53; staff nurse Shore Meml. Hosp., Somers Point, N.J., 1953-54, Ohio State U. Hosp., Columbus, 1954-55; instr. White Cross Hosp., Columbus, 1955-57; asso. dir. nursing service Riverside Meth. Hosp., Columbus, 1957-64; asst. exec. dir. Ohio Nurses Assn., Columbus, 1964-65; dean Capital U. Sch. Nursing, Columbus, 1965-72; dean Coll. Nursing, U. Ia., Iowa City, 1972—. Mem. Am., Ohio (pres. dist. 1966-68), Ia. nurses assns., Nat. League Nursing, Graceland Coll. Alumni Assn., Am. Assn. Higher Edn., Am. Assn. Colls. Nursing, Independence Hosp. Sch. Nursing Alumnae Assn., Ia., Johnson County women's polit. caucuses. Home: Rural Route 2 Timber Trails Iowa City IA 52240 Office: Coll of Nursing Univ of Iowa Iowa City IA 52240

BARRON, ELLA LILLIBRIDGE (MRS. BRYTON BARRON), author; b. Akron, Ia., Jan. 26, 1900; d. Lowell Stanton and Lottie (Eno) Lillibridge; student Sioux Falls Coll., 1917-19; A.B., U. Colo., 1921; m. Bryton Barron, Dec. 31, 1922; children—Bebe (Mrs. E. Carl Seward, Jr.), Roger. Head depts. English and psychology Ossining Sch. for Girls, Ossining-on-Hudson, N.Y., 1921-22; governess Chinor Hill, nr. Oxford, Eng., 1922-23; head English dept. All Saints Sch., Sioux Falls, S.D., 1924-25; tchr. high sch., Abra, P.I., 1925-26, P.I. Normal Sch., 1926; ofcl. insp. P.I. Bur. Edn., supr. English Acad. high schs., Manila, and asst. editor publs. bur., 1927-28; dir., owner Leewood Sch., Springfield, Va., 1942-49; owner, operator Leewood Remedial Service, Springfield, 1949-66; asst. mgr. pub. house, 1962-66. Mem. Nat. Council Tchrs. Math., Kappa Alpha Theta. Author: (with Bryton Barron) Mastery of English Fundamentals (4 vols.), rev. edit., 1960; The Inhumanity of Urban Renewal, 1965. Address: 7710 NW 8th St Pembroke Pines FL 33024

BARRON, MABEL AMMONS, ret. hosp. adminstr.; b. Somerset, Pa., Dec. 28, 1906; d. Edward C. and Carrie M. (Berkey) Barron; R.N., Western Pa. Hosp. Sch. Nursing, Pitts., 1928; student Tchrs. Coll., Columbia U., Summers, 1931-35; B.S., U. Pitts., 1943, M.A., 1944; D.H.L., Geneva Coll., 1962. Head nurse West Penn Hosp. Sch. Nursing, Pitts., 1928-30, med. supr., 1931-33, instr., 33-36, asst. prin., 1936-39; asst. adminstr., Magee Hosp., Pitts., 1939-52, dir. nursing, 1940-52; instr. U. Pitts. Sch. Nursing, 1940-43, asst. prof., 1944-53; adminstr. Ellwood City (Pa.) Hosps., 1952-73; spl. lectr. U. Pitts. Sch. Nursing, 1954-63. Bd. dirs. Ellwood City council Girl Scouts U.S.A., Lawrence County Mental Health Assn., Mental Health Clinic, Lawrence County Cancer Bd., Lawrence County Vis. Nurse Assn., 1966-73. Recipient Distinguished Service award, sr. citizen Jr. C. of C., Ellwood City, Pa., 1961; named Distinguished Dau. of Pa., Fellow Am. Coll. Hosp. Adminstrs., 1961; mem. Hosp. Assn. Pa. (past pres.; chmn. council hosp. auxs.), Middle Atlantic Hosp. Assembly (pres.), Pa. Assn. Hosp. Auxs. (counsellor 1967-74), Sigma Theta Tau. Presbyn. (trustee). Clubs: Zonta, Bus. and Profl. Women's. Home: Petrie Rd RD 2 New Brighton PA 15066

BARRON, ROS, artist; b. Boston, July 4, 1933; d. Louis and Ida (Tatelbaum) Myers; B.F.A., Mass. Coll. Art, 1954; fellow Radcliffe Inst., Harvard, 1966-68; m. Harris Barron, Apr. 19, 1953; children—Matt Lewis, Nina Rebecca. Exhibited in one-man show at Portland (Me.) Mus. Fine Art; exhibited in group shows Whitney Mus., 1971-72, Ward-Nasse Gallery, N.Y.C., de Cordova Mus., Lincoln, Mass., USIA Exhbn., Rotterdam, Holland, others; represented in permanent collections Addison Gallery Am. Art, Worcester Art Mus., Dartmouth Coll., Harvard, Syracuse Mus. Fine Arts, Boston Mus. Fine Arts, others; artist for media theater, dir. ZONE performance Guggenheim Mus., N.Y.C., 1972, others; asst. prof. U. Mass., Boston, 1972—. Recipient 1st prize in painting R.I. Arts Festival, 1964, 68, Design award U.S. Dept. Housing and Urban Devel., 1968, N.Y. Found. for Arts, Inc. award, 1972, Rockefeller Artist-in-TV grantee, 1968-69. Address: 30 Webster Pl Brookline MA 02146

BARRON, THEA ROSSI (MRS. MICHAEL O'N. BARRON), lawyer, city ofcl.; b. Detroit, May 17, 1939; d. Ernest Francis and Christine Marie (Zaffina) Rossi; A.B. in Polit. Sci., Barat Coll., 1961; J.D. (Clarence Burton scholar), U. Detroit, 1964; m. Michael O'N. Barron, Oct. 10, 1964; children—Michael, Christina, Stephen. Admitted to Mich. bar, 1964; practiced in Grand Rapids, 1965-67, Kalamazoo, 1968—; law clk. to judge of Mich. Ct. Appeals, Grand Rapids, 1964-65; asso. firm. Marcus, McCrosky Libner, Reamon, Williams & Dilley, 1965-67, Brown and Coleman, 1968-69; gen. counsel Kalamazoo County Community Action Program, 1971—; mem. firm Daudent and Barron, 1971—. Kalamazoo City commr., 1971—; sec. Kalamazoo County substance Abuse Bd., 1973—; mem. Dem. Com., Kalamazoo, 1972—; co-founder, chairperson Kalamazoo Women's Govt. Caucus. Mem. Kalamazoo County, Mich. State bar assns., Nat. Assn. Women Lawyers, Am. Judicature Soc., Am. Assn. U. Women, League of Women Voters. Mng. editor U. Detroit Law Jour., 1963-64. Home: 1420 Academy St Kalamazoo MI 49007 Office: 130 N Park Kalamazoo MI 49006

BARROW, ALACOQUE DANTZER (MRS. LESTER J. BARROW), assn. adminstr.; b. Detroit, July 29, 1906; d. Peter P. and Agnes (Raiter) Dantzer; student Detroit Comml. Coll., 1923-24, Coll. City Detroit, 1927-29, U. Detroit, 1954-55; m. Lester J. Barrow, July 20, 1940; 1 dau., Ruth Eleanore (Mrs. Carl Unholz). Admintrv. asst. to dir. U. Detroit Library, 1953-59; pub. writer Detroit Inst. Arts, 1960-61; exec. sec. Detroit Adventure, 1961—, editor Calendar, 1961—. Mem. Arts Com. New Detroit, 1972-73; active Girl Scouts, 1953-58; chmn. arrangements Program Planning Inst., 1972—. Bd. dirs. Children's Mus. Friends, 1973-74, Am. Women's Vol Services, 1941-45, Friends of WDET-FM, 1974—. Mem. Women in Communications, Detroit Press Club, Lambda Tau Delta. Home: 8100 E Jefferson Av Detroit MI 48214 Office: 100 W Kirby St Detroit MI 48202

BARROW, SADIE BELLE, educator; b. New Orleans; d. Sterling Bertel and Katie (Truss) Barrow; B.A. magna cum laude, Dillard U., 1946; M.A., Atlanta U., 1950; M.A. (hon.), Monrovia Coll., Liberia, W. Africa, 1953. High sch. instr. Gilbert Acad., New Orleans, 1946-49; teenage program dir. New Orleans br. YWCA, 1949-57, exec. dir., 1957-67; dep. dir. Irish Channel (Anti-Poverty) Center, 1967-68; community relations Coordinator Project 8 Children of Orleans Parish Sch. Bd., 1968—. Rep., Mid-Century White House Conf. on Children and Youth, 1950, Internat. YWCA, Seminar on Status Women, 13th UN Commn. on Status Women, 1959; mem. adv. com. New Orleans Juvenile Ct., 1953-57. Mem. Gen. Bd. A.M.E. Ch., 1956-60; trustee Union Bethel A.M.E. Ch., New Orleans, 1960—, honored as Pillar of Ch., 1973. Mem. bd. La. Council Chs. Named Citizen of Day, Radio Sta. WYLD, 1960. Mem. Nat. Council Negro Women (mem. La. conf. social welfare 1964—), La. Council on Human Relations (past sec.), Adult Edn. Assn. U.S.A., Acad. Certified Social Workers, Nat. Assn. Social Workers, Dillard U. Alumni Assn. (nat. pres. 1964-67), Alpha Kappa Alpha (past nat. personnel chmn.; chpt. grad. adviser 1973). Home: 1915 Peniston St New Orleans LA 70115 Office: 3820 St Claude Av New Orleans LA 70117

BARROW, SUSAN H. LUHRS (MRS. HENRY D. BARROW), mus. exec.; b. Chgo., July 6, 1907; d. John F. and Anne (Hill) Luhrs; student U. Ill., 1924-26, Northwestern U., 1927; B.A., U. Wash., 1958, postgrad., 1960; m. George W. Rickey, Apr. 1933 (div. June 1939); m. 2d, Henry D. Barrow, Apr. 17, 1942. Dir., Woodstock (N.Y.) Art Gallery, summers 1940-49; girls adviser Wrangell and Sitka (Alaska) Native Service, 1945-47; dir. Alaska State Mus., Juneau, 1964-66, Whatcom Mus. History and Art, Bellingham, Wash., 1966—. Mem. adv. bd. Center for Pacific Northwest Studies; mem. adv. bd. continuing study and symposiums for contemporary art Western Wash. State Coll.; mem. Alaska Bd. Geog. Names. Mem. Am. Anthropology Assn., Soc. for Am. Archeology, Am. Assn. Museums, Am. Assn. for State and Local History, Western Mus. League, Coll. Alaska Bd. Geog. Names, Nat. Trust Historic Preservation (bd. advisers), Am. Assn. Art Assn. Author: Whatcom Seascapes, 1970; Green Gold Harvest, 1969; Arts of a Vanished Era, 1968; An Alaska Traveler's Geography, 1961; Master Carvers of the Lummi and their Apprentices, 1971. Illustrator: Paradise North, 1956. Home: 2217 Walnut St Bellingham WA 98225 Office: Whatcom Mus History and Art Bellingham WA 98225

BARROWS, MARGARET BENTLEY HAMILTON, composer, lyricist, poet; b. N.Y.C., Sept. 6, 1920; d. David Osborne and Margaret (Bentley) Hamilton; grad. Sarah Lawrence Coll., 1941; Ph.D. (hon.), Colo. State Christian Coll., 1972; m. Dec. 16, 1944 (div. 1952); 1 son, David Osborne Hamilton. Composer, lyricist numerous compositions including Living with the Arts, Easter Carol, The Promised Land, To the Month of June, others. Staff asst. A.R.C. Fgn. Inquiry Service, Detroit, 1944; pres. Women's Farm Home Adv. Com. So. States Co-op., 1953. Chmn. life membership council Eastern Centre and World Poets Resource Center, 1971, also organizer, chmn. internat. poets workshop, 1971; bd. dirs. World Poets Resource Center Corp., 1970—; mem. lay jury Detroit Artists Market, 1953. Mem. United Republicans of Am., 1969—. Recipient essay award World Poets Resource Center, 1971. Life fellow Intercontinental Biog. Assn.; mem. Jr. League Detroit (stage design award 1941), Colonial Dames of Mich., Internat. Platform Assn., Columbia U. Acad. Polit. Sci., Regional Plan Assn. N.Y.C., Am. Guild Authors and Composers, Sarah Lawrence Alumnae Assn. Detroit (pres. 1943-44), Am. Conservative Union (life), Christian Crusade (mem. nat. adv. bd.), Am. Security Council (mem. nat. voter adv. bd.), Delta Omicron, Sigma Gamma (bd. dirs. 1944). Presbyn. (Help run children's library). Clubs: Capitol Hill (Washington); Quota of N.Y. Home: 500 E 77th St New York City NY 10021

BARROWS, MARJORIE, editor, author; b. Chgo.; d. Dr. Ransom Moore and Caroline (Dixon) Barrows; student Northwestern U., U. Chgo. Asso. editor Child Life, 1922-31, editor, 1931-38; co-editor Consol. Books, 1943-48; editor-in-chief Children's Hour, 1952-62; editor Treasure Trails, 1954-56, Jr. Treasure Chest, Family Weekly, 1954-62. Hon. mem. bd. govs. Heckscher Found. Nat. Council Radio Listeners. Recipient scroll for contbn. lit. heritage of Chgo., Chgo. Found. for Lit.; hon. scroll Rand McNally. Mem. Internat. P.E.N., Chgo. Drama League (past dir.), Soc. Midland Authors (bd.), Theta Sigma Phi, Zeta Phi Eta (hon.). Republican. Presbyn. Clubs: Drama; Cordon (past v.p., sec.); Arts (Chgo.). Author: Muggins, 1931, Fraidy Cat, 1941, Pirate of Pooh, Tut Tut! Tales, 1950, others. Compiler: 100 best Poems, 1931, 200 Best Poems, 1939, Organ Grinder's Garden, 1939, The Children's Treasury, 1947, 1000 Beautiful Things, 1947, 56, 57, 1000 American Things, 1948, 56, Read-Aloud Poems, 1957, 60, 62, 65, 70, Treasure Trail Parade, 1957; (with Bennett Cerf) A Treasury of Humor, 1955; A Treasury of Beauty and Romance 1959, The Family Reader, 1956, 61; Favorite Muggins Mouse Stories, 1965; The Parade, 1966; Muggins Takes Off, 1967; The Big Balloon, 1967; Hoppity, 1967; Little Red Boot, 1968; others. Home: 1615 Hinman Av Evanston IL 60201

BARRY, DIANNE KATHLEEN, lawyer; b. San Francisco, Dec. 5, 1944; d. Eugene Joseph and Helen Gertrude (Koch) Barry; B.A., San Jose State U., 1967; J.D., U. San Francisco, 1970. Admitted to Cal. bar, 1971; practiced in Oakland, 1971-73, San Francisco, 1973—; asso. firm Fletcher, Smith & Lasky, 1971-73; dep. city atty. City Atty.'s Office, San Francisco, 1973—. Arbitrator for expedited arbitration of steel industry, 1972—. Bd. dirs. Alameda County Dem. Lawyers, 1972. Mem. Cal. State Bar (com. on juvenile justice 1973), Am., San Francisco, Alameda County bar assns. Home: 2695 Greenwich St No 302 San Francisco CA 94123 Office: 206 City Hall San Francisco CA

BARRY, GAYLE EILEEN, state ofcl.; b. Bremerton, Wash., June 23, 1935; d. George E. and Helen N. (Torwick) Barry; B.A., U. Wash., 1957, LL.B., 1959; m. Darrell Malan Lee, Apr. 25, 1965; 1 dau., Laura Stephanie. Admitted to Wash. State bar, 1959; asso. firm Reaugh, Hart & Allison, Seattle, 1959-62; asst. atty. gen.-Seattle br., 1962—, adviser Wash. State Women's Council, 1971—. Home: 8043 NE 28th St Bellevue WA 98004 Office: 1266 Dexter Horton Bldg Seattle WA 98104

BARRY, JOSEPHINE STEWART, artist; b. Plattsburgh, N.Y., Jan. 17, 1899; d. Elmer Ellsworth and Hallie Phelps (Snyder) Stewart; tchrs. diploma Plattsburgh State Normal Sch., 1920; student N.A.O., 1924-25, Coll. City N.Y., 1923-24, Columbia, 1945-46; m. Lyman F. Barry, May 26, 1923; 1 son, L.F. Warren. Tchr. high schs., Oyster Bay, N.Y., 1920-21, Utica, N.Y., 1921-22, Patchogue, N.Y., 1922. Lectr. hist. field, 1947—; one-man shows N.Y. Pub. Library, 1951-53, Dry Dock Savs. Bank, N.Y.C., 1959, St. Johns Episcopal Ch., Bklyn., 1959-60, N.Y. Visitors Bur., N.Y.C. 1961, (graphics) Ch. Center for the UN, 1969, West Brighton Day Center, 1969; exhibited in group shows at Seton Hall U., 1956, S.I. Conf. House, 1970, Community Galleries, N.Y.C., 1970, S.I. Council Arts Gallery, 1973, regional art exhibit, Smithtown, N.Y., 1967. Vol., Serve orgn., 1972—. Recipient prize Raphael Tuck Internat. Art Contest, 1915, Plattsburgh Fair, 1917, 19, Nat. Art Week, Denton, Mo., 1938, 39. Mem. Am. Artists Profl. League, Plattsburgh State Tchrs. Coll. Alumnae Assn., Tottenville Unity Group (rec. sec. 1971—), D.A.R. (rep. Bicentennial workshop 1973). Club: N.Y.C. Womens Press. Contbr. poetry and articles to profl. and popular publs. Address: care Warren L Barry 106 Jefferson St Haskell NJ 07420

BARRY, SISTER MARY DAVID, former coll. pres.; b. N.Y.C., May 31, 1915; d. David R. and Mary (Creagh) Barry; A.B., Coll. Mount Saint Vincent N.Y.C., 1937; A.M., Columbia, 1946; postgrad. Cath. U. Am., Nat. U. Ireland, Dublin; D.H.L., Manhattan Coll., 1966 Joined Order of Sisters of Charity, 1938; tchr. English, Cathedral High Sch., N.Y.C., 1940-55; mem. faculty English, Coll. Mount Saint Vincent, 1955-56, dean students, 1956-63, pres., 1963-73. Co-founder Cath. Forensic League N.Y., 1944; bd. dirs. Commomn. on Ind. Colls. and Univs. N.Y.; pres. Race Relations Council N.Y.C., 1937. Past trustee Elizabeth Seton Coll., Yonkers, N.Y. Mem. Council Higher Ednl. Instns. N.Y.C. (dir., sec.), Nat. Cath. Ednl. Assn., Am. Assn. U. Women. Conf. Cath. Colls. and Univs. N.Y. (v.p.), Nat. Assn. Women Deans and Counsellors. Author articles, monograph. Address: Coll Mount Saint Vincent Riverdale NY 10471

BARRY, SISTER MARY MARTIN, educator; b. San Francisco; d. Charles James and Elizabeth (Regan) Barry; B.A., Dominican Coll., 1925; M.A., Cath. U. Am., Pacific Coast br., 1937; Ph.D., Cath. U. Am., Washington, 1947. Tchr. secondary schs., San Francisco and San Rafael, Cal., 1928-44; prof. English lit. Dominican Coll., 1944—, dean grad. div., 1950-72. Author: A Prosodic Study of Selected Poems of T.S. Eliot, 1968. Address: Dominican College San Rafael CA 94901

BARTEAU, BETTY ANNE (MRS. WILLIAM VANVELSOR BARTEAU), lawyer; b. Tennyson, Ind., Oct. 19, 1935; d. John Raymond and Mae Elizabeth (Burley) Scales; LL.B., Ind. U., 1965; m. William VanVelsor Barteau, Dec. 30, 1968; children—Brent, Raymond Bradley, Brian, Leslie, Laura Rector. Admitted to Ind. bar, 1965; practiced in Boonville, 1965-69, Indpls., 1969—; atty. Warrick County Boonville, 1966-68; atty. Park Bd., Boonville, 1967-69; town atty. Tennyson, 1967-69; dep. pros. atty., Boonville, 1965-67; judge Boonville City Ct., 1967-69; mem. firm Runnels, Barteau & Pontius, 1969—. Mem. Nat. Security Forum, 1973; mem. Ind. Employment Rev. Bd., 1969-72; chairperson Warrick County Young Democrats, 1966-68; county co-ordinator for Senator Bayh's re-election, 1966-68; mem. adv. council Govs. Commn. on status of women, 1973. Mem. Ind. State, Indpls. bar assns., Lawyers Assn., Bus. and Profl. Women, Nat. Women's Polit. Caucus, Greater Indpls. Women's Polit. Caucus, D.A.R., Hoosiers for Equal Rights Amendment, Order of Coif. Home: 4363 N Central Av Indianapolis IN 46205 Office: 3016 W 16th St Indianapolis IN 46222

BARTEL, NETTIE ROSE (MRS. HELMUT W. BARTEL), ednl. adminstr.; b. Truax, Can., Aug. 20, 1940; d. Jacob J. and Margaret (Kornelsen) Pankratz: came to U.S., 1961; B.A., Goshen Coll., 1961; M.S. in Edn. (U.S. Office Edn. fellow), Ind. U., 1966, Ph.D., 1968; m. Helmut W. Bartel, Sept. 5, 1960; children—Roxanne, Michael. Tchr. exceptional children, Winnipeg, Man., Can., 1959-60, Elkhart, Ind., 1961-65; asst. prof. spl. edn. Ind. U., Bloomington, 1968-69; asst. prof. spl. edn. Temple U., Phila., 1969-71, asso. prof., 1971-72, chmn. dept. spl. edn., 1972—. Mem. Bur. Edn. for the Handicapped. Cons. editor Exceptional Children, Arlington, Va., 1971—. Mem. Pa. Spl. Edn. Adv. Bd. Chmn. Nevil Sensory Disabilities Inst. Planning Bd. Mem. Am. Assn. on Mental Deficiency, Internat. Reading Assn., Council for Exceptional Children, Assn. for Children with Learning Disabilities. Author: (with D.D. Hammill) Educational Perspectives in Learning Disabilities, 1971, Teaching Children with Learning and Behavioral Problems, 1974. Contbr. articles on edn. to profl. publs. Home: 4708 Windsor Av Philadelphia PA 19143 Office: dept Special Education Temple U Philadelphia PA 19122

BARTELS, MARY ANN, ednl. adminstr.; b. Winnetka, Ill., Jan. 13, 1930; d. Albert Frederick and Matilda Florence (Levernier) Bartels; B.A., Coll. St. Francis, 1962, master certificate, 1965. Asst. to mgr. Technygraph Co., Techny, Ill., 1950-55; owner, operator N. Suburban Copy Service, Northbrook, Ill., 1955-57; high sch. tchr. St. Francis Acad., Joliet, Ill., 1960-64; bus. mgr. Coll. of St. Francis, Joliet, Ill., 1964-71, v.p., 1971-74; adminstr. Kennedy Job Tng. Center, Palos Park, Ill., 1974—. Trustee Coll. of St. Francis, 1964—. Mem. Am. Assn. U. Women. Club: Zonta (dir. Joliet 1973—). Home: 717 1/2 Buell Av Joliet IL 60435 Office: Kennedy Job Tng Center 123d & Wolf Rd Palos Park IL 60464

BARTER, ALICE K. SHAMLIAN, educator; b. Sivas, Turkey, Nov. 11, 1918; d. Harry and Marguerite (Seraderian) Shamlian; brought to U.S., 1921, naturalized, 1927; A.B., Eastern Mich. U., 1939; M.A., U. Mich., 1944, Ph.D., 1957, postdoctoral student, summers 1963, 67; m. Lloyd Barter, Aug. 18, 1940 (div. Aug. 1958); 1 dau., Andrea Marguerite. Tchr. English pub. schs., Mich., 1939-55; asst. prof. edn. U. Detroit, 1957-60; asst. prof. Miami U., Oxford, O., 1960-63, asso. prof., 1963-67; prof. English, Chgo. State U., 1967—. Mem. Am. Assn. U. Profs. (chpt. treas. 1962-64, chpt. sec. 1970—), Nat. Soc. Study Edn., Nat. Council Tchrs. English, Midwest Modern Lang Assn., Pi Lambda Theta. Contbr. articles in field to profl. jours. Home: 2216 Country Club Dr Apt 26 Woodridge IL 60515 Office: 95th and King Dr Chicago IL 60628

BARTH, DIANA cons. performing arts; b. Los Angeles, May 31, 1929; d. Harry and Sally (Pressman) Newman; B.A., U. Cal. at Los Angeles, 1950; m. Leslie Barrett, Nov. 22, 1951; 1 son, Randall. West Coast, European, Far East corr. Equity mag. Actors Equity Assn., 1959-70; sr. editor Simon & Schuster, N.Y.C., 1970-72; asst. to dir. Bklyn. Acad. Music, 1972-73; cons. theatre and dance N.Y. State Council of Arts, 1972—. Co-founder, adminstr. Equity Library Theatre West, Los Angeles, 1959-62; dir. prose and poetry series Beverly Hills Pub. Library, 1959-62, N.Y.C. Pub. Library, 1963-66. Mem. Dance Critics Assn. (chmn. publs. com. 1974—). Editor: The Use of Stanislavski Within Modern Dance (by Valentina Litvinoff), 1971; Proc. of 22d International Conference of Parapsychology Foundation, 1973. Contbg. editor Playbill, 1968—, Variety, 1958—, After Dark, 1968—, Backstage, 1959—, Christian Sci. Monitor, 1973—, Catalyst mag., 1974—; editorial bd., contbg. editor Standby mag. A.F.T.R.A., 1955-58. Home: 203 W 81st St New York City NY 10024

BARTH, EDNA ROSE SMITH (MRS. GEORGE FRANCIS BARTH), pub. co. exec.; b. Marblehead, Mass., Mar. 13, 1914; d. Charlton Lyman and Elizabeth (Bateman) Smith; B.A., Radcliffe Coll., 1936; B.S., Simmons Coll., 1937; m. Julius Weiss, Aug. 22, 1938; children—Elizabeth (Mrs. Richard Fein), Joel Peter, Paul Jeremy; m. 2d, George Francis Barth, Nov. 19, 1966. Br. librarian Jones Library, Amherst, Mass., 1937-39; children's librarian N.Y. Pub. Library, N.Y.C., 1940-41; tchr. Hillsboro (N.H.) Center Sch., 1948-50; asso. editor children's books McGraw Hill Book Co., N.Y.C., 1960-62, Thomas Y. Crowell Co., N.Y.C., 1962-64; editor children's books Lothron Lee & Shepard Co., N.Y.C., 1966-69, editor-in-chief, 1969—, v.p. parent co. William Morrow & Co., N.Y.C., 1970—. Mem. Children's Book Council (dir. 1970-73), Nat. Orgn. Women. Club: Radcliffe (N.Y.C.). Author: Sally Saucer, 1956; Truly Elizabeth, 1957; The Rainbow, 1960; Lilies, Rabbits, and Painted Eggs, 1970; I'm Nobody! Who are You?, 1971; The Day Luis Was Lost, 1971; Holly, Reindeer, and Colored Lights, 1971; Witches, Pumpkins, and Grinning Ghosts, 1972; Hearts, Cupids, and Red Roses, 1974; Jack-o'-Lantern, 1974. Home: 85 4th Av New York City NY 10003 Office: 105 Madison Av New York City NY 10016

BARTHOLET, CAROLYN LEARY (MRS. WILLIAM M. BARTHOLET), occupational therapist; b. Miami, Fla., May 7, 1939; d. Lewis and Mary Warren (Hudson) Leary; student U. Amsterdam (Netherlands), 1957-58, Chatham Coll., 1958-60; B.S., Columbia, 1962; m. William M. Bartholet, Nov. 24, 1960; children—Robin, Lynn. Sr. therapist Middlesex Rehab. Hosp., North Brunswick, N.J., 1965-66; head recreation program Francis F. Parker Meml. Home, New Brunswick, 1967; occupational therapist Middlesex Rehab. Hosp., 1971—. Charter mem. South County Hosp. Devel. Corp. Mem. Am., N.J. occupational therapy assns. Unitarian. Club: North Brunswick Racquet. Author: (with Lewis Leary and Catherine Roth) Articles on American Literature 1950-1967, 1970. Home: 24 Lansdowne Rd East Brunswick NJ 18816

BARTLE, ANNETTE GRUBER (MRS. THOMAS R. BARTLE), artist; b. Poland; d. Henry and Maria (Harczyk) Gruber; Bacheliere, Sorbonne, Paris, 1940; B.A., Elmira Coll., 1943; student Ecole des Beaux Arts (Paris), 1940, Art Student League (Art Student League scholar 1949), 1947-50; m. Thomas R. Bartle, Dec. 5, 1957; 1 dau.,

Eve Marie. Came to U.S., 1940, naturalized, 1943. Exhibited in one-man shows Midtown Galleries, N.Y.C., 1957, 60, 63, 66, Feingarten, Chgo., 1957, Wickersham Gallery, 1970; exhibited in group shows Am. Acad. Arts and Letters, 1963, Detroit Art Inst., 1958, 62, 65, 67, Pa. Acad., 1959, 60, 66, Butler Art Inst., 1960, 64, 65, Cin. Art Mus., 1960, 62, 67; represented in permanent collections Am. Internat. Underwriters, Union Carbide, Conn. Mut. Life, Mural Port Authority Heliport, N.Y. Worlds Fair. Active various community drives. Pan Am. Travelling fellow 1950. Recipient citation for outstanding achievements 90th U.S. Congress, 1968. Mem. Am. Fedn. Arts, Artists Equity. Address: 231 E 76th St New York City NY 10021

BARTLETT, AGNES VERNON, physician; b. Kyoto, Japan, Mar. 18, 1911 (parents Am. citizens); d. Samuel Colcord and Fanny Slater (Gordon) Bartlett; student Bradford Jr. Coll., 1929-31; B.A., Mt. Holyoke Coll., 1934; M.D., Yale, 1938. Intern Mass. Meml. Hosp., Boston, 1938-40, clin. instr., 1940-42, resident, clin. instr. obstetrics, 1942-44; with War Relocation Authority Relocation Centers, 1944-45; gen. practice medicine, Lyme, N.H., 1946-47; fellow in anesthesiology, clin. instr. pharmacology Dartmouth Med. Sch., 1948-50; resident anesthesiology Mary Hitchcock Meml. Hosp., Hanover, N.H., 1948-50; practice medicine specializing in anesthesiology, Springfield, Vt., 1950-61, Concord Hosp. (N.H.), 1961-64; chief sect. anesthesiology U.S. VA Hosp., White River Junction, Vt., 1964—; clin. asst. prof. surgery (anesthesiology) Dartmouth Med. Sch., 1972—. Trustee Brookhaven Home for Boys, Chelsea, 1967—. Diplomate Am. Bd. Anesthesiologists. Mem. A.M.A., N.H. Med. Soc., Am. Coll. Anesthesiologists, Am. (past dist. dir.), N.H. (pres. 1956, mem. com. on credentials 1961—) socs. anesthesiologists. Episcopalian (clk. of vestry 1969). Home: Box 349 Norwich VT 05055 Office: US VA Hosp White River Junction VT 05001

BARTLETT, DOROTHY LUCILLE WOOD (MRS. KENNETH FRANKLIN BARTLETT), librarian; b. Richmond, Va.; d. Wilfred Walton and Maude (Robins) Wood; B.A., Randolph-Macon Woman's Coll., 1932; B.A. in L.S., Emory U., 1933; m. Kenneth Franklin Bartlett, Oct. 20, 1945. Library asst., head children's dept. Richmond Pub. Library, 1933-40; map asst., archives div. Va. State Library, Richmond, 1940-42; chief circulation dept. City Library Assn., Springfield, Mass., 1942-43; map curator Nat. Archives, Washington, 1943-44; map analyst, chief map research sect. Fgn. Econ. Adminstrn., Washington, 1944-45; map analyst Dept. Agr., Beltsville, Md., 1946; chief reference sect., map library Dept. State, Washington, 1946-47; map librarian CIA, Washington, 1948-61; head reference and bibiography sect., geography and map div. Library Congress, Washington, 1962-70, bibliographer of div., 1970—. Mem. Spl. Libraries Assn. (chpt. vice chmn. geography and map group 1964-66, chmn. 1966-67, nominating com. 1967), Jamestowne Soc., U. D.C., Assn. Am. Geographers, Am. Assn. U. Women, Assn. Preservation Va. Antiquities, Carto-Philatelists, Va. Library Assn. Methodist. Contbr. articles to profl. jours. Home: 1713 Wainwright Dr Reston VA 22090 Office: Library Congress Washington DC 20540

BARTLETT, ESTHER ELIZABETH, physician, anesthesiologist; b. Somerville, Mass.; d. Frank Cavis and Dorothy (Kimball) Bartlett; B.A., U. Wis., 1930, M.A., 1931, M.D., 1934. Intern, Wis. Gen. Hosp., Madison, 1934-35; resident, Chgo. Lying-in Hosp. and Billings Hosp., Chgo., 1935-38; practice medicine specializing in anesthesiology, Boston, 1938-73; dir. dept. anesthesiology New Eng. Hosp., Roxbury, Mass., 1937-62; asso. anesthesiologist U. Hosp., Boston U. Sch. Medicine, 1963—, faculty mem., 1964-73; practice med. hypnosis, 1973—. Diplomate Am. Bd. Anesthesiology. Mem. Am. (sec. 1969-73), New Eng. (treas. 1965—) socs. clin. hypnosis, A.M.A., Am. Soc. Anesthesiology. Address: 181 Adams St Quincy MA 02169

BARTLETT, LYNN ROUNTREE (MRS. HENRY CHARLES BARTLETT), univ. ofcl.; b. Kinston, N.C., Aug. 1, 1908; d. Jack Robert and Clara (Wooten) Rountree; A.B., U. Cal. at Berkeley, 1930; M.A., Tchrs. Coll., Columbia, 1944, Ed.D., 1959; m. Henry Charles Bartlett, July 2, 1932; children—Linda Belle, Henry Charles. Advt. space salesman Fgn. Lang. Field Service Corp., N.Y.C., 1931-33; nat. advt. space salesman N.Y. Herald Tribune, N.Y.C., 1933-34; tchr. English and social sci. high sch. div. Scarborough (N.Y.) Sch., 1938-43, dean girls, 1943-46; exec. dir. Planned Parenthood, Kansas City, Mo., 1956-57; coordinator women's residence halls U. Miami, Coral Gables, Fla., 1958-68, coordinator residence halls programs, 1968-69, supr. office counseling men and women students, 1969—, mem. minority affairs com., 1971—, mem. women's commn., 1971—. Mem. ednl. planning com. to set up Dade County Planned Parenthood, bd. dirs., 1963-66; bd. dirs. YWCA Greater Miami, 1960-66, 68-71; group work Council Social Agys., Kansas City, 1955-57; mem. Com. on Edn. for Family Life and Human Sexuality, Dade County Dept. Health, 1970—; nat. adviser Phi Lambda Pi, 1968—; chmn. nat. screening com. All-Am. Family, 1971. Bd. dirs. San Francisco Protestant Orphanage, 1946-52, San Mateo County Family Service Agy., 1948-52, San Francisco chpt. A.R.C., 1951-52, Rec. for Blind, 1963; bd. mem. edn. Fedn. Protestant Welfare Agys., N.Y.C., 1952-54, mem. women's bd. dirs. Kansas City Philharmonic Symphony, 1955-57, women's guild Greater Miami Philharmonic Soc., 1968—; profl. adv. bd. Abortion study Assn. of Fla., 1968-70. Recipient award San Francisco chpt. A.R.C., 1952; named Woman of Achievement in World Affairs, Dist. II, Fla. Fedn. of Bus. and Profl. Clubs, 1965; Community Headliner award Theta Sigma Phi, 1970. Mem. Nat. Assn. Women Deans and Counselors, Am. Personnel and Guidance Assn., So. Personnel Assn., Mortar Bd. (sect. dir. 1964-67, nat. 2d v.p. 1967-70, named Woman of Distinction Nu Kappa Tau chpt. 1974), Intercollegiate Assn. Women Students (nat. adviser 1965-68), Council for Continuing Edn. Women (mem. exec. com. 1968-71, chmn. edn. sect. for My Lady Fair 1971), Sigma Kappa, Alpha Lambda Delta, Delta Sigma Rho, Kappa Delta Pi, Pi Lambda Theta. Episcopalian (vestry, sr. warden 1972). Club: Zonta (chmn. program com. Miami chpt. 1962-63). Home: 6401 SW 100th St South Miami FL 33143 Office: 1231 Dickinson Dr Coral Gables FL 33126

BARTLETT, MABEL, librarian, educator; b. Bklyn.; d. William Cushing and Mabel (Worman) Bartlett; B.A., Conn. Coll. for Women, 1930; B.S., Columbia, 1938. Cataloger, reference librarian L.I. Hist. Soc., Bklyn., 1940-43; reference and circulation asst. Pub. Library, New London, Conn., 1943-44; cataloger State U. Ia. Library, Iowa City, 1944-46; head catalog dept. Osterhout Free Library, Wilkes-Barre, Pa., 1946-48; head tech. processes dept. L.I. U. Library, Bklyn., 1948—, asst. prof., 1948-54, asso. prof., 1954-70, prof., 1970—. Mem. A.L.A., Am. Bible Soc., N.Y. Tech. Services Librarians, Am. Assn. U. Profs. L.I. U. (chpt. treas. 1966—). Republican. Episcopalian. Home: 143 Linden Blvd Brooklyn NY 11226

BARTMESS, DUCHESS MARIE (MRS. CHARLES E. BARTMESS), lawyer, state ofcl.; b. Denver, Dec. 15, 1939; d. Bill C. and Eva Marie (Black) Jett; B.A. in Humanities, U. Minn., 1961; J.D., Okla. City U., 1966; m. Charles E. Bartmess, Aug. 28, 1964. Admitted to Okla. bar, 1966; legal asst. to U.S. dist. judge, Oklahoma City, 1966-67; officer Okla. County Libraries, Oklahoma City, 1968-69; researcher and brief writer Pierce, Duncan Couch & Hendrickson Co., Oklahoma City, 1969-71; asst. atty. gen., Okla., Oklahoma City, 1971-72; staff atty. Okla. Legislative Council, 1972—. Named Outstanding Young Woman, 1967. Mem. Am., Okla. bar assns., Nat. Assn. Women Lawyers, Okla. Assn. Women Lawyers, Oklahoma City U. Law Alumni Assn., Iota Tau Tau, Alpha Omicron Pi. Home: 3408 Windsor Av Oklahoma City OK 73122 Office: State Capitol Bldg Oklahoma City OK 73105

BARTOL, KATHRYN MARIE, educator; b. Bellevue, Pa., Oct. 15, 1941; d. Walter Ray and Mary Amelia (Scherf) Ottinger; B.A., Marygrove Coll., Detroit, 1963; M.A. (fellow), U. Mich., 1966; Ph.D. (fellow), Mich. State U., 1972; m. Robert A. Bartol, Sept. 10, 1966. Advt. writer J.L. Hudson Co., retail dept. store, Detroit, 1963-64; system analyst, project leader Mich. Dept. Social Services, 1966-69; teaching asst. Mich. State U. Sch. Bus. Adminstrn., 1969-73; asst. prof. Sch. Bus. Adminstrn., U. Mass., Amherst, 1972-74; asso. prof. Syracuse (Mass.) U. Sch. Mgmt., 1974—. Mgmt. cons., 1972—. Mem. Amherst Republican Town Com., 1973—. Faculty growth and research grantee U. Mass., 1973-74. Mem. Acad. Mgmt. (chairperson com. status women in mgmt. profession 1973-74), Am. Inst. Decision Scis., Bus. and Profl. Women's Club, Phi Kappa Phi. Author: Male and Female Leaders of Small Groups, 1974. Contbr. articles to profl. jours. Office: Bldg 26 4950 Westbrook Hills Dr Syracuse NY 13215

BARTON, GAIL MELINDA (MRS. DUNCAN KRETOVICH), psychiatrist; b. Worcester, Mass., Apr. 20, 1937; d. Walter Earl and Elsa Viola (Benson) Barton; A.B. cum laude Jackson Coll. of Tufts U., 1959; M.D., Woman's Med. Coll. Pa., 1966; M.P.H., U. Mich., 1971; m. Duncan Kretovich, Aug. 31, 1968; 1 dau., Mariah Lynne. Rotating intern St. Joseph Mercy Hosp., Ann Arbor, Mich., 1966-67; resident psychiatry U. Mich. Hosp., Ann Arbor, 1967-71, chief resident, 1970-71, psychiat. cons. clin. research unit, 1969-71, clin. asst. prof. psychiatry, 1971—, adminstr. acute psychiat. ward, 1971, dir. after-care program, 1972—; dir. continuity of care program, 1971—. Mem. Founders Soc. Detroit Art Inst. Community mental health research asst. Sch. Pub. Health, U. Mich., 1971-72; psychiatrist after-care program Washtenaw County Community Mental Health Center, 1973—. Recipient physician's recognition award A.M.A., 1969, 71. Diplomate Nat. Bd. Med. Examiners. Mem. Am. Psychiat. Assn. (com. psychiatry and social work 1971-72, com. psychiatry and nursing 1973—), Am. Med. Women's Assn., Washtenaw County Med. Soc., Mich. Soc. Neurology and Psychiatry, Am. Psychiat. Art Assn., Ann Arbor Art Assn. Club: Ann Arbor Camera. Home: 1450 Westfield St Ann Arbor MI 48103 Office: University of Michigan Hospital Ann Arbor MI 48104

BARTON, NELDA ANN LAMBERT (MRS. HAROLD BRYAN BARTON), Republican nat. committeewoman; b. Providence, Ky., May 12, 1929; d. Eulis Grant and Rubie Lois (West) Lambert; student Western Ky. U., 1947-49; grad. Norton Meml. Sch. Med. Tech., 1950; m. Harold Bryan Barton, May 11, 1951; children—William Grant (dec.), Barbara Lynn, Harold Bryan, Stephen Lambert, Suzanne. Med. technologist, 1950-53; chmn. 5th dist. Rep. campaign, Ky., 1967; Whitley County (Ky.) Rep. chairwoman, 1968-72; del., mem. orgn. com. Rep. Nat. Com., 1968—; Ky. conf. chmn. Nat. Rep. Leadership Conf., 1972; mem. arrangements com. Rep. Nat. Conv., 1972, mem. rule 29 com.; mem. Gov.'s Ky. Commn. on Women, 1968-72; co-chmn. Urban Renewal and Community Devel. Agy. for City of Corbin, 1970-72; mem. Nat. Bipartisan Com. on Financing Convs., 1974—. Dist. chmn. P.T.A., 1958-59; pres. Corbin (Ky.) Central Elementary P.T.A., 1963-65; life mem. P.T.A., 1964—; mem. adv. com. Corbin City Commn., 1970—; mem. nursing adv. com. Cumberland Coll., Williamsburg, Ky., 1972—. Named Ky. Republican Woman of Year, 1968-69, Ky. Col., 1968, Ind. Sagamore, 1973. Mem. Ky. Fedn. Womens Clubs (dist. vice-gov. 1962-64), Ky. Fedn. Rep. Women (dist. gov. 1963-67, 2d v.p. 1968-70), Women's Aux. So. Med. Assn. (councilor 1965-66), Women's Aux. Ky. Med. Assn. (health career chmn. 1973-74) Women's Aux. Whitley County Med. Soc. (pres. 1959-60), Internat. Platform Assn. Mem. Christian Ch. Clubs: Corbin Republican Women's (pres. 1968), Ossoli Woman's (pres. 1961-62). Home: 1311 7th St Rd Corbin KY 40701

BARTON, VELDA MADGE (MRS. MERLE BARTON), banker; b. Bingham, Neb., Mar. 17, 1926; d. Diles Raymond and Eula Jane (Moon) Howell; grad. pub. schs., Edgemont, S.D., 1943; m. Merle Barton, Jan. 23, 1949; children—Marilyn (Mrs. Dennis Edward Mattingly), Marvin Marie (dec. June 1973). Bookkeeper, South Hills Bank, Edgemont, 1944-46, Casper Nat. Bank (Wyo.), 1946-53; bookkeeper Nat. Bank of Alaska, Anchorage, 1953-55, head bookkeeper, 1955-65, asst. cashier, 1965-71, asst. v.p., 1971—, operations officer, 1969—. Mem. Am. Inst. Banking, Nat. Assn. Bank Women. Mem. Hesperian Rebekah Lodge. Club: Altrusa (pres. 1968) (Anchorage). Home: Martin Arms 18-H Anchorage AK 99501 Office: National Bank of Alaska PO Box 600 Anchorage AK 99510

BARTON, VIRGINIA CAMPBELL (MRS. CHARLES CANNON BARTON), newspaper editor; b. Wilmington, Del., July 7, 1926; d. George Britton and Sallie Virginia (Powell) Campbell; grad. high sch.; m. Charles Cannon Barton, Sept. 14, 1946; children—Elizabeth Bonniwell (Mrs. James B. Shaw III), Philip Cannon, John Edward. With State Register, Laurel, Del., 1967—, editor, 1967—. Brownie leader Girl Scouts Am., Laurel, Del., 1960-61; den mother Cub Scouts Am., Laurel, Del., 1962-63. Mem. Md., Del., D.C. Press Assn. Episcopalian. Home: White Av Laurel DE 19956 Office: 225 E Market St Laurel DE 19956

BARTON, VIRGINIA GRACE ROCCA (MRS. E. EARL BARTON), supt. schs.; b. St. Maries, Ida., July 20, 1918; d. Philip Angelo and Angela Theresa (Torchia) Rocca; A.B., San Jose State Coll., 1940, M.A., 1952; m. E. Earl Barton, July 6, 1952. Tchr. pub. schs., Salinas, Cal., 1940-41, 43-44, prin., 1944-45, 46-47, supt. schs., 1947—. Mem. Salinas Congress for Community Progress, 1971—; mem. planning com. Civic Center, 1972—; mem. County Commn. on Recreation. Bd. dirs. Salvation Army, 1972—, YMCA, 1952-56, Crippled Children's Soc., 1948-53; bd. govs. 7th Agrl. Assn., 1960—. Named Boss of Year, Nat. Secs. Assn., 1966; Mentor scholar, 1969; recipient Continuing Service award P.T.A., 1969. Mem. C. of C., Assn. Cal. Sch. Adminstrs. (past sect. pres.; regional pres. 1973-74), Am. Assn. Sch. Adminstrs., N.E.A. (life), Bus. and Profl. Women's Club, Symphony Guild, Am. Assn. U. Women. Soroptimist. Club: Woman's. Home: 1231 Lamirada Dr Salinas CA 93901 Office: 1221 E Market St Salinas CA 93901

BARTON, MRS. WILLIAM P. (ELEANOR KEESE BARTON), newspaperwoman; b. Walhalla, S.C., May 31, 1901; d. John Perry and Soula T. (Reeder) Keese; B.A., Greenville Woman's Coll., 1921; postgrad. Cornell U., 1923; m. William P. Barton, July 19, 1924; 1 dau., Eleanor Sue (Mrs. John O. Allen). Instr. Greenville Woman's Coll., 1921-24, pub. relations work, 1921-29; woman's editor Greenville (S.C.) Piedmont, 1929-51, columnist, 1951-74, ret., 1974; feature writer, 1951-74; radio news commentator, 1956-62. Pres., Crescent Music Club, 1939-41, Community Concert Assn., 1953-55; mem. vol. corps U.S.O., 1951-63, chmn., 1959-61; chmn. Greenville County chpt. ARC, 1956-57; pres. Crescent Community Club, 1953-55; v.p. Better Govt. Assn., 1956-57; mem. Greenville Symphony Assn., 1949-65; mem. Greenville County Heart Council; adv. bd. S.C. div. Nat. Found.; bd. dirs. S.C. div. Am. Cancer Soc.; pres. Crescent Literary Club, 1961-63; v.p. Greenville County Fedn. Women's Clubs, 1965-66, chmn. Diamond Jubilee, S.C. Fedn. Women's Clubs; helped establish S.C. Commn. on Aging; adv. com. Palmetto Outdoor Hist. Drama Assn.; mem. S.C. Tricennial Adv. Com. Recipient Nat. Bus. and Profl. Women's Club award, 1932; Certificate Appreciation, Boys' Club Am., 1956; Nat. Recreation Assn. citation, 1961; Plaque from Greenville Symphony Assn., 1966. Gen., and State Fedns. Women's Clubs citation, 1955-56; Nat. Community Achievement citation, 1956. Mem. Nat. Fedn. Music Clubs (hon. life), Sigma Iota Chi. Baptist. Club: Woman's (director 1951-61, 63—). Author: History of the Crescent Music Club. 1956; History of Greenville Woman's Club. 1960; also papers, reports, brochures. Editor: U.S.O. Volunteer, 1959-61. Home: 208 McIver St Greenville SC 29601

BARTOSH, ELOISE THERESE CARROLL, librarian; b. Lackawanna, N.Y., Sept. 16, 1942; d. Joseph John and Angela Teresa (Gannon) Carroll; B.A., Marywood Coll., 1964, M.S., 1965; m. John Joseph Bartosh, June 28, 1969; children—Denise, John Joseph. Head librarian Lackawanna Jr. Coll., Seeley Meml. Library, Scranton, Pa., 1965-69; circulation librarian Marywood Coll., Scranton, 1969-70, lectr., 1973—; librarian, St. Mary's Mercedian Sch. Nursing, Scranton, 1970-72. Mem. Marywood Coll. Alumnae Assn. Home: 1023 Richmont St Scranton PA 18509

BARTUSIS, MARY ANN BABINSKY (MRS. D.J. BARTUSIS), physician; b. Palmer, Pa., Apr. 16, 1930; d. Steve and Ann K. (Polach) Babinsky; B.S., U. Pitts., 1952; M.D., Women's Med. Coll. Pa., 1956; m. Donald J. Bartusis, July 10, 1954; children—Joseph, Debbie, Monica, Michele. Intern, Phila. Gen. Hosp., 1956-57; resident psychiatry Trenton (N.J.) State Hosp., 1957-60, now cons.; asso. dir. guidance clinic Cath. Welfare Bur., Trenton, 1960-63, med. dir. guidance clinic, 1963-67; practice medicine, specializing in psychiatry, Trenton, 1960—; mem. staffs Mercer, St. Francis hosps., Trenton, Fairmount Farm, Phila.; asso. psychiatrist U. Pa. Med. Sch., Phila., 1968-69. Bd. govs. Greater Trenton Symphony. Named Woman Par Excellence, Trenton Trust Bank, 1969. Diplomate in psychiatry Am. Bd. Psychiatry and Neurology. Fellow Am. Psychiat. Assn.; mem. N.J. Neuropsychiat. Assn. (pres.-elect 1969-70). Club: Zonta International. Home and office: 1007 N Pennsylvania Av Morrisville PA 19067

BARZ, DIANE GAY (MRS. DANIEL J. BARZ), lawyer, county ofcl.; b. Bozeman, Mont., Aug. 18, 1943; d. John G. and E. Bernice (Johnson) MacDonald; student U. Heidelberg (Germany), 1964; B.A. magna cum laude, Whitworth Coll., 1965; J.D. (Bur. Nat. Affairs scholar), U. Mont., 1968; m. Daniel J. Barz, Nov. 28, 1970. Admitted to Mont. bar, 1968; law clk., research asst. Mont Supreme Ct., Mont. Criminal Commn., Helena, 1968-70; dep. county atty. Yellowstone County, Mont., 1970—; partner firm Poppler & Barz, Billings, Mont., 1973—. Account exec. United Way, Billings, 1973. Sec., Yellowstone County Republican Central Com., Billings, 1973. Bd. dirs. S. Central Mont. Regional Mental Health Center, Billings. Mem. Young Lawyers' Assn. (v.p., sec. 1970), Bus. and Profl. Women's Club (named Mont. Young Career Woman 1970), Mont., Yellowstone County bar assns., Jr. League Billings, Billings Jr. C. of C., Phi Delta (named Woman of Year 1970). Presbyn. (tchr., organist). Home: 2046 Av D Billings MT 59102 Office: Stapleton Bldg Billings MT 59101

BARZEL, ANN, dance critic; b. Mpls., Dec. 26, 1913; d. Nahum and Freda (Mirsky) Barzel; B.A., U. Chgo., 1931. Dance critic, writer on dance Chgo. Times, 1946-50, Chgo. Am. (now Chgo. Today), 1951—; writer reviews and articles for various nat. periodicals, including Dance mag., Dance News, Dance Index, Ballet Ann., London, Les Saisons de la Danse, Paris; dance cons., coordinator Ill. Arts Council, 1967—. Mem. adv. panel on dance State Dept. Cultural Presentations, 1956—; lectr. dance U. Chgo., 1950-55. Home: 3950 Lake Shore Dr Chicago IL,60613 Office: Chicago Today 445 N Michigan Av Chicago IL 60611

BASGALL, SISTER MARY RITA, hosp. adminstr.; b. Loretto, Kan., May 24, 1914; d. Alois G. and Anna Margaret (Basgall) B.; M.S. in Hosp. Adminstrn., Xavier U., 1967; B.S., Sacred Heart Coll., 1961. Joined Adorers of Blood of Christ, 1929; office mgr., St. Mary's Hosp., Enid, Okla., 1939-54; bus. mgr. St. Francis Hosp., Carlsbad, N.M., 1954-56; provincial treas. Provincial Motherhouse, Wichita, Kan., 1956-60; adminstr. St. Marys Hosp., Enid, 1960-68; provincial councillor, Provincial Motherhouse, Wichita, 1968-70; adminstr. St. Francis Hosp., Washington, Mo., 1970—. Bd. dirs. Sacred Heart Coll., Wichita, 1968-70, St. Mary's Hosp., 1960—, St. Josephs Villa, David City, Neb., 1968-70; mem. long range planning com. St. Mary's Hosp., St. Francis Hosp. Mem. Med. Record Librarian Assn., Bus. and Profl. Women's Club. Home: 1111 E 3d St Washington MO 63090 Office: 812 E 5th Av Washington MO 63090

BASH, EVELYN FLORENCE-FRENCH (MRS. HARRIS MITCHELL BASH JR.), writer; b. May 10, 1916; d. John William and Bertha (Glover) Cavileer; A.B., U. N.C., 1936; m. Harris Mitchell Bash Jr., July 1, 1944; children—Elaine Gyneath (Mrs. John Glandon), Harris Mitchell III. Mem. editorial staff Meth. Pub. House, Nashville, 1936-39; asst. office alumnae sec. U. N.C., Greensboro, 1940-42; radio script writer U.S. regional office Civil Def., Atlanta, 1942-43; asso. editor So. Dairy Products Jour., Atlanta, 1943-46; free-lance writer, Atlanta, 1946-49; columnist U.S. Tobacco Jour., Ice Cream Confectionary World, Radio and TV Weekly, Photo Weekly, 1949-60; staff corr. to Automotive News, 1954—; corr. Fairchild Publs., Inc., N.Y.C., 1960—. Instr., Lake Junaluska, N.C., 1937, YWCA, Nashville, 1938. Chief radio and newspapers Guilford County Office Civilian Def., Greensboro, 1941-42; radio, TV chmn., exec. bd. Girl Scouts U.S.A., Atlanta, 1956-57. Bd. dirs., rec. sec. bd. YWCA, Nashville, 1937-38. Recipient awards from profl. orgns. Mem. Nat. League Am. Pen Women (chmn. Fla. workshop, nat. scrapbook 1968-70, trade market editor Jour. 1966-68, chmn. pres. Clearwater br. 1964-66, parliamentarian 1968-70, pub. chmn. 1972-74, editor West Gulf Notes 1966-68), Nat. Soc. Arts and Letters (2d v.p. Clearwater chpt. 1968-69, historian 1965-68, 72-74; parliamentarian 1970-74, chmn. by-laws 1969-70), Nat. Writers Club. Democrat. Methodist. Address: 1427 Hunt Lane Clearwater FL 33516

BASILE, ABIGAIL JULIA ELLEN HERRON (MRS. JOSEPH BASILE), employment counselor, state ofcl.; b. St. Louis, June 15, 1915; d. Charles Arthur and Abigail (Edwards) Herron; student Kansas City Jr. Coll., 1948-50, U. Kan., 1959; B.S. in Bus. Adminstrn., Rockhurst Coll., 1965; M.Ed., Univ. Mo., 1967; m. Joseph Basile, Aug. 15, 1939. Employment security dep. Mo. Div. Employment Security, Kansas City, 1945-59, youth coordinator, employment counselor, 1959-65, counselor, supr., 1965—. Mem. com. on youth employment Mo. Council on Children and Youth, Mo. Assn. Social Welfare; mem. Kansas City Mayor's Com. on Employment of Handicapped; mem. citizen's adv. bd. Christian Inner City Council Youth Employment Service. Mem. Am. Personnel and Guidance Assn., Nat. Vocational Guidance Assn., Am. Vocational Assn., Internat. Assn. Personnel in Employment Security (pres. Mo. 1966-67, internat. sec. 1966). Nat. Rehab. Assn., Nat. Employment Counselors Assn., Interagy. Com. for Rehab. (sec. 1967), Urban League, Am. Legion Aux., Personnel Research Forum, Profl.

Counselors Assn. Democrat. Episcopalian. Home: 5221 N Wayne St Kansas City MO 64118 Office: 1411 Main St Kansas City MO 64105

BASILE, RUTH LEBARON RUTLEDGE, civic worker; b. Chgo., Nov. 25, 1912; d. William Askins and Bess (LeBaron) Rutledge; R.N., Evanston Hosp., 1934, A.B., Northwestern U., 1934; m. William B. Basile, July 25, 1935; children—Bette Claire (Mrs. William Eugene Kattmann), William Basil, Ralph Rutledge. Publicity work D.A.R., 1960—, also Women's Soc. Christian Service, North Shore Meth. Ch., 1960-64; ch. sch. sec. North Shore Meth. Ch., Glencoe, 1962—; cutting chmn. Infant Welfare Soc. Mem. Cultural Devel. Program, 1964. Mem. D.A.R. (jr. rep. 1965—, publicity chmn. 1967—), Evanston Hosp. Alumnae Assn., Northwestern Alumnae Assn. P.E.O. (treas. 1968—), U.S. Women's Golf Assn., Skokie Thistles. Clubs: Skokie Country, Woman's Library Club of Glencoe. Home: 501 Monroe Av Glencoe IL 60022

BASKETT, DOROTHY ADELINE THOMAS (MRS. CHARLES WILLIAM BASKETT), librarian; b. Benton, Tenn., July 27, 1940; d. Earl Jean and Grace Alleene (Willson) Thomas; B.A., U. Tenn., 1962; M.L.S., George Peabody Coll., 1967; m. Eldon Lee Davis Jr., Jan. 21, 1961 (div. May 1964); children—Michelle Alleene, Angela Thomas; m. 2d, Charles William Baskett, Apr. 14, 1972. Librarian, Polk County High Sch., Benton, Tenn., 1962-67; circulation librarian Columbia (S.C.) Coll., 1967-69; reference librarian Cleve. State Community Coll., 1969-71, acting dir., 1971-72, head librarian, 1973—. Library cons. for Polk County under Title III, 1966-67. Mem. Am., Tenn., Southeastern library assns., Tenn. Edn. Assn., Cleveland State Community Edn. Assn., Alpha Beta Alpha. Home: 2403 Rolling Hills Dr Cleveland TN 37311 Office: Box 1205 Cleveland TN 37311

BASKIN, MATTIE V., librarian; b. Stamford, Tex., Dec. 4, 1910; d. James Andrew and Lulu Laura (Sitton) McCuistion; student Tex. Women's U., Denton, 1928-30, Hardin-Simmons U., Abilene, Tex., 1931-32; B.A., West Tex. U., Canyon, 1934; M.S. in L.S., East Tex. U., Commerce, 1963; m. Henry Lee Roy Baskin, Feb. 22, 1947 (dec. 1956); 1 son, Roy Vee; stepchildren—Vashti B. Yonker, H.L. and M.L. Baskin (dec.) (twins). Tchr. country sch., Jones County, Tex., 1932-33; tchr. Stamford Pub. Schs., 1934-42; clk. Midland (Tex.) Bombardier Sch., 1942; tchr. Ector County (Tex.) Ind. Sch. Dist., 1942-64; librarian 1st Baptist Ch., Odessa, Tex., 1944-47; elementary librarian Ector County Ind. Sch. Dist., Odessa, 1964—. Librarian jungle mission hdqrs. Wycliffe Bible Translators, Yarinacocha, Peru, summer 1970. Mem. Am., Tex. library assns., N.E.A., Tex. State Tchrs. Assn., Am., Tex. classroom tchrs. assns., Order Eastern Star, West Tex. Genealogy Club, Wally Byam Internat. Airstream Club, Delta Kappa Gamma. Home: 1300 Parker Dr Odessa TX 79761

BASLER, MARIE LUCILLE (MRS. JOHN J. BASLER, SR.), owner title co.; b. Perryville, Mo., Mar. 1, 1915; d. Henry G. and Marie L. (McBride) Seitz; grad. high sch.; m. John J. Basler, Sr., Sept. 25, 1937; children—John J., James R., Joseph W., Marie L., Barbara A., Kathleen. Dep. recorder of deeds, Ste. Genevieve County, Mo., 1937-42; abstractor Vogt Abstract Co., Ste. Genevieve, 1935-52; owner, mgr. Old Settlement Title & Abstract Co., Ste. Genevieve, 1963—. Chmn. Municipal Cemetery Com., 1969-73, Landmarks Commn., 1969-73. Bd. dirs., sec. Found. for Restoration of Ste. Genevieve, 1966-73. Vice chmn. Ste. Genevieve Democratic Central Com., 1964-72. Mem. St. Louis Geneal. Soc., State Hist. Soc. Mo., St. Genevieve Bus. and Profl. Women's Club (charter mem., v.p. 1969-73). Writer hist. column in local publ., 1966—. Home: 50 N 5th St Ste Genevieve MO 63670 Office: 34 S 3d St Ste Genevieve MO 63670

BASS, BETTY ZOE PASSMORE (MRS. ERIC BASS), artist; b. Burlington, Wis., Mar. 26, 1926; d. Dempster Stewart and Bettina (Rakow) Passmore; student U. Ariz., 1943, U. Miami, 1944-47; B.A., U. Cal. at Los Angeles, 1955; M.A., Stanford, 1963; m. Eric Bass, Oct. 10, 1948. Designer, partner haute couture firm Eric Bass, Beverly Hills, Cal., 1949-53; fine art painting, Lakeside and Los Angeles, Cal., 1953—; exhibited U. Cal. at Los Angeles Art Galley, 1955, Art Center, LaJolla, Cal., 1957, So. Cal. Exposition, 1961; Oriental art research travel to Japan, Thailand, India, 1959-60. Chmn. opening night dinners San Diego Opera Guild, also chmn. La Jolla Assos.; mem. Asiatic arts com. Fine Arts Soc.; v.p. San Diego com. Los Angeles Philharmonic; v.p. Women's Assn. Salk Inst.; chmn. benefit ball San Diego Symphony, 1971; chmn. dinners Civic Light Opera. Bd. dirs. U. Cal. at San Diego Hosps. Aux.; bd. dirs. women's com. San Diego Symphony Assn. Named 1 of 11 San Diego Women of Elegance, 1972. Mem. Soc. Mayflower Descs., D.A.R., Social Service League, La Jolla Civic Orch. Assn., Old Globe Theater 400, Klee Wyk Soc. Mus. Man, La Jolla Mus. Contemporary Art, World Affairs Council, Country Friends, Starlight Women's Assn. (v.p.), Delta Gamma. Club: Stanford (San Diego). Home: 1351 Olivet LaJolla CA 92037

BASS, BEVERLY (MRS. SIDNEY N. BASS), pub. co. exec.; b. Bklyn., July 4, 1926; d. Benjamin and Eva (Breggin) Rutenberg; m. Sidney N. Bass, Oct. 28, 1945; children—Frederick, Barry. Asst. advt. mgr. Floyds Stores, Valley Stream, N.Y., 1964-68; with BFL Communications, Inc., Plainview, N.Y., 1968—, now v.p. Books for Libraries Press div. Office: 1 Dupont St Plainview NY 11803

BASS, FLORA GARDNER (MRS. HENRY C. BASS), lectr., writer; b. Manila, P.I., June 25, 1916; d. William Henry and Ceferina (de Castro) Gardner; student Philippine Coll. Commerce, 1929-31; m. Henry C. Bass, Nov. 5, 1933; children—Henry James, David, Robert, Richard (dec.). Lectr. on P.I., Hollywood Artists and Lecture Bur., Beverly Hills, Cal., 1952-63, Westbrook-Reeve and Asso. Artists, Laguna Beach, Cal., 1964-66, Nat. Artists and Lecture Service, Beverly Hills, Cal., 1966—; travel lectr. Eloise Fulmer Travels, Laguna Beach, 1971—; asso. editor Food Selling Digest, 1952-54; fgn. feature contbr. Philippines Free Press, 1948-70. Treas., Daus. Am. Vets., Manila, 1937-42; pres. women's aux. Filipino Catholic Club, 1947-51; area capt. Community Chest, 1950-54; sec. Los Angeles Archdiocesan Council Cath. Women, 1951-53, press chmn., 1953-54; vol. librarian St. Catherine's Library, Laguna Beach, Cal., 1956-62; press chmn. St. Catherine Council Cath. Women, 1960-65; vol. Escoda Meml. Fund, 1946-47, Am.-Philippine Guardian Assn., 1946-66; pub. relations asst. dir. Festival Arts, Laguna Beach, 1969—, Winter Festival, 1971-72. Pres. Philippine-Am. Republican Women's Study Club, 1950-54. Recipient 9 awards for top fgn. contbns. Philippines Free Press; certificate of merit Dict. Internat. Biography. Clubs: Ballet Pacifica, Laguna Chamber Music, Women's Internat. Home: Box 803 Laguna Beach CA 92652 Office: Mermaid Books Box 803 Laguna Beach CA 92652

BASS, KATHRYN FOSTER, educator; b. Knoxville, Tenn., Dec. 19, 1936; d. Adrian Carl and Sarah Alice (Bishop) Foster; B.S., U. Tenn., 1960; postgrad. George Peabody Coll., 1963-64, U. Tenn., 1967, 71; M.A. (Nat. Def. Edn. Act. fellow), Appalachian State U., 1970. Tchr., Martin (Tenn.) High Sch., 1960-61; asst. librarian Met. Library Nashville and Davidson County, 1961-67; reference and circulation librarian Emory and Henry Coll., Emory, Va., 1967-69; dir. learning resource center Walters State Community Coll., Morristown, Tenn., 1970—. Mem. A.L.A., Southeastern, Tenn., East Tenn. library assns., Tenn. Edn. Assn., Assn. Ednl. Communications and Tech., Community Coll. Assn. Instrn. and Tech., Am. Assn. Univ. Women (pres. chpt. 1972-74). Club: Pilot (Morristown). Home: 334 Redwood St Morristown TN 37814

BASS, MARY ALICE (MRS. GILBERT R. BASS), lawyer, county ofcl.; b. Niagara Falls, N.Y., Dec. 1, 1927; d. Arthur and Minnie (Hill) Toner; A.A., Phoenix Coll., 1965; A.B., Ariz. State U., 1967, J.D., 1970; m. Gilbert R. Bass, Jan. 14, 1950; children—Robert Nathan, Spencer Lorry, Admitted to Ariz. bar, 1971; makeup artist Metro Goldwyn Mayer Corp., Phoenix, 1959; actress television series, Buffalo, N.Y., 1956, Phoenix, 1960-61; criminal prosecutor dep. county atty. Maricopa County, Ariz., 1971; referee Maricopa County Juvenile Ct., Phoenix, 1973—. Mem. Gray Ladies, A.R.C., Buffalo, 1956. Mem. Am., Maricopa County bar assns., State Bar Ariz., Am. Trial Lawyers Assn., Nat. Dist. Attys. Assn. (sec. Maricopa chpt. 1972—). Home: 102 W Maryland Av Phoenix AZ 85013 Office: 3125 W Durango St Phoenix AZ 85009

BASS, SARA (MRS. ISIDORE MILLER), physician; b. N.Y.C., Mar. 15, 1905; d. Abraham and Fannie (Bruzel) Bass; A.B., Cornell U., 1926, M.D., 1929; m. Isidore Miller, Feb. 24, 1932. Intern, Montefiore Hosp., 1929-30; resident Sea View Hosp., 1932-39, Lenox Hill Hosp., 1940-42; practice medicine specializing in anesthesiology, N.Y.C., 1942—; attending asso. anesthesiologist Mt. Sinai Hosp., 1942—; asst. prof. anesthesiology Mt. Sinai Med. Sch., 1968—. Mem. A.M.A., N.Y. County Med. Soc., Am. Women's Med. Assn., Women's Med. Assn. N.Y. State, Women's Med. Assn. N.Y.C. Club: Cornell Women's. Author articles in field. Home: 55 East End Av New York City NY 10028

BASSETT, ANN KOBLITZ (MRS. RICHARD L. BASSETT), savs. assn. exec.; b. Cleve., May 31, 1917; d. Morris J. and Bert (Lederer) Koblitz; student Conn. Coll. for Women, 1934-35, Western Res. U., 1936; m. Richard L. Bassett, Apr. 24, 1965. Owner, Ann Koblitz Advt. Agy., Cleve., 1946-62; with Cuyahoga Savs. Assn., Cleve., 1962—, v.p. advt. and pub. relations, 1965—. Pres. Golden Age Center Cleve., 1968-69. Trustee Cleve. Hearing and Speech Center, 1971—; adv. bd. Salvation Army, 1957—. Recipient Certificate of Merit, Pub. Relations Com., Cleve. Welfare Fedn., 1957, Outstanding Service award for vol. activities United Appeal, 1958, Helping Heart award Women's Advt. Club Cleve., 1964, Silver medal award Advt. Fedn. Am., 1967. Mem. Am. Women in Radio and TV (pres. 1962-64), Fashion Group Cleve. (regional dir. 1966-68), Cleve. Women's Advt. Club, Bank Marketing Assn. Club: Oakwood (Cleve.). Home: 19601 Van Aken Blvd Cleveland OH 44122 Office: Cuyahoga Savings Assn One Erieview Plaza Cleveland OH 44114

BASSETT, JOSEPHINE ELIZABETH (MRS. EARL F. BASSETT), sportswear mfg. co. exec.; b. Nazareth, Pa., Aug. 28, 1921; d. Alex and Susan (Rosati) Company; student pub. schs.; m. Earl Francis Bassett, Mar. 4, 1944 (dec.); 1 son, Earl Francis. Sewing machine operator Phoenix Clothing, Allentown, Pa., 1942-52; owner, operator Dean's Motel and Cafe, Kenedy, Tex., 1952-59; wrestling promotor, Kenedy, 1959; interview program Wrestling Interviews with Josie, Kenedy, 1958-59; partner V.J. Fashions, Nazareth, 1963-65; pres., owner Jodi Fashions, Inc., Nazareth, 1966—. Mem. Atlantic Apparel Contractors Assn. Home: RFD 1 Hwy 191 Nazareth PA 18064

BASSETT, MARY GRACE, journalist; b. Spokane, Aug. 17, 1927; d. Joseph Elliott and Jane Olive (Jones) Bassett; B.A., Whitman Coll., 1947; M.S. in Journalism, Columbia, 1948; postgrad. U. Paris, U. Frankfurt, 1950-51. Free-lance writer, Europe, 1949-52; staff writer urban affairs Washington Post, 1952-57; Congl. corr. Washington Star, 1957-67; radio interview program, 1964-67; writer on politics, domestic and urban affairs King Features, Hearst News Service, Washington, 1969—. Asst. campaign mgr. Eugene McCarthy Presdl. campaign, 1968. Russell Sage Found. fellow, 1967; recipient Outstanding Polit. Writing citation Am. Polit. Sci. Assn.; Newspaper Guild prize. Home: 2704 N St NW Washington DC 20007 Office: Suite 510 1701 Pennsylvania Av Washington DC 20006

BASSETT, MILDRED AVIS, librarian; b. New Berlin, N.Y., Nov. 23, 1912; d. Sidney Skinner and Maude Etta (Allen) Coats; A.B., Cornell U., 1933; B.L.S., Columbia, 1934; m. Allen B. Bassett, Oct. 11, 1941; children—Carolyn (Mrs. Roger France), Emily. With Columbia Sch. Library Service, 1934-35, Scarsdale (N.Y.) Pub. Library, 1935-38, Bklyn. Pub. Library, 1938-49, New Berlin Central Sch., 1962-63, librarian Hartwick Coll., Oneonat, N.Y., 1963—. Mem. Am., N.Y. State library assns., D.A.R., League Women Voters, Hartwick Women's Club. Republican. Lutheran. Home: 33 Cedar St Oneonta NY 13820

BASSETT, SHIRLEY BRIGHTWELL, librarian; b. nr. Della, Va., July 19, 1914; d. Edgar Hill and Laura Edith (Thomas) Brightwell; B.S., Roanoke Coll., 1936; student Cornett Bus. Sch., Roanoke, 1943; m. George Walter Bassett, Apr. 19, 1946. Tchr. schs., Bassett, Va., 1937-42; sec. to dist. mgr. Standard Oil Co., Roanoke, Va., 1943-47; librarian Bassett Pub. Library, 1959—. Trustee Bassett Pub. Library. Mem. Henry County Hist. Soc. (preservation chmn. 1967—), Council Garden Clubs (pres. 1956-57). Home: PO Box 163 Bassett VA 24055 Office: RFD 5 Box 301 Bassett VA 24055

BASSMAN, ELEANOR CHANCIS (MRS. NATHAN JOSEPH BASSMAN), social worker; b. Bklyn., Mar. 2, 1918; d. Louis and Bessie (Sachs) Chancis; student Jt. Jons U., 1933-36; B.A., Hunter Coll., 1950; M.S. in Social Work (Nat. Assn. Jewish Women scholar), Columbia, 1952; m. Nathan Joseph Bassman, Dec. 19, 1937; 1 son, Arnold David. Psychiat. caseworker Bellevue Hosp., N.Y.C., 1952-53, VA Hosp., Bklyn., 1953-55; caseworker, family counselor Jewish Family Service, Bklyn., 1956-61; sr. social worker Jewish Hosp. Bklyn., 1961-63; adminstr. Family Ct. Mental Health Clinic, Westbury, N.Y., 1963-65; community mental health rep., program analyst N.Y. Dept. Mental Hygiene, 1965-68; chief social worker Hoch Psychiat. Hosp., West Brentwood, N.Y., 1968—. Instr., State U. N.Y., Salden; vis. lectr. U. N.Y. at Stony Brook, South Hampton (N.Y.) Coll. Mem. med. adv. com. Hampton S. Hosp. and Community Health Center, Westhampton Beach, N.Y. Mem. Nat. Assn. Social Workers, Am. Assn. U. Women, Acad. Certified Social Workers, Am. Pub. Health Assn., Am. Orthopsychiat. Assn., Hunter Coll., Columbia U. Sch. Social Work alumnae assns., Alpha Chi Alpha. Home: 52 Hicksville Rd Massapequa NY 11758 Office: Hoch Psychiatric Hospital West Brentwood NY 11717

BASULTO, HIGINIA CONTRERAS (MRS. SERGIO F. GROSSLING), anesthesiologist; b. Santiago, Chile, May 18, 1927; d. Victor Figueroa Contreras and Rosario Basulto Villalobos; M.D., U. Chile, 1945, B.S., 1946, M.D., 1954; postgrad. U. Concepcion Sch. Medicine, 1947-48; m. Sergio F. Grossling, Dec. 17, 1952; children—Lilie-Jean, Hans Christian, Paula Erika, Sylvia Shari, George Anthony, Mellita Jass (adopted). Came to U.S., 1962, naturalized, 1971. Anesthesiologist, U. Chile Hosp. Staff, Santiago, 1955-62; rotating intern Swedish Hosp., Mpls., 1963-64; resident anesthesiology U. Minn. Med. Center, Mpls., 1962-67; anesthesiologist VA Hosp., Mpls., 1968-69, Anesthesia Assn., Mpls., 1971-72, Mount Sinai Hosp., Mpls., 1973—. Recipient Recognition award Am. Med. Physicians, 1973. Mem. Am., Minn. Soc. Anesthesiologists, Am., Minn. med. assns., Hennepin County Med. Soc. Contbr. articles to profl. jours. Home: 1504 Windemere Dr Minneapolis MN 55421 Office: 1401 Silver Lake Rd New Brighton MN 55112

BATCHELDER, NORMA MAXINE BROWN (MRS. ROBERT F. BATCHELDER), civic worker; b. Kellerville, Ill., May 21, 1914; d. Elvin Otis and Lena (Selters) Brown; A.B., U. Cal. at Berkeley, 1935; postgrad. La. State U., 1950-51; m. Robert F. Batchelder, Aug. 18, 1959 (dec. May 1973). With Cal. Dept. Employment, Sacramento, 1936-43, 49-50; commd. ensign USN Res., 1943, advanced through grades to capt. Supply Corps, USN Res., 1972; extracurricular events chmn. La Jolla (Cal.) Newcomers' Club, 1963; chmn. La Jolla Sewing Group, Navy Relief Soc., 1962-66; mem. pink lady unit Scripps Meml. Hosp. Aux., 1963—; organizing chmn. San Diego County Women's Council Navy League U.S., 1966, pres., 1967-69, bd. dirs., 1969—, cruise chmn., 1969-72, editor Channelmarker, 1970—, mem. 11th region staff Navy League, 1969—, cruise vice chmn. San Diego area, 1970-71, cruise chmn. 11th region, 1971—, regional membership vice chmn. So. area, 1969—, nat. dir. of league, 1970—, mem. nat. membership com., 1970—, also life mem. league; adminstrv. officer Naval Res. Supply Co. 11-2, 1966-70, exec. asst. to C.O., 1970-73; nat. chmn. WAVES 25th Anniversary Reunion, 1967; mem. Supply Corps Assn., 1961—, Naval Officers Wives Club, Naval Supply Corps Officers' Wives Club, San Diego County Pan Hellenic Assn.; mem. Alpha Xi Delta, chmn. Province IX conv. 1969, nat. philanthropy chmn. 1968-71, pres. So. Cal. alliance 1970-71, membership v.p. San Diego alumnae 1970—, treas. Alpha Xi Delta Bldg. Corp. San Diego 1970-74; treas. Women's Assn. Mt. Soledad Presbyn. Ch., 1965-67. Mem. La Jolla Town Council. Recipient Meritorious award in Navy Relief, 1963; commendation Sec. Navy, 1973; numerous local, regional, nat. awards Navy League. Mem. Naval Res. Officers Assn., Freedoms Found. Valley Forge (life), Am. Soc. Mil. Comptrollers, Navy Supply Corps Alumni Assn. (life), Naval Inst., Internat. Platform Assn., Country Friends. Presbyn. Republican. Club: La Jolla Country. Editor Freedoms Found. Forge, 1972—. Home: 6186 Soledad Mountain Rd La Jolla CA 92037

BATCHELOR, LILLIAN LEWIS (MRS. HOWARD I. BATCHELOR), librarian; b. Camden, N.J.; d. Albert Kirk and Estella May (Finger) Lewis; B.S., U. Pa., 1930; postgrad. Drexel Inst., 1930; M.A., Columbia, 1946, Ed.D., 1952; m. Howard I. Batchelor, Dec. 30, 1942. Librarian, Ogontz Sch., Prospect Park, Pa., also Phila. pub. schs.; supr. secondary sch. libraries, Phila., 1948-62, supr. elementary and secondary libraries, 1962-66; dir. libraries Bd. Edn., Phila., 1966—. Adj. faculty Grad. Sch. Library Service, Drexel U., 1958—. Bd. dirs. YWCA, Camden, N.J., 1938-45. Recipient Alumnus of Distinction award U. Pa., 1966, award Drexel Alumni, 1967, citation of merit Pa. Sch. Librarians, 1971, award of merit Pa. Library Assn., 1971. Mem. Am. Assn. Sch. Librarians (pres. 1956), A.L.A. (mem. council 1956-62), Nat., Pa. edn. assns., Assn. Supervision and Curriculum Devel. (v.p., mem. exec. bd. 1960), Pa. Learning Resources Assn., U. Pa. Edn. Alumni (mem. exec. bd. 1960, pres. 1973—), Assn. Ednl. Communications and Tech., Beta Phi Mu. Author: School Library and the Gifted. Office: Bd Edn 21st and Parkway Philadelphia PA 19103

BATCHELOR, SHIRLEY STAGG, concert pianist, educator; b. Paterson, N.J.; d. Theodore and Janet (De-Witt) Stagg; student Oberlin Conservatory of Music, 1943-44; B.S., Juilliard Sch. Music, 1948; M.A., Columbia U., 1949; postgrad. N.Y. U.; student of Carl Friedberg, Edward Steuermann 1 dau., Martha Suzanne. Asst. prof., lectr. humanities Lebanon Valley Coll., Annville, Pa., 1950-54, Young Artists Series, Sta. WNYC, 1950-54; concert appearances throughout Eastern sect. of U.S., 1943; asst. prof. Trenton State Coll., 1962—; head music dept. and concert appearances summers at Les Chalets Francais, Deer Isle, Me., 1963—; reviewer books on keyboard harmony, piano pedagogy; chamber music and solo concerts, 1970—. Mem. Nat., N.J. edn. assns., Am. Assn. U. Profs., Music Educators Nat. Conf., N.J. Music Tchrs. Assn. (1st v.p. 1972—). Home: 261 State Rd Princeton NJ 08540 Office: Trenton State Coll Trenton NJ 08625

BATE, MARJORIE ELISE DUNLAP (MRS. LYAL HARRY BATE), coll. dean; b. Berkeley, Cal., Apr. 4, 1913; d. Luther Albert and Elsa Marie (Miller) Dunlap; B.S., U. Cal. at Berkeley, 1934, M.S. (Flood fellow), 1936; postgrad. Fresno State Coll., 1948-60; adminstrv. credential Hayward State U., 1969; m. Lyal Harry Bate, June 15, 1941; children—George Edward, Stephen Dunlap. Tchr., dept. chmn. Watsonville (Cal.) High Sch., 1936-42, Porterville (Cal.) High Sch., 1952-61; faculty Porterville Coll., 1961-64; faculty Contra Costa Coll., San Pablo, Cal., 1964—, dean of instruction, 1969—. Sec., Cella Vinyards, Fresno, Cal., 1949-51. Mem. Am. Assn. U. Women, Cal. Tchrs. Assn., Phi Beta Kappa, Beta Gamma Sigma, Phi Chi Theta, Kappa Phi. Democrat. Home: 16 Edwin Dr Kensington CA 94707 Office: 1600 Mission Bell Dr Contra Costa College San Pablo CA 94806

BATEMAN, BARBARA DEE, educator; b. Medford, Ore., June 15, 1933; d. Charles and Vivian (Coss) Bateman; student Reed Coll., 1950-51, U. Ore., 1951-52; B.S., U. Washington, 1954; M.A., San Francisco State Coll., 1958; Ph.D., U. Ill., 1962. Tchr., Wash. State Sch. for Blind, Vancouver, 1956; edn. intern Sonoma State Hosp. for Mentally Defective, Eldridge, Cal., 1957; research asst. U. Ill., 1957-59; spl. edn. tchr. Pub. Schs. Ashland, Ore., 1959-61; research asst., research asso., asst. prof. U. Ill., 1961-65; asso. prof. DePaul U., Chgo., 1965-66; asso. prof. U. Ore., Eugene, 1966-69, prof. edn., asso. dir. Nat. Center for Research and Devel. in Early Edn. Handicapped, 1969—. Cons. editor Dimensions in Early Learning, 1967—. Mem. Nat. Task Force on Children with Learning Disabilities. Mem. Am. Psychol. Assn., Am. Assn. on Mental Deficiency, Council on Exceptional Children, Assn. for Children with Learning Disabilities, Orton Soc., Internat. Reading Assn. Research, devel. cons. to Follett Pub. Co., 1966—. Editor, Jour. Learning Disabilities; asso. editor Exceptional Children. Contbr. articles to profl. jours. Home: 42 Rio Glen Eugene OR 97401

BATEMAN, BETTY LOUISE BELLINGER, librarian; b. Elkhart, Ind., Apr. 10, 1914; d. George Henry and F. Nina (Snook) B.; A.B., U. Akron, 1936; B.S. in L.S., Western Res. U., 1937; m. Bedford Byron Bateman, Dec. 12, 1946 (dec.); children—Barbara Lynn (Mrs. Gregory Cronin). Mgr. lab. libraries IBM, Poughkeepsie, N.Y. Mem. Southeastern N.Y. Library Resources Council (dir. 1965—). Contbr. tech. articles to profl. publs. Home: 8 Horizon Hill Dr Poughkeepsie NY 12603 Office: IBM Lab Libraries PO Box 390 Bldg 701 Poughkeepsie NY 12602

BATEMAN, DOTTYE JANE SPENCER, realtor; b. Athens, Tex.; d. Charles Augustus and Lillie (Freeman) Spencer; student Fed. Inst., 1941-42, So. Meth. U., Dallas Coll., 1956-58; m. George Truitt Bateman, 1947 (div. Apr. 1963); children—Kelly Spencer, Bethena Bateman; m. 2d, Joseph Eric Lindsley. Sec. to state senator, Tyler, Tex., 1941-42; sec. to pres. Merc. Nat. Bank, Dallas, State Fair of Tex., Dallas, 1942-48; realtor, broker, Dallas, 1956—; co-partner Play-Shade Co.; appraiser Asso. Soc. Real Estate Appraisers; auctioneer, 1963—; developer Stonewall Cave, 1964—. Pres., Central Elementary Sch. P.T.A., 1955-56, Bussey Jr. High P.T.A., 1956-57;

den mother Cub Scouts Am., 1957-59; chmn. Decent Lit. Com., 1956-58; chmn. P.T.A.'s council, 1958; bd. dirs. Dallas Heart Assn., 1960, local chmn., 1955-57, county chmn., 1957-60; spl. dir. Henderson County Red Cross, 1945; local chmn. March of Dimes, 1961-63; mem. Dallas Civic Opera Com., 1963-64; mem. homemaker panel Dallas Times Herald, 1955—. Former Republican precinct chmn., Garland, Tex. Named Outstanding Tex. Jaycee-Ette Pres., 1953, hon. Garland Jay-Cee-Ette, 1956, hon. Sheriff, Dallas County, 1963. Mem. Garland, Dallas (chmn. reception com., past dir.) real estate bds., Dallas Bd. Realtors (comml.-investment div.), Tex. Assn. Realtors (Make Am. Better Com. 1973-74), Internat. Real Estate Fedn., Auctioneers Assn., Nat. Inst. Farm and Land Brokers (spl. services com.), Dallas Women's (project chmn.), Garland (chmn. ministerial alliance com. 1955-56) chambers commerce, Consejo Internacional De Buena Vecindad, Delphian Study Club, Eruditis Study Club, Audubon Soc., Wilderness Soc., Tex. Hist. Assn., Kappa Chi (past pres.), Epsilon Sigma Alpha. Christian Scientist. Clubs: Garland (past v.p., pres.), Tex. (past treas., ofcl. hostess) Jaycee-Ettes, Garland Fedn. Women's (past pres.), Garland Garden, Trinity Dist. Fedn. Women's (past pres., chmn. scholarship com. 1974—), Pub. Affairs Luncheon, Press of Dallas (dir. 1973—, chmn. house com. 1973—). Home: 1140 Rock Creek Dr Garland TX 75040 Office: 5518 Dyer St Dallas TX 75206

BATEMAN, JEANNE CECILE NORDSTROM (MRS. ROY D. BATEMAN), physician; b. San Diego, June 16, 1908; d. David Algot and Joan C. (Olson) Nordstrom; A.B., George Washington U., 1938, M.D. cum laude, 1942; m. Roy D. Bateman, June 5, 1925 (dec. July 1947); children—John L., Fleur (Mrs. H. Franklin Byers). Intern, D.C. Gen. Hosp., Washington, 1942-43, resident, 1943-44; vis. physician 3d med. div. N.Y.U. Coll. Medicine, 1945-48, asst. medicine, 1944-45, instr. medicine, 1945-48; practice medicine, specializing in internal medicine and oncology, Alexandria, Va., 1966—; mem. staff Alexandria Hosp., Washington Hosp. Center; cons. Price Georges Hosp., Glen Dale Sanitarium, St. Elizabeth Hosp.; clin. instr. medicine George Washington U., 1949-68, asst. Lymphoma Clinic, Cancer Clinic, 1948-52. Diplomate Am. Bd. Internal Medicine. Fellow A.C.P.; mem. A.M.A., D.C. Med. Soc., A.A.A.S., N.Y. Acad. Sci., Washington Soc. Pathologists, Harvey Soc., Am. Fedn. for Clin. Research, Am. Assn. for Cancer Research, Internat. Hematology Soc., Am. Womens Med. Assn., Womans Med. Soc. D.C., Am. Soc. Internal Medicine, Smith Reed Russell Honor Soc., Royal Soc. Medicine (London, Eng.). Home: 1229 37th St NW Washington DC 20007 Office: 312 S Washington St Alexandria VA 22314

BATEMAN, MILDRED MITCHELL, psychiatrist, mental health adminstr.; b. Cordele, Ga., Mar. 22, 1922; d. S. Q. and Ella (McLeod) Mitchell; student Barber-Scotia Coll.; B.S., Johnson C. Smith U., 1941; M.D., Woman's Med. Coll. Pa., 1946; m.; 2 daus. Resident Menninger Sch. Psychiatry, Topeka, Kan., 3 years; former clin. dir., former supt. Lakin State Hosp.; supr. profl. services W.Va. Dept. Mental Health, 1960-62, acting dir. Dept. Mental Health, 1962, dir., 1962—. Mem. So. Regional Edn. Bd., Commn. on Aging, W.Va. Commn. Mental Retardation, Gov. W.Va. Commn. Status of Women; mem. commn. on mentally disabled Am. Bar Assn.; former Def. Adv. Com. Women in Services U.S., Dept. Def.; former med. adv. com. Vocational Rehab. Adminstr. U.S. Dept. Health, Edn. and Welfare. Bd. dirs. Nat. Assn. for Mental Health, Menninger Found. Mem. Acad. Religion and Psychiatry, Am. Psychiat. Assn. (v.p. 1973), Inst. Medicine-Am. Acad. Scis., Kanawha (W.Va.) County Mental Health Assn., Kanawha County Med. Soc., A.M.A., W.Va. Med. Assn., Group for Advancement Psychiatry (com. on pub. edn.), Council on Mental Health, Inst. Medicine of Nat. Acad. Scis., Am. Bar Assn. (commn. on mentally retarded). Presbyn. Office: State Capitol Charleston WV 25305

BATES, BARBARA J. NEUNER (MRS. HERMAN MARTIN BATES, JR.), town ofcl.; b. Mt. Vernon, N.Y., Apr. 8, 1927; d. John Joseph William and Elsie May (Flint) Neuner; B.A., Barnard Coll., 1947; m. Herman Martin Bates, Jr., Mar. 25, 1950; children—Roberta Jean, Herman Martin III, Jon Nicholas. Confidential clk. to supr. town Ossining (N.Y.), 1960-63; pres. BNB Assos., Briarcliff Manor, N.Y., 1963—, Upper Nyack Realty Co., Inc., Briarcliff Manor, 1966-71; receiver taxes Town of Ossining (N.Y.), 1971—. Vice pres. Ossining (N.Y.) Young Republican Club, 1958; pres. Young Womens Rep. Club Westchester County (N.Y.), 1959-60; regional committeewoman N.Y. State Assn. Young Rep. Clubs, 1962-62; mem. Westchester County Rep. Com., 1963—. Mem. Jr. League Westchester-on-Hudson, D.A.R., Hackley Sch. Mothers Assn. (pres. 1966-68), R.I. Hist. Soc. Conglist. Home: 78 Holbrook Lane Briarcliff Manor NY 10510 also RFD 2 Chepachet RI 02814

BATES, GLENDA WALKER (MRS. JOHN GILBERT BATES), civic worker; b. Mize, Miss., July 26, 1939; d. Thomas and Alice Rae (Howell) Walker; B.A. magna cum laude, Belhaven Coll., 1961; m. John Gilbert Bates, Sept. 3, 1960; children—Jennifer Lynn, John Paul. Personnel asst., surg. sec. Miss. Bapt. Hosp., Jackson, 1958-61; bookkeeper, sec., office asst. Dr. John Bates, Mendenhall, Miss., 1961-63; office nurse Elliott, Martin, Sills & Bates, Cuthbert, Ga., 1971-72. Active Women's Aux. to Med. Assn. Ga., 1963—, county officer and com. chmn., 1967—, state rural health chmn., 1967-69, rec. sec., 1969-71, chmn. membership, 1971-72, pres., 1973-74, councilor to So. Med. Assn., 1973—; chmn. community health A.M.A. Aux., 1974—. Recipient certificate of appreciation Easter Seal Soc., 1966, certificate of achievement Med. Assn. Ga., 1974. Mem. P.T.A. (com. chmn. 1973—). Baptist (ch. soprano soloist, 1957—, dir. Youth Sunday Sch., 1968—, dir. Woman's Missionary Union, 1968-71). Club: Camillia Garden (com. chmn. 1963-68). Home: 515 Court St Cuthbert GA 31740

BATES, GRACE ELIZABETH, educator; b. Albany, N.Y., Aug. 13, 1914; d. Walter M. and Julia (Dexter) Bates; B.S., Middlebury Coll., 1935, D.Sc., 1972; M.S., Brown U., 1938; Ph.D., U. Ill., 1946. Instr. math. George Sch., Pa., 1938-43, Sweet Briar Coll., 1943-44; from instr. to asso. prof. Mt. Holyoke Coll., 1946-56, prof. math., 1956—; vis. prof. math. Dartmouth, 1959-60; vis. mem. dept. math. statistics U. Cal. at Berkeley, summers 1951, 52, 54, 55. Trustee Tchrs. Ins. Annuity Assn. 1965-69. Mem. Am. Math. Soc., Math. Assn. Am. (chmn. Northeastern sect. 1964-65, commn. on undergrad. program in math.), Assn. Tchrs. Math. in New Eng. (pres. 1965-66). Address: 16 College View Heights South Hadley MA 01075

BATES, HARRIETT MARGARET GROSS (MRS. HOWELL A. BATES), civic worker; b. Cambridge, O., Mar. 29, 1920; d. Charles Frederick and Harriett (Allender) Gross; student Wellesley Coll., 1938-41, Katherine Gibbs Sch., 1941-42; m. Howell A. Bates, Mar. 6, 1943; children—Christopher French, Frederick Brainard. Pres., League Women Voters, Dover, Mass., 1961-63; mem. pub. relations com. Overseas Edn. Fund, League Women Voters U.S., 1963-65, now bd. dirs. fund; 2d v.p. League Women Voters Mass., Boston, 1965-67, pres., 1967-69; mem. Overseas Edn. Fund Inst. Com., 1967-72; mem. steering com. Mass. Civil Service Council, 1967-69; mem. Gov.'s Adv. Council Human Rights, 1967-69; mem. Boston Urban Coalition, 1968-69; mem. Gov.'s Adv. Council Comprehensive Health Planning Program Mass., 1968-74; mem. Boston-Suburban adv. council Mass. Commn. against Discrimination, 1968-73; mem. adv. council to Mass. Bd. Higher Edn. for Title I, 1969, 73; pres. World Affairs Council Boston, 1971-72. Bd. dirs. Harvard Community Health Plan. Home: Box 1216 Jupiter FL 33458

BATES, MARY JOYCE RENN (MRS. CARL L. BATES), broadcasting co. exec.; b. New Albany, Ind., Apr. 19, 1919; d. Raymond William and Mary Joyce (Austin) Renn; B.B.A., U. Cin., 1942; m. Carl L. Bates, Apr. 28, 1956 (dec. July 1970). Sec. advt. dept. Kroger Co., Cin., 1942; exec. sec. Ralph H. Jones Advt., Cin., 1943; writer, prodn. coordinator Bert Johnston Prodns., Inc., Cin., 1944-45; program adminstr. Avco Broadcasting Corp., Cin., 1955-60; account exec. Bob Long Assos., Indpls., 1961-63; pub. relations dir. Indpls. Symphony Orch., 1963-65; with Avco Broadcasting Corp., Cin., 1965—, v.p. pub. information, 1970-72, v.p. communications, 1972—. Mem. Pub. Relations Soc. Am. (dir. Cin. chpt. 1971-74), Women in Communications (Nat. Headliner award 1972), Broadcast Promotion Assn., Beta Gamma Sigma. Home: 1003 Grand Av Cincinnati OH 45204 Office: Provident Tower 1 E 4th St Cincinnati OH 45202

BATES-NISBET, (CLARA) ELISABETH, lawyer, sch. adminstr., piano tchr.; b. Houston, Dec. 4, 1902; d. William David and Kate Broocks (Arnall) Bates; B.A., U. Tex., 1940; M.A., U. Houston, 1941; LL.B., South Tex. Sch. Law, 1937. Tchr. pub. schs., Houston, 1923-49, prin., 1950-73, ret. prin. James Arlie Montgomery Elementary Sch.; admitted to Tex. bar, 1937; tchr. piano. Houston, 1928—. Mem. State Bar Tex., Houston Bar Assn., Tex. Tchrs. Assn., Tex. Geneal. Soc., Magna Charta Dames (organizing charter mem. East Tex. Colony 3d vice regent courier Round Table Tex. div. 1962-66), Tex. Hist. Assn. (patron, life), Colonial Dames XVII Century (chpt. registrar, mem. nat. com. on Am. history), Alston-Williams-Boddie-Hillard Soc. N.C., Colonial Order Crown, San Augustine County Hist. Soc. (charter), Daus. Republic Tex. (organizing charter mem. Ezekial Cullen chpt., recording sec. editor annuals 1963-65, 2d v.p. 1965-67), Soc. Descs. Charlemagne, U.D.C., D.A.R. (chpt. regent 1966-68, mem. nat. coms.), Daus. Am. Colonists (organizer charter mem. chpt.), Sovereign Colonial Soc. Ams. Royal Descent, Dames of Ct. of Honor, Founders and Patriots of Am., Delta Kappa Gamma (chpt. 1st v.p. 1966-68, life mem.). Address: 2305 Woodhead St Houston TX 77019 also PO Box 371 San Augustine TX 75972

BATINICH, MARY ELLEN (MRS. ALEX BATINICH), educator; b. Eveleth, Minn., Apr. 20, 1923; d. James Vincent and Mary (Noldin) Mancina; A.S., Eveleth Jr. Coll., 1943; B.M.E., Northwestern U., 1948, M.A., 1958, Ph.D., 1963; m. Alex Batinich, Apr. 20, 1946. Tchr. Yale Sch., Chgo., 1949-59, master tchr., 1961-63; instr. Chgo. Tchrs. Coll., 1961-63; prin. Walsh Elementary Sch., 1963-65, Carver Evening High Sch., 1966-68, Sbarbaro Elementary Sch., 1967-69, Schmid Sch., 1969-71. Lectr., Chgo. State Coll., 1963-65, 68-69; del. White House Conf. on Children and Youth, 1970. Chmn., Italian Library-Mus., Stone Park, 1969—. Recipient Eighth Note award Mu Phi Epsilon, 1968, Spl. citation in reading CARA, 1967, Woman of Year award Italics, 1971. Mem. Nat. Soc. for Study Edn., Dept. Elementary Sch. Prins., Internat., Chgo. Area (dir.) reading assns., Nat. Assn. Childhood Edn., Chgo. Area Kindergarten-Primary Assn., Gregorian Educators Soc. Chgo. (pres. 1965-67), Ill. Reading Council (treas. 1968-69, pres. 1970-71), Mu Phi Epsilon (editor alumnae newsletter 1963-68), Phi Lambda Theta. Club: Chicago Principals. Author, illustrator; Minnesota: Souvenir Coloring Book, 1965; Michigan: Coloring Book; author Invest in Your Future: A College Education; also author articles in field. Address: 9215 S Troy Chicago IL 60642

BATRA, SUZANNE WELLINGTON TUBBY (MRS. LEKH RAJ BATRA), entomologist; b. N.Y.C., Dec. 15, 1937; d. Roger Wellington and Anne W. (Williams) Tubby; B.A., Swarthmore Coll., 1960; Ph.D., U. Kan., 1964; m. Lekh Raj Batra, June 16, 1960; children—Mirabai Kuvi, Persaram Olitsky. Research asst. Archbold Biol. Sta., Fla., 1959; mem. Swarthmore Expdn. to Himalayas, 1960; research asst. entomology U. Kan., Lawrence, 1960-64, teaching asst. biology, 1961, research asso. entomology, 1964-70; collaborator entomology research div. U.S. Dept. Agr., Beltsville, Md., 1970—. Sr. research officer Punjab (India) Agrl. U., 1965. Recipient Research award Am. Philos. Soc., 1964. Mem. Entomol. Soc. Am., Bee Research Assn., Animal Behavior Soc., Bot. Soc. Am., Mycol. Soc. Am., Am. Inst. Biol. Scis., Kan. Entomol. Soc., Kan. Acad. Scis., Sigma Xi (Research award 1964). Contbr. articles to profl. jours. Research on wild bees, mycology, insect fungus symbiosis. Home: 2-Q Plateau Pl Greenbelt MD 20770

BATTELLE, PHYLLIS MARIE, columnist; b. Dayton, O., Jan. 4, 1922; d. Gordon S. and Marie (Sides) Battelle; B.A., Ohio Wesleyan U., 1944; m. Arthur Van Horn, Dec. 6, 1957; 1 son, Jonathan Gordon. Police reporter, feature writer, teen-age columnist The Dayton (O.) Herald, 1944-47; woman's editor, fashion editor Internat. News Service, 1947-54; writer daily syndicated column Assignment: America, King Features Syndicate, 1955—. Recipient ann. award for best domestic news coverage N.Y. Newspaperwomen's Assn., 1951; prizes ann. Ohio Newspaper Women's Assn., 1944-47. Mem. Delta Gamma. Methodist. Club: N.Y. Newspaperwomen's. Home: Old Church Lane Pound Ridge NY 10576 also Box 117 Frederiksted St Croix VI 00840 Office: 235 E 45th St New York City NY 10017

BATTEY, VIOLA VAN NICE (MRS. BLAINE L. BATTEY), social worker; b. Topeka; d. James Francis and Elsie (Furze) Van Nice; B.A., Washburn U., 1922; postgrad. Menninger Psychiat. Inst., 1923-24, U. Minn., 1934-36; m. Blaine L. Battey, June 9, 1923 (dec. Dec. 1968); children—Robert W., Andrea Blayne, Lowell V. Supr., Child Welfare Dept., St. Paul, 1934-44; supr., dir. Juvenile Ct. Services, St. Paul, 1944-59; asst. judge Juvenile Ct., St. Paul, 1959-63; cons. marital counseling Ct. Services, St. Paul, 1963-68; marital, personal, family counseling Central Presbyn. Ch., St. Paul, 1968—. Nat. lectr. in marital counseling, family life and corrections. Bd. dirs. Wilder Sr. Citizens Center, 1970-74. Mem. Delta Phi Delta. Episcopalian. Club: Womens City (v.p. 1969). Home: 20 E Exchange St St Paul MN 55101

BATTLE, ALICE HELEN KAVECKI (MRS. CHARLES BOB BATTLE), librarian; b. Cleburne, Tex., Dec. 29, 1933; d. Joseph and Jane Mary (Fenelon) K.; student Tex. Women's U., 1954, Tex. Christian U., 1956, summer 1958; B.S., U. Okla., 1959; M.S. in Library Services, N. Tex. State U., 1968; postgrad. U. Hawaii, 1969—; m. Charles Bob Battle, June 12, 1953; 1 son, Robert Charles. Elementary tchr. Birdville pub. schs., Ft. Worth, 1960-62, Albuquerque Pub. Schs., 1963-65; elementary sch. library media specialist, Albuquerque, 1965-68; high sch. library media specialist Hawaii Pub. Schs., 1968-69; head library media specialist Bishop Learning Center, Punahou Sch., Honolulu, 1969—. Cons. library facility planning, 1973—. Mem. steering com. Hawaii Task Force on Sex Bias, 1973—. Served with USAF, 1952-53. Mem. Am., Hawaii library assns., Am. Assn. Sch. Librarians (mem. instrnl. media com. 1972-73), Pacific Assn. for Communications and Tech. (exec. bd. 1971-73), Hawaii Assn. Sch. Librarians (pres. 1972-73), Hawaii Assn. Supervisory and Curriculum Devel., Assn. for Edn., Communication and Tech. Office: Bishop Learning Center Punahou School Honolulu HI

BATTLE, BARBARA HELEN, film co. exec.; b. Atlanta, Nov. 23, 1936; d. Charles Henry and Helen Elizabeth (Green) Battle; B.A., Agnes Scott Coll., 1956; M.A., U. N.C., 1958; postgrad. Union Theol. Sem., 1958, N.Y. U., 1963-64; Ph.D., Columbia U., 1969. Asst. prof. English and dramatic art Salem Coll., Winston-Salem, N.C., 1958-64; producer, dir. Film Centre Pty. Ltd., Perth, Western Australia, 1970-71; pres. Courtenay Prodns., Inc., N.Y.C., 1969—. Part time tchr. U. N.C., 1957-58, Columbia U., 1965-67, N.Y. U., 1965-67, Queens Coll., 1967-68. Dir. Religious Drama Workshop, Winston-Salem, N.C., 1963; dir. numerous plays for civic orgns. and chs. in N.Y. and N.C., 1958-63. Dodge Ayer Tileston Hoadley fellow Tchrs. Coll., 1964-65; recipient Golden Eagle award Council Internat. Nontheatrical Events, 1965, award Vancouver Film Festivals, 1965, LaPlata Film Festival, 1965. Mem. Am. Nat. Theatre and Acad., Am. Theatre Assn. Author: His Kingdom Cometh, 1958. Films: A Smashing Lady, 1971, Hello, World, 1965, A Question of Type, 1968. Home: 228 E 26th St New York City NY 10010 Office: 230 Park Av Suite 2801 New York City NY 10017

BATTON, DELMA-JANE HECK (MRS. JAMES HAROLD BATTON), librarian; b. Tampa, Fla., Dec. 10, 1915; d. William Claude and Myfanwy (James) Heck; student N.J. State Tchrs. Coll., 1935-36, Coll. of William and Mary, 1937-38, U. Pa., summer 1946; B.S. in L.S., U. Ill., 1950, postgrad., 1951; m. James Harold Batton, July 21, 1951; children—David Jeffrey, Nancy Janine, Thomas William. Asst., Princeton (N.J.) Pub. Library, 1930-32; librarian State Home for Girls, Trenton, N.J., 1934-35; asst. acquisitions and circulation Princeton U. Library, 1935-37; asst. children's and adult Free Library of Phila., 1938-43; asst. librarian U.S. Naval Hosp. Library, Phila., 1943-46; order librarian Principia Coll., Elsah, Ill., 1946-48; catalog asst. U. Ill. Library, 1948-51; field cons. State Library Commn., Dover, Del., 1961-68, acting state librarian, 1964-65, 67-68; dir. Dover Public Library, 1968—. Ednl. rep. Del. Assn. for Retarded Children, Dover, 1963-64; pres. Parents-Friends Assn. of Dover Day Care Center for Retarded, 1964-67; mem. State Adv. Council on Right to Read, 1973-74. Mem. Am. (adv. com. good reading project), Del. (editor Bull. 1965-66, 72—, pres. 1969-70, pres. pub. library div. 1970—) library assns., N.E.A., Am. Assn. U. Women. Club: Soroptimist of Dover (sec. 1973-74). Home: 1081 S Bradford St Dover DE 19901 Office: Dover Pub Library Dover DE 19901

BATTS, NATHALIE CATHERINE (MRS. WALTER M.P. BATTS), librarian; b. Balt., Nov. 3, 1918; d. Frank C. and Bertha M. (Prager) Chlan; A.B., Coll. of Notre Dame of Md., 1940; B.S., Columbia U., 1946, M.S., with honors, 1966; M.A., Mount Holyoke Coll., 1951; m. Walter M.P. Batts, June 16, 1952 (dec. July 1962). Jr. asst. Enoch Pratt Free Library, Balt., 1941-45; first asst. circulation Mount Holyoke Coll. Library, S. Hadley, Mass., 1945-49, order librarian, 1949-51; asst. reference librarian, Grad. Sch. of Bus. Library, Columbia, N.Y.C., 1951-55, reference librarian, 1955-62, serials cataloger Univ. Libraries, 1962—. Mem. Am. Econ. Assn., Am. Library Assn., Am. Numismatic Assn., Am. Soc. for Information Sci. (treas. met. N.Y. chpt. 1971-73), N.Y. Technical Services Librarians (sec., treas. 1968-69), Columbia U. Alumni Assn. (dir. 1972—), Beta Phi Mu. Club: Women's Faculty (corr. sec. 1970-72) (N.Y.C.). Author: Small Business, 1951. Editor: Library Service News, 1972—. Home: 21 Claremont Av New York City NY 10027

BATY, MARTHA ALDRIDGE, psychologist, educator; b. Hattiesburg, Miss., July 14, 1943; d. Oscar Emmett and Osie (Hosch) Aldridge; B.A., U. Miss., 1965; M.A., La. State U., 1967, Ph.D., 1970; m. Carl Franklin Baty, Jan. 19, 1969; 1 son, Christopher Cass. Chief psychologist Children's Mercy Hosp., Kansas City, Mo., 1970-71; staff psychologist, dir. psychol. tng. Johnson County Mental Health Center, Mission, Kan., 1971—; lectr. grad. sch. U. Kan., Lawrence, 1972—. Mem. Am., Mo., Southeastern, Southwestern Psychol. assns., Nat. Orgn. Women (mem. steering com.), Women's Polit. Caucus. Home: 4706 W 66th Terrace Prairie Village KS 66208 Office: 6000 Lamar St Mission KS 66202

BAUCOM, ELIZABETH ANN, stockbroker; b. Mt. Holly, N.C., May 14, 1931; d. Cleveland Winfred and Minerva Jane (Sanders) Baucom; B.A. in French, U. N.C., 1953; postgrad. Hunter Coll., 1966-68; certificate N.Y. Inst. Finance, 1970. Statistician pension and personal trust dept. Bankers Trust Co., N.Y.C., 1953-54; adminstrv. asst. to Am. Consul, U.S. Diplomatic Corps, Berlin, Germany, 1954-57; sales rep. internat. dept. Delta Airlines, Atlanta, 1959-68; bond analyst Merrill, Lynch, Pierce, Fenner & Smith, Inc., N.Y.C., 1968-71, stockbroker, 1971—. Lectr. Eng., Internat. House, N.Y.C., 1973-74, New Sch., 1974. Mem. Nat. Women's Stockbrokers Assn., U. N.C. Alumni Assn., Chi Omega. Democrat. Baptist. Home: 312 E 52nd St New York City NY 10022 Office: Merrill Lynch Pierce Fenner & Smith Inc 345 Park Av New York City NY 10022

BAUCOM, MARGARET DEAN (MRS. H. BASCOM BAUCOM), writer; b. Charlotte, N.C., Sept. 25, 1909; d. John Calvin and Lelia (Robinson) Dean; student pub. schs.; m. Hiram Bascom Baucom, Sept. 20, 1927 (dec. 1950); 1 dau., Joan Dean (Mrs. James Preston Brown, Jr.). Automobile dealer B & M Motor Co., Monroe, N.C., 1950-53; now columnist The Monroe Enquirer-Jour. Newspaper; write column Small Talk under name Margaret Baucom; also free-lance writer mags. and newspapers. Bd. dirs. Mecklenburg-Union Tb and Respiratory Disease Assn. Recipient Etta Caldwell Harris poetry award. Founder of Marshville Pub. Library. Mem. N.C. Hist. Soc., U.D.C. (pres. 1956-58, bd. mem. N.C. div.), Monroe Opera Guild, D.A.R. (publicity chmn.), Union County Hist. Soc., Little Theatre (v.p.), Women's Golf Assn., N.C. Lit. and Hist. Assn., N.C. Press Women Assn. (dist. chmn. 1965-66), Carolinas Geneal. Soc. (charter; co-editor bull.), Ill. Poetry Soc. (1st prize poetry award 1972), Nat. League Am. Pen Women, Cal. Chaparral Poetry Soc., Am. Poets Fellowship Soc., World Poetry Soc., Colonial Dames 17th Century, Daus. Colonial Wars, Huguenot Soc., Internat. Platform Assn. (publicity com.), Nat. Fedn. Press Women. Presbyn. (life mem. women of ch.). Clubs: Monroe Woman's (past pres.), Monroe Garden (past pres.), Monroe Music (past pres.), Silhouette Dance; Top of the Arch (St. Louis). Author: Mood Magic, 1974. Address: 710 S Hayne Monroe NC 28110

BAUER, ELIZABETH KELLEY (MRS. FREDERICK WILLIAM BAUER), govt. adminstr.; b. Berkeley, Cal., Aug. 7, 1920; d. Leslie Constant and Elizabeth Jeanette (Worley) Kelley; A.B., U. Cal. at Berkeley, 1941, M.A., 1943; Ph.D. (fellow), Columbia, 1947; m. Frederick William Bauer, July 5, 1944; children—Elizabeth Katherine (Mrs. Neil Hjalmar Berg), Frederick Nicholas. Instr. U.S. history and studies Barnard Coll., N.Y.C., 1944-45; lectr. history U. Cal. at Berkeley, 1949-50, 56-57; research asst. Giannini Found., 1946-49, asst. research agrl. economist, 1957-60; exec. sec. Internat. Conf. on Agrl. and Coop. Credit, U. Cal. at Berkeley, 1952-53; exec. sec. South Asia Project, 1955-56; registrar Holy Names Coll., Oakland, Cal., 1971-72; research asso. Brookings Instn. and nat. Acad. of Pub. Adminstrn., Washington, 1973; internat. relations officer Internat. Energy affairs, Fed. Energy Adminstrn. Washington, 1974—. Mem. Cal. Com. to Revise the Tchrs. Credential, 1961. Trustee Grad. Theol. Union, Berkeley, 1972-74; bd. dirs. St. Paul's Towers and Episcopal Homes Found, Oakland, 1971-72. Mem. Am. Assn. U. Women (Cal. chmn. for higher edn. 1960-62), Prytanean Honor Soc., P.E.O., Phi Beta Kappa, Pi Lambda Theta, Sigma Kappa Alpha, Phi Alpha Theta,

Pi Sigma Alpha, Mortar Bd. Author: Commentaries on the Constitution, 1790-1860, 1952; (with Murray R. Benedict) Farm Surpluses; U.S. Burden or World Asset?, 1960; (with Florence Noyce Wertz) The Graduate Theological Union, 1970. Editor: Proceedings of the International Conference on Agricultural and Cooperative Credit (2 vols.), 1953. Home: 7805 Radnor Rd Bethesda MD 20034 Office: New Post Office Bldg 12th and Pennsylvania Av NW Washington DC 20461

BAUER, MARJORIE FRANTZ (MRS. FRANZ K. BAUER), physician; b. New Orleans, June 2, 1916; d. Louis Theodore and Edna Florence (Stumpf) Frantz; B.A., Tulane U., 1936; M.D., La. Med. Sch., 1940; m. Franz K. Bauer, May 29, 1943; 1 dau., Anne. Intern Charity Hosp., New Orleans, 1942-43; resident in dermatology Los Angeles County-U. So. Cal. Med. Center, Los Angeles, 1946-48; pvt. practice medicine specializing in dermatology, Los Angeles, 1952-62; asst. prof. medicine U. So. Cal. Sch. Medicine, Los Angeles, 1962-69, prof., 1969—. Mem. Am. Acad. Dermatology, Los Angeles, Pacific dermatol. socs., A.M.A. Contbr. profl. jours. Office: Los Angeles County/U So Cal Med Center Women's Hosp 1200 N State St Los Angeles CA 90033

BAUGHMAN, ELMA MARIE, nurse; b. Buxton, Ia., Oct. 31, 1918; d. Newton Joel and Jennie Violet (McGowen) Scribner; student Chaffey Coll., 1938; R.N., Pasadena Coll., 1941; m. Don C. Baughman, 1941 (div. 1971); children—Harold, David, Jim. Supr. maternity and surg. nursing, Compton, Cal., 1941; indsl. nurse, Joshua Hendy County, 1941-42; pub. health and sch. nurse, Chino (Cal.) Unified Sch. Dist., 1945-48, 64—; supr. nursing Ontario (Cal.) Community Hosp., 1952-54, Central Meml. Hosp., Montclair, Cal., 1961-63. Newspaper corr. Pomona (Cal.) Progress, 1948-64; coordinator Allied Health Occupations Chino High Sch., 1974—. Mem. Chino Social Service Council; active Boy Scouts Am., 1950-60; rep. to White House Conf. on Domestic Affairs, 1961. Mem. City Council, Chino, 1960-61; commr. Police and Fire depts., Chino. Bd. dirs. Child Welfare, Am. Legion, 1946-49. Recipient certificates appreciation, Boy Scouts Am., adult edn., community work. Mem. N.E.A. (mem. dept. sch. nurses), Asso. Chino Tchrs., Cal. Tchrs. Assn., Cal. Sch. Nurses Orgn., Chino Gen. Hosp. Aux., Chino Bus. and Profl. Women (Woman of Year 1970), Quill and Scroll (hon. mem 1970). Home: PO Box 743 Chino CA 91710 Office: 5472 Park P Chino CA 91710

BAUM, HELEN SWARTENBERG (MRS. BERNARD CYRIL BAUM), pub. relations co. exec.; b. Perth Amboy, N.J.; d. Bram and Rachael (Zweigbaum) Swartenberg; student Syracuse U., 1934-36, Columbia, 1936-37; m. Bernard Cyril Baum, May 19, 1938; children—Karen (Mrs. Henry Crowell Alexander Jr.), Gail (Mrs. Zacharia Reike). Accounts exec. Robert Tapleiger Asso., N.Y.C., 1949-54, Hank Meyer Asso., Miami Beach, Fla., 1954-56, 67-72; pres. Helen Baum Asso., Miami Beach, 1956-67, 72—; living editor, columnist Miami Mag., 1973—. Active United Fund, Miami, 1967-72. Bd. dirs. Children's Center, Miami, 1970—. Recipient awards City of Miami, 1972, 73, Miami Dade Jr. Coll., 1969, 70, United Fund Dade County (Fla.), 1967. Fellow Nat. Home Fashions League (First Fellow award 1973); mem. Am. Inst. Interior Designers, Designers Guild, Fashion Group, Nat. Soc. Interior Design, Women in Communications. Author: Instant Publicity, 1967. Contbr. articles to profl. jours. and popular mags. Home and office: 4236 Alton Rd Miami Beach FL 33140

BAUM, INGEBORG RUTH, librarian; b. Berlin, Germany, Sept. 20, 1916; d. Ella Koch; Oberlyceum (scholar), Kassel, Germany, 1926-33; postgrad. Georgetown U., 1963-70; m. Albert Otto Baum, Feb. 16, 1938 (div. 1960); children—Harro Siegward, Helma Sigrun (Mrs. George Meadows). Came to U.S., 1951, naturalized, 1957. Export corr. Bitter-Polar, Germany, 1933-35, Hanschel Locs, Germany, 1936; exec. sec. Fieseler Airplane Mfrs., Germany, 1936-38; interpreter, sec. UNRRA, Germany, 1946-48; payroll supr., civilian dept. U.S. Army, Wetzlar PX, Germany, 1948-51; asst. librarian Supreme Council, Ancient and Accepted Scottish Rite, Washington, 1951-70, acting librarian and museums curator, 1970—. Free-lance contbr. to Pabelverlag, Rastatt, Germany, Harle, Ofcl. Publs., Inc., others. Mem. A.L.A. Mem. Ch. of Jesus Christ of Latter-day Saints. Home: 2480 16th St NW Apt 416 Washington DC 20009 Office: 1733 16th St NW Washington DC 20009

BAUM, MARY HELEN, home economist; b. Frankfort, Ind., Oct. 19, 1920; d. Henry Millenberg and Anna Michael Baum; B.S., Purdue U., 1948. Exec. sec. Hicks Body Co., Lebanon, Ind., 1943-46; sr. home economist So. Cal. Gas Co., Hollywood, Cal., 1953-54, consumer specialist, Monterey Park, 1972-74; tech. adviser TV commls., 1966—. Recipient Spl. commendation Industry-Edn. Council So. Cal., 1966. Mem. Am., Cal., Los Angeles Dist. (pres. 1961-62) home econs. assns., Los Angeles Home Economists in Bus. Assn. (chmn. 1954-55). Mem. Order Eastern Star. Home: 3521 W 84th Pl Inglewood CA 90305 Office: 810 S Flower St Los Angeles CA 90051

BAUM, SHARON ANN ENLOE (MRS. STEPHEN HUGH BAUM), bank exec.; b. Kansas City, Mo., Jan. 3, 1940; d. Herbert Samuel and Emma Bonnadell (Clibourn) Enloe; student, U. Stockholm, 1960-61; B.A., Randolph-Macon Woman's Coll., 1962; M.B.A., Harvard Bus. Sch., 1965; m. Stephen Hugh Baum, Mar. 16, 1969; 1 son, Benjamin Clibourn, Marketing asso. Eastern Airlines, N.Y.C., 1965-66; mgr. woman's promotion Pan Am. Airways, N.Y.C., 1966-69; with Chem. Bank, N.Y.C., 1969—, asst. v.p., dir. advt. and promotions, 1973—. Mem. Eastside Young Reps. Club. Mem. Am. Assn. U. Women, Zeta Tau Alpha. Clubs: Harvard, Radcliffe (N.Y.C.). Home: 215 E 73rd St New York City NY 10021 Office: Chemical Bank 20 Pine St New York City NY 10015

BAUMAN, CAROL DAWSON, writer; b. Indpls., Sept. 8, 1937; d. Ernest Eugene and Hilda Lou (Carroll) Dawson; B.A., Dumbarton Coll., Washington, 1959; m. Robert Bauman, Nov. 19, 1960; children—Edward Carroll, Eugenie Marie, Victoria Anne, James Shields. Exec. sec. Youth for Nixon-Lodge, 1959-60; legislative aide U.S. Congressman Donald C. Bruce of Ind., 1961-63; dep. dir. information Goldwater-Miller campaign, 1963-64; editor New Guard mag., Washington, 1965-66; dir. information Am. Conservative Union, 1967-68; news analyst Exec. Office President, 1969; staff reporter Easton (Md.) Star-Democrat, 1971; writer Md. Horse and Horse Play mag., 1972-73; free-lance writer, 1969—. Chmn. Talbot County (Md.) Right to Life Com., 1973-74. Pres. Dunbarton Coll. Young Republicans, 1958-59; co-chmn. Nat. Coll. Young Reps., 1959-60; bd. dirs. Young Americans for Freedom, 1960-64; vice chmn. Talbot County Rep. Central Com., 1970-74. Mem. 93d Congl., Rep. Congl. wives clubs, Talbot County Rep. Women's Club, Talbot County Kennel Club, Tidewater Pony Club (sponsor), Am. Assn. U. Women, Talbot County Horse Show Assn. Roman Catholic. Clubs: Talbot County Women's; Capitol Hill, Congressional (Washington). Home: Glebe House Route 5 Easton MD 21601 Office: 118 Cannon Bldg Washington DC 20515

BAUMAN, HELEN WOOD, ret. C.S. practitioner, editor, educator; b. St. Joseph, Mo., Nov. 17, 1891; d. Horace W. and Mary (Vance) Wood; mus. edn. with Arthur Foote, Boston; student Tobias Matthay Sch., London, Eng., 1928; master classes, Thomas Whitney Surette Sch., Concord, Mass., 1927; m. Oscar George Bauman, Jan. 1, 1922 (dec. 1960). C.S. practitioner, 1932—; asso. editor publs. C.S. Pub. Soc., 1948-59, editor in chief, 1959-70; tchr. normal class Mother Ch., 1958, pres. Mother Ch., 1963-64; editor C.S. Jour., 1959-70, C.S. Sentinel, 1959-70, C.S. Herald (in 11 langs. in Braille), 1948-70. Mem. D.A.R. Home: 274 Beacon St Boston MA 02116

BAUMAN, MARGARET ESTELLE LANG (MRS. ROGER ALAN BAUMAN), pediatric neurologist; b. New Haven, Aug. 6, 1938; d. Otto John and Margaret Pauline (Roney) Lang; grad. cum laude Emma Willard Sch., 1956; A.B., Smith Coll., 1960; M.D., Woman's Med. Coll. Pa., 1965; m. Roger Alan Bauman, May 11, 1968; children—Karen Lang, Margaret Sprague, David Westcott. Med. intern U. Md. Hosp., Balt., 1965-66, resident neurology, 1968-69; resident pediatrics Johns Hopkins Hosp., Balt., 1966-68; resident pediatric neurology Mass. Gen. Hosp., Boston, 1969-71, instr. pediatric neurology, 1973—; clinic physician for clin. evaluation and rehab. center Eunice Kennedy Shriver Labs., Waltham, Mass., 1971—; dir. EEG lab., neurol. cons. Cambridge (Mass.) Hosp., 1971—. Research fellow and spl. fellow grantee Nat. Inst. Neurol. Diseases and Stroke, 1969-73. Mem. D.A.R., New Eng. Hist. and Geneal. Soc., Am. Acad. Neurology (jr.), Child Neurology Soc., Mass. Med. Soc. Republican. Methodist. Home: 60 Wedgemere Av Winchester MA 01890 Office: Dept Pediatric Neurology Mass Gen Hosp Fruit St Boston MA 02114

BAUMAN, SISTER MARY BEATA, educator; b. Okarche, Okla.; d. Joseph and Mary (Ramharter) Bauman; nursing diploma Mercy Sch. Nursing, San Diego, 1928; B.S. in Nursing Edn., San Francisco Coll. for Women, 1936; M.S. in Nursing, St. Louis U., 1956; D. Nursing Sci., U. San Francisco, 1972. Joined Sisters of Mercy, 1931; supr. St. Mary's Hosp., San Francisco, 1931-34, teaching. supr. surg. and pediatric nursing, 1936-40, dir. nursing edn. and nursing service Sch. Nursing, 1945-46; nursing arts instr. Mercy Sch. Nursing, San Diego, 1940-42, dir. nursing edn., 1946-55; nursing arts instr., asst. ednl. dir. St. Joseph's Sch. Nursing, Phoenix, 1942-45; asst. prof. U. San Francisco Sch. Nursing, 1956, dean, prof., 1957-71; archivist Motherhouse, Burlingame, Cal., 1971—; cons. Zulia U., Maracaibo, Venezuela, summer 1965, 66. Active various civic nursing orgns., San Francisco, 1949—; mem. Cal. Bd. Nursing Edn. and Nurse Registration, 1948-57, 65-69, pres., 1955, 67-68. Mem. Am. Nurses Assn. Author: A Way of Mercy: Catherine McAuley's Contribution to Nursing, 1958. Contbr. articles to profl. jours. Home: 2300 Adeline Dr Burlingame CA 94010

BAUMANN, CAROL MAE EDLER (MRS. RICHARD J. BAUMANN), educator; b. Plymouth, Wis., Aug. 11, 1932; d. Clarence H. and Beulah (Weinhold) Edler; B.A., U. Wis., 1954, postgrad., 1954; Ph.D., U. London, 1957; m. Richard J. Baumann, Feb. 28, 1959; children—Dawn, Wendy. Mem. faculty U. Wis., Madison, 1957-62, Milw., 1962—, asso. prof. dept. polit. sci., 1967-72, prof., 1972—; dir. inst. world affairs U. Wis.-Milw., 1964—. Bd. dirs. Internat. Inst. Milwaukee County. Hon. Woodrow Wilson fellow, 1954-55, Marshall scholar, 1954-57. Mem. Am. Polit. Sci. Assn., Midwest Conf. Polit. Scientists, Adult Edn. Assn. U.S.A., Nat. Univ. Extension Assn., Nat. Com. Community world Affairs Orgns. (bd. dirs.), Soc. Citizen Edn. in World Affairs (sec.-treas.), Wis. Com. for Internat. Edn. (chmn.), UN Assn. U.S.A. (v.p. Wis. chpt.), Phi Beta Kappa, Phi Kappa Phi, Phi Eta Sigma. Democrat. Lutheran. Author: Western Europe: What Path to Integration, 1967; The Diplomatic Kidnappings, 1973; (monograph) Political Co-operation in NATO, 1960. Contbr. sect. to book, articles to publs. Home: 5109 N Woodburn St Milwaukee WI 53217

BAUMEISTER, MRS. CARL F. (ELEANOR H. BAUMEISTER), club woman; b. Lake Linden, Mich., Oct. 2, 1909; d. Thomas and Sarah (Madigan) Hoskins; B. Music Edn., U. Minn., 1930; m. Carl Frederick Baumeister, Apr. 19, 1930; 1 son, Richard. Co-founder, advt. mgr. The Corn Belt Livestock Feeder, trade mag., 1948-51. Publicity dir. Patron's Council, Riverside-Brookfield High Sch., 1951-53; pres. MacNeal Meml. Hosp. Women's Aux., 1956, mem. adv. bd., 1957; sec. High Sch. Dist., 208 Caucus, 1965-67. Dir., rec. sec. S.W. suburban chpt. Am. Cancer Soc., pres. central suburban unit, 1969-71, treas., 1972—; mem. citizens adv. com. Morton Coll. Sch. Nursing. Bd. dirs. Riverside Pub. Library, 1960-72, pres. bd., 1967-71, sec. bd., 1971-72. Mem. Gen. Fedn. Women's Clubs, P.E.O. (pres. Riverside chpt. 1955-56, Ill. corr. sec. 1956, rec. sec. 1957-58, financial officer Ill. home 1958-63, dir.). Presbyn. Clubs: Riverside Woman's (pres. 1954-56); Chicago Farmers. Republican. Home: 120 S Delaplaine Rd Riverside IL 60546

BAUMEISTER, MARGARET KILPATRICK (MRS. THEODORE BAUMEISTER), educator, artist; b. Marianna, Fla., Jan. 13, 1901; d. William Heard and Mary Beman (Guyton) Kilpatrick; B.S., Columbia Tchrs. Coll., 1922; m. Theodore Baumeister, Jan. 23, 1925; children—Theodore III, Heard Kilpatrick, Mary Berrien (Mrs. M.B. Parker). Tchr., Hoffman Sch., N.Y.C., 1923-25, Barnard Sch. Boys, 1930-40, Riverside Ch. Sch., 1943-46; supt., tchr. Christ Ch. Sch., 1947-54; illustrator childrens books Scott, Foresman, 1927-30, Macmillan, N.Y.C., 1930-33. Mem. Episcopal Diocesan Com. Religious Edn., N.Y.C., 1935-40. Mem. Huguenot Soc., Carolina Art Assn., S.C. Hist. Soc., D.A.R., Preservation Soc. Charleston, N.Y. Geneal. and Biog. Soc., Ladies Benevolent Soc., Charleston Artist Guild, Charleston Library Soc., Navy League, Nat. Ry. Hist. Soc., Delta Sigma. Episcopalian. Clubs: Riverdale Garden (pres. 1947-48), Shakespeare (pres. 1952-54) (N.Y.C.), Onteora (Tannersville, N.Y.); Century (Charleston). The Parsonage Willtown Bluff Yonges Island SC 29494

BAUMGARTNER, CHARLOTTE WOLFF (MRS. HELMUT WALTER BAUMGARTNER), educator; b. Liberty, N.Y., May 13, 1914; d. Anthony John and Jennie Helen (Wasilewski) Wolff; B.S., Rutgers U., 1935; M.A., Columbia Tchrs. Coll., 1940; M.A., Western Res. U., 1952; Ph.D. (Am. Home Econs. fellow), Ohio State U., 1961; m. Helmut Walter Baumgartner, June 22, 1957. Tchr., Davey Jr. High Sch., East Orange, N.J., 1938-40; instr. textiles and clothing Douglass Coll., Rutgers U., 1940-44; asst. prof. textiles and clothing Western Res. U., 1944-52; asso. prof., chmn. textiles and clothing U. Minn., 1952-61; prof., head, dept. textiles and clothing Cornell U., 1961-68; prof. consumer econs. State U. N.Y., Oneonta, 1973—. Recipient Anna Hallock award for home econs. Douglass Coll., 1935. Mem. Am. Home Econs. Assn., Am. Econ. Assn., Omicron Nu, Phi Upsilon Omicron. Research in socio-econ. aspects of clothing, 1956-61. Home: 107 West St Oneonta NY 13820

BAUMGARTNER, LEONA (MRS. ALEXANDER D. LANGMUIR), physician, adminstr., educator; b. Chgo., Aug. 18, 1902; d. William J. and Olga (Leisy) Baumgartner; A.B., U. Kan., 1923, M.S., 1925; postgrad. Kaiser Wilhelm Inst., Munich, 1928-29; Ph.D. (Univ. fellow, 1930-31, Sterling fellow, 1931-32), Yale, 1932, M.D., 1934, LL.D., 1970; D.Sc., Women's Med. Coll., 1950, N.Y.U., 1954, Russell Sage Coll., 1955, Smith Coll., 1956, Western Coll. for Women, 1960, U. Mass., 1963, MacMurray Coll., 1967, U. Mich., 1967, N.Y. Med. Coll., 1968, Clark U., 1969; LL.D., Skidmore Coll., 1959, Oberlin Coll., 1965; L.H.D., Keuka Coll., 1963; m. Nathaniel M. Elias, 1942 (dec. 1964); m. 2d, Alexander D. Langmuir, 1970. With Colby (Kan.) Community High Sch., Kansas City Jr. Coll., U. Mont., 1923-28; interne, asst. resident and asst. in pediatrics N.Y. Hosp. and Cornell Med. Coll., 1934-36, resident pediatrician N.Y. Hosp., 1942-56, asso. attending pediatrician, 1956—; faculty nursing edn. Columbia, 1939-42; with N.Y.C. Dept. Health, 1937-62, commr. health, 1954-62; exec. dir. N.Y. Found., 1953-54; asst. sec. state for tech. cooperation and research AID, Dept. State, 1962-65; asso. chief, cons. U.S. Children's Bur., 1949-56; faculty pub. health, pediatrics Med. Coll., Cornell, 1939-66, faculty dept. maternal and child health Harvard Sch. Pub. Health, 1948-62; vis. prof. social medicine Harvard Med. Sch., 1966—; lectr. Columbia Sch. Pub. Health and Adminstrv. medicine, 1957-67; exec. dir. regional med. programs and Med. Care and Edn. Found., Inc., 1968-72. Adviser to Indian Minister of Health, 1955, French Ministry Health, 1945; mem. ofcl. exchange mission to USSR, 1958; lectr. Tokyo Met. Govt., 1961; mem. nat. adv. council Peace Corps, 1961-63; pres. U.S. Conf. City Health Officers, 1961-62; chief U.S. delegation Colombo Plan Ministerial Conf., 1963, 1st Asian Population Conf., 1963, 17th All-Pakistan Sci. Conf. 1965. Bd. dirs. N.Y. Fund Children, New Sch. Social Research, Indsl. Areas Found., Sci. Museum. Recipient John Lovett Morse prize in pediatrics, New Eng. Pediatric Soc., 1934; Baby-Talk mag. award, 1945; Am. Design award, 1946; Kansas U. Alumni award, 1947; N.Y. Infirmary's Elizabeth Blackwell Citation, 1950; Albert Lasker award Am. Pub. Health Assn., 1954; William J. Schieffelen Pub. Service award Citizens Union, 1960; citation N.Y. State Med. Women's Soc., 1960; Elizabeth Blackwell award Hobart and William Smith Colls., 1961; Samuel J. Crumbine award Kan. Pub. Health Assn., 1961; Albert Einstein award 1964; N.Y. State Acad. Preventive Medicine award, 1964; Sedgwick Meml. medal Am. Pub. Health Assn., 1964; Modern Medicine award 1965; Haven Emerson award Public Health Assn., 1965; Chapin medal, 1966; Hermann M. Biggs award N.Y. State Pub. Health Assn., 1968; Wilbur Lucius Cross medal Grad. Sch. Assn. Yale, 1970. Diplomate Am. Bd. Pediatrics, Am. Bd. Preventive Medicine and Pub. Health. Fellow Am. Acad. Pediatrics, Am. Pub. Health Assn. (dir., pres. 1958-59), Royal Soc. Health (hon.); mem. Am. Acad. Arts and Scis., Am. Orthopsychiat. Assn., Am. Pub. Welfare Assn., Am., Oxford bibliog. socs., Harvey Soc., History of Sci. Soc., Am. Assn. History Medicine, Assn. Am. Indian Affairs (dir.), Am. Pediatric Soc., N.Y. Acad. Med., Child Welfare League Am. (dir.) Nat. Social Welfare Assembly (v.p.), Nat. Conf. Social Work (exec. com.), Nat. Health Council (pres. 1956), Phi Beta Kappa, Sigma Xi, Pi Beta Phi, Phi Sigma, Mortar Bd. Club: Cosmopolitan. Contbr. med. and sci. articles profl. jours. Home: 1010 Memorial Dr Cambridge MA 02138 Office: Harvard Med Sch 25 Shattuck St Boston MA 02108

BAUNE, JOAN MARIE HENNING (MRS. EDWARD JOHN BAUNE), home economist; b. Seattle, Aug. 12, 1943; d. Chester Edwin and Marion (Deja) Henning; B.S., U. Ida., 1965; m. Edward John Baune, May 20, 1966; children—Jyl Marie, Jan Michele, Jo Melissa. Extension home economist U. Ida., Lewis County, 1965-67, Boundary County, 1968-71, Bur. Indian Affairs, Nez Perce Nation, 1971—; library asst. Eastern Wash. State Coll., 1967-68. Mem. adv. com. on gerontology nutrition programs Community Action Program, Nezperce County (Ida.), 1971-72. Acting sec. Comprehensive Health Planning Council, Boundary County (Ida), 1970-71; educator Pre-Sch. and Slowlearner Project, Vista Workers, 1968-69; sr. troop leader Boundary County council Girl Scouts U.S.A., 1969-71. Mem. Am. Home Econs. Assn., Nat., Ida. home economists extension assns., Epsilon Sigma Phi. Home: 1103 Deakin Moscow ID 83843 Office: North Ida Agy Lapwai ID 83540

BAXTER, IDA MAE ALLEN (MRS. WALTER LAWRENCE BAXTER), educator; b. Morgan, Tex., Dec. 19, 1930; d. Joseph Flanary and Saphronia Anne (Womack) Allen; certificate Tarleton State Coll., 1950; B.B.A., Southwest Tex. State U., 1952; M.Ed., Colo. State U., 1967; m. Walter Lawrence Baxter, Apr. 21, 1951; children—Jessica Ann (Mrs. Douglas B. Hart), Dana Mae, Allen Lawrence. Stenographer Tex. Dept. Welfare, Glen Rose, 1949; typist Houston Power and Light Co., 1950; tchr. Mathis (Tex.) Ind. Sch. Dist., 1953-58, East Central Ind. Sch. Dist., San Antonio, 1958-59, New Caney (Tex.) Ind. Sch. Dist., 1959-60, Uvalde (Tex.) Ind. Sch. Dist., 1960-64; instr. data processing programming Southwest Tex. Jr. Coll., Uvalde, 1965—. Faculty adviser Bapt. Student Union, S.W. Tex. Jr. Coll., 1971—. Recipient Outstanding Faculty Mem. award Southwest Tex. Jr. Coll., 1972-73. Mem. Tex. State Tchrs. Assn., Tex. Jr. Coll. Tchrs. Assn., Soc. Data Educators, Tex. Assn. Ednl. Data Systems, Am. Assn. U. Women (rec. sec. 1972-74, corr. sec. 1968-70). Baptist (tchr. coll. and career dept. 1970—). Club: Music (Uvalde, Tex.). Home: 705 Skylane Dr South Uvalde TX 78801

BAXTER, LEONE (LEONE BAXTER WHITAKER), public relations exec.; b. Kelso, Wash., Nov. 20, 1913; d. Leon W. and Grace P. (Hayes) Smith; m. Alexander D. Baxter, June 16, 1930 (dec. 1931); m. 2d, Clem S. Whitaker, Apr. 15, 1938 (dec. 1961); stepchildren—Clem Sherman, Milton O., Patricia (Mrs. Harry Sanders), Burdette (dec.). Co-founder with Clem Whitaker, Campaigns, Inc., profl. mgmt. ballot issues and candidates, San Francisco, 1934; v.p. Whitaker & Baxter, pub. relations counselors to industry, San Francisco, 1934-58; co-founder, partner Whitaker & Baxter Internat., 1958-68, pres., 1962—; columnist 50 Cal. newspapers, 1936-50, created Women in the News, Uncensored, Sparks from the News Circuit columns; editor-pub. Cal. Feature Service, San Francisco, 1936-58; partner Whitaker & Baxter, advt., San Francisco, 1933-58; mng. editor San Francisco Record, 1940-45; pub. San Francisco Neighborhood Newspapers, 1940-45. Mgr. Earl Warren's campaign for gov. Cal., 1942, nat. campaign against compulsory health ins. for A.M.A., 1949-52; mem. Nat. Profl. Com. for Eisenhower and Nixon, 1952, Goodwin J. Knight's campaign for gov. Cal., 1954; polit. adviser Gov. Goodwin Knight, 1954-58; gen. mgr. Cal. host com. to Rep. Nat. Conv., 1956. Asst. mgr. Cal. campaign to create Central Valley Water Project, 1933. Trustee, Found. Pub. Relations Research and Edn., Presbyn. Med. Center, Meals for Millions, Dooley Found., San Francisco Opera Auditions, Met. Opera Auditions, Am. Cancer Soc., Nob Hill Assn., Cal. Heritage Council, Artists Embassy. Mem. Pub. Relations Soc. Am., San Francisco Opera Guild, DeYoung Mus. Soc., Internat. Pub. Relations Assn., U.S. People-to-People Com., Cal. Newspaper Pubs. Assn., Ballet Guild, Art Inst., San Francisco Symphony, Internat. Hospitality Center, Civic Light Opera. Clubs: Metropolitan, Lake Shore, San Francisco Press. Author, lectr. pub. relation aspects of govt., politics and industry. Home: 1250 Jones St San Francisco CA 94108 Office: Whitaker & Baxter Internat The Fairmont Nob Hill San Francisco CA 94108

BAXTER, MARILYNN RUTH, educator; b. Chgo.; d. George Byron and Ruth Quinn (Hurd) Baxter; B.A., State U. Ia., 1958; postgrad. U. Edinburgh, 1960, Sch. Actor's Co., N.Y.C., 1963; M.A., U. Wis.-Madison, 1965, Ph.D., 1973; postgrad. Lee Strasberg Dir.-Actor Workshop, 1968, Shakespeare Summer Sch., U. Birmingham (Eng.), 1973. Spl. events coordinator Marshall Field & Co., Chgo., 1958-60; with Barter Theatre, Abingdon, Va., 1962; instr., supr. dept. curriculum and instrn. U. Wis.-Madison, 1964-67; communications faculty, dir. Parkside Players, U. Wis. at Parkside, Kenosha, 1967-74. Mem. U. Wis. Arts Council, 1969-70, Greater Kenosha Arts Council, 1969-74. Ford Found. fellow, 1967. Mem. Am. Theatre Assn., Speech Assn. Am., Central States Speech Assn., Am. Assn. U. Profs., D.A.R. (chpt. regent 1974—), Kappa Alpha Theta (chpt. pres. 1957-58, chpt.

adv. bd. 1965-67). Home: Spring Brook Rd Rockford IL 61111 Office: 3812 5th Av Kenosha WI 53140

BAXTER, MERRY HART BUCHANAN (MRS. JOHN BANKS HARRIS, JR.), writer; b. Chattanooga, Mar. 16, 1921; d. William Lee and Cannie Belle (Ridge) Buchanan; student Nat. Acad. Broadcasting, 1950, Mag. Inst., 1953, Ventura Coll., 1956-60, Imperial Valley Coll., Laverne Coll., 1971, San Diego State U., 1973; m. John Banks Harris, Jr., Sept. 13, 1971. Freelance cartoonist, photojournalist, creative writer 1940—; pub. Tram Mag., 1957, Insight News Service, Merry Muse, El Centro, 1971—. Founder writers clubs, ESP study groups, metaphys. study group. Chmn., Nat. Employ Physically Handicapped Week, Bradley County, Tenn., 1950-53. Recipient state, nat. awards for journalism and creative writing; named Handicapped Woman of Achievement Dist. 14 Pilot Club, 1969. Mem. D.A.V. Aux. (chpt. founder, comdr. 1950-52), Quill and Brush (founder 1950), Am. Parapsychology Soc., Spiritual Frontiers Fellowship, Bus. and Profl. Women, V.F.W., Am. Legion Aux., Imperial Valley Art Assn., Nat. Cal. press women. Mem. Ch. Religious Sci. Clubs: Womens, Soroptomist (El Centro); Photography (founder 1950 Cleveland, Tenn.). Author: Terse Verse, 1943; Melancholy Muse, 1944; Stars Out of Heaven, 1946; Poetry Madrigals of a Modern Mystic, 1970. Contbr. poetry to anthologies. Home: PO Box 19 Calexico CA 92231 Office: Box 1556 El Centro CA 92244

BAXTER, VIRGINIA MACDONALD, librarian; b. Portsmouth, Va., June 28, 1918; d. Stephen Ashby and Kate (St. Clair) MacDonald; B.A. in L.S., Coll. William and Mary, 1940; m. Joe Warren Baxter, May 19, 1945; children—Elizabeth (Mrs. John Calvin Sugg), Stephen, Virginia, Howard. Librarian, Ruffner Jr. High Sch., Norfolk, Va., 1940-44; reference librarian Norfolk Pub. Library, 1941-44; library asst. U.S. Naval Sta., Norfolk, 1944-45; librarian Hinds County Library, Jackson, Miss., 1945-46; reference librarian Miss. Dept. Archives and History, Jackson, 1946-48; adminstrv. librarian Gunter AFB, Ala., 1956—. Mem. Am., Ala. library assns., D.A.R., U.D.C., Am. Assn. U. Women, Pilot Club. Presbyn. Home: 3561 N Georgetown Dr Montgomery AL 36109 Office: Base Library Bldg 850 Gunter AFB AL 36114

BAY, ZULA MAE (MRS. ELBA M. BAY), clothing co. exec.; b. Marietta, Okla., Feb. 23, 1920; d. Jess D. and Sally Ann (Swinney) Dickey; degree in textile and clothing Phila. Textile Inst., 1950; degree in mgmt. and bus. Hill's Bus. Coll., 1955; m. Elba M. Bay, Nov. 9, 1940; 1 son, Larry Eugene. With Mid American Mfg. Co., Ponca City, Okla., 1940-43; with Guy H. James, Inc., Midwest City, Okla., 1944—, exec. v.p., gen. mgr., 1960—. Co-chmn. cities div. United Appeal, Midwest City, 1967-74; mem. Okla. Bd. Pvt. Schs., State of Okla., 1973. Named Outstanding Bus. Woman, Theta Sigma Phi, 1970, Woman of Year, Pilots Club, 1971; Distinguished Service award Elks, 1972. Mem. Am. Legion Aux., Am. Bus. Womens Assn., Am. Mgmt. Assn., Am. Apparel Mfg. Assn., Okla. (dir. 1973—), Oklahoma City, Midwest City (dir. 1966— pres. 1974—) chambers of commerce. Baptist. Mem. Rebekah Lodge (mem. state assembly, past pres.). Home: PO Box 10698 Midwest City OK 73110 Office: PO Box 10698 Midwest City OK 73110

BAYARD, MARY IVY STECKER, librarian; b. Hazleton, Pa., Dec. 14, 1940; d. George Raymond and Mary Ivy (Ecker) Stecker; A.B., Wilson Coll., 1962; M.S. in L.S., Drexel U., 1963; m. Peter A. Bayard (div.); 1 dau., Mary Ivy. Head reference and adult services Montgomery County-Norristown (Pa.) Pub. Library, 1963-68, asst. dir., 1968-70; librarian Tyler Sch. Art, Temple U., Phila., 1970—. Lectr., Drexel U., 1964-65; mem. Pa. Library Master Plan Com., 1971—; tchr. in-service tng. classes Pa. State Library, 1967, 69, 72. Mem. A.L.A. (sec. art sect. 1973—), Pa. Library Assn. (2d v.p. 1971-72), Art Libraries Soc. N. Am., Booksellers Assn. Phila., Phila. Mus. Art, Alumnae Assn. Drexel U. (planning bd. 1974—), Beta Phi Mu. Presbyn. (elder 1974—). Club: Conversational (Norristown). Contbr. articles to profl. jours. Home: 3016 Old Arch Rd Norristown PA 19403 Office: Tyler School of Art Temple University Beech and Penrose Avs Philadelphia PA 19126

BAYER, HELEN T.M. (MRS. GEORGE H. BAYER, JR.), educator; b. Buffalo; d. Paul B. and Helen Tate; B.S., State U. N.Y. at Buffalo, 1950; M.S., Cornell U., 1952, Ph.D., 1955; m. George H. Bayer, Jr., July 1954. Instr., Lockport (N.Y.) Sr. High Sch., 1950-51; research asst. Cornell U., 1952-54, teaching asst., 1954-55, asst. prof. dept. child devel. and family relationships, 1955-60, asso. prof., extension leader, 1960-66, prof., 1966—. Fellow Am. Sociol. Assn.; mem. Am. Home Econs. Assn., Eastern Sociol. Soc., Nat., Tri-State councils on family relations, Soc. for Research in Child Devel., Omicron Nu, Pi Lambda Theta, Phi Upsilon Omicron, Epsilon Sigma Phi. Author: (with others) Personality Development: Infancy through Early Adolescence, 1966, American Families, the Impact of Social Change, 1965; also program materials, films. Home: 216 Forest Home Dr Ithaca NY 14850

BAYER, PATRICIA RUTH STEWART (MRS. JAMES THEODORE BAYER), food service assn. exec., editor; b. Zanesville, O., July 31, 1928; d. Hugh Leo Paul and Dorothy Maryjane (Shull) Stewart; B.S. in Journalism, U. Colo., 1948; m. James Theodore Bayer, Dec. 27, 1948; children—Jeffrey Thomas, Richard Stewart, Linda Suzanne. news editor EDN Mag., Cahners Pub., Denver, 1966-70, staff writer, 1965-66, also asst. art dir., 1964-65; editor School Foodservice Jour., dir. communications Am. Sch. Food Service Assn., Denver, 1970—. Pres., Instl. Food Editorial Council, 1974. Pres., Wallace Village Aux., 1957-58. Mem. Colo. Govs. Commn. on Status of Women., 1973—. Recipient Jesse H. Neal award for Outstanding Journalism Am. Bus. Press, 1965, Grand prize Western Soc. Bus. Publs., 1966. Mem. U. Colo. Alumni (dir.). Home: 3635 S Jersey St Denver CO 80237 Office: 4101 E Iliff Av Denver CO 80222

BAYES, BEVERLEY JOAN, physician; b. Regina, Sask., Can., Nov. 1, 1937 (came to U.S. 1968); d. Rev. Frederick Charles and Sylvia Mae (Hickling) Bayes; M.D., U. Toronto, 1961; m. Edgar Gibson Merson, May 25, 1968; children—Jennifer Alice, Andrew Charles. Intern Toronto Gen. Hosp., 1961-62; sr. intern U. Toronto Hosp., 1962-63; jr. resident pediatrics Hosp. Sick Children, Toronto, 1964, commonwealth registrar, Glasgow, Scotland, 1964-65; sr. resident, also asso. resident-in-chief Hosp. Sick Children, 1965-66, fellow hematology, 1966-67, fellow gastroenterology, 1967-68; fellow Cystic Fibrosis Soc. D.C., 1968-69; pediatrician Fairfax County (Va.) Health Dept., 1972—. Team capt. FISH (community vol. orgn.), 1969-72. Diplomate Am. Bd. Pediatrics. Fellow Royal Coll. Physicians (Can.).; mem. No. Va. Pediatric Soc., Fairfax County Med. Soc., Med. Soc. Commonwealth Va., Mt. Vernon-Lee Physicians Assn. Methodist. Address: 8309 Brewster Dr Alexandria VA 22308

BAYES, MARJORIE ANDRESS, psychologist, health services adminstr.; b. Chgo., Dec. 1, 1934; d. Allan Wallace and Mary (Nixon) Andress; B.A., U. Fla., 1956; M.A., U. Ky., 1959; Ph.D., U. Miami, 1970; children by previous marriage—Stephen Allan, Christopher Andrew. Psychol. cons. Mott Found. Community Programs, Flint, Mich., 1956; psychometrician Montanari Clin. Sch., Hialeah, Fla., 1963-65; asst. prof. psychology in psychiatry Yale, New Haven, 1970—; chief community consultation unit Conn. Mental Health Center, New Haven, 1971—. Lectr. U. Miami, Fla., 1970; cons. Tavistock Group Relations Conf., New Haven, 1973—. Bd. dirs. South Central Conn. Regional Mental Health Planning Council, 1973—. Mem. Am. Psychol. Assn., Phi Beta Kappa, Phi Kappa Phi, Sigma Xi. Democrat. Unitarian-Universalist. Office: 34 Park St New Haven CT 06519

BAYH, MARVELLA HERN (MRS. BIRCH E. BAYH, JR.), civic worker; b. Enid, Okla., Feb. 14, 1933; d. Delbert M. and Bernett (Monson) Hern; student Okla. State U., 1951-52, Ind. State U., 1952-54; B.S., Ind. U., 1960; m. Birch E. Bayh, Jr. (senator Ind.), Aug. 24, 1952; 1 son, Evan III. Tchr., Girls' State, Ind. U., Bloomington, 1962-74, Girls' Nation, Washington, 1965—; studied day care and child devel. centers, USSR, Japan, Eng., Netherlands, France; co-chmn. Ind. Easter Seal Soc., 1965, 66, 67; mem. Nat. Beautification Speakers' Com., 1966—; hon. chmn. Guttman Inst. Charity Ball, 1972; co-chmn. nat. crusade Am. Cancer Soc., 1974, co-chmn. Ind. div., 1973; sponsor mem. Citizen's Com. for Conquest Cancer, 1974. Mem. Speaker's Bur., Dem. Nat. Com., 1960—; campaign worker for husband, 1962, 68, 74. Recipient Matrix award, named Ind. Woman of Year, Indpls. chpt.; Pride of the Plainsmen award, 1967; Hoo's Hoo of Hoosier Women's award Ind. Soc. of Washington, 1968; elected to Theta Sigma Phi, 1964. Mem. Pi Beta Phi. Contbr. to Day Care Bull., McCall's mag., Today's Health, Nat. Enquirer. Home: 2919 Garfield St NW Washington DC 20008 Office: Senate Bldg Washington DC 20510

BAYLESS, MILDRED JOYCE MCLAUGHLIN (MRS. FREDERICK E. BAYLESS), guidance counselor; b. Channing, Tex., July 24, 1930; d. Ernest Van and Mildred Althea (Buffington) McLaughlin; B.A., E. Tex. State U., 1950, M.Ed., 1958; m. Frederick E. Bayless, May 27, 1951; children—Velma Lynette, Landis Eugene. Pvt. tchr. 3X Ranch, Victoria, Tex., 1958-50; tchr. Trinidad (Tex.) Ind. Schs., 1950-52; guidance counselor Rockdale (Tex.) Ind. Schs., 1956-73; dir. spl. edn. Milam County Schs., 1973—; spl. edn. cons. region VI Tex. Mem. Menninger Found., 1966—. Mem. Tex. (dist. pres. 1970-71), Milam County (sec.-treas. 1968-69) tchrs. assns., Am., Tex. personnel and guidance assns., D.A.R., Delta Kappa Gamma, Kappa Delta Pi, Sigma Tau Delta. Baptist. Contbr. articles, poems to various publs. Home: Route 1 Box 460 Rockdale TX 76567 Office: Box 632 Rockdale TX 76567

BAYLESS, VERNEDA KATHRINE BOYNTON (MRS. HENRY HINK BAYLESS), home economist; b. Pikeville, Tenn., Apr. 19, 1923; d. Arthur Alden and Nancy Lora (DeWeese) Boynton; B.S., Union Coll., 1967, B.A., 1968; m. Henry Hink Bayless, Aug. 18, 1944; children—Sandra Lou (Mrs. Roy Day), Macy Lamar. Sewer, cutter nurses uniforms Maryville (Tenn.) Coll. Sewing Shop, 1941-43; with Navy research lab. Nat. Cash Register Co., Dayton, O., 1943-44; cubicle operator Atomic Bomb Plant, Oak Ridge, Tenn., 1944; practical nurse Sequatchie County Gen. Hosp., Dunlap, Tenn., 1957-58; nurse aide expt. heart dept. Bryan Meml. Hosp., Lincoln, Neb., 1965-67; extension home economist N.M. State U., Las Cruces, N.M., 1969—. Tutor elementary, high sch., coll. students, 1953—. Mem. Nat. Assn. Extension Home Economists, Am., Albuquerque home econs. assns., Am. Forestry Assn., Nat. Parks Assn., Nat. Wildlife Found., Nat. Audubon Soc., Dale Carnegie Alumni Assn. Club: Land of Enchantment CB (Albuquerque). Home: Box 72 Corrales NM 87048 Office: Box 1667 Albuquerque NM 87103

BAYLEY, MONICA WORSLEY (MRS. EDWIN RICHARD BAYLEY), editor; b. Witten, S.D., Jan. 31, 1919; d. Thomas Roncetti and Mabel Gertrude (Stewart) Worsley; B.A., Lawrence U., 1940; m. Edwin Richard Bayley, Aug. 12, 1941; children—Mary (Mrs. Zachary Fisk), Thomas te Linde. Dir. news service U. Wis., Milw., 1953-59; asst. dir. Joint Office of Instl. Research, Washington, 1961-63; edn. research, publs. specialist U.S. Office of Edn., Washington, 1963-64; copy-editor McGraw-Hill Book Co., N.Y.C., 1964-69; East coast corr. Features & News, Inc., Chgo., 1966-69; editorial researcher, writer Determined Productions, Inc., San Francisco, 1969-72; editor, supr. graphic arts, 1972—. Publicity dir. Child Care Centers, Milw., 1947-57. Bd. dirs. U.N. Commn., Milw., 1958-59. Mem. Women in Communications, Wis. Acad. Scis., Arts and Letters, Alpha Delta, Kappa Alpha Theta. Democrat. Mem. Unitarian Ch. Author: The Black Africa Cook Book, 1971. Copy-editor: Dictionary of Art, 1970. Home: 25 Stonewall Rd Berkeley CA 94705 Office: Box 2150 San Francisco CA 94126

BAYLISS, SYLVIA JOYCE, editor, govt. ofcl.; b. Buffalo, Sept. 1, 1937; d. George Edgar and Ellen Sylvia (Suomela) Bayliss; B.S. in Journalism, Ohio U., 1959; M.S., Boston U., 1961. Writer, Editor U.S. Civil Service Commn., Washington, 1962-72, mag. editor, 1972—; mag. editor U.S. Dept. Commerce, Washington, 1972. Mem. Women in Communications, Fed. Editors Assn. (2d place award 1973), Tau Mu Epsilon. Home: 525 N Pollard St Arlington VA 22203 Office: 1900 E St NW Washington DC 20415

BAYNARD, MILDRED MOYER (MRS. ROBERT S. BAYNARD), business exec., club woman; b. Lincoln, Neb., May 10, 1902; d. Charles Calvin and Flora (Harter) Moyer; student Sullins Coll., 1921, U. So. Cal., 1922; B.A., U. Neb., 1925; m. Robert S. Baynard, May 24, 1927; 1 son, Lester B. Tchr. pub. schs., Lincoln, 1926-27, Crescent City, Fla., 1925-26; sec. Venice Land Co., Inc., 1949-69; sec. Fla. Bridge Co., 1960-68; partner Independent Parking, 1965-72; v.p. Venice-Nokomis Bank, Venice, Fla., 1947-63, dir., 1947-63; pres. Venice Land Co., 1969-72. Mem. Fla. State Dist. Welfare Bd., 1948-52; pres. bd. dirs. YWCA, 1953-56; Fla. chmn. Nat. Soc. Prevention Blindness, 1957-60, bd. dirs., 1960-67, v.p., 1963-66; nat. v.p., pres. Fla. Soc. Prevention Blindness, 1958-64, v.p., 1967-68, also mem. Fla. exec. com.; dir. Center for Blind, 1956; pres. Suncoast div. Arthritis Found. Inc., 1966-67; mem. nat. voter adv. bd. Nat. Security Council; pres. North Ward P.T.A., 1938; sec. St. Petersburg Woman's Club, 1945-46. Recipient Outstanding Citizen's award Pinellas County Commn., 1964. Mem. Internat. Platform Assn. (sec. So. region 1965), Stuart Soc., St. Petersburg Hist. Soc., Mus. Fine Arts, All Childrens Hosp. Guild, U. Neb. Alumni Assn. (bd. policy), Delta Gamma (province officer 1950-56, conv. chmn. 1964, Cable award 1964, Shield award 1973, house corp. 1969—, hon. fellow found. 1974—). Episcopalian. Clubs: Sorosis; Rotary Ann. (pres. Venice 1962); Yacht of St. Petersburg, Panhellenic, Women's, Interlock (sec. 1942-45) (St. Petersburg, Fla.), Innisbrook Country. Mem. editorial adv. bd. Florida Lives. Home: 627 Brightwaters Blvd NE St Petersburg FL 33704

BAYNES, BARBARA JEAN REYNOLDS (MRS. FREDERICK LOUIS BAYNES), educator; b. Salem, Ind., Aug. 20, 1936; d. Flavel Nicholson and Hazel Mae (Collins) Reynolds; B.S., Ind. U., 1958, M.B.A., 1962; m. Frederick Louis Baynes, Aug. 24, 1958. Tchr., Southwestern Sch. Corp., Shelbyville, Ind., 1958-64; tchr., dir. publs. Center Grove Sch. Corp., Greenwood, Ind., 1964-70; tchr., dir. pub. information, chmn. dept. bus. edn. Greenwood Community Schs., 1970—. Instr. dept. journalism Ind. U., Bloomington, summers 1963-72; cons. Central-Nine Vocational Tech. Sch., 1972. Recipient plaque Div. Vocational Edn. for Unity in Bus. Edn., 1971. Mem. Ind. (pres. 1969-71), North-Central (exec. bd. 1973) bus. edn. assns., Ind. High Sch. Press Assn. (pres. 1968), Ind. Vocational Assn. (v.p. 1969-71, Outstanding Service award 1973), Ind. Bus. Educators Club (v.p. 1973-74), D.A.R., Theta Sigma Phi. Club: Women's Press (Indpls.). Editor Ind. Vocational Edn. Assn. News and Views, 1971-73. Home: Rural Route 1 Box 54 D 11 Franklin IN 46131 Office: 615 Smith Valley Rd Greenwood IN 46142

BAZATA, ELEANOR JEANETTE, home economist; b. Elmhurst, L.I., N.Y., June 24, 1924; d. Henry Charles and Marie (Zeman) B.; B.A., Hunter Coll., 1945; M.A., Columbia, 1961. Dietetic intern, N.Y. Hosp.-Cornell Med. Coll., 1945-46, adminstrv. dietitian, 1946-50; home economist-dietitian Sealtest Foods div. Nat. Dairy Products Corp. (now Kraftco Corp.), N.Y.C., 1950-62, dir. consumer services, 1962-72; coordinator consumer service Dairy Council Met. N.Y., 1972—. Chairperson sch. breakfast com. Food and Nutrition Council Greater N.Y., 1972-74; nutrition services cons. N.Y. State Dept. Health, 1974—. Mem. N.Y. Regional Council Industry-Edn. Coop. Mem. Am., Greater N.Y. (pres. 1967-68) dietetic assns., Am. (treas. Southeastern dist.), N.Y. State home econs. assns., Am. Pub. Health Assn., Pub. Health Assn. N.Y.C., Home Economists in Bus. (mem. Navy food adv. com.), Instl. Food Editorial Council. Home: 160-17 29th Av Flushing NY 11358 Office: 2 World Trade Center New York City NY 10047

BEACH, BESSIE MAE, physician; b. Seymour, Ind.; d. Omer and Georgia May (Blumer) Beach; B.S., U. Cin., 1929, B.M., 1933, M.D., 1934. Intern U. Wis. Hosp., 1933-34; resident in pediatrics St. Christopher's Hosp. for Children, Phila., 1934-35, U. Cin., 1935-37; cons. pediatrics Bur. Maternal and Child Health, Wis. Bd. Health, 1937-39; asst. dir. Bur. Maternal and Child Health, Ala. Dept. Health, 1939-41; regional med. cons. U.S Children's Bur., 1941-43; practice medicine, specializing in pediatrics, Columbus, Ga., 1943-67; med. dir. Maternal and Infant Care Project, Greenville County (S.C.) Pub. Health Dept., 1967—. Mem. Am., S.C. med. assns., Greenville County Med. Soc., Am. Acad. Pediatrics, S.C. State Pediatric Soc., Am. Heart Assn., Am., S.C. pub. health assns., Am. Pub. Health Physicians Assn., Alpha Epsilon Iota. Baptist. Mem. Order Eastern Star. Home: 17 Balentine Dr Greenville SC 29605 Office: Maternal and Infant Care Project Greenville Pub Health Dept University Ridge Greenville SC 29602

BEACH, MARGARET GASTALDI (MRS. EDWARD WOODBRIDGE BEACH), nurse; b. Placerville, Cal., Aug. 10, 1915; d. Giovanni Batista and Josephine (Bisagno) Gastaldi; student Sacramento City Coll., 1934; grad. Mercy Coll. Nursing, 1938; m. Edward Woodbridge Beach, Feb. 15, 1946 (dec. Aug. 1968); children—Laura G. (Mrs. Robert L. Phillips), Edward Woodbridge, Margaret J. In charge urol. dept. Mercy Hosp., Sacramento, 1938-42; tchr. urology to student nurses, 1943-45. Treas., Germana M. Wilson Meml. Scholarship Found., 1967—. Mem. Woman's Aux. A.M.A., Sacramento County Women Med. Soc. Home: 6255 14th Av Sacramento CA 95820

BEACH, MARY LOUISE, sch. prin.; b. Fostoria, O., Feb. 24, 1938; d. Dawson Aart and Dorothy Mildred (Miller) Kortier; student Bowling Green State U., Toledo U. summers 1958-59; B.S., Capital U., 1960; M.A., Ohio State U., 1969, postgrad., 1969-70; children—Thomas Quentin, Michael Edward. Elementary tchr. Sylvania (O.) Schs., 1960, Columbus (O.) City Schs., 1961; substitute tchr., tutor, 1962-66; reading enrichment tchr. Westerville (O.) City Schs., 1966-68; supr. elementary edn. tchrs. Ohio State U., Columbus, 1969-70; state reading cons. S.C. Dept. Edn., Columbia, 1970-72; pub. elementary sch. prin. Brennen Elementary Sch., Columbia, 1972—. Instr., U. S.C., Columbia, 1971—; cons. reading, lang. arts S.C. Sch. Dists., 1970—. Den mother, mem. pack com. Boy Scouts Am., Columbia, 1972—. Nat. Defense Edn. Act fellow, 1968—. Mem. Nat., S.C. edn. assns., Nat., Am. assns. sch. adminstrs., Internat., S.C. reading assns., S.C. Elementary Prins. Assn. Editor: Teaching Children to Read, 1969; Children's Language, 1970; Learning Through Language, 1971; Building Elementary Reading Programs, 1972. Home: 3208 Montcrest Rd Columbia SC 29210

BEACH, ROSE MARY RANDALL, librarian; b. Waterloo, Ia., Dec. 11, 1921; d. Charles Warren Milton and Rose Ellen (MacDonald) Randall; B.A., State U. Ia., 1943; M.S., Drexel U., 1971; m. Thomas C. Beach, Jr., May 5, 1945; children—Charles Randall, Thomas Christopher Coffing, Murray MacDonald. Opinion researcher Audience Research, Inc., Princeton, N.J., 1944; radio news and feature writer A.P. Radio, Rockefeller Center, N.Y.C., 1944-47; instr. Green Mountain Jr. Coll., Poultney, Vt., 1951-54; instr. Goldey Beacom Coll., Wilmington, Del., 1956-69, head librarian, 1970—. Mem. Nat. Bus. Tchrs. Assn., Am., Del. library assns., Phi Beta Kappa, Beta Phi Mu, Kappa Tau Alpha, Sigma Delta Chi. Episcopalian. Home: RD 1 Landenberg PA 19350 Office: 4701 Limestone Rd Wilmington DE 19808

BEADLE, MURIEL MCCLURE BARNETT (MRS. GEORGE WELLS BEADLE), civic worker, writer; b. Alhambra, Cal., Sept. 14, 1915; d. Richard and Eunice L. (Bothwell) McClure; B.A., Pomona Coll., 1936, LL.D., 1973; D.H.L., Mundelein Coll., 1966; m. Joseph Y. Barnett, July 3, 1941 (dec. Feb. 1951); 1 son, Redmond James; m. 2d, George Wells Beadle, Aug. 12, 1953. Advt. copywriter Carson Pirie Scott & Co., Chgo., 1936-40, Bullock's Pasadena (Cal.), 1945-48; fashion editor, women's editor Los Angeles Mirror-News, 1948-58; free-lance writer newspapers and mags., 1958—. Lectr. on edn. and social welfare, cons. various educator groups, 1957—; v.p. Pasadena Com. on Pub. Edn., 1957-60; mem. Pasadena Library Bd., 1959-61; chmn. Harper Ct. Found., Chgo., 1962-72. Recipient citation City of Pasadena, 1960, citation for service to pub. edn. Pasadena Edn. Assn., 1959, award Chgo. Friends of Lit., 1962, Thomas Alva Edison Found., 1967, Delta Kappa Gamma, 1971. Mem. Phi Beta Kappa, Delta Kappa Gamma. Democrat. Club: Fortnightly, Friday (Chgo.). Author: These Ruins Are Inhabited, 1961; (with husband) The Language of Life, 1966; A Child's Mind, 1970; Where Has All the Ivy Gone?, 1972; The Fortnightly of Chicago: The City and Its Women, 1873-1973, 1973. Address: 5533 Dorchester Av Chicago IL 60637

BEAGLE, GAIL JOYCE, journalist; b. Beaumont, Tex., Nov. 25, 1935; d. Victor Leroy and Hazel (Block) Beagle; B.S., Tex. Woman's U., 1958; summer student U. Tex., 1959; student grad. program in legislative affairs George Washington U., 1973—. Reporter, San Antonio Light, 1957; mem. staff State Senator Henry B. Gonzalez, 1959, U.S. Senator Ralph W. Yarborough, 1959; adminstrv. asst. Tex. Methodist Student Movement, Austin, 1960-61; office mgr., press sec. U.S. Rep. Gonzalez, 1961-63, adminstrv. asst., press sec., 1963—. Mem. Tex. Soc. to Abolish Capital Punishment, Austin Council on Human Relations, Fed. Editors Assn., Women in Communications (Headliner award San Antonio chpt. 1968, v.p. Washington chpt. 1972, pres. 1972-74; nat. govt. action chmn.), Fedn. Orgns. for Profl. Women (1st alternate, governing bd.; rep. of nat. Women in Communications). Editor Meth. Student Movement NEWS, 1959-61, Austin Council on Human Relations newsletter Balance, 1960-61. Home: 2943 W Ashby Pl San Antonio TX 78228 also 526 4th SE Washington DC 20003 Office: 203 Fed Bldg San Antonio TX 78205 also 2446 Rayburn House Office Bldg Washington DC 20515

BEAHLER, ELECTRA CATSONIS (MRS. JOHN LEROY BEAHLER), lawyer; b. Washington, Aug. 6, 1933; d. Achilles and Anastasia (Carzis) Catsonis; B.A., Pa. State U., 1955; J.D., George Washington U., 1969; m. John Leroy Beahler, Feb. 7, 1973. Asst.

editor Aero Digest, Washington, 1955-56; editorial asst. adminstrv. sec. Fairchild Engine & Airplane Co., 1956-57; pub. relations, exec. suite sec. Kaiser Industries Corp., 1957-60; sec. to pres. George Washington U., 1960-62; legis. asst. to U.S. Congressman Donald D. Clancy, 1962-67; admitted to D.C. bar, 1970, also U.S. Ct. of Appeals for D.C. bar, U.S. Supreme Ct. bar. adminstrv. asst. to U.S. Congressman John M. Ashbrook, Washington, 1968-73; Mem. Am., D.C. Womens bar assns., Am. Womens Assn. of Kenya, Phi Beta Kappa, Kappa Beta Pi. Home: State Dept/Nairobi Washington DC 20521

BEAHON, MARY ANN (MRS. MICHAEL LEWIS BEAHON), editor; b. Manitowoc, Wis., Oct. 27, 1946; d. Joseph R. and Camillus (Justus) Eggers; B.J. (Gannett Newspapers scholar), U. Mo., 1968, postgrad, 1972—; m. Michael Lewis Beahon, June 6, 1970. Reporter, Times-Union, Rochester, N.Y., 1968-70; publs. specialist Greece (N.Y.) Central Sch. Dist., 1970-71; staff asst. pub. relations N.E. Mo. State Coll., Kirksville, 1971-72; asst. editor U. Mo., Columbia, 1972-73, editor internal publs., 1973—. Chmn. vol. com. Cerebral Palsy Telethon, Columbia, 1973; vol. March of Dimes, Cancer Fund, Multiple Sclerosis, United Way. Mem. Missourian Pub. Assn., Women in Communications (chmn. local membership 1971, sec. local chpt. 1967), Nat. Sch. Pub. Relations Assn. (sec. western N.Y. chpt. 1971), Mid-Mo. Press Club, Columbia Jaycees Wives (chmn. Aid-to Jaycees 1973, publicity chmn. 1974 Spokette award 1973, Sparkette award 1974), Theta Sigma Phi, Kappa Tau Alpha, Sigma Delta Chi, Kappa Alpha Mu, Alpha Chi Omega (pres. coll. alumnae club 1972-74, chmn. Mo. rush information 1973—, local editor mag. 1966-68, 70—, Ideal Sr. AN chpt. 1968, Outstanding Alumna 1974). Republican. Roman Catholic. Home: 804 Sycamore Lane Columbia MO 65201 Office: 223 Jesse Hall Columbia MO 65201

BEALE, BETTY (MRS. GEORGE K. GRAEBER), columnist; b. Washington; d. William Lewis and Edna (Sims) Beale; A.B., Smith Coll. Columnist Washington Post, 1937-40; reporter and columnist Washington Star-News, 1945—; weekly columnist Hall Syndicate, Washington, 1953-67, Pubs.-Hall Syndicate, 1967—; lectr. Address: 2926 Garfield St NW Washington DC 20008

BEALE, ELIZABETH ALTHEA, psychologist; b. Los Angeles, July 6, 1923; d. Lindsay D. and Beatrice Knowlton (Nourse) Beale; B.A. cum laude, U. Cal. at Los Angeles, 1946, M.A., 1948; Ph.D., U. Kan., 1956; m. James Francis, May 25, 1957; 1 dau., Bonnibeth Beale. Clin. psychologist Patton (Cal.) State Hosp., 1948-51, VA, Topeka, Kan., 1951-56, Cal. Youth Authority, Norwalk, 1956-57, Ore. State Hosp., Salem, 1957-58, Hacker Clinic, Beverly Hills, Cal., 1958-61, Los Angeles County Probation Dept., 1962-63, U. Cal. Counseling Center, Riverside, 1964-67, Camarillo State Hosp., Thousand Oaks, Cal., 1968—. Individual practice psychology, Los Angeles, 1961-67, Redlands, Cal., 1963-67, Thousand Oaks, 1968—. Mem. Am. Psychology Assn., Am. Orthopsychiat. Assn., Los Angeles Soc. Clin. Psychology, Cal. State, Ventura County psychol. assns., Americans for Democratic Action, Zonta Internat. Home: 2166 Moorpark Rd Thousand Oaks CA 91360 Office: PO Box 1846 Thousand Oaks CA 91360

BEALL, MELISSA LOUISE CHRISTENSEN (MRS. HUGH FULTON BEALL), educator; b. Pilger, Neb., June 4, 1944; d. Emil Peter and Olga Elizabeth (Hansen) Christensen; B.S., U. Neb., 1967, M.A. (Aksarben scholar), 1971; m. Hugh Fulton Beall, Mar. 13, 1971. Tchr. speech, drama, English, departmental chmn. Raymond (Neb.) Central High Sch., 1967-71; grad. student, instr. speech communication dept. U. Neb., Lincoln, 1971-74; tchr. English, drama, speech Lincoln S.E. High Sch., 1974—. Mem. Neb. Ednl. Theatre Assn. (sec. 1970-73, pub. relations dir. 1973—), Neb. Speech Communication Assn. (mem. tchr. preparation and certification standards com. 1972-74, chmn. forensics com. 1974—), Neb. Masquers, Central States Speech Assn., Speech Communication Assn., Nat., Neb., Lincoln edn. assns., Internat. Communication Assn. Democrat. Lutheran. Asso. editor Neb. Speech Communication Assn. and Neb. Ednl. Theatre Assn. Jour., 1973—. Home: 3802 South 37th St Lincoln NE 68506

BEALMEAR, PATRICIA MARIA, educator, immunologist; b. Dodge City, Kan., Oct. 23, 1929; d. John Morgan and Anna Margaret (Wilson) Bealmear; B.S. magna cum laude (coll. scholar), Mt. St. Scholastica Coll., Atchison, Kan., 1949; postgrad. (NSF fellow) Purdue U., 1957, (NSF and AEC fellow), U. Kan., 1959, St. Louis U., 1960; Ph.D. (NSF fellow, Arthur Schmitt fellow, NIH fellow), U. Notre Dame, 1965. Asst.-asso. faculty fellow U. Notre Dame, 1966-71; asst. prof. Baylor Coll. Medicine, Houston, 1971-74, asso. prof., 1974—. Nat. judge Elks Nat. Scholarship Contest, 1968-74; cons. NIH grants. Mem. A.A.A.S., Am. Assn. Immunologists, Am. Assn. U. Profs., Am. Soc. Exptl. Pathology, Assn. Gnotobiotics, Internat. Soc. Exptl. Hematology, N.Y. Acad. Scis., Radiation Research Soc., Transplantation Soc., Soc. Exptl. Biology and Medicine, Sigma Xi, Kappa Gamma Pi. Editor: Germfree Research-Biol. Effect of Gnotobiotic Environments, 1974. Contbr. articles to profl. jours. Home: 2815 Prescott St Houston TX 77025

BEAMGUARD, ELIZABETH PARKS (MRS. ELBERT STRODE BEAMGUARD), state ofcl.; b. Fayetteville, Tenn.; d. Joel Dodson and Emma Wenifred (Puckett) Parks; A.B., U. Tenn., 1931; B.S., Emory U., 1944; postgrad. U. Chattanooga;; m. Elbert Strode Beamguard, Nov. 24, 1930; 1 dau., Elizabeth (Mrs. Robert L. Swanson). Dir., Huntsville-Madison County Library, Huntsville, Ala., 1944-55; librarian U. Ala. Extension Center, Huntsville, 1953-54; field rep. Ala. Pub. Library Service, Montgomery, 1956-60, dir., 1960—. Instr. library course U. Ala., Tuscaloosa, summer 1962, 66; mem. legislative liaison com. Assn. State Library Agys., 1973. Mem. Mayor's Liaison Com., 1959, 71, Ala. Com. on Children and Youth, 1965, Ala. Sesquicentennial Coordinating Com.; mem. Pres.'s Com. Handicapped; mem. Ala. Environmental Quality Control Council, 1973. Recipient citation Ala. Legislature, 1963. Mem. Am., Ala. (mem. exec. council) library assns., Am. Soc. Pub. Adminstrn., Nat. League Municipalities, Ala. Hist. Assn., Am. Assn. U. Women, Ala. Bus. and Profl. Women. Club: Zonta (Montgomery, Ala.). Editor Am. Assn. U. Women Newsletter, 1970-71. Contbr. articles to profl. jours. Home: 3373 Dartmouth Circle Montgomery AL 36111 Office: Adminstrv Bldg Montgomery AL 36104

BEAN, ANNE ALEXANDER, ednl. therapist; b. N.Y.C., Feb. 27, 1927; d. Myron and Marian (Silverman) Alexander; B.A., Brown U., 1948; B.S. in Edn., Bank Street Coll. of Edn., 1960; postgrad. Columbia, 1962-70; m. Kenneth Bean, Sept. 12, 1948; children—Thomas, Douglas. Tchr. Temple Emanuel Nursery Sch., 1952-53; pvt. ednl. therapist for children with learning disabilities, Maplewood, N.J., 1965—. Mem. Am. Psychol. Assn., Orton Soc. Mem. Unitarian Ch. Address: 6 Lewis Dr Maplewood NJ 07040

BEAN, DENISE MARY HIDLEY (MRS. KENNETH FORTE BEAN), occupational therapist, clubwoman; b. Orange, N.J., Dec. 24, 1939; d. Ralph Emerson and Irene Elizabeth (Robinson) Hidley; B.A. in English Lit., Manhattanville Coll., 1961; certificate in occupational therapy Columbia Coll. Phys. and Surg., 1963; m. Kenneth Forte Bean, Nov. 7, 1964; children—Eric, Jason, Damon, Melissa. Occupational therapist, dir. male placement Connecticut Valley Hosp., Middletown, Conn., 1963-64; occupational therapy supr. in-patient psychiat. service Bristol (Conn.) Hosp., 1974—. Chmn. recreation study League Women Voters, Avon, 1969-71, program chmn. 1971-72; 1st v.p. Avon Jr. Women's Club, 1971-72, pres., 1973-74; mem. Avon Recreation Commn., 1972-74; pres. Manhattanville Coll. Alumnae Assn. Upper Conn., 1970-72. Mem. Am. Occupational Therapy Assn., Bristol Hosp. Aux., Women's Aux. Hartford County Med. Assn. Home: 183 Haynes Rd Avon CT 06001

BEAN, (MABEL) GLADYS, educator; b. Montreal, Que., Can., June 17, 1918; d. John Alfred and Mabel E. (Riddell) Bean; B.A., McGill U., 1940; M.A., Tchrs. Coll. Columbia, 1948; Ph.D., U. Mich., 1970. Dir. phys. edn., acad. tchr. Netherwood Sch. for Girls, Rothesay, N.B., Can., 1941-43; asst. prof. phys. edn. McGill U., Montreal, 1943—, dir. athletics, phys. edn. and recreation for women, 1966—. Cons. YWCA of Can., 1968-69. Mem. Canadian Assn. Health, Phys. Edn. and Recreation (v.p. phys. edn. 1969-71, R.T. McKenzie Honor award), A.A.H.P.E.R., Nat., Eastern assns. phys. edn. for coll. women, Royal Life Sav. Soc. Can. (Recognition Bar and Badge), Canadian Adult Edn. Assn., Adult Edn. Assn. Am., Internat. Assn. Phys. Edn. and Sports for Girls and Women (Canadian rep., sec.-treas. 1973—), Internat. Council Health, Phys. Edn. and Recreation, Canadian Amateur Synchronized Swimming Assn. (v.p. 1961-63, historian 1963—, sect. pres. 1961-64, 72—). Clubs: Prescott Golf, Royal Automobile. Home: 1400 Pine Av W Apt 1005 Montreal PQ H3G 1B1 Canada

BEAN, MARGARET JACKSON (MRS. EDWARD R. BEAN), banker; b. Jakin, Ga.; d. John J. and Ada (Taylor) Jackson; student St. Petersburg Bus. Coll., Am. Inst. Banking, 1950—; m. Edward R. Bean, July 20, 1943; 1 dau., Deborah Dell. With T.W. Rowland Used Cars, St. Petersburg, Fla., 1939-41; with First Nat. Bank, St. Petersburg, 1941—, asst. v.p., 1967—. Mem. Nat. Assn. Bank Women, Am. Bus. Women's Assn. (com. chmn. 1959). Methodist (mem. ofcl. bd. 1965—). Club: Bath. Home: 6221 4th Av N St Petersburg FL 33710 Office: PO Box 1689 St Petersburg FL 33710

BEAN, RUTH LOUISE, agy. exec.; b. Boston; d. Henry E.W. and Minnie (Schmeiser) Bean; S.B., Simmons Coll., 1933; Ed.M., Northeastern U., 1956. Accountant; Scovell, Wellington & Co., Boston, 1948-52; asst. dean Mass. Inst. Tech; Cambridge, 1952-60, 1st dean women, 1959-60; dean residence Brandeis U., Waltham, Mass., 1960-64; exec. dir. Women's Ednl. and Indsl. Union, Boston, 1964-74. Pres. Camp Fire Girls Greater Boston, 1968-72, mem. regional com., 1968-70, mem. nat. council, 1968—, 1st v.p. nat. council, 1971—; bd. dirs. Blue Hill council Girl Scouts Am., 1967-70, Back Bay Assn., 1967-71; pres. Ind. Credit Union, Boston, 1967-74. Mem. Mass. Commn. Status of Women, 1972-74. Trustee Hathaway House Bookshop, Wellesley. Recipient Top Hat award Nat. Fedn. Bus. and Profl. Women's Clubs, 1968. Mem. Am. Assn. U. Women, Nat., Mass. assns. women deans and counselors, Mass. Soc. for Univ. Edn. women (treas.). Home: 10508 Oak Ridge Dr Sun City AZ 85351

BEANE, DOROTHY GENE MOORE, med. editor; b. Ft. Worth, May 8, 1927; d. Elmer Harrison and Rossye Leila (Cornelius) Moore; A.B., N.M. Highlands U., 1950; grad. student, Chgo. Tchrs. Coll., 1958, Art Inst. Chgo., 1959; m. Ralph Clements Beane, May 22, 1964; 1 dau., Linda Alison Aldridge. Tchr. English and psychology, also librarian pub. sch. system, Newark and Hardy, Ark., 1949-51; practice accounting, Batesville, Ark., 1951-55; editor World Book Ency., Chgo., 1958-59; asst. editor U. Tex. M.D. Anderson Hosp. and Tumor Inst., Houston, 1959-65, asso. editor, 1965-67, 70—; asst. instr., editor radiology and neurophysiology Baylor Coll. Medicine, Houston, 1967-69; asst. prof. med. and tech. writing U. Tex. Health Scis. Center, Houston, 1971—, lectr. dental and tech. writing Dental Br., 1973; instr. piano, 1947-49, drawing and painting, 1951-55; editorial cons. Beane Photography and Advt., Houston, 1970—. Invited press relations officer ann. meetings Am. Assn. Cancer Research, 1963, 64; asst. investigator oncological word bank Nat. Cancer Inst. grant, 1967. Mem. Am. Med. Writers Assn., Bus. and Profl. Women's Club, Soc. Tech. Communications, Gulf Coast Lhasa Apso Club, Houston Cat Club, Conservative Arts Assn., Pi Beta Phi. Episcopalian. Home: 3902 Colerdige St Houston TX 77005

BEANE, KATHLEEN BURCH, advt. co. exec.; b. Salt Lake City, June 27, 1918; d. Roy Alton and Kathryn Francis (Allred) Burch; student U. Utah, 1935-37; m. Kenneth W. Beane, Oct. 8, 1937 (div. Dec. 1964); children—Patricia, Michael W., Christopher K. Accountant Harris & Love, Inc., Salt Lake City, 1956-70; media dir., 1970—, also corporate sec., 1969—. Active Salt Lake City Council Boy Scouts Am., 1970—, treas., 1971—. Mem. Advt. Club Salt Lake City. Republican. Presbyn. Home: 1870 Downington Av Salt Lake City UT 84108 Office: 1515 Walker Bank Blvd Salt Lake City UT 84111

BEAR, ELIZABETH MARIE, educator; b. Fort Totten, N.Y., Jan. 23, 1933; d. Charles Earl and Frances (DiLorenzo) Bear; B.S. with honors, U. Cal. at Berkeley, 1956; M.S., Wayne State U., 1958; certified nurse-midwife Cath. Maternity Inst., 1966. Staff nurse U. Cal. Med. Center, San Francisco, 1956-57; instr. U. Fla. Coll. Nursing, 1958-64; pub. health nurse Monterey County Health Dept., Salinas, Cal., 1964-65; asst. prof. U. N.M. Coll. Nursing, Albuquerque, 1966-70, asso. prof., 1970-72, chmn. maternal-child nursing, 1967-72; asso. prof., coordinator nurse-midwifery U. Ky. Coll. Nursing, Lexington, 1973—. Cons. Community Maternity Inst., Santa Fe, 1966-72. Mem. Am. Assn. U. Profs., Am., Ky. nurses assns., Am. Coll. Nurse-Midwifery, (com. on clin. practice), Nurses Assn. Obstetrics and Gynecology (mem. com. by-laws 1969-70, mem. com. on certification 1973—), Nat. League Nursing, Photog. Soc. Am., Albuquerque Childbirth Edn. Assn. (adv. bd. 1969—). Club: Sierra. Mem. editorial bd. Jour. Obstet. and Gynecol. Nursing, 1972—. Exhibited photography Sheldon Swope Art Gallery, Terre Haute, Ind., 1968. Home: 3260 Waterford Park Lexington KY 40502

BEARD, ALICE GAMBLE (MRS. OWEN WAYNE BEARD), educator; b. Rochester, Minn., Aug. 29, 1919; d. Joseph William and Isable Florence (Huggins) Gamble; B.S., U. Minn., 1942, M.D., 1944; m. Owen Wayne Beard, Apr. 9, 1944; children—Margaret (Mrs. Gary Wayne Cage), William King, Barbara Jo. Intern U. Tex. at Galveston, 1945-47, resident pediatrics, 1945-47; asst. prof. pediatrics U. Ark. Med. Center, Little Rock, 1948-58, asso. prof., 1958-70, prof., 1970—. Mem. Am. Acad. Pediatrics (com. fetus and newborn 1965-68), Alpha Omega Alpha. Contbr. articles to profl. jours. Home: 7008 Rockwood Rd Little Rock AR 72206

BEARD, ANNE KATHERINE ZIERDT, evaluator and research specialist criminal justice systems; b. Verona, Pa., Feb. 1, 1926; d. Conrad Henry and Leora (Harshberger) Zierdt; B.A., Pa. State U., 1947; M.S., Cal. State U. at San Jose, 1972; m. Joseph P. Brady, Nov. 16, 1946 (div. 1958); children—Jo Anne, Laurie Ann; m. 2d, William E. Melby, Oct. 23, 1964 (div. 1967); m. 3d, Samuel R. Beard, Apr. 27, 1968. Lab. technician Vernay Labs., Inc., Yellow Springs, O., 1955-56, research engr., 1956-62; systems engr. FMC Corp., Central Engring. Labs., Santa Clara, Cal., 1962-68, human factors and safety engr. Ordnance Engring. Div., San Jose, Cal., 1968-70; criminal justice systems analyst Regional Criminal Justice Planning Bd., Santa Clara County (Cal.), 1971-73; planner/evaluator criminal justice systems Chgo. regional office law Enforcement Assistance Adminstrn. Dept. Justice, Des Plaines, Ill., 1973-74; evaluation and research specialist Ill. Law Enforcement Commn., Chgo., 1974—. Mem. Human Factors Soc., Delta Gamma. Home: 2144 Lincoln Park West Apt 19B Chicago IL 60614 Office: 120 S Riverside Plaza Chicago IL 60606

BEARD, MARION LOIS PATTERSON (MRS. FRANCIS E. BEARD), artist, educator; b. nr. Vincennes, Ind., Nov. 3, 1909; d. George M. and Mattie (Purcell) Patterson; B.S., Ind. State U., 1931; M.F.A., U. Syracuse, 1942; m. Francis E. Beard, Dec. 22, 1963. Art supr. Knox County, Ind. 1930—; art supr. Vincennes City Schs., 1936—, now supr. art edn.; faculty mem. adult edn. art dept. Ind. U., Vincennes U., 1951; critic tchr. supervised teaching in art Ind. State Tchrs. Coll., 1957—, Ind. U., 1961-62; lectr. on travel, art. One woman show H. Lieber Art Gallery, Indpls., 1967; exhibited water colors Am. Water Color Soc., N.Y. Water Color Club, 1941, Hoosier Salon, yearly, 1942—, Ind. Artists-John Herron Art Museum, 1942-44, Nat. Assn. Women Artists, Swope Art Gallery, 1947-49, Ind. Artists, Inc., 1948, 2 paintings in 34th Nat. exhbn. Ogunquit (Me.) Art Center, 1954. Recipient Margaret George Bridwell Meml. prize, 1st award Hoosier Salon, 1942; hon. mention Ind. Artist, 1942; first award William H. Block prize, Hoosier Salon, 1948, 2d award Wabash Valley Artists, 1948, 1st in water color, 1950. Mem. Western Arts Assn. (state membership chmn. 1952-53), Nat. (state membership chmn. 1952-53), Ind. art edn. assns., Ind. Artists' Club, Inc., Art Assn. Indpls., Nat. Assn. Women Artists, N.E.A., Ind., Vincennes tchrs. Assn., Hoosier Art Salon, Am. Assn. U. Women, Marquis Bibliog. Soc., Psi Iota Xi. Presbyn. Home: Rural Delivery 1 Vincennes IN 47591 Office: 300 N 6th St Vincennes IN 47591

BEARD, MILDRED PAULENE, social worker; b. Frankfort, Ind.; d. Benjamin H. and Mae (Brammell) Beard; B.S. in Journalism, Butler U.; M.A., Ind. U., 1955. Supr. complaints and appeals Ind. Dept. Pub. Welfare, 1939-44, dir. pub. relations, editor 1944-53; dir. community relations, family counselor Family Service Assn. Indpls., 1953-61; dir. social services Methodist Hosp. of Ind,, Indpls., 1962—; writer-producer radio series People Are My Business, 1955-60, Friend of Family, 1957-60, weekly TV series Friend of Family, 1959-61, Bd. dirs. Meals on Wheels, Inc. also v.p., mem. exec. com. Nominated Peabody award; recipient 1st Pl. award for recognition outstanding achievement in developing pub. understanding of needs of families, 1963. Fellow Meth. Hosp. Found. Mem. Nat. Assn. Social Workers, Acad. Certified Social Workers, Soc. Hosp. Social Work Dirs., Am. Hosp. Assn., Theta Sigma Phi. Mem. Christian Ch. Mem. Order Eastern Star. Contbr. articles to nat. mags., profl. jours. Home 365 S Emerson Av Indianapolis IN 46219 Office: Social Service Dept Methodist Hosp 1604 N Capitol Av Indianapolis IN 46202

BEARDEN, MILDRED KING, educator; b. Jackson, Miss.; d. Leonard Decatur and Sue (King) Bearden; student Piedmont Coll., 1916-17; A.B. cum laude, Anderson Coll., 1921; student U. Va., 1923; M.A., U. S.C., 1936. Tchr. English, history Fruitland Inst., Hendersonville, N.C., 1921-22, and S.C. high schs. at Piedmont, 1922-24, Westminster, 1924-38, 58-63, pub. speaking coach, 1958-63; tchr. English and history, Walhalla, 1938-58; asst. prof. English, Lander Coll., Greenwood, S.C., 1963-65; prof. English, Anderson (S.C.) Coll., 1965-69; prof. Toccoa Falls (Ga.) Bible Coll., 1969-70; corr. Greenville (S.C.) News, 1945—; column writer Jour.-Tribune, Seneca, S.C., 1962—. Mem., sec. bd. women visitors U. S.C., 1940-50; adviser, sec. S.C. Scholastic Press Assn., 1960-63. Mem. Nat., Ga.-S.C. coll. English assns., Nat. Council Tchrs. English (S.C. judge achievement awards contest 1969, dir. 1957-59), S.C. Speech Assn., South Atlantic Modern Lang. Assn., Internat. Platform Assn., Am. Assn. U. Women. Democrat. Baptist. Clubs: Anderson College Campus; As You Like It (sec. 1958-60). Home: 201 Broad St Westminster SC 29693

BEARDMORE, DOROTHEA ALICE SPAULDING (MRS. ALFRED ANDREW BEARDMORE), vocational rehab. counselor; b. Fargo, N.D., Oct. 4, 1919; d. Charles Walter and Laura Bird (Young) Spaulding; student MacMurray Coll., 1937-38; B.A., U. Ia., 1941; m. Alfred Andrew Beardmore, Apr. 15, 1942; children—Laird (Mrs. Henry Fieger), Thomas Charles. Daycamp and established camp dir. Girl Scouts U.S.A., Waseca, Minn., 1944-47; center counselor Crestview Rehab. Center, State Dept. Pub. Instrn., Charles City, Ia., 1966-67, vocational rehab. field counselor Mason City dist. office, Div. Rehab. and Edn. Services, 1968—. Instr. water safety A.R.C., Charles City, Ia., 1948-52. Mem. Floyd County Republican Central Com., 1950-56, sec., 1954-56; del. Rep. State Conv., 1950-52. Bd. dirs. North Ia. council Girl Scouts U.S.A., also mem. regional camp com.; trustee Charles City Pub. Library. Mem. Nat., Ia. rehab. assns., Ia. Rehab. Counselor's Assn. (sec. 1971-72), Am. Assn. U. Women, D.A.R., P.E.O., Kappa Kappa Gamma. Conglist. Club: Women's (Charles City). Home: Cedar Crest Lane Charles City IA 50616 Office: 111 2d St Mason City IA 50401

BEARDSLEE, BETHANY, soprano; b. Lansing, Mich., Dec. 25, 1927; d. Walter and Ella (Simpson) Beardslee; B.Mus., Mich. State U.; student Juilliard Inst.; m. Godfrey Winham, July, 1957; children—Baird, Christopher. Singer modern music, contemporary vocal music, 1951—; appearances major contemporary festivals U.S. and Can., also Internat. Soc. Contemporary Music. League Composers, Composers Forum, B. de Rothschild Found, Fromm Found., Camera Concerts, Chgo. Contemporary Concerts, Caramoor Festival, Tanglewood, Library of Congress; singer in resident seminar advanced mus. studies Princeton, 1960; mem. N.Y. Pro Musica Antiqua, 1958-60; premier singer numerous young Am. composers; soloist with Boston, Minn., St. Louis, Detroit symphonies, N.Y., Buffalo philharmonics; recordings for Am. Recording Soc., Dial Records, Epic Records, Columbia Records, CRI Records, Acoustics Research Records. Recipient Laurel Leaf award Am. Composers Alliance, 1962; Concert Soloists award Ford Found. 1962. Address: River Rd Belle Mead NJ 08502

BEARDSLEY, M'LIZ MCLENDON (MRS. CHARLES HAROLD BEARDSLEY), writer, educator; b. Phoenix, Feb. 23, 1939; d. John Benjamin and Winzola (Poole) McLendon; A.A., Am. U., 1957, B.A., 1960; student Sorbonne, U. Paris, 1960; m. Charles Harold Beardsley, June 3, 1961; children—Charles Sean, Patrick Colin. Copy-girl, reporter Washington Post, 1955-58; teen editor U.S. Lady Mag., Washington, 1955-58; editorial staff asst. Washington Daily News, 1958; staff asst., asst. program dir. WRC, NBC-TV, Washington, 1959; writer Washington Post, U.S. Lady Mag., Paris, France, 1960; staff writer CBS, Washington, 1961-62; writer Am. and Brit. publs., Gmunden, Austria, 1965-67; writer, editor Diner's Choice column Sentinel Newspapers, Washington, 1968—; mem. teaching staff Georgetown Day Sch., Washington, 1967-71. Mem. Coll. Art Assn., Soc. Archtl. Historians, Alpha Chi Omega, Theta Sigma Phi, Pi Delta Epsilon. Home: 5315 Manning Pl NW Washington DC 20016

BEARE, MURIEL ANITA NIKKI BRINK (MRS. RICHARD AUSTIN BEARE), pub. relations co. exec.; b. Detroit, Mar. 7, 1928; d. Elbert Stanley and Dorothy Margaret (Welch) Brink; student Northwestern Mich. Community Coll., 1951, Miami-Dade Jr. Coll., 1970, 73; m. Richard Austin Beare, June 15, 1946; 1 dau., Sandra Lee

(Mrs. Joseph Johnston, Jr.). Writer Key West (Fla.) Citizen, 1959, Miami (Fla.) News 1967; field dir. Fla. Project Hope, 1967-68, southeastern area dir., 1968-69; asst. v.p. for pub. relations I/D Assos., Inc., Miami 1969-70; pres. Nikki Beare & Assos., Miami, Fla., 1971—; v.p. South Fla. office Cherenson, Carroll & Holzer, Livingston, N.J., 1973. Chmn. adv. bd. Met. Dade County Library, 1964; vice chmn. Met. Dade County Commn. Status Women, 1971-73; mem. Met. Gen. Land Use Master Planning Com., 1973, Govs. Com. Employment Handicapped, 1970-72. Mem. Dade County Dem. Exec. Com., 1972-74; founding mem. Nat. Women's Polit. Caucus, 1971—; candidate Fla. Senate, 1974. Recipient Silver Image award Fla. Pub. Relations Assn., 1967-68. Mem. Fla. Pub. Relations Soc. Am., Greater Miami, South Dade chambers commerce, League Women Voters, Nat. Orgn. for Women, Hist. Assn. So. Fla., Friends of Everglades, Antique Bottle Collectors Assn. Fla. Author: Pirates, 1961; Pineapples and People, Tales and Legends of Florida Keys From Turtle Soup to Coconuts, 1964; Bottle Bonanza, A Handbook for Glass Collectors, 1965. Editor: Feminist Directory, 1973. Home: 14301 SW 87th Av Miami FL 33158 Office: 7220 SW 61 Ct South Miami FL 33143

BEARMAN, JANE RUTH (MRS. SAUL FRANCES), artist; b. Mpls., Sept. 12, 1917; d. Arthur Samuel and Sarah Ruth (Berman) Bearman; student Mpls. Art Inst., 1932-37, Am. Acad. Art, 1934-35, Chgo. Inst. Art, 1935-36; B.A., U. Minn., 1937; m. Saul Frances, Nov. 2, 1941; children—David J., Sally Ann. Advt. artist, Mpls., 1937-41; art dir. N.Y.C. Dept. War Tng., 1941-45; author, illustrator children's books, N.Y.C., 1945-60; lectr. Seton Hall U., South Orange, N.J., 1969-70; exhibited in one-man shows Panoras Gallery, N.Y.C., 1966, Loyola U., Chgo., 1970-71, Brandeis U., Waltham, Mass., 1968-69, Hallmark Gallery, Kansas City, Mo., 1966-67, U. N.M., 1967-68, Montclair (N.J.) Coll., 1965, Paper Mill Playhouse Gallery, Millburn, N.J., 1970, Carver Mus., Tuskegee Inst., Ala., 1968-69, Caldwell (N.J.) Coll., 1974; represented in traveling exhibitions in Contemporary Am. Graphics, 1965-66, Thirty Artists in Watercolor and Casein, 1970-71, N.J. Printmakers, 1969-70, Impressions in Water Color, 1969-70, Old Testament, 1970—. Pres., Livingston (N.J.) P.T.A., 1960-61; pres. Am. Field Service, Livingston, 1960-61. Bd. friends Livingston Library, 1958-65. Recipient First in Graphics, Montclair Mus. Annual State Exhbn., 1962; First award, Medal of Honor, Painters and Sculptors Soc. Ann. Nat., 1962, Bainbridge award, 1974; First in Oils award Hunterdon Ann. State Exhbn., 1965; Mary Yelen prize Nat. Assn. Women Artists, 1970, Medal of Honor, 1973. Mem. Nat. Assn. Women Artists, Painters and Sculptors Soc. N.J., N.J. Water Color Soc., Artists Equity. Author and illustrator: Mother Goose ABC, 1946; Passover Party, 1966; David, 1966; Jonathan, 1966. Contbr. articles and works to profl. jours. and books. Home and office: 30 Spier Dr Livingston NJ 07039

BEASOM, NANCY ANN HIBBS (MRS. RONALD LIGHTNER BEASOM), craftsman, occupational therapist; b. Kansas City, Kan., Nov. 2, 1936; d. Albert Lawrence and Ruth Augusta (Badgley) Hibbs; student Pa. State U., 1954-56; B.S., U. Pa., 1958; m. Ronald Lightner Beasom, June 14, 1958; children—Kim Leslie, Jeffrey Craig, Bryn Ann. Silversmith, designer and creator silver jewelry, 1958—; lectr.-demonstrator design and creation of silver jewelry; vol. occupational therapist, rehab. div. Bryn Mawr Hosp. at Rush Hosp., Malvern, Pa., 1971; instr. gymnastics Harrison Gymnastic Sch., Cabrini Coll., Wayne, Pa., 1972, 73. Occupational therapy cons. for vol. services Easter Seal Soc., 1968; den leader Cub Scouts, 1968, 69. Campaign worker Rep. party, 1970-73. Mem. Am., Eastern Pa. occupational therapy assns., Gen. Alumni Soc. U. Pa., Pi Beta Phi. Lutheran. Home: 1614 Raewyck Dr West Chester PA 19380

BEATMAN, LILLIAN EILEEN PISETSKY (MRS. LESLIE HARVEY BEATMAN), lawyer; b. Hartford, Conn., Apr. 30, 1931; d. Benjamin and Mildred (Rozinsky) Pisetsky; A.A., Hartford Coll. for Women, 1951; student U. Hartford, 1955-56; B.S., St. Joseph Coll., 1956; postgrad. N.Y.U., 1957, 58; J.D., U. Conn., 1959; m. Leslie Harvey Beatman, Sept. 13, 1952; children—Joelle Carson, Matthew Krauss, Anthony Falperin, Bobbitt Solomon. Purchasing asst. Chandler Evans Control Systems div. Colt Industries, Inc., West Hartford, Conn., 1952-54; tchr. pub. schs., Hartford, 1956-57; partner Beatman & Beatman, Pub. Accountants, New Britain, Conn., 1957—; admitted to Conn. bar, 1959; practiced in New Britain, 1959—; mem. firm Lillian E. P. Beatman, 1959—; v.p., sec., dir. Cardinal Control Co., Inc., Kensington, Conn., J.B. Lewis & Co., Inc., Kensington; sec., dir, Towne House Motor Hotel, Inc. Worker lawyers div. A.R.C., New Britain, 1963-64; counselor Hartford Jewish Community Center, 1955; mem. camp com. New Britain YMCA, 1973—, corporator, 1974—. Mem. Am., Conn., Hartford County, New Britain bar assns., Comml. Law League. Club: Soroptimist (sec. New Britain 1961-62, v.p., 1962-64, pres. 1964-65, dir. 1965-66). Home: 12 W Normandy Dr West Hartford CT 06107 Office: 261 Kensington Rd Kensington CT 06037

BEATON, MAXINE BAILEY (MRS. WILLIAM BEATON), librarian; b. Belchertown, Mass., Apr. 13, 1915; d. Henry I. and Mabel (Ojier) Bailey; B.L.S., Simmons Coll., 1936; student Boston U., 1938; m. William Beaton, Nov. 9, 1947; 1 son, Bruce Bailey. Librarian, Mass. Gen. Hosp. Sch. Nursing Library, Boston, 1937-39; bibliotherapist N.E. Deaconess Hosp., Boston, 1936; asst. librarian Bellevue Hosp. Sch. Nursing Library, N.Y.C., 1939-41; med. librarian Burbank Hosp., Fitchburg, Mass., 1942-43; counselor Ft. Logan AAF Hosp., Denver, 1943-45; med. librarian Presbyn. Med. Center, Denver, 1951—. Cons., Colo. Assn. Nursing Homes, 1966—, Valley View Med. Center, 1971, Denver Med. Soc., 1971—; communication instr. Presbyn. Med. Center, 1962—, also editor monthly newsletter; library cons. Denver Clinic, 1963—. Mem. Colo. Council for Library Devel., 1968-70. Mem. Spl. Library Assn. (chmn. hosp. div. 1956-57, consultation officer Colo. chpt. 1971-72), Colo. Library Assn. (v.p. 1968-69). Home: 648 Albion St Denver CO 80220 Office: 1719 E 19th Av Denver CO 80218

BEATTIE, DIANA SCOTT (MRS. BENJAMIN HOWARD BEATTIE), biochemist, educator; b. Cranston, R.I., Aug. 11, 1934; d. Kenneth Allen and Lillian Francis (Barton) Scott; B.A., Swarthmore Coll., 1956; M.S., U. Pitts., 1958, Ph.D., 1961; m. Benjamin Howard Beattie, June 30, 1956; children—Elizabeth, Sara, Rachel, Ruth. Research asso. U. Pitts., 1961-67, VA Hosp., Pitts., 1967-68; asst. prof. Mount Sinai Sch. Medicine, N.Y.C., 1968-70, asso. prof., 1970—, mem. grad. faculty biomed. scis. City U. N.Y., 1968—, biochemistry, 1971—, biology, 1974—. NIH grantee, 1966—, NSF grantee, 1970—. Mem. Am. Soc. Biol. Chemists, Am. Soc. Cell Biology, Biophysics Soc. Contbr. articles to profl. jours. Research subcellular biochemistry, mitochondrial metabolism and biogenesis. Home: 141-21 33d Av Flushing NY 11354 Office: Dept Biochemistry Mount Sinai Sch Medicine Fifth Av and 100th St New York City NY 10029

BEATTIE, NORA MAUREEN, actuary; b. Bklyn., July 10, 1925; d. Robert G. and Eileen (Geaney) Beattie; B.A. summa cum laude, St. John's U., 1947, M.S., 1949. Asst. actuary N.Y. Life Ins. Co., N.Y.C., 1960-63, asso. actuary, 1963-67, actuary, 1967-71, 2d v.p., 1971-74, v.p., actuary, 1974—. Fellow Am. Acad. Actuaries, Soc. Actuaries; mem. Bus. and Profl. Women's Club (treas. Wall St. br. 1969-71, Woman of Year award N.Y. br. 1968). Club: N.Y. Actuaries. Home: 85 Livingston St Brooklyn NY 11201 Office: 51 Madison Av New York City NY 10010

BEATTY, BEULAH LEE COOPER (MRS. JOHN DAY BEATTY), club woman, genealogist; b. Louisburg, N.C., May 28, 1901; d. Willie Jackson and Annie Laura (Bowden) Cooper; student Louisburg Coll., 1918-19, 25-26; m. John Day Beatty, July 14, 1926; children—Laura Day (Mrs. Clyde Buchanan Rosser), Beulah Cooper (Mrs. Beulah B. Andrews), Neill McLaurin. Genealogist, 1959—. Historian Bladen County Hist. Soc., 1963—; pres. Bladen Star chpt. U.D.C., 1961-64, div. v.p., 1964-66, treas. N.C. div.; registrar Lord Craven chpt. Colonial Dames 17th Century, 1964-72. Active civic, polit. affairs Bladen County. Mem. Daus. Founders and Patriots Am. (state registrar 1970—), Huguenot Soc. S.C., Nat. Geneal. Soc., New Eng. Historic Geneal. Soc., D.A.R. (regent Battle of Elizabethtown chpt. 1971-73), N.C. Soc. County and Local Historians, Lost Colony. Democrat. Presbyn. Home: PO Box 905 Elizabethtown NC 28337

BEATTY, HAZEL MARIAN COWLES (MRS. CLARENCE EARL BEATTY), ret. educator; b. Cedar Springs, Mich.; d. Corwin Newell and Gracie (Story) Cowles; student Grand Rapids Jr. Coll., 1920; certificate Ferris State U., 1929; B.S., Wayne State U., 1946, M.E., 1955; m. Clarence Earl Beatty, Apr. 6, 1923 (dec. Mar. 1963); children—Richard Earl, Marianne (Mrs. Robert Morris Montgomery III). Tchr. rural schs. Kent County (Mich.), 1921-42, Macomb County, 1942-46; tchr. mentally handicapped Grand Rapids (Mich.) Pub. Schs., 1946-65. Recipient Distinguished Service award Mich. Congress P.T.A.'s Fellow Am. Assn. Mental Deficiency; mem. Am. Assn. U. Women, Mich. Edn. Assn., Nat., Grand Rapids edn. assns., Wayne State U. Alumni, D.A.R. Republican. Conglist. Mem. Order of Eastern Star. Author articles in field. Home: 2409 Southview Dr Lexington KY 40503

BEATTY, MARIAN CHANDLER, pub. relations exec.; b. Cleve., May 26, 1937; d. Robert and Alice Marian (Grinnell) Beatty; B.A., Pa. State U., 1958, M.A., 1962. News reporter WELM Radio, Elmira, N.Y., 1958-61, WHAM, Rochester, N.Y., 1962—; publs. editor Ayerst Labs., N.Y.C., 1962-69; communications specialist J.C. Penney Co., N.Y.C., 1969—. Mem. Am. Mgmt. Assn., Women in Communications, Phi Kappa Phi, Delta Gamma. Office: 1301 Sixth Av New York City NY 10019

BEATTY, PATRICIA JEAN (MRS. JOHN LOUIS BEATTY), author; b. Portland, Ore., Aug. 26; d. Walter Marcus and Jessie Pauline (Miller) Robbins; B.A., Reed Coll., 1944; postgrad. U. Ida., 1947-48, U. Wash., 1950; m. John Louis Beatty, Sept. 14, 1950; 1 dau., Ann Alexandra. Tchr. high sch., Portland, also Coeur d'Alene, Ida., 1947-50; tchr. creative writing U. Cal. at Riverside, 1967-69, U. Cal. at Los Angeles, 1968-69. Recipient Commonwealth Club of Cal. medal for children's novel, 1966, So. Cal. Council Lit. for Children and Young People's medal, 1967. Mem. Authors Guild, Cal. Writers Guild, Riverside Bus. and Profl. Women's Club, Riverside Roundtable Women's Orgns. (pres. 1972-73). Author: Bonanza Girl, 1962; At the Seven Stars, 1963; Nickel Plated Beauty, 1964; Campion Towers, 1965; Donkey for the King, 1966; Royal Dirk, 1966; Queen's Wizard, 1967; Me., California Perkins, 1968; Hail Columbia, 1970; Sea Pair, 1970; Long Way to Whiskey Creek, 1971; King's Knight's Pawn, 1971; O The Red Rose Tree, 1972; Holdfast, 1972; Red Rock over the River, 1973; Bad Bell of San Salvador, 1973; How Many Miles to Sundown, 1974; Master Rosalind, 1974. Home: 3113 Wendell Way Riverside CA 92507

BEATY, BETTY, ret. educator; b. Walnut Grove, Ky.; d. Henry H. and Mary Ann (Riddle) Beaty; B.S., U. Cin., 1942; A.M., U. Ky., 1951; Ed.D., Ind. U., 1956; postgrad. U. Southampton, U. London, summer 1960. Tchr. pub. elementary schs., Ky., 1926-44; exec. dir. Lexington, Fayette County council Girl Scouts U.S.A., 1944-50; cooperating tchr. U. Sch. U. Ky., 1950-53; teaching asso. Ind. U., 1953-54, lectr. edn., 1955-56; faculty U. Cin., 1956-71, now prof. emeritus Coll. Edn. and Home Econs. Mem. Nat. Council Tchrs. English, Am. Assn. Emeriti, Assn. Childhood Edn. Internat., Internat. Reading Assn., Kappa Delta Pi, Delta Kappa Gamma (pres. chpt. 1966-67, profl. affairs state com. 1971-73). Club: Zonta Internat. Mem. publs. com. Childhood Edn., 1966-68. Address: Rural Route 1 Box 401 Somerset KY 45201

BEATY, MARJORIE HECKEL (MRS. DONALD WILLIAM BEATY), educator; b. Buffalo, Jan. 21, 1906; d. Henry George and Josephine Mary (Fisher) Heckel; A.B., U. Rochester, 1928, M.A., 1929; postgrad. Brown U., 1929-31; Ph.D. (fellow), U. Colo., 1939; m. Donald William Beaty, Mar. 30, 1933; children—Debra (Mrs. Albert Baity Blanton II), Mary (Mrs. Joseph Ruey Edelen, Jr.). Grad. asst. Brown U., 1929-31, U. Colo., Boulder, 1935-38; instr. U. S.D., Vermillion, 1931-35, asst. prof. math., 1938-41, 56-58, acting dean of women, 1941, asso. prof. math., 1958-61, prof. math., 1961—, coll. lectr., 1965. Treas. ad hoc com. S.D. Modernization Cts., 1972—. Sec. Clay County Republican Central Com., 1950—. Mem. Am. Math. Soc., S.D. Ednl. Assn., Am. Assn. U. Women, P.E.O., Mortar Bd., Phi Beta Kappa, Sigma Xi, Pi Mu Epsilon, Delta Kappa Gamma, Alpha Lambda Delta, Chi Omega. Conglist. Mem. Order of Eastern Star. Home: 314 Canby St Vermillion SD 57069

BEAUCHAMP, MARGARET MCCLOSKEY, mus. ofcl.; b. Clenolden, Pa., Apr. 25, 1906; d. Samuel and Catherine (McGrath) Linnington; grad. high sch.; m. W.A. McCloskey, June 15, 1927 (dec.); children—Margaret (Mrs. Donald Deforrest), Marylou (Mrs. Elmer E. Miller), Kathleen (Mrs. James Inzerillo), Nancy (Mrs. Heiner Paetzold); m. 2d, Frank Beauchamp. Typist Pa. R.R. Co., Phila., 1924-27; clk. Sears Roebuck & Co., Chester, Pa., 1953-56; mgr. Downes Coal Yard, Chester, 1956-67; ofcl. Friends of the Caleb Pusey House, Swarthmore, Pa., 1968—. Home: 10 Race St Upland PA 19015 Office: Box P Swarthmore PA 19081

BEAUDREAU, ELIZABETH GOUVEIA (MRS. ARTHUR OLIVER BEAUDREAU), hosp. adminstr.; b. Fall River, Mass., Jan. 16, 1918; d. Joseph Fernandes and Gabriella (Andrade) Gouveia; grad. R.I. Hosp. Sch. Nursing, 1939; m. Arthur Oliver Beaudreau, Feb. 25, 1943; children—Arthur Oliver, David G., Mary E. (Mrs. David Ruggiero). Nurse operating room R.I. Hosp., Providence, 1939-42; Westerly (R.I.) Hosp., 1942-43; staff nurse and relief supr. S. County Hosp., Wakefield, R.I., 1946-54, day nurse and supr., 1954-63; nursing supr. Ladd Sch., N. Kingstown, R.I., 1963-68, supr. in-service edn., 1968-72, dir. nurses, 1972—. Supt. nurses jr. home nursing course Shannock (R.I.) V.F.W., 1969. Den mother Richmond Troop cub scouts, Boy Scouts Am., 1956-58; vol. nurse R.I. Spl. Olympics, 1969-72, adult leader, 1972. Served with Nurse Corps, AUS, 1943-45. Mem. R.I. Nurses Assn. (sec.-treas. Ladd Sch. unit 1969-72), R.I. Hosp. Alumnae Assn., Am. Assn. Mental Deficiency. Club: St. Mary's Ladies (Carolina, R.I.). Home: Lewiston Av Kenyon RI 02836 Office: Box 9 North Kingstown RI 02852

BEAUDREAU, THELMA FAY JACKSON (MRS. NED BEAUDREAU), musician, club woman; b. Kiowa, Okla., Nov. 12, 1907; d. George Edmond and Leona May (Harris) Jackson; student San Antonio Coll. Music, 1926-27, Kansas City Conservatory Music, 1929-30, San Angelo Coll., 1948, Tex. Coll. Arts and Industries, 1957-58, 60-61; m. Ned Willard Beaudreau, June 6, 1931; children—Vance Jackson, Marilyn Anne (Mrs. David B. Coulson). Dir., music instr. Lamesa (Tex.) High Sch. Orch., 1925-1926; music instr., Big Spring, Tex., 1927-29, 31-34, Corpus Christi (Tex.) Pub. Schs., 1948-50; tchr. Presbyn. Day Sch., 1952, charter mem. Corpus Christi Symphony, 1945, mem. string sect., 1945—; mem. Jackson-Wade Trio, Dallas, fall 1930; mem. String Ensemble Driscoll Hotel, Corpus Christi, 1941-42. Rec. sec. Harmony Music Club, 1945-47, pres., 1949-51, corr. sec., 1965-67, v.p., 1972—; jr. scrapbook chmn. 5th Dist. Fedn. Music Clubs, Tex., 1956-57; patron Thursday Music Club, Corpus Christi; rec. sec. Corpus Christi chpt. D.A.R., 1955-57, regent, 1958-60, parliamentarian, 1960-62, 74—; chmn. Am. Music com. Tex. Soc. D.A.R., 1961-64, chaplain Regents Club, 1964-66. Recipient 25 year award Corpus Christi Symphony. Mem. Internat. Platform Assn., Music Tchrs. Nat. Assn., Nueces County Hist. Survey Com., Nueces County Hist. Soc., Corpus Christi Symphony Guild, Corpus Christi Music Tchrs. Assn. Episcopalian. Club: Harmony Music (corr. sec. 1965-67, 74—, v.p. 1972-73, sec. past pres.'s assembly 1974—). Address: 109 E Vanderbilt St Corpus Christi TX 78415

BEAUDRY, YVONNE ANGELINA, free-lance writer; b. Claremont, N.H.; d. Alexis Joseph and Lillie Marie (Pratte) Beaudry; U. N.H.; Litt.B. in Journalism, Columbia; m. André D. Sennwald, (dec.). Editor, OWI, Washington, 1945; editor History War Psychiatry, med. history div. War Dept., 1945-46; spl. researcher, writer econ. devel. and fgn. aid plan U.S. Senate Appropriations Com., 1947-48; mem. U.S. Senate comms. missions making econ. survey of Western Europe, 1949-50; free-lance writer nat. and fgn. mags., newspapers, ednl. and religious publs., lit. quars.; translator French plays and scenarios for motion picture cos. Recipient letter of appreciation Govt. of Guatemala, 1971. Mem. Authors League Am., Alpha Chi Omega. Club: Overseas Press Am. (N.Y.C.). Address: Penthouse A 118 W 79th St New York City NY 10024

BEAUFORT, MARGARET, poet; b. Pitts., Jan. 30, 1907; d. Horace Jacob and Louise Rogan (Patterson) Miller; student Tusculum Coll., 1925-26; A.B., U. Tenn., 1929; postgrad. Appalachian State U., 1951-62. Tchr.-librarian Patterson Sch., Lenoir, N.C., 1951-53; tchr.-librarian George Washington Jr. High Sch., Guam, 1962-66; librarian Chalan Pago Elementary Sch., Guam, 1966-70; writer poetry for various publs. including Atlantic Monthly, Poetry Rev. of London, Christendon, Guam Times Weekly. Mem. Poetry Soc. S.C., S.C. Hist. Soc., Charleston Artist Guild. Home: 62 Broad St Charleston SC 29401

BEAUVOIR, SIMONE DE, author; b. Paris, France, Jan. 8, 1908; ed. U. of Paris. Prof. U. Paris, 1931-43. Author: L'Invitee, Le Sang des Autres, Les Bouches Inutiles; Tous les Hommes sont mortels; Pour un moral de l'Ambiguite; Les Mandarins (pub. in English translation), 1956, 1957; Memoirs of a Dutiful Daughter, 1959; Brigitte Bardot and the Lolita Syndrome, 1960; The Mandarins, 1960; The Prime of Life, 1962; Force of Circumstance, 1965. Recipient Prix de Goncourt, 1954. Address: Librarie Callimard 5 rue Sebastien-Bottin Paris 7 France

BEAVER, JOAN EVELYN HEIDEN (MRS. FRED EUGENE BEAVER), artist, educator; b. Detroit, Jan. 19, 1935; d. Frederick Otto and Evelyn (Tinsman) Heiden; B.S., U. Mich., 1957; M.A., Eastern Mich. U., 1965; m. Fred Eugene Beaver, Aug. 25, 1956; children—Michael, Jill. Exhibited one man show Eastern Mich. U., 1965; exhibited in group shows Detroit Artists Market, Rubiner Gallery, Royal Oak, Mich., Left Bank Gallery, Flint, Mich., Three Cities Show-Westland, Mich., others; represented in permanent collections United Meml. Hosp., Greenville, Mich., Luther Manor, Saginaw, Mich., Sinai Hosp., Detroit, Mich. Edn. Assn., Luther Home, Grand Rapids, City of Greenville, Luther Haven, Detroit; tchr. art Dearborn (Mich.) High Sch., 1957-58, Belleville (Mich.) High Sch., 1958, 59, Roosevelt Lab. Sch., Eastern Mich. U., 1959; art specialist Willow Run Pub. Schs., Ypsilanti, Mich., 1965-68, Ann Arbor Pub. Schs., 1968—. Recipient Graphics award Three Cities Show, 1967; 1st prize in graphics Danish Festival, Greenville, 1968, Purchase prize, 1969; Purchase prize Mich. Edn. Assn., 1969; named Outstanding Art Tchr. Mich., 1972. Mem. Nat., Mich. edn. assns., Ann Arbor Art Assn., Ann Arbor Women Painters. Republican. Lutheran. Home: 512 Fairview Circle Ypsilanti MI 48197 Office: 800 Soule Blvd Ann Arbor MI 48104

BEAVERS, DONNA GOETTSCHE (MRS. SHIRLEY CARLIN BEAVERS, JR.), editor; b. Miami, Fla., Aug. 28, 1946; d. Donald John and Peggy (Aper) Goettsche; B.A., High Point Coll., 1968; m. Shirley Carlin Beavers, Jr., Dec. 23, 1967. Editor, Nat. Consumer Finance Assn., Washington, 1968—. Occasional lectr. organized consumer groups, ednl. orgns. Mem. Pub. Relations Soc. Am., Soc. Nat. Assn. Publs. (mem. editorial com. 1972—), Alpha Gamma Delta. Home: 9712 Cymbal Dr Vienna VA 22180 Office: 1000 16th St NW Washington DC 20036

BEBBINGTON, MARGUERITE, librarian; b. Providence, May 16, 1922; d. John and Frances Isabel (Barnes) Bebbington; A.B., Upsala Coll., 1944; M.L.S., Pratt Inst., 1962. Lab. asst. Bakelite Corp., Bloomfield, N.J., 1944-46; with Internat. Nickel Co., N.Y.C., 1946-63; librarian titanium pigment div. N L Industries, Inc., South Amboy, N.J., 1963-70, lit. chemist patent dept., N.Y.C., 1970—. Instr. chem. lit. spl. program summers Montclair State Coll., 1969-72). Blood bank vol. Mountainside Hosp., 1948-58. Mem. Am. Chem. Soc., Spl. Libraries Assn., Am. Assn. U. Women. Clubs: Zonta (Newark); Upper Montclair (N.J.) Women's. Home: 211 Montclair Av Upper Montclair NJ 07043 Office: 111 Broadway St New York City NY 10006

BECCARI, NAN JUDITH HALL (MRS. ARMANO A. BECCARI), educator; b. Marietta, O.; d. Robert Earl and Bernice (Underwood) Hall; B.A. cum laude, U. Miami, 1958, M.Ed., 1961, postgrad., 1970—; m. Turner M. Hiers, Oct. 29, 1942 (div. Dec. 1973); m. 2d, Armano A. Beccari, Aug. 31, 1974. Tchr. pub. schs., Ga., Fla., 1935—; dir. Reading Center, Nova High Sch., Ft. Lauderdale, Fla., 1963—, Lauderdale Reading Clinic, 1965—. Mem. Internat. Reading Assn., Am. Ednl. Research Assn., Am. Assn. U. Women, Nat. Soc. for Study Edn., Kappa Delta Pi, Alpha Delta Kappa, Kappa Kappa Iota, Epsilon Tau Lambda, Phi Lambda Pl, Beta Sigma Phi. Home: 604 NE 9th Av Fort Lauderdale FL 33104

BECK, AUDREY PHILLIPS (MRS. CURT FREDERICK BECK), state legislator; b. Bklyn., Aug. 6, 1931; d. Gilbert Wesley and Mary (Reilly) Phillips; B.A. with high honors and distinction in econs., U. Conn., 1953, M.A., 1955; m. Curt Frederick Beck, Aug. 4, 1951; children—Ronald Pierson, Meredith Wayne. Instr. econs. U. Conn., Storrs, 1960-68; planning economist Windham Regional Planning Agy., 1968; mem. Conn. Ho. of Reps., 1969—, asst. minority leader, 1973—. Vis. prof. practical politics Center Am. Women and Politics, Eagleton Inst. Politics Rutgers U., 1973. Mem. liaison com. Mansfield (Conn.) U., 1967-68, mem. community devel. action program, 1968-71. Mem. Mansfield Bd. Finance, 1965-71, mem. town govt. study com., 1967-68; pres. Tolland County Democratic Assn.; del. Dem. nat. conv., 1972; mem. com. legislative ethics and campaign financing Nat. Legislative Conf., 1973. Recipient outstanding state ofcl. award, 1973. Mem. League Women Voters, Nat. Orgn. Women,

Women's Polit. Caucus. Alert, Women's Legislative Rev., Am. Assn. U. Women, Conn. Fedn. Dem. Women's Clubs Artus, Phi Beta Kappa, Phi Kappa Phi, Gamma Chi Epsilon, Delta Sigma Rho. Home: Dunham Pond Rd Storrs CT 06268

BECK, BETTY LIND (MRS. ROLAND L. BECK), educator; b. Newark, O., Jan. 16, 1907; d. John Huber and Elizabeth (Brooks) Shrock; B.A., DePauw U., 1927; postgrad. Central State Coll. Okla., 1942; M.A., U. Okla., 1951, Ph.D., 1963; m. Roland L. Beck, May 2, 1928; children—John Roland, Betty Beck (Mrs. Robert C. Palmer). Tchr. high sch., Montezuma, N.M., 1927-28, Piedmont, Okla., 1942-44; now chmn. English dept., head div. humanities Grand Canyon Coll., Phoenix. Active Camp Fire Girls, Cub Scouts; mem. North Central Evaluation Com. Secondary Schs., 1970—. Recipient spl. award as Grand Canyon Coll. Outstanding prof., 1973. Mem. Ariz. Intercollegiate Speech League (past pres.), Ariz. Edn. Assn. (pres. sect. 1970-71), Ariz. Coll. Assn. (council), Am. Assn. U. Women, Federated Women's Club, Phi Beta Kappa, Kappa Gamma Epsilon, Theta Sigma Phi, Alpha Phi, Delta Kappa Gamma. Baptist. Kiwani-Ann. Author: Rinsland Teaching Tests for Oklahoma, 1936, 39, 48, 53; co-author English tests. Home: 3631 W Pasadena Av Phoenix AZ 85019

BECK, CAROLYN RISON (MRS. ALAN ADAMS BECK), clubwoman; b. Providence, June 18, 1935; d. Clarence Herbert and Ebba Elvira (Rydberg) Rison; B.A., Smith Coll., 1957; m. Alan Adams Beck, June 28, 1958; children—James Alan, Laura Christina. Editorial asst., div. research and statistics Bd. Govs. Fed. Res. System, 1957-59, statis. asst., 1959-60; ways and means chmn. Alexandria Jr. Woman's Club, 1962, embassy tour chmn., 1962, Santa Claus shop chmn., 1962, treas., 1963-65; co-chmn. junior club Smith Coll. Club Washington, 1964-66, asst. treas., 1966-68, treas., 1968-70, pres., 1970-72, adviser to exec. bd., 1972-73, 74-75, chmn. nominating com., 1973-74, v.p., 1974-75; treas. Potomac Village Garden Club, 1972-73, program chmn., 1973-74; chmn. Lincoln Sch. Washington Alumnae Club, 1959—. Named Outstanding Jr. Clubwoman in No. Va., Va. Fedn. Woman's Clubs, 1963. Presbyn. Home: 10808 Stanmore Dr Potomac MD 20854

BECK, DOROTHY EPPLEY, editor; b. York, Pa., July 22, 1942; d. Alvin Leroy and Dorothy Elizabeth (Eppley) Beck; B.S., Western Md. Coll., 1964; M.A., Am. U., 1967. Journalism tchr. High Point High Sch., Beltsville, Md., 1964-65; mgmt. intern Dept. Army, Washington, 1966-67, writer Research and Devel. News mag., 1967-68, editor Ann. Report Chief Engrs. on Civil Works Activities, chief reports br. Directorate Civil Works, Office Chief Engrs., 1968—. Mem. Army Mgmt. Intern Assn. (pres. 1970-71), Audubon Naturalist Soc. Central Atlantic States (dir. natural history field studies 1973—). Home: 1010 25th St NW Washington DC 20037 Office: Chief Engrs DAEN-CWA-R Dept Army Washington DC 20314

BECK, EMILY MORISON (MRS. HARRY BROOKS BECK, JR.), editor pub. co.; b. Boston, Oct. 25, 1915; d. Samuel Eliot and Elizabeth (Shaw) Morison; B.A., Radcliffe Coll., 1937; postgrad. Newnham Coll., Cambridge, Eng., 1938-39; m. Harry Brooks Beck, Jr., June 1, 1946; children—Cameron Winslow, Gordon Morison, Emily Marshall. Mem. editorial dept. Harper & Bros., N.Y.C., 1939-42; editor Alfred A. Knopf, Inc., 1942-49; reviewer Book of the Month Club, 1950-52; editor Bartlett's Familiar Quotations, 13th edit., 1952-55, Atlantic Monthly Press, 1956-63, Bartlett's Familiar Quotations, 14th edit., 1963-67; asso. editor Atlantic Brief Lives, 1967-71; editor Atlantic Monthly Press, Boston, 1971—. Mem. ladies com. Inst. Contemporary Art, 1960-64. Mem. Phi Beta Kappa. Unitarian (parish com. 1964-67). Home: 4 Homans Lane Canton MA 02021 Office: 8 Arlington St Boston MA 02116

BECK, EVELYN TORTON (MRS. ANATOLE BECK), educator; b. Vienna, Austria, Jan. 18, 1933; d. Max and Irma (Lichtman) Torton; came to U.S., 1940, naturalized, 1945; B.A., Bklyn. Coll., 1954; M.A. (Ford Found. fellow), Yale, 1955; Ph.D. (E.B. Fred fellow), U. Wis., 1969; m. Anatole Beck, Apr. 10, 1954; children—Nina Rachel, Micah Daniel. Lectr. U. Md., College Park, 1971-72; asst. prof. comparative lit. and German U. Wis., Madison, 1972—. Am. Council of Learned Socs. grantee, 1970-71, Nat. Endowment for Humanities fellow, 1973. Mem. Modern Lang. Assn., Am. Comparative Lit. Assn., Am. Assn. U. Profs., Assn. Jewish Studies, Modern Lang. Caucus for Women. Author: Kafka and the Yiddish Theater: Its Impact on his Work, 1971. Translator short stories of Isaac Bashevis Singer, 1970. Home: 4221 Wanetah Trail Madison WI 53711

BECK, FRANCES JOSEPHINE MOTTEY (MRS. JOHN MATTHEW BECK), educator; b. Eleanora, Pa., July 12, 1918; d. George F. and Mary (Wisnieski) Mottey; B.S., Ind. State Tchrs. Coll., 1939; M.A., U. Chgo., 1955; m. John Matthew Beck, Aug. 23, 1941. Jr. visitor Pa. Dept. Pub. Assistance, 1940-41; asst. to the sec. Dept. Edn., U. Chgo., 1952-58, asst. dean of students Grad. Sch. Edn., 1958—; dir. MST Reading Cons. Program, 1968-70; reading instr. Central YWCA, Chgo., 1958-61. Mem. Nat., Ill. assns. women deans and counselors, Internat. Reading Assn., Am. Ednl. Research Assn., Pi Lambda Theta (nat. v.p. 1966-70, nat. 1st v.p. 1971—), Sigma Sigma Sigma, Delta Kappa Gamma. Contbr. articles to profl. jours. Office: 5835 Kimbark Chicago IL 60637

BECK, ISABELLE HERMONA DONLEY, clothing co. exec.; b. Lincoln, Neb., Apr. 16, 1921; d. Herman and Helga (Lindberg) Lindberg; student Knapps Bus. Coll., 1944; m. Frank Dudley Beck, Mar. 23, 1971; 1 son, James A. Asst. buyer Rhodes Dept. Store, Tacoma, Wash., 1944, sportswear buyer, 1945-51; buyer Peoples Dept. Store, Tacoma, 1951-52; buyer No. Comml. Co., Seattle, Wash., 1951-69, mdse. mgr., fashion and children's div., 1969—. Trustee Florence Crittenton Home, Seattle, also rec. sec., 1971—; trustee Ruth Sch. Girls. Soroptimist. Home: Route 6 Box 6745 Bainbridge Island WA 98110 Office: 419 Colman Bldg Seattle WA 98104

BECK, JOAN WAGNER, journalist; b. Clinton, Ia., Sept. 5, 1923; d. Roscoe Charles and Mildred (Noel) Wagner; B.S. in Journalism cum laude, Northwestern U., 1945, M.S. in Journalism, 1947; m. Ernest William Beck, Sept. 9, 1945; children—Christopher, Melinda. Radio script writer O.W.I., Voice of Am., 1945-46; copy writer Marshall Field & Co., 1947-50; feature writer Chgo. Tribune, 1950—, writer syndicated column about young people, 1956-61, writer syndicated column about children, 1961—. Hon. chmn. Mother's March of Dimes Met. Chgo., 1970-72. Exec. com., bd. dirs. Met. Chgo. chpt. March of Dimes-Nat. Found.; trustee Ill. Children's Home and Aid Soc. Recipient Helen Baker Cody award Chgo. Welfare Pub. Relations Bd., 1955; Trans-World Airlines Travel Feature award, 1954; Northwestern U. Alumni Merit award, 1965; Associated Press Feature Series award for Ill., 1964, single feature award, 1965. Mem. Theta Sigma Phi, Alpha Chi Omega (achievement award 1966). Methodist. Clubs: Chicago Press, Lake Forest. Author: How to Raise a Brighter Child, 1967; (with Virginia Apgur) Is My Baby All Right? A Guide to Birth Defects, 1972. Home: 905 Castlegate Ct Lake Forest IL 60045 Office: Chgo Tribune 435 N Michigan Av Chicago IL 60611

BECK, LEILA MAE GRAY (MRS. GEORGE ALFRED BECK), club woman; b. Cuba, Ill., Mar. 28, 1901; d. Frank Eldorado and Josephine (Witter) Gray; student Adrian Coll., 1919-22; m. George Alfred Beck, Sept. 4, 1922; 1 dau., Eleanor Eileen (Mrs. Jack Russell Maddy). Tchr. pub. schs., Ill., 1921-22. Mem. Duluth Campaign Rev. Council (Minn.), 1956—. Mem. Gen., Minn. fedns. women's clubs, Minn. and Duluth P.T.A., Nat. Congress P.T.A., Internat. Platform Assn., Nat. Wildlife Fedn., Matinee Musicale, Delta Delta Delta. Republican. Presbyn. Clubs: Twentieth Century, Women's Institute. Home: 1831 E 2d St Duluth MN 55812

BECK, MARILYN MOHR, editor; b. Chgo., Dec. 17, 1928; d. Max Mohr and Rose (Lieberman) Mohr; A.A., U. So. Cal., 1948; m. Roger Beck, Jan. 8, 1949; children—Mark Elliott, Andrea. Free-lance writer nat. mags., newspapers, Hollywood, Cal., 1959-63; featured Hollywood columnist Valley Times, Citizen News, Hollywood, 1963-65; West Coast editor Sterling Mags., Hollywood, 1963—; featured free-lance entertainment writer Los Angeles Times, 1965-67; Hollywood columnist Bell-McClure Syndicate, 1967-72, also chief West Coast bur.; Hollywood columnist NANA Syndicate, 1967-72; syndicated Hollywood columnist N.Y. Times Spl. Features, 1972—. Recipient Citation of Merit, Los Angeles City Council, 1973. Club: Hollywood Women's Press. Author: Marilyn Beck's Hollywood, 1973. Address: 19653 Wells Dr Tarzana CA 91356

BECK, MARY VIRGINIA, lawyer, assn. exec.; b. Ford City, Pa., Feb. 29, 1908; d. Michael and Anna (Woytowich) Beck; B.A., U. Pitts., 1929, LL.B., 1932; J.D., 1968. Admitted to Mich. bar, 1944; pavilion mgr. Century of Progress, Chgo., 1932-34; group social worker Internat. Inst., Detroit, 1934-35; probation officer, intake supr. Juvenile Ct., Detroit, 1935-47; practice law, Detroit, 1947-50; 1st woman mem. Common Council Detroit, 1950-70, pres. pro tem, 1952-58, pres., acting mayor, 1958-62; mem. Wayne County (Mich.) Bd. Suprs., 1950-69, chmn. ways and means com. 1955-58, port com., 1958-69; now exec. dir. Ukrainian Information Bur., Detroit Mem. Detroit Election Commn., 1958-62, Policemen and Firemen Pension and Retirement System, 1958-62, Gen. Retirement System, 1958-62; mem. Gov.'s Commn. on Status of Women, 1962, Gov.'s Commn. on Econ. Redevel., 1962; initiator establishment of Youth Commn., Detroit, 1955, D. J. Healy Center for non-delinquent children in Wayne County, 1960; sponsor World Wide Ukrainian Art Exhibit, Wayne State U., Detroit, 1960; founder Ukrainian Women's Literary award in field Ukrainian short stories, 1958. Mem. steering com. United Founds.; trustee Ukrainian Tech. Inst. N.Y. Named Detroiter of Week, Detroit Free Press, 1947, Women of Achievement, Detroit newspapers, 1953, Women of Year, Zeta Phi Beta, 1955, Ukrainian of Year, Ukrainian Grads. Club, 1963, Soroptimist Woman of Year, 1968; recipient Ruth Houston Whipple award Plymouth Bus. and Profl. Woman's Club, 1956, award Sports Guild, 1956, award Detroit Dental Soc., 1957, City of Hope award Detroit Cancer Fighters, 1959, Ukrainian Community Service award Ukrainians in Free World, 1960, Plaque award Detroit Am. Vets. World War II, 1967. Mem. Internat. Platform Assn. Club: Southfield Lions (hon.) (Detroit). Editor, pub. Woman World, Ukrainian and English lang. publ. Pitts., 1932-34; editor English sect. Ukrainian Star, Detroit. 1936-38. Address: 2026 Oakman Blvd Detroit MI 48238

BECK, NANCY MANN MCCONNICO (MRS. EARL C. BECK, JR.), clothing store exec.; b. Memphis, Aug. 31, 1931; d. John Davis and Pauline (Hilton) McConnico; grad. So. Sem. and Jr. Coll., 1949; m. Dean Carlton DuBois, Aug. 19, 1950 (div. Nov. 1963); children—Denise Hilton, Dean Carlton; m. 2d, Earl C. Beck, Jr.; 1 son, John Harrington. Asst. buyer, sportswear John Gerber Co., Memphis, 1949-50; fashion coordinator J. Hilton McConnico, Designer, Memphis, 1963-65; buyer, mgr. Bridal Salon, Goldsmiths, Memphis, 1965-70, French Room, 1970-71; partner, v.p. Beck Distbg. Co., Hughes, Ark., 1971—. Press relations Hunter Lane for mayor, 1967. Mem. Internat. Platform Assn., Memphis Arts Council, Memphis Symphony League. Episcopalian. Home: Casa Lorraine Plantation Hughes AR 72348 Office: Route 1 Box 50 Hughes AR 72348

BECK, PHYLLIS WHITMAN (MRS. AARON T. BECK), lawyer; b. N.Y.C., Oct. 7, 1927; d. Irving and Dora (Cukier) Whitman; A.B., Brown U., 1949; J.D., Temple U., 1967; m. Aaron T. Beck, June 4, 1950; children—Roy W., Judith S., Daniel T., Alice W. Admitted to Pa. bar, 1968; mem. firm Duane, Morris & Heckscher, Phila., 1970—; staff atty. Legal Aid of Phila., 1973—. Lectr. in law Temple U. Sch. of Law, Phila., 1972—. Dir. Alpha Corp., 1970—. Atty. Planned Parenthood of Southeastern Pa., Phila., 1971—. Dem. committeewoman, 1955-61. Bd. dirs. Greater Phila. Community Devel. Corp., 1968—, Green Tree Sch., 1972—, Montgomery County Mental Health Clinics, 1971-73. Mem. Am., Pa., Phila. (com. on womens rights 1972—, com. on abortion 1972—) bar assns., Phi Beta Kappa. Club: Cosmopolitan (Phila.). Home: 406 Wynmere Rd Wynnewood PA 19096 Office: 1600 Land Title Bldg Philadelphia PA 19110

BECK, SISTER RICHARD MARIE, coll. adminstr.; b. N.Y.C., May 19, 1935; d. Richard Joseph and Mary (Cody) Beck; B.A., Marymount Manhattan Coll., 1956; M.A., Marquette U., 1961. Registrar, dir. admissions Marymount Coll., Arlington, Va., 1958-60; tchr. Marymount Coll., Quebec, Que., Can., 1961-62; dir. admissions Marymount Coll., Tarrytown, N.Y., 1962-66; acad. dean Marymount Coll., N.Y.C., 1966-67; dean of admissions Marymount Coll., Boca Raton, Fla., 1967—. Mem. Coll. Entrance Exam. Bd. Mem. Fla. Personnel Guidance Assn., Assn. Coll. Admission Counselors, Am. Assn. Collegiate Registrars and Admission Officers. Address: Marymount Coll Boca Raton FL 33432

BECK, ROSEMARIE, painter; b. N.Y.C.; d. Samuel and Margit (Weisz) Beck; A.B., Oberlin Coll., 1944; student Inst. Fine Arts, N.Y. U., 1944-45, Columbia, 1944-45, Atelier Robert Motherwell, 1950; m. Robert Phelps, Sept. 14, 1945; 1 son, Roger. One man shows include Peridot Gallery, N.Y.C., 1953, 55, 56, 59, 60, 63, 65, 66, 68, 70, 72, Woodstock, N.Y., 1949, 50, 51, 52, Vassar Coll. Art Gallery, 1957, 61, Wesleyan U., Middletown, Conn., 1960, State U. N.Y. at New Paltz, 1962, Duke, 1970, Zachary-Waller, Los Angeles, 1971, Kirkland Coll., 1971; group shows include Chgo. Art Inst., 1962, Pa. Acad. Fine Arts, 1954, 66, Whitney Mus. Am. Art, N.Y.C., 1955, 57, 58, Am. Fedn. Arts, 1956, 57, 58, 59, 63, 64, 65, Tate Gallery, London, Eng., 1958, Butler Inst., Indpls., 1962. Kootz Gallery, N.Y.C., 1951, Felix Landau Gallery, Los Angeles, 1962, Am. Fedn. Arts, 1956, 57, 58, 59, 63, 64, 65, Vassar Coll., 1957-58, 61-62, 63-64, Middlebury (Vt.) Coll., 1958, 60, 63, U. Colo., 1960, 63, Nat. Inst. Arts and Letters, 1968, 69, 73; represented in permanent collections Whitney Mus. Art, State U. N.Y. at New Paltz, U. Neb., Lincoln. Grantee Ingram Merrill Found., 1966, Woodstock Found., 1951; Yaddo fellow 1954, 56, 58, 62, 64, 65, 66, 67. Address: 6 E 12th St New York City NY 10003

BECKER, SISTER BARBARA, educator; b. Chgo., Jan. 10, 1932; d. Frank Arthur and Margaret (Flannery) Becker; B.A., Marymount Coll., 1954; M.A., Catholic U. of Am., 1955; Ph.D., Georgetown U., 1965. Prof. chemistry Marymount Coll. of Va., Arlington, 1954-65, Marymount-Manhattan Coll., N.Y.C., 1965-66; prof. chemistry Marymount Coll., Tarrytown, N.Y., 1966-68, dean of students, 1968—. Mem. Am. Chem. Soc., A.A.A.S., Am. Assn. U. Women, Am. Personnel and Guidance Assn. Address: Marymount Coll Tarrytown NY 10591

BECKER, BARBARA KELLER, librarian; b. Findlay, O., Nov. 21, 1923; d. Louis Conrad and Margaret Belle (Holcombe) Keller; A.B., Oberlin Coll., 1945; A.B., U. Mich., 1948, postgrad., 1966-67; postgrad. Hillsdale Coll., 1970, Wayne State U., 1972; m. Jack Becker, Dec. 27, 1947 (div. Oct. 12, 1962); children—Nancy (Mrs. Kenneth Lee Johnson), Anne (Mrs. Frederick Kenneth Warneke), John. Librarian, Jones, Day, Cockley & Reavis, attys., Cleve., 1945-47; fgn. and internat. law acquisitions librarian U. Mich. Law Library, Ann Arbor, 1947-48; asst. librarian Findlay (O.) Pub. Library, 1951-52; librarian Mich. Municipal League, Ann Arbor, 1959-63; asst. librarian Parke, Davis & Co., Ann Arbor, 1963-69, research librarian, 1969—. Cons. Beth Israel Library, Ann Arbor, 1965-67, Planned Parenthood Clinic, Ann Arbor, 1965-66. Pres. Washtenaw County (Mich.) chpt. Muscular Dystrophy Assns. of Am., 1958-59; mem. adv. council Ann Arbor Pub. Library, 1958-63; cookie chmn. Huron Valley Girl Scout Council, Ann Arbor, 1963—. Washtenaw County (Mich.) del. Dem. State Conv., 1948; registered voters file chmn. Ann Arbor (Mich.) Rep. City Com., 1955-57. Mem. Spl. Libraries Assn. (pres. Mich. chpt. 1971-72, treas. pharm. div. 1972—), Med., Washtenaw County (v.p. 1960-61) library assns., Friends of the Ann Arbor Pub. Library (dir. 1963-68, pres. 1967), Women's Aux. Washtenaw County Bar Assn. (dir., treas. 1960-65), Met. Detroit Med. Library Group. Republican. Episcopalian (mem. vestry 1970-73). Mem. Order Eastern Star. Club: Huron Valley Swim (Ann Arbor). Home: 2761 Aurora Ann Arbor MI 48105 Office: 2800 Plymouth Rd Ann Arbor MI 48106

BECKER, BETTIE GERALDINE, artist; b. Peoria, Ill., Sept. 22, 1918; d. Harry Seymour and Magdalene Matilda (Hiller) Becker; B.F.A. cum laude, U. Ill., Urbana, 1940; postgrad. Art Inst. Chgo., 1942-45, Art Student's League, 1946, Ill. Inst. tech., 1948; m. Lionel William Wathall, Nov. 10, 1946; children—Heather Lynn (dec.), Jeffrey Lee. Dept. artist Liberty Mut. Ins. Co., Chgo., 1941-44; with Liberty-Palenskie-Young Studio, 1943-46; free lance illustrator N.Y. Times, Chgo. Tribune, Saturday Rev. Lit., 1948-50; pvt. tutor, tchr. studio classes. Exhibited one-man show Crossroads Gallery, Art Inst. Chgo., 1973; exhibited group shows including Critics' Choice show Art Rental Sales Gallery Art Inst. Chgo., 1972, Evanston-North Shore exhbns., 1964, 65, Chgo. Soc. Artists, 1967, 71, Union League, 1967, 72; represented in permanent collection Witte Meml. Mus., San Antonio; executed mural (with F. Wiater) Talbot Lab. U. Ill., Urbana, 1940. Active Campfire Girls, Chgo., 1968, 70; art chmn., mem. exec. bd. local P.T.A., 1959-60; active various art festivals, 1967—. Recipient Newcomb award U. Ill., 1940. Mem. Chgo. Soc. Artists (rec. sec. 1968—), Renaissance Soc. U. Chgo., Soc. Illustrators, Wis. Arts Council, Alumni Assn. Art Inst. Chgo. Republican. Unity Ch. Home: 1817 Asbury Av Evanston IL 60201

BECKER, BEVERLY J., educator; b. Paterson, N.J.; d. George L. and Adelaide (Hulse) Becker; A.B., Wellesley Coll., 1951; M.Ed. U. N.C., 1954; Ph.D., U. Ore., 1967; student Temple U., 1952-53. Instr., dept. phys. edn. U. Neb. at Lincoln, 1954-56, Mt. Holyoke Coll., South Hadley, Mass., 1956-59; prof., chmn. dept. phys. edn. Skidmore Coll., Saratoga Springs, N.Y., 1959—. Fellow Am. Coll. Sports Medicine; mem. Nat. Found. for Health, Phys. Edn. and Recreation, Nat. (chmn. finance com. 1974-75), Eastern (mem. exec. bd. 1968, 70—, pres. 1974-75), assns. phys. edn. for coll. women, A.A.H.P.E.R., N.Y. State Assn. Health, Phys. Edn. and Recreation, Assn. Women Phys. Educators N.Y., N.Y. State Council Adminstrs. Health, Phys. Edn. and Recreation, Am. Assn. U. Profs., North Am. Soc. Psychology of Phys. Activity and Sport. Home: PO Box 128 Haskell NJ 07420 Office: Phys Edn Dept Skidmore Coll Saratoga Springs NY 12866

BECKER, ELEANOR HOLDEN, mag. editor; b. Upland, Pa., Sept. 15, 1924; d. James Minshall and Elizabeth Catherine (Jones) Holden; B.A., Coll. William and Mary, 1946; m. Ernest Lovell Becker, July 12, 1922; 1 son, Frederick Holden Gernerd. Sr. editor Ladies' Home Jour., N.Y.C., 1953-62; fashion dir. B. Altman & Co., N.Y.C., 1962-63; dir. fashion publicity Monsanto Textiles, N.Y.C., 1965-66; exec. editor Bride's mag., N.Y.C., 1966—. Guest lectr. Drexel Inst. Tech., Phila., 1962, Phila. Mus. Sch. Art, 1970; instr. creative fashion writing Fashion Inst. Tech., N.Y.C., 1964-65. Recipient Best of Year awards for art direction Printing Week Graphics Arts Exhibit, 1959, 62. Mem. N.Y. Fashion Group, Home Fashions League, Assn. Interior Designers, Phila. Art Alliance, Kappa Alpha Theta. Presbyn. Club: Rose Valley (Pa.) Folk. Home: 530 E 72d St New York City NY 10021 Office: 350 Madison Av New York City NY 10017

BECKER, ELIZABETH ANN, reporter; b. LeMars, Ia., Aug. 19, 1947; d. Frank Prosper and Mary Catherine (Sage) Becker; B.A. in Journalism with honors, U. Ia., 1970. Reporter, LeMars Daily Sentinel, 1968-69; suburban reporter St. Paul Dispatch, 1970-71, reporter Action Line, 1971—. Mem. Women in Communications, Sigma Delta Chi. Roman Catholic. Office: 55 E 4th St St Paul MN 55101

BECKER, ESTHER RUTH, author; b. Hoboken, N.J.; d. Robert O. and Ida (Roedel) Becker; student N.Y. U., 1932-38, New Sch. for Social Research, 1938-41; m. Richard L. Lawrence, Apr. 1949 (dec.). Tng. within industry service U.S. Govt., 1941-44; research asst. Forstmann Woolen Co., Passaic, N.J., 1944-51; research asst., asst. editor, editor Mgmt. Information pub. Elliott Service Co., Mt. Vernon, N.Y., 1962-69; research cons. Kepner-Tregoe, Inc., Princeton, N.J., after 1969; now free-lance writer. Instr., Rutgers U., 1956—; guest lectr. Am. Mgmt. Assn. Seminars. Mem. Nat. Secs. Assn. Author: Secretaries Who Succeed, 1947; (with Richard L. Lawrence) Success and Satisfaction in Your Office Job, 1954; (with Eugene F. Murphy) The Office in Transition-Meeting the Problems of Automation, 1957; Dictionary of Personnel and Industrial Relations, 1958; How to Be an Effective Executive Secretary, 1962, paperback, 1966; (with Peggy Norton Rollason) The High Paid Secretary, 1967; The Successful Secretary's Handbook, 1970; (booklets) What the Secretary Should Know About Automation, Job Satisfaction and Memory, 1962-63. Contbr. chpt. Handbook of Business Adminstration, 1967. Contbr. articles to profl. jours. Home: Beachcomber Apts Venice FL 33595

BECKER, JANET AKE (MRS. FRED J. BECKER), clin. psychologist; b. Toledo, O., July 7, 1913; d. Alton Maurer and Mary Sedate (Fischel) Ake; B.A., U. Toledo, 1951, M.A., 1952; postgrad. Case Western Reserve U., 1957-59; m. Fred J. Becker, Mar. 20, 1933. Psychologist Longview State Hosp., Cin., 1952-57; clin. psychologist, coordinator community service unit Dayton (O.) State Hosp. (now Dayton Mental Health Center), 1959-69; clin. psychologist Toledo Mental Health Center, 1969—. Proctor, Am. Mensa, Toledo, 1973—. Mem. Am., Ohio psychol. assns., Am. Assn. U. Women, Ohio Civil Service Employees Assn. (mem. exec. bd. Anthony Wayne chpt. 1972—). Home: 3601 Hill Av Toledo OH 43607 Office: Toledo Mental Health Center 930 S Detroit Av Toledo OH 43614

BECKER, LAFOLLETTE, state ofcl.; b. N.Y.C., July 4, 1924; d. Frank and Friedy (Wegeli) Becker; ed. N.Y.U., Columbia. Asst. account exec. Ben Sackheim, Inc., 1951-53; editor, writer, translator George Fischer Ltd., Schaffhausen, Switzerland, 1953-57; pub. relations asst. Nat. Council Chs., 1958-61; editor, writer Pratt Inst., Bklyn., 1961-62; dir. pub. relations, advt. Incabloc Corp., N.Y.C., 1964; dir. pub. relations Franklin Soc. Fed. Savs. & Loan Assn., N.Y.C., 1965-68; cons. bank marketing, advt., pub. relations promotions for advt. agys. and banks, 1969-72; Empire Housing Found. coordinator N.Y. State Div. Housing and Community Renewal, 1972—. Cons. polit. pub. relations, 1960—. Founder, co-chmn. Community Action Council, 1970—. Republican candidate for State Assembly, 1964; 1st woman directly elected Rep. dist. leader, 1971—; mem. Rep. County Com., 1965-67, 69—; pres. Mid City Rep. Club, N.Y.C., 1964, 70, 71, v.p., 1962-63, 65-66, 68-69, dir., 1971—. Recipient Editorial award Am. Alumni Council, 1962; Marketing award Savs. Inst. Marketing Soc. Am., 1968; Freedoms Found. award, 1968. Mem. Am. Advt. Fedn., Pub. Relations Soc. Am., N.Y. U. Alumni Fedn., Citizens Union, Park Council, Washington Hdqrs. Assn., Financial Advt. and Marketing Assn. Met. N.Y., UN Assn., East Mid-Manhattan C. of C. (v.p., dir. 1972—). Contbr. articles to financial and other publs. Home: 305 E 88th St New York City NY 10028

BECKER, LOIS JOHNSON (MRS. BERNARD C. BECKER), author; b. Parkersburg, W.Va.; d. Robert Bruce and Carrie E. (Smith) Smith; student Marietta Coll., 1912-14; A.B. cum laude, Colo. Coll., 1916; postgrad. U. Cal. at Berkeley, 1941; m. George Virgil Johnson, June 29, 1920 (dec. Oct. 1929); children—Janet Elizabeth (Mrs. Russell Little), Marjorie Helen (dec.), William Bruce (dec.); m. 2d, Bernard Carl Becker, Oct. 16, 1971. Tchr. schs. Colorado Springs, 1916-18, Springfield, O., 1918-20, Monterey, Cal., 1930-43; with A.R.C., 1943-59, editor youth mags., 1946-59; free lance writer juvenile lit., 1959—. Mem. P.E.O. Sisterhood (chpt. pres. 1944-45, 51-53, 67-68), Children's Book Guild (pres. 1954), Women's Nat. Book Assn., Washington Press Club, Washington Bookseller's Assn., San Diego Hist. Soc., San Diego Zool. Soc., Phi Beta Kappa. Baptist. Author: Christmas Stories Round the World, 1960, rev., 1970; Happy Birthdays Round the World, 1963; Happy New Year Round the World, 1966; What We Eat, 1969; also short stories, articles. Home: 4164 Palisades Rd San Diego CA 92116

BECKER, LUCILLE FRACKMAN (MRS. ROBERT F. BECKER), educator; b. N.Y.C., Feb. 4, 1929; d. Mark and Sylvia (Schwartz) Frackman; B.A. magna cum laude, Barnard Coll., 1949; Diploma d'Etudes Francaises, U. d'Aix Marseille, France, 1950; M.A., Columbia, 1954, Ph.D., 1958; m. Robert F. Becker, Feb. 27, 1954; children—David, Daniel, Michael, Andrew. Instr. in French, Columbia, 1954-58; instr. in French, Rutgers U., Newark, 1958-68; asso. prof. French, Drew U., Madison, N.J., 1968—. Teaching fellow Columbia, 1954-58. Mem. Modern Lang. Assn., Am. Assn. Tchrs. of French, Am. Assn. U. Profs., Phi Beta Kappa. Clubs: Mt. Mansfield Ski, Berkeley Tennis, Watchung Riding. Author: Henry de Montherlant: A Critical Biography, 1970; Louis Aragon, 1971. Editor: Le Maitre de Santiago (Henry de Montherlant), 1965. Home: 82 Harding Dr South Orange NJ 07079 Office: Drew U Madison NJ 07940

BECKER, (MADGE) JOSEPHINE MOORE (MRS. HENRY C. BECKER, JR.), librarian; b. Portland, Ore., Sept. 1, 1928; d. Jesse William and Madge Johnson (Guthrie) Moore; B.A., Western Coll. Women, 1949; M.S., U. Ill., 1952; m. Henry C. Becker, Jr., Jan. 30, 1970. Gen. asst. New Castle-Henry County Library (Ind.), 1949-51; br. librarian Library Assn. Portland (Ore.), 1952-54; br. supr., adminstrv. asst. Yakima Valley Regional Library, Yakima, Wash., 1954-59; field librarian U.S. Army Spl. Service, Germany, 1959-61; county librarian Plumas County Free Library, Quincy, Cal., 1961-64; city librarian, Longview, Wash., 1964-71, City of Vallejo (Cal.) Pub. Library System, 1971-74; acting county librarian Solano County (Cal.), Fairfield, 1973-74, county librarian, 1974—. Mem. adv. bd. Lower Columbia Community Coll., 1969-70, Projects to Advance Creativity Edn., Elementary and Secondary Edn. Act, Cowlitz County, Cal., 1966-70; chmn. North Bay Coop. Library System, Santa Rosa, Cal., 1973-74. Bd. dirs., pres. bd. Lower Columbia Community Action Council, Office Econ. Opportunity, 1965-66, 67-69. Recipient Bess Sawhill Robertson award for excellence in English, Western Coll. for Women, 1949. Mem. Am., Pacific N.W., Cal., Wash. (1st v.p. 1969-70) library assns., Vallejo C. of C., Beta Phi Mu, Delta Kappa Gamma. Club: Soroptimist (pres. 1965-67) (Vallejo, Cal.). Home: 101 Hilborn Av PO Box 1917 Vallejo CA 94590 Office: 744 Empire St Fairfield CA 95833

BECKER, MARGARET PATERSON, educator; b. Mpls., June 12, 1930; d. Donald Gildersleeve and Margaret (Young) Paterson; B.A. cum laude, U. Minn., 1953; M.S. in Edn. (Nat. Def. Edn. Act fellow), U. Pitts., 1966, Ph.D., 1970; m. Robert C. Becker, June 17, 1952; children—William Paterson, Thomas Lyle, Nancy Katherine. Psychometrist, Hampton Twp. Schs., Allison Park, Pa., 1964-65; grad. asst. U. Pitts., 1966-68, instr. counselor edn., 1968-70, asst. prof., 1970—, dir. Day Master's Program Counselor Edn., 1973—. Scholarship Com. coordinator Hampton Twp., Pa., 1971—; chmn. Lawrenceville com. Cath. Social Service, 1973—. Bd. dirs. Cath. Social Service Allegheny County, Pa. Mem. Am., Pitts. psychol. assns., Am., Pa. personnel and guidance assns., Assn. Measurement, Evaluation and Guidance, Pa. Assn. Counselor Educators and Suprs. (sec.-treas. 1974—), Pi Beta Phi, Phi Delta Gamma. Clubs: Wildwood Golf, Wildwood Highlands. Mem. Editorial Bd. Leadership Tng. Inst./Pupil Personnel Services Jour., 1973—. Contbr. articles to profl. publs. Home: 4417 Maple Lane Oak Hill Farms Allison Park PA 15101 Office: Hill Bldg U Pitts Pittsburgh PA 15260

BECKER, MARY LOUISE, polit. scientist; b. St. Louis; d. W. R. and Evelyn (Thompson) Becker; B.S., Washington U., St. Louis, 1949, M.A. (Blewett fellow), 1951; Ph.D. (resident fellow 1952-56), Radcliffe Coll., 1957; postgrad. (Fulbright scholar) U. Karachi, Pakistan, 1953-54; married; children—James, John. Intelligence research analyst Dept. State, Washington, 1957-59; internat. relations officer AID, Washington, 1959-64, community relations officer, 1964-66, sci. research officer, 1966-71, UN relations officer, 1971—. Lectr. internat. relations civic orgns., student groups, 1954—. Mem. adv. bd., chmn. student placement Washington Citizenship Seminar, Nat. YMCA-YWCA, Washington, 1961—. Mem. Am. Polit. Sci. Assn., Am. Acad. Polit. and Social Sci., Assn. Asian Studies, Asia Soc., Am. Soc. Pub. Adminstrn., Am. Friends Middle East, Am. Assn. U. Women, Mo. Soc. Washington (sec. 1959-60), Mortar Bd., Chimes, Alpha Lambda Delta, Beta Gamma Sigma, Eta Mu Phi, Pi Sigma Alpha. Presbyn. Club: International (Washington). Author: Muhammed Iqbal, 1965. Contbg. editor: Concise Ency. of Middle East, 1973. Contbr. articles to govt. publs. Office: Agy for Internat Devel Washington DC 20523

BECKER, MILLIE ANNA, educator; b. Centralia, Ill.; d. Louis and Elizabeth (Mueller) Becker; student summers So. Ill. U., Eastern Ill. U.; grad. Chgo. Tchrs. Coll.; Ph.B., U. Chgo., 1936, postgrad., 1936-41. Tchr., Centralia Area Schs., 1919-24, Andrew Jackson Sch., Chgo., 1927-31, A.O. Sexton Sch., Chgo., 1931-53, Horace Mann Sch., Chgo., 1953-71. Mem. Nat. Soc. for Study Edn., Internat. Reading Assn., N.E.A., Ill. Edn. Assn., UN Assn., Chgo. Kindergarten Primary Assn., Chgo. Tchrs. Union, U. Chgo. Alumni Assn., Phi Beta Kappa. Mem. United Ch. of Christ. Address: 7637 S Loomis Blvd Chicago IL 60620

BECKER, NATALIE ROSE HARRITON (MRS. STANLEY M. BECKER), artist; b. Phila., Dec. 13, 1933; d. Frank and Zelda (Saltzman) Harriton; Asso. in Sci., Temple U., 1951; student Acad. Fine Arts, 1957-58, Art Students League, 1970-72; m. Stanley M. Becker, Oct. 27, 1957; children—Pamela Sue, Mitchell Douglas, Andrew David. One-man shows at Gallery 9, Chatham, N.J., 1969, Bloomfield Coll., 1971; exhibited in group shows at Fine Arts Mus., Carnegie Inst., Jersey City Mus., N.A.D., Nat. Arts Club, Bergen County Mus., Capricorn Gallery; represented in permanent collection at Bloomfield Coll. Recipient Leon Lehrer Meml. prize for landscape, 1972, Grumbacher award of merit, 1972, many others. Fellow Am. Artists Profl. League (N.J. dir. 1971-74); mem. Nat. Arts Club, Pen and Brush Club, Burr Artists N.Y., Catharine Lorillard Wolfe Art Club. Club: Salmagundi (N.Y.C.). Home: 97 Barchester Way Westfield NJ 07090

BECKER, PAULA LEE, pub. relations exec.; b. Denver, Mar. 29, 1941; d. Elmer Leroy and Beuna Pearl (Slater) Becker. Asst. dir. pub. relations Glendale (Cal.) Adventist Hosp., 1960-61; med. asst. Los Angeles County Hosp., 1962-64; asst. editor So. Pub. Assn., Nashville, 1964-68, dir. pub. relations, 1968-73; pres. Group II Pub. Relations, Inc., 1974—. Recipient Creative Communications awards (2) Religious Pub. Relations Council, 1969. Mem. Pub. Relations Soc. Am. (Mid.-Tenn. pres. 1972-73), Religious Pub. Relations Council (Nashville pres. 1970-71, nat. v.p. 1971-73, nat. pres. 1973—). Author: Adventures of Susan and Jimmy, 1968; Let the Song Go On, 1971. Home: 8207 Sawyer Brown Rd Nashville TN 37221 Office: Box 50563 Nashville TN 37205

BECKER, PAULINE RICCI (MRS. ALFRED G. BECKER), lawyer; b. Chgo., July 16, 1921; d. Eli Henry and Jeannette Cecelia (Kittridge) Phillips; B.A., De Paul U., 1943, J.D., 1952; m. David Ricci, Oct. 3, 1943 (dec. Jan., 1948); children—David, Pauline; m. 2d., Alfred G. Becker, Dec. 15, 1957; 1 son, Joel. Admitted to Ill. bar, 1952; practiced in Chgo., 1952-57, Evanston, Ill., 1957—; house atty. Raytheon Radio and TV Co., Chgo., 1952-54; with firm Ricci & Becker, 1957—; atty., corporate sec., dir. Becker Surg. Supply Co., Evanston, Ill., 1961—. Pres. Dawes P.T.A., Evanston, 1967-69, Chute P.T.A., Evanston, 1970-71; sec. Assn. for Children's Theatre. Mem. Women's Adv. Bd. Evanston YMCA, 1973—; mem. exec. com. Evanston Twp. High Sch. Adv. Council, 1972—. Mem. Ill., Women's bar assns., Lex Legio, Pi Gamma Mu. Home: 211 Dewey St Evanston IL 60202 Office: 815 Howard St Evanston IL 60202

BECKER, MRS. RALPH E. (ANN WATTERS BECKER), civic worker; b. N.Y.C., Apr. 26, 1922; d. William G. and Lucile (Miller) Watters; student pvt. schs., Harcum Jr. Coll., Child Edn. Found.; m. Ralph E. Becker; children—William Watters, Donald Lee, Pamela Rose, Ralph E. Chmn. spl. events D.C. chpt. Am. Cancer Soc., 1957-59, dir., 1959—, sec. exec. bd., 1962-64, 72—; trustee Washington Community Sch. Music, Washington Choral Arts Soc.; mem. Women's com. Nat. Symphony Orch., 1950—; bd. dirs. Nat. Symphony Orch., 1970—; mem. bd. Mother's Club of St. Albans Sch., 1958—, sec., 1962-63, pres., 1963-64; bd. govs. St. Albans Sch., 1970—; pres. Women St. Alban's Ch., 1965-66; founder, pres. Met. Washington chpt. Achievement Rewards for Coll. Scientists, 1969-72; organizing mem. Friends John F. Kennedy Center Performing Arts; exec. com. D.C. Commn. on Arts; rec. sec. League of Republican Women, 1955-57, exec. bd., 1955-59; women's com. Corcoran Art Gallery; women's bd. George Washington U. Hosp., 1954—; dir. D.C. chpt. ANTA; mem. Nat. Com. Sponsors for Margaret Sanger Inst. Human Reprodn. and Devel.; mem. exec. com. All Hallows Guild, Washington Cathedral, chmn. flower mart, 1972; chmn. distaff com. Textile Museum. Mem. Salvation Army Aux. (1st v.p. 1959-61, chmn. protocol com., bd. dirs. 1959-66, 74-75), Soc. Assos. Smithsonian Instn., World Affairs Forum (sec. 1960—), YWCA, League Women Voters, Daus. Utah Pioneers, Women's Aux. Soc. Cal. Pioneers. Decorated Order Stella Della Solidarieta Italiana 1st class, 1970. Episcopalian (vestry 1966-69). Clubs: Capitol Hill, Am. Newspaper Women's (asso.). Home: 2916 32d St Washington DC 20008

BECKER, SALLY ELECTA NORRIS (MRS. ALFRED D. BECKER), chem. cons.; b. Penn Yan, N.Y., Dec. 7, 1923; d. Ralph Thomas and Mary Leah (Post) Norris; A.B., Smith Coll., 1945; M.B.A., Northwestern U., 1964; m. Alfred D. Becker, Oct. 19, 1944; children—Stephen, Howard, Ralph. Owner, mgr. Chem. Bus. Consultants, Wilmette, Ill., 1964-69, Studio Research Assos., Kenilworth, Ill., 1972—. Home: 348 Sterling Rd Kenilworth IL 60043

BECKER, SARAH RUSKIN (MRS. IRVING BECKER), stockbroker; b. N.Y.C., May 4, 1914; d. Max and Bessie (Sirotkin) Ruskin; student Hunter Coll., 1931-34; B.A., Adelphi Coll., 1957; M.A. Hofstra Coll., 1961; m. Irving Becker, Dec. 11, 1938; children—Barbara Joan (Mrs. Martin Edward Kantor), Carol Doree (Mrs. Manny Goldberg). Tchr. math Nassau County, N.Y., 1957-59; grad. asst. Hofstra Coll., Hempstead, N.Y., 1958-60, lectr., freshman counsellor, 1964-65; sch. psychologist Union Free Sch. Dist. 2, East Williston, N.Y., 1959-68, Locust Valley (N.Y.) Sch. Dist., 1963-64, Central Sch. Dist. 4, Plainview, N.Y., 1967-71; stockbroker Liberty Securities Co., New Hyde Park, N.Y., 1971—. Active Girl Scouts U.S.A., 1952-56. Mem. Am., N.Y. State, Nassau County (treas. 1963-69) psychol. assns., Psi Chi, Pi Gamma Mu. Mem. B'nai B'rith (financial sec. 1952-54). Home: 1 Horseshoe Lane Roslyn Heights NY 11577 Office: 1604 Hillside Av New Hyde Park NY 11040

BECKET, MARTA (MRS. TOM WILLIAMS), dance mime, painter; b. N.Y.C.; d. Henry and Helen (Neidig) Becket; studied painting with Antonio Cortizes, dancing with Madame Toscaninni, Caird Leslie, Gluck Sandor, Am. Ballet Sch., Madame DuVal; m. Tom Williams, June 30, 1962. Cartoonist drama page N.Y. Herald-Tribune 1948-49; exhibited paintings Park South Gallery, N.Y.C.; 3 one-man shows; dance mime, appearing in solo concerts for concert assns., colls., univs. throughout nation, 1955—; appeared Town Hall, Carnegie Hall, Radio City Music Hall (N.Y.C.); Broadway appearances in Show Boat, A Tree Grows in Brooklyn, Wonderful Town; established, operator Amargosa Opera House and Gallery, Death Valley Junction, Cal. Illustrator: glossary for Complete Book of Ballets (Balanchine); Star Performance (Walter Terry). Address: PO Box 664 Death Valley Junction CA 92328

BECKETT, ADELE CECILIA MAAS STEVENS (MRS. GARNER A. BECKETT), civic worker; b. Chgo., May 8, 1900; d. Louis Herman and Mamie (Mayrhofer) Maas; student U. Wash., 1917-18, Washington U., St. Louis, 1922-23; m. Dillon Stevens, Apr. 11, 1918 (dec. Dec. 1953); 1 dau., Barbara (Mrs. John Albert Arnett); m. 2d, Garner A. Beckett, Oct. 28, 1967 (dec. Apr. 1974). Partner, Dillon Stevens & Co. Publicity chmn. John Burroughs Jr. High Sch. P.T.A., 1934, Los Angeles High Sch. P.T.A., 1936-37, Euterpe Opera Reading Club, 1937-38; pres. Glaides, 1946, v.p., 1963; finance chmn. Ebell of Los Angeles, 1955-57, sec. creative writing dept., 1962-63, asst. curator dept., 1971-72, chmn., 1973—, chmn. writer's workshop, 1972—; mem. California Club, Friends of Claremont Colls., Cal. Inst. Tech. Assos., Postscripts. Recipient award for blood bank work A.R.C., 1943, various awards for fiction. Mem. English-Speaking Union. Home: 706 N Elm Dr Beverly Hills CA 90210

BECKETT, FLOSSIE LEE EATON, educator; b. Mounds, Okla., Apr. 8, 1910; d. Danial J. and Mattie (Cumbey) Eaton; student Northeastern State Coll., Tahlequah, Okla., 1928-29; B.S. in Edn., East Central State Coll., Okla., 1947; M.Ed., U. Okla., 1951; postgrad. various colls., univs.; Ph.D. (hon.), Colo. State Christian Coll., 1973; m. Si Beckett, Sept. 1, 1929 (dec. Apr. 1969); children—Jo Anne (Mrs. Thomas L. Phillips), Peggy Jean Cochran, Si Dean. Tchr., prin. Tate Sch., Wewoka, Okla., 1943-48, Mountain View Sch., Seminole, Okla., 1948-49, Hilltop Sch., Wewoka, 1949-53; tchr. Central Elementary Sch., Wewoka, 1953-55, Lindsay (Okla.) Elementary Sch., 1955-67, elementary librarian, dir. instructional media center 1967—. Various positions N.E.A.-Okla. Edn. Assn. leadership workshops, 1951-67, N.E.A. Regional Classroom Tchrs. Confs., 1960-67; mem. Okla. Tchr. Edn. and Profl. Standards Commn., 1961-65, Okla. Curriculum Improvement Commn., 1961-66; mem. Gov.'s Phys. Fitness Council and Phys. Fitness Commn., 1965-69; mem. Okla. State Textbook Commn., 1973; del. tchr., edn. convs. Organizer various 4-H Clubs, Little Theatre groups; mem. state com. Oklahomans for Better Edn., 1964-65; pres. Okla. 4-H Club Leaders, 1970-71; mem. Okla. Dept. Edn. Profl. Practices Commn., 1965-73, vice chmn., 1969-70. Precinct insp. Seminole County (Okla.) Democratic Party, 1953-55; mem. Okla. Acad. for State Goals, 1966-69. Named Garvin County's Tchr. of Year, 1961, Okla. Tchr. of Year, 1961; Nat. Tchr. of Year Honor Roll, 1962. Mem. Am. Assn. U. Women (pres. Chickasha br. 1971-75), N.E.A., Garvin County Tchr. Assn., Internat. Reading Assn. (del. Conv. 1973), Okla. (sect. state pres. 1953-54, county unit treas. 1956-61, mem. constn. revision com. 1965-68, resolutions com. 1971—), Lindsay (chmn. pub. relations com. 1970-72) edn. assns., East Central Dist. (pres. 1959, chmn. program com. 1968-71), Lindsay (organizer 1957, exec. bd. 1957-67) classroom tchrs. assns., State (exec. com. 1961-67, state pres. 1964-66), South Central Regional (resolution com. 1966-68) depts. classroom tchrs., A.L.A., Audio-Visual Assn., Okla., Nat. aerospace edn. assns., Kappa Kappa Iota (state pres. 1969-70, projects com. 1966-69, mem. met. council; chmn. state empathy com. 1971-72, chmn. State pub. relations com. 1972-74), Gamma Theta (conclave treas. 1967-69). Mem. Rebekah Lodge (chmn. edn. com. 1960-61). Contbr. articles to publs. Home: 420 Garrett Av Lindsay OK 73052

BECKETT, GRACE, educator; b. Smithfield, O., Oct. 7, 1912; d. Roy M. and Mary (Hammond) Beckett; A.B., Oberlin Coll., 1934, A.M., 1935; Ph.D., Ohio State U., 1939. Grad. asst. econs. Ohio State U., 1936-39; asso. prof. econs. Ind. Central Coll., 1939-40; with U. Ill., 1941—, asst. prof. econs., 1945-51, asso. prof. econs., 1951—. Mem. Am. Midwest econ. assns., Music Educators Nat. Conf., Econ. History Assn., Music Tchrs. Nat. Assn., Am. Finance Assn., Ohio Hist. Soc., Interlochen (Mich.) Alumni Assn., Phi Beta Kappa, Pi Lambda Theta, Phi Chi Theta, Alpha Lambda Delta. Club: University of Illinois Women's. Author: Reciprocal Trade Agreements Program, 1941. Contbr. articles to profl. publs. Address: PO Box 386 Urbana IL 61801

BECKLAKE, MARGARET RIGSBY (MRS. MAURICE MCGREGOR), physician, educator; b. London, Eng., May 27, 1922; d. James T. and Dorothy (Mills) Becklake; M.B., B.Ch., U. Witwatersrand, South Africa, 1944, M.D., 1951; m. Maurice McGregor, Mar. 20, 1948; children—James A., Margaret J. Intern Johannesburg (South Africa) Gen. Hosp., 1945, tutorial registrar, 1950-54; intern Hammersmith Hosp., London, Eng., 1946, research registrar, 1949; jr. lectr. medicine U. Witwatersrand, 1950-54; physiologist Pneumoconiosis Bur., Johannesburg, 1954-57; mem. faculty McGill U., Montreal, Que., Can., 1961—, asso. prof. dept. exptl. medicine, 1965-71, prof., 1971—, dept. epidemiology, 1967-72, prof. epidemiology, 1972—; asso. Med. Research Council Can. Contbr. articles to profl. jours. Home: 7430 Bayard St Montreal PQ H3R 3A9 Canada Office: Royal Victoria Hosp Montreal PQ Canada

BECKMAN, GAIL MCKNIGHT, educator; b. N.Y.C., Apr. 8, 1938; d. Irland McKnight and Elizabeth (Hurlock) Beckman; grad. Baldwin Sch., 1955; B.A., Bryn Mawr Coll., 1959; J.D., Yale, 1963; diploma (Fulbright scholar), U. Tubingen (Germany), 1960; M.A., U. Pa., 1966. Admitted to Pa. bar, 1964, Ga. bar, 1972, D.C. bar, 1964, U.S. Supreme Ct. bar, 1968; counsel Legal Aid Soc. Phila., 1961; asso. firm Morgan, Lewis, Bockius, Phila., 1963-66; lectr. law U. Glasgow (Scotland), 1967-71; asso. prof. law Ga. State U., Atlanta, 1971—. Research asso. Am. Philos. Soc., 1966-69. Mem. Phila., Atlanta, Ga., Am. (chmn. com. internat. ct. of justice, 1968-72), Internat. bar assns., Am. Assn. U. Women, Jr. League Atlanta, Nat. Soc. Colonial Dames Am., Yale Club Atlanta, Bryn Mawr Club Phila., St. Andrew's Soc. Atlanta (co-founder, sec., 1971), Beta Gamma Sigma. Presbyn. Soroptimist (pres. 1973). Contbr. articles to profl. jours. Home: 1270 W Peachtree St Atlanta GA 30309

BECKMAN, JOY BULLOCK (MRS. FRED A. BECKMAN), journalist; b. Caldwell, Ida., Aug. 22, 1930; d. Claude Barton and Doris Alene (Whiffin) Bullock; student Nampa Bus. Coll., 1949-50; m. Fred A. Beckman, July 15, 1950; children—Paul Albert, Lynden Louise, Susan Camille. Sec., No. Life Ins. Co., Boise, Ida., 1951; sec., cashier First Fed. Savs. & Loan Co., Caldwell, 1951-52; teller Ida. First Nat. Bank, Wilder, 1953, Weiser, 1969-73; freelance writer-photographer Ida. Daily Statesman, Boise, 1958—; freelance writer, photographer Weiser Signal-American, 1964-68, editor, 1968-69. Active Boy Scouts Am., 1951-52, 4-H, 1964-66. Named Ida. Promoter of Week, Gov. Ida., 1966. Mem. Ida. Press Women (pres. 1971-74, v.p. 1970-71, treas. 1966), Nat. Fedn. Press Women. Mem. Community Ch. (dir. 1969-70). Home: Route 2 Box 97 Weiser IA 83672

BECKMANN, DOLORES JOAN, performing arts dir.; b. Moline, Ill., July 29, 1932; d. Arno and Alice M. (Smith) Beckmann; B.A., U. No. Ia., 1954. Tchr. speech John Deere Jr. High Sch., Moline, 1954-59, 61-62; tchr. speech, English, Beaumont (Tex.) High Sch., 1959-61; asst. dramatics dir. Moline (Ill.) High Sch., 1962-65, dramatics dir., 1965—. Dir. Playcrafters, Moline, 1972; cons. dir. Richmond Hill Players, Geneseo, Ill., 1968—; stage dir. Quad-City Music Guild, Moline, 1966, 74. Mem. Am. Theatre Assn., Speech Communications Assn., Ill. Speech and Theatre Assn., Internat. Thespian Soc. (sponsor 1962—), Theta Alpha Phi. Home: 2644 JFK Dr East Moline IL 61244 Office: 3600 23d Av Moline IL 61265

BECKNER, MARY KATHRYN, accountant; b. Mendota, Ill., Dec. 5, 1904; d. Edward J. and Mary (Hoerner) Cannon; student pub. schs.; m. Lester W. Beckner, Dec. 5, 1931. Pvt. sec., 1922-41; treas. Wayside Press, Inc., 1941—, also dir.; sec.-treas., dir. Kenneth B. Butler & Asso., 1944—; treas. Butler Typo-Design Research Center, 1951—; dir., treas. Packaging Digest Inc., 1964-70. Mem. Red Cross Canteen, Mendota Community Hosp. Aux.; bd. dirs. LaSalle County unit Am. Cancer Soc. Mem. Ill., Mendota chambers commerce, Nat. Council Catholic Women, Nat. Secs. Assn. (sec. of year Aishi chpt.). Roman Catholic. Elk. Clubs: Woman's (treas. pub. affairs dept.); Antique Automobile of America (sec.-treas. Mendota). Home: 1312 Burlington St Mendota IL 61342 Office: 700 14th Av Mendota IL 61342

BEDDALL, BARBARA GOULD (MRS. EDWARD A. BEDDALL), author, librarian; b. Tarrytown, N.Y., Oct. 28, 1919; d. Gerald Blenkiron and Anna Rosetta (Curtiss) Gould; B.A., Swarthmore Coll., 1941; B.S., Sch. Library Service, Columbia, 1942; M.S., Yale, 1962; m. Edward A. Beddall, Oct. 29, 1949; 1 son, Thomas. Research librarian Time, Inc., N.Y.C., 1944-52; with Sch. Bus. Library, Columbia, 1942-44, Stamford (Conn.) Pub. Library, 1952-53, Burndy Library, Norwalk, Conn., 1964-65, U. Bridgeport (Conn.) Library, 1965-66. Mem. A.A.A.S., Am., Brit. ornithologists unions, Assn. for Tropical Biology, Northeastern Bird-Banding Assn., Soc. for Bibliography of Natural History, Soc. Systematic Zoology, Wilson Ornithol. Soc., Fairfield Hist. Soc. (corr. sec. 1965-73). Author: Wallace and Bates in the Tropics, 1969; contbr. articles to profl. jours. Home: 2502 Bronson Rd Fairfield CT 06430

BEDDOE, RUTH M. DETWILER (MRS. WILBUR JOHN ENNIS), realtor; b. Toledo, Feb. 27, 1913; d. Charles Newton and Ethel J. (Wagoner) Detwiler; student pub. schs., Toledo; m. Arthur Waldo Holly, Jan. 19, 1935 (div.); 1 dau., Barbara Ann (Mrs. Lawrence J. Novak); m. 2d, Harry E. Beddoe, Sept. 29, 1948 (div. 1967); 1 son, Thomas Weston; m. 3d, Wilbur John Ennis, Feb. 14, 1974. Real estate salesman, broker Chas. N. Detwiler, realtor, Huntington Park, Cal., 1942-48, Harry E. Beddoe, realtor, Huntington Park and Downey, Cal., 1948-68; pres. Golden State Hawaiian Corp.; pres., dir. Land, Inc., Hilo, Hawaii; v.p., dir. Hawaii Home Developers, Inc.; sec., dir. Bayshore Towers. escrow officer Universal Escrow Co., Huntington Park, 1944, Advance Escrow Co., 1945-47. Treas., bd. dirs. Ainaloa Community Assn. Republican precinct capt., Buena Park, Cal., 1960, area chmn., 1962-70. Mem. Downey Bd. Realtors, Cal. Real Estate Assn. Clubs: Woman's (Downey); Hilo Yacht. Author (song): Aloha, Ainaloa. Designer residence plans. Home: Apt 506 2405 Kalanianaole Av Hilo HI 96720 Office: Suite 308 120 Pauahi St Hilo HI 96720

BEDELL, CATHERINE DEAN, govt. ofcl.; b. Yakima, Wash., May 18, 1914; d. Charles Henry and Pauline (Van Loon) Barnes; B.A., U. Wash., 1936, M.Edn., 1937; m. Donald W. Bedell, Nov. 14, 1970; children by previous marriage&-James C. May, Melinda E. May. Tchr., Chehalis, Wash., 1937-40; radio writer, commentator Sta. KMO, Tacoma, 1940-41, Sta. KOMO, Seattle, 1941-42; head radio dept. Strang-Prosser Advt. Agy., Seattle, 1942-43; radio writer WEAF, N.Y.C., 1944-46; radio broadcaster Sta. KIT, Yakima, 1948-56; mem. Wash. State Ho. of Reps., 1952-58; mem. 86th-91st Congresses; mem., incorporator Nat. R.R. Passenger Corp., Washington, 1970-71; chmn. U.S. Tariff Commn., Washington, 1971—. Mem. Nat. Commn. on Food Marketing, 1964-66. Active Washington Assn. for Retarded Children. Mem. Alpha Chi Omega. Republican. Home: 321 N 32d Av Yakima WA 98902 also 4101 Cathedral Av NW Washington DC 20016 Office: 8th and E Sts NW Washington DC 20436

BEDELL, GAYNELL PACK (MRS. F. KEITH BEDELL), C.S. practitioner; b. Paintsville, Ky.; d. William Reaves and Iuka D. (Welch) Pack; grad. W.Va. Bus. Coll.; m. Charles T. Skeer, 1931 (dec. 1949); children—William Thom, Zoe (Mrs. A. G. Vecchione); m. 2d, Frederick Haller, July 25, 1953 (dec. Apr. 1957); m. 3d, F. Keith Bedell, Nov. 21, 1966. Mgr. fashion shops, 1942-46; star Claire Angrist radio fashion show, Huntington, W.Va., 1942-46; fashion cons., resident rep. Goode-Bridgeman, Inc., N.Y.C., 1949-56; fashion and bridal cons.; mem. Christian Sci. Ch., practitioner, N.Y.C., 1931—. Pres., 1st Ch. of Christ Scientist, Huntington, W.Va., 1941-45, reader, Flushing, N.Y., 1953-56. Mem. Nat. Fedn. Bus. and Profl. Women's Clubs (pres. Huntington). Home: 60 Sutton Pl S New York City NY 10022 Office: 342 Madison Av New York City NY 10017

BEDELL, SUSANNA E., lawyer; b. Budapest, Hungary; d. Jozsef and Rosemarie (Kenyeres) Eszenyi; came to U.S., 1938, naturalized, 1948; A.B., Vassar Coll., 1940; J.D., Columbia, 1944; m. Wallace Canaday Bedell, Aug. 30, 1947 (div. 1967); children—Susanna Elizabeth, Wallace Canaday. Admitted to N.Y. bar, 1948, D.C. bar, 1953, U.S. Supreme Ct. bar, 1952; asso. with Shearman & Sterling & Wright, N.Y.C., 1944-51; practice law, Poughkeepsie, N.Y., 1951-52, 54—; asso. with Wilmer & Broun, Washington, 1953-54; of counsel Van De Water & Van De Water, Poughkeepsie, 1970—. Mem. Hoover Commn., 1948; panelist World Affairs Conf., U. Colo., 1968. Pres. W. W. Smith Center, 1956-58; treas., trustee Poughkeepsie Day Sch., 1958-65; area chmn. Columbia Campaign, 1968-69; legislative chmn. Region III, N.Y. State Mental Health Soc., 1966-67. Pres. Dutchess County Women's Republican Club, 1960-64; mem. Rep. County Com., 1962-73. Vice pres., bd. dirs. Astor Child Guidance Clinic, 1966—; bd. dirs. Dutchess County Mental Health Soc., 1962—; chmn. bd. trustees Dutchess County Supreme Ct. Library, 1968—; mem. women's aux. Dutchess County Med. Soc., 1951-67; treas., dir. Mid Hudson Meml. Soc., 1971—. Mem. Am., N.Y. State, Dutchess County bar assns., Bar Assn. City N.Y., League Women Voters, Jr. League, Asso. Alumnae Vassar Coll. (1st v.p., dir. 1954-57). Club: Poughkeepsie Tennis. Contbr. articles to periodicals. Home: 20 Sunrise Lane Poughkeepsie NY 12603 Office: 54 Market St Poughkeepsie NY 12601

BEDENBAUGH, ANGELA LEA OWEN (MRS. JOHN HOLCOMBE BEDENBAUGH), chemist; b. Seguin, Tex., Oct. 6, 1939; d. Wintford Henry and Nelia Melanie (Fischer) Owen; B.S. cum laude, U. Tex., 1961; Ph.D., U. S.C., 1967; m. John Holcombe Bedenbaugh, Dec. 27, 1961. Lab. instr. U. Tex. at Austin, 1960-61; research asso. in chemistry U. So. Miss., Hattiesburg, 1967—. Bd. dirs. Forrest-Stone Area Opportunity, Inc., 1970-72. Mem. Am. Chem. Soc., Sci. Research Soc. N. Am. (sec.-treas. U. So. Miss. br. 1967-69, pres. 1973-74), N.Y. Acad. Scis., Bus. and Profl. Women's Club, Sigma Xi, Delta Kappa Gamma (1st v.p. Alpha Beta chpt. 1972-74, pres. 1974—; chmn. Zeta state research com. 1973-75). Methodist. Contbr. articles to profl. jours. Patentee in field. Office: Box 466 Southern Station Hattiesburg MS 39401

BEDFORD, AMY ALDRICH (MRS. JOHN M. BEDFORD, JR.), pub. co. exec.; b. Pendleton, Ore., July 13, 1912; d. Edwin Burton and Elsie (Conklin) Aldrich; B.S., Ore. State U., 1933; m. John M. Bedford, Jr., May 1, 1937 (dec. Feb. 1949); 1 dau., Jacqueline (Mrs. David M. Brown). Corporate sec. East Oregonian Pub. Co., Pendleton, 1950—, also mgr. printing dept., 1951—. Vice pres. Pendleton River Parkway Found., Inc. Mem. Govs. Com. on Status of Women., 1970—. Mem. Am. Assn. U. Women, Women in Communications, Ore. Press Women, League of Women Voters, Pendleton C. of C. (dir. 1973). Club: Altrusa (pres. 1955-56). Home: PO Box 1456 Pendleton OR 97801 Office: 211 SE Byers Av Pendleton OR 97801

BEDFORD, LOUISE CHILDERS, librarian; b. Des Moines, May 6, 1917; d. Paul Carrington and Grace Pearl (Childers) Bedford; A.B., Drake U., 1938; M.S. in L.S., U. Ky., 1955. Tchr., Montgomery County, Ky., 1938-42; expediter Gen. Electric Co., Cin., 1942-50; tchr.-librarian Montgomery County, 1950-55; librarian Mt. Sterling (Ky.) schs., 1955—; summer instr. U. Ky., 1959, 61, 67, 73. Mem. Gov. Ky. Planning Com. for Libraries, 1968-71; mem. adv. media com. Ky. Dept. Edn., 1974—. Mem. Am., Ky. (rep. to exec. bd. Southeastern Library Assn. 1974-76), Central Ky. (pres. 1963-64) library assns., Ky. Assn. Sch. Librarians (sec., dir. 1971-72; pres. 1973-74), Nat., Ky., Central Ky. edn. assns., D.A.R. Clubs: Mt. Sterling Woman's; Woman's of Central Ky. (Lexington). Home: Jeffersonville KY 40337 Office: Sch Library N Maysville St Mt Sterling KY 40353

BEDFORD, MADELEINE ALANN PECKHAM (MRS. CHARLES FRANCIS BEDFORD), civic worker; b. Ontario, Cal., Jan. 25, 1910; d. Allen Lewis and Madeleine (Elliott) Peckham; A.B., U. Cal. at Berkeley, 1930, M.A., 1937; LL.D., Tex. Christian U., 1973; m. Charles Francis Bedford, Dec. 30, 1930; children—Madeleine Alann, Frances Ellen, Charlotte Jean. Supr. tchr. tng. and counseling, in charge testing Univ. High Sch., U. Cal. at Berkeley, 1931-38; tchr. English to fgn. born San Leandro (Cal.) Evening Schs., 1931-38; treas. Tarrant County Day Care Assn., 1953-54; pres. Ft. Worth and Tarrant County council Camp Fire Girls, 1961-63, pres. Nat. council, 1965-68, NGO rep. to UN, 1968—, nat. bd. dirs., 1960—, bd. dirs. Houston council, 1971-72; pres. Ft. Worth Lit. Council, 1963-65; v.p. Tarrant County United Fund and Community Council, 1963-66, mem. exec. com. bd. dirs., 1963—; pres. Ft. Worth chpt. Am. Field Service, 1964-66; chmn. budget sub-com. United Fund, 1959-68, chmn. met. div. Tarrant County, 1970; chmn. speakers tours, films div., United Way Tarrant County Campaign, 1973; sec. Tex. United Community Services, 1968-70, v.p., 1970-73, pres., 1973—; mem. Mid-Am. Regional Vol. Task group United Way Am.; Tex. state rep. for UNICEF, 1969—; chmn. Mayor's Council on Youth Opportunity, 1972—; del. White House Conf. on Children and Youth, 1970. Bd. dirs. Tarrant County chpt. A.R.C., United Cerebral Palsy, Tarrant County Community Action Agy., Tarrant County Community Council, Tex. Social Welfare Assn.; trustee Assn. Grad. Edn. and Research, 1971—. Recipient Gulick award, 1961, Wo-he-lo award, 1968 Camp Fire Girls; award of Excellence for Outstanding Leadership and Service Tarrant County Community Council, 1964, Civic award First Lady Ft. Worth Altrusa, 1966. Mem. Ft. Worth Lecture Found., Motar Board, Phi Beta Kappa (pres. Ft. Worth 1958-59), Alpha Chi Omega, Pi Sigma Alpha. Episcopalian. Club: Fort Worth Woman's (past pres. history sect.). Home: 7 Westover Rd Fort Worth TX 76107

BEDFORD, RUTH ALICE HAEDIKE (MRS. EDWIN GARRARD BEDFORD), librarian; b. Chgo.; d. William Henry and Alice (Lohr) Haedike; student Beloit Coll., 1932-33; B.S., U. Ill., 1936, M.S., 1954, postgrad.; m. Edwin Garrard Bedford, June 6, 1942; children—David Edwin, Ellen Louise. Instr. U. Ill. Library, Urbana, 1954-64; asst. prof. library sci. U. Utah Libraries, Salt Lake City, 1964-68; asso. librarian Butler Library, State U. Coll., Buffalo, 1968—, mem. faculty adv. council instructional resources, 1971-73. Mem. tech. services com. Western N.Y. Library Resources Council, 1968-73. Mem. State U. N.Y. Librarians' Assn., Am. Assn. U. Profs., A.L.A., Kenan Center (charter mem.), Delta Phi Alpha. Mem. Order Eastern Star. Home: 515 Locust St Lockport NY 14094 Office: 1300 Elmwood Av Buffalo NY 14222

BEDROSIAN, SARAH GARABED, educator; b. Harpoot, Turkey, June 5, 1919; d. Garabed and Aghavne (Maghakian) Bedrosian; brought to U.S., 1923, naturalized, 1947; A.B., Fresno State Coll., 1956, M.A., 1958; D.B.A., U. So. Cal., 1962. Accountant, Pacific Coll., Fresno, Cal., 1949-55; tchr. Roosevelt High Sch., Fresno, 1958-59; mem. faculty Fresno State Coll., 1962—, prof. quantitative studies and finance, 1966—. Commerce Assos. fellow, 1960-61; Royal Precision grantee, 1961-62; Ford Found. Doctoral Dissertation grantee, 1963-64. Mem. Am. Econ. Assn., Western Finance Assn., Phi Kappa Phi, Beta Gamma Sigma, Delta Pi Epsilon. Editor, Fresno Facts and Trends, 1962-68. Home: 3518 E Lowe Av Fresno CA 93702

BEDWELL, BETTY LEE, direct selling co. exec.; b. Los Angeles, Dec. 26, 1921; d. Roy B. and Pearl (Kelly) Springer; grad. Woodbury Bus. Coll., 1942; m. Wilbur S. Bedwell, Dec. 14, 1941. Sec. to controller Cal. Consumers Corp., Los Angeles, 1942-44; bookkeeper Fullerton Oil Co., Los Angeles, 1944-46, Brooks Clothier, Spokane, Wash., 1946, Berktown of Hollywood, Los Angeles, 1947-49; chief bookkeeper Ehrhart & Assos., engrs., Los Angeles, 1949-60; corporate sec. Con-Stan Industries, Inc., City of Industry, Cal., 1960—. Notary public, 1966—. Mem. Am. Bus. Women Assn. (rec. sec. 1970-71). Home: 1034 Van Horn Av West Covina CA 91790 Office: 19501 E Walnut Dr City Of Industry CA 91748

BEDWELL, ROSE LEONA, educator, librarian; b. Delmont, S.D., Mar. 18, 1923; d. John and Bertha (Fuerst) Bietz; B.S., U. S.D., 1956; M.A., U. Neb., 1958; M.L.S., U. Okla., 1972; m. Thomas Howard Bedwell, Dec. 21, 1956. Tchr., Ruff Sch., Douglas County, S.D., 1942-44, Wessington Springs (S.D.) Pub. Sch., Kimball (S.D.) Pub. Sch., Mitchell Pub. Sch., 1944-48, Wagner (S.D.) Pub. Sch., 1948-55, Canton (S.D.) Pub. Sch., 1956-57, Crete (Neb.) High Sch., 1959-60, Vermillion (S.D.) Jr. High, 1960-64; acquisitions librarian No. Ariz. U., Flagstaff, 1964-65; tchr.-librarian Flagstaff Pub. Sch., 1966—. Mem. Nat., Ariz., Flagstaff edn. assns., A.L.A., Am. Spl. Libraries Assn., Beta Phi Mu. Lutheran. Address: 2903 N Patterson St Flagstaff AZ 86001

BEEBE, GERTRUDE ANNA POTTER (MRS. JAMES BEEBE), mayor; b. Wheatland, Wyo., Aug. 9, 1903; d. Fredrick Lyman and Mae (Robertson) Potter; student U. Wyo., 1921-26; m. Joseph E. Travers, Nov. 9, 1928 (div. July 1937); children—Joseph E., Constance M. (Mrs. Dale L. Urquhart), John, Anita M. (Mrs. Hillebrandt); m. 2d, James Beebe, Dec. 4, 1943 (div. May 1949); 1 son, James A. Elementary sch. tchr., Wheatland, 1921-26; city treas., Signal Hill, Cal., 1942-68, city clk., 1966-68, city councilman, 1968-74, mayor, 1974-75, dir. Sanitation Dist. 3 and 29, Los Angeles County, 1972—. Clk. in charge Signal Hill br. sta. Long Beach P.O., 1956-68. Active A.R.C., Signal Hill, 1951-53. Mem. Municipal Treasurers Assn. U.S., Cal. Municipal Treasurers Assn., City Clks. Assn. So. Cal., Internat. Inst. Municipal Clks. Republican. Mem. Ch. of Jesus Christ of Latter Day Saints. Mem. White Shrine Jerusalem, Order Eastern Star. Home: 1751 E Hill St Signal Hill CA 90806 Office: 2175 Cherry Av Signal Hill CA 90806

BEEBE, JOSEPHINE PARISI, educator; b. New London, Conn., May 11, 1928; d. John and Nicasia (Di Bella) Parisi; B.A., Conn. Coll. Women, 1949; M.A., U. Conn., 1962, Ph.D., 1969; children—Susan Lynn, Edward Neil. Tchr. English New London High Sch., 1949-54; counselor Waterford (Conn.) High Sch., 1962-65; dir. pupil personnel services Norwich (Conn.) Bd. Edn., 1965-69; prof. central Conn. State Coll., 1969—, coordinator counselor edn. program, 1969—; cons. in field. Mem. Career Edn. com., East Lynne, Conn., 1973, Alcohol and Drug Awareness and Edn. com., East Lynne, 1974. Nat. Def. Edn. Act grantee, 1961, 63. Mem. Am. (council 1973—), Conn. (sec. 1970-73) psychol. assns., Conn. Counselor Educators (chmn. 1973—), New Eng. Measurement and Evaluation in Guidance Assn. (treas. 1973—), Am., Conn. personnel and guidance assns. Home: 9 Dodge Ct Niantic CT 06357 Office: Central Conn State Coll New Britain CT 06050

BEEBE, N. LORRAINE, state ofcl.; b. Kalamazoo; B.S., Western Mich. U.; M.S., Wayne State U.; postgrad. U. Mich.; m. 2 children. Former tchr. Henry Ford Community Coll.; mem. Mich. Senate 1966-71; chmn. Youth Parole and Review Bd., State of Mich., 1971—; chmn. Mich. Women's Commn., 1972. Cons. women's rights. Mem. Pres. Com. on Mental Retardation, pres. state conv. to study abortion reform; mem. Com. on Well-Being for Aged. Active A.R.C.; patron Menninger Found. Past mem. bd. Women's Republican State Fedn.; past chmn. Women's Republican Club 16th Dist., Mich.; mem. West Dearborn (Mich.), Redford (Mich.) Twp. Rep. clubs. Mem. ann. fund bd. Western Mich. U.; mem. bd. Hemophilia of Mich.; bd. dirs. Western Wayne YMCA, Clergy Counseling for Problem Pregnancy. Mem. Nat. (steering com.), Mich. (planning com.) women's polit. caucuses, Nat. Assn. Repeal Abortion Laws, Western State Alumni Assn., Dearborn Players Guild, Nomads, Am. Assn. U. Women. Episcopalian. Home: 24424 Fairmont Dr Dearborn MI 48124

BEEBEE, MARY ELIZABETH, librarian; b. Van Buren, Ark., Jan. 10, 1916; d. Sam Dent and Rose Anna (Meyer) Bell; student Lindenwood Coll., 1934-36; B.S. in Edn., U. Ill., 1938, postgrad., 1939; M.L.S., Rutgers U., 1957; m. C. Scripps Beebee, Dec. 25, 1939; children—William Scripps, Mary Elizabeth. Asst. librarian, tchr. English Centralia (Ill.) Twp. High Sch., 1938-39; clk. Columbia U. Library, N.Y.C., summer 1941; substitute tchr. East Orange (N.J.) High Sch., 1949-56; librarian, 1956-66; librarian Clifford J. Scott High Sch., East Orange, 1966—. Mem. Nat., N.J., Essex County, East Orange edn. assns., N.J., Essex County sch. media assns., Kappa Alpha Theta Alumnae Club No. N.J. Methodist. Home: 384 N Walnut St East Orange NJ 07017 Office: 129 Renshaw St East Orange NJ 07017

BEECHAM, MABEL ELIZABETH (MRS. SAMUEL C. DELANEY), mfg. co. owner; b. Oxmoor, Ala., Dec. 29, 1887; d. Samuel and Florence (Matheny) Mynhier; grad. high sch.; m. Samuel Carson Delaney, July 5, 1905; children—Ruth, Raymond, Carolyle, Kenneth, Josephine, Virginia. Owner, mgr., chmn. bd. Best Mattress & Furniture Co., West Columbia, S.C., 1932—. S.C. rep. People to People project, 1967; mem. Gov's Council for Aged, 1968-70; S.C. rep. on tour to USSR, 1967; dir. Women's Missionary Union, 1952-69; asst. treas. Youth Center, 1969-72; treas. Lexington Assn. 52 Churches, 1943-57. Trustee Connie Maxwell Orphan Home, Greenwood, S.C., 1960-72. Mem. C. of C., Bus. and Profl. Women's Club (pres. 1970-72). Baptist. Club: Woman's. Home: 800 B Av West Columbia SC 29169 Office: 713 Meeting St West Columbia SC 29169

BEECHER, MARGARET SMITH (MRS. HAROLD KLINE BEECHER), state ofcl., archtl. firm exec.; b. Salt Lake City, Sept. 15, 1909; d. Hyrum Mack and Ida Elisabeth (Bowman) Smith; student U. Utah, 1926-28, 60-61, U. Wis., summer 1929, Northwestern U., 1929-30, Brigham Young U., 1931, McCune Sch. Music, 1933-36, Banff Sch. Fine Arts, Can., 1941; m. Harold Kline Beecher, Aug. 15, 1936; children—Jane (Mrs. Kenneth W. Yeates III), Allyson. Tchr. creative arts and music Salt Lake City Schs., 1933-36, Rowland Hall, pvt. sch., Salt Lake City, 1936-41; pvt. tchr. music, art, Salt Lake City, 1936-50; v.p., sec. Harold K. Beecher & Asso. Architects, Salt Lake City, 1959—; interior decorator, color cons. H.K. Beecher Architect, Salt Lake City, 1965—, v.p., 1969—. Dir. University Heights Corp., Salt Lake City, Big Butte Ranch Corp., Sterling, Ida. Bd. dirs. Utah Div. Fine Arts, 1961—, vice chmn., 1966-70, chmn. bd., 1971-73; bd. dirs. Utah Symphony Orch., 1961—, mem. exec. com., 1961-66, 71-73; bd. dirs. Pioneer Craft House - Sch. Arts and Crafts. Chmn. lit. arts Utah State Arts Council, 1966—; state chmn. Women's fund raising U. Utah Med. Sch., 1958-59; organizer Utah Symphony Guild, 1953, v.p., 1953-55, pres., 1955-57, mem. adv. bd., 1958—; mem. Ballet West Guild, Salt Lake Art Center Guild, Pioneer Meml. Theatre Guild. Recipient Merit of Honor award U. Utah, 1973. Mem. Women's Archtl. League, Utah Poetry Soc. (hon. life), Utah League Writers, Nat. Orch. League. Clubs: Ambassador Athletic, Bonneville Knife and Fork (Salt Lake City). Home: 1098 Augusta Way Salt Lake City UT 84108 Office: 455 E 4th S Salt Lake City UT 84111 also 609 E South Temple Salt Lake City UT 84102

BEEMAN, ALICE LEE, assn. exec.; b. Gainesville, Tex., Sept. 16, 1919; d. William O. and Lucile M. (Anderson) Beeman; B.J., U. Tex., 1941; student Vanderbilt U., 1944-45; LL.D., Central Methodist Coll., 1969; L.H.D., Alderson-Broaddus Coll., 1973. Reporter U. Tex. News Service, 1941-43; asst. dir. dept. spl. services Vanderbilt U., 1943-46; asst. editor U. Mich. News Service, 1946-49; publs. editor, dept. univ. relations U. Mich., 1949-60, dir. univ. publs., 1960-64, dir. information services, 1964-69; gen. dir. Am. Assn. U. Women, Washington, 1969—. Mem. Mich. Ednl. Policies Commn., 1955-57; mem. adv. com. Center Am. Women and Politics, Rutgers U.; mem. adv. com. of nat. orgns. to Corp. Pub. Broadcasting. Mem. Am. Coll. Pub. Relations Assn. (editor quar., nat. dir. 1950-53), Am. Assn. U. Women (pres. Mich. 1955-57, v.p. Northeast Central region, nat. dir. 1957-61, mem. ednl. found. 1962-68, chmn. devel. com. 1964-69), Women in Communications. Home: 10213 Tyburn Terrace Bethesda MD 20014 Office: 2401 Virginia Av NW Washington DC 20037

BEEMAN, ELIZABETH ANN, educator; b. Barre, Vt., Aug. 12, 1916; A.B., Grinnell Coll., 1938; M.A., U. Chgo., 1939, Ph.D. in Behavior, 1947; M.A., Mt. Holyoke Coll., 1941. Asst. U. Chgo., 1941-44, asst. in biol. sci., 1944-45, instr., 1945-49, asst. prof., 1949-51; mem. sci. faculty Sarah Lawrence Coll., 1951-60; asso. prof. Mt. Holyoke Coll., 1960-70, prof. biol. scis., 1970—. NSF faculty fellow, 1959-60. Mem. A.A.A.S., Am. Soc. Zoology, Am. Ecol. Soc., N.Y. Acad. Scis. Office: Dept Biology Mt Holyoke Coll South Hadley MA 01075*

BEEMAN, HELEN MAE WILTSCHKO, physician; b. Carrington, N.D., Feb. 3, 1920; d. William and Nellie E. (Ewen) Wiltschko; B.S., U. Puget Sound, 1941; M.D., U. Ore., 1947; m. Joseph Beeman, Oct. 4, 1946 (div. Mar. 1953); children—Kolleen and Kelly I. (twins). Intern U. Ore. Med. Sch., 1954-55; resident pathology U. Ore. Med. Sch. and Providence Hosp., Portland, 1955-59; practice medicine specializing in pathology, Portland, 1959, Boise, Ida., 1960—; asso. pathologist Providence Hosp., 1959-60; asso. pathologist St. Alphonsus Hosp., Boise, 1960—, also mem. med. staff; cons. pathologist VA Hosp., Boise; mem. staff St. Lukes Hosp., Boise, Holy Rosary Hosp., Ontario, Ore. Partner, Treasure Valley Lab., Inc., Boise, 1967—; partner Pathology Services Profl. Assn., 1973—. Fellow Coll. Am. Pathologists, Am. Soc. Clin. Pathologists; mem. Pacific N.W. Soc. Pathologists, A.M.A., Ida., Ada County med. socs., Am. Med. Womens Assn., Am. Chem. Soc., Soc. Nuclear Medicine. Club: Altrusa (pres. Boise 1969-71, dist. XII community service chmn. 1971-73). Home: 5 Mesa Vista Dr Boise ID 83705 Office: 1055 N Curtis Rd Boise ID 83704

BEENE, BETTY STANLEY (MRS. WILLIAM MARVIN BEENE), assn. adminstr.; b. Texarkana, Ark., Oct. 6, 1946; d. Billy Lafon and Ruth Isabell (Burch) Stanley. A.A., Texarkana Coll., 1966; B.S., Ark. State U., 1968; m. William Marvin Beene, Sept. 7, 1968. Field adviser Crowley's Ridge council Girl Scouts U.S.A., Jonesboro, Ark., 1968-69, field adviser San Jacinto council, Houston, 1971-73, sr. field adviser, 1973-74, operations dir., 1974—. Mem. Assn. Girl Scout Profl. Workers (nat. communications com. 1973, sect. program chmn. 1974—), Assn. for Community Television, Nat. Orgn. Women. Alpha Omicron Pi. Democrat. Methodist (Women Soc. Christian Service, dir. youth group 1970). Home: 730 Seafoam St Houston TX 77058 Office: 1902 Commonwealth St Houston TX 77006

BEERMAN, MIRIAM (MRS. JULIAN JAFFE), artist; b. Providence, Nov. 11, 1923; d. William and Rose (Nochemson) Beerman; B.F.A., R.I. Sch. Design, 1945; postgrad. N.Y. Art Students' League, 1946; m. Julian Jaffe, Dec. 29, 1959; 1 son, William Benjamin. One artist shows Newport (R.I.) Art Assn., 1965, L.I. U., 1965, Chelsea Gallery, N.Y.C., 1968, Halpert Gallery, N.Y.C., 1970, Bklyn. Mus., 1971, Graham Gallery, N.Y.C., 1972, Montclair Art Mus., 1974; exhibited in numerous group shows in U.S., 1946—, also Am. embassy, Paris, France, 1955, Graham Gallery, 1970, New Sch. Social Research, 1968, 69, Am. Acad. Arts and Letters, 1968; represented in permanent collections Whitney Mus. Am. Art, N.Y.C., Squibb Bldg., Mpls., Downtown Gallery, N.Y.C., Andrew Dickson White Mus., Cornell U., Ithaca, N.Y., New Sch. for Social Research, N.Y.C., Bklyn. Mus., also numerous pvt. collections; instr. Miami U., Oxford, O., 1948-49; tchr. pub. schs. Roslyn, L.I., 1956-62, N.Y.C., 1967-68; lectr. Queensborough Community Coll., 1973-74, Jersey City State Coll., 1974. Recipient Providence Art Club award, 1943; Ives Prize for Painting, R.I. Sch. Design, 1944, Painting award 11th R.I. Arts Festival; Fullbright fellow, student of William Hayter, Atelier 17, Paris, France, 1953-55; McDowell Colony fellow, Peterborough, N.H., 1959; Creative Artists Pub. Service Program grantee Cultural Council Found., 1971. Editor, illustrator: The Enduring Beast, 1972. Address: 6 Macopin Av Upper Montclair NJ 07043

BEERS, CHARLOTTE RICE (MRS. DONALD CROCKER BEERS), advt. co. exec.; b. Beaumont, Tex., July 26; d. Glen Edison and Frances Ray (Bolt) Rice; B.S., U. Southwestern La., 1957; postgrad. U. Houston, 1958; m. Donald Crocker Beers, May 29, 1970; 1 dau., Lisa Lenore. Research mgr. Uncle Ben's Inc., Houston, 1958-60, group brand mgr., 1962-68; account rep. J. Walter Thompson Co., Chgo., 1969—, sr. v.p., 1973—. Bd. dirs. Better Bus. Bur., 1973—. Mem. Am. Marketing Assn. (v.p.), Chgo. Advt. Club (dir. 1973—). Club: Executives. Home: 2306 Lincolnwood St Evanston IL 60201 Office: 875 N Michigan Av Chicago IL 60611

BEERS, DORIS CREIGHTON, realtor; b. Enfield, N.H., Aug. 6, 1908; d. Harris Edgar and Ada (French) Creighton; grad. pub. schs.; m. Robert Clayton Beers, Sept. 22, 1934 (dec. Sept., 1965); children—Diane Elaine (Mrs. Edward C. Schmults), Bradford B. Head sec. to chmn. Democratic State Com., N.H., 1929-30; sec. Gen. Motors Acceptance Corp., 1930-32, J. R. Poole, Boston, 1932-36; saleswoman Town & Country Homes, Boston, 1956-58; owner Cedar Realty, Wellesley Hills, Mass., 1958—. Sec., Wellesley (Mass.) A.R.C. Fund Drive, 1955; pres. Melrose (Mass.) Jr. High Sch. P.T.A., 1953. Mem. Greater Boston Real Estate Bd., Nat. Assn. Realtors, Wellesley C. of C. Conglist. (past sec. guild). Club: Wellesley Women's. Home: 27 Livermore Rd Wellesley Hills MA 02181 Office: 33 Washington St Wellesley MA 02181

BEERS, HELEN CLARK (MRS. ROLAND FRANK BEERS), artist; b. Troy, N.Y.; d. James Wheelock and Lily (Smith) Clark; student Rudy Helmo Art Sch., 1949-59, Eliot O'Hara Sch. Painting (Ft. Lauderdale, Fla.), 1942-44, Robert Wite Sch. Art, 1960-64, Ann Schuler Sch. Arts (Balt.), 1965-67; m. Roland Frank Beers, Oct. 29, 1921; children—Roland Frank, Barbara Helen (Mrs. Herbert Trafford), Exhibited one man shows Rensselaer City Hist. Soc., Gallery-on-Mall, Alexandria, Va., Rehoboth (Del.) Art League; exhibited in group shows U. Va., Am. Pen Women Exhibit, Rehoboth Art League, Rensselaer County Hist. Soc., Albany (N.Y.) Artists Group, Troy (N.Y.) Art Guild; represented in many pvt. collections. Pres., Ramsay Alley Gallery, Alexandria, Va., 1964-67; mgr. gift shop Samaritan Hosp., Troy, 1955-60. Recipient 1st and 2d prize Rehoboth Art League, 1964. Mem. Rensselaer County Hist. Soc., Alexandria Assn. and Forum, Soc. for Preservation New Eng. Antiquities, Troy Art Guild, Albany Artists Group, Nat. League Am. Pen Women, So. Vt. Artists. Clubs: Wedgwood (Boston); Dallas Glass (pres. 1934); Boston Glass. Home: Birchwold-West Rd Manchester VT 05254

BEERS, THELMA SNEED, microbiologist, educator; b. Newport, Ky., June 6, 1913; d. Mayce Cannon and Edna (Dyer) Sneed; B.A. cum laude, U. Minn., 1934, M.A., 1936, B.S. in Edn., 1939, Ph.D. in Bacteriology, 1949; m. Russell James Beers, Dec. 27, 1950 (dec. July 1967); children—Barbara Lee, Shirley Kay. Tchr. biology Robbinsdale (Minn.) High Sch., 1939-45; research, teaching asst. U. Minn., 1945-48; bacteriologist Am. Crystal Sugar Co., St. Paul, 1948-49; instr. bacteriology Kan. State U., Manhattan, 1949-51; research asst. U. Ill., 1951-53; microbiologist Viobin Corp., Monticello, Ill., 1953-54; research in bacteriology Ia. State U., Ames, 1958-69; tchr. Edina (Minn.) Pub. Schs., 1969-70; microbiologist Kallestad Labs., 1970-71; research in microbiology U. Minn., 1971—. Mem. Am. Soc. for Microbiology, A.A.A.S., Am. Assn. U. Women, D.A.R., Women's Internat. Bowling Conf., Henrici Soc., Amateur Fencing League Am., Sigma Xi, Sigma Delta Epsilon, Iota Sigma Pi. Clubs: Ames Woman's (pres. 1968-69), Ames Rock and Mineral (pres. 1958-59), Iowa State University Faculty Women's; Women's Color Photo (pres. 1947-48), University Minnesota Faculty Women's (Mpls.). Home: 5500 Countryside Rd Edina MN 55436

BEETEN, CHARLOTTE LORAINE MALLONEE (MRS. LOUIS BEETEN), city ofcl.; b. Longmont, Colo., Feb. 27, 1911; d. Thomas Walter and Cynthia Jane (Dickenson) Mallonee; grad. Johnstown High Sch., 1929; m. Louis Beeten, Feb. 18, 1930; children—Robert Louis, Lynette (Mrs. Wayne Ashmore). Post office clk., Johnstown, Colo., 1930-34, 64-68; census taker, also with quality control U.S. Bur. Census, Greeley, Colo., 1960; census taker Weld County (Colo.) Irrigation Census, 1960-61; clk. Town Hall, Johnstown, 1958-70; clk. Burch Real Estate & Ins., Johnstown, 1958-72; scale lady Great Western Sugar Co., Johnstown, part-time, 1964-73; clk. Erickson's Greenhouse & Gift Shop, Greeley, part-time, 1965-73. Chmn. Glenn A. Jones, M.D., Meml. Library, Johnstown, 1970-74; chmn. Johnstown Cemetary Commn., 1968—. Clk., judge election bds., Longmont, Colo., 1942-50; council mem. Johnstown Town Bd., 1968—. Mem. Longmont Women's Club (pres. 1945-47), Johnstown Woman's Club (pres. 1954-56), Colo. Fedn. Women's Clubs (chmn. 1946-50), Women's Soc. Christian Service (life), P.E.O. Methodist (mem. bd. 1952-70, coordinator Wesleyan service guild 1968—). Club: DeMolay Mothers (pres. 1948-49). Home: 815 Charlotte St Johnstown CO 80534

BEETON, DIANA LAFAY, casting dir.; b. Washington, Oct. 17, 1934; d. John Ewing and LaFay (Gentry) Beeton; B.A., Coll. William and Mary, 1956. Asst. traffic mgr. Dancer, Fitzgerald & Sample, Inc., N.Y.C., 1956-57; with Batten, Barton, Durstine & Osborne, Inc., N.Y.C., 1957-62, Talent Assos., Ltd., N.Y.C., 1962-65; casting dir. Papert, Koenig & Lois, Inc., N.Y.C., 1965-67; sr. casting dir. Foote, Cone & Belding, Inc., N.Y.C., 1967-69; casting dir., prodn. asst. Alton/Melsky Prodns., Inc., N.Y.C., 1969-70; casting dir. Howard Zieff, Inc., N.Y.C., 1970-71; dir. casting Ogilvy & Mather, Inc., N.Y.C., 1972-74; free-lance casting The Casting Couch, N.Y.C., 1971-72, 74—. Mem. Nat. Acad. TV Arts and Scis. Home: 315 E 68th St New York City NY 10021 Office: 2 E 48th St New York City NY 10017

BEETS, VIRGINIA, museum exec.; b. Prentiss, Miss., Aug. 3, 1926; d. Virgil and Mary Elizabeth (Burkett) Beets; student Miss. Coll., 1945-46. Staff zoology dept. U.S. Nat. Museum, Smithsonian Inst., Washington, 1949-55, planning officer, 1955-57, officer dir. Museum of History and Tech., 1957-60, adminstrv. officer, 1960-72, registrar, collections mgmt. officer, 1972—. Recipient Outstanding Performance award, Mus. History and Tech., 1966. Office: The National Mus History and Tech Smithsonian Inst Washington DC 20560

BEFAME, JEANNETTE, reporter, writer; b. Wahpeton, N.D., July 15, 1919; d. Frederick and Sykea (Ashton) Befame; A.B., Stanford, 1941; m. John Allen Sontheimer. Reporter, San Francisco News, 1941, Sacramento Union, 1942; now newspaper feature writer-reporter San Jose (Cal.) Mercury-News; radio work, news reporter, interviews, San Francisco, 1947; TV guest appearances, 1956; during World War II wrote newscasts for overseas. Del. Asian-Am. Journalists Conf. at East-West Center in Hawaii, 1965. Sec. Santa Clara County unit Am. Cancer Soc. Recipient (only woman) Edward McQuade Meml. award for outstanding pub. service in journalism, 1955, Top Story award, met. dailies div. Cal. State Fair, 1956, Theta Sigma Phi Matrix award, 1964. Mem. Am. Assn. U. Women, Cal. Press Women (chartering pres. peninsula dist.), Stanford Alumni Assn. (sec. San Jose area 1962-63), Sigma Delta Chi (dir. No. Cal. chpt.), Theta Sigma Phi (chpt. organizer, 1st pres. 1960). Club: San Francisco Press. Home: 1615 Bel Air Av San Jose CA 95126 Office: San Jose Mercury-News San Jose CA 95125

BEGGS, LAURA MACMILLEN, assn. adminstr.; b. Newark, O., Mar. 9, 1902; d. Frank Leslie and Cora Anne (Styron) Beggs; student Shipley Sch., Bryn Mawr, Pa., 1920; grad. Abbot Acad., 1922; postgrad. Columbus Art Sch., 1925. Landscape designer Burwell Nursery, Columbus, O., 1938-54; pres. Styron Beggs Co., Newark, O. 1954-61. Exec. dir. Licking County (O.) Hist. Mus., Newark, 1966—. Recipient U.S. Treasury award, 1941-45, Service award A.R.C., 1947. Mem. Licking County Hist. Soc., Licking County Crippled Children Soc. (past pres.). Club: Newark Garden (Outstanding Gardener award). Home: 311 Granville St Newark OH 43055 Office: PO Box 535 Licking County Historical Society Newark OH 43055

BEGUE, LOUISE, educator; licence, diplome, d'et Sup., U. Aix (France); student Columbia. Tchr., Lycee Francaise, 1936-53, Columbia Grad. Sch., 1947-48, Coll. City N.Y., 1949-53, Sch. Gen. Studies, Columbia, 1949-51; faculty Sarah Lawrence Coll., 1953—, now prof. French; interpreter State Dept., 1947-53; recorded textbooks for schs. and colls. Author: Au pays de Soleil; Choix de Poesies; Au fil de l'eau; Poesie la vie entiere; co-author: Speak and Read French; La France Moderne. Editor novelette by Andre Dhotel. Address: care Dept French Sarah Lawrence Coll Bronxville NY 10708*

BEH, EDITH KESSEL (MRS. PHILIP CARLISLE BEH, JR.), govt. ofcl.; b. San Diego, Oct. 13, 1922; d. Frank John and Edith (Morrissey) Kessel; student Holton Adams Jr. Coll., 1941-43, Am. U., 1958-60; m. Philip Carlisle Beh, Jr., Oct. 13, 1952. With Nat. Tech. Information Service, U.S. Dept. Commerce, Springfield, Va., 1957—, chief document processing div., 1972—. Mem. Georgetown Citizens Assn. Recipient Bronze medal Dept. of Commerce, 1972. Mem. Am. Soc. Information Scis., Women In Communications. Home: 1229 29th St NW Washington DC 20007 Office: 5285 Port Royal Rd Springfield VA 22151

BEHAR, LENORE MARILYN BALSAM (MRS. VICTOR S. BEHAR), educator; b. Pitts.; d. Fred and Sara (Rosenzweig) Balsam; student U. Pitts., 1956-57; A.B. with honors, Duke, 1959, Ph.D. (USPHS fellow 1959-62), 1963; m. Victor S. Behar, Aug. 31, 1958 children—Marcy Lynn, Jeffrey Victor, Susan Rebecca. Research asso. dept. psychology Duke, 1962-63; staff psychologist Community Guidance Center, San Antonio, 1963-65, Robert B. Green Hosp., San Antonio, 1964-65; mem. faculty dept. psychiatry U. N.C. Sch. Medicine, Chapel Hill, 1965—, asst. prof. psychology, 1965—, coordinator pre-school services, 1968—, dir. Project Early-Aid, 1968—; chief child mental health services N.C. Div. Mental Health Services, Raleigh. U. N.C. faculty grantee, 1967-68, 69-70. Mem. Am., N.C. psychol. assns., Am. Orthopsychiat. Assn., Soc. Research in Child Devel. Jewish religion. Home: 1821 Woodburn Rd Durham NC 27705 Office: 325 N Salisbury St Raleigh NC 27603

BEHEL, BETTY SNYDER, town ofcl.; b. Springfield, O., Mar. 19, 1919; d. Henry Harrison and Cora B. (Lorton) Snyder; grad. Ohio Western Bus. Coll., 1937; student Coll. Marin, 1963, U. Cal. at Santa Cruz, 1973; m. Vernon W. Behel, Dec. 5, 1946 (dec. Nov. 1968); children—Tom, John, Nancy, Peter, Sandra. With First Nat. Bank, Springfield, O., 1938-41; sec. Air Service Command, Dayton, 1941-42; exec. sec. Arabian Am. Oil Co., San Francisco, 1942-49; sec. Corte Madera branch Crocker Bank, Corte Madera, Cal., 1963-64; town clk. Town of Corte Madera, 1964—. Mem. City Clks. Assn. Cal. Home: 87 Corte Madera Av Corte Madera CA 94925 Office: PO Box 159 Corte Madera CA 94925

BEHELER, LAURA FLO, educator, author; b. Ft. Worth, Apr. 21, 1921; d. Sherman Hite and Eva Florence (Larkin) Beheler; B.S., Tex. Christian U., 1943; postgrad. N.Y. U., 1945-46, George Washington U. 1960, U. N.M., 1963; M.A., N.M. Highlands U., 1955. Reporter, Ft. Worth Star Telegram, 1943-44; corr. McGraw Hill Pubs. N.Y.C., 1945; fashion copywriter Neiman-Marcus, Dallas, 1946; pub. sch. tchr., Santa Fe, 1946-63, counsellor, 1963—; also writer. Mem. Internat. Inst. Arts and Letters, Nat. Orgn. Women, C.G. Jung Found. for Analytical Psychology, N.E.A., Assn. to Advance Ethical Hypnosis. Democrat. Author: A Random Medley (poetry), 1955; The Paper Dolls (novel), 1956; Alegorias (poetry and short stories), 1969. Home: 3 Placita Rafaela Santa Fe NM 87501 Office: Harvey Sch Catron St Santa Fe NM 87501

BEHL, MARJORIE, painter; b. Pocahontas, Ark.; ed. Collins Sch. Art, Layton Art Inst., Cal. Coll. Arts and Crafts, Coll. William and Mary. Exhibited in shows at Gibbes Gallery, 1957, 58, Norfolk Mus. Art, 1959, 66, de Young Mus., San Francisco, 1957, Little Rock Art Mus., 1958, Va. Mus. Fine Arts, 1957, 59, 60, Fla. State Water Color Show, 1971, numerous others; represented in permanent collections at U. Va., Valentine Mus. Art, Richmond, Va. State Mus., Norfolk Mus., Va. Nat. Bank, Walter Chrysler Mus., U. Va., Charlottesville, numerous others; works represented in pub. and pvt. collections. Recipient 1st watercolor prize Ark. State Mus., 1957, Virginia Beach Boardwalk Exhbn., 1963, 64, Tidewater ann. Norfolk Mus., 1957, 65. Mem. Soc. Western Art, Virginia Beach Art Assn., Tidewater Art Assn., Sarasota Art Assn. Address: Villa 13 6308 Midnight Pass Sarasota FL 33581

BEHLES, JENNIE DEDEN (MRS. DANIEL J. BEHLES), lawyer; b. Longmont, Colo., May 8, 1946; d. Leroy O. and Kathryn B. (Ball) Deden; B.S.S., Northwestern U., 1967; postgrad. Loyola U., Chgo., 1967-69; J.D. cum laude, U. N.M., 1970; m. Daniel J. Behles, Aug. 31, 1968. Admitted to N.M. bar, 1970; practiced in Albuquerque, 1972—, Carlsbad, 1970-72; law clk. Menig and Sager, 1969-70; asso. counsel M. Rosenberg, atty., 1970-71; partner firm Behles and Behles, Carlsbad, 1971-72; mng. atty. Smiley Profl. Assn., Albuquerque, 1972—. Actress Carlsbad Community Theatre, 1971-72. Treas. Carlsbad chpt. Am. Field Service, 1971-72; mem. home interviewing com., 1971-72. Bd. dirs. Hacidenda de Esperanza, Inc., 1971-72. Mem. Am., Eddy County (law day chmn. 1971) bar assns., State Bar N.M. (continuing legal edn. com. 1970—, equal rights legislation adv. com. 1972-73), N.M. Fedn. Bus. and Profl. Women (state corr. sec. 1971-72), Carlsbad Bus. and Profl. Women Club (finance chmn. 1971-72, young career woman 1972), Carlsbad C. of C. (creative ideas com. 1971-72), Altrusa, Alpha Xi Delta, Kappa Beta Pi. Republican. Roman Catholic. Mem. Order Eastern Star. Contbr. articles to legal jours. Home: 2305 Camino de los Artesanos NW Albuquerque NM 87104 Office: 903 Public Service Bldg Albuquerque NM 87101

BEHMAN, SARA ATANASOFF, educator; b. Steelton, Pa., Mar. 2, 1923; d. Theodore and Spasia (Ilioff) Atanasoff; A.B. (Fels scholar), U. Pa., 1943, M. in Govt. Adminstrn., 1945; Ph.D., U. Cal. at Berkeley, 1966; m. Gerald A. Behman, July 1, 1944 (dec. May 1970); 1 son, Gerald A., Jr. Research analyst, senate finance com. Legislature, San Francisco, 1948-49; labor market analyst Dept. Employment, San Francisco, 1949-59; lectr. econs., research dir. Inst. Indsl. Relations U. Cal. at Berkeley, 1965-69; asst. prof. econs. San Jose (Cal.) State Coll., 1969-71; asso. prof. Cal. Poly. State U., San Luis Obispo, 1971-73, prof., 1973—. Cons. constrn. research Inst. Indsl. Relations, U. Cal. at Berkeley, 1969—. Mem. Indsl. Relations Research Assn. (sec.-treas. Central Coast Chpt.), Am., Western (exec. com. 1970-72) econs. assns. Editorial bd. Indsl. Relations, 1966—, Western Econ. Jour., 1969-73. Contbr. articles to profl. jours. Home: 587 Stanford Dr San Luis Obispo CA 93401

BEHMER, ELSIE ANN, pub. co. exec.; b. Plainfield, N.J., Sept. 30, 1943; d. John Henry and Elsie (Dietz) Behmer; student Cedar Crest Coll., 1961-63; B.A., U. Bridgeport, 1965; M.A. in Journalism, Syracuse U., 1966. Reporter, Long Br. (N.J.) Daily Record, 1966-67; writer, editor Nat. Cash Register, Dayton, O., 1967; asst. editor McGraw-Hill, Inc., N.Y.C., 1967-70; pub. relations mgr. Paillard Inc., Linden, N.J., 1970-74; pub. relations writer Merck & Co., Inc., Rahway, N.J., 1974—. Mem. Publicity Club N.Y., Nat. Women's Polit. Caucus, Nat. Orgn. Women (head pub. relations task force Middlesex County, N.J., 1971, 72, publicity coordinator N.J., 1972), N.J. State Women on Employment. Office: Merck & Co Inc Rahway NJ 07065

BEHREND, JEANNE, pianist, musical educator; b. Phila., May 11, 1911; d. Moses and Clara (Rosenbaum) Behrend; diploma Curtis Inst. Music, Phila., 1934; m. Alexander Kelberine, May 28, 1934; m. 2d, George S. MacManus, Mar. 31, 1950. Soloist; mem. faculty Curtis Inst. Music, 1936-43, Western Coll., Oxford, O., 1943-45, Juilliard Sch., 1946-52, Phila. Conservatory Music, 1949-54, Temple U., 1954, New Sch. Music, Phila., 1969—; rec. for RCA Victor, Allegro, M-G-M. Chmn. Phila. Composers Forum, 1954-66; founder, dir. Phila. Festival Western Hemisphere Music, 1959-60. Decorated Order So. Cross (Brazil), 1965; recipient Bearns prize, 1936; grantee State Dept. for concert tour S. Am., 1945. Mem. Am. Musicol. Soc., A.S.C.A.P. Editor: (Louis Moreau Gottschalk) Notes of a Pianist, 1964; Choral Music of the American Folk Tradition, 1956; Piano Music by Louis Moreau Gottschalk, 1956; The Unknown Foster, 1964. Composer works for piano, chamber music, orch., songs. Address: 2401 Pennsylvania Av Philadelphia PA 19130

BEHRENS, BERNICE (MRS. EARL C. BEHRENS), govt. ofcl.; b. Portland, Ore., July 5, 1910; d. Frank Kelly and Anita (Smith) Woodard; B.A. magna cum laude, Stanford, 1932; m. Jess A. Digman, May 9, 1935 (div. 1939); 1 dau., Diane (Mrs. James F. Dalton); m. 2d, Earl C. Behrens, July 11, 1963. Vice pres. d' Armigene Inc., N.Y.C., 1961-63; merchandising and fashion asst. to pres. Harry Camp Millinery Co., San Francisco, 1943-60; lectr., 1963-69; dir. U.S. Dept. State Reception Center, San Francisco, 1969—. Mem. Pres. Nixon's Women's Adv. Com., 1968—, Pres. Nixon's Commn. Observance 25th Anniversary UN, 1970—, regional panel Pres.'s Commn. White House Fellows. Decorated Officer's Cross Order Merit (West Germany). Mem. Fashion Group, Internat. Hospitality Center (dir.), People-to-People Program, Nat. Council Women U.S., Internat. Council Women, UN Assn. (dir.), World Affairs Council No. Cal., Am. Assn. U. Women, Am. Women Internat. Understanding (dir.), Phi Beta Kappa. Home: 2190 Washington St Apt 1206 San Francisco CA 94109 Office: Room 112 Fed Office Bldg 50 Fulton St San Francisco CA 94102

BEHRENS, JUNE YORK (MRS. HENRY WILLIAM BEHRENS), educator, author; b. Maricopa, Cal., Apr. 25, 1925; d. Mark Hannah and Aline (Stafford) York; B.A., U. Cal. at Santa Barbara, 1947; M.A., U. So. Cal., 1961; postgrad. U. Md., 1955, U. Cal. at Los Angeles, 1964-65, 73-74; m. Henry William Behrens, Aug. 23, 1948; children—Terry Lynne, Denise Noel. Tchr. Hermosa Beach (Cal.) City Schs., 1947-48, Torrance (Cal.) Schs., 1950-54, 56-58, Am. Dependent Schs., France and Germany, 1954-56; various positions as tchr., adminstr., reading specialist Los Angeles City Schs., 1958—; reading specialist Carson Sch., St. Bonita Sch., Carson, Cal., 1968-74, Park Western Pl. Sch., San Pedro, Cal., 1974—. Mem. Internat. Reading Assn., Nat. Assn. for Edn. of Young Children, N.E.A., Cal. Writers Guild, So. Cal. Council on Lit. for Children/Young People, Reading Specialists of Cal., Delta Kappa Gamma. Author: Soo Ling Finds A Way, 1965; Who Am I?, 1968; Walk In Neighborhood, 1968; Earth Is Home, 1971; Farm, 1971; Desert, 1973; Feast of Thanksgiving, 1974, others. Home: 3022 Hermosa Av Hermosa Beach CA 90254 Office: 1214 Park Western Pl San Pedro CA 90732

BEHRENS, ROSEMARY CONNOLLY (MRS. FRANK A. BEHRENS), investment co. exec.; b. Omaha, Neb., Sept. 1, 1917; d. Cornelius F. and Nelle Jane (Coulton) Connolly; LL.B., U. Omaha, 1940; m. Frank A. Behrens, June 10, 1967 (dec.). Sec., E.W. Nash Bldg. Co., Omaha, 1952—. Served with WAC, 1945-47. Mem. Women Lawyers Omaha (pres. 1960-73), Am. Legion. Democrat. Roman Catholic. Home: 6803 Minne Lusa Blvd Omaha NE 68112 Office: 1603 Farnam St Room 1222 Omaha NE 68102

BEHRENS, SUSAN MARY, educator; b. Appleton, Wis., Mar. 15, 1948; B.A., Eastern Mich. U., 1970; M.A., Ohio U., 1971. Faculty, U. Wis., Stevens Point, 1971-72; faculty speech Pan Am. U., McAllen, Tex., 1972—. Mem. Speech Communication Assn., S.W., Tex. speech assns., Tex. Assn. Coll. Tchrs., Civil Liberties Union, League Women Voters, Delta Zeta Alumni Assn. Office: 210 Southwick Hall Edinburgh TX 78539

BEHRMANN, JOAN METZNER (MRS. NICOLAS L. BEHRMANN), editor; b. N.Y.C., Mar. 9, 1936; d. Jerome and Jeanette (Silberman) Metzner; B.A., Queens Coll., 1956; M.S., Columbia, 1958; postgrad. U. Miami, 1970, U. Cal. at San Diego, 1971; m. R. Larry Jinks, Oct. 2, 1960 (div. Mar. 1970); children—Laura Beth, Daniel Carlton; m. Rabbi Nicholas L. Behrmann, Dec. 21, 1972. Editorial asst. Seventeen Mag., 1956-57; reporter, fashion editor Charlotte (N.C.) Observer, 1958-60; copy editor, reporter Miami Herald, 1960-61, 62-63; fashion editor Miami News, 1965-66; asst. prof. Miami Dade Jr. Coll. S., 1968-72; editor family living sect. South Middlesex Daily News, Framingham, Mass., 1973—. Mem. League Women Voters (state legislative chmn. Framingham chpt. 1973—), Women in Communications. Home: 6 Greenleaf Circle Framingham MA 01701 Office: 375 Cochituate Rd Framingham MA 01701

BEISNER, LILA LUCILE (MRS. LOUIS E. BEISNER), pub. co. exec.; b. Natoma, Kan., July 10, 1909; d. Samuel Benjamin and Grace Faye (McFadden) Hankins; student Grand Island Bus. Coll., 1927-28; m. Louis E. Beisner, June 30, 1930; children—Louis B., Faye Ellen (Mrs. Carol N. Anderson), Lila Lou (Mrs. Ralph E. Hoover Jr.). With Beisner Plumbing & Heating, Natoma, 1930-53; with Natoma Pub. Co., 1953—, editor, bus. mgr., 1968—. Sec., treas. Natoma Med. Center, 1963—. Municipal judge City of Natoma, 1957-73. Methodist. Mem. Order Eastern Star. Home: 817 N 2d St Natoma KS 67651 Office: 418 Main St Natoma KS 67651

BEISTLINE, MARY MOORE, lawyer; b. W.Va., Aug. 17, 1918; d. John William and Ada Grace (Daniels) Moore; A.B., W.Va. U., 1949; J.D., Am. U., 1958; m. William Edward Beistline, Nov. 2, 1963. Legal sec. to circuit judge, W.Va., 1940-46; tchr. chemistry Marlinton (W.Va.) High Sch., 1946-52; legal sec. Civil Service Commn., Washington, 1953-57; patent adviser Office Naval Research, Navy Dept., Washington and China Lake, Cal., 1957-72; cons. chem. prosecution of patent applications, 1972—. Mem. Am., Fed., W.Va. bar assns., Woman's Bar D.C., Woman Lawyers Assn., San Diego Floral Soc., Kappa Beta Pi. Republican. Presbyn. Mem. Order Eastern Star. Address: 12460 Grandee Rd San Diego CA 92128

BEITER, MARION, educator; b. Buffalo, Aug. 23, 1907; d. Edward Frederick and Kathryn (Kiel) Beiter; A.B., Canisius Coll., 1944; M.S., St. Bonaventure U., 1948, Ph.D., Cath. U. Am., 1960. Tchr. parochial and pvt. schs. and acads. N.Y., Washington, Ohio, 1925-39; prin., teaching prin. jr. and sr. high schs., 1939-52; chmn. math. dept. Rosary Hill Coll., 1952-71; sabbatical leave State U. N.Y. at Buffalo, 1971-72. Participant NSF programs, 1961, 62, 71, dir. insts., 1964, 65, 66. Parents Club Summer Study grantee, 1968. Mem. Assn. Math. Tchrs. N.Y. (council mem. 1965—, program chmn. ann. meeting 1970; mem. com. elementary math. 1965-73, chmn. 1972-73, chmn. summer workshop 1973), Am. Math. Soc., Math. Assn. Am., Nat. Council Tchrs. Math., Fibonacci Assn., Am. Assn. U. Profs., Sigma Xi. Home: 4380 Main St Buffalo NY 14226

BEITZEL, BARBARA ANN, army officer, occupational therapist; b. Chico, Cal., July 25, 1930; d. Richard Sherburn and Violet Margarite (Yuhnke) Beitzel; B.A. in Occupational Therapy, San Jose State Coll., 1953. Commd. lt. col. U.S. Army, 1969; occupational therapist, Washington, 1954, Honolulu, 1956-58, Denver, 1958-60, Ft. Riley, Kan., 1960-62, San Francisco, 1962-64, San Antonio, 1964, Phoenixville, Pa., 1965-67, Tokyo, Japan, 1967-69, chief occupational therapy, El Paso, 1969-71, 73—, Frankfurt/Main, Germany, 1971-73. Mem. Am., Tex. occupational therapy assns., Assn. Occupational and Phys. Therapists El Paso. Home: 5344 Cornell St El Paso TX 79924 Office: William Beaumont Army Med Center El Paso TX 79920

BEJENKE, CHRISTEL JOHANNA (MRS. GEORGE J. WITTENSTEIN), physician; b. Lodz, Poland; d. Karl Erich and Martha E. (Richter) Bejenke; M.D. cum laude, Ludwig Maxilimilan U., Munich, Germany, 1961; m. George J. Wittenstein, July 1, 1966. Came to U.S., 1961, naturalized, 1964. Intern U. Colo. Med. Center, Denver, 1963, resident anesthesiology, 1963-64; resident anesthesiology VA Hosp. and Nat. Jewish Hosp., Denver, Children's Hosp., Los Angeles, 1963-65; practice medicine specializing in anesthesiology, Denver, 1965-66, Santa Barbara, Cal., 1966; mem. staffs Santa Barbara Cottage Hosp., Santa Barbara Gen. Hosp., St. Francis Hosp., Goleta Valley Community Hosp., Santa Inez Valley Community Hosp. Fulbright travel grantee and exchange scholar U. Colo. at Boulder, 1956-57. Diplomate Am. Bd. Anesthesiology. Fellow Am. Coll. Anesthesiology; mem. Am., Cal. med. assns., Internat. Anesthesia Research Soc., Am., Cal. socs. anesthesiologists. Home: 4004 Cuervo Av Santa Barbara CA 93110 Office: 2235 Castillo St Santa Barbara CA 93105

BEK, DOROTHEA ELIZABETH HUDSON (MRS. PAUL HENRY BEK), librarian, civic worker; b. Arcadia, Neb., May 20, 1910; d. William Arnold and Mary (Murray) Hudson; student Duchesne Coll., 1927-29; B.A., U. Neb., 1931, M.A., 1957; postgrad. U. Wyo., 1941; m. Paul Henry Bek, June 14, 1944 (dec. Aug. 1959). Tchr. pub. schs., Arcadia, 1931-35, Hartington, Neb., 1935-41; tchr. fgn. langs. Seward (Neb.) Sch. Dist., 1941-51, librarian, 1951—. Adviser Seward Y-Teen Club, 1941-63; cons. Neb. Y-Teen clubs YWCA, 1962-66, bd. dirs. Neb. dist., 1946-52, 59-62, pres., 1949-51, bd. dirs., Seward, 1961-66; pres. Seward Mayor's Planning Commn., 1949-52; mem. Neb. Centennial Com. Seward County, 1966-68; mem. Neb. Gov.'s Commn. on Human Rights; mem. steering com. Neb. Gov.'s Confs. on Traffic Safety; counselor Cornhusker Girls' State, 1961; mem. Seward Library Bd., chmn., 1971-73; exec. dir. Neb. dist. Y-Teen Summer Conf., 1961, 62. Pres. Seward County Republican Women's Clubs, 1959-61; vice chmn. Seward County Rep. Central Com., 1962-64. Bd. dirs. Seward County Child Devel. Center, 1973—, sec., 1973—; charter mem. bd. dirs. Seward Arts Council, 1973—. Mem. A.L.A., Neb. Library Assn. (past chmn. sch. librarians sect.), N.E.A., Am. Assn. Sch. Librarians, Nat. Council Tchrs. English, Nat. Geog. Soc., Nat. Wildlife Fedn., Bus. and Profl. Women's Club (pres. Seward 1943-45, 60-62, internat. relations chmn. Neb. 1944-45), Nat. Council Adminstrv. Women in Edn., Am. Legion Aux., Seward County Hist. Soc. (charter, pres. 1968-69), Neb. Ednl. Media Assn. (charter mem., sec. 1969-71), Sch. Dist. Seward Edn. Assn. (chmn. profl. growth 1968-70), Neb. Sod House Soc. (life), Pi Lambda Theta, Delta Kappa Gamma (Neb. pres. 1963-65, membership chmn. 1965-67, rep. of Neb. at Pres.'s Regional Conf. on Traffic Safety, Chgo. 1965, mem. Internat. com. on profl. affairs 1968-70). Roman Catholic. Club: Seward Magazine. Home: 302 E Hillcrest Dr Seward NE 68434 Office: 532 Northern Heights Dr Seward NE 68434

BEK, NANCY ANN, educator; b. Worcester, Mass., Feb. 16, 1949; d. Stephen Stanley and Adeline Ann (Antkowiak) Bek; A.A., Worcester Jr. Coll., 1969; B.A., Suffolk U., 1971; certificate grad. studies Sorbonne, Paris, France, 1971; M.A. (Worcester Jr. Coll. scholar), Assumption Coll., 1973; postgrad. U. Edinburgh (Scotland), 1974. Dean of women Central New Eng. Colls., Worcester, Mass., 1971-73; asst. to dean of students Fitchburg (Mass.) State Coll., 1973-74; dean students Anna Maria Coll., Paxton, Mass., 1974—. Youth chmn. Republican party, Worcester County, 1972-74. Mem. Nat., Mass. assns. women deans, adminstrs. and counselors, Nat. Assn. Student Personnel Adminstrs. Home: Mumford Rd East Douglas MA 01516 Office: Anna Maria Coll Paxton MA 01612

BELAND, IRENE MARIE (MRS. THOMAS R. BELAND), paper products co. exec.; b. L'Erable, Ill., Apr. 21, 1913; d. John Benjamin and Mable Anna (Hougardy) Colombe; grad. high sch.; m. Thomas R. Beland, Nov. 5, 1938. Bookkeeper Edwin Pratt's Sons Co., Kankakee, 1930-38, Joseph Turk Mfg. Co., Bradley, Ill., 1938-46; office mgr., credit mgr. Amberg File & Index Co., Kankakee, 1946—. Mem. V.F.W. Aux., 1945—, Am. Legion Aux., 1964—; pres. Delphi Civic Orgn., Kankakee, 1956-58. Mem. Lady of the Moose, Elk. Club: Emblem. Home: 24 Lawrence Dr Kankakee IL 60901 Office: 1625 East Duane St Kankakee IL 60901

BELANGER, ESTELLE MARGARET, editor; b. Huntington, W.Va., Aug. 23, 1914; d. Anthony A. and Rosalie (Howard) Belanger; A.B., Marshall U., 1935, M.A., 1972. Reporter Huntington Pub. Co., 1942, asst. Sunday editor, 1942-45, Sunday city editor, 1945-60, asst. afternoon city editor, 1960-61, Sunday mag. editor, 1961-70, art and culture editor, 1970—. Arts corr. N.Y. Times, 1965—; judge art exhibits and competitions. W.Va., Ohio, Ky., 1965—. Mem. promotion com. Mountain State Art and Craft Fair W.Va., 1965. Bd. dirs. W.Va. Opera Theater, Greater Huntington Symphonic Band, Greater Huntington Arts Festival, Regional Arts Council W.Va. Recipient award Ohio Press Women, 1970-71, hon. award W.Va. Regional Authors, 1968. Mem. Nat. Fedn. Press Women, Ohio Press Women, Ohio Valley News Women (pres. 1970-71), W.Va. Press Women (pres. 1972—), Tri State Arts Assn., Huntington Galleries, Music Critics Assn. Am., Sigma Delta Chi. Home: 617 Riverside Dr Chesapeake OH 45619 Office: 946 5th Av Huntington WV 25720

BELCH, CAROLINE JEAN, librarian; b. Seattle, Nov. 5, 1916; d. William Edward and Evangeline Teresa (Cole) Ahrens; B.A., U. Wash., 1938, M.A. in Librarianship (William E. Henry scholar), 1960; m. Herbert James Belch, July 19, 1947; children—James Clifford, Paul Harris. Head tech. services Seattle Pacific Coll., 1967-68; head curriculum materials center U. Wash., 1968—. Author: Contemporary Games, 2 vols., 1973. Home: 5509 17th Av NE Seattle WA 98105

BELCHER, MARGARET LOUISE LYNCH (MRS. RALPH C. BELCHER), bus. exec., civic worker; b. Dallas; d. Samuel E. and Bessie Lee (Stokes) Lynch; student Carpenters Bus. Sch., 1951-52, La Salle Sch. Bus. and Accounting, 1956-58; m. Ralph C. Belcher, Sept. 1, 1940; 1 dau., Brenda Vernelle (Mrs. James Ancrum). Cashier, Afro Am. Life Ins. Co., 1951-62; bookkeeper ABC Bookkeeping Service, 1962-65; owner Belchers Bookkeeping & Secretarial Service, Columbus, Ga., 1965—. Hon. pres. Nat. Assn. Negro Bus. and Profl. Womens Clubs, 1967—; sec. N.A.A.C.P., Columbus, 1958—, bd. dirs. Columbus br., 1958—; bd. dirs. Columbus Council Human Relations, 1961—; pres. Columbus Club Bus. and Profl. Women, 1959-63; mem. exec. com. Leadership Conf. Civil Rights, 1967-69; bd. dirs. Nat. Council Women U.S.A., 1967-69, chpt. Am. Cancer Soc., 1965-73, Brookhaven br. YMCA, 1962—, sec. bd., 1965-69; sec., bd. dirs. Metro-Columbus Urban League; bd. dirs. Columbus chpt. Goodwill Industries, Fifth Av. Community Center, Columbus. Recipient Sojourner Truth award Bus. and Profl. Women's Club, 1963; Outstanding award for contbns. Youth of Am., Pres. L.B. Johnson, 1968; named Woman of Year, Iota Phi Lambda, 1959, Alpha Phi Alpha, 1960; Outstanding Career Woman, Chattachochee Valley Bus. and Profl. Women's clubs, 1971; Appreciation award U.S. Dept. Commerce, 1970; Community Service award Zeta Phi Beta, 1971; Outstanding Service award Nat. Found. March of Dimes, 1971; Nat. Appreciation award Nat. Assn. Negro Bus. and Profl. Womens Clubs, 1972. Mem. Ga. Council Human Relations. Baptist. Home: 2861 Urban Av Columbus GA 31907 Office: 1035 1st Av Columbus GA 31901

BELCHER, OPAL EARLENE, librarian; b. Belcher, Ky.; d. W.K. and Josephine (Bingham) Belcher; A.B., U. Ky., 1957, M.A., 1961, Edn. Specialist, 1974. Tchr. Elkhorn (Ky.) city schs., 1948-62, elementary librarian, 1962-64, high sch. librarian, 1964-67; dir. dist. instructional materials center Buchanan County, Grundy, Va., 1967-69; instr. Pikeville (Ky.) Coll., 1968, Murray (Ky.) State U., summer 1969, So. West Va. Community Coll., Williamson, 1971-72; dist. dir. libraries Pike County Schs., Pikeville, 1969-71; Title I librarian Magoffin County, Salyersville, Ky., 1972—. Mem. Southeastern, Ky. library assns., U. Ky. Alumni Assn. Mem. Christian Ch. Home: Route 1 Box 349A Elkhorn City KY 41522

BELEN, SISTER MARY JANICE, hosp. adminstr.; b. Lansing, Mich., Jan. 21, 1923; d. Louis M. and Amelia (Oyt) Belen; B.S. in Nurses Edn., Mercy Coll. Detroit, 1956; M.S. in Nursing Adminstrn., Wayne State U., 1957. Joined Sisters of Mercy, 1947; dir. Mercy Sch. Practical Nursing, Cadillac, Mich., 1950-51; dir. McAuley Sch. Practical Nursing, Detroit, 1951-56; adminstr. Mercy Hosp., Grayling, Mich., 1962-68; adminstr. St. Lawrence Hosp., Lansing, 1968—. Mem. Gov's. Adv. Council for Mental Health, 1971—, Lansing Planning Bd., 1972—. Bd. dirs. Mich. Catholic Social Services, 1971—. Recipient Distinguished Service award Grayling C. of C., 1967, Mayor's Certificate of Appreciation, Lansing, 1970; Distinguished Woman award Mich. Fedn. Bus. and Profl. Women's Clubs, 1973. Mem. Am. Coll. Hosp. Adminstrn., Am. Coll. Med. Adminstrn., Am. Mgmt. Assn., Nat. League Nursing, Am. Hosp. Assn. (Mich. del. 1974—), Nat. Assn. Mental Health, State Hosp. Assn., (mem. occupational safety com. 1973—), Zonta Club. Home: 627 Westmoreland St Lansing MI 48915 Office: 1210 W Saginaw St Lansing MI 48914

BELFORD, AILEEN LOUISE HIRSCHMAN, lawyer; b. N.Y.C., July 29, 1932; d. Sol R. and Rose (Korn) Hirschman; B.A., U. Va., 1953; J.D., Fordham U., 1955; m. Lloyd Earl Belford, Aug. 14, 1955; 1 dau., Kyle Alexandra. Admitted to Mass. bar, 1959, U.S. Supreme Ct. bar, 1967; partner firm Belford and Belford, Fall River, Mass., 1959—; asst. atty. gen. Mass., 1963-69; instr. McNeese Coll., 1955-56; tchr. pub. schs., Fall River, 1956-58; prof. criminal law Bristol Community Coll., Fall River, 1971—; corporator Fall River Five-Cents Savs. Bank, 1974—; civic and polit. leader, pub. speaker, lectr. Mem. Mass. Bd. Appeals on Motor Vehicle Liability Policies and Bonds, 1963-69. Del. UN Commn. on Human Rights, 1961, UN Social Commn., 1965; mem. Mayor's Task Force on Drug Abuse. Legal adviser Women's Union, Bristol Community Coll., 1973—. Republican state committeewoman, 1964—; parliamentarian Mass. Rep. Com., 1968—; mem. Fall River Rep. City Com.; pres. Fall River Women's Rep. Club; bd. dirs. Bristol County Rep. Club, Mass. Fedn. Rep. Women; del., mem. credentials com. Rep. Nat. Conv., 1972; chmn. rules com. Mass. Rep. Conv., 1972. Bd. dirs. Mass. Soc. Prevention Cruelty to Children, 1962—, Cerebral Palsy Found., Fall River chpt. A.R.C., Brandeis U. Nat. Women's Com.; mem. Truesdale Hosp. Women's Bd.; com. Heart Fund Ball. Recipient 1st Distinguished Alumnae award Mary Washington Coll. U. Va., 1966; named Most Outstanding Young Woman in Mass., 1968. Mem. Am., Mass. (bd. dels. 1969-70, com. criminal law 1973—), Bristol County, Fall River (sec. 1973—, Inter-Am. bar assns., Mass. (1st v.p. 1968, pres. 1969-70, chmn. jr. bar commn. 1965), Nat. (ed. bd. Law Jour. 1966—) assns. women lawyers, Internat. Fedn. Women Lawyers (chmn. domestic relations com.), Mass. Trial Lawyers Assn., Am. Assn. U. Women (legislation chmn. Fall River chpt.), Bus. and Profl. Women's Club, Fall River C. of C., Credit Women's Bus. Club, Fall River Hist. Soc., Mary Washington Coll. of U. Va. Alumni Assn. (past pres., dir. Mary Washington Coll.). Mem. B'nai B'rith (past v.p.). Club: Quota. Author series of articles on the importance of internat. understanding. Home: 1135 Highland Av Fall River MA 02720 Office: 279 N Main St Fall River MA 02722

BELING, HELEN (MRS. LAWRENCE R. KAHN), sculptor; b. N.Y.C., Jan. 1, 1914; d. Morris and Eva (Harrison) Beling; student N.A.D., 1930-37, Coll. City N.Y., 1931-32, Art Students League, N.Y.C., 1944-45; m. Lawrence R. Kahn, Sept. 30, 1937; children—Kathe (Mrs. James H. Mayer), Vicki (Mrs. Craig Hodgetts). One man shows Heller Gallery, N.Y.C., 1952, 54, Krasner Gallery, N.Y.C., 1959, 61, 64, 67, 69, 71; exhibited in group shows N.A.D., N.Y.C., 1938, 39, 40, 51, 52, 53, 58, Pa. Acad. Fine Arts, Phila., 1950, 51, 53, 54, 64, 66, Met. Mus., N.Y.C., 1951, Whitney Museum, N.Y.C., 1955, also various univs. and Sculptors Guild anns.; represented in permanent collections Butler Mus., Youngstown, O., Syracuse (N.Y.) U. Mus., Norfolk (Va.) Mus. Art, St. Lawrence U., N.Y. Tchr. sculpture Westchester (N.Y.) Workshop, 1950-66; tchr. sculpture Coll. New Rochelle, 1971—. Mem. Art Commn. City New Rochelle (N.Y.), 1958-63. Recipient award Sabena Airlines Internat. Competition, 1953, Silvermine Guild award, 1957, 60, medal of Honor, Audubon Artists, 1965. Mem. Sculptors Guild (pres.), Audubon Artists, Nat. Assn. Women Artists (medal of honor 1958, 68). Various home, sch., temple, hosp. archtl. commns. Home: 287 Weyman Av New Rochelle NY 10805

BELK, BEVERLY, physician; b. Macon, Ga., Sept. 19, 1937; d. Vilas Blue and Emily (Murray) Belk; A.B., Mercer U., 1959; M.D., Med. Coll. Ga., 1964. Rotating intern Ben Taub Gen. Hosp., Houston, 1964-65, pediatric resident, 1965-66; pediatric resident Med. Coll. Ga., Augusta, 1966-67; staff physician Sunland Tng. Center, Marianna, Fla., 1967-68; practice medicine specializing in pediatrics, Augusta, 1969-70; dir. children's unit Ga. Regional Hosp., Augusta, 1970-73, asst. prof. pediatrics Med. Coll. Ga., coordinator pediatric edn. U. Hosp., Augusta, 1973—. Fellow Am. Acad. Pediatrics; mem. A.M.A., Am. Women's Med. Assn., Med. Assn. Ga., Richmond County Med. Soc., Ga. Sheriffs Assn. (hon.). Home: 1723 1/2 Kissing Bower Rd Augusta GA 30904 Office: PO Box 5625 Augusta GA 30906

BELL, ALICE JULIETTE CRANDALL (MRS. E. JAMES BELL), assn. exec.; b. Salt Lake City, Apr. 19, 1910; d. Milan Lucian and Florence Mary (Robbins) Crandall; B.S., U. Utah, 1931; m. E. James Bell, July 6, 1935; children—Bonna (Mrs. George Hartmann), Kathleen (Mrs. Gregory Morgan). Tchr., Salt Lake City, 1929-30, 31-34, Latter Day Saints Bus. Coll., Salt Lake City, 1934-35; with Security Life & Accident Co., Denver, 1938-43, 44-45; asst. mgr. claims dept., 1942-43, sec. to chmn. bd. dirs., 1944-45; sec. to mgr. Internat. Minerals & Chem. Co., Carlsbad, N.M., 1943-44; exec. sec. Vallejo (Cal.) Gen. Hosp., 1955-67, adminstrv. asst., 1967-71; exec. dir. Solano County Med. Soc., Vallejo, 1971—. Bd. dirs. Found. for Med. Care Solano County, 1966-67. Mem. Napa-Solano Pan-Hellic Assn., Soroptimist Internat., Coll. Woman's Club, Delta Zeta. Home: 161 Edgemont Av Vallejo CA 94590 Office: 1520 Tennessee St Vallejo CA 94590

BELL, ARVINE, camp dir.; b. Little Rock, Aug. 18, 1925; d. Charles Wilkins and Edith Jewell (Goad) Bell; student Little Rock Jr. Coll., 1942-44; B.A., Ouachita Bapt. U., 1946; M.R.E., Southwestern Bapt. Sem., 1951; M.S., Ind. U., 1965. Tchr., Benton, Ark., 1946-47, Bauxite, Ark., 1948-50; instr. Ouachita Bapt. U., Arkadelphia, Ark., 1951-54; dir. Camp Crestridge for Girls, Ridgecrest, N.C., 1954—. Mem. recreational com. Woman's Aux. Salvation Army, Ashville, N.C., 1969—; mem. com. Home for Unwed Mothers, Asheville, 1969-70, com. on aid for Reynolds-Miller Chorale, Asheville, 1970—, recreation adv. com. S.W. Tech. Inst., Sylva, N.C., 1972-73; dir. pre-camp counselor course Carson-Newman Coll., Jefferson City, Tenn., 1957-65. Mem. Am. Camping Assn. (chmn. memberships com. S.E. sect. 1955-58), Christian Camping Internat. (Presdl. award 1969, mem. editorial com. mag. 1965-68, internat. sec. 1965-71). Baptist. Contbr. articles to camping, religious jours. Address: PO Box 128 Ridgecrest NC 28770

BELL, BARBARA, astronomer; b. Evanston, Ill., Apr. 1, 1922; d. George Irving and Hazel (Seerley) Bell; A.B., Radcliffe Coll., 1944, A.M., 1949, Ph.D., 1951. Mem. sci. staff Harvard Coll. Obs., Cambridge, Mass., 1951—, sci. asst. to dir., 1957-71, astronomer, 1971—. Mem. Am. Astronom. Soc., Internat. Astronom. Union, Am. Inst. Archaeology, Am. Center for Research in Egypt. Office: Harvard Coll Obs Cambridge MA 02138

BELL, BERTHA EWING (MRS. FRANCIS E. BELL), physician; b. Cleveland, Okla., May 9, 1913; d. Andrew and Bertha (Emory) Ewing; B.S., Baker U., 1936; M.D., U. Kan., 1943; m. Francis E. Bell, June 16, 1946 (dec. Apr. 1968); children—Steven Edward and Robert Frederick. Intern U. Kan. Med. Sch., 1943-44; resident internal medicine St. Mary's Hosp., Kansas City, Mo., 1944; asst. surgeon Mo. Pacific R.R., 1945-47; conducted Well Baby Clinic for City-County Health Dept., Wichita, Kan., 1950-53; physician to both homes for delinquent juveniles, Wichita, Kan., established, conducted 1st well baby clinics, Franklin County, Kan., 1956-64; student health physician U. Kan., 1964—; mem. staff Watkins Meml. Hosp., U. Kan., 1964—, sec., 1965-67; mem. courtesy staff Lawrence Meml. Hosp. Mem. Douglas County, Kan. State med. socs., A.M.A. Research on injuries to coll. students. Home: 3020 Iowa St H 17 Lawrence KS 66044 Office: Watkins Meml Hosp Lawrence KS 66045

BELL, BETTY JO, educator, nurse; b. Corsicana, Tex., Mar. 18, 1941; d. Daniel Joseph, Jr. and Ella Ruth (Sims) Bell; B.S. in Nursing (Clayton Fund scholar), U. Tex., Galveston, 1964; M.Nursing, U. Fla., Gainesville, 1965; certificate nursing care handicapped children, U. Wash., Seattle, 1973. Staff nurse John Sealy Hosp., Galveston, 1965-66; instr. pediatric nursing U. Tex., 1966-67; instr. nursing Child Devel. Center, U. Miami (Fla.), 1967-70; asst. prof. pediatric nursing, nursing coordinator clin. tng. projects Center Devel. and Learning Disorders, U. Ala., Birmingham, 1970—, guest lectr. spl. edn. and nursing classes, 1970—; cons., tchr. in field. USPHS Fed. Nursing trainee, 1964-65, 70-73. Mem. Am. Nurses Assn., Am. Assn. Mental Deficiency, Assn. Retarded Children, Phi Theta Kappa, Sigma Theta Tau. Methodist. Home: 1G Rue de Ville Homewood AL 35209 Office: 1720 7th Av S Birmingham AL 35294

BELL, BONNIE LOU ENGEL, art cons.; b. Elgin, Ill., Aug. 31, 1946; d. Earl Charles and Hazel Irene (Anderson) Engel; B.A., Carthage Coll., 1968; M.A., Bradley U., 1970; m. Carl Joseph Bell, June 10, 1972. Sch. psychologist Springfield (Ill.) Pub. Schs., 1969-71, Sangamon Area Spl. Edn. Dist., Rochester, Ill., 1971-72; asso. sch. psychologist W. Ga. Ednl. Services Center, Carrollton, 1972-73; v.p. Belbon Enterprises, Winter Park, Fla., 1971—; co-owner Art for the People, Winter Park, 1973—. Mem. faculty Lincoln Land Community Coll., Springfield, 1970-72; psychol. cons. pupil services dept. Ill. Office Supt. Pub. Instrn., 1971-72. Mem. Am. Assn. Univ. Women (program chmn. 1970-71), Council for Exceptional Children, Ill. Psychol. Assn., Nat., Fla., Ga. assns. sch. psychologists, Friends of Everglades, Kappa Phi Eta, Psi Chi. Author articles, songs. Office: Box 434 Winter Park FL 32789

BELL, CAROLYN SHAW (MRS. NELSON S. BELL), economist; b. Framingham, Mass., June 21, 1920; d. Clarence E. and Grace (Wellington) Shaw; A.B. magna cum laude, Mt. Holyoke Coll., 1941; Ph.D., London U., 1949; m. Nelson S. Bell Aug. 26, 1953; 1 dau., Tova Maria (by previous marriage). Economist OPA, Washington, 1941-42, San Francisco, 1943-45; research asso. Social Sci. Research Council, Harvard, 1950-53; economist U. P.R., 1952; instr. to asso. prof. Wellesley Coll. 1950-62, prof., 1962—, Katharine Coman prof. econs., 1970—. Pub. mem. Nat. Advt. Rev. Bd., 1972—; mem. U.S. Dept. Labor adv. com. status Women, 1973—; econs. commentator, radio and TV. Bd. overseers Amos Tuck Grad. Sch. Bus. Adminstrn. Dartmouth; mem. adv. bd. Pub. Interest Econs. Center, 1972—. Lucy Farr fellow Am. Assn. U. Women, 1961-62. Mem. Am. (com. on status women), Eastern econ. assns., Am. Assn. U. Profs., Am. Assn. Evolutionary Econs. (bd. dirs.), Nat. Orgn. Women, Am. Assn. U.

Women, Phi Beta Kappa. Unitarian. Author: Consumer Choice in the American Economy, 1966; The Economics of the Ghetto, 1970. Contbg. author: Marketing in Puerto Rico, 1955; Entrepreneurship Innovation and Social Change, 1966. Contbr. articles in field to profl., bus. and news jours. Bd. editors Challenge mag., 1973—. Home: Claybrook Rd Dover MA 02030 Office: Wellesley Coll Wellesley MA 02181

BELL, DOROTHY EILEEN, state ofcl.; b. Pontiac, Mich., Feb. 15, 1934; d. Russel Clyde and Mary Elizabeth (Fitzwater) Bell; B.S., Mich. State U., 1958, M.A., 1960; Ph.D., U. Ill., 1972. Tchr. Pontiac (Mich.) pub. schs., 1958-59, counselor, 1959-65; asst. dean of women, asst. prof. California (Pa.) State Coll., 1965-68; fellow Inst. for Advanced Study in Coll. Student Personnel Adminstrn., U. Ill., 1968-69, research asst., 1969-72; asst. dir. research and govtl. relations State of Ill. Bd. Higher Edn., Springfield, 1973—. Chmn. task force on alcoholism Champaign County Mental Health Bd., 1973. Mem. Nat. Assn. Women Deans, Adminstrs. and Counselors, Am. Assn. for Higher Edn., Kappa Delta Pi. Home: 1517 Grandview Dr Champaign IL 61820 Office: 500 Reisch Bldg 119 S 5th St Springfield IL 62701

BELL, ESTHER BERNICE, occupational therapist; b. Los Angeles, June 1, 1930; d. Clifford and Esther Mildred (Haug) Bell; B.S., U. Cal. at Los Angeles, 1951; certificate occupational therapy U. So. Cal., 1954; M.A., Tex. Woman's U., 1971. Staff therapist Tex. Rehab. Hosp., Gonzales, 1954-62, dir. occupational therapy, 1962—. Chmn. clin. council Tex. Woman's U., 1964—; mem. adv. com., occupational therapy asst. program St. Phillips Coll., San Antonio, 1973—. Mem. Am., Tex. (del. 1971—, Tex. Occupational Therapist of Yr. 1971), occupational therapy assns., Tex. Rehab. Assn., Beta Sigma Phi. Home: 111 N College St Gonzales TX 78629 Office: Box 58 Gonzales TX 78629

BELL, GRACE, govt. ofcl.; b. Rocky Ford, Colo., Dec. 4, 1908; d. Mark Adrian and Mary (Nancolas) Denson; A.B., U. Denver, 1929; M.A., Colo. State Coll. Edn., 1945; m. Rex Bell, May 28, 1930 (dec.); 1 adopted son, John. Tchr. elementary and high schs., Wyoming, Colo., Tex., Washington, 1930-49; dir. guidance Sunnyside (Wash.) Pub. Schs., 1952-58, chief staff services Wash. Dept. Licenses, 1958-60; cons. Office Emergency Planning, 1961-62, Office Civil Def., Dept. Def., 1962-65, chmn. tng. support dept. Western Tng. Center, 1963-65; edn. dir. 1st Strategic Aerospace div. SAC, Vandenberg AFB, 1965—. Mem. Bay Area bd. dirs. U. Denver; mem. bd. Lompoc Pub. Library, 1971—. Vice chmn. Wash. Democratic Central Com., 1959-61; del. Dem. Nat. Convs., 1956, 60. Mem. Am. Assn. U. Women (state bull. editor, publicity chmn. 1951-53, state sec. 1953-57, program chmn. Alameda br. 1963-64, pres. Alameda br. 1964-65, dir. Lompoc-Vandenberg br. 1966—), Washington Fedn. Dem. Women's Clubs (pres. 1959-61, state by-laws chmn. 1953-59, conv. del. 1956), Olympia Bus. and Profl. Women's Club, Mortar Bd., Alameda Conservation Assn. (founder), Air Force Assn., Women's Soc. Christian Service, Internat. Platform Assn., League Women Voters. Methodist (mem. adminstrv. bd.; mem. Wesleyan guild; steward). Club: Soroptimist (charter) (Lompoc). Home: Space 64 321 W North Av Lompoc CA 93436 Office: Edn Office (DPE) Vandenberg AFB CA 93437

BELL, GRACE WILLIAMS (MRS. D. LOCKE BELL), social worker; b. Cleveland, N.C.; d. Charles Wesley and Lula (Coon) Williams; A.B., U. N.C., 1934, M.S.W., 1940; postgrad. N.Y. Sch. Social Work, Columbia, 1935; m. D. Locke Bell, Jan. 10, 1942; children—Daniel L. II, Robert Neil. Cons. Bur. Family Services, Welfare Adminstrn., Dept. Health, Edn. and Welfare, Washington, 1956-68; chief community services sect. Nat. Center Alcoholism, Nat. Inst. Mental Health, Chevy Chase, Md., 1968-72; cons. on community services, 1972—. U.S. rep. on central com. Internat. Council Home-help Services; exec. sec. Conf. on Homemaker Services, Washington, 1964. Contbr. articles to profl. jours. Home: 3134 Barkley Dr Fairfax VA 22030

BELL, IRENE GEORGIANNA, town ofcl.; b. Ellis, Kan., Mar. 24, 1929; d. Philip Albert and Rose Elizabeth (Schuster) Aschenbrenner; grad. high sch.; m. George L. Bell, May 20, 1947; children—Karen (Mrs. Verle Dwight MacBain), Kay (Mrs. Kenneth Stone). Telephone operator Mountain States Telephone Co., 1950-52; radio dispatcher Colo. State Patrol, 1960-64; town clk., Limon, Colo., 1964—. Police matron, Lincoln County, Colo., 1960-64; acting asst. county clk. for voter registration Lincoln County, 1964—. Mem. Colo. Municipal League (sec. dist. 3). Home: 390 Cavenue St Limon CO 80828 Office: Box 8 Limon CO 80828

BELL, JANET TALLULAH JEWELL (MRS. WILLIAM WOOD BELL) (LEGAL AND PROFL. NAME JAY W. MACINTOSH), educator, actress; b. Gainesville, Ga., Jesse Dickson and Anna Louise (Dorough) Jewell; student U. Wis., 1955-57; B.F.A., U. Ga., 1961, M.A., 1962; postgrad., 1966; m. Darrell William MacIntyre, Aug. 17, 1957 (div. 1972); children—Tracy Lee, Craig Dickson, Blake William. Profl. model Manchesters, Inc., Madison, Wis., 1955-57; substitute tchr., grad. asst. U. Ga., 1961-62; instr. speech, drama Brenau Coll., Gainesville, Ga., 1962-65, acting head speech, drama, 1963; asst. prof. speech, acting chmn. div. humanities Gainesville Jr. Coll., 1966-68, founder dir. Coll. Players, 1966-68. Actress, dir. various local theatrical prodns.; guest star Bonanza, Gunsmoke, The FBI, Probe, also numerous films and commls.; mem. Adv. Com. Arts Program in Ga., 1965-68; co-founder Gainesville Civic Theatre, 1964, pres., 1965-68. Mem. Am. Ednl. Theatre Assn., ANTA, Am., So., Ga. (dist. 1966—) speech assns., Southeastern, Ga. (treas. 1965—) theatre confs., Artists Equity, A.F.T.R.A., Childrens Theatre Conf. Ga., Theatre Atlanta, U. Ga. Law Dames (pres. 1961-62), Gainesville Art Assn., Jr. Service League Gainesville (edn. and admissions com. 1967), Famous Artists Series, Thalian Blackfriars, Zodiac Scholastic Soc., Actors Studio, Screen Actors Guild, Phi Beta Kappa, Phi Kappa Phi, Zeta Phi Eta, Kappa Alpha Theta. Episcopalian. Clubs: Chattahoochee Study, Gainesville Federated Music, Chattahoochee Country. Home: 2399 Mandeville Canyon Rd Los Angeles CA 90049

BELL, MRS. J.O., JR. (MARY FRAZER KELLOGG), camp dir.; b. Athens, Ga., May 4, 1916; d. Forest Edwin and Allene (Hale) Kellogg; B.S. in Phys. Edn., U. Ga., 1937; m. Joseph Oscar Bell, Oct. 7, 1939; children—J.O. III, Edwin Kellogg, John Davis, Stephen Frazer. Radio advt. Richs, Inc., Atlanta, 1937-38; asst. dir. Camp Merrie Woode for Girls, Sapphire, N.C., 1938-39, Camp Arrowhead, 1939—; dir. Camp Glen Arden for Girls, 1950—; mem. Henderson County Sch. Bd., 1962-72. Mem. Jr. Welfare Club of Jr. League. Mem. P.T.A., Am. Camping Assn., P.E.O. Presbyn. Clubs: Woman's Jr. Woman's. Address: Snaggy Knob Tuxedo NC 28784

BELL, MARY ANNE HARDING (MRS. ROBERT MANNING BELL), educator; b. Rock Island, Ill., Oct. 22, 1922; d. Hydous William and Anna Elizabeth (Brown) Harding; B.Ed., Chgo. Tchrs. Coll., 1949, M.Ed., 1963; Ed.D., Loyola U., Chgo., 1974; m. Robert Manning Bell, April 27, 1947; children—Thomas Harding, Anthony Clifford. Tchr. elementary sch., Chgo., 1942-58; researcher, mental deficiency Chgo. Bd. Edn., 1958-60; tchr. secondary sch., Chgo., 1960-61; counselor Mary M. Dodge Sch., Chgo., 1961-67; mem. faculty Northeastern Ill. U., Chgo., 1967—, asst. prof. mental retardation, 1969-74, asso. prof. mental retardation, 1974—. Vice pres. adv. council Mary Thompson Hosp., Chgo., 1969-73, mem. corp., 1972—. Mem. Am. Assn. Mental Deficiency, Council for Exceptional Children, Am. Assn. U. Profs. Home: 1560 N Sandburg Terrace Chicago IL 60610

BELL, MARY KATHERINE, lawyer; b. Los Angeles, July 7, 1910; d. Weldon Branch and Vina (Cowan) Morris; B.A., Stanford, 1934; J.D. cum laude, George Washington U., 1942; m. Robert C. Bell, Jr., Mar. 22, 1941; children—Robert C. III, Marianne (Mrs. Thomas V. Reifenheiser, Jr.). Admitted to D.C. bar, 1942, N.Y. bar, 1952, Conn. bar, 1962; with Women's Bur. Dept. Labor and Dept. Justice, Washington, 1940-43; asso. firm Cummings & Lockwood, Stamford, Conn., 1944-45, Shearman & Sterling, N.Y.C., 1951—. Co-founder New Canaan (Conn.) Nursery Sch.; local chmn. Pace Com. Stanford; Counsel Resources Unltd., New Canaan. Mem. New Canaan Democratic Town Com.; Dem. candidate probate judge, New Canaan dist., 1958, 73. Bd. dirs. Conn. Planned Parenthood League. Mem. Am. Bar Assn., Assn. Bar City N.Y. (asst. exec. sec. 1949). Conglist. Clubs: Cosmopolitan of N.Y.C., Tokeneke of Darien, Conn. Author: Handbook of Indian Law, Personal Bankruptcy, Guide to Personal Finance. Home: New Cannan CT 06840 Office: Shearman and Sterling 53 Wall St New York City NY 10005

BELL, M(ARY) KATHLEEN, govt. ofcl.; b. Washington, July 7, 1922; d. Daniel W. and Sadie (Killeen) Bell; A.B., Smith Coll., 1943, M.A. (hon.), 1959. With Dept. of State, 1944-73, successively jr. profl. asst., post war program com., 1944-50, fgn. affairs officer, specialist in internat. orgn. affairs. Office Internat. Econ. and Social Affairs, Bur. Internat. Orgn. Affairs, 1950-66, officer in charge econ. and social council and gen. assembly affairs, 1964-66, chief div. instnl. devel. and coordination, 1966-71, dir. system coordination staff Office of UN, 1971-73, cons., 1973—. Asst. to exec. sec. U.S. delegation San Francisco Conf. UN, 1945; mem. staff prep. Commn. UNESCO, 1945-46; tech. asst to U.S. rep. to the 2d, 3d, 4th, 5th sessions ECOSOC, 1946-47, adviser to U.S. rep., 1948-70, alternate U.S. rep. ECOSOC, 1971-73, adviser U.S. delegation 56th session, 1973; U.S. mem. on com. on non-govtl. orgns., 1955-65, U.S. mem. interim com. on program of meetings, 1950-67, chmn., 1952-54; adviser to U.S. delegation to prep. commn. Internat. Atomic Energy Agy., 1957, adviser to U.S. conf. delegation, 1957, 58, 59, 60, 61; adviser to U.S. delegation 1st assembly Inter-govtl. Maritime Consultative Orgn., 1959, adviser U.S. Delegation to Council, 1960, U.S. del. ad hoc com. rules procedure, 1960; adviser to U.S. delegation 16th Gen. Assembly of UN, 1961; mem. spl. com. on coordination, 1964; adviser U.S. rep. Tech. Assistance Com., 1964; adviser U.S. delegation 9th, 10th and spl. session of governing council UN Devel. Program, 1970, dep. U.S. rep. to governing council, Geneva, Switzerland, 1973; alternate U.S. rep. to Joint Meeting Adminstrv. Com. on Coordination and Ednl. Com. on Coordination, 1971, 72; alternate U.S. rep. 1st Session Econ. Review and Appraisal Com., 1972. Trustee Washington Theol. Consortium. Decorated lady comdr. Equestrian Order Holy Sepulchre. Clubs: Internat., Sulgrave (Washington); Ponte Vedra (Fla.). Home: 3816 Gramercy St Washington DC 20016 Office: Dept State Washington DC 20025

BELL, MERTYS WARD (MRS. THOMAS EDWARD BELL), coll. dean; b. Arlington, Ga., July 13, 1917; d. Richard Christopher and Carol Odessa (Clements) Ward; A.B., Ga. Coll., 1937; B.S. in L.S., U. N.C., 1942, postgrad., 1966; m. Thomas Edward Bell, Dec. 12, 1942; children—John Bruce, Lisa Ann. Librarian, Douglas (Ga.) Pub. Schs., 1937-40; dist. library supr. WPA Ga., Savannah, 1940-42; dir. Athens (Ga.) Regional Library, Athens, 1942-43; br. library supr. King County Pub. Library, Seattle, 1943-46; cataloger Greensboro (N.C.) Pub. Schs., 1955-60; librarian Guilford Tech. Inst., Jamestown, N.C., 1963-66, dir. learning resources, 1969-72, dean learning resources, 1972—; librarian Rockingham Community Coll., Wentworth, 1966-68; acquisitions librarian U. N.C., Greensboro, 1968-69. Mem. vis. teams So. Assn. Colls. and Schs., 1968—; organizer Guilford County Nat. Library Com., 1970—. Pres., Learning Resources Assn., N.C. Community Coll., 1967-68. Mem. Am., N.C. vocational assns., Community Coll. Assn. Instrn. and Tech., Am., N.C. (sec.-treas. jr. coll. sect. 1973—), Southeastern library assns., N.C. Lit. and Hist. Assn. Presbyn. (ruling elder). Mem. Phi Rho Pi, Pi Gamma Mu. Club: Guilford Library (pres. 1973-74 Greensboro). Home: 5608 Scotland Rd Greensboro NC 27407 Office: PO Box 309 Jamestown NC 27282

BELL, MILDRED LECY, educator; b. Waxahachie, Tex., Apr. 23, 1924; d. John Clifford and Ineeta (Brooks) Bell; B.S. in Home Econs., North Tex. State U., 1949, M.S., 1951; Ph.D., U. Minn., 1959. Tchr. home econs. high sch., Milford, Tex., 1951-52; instr. home econs. Harding Coll., Searcy, Ark., 1952-54, prof. home econs., 1959-60, chmn. dept. home econs., 1960—. Mem. Am. Assn. U. Women, Am. Home Econs. Assn., Ark. Edn. Assn., Aminstrs. of Home Econs., Nat. Soc. for Study of Edn., Sigma Delta Epsilon, Iota Sigma Pi, Omicron Nu, Phi Upsilon Omicron. Home: 100 S Turner St Searcy AR 72143

BELL, NONA MARIE LITTLETON, educator; b. Dallas, Dec. 3, 1918; d. Daniel and Sarah Lily (Brookins) Littleton; B.S. in Edn., Prairie View A & M Coll., 1935; M.S. in Edn., Bishop Coll., 1950, LL.B., 1971; m. Rufus B. Bell, Nov. 23, 1944. Tchr. Lincoln High Sch., Dallas, 1943-47; prin. C.F. Carr Elementary Sch., Dallas, 1948-58; reading specialist Sequoyah Jr. High Sch., Dallas, 1959—, tchr., 1972—. Chmn. Beat 314, Dallas, 1973; vol. Bethlehem Center, Dallas, 1965-68. Recipient Citizenship award in edn. radio sta. KNOK, Dallas, 1967, Police Dept., 1973; Certificate of Merit A.R.C., 1952. Mem. Phi Delta Kappa. Club: Poetry (Dallas). Address: 4610 Baldwin St Dallas TX 75210

BELL, ROBINETTE NIXON (MRS. MURRAY NEIL ROTH), psychiatrist; b. N.Y.C., July 9, 1930; d. Laurence Allen and Virginia (Morris) Nixon; A.B., Smith Coll., 1951; postgrad. Albert Einstein Coll. Medicine, Yeshiva U., 1958-59; M.D., Columbia, 1962, postgrad. Psychoanalytic Clinic, 1966-73; m. Murray Neil Roth, July 16, 1971; children—Suzanne Elizabeth Bell, Donald Stuart Bell. Intern Bronx (N.Y.) Hosp., 1962-63; resident N.Y. State Psychiat. Inst., N.Y.C., 1963-66; practice medicine specializing in psychiatry, N.Y.C., 1966—; mem. staffs Presbyn. Hosp., Gracie Sq. Hosp., N.Y.C.; instr. psychiatry Columbia, 1966-67, 70—; asst. attending psychiatrist Vanderbilt Clinic, Presbyn. Hosp., N.Y.C., 1966-67, 70—. Mem. Am. Psychiat. Assn. (mem. com. interprofl. relations 1969—, dist. chmn. 1971-73), N.Y., N.Y. County med. socs. Address: 200 E End Av New York City NY 10028

BELL, WINIFRED, ednl. adminstr.; b. Detroit, Oct. 10, 1914; d. Rupert Benstead and Elizabeth Mary (Simmons) Bell; A.B., U. Mich., 1932, M.S.W., 1944; D.Social Welfare, Columbia, 1965. Faculty, U. Md., College Park, 1966-68; faculty State U. N.Y., Albany, 1968-72; co-dir. Center for Studies in Income Maintenance Policy, N.Y. U., N.Y.C., 1972—. Mem. Nat. Assn. Social Workers, Am. Pub. Welfare Assn., Council on Social Work Edn., Common Cause, Phi Beta Kappa. Author: (with Elizabeth Wickenden) Public Welfare: Time for a Change, 1961; Aid to Dependent Children, 1965; (with Robert Lekachman and Alvin L. Schorr) Public Policy and Income Distribution, 1974. Home: 2 Washington Sq Village New York City NY 10012 Office: 35 Fifth Av New York City NY 10003

BELLACERO, MARY ROSE DI RUSSO, investment co. exec.; b. Formia, Italy, Apr. 12, 1921; d. Joseph and Laura (CaraMadre) Di Russo; student Mchts. and Bankers Bus. Sch., 1942, U. B.C., 1952; m. Joseph Bellacero, Sept. 20, 1947 (div. Nov. 1961); children—Rosemarie, Joseph, Paul, Lauretta, Richard. With Union Carbide Corp., N.Y.C., 1939-51, F.H. Molitor & Co., Seattle, 1952-56; asst. treas. Di Russo Advt., Inc., N.Y.C., 1962-73; now controller Smilen & Safian, Inc., N.Y.C., 1973—. Mem. World Embrity Soc. (treas. 1968—), Advt. Women N.Y. Home: 739 Arnow Av New York City NY 10467 Office: 80 Broad St New York City NY 10004

BELLAIRS, BETTY RIVERS (MRS. RICHARD E. BELLAIRS), govt. ofcl.; b. Avera, Ga., Dec. 9, 1928; d. George E. and Sally (Dixon) Rivers; A.B., U. Ga., 1949, M.S.W., 1964; m. Richard E. Bellairs, Dec. 6, 1953. Social worker, Augusta, Ga., Louisville, Ga. and Macon, Ga., 1949-57; tchr. pub. schs., Porterdale, Ga., 1957-58; social worker, Newton County, Ga., 1958-62; quality control reviewer Ga. State Dept. Family and Children's Services, 1962-66, med. social reviewer, 1966, chief med. eligibility sect., 1966-69; asst. dir. div. social adminstrn. Ga. Dept. Human Resources, Atlanta, 1971-72, dir. div. benefits payments, 1972—. Mem. Nat. Assn. Social Workers, Am. Pub. Welfare Assn., Ga. Conf. on Social Welfare, Nat., Ga. (dir.) rehab. assns. Methodist. Home: 4126 Legion Dr Covington GA 30209 Office: Room 404-S 47 Trinity Av SW Atlanta GA 30334

BELLAMY, JEANNE (MRS. JOHN TURNER BILLS), banker; b. Bklyn., Nov. 15, 1911; d. Donald Lamont and Ethel Park (Houston) Bellamy; student Barnard Coll., 1928-29; A.B., Rollins Coll., 1933; m. John Turner Bills, Jan. 30, 1942. City hall and courthouse reporter Miami (Fla.) Tribune, 1935-37; reporter Miami Herald, 1937-49, asst. city editor, 1949-51, editorial writer, 1951-58, sr. editorial writer, 1958-73; chmn. bd. Sun Bank Midtown, Miami; 1973—; dir. Sun Bank of Coral Gables (Fla.). Commentator radio sta. WGBS, 1962-63; moderator We Want To Know, sta. WLBW-TV, 1961-63. Bd. dirs. Nat. Audubon Soc., 1963-69; trustee Fairchild Tropical Garden, Coral Gables, 1961—. Recipient ann. awards Fla. Bar, 1959, 62, Jose Marti Journalism award, 1966. Mem. Fla. Soc. Editors (pres. 1962), Hist. Assn. So. Fla., Opera Guild Greater Miami, Vizcayans, Women in Communications, Greater Miami C. of C. (chmn. environmental quality action com. 1971-73, v.p. 1973—), Kappa Alpha Theta. Episcopalian. Author: Taming the Everglades, 1947; Newspapers of America's Last Frontier, 1952; Communism: What It Means to You, 1961. Home: 2917 Seminole St Miami FL 33133 Office: 1400 NW 20th St Miami FL 33125

BELLAMY, LAURETTA CASILDA (MOLONEY), librarian; b. San Luis, Colo., Nov. 6, 1918; d. Alexis Ignatius and Casilda Genoveva (Salazar) Moloney; B.A., U. Colo., 1940, postgrad., 1940-68; postgrad. library sci. U. Denver, 1956; m. Kyle Y. Bellamy, Aug. 2, 1942 (div. Apr. 1946; 1 dau., Casilda (Mrs. Stanley W. Cazier. Tchr. high schs., Limon, Colo., 1940-41, Aurora, Colo., 1941-44, Monte Vista, Colo., 1945-47; instr., dir. lang. house U. Colo., Boulder, 1947-48; asst. prof. N.M. Western U., Silver City, 1948-49; catalog librarian U. Colo., 1949—. Mem. program com. Territorial Daus. Colo., 1958, 62, 72; ednl. dir. Boulder County unit Colo. Heart Assn., 1967—. Mem. Colo. Library Assn. (chmn. no. dist. 1955-56), Am. Assn. Univ. Profs. (sec.-treas. U. Colo. chpt. 1955-56, 62-63, 73—, Colo. Conf. 1962-65), Mortar Bd., Phi Beta Kappa. Club: University (Boulder). Home: 1510 13th St Boulder CO 80302

BELLEROSE, CECILIA AUREA, musical educator; b. Pembroke, N.H., Nov. 8, 1897; d. John Nathan and Elizabeth (Girard) Bellerose; Mus.B., Laval U., 1941, Mus.M. in Voice, 1946, Mus.D. in Composition, 1950. Joined Sisters of Holy Cross, 1914; prof. music elementary and secondary schs., N.H., 1920-37; prof. music Basile Moreau Coll., Montreal, 1937-50; prof. music, head dept. Notre Dame Coll., Manchester, N.H., 1950—; dir. rec. 101 Angels of Song, 1961. Mem. Met. Opera Guild, B.M.I., A.S.C.A.P. Composer ch. and secular music; cantata Concert d'Oiseaux; (choruses) Lux, La Fontaine, Lumiere et Joie, Dieu Nous Voit, Gradatim, O Vierge Radieuse, Cantique a Sant-Joseph. Address: 2321 Elm St Manchester NH 03104

BELLINGRATH, EILEEN GEARY (MRS. ROBERT G. BELLINGRATH), business ofcl.; b. Boston, Dec. 24, 1943; d. Patrick F. and Winifred T. (Grealish) Geary; B.A., Newton Coll., 1965; M.S., N.M. Highlands U., 1967; m. Robert G. Bellingrath, Sept. 30, 1973. Vocational counselor Action for Boston Community Devel., 1967-68; market research analyst Gillette Safety Razor Co., Boston, 1968-73; supr. brand research Personal Care div. Gillette Co., Boston, 1974—. Bd. dirs. Allston Mental Health Assn., 1968-71. Mem. Am. Marketing Assn., Am. Psychol. Assn. Home: 50 Presidential Dr Quincy MA 02169 Office: Gillette Co Gillette Park Boston MA 02106

BELLINI-SHARP, CAROL ANN (MRS. JOHN GORDON SHARP), educator, theatre dir.; b. Pitts., May 5, 1945; d. Albert R. and Mima S. (White) Bellini; B.A. with honors, Pa. State U., 1966, M.A., 1968; Ph.D. (Patrons fellow), Carnegie-Mellon U., 1971; m. John Gordon Sharp, Oct. 15, 1971. Asst. prof. English and theatre Pa. State U., McKeesport, 1967-69; adj. prof. English and speech Community Coll. of Allegheny County, Pa., 1969-73; asst. prof. speech and theatre LaRoche Coll., Pitts., 1972-73; asst. prof. drama, dir. theatre Kirkland Coll., Clinton, N.Y., 1973—. Dir. prodn. Underpants, Pitts., 1972, Ubu Roi, Atelier Theatre, Pitts., 1973, Beggars' Opera, Clinton, 1974; co-founder, dir. North Bank Theatre, Pitts., 1973—. Dir./tchr. creative dramatics Pitts. Model Cities, 1971-72; puppeteer Lovelace Marionette Theatre, Pitts., 1972-73. Mem. Am. Theatre Assn., Am. Civil Liberties Union. Home: 40 Utica St Clinton NY 13323

BELLMAN, BARBARA JOAN, occupational therapist; b. Richmond, Va., Sept. 28, 1930; d. William Henry and Avis Hillsman (Daprato) Bellman; student U. Md., 1949-51; B.S., Va. Commonwealth U., 1953, certificate in occupational therapy, 1954. Staff therapist Handicapped and Crippled Children's Clinic, Washington, 1954-56; asst. chief therapist C. Melvin Sharpe Health Sch., Washington, 1956-59; clin. dir. D.C. Gen. Hosp., Washington, 1959-69, chief therapist, 1969—. Recipient Outstanding Performance award D.C. Govt., 1961, 66. Mem. Am. (certification com. 1968—), D.C. (pres. 1958-60, dir. 1960-61, 65-66, 68-69) occupational therapy assns. Club: Quota (1st v.p. 1972-74 Prince George's County, Md., 2d v.p. 1974—). Mem. editorial bd. Am. Jour. Occupational Therapy, 1973—. Home: 1272 Palmer Rd Oxon Hill MD 20022

BELOTE, GLENDA ANN, coll. counselor; b. Detroit, Dec. 1, 1938; d. Richard Tyler and Virginia Mae (Carpenter) Belote; B.A., Western Mich. U., 1960; M.A., Mich. State U., 1969, Ph.D., 1973. Tchr. English, San Diego City Schs., 1960-62; tchr. English, chmn. lang. arts dept. Pontiac City Schs., 1963-66; resident adviser Mich. State U., 1966-69; dir. residence hall programs Grand Valley State Coll., Allendale, Mich., 1969-71, acting dir. counseling and student devel., 1972-73; dir. counseling and testing Counseling Center, S.W. Minn. State Coll., Marshall, 1973—. Mem. Am. Assn. Higher Edn., Nat. Assn. Women Deans and Counselors, Women's Equity Action League, Minn. Women's Polit. Caucus. Minn. Personnel and

Guidance Assn., Zonta Internat. Home: 904 Hackberry St Marshall MN 56258 Office: SW Minn State Coll Marshall MN 56258

BELSER, CAROLINE DICK MCKISSICK (MRS. IRVINE FURMAN BELSER), civic worker; b. Sumter, S.C., July 15, 1900; d. George William and Caroline (Hutchison) Dick; B.A., Winthrop Coll., 1921; postgrad. U. Wis., summer 1928-29, U. S.C., summer 1939-40; LL.D. (hon.), U. S.C., 1969; m. J. Rion McKissick, May 18, 1927 (dec. Sept. 1944); m. 2d, Irvin Furman Belser, June 21, 1947 (dec. Aug. 1969). Tchr. High Point (N.C.) Grammar Sch., 1921-23, Greenville (S.C.) High Sch., 1923-24, Sumter High Sch., 1924-26. Dir. Alice Mfg. Co., 1945—. Mem. Columbia Jr. League, 1929-40, sustaining mem., 1940—, founder Jr. League Book Club; pres. Dept. S.C., Am. Legion Aux., 1946-47, founder Palmetto Girls' State, 1947, pres. unit to Post 6, 1950-51, nat. v.p. So. div., 1953-54, only life mem. of Girls' State Com.; v.p. Garden Club S.C., 1956-59, chmn. Gardening Symposium, 1960-65. Vice chmn. Democratic Com. S.C., 1960-64. Charter mem. bd. assos. Converse Coll., 1962—; rep. Diocese Upper S.C., Nat. Cathedral Assn., 1962-65; mem. U. S.C. Found., Found. Chair Club, chmn., 1973-74; pres. U. S.C. Caroliniana Soc., 1954-60; chmn. bd. women visitors U. S.C., 1960—; mem. S.C. Am. Mother's Com. Recipient Algernon Sidney Sullivan award, 1951; Hon. S.C. State Mother award, 1968; past col. Gov.'s Staff; Distinguished Alumnus award U.S.C., 1972. Mem. English Speaking Union, Mus. of Art, Richland County, Sumter County hist. socs., League Women Voters; hon. mem. S.C. Press Assn. (pres. womens div. 1968-69), U. S.C. Aux., Mortar Board, Tau Kappa Alpha. Episcopalian (pres. Daus. of Holy Cross 1957-59). Clubs: Fortnightly Book (pres. 1944-45), New Century Book, Evening Music. Home: 15 Heathwood Circle Columbia SC 29205

BELSHAW, FRANCES RAYE, editor; b. LeRoy, Ill., Aug. 16, 1937; d. Raymond Clarence and Emma Lucille (Scott) Rippy; B.S., Ind. Central Coll., 1961; student Northwestern U., 1960-68; m. Terence W. Belshaw, Aug. 10, 1959 (div. July 1973); 1 son, Andrew E. With Libby McNeill, Eureka, Ill., 1959-60, Durkee Foods, Chgo., 1961-66; with Continental Coffee, Chgo., 1966-68; editor Putnam Pub., Chgo., 1968-74; editor Gorman Pub., Chgo., 1974—. Cons. marketing plans to various food industries. Pres. Park West Community Assn., Chgo., 1972—. Precinct capt. Ind. Precincts Orgn., 1969-71. Bd. dirs. Lincoln Park Conservation Assn., 1971-74. Mem. Inst. of Food Technologists. Episcopalian. Sect. editor: Food Processing Mag., 1968-74, Foods of Tomorrow, 1969-74; editor-in-chief Canner/Packer mag., Home: 2451 N Burling Chicago IL 60614 Office: 3460 John Hancock Center Chicago IL 60611

BELSHAW, YVONNE ELLEN, bakery and food service equipment co. exec.; b. Everett, Wash., Jan. 18, 1921; d. Lester Everett and Vida Leah (Stover) DeWitt; grad. Everett Bus. Coll., 1940; student U. Wash., 1956-57; m. Thomas Elwood Belshaw, Jan. 18, 1941; children—William Thomas, Mary Leah. With Belshaw Bros., Inc., Seattle, 1954—, sec., dir., 1961—, advt. dir., 1961—; pres., dir. Belshaw Internat., Inc.; dir. Food Tec Inc., Seattle. Mem. W. Seattle Com. Mgmt. YWCA, 1946-50; pres. W. Seattle Jr. Federated Women's Club, 1953-54. Mem. Japan Am. Soc. (2d place Haiku contest 1970, 1st pl. 1972), Seattle Art Mus. Conglist. Club: Swedish (Seattle). Author: Z is for Zucchini: 101 Recipes for Zucchini Squash, 1973. Home: 12649 Shorewood Dr SW Seattle WA 98146 Office: 1750 22d Av S Seattle WA 98144

BELTON, M. KATHLEEN, anesthesiologist; b. Grand Coulee, Sask., Can., Mar. 17, 1916; d. Alfred James and Gertrude Selina (Reed) Belton; B.A., U. Sask., 1936; M.D., C.M., McGill U., 1941. Came to U.S., 1954, naturalized, 1960; intern, then resident Montreal Gen. Hosp., 1941-43; resident anesthesia Toronto Gen. Hosp., 1943-44; chief resident anesthesiologist St. John (N.B.) Gen. Hosp., 1944-45; asst. dir. anesthesia Children's Meml. Hosp., Montreal, also asso. prof. anesthesiology McGill U. Med. Sch., 1945-47; mem. anesthesiology staff Vancouver (B.C.) Gen. Hosp., 1947-54; asst. dir. anesthesiology Children's Hosp., Los Angeles, also asst. prof. U. So. Cal. Med. Sch., 1954-60; anesthesiologist St. John's Hosp., Oxnard, Cal., 1960—; guest lectr. Colombian and Venezuelan socs. anesthesiologists, 1964; guest lectr. in Japan, 1967. Diplomate Am. Bd. Anesthesiology; certificate anesthesia Royal Coll. Physicians Can. Mem. Am. (del., chmn. com. communications 1965-66), Cal. (pres. 1967-68, editor bull. 1966, 69) socs. anesthesiologists, Am., Cal., Ventura County med. socs.; hon. mem. Colombian Soc. Anesthesiologists. Republican. Presbyn. (elder). Co-author: Pediatric Anesthesia, 1948; Pediatric Anesthesiology, 1960; also papers. Home: 639 Fernwood Dr Oxnard CA 93030

BELTON, SHEILA JOSELDA IMOGENE, nurse; b. Regina, Sask., Can., Nov. 17, 1947; d. Joseph George and Katherina Amalia Franziska (Miller) Seibel; diploma in nursing, R.N., Regina Gen. Hosp., 1968; m. Richard Robert Belton, Sept. 20, 1969. Nurse, Regina Gen. Hosp., 1968-70, 71-72; homemaker supr. Family Service Bur., Regina, 1970-71; nursing instr. Wascana Hosp., Regina, 1972-73, asst. dir. nursing, dir. inservice edn., 1973—. Del., Internat. Hosp. Congress, Montreal, Que., 1973. Mem. Sask. Registered Nurses Assn. (chmn. pub. relations com. Regina 1971, chmn. planning com. ann. meeting 1972-74 pres.-elect. 1974-75), Canadian Nurses Assn. (voting del. 1972, 74), Staff Nurses Assn. Wascana Hosp. (pres. 1972-73). Lutheran. Home: 59 Empress Dr Regina SK S4T 6M7 Canada Office: Wascana Hospital 23d Av and Av G Regina SK Canada

BELZ, MRS. HENRY (DOROTHY PERSHALL BELZ), ins. exec.; b. East St. Louis, Ill., Apr. 24, 1913; d. Estes Edward and Leita (Horton) Pershall; student Ohio State U., 1931-33, Washington U., St. Louis, 1936; m. Kenneth Dillman, June 3, 1932 (dec.); 1 dau., Nancy Wade (Mrs. William Peck); m. 2d, Frederick Carson Jones, Jan. 2, 1939 (div. Oct. 1949); children—Judith Pershall (Mrs. Louis Humes), Cynthia Pedley (Mrs. Michael Todorovich); m. 3d, Henry Belz, June 23, 1952; stepchildren—Henry III, Margartha Hager (Mrs. Alfred Kerth), John Ralph B. Spl. agt. Gen. Am. Inst. Co., St. Louis, 1959—; spl. rep. Gen. Am. Life Ins. Co. Mem. citizens com. St. Louis U. Expansion Fund, 1959—, women's com. Mo. Bot. Garden; city co-chmn. A.R.C. drive, 1952; maintenance fund chmn. St. Louis Symphony, 1940-41, now dir.; mem. promotion com. Art Mus. Ballot; mem. spl. gifts com. United Fund, Fine Arts Drive; mem. Camelot Auction Com. Bd. dirs. Washington U. Women's Assn. Mem. Women's Leaders Round Table, Life Underwriters Assn. (chmn. women's assn. 1962, mem. exec. com. Mo. assn.), Playgoers (dir.), Women for City Living, Jr. League Tearoom Womens Assn. (v.p.), St. Louis Symphony Assn., Nat. Quality Club, Qualified President's Club, Kappa Kappa Gamma. Methodist. Clubs: Sombrero Country (Maathon Shores, Fla.). Clayton for Women. Home: 14 Lenox Pl St Louis MO 16108 Office: 500 N Broadway Suite 1200 St Louis MO 63102

BEMIS, BEATRICE LUELLA BAILEY (MRS. OLIVER BERCY BEMIS), artist; b. Schnectady; d. Emmett and Mary Elizabeth (Harrison) Bailey; student N.Y. Sch. Fine and Applied Arts, 1927, also pvt. study; m. Oliver Bercy Bemis, Feb. 18, 1933; 1 son, Keith Oliver. One-man shows Columbus (O.) Gallery Fine Arts, 1960, Columbus Pub. Library, 1963, Springfield (O.) Art Center, 1963, Riverside Museum, N.Y.C., 1965, Studio II, Worthington, Worthington Pub. Library, 1969, Ohio Nat. Bank, 1972; Columbus City Hall, 1973, others; exhibited in group shows, 1939—, latest including Butler Inst. Am. Art, Youngstown, O., Nat. League Am. Pen Women, Washington, 1962, Royal Birmingham (Eng.) Soc. of Artists Galleries, 1964, Vera Cruz, Mexico, 1964, Mexico City, 1964, Guadalajara, Mexico, 1965, Everhart Museum, Scranton, Pa., 1966, Marathon (Fla.) Art Guild, 1966-70, Watkins Inst., Nashville, 1966, St. Joseph (Mo.) Art League, 1966, Artists, Unltd., Key West, Fla., Marathon Art Guild, 1966-70, 70, Central Ohio Water Color Soc., 1969-74), Worthington (O.) Art League, 1969, 74, Worthington Hist. Soc., 1969, Ohio State Fair, many times, Ohio Union of Ohio State U., 1967-74, Key West Art Center, 1969-72, Lazarus, 1973, 74, Columbus Festival of Arts, 1970, 73, Upper Arlington Municipal Bldg., 1973, Worthington Art Guild, 1973, Bexley Area Art Guild, 1970, 74, Artists Gallery, 1973, Springfield Art Center, 1974, Columbus Gallery Fine Arts, First Community Village, 1970, 73, also exhibited in France, Scotland, Japan, S.Am., numerous others; represented in numerous pvt. collections. Pvt. tchr. painting, art history, 1950—; lectr. art, history, travel, 1956—; asst. dir. fine arts Ohio State Fair, 1968. Recipient various prizes for paintings. Trustee Clintonville Woman's Club, 1961-65. Mem. Nat. Assn. Women Artists, Nat. League Am. Pen Women, Columbus Art League (pres. 1960-61, gov. 1962-63), Womens, Bexley Art guilds, Worthington Art League, Marathon Art Guild (sec. 1969-70) Daubers (past pres.), Columbus Gallery Fine Arts, Hossier Salon Patrons Assn., Central Ohio Water Color Soc. (prize 1967). Republican. Address: 44 E Torrence Rd Columbus OH 43214

BEMMANN, KATHRYN MARIE CHIZEK (MRS. IRVING STEWART BEMMANN), physician; b. Manitowoc, Wis., Oct. 29, 1931; d. Frank and Celia (Cigler) Chizek; B.S. in Medicine, Marquette U., 1953, M.D., 1956; m. Irving Stewart Bemmann, May 3, 1958. Intern St. Joseph Hosp., Milw., 1956-57; staff physician Milwaukee County (Wis.) Hosp. for Mental Disorders, 1957-58; resident Asso. Tng. Program in Psychiatry of Milw., 1958-61; staff psychiatrist Milw. Psychiat. Hosp., 1961-62; practice medicine specializing in psychiatry, Waukesha, Wis., 1962—; active med. staff Waukesha Meml. Hosp., 1962—, med. dir. psychiat. unit, 1968-70; asso. psychiat. staff Milw. Psychiat. Hosp.; instr. psychiatry Marquette U., Milw., 1960-64, asst. prof., 1964—, faculty moderator women med. students, 1964-69. Recipient CAROL award Wis. Jaycettes, 1961. Diplomate Am. Bd. Psychiatry. Mem. A.M.A., Wis., Waukesha County med. socs., Am., Wis. psychiat. assns., Am. Med. Women's Assn., Gamma Pi Epsilon. Home: S 46 W 22338 Tansdale Rd Waukesha WI 53186 Office: 251 W Broadway St Waukesha WI 53186

BENASUTTI, MARION ELVERA (MRS. FRANK I. BENASUTTI), writer; b. Phila., Aug. 2, 1908; d. Joseph E. and Elvera A. (Serafini) Gosette; student Temple U.; m. Frank I. Benasutti, Aug. 2, 1930; children—Noel I., Frank J. Feature writer Phila. Inquirer, Evening and Sunday Bull., Camden (N.J.) Courier-Post, Cath. Star Herald, Camden, to 1974; women's editor Italian-Am. Herald, Phila.; columnist, book reviewer Cath. Star Herald, 1974. Contbr. short stories and articles to mags., including Redbook, Reader's Digest, The Sign, Ford Times, Family Weekly (Eng.), The Horn Book, Mademoiselle, Farm Jour., Am. Home, Phila. Guide, Seventeen, Marriage, Today, The Rosary, The Lit. Rev. Mem. Nat. League Am. Pen Women. Author: No Steady Job for Papa, 1966. Editor: The Pen Woman, 1964-68. Home: Mt Vernon #6A3 885 Easton Rd Glenside PA 19038

BENCIVENGA, HILDA, optometrist; b. Waterbury, Conn.; d. Ciro and Josephine (Duccilli) Bencivenga; B.A., Albertus Magnus Coll.; D.Optometry, Mass. Coll. Optometry. Asso. practice optometry, Watertown, Conn., 1950—; pvt. practice optometry, Waterbury, Conn., 1953-71; v.p. Ciro Bencivenga Realty, Milford, Conn., 1966—. Bd. dirs. Josephineland, Day Camp for Childen, 1970, Tri-Beach Assn. Mem. Am. Optometric Assn., Conn. Optometric Soc. Club: Quota (pres. 1965-66) (Waterbury, Conn.). Home: 231 Broadway Milford CT 06460 Office: 678 Main St Watertown CT 06795

BENDER, RANDI LAINE (MRS. HOWARD JEFFREY BENDER), occupational therapist; b. Omaha, July 17, 1947; d. Kenneth Norman and Lois Elaine (Harmon) Anderson; B.S., U. Ill., 1970; postgrad. Manhattanville Coll., 1973; m. Howard Jeffrey Bender, May 22, 1971. Staff occupational therapist in psychiatry Grasslands Hosp., Valhalla, N.Y., 1970-72, sr. occupational therapist, 1972—. Mem. Am. Occupational Therapy Assn. Home: 5 Fieldstone Dr Apt 107 Hartsdale NY 10530 Office: Grasslands Rd Valhalla NY 10535

BENDER, SHIRLEY ADELAIDE BAILEY (MRS. HEINZ H. BENDER), exec. housekeeper; b. New London, Conn., Jan. 28, 1923; d. Louis Leroy and Margaret W. (Gunnison) Habryl; student Queens U. (Can.), 1941-42; m. George Bailey, May 12, 1942 (div. May 1949); children—George John III, Margaret Winifred (Mrs. M.W. Kroepel); m. 2d, Heinz H. Bender, Aug. 20, 1971. Exec. housekeeper Ritz Carlton Hotel, Boston, 1950-51, Williamsburg (Va.) Lodge, 1951-61, Internat. Inn, Floridan Hotel, Sheraton Tampa Motor Hotel, Tampa, Fla., 1961-64, Chase Park Plaza, St. Louis, 1964-67, Jack Tar Hotels, Galveston, Tex., Orange, Tex., Charleston, S.C., 1967-69; exec. housekeeper White House, Washington, 1970—. Part-time tchr. supervisory housekeeping Adult Edn., Hillsborough County Ednl. System, Tampa, 1962-63. Mem. Nat. Exec. Housekeepers Assn. (v.p. 1963-64). Home: 1220 Blair Mill Rd Silver Spring MD 20910 Office: 1600 Pennsylvania Av Washington DC 20005

BENDIT, DEVY JUDITH, lawyer, educator; b. Balt., June 8, 1943; d. Samuel and Rebecca (Zalis) Cohen; B.A., U. Md., 1964, J.D., 1968; postgrad. Johns Hopkins, 1973—. Admitted to Md. bar, 1969; rep. intergroup relations Community Relations Commn. Balt., 1968-69; pvt. practice law, Balt., 1969-70; asst. states's atty. Balt., 1970; law clk. for U.S. atty. Md., 1970; asst. prof. law Antioch Coll., Balt., 1971—. Cons. Nat. Paralegal Inst., Washington, 1973, Progressive Planning Systems Inc., Washington, 1973—. Bd. dirs. Mental Health Assn. Balt., 1971—. Mem. Md., Balt. City bar assns., Pub. Affairs Commn. (chmn. 1973—), Mental Health Assn. Balt., St. John's Council on Criminal Justice, Com. Review Proposed New Criminal Code, Parole Aid Vol. Commn.

BENEDEK, ELISSA PANUSH (MRS. RICHARD BENEDEK), physician; b. Detroit; d. Louis and Tillie (Lipsitz) Panush; M.D., U. Mich., 1960; m. Richard Benedek, June 20, 1958; children—David Manfred, Joel Abram, Sarah Ann, Dina Susan. Intern Sinai Hosp., Detroit, 1960-61; resident Gen. Psychiatry Neuropsychiat. Inst., U. Mich. at Ann Arbor, 1961-63; resident child psychiatry Children's Psychiat. Hosp., 1963-65; practice medicine specializing in child psychiatry, Ypsilanti, Mich., 1965—; asso. dir. York Woods Center, Ypsilanti State Hosp., 1965-74; tng. dir. Center for Forensic Psychiatry, Ypsilanti, 1974—; psychiat. cons. Huron Valley Child Guidance Clinic, Ypsilanti Family Service; instr. psychiatry U. Mich. Med. Center, Ann Arbor, 1965-72, clin. asst. prof. psychiatry, 1972—. Bd. dirs. Beth Israel Nursery Sch., 1966—. Fellow Am. Psychiat. Assn.; mem. A.M.A., Lawyers Wives, Alpha Epsilon Iota. Jewish religion. Contbr. articles in field to profl. jours. Home: 3607 Chatham Way Ann Arbor MI 48104 Office: PO Box 2060 Ann Arbor MI 48106

BENEDICT, NAN MAGRI (MRS. POWELL BENEDICT), artist, educator; b. Lynchburg, Va., July 27, 1937; d. John James and Jane (Wall) Magri; B.F.A., Pratt Inst., 1959, M.F.A., 1961; m. Powell Benedict, Aug. 31, 1957; children—Powell Allen Lucian, Amanda Jane, Jonathan Magri. Account asst. Paris & Peart Advt. Agy., N.Y.C., 1958; designer Quentin Flore Studios, N.Y.C., 1959-60; writer Information Services Pratt Inst., Bklyn., 1960-61; instr. graphics, 1960-61, instr. painting, 1961-62, asst. chmn. art edn. dept., 1961-62, asst. prof. art, 1964-67, asso. prof., 1968-71, prof., 1971—, asst. chmn. for grad. program, 1962-66, asst. dir. grad. programs in art and design, 1966-70, acting dir., 1970, asso. chmn. dept. grad. fine arts, 1966-70, acting chmn., 1970, acting chmn. dept. grad. art edn., 1970, chmn. grad. art div., 1971—. Exhibited in one-man show Golden Caravan in N.J., 1970, Monotypes show Pratt Graphics Center, 1972; exhibited in group shows Pratt Inst., Bklyn. Mus., Detroit Inst. Art, Gettysburg Coll., Jens-Risom Design N.Y.C., Betty Parsons Gallery; represented in permanent collections at Pratt Inst. Named one of outstanding Young Women of Am., 1969, 72. Mem. Am. Assn. U. Profs. Home: 183 Steuben St Brooklyn NY 11205

BENEDICT, SHIRLEY, b. Bklyn., July 30, 1935; d. Jack and Beatrice (Levy) Benedict; B.B.A., Baruch Sch. Bus. Adminstrn., City U. N.Y., 1958, postgrad., 1958-60; postgrad. N.Y. U., 1961, 68, 69, Lee Strassberg Inst., 1970, 71, New Sch. for Social Research, 1973-74; m. David Yanover, Jan. 31, 1954 (div. June 1971). Copywriter, Dancer-Fitzgerald-Sample, Inc., N.Y.C., 1961-65; freelance writer, N.Y.C., 1965-68; copywriter Avon Products, N.Y.C., 1968-69; with Vermilion Advt., N.Y.C., 1969—, creative dir., 1970—. Mem. Nat. Acad. TV Arts and Scis., Am. Advt. Fedn., Advt. Women N.Y. (asst. chmn. membership com. 1965-66, 66-67). Author: (juvenile TV film) Don Q, The Crusading Marshal Captures the Masquerading Bandits, 1967; (play) Special Privileges, 1973. Home: 68-37 Yellowstone Blvd Forest Hills NY 11375 Office: 145 E 69th St New York City NY 10021

BENEDIKT, LUCIE, social worker, health planner; b. Vienna, Austria; d. Benjamin and Stephanie (Politzer) Benedikt; B.A., Hunter Coll., 1948; M.S. S.W., Columbia, 1950, M.S. in Adminstrv. Medicine, 1969; postgrad. N.Y. U., 1969—. Caseworker social service dept. Columbia-Presbyn. Med. Center, N.Y.C., 1949-52, Beth Israel Hosp., Boston, 1952-55; sr. social worker social service dept. Maimonides Hosp., Bklyn., 1955-59; sr. social worker dept. home care, faculty Home Care Tng. Inst. Montefiore Hosp. and Med. Center, Bronx, 1959-63; asst. supr. social service dept. Maimonides Med. Center, Bklyn., 1963-67; program rep. N.Y. Met. Regional Med. Program, N.Y.C., 1969-70; social service exec. Barnert Meml. Hosp. Center, Paterson, N.J., 1971—. Vol. Internat. Center N.Y., Inc. Bd. dirs. N.Y. alumni Internat. House. Fellow Am. Pub. Health Assn.; mem. Nat. Assn. Social Workers, Acad. Certified Social Workers, Pub. Health Assn. N.Y.C., Soc. Hosp. Social Work, Am. Hosp. Assn., Sierra Club, Royal Soc. Health. Club: Appalachian Mountain. Contbr. articles to profl. jours. Home: 58 W 8th St New York City NY 10011

BENEDUCE, ANN, editor; b. Maplewood, N.J.; d. Elmer Schofield and Winnifred (Houghton) Keay; student Bryn Mawr Coll., 1934-36; A.B., Barnard Coll., 1946; postgrad. Columbia, 1946-47; m. Sanford L. Worth, Oct. 3, 1941 (div. Sept. 1946); m. 2d, Eugene J. Beneduce, May 30, 1947 (div. Sept. 1957); children—Wendy, Cynthia. Asst. editor gen. trade and religious books Doubleday & Co., 1957-59; asso. editor children's books J.B. Lippincott Co., N.Y.C. and Phila., 1960-63; editor children's books World Pub. Co., N.Y.C., 1963-69; v.p., editor-in-chief books for children and young people Thomas Y. Crowell Co., N.Y.C., 1969—, also dir. Mem. Children's Book Council (dir. 1969-71). Home: 25 E 92d St New York City NY 10028 Office: Thomas Y Crowell Co 666 Fifth Av New York City NY 10019

BENEKE, MILDRED STONG (MRS. ARNOLD W. BENEKE), civic worker; b. Prairie City, Ia., May 1, 1920; d. Rueben Ira and Lillian (Garber) Stong; student Wash. U., 1942-43, U. Minn., 1945-58, Mankato State Coll., 1951-54, 57, 64, 67; m. Arnold W. Beneke, Aug. 10, 1939; children—Bruce Arnold, Paula Rae, Bradford Kent, Cynthia Jane (Mrs. Daniel Berger), Lisa Patrice. Exec. sec. chmn. Vol. Services, St. Paul, Am. Red Cross, 1940-41; v.p. Pi House, St. Paul, 1972—; founder, bd. dirs., chmn. Project Interaction Boutique, Minn. Correctional Instn. for Women, Shakopee, 1971—. Republican chairwoman McLeod County (Minn.), 1969-73; mem. Rep. Minn. Platform com., 1970; McLeod County del. Rep. Minn. Central Com., 1969—; mem. Minn. Task Force Criminal Justice Commn., 1974—; mem. Rep. Women for Polit. Effectiveness; alderman Glencoe City Council, 1974—. Mem. Glencoe Bus. and Profl. Women, Grand Old Party Womens' Fedn., Minn. Womens' Polit. Caucus, Ripon Soc. Lutheran. Home: Glenview Woods Glencoe MN 55336

BENELL, FLORENCE BELLE, health educator; b. San Francisco; d. Charles and Anna (Slifkin) Benell; student Washington U., St. Louis, Mo., 1927-28, Wayne U., Detroit, 1928-30; A.B., U. Mich., 1931, M.S. in Pub. Health, 1933; Ph.D., U. Chgo., 1951. Tchr. Muskegon (Mich.) Pub. Schs., 1937-39; instr. hygiene State Tchrs. Coll., Milw., 1939-44; dir. health edn. Tb Inst. Chgo., Cook County, 1944-47; health coordinator Eastern Ill. Coll., Charleston, 1947-48; asso. prof. health edn. Fla. State U., 1950-51; asst. exec. dir. Ill. Social Hygiene League, 1953-59, asso. exec., dir., 1959-63; chief health educator venereal disease control sect. Chgo. Bd. Health, 1958-63; prof., chmn. dept. health and safety studies Cal. State U. at Sacramento, 1964—. Mem. Am. Pub. Health Assn., Am. Sch. Health Assn., Sacramento Lung Assn. (dir.), Pi Lambda Theta, Sigma Omega. Author: Behavioral Dynamics of Sex Education, 1967. Contbr. articles to health and edn. publs. Home: 5484 Carlson Dr Sacramento CA 95819

BENENSON, CLAIRE B., educator; b. N.Y.C.; d. Nathan H. and Alice E. (Zeisler) Berger; B.A., Wellesley Coll.; student N.Y. Inst. Finance; m. Lawrence A. Benenson; children—Harold, Gary. Lectr., N.Y. U. Mgmt. Inst.; research, security analyst, Conn. Coll., Merrill Lynch Pierce Fenner and Smith; now chmn. program, bus. and financial affairs New Sch., also coordinator Ann. Conf. for investors; creator also moderator, WNBC-TV series Wall St for Everyone. Dir. Burnham Fund. Bd. govs. Money Marketeers N.Y. U.; mem. adv. bd. First Women's Bank; bd. overseers Parsons Sch. Design. Mem., Am. Econ. Assn., Nat. Assn. Bus. Economists, Phi Beta Kappa. Clubs: Wellesley, Women's Bond, National Economists. Home: 60 Sutton Pl S New York City NY 10022 Office: 66 W 12th St New York City NY 10011

BENENSON, ESTHER SIEV (MRS. WILLIAM BENENSON), nursing home adminstr.; b. Jerusalem, Aug. 16, 1925; d. Joshua and Anna (Sanders) Siev; A.A.S., Queens Coll., 1957; B.S., Hunter Coll., 1972, M.S., 1974; m. William Benenson, Sept. 15, 1957; children—Michael J., Sharon G., Amy L., Blanche S. Exec. dir. Flushing (N.Y.) Manor Nursing Home, 1959—. Registered nurse; licensed X-ray technician. Mem. N.Y. State Bd. Examiners for Licensing Nursing Home Adminstrs.; mem. adv. council N.Y. State Health Planning Commn. Fellow Am. Coll. Nursing Home Adminstrs., Am. Assn. Med. Adminstrs.; mem. Am., N.Y. State, Met. N.Y. nursing home assns., Royal Soc. Health, Soc. Pub. Health Educators, Bus. and Profl. Women's Club Greater Flushing, Women's

Aux. Med. Soc. State N.Y., Women's Aux. A.M.A., Doctors Wives Aux. Flushing Hosp. and Med. Center. Home: 36-21 Parsons Blvd Flushing NY 11354 also 102 Ladder Hill Rd N Weston CT 06880 Office: 35-15 Parsons Blvd Flushing NY 11354

BENENSON, THEA FUCHS, psychologist, ednl. adminstr.; b. Karlsruhe, Germany, Mar. 27, 1936; d. Oscar H. and Hilde M. (Kahn) Fuchs; came to U.S., 1939, naturalized, 1946; B.A., Vassar Coll., 1957; M.A., Columbia, 1968, Ph.D. (U.S. Office Edn. Research Trainee fellow), 1971; m. Richard Benenson, June 16, 1957; children—Robert, Kim. Research psychologist New Rochelle (N.Y.) Bd. Edn., 1967-68; adj. asst. prof. psychology Queens Coll., N.Y.C., 1971-72; dir. devel. center Westchester (N.Y.) Community Coll., State U. N.Y., 1972; higher edn. officer office dean academic affairs, office instl. research Bronx (N.Y.) Community Coll., City U. N.Y., 1973—. Cons. evaluation ednl. programs, 1968—. Mem. Am., Eastern, N.Y. State Psychol. assns., Soc. for Research in Child Devel., Nat. Council on Measurement in Edn., A.A.A.S., Am. Assn. U. Profs., Am. Ednl. Research Assn., Sigma Xi. Office: University Av and 180th St Bronx NY 10453

BENEZRA, AUDREY GREENMAN (MRS. JOSEPH N. BENEZRA), lawyer, med. technologist; b. Seattle, July 13, 1926; d. Leon and Elizabeth (de Smith) Greenman; B.A., U. Wash., 1947, J.D., 1950, B.S., 1971; m. Joseph N. Benezra, Aug. 7, 1949; children—Cassandra Lee, Gail Leslie. Admitted to Wash. bar, 1950; credit adviser Bon Marche, Seattle, 1950-51, OPS coordinator, 1951-52; pvt. practice law, Seattle, 1952-54, 64-66; research technologist U. Wash., Seattle, 1972—. Cons., Group Health Coop. Puget Sound, 1964—. Mem. Wash., Seattle, King County bar assns., Am. Soc. Clin. Pathologists. Home: 7732 29th St NE Seattle WA 98115 Office: University of Washington Dept Medicine Div Nephrology Seattle WA 98195

BENEZRA, BARBARA BEARDSLEY (MRS. LEO L. BENEZRA), librarian; b. Woodman, Colo., Apr. 2, 1921; d. Earl and Alice (Smith) Beardsley; student Coll. of Pacific, 1943; A.B., U. Cal. at Berkeley, 1944; library degree San Jose State Tchrs. Coll., 1960; m. Leo L. Benezra, July 6, 1946; children—Heather, Paul, Judy, David. Librarian, Morse Elementary Sch., Sunnyvale, Cal., 1960-67; librarian Kennedy Jr. High Sch., Eastlake, O., 1967—. Mem. Am. Assn. U. Women, Delta Kappa Gamma. Author: Gold Dust and Petticoats, 1964; Nuggets In My Pocket, 1966; Fire Dragon, 1970. Home: 7170 Hawthorn Dr Mentor OH 44060 Office: 34050 Glen Dr Eastlake OH 44094

BENFORD, BEVERLY ANN DANIELS, univ. adminstr.; b. Denver, Aug. 4, 1945; d. Jodie and Willa Mae (Smith) Daniels; A.A., Contra Costa Coll., 1965; B.A., U. Ill., 1970; M.Ed., Loyola U., Chgo., 1974; m. Gerald J. Benford, Apr. 16, 1968 (div. Sept. 1972). Instr., counselor Project Upward Bound, U. Ill. at Chgo. Circle, 1969-71; coordinator coll. events Chgo. State U., 1970-71, asst. dir. student activities, 1971-72, dir. student union/student activities, 1972-73. Cons. Project Upward Bound, U. Ill. at Chgo. Circle, 1970-71. Recipient Black Merit Acad. Award, 1970. Mem. Nat. Assn. Women Deans, Adminstrs. and Counselors, Assn. Coll. Unions (mem. profl. devel. com. 1974). Home: 2515 Nason Av El Cerrito CA 94530

BENGSON, EVELYN MARGARET, occupational therapist; b. Esmond, N.D., Aug. 12, 1913; d. John J. and Stella Josephine (Jensen) Bengson; teaching certificate Presbyn. Coll., 1931; B.S., U. N.D., 1939; postgrad. U. Mont., 1941; certificate occupational therapy U. Puget Sound, 1954. Tchr. in elementary rural schs., N.D., 1932-35, 39-40; tchr. in secondary schs., Minn., 1940-42; staff therapist State Psychiat. Hosp., Salem, Ore., 1954-57; occupational therapy cons. Wash. Dept. Social and Health Services, Olympia, 1957—. Mem. Am., Wash. occupational therapy assns., Northwest Carvers. Republican. Home: 2213 Wilkins Place Olympia WA 98501 Office: PO Box 1788 Olympia Airport Olympia WA 98504

BENGTSON, CAROLYN SEAY, newspaper editor; b. Austin, Tex., Sept. 1, 1937; d. Henry Alexander and Minnie (Leifeste) Seay; student U. Hawaii, 1957; B. J., U. Tex. at Austin, 1958, postgrad. Sch. Law, 1959-60; m. Howard Bengtson, Aug. 22, 1958 (div. Dec. 1973); children—Avery, Bradley. Fashion editor Am.-Statesman, Austin, 1958-69, women's editor, 1969—. Recipient Headliner's awards, 1972, 73, A.P. award, 1974. Mem. Women in Communications, Alpha Delta Pi. Methodist. Home: 1404 Ethridge St Austin TX 78703 Office: 308 Guadalupe St Austin TX 78767

BENICE, SISTER MARY, provincial superior; b. Windber, Pa.; d. Stanley M. and Hedwig (Liss) Przywara; A.B., Canisius Coll., 1942; B.L.S., State U. N.Y. at Buffalo, 1944; M.A., Niagara U., 1950; postgrad. Syracuse U. 1954, State U. Coll., Geneseo, N.Y., 1965, D'Youville Coll., 1965—, Pius X Liturgical Sch. Music, Eastman Sch. Music U. Rochester, 1938, 65. Joined Felician Sisters, 1926; tchr. St. Augustine Sch., Depew, N.Y., 1929-30, St. John Gualbert Sch., Buffalo, 1930-32, St. Mary's, N.Y. Mills, N.Y., 1932-36, Sacred Heart Sch., Syracuse, 1936-38, St. Stanislaus Sch., Binghamton, N.Y., 1938-39; tchr. Immaculate Heart of Mary Acad., Buffalo, 1939-55, asst. prin., 1961-62; prin. Transfiguration Sch., Buffalo, 1955-61; instr. English, librarian Villa Marie Coll., Buffalo, 1961-64, became librarian 1964, also acad. dean, 1966-68; became supr. sch. libraries Felician Sisters Buffalo Province, 1960; provincial councilor Immaculate Heart Mary Convent, Buffalo, 1966-70, provincial superior, 1970—. Trustee Villa Maria Coll. Mem. Cath., Am., N.Y. library assns., Conf. on Coll. Edn., Nat. Cath. Ednl. Assn., Polish Arts Club, Western N.Y. Cath. Librarians Conf. (chmn. coll. sect. 1966—), Am. Assn. U. Women, Leadership Conf. of Women Religious, Pi Lambda Theta. Editor: Library Bull., 1956-58. Contbr. articles to profl. publs. Home and office: 600 Doat St Buffalo NY 14211

BENJAMIN, ANNA SHAW, educator; b. Phila., Aug. 6, 1925; d. Charles Dow and Grace (Shaw) Benjamin; A.B., U. Pa., 1946, M.A., 1947, Ph.D., 1955; Thomas Day Seymour fellow Am. Sch. Classical Studies, Athens, Greece, 1948. Fulbright fellow to Greece, 1949. Instr. Juniata Coll., 1951-52; asso. prof. classical langs. and archeology U. Mo., 1953-62, prof. classical langs., 1962-64, chmn. dept., 1958-64; prof. classics Rutgers U., Douglas Coll., 1964—, chmn., 1969-74; mem. staff Inst. Advanced Study, Princeton, N.J., 1960, research asso., 1966-67. Mem. Am. Philol. Assn., Archeol. Inst. Am., Am. Numismatic Soc., Am. Philos. Soc., Am. Oriental Soc., Phi Beta Kappa. Author: Arae Augusti: in Hesperia, 1958; Hadrian and His PanHellenic Program in Hesperia, 1963; Augustine's On Free Choice of The Will, 1964; Xenophon's Recollections of Socrates and Socrates' Defense Before the Jury, 1965. Editor: Archaeology, 1967-72. Home: 208 Cedar Av Highland Park NJ 08904 Office: Douglass Coll New Brunswick NJ 08903

BENJAMIN, BLANCHE STERNBERGER, civic worker; b. Mayesville, S.C., May 15, 1901; d. Emanuel and Bertha (Strauss) Sternberger; student Wellesley Coll., 1920-21; m. Edward B. Benjamin, Oct. 19, 1921; children—Edward B., W. Mente, Jonathan S. Formerly v.p. Starmount Co., Greensboro, N.C., Friendly Center, Inc., Greensboro, Benjamin Minerals, Inc. (New Orleans), now dir. Vice pres. New Orleans Garden Soc., 1927-30, New Orleans Philharmonic Soc., 1928-51; mem. orgn. com. Newcomb Preschool and Metairie Park Country Day Sch.; v.p. Benjamin Fund, New Orleans Symphony Soc.; co-founder (with husband) Sternberger Hosp., Starmount Forest Country Club; co-founder Emanuel Sternberger Ednl. Fund, Greensboro; bd. dirs. Greensboro Symphony; past trustee Delgado Art Mus.; hon. mem. Greensboro Jr. League. Clubs: Orleans (corr. sec. 1947-49), Garden Soc., New Orleans Country (New Orleans); Assembly, Dogwood Garden (Greensboro). Address: 383 Walnut St New Orleans LA 70118

BENJAMIN, EDITH WINIFRED, educator; b. Bloomington, Ill., Sept. 16, 1903; d. Frank Carothers and Louella (Bevan) Benjamin; B.Ed., Ill. State U., 1928; M.S., U. Ore., 1937; postgrad. U. Chgo., 1935-36, U. Wash., 1954, U. Buffalo, 1957, U. Ill., 1957-63. Tchr. math. high schs. Ill., 1925-66, Arlington Heights (Ill.) High Sch., 1960-66; tchr. math. Central YMCA Community Coll., Chgo., 1967—. Recipient award NASA, 1965, Outstanding Math. Tchr. award State Math. Meet, 1967; NSF grantee, 1954, 57, 63. Mem. D.A.R., Pi Lambda Theta, Kappa Mu Epsilon, Pi Kappa Delta, Kappa Delta Pi. Home: 55 W Chestnut St Chicago IL 60610 Office: 211 W Wacker Dr Chicago IL 60606 also Route 3 Bloomington IL 61701

BENJAMIN, MARYE DURRUM, broadcasting exec.; b. Hugo, Okla., May 14, 1913; d. William Landon and Effie Anne (Lear) Durrum; B.S. in Journalism, Tex. State Coll. Women, 1934; m. David Gleason Benjamin, Mar. 29, 1941; children—Margaret Anne (Mrs. James A. Keys), David Gleason, William Forbes. Adminstrv. sec. U. Tex. at Austin, 1939-43, script writer Radio House, 1943-45, lectr. radio, TV, film writing U. Tex., 1943-64, radio-TV script editor, 1945-67, supr. student projects sch. communication, 1966—, producer spl. programs communication center, 1967—; copy chief D. G. B., advt. agy., Austin, 1944-60; dir. spl. programs KLRN-TV S.W. Tex. Ednl. TV Council, 1964—; writer spl. radio series Tex. Sch. Air, 1942-52; writer-designer-researcher spl. series Nat. Ednl. TV and Radio Center, Nat. Assn. Ednl. Broadcasters (Tex.), 1955-56, films, 1964-67; producer-designer TV series on Am. lit. for high schs.; producer-designer-writer TV series How to Be Human, distributed nationally; producer Sashays in Am. Lit.; producer-designer-writer Program Devel. in the kindergarten, univ. extension course, 1970-71; asso. producer, editor TV series Educating a Nation, 1972; writer-designer nat. bilingual project, Ky. GED project, 1973; also free lance writer nat. and state agys., civic orgns., ednl., indsl., profl. assns., Tex., including ednl. TV series Hogg Found. Mental Health, 1966, 67-68, Tex. Dept. Pub. Welfare, 1967, Jr. League (Tex.), 1967, Tex. Edn. Agy., 1967; editorial cons. div. civil def. and disaster relief Tex. Gov.'s Office, 1943-57. Mem., program chmn. Austin P.T.A.'s; Cub Scout den mother Austin council Boy Scouts Am., 1952-55; Brownie troop leader Girl Scouts Austin, 1950-55. Recipient awards Am. Exhbn. Ednl. TV and Radio Programs, Columbus, 1948-60; Freedom Found., Valley Forge, Pa., 1956. Fellow Nat. Assn. Ednl. Broadcasters; mem. Alpha Epsilon Rho. Episcopalian. Club: Mary Eleanor Brackenridge (Tex. State Coll. Women), Ki-Anns. Author: Never the Twain Shall Eat, 1936, Symphony for Simple Simon, 1957. Home: 2305 Tower Dr Austin TX 78703

BENJAMIN, SARAH MAGDELENE WAESCHE (MRS. WILLIAM HERMAN BENJAMIN), editor; b. Frederick, Md., Apr. 24, 1923; d. Clinton Foreman and Sarah Magdelene (Greenwalt) Waesche; student Washington Coll., 1940-42, Strayer Bus. Sch., 1942; m. William Herman Benjamin, June 27, 1943; children—John Robert, Michael William, Richard Gary, Sally Lou, David Lee. Editor, Catoctin Enterprise, Thurmont, Md., 1965—. Sec., P.T.A., 1959. Recipient awards Lions Club, 1968, Cancer Found., 1969, Heart Assn., 1970. Mem. Thurmont Bus. and Profl. Women's Club (publicity chmn. 1970-71). Lutheran. Home: 307 E Main St Thurmont MD 21788 Office: 12 W Main St Thurmont MD 21788

BENNEDSEN, DORTE MARIANNE (MRS. JORGEN BENNEDSEN), ofcl. Danish govt.; b. Copenhagen, Denmark, July 2, 1938; d. Hans Harald and Bodil (Thastucm) Koch; degree U. Copenhagen, 1964; m. Jorgen Bennedsen, Sept. 27, 1961; children—Mettelene, Mads, Morten. Ordained to ministry; clergyman Navy Ch., Copenhagen, 1965-68; sec. gen. Danish Youth Council, Denmark, 1968-71; minister ecclesiastical affairs Danish Govt., 1971-73, Social Democrat. Home: 55 Tesdorpfsves Copenhagen 2000 F Denmark

BENNETT, ADELINE ROSALIE, physician; b. Worcester, Mass., Apr. 9, 1925; d. John and Rose (Zurowska) Bennett; B.S., Coll. Misericordia, 1945; D.O., Phila. Coll. Osteopathy, 1949; M.D., U. Cal., 1962; 1 son, Joseph L. Bennett. Intern, Los Angeles County Gen. Hosp., 1949-50, resident 1950; practice gen. medicine, Pico-Rivera, Cal., 1950-67, LaMirada, Cal., 1967—; adminstr., med. dir. Mirada Hills Convalescent and Rehab. Hosp., La Mirada, 1967—, corporate dir. 1967-72; pub. relations County Guardians and Vets. Adminstrn., La Mirada, 1967-72; mem. staff Los Angeles County Gen. Hosp.; clin. instr. U. Cal., 1951-54. Founder, La Mirada Community Hosp., 1960, extended hosp. campus Biola Sch. Nursing, La Mirada, 1967-72; mem. Joint Commn. on Accredition of Hosp., 1967—. Named Self-employed Prof. Woman of Year Bus. and Profl. Women's Club, La Mirada, 1969. Fellow Am. Geriatric Soc., Am. Acad. Gen. Practitioners; mem. Am. Cal., Los Angeles County med. assns., Am. Hosp. Assn., Acad. Am. Hosp. Adminstrs., Internat. Platform Assn., La Mirada C. of C. Home: 13978 Summit Dr Whittier CA 90602 Office: 2046 Hacienda Blvd Hacienda Heights CA 91745

BENNETT, BETTY BESSE, librarian; b. Omaha, Feb. 18, 1921; d. Gordon Stanley and Besse Harriet (Amos) Bennett; B.A., Municipal U. Omaha, 1942; B.S. in L.S., U. Ill., 1943; M.A., U. Ia., 1948; M.L.S., Tex. Woman's U., 1960. Asst. documents librarian U. Ia. Library, Iowa City, 1943-50; reference and documents librarian Kan. State Tchrs. Coll. Library, Pittsburg, 1950-57, reference librarian, archivist, 1957-67; reference and research librarian Stephen F. Austin State U. Library, Nacogdoches, Tex., 1967-72, govt. documents librarian, 1972—. Resource cons. Gov.'s Conf. on Libraries, Austin, Tex., 1974. Mem. Am. Assn. U. Women, Am. Assn. U. Profs., A.L.A. (state document classification com. 1974—, state documents task force) Tex. (chmn. elect govt. documents round table 1974-75), Southwestern library assns., Tex. Assn. Coll. Tchrs., Nacogdoches Friends of the Library, Alpha Xi Delta. Presbyn. (clk. of session 1967—). Home: 1525 Walnut St Nacogdoches TX 75961 Office: Stephen F. Austin State U Library Nacogdoches TX 75961

BENNETT, CAMILA ARMINTA SUAREZ (MRS. R. GORDON BENNETT), pub. relations exec.; b. Dayton, O., Nov. 6, 1917; d. Peter and Mary Arminta (Houghton) Suarez; B.J., U. Tex., 1966; M.S. in L.S., Our Lady of Lake Coll., 1971; m. R. Gordon Bennett, Mar. 14, 1942; children—Bonnie (Mrs. Robert Clinton Siddons), R. Gordon. With Nat. Cash Register, 1936-42, U.S. Dept. Agr., 1942, USAF, 1946-50; with U.S. Army, 1950—, information officer 8th Army Corps, Austin, Tex., 1962-68, pub. relations exec. 5th Army, Ft. Sam Houston, Tex., 1968-73, pub. information officer U.S. Berlin (Germany) Command, 1973; pub. relations exec. 5th Army, dep. information officer Ft. Sam Houston, Tex., 1974—. Instr. personnel mgmt. San Antonio Coll., 1971-72; guest lectr. pub. relations U. Tex. at Austin, 1960—. Reference source Library Human Resources, Am. Bicentennial Inst. Mem. Tex. Pub. Relations Assn. (dir. 1971), Pub. Relations Soc. Am., San Antonio Media Club, Govt. Information Orgn., A.L.A., Tex. Library Assn., Friends Austin Pub. Library, Tex. Press Women, Nat. Fedn. Press Women, Armed Forces Information Council, Armed Forces Mgmt. Assn., Austin Environmental Council, We Care Austin, Greater Austin Assn., Nat. Hist. Soc., Am. Heritage Soc., Zachary Scott Theater Center, Austin Ballet Theater, Am. Forestry Assn., Nat. Wildlife Fedn., Tex. Geneol. Soc., Am. Security Council, Tex. Fine Arts Assn., Laguna Gloria Art Mus., Elisabet Ney Guild, Am. Assn. U. Women, Am. Assn. U. Profs., Fedn. Orgns. for Profl. Women, Nat. Trust for Historic Preservation, Am. Hort. Soc., Nat. Geog. Soc., Nat. Audubon Soc. (Women's council, Austin), Travis County Audubon Soc., Austin Heritage Soc. and Guild, Austin Humane Soc. (life), Smithsonian Assos., U. Tex. Ex-Students Assn. (life), Alliance Francaise, Am. Mus. Nat. History, Nat. Parks and Conservation Assn., D.A.R., Women in Communications, Alpha Delta Sigma, Delta Zeta. Republican. Episcopalian. Clubs: Austin Woman's (life); Westwood Country, Forty Acres, Lost Creek Golf and Tennis (Austin); Berlin (Germany) Golf and Country. Home: 1703 Mohle Dr Austin TX 78703 Office: Information Office Ft Sam Houston TX 78234

BENNETT, CAROL ANNE BUENIK, trade assn. exec.; b. Chgo., Dec. 25, 1930; d. William George and Otillie Ann (ValChar) Buenik; student U. Colo., 1948-50; m. J. Bryan Bennett, Dec. 10, 1950 (div. Mar. 1964); children—Jeffrey Mark, Rodney Bryan, Julie Lynn. With Nat. Office Machine Dealers Assn., Elk Grove Village, Ill., 1964—, nat. adminstr., 1969—. Mem. Alpha Omicron Pi. Presbyn. Home: 600 S Owen St Mount Prospect IL 60056 Office: 1510 Jarvis Av Elk Grove Village IL 60007

BENNETT, DAPHNE MARY NICHOLSON (MRS. WILLIAM ERNEST BENNETT), psychologist, educator; b. Kent, Eng.; d. Thomas and Ingaborg (Sande) Nicholson; B.A., U. London (Eng.), 1942, diploma dramatic art, 1948; M.A., U. So. Cal., 1953, Ph.D., 1955; m. William Ernest Bennett, Dec. 22, 1945. Came to U.S., 1950, naturalized, 1960. Lectr. Dudley (Eng.) Coll. Edn., 1948-50; Fulbright lectr. Kan. State U., Manhattan, 1950-51; clin asst. U. So. Cal. at Los Angeles, 1952-55; practice psychology, Los Angeles, 1955-60; prof. speech and English, Mt. St. Mary's Coll., Los Angeles, 1960—. Author: Parents Should be Heard, 1972. Contbr. articles to profl. jours. Home: 1167 W 37th Pl Los Angeles CA 90007

BENNETT, DIANE TARLETON, editor; b. Pitts., Sept. 1, 1935; d. Owen H. and Altha (Cook) Tarleton; student New Sch. for Social Research, N.Y.C., 1968, Hofstra U., 1973; m. Charles J. Bennett, Mar. 10, 1954 (separated June, 1956); children—Patricia Anne, Elizabeth Anne. Editor Manhasset (N.Y.) Press, 1966-67, Roslyn (N.Y.) News, 1967-70, Glen Cove (N.Y.) Record, 1970-71; editor Westbury (N.Y.) Times, 1971—. Vol. tchr. Glen Cove High Sch., 1971. Mem. Roslyn Urban Renewal Adv. Com., 1968-69. Recipient awards N.Y. State Press Assn., 1965-69. Home: 214 Brown St Mineola NY 11501 Office: 57 Old Country Rd Westbury NY 11590

BENNETT, DOROTHY KEMLER, psychologist; b. Cambridge, Mass., June 1, 1935; d. Joseph Aaron and Rae (Shapiro) Kemler; B.S. magna cum laude, Tufts U., 1956; Ed.M., Harvard, 1957, Ed.D., 1970; m. Edward Martin Bennett, Apr. 1, 1959; children—James, Robert. Sch. psychologist Westwood (Mass.) Pub. Schs., 1969-73, dir. psychol. services, 1973-74; dir. spl. needs Winthrop (Mass.) Pub. Schs., 1974—; teaching fellow Harvard, 1958-59. Cons. religious edn. dept. Unitarian-Universalist Assn., Boston. Bd. dirs. Lexington (Mass.) Counseling Service, 1970-72. USPHS fellow Judge Baker Guidance Center, Boston, 1957-58. Mem. Nat. Assn. Sch. Psychologists, Am. Psychol. Assn., Sigma Xi, Pi Lambda Theta. Home: 10 Baskin Rd Lexington MA 02173 Office: Winthrop Pub Schs Winthrop MA 02152

BENNETT, ELEANOR GODWIN (MRS. WILLIAM MARSHALL BENNETT), assn. exec.; b. Meridian, Miss., July 12, 1931; d. Robert Leon and Virginia (Keller) Godwin; student Cecils Bus. Coll., 1954-55; m. William Marshall Bennett, Dec. 26, 1955; children—Robert Marshall, Kevin Godwin, William Marshall III. Bookkeeper, United Fund, Columbus, Ga., 1955-56, clk., bookkeeper, Charleston, S.C., 1958-62, head bookkeeper, Spartanburg, S.C., 1962-63, exec. dir., Colleton County (S.C.), Walterboro, 1963—; owner, sec.-treas. Med. Arts Pharmacy, Inc., Walterboro, 1964—. Active Colleton County Blood Mobile. Sec. Republican Com. Colleton County, 1970-71. Mem. S.C. Pharm. Aux. (sec.-treas. 1972-73), Beta Sigma Phi (pres. 1970). Home: Route 2 Box 340 Walterboro SC 29488 Office: 109 Webb St Walterboro SC 29488

BENNETT, ELEANOR MAXINE, med. educator; b. Beaver City, Neb., July 14, 1915; d. Irvin Allan and Mary Fay (Kline) Bennett; A.B., Hastings Coll., 1936; M.D., U. Neb., 1942. Intern Madison (Wis.) Gen. Hosp., 1942-43; med. dir. Wis. Bur. for Handicapped Children, Madison, 1950-53; asso. prof. surgery (otolaryngology) Med. Sch. U. Wis. at Madison, 1953-63, prof., 1963—, chmn. div. otolaryngology, 1958-68. Vis. prof. Columbia Coll. Phys. & Surgs., N.Y.C., 1968. Diplomate Am. Bd. Otolaryngology. Mem. Am. Acad. Opthalmology and Otolaryngology, Am. Laryngol., Rhinol. and Otol. Soc., Am. Council Otolaryngologists, Wis. Otolaryngol. Soc., A.M.A., Wis., Dane County med. socs., Soc. Univ. Otolaryngologists. Club: Altrusa, Centurion (founding). Home: Route 3 Madison WI 53713

BENNETT, ESTHER VORENA, naturalist; b. Columbia, S.C., July 2, 1921; d. Samuel R. and Amanda (Templeton) Bennett; B.A., U. N.C., 1942; certificate in mus. tng. Buffalo Mus. Sci., 1949; M.S., So. Ill. U., 1953; Ph.D., Cornell U., 1961. Jr. chemist Am. Enka (N.C.) Rayon Corp., 1942-44; asst. in biology U. N.C., Greensboro, 1944-48; asst. prof., curator edn. So. Ill. U. Mus., Carbondale, 1949-63; asst. prof. agronomy; asso. editor Wheat Abstracts, U. Neb. at Lincoln, 1964; city naturalist, dir. Chet Ager Nature Center, Lincoln, 1966—. Mem. Mid-Continent Regional Park and Recreation Conf., Wilson Ornithol. Soc., Am. Ornithol. Union, Neb. Ornithologists Union, Cornell Lab. Ornithology, Inland Bird Banding Assn., Assn. Interpretive Naturalists, Neb. Recreation and Park Assn., Sigma Xi, Phi Kappa Phi, Sigma Delta Epsilon (pres. chpt. 1968-69). Episcopalian. Clubs: Altrusa Internat. (rec. sec. Lincoln 1970-71, dir. 1973-75), Garden, Audubon Naturalists (v.p. 1965-66, pres. 1966-67) (Lincoln). Home: 600 S 33d St Lincoln NE 68510 Office: City Park Dept 2740 A St Lincoln NE 68502

BENNETT, EUDORA SMITH, hosp. adminstr.; b. W. Franklin, Pa., July 16, 1924; d. Merton Henry and Ruby-Estelle Grace (Allen) Smith; R.N., Robert Packer Hosp. Tng. Sch. Nurses, Sayre, Pa., 1945; m. Raymond Leslie Bennett, Dec. 21, 1946; children—Ann Marie, Donald Hasbrouck, Stanley Douglas. Gen. duty nurse Robert Packer Hosp., 1945-46, supr. pediatrics, 1947-48; pvt. duty nurse Carbondale (Pa.) Gen. Hosp., 1948-49; supr. Monmouth Meml. Hosp., Long Branch, N.J., 1950-51; adminstr. Montrose (Pa.) Med. Center, 1951—, also dir.; dir. Med. Arts Nursing Center, Montrose; a founder Med. Arts Clinic, Montrose, 1952. Mem. bd. N.Y.-Pa. Health Planning Council, 1969—, chmn. Susquehanna County chpt., 1971-72; mem. bd. Northeastern Human Parts Assn., 1971—; mem. Susquehanna County Ambulance and Emergency Services Assn., 1971—. Named Spirit of Nursing, Robert Packer Hosp., 1945. Mem. Am., Pa. hosp. assns., Health Care Facilities Assn. Pa. Republican.

Presbyn. Club: Y-Gradale (Montrose). Home: 42 Maple St Montrose PA 18801 Office: 3 Grow St Montrose PA 18801

BENNETT, FRANCES GRANT, wife of U.S. senator; b. Salt Lake City, Sept. 23, 1899; d. Heber J. and Emily (Wells) Grant; student Radcliffe Coll.; A.B., U. Utah, 1921; m. Wallace F. Bennett, Sept. 6, 1922; children—Wallace G., Rosemary (Mrs. Robert C. Fletcher), David W., Frances (Mrs. Lawrence S. Jeppson), Robert F. Author: Glimpses of a Morman Family, 1968. Home: 4201 Massachusetts Av NW Washington DC 20016

BENNETT, GERALDINE CARREL, civic worker; b. Mt. Carmel, Ill., Feb. 7, 1918; d. Benjamin Wilson and Bertha (Kays) Carrel; student Bradley U., 1938-41; R.N., Methodist Hosp., Peoria, Ill., 1941; m. Robert W. Bennett, July 4, 1941; children—Robert J., Mrs. Phillip C. Kosch, Kathleen J. Nurse Meth. Hosp., Peoria, 1941-42. Mem. citizens' com. Better Edn., Dunkirk, N.Y., 1951-52; mem. exec. bd. Brooks Hosp. Aux., Dunkirk, 1952-53; den mother Cub Scouts, Dunkirk, 1951-53; mem. exec. bd. troop com. Girl Scouts U.S., Niskayana, N.Y., 1954-55; organizer, dir. Niskayana Youth Center, 1957-59; mem. exec. bd. Niskayana Sch. and Community Assn., 1957-59; vol. nurse Schenectady Boys Club, 1960-62. Recipient award merit Schenectady Boys Club, 1960, 61. Methodist (tchr.). Club: Formal Dance (Columbus, O.). Home: 4154 Squires Lane Columbus OH 43220

BENNETT, GERTRUDE RYDER (MRS. FRANK CURTIS WILLIAMS), author, poet; b. Bklyn.; d. Edward and Nellie May (Ryder) Bennett; B.S., N.Y. U., 1925; M.A., Columbia, 1927; m. Frank Curtis Williams, June 21, 1942. Author: Etched in Words, 1938; The Harvesters, 1967; Ballads of Colonial Days, 1972; Fugitive, 1975. Recipient Arthur Davison Ficke award Poetry Soc. Am. 1960, 63, Carl Sandburg award N.C. Poetry Soc., 1968, Blanche Whiting Keysner Meml. award Pa. Poetry Soc., 1967, Evans Spencer Wall Meml. award, Fedn. State Poetry Socs., 1966; Fellowship of Me. award Pine Tree br. Nat. League Am. Pen Women, 1966, Norfolk prize Poetry Soc. Va., 1951, 52, Ruth Mason Rice award Nat. League Am. Pen Women, 1968. Mem. Poetry Soc. Am. (mem. exec. bd. 1973-74), Nat. League Am. Pen Women (pres. N.Y.C. br. 1974—), Pa., W.Va. Poetry socs., Women Poets N.Y., Bklyn. Poetry Circle, Long Island Hist. Soc. Home and office: 1669 E 22nd St Brooklyn NY 11229

BENNETT, HARRIET, painter; b. N.Y.C.; d. John and Henrietta (Jantzen) Bultman; student Art Students League N.Y., Bklyn. Mus., New Sch. for Social Research, Pratt Graphic Art Center. One-woman shows at Marino Gallery, N.Y.C., 1958, Condon Riley Gallery, N.Y.C., 1959, Cichi Gallery, Rome, Italy, 1964, Galerie de l'Université, Paris, France, 1962, Woodstock Gallery, London, Eng., 1965. Recipient Falmouth Artists Guild award, 1962. Mem. Long Beach Art Assn., Mus. Modern Art, Whitney Mus. Am. Art. Address: PO Box 225 Island Park NY 11558

BENNETT, JOAN HIERHOLZER, educator, artist; b. Grand Rapids, Mich., Sept. 26, 1928; s. Frank Rudolph and Bernice Henrietta (Cooper) Hierholzer; B.F.A. cum laude, U. Tex., 1952; M.F.A., Rutgers U., 1969; m. John Pine Bennett, Aug. 11, 1956 (div.); children—David Pine, Charles Cooper. Fashion illustrator Prost Bros., San Antonio, 1952-56, free-lance illustrator Joskes of Tex., San Antonio, 1954-56; substitute art tchr. Chatham-Summit (N.J.) Pub. Schs., 1969-72; tchr. Summit Art Center, 1970; one-woman exhbns. include Men of Art Guild, San Antonio, 1954-55, Marion Koogler McNay Art Inst., San Antonio, 1967, Chatham Library, 1971; two-man exhbn. Summit Art Center, 1965, 72; group exhbns. include Dallas Mus. Fine Arts, 1953-55, Mus. N.M., Santa Fe, 1955, Witte Mus., San Antonio, 1955, Bodley Gallery, N.Y.C., 1957-58, Fairleigh Dickinson U., 1957-58, Montclair (N.J.) Art Mus., 1963, N.J. State Mus., Trenton, 1968, Art Guild Gallery, Hempstead, N.Y., 1963, Gallery 9, Chatham, 1964, N.Y. Savs. Bank, N.Y.C., 1970; Nat. Acad., N.Y.C., N.Y.C., 1971, 73. Kappa Kappa Gamma scholar, 1950. Mem. Nat. Assn. Women Artists, Summit Art Center, P.E.O., Kappa Kappa Gamma. Christian Scientist. Home: 12 Johnson Dr Chatman NJ 07928 Office: 7 Waverly Pl Madison NJ 07940

BENNETT, (JULIA) MADALEINE GATES, research librarian; b. Great Bend, N.Y., Nov. 29, 1914; d. Ralph McClure and Ethel Nellie (Zapf) Gates; B.A., Mt. Holyoke Coll., 1935; M.A. in Edn., St. Lawrence U., 1936; M.Sc. in L.S., Simmons Coll., 1963; m. Edwin A. Bennett, Aug. 3, 1936; children—Gretchen (Mrs. Philip D. Blair), Edwin A. III, David M. Br. librarian, then readers asst. Pub. Library Youngstown and Mahoning County, O., 1951-59; clk., asst. librarian research div. Raytheon Co., Lexington, Mass., 1959-62, librarian, 1962—. Mem. Spl. Libraries Assn. Unitarian. Mem. Order Eastern Star. Home: 52 Grove St Lexington MA 02173 Office: 28 Seyon St Waltham MA 02154

BENNETT, LAURA MAE TRICK (MRS. EDWIN FAY BENNETT), editor; b. Anderson, Ind., July 12, 1929; d. Homer Forrest and Mertie Juanita (Turner) T.; grad. high sch.; m. Edwin Fay Bennett, Nov. 30, 1947; children—Carolyn (Mrs. John Raymond Rule), Edwin Forrest, John Randall. Ticket agt. Wallen Bus Line, DeSoto, Mo., 1945-47; bookkeeper Tru-Value Dress Shop, Alton, Ill., 1947; clk., bookkeeper Western Auto, Norton, Kan., 1947-48; asst. mgr. Norton Municipal Airport, 1954-62; dep. register deeds, Norton, 1962-63; co-owner, editor Jour. Adv. Jennings, Kan., 1963-67, Logan (Kan.) Republican, 1967—. Pres., P.T.A., Norton, 1963; pres. Title I Parents' Adv. Council, 1973; sec., Logan Pride Steering Com., 1972; adj. Civil Air Patrol, 1954-55; chmn. United Services Orgn., Logan, 1969—. Recipient 1st in Editorials, Kan. Better Newspaper Contest, 1970, 2d in Agr. and/or Commercial Coverage, 1973. Mem. Nat., Kan. press assns., Hansen Meml. Mus. Assn., Logan C. of C. (sec. 1972-73), Logan Bus. and Profl. Women (v.p. 1973). Republican. Mem. Christian Ch. Address: Box 97 Logan KS 67646

BENNETT, LOLA MILLER, real estate broker; b. Belmont, Miss., July 11, 1919; d. James Angelo and Helen Timothy (Richards) Miller; student Modesto Jr. Coll., 1942, McClellan AFB Post Sch., Sacramento, 1942; m. Herman Bennett, Dec. 30, 1936 (dec.); children—James M., Sharon Lynne (Mrs. Richard L. Saunders). Aircraft layout worker, Alameda, Cal., 1942-50; salesman Leuck Realty, Alameda, Cal., 1957-63; mgr. mortgage loan dept. Agnew-Copeland, Alameda, 1963-65; owner L.B. Enterprises, Alameda, 1967—. Mem. Alameda County Assessment Appeals Bd., 1972—. Sec., Chmns. adv. com. to Alameda County Democratic Central Com., 1964-66; alternate delegate to Dem. Nat. Conv., 1964; mem. Cal. Dem. Central Com., 1967, 69-71. Mem. Cal. Real Estate Assn. (chmn. equal rights com. 1966), Alameda Bd. Realtors (chmn. legislative affairs com. 1972, chairperson equal rights com. 1973-74), Nat. Assn. Real Estate Brokers. Home: 325 Laguna Vista Alameda CA 94501 Office: 550 Park St Alameda CA 94501

BENNETT, MAGGIE WAYNICK, author; b. Reidsville, N.C., Sept. 6, 1899; d. Pinkney Daniel and Jalia Ann (Smothers) Waynick; ed. Thompsonville Sch.; m. Charles Robert Bennett, Dec. 25, 1917; 1 dau., Sara Jeanette Bennett McArthur. Co-author: Stitchery, Creative Crayon Techniques, Printing Without a Press, Jewelry Anyone Can Make, Holiday Ideas, End and Odds to Art; also filmstrips including Creative Collages, Hand Puppets, Fingerpainting, Paper Mosaics, Cardboard and Collagraph Printing, Leaf and Clay Printing, Linoleum and Woodcut Printing, Silk Screen Printing, String and Glue Printing, Vegetable and Gadget Printing. Methodist. Address: 526 N Rainbow Dr Hollywood FL 33021

BENNETT, MARGUERITE ALTOMESE STANLEY (MRS. LORENZO DAVID BENNETT), coll. ofcl.; b. Waco, Tex.; d. Arthur Jackson and Bessie (Brown) Stanley; B.S., Paul Quinn Coll., 1950; postgrad. Prairie View U., 1962, 63, 69; hon. doctorate, 1973; m. Lorenzo David Bennett, Oct. 17, 1949 (dec. Sept. 1964). Accountant Waco Vocational Sch., 1947-49; coordinator vets. affairs Paul Quinn Coll., Waco, 1950-53, asst. registrar, 1953-55, registrar, 1955-64, dir. devel., 1964-65, dir. financial aid, 1965—. Vice pres. East Waco Improvement Orgn., 1963—. Sponsor Gamma chpt. Phi Beta Sigma; sustaining mem. local YWCA, YMCA; sec. Waco chpt. Links, Inc. Bd. dirs. Waco U.S.O. Council, 1967—. Recipient Employee of Year award Paul Quinn Coll., 1973. Mem. Tex. Assn. Coll. Registrars Orgns., Paul Quinn Coll. Alumni Assn. (state pres. 1963, nat. sec. 1956, nat. pres. 1973—), Nat., Tex., S.W. assns. student financial aid adminstrs., Nat. Assn. for Financial Assistance to Minority Students, Assn. Higher Edn., Nat. Assn. Coll. and Univ. Bus. Officers, Nat. Council Negro Women, Sigma Xi Sigma, Zeta Phi Beta (Woman of Yr. 1972, chpt. sponsor). Mem. A.M.E. Ch. (del. to Missionary Quadrennial A.M.E. Ch. 1960, del. gen. conf. 1972, bd. mem. Compilation com. 1972, co-chmn. legislation com. 10th Episcopal dist.). Home: 900 Turner St Waco TX 76704

BENNETT, OLGA, judge; b. Viroqua, Wis., May 5, 1908; d. John Henry and Olga (Omundson) Bennett; B.A., U. Wis., 1928, LL.B., 1935. Asst. cashier Farmers Bank, Viroqua, 1929-32; admitted to Wis. bar, 1935; practiced in Viroqua, 1941-70; law clk. to Justice of Wis. Supreme Ct., Madison, 1936-41; partner firm Bennett & Bennett, 1941-56; individual practice, 1956-70; city atty. City of Viroqua, 1946-48; county judge Vernon County, Viroqua, 1970—. Mem. Am., Vernon County bar assns., State Bar Wis., Am. Judicature Soc. Home: 322 N Dunlap Av Viroqua WI 54665 Office: 210 N Main St Viroqua WI 54665

BENNETT, SARA SHAW (MRS. CLYDE CICERO BENNETT), civic worker; b. Quincy, Fla.; d. Charles Richard and Olive (Sampson) Shaw; student Lucy Cobb Inst., 1922-23, Converse Coll., 1923-24, Fla. State U., 1924-25; m. Alexander Love Wilson, June 14, 1928 (dec. Oct. 1951); children—Alexandra Love (Mrs. Emmett Edward Johnson), Olive Shaw (Mrs. Roby Robinson, Jr.); m. 2d, Clyde Cicero Bennett, June 18, 1954. Vice pres. Women's Aux. Fish Meml. Hosp., DeLand, Fla., 1961-64; charter mem. Quincy Civic Music, 1952—; disaster chmn. Gadsden County chpt. A.R.C., 1951-53; mem. adv. com. Patriotic Edn. Inc., DeLand, 1956-66, hon. life member, 1973—. Mem. founding group DeLand chpt. Democratic Women's Club, 1957—, social chmn., 1957-58. Mem. D.A.R. (founders group), Ams. Royal Descent, Royal Order of Garter, Magna Charta Dames, Plantagenet Soc., Hemerocallis Soc., Nat. League Am. Pen Women, Fla. Hist. Soc. (charter mem.), West Volusia Artists, Loch Haven Art Center, Fla. Fedn. Arts, Met. Mus. Art, Internat. Platform Assn., Am. Security Council (nat. adv. bd.), Inst. Am. Strategy (bd. sponsors), Alpha Delta Pi. Clubs: Garden, Yacht, Country. Exhibited photography DeLand Mus. Art, 1965, oil paintings Volusia County Artists Exhbn., Stetson U., 1970, 71; exhibited Lock Haven Art Center, 1972; represented in permanent collection West Volusia Meml. Hosp. Recipient merit award DeLand Sidewalk Show, 1972. Home: 601 N Boston Av DeLand FL 32720

BENNETT, SARAH SALLY ISABEL (MRS. PAUL H. BENNETT), author, composer; b. Fountain Springs, Pa.; d. Franklin Daniel and Jennie Catherine (Bright) Neff; student, Banks Bus. Coll., 1940-41, Gwen Shock Modeling and Dramatic Sch., 1941-42, U. Pa., 1942; m. Paul H. Bennett, Nov. 1, 1947. Model, John Wanamaker's, Phila., 1942; legal sec. Dept. of Justice, Phila., 1945-46; writer, performer, disc jockey Radio and TV Sta. WLWA, Atlanta, 1954-56; playwrite, actress Karamu Little Theater and Lakewood Little Theater, Cleve., 1957-59; founder, pres. Composers Showcase Inc., 1965—. Mem. nat. council Met. Opera, N.Y.C., 1967—; mem. John F. Kennedy Center, 1967—; founder, pres. Animal Welfare Vols., Inc., Cleve., 1969—. Mem. Nat. League Am. Pen Women (pres. 1962-63), Am. Guild Authors and Composers, Am. Women in Radio and TV, Am. Guild of Variety Artists, Broadcast Music, D.A.R. Recipient numerous awards and honors. Clubs: Cleve. Yachting; Racquet Club Internat. Women's City Club of Cleve. Home: Winton Place 610 12700 Lake Av Lakewood OH 44107

BENNETT, SHERRELL LANSDON, banker; b. Opp, Ala., Apr. 28, 1931; d. Willie Preston Lansdon and Essie (Davis) Lansdon Woods; student Am. Inst. Banking, 1959, 60, 61, 63 children—(by previous marriage) Sherlene (Mrs. James E. Dyes), Karon; m. 2d, Robert Dale Bennett, Sept. 4, 1959; 1 dau., Jenifer. With 1st Nat. Bank, Columbus, Ga., 1954-57; with Nat. Bank, Fort Benning, Ga., 1957—, asst. v.p., 1967-71, v.p., 1971—. Mem. Am. Inst. Banking (dir. 1963-64), Ga. Women Bankers. Home: 6336 Fox Chapel Dr Columbus GA 31904 Office: PO Drawer J Fort Benning GA 31905

BENNETT, VIRGINIA CLIVER, educator; b. Asbury Park, N.J., Mar. 28, 1916; d. Samuel Leon and Ella (Dakin) Cliver; R.N., Ann May Sch. Nursing, 1940; B.S. in Elementary Edn., Rutgers U., 1956, M.Ed. in Ednl. Psychology, 1961, Ed.D., 1963; m. H. Malcolm Bennett, Oct. 17, 1940; children—Elizabeth (Mrs. Rex Gilbreath), Malcolm, Jr. Tchr. kindergarten, Wall Twp., N.J., 1952-60; intern Children's Psychiat. Center, Eatontown, N.J., 1961-63, Long Branch (N.J.) pub. schs., 1962-63; asst. prof. psychol. founds. Rutgers U., New Brunswick, N.J., 1963-67, asso. prof., 1967-72, prof., 1972—, coordinator sch. psychol. tng. program, 1967—. Cons. govt., pub. schs., profl. orgns., 1965—; chmn. Inter-Coll. Council Sch. Psychology Tng., 1965-69; mem. N.J. Bd. Psychol. Examiners, 1970—. Bd. dirs., v.p. Jour. Sch. Psychology, Inc., 1970-71. Grant Found. fellow, 1960-63. Diplomate Am. Bd. Profl. Psychology. Fellow Am. Orthopsychiat. Assn., Am. Psychol. Assn. (pres.-elect div. 16, 1973-74); mem. N.J. Assn. Sch. Psychologists (exec. bd. 1969-70), N.J. Psychol. Assn. (pres. 1972-73), N.E.A. (life), N.J. Edn. Assn., Soc. Projective Techniques and Personality Assessment, Am. Assn. U. Profs., Am. Ednl. Research Assn. Contbr. articles to profl. jours. Home: 10 Landing Lane New Brunswick NJ 08901

BENNETT, WILANNA FONTAINE, library cons.; b. Clarksdale, Miss., Sept. 1, 1938; d. Fontaine Gipson and Anna (Bufkin) Bennett; student Delta State Coll., 1958-60; B.S., Miss. State Coll. for Women, 1960-62; M.S. in L.S., La. State U., 1965. Cataloger Miss. Library Commn., Jackson, 1963-66, instnl. library cons., 1966—. Mem. A.L.A., Southeastern, Miss. (mem. membership com. 1972—) library assns. Presbyn. Editor: Here's What's Happening, quar. publ. Miss. Library Commn., 1969—. Home: 1315 N Jefferson St Apt 205 Jackson MS 39202 Office: Mississippi Library Commission PO Box 3260 Jackson MS 39207

BENNIGHT, KATHERINE COX (MRS. WILLIAM GEORGE EARL BENNIGHT), counseling exec.; b. Boyce, Ky., Oct. 27, 1916; d. Willis B. and Stella (Austin) Cox; B.S., E. Central State Coll., Okla., 1939; M.Ed., U. Md., 1968; postgrad. U. Ill., summer 1969; m. William George Earl Bennight, July 19, 1942 (dec. Oct. 1957); 1 son, William George Earl. Tchr., Cromwell (Okla.) High Sch., 1939-42; editor med. manuscripts W.F. Prior Pub. Co., Hagerstown, Md., 1948-55; employment interviewer Dept. Employment Security, Hagerstown, 1957-64, area counselor western Md., Hagerstown, 1964-69; state supr. counseling and testing Md. Employment Service, Balt., 1969—. Mem. Washington County Council on Alcoholism, 1968-69. Mem. Nat. Employment Counselors Assn. (nat. sec. 1974-75, pres. Md. chpt. 1971-72), Am., Md. (exec. bd. 1967-68) personnel and guidance assns., Nat. Vocation Guidance Assn., Nat. Rehab. Assn. Home: 75 Homeland Southway Baltimore MD 21212 Office: 1100 N Eutaw St Baltimore MD 21201

BENNINGHOFF, ANNE LOUISE STEVENSON (MRS. WILLIAM SHIFFER BENNINGHOFF), botanist; b. Shelby, O., Aug. 3, 1942; d. Clayton Cooper and Thelma Ruth (Kunkel) Stevenson; B.S. in Biology, Wittenberg U., 1964; M.S. in Botany, U. Mich., 1967, postgrad., 1967—; m. William Shiffer Benninghoff, June 14, 1969. Research asst. Parke-Davis & Co., Rochester, Mich., 1964-65; pollen analyst, research asst. dept. botany, dept. meteorology, U. Mich., Ann Arbor, 1966-67; teaching fellow dept. botany U. Mich., 1965-69; ind. researcher, 1969—. Mem. Ecol. Soc. Am., Bot. Soc. Am., Ohio Acad. Sci., Mich. Acad. Sci., Lit. and Arts, Internat. Assn. for Great Lakes Research, A.A.A.S., Women's Research Club U. Mich. (recording sec. 1973-74), Sigma Xi. Lutheran. Contbr. articles on paleoecology and phytocoenology of Western Lake Erie region to sci. jours. Home: 3315 Alton Court Ann Arbor MI 48105

BENNINGHOFF, EDITH LILLY AVERILL (MRS. HARRY MERRELL BENNINGHOFF), educator, speech therapist; b. Angelica, N.Y., Sept. 24, 1908; d. Clarence John and Frieda (Watkins) Averill; student pub. schs.; m. Harry Merrell Benninghoff, Aug. 21, 1929; 1 dau., Barbara (Mrs. David Ashley Shackelford IV). Instr. esophageal speech div. vocational rehab., Tallahassee, 1963—; instr. Internat. Assn. Laryngectomees; lectr. on cancer and smoking to schs., service clubs, nurse assns. Mem. Fla. Laryngectomee Assn. (editor state newsletter 1961-67, dir. 1961—, exec. 1st v.p. 1964, state pres. 1965-67), Nat. Rehab. Assn., Am. Cancer Soc. (service and rehab. com. Fla. div., mem. edn. com. Brevard County unit). Home: 300 W Vesta Circle Melbourne FL 32901

BENNION, LINDA ROLFE (MRS. PHILLIP J. BENNION), social worker; b. Rigby, Ida., May 12, 1942; d. Elwyn Walker and Nell Lucille (Balmforth) Rolfe; B.A., Brigham Young U., 1965; M.S.W., Portland State U., 1969; m. Phillip J. Bennion, Jan. 25, 1965. Social work aide Utah State Hosp., 1965-67; med. sch. social worker U. Ore., 1967; social worker Dept. Pub. Assistance, 1969-70; community services rep. Rainier Sch., Tacoma, Wash., 1970-72, supr. community services, 1972—. Program cons. Camas-Washougal Progress Center, Clark County, Wash., 1971-72; active in organizing local Meals on Wheels program, local family counseling services, reduced transit fares schedule for sr. and disabled citizens, adult activity center for developmentally disabled. Bd. dirs. Pierce County (Wash.) chpt. A.R.C. Recipient awards Community Awareness Task Force, Clark County chpt. Nat. Assn. for Retarded Children. Mem. Am. Assn. on Mental Deficiency (regional social work chmn.), Washington Assn. for Retarded Children (state dir.). Home: 126 S Normandy Rd Seattle WA 98148 Office: 2367 Tacoma Av S Tacoma WA 98402

BENOVITZ, MADGE KLEIN (MRS. BURTON S. BENOVITZ), civic leader; b. Wilkes-Barre, Pa., Nov. 26, 1934; d. Nathan and Esther (Miller) Klein; student Cornell U., 1952-54, U. Pa., 1954-55; B.A. in Econs., Wilkes Coll., 1956; m. Burton S. Benovitz, Sept. 5, 1954; 1 dau., Jane. Pres. League Women Voters Wilkes-Barre, 1964-65; bd. mem. League Women Voters Pa., 1967-69, 1st v.p., 1969-71, state pres., 1971-73; mem. Pa. Gov.'s Citizens Commn. on Basic Edn., 1972-73; mem. Nat. Orgn. Com. League Women Voters U.S., 1971-72; mem. Citizen Assembly Welfare Planning Council, 1966-72. Chmn. trustees League Women Voters Pa. Edn. Fund, 1971-73; mem. Home-Health Services Bd. Northeastern Pa., 1971—; mem. Homemaker Service Bd., 1966-71; 1st v.p. parents council Wyo. Sem. Day Sch., 1969; mem. Pa. State Adv. Council for Vocational Edn., 1973—, Flood Recovery Task Force, 1972-73; mem. citizens adv. com. Pa. Gov.'s Traffic Safety Council, 1973-74; mem. planning allocations and resources devel. com. United Way of Wyoming Valley, 1973—; treas. Parents Council of Wyoming Sem., 1973-74; mem. women's aux. Wilkes-Barre Gen. Hosp. Mem. Nat. Council Jewish Women, Women's Aux. Luzerne County Med. Soc., Jr. League Wilkes-Barre, Alpha Epsilon Phi. Jewish religion. Mem. Hadassah (v.p. Wilkes-Barre chpt. 1963-65). Clubs: Westmoreland (Wilkes-Barre); Valley Tennis and Swim (Trucksville). Home: 840 Nandy Dr Kingston PA 18704

BENSCOTER, CAROLYN MAE, ednl. cons.; b. Huntington Mills, Pa., Sept. 7, 1942; d. Freas W. and Mary Myrtle (Kishbaugh) Benscoter; B.S., Bloomsburg (Pa.) State Coll., 1964, M.Ed. in Spl. Edn., 1968; Tchr. jr. high sch. educable mentally retarded Clinton County (Pa.) Bd. Edn., 1964-66; tchr. trainable mentally retarded Berwick (Pa.) Area Bd. Edn., 1966-68; master tchr. trainable program Shiawasee County (Mich.) Intermediate Sch. Bd., 1969-73; tchr. cons. for severely impaired Tuscola County Intermediate Bd. Edn., Caro, Mich., 1973—. Organizer, dir. ch. program for mentally handicapped adults 1st Ch. of Christ, Owosso, Mich., 1972-73; mem. Owosso Mental Health-Mental Retardation Cons. Bd., 1972-73. Mem. Council for Exceptional Children (sec. Williamsport, Pa. area chpt. 1966, v.p. Thumb, Mich. area chpt. 1973, mem. Mich. gov. bd. 1972—), Am. Assn. Mental Deficiency, Columbia County (Pa.) Hist. Soc., Internat. Order King's Daus. and Sons. Home: 4572 Hill St Cass City MI 48726 Office: 207 E Grant St Caro MI 48723

BENSINGER, JUDITH SCHNEEBECK (MRS. PETER B. BENSINGER), physician; b. Klamath Falls, Ore., Dec. 16, 1941; d. Edwin Jacob and Bethel Jane (Crumbaker) Schneebeck; B.A. (with honors), Northwestern U., 1963; M.D., 1968; m. Peter B. Bensinger, July 25, 1969; 1 dau., Jennifer Anne. Intern Evanston Hosp., Ill., 1968-69; physician Head Start Health Services, Chgo., 1970—; clin. dir. for handicapped, Goodwill Industries, Springfield, Ill., 1970-73. Mem. com. on handicapped children State Ill. Commn. on Children, 1970-72; governing life mem. Art Inst. Chgo.; mem. women's bd. U. Chgo., Urban League Chgo.; chmn. inner-city sch. music programs Chgo. Symphony Orch., 1970-72, pres. Jr. governing bd., 1974. Trustee, Northwestern Meml. Hosp.; bd. dirs. The Villages (part of Karl Menninger Clinic). Mem. A.M.A., Cook County Med. Assn., Delta Gamma. Clubs: Lake Shore Country (Chgo.); Saddle and Cycle, Arts. Home: 1260 Astor St Chicago IL 60610

BENSKINA, MARGARITA O. (PRINCESS ORELIA), dancer, singer, musician; b. Colon, Panama, Mar. 16, 1915; d. Jose and Amelia Benskina; student parochial schs., Havana, Cuba, and Colon, Panama; Harren High Sch., N.Y.C.; diploma for instrs. in modeling, N.Y. Acad. Theatrical Arts, 1962; grad. N.Y. Sch. Floral Designing, 1971. Has appeared in theatres, night clubs, etc., in various cities of U.S.; in Dance with Your Gods, Calling All Stars, Broadway Parade, N.Y.C., 1935—; mem. Afro-Cuban dance team, Orelia and Pedro, 1942; toured with Osadata Dafara Dance Opera, Kykunkoi, 1947; now appearing with own ensemble; toured Canada with own dance co.,

Bacanal, 1950; starred in UN program Stars of the West Indies, also TV program Tropical Holiday, CBS; toured with Sam Manning Calypso Concert Co., 1954; personal mgr. for modern jazz group Rouse-Watkins-Les Modes Quintet, 1956, also dance and mus. groups; prod., dir. concerts, N.Y.C., 1959; produced, directed, starred in concert program, Princess Orelia's Pot Puree, Town Hall, N.Y.C., 1964. Recipient J.F. Kennedy for Minorities Heritage award, Am. Honorarium award, 1966. Mem. Broadcast Music, Inc., Synanon, Negro Women's Guild, Washington, Council Negro Am. Women (life). Ordained to ministry of Spiritual Science, 1956. Author: No Longer Defeated and Other Poems, 1972; The Inflammable Desire to Rebel, 1973. Contbr. to New Voices in American Poetry, 1972-73. Home: 192-22 100th Av Hollis NY 11423

BENSON, DOROTHY ANN DURICK (MRS. ROBERT BRONAUGH BENSON), psychologist, civic worker; b. Grand Forks, N.D.; d. William James and Grace (Johnson) Durick; B.S. with distinction, U. N.M., 1950; M.A. in Psychology, U. Minn., 1952; m. Robert Bronaugh Benson, May 8, 1954. Research asst. psychology dept., U. Minn., 1950-52; instr., counselor Student Counseling Service, Kan. State Coll., 1952-54; psychometrist, counselor Stephens Coll., 1957-58; exec. asst. Benson Bldg. Materials Inc. and Benson Lumber & Supply Co., Columbia, Mo., 1958—; partner Koti Krafts from Finland. Mem. exec. bd. U. Mo. YWCA, 1961-64; mem. Columbia Friends of Library; active League Women Voters, Columbia, 1955—, bd. dirs., 1955-61, pres., 1958-59. Mem. King's Daus., Phi Kappa Phi, Psi Chi Phi Sigma. Home: PO Box 3 Columbia MO 65201 Office: Benson Lumber Gen Office 710 Business Loop 70 W Columbia MO 65201

BENSON, HAZEL SARTWELL (MRS. ALFRED BENSON), librarian; b. Mooers, N.Y., Jan. 17, 1907; d. Edwin and Cora Anna (Rodden) Sartwell; A.B., Houghton Coll., 1927; A.M., Tchrs. Coll. Columbia, 1937; M.L.S., State U. N.Y. at Geneseo, 1962; postgrad. McGill U., summer, 1928; m. Alfred Benson, Apr. 1, 1939; children—Margaret Ann, James Kenneth Buck. Tchr. high sch. Bliss, N.Y., 1927-30, Tomkins Cove, N.Y., 1930-34, N.Y. Mills, N.Y., 1934-39, Montville, N.Y., 1955-60; dist. librarian elementary North Rockland Central Sch. Dist., Stony Point, N.Y., 1960-69, library coordinator K-12, 1969-72; librarian Faith Heritage Sch., Syracuse, N.Y., 1972—; librarian Tomkins Cove Pub. Library, 1947-72. Asst. leader Girl Scouts U.S.A., 1953-55; mem. P.T.A., Garnerville, 1960-67. Mem. Am. Assn. U. Women, Am. Assn. Retired Persons, N.Y. State Ret. Tchrs. Assn., N.Y. Library Assn., N.Y. State Sch. Library Media Suprs. Republican. Home: 860 James St Clayton NY 13624 also 837 Riviera St Venice FL 33595 Office: Box 130 Colvin Sta Syracuse NY 13205

BENSON, LINDA LOU MILLER (MRS. DELBERT LEE BENSON), editor; b. Martinsburg, W.Va., Feb. 2, 1942; d. Ralph Edgar and Alma Grace (Thomas) Miller; B.S., W.Va. U., 1964; m. Delbert Lee Benson, Sept. 5, 1964; 1 dau., Lesley Lorraine. Tchr. Khai Minh English Sch., Saigon, Vietnam, 1959-60; asst. librarian Inst. for Defense Analysis, Arlington, Va., 1964-65; editor Preston County Jour., Kingwood, W.Va., 1967—. Mem. cooperative extension com. W.Va. U., 1971—; mem. adv. bd. Salvation Army, Kingwood. Mem. W.Va. Press Assn., Kappa Tau Alpha, Theta Sigma Phi. Republican. Baptist. Club: Jr. Woman's. Home: 204 Brown Av Kingwood WV 26537 Office: 110 Main St Kingwood WV 26537

BENSON, MABLE A. RANSAW (MRS. EARLEE BENSON), social worker; b. Pitts., Nov. 23, 1926; d. Romie and Adellar (Edison) Ransaw; B.A., U. Pitts., 1948, M.S.W., 1960; Ph.D. (hon.), Colo. State Christian Coll., 1972 ; m. Earlee Benson, May 25, 1946; children—Dexter, Terrilena Elizabeth. Saleswoman, N.C. Life Mut. Ins. Co., Pitts., 1952-53; clk. Carnegie Inst. Tech. Engring. Library, Pitts., 1954-56; child care worker Western Psychiat. Inst. and Clinic, Pitts., 1956-58; social worker Dept. Pub. Welfare and Childrens Hosp., Pitts., 1957-59; out-patient supr. Mayview State Hosp., Pitts., 1960-63, psychiat. social worker Council House, 1963-64; med. and psychiat. social worker St. Margrets Hosp., Pitts., 1964-67; med. social worker cons., rodent control adminstr. Allegheny County Health Dept., Pitts., 1967-72, asst. chief community service, 1972, acting chief, 1972—, chief bur. community service devel., 1973—. A founder Homewood-Brushton Citizens Improvement Assn.; co-chmn. subcom. social services, com. home delivered services Area Wide Commn. on Services to Aged; cons. Multiple Purpose Program for Older Citizens; mem. community relations com. South Hill Council for Aged. Bd. dirs. Family Planning Council South-Western Pa. Mem. Nat. Assn. Social Workers, Assn. Black Social Workers, N.A.A.C.P., Internat. Platform Assn., Delta Sigma Theta. Baptist. Home: 7221 Kedron St Pittsburgh PA 15208 Office: Pittsburgh PA 15219

BENSON, MAXINE FRANCES, historian; b. Boulder, Colo., Sept. 5, 1939; d. Mac Walden and Frances (Ladwig) Benson; B.A. magna cum laude, U. Colo., 1961, M.A., 1962, Ph.D., 1968; M.A. in Librarianship, U. Denver, 1973. Dep. state historian State Hist. Soc. Colo., Denver, 1964-65, 66-67, state historian, also editor Colo. Mag., 1967-72, head librarian, 1972—. Vis. lectr. U. Denver, summers, 1969, 70, 71, Met. State Coll., Denver, spring, 1970; Nat. Hist. Publs. Commn. fellow in documentary hist. editing Smithsonian Instn., Washington, 1971-72. Mem. A.L.A., Spl. Libraries Assn., Am. Soc. for Information Sci., Western Hist. Assn., Orgn. Am. Historians, Colo. Authors League, Phi Beta Kappa, Phi Alpha Theta, Beta Phi Mu, Alpha Omicron Pi. Home: 805-B W Moorhead Circle Boulder CO 80303 Office: State Historical Society of Colo 200 14th Av at Sherman St Denver CO 80203

BENSON, (MILDRED) JUNE TOMPKINS, civic worker; b. Granite, Okla., Nov. 6, 1915; d. Elmer O. and Bessie (Stovall) Tompkins; A.B., U. Okla., 1937, A.M., 1954; m. Oliver Earl Benson, June 1, 1940; children—John, Megan (Mrs. Graydon Hale Doolittle). Mem. City Commn., Norman, Okla., 1953-61; 1st woman mayor City of Norman, 1957-58, 59-60; mem. Gov.'s Repeal of Prohibition Commn., 1958-62, Gov.'s Election Law Commn., 1965-67, Okla. Acad. State Goals, 1970—, Okla. State Commn. on Fiscal Structure and Procedures; mem. Norman Environmental Control Adv. Bd., 1973—. Pres. League Women Voters, Norman, 1951-53, mem. state bd., 1951-53, 62-70; past mem. bd. dirs. Okla. Municipal League; mem. Norman Civic Improvement Council, Nat. Municipal League. Former Camp Fire Girls leader, guardian and council mem. Mem. Am. Polit. Sci. Assn., Am. Soc. Pub. Adminstrn., C. of C., Urban League, Hilltop Guild, U. Okla. Faculty Club, Am. Civil Liberties Union, UN Assn., Colo. Mountain Club, Sierra Club, Common Cause, Scenic Rivers Assn., Pi Sigma Alpha, Alpha Delta Pi. Democrat. Presbyn. Author: (with others) Presidential Nominating Politics in 1952 (Okla. sect.), 1954; Let's Talk Taxes, 1961; The Capitol Letter (weekly newsletter 1964-70). Home: 640 E Boyd St Norman OK 73069 also Kingscourt Allenspark CO 80510

BENSON, SANDRA LORENE (MRS. RICHARD L. BENSON), journalist; b. Kansas City, Kan., Dec. 18, 1938 d. William M. and Rosalind Lorene (Muir) Kellner; B.S., Kan. State Coll., 1960; M.Edn., Kan. U., 1966; m. Richard L. Benson, Nov. 19, 1960; 1 dau., Laura Elaine. With Implement & Tractor Publ. Co., Kansas City, Mo., 1956-60; tchr. Leav (Kan.) pub. schs., 1960-61; publs. adviser Kansas City (Kan.) pub. schs., 1961-67; ch. and soc. writer Kansas City Star, 1967-68; journalism adviser Tulsa pub. schs., 1968—. Judge nat. yearbook Columbia Scholastic Press Assn., N.Y.C., 1973, lectr., 1973; lectr. U. Okla., 1972. Mem. Women in Communications (treas. 1970-71), Okla. Interscholastic Press Advisers Assn. (pres. 1972-73, rep. to nat. press assns. 1973—), Journalism Edn. Assn. (state dir. 1973-74), So., Okla. interscholastic press assns., Columbia Press Advisers Assn. Home: 6956 E 72nd St Tulsa OK 74133 Office: Edison School 2906 E 41st St Tulsa OK 74105

BENSTEAD, JOYCE, banker; b. Redcar, England, July 7, 1924; d. Albert Benstead and Lily (Lewis) Benstead Weatherill; came to U.S., 1948, naturalized, 1954; student Am. Inst. Banking, 1962. Bookkeeper, Benstead & Weatherill, Redcar, Eng., 1939-43, 46-48; with Am. Bank & Trust Co. Pa., Reading, 1948—, dir. tng., 1967—, asst. v.p., 1970-73, v.p. career devel. and tng., 1973—. Bd. dirs. Berks County Pa. Dutch Travel Assn. Served with Womens Royal Naval Service, 1943-46. Mem. Am. Inst. Banking (pres. 1963-64, bd. dirs. 1966-72), Adminstrv. Mgmt. Soc. (2d v.p. 1971-72, 1st v.p. 1972-73, pres. 1973-74), Nat. Assn. Bank Women (chmn. 1971-74). Presbyn. Home: 50 N 4th St Reading PA 19601 Office: 445 Penn St Reading PA 19601

BENT, MRS. FRANCES W., savs. and loan exec.; d.; Frank James and Elizabeth (Valley) Williams; grad. sch. financial pub. relations Northwestern U.; m. James Edward Bent, Sept. 26, 1936. Sec., Hartford Fed. Savs. & Loan Assn. (Conn.), 1937-70, exec. v.p., dir., 1958—; treas., dir. Hartford Stage Co. Regent, chmn. student affairs com. U. Hartford; past pres. Central Conn. Communities Cultural, Civic and Charitable Corp., Hartford Symphony Aux., Symphony Soc. Aux.; v.p. exec. com. St. Joseph's Coll. Bd. dirs. Symphony Soc. Greater Hartford; trustee Campfire Girls, Inc. Conn. Opera Assn.; past dir., mem. finance com. YWCA Greater Hartford; past dir. Greater Hartford Community Council. Mem. Women's Assn. U. Hartford (past dir.), Women Instituters Conn., Am. Assn. UN (bd. advisers Greater Hartford chpt.), Conn. Opera Guild (chmn. community affairs), Nat. League Insured Savs., Financial Pub. Relations Assn. (past dir.), Savs. Instns. Marketing Soc. Am. (dir., mem. exec. com.), Nat. League Insured Savs. Assns. (past gov.). Home: 343 N Steele Rd West Hartford CT 06117 Office: 50 State St Hartford CT 06103

BENTEL, MARIA-LUISE RAMONA AZZARONE (MRS. FREDERICK R. BENTEL), architect; b. N.Y.C., June 15, 1928; d. Louis and Maria-Teresa (Massaro) Azzarone; B.Arch., Mass. Inst. Tech., 1951; Fulbright scholar Scuola d'Architettura, Venice, Italy, 1952-53; m. Frederick R. Bentel, Aug. 16, 1952; children—Paul Louis, Peter Andreas, Maria Elisabeth. Partner, Bentel & Bentel, Architects, Locust Valley, N.Y., 1955—; pres. Tesstoria Realty Corp., N.Y.C., 1961—; treas. Correlated Designs, Inc., Locust Valley, 1961—. Adj. lectr. archtl. design, drafting Queensboro Community Coll., U. City N.Y. Founding mem. Locust Valley Bus. Dist. Planning Commn., 1968—; mem. Mass. Inst. Tech. Ednl. Council; chairperson Locust Valley Library Adv. Bd. Registered profl. architect, N.Y., N.J., Conn., Va., Vt., Nat. Council Archtl. Registration Bds. Mem. A.I.A. (design com. L.I. chpt.), N.Y. State Assn. Architects (design and awards com.), Nat. Council Archtl. Registration Bds., Mass. Inst. Tech. Alumnae Assn., Mass. Inst. Tech. Alumni L.I. (v.p., dir.). Contbr. chpt. to Time Saver Standards Reference Book, 1973. Archtl. works include Campus Union, Dome Auditorium, C.W. Post Coll. L.I. U., Hempstead Bank, Nassau Centre Exec. Hdqrs. Bldg. (award L.I. Assn. Architects, 1972), North Shore Unitarian Sch., Plandome, N.Y. (award L.I. Assn. Architects 1967, N.Y. State Assn. Architects award 1970), Shelter Rock Library, Searingtown, N.Y. (L.I. Assn. Architects award 1970), St. Anthony's Ch. (award N.Y. State Assn. Architects 1972), Nanuet, N.Y., Kinloch Farm, Va., Steinberg Learning Center-Woodmere (N.Y.) Acad. (N.Y. State Library Assn. award 1972), St. Francis de Sales Ch., Bennington, Vt., Amityville (N.Y.) Pub. Library (N.Y. State Assn. Architects-A.I.A. award 1973, L.I. Assn.-A.I.A. award 1973); Neitlich residence, Oyster Bay Cove, L.I. (N.Y. State Assn. Architects award 1971, L.I. Assn. award 1971). Home: 23 Frost Creek Dr Lattingtown NY 11560 Office: 22 Buckram Rd Locust Valley NY 11560

BENTLEY, ANTOINETTE COZELL (MRS. ROBERT D. BENTLEY), ins. co. exec.; b. N.Y.C., Oct. 7, 1937; d. Joseph Richard Cozell and Rose (LaFata) Vila; B.A., U. Mich., 1960; LL.B., U. Va., 1961; m. Robert D. Bentley, Aug. 28, 1960; children—Robert S., Anne W. Admitted to N.Y. bar, 1962, N.J. bar, 1971; atty. Sage, Gray, Todd & Sims, N.Y.C., 1961-65, Farrell, Curtis, Carlin, Davidson & Mahr, Morristown, N.J., 1971-73; sec. U.S. Fire Ins. Co., N.Y.C., 1973—, Crum & Forster, N.Y.C., 1973—, Internat. Ins. Co., Chgo., 1973—, Westchester Fire Ins. Co., N.Y.C., 1973—, N. River Ins. Co., Morris Twp., N.J., 1973—. Mem. N.J., Morris County bar assns., Order of the Coif, Lynchos Soc., Phi Delta Phi, Chi Omega. Mem. bd. editors U. Va. Law Review, 1959-61. Home: 16 Prospect St Mendham NJ 07945 Office: 305 Madison Av Morris Township NJ 07960

BENTLEY, GEORGIA MARIANNE, lawyer; b. Palmerston, Ont., Can., Nov. 9, 1929; B.A., U. Toronto, 1950; legal edn. Osgoode Hall Law Sch., Toronto. Admitted to Ont. bar, 1954, since practiced in Toronto; with firm Fasken & Calvin and predecessor. Mem. County of York (Ont.) Law Assn., Canadian Bar Assn. Office: Box 30 Toronto Dominion Centre Toronto ON Canada

BENTLEY, HELEN DELICH (MRS. WILLIAM ROY BENTLEY), govt. ofcl., journalist, TV producer; b. Ruth, Nev.; d. Michael and Mary (Kovich) Delich; student U. Nev., 1941-42, George Washington U., 1943; B.J., U. Mo., 1944; LL.D., U. Md., 1970, U. Alaska, 1973; L.H.D. (hon.), Bryant Coll., 1971, U. Portland, 1972; m. William Roy Bentley, June 7, 1959. Reporter, Ely (Nev.) Record, 1940-42; polit. campaign mgr. for late Senator James G. Scrugham in White Pine County, Nev., 1942; bur. mgr. United Press, Ft. Wayne, Ind., 1944-45; reporter Balt. Sun, 1945-53, maritime editor, 1953-69; chmn. Fed. Maritime Commn., 1969—; TV and film producer, world trade and maritime shows, 1950-64. Pub. relations adviser Am. Assn. Port Authorities, 1958-62, 64-67; only woman to trek Northwest Passage aboard SS Manhattan, 1969; Scripps lectr. journalism U. Nev., 1970; chmn. Am. Bicentennial Fleet, Inc., 1973—. Mem. bd. Church Home and Hosp., St. Scholastica Coll., United Seamen's Service, Oceanic Ednl. Found. Recipient numerous awards including Distinguished Service award North Atlantic Ports Assn., 1965; Meritorious Service award AFL-CIO Maritime Port Council Greater N.Y., 1965; Meritorious Service award Ironworkers and Shipbuilders Council, 1966; Am. Mcht. Marine Writers award Propeller Club of U.S., 1967, 68; Outstanding Woman Grad., U. Mo., 1968; Golden Anchor award Casa Mar de P.R., 1968; Woman of Year, Women's Advt. Club Balt., 1969; Order Maritime Merit, San Francisco Port Commn., 1970; George Washington Honor medal Freedoms Found. at Valley Forge, 1971; Adm. of Ocean Seas United Seamen's Service and South St. Mus., 1971; Man of Year award N.Y. Fgn. Freight Forwarders and Brokers Assn., 1972; GOP Woman of Year award, 1972; Distinguished Service medal Am. Legion, 1973; Robert M. Thompson award Navy League U.S., 1973. Mem. Md. Hist. Soc., Star-Spangled Banner Assn. Md., Am. Women in Radio and Television, Balt. Pub. Relations Council, Theta Sigma Phi. Republican (mem. bd. Rep. Women Washington). Greek Orthodox. Clubs: Am. Newspaper Women's, Press of Washington. Editor: Seaport Histories, Ports of Americas. Home: 408 Chapel Wood Lane Lutherville MD 21093 Office: Federal Maritime Commn 1100 L St NW Washington DC 20573

BENTON, EVELYN FLEMING, librarian; b. Ponchatoula, La., Aug. 10, 1921; d. Walter Raleigh and Mabel Magdalene (Varnado) Fleming; B.F.A. with high distinction and spl. mention in music, Okla. State U., 1943; student U. Tex. Grad. Sch. Library Sci., 1959-60; m. Douglas C. Benton, Aug. 25, 1942; children—Walter Bradford, Christopher Paul. Circulation asst. Tulsa Pub. Library, 1944, 1st asst. tech. dept., 1945; reference asst. Okla. State U., Stillwater, 1946-48, jr. reference librarian, 1948-50; piano tchr., Baytown, Tex., 1958-60; asst. librarian Lee Coll., Baytown, 1960-66; library dir. Deer Park (Tex.) Pub. Library, 1967—. Pres. San Jacinto Music Tchrs. Assn., 1960. Pres. Baytown Unitarian Fellowship, 1965. Mem. Am., Tex. (chmn. nominating com. 1971-72, chmn. reference roundtable 1972-73, sec. dist. V, 1969, treas. dist. VIII, 1971), Southwestern (conf. program com.), Pub. (editorial com.) library assns., Tex. Municipal Librarians Assn., Internat. Platform Assn., Phi Kappa Phi, Sigma Alpha Iota (treas. Iota Alpha chpt. 1942-43). Unitarian. Club: Houston Library. Home: 3401 Woodcrest St Baytown TX 77520 Office: 3009 Center St Deer Part TX 77536

BENTON, FLORA VIRGINIA HUFF, librarian; b. Roanoke, Va., Oct. 8, 1921; d. Thomas Franklin and Ethlind (Wertz) Huff; student Radford Coll., 1939-41, Ohio U., 1956-57; B.S., Ohio No. U., 1960; M.A., U. Toledo, 1964, postgrad., 1965-66; postgrad. Kent State U., 1971—; m. Stanley Theodore Benton, Dec. 24, 1942; children—Peggy Sue, Betty (Mrs. George Sarrica), Mary Jo (Mrs. Rick Vaillant), Lucy Lee. Reference asst. Roanoke (Va.) Pub. Library, 1939-42; catalog asst. Emory U. Library, Atlanta, 1942; sec. A.R.C., Atlanta, 1943; catalog asst. Pickerington (O.) Pub. Library, 1950-51; tchr. Celina (O.) pub. schs., 1957-62, Toledo pub. schs., 1962-64; library coordinator Oregon (O.) pub. schs., 1964—. Faculty U. Toledo, 1970; rep. Gov.'s Conf. on Libraries, Columbus, 1974; mem. evaluation team rep. Ohio Dept. Edn., 1973—. Vol. worker Am. Cancer Soc., 1946-48, Tb Soc., 1948-53; leader Girl Scouts U.S.A., 1969-71. Chmn., mem. adv. bd. library sci. dept. Com-Tech Coll., U. Toledo, 1965—. Mem. Nat., Ohio edn. assns., Am., Ohio library assns., Ohio Assn. Sch. Librarians (pres. 1972-73), Internat. Reading Assn. (local pres. 1966-67), Ohio Assn. for Supervision and Curriculum Devel., Ohio Sch. Suprs. Assn., Ohio Reading Assn., Ednl. Media Council Ohio, Delta Kappa Gamma, Pi Lambda Theta, Kappa Delta Pi, Phi Kappa Phi, Met. Toledo Ednl. Purchasing Assn. (chmn. 1967-68). Editor Ohio Assn. Sch. Librarians Bull., 1968-71. Home: Box 237 Fostoria Rd Curtice OH 43412 Office: Oregon Bd Edn 5721 Seaman Rd Oregon OH 43616

BENTON, HELEN DUNCAN (MRS. JOHN A. BENTON, JR.), counselor, psychometrist; b. Cameron, Mo., Apr. 6, 1918; d. Loren E. and Nan (Swartz) Duncan; A.B., U. Cin., 1940, B.E., 1941; M.Ed., Ohio State U., 1952; Ed.D., U. Fla., 1961; m. John A. Benton, Jr., June 1, 1962; 1 son, John A. III. Tchr., guidance counselor pub. schs. Cin., 1941-51, Fitzgerald, Ga., 1951-52; dean of women Ga. So. Coll., Statesboro, 1954-58; asst. prof. prin. guidance, coordinator undergrad. counseling U. Fla., Gainesville, 1960-63; vocational counselor U. South Fla., Tampa, 1966-70; vocational counselor Episcopal Counseling Center, Tampa, 1966—. Bd. dirs. Anclote Psychiat. Center, Tampa, Fla., 1974. Mem. Am. Psychol. Assn., Am. Personnel and Guidance Assn. Episcopalian. Home: 4230 Fairway Circle Tampa FL 33624 Office: Episcopal Counseling Center 240 Plant Av Tampa FL 33606

BENTON, KATHRYN M. BRADLEY (MRS. ROBERT E. BENTON), escrow co. exec.; b. Carnegie, Pa.; d. Charles A. and Mary (Halpin) Bradley; student U. Cal. at Los Angeles, 1929-35; m. Robert E. Benton, Sept. 14, 1935 (dec. Sept. 1965); 1 dau., Barbara A. (Mrs. Bernard P. Drachlis). Co-founder, pres. Eagle Rock Escrow Co., Los Angeles, 1962—. Charter exec. sec. United Orgns., 1966-68, N.E. Taxpayers Assn., 1966—. Bd. dirs., founder, sec. Robert E. Benton Meml. Found. Mem. Eagle Rock Bus. and Profl. Womens Club, Eagle Rock C. of C. Home: 5320 Vincent Av Los Angeles CA 90021 Office: 5012 Eagle Rock Blvd Los Angeles CA 90041

BENTON, LEVEVIAN MCDANIEL (MRS. NORMAN CHARLES BENTON), educator; b. Gary, Ind., Aug. 5, 1925; d. Lohney Lee and Geneva (Scott) McDaniel; A.B., Clark Coll., Atlanta, 1946; M.A., Atlanta U., 1957; m. Norman Charles Benton, Aug. 14, 1959. Camp counselor Karamu House, Cleve., 1946; tchr. Friendship Sch. for Mentally Retarded Children, Gary, 1947-49; elementary tchr. Dept. Interior, Ft. Totten, N.D., 1951-54, Indian Service, Macy, Neb., 1954-55, Cheyenne Agy., S.D., 1955-56, Oglala Community Sch., Pine Ridge, S.D., 1956-66; tchr. educable mentally handicapped Scottsbluff (Neb.) Pub. Sch., 1966—. Precinct committeeperson Republican Party, 1966-68. Mem. Nat., Neb., Scottsbluff (welfare com. and negotiation team 1970-73, profl. growth com. 1973—), Am. Assn. U. Women, N.A.A.C.P. (br. sec. 1966—), Bus. and Profl. Women's Clubs, Delta Kappa Gamma. Methodist (social concern chmn., treas. Wesleyan Service Guild). Home: 522 E 12th St Scottsbluff NE 69361

BENTON, MARGARET PEAKE, artist; b. South Orange, N.J.; d. James October and Elizabeth Maude (Peake) Benton; student N. Toronto Collegiate Inst., 1925, (Assn. Ont. Coll. Art scholar), Ont. Coll. Art, 1925-30, Victoria Coll., 1929-30. Exhibited in group shows Ont. Soc. Artists, Toronto, 1933, Royal Can. Acad. Art, 1938-40, 42, 45, 49, Royal Acad. London, Eng., 1950, Pa. Soc. Miniature Painters, 1940, 41, 45-51, Miniature Painters, Sculptors and Graver's Soc. Washington, 1943, 45-47, 51-73, Nat. Soc. Miniature Painters, N.Y.C., 1949, Miniature Art Soc. N.J., 1971-74, Frame House Gallery, Louisville, 1973; exhibited one-man shows in Victoria Coll. Library, Toronto, Eaton's Coll. St. Gallery, Toronto, Odeon Carlton, Toronto, St. Catharines (Ont.) Pub. Library, Oak Hall, Niagara Falls, Ont., Courthouse, Niagara-On-The Lake, Ont.; represented in permanent collections Queen's Pvt. Collection, Eng., King's Coll., Halifax, N.S., Can., United Ch. Bldgs., Toronto, Nurmanzil Psychiatric Clinic, Punjab, India, Pa. Acad. Art, Phila. Recipient Elizabeth Muhlhofer award Miniature Painters, Sculptors and Gravers Soc. Washington, 1962, Levantia White Boardman Meml. 2d prize, 1970, 72, R.V. Shope award Miniature Art Soc. N.J., 1971, 72, First award First Nat. Bank N.J., 1973. Mem. Miniature Painters, Sculptors and Gravers Soc. Washington D.C., Miniature Art Soc. N.J., Internat. Platform Assn., World's Woman's Christian Temperance Union, Women's Aux. Can. Bible Soc., Aux. Brit. and Fgn. Bible Soc. Home and office: Lansdowne Villa 14 Wesley Av Niagara-On-The-Lake ON L0S 1J0 Canada

BENZING, CONSTANCE CONSTANT (MRS. RAYMOND DONALD BENZING), resort mgr.; b. N.Y.C., July 12, 1908; d. Schuyler Colfax and Betsy Ann (Gallacher) Constant; student Spence Sch., 1921-26; B.A., Vassar, 1930; m. Raymond Donald Benzing, Dec. 12, 1934; 1 son, Joseph Constant. Owner-mgr. Five Chimneys Golf and Tennis Resort, Province Lake, N.H., 1957—. Mem. budget com. Town of Parsonsfield (Me.), 1970—; mem. Taxpayers' Assn., Parsonsfield, 1971—. Mem. Am. Hotel Motel Assn., N.H. Hotel Assn., New Eng. Innkeepers Assn., New Eng. Council. Clubs:

Womens (Effingham, N.H.); Women's (Forest Hills, N.Y.). Address: Route 153 Province Lake NH 03830

BENZINGER, MARIA GERHARTZ (MRS. THEODOR H. BENZINGER), physician; b. Bonn, Germany, Feb. 18, 1918; d. Heinrich and Elisabeth (Reineke) Gerhartz; came to U.S., 1950, naturalized, 1955; student Marburg U., 1936-37, Bonn U., 1937, Heidelberg U., 1937-38, U. Berlin, 1939, U. Innsbruck, 1939-41; M.D., Leopold-Franzens U., 1941; Dr.Med., U. Berlin, 1941; m. Dietrich Henke, Mar., 1946 (div. Sept. 1954); 1 son, Robert; m. 2d, Theodor H. Benzinger, Mar., 1960; 1 dau., Fay Ann. Intern, surg. resident Charite Hosp., Robert Koch Hosp., Berlin, Germany, 1941-50; practice medicine specializing in surgery, Berlin, 1947-50; intern, Port Chester, N.Y., Mt. Kisco, N.Y., 1950-53; resident in anesthesiology Bellevue Hosp., N.Y.C., 1952-54; instr. anesthesiology Albert Einstein Coll., N.Y.C., 1954-56; sr. instr. anesthesiology Western Res. U., Cleve., 1956-60; chief med. officer in anesthesiology D.C. Gen. Hosp., Washington, 1961—; clin. asst. prof. anesthesiology George Washington U., 1960—, Georgetown U., 1961—, Howard U. (all Washington). Mem. A.M.A., Am. Soc. Anesthesiologists, D.C. Med. Soc., Internat. Anesthesia Research Soc., Am. Med. Women's Assn. Home: 6607 Broxburn Dr Bethesda MD 20034 Office: D C Gen Hosp Washington DC 20003

BERANEK, BARBARA A., editor; b. Detroit, Aug. 6, 1927; d. George F. and Dorothy (Work) Beranek; B.A. Mich. State U. 1949, postgrad. 1949-50 student Interior Design, Art Inst. Chgo. Copywriter home furnishings, asst. div. advt. mgr. J.L. Hudson Co., Detroit, 1952-57; copywriter Campbell Ewald, Detroit 1957-58; home furnishings editor Gary (Ind.) Post-Tribune, 1958-61; asst. women's editor Detroit Free Press, 1961-65; women's editor Indpls. News, 1965—. Recipient Dorothy Dawe Home Furnishings award, 2 Casper awards Indpls. Community Service, award Nat. Fedn. Press Women. Mem. Woman's Press Club Ind. (various 1st place awards), Sigma Delta Chi, Theta Sigma Phi. Home: 2629 Cold Spring Manor Dr Indianapolis IN 46222 Office: 307 N Pennsylvania St Indianapolis IN 46204

BERANEK, PHYLLIS KNIGHT (MRS. LEO L. BERANEK), orgn. exec.; b. Boston, Oct. 18, 1917; d. Hardy Jay and Ethel (Beal) Knight; B. Dental Hygiene, Tufts U., 1937; m. Leo L. Beranek, Sept. 6, 1941; children—James Knight, Thomas Haynes. Fgn. students worker Mass. Inst. Tech., Cambridge, 1948-58, entertainment supr. spl. summer programs, 1953, 55, 57, 60, 64, 67, 72; chmn. ladies com. Internat. Congress Acoustics, Cambridge, 1958; chmn. ladies com. 1966 Meeting Acoustical Soc. Am., Boston, 1968 Meeting Audio Engring. Soc., N.Y., ladies com. Inter-Noise 72, Washington, 1972; sustaining sponsor Opera Co. of Boston, 1960—. Episcopalian. Clubs: Winton, Winchester Country; Murren (Switzerland) Ski, Great Britain Ski. Home: 7 Ledgewood Rd Winchester MA 01890

BERBEROVA, NINA (MRS. VLADISLAV KHODASEVICH), ret. educator, author; b. St. Petersburg, Russia, Aug. 8, 1901; d. Nikolai and Natalia (Karaulova) Berberova; student Inst. Art History, St. Petersburg, Russia, 1921-22, Sorbonne, Paris, France, 1926-27; m. Vladislav Khodasevich, June 1, 1922. Came to U.S., 1950, naturalized, 1958. Mem. staff Russian Daily, Paris, 1925-40; mem. faculty Yale, 1958-63; mem. faculty Princeton, 1963-71, asso. prof. Slavic dept. 1971-73. Guest prof. Columbia, 1973, U. Pa., Phila., 1972-73. Author: Alexandre Blok et son Temps, 1947; Commutation of Sentence, 1948; The Italics Are Mine, 1969. First biographer of Peter Chaikovsky, translated in 6 langs., 1937-48. Home: 44 Stanworth Lane Princeton NJ 08540

BEREND, MARGARET ROSENAK (MRS. BELA BEREND), violinist, educator; b. Budapest, Hungary, Sept. 23, 1903; d. Maximilian and Blanca (Behr) Rosenak; diploma, Prof. Violin, Franz Liszt Acad., Budapest, 1923; m. Bela Berend, Apr. 19, 1925 (dec. Sept. 1972); 1 dau., Anne Veronica (Mrs. John P.C. Allen). Came to U.S., 1954; naturalized, 1960. Faculty, Met. Music Sch., Budapest, 1946-53, Music Acad. Tel Aviv, Israel, 1953-54, Henry St. Settlement Music Sch., N.Y.C., 1955—, Music Sch. YMHA, Bklyn., 1955—. Mem. Am. String Tchrs. Assn. Author: Follow the Melody and Learn the Positions, 1969; Twentieth Century Shifting Studies, 1969. Contbr. articles to profl. jours. Home: 233 W 99th St New York City NY 10025

BERENDES, MARGRET MEYHOEFER (MRS. HEINZ BERENDES), physician; b. Munich, West Germany; d. Carl O. and Margret (Becker) Meyhoefer; came to U.S., 1953, naturalized, 1959; student U. Berlin, U. Freiburg, U. Munich, 1940-45; m. Heinz Berendes, May 23, 1952; children—Christoph M., Andrea M. Resident, City Hosp. Munchen Rechts der Isar, Munchen, Germany, 1945-49; research in poliomyelitis Red Cross Hosp., Wiessee, Bavaria, 1949-50; psychoanalyst Psychosomatic Inst., Heidelberg, Germany, 1950-52; research asst., med. dept. U. Minn. Hosp., Mpls., 1953-59; research in psychopharmacology Nat. Inst. Mental Health, Washington, 1961-62; trainee psychiatry and psychoanalysis George Washington U., Washington, 1962-65; practice psychiatry and psychoanalysis, Washington, 1965—. Contbr. articles to profl. jours. Home: 8613 Fenway Rd Bethesda MD 20034 Office: 4300 Fordham Rd NW Washington DC 20016

BERG, ERNESTINE HILLIARD (MRS. FRANK A. BERG), physician; b. Clinton, Ky., Apr. 4, 1922; d. Ernest A. and Gena (Finch) Hilliard; M.D., U. Louisville, 1953; m. Frank A. Berg, Apr. 24, 1954 (dec. Mar. 1968); children—Robert, Gena, Timothy, Leland, Donald, Sally. Intern, resident U. Ala., Birmingham, 1953-56; instr. anesthesiology Univ. Hosp., Birmingham, 1956-57, asst. prof., 1957-59; practice medicine, specializing in anesthesiology, Huntsville, Ala., 1959—; mem. staff Med. Center Hosp., Huntsville Hosp., Fifth Av. Hosp. Diplomate Am. Bd. Anesthesiology. Mem. Am., Ala. socs. anesthesiology, A.M.A., Madison County Med. Soc., Med. Assn. State of Ala. Baptist. Club: Huntsville Womans. Home: 714 Owens Dr Huntsville AL 35801

BERG, JEAN HORTON LUTZ (MRS. JOHN J. BERG), author; b. Clairton, Pa.; d. Harry Heber and Daisy (Horton) Lutz; B.S., U. Pa., in 1935, M.A., 1937; m. John Joseph Berg, July 2, 1938; children—Jean Horton, Julie Joanne, John Joel. Tchr. English and Latin, Bridgeville (Del.) High Sch., 1936-38; tchr. creative writing Radnor Twp. Adult Edn. lectr. in field; author: Three Mice and A Cat, 1950, The Jolly Jumping Man, 1950, The Noisy Clock Shop, 1950, The Playful Little Dog, 1951, Baby Susan's Chicken, 1951, The Big Jump-up Book of Farm Animals, 1952, Christmas In Song and Story, 1953, The Traveling Twins, 1953, It's Fun to Peek, 1955, The Big Jump-up Book of Trains, Trucks and Planes, 1955, Tuggy the Tugboat, 1958, The O'Learys and Friends 1961, Baby Raccoon, 1963, The Little Red Hen, 1963, The Wee Little Man, 1963, Big Bug, Little Bug, 1964, Bright Candle Light, 1966, There's Nothing to Do, So Let Me Be You, 1966, Miss Kirby's Room, 1966, Miss Tessie Tate, 1967, Nobody Scares a Porcupine, 1968, What Harry Found When He Lost Archie, 1970, Mr. Koonan's Bargain, 1971, others. Mem. exec. bd. Friends' Central Sch. Home and School Assn., 1965-67; bd. dirs. Wayne Art Center, 1950-57; bd. vols. Health and Welfare Council Phila., 1970-71; exec. bd. Infant Day Care Center of Young Great Soc., Phila.; bd. dirs. St. Davids Christian Writers Conf. Recipient Medallion of Phila. award, 1963, Follett award, 1961, Alumni Merit award U. Pa., 1969. Mem. Nat. League Am. Pen Women (pres. Chester County br. 1967-68), Parents Council Suburban Phila. (pres. 1966-67, exec. bd.), Radnor Hist. Soc., Gen. Alumni Soc. U. Pa. (exec. bd.), League Women Voters, A.S.C.A.P., Authors League, Phila. Childrens Reading Round Table, Authors Guild, Assn. Alumnae U. Pa. (officer, exec. bd.), Kappa Alpha Theta, Eta Sigma Phi, Pi Lambda Theta. Christian Scientist. Home: 207 Walnut Av Wayne PA 19087

BERG, MARIE MAJELLA, coll. pres.; b. Bklyn., July 7, 1916; d. Gustav Peter and Mary Josephine (McAuliff) Berg; B.A., Marymount Coll., Tarrytown, N.Y., 1938; M.A., Fordham U., 1948; D.H.L. (hon.), Georgetown U., 1970. Joined Sisters of The Sacred Heart of Mary, Roman Catholic Ch., 1934; tchr., registrar Marymount Manhattan Coll., 1948-57; registrar Marymount Coll. Va., Arlington, 1957-58, pres., 1960—; registrar Marymount Coll., Tarrytown, 1958-60; cons. in field. Mem. adv. com. ednl. TV, Va. Council Higher Edn., mem. exec. com. pvt. coll. adv. com., 1974—; mem. evaluation teams So. Assn. Colls. and Schs.; exec. com. Va. Coll. Fund, 1972-73, sec., 1973. Charter bd. dirs. Arlington chpt. Reading is Fundamental, 1975—. Kellogg Found. grantee 1961, U.S. Office Edn. grantee, 1962. Mem. Nat. Catholic Edn. Assn., Am. Council Edn., Am. Assn. Higher Edn., Assn. Va. Colls. (exec. com. 1968—), Council Ind. Colls. Va. (v.p. 1972-73, exec. com. 1973-74), Nat. Council Ind. Jr. Coll. (sec. 1969-72), So. Assn. Colls. Women (sec.-treas. 1969-72), Ch. Related Colls. South (pres. 1971-72), Arlington Citizens Participation Council, Arlington Chorus, Arlington Com. 100, League Women Voters, Am. Assn. U. Women, Arlington, Va. chambers commerce. Author articles, biographies. Address: 2807 N Glebe Rd Arlington VA 22207

BERG, MILDRED MARIE, banker; b. N.Y.C., Nov. 19, 1922; d. Edwin and Hanna Dorothea (Nielson) Berg; student pub. schs., N.Y.C. With Seamen's Bank for Savs., N.Y.C., 1943—, asst. sec., 1963-67, asst. v.p., 1968-70, corporate sec., 1971—. Mem. com. on adminstrn. and finance Lutheran Ch. Council in U.S.A.; trustee Lutheran Med. Center, Bklyn., Am. Lutheran Ch. (nat.). Mem. Nat. Assn. Bank Women, Savs. Bank Women N.Y. Club: Soroptimist. Home: 601 79th St Brooklyn NY 11209 Office: 30 Wall St New York City NY 10005

BERG, SUSAN MINDLIN (MRS. STANLEY PHILIP BERG), city planner; b. Chgo., Aug. 17, 1942; d. Joseph and Elfreda (Galantiere) Mindlin; A.B. in Polit. Sci., U. Cal. at Los Angeles, 1964, postgrad., 1964-66; m. Stanley Philip Berg, Sept. 10, 1967. Planning intern City of Baldwin Park (Cal.), 1965-66; planning intern City of Culver City (Cal.), 1965, asst. city planner, planning and community devel. div., 1966-70, asso. city planner, planning and community devel. div., 1970-72, city planner, 1972—. Mem. Am. Acad. Polit. and Social Sci., Am. Polit. Sci. Assn., Am. Inst. Planners. Home: 3732 Mentone Av Los Angeles CA 90034 Office: City Hall 9770 Culver Blvd Culver City CA 90230

BERG, VALBORG HANSING (MRS. LEIGHTON ARNOLD BERG), librarian; b. Thompson, Ia., Mar. 21, 1910; d. Henry Olaf and Marie Olivia (Dahl) Hansing; student Luther Acad. Bus. Coll., 1927-28; B.S., Mankato State Coll., 1966, M.S., 1973; m. Leighton Arnold Berg, Mar. 30, 1936; children—Roger, Jean (Mrs. Robert Brabec), Lowell. Stenographer, Queen Stove Works, 1928-29; stenographer, bookkeeper Olson Mfg. Co., 1929-39; tchr., Albert Lea (Minn.) Schs., 1966-67; librarian, Freeborn County Hist. Soc., Albert Lea, Minn., 1967—. Mem. Am. Assn. Museums, Nat. Audubon Soc., Minn. Archaeol. Soc., First Dist. Hist. Assembly, Sons Norway. Republican. Lutheran. Home: 214 N 2d Av W Albert Lea MN 56007 Office: Box 105 Bridge Av Albert Lea MN 56007

BERGAMO, DOROTHY JOHNSON, artist, art cons.; b. Chgo., Feb. 1, 1912; d. Glenn Van Ness Johnson and Alma (Sondeen) Johnson; Ph.B., U. Chgo., 1934; B.F.A., Art Inst. Chgo., 1937, resident fellow, 1938; M.A., Northwestern U., 1941; m. Ralph Bergamo, July 11, 1942 (div. Aug. 1947); 1 son, Ronald Johnson. Tchr. Municipal Jr. Coll., City Chgo., 1938-43; instr. Art Inst., San Antonio, 1943-46; asso. prof. Ariz. State Coll., 1948-51; dir. Art Center, Phoenix, 1951-56; spl. art tchr. Madison Schs., Phoenix 1956-57, Carl Hayden Sch., 1957-66; art cons. Phoenix Union High Sch. System, 1967—; exhibited group shows Chgo. Art Inst., Tex. Gen., Contemporary Art Gallery, N.Y.C.; represented in permanent collections Pub. Health Service Hosp., Lexington, Ky., Witte Mus., San Antonio, Olson Found., Guilford, Conn., Municipal, Grand Canyon Coll., Valley Nat. Bank, Phoenix. Mem. Am. Assn. U. Women, Nat. League Am. Penwomen (state pres.), Ariz. Watercolor Soc. Home: 8828 N 17th Av Phoenix AZ 85021 Office: 7402 W Catalina Dr Phoenix AZ 85033

BERGAN, CAROLYN WIDENER, civic worker; b. Crawfordsville, Ind., Oct. 1, 1928; d. Leslie F. and Mary Donnis (Saidla) Widener; B.S., Purdue U., 1950; M.S., Butler U., 1953; m. John J. Bergan, Aug. 4, 1951; children—Elizabeth, Margaret, John. Chmn. Ill. Day Care Standards Commn., 1965—; v.p. Welfare Council Met. Chgo., 1968-69, pres., 1969-71; v.p. Chgo. Commons Assn., 1969—, Girl Scouts U.S.A., Chgo., 1966-68; chmn. Chgo. Head Start, 1966-69; mem. Mayor's Commn. Sch. Bd. Nominations, 1969—; mem. vis. com. Sch. Social Service Adminstrn. U. Chgo., 1970—, mem. women's bd., 1970—; mem. Urban Dynamics-Inner City Fund, 1970. Trustee, Francis W. Parker Sch., Chgo., 1973—. Named Chicagoan of Year in Welfare, Jr. C. of C., 1971; recipient Phoenix award for civic leadership DePaul U., 1970. Mem. Mortar Bd., Kappa Gamma. Home: 2305 N Commonwealth Av Chicago IL 60614

BERGEN, CATHARINE MARY, ret. educator; b. Garden City, N.Y., Jan. 16, 1912; d. John Oldfield and Alice (Terry) Bergen; A.B., Wellesley Coll., 1933; M.A., Columbia, 1935, Ph.D., 1942. Elementary sci. cons. Garden City pub. schs., 1934-37; asst. in physics Hofstra Coll., 1939-40; elementary sci. Tchrs. Coll. Columbia, 1940-43; sci. workshop, extramural U. Chgo., Hastings, Mich., summer 1941; asso. prof. sci. Jersey City State Coll., 1941-54, prof. sci., 1954-69, prof. physics, 1969-72, chmn. sci. dept., 1954-58, ret., 1972, prof. emeritus, 1974—. Mem. Am. Phys. Soc., A.A.A.S., Am. Assn. U. Women (past pres. Jersey City br.; N.J. state bd. 1960-62), Am. Assn. U. Profs., N.E.A., Nat., N.J. (pres.) sci. tchrs. assns., Am. Inst. City of N.Y., Pi Lambda Theta, Kappa Delta Pi. Author: Children's Science Information, 1943. Home: 39 Duncan Av Jersey City NJ 07304

BERGEN, POLLY, actress; b. Knoxville, Tenn., July 14, 1931; d. William and Lucy (Lawhorn) Bergen; m. Freddie Fields, Feb. 13, 1956; children—Kathy, Pamela, Peter. Pres. Kam Enterprises, Ltd., 1956—, Apache Corp., 1955—; chmn. bd. Polly Bergen Co., Beverly Hills, Cal.; partner cosmetic firm Oil of the Turtle; v.p. Oil Fields, Unlimited, 1957—; pres., dir. Fashions of the Four Seasons, Inc., N.Y.C., 1959—; dir. F8 Prodns., Inc. Motion pictures include The Stooge, At War with the Army, That's My Boy, Cape Fear, The Caretakers, Move Over Darling, Kisses for My President, Guide for Married Men; star own show NBC-TV; panelist To Tell the Truth, CBS-TV, other TV appearances include Perry Como Show, Ed Sullivan Show, Playhouse 90, Andy Williams Show, Dean Martin Show, Red Skelton Show, Jack Benny Spl., Bell Telephone Hour, U.S. Steel Hour; recording artist Mercury, Columbia records. Mem. Share, Inc.; mem. women's guild Cedar-Sinai Med. Center. Bd. dirs. Peter Bruce Fields Found. Recipient Emmy award as best actress Nat. Acad. TV Arts and Scis., 1957-58; Troupers award Sterling Publs., 1957; Fame award Top Ten in TV, 1957-58; Editors and Critics award Radio and TV Daily, 1958; Nat. Outstanding Working Woman award Downtown St. Louis, Inc., 1968; named Best Dressed Am. Woman Entertainer, Costume Designers Guild, 1966; Golden Plate award Am. Acad. Achievement, 1969; Polly Bergen Cardio-Pulmonary Research Lab., Children's Research Inst. and Hosp., Denver, dedicated, 1970. Mem. Screen Actors Guild, Actors Equity, Am. Guild Variety Artists, A.F.T.R.A. Author: Fashion and Charm. Address: 190 N Canyon Dr Beverly Hills CA 90210 also 19 E 57th St New York City NY 10022

BERGEN, SARAH I. IVAN (MRS. JOHN F. BERGEN), banker; b. Woodbridge, N.J.; d. Joseph and Serena (Ur) Ivan; student pub. schs.; m. John F. Bergen, Jan. 10, 1942 (dec.). Sec. CIT Corp., 1940; sec. to exec. officer Perth Amboy (N.J.) Nat. Bank, 1941-61, asst. cashier, 1961-63, personnel officer, 1963-67, v.p., 1967-69, sr. v.p., 1969—. Recipient Women of the Year award Perth Amboy Bus. and Profl. Womans Group, 1967. Mem. Nat. Assn. Bank Women (group chmn. 1966-67, regional v.p. 1969-70). Home: 533 Gorham Av Woodbridge NJ 07095 Office: 313 State St Perth Amboy NJ 08861

BERGER, BETSY GREENBERG (MRS. LAWRENCE BERGER), lawyer; b. Bklyn., Nov. 8, 1929; d. Isidor and Martha (Partos) Greenberg; B.A., Rutgers U., 1950, J.D., 1952; m. Lawrence Berger, June 26, 1952; children—Nancy, Andrew, James. Admitted to D.C. bar, 1953, Neb. bar, 1965; asso. firm Healey & Healey, Lincoln, Neb., 1965-68; spl. asst. atty. gen. Dept. Justice, Lincoln, 1968-69; atty. Dorsey, Marquart, Windhorst, West & Halladay, Mpls., 1970; asst. atty. gen. Dept. Justice, State of Neb., Lincoln, 1970—. Office: State Capitol Lincoln NE 68509

BERGER, CHARNEY KIMMEL (MRS. MERTON B. BERGER), lawyer; b. N.Y.C., Dec. 25, 1934; d. Adolph and Lee (Hirsh) Kimmel; B.A. magna cum laude, Hunter Coll., 1956; M.A. in English Lit., Columbia, 1957; J.D. with distinction, Emory U., 1968; m. Merton B. Berger, Feb. 21, 1957; children—Adam Matthew, Stephen Charles, Richard Seth. Tchr., English, Rochester, N.Y., 1957-59; admitted to Ga. bar, 1967; practiced in Atlanta, 1968—; law asst. to judge Ga. Ct. Appeals, Atlanta, 1969; asso. firm Shoob, McLain and Jessee, 1970-72; asst. U.S. atty. Office of U.S. Atty. for No. Dist. Ga., Atlanta, 1972-73; internat. trademark atty. Coca-Cola Co., Atlanta, 1973—. Legal adviser James L. Riley Sch. P.T.A., Atlanta, 1970-72. Mem. Parent, Tchr., Student Assn. Riverwood High Sch., Atlanta, 1973—. Mem. State Bar Ga., Am., Fed., Atlanta (mem. pub. relations com. 1973-74) bar assns., Womens Aux. Med. Assn. Atlanta, Phi Beta Kappa. Asso. editor Jour. Pub. Law, 1967-68. Home: 1105 Crest Valley Dr Atlanta GA 30327 Office: 310 N Av NW Atlanta GA 30303

BERGER, EILEEN IDYLE (MRS. MARCUS BERGER), actress; b. Chgo., Oct. 29, 1947; d. David Joseph and Faye (Greenblott) Neiberg; student Loyola U., Chgo., 1968-69, Northwestern U., 1972-73; m. Marcus Berger, Aug. 29, 1971. Drama instr. Chgo. Park Dist., 1970; actress In-the-Round Dinner Playhouse, profl. children's theatre, Chgo., 1970-71; drama tchr. Hull House, Chgo., 1970; asst. buyer Evans Co., Chgo., 1973; actress appearing in numerous plays including Oedipus Rex, Death of Bessie Smith, Flower Drum Song, 1966, Women of Pellponesus, Red Shoes, 1970, Hansel & Gretel, 1971, The Inquisition, 1972, David, 1973, The Dybbuk, 1974. Recreation vol. Ill. State Children's Hosp., Chgo., 1969; mem. Mus. Soc. of U. Chgo., 1972-73; juror Chgo. Internat. Film Festival, 1970-71. Mem. Actor's Equity, Am. Ednl. Theatre Assn., U.S. Inst. Theatre Tech., Children's Theatre Conf., Audubon Soc. Club: Variety (dir. Chgo.). Home: 5702 N Kimball Chicago IL 60659

BERGER, EVELYN ELSIE, home economist; b. Cleveland, Wis., Mar. 15, 1920; d. Walter J. and Mattie (Lorfeld) Berger; B.S., U. Wis., 1942. Home economist Rural Gravure, Chgo., 1949-50; dir. home econs. Wilson & Co., Chgo., 1955-62; dir. home econs., marketing div. United Fruit & Food Corp., Boston, 1962-64; dir. home econs., account exec. McCann-Erickson Advt. Agy., Chgo., 1964-67; dir. Lipton Kitchens, Thomas J. Lipton, Inc., Englewood Cliffs, N.J., 1967—. Mem. Am. Home Econs. Assn., Home Economists in Bus., Am. Women in Radio and Television, Women's Advt. Club N.Y. Home: 1 Hudson Harbour Edgewater NJ 07020 Office: 800 Sylvan Av Englewood Cliffs NJ 07632

BERGER, HELEN HAZEL, banker; b. Bayou Current, La., July 13, 1920; d. William Holmes and Lillian Lottie (MaAdams) Berger; grad. Bus. Coll. Riverside, Cal., 1941; standard certificate Am. Inst. Banking, 1970. With Bank Am., San Bernardino, Cal., 1941—, lending officer, 1959-65, mgr., 1965—. Mem. br. mgrs. adv. council Bank Am., 1971-72. Chmn. Am. Nat. Red Cross, 1957-58; treas. March of Dimes, 1950-72, Cancer Soc., 1955-72, Heart Fund, 1955-72; hon. leader 4-H, 1963. Bd. dirs. Victor Valley Community Concert Assn., 1960—; trustee Karen Bender and Keith Gunn meml. scholarships, 1968-71. Named Woman of Year, Victor Valley Bus. and Profl. Women's Club, 1963, Hon. Future Farmers Am. farmer, 1964, 70, Hon. 4-H leader, 1963, Citizen of Year Apple Valley, 1967; Helen Berger Day, Victorville City Council, 1965; recipient Blue Ribbon award Western Fairs Assn., 1965. Mem. Victor Valley Bus. and Profl. Women's Club (pres. 1959-60), San Orco Dist. Bus. and Profl. Women (pres. 1965-66), Apple Valley C. of C. (bd. dirs. 1965-72; Citizen of Year 1971-72). Democrat. Presbyn. Home: PO Box 733 Yucalpa CA 92399 Office: 130 40th St San Bernardino CA 92307

BERGER, KAY SINGER, home economist; b. Pitts., Feb. 18, 1939; d. Alex and Eve (Lando) Singer; B.S., U. Cal., Los Angeles, 1961. Appliance counselor So. Cal. and So. Counties Gas Cos., Los Angeles, 1958-59; demonstrator Carl Byiors Pub. Relations, Los Angeles, 1960-61; appliance counselor Great Western TV & Appliances, Los Angeles, 1959-61; asst. dir. consumer relations Waste King Corp., Los Angeles, 1961-66; mgr. home econs. Calavo Tropical Produce, Los Angeles, 1966-69; home economist, v.p., group supr. Harshe-Rotman & Druck Pub. Relations, Los Angeles, 1969—. Recipient First Place award Nat. Council Farm Coops., 1967; 2 First Place Lulu awards Los Angeles Advt. Women, 1972. Mem. Home Economist in Bus. (Los Angeles group chmn. 1968-69), Am. Women in Radio and Television, Am., Cal. home econs. assns., Internat. Fedn. Home Econs. Home: 4305 Redwood Av Apt 3 Marina del Rey CA 90291 Office: 3345 Wilshire Blvd Los Angeles CA 90010

BERGER, MARJORIE ROSE (MRS. RICHARD C. BERGER), newspaper editor; b. Joplin, Mont., Apr. 8, 1934; d. George and Rose (LaCrosse) Johnston; grad. high sch.; m. Richard C. Berger, Apr. 23, 1953; children—Richard, Rosanne Mitchell, Robert, Rebecca, Carol Mary. Co-editor Cascade (Mont.) Courier, 1953—. Mem. Am. Legion Aux., Eagles Aux. Home: 17 1/2 N Front St Cascade MT 59421 Office: Cascade Courier Cascade MT 59421

BERGER, MIRIAM EASTON (MRS. PAUL D. BERGER), psychiat. social worker; b. N.Y.C., Apr. 4, 1924; d. Max and Tillie (Carlin) Easton; B.A., Queens Coll., 1946; M.S., Columbia U. Sch. Social Work, 1950; m. Paul D. Berger, Oct. 4, 1950; children—Suzanne, Elizabeth. Social investigator N.Y.C. Bur. Foster Care, 1946-49; caseworker Family Service Bur. Salvation Army, 1950-55, student supr., 1953-55; sr. psychiat. caseworker, psychotherapist L.I. Consultation Center, 1955-56, adult group therapist, 1964-66; pvt. practice, 1955— (all N.Y.C.); faculty Lehman Coll., 1972-73. Mem. Am. Assn. Marriage Counselors, Am. Group Psychotherapy Assn., Ethical Culture Soc. Queens (Sunday sch. dir. 1958-61, chmn. religious edn. com. 1963), Assn. Humanistic Psychology, Am. Acad. Psychotherapists, Am. Group Therapy Assn., Feminist Psychotherapy Referral Services. Contbr. articles to profl. publs. Address: 140-70 Burden Cresent Jamaica NY 11435

BERGER, SYDELLE ALICE, veterinarian; b. N.Y.C., Apr. 4, 1938; d. Juleus and Frieda (Zlatner) Berger; B.S. (Faculty Folk scholar, Hinman scholar), Mich. State U., 1959, D.V.M., 1961. Practice vet. medicine, Howell, Mich., 1961—. Bd. dirs. Give the Animals a Break Soc. Mem. Mich. Vet. Med. Assn., Livingston County Veterinarians Assn. (pres.). Address: 310 E Allen Rd Howell MI 48843

BERGERON, RITA MARIE, univ. dean, educator; b. Cloquet, Minn., Dec. 27, 1917; d. Ernest and Hermina (Meulendyke) Bergeron; B.S., Coll. St. Scholastica, 1940; M.S., Catholic U., Am., 1945, Ph.D., 1963. Instr. Coll. St. Scholastica, Duluth, Minn., 1945-46; supr. St. Mary's Hosp., Duluth, Minn., 1946-48; dir. Sch. Nursing and Nursing Service, Hibbing (Minn.) Gen. Hosp., 1948-52; prof. nursing, chmn. dept. nursing Coll. St. Scholastica, Duluth, 1952-68; prof. nursing Georgetown U., Washington, 1968—, dean Sch. Nursing, 1968—. Recipient NIH Profession Nurse Traineeship, 1960-63. Mem. Am. Assn. Colls. Nursing (mem. govt. affairs com. 1973-74, mem. finance com. 1974—), Nat. League for Nursing (mem. exec. com. council dept. degree programs 1971-73, conv. program com. 1973—), Am. Assn. for Higher Edn., Am. Nurses Assn., Sigma Theta Tau. Author: The Nursing Departmental Chairman in the Liberal Arts College, 1963. Home: 5101 River Rd Bethesda MD 20016 Office: 3700 Reservoir Rd NW Washington DC 20007

BERGEY, DOROTHY MABEL, librarian; b. Guernsey, Sask., Can., Apr. 7, 1913; d. Joshua Eldon and Gertrude Mabel (Hardy) Bergey; 2d class tchr.'s certificate Saskatoon (Sask.) Normal Sch., 1932; B. Commerce, U. Sask., 1949; B.L.S., U. Toronto (Ont., Can.), 1962. Tchr. elementary sch., Sask., Can., 1932-42; library clk. Defence Research Bd. of Can., Ralston, Alta., 1949-52, central registry clk., Halifax, N.S., 1952-54, sec., library clk. Canadian Joint Staff, Washington, D.C., 1954-60, library cataloger, Toronto, 1960-61, librarian, Halifax, N.S., 1962-69, librarian, Ottawa, Ont., 1969—. Served with Canadian Women's Army Corps, 1942-46. Decorated Brit. Empire medal. Mem. Spl. Libraries Assn., Canadian Assn. for Information Sci., Profl. Inst. of Pub. Service of Can. Mem. United Ch. Can. Club: University Women's (Ottawa, Ont.). Home: 330 Metcalfe St Ottawa ON K2P 1S4 Canada Office: Defence Sci Information Service Library Nat Defence Hdqrs Ottawa ON K1A 0K2 Canada

BERGH, HELEN JOYCE, mus. exec.; b. Aberdeen, S.D., June 5, 1908; d. Andrew Hans and Susanna Henrietta (Larson) Bergh; B.S., No. State Coll., 1943, M.S., 1956. Rural sch. tchr., Brown County, S.C., 1927-70, dir. music, 1945-70; supr. practice tchrs. No. State Coll., 1934-69, summer sch. instr., 1948-52, 62; mem. staff Dacotah Prairie Mus., Aberdeen, S.D., 1971—. Mem. Brown County Textbook Bd., 1950-69. Bd. dirs. Nat. Young Citizen's League; trustee Dacotah Prairie Mus. Mem. Am. Assn. U. Women (pres. 1966-68), Ambassadors Good Will S.D., Brown County Edn. Assn. (pres. 1945-48), Kappa Delta Pi, Delta Kappa Gamma. Republican. Lutheran. Club: Lyre Music (pres. 1964-65). Co-editor: Brown County History. Home: Rural Route 5 Box 337 Aberdeen SD 57401 Office: 21 S Main St Aberdeen SD 57401

BERGHUIS, SHARON LOUISE, psychologist; b. Chamberlain, S.D., Nov. 17, 1941; d. George Edward and Elnamae Augusta (Wickman) Sullivan; B.A. in Social Sci. (Ford Found. scholar), Mich. State U., 1964; M.S. in Clin. Psychology, Ohio U., 1966; m. Michael Bruce Berghuis, Apr. 6, 1974. Adj. therapist Haven Hosp., Rochester, Mich., summer 1965; clin. psychologist Pontiac (Mich.) State Hosp., 1966-68; sch. psychologist Lincolnwood (Ill.) schs., 1968-71; sch. psychologist Molloy (Ill.) Edn. Center, 1971-74. Mem. Am. Psychol. Assn., Nat. Assn. Sch. Psychologists, Niles Twp. Sch. Psychologists (chmn. 1971-73). Home: 1016 Carolyn Av Elkhart IN 46514

BERGLUND, HAZEL JEANETTE, physician; b. Chgo., Dec. 16, 1910; d. August J. and Ellen A. (Anderson) Berglund; R.N., Hinsdale (Ill.) Hosp., 1932; student Columbia Jr. Coll. (Md.), 1936-38; M.D., Loma Linda U., 1943. Intern, Los Angeles County Gen. Hosp., 1942-43, mem. staff, 1943-46; practice medicine, Armonk, N.Y., 1946-58, Greenwich, Conn., 1947-58; resident phys. medicine and rehab. White Meml. Hosp., Los Angeles, 1958-61; asst. phys. medicine and rehab. dept. Loma Linda U., 1961-64, mem. faculty, hosp. staff, 1964—; physiatrist Pacific State Hosp., Pomona, Cal., 1964—. Diplomate Am. Bd. Phys. Medicine and Rehab. Nat. Bd. Med. Examiners. Fellow Am. Acad. Phys. Medicine and Rehab.; mem. San Bernardino, Cal., Am. med. assns. Contbr. articles to profl. jours. Home: 11024 San Juan St Loma Linda CA 92354 Office: Pacific State Hosp Box 100 Pomona CA 91766

BERGLUND, SUE ANN, data processing co. exec.; b. Geneva, Ill., Aug. 18, 1947; d. Torston Gustav and Perdetta Ione (Todd) Berglund; grad. St. Charles High Sch., 1965. Clk. typist Dickey Mfg., St. Charles, Ill., 1965-66; clk.-typist Dukane Corp., St. Charles, 1966, Diamond Nat. Corp., St. Charles, 1967-68, Hoskins, Inc., Geneva, 1968; Keypunch operator Data Central Processing Corp., St. Charles, Ill., 1968—, supr., 1969—, corporate sec., 1971—, instr. keypunch operator, 1971—. Mem. Ladies Night Bowling League (pres. 1970-71). Home: 502 S 4th Av St Charles IL 60174 Office: PO Box 231 Batavia IL 60510

BERGMAN, RITA ELIZABETH, educator; b. Houston, O.; d. William J. and Emma (Broerman) Bergman; B.S., Ohio State U., 1946; M.E., U. Cin., 1954; Dr. Health and Safety, Ind. U., 1956, Ed.D., 1959; postgrad. U. Md., 1956-58, U. Wis., 1959-60, W.Va., U., 1961-62, Ind. U., 1964-65. Tchr., pub. schs., Ohio, 1946-55, U. Md., 1956-58; research asst. U. Wis., Madison, 1959-60; asso. prof. Wis. State U., 1960-61; health coordinator U. Detroit, 1962-63; dean students St. John Coll., 1964-65, prof. edn., 1964-65; dean women, prof. psychology West Liberty State Coll., 1965-66; prof. psychology Ashland Coll. (O.), 1966-71, Wilberforce U., 1971—. Cons. on children and youth, human devel., curriculum. Asst. to social worker Neighborhood House, Columbus, O., 1945-46; mem. Panhellenic Council, 1960-61; counselor, Immaculata High Sch., part-time 1962-63; worker W.Va. U., Guidance Clinic, 1961-62; caseworker in reading and study problem diagnosis, 1964-65; chmn. coms. on publicity, student and faculty health and welfare, departmental reorgn., health and dental hygiene curriculs; counselor in admissions, financial aids, reading and study aids; dir. student activities and residence hall, 1964-65; co-ordinator all campus student personnel services, 1964-65. Fellow Am. Sch. Health Assn.; mem. Nat. Assn. Women Deans and Counselors, Am. Coll. Personnel Assn., Am. Personnel and Guidance Assn., Assn. for Higher Edn., N.E.A. (life), Nat. Safety Council, A.A.H.P.E.R. (life; chmn. com. for standard coll. student accident report 1961-63; chmn. safety sect. Midwest 1962-63; sec. higher edn. sect.), U. Cin. Alumni Assn., Ind. U. Alumni Assn. (life). Editor: The Sociopath, 1968; Children's Behavior, 1969. Contbr. articles to ednl. jours. Home: Box 236 Houston OH 45333 Office: Wilberforce University Wilberforce OH 45384

BERGMAN, ROBERTA LESLIE ALLEN (MRS. HOWARD GERALD BERGMAN), educator; b. Chgo., Oct. 24, 1941; d. Arthur and Mynne (Leites) Allen; B.S. with high honors, U. Md., 1963, M.Ed., 1968; m. Howard Gerald Bergman, June 23, 1963; children—Elizabeth Lynn, Andrea Jeanne, Michael David, Stephanie Suzanne. Tchr., Prince Georges County Pub. Schs., Upper Marlboro, Md., 1963-64; dir. Bethesda-Chevy Chase Nursery Sch., Chevy Chase, Md., 1965-67; instr. early childhood edn. U. Md., College Park, 1969-71; coordinator early edn. project Prince Georges County Pub. Schs., Upper Marlboro, 1971-72; cons. Center for Human Services, Cleve., 1974—. Mem. Md. Community Coordinated Child Care Adv. Council, 1970-73, chmn. ad hoc com. for planning 3d ann. state spring meeting, 1973; pres. Md. Council Parent Participation Nursery Schs., 1970-72; grants chmn., jour. adviser Parent Coop. Preschs. Internat., 1970-73. Recipient Dist. Service award Parent Coop. Preschs. Internat., 1971. Mem. Nat. Assn. for Edn. Young Children, Phi Kappa Phi, Kappa Delta Pi, Phi Delta Gamma. Home: 3651 Gridley Rd Shaker Heights OH 44122 Office: 2084 Cornell Rd Cleveland OH 44106

BERGMAN, ROSELYN JUNE, pub. co. editor; b. Chgo., Mar. 23, 1929; d. Edward and Anna Elizabeth (Tichy) B. Bergman; student Beloit Coll., 1946-49; B.A., Drury Coll., 1950. Asst. editor Rand McNally & Co., Skokie, Ill., 1953-56, asso. editor, 1956-65, editor mass market dept., trade pub. div., 1966—. Mem. Children's Reading Round Table, Sokol Cechie, Kappa Delta. Presbyn. Home: 2141 Ridge Av 4E Evanston IL 60201 Office: Rand McNally & Co PO Box 7600 Chicago IL 60680

BERGMANN, WINOGENE LOUISE, library adminstr.; b. Milw.; d. William and Helen (Buck) Bergmann; B.A., Milw.-Downer Coll., 1931; certificate in econs. Univ. Coll., Exeter, Eng., 1931; M.S. in Library Sci., Columbia, 1952; postgrad. U. Wis., Milw., 1956—. Sch. librarian Juneau High Sch., Milw., 1932-56; coordinator print media, supr. libraries, Milw. pub. schs., 1956—. Pres. Inter-Group Council, Milw., 1965-66; mem. Mayor's Beautification Com., Milw., 1966—, vice chmn., 1969—; state exec. com. Nat. Library Week, 1970. Mem. A.L.A., Am. Assn. U. Women, Wis. Library Assn., Met. Milw. Library Council (exec. bd. 1972—), Internat. Platform Assn., Assn. Suprs. and Curriculum Devel., Wis. Assn. Suprs. and Curriculum Devel., WAC Vets., Delta Kappa Gamma. Club: Zonta. Contbr. articles to publs. Home: 709 E Juneau Av Milwaukee WI 53202 Office: 5225 W Vliet St Milwaukee WI 53208

BERGSTEN, BEBE, business exec.; b. New Bedford, Mass.; d. John Carl and Ines (Pietoff) Bergsten; grad. Katharine Gibbs Sch., N.Y.C., 1934. Sec., treas. Am.-Swedish News Exchange, N.Y.C., 1942-44, 49-54; v.p. James Brown Assos., N.Y.C., 1955-56, 60-61; dir. Ventures Cons. Corp., N.Y.C., 1957-62, Rochlin & Baran A.I.A. & Assos., Los Angeles; with Locare Research Group, Los Angeles, 1964—; pres. Hist. Films, Los Angeles. Mem. Spl. Libraries Assn. Author: The Great Dane and The Great Northern Film Company, 1974. Editor: Motion Pictures from the Library of Congress Paper Print Collection, 1894-1912; The First Twenty Years; Mary Pickford, Comedienne; One Reel A Week, Biograph Bulletins. Home: 2285 N Beachwood Dr Hollywood CA 90068 Office: 910 N Fairfax Av Los Angeles CA 90046

BERGSTROM, MARY LOUISE (MRS. OSCAR F. BERGSTROM), author; b. Leavonsworth, Wash., Oct. 29, 1941; d. William Basil and Mary Jane (Lewis) Simpson; student Ind. State Tchrs. Coll., 1932, Duff's Iron City Bus. Coll., 1933; m. Oscar Frederik Bergstrom, May 23, 1938; children—Loa Martha (Mrs. Quang Nguyen), Kristine Elizabeth (Mrs. John Choate). Author: Strange Legacy, 1968; Claudia's Secret, 1969; The Pink Camilla, 1969; Midsummer Eve, 1970; The Mockingbird Tree, 1971; The House of the Golden Dogs, 1971; The House of the Sphinx, 1972; The Mysterious Grotto, 1973. Address: 3308 Sunny Harbor Dr Punta Gorda FL 33950

BERGUM, SHIRLEY JEANNE FUNNELL (MRS. ROBERT LYSNE BERGUM), civic leader; b. Duluth, Minn., May 14, 1927; d. Leonard John and Hannah Clara (Hawkinson) Funnell; grad. high sch.; m. Robert Lysne Bergum, Nov. 1, 1947; children—R. Scott, John R., Thomas J. Chmn. cultural center feasability study com. Jr. League of Duluth, 1965-66, sec. interim cultural center com., 1966-67, co-chmn. interim cultural center com., 1967-69; dir., project coordinator Area Cultural Center Corp., Duluth, 1969-71, exec. sec., 1971—. Chmn. community arts Duluth Jr. League, 1965-66, del. regional conf., 1966, rec. sec., 1966-67; panel mem., reusing R.R. stas. conf. Nat. Endowment for Arts/Ednl. Facilities Labs., 1974. Bd. dirs. A.M. Chisholm Mus., 1965-71. Named Vol. of Yr., Jr. League Duluth, 1968; recipient Distinguished Service award A.M. Chisholm Mus., 1973. Lutheran (mem. ch. council 1967). Home: 208 Norton St Duluth MN 55803 Office: 506 W Michigan St Duluth MN 55802

BERGY, JOAN LEE IWERKS (MRS. GORDON G. BERGY), govt. ofcl.; b. Pontiac, Mich., Oct. 19, 1930; d. Charles Hiram and Alma (Mohn) I.; B.S. in Food and Nutrition, Mich. State U., 1952; m. Gordon Goodrich Bergy, July 19, 1958. Dietitian, King County Hosp., Seattle, 1953-54, clinic dietitian, 1955-57, home care dietitian, 1960-65; instr., U. Wash., Seattle, 1957-58; home economist Seattle Post-Intelligencer Newspaper, Seattle, 1958-60; consumer specialist FDA, Seattle, 1965-73; dir. U.S. Consumer Product Safety Commn., Seattle, 1973—. Clin. instr. Sch. Nursing U. Wash., Seattle, 1961-65; nutrition instr. Everett Jr. Coll., Everett, Wash., 1964; vis. lectr. U. Wash., Seattle, 1964; chmn. community service com. Seattle Fed. Exec. Bd., 1972-73. Recipient award of merit FDA, 1973. Mem. Am. Dietetic Assn., Am. Home Econ. Assn., Am. Pub. Health Assn., Seattle Dietetic Assn. (pres. 1963-64), Wash. Dietetic Assn. (community nutrition chmn. 1965-68), Wash. Home Econs. Assn. (consumer interest chmn. 1969—), Am. Home Econs. Assn. (mem. nat. consumer interest com. 1970-72). Contbr. articles to profl. jours. Home: 4114 78th SE Mercer Island WA 98040 Office: Consumer Product Safety Commn 1131 Federal Office Bldg Seattle WA 98104

BERING, HARRIET ALDRICH (MRS. EDGAR ANDREW BERING), civic worker; b. N.Y.C., Oct. 5, 1922; d. Winthrop Williams and Harriet (Alexander) Aldrich; student Mass. Inst. Tech., 1940-42; B.A., Barnard Coll., 1944; m. Edgar Andrew Bering, Nov. 3, 1944; children—Edgar A. III, Charles, Harriet. Chmn., United Fund, Brookline, Mass., 1961-62; treas. Audubon Naturalist Soc., 1964-68. Trustee Foxcroft Sch.; trustee Childrens Hearing and Speech Center, Washington, pres., 1971-74. Author: Foxcroft Cookbook, 1969. Home: Creek House Oxford MD 21654

BERKEY, HILDA GRACE, mezzo soprano; b. Berlin, Pa., Nov. 6, 1885; d. Jacob Maurer and Martha Jane (Lane) Berkey; ed. Pa. Coll. for Women (name changed to Indiana U. of Pa. Conservatory), 1913, Dr. Music (hon.), 1939; pvt. study voice, Europe. Debut as mezzo soprano France Fontainebleau Conservatory, 1922; concertized Europe and Am.; oratorio performances, Europe; head voice dept. Waynesburg (Pa.) Coll., 1921-42. Served with YMCA, 1918-19. Home: 200 Broaday Berlin PA 15530

BERKEY, RUTH MARGARET ANDERSON (MRS. BRUCE E. BERKEY), educator; b. Beverly, Mass., Nov. 17, 1935; d. Robert William and Helen (MacLachlan) Anderson; B.S., Pepperdine U., 1957; M.S., U. So. Cal., 1958; m. Bruce E. Berkey, Aug. 23, 1961; children—Bruce Robert, James Frederic. Instr. phys. edn. Pepperdine Coll., Los Angeles, 1958-59; tchr. pub. schs., Pasadena, Cal., 1959-60; instr. phys. edn. Occidental Coll., Los Angeles, 1960-72, asso. prof., 1972—, also chmn. dept., 1971—, dean of women, 1964-68. Del., Nat. Assn. for Intercollegiate Sports, Kan., 1973. Mem. Am., Cal. assns. health, phys. edn. and recreation, Am. Assn. U. Women. Home: 543 N Auburn Av Sierra Madre CA 91024 Office: 1600 Campus Rd Los Angeles CA 90041

BERKMAN, SARA LEE, social worker; b. Charleston, S.C., July 11, 1912; d. Samuel and Belle (Finklestein) Berkman; B.S., Coll. Charleston, 1934; M.S. in Social Work, Columbia, 1943. Home service dir. A.R.C., Columbia, S.C., 1943-46; adminstrv. supr. procedures dept. United Service for New Ams., N.Y.C., 1947-52; head community services dept. Nat. Council Jewish Women, N.Y.C., 1953-66; asso. exec. dir. Nat. Conf. on Social Welfare, N.Y.C., 1967—. Coordinator, mem. U.S. com. Internat. Council on Social Welfare, 1967—. Mem. Nat. Assn. Social Workers (charter), Nat. Conf. on Social Welfare, Council on Social Work Edn., Ams. for Democratic Action, Nat. Council Jewish Women, Advt. Club N.Y., Nat. Conf. Jewish Communal Services, Council Nat. Orgns. Adult Edn. Assn. (mem. exec. com., 1969-71), Internat. Conf. Jewish Communal Services, alumni assns. Coll. Charleston, Columbia U. Sch. Social Work, Social Work Vocational Bur. Home: 405 W 23d St New York City NY 10011 Office: 225 Park Av S New York City NY 10003

BERKMAN, SUSAN ANN, med. service exec.; b. Seattle, Jan. 5, 1945; d. Weaver and Fern (Ross) Berkman; student Grays Harbor Jr. Coll., 1963-64, U. Puget Sound, 1965, Inst. for Orgn. Mgmt., U. Santa Clara, 1969-70. With King County Med. Soc., Seattle, 1968-74, adminstrv. asst., 1968-69, exec. asst., 1969-70, acting dir., 1970-74; dir. Wash. State Profl. Standards Rev. Orgn., 1974—. Vol. Harborview Hosp., Seattle, 1973-74. Mem. citizens adv. com. Woodland Park Zoo, Seattle, 1973-74. Mem. Am. Assn. Med. Assts. (newsletter editor 1971), Exec. Secs., Inc., Am. Assn. Med. Soc. Execs., Washington Soc. Assn. Execs., Seattle Zool. Soc., Bus. and Profl. Women, Seattle Sailing Assn., Sierra Club. Club: Mountaineers (Seattle). Home: 2500 Gilman Dr W #400 Seattle WA 98119 Office: 2150 N 107th St Suite 504 Seattle WA 98133

BERKOWITZ, RHODA LAKRITZ (MRS. ROGER M. BERKOWITZ), librarian; b. N.Y.C., Nov. 6, 1939; d. David Eli and Edith (Fein) Lakritz; A.B., Mt. Holyoke Coll., 1960; LL.B., Yale, 1963; A.M. in Library Sci., U. Mich., 1970; m. Roger M. Berkowitz, Aug. 17, 1967. Admitted to D.C. bar, 1964, Mich. bar, 1968, practiced in Washington, 1963-68; law clk. to judges of D.C. Juvenile Ct., Washington, 1963-64; staff atty. Neighborhood Legal Services, Washington, 1965-68; chief reference librarian U. Mich. Law Library, Ann Arbor, 1969-74; asso. dir. Coll. of Law Library, U. Toledo, 1974—. Mem. Com. Friends of U. Mich. Mus. of Art, 1968-70; v.p. Friends of Ann Arbor Pub. Library, 1973-74. Bd. dirs. League of Women Voters of Ann Arbor, 1973, Washtenaw County Office of Econ. Opportunity, 1969-72. Mem. State Bar Mich., Am. Assn. Law Libraries, Beta Phi Mu. Democrat. Jewish religion. Home: 2200 Scottwood St Toledo OH 43620 Office: Coll of Law Library Univ Toledo Toledo OH 43606

BERLOWE, PHYLLIS HARRIETTE, pub. relations exec.; b. N.Y.C.; d. Louis and Rose (Jatchez) Berlowe; student Hunter Coll., 1939-41. Editorial asst. McGraw Hill Pub. Co., N.Y.C., 1953-55; dir. pub. relations Toscony Fabrics, Inc., N.Y.C., 1955-57; accounting exec. T.R. Sills & Co., N.Y.C., 1959-63, Harshe-Rotman & Druck, Inc., N.Y.C., 1963-65; sr. v.p. Edward Gottlieb & Assos., N.Y.C., 1965—. Mem. Pub. Relations Soc. Am. (mem. counselor's sect. 1969—), Am. Women in Radio and TV, Women Execs. in Pub. Relations, Publicity Club N.Y. (dir. 1960-69, rec. sec. 1961-63, 2d v.p. 1959-60, 1st. v.p. 1960-61, lectr. pub. relations, 1968—, distinguished service award 1960-64). Home: 201 W 77th St New York City NY 10024 Office: 485 Madison Av New York City NY 10022

BERMAN, ARIANE R. (MRS. MARIO LA ROSSA), artist; b. Free State Danzig, Mar. 27, 1937; d. Max and Riva (Gutmann) Berman; came to U.S., 1939, naturalized, 1945; B.F.A., Hunter Coll., 1959; M.F.A., Yale, 1962; study in Europe (Am. Assn. U. Women fellow, Fondation des Etats-Unis fellow); m. Mario La Rossa, June 17, 1965. One-man shows Fontana Gallery, Narberth, Pa., 1963, 71, 74, Center Gallery, New Haven, 1963, Philmont Country Club, Huntington Valley, Pa., 1965, Harry Salpeter Gallery, N.Y.C., 1966, Eileen Kuhlik Gallery, N.Y.C., 1971, 73, Galleria San Sebastianello, Rome, 1973, Graphic Art Gallery, Israel, 1973, Brentano's Gallery, N.Y.C., 1973, L.I., Shelter Rock, Bellmore, Huntington libraries, 1973, Wustum Mus. Fine Arts, Racine, Wis., 1974, Galleria d'Arte Helioart, Rome, 1974; exhibited in group shows Allied Artists of Am., Am. Color Print Exhbn., Silvermine, N.A.D., Yale Art Gallery, Art Alliance, Phila., USIA Traveling Exhibit to Europe, Albany (N.Y.) Print Biennial, Butler Inst. Am. Art, F 15 Gallery, Norway, Margo Feiden Galleries, N.Y.C., Asso. Am. Artists, N.Y.C., Gallery 500, Pa., Munson Gallery, Conn., Mass.; many others; represented in permanent collections Purdue U. Gallery Fine Arts, Phila. Mus. of Art, Fontana Gallery, Met. Mus. of Art, Am. Petroleum Inst., Seventeen Mag., Shipley Sch., Bryn Mawr, Pa., Charles E. Ellis Coll., Newtown Square, Pa., pvt. collections; commd. by Galleria d'Arte Helioart, Asso. Am. Artists, Fine Arts 260, Book of Month Club. Recipient Yale Painting prize 1960, Stella Drabkin Meml. award, purchase prize Am. color Print Soc., purchase award Purdue U., gold medal award Catharine Lorillard Wolfe Art Club, 1973; named to Hall of Fame, Alumni Assn. Hunter Coll., 1974 others. Mem. Am. Color Print Soc., Yonkers Art Assn., Silvermine Guild Artists, Hudson River Mus., League Present Day Artists, Met. Painters and Sculptors. Home: 161 W 54th St New York City NY 10019

BERMAN, CLAIRE GALLANT, author; b. N.Y.C., July 4, 1936; d. Max and Reva (Yarus) Gallant; A.B., Barnard Coll., 1957; m. Noel B. Berman, July 19, 1959; children—Eric, Mitchell, Orin. Sr. editor Cosmopolitan mag., N.Y.C., 1958-63; free-lance writer, editor with articles in McCall's, Good Housekeeping, Cosmopolitan, N.Y. Times Mag., Village Voice, New York; contbg. editor New York mag., 1971—; author: A Great City for Kids: A Parent's Guide to a Child's New York, 1969; We Take This Child: A Candid Look at Modern Adoption, 1974. Mem. children's entertainment com. 92d St YM-YWHA, 1969—; publicity mgr. Riverside Chamber Ensemble, 1972—; mem. editorial bd. Barnard Alumnae, 1973—. Address: 52 Riverside Dr New York City NY 10024

BERMAN, DOREEN HYAMS, neuropsychologist; b. London, Eng., Aug. 31, 1924; d. Sid and Cissie (Myers) Hyams; came to U.S., 1940; naturalized, 1952; B.Sc., McGill U., 1943, M.Sc. in Anatomy, 1946; Ph.D. in Neuropsychology, City U. N.Y., 1971; m. Aaron Joseph Berman, Sept. 14, 1943; children—Judith (Mrs. Philip Bukberg), Steven, Robert, Winifred. Neurophysiology research fellow Jewish Hosp. Bklyn., 1946-48; neurosurg. research asst. Queens Gen. Hosp., Flushing, N.Y., 1964-66; teaching asst. psychology Queens Coll., City U. N.Y., Flushing, 1968-69, lectr., 1971-73, asst. prof. psychology, 1973—; research psychologist Jewish Hosp. and Med. Center Bklyn., 1968-71, VA Hosp., Bronx, 1972—. Nat. Inst. Mental Health trainee, 1966-68. Mem. Am. Psychol. Assn. N.Y. Acad. Scis., Soc. for Neurosci., Internat. Soc. for Devel. Psychobiology, Sigma Xi. Contbr. articles to profl. jours. Office: Dept Psychology Queens College Flushing NY 11367

BERMAN, ELIZABETH A. (MRS. BRADLEY E. APPELBAUM), educator; b. Mpls., Feb. 27, 1937; d. Reuben and Isabel (Rosenstein) Berman; B.A. magna cum laude, U. Minn., 1958, M.A. (NSF fellow, Woodrow Wilson Found. fellow), 1959; Ph.D. (NSF fellow), U. Mo., Kansas city, 1970; m. Bradley E. Appelbaum, Aug. 8, 1957; children—James Steven, Sharon Rachel. Asst. prof. math. Rockhurst Coll., Kansas City, Mo., 1970—, acting chmn. dept., 1973—. Cons. Acad. Press, 1973—. Mem. Am. Math. Soc., Math. Assn. Am., Nat. Council Tchrs. Math., Am. Assn. U. Profs., Phi Beta Kappa. Contbr. articles to profl. jours. Home: 3016 W 73d St Prairie Village KS 66208 Office: Rockhurst Coll 5225 Troost Av Kansas City MO 64110

BERMAN, LOUISE MARGUERITE, educator, ednl. adminstr.; b. Hartford, Conn., July 6, 1928; d. Jacob and Anna Bertha (Woike) Berman; A.B., Wheaton Coll., 1950; M.A., Columbia, 1953, Ed.D., 1960. Instr., Central Conn. State Coll., New Britain, 1954-58; asst. prof., asso. prof., curriculum U. Wis., Milw., 1960-65; asso. sec. Assn. for Supervision and Curriculum Devel., Washington, 1965-67; prof. edn. U. Md., College Park, dir. U. Research Center for Young Children, 1967—. Vis. prof. U. P.R., summer 1969. Mem. U.S. Nat. Com. for Early Childhood Edn., 1969—. Mem. Am. Ednl. Research Assn., World Council on Curriculum and Instrn. (exec. com. 1971—), Assn. for Supervision and Curriculum Devel. (dir.), Common Cause, World Future Soc., Profs. Curriculum, Pi Lambda Theta, Kappa Delta Pi. Presbyn. Author: From Thinking to Behaving, 1967; New Priorities in the Curriculum, 1968; Supervision, Staff Development and Leadership, 1971; Beyond Confrontation: An Analysis of Power, 1973; Curriculum: Teaching the What, How and Why of Living, 1975. Home: 7333 New Hampshire Av Hyattsville MD 20783 Office: Coll Edn U Md College Park MD 20742

BERMAN, MONA S. (MRS. CARROLL Z. BERMAN), theatrical dir., producer; b. Jersey City, Jan. 17, 1925; d. Edward and Mary (Auster) Solomon; B.A., Beaver Coll., 1945; postgrad. Columbia, 1946; M.F.A., Boston U., 1959; m. Carroll Z. Berman, Sept. 9, 1947; children—Marcie S. (Mrs. Charles Parker Ries), Laura Jane. Tchr. English, drama Jersey City High Schs., 1945-47; actress Mass. Valley Players, Holyoke, 1947-49; owner, dir. The Theatre Sch. and Producing Co., Maplewood, N.J., 1964-74; chmn. drama edn. YM-YWHA of Met. N.J. Cons., Clark Center for Performing Arts, N.Y.C., 1965-66; instr. South Orange, Maplewood Adult Sch., 1967; artistic dir. Children's Theatre Co. Inc., Maplewood, 1968-70; cons. The Whole Theater Co., 1974—. Active Boston United Fund, 1955-59, chmn. Boston residential area, 1957. Bd. dirs. Greater Boston Girl Scouts Am., 1956-58, Tufts Med. Faculty Wives, 1956-58. Mem. Am. Theater Assn. Playwright: Hello Joe, 1967, That Ring in the Center, 1968, The Big Show, 1970; Interim, 1974. Producer, dir. A Night of Stars. Address: 92 Claremont Av Maplewood NJ 07040

BERMAN, MURIEL MALLIN (MRS. PHILIP I. BERMAN), civic worker; b. Pitts.; d. Samuel and Dora (Coopersman) Mallin; student U. Pitts., 1943, Carnegie Tech. U., 1944-45; B.S., Pa. State Coll. Optometry, 1948; postgrad. U. Pitts., 1950, Cedar Crest Coll., 1953, D.F.A., 1972; postgrad. Muhlenberg Coll., 1954; m. Philip I. Berman, Oct. 23, 1942; children—Nancy, Nina, Steven, Practice optometry, Pitts.; v.p., asst. treas., dir. Hess's Dept. Store, Allentown, Pa.; v.p., treas., dir. Fleet Ways, Inc., real estate, Philip and Muriel Berman Found. Active in UNICEF, 1959—, ofcl. non-govtl. orgns., 1964, 74; founder, donor Carnegie-Berman Coll. Art Slide Library Exchange; mem. Aspen (Colo.) Inst. Humanistic Studies, 1965, Tokyo, Japan, 1966; chmn. exhibit Great Valley council, Girl Scouts U.S.A., 1966; adminstrv. head, chmn. various events Allentown Bicentennial, 1962; vice chmn. Women for Pa. Bicentennial 1976; co-chmn. Lehigh County Bi-Centennial Liberty Bell-Trek, 1976; patron Art in the Embassies Program, Washington, 1965—; chmn. Lehigh Valley Ednl. TV, 1966—, programs Fgn. Policy Assn., Lehigh County, 1965-67; treas. ann. symphony ball Allentown Symphony, 1955—; mem. Dieruff High Sch. Art Adv. Com., Allentown, 1966—; producer weekly College Speak-Out, TV Channel 39, 1967—, producer, moderator TV program Guest Spot; chmn. art com. Episcopal Diocese Centennial Celebration, 1971; mem. Pa. Council on Status of Women, 1968-73; chmn. numerous art shows; mem. YWCA, Art Collectors Club Am., Am. Fedn. Art, Friends Whitney Mus., Mus. Modern Art, Mus. Primitive Art, Jewish Mus. Met. Mus., Kemmerer Mus., Bethlehem, Pa., Univ. Mus., Phila., Skirball Mus., Los Angeles (all N.Y.C.), Archives of Am. Art, Detroit, Allentown Art Mus., Phila. Art Mus., Reading Art Mus., Met. Opera Guild, N.Y.C., Lincoln Center, N.Y.C. Mem. Electoral College, 1968; mem. Democratic Platform Com., 1972; de. Dem. Nat. Conv., 1972. Bd. dirs. Pa. Ballet, Allentown Symphony (treas. ann. ball), Lehigh Valley Ednl. TV (chmn. program com.), Hadassah (nat. dir.), Heart Assn. Pa., Allentown Art Mus. Aux. (art appreciation dir.), Phila. Chamber Symphony, Baum Art Sch., Lehigh County Cultural Center, Women's Club (v.p., arts chmn. 1960—), Fgn. Policy Assn.; trustee Kutztown State Coll., 1960-66, vice chmn. bd., 1965; trustee Lehigh Community Coll., also sec. bd.; trustee Pa. Council on Arts, Smithsonian Art Council, Bonds for Israel. Named Woman of Valor, Israel, 1965; recipient Centennial Year Hon. citation Wilson Coll., 1969; Henrietta Szold award Allentown chpt. Hadassan; Outstanding Woman award Allentown YWCA, 1973. Mem. League Women Voters, Hist. Soc. Lehigh County, Lehigh, Phila. art alliances, UN We Believe. Jewish religion (past v.p. Temple sisterhood). Club: Wellesley. Good will tours to Latin Am. for U.S. Dept. State, 1965. Catalogs, research curator Berman (art) collection. Address: 20 Hundred Nottingham Rd Allentown PA 18103

BERMEL, CHARLOTTE GERTRUDE, investment co. exec.; b. Los Angeles, Nov. 22, 1919; d. Frank and Magdalena (Junker) Bermel; B.E., U. Cal. at Los Angeles, 1941. With R.H. Moulton & Co., Los Angeles, 1941—, head govt. securities trading dept., office mgr., corporate sec., 1973—. Mem. Am. Assn. U. Women (v.p. Los Angeles br. 1960-61), Los Angeles Assn. Investment Women (pres. 1972), Alpha Chi Delta. Office: 523 W 6th St Los Angeles CA 90014

BERMINGHAM, EVE DIANE (MRS. ARTHUR T. BERMINGHAM III), lawyer; b. N.Y.C., Nov. 20, 1946; B.A., Syracuse U., 1966; J.D. cum laude, Ariz. State U., 1971; m. Arthur T. Bermingham III, Mar. 18, 1966; children—Stacy Jennifer, Berry Ann. Admitted to Ariz. bar, 1971; asso. Deprima, Aranda, DeLeon & Lincoln, Phoenix, 1971-72; asso. counsel Ariz. Title Ins. & Trust Co., Phoenix, 1972-73; Simon & Jekel, attys., Scottsdale, Ariz., 1974—. Dir. Keyman Service Corp., Itinerations, Inc. Mem. docent com. Phoenix Art Mus., 1972—. Mem. State Bar Ariz., Maricopa County, Scottsdale bar assns., Am. Judicature Soc., Delta Theta Phi. Clubs: Scottsdale Raquet; University (Phoenix). Home: 6128 E Cactus Wren Rd Paradise Valley AZ 85253 Office: McCune Bldg 4320 N Scottsdale Rd Scottsdale AZ 85251

BERNARD, BETTY, physician, educator; b. St. Louis, Aug. 7, 1933; d. Raymond Francis and Mildred (Dowell) Bernard; student Ohio Wesleyan U., 1951-52, U. Mo., Columbia, 1953; B.A., U. Cal. at Los Angeles, 1956; M.D., U. So. Cal., 1960; m. Bascom Frank Anthony, June 17, 1961 (div. 1969); children—Peter Bernard, John Bascom. Intern, U. Minn. Hosp., Mpls., 1960-61, pediatric resident, 1961-63, med. fellow cystic fibrosis, 1963-64, NIH trainee in metabolism, 1965-67; sr. physician community medicine U. Cal. at San Diego, La Jolla, 1968-69, sr. physician pediatrics, 1968-69, clin. instr. pediatrics, 1968-70, fellow in neonatology, 1969-70; asst. prof. pediatrics Los Angeles County-U. So. Cal. Med. Center, 1970—, dir. pathology nursery of newborn service, 1970—. Diplomate Am. Bd. Pediatrics, Nat. Bd. Med. Examiners. Fellow Am. Acad. Pediatrics; mem. Los Angeles County Pediatric Soc., So. Cal. Perinatal Soc., Western Soc. Pediatric Research, Kappa Kappa Gamma. Contbr. articles to profl. jours. Home: 1866 Via Del Rey South Pasadena CA 91030 Office: Los Angeles County-U So Cal Medical Center Womens Hosp 1400 N State St Los Angeles CA 90033

BERNARD, JESSIE (MRS. LUTHER LEE BERNARD), author; b. Mpls., June 8, 1903; d. David Solomon and Bessie (Kanter) Ravage; B.A., U. Minn., 1923, M.A., 1924; Ph.D., Washington U., 1935; m. Luther Lee Bernard, Sept. 23, 1925 (dec. Jan. 1951); children—Dorothy Lee (Mrs. William Clay Jackson), Charles Henry Claude, David Hamilton. Statis. analyst Bur. Labor Statistics, 1938-40; prof. sociology Lindenwood Coll., St. Charles, Mo., 1940-47; prof. Pa. State U., 1947-64, research scholar honoris causa, 1964—; editorial bd. Jour. Marriage and Family, 1963—, Sociology and Social Research, 1960—, Jour. Conflict Resolution, 1967—, Internat. Jour. Sociology of the Family; cons. Spl. Operations Research Orgn., Am. U., Washington, 1965; del. White House Conf. on Youth, 1971; mem. com. on research Am. Council Edn.; cons. Nat. Conf. Commrs. Uniform State Laws, mem. com. uniform marriage and dir. legislation, 1968-70. Cons. Western Behavioral Scis. Inst., Center for Research on Acts of Man. Bd. dirs. Carver Found. of Tuskegee Inst., 1966—; mem. adv. bd. Internat. Inst. Women Studies, Am. Council on Edn., Commn. on Women in Higher Edn. Bd. dirs. Women's Center for Policy Studies, Internat. Inst. Sex Identities. Author: American Family Behavior, 1942; (with L. L. Bernard) Origins of American Sociology, 1942; American Community Behavior, 1949; Remarriage, 1956; Social Problems at Midcentury, 1957; Academic Women, 1964; Marriage and Family among Negroes in the United States, 1966; (with others) Dating, Mating and Marriage, 1959; The Sex Game, 1968; Women and the Public Interest, An Essay on Policy and Protest, 1971; The Future of Marriage, 1972; The Sociology of Community, 1973; The Future of Motherhood, 1974; Women, Wives, Mothers, 1975; Sociology and the Study of International Relations, 1932. Recipient award for best manuscript Pa. State U. Press for Acad. Women, 1964; award Delta Kappa Gamma, 1965; Distinguished Alumni award Washington U., 1966; Merit award Eastern Sociol. Soc., 1971; Distinguished Alumna award U. Minn., 1972; E.W. Burgess Research award Nat. Council Family Relations, 1972. Mem. Am. (v.p. 1953-54), Eastern (pres. 1953), D.C. (past pres., Stewart A. Rice award 1974) sociol. socs., Soc. for Study of Social Problems (pres. 1963), Sociologists for Women in Soc. (publs. com.), Sigma Xi, Phi Beta Kappa, Pi Gamma Mu, Alpha Kappa Delta. Mem. Society of Friends. Home: 4200 Cathedral Av NW Washington DC 20016

BERNARD, MARCELLE THOMASINE, physician; b. N.Y.C., Aug. 11, 1920; d. Rene Jules and Antoinette (Byrnes) Bernard; A.B. magna cum laude, Coll. of St. Elizabeth, 1941; M.D., N.Y. Med. Coll., 1944; m. Edmund D. Marinucci, Mar. 30, 1967. Intern, Flower and Fifth Av. Hosps., 1944-45; family practice medicine and geriatrics, N.Y.C., 1947—; attending physician St. Francis Hosp., Bronx, 1950-65, Union Hosp., N.Y.C., 1957—; attending staff Frances Schervier Home and Hosp., N.Y.C., 1952—, pres. med. bd., 1959-60, v.p., 1965; attending staff St. Patrick's Home, N.Y.C., 1954—, pres. med. bd., 1962; med. dir. St. Joseph's Heritage House, Danbury, Conn.; mem. med. bd. Notre Dame Convalescent Home, Norwalk, Conn.; mem. N.Y. Dept. Health Bd. Examiners of Nursing Home Adminstrs. Mem. exec. com. Bronx Tb and Health Assn., 1956-60; hon. surgeon Life Sav. Service N.Y.C., 1959—; v.p. Bronxboro Commn. on Aging, 1961-63; past chmn. 1st aid Bronx chpt. A.R.C.; chmn. profl. edn. com. Bronx chpt. Am. Cancer Soc., 1966-68, vice chmn. adv. bd., 1969—, bd. dirs. So. Fairfield Unit, mem. med. affairs com. Mem. Ladies of Charity; adv. bd. Salvation Army, 1964—. Named Lady Equestrian Order Holy Sepulchre Jerusalem. Served as lt., M.C. Women's Res., USN, 1945-47. Diplomate Nat. Bd. Med. Examiners. Fellow Am. Acad. Family Physicians (charter; pres. Bronx chpt. 1969-72), Am. Geriatrics Soc.; mem. N.Y. State (chmn. pub. med. care com. 1963-65, chmn. aging and nursing homes com. 1973—), Bronx County (pres. 1965-66, mem. bd. censors 1966-68, mem. comitia minora, mem. pub. relations, legislation coms.), Norwalk med. socs., Bronx Cath. Physicians Guild, Mil. Surgeons of U.S., Am. Med. Women's Assn., N.Y. State Acad. Family Physicians (legislation com.). Asst. editor Jour. Am. Med. Women's Assn., 1949-55. Contbr. articles on geriatrics to med. jours. Home: Appletree Lane Silvermine Norwalk CT 06850 Office: 635 E 211th St New York City NY 10467 also 156 East Av Norwalk CT 06851

BERNARD, SISTER MARIE, coll. dean; b. Del Norte, Colo., Jan. 8, 1927; d. Frank M. and Minnie (Borrego) Bernard; B.S. cum laude, St. Mary of Plains Coll., 1960; M.S., Ft. Hays Kan. State Coll., 1964; M.A. (student personnel grantee), U. Denver, 1971. Joined Community of Sisters of St. Joseph of Wichita, 1945; elementary tchr. St. Anthony Sch., Wellington, Kan., 1947-49, Sacred Heart Sch., Frontenac, Kan., 1949-50; tchr.-prin. St. Joseph Sch., Perry, Okla., 1950-55, St. Mary's Sch., Parsons, Kan., 1956-57, St. Paul Sch., Eugene, Ore., 1957-65; prin. Blessed Sacrament Sch., Wichita, Kan., 1965-68; intern in coll. adminstrn., freshmen adviser Wichita State U., 1968; adminstrv. asst. to pres., acting dean women, dir. student affairs St. Mary of Plains Coll., Dodge City, 1968-69; student personnel services staff Loretto Heights Coll., Denver, 1969-71; asso. dean students, dir. career planning and placement Kan. Newman Coll., Wichita, 1972—. Cons. Mid-Continent Regional Ednl. Lab., 1967-68; mem. sch. bd. Sisters of St. Joseph, 1967-69; mem. Wichita Diocesan Curriculum Council and Liturgical Commn., 1965-68. Founder, charter mem. Internat. U. of World, 1972. Local bd. dirs. YMCA, regional bd. dirs., 1967-69; bd. dirs. West Side Involvement Corp., Wichita. Mem. Nat. Assn. Women Deans, Adminstrs. and Counselors, Nat., Kan. assns. student personnel adminstrs., Rocky Mountain Coll. Placement Assn., Nat. Orientation Dirs. Assn., Kappa Delta Pi. Home: 855 S Sheridan St Wichita KS 67213

BERNARD, MARY ELIZABETH O'GORMAN, civic and polit. party worker; b. Dover, N.H.; d. Arthur Peter and Margaret (Donnelly) O'Gorman; R.N., Carney Hosp. Sch. Nursing, 1929; m. Albert O. Bernard, June 29, 1935. Real estate salesman, Albert O. Bernard, bldg. contractor, Dover, N.H., 1936-70; writer women's page Boston Globe, 1956-60. Active Cancer and Catholic Charities. Mem. Health and Welfare Com., 1967-71, N.H. State Instns. Com., 1967-73, Liquor Laws Com., 1973. Mem. Dover Democratic City Com., 1965-72, supr. check lists, 1963-72, chmn. bd. suprs. of checklists, 1973—, clk. Strafford County delegation and exec. com., 1973—, clk. Dover delegation, 1967-72; mem. N.H. Ho. of Reps., 1967-73; mem. Strafford County Dem. Exec. Com., 1969-73; clk. Strafford County Bldg. Com. Mem. St. Mary's Altar Soc., St. Mary's Rosary Soc., Cath. Daus. Am. (trustee). Club: Dover Point Community (treas. 1948-50). Address: 121 Portland Av Dover NH 03820

BERNARD, NAOMI DIANE RUDNICK (MRS. EDWARD R. BERNARD), pharmacist, pharm. cons.; b. New Haven, Nov. 18, 1925; d. Nathan Daniel and Sara (Gladstone) Rudnick; B.S. (B.A. Fox scholarship 1943), U. Conn., 1946; m. Edward Robert Bernard, June 29, 1947; children—Arthur, Ruth, Sidney, Frederic, David, Amy. Asst. instr. U. Conn. Sch. Pharmacy, New Haven, 1946-49, also pharmacist Melba Pharmacy, Milford; pharmacy cons. Golden Manor Convalescent Home, New Haven, 1966-68, Hawkins Convalescent Home; West Haven, Conn., 1966—, Orange (Conn.) Convalescent Home, 1966—, Arterburn Convalescent Home, 1969—, Montowese Convalescent Home, 1969—, Hewitt Meml. Convalescent Home, 1973—, Derby Convalescent Home, 1973—, Middlebury (Conn.) Convalescent Home, 1973—, United Methodist Convalescent Home, 1973—, Mary Wade Rest Home, 1974—; mem. pharm. adv. council Conn. Dept. Health, 1974—. Editor Corona Park Press, Milford, Conn., 1953-56. Pres. Jewish War Vets. Aux., Milford, Conn., 1956; co-chmn. Snow Ball, West Orange Assn., 1968; capt. Mothers March, 1965— Multiple Sclerosis Dr., 1965-67, Heart Fund, 1966-67. Mem. Am., Conn. (chmn. com. health care facilities 1971—), New Haven pharm. assns., Am. Soc. Cons. Pharmacists (Conn. dir.), Conn. Soc. Hosp. Pharmacists. Mem. editorial bd. Conn. Pharmacist, 1973—; editor Pharma-Conn., 1945-46. Contbr. articles to profl. jours. 406 Hilltop Rd Orange CT 06477

BERNARD, ROSE MARY (MRS. LAWRENCE BERNARD), educator; b. Coleridge, Neb., Apr. 7, 1909; d. Antone and Marie Julia (Solko) Ullsperger; B.S., Peru State Coll., 1959, M., 1962; postgrad. (scholar) Peabody Coll. for Tchrs., 1960, U. Neb., 1966; m. Lawrence Bernard, July 28, 1926; children—Marilyn (Mrs. Dan Sullivan), John, Connie (Mrs. Richard Tushla). Coordinator K-3, Neb. Sch. for Visually Handicapped, Auburn, 1958-66, elementary, 1970—; supr. campus sch. Peru (Neb.) State Coll., 1967-69, summers 1960-70. Salesman Bernard Real Estate, Auburn, summers. Mem. Neb. Democratic Central Com., 1962. Mem. Auburn C. of C., Assn. Childhood Edn. (v.p. Neb. 1965-72), Am. Assn. U. Women (pres. 1972-73), Faculty Women's Club. Democrat. Club: Auburn Country. Home: South J St Auburn NE 68305 Office: 912 Central Av Auburn NE 68305

BERNAY, BETTI (MRS. J. BERNARD GOLDFARB), artist; b. N.Y.C., Sept. 21, 1926; d. David Michael and Anna Gaynia (Bernay) Woolin; grad. costume design Pratt Inst., 1946; student Nat. Acad., N.Y.C., 1947-49, Art Students League, N.Y.C., 1950-51; m. J. Bernard Goldfarb, Apr. 19, 1947; children—Manette Deitsch, Karen Lynn. One-man shows at Galerie Raymond Duncan, Paris, France, Salas Municipales, San Sebastian, Spain, Circulo de Bellas Artes, Madrid, Spain, Bacardi Gallery, Miami, Fla., Columbia (S.C.) Mus., Columbus (Ga.) Mus., Galerie Andre Weil, Paris, France, Galerie Hermitage, Montecarlo, Monaco, Casino de San Remo (Italy), Galerie de Arte de la Caja de Ahorros de Ronda, Malaga, Spain, Centro Artistico, Granada, Spain, Circulo de la Amistad, Cordoba, Spain, Galerie Andre Weil, Paris, France, Studio Gallery H, N.Y.C., Walter Wallace Gallery, Palm Beach, Fla., Museo Bellas Artes, Malaga, Spain, Harbor House Gallery, Miami Beach, Fla., Crystal House Gallery, Miami Beach, Fla., Internat. Gallery, Jordan Marsh, Miami, Fontainebleau Gallery, Miami Beach, Fla.; exhibited in group shows at Painters and Sculptors Soc., Jersey City (N.J.) Mus., Salon de Invierno, Museo Malaga, Spain, Salon des Beaux Arts, Cannes, France, Nat. Acad. Gallery, N.Y.C., Salon des Artistes Independants, Paris, Salon des Artistes Francais, Paris, Salon Populiste, Paris, Salon de Otono, Madrid, Spain, Salamagundi Club, N.Y.C., Nat. Assn. Painters and Sculptors Spain, Madrid, Phipps Gallery, Palm Beach, Fla., Lever House, N.Y.C., Knickerbocker Artists, N.Y.C., Artists Equity, Hollywood (Fla.) Mus., Nat. Arts Gallery, N.Y.C., Springfield (Mass.) Mus., ACA Gallery, N.Y.C., Argent Gallery, N.Y.C., Nat. Acad. Gallery, N.Y.C., Gables Art Gallery, Miami, Gibralter Internat. Art Sch., Gault Gallery Cheltenham, Phila., Century Gallery, Miami, Fla., Lord & Taylor Gallery, N.Y.C., Pageant Gallery, Galerie 99 (both Miami); represented in permanent collections at Museo de Malaga, Circulo de la Amistad, Cordoba, Spain, I.O.S. Found., Geneva, Switzerland, others. Recipient Medal for artistic merit City of N.Y., Sch. Art Leagues, N.Y.C.; Prix de Paris, Raymond Duncan, 1958; others. Mem. Nat. Assn. Painters and Sculptors Spain, Nat. Assn. Women Artists, Societe des Artistes Francais, Societe des Artistes Ind., Fedn. Francais des Societes d'Art Graphique et Plastique, Artists Equity, Am. Artists Profl. League. Address: 5001 Collins Av Miami Beach FL 33140

BERNBAUM, MARJORIE EDNA (MRS. BERNARD BERNBAUM), banker; b. Dallas, Dec. 14, 1920; d. Paul Alfred and Jeanne (Isaacs) Swain; student Am. Inst. Banking, 1968-69; m. Bernard Bernbaum, Sept. 2, 1965; children (by previous marriage)—Mrs. Paula Barshop, Richard O. Amber. With Republic Nat. Bank, Dallas, 1967—, bond investment officer, 1971—. Mem. Am. Inst. Banking, Nat. Assn. Women Bankers, Nat. Assn. Bus. and Profl. Women. Mem. B'nai B'rith Women. Author: Federal Fund Practices, a Training Manual, 1971; Certificate of Deposit Procedure, 1972. Home: 6211-B Bandera St Pl Dallas TX 75225 Office: Republic National Bank Dallas TX 75222

BERNDT, MARION MAUER (MRS. DONALD WARREN BERNDT), librarian; b. Cleve., June 23, 1927; d. John Edward and Mary Lillian (Vrcek) Mauer; B.A., Notre Dame Coll., Cleve., 1949; M.L.S., Case Western Res. U., 1950; m. Donald Warren Berndt, Dec. 11, 1963. Children's librarian Lakewood (O.) Pub. Library, 1950-55; librarian U.S. Army, Japan, 1955-57; supervising librarian U.S. Army Korea, 1957-58; staff librarian U.S. Army Ryukyu Islands, 1958-61, U.S. Army So. Command, Panama Canal Zone, 1961-65; supervising librarian Ft. Hood, Tex., 1965-66; chief librarian USCONTIC, Ft. Bragg, N.C., 1967; chief librarian Spl. Services, Ft. Bragg, 1967-71; reference librarian, history br. CINCPAC Reference Library, Aiea, Hawaii, 1971-72; regional librarian Dept. of Navy in Pacific, Pearl Harbor, Hawaii, 1972-73; library resources coordinator Office Chief Naval Edn. and Tng. Support, Pensacola, Fla., 1973—. Guest lectr. U. Ryukyus, 1961, C.Z. Jr. Coll., 1962, Middle Mgmt. Workshop, Ft. Bragg, N.C., 1969. Recipient Sustained Superior Performance award U.S. Dept. Army, 1960, U.S. Navy Dept., 1972, 73, Outstanding Performance award, 1961, 64, 69, 70, 72, 73. Home: 3887 Durango Rd Pensacola FL 32504 Office: Chief Naval Edn and Tng Support Code N35 Pensacola FL 32509

BERNE, SHIRLEY MOSES, financial analyst; b. Mobile, Ala., June 4, 1924; d. Alfred G. and Birdie (Feld) Moses; student Washington U., 1941-42; A.B., U. Ala., 1945; postgrad. N.Y. Inst. Finance, 1953-54,

N.Y. U., 1956; m. Andrew Berne, Sept. 7, 1945; 1 son, Robert David. Security analyst Merrill Lynch, Pierce, Fenner & Smith, Inc., N.Y.C., 1951-57; contbg. investment editor Med. Econs., Inc., Oradell, N.J., 1961-67; pvt. practice as financial analyst, 1973—. Mem. finance com. Union Theol. Sem., N.Y.C., 1973—. Mem. N.Y. Soc. Security Analysts, Paramus Hist. and Preservation Soc., N.J., Bergen County hist. socs., League Women Voters, Sierra Club, Phi Beta Kappa, Alpha Kappa Delta. Home: 524 Jemco Pl Ridgewood NJ 07450

BERNER, EDITH MARGARET (MRS. WALTER A. BERNER), civic worker; b. St. Louis; d. Edward and Esther (Gurganus) Manss; student pub. schs., night sch. coll. courses; m. Walter A. Berner, Nov. 17, 1934; 1 dau., Barbara (Mrs. Harold R. Marsh, Jr.). Active P.T.A., 1944-56, pres. Rogers, Chgo., 1945-46, 1st v.p. North Side Council, Chgo., 1948-49, recreation chmn. Chgo. region, 1950-52, 1st v.p. Chgo., 1952-54, pres. Chgo., 1954-56; chmn. com. for wider use of schs., Chgo., 1950-54; administrv. asst. to dir. devel. U. Chgo., 1956-65; exec. dir. north shore unit Am. Cancer Soc., Evanston, 1965-69, asso. dir. income devel. Ill. div., 1970—. Recipient spl. life membership Chgo. region Ill. Congress P.T.A., 1956. Conglist. Home: 163 Asbury Av Evanston IL 60202 Office: 37 S Wabash Av Chicago IL 60603

BERNHAGEN, LILLIAN LOUISE FLICKINGER (MRS. RALPH JOHN BERNHAGEN), health educator, nurse; b. Cleve., Oct. 1, 1916; d. Norman Henry and Bertha (Rogers) Flickinger; student Ohio Wesleyan U., 1934-37; B.S., Ohio State U., 1940, M.A., 1958; m. Ralph John Bernhagen, Sept. 2, 1940; children—Ralph (dec.), Janet Elizabeth, Penelope Anne. Asst. dir. Kiwanis Health Camp for Underprivileged Children, Steubenville, O., 1940; asst. dir. nurses Jefferson Davis Hosp., Houston, 1940-41; home nursing instr. A.R.C., Ohio State U., Columbus, 1943; coordinator health services Worthington (O.) Pub. Schs., 1951-74, dir. health services, 1974—. Lectr., cons. in field; instr. A.R.C., 1961—. Bd. dirs. Columbus Hearing Soc., 1953-56, sec., 1956. Recipient Centennial award Ohio State U., 1970; named Tchr. of Year Worthington Pub. Schs., 1973. Fellow, Am. Sch. Health Assn. (chmn. com. health guidance in sex edn. 1963-67, 71-75, v.p. 1973-74, pres.-elect. 1974-75, pres. 1975—), Am. Pub. Health Assn.; mem. Am., Ohio (legislative com. 1960) nurses assns., Ohio State U. Hosp. Sch. Nursing Alumni Assn. (treas. 1948, pres. 1949-52), N.E.A., Central Ohio Tchrs. Assn. (chmn. sch. nurses sect. 1962), Worthington (v.p. 1961-62), Ohio edn. assns., A.A.U.W., Ohio U. Women's Golf Assn., Columbus Women's Dist. Golf Assn., Ohio State U. Women's Golf Assn. (vice chmn. 1971, chmn. 1972), Internat. Sertoma (Woman of Year 1972), Chi Omega (financial adviser Kappa Gamma chpt. 1964—), Pi Lambda Theta, Sigma Theta Tau. Methodist. Club: Ohio Wesleyan U. Monnett. Co-author: Growth Patterns and Sex Education, A Rationale for School Nurse Certification; author What A Miracle You Are, Boys, 1968; What A Miracle You Are, Girls, 1968. Contbr. articles to profl. jours. Home: 5916 Linworth Rd Worthington OH 43085 Office: 2341 Snouffer Rd Worthington OH 43085

BERNHEIM, HEATHER STANCHFIELD PETERSON (MRS. CHARLES BERNHEIM), civic worker; b. Houston; d. Weed and Mylla (Stanchfield) Peterson; student U. Tex., 1938-42; m. Charles A. Bernheim, July 18, 1973. Docent chmn. Harris County Heritage Soc., 1969-70, v.p., after 1970; vol. worker Hermann Hosp., 1968-69; team capt. Mus. Fine Arts Ball, Houston, 1969; maintenance fund drive worker Mus. Fine Arts, 1970. Bd. dirs. Planned Parenthood N.Y.C. Mem. Houston Country Club Womens Assn., Kappa Alpha Theta Alumni Assn. Club: Houston. Home: 33 E 70th St Apt S-E New York City NY 10021 also 4515 Briar Hollow Pl Houston TX 77027

BERNING, LOUISE JUSTINE NUMRICH (MRS. TERRENCE A. BERNING), banker; b. Scott City, Kan., Nov. 16, 1949; d. Paul William and Leona Mae (Macy) Numrich; B.S. in Econs., Tex. Woman's U., 1971; student U. Neb. Sch. Banking, 1974; m. Terrence A. Berning, June 21, 1969; children—Christopher Justin, Jonathan Tate. Residential asst. Tex. Woman's U., Denton, 1968-70; tchr. Sanger (Tex.) High Sch., 1970-71; substitute tchr. Scott City (Kan.) Jr. High Sch., 1971; teller Security State Bank, Scott City, 1971—. Vol., Kan. Assn. for Retarded Children, 1973-74; youth chmn. Anderson for Gov., 1972; active campaign for lt. gov. Owen, 1972; city chmn. Senator Dole's campaign, 1974; Republican committeewoman Scott County, 1974. Mem. Am. Assn. U. Women (legislative chmn. 1973-74), Tex. Woman's U. Alumnae Assn., Beta Sigma Phi (rec. sec. 1972-73, chmn. ways and means 1973-74, city council rep. 1972-73), Epsilon Rho, Phi Gamma Delta. Home: 812 College St Scott City KS 67871 Office: Box 188 Security State Bank Scott City KS 67871

BERNING, SUSIE MAXWELL (MRS. DALE P. BERNING), profl. golfer; b. Pasadena, Cal., July 22, 1941; d. Sheilds John and Isabelle Louise (Edwards) Maxwell; B.S. in Bus. Adminstrn., Oklahoma City U., 1963; m. Dale P. Berning, May 18, 1968; 1 dau., Robin Ann. On tour with Ladies Profl. Golf Assn., 1964—; sports adviser Dunlop Sporting Goods, 1964, Di Fini Clothing, 1964. Named Rookie of Yr., Ladies Profl. Golf Assn., 1964, Most Improved Player, 1967; named Athlete of Yr. Okla. Sports Writers, 1965, Nev. Sports Writers, 1969; winner Western Open tournament, 1965, U.S. Open tournament, 1968, 72, 73. Address: 400 Somers Loop Crystal Bay NV 89402

BERNINGER, EDITH RACHAEL, psychologist; b. Indpls., June 13, 1913; d. William Edward and Ursula Elizabeth (Morgan) Berninger; B.Ed., Ill. State Normal U., 1941; M.S., Ill. State U., 1964. Tchr., St. Anne (Ill.) Community High Sch., 1941-43; editorial sec. Instns. mag., Chgo., 1943-46; staff sec. Rohrer, Hibler & Replogle, indsl. psychologists, Chgo., 1946-62; psychologist Bur. Child Study, Chgo., 1964-66, Dist. 45, Villa Park, Ill., 1966—. Tchr. psychology evening high sch., Lakeview, Wells high schs., Chgo., 1958-62. Mem. Nat. Assn. Sch. Psychologists, Ill. Psychol. Assn., Nat., Ill., Villa Park edn. assns. Methodist. Home: 716 E Division St Lombard IL 60148 Office: 255 W Vermont St Villa Park IL 60181

BERNS, HAZEL MARJORIE SILVERSTEIN (MRS. MILTON BERNS), librarian; b. N.Y.C., Apr. 29, 1920; d. Morris and Amelia (Abrahams) Silverstein; LL.B. (Univ. scholar), St. John's U., 1941; M.L.S., Pratt Inst., 1959; m. Milton Berns, Jan. 31, 1941; children—Patricia (Mrs. Sheldon Weinrib), Neil. Librarian trainee Hewlett Woodmere Pub. Library, Hewlett, N.Y., 1956-59, jr. librarian, 1959-61, sr. librarian, 1961-63, asst. dir., 1963—. Mem. Nassau County Library Assn. (chmn. constitution and by-laws com. 1970-73), Beta Phi Mu, Pi Alpha Tau. Home: 1182 Frocan Ct Hewlett NY 11557 Office: Hewlett Woodmere Pub Library 1125 Broadway Hewlett NY 11557

BERNS, JACQUELINE (MRS. HARRY BERNS), health service adminstr.; b. London, Eng., Aug. 13, 1924; d. Zadik and Bertha (Brown) Heiber; came to U.S., 1946, naturalized, 1955; Diploma in Social Sci., London Sch. Econs., 1944; M.A., Ind. U., 1958; m. Harry Berns, Sept. 27, 1945; children—Leora (Mrs. Steven Zarit), Joanne, Beth. Psychiat. social worker Marion County Child Guidance Clinic, Indpls., 1958-66; dir. social services Marion County Assn. for Retarded Children, Indpls., 1966-72; dir. social services Community Hosp. of Indpls., 1972—. Bd. dirs. Damar Home, Indpls., 1967-73, also founder, pres., 1967-70. Fellow Am. Orthopsychiat. Assn.; mem. Nat. Assn. Social Workers. Home: 7980 N Illinois St Indianapolis IN 46260 Office: 1500 N Ritter Indianapolis IN 46202

BERNSTEIN, ANNE ELAYNE (MRS. RICHARD K. BERNSTEIN), psychoanalyst; b. N.Y.C., Jan. 1, 1937; d. Nathan and Edith (Leon) Hendon; A.B., Columbia, 1958, certificate psychoanalytic medicine, 1970; M.D., Albert Einstein Coll. Medicine, 1962; m. Richard K. Bernstein, Dec. 23, 1956; children—Julie Ann K., Laura Ann K., Jeffrey Milton K. Intern Bronx (N.Y.) Municipal Hosp. Center, 1962-63; resident Mt. Sinai Hosp., N.Y.C., 1963-66; research fellow physiology Albert Einstein Coll. Medicine, N.Y.C., 1963; practice gen. psychiatry, N.Y.C. and Mamaroneck, N.Y., 1966—, practice psychoanalysis, 1970—; instr. dept. psychiatry Mt. Sinai Sch. Medicine, N.Y.C., 1966-69; instr. Columbia Coll. Phys. & Surg., 1970—. Recipient award for continuing med. edn. A.M.A., 1970. Mem. A.M.A., Am. Med. Women's Assn., Am. Psychiat. Assn., N.Y. County Med. Soc., Assn. Psychoanalytic Medicine. Asst. editor Bull. Assn. Psychoanalytic Medicine. Home: 1160 Greacen Point Rd Mamaroneck NY 10543 Office: 1160 Fifth Av New York City NY 10028

BERNSTEIN, ARLENE ROBERTA LEZBERG (MRS. JERROLD GERSHON BERNSTEIN), lawyer; b. Boston, Oct. 31, 1940; d. Samuel and Jeanne C. (Milden) Lezberg; A.B. magna cum laude, Radcliffe Coll., 1961; J.D., Harvard, 1964; m. Jerrold Gershon Bernstein, Aug. 28, 1966; children—Janet Bracha, David Bennett. Admitted to Mass. bar, 1964; practice in Boston, 1973—; staff atty. Boston Legal Aid Soc., 1964-66; asso. firm Venable, Baetjer & Howard, Balt., 1966-68. Bd. dirs. Solomon Schechter Day Sch. Greater Boston, 1972—, pres. women's council, 1970-72. Mem. Am., Mass. bar assns., Mass. Assn. Women Lawyers. Office: 185 Devonshire St Boston MA 02110

BERNSTEIN, BERNICE LOTWIN, govt. ofcl.; b. Menomonie, Wis., Nov. 26, 1908; d. Charles and Fanny (Fein) Lotwin; Ph.B., U. Wis., 1930, LL.D., 1932; m. Bernard Bernstein, Aug. 4, 1938; children—Elinor (Mrs. S. Balka), Kate Louise, Anne Lisa. Admitted to Wis. bar, 1933; prin. atty. NRA, 1933-35; asst. counsel Social Security Bd., 1935-38; asst. gen. counsel FSA, 1938-42; asso. gen. counsel War Manpower Comm., 1942-45; asst. solicitor U.S. Dept. Labor, 1945-47; regional atty. FSA, U.S. Dept. Health, Edn., and Welfare, 1947-66, regional dir., 1966—. Pres. Fed. Bus. Assn. N.Y., 1969-70; chmn. Fed. Regional Council, 1970-71. Recipient 13th ann. Fed. Woman's award, 1973. Mem. Fed., Wis. bar assns., Nat. Council Jewish Women (mem. nat. bd. and nat. exec. com. 1950-63, nat. treas. 1955-59), Order of Coif, Phi Beta Kappa. Home: 34 Elm Ridge Rd Great Neck NY 11024 Office: 26 Federal Plaza New York City NY 10007

BERNSTEIN, BETTY JEAN, civic ofcl.; b. N.Y.C.; d. Julius A. and Esther (Simon) Bernstein; A.B., Bklyn. Coll., 1946; M.A., Columbia, 1948; Ph.D., N.Y.U., 1969. Research asst. prof. Irving Lorge Tchrs. Coll., Columbia U., summer 1943; with Citizens Com. for Children, N.Y.C., 1947—, successively research asst., research asso., 1947-62, asso. dir., 1962—. Vis. lectr. Baruch Coll., City U. N.Y., 1959, Columbia Sch. Pub. Health, Sloan Sch. Hosp. Adminstrn. at Cornell U., Fordham U. Sch. Social Services, N.Y. U. Grad. Program Pub. Health Nursing; cons. ofcl. govt. bodies and pub. ofcls. Mem. fiscal affairs com. Citizens Union; mem. Manhattan Borough Pres.'s Community Planning Bd. 5; mem. community council Greater N.Y. Health Task Force; mem. Mayor's Health Task Force, N.Y.C.; mem. personal health services com. Comprehensive Health Planning Agy. N.Y.C. Bd. dirs. Pub. Health Assn., N.Y.C. Fellow Am. Pub. Health Assn.; mem. League Women Voters, Am. Polit. Sci. Assn., Am. Soc. Pub. Adminstrn., Hermann Biggs Soc., Hadassah, Delpha Phi Epsilon (internat. v.p. 1946-48). Democrat. Club: Womens City. Contbr. articles to profl. and civic jours. Office: 2 Park Av Suite 2310 New York City NY 10016

BERNSTEIN, BEVERLY CHUCHIAN (MRS. ROBERT PAUL BERNSTEIN), educator; b. Los Angeles, Dec. 8, 1932; d. Melvin and Yevnike Mildred (Sabonjian) Chuchian; A.A., Bakersfield Coll., 1951; B.A., U. So. Cal., 1954; M.S., 1958; m. Robert Paul Bernstein, Nov. 18, 1961; children—Brenda Loren, Brigette Lynnelle. Tchr. Ventura (Cal.) Sr. High Sch., 1955-56, East Bakersfield (Cal.) High Sch., 1956-58, Adams Jr. High Sch., Los Angeles, 1958-62, Harding Elementary Sch., Bakersfield, 1972-73, McKinley Elementary Sch., Bakersfield, 1973—. Named Outstanding Woman grad. U. So. Cal., 1954. Mem. Cal. Tchrs. Assn., Bakersfield Elementary Tchrs. Assn., Theta Sigma Phi. Home: 3111 Linden Av Bakersfield CA 93305 Office: McKinley Elementary Sch 601 4th St Bakersfield CA 93304

BERNSTEIN, BLANCHE, economist; b. N.Y.C., Oct. 6, 1912; d. Henry and Annie (Goldstein) Bernstein; B.A., Hunter Coll., 1933; M.A., Columbia, 1936, Ph.D., 1940. Budget, research dir. Joint Distbn. Com., Paris, France, 1945-49; budget and research dir. N.Y. Assn. for New Ams., 1949-51; chief program planning staff Office for Europe FOA, 1951-53; dir. research Community Council, Greater N.Y., 1953-61; cons. to Social Security Adminstrn., 1960-61; chief social affairs br. Bur. Internat. Orgn. Affairs, State Dept., 1961-69; dir. research Center for N.Y.C. Affairs, New Sch. Social Research, 1969—. Mem. U.S. delegation to Social Commn. UN, 1962, 64, 65; U.S. del. to UN Children's Fund, exec. bd., 1962-68, UN Educational, Scientific, Cultural Orgn. 1962-63; mem. U.S. delegation UN Conf. on Prevention of Crime, 1965; chmn. U.S. delegation Latin Am. Conf. on Planning for Children and Youth; mem. task force on social services State Study Commn. for N.Y.C., 1972-73. Mem. Am. Econ. Assn., Am. Statis. Assn., Assn., Acad. Polit. Sci., Nat. Assn. Social Workers. Club: Women's City. Author: Pattern of Consumer Debt, 1940; Deterrents to Prenatal Care and Social Services, 1961; Welfare in New York City, 1970; Distribution of Income in New York City, 1970; Costs of Day Care, 1971; Welfare and Income in New York City, 1971; New York's Jewish Poor and Working Class, 1972; Income Tested Social Benefits in New York City: Adequacy, Incentives, Equity, 1973. Home: 207 E 74th St New York City NY 10021 Office: Center NYC Affairs 66 Fifth Av New York City NY 10011

BERNSTEIN, DOROTHY LEWIS, educator, mathematician; b. Chgo., Apr. 11, 1914; d. Jacob L. and Tillie (Lewis) Bernstein; B.A., M.A., U. Wis., 1934; Ph.D., Brown U., 1939. Instr. math. Mt. Holyoke Coll., 1937-40, U. Wis., 1941-42; research asso. U. Cal. at Berkeley, 1942-43; faculty U. Rochester, 1943-59, prof. math., 1957-59; prof. math. Goucher Coll., 1959—, chmn. dept., 1960-70, 73—; mem. Inst. Advanced Study, Princeton, 1950-51; vis. prof. U. Cal. at Los Angeles, 1957-58, Brown U., 1966-67. Mem. Am. Math. Soc., Math. Assn. Am. (1st v.p. 1972-73), Soc. Indsl. and Applied Math., Am. Assn. U. Profs., Phi Beta Kappa, Sigma Xi. Author: Existence Theorems in Partial Differential Equations, 1950; also articles. Office: Goucher Coll Towson Baltimore MD 21204

BERNSTEIN, FAYE, structural engr., archtl. designer; b. Detroit, July 22, 1943; d. Isadore and Lillian (Emmer) Bernstein; B.S. in Archtl. Engring., U. Miami (Fla.), 1967, 1968-69, 73. Grad. asst. U. Miami, 1968; structural designer Crain and Crouse, Inc., Miami, 1970; archtl. staff Met. Dade County Dept. of Housing and Urban Devel., Miami, 1971-73; archtl. project mgr. Carr Smith, Bechamps, Khoury, architects, engrs., Coral Gables, Fla., 1974—. Registered profl. engr., Fla. Mem. Am. Concrete Inst. Principal works include First Bapt. Ch. South Miami, 1968, Thornton Jr. Coll. Phase II, Chgo., 1970. Home: 6884 N Kendall Dr C-403 Miami FL 33156 Office: 123 Almeria Av Coral Gables FL 33134

BERNSTEIN, FLORENCE SCHNEIDERMAN (MRS. STANLEY JAMES BERNSTEIN), lawyer; b. N.Y.C., Apr. 3, 1929; d. Alexander and Rose (Rosenberg) Schneiderman; B.S. in Law, U. So. Cal., 1964, J.D., 1964; m. Stanley James Bernstein, Mar. 24, 1947; children—David Lee, Mark Daniel. Admitted to Cal. bar, 1965, U.S. Supreme Ct. bar; chief civil div. Los Angeles County Dep. Pub. Defender, 1965-67; consumer advocate Cal. Rural Assistance, 1967-68; practice law Los Angeles, 1968—; partner Rozner, Yorty, Landay, Gibbs, Hodges, Bernstein & Wagner, 1973—. Lectr. continuing edn. of bar, 1966-68; publs. cons., 1967-68. Mem. Am. Bar Assn., State Bar Cal. (mem. com. on debtor-creditor rights 1973—), Los Angeles Lawyers Club, Women's Lawyers Assn., Preventive Law Bar Assn. (pres. 1969), Legion Lex. Democrat. Jewish religion. Home: 3601 Wrightwood Dr North Hollywood CA 91604 Office: 10960 Wilshire Blvd Suite 1808 Los Angeles CA 90024

BERNSTEIN, IRVENE CLAYTON (MRS. NORRIS STANLEY BERNSTEIN), food mfg. co. exec.; b. San Francisco, July 21, 1930; d. Arthur Dan and Helen Ann (Goldstein) Clayton; B.A., U. Cal. at Berkeley, 1952; m. Norris Stanley Bernstein, Sept. 16, 1951; children—Perri Lynn, Robert Clayton. Trainee, Leibes' Dept. Store, San Francisco, 1948-52; with Bernstein's Restaurant, Long Beach, Cal., 1952-56; exec. v.p. Bernsteins' of Long Beach, Inc., Seal Beach, Cal., 1956—. Active A.R.C., United Crusade, United Jewish Appeal, P.T.A., Cub Scouts Am. Mem. Delta Phi Epsilon. Rotaryann. Home: 9309 Marina Pacifica Dr N Long Beach CA 90803 Office: PO Box 428 Seal Beach CA 90740

BERNSTEIN, LEEMARIE BURROWS NOVOGROD (MRS. MAURICE H. BERNSTEIN), editor; b. Stregowa, Russia, July 15, 1911; d. Isaac and Toby (Eidlitz) Novogrodsky; came to U.S., 1914, naturalized, 1927; student Hunter Coll., N.Y. U., Rabinovitch Art Workshop, Columbia, Mus. Modern Art, Coll. City N.Y.; m. Maurice H. Bernstein, Dec. 16, 1956. Exec. sec., adminstrv. asst. to pres. Fairchild Aerial Camera & Instrument Corp., Jamaica, N.Y., 1935-42, labor relations supr. for women, 1942-46; free lance photographer, 1946-52; art research, asst. to dir. design Look Mag., N.Y.C., 1952-72. Mem. Aux. to N.Y. State Optometric Assn. (pres. 1973—), Aux. to Greater N.Y. Optometric Soc. (pres. 1968-73), Columbia U. Sch. Social Work Alumnus. Fine arts editor Portrait of Jesus, 1972. Home: 349 E 49th St New York City NY 10017 Office: 318 W 56th St New York City NY 10019

BERNSTEIN, SYLVIA, artist; b. Bklyn., Apr. 11, 1920; student Arthur Covey, Gifford Beal, Sidney Dickinson at N.A.D. Exhibited in one-man shows at Columbia (S.C.) Mus., 1966, Ruth White Gallery, N.Y.C., 1956, 59, 60; exhibited in group shows at Butler Inst. Am. Art, 1957, 58, 68, Audubon Artists, 1957, Portland (Me.) Mus. Art, 1957, Exchange Exhbn., Berlin, Germany, Galerie Boss-Petrides, Paris, France, Silvermine Guild Artists, 1957, 58, 59, Chautauqua Inst., 1958, Am. Acad. Arts and Letters, Galerie Irla Kerk, others; represented in permanent collections at N.Y.U., Wadsworth Atheneum, Hartford, Ball State Tchrs. Coll., Norfolk Mus. Art, Hudson River Mus., Yonkers, N.Y., Adlai E. Stevenson Meml. Inst., Chgo., U. Me., Corcoran Gallery, Washington, Whitney Mus., N.Y.C., others. Recipient Jane C. Stanley Meml. award, 1954, 57; Samuel Mann Meml. award, 1960; New Haven R.R. Painting competition, 1956; Grumbacher award Silvermine Guild Artists, 1957; Laura M. Gross Meml. award, 1959; Soc. Four Arts award, 1960; Dawson Meml. medal; Aileen O. Webb award, 1972, medal of Honor, 1974 (both Nat. Assn. Women Artists); numerous others. Mem. N.Y. Soc. Women Artists, Audubon Artists, Phila. Watercolor Soc., Knickerbocker Artists. Address: 8 Circle Rd Scarsdale NY 10583

BERNSTEIN, THERESA, artist; b. Phila.; d. Isidore and Anne (Ferber) Bernstein; student Pa. Acad. Phila. Sch. of Design, Art Students League; m. William Meyerowitz, 1919. Mem. jury of awards Nat. Assn. of Women Artists, 1920-29; dir. Salons of Am., 1924-30; chmn. N.Y. Soc. of Woman Artists, 1935-36; dir. Independent Artists; life mem. Grand Central Art Galleries, N.Y.; represented in permanent collections U.S. Nat. Mus., Washington, Library of Congress, Phillips Meml. Art Gallery, Chgo. Art Inst., Met. Mus. Art, N.Y. Pub. Library, Bklyn. Mus., Cushing Acad. Mass., Philathea Coll. Mus. Modern Art, others, also pvt. collections; represented Art U.S.A. by painting Jazz Players; one-man shows Butler Inst. Am. Art, 1973-74, N.Y. St.-Pernenant Coll., 1974; exhbns. including Carnegie Inst., N.A.D., Cooper Union Mus., Boston Public Library, Philadelphia (Pa.) Museum; one-man show Nat. Mus., Smithsonian Instn., Fitchburg Art Mus., Doll & Richards, Inc., Boston, Publick House, Sturbridge, U. Me., Orono, 1963, Bar Harbor (Me.) Gallery, Columbus (Ga.) Mus., Gainesville (Ga.) Mus., Ogunquit Art Center, Norfolk, Va., others; dir. summer art course, Gloucester, Mass. Chmn. Meml. Exhibit Cape Ann Festival, 1958-64. Recipient Phillips prize for Progressive Painting, 1946; Margaret Cooper prize (oil portrait), Sarah, Nat. Assn. Women Artists, 1951, Jane Peterson prize, 1955, Robert Dain prize; Green traveling fellowship, John Sartain scholarship, Phila. Bd. Edn. scholarship; hon. mention, Soc. Am. Graphic Artists, 1954. Knickerbocker Artists, 1956; Matson prize Rockport Art Assn., 1967, New Eng. Artists award, 1967; Canterella prize Nat. Assn. Women Artists, 1968, Meml. prize, 1970, John A. Johnson Meml. award, 1971 (both North Shore Arts Assn.). Mem. jury of awards Nat. Assn. Women Artists, 1948-50, mem. jury of oil painting, 1959. Mem. Nat. Assn. Women Artists (nominating com. 1963-64), Boston Printmakers Assn., Cape Ann Soc. Artists, Nat. Assn. Women Artists, N.Y. Soc. Women Artists (hon. dir.), North Shore Arts Assn. (hon.), Cape Ann Soc. Artists, Conn. Acad. Fine Arts, Soc. Am. Color Prints, Audubon Artists Am. (mem. oil jury 1957-58), Allied Artists Am. Contbr. on art and graphic art mags., newspapers. Studio Address: 54 W 74th St New York City NY 10023 (summer) 44 Mt Pleasant Av East Gloucester MA 01930

BERRES, FRANCES S. BRANDES (MRS. GEORGE BERRES), psychologist, educator; b. Chgo., Oct. 30, 1915; d. Max and Anna (Gould) Brandes; B.A., U. Cal. at Los Angeles, 1937, M.A., 1940, Ph.D., 1967; m. George Berres, July 6, 1941; children—Barbara (Mrs. Francois M. LoMonaco). Tchr., psychology Clin. Sch., U. Cal. at Los Angeles, 1938-40, clin. psychologist, 1950-52, asso. dir. Fernald Sch., psychology dept. U. Cal., 1952-72; coordinator child related Programs information Project Neuropsychiat. Inst., U. Cal. Med. Sch., Los Angeles, 1972—; head remedial instrn. Huntington Beach U. High Sch., 1940-44; certified clin. psychologist, 1940—, marriage, family and child counselor. Cons. to sch. dists.; cons. to educationally-handicapped programs. Mem. Am. Psychol. Assn., Internat., Los Angeles (dir.) reading assns., Council Exceptional Children, Pi Lambda Theta. Author (with J.C. Coleman, W. Briscoe, F.M. Hewett) Deep Sea Adventure Series, 1958, 62, 71; Teacher's Manual for Deep Sea Adventure Series, 1959, 62, 71; also articles in profl. jours., chpts. in books. Office: 740 Westwood Blvd Los Angeles CA 90024

BERRY, ALMEDIUS BLANCHE, librarian; b. Chesterfield County, Va., June 25, 1920; d. Richard Cornelius and Maude (Patterson) Berry; B.S., Va. State Coll., 1941; B.S. in L.S., Syracuse U., 1945. Tchr., Evans Elementary Sch., Church Road, Va., 1942-44; asst. librarian Keney Br. Library, Hartford, Conn., 1945-47; asst. librarian Detroit Pub. Library, 1948; librarian Dinwiddie County Jr. High Sch., Dinwiddie, Va., 1949—. Rep. Dinwiddie County Edn. Fed. Credit Union, 1960—. Area v.p. Bapt. Gen. Conv. Va., 1970-73, sec. woman's aux., 1973—, woman's aux. Shiloh Bapt. Assn., 1966—. Mem. Am., Va. library assns., Nat., Va., Dinwiddie edn. assns., Alpha Kappa Alpha, Beta Phi Mu. Baptist (clk. 1958—). Mem. Order Eastern Star (dist. chmn., 1970—, sr. matron 1963-65), United Order of Tents (nat. grand sr. matron 1971-73), Heroines of Jericho of Va., Order Golden Circle, Nat. Ideal Benefit Soc. Home: 16900 Harrowgate Rd Colonial Heights VA 23834 Office: PO Box 364 Dinwiddie VA 23841

BERRY, BESSIE MAE THOMPSON, social worker; b. Memphis; d. Benjamin and Gertrude (Sanders) Thompson; B.S. in Bus. Edn., Tenn. A & I State U., 1956; postgrad. Syracuse U., Elmira Coll., 1974—; children—Theodore, Carmela. Protective service caseworker Chemung County Dept. Social Services, Elmira, N.Y., 1961-67; probation officer Chemung County Probation Dept., Elmira, 1967—. Mem. Elmira (N.Y.) Bd. Edn., 1966—. Mem. N.A.A.C.P. (dir. 1964-66), Chemung County Probation Officers Assn. (pres. 1971-72), Methodist (sec. trustee bd. 1972—). Home: 1300 W Church St Elmira NY 14905 Office: 203-209 William St Elmira NY 14901

BERRY, DOROTHY ANN, security co. exec.; b. Clinton, Mass., Sept. 12, 1943; d. Samuel J. and Frances (Heinig) Berry; A.B., Vassar, 1965; J.D., N.Y. Law Sch., 1973. Pres., Banner Personnel Cons., Inc., Worcester, Mass., 1965-66; account supr. Landco Labs, Inc., N.Y.C., 1966-67; office mgr., asst. v.p. Arnold Bernhard & Co., 1967-68, v.p., 1972—; v.p. adminstr. Value Line Securities, 1968—; pres., dir. Shareholders Services, Inc., 1974—; v.p., Arnold Bernhard & Co., Inc., 1974—. Mem. Am. Assn. U. Women, Nat. Assn. Security Dealers. Home: 160 E 48th St Apt 9J New York City NY 10017 Office: 5 E 44th St New York City NY 10017

BERRY, ESTHER FEATHERER (MRS. LOREN MURPHY BERRY), broadcasting co. exec., journalist; b. Phila., Dec. 8, 1939; d. Norman Peterson and Esther (White) Featherer; B.A. in Polit. Sci., Dickinson Coll., 1961; postgrad. U. Mo. Grad. Sch. Journalism, 1962-64; m. Loren Murphy Berry III, June 29, 1968. News writer sta. KOMU-TV, Columbia, Mo., 1963-64; news documentary research writer sta. WRCV-TV, Phila., 1965; news writer, reporter, producer sta. KXJB-TV, Fargo, N.D., 1965-66; news writer sta. WMAQ-TV, Chgo., 1966-71, Midwest network assignment editor, supr. news operations, 1971—. Mem. Am. Field Service, 1956—. Jr. governing bd. Chgo. Symphony Orch., 1972—, mem. exec. com. bd., 1972—. Mem. Women in Communications (v.p. 1973-74), Am. Women in Radio and TV, Radio and TV News Dirs. Assn., Nat. Acad. TV Arts and Scis. Methodist. Home: 6675 N Sioux Av Chicago IL 60646 Office: 19th floor Merchandise Mart Chicago IL 60654

BERRY, EVALENA HOLLOWELL POOL (MRS. HOMER L. BERRY), assn. exec.; b. Akron, O., Feb. 5, 1921; d. James E. and Theresa (King) Hollowell; B.A., Ark. Coll., 1942; M.S., U. Ark., 1954; m. Albert Allen Pool, Jr., Nov. 12, 1942 (dec. Nov. 1949); 1 son, Albert Allen III; m. 2d, Homer L. Berry, June 8, 1954 (dec. Dec. 1955). Tchr. pub. sch., Pulaski County, Ark., 1943-45, 50-52, Clarendon, 1948-49, Fayetteville, 1949-50, Little Rock, 1952-61; dir. publs. and editor Jour. Ark. Edn., Little Rock, 1961-68; asst. exec. sec. information and instrn. Ark. Edn. Assn., 1968—. Tchr. Capitol City Bus. Coll., Little Rock, part-time 1952-55, English courses, Little Rock AFB, 1956-57; speaker, cons. various edn. assns., 1961—. Mem. Ark. Womens Com. Pub. Affairs, 1966-67, edn. chmn., 1970-71, membership chmn., 1971-72; rep. to Ark. Council Children and Youth, 1961—, mem. exec. com., 1969-72; mem. Gov.'s Commn. Status Women, 1971-72; mem. State Title III Adv. Council, 1968—; mem. Ark. Ednl. TV Curriculum Steering Com., 1969—; mem. com. legislative orgn. Ark. Legislature, 1971; charter mem. Ark. Edn. Research and Devel. Council. Mem. N.E.A. (mem. adv. com. communications 1971-72), Nat. Staff Assn. for Improvement Instrn. (sec. 1973—), Ark. Edn. Assn., Am. Assn. U. Women (div. state bd. mem., br. chmn. edn. 1963-67, legislative chmn. Little Rock br. 1969-71, rep. edn. Ark. div. 1971-73, implementation chmn. edn. Ark. div. 1971-73, 1st v.p. 1973—), Ark. Congress Parents and Tchrs. (mem. state bd. 1965—, 5th v.p. edn. 1969-71, human relations chmn. 1971-73), Nat. Sch. Pub. Relations Assn. (charter mem. Ark. chpt., state coordinator 1972—), Women's Nat. Book Assn. (charter mem. Ark. chpt.), Nat. League Am. Pen Women, Kappa Delta Pi, Alpha Delta Kappa (chpt. charter mem., state bd. dirs. 1958—). Presbyn. Club: Little Rock Altrusa (pres. 1967-68). Editor: Ark. div. Am. Assn. U. Women Bull., 1963-68. Contbr. articles to publs. Home: 2724 Fair Park Blvd Little Rock AR 72204 Office: 1500 W 4th St Little Rock AR 72201

BERRY, JOHNNIE RENÉ CURTIS (MRS. EMMETT ALLISTON, JR.), home economist; b. Brookhaven, Miss., May 19, 1947; d. John William and Rene (Wright) Curtis; A.A., Copiah-Lincoln Jr. Coll., 1968; B.S., U. Miss., 1970; M.Ed. in Sch. Adminstrn., Miss. State U., 1974; m. Emmett Alliston, Jr., June 6, 1971. Asst. home economist Miss. Coop. Extension Service, Vicksburg, 1970-72, extension 4-H youth agt., 1972—. Cons. youth food-nutrition, Vicksburg, Warren County, Miss., 1970—, Food nutrition Meals on Wheels Program, Warren County, Miss., 1971—; guest lectr. U. So. Miss. Home Econs. Assn. Chmn. Urban Housing Task Force, 1971—; mem. Vicksburg Urban Housing Assn., 1971-73; asst. U. Miss. Alumni Found., 1970—; instr. YMCA, Warren County Mental Health Assn., 1972—, Miss. Boat and Water Commn.; active fund raising Heart Assn., Salvation Army, March of Dimes, Hemophilia Found.; safety fire arm instr. Miss. Fish and Game Commn.; mem. exec. bd. Community Services Youth Council; guest exhibitor Miss. Gem and Mineral Show, 1971, 72, 73. Recipient Outstanding Service award Warren County 4-H Adult Leaders Council, 1973. Mem. Am., Miss. home econs. assns., Nat., Miss. (pub. relations co-chmn. 1971-73) assns. extension home economists, Am., Miss. adult edn. assns., Nat., Miss. assns. 4-H youth agts., Nat. Bus. and Profl. Club, Vicksburg Bus. and Profl. Club (exec. com., corr. sec. 1972-73, Young Career Woman 1973), Miss. 4-H All Stars, Vicksburg Jaycetts, Am. Assn. U. Women (area rep. for Community devel.), Miss. 4-H Honor Club, Miss. Gem and Mineral Assn., Heart of Vicksburg Bus. Assn. Methodist. Home: Route 4 Box 245-V Vicksburg MS 39180 Office: Box 706 Vicksburg MS 89180

BERRY, JUNE EVANGELINE, educator; b. Torrington, Conn., June 1, 1925; d. Harold Kett and Marjorie Beatrice (Card) Berry; A.B., Brigham Young U., 1947; M.S., U. Utah, 1952; Ed.D., Brigham Young U., 1970. Librarian, Brigham Young U., Provo, Utah, 1948-68; instr. Coll. Ida., Caldwell, 1968-73; curriculum specialist Granite Sch. Dist., Salt Lake City, 1971—. Cons. to various libraries, Utah, Ida., Cal., Neb., N.M., Colo. Utah Library Assn. scholar 1968; Western States Small Schools Project grantee, 1970-71. Mem. Am., Utah (chmn. sch. sect. 1967-68) library assns., Am. Assn. U. Women (pres. Provo 1962). Mem. Ch. of Jesus Christ of Latter-day Saints (stake dir. libraries 1971—). Editor Utah Reading Rev., 1966-68. Home: RFD 1 Box 129 Payson UT 84651 Office: Webster Sch Magna UT 84044

BERRY, MARGARET C., coll. adminstr.; b. Dawson, Tex., Aug. 8, 1915; d. Winfred and Lillian (McCluney) Berry; B.A., U. Tex., 1937; M.A., Columbia, 1943, Ed.D., 1965. Tchr. El Campo (Tex.) High Sch., 1937-41, Freeport (Tex.) High Sch., 1941-42, Ball High Sch., Galveston, Tex., 1942-47; asst. dean-registrar Navarro Jr. Coll., Corsicana, Tex., 1947-50; dean of women East Tex. State U., Commerce, 1950-62; asso. dean women U. Tex., Austin, 1962-68, asst. dean students, 1968-69, asso. dean students, 1969-71, dir. research and devel. programs, office v.p. for student affairs, 1970—. mem. exec. bd. Austin Drug Control, 1971-73. Mem. Nat. (chmn. research com. 1969-71, editor jour. 1972—), Tex. (pres. 1953-55) assns. women deans, adminstrs. and counselors, Am. Coll. Personnel Assn., Am. Personnel and Guidance Assn., Nat., Tex. (v.p. 1971-73), assns. student personnel adminstrs., Alpha Lambda Delta (v.p. nat. exec. bd. 1971—), Delta Kappa Gamma (chpt. pres. 1957-59). Methodist. Home: 3705 Stevenson Av Austin TX 78703

BERRY, MARIE BRAUN, librarian; b. San Antonio, Tex., Aug. 15, 1913; d. Alois E. and Pauline Marie (Schattenberg) Braun; student San Antonio Jr. Coll., 1934-35, Tex. Lutheran Coll., Seguin, 1936, St. Mary's U., San Antonio, 1937-40; B.A. in L.S., Our Lady of Lake Coll., San Antonio, 1957; m. Clarence Matthew Berry, Feb. 3, 1942; 1 dau., Marie Suzette. Library asst. San Antonio Pub. Library, 1934-35, 37-42, reference librarian, 1954-58, head history, gen. reference and social sci. dept., 1958-68, reference librarian, 1969-73, head history, gen. reference and social sci. dept., 1974—. Mem. Tex., Am., Bexar library assns., Librarians Council San Antonio (chmn. 1958-59), San Antonio Pub. Library Staff Assn. (Outstanding Staff award 1968), Tex. (dir. 1967-68), San Antonio (dir. 1967-68) hist. assns., Am. Assn. U. Women, Assn. Tex. Pioneers, San Antonio Conservation Assn., Alpha Beta Alpha. Home: 213 Overhill Dr San Antonio TX 78228

BERRY, MARY FRANCES, educator; b. Nashville, Feb. 17, 1938; d. George Ford and Frances (Southall) Berry; student Fisk U., 1954-55; B.A., Howard U., 1961, M.A., 1962; Ph.D., U. Mich., 1966, J.D., 1970. Asst. prof. history Central Mich. U., 1966-68; asst. prof. history Eastern Mich. U., 1968-69, asso. prof., 1970; asso. prof. history U. Md., College Park, 1969-74, provost dir. behavioral and social scis., 1974—. Mem. adv. bd. Afro-Am. Bicentennial Corp., 1973; cons. Office Policy Planning, Dept. Housing and Urban Devel., 1972-73, Office Civil Rights, Dept. Health, Edn. and Welfare, 1973—. Civil War Round Table fellow, 1965-66. Mem. Assn. for Study Negro Life and History (mem. exec. council 1972—), Am. Hist. Assn. (com. on women historians), Orgn. Am. Historians, Am. Soc. Legal History, So. Hist. Assn., Phi Alpha Theta. Author: Black Resistance White Law: A History of Constitutional Racism in America, 1971. Home: 1656 34th St NW Washington DC 20007 Office: 2141 Tydings Bldg U Md College Park MD 20742

BERRY, NORMA NIERSTHEIMER (MRS. WILLARD DENNY BERRY), clubwoman; b. Pekin, Ill., Sept. 9, 1913; d. Adolph Casper and Anna Sophia (Beimfohr) Niersheimer; B.S., Northwestern U., 1934; m. Willard Denny Berry, July 2, 1938; children—Mrs. Barbara Bill Denny, Susan (Mrs. John Senner). Vice pres. W.D. Berry Shoe Corp., Tacoma, Wash., 1951-68. Regional dir. for Wash., Mont., B.C., Alpha Omicron Pi, 1964-69, internat. sec.-treas., 1969-71, internat. Panhellenic del., 1971-73, 1st alternate internat. Panhellenic del., 1973—. Leader Girl Scouts U.S.A., Seattle, 1951-54, 58-62; pres. Harriet Stimson Guild, Children's Orthopedic Hosp. and Med. Center, Seattle, 1955-57, chmn. ways and means com., 1957-69, charter mem. guild adv. com., 1964-68; mem. Assistance League Seattle, 1970—, chmn. scholarship com., 1973-74. Mem. North End Round Table (chmn. 1968-71, sec. 1971—). Clubs: Sand Point Golf, Washington Athletic (Seattle). Home: 3030 W Laurelhurst Dr NE Seattle WA 98105

BERRY, ROSE AUERSPERG (MRS. ROBERT NEWTON BERRY), educator; b. Hazen, Ark.; d. William and Rosa (Hansel) Auersperg; B.S.E., State Coll. Ark.; M.S., U. Ark.; postgrad. U. Md., U. Mich., Peabody Coll.; Ed.D., U. Ark., 1966; m. Robert Newton Berry; 1 son, Charles. Former tchr. elementary sch. Mississippi County Schs., Prairie County Schs., Little Rock Pub. Schs.; mem. summer staff U. Ark., Fayetteville, 1954-64; prof. edn., chmn. elementary and early childhood edn. dept. U. Ark., Little Rock, 1961—. Adviser, N.E.A., Assn. for Childhood Edn. Internat. Recipient Annie Webb Blanton Internat. Scholarship award for grad. study, 1966; named Tchr. of Year, Greater Little Rock Fedn. Women's Clubs, 1969, Outstanding Woman Educator, Bus. and Profl. Women's Clubs; J.L. Milton Children's Book award, 1972. Mem. N.E.A., Ark. Edn. Assn., Elementary Kindergarten and Nursery Edn. Assn., Assn. for Student Teaching, Assn. for Childhood Edn. Internat. (state pres. 1962-64, editorial bd. 1965-67, v.p. representing early adolescence 1970-73), Am. Assn. U. Women, So. Assn. for Children under Six, Am. Assn. U. Profs., Women's Nat. Book Assn., Ark. Library Assn., Internat. Reading Assn., Central Ark. Reading Council (pres. 1973-74), Am. Bus. Women's Assn., Altrusa, Delta Kappa Gamma (chpt. pres. 1956-58, state publicity and publs. chmn. 1972—, internat. chmn. com. on research 1972-74), Kappa Kappa Iota (state sec.), Delta Kappa Pi, Phi Mu (v.p. 1967). Home: 146 Ridge Rd Little Rock AR 72207

BERRY, SANDRA LEE, univ. adminstr.; b. Battle Creek, Mich., Aug. 3, 1947; d. Orvis Lynn and Edeth Lavon (Spaulding) Berry; A.A., Kellogg Community Coll., 1967; B.A. (Univ. scholar), Mich. State U., 1969, M.A., 1971, postgrad. U. Akron, 1973—. Resident hall dir. Western Mich. U., Kalamazoo, 1970-71; counselor, adviser students U. Akron (O.), 1971—, originator, univ. coordinator Center for Concern, U. Vol. Program, 1972-74, adviser Alpha Lambda Delta, 1974—. Mem. Nat. Assn. Women Deans, Adminstrs. and Counselors, Nat. Orgn. Women, Phi Beta Kappa. Home: 145-F W Overdale Tallmadge OH 44278

BERRYMAN, ALICE DAVIS (MRS. CECIL WELLS BERRYMAN), concert pianist, composer, educator; b. North Platte, Nebraska; d. George Warren and Alice (Clark) Davis; studied piano with August Borglum, Omaha, Wager Swayne, Paris, Rudolph Ganz, Switzerland, Me., Denver, N.Y.; mus. analysis Cecil Berryman; theory, harmony, composition and orchestration with Emile Schwartz, Paris; music course New Coll., Oxford, 1969; m. Cecil Wells Berryman, Dec. 19, 1916; children—Edward Davis, Warren Leigh, Rudolph Barton. Concert pianist, numerous concerts alone and jointly with husband and three sons, Paris, N.Y. and Midwest, 1912—; debut Princess Theatre, N.Y., 1915; accredited tchr. piano Berryman Piano Conservatory, 1916-60, U. Omaha, 1930-56; work shop tchrs. and players courses Presbyn. U., 1929; nat. judge of piano, Tex., Ia., Ohio, Va., Tenn., Wis., Alaska, 1939—; judge internat. record contests, 1954—. Mem. Hall of Fame, Piano Guild U.S.A. Mem. Am. Coll. Musicians (nat. membership com.), Nat., Neb. (exec. com.; certification chmn.), Omaha music tchrs. assns., Nat. Guild Piano Tchrs. (faculty mem.), P.E.O. Presbyn. Compositions for piano include Play Me a Story, Swinging on the High Trapeze, 1960. Home: 5018 Izard St Omaha NE 68132

BERRYMAN, DORIS LAVERNE, educator; b. Denver, June 23, 1926; d. Edward Hussen and Mable Laverne (Wilcoxson) Berryman; B.A., Denver U., 1948; M.A., Tchrs. Coll., Columbia, 1959; Ph.D., N.Y. U., 1970. Recreation worker Meml. Sloan-Kettering Cancer Center, N.Y.C., 1950-54, asst. dir., 1955-56, dir. recreation, 1956-59; research asso. Nat. Recreation Assn., 1959-61; research asso. Comeback, Inc., N.Y.C., 1963-65, asso. dir., 1965-67; research scientist, N.Y. U., N.Y.C., 1967-70; asso. prof. edn., 1970-73, prof., 1973—. Trustee Nat. Recreation and Park Assn., 1972—. Mem. Nat. Therapeutic Recreation Soc. (dir. 1969-72), Am. Ednl. Research Assn., Am. Assn. U. Profs., Am. Assn. Mental Deficiency, Nat. Rehab. Assn., Rehab. Internat. Assn., Soc. Park and Recreation Educators, Alpha Kappa Delta, Pi Lambda Theta. Editors: Therapeutic Recreation Annual, 1970; Therapeutic Recreation Jour., 1972—. Home: 100 Bleecker St New York City NY 10012

BERRY-TISDALE, EVELYN RUTH DANIEL (MRS. FLOYD W. TISDALE), bus. exec.; b. Corinth, Miss.; d. Robert Knight and Willie (Andrews) Daniel; student U. Tex., 1934; m. John Scott Berry, Jan. 22, 1936 (dec. Mar. 1964); 1 son, John Scott (dec. 1965); m. 2d, Floyd W. Tisdale, Jan. 5, 1973. Window decorator, mgr. personalized advt., sales and office Marie Antoinette, Austin, Tex., 1934-36; free-lance fashion model, N.Y.C., 1937; mgr., window dresser Ladies Dress Shops, Bklyn., and Hazelton, Pa., 1938; owner, mgr. Berry Engring. Co., 1964-65, 65-66, inc., 1966, sec.-treas., dir., 1966—; counsellor Snelling and Snelling Personnel Cons., 1966—. Active A.R.C., March of Dimes. Bd. dirs. Humane Soc. Harrison County, 1952-58, Miss. Gulf Coast chpt. A.R.C. Asso. chmn. Nat. Bible Week. Mem. Internat. Platform Assn., Am. Security Council (adv. com. 1970-73). Methodist. Home: 108 Sea Pine Av Long Beach MS 39560 Office: PO Box 342 Long Beach MS 39560

BERTELL, SISTER HELEN ROSALIE, nun, cancer researcher; b. Buffalo, Apr. 4, 1929; d. Paul G. and Helen J. (Twohey) Bertell; B.A. magna cum laude, (scholar 4 years), D'Youville Coll., 1951; M.A., Catholic U. Am., 1959, (NIH grantee 3 years), Ph.D., 1966. Joined Order Grey Nuns of Sacred Heart; asst. prof., registrar Sacred Heart Jr. Coll., 1958-68; coordinator high sch. math., Atlanta, 1968-69; asso. prof. D'Youville Coll., 1969-73; cancer research Roswell Park Meml. Inst., 1970—. Organist, Our Lady of Lourdes Parish; asst. research prof. Grad. Sch. State U. N.Y. at Buffalo; cons.; notary pub. Commonwealth Pa., 1966-70; mem. exec. bd. Sisters Assembly Buffalo, 1971—. Recipient Outstanding Civic Leader award, Atlanta, 1968, Outstanding Tchr. Am. award 1973. Mem. Nat. Assn. Women Religious (N.Y. state regional bd. 1973-74), Sigma Xi, Kappa Gamma Pi. Home: 422 West Av Buffalo NY 14213 Office: 666 Elm St Buffalo NY 14203

BERTELS, SISTER THOMAS MORE, educator; b. Ironwood, Mich., Jan. 8, 1918; d. Louis Henry and Elizabeth Malvina (LaForge) Bertels; B.A., Silver Lake Coll., 1943; M.A., Cath. U. Am., 1949, Ph.D., 1962. Joined Franciscan Sisters of Christian Charity, 1939; tchr. St. Francis High Sch., Hollandtown, Wis., 1943-44, St. Willibrord High Sch., Chgo., 1944-48, Cath. Meml. High Sch., Waukesha, Wis., 1949-58; faculty Silver Lake Coll., Manitowoc, Wis., 1960—, prof. history, 1967—, pub. relations dir., 1971—. Mem. com. for social devel. and world peace U.S. Cath. Conf., Washington, 1971-73. Mem. Manitowac (Wis.) Citizens Adv. Council, 1967-71; Pres. Manitowoc County Hist. Soc., 1966-68; mem. Manitowoc Selective Service Bd., 1972—; organizer Wis. Women for Agr., 1973. Bd. dirs. Nat. Cath. Rural Life Conf., 1965—. Recipient Gold Cross award Ind. Farmers Alliance, 1972. Mem. Orgn. Am. Historians, Wis. State Grange, League of Women Voters (dir. 1962—). Republican. Home and office: Rural Route 5 Manitowoc WI 54220

BERTHOLD, JEANNE SAYLOR, psychologist, nurse; b. Kansas City, Mo., June 4, 1924; d. Carl Richard and Ann Elizabeth (Wolfe) Saylor; R.N., Highland Hosp. Sch. Nursing, 1945; B.S., U. Cal. at Berkeley, 1953, M.S. in Psychiat. Nursing, 1955, Ph.D. in Counseling psychology, 1961. Pub. health staff nurse Vis. Nurse Assn., Los Angeles, 1945-46; sch. nurse, Los Angeles, 1946-47; staff asst. Sonoma County Hosp., Santa Rosa, Cal., 1947-51; psychiat. nurse Langley Porter Neuropsychiat. Inst., San Francisco, 1955-61; asst. prof. Francis Payne Bolton Sch. Nursing Case Western Res. U., 1961-63, asso. prof., 1963-64, prof., 1964-71; prof. U. Colo. Sch. Nursing, Denver, 1971-73; prof. community medicine and pub. health U. So. Cal. Sch. Medicine, 1973—; dir. nursing research Rancho Los Amigos Hosp., Downey, Cal., 1973—; instr., lectr. Sch. Nursing U. Cal. Med. Center, 1955-61; program dir. Regional Program Nursing Research and Devel., Boulder, Colo., 1971-73; participant numerous confs. and seminars. Mem. Highland Alumnae Assn., Nat. League Nursing, Cal. Alumni Assn., Am. Nurses' Assn., Am. Psychol. Assn., Am. Assn. U. Profs. Am. Ednl. Research Assn., Nat. Council Measurement Edn., N.Y.C. Acad. Scis., A.A.A.S., Common Cause, Pi Lambda Theta, Sigma Theta Tau. Contbr. articles to profl. jours. Home: 6121 Carpentero Lakewood CA 90713 Office: 7601 E Imperial Hwy Downey CA 90242

BERTLING, WILMA CHIDESTER (MRS. WALTER E. BERTLING), mus. ofcl.; b. Conklin, N.Y., July 26, 1929; d. David J. and Emily H. (Morris) Chidester; B.A., Syracuse U., 1951; m. Walter E. Bertling, Sept. 28, 1957. Mng. editor Alumni News Mag., Syracuse (N.Y.) U., 1951-52; printing coordinator Artcraft-Burow Printers, Buffalo, 1952-56; dir. publs. U. Buffalo, 1956-61; asst. publicity dir. Canisius Coll., Buffalo, 1962-63; curator edn. Buffalo and Erie County Hist. Soc., Buffalo, 1964-70, chief adminstrn., 1970—. Mem. Am. Assn. State and Local History. Home: 5 Georgetown Ct Williamsville NY 14221 Office: 25 Nottingham Ct Buffalo NY 14216

BERTON, ALBERTA DESIRÉE, med. librarian; b. Phila., Sept. 9, 1916; d. Albert Ernest and Marguerite Alma (Sutherland) Berton; student U. Pa., 1936. Free-lance lit. scientist, 1949-59; research librarian William H. Rorer, Ft. Washington, Pa., 1959-63, Nat. Drug Co., Phila., 1963-67; bus. mgr. COPNIP List, 1966—; dir. Med. Documentation Service Coll. Physicians, Phila., 1967—. Dir. Documentation Abstracts, Inc., 1971—, treas., 1973—. Mem. Montgomery County Rep. Com., 1949-52. Mem. Spl. Libraries Assn. (chpt. pres. 1969-71, membership chmn. 1971-72), Assn. Advancement of Sci. Information, Med. Library Assn., Nat. Microfilm Assn., Am. Med. Writers Assn., Drug Information Assn. (conf. chmn. 1973, editor Jour. 1973—), Pa. Library Assn., A.A.A.S. Author: (with Oliver H. Buchanan) History of Computers in Biomedicine, 1971. Editor: Proc. Nat. Colloquium on Information Retrieval: The Social Impact of Information Retrieval, 1970; Birth Defects, 1967-70, Cystic Fibrosis, 1967—, Bull. Phila. chpt. Spl. Libraries Assn., 1970-72, Newsletter Del. Valley chpt. Am. Soc. for Information Sci., 1970-72. Home: 913 County Line Rd Huntingdon Valley PA 19006 Office: 19 S 22d St Philadelphia PA 19103

BERTONI, MAE HENRIKSEN (MRS. DANTE H. BERTONI), artist; b. Bklyn., Dec. 17, 1929; d. Elias B. and Fanny (Hansen) Henriksen; student Parsons Sch. Design, 1948-51; m. Dante H. Bertoni, Oct. 18, 1952; children—Rachel, Irene. Artist, Norcross Greeting Card Co., N.Y.C., 1951-63; one man show at Grand Central Art Galleries, 1970; exhibited in group shows at Grand Central Art Galleries, Nat. Arts Club, Jersey City (N.J.) Mus., N.A.D.; represented in permanent collections at William Esty & Co.,

Columbia-Presbyn. Med. Center, N.Y.C., Dewey Ballantyne, N.Y.C. Recipient various 1st prize awards; Gold Medal of Honor, Catherine Lorillard Wolfe Art Club, 1966, 68, Grumbacher Artists Material award Nat. Arts Club, 1964, William Esty purchase prize, 1965, others. Mem. Am. Watercolor Soc., Knickerbocker Artists, Hudson Valley Art Assn., Painters and Sculptors Soc. N.J. Home: 5202 8th Av Brooklyn NY 11220

BERTRAM, JEAN DESALES, author, performing artist, educator; b. Burlington, Ia.; d. Val R. and Ruth C. (Gustafson) Bertram; A.B., U. N.C. at Greensboro; M.A., U. Minn., 1951; Ph.D. (Stanford-Wilson fellow), Stanford, 1963; div.; 1 son, Larkin. Founder, organizer pub. relations dept. Burlington Industries, exec. offices, Greensboro, N.C., 1943-49; dir. radio workshop Mpls. Vocational High Sch., 1951-52; instr. drama San Francisco State U., 1952-63, asst. prof. drama, 1963-66, asso. prof., 1966-72, prof. theatre arts, 1972—; lectr. in field; founder, dir. Jean De Sales Bertram Players; performer readings and impersonations. Drama cons. San Francisco council Girl Scouts U.S.A., 1954—. Author, dir. pageant nat. conv., 1955; recs. for blind Div. Blind and Handicapped, Library of Congress. Mem. Cal. Acad. Sci. Speech Communication Assn., Internat. Soc. Gen. Semantics, Phi Beta Kappa (pres. No. Cal. 1963-65), Delta Phi Lambda. Christian Scientist. Author: Blackbeard, The Pirate, 1951; The Oral Experience of Literature, 1967; also numerous articles on theatre history, speech, and child drama, poetry; co-author: The Emperor's New Clothes, 1953; Cosmorama, 1972; author, editor California Cameos, American Cameos, 1974. Home: 2 Varela Av San Francisco CA 94132

BERTRAM, MANYA MINNIE (MRS. BARRY BERTRAM), lawyer; b. Denver, July 21; d. Samuel and Ruby (Feiner) Boran; J.D. magna cum laude, Southwestern U., 1962; m. Barry Bertram, June 19, 1938; children—Neal, Carel (Mrs. Neal Snyder). Admitted to Cal. bar, 1963, since practiced in Los Angeles; partner firm Most and Bertram, 1963—. Trustee, Beverly Coll. Law, Los Angeles. Mem. Women Lawyers Assn., Internat. Women Lawyers, Am., Los Angeles County bar assns., State Bar Cal., Iota Tau Tau. Office: 9200 Sunset Blvd Los Angeles CA 90069

BERWALD, HELEN DOROTHY, educator; b. Lac Qui Parle County, Minn., Mar. 15, 1925; B.A., U. Minn., 1948, B.S., M.A., 1951, Ph.D., 1962. Tchr., Robbinsdale (Minn.) High Sch., 1951-52; mem. faculty Carleton Coll., Northfield, Minn., 1952—, now prof. edn. Dir. NSF video tape project. Mem. Phi Beta Kappa, Pi Lambda Theta, Delta Kappa Gamma. Home: 208 Elm St Northfield MN 55057

BERZINS, GUNDEGA, occupational therapist; b. Riga, Latvia, Nov. 21, 1942; d. Verners and Ilga Anna (Melngalvis) Fitins; came to U.S., 1952, naturalized, 1966; B.S. in Occupational Therapy, U. Pa., 1965; m. John G. Berzins, May 21, 1966; 1 dau., Elena Zinta. Coordinator pilot pulmonary research project Moss Rehab. Hosp., Phila., 1965-66, sr. therapist pulmonary rehab. research project, 1966-69, asst. chief therapist occupational therapy dept., 1969-70; cons. United Cerebral Palsy Assn. Phila. and vicinity, 1971—; tchr. Sch. Applied Health Professions Temple U., 1967—. Dept. Health, Edn. and Welfare evaluator grant evaluation needs cerebral palsied and epileptic, 1973-74. Mem. Am., Eastern Pa. occupational therapy assns., Assn. Mental Deficiency, Dzintra. Home: 37 A Brookside Dr Lansdale PA 19446 Office: United Cerebral Palsy Assn 4700 Wissahickon Av Philadelphia PA 19132

BESAHA, IRENE REGINA, orgn. exec.; b. East Vandergrift, Pa., Dec. 20, 1918; d. Otto and Mary Catherine (Jackamonis) Bulkowski; student Pa. State Coll.; m. Joseph E. Besaha, July 3, 1939 (dec.); children—Linda (Mrs. Michael Maxwell), Sandra A., Penny A. Various secretarial positions, 1937-60; sec. Kiski Valley United Fund, Vandergrift, Pa., 1960-72, exec. dir., 1972—. Sec., Vandergrift Democratic Com., 1956—; sec. bd. Westmoreland County Dem. Club; councilwoman Borough of Vandergrift, 1972—; sec. Vandergrift Recreation Bd., 1973-74. Roman Catholic. Club: Vandergrift Womans (pres. 1968-70). Home: 122 Jefferson St Vandergrift PA 15690 Office: 112 Grant St Vandergrift PA 15690

BESEN, JANE PHYLLIS TRIPTOW (MRS. IRVING BESEN), civic worker; b. Chgo., Aug. 6, 1921; d. Richard Herman and Rose (Krips) Triptow; student Northwestern U., 1946-47, E. Los Angeles Coll., 1967-68; m. Irving Besen, Mar. 25, 1951; children—Glenn, Allen. Exec. sec. Chgo. Ordance Dist., War Dept., 1941-46, Aubrey, Moore & Wallace, Advt. Agy., Chgo., 1946; exec. sec. sales office McGraw-Hill Pub. Co., Chgo., 1947-51. Publicity chmn. Am. Field Service, 1967-68; sec. Citizens Com. for Good Govt., 1961; capt. United Crusade, Monterey Park, Cal., 1967—; publicity chmn. Monterey Park Art Assn., 1966-67, corr. sec., 1968, dir., 1965—, past pres., dir. newsletter, 1970—; mem. Monterey Park Arts and Culture Com.; dir. in charge Bruggemeyer Library Shows, 1973-74. Dep. registrar voters Cal. State U., Los Angeles, 1971-74. Recipient Top award Alhambra Open Show, 1972. Mem. Nat. League Am. Pen Women (rec. sec., treas. 1961-65), League Women Voters (sec. Alhambra chpt. 1971-73 pres. Alhambra chpt. 1973-74). Home: 1540 Arriba Dr Monterey Park CA 91754

BESHEAR, RAMONA JOY, entomologist; b. Spalding County, Ga., Sept. 14, 1940; d. James Aldine and Laura Louise (Swaney) Beshear; student Ga. State Coll., 1958-65, U. Ga., 1967-68. Agrl. Research asst. III entomology dept. U. Ga. Coll. Agr., 1964—. Mem. Entomol. Soc. Am., Ga. Entomol. Soc., Bartram Trail Soc., Henry County Bus. and Profl. Women's Club (treas. 1963), Henry County Audubon Club, Southeastern Antique Bottle Club. Baptist. Author papers in field; described 4 insects new to sci. Home: Route 3 Box 356 McDonough GA 30253 Office: Univ Ga Coll Agr Experiment GA 30212

BESSANT, HELEN PEARL, educator; b. Waynesboro, Ga., Feb. 27, 1943; d. Oscar Scott and Josie Bell (Cotton) Bessant; A.A., Warren Wilson Jr. Coll., 1961; B.A., Berea Coll., 1963; M.Ed., Temple U., 1965; postgrad. (U.S. Office Edn. fellow), U. Ga., 1965-66; Ph.D. (So. Fellowships Fund fellow), U. Conn., 1972. Tchr. retarded educables, Phila., 1963-65, educable mental retardates, Atlanta, 1966-68; prof. spl. edn. Norfolk (Va.) State Coll., 1968—. Vis. prof. Atlanta U., 1968, Savannah (Ga.) State Coll., 1970; cons. Norfolk Pub. Schs., 1970, Phila. Pub. Schs., 1974, Va. State Sch. for Deaf and Blind, Hampton, 1974—. Mem. Task Force Southeastern Va. Tng. Center for Mentally Retarded, 1972—. Mem. alumni bd. dirs. Warren Wilson Coll., Swannanoa, N.C. Mem. Council for Exceptional Children (faculty adviser Norfolk State Coll. chpt.), Internat. (com. on minority groups, sec. mental retardation div.), Va. Fedn. councils for exceptional children, Am. Assn. Mental Deficiency, Am. Ednl. Research Assn., Sigma Gamma Rho. Mem. Order Eastern Star. Contbr. articles to profl. jours. Home: 944 Round Bay Rd G Norfolk VA 23502

BESSER, AMY (MRS. SAMUEL SINBERG), painter; b. N.Y.C., Nov. 21, 1900; d. Herman Carl and Ray (Hyman) Besser; student Nat. Acad. Art, 1916-18, Art Student League, 1923-25, Parson Inst. Design, 1918-20, Colorossi, Paris, France, 1926, 28; m. Samuel Sinberg, June 18, 1930; 1 dau., Amy. Easel artist, 1929—; exhbns. in U.S., Mexico, France, Monaco, S.Am. Recipient award Washington Art Assn., 1973. Mem. Nat. Assn. Women Artists, Artists Equity, Washington Art Assn. Home: 400 E 58th St New York City NY 10022 Studio: 10 E 23d St New York City NY 10010

BESSER, FANNIE BEAR (MRS. HYMAN BESSER), lawyer; b. Newark, Dec. 18, 1900; d. Max and Etta Bear; LL.B. with highest honors, Rutgers U., 1920, LL.M., 1940; m. Hyman Besser, Nov. 27, 1921; children—Albert G., Edith (Mrs. Harold A. Segall), Ann (Mrs. Gordon H. Scott). Admitted to N.J. bar, 1921, also U.S. Supreme Ct.; practice in Newark. Cons. in personal affairs br. Army Service Forces, 1945-50, Office of Econ. Opportunity, 1968-73. Mem. N.J. Com. for Refugee Relief; chmn. women's div. United Jewish Appeal, 1940; mem. Gov.'s Commn. on Landlords and Tenants. Recipient Outstanding alumnus award Rutgers U. Sch. Law, 1971, citation for meritorious service, Gen. Van Fleet, 1946, Gen. Robertson, 1947. Mem. N.J. Bar Assn. Club: Mountain Ridge Country. Home: 320 S Harrison St East Orange NJ 07018 Office: 744 Broad St Newark NJ 07012

BESSER, GRETCHEN ROUS (MRS. ALBERT GORDON BESSER), educator; b. Bklyn., Dec. 1, 1928; d. Ben and Sidonya (Menkes) Rous; B.A. (Coll. scholar) Wellesley Coll., 1949; postgrad. (Fulbright scholar) Sorbonne, Paris, France, 1949-50; M.A., Middlebury Coll., 1950; Ph.D., Columbia, 1967; m. Albert Gordon Besser, Dec. 28, 1952; children—James Mitchell, Neal Stuart, Brian Henry. Lectr. French, Fairleigh Dickinson U., Teaneck, N.J., 1955-57; preceptor Columbia, 1957-59, 63-67; asst. prof. Lehman Coll., City U. N.Y., 1967-70; lectr. Rutgers U., Newark, 1972-73. Nat. ski patroller, 1970—; instr. first aid A.R.C., 1970—, emergency med. technician, 1973—. Mem. Modern Lang. Assn., Am. Assn. Tchrs. French, Phi Beta Kappa. Jewish religion (trustee congregation). Clubs: Mt. Mansfield Ski; Stowe Tennis; Berkeley Tennis; B and G Riding. Author: Balzac's Concept of Genius, 1969. Translator: The Crossing of the "Copula", 1954; Journey to the Mountain Beyond, 1973; Aggression, 1973. Contbr. articles, book revs. to profl. jours. Home: 227 Tillou Rd South Orange NJ 07079

BESSERMAN, SISTER MARCELLITA, hosp. adminstr.; b. Streator, Ill., Sept. 22, 1913; d. John and Bertha (Turcik) Besserman; R.N., St. John's Sch. Nursing, Springfield, Ill., 1939; Ph.B., DePaul U., 1942; M.H.A., St. Louis U., 1963. Joined Hosp. Sisters of 3d Order of St. Francis, 1931; mem. faculty St. John's Sch. Nursing, 1941; supr. med. service dept. St. John's Hosp., 1942-46; tchr. St. Francis Convent High Sch., Springfield, Ill., 1942-46; adminstr. Our Lady of Ozarks Nursing Center, Carthage, Mo., 1956-61, Home Nursing Center, Carthage, 1956-61; adminstr. residency Providence Hosp., Kansas City, Kan., 1962-63; adminstr. St. Francis Hosp., Litchfield, Ill., 1963-69, Sacred Heart Hosp., Eau Claire, Wis., 1969-71, St. Anthony Meml. Hosp., Effingham, Ill., 1971—. Mem. Emergency Med. Services Com., Effingham; chmn. Effingham City-County Com. Aging; mem. com. Keep Christ in Christmas; mem. strategy com. Drug. and Alcohol Coordinating Council So. Ill. mem. health financing and resources com. sub-region IV, So. Ill. Health Services Coordination Program, Mem. Inter-Faith Prayer Group, Sisters Senate of Springfield Diocese; mem. apostolate com., community and parish council Springfield Diocese, also corr. sec. pastoral care com. Mem. Am., Ill., Cath. hosp. assns., Ill. Conf. Cath. Hosp., Diocesan Conf. Cath. Hosps. (pres. elect 1973), Am. Coll. Hosp. Adminstrs., St. Louis U. Alumni Assn. Address: 503 N Maple St Effingham IL 62401

BESSEY, CAROL HOSSNER (MRS. GRANT BESSEY), newspaper editor; b. Ashton, Ida., Dec. 17, 1919; d. Frederick and Luella Elmertie (Phillips) Hossner; ed. high sch.; m. Grant H. Bessey, Sept. 2, 1944; children—Helen (Mrs. Tom Hutchison), Herbert, Joyce, Jeanette. Editor weekly newspaper Ashton Herald, 1967—. Served with WAC, 1942-45. Mem. Ashton C. of C. (dir. 1973-74). Methodist. Home: Route 1 Ashton ID 83420 Office: 512 Main St Ashton ID 83420

BEST, BARBARA, pub. relations exec.; b. San Diego, Dec. 2, 1921; d. Charles Lewis and Leila Harrison (Sanders) Best; B.A., U. So. Cal., 1943. Publicist, 20th Century Fox, Los Angeles, 1943-49; with Stanley Kramer Co., Los Angeles, 1950-53; owner Barbara Best & Assos., Los Angeles, 1953-66; exec. v.p. Jay Bernstein Pub. Relations, Los Angeles, 1967; v.p., partner Freeman & Best, Inc., Los Angeles, 1967—. Bd. dirs. Vikki Carr Scholarship Found., 1970—. Mem. Hollywood Publicists Assn., Women in Communications, Hollywood Womens Press Club (pres. 1960-61). Home: 4948 Palo Dr Tarzana CA 91356 Office: 8732 Sunset Blvd Los Angeles CA 90069

BEST, LINDA LOUISE RICHMER, psychologist; b. Newark, O., Apr. 12, 1934; d. William Raymond and Mary (Price) Richmer; B.S., Ohio State U., 1959; M.S., U. Mich., 1963; postgrad. U. Toledo, 1970—; m. James R. Best, Aug. 8, 1959. Tchr., Miamisburg, O., 1955-56, Newark, O., 1956-59, Inkster, Mich., 1959-60, Livonia, Mich., 1960-62; psychologist Dearborn (Mich.) pub. schs., 1964-66, U. Toledo, 1971-73, Monroe County (Mich.) Intermediate Sch. dist., 1973—. Vol. Toledo Hosp., 1972-73. Mem. Am. Psychol. Assn. (asso.), Nat. Assn. Sch. Psychologists, Mich. Psychol. Assn., Kappa Delta Pi. Home: 3238 Hargo Rd Toledo OH 43606 Office: Monroe County Intermediate Sch Dist 1101 South Raisinville Rd Monroe MI 48161

BEST, RUTH ANDREW (MRS. GEORGE WASHINGTON BEST), sch. librarian; b. Newton, N.C., Oct. 15, 1915; d. James David and Flora Antoinette (Branson) Andrew; A.B., Catawba Coll., 1936; postgrad. George Peabody Coll. Tchrs., summer 1937; B.A. in L.S., U. N.C., 1940; postgrad. Appalachian State U., 1963; m. George Washington Best, May 12, 1940; children—George Washington, Elizabeth (Mrs. Michael Minier Sargent), Ruth (Mrs. Daniel Eugene Leeper). Librarian, Burlington (N.C.) City Schs., 1957—, Eastlawn Elementary Sch., 1958—. Children's librarian on staff Library/USA for A.L.A., N.Y. World's Fair, summer 1964. Mem. N.C. Assn. Sch. Librarians (dir. 1964-68), Burlington Bus. and Profl. Women's Club (pres. 1969-70), N.C., Alamance County art assns., Alamance County Hist. Soc., Alpha Delta Kappa. Mem. United Ch. of Christ (pres. Women of Ch. 1952). Home: 201 Tarpley St Burlington NC 27215

BESTBREURTJE, ANNIE MARTHA, physician; b. Rotterdam, Netherlands, Apr. 28, 1919; d. Anton Dirk and Hermanna Hendrieka (Worst) Bestebrevrtje; B.A., Freies Gymnasium, Zurich, Switzerland, 1937; candidate of medicine, U. Zurich, 1940; M.D., Johns Hopkins, 1943; m. William N. Fitzpatrick, Oct. 10, 1951; children—William N., Carol J., Hendrieka A., A. Dirk, Martha Wynn, Thomas Vaughan. Intern in pathology Duke Sch. Medicine, 1943-44, resident, instr. pathology, 1945-47, intern, asst. resident, chief resident in pediatrics, 1947-50; rotating intern U. Pitts. Med. Center, 1944-45; research fellow, pediatrician in charge Alfred I. duPont Inst., Wilmington, Del, 1950-51; practice medicine specializing in pediatrics and adolescent medicine, Balt., 1951—; asst. prof. pediatrics U. Md. Med. Sch., 1951—; instr. pediatrics Johns Hopkins, 1969—; pediatric cons. Rosewood State Tng. Sch., Balt., 1951-61; staff Johns Hopkins Hosp., Greater Balt. Med. Center, 1969, U. Md. Hosp., dir. health service Goucher Coll., Towson, Md., 1962—. Mem. Sigma Xi, Alpha Omega Alpha. Presbyn. (elder 1971—). Club: Johns Hopkins (Balt.). Home: 300 Somerset Rd Baltimore MD 21210 Office: 1515 Labelle Av Baltimore MD 21204

BETHEL, SHELBA JEAN, physician; b. Gans, Okla., Sept. 8, 1937; d. Earl Wilson and Pearl Juanita (Brunk) Henry; B.S., Northeastern State Coll., Tahlequah, Okla., 1960; M.D., U. Okla., 1965; m. Lander Bethel, June 2, 1955; children—Lander Louis, Lesa Jean, Steven Henry. Intern, St. Anthony Hosp., Oklahome City, 1965-66, resident pathology, 1966-67, resident obstetrics and gynecology, 1967-70; practice medicine, specializing in obstetrics and gynecology, Norman, Okla., 1970—; mem. staff Norman Municipal Hosp.; cons. Purcell (Okla.) Hosp., Moorse (Okla.) Municipal Hosp., Westinghouse Hosp., Norman, Cleveland County Health Dept. Jr. fellow Am. Fertility Soc., Am. Coll. Obstetrics and Gynecology; mem. Am. (Achievement award 1970), So., Okla. med. assns., Okla., Cleveland-McClain County med. socs., Oklahoma City Obstetrics and Gynecology Soc., Am. Med. Womens Assn., League Women Voters, Oklahoma U., Okla. U. Med. Sch. med. assns. Address: 500 E Robinson St Norman OK 73069

BETRUS, GLADYS WINTERSTEEN, nurse; b. Boise, Ida., Nov. 10, 1919; d. Ora and Olive Mae (Ogle) Barnes; diploma St. Lukes Sch. Nursing, Boise, 1941; student in sociology Ariz. State U.; m. Thomas A. Betrus, Nov. 22, 1947; children—Michael, Patricia. Nurse, U.S. Army, 1941-48; supr. St. Lukes Surgery, 1948; civil service nurse Army Hosp., LaRochelle, France, 1957-60; pub. health nurse Va. Dept. Health, 1961-64; sch. nurse Phoenix Union High Sch. Dist., 1965—. Mem. Am. Nurses Assn., Am. Sch. Health Assn., Ariz. Sch. Nurse Assn. (legislative chmn. 1971-72), Women's Overseas Service League (past local sec. and pres., nat. chmn. Save the Children).

BETTERIDGE, MAY ISABEL, writer, lectr.; b. Providence; d. James Thomas and Mary (Rostron) Betteridge; student Universidad Nacional de Mexico, 1945. Writer travel column Culver City (Cal.) Star News, 1953; contbg. editor What's Cookin' in New York mag., N.Y.C., 1956-58; land and housing promotion, Ore., 1959—. Research frost-resistant, high protein food plants, Fort Rock, Ore., 1959—; exhibitor collection of more than 300 pre-Columbian figurines; collector illustrated childrens books of world, 1794-1905; collector, exhibitor oil paintings and pencil sketches of Paul Puzinas; exhibitor color slides in internat. salons, color prints in art galleries. Established Indian museum, art gallery in Deschutes County Court House, Bend, Ore., 1960. Mem. Photog. Soc. Am. Club: Woman's Press (N.Y.C.). Address: 8927 1/2 Cattaraugus Av Los Angeles CA 90034

BETTINGER, MARY FRANCES LINKER, rental co. exec.; b. Louisville, July 10, 1923; d. Robert William and Antoinette Marie (Schlesinger) Linker; student Ursuline Acad., 1937-41; m. William George Weedman, Jr., Feb. 27, 1943 (div.); children—Susan, William G. III; m. 2d, Earl H. Bettinger, July 7, 1974. Exec. sec. dist. passenger agt. L&N R.R., Louisville, 1944-46; adminstrv. asst. Ky. Disabled Ex-Service Men's Bd., Louisville, 1947-49; exec. sec., adminstrv. asst. to pres. Louisville Textiles, Inc., 1951-68; adminstrv. asst., exec. sec. U. Louisville, 1968-74; exec. sec. Bettinger Barge Rentals, Tell City, Ind., 1974—. Mem. Nat. Secs. Assn. (chpt. pres. 1971-73; div. pres., 1974—). Home: 7 11th Av Tell City IN 47586 Office: Box 70 Tell City IN 47586

BETTINSON, BRENDA, artist, educator; b. King's Lynn, Norfolk, Gt. Britain, Aug. 17, 1929; d. Randall Cecil and Edith (Mitchley) Bettinson; came to U.S., 1960, naturalized, 1966; student St. Martins Sch. Art, London, 1946-48; Nat. Dipl. Design, Central Sch. Arts and Crafts, London, 1950; student Academie de la Grande Chaumiere, Paris, 1951; Eleve Titulaire de l'Ecole Pratique des Hautes Etudes, Ecole Pratique des Hautes Etudes, Sorbonne, Paris, 1952, postgrad., 1952-53. One-man shows including Interchurch Center, N.Y.C., 1961, 64, 67, Karilon Gallery, Provincetown, Mass., 1963, Immaculate Conception Sem., Ramsey, N.J., 1965, 66, Contemporary Christian Art Gallery, N.Y.C., 1966, 70, St. Joseph's Coll., Bklyn., 1966, Pace Coll., N.Y.C., 1967, Am. Bible Soc., N.Y.C., 1970, Dartmouth Coll., 1971; exhibited in group shows Vatican Pavillion, N.Y. Worlds Fair, 1965, Sacred Heart U., 1965, Nat. Arts Club, N.Y.C., 1966, Seton Hall U., 1966, also exhibited at Pacem in Terris Library, N.Y.C., 1966, 67, Am. Soc. Ch. Architecture, 1967, Bklyn. Pub. Library, 1967, Festival of Art and Religion, Chappaqua, N.Y., 1967, Contemporary Christian Art Gallery, N.Y., 1964—; represented in permanent collections Soc. Renewal Christian Art, N.Y.C., St. Mary's Benedictine Abbey, Morristown, N.J., St. Anselm's Abbey, Washington, Sem. of Our Lady of Angels, Albany, N.Y., also pvt. collections U.S., fgn. countries. Mem. faculty Pace U., Westchester, Pleasantville, N.Y., 1963—, asst. prof. fine arts, 1968-72, asso. prof., 1972—, chmn. faculty council, 1969-70, mem. Univ. senate, 1969—, dir. creative directions program, 1969-72; art dir. Riverside Radio WRVR-FM, N.Y.C., 1961-65; lectr. Katonah (N.Y.) Gallery, 1972—. Recipient Gold medal Nat. Arts Club, 1966; cons. Contemporary Christian Art Inc. and chmn. art com., 1966-68; book reviewer Liturgical Arts Jour., 1968—. Mem. Am. Assn. U. Profs., Liturgical Arts Soc. Episcopalian. Contbr. articles to publs. Home: 19 Horsechestnut Rd Briarcliff Manor NY 10510 Office: Pace University Westchester Bedford Rd Pleasantville NY 10570

BETTS, CAROLYN MCILVAINE WELCH, educator, author; b. Phila., Dec. 28, 1915; d. Wilbur Short and Eula May (McIlvaine) Welch; B.S., Beaver Coll., 1937; M.S., Pa. State U., 1942; m. Emmett Albert Betts, July 15, 1950 (dec. 1972). Tchr. pub. schs., Lewistown, Pa., 1937-39, 39-40; dir. reading clinic and supr. Benjamin Franklin Tng. Sch., State Tchrs. Coll., Bloomsburg, Pa., 1940-42; reading cons. Scott, Foresman & Co., N.Y., 1942-43; supr. reading clinic Lab. Sch., Reading Clinic, Pa. State U. Sch. Edn., 1943-45; acting supr. Reading Clinic, Balt. Dept. Edn., 1945-46; lectr., supr. publs. Reading Clinic, dept. psychology Temple U., Phila., 1946-54; supr. in-service tchr. edn. Betts Reading Clinic, Haverford, Pa., 1954-61; reading cons. Henry S. West Lab. Sch., U. Miami, Coral Gables, Fla., 1961—. Served as lt. USAF, 1952-57. Mem. Am. Assn. U. Women, Assn. for Childhood Edn., Internat. Reading Assn., Nat. Council Tchrs. English, Internat. Soc. for Gen. Semantics, Phi Kappa Phi, Pi Lambda Theta, Psi Chi, Delta Kappa Gamma. Author: Betts Basic Readers, 1965. Co-author: Betts New Reading-Study Program: Beginning Reading, 1970. Contbr. articles to profl. jours. Home and office: 12255 SW 73d Av Miami FL 33156

BETZ, JEAN (MRS. FRANK THEODORE BETZ), investment securities co. exec.; b. Utica, N.Y., Mar. 1, 1927; d. Walter John and Anna (Pomichowska) Haoanowicz; student Utica Free Acad., 1941-45; B.S., Rider Coll., 1949; postgrad. Beaver Coll., 1964-65; m. Frank Theodore Betz, Apr. 18, 1949; children—Frank, Eleanor Jean, Richard Walter. Editorial writer Book Publishers Projects, Inc., N.Y.C., 1967-68; sec., dir. Frank T. Betz & Co., Inc., investment securities, Phila., 1966—. Editor: The First Book of Magic, 1968. Home: 1554 Hower Rd Abington PA 19001 Office: Philadelphia National Bank Bldg Philadelphia PA 19107

BEVERIDGE, MARJORIE WINIFRED FAUQUET (MRS. ANDREW DONALD BEVERIDGE), former coll. adminstr.; b. Sioux Falls, S.D., Aug. 25, 1913; d. Arsene W. and Myrtle Ann (Fulmer) Fauquet; B.A., Sioux Falls Coll., 1935; postgrad. U. S.D., U. Ore.; m. Oswald Clifford Halverson, June 16, 1939 (dec. June 1956); children—John Clifford, Bruce Rogness, Christine Ann; m. 2d, Andrew Donald Beveridge, June 17, 1972. Tchr. elementary sch.,

Sioux Falls, 1935-39; bowling instr. Suburban Lanes, Sioux Falls, 1964-66; dir. student union Sioux Falls Coll., 1965-73, counselor to women, 1970-73, mem. women's bd., 1945—, pres., 1953-54. Den mother Cub Scouts, 1950-54; leader Brownie Scouts, 1953-54. Bd. dirs. Girls Club, 1971-72, YWCA, 1947-53; P.T.A. pres. grade sch., Sioux Falls, 1954-55, jr. high sch., 1956-57, high sch., 1961-62. Mem. S.D. Assn. Women Deans and Counselors (sec. 1971, 72), P.E.O. Baptist (mem. council 1973). Mem. Daus. of Nile. Club: Soroptimist (treas. Sioux Falls, 1972). Home: 903 North Dakota St Canton SD 57013

BEVERLY, LAURA ELIZABETH, educator; b. Glen Jean, W.Va., Nov. 26, 1935; d. Sidney and Alma Lee (Davis) Logan; B.A. in Elementary Edn., W.Va. State Coll., 1960; postgrad. Hofstra U., 1961-63, N.Y. U., 1967-70; M.S. in Edn. Retarded Children, Bklyn. Coll., 1969; m. Albert Beverly, 1962 (dec. 1970). Tchr. spl. children Nassau County Bd. Coop. Ednl. Services, Jericho, N.Y., 1963—; cooperating tchr. Hofstra U., 1973. Mem. Delta Sigma Theta. Home: 124 Terrace Av Hempstead NY 11550

BEVINGTON, HELEN, educator, author; b. Afton, N.Y., Apr. 2, 1906; d. Charles Wesley and Elizabeth (Raymond) Smith; Ph.B., U. Chgo., 1926; M.A., Columbia, 1928; m. Merle M. Bevington, June 1, 1928 (dec. Aug. 1964); children—David M., Philip R. Faculty, Duke U., 1943—, prof. English, 1970—. Recipient Roanoke-Chowan award, 1956, 62, N.C. award for lit., 1973. Mem. Am. Assn. U. Profs., Phi Beta Kappa. Author: Dr. Johnson's Waterfall, 1946; Nineteen Million Elephants, 1950; A Change of Sky, 1956; When Found, Make a Verse Of, 1961; Charley Smith's Girl, 1965; A Book and a Love Affair, 1968; The House Was Quiet and the World Was Calm, 1971; Beautiful Lofty People, 1973; poems pub. in popular mags. including New Yorker, Atlantic Monthly, N.Y. Times Book Review. Home: 4428 Guess Rd Durham NC 27705

BEVIS, LEURA DOROTHY, educator; b. Duluth, Minn.; d. Philemon and Leura (Palmer) Bevis; student Occidental Coll., 1923-25; B.A., Pomona Coll., 1927; B.S. in L.S., U. So. Cal., 1947; M.A., U. Wash., 1951; postgrad. Columbia, 1959-60. Researcher, buyer Dawson's Rare Book Shop, Los Angeles, 1929-39; dir. San Pasqual Press, Pasadena, Cal., 1939; editor U. Cal. Press, Berkeley, 1940-43; prof. Sch. Librarianship, U. Wash., Seattle, 1947-72, asso. dir., 1961-72, acting dir., 1963-64; dir. Norman Philbrick Library, Los Altos, Cal., 1972—. Adult services co-ordinator Glendale (Cal.) Pub. Library, 1948; reference librarian Long Beach (Cal.) Pub. Library, 1947; br. librarian Seattle Pub. Library, summer 1952; chmn. pub. relations council Pacific N.W. Library, Seattle, 1948-50; vis. prof. Sch. Library Sci. U. So. Cal., Los Angeles, 1951; judge Ohioiana Lit. award, 1954, N.W. Writers award, 1960; editor for acquisitions Library Resources and Tech. Services, Seattle, 1959—; vis. lectr. Columbia, N.Y.C., 1960; resources cons. Library Edn. Conf. U. Denver, 1960; adv. com. World Book Ency. 1962-63. Dir., United Good Neighbors Dr., Berkeley, 1942; pres. U. Wash. Women's Faculty Club, 1951; state dir. Nat. Library Week, 1958-59; mem. U. Wash. Student YWCA Bd., 1961; survey on all library services in Washington State. Served to lt. comdr. USCG, 1943-46. Mem. Am. Library Assn. (governing council), Wash. Hist. Soc., Assn. Am. Library Schs. (pres.), Am. Assn. Univ. Profs., Grolier Soc., Phi Beta Kappa, Beta Phi Mu. Club: Soroptimist (charter mem. N.W. dist.) (Seattle). Author: Silver Farthing, 1933; Changing Patterns of Reference Service, 1950; Virginia Woolf: Symbol and Thought, 1959. Asst. editor Jour. Edn. for Librarianship, 1960—; Survey Library Resources and Services, 1967. Contbr. articles to profl. jours. Home: 565 Arastradero Rd Palo Alto CA 94306

BEVLIN, MARJORIE KATHLEEN ELLIOTT (MRS. ERVIN W. BEVLIN), educator, artist; b. Dalles, Ore., May 9, 1917; d. John Arthur and Bess (Cornelius) Elliott; archtl. student U. Wash., 1936-37; B.F.A., U. Colo., 1938; M.S., N.Y.U., 1938; m. Ervin W. Bevlin, Jan. 8, 1948; children—Kathleen Anne (Mrs. Cruikshank), Jennifer Jane (Mrs. Cole). Draftsman, Gibbs & Cox, Inc., N.Y.C., 1942-44; faculty, founding chmn. fine arts dept., Otero Jr. Coll., La Junta, Colo., 1956—; one-man shows Koshare Kiva Mus., La Junta, 1958, Rocky Ford (Colo.) Floral Mus., 1959, Pioneer Mus., Pueblo, Colo., 1963; exhibited group shows Denver, 1959-61, Central City, 1962, Scotland, 1963, Eng., 1963, France, 1964, N.A.D., N.Y.C., 1963-65, 67-69, N.Y. World's Fair, 1965, Cal., 1972, Grand Prix International de Peinture, Deauville, France, 1972, Prix de Rome, 1972; represented in pvt. collections Ill., Tex., N.Y., Ind., Cal. Bd. dirs. Girl Scouts U.S.A., LaJunta, 1952-54; dir. Arkansas Valley Sch. Arts Festival, La Junta, 1956-72; organizer, mem. exec. bd. La Junta Council Arts and Humanities, 1972. N.Y.U. Sch. Retailing fellow, 1938-39. Mem. Nat. Assn. Women Artists, Delta Phi Delta, Alpha Chi Omega. Episcopalian. Author: Design Through Discovery, 1963, 2d edit., 1970. Contbr. articles to profl. jours. Home: 12 Cactus Dr La Junta CO 81050

BEYER, FRANCES ANN BRANDENBURG (MRS. J.W. BEYER, JR.), advt. exec.; b. Tulsa, July 26, 1929; d. Louis A. and Monica Mary (Steil) Brandenburg; student spl. courses, seminars and insts. in advt. and direct mail; m. Thomas P. Nolan, Sept. 6, 1948; children—Thomas P., Monica Louise, Meredith Ann; m. 2d, J.W. Beyer, Jr., Dec. 31, 1970. With Louis A. Brandenburg, advt., Tulsa, 1946-68; promotion mgr. Oil and Gas Jour., Tulsa, 1968-69; adv. dir. bus. services div. LVO Corp., Tulsa, 1969-70; owner Brandenburg-Beyer Advt., Tulsa, 1970—. Mem. Women's Steering Com. for Nixon, 1968; Republican Party precinct sec., 1970. Mem. Am. Marketing Assn. (past pres. Tulsa). Home: 1315 S Frisco St Tulsa OK 74119 Office: PO Box 696 1315 S Frisco Tulsa OK 74119

BEYER, MAY CATHERINE, charitable orgn. exec.; b. New Orleans, May 21, 1902; d. Thomas James and Mary Margaret (Clair) Hogan; grad. McNally Bus. Coll., New Orleans, 1918; m. Charles Roger Beyer, Dec. 15, 1926 (dec.); children—Charles Henry Michel, Elizabeth Collen (Mrs. Peter James Benvenutti), Margaret Mirian (Mrs. Norman Neal Burns). Exec. sec., adminstr. Hancock County United Fund, Bay St. Louis, Miss., 1964—. Mem. Bay St. Louis C. of C., Bay Waveland Garden Club (pres. 1963). Address: 410 Carroll Av Bay St Louis MS 39520

BEZCHLIBNYK, KALYNA ZORIANNA, pharmacist; b. Innsbruck, Austria, Sept. 17, 1947; d. Wasyl and Maria Josephine (Ruda) Solonynka; B.Sc. in Pharmacy, U. Toronto, 1970; m. Roman Michael Bezchlibnyk, June 6, 1970. Pharmacist, Queen St. Mental Health Centre, Toronto, 1970-72; dir. pharmacy Clarke Inst. Psychiatry, Toronto, 1972—. Mem. Canadian Pharm. Assn., Canadian Soc. Hosp. Pharmacists, Met. Toronto Dirs. Pharmacy. Home: 76 36th St Toronto ON M8W 3L2 Canada Office: 250 College St Toronto ON Canada

BIAGINI, MARY KATHRYN, educator; b. Charleroi, Pa., Nov. 30, 1942; d. George D. and Vera Jean (Lutz) Biagini; B.S., Cal. State Coll., 1963; M.L.S., Kent State U., 1965. Tchr., Akron (O.) Pub. Sch., 1963-64, librarian, 1965-68; reference librarian Stow (O.) Pub. Library, part-time 1965-67; asst. prof. Kent (O.) State U., Sch. Library Sci., 1968—, cons. materials specialist, 1967. Mem. Am., Ohio (mem. div. exec. bd. 1973-74) library assns., Am., Ohio assns. sch. librarians. Editor: Spotlight: Media Solution, vol. II, 1973. Home: 1350 N Howard St Akron OH 44310 Office: Kent State U Sch Library Sci Kent OH 44242

BIALEK, ILOMAE LILLIAN, sch. psychologist; b. Chgo., July 6, 1936; d. Edmund John and Marie Ida (Powers) B.; B.Ed., Chgo. Tchrs. Coll., 1958; M.A. in Psychology, DePaul U., 1967; supervision and adminstrn. endorsement Concordia Tchrs. Coll., 1972; m. John Walter, Feb. 27, 1960; children—Danita, John. Tchr., Chgo. Pub. Schs., 1958-61, 63-66; sch. psychologist, Morton Grove, Ill., 1966-68; supervising psychologist Leyden Area Spl. Edn., Franklin Park, Ill., 1968—. Leader, Girl Scouts, 1954-56, 70-72; mem. citizens com. Oak Park-River Forest (Ill.) High Sch., 1972—. Sec., 29th Ward Young Democrats, 1958-60; mem. Sch. Bd., River Forest, Ill., 1971—. Mem. Council for Exceptional Children (local pres. 1970-71), W. Suburban Sch. Psychologists (program chmn. 1972-73), Nat. Assn. Sch. Psychologists (charter). Home: 831 N William St River Forest IL 60305 Office: 10401 W Grand Av Franklin Park IL 60131

BIANCO, JUDITH ANN (MRS. PHILIP R. BIANCO), stock broker; b. Pittsfield, Mass., Nov. 5, 1945; d. Albert William and Margaret Mary (Lorette) Thomas; student U. Mass., 1964; B.S., Am. Internat. Coll., 1967; m. Philip R. Bianco, Aug. 7, 1965. Broker, G.H. Walker & Co., Inc., N.Y.C., 1967-68; v.p., dir., sec., stockbroker Culverwell & Co., Inc., Springfield, Mass., 1968—; v.p., dir. Bay State Growth Fund, 1969-71, Bay State Growth Mgmt. Co., 1969—. Recipient award Wall Street Jour., 1967. Mem. Boston Stock Exchange (1st woman; stock list com. 1971—), C. of C. (women's div.), Zonta Internat., Alpha Chi. Home: 25 Robin Ridge Dr Feeding Hills MA 01030 Office: Baystate West 1500 Main St Springfield MA 01115

BIANCO, PAMELA (RUBY) (MRS. GEORG T. HARTMANN), artist; b. London, Eng., Dec. 31, 1906; d. Francesco and Margery (Williams) Bianco; m. Robert Schlick, June 21, 1930 (div. June 1955); 1 son, Lorenzo Bianco; m. Georg T. Hartmann, July 25, 1955. Came to U.S., 1921, naturalized, 1930. Exhibited one man shows at Leicester Galleries, London, 1919, 20, Anderson Galleries, N.Y.C., 1921, The Print Rooms, San Francisco, 1922, Cannell and Chaffin, San Francisco, 1923, Art Inst. Chgo., 1924, Knoedler Galleries, N.Y.C., 1924, Rehn Galleries, 1926, Ferargil Galleries, 1937, David Herbert Gallery, 1961, Graham Gallery, 1969 (all N.Y.C.), Art Inst. Chgo., 1924, Internat. Gallery, Balt., 1964, Santa Barbara Mus. Art, 1970; exhibited group shows including Whitney Studio Club, N.Y.C., 1923-30, Contemporary Arts Mus., Houston, 1961, Pa. Acad., Phila., 1962, Albright-Knox Gallery of Art, Buffalo, 1964, Phila. Mus., 1966; represented in permanent collections including Mus. Modern Art, N.Y.C., Chase Manhattan Bank, N.Y.C., Queen's Coll., N.Y.C., N.Y. Pub. Library, also pvt. collections Joseph H. Hirshhorn, John de Menil, Gloria Vanderbilt and others; illustrated stories Harpers Bazaar mag., 1921-22, 27, Theatre Arts Mag., 1928-29 and others; illustrator books including Flora by Walter de la Mare, 1920; The Little Wooden Doll by Margery Bianco, 1925; Natives of Rock by Glenway Wescott, 1925, The Land of Dreams by William Blake, 1928, Three Christmas Trees by Juliana Horatia Ewing, 1930; The Skin Horse by Margery Bianco, 1927; The Birthday of the Infanta by Oscar Wilde, 1929; The Little Mermaid by Hans Andersen, 1935; The Easter Book of Legends and Stories by Hazeltine and Smith, 1947; Away to the Moon by John Symonds, 1956. Guggenheim fellow for creative painting abroad, 1930. Author: Sing a Song of Journeys, 1937. Author-artist: The Starlit Journey, 1933, Beginning with A, 1947, Playtime in Cherry Street, 1948, Joy and the Christmas Angel, 1949, Paradise Square, 1950, Little Houses Far Away, 1951, The Look Inside Easter Egg, 1952, The Doll in the Window, 1953, The Valentine Party, 1954, Toy Rose, 1957. Home: 430 Lafayette St New York City NY 10003 Studio 428 Lafayette St New York City NY 10003

BIBER, BARBARA (MRS. OSCAR BODANSKY), psychologist; b. N.Y.C., Dec. 20, 1903; d. William and Fanny (Stark) Biber; student Barnard Coll., 1920-22; Ph.B., U. Chgo., 1926; Ph.D., Columbia, 1942; m. Oscar Bodansky, May 31, 1929; 1 dau., Margery (Mrs. Raymond S. Franklin). Research asst. Bank St. Coll. of Edn., N.Y.C., 1928-31, chmn. child devel., chmn. student tchr. guidance program, 1931-49, dir. research, 1950-63, distinguished research scholar, 1963—, Blance F. Ittleson Research chair mental health and edn., 1971—; instr., dept. arly childhood and elementary edn. N.Y. U., 1938-48; lectr. child devel. Vassar Coll. Summer Inst., 1945-50; cons. Office Child Devel., Washington, 1971—, Inst. Rehab. Medicine, N.Y. U. Med. Center, 1971—. Mem. N.Y. Citizens Com. for Children, 1950—, Nat. Joint Commn. on Mental Health Children, 1967-69, tech. adv. bd. Inst. Tng. and Research in Child Mental Health, 1966—. Fellow Am. Psychol. Assn., Soc. for Psychol. Study Social Issues; mem. Soc. Research Child Devel. Author: Life and Ways of the Seven-to-Eight Year Old, 1942; co-author Psychological Impact of School Experience, 1969. Editor: School Begins at Two, 1936; Psychosocial Studies in Edn., 1969—. Contbr. articles to profl. jours., and books. Home: 535 E 86th St New York City NY 10028

BIBLE, JEAN PATTERSON (MRS. LLOYD EDWARD BIBLE), writer; b. Russellville, Tenn., Oct. 12, 1913; d. Hugh Graham and Lucy (Nenney) Patterson; A.B., Salem Coll., Winston-Salem, 1934; m. Lloyd Edward Bible, June 1, 1936; 1 dau., Laura Anderson Gould. Weekly columnist This and That, Standard-Banner and Grainger County News, Jefferson City, Tenn., 1959—; free-lance writer travel sect. N.Y. Times, 1961—, many others; feature article and photographs Atlanta Jour. and Constn. mag., Balt. Sunday Sun mag.; part-time Spanish tchr. high sch., Dandridge, Tenn., 1967; photo-journalist, 1968—. Mem. Tenn. Press Assn., Nat. League Am. Pen Women, Tenn. Press and Author's, Assn. for Preservation Tenn. Antiquities, E. Tenn. Hist. Soc., Nat. Trust Historic Preservation. Presbyn. Home: Dandridge TN 37725

BIBRING, GRETE LEHNER, psychiatrist, psychoanalyst; b. Vienna, Austria, Jan. 11, 1899; d. Moritz and Victoria (Stengel) Lehner; M.D., U. Vienna, 1924; L.H.D. (hon.), Brandeis U., 1968; m. Edward Bibring, Dec. 22, 1921 (dec. 1959); children—George L., Thomas. Came to U.S., 1941, naturalized, 1946. Resident, Neurol. Univ. Clinic, Vienna, also Psychiat.-Neurol. Univ. Hosp., U. Vienna, 1924-27; asst. dir. Vienna Psychoanalytic Out-Patient Clinics, 1926-30; tng. analyst, instr. Vienna Psychoanalytic Soc., 1933-38; tng. analyst Brit. Psychoanalytical Soc. and Inst., 1938-41, Boston Psychoanalytic Soc. and Inst., 1941—; spl. lectr. psychoanalytic psychology Simmons Coll. Sch. Social Work, Boston, 1942-64; head dept. psychiatry Beth Israel Hosp., Boston, 1946-55, psychiatrist-in-chief, 1955-65, emerita, 1965—; asso. psychiatry Harvard Med. Sch., 1946-50, asst. prof., 1950-55, asso. clin. prof., 1955-61, clin. prof. psychiatry, faculty medicine, 1961-65, clin. prof. psychiatry emerita, 1965—; research cons. psychoanalytic psychology Radcliffe Coll., Cambridge, Mass., 1965—; psychiat. cons. Children's Bur., Washington, 1949-54; chmn. ednl. com. Boston Psychoanalytic Soc. and Inst., 1952-54, pres., 1955-58; adv. com. psychol. counseling center Brandeis U., 1954—; vis. prof. psychiatry Sch. Medicine, U. N.C., 1955-56; cons. psychiat. service Faulkner Hosp., Boston, 1966—; adv. bd. psychiat. unit Mt. Auburn Hosp., Cambridge, Mass., 1956-58. Recipient medal Visitante Distinguido Consejo Consultive, Mexico City. Fellow Am. Acad. Arts and Scis., Am. Psychiat. Assn.; mem. A.A.A.S., Am. (councilor 1950-58, pres. 1962-63), Internat. (hon. sec. 1950-52, v.p. 1959-63), Boston (tng. analyst) psychoanalytic assns., Group Advancement Psychiatry (com. research 1960—, cons. in psychoanalytic psychology to Radcliffe Inst. 1965—), Mass. Med. Soc., N.Y. Acad. Sci., Alpha Omega Alpha (hon.). Contbr. articles to profl. jours. Editorial bd. Psychol. Problems in Medicine, 1960—, Jour. Geriatric Psychiatry, 1965—; editorial cons. Psychiatry in Medicine, 1970. Address: 47 Garden St Cambridge MA 02138

BICKFORD, CLARA LOUISE GEHRING (MRS. GEORGE P. BICKFORD), educator; b. Cleve.; d. Frederick William and Emma (Motz) Gehring; B.A. cum laude, Bryn Mawr Coll., 1925; m. George P. Bickford, Apr. 6, 1933; 1 dau., Louise (Mrs. Douglas K. Boyd). Tchr. piano Cleve. Inst. Music, 1929-33, tchr. adult classes in music appreciation, 1934—, trustee, 1934—, pres. bd., 1949-52. Pres. women's com. Cleve. Orch., 1939-41, trustee, 1944—; mem. vis. com. for humanities Western Res. U., 1959—; mem. jr. council Cleve. Mus. Art; pres. Women's City Club Found., 1960-62. Mem. Mu Phi Epsilon. Clubs: Bryn Mawr, Shaker Lakes Garden, Intown (Cleve.); Sulgrave (Washington). Home: 2247 Chestnut Hills Dr Cleveland OH 44106

BICKLEY, MARION THORNTON (MRS. WILLIAM P. BICKLEY, JR.), educator; b. Bklyn., Nov. 23, 1918; d. Charles and Edna Kate (Eckart) Thornton; B.A., Glassboro State Coll., 1963, M.A., 1965; Ed.D., U. Pa., 1968; m. William P. Bickley, Jr., Feb. 7, 1941; 1 son, William P. III. Tchr. Moorestown, (N.J.) Pub. Schs., 1957-65; faculty Glassboro (N.J.) State Coll., 1965—, prof. dept. spl. edn. services and instrn., 1971—; vis. lectr. edn. Grad. Sch. of Edn., U. Pa., 1970-71; cons. to schs. in N.J. and Del., 1965—; sch. psychologist, 1970—. Mem. N.J. Reading Tchrs. Assn. (bd. dirs. 1971—), Nat., N.J. edn. assns., Internat. Reading Assn., Council for Exceptional Children, Am. Assn. U. Profs., N.J. Assn. Learning Disability Tchr. Cons., Assn. Children with Learning Disabilities. Home: Hooten Rd Moorestown NJ 08057 Office: Glassboro State College Glassboro NJ 08028

BIDDLE, JANET ELIZABETH MAYO, financial cons. exec.; b. St. Paul, Nov. 6, 1912; d. Walter Lewis and Sarah (Joslin) Mayo; A.B., Vassar Coll., 1933; certificate photogrammetry Princeton, 1943; postgrad. Union Theol. Sem., 1955-57; certificate prins. life ins. Life Office Mgmt. Assn., 1963; m. Glenn L. Jepsen, June 14, 1934 (div. 1953); 1 dau., Katherine A.; m. 2d, Eric Harbeson Biddle, Oct. 24, 1957. Sec. field work office Union Theol. Sem., N.Y.C., 1954-57; office mgr. Council Social Work Edn., N.Y.C., 1958-59; sec. to sec. N.Am. Reassurance Co., N.Y.C., 1960-64; asst. to dir. internat. programs office Nat. Assn. State Univs. and Land-Grant Colls., 1965-69; asst. sec., asst. treas. Nat. Minerals Exploration, Inc., Washington, 1969—, dir., 1969-73; v.p., treas. Biddle Assos., Inc., N.Y.C., Washington, 1961—, also dir. Mem. Princeton (N.J.) Borough Bd. Edn., 1947-53, pres., 1951-53. Mem. UN Assn. U.S., Phi Beta Kappa. Democrat. Episcopalian. Home: 1200 N Nash St Arlington VA 22209 Office: 815 Connecticut Av NW Washington DC 20006

BIDDLE, LUCY BLINDON (MRS. CHRISTOPHER STARK BIDDLE), govt. ofcl.; b. Greenwich, Conn., Sept. 24, 1946; d. Montague and Lucy Mercer (Marbury) Blundon; student Sweet Briar Coll., 1964-66, Sorbonne, U. Paris (France), 1967, Louvre, Paris, 1967; A.B., George Washington U., 1968; postgrad. Harvard, 1971, Inst. in Arts Adminstn., 1971; m. Christopher Stark Biddle, May 20, 1972. Founder/adviser Folger poetry series Folger Shakespeare Library, Washington, 1969-73, bus. mgr. Folger theatre group, 1970-73; publs. specialist Nat. Endowment for Arts, Washington, 1974—. Mem. panel D.C. Commn. on Arts, 1971-73; mem. exec. com. Neighborhood Arts Council, 1971—; co. chmn. Nat. Poetry Center, Washington, 1970-73. Mem. Fed. Editors Assn., Nat. press Club, Woman's Nat. Democratic Club. Home: 2538 44th St NW Washington DC 20007 Office: National Endowment for the Arts Washington DC 20506

BIDEZ, THELMA CALHOUN (MRS. EARLE FELTON BIDEZ), club woman; b. Rockmart, Ga.; d. William Alexander and Eudora (Davitte) Calhoun; student pvt. schs.; m. Earle Felton Bidez, Sept. 4, 1916; children—Earle Calhoun (dec.), Miriam Elizabeth (Mrs. Lloyd E. Clark), William Alexander. Vice pres. Froebel Circle, 1953-54, pres., 1954-56; awards chmn. Garden Club of Savannah, 1954-57; sec., 1957-58, 1st v.p., 1958-60; librarian Savannah chpt. D.A.R., 1957-58; adv. mem. M.B.L.S.; mem. Am. Bicentennial Research Inst. Mem. Ga. Hist. Soc., Nat. Geneal. Soc., Daus. Am. Colonists (regent 1970), Magna Charta Dames, Plantagenet Soc., N.W. Ga. Hist. and Geneal. Soc., Ga. Geneal. Soc., Episcopalian (edited early marriage records of St. John's Ch.). Home: 116 E 53d St Savannah GA 31405

BIDLINGMEYER, EMILIE LADD, ednl. adminstr.; b. Cin., July 8, 1941; d. Charles John and Leah Dorothy (Ladd) Bidlingmeyer; B.A., U. Cin., 1963; M.A. (Nat. Def. Edn. Act fellow 1968-69), N.Y. U., 1969. Admissions counselor U. Cin., 1963-65; admissions officer, asso. dir. admissions U. Akron, 1965-68; orientat on adminstr. Inst. for Internat. Edn., N.Y.C., 1969-70; dir. admissions Pace U., N.Y.C., 1970—. Panelist to various profl. meetings and tng. seminars, 1964—; instnl. rep. Coll. Entrance Exam. Bd. Mem. Nat. Assn. Student Personnel Adminstrs., Am. Assn. U. Women, Am. Assn. Higher Edn., Phi Alpha Theta. Office: Pace Plaza New York City NY 10038

BIDWELL, KATHARINE KENNEDY (MRS. ROBERT REDDINGTON BIDWELL), civic worker; b. Omaha, Dec. 2, 1914; d. John Lauderdale and Marguerite (Pritchett) Kennedy; B.A., Stanford, 1938; m. Robert Reddington Bidwell, Oct. 26, 1940; children—Barbara Hanscom (Mrs. Robert Dunlap Hillman), Robert Reddington. Founder mem., 1st v.p. Cal. Hosp. Service Guild, Los Angeles, 1959-61; regional chmn. heart fund Los Angeles, 1959-60; regional chmn. heart fund Los Angeles County Heart Assn., 1959-60, county vice-chmn., 1961-62, mem. family service council, mem.-at-large Western Regional Council; co-ordinator jrs. Assistance League So. Cal., 1958-59, adv. bd., 1958—; mem. mayor's adv. council City of Los Angeles, 1963-64, Los Angeles County Mus. Assn. Bd. dirs. Family Service, Los Angeles, 1959-60. Recipient Award of Merit, Community Chest Los Angeles Area, 1948-49; award for meritorious service Los Angeles County Heart Assn., 1960, Exceptional Service award, Stanford U. service award. Mem. Affiliates U. Cal. Los Angeles, Stanford Alumni Assn. (mem. exec. bd. 1958-62, 2d v.p. 1961-62, bd. dirs. 1961-62), Internat. Platform Assn., Vivisection Investigation League, Nat. Cat Protection Soc., Stanford Assos., Dobbs Alumni Assn. (local chmn. 1960-62), Assos. of Stanford Libraries, Delta Delta Delta. Episcopalian. Clubs: Stanford Women's Los Angeles (bd. dirs. 1954-57, pres. 1956-57), Stanford of Los Angeles (dir. 1960-64), Westside Stanford (founder mem., dir. 1963). Home: 4009 Aladdin Dr Huntington Beach CA 92649

BIDWELL, VIRGINIA EMMONS (MRS. MYRON CHAPMAN BIDWELL), sci. researcher; b. Mpls.; d. Frank William and Myrtle Virginia (Thompson) Emmons; B.A., U. Minn.; Ph.D., U. Cal.; m. Myron Chapman Bidwell, July 2, 1944 (dec.). Employed in radio and script work, Chgo.; agt. U.S. Naval Intelligence, Los Angeles, 1942-48; cons. on atmospheric pollution, 1945—. Mem. Internat. Platform Assn., Alpha Xi Delta. Author: World of Milk, Honey and

Fall-out. Contbr. articles to various jours. and periodicals. Home: Box 1626 Beverly Hills CA 90213

BIEBER, BERNICE JEAN (MRS. RALPH GORDON BIEBER), pub. relations exec.; b. Newport, Ky., Feb. 7, 1920; d. Edward Griggs and Irene (Bird) Nieder; B.A. in Journalism, Ohio State U., 1942; m. Ralph Gordon Bieber, Oct. 2, 1942; children—Karen (Mrs. H. Stephen Downing), Gail Ellen, Sue Jill. Free lance writer, photographer Universal Trade Press Syndicate, N.Y.C., 1947-50; corr. Mental Health Dept., State of Ohio, Columbus, 1951-53; asst. editor Univ. Film Producers Jour., Columbus, 1955-58; dir. pub. relations and information Franklin County Soc. for Crippled Children, Columbus, 1959—. Mem. Women in Communications (pres. Columbus chpt. 1959-60), Am. Women in Radio and TV, Central Ohio Profl. Photographers. Baptist. Editor News Parade, 1963—. Home: 910 S Hague Av Columbus OH 43204 Office: PO Box 7166 565 Childrens Dr Columbus OH 43205

BIEBER, ELIZA DAVIS (MRS. ROBERT R. BIEBER), librarian; b. Stickney, Mo., Oct. 2, 1916; d. John Thomas and Emma (Berry) Davis; A. Library Sci., Community Coll. (Chgo.), 1966; student Chgo. Tchrs. Coll., 1966-67; B.A., Trinity Christian Coll., 1973; m. John Lewis Wyss, Sept. 21, 1940 (div. May 1969); 1 dau., Konda Eliza (Mrs. Jon Stanley Pulley; m. 2d, Robert Richard Bieber, Dec. 5, 1970. Librarian Bedford Park Library, Argo, Ill., 1964-65; head librarian Acorn Pub. Library, Oak Forest, Ill., 1967-72, South Stickney Pub. Library, Burbank, Ill., 1972—. Pres. P.T.A., Bedford Park, 1962. Mem. A.L.A., Ill. Library Assn., Library Adminstrs. No. Ill., So. Suburban Librarians Assn. (chmn. comn. on edn., sec. 1973-75). Home: 16621 Gaynelle Rd Tinley Park IL 60477

BIEBER, TOBY BENNETT (MRS. IRVING BIEBER), psychologist, educator; b. N.Y.C., Aug. 7, 1916; d. Barnet and Esther (Angel) Bennett; B.A., Hunter Coll., 1945; M.S., N.Y. Sch. Social Work, 1947; Ph.D., Columbia, 1963; m. Irving Bieber, Aug. 30, 1937. Pvt. practice psychology and psychoanalysis, N.Y.C., 1952—; clin. instr. N.Y. Med. Coll., 1968—. Recipient Hofheimer award Am. Psychiat. Assn., 1964. Mem. Am. Psychol. Assn., Am. Assn. Group Psychotherapy. Author: (with others) Homosexuality: A Psychoanalytic Study of Male Homosexuals, 1962; also articles in field. Home and office: 132 E 72d St New York City NY 10021

BIEBUSH, BARBARA ANN, librarian; b. Vallejo, Cal., Apr. 10, 1932; d. Frederick Calvin and Irma Mary (Hawkins) Biebush; A.A., Oceanside-Carlsbad Coll., 1952; A.B., Stanford, 1954; M.L.S., U. Cal. at Berkeley, 1957. Librarian, Santa Rosa Center, San Francisco State Coll., 1956-59, U.S. Army, Augsberg, Germany, 1959-60, Lenggris, Germany, 1960-61; base librarian March AFB, Cal., 1962; head reference librarian Cal. State Coll. at Sonoma, 1962—. Bd. dirs., sec. Cal. Orgn. to Acquire Access to State Tidelands, 1970-72. Mem. Cal. Library Assn., United Profs. Cal., Phi Beta Kappa, Beta Phi Mu. Democrat. Subscription editor Peace and Change, jour. peace research. Home: 1140 4th St Santa Rosa CA 95404 Office: 1801 E Cotati Av Rohnert Park CA 94928

BIEGEL, ANGENIETA ANNE, physician; b. Gorinchem, The Netherlands, July 18, 1928 (came to U.S. 1958, naturalized 1963); d. Hendrik J. and Hermina (van der Kint) Biegel; M.D., Rijks U., Leiden, The Netherlands, 1956. Asst. physician Amsterdam Clinic for Allergic Diseases, 1956-57; fellow medicine, instr. allergy Duke U. Med. Sch., Durham, N.C., 1958-60; intern medicine Ind. U. Med. Center, Indpls., 1960-61, resident medicine, 1961-63, USPHS fellow medicine and microbiology, 1963-65, instr. medicine, 1965-67, asst. prof., 1967-71, asso. prof., 1971—; staff physician Ind. U. Med. Center Hosps.; cons. allergy VA Hosp., Indpls., Marion County Gen. Hosp., Indpls. Mem. cons. com., transplantation-immunology br. Nat. Inst. Allergy and Infectious Diseases, 1971—. Mem. Am., Ind. med. assns., Am. Soc. Microbiology, Am. Acad. Allergy, Am. Soc. Clin. Research, Transplantation Soc., Am. Nephrology Soc., Ohio Valley Allergy Soc., Marion County Med. Soc. Office: 1100 W Michigan St Indianapolis IN 46202

BIELEY, PEGGY MOSES, economist; b. N.Y.C., June 5, 1929; d. Louis and Bella (Kenarik) Moses; B.S. magna cum laude N.Y.U. Sch. Commerce, 1950; M.A., Stanford U., 1953; student Columbia U., 1952-53; m. Alfred D. Bieley, Dec. 25, 1953; children—Harlan C., Lily B. Economist Nat. Indsl. Conf. Bd., N.Y.C., 1949; economist Jules Backman Asso., N.Y.C., 1949-50; teaching fellow Stanford, 1950-51; economist Nat. Manpower Council, Columbia, 1951-53; instr. econs. U. Miami, 1954-55; v.p., chief economist Julian Langner Research, Inc., Miami, Fla., 1955-60; pres., chief economist Bieley, Wagner & Assos. Miami, 1960-70, Econ. Data Bank, Inc., Miami, 1970-73; pres. Housing-Data-Bank, Miami, 1971-73; economist 1st Fed. Savs. and Loan Assn. of Tampa (Fla.), 1973—. Cons. economist savs. and loan assns., comml. banks. Mem. Am. Econ. Assn., Am. Statis. Assn., Econ. Soc. So. Fla., Beta Gamma Sigma Contbr. articles to tech. jours., nat. mags. Home: 11601 SW 64th Av Miami FL 33156

BIELING, MIRIAM ESTHER KOFF (MRS. HERMAN FREDERICK BIELING, SR.), tool mfg. co. exec.; b. Syracuse, N.Y., Feb. 2, 1917; d. Philip and Sonya (Gubberman) Koff; grad. high sch.; m. Herman Frederick Bieling, Sr., Mar. 24, 1934; children—Miriam (Mrs. George W. Barrows), Ann (Mrs. Anthony Fallonardo), Elizabeth (Mrs. John VanIderstine), Herman Frederick. Sec. home econs. div. Onondaga County Coop. Extension Service, 1950-52; sec. Autolite Battery Co., 1952-53; bookkeeper Easy Washing Machine Corp., 1953-55; machinist, bookkeeper Production Tool Mfg. Co., Tully, N.Y., 1948-63, pres., 1963—. Mem. Syracuse Peace Council, Tully Valley Grange (service and hospitality chmn. 1970—), Blodgett Vocational High Sch. Alumni Assn. (pres. 1956-57). Club: Syracuse (mem. exec. com. natural food assos. 1960—). Home: 2332 Cardiff Rd Lafayette NY 13084 Office: 29 Lincoln St Tully NY 13159

BIEMILLER, RUTH COBBETT (MRS. REYNARD BIEMILLER), writer; b. Morristown, N.J., June 5, 1914; d. Frederick Burford and Margaret (Dickison) Cobbett; B.A., Coll. William and Mary, 1935; postgrad. N.Y. U., 1947-48, 52-53, New Sch. for Social Research, 1963, 66; m. Reynard Biemiller, Nov. 5, 1938; 1 son, Christopher Cobbett. Mem. editorial staff Mut. Benefit Life Ins. Co., Newark, 1937-41; crossword puzzle editor N.Y. Herald Tribune, 1952-66; freelance writer and editor books, mags., corporate newsletters, 1966—; writer articles for mags. including N.Y. Mag., N.Y. Times, Sunday Book Rev., Chem. Week, Sat Rev., Retirement Living, 1966—; contbg. editor Family Bible Ency. Served to lt. (j.g.) USNR, 1942-44. Mem. Newspaper Women's Club N.Y. (dir. 1960-66), Overseas Press Club Am. (bd. govs. 1972—, chmn. bull. com. 1972-73), Mortar Board, Chi Delta Phi. Author: (with others) Nat. Fein's Animals, 1955; Dance: The Story of Katherine Dunham, 1969. Home: 3 Peter Cooper Rd New York City NY 10010

BIERDEMAN, JANE E., social worker; b. St. Louis, Nov. 7, 1922; d. Arthur E. and Adele (Bienvenu) Bierdeman; B.A., Maryville Coll., 1944; M.S.W., St. Louis U., 1949. Adminstrv. asst. Social Planning Council, St. Louis, 1949-55; psychiat. social worker, supr. St. Louis State Hosp., 1955-62; chief social worker Fulton (Mo.) State Hosp., 1962—; instr. social work U. Mo., 1966—. Mem. Govs. Com., Mo. White Ho. Conf. on Children and Youth, 1968—; delegate Govs. Conf. on Edn., 1966-67. Pres., Callaway County Human Devel. Corp., 1966-68. Mem. social concerns com. Mo. Cath. Conf., 1970—, state chmn., 1972-73; mem. Gov.'s Com. on Children and Youth. Mem. Nat. Assn. Social Workers (dir. 1968-71, chpt. pres. 1968-71), Mo. Council Social Workers (pres. 1966-68), Acad. Certified Social Workers, Delta Epsilon Sigma. Home: 1801 Dawson Pl Fulton MO 65251 Office: Fulton State Hosp Fulton MO 65251

BIERMAN, MARY MARGARET, librarian; b. Victoria, Tex., Aug. 6, 1916; d. Benjamin J. and Margaret Noble (Fox) Bierman; B.A., U. Tex., 1941, M.A., 1948, M.S. in L.S., 1969. Tchr., Victoria, 1941-48, Alamo Heights Sch., San Antonio, 1951-63; head librarian Victoria Intermediate Schs., 1963—. Mem. Tex. Library Assn., Tex. Tchrs. Assn., Tex. Assn. Sch. Librarians (pres. 1969-70), Tex. Assn. Ednl. Tech., Victoria County Hist. Soc. Home: 1101 Plantation Rd Victoria TX 77901 Office: 2502 Fannin St Victoria TX 77901

BIERNAT, LILLIAN M. NAHUMENUK (MRS. JOSEPH ANTHONY BIERNAT), interior designer; b. Phila., Apr. 27, 1931; d. Peter and Anna (Wolonick) Nahumenuk; student pub. schs.; m. Joseph Anthony Biernat, July 22, 1951; children—Joseph A., Daria Ann, Karen Marie, Mark Allen, Brent Hilary. Receptionist, sec. Mayer, Magaziner & Brunswick, lawyers, Phila., 1950-53; owner Town House Interiors, Columbia, Conn., Newton Square, Pa., 1956—. Mem. fund raising com. Girl Scouts U.S.A., 1968. Clubs: Womens, Garden (Newtown Square); Villagers Womens (Columbia). Address: 30 Hurdle Fence Dr Avon CT 06001

BIGBY, MARY FRANCES WILSON (MRS. LUTHER S. BIGBY), county ofcl., civic worker; b. Williamston, S.C.; d. James G. and Mary (Cason) Wilson; B.S., Greenville Woman's Coll., 1932; m. Luther S. Bigby, Oct. 12, 1935; children—Luther, James. Tchr. pub. sch., Pelzer, S.C., 1932-33; saleslady J. C. Penney Co., Greenville, 1933-34; caseworker Emergency Relief Adminstrn., Greenville, 1934-42; dept. head Greenville Army Air Base, 1942-45; retirement clk. Greenville County Dept. Edn., 1946-53; 1st clk., adminstrv. asst. Office County Supr., Greenville, 1953—. Corr. sec. S.C. Conf. on Status of Women, 1964-66, chmn. nominating com., 1966—, treas. 1969-70, 2d v.p. 1970-72, 1st v.p., 1972-74, pres., 1974—; mem. S.C. Council for Common Good, 1960—; mem. S.C. Gov.'s Commn. on Status of Women, 1965—; membership chmn. Greenville Forum on World Affairs, 1967—; residential chmn. Cancer Crusade, 1969; mem. Greenville County Mental Health, County Home Aux.; mem. Salvation Army Aux., chmn. camp. com., 1972-73, 1st v.p., 1974—; mem. bldg. solicitation com. Boys Home of South, 1972; mem. YWCA, Friends of Library. Mem. bd. Bus. and Profl. Womens Ednl. Found. Mem. Greater Greenville Women's Div. of C. of C. (1st v.p. 1965, pres. 1966), Nat. (contact chmn. 1959-60, bd. 1966—, rules com., credentials com. 1970), S.C. (corr. sec. 1959-61, rec. sec. 1961-62, 2d v.p. 1962-64, 1st v.p. 1964-66, pres. 1966-68, parliamentarian 1970-72, 73-74, chmn. ednl. found. conf. 1971-72, pres. ednl. found. conf. 1971-72, campaign mgr. 1974) fedns. bus. and profl. womens clubs, Greenville Bus. and Profl. Women's Club (pres. 1958-59, Woman of Year 1968), Nat. Secs. Assn. (parliamentarian 1968-69). Baptist (pres. Sunday Sch. class, leader Bible study group 1970-71, budget com. 1971-72, ch. flower chmn. 1972—, mem. fellowship com. 1972—). Mem. Order Eastern Star. Clubs: Altrusa (1st v.p. 1969-70, pres. 1970-72, parliamentarian 1972—), Blue Ridge (presiding partner 1970—). Home: 9 W Augusta Pl Greenville SC 29605 Office: 115 Courthouse Greenville SC 29601

BIGELOW, MARY ANN CAMPBELL (MRS. DANIEL SYLVESTER BIGELOW), artist; b. Olympia, Wash., Mar. 13, 1913; d. Laverne Russell and Hazel Aileen (Rich) Campbell; student U. Wash., 1930-32; m. Daniel Sylvester Bigelow, Oct. 16, 1935; children—George Campbell, John Douglas, David Harold, Timothy James. Exhibited one-man shows Capitol Art Mus., Olympia, Little Gallery, Olympia; exhibited in group shows Standforth Gallery, Tacoma, Town and Gown Gallery, Tacoma, Celebration Arts Gallery, Canoga Park, Cal.; represented in permanent collections Clinic Mall, Olympia, others; tchr. woodcarving portraiture, 1960—. Speaker creativity, 1965—. Ch. camp dir. First United Meth. Ch., Seattle, 1963-73; art cons. to various civic and community groups, 1970—; mem. Jr. Programs Honor Bd., 1960—; hon. mem. Am. Mother's Com., 1964-73, named Mother of Year, 1964. Mem. Olympia Jr. Woman's Club (v.p. 1940), Assos. State Capitol Mus., PEO, (chaplain 1970), Thurston-Mason County Bar Assn. Aux., Pioneer Assn. Methodist (lay speaker). Address: Bigelow House 918 Glass St Olympia WA 98506

BIGELOW, STEPHANIE SINEY (MRS. PAUL WHEELOCK BIGELOW), curator; b. Bklyn., Mar. 13, 1903; d. Edward Ferdinand and Clara Louise (Candidus) Siney; B.A., Wheaton Coll., 1924; m. Paul Wheelock Bigelow, May 7, 1927; children—Clare (Mrs. Thomas H. Sheppard), Nancy (Mrs. John B. Bird), Barbara (Mrs. Edward B. Doherty). Curator, Bellport-Brookhaven Hist. Soc. Mus., Bellport Lane, N.Y., 1967—. Lectr. garden clubs, women's clubs, lit. groups, others, 1954—. Mem. D.A.R. (regent 1956-59), Bellport-Brookhaven Hist. Soc., Am. Daffodil Soc., South Country Antiques Soc., Bklyn. Botanic Gardens. Republican. Methodist. Clubs: Fireplace Literary (Brookhaven, N.Y.); Community (Garden City, N.Y.); Garden City. Author: Bellport and Brookhaven, 1968. Home: 7 Thornhedge Rd Bellport NY 11713 Office: 31 Bellport Lane Bellport NY 11713

BIGGS, BARBARA ELLEN, clin. psychologist; b. Bayonne, N.J., Aug. 30, 1931; d. Joseph Michael and Sylvia (Rosenthal) Silverman; B.A., Adelphi U., Garden City, N.Y., 1952; M.A. in Speech Pathology, N.Y. U., 1953; M.A. in Psychology, U. Cal. at Los Angeles, 1966, Ph.D., 1971; m. Sidney Sonenbluh, Nov. 22, 1973; children—Michael Patrick Biggs, Michael Dietrich Preussner, Jonathan David Biggs. Asst. prof. communicative disorders U. Cal. at Northridge, 1968-69, 72; co-founder, acad. dir. Student Devel. Center, Mt. St. Mary's Coll., Los Angeles, 1969-71; condr. workshops in humanistic edn., U.S., Eng. and Holland, 1972-73, 75; vis. prof. psychobiology U. So. Cal., 1971-73; psychotherapist Center Interpersonal Studies, Los Angeles, 1971—; co-dir. Hearing Officer's Tng. program Los Angeles City Atty.'s Office, 1974. Cons. in field. Mem. Cal. State Democratic Central Com., 1964. Recipient Pub. Service award VA, 1968. Mem. Am., Cal., Los Angeles County psychol. assns., Los Angeles Soc. Clin. Psychologists (pres.-elect 1975), Group Psychotherapy Assn. So. Cal. (mem. bd. 1970—), Assn. Humanistic Psychology. Contbr. articles to profl. jours. Office: 11941 Wilshire Blvd Los Angeles CA 90025

BIGGS, ELECTRA WAGGONER (MRS. JOHN BIGGS), artist; b. Fort Worth; d. Edward Paul and Helen (Buck) Waggoner; student Columbia, 1930; hon. degree, Tex. Women's Coll., 1951; m. John Biggs, Apr. 25, 1942; children—Electra (Mrs. Charles Francis Winston), Helen Dale (Mrs. Gene Wade Willingham). One woman shows Seligman Gallery, N.Y.C., 1936, Corcoran Gallery, Washington, 1963; exhibited Tex. Mus. Fine Arts, Houston, 1951, Fort Worth, 1953; executed 3 equestrain statues Will Rogers, Fort Worth, Lubbock, Tex., Claremore, Okla. busts John N. Garner, Austin, Tex., Victor McLaglen, Los Angeles, Dwight D. Eisenhower, Abilene, Kan., Denison, Tex., Harry S. Truman, Mo., Herbert Marcus, Dallas, and others. Bd. dirs. E. Paul and Helen Buck Found., Vernon Tex Recipient 3d prize Salon d'Autumne, Paris, France, 1934. Address: Santa Rosa Ranch Vernon TX 76684

BIGGS, JUDITH LORRAINE BLACKFORD (MRS. FOWLER A. BIGGS), chem. economist; b. Mpls., Jan. 15, 1943; d. Harold George and Hazel Roberta (Mossberg) Akam; B.S. (Cal. State scholar, Zonta scholar), U. Cal. at Berkeley, 1964; m. Fowler A. Biggs, Nov. 7, 1969. Chemist, Dept. Navy Indsl. Lab., San Francisco, 1964-65; mgr. organic chems. Chem. Econs. Handbook, editor Directory of Chem. Producers, Stanford Research Inst., Menlo Park, Cal., 1965—. Mem. Am. Chem. Soc. (sec. chmn. marketing and econs. div. 1975), Chem. Marketing Research Assn., European Assn. Indsl. Marketing Research, Stanford Med. Faculty Wives, San Diego Zool. Soc., Nat. Orgn. Women. Editor: Directory Chemical Producers, 1969-74 edits.; So., Midwestern, Western, Eastern chem. producers directories, 1971. Home: 185 Waverley St Palo Alto CA 94301 Office: 333 Ravenswood Av Menlo Park CA 94025

BIGGS, KATE BRITT (MRS. FURMAN KENNETH BIGGS), genealogist, historian; b. Lumberton, N.C., Sept. 7, 1899; d. Angus Isley and Florence (Townsend) Britt; student Campbell Coll., 1917, Chowan Coll., 1918-19; m. Furman Kenneth Biggs, Feb. 16, 1921; children—Furman Kenneth, I. Murchison, John Duckett. Farmer, Lumberton, 1955—; pres. Katy Did Farms, Inc., 1968—. Chmn. Robeson County campaign A.R.C., Lumberton, N.C., 1944; chmn. bond sales, Lumberton, 1942-43; chmn. Robeson County Cancer Dr., 1953-54; mem. Robeson County Centennial Com. Mem. Am. Legion Aux. (N.C. v.p. 1947-48, dist. committeewoman 1944-46, pres. unit 42 1942-44, unit historian 1940-67, recipient 1st history prize N.C. 1956), U.D.C. (chmn. hist. markers N.C. 1948-54, historian 1950-67), D.A.R. (regent Col. Thomas Robeson chpt. 1950-52, geneal. chmn. 1944, recipient N.C. prize for records 1944, historian 1952-67), Colonial Dames 17th Century, Daus. Am. Colonists, Nat. Soc. Magna Charta Dames, Am. Camellia Soc. Baptist (historian 1950-67). Club: Pine Crest Country (chmn. local beautification 1930-54, bridge chmn. 1954—). Author: Progress on the Lumbee Since 1787, 1952 (pageant); The History of First Baptist Church, Lumberton, 1832-1955, 1953; The History of Lumberton's American Legion and Auxiliary, 1919-1955, 1955; The Musselwhites and Allied Families, 1961; Biggs-Britts and Allied Families, 1970. Died Nov. 22, 1972. Home: 1505 Elm St Lumberton NC 28358

BIGGS, MOLLY CLAIRE MCCARTHY (MRS. LARRY DEAN BIGGS), ednl. adminstr.; b. Des Moines, Nov. 5, 1941; d. Frank Eugene and Eunice Norine (McKenzie) McCarthy; B.A., Drake U., 1965, M.S., 1970; m. Larry Dean Biggs, Aug. 5, 1963; children—Kimberly, Robert. Editorial asst. Ia. Credit Union League, Des Moines, 1965-68; counselor, Molokai High and Intermediate Sch., Hoolehua, Hawaii, 1971—. Mem. Am. Personnel and Guidance Assn., Hawaii Fedn. Tchrs. (sec. Molokai unit 1972-74), Hawaii State Tchrs. Assn., Women in Communications, Inc. (pres. Des Moines chpt. 1968-70), Hawaii Personnel and Guidance Assn. Presbyn. Home: PO Box 92 Kualapuu Molokai HI 96757 Office: PO Box 158 Hoolehua Molokai HI 96729

BIGNER, BETTY PAUL (MRS. STERLING BURTON BIGNER), newspaperwoman; b. Shreveport, La., Mar. 21, 1931; d. Harry Walker and Elizabeth (Schaeffer) Paul; student Randolph Macon Woman's Coll., 1947-48; B.S. in Chemistry, Sophie Newcomb Coll., 1951; m. Sterling Burton Bigner, Dec. 31, 1954. Stewardess Braniff Airlines, 1953; sec. Jr. C. of C., Shreveport, 1954; staff writer woman's page Shreveport Jour., 1957-65, woman's editor, 1965-73, news feature editor, 1973—, mem. rev. com. profit-sharing trust fund. Capt., United Fund, 1952, 54. Recipient award Dallas Market Center, 1969, 1st place award, page make-up Nat. Fedn. Press Women, 1971, ann. awards women's pages, fashion, home furnishings, food and make-up La. Press Women; guest govt. Republic China in Taiwan representing Women in Communication Press Group, 1972. Mem. C. of C. (mem. edn. com. 1968-70), Jr. League, Pi Beta Phi, Sigma Delta Chi. Republican. Episcopalian. Club: Shreveport Country. Home: 472 Leo St Shreveport LA 71105 Office: 222 Lake St Shreveport LA 71120

BIJUR, HILDA REIS (MRS. WILLIAM BIJUR), photographer; b. Greenwich, Conn., Aug. 19, 1919; d. Arthur M. and Claire (Raphael) Reis; A.B., Vassar Coll., 1940; m. William Bijur, July 23, 1952 (dec. 1960); children—Victoria, Arthur William. Asst. editor Theatre Arts Mag., N.Y.C., 1940-43; writer, pub. information sect. A.R.C., Nat. Hdqrs. Washington, 1943-45; photographer, 1946—, including World Bank, UN; exhibited in Mus. Modern Art, Parents Mag. Gallery (N.Y.C.), Expo' 67 (Montreal, Que., Can.); appeared in various mags. and papers including N.Y. Times, Herald Tribune, N.Y. Jour. Am., Saturday Rev. Lit., Parents Mag., Life, others. Mem. womens aux. bd. Montefiore Hosp., 1958-64. Bd. dirs. Neighborhood Playhouse Sch. of Theatre, N.Y.C. Mem. Am. Soc. Mag. Photographers. Clubs: Cosmopolitan, Lexington. Democratic. Home: 190 E 72d St New York City NY 10021

BIKLE, HELEN VIRGINIA COX (MRS. AUSTIN H. BIKLE), fruit farm exec.; b. Hagerstown, Md., Dec. 17, 1902; d. Nesbitt and Bessie Virginia (Renner) Cox; tchrs. certificate Towson State Coll., 1923; B.A., Western Md. Coll., 1946, postgrad., 1966; M.A., U. Md., 1951; m. Austin H. Bikle, July 18, 1938; 1 son, Richard N. Tchr., librarian jr. high sch., Hagerstown and Smithsburg, Md., 1923-29, 1945-70; airplane pilot and hostess, 1929-34; social worker Washington County Social Services, 1934-44; partner, asst. mgr., finance officer Bikle's Fruit Farm, Smithsburg, Md., 1945—. Vice pres. P.T.A., 1960-65. Mem. The 99's (charter), Am. Assn. U. Women. Democrat. Episcopalian. Club: OX5. Home: Route 3 Smithsburg MD 21783

BIKOFSKY, ELAINE JOAN, educator; b. Boston, Apr. 2, 1938; d. Max D. and Lee R. (Riseman) Jacobson; B.S. in Edn., Tufts U., Boston Sch. Occupational Therapy, 1960; M.S. in Occupational Therapy, Boston U.-Sargent Coll., 1973; m. Aaron K. Bikofsky, June 18, 1960; children—Marjorie Dana, Deborah Lynne. Coordinator patient care Med. Services Corp. Am., Newton, Mass., 1969-71; coordinator, asso. prof. occupational therapy assts. program Quinsigamond Community Coll., Worcester, Mass., 1972—. Gerontol. cons. to social agys., nursing homes, 1967—, Mass. Fedn. Nursing Homes, Boston, 1973-74; guest lectr. Boston U., Assumption Coll., Worcester. Mem. Framingham (Mass.) Council Aging, 1970-72; mem. Com. to Study Housing Needs, Worcester, 1971; mem. social gerontology project Boston U. Sch. Social Work, 1973. Recipient Allied Health Spl. Projects grant, 1972-74; NIH trainee. Mem. Mass. Occupational Therapy Assn. (mem. bd. 1971-72), Am. Occupational Therapy Assn. (gerontology rep. New Eng. Council on Practice 1971-73). Home: 40 William J Heights Framingham MA 01701 Office: 640 W Boylston St Worcester MA 01605

BILBAO, MARCIA KEPLER (MRS. JOSEPH BILBAO), physician; b. Rochester, Minn., Jan. 14, 1931; d. Edwin John and Helen (Mackeen) Kepler; B.S., U. Minn., 1952; postgrad. Columbia, 1952-53, M.D., 1957; m. Joseph Bilbao, June 5, 1954; children—Joseph, Lauren, James. Intern, Roosevelt Hosp., N.Y.C., 1957-58 resident, 1958-59; resident U. Ore. Med. Sch., Portland, 1959-60, instr. radiology, 1961-63, asso. prof. radiology, 1963-69, prof., 1965—. Recipient awards, including Janeway prize Coll. Phys. & Surgs., 1957, Aesculapius award Ore. Med. Assn., 1967, award of merit A.M.A., 1968, 71. Patentee in field. Home: 7736 SW 10th Av Portland OR 97219 Office: 3181 SW Sam Jackson Park Rd Portland OR 97201

BILEK, MARY JEAN, univ. ofcl.; b. Marinette, Wis., Jan. 15, 1925; d. Loren Sedrick and Mary (Humphries) Miller; student Lawrence U., 1943-44; B.A. in Journalism, U. Wis.-Madison, 1947; m. Edward Joseph Bilek, May 28, 1947; 1 son, Edward Miller. Reporter, Capital Times, Madison, Wis., 1947-50; field dir., pub. relations dir. Lac-Baie Girl Scout Council, 1963-67; with U. Wis., 1967—, now asst. to dean U. Wis. Center, Marinette. Communications cons. Sea Grant projects Moss Landing Marine Labs., Cal. State U. and Coll. System, 1974; adminstrv. coordinator Theatre on the Bay. Bd. dirs. Lac-Baie Girl Scout Council. Mem. Women in Communication, Am. Field Service, State Congress on Aging, Marinette County Hist. Soc., Wis. Alumni Assn. (life mem., dir. Twin County alumni club), P.E.O., Kappa Alpha Theta. Republican. Presbyn. (trustee 1951-53). Home: 704 Chautauqua Rd Pine Beach Marinette WI 54143 Office: U Wis Center-Marinette County Bay Shore Marinette WI 54143

BILES, FAY REIFSNYDER (MRS. BEDFORD H. BILES), univ. adminstr.; b. Reading, Pa., Mar. 31, 1929; d. Thomas H. and Dora E. (Weaver) Reifsnyder; A.B., Duke, 1949; M.A., Kent State U., 1956; Ph.D., Ohio State U., 1968; m. Bedford H. Biles, Sept. 7, 1949. Tchr. biology and English, Coventry High Sch., Akron, O., 1950-56; prof. Kent (O.) State U., 1956-72, v.p. pub. affairs and devel., 1972—. Dir., City Bank, Kent. Cons., Presidents' Council on Phys. Fitness and Sports. Recipient Distinguished Teaching award Kent State U., 1970; named Outstanding Woman Alumna, Delta Phi Rho Alpha, 1949, Outstanding Delta Delta Delta Woman of Year, 1972. Mem. Am. (dist. chmn. phys. edn. sect. Midwest, state v.p. gen. div. Ohio, com. chmn., dir. Pepi project), Ohio (Meritorious award) assns. health, phys. edn. and recreation, Nat., Midwest (dir., pub. relations chmn., research project chmn.) assns. phys. edn. coll. women, Ohio Coll. Assn. for Phys. Edn. for Women (pres.), Am. Assn. Univ. Women, Northeastern Health Assn. (dir.), Am. Coll. Pub. Relations Assn. (nat. dir. 1973-74), Delta Psi Kappa, Delta Phi Alpha, Kappa Delta Pi, Alpha Lambda Delta, Delta Kappa Gamma. Home: 1151 Pin Oak Dr Kent OH 44242

BILINKAS, MARY THERESE LIVENGOOD (MRS. EDWARD W. BILINKAS), ednl. adminstr.; b. Oxford, N.C., Dec. 15, 1921; d. William S. and Martha Catherine (Cupp) Livengood; B.A., Juniata Coll., 1943; m. Edward W. Bilinkas, Jan. 15, 1961; children—Merrill (Mrs. Philip Hood), Barbara (Mrs. Ralph Prescuitti), William G., Barry C., Edward J. Reporter, Harrisburg (Pa.) Telegraph, 1941-43, Boise (Ida.) Statesman, 1943, Gowenfield (Ida.) Beacon, 1944-45; bur. mgr. Johnstown (Pa.) Tribune, 1945-46; reporter Pitts. Post Gazette, 1946-47; pub. relations dir. Cambrian County (Pa.) War Meml. Arena, 1950-53; owner John Everets, Inc., Johnstown, Pa., 1954-61; substitute tchr. Randolph (N.J.) High Sch., 1962-64; mng. editor Daily Advance, Dover, N.J., 1965-70; dir. coll. information services County Coll. Morris, Dover, N.J., 1970—. Dir. pub. relations Pro-Hockey Team, 1950-53. Pres., Meml. Hosp. Aux., Johnstown, 1952-53. Trustee Gen. MacArthur Mil. Acad., Mt. Freedom, N.J., 1973—. Pub. relations dir. Randolph Republican Club, 1961-64; dir. Morris County Woman's Rep. Club, 1964. Recipient 1st prize Nat. Aviation Newswriting, 1948; numerous news and feature writing awards N.J. Press Assn. and N.J. Press Womans Assn.; Distinguished Service award Lakeland Lodge, Patrolmens Benevolent Assn., 1972; named Woman of Year, Morris Cath. Mothers and Daus. Assn., 1970. Mem. N.J. Fraternal Order Police (life). Home: Radtke Rd RD 3 Dover NJ 07801 Office: County Coll Morris Route 10 and Center Grove Rd Dover NJ 07801

BILKER, IRIS JUNE, child psychiatrist; b. Phila., Aug. 2, 1927; d. Harry and Minnie Anna (Rosenberg) Bilker; R.N., Jewish Hosp. Phila., 1947; student Temple U., 1952-54; M.D., Woman's Med. Coll. Pa., 1958. Head nurse, supr. pediatrics Jewish Hosp., Phila., 1947-52; intern Albert Einstein Med. Center, Phila., 1958-59, pediatric resident, 1959-61, attending in pediatrics, 1961-72, resident in adult psychiatry, 1969-71, attending child psychiatry, 1973—; practice medicine, specializing in pediatrics, Phila., 1961-69, specializing in adult and child psychiatry, Wyncote, Pa., 1973—; resident in child psychiatry Hahnemann Med. Coll. and Hosp., Phila., 1971-73, clin. asst. asst. prof. child psychiatry, 1973—; clin. instr. pediatrics Woman's Med. Coll. Phila., 1961-72. Mem. Delaware Valley Regional Council Child Psychiatry. Nat. Inst. Mental Health grantee, 1969. Diplomate Am. Bd. Pediatrics. Fellow Am. Acad. Pediatrics; mem. Am. Med. Woman's Assn., Pa., Philadelphia County med. socs., A.M.A. Home: Cedarbrook Hill III Wyncote PA 19095

BILKEY, FRANCISCA ANGELICA ROMERO-MATOS, mental health research analyst; b. San Pedro de Macoris, Dominican Republic, Sept. 18, 1919; d. Eduardo and Angelica (Beltre) Romero-Matos; B.S. in Archtl. Engring., U. Santo Domingo (Dominican Republic), 1941; A.M. in Econs., Radcliffe Coll., 1949; tchrs. certificate U. Wis., 1968; m. Warren J. Bilkey, Sept. 10, 1949; children—Warren Jr., Christopher, Peter, Martin, Maria. Came to U.S., 1947, naturalized, 1968. Head sect. spl. studies dept. statistics Dominican Govt., Santo Domingo, 1941-47, vice minister of finance, 1963, tech. adviser Central Bank of Dominican Republic, 1963-66; faculty Madison Bus. Coll. (Wis.), 1966-68, 70; instr. econs. Edgewood Coll., Madison, 1968-70; research analyst Wis. Dept. Social Services, Madison, 1970—. Lectr. dept. econs. U. Santo Domingo, 1964-65; Dominican del. bd. govs. meeting IMF, 1948, UN Econ. Commn. for Latin Am., Brasilia, Brazil, 1964, UN Conf. on Trade and Devel., Geneva, 1964. Mem. Am. Econ. Assn. Home: 6310 Woodington Way Madison WI 53711 Office: 1 W Wilson St Madison WI 53702

BILL, DORA COX (MRS. RUSSELL W. BILL), pub. information ofcl.; b. Knoxville, Tenn.; d. Charles Fred and Imogene (Masters) Cox; student LaGrange Coll., 1928, 29; flower show judging degree, U. Ga., 1950; m. Ray Dodson, 1930; 1 dau., Jeanie Cox (Mrs. Jack Harris); m. 2d, Clayton Justin Cosse, Apr. 9, 1950; m. 3d, Russell W. Bill, June 20, 1969. Gen. mgr. So. office J. H. McGillvra Co. of N.Y., Atlanta, 1948-49; formed Dora Dodson Radio Rep. Agy., 1949; So. mgr. Forjoe Co., Atlanta, 1949; formed Dora-Clayton Agy., Inc., 1950, v.p., treas., 1950-69; pub. information specialist Office Econ. Opportunity, Washington, 1969—, U.S. Action, Region IV, Atlanta, 1971—. Active in Cerebral Palsy, A.R.C. drives; pres. Civitan Aux., 1955-56; mem. Atlanta Symphony Guild, mem. bd. 1959—; mem. Atlanta Opera Guild. Recipient Ann. Printers Ink Silver medal, 1968. Mem. Am. Women in Radio and TV (nat., local bds.; nat. pres. 1965-66), So. Council Internat. and Pub. Affairs, C. of C., Am. Fedn. Advt. Clubs, Atlanta Advt. Club, League of Women Voters, English Speaking Union, Soc. Pub. Adminstrn., Atlanta Arts Assn., Nat. Assn. Arts and Scis. Episcopalian. Clubs: Atlanta Women's Golf Assn. (mem. bd. 1959—), East Lake Golf Assn. (sec. 1956-58), Atlanta Press, Atlanta Variety (mem. women's com.), Parkwood Garden (sec.), Atlanta Athletic, East Lake Country; Ponte Vedra (Fla.) Country; Highlands (N.C.) Country. Home: 6851 Roswell Rd NE Apt B14 Atlanta GA 30328 Office: Action 730 Peachtree St Atlanta GA 30308

BILL, SHIRLEY AKERMAN (MRS. CHARLES A. BILL), educator; b. Chgo., Oct. 26, 1918; d. Bertel L. and Veronica (Bredt) Akerman; A.B., U. Chgo., 1941, M.A., 1942, Ph.D., 1950; m. Charles A. Bill, Nov. 2, 1936. Instr. history U. Ill., Chgo., 1947-51, asst. prof., 1951-60, asso. prof., 1960-66, prof. history, 1966—. Mem. Am. Hist. Assn., Orgn. Am. Historians, Am. Soc. 18th Century Studies, Phi Beta Kapp. Home: 2716 Sunnyside Chicago IL 60625

BILLER, MARY ANN, coll. pres.; b. Bronx, N.Y., June 20, 1935; d. George and Katharine (Bittl) Biller; B.S. in Edn., St. Thomas Aquinas Coll., 1958; M.A. in Philosophy, St. John's U., 1962, Ph.D., 1967; postdoctoral student State U. N.Y., U. Notre Dame. Joined Dominican Congregation, 1953; prof. philosophy, chmn. dept. St. Thomas Aquinas Coll., 1964—, pres., 1970—. N.Y. State Regents teaching fellow, 1959; Archdiocesan scholar, 1963; grantee State U. N.Y., 1969, U. Notre Dame, 1970, Wheeling Coll., 1968, U. Belgrade, 1972. Mem. Am. Catholic Philosophy Assn., Am. Assn. Higher Edn. Home: 3145 Decatur Av Bronx NY 10467 Office: St Thomas Aquinas Coll Sparkill NY 10976

BILLINGER, PATRICIA DONNA, clubwoman, writer; b. Chgo., July 10, 1934; d. Bryan B. and Lois (White) Billinger; student Oberlin Coll., 1953-54, Harvard, summers, 1957, 58; pvt. study piano; pvt. study voice with Joan Brainerd, 1968-72. Presented travel lectures with slides Bruce Mus., Greenwich, Conn., 1970, Norwalk Woman's Club, 1968, Dixie Club, N.Y.C., 1968, U.D.C. Programs, N.Y.C., 1964, Composers, Artists and Authors Am., N.Y.C., 1969, many others. Nat. pres. Shelby Hogge White Family Assn., 1962-64; chmn. bull. com. Norwalk (Conn.) Woman's Club, 1968-70; mem. sr. state bd. Children Am. Revolution, 1950-52; historian Margaret Fernald Dole Art Club, Greenwich, Conn., 1960-72, pub. relations chmn., 1968-72; mem. reception com. for Princess Margaret and Lord Snowden, English Speaking Union; active Multiple Sclerosis, Heart Fund drives. Mem. U.D.C. (1st v.p. N.Y.C. chpt. 1970-72, dir. radio and TV 1970-72), English-Speaking Union, Zeta Tau Alpha (mem. recommendation com. 1970-72). Club: Sprite Island Yacht (Norwalk, Conn.). Editor: Worth Remembering, 2d edit. U.D.C., 1972. Contbg. editor Northfield Lit. mag., 1950-52. Contbr. poetry to mags., including Child Life, Am. Poetry mag., Blue Moon Internat. Quar. Verse, Scimitar and Song, also various newspapers throughout U.S. Address: 40 France St Norwalk CT 06851

BILLINGS, JANE ELIZABETH KELLY (MRS. ROBERT EDWARD BILLINGS), librarian; b. Watertown, Wis., June 10, 1916; d. William Edward and Elizabeth Elydia (Knaak) Kelly; student Northwestern Coll., 1934-36; B.A., U. Wis., 1938, B.L.S., 1939, M.A. in L.S., 1962; m. Robert Edward Billings, Oct. 12, 1941. Librarian, Pub. Library of Clintonville (Wis.), 1939-49; supr. sch. libraries, Clintonville, 1949—. Faculty U. Wis. Library Sch., summers, 1963-71, chmn. adv. council, 1965-67. Mem. Gov.'s Council for Library Devel., 1965-71, chmn., 1969-70; mem. Legislative Library Laws Revision Com., 1970; chmn. library sect. Waupaca County Depressed Area Com., 1971; v.p. Clintonville chpt. Am. Field Service, 1969, sec., 1970-72, 74—, treas., 1972-74. Mem. Am. (chmn. Grolier scholarship com. 1968-69), Wis. (pres. 1948-50, dir. 1960-63) library assns., Nat., Wis. (pres. sch. library sect. 1956-57), Central Wis. (pres. 1973-74), Clintonville (pres. 1963-64) edn. assns., Am. (chmn. nominating com. 1970-71), Wis. (a founder) assns. sch. librarians, Am. Assn. Univ. Women (local pres. 1952), State Hist. Soc. Wis. (life), U. Wis. Alumni Assn. (life), Wis. Audio Visual Assn., U. Wis. Library Sch. Alumni Assn. (life mem., pres. 1949), Beta Phi Mu, Delta Kappa Gamma. Conglist. Mem. Order Eastern Star (worthy matron 1948-49). Contbr. articles to profl. jours. Home: 158 N Clinton Av Clintonville WI 54929 Office: 255 N Main St Clintonville WI 54929

BILLINGTON, LILLIAN EMILY, educator, author; b. Ashland, Wisconsin; d. Stephen and Ellen (Hawkins) Billington; Bachelor Arts, San Jose State U., 1931; M.A., Stanford U., 1934, Ed.D., 1946. Supr. elementary schs., Longview, Wash., 1929-30; faculty San Jose (Cal.) State U., 1934—, prof. elementary edn., 1950—. Cons in lang. arts to pub. sch. systems. Vol. work A.R.C. Recipient Honor award Eugene Field Literary Soc., 1951. Mem. Internat. Platform Assn., Nat. Writers Club, Speech and Hearing Therapy Club San Jose State U. (hon.), Pi Lambda Theta, Kappa Delta Pi, Delta Gamma. Author, Spelling Series: Using Words, 1941-68, Using Words With Power, 1972; Handwriting Series, 1945; Play and Learn books; Handwriting Series: Toward Better Writing, 1960. Home: Kingscote Gardens 586 Lomita Dr Stanford CA 94305

BILLOWS, GEORGETTE BRANIN, psychologist; b. Newark, Dec. 12, 1932; d. Everett and Louise (Cable) Branin; student Bowling Green U., Fairfield U.; A.B., Drew U., 1955; M.A., Ohio State U., 1959; postgrad. Tchrs. Coll., Columbia, 1974-75; m. Malcolm L. Billows, Nov. 25, 1965. Counselor, DePauw U., Greencastle, Ind.; clin. psychologist Mental Health Clinc, Bowling Green, O., Hawthorn Center, Northville, Mich.; sch. psychologist Greenwich (Conn.) Bd. Edn., 1966—. Mem. Am. Psychol. Assn., Conn. Assn. Sch. Psychologists, Pi Gamma Mu. Home: 66 Albin Rd Stamford CT 06902

BINDER, MARY JO AGETON (MRS. ROBERT HENRI BINDER), orgn. behavior specialist; b. San Diego, Jan. 20, 1939; d. Arthur Ainslie and Jo Lucille (Gallion) Ageton; A.B., Middlebury Coll., 1961; M.Ed., Antioch Grad. Sch. Edn., 1973; m. Robert Henri Binder, May 5, 1962; children—Ainslie Ann, Hilary Lyle, Robyn Meredith. Community aide/counselor D.C. Model Schs. Div., 1967-69; coordinator United Planning Orgn. Coalition Womens Orgns., Washington, 1967-71; project dir. Washington Opportunities for Women, 1970-71; policy/research/application fellow Center for Vol. Soc., 1971-73; program developer Human Resources Research Orgn., Washington, 1974—. Founding mem. D.C. chpt. Womens Polit. Caucus, 1970—. Mem. Nat. Orgn. Women (dir. D.C. chpt. 1974, chmn. D.C. chpt. volunteerism task force 1973-74, So. regional coordinator, 1974—), Profl. Womens Caucus, Internat. Transactional Analysis Assn., Assn. for Tng. and Devel., Nat. Tng. Labs. Orgn. Devel. Network. Home: 1824 Redwood Terrace Washington DC 20012 Office: 300 N Washington St Alexandria VA 22314

BINGAMAN, ANNE LENA KOVACOVICH (MRS. JESSE F. BINGAMAN JR.), educator; b. Jerome, Ariz., July 3, 1943; d. William Emil and Anne Ellen (Baker) Kovacovich; student London (Eng.) Sch. Econs. and Polit. Sci., 1964-65; A.B., Stanford, 1965; LL.B., Stanford, 1968; m. Jesse F. Bingaman Jr., Sept. 14, 1968. Admitted to Cal., Ariz., N.M. bars, 1969; law clk. Brown, Vlassis & Bain, Phoenix, 1968-69; atty. N.M. Bur. Revenue, Santa Fe, 1969-70; asso. Modrall, Sperling, Roehl, Harris & Sisk, Albuquerque, 1970; atty. N.M. Atty. Gen.'s Office, Santa Fe, 1971; asso. prof. law U. N.M. Law Sch., Albuquerque, 1972—. Legal counsel N.M. Planned Parenthood Assn., 1973—, atty. N.M. Commn. on Status of Women, 1973—. Mem. State Bar Cal., State Bar Ariz., State Bar N.M. (chmn. com. on community property 1973—), Am. Bar Assn. (chmn. com. on community property subcom. equal rights commn. on real property, probate and trust law 1974—). Home: 222 Camino Del Norte Santa Fe NM 87501 Office: U NM Law Sch 1117 Stanford NE Albuquerque NM 87131

BINGER, GRACE ELIZABETH GUNN (MRS. CARL E. BINGER), physician; b. Healdsburg, Cal.; d. George Lucius and Maude (Newland) Gunn; B.A., U. Cal., 1930, M.D., 1939; m. Carl E. Binger, Aug. 16, 1940; children—Nelson, Nancy, Jane. Intern, U. Cal. Hosp., San Francisco, 1938-39, asst. resident neurology, 1939-40; asst. resident anesthesiology Stanford U. Hosp., San Francisco, 1940-41, resident anesthesiology, 1941-42, staff anesthesiologist, 1942-48; practice medicine specializing in anesthesiology, San Jose, Cal., 1945-58; mem. staff San Jose, O'Connor hosps., Santa Clara Valley Med. Hosp., San Jose; staff anesthesiologist Kaiser Hosp., Santa Clara, 1968—. Diplomate Am. Bd. Anesthesiology. Fellow Am. Coll. Anesthesiologists; mem. Am., Cal. socs. anesthesiologists, Soc. Anaesthetists Gt. Britain and Ireland, Am., Cal., Santa Clara County med. assns., Delta Zeta. Episcopalian. Mem. Order Eastern Star. Home: 920 Pershing Av San Jose CA 95126 Office: Kieley Blvd Santa Clara CA 95051

BINGER, LYDIA THERING (MRS. RALPH E. BINGER), educator; b. Selm, Germany, Jan. 29, 1929; d. John and Bertha (Volker) Thering; B.S., State U. N.Y., 1951; M.S., Wash. State U., 1953; Ed.D., U. Tenn., 1969; m. Ralph E. Binger, Nov. 23, 1969. Tchr. phys. edn. Elba (N.Y.) Central High Sch., 1951-52; asst. Wash. State U., Pullman, 1952-53; asst. prof. U. N.Y., Oswego, 1953-54; asso. prof. phys. edn. U. Wis., Superior, 1954-74, prof., 1974—, dir. women's phys. edn. 1954—, supervising tchr., 1954-64, asso. athletic dir., 1974—. Mem. A.A.H.P.E.R., Nat. Assn. Phys. Edn. for Coll. Women (dist. rep. 1960-64), U. Wis. Women (pres. 1972-74), Lawyers Wives Wis., League Women Voters. Home: 193 Billings Dr Superior WI 54880

BINGER, PENELOPE ANDERSON (MRS. FORREST K. BINGER), bus. exec., civic worker; b. Omaha, May 1, 1926; d. Frank Wylie and Penelope (Hamilton) Anderson; student Cornell Coll., 1943-45, U. Omaha, summer 1945; B.A., U. Neb., 1946; postgrad. Sch. Religion U. Ia.; m. Forrest Keith Binger, Nov. 29, 1946; children—Penelope (Mrs. John A. Lawson), Virginia (Mrs. David F. Booth), James, Elizabeth, Paula, Julia. Office mgr. Constrn. and Indsl. Sales Co., Cedar Rapids, Ia., 1958—. Chmn. Mayor's Commn. on Status Women, Cedar Rapids, 1965-67; mem. sub-com. Gov.'s Commn. on Status Women, 1965-67; mem. com. to study Linn County Air Pollution Ordinance, 1969-70; mem. Gov.'s Child Labor Com., 1970—. Republican precinct committeewoman, 1953-67; vice chmn. 2d Dist. Young Republicans, 1954-57; vice chmn. Linn County Rep. Central Com., 1955-67; pres. Linn County Rep. Womens Club, 1958-60; Linn County campaign chmn. for David Stanley for U.S. Senate, 1968; vice chmn. Linn County Com. to re-elect Gov. Ray, 1972. Mem. Am. Assn. U. Women (pres. Cedar Rapids 1964-66; dir. Ia. div. 1969-73; mem. assn. program topic com. 1971-73), D.A.R., Common Cause, Assn. for Humanistic Psychology, Inner Peace Movement, Found. for Spiritual Understanding. Club: Altrusa (pres. 1971-73) (Cedar Rapids). Home: 1844 2d Av SE Cedar Rapids IA 52403 Office: 529 H St SW Cedar Rapids IA 52406

BINGHAM, ELIZA E. TURNER (MRS. LEONARD LAWRENCE BINGHAM), educator, psychol. examiner; b. Eden, N.C., Nov. 16, 1911; d. Joseph Platt and Myrtle (King) Turner; A.B., Meredith Coll., 1933; postgrad. High Point Coll., summers 1959-61; M.Ed., U. N.C., 1965; m. Leonard Lawrence Bingham, Sept. 6, 1952. Social worker Rehab. Center, Dept. of Army, Fort Jackson, S.C., 1943-44, psychol. asst., 1944-46, clin. psychologist U.S. Disciplinary Barracks, Camp Gordon, Ga., 1946-48, Fort Hancock, N.J., 1948-50, psychologist, Ft. Leavenworth, Kan., 1950-51; classroom tchr. Guilford County Schs., Greensboro, N.C., 1958-61, Greensboro City Schs., 1961-66; tchr. remedial reading Caldwell Sch., Greensboro, 1966-72; diagnostician Diagnostic Reading Center, Greensboro City Schs., 1972—; psychol. examiner, Greensboro, 1969—. Mem. N.C. Psychol. Assn. (asso.), Am. Childhood Edn. Internat., N.E.A., N.C. Edn. Assn., N.C. Classroom Tchrs. Assn., Internat. Reading Assn., N.C. Hist. Soc. Home: 801 Simpson St Greensboro NC 27401

BINGHAM, FRANCES WILMERE, biologist; b. N.Y.C., Apr. 14, 1913; d. Dr. Francis Elmer and Mary (Von Geissing-Hill) Bingham; B.S., Good Counsel Coll., 1933; M.S., Columbia, 1934. With Lederle Labs., Pearl River, N.Y., 1934—, dept. head biol. control services, 1962—. Active Girl Scouts U.S.A. Mem. Am. Soc. Microbiologists, N.Y. Acad. Scis., Am. Assn. U. Women, Rockland County Hist. Soc., Am. Inst. Biol. Scis. Office: Lederle Labs Pearl River NY 10965

BINGHAM, JUNE (MRS. JONATHAN BINGHAM), writer; b. White Plains, N.Y., June 20, 1919; d. Max J. H. and Mabel (Limburg) Rossbach; student Vassar Coll., 1936-38; B.A., Barnard Coll., 1941; m. Jonathan Bingham, Sept. 20, 1939; children—Sherrell (Mrs. James E. Bland), June Mitchell (Mrs. Erik C. Esselstyn), Timothy Woodbridge, Claudia Rossbach (Mrs. Thomas Meyers). Writer, editor War Finance div. U.S. Treasury, Washington, 1943-44; editorial asst. Washington Post, 1945-46. Vice pres. World Fedn. for Mental Health, U.S. Com., Inc., 1958-62; bd. dirs. African-Am. Inst., N.Y.C., Ittleson Center for Child Research, N.Y.C.; trustee Barnard Coll. Author: (with Dr. F. C. Redlich) The Inside Story; Psychiatry and Everyday Life, 1953; Courage to Change: An Introduction to the Life and Thought of Reinhold Niebuhr, 1961; U Thant: The Search for Peace, 1966; also booklets, mag. articles. Home: 5000 Independence Av New York City NY 10471 also 3308 Reservoir Rd Washington DC 20007

BINGHAM, LOIS A., art adminstr., author; b. Iowa Falls, Ia., July 8, 1913; B.A., M.A., Oberlin Coll.; postgrad. Yale Sch. Fine Arts, (Carnegie grantee) U. Paris (France). Arranged and supervised exhbns. of Am. art for circulation abroad including Modern Painting and Sculpture, Moscow, USSR, 1959, Biennials at Sao Paulo, Venice, Santiago, New Delhi, Paris, 1961—, numerous others; asso. curator for edn. Nat. Gallery of Art, Washington, 1943-54; chief fine arts div., exhbn. br. USIA, 1954-65; chief internat. art program Smithsonian Instn., Nat. Collection of Fine Arts, Washington, 1965—. Author: How to Look at Works of Art; Highlights of American Painting; contbr. articles to profl. jours. Home: 374 N St SW Washington DC 20024 Office: Nat Collection of Fine Arts Smithsonian Instn Washington DC 20560

BINGHAM, REBECCA JOSEPHINE TAYLOR (MRS. WALTER D. BINGHAM), librarian; b. Indpls., July 14, 1928; d. George Edward and Lalla (Bass) Taylor; B.S., Ind. U., 1950, M.L.S., 1969; M.A., U. Tulsa, 1962; m. Louis J. Simmons, July 28, 1950 (div. Dec. 1954); children—Gail Elaine, Louis Edward; m. 2d, Walter D. Bingham, Oct. 27, 1957. Asst. librarian Alcorn (Miss.) A. and M. Coll., 1950-51; asst. serials librarian Tuskegee (Ala.) Inst., 1952-53; asst. librarian Jarvis Christian Coll., Hawkins, Tex., 1955-57; librarian Carver Jr. High Sch., Tulsa, 1960-62; tchr. English, Russell Jr. High Sch., Louisville, 1962-63; librarian Jackson Jr. High Sch., Louisville, 1963-66; supr. library services Louisville Pub. Schs., 1966-70, dir. media services, 1970—. Bd. dirs. Louisville Children's Theatre, Christian Ch. Found.; mem. Louisville-Jefferson County Health and Welfare Council, Ky. Adv. Library Council; alumni trustee Grad. Library Sch., Ind. U. Named Outstanding Sch. Librarian, Ky. Library Trustees, 1969. Mem. A.L.A. (mem. council 1972-75, exec. bd. 1974—), S.E. Regional Library Assn. (sec.-treas. resources and tech. services div. 1973-75), Am., Ky. (editor Bull. 1967-68) assns. sch. librarians, Nat., Ky., Louisville edn. assns., Ky. Library Assn. (pres.

1971), Alumni Assn. Grad. Library Sch. Ind. U. (pres. 1974—), Pi Lambda Theta, Kappa Delta Pi. Episcopalian (pres. Episcopal Churchwomen 1969-70). Contbr. to Am. Educator Ency., Compton's Ency. Home: 3608 Dumesnill St Louisville KY 40211 Office: Brown Edn Center 4th St at Broadway Louisville KY 40202

BINGHAM, MRS. RUTHERFURD (KATHARINE CUNNINGHAM GRAY BINGHAM), civic leader; b. Brookline, Mass., Jan. 24, 1905; d. James Cunningham and Grace Elvira (Freeman) Gray; student pvt. schs., Boston, also Rome, Italy; m. Rutherfurd Bingham, May 24, 1941 (dec. Jan. 3, 1952); 1 stepson, Rutherfurd Glenn (dec.). Profl. singer Aborn Opera Co., Gilbert & Sullivan operas, NBC, many other concerts, etc., 1939-40. Served as 1st lt. A.R.C. Motor Corps, 1928-39. Treas. New Eng. Anti-Vivisection Soc.; mem. Mass. Revolutionary Bicentennial Commn. Mem. adv. bd. Salvation Army. Recipient citation Am. Legion; Freedom award Am. Inst.; citation Chelsea Naval Hosp. Mem. D.A.R. (regent Paul Revere chpt. 1958-61), Nat. Soc. Colonial Dames, Mass. Soc. Mayflower Descs., New Eng. Hist. Geneal. Soc., Dau. Colonial Wars (pres. Mass. 1962-65, nat. custodian 1965—), Am. Inst. (trustee), Trustees of Reservations (life), Daus. Founders and Patriots Am. (state v.p.), Soc. Descs. Colonial Clergy, Mass. Ct. Assts., Women Descs. Ancient and Hon. Arty. Co., Soc. Preservation New Eng. Antiquities, Nat. Trust Historic Preservation, Bunker Hill Monument Assn. (v.p.), Daus. of 1812 in D.C., Bostonian Soc. Episcopalian. Clubs: Capitol Hill (life) (Washington); College (Boston); Women's Republican (v.p. 1955-57, treas. 1957-59, pres. Mass.). Home: 65 Commonwealth Av Boston MA 02116

BINKLEY, MARGARET DELANO (MRS. PHILIP PACK), engring. geologist; b. Inspiration, Ariz., Sept. 24, 1914; d. Douglas Matthew and Gladys (Arnold) Delano; grad. U. Cal. at Berkeley, 1938; m. William G. Binkley, 1936 (dec.); children—Mary D. (Mrs. William Jadiker), Daniel Binkley; m. 2d, Phillip D. Pack, Aug. 30, 1965. Jr. geologist Standard Oil Co. Cal., Taft, 1942-43; petroleum engr. State Cal. Div. Oil and Gas, Taft and Bakersfield, Cal., 1943-53, Oceanic Oil Co., Bakersfield, 1953-56; engring. geologist U.S. Bur. Reclamation, Sacramento, Denver, 1957-65; geol. engr. U.S. AEC, Mercury and Las Vegas, Nev., 1965-74; geologist IRS, Washington, 1974—. Registered profl. engr., Cal. Mem. Assn. Engring. Geologists, Am. Assn. Petroleum Geologists, Geol. Soc. Am., U. Cal. Alumni Assn. Home: 4630 Norwood Dr Chevy Chase MD 20015 Office: IRS 1111 Constitution Av NW Washington DC 20224

BINNEBOSEL, ELINOR MARTHA (MRS. ALAN J. BROWN), pediatrician; b. Bklyn., Nov. 29, 1937; d. Erich W. and Katherine K. (Schick) Binnebosel; A.B. cum laude, U. Rochester, 1959; M.D., Albert Einstein Coll. Medicine, 1963; m. Alan J. Brown, May 3, 1963; children—Karen Rebecca, Beverly Lisa, Daniel. Intern Bronx (N.Y.) Municipal Hosp., 1963-64, resident, 1964-66; vis. pediatrician Lincoln Hosp., Bronx, 1966-71, dir. pediatric home care, 1966-68; asst. chief sect. pediatric neurology Grasslands Hosp., Valhalla, N.Y., 1971—, coordinator children's spl. meningomylocoele hydrocephalus program, 1971—; asst. attending pediatrician Flower Fifth Av Hosp., N.Y.C.; asst. clin. prof. pediatrics N.Y. Med. Coll., 1971—; cons. pediatrician Mental Retardation Inst., Valhalla, N.Y. Diplomate Am. Bd. Pediatrics. Mem. Phi Beta Kappa. Home: 6 Cohawney Rd Scarsdale NY 10583 Office: Dept Pediatrics Grasslands Hosp Valhalla NY 10595

BINNEY, JEAN BROWN (MRS. RONALD MORGAN BINNEY), occupational therapist; b. Panama City, Fla., May 10, 1948; d. William Samuel and Minnie Frances (Dalton) Brown; A.A. cum laude, Seminole Jr. Coll., 1968; B.S., U. Fla., 1970; m. Ronald Morgan Binney, Apr. 18, 1970. Occupational therapy cons. Tri-County Family Service Agy., Yuba City, Cal., 1972, Yuba-Sutter Home Health Agy., Yuba City, 1971-73; chief occupational therapy Eskaton Colusa Healthcare Center, Colusa, Cal., 1971-73; pediatric occupational therapist Shands Teaching Hosp., Gainesville, Fla., 1973—. Vice pres. Civinettes, Sanford, Fla., 1968; senator, honor ct. justice Coll. of Health Related Professions, U. Fla., Gainesville, 1970. Mem. Am. Occupational Therapy Assn., Archtl. Dames, Pi Beta Phi. Home: 1816 NW 10th St Gainesville FL 32601 Office: Dept Occupational Therapy Box 200 J Hillis Miller Health Center U Fla Gainesville FL 32601

BINNING, BETTE FINESE (MRS. GENE HEDGCOCK BINNING), athletic assn. ofcl.; d. Henry Josiah and Beatrice Victoria (Harrop) Ames; b. Brandon, Man., Can., Sept. 20, 1927 (father Am. citizen); grad. Brandon Collegiate, 1944; student Brandon, U., 1944-46; m. Gene Hedgcock Binning, May 3, 1952; children—Gene Barton, Barbara Jo, Bradford Jay. Exec. sec. to mgr. Gardner-Denver Co., Denver, 1950-52; mem. age group swimming com. Amateur Athletic Union U.S., 1966-68, 70-72, women's swimming com., 1968-69, 72-73, age group swimming objectives subcom., 1970-71, del. conv., 1971, 72, 73, 74, nat. chmn. swimming ofcl. certification, 1972-73, mem. nat. age group rules com., 1972-73, mem. nat. planning and orgn. com., 1972-73, dir. swimming records U.S., 1972—; Okla. state chmn. age group swimming Amateur Athletic Union, 1966-68, 70-72, chmn. women's swimming com., 1968-69, 72-75, mem. Okla. exec. bd. for all amateur sports, also registration com., 1971-75; Mem. U.S. Olympic Com., 1972—. Team capt. YMCA fund drives, 1966—; active Community Chest, Cancer, Muscular Dystrophy fund drives, Okla. Horse Shows. Mem. Kiwanis Ladies, Youth Study Club (treas. 1971-72). Presbyn. Clubs: Kerr-Mcgee Swim (dir. 1968—), Quail Creek Golf and Country, Oklahoma City Ski (Oklahoma City). Home: 3101 Rolling Stone Rd Oklahoma City OK 73120

BINNING, ROSALYN LUCILLE, physician; b. El Paso, Tex., Nov. 20, 1928; d. Robert Minor and Evelyn Lucille (Keith) Swafford; M.D., Cal. Coll. Medicine, 1952. children—Valerie Lyn, Karen Lee. Intern, Los Angeles County Gen. Hosp., 1952-53, resident internal medicine, 1953-54, resident anesthesiology, 1954-56, teaching fellow, 1957-58, asst. clin. prof. anesthesiology, 1966-67; mem. med. com. Pacific Hosp., Huntington Beach, Cal., 1971-72; practice medicine specializing in anesthesiology, Newport Beach, Cal., 1965—; teaching fellow anesthesiology Cal. Coll. Medicine, 1957-58. Mem. Analgesia and Anesthesia Research Soc., Am., Cal. med. assns., Orange County Med. Assn., Orange County Anesthesia Soc., Club: Lido Isle Woman's (Newport Beach). Home: 108 C Via Antibes Lido Isle Newport Beach CA 92660 Office: 2120 W 8th St Los Angeles CA 90057

BINTLIFF, ANN HUMPHREY, architect; b. Texarkana, Ark., Oct. 1, 1920; B.Arch. (scholar), Mass. Inst. Tech., 1941 Prin., Ann H. Bintliff, 1951-60; partner Bintliff & Bell, 1960-68, Bintliff, Bell & Holderness, Texarkana, Tex., 1969—. Pres., Episcopal Ch. Women, 1950, Bowie-Miller County Med. Aux., 1953-54. Sec., Texarkana Bd. Adjustment and Appeals, 1965-69, Texarkana Bldg. Standards and Housing Bd. Appeals, 1965-72. Bd. dirs. Texarkana Jr. League, 1951-55; treas., trustee St. James Day Sch., 1955-64, pres., 1964-67. Registered architect, Ark., La., Tex. Mem. A.I.A. (sec.-treas. N.E. Tex. chpt. 1961-62, dir. 1964-66), Tex. Soc. Architects (dir. 1970-72). Prin. works include: 1st Lutheran Ch., 1965, Texarkana Funeral Home, 1966, Coker Buick Agy., 1967, adminstrv. bldg. Texarkana Ind. Sch. Dist., 1968, Charcoal Broiler Restaurant, 1969 (all Texarkana). Home: 2529 N Robison Rd Texarkana TX 75501 Office: 707 W 12th St Texarkana TX 75501*

BIOCINI, WINNIE ANN ETEROVICH (MRS. GEORGE BIOCINI), owner real estate; b. San Francisco, Mar. 13, 1922; s. Ivan and Ana (Cvitanich) E.; student San Francisco State Coll., 1939-42; m. George Biocini, June 15, 1941; children—Linda (Mrs. Chad Schneller), Peggy, Georgia. Pres., owner Winnie Biocini, Realtor, Menlo Park, Cal., 1958—. Mem. C. of C., Jr. C. of C. (pres. 1950), Menlo Park Atherton Bd. Realtors (Million Dollar Club), Nat. Assn. Real Estate Bds., Cal. Real Estate Assn. Club: Commonwealth (San Francisco). Home: 145 Pineview Lane Menlo Park CA 94025 Office: 1150 El Camino Real Menlo Park CA 94025

BIONDI, MARY ESTHER HADLOCK (MRS. EDWARD BIONDI), historian; b. Potsdam, N.Y., May 4, 1919; d. Perry F. and Doris (Jones) Hadlock; student Bryant Coll., 1938; m. Murray R. Rodger, May 29, 1941 (dec.); children—Laurie D. (Mrs. Bruce W. Smith), Scott F. Biondi; m. 2d, Edward Biondi, Mar. 26, 1954. Exec. sec. Union Ch. Rio de Janeiro, 1951-54; tchr. English Instituto Brasil-Estados Unidos, Rio de Janeiro, 1951-52; adminstrv. asst. to pub. No. N.Y. Pub. Co., Ogdensburg, 1961-65; town historian, Hammond, N.Y., 1959-63, county historian dep., 1963-65, county historian, 1965—; sec. Hammond Bldg. Supplies, Inc. (N.Y.), 1963-70, v.p., 1968-70. Pres., Assn. Retarded children, 1967-70, v.p., 1970—; sec. Tb and Respiratory Disease Assn., 1970-73; Bd. dirs. Thousand Islands council Girl Scout U.S.A., 1961-65, 72-73, Seaway Area chpt. Heart and Tb Assn. (sec. 1969-73), Assn. Retarded Children, Adirondack Park Assn.; bd. govs. New York State Assn. Retarded Children, 1966-71; mem. N.Y. State Commn. for Bicentennial of Am. Revolution, 1969—. Recipient Thanks badge Girl Scout Troops on Fgn. Soil, Heidelberg, Germany, 1958. Mem. County Historians Assn. N.Y. State (pres. 1968-69; editor Newsletter 1969—), St. Lawrence County Hist. Assn. (sec. 1961-65; v.p. 1963; editor Quar. 1966—), Zonta Internat., Alpha Study Club Univ. Extension. Republican. Unitarian. Author: Take the Gray Basin, 1960; co-author Top O' the State, 1967. Contbr. articles to Adirondack Life, Yorkstate Tradition, Steelways, N.Y. Folklore Quar., county newspapers. Home: PO Box 648 Ogdensburg NY 13669 Office: Court House PO Box 43 Canton NY 13617

BIRCH, ALISON WYRLEY GREENBIE (MRS. RICHARD BIRCH), writer; b. N.Y.C., Mar. 11, 1922; d. Sydney and Marjorie (Barstow) Greenbie; student Western Conn. State Coll., 1962-63; m. Richard Wyrley Birch, Aug. 5, 1942; children—Wendy Wyrley (Mrs. Albert Martinez), Lorraine Wyrley (Mrs. Noel Kendall). Author: East of Manhattan (poems), 1965, A Little Of This And That, 1965, Say Ah-H, 1959. Columnist, Classroom Candids, Lakeville Jour., Lakeville, Conn., 1967—; lectr. poetry, radio readings. Bd. dirs. Soc. Prevention Drug Addiction, 1970—. Mem. Poetry Soc. N.H. Contbr. articles and poetry to maj. publs. Home and office: Macedonia Rd Kent CT 06757

BIRCH, LONAH KAY (MRS. C.E. BIRCH), govt. ofcl.; b. Columbia, Mo., Sept. 9, 1941; d. Orville Wayne and Mildred M. (Tate) Watt; B.J., U. Mo., 1963; m. C.E. Birch, May 22, 1971. Pub. relations dir. Metcalf South Shopping Center, Overland Park, Kan., 1967-69; nat. pub. affairs specialist Girl Scouts U.S.A., Kansas City, Mo., 1969-72; regional pub. information officer Small Bus. Adminstrn., Kansas City, Mo., 1972—. Named top nat. pub. information officer Small Bus. Adminstrn., 1973. Mem. Kansas City Pub. Relations Soc., Pub. Relations Soc. Am. (accredited), Women In Communications, Fed. Information Council. Republican. Home: 12905 W 77th St Lenexa KS 66216 Office: 911 Walnut St Room 2303 Kansas City MO 64106

BIRCH, MARGARET STEWART, provincial govt. ofcl.; b. Leamington, Ont., Can., June 13, 1921; d. Wallace Edward and Mary Jane (Ferguson) Stewart; grad. high sch.; m. Guy Birch, Sept. 27, 1941; children—Randy, Jane. Mem. Ont. Legislature, 1971-72, chmn. standing com. on social devel., 1972, mem. select com. on utilization of ednl. facilities, 1971-72; minister without portfolio Province of Ont., 1972-74, mem. Cabinet Bd. Mgt., 1972-74, mem. Cabinet Com. on Legislation, 1972-74, responsible for Ont. Youth Secretariat, 1972-74; provincial sec. for social devel. Province of Ont., 1974—, chmn. Cabinet Com. on Social Devel., 1974—, mem. Cabinet Policy and Priorities Bd., 1974—. Mem. steering com. to build Scarborough (Ont.) Centenary Hosp., 1963, charter mem. bd. govs., 1963—; mem. Scarborough Bd. Health, 1963-71, chmn., 1968-71; mem. Scarborough Social Planning Council, 1960-70. Named Citizen of Yr., Scarborough Rotary Club, 1970. Home: 53 Burnview Crescent Scarborough ON Canada Office: Queen's Park Toronto ON Canada

BIRCH, TERRIE R. HOLLOWED, former travel agy. exec.; b. Berwyn, Ill., Aug. 7, 1930; d. James Aloysius and Marie (Nohava) Hollowed; B.A. in Psychology, Rosary Coll., 1974; m. John E. Birch, Nov. 4, 1950 (div. Apr. 1969); children—John Edward, Christopher James, Terrie Johnice, Laurence Patrick. Sec.-treas., John Birch & Co., 1953-66, Terrie Birch & Co., 1953-66, Alert Carpentry, 1953-66, Durable Masonry, Inc., 1953-66, Cherrywood Homes (all Lombard, Ill.), 1953-66; travel counselor, 1969-71. Meml. and honor chmn., dir. Infant Welfare Soc., Chgo., 1963-65, pres. Western Springs Center, 1967. Mem. U. Ill. Alumni Assn., Pi Gamma Mu. Club: Village (Western Springs). Address: 5429 Caroline Av Western Springs IL 60558

BIRCKHEAD, MARY BUCHANAN, occupational therapist, artist; b. Towson, Md., July 24, 1914; d. Lennox and Mary Buchanan (Albert) Birckhead; B.A., Sarah Lawrence Coll., 1937; postgrad. U. Munich (Germany), 1938; certificate occupational therapy Phila. Sch. of Occupational Therapy, 1949. Tchr. painting Anneslic Sch., Towson, 1939-47; exhibited in one-man shows at Hotel Sans Souci, Port-au-Prince, Haiti, 1940-41, others; exhibited in group show at Balt. Art Mus., 1944; represented in pvt. collections; occupational therapist Trenton (N.J.) Psychiat. Hosp., 1949-74. Mem. Nat. Audubon Soc. Home: PO Box 161 Stockton NJ 08559

BIRD, CAROLINE, author, lectr.; b. N.Y.C., Apr. 15, 1915; d. Hobart Stanley and Ida (Brattrud) Bird; student Vassar Coll., 1931-34; B.A., U. Toledo, 1938; M.A., U. Wis., 1939; m. Edward A. Menuez, June 8, 1934 (div. Dec. 1945); 1 dau., Carol (Mrs. John Paul Barach); m. 2d, John Thomas Mahoney, Jan. 5, 1957; 1 son, John Thomas. Desk editor N.Y. Jour. Commerce, N.Y.C., 1943-44; editorial researcher Newsweek Mag., N.Y.C., 1942-43, Fortune Mag., N.Y.C., 1944-46; with Dudley-Anderson-Yutzy, pub. relations firm, N.Y.C., 1947-68; Froman Distinguished prof. Russell Sage Coll., 1972-73. Mem. Soc. Mag. Writers (sec. 1953), Am. Sociol. Assn., Nat. Orgn. Women (mem. nat. adv. com.), Equity Action League (dir.). Author: The Invisible Scar, 1966; Born Female, 1968, rev., 1970; The Crowding Syndrome, 1972; Everything a Woman Needs to Know to Get Paid What She's Worth, 1973; Women: Opportunity for Management, 1973; Is College Really Necessary?, 1975. Contbr. articles to nat. mags. others. Home: 60 Gramercy Park New York City NY 10010 and 31 Sunrise Lane Poughkeepsie NY 12603

BIRD, CHRISTINA MARIA, trust co. exec.; b. Ithaca, N.Y., July 3, 1942; d. Ignacio and Lucy (Jennette) Bird; B.A., Marymount Coll., 1964. Advt. and supply purchasing coordinator Jewel Box Stores Corp., Greensboro, N.C., 1964-65; portfolio mgr. Wachovia Bank & Trust Co., Winston-Salem, N.C., 1966-69, Trust Co. Ga., Atlanta, 1970—. Mem. Financial Analysts Fedn., Atlanta Soc. Financial Analysts, Am. Inst. Bankers, Greensboro Artist's League (corr. sec. 1968-69), Nat. Assn. Bank Women. Club: Gem and Mineral (Atlanta). Office: PO Box 4655 Atlanta GA 30302

BIRD, DOROTHY MABEL ANDREW (MRS. CHARLES BIRD), educator; b. Mpls., Nov. 11, 1909; d. George Lawrie and Maybelle (Howe) Andrew; B.A., U. Minn., 1930, M.A., 1931, Ph.D., 1935; m. Charles Bird, Mar. 16, 1944. Research asst. U. Minn. Employment Stabilization Research Inst., Mpls., 1931-33, teaching asst., 1933-35, faculty, 1946-49, 58—, prof. psychology dept. ind. study, 1968—; instr. psychology Chatham Coll., Pitts., 1935-37, asst. prof., 1937-43. Mem. Am. Psychol. Assn., Am. Acad. Polit. and Social Sci., Acad. Polit. Sci., Am. Assn. U. Women, U. Minn. Alumni Assn. (life), Sigma Xi, Pi Lambda Theta, Psi Chi. Club: University of Minn. Alumni. Author: (with D.G. Paterson, H.P. Longstaff) Minnesota Clerical Test, 1933; (with Charles Bird) Learning More by Effective Study, 1945. Contbr. articles to profl. jours. Home: 5836 Knox Av S Minneapolis MN 55419

BIRD, ETTA GERSTEIN, physician; b. N.Y.C., Nov. 22, 1916; d. Sol and Lena (Brenner) Gerstein; B.A., N.Y.U., 1934; M.D., U. Lausanne, 1943; m. Reuben Romalius Bird, Aug. 11, 1945 (div.); 1 dau., Beth. Gen. rotating intern Coney Island Hosp., 1945-46, resident, 1946-47; pvt. practice medicine, N.Y.C., 1948-52; resident psychiatry Rochester State Hosp., Manhattan State Hosp., 1952-55; practice medicine, specializing in psychiatry, Bklyn., 1955—; clin. asst. in psychiatry Am. Inst. for Psychoanalysis, 1954-58, Karen Horney Clinic, 1957-58, Coney Island Hosp., 1958-70, Kings County Hosp., 1970—; research in psychopharmacology Downstate Med. Sch., State U. N.Y., 1958-66, asst. prof. psychiatry, 1960—. Mem. A.M.A., Kings County Med. Soc., Am. Psychiat. Assn., Am. Soc. Psychoanalytic Physicians (mem. exec. bd.), Bklyn. Psychiat. Assn. Address: 207 Ocean Pkwy Brooklyn NY 11218

BIRD, HELEN PRIVETT, environmental cons.; b. Sarasota, Fla., Jan. 27, 1934; d. Joseph Hemphill and Helen (Mason) Privett; B.A., Wilson Coll., 1955; postgrad. Cornell U. extension, 1967; m. Paul Lloyd Bird, Apr. 6, 1963 (div.); 1 son, David Kennedy. Owner, founder Southeastern Environmental Services, Jacksonville, Fla.; lectr. in field; participant environmental confs. and seminars. Coordinator Fla. Citizens for Clean Water, 1966-67, Fla. League Conservation Voters, 1970; pres. S.E. Environmental Council, Inc., 1970—; regional v.p. Fla. Wildlife Fedn., 1970-73; chmn. energy com. Jacksonville Zero Population Growth, 1973—; mem. adv. council Duval County (Fla.) Environmental Edn. Trustee Lands for You, Inc., State of Fla.; bd. advisers Environic Found. Internat., Notre Dame, Ind. Recipient citation vol. service Fla. Pub. Co., 1969, county award Best Conservation Orgn., 1969, Pres.'s citation Fla. Fedn. Garden Clubs, 1970, Fla. Gov.'s award Outstanding Conservationist of Year, 1970; named Woman of Year for Conservation, 1970. Mem. Internat. Solar Energy Soc. Democrat. Episcopalian. Contbr. articles to conservation jours. Home: 7367 Pineville Dr Jacksonville FL 32210 Office: Box 31278 Yukon Br Jacksonville FL 32230

BIRD, MILDRED CRISTINE (MRS. DONALD JAMES BIRD), city ofcl.; b. Mt. Marion, N.Y., June 1, 1931; d. Edward and Kunigunde (Gohs) Willner; student Rutgers U. Extension, 1966, 71, Syracuse Extension, U. 1969-71; m. Donald James Bird, Apr. 10, 1955; children—Edward Kenneth, Alan Donald. Exec. sec. Johnston & Co., Inc., N.Y.C., 1948-61; sec. Bd. Health Borough of Bloomingdale, N.J., 1962-65, mem. dist. bd. elections, 1962-65; borough clk. Bloomingdale, 1966—, registrar vital statistics, 1970—. Exec. sec., mem. Youth Employment Service, Butler-Bloomingdale, 1969—, Youth Guidance Council, 1969—, Bloomingdale 50 Anniversary Com., 1968. Mem. N.J., Passaic County (corr. sec. 1970-71, rec. sec. 1969, v.p. 1974—) municipal clks. assns., Internat. Inst. Municipal Clks., Ladies Aux. Boy Scouts Am. Methodist (sec. ofcl. bd. 1959-60). Home: 43 Rafkind Rd Bloomingdale NJ 07403 Office: 101 Hamburg Turnpike City Hall Bloomingdale NJ 07403

BIRDCELL, GAIL ELAINE (MRS. JOHN JAMES BIRDCELL), librarian; b. Akron, O., Jan. 12, 1943; d. Herbert Marvin and Florence May (Strickland) Tabbut; B.A., Pa. State U., 1965; M. Librarianship, U. Wash., 1969; m. John James Birdcell, Feb. 23, 1973. Lit. searcher Pa. Tech. Assistance Program, University Park, Pa., 1967-68; field intern Nat. Lending Library for Sci. and Tech., Boston SPA, Great Britain, 1969; dir. libraries and learning resources devel. Ind. Vocational Tech. Coll., Indpls., 1970-73; dir. library and information services Am. States Ins. Cos., Indpls., 1973-74; head br. Lake County Pub. Library, Hobart, Ind., 1974—. Mem. librarians com. Consortium for Urban Edn., Indpls., 1972—. Mem. Am., Ind., Spl. library assns. Home: 771 Bowman Dr Crown Point IN 46307 Office: 100 N Main St Hobart IN 46342

BIRKHEAD, EUGENIA CLARKE MCCHESNEY (MRS. HERBERT CECIL BIRKHEAD), journalist; b. Louisville, Jan. 12, 1917; d. Hardin Field and Eugene Emile (McCulloch) McChesney; A.B., Western Ky. U., 1936; postgrad., Kan. U., 1957; m. Herbert Cecil Birkhead, May 26, 1939; children—Roy Field, David Logan, Herbert Douglas, John Andrew. Tchr. Frederick (Okla.) Jr. High Sch., 1937-39, 41-42, Frederick (Okla.) High Sch., 1946-48; librarian Frederick (Okla.) Pub. Library, 1948-51; asst. instr. Kan. U., Lawrence, 1956-57; tchr., testing specialist Ramstein Air Base, Germany, 1963-66; food editor Colorado Springs (Colo.) Free Press, 1968-70, womens editor, 1969-70; feature writer Colorado Springs Sun, 1970—. Mem. Red Cross Disaster Com., Colorado Springs, 1968—; mem. U.S.O. Council, Colorado Springs, Colo., 1969-74; Bd. dirs. Christmas Unlimited, 1972—, Community Vol. Center, 1973—. Mem. P.E.O. Democrat. Presbyn. (mem. bd. deacons 1967-68). Clubs: Pilot; Colorado Springs Press. Home: 1324 Alexander Rd Colorado Springs CO 80909 Office: 103 W Colorado Av Colorado Springs CO 80901

BIRKHOLZ, GERTRUD MARIA, lawyer, educator; b. Annaberg, Germany, 1922; d. Johannes and Gertrud Theresia (Sandmann) Birkholz; came to U.S., 1951, naturalized, 1957; R.N., Md., 1955; B.S., Johns Hopkins, 1962; J.D., Balt. U., 1970. Supr. nursing services Johns Hopkins Hosp., Balt., 1958-62; tchr. health occupation Balt. Pub. Schs., 1965-68; tchr., dir. practical nursing program Balt. County Pub. Schs., 1968—; admitted to Md. bar, 1970, since practiced in Balt. Mem. Am., Md. bar assns., Tchrs. Assn. Balt. County (faculty rep. 1971—), N.E.A., Iota Tau Tau. Address: 6205 The Alameda Baltimore MD 21239

BIRKIC, GERALDINE MARIA SCHIAFFINO, psychologist; b. N.Y.C., Dec. 4, 1941; d. John Dominick and Teresa (Torregrossa) Schiaffino; B.A., Ohio State U., 1963, M.S., 1965; Ph.D., St. John's U., 1969—; m. David G. Birkic, July 4, 1964. With Central Islip (N.Y.) Psychiat. Center, 1965—, clin. psychologist admission service, 1965-66, clin. psychologist drug addiction unit, 1966-68, clin. psychologist childrens unit, 1968-69, clin. psychologist alcoholism unit, 1969—; clin. psychologist Inst. for Research in Hypnosis and Hypnotherapy, Manhattan, N.Y., 1971-72. Lectr. South Oaks Hosp., Amityville, N.Y., 1972—; cons., mem. Islip Twp. Narcotic Addiction Program-Edn. Com., 1970. Mem. Am. Psychol. Assn., N.Y. State Psychologists in Pub. Service. Home: 20 Pequot Av Port Washington NY 11050 Office: Alcoholism Unit Central Islip State Hosp Central Islip NY 11722

BIRKLE, LYDIA SCHRACK BLOEDORN (MRS. DAVID L. BIRKLE), audiologist; b. Orleans, Neb.; d. Charles F. and Zoe (Schrack) Bloedorn; B.A., U. Denver, 1927, M.A., 1959; m. David L. Birkle, July 2, 1932 (dec. 1957). Tchr. high sch., Platteville, Colo., 1927-31; audiologist Colo. Hearing and Speech Center, Denver, 1959—. Mem. Acad. Rehabilitative Audiology, Am., Colo. speech and hearing assns., Am. Audiology Soc., Pi Beta Phi. Conglist. Home: 1901 Leyden St Denver CO 80220 Office: 4280 Hale Pkwy Denver CO 80220

BIRMINGHAM, MARGARET WEIR, educator; b. Jackson, Tenn., Mar. 16, 1948; d. Liberty Weir and Margaret (White) Birmingham; B.S., Union U., Jackson, 1970; M.S., U. Tenn., 1971. Asst., U. Tenn., Knoxville, 1970-71; instr. phys. edn. Carson-Newman Coll., Jefferson City, Tenn., 1970-71; instr. health and phys. edn. S.W. Bapt. Coll., Bolivar, Mo., 1971-72, Union U., 1972—. Mem. Am., Tenn. assns. health, phys. edn. and recreations, Chi Omega Alumni Assn. Baptist (dir. preschool Sunday sch. 1972—). Home: 517 Wisdom Av Jackson TN 38301 Office: Box 1067 Dept Health and Phys Edn Union U Jackson TN 38301

BIRNBAUM, AGNES MARTA BERENYI (MRS. HERBERT D. BIRNBAUM), editor; b. Budapest, Hungary; d. Emery and Barbara (Weiss) Berenyi came to U.S., 1950, naturalized, 1955; m. Herbert D. Birnbaum, June 16, 1958. Asst. editor Mag. Mgmt., 1960-61; editor Dell Pub. Co., 1961-63, Macfadden Publs., 1964-65; exec. editor TV Radio Mirror mag., 1965-67; editor-in-chief Award Books and Award House, 1968-69, editorial dir., 1969— (all N.Y.C.). Pres. Pub. Ventures Internat., Inc., pub. co., 1962—. Mem. N.A.A.C.P., Am. Civil Liberties Union. Home: 88 Bleeker St New York City NY 10012 Office: 235 E 45th St New York City NY 10017

BIRNBAUM, NATALIE CHOATE (MRS. ROBERT L. BIRNBAUM), lawyer; b. Boston, Dec. 22, 1945; d. Charles Francis and Jhan (English) Choate; B.A. cum laude, Radcliffe Coll., 1967; J.D., Harvard, 1970; m. Robert L. Birnbaum, Aug. 10, 1968. Admitted to Mass. bar, 1970; pvt. practice law, Boston, 1970—; asso. atty. Maloney, Williams & Baer, Boston, 1970-74, partner, 1974—. Mem. Mass., Boston Bar assns., Mass. Assn. Women Lawyers, Vincent Club. Home: 8 Newport Rd Cambridge MA 02140 Office: 1 Boston Place Boston MA 02108

BIRNBAUM, SHEILA L., lawyer, educator; b. N.Y.C., Mar. 5, 1940; d. Louis and Belle (Trotter) Lubetsky; B.A., Hunter Coll., 1960, M.A., 1962; LL.B., N.Y. U., 1965. Admitted to N.Y. bar, 1965; with Emile Z. Berman & A. Harold Frost, Attys., N.Y.C., 1965-72, partner, 1970-72; legal research asst. Supreme Ct., New York County, 1965; asso. prof. law Fordham U., 1972—; lectr. Practicing Law Inst., 1972—. Mem. Ins. Commn., 1970-72, Civil Ct. Com., 1973—. Mem. Assn. Bar City of N.Y., Am. Bar Assn. (vice chmn. faculty liaison com., ins., negligence and compensation sect.), N.Y. Women's Bar Assn. (2d v.p. 1971-72, 1st v.p. 1972, pres. 1974, chmn. judiciary com.), N.Y. State Bar Assn., Internat. Fedn. Women Lawyers, N.Y. County Lawyers, Phi Beta Kappa. Contbr. articles to profl. jours. Home: 220 Central Park South New York City NY 10019

BIRO, EVELYN DOROTHY (MRS. LOUIS LEO BIRO), ednl. adminstr.; b. Chgo., Aug. 31, 1921; d. James Kurt and Sara Bessie (Harris) Lindeman; B.S., Northwestern U., 1949; postgrad., St. Xavier Coll., 1963-65; m. Louis Leo Biro, Mar. 30, 1941; children—Barbara Ban (dec.), Richard Jay. Tchr. of deaf pub. sch., Chgo., 1949-56; prin. Park Lawn Sch., Oak Lawn, Ill., 1961—; instr. St. Xavier Coll., Chgo., 1968-71. Tchr. in tng. parents of deaf children Chgo. Hearing Soc., 1945. Recipient Service to Mankind award, named woman of year Highland Sertoma, 1966. Mem. Am. Speech and Hearing Assn., Am. Assn. on Mental Deficiency, Council Exceptional Children. Home: 9014 S Franciso Evergreen Park IL 60642 Office: 10833 S La Porte Oak Lawn IL 60453

BIRRELL, VERLA LEONE, educator; b. Tacoma, Nov. 24, 1903; d. James Walter and Elfie (Naylor) Birrell; B.S., U. Utah, 1928, postgrad. in anthropology, 1949-57; M.F.A., Claremont Colls., 1942; postgrad. pre-medicine Brigham Young U., 1942-47; postgrad. Art Students League, summers 1956-57; Ed.D., Columbia, 1967. Tchr. pub. schs. Salt Lake City, 1929-37; asst. prof. art, Brigham Young U., Provo, Utah, 1938-47, U. Utah, Salt Lake City, 1948-67, asso. prof. art in home econs, 1967-72, asso. prof. emeritus, 1972—. Pub. lectr. on topics including art, interior design, archeology, textiles, Utah, Ida., 1940—. Exhibited 12 one man art shows at local instns., 1933-64; exhibited in group shows western U.S., 1932—; numerous archael. study tours throughout U.S., Mexico, S. Am., 1942—; presented papers nat., internat. archaeology and anthropology congresses, 1951—. Recipient numerous art awards and purchase prizes Utah area, 1938—. Mem. Am. Anthropol. Assn., Soc. for Am. Archaeology, Federated Utah Artists, Am. Home Econ. Assn., U. Utah Faculty Women, Interior Designers Educators Council, Inter-Am. Club (past dir.), Nat. League Am. Pen Women, Asso. Utah Artists (pres. 1973-74), Am. Inst. Interior Designers, Reader's Guild, Alice Louise Reynolds Club, Spanish Club, Omicron Nu, Alpha Beta Theta, Alpha Delta Pi. Author: Book of Mormon Guide Book, 1948; The Textile Arts, 1959. Home: 2004 Wasatch Dr Salt Lake City UT 84108

BISBEE, PRUDENCE H., lawyer; b. Riverside, N.J., Oct. 31, 1941; d. Henry H. and Rebecca H. (Ridge) Bisbee; B.A., Ursinus Coll., 1963; M.S. in L.S., Drexel U., 1964; postgrad. State U. N.Y. at Buffalo, 1964-66; J.D., Rutgers U., Camden, 1969. Asst. law librarian Law Sch., State U. N.Y. at Buffalo, 1964-66; admitted to N.J. bar, 1969; dep. atty. gen. div. law N.J. Dept. Law and Pub. Safety, Trenton, 1969—, assigned state tax agy., 1969-70, assigned N.J. Div. Pensions, 1970—. Mem. Am., N.J., Burlington County bar assns., Nat. Assn. Women Lawyers. Home: 207 Wood St Burlington NJ 08016 Office: Atty Gen's Office State House Annex Trenton NJ 08625

BISCHOFF, CAROL LOUISE, editor; b. Flushing, N.Y., Apr. 25, 1943; d. Charles Thomas and Louise Josephine (Knaust) Bischoff; B.S., Wagner Coll., 1964. Editorial asst. Plenum Pub. Co., N.Y.C., 1964-67, prodn. editor, 1967-70, editor Plenum jour., 1970-72, asst. mng. editor, 1972—. Mem. Delta Zeta. Office: 227 W 17th St New York City NY 10011

BISCONER, BERNICE HAZEL BENSON (MRS. RAYMOND BISCONER), civic worker; b. Hurley, S.D., July 7, 1902; d. Andrew and Christine (Nelson) Benson; grad. high sch.; m. Raymond Bisconer, Oct. 27, 1920; children—Reynold M. (dec.), Andrea (Mrs. John Henninger), David S. Sr. partner Raymond and Bernice Bisconer Ranches, Raymond Bisconer and Sons. Valley sponsor San Joaquin Valley Town Hall, Inc., Fresno, Cal., 1965—; vol. nurse A.R.C., 1941; pink lady Tulare (Cal.) Dist. Hosp., 1959; charter mem. Fresno Symphony Orch., 1952—; charter mem., sponsor Tulare County Symphony and Women's Symphony League, 1960—; mem. Tulare-Kings Counties Civic Music Assn., 1935—. Mem. Tulare County Cotton Wives, Tulare County Hist. Soc., Tulare County Pioneers, Beta Sigma Phi (past sponsor). Democrat. Conglist. Clubs: Federated Woman's, Garden. Address: Elk Bayou Oaks 21201 Road 132 Tulare CA 93274

BISGYER, BARBARA GINETTE PEIERLS (MRS. ERIC M. COHN), artist; b. N.Y.C., June 7, 1933; d. Edgar S. and Betsy (Vogel) Peierls; student Northampton Sch. Girls (Mass.), 1951; Sarah Lawrence Coll., 1955; student Sculptors and Ceramic Workshop, N.Y.C.; m. M. Bisgyer; children—Marcia Louise, Ann Carol, Susan Jane; m. 2d, Eric M. Cohn, May 19, 1965; stepchildren—Andrew E., Lee Marbey. Sculptor, important works on view at Environment Gallery, N.Y.C.; exhbns. include Nat. Design Center, 1965-67, Audubon Ann., 1967-71, Iona Coll., 1968, Princeton, 1969, Jersey City Mus., 1969, New Haven Festival, 1969, Hudson River Museum, 1971, USIA 1st Traveling Sculpture Show, 1970—, and others; one man shows Environment Gallery, N.Y.C., 1966, 68, 70; represented in many prominent collections, U.S., Can. and Europe; cons. in field. Bd. dirs. Vogel Fund. Recipient award for sculptor, Victor D'amico, 1967, awards Mamaroneck Artists Guild, 1967, 69, 70, Westchester Art Soc., 1967, 68, Audubon Artists medal, 1968, Beaux Arts award, 1969, Today's Art medal Audubon Artists, 1971, awards New Rochelle Art Assn., 1970-71. Mem. Artist Craftsmen of N.Y. (bd. govs. 1964-69, 73, exhbn. chmn. 3 yrs., v.p. 1 yr., excellence award 1971), Mamaroneck Artists Guild (exhbn. chmn. 1972-73, awards 1970, 71), Westchester Art Assn. (awards 1967, 68), N.Y. Soc. Women Artists (exhbn. chmn. 1972-73), Am. Soc. Contemporary Artists. Address: 50 Lake Rd Rye NY 10580

BISHOP, AUDREY JUNE, editor; b. Balt.; d. Mark Zullinger and Viola Angela (Kornmann) Bishop; A.B., Bucknell U., 1945. Script writer WMAR-TV, Balt., 1947-48; feature writer Balt. Sun, 1948-59; specialist pub. relations E.I. du Pont de Nemours & Co., Inc., N.Y.C., 1959-70; feature writer Balt. News Am., 1971-73; editor News Am. Sunday mag., Balt., 1973—. Mem. Women in Communications, Sigma Delta Chi. Home: 3501 St Paul St Baltimore MD 21218 Office: News Am Baltimore MD 21203

BISHOP, D. VIRGINIA HILLAND (MRS. RANDOLPH B. BISHOP), civic worker; b. Washington, Oct. 25, 1929; d. Arthur Jonathan and Dorothy V. (Sheiry) Hilland; A.A. in Fashion Design, Stephens Coll., 1949; m. Randolph B. Bishop, Oct. 15, 1949; children—Valerie Ann, Randolph Hilland. Bd. mem. Jayncees, Washington, 1951-56; area chmn. sustaining drive Nat. Symphony, 1965—; nat. def. chmn. D.A.R., 1967—, mem. nat. mus. com., 1967-69, chpt. regent, 1968-69; mem. Ft. Lauderdale Boys Club Aux., 1971—. Pres. Chevy Chase (Md.) Republican Club, 1966-67, chmn. fund raising, 1967; mem. Women's Rep. Club, Fort Lauderdale, 1971—. Mem. Jean S. Cole circle Florence Crittenden Home, 1959-70. Mem. Lee Family of Va., D.A.R., Pachira Garden Circle, Stephens Coll. Alumnae Club. Presbyn. Home: 2864 NE 25th Ct Fort Lauderdale FL 33305

BISHOP, DOROTHY SWORD (MRS. HAROLD BISHOP), ret. educator, author; b. Chgo., Feb. 4, 1917; d. Gustaf Adolph and Edna Blanche (Grandin) Sword; B.A., William Jewell Coll., 1938; postgrad. Nat. Coll. Edn., summers 1957, 58, U. Costa Rica, San Jose, summer 1969; m. Harold B. Bishop, May 5, 1940; children—Barbara Anne (Mrs. George Cole), Margaret Ruth (Mrs. Allan Iverson). Tchr. Des Plaines (Ill.) Elementary Schs., 1957-61; Spanish coordinator Des Plaines Schs., 1961-72. Mem. Ill. (chmn. elementary sect. 1963-72), Central States (chmn. elementary sect. 1967-68) fgn. lang. tchrs. assns., Am. Assn. U. Women, Am. Assn. Tchrs. Spanish and Portuguese, Am. Council on Teaching Fgn. Langs., Delta Kappa Gamma. Author: Hablan los ninos, 1968; Habia una vez, 1969; Ya se leer, 1970; La primera fonetica, 1971; Hablan mas los ninos, 1971; Tina La Tortuga y Carlos El Conejo, 1972; Chiquita y Pepita, 1972; Leonardo el Leon y Ramon el Raton, 1972; Bienvenidos, 1972. Editor: Asi escribimos, 1971; Horas Encantadas, 1973. Home: 12646 Relindo Dr Rancho Bernardo San Diego CA 92128

BISHOP, ELIZA, journalist; b. Crockett, Tex., June 18, 1920; d. William Penn and Carey Ann (LeGory) Bishop; B.A., Mary Hardin-Baylor Coll., 1941. Editor, Crockett Democrat, 1941-43, 1947-48, news corr., 1944, staffwriter, 1948; Houston county commentator Radio KNET, Palestine, Tex., 1947-48; clk. Tri-County East Tex. Health Unit, Crockett, 1950-52; county news corr. Houston Chronicle, 1957-62, staff writer, photographer, 1962-66, reporter, 1967-73; news writer, commentator Radio Sta. KIVY, Crockett, Tex., 1960-62, 1970—; operator, mgr. Western Union, Crockett, 1962-65; office employee physicians office, Crockett, 1965—; reporter Houston Post, 1969—. Coordinator Houston County Civil Def., 1942-45; instr. first aid, 1942-47. Ct. dep. Houston County Commrs., 1944-45; tax clk. Houston County, 1946; dist. ct. dep. Houston County, 1956-60; sec. City Crockett, 1960-61; sec., mem. Charter Commn., 1961-62. Recipient Spl. service awards 4-H, 1967-69; award Am. Cancer Soc., 1969; Research award Daus. of Republic Tex., 1971; Distinguished Service award Houston County Devel. Found., 1972; awards Tex. Press Women, 1969, 70, 71, 72, Nat. Fedn. Press Women, 1970, 71. Mem. C. of C. (sec. 1952-55), Daus. Republic Tex. (chpt. pres. 1955), Women in Communication (regional chmn. 1950-52), Tex. Press Women (dist. pres. 1971-72), Nat. Fedn. Press Women, East Tex. Hist. Assn. (dir.), Am. Assn. State and Local History, Beta Sigma Phi. Episcopalian. Home: 629 N 4th St Crockett TX 75835

BISHOP, ELIZABETH, poet; b. Worcester, Mass., Feb. 8, 1911; d. William Thomas and Gertrude (Bulmer) Bishop; A.B., Vassar Coll., 1934; LL.D. (hon.), Smith Coll., Rutgers U., Brown U. Cons. poetry Library of Congress, 1949-50, hon. cons. in Am. Letters, 1958; lectr. English, Harvard, 1970—. Recipient Houghton Mifflin poetry fellowship award, 1945; Guggenheim fellowship, 1947; Lucy Martin Donnelly fellow (Bryn Mawr), 1951; Am. Acad. Arts and Letters award, 1951; Shelley Meml. award, 1952; Partisan Review fellowship, 1956; Pulitzer prize for poetry, Poems, 1956; Amy Lowell fellowship, 1957; Chapelbrook fellowship, 1961; Rockefeller grantee, 1966-67; Nat. Book award for poetry, 1969; Harriet Monroe award, 1974; decorated Order of Rio Branco (Brazil). Mem. Nat. Inst. Arts and Letters. Author: North & South (poems), 1946; Poems, 1955; A Cold Spring, 1956; Questions of Travel (poems), 1965; Complete Poems, 1969. Co-editor: An Anthology of Contemporary Brazilian Poetry, 1973. Contbr. poems, stories, mags. and anthologies. Office: care Farrar Straus & Giroux 19 Union Sq W New York City NY 10003

BISHOP, ISABEL (MRS. HAROLD G. WOLFF), artist; b. Cin., Mar. 3, 1902; d. John Remsen and Anna Bartram (Newbold) Bishop; student Wicker Art Sch., Detroit, 1917-18, N.Y. Sch. Applied Design for Women, 1918-20, Art Students League N.Y., 1920-22, 27-30; A.F.D. (hon.), Moore Inst., Phila.; m. Dr. Harold George Wolff, Aug. 9, 1934; 1 son, Remsen Newbold. Instr. life painting and composition Art Students League, N.Y.C., 1936-37. One man show Berkshire Mus., Pittsfield, Mass., 1957; 7 one man shows N.Y.C.; exhibited various group shows; represented in museums, art galleries, collections of Paul Sachs and others. Recipient prizes including W. A. Clark Prize bronze medal Corcoran Gallery, Washington, 1945; Mrs. H. S. Noyes and Am. Artists Group prizes, 1947; gold medal for painting N.A.D., 1966; Hallgasten prize N.A.D., 1967, Audubon Annual Creative Oil prize, 1972; 1st Altman prize N.A.D., 1973. Bd. govs. Showhegan (Me.) Sch. Painting and Sculpture N.A. Benjamin Franklin Fellow Royal Soc. Arts London; mem. Nat. Inst. Arts and Letters, Am. Acad. Arts and Letters, Am. Soc. Painters, Sculptors and Gravers. Soc. Am. Etchers, Am., Phila. Water Color Club, Am. Group. Clubs: Nat. Arts (Gold medal 1970), Cosmopolitan (N.Y.C.). Home: 355 W 246th St Fieldston NY 10471 Studio: 857 Broadway New York City NY 10003

BISHOP, JOAN FISS (MRS. ROBERT L. BISHOP), coll. adminstr.; b. Oshkosh, Wis.; d. Charles Ralph and Katherine (MacKinnon) Fiss; Ed.B., Wis. State Coll., 1931; A.M., Radcliffe Coll., 1935, certificate personnel adminstr., 1938, postgrad., 1942-43; postgrad. Syracuse U., 1935-36; m. Robert L. Bishop, Sept. 12, 1942. Asst. dir. appointment bur. Radcliffe Coll., dir. evening program in personnel adminstrn., 1943-44; dir. placement office Wellesley (Mass.) Coll., 1944—. Chmn. steering com., class rep. for Council Alumnae reps. Harvard-Radcliffe Program in Bus. Adminstrn., 1955-56, mem. adv. bd., 1956-63; mem. adv. com. 1st region U.S. Civil Service Commn., 1955-69; Resource attendant Pres.'s Commn. on Status Women, 1963-64. Recipient Distinguished Alumni award U. Wis.-Oshkosh, 1974. Mem. Am. Soc. Pub. Adminstrn. (nat. council 1970-73, exec. council Mass. chpt. 1971—, chmn. task force on women in pub. adminstrn. 1971-73, mem. nat. standing com. on women 1973—), Am. (chmn. placement steering com. 1952-56, mem. placement com. 1965-70), Mass. (mem. legislative com. 1968-72) personnel and guidance assns., Coll. Placement Council (research com. 1966-69), Eastern Coll. Personnel Officers (pres. 1947-48, program chmn. 1964-65), Nat. Assn. Prins. Schs. for Girls (mem. tchr. recruitment com. 1962-63), Am. Coll. Personnel Assn. (evaluation com. 1962-63), Nat. Council Guidance and Personnel Assns. (pres. 1948-49). Coll. Placement Publs. Council (v.p. 1953-55), Nat. (com. on careers 1949-53), Mass. (com. on careers 1953-58) leagues nursing, Women's Personnel Club Boston, Harvard Bus. Sch. Assn. Boston (mem. bd. govs. 1964-67). Club: College (pres. 1946-48 Boston). Home: 27 Amherst Rd Wellesley MA 02181

BISHOP, JULIE (MRS. WILLIAM BERGIN), actress; b. Denver; d. Will Wells and Blanche (Ferguson) Brown; student pvt. schs.; m. Clarence Shoop, July 24, 1944; children—Pamela Susan, Stephen Allen; m. 2d, William Bergin, Aug. 2, 1968. Featured in various films as Cinderella Jones, Rhapsody in Blue, Action in the North Atlantic, Sabre Jet, Westward the Women, Sands of Iwo Jima, The High and The Mighty, others; starred in plays as Holiday for Lovers, The Marquise, To Live Again, Tunnel of Love; opposite Bob Cummings in TV series of My Hero, many other TV shows. Pres. Los Angeles chpt. Achievement Rewards for Coll. Scientists Found., Inc., 1962-64, pres. ARCS Nat. Found., 1969-71. Recipient Eve award Mannequins of Assistance League So. Cal., 1973. Mem. Los Angeles Art Assn., U. Cal. at Los Angeles Art Council, Nat. Charity League, Los Angeles World Affairs Council, Les Dames de Champagne. Home: 1005 Laurel Way Beverly Hills CA 90210 also Casa Serena Puerto Vallarta Mexico

BISHOP, LUCY MOELING (MRS. LESLIE RALPH BISHOP), lawyer; b. Chgo., July 27, 1934; d. John Edward and Lucy Logwood (Maury) Moeling; B.A., U. Wis., 1956; LL.B., U. Va., 1958; m. Leslie Ralph Bishop, Aug. 22, 1959; children—John Leslie, Lucy Maury. Admitted to Ill. bar, 1958; pvt. practice law, LaGrange Park, Ill., 1959-68; mem. firm Bishop & Crawford, Ltd., Chgo., 1968—. Active West Suburban YMCA Swim Assn., 1969-72, McDonald's Hinsdale Swim Assn., 1972—. Mem. Chgo., Ill. bar assns., Village Field Club LaGrange Park, Phi Beta Kappa, Gamma Phi Beta. Episcopalian. Club: Oak Brook (Ill.) Women's. Home: 11 Croydon Lane Oak Brook IL 60521 Office: 1 First Nat Plaza Chicago IL 60670

BISHOP, MARIE, educator; b. Fort Smith, Ark., Aug. 26, 1911; d. Ray and Pansy Margaret Louise (Younger) Bishop; B.S., Northeastern State Coll. at Tahlequah, Okla., 1940; M.A., U. No. Colo., 1949; diploma Tchrs. Coll. Columbia U., 1958. Tchr. one room rural schs. Delaware County, Okla., 1932-39, Benton County, Ark., 1930-31; tchr. 1st grade Jay (Okla.) Pub. Schs., 1939-42; bookkeeper Douglas Aircraft, Tulsa, 1942-43; tchr. primary, kindergarten Euchee Boys Boarding Sch., Bur. Indian Affairs, Sapulpa, Okla., 1943-46; supr. elementary sch. Siloam Springs (Ark.) Pub. Schs., 1946-50; asst. prof. elementary edn., early childhood edn. specialist Bemidji (Minn.) State Coll., 1950—. Vice pres. Democratic Farm Labor Party Women, Beltrami County, 1967-68; vice chmn. League Women Voters, 1956-57. Bd. dirs. Bemidji Day Care, 1970—. Fulbright exchange lectr., Salisbury (Eng.) Tchr. Tng. Coll., 1952-53. Mem. N.E.A., Minn. Edn. Assn., Am. Assn. U. Women, Fedn. Bus. and Profl. Women, Nat., Minn. Assns. for edn. young children, Assn. for Childhood Edn. Internat., Minn. Fulbright (Exchange Tchrs. Club, Pi Lambda Theta, Alpha Delta Kappa. Democrat. Methodist. Author: (with Minn. Dept. Edn. Com.) Minn. Kindergarten Curriculum Guide, 1960-63. Home: 1611 Bixby Av Bemidji MN 56601

BISHOP, NOVA RHEA (MRS. CHESTER LEE BISHOP), ednl. adminstr.; b. Russellville, Ark., Jan. 13, 1911; d. Walter Granville and Arminda Belle (Henry) McGuire; student Ark. Tech. Coll., 1928-29, Coll. of the Ozarks, 1929-31; m. Chester Lee Bishop, Aug. 23, 1929; children—Robert, Patricia (Mrs. Carter), Michael, Dorothy (Mrs. Thomas Spencer), David. Tchr. Fairfax County (Va.) Schs., 1956-68; registrar Luther Rice Coll., Alexandria, Va., 1970—. Home: 6312 Roso St Springfield VA 22150 Office: 5912 Franconia Rd Alexandria VA 22310

BISHOP, OLGA BERNICE, educator, bibliographer; b. Dover, N.B., Can., June 24, 1911; d. Thomas Cochran and Minnie (Colpitts) Bishop; B.A., Mt. Allison U., 1938, M.A., 1951, LL.D., 1971; B. Pub. Adminstrn., Carleton U., 1946; A.M. in L.S., U. Mich., 1952, Ph.D., 1962. Sec., Mt. Allison Meml. Library, Sackville, N.B., 1932-40; asst. librarian 1946-53; sr. adminstrv. officer RCAF Record of Service, Can. Civil Service, Ottawa, 1940-46; gen. librarian U. Western Ont. (Can.) London, 1953-54, med. librarian, 1954-65; asso. prof. U. Toronto, 1965-70, prof., 1970—. Dir. Community Concert Assn., London 1963-66. Mem. Maritime (past 1st v.p.), Am., Canadian (councillor 1967-71, chmn. research and spl. libraries sect. 1967-68), Ont. (councillor 1966-67) library assns., Ont. (councillor 1963-71, chmn. 1966-67), Canadian (sec. 1965-66) assns. coll. and univ. libraries, Inst. Profl. Librarians of Ont. (dir. 1964-68, pres. 1966-67), Geosci. Information Soc., Spl. Libraries Assn., Med. Library Assn., Assn. Am. Library Schs., Canadian Assn. Library Schs. (pres. 1973-74), Bibliog. Soc. Can., Can. Assn. Univ. Tchrs., Ont. Hist. Assn., Beta Phi Mu (dir. 1973—). Mem. United Ch. of Can. Club: Faculty. Writer bibliog. govt. publs. Home: 1 Kilbarry Rd Toronto ON M5P 1K4 Canada

BISHOP, PATRICIA LYN, airline stewardess; b. Phila., Oct. 16, 1944; d. William Frederick and Mary Linda (Dawes) Bishop; B.A., Fla. State U., 1966. Editor, pub. relations Nat. Paint, Varnish and Lacquer Assn., 1966-69; pub. relations dir., editor Nat. Clean Up-Paint Up-Fix Up Bur., Washington, 1969-72; stewardess United Air Lines, Washington, 1972—. Hostess pub. relations N.Y. World's Fair Pavillion, Gen. Electric Co., 1965. Mem. Gamma Alpha Chi,

Delta Zeta. Democrat. Home: 1500 Arlington Blvd Arlington VA 22209

BISSELL, HILLARY RARDEN (MRS. WADSWORTH BISSELL), human relations adviser; b. Greenville, Mich., Dec. 24, 1912; d. W. H. and Nelle (Crowell) Rarden; A.B., U. Mich. (Earhart scholar 1933-34), 1934; postgrad. Ariz. State Coll., 1937-38, Mich. State U., 1958—; m. Wadsworth Bissell, May 9, 1936; children—Brereton, Torre, Trim. Social work Kent County (Mich.) Emergency Relief, 1934-35; supr. social research Nat. Youth Adminstrn., Grand Rapids, Mich., 1935-36. Mem. interracial com. Grand Rapids Council Social Agys., 1949-58; Grand Rapids bd. Mich. Com. on Civil Rights, 1952—, exec. sec., 1958—; mem. City of Grand Rapids Human Relations Commn., 1955-62; mem. casework com. Family Service Assn., 1956-58; mem. state steering com. Mich. Coordinating Council for Civil Rights, 1958—; mem. Mich. Civil Service Commn. Hearing Bd., 1960—. Asso. mem. Nat. Council for Social Action, Congl. Christian Chs., 1946-54, mem. nat. race relations com. Bd. Home Missions, 1952-54; state chmn. race relations Social Action Com., Mich. Congregation Christian Conf. Chs., 1949-53; del. Fed. Council Chs. Nat. Conf. on ch. and Econ. Life, 1950; vice chmn. social action dept. Mich. Council Chs., 1950-51, chmn. human relations, 1951-52. Candidate for Mich. Legislature, 1952; sec. Dem. State Central Com., 1952-54; mem. Dem. County Exec. Com., 1960—; candidate county treas., 1960; Barry County coordinator McGovern Campaign, 1972. Mem. pub. affairs com. YMCA. Recipient spl. achievement award Mich. Conf. N.A.A.C.P. Branches, 1959; Dale Carnegie Alumni Assn. honor citation 1962 Lambda Kappa Showcase award, 1968. Mem. Nat. Assn. Intergroup Relations Ofcls., League Women Voters. (dir. Grand Rapids 1939-42, Edgerton, Wis., 1944-46), N.A.A.C.P. (dir. Grand Rapids 1949—, v.p. Grand Rapids 1955-57, state treas. 1952-55, mem. nat. youth com. 1957-58, adviser Grand Rapids youth council, 1956-59, mem. Mich. youth work com., 1957-59, state v.p. 1959-62), Urban League, Women's Internat. League for Peace and Freedom, Am. Civil Liberties Union (dir. West Mich. chpt. 1970), Kappa Kappa Gamma. Club: Nautico (Boqueron, P.R.). Home: 1401 S Yankee Spring Rd Middleville MI 49333 also Box 326 Boqueron PR 00622

BISSELL, JEAN GALLOWAY (MRS. GREGG CLAUDE BISSELL), lawyer; b. Due West, S.C., June 9, 1936; d. Robert Stone and Clara Elizabeth (Agnew) Galloway; student Erskine Coll., 1952-54; B.S., U. S.C., 1956, LL.B., 1958; m. Gregg Claude Bissell, June 11, 1969. Admitted to S.C. bar, 1958; asso. firm Haynsworth, Perry, Bryant, Marion & Johnstone, Greenville, 1958-65, partner, 1965-71; partner firm McKay, Sherrill, Walker, Townsend & Wilkins, Columbia, 1971—. Lectr.-at-law Law Center, U. S.C., 1971—. Mem. adv. council S.C. State Library, 1971—, Furman U., 1972—, Columbia Coll., 1974—. Trustee Erskine Coll., 1971—, Greenville County Pub. Library, 1961-71, Daniel Found., 1968—, Richland County Pub. Library, 1973—. Mem. Am., S.C., Richland County bar assns., S.C. State Bar, S.C. Library Assn. (chmn. of trustee sect. 1966-67, award for distinguished service 1973), Am. Library Trustee Assn. (v.p., regional dir. 1965-66), Phi Beta Kappa. Clubs: Columbia Country; Greenville Country; Summit. Editorial Asst., Drafting Wills and Trust Agreements in South Carolina, 1971. Home: 3102 Keenan Dr Columbia SC 29201 Office: 1340 Bull St PO Box 447 Columbia SC 29202

BITKER, MARJORIE MARKS (MRS. BRUNO VOLTAIRE BITKER), writer; b. N.Y.C., Feb. 9, 1901; d. Cecil Alexander and Rachel (Fox) Marks; A.B. magna cum laude (Caroline Duror Meml. fellow), Barnard Coll., 1921; M.A. Columbia, 1922; m. James C. Jacobson, Dec. 12, 1922 (div. 1942); children—Emilie J. (Mrs. Frederick A. Jacobi), Margaret J. (Mrs. David Strange), Elizabeth J. (Mrs. Frank Hahn); m. 2d, John C. Mayer, Oct. 24, 1942 (dec. June 1945); m. 3d, Bruno Voltaire Bitker, Oct. 10, 1957. Free lance writer, 1922—; editor Farrar Straus, N.Y.C., 1946-47, G.P. Putnam's Sons, N.Y.C., 1947-53, David McKay Co., N.Y.C., 1953-55; now editorial cons., book reviewer, feature writer. Lectr., Hunter Coll., Coll. City N.Y., 1949-53. Bd. visitors U. Wis., 1962-68; alumnae trustee Barnard Coll., 1964-68; Barnard-in-Milw.; bd. dirs. Friends Wis. Libraries. Mem. Am. Assn. U. Women, Women's Nat. Book Assn., Nat. Book Com., Women in Communications, Bookfellows Milw. (pres. 1971-73, dir.), Council for Wis. Writers (bd. mem. 1971—), Phi Beta Kappa. Contbr. articles, and book revs. to popular mags. Address: 2330 E Back Bay St Milwaukee WI 53202

BITNEY, SUE, artist; b. Seattle, Nov. 3, 1942; d. Leslie W. and Lillian (Stai) Bitney; student San Jose State Coll., 1960-63; B.A., U. Cal. at Berkeley, 1966, M.A., 1967. Exhibited one man shows Studio Marconi, Milan, Italy, 1967, Galleria Deposito, Genoa, Italy, 1967, Galleria Foscherari, Bologna, 1968, Galerie B. Mommaton, Paris, France, 1968; exhibited in group shows Richmond Sculpture Ann., 1965, U. Cal. Art Mus., Berkeley, 1967, Inst. Contemporary Arts, Boston, 1968, Galleria Annuniciata, Milan, 1968; asso. instr. sculpture U. Cal., Berkeley, 1967; asst. prof. art Reed Coll., Portland, Ore., 1970—. Recipient Phelan award, 1966. Home: 5235 NE Cleveland Portland OR 97212

BITTEL, ANN LANNOM BRAMWELL (MRS. FERDINAND JOHN BITTEL), librarian; b. Nashville, Tenn., Aug. 9, 1944; d. Charles Robinson and Maggie Lee (Lannom) Bramwell; B.A., U. Miss., 1966, M.L.S., 1967; m. Ferdinand John Bittel, Aug. 23, 1969. Head librarian Northeast Ala. State Jr. Coll., Rainsville, 1967—. Mem. Ala. Jr. Coll. Library Assn. (sec., treas. 1970—), Am. Assn. U. Women, Jackson County Arts Council, N.E.A., Ala. Edn. Assn., Alpha Omicron Pi. Methodist. Home: 607 Benham Av Scottsboro AL 35768 Office: PO Box 159 Rainsville AL 35986

BIXBY, KATHERINE COSTLOW (MRS. E. REW BIXBY), charitable orgn. exec.; b. Lusk, Wyo., Feb. 8, 1920; d. Jesse Patrick and Anna (Thompson) Costlow; student Cottey Coll., 1937-38; B.A., Doane Coll., 1941; m. E. Rew Bixby, May 30, 1942; children—Patrick William, Jean (Mrs. Hennessy). Tchr. elementary schs., Lusk, Wyo., 1941-42; exec. dir. Vol. Bur. Voluntary Action Center, Los Angeles, 1971-74. Mem. Welfare Planning Council Bd., 1962-72, USO, 1965-71, Comprehensive Health Planning Los Angeles County, 1969-72, United Crusades Cal., 1968-72, Mayor's Com. on Aging, 1970-72, Los Angeles Mental Health Commn., 1967-72, Planned Protective Services, 1969-71, Camp Fire Girls, 1950-59. Bd. dirs. United Way, Inc., 1963-71. Recipient Gold Key United Way, 1963, Armed Forces Vol. award, 1966, Luther Gulick award Camp Fire Girls, 1959, Gold Medallion award USO, 1970. Home: 920 Crestview Av Glendale CA 91202 Office: 621 S Virgil St Los Angeles CA 90005

BIXEL, JANET KENNEDY (MRS. GORDON ARTHUR BIXEL JR.), physician; b. Columbus, O., Nov. 22, 1936; d. Harold William and Burnis Ruth (McKinstry) Kennedy; B.A. summa cum laude, Ohio State U., 1956, M.D. summa cum laude, 1959; m. Gordon Arthur Bixel, Jr., Sept. 15, 1956; children—Carl Adrian, Eric Arthur, Ronald Alan, Curtis Evan, Juanita Irene. Intern, White Cross Hosp., Columbus, O., 1959-60; resident internal medicine White Cross Hosp. and Riverside Meth. Hosp., Columbus, 1960-62, Ohio State U. Hosp., Columbus, 1962-63; practice medicine, specializing in internal medicine, Worthington, 1963-72, specializing in internal medicine and endocrinology, Columbus, 1972—; sr. attending staff, teaching staff, dir. endocrinology clinic Riverside Hosp., Columbus; courtesy staff, teaching in endocrinology clinic Univ. Hosp., Columbus; cons. staff Harding Hosp., Worthington; courtesy staff Grant & St. Anthony's Hosp., Columbus, 1972—; clin. instr. Ohio State U., Columbus, 1963-71, clin. asst. prof., 1971—. Mem. P.T.A., Worthingway Civic Assn., Worthington Human Relations Council. Diplomate Am. Bd. Internal Medicine. Mem. Am., Ohio med. assns., Am. Med. Women's Assn. (local sec. 1969), Am., Central Ohio heart assns., A.C.P., Am. Assn. U. Women, Columbus Acad. Medicine, Columbus Soc. Internal Medicine, Central Ohio Diabetes Assn., Ohio State Univ. Assn., Phi Beta Kappa, Alpha Lambda Delta, Alpha Epsilon Delta, Alpha Omega Alpha. Republican. Mem. United Ch. of Christ. Home: 410 Longfellow Av Worthington OH 43085 Office: Central Ohio Med Clinic 497 E Town St Columbus OH 43215

BIXLER, AGNES SEELYE (MRS. THOMAS KURTZ), educator; b. New Haven, Oct. 25, 1941; d. Herbert Edwards and Agnes Macauley (Rodgers) Rixler; A.B., Smith Coll., 1962, M.S., 1963; tchrs. certificate Chelsea Coll. Phys. Edn., Eastbourne, Eng., 1968; m. Thomas Kurtz, June 10, 1974. Faculty, Vassar Coll., Poughkeepsie, N.Y., 1963-67, U. Del., Newark, 1968-72; dir. women's athletics, coach field hockey, squash and lacrosse Dartmouth, Hanover, N.H., 1972—. Mem. touring lacrosse team to Gt. Britain and Ireland, 1964, 70; mem. U.S. Lacrosse team, 1963, 70, 71. Mem. U.S. Women's Lacrosse Assn. (2d v.p. 1970—). Editor Crosse-Checks, ann. lacrosse mag., 1970—, D.G.W.S. Lacrosse Guide, 1974—. Home: Blueberry Hill Hanover NH 03755

BIXLER, MARGARET MABEL TRIPLETT (MRS. ROLAND M. BIXLER), instrument co. exec.; b. Bluffton, O.; d. Ray L. and Etta (Lantz) Triplett; student Bluffton Coll., 1935-37; A.B., U. Mich., 1939; m. Roland M. Bixler, July 1, 1939; children—Katharine Anne, David Ray. Corporate sec., dir. J-B-T Instruments, Inc., New Haven, 1940—, 424 Chapel, Inc., New Haven, 1966—. Bd. dirs. YWCA, New Haven, 1954-68, 71—, pres., 1957-60; bd. dirs. United Fund of New Haven, Inc., 1962-65, Vis. Nurse Assn., New Haven, 1964-68; project dir. Women in Community Service, Inc., 1966—; finance chmn. YWCA, N.Y.C., 1969-70; bd. dirs. Profl. Children's Sch., N.Y.C., 1970—. Mem. Am. Assn. U. Women (local dir. 1950-53), Alpha Omicron Pi, Omega Upsilon. Mem. United Ch. of Christ (pres. Women's Assn. 1962-64). Home: 60 Wepawaug Rd Woodbridge CT 06525 Office: Box 1818 New Haven CT 06508

BIZETTE, JUSTINE RUTH LAMBERT (MRS. RUSSELL LAURENCE BIZETTE, SR.), home economist; b. Innis, La., Mar. 30, 1921; d. John Robert and Ruth Elizabeth (Humphreys) Lambert; B.S., Northwestern La. State U., 1942; m. Russell Laurence Bizette, Sr., Mar. 6, 1943; children—Russell Laurence, Justine Lambert, Pauline Ann, Thelma Darlene. Tchr. home econs. Morganza (La.) High Sch., 1942; asst. home demonstration agt. Vermillion Parish, Abbeville, La., 1943; tchr. home econs. St. Theresa's Parochial Sch., Coral Gables, Fla., 1948-52, cafeteria mgr., 1948-52; extension home econs. agt., 4-H coordinator Dept. Cooperative Extension Service, Dade County, Miami, Fla., 1961—. Ex-officio mem. Dade County Youth Fair Bd., Miami, 1965-72; charter mem. Mercy Hosp. Aux., A.R.C., Fla. Civil Def. Organizer, charter bd. dirs. Dade County 4-H Youth Found., Inc., 1966-72. Mem. Am., Fla. home econs. assns., Nat., Fla. (sec. 1965, dist. dir. 1972-73) assn. extension home econs. agts., Dade Bus. and Profl. Women's Club (dir. 1970-72, v.p. 1972), Epsilon Sigma Phi, Kappa Delta Pi, Delta Sigma Epsilon. Roman Catholic. Club: Zonta (charter mem., dir. 1971, 72) (Miami, Fla.). Home: 8463 SW 68th St Miami FL 33143 Office: 2690 NW 7th Av Miami FL 33127

BJORLIE, LIV BERGLIOT LUNDEBY (MRS. ELMER PEDER BJORLIE), adminstr.; b. Tolna, N.D.; d. Frederick and Anna (Samuelson) Lundeby; B.S., Valley City (N.D.) State Coll., 1972; m. Elmer Peder Bjorlie, Apr. 4, 1952; children—Peter, Anna, John, Paul, Laura. Exec. sec. real estate and ins. office; insp. N.D. Labor Dept.; now dir. Barnes and LaMoure Housing Authority, also coordinator Barnes County Sr. Citizens Council. Active Democratic Party, 1958—, county campaign mgr., 1960, county chmn. N.P.L. Women, 1958-60, dist. dir., 1959-61, pres., 1961-64; mem. Dem. Nat. Com., 1964-72; del., speaker Dem. Nat. Conv., 1964, 68, mem. credentials com., 1968, mem. site selection com., 1964-68; mem. Nat. Dem. Commn. on Rules, 1969-72; regional chmn. Women for Humphrey, 1968. Mem. Citizens Jud. Council N.D., Nat. Youth Adv. Council, Peace Corps Adv. Council, 1966-69, sr. citizens County Council. Mem. Am. Assn. U. Women. Lutheran (mem. Ladies Aid). Club: Zonta. Home: 1380 Central Av N Valley City ND 58072

BJORNLUND, GEORGIANA OSMOND MIRANDA (MRS. WILLIAM BRUCE BJORNLUND), lawyer, state ofcl.; b. Jamaica, N.Y., July 25, 1935; d. Nicholas Joseph and Georgiana Agnes (Osmond) Miranda; B.A., Coll. Notre Dame, 1957; LL.B., J.D., St. Johns U., 1964; m. William Bruce Bjornlund, Jan. 15, 1972. Admitted to N.Y. bar, 1965, Vt. bar, 1970; editorial clk. Long Island (N.Y.) Daily Press, 1952-56; bus. rep. N.Y. Tel. Co., Forest Hills, 1957-58; advt. copywriter B. Gertz Co., Jamaica, 1959-61, Arnold Constable Co., N.Y.C., 1961; law clk. Schneider & Kaufman Co., N.Y.C., 1961-62, Simpson Thacher & Bartlett, N.Y.C., 1962-64; claims examiner, N.Y.C. Comptroller's Office, 1964-65; asst. dist. atty. Queens County, N.Y., 1965-66; mng. atty. Casey, Lane & Mittendorf, N.Y.C., 1966; asst. U.S. atty., Eastern Dist. N.Y., Bklyn., 1966-69; asst. atty. gen. Vt., Montpelier, 1969—. Mem. Gov's Commn. Status Women Vt., 1969—; Mem. Jamaica Day Nursery Jr. League, 1957-61, pres. 1958-59; mem. Marian Guild Mary Immaculate Hosp., Jamaica, 1958-61, pres. 1958-59; co-chmn. Queen's County (N.Y.) Hosp. Week, 1958; chmn. United Hosp. Fund Dr., 1958. Mem. Vt., Queens County bar assns., Phi Alpha Delta. Roman Catholic (mem. parish council 1973-74). Home: Route 1 East Montpelier VT 05651 Office: 109 State St Montpelier VT 05602

BLACE, MARION AGNES RAWSON (MRS. JOHN L. BLACE), civic worker; b. Bridgeport, Conn., May 16, 1910; d. William Robertson and Beatrice (Garrity) Rawson; B.S., Columbia, 1938, M.A., 1951; m. John L. Blace, June 30, 1936; 1 dau., Joslyn (Mrs. Kirk A. Halstead). Tchr., Suffield, Conn., 1929-31, Leona, N.J., 1931-55; substitute tchr., Montvale, N.J., 1955-60. Park Ridge welfare Dir., 1966—; chmn. adjustment com. Park Ridge Youth Guidance Council, 1969-70; mem. Borough Council, 1959-65. Parliamentarian, Pascack Mental Health Center Aux., 1972-74; treas. N.J. Symphony League, 1972-74; chmn. spl. gifts expansion fund Pascack Valley Hosp., vol. worker, 1962-73; vol. worker Hackensack Hosp., 1952-73. Mem. Phi Lambda Theta. Mem. Dutch Reformed Ch. (treas. 1967-69). Clubs: Paskack Womans (v.p. 1969-70), Contemporary Women's (Parliamentarian 1973-74). Address: 29 Park Av Park Ridge NJ 07656

BLACK, ANITA (MRS. RUSSELL PAUL GAMBLE), journalist; b. Manitowoc, Wis.; d. Walter Herman and Else Henrietta Johanna (Kaems) Biesemeyer; B.A. in Journalism, U. Wis.; m. Russell Paul Gamble, June 8, 1971. Women's news editor The Daily Progress, Charlottesville, Va., 1949-62; fashion editor Times-Dispatch, Richmond, Va., 1962-65, asst. women's editor, 1962-63, women's news editor, 1963-65; men's fashion editor, women's news reporter Milw. Sentinel, 1965—. Recipient Lulu award Men's Fashion Assn., 1965, 66, 67, 69, 70, 71; Reporting award Caswell-Massey Men's Fashion, 1968. Mem. Nat. Fedn. Press Women (charter v.p. Va. chpt. 1958-65), Women in Communications, Sigma Delta Chi. Office: 918 N 4th St Milwaukee WI 53201

BLACK, ANNE FRANCES MONARCH, hosp. exec.; b. Mobile, Ala., Apr. 4, 1925; d. Charles James and Delma (Borders) Monarch; diploma Nazareth Sch. Nursing, St. Joseph Infirmary, 1945; B.S. in Nursing, Spaulding Coll., 1962; m. Donald Dale Black, July 27, 1948 (div.); 1 son, Stephen Dale. Staff nurse St. Joseph Infirmary, Louisville, 1945-46, 47, St. Anne's Maternity Hosp., Los Angeles, 1947, Quincy (Mass.) City Hosp., 1947-48, Scott AFB Hosp., Belleville, Ill., 1948-49, Herrick Meml. Hosp., Berkeley, Cal., 1951-54; pvt. duty nurse, Louisville, 1947; head nurse St. Joseph Infirmary, 1951-54, evening supr., 1957, asst. dir. nursing service, 1957-60; asst. exec. sec. Ky. Nurses Assn., Louisville, 1960-62; asst. exec. sec., dir. nursing staff devel. Williamson (W.Va.) Appalachian Regional Hosp., 1962-74; dir. nursing service Louisa (Ky.) Community Hosp., 1974—. Tchr. rehab. and inter-personnel classes to employees Williamson Regional Hosp., 1969-73. Active League Clean Voting W.Va., 1971-73. Mem. Ky. Nurses Assn. (pres. 1972, sec. 1974-75). Moose. (chmn. com. 1969-73). Home: 406 Franklin St Louisa KY 41230 Office: Box 769 Louisa KY 41230

BLACK, CAROLYN CROW (MRS. DOUGLAS R. BLACK), educator; b. Gilroy, Cal., Jan. 18, 1936; d. Harold Cornwell and Gwendolyn Jessie (Thomas) Crow; A.B., U. Cal. at Berkeley, 1958, M.A., 1962; Ph.D., Bryn Mawr Coll., 1967; m. Douglas R. Black, Dec. 30, 1969. Asst. prof. philosophy Cal. State U. at San Jose (Cal.), 1966—, Univ. fellow in instructional research, 1973-74. Mem. Am. Assn. U. Profs., Am. Philos. Assn. (Pacific div.), Mind Assn., Soc. for Women in Philosophy. Office: Philosophy Dept Cal State University at San Jose San Jose CA 95192

BLACK, ELIZABETH SEAY DEMERITTE, b. Birmingham, Ala., Jan. 23, 1908; d. James Elias and Elma Atkins (Austin) Seay; student pub. schs., Birmingham; m. Fred E. DeMeritte, Feb. 17, 1924 (div. Nov. 1956); 1 son, Frederick James; m. 2d, Hugo Lafayette Black, Sept. 11, 1957 (dec. Sept. 1971). Receptionist, Stokely, Scrivner, Dominick & Smith, attys., Birmingham, 1937-40; legal sec. and steno pool Reconstrn. Finance Corp., Birmingham, 1940-41; dep. clk. Dist. Ct. of U.S. for No. Dist. Ala., 1941-56; sec. to Justice Hugo L. Black, U.S. Supreme Ct., Washington, 1956-57. Democrat. Home: 1600 S Joyce St C-212 Arlington VA 22202

BLACK, HELEN LOUISE, newspaper feature editor; b. Pulaski, Va., June 14, 1927; d. Malcolm William and Annie Grace (Aust) Black; student The Coll. of William and Mary, 1944-48. Society and Women's editor Martinsville (Va.) Bull., 1949-73; writer enterprise feature articles A.P., 1957—. Chmn., Heart Fund, 1950-55; mem. Inter-Club Council, 1950; pres. Patrick Henry council Girl Scouts, 1951-52, mem. Piedmont council, 1952-54; home nursing chmn. Civil Def., 1954; active Ground Observer Corps Shelter, 1957, observer, 1954-57; instrumental in getting first sch. for mentally retarded children in Martinsville, 1957; vol. worker Christmas Cheer, 1950-55; gray lady A.R.C. Bd. dirs. Martinsville Henry County Mental Health Assn., 1960-63, Mental Hygiene Clinic, 1962-63, Martinsville Henry County chpt. Va. Heart Assn., 1967-72; trustee Meml. Pub. Library, 1971—. Recipient citation Cancer Soc., 1954, Polio Soc., 1956, Va. Fedn. Garden Clubs, 1969. Mem. Martinsville Henry County Civic Music Assn. (v.p. 1962-63), Va. Mus. Fine Arts, Friends of the Library, Va. Assn. Press Women, Henry County Autistic Soc. Mem. Christian Ch. Clubs: Music Study (founder; v.p. 1956-57), Va. Fedn. Music Clubs, Martinsville Henry County Woman's (sec. 1954-55), Martinsville Council Garden Clubs (pres. 1957), Longwood Garden (pres. 1962-63), Martinsville Business and Professional Women's (pres. 1957), Beta Sigma Phi, Xi Omega. Home and office: 102 Broad St Martinsville VA 24112

BLACK, IRYNE CODON (MRS. JOHN WOODLAND BLACK), lawyer; b. Los Angeles; d. Matthew M. and Eva (Levitt) Codon; B.A. cum laude, Stanford, 1950, LL.B., 1958; m. John Woodland Black, Sept. 3, 1959; children—Ian Andrew, Timothy Matthew. Ambassadorial sec. U.S. Fgn. Service, Berlin and Bonn, Germany, also Pusan, Seoul, Korea, 1950-53; social case worker Welfare Dept., Los Angeles County, Cal., 1954-55; employee relations officer U.S. Geol. Survey, Washington, 1955-57; dep. atty. gen. State of Cal., Colo. River Litigation, Los Angeles, 1958-59; admitted to Cal. bar, 1959, D.C. bar, 1969; atty., adv. Office of Solicitor, U.S. Dept. of Labor, Washington, 1959-62; staff atty. N.L.R.B., Washington, 1962; asst. gen. counsel Peace Corps, Washington, 1962-64; asst. gen. counsel Smithsonian Instn., Washington, 1967-69; cons., Tchr. Corps, Office of Edn., Dept. Health, Edn. and Welfare, Washington, 1968-69; dep. county counsel, Orange County, Cal., 1970—. Home: 1646 Irvine Av Newport Beach CA 92660 Office: 515 Sycamore St Santa Ana CA 92708

BLACK, JANET DOHERTY, educator; b. Doniphan, Mo., Jan. 14, 1930; d. Chester A. and Alma (Gerlach) Doherty; A.A., William Woods Coll., 1949; B.S. in Edn., U. Mo., 1951; M.Ed., Fla. Atlantic U., 1970. Tchr., St. Marks Episcopal Sch., Ft. Lauderdale, Fla., 1961-65; tchr. Fed. Program in Adult Edn., Ft. Lauderdale, 1965-66; tchr., counselor, adminstr. Adult Day High Sch., Ft. Lauderdale, 1966-69; registrar Ft. Lauderdale U., 1970-74, dir. counseling and testing, asst. prof. psychology, 1970-74. Vice chmn. Planning and Zoning Commn., City of Oakland Park, 1974—. Bd. dirs. Broward County Citizens for Environmental Preservation, 1972—. Mem. Zonta Internat. (v.p. Ft. Lauderdale 1974—), P.E.O., Ft. Lauderdale Panhellenic, Beta Delta, Gamma Phi Beta. Republican. Episcopalian. Home: 1401 NE 39th St Fort Lauderdale FL 33308 Office: 1401 E Broward Blvd Fort Lauderdale FL 33301

BLACK, MARCIA, sch. counselor; b. Boise, Ida., Mar. 30, 1937; d. Bryant Byron and Melba (Douglass) Black; B.A., Brigham Young U., 1959; M.A., San Jose State U., 1965. Tchr., Anaheim (Cal.) Sch. Dist., 1959-60; stock saleswoman Royal State Nat. Ins. Co., Honolulu, 1960; tchr. Honolulu Dept. Pub. Instrn., 1961; group sales dir. MGM and Twentieth Century Fox, Salt Lake City, 1961-62; tchr. Granite Sch. Dist., Salt Lake City, 1962-63, Sunnyvale (Cal.) Sch. Dist., 1963-67; counselor Oak Grove Dist., San Jose, 1967—. Owner, Bilmar Co.; partner Peruvian Treasures. Mem. Oak Grove Tchrs. Assn., Joyful Noise. Home: 18657 Ravenwood Dr Saratoga CA 95070 Office: 6061 San Ignacio St San Jose CA 95119

BLACK, MARGARET B. (MRS. HARRY E. FRISBIE), orthodontist; b. Mt. Vernon, Ind., Sept. 9, 1901; D.D.S., U. Cal., 1924, postgrad., 1926-27; m. Harry E. Frisbie, June 20, 1961. Pvt. practice orthodontics, Berkeley, Cal., 1927—. Fellow Am. Inst. Oral Biology; mem. Berkeley Dist. Dental Soc., Am. Cal. dental assns., Coll. Women's Club Berkeley, Nat. Assn. U. Women, Edward H. Angle Soc. Orthodontists, Charles H. Tweed Found. for Orthodontic Research, Upsilon Alpha, Omicron Kappa Upsilon, Epsilon Alpha. Home: Route 1 Box 192A2 Nevada City CA 95959 Office: 2300 Durant Av Berkeley CA 94704

BLACK, MARGARET JUNE (MRS. LEHMAN ERNEST BLACK, JR.), psychologist; b. Findlay, O., June 14, 1922; d. Clarence Alexander and Anna Augusta (Ward) Stewart; B.S. in Edn., Youngstown State U., 1962; M.S. in Edn., U. Akron, 1971; m. Lehman Ernest Black, Jr., Apr. 20, 1941; children—Paul, Karen (Mrs. James R. Hovell), Mary Anna (Mrs. Horace Stonework), Lynn (Mrs. H. L. Greene), Lehman Ernest III. Tchr. English Youngstown (O.) Bd. of Edn., 1962-67, psychology intern, 1970-71, sch. psychologist, 1971—. Tchr. English, Am. govt., econs., 1968-70. Mem. YWCA,

Youngstown, 1950—. Mem. Ohio Sch. Psychol. Assn., Kent-Akron Area Sch. Psychologists, Nat. Assn. Sch. Psychologists, Urban League, N.A.A.C.P., Mahoning County Mental Health Assn. (sec. 1973—), Alpha Kappa Alpha, Delta Kappa Gamma. Episcopalian (mem. bishop's com. 1955—). Home: 334 Tod Lane Youngstown OH 44504 Office: 1025 West Rayen Av Youngstown OH 44502

BLACK, MARIAN WATKINS, educator; b. Arcadia, Fla., Jan. 21, 1905; d. Richard Ellis and Bertha Marian (Parker) Watkins; A.B., Fla. State U., 1926; M.A., U. Fla., 1943; Ph.D., Northwestern U., 1953; m. Robert Franklin Black, Aug. 10, 1927. Tchr. pub. schs. Lee and De Soto counties, (Fla.), 1926-42; instr. University Sch., Fla. State Coll. for Women, Tallahassee, 1942-45; supr. schs. Calhoun and Liberty counties, (Fla.), Blountstown, 1945-48; asst. prof. Fla. State U., Tallahassee, 1948-52, asso. prof., 1952-65, prof. ednl. adminstrn., 1965—. Cons. McPherson Sch. for Delinquent Girls, Ocala, Fla., 1968-72. Recipient Achievement award Fla. chpt. Delta Kappa Gamma, 1971. Mem. Assn. Supervision and Curriculum Devel. (nat. bd. dirs. 1958-62, 65-66, 69-72), Phi Kappa Phi, Kappa Delta Pi (nat. presdl. adv. bd. 1964-68, Honor Key 1969), Phi Alpha Theta, Kappa Alpha Theta, Pi Lambda Theta, Delta Kappa Gamma. Contbr. profl. jours. Home: 1540 Colonial Dr Tallahassee FL 32303

BLACK, MARY ELIZABETH CHILDS, mus. adminstr., author; b. Pittsfield, Mass.; d. George and Isabelle (Merrill) Childs; A.B., U. N.C., 1943; postgrad. Cath. U., 1950; M.A., George Washington U., 1951; m. Richard Winthrop Black, Apr. 7, 1947 (div. 1970); 1 dau., Merrill Elizabeth. Research asst. Colonial Williamsburg, 1956-57; curator Abby Aldrich Rockefeller Folk Art Collection, Williamsburg, Va., 1958-60, dir., 1960-64, dir. Mus. Am. Folk Art, N.Y.C., 1964-69; curator painting, sculpture, decorative arts N.Y. Hist. Soc., N.Y.C., 1969—. Vis. lectr. Shelburne Mus., U. Vt., 1965, 72; cons. Smithsonian Inst., 1967. Author: (with Jean Lipman) American Folk Painting, 1967; (with Barbara and Lawrence Holdridge) Ammi Phillips, 1789-1865, 1969; Old New York in Early Photographs, 1973; Editor: (catalog) What is American in American Art, 1971; City of Promise: Aspects of Jewish Life in New York 1654-1970, 1971. Lectr., writer, asst. film producer, producer film strips on folk art. Contbr. articles to publs. Home: 149 W 94th St New York City NY 10025 Office: 170 Central Park W New York City NY 10024

BLACK, MAUREEN, newspaper feature editor; b. Manchester, Eng., Feb. 4, 1937; d. William Henry and Kathleen Mary (Cleaver) Jackson; came to U.S., 1957, naturalized, 1962; grad. Felt and Tarrant Comptometer Sch., Eng., 1953; student Alamogordo br. N.M. State U., 1959-60, 62-63; (div.); 1 dau., Karen Elizabeth Black. Office mgr., personnel dir. J.C. Penney Co., Alamogordo, N.M., 1958-66; exec. sec. to project mgr. Gen. Electric Co., Re-entry System div., Holloman AFB, 1967-68; soc. editor, columnist Alamogordo Daily News, 1968-73; regional corr. El Paso (Tex.) Times, 1968—; free lance writer and photographer; script writer Film Unit 505, Alamogordo, 1971—. Pres., Alamogordo Music Theatre, 1971-72. Mem. planning com. tourism, recreation, conventions, Gov. of N.M., 1965; Mem. N.M. State Film Commn., 1973-74. Life mem. Aux. of Zia Sch. for Handicapped Children. Recipient service award Nat. Found., March of Dimes, 1971; Americanism medal D.A.R., 1972; named Career Woman of the Year, Alamogordo chpt. Am. Bus. Women's Assn., 1971. Mem. N.M. Press Assn., N.M. Citizens for Clean Air and Water, Alamogordo C. of C. (chmn. conventions com. 1965—); hon. mem. Pan Am. Round Table of Alamogordo, Holloman AFB Officers' Wives Club. Home and office: 1206 Desert Eve Dr Alamogordo NM 88310

BLACK, NETTI PORTON (MRS. DAVID BLACK), artist; b. Phila., July 3, 1911; d. Rubin and Bluma (Morcell) Porton; A.A., Crane Coll., 1933; B.A., Chgo. Coll. Music, 1935; m. David Black, Dec. 29, 1936; children—Tobye (Mrs. Willard Peterson), Robert. Tchr. piano, music Pope Sch., Chgo., 1936-38, Holland Sch., Chgo., 1938-40; Ascension Sch., Oak Park, Ill., 1958-60; exhibited one-man shows Oak Park YMCA, 1968, 72, Esquire Gallery, Chgo., 1969, Garland Bldg., Chgo., 1970, Siegel Galleries, Ltd., Chgo., 1970, Presbyn.-St. Lukes Hosp., Chgo., 1971, 74, Unique Gallery, Oak Park, 1973, Oak Park Arms Hotel, 1974. Home: 919 S Lyman St Oak Park IL 60304

BLACK, PATRICIA CARR, museum curator; b. Sumner, Miss., May 18, 1934; d. Samuel Bismarck and Velma Miranda (Lewis) Carr; B.S., Miss. State Coll. for Women, 1955; M.A. (Univ. fellow), Emory U., 1968; 1 dau., Elizabeth Lewis. Research librarian, editorial asst. Miss. Dept. Archives and History, Jackson, Miss., 1957-62; catalog and art research librarian Met. Museum Art, N.Y.C., 1968-69; research librarian Time, Inc., N.Y.C., 1969-70; curator exhibits Miss. State Hist. Museum, Jackson, 1970—, project Miss. folk life series, 1971—. Instr. library sci. Univs. Center, Jackson, 1970—. Mem. planning com. Gov.'s Conf. on Edn., 1973. Founding mem., mem. bd. dirs. New Stage Theatre, 1965—; bd. dirs. Jackson Symphony League, 1963-64; adv. bd. Center So. Folklore, Memphis, 1973—. Mem. Miss. Hist. Soc., Miss. Folklore Soc., Miss. Art Assn. (dir. 1965-66), Beta Phi Mu. Episcopalian. Democrat. Designer Miss. Folk Architecture exhibit touring U.S. under auspices of Smithsonian Instn. Book reviewer Library Jour., 1968-71; music and drama reviewer Jackson Clarion-Ledger, 1973. Home: 1157 Quinn St Jackson MS 39202 Office: 100 N State St Jackson MS 39205

BLACK, PEGGY SHERIDAN, univ. exec.; b. Canyon, Tex., Sept. 16, 1926; d. Marion Samuel and Kathleen Grace (Stewart) Bishir; student W. Tex. State Coll., 1942-43; B.A., U. Wash., 1948; M.S., Ohio U., 1971; m. Sheppard Black, Dec. 27, 1969; children from previous marriage—Sue D. Sheridan, James F. Sheridan. Draftsman, Boeing Aircraft, Seattle, 1944-46; copywriter Weisfields, Inc., Seattle, 1948-51; dir. Service Club, U.S. Army Spl. Services, Hanau, Germany, 1951-53; writer, editor Office Pub. Information Ohio U., Athens, 1963-70, dir., 1970—. Pres., King County (Wash.) Young Democrats, 1950. Bd. dirs. Ohio Valley Summer Theater. Mem. Athens League Women Voters, Kappa Tau Alpha, Alpha Delta Sigma, Alpha Gamma Delta. Episcopalian. Home: Route 3 Peach Ridge Av Athens OH 45701

BLACK, SHIRLEY TEMPLE (MRS. CHARLES A. BLACK), civic worker, former actress; b. Santa Monica, Cal., Apr. 23, 1928; d. George Francis and Gertrude Temple; student pvt. tutors; grad. Westlake Sch. for Girls, 1945; m. John Agar, Jr., Sept. 19, 1945 (div. 1949); 1 dau., Linda Susan; m. 2d, Charles A. Black, Dec. 16, 1950; children—Charles Alden, Lori Alden. Began motion picture career playing leading roles at age of three and one-half yrs.; 1st of many successful full-length picture for Twentieth Century-Fox Film Corp., was Stand Up and Cheer; also made pictures for Paramount Studios, Warners, Enterprise, RKO, and was under contract to David Selznick; films include Little Miss Marker, Baby Take a Bow, Bright Eyes, Our Little Girl, The Little Colonel, Curly Top, The Littlest Rebel, Captain January, Poor Little Rich Girl, Dimples, Stowaway, Wee Willie Winkie, Heidi, Rebecca of Sunnybrook Farm, Little Miss Broadway, Just Around the Corner, The Little Princess, Susannah of the Mounties, The Blue Bird Kathleen, Miss Annie Rooney, Since You Went Away, Kiss and Tell, 1945; That Hagen Girl, War Party, The Bachelor and the Bobby-Soxer and Honeymoon, 1947; narrator, actress TV series Shirley Temple Storybook 1957-59, Shirley Temple Show, 1960. Dir. Del Monte Corp., Walt Disney Prodns. Candidate U.S. Congress, 1967. Mem. exec. com. San Francisco Irternat. Film Festival, 1965, 66; nat. chmn., dir. vols. Nat. Multiple Sclerosis Soc., 1963-66; internat. chmn. vols. Internat. Fedn. Multiple Sclerosis Socs., 1967-72; mem. Cal. Adv. Hosp. Council, 1968-70; U.S. del. to UN, 1969-70, mem. U.S. delegation to UN Conf. on Human Environment, Stockholm, Sweden, 1970-72, del., 1972; spl. asst. to chmn. Pres.'s Council on Environmental Quality, Washington, 1972—; mem. U.S.-USSR Joint Com. on Cooperation in Field of Environmental Protection, Moscow, 1972, Washington, 1973; mem. exec. com. U.S. commn. UNESCO, 1973—. Bd. dirs. Nat. Wildlife Fedn., 1973—, UN Assn. U.S.A., 1970-73, World Affairs Council No. Cal. Apptd. col. staff Gov. Ross of Ida., 1935; commd. col. Hawaiian N.G.; hon. col. 108th Reg. Ill. N.G. Decorations from 8 states in U.S.; decorated Cross of Malta, 1968. Mem. Bay Area Ednl. TV Assn. (dir. 1965-69), Acad. Television Arts and Scis., Wilderness Soc., League Women Voters, Cal. Tomorrow, Inc., Sierra Club, Planning and Conservation League.

BLACK, VERNA MAE, home economist; b. Marshalltown, Ia., May 31, 1914; d. Carey Floyd Crouse and Nona (Wiley) Crouse; B.S. (Tri-Delta scholar), Ia. State U., 1953; M.S., Ore. State U., 1961; m. James Edward Black, Aug. 30, 1936 (dec. 1945); 1 dau., Marilynn Ann (Mrs. Henry S. Saito). Home service adviser Ariz. Pub. Service Co., Globe, 1953-58; supr. Du-Par's Restaurants, Los Angeles, 1960-61; asst. prof. home econs. Linfield Coll., McMinnville, Ore., 1961-64; food scientist Western Farmers Assn., Seattle, 1965-71; specialist Sch. Food and Nutrition Services, Ore. Dept. Edn., Salem, 1971—. Mem. aux. Globe Community Hosp., 1957-58. Mem. Am. Home Econs. Assn., Bus. and Profl. Women's Club (v.p. 1958), Home Economists in Bus. (chmn. 1967-68), Single Adults Group (pres. 1966-67), Inst. Food Technologists, Am., Ore. sch. food service assns., Ore. Nutrition Council, Omicron Nu. Methodist (steward 1967-69). Clubs: Zonta (sec. 1958); Soroptimist. Home: 1925 Garfield St NE Salem OR 97303 Office: 942 Lancaster Blvd NE Salem OR 97310

BLACKBURN, ALICE KISER, librarian; b. La Junta, Colo., Feb. 2, 1917; d. Arthur Bertram and MaBelle (Sebree) Kiser; B.A., U. Wash., 1941, B.S. in Librarianship, 1942; M.S. in L.S., Columbia, 1971; m. Charles Edwin Blackburn, July 25, 1941; children—Julia MaBelle, Taft, MaryBeth. With Bur. Bus. Research, U. Wash., Seattle, 1942-47, reference div. Univ. Library, 1959-64; head librarian Pullman (Wash.) City Library, 1964—. Mem. Wash. State Adv. Council on Libraries, 1973—. Mem. Am., Pacific N.W., Wash. library assns., Am. Assn. U. Women, D.A.R., Phi Beta Kappa, Beta Phi Mu. Home: NW 605 Charlotte St Pullman WA 99163 Office: N 210 Grand St Pullman WA 99163

BLACKEY, MARY MADLYN MAKOWSKI (MRS. DONALD BLACKEY), artist; b. Glen Cove, N.Y.; d. Jacob and Adele (Kosciukiewicz) Makowski; B.S., Buffalo State Tchrs. Coll., 1953; certificate Albright Art Sch., 1952; postgrad. Columbia, 1953-55, Art Students League, 1962-67; m. Donald Blackey, June 5, 1955; children—Virginia, Robert. Tchr., Roslyn (N.Y.) Pub. Schs., 1953-54. Plainedge (N.Y.) Pub. Schs., 1954-55, Port Washington Pub. Schs., 1969-73, Roslyn Creative Arts Workshop, 1969-73. Group exhbns. include Nat. Arts Club Watercolor Ann., 1964, 67, 69, 71, Nat. Acad. Design Ann., 1965, 66, 68, Knickerbocker Artists, 1965-68, 70, 71, 73, 74 (award of merit medal 1971-73), L.I. Art League Ann., 1964-69 (1st prize 1968), Catherine Lovillard Wolfe Art Club Ann., 1965-69 (honorable mention 1966), Hecksher Mus., Huntington, N.Y., 1965, Hudson Valley Art Assn., 1965-73 (Mrs. John Newington award 1965), Am. Watercolor Soc., 1966, 68, 70, 72, 73 (Travel Award 1966-73), Butler Inst., 1966, Allied Artists, 1966-69, 70, 71, Coll. of New Rochelle (N.Y.), 1968, Modern Masters Gallery, 1966, N.Y. State Pavillion, 1967, 68, Audubon Artists Ann., 1969, 70, 72, Nat. Art League, 1969, 70, 71, Nat. Soc. Painters in Casein and Acrylic, 1973, Gregory Mus. Travel Exhbn., 1973-74, Watercolor U.S.A., 1973, Phila. Art Alliance, 1973, 74, others; one man shows Arts and Sci. Center, Nashua, N.H., Manchester Inst. Arts and Scis., Sharon (N.H.) Arts Center (all 1972); executed set designs for Green Mountain Playhouse, Poultney, Vt., 1954, Brander Matthews Theatre, N.Y.C., 1954, Fox Oak Players, Flushing, N.Y., 1959-61, 41st St. Theatre, N.Y.C., 1965. Mem. Hudson Valley, New Hampshire, Manhasset art assns., Nat. Soc. Painters in Casein and Acrylic, Knickerbocker Artists, Am. Watercolor Soc. Clubs: Philadelphia Water Color, Aquarelle. Home: 9 Benjamin St Glen Head NY 11545

BLACKHAM, ANN ROSEMARY (MRS. JAMES W. BLACKHAM, JR.), realtor; b. N.Y.C., June 16, 1927; d. Frederick Alfred and Letitia L. (Stolfe) DeCain; A.B., Ohio Dominican Coll., 1949; M.A., Ohio State U., 1950; m. James W. Blackham, Jr., Aug. 18, 1951; children—Ann C., James W. III. Mgr. br. store Filene & Sons, Winchester, 1950-52; broker Porter Co. real estate, Winchester, 1961-66; sales mgr. James T. Trefrey, Inc., Winchester, 1966-68; pres., founder Ann Blackham & Co. Realtors, Winchester, Mass., 1969—; corporator Charleston Savs. Bank. Mem. bd. econ. advisors to Gov., 1969-74; participant White House Conf. on Internat. Cooperation, 1965; mem. Presdl. Task Force on Women's Rights and Responsibilities, 1969; mem. exec. council Mass. Civil Def., 1965-69; chmn. Gov.'s Commn. on Status of Women, 1971—; regional dir. Interstate Assn. Commn. on Status of Women, 1971-73; mem. Gov. Task Force on Mass. Economy, 1972; mem. Mass. Emergency Finance Bd., 1974—; 2d v.p. Doric Dames, 1971-73. Pres. Mass. Fedn. Republican Women, 1964-69; sec. Nat. Fedn. Rep. Women, 1967-71, 3d v.p., 1972—; New Eng. regional dir., 1967—; pres. Women's Rep. Club Winchester, 1960-62; dep. chmn. Mass. Rep. State Com., 1965-66; sec. Mass. Rep. State Conv., 1970, del., 1960, 62, 64, 66; state vice chmn. Mass. Rep. Finance Com., 1970; alternate del. at large Rep. Nat. Conv., 1968, 72. Recipient Pub. Service award Commonwealth Mass., 1969, Merit award Rep. Party, 1969; Mass. Order Paul Revere Patriots; named Civic Leader of Yr. Mass. Broadcasters, 1962. Mem. Greater Boston Real Estate Bd. (dir. 1973—), Mass., Nat. (women's council) assns. realtors, Brokers Inst. Republican. Clubs: Capitol Hill (Washington); Winchester Boat, Winchester Country, Ponte Vedra. Home: 33 Canterbury Rd Winchester MA 01890 Office: 11 Thompson St Winchester MA 01890

BLACKLEDGE, ETHEL HALE (MRS. WALTER L. BLACKLEDGE), author; b. Mt. Vernon, Ky.; d. Wilburn and Allie (Allen) Hale; B.S., Ohio State U., 1949; postgrad. U. Okla., 1949-51; M.Ed., U. Tex. (Am. Assn. U. Women, grantee 1958-59), 1959; m. Walter L. Blackledge, Feb. 25, 1960; children—Walter Lloyd, Lawrence Allen. Sec., Wiesbaden, Germany, 1951-52; tchr. pub. schs., Ohio, 1954-57, U. Tex., Austin, 1957-59, So. Ill. U., Edwardsville, 1959-61. Cons. Tex. State Employment Service, 1959. Pres. Thomas Jefferson Elementary Sch. P.T.A., Alton, Ill., 1970-71, v.p., 1971-72; mem. auditing com. Dist. P.T.A. Council, 1970-71; v.p. East Jr. High Sch. P.T.A., Alton, 1974—. Served with WAVES, 1943-46. Mem. Phi Chi Theta, Pi Omega Pi. Club: Duplicate Bridge (Alton). Author: You and Your Job, 1967; The Job You Want-How to Get It, 1975. Contbr. articles to profl. jours. Home: 3620 Gary Av Alton IL 62002

BLACKMAN, EVELYN LUCILLE, educator; b. Eagle Grove, Ia., May 11, 1910; d. Warren O. and Almeda Heathman (Wood) Blackman; A.B., U. Wash., 1948; M.P.H. Edn. (Am. Cancer Soc. fellow), U. Cal. at Berkeley, 1949, Ed.D. (Rotary Internat. fellow), 1955. Health educator Stockton (Cal.) Dept. Pub. Health, 1949-52; dir. East Bay Assn. Retarded Children, Oakland, Cal., 1955-57; asst. prof. San Jose (Cal.) State Coll., 1957-59, Orange Coast Coll., Costa Mesa, Cal., 1960-61; prof. Sch. Edn., Cal. State U., Long Beach, 1961—. Research cons fed. and state, pub. sch. projects, 1965—. Mem. Am. Psychol. Assn., Am., Cal. ednl. research assns., Cal. Personnel and Guidance Assn., Coll. and Univ. Poetry Soc. Am., Phi Kappa Phi (life), Pi Lambda Theta, Theta Sigma Phi. Home: 16400 Saybrook Lane Huntington Beach CA 92649 Office: 6101 E 7th St Long Beach CA 90001

BLACKMEN, SARAH SIMKIN (MRS. FRED BLACKMEN), govt. ofcl.; b. Phila., Mar. 14, 1911; d. Philip and Minnie (Gorelick) Simkin; B.S., Temple U., 1932, M.S. summa cum laude, 1938; postgrad. U. Tenn., 1954-55, Temple U., 1962-65; m. Fred Blackmen, Mar. 23, 1941. Research analyst Nat. Research, Phila., 1936-41; statistician U.S. Bur. Census, Washington, 1941-43; economist, statistician U.S. Dept. Labor Dept. Employment Security, Balt., 1943-51; economist Econ. Stabilization Agy., Pitts., 1952-53; with U.S. Navy Dept. Aviation Supply Office, Phila., 1955—, supply systems analyst, 1965—. Speaker Bur. Employment Security, Balt., 1943-51. Mem. Am. Statis. Assn., Internat. Platform Soc., Phi Sigma Sigma. Contbr. articles to various jours. Home: 2010 Overlook Av Willow Grove PA 19090

BLACKMER, KATHLEEN JOAN CRISPELL (MRS. CHARLES W. BLACKMER), sportswear co. exec.; b. Sayre, Pa., June 4, 1945; d. Kenneth R. and Marjorie (Risk) Crispell; B.A., U. Mich., 1967; m. Charles W. Blackmer, July 30, 1966. Asst. women's editor Ann Arbor (Mich.) News, 1967, women's editor, 1967-69; publicity coordinator Head Ski & Sports Wear, Inc., Columbia, Md., 1969-70, advt. mgr., 1970—. Mem. Kappa Kappa Gamma, Kappa Tau Alpha, Theta Sigma Phi. Home: 10387 Barcan Circle Columbia MD 21044 Office: 9189 Red Branch Rd Columbia MD 21045

BLACKMORE, DOROTHY SMITH (MRS. EDWIN LESTER BLACKMORE), ednl. cons.; b. Willows, Cal., Nov. 19, 1914; d. Charles Leroy and Sarah Ella (Drew) Smith; A.B., Chico State Coll., 1937; M.S., Dominican Coll. San Rafael, 1957; Ed.D., U. Cal., 1963; m. Edwin Lester Blackmore, Sept. 2, 1935; children—Willis E., Margaret (Mrs. Michael Henwood). Demonstration tchr., head primary dept. Chico State Coll. Lab. Sch., 1939-41; prof. edn., dir. student teaching Dominican Coll. San Rafael, Cal., 1951-66; asso. head tchr. edn., lectr., supr. U. Cal. at Davis, 1966-69; coordinator tchr. recruitment, dir. Edn. Professions Devel. Act Rural Internship Project, Cal. State Dept. Edn., Sacramento, 1969-71, cons. early childhood edn., 1971—. Recipient Distinguished Achievement award for excellence Am. Assn. Colls. Tchr. Edn. Mem. N.E.A., Cal. Tchrs. Assn., Internat. Reading Assn., Cal. Assn. Edn. of Young Children, Assn. Tchr. Educators (state pres. 1962-64), Cal. Council on Edn. Tchrs. (bd. dirs. 1969-71, v.p. 1971-74, pres. 1974—), Delta Kappa Gamma, Pi Lambda Theta, Delta Phi Upsilon. Episcopalian. Author: (with Clark Robinson and G.W. Sowards) The Teaching Internship, 1960, (with (C. Richard McNair) A Rural Internship Program Model, 1971, Report of the Task Force on Early Childhood Education, 1972. Home: 620 Coolidge St Davis CA 95616 Office: 721 Capitol Mall Sacramento CA 95814

BLACKMORE, HELEN JOYCE MCVEY (MRS. FRANK PERCY BLACKMORE), educator; b. Rockton, Wis., Jan. 20, 1908; d. Edward Liola and Lillian May (White) McVey; B.A., U. Ariz., 1948, M.A., 1969; postgrad. U. Wis.-LaCrosse, 1972-73; m. Frank Percy Blackmore, Aug. 22, 1936; 1 son, Frank Edward. Tchr., Ontario, Wis., 1929-31, 34-36, 41-43, 54-58, Bisbee, Ariz., 1931-32, 38-41, LaFarge Wis., 1932-34, 44-54, Watertown, Wis., 1943-44; tchr. spl. edn. Norwalk-Ontario Area Schs., Ontario, 1958—. Mem. Bus. and Profl. Women's Club, Vernon County Tchrs. Assn., Allen McVey Women's Relief Corp., Delta Kappa Gamma. Methodist. Mem. Order Eastern Star. Home: Route 1 Box 188 LaFarge WI 54639

BLACKSHEAR, MARTHA JULE, librarian; b. Headland, Ala.; d. Robert Franklin and Martha (Vann) Blackshear; A.B., Samford U., 1937; M.L.S., Fla. State U., 1950, postgrad., 1951-52. Tchr. pub. schs., Clanton, Ala., 1937-41; field sec. Houston council Girl Scouts U.S.A., 1941-43, exec. sec. Columbus council, 1943; recreation dir. A.R.C., Station Hosp., Ft. Rucker, Ala., 1943-45; sch. librarian, Tallahassee, Fla., 1950-52; pub. librarian, Bainbridge, Ga., 1952-53; sch. library cons. Ala. Dept. Edn., Montgomery, 1953-67; library media specialist, Troy, Ala., 1967-69; instr. library sci. Fla. State U., U. Ala., Eastern Ky. U., 1969-70; librarian Wallace Jr. Coll., Dothan, Ala., 1970-71; field services rep. Ala. Pub. Library Service, Montgomery, 1971—. Dir. numerous library and media workshops throughout the Southeast U.S. Mem. A.L.A., Southeastern Library Assn., Ala. Library Assn. (v.p. 1959—, pres. 1960). Author: (with Pauline Foster) Building and Renovating School Libraries, 1956; School Administrators Ask Questions About School Libraries, 1957. Home: 103 E Church St Headland AL 36345 Office: Ala State Adminstrn Bldg Montgomery AL 36104

BLACKSTOCK, DOROTHY EVELYN LYONS, artist; b. Tacoma, Aug. 4, 1914; d. Frank and Mildred Aubrey (Potts) Lyons; student Whitman Coll., 1931, Coll. Puget Sound, 1932, U. Wash., 1933; m. Carl Mims Blackstock, July 12, 1942; children—Carl Lyons, Gregory Lee. One-man shows State Hist. Mus., Olympia, Wash., Handforth Gallery, Tacoma; exhibited art in group shows at Seattle Art Mus., Woessner Gallery, Kittredge Gallery, U. Puget Sound, Frye Art Mus., Frederick and Nelson Little Gallery and Exhbn. Hall, Puget Sound Area Shows, N.W. Watercolor Show, Nat. League Am. Pen Women Biennials, Wash. State Hist. Mus.; represented in permanent collections Wash. State Hist. Mus. at Tacoma, Wash. State U. at Pullman; illustrator two covers Tacoma News Tribune Mag. Section, five covers Seattle Times Mag. Section. Art chmn. Music and Art Found., Seattle, 1962-64, bd. trustees, 1958-64; mem. Seattle hospitality com. Allied Arts. Named Woman of Year in art, 1959. Mem. Nat. League Am. Pen Women (br. pres. 1966-68), Seattle Co-arts and Quad-A Art Club, Fedn. Women's Club, Women's Ednl. Club (pres. 1960-61), Women Painters Wash. (pres. 1972-74), Artist's Equity, Seattle Art Mus. Clubs: Golf (Seattle); Inglewood Golf and Country. Home: 5520 Coniston Rd NE Seattle WA 98105

BLACKSTOCK, MARY LILLIAN (MRS. PROCTOR L. BLACKSTOCK), author; b. Willowpoint, Tex., May 1, 1912; d. Charles Wesley and Lucy (Knox) Plumlee; student (scholar) Okla. Coll. for Women, 1932-33; m. Proctor L. Blackstock, June 24, 1936 (dec.); 1 son, Ronald Lee. Sec., Retail Mcht.'s Assn., Waurika, Okla., 1929-31, U.S. dep. R.R.A., Waurika, 1934-36; free lance reporter local newspapers, 1929-32; sec. pub. schs. Graham, Tex., 1949-51; columnist Rotary publ. Sec., Police Unit Civil Def. Named Poet Laureate, Graham; recipient Mayor's Service award Civil Def., Congress of Freedom award. Mem. Tex. Jr. Hist. Soc., Friends of Library (chmn. publicity), Graham C. of C., Graham Woman's Club, Garden Study Club (past pres.), Poetry Soc. Tex. (state councillor 1972-73; numerous awards), Okla. Poetry Soc., Internat. Platform Assn., Chatauqua, Literary and Sci. Club. Methodist. Author: Birds of the Bible, 1967; The Beachcomber, 1973; The Bride and Groom, 1974. Contbr. articles to newspapers and mags. Home and office: 1331 Edgewood Dr Graham TX 76046

BLACKSTOCK, VIRGINIA LEE LOWMAN (MRS. LEROY BLACKSTOCK), civic worker; b. Bixby, Okla., July 2, 1917; d. Joseph Arthur and Winifred (Lundy) Lowman; student Tulsa Coll. Bus., 1935-37; m. Leroy Blackstock, Dec. 29, 1939;

children—Vincent Craig, Priscilla Gay (Mrs. Richard S. Kurz), Birch Lee, Lore Anne, Trena Jan. Legal sec. law firm, Tulsa, 1937-41. Chmn. program Internat. Students in Tulsa, 1955-65; mem. Tulsa Council Camp Fire Girls, 1963-66; mem. youth com. Tulsa Philharmonic Soc., 1969-70; pres.Eliott Elementary P.T.A., 1961-62, Edison High Sch. P.T.A., 1971-72. Co-chmn. Democratic precinct No. 132, 1960-67. Mem. Tulsa County Bar Aux. (past pres., sec. 1962-63, chaplain 1966-67), Tulsa Opera Guild, Women's Assn. Tulsa Philharmonic. Baptist. Club: Summit Petroleum. Home: 3740 Terwilleger Blvd Tulsa OK 74105

BLACKWELL, LUCY WHITE, ret. govt. ofcl.; b. Jackson, Tenn., Apr. 22, 1912; d. William Francis and Ethel (White) Blackwell; A.B., Lambuth Coll., 1933; postgrad. W. Tenn. Bus. Coll., 1934-35. Stenographer, Tenn. Emergency Relief Adminstrn., Jackson, 1935; accounting clk. FSA, Jackson, Brownsville, Tenn., 1936-39; stenographer Tenn. Dept. Pub. Welfare, Jackson, 1939-40; clk., interviewer, local office mgr. Tenn. Dept. Employment Security, Jackson, 1940-73. Comdr. Am. Cancer Soc., Madison County, Tenn., 1943-54, dist. comdr. W. Tenn., 1947-48, rec. sec. Tenn. div., 1954-56, bd. dirs., 1945—, organizer Madison County unit, 1954, pres., 1954-55; bd. dirs. Jackson Community Chest, 1955-57; pres. League Women Voters, 1951. Treas., chmn. bd. trustees Jackson Free Library, 1948-57. Recipient R.E. Womack Alumni Achievement award Lambuth Coll. Alumni Assn., 1956; named Jackson-Madison Woman of Year, 1955. Mem. Internat. Assn. Personnel Employment Security (pres. Jackson chpt. 1956), Lambuth Coll. Alumni Assn. (pres. 1962-63). Presbyn. Clubs: Pilot Internat. (past pres. Jackson, dist. gov. Tenn., internat. dir. exec. com.). Altrusa Internat. (chmn.). Home: 111 Cherokee Dr Jackson TN 38301

BLADES, SARAH ELOISE HAND (MRS. JOSEPH H. BLADES), ins. exec; b. Jackson, Miss., Dec. 17, 1927; d. Thomas E. and Eloise (Wallace) Hand; B.A., Stephens Coll., 1947; B.B.A., U. Tex., 1949; m. Joseph H. Blades, July 11, 1953; children—Sarah Gaye, Robert H., Richard M., Barbara Lynn. Sec., Eddie Dyer Ins. Agy., Houston, 1949-53; sec. exec. J.H. Blades & Co., Houston, 1954—; owner Blades Ins. Agy., Houston, 1958—; v.p., dir. St. Johns Ins. Co. Ltd., Hamilton, Bermuda, 1969—. Com. chmn. Planned Parenthood, 1963-66; leader Blue Bird Girls, 1960, Camp Fire Girls, 1961-63. Mem. D.A.R., Blue Bird Circle, Womens Soc. Christian Service, Sigma Iota Epsilon, Alpha Delta Pi (pres. alumni 1959-60). Clubs: Women of Rotary, Houston, Houston Racquet, Houston Yacht. Home: 6155 Doliver Dr Houston TX 77027 Office: PO Box 22003 Houston TX 77027

BLAESING, DOROTHY ANNE, banker; b. Lyndhurst, N.J.; d. Paul H. and Laura (Oberwimmer) Blaesing; B.A., Wellesley Coll., 1936; postgrad. U. Heidelberg, summer 1936, Pace Inst., 1937. Chartist, Central Hanover Bank & Trust Co., N.Y.C., 1936-37; group analyst Equitable Life Assurance Soc. N.Y.C., 1937-38; asst. security analyst Brown Bros. Harriman & Co., N.Y.C., 1938-42; govt. bond analyst Fed. Res. Bank of N.Y., 1942-43; security analyst Am. Nat. Bank & Trust Co., Chgo., 1943-44; asst. v.p. Bankers Trust Co., N.Y.C., 1944—. Mem. N.Y. Soc. Security Analysts (program com. 1959-61), Nat. Assn. Bank Women. Republican. Methodist. Club: Women's Bond of New York (dir. 1960-62, v.p. 1966-68, pres. 1968-70). Home: 15 Dorset Lane Summit NJ 07901 Office: 51 Rockefeller Plaza New York City NY 10020

BLAGBROUGH, ELIZABETH MAY (MRS. HARRY PUTNAM BLAGBROUGH), fine art appraiser; b. Orlando, Fla., Sept. 8, 1926; d. Calvin Burr and Maud Alice (Wagner) McCaughen; B.A., Washington U., 1948; m. Harry Putnam Blagbrough, June 30, 1951; children—Helen (Mrs. Patrick L. Henderson), Harry Putnam, Alicia. Apprentice appraiser McCaughen & Burr, Inc. Fine Arts, St. Louis, 1948-70, appraiser, v.p., dir., 1970—. Pvt. appraisals by referral, 1970—; lectr. fine arts, art history; co-founder Valuers Consortium, Houston, 1972, vice chmn., bd. dirs., 1974—. Active local P.T.A. Mem. Am. Soc. Appraisers (sr., internat. bd. examiners, sec. St. Louis chpt., chpt. treas. 1974-75, del. internat. conf., preparator lectr. presentations), Methodist. Home: 340 S Elm St Louis MO 63119 Office: 5 Maryland Plaza St Louis MO 63108

BLAINE, SISTER MARIE CATHARINE, hosp. exec.; b. S.I., N.Y., Aug. 11, 1904; d. Thomas Joseph and Catharine (McBreen) Blaine; B.A., Coll. Mt. St. Vincent-on-Hudson, 1934; M.S. in Social Work, Catholic U. Am., 1936. Joined Sister of Charity, 1926; tchr. elementary and secondary schs., 1924-39; dir. boarding dept. N.Y. Foundling Hosp., N.Y.C., 1939-56, asst. adminstr., 1956-57, adminstr., treas., 1957-67; adminstrv. cons. dept. child care Cath. Charities, Archdiocese of N.Y., 1967—. Bd. mgrs. St. Agatha Home for Children. Mem. Acad. Certified Social Workers. Home: 1175 3d Av New York City NY 10021 Office: 1011 1st Av New York City NY 10022

BLAIR, ANNE D., broadcasting journalist; b. Oakmont, Pa.; d. Hal P. and Eliza Russell (Peachy) Denton; ed. Bryn Mawr Coll.; m. Robert F. Blair (div.); 1 son, Farnham. Women's program dir. Good Music Sta., Washington, 1948-58; dir. radio and TV, Met. area chpts. A.R.C., Washington, 1958-62; Washington corr. Triangle Publs., Inc., 1962-72; Washington corr. Teleprompter Cable TV, 1972-73; commentator programs including Capital Shopping, Music for Moderns, Window on Washington; cons. on pub. affairs Environmental Protection Agy., 1973—. Recipient Distinguished Pub. Service award 21 Jewel Sq. Club, Phila., 1964. Mem. Am. Newspaper Woman's Club (pres. 1963-65), Am. Women in Radio and TV. Clubs: Washington Press, Sulgrave (Washington); Cosmopolitan (N.Y.C.). Home: 3315 Dent Pl NW Washington DC 20007 Office: 3315 Dent Pl NW Washington DC 20007

BLAIR, BARBARA BOWMAN (MRS. BYRON O. BLAIR), educator; b. Salina, Kan., June 10, 1925; d. Lee L. and Lenna E. (Odle) Bowman; B.A., Ft. Hays State Coll., 1950; postgrad. U. Ariz., 1950-51, Ind. U., 1957; pvt. studies, 1951-60; m. Byron O. Blair, Sept. 1, 1946; 1 dau., Barbara Lee. Tchr. pub. schs., Kan., 1943-46, N.Y., 1951-54; dir. U. Ariz. Glee Club, Tucson, 1950-51; owner, instr. Blair Studio of Voice, Lafayette, Ind., 1954—. Supr., broadcaster elementary sch. music WBAA radio, Purdue U., Lafayette, 1955-63, pvt. tutor English as 2d lang. to fgn. students, tchr. Japanese, 1972—; minister music Lafayette Meth. Ch., 1956—; lectr. on Japan to service, internat. groups, 1969—; tchr. English lang. tng. dept. Matsushita Electric Corp. Ltd., Osaka, Japan, 1971-72. Mem. women's found. com. Internat. Christian U., Tokyo, Japan, 1968—. Mem. Fellowship United Meth. Musicians (sec. 1965-69), Nat. Assn. Tchrs. Singing, Sigma Alpha Iota, Phi Kappa Phi, Alpha Delta Pi. Methodist (del. world conf. 1966, dir. music N.W. Ind. conf. 1958-68). Home: 46 Thise Ct Lafayette IN 47905

BLAIR, JEAN DODDS (MRS. LLOYD JOSEPH BLAIR), drug store asst.; b. Gouverneur, N.Y., Mar. 27, 1919; d. Keith Alexander and Emma Edna (Broeffle) Dodds; grad. Watertown (N.Y.) Sch. of Commerce, 1936; m. Lloyd Joseph Blair, Mar. 28, 1937; children—Paul Joseph, Joan (Mrs. Christopher Orr Morrell). Tissue wrapper Rushmore Paper Mill, Natural Dam, N.Y., 1936-38; mender Hosiery Mills, Gouverneur, 1938-39; with J.C. Penney Co., Gouverneur, 1949-57; dept. mgr. W.T. Grant Store, Gouverneur, 1957-63; acting librarian Pub. Library, Gouverneur, 1963; asst. to editor Tribune Press, Gouverneur, 1963-67, acting editor, 1967, editor, 1967-72; various office positions Eckerd's Drug Store, Dunedin, Fla., 1972—. Recipient Good Citizenship award V.F.W., 1972. Mem. Sigma Delta Chi. Republican. Roman Catholic. Home: 2242 US Alternate 19 Palm Harbor FL 33563 Office: Eckerd's Causeway Inc 2600 Bayshore Blvd Dunedin FL 33528

BLAIS, MARGARET ELIZABETH, pub. relations ofcl.; b. Acton, Ont., Can., Oct. 10, 1919; d. Hugh Thomas and Myrtle Olive (Gammon) Johnson; diploma in hosp. adminstrn., U. Sask., 1969; m. Aime Blais, Oct. 30, 1948 (dec.); children—David, Donald, Paul, Michele, Douglas, Nicole. With Strathroy (Ont.) Middlesex Gen. Hosp., 1954—, pub. relations ofcl., dir. med. records, mem. exec. council. Trustee Strathroy Community Credit Union, 1973—. Served with RCAF, 1943-46. Mem. Ont. Hosp. Record Assn., Pub. Relations Assn., Canadian Assn. Med. Record Librarians (pres. regional record assn. 1969-70), Scribes. Contbr. articles to newspapers, mags. Home: 40 Kittredge St Strathroy ON N7G 2A6 Canada Office: 395 Carrie St Strathroy ON N7G 3I4 Canada

BLAISDELL, FAUSTENA, educator; b. Arlington, Mass.; d. Fred Wilson and Gertrude (Nicoll) Blaisdell; B.S., Columbia Tchrs. Coll., 1939, Ed.D., 1960; M.Litt., U. Pitts., 1946. Instr., asst. prof., asso. prof., prof. nursing U. Pitts., 1942-54; prof. nursing in charge masters program Wayne State U., Detroit, 1955-58; prof. nursing Tex. Womans U., Denton, 1959-65; prof. nursing, acting dir. pub. health nursing tchr. preparation program U. N.C., Chapel Hill, 1965-67, prof., dir. masters program Sch. Nursing, 1967-70; prof. nursing, asso. dean charge masters program Sch. Nursing, U. Miss. Med. Center, Jackson, 1970—. Vice pres. Denton County Heart Assn., 1964-65. Mem. Am. (bd. dirs. 1952-54), Miss. nurses assns., Nat. League for Nursing, Am. Assn. U. Profs., Am. Heart Assn. Office: 2500 N State St Jackson MS 39216

BLAKE, DOROTHY WAGER, librarian; b. Heflin, Ala., Sept. 16, 1928; d. Clellon Leon and Minnie (Adams) Wager; B.S., Jacksonville State U., 1949; M.A., George Peabody Coll. Tchrs., 1953; diploma advanced studies in librarianship Emory U., 1967; m. Bruce Blake, July 30, 1946; children—Allan Adam, Elizabeth Mitchell. Tchr., Huntsville, Ala., 1949-51; high sch. librarian, Decatur, Ga., 1951-54, tchr., 1955-57; elementary sch. librarian Atlanta Pub. Schs., 1958-61, resource librarian, 1961-64, coordinator libraries, 1964—. Mem. League Women Voters, Am. Assn. Univ. Women, Southeastern, Ga., Met. Atlanta library assns., Am. Assn. Sch. Librarians (sec. suprs.' sect. 1974—), A.L.A., Nat. Edn. Assn., Ga., Atlanta assns. educators, Kappa Delta Pi (past chpt. pres.), Delta Kappa Gamma (past chpt. pres.). Club: Reserve Officers Assn. Ladies. Home: 232 Daniel Av SE Atlanta GA 30317 Office: 2930 Forrest Hill Dr SW Atlanta GA 30315

BLAKELY, CAROLINE MILLER (MRS. DURWARD E. BLAKELY), newspaper editor; b. Legrande, Ky., Apr. 12, 1924; d. John Bryson and Mary Brown (Elliott) Miller; B.A., Bethel Coll., 1958; M.A., Syracuse U., 1961; m. Durward E. Blakely, Aug. 25, 1948 (dec. Feb. 1952); children—Carol (Mrs. John Berry), Charles Lynch, Donna (Mrs. Dean Pohl), John, David. Editor, News for You, New Readers Press, Laubach Literacy, Inc., 1960-71, editorial dir. New Readers Press, 1971—. Mem. Council for Exceptional Children, Adult Edn. Assn., Women in Communications. Editor: Our United States, 1965; Occupations, 1973. Home: 238 Greenwood Place Syracuse NY 13210 Office: Box 131 Syracuse NY 13210

BLAKELY, ELEANOR WHITE, editor; b. Balt., July 20, 1919; d. Park Jerald and Maria (Bain) White; student Radcliffe Coll., 1936-38; M.A., U. Chgo., 1957; m. Robert John Blakely, Dec. 26, 1938 (div. July 1964); children—Susan (Mrs. Paul Shurin), Craig Baird, Stephen Bush. Mgmt. cons. Nelson Assos., N.Y.C., 1963-65; publs. writer continuing edn. Pa. State U., University Park, 1965-70, asst. editorial specialist, editor newsletter Inst. Research on Land and Water Resources, 1970—. Freelance writer on community colls., higher edn. Mem. Am. Assn. Agrl. Coll. Editors, Adult Edn. Assn., Nat. Pilots Assn., Women in Communications, Inc. Episcopalian. Club: University Athletic (Iowa City, Ia.). Author tech. articles. Editor: Perspectives of Property, 1972. Home: 409 S Atherton St State College PA 16801 Office: Agrl Adminstrn Pa State U University Park PA 16802

BLAKELY, FLORENCE ELLA, librarian; b. Clinton, S.C., Sept. 3, 1923; d. Ralph Royd and Lois (Newkirk) Blakely; B.A. magna cum laude, Presbyn. Coll., 1943; B.S in L.S., George Peabody Coll., 1945, M.A. in L.S., 1960. Asst. librarian Presbyn. Coll., Clinton, S.C., 1943-44; reference librarian Greenville (S.C.) Pub. Library, 1945-47, br. librarian, 1947-48; reference librarian Duke U., Durham, N.C., 1948-56, head reference dept., 1956—. Vis. lectr. U. N.C. Library Sch., summer 1962. Council on Library Resources fellow, 1970. Mem. Am. Assn. U. Women (br. pres. 1965-67), A.L.A. (life), Am. Assn. U. Profs., Soc. Mayflower Descs., Delta Kappa Gamma, Beta Phi Mu. Episcopalian. Home: 709 W Club Blvd Durham NC 27701 Office: Perkins Library Duke U Durham NC 27706

BLAKELY, NELL ELIZABETH ROBERTSHAW (MRS. JULIAN GRIER BLAKELY), educator; b. Greenville, Miss., Apr. 18, 1919; d. Frank Newell and Hannah Mary (Aldridge) Robertshaw; B.A., La. State U., 1940; M.A., E. Tex. State U., 1966; postgrad. U. Ia., 1968; m. John Earle Uhler, Jr., Nov. 23, 1940; children—Ellen (Mrs. Robert Louis Erwin), Jan (Mrs. Jay Turner); m. 2d, Julian Grier Blakely, May 6, 1951; children—Melanie (Mrs. William Alan Liston), Mary Catherine, Hannah Paxton. Co-owner Uhler Studios, Inc., Greenville, 1945-51; partner Blakenell Studios, Greenville, 1951-61; pub. relations photographer Miss. State Coll. for Women, Columbus, 1961-65; instr. photography E. Tex. State U., Commerce, 1966—; cons. workshops in photography, 1970—. Supr. mag. ETSU Spl., 1971—. A founder Cerebral Palsy Sch. for Handicapped Children, Greenville, Miss., 1956; dir. publicity Companion Collies, Columbus, 1962-65; mem. Commerce Humane Soc., 1971—. Recipient Pub. Service award Am. Radio Relay League, 1952. Mem. Women in Communications, Chi Omega. Home: 1605 Jackson St Commerce TX 75428

BLAKEMAN, MARIE BARBARA (MRS. HARRY JOSEPH BLAKEMAN), mfg. co. exec.; b. Iowa City, Oct. 10, 1917; d. Rudolph and Louise Elizabeth (Olhoeft) Wegmiller; grad. Platt-Gard Bus. Coll., St. Joseph, Mo., 1936; m. Harry Joseph Blakeman, July 24, 1938; children—Barbara Ann (Mrs. James K. Richardson, Jr), Rudolph Joel. Sales analyst Strutwear Knitting Co., St. Joseph, 1936; sec. Quaker Oats Co., Southall, Middlesex, Eng., 1937; sec.-treas. Nor-Lake, Inc., Hudson, Wis., 1947—. Pres. Lutheran Women's Missionary League, 1963, chmn. Christian growth com., 1966; sec.-treas. Hudsonites for Good Govt., 1962-66. Named Outstanding Citizens of Hudson, 1966. Mem. Hudson C. of C. (dir. 1962-66), Twin City Choirmasters Assn., St. Croix Hist. Soc. (life), St. Paul's Women's Civic Opera Guild, Tyrone Guthrie Stagehands, Trinity Guild, Hudson Meml. Hosp. Assn., Hudson Meml. Hosp. Aux., Hudson Band Parents, Hudson P.T.A. Lutheran (choir dir., Sunday sch. tchr.). Clubs: Hudson Country, Woman's, Nor-Lake (life) (Hudson). Home: 727 12th St Hudson WI 54016 Office: Nor-Lake Inc 2d and Elm Sts Hudson WI 54016

BLAKEY, LILLIAN LUELLA (MRS. PAUL BLAKEY), educator; b. Lake City, Ia., Feb. 17, 1909; d. Axel M. and Nellie (De Burgh) Halvorsen; Two Year certificate, Buena Vista Coll. (Storm Lake, Ia.), 1949; B.S. in Edn., Drake U., 1952, M.A., 1957, postgrad., summers 1959-68, 70; m. Paul Blakey, Sept. 19, 1942. Tchr. pub. schs., Lytton, Ia., 1936-46; mgr., councilor children's books C.K. Wilson Book Store, Quincy, Ill., 1946-47; tchr. pub. schs., Vinton, Ia., 1947-49, Glick Sch., 1949—. Math. adviser Ia. Council Tchrs. Math., 1970-72, mem. program com., 1974. Rep. Am. Assn. Childhood Edn. and Alpha Delta Kappa to Gov.'s Conf. on Traffic Safety, 1966, rep. Marshalltown Bus. and Profl. Women, 1967. Mem. Ia. Fedn. Republican Women, 1965—. Named Marshalltown Elementary Tchr. Year, 1967; recipient Fisher Ednl. award Fisher Found., Fisher Gov. Co., 1967, Willard J. Combs Aerospace award Aerospace Edn. Council Ia., 1970. Mem. N.E.A. (life), Ia. Edn. Assn., Am. Assn. Childhood Edn., Bus. and Profl. Women's Assn., Ia. Ornithologists Assn. (charter mem.), Alpha Delta Kappa (life mem.; internat. regional grand v.p. 1965-67, chmn. internat. credential com. 1971—, chmn. internat. balloting com. 1969, mem. internat. bldg. expansion com., rep. North Central region 1973-74). Home: 301 S 9th St Marshalltown IA 50158 Office: 301 S 9th St Marshalltown IA 50158

BLALOCK, CARY STARKE (MRS. JESSE P. BLALOCK), occupational therapist; b. Birmingham, Ala., Feb. 9, 1932; d. John M. and Elizabeth (Jones) Starke; B.S., Tex. Womans U., 1952; m. Jesse P. Blalock, Oct. 16, 1953; children—Laurie, Price, William, Brian, John, Virginia. Rehab. dir. Austin (Tex.) State Hosp., 1952-53; therapy dir. Portsmouth (Va.) Rehab. Center, 1956; occupational therapy dir. Holy Cross Hosp., Austin, 1964; rehab. dir. St. Josephs Mental Health Center, 1964-66; instr., dir. occupational therapy Sch. Allied Health Sci., U. Tex. Med. Br., Galveston, Tex., 1967-70; occupational therapy dir. Bellaire (Tex.) Hosp., 1971; pres., dir., chmn. bd. Community Living Center, Houston, 1971—. Mem. adv. com. allied health Houston Community Coll.; regional mental health cons. Author, recipient Regional Med. Programs grant, 1969. Mem. Nat., Tex., Houston occupational therapy assns., Nat. Assn. for Retarded Children, Nat. Rehab. Assn., S.W. Regional Partial Hospitalization Assn. Methodist.

BLALOCK, JOYCE, lawyer, assn. exec.; b. Huntsville, Tex., Dec. 5, 1929; d. William Ben and Minnie Sue (Robbins) Blalock; B.A., Tex. U., 1946; LL.B., U. Denver, 1963; LL.M., Columbia, 1968; m. D.B. Cocovinis, June 18, 1949 (div. Dec. 1962); children—Dean, Derek, Dwight. Admitted to Mass. bar, 1963, N.M. bar, 1969; practiced in Boston, 1963-67, Santa Fe, N.M., 1969-74; asso. firm Choate, Hall and Stewart, Boston, 1963-67; police legal adviser, atty. N.M. State Police, Santa Fe, 1969-74; supervising atty. Internat. Assn. Chiefs Police, Gaithersburg, Md., 1974—. Asst. prof. criminal law Coll. of Santa Fe, 1973—; mem. Steering Com. of Community Criminal Justice Agys. U. Albuquerque, 1973—, asst. prof. criminal trials, 1974. Bd. dirs. Santa Fe Community Theatre, bus. mgr., 1971-73; mem. La Tierra Profl. Adv. Bd., Coll. Santa Fe. Mem. Bar of Commonwealth of Mass., Bar of State N.M., Am., N.M. bar assns., Nat. Dist. Attys. Assn., Internat. Assn. Chiefs of Police (mem. legal sect. 1970—). Author: Civil Liability of Law Enforcement Officers, 1973. Contbr. numerous articles to legal publs. Home: 4620 De Russey Pkwy Chevy Chase MD 20015 Office: 11 Firstfield Rd Gaithersburg MD 20760

BLANCHAR, MRS. DONALD W. (GLADYS M. BLANCHAR), state ofcl.; b. Madison, Wis., Sept. 12, 1917; d. G. W. and Alma (Mahnke) Fehlau; Ph.B., U. Wis., 1938; m. Donald W. Blanchar, Apr. 8, 1950. Asst. dist. manpower dir. Wis. State Employment Service. Mem. Madison Personnel Assn., Phi Chi Theta (nat. v.p. 1946-48, nat. sec.-treas. 1956-58, treas. Madison 1962-64, sec. 1968-69, 72-73, Internat. Assn. Personnel in Employment Security. Home: 708 Butternut Rd Madison WI 53704 Office: 206 N Broom St Madison WI 53704

BLANCHARD, CORA IRENE, banker; b. Danvers, Mass., May 18, 1904; d. Fred Monroe and Melita G. (MacPhetres) Blanchard; student Lynn Burdett Coll., 1923-25. With Suffolk Franklin Savs. Bank (formerly Suffolk Savs. Bank for Seaman and Others), Boston, 1925—, asst. treas., 1942-63, asst. v.p., 1963-66, v.p., 1966-69, corporator, trustee, 1967—. Mem. Savs. Bank Women of Mass. (pres. 1941-43), Nat. Assn. Bank Women (pres. 1954-55), Danvers Hist. Soc., Women's Ednl. and Indsl. Union of Boston, Conglist. (treas. 1956-62, chmn. bd. trustees 1966-69). Clubs: Zonta (pres. Boston 1950-51, gov. dist. I 1953-54). Home: 39 Otis St Danvers MA 01923 Office: 45 Franklin St Boston MA 02110

BLANCHARD, HELEN MARGARET KANSAS (MRS. ROBERT BLANCHARD), obstretrician; b. Amsterdam, N.Y., Feb. 24, 1932; d. Thomas Christ and Margaret (Smith) Kansas; B.A., U. Rochester, 1953; M.D., Med. Coll. Pa., 1957; m. Robert Edwin Blanchard, July 26, 1958; children—Thomas Edwin, John Kenneth, Robert Allen. Intern Rochester Gen. Hosp., 1957-58, resident, 1958-59; resident Park Av. Hosp., Rochester, 1959-60; practice medicine specializing in obstetrics, Amsterdam, N.Y., 1960—; mem. staffs St. Mary's Hosp. (sec.-treas. staff 1964-66), Amsterdam Meml. Hosp. (both Amsterdam, N.Y.). Chmn. youth com. YMCA, 1968—; mem. Greater Amsterdam Bd. Edn., 1969—, v.p., 1972-73, pres., 1973—. Bd. dirs. (1st woman) YMCA, 1972-73. Mem. A.M.A., N.Y. State, Montgomery County (sec. 1964-66, treas. 1966-69) med. socs., Montgomery County Assn. for Retarded Children, Amsterdam Bus. and Profl. Womens Club. Episcopalian (vestryman 1972—). Mem. Order Eastern Star. Home: Box 236 Hagaman NY 12086 Office: 192 Market St Amsterdam NY 12010

BLANCHARD, MARGARET ANN, educator; b. Schenectady, Sept. 4, 1943; d. Earl C. and Gladys M. (Hickok) Blanchard; A.A., Palm Beach Jr. Coll., 1963; B.S., U. Fla., 1965, M.A., 1970. Reporter, Miami Herald, 1966-69, women's editor Broward edit., 1966-68; asst. prof. journalism E. Carolina U., Greenville, N.C., 1970-74; instr. Sch. Journalism, U. N.C., Chapel Hill, 1974—. Sec., treas. Greenville chpt. N.C. Civil Liberties Union, 1970-74; dir. human resources Pitt-County League Women Voters, Greenville, 1971-74; dir. human resources N.C. League Women Voters State Bd., 1973—. Mem. Women in Communication, Assn. for Edn. in Journalism, Sigma Delta Chi, Phi Kappa Phi, Kappa Tau Alpha. Home: Kingswood Apts Chapel Hill NC 27514

BLANCHARD, ORA LOUISE, journalist; b. Roswell, N.M., Nov. 18, 1922; d. Francis Lincoln and Ora Hardin (Wallace) Blanchard; grad. N.M. Coll. Agrl. and Mechanic Arts, 1946; postgrad. U. Miami, 1947-49. With Roswell (N.M.) Record, summers, 1943-46, Las Cruces (N.M.) Sun News, 1946-47; with Miami (Fla.) News, 1949—, edn. writer, 1954-68, 73—, urban affairs writer, 1968-72; dir. Model City Journalism Project, 1972-73. Vol., Dade County Mental Health Soc., 1963-66. Recipient School Bell award Dade County Classroom Tchrs. Assn., 1964, 66, 67. Office: Box 615 Biscayne Annex Miami FL 33152

BLANCHFIELD, NINA MARIE (MRS. JAMES JOSEPH BLANCHFIELD), editor; b. Paterson, N.J., Sept. 25, 1914; d. Joseph and Maria (Retiro) Marchese; ed. Spencer Bus. Sch., Paterson; m. James Joseph Blanchfield, July 9, 1933; children—Thomas J., Joseph P. With IBM-Poughkeepsie News (N.Y.), 1956—, asso. editor, 1964-70. Chmn. women's div. Beacon (N.Y.) Golden Jubilee Celebration, 1963. Democratic committeeman, 1st ward, 2nd dist., Beacon, 1940-66; vice chmn. Beacon Dem. Com., 1945-59; vice chmn. Dutchess County Dem. Com., 1950-65; alternate del. Dem. nat. conv., Atlantic City, 1964, del. N.Y. State conv., 1958, 62; v.p. Dutchess County Women's Dem. Club, 1960-66. Mem. Beacon Jr. Social League, Franklin D. Roosevelt Home Club, Cath. Daus. Am. Roman Catholic. Home: 3 Deerfield Place Beacon NY 12508

BLANCO, JULIA DIANE KEITH (MRS. VICTORINO SEVERO BLANCO), ednl. adminstr.; b. Mobile, Ala., July 17, 1946; d. Morris Olen and Mary (Dean) Keith; B.S. in Edn., U.S. Ala., 1967; M.Ed., Auburn U., 1969; m. Victorino Severo Blanco, June 1, 1968. Tchr. John Shaw High Sch., Mobile, Ala., 1967-68; counselor Alexander City State Jr. Coll., 1969-70; counselor Va. Poly. Inst. and State U., 1970-72, dean of women, 1972; dir. student devel. Tex. A. and I. Univ., Kingsville, 1973—. Vocational Rehab. fellow Auburn U. Mem. Am. Personnel and Guidance Assn., Nat. Assn. Women Deans and Counselors, Am. Assn. U. Women (v.p. 1973-74), Southwest Assn. Coll. and Univ. Housing Officers, Tex. Assn. Coll. Tchrs., Tex. Assn. Student Personnel Adminstrs., Zonta Internat. Club: Kingsville Women's. Home: Route 1 Box 540 N Kingsville TX 78363 Office: 225 College Hall Texas A & I Kingsville TX 78363

BLANCPAIN, JOAN BEATRICE BONVICINI (MRS. PHILIPPE BLANCPAIN), gen. contractor; b. Torrington, Conn.; d. Julius and Louise (Paganini) Bonvicini; student Purdue U., 1954-56, U. Conn., 1956-58; m. Philippe Blancpain, Sept. 12, 1970; children—Erica, Paul. Vice pres., sec., dir. Bonvicini Bldg. Co., Inc., 1959-70, pres., treas., dir., 1970—; dir. v.p., sec. Torrington Bldg. Supply Co., Inc., bldg. material retailers. Mem. Beta Sigma Phi, Chi Epsilon. Home: 909 Torringford West St Torrington CT 06790 Office: 1500 S Main St Torrington CT 06790

BLAND, HESTER BETH, cons. health edn.; b. Sullivan, Ind.; d. Hudson A. and Dessie (Denney) Bland; B.S., Ind. State Tchrs. Coll., 1942; M.S., Butler U., 1949; Dr. Health and Safety, Ind. U., 1956; LL.D., Ind. State U., 1973. Tchr. Sullivan County Pub. Schs., 1930-43; aux. Allison div. Gen. Motors, 1943-44; tchr. Speedway Pub. Schs., 1945-47; cons. health and phys. edn. Ind. Bd. Health, 1947-71; lectr. Div. Allied Sci., Ind. U. Med. Sch., 1950-71; vis. prof. Utah State U., 1962, 65, 66, 69, 70, 72, 73, Madison Coll., Va., 1965, Union Coll., Ky., 1965, 66, 69, 70, 71, 72; adj. prof. Ind. State U., 1972, Kent State U., 1972. Rep. to Am. Assn. for Health, Phys. Edn. and Recreation from Midwest, 1957-60; coordinator drug edn. project Am. Sch. Health Assn.-Pharm. Mfrs. Assn., 1969-70. Recipient Ind. State U. Alumni Distinguished Service award, 1962; Distinguished Service award Ind. Assn. Health, Phys. Edn. and Recreation, 1957, Ind. Pub. Health Assn., 1965. Fellow Am. Pub. Health Assn., Am. Sch. Health Assn. (governing council, mem. com. on drugs, pres. 1972-73; Distinguished award 1970), A.A.H.P.E.R. (pres. Ind. 1954-55, honor award 1967), Ind. Assn. Health, Phys. Edn. and Recreation (pres. 1954-55); mem. Midwest Assn. for Health, Phys. Edn. and Recreation (pres. 1956), Delta Psi Kappa, Eta Sigma Gamma. Methodist. Author filmstrips in field; (with others) Healthful Living in Your Environment, 1972. Home: 2511 Parkwood Dr Speedway IN 46224

BLANDFORD, SISTER MARGARET VINCENT, hosp. adminstr.; b. Lebanon, Ky., Oct. 27, 1920; d. John Martin and Mary Lyda (O'Daniel) Blandford; R.N., St. Joseph's Sch. Nursing, 1941; B.S. in Nursing Edn., Spalding Coll., 1952; postgrad. Sloan Inst. Hosp. Adminstrn., Cornell U., 1962. Asst. adminstr. St. Joseph's Hosp., Lexington, Ky., 1949-54; adminstr. St. Vincent Infirmary Little Rock, 1955-61, pres. bd., chief exec. officer, 1971—. trustee, hosp. coordinator, hosps. of Sisters of Charity, Nazareth, Ky., 1961-71. Chmn. bd. govs. Am. Health Congress, 1971-72. Named Woman of Year, Greater Little Rock, 1960. Fellow Am. Coll. Hosp. Adminstrs.; mem. Ark. Conf. Cath. Hosps. (pres. 1957-59), Little Rock Hosp. Council (pres. 1960-61), Cath. Hosp. Assn. (sec. bd. trustees 1961-65, trustee 1966-69, pres. elect 1970-71, pres. 1971-72). Home and office: St Vincent Infirmary Markham and Univ Avs Little Rock AR 72201

BLANEY, DORIS RUTH (MRS. KARTER ROBERT BLANEY), ednl. adminstr.; b. Gary, Ind., Sept. 5, 1932; d. Frank Albert and Ruth Elnora (Carlson) Papke; B.S. in Nursing, Ind. U., 1955, Ed.D., 1973; M.A. in Edn., U. Chgo., 1959; m. Karter Robert Blaney, Mar. 10, 1956; children—James Michael, Thomas Karter. Asst. prof. nursing, Ind. U., Gary, 1966-67, asso. prof., 1970-74, prof., 1974—, dir. div. nursing, 1967—. Mem. N.W. Ind. Home Health Services; mem. exec. com. N.W. Ind. Comprehensive Health Planning Council, 1970-72. NIH fellow, 1972, 73. Mem. Am., Ind. (dir. 1971—) nurses assns., Nat. League for Nursing, Am. Assn. for Higher Edn., Am. Ednl. Research Assn., Altrusa, Pi Lambda Theta, Sigma Theta Tau, Alpha Chi Omega. Lutheran. Author: (with others) A Study of Nursing Needs in Indiana, 1973. Home: 358 N Kelly Hobart IN 46342 Office: 3400 Broadway Gary IN 46408

BLANK, ANNETTE CHOTIN (MRS. FRANKLIN BLANK), librarian; b. N.Y.C., June 1, 1925; d. Solomon and Frances (Freifeld) Chotin; B.S., Wilson Tchrs. Coll., 1948; M.S., U. So. Cal., 1951; m. Franklin Blank, Dec. 25, 1952; 1 dau., Emily Celia. Library clk.-aide Los Angeles County Gen. Hosp. Library, 1948-50; sch. librarian Towson (Md.) Jr. High Sch., 1951-52; children's librarian D.C. Pub. Library, Washington, 1953; children's librarian Enoch Pratt Free Library, Balt., 1957—, head central children's dept., 1973—; book reviewer Children's Book Rev. Service, 1973—. Mem. Am. (Md. membership chmn. 1973—), Md. library assns., Women's Internat. League for Peace and Freedom (rec. sec. 1973—), Soc. Israel Philatelists. Jewish religion. Home: 5477 Cedonia Av Baltimore MD 21206 Office: Enoch Pratt Free Library 400 Cathedral St Baltimore MD 21201

BLANK, BLANCHE DAVIS (MRS. JOSEPH S. BLANK, JR.), educator; b. N.Y.C.; d. Joseph B. and Matilda (Markendorff) Davis; B.A., Hunter Coll., 1944; M.A., Maxwell Sch., Syracuse U., 1945; Ph.D., Columbia, 1951; m. Joseph S. Blank, Jr., Oct. 10, 1945; children—Laura, Barbara, Alice. Research asso. Tax Found., 1945-46; instr. Coll. City N.Y., 1946-49; lectr. New Sch. Social Research, 1950-53; mem. faculty Hunter Coll., 1953—, prof. polit. sci. and pub. adminstrn., 1967-72, dean social scis., 1972—; cons. in field. Exec. dir. Mayor N.Y.C. Task Force City Personnel, 1966. Past village chmn. and county mem. Greenville (N.Y.) Democratic com. Past mem. regional bd. Woodrow Wilson Found. Recipient Service award Manhattan Community Coll., 1954. NSF grantee, 1966-68, City U. N.Y., 1965, 69; Legislative Research grantee, 1963. Mem. Am. Assn. U. Profs., Am. Polit. Sci. Assn., Pub. Adminstrn. Soc., Comparative Adminstrn. Group, Phi Beta Kappa. Author: American Government and Politics: A Critical Introduction, 1973. articles to profl. jours. Home: 13 Withington Rd Scarsdale NY 10583 Office: 695 Park Av New York City NY 10021

BLANK, CYNTHIA FISHER (MRS. SANFORD BLANK), lawyer; b. N.Y.C., Mar. 5, 1925; d. Irwin and Rose (Spiro) Fisher; A.B., Cleve. Coll. of Western Res. U., 1944; J.D., Chase Coll. of Law, 1956; LL.M. in Taxation, N.Y. U., 1973; m. Sanford Blank, Feb. 24, 1943; children—Leslie Margaret, Claudia Ellen. Admitted to Ohio bar, 1956; pvt. practice, Cin., 1956-64; dir. Domestic Relations Ct., Hamilton County, Cin., 1964-69; asso. firm Taft, Stettinius & Hollister, Cin. 1969—. Tchr., S.P. Chase Coll. of Law, instr. No. Ky. State Coll., Cin., 1974—; guest lectr. alumni seminars in estate planning U. Cin., 1973-74. Propr., dir. Circle Gallery, Cin., 1967—. Mem. auxs. Providence, Jewish hosps., Cin.; mem. Estate Planning Council of Cin., 1973—; mem. Women's Polit. Caucus, 1972—. Mem. Cin. Bar Assn., Council Jewish Women, Order of Curia, United Order of True Sisters, Hadassah. Club: Women's City. Home: 177 Lafayette Circle Cincinnati OH 45220 Office: Dixie Terminal Bldg Cincinnati OH 45202

BLANK, MARIE LATZ, social work cons.; b. Atlantic City, Nov. 26, 1918; d. Milton Cadet and Evalyn Rose (Loewy) Latz; B.S., Drexel U., 1942; M.S.W., U. Pa., 1947. Dir. social service Commonwealth Mental Health Center, Phila., 1957-62; project dir. priority project Pa. Dept. Pub. Welfare, Harrisburg, 1962-65; cons. social work sect. on mental health of aging Nat. Inst. Mental Health, Rockville, Md., 1968—. Mem. Am. Orthopsychiat. Assn. (chmn. task force on aging), Gerontology Soc., Nat. Assn. Social Workers. Home: 3001 Veazey Terrace NW Washington DC 20008 Office: Sect on Mental Health of Aging Nat Inst Mental Health 5600 Fishers Lane Rockville MD 20852

BLANKENSHIP, BARBARA ELAINE STRICKLIN (MRS. THOMAS LARRY BLANKENSHIP), univ. adminstr.; b. Arkadelphia, Ark., June 17, 1945; d. Maurice Shepard and Marnine Elizabeth (Allison) Stricklin; B.S., Henderson State Coll., 1967; M.S., U. Ark., 1969; m. Thomas Larry Blankenship, Feb. 13, 1970; 1 dau., Michele Kathleen. Tchr. math. Clay County Jr. High Sch., Green Cove Springs, Fla., 1967, Pine Bluff (Ark.) Jr. High Sch., 1967-68; grad. asst. U. Ark., Fayetteville, 1968-69; program dir. Miss. State U. Union, Mississippi State, 1969—. Mem. Nat. Assn. Women Deans, Adminstrs. and Counselors, Am. Personnel and Guidance Assn., Assn. Coll. Unions-Internat. (regional arts coordinator 1972-74), Starkville C. of C., Starkville Jaycettes, Alpha Xi Delta, Alpha Chi, Kappa Delta Pi, Phi Lambda Pi. Baptist. Home: PO Box 532 Mississippi State MS 39762 Office: PO Box 5368 Mississippi State MS 39762

BLANKENSHIP, MARTHA ELISE, educator; b. Baton Rouge, La., July 4, 1933; d. Macon O'Bryant and Louise Aimee (Jackson) Blankenship; B.S., Centenary Coll., 1955; M.Ed., U. Md., 1958; certificate of Advanced Studies, (Nat. Inst. Mental Health grantee), Syracuse U., 1966; Ed.D. (Delta Kappa Gamma scholar, Alpha Epsilon Phi scholar), U. Houston, 1969. Elementary tchr. gifted and learning disabilities children, Caddo Parish Sch. Bd., Shreveport, La., 1955-67; asst. dir. Clin. Edn. Program, U. Houston, 1967-68, teaching fellow, 1967-69; ednl. diagnostician pediatric and child psychiatry depts. John Sealy Hosp., Galveston, Tex., 1968-69; asso. prof. spl. edn. Northern Ill. U., DeKalb, 1969—. Cons. Bay City-Wharton Counties Project, Bay City, Tex., 1968-69, evaluator Elementary Secondary Edn. Act Title III Projects in the State of Ill., Edwardsville and Wilmette, 1970-71, Inst. for Higher Edn. and State Depts. of Spl. Edn. Personnel, Chgo., 1971—; asso. evaluator residential program for emotionally disturbed children Chgo. Pub. Sch. Bd., 1971—. NSF grantee Eastern Mich. U., 1962; vis. scholar Northwestern U., summer 1971. Mem. Council for Exceptional Children, Assn. for Children with Learning Disabilities, Am. Psychol. Assn., A.A.A.S., Am. Assn. U. Profs., Am. Assn. U. Women, Delta Kappa Gamma, Kappa Delta Pi. Editor: Reciprocity Special Education Personnel, 1972. Contbr. articles to profl. jours. Home: 721 Hillcrest Dr DeKalb IL 60115 Office: Dept of Special Education Northern Illinois University DeKalb IL 60115

BLANKENSHIP, MRS. WAYNE GOVAN, club woman; b. Pensacola, N.C., Dec. 25, 1906; d. Welzie Hampton and Emma (Wilson) Hensley; grad. Opportunity Bus. Coll., 1931; m. Wayne Govan Blankenship, May 3, 1930; children—Emma Mae, Wayne Govan. Tchr. Pensacola High Sch., N.C., 1926-30; sec. Home Fed. Savs. and Loan Assn., Knoxville, Tenn., 1937-40, sec. to pres., 1940—. Mem. ways and means com. Ossoli Circle Club, 1964-65, 74-75; rec. sec. Knoxville Woman's Club, 1951-52, v.p., 1964-65, pres., 1965-66, dist. treas. federated clubs, 1960-62; treas. Knoxville chpt. Am. Assn. UN, 1962-64; conservation chmn. Flower Lovers Club, 1963-64, treas., 1970-71, v.p., 1974-75; state rec. sec. Tenn. W.C.T.U., 1959-62, dist. chmn., 1961-62, corr. sec., 1962-64, promotion sec., 1965-66, 67-68, v.p., 1969-70, pres., 1971-73; v.p. Tuesday Morning Musical Club, 1960-62, pres., 1962-64; dist. sec. Christian Social Relations Woman's Soc. Christian Service 1961-64, local pres., 1959-60, dist. treas., 1964-65; v.p. City Assn. Women's Clubs, 1964-65; v.p. E. Tenn. of Tenn. Fedn. Music Clubs, 1964-66, 68-70, corr. sec., 1966-68; music chmn. Tenn. Fedn. Women's Clubs, 1962-64; parliamentarian Exchangette Club, 1965-66, pres., 1968-69. Methodist (steward). Home: 5107 Holston Dr Knoxville TN 37914

BLANKS, MARY ANN THOMPSON (MRS. THOMAS R. BLANKS, JR.), lawyer; b. Nashville, Nov. 3, 1934; d. William Terry and Gladys (Mitchell) Thompson; student U. Chattanooga, 1954-58; LL.B., Cumberland U., 1960, J.D., 1969; m. Thomas R. Blanks, Jr. Office mgr. Lookout Beverages, Inc., Chattanooga, 1961-63; admitted to Tenn. bar, 1961; asso. counsel Provident Life & Accident Ins. Co., Chattanooga, 1963—. Bd. dirs., treas. Big Bros.-Big Sisters, Inc.; mem. day care com. Orange Grove Sch.; active Nat., Tenn., Chattanooga retarded children's assns. Mem. Am., Tenn., Chattanooga, Hamilton County bar assns., Zonta Internat. (pres. Chattanooga club), Alpha Lambda Delta, Pi Gamma Mu, Iota Tau Tau (dean Zeta chpt. 1959-60). Republican. Episcopalian. Home: 909 S Crest Rd Chattanooga TN 37404 Office: Provident Life & Accident Ins Co Fountain Sq Chattanooga TN 37402

BLANTON, GLORIA HORTENSE, educator; b. Teachey, N.C., Sept. 19, 1924; d. Johnnie J. and Fannie (Wadsworth) Blanton; B.A., Wake Forest U., 1947; M.A., Columbia, 1950; Ph.D., U. N.C. at Chapel Hill, 1967. With Bapt. State Conv. N.C., 1947-61, asso. state dir. dept. student work, Raleigh, 1959-61; asso. dean students St. Andrews Presbyn. Coll., Laurinburg, 1962-64, devel. asso., 1961-62; coordinator long-range planning, asst. prof. psychology, 1967-69, asso. prof. psychology Meredith Coll., Raleigh, 1969—. Counselor guidance and testing center U. N.C., Chapel Hill, part-time 1965-67. Active various community drives; mem. exec. bd. Scotland County Mental Health Assn., 1963-64. Recipient Danforth Campus Ministry grant, 1957-58; Elizabeth Avery Colton fellow Am. Assn. U. Women, 1966-67. Mem. Am., N.C. (status of Women com.) psychol. assns., Am. Assn. U. Women (pres. N.C div. 1974—), Am. Assn. U. Profs., Am. Personnel and Guidance Assn., Nat. Assn. Women Deans and Counselors, Am. Coll. Personnel Assn., Raleigh Bus. and Profl. Women's Club, N.C. Adult Edn. Assn. (exec. bd. 1969-71), N.C. Personnel and Guidance Assn. (exec. council 1971-72), N.C. Coll. Personnel Assn. (pres. 1971-72). Baptist. Home: 1322 Dogwood Lane Raleigh NC 27607 Office: Box X113 Meredith Coll Raleigh NC 27611

BLASER, BARBARA ANGELA, customhouse broker; b. Findlay, O.; d. John Charles and Emma Elizabeth (Dondelinger) Blaser; student parochial schs. Pres., Blaser & Mericle, Inc., Cleve., 1955—; 1st v.p. Womens Fed. Savs. & Loan Assn., Cleve., 1968—. Mem. Womens Traffic Club Cleve. (past treas.), Cleve. World Trade Assn. (past sec.). Address: 4157 Ruple Av South Euclid OH 44121

BLASKOWER, MARJORIE ANDREWS (MRS. RICHARD BROOKS BLASKOWER), research co. exec.; b. Sanford, Fla., Dec. 22, 1922; d. Philip Roy and Margaret Bonita (Lockwood) Andrews; student Fla. State U., 1944; m. Richard Brooks Blaskower, Mar. 15, 1944; children—Patricia, Melanie (Mrs. Charles Buxton), Cynthia (Mrs. Sean Griffin), Richard Brooks. Supr. market research Blaskower Research Co., Ross, Cal., 1962-66, owner, 1971—; dir. research Dalaba Asso., San Francisco, 1967-69, Towers, Perrin, Forster & Crosby, San Francisco, 1970-71. Mem. Am. Marketing Assn., Sunny Hills Jr. Aux., Club: Lagunitas Country (dir.). Address: 38 Southwood Av Ross CA 94957

BLATT, ELEANOR STEINGISSER (MRS. RONALD BLATT), pediatrician; b. N.Y.C., Oct. 27, 1935; d. Sigmund and Lillian (Genad) Steingisser; B.S., Kan. State U., 1956; M.D., U. Kan., 1960; m. Ronald Blatt, Feb. 7, 1963; children—Geoffrey Leigh Siegel (by a previous marriage), Michelle, Nicole. Intern, Cedars of Lebanon Hosp., Los Angeles, 1960-61; resident pediatrics Los Angeles County Harbor Gen. Hosp., 1961-63; practice medicine specializing in pediatrics, Huntington Beach, Cal., 1963—; chmn. dept. pediatrics Huntington Intercommunity Hosp., Huntington Beach, 1971; mem. staffs Huntington Intercommunity Hosp., Westminster Hosp., Pacifica Hosp. Diplomate Am. Bd. Pediatrics. Fellow Am. Acad. Pediatrics. Home: 4021 Figaro Circle Huntington Beach CA 92649 Office: 17822 Beach Blvd Huntington Beach CA 92647

BLATT, LISA IRENE, univ. ofcl.; b. Chgo., Apr. 1, 1950; d. Bernard Morton and Marilyn Elaine (Rosenberg) Blatt; B.S. in Elementary Edn., So. Ill. U., 1972; M.S. in Coll. Student Personnel Adminstrn., Ind. U., 1974. Resident fellow So. Ill. U., 1970-72; resident asst. dept. residence life Ind. U., 1972-73, tutor-counselor Upward Bound project, 1973-74, asst. coordinator for residence life, 1973-74; head resident adviser Western Ill. U., Macomb, 1974—. Mem. Nat. Assn. Student Personnel Adminstrs., Nat. Assn. Women Deans, Adminstrs. and Counselors, Ind. U. Student Personnel Assn. (sec. 1973), Pi Lambda Theta. Home: 2944 Central Av Wilmette IL 60091 Office: Bayliss Hall Western Ill U Macomb IL 61455

BLAU, ZENA SMITH, educator; b. N.Y.C.; d. Joseph and Lena (Kretchzmer) Smith; A.B., Wayne State U., 1943, M.S.W., 1946; Ph.D., Columbia, 1957; m. Peter M. Blau, Aug. 7, 1948 (div. July 1969); 1 dau., Pamela. Instr. sociology Adelphi Coll., Garden City, N.Y., 1948, Wayne State U., Detroit, 1950-52; asst. prof. U. Ill., Chgo., 1958-62, Grad. Sch., U. Ill., Chgo., 1963-65; lectr. U. Chgo., 1967-69; asso. prof. sociology Northwestern U., Evanston, 1969-74; prof. sociology Richmond Coll. City U. N.Y., 1975—. Sr. research scientist Inst. for Juvenile Research, Chgo., 1965—; cons. Mayor's Office for Sr. Citizens, Chgo., 1971—. Recipient research fellowship Cornel U., 1953-54, research grant Nat. Inst. Mental Health, 1962-64, Social and Rehab. Service, Dept. Health Edn. and Welfare, 1967-72. Mem. Am. Sociol. Assn. (mem. nominations com. 1972-73), Soc. Study Social Problems, Sociologists Women in Soc., Assn. for Sociol. Study of Jewry (mem. exec. com. 1972-73, 74-75, chmn. nominations com. 1973). Author: Old Age in a Changing Society, 1973. Asso. editor Am. Sociologist, 1970—. Home: 5737 S Dorchester Av Chicago IL 60637 Office: Richmond Coll City U NY Staten Island NY 10301

BLAWIE, MARILYN-JUNE BEYERLE (MRS. JAMES L. BLAWIE), lawyer, educator; b. Danbury, Conn., Apr. 11, 1930; d. Christian W. and Marion (Brown) Beyerle; B.A., U. Conn., 1952; J.D., U. Chgo., 1955; student U. Lund (Sweden), summer 1952, London Sch. Econs. and Polit. Sci. (Rotary Internat. Found. fellow), 1952-53; m. James L. Blawie, May 30, 1952; children—Elias James, Cecelia Ruth, Christiana Lyn. Research and sci. writer, news editor Mich. State U., Lansing, 1956; personnel counsellor Buckeye Personnel Service, Akron, O., 1956-57; legal research, and editor Columbia U., N.Y.C., 1957-58, part-time analyst, asso. editor, 1958-59; asst. prof. Cal. State U. at Hayward, 1959-62, asso. prof. 1962-66, prof. polit. sci., 1966—; admitted to Conn. bar, 1956, Cal. bar, 1970; practiced in Fremont, Cal., 1970—; mem. firm Blawie & Blawie, 1970—. Mem. Univ. Centers for Rational Alternatives. Trustee, Ohlone Community Coll., 1965-68, Gemco Charitable and Ednl. Found., 1973—. bd. dirs. Cal. State U. Bill of Rights Workshops, 1966-67; adviser Blackstone Soc., Hayward; bd. dirs. Citizen's Com. for a Sensible Environment, Washington Twp., Cal.; mem. Hayward Women's Studies Adv. Commn., 1972—. Mem. Law and Soc. Assn., Am., Western polit. sci. assns., Conn., Cal., Alameda, San Francisco bar assns., Am. Assn. U. Profs., Nat. Municipal League, Am. Judicature Soc., Queen's Bench, Phi Kappa Phi, Gamma Chi Epsilon. Democrat. Club: Commonwealth of Cal. Co-author 3 books. Contbr. articles to profl. jours. Home: 41752 Marigold Dr Fremont CA 94538 Office: Dept Polit Sci Cal State Univ Hayward CA 94535 also 40587C Fremont Blvd Fremont CA 94538

BLAZER, SONDRA KAY GORDON (MRS. CHARLES M. BLAZER), free lance journalist, writer; b. Middletown, O., June 2, 1937; d. John Charles and Ora Lillie (Stewart) Gordon; student U. Cin., evenings 1955—; m. Ralph J. Bays, Feb. 17, 1956 (dec. 1969); children—Sherry Kay, Cynthia Rae, Robert Jay; m. 2d, Charles M. Blazer, July 22, 1972. Reporter, ch. editor Middletown (O.) Jour., 1955-56; mng. editor Warren County Reporter, Lebanon, O., 1966-72; contbg. editor Franklin (O.) Chronicle, Miami Gazette, Waynesville, O., 1972—; free lance journalist, 1973—. Mem. Ohio Gov. Gilligan's Traffic Safety Com., 1972—, Warren County Bd. Mental Health and Retardation, 1972—, now pres.; mem. citizen's adv. com. Lebanon Correctional Instn., Lebanon, 1971—; sec. Warren County Safety Council, 1972—, Warren County com. Ohio Easter Seal Soc. for Crippled Children and Adults, 1967—, now vice chmn.; mem. Warren County Bd. Elections, 1974—. Sec., Warren County Democratic Womens Club, 1963-67, Warren County Dem. Central and Exec. Com., 1965—; precinct committeeman Dem. party, 1964—; mem. Ohio Dem. Century Club. Mem. Ohio Corrections and Ct. Assn., Am. Police and Fire Reporters Assn., Nat. Council Crime and Delinquency, Internat. Platform Assn., Phi Kappa Epsilon, Alpha Sigma Lambda. Methodist (Sunday sch. tchr. 1963-72, sec. worship commn. 1972—). Address: 3730 Beatrice Dr Franklin OH 45005

BLEAKNEY, CHERYL ANNE (MRS. THOMAS P. BLEAKNEY), city ofcl.; b. Salt Lake City, Aug. 28, 1931; d. Edward Dale and Ruth (Platt) Hoggan; student U. Utah, 1948-51; m. Thomas Paul Bleakney, Feb. 21, 1953; children—Paul, Sheila, Eileen, Ross, Scott. Sec., law firm Halliday & Halliday, Salt Lake City, 1952; sec. Equitable Life Assurance, Salt Lake City and N.Y.C., 1952-53; mem. Seattle League Women Voters, 1958—, sec., 1965-68; bd. dirs. League Women Voters Wash., 1971-72; mem. Seattle Bd. Adjustment, 1968-72; mem. Seattle Sch. Bd., 1972—. Mem. Washington Environmental Co., Seattle Citizens for Quality Integrated Edn., Seattle Municipal League, Wash. (communications com. 1974—),

King County (treas. 1974—) sch. dirs. assns. Home: 3434 Perkins Lane Seattle WA 98199

BLEDSOE, ERNESTINE, educator; b. Ft. Valley, Ga., Jan. 16, 1912; d. James Ernest and Emma Louise (Anderson) Bledsoe; A.B., Wesleyan Coll., 1933; M.Ed., U. Ga., 1948; Ed.D., Columbia, 1954. Dir. young peoples work Vineville Meth. Ch., Macon, Ga., 1933-37; v.p. in charge personnel Ga. Basket & Lumber Co., Ft. Valley, 1937-42; supr. personnel unit Warner Robbins Air Depot (Ga.), 1942-45; tchr. Decatur (Ga.) Girls High Sch., 1945-48; asst. prof., dir. field services in guidance U. Ga. Coll. Edn., Athens, 1948-54; prof. edn., dir. tchr. edn. Wesleyan Coll., Macon, 1954—. Mem. Nat., Ga. edn. assns., Am. Assn. Higher Edn., Am. Personnel and Guidance Assn., Nat. Vocational Guidance Assn., Am. Assn. U. Women, Ga. Council Tchr. Edn., Kappa Delta Pi, Kappa Delta Gamma, Phi Kappa Phi. Methodist. Club: Pilot (Macon). Home: 405 Persons St Fort Valley GA 31030 Office: Wesleyan Coll Macon GA 31201

BLEISCH, NADYA FRANCES KONIKOV (MRS. VIRGIL ROLAND BLEISCH), pathologist; b. Boston, Sept. 24, 1927; d. William Morris and Henrietta (Fink) Konikov; B.S., Boston U., 1947, M.D., 1950; m. Virgil Roland Bleisch, Nov. 1, 1952; children—William, Sabrina, Barbara, Pamela. Intern, Grace-New Haven Hosp., 1950-51; resident, Mallory Inst. Boston City Hosp., 1952-53, Beth Israel Hosp., Boston, 1953-55; instr. pathology Washington U. Med. Sch., 1955-58; owner pvt. lab., Alton, Ill., 1957-60; cytopathologist St. Louis City Hosp., 1960-65, Barnes Hosp., 1965-69; cons. cytology City Hosp., St. Louis, 1969—; asst. prof. pathology Washington U. Med. Sch., St. Louis, 1969—. Bd. dirs. Univ. City Day Care Center, 1969-71. Recipient fellowship Am. Cancer Soc., 1957. Diplomate Am. Bd. Pathology. Fellow Am. Coll. Pathologists; mem. St. Louis Med. Soc., Royal Soc. Health, Common Cause, Am. Civil Liberties Union, League Women Voters, Mensa Internat., Phi Beta Kappa. Presbyn. (deacon 1971-74). Home: 524 Midvale St St Louis MO 63130 Office: 1606 Grattan St St Louis MO 63111

BLEMING, MARY ELIZABETH (MRS. ROSS ABERNATHY BLEMING), trucking and warehouse co. exec.; b. Phoenix, July 18, 1911; d. Ernest Foss and Ethel Ione (Hanger) Bishopp; grad. high sch.; m. Ross Abernathy Bleming, Feb. 22, 1936; 1 dau., Janet Elizabeth (Mrs. Donald Paul Swartz). Owner S & N Transp. Co., Long Beach Cal., 1936, formerly v.p., pres. Bleming Warehouse and West Coast Warehouse Corp., 1958-74. Active P.T.A., 1957-61. Chmn. election bd., Palm Springs, Cal., 1968-72. Mem. Long Beach C. of C., Fgn. Trade Assn. of Los Angeles, Los Angeles World Affair Council, P.E.O. (pres. Palm Springs chpt. 1958-60). Republican. Presbyn. Clubs: Seven Lakes Country (Palm Springs); Women's Traffic (transp. chmn. 1943) (Los Angeles). Home: 1094 Palo Verde Av Long Beach CA 90815 Office: Pier A Berth 7-8-9 Warehouse No 1 Long Beach CA 90801

BLETTE, PATRICIA ANN ORMSBY (MRS. JOHN BLETTE III), univ. adminstr.; b. Niagara Falls, N.Y., Mar. 24, 1941; d. Linus Lambert and Barbara Elizabeth (Wallace) Ormsby; student Niagara U., 1960-62; B.A., U. Tex., 1964; M.A., U. N.M., 1972, postgrad., 1972—; m. John Blette III, May 4, 1963; children—Veronica Lynn, David John, Steven James. Tchr., Sandoval County Indian Community Action Program. N.M., 1969-72; intern staff psychologist Alcoholic Treatment Program, Albuquerque, 1972; intern financial aid officer U. N.M., Albuquerque, 1973, spl. acad. adviser, 1973—. Substitute tchr. El Paso (Tex.) Pub. Schs., 1964-66. Recipient scholarship U. N.M, 1973. Mem. Am. Assn. Higher Edn., Am. Personnel and Guidance Assn., Am. Coll. Personnel Assn., Nat. Assn. Women Deans and Counselors (regional rep. 1973—). Home: 2937 Montclaire Dr NE Albuquerque NM 87110

BLEVINS, JUNE MADLOM (MRS. KENDRICK BLEVINS), city ofcl.; b. Williamson, W.Va., Sept. 12, 1926; d. Mohammed Ali and Ida Belle (Curnutte) Madlom; grad. high sch.; b. Kendrick Blevins, Oct. 29, 1965; children—Bobbie Gayle (Mrs. James R. Corea), Beth Ann. Billing clk. Williamson Supply Co., 1944, Persinger Supply Co., 1945; sec. Acme Machinery Co., 1950; records clk. Mingo County Circuit Ct., 1959; Mingo County maintenance clk. W.Va. Dept. Hwy., 1962; city clk., City of Williamson, W.Va., 1965—. Del., Mingo County Young Democrats Conv., 1963, poll clk., commr., 1963. Mem. Beta Sigma Phi. Presbyn. Mem. Order Eastern Star. Home: Box 814 Williamson WV 25661 Office: Box 1517 Williamson WV 25661

BLEVINS, MARY FRANCES DOBBS (MRS. J. CLARENCE BLEVINS), banker; b. Wilmore, Ky.; d. Charles Alvin and Rosa Lee (Bishop) Dobbs; grad. high sch.; m. J. Clarence Blevins, July 11, 1950. With 1st Nat. Bank, Nicholasville, Ky., 1942—, asst. cashier, 1963-66, asst. v.p., 1966—, auditor, 1964-66; collection agt. Gen. Tel. Co. Ky., 1960-65; bookkeeper Blevins Paint & Wallpaper Store, Lexington, Ky., 1956—. Treas., Jessamine County Bd. Edn., Nicholasville, 1945-49; treas. Jessamine County Library, 1961—, also mem. adv. bd.; treas. Jessamine County Salvation Army Fund Drive, 1960; solicitor Jessamine County chpt. A.R.C., 1951, Arthritis Drive, 1967. Named Ky. col., 1963. Mem. Nat. Assn. Bank Women, Lena Madesin Phillips Bus. and Profl. Women's Club (treas. 1962), Nat. Audubon Soc. Mem. Christian Ch. (treas. Christian Womens Fellowship 1953, deaconess 1971-74, chmn. deaconess 1971). Home: 312 Hickory Hill Rd Nicolasville KY 40356 Office: 307 N Main St Nicholasville KY 40356

BLEWER, GLENDA GLORIA (MRS. ALTON GEORGE BLEWER), banker; b. Higgins, Tex.; Mar. 2, 1927; d. Lee Roy and Lillie Mae (Reimer) Goettsche; student Draughon's Bus. Coll., 1944-45, Tex. Tech. U., 1952; m. Alton George Blewer, Apr. 7, 1946; 1 dau., Alison (Mrs. David Little King). Tchr. typing and machine practice Draughon's Bus. Coll., Lubbock, Tex., 1945; billing clerk Lubbock (Tex.) Sash and Door Co., 1946; bookkeeper First Nat. Bank, Lubbock, 1948-49, teller, 1950-55, asst. cashier, 1965-71, asst. v.p., 1972—. Vice pres. Lubbock P.T.A., 1957-58; electoral mem. YWCA, 1959—; life mem. Tex. Congress Parents and Tchrs., 1959—. Mem. Nat. Assn. Bank Women, Inc., Am. Inst. Banking (sec. 1965), Bank Adminstrn. Inst. Baptist. Home: 2308 53d St Lubbock TX 79412 Office: 1500 Broadway St Lubbock TX 79401

BLEY, CARLA BORG (MRS. MICHAEL MANTLER), composer jazz music; b. Oakland, Cal., May 11, 1938; d. Emil C. and Arlene (Anderson) Borg; ed. schs., Oakland; m. Paul Bley, Jan. 27, 1959 (div. Sept. 1967); m. 2d, Michael Mantler, Sept. 29, 1967; 1 dau., Karen. Mem. Jazz Composer's Orch., N.Y.C., 1964—, co-leader, pianist orch., quintet, 1963-65, tours Europe, 1965, 66; free-lance jazz composer, 1956—. Named winner internat. jazz critics poll, Down Beat mag., 1966, 71, 72. Mem. Jazz Composer's Orch. Assn. (adviser 1967—). Composed, recorded: A Genuine Tong Funeral, 1967; (with Charlie Haden) Liberation Music Orch., 1969; (opera) Escalator Over the Hill, 1970-71. Home: 1476 Lexington Av New York City NY 10028

BLICK, NAOMI TRUEBLOOD (MRS. MILTON HAROLD BLICK), govt. ofcl.; b. Portsmouth, Va., Oct. 14, 1921; d. Hansa L. and Susan Stuart (Wichert) Trueblood; student Fgn. Service Inst., Washington, 1964; m. Milton Harold Blick, Mar. 17, 1949; children—James Walter, Carol Lea. Personnel asst. RFC, Washington, 1943-46; personnel asst. ECA, 1948-50; adminstrv. asst. OPS, 1950-51, Fed. Civil Def. Adminstrn., 1951-52; adminstrv. officer, exec. dir. Bd. Contract Appeals, AID, 1954-61, exec. officer AID, 1961-65; adminstrv. officer directing mgmt. Vol. in Services to Am. (VISTA), Office Econ. Opportunity, 1965-68, spl. asst. to dir. adminstrn., 1968-71; asst. dir. for nat. councils and orgns. Environmental Protection Agy., Washington, 1971—. Home: 9218 Laurel Oak Dr Bethesda MD 20034 Office: Environmental Protection Agy Washington DC 20460

BLICKENSDERFER, KATHERINE JOSEPHINE PIERCE (MRS. G. LYMAN BLICKENSDERFER), bus. exec.; b. Denver, Sept. 6, 1913; d. William Henry and Laura (McClay) Pierce; student Denver U., 1943, San Diego State Coll., 1944; m. G. Lyman Blickensderfer, Dec. 28, 1944; 1 son, G. Lyman. Accountant B and B Mfg. and Supply Co., Westminster, Colo., 1957-58, Hopkins and Co., Denver, 1958-62, Hopkins Constrn. Co., Denver, 1958-62; accountant Union Supply Co., Denver, 1962-65, corporate sec., 1963-65; accountant Bosworth, Sullivan & Co., 1965-67, Am. Nat. Cattlemen's Assn., 1967-69; accountant Vis. Nurse Assn., Denver Area, 1969-73, bus. mgr., 1973—. Mem. Am. Soc. Women Accountants (v.p. 1961-62, pres. Denver chpt. 1962-63, bull. editor 1960-61, 1963-64), Bus. and Profl. Women's Club, Colo. Fedn. Bus. and Profl. Women's Clubs (state treas. 1974-75), Adminstrv. Mgmt. Soc., Denver Symphony Soc., Denver Artists Guild. Methodist. Club: Altrusa. Home: 7700 Lowell Blvd Westminister CO 80030 Office: 659 Cherokee St Denver CO 80204

BLINDER, BEULAH BERNARDIK, psychologist; b. N.Y.C., Nov. 24, 1923; d. Alexander and Ida (Forstein) Bernardik; B.A. with honors, Cal. State U., 1953; M.Ed. (grad. fellow), U. Md., 1968; m. Herbert I. Blinder, Jan. 24, 1944, children—Joshua Andrew, Judith Naomi. Sch. psychometrist San Juan Unified Sch. Dist., Sacramento, Cal., 1954-61; personality researcher Nat. Inst. Mental Health, Bethesda, Md., 1965-66; cons. early childhood research Urban Service Corp., Washington, 1963-66, Washington pub. schs., 1963-66; counselor adult basic edn. Washington Pub. Schs., 1968-69; diagnostician and dir. spl. projects Kingsbury Center, Washington, 1969-71; sch. psychologist The Acton Sch., Washington, 1973—. Counseling therapist Rockville Free Clinic and Ken-gar Mobile Med. Care, 1971—. Mem. Am. Psychol. Assn., Am. Personnal and Guidance Assn., Washington Ethical Soc. (dir. 1969-72). Home: 6214 Crathie Lane Bethesda MD 20016 Office: The Acton School 7750 16th St NW Washington DC 20012

BLISS, ALICE WITHERSPOON, author, composer; b. Atlanta, Jan. 9, 1925; d. Fred James and Ruth Evelyn (Lee) Witherspoon; B.A. in English and History, U. Ga., 1943, M.A., 1944; student music composition and organ, Akademie der Musik und darstellende kunst, Vienna, Austria, 1956-57; student music composition U. Ill., 1957-58, Ind. U., 1959; m. Frank W. Bliss, Jr., Apr. 14, 1945 (div. Mar. 1952). Program mgr. sta. WFOM, Marietta, Ga., 1952-53; woman's editor sta. WDEC, Americus, Ga., 1953-54; TV traffic mgr. sta. WALB-TV, Albany, Ga., 1954; tchr. English and music Alice Lloyd Coll., Pippa Passes, Ky., 1959-60, 62-63, Cumberland (Ky.) Coll., 1960-61; tchr. English, No. Ill. U., 1961-62, Maryville (Tenn.) Coll., 1963-64; music critic Atlanta Constitution, 1964-65. Recipient 1st prize short story U. Ala. Festival of Arts, 1967. Author: (poems) Words for Dancing, 1958; Ellipse of Sonnets, 1960; The Sun in Splinters, 1972; Pinned, Pinnioned, 1974; (novella) Spring in the Bishop's Palace, 1969. Founder, Editor Sahara Lit. Mag., 1973. Composer: (operas) The Music Club, 1954; The School Board, 1965. Founder, dir. Atlanta Contemporary Opera Soc., 1966, Opera Inc., 1973. Address: 239 Mountain View St Decatur GA 30030

BLISS, AUDREY PRATT (MRS. WALTER ERNEST BLISS), real estate agt.; b. Phila., June 20, 1919; d. Joshua Dickson and Marion Claudine (Grignard) Pratt; student Mills Coll., 1936-37; B.A., U. Colo., 1940; m. Walter Ernest Bliss, Nov. 10, 1945; children—Walter Ernest, Wendy Marie (Mrs. Gregory Stuart Martin). Tchr., Schofield Barracks, Hawaii, 1940-41; teller Bank Hawaii, Honolulu, 1942-45; salesman real estate Fearon-Cross, Inc., Honolulu, 1959-60; salesman real estate A.D. Castro & Co., Honolulu, 1960-62, broker, 1962; ind. real estate broker, Honolulu, 1963—. Mem. State Ethics Commn., Honolulu, 1971—; active Girl Scouts Am., 1957; div. chmn. Punahou P.T.A., 1957. Bd. dirs. Jr. League Honolulu, 1947, Children's Aid Assn., 1954. Mem. Daus. Hawaii, Hawaiian Mission Children's Soc., Lawyers Wives Hawaii (past dir.), Outdoor Circle, Delta Gamma (del. Panhellenic Council 1967). Club: Garden of Honolulu (dir. 1973—). Home: 44-023 Kaimalu Place Kaneohe HI 96744

BLISS, DOROTHY LOUISE CRANDALL (MRS. PAUL D. BLISS), educator; b. Westerly, R.I., Feb. 20, 1916; d. Frank Henry and Alice (Arnold) Crandall; B.S., U. R.I., 1936, M.S., 1938; Ph.D., U. Tenn., 1957; m. Paul D. Bliss, Mar. 6, 1969. Sci. instr. Westerly Jr. High Sch., R.I., 1936-37; sci. and math. instr. Greenbrier Coll., Lewisburg, W.Va., 1941-43, So. Sem., Buena Vista, Va., 1943-47; instr. botany U. Wyo., Laramie, 1947-49; asst. prof. biology Randolph-Macon Woman's Coll., Lynchburg, Va., 1949-59, asso. prof. biology, 1959-68, prof. biology, 1968—. Recipient So. Fellowships Fund award, 1955-56; J. Shelton Horsley Research award Va. Acad. Sci., 1959. Mem. Am. Bot. Soc., Ecol. Soc. Am., Am. Inst. Biol. Scis., Am. Fern Soc., Assn. Southeastern Biologists (sec. 1967-70), Va. Acad. Scis., So. Appalachian Bot. Club (past pres.), Sigma Xi, Delta Kappa Gamma, Phi Kappa Phi. Contbr. articles to profl. jours. Research on ecol. studies in spruce-fir areas of Smokies, ferns of R.I.; bot. studies in Blue Ridge Mountains. Home: 322 Sumpter St Lynchburg VA 24503

BLITZER, CAROL BETTINA GOODKIN (MRS. ROY JULIAN BLITZER), journalist; b. Maywood, Cal., Apr. 6, 1946; d. Reuben Jacob and Lillian (Sheffner) Goodkin; B.A. with honors, U. Cal. at Berkeley, 1967; M.A. (Ford Found. fellow), Stanford, 1969; m. Roy Julian Blitzer, June 15, 1969. Editorial asst. Lane Mag. & Book Co., Menlo Park, Cal., 1969-70; copy editor George Pfeiffer & Asso., Palo Alto, Cal., 1970-71; editor Sci. & Behavior Books, Palo Alto, 1971-72; news editor Peninsula Electronics News, Palo Alto, 1973-74. Women in Communications. Democrat. Author: Papier Mache, 1970; also articles. Home: 818 B Live Oak Av Menlo Park CA 94025

BLOCH, LENORA RENAULT (MRS. ALAN BLOCH), controller; b. N.Y.C., Oct. 22, 1921; d. Jacob and Mary (Factor) Renault; B.A. in Math., Hunter Coll., 1941; m. Arthur Lerner, June 11, 1942 (dec. Oct. 1964); children—Jane and Margaret (twins); m. Alan Bloch, Dec. 16, 1967. N.Y. News, N.Y.C., 1941-46; with Met. Sunday Newspapers, N.Y.C., 1946—, controller, 1960—, research dir., 1956—. Mem. Am. Marketing Assn., Media Research Dirs. Assn. Home: 333 E 30th St New York City NY 10016 Office: 260 Madison Av New York City NY 10016

BLOCK, AMANDA ROTH (MRS. MAURICE BLOCK, JR.), artist; b. Louisville, Feb. 20, 1912; d. Albert S. and Helen (Bernheim) Roth; student Smith Coll., 1929, U. Cin., 1930-31, Art Acad. Cin., 1933-40, 46-47; B.F.A., Ind. U. Herron Sch. Art, 1960; m. Gordon J. Wolf, June 16, 1931 (div. May 1948); 1 son, Joseph G.; m. 2d, Maurice Block, Jr., July 15, 1949. One man shows 1444 Gallery, Indpls., 1962, Sheldon Swope Art Gallery, Terre Haute, Ind., 1963, 73, Orange County Coll., Middletown, N.Y., 1964, Park Av. Gallery, Indpls., 1944, Revel Gallery, N.Y.C., 1964, Harriet Crane Gallery, Cin., 1965, Talbot Gallery, Indpls., 1967, Merida Gallery, Louisville, 1967, Herron Mus. Art, Indpls., 1969, Editions Ltd. Gallery, Indpls., 1971, 72, Franklin Coll., 1973; exhibited group shows in large cities, including Soc. Am. Graphic Artists Exhbn. AAA Gallery, N.Y.C., 1964, 65, 66, travelling show, Europe, India, 1973-74, Isetan Gallery Print Exhbn., Tokyo, Japan, 1966, Imprint Gallery, San Francisco, 1972, McWay Inst., San Antonio, 1972, Van Straaten Gallery, Chgo., 1973; represented in permanent collections at DePauw U., Greencastle, Ind., Ind. State Coll., Terre Haute, Ind. Med. Soc., Indpls., Sheldon Swope Art Gallery, Stevens Coll., St. Louis, USIS, Lafayette (Ind.) Art Center, Speed Mus., Louisville, Phila. Mus. Art, Cin. Mus. Art, Bklyn. Mus. Art, Boston Pub. Library, N.Y.C. Pub. Library; mem. faculty Herron Sch. Art, Ind. U., Purdue U. at Indpls., 1970-73. Mem. State House Art Salon Com., Indpls., 1967-68. Recipient Catherine Mattison Water Color prize Ind. Artists Exhbn., 1963; Purchase prize DePauw U. Nat. Print Exhbn., 1963; Water Color prize Wabash Valley Exhbn., 1963, 64; Fifty Ind. Prints Exhbn., Stone Stafford and Stone Purchase prize, 1964; Purchase prize Lafayette Art Center, 1966; Ben and Beatrice Goldstein Found. award, Soc. Am. Graphic Artists, 1971. Address: 6000 Springmill Rd Indianapolis IN 46208

BLOCK, AMIE WILLARD (MRS. HUNTINGTON T. BLOCK), civic worker; b. Washington, Nov. 4, 1930; d. William Bradley and Florence Fazio (Keys) Willard; A.B. in English Lit., Sweet Briar Coll., 1952; m. Huntington T. Block, Sept. 21, 1952; children—Huntington Macdonald, Florence Willard, William Bradley, Willard, Amie Keys. Dance chmn. Jr. League, Washington, 1962, sec., 1965-66; mem. women's com. Corcoran Gallery, Washington, 1956—, ball chmn., 1967, asst. treas., 1962, v.p., 1964; mem. women's com. Smithsonian Instn., Washington, 1967—, chmn. projects com., 1970, chmn. Christmas Dance, 1971. Bd. dirs. Travelers' Aid, 1961-64, Friends Nat. Zoo, 1971-73, Arena Stage, 1973—, Nantucket Arts Council, 1974—. Club: Sulgrave (dir. 1967—). Home: 1312 30th St Washington DC 20007

BLOCK, BARBARA ALEEN, advt. exec.; b. St. Louis, Aug. 15, 1925; d. Alexander Ellisworth and Dorothy Elizabeth (Burgard) Block; B.A. in English, Fontbonne Coll., 1945. Prodn. mgr., copywriter, TV producer Westheimer and Block Advt. Agy., St. Louis, 1945-53; radio and TV dir. Prater Advt. Agy., St. Louis, 1953-60; media dir., writer-producer Horan Daugherty Advt. Agy., 1960-62; account exec., v.p. bd. Winfield Advt. Agy., St. Louis, 1963-73; advt. dir. Falls City Brewing Co., Louisville, 1973—. Sec. St. Louis chpt. Nat. Acad. TV Arts and Scis., 1969-70, gov., 1971. Mem. Friends St. Louis Art Museum, Fontbonne Alumnae Assn. (v.p. 1948-49). Roman Catholic. Clubs: Women's Advertising, St. Louis; Louisville Advertising. Home: 5100 Brownsboro Rd Louisville KY 40222 Office: 3050 W Broadway Louisville KY 40201

BLOCK, JANET JACOBS, occupational therapist; b. N.Y.C., Oct. 3, 1937; d. Barrett and Paula (Herling) Jacobs; B.S., Tufts U./Boston Sch. Occupational Therapy, 1960; M.A., N.Y. U., 1963; m. Bartley C. Block, May 26, 1963; children—Kenneth Joseph, Deborah Marion, Steven Michael. Mem. staff Inst. Phys. Medicine and Rehab., N.Y.C., 1960-62, sr. occupational therapist, 1962-63; chief occupational therapist Jefferson Med. Coll. Hosp., Phila., 1963-65; cons. Soundview Convalescent Home, West Haven, Conn., 1966-67; cons. Laurel Heights Hosp., Shelton, Conn., 1969—; lectr. in field. Mem. Am., Conn. occupational therapy assns. Home: 233 Plains Rd Milford CT 06460 Office: Laurel Heights Hosp Shelton CT 06457

BLOCK, PHYLLIS SUSAN ROBINOVE (MRS. IRVING J. BLOCK), editor; b. N.Y.C., May 13, 1927; d. Herman and Belle Rose (Bersoff) Robinove; B.A. cum laude, Hunter Coll., 1947, M.A., Columbia, 1948, Ph.D., 1955; m. Irving J. Block, Feb. 23, 1964; 1 son, Herbert. Lectr. French, Sch. Gen. Studies, Columbia, N.Y.C., 1949-50; instr. French and Spanish, Newark Coll., Rutgers U., 1951-54; translator, press and information div. French embassy, N.Y.C., 1956-58; editor fgn. lang. dept. Holt, Rinehart & Winston, N.Y.C., 1958-64; free-lance editor fgn. lang. textbooks, 1958—. Mem. Modern Lang. Assn. Am., Am. Assn. Tchrs. French, B'nai B'rith Women, Phi Beta Kappa. Mem. Hadassah. Author two high sch. French workbooks. Home: 79 W 12th St New York City NY 10011

BLOCK, RUTH ANN (MRS. NORMAN BLOCK), ins. co. exec.; b. N.Y.C., Nov. 7, 1930; d. Albert and Celia (Shapiro) Smolensky; B.A., Adelphi U., 1952; m. Norman Block, Apr. 5, 1952. With The Equitable Life Assurance Soc. U.S., N.Y.C., 1952—, asst. v.p., 1969-72, 2d v.p., 1972-74, v.p., 1974—; dir. Informatics, Inc., Cal. Mem. Assn. for Computing Machinery, Data Processing Mgmt. Assn. Home: 81 Blackwood Lane Stamford CT 06903 Office: 1285 Av of the Americas New York City NY 10019

BLOCKI, PHYLLIS CRANE, pub. co. exec.; b. Chgo., Sept. 6, 1923; d. Merrill Leslie and Mabel Olive (Dedrick) Crane; student Woodrow Wilson Jr. Coll., 1943; m. William George Blocki, Feb. 6, 1943 (div.); children—Phyllis M. (Mrs. Alvin Somerville), Kay M. (Mrs. Barry Thompson), Barbara J., Susan P. Reporter Hyde Park Herald, Chgo., 1940-43; sec. to sales mgr. Mac Tac Adhesives, Stow, O., 1960-62; promotion mgr. CBS-TV affiliate, Harrisburg, Pa., 1963-65; promotion dir. Stackpole Books, 1965-74; mgr. sales promotion Open Ct. Pub. Co., LaSalle, Ill., 1974—. Mem. A.L.A., Woman's Nat. Book Assn. Methodist. Home: 516 Columbia Av Oglesby IL 61348 Office: 9th and Sterling Sts LaSalle IL 61301

BLOCKLINGER, MARIE HAZEL (MRS. EDWARD JOSEPH BLOCKLINGER), real estate broker; b. Rock Island, Ill., Mar. 10, 1918; d. Sam Mack and Wenona Gilmore (Ewing) Sible; student Am. Inst. Commerce, 1962, Weaver Real Estate, 1962; m. Edward Joseph Blocklinger, June 9, 1934; children—Dale, Janice (Mrs. Ronald Johnson), Lisa. Saleslady DeBois, Realtor, Rock Island, Ill., 1960-65; owner Blocklinger Realty, Rock Island, Ill., 1965—. Dir. A.R.C., 1950-58, chmn. nurses aides, 1945-59; mem. council P.T.A., Frances Willard Sch. and Franklin Jr. High Sch., 1945-57. Bd. dirs. City of Hope, Rock Island, 1972—, also v.p. Mem. C. of C., Nat., Ill. assns. real estate bds., D.A.R. (sr. pres. Children Am. Revolution 1954-58). Presbyn. (trustee 1970-72). Mem. Rebekah (Noble Grand 1942). Clubs: Pilot (v.p. 1972-73), Woman's. Home: 1409 32d Av Rock Island IL 61201 Office: 1600 18th Av Rock Island IL 61201

BLODGETT, MARGARET CORNELIA SHEEHAN (MRS. ROBERT FULLER BLODGETT), lawyer, ins. analyst; b. Manchester, N.H., Oct. 13, 1897; d. John Aloysius and Georgia Mary (Beebe) Sheehan; A.B. magna cum laude, Trinity Coll., 1919, M.A., 1920; LL.B., Portia Law Sch., 1924; m. Robert Fuller Blodgett, Jan. 25, 1934. Instr. calculus Trinity Coll., Washington, 1919-20; ins. analyst John A. Sheehan Ins. Agy., Manchester, 1919-45, 46—; admitted to Mass. bar, 1924, N.H. bar, 1925; practice law, Manchester, State Mass., 1925—; mgr., Cypress Restaurant, Manchester, 1925-28; coach basketball Manchester High Sch., 1921-25. Co-author city charter Manchester, 1925-26; territorial chmn. Manchester Community Chest drive, 1934-36; active A.R.C., 1917-46; mem. N.H. Selective Service Bd., 1945—. Mem. Mass.,

N.H. bar assns., Sacred Heart, Cape Cod hosp. assns., Manchester (pres. 1970-71), Cape Cod (sec. 1967-70) duplicate bridge clubs, N.H. Assn. Ins. Agts. Club: Beach (Centerville, Mass.). Editor: The Trinilogue, 1919. Contbr. articles to profl. jours. Home: 49 Sagamore St Manchester NH 03104 Office: 62 Stark St Manchester NH 03101

BLODGETT, VIRGINIA JUNE BALLARD (MRS. RALPH WESLEY BLODGETT), ednl. adminstr.; b. Detroit; d. William King and Marie (Crossley) Ballard; A.B., Asbury Coll., 1935; M.S., Butler U., 1967; postgrad. U. Louisville, Ind. State U., Ball State U., Ohio State U., San Francisco State U.; m. Ralph Wesley Blodgett, Sept. 25, 1935; children—Vivian Sue (Mrs. William E. Shields), Rebecca June Downing, Judith Elaine (Mrs. David Purvis). Tchr. Dependent Schs., Europe, 1951-54, English various high schs., Ind., Va., Fla., 1942—, chmn. English dept. Woodview Sch., Indpls., 1961—, dean girls, 1964—. Instr. evening div. Ind. Central Coll., Indpls., 1964-69, adult counselor, 1965—. Active various community drives. Gen. Electric Co. fellow, 1967. Mem. Am., Ind. (sec. 1969) assns. women deans and counselors, N.E.A., Ind. State Tchrs. Assn., Warren Twp. Classroom Tchrs., Central Ind., Ind. personnel and guidance assns., Alpha Delta Kappa. Methodist (tchr. ch. schs. 1935—). Home: PO Box 21 Willow Branch IN 46187 Office: 901 N Post Rd Indianapolis IN 46219

BLOEDE, MERLE HUIE (MRS. VICTOR G. BLOEDE III), club woman; b. Brady, Tex., May 4, 1921; d. Hulon William and Anna (Lohn) Huie; student San Angelo Bus. Coll., 1944; m. Victor G. Bloede III, Mar. 11, 1945; children—Dee Anna Smith (Mrs. Gene Donald Bratton), Victor G. IV, Susan Lohn. Asst. supr. Office Censorship, San Antonio, 1942-43. Patroness North Shore Hosp., Manhasset, N.Y., 1954-56, 67-68; vol. Waldorf Sch. Scholarship Fund, Garden City, N.Y., 1957; mem. art com. Meml. Sloane-Kettering Cancer Center, N.Y.C. Mem. North Shore So. Soc. (pres. 1963-65). Republican. Presbyn. Clubs: Coral Beach and Tennis (Bermuda); Sands Point Bath and Tennis, Sands Point Golf (Sands Point, N.Y.); Flower Hill Garden (chmn. community service com. 1967); Manhasset Bay Yacht. Home: 440 E 56th St New York City NY 10022 also 160 Bayview Rd Plandome Manor NY 11030

BLOMBERG, MILDRED MCKIBBEN (MRS. CHARLES R. BLOMBERG), ednl. adminstr.; b. Dove Creek, Colo., Aug. 16, 1919; d. Ivan S. and Hedrick Cecilia (Carlson) McKibben; student U. Denver, 1937-41; m. Charles R. Blomberg, July 6, 1941;children—Karen (Mrs. Herbert Jahncke, Jr.), Marcia Christine, Charles Martin. Sec. Retail Credit Men's Assn., 1937-41; sec. Trinity Episcopal Sch., 1960-72. Mem. Orleans Parish Sch. Bd., 1969—, v.p., 1972, pres., 1973; past La. rep. Nat. Com. Support Pub. Schs. Bd. dirs. League of Women Voters of La., 1955-57, edn. chmn., 1962-68; bd. dirs. League of Women Voters of New Orleans, from 1958; bd. dirs. Operation Upgrade, also tchr. Mem. Phi Chi Theta, Sigma Kappa. Episcopalian. Home: 2420 Prancer St New Orleans LA 70114 Office: 703 Carondelet St New Orleans LA 70130

BLOMO, CHRISTINE JOHNSON (MRS. JAMES HARRY BLOMO), precision products co. exec.; b. Pasadena, Cal., Sept. 13, 1916; d. Albert John and Mabel (Francis) Johnson; grad. high sch.; m. James Harry Blomo, Aug. 7, 1937; children—Donald J., Linda Jean (Mrs. Dale R. Hersh), Patricia Harrison. Legal sec. Judge John J. Craig, Los Angeles, 1935-38; sec.-treas. King Precision Products Corp., Montebello, Cal., 1953—. Active Girl Scouts, 1950-55. Clubs: Bahia Corinthian Yacht (Corona Del Mar, Cal.); Porsche Owners, Porsche of Am. Home: 1323 W Bay Av Newport Beach CA 92660 Office: 1024 S Vail Av Montebello CA 90640

BLOMQUIST, JANE MARGARET, advt. and art cons.; b. Phila., Aug. 20, 1943; s. Frank Ernest and Willamay Jane (Moore) Blomquist; ed. Phila. Coll. Art, Charles Morris Price Sch. Advt. and Journalism, Samuel Fleisher Sch. Art. Formerly various positions advt. and pub. relations firms, Phila.; advt. sales mgr. Thursday's Drummer, 1971-72; operator art and advt. cons. firm, N.Y.C., 1973—, art cons. Manhattan Life Ins. Corp. Ward leader congl. campaign, Phila., 1971-72; art dir. McGovern presdl. campaign Pa., 1972; mem. Phila. Ref. Democrats. Mem. Museum Modern Art, Phila. Mus. Art, Nat. Geog. Soc., Center City Residents Assn. Address: 42 W 13th St New York City NY 10011

BLONDELL, JOAN, actress; b. N.Y.C., Aug. 30, 1912. Appeared on Broadway in Tarnish, Trial of Mary Dugan; appeared in 97 motion pictures including: Three on a Match, Gold Diggers, East Side of Heaven, Two Girls on Broadway, Model Wife, Three Girls About Town, Lady for a Night, Corpse Came C.O.D., Christmas Eve, Nightmare Alley, For Heaven's Sake, Blue Veil (Oscar nomination), Opposite Sex, Desk Set, This Could Be The Night, The Cincinnati Kid, A Tree Grows in Bklyn., Waterhole No. 3, Stay Away, Joe; numerous TV appearances including Studio One, Playhouse 90, Hallmark Hall of Fame, G.E. Theater, Carroll O'Connor Spl., others; appeared in TV series Here Comes the Brides, Love Am. Style, Medical Center, Dick Van Dyke Show, Rookies, Banyon; road company appearances in Come Back Little Sheba, Happy Birthday, The Dark at the Top of the Stairs, Time of the Cuckoo, Bye-Bye Birdie, Gamma Rays on the Moon Marigolds. Author: (novel) Center Door Fancy, 1972. Address: care Flora Marks 1416 Havenhurst Dr Los Angeles CA 90046

BLOOM, CLAIRE, actress; b. London, Eng., Feb. 15; d. Edward Max and Elizabeth (Grew) Blume; student Badminton Sch., Bristol, Eng., Fern Hill Manor, New Milton, Eng.; pub. schs., Fla., N.Y.; 1 dau., Anna. Appeared as Ophelia, Stratford-Upon-Avon, 1948; plays include Lady's Not for Burning, Ring Around the Moon, London, 1949-51; in Romeo and Juliet, others, for Old Vic, also as Juliet in Old Vic tour of U.S.; film roles in Limelight, Man Between, Richard III, Alexander the Great, Brothers Karamazov, Buccaneer, Look Back in Anger, Three Steps to Freedom, 1960; The Brothers Grimm, The Chapman Report, The Haunting, 1962; 80,000 Suspects, 1963, Alta Infidelita, 1963, Il Maestro de Vigevana, 1963, The Outrange, 1964; appeared Broadway in Rashomon, 1959, at Royal Court Theatre, London, in Altona, 1960. Address: care Ashley-Steiner 579 Fifth St New York City NY 10017

BLOOM, EVELYN MAE DEUTSCH, editor; b. Detroit, July 6, 1917; d. Simon and Cecilia (Borg) Deutsch; student St. Mary's, Notre Dame, 1931-35, U. Wis., 1935-37, Ohio State U., 1958-59, 63-64; m. Howard A. Bloom, Jan. 3, 1939; children—Gary S., Phillip Jeffrey, Cecilia Dee. Founder, exec. dir. Columbus (O.) Jr. Theatre of Arts, 1963-65, bd. dirs., mem. adv. staff, 1964—; asst. continuity dir. WBNS Radio, Columbus, 1959-63; publicity dir. WLWC TV, Columbus, 1964-66; continuity dir. WBNS Radio, Columbus, 1966-67; promotion mgr. WTVN-TV, Columbus, 1967-70; dir. pub. relations, pub. information Central Ohio Heart Assn., Columbus, 1970-72; editor Fine Print, dir. closed circuit TV programming, script writer Motorists Ins., Columbus, 1972—. Mem. Columbus Arts Council, 1966-71; Columbus Gallery Fine Arts, 1963—. Publicity dir. Save the Ohio Theatre. com., 1969-71. Mem. Columbus Advt. Fedn., Broadcasters Promotion Assn. (mem. com. 1967-70), Nat. Acad. TV Arts and Scis. (chpt. pres. 1964-71), Am. Women in Radio and TV, Press Club Ohio. Presbyn. Writer, producer Who's Horace (mus. prodn. for children), 1970. Home: 184 S Stanwood Rd Columbus OH 43209

BLOOM, LILLIAN DORIS (MRS. EDWARD A. BLOOM), educator; b. N.Y.C., July 20, 1920; d. Benjamin A. and Frances (Eisenberg) Blumberg; B.A., N.Y. U., 1941, M.A., 1942; Ph.D., Yale, 1946; m. Edward A. Bloom, June 17, 1947. Instr. English, U. Ill., 1945-46, Queens Coll., 1946-47; asst. prof., U. R.I., 1947-50; mem. faculty R. I. Coll., 1956—, prof. English, 1964—. Am. Council Learned Socs. grantee, 1967. Mem. Am. Assn. U. Profs., Modern Lang. Assn., Phi Beta Kappa. Author: Willa Cather's Gift of Sympathy, 1962; The Variety of Fiction, 1968; Addison's Sociable Animal, 1972. Co-editor: Fanny Burney's Camilla, 1972; The Journals and Letters of Fanny Burney (Mme. D'Arblay), 1974. Home: 82 Laurel Av Providence RI 02906

BLUE, JANET L. ROBERTS (MRS. SHERWOOD BLUE), lawyer; b. Hamilton, O., June 21, 1933; d. Sam G. and Jessie (Weybright) Roberts; A.B., Ind. U., 1954, J.D., LL.B., 1957; m. Sherwood Blue, Apr. 9, 1961. Admitted to Ind. bar, 1957; practiced in Indpls., 1957—; mem. firm Sherwood Blue, 1957-63; partner Blue & Roberts, 1964—; mem. staff Appellate Ct. of Ind., 1967—, commr.-adminstr. 1970-72; commr., adminstr. Ct. of Appeals, 1972—. Mem. Meth. Hosp. Vols. Corps, 1963—, Indpls. Symphonic Choir, Indpls. Matinee Musicale. Fellow Meth. Hosp. Found.; mem. Internat., Am., Ind., Indpls. bar assns., Indpls. Legal Aid Soc., Indpls. Lawyers Assn., Am. Judicature Soc., Art Assn. Indpls., Meth. Hosp. White Cross Guild, Ind. U. Sch. Law Alumni Assn. Republican. Methodist. Clubs: Indianapolis Athletic, Athenaeum Turners, Riviera, Indianapolis Press. Home: 1460 E 77th St Indianapolis IN 46240 Office: Ill Bldg Indianapolis IN 46204

BLUE, JOAN RUINE, assn. ofcl., b. Columbus, O., June 21, 1925; d. George Edward and Florence Nell (Patterson) Ruine; B.A., Ohio State U., 1947; M.A., Georgetown U., 1950; m. William Lacy Blue, Oct. 16, 1954. With State Dept., Washington, 1949-54; v.p. Am. Horse Protection Assn., Great Falls, Va., 1969—. Mem. Kappa Kappa Gamma. Club: City Tavern (Washington). Home: 3316 N St NW Washington DC 20007 Office: 629 River Bend Rd Great Falls VA 22066

BLUE, ROSE, author, educator; b. N.Y.C., Dec. 3, 1931; d. Irving and Frieda (Rosenberg) Bluestone; B.A., Bklyn. Coll., 1953; postgrad. Bank St. Coll. Edn., 1967. Tchr., N.Y.C. pub. schs., 1955—. Mem. Authors' Guild Am., Authors' League Am., MENSA, Profl. Women's Caucus, Broadcast Music, Inc. Author: A Quiet Place, 1969, Black, Black Beautiful Black, 1969, How Many Blocks in The World, 1970, Bed-Stuy Beat, 1970, I Am Here (Yo Estoy Aqui), 1971; A Month of Sundays, 1972; Grandma Didn't Wave Back, 1972; Nikki 108, 1973; We Are Chicano, 1973. Lyricist: Drama of Love, 1964, Let's Face It, 1961, My Heartstrings Keep Me Tied To You, 1963, Give Me A Break, 1962, Homecoming Party, 1966. Home and office: 1320 51st St Brooklyn NY 11219

BLUESTEIN, CLAIRE KRAIMAN (MRS. BERNARD R. BLUESTEIN), chemist; b. Phila., May 3, 1926; d. Louis A. and Bessie (Millstein) Kraiman; A.B., U. Pa., 1947; M.S. (univ. fellow, U.S. Rubber Res. fellow), U. Ill., 1948, Ph.D., 1950; m. Bernard R. Bluestein, June 22, 1947; children—Rhona C., Sherrie L., Hazel M., Carol J. Instr. chemistry Pa. State U. Extension Service, 1958-59; sr. research chemist Sonneborn Chem. & Refining Corp., Petrolia, Pa., 1959-62; mgr. research and devel. dept. Witco Chem. Corp., Oakland, N.J., 1962—. Postdoctoral fellow Purdue U., 1951-52. Mem. Am. Chem. Soc., Am. Inst. Chemists, Phi Beta Kappa, Sigma Xi. Contbr. chpts. to Ency. of Polymer Sci. and Tech., 1968, Anionics Surfactants, 1974. Contbr. articles to profl. jours. Patentee in field. Home: 358 Dunham Pl Glen Rock NJ 07452 Office: 100 Bauer Dr Oakland NJ 07436

BLUESTEIN, JUDITH ANN, diversified industry exec.; b. Cin., Apr. 2, 1948; d. Paul Harold and Joan Ruth (Straus) Bluestein; B.A., U. Pa., 1969; postgrad. Am. Sch. Classical Studies, Athens, Greece, 1968, Vergilian Soc., Italy, 1970, Hebrew Union Coll. Jewish Inst. Religion, Jerusalem, 1971; M.A. in Religion (Univ. fellow), Case Western Res. U., 1973, M.A. in Latin, 1973. Sec., Paul H. Bluestein & Co., Cin., 1964—; v.p. Panel Machine Co., 1966—, Blujay Corp., 1966—, Ermet Products Corp., 1966—; partner Companhia Engenheiros Industrial Bluestein do Brasil, Cin., 1971—; tchr. Latin, Cin. Pub. Schs., 1973—. Mem. Soc. Hist. Archaeology, Soc. Post Medieval Archaeology, Archeol. Inst. Am., Classical Assn. Middle West and South, Am. Classical League, Ohio Classical Conf., Vergilian Soc., Soc. Bibl. Lit., Cin. Assn. Tchrs. Classics, Am. Philol. Assn., Philo. Inst., Ohio Edn. Assn., Cin. Tchrs. Assn. Address: 3420 Section Rd Cincinnati OH 45237

BLUESTEIN, VENUS WELLER, psychologist; b. Milw., July 16, 1933; d. Richard T. and Hazel (Beard) Weller; B.S., U. Cin., 1956, M.Ed., 1959, Ed.D., 1966; m. Marvin Bluestein, Mar. 7, 1954. Psychologist in tng. Longview State Hosp., Cin., 1956-58; sch. psychologist Cin. Pub. Schs., 1958-65; asst. prof. psychology U. Cin., 1965-70, asso. prof., 1970—; coordinator sch. psychology program, 1965-70, co-coordinator, 1970—; cons. child psychologist. Sec., U.S. exec. com. research Children's Internat. Summer Villages, 1964-68; chmn. Ohio Interuniv. Council on Sch. Psychology, 1967-68. Diplomate Am. Bd. Examiners in Profl. Psychology. Mem. Am., Cin. (sec. 1961-62), Ohio (editor Ohio Psychologist 1961-68, recipient of Distinguished Service award 1968) psychol. assns., Sch. Psychologists Ohio, Am. Assn. Univ. Profs., Am. Mental Health Assn., Nat. Assn. Sch. Psychologists. Contbr. articles to profl. pubs. Co-editor Ohio Psychologist. Home: 1049 Newcastle Dr Cincinnati OH 45231

BLUITT, JULIANN STEPHANIE (MRS. ROSCOE C. FOSTER, JR.), ednl. adminstr.; b. Washington, June 14, 1938; d. Stephen Bernard and Marion Eugene (Hughes) Bluitt; B.S. (LaVerne Noyes Found. fellow), Howard U., 1958, D.D.S., 1962; m. Roscoe C. Foster, Jr. Clin. instr. Dept. Oral Medicine, Howard U., 1962-63; dentist Chgo. Bd. Health, 1964-67; supr. dept. dental hygiene Northwestern U. Dental Sch., Chgo., 1967-70, asst. dean aux. and community programs, 1970; now asso. dean. Cons. FDA, 1971-72. Bd. dirs. Johnson Rehab. Home, Harvey Pre-Sch. for Exceptional Children. Recipient Louise Ball award, 1962, citation Chgo. Bd. Health, 1971, Great Guy award Sta. WGRT, 1968. Mem. Am. Assn. Dental Schs., Nat., Am. dental assns., Am. Assn. U. Profs., Am. Soc. Preventive Dentistry, Fedn. Dentaire Internat. Club: Coiterie (Chgo.). Author: Hector and Timmy Coloring Book, 1971. Contbr. articles to profl. pubs. Home: 4747 S Kenwood Av Chicago IL 60615 Office: Northwestern University Dental School 311 E Chicago Av Chicago IL 60611

BLUM, ETHEL WIDLUS (MRS. MILTON R. BLUM), editor; b. Cleve., Aug. 16, 1921; d. Abe and Minnie (Cherlin) Widlus; student Ohio State U., 1942; m. Milton R. Blum, Feb. 23, 1942; children—Carol Gould, Jeffrey, Roger. Editor, Gen. MacArthur's staff, Japan, 1947-50; free lance writer, 1950—; travel editor, women's editor Miami Beach (Fla.) Daily Sun, 1964-69; radio commentator Talking About Traveling, WKAT, Miami; editor Travel Publs., Inc., 1970—; editor, author Travel Guides, 1970—; asso. editor Miami Beach (Fla.) Daily Sun, 1969-71; travel editor Miami Mag. and Gold Coast Pictorial, 1972—; bur. chief Travel Agt. mag., 1972—; editor Cruise Guides, 1971—; syndicated columnist, 1974—. Pres., Cancer Inst. Miami. Mem. Dade County Democratic Exec. Com., 1972—. Recipient Fla. Press Womens awards for feature writing, for best series articles written by woman in Fla., best newspaper photography, 1966, 67, 68. Mem. Fla. Press Womens Assn., Soc. Am. Travel Writers (chmn. Southeastern U.S.-Caribbean chpt.). Home: Apt 10B 5838 Collins Av Miami Beach FL 33140 Office: One Lincoln Rd #222 Miami Beach FL 33139

BLUM, LUCILE JACOBY (MRS. EDWIN H. BLUM), civic worker; b. New Orleans, Jan. 5, 1904; d. Martin and Henrietta (Landauer) Jacoby; B.A., Tulane U., 1936; L.H.D., La. State U., 1973; m. Edwin Henry Blum, Nov. 27, 1923, (dec. June 1952); 1 dau., Margaret (Mrs. Joseph H. Epstein, Jr.). Cotton planter, Newellton, La., 1935—. Founder, pres. La. Council for Music and Performing Arts, Inc., 1965—; hon. pres. Women's Guild, New Orleans Opera House Assn., 1963—; La. chmn. Friends of John F. Kennedy Center for Performing Arts, Washington, 1967—; hon. chmn. Lucile J. Blum Opera Library 1963—; mem. exec. com. 250th Anniversary Founding of New Orleans, 1967—; mem. meml. selection com. La. Ednl. Hall of Fame, 1967—; mem. Task Force for Preservation and Promotion of Quality Education in Louisiana, 1970—; charter mem. adv. council Coll. Music, Loyola U. Gulf Coast regional dir. Central Opera Service; mem. council Met. Opera. Bd. founders Repertory Theatre, New Orleans; bd. dirs. New Orleans Opera House Assn., Fgn. Relations Assn. New Orleans, women's com. New Orleans Philharmonic Symphony Soc., Friends of New Orleans Pub. Library, English Speaking Union New Orleans; hon. mem. La. assn. Future Music Leaders Am. Decorated Knight Order of Leopold II (Belgium); named Outstanding Humanitarian of Year, Acadian Dairy Industry, 1972. Address: 7524 St Charles Av New Orleans LA 70118

BLUM, REBECCA ANNE MULHOLLAND (MRS. DAVID NORMAN BLUM), food editor; b. Indpls., Feb. 10, 1944; d. Ramon Alfred and Ruthe Joanna (Felkins) Mulholland; B.S., Bradley U., 1965; m. David Norman Blum, Feb. 6, 1965. Home service rep. Peoples Gas Light & Coke Co., Chgo., 1965-66; asst. food editor Chgo. Sun-Times, 1966-68; account exec. Pub. Relations Bd., Chgo., 1968-70; home economist Jewel Food Stores, Melrose, Park, Ill., 1970-73; food editor Knoxville (Tenn.) mag., 1973—. Cons. Mogen David Wine Corp., Chgo., 1970—, Super Dollar Markets, Greeneville, Tenn., 1973—. Chmn. pub. relations Mental Health Assn. Knox County, 1973. Mem. Am. Assn. U. Women, Am., Tenn. home econs. assns., E. Tenn. Home Economists in Bus. Home: 614 Blows Ferry Rd Knoxville TN 37919

BLUM, ROSALIND F., psychologist; b. N.Y.C., Mar. 30, 1910; d. Charles B. and Jennie (Prince) Blum; B.S., Tchrs. Coll., Columbia, 1940, M.A., 1943; m. Saul T. Schulman, Oct. 16, 1934 (dec. Nov. 1959); children—Donald, Susan. Dir. Psychol. Testing Center, N.Y.C., 1941—; instr. Tchrs. Coll. Columbia, N.Y.C., 1942-58, asso. guidance lab., 1933-41. Cons. psychologist to several pvt. schs. in N.Y.C., 1941—. Chmn. Day Sch. Com. of Rodeph Sholom Day Sch., N.Y.C., 1970—. Diplomate in sch. psychology Am. Bd. Profl. Psychology. Mem. Am., N.Y. State psychol. assns., Am. Personnel and Guidance Assn., N.Y.C. Soc. of Clin. Psychologists, Kappa Delta Pi, Pi Lambda Theta. Address: 40 West 86th St New York City NY 10024

BLUMBERG, BARBARA SALMANSON (MRS. ARNOLD G. BLUMBERG), civic worker; b. Bklyn., Oct. 2, 1927; d. Sam and Mollie (Greenberg) Salmanson; B.A., DePauw U., 1948; postgrad. New Sch. for Social Reserach, N.Y.C.; m. Arnold G. Blumberg, June 19, 1949; children—Florence Ellen (Mrs. Schwartz), Martin Jay, Emily Anne. Pub. relations Nate Fein & Co., N.Y.C., 1948-51; free lance, 1960—. Pres., UN Assn. Great Neck, N.Y., 1967—, chmn. China Study Workshop, 1966-67; leader Fertile Crescent Study Group; pres. Shalom chpt. Hadassah, 1955-57; exec. v.p. Lakeville P.T.A., Great Neck, 1963-65; exec. v.p. Great Neck South Jr. High Sch., 1965-66; co-chmn. Great Neck com. for UNICEF. Area co-chmn. Nassau County McGovern for Pres., 1972; v.p. Reform Democratic Assn. of Gt. Neck; bd. dirs. New Dem. Coalition of Nassau; Dem. candidate for North Hempstead Town Council. Bd. dirs. Citizen's Sch. Com., Great Neck. Mem. N.Y. Alumni Club DePauw U. (trustee), North Shore Archael. Soc., Alpha Lambda Delta, Theta Sigma Phi. Club: Glen Oaks. Home: 12 Birch Hill Rd Great Neck NY 11020

BLUMBERG, BEATRICE (MRS. HERMAN BLUMBERG), retail trade exec., motel exec.; b. N.Y.C., Oct. 15, 1910; d. Morris Gabrial and Marie (Schein) Rosenberg; B.A., Fla. State U., 1931; m. Herman Blumberg, Jan. 17, 1933; children—H. Leslie, Beverly (Mrs. S.M. Erdreich, Jr.). Partner, exec. mgr. Quality Inn Carousel, Dothan, Ala., 1969—; partner Antique Corner, Dothan, 1967—. Chmn. Concert Assn., Dothan, 1950-52; publicity chmn. Red Cross dr., 1945-46; chmn. steering com., univ. center U. Ala., Dothan, 1955-58. Named Woman of Year, Bus. and Profl. Women's Club, 1955. Mem. Nat. Assn. Antique Dealers, Univ. Women Assn. (pres. 1960-62). Clubs: Cherokee Garden, Fine Arts. Home: 308 West Woodland Dr Dothan AL 36305 Office: Quality Inn Carousel 231 North and Ross Clark Circle PO Box 1405 Dothan AL 36301

BLUMBERG, JANE W. (MRS. ROLAND K. BLUMBERG), banker, ind. oil producer, mem. Democratic Nat. Com.; b. Sequin, Tex., Sept. 24, 1917; d. Hilmar Herman and Hilda (Blumberg) Weinert; B.A., U. Tex., 1937; M.A., Northwestern U., 1938; m. Roland K. Blumberg, Apr. 20, 1940; children—Carla Ann, Hilmar Daniel, Edward Austin. Chmn. bd., dir. Seguin State Bank & Trust Co. Sec., Seguin Sch. Bd., 1957-65; mem. Tex. Hosp. Adv. Commn., 1960-64; dir. Seguin United Fund, 1959, 67—; bd. regents Tex. Lutheran Coll., 1965—. Mem. Dem. Nat. Com. from Tex. Mem. Phi Beta Kappa, Kappa Kappa Gamma. Democrat. Lutheran. Club: Seguin Shakespeare. Home: RFD 2 Box 236 Sequin TX 78155 Office: PO Drawer 231 Seguin TX 78155

BLUMBERG, JULIA BAUM (MRS. LEO BLUMBERG), club woman; b. Hazelton, Pa.; d. Benjamin and Ida Ruth (Lurie) Baum; Ph.B. summa cum laude, Muhlenberg Coll., Allentown, Pa., 1937; grad. student N.Y.U., Columbia; m. Dr. Leo Blumberg, Aug. 9, 1938. Mem. faculty Bethleham (Pa.) Sr. High Sch., dir. placement coml. grads., 1938-46. Organizer B'nai B'rith Women, Bethlehem, 1938; pres. Bethlehem, 1938-39, pres. Dist. 3, 1945-46, mem. nat. exec. bd., 1957-59, rep. nat. orgn. 1957-59, chmn. nat. vocational guidance, 1957-59, chmn. dist. 3 Klutznick scholarship award, 1966-69, mem. bd. B'nai B'rith Women of Wilmington, pres. vocational service bd., 1962-64; mem. bd. Temple Beth Emeth Sisterhood, 1949-59, 70-74; treas. Dist 8, Nat. Fedn. Temple Sisterhoods, 1952-56; mem. exec. bd. nat. fedn., 1953-57; gen. chmn. Dist. 8 conv., Wilmington, 1957; mem. bd. Wilmington City Fedn. Women's Clubs and Allied Orgns., 1951—, 1st v.p., 1961-63, pres., 1963-65; mem. bd. mgrs. Florence Crittendon Home of Del., 1955-61; mem. Women's div. Brandeis U.; mem. aux. Kutz Home for Aged, also bd. dirs. aux., v.p., 1972-74; mem. Nat. Commn. Vocational Service, 1957-59, Recreation, Promotion and Service, Inc., Mayor's Com. for Christmas, Mayor's Com. for UN; mem. bd. UNICEF, 1972—; mem. steering com. CARE, Inc., 1971—; mem. Del. Nature Edn. Center, Inc., Del. Council on Crime and Justice; bd. dirs. Hillel Found. Bldg. Fund Corp. Pa., chmn. bldg. and furniture com., dedication com. Hillel Found. at

U. Del., 1963-64; mem. women's div. Jewish Fedn. Del.; mem. bldg. fund com. St. Francis Hosp., 1973. Mem. Nat. Council Jewish Women, Greater Wilmington Fedn. Women's Orgns. (dir. 1965-69, 69-73, pres. Past Officers Club 1965-67, historian 1973-75), Del. Mental Health Assn., Crippled Children and Adults Soc. Del., Phi Sigma Iota. Jewish religion (pres. Sisterhood 1952-53, mem. bd. 1971—, dir. temple 1952-55). Mem. Hadassah. Club: New Century (dir., program com. 1955-64, chmn. admissions com. 1968-70). Home: 4 E 14th St Wilmington DE 19801

BLUME, LOIS BETH WEINBERG (MRS. ARNOLD BLUME), univ. ofcl.; b. N.Y.C., Mar. 25, 1930; d. Louis B. and Beatrice (Fishel) Weinberg; B.A. with honors in Polit. Sci., Hunter Coll., 1951, M.A. in Polit. Sci., 1966; m. Arnold Blume, Apr. 10, 1949; children—Michael Harris, Judith Allison. Research aide Fair Campaign Practices Com., N.Y.C., 1959-60; intern Nat. Center Edn. in Politics, 1962; research analyst Office of County Exec., Nassau County, Mineola, N.Y., 1962-66, fed. and state aid coordinator, 1966-70; exec. dir. Nassau County Drug Abuse and Addiction Commn., 1970-71; dir. Center for Bus. and Urban Research, Hofstra U., Hempstead, N.Y., 1971-72; dean continuing edn. Adelphi U., Garden City, N.Y., 1972-74; prof. urban affairs, dir. program devel. for N.Y.C. affairs New Sch. for Social Research, N.Y.C., 1974—. Former cons. Nat. Assn. Counties, Arden Hill Hosp., Goshen, N.Y., Nat. League Cities, Catholic Charities. Former mem. Manpower Task Force, Nassau County Econ. Opportunity Commn. Mem. Women's Polit. Caucus North Shore. Bd. dirs. Big Bros. Assn. Nassau County, Nassau County, Council Univ. Insts. Urban Affairs; mem. citizens adv. com. Roslyn Urban Renewal Assn., 1968—, Nassau County Crime Council, 1968-70, Nassau County Area Manpower Planning Council, 1968-71. Mem. Nat. Assn. County Devel. Coordinators (pres. 1968-69, dir. L.I. chpt.), Am. Soc. Pub. Adminstrn. (pres. elect), Regional Plan Assn., Hunter Coll. Alumni Assn., Women's Task Force, Am. Jewish Com., Phi Beta Kappa. Contbr. articles to profl. jours. Home: 850 Bryant Av Roslyn Harbor NY 11576

BLUMENTHAL, MONICA DAVID (MRS. FRANK S. BLUMENTHAL), physician; b. Tubingen, Germany, Sept. 1, 1930 (came to U.S. 1936, naturalized 1949); d. Hans Theodore and Frances (Heidenhain) David; B.A. with honors and distinction, U. Mich., 1952, M.S., 1953, M.D., 1957; Ph.D., U. Cal. at Berkeley, 1962; m. Frank S. Blumenthal, June 6, 1954; children—Martin Benno, Holly Patricia. Intern San Francisco Gen. Hosp., 1957-58; resident psychiatry U. Mich. Med. Center, 1963-66; research asst. U. Mich. Lab. and Vertebrate Biology, 1952, dept. physiology, 1953, dept. zoology, 1953, dept. pharmacology, 1954-55, asso. research clin. biochemist, schizophrenia and psychopharmacology project, 1962, asst. research scientist mental health research inst., 1963—, instr. psychiatry, 1965-66, asst. prof., 1967-71, asso. prof., 1971—, research asso. Inst. Social Research, 1969-71, program dir., 1971—. Cons. to Washtenaw Community Mental Health Center, Ann Arbor, Mich., 1968-69; mem. subcom. police tng. Mayor's Ad Hoc Com. on Police Community Relations, Ann Arbor, 1969; staff cons. Mass Media Task Force, Pres.'s Violence Commn., 1969; cons. psychiatry tng. br. Nat. Insts. Mental Health, 1971; mem. NRC, 1973—. Fellow Nat. Inst. Mental Health, 1959-62, research grantee, 1964-66, grantee, 1971-73, career investigator devel. award, 1962-68; NSF research grantee, 1969-71, 71-73. Mem. A.A.A.S., Women's Research Club (faculty curriculum com. 1968-69), Am. Psychiat. Assn. (research award 1972), Soc. Biol. Psychiatry, Am. Assn. U. Profs., Phi Beta Kappa, Sigma Xi, Alpha Epsilon Iota. Co-author: Justifying Violence Attitude of American Men. Contbr. articles to profl. pubs. Home: 4231 Shetland Dr Ann Arbor MI 48104 Office: 4009 Institute for Social Research Ann Arbor MI 48106

BLUMERFIELD, CELIA FOWLER (MRS. MICHAEL BLUMERFIELD), lawyer; b. Chelsea, Mass., Aug. 12, 1900; d. Morris and Lena (Seltzer) Fowler; J.D., Portia Law Sch., 1937, LL.M., 1939; m. Michael Blumerfield, June 15, 1921; 1 dau., Paula B. (Mrs. Robert H. Roberts). Admitted to Mass. bar, 1939, U.S. Supreme Ct., 1958; mem. draft bd. Home Service A.R.C., Everett, Mass., 1920, with legal dept., 1919-25; legal dir. land lease program United Ship Bldg. Corp., East Boston, Mass., 1937-45; practice law, Boston, 1939—; Mass. Land Ct., 1958—. Mem. ladies com. New England Med. Center, Boston, 1940—. Mem. Nat. Assn. Women Lawyers, Mass. Bar Assn. (del. 1965, pres. 1965-66), Internat. Women Lawyers. Home and office: 20 Hammond Pond Pkwy Chestnut Hill MA 02167

BLUNT, SARA CONRAD, civic and community worker; b. Detroit, July 10, 1942; d. Winthrop Brown and Dolores Joan (Millard) Conrad; A.A., Pine Manor Jr. Coll., 1962; certificate N.Y. Sch. Interior Design, 1963-64; m. William Williams Blunt, Jr., Sept. 8, 1962; children—Dorsey Conrad, William Winthrop. Propr. Sara C. Blunt Interior Design, N.Y.C., also Washington, 1965—. Mem. Com. 100 on the Fed. City, Washington, 1972—; mem. spl. events com. Fresh Air Fund, N.Y.C., 1968-69; mem. exec. com. for benefits Northwest Settlement House, Washington, 1971-73; mem. scholarship benefit com. Potomac Sch., McLean, Va., 1974. Trustee Citizens Assn. Georgetown, 1972—, West Side Day Nursery, N.Y.C., 1966—. Mem. N.Y. Jr. League. Republican. Episcopalian. Address: 3200 P St NW Washington DC 20007

BLUST, MARIAN ALMGREN, osteo. physician; b. Stark County, Ill., June 9, 1910; d. Carl George and Louella May (Williams) Almgren; D.O., Kirksville Coll. Osteopathy and Surgery, 1932; m. James Francis Blust, Aug. 6, 1936; children—Larry David, Sally (Mrs. Charles Busenhart, Jr.). Practice osteo. medicine, LaFayette, Ill., 1933-35, Galva, Ill., 1935—. Mem. Am. Osteo. Assn., Order Eastern Star. Methodist. Address: 415 NW 2nd St Galva IL 61434

BLYTHE, PEGGY JANE, physician; b. Pitts., Oct. 9, 1919; d. Shanor Reese and Edith (Robison) Blythe; B.S., Westminster Coll., 1941; M.D., U. Pitts., 1944. Intern, Pitts. U. Hosp. Med. Center, 1944-45; chief resident Presbyn. and Women's Hosp., chief resident internal medicine, 1945-46; sch. physician, Charleroi, Pa., 1948-52, gen. practice and allergy, 1946—; clin. instr. U. Pitts. Sch. Medicine, 1944-46, instr. dept. medicine-allergy and immunology clinic, 1946-64. Aviation med. examiner FAA, 1960—. Mem. A.M.A., Pa., Washington County med. socs., Charleroi Bus. and Profl. Women's Club (charter), Am. Med. Women's Assn., Am. Acad. Allergy, Pa. Allergy Soc., Pitts. Soc. Allergy, Alpha Gamma Delta. Mem. Order Eastern Star. Home: Locust St Craven Hill Charleroi PA 15022 Office: 539 Fallowfield Av Charleroi PA 15022

BOAGNI, ETHEL ELIZABETH HAAS (MRS. EDWARD MILLARD BOAGNI III), physician; b. Madisonville, La., May 17, 1933; d. Edward Rudolph and Ethel Eva (Ouilliber) Haas; B.S., La. State U., 1954, M.D., 1956; m. Edward Millard Boagni, III, July 7, 1962; children—Thomas Jonathan, Nancy Ann, Robert Edward, Mary Elizabeth. Intern, Touro Infirmary, New Orleans, 1956-57; resident Ochsner Clinic, New Orleans, 1957-59, mem. staff, 1959-64; practice medicine specializing in anesthesiology, Baton Rouge, 1964-71; mem. La. State U. Med. Sch. staff Earl Long Hosp., 1971—. Bd. dirs. Baton Rouge Found. for Hist. La., 1967-71. Mem. A.M.A., La., East Baton Rouge Parish med. socs., Am., La. socs. anesthesiologists, Baton Rouge Symphony Guild, Baton Rouge Art League, Guild La. Arts and Scis. Center, East Baton Rouge Parish Med. Aux., Alpha Chi Omega. Roman Catholic. Clubs: Passe Bon Temps, Bocage Racquet, Achilles Carnival Krewe (Baton Rouge). Home: 3156 McCarroll Dr Baton Rouge LA 70809 Office: Earl Long Hosp Baton Rouge LA 70810

BOAN, VURLYNE ELLSWORTH, nursing educator; b. Hillsboro, N.H.; d. James L. and Nellie E. (Whitcomb) Ellsworth; B.S., Ariz. State U., 1949, M.A., 1950, Ph.D., 1972; m. Bobby Marion Boan, Aug. 29, 1949. Dentist asst., 1935; staff nurse, head nurse Margaret Pillsbory Gen. Hosp., Concord, N.H., 1939-40; high sch. sci. tchr., 1950; head nurse St. Monica Hosp. and St. Joseph Hosp., Phoenix, 1951-52, Good Samaritan Hosp., Phoenix, 1951-73; with regional med. program U. Ariz., Phoenix, 1973—. Ednl. cons., spl. rep. Nat. League for Nursing. Chmn. exec. com. Ariz. Cancer Soc. Recipient Achievement Award, State Ariz., 1961. Served with nurses corp Army U.S., 1941-44. Mem. Bus. and Profl. Women's Club, Nat. Assn. Parliamentarians, Am. (occupational area rep.) Ariz. (conv. chmn. 1962, chmn. continuing edn. 1971—) nurses assns., Ariz. League Nursing (pres. 1959-61), Western Council State Leagues for Nursing (chmn. 1959-61), Am. Assn. U. Women, Am. Edn. Assn., Maricope Mental Health Assn., Kappa Delta Pi. Home: 837 W Thomas Rd Phoenix AZ 85013 Office: 4750 Central Av Phoenix AZ 85012

BOARDMAN, ELEANOR SUSAN PENNIMAN (MRS. JOHN K. BOARDMAN), editor; b. Enid, Okla.; d. William B. and Victoria (Fisher) Penniman; B.S., Ohio State U., 1927; m. John K. Boardman, Nov. 24, 1928; children—John K., William P. Radio editor Ohio State Jour., 1927-28; soc. editor Tri-Village Pub. Co., Columbus, O., 1948-52, news editor, 1956-68, exec. editor, 1968—. Bd. dirs. Instructive Dist. Nursing Assn., 1950-56, pres. bd., 1952-56. Recipient awards City Grandview Heights (O.), 1967, Upper Arlington (O.), 1963; Am. Press award Tri-village Jr. C. of C., 1966; Big Wheel award Upper Arlington Civic Assn., 1967; Outstanding Alumnae Achievement award Kappa Kappa Gamma, 1966. Mem. Theta Sigma Phi (pres. Columbus chpt. 1942-43), Kappa Kappa Gamma. Episcopalian (pres. of women 1957-58, mem. vestry 1963-65, chmn. fellowship commn. 1964-65). Home: Apt B-11 1631 Roxbury Rd Columbus OH 43212 Office: 1302 Grandview Av Columbus OH 43212

BOARDMAN, EUNICE LOUISE (MRS. DELMAR C. MESKE), educator; b. Cordova, Ill., Jan. 27, 1926; d. George Hollister and Anna Bryson (Feaster) Boardman; B. Music Edn., Cornell Coll., Mt. Vernon, Ia., 1947; M. Music Edn., Columbia, 1951; Ed.D., U. Ill., 1963; m. Delmar C. Meske, June 24, 1972. Tchr. vocal music Postville, Ia., 1947-51, Maquoketa, Ia., 1951-53; supr. elementary music Clinton (Ia.) Pub. Schs., 1953-54, Grinnell, Ia., 1952-55; instr. music edn. No. Ill. U., DeKalb, 1955-56; prof. music edn. Wichita (Kan.) State U., 1956-72; adj. prof. music edn. Ill. State U., Normal, 1972-74; prof. music edn. Roosevelt U., Chgo., 1974—. Del. Internat. Curriculum Conf., Oxford, Eng., 1968. Recipient CMP-Ford Found. grants, 1963, 64. Mem. Music Educators Nat. Conf. (mem. nat. commn. on instrn. 1970—), Mu Phi Epsilon. Co-author: Musical Growth in Elementary School, 1963-70, Exploring Music, 1966-71. Home: 6212 Kilkenny Dr Crystal Lake IL 60014 Office: Music Edn Dept Chicago Musical College Roosevelt University Chicago IL 60600

BOATNER, MAXINE TULL (MRS. EDMUND BURKE BOATNER), writer, lectr.; b. Kentwood, La., Feb. 23, 1903; d. James Porter and Mai (Bailey) Tull; B.A., Millsaps Coll., 1924; M.A., Gallaudet Coll., 1926, L.H.D., 1960; M.A., Yale, 1951, Ph.D., 1952; m. Edmund Burke Boatner, July 19, 1928; 1 dau., Emma Barbara. Tchr. pub. schs., Belzoni, Miss., 1925-26, Miss. Sch. for Deaf, Jackson, 1926-28; writer Cleve. Plain Dealer, Cleve. News, 1928-31; tchr. Kendall Sch. for Deaf, Washington, 1932-33, N.Y. Sch. for Deaf, N.Y.C., 1933-35, Am. Sch. for Deaf, Hartford, Conn., 1935-49; writer, lectr., 1935—. Project dir. V.R.A., Dept. Health, Edn., Welfare, 1962-66. Dir. Hartford Symphony Soc. Hartt Opera-Theater Guild U. Hartford, Mark Twain Library and Meml. Commn., Hartley-Salmon Child Guidance Clinic; mem. woman's bd. Hartford Sem. Found.; dir. Conn. Opera Guild. Dir. hist. research Conf. Execs. of Am. Schs. for the Deaf, hon. mem. Recipient Amelia Earhart Medal for Service to Humanity, N.Y. br. Am. Pen Women, 1960; Edward Allen Fay award Conf. Execs. Am. Schs. for Deaf Centennial, 1968.; named Woman of Year, Gallaudet Coll. Women's Recreation Com., 1970. Mem. Trinity Coll. Library Assos., Yale U. Library Assos., West Hartford League Women Voters, Am. Assn. U. Women (1st v.p. Greater Hartford), Nat. Soc. Arts and Letters, Nat. League Am. Pen Women (pres. Greater Hartford br.), Alumni assns. Millsaps Coll., Gallaudate Coll., Yale, Chi Delta Phi, Kappa Delta. Clubs: Town and County (Hartford), Pilot; Woman's Press (N.Y.C.). Author: Voice of the Deaf, A Biography of Edward Miner Gallaudet, 1959; Dictionary of Idioms for the Deaf, 1966; also articles in profl. mags. and book reviews in newspaper. Home: 2 Linbrook Rd Rd West Hartford CT 06107

BOAZ, RUTH LAVONNE, librarian; b. Water Valley, Ky., Mar. 27, 1926; d. Richard Murray and Eula Lee (Bennett) Boaz; B.S., Memphis State Coll., 1948; M.A., George Peabody Coll. for Tchrs., 1953; postgrad. Vanderbilt U., 1955-56. Asst. librarian Ill. Wesleyan U., Bloomington, 1953-54; librarian San Francisco State Coll., 1954-55; cataloger Meth. Pub. House, Nashville, 1956-59; dean women's staff Vanderbilt U., Nashville, 1959-60; circulation asst. Memphis Pub. Library, 1960-64; asst. librarian N.Y. State Edn. Dept., Albany, 1964-66, sr. library supr., 1966-68; edn. program specialist U.S. Office Edn., Washington, 1968-73; adult services specialist Ohio Valley Area Libraries, Wellston, O., 1973—. Mem. Am. Assn. U. Women, A.L.A., D.A.R. Contbr. articles to profl. publs. Home: 11 Oak St Jackson OH 45640 Office: 8 S Ohio St Wellston OH 45692

BOBEAR, JEAN BARRY, educator; b. Schenectady, N.Y.; d. William H. and May (Barry) Bobear; B.S., Coll. Saint Rose, 1948; M.S., Cornell U., 1954; Ph.D., U. Dublin, 1964 Engring. asst. Gen. Electric Co., Schenectady, 1948-53; asst. prof. State U. Coll., Brockport, N.Y., 1956-58, asso. prof., 1958-62; research student U. Dublin, Ireland, 1962-64; prof. State U. College, Brockport, N.Y., 1964—. State U. Faculty fellowship, 1967-68, Smithsonian Instn. Systematics Inst. participant. Mem. A.A.A.S., Am. Inst. Biol. Sci., Am. Soc. Plant Taxonomists, Bot. Soc. British Isles, Bot. Soc. Am., Internat. Assn. Plant Taxonomy. Author series documentary films on Bergen Swamp. Contbr. articles to profl. jours. Home: 28 Monroe Av Brockport NY 14420

BOBEN, MARIAN STEVENS, librarian; b. Kingston, Pa., June 27, 1941; d. Russell Alvin and Rosa (Healy) Stevens; student Mt. Holyoke Coll., 1959-60; B.A., U. Pa., 1963; M.L.S., Drexel Inst., 1967; m. William R.A. Boben, Jr., July 20, 1960; 1 son, William R.A. III. Librarian Wolfsohn Meml. Library, King of Prussia, Pa., 1967-70; head librarian Tredyffrin Pub. Library, Berwyn, Pa., 1970—. Home: 254 Old Eagle School Rd Strafford-Wayne PA 19087 Office: Tredyffrin Pub Library Box 576 Berwyn PA 19312

BOBER, PHYLLIS PRAY, coll. dean; b. Portland, Me., Dec. 2, 1920; d. Melvin Francis and Lea Arlene (Royer) Pray; B.A., Wellesley Coll., 1941; M.A., N.Y. U., 1943, Ph.D., 1946; m. Harry Bober, Aug. 11, 1943 (div. 1973); children—Jonathan Pray, David Hall. Instr. Wellesley (Mass.) Coll., 1947-49, lectr., curator of mus., 1951-54; instr. N.Y. U., 1949-50, adj. asso. prof., 1965-67, chmn. fine arts dept., 1967-73, prof., 1970-73; teaching asst. Sch. Architecture, Mass. Inst. Tech., Cambridge, 1951-53; dean Grad. Sch. Arts & Scis., Bryn Mawr (Pa.) Coll., 1973—. In charge research project Census of Antique works of Art Known to Renaissance Artists sponsored by Warburg Inst., U. London, 1949—; also jointly by Inst. Fine Arts, N.Y. U., 1954—. Fellow German Archeol. Inst. (corr.); mem. Internat. Assn. for Classical Archaeology, Archeol. Inst. Am., Renaissance Soc. Am., Coll. Art Assn. Am., N.Y. Mycological Soc. Author: Drawings After the Antique by Amico Aspertin, 1957. Home: 29 Simpson Rd Ardmore PA 19003 Office: Bryn Mawr College Bryn Mawr PA 19010

BOCK, D(OROTHY) JOLEEN WESSEL, librarian; b. Bennington, Kan., Sept. 30, 1925; d. Ralph Morgan and Helen (Leonard) Wessel; B.A., U. Denver, 1947, M.A., 1948; M.S. in L.S., U. So. Cal., 1963. Asst. coordinator tchr. in-service tng. program, instr. creative dramatics, extension div. U. Neb., Lincoln, 1952-55; cataloger Whittier (Cal.) Union High Sch., 1958-60; librarian Whittier High Sch., also instr. creative dramatics Whittier City Recreation Dept., 1960-63; dir. library services Rio Hondo Coll., Whittier, 1963-69; dir. instrnl. resources Coll. of Canyons, Valencia, Cal., 1969—. Mem. joint com. for jr. coll. libraries A.L.A.—Am. Assn. Jr. Colls., 1970-73; mem. adv. com. for library tech. asst. curriculum project U.S. Office Edn., 1971-72. Mem. A.L.A. (chmn. jr. coll. library sect. 1970-71), Am. Assn. Jr. Colls. (mem. adv. com. on microforms 1972). Contbr. articles to profl. jours. Home: 1306 Armacost St Los Angeles CA 90025 Office: 25000 W Valencia Blvd Valencia CA 91355

BOCK, JANE ANN HASKETT (MRS. CARL E. BOCK), educator; b. Rochester, Ind., Oct. 3, 1936; d. Carlton H. and Viola (Jones) Haskett; B.A., Duke, 1958; M.A., Ind. U., 1960; Ph.D., U. Cal. at Berkeley, 1966; m. Carl E. Bock, June 13, 1964. Asst. prof. biology dept. Cal. State Coll., Hayward, 1967-68; vis. lectr. U. Colo., Boulder, 1968-69, asst. prof. biology dept., 1969-73, asso. prof., 1973—. Mem. A.A.A.S., Brit. Ecol. Soc., Ecol. Soc. Am., Bot. Soc. Am., Am. Soc. Plant Taxonomists, Assn. for Tropical Biology, Bot. Soc. Brit. Isles, Sigma Xi, Phi Sigma. Contbr. articles to profl. jours. Home: 665 Northstar Ct Boulder CO 80302

BOCK, SADIE GWENDOLYN PATTERSON, newspaper editor, freelance writer; b. Dane, Wis.; d. Frank Walter and Elsie (Mahaney) Patterson; B.J., Newspaper Inst. Am. 1948; m. Wayne Sidney Padley, Jan. 30, 1918, (dec. Mar. 1960); children—Dorothy (Mrs Ralph Ullring), Wayne. Carol (Mrs Donald Manke), Donovan S., Howard E., Ireta (Mrs. Delbert Ryan), Richard A.; m. 2d, Walter E. Bock, May 10, 1963 (dec. 1969). Free-lance writer, 1930—; editor Lodi Enterprise, 1959-64, now weekly columnist; creator, writer column Sadie Cues, 1959—; columnist Portage Daily Register. Outreach supr. Community Action Program Central Wis. Office Econ. Opportunity. Active A.R.C.; publicity dir., sec. chpt., pub. relations dir. Columbus Community Chest, 1964-65; mem. adv. bd. Columbia County Social Services, Commn. of Aging. Mem. Columbia County, (v.p.), Wis. hist. socs., Lake Wisconsin C. of C. (sec., pub. relations 1959-65). Lutheran. Club: Columbus Women's Civic (past pres.). Author: Safari with Sadie, vol. 1, vol. 2. Address: 236 W James Columbus WI 53925

BODDIE, GRACE COLLINS, lawyer; b. Charlotte County, Va., Jan. 15, 1917; d. Flavius Overton and Grace Comfort (Crews) Collins; B.S. cum laude, Longwood Coll., 1943; J.D., Duke, 1951; m. Richard Franklin Boddie, Mar. 20, 1948; children—Mary (Mrs. Philip E. Dayvault), Needham James II. Elementary sch. tchr. and prin., Charlotte County, Va., 1935-43; admitted to N.C. bar, 1951; staff atty. Duke Legal Aid Clinic, 1951-53; controller, chief research support mgmt. U.S. Army Research Office, Durham, N.C., 1953-72; sr. contract adminstr. Research Triangle Inst., Research Triangle Park, N.C., 1972—. Served to lt. comdr. USNR, 1943-48. Recipient Meritorious Civilian Service award U.S. Army, 1964. Mem. Am. Bar Assn., N.C. State Bar. Home: 1101 Vickers Av Durham NC 27707 Office: Hanes Bldg Research Triangle Inst Research Triangle Park NC 27709

BODDY, MARGARET PEARSE, educator; b. Owen Sound, Ont., Can., Apr. 10, 1909; d. James Newton and Eva (Pearce) Boddy; B.A., U. Minn., 1931, M.A., 1932, Ph.D., 1935, Am. Assn. U. Women fellow, 1935-36. Asst. prof. Duchesne Coll., 1936-37, N.M. State Coll., 1937-39; instr. U. Mont., 1940; tchr. Winsor Sch., Boston, 1940-43; chmn. English dept. Kent Sch., Denver, 1943-44, Park Sch., Buffalo, 1944-46, Columbia Sch. for Girls, Rochester, N.Y., 1946-50; asso. prof. Winona (Minn.) State Coll., 1950-56, prof. English, 1957—. Mem. Minn. Gov.'s Comm. on Status of Women Minn., 1963-67; mem. women's adv. com., chmn. com. on employment of women Minn. Dept. Human Rights, 1972—. Bd. dirs. Minn. Civil Liberties Union, D.F.L. Feminist Caucus. Mem. Am. Assn. U. Women (pres. Winona br. 1954-56), Modern Lang. Assn. Am., Renaissance Soc. Am., Am. Assn. U. Profs. (v.p. Minn. conf. 1960-61, pres. 1963-64, council 1960-66, 71—, exec. com. 1973—, chmn. conf. com. on coll. and univ. govt. 1960-66, 71—, nat. com. 1962-66; pres. Winona chpt. 1965-66), Milton Soc. Am., Am. Studies Assn., Modern Humanities Research Assn., Vergilian Soc., Women's Equity Action League, Phi Beta Kappa. Contbr. articles to learned Jours., also articles on coll. and univ. govt., problems of women. Home: Homer Rd Route 3 Winona MN 55987

BODE, FRANCES LOUISE MAINO (MRS. WILLIAM THEODORE BODE), author, lectr.; b. San Luis Obispo, Cal., Mar. 1, 1920; d. Theodore Michael and Eleanor Elizabeth (Hazard) Maino; B.A., Mills Coll., 1940; postgrad. U. Cal. at Berkeley, 1941; M.A., Sacramento State U., 1958; m. William Theodore Bode, Dec. 25, 1942; children—Eleanor (Mrs. Charles Caudwell), Catherine (Mrs. Leo Appel), William T. II. Tchr. Ceres Union High Sch., 1941-43, Sacramento State Coll., 1958; free-lance tchr. flower arrangement, 1946—; lectr. on flower arrangements to various orgns. throughout U.S. Teaching specialist Ala. Judges Council, 1971, Ohio Judges Council, 1971; dir. Sacramento Garden and Art Center, 1958-68. Recipient Exec. Com. award Cal. Expn., 1969. Mem. Profl. Arrangers No. Cal. (pres. 1968-69), Am. Horticultural Council, Cal. Writers Club, Garden Writers Assn. Am., Carmichael, Sacramento arrangers guilds, Kingsley Art Club, Nat. Council State Garden Clubs, Cal. State Garden Clubs, Inc., Mignonette Garden Club. Author: Creativity in Flower Arrangement, 1967; New Structures in Flower Arrangement, 1968. Contbr. pictures of arrangements to various mags. Home: 2800 Huntington Rd Sacramento CA 95825

BODEAU, VIVIENNE ROSE FITZSIMMONS-TRACEY, writer, publisher; b. Indpls.; d. Robert C. and Lenora (Sterling) Fitzsimmons; student Ohio No. U., Boston U., Cin. U.; m. Edward Bodeau, May 14, 1947; children—Pierre Philippe, Michelle Colette, Andre. Social worker Grace Meth. Ch., Dayton, O., 1939-41; counselor Kelly AFB, San Antonio, 1944-45, Hdqrs. 24th Corps. USAAF, Seoul, Korea, 1946-47, Nagoya, Japan, 1947-48; free-lance mil. writer, Washington, 1949-51; mil. editor Gazette Telegraph, Colorado Springs, Colo., 1951-54; mil. writer and corr. U.S. Lady Mag., Europe, Africa, 1954-58, publisher, Stuttgart, Germany, 1955-58; mil. columnist, editor No. Va. Sun newspaper, Arlington, Va., 1959-63; editor, pub. Nat. Byline newspaper, Washington, 1963—; pres. Nat. Byline Corp.,

Arlington, Va., 1963—, Bodeau News Bur.; sometimes lectr.; pub. relations Le Doux Cons. Internat., Inc., Action Printing Service, Inc., others. Recipient numerous mil. citations; 1st prize news story Va. Assn. Press Women, 1962, 63, 1st prize for interview, 1st prize for news story in weekly, 1964, 1st prize for editorial, 1963, 67, 68, 1st prize for page regularly edited by woman, 1965, 66, 1st prize for page layout, 1966, 67, 1st prize for feature story, 1968, 1st prize for page makeup, 1968, 74, 1st prize for personal column, 1973, 74, 1st prize for news-feature story, 1974; 2d prize for editorial Nat. Fedn. Press Women, 1967, 68, also named Woman of Achievement 1964; Outstanding Woman award No. Va. Altrusa Club, 1964; 1st award news feature Va. Press Assn., 1974. Mem. Am. Newspaper Women's Club, Nat. Fedn. Press Women, Va. Assn. Press Women, Ind. Soc. Washington, Internat. Platform Assn., No. Va. News Assn., McLendon Press Briefing Group, Greater Rosslyn Bus. and Profl. Assn. Club: Altrusa. Home: 6209 Lakeview Dr Falls Church VA 22041 Office: 1400 Wilson Blvd Arlington VA 22209

BODEL, MARY GIBNEY (MRS. JOHN KNOX BODEL, JR.), coll. adminstr.; b. Balt., Dec. 5, 1921; d. Robert Alexander and Mary-Garrett (Bartlett) Gibney; A.B., Vassar Coll., 1943; M.A., U. Pa., 1948; m. John Knox Bodel, Jr., June 24, 1955; children—John Putnam, Mary-Garrett. English tchr. Baldwin Sch., Bryn Mawr, Pa., 1943-47; English tchr. Oxford Sch., Hartford, Conn., 1948-55; adminstrv. asst. Admission Office, Vassar Coll., Poughkeepsie, N.Y., 1962-69, asst. dir. Vocational Bur., 1970-71, dir. Office Career Planning, 1971—; English tchr. Webutuck Central High Sch., Amenia, N.Y., 1969-70. Trustee Garrison Forest Sch. (Md.), 1960-65, 68-73. Mem. Asso. Alumnae Vassar Coll. (dir. 1965-68). Home: Indian Mountain Rd Lakeville CT 06039 Office: Vassar Coll Poughkeepsie NY 12601

BODEN, SUZANNE MARIE BOHNEN, lawyer; b. Chgo.; d. Fred George and June (Gafford) Bohnen; B.A., U. Chgo.; m. Paul Boden, Sept. 10, 1966. Asst. sec. Chgo., North Shore & Milw. R.R., 1952-56; practiced in Chgo., 1961—; mem. firm Clinch & Boden, Chgo., 1966-73, Jenner and Block, Chgo., 1973—, Gould, Cooksay, Fennell, Appleby and McKinnon, Vero Beach, Fla., 1973—. Bd. mgrs. Mary Bartelme Home Girls Met. Chgo., North Av. Day Nursery. Mem. Am., Chgo., Womens bar assns. Home: 910 N Lake Shore Dr Chicago IL 60611 Office: 1 IBM Plaza Chicago IL 60610 also PO Box 760 Vero Beach FL 32960

BODIFORD, DOROTHY LOUISE HINES, librarian; b. Selmer, Tenn., Jan. 5, 1921; d. James Arlie and Mary Drulah (Cox) Hines; B.S., Ark. State Tchrs. Coll., 1961; M.L.S., U. Miss., 1967; m. Edward Paul Bodiford, June 21, 1936; children—Larry, Robby (dec.), Eldon (dec.), Paulette (Mrs. Cletis Guest), Ricky, Sandra. Tchr., Good Luck Sch., Marvell, Ark., 1956-60; librarian Marvell High Sch., 1960-69, McNairy Central High Sch., Selmer, Tenn., 1969—. Mem. Tenn., West Tenn. edn. assns., McNairy County Tchrs. Assn., Tenn., West Tenn. library assns. Mem. Ch. of Christ. Home: Route 1 Selmer TN 38375 Office: McNairy Central High Sch Selmer TN 38375

BODKIN, ALLIE SUE GOTTWALD, home economist; b. Luling, Tex., June 2, 1940; d. Norwood Henry and Artie (Hoover) Gottwald; B.S., U. Tex., 1962; postgrad. U. N.M., 1971; m. Robert Bodkin, Sept. 28, 1962 (div. Dec. 1967). Kendall County home demonstration agt., Boerne, Tex., 1962-67; program coordinator Dairy Council, Inc., Lubbock, Tex., 1968-69; extension home economist Expanded Nutrition Program, Albuquerque, 1970—. Ex-Officio dir. Kendall County Fair Assn., 1962-67; mem. steering com. women's div. San Antonio Livestock Expn., 1963-67; mem. N.M. Com. on Foods, Nutrition and Health. Mem. Nat., N.M. (sec. 1972-73, pres. 1975) assns. extension home economists, N.M. Fedn. Extension Assns. (pres. 1974—), Am., N.M. (newsletter editor 1972-74, v.p. for program planning 1974—) home econs. assns., West Tex. Home Economists in Bus. (chmn. elect 1969-70), N.M. Pub. Health Assn., Albuquerque Home Economists. Democrat. Baptist. Mem. Order Eastern Star. Home: 1111 Cardenas Dr SE Albuquerque NM 87108 Office: Box 6548 Albuquerque NM 87107

BODMAN, HELENE DUNN (MRS. RICHARD S. BODMAN), social worker; b. N.Y.C., Nov. 22, 1936; d. Kempton and Susan Barret (Gill) Dunn; student New Eng. Conservatory Music, 1957-60; Mus.B., San Francisco Conservatory Music, 1968; m. Richard S. Bodman, Jan. 28, 1961; children—Taylor, James Martyn. Instr. piano, music theory, San Francisco, 1969-71; bus. mgr. Potomac chpt. Bull., Sierra Club, 1972-73; caseworker to U.S. Rep. William S. Mailliard, Washington, 1973—. Republican precinct capt., San Francisco, 1967-71. Bd. dirs. Jr. League of San Francisco, 1966-67, 68-69, chmn. previews and publicity coms.; bd. dirs. Spring Opera of San Francisco, 1967-70, Wilmington (Del.) Music Sch.; trustee San Francisco Conservatory Music, 1967-71. Club: Francisca (San Francisco). Mem. steering com. Here Today: San Francisco's Architectural Heritage, 1969.

BODNAR, ELEANOR ELIZABETH (MRS. JOHN WILLIAM BODNAR), optometrist; b. McKeesport, Pa., June 14, 1926; d. Alex S. and Elizabeth (Phillips) Kaszonyi; D. Optometry, Pa. Coll. Optometry, 1947; m. John William Bodnar, Aug. 2, 1952; children—John Alex, Lisa Lynn, Susan Marie, David Phillip. Pvt. practice optometry, McKeesport, Pa., 1948—. Bd. mem. for parents Serra High Sch., McKeesport. Mem. Am., Western Pa. optometric assns., Pa. Optometric Soc., Pa. Coll. Optometry Alumni Assn., Phi Beta Rho. Democrat. Club: Altrusa (pres. 1956-57). Office: 333 1/2 6th Av McKeesport PA 15132

BODNER, AUDREY GISELLE MILLER (MRS. ANDREW E. BODNER), artist, author; b. Sedalia, Mo.; d. Charles Edward and Elizabeth Jane (Johnson) Miller; B.M., U. Ill., 1927, M.Mus., Northwestern U., 1939; postgrad. Kansas City Art Inst., 1953, 55-56, U. Hawaii, 1954; m. Andrew E. Bodner, Dec. 28, 1957. One-man shows C. C. Carstenson Studio, Rock Hill Club, Am. Assn. U. Women, 1955, 56, 66, 74; represented in permanent collections U. Kansas City, Western Electric Offices Santa Fe; supr. music Woodstock Ill., 1930-44; tchr. art, art cons., Kansas City, Mo., 1944-59; tchr. French and German, Kansas City, Mo., 1959-73; lectr. in edn. U. Kansas City, 1956; producer, narrator Art for Everyone, KMBC-TV, 1954-57, Portrait, KCMO-TV, 1957-60, Treasure, Pride in Kansas City, WDAF-TV, 1957, Three Star Gifts for Halls Inc., Sta. KCMO-TV, 1958. Recipient 1st pl. award in watercolor Nat. League Pen Women State Contest, 1967, 73; 1st pl. award ink and pencil drawing state contest, 1969; 1st pl. award State Free Verse Contest. Mem. Nat. League Am. Pen Women, Am. Women in Radio and TV, Friend of Art of Nelson Gallery, People to People Greater Kansas City, Friends Seville-Kansas City Sisters City Commn., Federated Women's Clubs Mo., Women's Kansas City Mayor's Commn. of Assn. Internat. Relations and Trade, Gamma Phi Beta, Gamma Alpha Chi. Republican. Episcopalian. Address: 8104 Dearborn Dr Prairie Village KS 66208

BODOR, ROSE EMMA FONYAD (MRS. EDWARD ELEMER BODOR), architect and artist; b. Paks, Hungary, Jan. 30, 1934; d. Gyula and Rozsa (Marosi) Fonyad; Architect, Indsl. and Trans. Tech. U. (Budapest, Hungary), 1956; m. Edward Elemer Bodor, Nov. 12, 1955; children—Suzanne, Richard. Came to U.S., 1956, naturalized, 1961. Archtl. designer Schurect, Inc., Chgo., 1957-59, K.W. Malmgren Inc., Chgo., 1959-62; free lance architect, interior and comml. art, 1962—; comml. artist Welch Sci. Co., Skokie, Ill., 1962-73; architect Langson Bros. Constrn. Co., 1973—. Address: 8805 Merlin Dr Houston TX 77055

BOE, BARBARA LOUISE LAMPHERE (MRS. DONALD O. BOE), educator; b. Newport, N.H., Sept. 26, 1935; d. F. Wilson and Rose M. (Sankovich) Lamphere; B.Ed., Keene State Coll., 1957; postgrad. Boston Coll., 1958-60; M.S. in Teaching, U. N.H., 1962; Ph.D., U. Wis., 1966; m. Donald O. Boe, Apr. 30, 1966; 1 son, David. Tchr. math. Hampton (N.H.) sch. dist., 1957-58; chmn. math. dept. coop. sch. dist. 21, Hampton, 1958-62; part-time instr. U. Wis., Extension Div., Madison, 1963-66; instr. math. Viterbo Coll., La Crosse, Wis., summer 1964; research asst., research and devel. center for learning and re-edn., U. Wis., 1965-66; asst. prof. math., acting dept. chmn. Milton (Wis.) Coll., 1966-68, asso. prof., 1968-71, prof. math., 1971—, chmn. dept., 1967—, chmn. sci. and math. div., 1970—. Cons. math. elementary sch., Hampton, N.H., 1959-61. Named Outstanding Young Woman of Am., 1966. Mem. Am. Assn. U. Profs., Math. Assn. Am., Nat. Council Tchrs. Math., Wis. Math. Council, Southeastern N.H. Assn. Tchrs. Math. (pres. 1960-62), Tri-State Math. League (pres. 1959), A.A.A.S., Phi Delta Gamma, Pi Lambda Theta (chpt. sec. 1969-70, v.p. 1970—). Home: 1402 Winslow Lane Madison WI 53711 Office: Milton Coll Milton WI 53563

BOE, DOROTHY VIRGINIA CHRISTENSON (MRS. ROBERT N. BOE), city ofcl.; b. Concordia, Kan., Jan. 19, 1925; d. Arthur Julius and Frances Virginia (Sansom) Christenson; grad. high sch.; m. Robert N. Boe, Oct. 25, 1947; children—Steven, Nancy (Mrs. Ronald J. Dahl), Christopher. Bookkeeper, Dickinson Lumber Co., Bemidji, Minn., 1945-50, Lakeside Furniture Co., Bemidji, 1945-50; city clk.-treas. City of Bemidji, 1972—. Leader Camp Fire Girls, Sault Ste. Marie, Mich., 1961-64, Cub Scouts, Bemidji, 1957-59; pres. McKinley P.T.A., Sault Ste. Marie, 1960-62. Office: 401 Minnesota Av Bemidji MN 56601

BOECKLIN, PEG PITMAN (MRS. ROLAND BOECKLIN), univ. adminstr.; b. Bisbee, Ariz., Dec. 11, 1910; d. Laurence Minot and Elise Maude (Aztle) Pitman; B.A., Smith Coll., 1933; m. Roland Boecklin, June 16, 1941 (dec.); 1 son, Arnold Pitman. Mng. editor Intercollegiate Daily News, 1933-34; personnel dir. Jordan Marsh Co., Boston, 1935-36; circulation cons. Pubs. Service, Inc., 1937-40; placement dir., instr. Fisher Bus. Schs., Boston, 1940-41; vocational cons. Ohio Wesleyan U., Delaware, 1949-50, placement dir., 1950-68, dir. career planning and placement center, 1968—. Mem. Am. Soc. Personnel Adminstrn., Internat. Assn. Personnel Women, Am. Inst. Mgmt., Midwest Coll. Placement Assn., Assn. for Sch. Coll. and U. Staffing (pres. Ohio sect. 1968-69), Am. Assn. Univ. Adminstrs. Contbr. articles to mags. Home: 52 Westgate Dr Delaware OH 43015

BOEHM, ALICE EVELYN, psychologist; b. Prague, Czechoslovakia; d. Leopold and Bertha Boehm; Ph.D., German U. in Prague, 1938; postdoctoral study Oxford (Eng.) U., 1940-41. Came to U.S., 1941, naturalized, 1946. Research asst. N.J. State Hosp., Trenton, 1941-42; ind. psychol. research, N.Y.C., 1947—. Fellow A.A.A.S., Internat. Council Psychologists; mem. Am., Eastern, N.Y. State psychol. assns., N.Y. Acad. Scis., World Fedn. Mental Health (asso.). Contbr. articles to profl. jours. Home: 30 E 81st St New York City NY 10028

BOEHM, LEONORE EVA DEUTSCH, psychologist, educator; b. Berlin, Germany, Jan. 1, 1911; d. Herman and Dorothea (Gradenwitz) Deutsch; came to U.S., 1938, naturalized, 1943; Ph.D., Geneva U., 1952. Instr. Bennington (Vt.) Coll., 1940-42; psychiat. case worker, supr. New Eng. Home Little Wanderers, Boston, 1942-47; head dept. child study Garland Jr. Coll., Boston, 1947-52; asst. prof. edn. dept. Bklyn. Coll., 1952-62, asso. prof., 1962-70, prof. psychology, child psychology, 1970-73, emerita, 1973—. Nat. Inst. Mental Health research grantee, 1958-61. Mem. Am. Psychol. Assn., Soc. Research Child Devel. Author: Les Tendances Nouvelles de L'Education Prescolaire aux Etats—Unis et Leurs Aspect Psychologiques, 1952. Address: 60 Longwood Av Apt 908 Brookline MA 02146

BOEHM, VIRGINIA RUTH, indsl. psychologist; b. Berwyn, Ill., Sept. 25, 1941; d. Myron Peter and Doris Ruth (Kinney) Boehm; B.A., Hanover (Ind.) Coll., 1962; Ph.D., Columbia, 1966; m. Barry Lee Coyne, Aug. 7, 1971. Personnel psychologist N.Y. State Labor Dept., N.Y.C., 1966-72; personnel supr. research Am. Tel. & Tel. Co., N.Y.C., 1972—. Cons. in field. Mem. Am. Psychol. Assn., Soc. Psychol. Study Social Issues, Met. Assn. Applied Psychology, Am. Acad. Polit. and Social Scis., Women's City Club. Home: 166 W 76th St New York City NY 10023 Office: 195 Broadway New York City NY 10007

BOEHME, LILLIAN RODBERG, indsl. landscape co. exec., author; b. Vineland, N.J., Apr. 15, 1936; d. Henrik Nils and Katherine (Nitsch) Rodberg; student Rutgers U., 1953-54; m. Walter K. Boehme, Jan. 1954 (separated Sept. 1971); children—Kathleen Anne, Carroll Stephen, Kirsten Yvonne. Editor, co-pub. Libertarian, Wenonah, N.J., 1965-71; office mgr. Indsl. Landscape Maintenance Co., Wenonah, 1966-71; editorial asst. Rev. of News, Belmont, Mass., 1971-72; mgr. designer Grounds Care, Wenonah, 1972—. Free lance writer, 1970—; econs. cons. Rev. of News; contbg. reviewer Books for Libertarians, Washington, 1972—. Author: Carte Blanche for Chaos, 1970. Home: Cohawkin Rd Clarksboro NJ 08020 Office: Box 36 Wenonah NJ 08090

BOEHNE, PATRICIA CALLISTER (MRS. BILLY L. BOEHNE), ednl. adminstr., b. Kenyon, Minn., Feb. 10, 1933; d. Stanley D. and Margaret O. (Salzwedel) Callister; B.S. with distinction in Occupational Therapy, U. Minn., 1955; m. Billy L. Boehne, Oct. 23, 1954; children—Alan, Brian, Scott. Dir., Bloomington (Minn.) Nursery Sch., 1970—. Mem. Am., Minn. occupational therapy assns. Republican. Presbyn. (deacon 1968—). Home: 10201 Nesbitt Rd Bloomington MN 55437 Office: 10155 Penn Bloomington MN 55431

BOEKER, ELISABETH H., nurse; b. St. Louis, Sept. 25, 1912; d. Rev. L. C. and Caroline (Kamm) Boeker; Diploma, U. Colo., 1933, student, 1937-39; B.S., Wash. State Coll., 1941; M.S., U. Wash., 1943; M.S., U. Rochester, 1960. Hosp. nurse Colo. Gen. Hosp., Denver, 1933-35; Tb nurse, Fitzsimmons Gen. Hosp., Denver, 1935-37; pub. health nurse King County Health Dept., Seattle, 1943-45; supr., pub. health nursing Territorial Bd. Health, Honolulu, 1945-47; commd. officer USPHS, dir. pub. health nursing Cowley County Health Dept., Winfield, Kan., 1947-49, ednl. dir. pub. health nursing Me. Dept. Health, Augusta, 1949-51, asst. chief nurse, cancer nursing Nat. Cancer Inst., Bethesda, Md., 1951-53, chief nurse U.S. Operations Mission to Iraq, Baghdad, 1953-55, acting chief nurse Div. Internat. Health, USPHS, Washington, 1955-58, cons. Div. Radiol. Health, 1958-60, radiol. physicist tng. br., div. radiol. health, USPHS, 1960-63, chief biomed. radiol. health tng. sect., tng. br., 1963-66, dir. tech. tng. services tng. br., 1966-70, asso. dir. tng. inst., environmental control adminstrn., 1970-71, dir. Office of Tng. Bur. Radiol. Health, 1971-72, asst. to dir. Bur. Radiol. Health, 1972—. Recipient of the Commendation medal USPHS, 1968. Fellow Am. Pub. Health Assn.; mem. Am. Nurses Assn., Nat. League Nursing, Health Physics Soc. Home: 5101 River Rd Chevy Chase MD 20016 Office: Bur Radiol Health USPHS 12720 Twinbrook Pkwy Rockville MD 20852

BOELK, PATRICIA JO MCNAMER (MRS. NORMAN LEE BOELK), occupational therapist; b. Dubuque, Ia., May 3, 1946; d. Robert Glenn and Virginia Francis (Ney) McNamer; B.S. in Occupational Therapy (scholar 1966-68), State U. Ia., 1969; m. Norman Lee Boelk, Nov. 23, 1968; 1 dau., Beth Ann. Occupational therapist Mercy Mental Health Center, Dubuque, 1967; staff therapist Mercy Hosp., Davenport, Ia., 1969-70, dir. occupational therapy, 1970-73, rehab. therapist, 1973—. Cons. occupational therapy Scott County Community Mental Health Center, Davenport, 1972-73. Mem. Am., Ia. occupational therapy assns. Lutheran. Elk. Office: Mercy Hosp 1326 W Lombard Davenport IA 52803

BOERSMA, WILHELMINA, lawyer; b. Detroit, June 17, 1919; d. Gerlof and Regina (Zondergeld) Boersma; J.D., Wayne State U., 1941. Admitted to Mich. bar, 1941, since practiced in Detroit; asso. firm Clark, Klein, Winter, Parsons & Prewitt, 1941-69, partner, 1970—. Dir. Kel Truck Service, Inc., Lyons Transport, Inc. Arbitrator Am. Arbitration Assn., 1969—. Mem. adv. bd. women United Found. Mem. Am., Mich., Detroit bar assns., Motor Carrier Lawyers Assn., ICC Practitioners, Phi Delta Delta. Clubs: Zonta (pres. 1958-59, 61-62), Women's City (dir. 1971—). Home: 20020 Holiday Rd Grosse Point Woods MI 48236 Office: 1600 First Federal Bldg Detroit MI 48236

BOESCH, BERTHA (MRS. FERDINAND BOESCH), mus. ofcl.; b. Haines, Ore., Mar. 20, 1913; d. Artimus Arthur and Susan (Saunders) Warfield; grad. high sch.; m. Ferdinand Boesch, June 8, 1932; children—Anna Belle, Bonnie Lee (Mrs. Kenneth L. Sipes, Jr.), Donald Glen, Dora Mae (Mrs. Stanley E. Wells). Dir. Eastern Ore. Mus., Haines, 1960—, sec., 1962—. Pres., Muddy Creek P.T.A., Haines, 1944-48. Republican. Club: Mutual Improvement (pres. 1952-56) (Haines). Address: Rural Route 1 Box 109 Haines OR 97833

BOESE, ELSIE JEAN MCGIVNEY (MRS. HERMAN LAMAR BOESE), mem. Republican Nat. Com.; b. New Orleans, Jan. 19, 1925; d. John Roderick and Elsie (Buist) McG.; B.A., Sophie Newcomb Coll., 1945; m. Herman Lamar Boese, May 20, 1946; 1 son, Robert Lamar. Caseworker A.R.C., 1945-46; script writer Tulane U. Ednl. TV, 1954-55; tchr. Sunny Ct. Sch. For Retarded Children, 1954-55. Mem. La. Gov.'s Commn. Indian Affairs, 1972—, steering com. Gov.'s Conf. on Libraries; mem. Gov.'s Commn. on Compensation for Elected Statewide Ofcls., 1974—. Vice chmn. Republican State Central Com. La., 1964—, vice chmn. Rep. polit. action council of La., 1965—, del. nat. conv., 1964, 68; Rep. nat. committeewoman from La., 1968—. Legislative chmn. St. Frances Cabrini Hosp. Aux., 1963—. Recipient Freedom award La. State Farm Bur. Fedn., 1965, Freedom award in religion, 1969. Mem. Central La. Community Theatre, Poets' Circle, Woman's Aux. Rapides Parish Med. Soc. (pres.), La. Med. Aux. (state legislative chmn. 1967-68), Alpha Delta Pi. Roman Catholic. Home: 831 City Park Blvd Alexandria LA 71301

BOESE, VIRGINIA ELLEN (MRS. CARL WIMMLER BOESE), curator; b. Troy, O., July 16, 1907; d. William Harry and Virginia Grace (Meeker) Gilbert; student Western Coll. for Women, Oxford, O., 1924-26; B.A., Ohio Wesleyan U., Delaware, 1928; m. Carl Wimmler Boese, Aug. 5, 1929. Tchr. Latin and English, Concord Twp. Sch., Miami County, O., 1928-29; legal sec. to William Harry Gilbert, Troy, 1931-45; dir. Troy Hist. Soc., 1965—, archivist-librarian, genealogist, 1966—; dir., curator Overfield Log Tavern Mus., 1966—. Pres., violinist Troy Music Club, 1932-33; pres. Troy Altrurian Club, 1933-34; pres. Current Events Club, 1954-55. Co-recipient, with husband, Community Service award Troy Jr. C. of C., 1972. Mem. D.A.R., League Women Voters, Phi Mu, Kappa Delta Pi. Republican. Presbyn. (deacon). Author: Overfield Genealogy Research Notes, 1968, rev., 1970. Compiler, Index to Beers 1880 History, 1973. Home: 106 S Plum St Troy OH 45373 Office: 201 E Water St Troy OH 45373

BOESHORE, ELINOR FRANCES STRAUSS, librarian; b. Lebanon County, Pa., Aug. 2, 1925; d. Russell Gerhart and Florence Anita (Swanger) Strauss; B.S. in Music Edn., Lebanon Valley Coll., 1947, elementary certificate, 1958-60, library sci. certificate, 1968; m. Robert Leon Boeshore, June 21, 1947; children—Barry Craig, Beryl Gaye (Mrs. Earl M. Stoddard). Pvt. music tchr., 1945-55; pvt. tutor, 1955-58; tchr. Jonestown (Pa.) Elementary Sch., 1958-64; elementary librarian No. Lebanon Sch. Dist., Fredericksburg, Pa., 1965—. Mem. Jonestown Planning Commn., 1969-71; mem. Lebanon County Library Bd., 1970-72. Mem. Am., Pa. library assns., Nat., Pa., No. Lebanon edn. assns., Am. Assn. Univ. Women, Bus. and Profl. Women's Clubs (past pres.), Delta Kappa Gamma (exec. bd.). Mem. Order Eastern Star, Club Women's of Lebanon. Home: 131 N King St Jonestown PA 17038 Office: Route 2 Annville PA 17003

BOESKE, MARGARETE HELENE (MRS. JOHN BOESKE), physician; b. Goettingen, Germany, Jan. 15, 1921; d. Wilhelm Adolph and Margarete Lina (Heuer) Ziegenbein; Staatsexamen, M.D., U. Göttingen, 1944; m. John Boeske, Aug. 27, 1950; 1 son, John. Came to Can., 1950, naturalized, 1956. Intern, Royal Alexandra Hosp., Edmonton, Alta., Can., 1954-55, resident, 1952-56, now mem. staff; practice gen. medicine, Edmonton, 1957—. Mem. Canadian, Alta. med. assns. Mem. Ch. of Jesus Christ of Latter-day Saints (vis. tchr. 1971—). Home: 4634 Ada Blvd Edmonton AB T5W 4M8 Canada Office: 6414-118 Av Edmonton AB T5W 1G3 Canada

BOESZ, CHRISTINE CLARK (MRS. DANIEL L. BOESZ), statistician; b. Bridgeton, N.J., May 26, 1944; d. Stanley Marion and Cecilia Marie (Cantillon) Clark; B.A., Douglas Coll., 1966; M.S., Rutgers U., 1967; m. Daniel L. Boesz, June 26, 1965. Asst. prof. math. Valdosta (Ga.) State Coll., 1968-69; statis. analyst Alamo Area Council of Govts., San Antonio, 1969-71; statis. dir. Bexar County Med. Found., San Antonio, 1971—. Cons. in statistics ACTION. Mem. Am. Statis. Assn., Ninety-Nines Pilot Assn., Pi Mu Epsilon. Home: 203 Lost Forest San Antonio TX 78233 Office: 202 W French Place San Antonio TX 78212

BOETTCHER, BETTY JANE, ins. co. exec.; b. Indpls.; d. John Edward and Mildred (Williams) Boettcher; student Butler U., 1937-39; certificate in advanced personnel mgmt. Ind. U., 1943. Owner, Boettcher Employment & Recruiting Services, Indpls., Kokomo, Ind., 1950-62; personnel mgr. Indpls. Life Ins. Co., 1962—. Vol., adviser Jr. Achievement, Indpls., 1966. Mem. Asso. Employment Agys. Ind. (hon. life mem., pres. 1953-54), Internat. Assn. Personnel Women, Am. Soc. for Personnel Adminstrn., Altrusa Internat., Indpls. C. of C. (Bus. Woman Achievement award 1962, dir. women's council 1964), Kappa Alpha Theta. Presbyn. Home: 6386 Broadway St Indianapolis IN 46220 Office: 2960 N Meridian St Indianapolis IN 46208

BOETTLER, BETTY LORRAINE (MRS. JAMES HERBERT BOETTLER), printing co. exec.; b. Canton, O., Mar. 31, 1930; d. John Reader and Nadine Mabel (Snyder) Gray; grad. high sch.; m.

James Herbert Boettler, Sept. 22, 1962; 1 dau., Beth Lorraine. Sec. to mgr. Borden Ice Cream Co., Canton, O., 1948-57; sec. to pres. Danner Press Corp., Canton, 1957-64, exec. asst. to pres., 1964-69, corporate sec., 1969—, dir., 1973—; corporate sec. Akron (O.) Typesetting Co., 1968—, also dir.; corporate sec., treas. Photo-Matic Typographers, Inc., North Canton, 1965—, also dir., sec. treas. Danart Enterprises, North Canton, 1968—, also dir. Bd. dirs. Danner Found. Mem. Am. Bus. Women's Assn. Home: 2588 Hyacinth Dr North Canton OH 44720 Office: 7555 Freedom Ave NW North Canton OH 44720

BOEVE, ERVINA (MRS. EDGAR GENE BOEVE), educator; b. Holland, Mich., Dec. 24, 1924; d. Gerrit J. and Janna Cornelia (Van Tatenhove) Van Dyke; B.A., Calvin Coll., 1946; M.A., U. Mich., 1954; m. Edgar Gene Boeve, Aug. 13, 1955. Tchr. speech and English, Holland Christian High Sch., 1946 53; dir. drama Calvin College, Grand Rapids, Mich., 1954—. Instr. drama Interlochen Arts Camp, summers 1957-59. Mem. Am. Theater Assn. Home: 2228 Thornapple River Dr Grand Rapids MI 49506

BOGAEV, RONNI (MRS. ELEAZER GREENSTEIN), artist; b. Phila., Nov. 13, 1924; d. David and Luba (Voloshin) Bogaev; student Hussian Sch. Art, Phila., 1944-47; m. Eleazer Greenstein, Nov. 28, 1964; children—Felicia, Dana. Head, Bogaev Sch. of Art, Coconut Grove, Fla., 1963-69; one man shows Old Schoolhouse Gallery, Coconut Grove, 1964, 68, Fort Lauderdale (Fla.) Mus. Fine Arts, 1967, Emerald Gallery, Miami Beach, Florida, 1970, Galerie 99, 1972, 74, LeMoyne Art Found., Tallahassee, 1974; exhibited group shows at Soc. 4 Arts, Palm Beach, 1963, 64, 66, 67, 68, 70, Miami Art Center, 1969, 71, Rogue's Gallery, Coral Gables, Fla., 1963, Bass Mus., Miami Beach, Fla., 1965, Contempora Galleries, Fort Lauderdale, 1966, Playhouse Gallery, Coconut Grove, 1965, 66, Le Moyne Art Found., 1967, 68, Emerald Gallery, Miami Beach, 1968, Mint Mus., N.C., 1972, 73, Harmon Gallery, Naples, Fla., 1972, Benedek Gallery, N.Y.C., 1973, Aronson Gallery, Atlanta, 1972, 73, others; represented in permanent collections Fort Lauderdale Mus. Fine Arts, Temple Beth Am., Miami, Old Schoolhouse Gallery, Coconut Grove, Playhouse Gallery, Coconut Grove, Le Moyne Art Found., Tallahassee. Sec. Artists Equity, 1966-67, bd. dirs. Home: 3845 Park Av Coconut Grove FL 33133

BOGARD, BRIDGET, art gallery exec.; b. Vienna, Austria, Aug. 24, 1930; d. Ernest and Bertha (Jefroykin) Angel; student Hunter Coll., New Sch. for Social Research; div.; 1 son, David. Asst. to pres. Warren, Muller & Dolobowsky Advt. Agy., N.Y.C., 1965-71; asst. dir. Max Hutchinson Gallery, N.Y.C., 1971—. Home: 535 E 14th St New York City NY 10009 Office: 127 Greene St New York City NY 10012

BOGART, HARRIET (MRS. ALBERT BOGART), advt. co. exec.; b. Bklyn., Nov. 24, 1931; d. Murray Bernard and Claire Rose (Suris) Galan; student Bklyn. Coll., 1948-50; m. Albert Bogart, Aug. 9, 1970; children—Jeffrey, Dale, Leslie. Traffic mgr. WBNS-TV, Columbus, O., 1962-68; account exec., v.p. Hameroff & Assos., Columbus, 1968—. Leader Girl Scouts U.S. Mem. Columbus Advt. Fedn. (co-chmn. achievement and recognition commn. 1973), Nat. Council Jewish Women (Columbus sect. chmn. pub. affairs com.). Mem. Order of Eastern Star. Home: 1190 Stone Ridge Dr Apt E Columbus OH 43213 Office: 250 E Town St Columbus OH 43215

BOGART, JUDITH ANNE SAUNDERS (MRS. WILLIAM ROBERT BOGART), pub. relations exec.; b. Batesville, Ind., Nov. 16, 1936; d. David Rodman and Anna Eva (Kohles) Saunders; B.A. in Psychology, Baldwin-Wallace Coll., 1958; m. William Robert Bogart, Oct. 22, 1971. Pub. relations dir. Girl Scout Council of Nation's Capital, Washington, 1963-65, Great Rivero Girl Scout Council, Cin., 1965-67; regional account exec. Edn. Funds, Inc., Providence, 1967-68; community relations dir. Cin. Human Relations Commn., 1968—. Guest lectr. U. Cin., 1972—. Mem. Pub. Relations Soc. Am. (treas. Cin. chpt. 1973, v.p. 1974), Women in Communications (sec. 1969). Mem. Unitarian Ch. (v.p. 1972). Club: Woman's City. Home: 1050 Hatch St Cincinnati OH 45202 Office: 110 City Hall Cincinnati OH 45202

BOGATIN, NANCY ERDMAN (MRS. IRVIN BOGATIN), advt. exec.; b. N.Y.C., Oct. 26, 1925; d. Mark Albert and Elizabeth (Baum) Erdman; B.J., U. Mo., 1946; m. Irvin Bogatin, Jan. 24, 1952; children—Mark John, Liz. Copywriter, continuity dir., radio personality WMPS, Memphis, 1946-47; nat. retail fashion coordinator Sears Robuck Co., N.Y.C., 1947-50, buyer retail sportswear, 1950-52; free lance pub. relations advt. copywriter, Memphis, 1952-53; owner, operator Casuals, Memphis, 1953-56; partner Studio of Advt. and Art, Memphis, 1956—; mng. editor, gen. mgr. Delta Rev. Mag., Memphis, 1967-69. Mem. profl. adv. council Memphis State U. Sch. Journalism, 1972—. Memphis advt. campaign coordinator Senator Albert Gore, 1970, George McGovern 1972. Mem. exec. com. bd. dir. Arts Council, Memphis, 1973—. Mem. Women In Communications (v.p. 1972—), Women in Cable TV (charter, dir.). Home: 5169 Shady Grove Memphis TN 38117 Office: 1468 Vinton St Memphis TN 38104

BOGGS, CORINNE CLAIBORNE, congressman; b. Brunswick Plantation, La., Mar. 13, 1916; d. Roland and Corinne (Morrison) Claiborne; B.A., Newcomb Coll., Tulane U., 1935; m. Thomas Hale Boggs, Jan. 22, 1938 (dec.); children—Barbara (Mrs. Paul E. Sigmund, Jr.), Thomas Hale, Corinne (Mrs. Steven V. Roberts). Tchr. history and English, St. James Parish, La., 1936-37; mem. 93d Congress to fill vacancy caused by death of husband, 1973—. Pres., Dem. Congl. Wives Forum, 1955-56, Womans Nat. Democratic Club, 1957-58, Congl. Club, 1970-72; co-chmn. Inaugural Balls for Presidents John F. Kennedy, Lyndon Johnson, 1961-65. Bd. dirs. La. Council for Music and Performing Arts. Mem. Nat. Soc. Colonial Dames, League Women Voters, Internat. Fedn. Catholic Alumni. Home 2801 St Charles Av New Orleans LA 70130 Office: 1519 Longworth Bldg Washington DC 20515

BOGRAD, HARRIET MARY, lawyer; b. Paterson, N.J., Apr. 6, 1943; d. Samuel and Pauline (Klemes) Bograd; A.B., Bryn Mawr Coll., 1963; LL.B., Yale Law Sch., 1966. Admitted to N.Y. bar, 1967; lawyer Dr. Martin Luther King Health Center, Bronx, N.Y., 1966-70; project dir. Children's Circle Planning Corp., Bronx, 1970-71; research asso. Center for the Study of Edn., Yale, 1971-72; asso. dir. edn. Improvement Center, New Haven, 1971-72; tng. asso. Drug Dependence Inst., New Haven, 1972-74; cons., 1974—. Lectr. dept. psychiatry Yale U. Sch. Medicine, 1972—; instr. dept. community health Albert Einstein Coll. Medicine, Bronx, 1967-71. Bd. dirs. Tchrs. Center, Inc., New Haven, 1971—. Mem. N.Y. Bar Assn. Home: 40 Foster St New Haven CT 06511

BOGRAD, MILDRED GABY, apparel co. exec.; b. Scranton, Pa., Nov. 25, 1930; d. Simon and Frieda (Golnick) Gaby; grad. high sch.; children—Paul Gary, Sandra Lynn. With Hammarlund Mfg. Co., N.Y.C., 1962-63; controller Morton Rothenberg, Atty., Miami Beach, Fla., 1963-65; office mgr. Brentwood Sportswear, Inc., Phila., 1966-70, controller, 1970—. Mem. Nat. Assn. Accountants (dir. ednl. activities 1969-70, dir. pub. relations 1970-71), Am. Inst. Corporate Controllers. Home: Towers of Windsor Park Cherry Hill NJ 08034 Office: 4411 Whitaker Av Philadelphia PA 19120

BOGUE, ELIZABETH MCCORMICK (MRS. ARTHUR BOGUE), social worker; b. Harrisburg, Pa., Feb. 25, 1896; d. Harris Barton and Ellen Martin (Vaughan) McCormick; B.S., U. Mich., 1920; postgrad. U. Chgo., 1929-30; M.S.W. (Bus. and Profl. Women's Club scholar), Mich. State U., 1954; m. Arthur Bogue, Sept. 13, 1920; children—Bernard Madison, Elizabeth Vaughan (Mrs. Harry Obertreis). Ednl. sec. Detroit League of Nations, 1927-29; exec. sec. A.R.C., Lansing, Mich., 1934-43, dir. officer clubs A.R.C., Europe, 1943-45; med. social worker VA Hosp., Shumount, N.Y., 1946-48; med. social worker County of Los Angeles, 1954-58; cons. aid to totally disabled persons State of Cal., 1958-68. Mem. Am. Assn. Social Workers (charter), Women's Overseas League (San Diego corr. sect. 1970-73), Foothills Art Assn. Home: 7346 Vassar Av La Mesa CA 92041

BOGUE, PAULINE AVIS HEIDEMANN (MRS. OREL EDWIN BOGUE), bus. exec.; b. Cushing, Okla.; d. John Henry and Reba (Savage) Heidemann; grad. high sch.; m. Orel Edwin Bogue, Aug. 29, 1935; children—Ronald Ray, Judith Louise (Mrs. Donald W. Ringgold), Lewis Claude. Classified display advt. mgr., legal advt. mgr. Okmulgee (Okla.) Daily Times, 1950-52; sec. to supt. schs., clk. bus. office Bd. Edn., Pryor, Okla., 1952-54; bookkeeper, asst. cashier Miami Savs. & Loan Assn. (Okla.), 1954-59; asst. sec., asst. treas., investments and accounting supr. Thurston Nat. Life Ins. Co. (name now Profl. Investors Life Ins. Co), Tulsa, 1961—, also Thurston Nat. Ins. Co. (name now Thurston Fire & Casualty Ins. Co.), 1961—; asst. sec., asst. treas. Nat. Funding Corp., Tulsa. Chmn., P.T.A., 1940-59. Mem. Christian Ch. Home: 10625 E 1st St Tulsa OK 74128 Office: PO Box 2888 Tulsa OK 74101

BOHANNAN, LAURA M. SMITH (MRS. PAUL JAMES BOHANNAN), anthropologist, educator; b. N.Y.C., July, 1922; d. Hanson Ambrose and Elenore (Altman) Smith; B.A., U. Ariz., 1943, M.A., 1947; postgrad. Brown U., 1943-44; Ph.D., Oxford U., 1951; m. Paul James Bohannan, May 15, 1943; 1 son, Denis Michael. Lectr. anthropology Northwestern U., Evanston, Ill., 1959-62; lectr. social sci. U. Chgo., 1962-65; asso. prof. anthropology U. Ill. at Chicago Circle, 1965-67, prof., 1970—. Sr. research fellow East African Inst. for Social Research, Kampala, Uganda, 1954-56; Guggenheim fellow, 1974. Fellow Am. Assn. Anthropologists, Royal Anthrop. Inst., A.A.A.S., African Studies Assn. (mem. exec. bd. 1972—), Internat. African Inst.; mem. Brit. Assn. Social Anthropologists, Am. Assn. Ethnology. Author: (with Paul Bohannan) Tiv Economy (Herskovits) award for best book on Africa 1968), 1968; (as Elenore Smith Bowen) Return to Laughter, 1951; The Frightened Witch, 1960; (with Paul Bohannan) Three Source Notebooks in Tiv Ethnography, 1958, Tiv of Central Nigeria, 1953. Five Source Notebooks in Tiv Religion, 1969. Editor: Am. Anthropologist, 1970-73. Home: 405 Deerfield Rd Deerfield IL 60015 Office: Dept Anthropology U Ill at Chgo Circle Box 4348 Chicago IL 60680

BOHLE, SUE (MRS. JOHN BERNARD BOHLE), pub. relations exec., journalist; b. Austin, Minn., June 23, 1943; d. Harold Raymond and Mary Theresa (Swanson) Hastings; B.S. in Journalism (univ. scholar 1961-64, Panhellenic scholar 1964-65), Northwestern U., 1965, M.S. in Journalism, 1969; m. John Bernard Bohle, June 22, 1974. Tchr. pub. high schs., Englewood, Colo., 1965-68; account exec. Burson-Marsteller Pub. Relations, Los Angeles, 1969-73; account supr. pub. relations dialog div. J. Walter Thompson Co., Los Angeles, 1973—. Free lance writer, 1972; instr. communications Cal. State U. at Fullerton, 1972-73. Dir. pub. relations Los Angeles Jr. Ballet, 1971-72; pres. Panhellenic Advisers Council U. Cal. at Los Angeles, 1972-73. Adv. bd. Los Angeles Valley Coll., 1974—. Mem. Women in Communications, Shi-ai, Delta Zeta, Kappa Alpha Tau. Contbr. articles to trade mags. Home: 8035 Briar Summit Dr Los Angeles CA 90046 Office: 6505 Wilshire Blvd Los Angeles CA 90048

BOHLER, CLORINDA SCARPA-SMITH (MRS. T. GORDON BOHLER), physician; b. Buenos Aires, Argentina; d. Jose and Maria (Smith) Scarpa; M.Teaching, Ministerio Nacional de Educacion de la Nacion (Buenos Aires), 1941, B.A., 1942; M.D., U. Buenos Aires, 1949; m. T. Gordon Bohler, Jan. 4, 1959. Intern Hosp. Argerich, Buenos Aires, 1946-47, resident 1948-51; instr. anatomy U. Buenos Aires, 1946-47, asst. physician, dept. medicine, 1949-57; chief of colpocitology sect. Instituto Nacional de Endocrinologia, Nat. Ministry of Health, Buenos Aires, 1950-56; prof. specialties of medicine Red Cross Sch. for Nurses, Buenos Aires, 1952-56; practice medicine, specializing in endocrinology, Buenos Aires, 1950-56; asst. physician Dr. Fred A. Simmons, Mass. Gen. Hosp., Harvard Med. Sch., Boston, 1957; clin. and research fellow Mass. Gen. Hosp., 1957; head sect. of Gonads and infertility NIH, Buenos Aires, Argentina, 1958; research fellow, dept. endocrinology Med. Coll. Ga., Augusta, 1958, cardiovascular research, 1959-60, research asso., 1960-63; research asso., dept. physiology and hemodynamic unit, dept. medicine Eugene Talmadge Meml. Hosp., Med. Coll. Ga., Augusta, 1963-65, asst. prof., dept. obstetrics-gynecology, instr. dept. physiology, 1965-70; research fellow endocrinology Med. Coll. Ga., 1970-71, clin. prof., 1972—; practice medicine specializing in endocrinology and metabolism, Augusta, 1971—. NIH and Ga. Heart Assn. grantee, 1966-69. Baptist. Author: Nociones de Especialidades Medicas para Enfermeras, 1954. Contbr. articles to profl. jours. Home: 1434 Anthony Rd Augusta GA 30904

BOHLIN, BETTY JEAN (MRS. JOHN RAYMOND BOHLIN), data processor; b. Graham, Tex., Dec. 20, 1921; d. Horace Greely and Kathryn Henrietta (Thomas) Secrest; B.S., Mary Hardin-Baylor Coll., 1942; postgrad. N. Tex. State U., 1960, U. Ark., 1970; m. John Raymond Bohlin, Dec. 20, 1946; children—Kathryn Sue, Lucia Marie (Mrs. Bill Saunders), Joe Raymond, John Robert. Civil service instr. Brooke Army Med. Center, Ft. Sam Houston, Tex., 1942-46, Q.M. Med. Center, Ft. Worth, 1952-54, Ft. Wolters, 1954-60; tchr. Mineral Wells High Sch., 1965-66; financial aid officer Mary Hardin-Baylor Coll., 1966-72, San Antonio Coll., 1972-73; civil service data processor Army Dept., Ft. Hood, Tex., 1973—. Sec., Baptist Student Union, 1940-42; sponsor Hist. Phila. and Bapt. Student Union, Mary Hardin-Baylor Coll., 1966-72. Mem. Tex. Assn. Student Financial Aid Adminstrs. (treas.), Bus. and Profl. Womens Club (sec.), Am. Legion Aux. (v.p.), Alumni Assn. Mary Hardin-Baylor Coll. (exec. council). Mem. Order Eastern Star. Home: PO Box 111 Belton TX 76513 Office: III Corps Test Hdqrs Fort Hood TX 76544

BOHLS, CLEO EVELYN EVANS (MRS. LOUIS F. BOHLS), heavy machinery mfg. co. exec.; b. Little Rock, Dec. 2, 1924; d. William Roy and Edna Mae (Gray) Evans; student Draughon's Bus. Sch., 1942; m. Louis F. Bohls, Mar. 8, 1944; children—Linda (Mrs. Don R. Ellis), Louis David. Sec.-treas. Bohls Equipment Co., San Antonio, 1960—. Pres., N.E. Council P.T.A.'s, 1965-67; mem. steering com. Citizens Adv. Council to Alamo Area Council Govts., 1972; mem. citizens' adv. com. Tex. Constl. Revision Commn., 1973; mem. local draft bd., 1972—; pres. Tex. Fedn. Republican Women, 1969-71; 2d v.p. Nat. Fedn. Rep. Women, 1973—. Bd. mgrs. Bexar County Hosp. Dist. Mem. Nat. Assn. Parliamentarians, League Women Voters (dir. San Antonio 1960-64). Methodist. Home: 123 Meadowood St San Antonio TX 78216 Office: 201 Probandt St San Antonio TX 78204

BOHN, MARIE HANNAH, psychiatrist; b. Bklyn., Oct. 3, 1909; d. Edward A. and Marie (Folmer) Bohn; B.S., St. Xaviers Acad. for Women, Chgo.; M.D., Loyola U., 1934. 2 adopted children—Michelle Marie, John Stewart. Intern Little Company of Mary Hosp., Evergreen Park, Ill., 1934-35; resident psychiatry Manteno State Hosp., Inst. for Juvenile Research 1935-37; supt. Grand View Hosp., LaCrosse, Wis., 1937-42; gen. practice medicine and surgery, Freeport, Ill., 1942-62; staff physician U. Okla. Student Health Service, Norman, 1962-65; asst. dir. health service U. Okla. Med. Center, 1965-67; practice psychiatry, Norman, 1965-67; staff psychiatrist Ariz. State Hosp., Phoenix, 1967-70; med. dir. Tri City Mental Health Center, Mesa, Ariz., 1970-72, clin. supr., 1971-72; pvt. practice psychiatry, 1971—; psychiatrist Student Health Service, Ariz. State U., Tempe, 1972-74. Cons., Tri City Cath. Social Services, Cultural Environment Inst., Inc., 1974—. Diplomate Nat. Bd. Med. Examiners. Mem. A.M.A., Stephenson County (past pres.), Ill., Ariz., Maricopa County med. socs., Ill. (pres. No. Ill. chpt. 1958), Am., Ariz. acads. gen. practice, Am. Psychiat. Assn. (asso.), Ariz. Psychiat. Soc., Phoenix Psychiat. Council, P.E.O. Home: 6202 N Palo Cristi Rd Paradise Valley AZ 85253 Office: 500 W 10th Pl Phoenix AZ 85201

BOHNER, GRACE LILLIAN ERB (MRS. WILLIAM R. BOHNER), banker; b. New Berlinville, Pa., May 3, 1919; d. Wallace Henry and Annie Cora (Dierolf) Erb; certificates Am. Inst. Banking, 1964-72; m. William Roland Bohner, Nov. 28, 1946. With Nat. Bank of Boyertown (Pa.), 1948—, successively bookkeeper, teller, asst. to loan officer, sec. to pres., asst. sec. to bd., 1948-68, asst. v.p., 1968—. Leader Girl Scouts U.S.A., 1946-56. Mem. Am. Inst. Banking. Lutheran. Home: 13 N Monroe St Boyertown PA 19512 Office: PO Box 547 Boyertown PA 19512

BOHR, AUDREY EMERY, social worker; b. Montgomery, Pa., July 29, 1937; d. Edson Harman and Grace (La Forme) Emery; B.A., Wagner Coll., 1959; student State U. N.Y. at Buffalo, 1961-62; M.S.S., Bryn Mawr Coll., 1965; m. Ronald H. Bohr, June 10, 1961; children—Christopher David Emery, Benjamin Daniel Emery. Caseworker, Phila. County Bd. Pub. Assistance, 1960-61, Buffalo State Hosp., 1961-63; sr. psychiat. social worker Child Study Center Phila., 1965-70, Northeast Phila. Community Mental Health Center, 1970—; field instr. dept. social work and social research Bryn Mawr Coll., 1968-70; pvt. practice, 1973—. Mem. Nat. Assn. Social Workers, Acad. Certified Social Workers, Am. Group Psychotherapy Assn., Pa. Soc. for Clin. Social Workers Am. Assn. U. Women, Alpha Psi Omega. Republican. Lutheran. Home: 613 E Wadsworth Av Philadelphia PA 19119 Office: Northeast Community Mental Health Center Roosevelt Blvd at Adams Av Philadelphia PA 19124

BOIKESS, OLGA SHNIPER, lawyer; b. Jamaica, N.Y., Dec. 25, 1938; d. Robert and Bella (Jarus) Shniper; B.A., Barnard Coll., 1960; J.D., U. Cal. at Los Angeles, 1964. Admitted to Cal. bar, 1964, D.C. bar, 1969; law clk. U.S. Dist. Ct. for So. Dist. Cal., 1964-65; atty. gen. counsel's office, Office Econ. Opportunity, Exec. Office President, Washington, 1965-68; asso. firm Galland, Kharasch, Calkins & Brown, Washington, 1968—. Cons. in health services and econ. devel. for fed. agys. and govt. contractors, 1968—. Mem. Am. Civil Liberties Union (vol. atty. 1968—), Health and Welfare Council (mem. nat. capital area membership com. 1970-73, budget com. 1970-73), Sierra Club (vol. atty. 1970—). Home: 1605 22d St NW Washington DC 20008 Office: 1054 31st St NW Washington DC 20007

BOISCLAIR, REGINA ANN, sem. librarian; b. Lynn, Mass., Oct. 9, 1944; d. Ernest Napoleon and Eva Elmire (Baron) Boisclair; A.B., Anna Maria Coll., 1966; M.S., Simmons Coll., 1967; certificate (Higher Edn. Act grantee), U. Wis. Sch. Library Scis., 1968. Library asst. Mass. Dept. Edn. Bur. Library Extension, Boston, 1964-67; asst. librarian N. Shore Community Coll., Beverly, Mass., 1967-69; asst. librarian R.I. Coll. Adams Library, Providence, 1969-71; dir. librarian Sem. Coll. of Our Lady of Providence, Warwick, R.I., 1971—. Profl. cons. Assumption Sch. Library, Providence, 1970-72, St. Patrick's Word of God Sch., Providence, 1972—. Co-head Book-Tape Ministry, Word of God Community, Providence, 1971—. Mem. Am., Cath., New Eng. (sec. coll. sect. 1972, 73), R.I. library assns., Lambda Iota Tau, Delta Psi Omega. Roman Catholic. Editor: (with Helen P. Hawkinson): In God's Providence the Birth of a Catholic Charismatic Parish (John Randall), 1973. Home: 12 W Park St Providence RI 02908 Office: Rural Route 1 Warwick Neck Av Warwick RI 02889

BOISSE, JOSETTE ANNE (MRS. JOSEPH ADONIAS BOISSE), librarian; b. Elmhurst, N.Y., June 29, 1942; d. Joseph Leon and Georgette Constance (Chapellier) Smongeski; A.B., Stonehill Coll., North Easton, Mass., 1964; M.S., Simmons Coll. Sch. Library Sci., 1967; m. Joseph Adonias Boisse, Aug. 28, 1965. Children's services cons. Vt. Free Pub. Library Service, Montpelier, 1967-68; head extension service Oshkosh (Wis.) Pub. Library, 1968-71; librarian Spaulding High Sch., Barre, Vt., 1971—; instr. U. Wis. extension, 1968-69; co-exec. dir. Wis. Nat. Library Week, 1971; reviewer Library Jour., 1969—, LJ/SLJ Previews, 1972—. Mem. Gov. Vt. Com. Children and Youth, 1967-68. Mem. adv. bd. Oshkosh Boys Club, 1970-71. Mem. Am. (mem. com. nat. orgns. serving the child) New Eng., Vt. library assns., Vt. Ednl. Media Assn. (exec. bd., pres. elect 1974—). Designed, established county-wide bookmobile service for Winnebago County, Wis., 1968-71. Home: PO Box 214 Montpelier VT 05602 Office: Spaulding High Sch Ayers St Barre VT 05641

BOJALAD, JUNE BRANNAN, photog./lithographic co. exec.; b. Beaver Springs, Pa., Aug. 16, 1921; d. Fern Ralph and Lulu Elizabeth (Lepley) Brannan; grad. high sch.; m. Richard John Bojalad, Jan. 2, 1944; children—Maureen Ann (Mrs. Paul R. Blossey, Jr.), Cynthia Louise (Mrs. Kenneth G. Truesdale). Spl. corr. Pa. Dept. Revenue, Bur. Motor Vehicles, Harrisburg, 1939-45; sec., bookkeeper Kline Motors, Beaver Springs, Pa., 1958-62; office mgr. finance, pub. relations R. J. Bojalad Printing Co., Inc., Beaver Springs, Pa., 1962—, sec.-treas., 1964—, also dir. Dist. chmn. Heart Fund, 1953—; active P.T.A. Roman Catholic. Home: W Snyder Av Beaver Springs PA 17812 Office: Box 107 Beaver Springs PA 17812

BOLAND, GERTRUDE CATHERINE, educator, economist, psychologist; b. Buffalo, July 26, 1914; d. Joseph Anthony and Katherine Irene (Reilly) Boland; A.B. magna cum laude, Mt. St. Mary's Coll., 1936; B.S. in Fgn. Service, Georgetown U., 1948; A.M., Cath. U. Am., 1950; Ph.D. (Claremont scholar, Haynes Found. fellow), Claremont Grad. Sch., 1961; Ph.D., St. Louis U., 1970. Tchr. elementary schs., Los Angeles, 1937-44; instr. econs. Manhattanville Coll. of Sacred Heart, N.Y.C., 1949-50; group leader, statistician Aerojet-Gen. Corp., Azusa, Cal., 1951-56; prof. econs. Cal. State Poly. U., Pomona, 1957—, acting chmn. dept. econs., 1971-72, chmn. dept. econs., 1972—; asso. clin. prof. psychology Fuller Theol. Sem., Pasadena, Cal., 1971-72; staff psychologist St. John's Hosp., Santa Monica, Cal., 1971-72; clin. psychologist in pvt. practice, Santa Monica, 1972—; psychology intern Kennedy Child Study Center, Santa Monica, 1967-68, David P. Wohl Meml. Mental Health Inst., St. Louis, 1968-69, psychology resident St. John's Hosp., Santa Monica, 1970-71. Served with USNR, 1944-46. Mem. Am. Econ. Assn., Assn. Asian Studies, Am. Assn. U. Profs., A.A.A.S., Pi Gamma Mu, Psi Chi. Research and publs. in psychol. field. Office: Economics Dept Cal State Polytechnic Univ Pomona 3801 W Temple Av

Pomona CA 91768 also 2021 Santa Monica Blvd Santa Monica CA 90404 PO Box 213 Glendore CA 91740

BOLAND, JANET LANG (MRS. JOHN B. BOLAND), judge; b. Kitchener, Ont., Can., Dec. 6, 1924; d. George William and Miriam Janet (Geraghty) Lang; B.A., Waterloo Coll., 1946; law degree, Osgoode Hall, 1950; m. John Brown Boland, Oct. 1, 1949; children—Michael, Christopher, Nicholas. Called to Ont. bar, 1950; mem. firm White, Bristol, Beck & Phipps, Toronto, Ont., 1959-69; partner Lang Michener, Toronto, 1969-72; county ct. judge, Toronto, 1972—. Queen's Counsel, 1965; co-chmn. Penal Reform for Women Joint Com., 1956-58. Mem. Jr. League Toronto. Roman Catholic. Home: 164 Inglewood Dr Toronto ON Canada Office: New Court House University Av Toronto ON Canada

BOLD, FRANCES ANN, librarian; b. Evansville, Ind., May 30, 1930; d. John D. T. and Frances (Wilson) Bold; B.A., Mary Washington Coll. of U. Va., 1952; M.S. in L.S., U. N.C., 1956. Library asst., Falls Church (Va.) Pub. Library, 1952-53, Hollins Coll. (Va.) Library, 1953-54; asst. br. librarian Arlington County (Va.) Pub. Library, 1957-58, br. librarian, 1958-64; library dir. Pottstown (Pa.) Pub. Library, 1964-67; dir. Free Pub. Library, New Bedford, Mass., 1967-69; dir. Meml. Hall Library, Andover, Mass., 1969-70; decimal classification specialist Library of Congress, Washington, 1971—. Fulbright scholar, 1956-57. Mem. Va., Am. library assns., Library Assn. Gt. Britain, Bibliog. Soc. U. Va., Phi Sigma Iota, Beta Phi Mu. Democrat. Episcopalian. Home: 210 E Fairfax St Apt 614 Falls Church VA 22046 Office: Decimal Classification Div Library of Congress Washington DC 20540

BOLDER, DOROTHY MARIE, univ. exec.; b. Dunnington, Ind., Sept. 11, 1923; d. Charles Joseph and Anna Cordelia (Hardebeck) A.; student Carnegie Inst. Tech., 1954-60; m. Roland Walter Bolder, Oct. 5, 1943; children—Rolanda (Mrs. Joseph A. Schalburg), Diane (Mrs. William Martin), Carolanne (Mrs. William S. Robinson III). Clk., Ind. Hwy. Dept., 1956-60; adminstr. asst. v.p. Purdue U., 1962-66, financial aids counselor, 1966—. Exec. asst. to pres. Assn. N.R.O.T.C. Colls., 1970—, asst. sec.-treas., 1962-70; mem. spl. adv. com. to sec. navy for N.R.O.T.C. affairs, Mem. Tippecanoe Area Manpower Planning Council, 1968—. Treas. Fedn. Republican Women, Benton County, Ind., 1952-56. Mem. Midwest Assn. U. Student Employment Dirs. (pres. 1972-73, exec. bd. 1972-74), Fedn. Bus. and Profl. Women (pres. Tippecanoe 1966-67, 73-74, Ind. legislative chmn. 1969-71, dist. legislative chmn. 1973-74), Sigma Lambda Sigma. Home: 3528 Indianbrook St Lafayette IN 47905 Office: Purdue Univ West Lafayette IN 47907

BOLDING, AMY AGNESS (MRS. JAMES TARPLEY BOLDING), author; b. Shawnee, Okla., Jan. 28, 1910; d. John Bascom and Monnie Maria (Donnell) Ward; student Burleson Coll., 1926-28, Hardin Simmons U., 1929-30, Southwestern Bapt. Theol. Sem., 1937-40; m. James Tarpley Bolding, May 21, 1928; children—Genelle (Mrs. Roy Wayne Carpenter), James, Rebecca (Mrs. Joseph Howard Greer. Tchr. pub. sch., Wake, Tex., 1928-29; operator Amy's Sch., Leonard, Tex., 1945-46. Mem. Lubbock Women's Mission Soc. (pres. 1960-61). Democrat. Baptist. Clubs: South Plains Writers (Lubbock, Tex.). Author: Please Give A Devotion Series, 1965; Installation Services For All Groups, 1969; Series Fingertip Devotions, 1970; Contbr. articles to Home Life Mag. Home: 4802 10th St Lubbock TX 79416

BOLDING, LAURA HELEN BYRD (MRS. SAMUEL MCCONNELL BOLDING), librarian; b. Vimville, Miss., Sept. 8, 1913; d. Albert Sidney and Annie (Campbell) Byrd; B.A. cum laude, Millsaps Coll., 1935; certificate L.S., U. Ala., 1940; postgrad. Auburn U., 1958; m. Samuel McConnell Bolding, Aug. 21, 1939; 1 dau., Betty. Tchr. pub. high sch., Miss., 1936-37, librarian, 1937-38; librarian pub. high sch., Ala., 1939-42; asst. librarian U. Ala. Coll. Edn. Library, University, 1945-46; head popular lit. dept. Birmingham (Ala.) Pub. Library, 1948-50; reference librarian Montgomery (Ala.) Pub. Library, 1959-68, reader's adviser, supr. outreach to aging, 1968—. Mem. Ala. Adv. Com. for Sch. Library Service, 1968-69. Mem. adv. com. Montgomery Area Commn. on Aging, 1972—. Mem. Ala. Library Assn. (awards com. 1972-73, recruitment com. 1973-74), Am. Assn. U. Women, Ala. Bus. and Profl. Women's Club (state exec. bd. 1950-51), Kappa Kappa Iota, Kappa Delta Pi, Beta Sigma Omicron. Methodist (librarian 1959-68, mem. commn. on edn. 1960-68). Clubs: Montgomery Music Study (pres. 1964-65); Soroptimist (Montgomery). Home: 620 Ponce De Leon Av Montgomery AL 36106 Office: 445 S Lawrence St Montgomery AL 36104

BOLDT, MABELLE WILHELMINA, educator; b. Schenectady, N.Y.; d. William Frederick and Isabel (Eckerson) Boldt; B. Interior Design, Syracuse U.; grad. Parsons Sch., 1946; m. Arthur Goold, Apr. 1930 (div. Dec. 1947); children—Peter Boldt Goold (dec.), David William Boldt; m. 2d, Dale Cordell Hull, July 1955; children—Dale (dec.), Condra (Mrs. Robert Mustain). Founder, pres. Internat. Inst. Interior Design, Inc., Washington, 1957—. Mem. Dupont Circle Citizens Assn., Kalorama Citizens Assn. Mem. Nat. Soc. Interior Designers, Internat. Soc. Edn. through Art, Nat. Home Fashions League, Interior Design Educators Council. Home: 2225 R St NW Washington DC 20008

BOLEN, ELIZABETH WEBB (MRS. W.L. BOLEN), city ofcl.; b. Charleston, Tenn., Sept. 6, 1918; d. Jake H. and Dollie E. (Haney) Webb; grad. Charleston High Sch., 1937; student Ayre Sch. Bus., 1938; m. W.L. Bolen, Dec. 23, 1966. Teller, asst. cashier Hiwasse Bank, Charleston, Tenn., 1939-48; sec. Duplan Corp., Cleveland, Tenn., 1948-71; city recorder City of Charleston, 1968—. Pres. Wesleyan Service Guild, 1941-42. Methodist (mem. adminstrv. bd. 1950—). Mem. Order Eastern Star. Club: Cleveland Pilot (pres. 1956-57, sec. 1953-54). Home: Route 1 Box 4 Charleston TN 37310 Office: City Hall Charleston TN 37310

BOLEN, JEAN MIYE SHINODA (MRS. JAMES GRAYSON BOLEN), psychiatrist, educator; b. Los Angeles, June 29, 1936; d. Joseph and Megumi (Yamaguchi) Shinoda; student U. Cal. at Los Angeles, 1954-55, Pomona Coll., 1955-57; B.A., U. Cal. at Berkeley, 1958; M.D., U. Cal. at San Francisco, 1962; m. James Grayson Bolen, May 21, 1966; children—Melody Jean, Andre Joseph. Intern Los Angeles Gen. Hosp., 1962-63; resident psychiatry Langley Porter Neuropsychiat. Inst., U. Cal. Med. Center, San Francisco, 1963-66; pvt. practice psychiatry, San Francisco, 1967—; mem. staff U. Cal. Hosp., San Francisco; clin. instr. psychiatry U. Cal. Sch. Medicine, San Francisco, 1967-69, Langley Porter Neuropsychiat. Inst., San Francisco, 1967-69; asst. clin. prof., 1969—; candidate C.G. Jung Inst. Tng. Program, San Francisco. Exec. v.p., dir. Psychic Mag., Inc., San Francisco, 1968—. Named Outstanding Young Women of Am., 1968. Diplomate Am. Bd. Psychiatry and Neurology. Fellow Am. Psychiat. Assn.; mem. No. Cal. Psychiat. Soc., A.M.A., Cal., San Francisco med. socs., Am. Soc. Clin. Hypnosis, Med. Center Faculty Club, Royal Soc. Medicine, Acad. Parapsychology and Medicine. Chmn. editorial adv. bd. Psychic mag., 1969—. Home: 688 Hawthorne Dr Tiburon CA 94920 Office: 2021 Webster St San Francisco CA 94115

BOLENE, MARGARET ROSELIE STEELE (MRS. ROBERT V. BOLENE), bacteriologist, civic worker; b. Kingfisher, Okla., July 11, 1923; d. Clarence R. and Harriet (White) Steele; student Ore. State U., 1943-44; B.S., U. Okla., 1946; m. Robert V. Bolene, Feb. 6, 1948; children—Judith Kay, John Eric, Sally Sue, Janice Lynn, Daniel William. Technician bacteriology dept. Okla. Dept. Health, Oklahoma City, 1946-48; asst. bacteriologist Henry Ford Hosp., Detroit, 1948-49; bacteriological cons., also asst. bus. mgr. Ponce Gynecology and Obstetrics, Inc., 1956—. Organizing dir. Bi-Racial Council, 1963; lay adviser Home Nursing Service, 1967-68; mem. exec. bd. P.T.A., 1956-71; active various community drives; sponsor Am. Field Service; patron Ponce Playhouse. Republican precinct organizer, 1960. Mem. Am. Assn. U. Women (treas. 1964-66), D.A.R. (sec.-treas. 1961-67, 1st vice regent 1972-73), Kay-Noble County Med. Aux. (treas. 1957-58, 66-67), Ponca City Art Assn., Pioneer Hist. Soc., Lambda Tau, Phi Sigma, Alpha Lambda Delta. Presbyn. Club: Ponca City Country. Home: 2116 Juanito St Ponca City OK 74601

BOLIN, JANE M. (MRS. WALTER P. OFFUTT, JR.), judge; b. Poughkeepsie, N.Y., Apr. 11, 1908; d. Gaius C. and Matilda I. (Emery) Bolin; A.B., Wellesley Coll., 1928; LL.B., Yale, 1931; LL.D., Morgan State Coll., Tuskegee Coll., Western Coll.; m. Walter P. Offutt, Jr.; 1 son, Yorke B. Mizelle. Admitted to N.Y. bar, 1932; practiced in N.Y.C., 1932-37, mem. firm Mizelle & Bolin; asst. corp. counsel City of N.Y., 1937-39; judge Family Ct. State N.Y., N.Y.C., 1939—. Mem. N.Y.C. Assn. Family Ct. Judges, Nat. Bar Assn., Assn. Bar City N.Y., Harlem Lawyers Assn. Office: 135 E 22nd St New York City NY 10010

BOLIN, LILLIAN GRACE (MRS. EVERT PILGRIM BOLIN), banker; b. Lewisville, Tex., Dec. 11, 1927; d. Charlie and Ora Effie (Morriss) Stockard; student Am. Inst. Banking, 1965-71; m. Evert Pilgrim Bolin, Jan. 1, 1946; children—Jacqueline Sue (Mrs. John W. Alcoze, Jr.), Thomas Evert. Bookkeeper, First Nat. Bank, Lewisville, 1944-46; bookkeeper, teller Lewisville State Bank, 1957-61; bookkeeper, teller, cashier, loan officer Lewisville Nat. Bank, 1963—, v.p., 1970—. Pres. Lewisville P.T.A., 1961-63; treas. March of Dimes, 1972; mem. Planning and Zoning Commn, 1971—. Named Woman of Year, Lewisville Bus. and Profl. Women, 1971. Mem. Am. Cancer Soc. (treas. 1970—), Nat. Assn. Bank Women, Am. Inst. Banking (chpt. bd. govs. 1971-72). Methodist (sec. bd. stewards 1971-72), Bus. and Profl. Women's Club of Lewisville (treas. 1971-72). Home: 556 Richland St Lewisville TX 75067 Office: 250 Stemmons St S Lewisville TX 75067

BOLING, CATHERINE AUGUSTA, state ofcl., social worker; b. Columbia, S.C., Sept. 14, 1924; d. John Radford and Mary Ethel (Fitzmaurice) Boling; student Fla. State Coll. for Women, 1942-44; A.B., U. N.C., 1946. Social Work, Tulane U., 1951. Caseworker, Children's Center of Met. Atlanta (formerly Child Welfare Assn. Fulton and DeKalb Counties), 1951-53, supr., 1954-55, asst. dir. casework, 1955-56, dir. caseworkers, 1957, exec. dir., 1957-64; exec. dir. Children's Center, Atlanta, 1964-68; asst. dir. Community Council Atlanta, 1969-71; regional adminstr. Ga. Dept. Human Resources, Atlanta, 1971-74, supr. community social service, 1974—. Del., White House Conf. on Children and Youth, 1960. Membership com. Child Welfare League Am.; steering com. Atlanta Community Chest; bd. dirs. Community Council of Atlanta Area, Catholic Social Services, Medicaid Adv. Council of Ga. Dept. Pub. Health. Mem. Nat. Assn. Social Workers, Acad. Certified Social Workers, Ga. Conf. on Social Welfare (pres. 1959-60), Atlanta Jr. League. Home: 128 Winona Dr Decatur GA 30030 Office: State Office Atlanta GA 30334

BOLING, CLAUDIA (MRS. PAUL BOLING), banker; b. Denver, Feb. 8, 1943; d. Jack and Jessie Marie (Cholvin) Harrison; student U. Colo., 1960-61, Am. Inst. Banking, 1963-64; m. Paul D. Boling, May 21, 1960; children—Scott Taylor, Robert Joseph. Trust clk. Denver U.S. Nat. Bank, 1962; with Aurora Nat. Bank (Colo.), 1965—, head bookkeeper, to 1968, asst. cashier, 1968-73, asst. v.p., 1973—. Mem. adv. com. on accounting Aurora Pub. Schs., 1973-74. Treas. Aurora Jaycettes, 1972-73. Mem. Aurora C. of C. (membership com. 1970-73). Baptist (financial sec. 1972—, treas. 1973—). Office: PO Box 128 Aurora CO 80010

BOLING, CONNIE SUE BARTLES (MRS. ROBERT GUY BOLING), paint mfg. co. exec.; b. Emporia, Kan., Oct. 20, 1937; d. Roy Albert and Pearl Lucille (Bangerter) Bartles; Asso. Applied Sci., Wichita State U., 1957; m. Robert Guy Boling, July 27, 1957; children—Eric Christopher, Angela Susanne. Corp. sec., dir. Kan. Paint & Color Corp., Wichita, 1957—, treas., 1973—. Tag Day co-chmn. Cystic Fibrosis Found., 1971. Mem. Profl. Engrs. Wives Aux., Alpha Chi Omega. Republican. Lutheran. Home: 6519 Marjorie Lane Wichita KS 67206 Office: 132 N Mosley St Wichita KS 67202

BOLING, JEWELL, govt. ofcl.; b. Randleman, N.C., Sept. 26, 1907; d. John Emmitt and Carrie (Ballard) Boling; student Women's Coll., U. N.C., 1926, Am. U., 1942, 51-52. Interviewer, N.C. Employment Service, Winston-Salem, Asheboro, 1937-41; occupational analyst U.S. Dept. Labor, Washington, 1943-57, placement officer, 1957-58, employment service adviser, 1959-61, occupational analyst, 1962, employment service specialist counseling and testing, 1963-69, manpower devel. specialist, 1969—. Recipient Meritorious Achievement award U.S. Dept. Labor, 1972. Mem. A.A.A.S., Am. Personnel and Guidance Assn. (profl. mem. nat. vocational guidance assn.), Am. Rehab. Counseling Association (archivist 1964-68), Assn. Measurement and Evaluation in Guidance, Assn. Humanistic Psychology, Smithsonians, Sierra Club, Internat. Platform Assn. Audubon Naturalist Soc., Nat. Capital Astronomers (editor Star Dust 1949-58). Author: Counselor's Handbook, 1967; Counselor's Desk Aid, Eighteen Basic Vocational Directions, 1967; Handbook for New Careerists in Employment Security, 1971. Contbr. articles to profl. publs. Home: 1514 17th St NW Washington DC 20036 also Route 2 Randleman NC 27317 Office: Patrick Henry Bldg 601 D St NW Washington DC 20001

BOLING, LENORE A. (MRS. ELDON A. BOLING), physician; b. N.Y.C., Nov. 25, 1919; d. Isaac J. and Bessie (Schwartz) Altschule; B.A., Barnard Coll., 1939; M.A., Columbia, 1942; M.D., U. Cal. at San Francisco, 1949; m. Eldon A. Boling, Feb. 13, 1948; children—Peter Avery, Alice, Lucy, Sarah, Deborah, Eli. Intern San Francisco Gen. Hosp., 1949-50; research fellow Inst. for Metabolic Research, Highland Alameda County Hosp., 1950-52; resident Boston Psycopathic Hosp., 1952-54; research fellow, 1953-55, research staff, 1955-57; staff psychiatrist Community Extension Service of Mass. Mental Health Center, Boston, 1959-60, research staff, 1960—, asst. clin. dir., center, 1973—; asst. clin. prof. psychiatry Harvard Med. Sch. Mem. A.M.A., Mass. Med. Soc., Am. Psychiat. Assn., Am. Fedn. Clin. Research, N.Y. Acad. Scis. Contbr. articles to profl. jours. Office: Mass Mental Health Center Boston MA 02114

BOLINGER, SHIRLEY GOODWIN (MRS. JOHN RANDOLPH BOLINGER), clubwoman, former librarian; b. Seattle, July 11, 1907; d. Ervin Shirley and Eda (Hague) Goodwin; B.S. in Library Sci., U. Wash., 1931; m. John Randolph, Feb. 20, 1932; 1 son, Ervin Michael. Librarian elementary schs., Arlington, Va. until 1972. Mem. bd., v.p., Seattle YWCA, 1947-49; bd. mem. Travelers Aid Soc. of Tacoma, 1940-41, Travelers Aid Soc. of D.C., 1958-59; mem. bd., admission chmn. Washington Home for Incurables, 1952-59; mem. bd., program chmn. Rock Springs Garden Club of Arlington, 1952-58. Mem. Jr. League of Washington Nat. Symphony Orch. (women's com.), English Ceramic Circle, Antique Porcelain Soc. of Washington (founder), Smithsonian Assos., Nat. Trust for Historic Preservation, Friends of Kennedy Center, Kappa Kappa Gamma. Episcopalian. Clubs: Farmington Country (Charlottesville, Va.); Neighbors (Arlington). Home: 3224 N George Mason Dr Arlington VA 22207

BOLLEY, IRMA SAILA (MRS. DON S. BOLLEY), artist, designer; b. Turku, Finland; d. Frans W. and Ida (Jumisko) Saila; grad. Mass. Coll. Art, 1931;; m. Don S. Bolley, Sept. 18, 1943; 1 son, Henry S. Art dir. Gilchrist Co., Boston, 1936-40; free lance artist, 1940-41; art dir. Gray Advt. Agy., N.Y.C., 1941-44; free lance designer, N.Y.C., 1944—; designer-cons. McCall Needlework and Crafts mag., N.Y.C., 1950—; lectr. on creative stitchery and crafts; exhibited one man shows at Swain's Art Gallery, Plainfield, N.J., Summit (N.J.) Art Center; exhibited in group shows including Riverside Mus., N.Y.C., Newark Mus. Arts Festival, Montclair (N.J.) Mus.; represented in pvt. collections. Vol., Green Thumb Corp., Lyons VA Hosp., N.J. Recipient Silver medal N.J. Water Color Soc., 1955, also numerous other awards. Mem. Nat. Assn. Women Artists, N.J. Water Color Soc., Summit Art Center, World Crafts Council. Home: 79 Redmont Rd Watchung NJ 07060

BOLLINGER, ESTHER HELEN BAKER (MRS. EDWARD ARTHUR BOLLINGER), artist; b. Melvern Sq., N.S., Can., July 5, 1907; d. Joseph Edwin and Kathryn (Buchanan) Baker; student Provincial Normal Coll., Truro, N.S., Can., 1924-25, Albright Art Sch., 1926-28, Scott Carbee Sch. Art, 1929-30; m. Edward Arthur Bollinger, July 15, 1933; 1 son, Wynn Buchanan. Comml. artist Boston Herald, 1929-30; fashion illustrating Simpson's, Halifax, N.S., 1931-32; free lance fashion illustrator stores in Buffalo, 1934-39; exhibited in one-man shows at Zwicker Gallery, Halifax, 1963, Halifax Meml. Library, 1963, 64, Halifax Shopping Center, 1965, 67, Neate Gallery, Halifax, 1970; exhibited in two-man show at Chase Fed. Bank, Miami Shores, Fla., 1970; also exhibited in groups shows at Miami Art League's ann. shows, 1960—, Am. Artists Profl. League's ann. shows, Miami, 1962—, Allied Arts of North Miami ann. shows, 1958—, Nat. League Am. Pen Women ann. shows, Miami, 1960—. Recipient numerous art awards including blue ribbons Miami chpts. Nat. League Am. Pen Women, Am. Artists Profl. League. Fellow Am. Artists Profl. League (dir. 1967—; v.p. Miami 1968); mem. Allied Arts North Miami (pres. 1962), Miami Art League (treas 1963; dir. 1967—), Nat. League Am. Pen Women (membership chmn. 1962-64; telephone chmn. 1967-68, art chmn. 1970-71). Republican. Home: 1100 NE 153rd Terrace North Miami Beach FL 33162

BOLLINGER, EVANGELINE GRACE, educator; b. Detroit, Nov. 30, 1922; A.B., Madison Coll., 1944; M.A., U. Mich., 1945, Ph.D. in English (Fellow), 1951. Instr. English, Stephens Coll., 1945-46, U. Mich., 1950-51, St. Joseph Coll., Conn., 1951-54; instr. U. Dayton, 1954-55, asst. prof., 1955-57; asst. prof. English, St. Xavier Coll., Chgo., 1957-58, prof., head dept., 1958—, chmn. div. liberal arts and humanities, 1961-66, dean, 1967—, v.p., dean faculty, 1970—. Mem. Modern Lang. Assn., Coll. English Assn., Nat. Council Tchrs. English. Research on Dante. Home: 10230 S Walden Pkwy Chicago IL 60643

BOLLINGER, JANE ASHLEY KETCHUM (MRS. HENRY R. BOLLINGER), civic worker; b. Glens Falls, N.Y., Mar. 31, 1910; d. Harold B. and Bertha (Mason) Ketchum; B.A., Vassar Coll., 1932; M.A., Middlebury Summer Spanish Sch., 1933; postgrad. Escuela De Estudios Historicos, Madrid, Spain, 1932-33; m. Albert J. Drake, June 23, 1934 (dec. Apr. 1958); children—Diana Ashley (Mrs. Jose Abizaid), Alan Ward; m. 2d, Henry R. Bollinger, Jan. 11, 1959; stepchildren—Elizabeth Louise (Mrs. Thomas Green), H. Robb. Nat. life mem. P.T.A.; chpt. regent D.A.R., 1959-62, state vice chmn. Nat. def. dist. IX, 1965-71, state dir. dist. IX, 1971—, chpt. registrar, 1962—; chpt. regent Duchess of York chpt. Daus. Am. Colonists, 1963-67, state chmn. of flag, 1963-66, state registrar, 1966-69, state 1st vice regent, 1970-73, N.Y. State regent, 1973—; editor newsletter N.Y. State Fedn. Womens Clubs, 1962-64, chmn. nat. mag., 1964-66, chmn. inter-Am. relations, 1966-68, chmn. community improvement dist. IX, 1968-72, chmn. Dutchess County, 1970-74; councillor N.Y. State chpt. Daus. of Founders and Patriots, Nat. Soc. New Eng. Women (past chpt. pres.), Vassar Bros. Hosp. Women's Aux., Vassar Bros. Assn. (sec. 1960-66), Am. Assn. U. Women (past br. pres.), Alumnae Assn. Vassar Coll. (past pres. Poughkeepsie), Vt. Soc. Colonial Dames, Daus. Colonial Wars (chmn. nat. def. N.Y. State chpt. 1971-73, N.Y. State registrar 1973—), soc. Hawley Family (gen. sec. 1963—), Ashleys of Am. Huguenot Soc. Conn., Descs. Colonial Tavern Keepers. Clubs: Art Study, Women's City and County (Poughkeepsie and Dutchess County), N.Y. State Officers (D.A.R., Daus. Am. Colonists pres. 1969-73, Fedn. Womens Clubs). Home: 74 Ferris Lane Poughkeepsie NY 12601

BOLLS, IMOGENE LAMB, educator; b. Manhattan, Kan., Sept. 25, 1938; d. Donald Quincy and Helen Letson (Keithley) Lamb; B.A. in English, Kan. State U., 1960; M.A. in English and Comparative Lit., U. Utah, 1962; m. Nathan Johnson Bolls, Jr., Nov. 24, 1962; 1 dau., Laurel Helen. Teaching positions Kan. State U., Manhattan, 1960, extension div., 1960, 61, U. Utah, 1960-62, Ft. Riley, Kan., 1962-63; tchr. lit., creative writing, journalism Wittenberg U., Springfield, O., 1963—. Cons., Midwest English Conf., Ball State U., 1972; condr. workshops in poetry and creative writing. Mem. Modern Lang. Assn., Ohio Poets Assn., Women in Communications, P.E.O., Alpha Lambda Delta, Phi Kappa Phi, Kappa Kappa Gamma. Democrat. Methodist. Contbr. poetry to jours, and anthologies. Home: 1738 Crescent Dr Springfield OH 45504

BOLSTER, ELLA S., artist; b. Helena, Mont., Dec. 8, 1906; d. Fred and Eva (Goetz) Schimpf; student Mont. State U., Colo. State U., Haystack Mountain Sch. Crafts, Me., others; m. Horace Goodwin Bolster, Sept. 14, 1930; children—Archie Milburn, Robert Neil. Instr. adult classes in canvas stitchery and macrame Central YWCA, Tucson, East Side YWCA, Tucson, U. Ariz., Davis-Monthan AFB Officers Wives Club, Tucson, An Art Gallery, Mesa, Ariz. Recipient numerous nat. and internat. awards. Mem. Nat. League Am. Pen Women (state pres. 1970-72, state art chmn. 1972-74, nat. art bd.), Alpha Gamma Delta. Home: 6391 E Printer Udell St Tucson AZ 85710

BOLSTER, JACQUELINE NEBEN (MRS. JOHN A. BOLSTER), advt. exec.; b. Woodhaven, N.Y.; d. Ernest W. B. and Emily (Guck) Neben; student Pratt Inst., Columbia; m. John A. Bolster, May 8, 1954. Promotion mgr. Photoplay mag., 1949-53; merchandising mgr. McCall's, 1953-64; dir. promotion and merchandising Harper's Bazaar, N.Y.C., 1964-71; dir. advt. and promotion Elizabeth Arden Salons, N.Y.C., 1971—. Recipient Art Director's award 1961, 66. Mem. Fashion Group, Inner Circle, Advt. Women N.Y. (life). Home: 8531 88th St Woodhaven NY 11421 also Halsey Neck Lane Southampton NY Office: Elizabeth Arden Salons 691 Fifth Av New York City NY 10022

BOLTON, ANN D., govt. ofcl.; b. Stamford, Conn., Apr. 4, 1930; d. Frank and Paula (Pepe) D'Elia; grad. Merrill's Jr. Coll., 1950; div.; children—Jamie Lynn, Keith Patrick. Legal, personal sec. Moore and Epifanio, attys., Stamford, Conn., 1949-52; personal sec. to mem. Congress, Washington, 1952-59; adminstrv. asst. to mem. Congress, Washington, 1960—. Mem. Congl. Staff Club (dir. 1969—, v.p. 1972—, pres. 1975—). Republican. Home: 6031 N 22nd Rd Arlington VA 22205 Office: 1401 House of Representatives Washington DC 20515

BOLTON, BARBARA WEEKS (MRS. JOHN DICKSON BOLTON, JR.), pub. relations and devel. cons.; b. Oil City, Pa., Jan. 16, 1930; d. Charles Raymond and Edna Alice (Baumbach) Weeks; B.A., Muskingum Coll., 1951; postgrad. U. Pitts., 1951-52, N.Y. U., 1954, Columbia, 1963; m. John Dickson Bolton, Jr., Nov. 29, 1952. Columnist, feature writer, corr. Zanesville News, New Concord Enterprise, 1948; dir. radio, television, films Community Chest of Allegheny County, 1951-54; fund raising and pub. relations dir. Western Pa. Heart Assn., 1954-67; exec. dir. Western Pa., Nat. Cystic Fibrosis Research Found., 1967-69; free lance pub. relations and devel. cons., 1969-72; asso. dir. Inst. for Ednl. Research, Pitts., 1972-74; pub. relations cons. Nat. Poison Center Network, Pitts., also free lance writer, 1974—. Mem. community relations com. Goodwill Industries Pitts. Mem. Sigma Tau Delta. Club: Zonta of Pittsburgh. Office: 832 Graham Blvd Pittsburgh PA 15221

BOLTON, ELIZABETH GRIER, librarian; b. Charlotte, N.C., July 9, 1912; d. Robert Louis and Lizzie Gary (Griffith) Bolton; B.A., U. N.C., 1933; M.A. in Guidance and Personnel, Columbia, 1943; B.S. in L.S., U. N.C., 1953. Tchr. high schs., N.C., govt. schs., Italy and Izmir, Turkey; coll. personnel ofcl.; librarian U. N.C. Library, Chapel Hill, 1959—. Mem. N.C. Library Assn., U. N.C. Librarians Assn., Chi Omega. Baptist. Author poetry, short stories, articles. Home: 224 McCauley St Chapel Hill NC 27514

BOLTON, ELIZABETH MCLUNDIE, civic worker; b. Chattanooga, Aug. 19, 1917; d. Archibald Stevenson and Elizabeth Agnes (Griffiths) McLundie; A.A., Stephens Coll., 1936; student La. State U., 1936-37; m. Robert Harvey Bolton, Apr. 14, 1939; children—Robert Harvey, Elizabeth McLundie (Mrs. Robert Conery Hassinger), Mary Calderwood (Mrs. James Kelly Jennings, Jr.). Dir., Citizens Finance Service, Baton Rouge. Chmn. bd. Kent Plantation House, Inc., 1971-73, pres. 1968-71; chmn. bd. Central La. Art Assn., Inc., 1972-74, pres. 1968-72; chmn. Kent House Festival, 1973; mem. La. Adv. Council Dept. Art, Hist. and Cultural Preservation, 1973-74; chmn. subcom. hist. preservation and tourism Rapides Area Planning Commn.; v.p. Anglo-Am. Mus., Baton Rouge; mem. bd. La. Council Music and Performing Arts, chmn. traveling art exhibit; mem. La. Am. Revolution Bicentennial Commn., chmn. art exhbn.; exec. bd. Rapides Arts Council; chmn. steering com. Alexandria Mus.; bd. mem. Alexandria Hist. Library, La. Outdoor Drama Assn., Natchitoches; mem. trustees com. Am. Assn. Museums; mem. Nat. Trust, La. Landmarks Soc., La. Hist. Assn., La. Hist. Found. Recipient Outstanding Sustainer award Alexandria Service League, 1971; Harnett Kane award La. Landmarks Soc., 1973. Home: 3200 Parkway Dr Alexandria LA 71301

BOLTON, EMILY BARBARA TURANSKI (MRS. HARVEY NEIL BOLTON), nurse; b. Vernon, B.C., Can., Sept. 11, 1937; d. George and Mary (Sawicki) Turanski; diploma in nursing Royal Columbian Hosp. Sch. Nursing, New Westminster, B.C., 1959; student Winnipeg Gen. Hosp., 1961; m. Harvey Neil Bolton, Sept. 5, 1964. Gen. duty nurse Vernon Jubilee Hosp., 1959-61, 62-64, Royal Columbian Hosp., New Westminster, 1961-62; operating room head nurse Chariboo Meml. Hosp., Williams Lake, B.C., 1964-68; operating room supr. Mills Meml. Hosp., Terrace, B.C., 1968-73; nurse Peel Meml. Hosp., Brampton, Ont., 1974—. Mem. R.N. Assn. B.C., United Ch. Women (v.p. Williams Lake 1967). Mem. Order Eastern Star. Clubs: Terrace Health, Terrace Curling. Home: 26 Grand Rapids Sq Bramalea ON L6S 2J1 Canada Office: Peel Meml Hosp 20 Lynch St Brampton ON Canada

BOLTON, MIMI DUBOIS, artist, author; b. Gravlotte, France, Dec. 12, 1902; d. Paul Traugott and Anna (Yhan) Hoffman; brought to U.S., 1904; student Marquette U.; m. George W. Bolton, Oct. 5, 1932. Exhibited in numerous one man and group shows in U.S. and abroad, 1933—. Recipient numerous prizes and awards for paintings. Mem. Artist Equity, Soc. Washington Artists. Author: Merry-Go-Round-Family (N.Y. Times list of 100 best childrens books, also Jr. Lit. Guild). Home: 3301 W Esplanade Apt 18291-B Metairie LA 70002

BOLTON, RUTH ANNE, hosp. adminstr.; b. Trenton, N.J., May 14, 1925; d. Guy Levon and Elsie (Fisher) Bolton; R.N., St. Francis Hosp. Sch. Nursing, 1945; B.S., Villanova U., 1954; M.H.A., St. Louis U., 1960. Supr., St. Francis Hosp., Trenton, 1945-46, Our Lady of Angels Geriatric Infirmary, 1946-50; supr. St. Joseph's Hosp., Balt., 1950-53, asst. adminstr., 1954-58, 60-61; adminstrv. asst. Kaiser Found. Hosps., Oakland, Cal., 1961-62; adminstr. Tracy (Cal.) Community Meml. Hosp., 1962—. Cons., lectr. Mem. adv. bd. Delta Coll., Stockton, Cal. Mem. Am. Coll. Hosp. Adminstrs., Am. Hosp. Assn., Assn. Western Hosps., Hosp. Council Central Cal., San Joaquin Valley Regional Health Council, N. San Joaquin Valley Hosp. Conf. (pres. 1965-66), Vis. Nurses Assn. (dir.), Tracy C. of C. Club: Soroptimist. Home: 1650 Tracy Blvd Tracy CA 95376 Office: 525 W Eaton Av Tracy CA 95376

BOLWELL, SUZANNE POLJACIK (MRS. HARRY J. BOLWELL), civic worker; b. Pittsford, Vt., Aug. 14, 1927; d. Andrew P. and Helen (Suchan) Poljacik; B.S., U. Vt., 1949; R.N., U. Vt. Sch. Nursing, 1949; M.A., U. Toledo, 1967; m. Harry James Bolwell, Sept. 24, 1949; children—Brian James, Suzanne Carr. Instr. med. and surg. nursing Presbyn. Hosp., Newark, 1949-51; instr. A.R.C., S.C., 1952; clin. instr. East Tenn. Bapt. Hosp., Knoxville, 1953, White Plains Hosp. (N.Y.), 1954; instr. psychology and psychiat. nursing Kirkman Tech. High Sch., Chattanooga, 1961; part time instr. psychology Cuyahoga Community Coll., Cleve. 1969—. Bd. mem. womens com. Boys Club Cleve; bd. examiners United Fund, Chattanooga, 1959-61. Mem. bd. Women's Orch. League Toledo, 1962-67, Health Hill Hosp., Cleve., 1968; mem. bd. Toledo Orch. Assn., 1965-67, mem. bd. women's com. Cleve. Orch., 1967—; mem. nat. com. sponsors Margaret Sanger Inst. Human Reprodn. and Devel., 1967—. Mem. Tenn. (past treas.), Chattanooga (past pres.), Greater Toledo leagues of women voters. Episcopalian (Sunday Sch. tchr.). Clubs: Country, Clevelander, Cleveland Athletic; Country, Cleveland Racquet; Garden. Home: Roundwood Rd Hunting Valley Chagrin Falls OH 44022

BOLYARD, JUDITH LYN, naturalist; b. Springfield, Ill., Oct. 16, 1949; d. Joseph D. and Aritha Joyce (Oliver) Bolyard; student U. Oslo, 1970, U. Copenhagen, 1970; B.A., Earlham Coll., 1971. Mem. staff Joseph Moore Mus., Richmond, Ind., 1969-71; naturalist Aullwood Center, Nat. Audubon Soc., Dayton, O., 1971—. Instr. summers Miami U., Oxford, O., 1972, Wright State U., Dayton, 1973, 74. Mem. Dayton Audubon Soc. (hon. mem., dir., chmn. edn. com.). Address: 1000 Aullwood Rd Dayton OH 45414

BOLYARD, ROCHELLE HARRISON (MRS. MARION BURL BOYLARD), assn. exec.; b. Clayton, N.C., Nov. 6, 1921; d. Brenton and Bettie (Coates) Harrison; student various bus. schs. and colls.; m. Marion Burl Bolyard, Apr. 5, 1947; children—Robert Burl, Richard Harrison. With Glenn L. Martin Co., Balt., 1946-47, N.C. Revenue Dept., Raleigh, 1946-47, Budd Co., Detroit, 1947-55, Electric Storage Battery Co., Raleigh, 1964-65, Investors Diversified Services, Raleigh, 1965-66; state sec. N.C. Pork Producers Assn., Raleigh, 1967-68; sec. to owners R. & R. Brokerage Co., Raleigh, 1969; exec. sec. Clayton (N.C.) C. of C., 1970—. Exec. sec. Human Relations Council Clayton, 1971—; pres. So. Belles chpt. Clayton Centennial, 1969; mem. Clayton Community Improvement Council, 1971—. Recipient Pres.'s plaque Clayton C. of C., 1971, 73, Gov.'s award, 1972. Mem. Clayton C. of C. (mem. exec. bd. 1970—). Home: Route 2 Box 274 Clayton NC 27520 Office: PO Box 246 Clayton NC 27520

BOLYARD, STARLYN MARIE, theater adminstr.; b. Morgantown, W.Va., Nov. 7, 1947; d. Charles A. and Marie Victoria (Orlando) Bolyard; B.F.A. (Rotary Scholar), W. Va. U., 1968, M.A., 1970. Dir. puppetmobile, W.Va. U., 1970-71; adminstrv. asst. Knoll Internat., Washington, 1971; adminstrv. asst., bus. mgr. Am. U., Washington, 1971—, instr., 1971-73, mem. Center for Liberal Studies, 1971-73; asst. house mgr. Arena Stage, Washington, 1973-74; interim dir. operations Am. U. Wolf Trap Acad. Performing Arts, 1973-74. Del. White House Conf. Children and Youth, 1970; ednl. tours with puppets. W. Va. Arts and Humanities Council grantee, 1970-71. Mem. Am. Coll. Theatre Assn., Am. Theatre Assn. (del. Conv. 1970), Speech. Assn. Eastern States, W. Va. Speech Assn., Catholic Daus. Am., Nat. Collegiate Players. Author: Punch and Judy and the Three Wishes, 1969, The Christmas Ogre, 1970. Home: 2701 S 16th St Arlington VA 22204 Office: American U McCabe Hall Washington DC 20016

BOLZ, HARRIETT HALLOCK (MRS. HAROLD A. BOLZ), musician; b. Cleve; d. Roscoe Scott and Anna (Griffith) Hallock; B.A., Western Res. U., 1933; M.A., Ohio State U., 1958; m. Harold A. Bolz, Aug. 7, 1937; children—William Scott, Everett Arthur, Eric Harold. Composer, pianist numerous compositions; lectr.; songs with piano, with string accompaniments, religious anthems, sonata for cello and piano, sonata for string and woodwind septet, cantata for chorus and orch., sonatina for clarinet and piano; pub. Four Christmas Songs, Carol of the Flowers, 1967; Two Madrigals for Christmas, 1968; That I May Sing, 1970; Sweet Jesus, anthem, 1974; performances Chgo., Cleve., Indpls., Lafayette, Kokomo, Ind., Columbus, O., Toledo, Miami Beach, Fla., Salt Lake City, Detroit, Cin., N.Y.C. at Lincoln Center. Recipient 1st prize for piano compostion Nat. Fedn. Music Clubs Adult Contest, 1965; 1st prize religious anthem, Nat. League Am. Pen Women, 1970, Biennial awards, 1972, two 1st prizes, 1974. Mem. A.S.C.A.P., Nat. League Am. Pen Women, Women's Aux. Am. Soc. M.E., Women's Music Club Columbus Nat. Assn. Am. Composers and Condrs., Ohio Fedn. Music Clubs (chmn. jr. and adult composers), Theta Lambda Phi, Phi Beta (Pi Nu chpt). Club: Ohio State University Women's. Home: 3097 Herrick Rd Columbus OH 43221

BOMAR, CORA PAUL, library educator; b. Memphis, Sept. 8, 1913; d. Paul C. and Rosa (Adams) Bomar; B.S. in Edn., U. Tenn., 1939; B.S. in L.S., George Peabody Coll., 1946; M.A., U. N.C., 1950. Tchr. elementary sch. Trezevant, Tenn., 1932-39; tchr., librarian pub. schs., Bruceton, Tenn., 1939-41; librarian high sch., Milan, Tenn., 1941-42; librarian and audio-visual program, Jr. high sch., Atlanta, 1945-46; reference librarian U. Tenn. Jr. Coll., Martin, 1946-47; elementary librarian, Chapel Hill, N.C., 1947-49; instrnl. supr., Orange County, N.C., 1949-51; supr. State Sch. Library Services, N.C. Dept. Pub. Instrn., 1951-66; dir. ednl. media N.C. Dept. Pub. Instrn., 1966-69; asst. prof. library edn. U. N.C. at Greensboro, 1969—; vis. faculty U. N.C. Library Sch., 1950, 53-55, 61, 64, 72, U. S.C., 1955; mem. U.S. Office Edn. adv. com. on new ednl. media, 1966-68, dir. Ednl. Media Selection Centers research project, 1970-71; mem. Nat. Cath. Edn. Assn. adv. Council, 1968-70. Mem. State Sch. Library Suprs. (chmn. 1957), Am. Assn. Sch. Libraries (exec. bd. 1958-60, pres. 1962-63), Am. (com. legislation 1960-66, adv. com. recruitment, 1963-65, Econ. Opportunity Act 1965-68, pres. Library Edn. div. 1969-70), Southeastern (mem. exec. bd. 1958-62, v.p. 1966-67, pres. 1967-68), N.C. (exec. bd. and Ala. councilor 1964—) library assns., Am. Assn. U. Women, N.C. Edn. and Library Assn., Delta Kappa Gamma, Beta Phi Mu (nat. v.p., nat. pres. 1965-66), Pi Gamma Mu. Democrat. Baptist. Club: Altrusa. Author articles profl. jours.; also author and co-author profl. bulls. Home: 107 W Avondale Dr Greensboro NC 27403

BOMBECK, ERMA LOUISE (MRS. WILLIAM BOMBECK), author; b. Dayton, O., Feb. 21, 1927; d. Cassius Edwin and Erma (Haines) Fiste; B.A., U. Dayton, 1949; m. William Lawrence Bombeck, Aug. 13, 1949; children—Betsy, Andrew, Matthew. Syndicated columnist Newsday Syndicate, 1965-70, Pubs.-Hall Syndicate, 1970—; contbg. editor Good Housekeeping Mag., 1969—. Mem. Theta Sigma Phi (Headliner award 1969), Sigma Delta Chi. Author: At Wit's End, 1967; Just Wait Till You Have Children of Your Own, 1971; I Lost Everything in the Post-Natal Depression, 1973. Home: 6301 N 38th St Paradise Valley AZ 85253

BOMPANE, PHYLLIS JOSEPHINE (MRS. FRANK WILLIAM BOMPANE), advt. agy. exec.; b. N.Y.C., Jan. 25, 1919; d. Benjamin and Adelaide (Bergmann) Rothman; B.A., Hunter Coll., 1938; m. Frank William Bompane, Feb. 8, 1941; children—Richard, Arthur, Ellen (Mrs. Walter Taurins). Coordinator radio-TV traffic Emil Mogul Advt. Co., N.Y.C., 1951-56; exec. sec. Frank B. Sawdon Advt. Co., 1956-61; adminstrv.-exec. sec. RKO Gen. Broadcasting WOR-TV, N.Y.C., 1961-68; corporate sec. Sawdon & Bess, Inc., N.Y.C., 1968—. Home: 277 Van Cortlandt Av E New York NY 10467 Office: 555 Madison Av New York NY 10022

BONAR, DOROTHY LOUISE (MRS. FREDERICK WOOD BONAR), retail exec.; b. Cleve., Apr. 14, 1918; d. Harry Daniel and Margaret Vera (Hartmeyer) Beutlich; student Carroll Coll., 1935-37; B.S., Northwestern U., 1940; Ed.M., U. Denver, 1942; m. Frederick Wood Bonar, June 25, 1940; 1 dau., Sharon Louise (Mrs. Fred Joe Gray). Collection corr. Cherry Creek, Sears-Roebuck Co., Denver, 1960-62; collection mgr. Fashion Bar, Denver, 1963-66, Dave Cook Sporting Goods Co., Denver, 1967; credit and collection mgr. Bonar Custom Tailors, Denver, 1967-73; collection mgr. Lane Bryant, Denver, 1973—. Mem. Gov.'s Com. on Edn., 1955-57; organizer, chmn. Mother's March for Polio, Denver, 1952-53; mem. membership com. Bonfils Meml. Theatre, Denver, 1940-52; mem. adv. budget com. Denver Pub. Schs., 1968-70. Bd. dirs. Emily Griffith Opportunity Sch., 1954-57, Sta. KRMA, 1955-58. Mem. Credit Women-Internat., Colo. Congress of P.T.A., Theta Sigma Phi, Women In Communications, Chi Omega. Republican. Presbyn. Mem. Order Eastern Star. Writer TV show Who Said It, Sta. KRMA, 1957. Home: 665 Monaco Parkway Denver CO 80220 Office: 808 16th St Denver CO 80202

BONAVENTURA, MARIA MIGLIORINI, educator; b. Somerville, Mass., June 29, 1938; d. Andrew and Maria Civita (Gallinaro) Migliorini; B.A. cum laude, Regis Coll., 1960; Ph.D., Tufts U., 1965; m. Andrew Salvatore Bonaventura, June 9, 1963. Research asst. Tufts U , Medford, Mass., 1960-64, research asso., 1965-66; asst. prof. Suffolk U., Boston, 1965-68, asso. prof., 1968-71, prof., 1971—, chmn. dept. chemistry, 1972—; research asso. Bio-Research Inst., Cambridge, Mass., 1968. Faculty rep. to trustees Joint Council on Univ. Affairs, Suffolk U., 1973-75, convenor president's Com. on Status of Women, 1974—, speaker Ednl. Policy Com., 1972-73. Mem. Am. Chem. Soc., The Chem. Soc. (London), New Eng. Assn. Chemistry Tchrs., Boston Malacological Soc., Am. Assn. Univ. Profs. (pres. chpt. 1970), Sigma Xi (pres. chpt. 1972-73), Sigma Zeta (sec. chpt. 1970—), Alpha Lambda Delta, Delta Epsilon Sigma. Contbr. articles to profl. jours. Home: 28 Lawndale Rd Stoneham MA 02180 Office: Suffolk University Beacon Hill Boston MA 02114

BONAZZI, ELAINE CLAIRE (MRS. JEROME ASHE CARRINGTON), mezzo soprano; b. Endicott, N.Y.; d. John Dante and Zina (Rossi) Bonazzi; B.Mus. (George Eastman scholar), Eastman Sch. Music; m. Jerome Ashe Carrington, Sept. 21, 1963; 1 stepson, Christopher. Made debut with Santa Fe Opera, 1958, Opera Soc. Washington, 1960, N.Y.C. Opera, 1965, Opera Internacional, Mexico City, Mexico, 1966, West Berlin Festival Opera, 1961, Spoleto Festival, 1974; mem. faculty Peabody Conservatory; soloist with several major Am. orchs., Canadian Broadcasting Corp., NBC-TV, ABC-TV; prin. roles include Baba in Rake's Progress, Augusta in Ballad of Baby Doe, Countess Geschwitz in Lulu, Genevieve in Pelleas, title role in Grande Duchesse de Gerolstein, La Vieja in Yerma, Carmen, Spy in Labyrinth, The Trial of Mary Lincoln; recs. on Vox, Columbia, Vanguard, Folkways, CRI records. Named One of 6 Honored Alumni, Eastman Sch. Music 50th Anniversary Year, 1971; chosen by Stravinsky, Hindemith, Menotti, Chavez, Rorem and Thomson for premiers of their works. William Matheus Sullivan grantee. Mem. Mu Phi Epsilon. Home: 650 West End Av New York City NY 10025 Office: care Thea Dispeker 59 E 54th St New York City NY 10022

BOND, ALISON MARY, editor; b. Surrey, Eng., Jan. 2, 1935; d. Cyril Edgar and Dorothy (Wood) Bond; B.A. with honors in Modern Langs., U. London, 1957; diploma U. Marburg (Germany), 1955. Came to U.S., 1960. Manuscript editor Oxford U. Press, Inc., N.Y.C., 1960-67; editor Charles Scribners, N.Y.C., 1967-68; trade editor Holt, Rinehart & Winston, Inc., N.Y.C., 1968-72; exec. editor Peter H. Wyden, Publishers, N.Y.C., 1973—; also free-lance editor, cons.; fgn. lang. reader pub. houses. Tchr. English as 2d lang. Midtown Center, N.Y.C., 1966-67. Vol. campaign worker McGovern for Pres., 1972. Club: University Women's (London). Editor: (A. Tucker) The Woman's Eye, 1973. Home: 125 E 93d St New York City NY 10028 Office: 750 3d Av New York City NY 10017

BOND, DOROTHY ANN, cartoonist; b. Chgo.; d. William George and Helga (Hansen) Peterson; student Chgo. Acad. Fine Arts, also pvt. tutoring; m. John Delmar Bond (div.); children—John Delmar, Raleigh V. Civilian exec.-sec. to Rear Adm. Alex M. Charlton, USN, 1940-44; syndicated cartoonist, 1945—; active in Realemon ad campaign, 1967-68; lectr. Hon. mem. Nat. Secs. Assn., Toastmistress Club, Chgo. Boys' Clubs, numerous other nat. and local orgns.; bd. sponsors Easter Seal Society, 1964—. Author cartoon books; Goverment Gertie, 1944; Navy Nora, 1945; Office Daze, 1945; The Second Baby, 1946; Life With the Boss, 1947; Mama, The Unsung Hero, 1948; Meet Me in The Ladies Room, 1948; All Men Are Dogs, 1950; Let's Have a Baby, 1950; Your First or Second Baby, 1956; Life With The Doctor n' Nurse, 1960; With Love, Bobbi Borcherdt, 1961; Bobbi Borcherdt Presents, 1962; Heartwarmers, 1963. Creator of Dietstickers, 1965; newspaper feature Delightful Diettips, 1966. Home: Dorothy Bond Enterprises 2450 N Washtenaw Av Chicago IL 60647

BOND, GLADYS BAKER (MRS. FLOYD J. BOND), author; b. Berryville, Ark., May 7, 1912; d. Coy Ernest and Clara (Clark) Baker; grad. Blair Bus. U., 1933; student Mont. State U., 1954-56; m. Floyd J. Bond, Sept. 3, 1934; 1 son, Nicholas Peter. Free-lance short story writer, newspaper writer, 1945-48; editor Leagazette Mag., 1971-72. Creative writing classes YWCA; mem. staff Pacific N.W. Writers Conf., 1970; tchr. art extension program Walla Walla Community Coll., 1974. Named Ida. Writer of Year, 1967. Lutheran. Mem. Art Assn. (pres. 1966-67), Valley Art Center. Club: Lewis-Clark Writers. Author: Blue Chimney, 1959; Little Stories on Big Subjects, 1957; The Special Secret, 1961; The Cottage Holiday, 1962; A Head on Her Shoulders, 1963; Here Comes A Friend, 1963; Tom and the Dickie-Bird, 1964; Here Come the Tuckers, 1964; Toby Tucker, 1964; That Kitten Again, 1964; The Secret at Rocky Ridge, 1965; Chap and Chirpy Chipmunk, 1965; Adventures with Hal, 1965; Fawn Baby, 1966; Patrick Will Grow, 1966; Animal Babies Wild and Free, 1966; Meg and the Disappearing Diamonds, 1966; The Mystery of Far Reach, 1967; On the Stranger's Mountain, 1968; Magic Friend Maker, 1966; Lassie and The Four White Ducks, 1968; My Widening World, 1969; Corey Baker's Show and Tell, 1969; Buffy and the New Girl, 1969; Buffy Finds a Star, 1970; Album of Cats, 1971; Boy in the Middle, 1972. Home: 1425 8th St Clarkston WA 99403

BOND, KAREN RUTH LAMBERT (MRS. DEWAYNE BOND), banker; b. Albuquerque, Nov. 10, 1942; d. Alazada M. and Betty (Engh) Lambert; student Am. Inst. Banking, 1961-63; m. Dewayne Bond, Nov. 26, 1961; 1 son, Dewayne Eric. Sec. to pres. First Security Bank, Mesa, Ariz., 1961-63, Central Ariz. Bank, Casa Grande, 1963-64; sec. to pres. Thunderbird Bank, Phoenix, Ariz., 1964-69, asst. cashier, 1968—, asst. v.p., 1972—; sec.-treas. Thunderbird Capital Corp., 1968—. Named Young Career Woman, Ariz. Bus. and Profl. Women's Clubs, 1969. Mem. Am. Inst. Banking (ednl. adviser 1969—), Nat. Assn. Bank Women (sec. 1971-72, vice chmn. 1973-74), Glendale Bus. and Profl. Women's Clubs (pres. 1969-70). Republican. Methodist. Home: 6425 N 44th Av Glendale AZ 85301 Office: PO Box 11856 Phoenix AZ 85061

BOND, RUTH CLEMENT (MRS. J. MAX BOND), club woman, educator; b. Louisville, May 22, 1904; d. George Clinton and Emma Clarissa (Williams) Clement; student Livingstone Coll., 1921; A.B., Northwestern U., 1925, M.A., 1930; postgrad. U. So. Cal., summer 1932; m. J. Max Bond, Aug. 5, 1931; children—Jane Emma, J. Max, George Clement. Tchr. English, Central High Sch., Louisville, 1927-30; head English dept. Ky. State Coll., Frankfort, 1930-32; prof. English L'Ecole Normale de Martissant, Port-au-Prince, Haiti, 1945; head English dept. U. Liberia, West Africa, 1951-54. Mem. bds. YWCA, Louisville, Knoxville, Tenn., New Orleans, Atlanta, and Liberia; co-founder Antoinette Tubman Children's Welfare Assn., Liberia, 1953; chmn. Research Com. on Status of Women in Liberia, World YWCA, Geneva, 1952; organizer World Day of Prayer Service, United Ch. Women, Kabul, Afghanistan, 1956, Tunis, Tunisia, 1958; chmn. Tunisian Projects Com., Am. Women's Club, Tunisia, 1958-59, chmn. com. aid to Algerian refugees Djilma Camp, Tunisia, 1959; sec. African Am. Inst., Malawi, Central Africa, 1963-64; pres. Women's Faculty Club, U. Liberia, 1951-54; mem. steering com., Widening Horizons D.C. Pub. Schs.; mem. Health and Welfare Council of Greater Washington; mem. met. bd. Boys' Clubs Greater Washington. Mem. Am. Assn. Fgn. Service Women (1st v.p. 1970-71, chmn. community relations com. 1971—, liaison rep. to Nat. Council Women), Nat. Council Women U.S., Church Women United (bd. mgrs.; exec. com., chmn. ecumenical and internat. coms., mem. Conf. Ch. and Synagogue Women), African-Am. Women's Assn.

(pres.), Delta Sigma Theta. Methodist. Home: 622 A St NE Washington DC 20002

BOND, SHIRLEY ARLENE PURDY (MRS. ELLWOOD WAYNE BOND), editor; b. Greenfield, Ia., Apr. 26, 1927; d. Clifford Floyd and Juanita Marie (Cox) Purdy; student West Tech. Coll., 1944; m. Ellwood Wayne Bond, Dec. 16, 1944; 1 son, Tim A. Salesgirl Montgomery Ward, Des Moines, 1944; owner, operator Home Cafe, Fontanelle, Ia., 1959-61; office mgr. Fontanelle Observer, 1961-69, editor, 1969—. Mem. Businessmen's Club (v.p. 1973). Democrat. Methodist. Club: Enterprise (sec.-treas. 1963-64) (Fontanelle). Home: Rural Route 2 Fontanelle IA 50846 Office: 313 5th St Fontanelle IA 50846

BOND, SHIRLEY REBECCA RILEY (MRS. RICHARD WILLIAM BOND II), county extension agt.; b. Martinsburg, W.Va., Feb. 3, 1944; d. Jesse Harrison and Eleanor Irene (Lord) Riley, Sr.; B.A., Shepherd Coll., 1967; M.A. in Child Devel., W.Va. U., 1973; m. Richard William Bond II, Mar. 31, 1973. County Extension agt. 4-H, W.Va. U. Cooperative Extension Service, Jefferson County, W.Va., 1967-73; home econs. agt. expanded nutrition program U. Fla. Coop. Extension Service, 1973, Dade County Coordinator 4-H Clubs, 1974—. Alumnae advisory bd. Sigma Sigma Sigma Sorority Shepherd Coll., 1969-71. Membership adviser 4-H All Stars, W.Va., 1962-72; mem. Shenandoah Concert Assn. Mem. Nat. (nat. com. to plan Nat. 4-H Week kit 1971, mem. policy and resolution com. 1972), W.Va. (pres. 1972) assns. extension 4-H agents, W.Va. Extension Women's Assn. (policy and resolutions com. 1971), Am. Assn. U. Women, Nat. Council on Family Relations, W.Va. Extension Workers Assn., Beta Sigma Phi, Sigma Sigma Sigma Alumnae. Home: 10791 N Kendall Dr Apt B102 Miami FL 33156 Office: 2690 NW 7th Av Miami FL 33127

BONESATTI, TERESA BERNARDEZ (MRS. JORGE BONESATTI), psychiatrist; b. Buenos Aires, Argentina, June 11, 1931 (came to U.S. 1957, naturalized 1963); d. Francisco and Dolores (Novoa) Bernardez; B.A., Liceo No 1 de Senoritas, 1948; M.D., U. Buenos Aires, 1956; m. Jorge Bonesatti, Dec. 26, 1956; 1 son, Diego. Intern hosps., Buenos Aires, 1956; psychiat. resident Topeka State Hosp., Menninger Sch. Psychiatry, 1957-60; postgrad. fellow in adult psychiatry C. F. Menninger Meml. Hosp., 1960-62, staff psychiatrist, 1962-65; staff psychiatrist The Menninger Found., Topeka, 1965—; practice medicine specializing in psychiatry, Buenos Aires, 1956, Paris, 1957, Topeka, 1957; cons. Topeka State Hosp., Office Econ. Community programs; instr. Menninger Sch. Psychiatry, 1965-71; asso. prof. psychiatry Mich. State U., 1971—. Diplomate Am. Bd. Psychiatry and Neurology. Mem. Am. Psychiat. Assn., Mich. Psychiat. Soc., N.Y. Acad. Scis. Home: 835 Westlawn East Lansing MI 48823 Office: Coll Human Medicine Mich State U East Lansing MI 48823

BONFIELD, GENEVIEVE KRIESEL (MRS. CHARLES EDWARD BONFIELD), securities broker; b. Michigan City, Ind., Dec. 23, 1913; d. Gustav Herman and Clara Mae (Brodersen) Kriesel; B.A., Eastern Mich. U., 1934; postgrad. Ind. U., 1938, Ariz. State U., 1955, Purdue U., 1962; m. Charles Edward Bonfield, Jan. 26, 1941 (dec.); children—Claire (Mrs. William G. Baldry, Jr.), Phyllis (Mrs. Phillip Keidaish), Charles Edward (dec.). Tchr. English, Elston Sr. and Jr. High Schs., Michigan City, 1934-41, 60-69; editor, pub. Shorelines, Michigan City, 1939-40; owner, operator Bonfield Speakers Agy., Michigan City, 1942-54; pres. Bonfield Motor Co. and Bonfield Farm Implement Corp., Michigan City, also La Porte, Ind., 1964-68; sec., broker Investors Diversified Services, Michigan City, 1969-73. Bd. dirs. LaPorte County Mental Health Assn. Recipient Dist. Service award Ind. Mental Health Assn., 1971, Outstanding Service award Ind. Fedn. Bus. and Profl. Women's Clubs, 1971. Mem. Ind. Congress Parents and Tchrs. (life mem.), Ind. Fedn. Bus. and Profl. Women's Clubs (dir. 1969-71, 72—), Am. Assn. U. Women (dir. Ind. div. 1971—, charter pres. Beverly Shores br. 1972—), League Women Voters (area pres. 1970—), Kappa Delta Pi. Presbyn. (pres. Womens Assn. 1952-54). Home: 2005 Lake Shore Dr Long Beach Michigan City IN 46360

BONHAM, KATHY P., lawyer; b. Bluefield, W.Va., Nov. 6, 1944; d. Jack Russell and Eva Arline (Cole) Bonham; B.A., U. Colo., 1966; J.D., U. Miami, 1969; Reginald Heber Smith Community Lawyer fellow U. Pa. and Howard U., 1969-71; postgrad. U. Ariz., 1971. Reporter, Coconut Grove (Fla.) Village Post, 1966; law clk. Office Econ. Opportunity, Miami, Fla., 1968-69; admitted to Fla. bar, 1970, Ariz. bar, 1971, Colo. bar, 1971; atty. Legal Services, Window Rock (Ariz.) Navajo Reservation and Papago Reservation, 1969-71; practice law, Denver, 1971—; part time faculty U. Denver Law Sch., 1972-73. Bd. dirs. Granfalloon Ednl. Broadcasting Inc., Capitol Hill Tenants Union, Community Econ. and Human Devel. Inc., Rocky Mountain Law Sch. Mem. Nat. Lawyers Guild, Fla., Ariz. bar assns., Bar and Gavel, Theta Sigma Phi, Kappa Beta Pi. Home: 2332 Emmerson St Denver CO 80205 Office: 1452 Pennsylvania St Denver CO 80203

BONHAM, LEAH ADRIANNE, religious orgn. adminstr.; b. Port Arthur, Tex., June 15, 1938; d. Stanley and Ione (Graves) Bonham; B.A., Mary Hardin Baylor Coll., 1960; M.R.E., Southwest Bapt. Theol. Sem., 1968. Editorial asst. press relations So. Baptist Fgn. Mission Bd., Richmond, Va., 1960-62; manuscript editor Baptist Sunday Sch. Bd., Nashville, 1964-66, editor childrens leisure reading materials, 1967-70; cons. gen. adminstrn, research, program design So. Baptist Woman's Missionary Union, Birmingham, Ala., 1970, dir. editorial services dept., 1970-73, supr. adult dept., 1973—. Mem. Women in Communications (treas. Birmingham chpt. 1972-73). Baptist (tchr. Sunday sch. 1964—, v.p. women's orgn. 1973-74). Author: Yes: A Woman's View of Mission Support, 1974. Contbr. articles to religious publs. Home: 2845 Carlisle Rd Birmingham AL 35213 Office: 600 N 20th St Birmingham AL 35203

BONN, ETHEL MAY, hosp. adminstr.; b. Cin., Oct. 14, 1925; d. Stanley Ervin and Ethel May (Cliffe) Bonn; B.A., U. Cin., 1947; M.D., U. Chgo., 1951. Intern, Strong Meml. Hosp., Rochester, N.Y., 1951-53; resident psychiatry VA Hosp., Topeka, Kan., 1953-55, asst. chief women's psychiat. sect. 1956-57, chief, 1957-61, chief N. psychiat. service, 1961-62; practice medicine specializing in psychiatry, Topeka, 1956-62, Denver, 1962—; mem. staff; asst. hosp. dir. Ft. Logan Mental Health Center, Denver, 1962-67, dir., 1967—; cons. staff Fitzsimons Army Gen. Hosp., Denver, Ft. Lyons (Colo.) VA Hosp. Clin. instr. psychiatry U. Colo., 1964—. Fellow Am. Psychiat. Assn.; mem. Am. Coll. Hosp. Adminstrs., Assn. Med. Supts. Mental Hosps., Assn. Mental Hosp. Adminstrs., Am. Hosp. Assn. Club: Altrusa (Denver). Home: 6636 W Glasgow St Littleton CO 80123 Office: 3520 W Oxford St Denver CO 80236

BONNELL, BARBARA JOHNSON (MRS. ROBERT OWEN BONNELL, JR.), pub. adminstr.; b. Balt., Feb. 27, 1931; d. Edward Sooy and Lillian (Diehl) Johnson; B.A. cum laude, Wellesley Coll., 1952; Certificat d'Etudes Politiques, U. Paris, 1953; M.A., Johns Hopkins, 1954, postgrad., 1955; m. Robert Owen Bonnell, Jr., June 18, 1966; 1 dau., Lila Johnson Hazlett. Instr. polit. sci. Johns Hopkins, 1953-54, 55-56, Goucher Coll., 1954-55; research asst. Ford Found. sponsored Com. on Govt. and Higher Edn., 1957-58; asst dir. Greater Balt. Com., 1958-60; dir. information Charles Center—Inner Harbor Mgmt. Inc., Balt., 1961—; dir. Waverly Press, Inc., 1974—. Pres. Assn. Jr. Leagues Am., 1962-64, dir., 1959-62; 2d v.p. Nat. Conf. on Social Welfare, 1964-65; dir. Nat. Health Council, 1965-68, YWCA Internat. Center, 1967-68; mem. U.S. Nat. Commn. for UNESCO, 1962-64; mem. pres. Commn. on Employment of the Handicapped, 1962-64; mem. Mayor's Charter Revision Commn., Balt., 1964; mem. citizens adv. com. Inst. for Polit. Edn., Morgan State Coll., 1961-69; sec. Md. Citizenship Commn., 1958; bd. mgrs. Bryn Mawr Sch., 1956-59; dir. UN Assn. Md., 1948-68; mem. Commn. of the Future of Coll. Wellesley Coll., 1969-71. Trustee St. Paul's Sch. for Girls, 1957-72, Union Meml. Hosp., 1970—; bd. dirs. Family and Children's Soc., 1966—, pres., 1973—; bd. dirs. Md. Soc. for Prevention of Blindness, 1965—, Met. Sr. Citizens Center, 1967—, Community Chest Met. Balt., 1971-72; bd. dirs. Balt. city com. Md. Hist. Trust, 1973—. Fulbright scholar, 1953-54, Horton-Hallowell fellow, Wellesley Coll., 1959-60, Univ. scholar Johns Hopkins, 1953-55. Club: Baltimore Wellesley (pres. 1971-74). Home: 5 Stratford Rd Baltimore MD 21218 Office: One Charles Center Baltimore MD 21201

BONNER, ALICE AMELIA, lawyer; b. Slidell, La., Apr. 11, 1941; d. Ernest B. and Eunice Amelia (Ducre) Wilkerson; B.A., Tex. So. U., 1963, J.D. with honors, 1966; m. Alfred Bonner, Mar. 30, 1966; children—Yvonne, Bernard, LaMont. Admitted to Tex. bar, 1967; partner firm Bonner & Bonner, Houston, 1967—; judge municipal ct., Houston, 1974—. Sec., dir. Bonmore Corp., 1969-72; pres., dir. AlBon 2000, Inc., 1973—; counsel Riverside Nat. Bank, Forward Times Newspaper, Judson Robinson & Sons Mortgage. Bd. dirs. West MacGregor Protective Assn., 1970-72, Citizens for Good Schs., 1972-73, Florence Crittenton Services, 1973—, Mt. Hope Bible Coll. Named Outstanding Alumni, Tex. So. U., 1970. Mem. Am., Nat. (exec. bd. 1974—, jud. council 1974—), Tex., Houston Jr. bar assns., Nat. Assn. Women Lawyers, Houston Lawyers Assn., Pivots of Houston, Nat. Council Negro Women (chpt. 2d v.p.) YWCA (life), Friends of Youth Soc. (life), Eta Phi Beta. Home: 4111 Roseneath Dr Houston TX 77021 Office: 2411 Southmore St Houston TX 77004

BONNER, CONNIE JEANNE GREER, pharmacist; b. Chgo., Mar. 24, 1939; d. William and Delores Ethel (Carlson) Greer; B.S. in Pharmacy, Purdue U., 1961; 1 son, Bret Jason. Pharmacist, Brunt-Schultz Drugs, 1961-63, 65, Med. Arts Pharmacy, New Orleans, 1963-64, Village Pharmacy, 1965-66, Needham Pharmacy, 1965-73, Med. Arts Pharmacy, 1973—, South Suburban Hosp., 1972—, Hermans Prescription Shop, 1973—. Mem. Am. Bus. Women's Assn. (program chmn. 1972-73, corr. sec. 1973-74, ways and means chmn. 1973-74, local chpt. Woman of Year 1974, charter chpt. pres. 1974), Chgo. Retail Druggists Assn. Presbyn. (Sunday sch. supt., trustee). Home: 618 Dundee Av Flossmoor IL 60422 Office: 3450 Chicago Rd Steger IL 60475

BONNER, EVELYN KELSAW (MRS. DAVID BENJAMIN BONNER III), librarian, archivist; b. nr. Camden, Ala., Mar. 3, 1940; d. James Thomas and Corine Eleanor (Tolbert) Kelsaw; A.A., Mary Holmes Jr. Coll., 1961; B.A., Johnson C. Smith U., 1965; M.S., Atlanta U., 1972; certificate U. Md., 1974; m. David Benjamin Bonner III, Dec. 30, 1962; 1 dau., Davita Bennetta. Instr. English, Teamer High Sch., Charlotte, N.C., 1963-65; asst. instr. speech Johnson C. Smith U., Charlotte, 1963-64; dir. adult edn., adminstrv. asst. Gillespie-Selden Inst., Cordele, Ga., 1966-67; instr. Sheldon Jackson Coll., Sitka, Alaska, 1967-72, dir. library, archivist, 1972—. Historian, Sitka Council on Arts. Bd. dirs. Sitka Concert Assn. Named Best All Around Woman on Johnson C. Smith campus, 1964. Mem. Am., Alaska library assns., Sitka Hist. Soc., Internat. Fedn. Bus. and Profl. Women (v.p.), Am. Assn. Univ. Women (edn. chmn.). Presbyn. (elder). Club: Soroptimist of Sitka (v.p.). Home: 836 Hillcrest Dr Sitka AK 99835 Office: Box 479 Sitka AK 99835

BONNER, JOAN ELIZABETH, med. social worker; b. Balt., Aug. 29, 1920; d. James Michael and Elizabeth (Lukes) Bonner; B.A., Rosemont Coll., 1941; M.S. in Social Work (A.R.C. scholar 1943), Cath. U. Am., 1943; advanced certificate social work adminstrn. U. Pa., 1967, postgrad., 1967—; m. Thomas Agnew Conway, Jan. 6, 1968 (dec. July 1968). Med. social worker, then asst. casework supervisor for the American Red Cross, 1943-48; psychiat. social worker VA, 1948-50; med. social worker U. Pa. Hosp., Phila., 1950-53, Misericordia Hosp., Phila., 1953-55; Albert Einstein Med. Center, Phila., 1957-58; dir. social service dept. Magee Meml. Hosp. for Convalescents Rehab. Center, Phila., 1958-71; dir. social service dept. Hosp. of U. Pa., 1971—. Tchr. history Collegio Americana. Caracas, Venezuela, 1956, Merici Acad., 1956-57. Mem. Council for Internat. Visitors Phila., 1957—; mem. St. Vincent's Aux., 1948—; mem. sch-agy. relations com. U. Pa. Sch. Social Work, 1962-65; mem. rehab. com. S.E. Pa. chpt. Am. Heart Assn., 1972-74. bd. dirs. Main Line Council Alcoholism, 1961-67. Mem. Nat. Assn. Social Workers (charter mem., chmn. med. social work Phila. 1962-64, chmn. nat. com. local council relationship com. 1963-64, chmn. nominating com. 1964-66, 1st vice chmn. exec. com. 1971-73, chmn.-elect Phila. area chpt. 1973-74, chmn. 1974—), Nat. Rehab. Assn., Pan Am. Assn., Alumni Assn. Cath. U. Am., Council on Social Work Edn., Acad. Certified Social Workers, Rosemont Coll. Alumnae Assn. (rec. sec. 1964-66, pres. Phila. 1969-70, 2d v.p. gen. assn.), Am. Hosp. Assn., Nat. Conf. on Social Welfare, Am. Soc. Hosp. Social Work Dirs. (charter mem., area rep. Phila. and Eastern Pa. region 1968-70, chmn. Phila. area chpt. 1971-73). Home: 603 Ballytore Rd Wynnewood PA 19096 Office: 34th and Spruce Sts Philadelphia PA 19104

BONNER, LILLY ANNELLE, educator; b. Toxey, Ala.; d. Martin C. and Lilly (Moseley) Bonner; B.S., U. So. Miss., 1946, M.A., 1954; Ed.D., Ind. U., 1964. Sec., U.S. Dept. Agr., Hattiesburg, Miss., 1946-48; tchr. New Augusta High Sch., New August, Miss., 1942-43, Houston Pub. Schs., (Miss.), 1943-44, Moselle (Miss.) Consol. High Sch., 1948-51, Sumter County High Sch., York, Ala., 1951-52, Soso (Miss.) Consol. High Sch., 1952-54, Quitman (Miss.) Consol. High Sch., 1954-58; instr. dept. bus. edn. U. So. Miss., Hattiesburg, 1958, asst. prof., 1959-65, acting chmn., 1963-64, asso. prof., 1965-68, prof., chmn. dept., 1968—. Mem. Hattiesburg Community Concert Assn., 1960—. Named Woman of Achievement, Bus. and Profl. Women's Club, Hattiesburg chpt., 1972. Mem. Am. Bus. Communication Assn., Am., Miss. vocational assns., Nat. (editor, mem. publs. com. 1973—), So. (sec. 1974), Miss. (pres. 1967-68, profl. awards com. 1974) bus. edn. assns., Miss. Edn. Assn., Hattiesburg Bus. and Profl. Women's Club (chmn. scholarship com. 1970-71), Pi Tau Chi, Phi Kappa Phi, Delta Pi Epsilon, Pi Omega Pi, Delta Kappa Gamma. Baptist. Home: 1115 Adeline St Hattiesburg MS 39401

BONNER, MERLINE CASE (MRS. JERRY JACKSON BONNER), dist. judge; b. Bentley, Okla., Jan. 25, 1924; d. Jeff David and Lizzie Lovel (Towry) Case; B.A., Okla. Coll. Women, 1944; M.A., U. Ia., 1945; LL.B., Okla., 1964, J.D., 1970; m. Jerry Jackson Bonner, Aug. 5, 1946; children—Frances (Mrs. Mason Mungle), Robert, Jerri (Mrs. Thomas B. Gordon III), Charles. Tchr. pub. sch., Atoka, Okla., 1945-46; admitted to Okla. bar, 1964; practiced in Atoka, 1964-71; judge, Atoka, 1971—. Mem. Am., Okla. bar assns., Am. Judicature Soc., Atoka C. of C., Zeta Phi Eta. Home: 11th St and Choctaw St Atoka OK 74525 Office: Courthouse Atoka OK 74525

BONNER, PATRICIA JANE, educator; b. Painesville, O., Apr. 8, 1935; d. Charles Leonard and Marie Estelle (Burridge) Bonner; B.A., Milligan Coll., 1957; M.Ed., U. Ariz., 1963; postgrad. U. Colo., 1961, Pepperdine Coll., 1966; M.Religious Edn., Emmanuel Sch. Religion, 1970. Tchr., Riverside High Sch., Painesville, O., 1957-62; grad. asst. U. Ariz., 1962-63; tchr. high sch., Los Angeles, 1963-64; instr. Fullerton (Cal.) Jr. Coll., 1964-65; personnel and credit office worker Broadway Dept. Stores, Downey, Cal., 1965-66; prof. phys. edn., Coach Milligan (Tenn.) Coll., 1966—. Dir. women's and girl's activities YMCA, Painesville, 1957-58; dir. religious edn. Norwalk (Cal.) Christian Ch., 1964-66; tennis clinician Lifetime Sports Found., 1967—. Mem. N.E.A., Tenn., East Tenn. edn. assns., Am., Tenn. assns. health, phys. edn. and recreation, Tenn. Coll. Phys. Edn. Assn., Nat. Intramural Sports Council (Tenn. rep. 1967-69, exec. sec. 1969-72), Tenn. Coll. Women's Sports Fedn. (sec.-treas. 1968-71, eastern rep. 1971-73), Am. Assn. U. Women, Milligan Coll. Alumni Assn. (sec. 1969-71), Milligan Faculty Club (treas. 1968), Delta Kappa Gamma, Pi Lambda Theta. Mem. Christian Ch. (Sunday sch. tchr. 1957—). Home: PO Box N Milligan College TN 37682

BONNET, WANDA GAIL WEHNER (MRS. BENNIE OLIVER BONNET), hotel exec.; b. Del Rio, Tex., Apr. 30, 1928; d. Herman Henry and Thelma Oralie (Thorgeson) Wehner; B.S. in Home Econs., U. Tex. at Austin, 1949; postgrad. Tex. A. and M., 1969; m. Bennie Oliver Bonnet, Sept. 3, 1949; children—Steve, Ted, Gary, Craig, Brian. Tchr., Willis (Tex.) High Sch., 1967-68, Del Rio Jr. High Sch., 1969-70, Garfield Elementary Sch., Del Rio, 1970-71; owner and mgr. Roswell Hotel, Del Rio, 1971—, Roswell Restaurant, 1972. Chmn. house-to-house crusade Val Verde County chpt. Am. Cancer Soc., 1973, 74. Mem. Tex. State Tchrs. Assn. (pres. 1972-73), Parent Tchr. Student Assn. (pres. 1972-73), North Heights P.T.A. (pres. 1964), U. Tex. Ex-Students Assn., Tex. A. and M. Mother's Club (sec. 1969-70, v.p. 1970-71, 73-74, pres. 1974-75). Methodist (pres. Womens Soc. Christian Service 1955-56, 65, sec. 1958, 72, 73). Club: Cactus Twirlers Square Dance. Home: PO Box 669 Hamilton Lane Del Rio TX 78840 Office: 137 W Garfield St Del Rio TX 78840

BONNETT, ALICE HERRING, newspaper editor; b. Marlin, Tex., Mar. 15, 1905; d. William E. and Cora Lee (Beal) Herring; grad. high sch.; m. Ralph G. Bonnett Aug. 25, 1929 (dec.). Asst. society editor San Antonio Eve. News, 1924-39; society editor San Antonio Express, 1954-70; society columnist N. San Antonio Times, 1970—. Mem. Women in Communications. Home: 2909 Fredericksburg Rd San Antonio TX 78201 Office: 5307 Broadway San Antonio TX 78209

BONNETTE, JEANNE DE LAMARTER (MRS. ARTHUR EDWARD BONNETTE), poet; b. Wausau, Wis., Dec. 19, 1907; d. Eric and Rubee (Wilson) De Lamarter; student Hazel Sharp Sch. of Ballet, 1921-27; student U. Chgo., 1927; certificate Cosmopolitan Sch. Music and Dramatic Art, 1927-29; m. Arthur Edward Bonnette, Dec. 29, 1957; children from previous marriage—Judith Best (Mrs. W.W. Barrick IV), Haven Best (Mrs. Henry J. Tobias). Free lance writer, 1924—; producer of the Creative Process series for TV Sta. KNME, Albuquerque, 1969—. Tchr. ballet, Bensenville, Ill., 1927-30; composer orchestral music for U. Chgo. Blackfriars and Mirror shows, 1926-28. Recipient Zia award N.M. Press Women, 1970, numerous others. Mem. Nat. Fedn. of State Poetry Socs. (sec. 1968-74), Poetry Soc. Am., N.M. Poetry Soc. (v.p. 1973-74), Nat. League Am. Pen Women (state letters chmn. 1972-73), World Poetry Soc., Poetry Soc. Am. Author: Colored Sails (poems), 1930; Seven Stars (poems), 1939; Chess Game and Other Poems, 1952; Oh, the Wide Sky (poems), 1968; In This Place (poems), 1971. Editor Some Haystacks Don't Even Have Any Needle; Poetry of the Desert Southwest, others. Address: 235 Coronado Village 8901 West Frontage Rd NE Albuquerque NM 87113

BONNEY, JEAN COZZA (MRS. RUSSELL NORWOOD BONNEY, JR.), ednl. adminstr.; b. Orange, N.J., Sept. 9, 1940; d. Stanley and Margaretta (Meyer) Cozza; B.A. in Math., U. Del., 1962; M.S. in Math., Stevens Inst. Tech., 1967; m. Russell Norwood Bonney, Jr., Sept. 14, 1963; children—Lesley Suzanne, Andrea Kay. Mem. tech. staff Bell Labs., Whippany, N.J., 1962-71; asst. dir. computer center Rutger's U., New Brunswick, N.J., 1971—. Active YMCA, Madison, N.J. Mem. Assn. for Computing Machinery (spl. interest groups-computers in edn., programming langs., univ. computer centers), Mortar Bd., Kappa Delta Pi. Presbyn. (Sunday sch. tchr. 1973—). Home: 55 Crestview Av Madison NJ 07940 Office: CCIS Hill Center Rutgers U New Brunswick NJ 08903

BONNEY, MARILYN JANE BARKELEW (MRS. GEORGE EDWIN BONNEY), educator; b. Syracuse, N.Y.,; d. Peter VanOrdan and Norma (Burdick) Barkelew; B.A., U. N.C., 1942; M.A., U. Pa., 1944; postgrad. State U. N.Y. Albany, 1967—; m. George Edwin Bonney, Aug. 17, 1945; 1 son, Russell Dean. Instr. Latin U. N.C., Greensboro, 1943-45; caseworker Jefferson County Pub. Welfare Dept., Watertown, N.Y., 1950-53, sr. caseworker, 1953-55; tchr. N.Y. pub. schs., Adams Center, 1955-57, Watertown, 1959-60, Dexter, 1962-63; asst. prof. English Jefferson Community Coll., Watertown, N.Y., 1963-66, asso. prof., 1966-69, prof., 1969—, also head dept., 1967—, chmn. liberal arts div., 1970—, affirmative action coordinator, 1973—. Mem. N.E. Regional Conf. English in Two-Yr. Coll. Mem. bd. South Jefferson Central Sch., 1957-69. Mem. Nat. Council Tchrs. English, N.Y. State English Council, N.Y. State Jr. Coll. Assn. (exec. bd. 1970-72). Home: Massey Rd RD 1 Watertown NY 13601

BONNIFIELD, PATRICIA PEARL GENTRY, librarian; b. Pirtle, Ore., Oct. 11, 1921; d. Henry Thomas and Frieda Edna (Gierre) Gentry; student Holy Names Coll., Spokane, Wash., 1940, Fla. State U., 1960, C.Z. Coll., 1961; A.A., Centralia Coll., 1965; B.A., St. Martins Coll., 1967; M.Librarianship, U. Wash., 1968; m. Jon Bonnifield, Jan. 30, 1943; 1 dau., Patricia. Fiscal office asst. Wash. Dept. Licenses, 1956-59; office asst. Gorgas Hosp., C.Z., 1961; library asst. C.Z. Library and Mus., Ancon, 1961-62; dir. library St. Martins Coll., Olympia, Wash., 1968—. Tchr., St. Michael Sch. Religion, Olympia, 1950-59, St. Marys Sch., Balboa, C.Z., 1959-60. Charter mem. St. Peter Hosp. Aux., Olympia, 1955—, treas., 1959; mem. Evergreen Orthopedic Guild, 1955-59; sec. Jr. Women, Olympia, 1955; leader Girl Scouts Am., Olympia, 1955; mem. exec. bd. Seattle Archdiocesan Council Catholic Women, 1955-59; mem. Wash. Adv. Council on Libraries, 1973—. Mem. Wash. Assn. Acad. and Research Librarians (pres. elect 1974—, charter mem.), N.W. Assn. Pvt. Coll. and Univ. Librarians (sec. 1969), Wash., Pacific N.W. library assns., Am. Assn. Univ. Women, C.Z., Olympia (legislative chmn. 1955), Catholic daughters Am. Democrat. Home: 1002 S Lybarger St Olympia WA 98501 Office: Library St Martins Coll Olympia WA 98503

BONNY, HELEN LOUISE LINDQUIST (MRS. OSCAR E. BONNY), music therapist; b. Rockford, Ill., Mar. 31, 1921; d. Gustavus Elmer and Ethel (Geer) Lindquist; Mus.B., Oberlin Coll., 1943; B. Music Edn., Kan. U., 1964, M. Music Edn., 1968; m. Oscar E. Bonny, Aug. 17, 1943; children—Beatrice Helen (Mrs. Gary Starrett), Erich Lind, Francis Albert. Developer stringed instrument dept., pub. schs., Anthony, Kan., 1949-51; instr. stringed instruments St. Mary's Coll., Xavier, Kan., 1958-60; music therapist VA Hosp.,

Topeka, Kan., 1963-64, Parsons (Kan.) State Hosp., 1965; research investigator VA Hosp., Topeka, Kan., 1966-68; coordinating sec. Nat. Assn. for Music Therapy, Lawrence, Kan., 1967-68; music therapist Md. Psychiat. Research Center, Balt., 1969—. Cons. music therapy Friends of Psychiat. Research, Balt., 1969; co-founder, pres. Inst. for Consciousness and Music. Mem. adv. bd. Assn. Transpersonal Psychology Palo Alto, Cal., Inst. for Consciousness Research, Iceland. Mem. Nat. Assn. for Music Therapy (regional v.p. 1972), Assn. Humanistic Psychology, Pi Kappa Lambda, Sigma Alpha Iota. Co-author: Music and Your Mind, 1973. Home: 721 St Johns Rd Baltimore MD 21210 Office: Box 3235 Md Psychiat Research Center Baltimore MD 21228

BOOCOCK, SARANE SPENCE (MRS. C. BRETT BOOCOCK, JR.), sociologist; b. Evanston, Ill., May 7, 1935; d. William Kenneth and Barbara (Gilbreath) Spence; B.A., Vassar Coll., 1957; M.A., Rutgers U., 1961; Ph.D., Johns Hopkins, 1966; m. C. Brett Boocock, Jr., Dec. 22, 1957; 1 son, Paul Morris. Cost analyst Prudential Life Ins. Co., Newark, 1957-58; social caseworker, child welfare analyst N.J. Bd. Child Welfare, New Brunswick, 1958-59; group leader European Traveling Seminar, 1959; instr., research asst. Rutgers U., 1959-62; asso. Center for Study Social Orgn. Schs., research asso. dept. social relations Johns Hopkins., 1962-68; asst. prof. sociology U. So. Cal., Los Angeles, 1968-70, asso. prof., 1970-73; sociologist Russell Sage Found., N.Y.C., 1973—. Co-founder Acad. Games Assos., Balt., 1968, also dir.; vis. prof. Hebrew U., Jerusalem, Israel, 1973; vis. lectr. U. Stockholm (Sweden), U. Göteborg (Sweden) 1973. Grantee Carnegie Corp., 1965, U.S. Office Edn., 1967, NASA, 1969, ESSO Edn. Found., 1972-73, U.S. Office Child Devel., 1972-73, Russell Sage Found., 1974-75. Recipient Dart award, 1970. Mem. Am. Sociol. Assn. Author: (with Matilda W. Riley) Sociological Research Methods, 2 vols., 1963; contbg. author, co-editor: Simulation Games for Learning, 1968; An Introduction to the Sociology of Learning, 1972. Asso. editor Sociology of Edn., 1969—; co-founder, editorial bd. Simulation and Games, 1969—, editor, 1973—; contbg. editor Ednl. Tech., 1967-69. Contbr. articles to profl. jours. Home: 320 E 72d St New York City NY 10021 Office: Russell Sage Found 230 Park Av New York City NY 10017

BOODY, SARAH VANETTA, nursing adminstr.; b. Auera, Miss., Jan. 23, 1946; d. William Donald and Helen Geneva (Roberts) Polen; A.A. in Nursing, Jones County Jr. Coll., 1966; B.A. in Christian Edn., Lee Coll., 1971; m. Robert Antonious Boody, Dec. 25, 1971. Staff nurse Jones County Community Hosp., Laurel, Miss., 1966-68; sch. nurse Lee Coll., 1968-71; dean women West Coast Bible Coll., Fresno, Cal., 1971-73; dir. nursing Fresno Care and Guidance Center, psychat. nursing home, 1973—. Pres., Sem. Women's fellowship Mennonite Brethren Bibl. Sem., Fresno, 1972—. Mem. Pi Delta Omicron. Home: 435 S Maple Av Fresno CA 93702 Office: 1715 S Cedar Av Fresno CA 93727

BOOG, JANET MARGARET, physician; b. Cin., Mar. 4, 1913; d. Fredrick Anthony and Gertrude (Petit) Boog; student U. Cin., 1931-33; M.D., N.Y. Med. Coll., 1939. Intern, Good Samaritan Hosp., Cin., 1939-40; resident N.Y. Infirmary for Women and Children, N.Y.C., 1940-41, Margaret Hague Hosp., Jersey City, 1942-43, Univ. Hosp., Ann Arbor, Mich., 1943-44, Omaha, 1945-46; cons. obstetrics Dept. of Health, Honolulu, 1946-48; practice medicine specializing in gynecology and obstetrics, Lawrence, Mass., 1949-52, Detroit, 1953-57; resident neuropsychiatry VA Hosp., N.Y.C., 1959-62; staff psychiatrist Longview State Hosp., Cin., 1962-66; unit chief psychiatry VA Hosp., Lexington, Ky., 1966—; clin. instr. psychiatry U. Ky., 1968—. Diplomate Am. Bd. Obstetrics and Gynecology. Fellow Am. Coll. Obstetrics and Gynecology; mem. Am. Psychiat. Assn., Cin. Soc. Neurology and Psychiatry, Wilderness Soc. Club: Sierra. Contbr. articles to obstet. and gynecol. jours. Home: 1545 Alexandria Dr Lexington KY 40504 Office: Leestown Pike Lexington KY 40507

BOOHER, OLGA BONKE (MRS. NORMAN R. BOOHER), physician; b. Indpls., Aug. 14, 1907; d. Robert R. and Margaret C. (Gommel) Bonke; A.B., Butler U., 1929; M.D., Ind. U., 1932, M.D. cum laude, 1933; m. Norman R. Booher, Oct. 7, 1934; children—Alice Ann, Philip Norman, John Holliday and Robert Bonke (twins). Rotating intern Ind. U. Hosps., 1932-33; asst. resident pediatrics Riley Hosp. for Children, Indpls., 1933-34, chief resident pediatrics, 1934-35; practice medicine specializing in pediatrics, Indpls., 1935—; mem. staffs Ind. U. Hosps., Meth. Hosp., St. Vincent Hosp., Community Hosp., Marion County Gen. Hosp.; mem. Ind. State Nutrition Council, 1947—. Adviser Med. Explorer Girls. Bd. dirs. Met. YWCA. Recipient outstanding achievement award Indpls. C. of C., 1969. Diplomate Am. Bd. Pediatrics. Fellow Am. Acad. Pediatrics; mem. A.M.A., Ind., Marion County med. socs., Ind. U. Sch. Medicine Alumni Assn. (pres. 1962-63, sec. 1963—, Mortar Bd., Zeta Tau Alpha, Nu Sigma Phi. Presbyn. Club: Zonta (city pres. 1958-60). Home: 2818 Barbary Lane Indianapolis IN 46205 Office: 447 E 38th St Indianapolis IN 46205

BOOK, ANITA-BAKER (MRS. WILLIAM S. BOOK), store owner, designer; b. Essex, Ill.; d. John Benjamin and Dora (Greenwald) Baker; student Chgo. Bus. Coll., Columbia Conservatory, 1921-23, Am. Acad. Fine Arts; grad. Herzl Jr. Coll., 1936; student N.Y. U., 1936; U. Chgo., 1937-39, 40-41, U. Neb., 1941; m. William Ship Book, Mar. 14, 1941. Tchr. dramatic art, Chgo., 1926-32; appeared various radio plays. Chgo., 1926-37; secretarial position, receptionist, Chgo., 1927-32; mgr. N.Y. import office, 1933-34; lectr. throughout U.S. with exhbn. wood carvings and handicrafts from Dutch East Indies, 1934-41; secretary Consairways, Fairfield, Cal., 1945; owner exec. dir., designer Binita Fruit & Gift Wares, Skokie, Ill., 1945—, exhbns. major gift and trade shows throughout U.S.; ex-treas. Natural Hygiene Press. Commr., Skokie Beautification and Improvement Commn.; mem. Skokie Bicentennial Commn. Mem. nat. women's com. Brandeis U. Mem. Natural Hygiene Assn., Gift and Decorative Arts Assn., Natural Food Assns., Organic Growers No. Ill., League Women Voters (dir. local chpt., chmn. pub. relations, chmn. observation program publs.), Nat. Health Fedn., Skokie C. of C. (chmn. beautification com. 1968). U. Chgo. Alumni Assn. (life), Art Inst. Chgo. (life), Skokie Valley Symphony Orch. and Women's Guild, Skokie Valley Bus. and Profl. Women's Club, Nat. Fedn. Ind. Bus's Inc., Poets and Patrons, Nat. Geog. Soc., Smithsonian Assos., North Shore Pub. Relations. Home: 3811 Wright Terrace Skokie IL 60076 Office: 8100 N Lawndale Av Skokie IL 60076

BOOK, CASSANDRA LOU, educator; b. Aurora, Ill., Nov. 6, 1948; d. Allan Lavern and Florence Marie (Harvey) Book; B.A., Mich. State U., 1970; M.A., Northwestern U., 1971; postgrad. Purdue U., 1972—. Program dir., counselor-in-tng. dir. Camp Watervliet (Mich.), summers 1968-71; grad. asst. Northwestern U., Evanston, Ill., 1970-71; instr. U. Wis., Whitewater, 1971-72; grad. teaching asst., speech communication Purdue U., West Lafayette, Ind., 1972-74; instr. Mich. State U., East Lansing, 1974—. Mem. Speech Communication Assn., Central States Speech Communication Assn., Mich. Speech Assn., Internat. Communication Assn., Mortar Bd., Delta Delta Delta. Methodist. Author: (with Kathleen Galvin) Speech Communication: An Interpersonal Approach for Teachers, 1972, Person-to-Person: An Introduction to Speech Communication, 1973. Office: Dept Communication Mich State U East Lansing MI 48823

BOOK, IMOGENE IRIS CLARK (MRS. WILTZ ALONZO BOOK), librarian; b. Mt. Vernon, Ill., Dec. 12, 1924; d. Keith and Mona (Hawkins) Clark; B.S., So. Ill. U., 1946, postgrad., 1955, summer 1956; M.S., U. Ill., 1960, certificate of advanced study in librarianship, 1966; m. Wiltz Alonzo Book, Aug. 18, 1946; children—Douglas Keith, Karen Lynn. Tchr. secondary schs., Bellmont, Ill. 1946-47, Marissa, Ill., 1947-48, Bluford, Ill., 1955-56; tchr. Mt. Vernon Twp. High Sch., 1954-55, 56-57, librarian 1958-62; librarian Mt. Vernon Community Coll., 1956-67, mem. adv. council, 1961-69; librarian Rend Lake Coll., Ina, Ill., 1967—. Cons., Student Ill. Edn. Assn., 1964-70; mem. adv. council U. Ill. Grad. Sch. Library Sci., 1962-64, Ill. Commn. Tchr. Edn. and Profl. Standards, 1966-70. Mem. Ill. (legislative devel. com. 1965-69), Jefferson County (sec. 1964-65, pres. 1965-66), Mt. Vernon (pres. 1959-60) edn. assns., N.E.A., Ill., Mt. Vernon (sec. 1962-63, v.p. 1963-64, pres. 1964-65) library assns., Ill. Assn. Sch. Librarians (sec. 1958-59), Ill. Audiovisual Assn., Ill. Assn. Coll. and Research Libraries (com. on guidelines for community colls. 1974—), Delta Kappa Gamma (chpt. v.p. 1964-66, rec. sec. 1966-68, pres. 1968-70). Home: 912 S 21st St Mount Vernon IL 62864 Office: Rend Lake College Rural Route 1 Ina IL 62846

BOOKER, HARRIET JEAN ANDERSON, writer, home economist; b. Craftsbury Common, Vt., July 8, 1918; d. William W. and Helen (Stuart) Anderson; B.S., U. Vt., 1939; student Columbia U. Sch. Journalism, 1946-47, N.Y. U. Writing Workshop, 1947-48; m. William Edward Booker, Dec. 12, 1955. Tchr. home econs. Buckley High Sch., Hartford, Conn., 1939-41; home demonstration agt. Windham County, Vt., 1941-42; dir. A.R.C., First Gen. Hosp., Eng., France and Germany, 1942-45; food editor N.Y. Herald Tribune, food writer for This Week Mag., 1947-50; dir. N.Y. Herald Tribune Home Inst., N.Y.C., 1950-53; dir. home econs. Am. Can Co., N.Y.C., 1953-56, Winter Garden Co., Inc., 1956-70; pres., propr. Booker Trading Co. Co-chmn. publicity and pub. relations Knoxville Met. Opera Com.; chmn. pub. relations Dulin Gallary Art; mem. steering com. United Community Services; mem. adv. bd. Knox County Juvenile Ct.; mem. exec. res. corps Dept. Labor, 1970—; asst. chmn. pub. relations Knoxville Heritage. Mem. adv. bd. Nixon-Agnew Campaign Com., 1968-72. Bd. dirs. Helen Ross McNabb Mental Health Center, Knoxville. Recipient W.J. Stone award U. Vt. Mem. bd. Soc. for Preservation Tenn. Antiquities. Mem. N.Y. Women's Newsppaer Club, Am. Women in Radio and Television, Am. Home Econs. Assn., Home Econs. in Bus., Mortar Board, Knoxville Art League, Knoxville Symphony Soc. (dir. pub. relations), Assn. for Preservation Tenn. Antiquities, Omicron Nu. Clubs: Cherokee, Ossolli, Republican Women's. Compiler: American Cook Book, 1952. Author: How to Eat Better and Save Money, 1953. Home and office: 3039 Kingston Pike Knoxville TN 37919

BOOKER, JANICE LEKOFF (MRS. ALVIN E. BOOKER), editor; b. Phila., July 25, 1929; d. Max and Betty (Cohen) Lekoff; B.S., Temple U., 1951; m. Alvin E. Booker, Dec. 16, 1951; children—Ellis Carl, Susan Barbara. Editor, Shopper Publs., Inc., Jenkintown, Pa., 1951-58; dir. information Oak Lane Day Sch., Blue Bell, Pa., 1963—. Free lance writer, editor in edn. and social scis., 1960—; columnist Phila. Jewish Exponent, 1969-72; feature writer Suburban Life, 1970-73; research writer Phila. Bd. Edn., 1973-74; reporter Times Chronicle, 1974—. Mem. Women in Communications. Home: 530 Elkins Av Elkins Park PA 19117

BOOKER, NANA LAUREL, educator; b. Waco, Tex., Aug. 5, 1946; d. Karl and Helen Dorothy (Keene) Booker; B.A. (Forensic scholar), Baylor U., 1968; M.A. (fellow), U. Fla., 1970, postgrad., 1970—. Instr., La. State U., New Orleans, 1970-71, asst. prof., dir. lab. theatre, 1971—, coach debate team, 1971-72, adviser student publs., 1972-74; account exec. advt. and pub. relations E. Allen Davis & Assos., New Orleans, 1974—. Formerly co-producer children's radio show; cons. in creative dramatics to schs. and kindergartens. Vol. services to various charities, 1970—. Research grantee La. State U., 1972. Mem. Am. Assn. U. Profs., Puppeteers of Am., Am. Ednl. Theatre Assn., Speech Communication Assn., Am. Theatre Assn., Columbia Scholastic Press Assn., Nat. Council Coll. Publ. Advisers, Pi Kappa Delta, Kappa Delta Pi. Office: 811 International Bldg New Orleans LA 70130

BOOMSLITER, JEAN R. MORRIS, bus. exec., librarian, ednl. communications technologist; b. Syracuse, N.Y., Apr. 15, 1934; d. Seymour L. and Ruth (Harrison) Morris; student Northwestern U., 1951-53; A.B., State U. N.Y., Albany, 1958, M.L.S., 1968; postgrad. Harvard; m. Paul C. Boomsliter, June 10, 1958 (div. Aug. 1963); 1 son, P. Lon Harrison. Drama dir. Gloversville (N.Y.) High Sch., 1955-58; asst. to curator Drama Collection Houghton Library Harvard, 1957; instr. pub. speaking Jr. Coll. Albany br. Russell Sage Coll., 1958-59; librarian New Lebanon Central, Lebanon Springs, N.Y., 1965-67; instr. English, Fulton-Montgomery Community Coll., 1967—; media specialist Amsterdam Sch. Dist., 1968—; chief copywriter Seymour Morris Assos., Inc., Gloversville, 1962—. Trustee Albany Civic Theatre, dir. Do a Revue, 1963, Named col. a.d.c. staff Gov. N.M., 1965. Mem. Am., N.Y. library assns., Am. Assn. U. Women, N.Y. State Tchrs. Assn., Assn. Ednl. Communications and Technology, Capitol Region, N.Y. State ednl. communications associations, also Alpha Epsilon Phi. Author, dir. (with Vincent Cresanti) So Young and Fair, three-act mus. comedy, 1957; author Alice in Leatherland, 1965. Home: 136 Prospect Av Gloversville NY 12078 Office: 42 N Main St Gloversville NY 12078

BOONE, BETTY EVANS (MRS. ELBERT JAMES BOONE), lawyer, county ofcl.; b. Baton Rouge, La., Oct. 4, 1928; d. Charles Hadley and Pearl (Grubbs) Evans; B.S., Centenary Coll. of La., 1950; postgrad. Tex. Christian U., 1958-59; J.D., U. San Diego, 1964; m. Elbert James Boone, Dec. 27, 1950; children—Evan Patrick, Karsten Scott. Legal sec. firm Carstarphen & Carstarphen, Shreveport, La., 1947-50, Birkhead, Beckman, Stanard, Vance & Wood, San Antonio, 1951-52, Clayton, Arnow, Duncan & Johnston, Gainesville, Fla., 1950-51, Higgs, Fletcher & Mack, San Diego, 1960-65; admitted to Cal. bar, 1965; asso. trust counsel San Diego office, Title Ins. and Trust Co., 1965-67; dep. county counsel Office of County Counsel of San Diego County, 1967—, chief of sect. on schs., elections and retirement, 1973—. Bd. dirs. Women's Aux., Univ. Hosp., San Diego, 1968-70. Grad Teaching fellow, 1958-59. Mem. State Bar Cal., Dist. Attys. and County Counsels Assn. of Cal. (state sect. chmn. 1973-74), San Diego County Bar Assn., Nat. Orgn. on Legal Problems of Edn., League of Women Voters. Republican. Mem. Unitarian Ch. (dir. 1965-68, chmn. bd. 1967-68, ch. historian 1973-74). Club: Altrusa of San Diego. Home: 4375 Loma Riviera Court San Diego CA 92110 Office: 302 County Administration Center 1600 Pacific Hwy San Diego CA 92101

BOONE, CHARLOTTE JACKSON, geologist; b. Springdale, Ark., Sept. 28, 1914; d. Roy Weeks and Mollie (Jones) Jackson; B.A., Oklahoma City U., 1953; postgrad. U. Okla., 1953; m. Francis Maynard Boone, Dec. 7, 1935(div. Oct. 1961; 1 dau., Nancy Marie (Mrs. Michael David Denton). Exploration geologist Parker Petroleum, Inc., Ponca City, Okla., 1954-57; staff geologist Okla. State Corp. Commn., Oklahoma City, 1958—. Certified profl. geologist, Okla. Mem. Am. Assn. Petroleum Geologist, Soc. Econ. Paleontologists and Mineralogists, Inst. Profl. Geologists, Oklahoma City Geol. Soc. Home: 1310 Whitehurst Lane Nicoma Park OK 73066 Office: Jim Thorpe Bldg Oklahoma City OK 73105

BOONE, GRAY DAVIS (MRS. JAMES BUFORD BOONE, JR.), publisher; b. Houston, Aug. 27, 1938; d. Edwin Theodore and Martha Lucille (Scholl) Davis; student U. Tex., 1956-59, U. Geneva, Switzerland, 1959; m. James Buford Boone, Jr., June 30, 1961; children—Kenneth Scholl, James Buford III, Martha Frances. Legal sec. to dist. atty. in Harris County, Tex., 1960-61; founder, propr. Antique Monthly publ., Tuscaloosa, Ala., 1967—. Tchr. French pub. schs., Suffolk, Va., 1963-64. Mem. Jr. Vol. Service Corps, Suffolk, Va., v.p., 1964-65, pres. 1966-68. Mem. adv. bd. Tuscaloosa County Preservation Authority. Bd. dirs. Devel. of New Coll., U. Ala., 1970. Mem. Tuscaloosa Preservation Soc. Episcopalian. Home 8 Central Highlands Tuscaloosa AL 35401 Office: PO Drawer 2 Tuscaloosa AL

BOONE, MARY GRACE, lawyer; b. Lansing, Kan., Jan. 2, 1898; d. Thomas John and Theresa Henrietta (Lin) Boone; B.S., Kan. State U., 1924, M.S., 1937; postgrad. San Jose State Tchrs. Coll., 1925; LL.D., Kan. U., 1957. Tchr., Lansing, 1918-1921, Leavenworth, Kan., 1921-22, 27-73, Turner, Kan., 1924-27; admitted to Kan. bar, 1957; mem. firm Boone, Boone & Boone, Leavenworth, 1957—; police judge City of Leavenworth, Kan., 1965-69, municipal judge, 1969-73. Mem. Bar Assn. Kan., Leavenworth County Bar Assn. (pres. 1966), Cath. Lit. Soc., Ret. Tchrs. Assn. (pres. 1972), Daus. of Isabella, Phi Delta Delta, Phi Alpha Delta. Home: 110 Kay St Lansing KS 66043 Office: Axa Bldg Delaware St Leavenworth KS 66048

BOONE, WILLIE CATHERINE GODFREY (MRS. ROBERT SILLS BOONE), librarian; b. Morganton, N.C., Aug. 26, 1913; d. William Wesley and Fannie (Quinn) Godfrey; A.B., Wake Forest Coll., 1935; M.Ed., U. N.C., 1958; m. Robert Sills, William Herbert. Tchr. English and history Murphy High Sch., 1935-40, Shelby High Sch., 1941-46, Winecoff High Sch., Concord, 1947-51, Clinton High Sch., 1952-56, So. High Sch., Durham, 1957-59 (all N.C.); head librarian Durham High Sch., 1960-74; asst. prof. library sci. dept. Appalachian State Tchrs. Coll., summers 1959-67. Exec. sec. N.C. High Sch. Library Assn. Mem. N.E.A., N.C. Edn. Assn., Am. Assn. U. Women, Classroom Tchrs. Assn., Am., N.C. library assns., Bus. and Profl. Women's Club (past pres.). Baptist. Mem. Order Eastern Star (past matron). Home: 2918 University Dr Durham NC 27707

BOONIN, TOBYANN AUERBACH (MRS. LAWRENCE I. BOONIN), civic worker; b. Phila., Dec. 28, 1927; d. Philip and Rose (Levin) Auerbach; student Temple U., Neighborhood Playhouse Sch. Theatre, N.Y.C.; m. Lawrence I. Boonin, Mar. 4, 1948; children—Nicholas, David, Robert. Mem. Pa. Sch. Bds. Assn., Nat. Sch. Bds. Assn., League Women Voters, Orgn. for Rehab. through Tng., Alliance of Bus., Academe and Commerce in U.S.; bd. dirs. Phila. Bd. Edn., Anti-Defamation League B'nai B'rith, Oak Lane Civic Assn.; liaison Sch. Dist. Phila. and Boy Scouts Am.; mem. bd. Dropsie U., Phila., Crime Prevention Assn. Recipient Woman of Valor award Phila. Home and Sch. Council, 1970, Humanitarian award Adult Trainees Assn. Retardates, 1970. Jewish religion. Home: 1243 65th Av Philadelphia PA 19126 Office: Administration Bldg 21st and Parkway Philadelphia PA 19103

BOORSTEIN, BEVERLY WEINGER, lawyer; b. Chgo., Apr. 25, 1941; d. Morris Aaron and Bess (Meisel) Weinger; B.A., Brandeis U., 1961; J.D., Boston U., 1964; m. Sidney Lester Boorstein, July 3, 1962; children—Robin Anne, Michelle Loren. Admitted to Mass. bar, 1964; with firm Siskind & Siskind, Boston, 1965-68; pvt. practice, Boston, 1969—. Mem. women's council Solomon Schechter Day Sch.; women's aux. West End House Boys Club. Bd. dirs. young women's div. Combined Jewish Philanthropies, 1968-70, bd. dirs. lawyers div., 1971—; contbg. asso. Weizmann Inst. Sch.; president's councillor Brandeis U. Mem. Am., Mass., Boston bar assns., Mass. Assn. Women Lawyers (rec. sec. 1969-70), Brandeis U. (nat. reunion chmn. 1971, v.p., bd. dirs. Greater Boston chtp. 1970, rec. sec. nat. exec. bd. 1967-69), Boston U. Law Sch. alumni assns., Mass. Audubon Soc., Nat. Council Jewish Women, Am. Jewish Com., Boston Zool. Spc., Hadassah. Home: 213 Waltham St West Newton MA 02165 Office: 185 Devonshire St Boston MA 02110

BOOSE, BEATRICE JORDAN (MRS. SIDNEY S. BOOSE), psychologist, educator; b. Waynesboro, Miss., May 4, 1924; d. Willie Lester and Dorothy (Robinson) Jordan; B.S., Alcorn Coll., 1947; M.S., U. Ill., 1950; Ph.D., U. Ia., 1962; m. Sidney S. Boose, Aug. 2, 1948; children—Debra, Keela. Instr. Alcorn Coll., Lorman, Miss., 1947-52; counsellor Ind. U., Bloomington, 1952-54; asst. prof. Grambling, (La.) Coll., 1954-60, asso. prof., 1962-63; prof. Ala. State U., Montgomery, 1963-65; prof. Norfolk (Va.) State Coll., 1965—. Cons. sch. psychol. services; adviser parents of exceptional children. Diplomate Sch. Psychology. Mem. Am., Va. psychol. assns., Am. Assn. Mental Deficiency, Am. Edn. Research Assn. Roman Catholic. Author: Curriculum Guide for Teaching the Retarded Child, 1964. Home 1936 Springfield Av Norfolk VA 23523

BOOTH, ANN MADSEN, social worker; b. Tacoma, July 27, 1910; d. Mads Peter and Anne (Villadson) Madsen; B.A., Wash. State U., 1935. Case worker Family Service Soc., Tacoma, 1934; supr. Wash. State Dept. Pub. Welfare, 1935; state supr. intake and certification Fed. Relief Works Agy., Wash., 1935-41; dir. Seattle War Chest, 1941-45; dep. dir. Brit. Zone of Austria, UNRRA, 1945-48; dir. health div. Community Council of Greater N.Y., 1948-55; dir. Plays for Living, Family Service Assn. Am., N.Y.C., 1960—. Mem. Nat. Assn. Social Workers, Nat. Conf. on Social Welfare, Ethical Culture Soc., League of Women Voters. Home: 17 W 67th St New York City NY 10023 Office: 44 E 23d St New York City NY 10010

BOOTH, BARBARA R. (MRS. MITCHELL B. BOOTH), civic worker; b. N.Y.C., May 2, 1928; d. Benjamin C. and Ceclia (Lowe) Ribman; A.A., Centenary Jr. Coll., Hackettstown, N.Y., 1948; B.A., Barnard Coll., 1950; m. Mitchell B. Booth, July 13, 1952; 1 son, Brian S. Pres. women's alliance, chmn., Christmas fair 1st Congl. Ch. of City of N.Y., 1959-63; mem. vol. com. Sheltering Arms Children's Service, N.Y.C.; trustee Florence K. Griswold Meml. Fund. Com., All Souls Unitarian Ch., N.Y.C.; dir. women's div. Jefferson Dem. Club. N.Y.C.; committeewoman N.Y. County Dem. Com.; bd. govs. v.p. N.Y. Fruit and Flower Mission, Inc.; del. city conv., chmn. East Manhattan br. League of Women Voters. Home: 75 East End Av New York City NY 10028

BOOTH, CAROLEE, state ofcl.; b. Vallejo, Cal., Sept. 14, 1940; d. Ernest Kenneth and Leila Mae (Wood) Booth; student U. N.H., 1959; B.A., San Jose State Coll., 1963; postgrad. U. Cal. at Berkeley, 1964, Chico State Coll., 1966-69; M.A. in Counseling, Cal. State U. at Fresno, 1973. With Macy's, Sacramento, 1963-64; employment counselor Cal. Dept. Employment, Sacramento, 1964-65, Redding, 1964-69; supervising employment counselor Cal. Employment Devel. Dept., Fresno, 1969—. Mem. Am., Cal. personnel and guidance assns., Nat., Cal. (editor newsletter 1969-71; sec. 1970-72, trustee 1974-75) employment counselors assns., Cal. Council on Criminal Justice. Episcopalian (mem. No. Cal. diocese youth council 1967-68). Home: 1050 O St Fresno CA 93721

BOOTH, CHARLENE WARREN, assn. ofcl.; b. Olney, Ill., Dec. 27, 1930; d. Charles Jerome and Dorothy Mae (Daubs) Warren; A.A., Stephens Coll., 1949; B.J., U. Tex., 1951; m. Crawford H. Booth, June 21, 1952 (div. 1965); children—Lisa (Mrs. Daniel L. Rundberg), Martha Alison. Advt. copywriter Radio Sta. KTAE, Taylor, Tex., 1952; with Hogg Found., U. Tex., Austin, 1965—, editor Hogg Found. News, 1971—. Editorial cons. Tex. Assn. of Homes for the Aging, 1970. Active in various fund raising drives. Mem. Women In Communications, Alpha Chi Omega. Methodist (mem. adminstrv. bd. 1966-67). Home: 5802 Marilyn Dr Austin TX 78731 Office: Box 7998 University Station Austin TX 78712

BOOTH, DELORES COSTELLO, ednl. adminstr.; b. Detroit; d. James and Lillian (Wallace) Booth; B.S., Wayne State U., 1954; postgrad. San Francisco State Coll., 1956; M.A., U. Cal. at Berkeley, 1959, postgrad., 1961-67. Tchr., Patrick Henry Elementary Sch., 1955, Pacific Heights Elementary Sch., 1956-59; tchr., counselor Pelton Jr. High Sch., San Francisco, 1959-67, asst. prin., 1967-71; asst. prin. for curriculum A.P. Gianini Jr. High Sch., San Francisco, 1971-72; prin. Claremont Jr. High Sch., Oakland, Cal., 1973—; asst. head tchr. Herbert Hoover Jr. High Sch., 1965; owner, designer Kostello's Design Co., Oakland, 1970—. Demonstration tchr. for student observers, student tchrs., 1956-60. Mem. Am., San Francisco assns. sch. adminstrs., Cal. Tchrs. Assn. (sec. salary com. 1962-63), Nat. Council Adminstrv. Women in Edn., Cal. Alumni Assn. U. Cal. at Berkeley, Sch. Edn. Alumni Soc., Pacific Arts Assn., Wayne State Coll. Edn. Alumni, Pi Lambda Theta. Home: 6604 Tremont St Oakland CA 94609 Office: 5750 College Av Oakland CA 94618

BOOTH, DOLA, physician; b. Belfalls, Tex., Jan. 3, 1906; d. Zachary Alphonso and Susannah (Bryant) Booth; A.B., U. Tex., 1927, M.O. (Eleanor Brackenridge scholar 1930) 1930; m. J. Harriss Williams, Dec. 23, 1931; 1 dau., Su Alice (Mrs. Lynwood C. Jostes). Intern, resident John Sealy Hosp., Galveston, Tex.; practice medicine, Austin, Tex., 1936-43; med. cons. for State Dept., 1959-74, Disability Determination div. Social Security Adminstrn., Austin, 1974—. past mem. staff St. David, City hosps. Dir. Riesel State Bank. Past mem. bd. Planned Parenthood Clinic, City Charity Clinic. Bd. dirs. Austin Symphony League. Mem. Women's Aux. Travis County Med. Soc., Austin Symphony Soc., Fine Arts Assn., Alpha Epsilon Iota, Alpha Delta Phi Mother's Club. Presbyn. Clubs: Settlement, University Ladies, Austin Country, Westwood Country, Austin (Austin). Home: 2413 Pemberton Pl Austin TX 78703 Office: 7700 Chevy Chase Dr Austin TX 78753

BOOTH, ESTELLA PERRY, retail trade co. exec.; b. Pearl, Ill., Nov. 20, 1923; d. Raymond Wesley and Jeanette Anne (Davis) Perry; student Springfield Jr. Coll., 1968; m. Robert Meredith Booth, Oct. 5, 1968 (dec. Apr. 1971). Office mgr. to physician, Springfield, Ill., 1942-64; office mgr. and saleswoman Comml. Steel Fabricators Co., Jacksonville, Ill., 1964-71; propr., mgr. Aardvark Clocks & Antiques Co., Springfield, 1972—. Tchr. antiques to adult classes South East High Sch., Springfield, 1973—. Mem. Springfield Symphony Guild, St. Johns Hosp. Aux., Springfield; pres. Circus Fans Am., 1970-72; mem. Lake Shore Improvement Assn. Pres. Republican Women of Sangamon (Ill.) County, 1973-74. Mem. Am. Bus. Womens Assn. of Springfield (pres. Carillon chpt. 1973-74, named woman of the year 1972), Lincoln Land Antique Dealers Assn., Bus. and Profl. Womens Assn., Sangamon County Farm Bur., Ill. State Mus. Assn., Ill. State Hist. Soc. Club: Altrusa of Springfield. Home: 95 Maple Grove Springfield IL 62707 Office: 1406 South Fifth St Springfield IL 62703

BOOTHBY, EVELYN ELIZABETH VAN ALSTINE (MRS. CHARLES R. BOOTHBY), educator, clubwoman; b. Greenwich, Conn.; d. C. Ralph and Mary (Husted) Van Alstine; A.B., Syracuse U., 1924; M.A., N.Y. U., 1935; m. Charles R. Boothby, July 14, 1938. Tchr. pub. schs. Plainfield, N.J., 1924-27; tchr. Am. history Port Chester (N.Y.) Sr. High Sch., 1931-67, head social studies dept., 1954-67. Mem. N.Y. Bicentennial Com. from Westchester County. Mem. P.T.A. (hon. life), Westchester Council for the Social Scis. (pres. 1954-55), Westchester County, Port Chester (founder, pres. 1969—) hist. socs., D.A.R., (chpt. regent, nat. vice chmn. sch. com. 1974—dist. dir.), D.A.R. ExRegents Assn. (pres. Westchester County chpt. 1974-75), Daus. Am. Colonists (chpt. v.p. 1974-76, state chmn. bicentennial com. 1974-76), Delta Kappa Gamma. Baptist (historian for centennial book 1960). Co-author: Port Chester Centennial Book, 1968. Home: 49 Upland St Port Chester NY 10573

BOOZ, VIRGINIA ADAMS (MRS. FRANCIS FREEMAN BOOZ), real estate counselor; b. Clinton, Ind., Mar. 1, 1914; d. John Franklin and Martha Louella (Merriman) Adams; B.A., Ind. State Coll., 1935; postgrad. Northwestern U., 1937, Pasadena City Coll., 1962-74; m. Francis Freeman Booz, Aug. 29, 1937; children—Martha (Mrs. James Ullrey), Katherine (Mrs. Douglas L. Mann), Nancy (Mrs. Kenneth Lynn Macy). Dept. mgr. Robinsons Dept. Store, Pasadena, Cal., 1958-60; real estate salesman Henry Wolcott, Pasadena, 1960-63; real estate broker, realtor Virginia A. Booz, Pasadena, 1963—; real estate investment counselor, Pasadena, 1970—. Pres. Bd. Realtors, Pasadena, 1973; dir. Multiple Listing Service. Pres. local P.T.A., Pasadena, 1952-53; Pasadena area Girl Scout leader, 1946-62; vice chmn. Task Force on Communications Pasadena Sch. Dist., 1971-72. Area precinct leader Pasadena Republican Club. Mem. Cal. Real Estate Assn. (state dir. 1970-74). Club: Wilshiere Women's of Los Angeles. Home: 1160 Cordova No 1 Pasadena CA 91106 Office: 380 East Green St No 113 Pasadena CA 91101

BOOZER, DARLING GERALDINE RAKESTRAW, psychologist; b. N.Y.C., July 15, 1918; d. Henry Clay and Lee (Hurdus) Rakestraw; certificate diploma N.Y. U., 1939; B.B.A., U. Miami, 1954, M.S., 1957; Ph.D., La. State U., 1961; m. James Corkern Boozer, Apr. 24, 1948 (div. 1966); 1 son, James Corkern. Asst. clin. psychologist Child Clinic, Baton Rouge, 1957-58; Psychology fellow S.E. La. State Hosp., Mandeville, 1958-59; psychology intern La. State Med. Sch. and Charity Hosp., New Orleans, 1958-59; Research fellow USPHS, 1960-61; mem. clin. psychologist staff S. Fla. State Hosp., Hollywood, 1960-65, 1966—, dir. Rehab. Program for Criminal Sex Offenders, 1972—; forensic psychologist, 1966—; pvt. practice clin. psychology, Miami and Hollywood, Fla., 1961—; clin. asst. prof. psychology U. Miami, Coral Gables, Fla., 1962-66; staff cons. Fla. Gardens Children's Center, Hallandale, 1965—. Cons. various orgns., 1960—; discussant, lectr., panel mem. various groups; exhibited in group art shows at Miami Beach, Fla.; comml. artist Advt. Co., Miami, 1954-63; legal, exec. sec. various attys., N.Y.C. Instr. water safety A.R.C., Miami, 1945-46. Mem. Am., S.E. psychol. assns., Mental Health Soc. Greater Miami, Fla. Council Crime and Delinquency, Internat. Platform Assn., Art Student's League N.Y., Psi Chi. Home: 3419 Acapulco Dr Hollywood FL 33023 Office: South Fla State State Hosp West Hollywood FL 33023

BOQUIST, NORMA FAYE MARTIN (MRS. ARTHUR W. BOQUIST), journalist; b. Wilbur, Wash., Mar. 11, 1922; d. Henry Theodore and Lela Derissa (Perkins) Martin; student Holy Names Coll., 1940-42; m. Arthur W. Boquist, Feb. 20, 1942; children—Barry, Scott, April, Matt. Women's editor Sunnyvale (Cal.) Daily Standard, 1961-69; reporter Lewiston (Ida.) Morning Tribune, 1970-71; food and feature editor Valley Jour., Sunnyvale, 1971-73; reporter San Jose (Cal.) Mercury, 1973—. Pres. Sweet Adelines, Yakima, Wash, 1955-56, pub. relations editor Little Theatre, Yakima, 1955-59, Sunnyvale Little League, 1959-62. Mem. Fedn. Women's Club, Beta Sigma Phi. Club: Altrusa (Sunnyvale). Contbr. articles to mags. Home: 909 Rose Blossom St Cupertino CA 95014 Office: 755 Ridder Park Dr San Jose CA 95131

BORAKS, JACQUELINE, editor; b. Bklyn., Dec. 19, 1928; d. Burt and Ruth (Ginzburg) Mirken; student Davis and Elkins Coll., 1946-48; m. Malcolm Jay Boraks, June 24, 1961 (div. May 1967). Editorial asst., asst. editor Physics Today, Am. Inst. Physics, N.Y.C., 1955-61; editorial asst. The Physics of Fluids, 1961-62; asst. to mng. editor applied optics Optical Soc. Am., Washington, 1962-64; prodn. editor, copy editor Nat. Acad. Sci. Printing and Pub. Office, Washington, 1965-67, chief copy editor, 1967-69, editor div. phys. scis., 1969—; also free-lance redactor. Contbr. poetry to mags., photos to books. Home: 416 E Capitol Washington DC 20003 Office: 2101 Constitution Av Washington DC 20418

BORCHERS, GLADYS LOUISE, educator; b. La Valle, Wis., July 4, 1891; d. August and Sophie (Gross) Borchers; student Whitewater State Coll., 1918; B.A., U. Wis., 1921, M.A., 1925, Ph.D., 1927. Instr. to asso. prof. Rockford (Ill.) Coll., 1921-24; prof. speech U. Wis., Madison, 1927-62; vis. prof. Northwestern U., Evanston, Ill., summers 1935, 37, U. Minn., Mpls., summers, 1928, 31, 68, Taylor U., Upland, Ind., 1964, 67, La. State U., Baton Rouge, 1939, 46-47, Brigham Young U., Provo, Utah, 1964, 68, 69, U. Utah, Salt Lake City, 1936, U. Colo., Boulder, 1962-63, U. Ill. at Normal, 1967-68, Eastern Wash. U., Pullman, summers 1965-68, Western Wash. U., Bellingham, 1965-66, U. Hawaii, Honolulu, 1949-50; cons. speech U. Wis., Oskosh, 1964; scholar in residence Whitewater U., 1973—. Recipient Distinguished Alumni award Whitewater State Coll., 1958; Andrew T. Weaver award for outstanding speech tchr. Wis. Communication Assn., 1973-74. Mem. Nat. Collegiate Players, German Nat. Speech Assn., Internat. Inst. Arts and Letters, Central, Western, Wis. Speech assns., Nat. Ret. Tchrs. Assn., Am. Assn. Univ. Women, Am. Assn. Univ. Profs., Nat. Assn. Communication Arts, Mortar Board, Delta Sigma Rho, Pi Lambda Theta, Zeta Phi Eta, Phi Beta. Club: Presidents of U. Wis. Found. (trustee). Author: The New Better Speech, 1937; Living Speech, 1938; (with Wilbur Hatfield) English Activities, 1938; (with Andrew T. Weaver) Speech, 1946; (with Claude M. Wise) Modern Speech, 1947; (with others) Teaching Speech, 1952; (with Karl Wallace) History of Speech Education in America, 1954; (with others) Speaking and Listening, 1956; (with Joseph V. Totaro) Women in College and University Teaching, 1963; (with John Wilson) In Honor of Harry Caplan, 1965; (with Keith Brooks) Communicative Arts and Sciences of Speech, 1967; Editor: Speech Teacher, 1961-64. Home: Apt 246 4725 Sheboyan Av Madison WI 53705

BORCHERS, SISTER JEANNETTE FRANCES, educator; b. Dayton, O., Jan. 8, 1914; d. Bernard John and Eleanor (Schenk) Borchers; student Sister of Charity Coll. Mt. St. Joseph, Ohio, 1932, B.S., 1936; M. Ed., U. St. Louis, 1956; postgrad. Xavier U., So. Colo. State Coll.; M. Social Work, Ohio State U., 1971. Dietetic intern Good Samaritan Hosp., 1936-37, dietitian, 1937-38, St. Joseph Hosp., Mt. Clemens, Mich., 1938-41; instr. chemistry, home econs. Acad. Mt. St. Joseph, O., 1941-46; instr. biology, home econs. St. James High Sch., Bay City, Mich., 1947-55; edn. dir. dietetic internship Good Samaritan Hosp., 1955-57, dir. dept. nutrition 1957-64; dir. dietary dept. St. Mary-Corwin Hosp., 1964-65, coordinator hosp. in service edn., 1965-66; adminstr. El Pomar Retreat Center, Colorado Springs, 1966-69; social work adminstrv. resident U. Cin. Med. Center, 1971; social counselor St. Joseph Hosp., Mt. Clemens, Mich., 1972—. Exec. sec. Nat. Cath. Council on Home Econs., 1957-59, regional chmn., 1959-61; chief nutrition services Med. and Health Div. Ohio Valley Civl Def. Authority, 1959-61; former mem. nutrition council Cin. Pub. Health Fedn. Bd. dirs. Sister Romuald Merit award Meml. Fund, 1957-64. Mem. Am. Home Econs. Assn., Am. (chmn. corr. course for food service suprs. Colo.), Cin. (life mem., pres. 1963-64), Colorado Springs (pres.), Detroit dietetic assns., Nat. Cath. Council on Home Econs., Nat. Assn. Social Workers, League Women Voters. Contbr. articles in profl. jours. Address: St Joseph's Hosp Mount Clemens MI 48043

BORDALLO, MADELEINE MARY (MRS. RICARDO JEROME BORDALLO), mem. Democratic Nat. Com.; b. Graceville, Minn., May 31, 1933; d. Christian Peter and Mary Evelyn (Roth) Zeien; student St. Mary's Coll., S. Bend, Ind., 1952; A.A., St. Katherines Coll., St. Paul, 1953; hon. degree U. Guam, 1968; m. Ricardo Jerome Bordallo, June 20, 1953; 1 dau., Deborah Josephene. Presented in voice recital Guam Acad. Music, Agana, 1951, 67; mem. Civic Opera Co., St. Paul, 1952-53; mem. staff KUAM Radio-TV sta., Agana, 1954-63; free-lance writer local newspaper, fashion show commentator, coordinator, civic leader, 1963—; nat. Democratic committeewoman for Guam, 1964—; del. Nat. Dem. Conv., 1964, 68; pres. Women's Dem. Party Guam, 1965-70; Dem. rep. Presdl. Inauguration, Washington, 1965; del. campaign conf. for Dem. Women, Washington, 1966; sec. Dem. Western States Conf., 1968—. Pres. Guam Women's Club, 1958-59; del. Gen. Fedn. Women's Clubs Convs., Miami Beach, Fla., 1961, New Orleans, 1965, Boston, 1968; v.p. Fedn. Asian Women's Assns., 1964-67, pres., 1967—, del. convs., Manila, P.I., 1959, Taipei, Formosa, 1960, Hong Kong, 1963, Agana, 1964; chmn. Guam Christmas Seal Drive, 1961; sec. Guam chpt. A.R.C., 1963—. Pres. Marianas Assn. for Retarded Children, 1968-70, 73—, Guam Symphony Soc., 1966—, Acad. of Our Lady Sch. P.T.A., 1969-71, St. Francis Sch. P.T.A., 1967-68; bd. dirs. Guam Theatre Guild, pres. Guam Meml. Hosp. Vols. Assn., 1969-71, Guam Rehab. Assn. and Workshop Center; chmn. Guam Civic Auditorum Bldg. Com., 1969—; pres. Beauty World Guam Ltd., 1971-73. Club: Spanish. Address: PO Box 1458 Agana Guam 96910

BORDELEAU, NANCY VIVIAN MCINTOSH (MRS. ROLAND J. BORDELEAU), pub. welfare exec.; b. Boston, Aug. 30, 1934; d. Edmund and Dorothy (Goldstein) McIntosh; B.Ed., R.I. Coll. Edn., 1955; m. Roland J. Bordeleau, June 18, 1955; children—John Michael, Lisa Marie, Michele Denise. Tchr., Hugh B. Bain Jr. High Sch., Cranston, R.I., 1955-57; social caseworker R.I. Div. Pub. Assistance, Dept. Social Welfare, 1957-60; substitute tchr. secondary schs., Cranston, 1965; dir. Pub. Welfare, Cranston, 1966—; cons. Legislative Commn. to Study Day Care in R.I., 1968-73, chmn. Community Action Program Com. Cranston, 1969-70. Chmn. Cranston Heart Fund, 1969. Past pres. Cranston Community Mental Health Bd., Cranston Council P.T.A.'s, D.D. Waterman P.T.A.; bd. dirs. Cranston Dist. Nursing Assn., Cranston Day Care Com., Inc.; trustee Butler Hosp. Charter mem. Cranston Community Caucus. Named Woman of Year, Cranston Bus. and Profl. Women's Club, 1966, Outstanding Young Woman of R.I., 1967. Mem. R.I. Dirs. Pub. Welfare Assn. (pres.), R.I. Conf. Social Work, Nat. Conf. Social Welfare, Am. Pub. Welfare Assn., Kappa Delta Pi. Baptist (sec. diaconate bd. 1973, v.p. 1974). Home: 70 Poppy Dr Cranston RI 02920 Office: 1090 Cranston St Cranston RI 02920

BORDEN, BARBARA LEVY (MRS. RONALD JOEL BORDEN), family counselor; b. Wilmington, Del., Jan. 17, 1945; d. Norman Benjamin and Edith Ruth (Cohodas) Levy: B.S., U. Wis., 1967; M.Teaching, Nat. Coll. Edn., 1971; certificate in child guidance and family counseling Alfred Adler Inst., 1972; m. Ronald Joel Borden, Aug. 2, 1969; 1 dau., Mara Rae. Psychiat. occupational therapist gen. hosps., Chgo., 1967-69; remedial tchr., Evanston, Ill., 1970; occupational therapist Spalding Sch., Chgo. Pub. Schs., 1971-73; child guidance and family counselor Family Edn. Assn., Chgo., 1971—. Mem. Am. Occupational Therapy Assn., Am. Soc. Adlerian Psychology. Home: 440 Dell Lane Highland Park IL 60035

BORDEN, CONSTANCE, landscape architect; b. Scarsdale, N.Y., July 13, 1906; d. Glentworth DeGrauw and Velma (Mote) Borden; student Wells Coll., 1925-26; grad. Lowthorpe Sch. Landscape Architecture, 1929; student R.I. Sch. Design. Pvt. practice as landscape architect, Greenwich, Conn., 1929—. Active Greenwich Red Cross Motor Corps, World War II. Recipient Mrs. Oakleigh Thorne medal Garden Club Am., 1961. Mem. Am. Soc. Landscape Architects. Clubs: Hortulus (Greenwich); Garden of Am. (N.Y.C.); Federated Gardens Clubs Conn. (Hartford). Address: 41 Pheasant Lane Greenwich CT 06830

BOREA, PHYLLIS GILBERT, author; b. Chgo., Oct. 12, 1924; d. Clinton Wallace and Pauline (Clarke) Gilbert; ed. Bryn Mawr Coll., New Sch. for Social Research, Sch. Visual Arts; m. Raimondo Borea; children—Roberto, Carla. Editor, artist Dell Pub. Co., N.Y.C.; partner Raimondo Borea Assos., N.Y.C., 1957—. Mem. Authors Guild, Inc., Am. Soc. Picture Profls. (asso. editor 1971-73). Author: First Thing in the Morning, 1970; Tino and Jamie, 1972; Seymour, A Gibbon, 1973. Illustrator: Children Discover Arithmetic (Catherine and Margaret B. Stern), 1971. Address: 245 W 104th St New York City NY 10025

BORER, KATARINA BRANKA TOMLJENOVIC (MRS. ROBERT C. BORER, JR.), univ. research scientist; b. Tuzla, Yugoslavia, Sept. 17, 1940; d. Juraj and Borka (Jovanovic) Tomljenovic; student U. Zagreb Sch. Natural Sci. and Math., 1959-61; B.A. with distinction, U. Pa., 1962, Ph.D. (Orville Paul Phillips, Bloomfield Moore, Am. Assn. U. Women fellow), 1966; postgrad. (NIH fellow), U. Miami Rosenstiel Sch. Marine and Atmospheric Sci., (Fla.), 1969-70, U. Mich., 1971-73; m. Robert C. Borer, Jr., Apr. 11, 1964; children—Elizabeta Helena, Robert C. III, Richard C. Came to U.S., 1961, naturalized, 1969. Lectr., Alaska Meth. U., Anchorage Comml. Coll. U. Alaska (both Anchorage), 1968-69; guest investigator Scripps Inst. Oceanography Physiol. Research Lab., 1970-71; asst. research scientist U. Mich. Neurosci. Lab., Ann Arbor, 1973—. Pres.-elect Angell Elementary Sch. Parent Tchr. Orgn., 1973-74. Weight Watchers Found., U. Mich. Office Research Adminstrn. grantee. Mem. Am. Soc. Zoologists, Animal Behavior Soc., Am. Inst. Biol. Scis., A.A.A.S. Contbr. articles to sci. jours. Home: 1724 S University Av Ann Arbor MI 48104

BORG, DOROTHY, educator, author; b. Elberon, N.J., Sept. 4, 1902; d. Sidney C. and Madeleine (Beer) Borg; A.M., Ph.D., Columbia. Research asso. Am. Inst. of Pacific Relations, 1939-58, East Asian Research Center, Harvard, 1960-61; research asso. East Asian Inst., mem. faculty, Columbia, N.Y.C., 1962—, now lectr., sr. research asso.; lectr. Peking (China) Nat. U., 1947. Recipient Bancroft prize, 1965. Mem. Am. Hist. Assn., Assn. Asian Studies, Acad. Polit. Scis. Author: American Policy and the Chinese Revolution 1925-28, 1947; The United States and The Far Eastern Crisis 1933-38, 1964. Co-editor: Pearl Harbor as History: Japanese-American Relations 1931-1941, 1973. Home: 22 Riverside Dr New York City NY 10023

BORG, ESTHER CLAREISSE (MRS. EDWARD BORG), soc. ofcl.; b. Lopez, Wash., Nov. 26, 1908; d. Joseph Fargie and Susie May (Cochran) Gallanger; grad. high sch.; m. Percival Williamson, Sept. 7, 1929 (div. May 1938); 1 dau., Bonnie May (Mrs. Elton Atkinson); m. 2d, Edward Borg, Dec. 20, 1947. Various positions in restaurants, Portland and Astoria, Ore., 1925-26, 29, Seattle, 1937-38, 45-47, Cordova, Alaska, 1935-36; owner, mgr. chicken farm, San Juan, Wash.; mgr. ranch, Port Stanley; 1939-44; organizer Lopez Island Hist. Soc., 1966, pres., 1967—. Mem. Am. Legion Aux. (pres., 1966, 67, 71). Home: Lopez WA 98261 Office: Lopez Island Hist Soc Lopez WA 98261

BORGATTA, ISABEL CASE (MRS. ROBERT EDWARD BORGATTA), sculptor, educator; b. Madison, Wis., Nov. 21, 1921; d. Harold Clayton and Naomi (Newburn) Case; student Smith Coll., 1939-40; B.F.A., Yale, 1944; postgrad. New Sch. for Social Research, 1944-45; m. Robert Edward Borgatta, Apr. 24, 1948; children—Francesca Naomi, Paola Case, Alice Mia. Art dir. Nat. Bapt. Conf. 1946; art tchr. Halsted Sch., Yonkers, N.Y., 1946-48; instr. sculpture Coll. City N.Y., 1958—, instr. Coll. of New Rochelle (N.Y.), 1973—, asso. prof., 1974—; sculpture exhibited one-man shows Village Art Center, N.Y.C., 1947-51, Galeris St. Etienne, N.Y.C., 1954, Tyringham (Mass.) Gallery, 1955, Gallery 10, N.Y.C., 1960, Frank K. M. Rehn Gallery, N.Y.C., 1968, Frank Rehn Gallery, 1971, 74, Briarcliff Coll., 1970, Briarcliff Coll. Mus., 1971, Overseas Press Club, 1972, Coll. of New Rochelle, 1973, Seton Coll., 1974; exhibited in group shows Village Art Center, Audubon Artists Anns., Nat. Acad. anns., Pa. Acad. Fine Arts, Whitney Mus., Riverside Mus., N.Y.C., Roko Gallery, N.Y.C., Laurel Gallery, N.Y.C., Van Loen Gallery, N.Y.C., Ann Ross Gallery, N.Y., Sculptors Guild, Sculptors League; represented in permanent collections Hartford (Conn.) Atheneum, Norfolk (Va.), Yeshiva U., Krannert Mus., U. Ill. Mus., U. Conn., Boston Mus. MacDowell fellow, 1968, 70, 73; Yaddo fellow, 1971-73; recipient sculpture prize Village Art Center, 1946, 51; Peabody prize Nat. Assn. Woman Artists, 1952; Dorsay prize Silvermine Guild Conn., 1957; Zell prize, 1960; Jacques Lipchitz award, 1960; 1st prize Hudson River Mus., Yonkers, N.Y., 1960. Mem. Sculptors Guild, Sculptors League, Women in Arts. Democrat. Presbyn. Home: 320 Clinton Av Dobbs Ferry NY 10522 Office: Frank M Rehn Gallery 655 Madison Av New York City NY 10021

BORGSTEDT, AGNETA DAGMAR, med. educator; b. Hamburg, Germany, May 31, 1931 (came to U.S., 1956, naturalized, 1962); d. Werner and Else C. (Scherer) von Rehren; M.D. summa cum laude, U. Hamburg, 1955; m. Harold H. Borgstedt, May 11, 1957; children—Eric, Astrid. Practice medicine, specializing in pediatric-neurology, Rochester, N.Y., 1960—, neurol. pediatrics, 1964—; dir. muscular dystrophy clinic, 1960-72, clin. asst. prof. pediatrics U. Rochester Med. Sch., 1969—. Mem. med. adv. bd. Monroe County Assn. Brain Injured Children; mem. coordinating com. mental retardation of Health Council Monroe County; mem. med. adv. bd. Greater Rochester chpt. Muscular Dystrophy Assn. Am.; mem. regional com. N.Y. State for Handicapped. Mem. A.M.A., Med. Soc. Monroe County, State N.Y., Rochester Acad. Medicine, Rochester Pediatric Soc., Am. Acad. Pediatrics, Rochester Neurol. Soc., Am. Med. Womens Assn. Address: 88 Church Hill Rd Henrietta NY 14467

BORITZ, MYRA ARLENE FREILICH, med. editor, writer; b. N.Y.C., Dec. 27, 1942; d. Louis and Gertrude (Staff) Freilich; B.S. cum laude, Coll. City N.Y., 1963; M.D., State U. N.Y. Upstate Med. Center, 1963-67; m. Pepi Isaac Boritz, Dec. 25, 1967. Research asst. anatomy Columbia Coll. Phys. and Surg., 1961-63; summer fellow Syracuse (N.Y.) Psychiat. Hosp., 1965; profl. asso. Media Medica, Inc., N.Y.C., 1968-69; asst. to pubs. Medcom, Inc., N.Y.C., 1969-73, exec. producer, writer 8 filmstrip library on care of newborn; med. cons. slide series Famous Teachings in Modern Medicine; dir. med.

copy Synapse Communication Services, Inc., Old Greenwich, Conn., 1973—. Mem. Am. Med. Women's Assn., Am. Med. Writers Assn., Am. Pub. Health Assn., Met. Mus. Art, Mus. Modern Art, Phi Beta Kappa. Democrat. Jewish religion. Contbg. editor tech. monographs. Chief contbg. writer to teaching manuals on Med. gynecology, gastro-enterology and infant nutrition for pharm. salesmen. Address: 945 Fifth Av Apt 10 E New York City NY 10021 Office: PO Box 318 Old Greenwich CT 06870

BORLAND, ZELLE WILLIAMS (MRS. ANDREW H. BORLAND), club woman; b. Sanford, N.C., Oct. 5, 1908; d. James Crockett and Henrietta (Frizelle) Williams; A.B., Duke, 1931; m. Andrew Hoyt Borland, Dec. 12, 1934; 1 son, Andrew Hoyt. Pres., Margaret Brawley Garden Club, 1946-47, 52-53, 55-56, 66-68; pres. Durham (N.C.) Council Garden Clubs, 1946-47, 59-60; parliamentarian Garden Club N.C., 1959-61; bd. dirs. Family Service, 1943-48, treas., 1946-48. Mem. Am. Assn. U. Women, United Meth. Women, Nat. Assn. Parliamentarians, Kappa Alpha Theta (alumnae dist. pres. 1963-68, supr. alumnae chpt. by-laws 1973—). Methodist (tchr. bible class 1953-71). Home: 1600 High St Durham NC 27707

BORMAN, SUSAN DOLINER, judge; b. Elizabeth, N.J., June 30, 1941; d. Manuel Frederick and Pauline (Grossman) Cohen; A.B., Smith Coll., 1963; postgrad. Columbia, 1963-64; J.D., U. Detroit, 1969; 1 dau., Johanna. Admitted to Mich. bar, 1969; dep. defender Legal Aid and Defender Assn. of Detroit, 1970-73; judge recorders ct., Frank Murphy Hall of Justice, Detroit, 1973—. Mem. State Bar Com. on Standard Jury Instrns. Bd. dirs. Anti-Defamation League. Mem. State Bar of Mich., Women Lawyers Assn. of Mich., Am. Bar Assn. Democrat. Jewish religion. Office: 1441 St Antoine Detroit MI 48226

BORMANN, SISTER MARY CLARA, librarian; b. Cedar Rapids, Ia., Sept. 17, 1914; d. John Henry and Gertrude (McLaughlin) Bormann; A.B., Clarke Coll., 1940; B.L.S., Coll. St. Catherine, 1944; M.L.S., U. Mich., 1954. Tchr., Gesu Sch., Milw., 1937-38; library asst. Mundelein Coll., Chgo., 1938-44, asst. librarian, 1944-50, librarian, 1950—. Mem. Am., Ill., Catholic (com. chmn.) library assns. Democrat. Editor: Periodical Holdings in Eleven College Libraries in the Chicago Area, 1962. Address: 6363 Sheridan Rd Chicago IL 60626

BORN, SISTER MARY VERONICE, ednl. adminstr.; b. Parsons, Kan., Feb. 15, 1931; d. John Phillip and Anna Frances (Paulie) Born; B.A., Sacred Heart Coll., St. Mary of Plains, 1960; M. in Spl. Edn., St. Louis U., 1964; adminstrs. certificate Wichita (Kan.) State U., 1969. Tchr. elementary schs., Wichita and Perry, Okla., 1948-60; tchr. retarded children St. Mary's Spl. Sch., Wichita, 1960-65; dir. Holy Family Center, Wichita, 1965—. Mem. Nat. Apostolate for Mentally Retarded, 1970-73, sec. 1973-74. Speaker Nat. Whitehouse Conf. Youth, 1969, State Assn. Retarded Children, 1960-74; panel mem. Nat. Cath. Edn. Assn. Conv., 1971—; Keynote speaker State Cath. Youth Orgn. Conv., 1973—. Trustee St. Mary of Plains Coll., Dodge City, Kan., 1960-73. Mem. Am. Assn. Mental Deficiency, Council Exceptional Children, Nat. Assn. Retarded Children, Okla. Kindergarten Assn. (pres. 1952-53). Home: Rural Route Viola KS 67149 Office: 619 S Maize Rd Wichita KS 67209

BORNHOLDT, LAURA ANNA, found. exec.; b. Peoria, Ill., Feb. 11, 1919; d. John and Barbara (Kohl) Bornholdt; A.B., Smith Coll., 1940, A.M., 1942; Ph.D., Yale, 1945; L.H.D., MacMurray Coll., 1964. Asst. prof. history Smith Coll., Northampton, Mass., 1945-52; asso. for internat. relations Am. Assn. Univ. Women, Washington, 1952-57; dean of coll. Sarah Lawrence Coll., Bronxville, N.Y., 1957-59; dean of women U. Pa., Phila., 1959-61; dean Wellesley Coll., 1961-64; v.p., specialist in higher edn. for grants and programs Danforth Found., St. Louis, 1964-73; coordinator ednl. research Lilly Endowment, Inc., Indpls., 1973—. Trustee Wooster Coll., St. Louis U. Mem. Am. Assn. for Higher Edn. (bd. dirs. 1970-73), Yale U. Alumni Assn. (dir. 1969-73), Nat. Coalition for Research on Women's Edn. and Devel. (dir. 1971—), Phi Beta Kappa. Mem. editorial bd. Jour. Higher Edn., 1970—. Office: 2801 N Meridian St Indianapolis IN 46208

BORNMANN, MARGARET ALICE EHM, alumnium co. exec.; b. Phila., June 9, 1943; d. John Aloysius and Margaret Carmencita (Garvin) Ehm; grad. high sch.; m. Sept. 7, 1963; children—Rusty, John A., Margaret R., Keleen E. Sec., Bornmann Aluminum Co., Inc., Williamstown, N.J., 1968-72, v.p., 1972—, also dir. Mem. Another Mother for Peace. Home 292 S Almonesson Av Deptford NJ 08096 Office: Black Horse Pike Williamstown NJ 08094

BOROCHOFF, IDA SLOAN (MRS. CHARLES Z. BOROCHOFF), real estate exec., artist; b. July 29, 1922; d. Louis and Eva (Bistrick) Sloan; ed. U. Ga., 1939-40, Ga. State U., 1940, Chgo. Sch. Interior Decorating, 1966, Allegro Sch. Bailet, Chgo., Atlanta Ballet, 1948-54, Emory U., 1971-72; m. Charles Zachary Borochoff, Jan. 11, 1942; children—Lynn (Mrs. Myles J. Gould), Jean Sue, Toby Ann (Mrs. Stanley E. Galkin), Lance Mark. Investor and owner real estate, 1941—; v.p. Designs Unltd., Inc., Atlanta, 1964—; pres. Sloan Borochoff Gallery, Atlanta, 1970—; art lectr. Met. Ednl. Service; tchr. Ga. Inst. Tech. - Free U.; exhibited several one-woman shows, 1961-71, one-woman show Lovett Sch., 1972, 75, Ga. Inst. Tech., 1972, 75. Bd. dirs. Atlanta Ballet, 1950-57; bd. dirs. Atlanta Music Club, also co-editor Newsletter; hostess Atlanta Arts Festival; capt. Heart Fund, 1968-73; active various multi-media groups, Atlanta Playhouse Theatre, Dogwood Festival; chmn., trustees Atlanta Playhouse Theatre. Recipient several art awards; named hon. alumnus Atlanta Art Inst., 1968. Mem. Atlanta Press Club, Atlanta Writers Club (membership com.), Atlanta Artists Club, League Women Voters, High Mus. Art, Ga. Writers Assn. Mem. B'nai B'rith Women (pres. chpt. 1975). Clubs: Jockey, Progressive. Home: 3450 Old Plantation Rd NW Atlanta GA 30327 Office: 795 Glendale Rd Scottdale GA 30079

BOROFSKY, RUTH BRAVERMAN (MRS. ISADORE N. BOROFSKY), psychologist, educator; b. Boston, Nov. 24, 1910; d. Philip and Sarah (Jackson) Braverman; R.N., Beth Israel Hosp., Boston, 1935; B.S., Simmons Coll., 1960; M.S., Boston U., 1962, Ed.D., 1969; m. Isadore N. Borofsky, Sept. 15, 1930; children—Gerald, Richard, Robert. Pvt. practice clin. psychology, Brookline, Mass., 1960—; psychologist pub. schs., Southborough, Mass., 1964-70; prof. psychiatry Boston U. Sch. Nursing, 1970—, chmn. psychiatry program, 1971—. Nat. Inst. Mental Health grantee, 1960-62. Mem. Am., Mass. psychol. assns., Am. Psychosomatic Soc., Am. Orthopsychiat. Assn., Assn. Marriage and Family Counseling, Soc. for Family Therapy and Research, Am. Soc. Clin. and Exptl. Hypnosis, Am. Soc. Psychotherapists, Am. Nurses Assn., Theta Beta Tau. Research in experiential structure of therapeutic dialogue, using referral opinion poll to plan for comprehensive child care services. Home: 21 Payson Rd Brookline MA 02167 Office: Boston U 635 Commonwealth St Boston MA 02215

BORROFF, MARIE, educator; b. N.Y.C., Sept. 10, 1923; d. Albert Ramon and Marie (Bergersen) Borroff; Ph.B., U. Chgo., 1943; M.A., 1946; Ph.D., Yale, 1956. Teaching asst. U. Chgo. Coll., 1946-47; instr. dept. English, Smith Coll., 1948-51, asst. prof., 1956-59, asso. prof. 1959; vis. asst. prof. English, Yale, 1957-58, vis. asso. prof., 1959-60, asso. prof., 1960-65, prof., 1965-71, William Lampson prof., 1971—. Fellow Ezra Stiles Coll., Yale; Phi Beta Kappa vis. scholar, 1973-74. Recipient John Billings Fiske poetry prize U. Chgo., 1943, Eunice Tietjens Meml. prize Poetry Mag., 1945, Margaret Lee Wiley fellowship Am. Assn. U. Women, 1955-56; Guggenheim fellow, 1969-70. Mem. Modern Lang. Assn. Am., Mediaeval Acad. Am., Phi Beta Kappa. Author: Sir Gawain and the Green Knight; A Stylistic and Metrical Study, 1962; Sir Gawain and the Green Knight: A New Verse Translation, 1967. Editor: Wallace Stevens: A Collection of Critical Essays, 1963. Home: 311 St Ronan St New Haven CT 06511

BORSCHEL, JACQUELINE ANNETTE RANKIN, educator; b. Omaha, May 19, 1925; d. Arthur C. and Virdie (Gillispie) Rankin; student U. Ia., 1943-45; B.A., Cal. State U., 1964, M.A., 1966; m. Howard C. Borschel, May 16, 1945 (div. 1973); children—Michael, Richard. Tchr., Rowland High Sch., Walnut, Cal., 1964-66, Lowell High Sch., La Habra, Cal., 1966-69, Pomona (Cal.) High Sch., 1969—. Faculty evening div. Mt. San Antonio Jr. Coll., Walnut, part-time 1965—. Covina (Cal.) chmn. Hollywood Bowl, 1961-63; v.p. Friends of Library, Covina, 1961-65; treas. Pomona High Sch. P.T.A., 1969—; soloist Collegium Musicum Claremont Colls., 1971—. Precinct orgn. chmn. Democratic Council, 25th Congl. Dist., 1960-65; publicity chmn. United Valley Democrats, 1970—. Mem. Am. Assn. U. Women (Ia. dir. 1950-51), Speech Assn. Am., Western Speech Assn. (lectr. 1965 conv.), Asso. Pomona Tchrs. (2d v.p.), N.A.A.C.P., Am. Civil Liberties Union, Pi Lambda Theta, Alpha Delta Pi. Unitarian-Universalist (lectr.). Club: Federation of Womens (dist. pub. speaking chmn. 1958-64). Writer, producer, actress ednl. films Cal. State Coll., Los Angeles. Home: 641-D S Indian Hill Claremont CA 91711 Office: 875 Bangor St Pomona CA 91767

BORST, BEATRICE, realtor; b. Pawling, N.Y.; d. Charles Austin and Grace Maria (Olmstead) Borst; B.A. (Campbell scholar), U. Cal. at Los Angeles, 1932; grad. Sawyer's Sch. Bus., 1934; M.A., U. Mich., 1940; profl. diploma Columbia Tchrs. Coll., 1952; postgrad. U. So. Cal., 1958, Lumbleau's Real Estate Sch., 1959, 65. Sec. to asst. dean Columbia Sch. Journalism, 1935-36; sec. advt. dept. Fortune Mag., N.Y.C., 1936-37; with research dept. CBS, N.Y.C., 1943; sec., asst. to dir. of publicity Research Inst. Am., 1944; with sales dept. Doubleday Book Shops, N.Y.C., 1945-47; free lance writer, 1947; real estate saleswoman, 1959; realtor, asso. Culver Nichols, Realtor, Palm Springs, Cal., 1965—. Travel, Far East, Australia, New Zealand, 1948-49, Europe, 1957, 63, 66, Spain, Morocco, 1968. Recipient Avery Hopwood award U. Mich., 1941. Mem. Cal. Real Estate Assn., Nat. Assn. Real Estates Bds., Palm Springs Bd. Real Estate (dir., 1966-68), Phi Beta Kappa (1st prize essay contest, 1931). Republican. Presbyn. Author: Nearer the Earth, 1941. Home: 643 Thornhill Rd Palm Springs CA 92262 Office: Culver Nichols Realtor 899 N Palm Canyon Dr Palm Springs CA 92262

BORTH, AUDREY MARY, psychologist, educator; b. Buffalo, Sept. 10, 1926; d. Ervin Jacob and Alice Grace (Haggerty) Borth; B.A., Mich. State U., 1948; M.A., U. Mich., 1950; Ph.D., U. Chgo., 1969. Instr., Grad. Sch. Edn. and Lab. Schs., U. Chgo., 1954-66, research asst. dept. edn., 1966-69; asso. prof. psychology, chmn. dept. edn. Barat Coll., Lake Forest, Ill., 1970-72, now research and evaluation cons.; postdoctoral fellow Harvard, 1972-73; asso. prof. Northeastern Ill. U., Chgo., 1973-74; asso. prof., head dept. edn. Lake Forest Coll., 1974—. Adv. council Interlochen (Mich.) Center for Arts. Mem. Am. Ednl. Research Assn., Am. Assn. Higher Edn., Am. Psychol. Assn., Pi Lambda Theta. Author publs. in field. Home: 70 W Burton Pl Chicago IL 60610

BORTNICK, JOAN SCHOEN KATZ (MRS. LEON BORTNICK), motor co. exec.; b. N.Y.C., Apr. 26, 1930; d. Abraham Maurice and Elsie Jane (Perlmutter) Katz; B.A., Mary Washington Coll., 1951; M.S. in Edn., Hofstra Coll., 1958; m. Leon Bortnick, Nov. 25, 1964 (dec.); children—Lawrence Schoen, David Schoen. Tchr., Shore Rd. Sch., Bellmore, L.I., 1957-58, P.S. 6, Manhattan, N.Y., 1959-64, Louise Archer Sch., Vienna, Va., 1965-70; pres. Rockville (Md.) Motor Co., Inc., 1969—. Mem. Rockville (Md.) Civic Assn., 1969—. Mem. Nat. Auto Dealers Assn. Home 8014 Birnam Wood Dr McLean VA 22101 Office 718 Rockville Pike Rockville MD 20852

BORTOLUSSI, VICKI HYMAN (MRS. JOHN BORTOLUSSI, JR.), journalist, educator; b. Chgo., Feb. 14, 1948; d. Alvin and Gladys Lee (Jaffe) Hyman; student Phoenix Coll., 1965-66, Ariz. State U., 1966-67; B.A. in Journalism (univ. scholar, Theta Sigma Phi scholar), U. So. Cal., 1968, M.S. in Journalism, 1970; m. John Bortolussi, Jr., Aug. 29, 1970. Tchr. journalism and Eng., Foshay Jr. High Sch., Los Angeles, 1968-70; dir., also instr. communications workshop U. So. Cal., Los Angeles, 1969, 70; pub. relations dir. San Fernando High Sch., Los Angeles, 1971; dir. journalism Agoura (Cal.) High Sch., 1971—. Gen. news editor Las Virgenes Enterprise, Calabasas, Cal., 1972, 73, columnist, 1973—; columnist Phoenix Jewish News, 1964-66; faculty grad. workshop Am. Inst. Family Relations, Los Angeles, 1970. Recipient, Nat. Hearst Feature Writing award, 1968, Journalism Edn. award, Cal. Newspaper Pubs., 1969. Mem. Cal. Tchrs. Assn., Nat. Ednl. Assn., Women in Communications. Democrat. Jewish religion. Office: 28545 Driver Av Agoura CA 91301

BORUM, ELIZABETH ANN, psychologist; b. Newman, Cal., May 4, 1930; d. John Allen and Helen E. (Sheedy) Borum; B.A. with honors, U. Cal. at Berkeley, 1951, M.A., 1953; m. Robert Arthur Arey, Jan. 27, 1951 (div. Jan. 1960). Research psychologist Inst. Child Welfare, U. Cal. at Berkeley, 1951-53, grad. research psychologist Inst. Human Devel., 1957-60; chief psychometrist, vocational counselor YMCA Vocational Service Center, N.Y.C., 1953-57; research psychometrist Inst. Med. Scis., San Francisco, 1961-67; psychologist Contra Costa Probation Dept., Pleasant Hill, Cal., 1967—. Sec. counseling cabinet YMCA City, N.Y., 1956-57; chmn. West Coast Council for Ethical Culture, 1965-67, San Francisco Ethical Forum, 1966-67; pres. Bay Area Fellowship for Ethical Culture, 1960-64, 66-67; mem. com. non-govt. orgns. adv. San Francisco's Mayor Com. for UN 20th Anniversary Celebration, 1964-65; chmn. spl. sessions UN Day Conf., Oakland, 1971. Mem. Am., Western, Cal., Contra Costa County (v.p. 1973-74) psychol. assns., A.A.A.S., Berkeley Bus. and Profl. Women's Club (pres. 1967-68), United World Federalists, UN Assn., Am. Civil Liberties Union, Soc. for Psychol. Study Social Issues, Oakland Mus. Assn., Am. Acad. Polit. and Social Sci., Am. Correctional Psychologists Assn., People to People. Home: 1830 Lakeshore St Apt 304 Oakland CA 94606 Office: Psychological Clinic 2265 Contra Costa Blvd Pleasant Hill CA 94523

BOSANKO, LYDIA ANN, educator; b. Madras, India, 1928 (parents Am. citizens); d. Arthur Kingsley and Ethelyn (Staples) Bosanko; A.B., Syracuse U., 1950; B.S. in Nursing, Columbia, 1958, M.A., Tchrs. Coll., 1963; postgrad. Boston Coll., Northeastern U. Sec. Herald Tribune Fresh Air Fund, N.Y.C., 1950-52, A. E. Nettleton Co., Syracuse, N.Y., 1952-55; staff and head nurse Presbyn. Hosp., N.Y.C., 1958-59; instr., asso. in nursing Faculty of Medicine, Columbia, N.Y.C., 1959-64; asst. prof. Northeastern U. Coll. Nursing, Boston, 1964-67, asso. prof., 1967-71, asst. dean, 1971—, also coordinator and chmn. med. surg. nursing courses, 1966-71, mem. adv. bd. pediatric nurse practitioner program, Somerville Hosp. Sch. Nursing. Mem. sustaining faculty New Eng. Council on Higher Edn. for Nursing intensive workshop program for teaching, summers 1967-68. Mem. Am. Nurses Assn., Nat. League Nursing (vice-chmn. steering com., dept. asso. degree programs 1966-67), New Eng. Council on Higher Edn. for Nursing, Am. Assn. U. Profs., Nursing Edn. Alumni Assn. Columbia, Presbyn. Hosp. Sch. Nursing Assn. (editorial bd. alumnae mag. 1959-63), Nat. Multiple Sclerosis Soc., Sigma Theta Tau, Kappa Delta. Contbr. articles to profl. jours and books.

BOSCH, GULNAR KHEIRALLAH, Islamicist, art historian; b. Lake Preston, S.D., Oct. 31, 1909; d. George I. and Anna (Griewisch) Kheirallah; B.F.A., Art Inst. Chgo., 1929; M.A. (Carnegie scholar) in Art History and Archaeology, N.Y.U., 1940; Ph.D. in Oriental Langs. and Lit., U. Chgo., 1952; m. Gerhard Bosch, Dec. 23, 1932; (div. 1964); children—hild, Jarir (dec.). Carnegie fellow Inst. Art and Archaeology, U. Paris, summer 1939; Am. Council Learned Societies fellow Princeton Grad. Coll. Islamic Seminars, 1938, 41, research asst. Oriental Inst., U. Chgo., 1943-45; asst. prof. art Fla. State Coll. for Women, 1940-43, Catherine Comer prof. art history, chmn. dept. art Wesleyan Coll., 1945-57; prof. art history, chmn. dept. fine arts La. State U., 1957-60; prof. art history, head art dept. Fla. State U., 1960—, dir. Study Center, Florence, Italy, 1967-68. Research grantee La. State U., XXV Internat. Congress Orientalists, Moscow, grantee Fla. State U. TO XXVI congress, New Delhi, XXIX congress, Paris. Mem. Am. Oriental Soc., Nat. Southeastern Coll. art assns., La. Coll. Conf. (sec. art sect. 1959), Southeastern Coll. Art Conf. (pres. 1957-58, v.p. 1965-67), Am. Assn. U. Profs. Contbr. articles profl. jours. revs., encys. Home: 1501 Hilltop Dr Tallahassee FL 32303

BOSCH, PATRICIA CARROLL (MRS. GEORGE ALEXANDER BOSCH), journalist; b. Jackson, Miss., Apr. 16, 1937; d. William Womack and Sudie Lee (Pierce) Ferguson; A.A., Stephens Coll., Columbia, Mo., 1956; student Lamar U., 1969-70; m. George Alexander Bosch, Dec. 30, 1956; children—William Alexander, George Michael. Tchr., Stephens Coll., 1956, Patricia Bosch Acad. of Charm, 1960; profl. model, 1960-62; v.p. Richey Bosch Assos., Beaumont, Tex., 1961—; dir. Hobby Horse Farms Enterprises. Publicity dir. Sr. Citizen Hobby Show, 1973. Bd. dirs. William Alexander Bosch Trust, George Michael Bosch Trust. Recipient Fair Face of Fashion award, 1964; named, with husband, Extraordinary Couple, Alpha Omega, 1962. Mem. Am. Women in Radio and Television, Women Broadcasters Am., Nat. Acad. Television Arts and Scis., Internat. Radio and Television Soc., Womans Aux. Med. Soc. Club: International. Author series newspaper columns (with Dorothy Richey) First Lady in Your Home, 1962, How To Be Rich and Beautiful, 1965, Today's Woman in Today's World, 1973. Home: 1880 Karen Lane Beaumont TX 77706 Office: PO Box 5201 Beaumont TX 77706

BOSLEY, PHYLLIS BUNKER (MRS. KENNETH T. BOSLEY), educator; b. Kansas City, Mo., July 28, 1931; d. Eng and Wilda (Dobbin) Bunker; B.A., Southwestern Coll., Winfield, Kan., 1953; M.A., U. Neb., 1955; postgrad. Harvard, 1955-56, U. Md., 1956-58, Syracuse U., 1969; m. Kenneth T. Bosley, Dec. 23, 1954; children—Kenneth Webster, Kerry Hopkins. Instr. U. Md., College Park, 1955-56; home economist Am. Sheep Producers Council, Balt.-Washington, 1958-63; instr. Villa Julie Coll., Balt., 1961-63; pub. relations cons. Infoplan Internat., Inc., 1959—; faculty mass. communications and speech Towson State Coll., Balt., 1963—, asso. prof., 1973—. Dir. ann. Newspaper in Classroom Curriculum Devel. Conf., 1973—; cons. speech communication and pub. relations to various orgns. and industries. Judge home arts Md. State Fair, 1963—; mem. pub. information com. Am. Cancer Soc., 1973-74. Mem. Speech Communications Assn., Am. Forensics Assn. (asso. editor calendar publ. 1968—), Balt. Pub. Relations Council, Pi Kappa Delta. Editor: (with Sies, Bosley, Beitzel and Stone) Fundamentals of Speech, 1965. Asso. editor various nat. profl. publs. Home: Route 2 Box 7 Sparks MD 21152 Office: Towson State College Baltimore MD 21204

BOSNER, JANE POTTER, ednl. adminstr.; b. Atlantic City, Mar. 17, 1927; d. Floyd Arthur and Olga (Gutleher) Potter; A.B., Middlebury Coll., 1948; M.Ed., Temple U., 1952; postgrad. Rutgers U., 1955-63, Monmouth Coll., 1973—; m. Stanley Bosner, Sept. 13, 1958. Placement officer pub. schs., Atlantic City, 1949-52, sch. psychologist, 1952-57; sch. psychologist pub. schs., Red Bank, N.J., 1957-70, dir. child study services, 1970—. Dir. Atlantic City Easter Seal Speech Clin., 1954-57; dir. Community Mental Health Center, Red Bank, since 1973—. Mem. Am., N.J., Monmouth-Ocean County psychol. assns., N.J. Assn. Sch. Psychologists (exec. sec. 1969—), Soc. for Personality Assessment, N.E.A., N.J. Edn. Assn. Home: 121 Horseneck Pt Rd Oceanport NJ 07757 Office: 76 Branch Av Red Bank NJ 07701

BOSS, MAHALEY ANN, nurse; b. Harrisonburg, La., Feb. 21, 1919; d. William Aaron and Katherine Evelyn (Smith) Davis; grad. St. Francis Hosp. Sch. Nursing, Monroe, La., 1941; m. Robert Vaughn Boss, Apr. 11, 1947; children—Robert Aaron, Thomas Vaughn. Asst. supr. women's ward St. Francis Hosp., 1941-42; obstet. nurse Akron (O.) City Hosp., 1947-65, head nurse gynecology dept., 1965—. Served to 1st lt. Army Nurse Corps, 1942-47; ETO, PTO. Mem. La., Ohio nurses assns., Women's Overseas Service League. Home: 5741 Dailey Rd Akron OH 44319 Office: 525 E Market St Akron OH 44304

BOSS, PATTI JUNE JACKSON (MRS. FREDERICK L. BOSS, JR.), lawyer; b. Hobbs, N.M., Feb. 1, 1938; d. Lester Arthur and Nada Ferne (Morse) Jackson; B.S., Tulsa U., 1961, J.D., 1970; m. Frederick L. Boss, Jr., Aug. 30, 1966; children—Amie Anne, Frederick L. III. Admitted to Okla. bar, 1970; mem. firm Boss & Boss, Tulsa, 1970—. Cons. (with husband) Tulsa chpt. Parents without Partners, 1970—. Mem. finance com. Tulsa Philharmonic Soc., 1973—. Mem. Am., Okla., Tulsa County (pub. relations com. 1973—) bar assns., Tulsa County Bar Aux. (exec. bd. 1970-74, chmn. law week com. 1974—), Alumni Assn. Tulsa U., Alumni Assn. Ark. U., Pi Gamma Mu, Phi Alpha Delta, Alpha Delta Pi. Republican. Episcopalian. Club: Southwood. Home: 2994 E 78th St Tulsa OK 74136 Office: 4401 S Harvard Av Tulsa OK 74135

BOSSE, DELORES JEAN SNYDER (MRS. GEORGE S. BOSSE), assn. exec., b. Grand Haven, Mich., Apr. 20, 1929; d. Joseph Frank and Anne Mary (Jurak) Snyder; B.S., Western Mich. U., 1951; postgrad. U. Mich., 1952-53; m. George S. Bosse, June 7, 1953; 1 stepdau., Charel (Mrs. Robert Anderson); children—DeAnne (Mrs. Paul D. Sherd), Blayne, Janelle, Jodi, Melanie, Lynnette. Homebound occupational therapist Western Area of Mich., Mich. Soc. for Crippled Children and Adults, 1951-52; exec. sec., occupational therapist Berrien County Soc. Crippled Children and Adults, St. Joseph, Mich., 1952-53; occupational therapist, bookkeeper Easter Seal Soc. Crippled Children and Adults of Grand Valley, Inc., Grand Rapids, Mich., 1965-69, acting exec. dir., 1969-71; occupational therapist Easter Seal Soc. for Crippled Children and Adults N.E. Fla., Jacksonville, 1971-73, acting exec. dir., 1974—, vol. bookkeeper, 1971—. Mem. Am., Fla. occupational therapy assns., Service Orgn. of the Shores (treas. 1972-73). Mem. Order Eastern Star. Home: 8114 Madeira Dr Jacksonville FL 32217 Office: 835 N Main St Jacksonville Fl 32202

BOSSERT, EDYTHE HOY, artist, educator; b. Jacksonville, Pa., July 18, 1908; d. George Nevin and Minnie Elizabeth (Swope) Hoy; tchrs. certificate Lock Haven (Pa.) State Coll., 1928; student oil painting and art Carnegie Inst. Tech., 1930, Lock Haven State Coll., 1960; m. Willard Max Bossert, Oct. 24, 1931; children—Jane Rebecca (Mrs. Frank J. Schwab), B. Susan (Mrs. Robert Hannegan), Thomas Hoy, Willard Max, Bethany Ann. Elementary sch. tchr., Lock Haven, 1958-68; tchr., supr. pub. sch. art Keystone Central Sch. Dist., Lock Haven, 1969-71; exhbns. include ann. Nat. Acad. Design, 1944, ann. Nat. Assn. Women Artists, 1945-74, North Shore Art Assn.; group shows Millbrook Art Gallery, Ogunquit, Me., Terry, Fla. Parkersburg Fine Arts Exhbn., Bucknell U.; one man show Lock Haven State Coll., Ross Library, Lock Haven, 1968, three-man exhbns. Britts Gallery, Williamsport, Pa., 1967. Chmn. Clinton County Mother's March of Dimes, 1952-74; pres. bd. dirs. Crafts, Inc. for mentally retarded, 1973. Mem., sec. Bald Eagle Mittany Bd. Edn., Mill Hall, Pa., 1935-50; pres. Bald Eagle Council Republican Women, 1968-70. Sec. bd. trustees Annie Halenbake Ross Library, Lock Haven, 1958—; charter mem. Millbrook Playhouse Bd.; Clinton Lycoming Mental Health Mental Retardation Adv. Bd., 1974—. Mem. Nat., Pa. edn. assns., Nat. Assn. Women Artists, Delta Kappa Gamma. Republican. Presbyn. (elder). Address: Old Beech Creek Rd Beech Creek PA 16822

BOST, CECILE ELIZABETH, journalist; b. Newton, N.C., Nov. 28, 1924; d. Marcus Marion and Myrtle Cidy (Gross) Rowe; A.B. cum laude, Catawba Coll., 1946; m. Robert Preston Bost, Apr. 28, 1946; 1 son, William Stephen. Instr. English, Rock Springs High Sch., Denver, N.C., 1947-48; women's editor radio sta. WNNC, Newton, N.C., 1948-53; continuity editor, air personality sta. WIRC, Hickory, N.C., 1953-63; free-lance broadcaster, writer, producer Cecile Bost Reporting, 1963—. Corr., WBTV News, Charlotte, N.C., 1970—; lectr. in field. Recipient N.C. Sch. Bell award, 1966; N.C. A.P. 1st place awards women's news, 1966, 68, 70, state news, 1968, documentary-pub. affairs, 1970; named Catawba County's Leading Citizen in Communications, Catawba News-Enterprise. Mem. Catawba Coll. Alumni Assn. (pres. 1964-66), Am. Women in Radio and TV (pres. N.C. chpt. 1964-66), N.C. Lit. and Hist. Soc., Internat. Platform Assn. Club: Catawba Valley Executives. Author short stories, one-act plays; contbr. articles to mags. Home: 503 E Herman St Newton NC 28658 Office: 503 E Herman St Newton NC 28658

BOSTDORF, MARY GALLOWAY (MRS. FLOYD MILTON BOSTDORF), lawyer; b. Balt., Md., Feb. 8, 1903; d. John Adam and Sarah Ellen (Parks) Galloway; student U. Balt., 1930-33; LL.B., Johns Hopkins, 1934; m. Floyd Milton Bostdorf, June 28, 1940; 1 dau., Donna Mae (Mrs. John Walter Sippel). Admitted to Md. bar, 1933, since practiced in Towson; with firm Smalkin & Hessian, 1951-57, Milton J. Dance Co., 1957-62. Methodist (sec. adminstrv. bd. 1966—). Address: Williams Rd Hyde MD 21082

BOSTIAN, IRMA RUTH (MRS. J. CALVIN BOSTIAN), editor, state ofcl.; b. De Kalb, Ill., Mar. 27, 1929; d. Arthur F. and Caroline M. (Weiherman) Carstedt; student No. Ill. U., 1946-50, U. Ill., 1962-63; m. J. Calvin Bostian, May 28, 1949; children—Laurence, Sandra (Mrs. David Colee), Cheryl (Mrs. Lawrence Lottino). Head art services Ill. State Library, Springfield, 1959-65, head publs. unit, 1965—, editor Ill. Libraries, 1965—. Recipient H.W. Wilson Periodical award, 1972. Mem. Am., Ill. (mem. exec. bd. 1968—) library assns., Lawyers Wives Assn., Delta Zeta, Pi Kappa Delta. Lutheran. Club: Springfield Women's. Editor: In Our Opinion, 1973. Home: 15 Timber Hill Springfield IL 62704 Office: Illinois State Library Springfield IL 62756

BOSTON, LUCYANN MUELLER (MRS. ALLEN SPENCER BOSTON), journalist; b. St. Louis, July 9, 1943; d. Arthur Bode and Lucy (Scott) Mueller; B.S. in Journalism, Northwestern U., 1965; m. Allen Spencer Boston; 1 son, Scott Spencer. Text book editor C. V. Mosby Co., St. Louis, 1965-66; staff writer St. Louis Globe-Democrat, 1966-67, Sunday Women's editor, 1967-73, fashion columnist, 1974—; broadcaster KMOX-CBS radio, St. Louis, 1967—; instr. feature writing Washington U., St. Louis, 1973—. Mem. Northwestern U. Alumni Assn., Fashion Group, Press Club Met. St. Louis (dir.), Jr. League St. Louis, Women in Communications, Sigma Delta Chi, Chi Omega. Presbyn. Home: 306 Sylvester Av Webster Groves MO 63119

BOSTON, OLIVE MAY (MRS. ROBERT M. BOSTON), educator, ednl. adminstr.; b Pitts., Mar. 5, 1914; d. George Joseph and Lillie May (Findley) Miller; student Morton's Bus. Coll., Pitts., 1933; certification early childhood edn. Drexel U., 1957; certificate early childhood edn. Pa. State U., 1969, certificate Gesell Inst. Child Devel. Readiness and Devel. Placement, 1970; courses Pa. State U., summer 1971; m. Robert M. Boston, June 8, 1940; children—Judith (Mrs. Dean S. Skillman), Olive (Mrs. Steven C. Davidson). Welfare worker WPA, Pitts., 1934-35; interviewer Family Soc. Allegheny County, Pitts., 1934-40; asst. to pediatrician, Phila., 1941-42; asst. tchr. nursery lab. sch. Drexel U., 1954-57; head tchr. nursery sch., instr. Harcum Jr. Coll. students Mildred Sullivan Sch., Rosemont, Pa., 1957-58; teaching prin., adminstr. Merion Friends Sch., nursery sch., Merion Station, Pa., 1958—. Instr., Harcum Jr. Coll., part time 1963-65; cons. St. Peters Sch. Boys, Phila., Overbrook Presbyn. Sch., Byberry Friends Sch., 1969-70. Mem. Friends Council Edn. (mem. prin. group 1960-74), Child Study Assn. Am., Nat., Delaware Valley (membership com. 1970-71) assns. edn. young children, Buten Wedgewood Mus. Soc. Presbyn. (deacon 1968-70). Clubs: Bala Cynwyd Womens, Republican Women. Home: 120 Birch Av Bala Cynwyd PA 19004 Office: 615 Montgomery Av Merion Station PA 19066

BOSTWICK, MARGERY FLORENCE NUTTALL (MRS. HENRY HOLDING BOSTWICK), personnel exec.; b. Millville, N.J., Jan. 6, 1937; d. John William and Rhoda Susanne (Stauffer) Nuttall; grad. high sch.; m. Henry Holding Bostwick, Feb. 25, 1956; children—Terry Lynn, Cynthia Louise, Greta Lorraine. Varitypist, Glendale Press, Vineland, N.J., 1955-57; debit clk. Prudential Inst. Co., Millville, 1957-59; with Vineland Labs., Inc., 1963—, personnel mgr., 1973—. Home: 1724 Washington Av Vineland NJ 08360 Office: 2285 E Landis Av Vineland NJ 08360

BOSWELL, SARA JANE ZIMMERMAN (MRS. WILLIAM B. BOSWELL), advt. exec.; b. Rochester, Ind., June 17, 1918; d. Lon and Fern (Bryant) Zimmerman; student Ball State Tchrs. Coll., 1936-38; m. William B. Boswell, Dec. 24, 1938; children—Judith (Mrs. Charles D. Reece), Jeffrey W. Tchr., Woodrow Elementary Sch., Rochester, 1938-39; grinder operator Warner Gear div. Borg Warner, 1943-45; accounts receivable Ball Bros. Co., Muncie, 1949; dir. radio and TV, account exec., v.p. R. J. Poorman & Assos., Inc., Advt. Agy., 1954-66; asso. dir. advt. and pub. relations Indsl. Trust and Savs. Bank, Muncie, 1967—. Pres. Community Services Council Delaware County. Vice committeeman Del. County Republican Central Com., 1946-48, del. to state conv., 1964. Bd. dirs. Family Counseling Service, 1964, 65, 66, Nat. Found. for Infantile Paralysis, 1955-57, Muncie Area chpt. A.R.C., 1967-70, Community Services Council, 1971-74 (pres. 1973-74), United Fund Delaware County, 1971-74. Mem. Altrusa Internat. (editor dist. service bull. 1967-69, pres. Muncie 1970-71), Nat. Assn. Am. Pen Women, Theta Sigma Phi. Methodist. Club: Altrusa of Muncie. Home: Hamilton Village Rural Route 13 Box 366 Muncie IN 47302 Office: 117 E Adams St Muncie IN 47305

BOSWORTH, PHYLLIS RUTH, broadcasting exec.; b. Long Beach, N.Y., June 5, 1934; d. Louis and Natalie Rose (Jacobs) Bosworth; B.S., Cornell U., 1956. Researcher, CBS News, N.Y.C., 1961-72, asso. producer documentary films, 1972—. Mem. Writers Guild Am. East. Home: 150 West End Av New York City NY 10023 Office: 524 W 57th St New York City NY 10019

BOTDORF, RUTH GRAYBILL, chemist, educator; b. Freeburg, Pa., Dec. 13, 1923; d. George Allen and Elizabeth Mable (Graybill) Botdorf; A.B. cum laude, Susquehanna U., 1945; M.S., Columbia, 1948; Ph.D (NSF fellow), Pa. State U., 1969. Instr. chemistry Pa. State U. at Du Bois, 1948-51, Ogontz, 1951-61, University Park, summer, 1958, 65, McKeesport, 1965-69; asst. prof. chemistry Pa. State U. at Berks, Reading, 1969—. Mem. Exec. Com. Reading-Berks Sci. and Engring. Fair, 1970—, chmn. Awards Com., 1970—. NSF faculty fellow. Mem. Am. Chem. Soc., N.Y. Acad. Sci., A.A.A.S., Reading Chemists Club, Pi Gamma Mu, Pi Lambda Theta, Kappa Delta Pi, Sigma Pi Sigma, Iota Sigma Pi, Sigma Delta Epsilon. Republican. Lutheran. Contbr. articles on inorganic chemistry; chem. edn., X-ray crystallography to sci. jours. Home: RD 1 Box 79 Harrisburg PA 17111 Office: RD 5 Tulpehocken Rd Reading PA 19608

BOTELHO, PATRICIA ANN, assn. adminstr.; b. Providence, July 19, 1943; d. Alfred and Mary Elizabeth (Corey) Botelho; Ed.B. in Elementary Edn., R.I. Coll., 1965, Ed.M. in Elementary Adminstrn., 1971. Tchr., Scituate (R.I.) Schs., 1965-74; membership specialist R.I. Edn. Assn., Providence, 1973—. Chairwoman, Women Educators' Legislative Com., 1972—. Mem. Nat., R.I. (pres. 1969-70, dir. 1969, 70-73) edn. assns., Scituate Tchrs'. Assn. (pres. 1972-73), Edn. assns., R.I. Coll. Alumni Assn., Scituate P.T.A. (pres. 1973-74). Home: 149 Fort St East Providence RI 02914 Office: 300 Hennessey Av North Providence RI 02911

BOTHE, ELSBETH LEVY (MRS. BERTHOLD BOTHE), lawyer; b. Balt., Oct. 17, 1927; d. Milford and Elsa Belle (Kraus) Levy; B.A., U. Chgo., 1947; postgrad. U. Zurich (Switzerland), 1948-49; LL.B., U. Md., 1952; m. Berthold Bothe, July 24, 1965. Indsl. editor Lock Insulator Corp., Balt., 1949; editor United Auto Workers, Balt., 1952; admitted to Md. bar, 1952; staff atty. Legal Aid Bur., Balt., 1953-54; practiced in Balt., 1952-72; asst. state pub. defender Balt., 1972—. Cons., Am. Civil Liberties Union Md., 1966—. Mem. Constl. Revision Commn. 1966-68; Democrat del. Md. Constl. Conv., 1968. Bd. dirs. Patuxent (Md.) Inst., 1964-72; bd. govs. Citizens Planning and Housing Assn. Md., 1967—. Mem. Am., Md., Balt. bar assns. Women's Law Center. Home: 208 Kemble Rd Baltimore MD 21218 Office: 410 Maryland Trust Bldg Calvert St and Redwood St Baltimore MD 21202

BOTHWELL, DORR, artist; b. San Francisco, May 3, 1902; d. John Stuart and Florence Isabel (Hodgson) Bothwell; student Cal. Sch. Fine Arts, Rudolph Schaeffer Sch. Design, U. Ore. Painter, Tau, Mau'a, Am. Samoa, 1928-29, France, 1930-31; instr. Cal. Sch. Fine Arts, San Francisco, 1945—, Rudolph Schaeffer Sch. Design, 1960—, Mendocino (Cal.) Art Center, 1962—; prof. U. Cal., Mendocino Art Center, summers 1965-67; exhibitor West Coast exhbns., 1927—; 3d biennial Sao Paulo, Brazil, Pitts. Internat., 1952, 55, Art: U.S.A., 1958; works in permanent collection San Diego Gallery Fine Art, Crocker Gallery, Sacramento, San Francisco Mus. Art, Whitney Mus. Am. Art, Bklyn. Mus., Mus. Modern Art, Fogg Mus., Met. Museum, Victoria and Albert Museum, London, Eng., Bibleotheque Nationale, Paris, France; one-man show De Young Meml. Mus., San Francisco, 1963. Instr. San Francisco Art Inst., 1961, Rudolph Sch. Design, San Francisco, 1961; prof. Sonoma State Coll., Mendocino, summer session, 1964. Recipient 1st prize, 4th ann. exhbn. San Francisco Soc. Women Artists, 1929, Pres.'s purchase prize, 1941; Leisser-Farnham award 7th ann. exhbn. San Diego Art Guild, 1932; hon. mention 7th ann. exhbn. So. Cal. Artists, 1933, spl. prize 9th ann. exhbn., 1937; Artists Fund prize ann. exhbn. drawings and prints San Francisco Art Assn., 1943; hon. mention 2d spring ann. Cal. Palace Legion of Honor. San Francisco, 1947. Notan: The Principle of Dark-Light Design, 1968. Home and studio: PO Box 27 Mendocino CA 95460

BOTKIN, DOROTHY VIRGINIA, educator; b. Lexington, Ky.; d. Daniel Robert and Dooley (Welch) Botkin; B.A., U. Louisville, 1947; B.S., Juilliard Sch. Music, 1950; M.Mus., Ind. U., 1951; postgrad. North Tex. State U., summer 1954, Mozarteum, Salzburg, Austria, summers, 1956, 66, Eastman Sch. Music, summers 1960-61, Music Acad. West, 1963. Faculty, Mary Hardin-Baylor, Belton, Tex., 1951-53, Del Mar Coll., Corpus Christi, Tex., 1954-58; asst. prof. North Tex. State U., Denton, 1958-70, asso. prof., 1970—. Concert tour, Asia, summers 1967-69; performer Dallas symphony, Ft. Worth Opera Co., Corpus Christi Symphony, Midland-Odessa Symphony, Monroe Symphony Orch., numerous choral socs.; held concerts in Austria, Mexico, Malaysia, West Malaysia, Viet-Nam, U.S.; toured Viet-Nam and sang in mil. hosp. wards, chapels, hdqrs. spl. forces camps; gave concerts mission stas., chs. Mem. Tex. Assn. Coll. Tchrs., Am. Assn. U. Profs., Nat. Assn. Tchrs. Singing, N. Tex. Juilliard Assn., Music Tchrs. Nat. Assn., Tex. Music Tchrs. Assn., Am. Assn. U. Women, Mu Phi Epsilon (faculty adviser 1959—), Mu Phi Epsilon Alumni, Pi Kappa Lambda (chpt. pres. 1964-66). Republican. Office: Box 5331 North Tex Sta Denton TX 76203

BOTSKO, LISSANTE HILL POWELL, mgmt. exec.; b. Washington, July 13, 1939; d. W. Royce and Louise (Hill-Conkey) Powell; B.S., Am. U., 1967, postgrad., 1968-69; m. Francis V. LoBianco, July 9, 1960 (dec. July, 1965); children—Royce Powell, Lissante Louise; m. 2d, Richard G. Botsko, May 12, 1973. Adminstrv. asst. Surveys and Research Corps, Washington, 1960-65; adminstr. Am. U., 1966-67; with Sears Roebuck & Co., White Oak, Md., 1967-71, mgmt. tng. exec., 1967-71, personnel exec., Arlington, Va., 1971-73, mdse. mgr., 1973-74, asst. mgr. operating supt. exec. tng., 1974, asst. mgr., operating supt., Rochester, N,Y., 1974—. Election ofcl. Republican Party, Alexandria, Va., 1964-65, 72, Washington, 1964-65; precinct chmn. Montgomery County (Md.) Rep. Party, 1970-74. Recipient Distributive Edn. award, 1972. Mem. Magna Charta Dames, Alpha Chi Omega. Club: International (Washington). Home: 63 Stuyvesant Rd Pittsford NY 14534 Office: 259 Monroe Av Rochester NY 14607

BOTT, DOROTHEA ROSALIE, occupational therapist; b. Deloraine, Australia, Feb. 16, 1940; d. George Walter and Jean (Wilson) Bott; student Methodist Ladies Coll., Launceston, Australia, 1949-57; Diploma in Occupational Therapy, Victorian Sch. Occupational Therapy (Australia), 1960. Came to Can., 1964. Staff therapist Heidelberg Repatriation Hosp., Melbourne, Australia, 1961-62, Bethelem Day Hosp., London, Eng., 1962-63; staff therapist Glenrose Hosp., Edmonton, Alta., Can., 1964-65, supt. occupational therapy, 1966—. Mem. Canadian Assn. Occupational Therapists (provincial rep. clin. tng. com. 1973-74), Edmonton Rehab. Soc. (dir. 1972-74). Mem. United Ch. Can. Home: Suite 606 10185 115th St Edmonton AB T5K 1T4 Canada Office: 10230 111th Av Edmonton AB Canada

BOTTEL, HELEN, columnist, pub. speaker; m. Robert Bottel; 4 children. Newspaper columnist King Features Syndicate columns Helen Help Us!, also (with dau.) Generation Rap; author; speaker social fraternal, profl. orgns., schs., colls. Mem. Grants Pass (Ore.) Juvenile Adv. Com., 1960-62. Bd. dirs. Ill. Valley Med. Center, 1958-62, Childrens Center Sacramento, 1969, Students League Against Narcotics Temptation; charter patron Cosumnes River Coll. Recipient 1st place award for books Cal. Press Women, 1969; also 4 newspaper feature writing awards Western Timbermen's Assn.; citation for aid to U.S. servicemen in Vietnam, Gov. of Ga.; Distinguished Merit citation Nat. Conf. Christians and Jews. Mem. Soc. Mag. Writers, Cal. Writers Club, Nat. Platform Assn. Author: To Teens With Love, 1969; Helen Help Us, 1970. Parent Survival Kit, 1974. Contbr. articles to nat. mags., newspapers. Address: 2060 56th Av Sacramento CA 95822*

BOTTICHER, WILHELMINA WOTKYNS (MRS. WILHELM KARL E. BOTTICHER), microbiologist; b. Pasadena, Cal.; d. Grosvenor Libeneau and Wilhelmina (Eliot) Wotkyns; certificate Pasadena City Coll., 1933-35; A.B., U. So. Cal., 1944, M.S., 1945; m. Wilhelm Karl E. Botticher, Jan. 19, 1946. Lab. technician U. Cal. Med. Center, 1952; pub. health bacteriologist Los Angeles County Health Dept., 1953-56; pub. health microbiologist Solano County Health Dept., 1956-60, lab. dir., 1960-62; supervisory microbiologist Travis AFB, Cal., 1962-67; microbiologist Peralta Hosp., Oakland, Cal., 1969-70; supervisory microbiologist VA Hosp., Martinez, Cal., 1970—. Diplomate Nat. Acad. Med. Technologists. Fellow Royal Soc. Health; mem. Med. Mycology Am., Am. Pub. Health Assn., Am. Assn. Microbiologists. Author: A Rapid Method for the Identification of Candida albicans and Other Candida, 1963; Alternaria as a Possible Human Pathogen, 1965; Serratia Studies, 1970. Home: 3151 Mt Veeder Rd Napa CA 94558

BOTTOMLEY, SYLVIA STAKLE (MRS. RICHARD HAROLD BOTTOMLEY), physician, educator; b. Riga, Latvia, Mar. 9, 1934; d. John Waldemar and Leontine (Miluns) Stakle; brought to U.S., 1950, naturalized, 1955; B.S., Okla. State U., 1954; M.D., U. Okla., 1958; m. Richard Halrold Bottomley, June 5, 1958; children—Astrid Elizabeth, Ian Philip. Intern, Salt Lake City Gen. Hosp., 1958-59; resident U. Okla. Health Scis. Center, Oklahoma City, 1959-61, fellow in hematology, 1961-64; asst. prof. medicine U. Okla. Sch. Medicine, Oklahoma City, 1967-71, asso. prof. medicine, 1971—, asso. prof. pathology, 1973—; mem. staff VA Hosp., Oklahoma City, 1969—, asst. chief hematology, 1969—. Investigator VA Clin. Research, 1965-69. Diplomate Am. Bd. Internal Medicine, Am. Bd. Hematology. Fellow, Am. Coll. Physicians; mem. Am. Fedn. for Clin. Research, Am. Soc. Hematology, Central Soc. for Clin. Research, So. Soc. for Clin. Investigation, Sigma Xi, Phi Kappa Phi, Alpha Omega Alpha. Research in erythropoiesis and hemesynthesis. Home: 1325 NE 54th St Oklahoma City OK 73111 Office: VA Hosp 921 NE 13th St Oklahoma City OK 73104

BOTTRELL, HELEN KNOLLENBERG, psychologist; b. Augusta, Kan., Sept. 17, 1919; d. Will J. and Nonie (Barnes) Knollenberg; B.S. in Edn., U. Neb., 1930, B.A. in Social Scis., 1932, M.A., 1933; Ed.D., U. Houston, 1954; m. Harold R. Bottrell, Apr. 8, 1944; children—Robert, David. Tchr. pub. schs., Neb., 1930-43; tchr. pub. speaking Northwestern U., 1943; tchr. communications Stephens Coll., Columbia, Mo., 1943-45; nursery sch. tchr., Evansville, Ind., 1948-49; tchr. pub. schs., Houston and Pasadena, Tex., 1950-64; faculty San Jacinto Jr. Coll., Pasadena, 1964-67; faculty S. Tex. Jr. Coll., Houston, 1967-74, prof. humanities and social scis.; staff psychologist Tex. Rehab. Commn., 1974—. Ford fellow, 1955-56. Mem. Nat. Council Tchrs. English, Nat. Assn. Tchrs. Speech, Am., Tex., Houston personnel and guidance assns., Am. (asso.), Tex., Houston, Southwestern psychol. assns., Tex. Jr. Coll. Classroom Tchrs. Assn., U. Houston Faculty Women's Assn., S. Tex. Faculty Assn., League Women Voters, Internat. Platform Assn., Kappa Delta Pi (past chpt. sec.), Delta Kappa Gamma. Home: 4370 Wheeler St Houston TX 77004

BOUCHARD, SISTER JEANNE, sch. adminstr.; b. St. Agathe, Me., Apr. 1, 1924; d. Alphonse and Agnes (Tardif) Bouchard; B.S. in Edn., St. Joseph's Coll., North Windham, Mo., 1962; M.A., Catholic U. of Am., 1967. Joined Daus. of Wisdom, 1943; tchr. elementary schs., Me., 1943-56, prin., 1957-62; prin. elementary schs. Va., 1962-65; adminstr. Maryhaven Sch., Port Jefferson, N.Y., 1965—. Cons. provincial govt. Daus. of Wisdom, 1967-70; rep. to Sisters Adv. Council, Rockville Centre Diocese, 1971—. Bd. dirs. St. Charles Hosp., Port Jefferson, 1965—, Respite Lodge, Glen Spey, N.Y., 1972—, Consultative Services Inc., Rockville Centre, 1972—, Regional Task Force for Mental Retardation, 1971-72. Recipient award for service in mental retardation Mother Yvonne chpt. Friends of Maryhaven, 1971. Mem. Nat. Rehab. Assn., Nat. Cath. Edn. Assn., Nat. Cath. Guidance Assn., N.Y. State Tchrs. Mentally Retarded, Am. Assn. Mental Deficiency, Council for Exceptional Children, L.I. Assn. Spl. Edn. Adminstrs. Home: 110 Hawkins St Port Jefferson NY 11777 Office: 450 Myrtle Av Port Jefferson NY 11777

BOUCHER, DOROTHY BUCK (MRS. RALPH EMERSON BOUCHER), lawyer; b. Abingdon, Va., Mar. 24, 1924; d. Frederick Carlyle and Mattie Newell (Dyer) Buck; grad Va. Intermont Coll., 1942; B.A., Emory and Henry Coll., 1944; LL.B., U. Va., 1946; m. Ralph Emerson Boucher, June 17, 1950; children—Frederick Carlyle, Dorothy Anne. Admitted to Va. bar, 1945; asso. Ralph E. Boucher, Abingdon, 1947-50; partner Boucher & Boucher, Abingdon, 1950—. Vice pres., dir. Crabtree Buick-Pontiac, Inc.; sec., dir. Abingdon Real Estate & Auction Co., Inc.; mem. adv. bd. Va. Nat. Bank. Mem. Abingdon Planning Commn., 1947—, chmn., 1957—; mem. Abingdon Archtl. Bd. Rev., 1972—; commr. accounts Circuit Ct. Washington County, Va., 1950—. Sec., Washington County Electoral Bd., 1964-71, Washington County Democratic Com., 1973—. Bd. dirs. Holston Meth. Homes for Ret. Mem. Va., Washington County bar assns., Washington County Hist. Soc., D.A.R., Am. Assn. U. Women, Kappa Delta. Methodist (trustee). Club: Mattie Rountree Stephenson Womans (past pres.). Home: 107 W Main St Abingdon VA 24210 Office 188 E Main St Abingdon VA 24210

BOUEY, MELICENT VYOLA, investment specialist; b. Monrovia, Liberia, Jan. 17, 1924 (parents Am. citizens); d. Edward H. and Elizabeth (Coles) Bouey; B.A., Va. Union U., 1938-42; postgrad. Pratt Inst., 1943-45, Columbia, 1945-46, U. Cal. at Los Angeles, 1961-65, Law Sch., LaSalle Extension U., 1966—. Designer-patternmaker with motion picture studio, also fashion houses, 1946-56; mfr. own designs of high fashion loungewear, 1956-59; real estate broker, Los Angeles, 1961-67; with various investment cos., Washington, 1967-69; prin. Bouey Investment Co., Washington, 1969-73, Bouey Internat. Inc., N.Y.C., 1973-74; prin. Bouey Found., N.Y.C., 1974—. Mem. Nat. Assn. Securities Dealers Conglist. (trustee 1969-71, mem. investment com. 1969—). Home: 80 Park Av New York City NY 10016

BOULANGER, CAROL SEABROOK, lawyer; b. N.Y.C., Sept. 14, 1942; d. John M. and Anne S. (Schlaudecker) Seabrook; B.A., Swarthmore Coll., 1964; LL.B., U. Pa., 1969; m. Jacques P. Boulanger. Admitted to N.Y. bar, 1970, U.S. Tax Ct., 1970; asso. Baker & McKenzie, N.Y.C., 1969-71, Wender, Murase & White, N.Y.C., 1971—. Founding mem., sec. ARCS Found., Inc., N.Y. chpt., 1973—.

Mem. Am. Bar Assn., Assn. Bar City N.Y., N.Y. Council Law Assos., Law Alumni Sec. U. Pa. (bd. mgrs.), Swarthmore Coll. Alumni Council. Office: 350 Park Av New York City NY 10022

BOULTON, GRACE, Republican nat. committeewoman; b. Ardmore, Okla., Oct. 4, 1926; d. William T. and Grace (Johnson) Ward; student Vassar Coll., 1944-46; B.A., U. Okla., 1948; m. Don C. Boulton, Aug. 14, 1948; children—Anne Elaine, Scot William. Vice chmn. 5th Congl. district Okla. Republican party, 1967-71, state vice chmn., 1971-72; mem. Rep. nat. com. from Okla., 1972—. Pres. Millwood Bd. Edn., 1967-70. Mem. Alpha Chi Omega, Sigma Iota Pi. Mem. Disciples of Christ. Home: 1701 NE 63d St Oklahoma City OK 73111

BOULTON, MARY HOLZMAN BANCROFT (MRS. SCHROEDER BOULTON), psychotherapist; b. Cin.; d. Wallace and Claire (Workum) Holzman; B.S., U. Cin., 1932; M.S.W., U. Pa., 1935; Ph.D. in Human Relations, Ind. No. U., 1973; m. Frank Carter Bancroft, Aug. 30, 1935 (dec. 1959); children—Carter, Michael, Janet, Nancy, John; m. 2d, Schroeder Boulton, Feb. 27, 1965. Pvt. practice of psychotherapy, individual, family and group therapy, N.Y.C., 1969—; clin. dir. N.Y. Transactional Analysis Seminar, Eastern Inst. for Transactional Analysis. One man shows of oil paintings at Panoras Gallery, N.Y.C., La Galleria, Mahopac, N.Y.; exhibited in group shows at Downstairs Gallery, Westchester Arts Council, Mahopac Art Show. Fellow Soc. Clin. Social Workers; mem. Nat. Assn. Social Workers, Am. Group Psychotherapy Assn., Eastern Group Psychotherapy Soc., Am. Orthopsychiat. Assn., Internat. Transactional Analysis Assn. (clin. and teaching mem., trustee, editorial bd. T.A. Jour.). Home: Penthouse 136 Waverly Pl New York City NY 10014

BOUNDS, DORIS SWAYZE (MRS. ROGER J. BOUNDS), banker; b. Muskogee, Okla., Oct. 26, 1904; d. Frank B. and Anna (Miller) Swayze; B.A., Leland Stanford Jr. U., 1926; student Columbia, 1926-27; m. Roger Jackson Bounds, Sept. 15, 1931; 1 son, Roger Swayze. Adminstrv. asst. to U.S. Senator, Washington, 1927-38, 39, also Gen. Lucius Clay, 1940-41, asst. sec. commerce, 1941; specialist Nat. Housing Agy., 1942-45; Washington rep. Stanford U., 1946-47; sec. First Nat. Bank, Hermiston, Ore., 1947-53; dir. Inland Empire Bank, Umatilla and Hermiston, 1948—, exec. v.p., 1960-72, chmn. bd., 1972—. Mem. Ore. Arts Commn., State Rural Areas Devel. Com. Pres., Roger J. Bounds Indian Found. Trustee Umatilla County Library, Pacific N.W. Indian Center, Inc., Indian Festival Arts. Mem. Nat. Assn. Bank Women (exec. com. 1962-63), Ind. Bankers Ore. (dir. 1972-75), Western Ind. Bankers, Ore. Bankers Assn. (treas. 1962-63; exec. council 1964-65), Bus. and Profl. Women's Club, Am. Assn. U. Women, Chi Omega, Arts in Ore. Assn. (bd. dirs. 1966-67, treas. 1966-67), Internat. Platform Assn., Pendleton Round Up Assn., Acad. Polit. Sci., P.E.O. Republican. Episcopalian. Clubs: McNary Yacht, Pendleton Country. Home: Box F Hermiston OR 97838 Office: 101 Main St Hermiston OR 97838

BOURAS, ARLENE MARIE AKLIN (MRS. HARRY D. BOURAS), editor; b. Rochester, N.Y., Mar. 9, 1930; d. George Harry and Mary Etta (Shafer) Aklin; student U. Rochester, 1949-51; m. Harry D. Bouras, Aug. 18, 1951; 1 dau., Lorraine Ann. Proofreader Scott, Foresman & Co., Chgo., 1956-57; copy editor Playboy mag. Playboy Enterprises, Inc., Chgo., 1957—. Home: 814 Sheridan Rd Evanston IL 60202 Office: 919 N Michigan Av Chicago IL 60611

BOURGEOIS, LOUISE, sculptor; b. Paris, France, Dec. 25, 1911; d. Louis and Josephine (Fauriaux) Bourgeois; baccalaureat Ecole des Beaux Arts, U. Paris, 1934; postgrad. Ecole du Louvre, 1936, 37, 38, Academie Ranson (Atelier Bissiere), 1936-37, Academie de la Grand Chaumiere (Atelier Wlerick), 1937-38, Academie Julian, also with Fernand Leger, 1938; m. Robert Goldwater, Sept. 12, 1938; children—Michel, Jean-Louis, Alain. Came to U.S., 1938, naturalized, 1953. Docent, Louvre, 1937-38; teaching asst. Atelier Yves Brayer, Grande Chaumiere, 1937, 38; tchr. Great Neck (N.Y.) Schs. Program, 1960, Bklyn. Coll., 1963-68, Pratt Inst., 1965-67, Goddard Coll., 1970; one-man shows Norlyst Gallery, 1947, Peridot Gallery, 1949, 50, 53, Allan Frumkin Gallery, Chgo., 1953, White Art Mus., Cornell U., 1959, Stable Gallery, 1964, Rose Fried Gallery, 1964; exhibited in numerous group shows in U.S., Europe; represented in collections Mus. Modern Art, N.Y.C., Whitney Mus., N.Y.C., R.I. Sch. Design, N.Y.U., also pvt. collections; works reproduced in Contemporary Sculpture (Giedion Welcker), 1955, Sculpture of This Century (Michel Seuphor), 1959, Form and Space (Trier), 1961, A Concise History of Modern Sculpture (Herbert Read), 1964, Modern American Sculpture (Dore Ashton), 1968, History of Modern Art (H.H. Arnason), 1968, What is Modern Sculpture, 1969, Sculpture in Wood (J.C. Rich), 1970, also various mags. Mem. Sculptors Guild, Am. Abstract Artists, La Jeune Sculpture, Paris. Address: 347 W 20th St New York City NY 10011

BOURGEOIS, SISTER MARY DENISE, educator; b. Baton Rouge, Oct. 9, 1930; d. Eugene Oliver and Una Sara (Chauvin) Bourgeois; B.A., St. Mary's Dominican Coll., 1959; M.A., La. State U., 1961; Ph.D., St. Louis U., 1969. Joined Order St. Mary's Dominican Congregation of New Orleans, 1947; tchr. parochial schs. New Orleans, 1949-59, Dominican High Sch., 1959-60; instr. St. Mary's Dominican Coll., New Orleans, 1962-65, prof. math., 1969—, chmn. dept., 1969—, dir. summer sessions, 1974. Mem. adv. com. elementary math specialist program Consortium Loyola, Xavier and Dominican colls., New Orleans, 1971-72. NSF fellow, 1960-61. Mem. Sigma Xi. Address: 7214 St Charles Av New Orleans LA 70118

BOURGUIGNON, ERIKA EICHHORN (MRS. PAUL BOURGUIGNON), anthropologist; b. Vienna, Austria, Feb. 18, 1924; d. Leopold H. and Charlotte (Rosenbaum) Eichhorn; B.A., Queens Coll., 1945; grad. study U. Conn., 1945; Ph.D., Northwestern U., 1951; m. Paul H. Bourguignon, Sept. 29, 1950. Field work Chippewa Indians, Wis., summer 1946; field work, Haiti, anthropology Northwestern U., 1947-48; instr. Ohio State U., 1949-56, asst. prof., 1956-60, asso. prof., 1960-66, prof., 1966—, acting chmn. dept. anthropology, 1971-72, chmn. dept., 1972—; dir. Cross-Cultural Study of Dissociational States, 1963-68. Fellow Am. Anthrop. Assn.; mem. Central States Anthrop. Soc. (treas. 1953-56), Ohio Acad. Sci., Am. Assn. U. Profs., Am. Ethol. Soc., Assn. Current Anthropology, Sigma Xi. Co-author: Diversity and Homogeneity in World Societies, 1973. Editor, co-author: Religion, Altered States of Consciousness and Social Change, 1972. Contbr. articles to profl. jours. Home: 193 E Broadway Columbus OH 43214

BOURISSEAU, WHITFIELD STALLINGS (MRS. WILLIAM JOHN DEGUERRE), sch. psychologist; b. Detroit, Sept. 3, 1917; d. George Whitfield and Laura Hodges (Hughes) Stallings; A.B., Hillsdale Coll., 1939; M.A., Kent State U., 1964; m. William John DeGuerre, July 21, 1973; children by previous marriage—Joie (Mrs. Karl Kirke Harper), John W., Virginia. Kindergarten tchr., Grand Blanc, Mich., 1939-42; exec. Girl Scouts, Waukegan, Ill., 1942-43; kindergarten tchr., Chagrin Falls, O., 1960-63; sch. psychologist, East Cleveland, O., 1963-67, Mayfield, O., 1967-73. Cons., Sci. Research Assos. Mem. Nat., Ohio (sec.), Cleve. Area (gov. bd.) assns. sch. psychologists, Pi Beta Phi. Author: Manual of Psychological Services for the Hearing Impaired, 1974; contbr. chpt. to Child and His Image, 1972. Home: 135 Union St Simcoe ON N3Y 4L5 Canada

BOURNE, AVIS COTTRELL (MRS. C. FRED BOURNE), educator; b. Boston, Sept. 1, 1905; d. Charles T. and Carolyn (Frink) Cottrell; A.B., Boston U., 1927, A.M., 1931; certificate U. Grenoble, 1927; m. Charles Fred Bourne, Aug. 14, 1932; 1 son, Richard Cottrell. Tchr. Sterling, Mass., 1927-28, 34—, asst. prin., 1948-62, dir. guidance, 1962-71, certified psychometrist, 1962—; tchr., Walpole, Mass., 1928-31, Norwood, Mass., 1931-32. Adv. council women's div. Mass. Dept. Commerce. Mem. Wachusett Regional Sch. Dist. Com., 1955-67, chmn., 1958-59; mem. Sterling Hist. Commn, 1968—. Mem. Am. Assn. U. Women (pres. No. Mass. br. 1957-61), Mass. Fedn. Bus. and Profl. Women's Clubs (various com. chairmanships and offices, state pres. 1957-59, dist. chmn. 1965-67, state parliamentarian, 1969-71), Daughters of Colonial Wars, Daus. Am. Colonists (Mass. regent 1973—), D.A.R., Mass. Tchrs. Assn., N.E.A. (legislative agt. for Worcester County), Sterling (founder, trustee, charter pres.), Waterville hist. socs., Lancaster League Hist. Socs. (treas. 1972—), Mass. Sch. Counselors Assn. (trustee), Am. Personnel and Guidance Assn. (sec. Worcester County chpt.), New Eng. Guidance and Personnel Conf. (rep.), Mass. North Central Guidance Assn. (hon. life, pres. 1967-68, dir. 1968—), Belgrade Lakes C. of C., Pi Lambda Theta, Phi Sigma Pi. Theta Upsilon, Delta Kappa Gamma (state com. on personal growth and services). Club: Waterville Community Garden. Home: Clinton Rd Sterling MA 01564 also Box 167 Belgrade Lakes ME

BOURNE, BERNADETTE BOCKLAGE, chemist; b. Mo., Oct. 18, 1921; d. George Henry and Marie (Roesner) Bocklage; B.A., S.E. Mo. State Coll., 1945, B.S., 1946; Ph.D. (fellow 1947-52), St. Louis U., 1952; m. William Hunt Bourne, Aug. 5, 1959; children—William, Patricia, Barbara. Mem. faculty biochemistry dept. St. Louis U., 1952-59, depts. neurology and biochemistry U. Miami (Fla.), 1959-67; dir. clin. chem. labs. City Hosp., St. Louis, 1957-59; dir. Morton F. Plant Hosp. Clin. Chemistry Lab., Clearwater, Fla., 1967-68, Mercy Hosp. Clin. Chem. Lab., Miami, 1968—. Mem. Dade County Pollution Control Hearing Bd., 1970-73; adv. com. diagnostic products FDA, 1973—. Mem. Am. Assn. Clin. Chemists (dir. 1973—), Nat. Registry in Clin. Chemistry, Am. Chem. Assn. Res. Officers Assn. Ladies. Home: 441 San Servando Av Coral Gables FL 33143 Office: 3663 S Miami Av Miami FL 33133

BOURNE, ROSEMARY ELIZABETH, financial exec.; b. Freeport, N.Y., Aug. 17, 1938; d. George A. and Elizabeth Halligan) Bourne; student U. So. Cal., 1958-59; B.A., Skidmore Coll., 1960; postgrad. N.Y. U., 1962-63. Security analyst Savs. Banks Trust Co., N.Y.C., 1961-67; security analyst, stock trader Ford Found., N.Y.C., 1967-71; portfolio mgr. Capricorn Growth Co., N.Y.C., 1971—. Mem. N.Y. Soc. Security Analysts, Inst. Chartered Financial Analysts. Home: 301 E 73d St New York City NY 10022 Office: 488 Madison Av New York City 10022

BOUTTE, MARGARET ANN, psychologist; b. Eunice, La., Dec. 22, 1946; d. Charley and Euna (Young) Boutte; student U. Southwestern La., 1965, summer 1966; B.A., La. State U., 1968; postgrad. U. So. Miss., 1968-69; M.S., N. Tex. State U., 1970; postgrad. Tex. Woman's U., 1973—. Psychometrist, Lafayette (La.) Parish Sch. Bd., 1968; cons. asso. sch. psychol. asso., Ednl. Service Center, Austin, Tex., 1970-71; instr. La. State U., Eunice, 1971-72; grad. fellow Tex. Woman's U., Denton, 1973—. Psy Chi fellow, 1973-75. Mem. Nat. Assn. Sch. Psychologists, Southwestern Psychol. Assn. Democrat. Roman Catholic. Home: 2505 Louise St Denton TX 76201 also 305 6th St Mamou LA 70554

BOUVIER, HELEN SCHAEFER (MRS. JOHN A. BOUVIER, JR.), leasing co. exec.; b. McAlester, Okla., Sept. 11, 1910; d. William John and Anna (Perrin) Schaefer; student U. Fla., 1928-29, Northwestern U., 1929-30; m. John A. Bouvier, Jr., June 6, 1928; children—Helen (Mrs. William Spencer), John A. III, Thomas R. Sec., Sunset Rock & Sand Co., Miami, Fla. 1939-45, Coral Rock & Sand Co., 1945-48; dir. Knight Manor, Inc., West Kingsway, Inc., East Kingsway, Inc., South Kingsway, Inc., Fiftieth St. Heights, Inc. (all Miami, Fla.), Karen Garden, Inc. (Ft. Lauderdale, Fla.); dir., pres. Nat. Leasing Corp., Miami, Fla. and N.Y.C., 1954-64; sec., dir. Nat. Leasing, Inc.; pres., dir. Miami Service Co., Knight Manor No. One, Inc., Knight Manor No. Two, Inc., South Central Manor, Inc.; also mgmt. cons., Miami, Fla. and N.Y.C., 1945—. Trustee Ella R. Bouvier Fund. Presbyn. (pres. womens aux., pres. womens aux. synod). Clubs: Corinthian (Syracuse, N.Y.); Skaneateles Country, Riviera Country (Coral Gables, Fla.); Surf (Surfside, Fla.); Beach Colony (Miami Beach, Fla.). Home: 2756 NE 17th St Fort Lauderdale FL 33305 also Bienvenue Blowing Rock NC Office: 6888 NW 7th Av Miami FL 33150

BOVE, JUNE BURNS (MRS. JOHN LOUIS BOVE), assn. exec.; b. Bklyn., June 11, 1930; d. Roy Wilbur and Althea Hortense (Hoffmann) Burns; A.B., Bucknell U., 1952; m. John Louis Bove, Dec. 28, 1957; children—Adele June, Catherine Louise. Mem. Bicentennial Commn. Com. Village Ridgewood, N.J., 1973—; chmn. ways and means com., trustee Friends of the Hermitage, Ho-Ho-Kus, N.J., 1972—; vol. staff Met. Mus. Art Costume Inst., N.Y.C. Mem. camp com. Ridgewood YWCA, 1969-72. Mem. Womens Nat. Book Assn., Woman's Club Ridgewood (chmn. pub. relations 1967-68), Paramus Hist. and Preservation Soc., D.A.R., Daus. of Revolution 1776, Kappa Kappa Gamma. Episcopalian (pres. Churchwomen 1970-72). Home: 216 California St Ridgewood NJ 07450

BOWDEN, ANN (MRS. WILLIAM B. TODD), library adminstr.; b. Orange, N.J., Feb. 7, 1924; d. William and Anna Elisabeth (Herrstrom) Haddon; B.A., Radcliffe Coll., 1948; M.S. in L.S., Columbia, 1951; m. Edwin T. Bowden, June 12, 1948 (div. Aug. 1969); children—Elisabeth, Susan, Eric; m. 2d, William B. Todd, Nov. 23, 1969. Descriptive cataloger Yale Library, 1948-49, reference asst. in charge H.L. Stimson collection, 1951-53; manuscript cataloger Humanities Research Center, U. Tex. Library, Austin, 1958-60, Humanities Research Center librarian, 1960-63, acad. center librarian, 1963, lectr. Grad. Sch. Library Sci., 1964—; dir. films, recs. Austin Pub. Library, 1963-65, coordinator adult services, 1965-67, asst. dir. libraries, 1967-71, dep. dir. libraries, 1971—. Served with USMC Womens Res., 1944-46. Mem. Bibliog. Soc. Am., A.L.A. (membership com. Tex. 1965-72, chmn., 1968-72, chmn. regional membership com. 1972-74, assn. coll. and research libraries, exec. bd. rare book and manuscript sect. 1971-73, vice-chmn., chmn. elect rare book and manuscript sect., 1974-75, mem. manuscript collection com. 1971-73), Southwestern (mem. scholarship endowment com. 1971-72, state chmn. Nat. Endowment Humanities S.W. project 1974-75), Tex. (chmn. publs. com. 1965-71, chmn. intellectual freedom com. 1972-74, mem. legislative com. 1971-73) library assns., Austin Soc. Pub. Adminstrn., Kappa Tau Alpha. Author: An Exhibition of Manuscripts and First Editions of T.S. Eliot, 1961; T.E. Lawrence/Fifty Letters: 1920-1935, 1962. Asst. editor: Papers of Bibliographical Soc. Am. quar. jour., 1967-68, asso. editor, 1968—. Contbr. articles to profl. jours. Home: 2424 Wooldridge Austin TX 78703 Office: 401 W 9th St Austin TX 78701

BOWDEN, ELEANOR MAY, librarian; b. Sextonville, Wis., Nov. 13, 1914; d. Bernard Ray and Marcella M. (Draper) Bowden; B.E., No. Ill. U., 1938; M.S., U. Wis., 1958. Tchr. pub. schs., Crandon, Wis., 1940-43, Blue Island, Ill., 1943-45, Reedsburg, Wis., 1945-52, Crandon, Wis., 1952-56; librarian Craig Sr. High Sch., Janesville, Wis., 1957-59; with East High Sch., Madison, Wis., 1969—, head instructional materials center, 1959-73, library cons., 1973—. Mem. Nat., Wis., So. Wis. (chmn. sch. library div. 1960) edn. assns., Madison Tchrs., Inc., Wis. Library Assn. (treas. sch. library div. 1961), U. Wis. Library Sch. Alumni Assn. (treas. 1970-74), Beta Phi Mu. Home: 921 High St Madison WI 53715 Office: 2222 E Washington Av Madison WI 53704

BOWDEN, MARIE B. (MRS. MARVIN BOWDEN), business exec., assn. exec.; m. Marvin Bowden. With Minute Maid Co., 25 years; now comptroller Leesburg (Fla.) Gen. Hosp. Mem. membership com. Internat. Fedn. Bus. and Profl. Women, 1962-68, chmn. hemispheric friendship com., 1958-62, 64-65, chmn. world affairs com., 1963-64, chmn. finance com., 1965-66, chmn. 1st Conf. Bus. and Profl. Women of Americas, 1961; sec. Nat. Fedn. Bus. and Profl. Women's Clubs, 1970-71, 2d v.p., 1971-72, 1st v.p., 1972-73, pres.-elect, 1973—. Former mem. spl. adv. com. pub. opinion Dept. State. Bd. dirs. United Appeal of Lake County, Inc., So. Scholarship and Research Found., Inc.; founding pres., bd. dirs. Edn. Found. of Fla. Fedn. Bus. and Profl. Women's Clubs, Inc.; trustee, pres. Lake-Sumter Jr. Coll.; trustee, officer Bus. and Profl. Women's Found., Inc., 1970-72. Mem. Leesburg C. of C. (past pres.), Soroptimist Internat., Delta Kappa Gamma. Methodist (mem. bd. evangelism Fla. Conf. 9 yrs). Address: PO Box 3 Leesburg FL 32748

BOWDITCH, ANNA HALE (MRS. E. FRANCIS BOWDITCH), sch. headmistress; b. Haverhill, Mass., Mar. 28, 1912; d. Edward Russell and Ethel Frost (Mitchell) Hale; student Bradford Acad., 1925-30; A.B., Wellesley Coll., 1934; m. E. Francis Bowditch, Aug. 3, 1935; children—E. Francis, Susan (Mrs. David S. Badger), Elizabeth Shoemaker (Mrs. James O. Watt), Nathaniel Hale. Tchr., Shady Hill Sch., Cambridge, Mass., 1934-35, Milton (Mass.) Acad., 1935-37, Park Sch., Indpls., 1939-41; dir. devel. Walnut Hill Sch., Natick, Mass., 1960-63; headmistress Day Prospect Hill Sch., New Haven, Conn., 1963-72; asst. head Hammonasset Sch., Madison, Conn., 1972—. Mem. nat. assembly Assn. Coll. Admissions Counselors, 1969—; mem. standing com. on devel. Nat. Assn. Ind. Schs., 1970-74; mem. sch. and coll. conf. com. New Eng. Assn. Colls. and Secondary Schs., 1967-70. Chmn. vols. A.R.C., Boston, 1953-57. Bd. dirs. St. Luke's Presbyn. Hosp., Chgo., 1944-51; hon. trustee Bradford Jr. Coll. Mem. Headmistresses Assn. of the East, Nat. Assn. Prins. Schs. for Girls, League of Women Voters, Jr. League, New Eng. Assn. Coll. Admissions Counselors (pres. 1973-74), Nat. Soc. Colonial Dames Am. Clubs: Yale Faculty (New Haven); Vincent (show chmn. 1957-59) (Boston). Author: Professional Audit for Secondary School Counselors, 1974; also articles in profl. pubs. Home: RFD 3 River Rd Killingworth CT 06417 Office: Hammonasset Sch Madison CT 06443

BOWEN, ADA MAY SELTZER (MRS. JOHN WESLEY BOWEN), librarian; b. Kempton, Pa., June 7, 1942; d. Clayton Franklin and Dorothea Anna (Oldt) Seltzer; B.S., Kutztown State Coll., 1964; M.S., Fla. State U., 1965; M.A., U. S. Fla., 1971; m. John Wesley Bowen, Dec. 24, 1965. Asst. reference librarian U. S. Fla., Tampa, 1965-68, asso. reference librarian, 1969-71, reference librarian Med. Center Library, 1971-74, head pub. services, 1974—. Fla. Library Assn. rep. to Fla. Council on Aging, 1973-74; project editor of grant to compile statewide union serials list, 1969-73. Mem. Am., Fla. (chmn. reference roundtable 1969-70, chmn. intellectual freedom com. 1974—) library assns., Med. Library Assn., Fla. Med. Librarians, Kappa Delta Phi, Beta Phi Mu. Home: 8014 Hiawatha St Tampa FL 33615 Office: Medical Center Library U South Florida Tampa FL 33620

BOWEN, BEVERLY GIFFORD (MRS. WILBUR L. BOWEN), ednl. adminstr.; b. Madison, N.Y., Dec. 10, 1931; d. Barton Lucas and Thelma Mae (Parks) Gifford; B.S., Beaver Coll., 1953; m. Richard D. Gifford, June 12, 1953 (div.); children—David, John, Amy, Stephen; m. 2d, Wilbur L. Bowen, Feb. 8, 1974. Edn. writer Ohio Edn. Assn., Columbus, 1966-74; dir. pub. info. Columbus Pub. Schs., 1974—. Recipient All-Am. awards Ednl. Press Assn. Am., 1970, 71, 72. Mem. N.E.A. (state staff liaison womens caucus). Contbr. articles to newspapers, profl. jours. Home: 60 Kenyon Brook Dr Worthington OH 43085 Office: 270 E State St Columbus OH 43215

BOWEN, CHARLOTTE KIRK LAZELL (MRS. ALBERT ARTHUR WRIGHT, JR.), lawyer; b. Goshen, N.Y., July 1, 1945; d. Joseph Arthur and Ruth Lyon (Preston) Lazell III; A.B., Marshall U., W.Va., 1967; J.D., W.Va. Coll. Law, 1970; m. James A. Bowen II, Aug. 16, 1963 (div. Aug. 1968); 1 son, Andrew Courtenay; m. 2d, Albert Arthur Wright, Jr., Dec. 22, 1972. Admitted to W.Va. bar, 1970; practiced in Huntington, 1970—; mem. firm Bowen & Colburn, 1973—. Vice pres. Wright Rental Mgmt. Co., 1972—. Mem. State Exec. Com. Young Democrats, 1972—. Bd. dirs. Family Services; bd. dirs. W.Va. Heart Assn., chmn. bd. southwestern div., 1973—. Mem. Am., W.Va. bar assns., Am. Trial Lawyers Assn., W.Va., Cabell County bars. Club: Pilot International. Office: 452 5th Av Huntington WV 25701

BOWEN, HELEN EAKINS, artist; b. Bluefield, W.Va., June 30, 1915; d. Reuel and Varinda (Pruett) Bowen; student Art Students League, 1959-65, N.A.D. Sch. Fine Art, 1965-66. Exhibited one artist shows, N.Y.C.; exhibited group shows Catherine Lorillard Wolfe Art Club, Nat. Arts Club, Am. Artists Profl. League, Duncan Gallery, Wickersham Gallery, Chapellier Gallery, Art Students League, N.A.D., Hunterton Art Center, Hawthorne House, Cooperstown Art Assn., Berkshire Art Assn., Mystic Art Festival, Herbert E. Feist Gallery; represented in collections Chrysler Mus. Art, Finch Coll. Mus., Miami Mus. Modern Art, Syracuse U., Nat. Collection Fine Arts, U.S. Dept. State, Gibbes Art Gallery, Charleston, S.C., also numerous pvt. collections. Mem. adv. council Sch. Visual and Performing Arts, Syracuse U. Recipient Alma Guillet award, 1962, Louis Jambor Meml. award, 1962, James A. Suydam bronze medal N.A.D., 1966. Ivy B. Clifford, Louise Kohler, Carese Crosby grantee; Mark Trafton Fowler fellow, Prof. Homer Cree Vaughan fellow, Dr. Jorge Gasteazoro fellow; Alexander Dobkin scholar. Mem. Art Students League (life), Gibbes Art Gallery, Met. Mus., Mus. Natural History, Mus. Modern Art. Methodist. Home: 531 W 122d St New York City NY 10027

BOWEN, (LILLIAN) ANN (MRS. THEODORE BOWEN), lawyer; b. Alliance, Neb., Oct. 26, 1926; d. William Shepherd and Barbara Rebecca (King) Neill; B.A., U. Colo., 1959; M.A., U. Wyo., 1961; J.D., U. Ariz., 1967; m. Allen Grant Alter, June 12, 1947 (div. 1957); 1 son, Warren McClure; m. 2d, Theodore Bowen, Mar. 4, 1961. With Gen. Electric Co., Denver, 1948-51; sec. Lawson AFB, 1952; sec. Psychol. Warfare Center, Dept. Army, Ft. Bragg, N.C., 1953, post engr., 1957; grad. asst., English instr. U. Wyo., Laramie, 1960-61; tchr. English lit., composition Amphitheater High Sch., Tucson, 1963-64; admitted to U.S. Ct. of Claims, 1967; gen. atty. Ct. of Claims sect., civil div. U.S. Justice Dept., Washington, 1967-68, trial atty., 1968-69; asst. U.S. atty. Office of U.S. Atty., Dist. of Ariz., Tucson,

1969—, chief criminal sect., 1972—. Den mother Cub Scouts Am., Tucson, 1963-64; mem. Mayor's Com. on Morningside St. Lighting Improvement Dist., Tucson, 1965-66. Recipient Hats Off award for meritorious services Order of DeMolay, 1973; Spl. Achievement award U.S. Dept. Justice, 1972. Mem. Am., Fed. bar assns., State Bar Ariz., Am. Judicature Soc., Phi Kappa Phi, Kappa Beta Pi, Chi Omega. Club: DeMolay Mothers (pres. 1973—, treas. So. dist. 1973—) (Tucson). Home: 2233 E Waverly St Tucson AZ 85719 Office: 110 S Scott Tucson AZ 85702

BOWEN, PEGGY LEAR, educator; b. Portsmouth, Va., Sept. 27, 1949; d. Cliffton Smith and Virginia Lear (DeLotche) Bowen; B.A., U. Nev., 1972. Tchr., Nev. Youth Tng. Center, Elko, 1972-74, dir. audio-visual dept., 1974; now tchr. McDermitt (Nev.) sch. Mem. Nat., Nev. edn. assns., Nev. Secondary English Assn., Speech Communication Assn., Nat. Council Tchrs. English, U. Nev. Alumnus Assn., Grad. Students Assn. (mem. pub. occasions bd. 1967-72), Alpha Psi Omega. Home: Box 44 McDermitt NV 89421 Office: McDermitt Sch McDermitt NV 89421

BOWENS, EDNA DEVLIN, lawyer; b. St. Catharines, Ont., Can.; d. Patrick J. and Mary Ann McNamara (Breen) Devlin; student St. Catharines Collegiate Inst., 1905-10, U. Toronto, 1910, Northwestern U. Sch. Commerce, 1918-20; LL.B., Loyola U., 1930, LL.M., 1931; m. Martin J. Bowens, Oct. 17, 1934. Exec. sec. to A.M. Johnson, Death Valley, Cal.; exec. offices Nat. Life Ins. Co. U.S.A., 1913-33; asst. to Patrick J. Lucey, receiver, Nat. Life Ins. Co. U.S.A., 1933-38; admitted to Ill. bar, 1930, since practiced in Chgo. Dir. Citizens of Greater Chgo. and Cook County Fedn. Women's Orgns. (pres. 1949-53), Civic Auditorium Com. Trustee and pres. woman's bd. Mary Thompson Hosp. Mem. Am., Ill., Chgo. bar assns., Women's Bar Assn. Ill. (pres. 1934-35), Cath. Lawyers' Guild, Our Lady's Sodality St. Ignatius Parish (pres. 1947-50), Ill. Club Cath. Women. Club: Glenola (Chgo. pres. 1950-52). Home: 6608 N Newgard Av Chicago IL 60626

BOWER, EVELYN MARSH (MRS. LENNOX CORLEY BOWER), educator, poet; b. Bobo, Ind., Jan. 7, 1910; d. Chester Lawrence and Katie Lou (Harbaugh) Marsh; B.A. cum laude, Southwestern U., 1929; M.Ed., U. Houston, 1958; m. Lennox Corley Bower, Mar. 25, 1935; children—Marsha (Mrs. David Watson), Lennox C. Tchr. elementary sch. Houston Ind. Sch. Dist., 1954—. Circle chmn. Woman's Soc. Christian Service, 1968-70. Recipient Internat. Poetry-Moon Contest winner award, 1970. Mem. N.E.A., Houston, Tex. tchrs. assns., Poetry Soc. Tex. (Critics award 1970-73, sec. Houston chpt. 1969-70), Internat. Poetry Inst. (Travel award 1971), Scribblers Club, League of Women Voters (chmn. 1970-72). Methodist (Sunday sch. tchr. 1965-67). Contbr. poems to lit. publs. Home: 8406 Glencross Houston TX Office: 7185 Santa Fe Houston TX 77017

BOWER, MARGE EMILY, educator; b. Chgo., June 8, 1941; d. Elmore Arthur and Elsie Ruth (Sauer) Bower; B.A., U. Mich., 1963; M.A., Loyola U., Chgo., 1967; postgrad. Bradley U., Western Mich. U., U. Mich. Tchr. English, South Shore High Sch., Chgo., 1963-67; guidance counselor Elmwood Park (Ill.) High Sch., 1967—. Chmn nat. alumnae com. on out-of-state admissions and scholarships U. Mich., 1972—, governing bd. U. Nat. Alumnae Council, 1972—. Newspaper Fund fellow Wall St. Jour., 1967. Mem. Personnel and Guidance Assn., Ill. Guidance and Personnel Assn., Am., Ill. sch. counselors assns., Nat., Ill. assns. women deans, adminstrs. and counselors, Nat., Ill. edn. assns., U. Mich. Alumni Assn. Home: 520 W Aldine Av Chicago IL 60657 Office: 8201 W Fullerton Av Elmwood Park IL 60635

BOWER, SHIRLEY MAE (MRS. JAY R. BOWER), realtor; b. Marshfield, Mo., Apr. 2, 1935; d. James Oliver and Ruth Irene (Hyde) Day; B.A. in Speech and Dramatics cum laude, Culver-Stockton Coll., 1957; grad. Ill. Inst. Real Estate Brokers, 1972; m. Jay R. Bower, Aug. 5, 1956; 1 dau., Lisa Lynne. Tchr. speech, drama and English Quincy (Ill.) Jr. High Sch., 1951-58; tchr. speech and drama Central High Sch., Camp Point, Ill., 1958-60, 65-66; real estate broker, saleswoman, 1967; co-owner Bower Gallery of Homes, Quincy, Camp Point and Mt. Sterling, Ill., 1967—. Co-dir. Quincy Jr. Theater, 1957-58, bd. dirs.; bd. dirs. Family Service Agy., Quincy, 1967-68, Quincy Jr. High Sch. P.T.A., 1973; alumni bd. dirs. Culver-Stockton Coll., 1967—, pres., 1965-66. Mem. Quincy Bd. Realtors, Nat. Assn. Real Estate Brokers, Nat. Inst. Real Estate Brokers, Pan-Hellenic Council Quincy, Chi Omega. Mem. Order Eastern Star. Mem. Christian Ch. Club: Spring Lake Country (Quincy). Home: 3 Curved Creek Rd Quincy IL 62301 Office: 503 Maine St Quincy IL 62301

BOWERS, (ALICE) ELIZABETH ADCOCK (MRS. LESLIE L. BOWERS), librarian; b. Riverton, Wyo., Nov. 7, 1917; d. Warner and Alice Minder (Farnsworth) Buckman; B.A., U. No. Colo., 1937; B.S. in L.S., U. Denver, 1939; m. Harold Wayne Adcock, Aug. 16, 1940 (dec. 1968); children—Donald G., Kathleen A. (Mrs. Richard G. Rosecrans); m. Leslie L. Bowers, Jan. 20, 1974. Circulation and asst. cataloger DePauw U. Library, Ind., 1938-40; librarian Greeley (Colo.) High Sch., 1942-43; reference and cataloging asst. U. No. Colo., part-time, 1946-53; dir. Weld County Library, Greeley, Colo., 1954—. Recipient Certificate of Merit, Colo. Library Assn., 1966; Business Woman of Yr., Greeley, 1966; Beautiful Activist Colo., 1972. Mem. Am. (mem. council 1972-74), Colo. (pres. 1961-62), Mt. Plains (sec. 1960, pres. pub. library div. 1961) library assns., Colo. Council Library Devel. (chmn. 1966, 67), P.E.O., Altrusa, Delta Kappa Gamma. Democrat. Mem. Christian Ch. Home: 1808 Lakeside Dr Greeley CO 80631 Office: 2227 23d Av Greeley CO 80631

BOWERS, CAROLYN, editor; b. Ottawa, Kan., Oct. 7, 1949; d. William Sheldon and Virginia Jean (Ott) Bowers; student Colo. Coll., 1967-68; B.S., Kan. U., 1971; m. Richard Lee Hull, Aug. 28, 1971 (div.). Editorial asst. U. Kan. Alumni Publs., Lawrence, 1971; asst. editor Vance Pub. Corp., Kansas City, Kan., 1971-72; news editor, 1972-74; press asst. consumer affairs office Giant Food Inc., Washington, 1974—. Recipient awards Kan. Press Women, 1972-73. Mem. Women in Communications (spl. projects dir. 1973), Nat. Press Women's Assn. (2d pl. award 1972, 1st pl. award 1974), Sigma Delta Chi. Home: 207 A St NE Washington DC 20002 Office: Box 1804 Washington DC 20013

BOWERS, ELLEN EVELYN, univ. dean; b. Prescott, Ariz., Sept. 5, 1909; d. Charles H. and Paulina (Herreford) Bowers; B.A., Pomona Coll., 1931; M.A., Claremont Grad. Sch., 1933; postgrad. personnel adminstrn. Columbia Tchrs. Coll., 1941-42. Asst. to dean women Pomona Coll., 1934-41; dir. Ida. Hall, residence hall civilian govt. women employees, Washington, 1943-47; faculty U. Cal. at Santa Barbara, 1947—, asso. dean students, dean women, 1960—. Contbg. mem. UN Assn. U.S., Cal. Tomorrow, Planned Parenthood League, Goleta Valley Girls Club, Santa Barbara Symphony, Community Arts Music Assn. Santa Barbara, Youth Theatre, Pomona Coll. Assos., Claremont Grad. Sch. Assn.; mem. Santa Barbara Mental Health Assn. Bd. dirs. Channel City Women's Forum, Santa Barbara. Mem. Nat. Assn. Women Deans and Counselors, Cal. Assn. Women Deans and Vice Prins. (treas. 1949-51, chmn. So. region 1956-58, citation 1963, chmn. coll. and univ. div. 1967-69), Am. Assn. U. Women, Delta Kappa Gamma (1st pres. Delta Eta chpt. 1956-58). Home: 3529 San Jose Lane Santa Barbara CA 93105

BOWERS, PATRICIA ELEANOR FRITZ, economist; b. N.Y.C., Mar. 21, 1928; d. Edward and Eleanor (Ring) Fritz; student (scholar) Goucher Coll., 1946-48; B.A., Cornell U., 1950; M.A., N.Y. U., 1953, Ph.D., 1965. Statis. asst. Fed. Res. Bank N.Y., N.Y.C., 1950-53; lectr. Upsala Coll., East Orange, N.J., 1953-59; researcher Fortune Mag., N.Y.C., 1959-60; teaching fellow N.Y. U., N.Y.C., 1960-62, instr., 1962-64; economist Bklyn. Coll., City U. N.Y., 1964—. Teaching fellow N.Y. U., 1960-62. Mem. Am. Econ. Assn., Econometric Soc., Met. Econ. Assn. (sec. 1963-68, pres. 1974—), Am. Statis. Assn. (univs. chmn. annual forecasting confs. 1970-71, 71-72). Club: Women's Bond (N.Y.C.). Author: Private Choice and Public Welfare, 1974. Home: 145 E 16th St New York City NY 10003 Office: Dept Econs Brooklyn Coll City U N Y Brooklyn NY 11210

BOWERSOCK, MARGARET EMMA (MRS. RALPH EDWARD BOWERSOCK), mayor; b. New Brighton, Pa., Sept. 29, 1917; d. George Clayton and Ida Belle (Kincaid) Frame; student pub. schs.; m. Ralph Edward Bowersock, July 18, 1937; children—Earl Dean, Vernon Kaye, Carolyn Laverne (Mrs. Walter Edward Lonas). With Am. Viscose Co., Parkersburg, W.Va., 1936-38, S.S. Kresge Co., Parkersburg, 1951-52; operator Bowersock's Ashland Bookkeeper & Service Sta., 1956-71. Mayor, Belpre, O., 1972—. Mem. Washington County Exec. Com., 1971-72. Mem. Bus. and Profl. Womens Club, V.F.W. Aux. Home: 503 Beach Dr Belpre OH 45714 Office: 201 Washington Blvd Belpre OH 45714

BOWES, FLORENCE (MRS. WILLIAM DAVID BOWES), editor; b. Salt Lake City, Nov. 19, 1925; d. John Albreckt Elias and Alma Wilhelmina (Jonasson) Norborg; student U. Utah, 1941-42, Columbia, 1945-46, N.Y. U., 1954-55; grad. N.Y. TV Workshop, 1950; m. Samuel Ellis Levine, July 15, 1944 (dec. July 1953); 1 son, Alan Richard; m. 2d, William David Bowes, Mar. 15, 1958. Actress, writer Hearst Radio Network, WINS, N.Y.C., 1944-45; personnel and adminstrv. exec. Mut. Broadcasting System, N.Y.C., 1946-49, free-lance editor, writer, 1948-49; freelance writer Nat. Broadcasting Co., Am. Broadcasting Co., 1949-53; script editor, writer Robert A. Monroe Prodns., N.Y.C., Hollywood, Cal., 1953-56; script and comml. dir. KUTV-TV, Salt Lake City, 1956-58; spl. editor, writer pub. relations dept. U. Utah, Salt Lake City, 1966-68, editor, writer U. Utah Rev., 1968—. Mem. Beta Sigma Phi. Home: 338-K St Salt Lake City UT 84103

BOWIE, B(LANCHE) LUCILE, educator; b. LaPlata, Md., 1910; d. Henry Clay and Blanche (Garner) Bowie; B.S., in Elementary Edn., U. Md., 1942, Ed.D. (Grant Found. fellow), 1957; M.A., Columbia, 1946. Tchr. elementary schs., Charles County, Md., 1929-43, supr., 1943-54; instr. human devel. edn. Inst. Child Study, U. Md., College Park, 1956-57; asst. prof., 1957-59, asso. prof., 1959-67, prof., 1967-73, prof. emerita, 1973—, asso. dir. doctoral program in ednl. adminstrn., 1970-72; cons. speaker various local, nat. sch. systems. Mem. Prince George's County Mental Health Assn. Mem. Charles County Hist. Soc., A.A.A.S., Am. Assn. U. Profs., Assn. Supervision and Curriculum Devel. (sec. Md. chpt. 1950-52), N.E.A., Assn. Higher Edn., Soc. Research in Child Devel., U.S. Nat. Com. Childhood Edn., Internat. Platform Assn., Am. Acad. Sci., Soc. Profs. Edn., Delta Kappa Gamma (pres. Iota chpt. 1962-64, pres. Epsilon chpt.), Phi Delta Gamma (sponsor, 1st pres. Sigma chpt. 1955-57, nat. council rep. 1968-72, nat. treas. 1968-70). Contbr. articles profl. jours. Home: 9308 Cherry Hill Rd College Park MD 20740

BOWLES, HELOISE journalist; b. Ft. Worth; d. Charles L. and Amelia (Harrison) Bowles; grad. Felt and Tarrent Bus. Coll.; student Tex. sch. Fine Arts, 1938; grad. Draughn's Bus. Coll., 1939; Dr. Humanities, Nat. Christian U., 1972; children—Louis D., Ponce K. Columnist, Honolulu Advertiser, 1959-62; writer Hints from Heloise, King Features Syndicate, N.Y.C., 1962—. Active A.R.C. Recipient Silver Lady Banshee award for outstanding columnist Actors and Writers Profl. Orgn., 1964; writer's award Headliners Club, Austin, Tex., 1964; Headliner's award, San Antonio, 1968; Howe Press award for work with blind, 1971; Trophy Internat. Perkins Sch. Blind, Boston, 1972; Internat. Ecology award, Paris, France, 1973, Mental Health trophy McLennan County Assn. Mental Health, 1973, ALMA award, Dallas, 1973. keys to city, Ft. Worth, 1965, New Orleans, 1971, Waco, Tex., 1971; Outstanding Service award San Antonio Press Club, 1966; NIRC recognition for distinguished service, 1969; numerous citations; named Woman of Achievement, Theta Sigma Phi (now Women in Communications), 1962, Ecology Woman of Year, 1972, 73. Mem. Order Eastern Star, Lady Shriner. Author: Heloise Housekeeping Hints, 1963; Heloise Kitchen Hints, 1964; Heloise All Around the House, 1965; Heloise's Work and Money Savers, 1967; Heloise's Hints for the Working Woman, 1970; Heloise in China, 1972. Office: care King Features Syndicate 235 E 45th St New York City NY 10017

BOWLES, JEAN KERCHEVAL (MRS. DONALD RAY BOWLES), pub. relations exec., county ofcl.; b. Indpls., June 9, 1921; d. Leonard Cranston and Joyce (Morris) Kercheval; B.S. in Journalism. Butler U., 1944; m. Donald Ray Bowles, Aug. 18, 1945; 1 son, Bruce Cranston. City desk reporter Indpls. Times. 1944-45; editorial asso., editor United Christian Missionary Soc., Indpls., 1960-63; news asst. Office of Interpretation Christian Ch., internat. hdqrs., Indpls., 1963-67; head Pub. Relations Office, Indpls.-Merion County Pub. Library, 1968—. Mem. Women in Communications, Soc. of Ind. Pioneers, Kappa Tau Alpha. Mem. Disciples of Christ. Home: 5138 University Av Indianapolis IN 46219 Office: 40 East Saint Clair St Indianapolis IN 46204

BOWLES, MINNIE REDMOND (MRS. E. MILTON JOHNSON), librarian; b. Clarksville, Tenn., Feb. 27, 1911; d. Dr. Robert L. and Julia Percy (Thomas) Redmond; B.A., Fisk U., 1932; B.L.S., Atlanta U., 1944; M.A., U. Chgo., 1945; m. Arthur E. Bowles, Feb. 4, 1939 (div. Aug. 1941); m. 2d, Dr. E. Milton Johnson, Dec. 20, 1959. Tchr. Memphis city schs., 1933-37; librarian man. tng. sch, Bordentown, N.J., 1937-43; instr. sch. library service Atlanta U., 1945-46; asst. librarian Fisk U., 1946-49, 50-52, acting librarian, 1949-50; head librarian Hampton Inst., 1952-58; librarian Crane br. Ill. Tchrs. Coll., Chgo.-South, 1958-67, Chgo. State Coll., West Center, 1967-70; catalog librarian Chgo. State U., 1970-72, head catalog dept., 1972-73, acting dir. libraries, 1973—. One of area chmn. WTTW Channel 11 ann. fund dr., 1963-65; dir. Hampton Book Fair, 1956-58. Mem. League Women Voters, N.A.A.C.P., Am., Ill. library assns, Am. Assn. U. Profs., Assn. Coll. and Reference Libraries, Alpha Kappa Alpha, Delta Kappa Gamma. Clubs: Chicago Fisk (chmn. exec. com. 1967-69). Chicago Library. Home: 501 32d St Chicago IL 60616 Office: Chgo State U 95th at King Dr Chicago IL 60628

BOWLES, PAULINE MARGUERITE (MRS. JAMES ARTHUR BOWLES), mayor; b. Eagle, Colo., Dec. 23, 1933; d. Leo Peter and Rachel (Clardy) Daugherty; B.A. in Dietetics and Bus., U. No. Colo., 1955; m. James Arthur Bowles, Nov. 26, 1955; children—Jacque Lynn and Jill Lee (twins). Owner, mgr. Woods Lake Resort, Basalt, Colo., 1958-71; mayor of Basalt, 1972—. Chmn. region 12 Criminal Justice Council, Colo., 1973—; mem. Colo. Municipal League Legislative Com., 1972-73, Colo. Municipal League Resolution Com., 1973, Exec. Bd., 1973—; chmn. dis. 3 Colo. Centennial-Dicentennial Hospitality Com., 1972; alternate mem. Colo. Big Country Resource Convervation and Devel. Council., 1972—. Mem. adv. bd. Mountain Coll. Continuing Edn. Adv. Bd., 1972-73. Mem. Tri-County Fedn. Women's Clubs (pres. 1973-74), Basalt Literary Sorosis Club, League Women Voters. Republican. Roman Catholic. Home: PO Box 1040 Basalt CO 81621 Office: PO Box 1046 Basalt CO 81621

BOWLUS, ALEEN RUTH, ret. pub. health lab. dir.; b. Wichita, Kan., July 26, 1918; d. Pearl Arthur and Florence (Dabney) Bowlus; A.B., U. Cal., Los Angeles, 1943; J.D., Ventura Coll. Law, 1974. Clin. technologist Sansom Clinic, Santa Barbara, Cal., 1944; microbiologist license Los Angeles Health Dept., 1945; lab. dir. Ventura County Health Dept., Ventura, Cal., 1945-71. Mem. emeritus Conf. State and Provincial Pub. Health Lab. Dirs. Home: 144 N Aliso St Ventura CA 93001

BOWMAN, C. DALE (MRS. ROBERT EUGENE BOWMAN), univ. adminstr.; b. Marshall, N.C., July 16, 1936; d. Eldridge Millard and Cora Lee (Fender) Wild; B.S., Berea Coll., 1958; M.S., Ind. U., 1960; m. Robert Eugene Bowman, July 27, 1963; 1 son, Brett Eugene. Dir. residence hall Berea (Ky.) Coll., 1958-59; asst. head counselor Ind. U., Bloomington, 1959-60; residence dir. Ball State U., Muncie, Ind., 1960-63, asst. dir. student programs, 1963-67, asst. to dean students, v.p. for student affairs, 1969—. Mem. Nat. (adv. council for univ. sect. 1973-75), Ind. (pres. 1974-75) assns. of women deans, adminstrs. and counselors. Lutheran (mem. ch. council 1973-77). Home: 1205 Brentwood St Muncie IN 47304

BOWMAN, DOROTHY LOUISE, artist; b. Hollywood, Cal., Jan. 20, 1927; d. Bruce L. and Dorothy L. (Kalkman) Bowman; ed. Chouinard Art Inst., Cal., Jepson Art Inst., Los Angeles; m. Howard Hugh Bradford, Dec. 30, 1949 (div. 1965); children—Brock, Cyndra, Tal Scot, Heather, Delia, Callia. Serigrapher, printmaker, painter; represented in permanent collections Immaculate Heart Coll., Los Angeles County Mus., Bklyn. Mus., Long Beach Mus., Crocker Art Gallery, Mus. Modern Art, Phila. Mus. Fine Arts, San Jose State Coll., De Cordova and Danna Mus., Boston Pub. Library, Boston Mus. Fine Arts, N.Y. Pub. Library, Rochester Meml. Gallery, U. Wis., U. Hawaii, U. Ill., Santa Barbara Mus., Achenbach Found. Legion of Honor, U. Kan., Mus. Modern Art, Monterey, Cal., Library of Congress, Cal. State Library Archieves, Aravivos Historicos de Arte Contemporanea, Sao Paulo, Brazil. Address: Big Sur CA 93920

BOWMAN, ELIZABETH CLARK, reporter; b. Willard, O., Feb. 13, 1949; d. John Benjamin and Constance (Judkins) Bowman; B.A., Wellesley Coll., 1971; M.S. in Journalism, Columbia, 1972. Reporter, Congl. Quar., Washington, 1972—. Participant Internat. Fellows program Columbia, 1971-72, Pulitzer travelling fellow, 1972. Mem. U.S. Senate and House Press Gallery, Phi Beta Kappa. Office: 1414 22d St NW Washington DC 20037

BOWMAN, GARDA BROWN WISE, educator; b. N.Y.C., Dec. 13, 1900; d. Willard and Stella (Drake) Brown; B.A., Barnard Coll., 1923; M.A., N.Y. U., 1958, Ph.D., 1962; m. Edward E. Wise, Apr. 2, 1923 (dec. 1940); children—Edward E., Timothy J.W.; m. 2d, LeRoy Bowman, Sept. 23, 1942 (dec. 1971). High sch. tchr., N.Y.C., 1923-25; exec. dir. Boston League Women Voters, 1938-40; dir. Vol. Service Bur., Boston Council Social Agencies, 1940-42; supr. edn. and welfare projects region I, WPA, 1942-43; asst. dir. N.Y. State Child Care Program, 1943-45; asso. dir. edn. N.Y. State Commn. Human Rights, 1945-62; dir. merit promotion Nat. Conf. Christians and Jews, 1963-64; program analyst, cons. Bank St. Coll. Edn., N.Y.C., 1965—; cons. in field. Mem. N.Y.C. Youth Bd., 1960—. Mem. exec. com. Mass. Democratic Com., 1928-36; mem. nat. speaker F.D. Roosevelt campaigns, 1932-36; v.p. Kings County (N.Y.) Liberal Party, 1952-71, mem. N.Y. State exec. bd., 1958-71. Mem. Individual Psychology Assn. (sec. 1950-72), SANE (v.p. Bklyn. Heights chpt. 1960-68), UN Assn. (dir. N.Y.C. chpt. 1964-68), Phi Beta Kappa, Kappa Delta Pi. Mem. Community Ch. (chmn. adult edn. com. 1950-52). Author: Self Education for Merit Promotion, 1963; (with Gordon J. Klopf) Education in a Social Context, 1966, New Careers and Roles in the American School, 1969; (with others) A Learning Team: Teacher and Auxiliary, 1969; also chpts. in books, articles, reports. Home: 1 Sherman Sq New York City NY 10023

BOWMAN, GEORGIA BESSIE, educator; b. Bonne Terre, Mo., May 20, 1914; d. John J. and Betty (Hill) Bowman; A.B., William Jewell Coll., 1934; B.J., U. Mo., 1937; M.A., U. Ia., 1941, Ph.D., 1956; postgrad. Denver U., Northwestern U. Tchr. high sch., Liberty, Mo., 1934-37, Hannibal, Mo., 1937-40; instr. U. Mo. Sch. Journalism, 1942-44; radio chief Midwestern area A.R.C., 1944-45; lectr. Bklyn. Coll., 1946; faculty William Jewell Coll., Liberty, 1947—, chmn. dept. communications, 1965—. Mem. Mo. Com. for Humanities. Recipient Tchr. of Year award Liberty C. of C., 1962. Mem. Speech Communications Assn. (legislative assembly 1964-66, 68-70), Central States Speech Assn., Speech and Theatre Assn. Mo. (pres. 1961, dir. 1971—), Am. Assn. U. Women, Women in Communication, Soroptimists (local pres. 1973), Delta Kappa Gamma, Zeta Phi Eta, Zeta Tau Alpha, Beta Sigma Omicron (nat. editor 1936-42, pres. 1942-46), Pi Kappa Delta (nat. council 1957-69, pres. 1965-67, nat. editor 1971—). Home: 716 Ridgeway Dr Liberty MO 64068 Office: William Jewell College Liberty MO 64068

BOWMAN, HAZEL LOIS, educator; b. Plant City, Fla., Feb. 18, 1917; d. Joseph Monroe and Annie (Thoman) Bowman; A.B., Fla. State Coll. for Women, 1937; M.A., U. Fla., 1948; postgrad. U. Md., 1961—. Tchr., Lakeview High Sch., Winter Garden, Fla., 1939-40, Eagle Lake Sch., Fla., 1940-41; welfare visitor Fla. Welfare Bd., 1941-42; specialist U.S. Army Signal Corps, Arlington Hall, Va., 1942-43; recreation worker, asst. procurement officer A.R.C., CBI Theater, 1943-46; lab. technician Am. Cyanamid Corp., Brewster, Fla., 1946-47; instr., asst. prof. gen. extension div. U. Fla., Fla. State U., 1948-51; free-lance writer, editor, indexer, N.Y., Fla., 1951-55; staff writer Tampa (Fla.) Morning Tribune, 1956; staff writer, telegraph editor Winter Haven (Fla.) News-Chief, 1956-57; registrar/admissions officer U. Tampa, 1957-59; coll. counselor, Atlantic states, 1959-60; registrar/freshman adviser Towson State Tchrs. Coll., Balt., 1960-62; dir. student personnel, guidance, admissions Harford Jr. Coll., Bel Air, Md., 1962-64; instr. York (Pa.) Coll., 1965-66, asst. prof. English, journalism, 1966-69; tchr. S.W. Jr. High Sch., Lakeland, Fla., 1969-70; tchr. learning disabled Vanguard Sch., Lake Wales, Fla., 1970—. Mem. Am. Assn. U. Profs., Am. Assn. U. Women, Am. Assn. for Higher Edn., Am. Coll Personnel Assn., Assn. for Supervision and Curriculum Devel., Assn. for Measurement in Edn. and Guidance, Internat. Reading Assn., Nat. Council Tchrs. English, Fla. English Assn., Mortar Bd., Alpha Chi Alpha, Chi Delta Phi. Club: Altrusa. Editor: Tampa Altrusan, 1958-60. Home: 511 NE 9th Av Mulberry FL 33860 also 2549 S George St York PA 17403

BOWMAN, JACQUELINE BONNIE (MRS. ROBERT JULIAN BOWMAN), ednl. adminstr.; b. Los Angeles, Dec. 28, 1936; d. John and Margaret Eleanor (Hagen) Glatz; B.A., LaVerne Coll., 1959; M.A., Pasadena Coll., 1965; postgrad. U. So. Cal., 1974; m. Robert Julian Bowman, Aug. 19, 1961. Tchr., Charter Oak (Cal.) Unified Sch. Dist., 1958-63, counselor psychometrist, 1963-66, psychologist, 1966-69, coordinator spl. edn., 1969-72, dir. pupil personnel services,

1972—. Prof. edn. U. Cal. at Los Angeles, 1961-62, LaVerne Coll., 1973-74. Founder, Parent Ednl. Programs, Spl. Edn., Charter Oak and P.T.A. Scholarship awards, 1968. Bd. dirs. Perceptual Learning Center. Mem. Nat., Cal. assns. sch. psychologists, Assn. Sch. Adminstrs., Cal. Assn. for Gifted, Univ. Women, Dirs. of Spl. Edn. (chmn. 1971-73), Assn. Sch. Adminstrs. (sec. 1971-73), Native Daus. Golden West, Pi Lambda Theta. Lutheran. Home: 938 Arrow Hwy San Dimas CA 91773

BOWMAN, MARY BLANCHE (MRS. RICHARD A. SHAHEEN), banker; b. Cedar Rapids, Ia., July 1, 1939; d. Roy Roland and Margaret Grace (Wehmer) Bowman; B.A., Cornell Coll., Mt. Vernon, Ia., 1961; m. Richard A. Shaheen, May 26, 1973. Admissions counselor Cornell Coll., 1961-64, with personal banking div. Harris Trust and Savs. Bank, Chgo., 1964—, personal banking officer, 1970-73, asst. v.p. 1973—. Home: 910 N Lake Shore Dr Chicago IL 60611 Office: 111 W Monroe St Chicago IL 60690

BOWMAN, MARY JEAN (MRS. C. ARNOLD ANDERSON), educator; b. N.Y.C.; d. Harold Martin and Mary Catherine (Kauffman) Bowman; B.A., Vassar Coll., 1930; M.A., Radcliffe Coll., 1932; Ph.D., Harvard, 1938; m. Charles Arnold Anderson, July 18, 1942; 1 son, Lloyd Barr. City dir. U.S. Bur. Labor Statistics, N.H., 1934, sr. economist, Washington, 1944-46; instr., asst. prof. econs. Ia. State Coll., Ames, 1935-44; N.W. central regional dir. U.S. Dept. Agr. Study Consumer Purchases, Grinnell, Ia., 1935-36; lectr. econs. U. Cal. at Berkeley, 1949; contract researcher Resources for Future, Lexington, Ky., 1957-60; research asso. prof. U. Chgo., 1958-69, prof. econs. and edn., 1969—. Cons. various nat., internat. govt. and pvt. agys., 1958—. Mem. tech. adv. com. U.S. Population Census, 1966—. Fulbright fellow, Sweden, 1955-56. Mem. Am. Econ. Assn. (nominating com. 1953, exec. com. 1969—), Internat. Assn. for Research Income and Wealth, Univs. Nat. Bur. Com. for Econ. Research, Internat. Econs. Assn. (com. on econs. of edn. 1962-63). Author: Economic Analysis and Public Policy, 1943, 49; Resources and People in East Kentucky, 1963; (with H.D. Plunkett) Elites and Change in the Kentucky Mountains, 1973; (with Anderson and Tinto) Where Colleges Are and Who Attends, 1972. Editor: Expectations, Uncertainty and Business Behavior, 1958; (with C.A. Anderson) Education and Economic Development, 1965. Contbr. articles to profl. jours. Home: 5650 Dorchester Av Chicago IL 60637

BOWMAN, NELMA JEAN (MRS. KENNETH H. BOWMAN, JR.), banker; b. Parkersburg, W.Va., Dec. 10, 1932; d. H. Everett and Ethel B. (Cline) McKown; grad. Mountain State Bus. Coll., 1951; student Am. Inst. Banking, 1967; m. Kenneth H. Bowman, Jr., Sept. 20, 1953; children—Marta Jo (Mrs. Steven R. Masters), Lois Ann. Sec. to sales mgr. Pa. Metal Co., Vienna, W.Va., 1951-53; postal clerk Bartlett (Ohio) Post Office, 1959-60; bookkeeper The Bartlett Farmers Bank, 1960-68, asst. sec., treas., 1968—, loan officer, 1971—; twp. clerk, 1964—. Mem. Nat. Assn. Bank Women, Washington County Assn. Twp. Trustees and Clks. (sec.), Nat. Assn. Bank Women (sec., charter mem. Southeastern Ohio group), D.A.R., Bartlett Grange. Republican. Methodist. Home: Box 116 Bartlett OH 45713 Office: Box 57 Bartlett OH 45713

BOWMAN, PEGGY COCHRANE (MRS. HUGH BOWMAN), architect; b. Alhambra, Cal., July 9, 1926; d. Earl Elliott and Gladys S. (Moran) C.; B.A., Scripps Coll., 1946; postgrad. U. So. Cal., 1952, Columbia U., 1954; m. Hugh Bowman, Nov. 24, 1954. With Kahn and Jacobs, architects, N.Y.C., 1954-57, Litchfield, Whiting, Panero and Severud, Teheran, Iran, 1956-57, individual practice architecture, Los Angeles, 1958—. Mem. Assn. Women in Architecture (pres. 1970-72), A.I.A. (com. chmn. 1960-61), Union Internationale des Femmes Architectes, Scripps Alumnae Assn. (chpt. chmn. 1960). Episcopalian (chmn. guild 1961). Author: Witch Doctor's Manual. Composer musicals: Cable Car, 1958; Yucatan, 1970. Contbr. articles to profl. pubs. Address: 3888 Sherview Dr Sherman Oaks CA 91403

BOWMAN, RUTH, museum educator; b. Denver, June 14, 1923; A.B., Bryn Mawr Coll.; studied Columbia U. Sch. Architecture; M.A. N.Y. Inst. Fine Arts. Asst. curator Jewish Mus., N.Y.C., 1962-63; curator N.Y.U. Art Collection, N.Y.C., 1963-74; dir. edn. Los Angeles County Mus. Art, Los Angeles, 1974—; lectr. art history Washington Sq. Coll. N.Y.U.; adj. asst. prof. Sch. Edn. N.Y.U., 1965—. Staff lectr. Gallery Passport, Ltd., 1962-68; vis. lectr. Mus. Modern Art, N.Y.C., 1964-69; condr. weekly radio and TV art programs Sta. WNYC, from 1967. Mem. N.Y.C. Cultural Council. Mem. Am. Fedn. Arts (nat. exhbns. com.). Home: 10701 Wilshire Blvd Los Angeles CA 90024

BOWNESS, LAVERNE EMILY (MRS. WILLIAM A. BOWNESS), banker; b. Albion, Neb., Nov. 29, 1915; d. Theodore Louis and Louise (Kolm) Stejskal; grad. high sch.; m. Joseph L. Sup, Aug. 10, 1937 (dec. 1960); children—Gale Lynn, Ted J.; m. 2d, William A. Bowness, Sept. 9, 1968. Tchr., elementary sch., Loretto, Neb., 1934-37; asso. Sup's Hatcheries, St. Edward, Albion, and Wilber, Neb., 1937-62; teller First Nat. Bank, Lincoln, Neb., 1964; salesman Gateway Realty, Lincoln, 1964-68; dir., v.p., sec. Sherman County Bank, Loup City, Neb., 1968—; dir., 1st v.p., treas. Sherman County Mgmt., Inc., Loup City, 1968—; acting sec. to pres. Loup City Devel. Corp., 1969—. Mem. Loup City C. of C. (pres. 1975), P.E.O. Lutheran. Clubs: Woman's (St. Edward); Extension (Albion). Home: 540I St Loup City NE 68853 Office: 734 O St Loup City NE 68853

BOWSER, BETTY ANN, news commentator; b. Norfolk, Va., 1944; d. John and Elizabeth (Martin) Bowser; B.A. in English and Journalism, Ohio Wesleyan U., 1966. Reporter, Cleve. (O.) Press, 1967; reporter WAVY-TV, Portsmouth, Va., 1967-68, night news dir., 1968-69; polit. corr. radio-TV news WTAR, Norfolk, 1969-74, anchor woman 11 P.M. news, 1969-74; producer Newsmakers weekly interview program, 1970-74; reporter CBS News, N.Y.C., 1974—. Home: Apt 7-D 219 E 84th St New York City NY 10019 Office: 524 W 57th St New York City NY 10019

BOYAJIAN, JOANNE VIRGINIA FISH (MRS. ARMON K. BOYAJIAN), real estate broker; b. Dinuba, Cal., Oct. 3, 1931; d. Alfred Lafayette and Edwina L. (LaRue) Fish; student Reedley Coll., 1950-51; m. Armon Kaye Boyajian, May 26, 1961; stepchildren—Carol Louise (Mrs. Jeffrey S. Schainen), Janice Lynn. Office mgr., bookkeeper Josephine Furniture Co., Fresno, Cal., 1951-60; sec., treas. Herald Realty Co., Fresno, 1961-71, v.p., 1972—; owner Herald Investment Co., Fresno, Cal., 1971—, sec., treas., gen. mgr. 1971—, also dir.; partner House of Treasures Gift Shop, Fresno, 1973—; dir. Fashion Furniture Co., Fresno, 1961—. Mem. womens league Fresno Art Center, 1970—. Mem. Colonial Dames of the Seventeenth Century, Fresno Hist. Soc., Beta Sigma Phi, Xi Zeta Omicron. Home: 1201 W Sierra Av Fresno CA 93705 Office: 4935 N Blackstone Fresno CA 93726

BOYCE, EMILY HUGHES (MRS. JOSEPH C. BOYCE), ret. astronomer; b. Oxford, O., July 3, 1906; d. Raymond Mollyneaux and Ella (Rogers) Hughes; A.B., Miami U., Oxford, O., 1927; A.M., Radcliffe Coll., 1932; m. Joseph C. Boyce, June 15, 1934; children—Mary (Mrs. Nelson Gelfman), Emily (Mrs. Thomas White), Elizabeth (Mrs. Samuel DiPiero), Frances (Mrs. Ronald Swann), Katherine (Mrs. Fred Hinman). Research asst. Harvard Coll. Obs., Cambridge, Mass., 1931-34, part-time, 1934-44; assisted in computing data for devel. jet engines United Air craft, 1944-45; collaborator Internat. Astron. Union Bibliography all articles on astron. subjects, 1963-64; research contbr. asst., librarian Georgetown Coll. Obs., Washington, 1964-72; ret., 1972. Legislative chmn. P.T.A., 1957-61. Mem. Am. Assn. U. Women (legislative chmn. Hinsdale, Ill. br. 1955-59, Washington br., 1964-65, 66-67, edn. chmn. 1959-61, treas. 1953-55, legislative program chmn. Ill. 1957-61), League Women Voters (mem. bd. Hinsdale 1952-60), Am. Astron. soc., Phi Beta Kappa. Contbr. articles to profl. jours. Home: 2500 Q St NW Washington DC 20007

BOYD, CAROL KNESS, casket co. exec.; b. Oregon, Ill., Sept. 5, 1932; d. Carl Henry and Hannah Irene (Fruit) Kness; student Frances Shimer Coll., 1949-50; m. Allan James Boyd, Aug. 14, 1964. Tchr., Franklin Grove (Ill.) Grade Sch., 1954-55; with Nat. A.J. Boyd Casket Co., Prophetstown, Ill., 1964—; div. adminstrv. mgr., 1971—, sec.-treas., 1964—, also dir. Mem. Whiteside County Republican Women. Home and office: 109 E Railroad St Prophetstown IL 61277

BOYD, DOROTHY LUCILLE DAVIS (MRS. CHARLES FRANKLIN BOYD), educator; b. Luling, Tex., July 28, 1930; d. John James and Lucille (Andrewartha) Davis; B.S., U. Tex., 1959, M.Ed., 1961, Ph.D., 1965; m. Charles Franklin Boyd, July 10, 1948;children—Sandra Kay, Russell Franklin. Sec. State Offices, Austin, Tex., 1947-52; teaching asst. U. Tex., Austin, 1959-62, vis. asst. prof., 1967; tchr. Austin pub. schs., 1962-65, mem. curriculum revision com., 1963-65; asst. prof. edn. S.W. Tex. State U., San Marcos, 1965-68, asso. prof., 1968—; cons. in field elementary edn. Mem. Am. Assn. U. Profs., Assn. Childhood Edn. Internat., History of Edn. Soc., N.E.A., Nat., Southwestern philosophy of edn. socs., Tex. Assn. for Improvement Reading, Tex. Assn. Coll. Tchrs., Tex. State Tchrs. Assn., Delta Zeta, Kappa Delta Pi, Pi Lambda Theta (chpt. v.p. 1961), Delta Kappa Gamma. Contbr. articles to profl. Jours. Home: 1425 Highland Dr San Marcos TX 78666

BOYD, ELIZABETH MARGARET, ret. educator; b. Liverpool, Eng., July 8, 1908; d. John William Parker and Christianna (Ker) Boyd; B.Sc. with honors (Vans Dunlap scholar), Edinburgh U., Scotland, 1930; M.A., Mt. Holyoke Coll., 1933; Ph.D. (Olmstead fellow), Cornell, 1946. Came to U.S., 1937, naturalized, 1953. Demonstrator zoology Edinburgh U., 1930-31; asst. Mt. Holyoke Coll., 1931-33, McGill U., Montreal, Que., Can., 1933-37; faculty Mt. Holyoke Coll., South Hadley, Mass., 1937-73, asso. prof., 1948-58, prof., 1958-73, Alumnae Found. prof., 1964-73, chmn. dept. biol. scis., 1967-70. Bd. dirs. Mass. Audubon Soc., Arcadia Wildlife Sanctuary, Northhampton, Mass. USPHS grantee, 1954, 63; NIH fellow, 1964. Fellow A.A.A.S.; mem. Ornithol, Lab. Cornell U., Am. Soc. Parasitologists, Am. Soc. Zoologists, Am. Ornithol. Union, Helminthological Soc. Washington, Entomol. Soc. Washington, Am. Inst. Biol. Sci., Sigma Xi. Contbr. articles to profl. jours. Home: 23 Jewett Lane South Hadley MA 01075

BOYD, FANNIE LEE, educator; b. Gainesville, Ga., Nov. 19, 1916; d. William Leonard and Eula (Light) Boyd; student Young Harris Jr. Coll., 1934-36; B.S., Ga. State Coll. Women, 1939; postgrad. Emory U., summer 1947; M.Ed. (Gen. Mills. fellow), U. Ga., 1950, Edn. Specialist degree, 1955; Ed.D., Columbia, 1958. Tchr. vocational high sch. home econs., Concord, Ga., 1939-42; tchr. vocational home econs. Chamblee (Ga.) High Sch., 1942-48; asst. prof. U. Ga., Athens, 1949-51, 55-56, asst. prof. edn., 1958-63, asso. prof. edn., 1963—; curriculum dir. Clarke County Schs., Athens, Ga., 1951-55; research asst. Columbia, N.Y.C., 1956-58. Chmn. adult adv. council Ga. Teen-Age Nutrition Program, 1964-65. Mem. Am., Ga. (pres. 1962-63) home econs. assns., Am. Vocational Assn., N.E.A., Assn. Supervision and Curriculum Devel., Soc. for Nutrition Edn., Nat. Sch. Food Service Assn., Ga. Assn. Supervision and Curriculum Devel. (pres. 1954-55), Nat. Assn. Tchr. Educators of Home Econs. (pres. 1974—), Assn. Orgns. Tchr. Edn. (mem. nat. adv. council 1973—), Kappa Delta Pi, Omicron Nu, Phi Lambda Theta, Delta Kappa Gamma. Methodist (mem. adminstrv. bd. 1963-67, 70-74). Home: 175 Baxter Dr Athens GA 30601 Office: Aderhold Hall U Ga Athens GA 30601

BOYD, HELEN MCPHERSON (MRS. DEWARD GASTON BOYD, JR.), mathematician; b. Marks, Miss., Jan. 27, 1937; d. William Joseph and Miriam (Till) McPherson; student Miss. State Coll. Women, 1954-55; B.A. with distinction, U. Miss., 1958, M.A., 1959; postgrad. U. Ala., 1967; m. Deward Gaston Boyd, Jr., June 1, 1963. Instr. math Miss. State U., State College, 1959-64, asst. prof., 1964-65; release chemist Baxter Labs, Mountain Home, Ark., 1965; mathematician Army Missile Command, Redstone Arsenal, Ala., 1967—. Mem. Southeast Huntsville Civic Assn., 1972—; vol. mem. Madison County Local Govt. Study Commn., 1972—. Recipient Taylor medal math. U. Miss., 1958; So. Fellowships Fund fellow, 1958-59. Mem. Math. Assn. Am., Assn. U.S. Army, Am. Meteorol. Soc., Phi Kappa Phi, Gamma Sigma Epsilon. Presbyn. Toastmistress. Home: 703 Dellwood Rd SE Huntsville AL 35802 Office: US Army Missile Command AMSMI-RRA Redstone Arsenal AL 35809

BOYD, INA HELENE (MRS. PAUL RODDA COOK), physician; b. Houston, Dec. 12, 1911; d. William T. and Ina (Reeves) Boyd; B.A., Rice U., 1932; M.D., U. Tex., 1936; m. Paul Rodda Cook, Jan. 30, 1949; children—Paulina Cook (Mrs. John McMurray), Rodda Ruth. Intern John Sealy Hosp., Galveston, Tex., 1936-37; resident N.J. State Hosp., 1939-42, in psychiatry Greystone Park, N.J., 1939-42, Galveston (Tex.) Psychopathic Hosp., 1942-43; staff psychiatrist San Antonio State Hosp., 1943-49, VA Hosp., Houston, 1949—, asst. chief psychiatry and neurology, 1955—, dir. Day Hosp., 1967—; asso. prof. clin. psychiatry Baylor U., 1963—. Mem. Am. Psychiat. Assn., Am. Group Psychotherapy Assn. Contbr. articles in field to profl. jours. Home: 12339 Longworth Houston TX 77024 Office: 2002 Holcombe St Houston TX 77031

BOYD, JANE REID (MRS. JOHN THOMAS BOYD), real estate broker; b. Hickman, Ky., Feb. 24, 1918; d. John McGruder and Kate (Hackett) Reid; student Southwestern U., 1936-38, U. So. Ill., 1938-39, Ga. Tech., 1942, Orange Coast Coll., 1967-69; m. John Thomas Boyd, Apr. 6, 1941; children—John Thomas, Robin Reid, Stephen L. Real estate saleswoman Paul-White Carnahan Co., Costa Mesa, Cal., 1967; real estate broker Boyd Realtors, Corona del Mar, Cal., 1969—. Founding mem. Womens Council of Realtors Newport Harbor, v.p., 1973-75; pres. Assistance League of Newport Beach, 1960-61; v.p. Nat. Assistance League, 1966-70. Mem. Costa Mesa and Newport Harbor Bd. Realtors, Grad. Realtors Inst. Presbyn. Home: 2512 Lighthouse Lane Corona del Mar CA 92625 Office: 3637 E Coast Hwy Corona del Mar CA 92625

BOYD, JUANITA JOAN, photog. artist; b. Ft. Wayne, Ind., Mar. 13, 1932; d. Howard Nicholas and Pauline Cecilia (Hubartt) Funk; student Winona Sch. Profl. Photography, also courses Profl. Photographers Am.; m. Garland Dewitt Boyd, Oct. 7, 1951; children—Karen Sue, Beverly Ann. Free lance photog. artist, 1963—. Recipient 1st pl. awards in brush oil photog. painting Profl. Photographers Ind., 1971-73; named Ind. Artist of Year, 1973. Mem. Profl. Photographers Ind. (dir.), Profl. Photog. Artists Ind. (chmn. 1973-74), Psi Iota Xi (chpt. v.p. 1972-73). Introduced craft process of pressing photographs on wood. Home 3109 Southwin Dr Fort Wayne IN 46816

BOYD, JUDITH SIKES (MRS. ELBERT MOYE BOYD), food products research co. exec.; b. nr. Charlotte, N.C., Feb. 11, 1943; d. Ralph Farrell and Maxine (Babbitt) Sikes; B.S. in Home Econs., East Carolina U., 1964; m. Elbert Moye Boyd, Apr. 21, 1972. Home economist N.C. Egg Marketing Assn., Raleigh, 1964-69; dir. pub. relations Raeford Turkey Farms, Raleigh, 1969-71; dir. food research BTR Mgmt. Corp., Raleigh, 1971—. Mem. Home Economists in Bus., Am. Women in Radio/TV (past v.p.). Home: 3304 Milton Rd Raleigh NC 27609 Office: 3900 Merton Dr Raleigh NC 27609

BOYD, SYDNEY WILSON (MRS. FRANCIS T. BOYD), pub. relations cons.; b. Phila., May 23; d. Joseph Robert and Cora (Shaw) Wilson; student spl. courses N.Y. U., 1944; student art course; m. Francis Thibault Boyd, June 3, 1931. Asst. dir. personnel Burchell Products, N.Y.C., 1943-44; asst. to manpower supr. Sperry Gyroscope Co., Lake Success, N.Y., 1944-45; dir. pub. relations Meml. Cancer Center, N.Y.C., 1945-50; dir. centennial and 2d century devel. program The Gunnery Sch., Washington, Conn., 1950-52; pub. relations rep. for 10th Anniversary Yr., Pub. Relations News, N.Y.C., 1953-54, pub. relations cons., N.Y.C., 1955-57; dir. pub. relations Leake and Watts Children's Home, Inc., Yonkers, N.Y., 1957-67, Bd. dirs. West Side Day Nursery, N.Y.C., 1932-61, hon. life mem. 1962—, pres. bd., 1937-40; bd. mem. Nat. Assn. Day Nurseries, 1939-42, v.p., 1940-42, chmn. ann. conf., 1939-40; mem. exec. com. Women's Adv. council N.Y. World's Fair, 1964-65; mem. nat. bd. Am. Mothers Com., Inc., 1968—; nat. chmn. A Chapel in Every Home, 1968—. Mem. Pub. Relations Soc. Am. (chmn. women's activities com. ann. conf. 1958), Women Execs. in Pub. Relations, English-Speaking Union, Nat. Inst. Social Scis., Gunnery Alumni Assn. (hon. 1965), Nat. Council Women U.S. Episcopalian. Home: Nettleton Hollow Rd Washington CT 06793

BOYDEN, ANN MARIE, advt. agy. exec.; b. Salt Lake City, July 20, 1939; d. Walter Everett and Frances (Nuttall) Boyden; B.A., U. Utah, 1961. Promotion dir. radio sta. KUER and KUED-TV, U. Utah, 1960-61; asst. promotion dir. KSL-TV, Salt Lake City, 1961-64; writer, producer Ross Jurney & Assos., Inc., Salt Lake City, 1964—; dir. advt., pub. relations Gorgoza, Inc., 1968; pres. Advt. et al, Inc., 1969—. Mem. alumni bd. control U. Utah, 1967-68. Sec., Salt Lake County Young Democrats, 1962. Dir. state bd. Campfire Girls Am., 1962-63; bd. dirs. Community Tng. Center Retarded Adults, 1970-71. Recipient Internat. Broadcasting award Hollywood Radio and TV Soc., 1966. Mem. Am. Women in Radio and Television, Intermountain Assn. Indsl. Editors, Soc. Mayflower Descendants, Jr. League Salt Lake City, Intermountain Kennel Club, Great Salt Lake Dog Tng. Club, Pi Beta Phi, Zeta Phi Eta, Tau Beta Sigma. Club: Salt Lake Advertising (dir.). Office: 555 East South Temple Salt Lake City UT 84102

BOYDSTON, JO ANN (MRS. DONALD N. BOYDSTON), educator; b. Hugo, Okla., July 2, 1924; B.A. with high distinction, Okla. State U., 1944, M.A., 1947; Ph.D., Columbia U., 1950; m. Donald N. Boydston, May 8, 1943. Tchr. high schs., instr. jr. coll., Poteau, Okla., 1944-45; lectr. Spanish, Columbia U., N.Y.C., 1947-49; asst. prof. Spanish, U. Miss., University, 1950-51, asso. prof. Sch. Edn., supr. student tchrs., 1952-55; asst. dir. tchr. tng. So. Ill. U., Carbondale, 1955-61, asso. dir., 1961-66, project dir., 1966—, asso. prof. library affairs-adminstrn., 1969-73, prof., 1973—. Mem. John Dewey Soc. (sec.-treas. 1962-70, pres. 1970-72), Modern Lang. Assn. Am., Bibliog. Soc. Am., Manuscript Soc., Am. Assn. U. Profs., Bibliog. Soc. U. Va., Philosophy Edn. Soc., Midwest Modern Lang. Assn., Midwest Philosophy Edn. Soc., Mortar Bd., Phi Kappa Phi. Editor: The Early Works of John Dewey, Vols. I, II, III, IV, V; (with Robert E. Andresen) John Dewey: A Checklist of Translations, 1900-1967, 1969; Guide to the Works of John Dewey, 1970; Dewey Newsletter, 1967—; gen. editor The Collected Works of John Dewey. Contbr. articles to edn. and bibliog. jours. Home: 1190 W Sycamore St Carbondale IL 62901

BOYDSTON, KATHRYN ESTELLE TENNEY (MRS. T. WALTER BOYDSTON), cultural center adminstr.; b. Denver, Oct. 12, 1897; d. George Lee and Adelaide Brown (Miller) Tenney; student Lewis Inst., 1916-18; B.A., U. Wis., 1920; m. T. Walter Boydston, Oct. 29, 1921; children—Robert Walter, Barbara (Mrs. Harry Johnson), Donald Wayne. Dir. Fernwood, Inc., Niles, Mich., 1964—. Recipient certificate of merit in recognition of hort. achievement Mich. Hort. Soc., 1962, award in recognition of accomplishments achieved in field of landscape gardening, 1969; citation for outstanding contbn. to profl. hort. Am. Hort. Soc., 1971; distinguished service certificate for research and hybridization ferns Nat. Council Garden Clubs, 1969. Address: 1720 Range Line Rd Niles MI 49120

BOYER, ELIZABETH MARY, lawyer, educator; b. Fremont, O.; d. Clyde S. and Lydia (Miller) Boyer; B.S., Bowling Green State U., 1937; J.D., Cleve. Marshall Law Sch., 1947; LL.M., Western Res. U., 1956. Admitted to Ohio bar, 1947, since practiced in Cleve.; tchr. area schs., Cleve., 1955—; prof. bus. law Cuyahoga Community Coll. Pres. bd. alumni trustees Bowling Green State U., 1952; founder, 1st pres. Women's Equity Action League, 1969, nat. bd. dirs., 1970-72, trustee Edn. and Legal Def. Fund; bd. dirs. Ohio Coalition for Equal Rights Amendment. Named Woman of Achievement, Interclub Council Greater Cleve., 1972. Mem. Am. Assn. U. Profs., Nat. Assn. Women Lawyers, Cuyahoga County Bar Assn., Cleve. Women Lawyers Assn., Bus. and Profl. Womens Clubs, Zonta Internat., Nat. Women's Party, Ohio Commn. on Status Women, Delta Gamma. Home and office: 7657 Dines Rd Novelty OH 44072

BOYER, GENE THELMA COHEN (MRS. BURTON L. BOYER), furniture co. exec., civic worker; b. Milw., July 11, 1925; d. Nathan and Rene (Hiller) Cohen; student U. Wis., 1942-45; m. Burton L. Boyer, Mar. 21, 1945; 1 dau., Bari Lynn. Various positions in sales, secretarial work, journalism, 1945-49; partner, v.p. Matlin's Furniture Stores, Beaver Dam and Fond du Lac, Wis., 1951—. Rep., Gov.'s Conf. on Status of Women, 1964, 65; chmn. Dodge County Com. for Brotherhood Week, 1960-61, Beaver Dam Mayor's Commn. on Status of Women, 1965—; vice chmn. Beaver Dam Human Relations Council, 1968-70; mem. Beaver Dam Housing Authority, 1968—; mem. Gov.'s Commn. Status of Women, 1971—, treas., 1974—; mem. Beaver Dam Planning Commn., 1971—, Beaver Dam Landmarks Commn., 1973—; del. White House Conf. on Children, 1970. Founding mem. Wis. Women's Polit. Caucus, 1971; v.p. Wis. Feminist Projects Fund, 1973—. Bd. dirs. Center for Pub. Representation, 1974—. Named Woman Activist of Year, Wis. Zero Population Growth, 1972. Mem. Am. Assn. U. Women, Beaver Dam C. of C. (founder, past pres. women's div.), Am. Acad. Lighting Arts, Wis. Retail Furniture Assn., League Women Voters (sec. 1958-59), Nat. Orgn. Women (a founder, bd. dirs. 1968-70, nat. treas. 1970-71, nat. v.p. finance 1971—), Wis. Equal Employment Opportunity Assn. (bd. dirs. 1971—). Clubs: Toastmistress (charter mem.), Wisconsin Alumni. Writer, Decorating Corner weekly column Beaver Dam Daily Citizen, 1960-65; contbr. articles to profl. jours. Home: 1012 Lakeshore Dr Beaver Dam WI 53916 Office: 218 Front St Beaver Dam WI 53916

BOYER, GWEN ROBERTS, librarian; b. East Chicago, Ind., Nov. 7, 1910; d. David John and Maude (Lewis) Roberts; student Moody Bible Inst., 1933-34, Ind. U., 1934-36; L.H.D. (hon.), Free U. of Asia, Karachi, Pakistan, 1969; m. Frank Allen Boyer, Dec. 7, 1939; 1 son, David Keith. Head librarian Lake County (Ill.) Pub. Library; poetry editor WCAE Jour., WCAE-TV, St. John, Ind., 1971-73; dir., editor monthly newsletter Dyer (Ind.) C. of C., 1973—. Co-chmn., Dyer Salvation Army; past treas. chaplain Nat. Council for Encouragement of Patriotism, Inc., Munster, Ind. Trustee A.K. Brewer Library Found. Recipient award of honor UN Day, Philippines, 1967, Outstanding Citizenship award Dyer Lions Club, 1969, certificate of merit for distinguished contbns. to poetry London, Eng., 1969, 71. Poet laureate Ind. State Poets, 1957-58. Mem. Am. Bus. Womens Assn., Lake County Poetry Club, Ind. Library Assn. Composer: I Live To Do Thy Will, 1948. Contbr. to numerous poetry anthologies. Home: 418 Keilman St Dyer IN 46311

BOYER, HELEN KING, designer; b. Pitts.; d. Ernest Wilson and Louise Rive King (Miller) Boyer; ed. privately fine arts and crafts techniques. Designer, owner bus. specializing hand crafted silks and accessories, also free lance designer, 1949-54; designer home patterns Reader Mail Co., N.Y.C., 1955; designer toys My Toy Co., Bklyn., 1956-57; designer toys A & L Novelty Co., 1957-60, Gund Mfg. Co., 1960, Beloved Toy Co., 1968—; with Columbia Toy Co., Kansas City, 1960-64; now pvt. practice; cartoonist; dir. Parkville Fine Arts Assn. Country Gallery, 1969-72; art coordinator Fedn. Earth Sci. Clubs Kansas City. Exhibited one man shows Arts and Crafts Centre, Pitts., 1951, Witte Mus., San Antonio, 1956, Kansas City, 1964, Plaza Bank Gallery, Kansas City, 1966, Marillac Coll., St. Louis, 1970, Unity Gallery, Kansas City, 1971, Independence (Mo.) RLDS Gallery, 1973, Johnson County Community Coll., 1973; two-man shows Bache & Co. Gallery, 1973, Riverside Midcontinent Library, 1973, 74. exhibited in group shows at Pennel Fund, Seattle Ann., all major print shows in U.S., Soc. Am. Graphic Artists to Eng., Parkville Fine Arts Assn., 1969-71; represented in permanent collections Pennell Fund, Library of Congress, Carnegie Mus., Pitts., Met. Mus., N.Y.C., Nelson-Atkins Mus., Kansas City, Mo., 5-county chmn. Greater Kansas City area State Council on Humanities. Trustee Kansas City Mus. Sci. and History. Recipient first prize N.J. Fedn. Women's Clubs, 1951, 52, 53, Phila. Sketch Club Print Ann., 1956; 2d prize sculpture Greater Kansas City Art Assn., 1968, 1st prize, sculpture, 1969, 3d prize wall hangings, 1972; Best of Show, City-wide Arts and Crafts show, 1973. Mem. Greater Kansas City Art Assn. (3d prize in graphics 1971, v.p. 1973-74). Club: Kansas City Lapidary (pres. 1974). Address: 3242 Norledge Pl Kansas City MO 64123

BOYER, RUTH GASINK, educator; b. Mpls., May 18, 1913; d. Edward James and Lulu (Townsend) Gasink; B.A., U. Minn., 1934; M.Social Sci., Smith Coll., 1936; D.S.W., Cath. U. Am., 1966; m. Welch Hall Boyer, Dec. 20, 1944 (div. 1952); children—John Thomas, Eva Fann, William Barton. Asso. prof., chmn. field instrn. Ariz. State U. Sch. Social Work, Tempe, 1963-66; asso. prof., chmn. behavior sequence U. Ga. Sch. Social Work, Athens, 1967-68; prof., coordinator curriculum dept. social work Fla. State U., Tallahassee, 1967-68; prof. U. Ark. Grad. Sch. Social Work, Little Rock, 1968—. Cons. U.S. Dept. Health, Edn. and Welfare, 1961, Cuban Refugee Children's Program, 1962, Atlanta Community Council, 1967-68, U. Ga. Council on Gerontology, 1967-68; cons. evaluator Pima Indian Reservation project on delinquency, 1966; faculty S.W. Regional Conf. on Aging, Hot Springs, Ark., 1970; tng. coordinator CONTACT, Little Rock, 1969. Asst. field dir. hosp. service A.R.C., Italy, 1943-45. Mem. Minn. Edn. Assn. (pres. student personnel sect. 1955-57), Acad. Certified Social Workers, Ark. Gerontological Soc. (pres. 1974-75), Council on Social Work Edn., Alpha Omicron Pi (pres. Milw. alumnae 1938). Republican. Conglist. Author: Tomorrow is Living, 1968. Contbr. articles, poetry to profl. jours. Home: 1507 Garland St North Little Rock AR 72116 Office: 33d and University Little Rock AR 72204

BOYES, MADALINE MARCIA (LINDY), travel promotion ofcl.; b. San Francisco, June 17, 1926; d. Bedford Walker and Marcia Isadora (Edwards) Boyes; B.A., U. Cal., 1950. Aviation writer Oakland (Cal.) Tribune, 1951-57; asso. editor Skyways Mag., N.Y.C., 1957-59; free lance pub. relations cons., writer, Piedmont, Cal., 1960-63; vol. Peace Corps, Brazil, 1963-65; asst. editor Jour. Med. Entomology, Honolulu, 1966-68; sr. communications specialist Hawaii Visitors Bur., Honolulu, 1969—. Active Civil Air Patrol, 1950—, information officer, Hawaii, 1970—. Recipient award of merit Hawaii Dept. Transp., 1967, outstanding service award Hawaii wing Civil Air Patrol, 1970. Mem. Aviation/Space Writers Assn., 99's, Honolulu Symphony Soc., Honolulu Press Club, Variety Club Women. Author: (with David McCallister) Sabres Over Brandywine, 1961; Pilots Weather Guide, 1962, rev. edit., 1972; also articles. Home: 1619 Kamamalu Av Honolulu HI 96813 Office: 2270 Kalakaua Av Honolulu HI 96815

BOYHAN, CYNTHIA ANNE (MRS. JOHN H. BOYHAN), journalist; b. nr. Elberton, Ga., June 23, 1934; d. John Wayne and Flo (Haynes) McCalla; A.B., Coll. William and Mary, 1956; m. John H. Boyhan, Nov. 8, 1958; children—Wayne Michael, Leslie Anne, Stephen Kelly. Social worker Laramie County Welfare Dept., Cheyenne, Wyo., 1957-58, Lander, Wyo., 1958-60; journalist Wyo. Eagle, Cheyenne, 1956-57; tchr. pub. schs., Dubois, Wyo., 1967-70; journalist Wyo. State Jour., Lander, 1972—. Mem. State Nursing Adv. Com., 1973—. Justice of peace, Dubois, Wyo., 1961-70; mem. Fremont County Democratic State Com., 1962-73; police judge, Dubois, 1967-70; del. Dem. Nat. Conv., 1972. Bd. dirs. Big Horn Basin Children's Center, 1973—; trustee Dubois Sch. Bd., 1971—. Home: Box 571 Dubois WY 82513

BOYLE, ANN PETERS, author; b. Independence, Mo., Jan. 21, 1916; d. Robert Mize and Lucy Turpin (Conway) Peters; A.A., Chevy Chase Jr. Coll., 1936; B.A., U. Mo. at Kansas City, 1938; m. James Hancock Boyle, Dec. 26, 1938; children—Eleanor (Mrs. Richard Riley), Lucy (Mrs. Robert E. Buschmann), Jean (Mrs. Alan Doyle Dannenberg). Tchr. primary grades Barstow Sch., Kansas City, Mo., 1938-39; freelance fiction writer children's mags., 1953-69; freelance writer novels, Tustin, Cal., 1969—. Capt. Community Chest campaign, Kansas City, Mo., 1938-41; vol. A.R.C., VA, 1940-50; leader, tchr. leadership tng. U.S. Forces, Austria and Calumet Councils Girl Scouts Am., 1946-60. Mem. Lambda Beta Writers Workshop (co-founder), Newport Writers Group, Cal. Writers Guild, Assn. Jr. Leagues Am. Club: Quill Pen (pres. 1971-72) (Tustin). Author: Stormy Slopes, 1971; Sundown Girl, 1971; The Well of Three Echoes, 1972; Rim of Forever, 1973; One Golden Earring, 1974. Home: 15991 Bliss Lane Tustin CA 92680

BOYLE, BARBARA DORMAN (MRS. KEVIN BOYLE), lawyer; b. N.Y.C., Aug. 11, 1935; d. William and Edith Dorman (Kleiman) Dorman; B.A. with honors, U. Cal. at Berkeley, 1957; LL.B., U. Cal. at Los Angeles, 1960; m. Kevin Boyle, Nov. 26, 1960; children—David Eric, Paul Coleman. Admitted to Cal. bar, 1961, N.Y. bar, 1964, U.S. Supreme Ct. bar, 1973; atty. Am. Internat. Pictures, Los Angeles, N.Y.C., 1960-65, corporate asst. sec., 1962-65; partner firm Cohen & Boyle, Hollywood, Cal., 1967—. Bd. dirs. New World Pictures, Inc., Murakami-Wolf Prodns., Inc., Fafinta, Inc., Los Angeles. Mem. vol. com. Marquez Elementary Sch., Pacific Palisades, Cal., 1970—, chmn. resource com., 1972—; chartermem. women in films, 1973—. Legal adviser Park Century Sch., Santa Monica, Cal., 1973—. Mem. N.Y., Cal., Hollywood, Los Angeles bar assns. Home: 560 Muskingum Av Pacific Palisades CA 90272 Office: 6430 Sunset Blvd 1500 Los Angeles CA 90028

BOYLE, JUNE, mem. Democratic Nat. Com.; b. Greeley, Colo., Sept. 30, 1917; d. Walter J. and Millicent (Williamson) Ott; B.F.A., U. Colo., 1939; postgrad. U. Wyo., 1949-52; m. James M. Boyle, Sept. 2, 1939; children—Kathleen (Mrs. John G. Champlain), Michael John. Mem. Wyo. Ho. of Reps. from Albany County, 1963, 65, 67, 69, 71, Wyo. Senate, 1973—. Chmn., Albany County Dem. Com., 1960-62; mem. Nat. Dem. Com. for Wyo., 1964—. Mem. Wyo. Commn. on status Women, 1969—. Bd. dirs. S.E. Wyo. Mental Health Center. Mem. League Women Voters, Nat. Order Women Legislators, Alpha Phi, Delta Phi Delta. Address: 706 S 14th St Laramie WY 82070

BOYLE, KATHRYN MARION (MRS. FREDERICK ARTHUR BOYLE), real estate broker; b. North Adams, Mass.; d. John Henry and Mary Frances (Harrington) Smith; student Burdett Bus. Coll., 1925; grad. hairdressing course, 1926, Dale Carnegie course, 1952; m. Frederick Arthur Boyle, Sept. 1, 1928; 1 dau., Beverly A. (Mrs. William J. Tabor). Beautician, Boston, 1932-34, Billercia, Mass., 1935-45; rep., then field mgr. Avon Products, Boston, 1946-48; distbr. Tupper Corp., Farnumsville, Mass., 1948-50; owner, operator Better Products, Inc., Dorchester, Mass., 1951-58; leader, sales promotion meetings, various cities in New Eng., 1950-58; sales mgr. Mutual Toy Co., Boston, 1958-62; realtor, broker Elouise A. Troup, Realtor, Braintree, Mass., 1962—; guest speaker realty meetings. Mem. com. Make Am. Beautiful, Mass., 1970-71. Mem. Quincy and South Shore Bd. Realtors (chmn. hospitality 1970-71, alternate mem. com. profl. ethics 1972—), South Shore Bd. Realtors (chmn. publicity 1970-71). Christian Scientist (Sunday Sch. tchr. 1957-71, asst. to com. on publ. for Mother Ch. 1966, 69). Home: 6 Colonial Club Dr Apt 203 Boynton Beach FL 33435

BOYLE, SISTER MARIA LUCY, educator; b. Bethleham, Pa.; d. P.F. and S.J. (Ward) Boyle; student Moravian Coll., 1921-22; B.A., Immaculata Coll., 1925; M.A., U. Pa., 1933; Ph.D., U. Laval, 1944. Tchr. secondary sch., Phila., 1928-40; faculty Immaculata (Pa.) Coll., 1940—, now prof., chmn. modern fgn. lang. dept. Recipient scholarship for ind. study and research in France, summer 1966. Decorated Chevalier dans l'Ordre des Palmes Academiques, 1968. Mem. Alliance Francaise, Société des Professeurs Francais en Amerique, Am. Assn. Tchrs. French, Nat. Catholic Renascence Soc. (past pres., dir.), Internat. Fedn. Cath. Alumnae, Immaculata Coll. Alumnae Assn. (faculty del. 1959—), Am. Assn. U. Women, Modern Lang. Assn., Assn. des Membres de l' Ordre des Palmes Academique. Address: Immaculata Coll Immaculata PA 19345

BOYLE, SISTER MARY MAURICE, educator; b. Phila., Dec. 27, 1922; d. Malachy and Bridget (O'Donnell) Boyle; B.A. in Math., Villanova U., 1952; M.S. in Physics, Cath. U. Am., 1959; Ph.D. in Physics and Biophysics, St. Thomas Inst. Advanced Study, Cin., 1969. Joined Sisters of Mercy, Merion, Pa., 1940; elementary sch. tchr. in Ardmore, Pa., 1943-45; secondary sch. tchr. in Phila., 1946-49, Merion, 1949-59; mem. faculty Gwynedd Mercy Coll., Gwynedd Valley, Pa., 1959-73; allied health coordinator Mercy Cath. Med. Center, Lansdowne, Pa., 1973—, Cancer research grantee in nuclear medicine Mercy Cath. Med. Center, 1970—. Mem. Jr. Cath. Round Table Sci. (sec., treas. 1957), Franklin Inst. (sci. fair com. 1956-57), Optical Soc. Am., Radiation Research Soc., Am. Physics Tchrs. Assn., Cath. Round Table Sci., Assn. Schs. Allied Health Professions. Author research papers. Address: Mercy Catholic Med Center Lansdowne Av Darby PA 19023

BOYLE, VIRGINIA HILL (MRS. FRANK GORDON BOYLE), banker; b. Tishomingo, Okla., Nov. 6, 1942; d. Johnie Lee and Rose (Stewart) Hairell; grad. high sch.; m. Frank Gordon Boyle, Aug. 6, 1966. Sec., Pacific Finance, Wichita Falls, Tex., 1961-64; sec. Meml. Bank, Houston, 1964-67, asst. cashier, 1967-69, asst. v.p., 1969-73; retail loan officer Corpus Christi State Nat. Bank, 1974—. Mem. Meml.-Spring Branch C. of C. (dir. 1972—), Nat. Assn. Bank Women, Am. Inst. Banking, Bank Adminstrv. Inst. Club: Bank Women's (project chmn. 1969-70, publicity chmn. 1970-71, by-laws chmn. 1971-72, v.p. 1972, pres. 1973). Home: 6628 Sahara Pharoah Valley Corpus Christi TX 78412 Office: PO Box 301 Corpus Christi TX 78403

BOYLES, MARCIA VIRGINIA, assn. exec.; b. Oak Park, Ill., July 4, 1936; d. Howard B. and Virginia (Parshall) Boyles; B.S., Mary Washington Coll. of U. Va., 1958; M.S., Ohio U., 1960; Ph.D., Northwestern U., 1969. Mem. faculty Grand Valley State Coll., Allendale, Mich., 1965-73, asso. prof. biology, 1969-73, dir. sch. health scis., 1970-73; dir. health related program devel. Am. Assn. State Colls. and Univs., Washington, 1973—. Mem. Assn. Schs. Allied Health Professions, Am. Soc. Biol. Scis., Sigma Xi. Home: 707 S Pitt St Alexandria VA 22314 Office: Suite 700 1 DuPont Circle Washington DC 20036

BOYNTON, ELIZABETH K. (MRS. BEN LYNN BOYNTON), civic worker; b. Princeton, Ky., Jan. 30, 1911; d. William Roy and Jessie (Rooks) Katterjohn; student Murray State Tchrs. Coll., 1929; B.S., Northwestern U., 1933; m. Ben Lynn Boynton, Aug. 19, 1933; children—Lynn William, Irvin Parker, Sylvia Wells (Mrs. Darrell McGuire), Melbourne Roy, Elizabeth Helen (Mrs. Karl Kubler). Treas., Woman's Soc. Christian Service, Houston, 1951-53, spl. mem., 1953, circle chmn., Glen Ellyn, Ill., 1955, spiritual life sec., 1956-58, missionary edn. sec., 1958-60, dist. treas., Akron, O., 1962-67, circle chmn., 1961-62, sec., 1968-69, spl. mem., 1970, hon. life mem., dist. speaker-at-large, 1967—, active Boy Scouts Am.; health chmn. Litchfield Jr. High Sch. P.T.A., Akron, O., 1961-62; mem. Woman's Aux. A.M.A., Service League Akron Gen. Hosp., Stan Hywet Found., Rotary Anns (social service chmn. 1967-68, treas. 1969, Appreciation award 1970), Gt. Books Found. Recipient spl. family plaque Bethany Meth. Ch., Houston, 1953; named Meth. Family of Year, First Meth. Ch., Glen Ellyn, 1958; award Woman's Soc. Christian Service. Mem. Nat. Audubon Soc. Home: 2302 O'Henry Dr Panama City FL 32401 summer Route 3 Box 535 Shelby MI 49455

BOYUM, JOY GOULD (MRS. ASMUND BOYUM), educator; b. N.Y.C., Dec. 8, 1934; d. David and Beatrice (Levine) Gould; B.A., Barnard Coll., 1955; M.A., N.Y. U., 1957, Ph.D., 1962; m. Asmund Boyum, Sept. 5, 1960; children—David, Ingrid. Prof. English, N.Y. U., N.Y.C., 1960—; film critic Wall St. Jour., 1971—. Mem. Modern Lang. Assn., Nat. Council Tchrs. English, N.Y. Film Critics, Nat. Soc. Film Critics. Author: (with Adrienne Scott) Film as Film, 1971. Contbr. articles to Ency. Brit., World Book Yearbook. Home: 45 Remsen St Brooklyn NY 11201 Office: Washington Square New York City NY 10003

BOZEMAN, ADDA BRUEMMER (MRS. ARNE BARKHUUS), educator, author; b. Geistershof, Latvia, Dec. 17, 1908 (came to U.S. 1936, naturalized 1941); d. Leon and Anna (von Kahlen) von Bruemmer; diplomee Ecole Libre des Scis. Politiques, Paris, France, 1934; barrister at law, Middle Temple Inn of Ct., London, Eng., 1936; J.D., So. Meth. U., 1937; postgrad. student Stanford, Hoover Inst.; m. Virgil Bozeman, Mar. 26, 1937 (div. 1947); 1 dau., Anya (Mrs. Mark Taylor); m. 2d, Arne Barkhuus, Feb. 8, 1951. With law offices Charles H. Huberich, Berlin, Paris, The Hague, London, 1933-36; asso. prof. history Augustana Coll., 1943-47; prof. internat. history Sarah Lawrence Coll., 1947—; vis. prof. Northwestern U., 1945, N.Y.U., 1948, 49, Grad. Faculty New Sch. Social Research, 1954, 55, 63; mem. faculty seminar study peace Columbia, 1953—. Research grantee Carnegie Endowment Internat. Peace, 1952, Rockefeller Found., 1960. Mem. Am. Soc. Internat. Law, Am. Polit. sci. Assn., Internat. Studies Assn., Am. Hist. Assn., Internat. Law Assn., Am. Soc. Legal History. Author: Regional Conflicts Around Geneva, 1948; Politics and Culture in International History, 1960; The Future of Law in a Multicultural World, 1971; also articles, essays. Home: 24 Beall Circle Bronxville NY 10708

BOZONE, BILLIE RAE, librarian; b. Norphlet, Ark., Oct. 7, 1935; d. Guy Samuel and Vera (Jones) Bozone; B.S. in Library Sci., Miss. State Coll. for Women, 1957; M.A., George Peabody Coll. for Tchrs., 1958. Asst. ref. librarian Miss. State U., State College, 1958-61, serials librarian, 1961-63; asst. ref. librarian U. Ill. at Urbana, 1963-65; asst. librarian New Eng. Mut. Life Ins. Co., Boston, 1965-67; sr. ref. librarian U. Mass., Amherst, 1967-68; head circulation dept. Smith Coll., Northampton, Mass., 1968-69, asst. librarian, 1969-71, librarian, 1971—. Sec., bd. dirs. Hampshire Inter-library Center, Amherst, 1971—. Mem. Alpha Beta Alpha, Alpha Psi Omega. Club: Zonta (Northampton, Mass.). Home: 42 Greenwich Rd Amherst MA 01002 Office: Smith Coll Library Northampton MA 01060

BRACE, MARY MICHAEL (MRS. KENNETH M. BRACE), educator; b. Aliquippa, Pa., Nov. 2, 1918; d. John E. and Catherine (Bailey) Michael; B.S., Mansfield State Coll., 1940; M.Ed., Pa. State U., 1956, postgrad. Delta-Kappa Gamma scholar, (Family Finance Workshop scholar), 1961-71, Ed.D., 1971; m. Kenneth M. Brace, Nov. 26, 1942; children—John Michael, Jean Ann, Thomas H. Tchr. high schs., New Albany, Pa., 1940-43, Mansfield, Pa., 1949-64; co-op. student tchr. supr. Mansfield State Coll., 1941-43, 49-64, asso. prof. home econs., 1964-70, prof., 1970—, also supr. student tchrs. Judge, Pa. Farm Show, 1966-68. Active fund raising A.R.C., Heart Fund, Polio; pres. Holy Child Parish Women's Guild, 1962-64. Mem. Nat., Pa. edn. assns., Pa., Middle States (evaluation teams), Am., Pa. home econs. assns., Am. vocational assns., Am. Legion Aux. (pres. 1952), Blossburg Hosp. Aux., Pi Lambda Theta, Delta Kappa Gamma (corr. sec. 1966—, pres. Pi chpt. 1971-73), Delta Zeta (program chmn., coll. chpt. and co. province dir.). Home: 50 Mann St Mansfield PA 16933

BRACELIN, ELIZABETH JANE, lawyer; b. Seattle, Apr. 2, 1945; d. Raymond Francis and Mary M. (Sippely) Bracelin; B.A. in History, U. Wash., 1967, J.D., 1969. Admitted to Wash. bar, 1969; since practiced in Seattle; mem. firms Keller, Rohrbach, Waldo, Moren & Hiscock, 1969-73, Peterson, Bracelin, Creech & Young, 1973—. Tchr. criminal evidence Shoreline Community Coll., 1973—; tchr. women and law Seattle U., 1974. Mem. Wash. Women's Political Caucus, 1973. Bd. trustees Pub. Defenders, 1972-74. Mem. Wash., Seattle-King County (vice chmn. young lawyers sect. 1972-73, chmn., 1973-74, trustee, 1970—), Am. bar assns., Wash. Women Lawyers, Wash. Trial Lawyers, Phi Beta Kappa, Phi Alpha Theta, Alpha Delta Pi. Democrat. Editor: Wash. Law Review, 1968-69. Home: 2300 11th St E Seattle WA 98102 Office: 2500 Smith Tower Seattle WA 98104

BRACKEBUSCH, FRIEDA, ret. social worker, educator; b. Bingham, Ill., Oct. 7, 1907; d. Andrew and Rose (Kettelkamp) Brackebusch; B.S., Ill. Wesleyan U., 1932; M.S., U. Ill., 1933; M.A., U. Chgo., 1939. Tchr. elementary sch., Fillmore, Ill., 1927-29; dir. Fayette County Emergency Relief, Vandalia, Ill., 1934-36; caseworker disaster relief A.R.C., Cairo, Ill., 1937; med. social worker Vanderbilt U. Hosp., Nashville, 1939-40; dir. social service Ellis Fischel State Cancer Hosp., Columbia, Mo., 1940-42, St. Louis County Hosp., Clayton, Mo., 1942-43; exec. sec. Health and Hosp. div., Social Planning Council, St. Louis, 1943-56; exec. dir. St. Louis City and County unit Am. Cancer Soc., 1956-58; asso. prof. Sch. Social Service, St. Louis U., 1958-73, asst. prof. community medicine, 1969-73, emerita, 1973—; dir. social service St. Louis U. Hosps., 1962-73. Mem. mayor's adv. com. on survey of health and hosp. facilities, 1956-59. Fellow Am. Pub. Health Assn.; mem. Nat. Assn. Social Workers, Am. Soc. Hosp. Social Work Dirs., Phi Kappa Phi. Conglist. Club: Zonta. Home: 4475 W Pine Blvd St Louis MO 63108

BRACKEN, DOROTHY KENDALL (MRS. CLIFFORD FREDRICK BRACKEN), educator; b. Dallas, May 16, 1910; d. James Romulus and Robbie (Goodwin) Kendall; A.B., Daniel Baker Coll., 1929; M.A., So. Meth. U., 1932; postgrad. U. Chgo., 1933, Columbia U., 1935, 45; m. Clifford Fredrick Bracken, June 3, 1938; 1 dau., Brenda (Mrs. James T. Whorton). Tchr., Dallas Ind. Sch. Dist., 1930-38, Highland Park (Tex.) Ind. Sch. Dist., 1940-42, U. Tex., 1945; mem. faculty So. Meth. U., Dallas, 1947—, prof. grad. courses dept. edn., dir. Reading Clinic, 1947—. Vis. lectr. Tchrs. Coll., Columbia U., summers, 1953-55, U. Chgo., summer, 1958, U. Alta. (Can.), summer, 1962; reading workshop leader in U.S., Australia, New Zealand, S. Africa; reading cons. pub., pvt. schs. and industry; co-chmn. 2d World Congress on Reading, Copenhagen, 1968, speaker world congresses, Paris, 1966, Copenhagen, 1968, Sydney, Australia, 1970, Buenos Aires, 1972; mem. Lang. Arts Commn., Tex. Edn. Agy., 1958; chmn. subcom. on reading and lit., 1958; chmn. Doubleday Young Readers Adv. Com., 1964-66. Recipient distinguished award Internat. Reading Assn., 1970. Mem. Internat. Reading Assn. (dir. 1962-65, pres. 1965, ednl. tours coordinator, 1965—), Nat. Reading Conf. (dir. 1969-71), Tex. Assn. Improvement Reading (dir., editor newsletter 1962—), Tex. Assn. Coll. Profs. Reading (pres. 1973), Delta Kappa Gamma. Methodist. Author or co author numerous textbooks. Contbr. articles to periodicals, yearbooks, tchr. manuals. Co-editor: Third World Congress Procs., Sydney, Australia, 1970 (listed as distinguished book on edn. 1972). Home: 3230 Daniel Ave Dallas TX 75205 Office: 308 Clements Hall So Methodist U Dallas TX 75275

BRACKEN, HARRIET MARIE OELGOETZ (MRS. GEORGE F. BRACKEN), public relations exec.; b. Columbus, O., May 20, 1919; d. Joseph Frank and Ida (Kauderer) Oelgoetz; B.S., Ohio State U., 1941; m. George F. Bracken, Sept. 19, 1947; children—Carol Lee, Drew Joseph. With F & R. Lazarus Co., Columbus, 1942-48, 51-66; v.p., Huntington Nat. Bank, Columbus, 1966—. Mem. citizen's council bd. Franklin County Children's Services 1966-68. Godman Guild, 1971—. Mem. Nat. Assn. Bank Women, Columbus C. of C. (downtown area com. 1971—), Columbus Advt. Fedn., Pub. Relations Soc. Am., Gamma Alpha Chi. Clubs: Zonta (Columbus). Home: 1430 Zollinger Rd Columbus OH 43221 Office: 17 S High St Columbus OH 43216

BRACKEN, PEG, author; b. Twin Falls, Ida., Feb. 25, 1918; d. John Lewis and Ruth (McQuesten) Bracken; A.B., Antioch Coll., 1940; m. Parker Edwards, Mar. 17, 1966; 1 dau., Johanna Kathleen. Author: The I Hate To Cook Book, 1960; The I Hate To Housekeep Book, 1962; I Try to Behave Myself, 1963; Peg Bracken's Appendix to the I Hate To Cook Book, 1966; I Didn't Come Here To Argue, 1969; But I Wouldn't Have Missed It for the World, 1973. Mem. A.F.T.R.A.,

Screen Actors Guild, Authors Guild, P.E.N. Address: Box 35 Bolinas CA 94924

BRACKETT, LEIGH DOUGLAS (MRS. EDMOND HAMILTON), writer; b. Los Angeles, Dec. 7, 1915; d. William Franklin and Margaret Leigh (Douglass) Brackett; privately ed.; m. Edmond Hamilton, Dec. 31, 1946. Screenplay credits include; (with William Faulkner) The Big Sleep, 1944, Rio Bravo, 1957, Hatari!, 1963, El Dorado, 1965, The Long Goodbye, 1971. Recipient Jules Verne Fantasy award, 1953, Golden Spur award Western Writers Am., 1963; Nova award (with husband), 1969. Mem. Authors Guild, Writers Guild Am. West, Western Writers Am., Sci. Fiction Writers Am., Western Hist. Assn., Internat. Platform Assn. Author books, including: The Starmen, 1952; The Long Tomorrow, 1955; The Tiger Among Us, 1957; Eye for An Eye, 1957; Follow the Free Wind, 1963; Silent Partner, 1970. Address: RD 2 Kinsman OH 44428

BRACKETT, PEARL COLE, sch. adminstr.; b. Balt., Jan. 6, 1919; d. Richard B. and Esther Rosina (Thompson) Cole; certificate teaching Coppin State Coll., 1936; B.S. in Edn. summa cum laude, Morgan State Coll., 1941; M.A. cum laude, N.Y. U., 1945; postgrad. U. Vt., 1957, Johns Hopkins, 1968, U. Md.; divorced. Tchr. Balt. City Pub. Schs., 1938-42, demonstration tchr., 1942-44, supervising tchr., 1945-55, asst. prin., 1955-68, area dir., 1968, asst. supt. community schs. div., 1968—. Cons. Open Communications Project, Washington, U. Va. Cultural Relations. Dir. Waverly Press, Inc. Mem. Mayor's Group Tourism, Balt., 1969—; mem. adv. bd. Jr. League Balt. Inc., Childhood Assn. Inc. Md.; mem. adv. com. Mayor's Ball; mem. Balt. Promotion Council, v.p. in charge spl. events. Bd. dirs. Urban League, 1962-68, A.R.C., Balt., 1970-73, Md. Ballet Co., Soc. for Prevention Blindness; trustee Balt. Mus. Art, 1970-73, chmn. edn. com.; mem. Gov.'s Commn. Negro History and Culture. Recipient Valuable Service award Balt. Urban League, 1964; Appreciation award Com. Sponsor Better Race Relations, 1968; Outstanding Service in Field Edn., Nat. Assn. Negro Bus. and Profl. Women's Club, Inc., 1969; Outstanding and Meritorious Service in Edn. United Negro Coll. Fund Woman's div., 1970; Outstanding Leadership award Girl Scouts, 1971; Balt. Mayoral citation, 1973. Mid Career program City Sch. Adminstrn. fellow Yale, 1973-74. Mem. Parent-Tchr. Community Assn., Pub. Sch. Supt.'s Assn. Md., Md. Acad. Sci. (mem. women's com.), Nat. Community Sch. Edn. Assn. (dir.), Prins. Assn. U.S. (vice chmn. com. large cities, editor Prins. Assn. Communique), Am. Assn. Sch. Adminstrs. (leader Nat. Acad. Sch. Execs.), Zonta, Delta Sigma Theta, Delta Kappa Gamma. Mem. A.M.E. Ch. Club: Short Club Bridge (Balt.). Home: 1 University Pkwy East Baltimore MD 21218 Office: 3 E 25th St Baltimore MD 21218

BRACKI, MARIE ANNE, psychologist; b. Chgo., Nov. 29, 1942; d. Roy and Helen (Van der Meeren) Fisher; B.A. in Sociology, De Paul U., 1964, M.A., 1972; m. Robert F. Bracki, July 4, 1966; children—Karen, Michael. Grad. asst. De Paul U., Chgo., psychometrist VA Guidance Center, 1965-66; psychologist U.S. Army Mental Hygiene Clin., Ft. Sill, Okla., 1967-68; cons., coordinator youth program Police Dept., Elmhurst, Ill., 1972—; asso. psychologist Elmhurst Psychol. Center, 1972—; instr. in Parent Effectiveness Tng. Courses, Lombard, Ill., 1973—. De Paul U. scholar, 1960-61; Dept. Health, Edn. and Welfare grantee, 1968-69. Mem. Am. Personnel and Guidance Assn., Am. (asso.), Ill. psychol. assns., Lombard Jr. Woman's Club (publicity chmn. 1971-72, service chmn. 1972-73), Psi Chi, Pi Delta Phi. Home: 249 N Lombard St Lombard IL 60148 Office: 533 W North Av Elmhurst IL 60126

BRACKMAN, SELMA (MRS. ARTHUR BRACKMAN), picture service exec.; b. N.Y.C.; d. Gedalia and Anna (Jacobs) Rabinowitz; student Hofstra U., 1940-44; B.A., Mich. U., 1945; postgrad. U. Ariz., 1946; m. Arthur Brackman, Oct. 13, 1947; children—Jacob, Rebecca, Deborah, Susanna, Jessica. Picture researcher, librarian Free Lance Photographer's Guild, 1955—, v.p., 1954—; researcher, librarian Alpha Photo Assos., European Picture Service, N.Y.C., 1955—. Candidate to World Constl. Conv., 1968; Peace worker Women Strike for Peace; exec. dir. Nat. Teach-In on World Community, Columbia, 1969. Bd. dirs. Council for Dept. Peace, 1971—; Coalition Against Pollution, Irasburg, Vt., Center for Energy Information, N.Y.C. Co-editor Man, instl. newspaper for peace; asso. editor Propaganda Analysis Newsletter; Editor Media Performance Reports. Home: 14 Bromley Lane Great Neck NY 11023 Office: 251 Park Av S New York City NY 10010

BRADAC, MARY FRANCES MARINELLI (MRS. JOSEPH BRADAC), librarian; b. Chisholm, Minn.; d. John and Clara (Varriano) Marinelli; B.S. Coll. St. Catherine, 1932; M.A., U. Mich., 1945; postgrad. Columbia; m. Joseph Bradac, Mar 29, 1948; children—Jane, John. Nurses aide Army Hosp., New Orleans, 1938-39, Hibbing (Minn.) Gen. Hosp., 1940-41, librarian La Guarde Hosp. U.S. Army, Cheyenne, Wyo., 1942-44; reference librarian Hibbing High Sch., 1932-45; head circulation dept. U. N.D., Grand Forks, 1945-48; head communication library Stephens Coll., Columbia, Mo., 1948-50; edn. librarian Central Mich. U., Mt. Pleasant, 1963—. Mem. Am., Mich. library assns., Am. Assn. Sch. Librarians, Mich. Assn. for Media in Edn., Am. Assn. U. Women. Club: Youth Study (Mt. Pleasant). Home: 628 W Preston St Mount Pleasant MI 48858 Office: Edn Library Central Mich U Univ Park Library MI 48858

BRADBURY, MAXINE DOROTHY (MRS. THEOPHILUS BRADBURY), newspaper pub.; b. Cresbard, S.D., Aug. 14, 1924; d. Lawrence Lamar and Pansie Ethel (Connell) Harrington; grad. high sch.; m. Theophilus Bradbury, July 8, 1944; children—Richard, Kathleen (Mrs. Dean Frelk), Marileen Bradbury, Randy, Cynthia. Bookkeeper, Burke Ins., Aberdeen, S.D., 1942; with McClintock Def. Plant, Mpls., 1943; sec. Socony Vacuum Oil, Aberdeen, 1944; sec., bookkeeper Farm Home Adminstrn., Faulkton, S.D., 1956; co-pub., editor LaMoure (N.D.) Chronicle, 1971—. Pres. Civic League, Howard, S.D., 1968; organizer Civic League, Volga, 1969, pres., 1969-70; mem. parents council S.D. State U., Brookings. Mem. Am. Legion Aux. (pres. 1954, 61), 40 and 8, Women's Soc. Christian Service (v.p. 1967-68), Sigma Delta Chi. Presbyn. (elder). Rebekah. Clubs: Fortnightly Study (LaMoure); Home Extension (Howard, S.D.). Home: 516 1st St W LaMoure ND 58458 Office: 10 S Main St LaMoure ND 58458

BRADEN, BARBARA LOUISE, city ofcl.; b. Phoenix, Apr. 24, 1938; d. Forrest Clifford and Margaret Frances (Mize) Braden; student Radcliffe Coll., 1955-57; A.B., Boston U., 1960; postgrad. Brandeis U., 1960-61, (A.D. Simpson fellow) Harvard, 1969-71; M.Ed., Northeastern U., 1968; Ed.D., Harvard, 1973. Tchr., math. coordinator Avon (Mass.) Pub. Schs., 1962-67; adminstrv. asst. to asso. commr. Mass. Dept. Edn., 1967-68; asst. to supt., Concord (Mass.) Pub. Schs., 1968-69; dir. ednl. and social welfare planning N.Y.C. Planning Commn., 1971—. Bargaining rep. Mass. Tchrs. Assn., 1966-67; clin. prof. Stonehill Coll., 1966-68; asst. prof. Lowell State Coll., 1970-71. Mem. Am. Assn. Sch. Adminstrs., Pi Lambda Theta, Alpha Delta Pi. Home: 35 Ellicott Pl Staten Island NY 10301 Office: NYC Planning Commission 2 Lafayette St New York City NY 10007

BRADEN, JANE HOLMES, psychologist, educator; b. N.Y.C., June 27, 1946; d. Lucian Joseph and Mary (Holmes) Braden; B.A., Barnard Coll., 1967; M.A. (N.Y. State Tchrs. fellow, Columbia Faculty fellow), Columbia, 1969, Ph.D., 1972. Asst. prof. psychology Fairleigh Dickinson U., Teaneck, N.J., 1971—. Mem. Am., Eastern psychol. assns., Sigma Xi. Research in visual perception. Home: 2100 Linwood Av Fort Lee NJ 07024

BRADEN, LOUISE CATHERINE WEBER (MRS. FORREST H. BRADEN), real estate exec.; b. Milw.; d. Adam George and Frances (Lehrbaummer) Weber; student U. Wis., 1926-28; m. Forrest H. Braden, 1941; 1 dau., Barbara L. adminstrv. personnel asst. U.S. Forest Service, Milw., 1933-51; pres. Braden Realty Co., Sheboygan, Wis., 1951—; real estate cons., 1953—; residential builder, 1963—. Mem. com. Sheboygan County Community Fund, 1954-59; vol. Sheboygan United Fund. Mem. Sheboygan Bd. Realtors (sec.-treas. 1965-67, 1st woman pres. 1967-68; named Realtor of Year 1966), Internat. Platform Assn., Wis. Realtors Assn., Nat. Assn. Real Estate Bds. (exec. officers council), Nat. Inst. Real Estate Brokers, Wis. State-wide Multiple Listing Service, Sheboygan Area C. of C. Mem. Order Eastern Star. Club: Sheboygan Woman's. Address: 1316 Eisner Av Sheboygan WI 53081

BRADFIELD, KATHRYN NUSBAUM (MRS. LLOYD EUGENE BRADFIELD), psychologist, educator; b. Park Falls, Wis., Aug. 8, 1930; d. Daniel V. and Mabel (Gorsuch) Nusbaum; B.A., U. Wis., M.A., 1960; Ph.D., U. Colo., 1963; m. Lloyd Eugene Bradfield, July 2, 1965. Research asso. U. Wis. at Madison, 1960-61; post-doctoral fellow N.D. State Hosp., Jamestown, 1963-64; asst. prof. U. N.D. at Grand Forks, 1964-66; asst. prof. psychology Bemidji (Minn.), State Coll., 1966-67, asso. prof., 1967-70, prof., 1970—, chmn. dept. psychology, 1968—. Cons., N.D. State Hosp., 1964-66, Opportunity Tng. Center for Retarded, Grand Forks, 1964-66. Mem. Am., Midwestern psychol. assns., A.A.A.S., Phi Beta Kappa. Home: Route 3 Bemidji MN 56601

BRADFORD, BARBARA TAYLOR (MRS. ROBERT BRADFORD), journalist; b. Leeds, Eng., May 10, 1933; d. Winston and Freda (Walker) Taylor; student pvt. schs., Eng.; m. Robert Bradford, Dec. 24, 1963. Came to U.S., 1964. Columnist, London Evening News, 1955-57; exec. editor London Am., 1959-62; editor Nat. Design Center Mag., 1965-69; syndicated columnist Newsday Specials, L.I., 1968-70; nationally syndicated columnist Chgo. Tribune/N.Y. News Syndicate, N.Y.C., 1970—. Recipient Dorothy Dawe award Am. Furniture Mart, 1970, 71. Mem. Authors Guild, Nat. Home Fashions League, Nat. Soc. Interior Designers (Distinguished Editorial award 1969, Nat. Press award 1971), Am. Inst. Interior Designers. Author: The Innocent Are Wise, 1963; Complete Encyclopedia Homemaking Ideas, 1968; A Garland of Children's Verse, 1968; How to be the Perfect Wife, 1969; Easy Steps to Successful Decorating, 971. Home: 135 E 83d St New York City NY 10028 Office: Daily News 220 E 42d St New York City NY 10017

BRADFORD, LOUISE MATHILDE, social worker; b. Alexandria, La., Aug. 3, 1925; d. Henry Aaron and Ruby (Pearson) Bradford; B.S., La. Poly. Inst., 1945; certificate Social Work, La. State U., 1949; M.S., Columbia, 1953; postgrad. Tulane U., 1962, 64, La. State U., 1967; certificate U. Pa., 1966. With La. Dept. Pub. Welfare, Alexandria, 1945—, welfare caseworker, 1950-53, children's caseworker, 1957-59, child welfare cons., 1959-73, social services cons., 1973—, state cons. day care, 1963-66. Del., Nat. Day Care Conf., Washington, 1964; mem. early childhood edn. com. So. States Work Conf., Daytona Beach, Fla., 1968; mem. La. adv. com. 1970 White House Conf. on Children, also del.; mem. So. region planning com. Child Welfare League Am., 1970-73; mem. profl. adv. com. Cenla chpt. Parents Without Partners, 1970; instr. family and child welfare services La. Coll., Pineville, lectr. Kindergarten workshop, 1970-72; mem. La. 4-C Day Care Licensing Rev. Com., Central La. 4-C Steering Com. Pres., Les Soignees, Alexandria, 1947-48. Bd. dirs. Cenla Community Action Com., Alexandria, 1966-68. Mem. Acad. Certified Social Workers, Nat. Assn. Social Workers, So., La. assns. children under six, La. Conf. Social Welfare, Am. Pub. Welfare Assn. (S.W. region planning com. 1965), D.A.R., Central La. Pre-Sch. Assn. (dir. 1967-70), Day Care and Child Devel. Council Am., Marquis Biog. Library Assn. (adv.). Methodist (kindergarten bd. 1967—, ofcl. bd. 1974—). Clubs: Rapides Golf and Country, Pilot (Alexandria). Home: 5807 Joyce St Alexandria LA 71301 Office: PO Box 832 Alexandria LA 71301

BRADFORD, MARY (MRS. BERNARD MICHAEL ROTH), physician; b. Tilbury, Ont. Can., Dec. 8, 1922; d. Magnus Andrew and Mary (Megaw) Bradford; came to U.S., 1926, naturalized, 1944; A.B., Barnard Coll., 1943; M.D., Temple U., 1950; m. Bernard Michael Roth, May 17, 1957; stepchildren—Paul, Rodney, Stephanie, Thomas. Intern, Los Angeles County Gen. Hosp., 1950-51; asst. health officer, Madera, Cal., 1951-52; staff physician Tb Hosp., San Diego, 1952-53; gen. practice medicine, LaMesa, Cal., 1953-59; physician Pub. Health Dept. San Diego, 1959-66, Cal. State U. at San Diego, 1966—. Served to lt. (j.g.) USNR, 1944-46. Mem. Am., Cal. med. assns., Am. Med. Women's Assn. (br. pres. 1956-58, 69-70), San Diego County Med. Soc. Office: Health Service San Diego State 5402 College St San Diego CA 92115

BRADFORD, SUSAN ELLEN, physician; b. Springfield, Mass., July 21, 1943; d. Donald Robert and Shirley Elizabeth (Wood) Bradford; B.A., Boston U., 1967, M.D., 1967; m. Philip R. Elia, June 4, 1966 (div. Dec. 1972); children—Cheryl Lesley, Valerie Beth. Intern, Framingham (Mass.) Union Hosp., 1967-68, Hosp., 1967-68, resident in pathology, 1970-71; resident in psychiatry U. Hosp., Boston, 1968-69; physician Planned Parenthood, Albany, N.Y., 1972—; ophthalmology fellow Tulane U., New Orleans, 1974—. Recipient Macy fellowship in medicine Radcliffe Inst., 1970-71. Mem. Benjamin Waterhouse Med. History Soc. (v.p. 1967). Home: 206A Executive Dr Guilderland NY 12084

BRADL, ELAINE MARIE, coll. adminstr.; b. Buffalo, Sept. 20, 1947; d. Henry J. and Verna R. (Wiser) Bradl; B.S., Russell Sage Coll., 1970; M.Ed., Pa. State U., 1971; postgrad. Syracuse U., summers 1972-73. Admissions counselor Fisher Jr. Coll., Boston, 1971-74; admissions counselor Lesley Coll., Cambridge, Mass., 1974—. Mem. Am. Assn. Women in Community and Jr. Colls., Mass. Assn. Women Deans, Adminstrs. and Counselors, Russell Sage Coll. Alumnae Club, Iota Alpha Delta. Office: 29 Everett St Cambridge MA 02138

BRADLEY, BETTY MAY HUNT, psychologist; b. Oelwein, Ia., Dec. 17, 1932; d. Hollis N. and Mildred (Wilkins) Hunt; B.A., Coe Coll., 1954; M.A., Ohio State U., 1955; m. Raymond Patrick Bradley, Apr. 21, 1962; 1 dau., Teresa. Psychologist, Columbus (O.) State Inst., 1955—. Mem. Phi Beta Kappa, Phi Kappa Phi. Author: Teaching Moderately and Severly Retarded Children, 1971. Contbr. articles to profl. jours. Home: 90 E Henderson Rd Columbus OH 43214 Office: 1601 W Broad St Columbus OH 43223

BRADLEY, BOBBIE JEAN (MRS. J.L. BRADLEY), state ofcl.; b. Madison, Ill., June 30, 1936; d. John Calvin and Victoria (Gray) Davenport; B.S. in Edn., No. Ill. U., 1960; M.S. in Edn., Ind. U., 1968; m. Jimmy L. Bradley, Apr. 21, 1962; children—Cynthia Marie, Karen Louise. Tchr. Chgo. Bd. of Edn., 1960-64; case worker Cook County Pub. Aid, Chgo., 1964-65; employment interviewer Ill. State Employment Service, 1965; employment counselor Ill. Dept. Labor, Chgo., 1966-70; state counseling specialist Ill. Dept. of Labor, Chgo., 1970—. Cons. counseling. Gen. Electric fellow, 1972. Mem. Am. Personnel and Guidance Assn., Ill. Employment Counselor Assn. (trustee 1974-75). Home: 8025 S Phillips Chicago IL 60617 Office: 165 N Canal Chicago IL 60606

BRADLEY, DEBORAH RALPH, educator; b. Auburn, N.Y., July 31, 1916; d. Roy Alson and Dora (Lincoln) Ralph; A.B. in Math., William and Mary Coll., 1937; M.Ed., U. Va., 1966; m. Thomas Glynn Bradley, June 26, 1941; children—Thomas Glynn; 1 foster dau., Martha B. Rickman (Mrs. John C. Rudd). Tchr., Bedford County, Va., 1937-42, 45-47, Norfolk County, Va., 1942-44; tchr., Lynchburg, Va., 1958-65, 66-67, counselor, 1967—. Mem. Nat. (life), Va. (pres. dist. J guidance sect. 1967-69, state guidance sect. 1969-70), Lynchburg edn. assns., Am., Va. (treas. 1970-72), Lynchburg (pres. 1972-73) personnel and guidance assns., Am. Sch. Counselors Assn., Delta Kappa Gamma, Beta Gamma, Chi Omega. Episcopalian (Sunday sch. tchr. 1957-62, sec. 1965-69). Club: Book Mark (pres. Bedford 1970-71). Home: 1403 Oakwood St Bedford VA 24523 Office: Dunbar High School 12th and Polk Sts Lynchburg VA 24504

BRADLEY, DOROTHY MAYNARD, state legislator; b. Madison, Wis., Feb. 24, 1947; d. Charles Crane and Maynard (Riggs) Bradley; B.A. cum laude, Colo. Coll., 1969; m. Rick Applegate, 1973. Mem. Mont. Ho. of Reps., 1971—, vice chmn. natural resources com. Mem. Phi Beta Kappa. Home: PO Box 931 Bozeman MT 59715

BRADLEY, DOROTHY WINCHESTER (MRS. JOHN D. BRADLEY), govt. ofcl., social worker; b. Hutchinson, Kan., Feb. 7, 1909; d. Stanley Allen and Edith (Carey) Winchester; A.B., U. Ia., 1932; M.A., U. Chgo., 1938; m. John D. Bradley, Feb. 26, 1946 (dec. Dec. 1968). Social worker Reno County, Hutchinson, 1933-34; supr. Family Transient Service, Kansas City, Kan., 1934-36; child welfare worker, cons., supr. Kan. Dept. Social welfare, 1938-42; dist. child welfare supr. Indpls., Dept. Pub. Welfare, 1942-45; dir. Div. Children, Youth and Their Families, Kan. Dept. Social and Rehab. Services, Topeka, 1945—. Dir., Winchester Packing Co. Mem. Kan. Gov's. Interagy. Council on Children and Youth, Kan. Gov.'s Adv. Com. on Mental Retardation; mem. Kan. Gov.'s com. attending White House Conf. on Children and Youth, 1950, 60, State White House Planning Com., 1970. Mem. Am. Pub. Welfare Assn., Child Welfare League Am., Nat., State confs. social welfare, Nat. Assn. Edn. Young Children, Nat., Kan. (dir.) rehab. assns., Kan. Council for Children and Youth, P.E.O., Kappa Kappa Gamma. Home: 2078 Lincoln St Topeka KS 66604 Office: State Office Bldg Topeka KS 66612

BRADLEY, EARLINE (MRS. ROBERT G. BRADLEY), real estate broker; b. Camden, Ark., June 16, 1923; d. Lee Frank and Dovie Frances (Nix) Dawson; student Ouachita Coll., 1948-50, Southwestern Baptist Sem., 1950-51, Fullerton Jr. Coll., 1963-64, U. Cal. at Los Angeles, 1964-65, Santa Barbara City Coll., 1969-71; m. Norman B. Short, Nov. 26, 1939 (dec. Jan. 1966); children—Reba (Mrs. Rolf Froelich), Derrell R., Gail (Mrs. Bobbie Cole), Nelda (Mrs. George Sisk). Advt. mgr. Fornicari Co., Los Angeles, 1960-61; partner, designer Norman Short & Assos., Santa Ana, Cal., 1962-66; owner, real estate broker Earline Bradley, Realtor, Santa Barbara, Cal., 1968—. Mem. Nat. Assn. Real Estate Brokers, Nat. Inst. Real Estate Brokers, Cal. Real Estate Assn., Nat. C. of C., Better Bus. Bur., Nat. Fedn. Ind. Bus., Santa Barbara C. of C. Home: 1104 La Vista Rd Santa Barbara CA 93100 Office: 215 W Mission Santa Barbara CA 93101

BRADLEY, FLORENE JORDAN (MRS. STEVE BRADLEY), librarian; b. Magnolia, Ark., Aug. 18, 1917; d. Thomas Scott and Nellie (Nipper) Jordan; student So. State Coll., Ark., 1935-37; B.A., Henderson State Tchrs. Coll., 1939; B.S. in L.S., Peabody Coll., 1947; m. Steve Bradley, Nov. 23, 1966. Librarian, tchr. Burdette High Sch., 1939-42, Calhoun High Sch., 1942-43, Magnolia High Sch., 1943-51; regional librarian Columbia-Lafayette-Ouachita-Calhoun Regional Library, Magnolia, 1951—. Sec. City Planning Commn., Columbia County Fair Bd. Named Magnolia Woman of the Year service and civic clubs, 1963; Citizen of Yr., 1968. Mem. Magnolia Bus. and Profl. Women's Club, Am. Assn. U. Women, Magnolia League Women Voters, Ark. (past pres.), Southwestern (past chmn. pub. library div.) library assns., A.L.A. (mem. notable books council adult services div. 1962-64), C. of C. (dir.), Delta Kappa Gamma. Methodist. Club: Quota. Home: 405 W Calhoun St Magnolia AR 71753 Office: 220 E Main St Magnolia AR 71753

BRADLEY, GAIL SOULES (MRS. DAVID GILBERT BRADLEY), civic worker; b. Long Beach, Cal., Apr. 8, 1917; d. John B. and Margaret (Emory) Soules; B.A., U. Cal. at Los Angeles, 1940; M.A., 1940; m. David Gilbert Bradley, Mar. 18, 1940; 1 dau., Katherine Ann. Pres. League of Women Voters of N.C., 1962-65, dir. nat. orgn., 1966-70, v.p. nat. orgn., 1970-74. Dir. Nat. Inst. for Consumer Justice, Washington, 1971-74; mem. Nat. Com. on U.S.-China Relations, 1972—. Mem. Nat. Orgn. Women. Home: 2507 Sevier St Durham NC 27705

BRADLEY, HASSELL GRIMES (MRS. JOE ALLEN BRADLEY), editor, educator; b. Paris, Tex., June 29, 1930; d. William F. and Kathryn Lynn (Ellis) Grimes; B.A. in Journalism, U. Okla., 1951; postgrad. U. Cal. at Berkeley, 1953, Wichita State U., 1966; m. Joe Allen Bradley, July 8, 1951; children—William Stanton, Margaret Lynn. Reporter Paris (Tex.) News, 1949; society editor Woodward (Okla.) Daily Press, 1950; feature writer Wichita (Kan.) Eagle and Beacon, 1965-66; home and garden writer Oklahoman and Times, Oklahoma City, 1968; editor University Park News, Denver, 1971-72; area mgr. Luzier Cosmetics Co., Littleton, Colo., 1971-72; foods editor Sentinel Newspaper, Denver, 1972—. Cons. pub. relations, 1971; tchr. adult edn. in foods and creative writing Arapahoe Community Coll., Littleton, Colo., 1973—. Bd. dirs. Bethesda Community Mental Health Center Half-Way House, Denver, 1973. Recipient awards Kan. Press Women, 1966, Nat. Press Women, 1967. Mem. Women in Communications, Nat., Colo. press women, Home Economists in Bus., Am. Home Econs. Assn., Denver Woman's Press Club, Alpha Chi Omega. Home: 6474 S Sycamore Littleton CO 80120 Office: 3434 S Acoma Englewood CO 80110

BRADLEY, IDA FLORENCE, artist, educator; b. Johnstown, Pa., Oct. 24, 1908; d. Park Orlanda and Minerva (Parks) Custer; student Puzzletown Art Sch., 1950-52, Arts League of Ligonier Valley, 1955-59; m. Joseph Bradley, Oct. 10, 1927; children—Judy (Mrs. James Adams), Joanne. Pvt. sch. instr., 1948—; tchr. Westmont Sr. High Sch., 1957-58; substitute tchr. elementary schs., 1958-60; vol. instr. for sr. citizens, Johnstown, 1963—. Recipient Best of Show, St. Vincent Coll., 1971. Mem. Arts Assn., Allied Artists of Johnstown (Best of Show 1950, 59), Am. Artists Profl. League of N.Y., Johnstown Area Arts Council, Ind. Art Assn. Home: 2139 Pitt Av Johnstown PA 15905

BRADLEY, LISA (MRS. MICHAEL UTHOFF), ballerina; b. Elizabeth, N.J.; d. Robert M. and Florence (Wilsey) Bradley; student pub. schs.; m. Michael Uthoff, Mar. 5, 1966; one dau., Michelle. Dancing lead Carousel, Chautauqua, N.Y., 1960, N.Y.C. Center Opera, Dallas Civic Opera, 1960; tours U.S., 1961, 62, 64, Near and Middle East, 1962, 63, Russia, 1963; star Stage Two, CBS, 1964; spl. dance program Nat. Edn. TV, 1965, Jacobs Pillow Dance Festival, 1965, N.Y.C. Center Theatre, 1966, 67; leading dancer City Center Joffrey Ballet, N.Y.C., 1964—; dancer, actress film short Sea Fall, 1968; leading dancer N.Y.C. Opera, 1968—, 1st Chamber Dance Co., N.Y., 1969; toured U.S.A., 1968; appeared at White House, 1968; lead roles Aida and Cinderella with Honolulu Symphony Soc., 1972; tchr., coach dancers Hartford Ballet Co., permanent guest artist, 1973—.

BRADLEY, LORETTA JEAN DIXON (MRS. CHARLES ALLEN BRADLEY), educator; b. Ashland, Ky., Dec. 21, 1941; d. Benjamin Arthur and Edith Belle (Hutchinson) Dixon; B.A., U. Ky., 1963, M.A., 1965; Ph.D., Purdue U., 1971; m. Charles Allen Bradley, Aug. 20, 1961; 1 son, Brian Allen. Tchr. pub. schs., Lexington, Ky., 1966-67; tchr., counselor Wichita (Kan.) pub. schs., 1967-68; counselor Winchester (Ky.) pub. schs., 1968-69; grad. asst. Purdue U., West Lafayette, Ind., 1969-71, profl. counselor, 1971—. Guest lectr. Ind. U., Kokomo, 1969—. Mem. aux. bd. Home Hosp. Recipient fellowship Nat. Vocational Rehab. Assn., 1965-67. Mem. Am., Ind. (mem. exec. council 1972—, sec.-treas. 1974—), N.W. Central Ind. (pres. 1973-74) personnel and guidance assns., Am. Coll. Personnel Assn., Am. Assn. for Measurement and Evaluation in Guidance, N.E.A., Nat. Assn. Women Deans, Adminstrs. and Counselors, Am. Assn. Univ. Women. Club: Dames (Lexington). Author: Career Education: Implications for the Biological Sciences, 1974. Home: 1301 Palmer Drive West Lafayette IN 47906

BRADLEY, MADGE, ret. judge; b. Ukiah, Cal., Nov. 14, 1904; d. Hugh and Bertha (Shaw) Bradley; pvt. study of law. Admitted to Cal. bar, 1933; dep. county clk. San Diego County, Cal., 1927-40; pvt. practice law, 1940-53; judge Municipal Ct., San Diego Jud. Dist., 1953-71; judge pro tem Superior Ct., 1952 (1st woman San Diego County). Mem. various coms. Community Welfare Council. Named Woman of the Year, San Diego, 1953; recipient Woman of Valor award B'nai B'rith, 1959, Regional award Nat. Conf. Christians and Jews, 1974. Mem. State Bar Cal., Bar Assn. San Diego County, Conf. Cal. Judges, Republican. Club: Altrusa (pres. 1945-46). Home: 1595 Chatsworth Blvd San Diego CA 92107

BRADLEY, SISTER RITAMARY, educator; b. Stuart, Ia., Jan. 30, 1916; d. James Francis and Alice (Muldoon) Bradley; Ph.B., Marygrove Coll., 1938, M.A., 1945; Ph.D., St. Louis U., 1953; LL.D., (hon.), Marquette U., D.H.L., Fordham U., 1960. Asst. prof. dept. English, Marycrest Coll., 1940-56; instr., novitiate, juniorate Sisters of Humility of Mary, Ottumwa, Ia., 1957-61; asst. exec. sec. Sister Formation Conf., Nat. Cath. Ednl. Assn., Washington, 1961-64; hon. fellow, dept. English, U. Minn., 1964-65; prof. English, St. Ambrose Coll., Davenport, Ia., 1965—. Dir. Seminars in Philosophy, Cath. U. Am., 1963, 64; asst. dir. Workshop for Sisters, Marquette U., 1964. Mem. Modern Lang. Assn., Religious Edn. Assn. Contbr. articles profl. jours., chpt. to book. Editor: Sister Formation Bull., 1954-64. Address: 2317 Western Av Davenport IA 52803 also 518 W Locust Davenport IA 52803

BRADSHAW, LILLIAN MOORE, librarian; b. Hagerstown, Md., Jan. 10, 1915; d. Harry M. and Mabel E. (Kretzer) Moore; B.A., Western Md. Coll., 1937; B.S. in L.S., Drexel U., 1938; m. William Theodore Bradshaw, May 19, 1946. Asst. adult circulation dept. Utica (N.Y.) Pub. Library, 1938-41, asst. head, 1941-43; adult librarian Enoch Pratt Free Library, Balt., 1943-44, asst. coordinator work with young adults, 1944-46; br. librarian Dallas Pub. Library, 1946-47, readers adviser, 1947-52, head dept. circulation, 1952-55, coordinator work with adults, 1955-58; asst. dir., 1958-62, dir., 1962—. Chmn., H.W. Wilson Library Periodical Award Jury, 1968-69; steering com. Nat. Library Week, 1967-70; mem. library edn. adv. com. Tex. Coll. and U. System Coordinating Bd.; mem. adv. com. U. Tex., Dallas; mem. U.S. Com. for Am. Library in Paris, 1970-71. Mem. Gov.'s Commn. Status Women; bd. publs. So. Methodist U., 1970-73; dir. Dallas County Community action com. Office Econ. Opportunity, conferee, asst. leader task force; chmn. goals achievement com. for continuing edn. Goals for Dallas, 1972, com. to plan future, 1973—; mem. profl. adv. com. Greater Dallas Community Relations Commn. Bd. dirs. Tex. Municipal League, 1966-68, Com. of Future, 1971—, Hoblitzelle Found. Named Tex. Librarian of Yr., 1961; one of 6 most prominent personalities among Am. Women to visit France, by French Govt., 1970; recipient Titche's Arete award, 1970, Distinguished Alumnus award Drexel U., 1970. Mem. Assn. Grad. Edn. and Research in North Tex. (trustee, adv. council), Am. (v.p. adult services div., 1966-67, dir. exec. com. pub. relations sect. library adminstrn. div. 1964-66, pres. adult services div. 1967-68, council 1968-69, pres. 1970-71, chmn. membership com. 1973-74, trustee Freedom to Read Found. 1969-71), Tex. (chmn. pub. libraries div. 1955-56, pres. 1964-65, chairperson awards com. 1973-74) library assns., Internat. Fedn. Library Assns. (rep. on working com. to revise standards for pub. libraries 1970-72), Friends Tex. Libraries (adv. bd. 1963-70), Nat. Reading Council, League Women Voters, Am. Assn. U. Women, Beta Phi Mu. Club: Zonta. Bd. consultants Library Jour., 1962-63. Contbr. articles to profl. jours. Home: 6318 E Lovers Lane Dallas TX 75214 Office: 1954 Commerce St Dallas TX 75201

BRADSHAW, OTABEL PETERSON (MRS. CHARLES HOWARD BRADSHAW), educator; b. Magnolia, Ark., Oct. 27, 1922; d. Grover Cleveland and Mae (Staggs) Peterson; B.S. in Edn., So. State Coll., 1953; postgrad. Ouachita Bapt. U., 1967, U. Ark., 1971; m. Charles Howard Bradshaw, Aug. 14, 1948; children—Mary Rogers, Michael Howard, Susan Charla. Tchr., Walkers Creek Sch., Taylor, Ark., 1945, Locust Bayou Sch., Camden, Ark., 1946-52, Fairview Sch., Camden, from 1961, now at Harmony Grove Sch., Camden. Sec. P.T.A., 1960, now life mem. Kazanjian winner; recipient Tchr.'s medal, George Washington medal Freedoms Found. Mem. Nat., Ark. edn. assns., Alpha Delta Kappa. Methodist. Club: Tate Park Garden (sec. 1958) (Camden). Home: Roseman Rd Camden AR 71701

BRADSHER, MILDRED MARY STEWARD, extension home economist; b. Lowndes, Mo., Nov. 16, 1917; d. Elonzo Lewis and Bertha Pink (Harty) Steward; B.S. in Edn., S.E. Mo. State Coll., 1940; M.S., U. Mo., 1963; m. Thomas Alfred Bradsher, May 28, 1950 (dec. July 1956); children—Bonnie Ruth, Trudy Ellen. Tchr. elementary sch., S.E. Mo., 1937-40; home supr. Farmers Home Adminstrn. Mo., Charleston, 1940-47; extension home economist Mississippi County, Charleston and Monroe County, Paris, 1947-51; extension consumer marketing specialist Marion County, Hannibal and Buchanan County, St. Joseph, 1957-61; state extension specialist food and nutrition, asso. prof. food and nutrition U. Mo. at Columbia, 1962—. Cons. homemaker programs U.S. Office Econ. Opportunity, 1965-67. Mem. Altrusa Internat., Mo. Pub. Health Assn., Mo. Assn. Social Welfare, Am., Mo. home econs. assns., Am. Assn. U. Profs., Epsilon Sigma Phi, Kappa Omicron Phi, Gamma Sigma Delta. Baptist. Mem. Order Eastern Star. Home: 1900 Vassar Dr Columbia MO 65201 Office: Cooperative Extension Service U Mo Columbia MO 65201

BRADY, ADELAIDE MARY, pub. relations agy. exec.; b. N.Y.C., June 27, 1926; d. Earl Victor and Audrey Sylvia (Calvert) Burks; B.S., Boston U., 1947; m. James Francis Brady, Jr., June 22, 1946 (div. 1953); 1 son, James Francis III. Dir. group relations Save the Children Fedn., N.Y.C., 1955-59; dir. pub. affairs div. Girl Scouts U.S.A., N.Y.C., 1959-69; pres. Communication Internat., Inc., Washington, 1969—; pres. Burks Brady Communications, N.Y.C.. 1973—; exec. v.p. Arts in the Parks, Inc.. Washington, 1971—. Mem. Nat. Women's Republican Club, 1968—. Recipient Silver Reel award for film The Children of Now, Save the Children Fedn., 1968. Mem. Pub. Relations Soc. Am., Am. Assn. U. Women, N.E.A., Am. Women in Radio and TV, Nat. Ednl. Broadcasters Assn., Am. Legion Aux. Roman Catholic. Club: Capitol Hill (Washington). Office: 6 E 78th St New York City NY 10021

BRADY, BARBARA ROSEWATER (MRS. WILLIAM WEBB BRADY), civic worker, writer; b. Omaha, Feb. 27, 1918; d. Stanley M. and Barbara (McAlvay) Rosewater; A.B., U. Neb., 1939; m. William Webb Brady, Sept. 28, 1940; children—Barbara Leslie (Mrs. Richard K. Karchmer), Nanch Webb (Mrs. Scott W. Shafer), Katherine Anne, Margaret Louise. Fashion editor Chgo. Daily News, 1941-43; reporter Omaha World-Herald, 1944; instr. journalism Judson Coll., Elgin, Ill., 1969-70. Commentator Meet the Churches program Sta. WRMN, Elgin, 1950-51. Mem. Elgin Jr. Service Bd., 1947-52; mem. exec. bd. Friends of Judson Coll., 1963—, pres., 1967-68. Bd. dirs. YWCA, Elgin, 1951-52. Named Woman of Year, Altrusa Club, Elgin, 1968. Mem. League Women Voters (dir. Elgin 1962-63), Theta Sigma Phi, Alpha Xi Delta. Republican. Baptist. Club: Elgin Country. Author: Come See Where Jesus Lived, 1954. Contbr. articles to Read, Woman's Day, Sunday Digest, Mother's Mag., Christian Mother, New Century Leader, Sunday Pix. Home: 332 Vincent Pl Elgin IL 60120

BRADY, BERNICE LUELLA, library exec.; b. Wichita, Kan., Mar. 19, 1928; d. Hobert Chalmer and Lillian Luella (Cheatum) Brady; B.S., U. Kan., 1950, M.S., 1955; M.L.S., Kan. State Tchrs. Coll., 1971. High sch. tchr., Lawrence, Kan., 1950-53; instr. U. Kan., Lawrence, 1954-60; pub. relations dir. Library, Hutchinson, Kan., and South Central Kan. Library System, 1971—, now at Elementary Attendance Centers, Harveyville and Eskridge, Kan. Camp dir. Kaw Valley council Girl Scouts, 1954. Winner Charlotte Chorpenning Cup, Children's Theatre, 1959. Mem. Am., Kan. library assns., League Am. Pen Women, Press Women of Kan., Gamma Phi Beta, Pi Lambda Theta. Club: Kan. Authors (dist. historian 1967). Author plays. Contbr. articles to profl. publs. Home: PO Box 154 Harveyville KS 66431

BRADY, BETTY ANN, librarian; b. Salem, Mass., May 9, 1936; d. Claren Leigh and Mary Emily (Abbott) Brady; A.A., Orlando Jr. Coll., 1956; B.A., Fla. State U., 1960. Page, Orlando (Fla.) Pub. Library, 1956-57, clk., 1957-59, librarian, 1960—. Mem. Am., Southeastern, Fla. library assns. Democrat. Presbyn. Home: 1122 W Yates St Orlando FL 32804 Office: 10 N Rosalind St Orlando FL 32801

BRADY, HELENA REAL (MRS. GENE PAUL BRADY), educator; b. Havana, Cuba (parents Am. citizens); d. Francis Alexander and Ofelia (Hernandez Oliva de Nordarse) Real; B.S. with honors, Fordham U., 1952, M.A., 1954; Ph.D., U. Pa., 1960; m. Gene Paul Brady, Feb. 1, 1958. Acting chmn. social sci. dept. St. Walbarga's Acad., Purchase, N.Y., 1953-54; asst. prof. history econs. Rosemont (Pa.) Coll., 1954-57; research fellow U. Pa., Phila., 1957-59; asso. prof. history polit. sci. Marymount Coll., Tarrytown, N.Y., 1960-66; adj. asso. prof. Coll. White Plains (N.Y.), 1963-66, chmn. dept. history and social scis., prof. history and internat. studies, 1966—; adj. asso. prof. Fordham U., summers, 1963-64. Chmn. or adviser confs. on fgn. policy Dept. Def., Dept. Army, U.S. Mil. Acad., 1963—; cons. lectr. internat. affairs; staff tng. cons. Westchester County Dept. Social Services, summer 1970; cons. adult edn. center White Plains Bd. Edn., 1971—. Mem. com. seminars at UN for coll. students, 1956—. Bd. dirs. Monument Com. of White Plains, 1968—. Recipient Gold medal Fordham U., 1952; The Gannon Council of Debate Trophy, 1951-52. N.Y. State Faculty Scholar, 1965-69. Mem. Am. Polit. Sci. Assn., Am. Hist. Assn., Assn. Am. U. Profs., Latin Am. Studies Assn., Am. Geog. Soc., Middle East Inst., Phi Alpha Theta (internat. councillor 1972—). Home: Scarborough Rd Scarborough NY 10510

BRADY, SISTER MARION, librarian; b. Denver, Apr. 5, 1919; d. John Joseph and Esther Marie (Fassett) Brady; B.A., Fontbonne Coll., 1953; M.A., Coll. St. Catherine, 1959. Tchr., St. Joseph's Inst. for Deaf, St. Louis, 1942-47; tchr. elementary sch. Immaculate Conception Sch., St. Joseph, Mo., 1947-50, Nativity Sch., St. Louis, 1950-52, St. Cecelia Sch., Peoria, Ill., 1952-54, St. Mary's Sch., Peoria, 1954-58; tchr., librarian Reicher High Sch., Waco, Tex., 1958-67; head librarian St. Joseph's Acad., St. Louis, 1967—. Fellow Found. for Econ. Edn., Inc., Irvington-on-Hudson, N.Y., summer 1973. Mem. Am., Cath., Mo. library assns., Greater St. Louis Library Club (vice chmn. 1970-72). Address: 2307 S Lindbergh Blvd St Louis MO 63131

BRADY, MARY LAURA (MRS. ROBERT J. O'BRIEN), educator; b. N.Y.C., Mar. 28, 1912; d. Dr. Joseph A. and Anna Eva (Wagner) Brady; A.B., Coll. Mt. St. Vincent, 1933; Ph.D., Fordham U., 1945; m. Robert J. O'Brien, July 16, 1962. Instr. math. Coll. Mt. St. Vincent, Riverdale, N.Y., 1935-45, asst. prof. philosophy, 1945-55, chmn. dept. 1968-71, prof. philosophy, 1970—; mem. evening faculty Hunter Coll., also mem. summer faculty Bklyn. Coll., 1944-49. Recipient Tchr. of Year award Mt. St. Vincent Coll., 1967. Mem. Am. Assn. U. Profs., Am. Philos. Assn., Metaphys. Soc., Am. Cath. Philos. Assn., N.Y. Round Table Philosophers, Existential Phenomenology Assn. Home: 525 W 238th St Bronx NY 10463 Office: College Mount St Vincent Riverdale NY 10471

BRAESSLER, ROBERTA PIPER, advt. co. exec.; b. Cleve., Jan. 17, 1940; d. Robert and Katherine (Eisenmann) Piper; student Dyke Coll., 1958-59, 61, Fenn Coll., 1960. Pub. relations sec. Bayless-Kerr Advt. Co., Cleve., 1961-66; sec. Clevite Corp., Cleve., 1967; exec. sec. Med. Mut. of Cleve., Inc., pres., 1968-69; account exec. Carr Liggett Advt. Inc., Cleve., 1971—, also traffic mgr., 1969-70. Home: 1701-F 12th St Cleveland OH 44114 Office: 815 Superior Av NE Cleveland OH 44114

BRAFF, RHODA ADRIAN (MRS. GEORGE BRAFF), psychologist; b. N.Y.C., Oct. 3, 1944; d. Henry L. and Lillian (Rosenshein) Ruderman; B.A. cum laude, Cornell U., 1965; M.A. in Ednl. Psychology (Anderson fellow 1965-72), N.Y. U., 1967, Ph.D., 1972; m. George Braff, July 23, 1967. Psychologist Escuela Hispana Nursery Sch., N.Y.C., 1967-68, Bur. of Child Guidance, N.Y.C., 1968-69, Highland Park (Mich.) pub. schs., 1969-71, Garden City (N.Y.) pub. schs., 1971—. Certified psychotherapist, N.Y. Recipient Brian Tomlinson Meml. award, 1971. Mem. Am. Psychol. Assn., Assn. for the Advancement of Psychology, Psi Chi. Home: Great Neck NY

BRAGG, NANCY ANN ALDEN, lawyer; b. Des Moines, Oct. 3, 1942; d. Frederick George and Esther Mildred (Patterson) Alden; B.A., State U. Ia., 1964, M.A., 1965; J.D., U. Colo., 1968; m. Douglas Earl Bragg, Dec. 24, 1966 (div.); 1 dau., Ann Michelle. Admitted to Ia. bar, 1968, Colo. bar, 1969; atty. Ia. Civil Rights Commn., Des Moines, 1968-69, Colo. Civil Rights Comn., Denver, 1969-72; trial atty. Denver Litigation Center, Equal Employment Opportunity Commn., 1973—. Mem. Ia. Bar Assn., Am. Assn Women Lawyers, Phi Beta Kappa. Home: 2453 Briarwood Dr Boulder CO 80303 Office: 1531 Stout St Denver CO 80202

BRAINARD, EDITH MAE, ret. librarian; b. Guthrie County, Ia.; d. Charles W. and Henrietta (Martin) Brainard; B.A., U. Ia., 1927, M.A., 1928; B.S., U. Minn., 1932; U. Chgo. Library Sch., 1944-45. Tchr. high sch. and jr. coll., St. Johns, Ariz;, Waukon, Ia., 1928-31; librarian Eldora (Ia.) Pub. Library, 1933-36, Southwestern Coll., 1936-42, Itasca Jr. Coll., 1942-43, Gustavus Adolphus Coll., 1943-44, Ill. Wesleyan U., 1945-47, James Millikin U., 1947-51; asst. librarian Portland (Ore.) State Extension Center, 1951-52; head circulation and reference John McIntire Library. Zanesville, O., 1952-53; head librarian McKinley Meml. Library, Niles, O., 1953-69. Lectr. U. Minn. Library Sch., summers 1937-42. Mem. Niles Mayor's Com. on Comic Books; mem. Niles Council Girl Scouts U.S.A., 1964. Mem. Am., Ohio, Kan., (past pres.) library assns., Bus. and Profl. Women's Club (past pres. Eldora, Niles 1959-60). Conglist. Club: Trumbull Toastmistress (v.p.). Contbr. articles profl. and ednl. jours. Home: 333 W Park Av Niles OH 44446

BRAINARD, JAYNE DAWSON (MRS. ERNEST SCOTT BRAINARD), civic worker; b. Amarillo, Tex., Nov. 1; d. Bill Cross and Evelyn (McLane) Dawson; A.B., Oklahoma City U., 1950; m. Ernest Scott Brainard, Nov. 26, 1950; children—Sydney Jane, Bill Dawson. Guardian, Camp Fire Assn., 1960—; vol. Northwest Tex. Hosp. Aux., 1960-63; state chmn. Am. Heritage, D.A.R., 1963-67, regent chpt. 1966-67, state historian, state chmn. marshalls, 1967-70, 73—, mem. state organizing com., 1967-70, nat. vice chmn. marshalls, 1969—, state rec. sec., 1970-73, editor cookbook 1972, nat. vice chmn. motion picture com., 1971—, mem. Tex. speakers staff, 1972—, state chmn. state regents project, 1973—, mem. state by law com., pres. chpt. regents Club, 1973-74, organizing pres. Children Am. Revolution, 1963-65; organizing regent Daus. Am. Colonies, 1972; pub. relations Amarillo Little Theater, 1965-69, pres., 1968-69, dir., 1966-69; bd. mem., program com. chmn. Amarillo Camp Fire Council, 1965-67; chmn. Camp Fire Leaders Assn., 1964-65; br. pres. Am. Assn. U. Women, 1963-65, pub. relations, 1965-67, world affairs rep., 1965-67; sec.-treas. group League Democratic Women, 1964; pres. Panhandle Geol. Soc. Aux., 1959, Starlighters Dance Club, 1963-64; pres. Speaking of Living Study Club, 1962-63, sec., 1973-74; pres. Republican Womans Club, 1968, 73, v.p., 1972; steering com. Nat. Library Week, 1966, 67, 68, Amarillo Chischom Trail Centennial, 1967; mem. Revitalize Amarillo Com., 1972, Amarillo Heart Bd., 1972-73, Historic Markers Task Force. Mem. Internat. Platform Assn., U.D.C. (rep. to Amarillo Geneal. adv. bd. 1973-74). Mem. Christian Ch. (bd. parliament 1965-66). Home: 2119 S Lipscomb St Amarillo TX 79109 Office: Box 1101 Amarillo TX 79105

BRAITHWAITE, MARY ANNE KNUTH (MRS. DALE EDWARD BRAITHWAITE), librarian; b. Pitts., July 7, 1936; d. John George and Ethel Ann (Lemak) Knuth; B.S., Chatham Coll., 1958; M.L.S., U. Pitts., 1967; m. Dale Edward Braithwaite, Mar. 18, 1964; children—Jeanine Ann, Dale George. Jr. engr. Westinghouse Research Center, Pitts., 1958-59; research asst. Pa. State U., State College, 1960-61; acting librarian PPG Industries, Glass Research Center, Pitts., 1962-64, free-lance librarian, information systems developer, 1967-73; cons. Westinghouse Research Center Library, Pitts., 1973—. Library chmn. Berkeley Hills Parents Assn., 1965-70; sec. AWARE Citizan's Group, 1971-72; mem. ednl. council North Hills Sch. Dist., 1970-73, mem. community adv. council, 1973-74, publicity chmn. sch. bd. election, 1973. Mem. Spl. Libraries Assn., Beta Phi Mu, Pi Sigma Alpha. Republican. Roman Catholic (mem. steering com. ch. council 1969-70). Home: 441 Woodland Rd Pittsburgh PA 15237 Office: Westinghouse Research Center Library Beulah Rd Pittsburgh PA 15235

BRAKEFIELD, LUCY ANN BORDERS (MRS. JACK BRAKEFIELD), univ. dean; b. Carrollton, Ga., Dec. 10, 1937; d. William Emmett and Katie Ruth (Hilley) Borders; student Mercer U., 1956-58; B.A., Miss. Coll., 1959-62; m. Jack Brakefield, Nov. 26, 1970. Social worker Buckner Bapt. Benevolences, Dallas, 1965-67, Crittenton Services, Houston, 1967-70; faculty, dean of women Okla. Bapt. U., Shawnee, 1970—. Democrat. Home: 737 W University Shawnee OK 74801

BRAKONECKE, HELEN ELIZABETH (MRS. EDWARD STANLEY BRAKONECKE), prodn. analyst, state ofcl.; b. Nile, O., Mar. 2, 1931; d. Joseph N. and Elizabeth (Kovacs) Kuhn; student Am. Inst. Banking, 1962; m. Edward Stanley Brakonecke, Nov. 5, 1949; children—Patricia Ed (Mrs. Tim Thompson), Sandra Marie (Mrs. Thomas Babcock). Adminstr. asst. So. Wayne County C. of C., Wyandotte, Mich., 1969, 70-71; prodn. analyst Prodn. Finishing Corp., Wyandotte, 1971—. Commr., Mich. State Crippled Children's Commn., 1965—; mem. Mrs. Mich. Panel for Consumer Affairs, 1965-67; hon. chmn. Wayne Assn. Retarded Children, 1965-66. Chmn. or co-chmn. Torch drive, 1964-65, Mother's March on Polio, 1963-64, Muscular Dystrophy, 1962-63, Cancer Found., 1964-65. Precinct del. Republican Party, 1963—; bd. dirs. Trenton Republican Club, 1968—; candidate State Rep., 1966. Named Mrs. Mich., 1965-66. Mem. League of Women Voters. Moose. Home: 5037 Argonne Blvd Trenton MI 48183 Office: 4261 13th St Wyandotte MI 48192

BRALEY, JESSIE ELLEN MCAULAY, auditor; b. Upton, Wyo., July 23, 1927; d. Raymond Paul and Maggie Sophia (George) McAulay; student U. Wyo., 1945-47, Colo. Sch. Banking, 1969, 70, 71; diploma Grad. Sch. Banking, 1971; m. Earl W. Braley, Oct. 14, 1956 (dec. July 1967). Teller, sec. Union State Bank, Upton, 1947-56; office receptionist Gillette, Wyo., 1956-57; with Stockmens Bank, Gillette, 1958—, auditor, 1971—. Active fund drives March of Dimes, Heart Fund. Recipient state citation Wyo. Heart Fund, 1971. Mem. Bus. and Profl. Women's Club (2nd v.p. 1972, pres. 1973-74), Wyo. Bank Adminstrs. Inst. Presbyn. (sec. 1969—). Mem. Order Eastern Star (sec. 1972—), Daus. of Nile. Home: Box 234 Gillette WY 82716 Office: Box 720 Gillette WY 82716

BRAM, MARJORIE, orch. condr., educator, author; b. Phila., June 28, 1919; B.S., Temple U., 1940; student Juilliard Sch. Music, summer 1945, Tanglewood, 1950; M.A., Columbia, 1951; certificate in conducting Internat. Acad. of Mozarteum, Salzburg, Austria, 1957. Instrumental music South Orange (N.J.)-Maplewood Sch. Dist., 1942—; condr. South Orange Community Orch., 1949-69; founder, mus. dir. Friends Early Music (N.J.) 1964—. 1st desk viola N.J. Symphony Orch., 1945-48; 1st chair viola Am. Symphony Orch. League Workshop for Condrs. and Composers, Asilomar, Cal., 1959, condr., Sewanee, Tenn., 1959. Mem. Am. Symphony Orch. League, Internat. Soc. Music Educators, Music Educators Nat. Conf., Am. String Tchrs. Assn. (coach chamber music Pa. chpt. 1962-63), N.E.A., Brit. Gamba Soc., Viola de Gamba Soc. Am. (dir. 1966-70, pres. 1970—), Am., Brit. recorder socs., Dolmetsch Found. Author: Sound Dimensions for New Players, 1971. Contbr. articles, revs. to periodicals. Home: 332 Vose Av South Orange NJ 07079 Office: 70 N Ridgewood Rd South Orange NJ 07079

BRAM, PAULA LEVINE, med. psychologist; b. Pitts., Jan. 9, 1934; d. Samuel H. and Anne (Klein) Levine; A.B., Antioch Coll., 1956; postgrad. U. N.M., 1958-60; M.S., Med. Coll. Pa., 1970, Ph.D., 1973; m. Harold Bram, Oct. 23, 1955 (div. May 1972); children—Aaron, Adam. Psychologist, Albuquerque Child Guidance Center, 1959-63; psychotherapist Devereux Schs. Found., Devon, Pa., 1964-69; med. psychologist, dept. psychiatry Jefferson Med. Coll., Phila., 1972—; pvt. practice psychotherapy and behavior therapy, Phila., 1972—. Mem. West Chester (Pa.) Human Relations Council, 1967—. Bd. dirs. Sky Found., Phila.; bd. dirs. West Chester YWCA, 1968-70, chmn. human concerns com., 1968-69. Falk Found. fellow, 1969-70; Schweppes Found. grantee, 1971. Mem. Am. Psychol. Assn., Am. Assn. for Advancement of Behavior Therapy, Assn. for Behavior Therapy and Exptl. Psychiatry, Biofeedback Research Soc. Home 402 W Barnard St West Chester PA 19380

BRAMBLETT, VIANNA DIZMANG, educator; b. Xenia, Kan., Dec. 8, 1908; d. John Kirk and Carrie B. (Hammons) Dizmang; B.S. in Home Econs., Kan. State U., 1929; M.S., Purdue U., 1933; postgrad. U. Mo., 1933-34; m. Ardrey Marvin Bramblett, Aug. 3, 1935; 1 son, James Kirk. Tchr. pub. high sch., Linwood, Kan., 1929-31; instr. Purdue U., 1931-33; supr. home econs. consol. schs., Wamego, Kan., 1934-36; food lectr. ednl. dept. Ball Bros. Co., Muncie, Ind., 1934-43; instr. Pratt Inst., Bklyn., 1937-40; supr. test kitchen Eastern Coop Wholesale, Bklyn., 1938-40; nutrition cons. radio sta. WLW, Cin., 1943-46, Nat. Aluminum Mfg. Co., Peoria, Ill., 1950-56; faculty Purdue U., West Lafayette, Ind., 1956—, now prof. food and nutrition. Mem. Am. Assn. U. Profs., Am. Meat Sci. Assn., Am. Soc. Animal Sci., Am. Assn. U. Women, A.A.A.S., Am. Home Econs. Assn., Inst. Food Technologists, Internat. Platform Assn., Sigma Xi, Omicron Nu, Iota Sigma, Sigma Delta Epsilon, Zeta Tau Alpha, Gamma Sigma Delta, Phi Tau Sigma. Methodist. Mem. Order Eastern Star, Rebekahs. Home: 2107 Fairway Lane West Lafayette IN 47906

BRAMHALL, JANET NATALIE, statis. analyst; b. Washington, Dec. 19, 1931; d. William Archibald and Gertrude Mary (Potzler) Bramhall; student Villanova Coll., 1949-51, Dunbarton Coll. of the Holy Cross, 1953-54; A.A., George Washington U., 1958, B.S., 1962. Tchr., elementary sch., N.J., 1951-52, Pa., 1952-53, Washington, 1953-54; sec. Aeronautical Radio, Inc., Washington, 1954-57; tchr. pub. schs. Md., 1957-58; sr. mathematician Applied Physics Lab., Johns Hopkins, Silver Spring, Md., 1959—, dir. med. computing center Johns Hopkins Med. Insts., Balt., 1963-64. Mem. Inst. Math. Statistics, Am. Statis. Assn. Contbr. articles to profl. jours. Home: 4600 29th St Mount Rainier MD 20822 Office: 8621 Georgia Av Silver Spring MD 20910

BRAMLETTE, SELMA GEORGIA MITCHELL (MRS. JAMES D. BRAMLETTE), librarian; b. Center Hill, Ark., July 22, 1893; d. Virgil B. and Sarah L. (Adams) Mitchell; B.A., Tex. Coll. Arts and Industries, 1930; B.S., in L.S., Tex. Woman's U., 1946, M.L.S., 1950; m. James D. Bramlette, July 24, 1912 (dec. Oct. 1967); children—Sarah J. (Mrs. C. A. Buenning), James D., Mary Jane (Mrs. W. D. Hughart). Social studies tchr., Stephenville, Tex., 1924, Waco State Home, 1943-46, Sinton, Tex., 1945-46; librarian Sinton (Tex.) High Sch., 1946-49; supr. libraries Sinton Ind. Sch. Dist. 1949-62; librarian Refugio County Pub. Library, Refugio, Tex., 1962—. Recipient certificate of merit Sinton Pub. Schs., 1962. Mem. N.E.A. (life), Tex. Coastal Bend (pres. 1952-53) library assns., Alumni Assn. Tex. Coll. Arts and Industries, Delta Kappa Gamma, Alpha Beta Alpha. (life). Clubs: Sinton Faculty; Century (Stephenville, Tex.). Democrat. Baptist. Home: 214 W Heard St Refugio TX 78377 Office: Commerce St Refugio TX 78377

BRAMLEY, VIVIAN LUCILE, adminstr. disabled persons; b. Wowata, Okla., Jan. 9, 1921; d. Ira Lee and Ruth Truman (Swinney) Bitters; R.N., William Newton Meml. Hosp., Winfield, Kan., 1945-48; B.S. in Nursing, U. Colo., 1952, M.S. in Nursing Sch. Adminstrn., 1967; seminar student U. Cal. at Los Angeles, 1959-63; m. Ralph A. Wakefield, June 10, 1941 (dec. 1945); 1 son, Ralph A.; m. 2d, Frank Burdell Bramley, June 29, 1962. Asso. prof. U. Okla. Sch. Nursing, 1955-56; instr. U. Denver Sch. Nursing, 1957-61; vol. faculty mem. U. Colo.-Western Interstate Commn. Higher Edn. in Nursing, Boulder, 1958-63; dir. inservice tng. dept. State Home and Tng. Sch., Wheat Ridge, Colo., 1961-70; coordinator staff devel. and grants, div. mental retardation Colo. Dept. State Instns., Sherman, 1970—; tchr. leadership practice to grad. nurses in Colo., Wyo. and N.M., 1958—; cons. in field. Mem. Am. Assn. Mental Deficiency, Colo. Assn. Retarded Children, Colo. Assn. Pub. Employees, Am. Nurses Assn. (legislative com. 1971), Nat. League Nursing (bd. dirs. 1971), Am. Assn. U. Profs. Author: Participant's Guide, 1965; A Road to Main Street, 1970. Home: 5909 S Windemere St Littleton CO 80120 Office: 306 State Services Bldg 1525 Sherman St Denver CO 80203

BRANCH, CAROLINE WILBUR (MRS. JOHN WELLS BRANCH), judge; b. Franklin, N.J., Nov. 10, 1911; d. Frederick Petheram and Caroline Frederica (Laick) Wilbur; A.B., N.J. Coll. Women, 1933; J.S.D., Cornell U., 1933; m. John Wells Branch, May 29, 1937. Admitted to N.Y. State bar, 1938, U.S. Dist. Ct. bar, 1939; partner firm Branch, Jefferson, Mort, Friedman & Branch and predecessors, Rochester, N.Y., 1940—; family ct. judge Monroe County, Rochester, 1965—. Vice pres. YWCA, 1960—, Contact, Inc., 1967—. Pres., Women's Republican Club, East Rochester, N.Y., 1950-62. Recipient Helen Jones Civic award. Mem. Am., N.Y. State, Monroe County bar assns., Nat. Assn. Women Lawyers, Family Ct. Judges Assn. Republican. Methodist. Club: Zonta. Author: Blue Book for Jurors, 1945. Home: 68 Green Valley Rd Pittsford NY 14534 Office: Hall of Justice Rochester NY 14614

BRANCH, KAY EILEEN MOORE (MRS. JOHN THOMAS BRANCH), advt. exec.; b. Elkhart, Ind., July 9, 1945; d. Clarence Cecil and Ruby (Clyde) Moore; B.A., Bethel Coll., 1967; m. John Thomas Branch, June 10, 1967. Sr. copywriter WCMR and WXAX radio stas., Elkhart, 1962-68; v.p., dir. Branch Advt. Agy., Elkhart, 1968—. Promotional cons. Progressive Broadcasting System, Elkhart, radio stas. WFWR and WCMX, Fort Wayne, 1969—. Home and office: 4112 Vistula Rd Mishawaka IN 46544

BRANCH, MARJORIE BEATRICE, ednl. adminstr.; b. Chgo., Mar. 31, 1927; d. Foster Raymond and Josephine Beatrice (Statum) Branch; B.A. in Christian Edn., Wheaton Coll., 1955; M.A. in Edn., U. Chgo., 1959; student Northwestern U., 1946-48; postgrad. Chgo. Tchrs. Coll., 1959-61. Instr., Carver Bible Inst., 1955-57; tchr. Chgo Bd. Edn., 1957-66, adminstr. dept. human relations, 1966-72, adminstr. dept. govt. funded programs, 1972-73, prin. Leif Ericson Elementary Sch., 1973—. Instr. community organizing and citizenship tng., 1966-71. Adv. council Met. Comprehensive Health Care Orgn., 1970-71. Bd. dirs. League Women Voters Citizen Information Service, 1966-72, Tri-Community Day Care Center, Chgo., 1973—. Mem. Assn. Adminstrv. Women (dir. Met. Chgo. chpt.), Chgo. Prins. Assn. Mem. Christian Ch. (dir. religious edn. 1969-72). Home: 3021 S Michigan Av Chicago IL 60616 Office: 3600 W 5th Av Chicago IL 60624

BRANCH, OLIVE HARLLEE, librarian; b. Clinton, S.C.; d. James Bennett and Nora (Pryse) Branch; A.B., Converse Coll., 1933; B.A. in L.S., Emory U., 1934. Librarian, La Follette (Tenn.) High Sch., 1934-35, Spartanburg (S.C.) High Sch., 1935-41; cataloging librarian Duke, 1941-42; librarian U.S. Army, Ft. Moultrie, S.C., 1942-45, Europe, 1945-46; bookmobile librarian, Spartanburg, S.C., 1947; asst. circulation librarian U. Tenn., Knoxville, 1948, head order dept., 1949-62, acquisition librarian, 1962—. Mem. A.L.A., Southeastern, Tenn. library assns. Home: 1400 Kenesaw Av Knoxville TN 37919

BRAND, RENEE, psychologist; b. Berlin, Germany; d. Philipp and Henriette (Wolly) Brand; student U. Berlin; Ph.D., U. Basel, 1943; m. Andrew Sommerfield (div.); 1 son, Peter Sommerfield. Came to U.S., 1941, naturalized, 1947. Instr. U.S. Army spl. tng. program Stanford, 1943-44; pvt. practice, specializing in Jungian psychology, Los Angeles, 1945-49, San Francisco, 1949—. Mem. Soc. Jungian Analysts, Internat. Assn. for Analytical Psychology, Am., Western, Cal. psychol. assns. Author: Short Days Ago, 1941; Niemandsland, 1940; Ackermann aus Boehmen, 1934. Contbg. author: Current Trends of Analytical Psychology, 1961; Contact with Jung, 1963. Address: 3435 Clay St San Francisco CA 94118

BRANDENBERG, EDITH CAMILLA ENEMARK (MRS. FERNANDO THEODORE BRANDENBERG), artist; b. Portland, Me.; d. Hans Jacob and Camilla Marie (Molback) Enemark; student Farmington Tchrs. Coll., 1931-33, Guiseppe Trotta Art Sch., Fliegal Art Sch., Art League of L.I. Sch., 1947-51, Hofstra Coll., 1955-56; m. Fernando Theodore Brandenberg, Nov. 9, 1935; children—Theodore Thomas, Robert Roger. One man shows at Little Gallery, Baldwin, N.Y., Drs. Hosp. Gallery, N.Y.C., Hand Gallery, Poughkeepsie, N.Y., Art Depot Gallery, LaGrangeville, N.Y.; Southeast Mus., Brewster, N.Y., 1968, Lathrop Gallery, Pawling, N.Y., IBM Main Gallery, Poughkeepsie, 1969-70, Washington (Conn.) Art Gallery, 1971, Akin Mus. Gallery, Pawling, N.Y., 1972, Annex Gallery, Pawling, N.Y., 1974, St. Francis Gallery, Poughkeepsie, 1973, Bethlehem Gallery, Newburgh, N.Y., 1974; exhibited group shows at Smithsonian Instn., Pen and Brush Art Gallery, N.Y.C., Hofstra Coll. Art Gallery, Nat. Arts Gallery, Cornell U. Art Gallery, Berkshire Gallery, Mass., S.I. Mus., Biltmore Hotel Art Gallery, N.Y. Transp. Bldg., N.Y. State Bldg. World Fair; numerous others; represented in permanent collections at Drs. Hosp., New Milford (Conn.) Hosp., Art Depot Gallery, N.Y., Office Victor Meyer, Geneva, Switzerland, St. Francis Hosp., Poughkeepsie, Pawling Savs. Bank. Tchr., Bayside (N.Y.) Art Studio, 1947-60, Art League of L.I. Sch., 1950-52, Clearview (N.Y.) Art Center, 1954-56, Baldwin Art Gallery, N.Y., 1956-58, Bayside (N.Y.) Evening High Sch., 1957-60, Drs. Hosp. Art Studio, 1959-61, Holiday Hills YMCA Art Center, 1961-68, New Milford Hosp. Galler, Greater N.Y. YMCA, Pawling. Dir. art sect. Flushing Council Womens Orgns., N.Y.C., 1955-57; art dir., lectr., demonstrator Lathrop Meml. Center Art Gallery, Pawling, N.Y., 1968. Mem. ednl. com. Greater N.Y. YMCA, Pawling; mem. Dutchess County Philharmonic Fund Com. Recipient 1st prize awards Art League of L.I., 1950, Queensboro Art Soc., 1953, Queens Nat. League Am. Pen Women, 1954, Kent Art Assn., 1967, 68, Hyde Park Library, 1968, Art Depot Gallery, 1969; named Woman of Yr., YMCA Greater N.Y., 1973-74. many others. Mem. Art League of L.I. (dir. 1951-60, pres. 1953-55), Island Art Guild (founder, pres., dir. 1958-67), Queens Nat. League Am. Penwomen (v.p., dir. 1954-55), Dutchess County Art Assn. (dir. and v.p. 1967-69), Dutchess County Art Council Art Depot Guild of Artists (dir. 1967, pres. 1969-70), Nat. Art League (past pres., dir.), Nat. Council Arts and Govt. (asso.), Kent (Conn.) Art Assn. (mem. jury, dir., mem. arts com.), Am. Artists Profl. League, Art League Hudson Valley (pres. 1971-74). Clubs: Pawling Garden; Bayside Mothers (sec., v.p. 1947-49). Home: 134 E Main St Pawling NY 12564 Office: 41-25 Bell Blvd Bayside NY 11361

BRANDENBURG, DOROTHY BERNINGHAUS (MRS. JOHN BRANDENBURG), civic worker; b. St. Louis, July 8, 1902; d. Oscar Edmund and Emilia (Miller) Berninghaus; A.B., Washington U., St. Louis, 1925; m. John Peter Brandenburg, Aug. 27, 1927; 1 dau., Barbara (Mrs. John M. Brenner). Dir. First State Bank Taos, (N.M.), 1940-72. Pres. N.M. Congress Parents and Tchrs., 1958-60; active numerous civic and charitable actiVities. Bd. dirs. Opera Assn. N.M., 1966—, Harwood Found. U. N.M.; bd. regents U. N.M., 1960-64, now mem. pub. adv. council; mem. adv. bd. Albuquerque Symphony. Mem. Delta Gamma. Republican. Presbyn. Home: PO Box 857 Valdez Rd Taos NM 87571

BRANDES, ANNETTE THERRIEN, educator; b. Cokato, Minn., Nov. 6, 1940; d. Frederick George and Geneva Orcella (Therrien) Brandes; B.S., U. Minn., 1962, M.A., 1967; postgrad. Ariz. State U., 1969, U. Chgo., 1974—. Tchr. phys. edn. Meml. High Sch., Eau Claire, Wis., 1962-64; phys. edn. specialist Stillwater (Minn.) Schs., 1964-66; counselor Centennial High Sch., Circle Pines, Minn., 1966-68, St. Louis Park (Minn.) Schs., 1968-69; dir. counseling Rhein-Main Am. Schs., Frankfurt, West Germany, 1969-71; asst. dean of women Westminster Coll., Salt Lake City, 1971-72; head counselor, instr. dept. psychology St. Scholastica Coll., Duluth, Minn., 1972-74. Cons. edn. and human relations, Duluth. Leader, Girl Scouts U.S.A., Duluth, 1972-74. Mem. Nat. Assn. Women Deans, Adminstrs. and Counselors, Am. Assn. Univ. Adminstrs., Am. Assn. Univ. Profs. Club: Zonta International (Duluth). Home: 629 Martin Rd Duluth MN 55803

BRANDINGER, ALICE (MRS. JAY JEROME BRANDINGER), educator; b. N.Y.C., Nov. 23, 1929; d. Max M. and Lydia J. (Schwartz) Levite; B.A., Hunter Coll., 1949; M.A., Trenton (N.J.) State Coll., 1963; Ed.D., Rutgers U., 1970; m. Jay Jerome Brandinger, Dec. 25, 1949; children—Paul, Norman, Donna. Tchr. reading N.J. Sch. for Deaf, Trenton, 1963-66; reading specialist Cranbury (N.J.) Sch., 1966-67; prof. in spl. edn. Trenton State Coll., 1967—, chairperson, 1974—. Cons. to various schs., 1966—. Mem. Internat. Reading Assn., Assn. Children with Learning Disabilities, Am. Assn. Univ. Profs., N.J., Nat. edn. assns. Editor: A Candle in the Mist (F. Means), 1968. Home: 19 Carnation Place Trenton NJ 08638 Office: Trenton State College NJ 08625

BRANDON, ELIZABETH KAPLAN (MRS. SYLVAN BRANDON), educator; b. Volkovysk, Poland, Oct. 18, 1913; d. Samuel and Chasia (Salman) Kaplan; came to U.S., 1939, naturalized, 1944; Magister Philosphiae in French, U. Warsaw, Poland, 1936; diploma U. Paris, 1938; Ph.D., Laval U., 1955; m. Sylvan Brandon, Sept. 8, 1935; children—Anne, Michael. Substitute tchr. Alliance Francaise de Paris, 1938-39; instr. U. Houston, 1947-50, asst. prof., 1950-55, asso. prof., 1955-61, prof., 1961—, head dept. French, 1956-69; cons. Houston Ind. Sch. Dist., Spring Branch Sch. Dist. Recipient Honorary Citizenship Abbeville, La., 1954, teaching Excellence award U. Houston, 1967-68; decorated chevalier des Palmes Academiques French Ministry Edn., 1960; U. Houston Research Found. grantee, 1965, 67. Mem. Internat. Folk-Narrative Research Orgn. (charter), Internat. Folk Music Council, Societe Internat. de Linguistique Appliquee, Am. Assn. U. Profs., Am. Assn. Tchrs. French, Modern Lang. Assn., Am. Council Tchrs. Fgn. Langs., South Central Modern Lang. Assn., Tex. Assn. Coll. Tchrs., Tex. Fgn. Lang. Assn., Tex. Edn. Agy., Tex., La. folklore socs., Houston Area Tchrs. Fgn. Langs., Alliance Francaise de Houston, U. Houston Faculty Assn., Pi Delta Phi, Sigma Delta Pi, Phi Kappa Phi. Home: 2330 Maroneal St Houston TX 77025

BRANDON, PHYLLIS DILLAHA (MRS. JAMES WILLIAM BRANDON), county ofcl.; b. Little Rock, July 31, 1935; d. Calvin Arthur and Vera (Burt) Dillaha; B.A., U. Ark., 1957; m. James William Brandon, Nov. 30, 1957; children—James Alexander, Philip Dillaha. Reporter, Ark. Democrat, 1957; asst. food and home editor Ark. Gazette, 1958-60; election commr., Pulaski County, Ark., 1970—. Host, TV show on gardening KARK-TV, 1970. Pres., Brady Sch. P.T.A., 1971, Little Rock P.T.A. Council, 1973. Del., Democratic Nat. Conv., 1968, 72; mem. Dem. Com. Pulaski County, Ark., 1968-74. Mem. Ark. Women's Polit. Caucus, Kappa Kappa Gamma. Episcopalian (pres. ch. women 1974—). Club: Garden (pres. 1970) (Little Rock). Home: 14 Wingfield Circle Little Rock AR 72205

BRANDT, DOROTHEA EDNA (MRS. GUNNAR NELSON), composer; b. Frewsburg, N.Y.; d. Samuel Otis and Hannah Erica (Venman) Brandt; pvt. studies in piano, organ, composition; m. Gunnar Nelson, May 7, 1930; 1 son, Robert Brandt. Tchr. piano McLagan Sch., Yakima, Wash., 1925-29; pvt. piano tchr., Washington, 1918-29, Cal., 1930—. Mem. Nat. League Am. Pen Women, Musicians' Club Pomona Valley. Composer: Wagon Train 1954; Japanese Print, 1955; Zapateado, 1955: Dancing Japanese Marionettes, 1960; Little Donkey In the Snow, 1964; Chinese Woodcutter, 1964; Christmas Anthem The Star, 1967; Arietta, 1968; Calico Mountain Trail in Sparklers, 1968; anthem-Jesus Abides In My Heart, 1973; As I Kneel to Pray, 1973. Home and office: 2934 N Towne Av Claremont CA 91711

BRANDT, IRENE M., assn. adminstr.; b. Burlington, Ia.; d. Roy W. and Gladys L. Brandt; B.S., U. Ia., 1957; M.S. in Bus. Mgmt., George Washington U., 1972. Asst. govt. relations Eli Lilly & Co., Washington, 1957-62, dir. govt. relations, Washington, 1964—; legislative case worker Jack Miller, U.S. senator, Washington, 1962-64. Instr. Strayer Coll., Washington, 1966-69. Chmn. volunteers, St. Elizabeth's Hosp., 1963-65. Mem. Pub. Relations Soc. Am., Nat. Women's Polit. Caucus, U.S. Senate Staff Club, Nat. Fedn. Press Women, Iowans of Washington Area (pres. 1971), U. Ia. Alumni Club (pres. met. Washington chpt. 1973-74). Home: 1900 S Eads Arlington VA 22202 Office: Eli Lilly and Co 1030 15th St NW Washington DC 20005

BRANDT, JANET CORRINE (MRS. CHARLES LYNN BRANDT), home economist; b. Park Falls, Wis., Feb. 3, 1946; d. Adolph Frank and Irene Louise (Kapustka) Slanovich; B.S., Stout State U., 1968; m. Charles Lynn Brandt, Aug. 24, 1968; children—David Lynn, Jonathan Lynn. Tchr. home econs. West Bend (Wis.) High Sch., 1968; substitute tchr. Clovis (N.M.) High Sch., 1968-69; extension home economist Sawyer County, Hayward, Wis., 1969—. Recipient award Am. Legion. Mem. N.E.A., Am., Wis. home econ. assns., Nat., Wis. home econ. educators, Wis., Nat. assns. extension home economists, Phi Upsilon Omicron, Alpha Omicron Pi. Home: Route 1 Hayward WI 54843 Office: Box 486 Hayward WI 54743

BRANDT, KANDY BETH, librarian; b. Madison, Wis., Sept. 4, 1944; d. Uclair William and Beth Virginia (Wiedenhoeft) Brandt; student Beloit Coll., 1962-63; B.S., U. Wis., 1970, M.L.S., 1971. Asst. librarian Madison (Wis.) Pub. Library, 1967-71, librarian, 1971-72, audiovisual librarian, 1972—, editor staff newspaper, 1969-73. Home: 4715 Sheboygan Av Madison WI 53705 Office: 201 W Mifflin St Madison WI 53703

BRANDT, LINDA SUZANNE, food co. exec.; b. Indpls., June 28, 1940; d. Ralph Samuel and Mariamelia (Schmidt) Brandt; B.A., Butler U., 1962; M.A., U. Wis., 1968. Reporter, Ill. State Jour.-Register, Springfield, 1962-63; publs. dir. Crown Point (Ind.) Pub. Schs., 1964-65; tchr. Proviso East High Sch., Maywood, Ill., 1966-67; dir. pub. relations Peavey Co., Mpls., 1968—. Mem. information task force Mpls. Urban Coalition, 1969; tutor Indian Upward-Bound, 1973. Mem. Pub. Relations Soc. Am., Women in Communication--Nat. Task Force for Long Range Devel. (pres. Minn. 1971-72), Minn. Arboretum, Walker Art Center, Minn. Zool. Soc., Internat. Assn. Bus. Communicators (sec. Minn. 1970, dir. 1971), Delta Delta Delta. Club: Minn. Press. Home: 15406 Abbott Pl Edina MN 55410 Office: 730 E 2d Av S Minneapolis MN 55402

BRANDT, MARY ATLEE, occupational therapist; b. White Plains, N.Y., Oct. 17, 1919; d. Porter Falconer and Harriet Delarue (Kipling) Atlee; B.A., Wellesley Coll., 1941; certificate occupational therapy Columbia, 1943; m. William Reed Brandt, Mar. 7, 1944; children—Harriet A., Margaret C., Sarah R. Dir. occupational therapy N.Y. Orthopaedic Hosp. (now Columbia Presbyn. Med. Center), N.Y.C., 1944-50; cons. Park View Health Center, Winnebago, Wis., 1971-72, dir. occupational center, 1971—. Plan commr. City of Ripon, sec., chmn. zoning com., 1965-73; mem. Ripon Pub. Library Bldg. Com., 1969-73; mem. Ripon dr. recruitment (DOC) com., 1970—. Recipient Distinguished Service award Ripon Jaycees, 1969. Mem. Am., Wis. occupational therapy assns., League Women Voters, UN Assn., Wis. Fedn. Handweavers, Arthritis Found. Wis. Home: 234 Elm St Ripon WI 54971 Office: Park View Health Center Winnebago WI 54981

BRANDT, RUTH ANNE WAGNER (MRS. HERBERT W. BRANDT), bus. exec., civic worker; b. Sandusky, O., June 6, 1923; d. Clarence E. and Anna (Kopp) Wagner; B.S., Seton Hill Coll., 1945; M.S., Case Western Res. U., 1970; m. Herbert W. Brandt, Aug. 12, 1952; 1 dau., Martha Ann. Dietetic Intern Univ. Hosps., Cleve., 1946, clinic dietitian, 1946-49; clinic dietitian Henry Ford Hosp., Detroit, 1949-51; chief nutrition clinic VA Regional Office, Cleve., 1951-53; owner Branlon Studio, Shaker Heights, O., 1953—; adj. instr. Case Western Res. U., 1970—; dir. Mayfair Mgmt., Inc., Sandusky, O.; sec., dir. Stellen, Inc., Sandusky; dir. Wagner Realty Co., Sandusky. Nutrition cons. Golden Age Center Cleve., 1956-59, bd. dirs., 1958-59; puppet workshop chmn. Jr. League, 1959-60; bd. dirs., mem. women's com. Cleve. Inst. Music, 1967—; mem. women's com. Natural Sci. Mus., 1965-70, Shaker Lakes Regional Nature Center, 1968-70; chmn. adv. bd. Community Nutrition Service, 1973—; trustee Cleve. Health Mus. and Edn. Center, 1973—. Mem. Am., Cleve. (pres. 1954-55) dietetic assns., Council on World Affairs (internat. student housing com. 1961-63). Clubs: Cleveland Skating, Cleveland Playhouse, Junior League Garden (Cleve.). Home: 2626 West Park Blvd Shaker Heights OH 44120 Office: Dept Nutrition 2121 Abington Rd Cleveland OH 44106

BRANDWYNNE, JACQUELINE BALBINA, advt. agy. exec.; b. Bienne, Switzerland, 1937; diploma in Liberal Arts, Hochere Toechterschule der Stadt Zurich, 1955; postgrad. New Sch. Social Sci., 1958-60. Reporter, Annabelle & Die Weltwoche, Zurich, 1955-58; pub., asst. editor-in-chief Alfred A. Knopf, N.Y.C., 1958-60; dir. internat. promotions Helena Rubinstein, Inc., N.Y., 1960-62; free lance writer contbr. Vogue, Harpers Bazaar, Cosmopolitan mag., 1960—; v.p., creative dir. Yardley London Inc., N.Y.C., 1964-69; pres., chief exec. Brandwynne, Burr. Giordano Advt., Inc., N.Y.C., 1969—. Mem. White House Adv. Com. on Econ. Role of Women, 1972. Recipient Advt. and Poetry awards. Mem. Fashion Group,

Child Study Assn./Wel-Met. Home: 8 E 83d St New York City NY 10022 Office: Brandwynne Burr Giordano Advt Inc 620 Fifth Av New York City NY 10020

BRANHAM, JANET LILLIAN, editor; b. Grundy County, Mo., Jan. 10, 1910; d. Robert E. and Addie Grove (Fleshman) Craig; student Central Bus. Coll., Kansas City, Mo., 1929, Emily Griffith Sch., Denver, 1940, Am. U., 1943; m. Adam Branham, June 20, 1931; 1 son, Donald. Clk.-typist, Pentagon, Washington, 1941-43; reporter Trenton (Mo.) Republican-Times, 1946-49, editor, 1949—. Mem. Friends of Arts Council. Named Mo. press Woman of Year, 1974. Mem. Nat. Fedn. Press Woman, Mo. Press Women's Assn. (pres. 1967-69). Republican. Baptist. Author: Bret Harte: Young Storyteller, 1969. Contbr. articles to mags. Home: 715 Main St Trenton MO 64683 Office: 122 E 8th St Trenton MO 64683

BRANIN, JEANNETTE WELLMAN (MRS. PATRICK IRVING BRANIN), journalist; b. Sterling, Kan., May 11, 1909; d. Edward Chauncey and Jessica (Coyle) Wellman; student Sterling Coll., 1925-27; B.A., U. Kan., 1929; m. Patrick Irving Branin, May 1, 1947; 1 son, Patrick Coyle. Publicity dir. Red Cross Blood Donor Service, San Diego, 1943-45; mgr. publicity dept. San Diego C. of C., 1945-47; co-owner, mgr. Branin Advt. Agy., San Diego, 1947-53; womens editor San Diego Ind., 1953-68; club editor San Diego Union, 1968—; producer, hostess weekly radio program Spanish Town, 1945-47; producer, hostess daily TV Ind. Woman, 1955-57; TV news commentator, 1957-58. Bd. dirs. San Diego Soc. for Crippled Children, Childrens Hosp. Recipient numerous awards for excellence in writing Cal. Press Women and Nat. Fedn. Press Women, 1964—. Mem. Mortar Bd., Chi Omega, Theta Sigma Phi, Sigma Delta Chi. Home: 4957 Pacifica Dr San Diego CA 92109 Office: 350 Camino de la Reina San Diego CA 92112

BRANNAN, LINDA LEE MYERS (MRS. DAVID A. BRANNAN), librarian; b. Wilmington, Del., Aug. 26, 1940; d. Ward Ralston and Beulah Evelyn (Thomas) Myers; B.A., Coll. Wooster, 1962; M.S. in L.S., Drexel U., 1963; m. David A. Brannan, Jan. 9, 1971. Research librarian Tech. Library, DuPont Co., Wilmington, Del., 1963-66, 69-71, circulation librarian, 1971—, br. librarian Newport (Del.) Devel. Lab., 1966-69. Mem. Del. Library Assn., Brandywine Valley Assn., Phi Kappa Phi. Republican. Presbyn. Home: 2513 Teal Rd Wilmington DE 19805 Office: 3145 DuPont Bldg Technical Library DuPont Co Wilmington DE 19898

BRANNAN, PHYLLIS JEANNE, educator; b. Suttons Bay, Mich., Nov. 20, 1935; d. Herman Austin and Elizabeth Lovenia (Fox) Brannan; B.S., Central Mich. U., 1958, M.A., 1966; M.S.T. (Carnegie Found. fellow), U. Chgo., 1969. Tchr. Buchanan Sch., Grand Rapids, Mich., 1958-59, Adams Sch., Pullman, Wash., 1959-60; tchr. Army Schs., Okinawa, 1960-61, Ludwigsburg, Germany, 1961-63; tchr. Sterling Sch., Utica, Mich., 1963-64, Jefferson Sch., DeKalb, Ill., 1964-66, Charlevoix (Mich.) Elementary Sch., 1967-68; reading cons., Washtenaw Intermediate Schs., Ann Arbor, Mich., 1969—. Vis. lectr. Eastern Mich. U., 1969-73. Mem. Internat. Reading Assn., Washtenaw Reading Council (pres. 1973-74), Zonta Club. Home: 1511 Pine Valley Blvd A-18 Ann Arbor MI 48104 Office: 1819 S Wagner Rd Ann Arbor MI 48106

BRANNON, JOAN CAGE (MRS. WILLIAM LOVE BRANNON), banker; b. Sinton, Tex., Oct. 12, 1930; d. James Bailess and Leola (Moss) Cage; student Southwestern U., 1947-48; B.A., U. Tex., 1951; m. William Love Brannon, Oct. 5, 1963; children—William Love, Lea. Legal sec. Shell Oil Co., Corpus Christi, Tex., 1953-56, Am. Petrofina Oil Co., Dallas, 1956-58, Union Oil Co. of Cal., Houston, 1958-63; oil operator Cage Prodn. Co., Taft, Tex., after 1958; adv. dir. First State Bank, Taft; rancher and farmer, nr. Taft and Llano, Tex, 1958—. Home: 11511 Raindrop Dr San Antonio TX 78216 Office: care William Carter 1835 W Hunt St McKinney TX 75609

BRANNON, MARIANNA GREER (MRS. PAUL JONES BRANNON), ednl. editor; b. Woodville, Miss., Oct. 4, 1920; d. Clarence Clifton and Grace (Pope) Greer; student Belhaven Coll., 1938-40; B.A., Kent State U., 1942; m. R. L. Ledbetter, May 10, 1940 (div. Sept. 1950); 1 son, Robert Christian; m. 2d, Paul Jones Brannon, May 30, 1952; 1 step-son, Johnny. Free lance photographer and darkroom technician, 1944-46; continuity writer, traffic mgr. Radio Sta. WRBC, Jackson, Miss., 1947-59; mng. editor Miss. Ednl. Advance, Jackson, 1951—. Recipient Nat. Safety Council award, 1959; 1st pl. awards for best mag. Miss. Press Women, 1962-69, 71, 72, 73; 3d pl. award for best mag. Nat. Fedn. Press Women, 1968, 1st pl., 1969; Excellence award Indsl. Editors Assn. Miss., 1966; two All-Am. awards Ednl. Press Assn. Am., 1969. Mem. Ednl. Press Assn. Am. (regional v.p. 1961), Nat. Fed. Press Women, Indsl. Editors Assn. Miss., Miss. Press Womens Assn., Theta Sigma Phi. Club: Harvard Parents. Home: 2022 Paden St Jackson MS 39204 Office: 219 N President St Jackson MS 39205

BRANSCOM, MARGARET ELLEN, psychiatrist; b. Iola, Kan., Sept. 2, 1920; d. Guy L. and Hazel (Howard) Branscom; A.B., U. So. Cal., 1941; M.A., U. Ia. 1942; M.D., U. So. Cal., 1945; m. Nathan E. Carl, Dec. 26, 1948; children—Lisa M., Scott E. Am. Research fellow U. Ia., 1941; Commonwealth Fund fellow John Hopkins Sch. Medicine, 1946-48; resident psychiatry Henry Phipps Clinic, Johns Hopkins Hosp., 1946-48, Bellevue Hosp., 1948-49; pvt. practice, 1949—; attending staff Encinitas Hosp.; courtesy staff Palomar Meml. Hosp. Mem. Am., Cal., San Diego County med. assns., Am. Bd. Neurology and Psychiatry, Am. Women's Med. Assn., Am. Psychiat. Assn. Office: 360 Santa Fe Dr Encinitas CA 92024

BRANSCOMB, LOUISE, physician; b. Birmingham, Ala., Mar. 25, 1901; d. Lewis Capers and Minnie (McGehee) Branscomb; A.B., Huntingdon Coll., 1921; M.D., Johns Hopkins U., 1928. Intern Women's Hosp. of Md., 1928-29, Phila. Women's Hosp., 1929-30; resident Franklin Square Hosp., 1930-31; practice medicine specializing in gynecology, Birmingham, 1945—; mem. staff. Univ. Hosp., Birmingham Bapt. Med. Center, Birmingham Bapt. Hosp.; asso. prof. U. Ala. Med. Sch., Birmingham, 1944—. Vis. prof. Vellore (South India) Christian Med. Coll., 1944. Mem. Interracial Council Jefferson County, 1951-56, Mayor's Interracial Com., 1963; pres. Jefferson County Mental Health Assn., 1963-64; mem. exec. com., Jefferson County Com. for Econ. Opportunity, 1967—; mem. exec. bd. woman's div. Bd. Missions, United Methodist Ch., World Div., Bd. Missions, Meth. Ch., 1964-72; mem. commn. on status and role women United Meth. Ch., 1972—, commn. to study episcopacy and dist. superintendency, 1972—; bd. dirs. Miles Coll., Birmingham, 1965—, Greater Birmingham Ministries United Methodist Ch., 1969—, Birmingham Crisis Intervention Center, 1969—, Ewha Women's U., Seoul, Korea, 1969-72. Recipient Huntingdon Achievement award Huntingdon Coll., 1941. Diplomate Am. Bd. Obstetrics and Gynecology. Fellow A.C.S.; mem. Am. Coll. Obstetrics and Gynecology, Am. Fertility Soc., A.C.S., A.M.A., Ala. Med. Assn., Jefferson County Med. Soc., Birmingham Soc. Obstetrics and Gynecology. Club: Altrusa. Home: 1225 Greensboro Av Birmingham AL 35208 Office: 944 S 18th St Birmingham AL 35205

BRANSCOMB, MARJORIE BERRY STAFFORD (MRS. LEWIS CAPERS BRANSCOMB, JR.), accountant, mfg. co. exec.; b. Birmingham, Ala., Jan. 13, 1915; d. George T. and Margaret (Berry) Stafford; B.S., U. Ala., 1936; M.S., U. Ill., 1947; postgrad. Ohio State U., 1964; m. Lewis Capers Branscomb, Jr., Jan. 15, 1938; children—Lewis C. III, Ralph Stafford, Carol Jean, Lawrence McGehee. Statis. clk. Gen. Motors Acceptance Corp., Birmingham, 1936-38; asst. regional supr. Bur. Labor Statistics, Atlanta, 1939-40; v.p., dir. Birmingham Mfg. Co., 1955—; treas. Birmingham Totem-All Inc., 1965—. Cons. taxes, accounting problems. Mem. Columbus Gallery Fine Arts, 1956—. Mem. Tri Village Women's Democratic Club, Upper Arlington, O.; Dem. precinct chmn. Mem. Common Cause (activator), UN Assn. (treas. 1965-66, mem. finance com. 1963-66), Alpha Omicron Pi, Democrat. Episcopalian. Clubs: Crichton Columbus, O.; Ohio State University Women's (pres. 1970-71). Home: 3790 Overdale Dr Columbus OH 43220

BRANSCOMBE, GENA (MRS. JOHN FERGUSON TENNEY), composer, condr.; b. Picton, Ont., Can., Nov. 4, 1881; d. Henry W. and Sara (Allison) Branscombe; ed. high sch.; grad. Chgo. Mus. Coll. (gold medalist); studied piano with Rudolph Ganz and Hans von Schiller, composition with Felix Borowski and Prof. Engelbert Humperdinck, in Berlin, conducting with Frank Damrosch, Walter Rothwell, Chalmers Clifton and Albert Stoessel; M.A. (hon.), Whitman Coll., Washington, 1932; m. John Ferguson Tenney, Oct. 1910 (dec.); children—Gena, Vivian Allison, Betty (dec.), Beatrice (dec.). Condr. Branscombe Choral of N.Y., MacDowell Chorus of Mountain Lakes, N.J.; lectr. music, architecture; condr. State Chorus of N.J., 1940-42; condr. first organized Glee Club, Am. Women's Voluntary Services, 1942-44; condr. Contemporary Club Choral, Newark, 1940-45; conducted chorus of 1,000 for festival celebrating 50 years of women's achievements Gen. Fedn. Women's Clubs, Atlantic City, 1941. Nat. chmn. of Am. Music and folksong, Gen. Fedn. Women's Clubs, 1930-35. Mem. MacDowell Colony. Recipient citation for achievement Beta Sigma Phi, 1958; citation Nat. Assn. Am. Composers and Condrs., 1967. Mem. numerous profl. assns. Author texts, lyrics, translations for own music and arrangements. Composer numerous music items, latest being: American Suite for French horn and piano, 1959; Old Woman Rain, Gift at Parting, Across the Blue Aegean Sea, 1960; Arms That Have Sheltered Us (hymn adopted for use by Royal Canadian Navy), 1961, 91st Psalm (for chorus and orch.), 1962, Island Night, Wings, Just in the Hush Before the Dawn (orch.), 1963; orch. work Procession from (orch.) Que. Suite performed N.Y.C., San Francisco, Manila, 1962, Voice of Am. broadcasts, 1965; choral work Prayer for Song performed in Pitts., 1963; orch. manuscripts displayed at N.Y. Pub. Library, 1963; Bridesmaid's Song (for chorus) performed Boston Symphony Pops concert, 1965; The Sun Dial (cycle), Musicians Club of Women, Chgo., 1965; Pilgrims of Destiny (solo voices, chorus and orch.; manuscript, score and parts now in Library of Congress), 1965; Youth of the World (cycle for Women's voices and orch., performed U.S., Can., Eng., Philippines; manuscript, score and parts now in Nat. Library Can., Ottawa); Coventry's Choir (chorus), 1944; A Joyful Litany, 1967; Soldier, Soldier, Come from the Wars (men's chorus), 1969; The Lord is Our Fortress; Introit, Response, Amen for Choir of Riverside Ch., 1973. Published over 150 songs, 60 choral arrangements. Contbr. Showcase mag. Condr. own compositions in U.S., Can. and Europe, 1957. Home: 90 La Salle St New York City NY 10027

BRANSFIELD, ANNE HUNT, educator; b. New Hope, Pa., May 28, 1940; d. Maurice John and Irvina Fawly (Wood) Bransfield; student St. Francis Hosp. Sch. Nursing, Trenton, N.J., 1957-60; B.S. cum laude, Boston Coll., 1964; M.S., Boston U., 1966, D.Nursing Sci., 1969. Head nurse pediatrics Princeton (N.J.) Hosp., 1960-61; pvt. duty intensive care Mass. Gen. Hosp., Boston, 1961-63; pub. health practitioner, Lynn, Mass., 1963-64; mental health counselor Guidance Camps, Inc., Boston, 1965; asso. prof. nursing in child psychiatry Boston U., 1969-70; asso. prof., chmn. mental health nursing State U. N.Y., Stony Brook, L.I. Health Sci. Center, 1970-73, sr. coordinator Coll. Nursing and Health Scis. Center, 1971-72; writer, cons. in community health and research, 1974—. Spl. cons. nursing div. Mass. Dept. Mental Health, 1970-72; research coordinator, Belfast, No. Ireland, summer 1972. Mem. Internat. Platform Assn., Nat. League Nursing, Am. Nurses Assn., Sigma Theta Tau. Contbg. editor Nursing in Child Psychiatry, 1969. Home: 293 S Logan Av Trenton NJ 08629

BRANSON, BARBARA PHYLLIS, pub. co. exec.; b. Chgo., Mar. 28, 1937; d. Joseph Sherol and Ethel (Rauch) Branson; student Northwestern U., 1962-63. Sec., A. Stein & Co., Chgo., 1954-63; copywriter Harrison Wholesale Co., 1965-66, Kay Musical Instruments, Elk Grove Village, Ill., 1966, Howard Sheldon Advt., Niles, 1966-67; copy chief David L. Brody & Assos., comml. art studio, Chgo., 1967; trade advt. mgr. Rand McNally & Co., Skokie, 1967—. Clubs: Copywriter's, Women's Advertising (Chgo). Home: 7943 Oconto St Niles IL 60648 Office: 8255 N Central Park Skokie IL 60076

BRANSON, MARGARET INEZ STIMMANN (MRS. RODNEY B. BRANSON), educator; b. Modesto, Cal., Aug. 7, 1922; d. George August and Dora (Schramm) Stimmann; A.B. with high honors, U. Pacific, 1944; M.A. in edn., U. Cal., 1952; M.A. in history, Coll. of Holy Names, 1962; m. Rodney B. Branson, June 15, 1946; children—Rodney Thomas, Martha Elizabeth (dec.), David George. Tchr., counselor, curriculum asst. Oakland (Cal.) Pub. Schs., 1945-59, vice prin., 1959-64, supr. secondary social scis., 1964-69; asso. prof. Holy Names and Mills Coll., 1970—. Spl. lectr. various colls. and univs.; cons. social scis. Civil Rights Inst., U. Cal., 1965-66; spl. cons. to Law in a Free Soc. project, Cal. Dept. Edn. and Cal. State Coll., 1965—; sr. staff Inst. Study Comparative Communisms, U. Cal. at Davis, 1967, 68; participant Nat. Com. Study of History, Amherst Coll., 1965—, Nat. Conf. Fgn. Policy for Educators, U.S. Dept. State, 1966, 67; mem. Cal. Gov.'s Conf. on Edn., 1956; mem. Nat. Task Force To Develop Guidelines for Ednl. Profl. Devel. Act; editorial cons. Ginn & Co., Cal. Almanac, Zenith Books; hon. life mem. P.T.A. Bd dirs. Oakland Mus. Assn., Oakland Symphony Assn. Mem. Nat., Cal. councils social studies, Am. Hist. Assn., Am. Acad. Polit. and Social Sci., League Women Voters (dir. Oakland 1954-56), P.E.O., Pi Lambda Theta, Alpha Delta Kappa, Delta Kappa Gamma, Delta Delta Delta. Lutheran. Club: Zonta (Oakland). Author: American History for Today, 1970; Inquiry Experiences in American History, 1970; (with Evarts Erickson) Urban America, 1970; (with Edward E. France) The Human Side of Afro American History, 1972; (with Roy Calkins and Charles Quigley) The Environment We Live In, 1972; (with June Chapin) Women: the Majority-Minority, 1973; Land of Challenge, 1974. Home: 523 Hampton Rd Piedmont CA 94611 Office: 3900 Mountain Blvd Oakland CA 94619

BRANT, MARGARET G., ednl. adminstr.; b. Davenport, Neb., Sept. 22, 1924; d. Charles Robert and Bessie Louise (Moore) Brant; student Midland Coll., 1943-44; diploma Cal. Hosp. Sch. Nursing, 1949; B.S. in Nursing, U. So. Cal. at Los Angeles, 1949, M.S. in Nursing, 1961. Staff nurse Cal. Hosp., Los Angeles, 1949-54, Hawthorne (Cal.) Community Hosp., 1954-57; operating room supr. Pacific View Hosp., Hermosa Beach, Cal., 1957-58; staff nurse VA Hosp., Los Angeles, 1958-60; instr. Los Angeles City Coll., 1961-62; instr. El Camino (Cal.) Coll, 1962-64, coordinator of nursing, 1964—. Mem. adv. com. health cocupations Los Angeles Trade Tech. Coll., 1969—. Bd. dirs. Los Angeles County Heart Assn., Health Services Ednl. Activity, regional med. programs, Los Angeles. Recipient Merit award Los Angeles County Heart Assn., 1968—. Mem. Western Council on Higher Edn. for Nursing, Cal. Tchrs. Assn., Nat. League for Nursing, Vocational Nurse Educators Assn., Am., Cal. (chmn. ednl. adminstrs. sect. 1969-73, treas. 1973—) nurses assns. Lutheran. Home: 2503 West 115th St Inglewood CA 90303 Office: El Camino Coll Via Torrance El Camino College CA 90506

BRANTL, VIRGINIA MUIR, nurse educator; b. Woodhaven, N.Y., Mar. 20, 1925; d. Charles Justin and Edna Maria (Muir) Brantl; A.B., Albertus Magnus Coll., New Haven, 1945; M.A. in Psychology, Fordham U., 1947; M.Nursing, Yale, 1951; Ph.D. in Human Devel., U. Chgo., 1969. Staff nurse N.Y.-Cornell Med. Center, 1951-52; instr. med.-surg. nursing Yale, 1952-56; asso. prof., chmn. dept. med.-surg. nursing U. Tex., Galveston, 1956-59; lectr. U. Cal. at Los Angeles, 1960-62, 64-66; prof. nursing, asso. chmn. grad. studies U. Rochester (N.Y.), 1968-71; prof. nursing, dir. nursing and nursing edn. Pa. State U., Hershey Med. Center, 1971—; cons. in field. USPHS predoctoral fellow, 1959-60, 62-64; recipient Outstanding Prof. award Asso. Students Orgn. U. Cal. at Los Angeles, 1971; citation Nat. Commn. Study Nursing and Nursing Edn., 1969. Mem. Am. Psychol. Assn., Am. Assn. U. Profs., Am. Nurses Assn., Nat. League Nursing, Am. Med. Anthrop. Assn. Co-author: Readings in Gerontology, 1973. Contbr. articles to profl. jours. Home: 25 Townhouse Briarcrest Gardens Hershey PA 17033

BRANTLEY, ALICE VIRGINIA SINGER (MRS. EDWARD FITZROY BRANTLEY), civic worker; b. Muncie, Ind.; d. Harry Dwight and Dessa (Slater) Singer; student Muncie Conservatory Music, 1912-20, Met. Sch. Music, 1920-22; studied harp with Louise Schelschmidt Koehne, Indpls., 1917-22, Henriette Renie, Paris, France, 1922-26, 50; m. Edward Fitzroy Brantley, Sept. 19, 1956. Concert debut, Paris, 1925; mem. Septuor Renie, 1923-26; concerts in Paris, N.Y.C., Chgo., Ft. Wayne, Indpls., St. Petersburg, Fla, 1920-63; with Alice Singer Trio, St. Petersburg, 1933-56; performed with St. Petersburg Symphony, Jacksonville (Fla.) Symphony, Tampa (Fla.) Philharmonic, Fla. Philharmonic, 1950-66; radio program WSUN, St. Petersburg, 1933. Ambassador, People-to-People Goodwill Mission from St. Petersburg to Europe and Middle East, 1960, to Soviet Union and satellites, 1965; mem. Fla. Art Commn., 1964-67; v.p. Suncoast Goodwill Industries, 1965-69, v.p. Aux. Guild, 1965-66; mem. St. Anthony's Hosp. Guild, 1961—, Children's Home Soc., 1963—, Suncoast Heart Assn., 1966; chmn. Queen of Hearts Ball, St. Petersburg, 1968; Heart Sunday chmn., 1963. Bd. dirs. Pinellas County Mental Health Assn., Mound Park Hosp. Aux., All Children's Hosp. Guild. Recipient Renie Harp award Paris, 1926, citation Radio Sta. WDAE, Tampa, 1965; named Princess of Royal Ct., St. Petersburg Heart Assn., 1963, Queen of Hearts, 1967; Contessa of Year, Fla. Suncoast Opera Guild, 1970. Mem. Fla. Philharmonic Soc. (charter pres. 1954), Chamber Music Soc. (charter pres. 1966-68), Bel Canto (charter 1956), St. Petersburg opera assns., Fla. Art Council (charter 1963), Lions Club Aux. (past pres.), Soroptimist Internat. (pres. St. Petersburg 1962-63), St. Petersburg Hist. Soc., Mus. Fine Arts. Home: 1910 Brightwaters Blvd NE St Petersburg FL 33704

BRANTLEY, ANNABEL MOFFAT, educator; b. Miami, Fla., June 9, 1924; d. Victor Robert and Edith Earle (Moore) Moffat; B.A., Queen's Coll., N.Y., 1948; M.S.W., Fla. State U., 1961; m. Melvin Harry Brantley, Feb. 14, 1950 (div. Sept. 1955); children—Patricia (Mrs. Sam Casey, Jr.), Victoria. Clk. stenographer USN Dept., Key West, Fla., 1941-44, 48-50; tchr. elementary sch. Key West, 1955-59; vis. tchr., sch. social worker, Key West, 1961-66; cons. to Dept. Edn. Tallahassee, 1966—. Mem. adv. bd. Leon County Health Assn., 1971—. Recipient Achievement award Fla. Mental Health Assn., 1966. Mem. Acad. Certified Social Workers, Am. Orthopsychiat. Assn., Nat., Fla. edn. assns., Alpha Delta Kappa. Home: 1237 Halifax Ct Tallahassee FL 32303 Office: Pupil Personnel Sect Div Elementary and Secondary Dept Edn Tallahassee FL 32304

BRAS, SISTER BENVENUTA, educator; b. Mitchell, S.D.; d. Clarence Charles and Katherine (Ward) Bras; B.S., U. Washington at Seattle, 1924; Ph.D., U. Fribourg (Switzerland), 1936. Mem. faculty Rosary Coll., River Forest, Ill., 1935—, prof. French dept., 1948—, chmn. dept., 1949-55, 72—, dir. jr. yr. abroad, Fribourg, Switzerland, 1955-61. Mem. Am. Assn. Tchrs. French, Am. Translators Assn. Writer children's stories in French; contbr. articles to French Review; numerous translations, book reviews to mags. Address: Rosary Coll River Forest IL 60305

BRASSELL, ROSELYN STRAUSS, lawyer; b. Shreveport, La., Feb. 19, 1930; d. Herman Carl and Etelka (McMullan) Strauss; B.A., La. State U., 1949; J.D., U. Cal. at Los Angeles, 1962. Legal sec. Welton P. Mouton, Lafayette, La., 1949-50; office sec. Leake, Henry, Golden & Burrow, Dallas, 1950-57; admitted to Cal. bar, 1963; atty. CBS, Los Angeles, 1962-68, sr. atty., 1968—. Mem. Cal., Los Angeles County (exec. com. 1970—), Beverly Hills bar assns., Los Angeles Copyright Soc., Am. Women in Radio and TV (nat. dir.-at-large 1971-73), Nat. Acad. Television Arts and Scis., U. Cal. Law Alumni Assn. (dir.), Order of Coif, Alpha Xi Delta, Phi Delta Delta. Republican. Bd. editors: U. Cal. Law Rev., 1960-62. Home: 6100 Canterbury Dr Culver City CA 90230 Office: 7800 Beverly Blvd Los Angeles CA 90036

BRASSIL, JEAN ELLA, clin. psychologist; b. New Haven, June 4, 1933; d. Joseph Eugene and Ella Eve (Lindhardt) Brassil; B.S., So. Conn. State Coll., 1955; M.A., Tchrs. Coll., Columbia U., 1958; Ph.D. (USPHS fellow), Adelphi U., 1971. Tchr., North Haven, Conn., 1955-58, 60-62, Caspar, Wyo., 1958-59, Montebello, Cal., 1959-60; sch. psychologist Meriden, Conn., 1962-63, Elmont, N.Y., 1964-66, Belport, N.Y., 1967, Fairfield, Conn., 1973—; clin. psychologist Child Guidance Clinic, Bridgeport, Ct., 1968-74; lectr., Adelphi U., 1966-67; asst. prof. psychology So. Conn. State Coll., New Haven, 1967-68; cons. learning disabilities program Rehab. Center Eastern Fairfield County, Bridgeport, 1970-73. Mem. Am., New Eng., Conn. Psychol. assns. Home: 7 Orangewood W Derby CT 06418 Office: Timothy Dwight Sch Fairfield CT 06430

BRASWELL, EMMA MARGUERETE BOND (MRS. FRANK AMOS BRASWELL), former pipeline co. exec.; b. Atoka, Okla., Aug. 26, 1890; d. Walker Julian and Eva Elizabeth (Conrad) Bond; student Mill's Bus. Coll., Oklahoma City, 1905-06, Oklahoma City Coll., 1906; m. Frank Amos Braswell, Mar. 8, 1922. Office employee, Oklahoma City, 1906-15; employee State of Okla., 1915-17; with Prairie Pipe Line Co., Tulsa, 1917-18; with Service Pipe Line Co. subsidiary Standard Oil Co. (Ind.), Tulsa, 1923-26, chief clk., 1926-46, adminstrv. asst., right of way dept., 1946. Active fund drives United Community Chest; active A.R.C., 1918. Mem. Women's Overseas Service League, Service Pipe Line Alumni. Baptist. Rebekah. Home: 1511 E 36th St Tulsa OK 74105

BRASWELL, JEFF SUTHERLAND ARMSTRONG (MRS. T. EDWARD BRASWELL, JR.), social worker; b. Mpls., June 4, 1928; d. Harry George and Mary (Sutherland) Armstrong; student

Randolph-Macon Womens Coll., 1945-47; B.A., Incarnate Word Coll., 1949; m. T. Edward Braswell, Jr., Dec. 8, 1953; children—John McCauley, Harry Armstrong, Thomas Edward III, Andrew Sutherland. Adminstrv. sec. Inter-Am. Def. Bd., Washington, 1950-51; sec. to dir. legislative liaison Office of Sec. Air Force, Washington, 1951-54; salesman Goddin Real Estate Co., Alexandria, Va., 1958-62; social worker-technician Alexandria (Va.) Dept. Pub. Welfare, 1969—; exec. dir. Va. Assn. for Retarded Children, 1971; cons. for grants and funding Alexandria Pub. Sch., 1972. Vol. researcher Am. Cancer Soc., 1959-64; mem. 10th Dist. Mental Health Study Comm., 1963-64, Alexandria Mental Health Study Commn., 1964; mem. budget com. Met. Area Health and Welfare Council, 1965-66; chmn. city Alexandria Mental Retardation Com., 1963-66; pres. Alexandria Assn. Retarded Children, 1960-62, No. Va. Assn. Retarded Children, 1963-64; mem. Alexandria Hosp. Corp., 1964-66; dir. Sheltered Occupational Workshop No. Va., 1961-64; mem. profl. adv. bd. Va. Hosp. Bd., 1971-73. Bd. dirs. Va. chpt. A.R.C., 1972. Mem. Va. Council Social Welfare, Council Execs. Assns. for Retarded Children, Am. Assn. on Mental Deficiency, Kappa Alpha Theta. Episcopalian. Home: 820 S Washington St Alexandria VA 22314 Office: 110 N Royal St Alexandria VA 22314

BRASWELL, THELMA, ednl. adminstr.; b. Tuskegee, Ala., July 10, 1940; d. Joseph Waldo and Thelma Elizabeth (Baird) Braswell; B.A., Huntingdon Coll., 1962; M.Ed., Auburn U., 1967. Tchr. math. Sidney Lanier High Sch., Montgomery, Ala., 1962-70; dir., tchr. govtl. relations Ala. Edn. Assn., Montgomery, 1970—. Mem. Nat., Ala. edn. assns., Alpha Delta Kappa, Delta Kappa Gamma. Democrat. Methodist. Home: 3535 Carter Hill Rd Montgomery AL 36111 Office: PO Box 4177 Montgomery AL 36101

BRATAAS, NANCY OSBORN, mgmt., data processing cons., state senator; b. Mpls., Jan. 19, 1928; d. John Draper and Flora Losier (Warner) Osborn; student U. Minn., 1945-47; m. Mark Gerald Brataas, Nov. 27, 1948; children—Mark, Anne. Data processing cons. Kan. gubernatorial primary election, 1970; polit. cons. Irwin Mgmt. Co., Columbus, Ind., 1971; dir. nat. telephone campaign Com. for Re-election of Pres., Washington, 1972; pres. Nancy Brataas Assos., planning and mgmt. vol. telephone campaigns, Rochester, Minn., 1973—; planning and mgmt. cons. Mich. Gov.'s Statewide Voter Contact Program, 1974; data processing and mgmt. cons. Northeast chpt. March of Dimes, Cleve., 1974. Founding pres. Olmsted County Republican Workshop, 1957-58; city chmn. Rochester Republican Party, 1957-59; chmn. Olmsted County Rep. Party, 1960-61; vice chmn. Minn. Rep. Party, 1963-69, finance chmn., 1969-71; state chmn. Rep. gubernatorial campaign Minn., 1970; del. Rep. Nat. Conv., 1960, 64, 68, county, dist. and state convs., 1958-70; mem. Minn. senate, 1975—, mem. edn., labor and commerce com., also select com. on nursing homes. Mem. Am. Assn. U. Women (chmn. recent grads. 1953, co-chmn. ways and means com. 1955). Episcopalian (past tchr. ch. sch.). Home: 839 10 1/2 St SW Rochester MN 55901 Office: 113 State Office Bldg St Paul MN 55155

BRATCHER, TWILA LANGDON (MRS. FORD F. BRATCHER), conchologist, malacologist; b. Smoot, Wyo., Nov. 29, 1916; d. Willis G. and Pearl (Graham) Langdon; m. Ford F. Bratcher, Sept. 10, 1942. Research asso. Los Angeles Museum of Natural History, 1965-71; musuem asso. Los Angeles County Museum Natural History, 1972—; mem. Ameripagos Sci. Expedition to Galapagos Islands, 1971; author stories for blind children about skin diving, sea shells, creatures of the sea pub. Braille Inst., 1964-72; work with schs. for blind. Mem. Conchological Club So. Cal. (pres., 1966), Am. Malacological Union (counsilor at large 1971), Western Soc. Malacologists (pres. 1973), Hawaiian Malacological Soc., San Diego Shell Club, Santa Barbara Malacological Soc., Pacific Shell Club. Contbr. articles to sci. jours. Home: 8121 Mulholland Terrace Hollywood CA 90046

BRATEK, DARLENE RUTH BRIGGS, educator; b. Shawnee, Okla., Aug. 2, 1923; d. Frank Parks and Catherine Allen (Shull) Briggs; student Central Mo. Methodist Coll., 1941-42; B.J., U. Mo., 1945, M.A., 1964; m. Joseph Thomas Bratek, Oct. 2, 1947 (div. Mar. 1961); 1 dau., Catherine Joanne. Display advt. rep. St. Joseph (Mo.) News Press & Gazette, 1945-46; advt. and bus. mgr. West Plains (Mo.) Daily and Semi-Weekly Quill, 1947; asst. advt. mgr., Macon (Mo.) Chronicle Herald, 1948-49; mem. faculty U. Mo., Columbia, 1956—; asso. prof. journalism, 1971—; acting advt. dir. Columbia Missourian, 1956—; v.p., dir. Chronicle-Herald Pub. Co., Macon, 1962-72. Mem. Internat. Newspaper Advt. Execs. Assn. Mem. Order Eastern Star. Home: 1401 Marylee Dr Columbia MO 65201

BRATEL, BARBARA RIGGINS, journalist; b. Akron, O., July 22, 1934; d. Claud Howard and Carrie (Poling) Riggins; B.S., Kent State U., 1956; postgrad. Western Res. U., 1958-59, 61. Home service rep. East Ohio Gas Co., Akron and Cleve., 1956-61; regional home economist E.I. DuPont Co., Cleve., 1961-62; regional home economist Mpls. Honeywell, Inc., Cleve., 1962-64; asst. foods editor Cleve. Press, 1964-66, home econs. and foods editor, 1966—. Recipient 1st prize for state ednl. story Am. Heart Assn., 1st prize all categories, 1971. Mem. Am., Ohio home econs. assns., Home Economists in Bus., Ohio Newspaper Womens Assn., Cleve. Art Mus., Garden Center Greater Cleve., Newspaper Food Editors and Writers Assn., Sigma Delta Chi. Home: 1011 Trevitt Circle North Cleveland OH 44143 Office: 901 Lakeside Av Cleveland OH 44114

BRATTON, BEULAH O'KELLEY, educator; b. Weatherford, Tex., Oct. 2, 1906; d. Charles Edward and Ethel Virginia (Pickard) B.; B.S., Tex. Wesleyan Coll., 1938; postgrad. Tex. Technol. U., U. Tex., 1961; m. John Bratton, Sept. 1, 1927. Tchr. Benbrook Sch., Tarrant County, Tex., 1926-36, prin., 1936, Castleberry Sch., Tarrant County, 1936-40; chmn. English dept., publs. sponsor W.C. Stripling Jr. High Sch., Fort Worth, 1943-72; producer newspaper Hornet Herald, 1944-72; staffer various newspapers; engaged in real estate, 1972—. Chmn. planning bd. Tex. High Sch. Press Conf., 1950; mem. bd. judges Columbia Scholastic Press, 1968-72, recipient Gold Key award, 1967. Recipient Proficiency citation Tex. Interscolastic Press, 1955; Edith King award merit U. Tex., 1972. Wall St. Jour. fellow, 1961. Mem. Ft. Worth Classroom Tchrs. (exec. bd.), Tex. Tchrs. Assn., Tex. P.T.A. (life), Women in Communications (Journalism Tchr. of Year 1972), Columbia Scholastic Press Sponsors Assn., Alpha Delta Kappa, Delta Kappa Gamma. Home: 2117 Carleton St Fort Worth TX 76017 Office: 747 Parkway PL Arlington TX 76012

BRATTON, VIRGINIA LOUISE, educator; b. Bridgeport, Conn., June 6, 1925; d. Robert Bernard and Ethel (Plummer) Bratton; B.S., Simmons Coll., 1947. Editorial and prodn. asst. Am. Physiol. Soc., Washington, 1947-48; freelance writer, editor, designer, Boston, 1948-51; co-owner Gaye Press, 1953-56; instr. graphic arts Simmons Coll., Boston, 1951-54, asst. prof., 1955-62, asso. prof., 1963-73, prof., 1973—, dir. Simmons Coll. Press, 1962-71, adviser design and prodn. Simmons Coll. Press, 1971—. Mem. Am. Inst. Graphic Arts, Internat. Graphic Arts Edn. Assn., Am. Assn. U. Profs., Bookbuilders of Boston, Am. Civil Liberties Union. Democrat. Office: 300 The Fenway Boston MA 02115

BRAUCHER, JANE ALBERTA ELLIOTT, librarian; b. N.Y.C.; d. Rachel G. (Dinsmore) Elliott; diploma nursing U. Pa., 1950; B.S. (USPHS grantee), Duke, 1957; M.S., Cath. U., 1962; postgrad. Washington Coll. Law, 1962-64, (govt. grantee) U. Cal. at Berkeley, 1966, 71. Examiner, United Mine Workers Welfare Fund, Washington, 1950-54; researcher Nat. Inst. Mental Health, Bethesda, Md., 1954-55; pub. health nurse D.C. Pub. Health, 1957-58; librarian Fgn. Affairs Inst., Washington, 1958-59, SEC, Washington, 1959-62, Army Library, Pentagon, Washington, 1962-68, Dept. Transp., Washington, 1968—. Instr. library sci. and legal research Grad. Sch. Dept. Agr., Washington, 1967—. Mem. Am. Assn. Law Librarians (editor 1963), Spl. Libraries Assn. (life mem., local chmn.), A.L.A. Clubs: Kenwood Golf and Tennis, Aero, Nat. Aviation (Washington). Author: Transportation, 1973. also RD 4 Carlisle PA 17013 Office: Dept Transp Washington DC 20590

BRAUCHT, JUNE ELDER (MRS. JESS WILLIAM BRAUCHT), mus. dir.; b. Berkeley, Cal., Aug. 26, 1918; d. Edwin Thomas and Gertrude Rose (Haws) Elder; B.A., U. Cal. at Berkeley, 1939; postgrad. Livingston Sch. Advt. Art, 1939-40; m. Jess William Braucht, June 2, 1940. Owner-mgr. decorative-arts shops, Oakland, Cal., 1947-52; with Oakland Art Mus., 1959; chmn. art tours, artist's studio tour, workshops, exhibitions Monterey Peninsula chpt. Am. Fedn. Art, 1960-62, pres., 1962, dir.-curator, 1963-66; organizer, mgr. Rental Gallery, Monterey Peninsula Mus. Art, Monterey, Cal., 1971-72, dir.-curator, 1972—. Vol. Oakland Recreation Dept., 1953-57, Oakland Art Mus., Rental Gallery, 1957-59. Mem. Am. Assn. U. Women (program chmn. 1961-62), Alpha Xi Delta, Delta Epsilon. Home: 26074 Mesa Dr Carmel CA 93921 Office: 559 Pacific St Monterey CA 93940

BRAUDE, ADELE COVY (MRS. JACOB M. BRAUDE), designer; b. Cin.; d. Tobias and Martha (Rosenberg) Covy; student U. Cin. Coll. Music; m. S. Henry Englander, Feb. 10, 1927 (dec. Aug. 1944); children—Ann Englander, Jane E. Berkson; m. 2d, Jacob M. Braude, Feb. 22, 1946 (dec. Dec. 1970). Sec.-treas. Nordell Co., 1931-44, pres., 1944-47; dir. Gidding Co., 1946-58. Pres., Cin. chpt. Los Angeles Sanitorium, 1935; v.p. Jr. Council Jewish Women, Cin., 1936; pres. nat. women's com. Greater Chgo. chpt. Brandeis U., 1956; mem. Com. for Restoration of Hull House; bd. dirs. Chgo. Women's Aid, Deborah Women's Club; active fund drives A.R.C., Community Fund. Mem. Internat. Platform Assn. Designer, builder miniature rooms done to scale, reprodns. of ancient, period and historic rooms and bldgs. Address: 1000 Lake Shore Plaza Chicago IL 60611

BRAUDY, SUSAN ORR, editor; b. Phila., July 8, 1941; d. Bernard and Blanche (Malin) Orr; B.A., Bryn Mawr Coll., 1963; postgrad. U. Pa., 1963-64. Asso. editor, contbg. editor New Jour., Yale, 1967-69; contbg. editor Glamour Mag., 1970-71; asso. editor Newsweek Mag., 1971-72; contbg. editor Ms. Mag., N.Y.C., 1973—. Cons. Ford Found., 1973. Contbr. articles to profl. jours. Office: 370 Lexington Av New York City NY 10017

BRAUEL, PATRICIA ANN, coll. dean; b. Detroit, Apr. 22, 1924; d. Charles E. and Mary (Butts) Brauel; B.A., Pomona Coll., 1944; M.A., Stanford, 1946; postgrad univs. of Ind., N.Y., State Ia., Cal. at Berkeley. Asst. dir. Lagunita Ct., Stanford, 1946-47; resident counselor, faculty asso. Ind. U., 1947-48; dir. Williston Hall, asst. dean women No. Ill. State U., DeKalb, 1948-54; asst. dean students U. Cal. at Berkeley, 1954-58; dean students Mills Coll., Oakland, 1958-74. Mem. Am. Assn. U. Women, Nat. Assn. Women Deans and Counselors, Am. Personnel and Guidance Assn., Cal. Assn. Women Deans and Vice Prins., Pacific Coast Coll. Health Assn. Home: Mills Coll Oakland CA 94613

BRAUER, RIMA LOIS RUBENSTEIN (MRS. LEE DAVID BRAUER), child psychiatrist; b. Bklyn., Feb. 5, 1938; d. Gerald and Freeda (Rubin) Rubenstein; B.A. (Dietches scholar, Goucher scholar), Goucher Coll., 1959; M.D., U. Md., 1964; m. Lee David Brauer, Dec. 29, 1959; children—Samuel, Jennifer, Nathan. Biochemistry research asso. Sinai Hosp., Balt., 1960; psychiatry fellow U. Md., summer 1961, Conn. Valley Hosp., summer 1969; intern Montefiore Hosp., Bronx, N.Y., 1964-65; resident in psychiatry and fellow in child psychiatry, Yale, New Haven, 1966-72; practice medicine specializing in child psychiatry, New Haven, 1969—. Mem. Conn. Council of Child Psychiatrists. Home: Old Gate Rd Wallingford CT 06492 Office: 291 Whitney Av New Haven CT 06511

BRAUMAN, SHARON K., chemist; b. Elizabeth, N.J., Apr. 14, 1939; d. Clare Henry and Ilaine (Wagenshutz) Kruse; B.A. magna cum laude, Mt. Holyoke Coll., 1961; Ph.D. in Organic Chemistry, U. Cal. at Berkeley, 1965; m. John I. Brauman, Aug. 22, 1964. Sr. chemist Stanford Research Inst., Menlo Park, Cal., 1965—; chmn. Frenchmen's Hill exec. com. Stanford, 1972-73; dist. rep. Stanford Campus Homeowners Assn., 1973—. NIH postdoctoral fellow, 1961-65. Mem. Am. Chem. Soc., Chem. Soc. London, A.A.A.S., Phi Beta Kappa, Sigma Xi. Contbr. profl. jours. Home: 849 Tolman Dr Stanford CA 94305 Office: Stanford Research Inst Menlo Park CA 94025

BRAUN, ALMA MARY SCHMIDT (MRS. WILLIS H. BRAUN), city ofcl.; b. Portage, Wis., July 15, 1926; d. Frank Arthur and Jean Marie (Learmonth) Schmidt; student Madison Bus. Coll., 1944-45; m. Willis H. Braun, Mar. 29, 1950. Legal sec. Bogue & Sanderson, Portage, Wis., 1945-67; dep. city clk., Portage, 1967-69, city clk., 1969—. Mem. Internat. Inst. Municipal Clks. Home: 810 Dunn St Portage WI 53901 Office: 309 W Wisconsin St Portage WI 53901

BRAUN, CONSTANCE TODD (MRS. LOUIS CARL BRAUN), educator; b. Flushing, N.Y., July 12, 1931; d. Wallace Kirkum and Beatrice May (Carroll) Todd; student Indiana (Pa.) State Coll., 1949-51; B.S., Geneva Coll., 1965; M.L.S., U. Pitts., 1968; postgrad. Westminster Coll., 1973—; m. Louis Carl Braun, Oct. 30, 1950; 1 dau., Catherine Lee (Mrs. Kenneth Blanchard). Elementary librarian Highland Suburban Sch. Dist., Beaver Falls, Pa., 1966-67; referemce librarian Edn. Curriculum Center dir. Geneva Coll., Beaver Falls, 1972, instr., Center, 1972—, dir. reading clinic, 1973, 74. Leader, Girl Scouts U.S.A., Beaver Falls, 1959-63. Mem. Am. Assn. U. Profs. (exec. bd. 1973), Internat. Reading Assn., Pa. Edn. Assn., Beta Phi Mu, Delta Sigma Epsilon. Presbyn. (treas. 1971). Home: 128 McLanahan Dr Beaver Falls PA 15010

BRAUN, NORMA MAI TSEN WANG (MRS. CARL W. BRAUN), physician; b. Shanghai, China, Oct. 30, 1937 (came to U.S., 1949, naturalized 1956); d. Joseph K.C. and Jean (Soltys) Wang; A.B., U. Pa., 1959; M.D., Columbia, 1963; m. Carl W. Braun, June 11, 1961; children—Erich H.P., Aimee C.H. Intern, Bellevue Hosp. Columbia div., N.Y.C., 1963-64, resident 1964-65; fellow St. Luke's Hosp. Center, N.Y.C., 1967-69; practice medicine, specializing in pulmonary diseases, N.Y.C.; mem. attending staff cardiology Grasslands Hosp., Valhalla, N.Y., 1969-70; mem. clin. attending staff medicine Columbia U. at Harlem Hosp. Center, N.Y.C., 1970—; instr. medicine Columbia U., 1971—, asso. in medicine, 1973—. Diplomate Am. Bd. Internal Medicine. Mem. Am. Med. Womens Assn., A.A.A.S., N.Y. Trudeau Soc., Am. Thoracic Soc., N.Y. State, N.Y. County med. socs., Am. Heart Assn. Home: 733 Old Kensico Rd Thornwood NY 10594 Office: Harlem Hosp Center Lenox Av and 136th St New York City NY 10037

BRAUNSCHWEIGER, HELEN REBECCA RAYMOND (MRS. WALTER J. BRAUNSCHWIEGER), artist; b. Norwich, Conn.; d. George Clark and Helen (Smith) Raymond; student Boston U. Art Sch., 1927-29, also pvt. study; m. John S. Lapp, Apr. 12, 1933 (dec. May 1953); 1 son, Sumner Philip; m. 2d, Walter J. Braunschweiger, Apr. 19, 1955. One man shows at DeBreaux Gallery, N.Y.C., 1957, La Fontanella Gallery, Rome, Italy, 1959, Iolas Gallery, N.Y.C., 1959, Scorpio Gallery, Los Angeles, 1961, Desert Art Center, Palm Springs, Cal., 1966, Zulch Gallery, Costa Mesa, Cal., 1968, San Gabriel Fine Arts Soc., 1974, Brentwood Savs. and Loan, 1974; exhibited in group shows at Cal. Art Club, Greek Theater, 1961, Valley Artists Guild, Los Angeles, 1964, Glendale Fed. Savs. (Cal.), (1964), Artists of S.W., Greek Theater, 1964, Waldorf Astoria, N.Y.C., 1964, Cal. Festival, 1964; represented in permanent collections City of Los Angeles City Hall, Occidental Life Ins. Co., Los Angeles, also numerous others. Mem. costume council Los Angeles County Mus.; mem. womens bd. Cal. Inst. Arts. Recipient two 2d prizes Nat. Assn. Am. Pen Women, 1960. Fellow Am. Profl. Artists League, Am. Inst. Fine Arts; mem. Cal. Council Traditional Artists (v.p., dir.), Valley Artists Guild, Laguna Beach Art Assn., Artists of S.W., Palm Springs Civic Art Assn., Palm Springs Pathfinders, Cal. Art Club (dir.), San Gabriel Fine Arts Assn., Los Angeles Opera Guild, Mus. Assos., Muses. Address: El Royale Apts 450 N Rossmore Av Los Angeles CA 90004

BRAUNSTEIN, RUTH (MRS. THEODORE H. BRAUNSTEIN), art gallery adminstr.; b. Mpls., July 20, 1923; d. Abe and Pauline (Kestenberg) Gershkow; student U. Minn., 1941-42; m. Theodore H. Braunstein, July 13, 1943; children—Mark, Marna (Mrs. Donald Clark). Founder Quay Gallery, Tiburon, Cal., 1961, propr., dir. Quay Gallery, San Francisco, 1965—. Founder Collectors Press, San Francisco, 1966, v.p., 1966-69. Vice pres. Hadassah, Central Pacific Coast Region, 1971—. Mem. San Francisco Art Dealers Assn. (dir. 1973—), Modern Dance Council (founder 1952). Home: 2892 Bryant St Palo Alto CA 94306 Office: 560 Sutter St San Francisco CA 94102

BRAUNWALD, NINA STARR (MRS. EUGENE BRAUNWALD), surgeon; b. N.Y.C., Mar. 2, 1928; d. Morris and May (Levine) Starr; B.A., N.Y.U., 1949, M.D., 1952; M.S. in Surgery, Georgetown U., 1957; m. Eugene Braunwald, May 25, 1952; children—Karen, Denise, Adrienne. Intern Bellevue Hosp., N.Y.C., 1952-53, asst. resident in surgery, 1953-55; resident in surgery Georgetown U. Hosp., Washington, 1955-58; staff Clinic of Surgery, Nat. Heart Inst., Bethesda, Md., 1958-65, dep. chief surgery 1965-68; surg. staff Georgetown U. Med. Sch., Washington 1960-64; asso. prof. dept. surgery U. Cal. at San Diego, 1968-72; asso. prof. surgery Harvard Med. Sch., Boston, 1972—. Diplomate Am. Bd. Surgery, Am. Bd. Thoracic Surgery. Fellow A.C.S.; mem. Am. Soc. Artificial Internal Organs, Am. Assn. Thoracic Surgery, Internat. Cardiovascular Soc., Am. Heart Assn. (adv. council on surgery), Soc. Thoracic Surgeons, Am. Coll. Cardiology. Soc. for Vascular Surgery. Research on cardiovascular surgery, artificial heart valves; 1st woman engaged in open heart surgery. Home: 75 Scotch Pine Rd Weston MA 02193 Office: Dept of Surgery Peter Bent Brigham Hospital 721 Huntington Av Boston MA 02115

BRAVERMAN, JOAN LYDIA, interior designer; b. Phila., June 23, 1938; d. Louis Philip and Jane M. (Farrell) Kohl; student Moore Coll. Art, 1961-63, Interior Design Sch. Phila., 1963-64; m. Merrill Braverman, Sept. 22, 1971; children—Garfield Harrison, Jonathan Louis. Designer, Interior Decorators Guild, Phila., 1964-65; partner Zelda of Yorktown, Moorestown, N.J., 1965-66; prin. Joan Lydia Interiors, Cherry Hill, N.J., 1966-72, Asbury Park, N.J., 1972—. Mem. Nat. Home Furnishings League. Office: 1200 Memorial Dr Asbury Park NJ 07712

BRAVERMAN, MILLICENT LENORE VON GLUBT, advt. and pub. relations agy. exec.; b. N.Y.C.; d. Joseph and Rose (Alpert) von Glubt; student U. Pa., 1949-50, Temple U., 1951-53; m. Irving D. Braverman (div. 1972); children—Kate Ellen, Harry Andrew. With Braverman Mirisch, Inc., Los Angeles, 1962—, pres., 1967—; radio syndicated lit. critic KFI, Los Angeles, 1973—. Frequent speaker, lectr. on books, 1968—; cons. Jewish Fedn. Council-United Jewish Welfare Fund Greater Los Angeles, 1974—. Conductor various Democratic polit. campaigns. Recipient 1st award for pub. service campaign Los Angeles Advt. Women, 1968; pub. service award Los Angeles City Council, 1973. Office: 9255 Sunset Blvd Los Angeles CA 90069

BRAY, DORIS, newspaper pub.; b. Santa Monica, Cal., July 2, 1905; B.A., U. Cal. at Los Angeles, 1926, postgrad., 1932-33; m. Emmett W. Bray, May 17, 1955. Self-employed adminstrv. cons., 1932-55; newspaper corr., 1956—; pub. Trona (Cal.) Argonaut, 1964—. Chmn. San Bernardino County Mental Health Adv. Bd., 1969-74, mem. 1974—; exec. dir. Searles Valley Community Services Council, 1970—; commr. County Service Area 22, 1962—. Bd. dirs. Community Chest, 1956—; chmn. adv. bd. for mentally retarded Patton State Hosp., San Bernardino, 1971—. Named Citizen of Yr., Trona Elks Club, 1973. Mem. Trona Bus. and Profl. Women (pres. 1973-74), Am. Assn. U. Women, V.F.W. Aux. Mem. Order Eastern Star. Home: 84639 11th St Trona CA 93562 Office: 13193 Main St Trona CA 93562

BRAY, ELIZABETH ANN, health service adminstr.; b. Washington, Sept. 15, 1940; d. Francis Robert and Dorothy Virginia (Kidd) Bray, Sr.; student Mary Washington Coll., 1958-60; B.S. in Nursing, U. Va., 1963; M.S. in Nursing, Boston U., 1968, postgrad., 1969. Asst. head nurse med. surg. unit Georgetown U. Hosp., Washington, 1966, head nurse, 1966-67; pvt. duty nurse, Arlington, Va., 1965-66; dir. nursing service Great Oaks Center, Silver Spring, Md., 1970-73, unit dir. nursery infirmary program, 1971-73, dir. residential care, 1973—. Flight nurse, capt. USAF Res., 1970—. Mem. Am. Assn. on Mental Deficiency, Sigma Theta Tau (pres. Tau chpt. 1971-72). Home: 2801 Maple Lane Shady Knolls Fairfax VA 22030 Office: Great Oaks Center 12001 Cherry Hill Rd Silver Spring MD 20904

BRECH, MARIA JULIA KENNY (MRS. MARTIN BRECH), librarian; b. N.Y.C., July 22, 1931; s. Gerard and Grace (McCarthy) Kenny; A.B., Coll. Mt. St. Vincent-on-Hudson, 1960; M.S., Columbia, 1963; media certificate State U. N.Y. Brockport, 1967; m. Martin Brech, July 29, 1969. Tchr. elementary and high sch., N.Y.C., 1952-63; librarian, sr. high sch., N.Y.C., 1963-67; asso. Bur. Sch. Libraries, State Edn., Dept., N.Y.C., 1968-69; library dir. Briarcliff Coll., Briarcliff Manor, N.Y., 1969—; owner Phoenix Books 'n Things, Phoenicia, N.Y., 1972—. Cons. sch. dists., library funding. Recipient Nat. Def. Edn. Act grant, 1967, 68. Mem. N.Y., Westchester (v.p., pres. coll. librarians sect. 1973—) library assns., Teilhard de Chardin Assn., Audubon Soc., N.E.A., Am. Booksellers Assn. Democrat. Roman Catholic. Author: English as a Second Language, 1969; Performing Arts, 1968; Dance, 1969. Home: RD 2 Chestnut Ridge Rd Mount Kisco NY 10549 Office: Tead Library Briarcliff Coll Briarcliff Manor NY 10510

BRECHEISEN, GENEVIEVE BURNETT (MRS. RICHARD STOUFFER BRECHEISEN), civic worker; b. Atwood, Okla., Dec. 5, 1911; d. Oliver and Emma (Hauert) Burnett; grad. Arlington Hall, Washington, 1931; m. Richard Stouffer Brechelsen, Oct. 22, 1932;

children—Richard Burnett, John Edward. Vol. worker A.R.C., 1940-44; active bds. P.T.A., 1946-49; founding mem. Phoenix Symphony Guild, 1947—; bd. dirs. Kiwani-Anns, Phoenix, 1950-55; founding mem. Phoenix Mus. Theater, 1954, Goodwill Industries, 1953-62, Phoenix Fine Arts Assn., 1948—, Phoenix Art Mus., 1948—, founding bd. mem. Phoenix Cotillion, 1959; founding mem. Western Art, 1968—, Friends of Art, 1962—, Heart Assn., Phoenix, 1961—; active Reading Reform Found., 1962—; mem. Am. Cancer Soc., Phoenix, 1961—; founding mem. women's bd. Barrows Neurol. Found., 1965—, Rec. and Guide Dog for Blind, 1961—, Paraplegia Found., 1969—, Friends of Stratford, 1961, Ariz. State U. Library Assos., 1969—; bd. dirs. United Cerebral Palsy Assn. Central Ariz., Ariz. Costume Inst. Phoenix Art Mus. Mem. English Speaking Union. Republican. Presbyn. Clubs: Phoenix Country, Kiva. Address: 201 W Montebello Av Phoenix AZ 85013

BRECHNER, BEVERLY LORRAINE, mathematician, educator; b. N.Y.C., May 27, 1936; d. Herman and Goldie (Zimmerman) Brechner; B.S., U. Miami, 1957, M.S., 1959; Ph.D., La. State U., 1964. Instr., La. State U., New Orleans, 1962-64, asst. prof., 1964-68; asst. prof. U. Fla., Gainesville, 1968-71, asso. prof. math., 1971—. Vis. lectr. La. Acad. Sci., New Orleans, 1967-68. Mem. Inst. for Advanced Grad. Students in Topology, Topology of Manifolds Inst., U. Ga., Athens, 1961. Mem. Am. Math. Soc., Math. Assn. Am., A.A.A.S., Fla. Found. Future Scientists (dir. 1970-73), Sigma Xi. Democrat. Jewish religion. Contbr. articles to profl. jours. Reviewer papers for Zentralblatt for Mathematik, 1968—, Math. Revs., 1971—. Home: 4003 NW 17th Av Gainesville FL 32605 Office: Dept of Math U Fla Gainesville FL 32611

BRECHT, JOYCE SOUTHARD (MRS. WARREN F. BRECHT), educator; b. Toledo, Sept 1, 1932; d. Frederick Reynolds and Eleanor M. (Plumb) Southard; B.A., DePauw U., 1954; Ed.M., Boston U., 1962; m. Warren F. Brecht, July 3, 1954; children—Amy, Stephen, David, Peter. Tchr. pub. schs., Fairborn, O., 1955-57, Weston, Mass., 1957-61, Montgomery County, Md., 1973—; pres. Joyce Brecht Enterprises, Inc. (pub.), Rockville, Md., 1974—. Bd. dirs. Southlawn Child Care, Rockville. Mem. Harvard Bus. Sch. Wives Assn. (bd. dirs. 1958-59), Pi Lambda Theta, Pi Beta Phi. Episcopalian. Author: Sing Noel, 1974. Composer: Talitha (an opera), 1968. Home: 9 Orchard Way North Rockville MD 20854 Office: Luxmanor Sch Tilden Lane Rockville MD 20852

BRECHTEL, IDA MARGARET, physician; b. Lena, Ill., June 13, 1915; d. Frank Howard and Cora Elizabeth (Strunk) Brechtel; R.N., Swedish Am. Hosp., Rockford, Ill., 1937; B.S., Rosary Coll., River Forest, Ill., 1943; M.D., U. Ill., 1946. Intern, Cook County Hosp., Chgo., 1946-47; resident Chgo. Lying In Hosp., 1947-48, City Hosp., Columbus, Ga., 1948-49; practice medicine specializing in obstetrics and gynecology, Rockford, 1950—; mem. staff Swedish Am. Hosp., Rockford. Mem. Am. Coll. Obstetrics and Gynecology. Contbg. author: American Marriage - A Way of Life, 1959. Home: 2526 Chickadee Trail Rockford IL 61107 Office: 1215 N Alpine Rd Rockford IL 61101

BRECKA, JUDITH ANN, lawyer; b. Council Bluffs, Ia., Apr. 24, 1944; d. Louis V. and Anne Marie (Bejvancesky) Brecka; B.S., U. Neb., 1967, J.D., 1970. Admitted to Neb. bar, 1970, Cal. bar, 1971; chmn., pres. Potrero Hill Community Law Firm, Inc., San Francisco, 1971—. Dir. S.F. Local Devel. Corp., Goat Hill, Inc., sec.-treas., 1972-73. Mem. adv. bd. Potrero Hill Youth Council, 1972—, San Francisco Renaissance Assn.; chairwoman Interagy. Com., Potrero Hill, 1972—; co-founder Potrero Players, 1972; mem. Citizens Council on Criminal Justice. Bd. dirs. Arts and Scis. Corp., San Francisco. Mem. Am., Cal., San Francisco bar assns., Nat. Lawyers Guild, Lawyers Club San Francisco. Home: 664 Carolina St San Francisco CA 94107 Office: 953 DeHaro St San Francisco CA 94107

BRECKENRIDGE, CHARLOTTE THOMAS, economist, govt. ofcl.; b. Roanoke, Va., Feb 15, 1925; d. Charles Herbert and Ann Frances (Moody) Thomas; B.A., Antioch Coll., 1949; postgrad. George Washington U., 1952-54, London Sch. of Econs., 1959. Research asst. Fed. Reserve Bd., Washington, 1952-56, 1965-66; research analyst Md. State Planning Commn., Balt., 1956-59; economist U.S. Dept. Commerce, Washington, 1967—. Mem. Regional Sci. Assn., Nat. Economists Club. Editor The Research Rev. Home: 3020 Q St Washington DC 20007 Office: 14th and Constitution Washington DC 20230

BRECKENRIDGE, MARGARET ANN, communications cons.; b. Whittier, Cal., July 11, 1936; d. Eugene Walter and Georgia Lou (Barron) Breckenridge; B.A. in English, Whittier Coll., 1958. Tchr., La Puente (Cal.) High Sch., 1959-60; copywriter Kenyon & Eckhardt Advt., N.Y.C., 1960-62; editor systems and procedures dept. Gen. Dynamics Corp., N.Y.C., 1962-63; editorial and research asst. for book My Years With General Motors, 1963; promotion dir. McClatchy Newspapers, Sacramento, 1964-67; mgr. media relations Whittaker Corp., Los Angeles, 1967-71; corporate communications cons., Los Angeles, 1971—. Active Los Angeles Region Vol. Bur. Mem. Pub. Relation Soc. Am. Home: 6075 Alcott St Los Angeles CA 90035 Office: 2322 Loma Vista Pl Los Angeles CA 90039

BREDBENNER, YVETTE HELENE, educator; b. Boston, Feb. 25, 1922; d. James Andre and Rose Violet (Wolff) Mojon; certificate dietetics N.Y. Inst. Dietetics, 1941; B.A. cum laude in French, U. Bridgeport, 1961; M.A., U. Okla., 1965, M.L.S., 1975; postgrad. U. Grenoble (France), 1968; m. Phillip Clyde Bredbenner, July 30, 1949 (dec.); children—Richard James, Lee Allen. Dietitian Sharon (Conn.) Hosp., 1946-49; instr. U. Okla., 1962-63, Midwest City (Okla.) High Sch., 1966-71; prof. modern langs., supr. library Hillsdale Free Will Baptist Coll., Moore, Okla., 1971—; cons. in field. Mem. Tchrs. Polit. Action com., Midwest City, 1968-71. Served with U.S. Army, 1943-45. Nat. Def. Edn. Act fellow, 1961-65. Mem. Am. Tchrs. French, Okla. Fgn. Lang. Tchrs., Okla. Library Assn., A.L.A., Kappa Kappa Iota. Republican. Mem. Disciples of Christ (deaconess). Home: 1729 Parkview Terrace Norman OK 73069 Office: Box 6343 Moore OK 73160

BREDESEN, DOROTHY LOUISE ANTIL, vocational rehab. counselor; b. N.Y.C., July 20, 1929; d. Michael Charles and Mary (Holman) Antil; B.A., Syracuse U., 1951, M.A., 1956; postgrad. U. Chgo., 1962-64; m. Norman Bjorne Bredesen, Nov. 1, 1952 (div. Dec. 1972); children—Karen Louise, Mark Jon, Eric Tod. Social worker Maricopa County Welfare Dept., Phoenix, 1957; lectr. speech Ariz. State U., Tempe, 1957-59; instr. speech Memphis State U., 1960-62; vol. worker Christ Child Settlement House, 1964-65; vocational rehab. counselor, D.C. Bur. Rehab. Services, Washington, 1965—. Chmn. working adv. com. New Brent Sch., 1967-68; mem. exec. com. Brent Elementary Sch., 1965-68. Panel chmn. Dist. Tng. Sch.'s 9th ann. conf. Mental Retardation, 1968—; mem. counselor adv. com. Occupational and Tng. Center, 1971-74. Recipient certificate of appreciation, Help for Retarded Children, Inc., 1967, D.C. Dept. Vocational Rehab., 1968. Mem. Rehab. Internat. U.S.A., Adult Edn. Assn. Greater Washington (dir. 1967-68, rec. sec. 1968-69 2d v.p. 1970-71), Am. Civil Liberties Union, Am. Sociol. Assn., Nat. Rehab. Assn., Nat. Rehab. Counseling Assn. (dir. D.C. chpt. 1971-72), Capitol Hill Community Council (pres. 1968-69), Common Cause, Gordon Jr. High P.T.A. (2d v.p. 1968-69), Nat. Soc. for Study of Edn., Center for Study Democratic Institutions, Soc. for Psychol. Study Social Issues, Ralph Nader's Public Citizens, Inc., Delta Sigma Rho. Democrat. Roman Catholic. Home: 11180 Forest Edge Dr Reston VA 22090 Office: 122 C St NW Room 205-C Washington DC 20001

BREEDLOVE, LOUELLA ROTE (MRS. ALLISON EARL BREEDLOVE), policewoman; d.; Niels Peter and Marie (Hansen) Nielsen; B.S. in Police Adminstrn., U. Houston, 1958; D.C.I., U. So. Cal; postgrad. Mich. State U.; m. Orville Winn Rote, (dec. 1944); children—Jean Jacquies (Mrs. Harold William Schmid), Orville W., Ruth Estelle (Mrs. Kenneth Wayne Urmy), Laura Bridget (Mrs. Alvin Leo Jensen); m. 2d, Allison Earl Breedlove, June 29, 1959. Policewoman, Houston Police Dept., 1945-50, supr. policewomen, 1950-55, detective, 1955—. Lectr. to various groups. Pres., Planned Parenthood Fedn. Houston, 1949-50; gen. chmn. 16th Ann. Interfaith Workshop, 1973-74. Bd. dirs. Magnolia Park YWCA, 1956-60, Protestant Charities; exec. bd. Community Council Child Welfare, 1959-61; nominating com. Houston Community Council and United Fund; personnel chmn. Houston Met. bd. YWCA, 1965, past pres. bd. dirs., distinguished service award, 1967, co-chmn. nat. conv., 1970; pres. Ch. Women United Greater Houston; mem. Houston Civic Ballet bd.; charter mem. Freedom's Found., Houston; former chmn. bd. dirs. Lutheran Student Found. Harris County; mem. nat. com. on criminal justice and penal reform Luth. Ch. Am.; state bd. dirs. Luth. Ch. Women, 1973—, treas. local unit. Recipient Service award City of Houston, Louella Breedlove Day, 1971; Service award Ch. Women United in Tex., 1972; B'nai B'rith Brotherhood award; named Woman of Yr., Alpha chpt. Gamma Sigma. Mem. Tex. Social Welfare Assn., Internat. Juvenile Officers Assn., Council Human Relations, Tex. Municipal Police Assn., Tex. Probation and Parole Assn., Alumni Assn. U. Houston, Houston Police Officers Assn., Bus. and Profl. Women's Clubs (dir. 1965-67, membership chmn. Houston), Milford House, Action for Youth in Tex. Clubs: Altrusa (past pres., Houston Altrusan Yr. 1972), Houston Farm and Ranch, Noonday Toastmistress (sec. 1974—), Gulf Coast Scandinavian. Home: 726 W 18th Av Houston TX 77008 Office: 3540 W Dallas St Houston TX 77019

BREEN, CATHERINE PATRICIA, retail trade co. exec.; b. N.Y.C., Sept. 19, 1919; d. Patrick Joseph and Elizabeth Josephine (Kiernan) Breen; B.S., Fordham U., 1951; M.A., Columbia, 1960. Tng. specialist J.C. Penny Co., N.Y.C., 1958-61; asst. product sales tng. mgr. Montgomery Ward Co., Chgo., 1961-66, corporate tng. dir., 1966—. Lectr. adult psychology Fordham U., 1954-62, Fashion Inst. of Tech., 1963-66. Mem., Pres. Johnson's Task Force on Occupational Tng. in Industry, 1967-68; mem. nominating com. YWCA, 1969; mem. adv. com. TV Coll. of Chgo.; mem. Nat. Adv. Com. for Handicapped, 1971-74. Bd. dirs. Sr. Centers of Met. Chgo., 1970, Camp Fire Girls, 1967. Mem. Am. Psychol. Assn., Am. Soc. for Tng. and Devel. (v.p. 1970-73), Am. Guidance and Personnel Assn., Ill. Tng. Dirs. Assn., Soc. for Communicating Arts, Advt. Women's Club of Chgo. Club: Altrusa Chgo. Home: 1400 Lake Shore Dr Chicago IL 60610 Office: Montgomery Ward 535 West Chicago Av Chicago IL 60607

BREESKIN, ADELYN DOHME, art mus. dir.; b. Baltimore, July 19, 1896; d. Alfred R. L. and Emmie (Blumner) Dohme; grad. Sch. Fine Arts, Crafts and Decorative Design, Boston, 1918; L.D., Goucher Coll., 1953; D.F.A. (hon.), Washington Coll., 1961, Wheaton Coll., 1963, Hood Coll., 1966, Morgan Coll., 1966; m. Elias Breeskin, Apr. 12, 1920; children—Jean (Mrs. Clayton Timbrell), Dorothy (Mrs. Samuel E. Brown, Jr.), Gloria (Mrs. Cornelius Peck). Asst. print dept. Met. Mus., N.Y.C., 1918-20; with Balt. Mus. Art, 1930-62, acting dir., 1942-47, dir., 1947-62, also curator graphic art; dir. Washington Gallery Modern Art, 1962-64; spl. cons. Nat. Collection Fine Arts, Smithsonian Instn., Washington, 1964-68, curator contemporary painting and sculpture, 1968—; lectr. U.S. and abroad. Decorated Star of Solidarity by Italian Govt., 1954. U.S. Commnr. Am. Pavilion, Venice Exhbn., 1960. Mem. Assn. Art Museum Dirs. (pres. 1956-57; hon. mem.) Internat. Graphic Arts Soc. (mem. Am. jury of selection 1955-64), Print Council of Am. (sec. 1956-62). Author: Catalogue Raisonne, Graphic Works of Mary Cassatt, 1949; Mary Cassatt: Catalogue Raisonne of the Oils, Pastels, Watercolors and Drawings, 1970. Home: 1254 31st St NW Washington DC 20007 Office: Nat Collection Fine Arts Smithsonian Instn Washington DC 20560

BREIDINGER, HELEN ELIZABETH (MRS. W. WILSON BREIDINGER), banker; b. South Williamsport, Pa., Dec. 19, 1928; d. David C. and Madge E. (Goldy) Dangle; grad. high sch.; m. W. Wilson Breidinger, Oct. 27, 1952. With Bank Central Pa. (name formerly Bank of South Williamsport), 1945—, v.p., 1971-74, v.p., asst. mgr. S. Williamsport office, 1974—, sec. to bd. dirs., 1964—. Chmn. S. Williamsport area United Fund Campaign, 1974; treas. North Central chpt. Am. Heart Assn., 1974—. Named Woman of Year, Penn Laurel chpt. Am. Bus. Women's Assn., 1971. Mem. Am. Bus. Women's Assn. (chpt. treas. 1969), Nat. Assn. Bank Women (corr. sec. chpt. 1971), United Comml. Travelers (sr. counselor). Mem. Order Eastern Star. Home: RD 1 Montgomery PA 17752 Office: 251 Market St South Williamsport PA 17701

BREIHAN, EDNA MARIA THIES (MRS. ARMIN HENRY BREIHAN), educator; b. Flossmoor, Ill., Jan. 22, 1911; d. Henry Frederick and Anna (Cohrs) Thies; student Valparaiso U., 1928-30; A.B., Coll. of St. Francis, 1953; M.Ed., De Paul U., 1957; certificate advanced study in reading U. Chgo., 1966; m. Armin Henry Breihan, June 26, 1937; children—Joanne, James. Tchr., Lutheran Parochial Schs., Detroit, Chgo., 1930-37; pvt. tchr. remedial reading, Homewood, Ill., Flossmoor, 1945-51; tchr. Culbertson Sch., Joliet, Ill., 1953-57, Central Sch., Lockport, Ill., 1955-58; reading cons. Lockport Twp. High Sch. 1958-66; reading coordinator Lockport Twp. Sch. Dist. 205, 1966-71, chmn. reading dept., 1971—. Mem. Lockport Woman's Club (hon.), N.E.A., Nat. Soc. for Study Edn., Internat. Reading Assn. (past pres. Will County council), Ill. Edn. Assn., Internat. Platform Assn., Lockport Bus. and Profl. Women's Assn., Assn. Supervision and Curriculum Devel., Delta Kappa Gamma, Chi Sigma Xi. Lutheran. Club: Joliet Country. Home: 1512 Briggs St Lockport IL 60441

BREILAND, MILDRED EILEEN SCHUBERT (MRS. JOHN G. BREILAND), librarian; b. Rock Port, Mo., July 6, 1915; d. Otto Hugo and Eva Augusta (Marlatt) Schubert; B.A. in Edn., Neb. State Tchrs. Coll., 1937; B.A. in L.S., U. Mich., 1940; m. John G. Breiland, Dec. 19, 1942; children—John Robert, William George. Tchr., Atlanta Sch., 1937-39; cataloger U. Mich. Library, Ann Arbor, 1940-41; head serials U. N.M. Library, Albuquerque, 1941-43; cataloger U. Cal. at Los Angeles Library, 1947-48; reference librarian Albuquerque Pub. Library, 1951-53; librarian Albuquerque High Sch. Library, 1953-63; dir. library processing center Albuquerque Pub. Schs., 1963—. Mem. Am., N.M. (pres. 1964-65), Southwest, Greater Albuquerque (pres. 1955-56) library assns., P.E.O. Home: 908 Georgia St SE Albuquerque NM 87108 Office: 606 Maple St SE Albuquerque NM 87106

BRELAND, WILLA MURRAY (MRS. ROBERT MILTON BRELAND), ret. social work adminstr.; b. Cin., Dec. 4, 1893; d. William C. and Rose E. (Darst) Murray; B.A., U. Cin., 1928; M.A., Am. U., 1930; diploma grad. sch. social adminstrn. U. Chgo.; m. Robert Milton Breland, May 10, 1949. Dir. social service dept. Mayo Clinic, 1917-23; dir. psychiat. social service VA Hosp., Little Rock, Ark., 1924-26; dir. social service dept. Municipal Hosp., Washington, D.C., 1926-31; instr. social work grad. sch., U. Akron, 1934-35; dir. social service dept. George Washington U. Hosp., Washington, 1935-43; phychiat. social work adminstr. Dept. of Health Hawaii, 1943-56; dir. social service dept. Queen's Hosp., Honolulu, 1956-58, Gallipolis (O.) State Inst., 1959-74; ret., 1974. Fellow Am. Orthopsychiat. Assn.; mem. Am. Assn. U. Women, Mental Health Fedn. Ohio, Nat. Assn. Social Workers, Nat. Mental Health Assn. Am. Assn. for Mental Deficiency, Royal Soc. Health (London), Academy of Certified Social Workers, Arkansas Psychol. Assn., Ohioana Library Assn., American Academy Clinical Socialogists, Business and Profl. Women's Club, Phi Delta Gamma. Mem. Order Eastern Star. Club: Zonta. Author articles in field. Home: 1709 Waltham Rd Columbus OH 43221

BRELSFORD, ELINOR BALE (MRS. HARRY WATSON BRELSFORD), educator; b. Cleve., Nov. 18, 1916; d. Lester Snow and Laura (Stiles) Bale; student Ohio Wesleyan U., 1934-35; B.A., U. Mich., 1938, M.S., 1940; postgrad. U. Cal. at Los Angeles, 1955-66; m. Harry Watson Brelsford, Sept. 14, 1940; children—Marcia, John Bale. Psychology asst. U. Mich., 1939-40; dir. Parent-Child Workshop, Santa Barbara (Cal.) City Coll., 1950—, also tchr. parent classes adult edn. dept.; mem. faculty U. Cal. extension, Santa Barbara, 1965—, also dir. orientation programs for tchrs. Head Start Programs, U. Cal. at Santa Barbara, 1965, 66, 67, psychologist, summer, 1967. Mem. adv. bd. Nursery Sch., Santa Barbara, 1966—. Mem. Nat. Assn. Edn. Young Children (state dir. 1964-68, local pres. 1964-65), Phi Beta Kappa, Sigma Xi, Kappa Alpha Theta, Phi Kappa Phi, Alpha Kappa Delta, Pi Lambda Theta, Delta Kappa Gamma. Republican. Unitarian-Universalist. Home: 1413 Alameda Padre Serra Santa Barbara CA 93103

BREME, MARY GOTTLIEB, physician; b. Chgo., Jan. 25, 1914; d. John Francis and Julia Ann (Zorc) Gottlieb; student Ill. Inst. Tech., 1935-39; B.S., U. Ill., 1940, M.D., 1942; postgrad. Menninger Sch. Psychiatry, 1964-66; m. John T. Breme, Aug. 17, 1935 (div. Jan. 1948); 1 dau., Mary Ellen (Mrs. Taghi Rezaian). Intern, Cook County Hosp., Chgo., 1943-44; resident Topeka State Hosp., 1964-66; resident in psychiatry Loyola U. Stritch Sch. Medicine, 1970-71; gen. practice medicine, Warrenville, Ill., 1943-64, specializing in psychiatry, Warrenville, 1966—; med. dir. Warrenville Clinic; staff psychiatrist Chgo. Alcoholic Treatment Center, 1971-72. Mem. Warrenville Plan Commn., 1968—; pres. Christian Counseling Found., 1963—. Mem. Am. Psychiat. Assn., Acad. Psychosomatic Medicine, Am. Soc. Clin. Hypnosis, A.M.A. Research on effect of pregnanediol on premenstrual syndrome. Home: 3S124 Winfield Rd Warrenville IL 60555 Office: PO Box K Warrenville IL 60555

BREMER, ROSLYN, communications cons.; b. N.Y.C., June 9, 1926; d. Abraham Samuel and Rae (Breitstein) Bremer; B.A. cum laude, Bklyn. Coll., 1948; M.A., N.Y. U., 1949, Ph.D. candidate; m. Carl Spielvogel, July 29, 1953; children—David, Rachel, Paul. Tchr. speech, dramatic coach High Sch. Music and Art, N.Y.C., also speech examiner N.Y.C. Bd. Edn. and instr. Baruch Sch. of Coll. City N.Y., 1951-56; part-time instr. speech Fairleigh Dickinson U., 1956-67, instr. communications Dental Sch., 1963—; asst. adj. prop. communications to people who speak English as a 2d lang. Am. Lang. Inst., N.Y. U., 1970—; propr. Communi-Vu, N.Y.C., 1972—; cons., speaker in field; dir. mgmt. tng. programs in communications. Bd. dirs. women's div. Anti-defamation League. Mem. Internat. Communication Assn., Indsl. Communications Council, Am. Soc. Tng. and Devel., Alpha Psi Omega. Contbr. articles to publs. Home: 26 Bradford Rd Scarsdale NY 10583 Office: 58 W 58th St New York City NY 10019

BREMERS, JEAN L. MCMAHON (MRS. HAROLD HENRY BREMERS), physician; b. Colorado Springs, Colo., Apr. 15, 1916; d. Louis F. and Lenore (Gillis) McMahon; B.S., U. Denver, 1938; M.D., U. Colo., 1942; m. Harold Henry Bremers, 1949; children—Henry, Ann, Robert. Intern, Denver Gen. Hosp., 1941, Colo. Gen. Hosp., Denver, 1942-43, N.Y. Hosp., N.Y.C., 1943, New Haven Hosp., 1944; resident Univ. Hosp., U. Minn., 1944-45; practice medicine specializing in pediatrics, Denver, 1945-50; dir. developmental and evaluation clinic Children's Hosp., Denver, 1956—; mem. staff St. Joseph's Hosp., St. Lukes Hosp.; asst. clin. prof. pediatrics U. Colo., 1968—. Diplomate Am. Bd. Pediatrics. Fellow Am. Acad. Pediatrics, Am. Assn. Mental Deficiency; mem. Am. Acad. Cerebral Palsy, Rocky Mountain Pediatric Soc., Denver County Med. Soc., Assn. Children with Learning Disabilities, Denver Assn. Mental Health (profl. adv. bd. 1967-70). Contbr. articles to profl. jours. Home: 2292 E Dartmouth Av Englewood CO 80110 Office: 19th Av and Downing St Denver CO 80218

BRENDEL, BETTINA, painter; b. Luneburg, Germany; d. Robert and Xenia (Bernstein) Brendel; B.A., Oberschule a. Lerchenfeld, Hamburg, Germany, 1940; postgrad. Kunstschule Schmilinsky, 1941-43, Staatliche Hochschule fur bild. Künste, Hamburg, 1945-47, U. So. Cal., 1955-58, New Sch. for Social Research, 1968-69; m. Arthur Spitzer, 1949 (div. July 1965); 1 dau., Violet Spitzer. Came to U.S., 1951, naturalized, 1957. One-woman shows at Los Angeles Art Assn., 1954, Esther Robles Gallery, Los Angeles, 1957, 60, 61, Long Beach Mus. Art, 1958, Wittier Art Gallery, 1958, Downew Mus. Art, 1959, Dana Br. Library, Long Beach, 1959, Art Center La Jolla, 1962, Pasadena Art Mus., 1962, Santa Barbara Mus. Art, 1966 (preceding all Cal.), Spectrum Gallery, N.Y.C., 1967; exhibited in numerous group shows in U.S., also in Hamburg, 1947, Munich, Germany, 1949, 50, Turin, Italy, 1965, Milan, Italy, 1969; represented in permanent collections at Long Beach Mus. Art, La Jolla Art Mus., Santa Barbara Mus. Art, Pasadena Art Mus., San Francisco Mus. Art, Internat. Center for Aesthetic Research, Turin. Faculty, U. Cal. at Los Angeles extension, 1958-61; lectr. Los Angeles Art Assn., 1955, 65, Inst. of Optics, Rochester, N.Y., 1971. Recipient awards La Jolla Art Mus., 1958, 59, Downey Mus., 1959, Long Beach Mus. Art, 1960, 61, San Francisco Mus., 1966. Mem. Artists for Econ. Action, Am. Fedn. Art, Cal. Art Assn. Am., Univ. Cal. Los Angeles Art Council. Address: 1061 North Kenter Av Los Angeles CA 90049

BRENDELL, GWILLI GOFF (MRS. FRED D. BRENDELL, JR.), home economist; b. Ft. Wayne, Ind., Aug. 9, 1936; d. Earl Edward and Dorothy Jane (Baker) Goff; student Jordan Conservatory Music, 1954-55; B.S., Ball State Tchrs. Coll., 1959; M.A., Western Carolina U., 1969; m. Fred D. Brendell, Jr., Feb. 22, 1957; children—David Edward, Janna Kay, Bradley. Tchr. home econs. Erwin High Sch., Asheville, N.C., 1959-60, 61-62; home econs. extension agt. Agrl. Extension Service, Waynesville, N.C., 1962—. Recipient Distinguished Service award U.S. Dept. Agr., 1973. Mem. Am., N.C. home econs. assns., Nat., N.C. (pres. 1974—) assns. extension home economists, N.C. Assn. Extension 4-H Agts., N.C. Family Life Council, Epsilon Sigma Phi. Baptist (county dir. Woman's Missionary Union work 1971-74, dir. youth choir 1970—). Home: Route 2 Canton NC 28716 Office: Box 102 Waynesville NC 28716

BRENEMAN, LUCILLE NIX (MRS. ALDYNE D. BRENEMAN), educator; b. Plainview, Tex., Mar. 26, 1914; d. John Franklin and Bertha Lee (Whitlock) Nix; student Wayland Coll., 1932, 33; A.B., Baylor U., 1935; postgrad. Ia. U., 1936, U. Colo., 1937, U. So. Cal., 1938-39, U. Birmingham (Eng.), 1963; M.A., U. Hawaii, 1949; m. Aldyne Derald Breneman, Sept. 24, 1938; children—Aldyne Derald, Steven Bret, John Austin, Beverly Nix. Tchr. secondary schs., Hemet, Cal., 1940-44, San Bernadino, Cal., 1944-45; mem. faculty U. Hawaii, Honolulu, 1947—, prof. speech and interpretation, 1972—, chmn. interpretation, 1966—, chmn. Univ. Reading House, 1966—. Cons. storytelling Fine Arts of Hawaii, 1966, Friends of Library, Honolulu, 1974; cons., performer Honolulu Drama Study Group, 1959—. Mem. Speech Communication Assn., Pacific Speech Assn. (pres. 1965, Speech Tchr. of Year award 1969), N.E.A., Am. Assn. U. Women, Phi Kappa Phi, Delta Kappa Gamma. Contbr. articles to profl. jours. Home: 5328 Malu Pl Honolulu HI 96816

BRENMAN-GIBSON, MARGARET, psychoanalyst; b. Denver, Jan. 14, 1918; d. Leo John and Janet (Siegal) Brenman; B.A., Bklyn. Coll., 1938; M.A., Columbia, 1939; Ph.D., U. Kan., 1942; m. William Gibson, Sept. 6, 1940; children—Thomas Eli, Daniel Jonah. Sr. psychologist Menninger Clinic, Topeka, 1943-44; dir. psychology div. dept. clin. service Menninger Found., Topeka, 1946-48, prof. psychology, 1946-48; sr. staff mem. Austen Riggs Center, Stockbridge, Mass., 1948—. Cons., Winter VA Hosp., 1946-48; cons. dept. student mental hygiene Yale, 1951. Recipient C.P. Menninger Meml. award, 1960; Founds. Fund grantee for research in psychiatry, 1968-71; Guggenheim Found. fellow, 1969; Nat. Endowment for Humanities fellow, 1969; Morton Prince award for research in hypnosis and altered states of consciousness, 1972; Am. Assn. U. Women fellow, 1973. Diplomate Am. Bd. Examiners in Clin. Psychology. Mem. Am. Psychol. Assn., Am. Orthopsychiat. Assn., Topeka, N.Y. psychoanalytic socs., Western New Eng. Inst. Soc. Psychoanalysis (tng. analyst 1954-67), Mass. Psychol. Assn., Sigma Xi. Author: (with Merton M. Gill) Hypnotherapy, 1947, Hypnosis and Related States, 1959. Office: Austen Riggs Center Inc Stockbridge MA 01262

BRENNAN, DOROTHY TERESA OLIVER (MRS. MELVIN GEORGE BRENNAN), polit. party ofcl.; b. Phila., Apr. 30, 1916; d. Murray Sylvester and Sarah Edith (Cannon) Oliver; grad. high sch.; m. Melvin George Brennan, Sr., July 3, 1933; children—Melvin George, Sarah, Arlene. Committeeman Dem. Party, 1950; ward leader Third Dem. Ward, Phila., 1965-68, 1970—; clk. Marriage Bur., 1964-68; del. Dem. Nat. Conv., 1968; chief probate clk. Register of Wills, 1968-72, 2d dep. to registrar, 1972—; v.p. party liaison Dem. Women's Forum, 1972—. Bd. dirs. Community Nursing Service, YMCA. Mem. Community Action Dem. Women's Forum (v.p.), Concern Women Group (chmn.), Phila. Com. for Aid to Biafran Children (co-chmn.). Methodist Episcopalian. Home: 5917 Osage Av Philadelphia PA 19143

BRENNAN, ELEANOR LEE OLSEN, polit. orgn. exec.; b. Salt Lake City, Jan. 10, 1940; d. Lawrence S. and Eleanor (Stewart) Olsen; B.S., U. Utah, 1962; m. Patrick J. Brennan, June 16, 1962 (dec.); children—Patrick John, Coralee. Conf. group leader Olympus Research Corp., 1972. Trainer, cons. vols. Voluntary Action Center, 1972. Bd. dirs. Salt Lake City chpt. League Women Voters, 1964-69; pres. League of Women Voters of Utah, 1971—. Mem. Jr. League, Phi Mu (pres. 1969-61). Home: 1218 S 13th St E Salt Lake City UT 84105 Office: 211 E 3d St S Salt Lake City UT 84111

BRENNAN, SISTER M. JOSEPHINE, educator; b. Green Bay, Wis., Feb. 12; d. James J. and Mary Therese (Dormeaux) Brennan; B.A., Marywood Coll., 1926; M.A., Catholic U. Am., 1927, Ph.D., 1947; student Duquesne U., 1930-35, U. Pitts., 1938-40, N.Y.U., 1963—. Tchr. secondary schs., Pitts., 1929-44; instr. Tchrs. Knights Columbus Extension Sch., Pitts., 1938-42; instr., asst. prof., asso. prof. Marywood Coll., 1947-54, prof. classics dept., 1954—, chmn. classics dept., 1962—, dean Grad. Sch. Arts and Scis., 1970—. Mem. Am. Classical Assn., Classical Assn. Atlantic States, Pa. State Assn. Classical Tchrs., Am. Assn. U. Women, Marywood Alumni Assn., Cath. U. Alumni Assn., Am. Assn. U. Profs., N. Am. Patristic Soc. Editorial bd., translator Fathers of the Church. Address: Marywood Coll Scranton PA 18509

BRENNAN, SISTER MARY JUDINE, educator; b. Richmond, Ind., Oct. 20, 1911; d. Thomas F. and Anna I. (Walz) Brennan; R.N., W. Suburban Hosp., Oak Park, Ill., 1933; B.S. in Edn., Alverno Coll., 1944; M.A., Notre Dame U., 1957; Ph.D., Western Colo. U., 1973. Joined Sch. Sisters of St. Francis, 1934; tchr. elementary sch., Kenosha, Wis., 1938-40, Racine, Wis., 1940-42, Hartford, Wis., 1942-44; tchr. sr. high schs., Pius XI High Sch., Milw., 1944-56, St. Benedict High Sch., Chgo., Madonna High Sch., Aurora, Ill., 1959-67; instr. drama and speech Waubonsee Community Coll., Sugar Grove, Ill., 1967—. Trustee Western Colo. U., 1973—. Recipient Award of Honor placque Western Colo. U., 1973. Mem. Ill. Speech Assn., Am. Theatre Assn., Assn. Collegiate Players, Western Colo. U. Alumni Assn. (sec. 1973—). Home: 314 Pierce St Aurora IL 60505 Office: Route 47A Harter Rd Sugar Grove IL 60554

BRENNAN, MARY M. (MRS. HENRY T. BRENNAN), lawyer; b. Boston, Dec. 13, 1919; d. Cornelius J. and Julia A. (Hayes) Murphy; A.B., Regis Coll. for Women, 1942; certificate mgmt. tng. program Radcliffe Coll., 1943; Ed.M. in Vocational Guidance, Harvard, 1943; LL.B., Boston Coll. Law Sch., 1950; m. Henry T. Brennan, Sept. 22, 1945; children—Judith Marie, Mary Patricia. Admitted to Mass. bar, 1950, U.S. Ct. Mil. Appeals, 1970; atty. Town & Country Homes, Inc. and affiliated cos., 1950-52; pvt. practice of law, 1952-67; asst. U.S. atty. for Dist. of Mass., Boston, 1967—. Sec. Community Action Council, John F. Kennedy Meml. Center, March Dimes Maj. 1963 Drive; sec. Fedn. Charlestown. Orgns. (aid culturally deprived children); established Henry T. Brennan Meml. Scholarship Fund, Boston City Hosp. Sch. Nursing, 1969. Served as lt. (j.g.) USNR, 1943-46. Mem. Mass., Boston bar assns., Harvard Bus. Sch. Assn. Boston, Regis Coll., Radcliffe Coll., Harvard Coll., Boston Coll. Law Sch. (mem. adv. council) Regis Coll. (alumnae bd. 1967—) alumni assns., Am. Legion, Nat. Assn. Cath. Women, Girls' Latin P.T.A., Delta Epsilon Sigma. Roman Catholic (chmn. legal div. local Nat. Council Cath. Women). Club: Radcliffe (Boston). Home: 117 Rutherford Av Charlestown MA 02129 Office: Post Office and Ct House Bldg Boston MA 02108

BRENNAN, PATRICIA ANN CONLON (MRS. RALPH C. BRENNAN), microbiologist; b. Chgo., Nov. 20, 1932; d. John Thomas and Frieda Lucille (Bell) Conlon; B.A., Albion Coll., 1954; M.S., U. Wis.-Madison, 1957; Ph.D., Loyola U. Chgo., 1968; m. Ralph Charles Brennan, Feb. 1, 1958; children—Daniel, Timothy, Margaret. Bacteriology technician G.D. Searle & Co., Skokie, Ill., 1954-56; microbiologist Animal Disease Diagnostic Lab. Wis. Dept. Agr., 1957-58, U. Chgo. Hosps. and Clinics, 1960-63; sci. asst. Argonne (Ill.) Nat. Lab., 1963-68, asst. biologist, 1968-73, biologist, 1973—. Mem. adv. com Inst. Lab. Animal Resources Nat. Acad. Scis. Mem. Am. Soc. for Microbiology, Radiation Research Soc., N.Y. Acad. Sci., Chgo. Assn. Immunologists, Phi Beta Kappa, Sigma Delta Epsilon, Alpha Xi Delta. Roman Catholic. Contbr. numerous articles to profl. jours. Home: 225 Brewster Lombard IL 60148 Office: 9700 S Cass Av Argonne IL 60439

BRENNEMAN, FREDERICA SHOENFIELD (MRS. RUSSELL L. BRENNEMAN, JR.), judge; b. Ann Arbor, Mich., July 10, 1926; d. Allen and Kate (Friedman) Shoenfield; A.B. magna cum laude, Radcliffe Coll., 1947; LL.B., Harvard, 1953; m. Russell L. Brenneman, Jr., July 14, 1951; children—Matthew Charles, Andrew Stearns, Amy Frederica. Admitted to Conn. bar, 1956; practiced in Torrington, 1956-61, Essex, 1961-66; asso. firm Greene & Cook, Torrington, 1956-61, Copp, Brenneman & Tighe, New London, 1961-66; atty. U.S. Dept. Justice, Washington, 1955-56; law clk. judiciary com. Conn. Gen. Assembly, Hartford, 1967; juvenile ct. judge, Hartford, 1967—. Bd. dirs. Amistad House, Hartford, 1972—, Big Bros., Hartford, 1971—, Conn. Prison Assn., 1971—. Mem. Am., Conn. bar assns., Nat. Council Juvenile Ct. Judges, Nat. Council on Crime and Delinquency, Phi Beta Kappa. Democrat. Conglist. Club: Woodledge (Glastonbury, Conn.) Home: 244 Carriage Dr Glastonbury CT 06033 Office: 322 Washington St Harford CT 06106

BRENNEMAN, HELEN GOOD (MRS. VIRGIL JOHN BRENNEMAN), author; b. Harrisonburg, Va., Nov. 26, 1925; d. Lewis Christian and Lois Elizabeth (Eby) Good; student Eastern Mennonite Coll., 1944-45, Goshen Coll., 1948-50; m. Virgil John Brenneman, Nov. 3, 1947; children—Don, Lois, John, Rebecca. Clk. U.S. Dept. Agr., Washington, 1942-44, 46-47; sec. Mennonite Central Com., Gronau, Germany, 1947-48; sec. to dean Goshen (Ind.) Coll. Bibl. Sem., 1948-50. Chmn., Creative Writing Group, Goshen, 1969-72. Hon. mem. Mark Twain Lit. Soc. Democrat. Mennonite. Club: Phalo Book Review (Goshen). Author: Meditations for the New Mother, 1953; But Not Forsaken, 1954; My Conforters, 1966; Meditations for the Expectant Mother, 1968; The House by the Side of the Road, 1971; Ring a Dozen Doorbells, 1973. Home: 516 E Waverly St Goshen IN 46526

BRENNEMAN, MARY LOUISE BLACK, psychiatrist; b. Sewickley, Pa., Oct. 14, 1923; d. George Edward and Laura Marjorie (Dryden) Black; M.D., U. Toronto, 1947; M.P.H., U. Pitts., 1956; m. Richard Henry Brenneman, Dec. 17, 1949 (div. Jan. 1973); children—Gayne Marie, James Richard, Donna Lee, Heidi Kean. Rotating intern W. Pa. Hosp., Pitts., 1947-48, resident pediatrics, 1948-49; resident pediatrics Children's Hosp., Pitts., 1949-50; with Pitts. Pub. Health Dept., 1950-57; clin. instr. pediatrics U. Pitts., 1950-57, U. Cal. at Los Angeles, 1957-68; practice psychiatry, Santa Monica, Cal., 1971—; sch. physician Los Angeles Bd. Edn., 1962-68; attending staff Rancho Los Amigos Hosp., Los Angeles; mem. psychiat. staff St. John's Hosp., Santa Monica, 1973—; staff psychiatrist Camarillo State Hosp., 1971-73. Co-investigator Moonwalker research grant to U. Cal. at Los Angeles Med. Center, 1963-65. Mem. Am., Cal., So. Cal. psychiat. assns., So. Cal. Soc. for Adolescent Psychiatry. Home: 16 Outrigger A Marina del Rey CA 90291 Office: 427 N Camden Dr 105 Beverly Hills CA 90210

BRENNER, ARLINE ROSLYN, educator; b. N.Y.C., Jan. 14, 1943; d. Charles and Frieda (Mazoff) Brenner; B.A., N.Y. U., 1964; M.A., U. Toledo, 1965; Ph.D., Wayne State U., 1968. Grad. asst. dept psychology U. Toledo, 1964-65; teaching asst. Wayne State U., Detroit, 1965-67; instr. Upsala Coll., East Orange, N.J., 1967-68, asst. prof., 1968-69; adj. asst. prof. Herbert H. Lehman Coll., City U. N.Y., 1969-70, asst. prof. John Jay Coll. Criminal Justice, 1970—, also lectr. City Coll., 1969-70. Lectr. European div. U. Md., 1973-74. Mem. Am., Eastern psychol. assns., A.A.A.S., Psi Chi, Iota Alpha Pi. Contbr. numerous articles to profl. jours. Office: Dept Psychology John Jay College of Criminal Justice 445 W 59th St New York City NY 10019

BRENNER, SISTER BARBARA ANN, hosp. adminstr.; b. Wenatchee, Wash.; d. Alphonse A. and Mary (Roediger) Brenner; B.S., Seattle U., 1951; M.Hosp. Adminstrn., St. Louis U., 1970; Dietetic intern King County Hosp., Seattle, 1954-55; dir. dietary dept. Sacred Heart Hosp., Spokane, Wash., 1955-68, asst. adminstr., 1966-68, nutrition instr. Sch. Nursing, 1961-63; resident hosp. adminstrn. Carney Hosp., Boston, 1969-70; adminstrv. asst. Columbus Hosp., Great Falls, Mont., 1970; adminstr. St. Clare Hosp., Ft. Benton, Mont., 1971—. Entered Sisters of Charity of Providence, Seattle, 1951, now del. provincial chpt. Pres.-elect, sec. Comprehensive Health Planning, 1971-73. Trustee Coll. of Great Falls. Mem. Am. Coll. Hosp. Adminstrs., Am., Western, Mont. (dist. pres. 1972-73), Cath. (com. mem.) hosp. assns., Wash. Dietetic Assn. (past officer). Address: St Clare Hospital Fort Benton MI 59442

BRENNER, RENA LOURETTA MORGAN CLAUDY, business exec.; b. Camden, N.J.; d. John Lawler and Louretta (DuFresene) Morgan; certificate Am. Mgmt. Assn., 1967; m. Edgar W. Claudy, June 22, 1940 (div. 1968); 1 dau., Renee May; m. 2d, Millard M. Brenner, Nov. 6, 1971. With Camden Courier, 1937-39, Salt Lake Telegram, 1943-45, Jenkintown Times Chronicle, (Pa.), 1950-55, Suburban Rev., Roxborough, Pa., 1959-60; free lance pub. relations, 1955-60; pub. relations dir., advt. mgr. Gen. Atronics Corp. subsidiary Magnavox Co., Phila., 1960-70; pub. relations mgr. I-T-E Imperial Corp., Phila., 1970-73, dir. corporate communications, 1973—. Publicity adviser adv. bd. Temple U. Community Coll., 1953; chief dep. Women's Civil Def. Unit, Springfield Twp., Pa., 1953-54; pres. Enfield (Pa.) P.T.A., 1954; a founder League Women Voters, Whitemarsh Twp., Pa., 1956; publicity chmn. edn. com. Suburban Phila. chpt. Am. Cancer Soc., 1957. Mem. Phila. Pub. Relations Assn., Assn. Indsl. Advertisers, Am. Mgmt. Assn., Phila. Press Assn., Delaware Valley Assn. Communicators. Club: Poor Richard. Home: 6032 Sheaff Lane Fort Washington PA 19034 Office: 1900 Hamilton St Philadelphia PA 19130

BRENNER, RUTH MARIE ERIKSON (MRS. WOODROW BRENNER), advt. co. exec.; b. West Nyack, N.Y.; d. Erik Emanuel and Marie (Erikson) Erikson; B.S., Pace U., 1939; mgmt. inst. certificate N.Y. U., 1968; m. Woodrow Brenner, Jan. 14, 1942. With Ted Bates & Co., Inc., N.Y.C., 1943—, dir. spl. projects media information and analysis, 1965—, v.p., 1966—. Named Alumnus of Month, Pace U., 1967. Mem. Pace Alumni Assn., Internat. Radio and TV Soc. Home: 67 Demarest Av West Nyack NY 10994 Office: 1515 Broadway New York City NY 10036

BRENNER-WORMSER, EVELYN ROZELLA, nurse therapist; b. Los Angeles, Apr. 3, 1929; d. Frank R. and Anne Louise (Kessler) Brenner; R.N., Baptist Meml. Hosp., San Antonio, 1949; B.S. in Nursing Edn. summa cum laude, Incarnate Word Coll., San Antonio, 1954; M.S. in Psychiat. Nursing summa cum laude, Tex. Woman's U., 1971; m. Joseph Julius Wormser, Nov. 19, 1955; children—Alan Joseph, Deborah Anne, Lisa Michelle. Staff nurse, charge nurse Robert B. Green Hosp., San Antonio, 1949-50; charge and staff nurse obstetrics Brooke Army Hosp., San Antonio, 1950-53; instr. nurses Bapt. Meml. Hosp. Sch. Nursing, 1954-55, Tex. Women's U. Coll. Nursing, 1971, El Centro Coll. Nursing, Dallas, 1972, U. Tex. Sch. Nursing, 1974; pilot project instr. fgn. nurses Dept. Health, Edn. and Welfare, 1972; parent educator, expectant parent educator Dallas Assn. Parent Edn., 1964—; pvt. practice as mental health nurse therapist, Dallas, 1972—. Mem. counseling task force Women for Change Center, Dallas, 1973—. Mem. nurses orgn. Am. Coll. Obstetricians and Gynecologists. Study grantee Nat. Inst. Mental Health. Mem. Am., Tex., Dallas Area nurses assns., Nat. League Nursing (2d v.p. Dallas 1972-73), Am. Orthopsychiat. Assn., Bapt. Meml. Hosp. Sch. Nursing Alumnae Assn. (pres. 1951), League Women Voters, Sigma Theta Tau. Address: 7106 Meadow Rd Dallas TX 75230

BRENT, JOLEENE ADALIE, arts and sci. center adminstr.; b. Dallas, Nov. 27, 1920; d. Joseph Herman and Bertha B. (Raphiel) Margules; B.A., U. Cal. at Los Angeles, 1941, postgrad., 1942-43; postgrad. La. State U., 1953-54; m. Allan Rudolph Brent, Dec. 19, 1941; 1 dau., Joanna Raphiel. Art tchr., supr. Los Angeles Pub. Sch. System, 1941-42; instr. La. State U., 1947-51; art tchr. St. Joseph Acad., Baton Rouge, 1955-63; dir. La. Arts and Sci. Center, 1963—. Designed stained glass windows La. State U. Law Center, 1971, murals Catholic Life Center, Baton Rouge, 1967-72, stained glass windows St. Joseph Cathedral, Baton Rouge, 1968, murals Am. Bank and Trust Co., Baton Rouge, 1971, stained glass windows Cath. Life Center, Our Lady of Mercy (both Baton Rouge), Eglise Assumption, Plattenville, La., mural Convent St. Aloysius, Baton Rouge. Mem. adv. council Jr. Sci. and Humanities Symposium, 1970—; mem. art council Bur. Indian Affairs, U.S. Dept. Interior, Albuquerque, 1969—, Baton Rouge Bicentennial Commn., 1972—, capital dist. drug edn. adv. com. Recipient Alex Weissburg award Dallas Mus. Fine Arts. Mem. Royal Soc. Arts (London), Kappa Delta, Delta Kappa Gamma. Author: A Child Likes, 1970. Home: 3930 Floyd Dr Baton Rouge LA 70808 Office: 502 N Blvd Baton Rouge LA 70802

BRENT, JOSEPHINE STRESEN-REUTER, poet, lectr.; b. Chgo., Aug. 30, 1911; d. Frederick Arthur and Irene Elizabeth (Procter) Stresen-Reuter; student U. Chgo., 1935-36, Down Town Coll., 1935-36, Lewis Inst., 1935-36; B.A., Art Inst. Chgo., 1936; m. Stuart Brent, Mar. 21, 1936 (div. 1947); children—Barbara Jo (Mrs. William Peyton Brower), Robert Leo. Art supr. St. Sabina Sch., Chgo., 1946-49, St. Basals Sch., Chgo., 1947-49; tchr. art and English Chgo. pub. high schs., 1949-52; tchr. art Holland, Mich., 1953-55; lectr. on antiques. Girl Scout leader, Chgo., 1949-52. Recipient 1st prize humorous poem Peninsula Poets, 1970; 3rd prize poetry contest Argentine, Mich., 1962. Mem. Poetry Soc. Mich., Internat. Platform Assn. Contbr. poetry to profl. jours. Home and office: 600 Midway Av Holland MI 49423

BRENT, LISELLE WOLF, editor; b. Europe; d. Willibald and Paula (Dewald) Wolf; student Columbia U., 1944; m. Rudolph Brent, Nov. 9, 1946. Came to U.S., 1938, naturalized, 1944. Designer's asst. Amrose, Inc., Oriole, Inc., Evette Hats, N.Y.C., 1944; millinery designer Miss Bobs, N.Y.C., 1944-46, L. de Valle, Inc., N.Y.C., 1946-49; womans editor United Overseas Press, N.Y.C., 1949-66, editor, 1966—. Named Hon. Citizen State Tenn., 1963. Mem. Fgn. Press Assn., Internat. Platform Assn. Club: Overseas Press America (N.Y.C.). Home 12 E 97th St New York City NY 10029 Office: 663 Fifth Av New York City NY 10022

BRENTON, PEARL YETIVE STEERS (MRS. BYRON HUNTER BRENTON), editor; b. Indpls., Nov. 27, 1911; d. Edwin McMaster Stanton and Leila Edith (Kemp) Steers; A.B., Ind. U., 1933; m. Byron Hunter Brenton, Oct. 25, 1935. Social worker State and County Welfare Depts., 1933-42; editor, columnist Indpls. Star, 1963—. Pres., 4th Ward Women's Republican Club, 1956-60. Recipient medal of Appreciation, S.A.R., 1971. Mem. League Am. Pen Women (treas. Indpls. br. 1966-72), Ind. Pioneer Soc. (membership chmn. 1970—), D.A.R. (treas. 1960-62), Magna Charta Dames, Ind. Mayflower Descs. (mem. bd. assts. 1959—), Koskiusco County Hist. Soc., Psi Iota Xi. Author, compiler: Hoosier Ancestors Indexes. Patentee in field. Home: Rural Route 1 Box 99 Leesburg IN 46538 Office: 3686 E Fall Creek Pkwy N Drive Indianapolis IN 46205

BRENTZEL, WANDA WENIGER (MRS. WILLIAM E. BRENTZEL), botanist, plant pathologist, civic worker; b. Milw., Dec. 5, 1895; d. Wilhelm and Caroline (Taubert) Weniger; B.S., Ore. State U., 1915; M.S., U. Wis., 1916; Ph.D. (Teaching fellow), U. Chgo., 1918; m. William E. Brentzel, July 30, 1925; 1 son, Edward Reese. Instr., William and Vashti Coll., Aledo, Ill., 1918; plant pathologist N.D. Exptl. Sta., Fargo, 1918-25; pvt. researcher cereal diseases, 1925—. Mem. adv. bd. Fargo Nursery Sch., 1942-55; mem. Fargo Bd. Edn., 1942-51, pres., 1945-46; mem., vice chmn. Cass County (N.D.) Sch. Dist. Reorgn. Bd., 1947-62; mem. N.D. Status of Women Commn., 1963-70. Recipient Citation for pub. service U. Chgo., 1954; Citation for outstanding service N.D. Fedn. Women's Clubs, 1960. Fellow A.A.A.S.; mem. Biol. Stain Commn., Bot. Soc. Am., N.D. Council Edn. (founder 1947; pres. 1950-52), Am. Assn. U. Women (br. founder 1922, state chmn. fellowships 1930-38, state pres. 1948-52, state chmn. edn. 1942-48), Nat. Assn. Parliamentarians, N.D. Mental Health Assn. (founder 1952, sec. 1952-54; bd. dirs. 1952-58), N.D. Fedn. Women's Clubs (bd. dirs. 1947-54; state pres. 1952-54), Gen. Fedn. Women's Clubs (bd. dirs. 1952-58, 62-64), Sigma Xi. Editor, writer N.D. Clubwoman, 1944-49; abstractor Biol. Abstracts, 1940—, other plant sci. jours. Contbr. numerous articles to various publs. Address: 1125 N 12th St Fargo ND 58102

BRENZ, ELIZABETH ANN, diversified business co. ofcl.; b. Arkansas City, Kan., Apr. 4; d. Louis Edward and Margaret (MacDonald) Brenz; grad. Arkansas City Jr. Coll., 1939; student Kan. State Coll., 1939-41; B.A., U. Okla., 1946. With advt. dept. El Reno (Okla.) Daily Tribune, 1946-47; editor Kermac News, employee publ., pub. relations work Kerr-McGee Corp., Oklahoma City, 1948-72, creative services adminstr., 1972—. Lectr. journalism classes, served on panel discussions U. Okla., Norman, Okla. State U., Stillwater. Recipient Freedoms Found. at Valley Forge award, 1966, 71. Mem. Internat. Assn. Bus. Communicators (past nat. dir., Oklahoma City chpt. Editor of Year 1956, past pres.), P.E.O., Alpha Xi Delta. Episcopalian. Home: 1902 N Robinson St Oklahoma City OK 73103 Office: Kerr-McGee Center 123 Robert S Kerr Av Oklahoma City OK 73102

BRESENHAN, KAROLINE PATTERSON (MRS. MAURICE L. BRESENHAN, JR.), pub. relations exec.; b. Gilmer, Tex., Feb. 6, 1942; d. Clovis C. and Jewel Estelle (Pearce) Patterson; student U. Mo., 1960-61; B.S., Sam Houston State U., 1962; M.A., U. Tex., 1968; m. Maurice L. Bresenhan Jr., Aug. 31, 1963. Tchr. journalism and speech Huntsville (Tex.) Schs., 1963-65; editor convs. Tex. Med. Assn., Austin, 1963-67; dir. informational services Tex. Classroom Tchrs. Assn., Austin, 1965-68; partner Capitol Ideas, Austin, 1967; editor Houston Tchrs. Assn., 1968-71, Tex. Spectator Mags., 1968-69, Tex. Music Educators Assn., 1969-70; account exec. Ruder & Finn, pub. relations, Houston, 1969—, now v.p. Free lance writer. Cons. foster home div. Harris County Child Welfare Unit, 1971-72, Job Fair, 1973. Recipient Nat. Writing award Ednl. Press, 1966, 68. Mem. Women in Communications (pres.-elect), Pub. Relations Soc. Am. (accredited), Sales and Marketing Execs., Am. Marketing Assn., Zeta Tau Alpha. Office: 647 Capital National Bank Bldg Houston TX 77002

BRESHEARS, GLENDENE LOUISE (MRS. PAUL E. BRESHEARS), town ofcl.; b. Magnet, Tex., Oct. 11, 1920; d. Glen Eric and Vera Ann (Bell) St. John; student Ross Bus. Coll., 1939; m.

Paul E. Breshears, Dec. 22, 1941; children—Paul E., Linda (Mrs. D.A. Kinney). Bookkeeper, Comstock Enterprises, Rangely, Colo., 1957; bookkeeper, parts mgr. Comstock Motors, Rangely, 1958-64; accountant H.O. West, Rangely, 1965; bookkeeper Town of Rangely, 1965-66, town clk., treas., 1966—, clk. municipal ct., 1970—. Mem. Colo. Assn. City Clks., Municipal Finance Officers Assn. So. Baptist (treas. 1962—, ch. clk. 1972—). Home: 206 S Grand St Rangely CO 81648 Office: 209 E Main St Rangely CO 81648

BRESKIN, ARLINE FRIEDMAN (MRS. KENNETH JAY BRESKIN), occupational therapist; b. Mt. Vernon, N.Y., Oct. 3, 1932; d. Charles Stodel and Jeanette (Holczer) Friedman; B.S., Tufts U., 1955; certificate Boston Sch. Occupational Therapy, 1955; certificate Vanderbuilt U. Grad. Sch. Mgmt., 1973; m. Kenneth Jay Breskin, Sept. 21, 1955; children—Douglas Breskin, Gregory, Erica. Chief occupational therapist Mass. Hosp. Sch., 1955-56, Children's Hosp., Washington, 1957-58; occupational therapist Mobility, Inc., New Rochelle, N.Y., 1959-61; cons., United Home Aged Hebrews, New Rochelle, N.Y., 1971—. Chmn. R.J. Bailey P.T.A., 1968; producer Woodlands Scholarship Fund Show, 1971-73; mem. profl. adv. bd. Asso. Vis. Nurses, Westchester County, N.J., 1969—; chmn. Greenburgh Central No 7 Sch. Dist. Transp. Com., 1972—. Mem. Greenburgh Democratic Town Com., 1961-69; sec., Greenburgh Dem. Club, 1967-69. Mem. Westchester Council Aging, Westchester Coalition on Crime and Delinquency, Nat. Council Jewish Women (v.p. community services Greater Westchester sect. 1963-67, pres. 1971-73), Westchester Fedn. Women's Clubs (dir. 1969-71). Bull. editor Northeastern Dist. Bull. Nat. Council Jewish Women, 1972-74. Home: 18 Old Farm Lane Hartsdale NY 10530

BRESLIN, MARIANNE SONNENBRODT, med. educator; b. Buendheim, Germany, Dec. 10, 1918; d. Albert Robert and Alice (Meyer) Sonnenbrodt; M.D., Duesseldorf (Germany) Med. Acad., 1946; m. Lou Eugene Breslin, Nov. 21, 1951 (dec. 1956); 1 dau., Louanne Virginia. Came to U.S., 1951, naturalized, 1960. Intern, City Hosp. I, Hannover, Germany, 1946-47; resident internal medicine City Hosp. III, Hannover, 1947-49; resident surgery City Hosp. Bremen (Germany), 1949-51; fellow Presbyn. Hosp., N.Y.C., 1951-52; resident psychiatry Dorothea Dix Hosp., Raleigh, N.C., 1955-57, N.C. Meml. Hosp., Chapel Hill, 1958-59; staff physician Dorothea Dix Hosp., 1955-59, dir. female service, 1959-60; asst. dir. adult psychiat. outpatient clinic N.C. Meml. Hosp., 1961-68; pvt. practice, Chapel Hill, N.C., 1961-68; mem. staff U. N.C.-Duke Psychoanalytic Inst., 1964—; abstractor Psychosomatic Medicine, 1964-68, asso. prof. psychiatry Duke Med. Center, 1968—, head psychosomatic div., dept. psychiatry, 1973—; pvt. practice psychiatry and psychoanalysis, Durham, 1968—; cons. John Umstead Hosp., Butner, N.C., Durham VA Hosp., Watts Hosp., Durham. Chmn. liaison com. Sch. of Blind, Raleigh, 1955-57; chmn. N.C. Cancer Assn. Drive, 1958. Mem. parent's com. Vardell Hall, Red Springs, N.C., 1968-69. Recipient Distinguished Merit award Am. Cancer Soc., 1958. Diplomate Am. Bd. Psychiatry and Neurology. Fellow Am. Psychiat. Assn.; mem. N.C. Med. Soc., N.C. Neuropsychiat. Assn., Am. Psychoanalytic Assn., Assn. Am. Med. Colls. Lutheran (chmn. stewardship com. 1966-69, mem. council 1968-69). Clubs: Carolina Caribbean (Beech Mountain, N.C.); Chapel Hill Country. Author chpt. in book. Home: 1604 Michaux Rd Chapel Hill NC 27514 Office: Box 3837 Duke Med Center Durham NC 27706

BRESSLER, (MAYBELLE) JEAN, educator; b. Oakland, Neb.; d. Daniel Arthur and Maybelle Blanche (Guss) Bressler; B.A., U. Neb., 1950, M.A., 1958, Ph.D., 1965. Tchr. English, Pacific Beach Jr. High Sch., San Diego, 1950-52; tchr. English, Spanish, South High Sch., Omaha, 1952-59; teaching asst. English, U. Neb., 1959-61; tchr. English, Spanish, South High Sch., Omaha, 1961-63, chmn. English and fgn. lang. dept., 1963-66; instr. English, U. Neb., 1964, asst. prof. English edn., 1966-69, asso. prof., 1969—. Pilot tchr. Project English, Omaha Pub. Schs., 1962-66; co-dir. Workshop in English for Tchrs. in Dist. 66 Schs., 1967; mem. North Central Assn. Evaluation Team, 1969—; co-dir. workshop in linguistics, 1970-71; docent chmn. Henry Doorly Zoo; chmn. Zoo Edn. Task Force. Mem. N.E.A., Nat. Council Tchrs. English, Tchrs. English to Speakers of Other Langs., Modern Lang. Assn., Internat. Reading Assn., Am. Dialect Soc., Assn. Supervision and Curriculum Devel., Neb. Council Tchrs. English, Conf. English Edn., Conf. Coll. Composition and Communication, Henry Doorly Zoo Guild, Fund for Animals, Nat. Mustang Assn., Nat. Cat Protection Soc., Pet Pride, Nat. Wildlife Fedn., Defenders Wildlife, Kappa Delta Pi, Republican. Conglist. Home: 12724 Arbor St Omaha NE 68144

BRETT, GRACE NEFF (MRS. GILBERT JAMES BRETT), author; b. Chgo., Feb. 11, 1900; d. George Gottlob and Sophia Maria (Bach) Neff; B.A., U. Ill., 1925; postgrad. New Sch. Social Research, N.Y.C., 1936, Columbia, 1937, 38; m. Gilbert James Brett, Oct. 15, 1942. Advt. copy exec. Women's Wear Daily, Fairchild Publs., Chgo., 1925-29; owner advt. service studio, Chgo., 1929-31; v.p., stylist Sportswear Mag., N.Y.C., 1931-33; writer, designer, lectr. Fashion Acad., N.Y.C., 1935-42, also lectr.; creator house furnishings promotion Nat. Kate Greenaway, N.Y.C. and Chgo., 1942-52; lectr., designer Ray Vogue Sch., Chgo., 1942-52; writer, contbr. religious art Am. Peoples Ency. Yearbook, 1956-62; writer, contbr. Follett Pub. Co. Great Books leader Chgo. Pub. Library, 1959-64. Mem. Women in Communications, Soc. Midland Authors, Nat. League Am. Pen Women, Chgo. Childrens Reading Roundtable, Alpha Delta Kappa. Club: Univ. Ill. Author: Squiffy the Skunk, 1953; The Runaway, 1958 (Book of Month, Parents Mag. 1959, prize for best children's book Lowell Sch. 1959); That Willy and Wally, Albert Whitman, 1964; Tom Paine-a Biography, 1965; Hatsy Katsy, 1969. Address: 1566 Grove St Clearwater FL 33515

BRETZ, GISELLE TAKACS (MRS. G. WILLIAM BRETZ), physician; b. Gyomore, Hungary, Sept. 20, 1939; d. Istvan and Gizella (Nagy) Takacs; M.D., Med. U. Budapest, Hungary, 1963; m. G. William Bretz, Aug. 11, 1962; children—Julie Camilla, Stephen William. Came to U.S., 1964, naturalized, 1969. Intern, Union Meml. Hosp., Balt., 1966-67; resident John's Hopkins Hosp., Balt., 1967-71; practice medicine, specializing in radiotherapy, Dayton, O., 1971—; clin. asst. prof. radiology Ohio State U., 1971—. NIH fellow, 1964-66. Mem. Am. Assn. Therapeutic Radiologists, Am. Coll. Radiology. Home: 648 Murrell Dr Dayton OH 45429 Office: Miami Valley Hosp Dayton OH 45409

BREWER, CLYDE SAVAGE (MRS. CLAUDE A. BREWER), educator, civic worker; b. Whitewright, Tex.; d. Charles Edward and Flora Belle (Payne) Savage; grad. North Tex. State U., 1917; B.S., So. Meth. U., 1951; m. Claude A. Brewer, Jan. 13, 1918 (dec. Jan. 1, 1970); children—Bette Belle (Mrs. Carl H. Ingwer, Jr.), James Ashley II, Claude A. Tchr., Jefferson, 1914-15, Sherman, Tex., 1917-18, Dublin, Tex., 1920-21, Ranger, Tex., 1921-22, Big Springs, Tex., 1922-23, Cumby, Tex., 1925-27, Dallas, 1935-38, 1943-44, Dallas Pub. Schs., 1942-43, 1953-54; substitute tchr. Dallas Schs., 1967—. Publicity chmn. Dallas Woman's Forum, 1967—; mem. Local History and Geneal. Soc.-Dallas Pub. Library, 1955—, dir., 1963-69; pres. Clionean Study Club, 1964-65; del. State Federated Clubs, 1915-17; pres. Christian Woman's Fellowship Fowler Homes, 1966-67, 1967-68; mem. P.T.A., Robert E. Lee Elementary Sch., 1927-43, J.L. Long Jr. High Sch., 1933-35, Woodrow Wilson High Sch., 1932-40, Spence Jr. High Sch., 1941-45, North Dallas High Sch., 1946-50; active various fund drives. Mem. D.A.R. (com. chmn. 1965-69), Nat. Soc. China Painters, So. Meml. Assn. (v.p. Dallas chpt. 1973-74), Cosmos Rev. Class (1st v.p. 1972-73). Mem. Christian Ch. (pres. Lida C. Walls Bible Class 1956, v.p. 1973-74, corr. sec. Christian Women's Fellowship 1969-70). Clubs: Palm (pres. 1956-57), Mary Arden. Address: 6824 Dalhart Lane Dallas TX 75214

BREWER, DEBORAH, artist, tchr.; student Hayter Studio 17, N.Y.C.; B.F.A., Cranbrook Acad. Art. Tchr. art, supr. practice teaching, seminars Smith Coll., 1945-47; tchr., adminstr. Del. Art Center, 1947-49; tchr. painting, exptl. plastics workshop Pasadena (Cal.) Art Museum, 1961-68, coordinator U. Cal. at Los Angeles extension class, summers 1969-71, program coordinator, 1969-72; research specialist to Los Angeles Sch. Bd., 1972—; tchr. art Watts Towers Art Center, Los Angeles, 1964-67, dir., 1966, organizer Watts Art Festival (now Watts Summer Festival), 1965; tchr. Los Angeles County Mus. Art, 1966-68; works exhibited Detroit Art Mus., Smith Coll., Cranbrook Mus., Del. Art Mus., Gallery Modern Art, Washington. Address: 952 S Marengo St Pasadena CA 91106

BREWER, DOROTHY (MRS. NILES CHUBB), physician; b. San Antonio, Apr. 6, 1920; d. Leo and Dorothy (Swearingen) Brewer; A.B., U. Tex., 1940; M.D., Columbia, 1943; m. Niles Chubb, June 17, 1955. Intern, Charity Hosp., New Orleans, 1944-45; resident Bellevue Hosp., N.Y.C., 1945-48; practice medicine specializing in internal medicine, San Antonio, 1949—. Diplomate Am. Bd. Internal Medicine. Mem. Tex. Acad. Internal Medicine, Am. Heart Assn., Am., Tex., Bexar County med. assns., San Antonio Club Internal Medicine (past pres.), Jr. League, Pi Beta Phi. Home: 308 Torcido Dr San Antonio TX 78209 Office: 124 Dallas St San Antonio TX 78205

BREWER, ELAINE CATHERINE, educator; b. N.Y.C., Aug. 24, 1946; d. Donald Macdermid and Mary Edwina (Riley) Brewer; A.B., West Liberty State Coll., 1967; M.A., W.Va. U., 1970. Social worker W.Va. Dept. Welfare, Moundsville, 1967-69; head tchr. Monmouth County Vocational Sch., West Long Branch, N.J., 1970-71; tchr. Middletown (N.J.) Twp. Bd. Edn., 1971—. Mem. Nat., N.J., Monmouth County, Middletown Twp. edn. assns., Council for Exceptional Children, Am. Assn. on Mental Deficiency, Mensa, Alpha Psi Omega, Kappa Pi. Home: Beacon Hill PO Box 152 Atlantic Highlands NJ 07716

BREWER, JULIET GODDARD, historic restoration dir., museum coordinator; b. Harrodsburg, Ky., Apr. 23, 1898; d. Rebel E. and Katherine Bruce (Edelen) Goddard; student Beaumont Coll., Harrodsburg, 1917; m. Lawrence Brewer, Oct. 20, 1920 (dec.); children—Katherine Dade (dec.), Robert McAfee. Active in establishment Waveland (Ky.) Life Mus., 1956-60, Shakertown at Pleasant Hill Mus. Village, 1959—, Hunt Morgan Mus., 1960—, Liberty Hall Mus., 1961—, Henry Clay Law Office Mus., 1968—; cons. on historic restoration to various Ky. orgns., including Commonwealth of Ky. Heritage Commn.; dir. Ky. Heritage Commn., asst. to regional state hist. socs. in planning restoration projects. Trustee Shakertown at Pleasant Hill, Blue Grass Trust for Historic Preservation, Short St. Orphan's Home. Recipient awards Colonial Williamsburg, Blue Grass Trust for Historic Preservation, U. Ky. Mem. Nat. Trust for Historic Preservation, Ky. Hist. Soc., Colonial Dames Am. (trustee Ky.), Garden Club Am., Garden Club Ky. Democrat. Presbyn. Club: Idle Hour. Author articles on restoration mus. houses, growth and prodn. tobacco. Home: 221 Henry Clay Blvd Lexington KY 40502 Office: PO Box 353 Lexington KY 40501

BREWER, LIS KAMMA (MRS. SAM POPE BREWER), pub. relations exec.; b. Cnia, Sarmiento, Argentina, Sept. 24, 1924 (came to U.S. 1959, naturalized 1967); d. Hans Lauritz and Kamma Sylvia (Schou) Wange; grad. Normal Sch., Buenos Aires, 1941; writing courses N.Y. U., 1960; m. Sam Pope Brewer, June 11, 1965. Pub. relations rep. Braniff Internat., Lima, Peru, 1953-59; promotion mgr. St. Louis Globe Democrat, 1959; pub. relations officer Brit. Overseas Airways Corp., N.Y.C., 1961-64; dir. pub. relations Hilton Internat., N.Y.C., 1964—. Mem. Soc. Am. Travel Writers, Women in Pub. Relations. Presbyn. (trustee). Home: 201 E 21st St New York City NY 10010 Office: Hilton Internat 301 Park Av New York City NY 10022

BREWER, MABEL STRICKLIN (MRS. WILLIAM WALTER BREWER), city ofcl.; b. Clifton, Tenn., Jan. 18, 1908; d. Iley Amos and Flora Ethel (Brewer) Stricklin; certificate interior decorating Murfreesboro (Tenn.) State U., 1958; m. William Walter Brewer, May 21, 1926 (dec. 1945); children—William Walter, Charles E., Rita (Mrs. Harold Bell), Gene S., Patsy (Mrs. Allen Barnett). Sheriff, Wayne County, Tenn., 1945-46; elementary tchr. Wayne County Sch. System, Waynesboro, 1946-50; owner Waynesboro Motel, 1951-68; commr. Waynesboro City Bd. Commrs., 1969—. Mem. Am. Legion Aux., Waynesboro Hist. Soc. Methodist (sec. United Women's Soc. 1972—), Order Eastern Star, Waynesboro Garden Club. Home: S Main St Waynesboro TN 38485

BREWER, MAXINE REGINA ROSENTHAL (MRS. GEORGE E.F. BREWER), artist; b. Toledo, Aug. 31, 1909; d. Edwin M. and Ester (Loeb) Rosenthal; student Wicker Art Sch., Detroit, 1922-27, Andre L'Hote Atelier, Paris, France, 1930-31, Art Sch. Soc. Arts and Crafts, Detroit, 1945-47; m. Hoke Levin, Sept. 14, 1933 (dec. 1960); children—Barbara (Mrs. Reuben Bergman), Frances (Mrs. F. Koerner), Margaret (Mrs. John Larcade); m. 2d, George E.F. Brewer, Mar. 4, 1967. Dir., Newman Devel. Co., Detroit, 1935-45, Hadley of Worcester (Mass.), 1960-63, Hadley of Springfield (Mass.), 1960-63; one-man show Detroit Artists Market, 1933; exhibited in group shows at Mich. Artists Annual Exhbn., Am. Painting and Sculpture, Chgo., Pa. Acad. Fine Arts, South Bend Art Assn., Mich. Regional, Mich. Watercolor Soc., Toledo Area Artists, Scarab Club Watercolor Exhbn; represented in permanent collections at Northwood Inst., Midland, Mich. Pres., Balmoral Found., Detroit, 1956-58, Hoke and Maxine Levin Found., Detroit, 1958—; 1st pres. Detroit City Theater, 1967-68, bd. dirs., 1969—; sec. bd. trustees Art Sch. Soc. Arts and Crafts, Detroit, 1957-69, v.p., 1970—; mem. bd. advisers Wayne State U. Press, v.p., 1974—. Recipient 1st prize oils Detroit Soc. Women Painters and Sculptors, 1956, 58, 59, 60. Mem. Detroit Symphony Soc., Founders Soc. Detroit Inst. Arts, Archives Am. Art, Council Jewish Women, Friends Detroit Pub. Library, Livingston Co. Art Assn., Detroit Soc. Women Painters and Sculptors, Mich. Acad. Arts, Scis. and Letters. Address: 11065 E Grand River Rd Brighton MI 48116

BREWER, WENONAH GOSHORN, educator; b. Clay City, Ind., Dec. 1, 1906; d. Martin Riley and Mae (Shonkwiler) Goshorn; B.S., Ind. State Tchrs. Coll., 1939, M.S., 1940; Ed.D., Ind. U., 1950; m. Alza Alton Brewer, June 14, 1952 (dec.). Tchr., Mishawaka (Ind.) Pub. Schs., 1926-39; tchr. Lab. Sch. Ind. State U. at Terre Haute, 1939-42, dean of students, 1942-46, asst. prin., 1946-50; prof. edn., asst. dir. teaching div. Ind. State U., 1950—. Chmn. adv. com. St. Anthony Hosp. Sch. Nursing, 1948-56; chmn. Ind. Tchr. Edn. Workshops, steering com., 1952—. Mem. Edinburg Community Sch. Bd., 1962-67. Mem. Ind. Tchrs. Assn. (sec., pres.), Nat. (clinics steering com., 1960-66, workshops steering com., 1966—), Ind. (sec., pres.) assns. student teaching, Nat. Assn. Higher Edn., Nat. Assn. U. Profs., Am. Assn. U. Women, N.E.A., Ind. State U. Alumni Assn., Ind. U. Alumni Assn., Daughters Am. Colonists, Kappa Delta Pi, Pi Lambda Theta, Kappa Pi. Clubs: Franklin (Ind.) Hillview Country; Terre Haute (Ind.) Women's Department. Home: Rural Route 5 Box 211 Franklin IN 46131

BREWSTER, ETHEL CRAIG, city ofcl.; b. Mifflinburg, Pa., July 30, 1889; d. Benjamin Keller and Anna Belle (Young) Heisler; student pub. schs., Mifflinburg; m. Harry S. Brewster, Dec. 31, 1923 (dec.). Dep. county clk., 1914-22, sec., county supt. hwys., 1922-23; with Abstract Office, Freeport, Ill., 1928-37; dep. circuit clk., Stephenson County, Ill., 1937-43, circuit clk., 1943-45; city treas., Freeport, 1945—. Pres., Stephenson County Humane Soc., 1954—; v.p. Stephenson County Nursing Home Aux., 1967; treas. Stephenson County Council for Aging; mem. adv. bd. 9 county area Northwestern Area Agy. on Aging; chmn. March of Dimes Stephenson County. Mem. Freeport C. of C. (pres. womens div., treas.), Am. Bus. Womens Assn. (elected 1st Woman of Year 1962), Am. Legion Aux. (50 Year pin). Club: Quota (pres. 1955-57) (Freeport). Home: 725 W Galena Av Freeport IL 61032 Office: City Hall Freeport IL 61032

BREYTSPRAAK, CHARLOTTE JANET HELFAND (MRS. JOHN BREYTSPRAAK, JR.), psychologist; b. Woonsocket, R.I.; d. Samuel and Mary (Kahn) Helfand; B.S., Simmons Coll., 1952; M.A., Columbia, 1953, Ed.D., 1964; m. John Breytspraak, Jr., Dec. 27, 1958. Counselor, Hunter Coll. Guidance Center for Adults, N.Y.C., 1954-55; rehab. counselor Bklyn. Tb and Health Assn., 1955-56; asso. dir. career counseling and placement bur. Hunter Coll., 1956-59; psychology intern VA, N.Y.C., 1959-62; counselor Hunter Coll., 1962-63; psychologist counseling center, Hofstra U., 1963-65; supr. tng. Vocational Adv. Service, N.Y.C., 1965-66, asst. dir., 1966-67; psychologist Marymount Coll., Tarrytown, N.Y., 1967—; pvt. practice, 1968—. Testing cons. Lane Bryant, Inc., N.Y.C., 1957-59. Mem. World Mental Health Assn., Am., N.Y. State psychol. assns., N.Y. Soc. Clin. Psychologists, Internat. Council Psychologists, Kappa Delta Pi, Pi Lambda Theta. Home: 315 W 70th St New York City NY 10023 Office: Marymount Coll Tarrytown NY 10591

BRIAN, MARGARET PAXSON (MRS. HARRY F. BRIAN), physician; b. Phila., Sept. 23, 1913; d. Charles Small and Martha (Dunning) Paxson; B.S., Ursinus Coll., 1935; M.D., Temple U., 1939; postgrad. Wayne State U., 1944-46; m. Harry F. Brian, Aug. 17, 1940; children—Bonnie Paxson, Penny Paxson, Terry Paxson. Intern Pottsville (Pa.) Gen. Hosp., 1939-40; obstetric residency Hosp. for Women of Md., Balt., 1943-44, gynecology residency City of Detroit Receiving Hosp., 1944-46; clinician, bd. med. dirs. Planned Parenthood Assn. of Md., 1958—; family planning clinician Cecil, Howard, Baltimore County Dept. Health, 1964—. Mem. Balt. Planning and Housing Assn., A.M.A., Am. Med. Women's Assn., Baltimore County Med. Soc., Assn. Planned Parenthood Physicians. Republican. Methodist. Home: Box 13 Riderwood MD 21139 Office: 517 N Charles St Baltimore MD 21201

BRIANSKY, RITA, artist; b. Grajewa, Poland, July 25, 1925; ed. Montreal Mus. Fine Arts, Ecole des Beaux-Arts, Art Students League, N.Y.C. One-man shows at Montreal Mus. Fine Arts, 1958, 60, Upstairs Gallery, Toronto, 1959, Elca London Studio, Montreal, 1963, 65, Gallery Pascal, Toronto, 1964, 66, 69, 72, Artlenders, Montreal, 1964, Alice Peck Gallery, Burlington, Ont., Can., 1964, Glynhyrst Arts Council, Brantford, Ont., 1965, West End Art Gallery, Montreal, 1967, Gallery 1640, Montreal, 1969, Waddington Galleries, Montreal, 1971, 73, Gallery Fore, Winnipeg, Man., 1971, Wallack Galleries, Ottawa, Ont., 1972; exhibited in group shows, 1949—, including Canadian Soc. Graphic Artists, 1958-61, Women's Internat., Vichy, France, 1960, Internat. Prints, Tokyo, 1960, Phila. Art Alliance, 1965, UN, 1965, Internat. Exhbn. Miniature Graphic, Fredrikstad, Norway, 1973; works represented in permanent collections including McMaster U., Willistead Art Gallery, Vancouver Art Gallery, Canadian Nat. R.R., Alta. Coll. Art; pub. etchings portfolio based on Shakespeare's sonnets. Recipient various awards. Mem. Canadian Soc. Graphic Artists, Canadian Painter-Etchers and Engravers, Assn. de Graveurs du Que. Address: 4832 Wilson Av Montreal 253 PQ Canada

BRICHANT, COLETTE DUBOIS (MRS. ANDREW BRICHANT), educator, author; b. Noisy le Sec, Seine, France, July 9, 1926; d. Henri and Suzanne (Aubourg) Dubois; License en Lettres, U. Paris, 1947, diplome d'Etudes Superieures, 1948, Doctorat, 1952; m. Andrew Brichant, Sept. 8, 1955; 1 son, Stephen. Instr. Russell Sage Coll., 1950, Middlebury Coll., 1950-58; lectr. U. Cal. at Los Angeles, 1958—. Instr. Peace Corps Program, 1963-65. Fulbright scholar, 1949; Ford Found. grantee. Author books: Tableaux d'histoire, 1964, L'Heritage Cultural, 1964; La France au travail, 1965, Arts de France, 1965; French Grammar, Key to Reading, 1969; French for the Humanities, 1968; French for the Social Sciences, 1968; French for the Sciences, 1968; Charles de Gaulle, artiste de l'action, 1968; La France au cours des Ages, Grands jours et Vie Quotidienne, 1973; others. Home: 3232 Glendon Av Los Angeles CA 90034

BRICK, KATHERINE ADAMS MENGES (MRS. FRANK REEVE BRICK), powder puff derby ofcl.; b. Dixmont, Me.; d. Oliver Adelbert and Ruth (Swift) M.; grad. Sargent Coll., 1927-30; B.S. in Edn., Boston U., 1931; M.A., N.Y. U., 1938; postgrad. Columbia, 1939; m. Frank Reeve Brick, Feb. 28, 1948; 1 dau., Ruth Canivet. Bd. dirs. Powder Puff Derby, Teterboro Airport, N.J., 1951—, chmn. bd., 1961—. Cons. FAA Women's Adv. Com. on Aviation, 1968-71; safety counselor FAA, 1972-74; participant numerous air races including Power Puff Derbies, 1955-59; mem. electoral com. Teterboro Aviation Hall of Fame, 1972. Institutor, co-chmn. Colt for Kim and Women of Korea, 1962-63. Served to capt. WASP, 1943-45. Recipient awards including spl. award for outstanding contbn. to humanity Boston U. Sargent Coll. Alumni, 1967; certificate commendation FAA, 1966; Paul Tissandier diploma Fedn. Aeronautique Internat., 1973. Mem. Ninety-Nines (Amelia Earhart medals 1949, 60, internat. pres. 1950-51, exec. bd. 1951-53), Nat. Pilots Assn. (sec. bd. 1958-59, 68—, bd. dirs.), Aviation Space Writers Assn., Thunderbolt P-47 Pilots Assn. (sec. 1970—), Nat. Aeros. Assn., Air Force Assn., Am. Aviation Hist. Assn., Australian Women Pilots Assn., San Diego Aerospace Mus., Airplane Owners and Pilots Assn. Clubs: Silver Wings; Wings (N.Y.C.); Teaneck College (N.J.). Author booklet: Thirty Sky Blue Years, 1959. Contbr. articles to newspapers, profl. publs. Home: 820 Blanch Av Norwood NJ 07648 Office: Teterboro Airport Teterboro NJ 07608

BRICK, SISTER RAPHAEL, educator; b. Lindsay, Ont., Can., Apr. 4, 1914; d. Herbert Maurice and Catherine Frances (Shannon) Brick; B.S. in Edn., Mt. St. Joseph Tchrs. Coll., 1942; M.A., Northwestern U., 1947. Tchr., Cathedral Elementary Sch., Buffalo, 1934-40, Mt. St. Joseph Pvt. Grade Sch., Buffalo, 1940-49; faculty, edn. div. Medaille Coll., Buffalo, 1950—, asso. prof. 1955—; dir. pub. relations, 1960—. Tchr. ednl. TV, Buffalo, 1959-67. Recipient Gibbons award for outstanding service Diocese Buffalo, 1963. Mem. Western N.Y. Edn. Communication Council. Author: (with Sister Monica Marie Lahiff) Science and Living in Today's World, grade 7, 1954, grade 8, 1954. Home 1 Agassiz Circle Buffalo NY 14214 Office: 18 Agassiz Circle Buffalo NY 14214

BRICKELL, MARGARET ANN BRADY, prodn. agy. exec.; b. Chgo., July 1, 1933; d. Michael Nugent and Margaret LaVallon (Barry) Brady; B.A., U. Miss., 1957; m. Robert Vreeland Brickell, Aug. 8, 1953 (div. Oct. 1970); children—Kimberly Ann, Jennifer, David, Kate. Airline stewardess Delta Airlines, 1952-53; airline reservationist Pan Am., Seattle, 1953-55; romper room tchr. WRAL-TV, Raleigh, N.C., 1959-61; kindergarten tchr. Ravenscroft Sch., Raleigh, 1963-65; woman's editor, broadcaster radio sta. WPTF, Raleigh, 1964-69; dir., radio-TV broadcaster Prodn. Agy. of N.C., Raleigh, 1969—; free-lance broadcaster, 1969—. Judge N.C. beauty pageants, 1959-69; judge P.T.A. Oak Leaf Award, 1971, 72. Recipient mental health awards Wake County Mental Health Assn. and N.C. Mental Health Assn., 1966, 68. Mem. Am. Women in Radio and TV (N.C. pres. 1972-74), Delta Delta Delta. Episcopalian (chmn. Altar Guild 1973—). Wirter, producer, narrator ednl. tapes. Address: 4501 Keswick Dr Raleigh NC 27609

BRICKMAN, DOROTHY, educator; b. Vineyard Haven, Mass., June 1, 1916; d. Judal and Eudice (Midzuk) Brickman; B.S., Simmons Coll., 1938; postgrad N.Y. Sch. Social work, 1956-57; M.A., Tchrs. Coll., Columbia, 1958, 64. Asst. dir., dir. activities U.S.O., Augusta, Ga., 1943-46, Balboa, C.Z., 1946, 52-56; dir. vol. service dept. Beth Israel Hosp., Boston, 1946-50; dir. Christmas Holiday Center for Fgn. Students, N.Y.C., 1958-59; acting dir. U.S.O., Tokyo, Japan, 1962-63, asso. dir., program dir., 1958-63; mem. dean of womens staff U. Cin., 1965-66; fgn. student adviser Western Coll. for Women, Oxford, O., 1966—, instr. edn., 1968-69, prof., 1973—, dir. study abroad program, 1971—. Chmn., Internat. Dialogue Series, 1969—, pres., 1971—. Mem. Nat. Assn. Fgn. Student Affairs (chmn. region VI 1973—), N.Y. Internat. House Alumni Assn., Comparative and Internat. Edn. Soc., Japan Soc., Am.-Japan Soc., Internat. House Japan, Am. Assn. UN, Am. Assn. Higher Edn., Am., Ohio personnel and guidance assns., Nat. (chmn. internat. students and programs com. 1973—), Ohio assns. women deans, adminstrs. and counselors, Am. Acad. Polit. and Social Sci., Ohio Coll. Assn. (v.p. internat. edn. sect. 1971-72, pres. 1972-73, dir. 1973—), Am. Assn. U. Women (dir. Oxford br. 1969-71, chmn. pub. information com. 1973—), Cin. Council World Affairs, Columbia U. Sch. Social Work, Simmons Coll. Sch. Social Work, Simmons Coll., Tchrs. Coll., Columbia U. alumni assns., Am. Coll. Personnel Assn., Internat. Conf. Jewish Communal Service, Internat. Platform Assn., Dukes County Hist. Soc., Archaeol. Inst. Am. (asso.), Pi Lambda Theta, Kappa Delta Pi. Delta Kappa Gamma. Home: Vineyard Haven MA 02568 Office: Western Coll for Women Pi, Oxford OH 45056

BRICKUS, SISTER HILDA R., educator; b. Bklyn.; d. Eugene and Etta (Byrdsong) Brickus; B.S. in Radiologic Tech., St. Louis U., 1954, M.A., 1968, postgrad. Joined Sisters of St. Mary, 1946; adminstrv. supr. dept. radiology and ednl. dir. sch. radiologic tech. St. Mary's Infirmary Hosp., St. Louis, 1954-63, St. Joseph's Hosp., St. Charles, Mo., 1963-66; mem. faculty St. Louis U., 1956, 65—, asst. chmn. dept. radiologic tech., 1968—. Mem. Commn. on Human Rights of Archdiocese of St. Louis, 1968—, radiologic tech. adv. com. Jr. Coll. Dist. St. Louis-St. Louis County, 1968—. Mem. Assn. U. Radiologic Technologists, Am. Registry Radiologic Tech., Am., Mo. (mem. edn. com. 1968) socs. radiologic tech., N.A.A.C.P., Nat. Black Sisters Conf., Alliance for Regional Community Health. Home: 2904 Lawton Pl St Louis MO 63103

BRIDGE, ALMA NIELSEN STANLIS, librarian; b. Detroit; d. Harold E. and Klara (Fredericksen) Nielsen; B.A., U. Mich., 1945, B.A. in Library Sci., 1948; m. Peter J. Stanlis, Aug. 16, 1945 (div. Feb. 1970); children—Ingrid Alma (Mrs. Peter R. Russell), Eleanor Marie (Mrs. Eric Johnson); m. George H. Bridge, Oct. 13, 1974. Instr. English, U. Mich., Ann Arbor, 1946-47, cataloging asst., Clements Library, 1947-48; librarian Detroit Pub. Library, 1948-50; high sch. librarian, Riverview (Mich.), 1956-61, dir. sch. libraries, 1961-68; head social scis. div. Rockford (Ill.) Pub. Library, 1969, coordinating supr. supporting services, 1970—. Mem. faculty Nat. Def. Edn. Act Inst. for Sch. Library Suprs., Case Western Res. U., Cleve., summer 1966; chmn. Trenton (Mich.) Pub. Library Adv. Commn., 1962-67. Mem. A.L.A., Am. Soc. for Personnel Adminstrn., Ill. Library Assn., Republican. Episcopalian. Club: Zonta of Rockford. Home: 2205 Denver Drive Rockford IL 61108 Office: Rockford Pub Library 215 N Wyman Rockford IL 61101

BRIDGEMAN, FRIEDA ESTES (MRS. GARVEY BRIDGEMAN), educator; b. Dexter, Mo.; d. Harley Sylvester and Cleopatra (White) Estes; B.S., Southeast Mo. State Coll., 1956; M.S., U. Wis., 1958, Ph.D. in Theatre Design, 1971; m. Harry E. Keener, Jr., Oct. 10, 1943; children—Mallory Kay, Harry Eliott, III; m. 2d, Garvey Bridgeman, Mar. 28, 1959. Instr. art. No. Kansas City pub. schs., 1956-60; instr., designer, tech. dir. Univ. Playhouse, U. Mo. at Kansas City, 1960-63; grad. asst., lectr. U. Wis.-Stevens Point, 1963-65, asso. prof. theatre, theatre designer, 1965—. Coordinator judges Wis.-Am. Coll. Theatre Festival, 1974-75. Bd. dirs. Wis. Theatre Assn., 1971-72, chmn. spl. service com., 1972—; chmn. bd. dirs. Wis. Repertory Theatre Co., 1973-74. Mem. United Scenic Artists Assn., U.S. Inst. Theatre Tech., Am. Theatre Assn., Am. Assn. U. Profs., Wis. Acad. Letters, Arts and Sci., Assn. U. Wis. Faculties. Home: 1401 4th Av Stevens Point WI 54481

BRIDGES, ANN MIDDLEBROOKS, city ofcl.; b. Josephine, Tex., Dec. 17, 1930; d. William Arthur and Lela May (Buck) Middlebrooks; student So. Methodist U., 1947-48; m. Doyle L. Bridges, July 20, 1948 (div. Apr. 1949); 1 son, Larry M. Charge campaign materials Dallas Community Chest, 1948-49; bookkeeper Wilcoxson & Burns Ins. Agy., Farmersville, Tex., 1953-55; dep. company clk. Collin Co., McKinney, Tex., 1955-61; city sec. Farmersville, 1961—. Active United Fund, 1963—; sec. Centennial Celebration, 1973; chmn. Cystic Fibrosis drive, Farmersville, 1973. Mem. City Secs. Assn. Tex., Wesleyan Service Guild (past pres., treas., v.p. 1972—). Methodist (youth leader, mem. choir, bd. stewards). Home: 307 S Washington St Farmersville TX 75031 Office: 303 S Main St Farmersville TX 75031

BRIDGES, CONSTANCE LOUISE, pub. relations exec.; b. Bklyn., Mar. 7, 1935; d. Robert Wallace and Eleutheria (Bezas) Bridges; B.B.A., Hofstra U., 1956. Tchr. Uniondale (N.Y.) High Sch., 1956-58; sec. Am. Bosch Arma Corp., Garden City, N.Y., 1958-63; exec. sec. to v.p. Republic Aviation, Farmingdale, N.Y., 1963-64; exec. appointments sec. to pres. Diebold Group, N.Y.C., 1965-66; bus. mgr., corporate treas. L.I. Bus. Review, Syosset, N.Y., 1966-69; pub. relations dir., books dept. dir. Townsend Communications Bur., Syosset, 1969-70; pub. relations dir. L.I. Airports Limousine Service Corp., Farmingdale, 1970-72; pub. relations specialist Nassau Hosp., Mineola, N.Y., 1972-74; mgr. community relations, marketing and promotions Met. Suburban Bus. Authority, Carle Place, N.Y., 1974—. Tchr. adult edn. program Uniondale (N.Y.) High Sch., 1956-57. Alumni Assn. scholar, 1952-56; Nat. Secs. Assn. scholar, 1953-54. Mem. Am. Assn. U. Women (pub. information officer 1972—), L.I. Pub. Relations Assn., L.I. Communicators Assn., Solon Soc. Home: 2040 Valentines Rd Westbury NY 11590 Office: One Old Country Rd Carle Place NY 11514

BRIDGES, LUCILE HUDSON (MRS. MARK JAGOE BRIDGES), psychologist, educator; b. Eatonton, Ga., July 28, 1914; d. John Rees and Minnie Lucile (Burruss) Hudson; A.B., Smith Coll., 1934; M.A., Duke, 1936; Ph.D., U. Ky., 1939; m. Mark Jagoe Bridges, Dec. 23, 1936 (dec. Nov. 1965); children—Mark Jagoe, John Hudson. Sch. psychologist, Lexington, Ky., 1937-39; instr. psychology Louisville City Hosp., 1941-42; tchr. kindergarten, Prattville, Ala., 1954-55; asso. prof. psychology Huntingdon Coll., Montgomery, Ala., 1955—. Psychology cons. Halsted Surg. Pavillion, P.R., 1974—. Bd. dirs. Reading Is Fundamental, Montgomery, 1973-74. Mem. Am. Psychol. Assn., Prattville Service League, Psi Chi. Republican. Episcopalian. Club: Montgomery Country. Home: 472 Pinecrest St Prattville AL 36067 Office: Huntingdon Coll Montgomery AL 36106

BRIETZKE, JUNE ONESON (MRS. CHARLES H. BRIETZKE), musician; b. Racine, Wis., June 1, 1917; d. Irvin and Bess (Hannon) Oneson; student Carre Mus. Coll., 1934-35, Chgo. Mus. Coll., 1936-37; m. Charles H. Brietzke, Jan. 25, 1946. Harpist with Racine (Wis.) Symphony Orch., 1935—; organist 1st Presbyn. Ch., Racine. Mem. Am. Guild Organists, Am. Harp Soc., Sigma Alpha Iota. Home: 4300 Lighthouse Dr Windsong Village of Wind Point Racine WI 53402

BRIFFAULT, HERMA HOYT (MRS. ROBERT BRIFFAULT), ghost writer, translator; b. Reedville, O., May 4, 1898; d. Ezra Otis and Sarah-Anne (Hetzer) Hoyt; ed. Columbus (O.) Normal Sch.; m. J. Eugene Mullins, Dec. 5, 1921 (div. 1931); m. Robert Briffault, Feb. 4, 1931. Ghost author Fulland By, 1936; Cesar Ritz, Host to the World, 1938; Cooking with a French Touch, 1951; The Face of the Arctic, 1952; editor: Reasons for Anger, 1936; The Memoirs of Doctor Felix Kersten, 1946; Youth in Despair, 1948; Beyond Time, 1964; translator The Sea Wall, 1952; House of Lies, 1957; Pascual Duarte and his Family, 1965; The Witches, 1969; The Pure and the Impure, 1967. Home and office: 137 W 12th St New York City NY 10011

BRIGGS, CATHERINE ALLEN (MRS. FRANK P. BRIGGS), pub. co. exec.; b. Gower, Mo., July 16, 1895; d. Aytchmonde Perrin and Catherine Rebecca (Allen) Shull; A.A., Central Coll., Fayette, Mo., 1914; m. Frank P. Briggs, May 28, 1916; children—Thomas F., Eugene A., Ruth (Mrs. Bratek), Betty, Dorothy (Mrs. M.R. Ramon). Corp. sec. Chronicle Herald, Macon, Mo., 1926—. Mem. A.R.C. Workers, 1945. Mem. D.A.R. (regent 1965-66), U.D.C. (pres. 1917-18), P.E.O., U.S. Senate Ladies. Democrat. Baptist. Mem. Order Eastern Star. Home: 1132 N Jackson St Macon MO 63552 Office: 217 W Bourke St Macon MO 63552

BRIGGS, CHARI COUCH HERENDEEN (MRS. JOHN WALKER BRIGGS), psychologist, educator; b. Flushing, N.Y., Nov. 29, 1938; d. James Hallett and Mary Louise (Couch) Herendeen; B.A. cum laude, William Smith Coll., 1960; M.A., Johns Hopkins, 1961; Ph.D., U. Minn., 1966; m. John Walker Briggs, Aug. 13, 1960; children—Marissa, Vania. Asst. prof. edn. psychology U. Minn., 1966-69; asst. prof. spl. edn. U. Md., College Park, 1969-70; sch. psychologist BOCES, Spencerport N.Y., 1970-71; asst. prof. psychology U. Rochester (N.Y.), 1971—. Mem. Am. Psychol. Assn., Council Exceptional Children, Soc. Research Child Devel. Home: 330 Aberdeen St Rochester NY 14619

BRIGGS, JOAN KRAFFT, educator; b. Kansas City, Mo., Sept. 13, 1927; d. Louis Phillip and Annie Margaret (Rush) Krafft; A.B., B.S., S.W. Mo. State Coll., 1947; M.A., Northwestern U., 1948; postgrad. S.E. Mo. State Coll., No. Ill. U., Western Mich. U.; m. David H. Briggs, May 20, 1949; 1 dau., Margaret Evon. Mem. faculty Northwestern U., 1947-48, S.W. Mo. State Coll., 1948-50, Glenwood Sch. for Boys, 1952-54, Lyons Twp. (Ill.) Jr. Coll., 1959-66; prof. theatre and speech Coll. of DuPage, Glen Ellyn, Ill., 1966—. Mem. Speech Communications Assn., Ill. Speech Assn., Phi Rho Pi (readers theatre com. 1973-74). Presbyn. (Sunday sch. tchr.). Home: 108 Woodstock St Clarendon Hills IL 60514 Office: College of DuPage Lambert Rd Glen Ellyn IL 60137

BRIGGS, SHIRLEY ANN, orgn. exec.; b. Iowa City, Ia., May 12, 1918; d. John E. and Nellie (Upham) Briggs; B.A. with highest distinction, U. Ia., 1939, M.A., 1940. Instr. art N.D. State Coll., Fargo, 1941-43; illustrator Glenn L. Martin Co., Balt., 1943-45; information specialist U.S. Fish and Wildlife Service, Washington, 1945-47; chief graphics sect. Bur. Reclamation, 1948-54; painter habitat group backgrounds Smithsonian Instn., 1954-55; diorama prodn. Nat. Park Service, 1956-57; editor Atlantic Naturalist, 1948-69; sec. Rachel Carson Trust for Living Environment, 1966—, exec. dir., 1970—. Mem. Audubon Naturalist Soc. Central Atlantic States (dir. 1948-49, v.p. publs. 1956-69), Am. Assn. U. Women (arts chmn. D.C. chpt. 1956-57), Am. Ornithol. Union, Wilson Ornithol. Soc., Phi Beta Kappa, Pi Beta Phi, Presbyn. Illustrator: The Pronghorn Antelope, 1948; The Wonders of Seeds, 1956; Insects and Plants, 1963; editor, illustrator The Trumpeter Swan, 1960; Landscaping for Birds, 1973; also spl. assignments writing and illustrating. Home: 7605 Honeywell Lane Bethesda MD 20014

BRIGHAM, MARIANNE DIMOCK (MRS. WENDELL P. BRIGHAM), psychiat. social worker; b. Chgo., Feb. 26, 1934; d. Marshall Edward Dimock and Lucy (Stotesbury) Dimock Rhodes; B.A., Pomona Coll., 1956; M.S.W., U. Conn., 1961, postgrad., 1966-67; student Smith Coll., 1967-68; m. Wendell Phillips Brigham, Mar. 17, 1972. Social worker Orange County Welfare Dept., Santa Ana, Cal., 1956-57; child welfare worker Vt. Dept. Social Welfare, 1957-60; caseworker Family Service, New Haven, 1961-63; psychiat. social worker VA Hosp., Northampton, Mass., 1963-70; dir. social service Gifford Meml. Hosp., Randolph, Vt., 1970-72; psychiat. social worker VA Hosp., White River Junction, Vt., 1972—, acting chief, 1973-74. Field work instr. U. Conn., 1966-70. Solicitor, Cancer Crusade, 1958, United Fund, 1962, 64, 68, United Service and Health Agys., 1965; mem. Community Council, Hampshire County, Mass., 1964-70, sec., 1967. Mem. Nat. Assn. Social Workers (officer 1964-69, chmn. subcom. on adv. council to welfare dept. Vt. Chpt. ombudsman com. 1972-73, chpt. dir. 1974—), Acad. Certified Social Workers, New Haven Social Workers Club (sec. 1963), Council on Social Work Edn. Democrat. Unitarian. Home: Christian Hill Bethel VT 05032 Office: VA Hosp White River Junction VT 05001

BRIGHAM, MARY LUCILLE WILLIAMS (MRS. WILLIAM H. BRIGHAM), educator; b. Waco, Tex., Oct. 10, 1931; d. Walter Jefferson and Lucy Sue (Abney) Williams; B.A., Baylor U., 1952, M.A., 1953; m. William H. Brigham, Nov. 27, 1952; children—Mary Sue, Shari Lynn, John Edwin. Tchr. pub. schs., Waco, 1952-53; asst. prof. math. Baylor U., Waco, 1957—. Mem. McLennan County Democratic Women, 1962—. Mem. Math. Assn. Am., A.A.A.S. Home: 2431 Starr Dr Waco TX 76710

BRIGHT, ALICE M., lawyer; b. Homewood, Ill., Sept. 18, 1917; d. Orville T. and Mary C. (Griggs) Bright; A.B., U. Chgo., 1939, J.D. cum laude, 1941. Admitted to Ill. bar, 1941; asso. Sidley & Austin, Chgo., 1942—, partner, 1956—. Mem. Chgo. (chmn. probate practice com. 1956), Ill., Am., Women's (pres. 1955-56) bar assns., Am. Coll. Probate Counsel, Am. Judicature Soc., Bar Assn. 7th Circuit. Home: 1514 Lake Av Wilmette IL 60091 Office: 1 First Nat Plaza Chicago IL 60670

BRIGHTWELL, JUANITA SUMNER (MRS. LOUIE BRIGHTWELL), librarian; b. Sylvester, Ga., Jan. 4, 1918; d. Robert Beauregard and Lottie (Davis) Sumner; tchrs. certificate in piano Kate Land Sch. Mus., 1935; normal diploma Ga. Southwestern Coll., Americus, Ga., 1936; B.S. in Edn., Woman's Coll. Ga., 1938; M.Librarianship, Emory U., 1965; m. Louie Brightwell, June 30, 1938; 1 dau., Claire (Mrs. Charles W. Shaeffer, Jr.). Elementary tchr. Weston (Ga.) High Sch., 1937-38; tchr. English, also librarian Smithville (Ga.) High Sch., 1941-42, Americus High Sch., 1942-43; operator Brightwell's Nursery, Americus, 1946-52; asst. librarian Lake Blackshear Regional Library, Americus (formerly Americus Carnegie Library), 1952-55, dir. library services in Sumter County, 1962—, Crisp County, 1964—, Schley and Dooly Counties, 1970—; tchr. New Era Elementary Sch., Americus, 1955-56; tchr. English, also library asst. Americus High Sch., 1956-62. Mem. Middle Flint Council on Aging. Tchr. Merit scholar Ga. Dept. Edn., 1962-65. Mem. Am., Southeastern, Ga. (chmn. pub. library sect. 1969-71) library assns., Am. Assn. U. Women, D.A.R., Am. Camellia Soc., Azalea Garden Club (pres. 1955), S.W. Ga. Camellia Soc., Federated Garden Clubs, Ga. (del. 1951-52), Ga. Coll. at Milledgeville (dist. dir. 1965-67), Americus and Sumter County Bus. and Profl. Woman (pres. 1968-69, Woman of Year 1968), U.D.C., Delta Kappa Gamma. Alpha Chi Omega. Baptist. Author: The Organization of the American Library Association, 1965. Home: 1307 Hancock Dr Americus GA 31709 Office: 111 S Jackson St Americus GA 31709

BRILLHART, MAXINE T. (MRS. ROY W. BRILLHART), physician; b. Coffeyville, Kan., Nov. 11, 1915; d. Forest C. and Rena H. (Huffman) Thornton; M.D., U. Kan., 1950; m. Roy William Brillhart, Nov. 15, 1935; children—Robert Allen, Roy William. Intern Providence Hosp., Kansas City, Kan., 1950-51, now staff; pvt. practice medicine, Kansas City, 1951—; staff Bethany, St. Margaret, Providence hosps. Dir., sec. Allied Investors, Inc.; dir., v.p. sec. Med. Offices Lab. Mem. Kan. Commn. on Status of Women, 1966. Recipient Matrix award Theta Sigma Phi, 1969. Mem. Am., Kan., Wyandotte County (sec.-treas. 1957-58) acads. gen. practice, World, Am. Women's med. socs., S.W. Clin. Soc., English-Speaking Union, Internat. Personnel Research Soc., Am. Biog. Inst., Internat. Platform Assn. Methodist. Clubs: Women's City, Around-The-World, Soroptimist (pres. Kansas City 1965-66, Woman of Year 1962). Home: 4540 County Line Rd Kansas City KS 66106 Office: 1610 Washington Blvd Kansas City KS 66102

BRILLIANT, JUDITH FEINBERG (MRS. SIDNEY N. BRILLIANT), real estate broker; b. St. Louis, Nov. 21, 1938; d. Adolph Katts and Virginia Campbell (Burke) Feinberg; student Barry Coll., 1956-58; B.A., U. Miami, 1960; postgrad. Washington U. Law Sch., 1960-61; m. Sidney N. Brilliant, Dec. 31, 1969. Stock broker A.G. Edwards & Sons, St. Louis, 1961-62; agt. commd. works Sculptors Gallery, St. Louis, 1963-64; office mgr., real estate broker Adolph K. Feinberg Real Estate Co., Inc., St. Louis, 1963-69; pvt. practice as real estate broker, comml. and residential developer, 1971—. Trustee, St. Louis Pub. Library; v.p. St. Louis council Expt. in Internat. Living. Mem. Friends of St. Louis Art Mus., Mo. Botanical Garden, Am., Mo. library assns., Council St. Louis, Chgo. Council Fgn. Relations, Nat. Trust Historic Preservation. Home: 1 Glen Forest St St Louis MO 63124 Office: Wentzville Devel Corp PO Box 202 O'Fallon MO 63366

BRIMACOMBE, DOROTHY DARTMOUTH REDENBAUGH (MRS. ALFRED JOHN BRIMACOMBE), printing, stationery co. exec.; b. Quincy, Ill., Oct. 30, 1901; d. William Alfred and Mary Louise (Farr) Redenbaugh; tchrs. diploma Ellensburg (Wash.) Normal Sch., 1922; B.S. in Edn., Ore. State U., 1926; m. Alfred John Brimacombe, Aug. 2, 1935. Tchr. pub. schs., Wapato, Wash., 1922-23, Seattle, 1923-25, 26-28; instr. journalism Ellensburg Normal Sch., 1928-31; receptionist Six Cos., Inc., Boulder City, Nev., 1931; co-owner, asso. editor Las Vegas Age, Nev., 1933-44; co-owner Brimmies Comml. Printing & Stationery, Las Vegas, 1944—. Sec., Nev. Safety Council, 1968—. Bd. dirs., exec. com. Nev. Safety Council, 1967—; Nev. mem. Nat. Assn. Women Hwy. Safety Leaders, 1969-71; bd. dirs. So. Nev. Drug Abuse Council, 1972—; founder Nike House, home for girls, 1972, pres. bd. dirs., 1972—. Pres., Nev. Fedn. Republican Women, 1952-53. Mem. Am. Assn. U. Women (pres. Las Vegas sect. 1940-42, Nev. div. 1946-47), Las Vegas Bus. and Profl. Womens (pres. 1940-42), Nev. (pres. 1943-44), Nat. (treas. 1956-60) fedns. bus. and profl. women, Nat. Fedn. Press Women (regional v.p. 1946), Alpha Gamma Delta. Clubs: Mesquite (pres. Las Vegas 1940), Las Vegas Altrusa. Home: 2812 Mason Av Las Vegas NV 89102 Office: PO Box 150 Las Vegas NV 89101

BRIN, ANNETTE SARA (MRS. FOSTER BLAKE BRIN), editor, journalist; b. Miami, Fla., Jan. 25, 1948; d. Harold Orville and Jean (Bulafkin) Van Dam; B.S. in Journalism, U. Fla., 1970; m. Foster Blake Brin, Mar. 28, 1970. Reporter, Coral Gables (Fla.) Times, also The Guide, Coral Gables, 1970-71, women's editor, 1971-72, edn. editor, 1972—. Mem. Fla. Women's Polit. Caucus, 1970-71. Recipient Sch. Bell award Fla. Edn. Assn., 1973, 74; Number Two Suburban Journalist in U.S. award Suburban Newspapers Am., 1973. Mem. Women in Communications (corr. sec. 1972-73, rec. sec. 1973-74), Fla. Press Club, Sigma Delta Chi, Phi Delta Epsilon Wives Club (treas. 1972-73, v.p. 1973-74, pres. 1974-75). Democrat. Jewish religion. Office: 4627 Ponce de Leon Blvd Coral Gables FL 33146

BRINCEFIELD, DOROTHY ANN, diversified industry exec.; b. White Plains, N.Y., July 24, 1935; d. Charles R. and Mary L. (Corbett) Brincefield; student State U. N.Y. Tchrs. Coll., 1953-55, Columbia, 1955-56. Tchr., Colonial Nursery Sch., Larchmont, N.Y., 1956-57; community relations mgr. ITT Continental Baking Co., Rye, N.Y., 1959-73; mgr. equal employment opportunity affairs ITT Corp., N.Y.C., 1973—. Sec., Westchester Residential Opportunities, 1973—; v.p. Port Chester Carver Center, 1972; adv. council Pace U. Inst. for Sub/Urban Governance. Bd. dirs. George Washington Carver Community Center, chmn., 1971—; trustee Council for Arts in Westchester. Recipient Afro-Am. Cultural Found. award, 1973. Mem. Pub. Relations Soc. Am. (sec. Westchester chpt. 1972—), Nat. Urban Affairs Council, Nat. Council Negro Women (sec. 1972), Publicity Club N.Y. Baptist. Home: 9-5 Wyndover Woods White Plains NY 10603 Office: 320 Park Av New York City NY 10022

BRINDLEY, FERN BELLE, educator; b. Lorain, O., May 27, 1912; d. Clyde J. and Anna Marie (Hackett) Brindley; A.B., Mather Coll., Western Res. U., 1934; M.A., Western Res. U., 1950; Ed.D., Case Western Res. U., 1970. Sec., Banks Baldwin Law Pub. Co., Cleve., 1934-35, Johnson-Jennings Co., Cleve., 1935-36; tchr. French and English, North Olmsted Schs., 1936-41; asst. office mgr., factory employment TRW, Cleve., 1941-42; chmn. bus. edn. dept. Mayfield City Schs., Cleve., 1942-60, guidance counselor, 1960—. Active worker United Fund, 1956-60. Mem. Nat. (life), Ohio (life), Mayfield (pres. 1959-60) edn. assns., Am. Personnel and Guidance Assn., Am. Sch. Counselors Assn. (life), Vocational Guidance Assn., Nat. Assn. Women Deans, Adminstrs. and Couselors, Am. Assn. U. Profs., Phi

Delta Gamma, Delta Kappa Gamma. Home: 895 Richmond Rd Lyndhurst OH 44124

BRINKER, JUNE MARIE, advt. co. exec.; b. Butte, Neb., June 5, 1926; d. Harvey H. and Blanche M. (Staples) Story; grad. high sch.; m. William R. Brinker, Oct. 8, 1944 (div. 1946); 1 dau., Patricia. Account exec. Pleskach & Smith Advt., Omaha, 1950-62; with Lloyd Advt., Omaha, 1962—, v.p., gen. mgr., 1970—. Home: 1606 N 72d St Omaha NE 68114 Office: 7171 Mercy Rd Omaha NE 68106

BRINKLEY, LILLY INEZ, sch. psychologist; b. Rover, Ark., Mar. 10, 1922; d. William Ernest and Lillie (Morse) Brinkley; diploma with honors Ark. Poly. Coll., 1942; B.A., Redlands U., 1952; M.A., Cal. State Coll., Los Angeles, 1964; postgrad. U. So. Cal., U. Cal. at Los Angeles and Riverside, Cal. State Coll., Santa Clara; divorced. Elementary tchr. Plainview-Rover Consol. Sch., 1942-43, Tanona (Okla.) Sch., 1943-45, Cucamonga (Cal.) Sch., 1946-51, Temple City (Cal.) Sch. Dist., 1952-64; coordinating sch. psychologist Ontario-Montclair Sch. Dist., Ontario, Cal., 1964-68; sch. psychologist Riverside (Cal.) Unified Sch. Dist., 1968—. Leader, Girl Scouts, Cucamonga, 1947-51; mem. Civic Improvement Com., Ontario. Mem. N.E.A., Cal. Tchrs. Assn., Nat. Assn. Sch. Psychologists (charter), Cal. Assn. Sch. Psychologists and Psychometrists, S.E. Counties Sch. Psychologists Assn., Council for Exceptional Children, Riverside City Tchrs. Assn., Riverside Mental Health Assn., Epsilon Psi (charter), Delta Kappa Gamma, Zonta Internat. Home: 5345 Greenbrier Dr Riverside CA 92504

BRINKLEY, RUTH ELIZABETH, ret. librarian; b. Lincoln, Neb., Dec. 8, 1890; d. L. Robert and Ellen Carolyn (Nichols) Wilhelm; A.B., U. Kan., 1911; m. Joseph Arthur Brinkley, Oct. 31, 1912 (dec. 1968); children—Joseph Wilhelm, Robert Alexander, Ellen Rebecca Swenson, Ruth Kathleen Richards. Tchr. sci. Lawrence (Kan.) High Sch.; librarian Anacortes (Wash.) Pub. Library, now ret.; writer children's books. Named Anacortes Woman of Yr. Mem. Am. Assn. U. Women. Methodist. Mem. Order Eastern Star. Clubs: Federated Women's, Soroptimist. Author articles and lectr.; initiated hobby exhbns., adult edn. and craft classes in library. Home: 5918 Sunset Dr Anacortes WA 98221

BRISCOE, KATHLEEN ELLEN (MRS. EDWARD MCDONALD), physician, educator; b. Alameda, Cal., Dec. 10, 1941; d. Charles Arthur and Leitha Mary (Delavan) Briscoe; student U. Wash. at Seattle, 1959-62; M.D., U. Cal. at San Francisco, 1966; m. Edward Allen McDonald, July 13, 1968; 1 dau., Stephanie Winters. Rotating intern U. So. Cal.-Los Angeles County Med. Center, 1966-67, resident in medicine, 1967-68; resident in pathology U. Cal. at San Diego, 1968-69, resident in medicine, 1969-70; med. dir. San Ysidro Health Center, 1970—; clin. instr. U. Cal. Sch. Medicine, San Diego, 1970-71, asst. clin. prof. medicine, 1971—, clerkship coordinator medicine dept., 1970-72; mem. dept. internal medicine So. Cal. Permanente Med. Group, San Diego, 1971-72; clin. investigator Eli Lilly & Co., Indpls., 1973—. Diplomate Am. Bd. Internal Medicine. Mem. A.C.P., Delta Gamma. Home: 4619 Somerset Way S Carmel IN 46032 Office: 306 E McCarty Indianapolis IN 46206

BRISCOE, MAY ELIZABETH, psychologist; b. Lexington, Ky., July 23, 1939; d. U.G. and Carmen Lucille (Quillin) Briscoe; student Stephens Coll., 1956-57, Transylvania Coll., 1957-58; B.A. with distinction and honors, U. Ky., 1960; M.A., U. Fla., 1964, Ph.D., 1970. Research asst. psychol. dept. U. Fla., Gainesville, 1965-66; research dir. Ky. Child Welfare Research Found., Frankfort, 1966-68; home health coordinator Whitesburg (Ky.) Appalachian Regional Hosp., 1969-70; research asso. Appalachian Regional Hosp., Lexington, Ky., 1970—. Cons. W.Va. Regional Med. Program Pharmacy Home Health Project, HEW Project on Improved Utilization of the Outpatient Pharmacist, 1972-74. Mem. citizens adv. council Dept. Edn. Commonwealth Ky., 1971-73; mem. Ky. Statewide Family Planning Rev. Com., 1972-74, chairperson tng. subcom., 1973-74. So. Fellowship Fund Teaching fellow, 1960-62; Nat. Rehab. trainee, 1963-64. Mem. Am., Ky. psychol. assns., Am. Pub. Health Assn., Assn. for Women in Psychology, Am., Ky. Audobon socs., Phi Beta Kappa, Kappa Delta. Methodist. Home: 418 Plymouth Dr Lexington KY 40503 Office: Box 8086 1220 Harrodsburg Rd Lexington KY 40503

BRISKY, MARY OWEN, city ofcl.; b. Anniston, Ala., May 19, 1930; d. Ozie Whitton and Melinda Everlina (Welchel) Owen; grad. high sch.; 1 son, James E. Asst. to city clk., Anniston, Ala., 1956-62, dep. city clk., 1962-66, city clk., 1966—. Recipient Municipal Accounting award Ala. Soc. C.P.A.'s, 1966. Baptist. Home: 1520 E 10th St Anniston AL 36201 Office: PO Box 670 Anniston AL 36201

BRISLIN, GENE (MRS. J. HAROLD BRISLIN), newspaper editor; b. Blakely, Pa.; d. Charles Augustus and Helen Barbara (Gray) O'Boyle; student Bucknell U., 1934-36; B.A., Marywood Coll., Scranton, Pa., 1938, postgrad., 1940-42; postgrad. U. Scranton, 1938-40; m. J. Harold Brislin, Aug. 9, 1946. Gen. assignment reporter Scrantonian-Tribune, 1943-47, woman's page editor, 1947—. Mem. Scranton Mayor's Adv. Com., 1959—. Bd. dirs. Scranton Philharmonic Orch., 1948-50, Abington Heights Student Aid Assn., Heart Assn., Cancer Soc., Mus. Assn. Recipient numerous state and nat. awards for excellence in writing. Mem. Nat. Fedn. Press Women, Pa. Women's Press Assn. (named outstanding newswoman of the year 1951, 62, pres. 1958-59), Am. Newspaper Guild (pres. Scranton Chpt. 1952-50), Theta Sigma Chi. Roman Catholic. Home: Glenburn Pond Clarks Summit Rd 1 PA 18411 Office: Scrantonian-Tribune 325 N Washington Av Scranton PA 18501

BRISTOL, DIXIE DUMMIT (MRS. FAYETTE INGALLS BRISTOL), silica co. exec.; b. Arlington, Tex., Aug. 27, 1920; d. Bert and Hattie (Boucher) Dummit; student Hockaday Jr. Coll., Dallas, 1937-38; B.S., U. Tex., 1941; m. Charles H. Read, Nov. 15, 1940 (dec. Mar. 1959); children—Mary Kathleen, Charles Robert; m. 2d, Fayette Ingalls Bristol, Nov. 27, 1970. Bus. mgr. Stewart Bldg. Supply, Walnut Creek, Cal., 1945-49; gen. motors dealer's accountant Rector Motor Co., Jurs Motor Co., Walnut Creek, Cal., 1949-51; law office mgr. firm McCarty & Swindells, Portland, Ore., 1953-72, also sec. client assns.; partner, owner Bristol N.W. Silica, 1972—; sec.-treas. Bristol Chem. Co. Mem. Gamma Phi Beta (past pres.) Episcopalian. Republican. Clubs: American Federated Women's, Diablo Country, Multnomah Athletic, Portland Yacht. Home: 3800 SW 48th Pl Portland OR 97221

BRISTOL, JOAN ELLEN MCVETTY (MRS. LOUIS G. BRISTOL), ednl. adminstr.; b. N.Y.C., Nov. 4, 1946; d. George Joseph and Marion (Welsh) McVetty; A.A., Nassau Community Coll., 1966; B.S., State U. Brockport, 1968; M.S., State U. N.Y., 1969; m. Louis G. Bristol, Jan. 3, 1970. Asst. dean residence State U. N.Y. Coll. at Geneseo, 1969-71; asst. dir. student activities, residence dir. Wilmington (O.) Coll., 1971-72; dean students Coll. New Rochelle (N.Y.), 1972—. Mem. Nat. Assn. Student Personnel Adminstrs., Am. Personnel and Guidance Assn., Nat. Assn. Women Deans and Counselors. Home: 230 Pelham Rd New Rochelle NY 10805

BRISTOW, MABEL MORROW, mfg. co. exec.; b. Roland, N.C., Feb. 25, 1914; d. Marion C. and Alice Lucile (Curlee) Bristow; grad. high sch., Lakeland Bus. Coll. Supr. applications crop subsidy Agrl. Dept., Florence, S.C., 1940-42; civilian supr. property and accounting Chief Clk. Base Supply, Florence AFB, 1942-46; gen. office mgr. Vulcraft, steel joists mfg., Florence, S.C., 1947-52; civilian supr. monetary accounting and appropriation accounting, dir., sec. credit union Shaw AFB, S.C., 1953-57; controller, Vulcraft div. Nucor Corp., Florence, 1957—, asst. sec. home office, Charlotte, 1962—. Recipient Civilian Worker award U.S. Air Force, 1956, award of excellent efficiency rating, 1943-46, Meritorious Service award, 1945, spl. commendation and award, 1955. Mem. Florence C. of C. (sec. woman's div. 1964). Baptist. Club: Business and Professional Womens. Home: 1810 Marsh Av Florence SC 29501 Office: PO Box 3009 Florence SC 29501

BRITAIN, RADIE, composer; b. Amarillo, Tex., Mar. 17, 1903; d. Edgar Charles and Katie (Ford) Britain; student U. Chgo., 1920-21; B.M., Am. Conservatory, Chgo., 1924; Mus.D. (hon.), Mus. Arts Conservatory, 1958; m. Ted Morton; 1 dau., Lerae. Composer orchestral, piano and vocal music, debut as composer, Munich, Germany, 1925; represented by string quartet at White House. Awarded nat. prizes for orchestral and vocal compositions; Internat. prize Heroic Poem for orch.; Juilliard Publ. Prize, 1945; first Nat. prize for We Believe, and for Suite for Strings; award merit Nat. League Am. Pen Women, 1957; Internat. award for Nisan for chorus and orch. Delta Omicron; 1st Nat. prize for Fantasy for Flute and Piano. Mem. A.S.C.A.P., League Am. Penwomen; hon. mem. Gamma Chpt. S.A.I., Tex. Fed. of Music Clubs; life hon. mem. Tex. Music Tchrs. Assn. Clubs: Etude (hon.), Schubert, Los Angeles Press (Los Angeles); Philharmonic (Amarillo, Tex.). Home: 1945 N Curson St Hollywood CA 90046

BRITT, RUTH EVANGELINE BURGIN (MRS. JAMES T. BRITT), civic worker; b. Fayette, Mo., Mar. 15, 1907; d. Samuel Herschel and Lora (Miller) Burgin; student Wesleyan Woman's Coll., 1926-27; A.B., Tallahassee Woman's Coll., 1928; m. James T. Britt, Sept. 18, 1930; children—Thomas Burgin, Robert McCammon. Bd. dirs. Spofford Home for Children, 1937-38, Della Lamb Neighborhood House, 1937-38, YMCA, 1938-39; mem. Woman's City Club, Kansas City, Mo., 1931—, chmn. hosp. com., 1931-35; mem. Guild Friends Art at William Rockhill Nelson Gallery, 1961—; mem. fireside com. Kansas City Art Inst., 1948-49; mem. women's div. Kansas City Philharmonic Assn., 1966—, Kansas City Mus. Assn., 1966—; bd. mgrs. George H. Nettleton Home for Aged Women, 1968—. Chmn. Christian-social relations Women's Soc. Christian Service, 1946-48, pres., 1937-38, chmn. missions, 1961-63; chmn. St. Francis Aux. of St. Francis Home for Boys, Salina and Ellsworth, Kan., 1946-48, supplies com. Community Chest Dr., 1951; vol. visitor for aged Mattie Rhodes Settlement House, 1948; Hosp. Gray Lady, 1948-50. Pres., Young Women's Democratic Club, 1931-33. Mem. U.D.C., D.A.R. (regent 1942-43). Methodist (mem. adminstrv. bd.). Address: 409 W 58th Terrace Kansas City MO 64113

BRITTON, ETHEL CHURCHILL (MRS. ALEXANDER M. BRITTON), club woman; b. Yakima, Wash.; d. Edward B. and Nettie B. (Sharon) Churchill; student St. Joseph's Acad., Yakima, 1919-20; m. Homer R. Rutherford (dec.); children—Lorraine (Mrs. Joseph J. McKay), James; m. 2d, Alexander M. Britton, Feb. 28, 1929; 1 son, William E. Pres. Daus. of Pioneers, 1960-62, treas., 1968—; dist. chmn. Tb Christmas Seals, 1937-45. Mem. D.A.R. (regent Narcissa Prentiss chpt. 1950-52, 58-60, chpt. corr. sec. 1969, state regent Wash. 1962-64, state historian 1952-54, 64—, state chmn. by laws, hon. state regent), Daus. Am. Colonists (corr. sec. 1952-54), Colonial Dames 17th Century. Clubs: Christian Women's (adviser); Walla Walla Garden (pres. 1969-71). Home: 636 Francis Av Walla Walla WA 99362

BRITTON, GWENDOLYN AUDREY, librarian; b. Muskogee, Okla., Feb. 28, 1917; d. Otto Lawrence and Nelle (McKee) Britton; grad. Muskogee Jr. Coll., 1936, Okla. Baptist U., 1938; postgrad. George Peabody Coll. for Tchrs., summers 1942-44. Girl res. sec. Muskogee YWCA, 1938-41; librarian West Jr. High Sch., Muskogee, 1942—. Recipient Life Beautiful award Okla. Bapt. U., 1938. Mem. Nat., Okla., Muskogee edn. assns., Okla. Sch. Librarians Assn., D.A.R., Nat. Honor Soc., Kappa Delta Pi. Baptist. Contbr. articles to local newspaper. Home: 1218 Boston Av Muskogee OK 74401 Office: 200 N 16th St Muskogee OK 74401

BRITTON, HELEN HENDERSON, librarian; b. Tuskegee, Ala., Nov. 20, 1922; d. John Lindsay and Hettie (Code) Henderson; B.A. in Edn., Leland Coll., 1943; M.A., U. Ia., 1945; M.A. in L.S., U. Mich., 1953; m. Oscar S. Copeland, Aug. 2, 1943 (dec. Jan. 1957); m. Albert J. Britton, Feb. 14, 1958 (d. Oct. 1970). Instr., Leland Coll., Baker, La., 1943-44, Bishop Coll., Marshall, Tex., 1945-46, Tuskegee Inst., 1946-47, So. U., Baton Rouge, 1947-50; tchr. Boston High Sch., Lake Charles, La., 1950-51; librarian Free Library of Phila., 1953-55; asst. prof. Grambling (La.) Coll., 1955-56; librarian La. State Library, Baton Rouge, 1956-62; cataloger Ohio State U. Library, Columbus, 1962-63, circulation desk and bookstack librarian, 1963-66, cataloger, 1966-68, sr. catalog librarian, asst. catalog reviser, 1968-71, also asst. prof.; sr. cataloger, asst. prof. Tex. A & M U., College Station, 1971-72, documents librarian, 1972-74; asso. prof., head cataloging dept. U. Houston, 1974—. Mem. A.L.A., Tex., S.W. library assns., Houston Library Club, Am. Assn. U. Profs., Tex. Assn. Coll. Tchrs., Assn. Coll. and Research libraries, Am. Assn. U. Women, Episcopal Ch. Women, Alpha Kappa Alpha, Pi Lambda Theta, Phi Delta Gamma. Episcopalian. Office: U Houston Libraries Cullen Blvd Houston TX 77004

BRITZ, ALVINA MARY, television co. exec.; b. Royalton, Minn., Sept. 22, 1919; d. Henry J. and Theresa (Zormeier) Britz; grad. high sch. Sec., auditor Hotel Androy, Superior, Wis., 1937-42; sec. P.O. B. Montgomery, Dallas, 1942-43; sec. to mgr., asst. mgr. Stoneleigh Hotel and Maple Terrace Apts., Dallas, 1943-47; sta. mgr., treas., dir. Bermac Radio, Inc., La Crosse, Wis., WBIZ, Inc., Eau Claire, Wis., 1947-54; bus. mgr., treas., dir. KTVO-TV, Inc., Ottumwa, Ia., 1954-68, gen. mgr., 1968—; gen. mgr. KBIZ Radio, 1968—. Bd. dirs., sec. Ottumwa council Campfire Girls, 1955-58; bd. dirs. Community Players, Ottumwa, 1959-60; bd. dirs. Civic Music Assn., Ottumwa, 1960-62. Mem. Am. Women in Radio and Television (pres. Hawkeye-Iowa chpt. 1968-69, area v.p. 1972-74, nat. bd. dirs. 1972-74), Saint Joseph Hosp. Aux., P.E.O., Catholic Daus. Am. (pres. 1957-59), Ottumwa C. of C. (dir. 1970—, pres. 1974), Beta Sigma Phi (pres. Dallas 1944-45). Republican. Clubs: Quota (dir., sec., pres., dist. gov. 1968-69), Ott Country. Home: 128 E 5th St Ottumwa IA 52501 Office: 211 E 2d St Ottumwa IA 52501

BROADD, MARY JANE, counselor; b. Milw., Nov. 14, 1943; d. Arthur Carl and Mary Agnes (Drobeck) Tesch; student Milw. Area Tech. Coll., 1963-64; B.S. in Psychology, U. Wis.-Milw., 1967-69, M.S. in Ednl. Psychology, 1969, postgrad., 1974—; m. Gregory Andrew Broadd. Counselor Goodwill Rehab. Center, Milw., 1969-71, acting chief counselor, 1970-71; rehab. counselor Wis. State Div. Vocational Rehab., Milw., 1971—; lectr. dept. ednl. psychology U. Wis.-Milw., also rehab. counselor dept. psychol. services, 1971—. Mem. Wis. Gov.'s Task Force Problems People with Phys. Handicaps, 1973-74. Mem. Wis. (sec.-treas. 1971-73), Nat. rehab. counseling assns.; Am. Personnel and Guidance Assn., Am. Psychol. Assn., Nat. Paraplegia Found., Am. Assn. U. Women (scholar). Contbr. articles to profl. jour. Office: 819 N 6th St Milwaukee WI 53203

BROADHURST, FRANCES NEILL, educator; b. Kansas City, Mo., Mar. 27, 1920; d. Thomas Franklin and Radah Agnes (Carbaugh) Broadhurst; B.A., Park Coll., 1942; M.A., McCormich Theol. Sem., 1953; M.Ed., Kan. U., 1968. Tchr. pub. sch., Easton, Mo., 1942-43; mgr., partner Broadhurst Grocery & Mdse. Co., Parkville, Mo., 1942-51; dir. Christian edn. Southridge Presbyn. Ch., Shawnee Mission, Kan., 1953-57, The Village Ch., 1957-60; instr. Park Coll., 1960-62; instr. dept. religion and philosophy Coll. Emporia (Kan.), 1962-63, asst. prof., 1963-70, asso. prof., 1970-74, head dept., 1970-74; dir. United Campus Ministry, chaplain Western N.M. U., Silver City, 1974—. Recipient Outstanding Faculty award Jewish Students Assn., Coll. Emporia, 1971. Mem. Am. Assn. U. Profs., Am. Assn. U. Women (dir. Emporia br. 1966-71), Nat. Campus Ministry Assn. (dir. 1965-74), United Ministry in Higher Edn. (dir. 1968-73, sec. bd. 1968-73). Home: 1402 W 8th St Silver City NM 88061

BROADSTON, ELIZABETH JEANNETTE HERRNSTEIN (MRS. JAMES ANDREW BROADSTON), nutritionist, author; b. Chillicothe, O., June 7, 1908; d. Edward Jacob and Anna (Schmieder) Herrnstein; B.S. in Nutrition, U. Cin., 1930; postgrad. U. So. Cal., 1951-52, U. Cal. at Los Angeles, 1950-51, Cal. State U., 1967-68; m. James Andrew Broadston, Nov. 25, 1936; children—Donald, Susan (Mrs. William Nichparenko), LoAnne (Mrs. Laurie E. Koykka). Asst. dietitian Proctor & Gamble Co., Cin., 1930-32, Good Samaritan Hosp., Los Angeles, 1938-39; free lance writer Let's Live Mag., Los Angeles, 1953—, Health Food Age Mag., 1971—. Lectr. nutrition to schs., social clubs, YMCA, chs., TV., 1950—; lectr. Everywoman's Village, 1964-68, sta. KPFK-FM, Los Angeles, 1967-68, sta. KPFA-FM, Berkeley, Cal., 1967-68; tchr. Tulsa Town Hall, 1971. Pres. women's fellowship valley com. Los Angeles Philharmonic, 1970—. Mem. Opera Guild of So. Cal., 1971—. Vice pres. Woodland Hills Republican Women Fedn., 1958-60. Named Cal. Merit Mother, Am. Mothers Com., Inc., 1971. Mem. Am. Assn. Univ. Women, Am. Home Econs. Assn., Soc. Nutrition Edn., Nat. Health Fedn., Natural Foods Assn., Am. Nutrition Soc. (nat. dir. 1963—), Soc. Nutritional Research, Alpha Chi Omega. Conglist. Home and office: Sprague St Tarzana CA 91356

BROCARD, TULA SALPAS (MRS. JAMES C. BROCARD), govt. ofcl.; b. Chgo., Mar. 1, 1922; d. Spero and Mary (Koursoumis) Salpas; student Northwestern U., 1940-46; m. James C. Brocard, Aug. 30, 1949; children—John Philip, Mary Catherine. Regional radio officer OPA, Chgo., 1944-46, asst. chief field br. Office Information, Washington, 1946-47; information officer div. occupational health USPHS, Washington, 1947-65; information officer Nat. Inst. Dental Research, NIH, Bethesda, Md., 1965—. Recipient Superior Work Performance award USPHS, 1959, 64. Mem. Pub. Relations Soc. Am., Washington Press Club. Home: 12112 Whippoorwill Lane Rockville MD 20852 Office: 9000 Rockville Pike Bethesda MD 20014

BROCK, LAURA HANDLY (MRS. WILLIAM EMERSON BROCK III), wife U.S. senator; b. Hamilton County, Tenn., Mar. 15, 1936; d. Oscar and Laura Thatcher (Hutcheson) Handly; ed. Briarcliff Jr. Coll.; m. William Emerson Brock III, Jan. 11, 1957; children—William Emerson IV, Oscar Handly, Laura Hutcheson, John Kruesi. Home: 2740 32d St NW Washington DC 20008

BROCKLAND, SISTER MARY DIONYSIA, librarian; b. Shrewsbury, Mo., Dec. 3, 1916; d. George Henry and Margaret (Meierotto) Brockland; student Notre Dame Coll., 1934-38, St. Louis U., 1935-39, Loyola U., New Orleans, 1939; B.A., Mt. Mary Coll., 1947; postgrad. LeClerc Coll., 1948; M.S., La. State U., Baton Rouge, 1970. Joined Sch. Sisters Notre Dame; tchr., Our Lady of Perpetual Help, St. Louis, 1937-38, Notre Dame Acad., Belleville, Ill., 1938-39, St. Francis Sch., Aviston, Ill., 1939-50, St. Dominic High Sch., Breese, Ill., 1940; tchr., librarian St. Joseph Grade and High Schs., Farmington, Mo., 1950-69, St. Francis de Sales High Sch., 1969-72; head librarian Notre Dame Coll., St. Louis, 1972—. Mem. Am., Catholic, Mo. library assns. Home: 320 E Ripa St St Louis MO 63125

BROCKMAN, LOIS MARGARET (MRS. RONAL T. HASTIE), psychologist, educator; b. Humboldt, Sask., Can., Oct. 17, 1931; d. Henry J. and Agnes (Gieselman) Brockman; B.A., U. Sask., 1953; M.A., U. Windsor, 1962; Ph.D., Cornell U., 1966; m. Ronal T. Hastie. Social worker Dept. Social Welfare, Saskatoon, Sask., Can., 1953-54; tchr. elementary pub. schs., St. Catherines, also Toronto, Ont., Can., 1955-59; asst. prof. psychology dept. U. N.D., Grand Forks, 1967-70; asso. prof. dept. family studies U. Man., Winnipeg, 1970—. Mem. Am., Canadian psychol. assns., A.A.A.S., Soc. for Research in Child Devel., Canadian Assn. for Advancement of Research in Child Devel. (dir. 1972—), Sigma Xi, Sigma Delta Epsilon.

BROCKMAN, VIVIAN WATSON, ednl. adminstr.; b. Cheraw, S.C., Jan. 10, 1923; d. Silas E. and Matilda R. (Bowman) Watson; A.B., Claflin Coll., 1943; B.L.S., U. Wis., 1949; postgrad. U. Colo., 1962—; div.; children—Karen, Sandrena, Rushane Alvita. Tchr. Reed St. High Sch., Anderson, S.C., 1943-44, Sterling High Sch., Greenville, S.C., 1944-48; librarian Benedict Coll., Columbia, S.C., 1949-50; librarian Denver Pub. Library, 1953-59; sr. high librarian Denver Pub. Schs., 1960-68; dir. learning materials center Community Coll. Denver, 1968—. Active Girl Scouts, 1959—. Mem. A.L.A., Mountain Plains, Colo. library assns., Assn. Colo. Community Coll. Learning Resources (pres. 1971-72), Colo. Council Library Devel. Methodist (lay speaker 1950). Home: 3250 Fillmore St Denver CO 80205 Office: 1201 Acoma St Community College of Denver Denver CO 80204

BROCKMANN, JEANNE BORCHERS, educator; b. Mt. Kisco, N.Y., July 25, 1928; d. H. William and Elsie (Borchers) Brockmann; B.A., Beaver Coll., 1950; postgrad. City Coll. N.Y., 1952, U. Mass., 1973—; student Phila. Conservatory Music, 1946-49, Am. Inst. Banking, 1952-54. Asst. to dir. pub. relations dept. Beaver Coll., Jenkintown, Pa., 1946-50; br. operational floater and personnel service rep. Hanover Bank, N.Y.C., 1950-55; group leader, incoming program asso. Expt. in Internat. Living, Putney, Vt., 1955-58; exec. sec., registrar Am. Lang. Center, Columbia U., N.Y.C., 1958, Yale Fgn. Student Inst., Yale U., New Haven, 1959; asst. dir. Herald Tribune World Youth Forum, N.Y.C., 1958-59; exec. sec. Nat. Assn. Fgn. Student Affairs, N.Y.C., 1959-65; asst. to univ. dean, asso. dir. overseas acad. programs State U. N.Y., Albany, 1965-71; asst. to pres., exec. v.p., dir. internat. programs Empire State Coll., State U. N.Y., Saratoga Springs, 1971—. Vis. lectr. Tchrs. Coll., Columbia, 1968-72; also Mohonk Eastern Europe study program coordinator, 1969; cons., del., workshop coordinator World Conf. Internat. Houses and Centers Paris, 1961, cons., 1969—; mem. Nat. Endorsement and Sponsoring com. Am. Youth Hostels, 1961-67; mem. Pres. Kennedy's Task Force on exchange of persons, 1960, Experimenters Adv. Bd., 1960-71, Speakers Bur., 1967-69; study tour German Internat. House and Centers grantee, 1961; del. 25th Internat. meeting Expt. in Internat. Living; cons. Eastern States Fulbright Conf., 1973. Mem. nat. com. Women for Nixon. Recipient Golden Disc award for profl. achievement Beaver Coll., 1970. Mem. Nat. Assn. for Fgn. Student Affairs (Comsec. exec. com. 1967-70, 73-74, publs. com. 1966-70, commn. on internat. services 1972-74, regional conf. elections chmn., mem. U.S. students abroad com. 1966-71, profl. devel. com. 1967-70, personnel com. 1966-71, mem. regional conf. com. 1967-71, chmn. 1967-68), Council Internat. Ednl. Exchange (dir. 1968-71, sec. bd. 1969-71, membership com. 1969-71, exec. com. 1970-71, overseas acad. program com. 1968-70), State U. N.Y. Dirs. Internat. Edn. (chmn. intercampus communications com. 1971-72, chmn. overseas study program evaluation com. 1972-74). Presbyn. Home: 12 Valencia Lane Elnora NY 12065 Office: Empire State College State University of NY 2 Union Av Saratoga Springs NY 12866

BRODERICK, GRACE NOLAN (MRS. FRANCIS BYRNE BRODERICK), phys. scientist; b. Niagara Falls, N.Y.; d. Emmett Robert and Edna (Burnett) Nolan; student U. Mo., summer 1946; B.A., U. Buffalo, 1947; M.A., Brigham Young U., 1950; J.D., Georgetown U., 1956; postgrad. U. Wyo., 1947, Pa. State U., 1950-52, Am. U., 1959-60; m. Francis Byrne Broderick, Aug. 5, 1959; 1 dau., Grace Margaret. Export clk., translator Carborundum Co., Niagara Falls, N.Y., 1947-48; asst. in geology Brigham Young U., Provo, Utah, 1948; asst. in mineralogy Pa. State U., University Park, 1950-52; geologist U.S. Geol. Survey, Washington, 1952-67; acting research coordinator, phys. scientist div. mineral econs. U.S. Bur. Mines, Washington, 1967—. Fellow A.A.A.S.; mem. Am. Assn. Petroleum Geologists, Geol. Soc. Washington, Delta Phi Alpha, Sigma Delta Epsilon, Kappa Beta Pi, Phi Delta Gamma. Home: 4141 N Henderson Rd Arlington VA 22203 Office: US Bur of Mines Washington DC 20240

BRODIE, DOROTHY RAY MAUPIN (MRS. LOY H. BRODIE, JR.), govt. ofcl., physician; b. Atlanta, Sept. 30, 1927; d. Arthur Ray and Gladys Lois (Haskin) Maupin; B.S., George Washington U., 1949, M.D., 1953; m. Loy H. Brodie, Jr., July 1, 1950; children—William Massie, Robin Elizabeth. Intern, Emergency Hosp., Washington, 1953-54; resident in radiology Mt. Alto VA Hosp., Washington, 1954-57; med. officer diagnostic radiology NIH, Bethesda, Md., 1957-66, program adminstr. radiology tng. program Nat. Inst. Gen. Med. Scis., 1966—, program adminstr. surgery tng. program, 1971-73, sci. adminstr. diagnostic radiology, 1973—. Diplomate Am. Bd. Radiology. Mem. Am. Coll. Radiology, Am. Med. Women's Assn., Radiol. Soc. N.Am., Med. Soc. D.C. (asso.). Home: 1544 Bruton Ct McLean VA 22101 Office: Westwood Bldg 5533 Westbard Av Bethesda MD 20014

BRODIE, FAWN MCKAY (MRS. BERNARD BRODIE), biographer, historian; b. Ogden, Utah, Sept. 15, 1915; d. Thomas E. and Fawn (Brimhall) McKay; B.A., U. Utah, 1934; M.A., U. Chgo., 1936; m. Bernard Brodie, Aug. 28, 1936;children—Richard, Bruce, Pamela. Prof. history U. Cal. at Los Angeles, 1968—. Recipient medal in history Commonwealth Club of Cal., 1959; named Fellow of Year, Utah Hist. Soc., 1967. Alfred A. Knopf fellow, 1943. Mem. Am. Hist. Assn. Author: No Man Knows My History, the Life of Joseph Smith the Mormon Prophet, 1945; Thaddeus Stevens, Scourge of the South, 1959; (with Bernard Brodie) From Crossbow to H-Bomb, 1961; The Devil Drives, a Life of Sir Richard Francis Burton, 1967; Thomas Jefferson, an Intimate History, 1974. Editor: Route from Liverpool to Great Salt Lake Valley, 1962; The City of the Saints, 1963. Contbr. to N.Y. Times Mag., Ency. Brit. Home: 619 Resolano Dr Pacific Palisades CA 90272 Office: Dept History U Cal Los Angeles CA 90024

BRODIE, MAUD RUTH PYE (MRS. JACK BRODIE), journalist; b. Windsor Mills, Que., Can., Aug. 27, 1915; d. George Peter and Margaret Eleanor (Lefebvre) Pye; student Stanstead Coll., 1930, 33; m. Jack Brodie, Apr. 7, 1958. Tech. librarian Aluminum Co. Can., 1942-50; sales promotion asst. dept. store sales promotion James Ogilvy's, Montreal, Que., Can., 1951-55; women's editor, fashion and beauty editor Montrealer Mag., 1956-60; editor Current Events in Toronto, 1961-70; feature writer Key to Toronto (Ont., Can.), 1970—; pub. relations officer Whitby Psychiat. Hosp., Whitby, Ont., 1973—. Mem. Fashion Group Toronto, Inc. (publicity staff 1966-70). Address: PH8 45 Balliol St Toronto ON M4S 1C3 Canada

BRODIE, ROSEMARY ELIOT, physician; b. Evanston, Ill., Aug. 28, 1926; d. Thomas and Sigrid (Wijnbladh) Eliot; B.A., Reed Coll., 1948; M.D., Northwestern U., 1952; m. William G. Bosworth, Oct. 25, 1973; children (by previous marriage)—Ann Brodie, Carol Brodie, Walter Brodie. Intern St. Francis Hosp., Evanston, 1952-53; resident neurology Good Samaritan Hosp., Portland, Ore., 1962-67; pvt. practice medicine, specializing in neurology and gen. medicine, 1953-62, in neurology and electromyography, Portland, Ore., 1967—; mem. staff Med. Center Hosp., Holladay Park Hosp., Good Samaritan Hosp. (all Portland). Mem. Am. Acad. Neurology, N. Pacific Soc. Neurology and Psychiatry, Ore. Neuropsychiat. Soc. (v.p. 1971-72). Unitarian (trustee). Home: 3633 SE Henderson St Portland OR 97202 Office: Portland Med Center Portland OR 97205

BRODINE, VIRGINIA DARE WARNER (MRS. RUSSELL V. BRODINE), writer, editor; b. Seattle, Feb. 18, 1915; d. Hayward Dare and Grace (McKibben) Warner; student Reed Coll., 1933-34, 37-38, Cornish Sch. Arts, Seattle, 1936; m. Russell V. Brodine, Oct. 19, 1941; children—Cynthia (Mrs. Roger L. Snow), Marc Russell. Free lance writer, newspaper articles, short stories, various jobs, Seattle, 1939-41, Los Angeles, 1942-49, St. Louis, 1949-51; copy editor Surgery Jour., Mosby Pub. Co., St. Louis, 1951-52; pub. relations dir. central states region, Internat. Ladies Garment Workers Union, St. Louis, 1954-61; editor Scientist and Citizen, St. Louis, 1962-69, cons. editor Environment, 1969—; editor Scientists' Inst. Pub. Information Environmental Workbooks, 1970. Founder Com. for Nuclear Information, now Com. for Environmental Information, 1958, bd. dirs., 1958-62, 69—; vice chmn. Scientists Inst. for Pub. Information, 1973—. Mem. Women's Internat. League for Peace and Freedom. Author: Air Pollution, 1973; Radioactive Contamination, 1974. Editor: (with Mark Selden) Open Secret, The Kissinger-Nixon Doctrine in Asia, 1972. Home: 4393a Westminster Pl St Louis MO 63108 Office: 438 N Skinker St Louis MO 63130

BRODKEY, GERTRUDE ELAINE (MRS. DONALD BRODKEY), lawyer; b. Omaha, Apr. 30, 1914; d. Harry Mendel and Frances (Stock) Rothkop; B.S. cum laude, Creighton U., 1936, postgrad., 1969; LL.B. with honors, U. Omaha, 1940; J.D., U. Neb., 1969; m. Donald Brodkey, May 30, 1943; children—Bruce Harrison, Amy Catherine, Frank D. Admitted to Neb. bar, 1940, U.S. Supreme Ct. bar, 1967; practiced in Omaha; with Prudential Ins. Co., Omaha, 1938-46, Joseph T. Votava, Omaha, 1960-67, Joseph H. McGroarty, Omaha, 1969—, Legal Aid Soc., Omaha, 1970—. Lectr. on gifted children, family law, and legal services, 1970—. Mem. task force on higher edn. Riverfront Devel., Omaha, 1973-74, Neb. Women Under Law Com., 1972-73, Neb. Gov's. Commn. on Status of Women, 1971, Neb. Govs. Commn. on Edn., 1965, Omaha Mayor's Commn. on Status of Women, 1970-73, Citizens Adv. Com. Omaha Pub. Schs., 1965-68. Bd. dirs. Neb. Assn. for the Gifted; trustee Neb. Diabetes Assn.; bd. regents commn. U. Neb. Named to Hall of Fame Creighton U., 1935; recipient Bnai Brith Citizenship award, 1966, Omaha Pub. Schs. award, 1966, Woman of Year award Sun Newspaper, 1964. Mem. Am. (family law sect.), Neb. (com. on legal services), Omaha (com. family law, constn. by-laws) bar assns., Nat. Assn. Women Lawyers, Women Lawyers Neb. (pres. 1964-68), Nat. Congress Parents and Tchrs. (state life mem.), Nat. Orgn. Women (nat. def. and edn. task force 1971-72), Omaha Council Parents and Tchrs. (pres. 1966-67), Nat. Women's Polit. Caucus (Neb. policy adv. bd. 1971—), Altrusa Internat. Club, Iota Tau Tau (pres. 1939-40). Jewish religion. Mem. Shrine Aux. Home: 1001 S 55th St Omaha NE 68106 Office: Farnam Bldg 1613 Farnam St Omaha NE 68102

BRODMAN, ESTELLE, librarian, educator; b. N.Y.C., June 1, 1914; d. Henry and Nettie (Sameth) Brodman; A.B., Cornell U., 1935; B.S., Columbia, 1936, M.S., 1943, Ph.D., 1954, D.Sc., 1974; postdoctoral study U. Cal. at Los Angeles, 1959, U. N.M., 1960. Asst. librarian Cornell U. Sch. Nursing Library, N.Y.C., 1936-37; asst. med. librarian Columbia U. Libraries, N.Y.C., 1937-49; asst. librarian for reference services Nat. Library Medicine, Washington, 1949-61; librarian, asso. prof. med. history Washington U. Sch. Medicine, St. Louis, 1961-64, librarian, prof. med. history, 1964—. Documentation expert UN Tech. Assistance Program, New Delhi, 1967-68; expert tech. assistance program S.E. regional office WHO, New Delhi, 1970, UN Econ. Agy. for Asia and Far East, Bangkok, 1973. Mem. Pres.'s Commn. Libraries, 1966-68. Instr., Columbia, 1946-52, Cath. U. Am., 1957, Kelo U., Tokyo, Japan, 1962, U. Mo., 1971, 73; cons. Am. Hosp. Assn., NIH, others. Mem. Am., Med. (spl. award 1957, Noyes award 1971; pres. 1964-65), library assns., Spl. Libraries Assn. (dir. 1949-52), Bibliog. Soc. Am., Am. Assn. History Medicine. Author: Development of Medical Bibliography, 1954; Bibliographical Lists for Medical Libraries, 1950. Editor: Bull. Med. Library Assn., 1947-57. Home: 4464 W Pine Blvd St Louis MO 63108

BRODSKY, ANNETTE, advt. exec.; b. N.Y.C.; d. Norman and Bella (Gofsaof) Brodsky; B.A., N.Y. U., 1950. Co-owner, exec. v.p. Accredited Mailing Lists, Inc., N.Y.C., 1960, Mem. Direct Mail Marketing Assn., Mailing List Brokers Profl. Assn., Mail Advt. Services Assn., Women's Direct Response Group (exec. com. 1973-74), Washington Direct Marketing Club. Home: 360 E 72d St New York City NY 10021 Office: 15 E 40th St New York City NY 10016

BRODY, ELAINE, music historian, educator; b. N.Y.C., Apr. 21, 1923; d. S. Lawrence and Helen (Golding) Brody; A.B., Washington Square Coll., N.Y. U., 1944; A.M., Columbia U., 1960; Ph.D., N.Y. U., 1964; m. David Silverberg, July 4, 1966; 1 dau., Sue. Instr. N.Y. U., N.Y.C., 1963-65, asst. prof., 1965-67, asso. prof., 1967-70, prof. music, 1970—, chmn. dept. music, 1966-73. Mem. Am., Internat. musicol. socs., Music Library Assn., Internat. Music Library Assn., Internat. Comparative Lit. Soc., Phi Beta Kappa. Author: Music in Opera, 1970; (with W. Robert A. Fowkes) German Lied and Its Poetry, 1971; (with Claire Brook) Music Guide to Europe, 1974. Home: 35 E 84th St New York City NY 10028

BRODY, SELMA BLAZER (MRS. DAVID M. BRODY), physicist, educator; b. N.Y.C., May 2, 1914; d. Benjamin and Rose (Halle) Blazer; A.B., N.Y. U., 1934; M.A. (DuPont fellow), U. Va., 1935; Ph.D., Bryn Mawr Coll., 1942; m. David M. Brody, Dec. 1939. Indsl. physicist Bliley Electric Co., World War II; faculty Sarah Lawrence Coll., 1946-47, Bklyn. Coll., 1947-53, U. Conn., 1953-55, Bard Coll., 1955-57; prof. physics St. Johns U., Jamaica, N.Y., 1957—. Huff post-doctoral fellow Bryn Mawr Coll., 1964-65. Mem. Am. Crystallographic Assn., Assn. Physics Tchrs., Am. Assn. U. Profs., Phi Beta Kappa, Sigma Xi, Pi Mu Epsilon. Contbr. articles to profl. jours. Home: 53 Country Club Dr Port Washington NY 11050 Office: St Johns U Jamaica NY 11432

BROEDLING, LAURIE ADELE (MRS. TIMOTHY J. BROEDLING), psychologist, govt. ofcl.; b. Plainfield, N.J., Aug. 1, 1945; d. Dana Adams and Olga (Goerke) Griffin; B.A., Brown U., 1967; M.A. (Teaching fellow), George Washington U., 1969, Ph.D., 1973; m. Timothy J. Broedling, Sept. 9, 1967. Social worker Kern County Welfare Dept., Ridgecrest, Cal., 1969; research psychologist Naval Personnel Research and Devel. Lab., Washington, 1970-73, San Diego, 1973—. Instr., Bakersfield Jr. Coll., China Lake, Cal., 1969, Navy Electronics Lab. Center Tutorial Program, San Diego, 1973-74. Mem. La Jolla Civic Assn., 1973-74. Mem. Am., Western psychol. assns., Am. Statis. Assn., Acad. Mgmt., Psi Chi. Home: 5721 Bellevue Av La Jolla CA 92037 Office: Navy Personnel Research and Devel Center San Diego CA 92152

BROEKEMA, MARILYN KAY CHAPMAN (MRS. VICTOR JON BROEKEMA), occupational therapist; b. Detroit, Apr. 26, 1944; d. Lloyd George and Lois Margaret (DePree) Chapman; B.S. with high distinction, Wayne State U., 1966; m. Victor Jon Broekema, Aug. 28, 1965; children—David Victor, Wendy Marie. Supr. adult occupational therapy and clin. training supr. Lafayette Clinic, Detroit, 1967-69; instr. Wayne State U., Detroit, 1967-70, U. Wis., Madison, 1972—; therapist, Dane County Mental Health Center, Madison, 1973—. Recipient Scholarship, Nat. Health Found., 1962-66, Sister Elizabeth Kenny award Wayne State U., 1966. Mem. World Fedn. Occupational Therapy, Am., Wis. occupational therapy assns., Wis. Council Edn.-Occupational Therapy (mem. steering com. 1973-74). Presbyn. Home: 1522 Jefferson St Madison WI 53711 Office: 1308 W Dayton St Madison WI 53706

BROGDEN, HELEN SIDENER (MRS. KARL PHILIP STERN), physician; b. Cin., Feb. 24, 1904; d. Thomas Taylor and Miriam Belle (Lippincott) Sidener; A.B., Ohio State U., 1925, M.D., 1928; m. Karl Philip Stern, June 5, 1936; 1 son, Philip. Intern, Northwestern Gen. Hosp., Phila., 1928-29, resident, 1929-31; gen. practice medicine, Canton, O., 1931-42, specializing in internal medicine, 1943—; tchr. Sch. Nursing, Aultman Hosp., Canton, 1935-50, tchr. interns and residents, 1940-55, sr. active staff, 1932—; courtesy staff medicine Timken Mercy Hosp., Canton; chmn., dir. Stern & Mann Co., Canton; dir. Computerized Components, Inc., Alliance. Fellow Am. Coll. Chest Physicians, Am. Geriatrics Soc.; mem. Pan Am. Cancer Cytology Soc., A.M.A., Ohio Med. Soc., Stark County Acad. Medicine, World Med. Orgn. (asso.), Stark County Hist. Soc. Republican. Episcopalian. Home: 1055 Chelmsford St NW Canton OH 44720 Office: 200 Tuscarawas St W Canton OH 44702

BROGDON, HELEN DELOACH (MRS. WALLACE M. BROGDON), educator; b. Columbia, S.C., May 8, 1923; d. Eugene K. and Annie Mae (Olliff) DeLoach; B.S., U. Md., 1945; M.S., Fla. State U., 1959; m. Wallace M. Brogdon, Aug. 20, 1947; children—Anne (Mrs. Glenn L. Shuman), Rowe. Faculty, U. Md., College Park, 1945-47, Uvalda (Ga.) Elementary Sch., 1948, Hazelhurst (Ga.) High Sch., 1956-58, U. Ga., Athens, 1959; head phys. edn. for women Ga. So. Coll., Statesboro, 1960—. Cons. State of Ga. Phys. Edn. Guide for High Sch. Mem. Am., Ga. (So. dist. chmn. div. girls and womens sports 1960-66, state chmn. health sect. 1972, Outstanding Phys. Educator of Ga. 1970) assn. health, phys. edn. and recreation, So. Assn. Phys. Edn. for Coll. Women, Delta Kappa, Kappa Delta, Delta Psi Kappa. Home: 406 Wilburn Circle Statesboro GA 30458

BROKAW, ROBERTA MIRIAM, pub. co. exec.; b. Kobe, Japan, June 15, 1917 (parents Am. citizens); d. Harvey and Olivia (Forster) Brokaw; LL.D., Wilson Coll., 1966. Editor religious mags. and papers Westminster Press, Phila., 1937-43; free lance editor, Prentice Hall, N.Y.C., 1944-45; proofreader Princeton U. Press (N.J.), 1946-48, editor, 1948-50, mng. editor, 1950-66, asso. dir., editor, 1966—; editor Tokyo (Japan) Press, 1965-66. Fulbright Found. grantee translation program Tokyo U. Press, 1965-66. Mem. Am. Hist. Assn., Modern Lang. Assn., Asian Assn. Am. U. Presses. Home: 4674 Province Line Rd Princeton NJ 08340 Office: Princeton University Press 41 William St Princeton NJ 08540

BROMAGE, MARY COGAN (MRS. ARTHUR W. BROMAGE), author, educator; b. Fall River, Mass., Oct. 13, 1906; d. James Joseph and Edith (Ives) Cogan; A.B., Radcliffe Coll., 1928; M.A., U. Mich., 1932; m. Arthur W. Bromage, July 5, 1928; 1 dau., Susanna Sarah (Mrs. John Paterson). Dep. dir. tng. div. UNRRA, 1944-45; asso. dean women U. Mich., Ann Arbor, 1945-50, mem. faculty Sch. Bus. Adminstrn., 1955—, now prof. written communication. Cons. in field. Past pres. Ann Arbor Community Fund; active YWCA. Mem. Am. Com. Irish Studies, Conf. Brit. Studies. Bd. govs. Mich. League, U. Mich. Recipient certificate editorial writing Freedoms Found.; award merit Interagy. Auditor Tng. Center Dept. Commerce, 1971. Mem. Pub. Health Nursing Assn., Willow Run Community Council, Family Welfare Assn., Am. Bus. Writing Assn., League Women Voters, Women of U. Faculty Club, Research Club, Am. Assn. U. Women, Phi Beta Kappa (dir.). Club: Radcliffe. Author: De Valera and the March of a Nation, 1956; Churchill and Ireland, 1964; Writing for Business, 1964; Cases in Written Communication, 1964; (with Bruce A. Nelson) Cases on Written Communication II. Home: 2300 Vinewood Blvd Ann Arbor MI 48104

BROMAN, KATHRYN FLYNN, broadcasting exec.; b. Pitts.; d. F.A. and Florence (Morgan) Flynn; student student Carnegie Inst. Tech., 1937-38; m. Paul Broman; children—Karen E., Paul Richard, Morgan Andrew, Erica Ann. Broadcaster, hostess program At Home with Kitty, 1954—; dir. women's programs WWLP-TV, Sringfield, Mass., 1955—; asst. to pres. Springfield TV Broadcasting Corp., 1960—, v.p., 1970—. Mem. Nat. Assn. Broadcasters (dir. 1974—). Home: 214 Converse St Longmeadow MA 01106 Office: Box 2210 Springfield MA 01101

BROMBERG, RACHEL BEREZOW (MRS. BENJAMIN BROMBERG), writer, educator; b. Bklyn., July 24, 1917; d. Samuel and Lena (Jacobson) Berezow; B.A., N.Y. U., 1940; M.A., U. Wis., 1942; postgrad. (univ. fellow) Bryn Mawr Coll., 1942-44; m. Benjamin Bromberg, Dec. 24, 1964. Instr. advanced Spanish lit. U. Md., College Park, Md., 1945-50; English as 2nd lang. Spanish-Am. Inst., N.Y.C., 1966—. Mem. Modern Lang. Assn., Am. Assn. U. Profs. Author: Three Pastoral Novels, 1970. Contbr. articles to profl. jours. Home: 137-57 228th St Laurelton NY 11413 Office: 215 W 43rd St New York City NY 10036

BROMER, ANNE CELIA EPSTEIN (MRS. DAVID J. BROMER), state ofcl.; b. Winthrop, Mass., Apr. 1, 1942; d. Bernard Lewis and Florence (Block) Epstein; A.B., Emerson Coll., 1963; M.S., Simmons Coll., 1965; m. David J. Bromer, June 16, 1962; 1 dau., Juliet Sara. Adult librarian Boston Pub. Library, 1965-66; chmn. Watertown Fair Housing Com., 1967-68; suburban housing specialist Fair Housing, Inc., 1969; tenant selection, relocation and mgmt. specialist Mass. Housing Finance Agy., Boston, 1971-73, sr. mgmt. analyst, 1973—. Research fellow Simmons Coll., Sch. Library Sci., 1964-65. Recipient Community Service award Nat. Conf. Christians and Jews, 1970. Home: 127 Barnard Av Watertown MA 02172 Office: 45 School St Old City Hall Boston MA 02108

BRONER, ESTHER MASSERMAN (MRS. ROBERT BRONER), writer, educator; b. Detroit; d. Paul and Beatrice (Weckstein) Masserman; B.A., Wayne State U., 1950, M.A., 1962; m. Robert Broner; children—Sari, Adam, Jeremy, Nahama. Asso. prof. Wayne State U., Detroit, 1964—, writer-in-residence, 1973—. Vis. prof. in Israel, 1972. Mem. Com. for Soviet Jewry; mem. Miles Modern Poetry Com., 1963—. Recipient 2d prize O. Henry Prize Stories, 1968; Faculty Research grantee Wayne State U., 1966, 70. Mem. Am. Civil Liberties Union, Am. Fedn. Tchrs. Author: Summer Is a Foreign Land, 1966; Journal/Nocturnal and Seven Stories, 1968. Contbr. articles and fiction to lit. mags. Home: 18244 Parkside St Detroit MI 48221

BRONKEY, JUDY PACKARD (MRS. GARY LEE BRONKEY), coll. dean; b. Portland, Ore., Dec. 22, 1935; d. Frank Bayley and Darthea (Peniston) Packard; A.B., Whitman Coll., 1958; postgrad. Cornell U., 1959; M.A., Columbia, 1961; m. Gary Lee Bronkey, Mar. 18, 1972; children—Tameem, Jeffery, Shelly. Asst. dean students State U. N.Y., Cortland, 1958-60; asst. to dir. financial aids Columbia, 1960; sec. to pres., instr. English, Kabul (Afghanistan) U., 1962-63; asst. to dean students, counselor Portland (Ore.) State U., 1968-69; dean women Ore. Inst. Tech., Klamath Falls, 1969-70, asst. dean students, internat. student adviser, 1971—, mem. faculty senate, 1970-72, coordinator new student orientation, chmn. student awards com., 1970—, chmn. student publs. adv. com., 1971—, also commencement co-chmn. Mem. Rotorua, New Zealand Sister City Com., 1970-72. Mem. Nat. Assn. Fgn. Student Affairs (co-chmn. Region 1 Conf. 1972, chmn. Ore. 1974—), N.W. Coll. Personnel Assn. (sec.), Nat. Assn. Women Deans, Adminstrs. and Counselors, Klamath Falls C. of C., Kappa Kappa Gamma, Kappa Delta Pi, Pi Lambda Theta. Club: Soroptimist (judge Citizenship award). Home: 109 Dahlia St Klamath Falls OR 97601 Office: Ore Tech Br Post Office Klamath Falls OR 97601

BROOK, JUDITH SUZANNE, psychologist; b. N.Y.C., Dec. 31, 1939; d. Robert Edward and Helen (Zimmerman) Muser; B.A., Hunter Coll., 1961; M.A., Columbia, 1962; Ed.D., 1967; m. David Brook, Dec. 15, 1962; children—Adam, Jonathan. Asst. prof. Queens Coll., Flushing, N.Y., 1967-69; research asso. Inst. for Developmental Studies, N.Y. U., 1969-71; research asso. Columbia, 1971-73, sr. research asso., 1973—. Mem. Am., Eastern psychol. assns., Am. Ednl. Research Assn., Psi Chi, Kappa Delta Pi. Author: Study of Relationships Between Formal Organizational Structure and Organizational Climate in Selected Schools, 1972. Research and publs. in child devel. Home: 350 Central Park W New York City NY 10025

BROOKER, CYNTHIA CROCKER (MRS. ROBERT MORRIS BROOKER), educator; b. Elmira, N.Y., Apr. 1, 1909; d. Frederick William and S. Mabel (Allen) Crocker; B.S. in Sci., Elmira Coll., 1930; M.A. in Psychology and Secondary Edn., Am. U., 1933; m. Harold E. Warner, June 30, 1933 (dec. Mar. 1958); children—Richard Allen, Nancy Jane; step-children—Elizabeth Anne Stiles, William Claflin, Robert Newell; m. 2d, Robert Morris Brooker, Oct. 15, 1959; stepchildren—R. Alexander, Susan Gay. Instr. dietetics and dietotherapy Sibley Hosp., Washington, 1930-33; tchr. Lady Margaret Sch., Washington, 1933-34; founder Cynthia Warner Sch., Ltd., Takoma Park, Md., 1934, also dir.; founder Kamp Kilmarock, Takoma Park, Md., 1940. Ambulance driver A.R.C., 1944-46; mem. sch. com. for funds Holy Cross Hosp.; neighborhood chmn. Girl Scouts U.S.A., Silver Spring, Md., 1955-57. Recipient Golden Eaglet award Girl Scouts Am., 1926. Mem. Am. Camp Assn. (treas. Washington 1957-58, sec. 1961, chmn. sect. standards 1970-72), Assn. Ind. Schs. Greater Washington (mem. at large 1973-75), Ind. Sch. Assn. Montgomery County (sec.-treas. 1955-62), D.A.R. (regent Ft. McHenry chpt. 1972-74), Phi Delta Gamma (sec. 1937-39, 1st v.p.

1970-71, treas. 1974—). Conglist. Clubs: Soroptimist (corr. sec. Washington 1941), Elmira College (pres. 1939-40, sec. Washington 1961-62), Abracadabra Literary (program chmn. 1969-71, pres. 1971-73) Contbr. numerous articles on edn. to profl. jours. Address: 8114 Carroll Av Takoma Park MD 20012

BROOKER, MARIE LARSON, health service adminstr.; b. Manistee, Mich., Nov. 18, 1934; d. Gordon P. and Josephine D. (Smith) Larson; B.S., Eastern Mich. U., 1957; M.S.W., U. Ill., 1964. Dir. social work Loyola U., Chgo., 1965-68; dir. patient service Planned Parenthood Assn. of Chgo., 1968-69; asst. prof. social work Loyola U., Chgo., 1969-72; asst. dir. children's services Dept. of Mental Health, Region 2, Chgo., 1972-73; dir. children's services Div. of Devel. Disabilities, Chgo., 1973—. Cons. in sch. of social work; lectr. Loyola U. Grad. Sch. Social Work, 1972—. Mem. Mid-North Community Council, Chgo., 1969-70, Rogers Park Community Orgn., Chgo., 1970-73. Mem. Near North Joint Youth Devel. Com. Adv. Bd., 1967-68. Nat. Inst. Mental Health fellow, 1962-64. Fellow Am. Orthopsychiat. Assn.; mem. Acad. Certified Social Workers, Nat. Assn. of Social Workers, Am. Civil Liberties Union, Common Cause, Kappa Delta Pi. Home: 6033 N Sheridan Rd Chicago IL 60660 Office: 160 N LaSalle St Chicago IL 60616

BROOKE-ROSE, CHRISTINE (MRS. JERZY PETERKIEWICZ), novelist, educator, critic; b. Geneva, Switzerland; B.A., Somerville Coll. Oxford (Eng.) U., 1949, M.A., 1953; Ph.D., U. Coll. U. London (Eng.), 1954; m. Jerzy Peterkiewicz. Author books, radio plays, other; lectr. U. Paris VIII, Vincennes, 1969—. Recipient James Tait Black Meml. Book prize for work Such, 1966. Author: The Languages of Love, 1957; The Sycamore Tree, 1958; The Dear Deceit, 1960; The Middlemen, 1961; Out, 1964; Such, 1966; Between, 1968; Go When You See the Green Man Walking (collection short stories), 1970; author critique A Grammar of Metaphor, 1958, A ZBC of Ezra Pound, 1971. Contbr. short stories, essays to newspapers, mags., lit. rev. Address: care Hamish Hamilton 90 Great Russell St London WC 1 England

BROOKFIELD, KATHARINE KINSMAN SNOW, counseling psychologist; b. Newburyport, Mass., Oct. 31, 1917; d. William Abbot and Edith May (Corey) Kinsman; B.A., Vassar Coll., 1938; M.A., Columbia Tchrs. Coll., 1960, profl. diploma, 1962, Ph.D., 1969; m. William Lord Brookfield, June 26, 1960; children—Abbot Kinsman Snow, Katharine V. Snow (Mrs. Martin J. Denny-Brown), Norman Nicoll Snow. Counseling psychol. intern Vocational Adv. Services, N.Y.C., 1960-61, Burke Found. Rehab. Center, White Plains, N.Y., 1961-62, VA Hosp., Bronx, N.Y., 1963-65; psychologist Psychiat. Clinic, Charlotte Hungerford Hosp., Torrington, Conn., 1969—. Treas. Norfolk (Conn.) Sr. Housing Corp., 1972—. Bus. mgr. scholarship funds raising Fairfield County, Vassar Coll., 1955-57, chmn., 1958-59, class pres., 1963-68. Vocational Rehab. Adminstrn. grantee, 1963, 65-67. Mem. Am., Conn. psychol. assns., Nat. Soc. Colonial Dames Am., Squadron A Assn., Vassar Club Northwestern Conn. Episcopalian. Clubs: Wee Burn Country (Darien, Conn.); Norfolk Country. Home: Greenswoods East Norfolk CT 06058 Office: Psychiat Clinic Charlotte Hungerford Hosp Torrington CT 06790

BROOKHOUSE, BARBARA ANN KENNEDY (MRS. JACK A. BROOKHOUSE), occupational therapist; b. Windsor, Ont., Can., June 25, 1938; d. Hugh John and Marion Rose (Massard) Kennedy; came to U.S., 1961; B.S. in Occupational Therapy, Wayne State U., 1960; m. Jack A. Brookhouse, May 6, 1961; children—Patricia, Brian, Marion. Staff therapist Rehab. Inst., Detroit, 1960-61, Municipal Tb Sanitarium, Chgo., 1961-62; staff therapist St. Luke's Meth. Hosp., Cedar Rapids, Ia., 1969-70, dir. occupational therapy, 1971—. Mem. adv. bd., occupational therapy asst. program Kirkwood Community Coll., Cedar Rapids, 1972-74; occupational therapy cons. Asbury Day Care Center, Cedar Rapids, 1973—. Mem. Am., Ia. occupational therapy assns., Am. Assn. U. Women, St. Luke's Meth. Hosp. Aux., Wayne State U. Occupational Therapy Assn. Presbyn. (supt. Sunday sch. 1965-66). Home: Rural Route 1 Ely IA 52227 Office: 1026 A Av NE Cedar Rapids IA 52402

BROOKS, ANITA HELEN SAYLE, pub. relations exec.; b. N.Y.C.; d. Arthur and Bertha (Stewart) Sayle; B.A., Hunter Coll., 1950; M.A. Columbia, 1952, M.L.S., 1954; m. Arnold Brooks, July 1, 1954 (div.). Tchr. Latin Hunter Coll. High Sch., 1955; publicity WOR, 1955; writer King Features Syndicate, 1955-59; pub. relations NBC, 1956; dir. pub. relations N.Y. State Mental Health Fund Campaign, 1956, WMCA, 1957; account exec. Dick Taplinger, pub. relations, 1957-59, Ted Deglin, pub. relations, N.Y.C., 1959-61, Marianne Strong Assos., 1961-63, Ted Howard Assos., pub. relations, N.Y.C., 1963-65; pres. Anita Helen Brooks Assos., pub. relations, N.Y.C., 1965—; lit. agt. Anita Brooks, Lit. Agt., 1956—; writer radio-TV shows. Decorated dame Knights of Malta; named hon. citizen Venezuela. Mem. Am. Women in Radio and Television, Pub. Relations Soc. Am., Internat. Radio-Television Soc., Publs. Publicity Assn., Asso. Motion Picture Advertisers, Mystery Writers Am., Columbia U. Alumni Assn., Publicity Club N.Y., Smithsonian Assos., Intercontinental Biog. Assn. Address: Anita Helen Brooks Assos 155 E 55th St New York City NY 10022

BROOKS, BARBARA TAIT (MRS. J. LORING BROOKS), investment co. exec.; b. Springfield, Mass.; d. James C. and Mary Emily (Dana) Tait; student LaSalle Seminary, 1927, Skidmore Coll., 1929; m. J. Loring Brooks, Oct. 10, 1930; 1 dau., Grace (Mrs. Robert I. Knibb). Owner, dir. Brookmont Farms, Lebanon, Tenn., 1950—; sec. Brooks Co., Springfield, 1950-57, v.p., 1950-57; sec. Brookmont Assos., Wilbraham, Mass., 1958—, exec. v.p., 1955-70, pres., dir., Wilmington, Del. and Lebanon, 1971—. Chmn. Well Child Clinic, Wilbraham, 1950-58, Wilbraham Horse Show, 1938-55, Eastern States Horse Show, 1960-71; corporator Vis. Nurse Assn., 1959-65. Bd. dirs. Mass Horse Show Council, 1939-50; trustee J. Loring Brooks Found., 1950—. Mem. Am. Horse Shows Assn. (life), Am. Hackney Horse Soc. (life), Tenn. Tenn. Horsemens Council (dir. 1973—). Republican. Methodist. Clubs: Lebanon Golf and Country; Ocean of Fla. (Delray Beach). Composer: Million Yards of Ribbon, 1954; Why Does Santa Have a Red, Red Nose, 1960; Greetings from the Moon, 1960; The Legend of the Red Bird, 1969; A Little Christmas Shop, 1969. Home: 2170 Ibis Isle Palm Beach FL 33480 Office: Route 4 Lebanon TN 37087

BROOKS, MRS. BERRY BOSWELL (VIRGINIA FEILD WALTON BROOKS), writer, explorer; b. Jonesboro, Ark.; d. Allan and Virginia W. (Feild) Walton; student Lindenwood Coll., 1922-24; m. Berry Boswell Brooks, Apr. 27, 1929; 1 dau., Virginia Walton (Mrs. Allen Martin). World traveler, explorer with husband, 1937-49; hunting and photographic expdns. Africa, 1947, 49; fgn. corr. Cotton Trade Jour., 1947-49, Memphis Comml. Appeal, 1949, Blytheville (Ark.) Courier News, 1947; world fight for photog. essay, 1956, world circum navigations, 1956, 1961, 1962. Dir., Brooks Meml. League; adviser Memphis Mus.; Recipient golden key to City of Memphis, 1955, 67, 69, Royal Duchess Mystic Soc. of Memphi Ct., 1953, Royal Club of Memphis Cotton Carnival Assn. of which Mr. Brooks was King, 1957; Fellow Intercontinental Biog. Assn.; mem. Nat. Soc. Children Am. Colonists (hon. life pres. nat. and Tenn.), Huguenot Soc. Founders of Manakin in Colony Va. (past nat. historian; hon. Tenn. pres. for life), Tenn. Geneal. Soc. (hon. life pres., founder), Nat. League Am. Pen Women (past pres. Tenn.), Magna Charta Dames (dist. pres.), Daus. Barons Runnemede (councillor 1962-67), Ams. Royal Descent, La. Colonials, Memphis Glass Collectors Club, Brit.-Am. Soc. Am. (adv. bd.), Soc. Descs. King William I, The Conqueror (adv. bd.), Soc. Descs. Colonial Clergy, Half Million Miler Club, Order First Three Crusades, D.A.R., U.D.C., Order First Families of Va., Daus. of 1812, Descs. Lords of Md. Manors (councillor), Nat. Soc. Dames Ct. of Honor (hon. life nat. 1st v.p., founder Tenn. soc.), Daus. Am. Colonists (2d vice regent), Plantagenet Soc., Ams. Armorial Ancestry Jamestown Soc. (founder Tenn. company; organizing dep. gov. Tenn. co.), Brooks Art Gallery League (dir.), Order of Crown Charlemagne U.S.A., Nat. Soc. Daus. of Founders and Patriots Am. (past pres. Tenn.), Internat. Soc. Descs. Woden in N.Am. (founder, pres. Tenn. soc.), Order of Crown in Am., Colonial Dames Am., Descs. Knights of Most Noble Order of Garter St. George's Chapel Windsor Castle (Am. dir.), Soc. Lees Va., Bates Family Old Va., Memphis Cotton Wives (charter), Assn. for Preservation Tenn. Antiquities (charter mem. patron), Kappa Delta (hon., local chpt. alumna 1953), Order Descs. Colonial Govs. Clubs: Shikar-Safari Internat. (charter mem., past v.p.); Tenn. Women's Press and Author's (life, 2d v.p., curator); Memphis Country; Clipper; 100,000 Mile; Hellenic (London, Eng.). Author: Screed of Safari Scribe, 1947; Spate of Safari Scribe, 1949. Home: Epping Forest Manor 3661 James Rd Memphis TN 38128

BROOKS, BETTY WATT, ret. govt. ofcl., writer, educator; b. Wellesley, Mass.; d. Thomas Thompson and Barbara (Hunter) Watt; A.B., Wellesley Coll., 1922; M.A., 1923; Ph.D., U. Pitts., 1934; m. Stanley Truman Brooks, Apr. 30, 1927 (dec. Apr. 1958); children—Stanley H.W., Barbara (Mrs. Richard E. Andersen), Anne, (Mrs. Clyde W. Kenyon). Research asst. Carnegie Instn. Washington, Cold Spring Harbor, L.I., N.Y., 1923-25; instr. U. Pitts., 1925-28; asst. prof. dept. biology Pa. Coll. Women, 1928-30; research asso. sect. recent invertebrates Carnegie Mus., Pitts., 1930-45; sci. editor Biol. Abstracts, Inc., Phila., 1945-46; document analyst Tech. Indsl. Intelligence div. U.S. Dept. Commerce, 1946; tech. editor Field Information Agy., Germany, 1946-47; research analyst div. state grants USPHS, Washington, 1951-52, research analyst pub. health div. hosp. and med. facilities, 1957-65, pub. health analyst, div. hosp. and med. facilities, 1965-66; exec. sec. health facilities demonstration grants adv. com., also fed. hosp. council research and demonstration grants br., 1966-68; exec. sec., pub. health analyst Office Grants and Contracts, Health Services and Mental Health Adminstrn., Nat. Center Health Services Research and Devel., 1968-69, retired, 1970; dist. dir. and dir. Camp Pocahontas, Girl Scouts, Richmond, Va., 1953-55. Social worker Va. Bd. Registration Social Workers, 1954-64. Mem. Girl Scout council of Nation's Capital, 1958—, Montgomery County Mental Health Assn., 1958—; treas. Montgomery County Com. on Aging, 1952-53; chmn. vols. Attic Thrift Shop, 1970—; chmn. Com. for Preserving Town Records, Washington Grove, Md., 1970—. Fellow A.A.A.S.; mem. Fed. Profl. Assn., Am. Mus. Natural History, Am. Pub. Health Assn., Royal Soc. Health, N.Y. Acad. Scis., Wellesley Coll. Alumnae Assn., Internat. Platform Assn., Am. Forestry Assn., UN Assn., Am. Acad. Polit. and Social Scis., Wilderness Soc., Wildlife Fedn., Am. Assn. Ret. Persons, Nat. Assn. Ret. Fed. Employees, Postal Commemorative Soc., Marquis Biog. Library Soc. (adv.), Chi Omega, Phi Sigma. Episcopalian. Clubs: Nat. Travel, Wellesley (Washington), Wayfarers, Washington Grove Woman's (chmn. nominating com. 1972—), Homemakers of Washington Grove (historian), Birthday Luncheon of Washington Grove; Gaithersburgh Senior Citizens. Contbr. articles to profl. publs. Home: 319 Grove Av Washington Grove MD 20880

BROOKS, CAROLINE VOGEL (MRS. KENNETH LEE BROOKS), pub. relations exec., journalist; b. Wichita Falls, Tex., June 10, 1938; d. Irvin John and Mary Caroline (Meredith) Vogel; student Midwestern U., 1956-58; B.J., U. Tex., 1960; m. Kenneth Lee Brooks, Mar. 31, 1961; children—Amelia Louise, Mary Caroline. Reporter Wichita Falls (Tex.) Times, 1960-61; editorial asst. U. Denver, 1961-62; dir. pub. relations William Jewell Coll., Liberty, Mo., 1962-65, 70-71; interim editor Liberty (Mo.) Tribune, 1969; instr. journalism Maple Woods Community Coll., Kansas City, Mo., 1971, asst. to pres. for information services, 1971—. Free lance writer, 1969—; pub. relations cons., 1971—. Recipient 1st Place award Nat. Fedn. Press Women, 1971, 72, 1st Place award Mo. Press Women, 1970, 71, 72, 73. Mem. Women in Communications, Nat. Fedn. Press Women, Mo. Press Women, Kansas City Pub. Relations Soc., Pub. Relations Soc. Am., Am. Coll. Pub. Relations Soc. Editor Progress Edit. Townsend Communications, 1971—. Home: 6107 NW Karen Rd Kansas City MO 64151 Office: 2601 NE Barry Rd Kansas City MO 64156

BROOKS, EVELYN MATHIS, home economist; b. Rocky, Okla., Apr. 8, 1921; d. Claude Lee and Inez Dexter (Sipes) Mathis; student Okla. State U., 1939-41, B.S., 1969; now postgrad. (Norma Brumbaugh scholar); student North Tex. State U., summer 1967; m. Clare Dale Brooks, Jan. 29, 1942 (div. 1969); children—Lynn Dale, Larry Dee, Lanny Don, Layne Darrell. Teller, First Nat. Bank, Lancaster, Tex., 1965; extension home economist Okla. State U. Extension Center, Pauls Valley, 1969—. Chmn. Garvin County, Keep Okla. Beautiful. Mem. Am., Okla. home econs. assns., Nat. (mem. profl. improvement com. 1972-73, winner State solo radio tape competition 1973), Okla. (state chaplin 1970-71, winner scholarship, 1973) assns. extension home economists, Okla. Christian Coll. Asso. Women's Orgn. (v.p. 1974—), Pauls Valley C. of C. (dir. 1974—), Am. Assn. U. Women. Democrat. Mem. Ch. of Christ. Home: Route 3 Box 305A Pauls Valley OK 73075 Office: PO Box 271 Pauls Valley OK 73075

BROOKS, GLADYS SINCLAIR, city ofcl.; b. Mpls., June 8, 1914; d. John Franklin and Gladys (Phillips) Sinclair; student U. Geneva (Switzerland), 1935; B.A., U. Minn., 1936; LL.D., Hamline U., 1966; m. Wright W. Brooks, Apr. 17, 1941; children—Diane (Mrs. Peter Tischendorf), John, Pamela. Lectr. on world affairs, 1939—; mem. Mpls. City Council, 1967-73; dir. Farmers & Mechanics Bank, 1973—. Lectr. on world tours as Am. specialist U.S. Dept. State; mem. Mpls. Charter Commn., 1948-51, met. Airports Commn., Met. Sound Abatement Council; pres. Mpls. Bd. Estimate and Taxation, 1970-71; pres. YWCA, 1953-57, mem. nat. bd., 1958-70, del. world meeting, Denmark; pres. Minn. Internat. Center, 1953-63; chmn. Minn. Women's Com. for Civil Rights; mem. U.S. Com. for UNICEF, 1961-70; mem. Gov.'s Adv. Com. Children and Youth, Minn. Adv. Com. Employment and Security; mem. Midwest adv. com. Inst. Internat. Edn.; mem. nat. com. White House Conf. Children and Youth, 1960; chmn. Gov.'s Human Rights Commn., 1961-65; bd. mem. Hennepin County League Municipalities; bd. mem. Mobilization Econ. Resources, 1967-69; mem. Adv. Commn. on Delinquency and Crime. Del. Republican Nat. Conv., 1952; state chmn. Citizens for Eisenhower, 1956; founder, pres. Rep. Workshop; Rep. candidate for Mayor, 1973. Pres. Internat. Center for Fgn. Students, 1953-63; chmn. Minn. Child Care Trust Fund; mem. adv. bd. Travelers Aid; trustee United Theol. Sem.; area bd. dirs. Nat. Orgn. Interested Sound Environment (Noise). Recipient Centennial Women of Minn. award Hamline U., 1954; Woman of Distinction award Am. Assn. U. Women (Mpls.), 1956, Outstanding Achievement award U. Minn., 1962. Mem. World Affairs Council (pres. 1942-44), Minn. League Women Voters (dir. 1940-45), Mpls. Council Ch. Women (pres. 1946-48), Nat. (gen. bd. v.p.), Minn. (1st woman pres., Christian service award 1967), Mpls. (v.p. 1946-48) councils chs., United Ch. Women (bd. mgrs.), Minn. UN Assn. (dir.), Am. Acad. Polit. Sci., Am. Assn. U. Women, Women's Symphony Assn., Minn. Alumni Assn. (bd.), Delta Sigma Rho. Presbyn. Clubs: Women's (Mpls.); Lafayette. Home: 5056 Garfield Av S Minneapolis MN 55419

BROOKS, GWENDOLYN, author; b. Topeka, June 7, 1917; d. David Anderson and Keziah Corinne (Wims) Brooks; grad. Wilson Jr. Coll., Chgo., 1936; 10 hon. doctorates; m. Henry L. Blakely, Sept. 17, 1939; children—Henry L., Nora. Named One of 10 Women of Year, Mademoiselle mag., 1945; recipient award for creative writing Am. Acad. Arts and Letters, 1946, Pulitzer prize for poetry, 1950; Friends of Lit. award for poetry, 1964; Thormod Monsen award for lit., 1964; others; named poet laureate of Ill., 1968. Guggenheim fellow in creative poetry, 1946-47. Mem. Soc. Midland Authors. Author: Harper: A Street in Bronzeville, 1945; Annie Allen (poetry), 1949; Maud Martha (novel), 1953; Bronzeville Boys and Girls (book for children), 1956; (poetry) The Bean Eaters, 1960, Selected Poems, 1963, In the Mecca, Riot, 1969, Family Pictures, 1970, Aloneness, 1971; Report from Part One, 1972. Address: 7428 S Evans Chicago IL 60619

BROOKS, HARRIETT BURCH (MRS. FRANCIS EARL BROOKS), nursing adminstr.; b. Deland, Fla., May 24, 1924; d. William A. and Mary (Cadwallader) Burch; diploma Grady Meml. Hosp. Sch. Nursing, Atlanta, 1945; B.S. in Pub. Health Nursing, U. N.C., 1962; m. Francis Earl Brooks, Mar. 6, 1946; children—Mary Anne, Eleanor Susan. Inst. staff nurse Hernando County Hosp., Brooksville, Fla., 1945-47; staff pub. health nurse Citrus County Health Dept., Inverness, Fla., 1951-60; field supr. pub. health nursing Palm Beach County Health Dept., West Palm Beach, Fla., 1962-64; dir. nursing service Leon County Health Dept., Tallahassee, 1964—; asst. prof. Fla. State U., 1972-73. Sec. continuing edn. com. Fla. Bd. Health, 1966-69, chmn. conf. adminstrs., suprs. and educators, 1969—. Bd. dirs. Tallahassee-Leon County Community Action Program, 1967-72. Mem. Fla. Nursing Assn. (dist. 1st v.p. 1967-68), Fla. Pub. Health Assn. (sec. 1969, 1st v.p. 1972, dir. 1973-74), Leon County Assn. Community Services. Baptist. Home: 4113 N Monroe St Tallahassee FL 32301 Office: PO Box 2745 Tallahassee FL 32304

BROOKS, HELEN DWIGHT, lawyer, editor; b. Rochester, N.Y., Oct. 17, 1924; d. George S. and Helen (Clark) Brooks; A.B. with honors, Bryn Mawr Coll., 1946; LL.B., Cornell U., 1949. Admitted to N.Y. bar, 1949; editor legal textbook writing Lawyers Co-op Pub. Co., Rochester, 1950-71, sr. editor, 1971—. Address: Lawyers Co-op Publishing Company Aqueduct Bldg Rochester NY 14603

BROOKS, HELEN LOUISE, educator; b. Portage, Me., July 10, 1932; d. Charles A.H. and Viola (Orcutt) Brooks; B.A., Ricker Coll., 1954; postgrad. U. Me., 1955-56, U. Minn., 1955-56, U. Ark., 1962-63, Ohio U., 1962-63; m. Neil E. Bishop, Nov. 3, 1949 (div. Apr. 1954); 1 dau., Connie Elizabeth. Tchr., phys. edn. dir., basketball coach Skowhegan (Me.) Pub. Schs., 1954-55; tch., coach, phys. edn. dir. Caribou (Me.) Pub. Schs., 1955-56; counselor for blind children Me. Div. Services for Blind, 1956-58; reporter Portland (Me.) Sunday Telegram, 1959; tchr., coach, girls athletic dir. Presque Isle (Me.) High Sch., 1959-66; tchr. English, dir. women's phys. edn. Prince of Wales Coll., Charlottetown, P.E.I., 1966-67; dir. girls phys. edn. Provincial Vocational Inst., Charlottetown, 1967-70; tech. writer P.E.I. Newstart, Inc., Montague, 1970—; founder, adminstr. Golden Gaits Ranch, 1971—; P.E.I. local initiatives coordinator Can. Dept. Manpower and Immigration, 1973—; founder, research coordinator High Hopes, aid to ednl. disadvantaged, 1974—; tchr., coach Limestone (Me.) High Sch., 1958-59. Pub. relations dir. No. Me. Fair, 1956—; program dir. Aroostook Raceways, 1958-60; trainer harness horses, 1960—; free-lance writer, photographer, 1954—; trainer, exhibitor show dogs, 1955—, show horses, 1958—; founder, owner Jolly Yankee Stockfarm. Exec. council No. Me. High Sch. Girls Olympics, 1963-64, Me. Girls Athletic Assn., 1960-61. Vice pres. Houlton Riding Club, 1955-58; sec. Aroostook Riding Club, 1954-55; sec. No. Me. Fair Jr. Dog Obedience Orgn., 1957—; founder, instr., dir. Golden Gaits Jr. Mounted Patrol, 1967—. Mem. N.E.A., Me. Tchrs. Assn., Me. Assn. for Health, Phys. Edn. and Recreation, Ricker Coll. Alumni Assn., Obedience Assos. (hon. award for distinguished service to children and animals 1962), Lewiston-Auburn Kennel Club (hon.), Nat. Honor Soc., Sch. Adminstrv. Dist. 1 Tchrs. Club, Amateur Athletic Union Can. (mem. P.E.I. br. gymnastic com.), U.S. Trotting Assn., Maritime Harness Breeders Assn., P.E.I. Horsemen's Assn. (sec.), P.E.I. Harness Breeders Assn., Internat. Platform Assn. Clubs: Charlottetown Driving; Abequeit Kennel (dir.). Home: Jolly Yankee Stockfarm PO Box 1032 Charlottetown PE Canada Office: Newstart Box 1000 Montague PE Canada

BROOKS, IVY OPHELIA (MRS. ALFRED DETROY BROOKS), radiologist; b. Bklyn., June 21, 1918; d. James Christopher and Mabel (Shepherd) Roach; B.A., Hunter Coll., 1940; M.S., 1944; M.D., Meharry Med. Coll., 1954; m. Alfred Detroy Brooks, Aug. 30, 1945; children—Mary Elizabeth, Alfred Christopher, Stephen Conrad. Intern Kings County Hosp., Bklyn., 1954-55; resident VA Hosp., Tuskegee, Ala. and East Orange, N.J., 1955-58; practice medicine, specializing in radiology, Tuskegee, 1958—; chief of radiology VA Hosp., Tuskegee, 1955—; instr. Spelman Coll., Atlanta, 1944-45; cons. Tuskegee Inst., 1959—. Commr. Tuckabatchee council Boy Scouts Am., 1972—. Served with M.C., AUS, 1945-46. Mem. A.M.A., Nat. Med. Assn., Radiol. Soc. N.Am., Zeta Phi Beta. Mem. Order Eastern Star. Home: 226 Bibb St Tuskegee Institute AL 36088 Office: Box 511 Veterans Hosp Tuskegee AL 36083

BROOKS, JEAN BAILEY (MRS. JAMES TAYLOR BROOKS), physician; b. Jacksonville, N.C., Aug. 2, 1920; d. Isaac Mayo and Ida Augusta (Thompson) Bailey; A.B., Duke, 1941; M.D., Bowman Gray Med. Sch., 1944; m. James Taylor Brooks, July 10, 1948; children—James Taylor, Helen Elizabeth. Intern N.C. Bapt. Hosp., Winston-Salem, 1945, resident obstetrics and gynecology, 1948; intern L.I. Coll. Hosp., Bklyn., 1946; practice medicine, specializing in gynecology, Greensboro, N.C., 1948—; med. dir. Greensboro Maternity Clinic, 1948-52; mem. staff Wesley Long Community Hosp., Moses H. Cone Meml. Hosp. Mem. alumni adv. council Bowman Gray Med. Sch., 1960-73. Bd. dirs. Family Service-Travelers Aid, Greensboro, Greensboro Com. on Alcoholism, Greensboro Community Council, Childrens Home Soc. N.C. Named Mother of Yr. Greensboro Mchts. Assn., 1969. Mem. A.M.A., Am. Coll. Obstetricians and Gynecologists, Am. Fertility Soc., Am. Hearing Soc. (nat. dir. 1958-62), N.C., Guilford County med. socs., Bowman Gray Med. Alumni (sec.-treas. 1967-73, pres. 1973-74), Greensboro Acad. Medicine, Colonial Dames U.S.A., Greensboro Jr. League, Hist. Book Club N.C. Clubs: Quota, Women's Investment (Greensboro, N.C.). Home: 609 W Cornwallis Dr Greensboro NC 27408 Office: 1100 N Elm St Greensboro NC 27401

BROOKS, JEANETTE DORIS JENKINS (MRS. WILLIAM KERR BROOKS), ednl. adminstr.; b. Mellen, Wis., Mar. 4, 1932; d. Carl Edward and Doris Catherine (Pierrelee) Jenkins; B.A., Alaska Meth. U.; m. William Kerr Brooks, Jan. 6, 1954; 1 son, William Carl

Randall. Sec. to dean Alaska Meth. U., Anchorage, 1961-62; asst. for registration, 1962-65, registrar, 1965—. Mem. financial aids com. Alaska Meth. U., chmn. personnel search com., 1970-71. Recipient Faculty award Alaska Meth. U., 1971. Mem. Am. Assn. Collegiate Registrars and Admissions Officers, Phi Alpha Theta. Home: 1518 K St Anchorage AK 99501

BROOKS, JOANNE FERGUSON, sch. adminstr.; b. Hyannis, Mass., Mar. 29, 1930; d. Robert Allen and Helen Paulina (Pelton) Sherman; B.S., Bridgewater (Mass.) State Coll., 1951, M. Ed., 1971; children—Peter, Dwight, Karen. Tchr. sci., math, Norton (Mass.) High Sch., 1951-53, Harwich, Mass., 1953-55; tchr. Riverview-Hopefields Sch., East Sandwich, Mass., 1964-66, supr., 1966-69, asst. head of sch., 1969—, bd. dirs., 1967—, clk. of corp., 1971—. Mem. Sandwich Hist. Soc., (com. mem. 1972), Mass. Sch. Prins. Assn., Internat. Reading Assn., Baptist (supt. Sunday sch. 1964-65). Home: Connors Rd Centerville MA 02632 Office: Route 6A East Sandwich MA 02537

BROOKS, LUCY WADLINGTON (MRS. EDWARD ALLEN BROOKS), motel owner; b. Cadiz, Ky., July 17, 1926; d. Reginald Cooper and Sarah Alice (Mitchell) Wadlington; student E. Carolina Tchrs. Coll., 1944; m. Edward Allen Brooks, Dec. 7, 1946; children—Edward Allen, Sharon Kay. Office mgr., owner Mericana Motor Lodge, Ft. Madison, Ia.; office mgr. Brooks Erection, 1963—; owner Keokuk (Ia.), 1967—, Friendship Inn Knotty Pine Motel, Keokuk, 1971—. Active South Souix City (Neb.) P.T.A., 1957-65; life mem. Neb. P.T.A. Methodist. Mem. Order Eastern Star. Home: Main Street Rd Keokuk IA 52632

BROOKS, MARGARET ELIZABETH SHEPHERD (MRS. HERBERT EDMUND BROOKS, JR.), mus. ofcl.; b. Phila., Dec. 7, 1922; d. James Edward and Emily (Stevenson) Shepherd; grad. Peirce Bus. Sch., 1943; m. Herbert Edmund Brooks, Jr., Mar. 6, 1961. Sec. med. research Nat. Drug Co., Phila., 1943-52; sec. Merck Sharp & Dohme, West Point, Pa., 1952-61; asst. curator Atlantic County Hist. Soc., Somers Point, N.J., 1971—. Mem. Atlantic County Council Environment, Inc., Pleasantville, N.J., 1971-74. Mem. The Questers, Inc. Ref. Episcopalian. Mem. Order Eastern Star. Club: Antique Collectors (Linwood, N.J.). Home: 108 Carol Rd Linwood NJ 08221 Office: Atlantic County Hist Soc 907 Shore Rd Somers Point NY 08244

BROOKS, SISTER MARY, hosp. adminstr.; b. Des Moines, June 29, 1933; d. William James and Kathryn Eleanor (McDonough) Brooks; B.S. in Nursing, St. Mary's Coll., Ind., 1960; diploma Holy Cross Sch. Nursing, South Bend, Ind., 1957; M.H.A., St. Louis U., 1967. Asst. adminstr. St. Joseph's Hosp., South Bend, 1963-65; adminstr. Holy Cross Hosp., Jacksonville, Ill., 1967-68; asst. adminstr. Holy Cross Hosp., San Fernando, Cal., 1968-69; adminstr. St. John's Hickey Meml. Hosp., Anderson, Ind., 1969—, also trustee. Mem. Council on Alcohol Abuse, Center for Mental Health; v.p. United Way; coordinator Christian dialogue Ind. Reformatory; mem. Anderson Commn. on Status Women's Affairs. Trustee St. Joseph's Hosp., South Bend. Mem. Am. Coll. Hosp. Adminstrs., Am. Mgmt. Assn., Am., Ind., Eastern Ind. (sec.), Cath. (chmn. council on hosp. orgn. and adminstrn.) hosp. assns., St. Louis U. Alumnae. Address: St John's Hickey Memorial Hospital 2015 Jackson St Anderson IN 46014

BROOKS, MARY ELIZABETH, govt. ofcl.; b. Colby, Kan.; d. John and Florence Thomas; student Mills Coll., Oakland, Cal.; B.A., U. Ida.; m. A.J. Peavey, Jr., 1939; children—John Thomas, Betty Ann (Mrs. Gordon Eccles); m. 2d, C.W. Brooks, 1945. Adminstrv. asst. to U.S. Senator John Thomas of Ida., 1941-44; vice chmn. Republican Nat. Com., Washington, 1960-65, asst. chmn., 1965—. Owner, mgr. Flat Top Livestock Co., Muldoon, Ida. Mem. Pres.'s Commn. on Sch. Finance, 1971-72. Ofcl. hostess Rep. Nat. Conv., Chgo., 1960; vice chmn. Com. on Big City Politics, 1961; mem. Ida. Senate, 1964-68. Bd. dirs. Ida. Youth Ranch. Recipient Exceptional Service award Treasury Dept., 1972; named Woman of Year, N.Y. Womens Nat. Rep. Club, 1969, Ida.'s Woman of Year and elected to U. Ida.'s Hall of Fame, 1970. Mem. Am. Legion Aux., Am. Newspaper Women's Club, Kappa Kappa Gamma. Home: 2710 Virginia Av Washington DC 20037 Office: 15th and Pennsylvania Av Washington DC 20037

BROOKS, MARY THOMAS, govt. ofcl.; b. Colby, Kansas; d. John and Florence Jessie (Johnson) Thomas; student Mills Coll., 1926-27; B.A., U. Ida., 1929; m. Arthur J. Peavey, Jr., July 28, 1939 (dec.); children—John Thomas, Betty Anne (Mrs. Gordon Eccles); m. 2d, C. Wayland Brooks, May 8, 1945 (dec. 1957). Formerly bus. mgr. Mills Coll.; mem. Republican Nat. Com., 1956-63, asst. chmn., 1965-69; mem. Ida. Senate, 1964-69; dir. U.S. Mint, Washington, 1969—. Mem. bd. Immigrants Service League, 1957-64, Children's Home and Aid Soc., Chgo., 1957-64, Lighthouse for the Blind, 1959-64; mem. Def. Adv. Com. on Women in Services. Named Republican Woman of Yr., Women's Nat. Rep. Club N.Y., 1969, Ida. Woman of Yr., Ida. Press Assn., 1970; named to U. Ida. Alumni Hall of Fame, 1970; recipient exceptional service award Treasury Dept., 1972; certificate of merit Cal. Hist. Soc., 1973; Laura Bride Powers award San Francisco Birthday Celebration Com., 1974. Mem. Am. Assn. U. Women, Am. Newspaper Women's Club (dir.), Am. Legion Aux., Kappa Kappa Gamma (Achievement award 1974). Home: Apt 1110 Watergate West 2700 Virginia Av NW Washington DC 20037 Office: US Treasury 15th and Pennsylvania Av Washington DC 20220

BROOKS, PEGGY JONES (MRS. JOHN BENSON BROOKS), pub. co. exec.; b. Orange, N.J., June 19, 1919; d. T. Catesby and Louisa R. (Brooke) J.; B.A., Vassar, 1940; m. John Benson Brooks, Apr. 8, 1961. Account exec. Franklin Spier, Inc., N.Y.C., 1944-47; promotion head Thomas Y. Crowell Co., N.Y.C., 1947-49; advt. mgr. E.P. Dutton & Co., Inc., N.Y.C., 1953-57, editor 1957-68, exec. editor, 1968-70; sr. editor Coward McCann & Geoghegan, Inc., N.Y.C., 1970—, sec., 1974—. Mem. P.E.N. Clubs: Editor's Lunch, Cosmopolitan (N.Y.C.). Home: 9 Gay St New York City NY 10014 Office: 200 Madison Av New York City NY 10016

BROOKS, PHYLLIS FEATHERSTONE, artist, educator; b. Mpls.; d. James Wesley and Eleanor (Maloney) Featherstone; student Coll. William and Mary, 1958-59; B.A., Am. U., 1965; m. Henry S. Brooks, Aug. 21, 1965; children—Edwin Featherstone, Helen Ruth, Benjamin Levi. Exhibited one-woman shows Fed. Res. Bd., Washington, 1964, London Sch. Azalea Festival, Bethesda, Md., 1965, Watkins Gallery, Washington, 1965; exhibited juried shows No. Va. Fine Arts Assn., 1972, 73; instr. art Alexandria (Va.) Pub. Schs., 1965-66; instr. pvt. painting classes, Heidelberg, West Germany, 1969-71. Mem. No. Va. Fine Arts Assn., Art League Alexandria. Home: 319 S Pitt St Alexandria VA 22314

BROOKS, ROBERTA DELORES, psychologist; b. Kitts Hill, O., July 9, 1933; d. Goerge L. and Alma (Chafin) Brooks; Asso. Liberal Arts, Ashland Jr. Coll., 1952; B.S., Ohio State U., 1954; M.A., Marshall U., 1964; Ed.D., U. Cin., 1974. Tchr., Rock Hill High Sch., Pedro, O., 1955-57; tchr. history Ironton High Sch., 1957-59, tchr. English and history, 1963-67; tchr. history Ironton Jr. High Sch., 1959-63; intern sch. psychology U. Cin., 1967-68; counselor, sch. psychologist Ironton City Schs., 1968—. Social scientist Lea-Mendota Research Group, Ambler, Pa., part-time 1964-67; psychologist Head Start Program, Lawrence County, O., 1965; instr. Ironton br. Ohio U., 1966-67; mem. Lawrence County Mental Health Clinic Task Force, 1974—, Nelsonville Children's Service Bd., 1974—; co-chmn. Lawrence County br. Arthritis Found., 1973-74. Recipient Outstanding Young Educator award Jr. C. of C. Ironton, 1967. Mem. Nat. Assn. Sch. Psychologists (charter), Ohio, Southeastern Ohio, Ironton (pres. 1965-67) edn. assns., Ohio Psychol. Assn., Ohio (mem. com. on profl. problems 1971—), Southeastern Ohio sch. psychologists assns., Lawrence County Guidance Assn., Lawrence County Sch. Ofcls. Assn., Am. Assn. U. Women (pres. Ironton 1965-67). Home: 2207 N 2d St Ironton OH 45638 Office: 105 S 5th St Ironton OH 45638

BROOKS, RUTH CLAUDIA (MRS. JOE FELIX BROOKS), educator; b. Pasadena, Md., Sept. 27, 1934; d. Francis Aldelbert and Catherine Claudia (Wigley) Hutchins; student U. Alaska, 1962-64, New Haren Coll., 1964-65, U. Bridgeport, 1965, Anne Arundel Coll., 1967-68; B.S., So. Conn. U., 1968; postgrad. Hood Coll., 1973, Towson State Coll., 1970; m. Joe Felix Brooks, Mar. 4, 1951; children—Joe Francis, Catherine Claudia. Tchr., Anne Arundel County Bd. Edn., Annapolis, Md., 1967-73, resource tchr. in continuum spl. edn., 1973—. Lectr., Assn. for Retarded Children, 1966-67. Active Boy Scouts Am., 1961-63, Girl Scouts Am., 1965-67, Pioneer Girls Am., 1968-72. Recipient Den Mother's award, Boy Scouts Am., 1963, Certificate Appreciation, Pioneer Girls Am., 1972. Mem. N.E.A., Md. State Tchr. Assn., Council for Exceptional Children (chmn. membership 1971-72), Am. Assn. on Mental Deficiency, Tchrs.' Assn. Anne Arundel County, Royal Soc. Health, Alpha Delta Kappa (program chmn. 1972-73, parliamentarian 1974-75). Mem. Jobs Daus. Home: 800 Stewart Av Glen Burnie MD 21062 Office: Brooklyn Park Elementary School 14th Av Baltimore MD 21225

BROSIUS, EVA REID (MRS. ARTHUR JAMES BROSIUS), educator; b. Birmingham, Mich., Aug. 9, 1913; d. Wilson and Annie (O'Beirne) Reid; student Ashland Coll., 1931-33; B.A., Westminister Coll., 1935; M.Ed., U. Pitts., 1967; m. Carter Branch Grundy, Aug. 29, 1944 (dec. Sept. 1955); m. 2d, Arthur James Brosius, Aug. 23, 1969. Dir. womens work Covenant Presbyn. Ch., Cin., 1936-37; asst. to minister 6th U.P. Ch., Pitts., 1937-66; dean released time religious edn. Peabody High Sch., Pitts., 1956-66; dean of women, asst. dean students Thiel Coll., Greenville, Pa., 1966-69, dir. placement, 1967-69; asso. dir. devel. U. Pitts., 1969—, clk. Univ. Senate, 1971—. Mem. Nat., Pa. assns. women deans and counselors, N.E.A., Am. Assn. U. Women, Middle Atlantic Placement Assn., Am. Assn. Higher Edn., Delta Kappa Gamma. Home: 154 N Bellefield Av Pittsburgh PA 15213

BROSKY, CATHERINE M., librarian; b. Pitts., Apr. 2, 1926; d. Ignatius Joseph and Veronica (Szacowna) Brosky; B.S., Carnegie Inst. Tech., 1946, B.S. in L.S., 1947. Librarian Carnegie Library, Pitts., 1947-52; asst. librarian, region V, U.S. Bur. Mines, Pitts., 1952-55; librarian Grad. Sch. Pub. Health, U. Pitts., 1955—; dir. Western Pa. Regional Med. Program Library System, 1968—. Mem. N.Y. Acad. Scis., Am., Med. (treas. Pitts. chpt.) library assns., Spl. Libraries Assn. (pres. chpt. 1961-62), Am. Soc. Indexers, Am. Soc. Information Sci. (chpt. sec.-treas. 1962-64). Home: 4614 5th Av Pittsburgh PA 15213 Office: Grad Sch Pub Health U Pitts Pittsburgh PA 15261

BROSMAN, CATHARINE HILL SAVAGE (MRS. PAUL W. BROSMAN, JR.), educator; b. Denver, June 7, 1934; d. Paul Victor and Della Leota (Stanforth) Hill; B.A., Rice U., 1955, M.A., 1957, Ph.D., 1960; postgrad. U. Grenoble, 1957-58; m. Patric Savage, Apr. 7, 1955 (div. July 1964); m. 2d, Paul W. Brosman, Jr., Aug. 21, 1970; 1 dau., Katherine Elliott. Instr. French, Rice U., 1960-62; asst. prof. Sweet Briar Coll., 1962-63, U. Fla., 1963-66; asso. prof. Mary Baldwin Coll., 1966-68; asso. prof. French dept. French and Italian Tulane U., New Orleans, 1968-72, prof., 1972—. Recipient grants-in-aid Am. Council Learned Socs., 1962, Bd. Edn., Presbyn. Ch. U.S., 1967. Mem. Modern Lang. Assn. (mem. commn. on status of women in profession 1969-70), South-Central (v.p. 1973-74), South Atlantic modern lang. assns., Phi Beta Kappa. Home: 7834 Willow St New Orleans LA 70118

BROSNAHAN, CAROL SIMON (MRS. JAMES JEROME BROSNAHAN JR.), lawyer; b. Bklyn., Dec. 4, 1934; d. Alfred Joseph and Celia (Aland) Simon; A.B. cum laude, Wellesley Coll., 1955; LL.B., Harvard, 1959; m. James Jerome Brosnahan Jr., Nov. 8, 1959; children—Amy, James Jerome III, Lisa. Asst. investment counselor Bank of N.Y., N.Y.C., 1955-56; admitted to Ariz. bar, 1960; practiced in Phoenix, 1960-62; with Cal. Continuing Edn. of the Bar, U. Cal. at Berkeley, 1965—, supervising atty. 1972—. Mem. Am. Bar Assn., State Bar Cal., State Bar Ariz. Editor: Attorney's Guide to Family Law Act Practice, 1970, rev. edit. 1972; Attorney's Guide to Cal. Profl. Corporations, 1969, rev. edit., 1973; Personal Bankruptcy and Wage Earner Plans, 1971; Attorney's Guide to Trade Secrets, 1971; California Debt Collection Tort Practice, 1971; Creditor's Remedies and Debtor's Rights, 1973; Liability of Lawyers and Accountants, 1972; CEB Legal Services Gazette, 1967-69. Home: 2808 Oak Knoll Terrace Berkeley CA 94705 Office: 2150 Shattuck Av Berkeley CA 94704

BROSS, MARY DIANE, sch. adminstr.; b. Milw., July 26, 1933; d. Henry John and Diane Clara (Carney) Bross; B.S., Cardinal Stritch Coll., 1967; postgrad. U. Wis., 1973-74. Tchr. elementary sch. St. Sebastian's Sch., Milw., 1953-55, St. Mary's Sch. Random Lake, Wis., 1955-57, St. Bernard's Sch., Middleton, Wis., 1957-59, St. Mary's Sch., South Milw., 1959-60; spl. edn. tchr. Cardinal Cushing Sch. and Tng. Center, Hanover, Mass., 1960-63, St. Coletta Sch., Jefferson, Wis., 1963-64, Lt. Joseph Sch. for Exceptional Children, Palos Park, Ill., 1964-70; prin., spl. edn. tchr. St. Francis' Children's Activity and Achievement Center, Milw., 1970—. Instr., Cardinal Stritch Coll., 1970-72. Mem. Am. Assn. Mental Deficiency, Council for Exceptional Children, Wis. Assn. for Children with Learning Disabilities, Wis. Soc. for Brain-Injured Children. Home: 8330 N 46th St Brown Deer WI 53223 Office: PO Box 3717 Milwaukee WI 53217

BROSTOFF, PEARL KALB, clin. psychologist; b. Pitts., June 22, 1927; d. George and Minnie (Bergman) Kalb; student Pa. State U., 1944-45; B.S., U. Pitts., 1948, M.S., 1969, Ph.D., 1971; m. Gerald Brostoff, June 29, 1947; children—Janet (Mrs. Lee Beerman), Diane, George, Myer. Cons. psychologist, spl. edn. Allegheny Intermediate Unit #3, Pitts., 1971-73; psychologist Vocational Rehab. Center, Pitts., 1971—; clin., sch. psychologist Churchill Area Sch. Dist., Pitts., 1973-74. Mem. Am., Pa., Pitts. psychol. assns. Democrat. Jewish religion. Home: 2301 Marbury Rd Pittsburgh PA 15221

BROTCHNER, DOROTHY GOLDBLUM (MRS. ROBERT BROTCHNER), civic worker; b. Mpls.; Hal and Emma (Shapere) Goldblum; student Macalester Coll., 1935-36, U. Minn., 1936-38; m. Robert Brotchner, Apr. 3, 1943; children—Richard Raymond, Leslie Alison. Mem. bd. Ramsey County (Minn.) Med. Aux., 1947-51, rec. sec., 1950-51; mem. bd. Rheumatic Diagnostic Clinic, St. Paul, 1949-51; unit chmn. League Women Voters, St. Paul, 1950; mem. U. Minn. Faculty Wives' Club, 1949-51; mem. bd. univ. sect. Newcomers, 1949-51; mem. various local and council bds. Cal. P.T.A., 1951-64, hon. life mem., 1956—; mem. aux. bd. Queen of Angels Hosp., Los Angeles, 1953-62; den mother Cub Scouts, Los Angeles, 1952-54; patrol sponsor Boy Scouts Am., Los Angeles, 1954-55; Brownie leader Girl Scouts U.S.A., Los Angeles, 1954-58, troop leader, 1959; mem. U. So. Cal. Med. Faculty Wives' Club, 1960—; mem. bd. met. sect. Los Angeles County Med. Aux., 1960, mem. bd. W. Valley sect., 1969—; pres. Gamma Phi Beta Mothers' Club, 1963-64, asso., 1969—; mem. bd. U. Cal. at Los Angeles Intersorority Mothers' Club, 1964-69; mem. Los Angeles County Mus. Art, 1969—; mem. U. Cal. at Los Angeles Arts Council, 1974—, Natural History Mus., Los Angeles, 1973—. Mem. Encino (Cal.) Republican Women's Club, 1965—, bd. dirs., 1969-70. Mem. alumni council U. Cal. at Los Angeles, 1972—, exec. bd., 1973-74. Recipient certificate for Outstanding Pub. Service, Civil Def. and Disaster Corps, City of Los Angeles, 1955. Mem. U. Cal. at Los Angeles (life), Westside Trojan alumni assns. Clubs: Braemar Country (Tarzana, Cal.), The Affiliates U. Cal. at Los Angeles (life, dir. 1973—, pres. 1974-75) Town and Gown of U. So. Cal., Westwood Women's Bruin (exec. bd. 1970—, pres. 1972-74) (Westwood, Cal.); Riviera Country (Pacific Palisades); U. Cal. at Los Angeles Faculty Women's (hon.), Westside Bruins Home: 15604 Royal Woods Pl Sherman Oaks CA 91403

BROTHER, MIRIAM HOFFMEIR (MRS. EDWARD BROTHER), pub. relations cons.; b. N.Y.C.; d. Harry J. and Anna Florence (Kimberly) Hoffmeir; student Columbia, 1929-31, N.Y. U., 1931-32; m. Edward B. Brother, Apr. 15, 1933; children—Katherine A. (Mrs. Roland J. Allen), Elizabeth D. Writer continuity dept. NBC, N.Y.C., 1930-35, program analysis dept., 1935-42, mgr. program analysis dept., 1942-73. Freelance pub. relations cons., 1973—. Bd. dirs. Wilton Playshop, 1945-56, pres., 1956-58, now trustee; bd. dirs. United Fund Wilton; trustee Mid-Fairfield Child Guidance Center. Membership chmn. Democratic Town Com. Wilton, 1974—. Mem. Am. Women in Radio and Television (pres. N.Y.C. chpt. 1959-60, chmn. bd. trustees Ednl. Found. 1968-70), Town Assn. Wilton, Wilton Garden Club, Internat. Radio and TV Soc. Democrat. Episcopalian. Home: 56 Grumman Hill Rd Wilton CT 06897

BROTHERS, HOPE RICHARDS, coll. adminstr.; b. Providence, Mar. 14, 1923; d. Clarence and Ellen Jane (Parker) Richards; A.B., Brown U., 1944; 1 son, Richard Stephen. Asst. to recorder Brown U., 1944-46, acting dir. sr. placement, 1950-51, dir. placement-The Coll., 1951-71, asst. dir. univ. placement, 1971-72; dir. career counseling Williams Coll., 1972—; sec. to gen. mgr. radio sta. WPRO, 1946-47. Co-chmn. elect Women's Forum, 1972-73. Past sec. East Providence Republican Club. Bd. dirs. East Providence Citizens League, 1960. Mem. N.E. Assn. Pre-Law Advisers (chmn. 1973—), Eastern Coll. Personnel Officers (pres. 1959-60, rep. Coll. Placement Council 1959-60), Am. Personnel and Guidance Assn., Eastern Coll. Personnel Officers, Am. Coll. Personnel Assn. Club: Williams College Faculty (bd. govs. 1974—). Home: Green River Rd Williamstown MA 01267

BROTHERS, JOYCE DIANE BAUER (MRS. MILTON BROTHERS), psychologist; b. N.Y.C.; d. Morris K. and Estelle (Rapoport) Bauer; B.S., Cornell U., 1947; M.A., Columbia, 1949, Ph.D., 1953; L.H.D., Franklin Pierce Coll., 1969; m. Milton Brothers, July 4, 1949; 1 dau., Lisa Robin. Mem. faculty Hunter Coll., 1948-53, Columbia U., 1948-53; research fellow UNESCO, 1949-50; TV program Dr. Joyce Brothers WNBC, 1958-63, Consult Dr. Brothers syndicated by ABC, 1961-66, Tell Me, Dr. Brothers syndicated by Triangle Films, 1964-70; syndicated on TV by Gen. Foods Co., Kohner Bros., 1972—; Living Easy with Dr. Joyce Brothers syndicated by Trevira, 1972—; radio program ABC, 1963-68; program Call Dr. Brothers, WNBC Radio, 1966-69, WMCA, 1969-71, NBC Radio Emphasis, 1966—, NBC Monitor, 1966—; newspaper column North Am. Newspaper Alliance, 1961-72; columnist Good Housekeeping mag., 1964—, King Features Syndicate, 1972—; cons. Magee Carpet Co., Sperry and Hutchins Co., ABC Films, Greyhound Corp., Hoechst Fibers, Inc., Reading Devel. Center. Recipient wisdom award of honor, 1965; named Woman of Achievement, Fedn. Jewish Women's Orgn., 1964; Justice Lodge citation for unselfish devotion and inspired leadership and service to community, 1963; named Profl. Woman of Year dist. 1 Bus. and Profl. Womens Clubs, 1968; Merit award Bar-Ilan U., Ramat, Israel, 1968, award Parkinson Disease Found., 1971, Deadline award for excellence in broadcasting radio news Sigma Delta Chi, 1971. Mem. Sigma Xi. Author: Ten Days to a Successful Memory, 1960; Woman, 1962; The Brothers System for Liberated Love and Marriage, 1972. Home: 305 E 86th St New York City NY 10028 Office: NBC 30 Rockefeller Plaza New York City NY 10020

BROTMAN, PHYLLIS BLOCK (MRS. DON N. BROTMAN), public relations exec.; b. Balt., Mar. 22, 1934; d. Sol George and Delma (Herman) Block; ed. Balt. Jr. Coll., U. Va., Mary Washington Coll.; m. Don N. Brotman, Aug. 16, 1953; children—Solomon G., Barbara Gay. Asso., Channel 13 TV, 1953-55; free-lance pub. relations, 1960-66; coordinator pub. relations Md. Council Ednl. TV, 1965-66; pres. Image Dynamics, Inc., Balt., 1966—. Lectr., cons.; lectr. pub. relations Johns Hopkins; spl. lectr. pub. schs., Balt. County; cons. legislative information program Md. Gen. Assembly, 1970; former coordinator spl. events Balt. Jr. Coll.; former program coordinator Wine Inst. Internat. pres. B'nai B'rith Girls, 1952-53. Bd. dirs. Nat. Council Jewish Women, 1969-71, former coordinator pub. affairs, chmn. coll. program, program intellectual enrichment; bd. dirs. Levindale Home and Infirmary Ladies Aux., 1963-64, Asso. Placement and Guidance Bur., 1964-65, Sinai Hosp. Aux., 1964-65; former bd. dirs. Asso. Jewish Charities, Nat. Jewish Welfare Fund Recipient certificate of achievement Md. Ho. of Dels., Md. Senate, Asso. Jewish Charities, 1965, award for outstanding community service Beta Omega Kappa, 1952. Mem. Pub. Relations Soc. Am. (asso. mem., sec. Balt. chpt., certificate of achievement Md. chpt.), Am. Assn. Polit. Consultants (dir.), Internat. Assn. Polit. Cons., McDonough-Field Assn. (pres.), Balt. Council Pub. Relations, Md.-Del.-D.C. Press Assn., Council State Govts., Chesapeake Bay Flyers, Advt. Club D.C., Beta Omega Kappa (past pres.). Democrat. Jewish religion (pres. parents assn. 1968-70, mem. religious sch. com., bd. congregation). Mem. B'nai B'rith Women (v.p. Balt.), Hadassah (past chmn., speaker rep.). Instrumental in legislation to create state-wide ednl. television network. Home: McDonogh Lane RFD 7 Box 554 Baltimore MD 21208 Office: Horizon House Calvert at Chase Sts Baltimore MD 21202

BROUGH, ALBERTA KATHLEEN (MRS. ROBERT FORSYTH OLDHAM), physician; b. Terre Haute, Ind., Nov. 17, 1938; d. John Thomas and Maxine (Ames) Brough; A.B., Ind. State U., 1960; M.D., Ind. U., 1964; m. Robert Forsyth Oldham, Nov. 1, 1970; 1 son, John Thomas. Intern, St. Vincents Hosp., Indpls., 1964-65; med. chief of staff Marion County Home and Julietta Convalescent Center, Indpls., 1965-72; resident Jewish Meml. Hosp., Boston, 1967-68; supervising physician Ind. Dept. Pub. Welfare, 1973-74; physician Student Employee Health Service, asst. prof. family practice Ind. U. Med. Center, 1974—. Mem. Am. Geriatric Soc., A.M.A., Ind., Marion County med. socs. Mem. Christian Ch. Home: 505 W 106th St Carmel IN 46032 Office: 1100 W Michigan St Indianapolis IN 46202

BROUSSARD, ELSIE RITA (MRS. LLOYD COOPER), med. educator; b. Baton Rouge, Jan. 30, 1924; d. Arney L. and Elsie M. (Parent) Broussard; B.S., La. State U., 1942, M.D., 1944; M.P.H., U. Pitts., 1962, Dr.P.H., 1964; m. Francis P. Cassidy, Jan. 30, 1945; children—Jude Anne, Francis P.; m. 2d, Lloyd Cooper, Jan. 1, 1972. Rotating intern Hotel-Dieu Hosp., New Orleans, 1944-45; admitting physician Charity Hosp., New Orleans, 1945-46, 48-49; resident surgery Children's Hosp., San Francisco, 1946; resident pub. health Fla. Bd. Health, Pensacola, 1959-61; teaching fellow gen. psychiatry Western Psychiat. Inst. and Clinic, U. Pitts., 1965-67, mem. adj. staff, 1967-68, mem. staff, 1969—; teaching fellow child psychiatry Pitts. Child Guidance Center, 1965-67; asso. psychoanalysis Pitts. Psychoanalytic Inst., U. Pitts., 1968—; individual practice pediatrics, New Orleans, 1949-51; asst. health officer, dir. mental health and maternal-child health programs Escambia County Health Dept., Pensacola, 1952-61; asst. prof. child psychiatry U. Pitts. Sch. Medicine, 1967—, asso. prof. pub. health psychiatry, head community mental health program Grad. Sch. Pub. Health, 1967-71, prof. pub. health psychiatry, head community mental health program, 1972—, cons. in field. Commr. Pitts. Model Cities, 1972-74. Diplomate Am. Bd. Preventive Medicine splty. Pub. Health; Am. Bd. Psychiatry and Neurology, also sub-splty. Child Psychiatry. Fellow Am. Pub. Health Assn.; mem. Am., Pa. med. assns., Allegheny County Med. Soc., Am. Psychiat. Assn. (Hofheimer award for outstanding research 1973), Pa. Psychiat. Soc., Am. Acad. Child Psychiatry. Home: 201 Lytton Av Pittsburgh PA 15213

BROUSSARD, NORMAJ (MRS. LEE R. BROUSSARD), artist, journalist; b. Lake Providence, La., Aug. 28, 1931; d. C. Thomas and Hazel Valli (Ainsworth) Edwards; student Stephen F. Austin State Coll., 1951-52, U. Tex., 1973—; mem. Internat. Workshop Danish Sch. Design, Copenhagen, 1973; m. Lee R. Broussard, Dec. 31, 1958; 1 dau., Cherie Antoinette; children from previous marriage—Bonnie Greening (Mrs. Allen P. Bennett), Billy E. Greening. Owner, The Chateau, Port Arthur, Tex., 1968—, Broussard's Mobile Village, Port Arthur, 1960—, Studio Normaj, 1972—; journalist column Arts and Artists, Port Arthur News, 1971—; organizer, sponsor Gulf Coast Arts and Crafts Festival, 1970, Jefferson County (Tex.) Arts and Crafts Festival, 1972, Diamond Jubilee Fine Arts Show, 1973; tchr., lectr. in field. Founder, Tex. Artists Mus. Soc., 1972, pres., 1973-74; mem. com. Tex. Constl. Rev. Commn., 1973—. Recipient numerous awards local and state art competitions including La. Art and Folk Festival, 1970-73, Sabine Area Art Show, 1972. Mem. Port Arthur Art Assn. Fine Arts Guild (pres. 1971), Diocesan Council Cath. Women (pres. 1965), Noon Bus. and Profl. Women's Club, Internat. Platform Assn., Tex. Fedn. Women's Clubs, Tex. Poetry South and Major Poets Club, S.E. Area Arts Council (treas.), Port Arthur C. of C., Zeta Phi Delphians (pres. 1967), Beta Sigma Phi. Roman Catholic (pres. altar soc. 1965, 66). Club: Heritage Antique Study (pres. 1973-74). Address: 4801 7th St Port Arthur TX 77640

BROWER, BERNICE MORRISON (MRS. WILLIAM SEAMAN BROWER, JR.), editor; b. Bklyn., Sept. 15, 1926; d. Milton Aaron and Tillie (Metz) Morrison; student William Smith Coll., 1945-47; m. William Seaman Brower, Jr., June 15, 1947 (dec.). Copy chief Shevlo, Inc., advt., N.Y.C., 1951-55; copy chief Oppenheim Collins stores, N.Y.C., 1955; sr. writer Seventeen mag., N.Y.C., 1956-67, copy chief, travel editor, 1967—. Mem. Soc. Am. Travel Writers, N.Y. Travel Writers Assn. Home: 414 E 52d St New York City NY 10022 Office: 320 Park Av New York City NY 10022

BROWER, DIANA RAE REMBOLT (MRS. LESLIE FRANKLIN BROWER), occupational therapist; b. Lincoln, Neb., July 6, 1942; d. Raymond Ralph and Mae Ione (Street) Rembolt; B.S., U. Ia., 1964; m. Leslie Franklin Brower, June 7, 1964; children—Jennifer, Andrew. Intern, Mpls. VA Hosp., 1964-65; occupational therapist Fairview Hosp., Mpls., 1965-69; occupational therapy cons. Heritage Manor Nursing Home, Dubuque, Ia., 1970, Mitchell County Homemaker Health Aide Service, Osage, Ia., 1972—; co-owner Brower Drug Co., St. Ansgar, Ia., 1971—; co-owner, mgr. The Gift Barrel, St. Ansgar, 1973—. Bd. dirs. St. Ansgar Presch., 1973—. Mem. Am., Ia. occupational therapy assns., Pi Beta Phi, Gen. Fedn. Women's Club. Methodist. Republican. Home: PO Box 308 St Ansgar IA 50472 Office: 308 W 4th St Ansgar IA 50472

BROWER, IRENE CIOCHINE (MRS. JAMES ORIS BROWER III), educator; b. New Haven, Jan. 1, 1922; d. Joseph A. and Rose (Crotta) Ciochine; student Albertus Magnus Coll., 1939-41; B.A., Western Res. U., 1943; postgrad. Pa. State Extension Coll., 1945, Columbia, 1967; M.S.W., U. Denver, 1948, postgrad., 1949, 66; Creative Problem Solving Inst., State U. N.Y. at Buffalo, 1973; m. James Oris Brower III, Sept. 5, 1948; children—Deborah Jean, James Oris IV. Field dir. Girl Scouts U.S.A., Lancaster County, Lancaster, Pa., 1943, exec. dir., 1944-46; group worker Grace Community Center, Denver, 1949; supr. grad. students, field dir. Girl Scouts U.S.A., Met. Denver, 1948-49; camp intake worker New Haven Council Social Agcys., 1955; personnel dir., field dir. New Haven council Girl Scouts U.S.A., 1956-57, exec. dir. Laurel Trail council, New Haven, 1957-63, Conn. Trails council 1964-66; asst. prof. So. Conn. State Coll., New Haven, 1966—. Bus. mgr., corp. sec. Brower Art Enamel Studios, Inc., 1951-55. Agy. del. groupwork council New Haven Council Social Agcys., 1951-53; mem. stage settings com. Theater Group, Cheshire, Conn., 1954; U.S.O. recreation leader Lancaster YWCA, 1944-46; club leader Alta House, Cleve., 1942-43; mem. Orange (Conn.) Human Relations Council. Bd. dirs. New Haven, Cheshire councils Girl Scouts U.S.A., West Haven Community House, Soc. Conn. Craftsmen. Recipient Thanks Badge New Haven council Girl Scouts U.S.A., 1953, news salute WNHC-TV, 1966. Mem. Acad. Certified Social Workers, Nat. Assn. Social Workers (chpt. social work month com. 1967, nominating com. 1971-72), Consortium on Systems Edn., N.E.A., Conn. Edn. Assn., So. Conn. State, Four State coll. faculty assns., Internat. Platform Assn., Delta Psi Omega. Republican. Episcopalian (vestrywoman 1969-71; del. diocesan conv. and deanarie; mem. calling, nominating coms.). Home: 838 Oakwood Rd Orange CT 06477

BROWIN, FRANCES WILLIAMS, editor, author; b. Media, Pa.; d. John J. and Alice (Roberts) Williams; A.B., Swarthmore Coll.; m. Beverly M. Browin (dec. 1962). Editor Rotogravure Publs., Phila., 1929-32; editor Pa. Dept. of Welfare, Harrisburg, 1932-35; asst. editor Friends Intelligencer, Phila., 1938-44; copy editor J.B. Lippincott Co., Phila., 1944-46; editor Friends Jour., Phila., 1962-68, contbg. editor, 1968—. Mem. Authors' Guild. Mem. Soc. of Friends. Author: Pennsylvania: An Inventory, 1936; Ginger's Cave, 1954; Captured Words, 1954; The Whozits, 1955; Big Bridge to Brooklyn, 1956; Looking for Orlando, 1961; Coins Have Tales to Tell, 1966; (with Seale Harris) Banting's Miracle, 1946; Woman's Surgeon, 1950; (with Florence Aiken Banks) Coins of Bible Days, 1955. Home: 1321 Spruce St Philadelphia PA 19107

BROWN, ADELINE HELEN LUSTRI (MRS. JAMES EDWARD BROWN), borough ofcl.; b. Oakmont, Pa., Apr. 27, 1927; d. Angelo and Ernestine (Liberati) Lustri; student pub. schs., Oakmont; m. James Edward Brown, Sept. 13, 1947; 1 son, Richard Edward. Sec., Red Raven Corp., 1945-47; with Borough of Oakmont, 1947—, borough mgr., 1968—. Active numerous civic activities. Mem. Internat. City Mgrs. Assn., Pa. Municipal Mgrs. Assn., Pa. (Sec. of Year award 1971), S.W. Pa. (v.p.) municipal secs. assn. Home: 650 8th St Oakmont PA 15139 Office: City Hall 5th St and Virginia Av Oakmont PA 15139

BROWN, ALICE ELAINE (MRS. LAURENCE I. ASCHER), pediatrician; b. Lynbrook, N.Y., Aug. 1, 1923; d. Irving and Sadie Jeannette (Berlinger) Brown; ed. U. Mich., 1941-44, N.Y. Med. Coll., 1944-48; m. Laurence I. Ascher, Dec. 11, 1955; children—Herman H., Stephen J. Intern Coney Island Hosp., N.Y.C., 1948-49; resident Queens Gen. Hosp., Jamaica, N.Y., 1950-52; practice medicine, specializing in pediatrics, Valley Stream, N.Y., 1952—; mem. staff Franklin Gen. Hosp., Valley Stream, L.I. Jewish Hosp., Glen Oaks, N.Y. Diplomate Nat. Bd. Med. Examiners. Mem. A.M.A., Nassau Pediatric Soc. Address: 115 N Cottage St Valley Stream NY 11580

BROWN, ALICE EMMERT, library adminstr.; b. Sunnyside, Wash., Mar. 7, 1911; d. George C. and Harriet Jane (Lamb) Emmert; A.B., Mt. Morris Coll., 1932; M.A. in French, U. Ill., 1933; M.A. in Library Sci., Drexel U., 1962; m. Donald Fowler Brown, June 17, 1935; children—Timothy, Sarabeth Clevenger, Abigail, Prodence Jacobs, Anthony. Children's librarian Wolfsohn Meml. Library, King of Prussia, Pa., 1963-66; head W. Phila. br. Free Library of Phila., 1966-68, asst. head stas. dept., 1968—. Mem. A.L.A. (com. fgn. children's lit.). Home: 108 Wooded Lane Villanova PA 19085 Office: 236 N 23d St Philadelphia PA 19103

BROWN, ALLISON TRAVIS (MRS. DEAN E. BROWN, JR.), author, illustrator, assn. exec.; b. Bklyn., Feb. 5, 1914; d. George Morton and Blanche (Sherry) Travis; student Beaver Coll., 1931, Parsons Sch. Design, 1932-35; m. Dean Edgar Brown, Jr., Nov. 24, 1939; children—Dean Edgar III, Travis Bliss. Asst. decorator Tate & Hall, N.Y.C., 1936-37, McMillan, Inc., N.Y.C., 1937-38; sr. decorator Lord & Taylor, N.Y.C., 1938-39; instr. interior design, lectr. survey of art history U. Md., College Park, 1941-53; exec. dir. Internat. Visitors Service Council, Washington, 1966-67, vice chmn., 1965-66, sec., 1966—, dir., 1965—. Mem. exec. com. Mayor's Com. for Internat. Visitors, Washington, 1969—; Washington rep. Nat. Council Women of U.S., 1969-71; sec. Hospitality and Information Services for Diplomatic Families, 1965-67, treas., 1967-69, dir., 1962—; mem. steering com. Internat. Youth Hostel, 1968-70; mem. D.C. Bicentennial Assembly, 1972—. Bd. dirs. Fgn. Student Service Council, Meridian House Found.; bd. dirs. Nat. Council for Community Services to Internat. Visitors, treas., 1969-71. Mem. Am. Assn. U. Profs. Democrat. Unitarian. Author, illustrator: Heritage: An Illustrated History of Western Culture, 1956. Editor, illustrator: Come to Washington, 1964; illustrator Religious Services in Foreign Languages in the Washington Area, 1966, 67; editor News from IVIS, 1959-64; Directory of Orgns. serving Internat. Visitors in the Nation's Capital, 4th edit., 1972; News for Volunteers, Fgn. Student Service Council, 1962. Home: 4530 Connecticut Av NW Washington DC 20008

BROWN, ANN CHRISTINE HINDMAN, journalist; b. Columbus, O., June 23, 1950; d. William Murphy and Vivien Eileen (McLaughlin) Hindman; B.A. in Journalism cum laude and with distinction, Ohio State U., 1972, M.A., 1973; m. Charles Wayne Brown, Aug. 7, 1971 (div. Jan. 1974). Promotion writer WBNS-TV, Columbus, 1969-71; copy editor and writer, The Dispatch, Columbus, 1971-74; entertainment writer The Free Press, Detroit, 1974—. Lectr., Ohio State U., 1973-74. Glenna Joyce scholar, 1968-72, Columbus Dispatch Internship scholar, 1971. Mem. Pub. Relations Student Soc. Am. (v.p. Ohio State U. chpt. 1972-73), Mademoiselle Mag. Coll. Bd., Mortar Board, Women in Communications, (program dir. Columbus chpt. 1972-73), Kappa Tau Alpha, Sigma Delta Chi, Phi Mu (treas. 1970-71). Home: 48910 Denton Rd Apt 36 Belleville MI 48111 Office: 321 W Lafayette Blvd Detroit MI 48231

BROWN, ANNA ELIZABETH MELLO (MRS. WILLIAM R. BROWN), town ofcl.; b. Bridgewater, Mass., May 13, 1918; d. Manuel M. and Mary (Perry) Mello; grad. high sch.; m. William R. Brown, May 30, 1938; children—Patricia (Mrs. Thomas Dawson), William R., Judith (Mrs. Ralph Souza), Kathryn (Mrs. Michael McLaughlin). Asst. to town clk. West Bridgewater, Mass., 1936-49, town clk., 1949—; clk. Bd. Registrars West Bridgewater, 1949, Bd. Health, 1966—. Mem. Tri-County (pres. 1962-63), N.E. (mem. com. 1968—), Mass. clks. assns., Legion Aux. (1st v.p. 1966), Bridgewater Vis. Nurse Assn. (mem. com. 1974—), Internat. Municipal Clks. Assn. Club: Mothers (West Bridgewater). Home: 178 S Main St West Bridgewater MA 02379 Office: Town Hall N Main St West Bridgewater MA 02379

BROWN, ANNE LEAH KRAMER (MRS. FRANK J. BROWN), realtor, developer; b. Latvia; d. Robert Louis and Rachael (Elsberg) Kramer; came to U.S., 1907, naturalized, 1940; grad. Manhattan Sch. Applied Arts, 1918; m. Frank J. Brown, Dec. 22, 1921; children—H. Harding, N. Bruce, C. Theodore. Partner Brown & Brown, realtors, indsl. developers, Elizabeth, N.J., 1930—. Chmn. comml. div. A.R.C., 1958-59, United Fund, 1960-62. Recipient citations Internat. Traders Club, Nat. Inst. Real Estate Brokers, Eastern Union County Bd. Realtors, also others. Mem. Nat. (state pres. woman's council 1949-50, chmn. library policy com. 1970; vice chmn. comml. indsl. div., mem. ednl. com., profl. standards and practices com.), N.J. (dir. 1961-63, 67-68, 71—, chmn. spl. gifts com.) assns. real estate bds., Internat. Real Estate Fedn., Nat. Inst. Real Estate Brokers (v.p. 1957-58, librarian 1962-63, ednl. com. 1967-68, gov. 1967-68, vice chmn. comml. investment div.), Eastern Union County Bd. Realtors (pres. 1961, chmn. human rights com. 1967), Soc. Indsl. Realtors, Nat. Council Jewish Women (chpt. pres. 1949-50). Club: Internat. Traders (pres. N.J. 1962). Author articles in field. Home: 231 Canterbury Rd Westfield NJ 07090 Office: 160 Elmora Av Elizabeth NJ 07202

BROWN, ANNE SEDDON KINSOLVING (MRS. JOHN NICHOLAS BROWN), author, hist. collector; b. Bklyn., Mar. 25, 1906; d. Arthur B. and Sally (Bruce) Kinsolving; grad. Bryn Mawr Sch., Balt., 1924; L.H.D., Brown U., 1962, fellow Co. Mil. Historians, 1956; m. John Nicholas Brown, Oct. 18, 1930; children—Nicholas, J. Carter, Angela (Mrs. Edwin G. Fischer). Feature writer, columnist, music critic Balt. News, 1924-30; contbr. mil. and hist. periodicals, 1936—; curator Anne S.K. Brown Mil. Collection, Brown U.; lectr. in mil. history U. Cal., 1965. Mem. adv. com. U.S. Army Mil. History Research Collection, 1970-73. Pres., Providence Community Concert Assn., 1931-36; pres. Newport Music Festival, 1970-73, bd. dirs., 1974—; mem. nat. adv. bd. Met. Opera, 1960-63. Bd. dirs. Robert E. Lee Meml. Found., 1933-39, bd. mgrs. Providence Lying-In Hosp., 1932-46, St. Mary's Home for Children, 1932-51; mem. adv. bd. Ft. Ticonderoga, N.Y., 1959-63. Recipient Chinard prize Institut Français de Washington-Soc. for French Hist. Studies, 1973; Merit award Am. Assn. for State and Local History, 1973; medal of honor D.A.R., 1973. Mem. Co. Mil. Historians (founder, v.p. 1953, treas 1951-63, pres. 1963-65, gov. 1951—), Nat. Soc. Colonial Dames, Société de la Sabretache, d'Honneur Musee de L'Armee (Paris), Army Hist. Research Soc. London, Gesellschaft für Heereskunde (Berlin), Phi Alpha Theta. Co-author: The Anatomy of Glory: the Story of Napoleon and his Guard, 1961; The American Campaigns of Rochambeau's Army: 1780-1783, 1972; collaborator Index to British Military Costume Prints, 1500-1914, 1972. Home: Harbour Ct Newport RI 02840 Office: 357 Benefit St Providence RI 02903

BROWN, ARLYSS ELAINE (MRS. VINCENT DON BROWN), lawyer; b. Ashland, Neb., Aug. 3, 1935; d. Earl Leonard and H. Pauline (Michel) Welch; B.A. cum laude in Govt. and Speech, U. Omaha, 1956; J.D., U. Neb., 1959; m. Vincent Don Brown, Mar. 19, 1965; 1 son, Jeffrey Michael. Admitted to Minn. bar, 1959, Neb. bar, 1959, practiced in Mpls., 1960, Omaha, 1961-63, Lincoln, 1963—; asso. firm Peterson, Engberg, Curry and Peterson, 1960; real estate atty. U.S. Army Corps Engrs., 1961-63; asst. city atty., Lincoln, 1963-67; atty. Woodmen Accident & Life Co., 1967—. Tchr. legal ins. claims course, Lincoln, 1967, life ins. courses Lincoln Soc. Life Ins. Co. Lawyers, 1973—. Cornhuskers Girl's State adviser, 1967-68; active P.T.A. Vice chmn. Mayor's Air Pollution Adv. Com., Lincoln, 1964-66; adviser Uniform Bldg. Com., Lincoln, 1966. Sec., Lancaster County Young Republicans, 1965; precinct chmn. Rep. Com., 1972-73. Mem. Am., Fed., Lincoln, Minn., Neb. bar assns., Neb. State Bar (mem. pub. relations com. 1971—), Order of Coif, Pi Kappa Delta (pres. 1955-56), Pi Gamma Mu. Mem. First Covenant Ch. Home: 5800 The Knolls Lincoln NE 68512 Office: 1526 K St Lincoln NE 68501

BROWN, BERTHA OLIVIA MALLARD (MRS. WILLIAM NOWEL BROWN), home economist; b. nr. Trenton, N.C., Aug. 16, 1924; d. William Grover and Hattie (Banks) Mallard; A.B., East Carolina U., 1945; m. William Nowell Brown, Apr. 2, 1949; 1 dau., Nell Roberta. Asst. home demonstration agt. Agrl. Extension Service, Wilson County, Wilson, N.C., 1945-47, home demonstration agt., Gates County, Gatesville, 1947-51; sec.-bookkeeper Miller Equipment Co., Gatesville, 1953-55; kindergarten tchr. While-Away Pvt. Sch., Newport News, Va., 1956-57; extension agt. home econs. Coop. Extension Service, City of Newport News, 1959—, dept. dir., 1972—. Co-chmn. fund drive Gates County unit Am. Cancer Soc., 1948-50; bd. dirs. Gatesville Pub. Library, 1947-50. Mem. Nat. (Distinguished Service award 1966, chmn. nat. registration com. 1971), Va. (mem. bd. 1966—, pres. 1970) extension home econs. assns., N.E. Dist. Extension Home Econs. (pres. 1966-68), Am. Legion Aux., Va. Extension Service Assn., Am., Va. home econs. assns., Epsilon Sigma Phi. Baptist. Home: 2 Jules Circle Newport News VA 23601 Office: 108 Main St Newport News VA 23601

BROWN, BETSY CLARK, librarian; b. Shelbyville, Ky., Aug. 25, 1924; d. Weston Victor and Emma Rowena (Jennings) Brown; student Eastern Ky. State Tchrs. Coll., 1942-44; B.A., U. Ky., 1946. Children's librarian Youngstown (O.) Pub. Library, 1946-48; librarian U.S. Armed Forces, Germany, 1948-51, Ft. Knox, Ky., 1951-53; supr. br. libraries Kenosha (Wis.) Pub. Library, 1954—. Mem. Am., Wis. library assns., Am. Assn. U. Women, Delta Kappa Gamma. Home: 2418 73d St Kenosha WI 53140 Office: 2419 63d St Kenosha WI 53140

BROWN, BETTY BEAUMONT (MRS. C. PRATT BROWN), artist; b. San Saba, Tex., Oct. 23, 1913; d. Edgar Chetwyn and Jimmie (Clark) Beaumont; student Miss. State Coll. for Women, 1932-33, U. Miss., 1933-34, Am. U., 1956-58; m. C. Pratt Brown, June 29, 1941. Exhibited at Seecelo Gallery, Burnsville, N.C., 1949-58, Dayton (O.) Mus., 1953, Corcoran Art Gallery, Washington, 1957, Smithsonian Instn., 1955-57, 59, 64, Balt. Mus. Art, 1964, Columbus (Ga.) Mus. Arts and Crafts, 1963, Watkins Art Gallery, Am. U., 1959; represented in permanent collections Columbus Mus. Arts and Crafts, Episcopal Center, N.Y.C., Air Force Acad., Colo., Am. U., Pentagon, Maryville Coll., Tenn., Ohio Wesleyan U., George Mason U. (Va.), St. Patricks Ch., Washington, SAC Hdqrs., Omaha, U.S. Capitol, also in pvt. and bus. collections. Mem. ladies bd. House of Mercy, Washington, 1955—; mem. Salvation Army Aux., Washington, 1954. Mem. Delta Delta Delta. Episcopalian. Home: 6800 Melody Lane Bethesda MD 20034

BROWN, BETTY RUTH, lawyer, govt. ofcl.; b. Racine, Wis., Feb. 15, 1926; d. Lawrence Angell and Blanche Eunice (Jansa) Brown; B.A., U. Wis., 1946, LL.B., 1948, postgrad. (Wis. Legal History Fund fellow), 1948-49. Admitted to Wis. bar, 1948, U.S. Supreme Ct. bar, 1972; practiced in Eau Claire, 1948-52; asso. firm Wilcox & Sullivan, 1948-52; policewoman Madison (Wis.) Police Dept., 1954-58; cons. juvenile law enforcement, juvenile ct., and legal depts. Wis. Dept. Pub. Welfare, Madison, 1958-63; asst. atty. gen. Wis. Dept. Justice, Madison, 1963—; solicitor gen. Wis. Dept. Justice, Madison, 1973—. Bd. dirs. Madison Welfare Council, 1964-67. Served with USAF, 1952-53. Mem. Wis., Dane County Bar assns., Order of Coif. Author: The Wisconsin District Attorney and the Criminal Case, 1971, cumulative supplement, 1973. Editor: Wisconsin Handbook for Juvenile Court Services, 1959; exec. editor: Wis. Law Review, 1947-48. Contbr. articles to profl. jours. Home: Route 1 Waunakee WI 53597 Office: 114 E State Capitol Madison WI 53702

BROWN, BRENDA LEE LAWSON (MRS. JOHN SCOTT BROWN), univ. adminstr.; b. Louisville, Sept. 3, 1938; d. LaMont Harris and Charlotte Jeannette (Hughes) Lawson; B.A., Howard U., 1960; postgrad. U. Md., 1960, D.C. Tchrs. Coll., 1960-63; m. John Scott Brown, June 17, 1961; children—Courtney Hughes, Leigh Melle. Speech therapist, tchr. D.C. pub. schs., 1960-64; program asst. U.S. Dept. Justice Community Relations Service, 1964-66, program devel. officer, 1970-71; dir. alumni affairs Howard U., Washington, 1967—. Vis. lectr. D.C. Tchrs. Coll., 1962-64. Bd. dirs. Regional Nat. Conf. Christians and Jews, 1969-73, Met. YWCA, 1970-71. Mem. Am. Coll. Pub. Relations Assn., Nat. Soc. Fund Raisers, Am. Alumni Council, Washington Urban League (dir. 1970-73). Alumni editor Howard U. mag., 1966-68. Home: 4225 17th St NW Washington DC 20011

BROWN, CHARLOTTE MARCUS (MRS. MORTON BROWN), artist; b. Bklyn., July 17, 1932; d. Irving and Zella (Nathan) Marcus; student Bklyn. Coll., 1950, Queen's Coll., 1952; B.F.A., Pratt Inst., 1956; m. Morton Brown, Dec. 30, 1951; children—Alison Carol, Jonathan. Exhibited one-man show Central Hall Gallery, Port Washington, N.Y., 1973; exhibited group shows Hechscher Mus., Huntington, N.Y., 1963, 68, Mus. Fine Arts Springfield, Mass., 1965, Suffolk Mus., Story Brook, N.Y., 1968, 72, Hofstra Coll., 1963-65, Nassau Community Coll., Garden City, N.Y., 1967, 73, Larry Aldrich Mus., Ridgefield, Conn., 1974, others; represented in permanent collections C.W. Post Fine Arts Mus., Greenvale, N.Y., also corp., pvt. collections; tchr. Jericho (N.Y.) Elementary Sch., 1961-62; art dir. Woodbury (N.Y.) Country Club Assn., 1962-70, Art in Am. Sch., Great Neck, N.Y., 1964-68, North Shore Community Art Center, Great Neck, N.Y., 1969-70, Cultural and Performing Arts Center, Syosset, N.Y., 1970—; lectr. Nassau County Office of Cultural Devel., 1972—, tchr. class for gifted children, 1973—; lectr. Nassau County art tchrs., 1972-73. Recipient awards Hofstra U., Garden City, 1965; Hechscher Mus., Huntington, 1969; Silvermine Guild Artists, New Canaan, Conn., 1969, 70. Mem. Women in Arts, Profl. Artist Guild (charter mem., v.p. 1973), Nat. Assn. Women Artists (Molly Morpeth Carady award 1973, ad hoc com. 1973-74). Address: 11 Hunting Hill Rd Woodbury NY 11797

BROWN, CLARE WADE (MRS. JOE H. BROWN), home economist; b. Sellersburg, Ind., Nov. 3, 1920; d. Ernest E. and Lorene M. (Pass) Wade; B.S., Mich. State U., 1942, M.A., 1954; postgrad. (Ford Found. fellow), Cranbrook Acad. Art, 1954-55; m. Joe H. Brown, Nov. 19, 1944; children—Marcella (Mrs. Curtis Remington), Thomas Wade. Tchr., Ionia (Mich.) High Sch., 1942-43, Gila Bend (Ariz.) High Sch., 1944-46, East Jordan (Mich.) High Sch., 1948-54; asst. dietitian Sparrow Hosp., Lansing, Mich., 1943-44; instr. Central Mich. U., Mt. Pleasant, 1955-56; home economist Coop. Extension Service, Mich. State U., Mt. Pleasant, 1956—. Recipient Distinguished Service award Mich. Coop. Extension, 1967, Nat. Coop. Estension, 1970. Mem. Nat. (mem. exhibits com. 1971-72), Mich. (pres. 1973-74) assns. extension home economists, Mich. Council Extension Assn. (mem. exec. bd.), Nat., Mich. home econs. assns., Mich. Council Family Relations, Clare Bus. and Profl. Womens Club (corr. sec. 1969-71). Mem. Order Eastern Star. Home: 108 W 5th St Clare MI 48617 Office: Courthouse Annex Mount Pleasant MI 48858

BROWN, DIANA LYNN, advt. agy. exec.; b. Grosse Point, Mich., Sept. 13, 1944; d. Samuel L. and Billie (Moss) Brown; student Columbia State Community Coll., 1971. Office sec. LIN Broadcasting Corp., Nashville, 1964-69; coordinator Miss Teenage Am. Pageant, Nashville, 1967-69; with Trans World Airlines, Chgo., 1970; asso. media dir. Noble-Dury Advt., Nashville, 1971-73; media dir. Buntin Advt., Inc., Nashville, 1973—. Mem. Am. Women in Radio and TV, Nashville Advt. Fedn. Home: Apt 79 3000 Hillsboro Rd Nashville TN 37215 Office: 900 Division St Nashville TN 37203

BROWN, DIANE PATRICIA (MRS. LAFAYETTE BROWN JR.), coll. adminstr.; b. Newark, Aug. 11, 1944; d. Eugene Jasper and Mary Rochelle (Davis) Robinson; A.B., Ind. U., 1966; M.A., U. Mass., 1968; postgrad. (Mellon fellow) Mass. Inst. Tech., 1971-72; m. Lafayette Brown Jr., July 29, 1972. Systems engr. IBM, Cambridge, Mass., 1968-69; research cons. Circle Assos., Roxbury, Mass., 1969-70; information coordinator Model Cities, Newark, 1970-72; spl. asst. to provost for student services Mass. State Coll. System, Boston, 1972—. Mem. Com. to Save "Say Brother", Roxbury, 1969-70; del. to Nat. Black Polit. Conv., Gary, Ind., 1972. Mem. Am. Sociol. Assn., Am. Soc. Planning Ofcls., Nat. Assn. Student Personnel Adminstrs., Black Women's Assn. for Civic and Cultural Activities. Author: Consider College, 1973. Home: 4 Donna Rd Peabody MA 01960 Office: 53 State St Boston MA 02109

BROWN, DOROTHEA NELL WILLIAMS (MRS. IRA H. BROWN), ednl. adminstr.; b. Kansas City, Kan., Dec. 23, 1918; d. Van Wilford and Ethel Lee (Connor) Williams, Sr.; student Prairie View Coll., 1936-37; B.S., Huston-Tillotson Coll., 1939; postgrad. Fenn Coll., 1952-54; M.A., John Carroll U., 1959; postgrad. Ohio State U., 1960, Western Res. U., 1967; m. Ira H. Brown, Aug. 28; 1 dau., Michele. Tchr., Trinity (Tex.) Ind. Schs., 1939-41, Austin (Tex.) Pub. Schs., 1941-43; asst. mgr. Youngstown Met. Housing Authority, 1947-51; with Cleve. Pub. Schs., 1951-71, asst. prin. Harry E. Davis Jr. High Sch., 1962-64, Charles W. Eliot Jr. High Sch., 1964-71; coordinator tchr.-leader program Martha Holden Jennings Found., Pace Assn., Cleve., 1969—. Coll. counselor Glenville High Sch., 1969-71; in-service tchr. human relations Cleve. Bd. Edn., 1966-70; resource person to Ind. Schs. Talent Search Program, Boston, 1964-70; edn. cons. Cleve. Commn. on Higher Edn., 1971-72; coordinator extended learning program Ohio U., Athens, 1972-73; program officer KEDS Gen. Assistance Center, Coll. Edn., Kent (O.) State U., 1973—. Formerly active Girl Scouts U.S.A. Trustee Harvard Community Services Center, Cleve., Goodrich Social Settlement, Cleve. Internat. Program. Mem. Nat., Ohio, Cleveland edn. assns., Nat. Ohio assns. women deans and counselors, Am. Personnel and Guidance Assn., Am. Assn. Higher Edn., Ohio Sch. Counselors Assn., Northeastern Assn. Women Deans Adminstrs. and Counselors, Human Relations Council (sec. 1966-71, trustee), Women's Civic League Cleve., Jack and Jill Inc., N.A.A.C.P., Urban League, United Negro Coll. Fund, Alpha Kappa Alpha (chpt. pres. 1957-60). Episcopalian. Clubs: Links; Women's City (Cleve.). Contbg. editor New Lady Mag., Hayward, Cal., 1967—. Home: 3061 Albion Rd Cleveland OH 44120 Office: 304 Wright Hall Coll of Edn Kent State U Kent OH 44240

BROWN, DOROTHY DODD (MRS. WILLIAM KENNETH BROWN), govt. ofcl.; b. Brush, Colo., Feb. 2, 1913; d. William Wilson and Ammie Flora (Royse) Dodd; B.S., Chadron State Coll., 1963, postgrad., 1966-72; m. William Kenneth Brown, Sept. 8, 1933; children—Jeanne Ann (Mrs. Joe Neal Nay), Lloyd Kenneth. Office mgr. W. Neb. Gen. Hosp., Scottsbluff, 1954-57; asst. dir. Scottsbluff C. of C., 1957-59; broadcaster, producer KOLT Radio, Scottsbluff, 1959-69; dir. pub. relations Hiram Scott Coll., Scottsbluff, 1969-72; sch. cons. pub. relations, Scottsbluff, 1970; telecaster KSTF-TV, Scottsbluff, 1972; resource coordinator, children family resource program Dept. Health, Edn. and Welfare, Gering, Neb., 1973—. Membership chmn. P.T.A., Haig, Neb., 1954-55; mem. Gov.'s Commn. on Status of Women, 1965-69, Panhandle Regional Library Commn., 1973—; mem. ad hoc com. Panhandle Hosp. Commn., 1973—. Recipient State 4-H Alumni award, 1965; Neb. Centennial Good Neighbor award, 1967. Mem. Am. Assn. U. Women (localist v.p. 1964-65), Am. Women in Radio and TV (treas. 1963-66), Wesleyan Service Guild (regional chmn. 1969-70), Women's Council C. of C. Methodist. Mem. Order Eastern Star. Clubs: Women's (pres. 1935-36) (Mitchell, Neb.); Soroptimist (dir. Scottsbluff 1973). Home: 1 Rural Route Mitchell NE 69357 Office: 1840 7th St Gering NE 69341

BROWN, DOROTHY LAVINIA, physician; b. Phila., Jan. 7, 1919; d. Frank Brown and Emma Brown Bates; foster parents Samuel Wesley and Lola Redmon; B.A., Bennett Coll., Greensboro, N.C., 1941; M.D., Meharry Med. Coll., Nashville, 1948. 1 adopted dau., Lola Denise. Intern Harlem Hosp., N.Y.C., 1948-49; surg. residency Hubbard Hosp., Nashville, 1949-54; clin. prof. surgery Meharry Med. Coll.; chief surgery Riverside Hosp.; attending surgeon Hubbard, Met.-Gen., Riverside hosps. Mem. So. Regional Edn. Bd., 1967—, Tenn. Youth Guidance Commn., Nashville Met. Health Bd., Tenn. Consumer Protection Com. Former mem. Tenn. Ho. Reps. Trustee Bennett Coll. Recipient Outstanding Achievement award Delta Sigma Theta, 1963, Negro Bus. and Profl. Women's Club, 1967; named Citizen of Year, WVOL, 1959, Davidson County Bus. and Profl. Women's Club, 1965, Frontiers Internat., 1967; recipient Centennial Medallion, Hampton Inst., 1968, Woman Doer citation Democratic Nat. Com., 1967; other honors; Dorothy L. Brown Women's Bldg. at Meharry Med. Coll. named in her honor, 1969. Fellow A.C.S.; mem. A.M.A., Am. Assn. U. Women, Nat. Council Negro Women (hon.), Nashville Acad. Medicine, R. F. Boyd Med. Soc., Nat. Med. Assn., Assn. Am. Med. Colls., Negro Bus. and Profl. Women's Clubs, Internat. Platform Assn., N.A.A.C.P. (life), Delta Sigma Theta, Kappa Delta Pi (hon.). Methodist. Home: 3109 Centennial Blvd Nashville TN 37209

BROWN, ELISE ANN BRANDENBURGER (MRS. ARTHUR BRICKMAN BROWN), pharmacologist; b. Jacksonville, Fla., Dec. 5, 1928; d. Oscar Louis and Inee Marie (Peterson) Brandenburger; B.S. in Chemistry, George Washington U., 1949, M.S. in Biochemistry, 1950, Ph.D. in Pharmacology (Nat. Cancer Inst. fellow), 1956; m. Arthur Brickman Brown, June 14, 1952; children—Barron Brandenburger, Terrence Leon Brickman, Roderick Scott Kjelmyr. Post doctoral fellow Johns Hopkins U., Balt., 1957-59; research pharmacologist Nat. Heart and Lung Inst., NIH, Bethesda, Md., 1962—. Lt. Civil Air Patrol, 1971—, med. officer, 1968—. Mem. Am. Soc. Pharmacology and Exptl. Therapeutics, Internat. Soc. for Biochem. Pharmacology, Am. Chem. Soc., Soc. Gen. Physiologists, N.Y. Acad. Scis., D.A.R. (regent local chpt. 1971-73), Sigma Xi, Sigma Delta Epsilon, Sigma Kappa. Home: 6811 Nesbitt Place McLean VA 22101 Office: Bldg 10 Room 5N325 National Institute of Health Bethesda MD 20014

BROWN, ELIZABETH HENSHAW GASPAR (MRS. DOUGLAS STEWART BROWN), lawyer; b. Chgo., Nov. 24, 1913; d. Vernon Moore and Marguerite Elizabeth (Henshaw) Gaspar; A.B., Rockford Coll., 1935; J.D., U. Wis., 1952; m. Douglas Stewart Brown, Dec. 11, 1937 (dec. Nov. 1956); 1 dau., Louise (Mrs. Ross N. Pearson, Jr.). Admitted to Wis. bar, 1952, Mich. bar, 1957; instr. in econs. Pa. State Coll., University Park, 1946-50; research asst. in law U. Mich., Ann Arbor, 1951-57, research asso., 1957—. Sec. Ann Arbor Bldg. Authority, 1965—, asst. treas., 1970—. Bd. dirs. Ann Arbor Hills Homes Assn., 1963—, Old Ladies Home Assn., 1973—. Mem. Phi Beta Kappa. Republican. Episcopalian. Author: Digest of Procedural States and Court Rules, 1954; Legal Education at Michigan 1859-1959; British Statutes in American Law 1776-1836, 1964. Contbr. articles to profl. jours. Office: Legal Research Bldg Michigan Law School Ann Arbor MI 48104

BROWN, ELIZABETH LOUISE, librarian, b. Toledo, May 18, 1918; d. James Hall and Bertha (Peck) Brown; B.A., U. Toledo, 1941; B.L.S., Western Res. U., 1942; M.A., U. Toledo, 1952. Young poeple's asst. Toledo Pub. Library, 1942-48; br. librarian Lucas County Library, 1948-60; high sch. librarian overseas schs. Dept. Def., Japan, 1960-62, coordinator Chofu (Japan) sch. libraries, head mediatrician high sch. library, 1963-74, adminstrv. librarian, security services, Japan, 1974—; high sch. librarian Scott High Sch., Toledo, 1962-63. Lectr. library courses U. Md.; instr. Ikebana; adult edn. instr. speed reading, research writing. Office Edn. scholar U. Hawaii, 1968. Mem. Ikebana Internat., Internat. House of Japan, Delta Kappa Gamma. Republican. Episcopalian. Home: care Northup 2838 Emmick Dr Toledo OH 43606 Office: 6920th Air Base Group PSC 4268 APO San Francisco CA 96519

BROWN, ELIZABETH MYERS (MRS. KENT LOUIS BROWN), publishing co. exec.; b. Bklyn., Dec. 31, 1915; d. Garry Cleveland and Caroline (Clark) Myers; B.S., Cornell U., 1937; M.A., Case Western Res. U., 1960; m. Kent Louis Brown, June 26, 1940; children—Karen Elizabeth (Mrs. Lyman Anders Johnson), Kent Louis, David Stuart, Garry Myers. Tchr., Walden, N.Y., 1937-38, Auburn, N.Y., 1938-39, Cleveland Heights, O., 1939-40; asst. Erie County (N.Y.) home demonstration agt. govt. extension service Cornell U., Ithaca, N.Y., 1940-42; editorial asst. Highlights for Children, Columbus, O., 1962-64, asst. editor, 1964-66, asso. editor, 1966—, asst. sec., 1968—, dir., 1960—; dir. Zaner-Bloser Co., 1972—. Mem. Metro Writers Workshop, 1970—; trustee New Day Press, 1972— (both Cleve.). Bd. dirs. Fedn. Cornell Women's Clubs, 1955-57, pres. Cornell Women's Club Cleve., 1953-55; bd. dirs. Nutrition Assn. Greater Cleve., 1964-68. Mem. Women's Assn. of Univ. Center for Continuing Edn. (treas. 1959-61, pres. 1961-63), Women's Aux. Acad. Med. of Cleve. (pres. 1969-70), Woman's Aux. Ohio Med. Assn. (chmn. mems.-at-large com. 1970-71, mem. state bd.). Home: 2861 Kersdale Rd Cleveland OH 44124 Office: 803 Church St Honesdale PA 18431

BROWN, ELSA CLARA LUSEBRINK (MRS. HERBERT A. BROWN), ednl. adminstr.; b. Bridgeport, Conn., Sept. 21, 1920; d. Herman Joseph and Elsa Anna (Wendler) Lusebrink; A.S., Jr. Coll. Conn., 1939; diploma Bridgeport Hosp. Sch. Nursing, 1942; B.S. in Nursing Edn., Tchrs. Coll., Columbia, 1945, M.S., 1951; postgrad. U. Toledo, 1972—; m. Herbert A. Brown, Oct. 11, 1958, 1 dau., Martha Ann. Asso. exec. dir. Bridgeport (Conn.) Hosp. Sch. Nursing, 1942-53; dir. Sch. Nursing and Nursing Services, Danbury (Conn.) Hosp., 1953-57, asst. adminstr., 1957-61; asso. prof. nursing U. Bridgeport, 1961-65, prof. nursing, 1966--70; dean Jr. Coll. Conn., Bridgeport, 1969-70; dean Med. Coll. Ohio, Toledo, 1970—. Cons. Asso. nursing programs, 1942-70. Recipient Alumni award U. Bridgeport, 1954; Lusebrink scholar U. Bridgeport, 1969. Mem. Ohio Nurse Assn. (chmn. com. 1972—), Am. Assn. Community and Jr. Colls., Am. Assn. Allied Health Profs., Am. Nurses Assn., Ohio League Nurses, Nat. League Nursing (liaison com.), N.E.A., Internat. Congress Nurses. Home: 2703 Densmore Dr Toledo OH 43606 Office: Med Coll O PO Box 6190 Toledo OH 43614

BROWN, ELSIE BLANCHE RAMBO (MRS. CHARLES W. BROWN), educator; b. Cleve., Sept. 15, 1912; d. Albert W. and Elsie (Datzel) Rambo; B.S., Western Res. U., 1934, M.A., 1955; m. Charles W. Brown, Nov. 25, 1937; 1 dau., Anne (Mrs. Robert A. Chapman). Tchr., Wade Park Elementary Sch., 1946-53; asst. prin. Gracemount Elementary Sch., 1953-55; prin. Alfred A. Benesch Elementary Sch., 1955-66, William Rainey Harper and Mark Twain Elementary Schs., 1966— (all Cleve.). Prin. Willard Reading Improvement Summer Sch., 1957-60; instr. Cleve. In-Service Reading Courses for Tchrs., 1963-65. Recipient Am. Educator Nat. award Freedoms Found. at Valley Forge, 1966. Mem. Council of Human Relations, N.E.A., Ohio Elementary Sch. Prins., Dept. Elementary Sch Prins., Council Tchrs. English, Cecil Sharp English Folk Dance Soc. (pres. 1940-46), Western Res. Hist. Soc., Delta Kappa Gamma (chpt. v.p. 1956-58). Home: 6965 Pearl Rd Middleburg Heights OH 44130 Office: 6000 Memphis Av Cleveland OH 44144

BROWN, ERLINE GORE, home economist; b. Embry, Miss., Jan. 20, 1919; d. Solon Streeter and Elizabeth (McGahey) Gore; B.S. in Home Econs., Miss. State Coll. for Women, 1939; m. S.N. Brown, Jr., June 29, 1939; children—Lynn (Mrs. Joseph F. Wampler), Steven Neely. Tchr. home econs. Belzoni (Miss.) High Sch., 1944-64, Miss. Delta Jr. Coll., Moorhead, 1964-66; with Miss. Dept. Pub. Welfare, Belzoni, 1966-68; home economist Miss. Coop. Extension, 1968-71; coordinator expanded food nutrition edn. program Miss. State U., 1971—. Mem. Am., Miss. home econs. assns., Delta Kappa Gamma. Home: 2706 Maple St Starkville MS 39759 Office: Miss State Univ State College MS 39762

BROWN, GLADYS MUNGEN, writer; b. Alexandria, Va., Feb. 21, 1926; d. Howard Loyola and Elizabeth Mae (Mungen) Youngs; diploma Alexandria Music Inst., 1944, Am. Acad. Dramatic Art, 1949, Sorbonne, 1951; ed. music and pipe organ, composition and poetry, Columbia, 1949-50; pupil Malvina Hoffman, Harry Hazzard; m. Charles Lefferts Brown, June 28, 1946. Asst. soc. editor Bklyn. Daily Eagle, 1952; screen writer Laurel Films, Inc., 1952; feature writer King Features, 1953; rewrite A.P., 1954; drama critic Am. Rev. mag., 1972—; dir. plays and musicals South St. Seaport, 1974—. Vice pres. So. Molasses Co., Scripts Inc. Pres. Little Gardens Club, 1947; publicity dir. Outdoor Art Show, 1947; mem. N.Y.C. Tree Planting Commn., 1947. Served with USNR. Poetry scholar U. Madrid, 1973. Mem. Actors Equity Assn., A.S.C.A.P., Poetry Soc. Am., N.Y. Poetry Forum (award 1974), Shelley Soc. N.Y., Composers, Authors and Artists Am. (award 1973). Republican. Episcopalian. Author: Gilfillan Method, It's Your Face, 1973; also poems in anthologies; author, producer musical play Homespun Hero, 1974. Composer songs, including Earth Day Anthem, 1974. Address: 60 Gramercy Park N #6K New York City NY 10010

BROWN, GOLDIE FERN ROUSE (MRS. FREDERICK R. BROWN), civic worker; b. Ayrshire, Ia., Mar. 1, 1927; d. John Fremont and Ada Beatrice (Eaton) Rouse; B.S. in Home Econs., Ia. State U., 1948; postgrad. (Danforth fellow) U. N.M., 1948-49, Eastern N.M. U., 1961; m. C. Claberon Buckner, July 16, 1949 (dec.); children—C. Claberon, Ronald Ray, William Wayne; m. 2d, Frederick R. Brown. Home service adviser Southwestern Pub. Service Co., Roswell, N.M., also Amarillo, Tex., 1950; asst. in husband's ins. firm, Roswell, 1951-67; nutrition cons. fed. govt., 1967—; area home economist S.E. N.M. program HELP, Office Econ. Opportunity, 1967-68. Organizer, pres. Chaves County Assn. for Retarded Children, 1955; an organizer, pres. N.M. Assn. for Retarded Children, 1957, bd. dirs., 1957-60; publicity chmn. Nat. Assn. for Retarded Children, 1958-61, conv. del., 1955; del. White House Conf. on Children and Youth, 1960, mem. Permanent N.M. Com. on Children and Youth, 1960-66; sec. bd. dirs. N.M. Mental Retardation Project, 1957-59; bd. dirs. family life com. N.M. conf., Methodist Ch., 1960-64. Recipient Jane Addams Centennial award for outstanding community service, 1960; internat. hon. mention for community service Sertoma Internat., 1964; Alumni Merit award Ia. State U., 1964; named Roswell Citizen of Year, Bd. of Realtors, 1964. Mem. P.E.O. (chpt. pres. 1964, nat. del. 1969), United Ch. Women, Internat. Fedn. U. Women, Am. Assn. U. Women (1st v.p. 1966-67), Am. Home Econs. Assn. (N.M. del. to nat. conv. 1971), Chaves County Hist. Soc. (sec. 1964, pres. 1966-67, 72-73), Mortar Bd. (past pres.), N.M. Folklore Soc. (1st v.p. 1966-67), Phi Upsilon Omicron, Omicron Nu. Methodist (lay speaker). Author: Tell the Happy of It, 1964; The Alexander Rouse Family, 1964; also articles in various mags. Editor: Family Faith, quar. newsletter Methodist Ch., 1960-64. Address: 3949 E Easter Dr Littleton CO 80122

BROWN, HELEN GURLEY, author, editor; b. Green Forest, Ark., Feb. 18, 1922; d. Ira M. and Cleo (Sisco) Gurley; student Tex. State Coll. for Women, 1939-41, Woodbury Coll., 1942; m. David Brown, Sept. 25, 1959. Exec. sec. Music Corp. Am., 1942-45, William Morris Agy., 1945-47; copywriter Foote, Cone & Belding, advt. agy., Los Angeles, 1948-58; advt. writer, account exec. Kenyon & Eckhardt, advt. agy., Hollywood, Cal., 1958-62; editor-in-chief Cosmopolitan mag., 1965—, editorial dir. Brit. Cosmopolitan mag., 1972—, also 13 other overseas edits.; supervising editor EYE mag., 1967-68. Recipient Francis Holmes Achievement award for outstanding work in advt., 1956-59, Distinguished Achievement award U. So. Cal. Sch. Journalism, 1971, ann. awards Am. Newspaperwomens Assn., 1972, Am. Soc. Journalism Sch. Adminstrs., 1972. Mem. Authors League Am., A.F.T.R.A., Eta Upsilon Gamma. Author: Sex and the Single Girl, 1962; Sex and the Office, 1965; The Outrageous Opinions of Helen Gurley Brown, 1967; Helen Gurley Brown's Single Girl Cookbook, 1969; Sex and the New Single Girl, 1970. Home: 605 Park Av New York City NY 10021 Office: Hearst Corp 224 W 57th St New York City NY 10019

BROWN, HELEN MARGARET, librarian; b. Troy, N.Y., July 17, 1912; d. Edwin Nelson and Margaret Jane (Walker) Brown; A.B., Vassar Coll., 1933; B.S., Columbia, M.S., 1942. Mem. library staff Vassar Coll., 1934-44; librarian MacMurray Coll., Jacksonville, Ill., 1944-47, Skidmore Coll., Saratoga Springs, N.Y., 1947-53, Wellesley (Mass.) Coll., 1953—. Mem. A.L.A. (mem. council 1960, 66-68), Assn. Coll. and Research Libraries (pres. 1965-66), Am. Assn. U. Profs., Am. Assn. U. Women, League of Women Voters. Club: Vassar (Boston). Address: Fiske House Wellesley Coll Wellesley MA 02181

BROWN, MRS. JAMES ROBERT (JOSEPHINE M. BROWN), educator, lawyer; b. N.Y.C.; d. Antonio and Josephine C. (Walsh) Pisani; B.A. (Regents scholar), St. Joseph's Coll. for Women, N.Y.C., 1934; LL.B., Fordham U., 1936, Ph.D., 1941; M.A., Columbia, 1937, postgrad., 1949-50; postgrad. Laval U., P.Q., Can., Mexico City Coll.; m. James Robert Brown, Aug. 20, 1955; 1 son, John Francis. Admitted to N.Y. bar, 1936, Wis. bar, 1958, Conn. bar, 1970; pvt. practice, N.Y.C., 1936-56; instr., then asst. prof. polit. sci. Queens Coll., Flushing, 1942-55; vis. lectr. Marymount Coll., 1941-42, Sarah Lawrence Coll., 1944, Fordham U., 1948, Albertus Magnus Coll., 1955; vis. prof. St. Joseph Coll., 1960-63, Central Conn. Coll., 1963-66; asso. prof. history and polit. sci. Mount Mary Coll., 1958-60; non-governmental observer UN for women lawyer assns., 1953-57; past chmn. parties com. Citizen's Union N.Y.C.; pres. Greater Hartford chpt. Citizens for Educational Freedom, 1965; legislative legal adviser Legislative Commrs. Office, Hartford, Conn., 1967—. Mem. Hartford Archdiocesan Sch. Bd., 1965-69. Mem. Dem. State Com., N.Y., 1946-50, founder youth div., 1946, chmn. 1946-50. Mem. Am. Polit. Sci. Assn. (past dir. N.Y.), Am. Bar Assn., Nat. Assn. Women Lawyers (chmn. law year com. 1964-65, v.p. 1965-66), Council Cath. Women (past internat. relations chmn. Hartford Archdiocesan council), Conn., Hartford County bar assns., U. Hartford Women's League (pres. 1972-73), Orgn. for Study in France and Am. (v.p.), Phi Delta Delta (past chmn. UN com.). Editor Women Lawyers' Jour., 1954-55, 61-63; asst. editor Tax Rev. Series (Harvard), 1957; asst. book rev. editor Am. mag., 1947. Address: Legislative Commrs Office State Capitol Hartford CT 06115

BROWN, JANE FRANCES, ct. reporter, civic worker; b. Wichita Falls, Tex., Aug. 25, 1924; d. Charles E. and Thresa (Trinkley) Brown; student Hardin Jr. Coll., 1941-43, Hunter Coll., 1944, Okla. A. and M. Coll., 1945; B.A., U. Colo., 1947. With claims dept. Employers Casualty Co., 1943-44; ct. reporter, owner, operator reporting services, Wichita Falls, Tex., 1950—. Bd. dirs. Confrat. Christian Doctrine, 1959-73, dir.-coordinator, 1973—; tchr. retarded children, 1961-64, tchr. deaf children, 1962-63, nat. sec. dir. Council Retarded Children, 1962-63; founder, exec. sec. Wichita Falls Eye Bank, 1960-65. Sec., Wichita County Democratic Com., 1960. Bd. dirs. Cath. Charities. Served with WAVES, 1944-46. Recipient Outstanding service award Kiwanis, 1963, Humanitarian award A.R.C., 1964. Mem. Tex. Shorthand Reporters Assn. (dir. 1957-59), Wichita Falls Legal Sec. Assn. (dir. 1959-61), Okla. Beekeepers Assn., Cath. War Vets. (dir. 1947-48), Amvets (state sec. 1949-52), St. Vincent de Paul Soc. (sec. 1968—), Tex. Beekeepers Assn. Roman Catholic. Club: Soroptimist (dir. 1958-60, 63-65, pres. 1962-63, regional steward 1963-64). Home and office: 612 Van Buren St Wichita Falls TX 76301

BROWN, JANET C., lawyer; b. Balt., Mar. 16, 1927; B.A., Wellesley Coll., 1949; LL.B., Yale, 1952. Admitted to N.Y. State bar, 1953, U.S. Supreme Ct. bar, 1965; mem. firm Chadbourne, Parke, Whiteside & Wolff, N.Y.C. Mem. Am., N.Y. State bar assns., N.Y. County Lawyers Assn., Phi Beta Kappa, Sigma Xi. Office: Chadbourne Parke Whiteside & Wolff 30 Rockefeller Plaza New York City NY 10020

BROWN, JANET LOUISE, psychologist; b. Phila., July 21, 1930; d. Aubrey Lee and Mabel (Bock) Brown; B.A., Mt. Holyoke Coll., 1950; M.A., Yale, 1951, Ph.D., 1955. Research asst. Yale Child Study Center, 1954-57; psychologist Putnam Children's Center, Boston, 1957-70, chief psychologist, 1970—, dir. research, 1970—. Asst. prof. psychiatry Boston U. Med. Sch., 1967—. Fellow Am. Orthopsychiat. Assn.; mem. Soc. for Research in Child Devel., Mass. Psychol. Assn. Contbr. articles on etiology and prognosis in autistic children and normal children to profl. jours. Home: 220 Wolcott Rd Brookline MA 02167 Office: 244 Townsend St Boston MA 02121

BROWN, JEAN ELAINE, assn. recreation adminstr.; b. Pitts., Feb. 13, 1927; d. Willard Edwin and Grace Elizabeth (King) Brown; B.A., Geneva Coll., 1949; M. Letters, U. Pitts., 1952. Social worker State of Pa., Rochester, 1949-50; tchr. speech, theatre Geneva Coll., Beaver Falls, Pa., 1953-56; tchr. theatre and communications Allegheny

Coll., Meadville, Pa., 1956-59; camp adminstr. Lake Erie Girl Scout Council, Cleve., 1959-66; program services dir. Lone Tree Area Girl Scout Council, Oak Park, Ill., 1966—. Tchr. Camp Dirs. Tng. for Nat. Girl Scouts of U.S., 1973. Bd. dirs. River Forest Civic Theatre. Mem. Am. Camping Assn. Home: 408 Scoville 3S Oak Park IL 60302 Office: 1048 Pleasant St Oak Park IL 60302

BROWN, JOAN HELEN FRANKS (MRS. JOHN T. BROWN), editor; b. New Bremen, O., Oct. 24, 1932; d. John Paul and Evelyn L. (Arkenberg) Franks; student Ashland Coll., 1964; m. John T. Brown, Dec. 2, 1950; children—James, John, Jeffrey. Religion editor, feature writer Mansfield (O.) News Jour., 1969—. Bd. dirs. YWCA, 1964, Community Players, 1963, Inter-Service Club Council, 1963, United Arts Council, 1964, Mansfield Symphony. Recipient Drama award Community Players, 1961, award A.P., 1972. Mem. Ohio Newspaper Women's Assn., Richland County Bar Aux. (pres. 1963), Fine Arts Guild, Little Theatre, Community Players. Republican. Conglist. (deaconess 1964). Clubs: Colony (pres. 1962), Prometheus Study, Los Leidos (Mansfield); Mensa (Cleve.). Home: 1200 Millsboro Rd Mansfield OH 44906 Office: 70 W 4th St Mansfield OH 44901

BROWN, JOAN VIVIEN BEATTY, artist; b. San Francisco, Feb. 13, 1938; d. John W. and Vivien (Beck) Beatty; B.F.A., San Francisco Art Inst., also M.F.A., 1960; m. divorced; 1 son, Noel Neri. Exhibited in shows at Staempfl Gallery, N.Y.C., 1960, 61, 62, 64, 65, Stuart Gallery, Los Angeles, 1961, 62, 64, Hansen Gallery, San Francisco, 1967; represented in permanent collections at Mus. Modern Art, N.Y.C., Albright Knox Gallery, Buffalo; tchr. painting, drawing. Mem. San Francisco Zool. Soc., YWCA. Home: 37 Saturn St San Francisco CA 94114 Office: 800 Chestnut St San Francisco CA 94133

BROWN, JUANITA CARSON, fine arts appraiser; b. Holdenville, Okla., Jan. 17, 1922; d. Robert Lee and Nora Maybell (Hooter) Carson; grad. high sch.; 1 dau. by previous marriage, Lisa Lee. Sec.-bookkeeper Ligon Furniture Co., Wewoka, Okla., exec. sec. Ligon Oil Co., 1940-46; ind. lease broker H.M. Barnes Co., Casper, Wyo., 1949-53, Delhi Oil Co., Casper, 1949-52; office mgr. Heldenbrand Auctioneering Co., Oklahoma City, 1958-70; ind. fee appraiser and estate liquidator Don Juan Antiques, Oklahoma City, 1963—. Mem. Oklahoma City Better Bus. Bur. Mem. Am. Soc. Appraisers (pres. Oklahoma City chpt. 1972-73), Appraisers Assn. Am., Valuers Consortium, Fashion Group, Oklahoma City C. of C., Nat. Assn. Dealers Antiques, Doberman Pinscher Club Am., Doberman Pinscher Club Indian Nation, Am. Arbitration Assn. (mem. panel arbitrators 1973). Home: 4401 NE 36th St Oklahoma City OK 73111 Office: Route 4 Box 532 Oklahoma City OK 73111

BROWN, JUDITH ELLEN WILLIAMS (MRS. ROBERT WINFIELD BROWN), univ. adminstr.; b. N.Y.C., Sept. 5, 1920; d. David and Irene (Gottlieb) Williams; B.A. summa cum laude (N.Y. State Regents scholar 1937-41), Syracuse U., 1941; m. Robert Winfield Brown, June 2, 1941; children—Philip Carlton, Jonatha Anne, David Winfield. Jr. account exec. Ed Wolff & Assos., Rochester, N.Y., 1943-46; free-lance writer, 1946-58; with U. Rochester, 1958—, asst. dir. pub. relations, 1960-68, asso. dir. pub. relations, 1968-71, dir. pub. information, 1969-71, dir. pub. relations, 1971—. Bd. dirs. Family Service Rochester, 1963-69; trustee Harley Sch. Rochester. Mem. Women in Communications, Phi Beta Kappa (prize Syracuse U. 1941). Club: Faculty (Rochester, N.Y.). Author: (with Donald Grossfield) I Wish I'd Known That Before I Went to College, 1966. Editor Rochester Rev., 1963-72. Contbr. articles to profl. jours. and mags. Home: 44 Parker Dr Pittsford NY 14534 Office: U Rochester Rochester NY 14627

BROWN, KATHLEEN OLDER (MRS. CARL M. BROWN), anthropologist; b. Charleston, W. Va., Oct. 21, 1922; d. Otto Brown and Dora Bernice (Lewis) Older; B.S. in Edn. summa cum laude, Morris Harvey Coll., 1949; M.A. in Counseling and Guidance, Marshall U., 1952; Ph.D. in Ednl. Anthropology, Am. U., 1970; m. Carl M. Brown, Feb. 22, 1960. Tchr. Kanawha County pub. schs., Charleston, 1949-62; tchr. enrichment program specializing in African Anthropology Fairfax County Pub. Schs., Fairfax, Va., 1962—. Cons. on Africa, Fairfax County, 1965—; lectr. on Africa to community and church groups and service clubs, 1965—. Judge, Optimist Club Oratorial Contest, Fairfax County, 1972. Fellow Am. Anthrop. Assn., A.A.A.S.; mem. African Studies Assn., Applied Anthropology Soc., Council on Anthropology and Edn., Ethnology Soc. of Washington, Nat., Va., Fairfax Edn. assns., Phi Delta Gamma (recipient gold emblem award 1970). Author: (edn. filmstrip) The Bushmen Hunters-Gathers of Botswana, 1973; also article. Home: 13713 Pennsboro Dr Chantilly VA 22021 Office: 3710 Bevan Dr Fairfax VA 22030

BROWN, LAURA VENTRESCA (MRS. GEORGE BERDINE BROWN), arts coordinator; b. Washington, Oct. 2, 1915; d. Francesco and Florence Vendla Elizabeth (Olson) Ventresca; B.A., U. Ill., 1936, B.S. in L.S., 1941; postgrad. U. Md., 1961-62; m. George Berdine Brown, July 17, 1938; children—David Alan, Donald Kent, Douglas Scott. Librarian, Falls Church, Va., 1952-53; arts coordinator Anne Arundel County Dept. Recreation and Parks, Annapolis, Md., 1972—. Dir. Cultural-Edn. Centre, Inc., Annapolis. Membership chmn. Arlington County Womens Com. for Nat. Symphony, 1953-54; fine arts chmn. Marshall Sch. P.T.A., 1953-54; membership chmn. Anne Arundel County Concert Assn., 1959; chmn. symphony com. Anne Arundel County Gen. Hosp. Aux., 1959-69; v.p. Md. Com. for Arts; bd. dirs. Anne Arundel Arts Assn., also pres. 1970-72; patron Annapolis Symphony Orch., Annapolis Colonial Players, Md. Fedn. Arts, Annapolis Summer Garden Theatre, Annapolis Childrens Theatre, Annapolis Opera Soc., Historic Annapolis, Balt. Mus. Mem. Pi Delta Pi. Home: 200 Riggs Av Severna Park MD 21146

BROWN, LILLIAN BROOKS, ednl. broadcaster; b. Huntsville, O., Aug. 8, 1914; d. James Irwin K. and Nelly Blanche (Haynes) B.; diploma elementary edn. Bowling Green State U., 1933; student Ohio State U., 1933-36; children—Carla (Mrs. Richard Gorrell), Kristi, Kimberly. Tchr. elementary schs., Ohio, 1933-38; dir. radio and TV, George Washington U., Washington, 1956-66; dir. radio and TV programming Am. U., Washington, 1966—. Recipient Golden Mike award McCalls, 1959, Emmy award Nat. Acad. TV Arts and Scis., 1966, award Internat. Broadcasters Soc., 1967, Golden Mike award Am. Legion, 1972. Mem. Am. Women in Radio and TV, Nat. Assn. Ednl. Broadcasters, Nat. Acad. TV Arts and Scis., Am. Newspaper Women's Club. Author: A Living Centennial, 1968. Home: 1003 Gelston Circle McLean VA 22101 Office: American U Washington DC 20016

BROWN, LOIS ANNE SULLIVAN, editor; b. San Francisco, Oct. 3, 1926; d. Edward Francis and Jennie Gergine (Garstad) Sullivan; student U. S. Fla., 1968; m. William L. Brown, Apr. 22, 1946 (div.); children—Katherine (Mrs. Richmond McDavid), William M., Michael J., Ronald F. Mem. editorial staff Fla. Grower Publs., Tampa, 1956-57; owner, editor Penny Saver North Tampa News, 1957—; mem. adv. com. Northside Bank, Tampa, 1973—. Adv. com. Franciscan Center, Tampa, 1972—; sec. Hillsborough County Council Civic Club, 1969, North Tampa 100, 1971. Bd. dirs. North Tampa Improvement Assn., 1970-72. Mem. North Tampa C. of C. (pres. 1972-73, dir.). Club: Women's (v.p. 1970-71 Tampa). Home: 320 W Waters Av Tampa FL 33604 Office: PO Box 8395 Tampa FL 33604

BROWN, MABEL WELTON, lawyer; b. Geneseo, Ill., Dec. 7, 1916; d. Harry E. and Mabel (Welton) Brown; B.A., Oberlin Coll., 1938; J.D., U. Chgo., 1941. Partnership with father, Harry E. Brown, atty., 1941-44, sole owner, 1944—; atty. for Green River Spl. Drainage dist., Henry and Bureau counties (Ill.). Chmn. Geneseo Planning Commn., 1961-68. Mem. Am., Ill., Henry County pres. 1973—) bar assns., Am. Judicature Soc., Kappa Beta Phi. Republican. Methodist (trustee). Home: 115 E North St Geneseo IL 61254 Office: 115 N State St Geneseo IL 61254

BROWN, MARGARET ANN ALEXANDER (MRS. JOHN RICHARD BROWN), newspaper pub.; b. Norborne, Mo., Oct. 30, 1925; d. James Robert and Daisy Bertha (Summers) Alexander; grad. high sch.; m. John Richard Brown, Aug. 28, 1944; children—Judith Ann (Mrs. Charles R. Dover), John Richard. Tchr. Stamm Elementary Sch., Norborne, 1944; linotype and press operator Norborne Democrat-Leader, 1957-68, owner, editor, pub., 1968—; reporter, news writer Carrollton (Mo.) Daily Democrat, 1960. Methodist. Mem. Order Eastern Star. Home: 501 E 2d St Norborne MO 64668 Office: 106 S Pine St Norborne MO 64668

BROWN, MARILYN JANE (HAHN), banker; b. Huron, O., Oct. 23, 1920; d. Henry Conrad and Cora Oleta (Zimmerman) Hahn; student Sandusky (O.) Bus. Coll., 1938-39, Ohio Sch. Banking, 1968-69; m. Wayne Victor Brown, Dec. 19, 1942 (dec. 1968); children—Gary Wayne, David Victor. Bookkeeper, sec. Erie County Title Co., 1940-42; pub. accountant, 1951-57; office mgr. Consolo Supermarket, 1957-60; receptionist, clk. Luster Corp., 1962-64; receptionist, sec. Firelands Community Bank, Huron, 1964-66, asst. cashier, 1966-67, cashier, 1968-69, asst. v.p., sec. to bd. dirs, 1969—. Sec. Huron Booster Club, 1962; chmn. Citizen's Sch. Adv. Com. for Operating Levy, 1973. Mem. Nat. Assn. Bank Women, Ohio Bankers Assn. (activities com. 1969-71), Am. Inst. Banking (chpt. sec. 1968-69, gov. 1970-71). Episcopalian (treas. 1972-73, mem. Vestry 1973—). Club: Sandusky Altrusa (treas. 1967-71). Home: 107 Miami Pl Huron OH 44839 Office: 357 Main St PO Box 457 Huron OH 44839

BROWN, MARILYN KATHERINE VOLKER, stock brokerage co. exec.; b. Somerville, N.J., Aug. 8, 1937; d. Harry Charles and Evelyn Cornelia (Wilson) Volker; A.B. cum laude, Mt. Holyoke Coll., 1958; postgrad. Duke U., 1958-59. Asst. investment counselor Bank of N.Y., N.Y.C., 1959-60; research economist Nat. Econ. Research Assos., N.Y.C., 1960-61; securities analyst DeVegh & Co., N.Y.C., 1961-62, Investors Diversified Services, Mpls., 1962-63, Daln, Kalman & Quail, Mpls., 1963-69; asst. dir. research Equity Research Assos., N.Y.C., 1969-70; supervisory securities analyst Drexel Burnham & Co., Inc., N.Y.C., 1970-73, v.p., 1972—, asst. research dir., 1973—. Chartered financial analyst. Mem. N.Y. Soc. Securities Analysts, (edn. com. 1971-72), Financial Analysts Fedn. (accounting policy com. 1971-72, chmn. program com. 1972-74), Mt. Holyoke Alumnae Assn. (dir. 1974—, pres. Minn. chpt. 1968-69, state fund raising chmn. 1967; mem. finance com. 1972—, chmn. 1974). Editor: Drexel Burnham View, 1970-74. Home: 145 E 16th St New York City NY 10003 Office: 60 Broad St New York City NY 10004

BROWN, MARION RHODES (MRS. JOHN ALBERT BROWN, JR.), educator; b. N.Y.C., Apr. 8, 1909; d. William Milton and Nora (Coughlin) Rhodes; B.A., Barnard Coll., 1930; M.A., Columbia, 1933, Ph.D., 1958; m. John Albert Brown, Jr., June 12, 1943; 1 dau., Valerie Anne. Tchr. social studies secondary schs., N.Y.C., 1930-46; lectr., supr. student teaching Hunter Coll., N.Y.C., 1951; asso. personnel research Herrold Assos., N.Y.C., 1958-60; asso. prof. edn. Coll. City N.Y., 1961-73. Sec., 2d Internat. Edn. Conf., 1957, 3d, 1958; v.p. N.Y.C. chpt. World Edn. Fellowship, Fellowship rep. to UN, 1972—. Mem. Morningside Citizens Com. Fellow Internat. Council Psychologists; mem. Am. Psychol. Assn. (divs. ednl. psychology and social psychology), Soc. for Psychol. Study Social Issues, A.A.A.S., Am. Acad. Polit. and Social Scis., N.Y. Acad. Scis., Am. Ednl. Research Assn., Am. Assn. for Higher Edn., N.E.A., Am. Assn. U. Women (corp. del., cons., area rep., implementation chmn. on world problems N.Y.C. 1963-68), Columbia Grad. Faculties Alumni Assn., Pi Lambda Theta (treas., pres. Alpha Epsilon chpt. 1956-57, nat. v.p. 1963-67), Kappa Delta Pi (v.p. Kappa chpt.). Editor: Tchr. Edn. News and Notes, 1964-66. Home: 404 Riverside Dr New York City NY 10025

BROWN, MARJORIE MODELLE, educator; b. Thompsonville, Tex., July 16, 1914; d. Albert Thomas and Ella May (Diddle) Brown; B.S., S.W. Tex. State Coll., 1936; M.Ed., Colo. State U., 1944; Ed.D., U. Ill., 1954. Tchr. Tex. high schs. throughout Tex., 1936-49; instr. U. Ill., Urbana, 1949-51; asst. prof. Colo. State U., Fort Collins, 1951-59; prof. home econs. edn. U. Minn., St. Paul, 1959—. Home demonstration agt. Tex. Agrl. and Mech. Coll. Extension Service, 1941-43; cons. U.S. Office Edn., 1957-58, Nat. Assessment in Edn., 1969. Block leader United Fund, St. Paul, 1967-68. Vol. worker Democratic Party, 1968, 72. Minn. Dept. Edn. grantee, 1968, 69, 70. Mem. League Women Voters, Am. Home Econs. Assn. (mem. com. 1970-72), Am. Ednl. Research Assn., Am. Assn. U. Profs. (chpt. v.p. 1957-58; chpt. exec. com. 1972-73), Nat. Assn. Home Econs. Tchr. Educators (pres. 1955), Am. Vocational Assn., Kappa Delta Pi, Omicron Nu, Pi Gamma Mu. Author: Home Learning Experiences, 1963; Evaluation Materials for Use in Teaching Child Development, 1966; Physicial Home Environment and Psychological and Social Factors, 1969. Editorial bd. Home Econs. Research Jour., 1971-73. Home: 734 LaBore Rd St Paul MN 55117

BROWN, MARY ELEANOR, physical therapist, educator; b. Williamsport, Pa., Jan. 1, 1906; d. Sumner Locher and Mary Kate (Eagles) Brown; student U. Wis. at Madison, 1927-28; B.A., Barnard Coll., 1931; M.A., N.Y.U., 1941; student N.Y.U., 1942-45, Western Reserve U., 1960-61; postgrad. U. Miami, Miami-Dade Jr. Coll., 1971-72. Supervising phys. therapist, research asst. Inst. for Crippled and Disabled, N.Y.C., 1941-46; instr. edn. N.Y.U., 1942-46; phys. therapist Childrens Rehab. Inst., Cockeysville, Md., 1946; organizing dir. phys. edn. State Rehab. Hosp., West Haverstraw, N.Y., 1946-47; phys. therapy cons. Nat. Soc. for Crippled Children and Adults, Chgo., 1947-49; physical therapy cons., dir. prof. services, dir. cerebral palsy sch. N.Y. State Dept. Health, Albany, N.Y. and Eastern N.Y. Orthopedic Hosp. Sch., Schenectady, N.Y., 1949-53; chief phys. therapist Bird S. Coler Hosp. for Chronic Diseases, N.Y.C., 1953-54; chief phys. therapist, instr. edn. St. Vincents Hosp. and N.Y.U., 1954-58; chief research asso. hand research Highland View Hosp., Cleve., 1958-64, cons. on kinesiology, hand research, 1964-65; supr. continuing edn. for phys. therapists, asst. prof. phys. therapy Case Western Res. U., Cleve., 1964-68; dir. phys. therapy Margaret Wagner House of Benjamin Rose Inst., Cleve., 1968-70; free lance writer, 1970—. Recipient Award of Merit, Case-Western Res. U., 1970. Mem. Inst. Gen. Semantics, World Confedn. Phys. Therapy, Am. Phys. Therapy Assn., Soc. for Behavorial Kinesiology (charter), Monhegan (Me.) Assos. Club: Barnard College. Contbr. articles in field to profl. jours. Home: 684 Bernardo Av Morro Bay CA 93442

BROWN, MARY FRIEL, librarian; b. Birmingham, Ala., Sept. 22, 1914; d. Waldo Marvin and Theresa Agnes (Regan) Brown; B.A., Vanderbilt U., 1936; B.S., George Peabody Coll., 1939. Tchr., Nashville City Schs., 1936-38, librarian Cohn High Sch., 1938-40, N. Nashville High Sch., 1940-67; tech. processes librarian I Vanderbilt U. Med. Center Library, 1967—. Mem. Womens Nat. Book Assn. (recording sec. 1971-73), Med., Tenn. library assns., Nashville Library Club, Legion of Mary (rec. sec. 1963-68), Gamma Phi Beta. Home: 6112 Jocelyn Hollow Rd Nashville TN 37205

BROWN, MARY LORETTA THERESE, pub. relations exec., author; b. N.Y.C.; d. John J. and Caecilia (Reynolds) Brown; ed. Blessed Sacrament Acad., Goshen, N.Y., and Columbia. Account exec., publicity and pub. relations dir. Harriet Hubbard Ayer, 1948-55; creative coordinator Lux products Lever Bros., 1955-56; account exec. Hill & Knowlton, Inc., N.Y.C., 1956-60, women's dir., 1960-66, v.p., 1966—; author short stories, poetry, book revs.; columnist on grooming. Mem. adv. council Jr. Achievement N.Y. Recipient gold key City N.Y., 1965; named Woman of Month, Sign mag., 1967, Lady Holy Sepulchre, 1972, Dame Order Collar St. Agatha, 1972. Mem. Fashion Group (bd. govs. 1970-72), Parliament of Women (founder), Women Execs. in Pub. Relations, English-Speaking Union, Lapidary and Gem Soc. N.Y., Oriel Soc., N.Y. Geneal. and Biog. Soc. Republican. Roman Catholic. Club: York (N.Y.C.). Author: Angela in Public Relations, 1965; The Gift, 1968 (St. Thomas More award 1969); Gems for the Taking, 5th printing, 1971. Home: 1025 Park Av New York City NY 10028 Office: 633 3d Av New York City NY 10017

BROWN, MARY RUTH, librarian; b. Lexington, Ky., May 3, 1925; d. Jesse Edward and Kathryn (Prather) Ballard; A.B. in Edn., U. Ky., 1947, M.S. in L.S., 1960; m. George W. Brown, Nov. 10, 1948; 1 dau., Jessica (Mrs. Lewis Young). Tchr.-librarian Joseph (Ore.) High Sch., 1951-56; asst. librarian Reno High Sch., 1956-59; cataloger U. Ky., Lexington, 1960-66, head librarian Agr. Library, 1966—, asso. dir. for operations U. Ky. System Libraries, 1973-74, asso. dir. libraries, 1974—. Library adviser N.E. Thailand Agrl. Research Center, 1967-72; library devel. cons. Universidad de Oriente, Cumana, Venezuela, 1972; treas. Assos. of Nat. Agrl. Library, 1973-74. Recipient citation spl. recognition Assos. Nat. Agrl. Library, 1974. Mem. Internat. Assn. Agrl. Librarians and Documentalists, Ky. Library Assn., Asociacion Interamericana de Bibliotecarious y Documentalistas Agricolas, Beta Phi Mu. Baptist. Author: (with E.L. Moss, K.D. Bright) Agricultural Education in a Technical Society, 1973. Contbr. articles to profl. jours. Home: Route 1 Box 93 Winchester KY 40391 Office: U Ky Lexington KY 40506

BROWN, META SUCHE (MRS. SIDNEY OVERTON BROWN), educator; b. San Antonio, Nov. 21, 1908; d. Edward and Amanda (Meyer) Suche; student San Antonio Coll., 1926-28, Our Lady of the Lake Coll., 1928-29; B.A., U. Tex., 1931, M.A., 1933, Ph.D., 1935; m. Sidney Overton Brown, Aug. 27, 1938; 1 dau., Lorelei. Research asso. dept. zoology, U. Tex., 1935-38; cytologist dept. agronomy Agrl. and Mech. Coll. Tex., 1940-48, asso. prof., 1948-55; prof. Tex. A. and M. U., College Station, 1955—. Instr. biology East Tex. State Coll., summers, 1935-36. Mem. Brazos Valley Arts Council, 1972—. Recipient Faculty Distinguished Achievement award for research, 1964, Cotton Genetics Research award, 1964. Mem. Genetics Soc. Am., Bot. Soc. Am., Genetics Soc. Canada, Am. Soc. Naturalists, Am. Genetics Assn., Soc. for Study Evolution, Tex. Acad. Sci., Tex. Soc. for Radiation Research, Am. Assn. U. Women (corp. del., 1972-74), Bus. and Profl. Women (pres., 1972-73), Sigma Xi, Sigma Delta Epsilon, Phi Kappa Phi, Gamma Sigma Delta. Home: 700 Gilchrist St College Station TX 77840

BROWN, MURIEL WHITBECK, cons. psychologist; b. Brighton, N.Y., Oct. 29, 1892; d. William Mortimer and Helen (Hood) Brown; B.A., Wellesley Coll., 1915; M.A., Stanford, 1924; Ph.D., Johns Hopkins, 1926. Tchr.-counselor Phila. Pub. Schs., 1916-20; spl. edn. supr. Pa. State Dept. Pub. Instrn., 1920-22; dir. child study dept. and mental health program Soc. Prevention Cruelty to Children, Rochester, N.Y., 1927-33; research asst. Nat. Council Parent Edn., N.Y.C., 1933-35; regional parent edn. supr. Cal. Dept. Edn., San Francisco, 1935-37; parent edn. specialist Tulsa Pub. Schs., 1937-40; asst. prof. psychology U. Tulsa, 1937-40; specialist parent and family life edn. and community devel. U.S. Dept. Health, Edn. and Welfare, Office of Edn., Washington, 1940-56, Children's Bur., 1956-62; cons. psychologist, Stephens City, Va., 1962—. Cons. U.S. Mil. Govt., Germany, 1949, World Fedn. for Mental Health, Germany, 1951, 52-53, Mental Health Materials Center, N.Y.C., 1951-68, ICA, Egypt, 1953, Okla. State U.-Ford Found Team, Pakistan, 1957, Ministry Health, Guyana, S. Am., 1968, Northwestern Mental Health Assn., Winchester, Va., 1965—; mem. steering com. nat. vol. orgns. Nat. Council on Aging, 1971—; conf. cons. Caribbean Fedn. for Mental Health, Trinidad, 1969; conf. cons. Internat. Fedn. for Parent Edn., Caracas, 1970, Sopron, Hungary, 1971, Neuchatel, Switzerland, 1972, rep. on non-govtl. orgns. com. for UNICEF, mem. adv. com. experts, 1972—; chmn. task force on aging Nat. Council on Family Relations, 1973—. Bd. dirs. Sheltered Workshop, Winchester; trustee Research Inst. Toy Mfrs. of Am. Fellow A.A.A.S.; mem. Am. Civil Liberties Union, Am. Home Econs. Assn., Am. Social Health Assn. (hon. life), Nat. Council Family Relations, Soc. Women Geographers, Caribbean Fedn. for Mental Health, World Fedn. Mental Health, World Federalists, Phi Beta Kappa, Sigma Xi, Omicron Nu (hon. life). Contbg. author Modern Marriage and Family Life, 1957; Handbook on Marriage and Family Living, 1964; History of the American Home Economics Association, 1972. Author: Prenatal Care, 1962; (with Margaret Mead) The Wagon and The Star: A Study of American Community Initiative, 1967. Contbr. articles to profl. jours. Address: RFD 1 Stephens City VA 22655

BROWN, MYRTLE IRENE, nursing educator; b. East Peoria, Ill., Feb. 1, 1915; d. Clifford Richard and Sarah (Scoville) Brown; B.A., Eureka Coll., 1939; B.S., U. Minn., 1942, M.S., 1947; Ph.D., N.Y.U., 1961. Instr., supr. pediatric nursing Mont. State Coll., Great Falls, 1939-41; instr., supr. pediatric nursing U. Minn., 1942-46, instr. advanced pediatric nursing, 1947-49; nursing cons. maternal and child health team, WHO, India, 1949-50; pub. health staff nurse Wayne County Health Dept., Eloise, Mich., 1950-52; asst. prof. maternal, child health Johns Hopkins U., Balt., 1952-55; instr. introductory epidemiology, sr. clin. nursing, maternal and children's nursing, N.Y.U., 1955-61; research cons. Am. Nurses' Found., N.Y.C., 1961-64; asso. prof. community health and med. practice U. Mo. Sch. Medicine, Columbia, 1964-67, asso. prof. Sch. Nursing, 1966-67; dean Sch. Nursing, Duke, 1967-70, prof., 1967-70, dir. patient care Med. Center, Duke, 1967-70; prof., dir. grad. studies Coll. Nursing, U. S.C., Columbia, 1970—. Mem. maternal and child health and crippled children's services research com. Dept. Health, Edn. and Welfare, 1971—. Mem. Trained Nurse Assn. India (life), Am. Sociol. Assn., Am. Pub. Health Assn., Am., S.C. nurses assns., Kappa Delta Pi, Alpha Kappa Delta, Sigma Theta Tau. Home: 5400 Lake Shore Dr Columbia SC 29206

BROWN, NELDA JEAN, advt. co. exec.; b. Monette, Ark., Dec. 5, 1938; d. Ewel Wayne and Lois (Jacks) Herrod; student Ark. State U., 1956-57; children by previous marriage—Wendell Carl, Tammy Lynn, Christopher Lloyd. Copywriter radio sta. KDRS, Paragould, Ark., 1959-62, 1964-68, disc jockey, 1964-68; copywriter KFRU Radio, Columbia, Mo., 1963-64; copywriter Cranford, Johnson, Hunt & Assos., Little Rock, 1968, account exec., 1969, dir. plans and recommendations, 1973—. Mem. pub. com. United Way of Pulaski County, Ark., 1973. Recipient awards copywriting Little Rock Advt. Fedn., 1969, 72. Mem. Discover Am. Travel Orgn. Baptist. Contbr. poetry to popular mags. Home: 5900 Hacienda Dr N Little Rock AR 72118 Office: 1st National Bank Bldg 3rd St and Louisiana St Little Rock AR 72201

BROWN, NELLIE KATHERINE (MRS. WALTER EDWARD BROWN), real estate broker; b. Pinesburr, Miss., July 3, 1917; d. Palma George and Eva G. (Patterson) Perry; grad. Mobile High Sch., 1935; m. Walter Edward Brown, Mar. 14, 1940; children—Lana Marie (Mrs. James Sullivan), Larry Edward, Linda Mae (Mrs. Royal Stanton Clark, Jr.). Real estate broker, owner Three Worlds-A & B Brokers, Norwalk, Cal., 1968—. Mem. Women's Council, Norwalk, 1968—. Mem. Norwalk Bd. Realtors, Order Eastern Star. Home: 14505 Corby Apt 1 Norwalk CA 90650 Office: 14515 S Pioneer Blvd Norwalk CA 90650

BROWN, NONA BALDWIN (MRS. CLINTON B.D. BROWN), writer, editor; b. N.J., May 11, 1918; d. Allen Thomas and Helen Pugh (Smitheman) Baldwin; A.B., Vassar Coll., 1939; M.S. in Journalism (Pulitzer fellow), Columbia, 1940; m. Clinton B.D. Brown, Mar. 25, 1944. With N.Y. Times, 1940-42, 46-73, Sunday staff writer Washington bur., 1946-63, Sunday corr. Washington bur., 1963-73; free lance writer, editor, 1973—. Served to lt. USNR, 1942-45. Mem. Soc. of Friends. Club: Washington Press. Home: 3801 Kanawha St NW Washington DC 20015

BROWN, NYDA WILLIAMS, psychiatrist; b. Tampa, Fla., Dec. 31, 1933; d. Maynard Oliver and Irene Helen (Patton) Williams; A.B., Emory U., 1957; M.D., Med. Coll. Ga., 1963; m. Julian E. Howell, Nov. 24, 1952 (div. May 1957); children—Julian, Evan; m. 2d, C. William Brown, Aug. 5, 1960 (div. Aug. 1971); children—Ian, Margaret. Intern, E. Talmadge Meml. Hosp., Augusta, Ga., 1963-64, resident psychiatry, 1964-67; practice medicine specializing in psychiatry, Atlanta, 1967—; mem. staffs Northside Hosp., Parkwood Hosp., Peachtree Hosp.; pres. Clown Enterprises, 1971-72. Mem. Am., Ga. psychiat. assns., Am. Med. Women's Assn. (br. pres. 1965-67), Med. Assn. Ga., Fulton County Med. Assn. Home and office: 5075 Green Pine Dr NE Atlanta GA 30342

BROWN, OLLIE MAE HULL (MRS. ALLEN HAUTENTS BROWN), educator; b. Charlotte, N.C., Feb. 7, 1926; d. John Henry and Alberee (Thomas) Hull; student Livingstone Coll., 1943; B.S., Johnson C. Smith U., 1947; M.S., Mont. State U., 1961; postgrad. Ore. State U., 1963, Ill. State U., 1968, 71-72; m. Allen Hautents Brown, Sept. 10, 1947; children—Marquessa Vonberee, Carlton Allen. Tchr., Bluefield (Va.) pub. schs., 1955-58; faculty Jackson (Miss.) State Coll., 1958—, asst. prof. phys. edn., 1967—. Choreographer local theatrical prodns.; cons. Juvenile Detention Center, Jackson, 1969-70. Mem. Am., Miss. (pres. elect dance sect.) assns. health, phys. edn. and recreation, Am. Assn. Univ. Profs., Jack and Jill of Am., Delta Sigma Theta. Presbyn. Home: 3602 Westchester Dr Jackson MS 39213

BROWN, PATRICIA ANN CHARLTON (MRS. JOHN FRANKLIN BROWN), librarian; b. Ft. Sumner, N.M., Oct. 21, 1930; d. William Edmund and Elnora Marthalee (Plaster) Charlton; B.A., N. Tex. State U., 1951; postgrad. Tex. Western Coll., Odessa Coll., Our Lady of Lake Coll., Tex. Tech U., Tex. Woman's U.; m. John Franklin Brown, Aug. 3, 1952; 1 dau., Cynthia Ann. Elementary librarian Odessa (Tex.) pub. schs., 1952-55, 59-66; children's librarian Midland (Tex.) Pub. Library, 1957-59; librarian Ector High Sch., Odessa, 1966—. Mem. budget com. United Fund, 1972. Mem. Am., Tex. (life) library assns., Tex. Assn. Sch. Librarians, Odessa Bapt. Assn. (dir. 1973-74), Associated Ch. Librarians Orgn. (pres. 1973), Beta Sigma Phi, Kappa Kappa Iota. Club: Altrusa (Odessa, Tex.). Home: 1702 Palomar Lane Odessa TX 79763 Office: PO Box 3912 Odessa TX 79760

BROWN, PATRICIA EDWINA RHINE (MRS. EDWARD EZELL BROWN), civic worker; b. Thornton, Ark., Feb. 7, 1928; d. Thomas Edwin and Naneitta (Raines) Rhine; student Ward Belmont Jr. Coll., 1945-47; B.A., U. Ark., 1949; m. Edward Ezell Brown, Oct. 6, 1951; children—Thomas Edward, Patricia Ann, Richard DuPree, David Rhine, Virginia Marks. Mem. League Women Voters, 1952—, pres., 1954-57, mem. state bd., 1959-63, state v.p., 1961-63; mem. Jr. Aux., 1954-62, pres., 1959; pres. Lutheran Elementary Sch. Christian Edn. Assn., 1958; chmn. Kindergarten Mothers Com., 1963, 67, pres., 1969-70; vol. tchr.'s aid at deprived sch.; mem. bd. Lakeside P.T.A., 1968-70; host family for Am. Field Service fgn. exchange student, 1969-70; mem. Mental Health Assn., 1960—, v.p., 1960; chmn. Citizens Com. for a Mental Health Center, 1963; 1st pres. Little Firehouse Community Art Center, 1966; mem. bd., v.p. S.E. Ark. Mental Health Center, chmn. bd., 1972-73; mem. alumni bd. U. Ark., 1956-58; mem. steering com. Youth Homes, Inc., 1972, bd. dirs., 1972—; chmn. steering com. Vols. in Pub. Schs., 1973, chmn. bd., 1973—. Trustee Marks Family Cemetery. Vice chmn. Jefferson County Democratic Central Com., 1964—. Mem. Pine Bluff Jr. League (sustaining), Chi Omega, Sigma Alpha Iota, Phi Theta Kappa. Presbyn. (extension com. 1969—). Clubs: Mathontes (past pres.); Alumnae. Home: 1 Southern Pines Pine Bluff AR 71601

BROWN, PATRICIA IRENE, librarian; b. Boston; d. Joseph Raymond and Harriet T. (Taylor) Brown; A.B., Suffolk U., 1955, J.D., 1965, M.B.A., 1970; postgrad. Gordon-Conwell Theol. Sem., 1972—. Typist, Rustcraft Pub. Co., Boston, 1948-50; pitcher All-Am. Girls Baseball League, Chgo., 1950-52; asst. librarian Suffolk U., Boston, 1955-65, asst. law librarian Law Library, 1966—. Adv. bd. dirs. Children's Haven, Inc., East Douglas, Mass. Mem. Am. Judicature Soc., Am. Assn. Law Libraries, Mass., Boston bar assns., Phi Alpha Theta. Conglist. (librarian 1969—).

BROWN, PATRICIA LAVERNE, educator; b. Chgo., Mar. 10, 1942; d. Edward H. and Anna Mae (Martin) Brown; B.A. in English, Loyola U., Chgo., 1964, M.A., 1969. Asst. dir. advt. dept. Callaghan & Co., Chgo., 1964-65; staff writer Charles A. Davis & Assos., Chgo., 1965-66; pub. information officer Chgo. Com. on Urban Opportunity, 1966-69; instr. lit., communications Malcolm X Community Coll., Chgo., 1969-73; vis. lectr. U. Mass., Boston, 1973—. Bus. mgr. Kuumba Workshop, 1969-73; mem. exec. council Afrikan Heritage Inst. Mem. Welfare Pub. Relations Forum, 1969-70. Mem. African Heritage Studies Assn., Inst. of Black World, Nat. Assn. for Community Devel., Modern Lang. Assn., Congress of African People (communications council), Kappa Beta Gamma (editor nat. news 1963-64, chpt. v.p. chpt. 1965-66, pres. 1966-67, dir. 1967-68). Editor: To Gwen with Love, 1970. Home: 186 Commonwealth Av Apt 11 Boston MA 02116 Office: Harbor Campus U Mass Boston MA 02125

BROWN, PATRICIA LYNN, information scientist; b. Lafayette, La., Oct. 1, 1928; d. William Madison and Maude Juanita (Thomas) Brown; B.S. in Chem. Engring., U. Southwestern La., 1947; M.A. in Chemistry, U. Tex., 1949. Instr. analytical chemistry Smith Coll., Northampton, Mass., 1949-50; chemist R&M Labs., Peabody, Mass., 1950; research asso. indsl. toxicology Albany (N.Y.) Med. Coll., 1950-51; information services Ethyl Corp., Ferndale, Mich., 1951-55; sr. tech. writer, editor, staff engr. Westinghouse Atomic Power Div., Pitts., 1955-57; supr., then mgr. information services, tech. information cons. Tex. Instruments, Dallas, 1957-66; sr. information scientist, asso. adviser, sr. adviser for information systems design Battelle Columbus (O.) Labs., 1966—. Loaned exec. United Way Campaign, 1972, 73. Bd. dirs. Engring. Socs. Library, 1961-63, 66-71. Mem. Soc. Women Engrs. (pres. 1961-63), Am. Chem. Soc., Spl. Libraries Assn., Soc. Applied Learning Tech., Am. Soc. Information Sci., Soc. Tech. Communication, Altrusa. Author publs. in field. Home: 1567 Northcrest Av Columbus OH 43220 Office: 505 King Av Columbus OH 43201

BROWN, PATRICIA MARIE, educator; b. Beech Grove, Ind., Jan. 8, 1949; d. Robert Francis and Mary Louise (Daufel) Brown; B.S., Ball State U., 1971. Tchr., head drama dept. Roncalli High Sch., Indpls., 1972—. Active summer stock profl. theatre cos. Mem. Delta Gamma, Alpha Psi Omega. Roman Catholic. Home: 2528 S Delaware St Indianapolis IN 46225 Office: 3300 Prague Rd Indianapolis IN 46227

BROWN, PHYLLIS JOEANNE SMITH (MRS. FREMONT VIRGIL BROWN II), office supply co. exec.; b. Edgerton, O.; d. John Rupert and Elva (Rohrbaugh) Smith; student U. Toledo, 1945-47, Bowling Green State U., 1947-48; m. Fremont Virgil Brown II, Jan. 28, 1950; children—Fremont Virgil III, Thomas Michael. Owner, Brown's Office Supply, Ft. Lauderdale, Fla., 1956—. Mem. Am. Bus. Womens Assn., Broward Geneal. Assn. (founding mem.), D.A.R., Nat. Geneal. Soc. Episcopalian. Club: Altrusa (pres. Ft. Lauderdale club 1963-65). Author: Thaddeus and Theresa Smith, Their European Ancestry and American Descendants, 1502-1971, 1971. Home: 724 Holly Lane Plantation FL 33313 Office: 1813 S State Rd 7 Fort Lauderdale FL 33314

BROWN, RHEA PETTIT BANGERT, judge; b. Logan, O., Apr. 29, 1904; d. John C. and Louisa (Wetzler) Pettit; student Ohio U., 1922-24; J.D., Ohio State U., 1928; m. Archie Bangert, 1932 (dec. 1950); m. 2d, O. Every Brown, Nov. 14, 1954 (dec. 1970). Admitted to Ohio bar, 1927, Fed. bar, 1934; gen. practice law, Logan, 1927-34; asst. state counsel Home Owners Loan Corp., 1934-37; common pleas judge, Hocking County, O., 1945-47, probate and juvenile judge, 1949—. Chmn. Ohio Probation and Parole Com. on Detention Home Standards. Adminstr., Crippled Children, 1949-64; past chmn. Hocking County Heart Drive, Crippled Children, Blood Recruitment, Easter Seals; trustee Community Chest, 1956; mem. Child Welfare Bd. Hocking County; past mem. state exec. bd. Ohio Welfare Conf.; exec. bd. State Mental Health Assn.; adviser Girl Scouts; Chmn. Women's Democratic Orgn., 1947—. Mem. Hocking County Bar Assn. (past pres.), Ohio Probate Ct. Judges Assn. (treas.), Nat. Council Juvenile Court Judges, Ohio Juvenile Judges Assn. (sec.-treas. 1954-58, mem. state exec. bd., past pres.), Ohio Probation and Parole Assn. (mem. legislative com., state exec. bd.), Ohio Citizens Council for Health and Welfare (v.p.), Logan, Ohio (chmn. Florence Allen scholarship fund, 1954-55, trustee 1956; mem. state exec. bd., legislative com.) bus. and profl. women's clubs, Am. Judicature Soc., Am. Assn. U. Women, Nat. Assn. Women Lawyers, Internat. Toastmistress, Kappa Beta Pi. Mem. Order Eastern Star (past matron), White Shrine of Jerusalem. Presbyn. Club: Hocking Hills Country. Home: 248 Florence Av Logan OH 43138 Office: Ct House Logan OH 43138

BROWN, ROWINE HAYES, pediatrician, lawyer; b. Harvey, Ill., Feb. 15, 1913; d. Robert and Nancy Detrich (Steel) Hayes; student Stanford, 1931-32; B.S., U. Ill., 1938, M.D., 1938; J.D., Chgo. Kent Coll. Law, 1961; m. William J. Brown, June 12, 1943 (dec.). Intern, then resident; asst. supt. Municipal Contagious Disease Hosp., Chgo.; asst. med. supt. in charge children's div. Cook County Hosp., Chgo., 1950-73, dir. pediatrics, med. director, 1973—; admitted to Ill. bar, 1961; clin. prof. pediatrics U. Ill. Coll. Medicine; adj. prof. law Chgo. Kent Coll. Law; lectr. in field. Bd. dirs. YWCA Met. Chgo.; bd. dirs., sec. Chgo. Kent Coll. Law, Chgo. Foundlings Home. Named Woman of Year YWCA Met. Chgo. and Women's Share in Pub. Service, 1973. Diplomate Am. Bd. Pediatrics. Mem. A.M.A., Am. Acad. Pediatrics, Chgo. Pediatric Soc., Ill. Bar Assn., Ill., Chgo. med. socs., Women's Bar Assn. Ill., Am. Coll. Legal Medicine. Contbr. articles specializing in the problem of battered children to med. and legal jours. Address: 1700 E 56th St Chicago IL 60615

BROWN, RUTH CUNNINGHAM (MRS. WILLIAM RUSSELL BROWN), club woman; b. Brooksville, Miss., Jan. 6, 1914; d. George William and Ruth (Hambrick) Cunningham; student Sophie Newcombe Coll., 1933-34, U. Tex., 1934-36; m. William Russell Brown, Apr. 19, 1941; children—Betsy (Mrs. Thomas M. Smith III), Virginia (Mrs. Fred E. Riddle, Jr.), Russell. Bd. dirs. Houston Community Council, 1962-63, mem. women's aux. Houston Bar Assn., 1956; bd. dirs., horticulture chmn. Garden Club of Houston, 1955-57; bd. visitors Sullins Coll., Bristol, Va., 1966-67, 69—. Mem. D.A.R. (dir. John-McKnitt chpt. 1963), Kappa Kappa Gamma (v.p. Houston alumnae assn. 1961). Republican. Episcopalian. Clubs: Houston, Houston Country. Address: 5816 Bayou Glen Rd Houston TX 77027

BROWN, RUTH ELEANOR, pharmacist; b. Phila., Sept. 10, 1906; d. Elmer Haines and Clara (Potter) Brown; Ph.G., Phila. Coll. Pharmacy and Sci., 1926. Asst. mgr. Jones Drug Store, Florence, Ariz., 1929-32; asst. mgr. Western Thrift Drug Chain, Eugene, Ore., 1933-40; became dir. pharmacy services Group Health Hosp. and Med. Centers, Seattle, 1941; now pharmacy cons. Group Health Am.; clin. instr. hosp. pharmacy U. Wash., 1967—. Mem. adv. bd. USV Pharm., Inc. Mem. Am. Pharm. Assn., Am. Soc. Hosp. Pharmacists, Fedn. Internat. Pharmacists, Washington State Soc. Hosp. Pharmacists (pres., 1961, treas., 1968), Acad. Gen. Practice Pharmacy, Internat. Platform Assn., Christian Bus. and Profl. Women (dir., pres. 1951), Matrix Table. Clubs: Soroptimist (dir.) (Met. br. Seattle); Faculty Womens. Contbr. articles to profl. jours. Home: 3821 Whitman Av N Seattle WA 98103 Office: 1507 E John St Seattle WA 98102

BROWN, SARA MAE, educator; b. Monessen, Pa., Aug. 11, 1927; d. Clark P. and Grace E. (Allen) Brown; B.A., Wellesley Coll., 1949; Ed.B., U. Miami, 1952; M.S., U. Pa., 1961, Ed.D., 1964. Secondary sch. tchr. Ardmore, Pa., 1957-62; research asst. Carter Found., U. Pa., Phila., 1962-64; asst. prof. ednl. psychology U. Del., Newark, 1964-67; asso. prof. So. Conn. State Coll., New Haven, 1967-70, prof. psychology, 1970—. Mem. Am. Psychol. Assn., Am. Statis. Assn., Am. Ednl. Research Assn., Am. Personal and Guidance Assn., Pi Lambda Theta, Psi Chi. Home: 279 Oak Av Cheshire CT 06410 Office: Southern Conn State Coll 501 Crescent St New Haven CT 06515

BROWN, SARAH COLE (MRS. STERLING F. BROWN), librarian; b. Conway, Ark.; d. Russell T. and Mary (Craig) Cole; B.A., Hendrix Coll., 1934; B.S. in L.S., U. Ill., 1939; m. Sterling F. Brown, Oct. 25, 1941; 1 son, Sterling Russell. Asst. librarian Ala. Coll., 1939-41, Air Corps Tactical Sch., 1941-43; cataloger, asso. librarian U. Ala. Med. Center, Birmingham, 1949-55, librarian, 1955-72, prof. library sci., dir. Lister Hill Library Health Scis., 1973—. Cons. to comprehensive health planning office Ala. Dept. Pub. Health, 1968-69; cons. Montgomery Regional Med. Found., 1969; mem. adv. council Southeastern Regional Med. Library, 1969—; mem. So. Assn. Colls. and Schs. vis. com. evaluators Va. Commonwealth U., 1973. Mem. Med. Library Assn. (dir. 1967-70, v.p., pres.-elect 1972-73, pres. 1973-74; chmn. liaison com. with Nat. Library Medicine 1968-69), Spl. Libraries Assn., Am., Ala. (pres. 1969-70, mem. exec. council 1970-71) library assns., Assn. Am. Med. Colls., Am. Assn. Dental Schs. (chmn. sect. learning resources, chmn. sect. dental libraries and information services 1970-71), Am. Assn. for History of Medicine, Am. Acad. History of Dentistry, Birmingham Library Club. Contbr. articles profl. jours. Home: 2100 Mountain View Dr Birmingham AL 35216 Office: Lister Hill Library Health Scis Univ Sta Birmingham AL 35294

BROWN, SARAH E. (MRS. RALPH JASON TEMPLE), lawyer; b. Topeka, Kan., Aug. 9, 1936; d. Paul Shannon and Alice (Rafter) Brown; A.B., Vassar Coll., 1958; student George Washington U., 1959-61, LL.B., Georgetown U., 1963; m. Ralph J. Temple, July 17, 1960; children—Katherine Esme, John Anthony. Admitted to D.C. bar, 1964; staff mem. U.S. Senator Estes Kefauver, Washington, 1958; legislative aide U.S. Senator Vance Hartke, Washington, 1959-60; asst. to dir. compliance surveys and research Pres. Com. on Equal Employment Opportunity, Washington, 1961-65; cons. Migrant div. Office Econ. Opportunity, Washington, 1965-66; practiced in Washington, 1968-71; staff atty. Pub. Defender Service, Washington, 1971—. Adj. prof. criminal law George Washington U. Grad. Sch., Washington, 1974—. Treas., dir. N.W. Investment Co., Washington, 1964-66; atty. Am. Civil Liberties Union, Washington, 1969—. Mem. D.C., Women's bar assns., D.A.R., Kappa Beta Pi. Club: Vassar. Home: 1520 Locust Rd NW Washington DC 20012 Office: 601 Indiana Av NW Washington DC 20004

BROWN, STELLA CHANEY, advt. agy. exec.; b. East St. Louis, Ill., Apr. 1, 1924; d. James Oscar and Lela Elizabeth (Hartill) Chaney; student Northwestern U., 1941-42, Jefferson Coll., 1942-45; m. A. Harvey Brown, Nov. 1, 1946 (div. Nov. 1960); children—Wendy Alexandra, Deborah Elisabeth. Advt. mgr. Sonnenfelds, St. Louis, 1943; dir. men's wear advt. Stix, Baer & Fuller, St. Louis, 1944; account exec., copy writer Hillman Shane Breyer Agy., Los Angeles, 1945; copy dir. Harry Serwer Agy., N.Y.C., 1945-46; advt. mgr. Libson Shops, St. Louis, 1946-47; asst. advt. dir. Edison Bros. Stores, Inc., 1947-53; copy dir., account exec. Hirsch-Tamm & Ullman Agy., 1957-58; pres. Stella Chaney Brown Advt., Inc., Clayton, Mo., 1959—; dir. St. Louis Broadcasting Co., Inc.; fashion editor Prom Mag., 1946—. Mem. Am. Fedn. Astrologers. Author: Wheelspin, 1953-58, Parents Without Partners Newsletter. Address: 9180 Ladue Rd Saint Louis MO 63124

BROWN, SUSAN LYNN LANGE (MRS. WILLIAM LYMAN BROWN III), educator; b. Lebanon, Ind., Aug. 29, 1946; d. Frank John and Dorothea Esther (Chavers) Lange; B.A. in Math., DePauw U., 1968; M.A. in Teaching in Math., Ind. U., 1969; m. William Lyman Brown III, June 9, 1973. Tchr. math. Frankfort (Ind.) community schs., 1969-70, Lebanon community schs., 1970-73, Ridgewood (N.J.) schs., 1973—. Mem. Nat. Fedn. Republican Women. Recipient Curved Bar award Girl Scouts Am., 1962, Grand Cross of Color Order of Rainbow for Girls in Ind., 1964, Young Career Woman award Bus. and Profl. Women, 1971. Mem. Nat. Council Tchrs. Math., N.E.A., Jordan Coll. Music (life), Am. Legion Aux., Order Rainbow for Girls in Ind., Internat. Women in Communications, DePauw U., Ind. U. alumni assns., Bus. and Profl. Women (corr. sec. 1970-73), Epsilon Sigma Alpha (First Pearl award 1971). Mem. Order Eastern Star. Mem. Christian Ch. Club: International Travel Study (corr. sec. Indpls. 1970-73). Home: 23 B Lakeview Av Leonia NJ 07605 Office: Benjamin Franklin Jr High Sch Van Dien St Ridgewood NJ 07451

BROWN, SUSAN ROSENZWEIG, psychologist; b. Newark, Mar. 1, 1939; d. Herbert and Ethel (Hinkes) Rosenzweig; Ph.D. in Psychology, U. So. Cal., 1971; div.; children—Jonathan, Jennifer. Psychologist, treatment dir. Cedars Sinai Med. Center, Los Angeles. Mental health cons. Headstart, Los Angeles City Schs., Pacific Oaks Coll. Bd. dirs. Cal. Sch. Profl. Psychology. Mem. Am., Cal., Los Angeles County psychol. assns., Am. Orthopsychiat. Assn., Soc. for Psychol. Study Social Issues. Research on eye contact in infants. Home: 2008 La Brea Terrace Los Angeles CA 90046 Office: 8730 Alden Dr Los Angeles CA 90048

BROWN, TOMMIE FLORENCE, social worker, educator; b. Rome, Ga., June 25, 1934; d. Phillip and Louise (Murden) Brown; B.A. cum laude, Dillard U., 1957; postgrad. Atlanta U., 1957-58; M.S.W., Washington U., St. Louis, 1964. With Tenn. Dept. Pub. Welfare, 1957-71, child welfare trainee Hamilton County Office, 1957, child welfare worker, 1958-61, sr. child welfare worker, 1961-66, field supr. I, Chattanooga Tng. Center, 1966-68, field supr. II, 1968-71; asst. prof. sociology U. Tenn. at Chattanooga, 1971—. Mem. mission council St. Mary the Virgin Episcopal Mission, 1968—; mem. human resources and membership com. League Women Voters, 1968—; mem. Chattanooga Model Cities Bd., 1969—, mem. exec. com., 1969—. Mem. Nat. Assn. Social Workers (sec. southeastern Tenn. chpt. 1967-68, v.p. 1968-69, pres. 1969-70, nat. sec. 1972-73, merit certificate 1968, Nat. Social Worker of Year, 1970, Howard Gustafson Meml. award 1970, Social Worker of Year Southeastern Tenn. chpt. 1970), Acad. Certified Social Workers, N.A.A.C.P. (sec. Chattanooga br. 1962-63, 64-68, merit certificate 1968, 1st v.p. 1969—), Alpha Kappa Alpha (Woman of Year award Pi Omega chpt. 1968-69, chmn. publicity and human relations 1968-70). Home: 603 N Highland Park Av Chattanooga TN 37404

BROWN, V. JEAN, pharmacist, educator; b. Laclede, Mo., Dec. 22, 1902; d. James Henry and Dovie (Trippeer) Brown; Ph.G., U. Kan., 1923; B.A., U. Okla., 1928, M.S., 1947; postgrad. Purdue U., 1951.Pharmacist, Mo. Methodist Hosp., St. Joseph, 1924-30, Bethany Hosp., Kansas City, Kan., 1930-33, Browns Pharmacy, Laclede, 1934-43; instr. pharmacy U. Okla. Coll. Pharmacy, Norman, 1946-47, asst. prof., 1949-61, asso. prof., 1961-69, prof., 1969—; asst. prof. Coll. Pharmacy, Med. Coll., Charleston, S.C., 1947-48; asso. prof. U. Miss. Coll. Pharmacy, Oxford, summers 1958, 59. Dist. dir. Gosselin Prescription Survey, Ray A. Gosselin Co., 1965-66, KETA-TV programs, 1960, 61, 65. Recipient Prof. of Month award Drug Topics mag., 1960, Lederle Faculty award, 1972, Standard Oil Found. Teaching award, 1972, Okla. U. Sr. Class Coll. Pharmacy award as outstanding tchr., 1972, 73. Walgreen fellow, 1967. Mem. Am. Assn. U. Women (br. pres. 1954-56), Am. Assn. Colls. of Pharmacy, Acad. Pharm. Scis., Am. (sect. chmn. 1965), Okla. pharm. assns., Okla. Edn. Assn., P.E.O., Mortar Bd., Sigma Xi, Lambda Kappa Sigma, Sigma Iota Pi, Delta Kappa Gamma (pres. Eta chpt. 1974), Gamma Phi Beta, Alpha Lambda Delta, Rho Chi. Methodist. Co-author Husa's Pharm. Dispensing, 1959, 66 (now entitled Martin's Dispensing of Medication), 1971. Contbr. articles to profl. jours. Home: 1357 Tarman Circle Norman OK 73069

BROWN, VANESSA (SMYLLA SANDRICH) (MRS. MARK R. SANDRICH, JR.), actress, author; b. Vienna, Austria, Mar. 24, 1928; d. Nah and Anna (Butterman) Brind; B.A. in English, U. Cal. at Los Angeles, 1949; m. Mark R. Sandrich, Jr., Nov. 29, 1950; children—Cathy Lisa, David Michael. Appeared in numerous motion pictures, 1941-67, including Youth Runs Wild, 1941, Concerto, 1943, The Late George Apley, 1945, The Heiress, 1948, Three Husbands, 1949, The Basketball Fix, 1950, The Fighter, 1951, The Bad and The Beautiful, 1952, Rosie, 1967; co-star Broadway play the Seven Year Itch, 1953; appeared as Celia in As You Like It, 1950; starred in Gigi, 1959, Pygmalion, 1959; appeared in numerous dramatic television and radio shows; corr. Voice of Am., 1962-73, Los Angeles Times Service, 1970-74; writer KTLA-TV, 1972-74. Lectr., Clark U., Worcester, Mass., 1953, Fall Joint Computer Conf., Las Vegas, 1956, U. Cal. at

Los Angeles, 1960, SWAP, Los Angeles, 1961, also Los Angeles elementary schs. Alternate del. Democratic Nat. Conv., 1956. Recipient Citizenship awards B'nai B'rith, 1959, Bonds for Israel, 1960, Hadassah, 1961. Office: care Braverman & Cordon 233 S Beverly Dr Beverly Hills CA 90212

BROWN, VERA DAWSON VINOGRADOFF (MRS. ARTHUR A. BROWN), psychologist, govt. ofcl.; b. Pitts., Jan. 12, 1912; d. Wilson C. and Elsa D. (Tracy) Dawson; A.B., Allegheny Coll., 1931; certificate U. Paris, France, 1936; Ph.D., U. Pitts., 1934; postgrad. Am. U., 1954-58, George Washington U., 1954-58, Washington Sch. of Psychiatry, 1956-62, Yale, 1961; m. Arthur A. Brown, Aug., 1970; children of previous marriage—E.D. Vinogradoff, Vera (Mrs. T. Reilly). Dir. psychol. services Alexandria (Va.) city schs., 1954-65; staff psychologist Peace Corps, Washington and overseas, 1966-72; dir. Fed. Women's Program, Dept. of Health, Edn. and Welfare, Washington, 1972—. Cons. child devel., 1965—; practice psychology, Washington, 1962—. Co-founder Alexandria Mental Hygiene Clinic, 1950. Recipient Outstanding Woman of No. Va. award No. Va. Civic Assn., 1962, Superior Service in Govt. award, 1967, 74. Mem. Am. Psychol. Assn. Home: 1101 New Hampshire Washington DC 20037 Office: Health Education and Welfare Room 4758N Washington DC 20201

BROWN, VERNON KIMBALL (MRS. MADISON B. BROWN), pub. relations dir.; b. Macon, Ga.; d. Wilmer Atkinson and Maude (Deale) Kimball; student Fla. State Coll. for Women; m. Dr. Madison B. Brown, July 12, 1958. Writer Newspaper Enterprise Assn. Syndicate, 1943-46; picture editor UNRRA, N.Y.C., 1946-47; mag. dir. UN Appeal for Children, N.Y.C., 1947-49; writer United Hosp. Fund, N.Y.C., 1949-50; pub. relations dir. Roosevelt Hosp., N.Y.C., 1950-53, Nat. Arthritis and Rheumatism Found., 1953-55, Phila. Blue Cross, 1956, Passavant Meml. Hosp., Chgo., 1957-72; asst. to v.p., devel. and pub. relations Northwestern Meml. Hosp., Chgo., 1972-73; exec. dir. Acad. Hosp. Pub. Relations, Chgo., 1974—. Fellow Acad. Hosp. Pub. Relations (pres. 1969-70); mem. of the Am. Soc. Hosp. Pub. Relations Dirs., Am. Med. Writers Assn., Chgo. Jr. League, Delta Delta Delta. Presbyn. Club: New York Fencers. Co-author: How to Fence, 1956. Home: Apt 4516 175 E Delaware Pl Chicago IL 60611 Office: 244 E Pearson St Suite 1903 Chicago IL 60611

BROWN, VIRGINIA MAE BROWN (MRS. JAMES V. BROWN), govt. ofcl.; b. Pliny, W.Va., Nov. 13, 1923; d. Felix Melville and Hester (Crandall) Brown; A.B., W.Va. U., 1945, J.D., 1947; m. James V. Brown, Apr. 8, 1955; children—Victoria Anne, Pamela Kay. Tchr., Winfield High Sch., Putnam County, W.Va., 1943-44; admitted to W.Va. bar, 1947; law clk. to W.Va. atty. gen., Charleston, 1947-50; exec. sec. W.Va. Jud. Council, Charleston, 1950-52; asst. atty. gen. State of W.Va., Charleston, 1952-61; counsel to gov. of W.Va., 1961; ins. commr. State of W.Va., 1961-62; mem. W.Va. Pub. Service Commn., 1962-64; commr. ICC, Washington, 1964—, vice chmn., 1968, chmn., 1969—. Mem. W.Va. Commn. Status of Women. Mem. Am., W.Va. bar assns. Home: 9733 Lookout Pl Montgomery Village Gaithersburg MD 20760 Office: ICC Washington DC 20423

BROWN-AZAROWICZ, MARJORY FRANCES, educator; b. Calgary, Alta., Can., Nov. 10, 1922; d. Charles and Isabella M. Lascelles (Glenday) Brown; B.A., U. B.C., 1950; B.Ed., U. Alta., 1953, A.Mus., 1954; A.R.C.T., U. Toronto, 1953; M.A., U. Wash., 1956, Ph.D., 1961; children—Calvin, Edward, Diane (Mrs. James Black). Came to U.S., 1956, naturalized, 1966. Tchr., Calgary, 1941-56; asso. prof. State U. N.Y. Coll., Buffalo, 1960-66; tchr., Fairfax (Va.) Pub. Schs., 1966-67, also coordinator secondary edn.; prof. edn. George Mason U., Fairfax, 1967—. Piano tchr., Fairfax, 1936—. Recipient Gov's. Gold Medal in Music, U. Alta., 1954. Mem. Nat. Guild Piano Tchrs., Pi Lambda Theta, Kappa Delta Pi, Phi Delta Kappa. Author: A Handbook of Creative Choral Speaking, 1970. Home: 4406 Middle Ridge Dr Fairfax VA 22030

BROWNE, ELIZABETH WINGREENE (MRS. WILLIAM S. FORT), state senator; b. Mpls., Apr. 4, 1926; d. William Alexander and Margaret Muriel (Blackwood) Wingreene; B.A., U. Minn., 1948; M.A., U. Chgo., 1951; J.D., U. Ore., 1966; m. Colbert Hughes Browne, Nov. 13, 1949; children—Claudia, Scott, Paula Jane, Christopher; m. 2d, William S. Fort, 1973. Tchr. secondary schs. Dade County, 1951-58; admitted to Ore. bar, 1966; dep. dist. atty. Lane County (Ore.), 1966-68, atty., 1969-72; referee Lane County Circuit Ct., 1969; mem. Ore. Ho. of Reps., 1969-70; mem. Ore. Senate, 1970—, majority leader, 1971—, chmn. judiciary com.; instr. law enforcement Lane Community Coll. Bd. dirs. Lane County Auditorium Assn., Lane County Family Planning Assn. Mem. Am., Ore., Lane County bar assns., Nat. Dist. Attys. Assn., Legal Aid and Defenders Assn., Am. Judicature Soc., Council State Govts. (chmn. law and criminal justice com. Western conf., Pres. elect Western conf.). Democrat. Editor: Juvenile Court Digest, Family Law Newsletter. Home: Laurel Butte Dr Oakridge OR 97463 Office: PO Box 737 Oakridge OR 97463

BROWNE, GWENNETH LORRAINE, educator; b. Santa Monica, Cal., Nov. 1, 1934; d. Maitland Arthur and Georgie Parker (Ferguson) Browne; B.A. summa cum laude, Queens Coll., 1960; postgrad. U. Heidelberg (Germany), 1961; Ph.D. (Columbia Tuition scholar), Columbia, 1968. Tutor, Queens Coll., Flushing, N.Y., 1961-62, lectr., 1962-64; instr. Washington Coll., Chestertown, Md., 1964-65; asst. prof. Bradley U., Peoria, Ill., 1966-68; asso. prof. philosophy U. Pacific, Stockton, Cal., 1968-73, prof., 1973—. Bd. dirs. Anderson Y Center, Stockton, 1969-73, pres. bd., 1970-71; bd. dirs. Opportunities Industrialization Center, Stockton, 1973—. Served with USAF, 1952-55. Recipient Fulbright fellowship, 1960-61, Gertz fellowship, 1960. Mem. Am. Assn. U. Profs. (chpt. v.p. 1971-72), Am. Civil Liberties Union (dir.), Center for Study Democratic Instns., Phi Beta Kappa, Delta Phi Alpha, Phi Sigma Tau. Home: 5153 Leonardini Rd Stockton CA 95205 Office: Dept Philosophy U Pacific Stockton CA 95204

BROWNE, HELEN EDITH, nursing service exec.; b. Bury St. Edmunds, Eng., Feb. 3, 1911; d. Phil and Agnes (Rice-Capon) Browne; State Registered Nurse, St. Bartholomew's Hosp. Sch. Nursing, London, Eng., 1934; State Certified Midwife, Brit. Hosp. for Mothers and Babies, London, 1935. Nurse-in-charge St. Bartholomew's Hosp., 1936; midwifery supr. Brit. Hosp. for Mothers and Babies, 1937; dist. nurse-midwife Frontier Nursing Service, Wendover, Ky., 1938-40, asst. dir., 1949-55, asso. dir., 1955-65, dir., 1965—; midwifery supr. Hyden (Ky.) Hosp., Frontier Nursing Service, 1941-47, supt., 1948; dir. Southeastern Ky. Health Demonstration Corp., Lexington, 1967—. Decorated officer Most Excellent Order of Brit. Empire. Mem. Am., Ky. (dir. 1954-58) nurses assns., Am. (dir.), Royal (Eng.) colls. nurse-midwives, Nat. League Nursing. Episcopalian. Club: Cosmopolitan (N.Y.C.). Address: care Frontier Nursing Service Wendover KY 41775

BROWNE, JANE COTTON, family planning cons.; b. St. Paul, Nov. 19, 1912; d. Donald Reed and Grace (Gillette) Cotton; student Wells Coll., 1930-32; m. Harry C. Browne, May 17, 1941 (div. May, 1954); 1 son, Marshall Gillette. Adminstrv. asst. Cargill, Inc., Mpls., 1944-45; office mgr., dir. spl. gifts Am. City Bur., Portland, Ore., 1947-48; dir., field cons. Planned Parenthood, N.Y. State (Eastern League), 1956-58, exec. dir., Mpls., 1951-56, Chgo., 1958-69, sr. fellow Adlai Stevenson Inst. Internat. Affairs, 1969; chmn. exec. dirs. council Planned Parenthood-World Population, 1965-68; mem. steering com. N. Cook County Office Econ. Opportunity, 1966-69; gov. bd. Cook County, Office Econ. Opportunity, 1966-69, founder, mem. Family Planning Coordinating Council Met. Chgo., 1967-71; mem. health com., welfare com., Evanston Anti-Poverty Council, 1967-69; mem. Gov.'s State-Wide Adv. Council Ill. Div. Health Planning and Resource Devel., Com. Health Care Facilities, 1968-71; mem. profl. adv. panel Welfare Council Met. Chgo., 1969-71; adv. council Comprehensive Health Planning, Inc., Met. Chgo., 1969-71; family planning cons., research asso. Center for Population Studies, U. Minn., 1970—. U.S. del. Internat. Planned Parenthood Conf., Singapore, 1963 Bangdung, Indonesia, 1969; cons. Near East South Asia div. AID, 1968; project dir. Ark. Family Planning Council, 1970-71, spl. cons., 1971—; family planning cons. Office Econ. Opportunity, Washington, 1970—; cons. Nat. Center Family Planning Services, Region VIII, Dept. Health, Edn. and Welfare, 1972-73; program adviser Naomi Gray Assos., 1970—; internat. traveler, lectr. Bd. dirs. Opportunity Workshop, Mpls., 1972—; budget allocations com. United Way of Mpls., 1974—. Mem. Mpls. Bd. Realtors (asso.), Am. Pub. Health Assn., Nat. Conf. Social Welfare. Republican. Episcopalian. Home: 978 Shady Lane Wayzata MN 55391

BROWNE, MARIE JULIA, physician; b. N.Y.C., Jan. 16, 1923; d. William Joseph and Marie Anna (Young) Browne; B.A., Hunter Coll., 1944; M.A., Syracuse U., 1949; M.D., State U. N.Y. at Syracuse, 1953. Intern, Hahnemann Med. Coll. and Hosp., Phila., 1953-54; resident pediatrics Children's Hosp. of Phila., 1954-56, fellow pediatric cardiology, 1956-57; fellow pediatric cradiology Harriet Lane Home, Johns Hopkins, Balt., 1957-58; attending pediatric cardiologist Yale New Haven Med. Center, New Haven, Milford (Conn.) Hosp., New Britain (Conn.) Hosp.; faculty Yale U. Sch. Medicine, 1958—, asso. prof. pediatrics, 1967—. Dir. health Town of Bethany, 1970—. Chmn. Health Careers Day Greater New Haven Heart Assn., 1971-72. Recipient Francis Gillman Blake award Yale U. Sch. Medicine, 1965. Diplomate Am. Bd. Pediatrics. Fellow Am. Acad. Pediatrics, Am. Coll. Cardiology; mem. Am., Conn., New Haven heart assns. Home: Bethany Wood Bethany CT 06525 Office: 333 Cedar St New Haven CT 06510

BROWNE, ROSALIND BENGELSDORF (MRS. BYRON BROWNE), artist; b. N.Y.C., Apr. 30, 1916; d. Isidore and Sadie (Bengelsdorf) Bengelsdorf; student Art Students League N.Y.C., 1930-34, Annot Art Sch., 1934-35, Hans Hofmann Art Sch., 1935-36, N.Y. U., 1956-58, New Sch. for Social Research, 1968; m. (George) Byron Browne, July 16, 1940; 1 son, Stephen Bernard. Executed murals, N.Y.C., 1936-39; exhibited nationally, 1936-40; exhibited Am. Fedn. Arts Exhbn., 1972-73; art critic, reviewer Pictures on Exhibit, 1946-51, N.Y. Star, 1948-49, Art News, 1949, 64-72; art tchr., lectr., 1935—; art perception tchr. New Sch. for Social Research, N.Y.C., 1966—; cons., writer Nat. Endowment for Arts project, 1968-72; lectr. Drew U., 1970, Wagner Coll., 1969, many others exhibited in group shows Am. Abstract Artists anns., 1937-40, ACA Gallery, N.Y.C., 1939, Zabriskie Gallery, N.Y.C., 1972, Washburn Gallery, N.Y.C., 1974, Mus. U. N.M., 1974, others. Mem. Am. Abstract Artists (charter mem., chmn. exhbn. com. 1936-39), Artists Equity Assn. N.Y., Coll. Art Assn. Am. Contbr. many articles to various publs. Address: 203 W 86th St New York City NY 10024

BROWNELL, BERYL ANN, editor; b. Valparaiso, Ind., Aug. 28, 1919; d. Walter Ezra and Floy Gladys (Binyon) Bromwell; A.B., Ind. U., 1942. Sports editor Vidette-Messenger, Valparaiso, 1942; editor women's dept. Gary (Ind.) Post-Tribune, 1942—. Recipient J.C. Penny-U. Mo. award, 1960, 70, First Place award Nat. Fedn. Press Women, 1967, Kate Milner Rabb award Women's Press Club Ind., 1971. Mem. Ind. Women's Press Club (pres. 1968-70). Home: 703 Washington St Valparaiso IN 46383 Office: 1065 Broadway Gary IN 46402

BROWNELL, WINIFRED WATSON, educator; b. Dayton, O., June 21, 1945; d. Eric Raymond and Ethel Roberta (Blankenship) Watson; B.A., State U. N.Y. at Buffalo, 1967, M.A., 1970, Ph.D., 1973; m. Gary Grant Brownell, Mar. 30, 1968. Asst. prof. communication theory U. R.I., Kingston, 1971—. Mem. R.I. Gov.'s Adv. Commn. on Women's Legal Rights, 1971—. NSF fellow, 1971. Mem. Eastern, Internat., Speech communication assns., Am. Ednl. Research Assn., Am. Assn. U. Profs. Author: (pamphlet) Before You Buy; contbg. author Speech Monographs, 1973. Address: Dept Speech University of Rhode Island Kingston RI 02881

BROWNFIELD, LILLIAN THOMAS (MRS. WILLIAM BROWNFIELD), editor; b. Columbus, O., Nov. 29, 1916; d. Charles Alfred and Mary Jane (Evans) Thomas; grad. high sch.; m. C. William Brownfield, Nov. 29, 1938 (dec. Feb. 1971); children—C. William, Thomas A., Stephen C., John R., Margaret A. Editor, spl. writer High Spots, biweekly newspaper Ohio Credit Union League, Columbus, 1967—. Recipient awards Credit Union Nat. Assn., 1968-71. Mem. Internat. Assn. Bus. Communicators (state bd. govs. 1967—), Women in Communications, Ohio Consumers Assn. (trustee 1971), Columbus League of Women Voters (legislative chmn. 1945-46). Conglist. Home: 969 Woodhill Dr Columbus OH 43212 Office: 1201 Dublin Rd Columbus OH 43215

BROWNING, COLLEEN (MRS. GEOFFREY WAGNER), artist; b. Ireland; d. General Langley and Violet (Cairnes) Browning; student Franham Sch. Art, Slade Sch., London; m. Geoffrey Wagner, June 15, 1949. Came to U.S., 1949, naturalized, 1956. Exhibited in one-man shows at Hewitt Gallery, 1951, 54, 57, Isaacson Gallery, 1960, 62, Jacques Seligmann Gallery, 1965, Kennedy Galleries, 1969, 71; exhibited in group shows at Whitney Mus., Art. Inst. Chgo., Pa. Acad., Detroit Art Inst., U. Ill., Cleve. Inst. Art; represented in permanent collections San Francisco Palace of Legion of Honor, Detroit Art Inst., Butler Art Inst., Columbia (S.C.) Mus., Wichita Art Inst., Rochester Art Gallery, Williamstown (Mass.) Mus., Randolph Macon Women's Coll. Instr., City Coll. N.Y., 1961—. Recipient fellowship and grants Tupperware, Edwin Austen Abbey, Stacey, 1958, Yaddo, 1955, McDowell, 1956; awards N.A.D. 1953, 57, 63, Butler Art Inst., 1954, 55, 60, Stanford U., 1954, Carnegie Internat., 1953, Los Angeles County Fair, 1956, Turck and Renfield awards for best fiction book jackets, 1959, 65; Adolph and Clara Obrig prize N.A.D., 1970. Academician, N.A.D. (council 1969—). Illustrator: Best in Children's Books; Portrait of A Lady, 1966, Pioneers and Patriots, 1966, Worth Fighting For, 1965; Every Man Heart Lay Down, 1970. Home: 100 La Salle St New York City NY 10027

BROWNING, NORMA LEE (MRS. RUSSELL J. OGG), journalist; b. Spickard, Mo., Nov. 24, 1914; d. Howard R. and Grace (Kennedy) Browning; B.J., U. Mo., 1937, A.B. with distinction in English, 1937; M.A., Radcliffe Coll., 1938; m. Russell J. Ogg, June 12, 1938. Reporter-feature writer Chgo. Tribune, 1944—; contbr. to Sat. Eve. Post, Reader's Digest mags.; lectr. news and travel Colston Leigh Bur., 1957—. Editorial cons. Nat. Music Camp, Interlochen (Mich.) Arts Acad., 1960—, also faculty adviser in journalism; editorial cons. Interlochen (Mich.) Art Acad. Recipient E. S. Beck award in reporting Chgo. Tribune for series investigating med. quacks, 1949. Mem. Mortar Bd. (pres. 1937), Theta Sigma Phi, Kappa Tau Alpha, Alpha Chi Omega. Author: City Girl in the Country, 1955; Joe Maddy of Interlochen, 1963; (with W. Clement Stone) The Other Side of the Mind, 1965. Contbr. to nat. mags. Home: 226 Marongo Rd Palm Springs CA 92292 Office: The Chgo Tribune Chicago IL 60611

BROWNLEE, GWYN SCOTT (MRS. GEORGE H. BROWNLEE), ednl. adminstr.; b. Lakeview, Tex., July 5, 1928; d. James Robert and Prudie Beatrice (Crowder) Scott; B.S., Howard Payne Coll., 1948; M.Ed., N. Tex. State U., 1963; m. George H. Brownlee, May 30, 1946; children—Susan (Mrs. Don Snowden), Sarah (Mrs. Pat Tynes), Lynnlee. Tchr. pub. schs., Rosebud, Tex., 1948-50, Weatherford, Tex., 1951-53, Pearsall, Tex., 1953-55, Lancaster, Tex., 1955-61; elementary supr. Lancaster (Tex.) Pub. schs., 1962-63, dir. curriculum, 1963-65, dir. fed. programs, 1965-67; dir. acad. services Region X Edn. Service Center, Richardson, 1967—, dir. Title III grant, 1965-67. Mem. N.E.A., Assn. Supervision and Curriculum Devel. (rep. 1970-72, bd. dirs.), Nat. Elementary Sch. Prins., Tex. Tchrs. Assn., Tex. Assn. Supervision and Curriculum Devel. (dir. 1969-72). Baptist. Author: Our Family of Men, social studies series K-6, 1971. Home: 4018 Williamsburg St Dallas TX 75220 Office: Box 1300 Richardson TX 75080

BROWNSON, ANNA LOUISE HARSHMAN (MRS. CHARLES B. BROWNSON), editor; b. Indpls., May 4, 1926; d. Walter W. and Jennie Andrea (Jensen) Harshman; B.A., Butler U., 1949, postgrad., 1950-51; m. Charles B. Brownson, Nov. 23, 1966; children—Dwight, Bruce, David, Catharine, Scott. Asst. biochemistry lab. Ind. U. Med. Sch., Indpls., 1944-47; grad. asst. Butler U., Indpls., 1949-51; adminstrv. asst. to U.S. congressman from 11th Dist. Ind., Indpls., 1951-58; asso. editor, treas. Congl. Staff Directory, Washington, 1959—; asso. Charles Brownson Assos., govtl. and assn. counselors, Washington, 1959—; pub., owner, editor (with husband) Advance Locator for Capitol Hill, 1963—, Election Index, 1966—. Mem. Washington Butler Alumni (sec. 1950—), Former Mems. Congress Aux., Corcoran Art Gallery, Smithsonian Assos., Internat. Oceanographic Found., Kappa Alpha Theta. Presbyn. Home: 1261 S Alhambra Circle Coral Gables FL 33134 Office: 4748 Neptune Dr Alexandria VA 22309

BROWNSON, SHIRLEY MARIE BREMAN (MRS. WAYNE ALAN BROWNSON), mus. ofcl.; b. Syracuse, N.Y., Aug. 8, 1950; d. Donald Frank and Helen Marie (Lutz) Breman; B.A. in History, Hartwick Coll., 1972; m. Wayne Alan Brownson, Apr. 8, 1972. Sec. Gallery Assn. N.Y. State, Inc., Syracuse, 1972; asst. for edn. Canal Mus., Syracuse, 1972-73, asso. for edn., 1973—. Del. N.Y. State Square and Round Dance Fedn., 1973. Mem. N.E.A., Nat. Hist. Soc., Phi Alpha Theta. Club: Paris N Squares Modern Square Dance (Syracuse). Home: 8114 Brook Hollow Bridgeport NY 13030 Office: Canal Mus Weighlock Bldg Erie Blvd East Syracuse NY 13202

BROYHILL, ARLINE W. STEWART (MRS. ROY F. BROYHILL), business exec.; b. Sholes, Neb., Feb. 2, 1921; d. Clarence A. and Sophia (Wriedt) Stewart; student pub. schs., South Sioux City, Neb.; m. Roy F. Broyhill, Jan. 30, 1943; children—Lynn Diann (dec.), Craig G., Kent B., Bryce A. Legal sec. Malcolm R. Smith, Dakota City, Neb., 1940-46; v.p. Broyhill Co., Dakota City, 1946-66, exec. v.p., 1966—; pres. Broyhill Corp., 1953—; sec. Star Printing and Pub. Co., Inc., South Sioux City, 1949—. Publicity chmn. Dakota County Republican Com. Mem. Farm Equipment Mfrs. Assn., P.E.O. Republican. Mem. Order Eastern Star, Shrine Aux. Home: 1610 Broadway Dakota City NE 68731 Office: Broyhill Co N Market Sq Dakota City NE 68731

BROYLES, IRENE MARIE, coll. adminstr.; b. Chgo., Apr. 12, 1922; d. Thomas William and Mary (Safranek) Krenek; B.S. in Edn., Miami U., Oxford, O., 1944, M.A. in History, 1945; m. Carlos William Broyles, June 20, 1948; children—James W., Barbara Ellen. Tchr. bus. Richmond (Ind.) High Sch., 1944-46; with Nat. Park Service, 1946-47, U.S. Naval Supply Center, Oakland, Cal., 1947-49; tchr. adult edn., Alameda, Cal., 1947-49; adult edn. tchr., substitute tchr. San Diego pub. schs., 1952-54; mem. faculty San Diego City Coll., 1954-64, asst. dean students, 1962-64; instr. bus., also counselor Mesa Coll., San Diego, 1964-66, counselor, coordinator student affairs, 1966—. Treas. Farragut Sch. P.T.A., 1950-51; sec. Linda Vista Improvement Assn., 1955-56; bd. dirs. San Diego Jr. Theatre, 1959-67, box office chmn., 1962-67, sec., 1961-63. Recipient Woman of Year award Mesa Assn. Women Students, 1972. Mem. Cal. Assn. Women Adminstrs. and Counselors (newsletter editor 1973-74, chmn. So. region 1974-76), San Diego Am. Assn. U. Women (chpt. newsletter editor 1973-75), Am., Cal. personnel and guidance assns., Cal. Tchrs. Assn., N.E.A., Miami Alumni Assn. San Diego (pres. 1974-76), Faculty Assn. Cal. Community Colls., Cal. Community Colls. Activity Adminstrs. Assn., Nat. Assn. Women Deans, Adminstrs. and Counselors, Zeta Tau Alpha (pres. San Diego 1959-61), Delta Kappa Gamma, Theta Alpha Delta. Presbyn. (elder 1967-70). Mem. Order Eastern Star. Home: 2414 Murray Ridge Rd San Diego CA 92123

BROYLES, MABEL ELIZABETH GRUBBS, writer; b. Hopkinsville, Ky., Apr. 2, 1916; d. Andrew Jackson and Georgia Anne (Burke) Grubbs; student pub. schs.; m. Horace Clinton Broyles, Jr., Nov. 30, 1933 (dec. 1958); children—Anne (Mrs. Harry Stroman Bagnal), Julia (Mrs. James Ellis Chandler). Co-owner Davidson Printing Co., Davidson, N.C., 1947-58, owner, 1958-67; editor Mecklenburg Gazette, Davidson, 1948-67, asso. editor, 1967-70; editor TarHeel Woman state mag. Bus. and Profl. Women's Club, N.C., 1957-58; free lance writer, 1970—. Vice chmn. Republican party, Davidson, 1970-72. Address: 3231 Moorewood Dr Nashville TN 37207

BRUCE, CAROLINE HAGEMAN (MRS. HENRY A. BRUCE), ret. army officer, artist; b. Woodward, Okla., Sept. 1, 1907; d. John and Caroline (Obringer) Hageman; student Ark. A. and M. Coll., 1926-29; diploma St. Bernard's Sch. Nursing, 1929; certificate Nat. Art Sch., Washington, 1949; postgrad. Corcoran Art Sch., 1951-52, Student Art Students League, 1954-56, Nat. Acad. Art Sch., N.Y.C., 1957-58; m. Henry A. Bruce, Dec. 24, 1949. Commd. 2d lt. U.S. Army, 1930, advanced through grades to lt. col., 1947, chief nurse Nurses Tng. Center, Ft. Rucker, Ala., 1943-45, ret., 1947; artist portraits, Washington, 1958—; exhibited in shows at Masters Art Gallery, N.Y.C., 1956, 57, 58, Colonial Art Gallery, Alexandria, Va., 1960, 61, Miami Beach Art Gallery, 1954, 55. Decorated Commendation medal. Mem. Art Students League, No. Va. Art League, Nat. League Am. Pen Women (past nat. auditor), Am. Legion. Republican. Roman Catholic. Home: 110 Center St Winter Haven FL 33880 also 2020 N Atlantic Av Cocoa Beach FL 32931

BRUCE, LEONA BANISTER (MRS. CHARLES DANIEL BRUCE), author; b. Santa Anna, Tex., July 11, 1899; d. John Riley and Emma Daugherty (Dougherty) Banister; grad. high sch.; m. Charles Daniel Bruce, Apr. 22, 1923; children—Margaret (Mrs. Tom Robin), Evelyn (Mrs. Jack Kingsbery), Barbara (Mrs. Tom Kingsbery). Acting dep. sheriff Coleman County, Tex., 1916-18; tchr. rural schs., Coleman and Junction, Tex., 1918-23; acting postmaster, Santa Anna, Tex., 1955-58. Pres., P.T.A., 1936-38. Dist. vice-chmn.

Tex. Republican party, 1953-54; vice-chmn. Coleman County Rep. Com., 1950-53. Mem. Am. Legion Aux. (sec. 1920-21), West Tex., Edwards Plateau (pres. 1973-75) hist. assns., Tex. Fedn. Women's Clubs (dist. pres. 1942-45), Delta Kappa Gamma. Baptist (dir. pre-sch. 1934-74). Author: Trickham, Texas, 1966; Banister Was There, 1968; They Came in Peace, 1970; First Lady on Home Creek, 1973. Home: Box 335 Santa Anna TX 76878

BRUCE, MARCELLA FRANCES MARTIN (MRS. KENNETH BAIRD BRUCE), newspaper pub.; b. Pino Grande, Cal., Aug. 12, 1916; d. Wallace Perry and Ida Camille (Tripp) Martin; Asso. Fine Arts, Cottey Coll., 1935; Mus.B., Bethany Coll., 1937, B. Music Edn., 1937; pvt. study voice Sherwood Music Sch., Chgo., 1937-38; m. Kenneth Baird Bruce, June 28, 1941; children—Kenneth Martin, Marcia Sue (Mrs. Glenn Wiederstein). Tchr. music Sedgwick (Kan.) pub. schs., 1939-41, Marquette (Kan.) pub. schs., 1943-44, 47-50; co-editor, pub. Marquette (Kan.) Tribune, 1946-53, Hillsboro (Kan.) Star-Jour., 1954—. Sec. Kan. Fedn. Rep. Women, 4th Dist., 1974—. Mem. Kan. Press Assn., Kan. Press Women (sec. 1972-74), C. of C. Hillsboro (dir. 1973—), Sigma Alpha Iota (life). Methodist. Mem. Order Eastern Star. Club: Mentor Study (pres. 1956-58) (Hillsboro, Kan.). Home: 809 W Grand St Hillsboro KS 67063 Office: 104 S Main St Hillsboro KS 67063

BRUCE, MRS. RUDOLPH (PEGGY BRUCE), civic leader; b. Boston, Sept. 3, 1912; d. Charles Bartholomew and Mary (Days) O'Neil; A.B., Boston U., 1933; m. Rudolph Bruce, Apr. 9, 1937 (dec. 1964); children—Robert B., Douglas S., Heather. Pub. realtions dir. Longy Sch. Music, Cambridge, Mass., 1966-70. Bd. dirs., pres. League Women Voters, Wayland, Mass., 1948-55, sec. Mass. chpt., 1953-55, pres., 1955-57, mem. bd., 1957-65; pub. relations Vokes Theatre, Inc., 1959—; bd. dirs. Weston Drama Workshop, 1964-66; judge Mass. UN Essay Contest, 1956; guardian Sponsor Campfire Girls; mem. Wayland Com. Fair Housing Practices, 1962—; mem. Gov.'s Adv. Com. Mass. Mental Health Planning Project, 1964-65. Mem. Wayland Democratic Town Com., 1968—. Trustee L. William Bertelsen Meml. Scholarship Fund Minority Students, 1974—. Mem. Sigma Kappa. Author: (with others) Massachusetts State Government, A Citizen's Handbook, 1956; The First Fifty, 1970; also TV scripts. Home: 46 Plain Rd Wayland MA 01778

BRUCH, VIRGINIA IRENE SULLIVAN (MRS. TRUMAN ELWOOD BRUCH), librarian; b. Hickman, Ky., May 26, 1921; d. Thomas Terrell and Virginia Irene (Helm) Sullivan; B.S., Murray U., 1943; m. Truman Elwood Bruch, Feb. 18, 1944; 1 dau., Susan Irene (Mrs. Richard Lyons Rose). Librarian, Union City (Tenn.) High Sch., 1943-44; librarian, cataloger FTC, Washington, 1949-55; librarian, cataloger Army Library, Washington, 1955-65, chief catalog sect., 1965-71, chief tech. services br., 1971—. Recipient prize Fed. Poet, 1956. Mem. Spl. Libraries Assn., A.L.A. Mem. Christian Ch. (librarian 1960-72). Contbr. to Am. Poetry mag., Poet Lore, Driftwood, Christian Herald, Fed. Poet, Badge of Honor. Home: 15 W Howell Av Alexandria VA 22301 Office: Army Library Room 1A522 Pentagon Washington DC 20310

BRUEMMER, MARY ADELE, univ. ofcl.; b. Madison, Ill., Feb. 26, 1920; d. Ignatius George and Adele M. (Bergrath) Bruemmer; A.B. in Edn., St. Louis U., 1938-42, M.Ed., 1960. Dir. Cath. Youth Orgns., Springfield, Ill., 1943-48; dir. continuity dept. Radio Sta. WCVS, 1948-53; dir. publicity Lincoln Library, 1953-55; dir. adult edn. dept. Springfield Coll. in Ill., 1955-56; dir. Marguerite Hall, St. Louis U., 1956-59, dir. women's housing, 1959-67, dean of women, 1967-73, asst. v.p. student devel., dean of women, 1973—. Mem. Nat. Mo. (sec.-treas. 1958-64, pres. 1971—) assns. women deans and counselors, Am. Assn. U. Women, Assn. Coll. Personnel Adminstrs., Am. Personnel and Guidance Assn., Am. Assn. for Higher Edn. Roman Catholic. Address: 300 Mansion House Center St Louis MO 63102

BRUÈRE, KATHARINE JANE BECKER (MRS. RICHARD T. BRUÈRE), librarian; b. Chgo., July 2, 1918; d. Robert Wilson and Katharine Eaton (Critchell) Morris; B.S., U. Chgo., 1940; M.S., U. Wis., 1966; m. Richard T. Bruère, Mar. 17, 1973; 1 dau. by previous marriage, Katharine Elizabeth. Asst. to dir. adminstrn. U. Chgo., 1940-48; asst. dir. alumni placement bur. Mass. Inst. Tech., Cambridge, 1948-49; library cons., dir. instructional materials center Abraham Lincoln Middle Sch., Madison, Wis., 1966—, also mem. book selection com. Madison Sch. System, 1966—. Vol., Madison Gen. Hosp. Aux., 1953-60; fund raiser Community Chest, also March Dimes, Mental Health Assn., 1952-70. Mem. Madison Art Assn., Am., Wis. library assns., Nat., Wis., Southeastern Wis. (head library sect. 1971-73) edn. assns., Wis. Audiovisual Assn., League Women Voters (dir. pub. relations Madison area 1955-60), Madison Tchrs., Phi Beta Kappa. Methodist. Club: Civics (Madison). Home: 4015 Hammersley Av Madison WI 53705 Office: Abraham Lincoln Middle School 909 Sequoia Trail Madison WI 53713

BRUFF, BEVERLY OLIVE, assn. adminstr.; b. San Antonio, Dec. 15, 1926; d. Albert Griffith and Hazel Olive (Smith) Bruff; B.A., H. Sophie Newcomb Coll., 1948; postgrad. Our Lady of the Lake Coll., 1956, Okla. Center for Continuing Edn., 1960-70. Asst. dir. New Orleans Theatre Guild, 1948-50; dist. dir. San Antonio Area Council, Girl Scouts U.S.A., 1958-70, pub. relations dir., 1970—. Mem. Council of Presidents, 1971, Council of Internat. Relations, 1971. Zoning commr. Hill Country Village, Tex., 1973—. Mem. Assn. Girl Scout Profl. Workers (mem. exec. bd. 1963-72, pub. relations chmn. 1964-69, v.p. 1969-72, mem. nat. bd. dirs. 1972—, communications chmn. 1972), Tex. Pub. Relations Assn., Women in Communications (historian 1969-70, v.p. 1970-71, treas. 1971-73), Tex. Press Women (recipient state writing contest awards 1971, 72, 73, 74, mem. exec. bd. dirs. 1970-71, dist. treas. 1972-73, dist. v.p. 1973), Nat. Fedn. Press Women, Alamo Indsl. Editors Assn., Speech Arts of San Antonio (v.p. 1963-64, pres. 1964-66, 70-72, dir. 1964-72, chmn. bd. dirs. 1966-69), Am. Women in Radio and TV. Home: 508 Tomahawk Trail San Antonio TX 78232 Office: 335 King William St San Antonio TX 78204

BRUGGEMAN, MARSHA LEE, educator, b. Ft. Wayne, Ind., May 1, 1944; d. Anthony and Barbara Ann (Gordon) Bruggeman; B.S. in Eng., Ball State U., 1964, M.A., 1965; postgrad Purdue U., 1967-68. Tchr., W. Lafayette (Ind.) Sr. High Sch., 1965-66; instr. Valparaiso (Ind.) U., 1968-71; instr. Ball State U., Muncie, Ind., 1971—. Investment analyst Lincoln Life Security Co., Ft. Wayne, 1969. Mem. Am. Assn. U. Women (chmn. lit. study Valparaiso chpt. 1969-71, banquet chmn. 1970-71), Internat. Platform Assn., Kappa Delta Pi, Pi Gamma Mu, Lambda Tau Delta. Presbyn. Club: Woman's Bd. of Muncie. Home: 404 Riverside St Muncie IN 47303

BRUHN, FLORENCE MARIE CHRISTINE, educator; b. Yankton, S.D., Sept. 18, 1910; d. Henry J. and Elisabeth (Thaisen) Bruhn; B.A., U. S.D., 1939, M.A., 1942; postgrad. Temple U., Denver U., Wyo. U., Man. U., Yankton Coll. Tchr., Platte (S.D.) Rural Schs., 1933-35, Armour (S.D.) Jr. High Sch., 1935-38; tchr. English, dramatics art Watertown (S.D.) Sr. High Sch., 1939—. Tutor speech rehab., 1956-64; tchr. adult oil painting classes, 1964—. Chmn., Watertown Area Arts Council, 1970-74, S.D. Arts Council, 1971-74; designer, dir. Watertown Santa Land, 1969-74; designer Bicentennial display, 1975—. Mem. Nat., S.D. art edn. assns., Nat., Western, S.D. edn. assns., P.E.O. (local pres. 1955-57), Delta Kappa Gamma (state pres. 1973-75), Alpha Xi Delta. Home: 208 5th Av NE Watertown SD 57201

BRUKARDT, DIANE THERESE, physician, educator; b. Dearborn, Mich., Sept. 7, 1929; d. Arthur M. and Mae E. (Ayotte) Brukardt; A.B., U. Mo., 1950; B.S. in Medicine, 1952; M.D., Harvard, 1954. Intern Kansas U. Med. Center, Kansas City, Kan., 1954-55, resident 1955-57; resident U. Mo. Med. Center, Columbia, 1957-58; practice medicine specializing in internal medicine, Columbia, 1957—; physician Student Health Service U. Mo., Columbia, 1959—, asso. dir., 1968—, asst. prof. medicine, 1966—. Diplomate Am. Bd. Internal Medicine. Mem. Am., Mo. State, Boone County, So. med. assns., A.C.P., Phi Beta Kappa. Club: Altrussa (pres. 1972-73). Home: 901 Mikel Columbia MO 65201 Office: Univ of Missouri Columbia MO 65201

BRUMFIELD, BETTY JANE DIAL (MRS. ROBERT L. BRUMFIELD), newspaper editor; b. Wabash, Ark., Mar. 20, 1927; d. David McCoy and Rosalie Eggleston (Denio) Dial; grad. high sch.; m. Robert L. Brumfield, Aug. 22, 1948; children—Patricia Rosalie, E. Susan, William A. With Enterprise Jour., McComb, Miss., 1963—, woman's page editor, 1967—. Recipient awards Nat. Press Women, 1967, 70, 72. Home: 315 Burke St McComb MS 39648 Office: 109 Broadway McComb MS 39648

BRUMFIELD, MIRIAM DELORES, educator; b. Prichard, Ala., May 26, 1932; d. Earl Henry and Miriam McKay (Turner) Brumfield; B.S., Ala. Coll., 1954; M.S., U. So. Miss., 1959, Ed.D., 1969. Profl. player Am. Girls Baseball League, Ind., Wis., 1947-53; high sch. coach Shaw (Miss.) High Sch., 1954-56; instr. phys. edn. Copiah-Lincoln Jr. Coll., Wesson, Miss., 1956-63; asso. prof. dept. health, phys. edn. and recreation Henderson State Coll., Arkadelphia, Ark., 1963—. Chmn., City Recreation and Park Commn., Arkadelphia, 1972-73. Recipient Outstanding Contbns. award City of Arkadelphia chpt. Nat. Recreation and Park Assn., 1972. Mem. Am., Ark. assns. health, phys. edn. and recreation, So. Assn. Phys. Edn. for Coll. Women. Home: 1510 Evans St Arkadelphia AR 71923

BRUMMETT, CLAUDIA MAE, steel co. exec.; b. Amarillo, Tex., Feb. 28, 1927; d. Claude Jamieson and Mae (Kight) Brummett; student Amarillo Coll., 1944-46, U. Coll., 1946-48. Chief diversion and tracer clk. Santa Fe Rwy. Co., 1948-68; partner, JAL Co., JAL Ranch, Alvarado, Tex., 1968—; corp. sec., J & M Steel Co., Inc., Fort Worth, 1971—; one-man shows at Simpson Gallery, Amarillo, Tex., Square House Mus., Panhandle, Tex.; exhibited in group shows at Tex. Tech. Mus., Wichita Falls, Tex. Mus., Pan-Am. Mus., McAllen, Tex.; represented in permanent collection Carlin Gallery, Ft. Worth. Mem. State Democratic Exec. Com., 1962-70, mem. dist. exec. com., 1962-70; del. Dem. Nat. Conv., 1964, 68, 74, mem. rules com., 1964, mem. credentials com., 1968, 72; mem. del. selection commn. Dem. Nat. Com., 1973-74; co-chmn. Briscoe Campaign for Gov., 1972. Mem. Tex. Designer Craftsman, Tex. Artist, Craftsman Guild, W. Tex. C. of C., Tex. Exec. Club, Nat. Fedn. Democratic Women (2d v.p. S. Central region 1972—). Baptist. Address: JAL Ranch Box 308 Alvarado TX 76009

BRUNAUER, DALMA MARIA HUNYADI (MRS. STEPHEN BRUNAUER), educator; b. Budapest, Hungary; d. Laszlo and Dalma (Benke) Hunyadi; Ph.D. in English, U. Budapest, 1948; m. Stephen Brunauer, Jan. 6, 1961. Came to U.S., 1949, naturalized, 1955. Instr., DePaul U., Chgo., 1949-53; lectr. U. Chgo., 1953-57; asst. prof. Lewis Coll., Lockport, Ill., 1953-58, chmn. dept. English, 1955-57; instr., asst. prof., asso. prof. English, Amundsen-Mayfair br. Chgo. City Jr. Coll., 1958-65; asso. prof. humanities Clarkson Coll. Tech., Potsdam, N.Y., 1965—. Tchr., Sta. WTTW-TV, Chgo., 1960, 63, 65, Sta. WIND, Chgo., 1962-63. Sec., Conf. on Christianity and Lit., 1973—. Mem. Modern Lang. Assn., Am. Assn. U. Profs., Modern Humanities Research Assn., Soc. for Arts, Religion and Contemporary Culture, Internat. Platform Assn. Author: World Literature in Translation, 1960. Editor: Literature and Religion: Albee and Beckett, 1971; (with David Stouck) Willa Cather 1873-1973, 1973. Contbr. to New Catholic Ency., 1967, articles to profl. jours. Home: 39 Chestnut St Potsdam NY 13676

BRUNDAGE, GLORIA MARGUARITE, educator; b. Kansas City, Kan.; d. Eugene Henry and Sibyl (Betts) Swegman; student Washburn U., 1946-49; B.S., Columbia, 1951, M.S., 1952; postgrad. Am. Theater Wing, 1951, South Tex. Coll. Law, 1963-64; Ph.D., N.Y. U., 1969; m. Harrison T. Brundage, Apr. 5, 1957 (div. Dec. 1966); 1 son, Bruce Harrison. Traffic asst. program dept. NBC, 1943-44; information specialist U. Md. Extension, 1944; trainee Am. Newspaper Guild, 1944-45; staff various newspapers, 1945-49, 52-53; research asst. citizenship edn. project Columbia U., 1950-51; instr. journalism Miss. So. Coll., 1953-54; textbook editor Am. Inst. Banking, 1955-56; copywriter Doremus & Co., 1956; adminstrv. asst. pres.'s office L.I.U., 1958; ednl. TV coordinator Smithtown (N.Y.) sch. dist., 1958-59; sr. engring. writer Rep. Aviation, 1959-60; free lance writer, Houston, 1960-64; asst. prof. State U. Coll. N.Y. at Potsdam, 1964-67; asst. prof. pub. relations Boston U., 1967-69, U. Dayton (O.), 1969-71; asst. prof. journalism Marquette U., Milw., 1971—. Vis. prof. community edn. program for dental hygienists Tufts U., 1967-68; producer ednl. TV series, 1954; mem. Nat. Ednl. Adv. Council, exec. bd. Grad. Students Orgn. Com. mem. Boy Scouts Am., Brookline, Mass., 1967-69; sec. CLEAN, Inc., 1972—. Mem. state bd. Kan. Young Republicans, 1948-49; writer Citizens for Eisenhower, 1952. Mem. Assn. Edn. in Journalism, Am. Assn. U. Profs., Speech Communications Assn. (sec. polit. communications div.), Internat. Communications Assn. (officer polit. communications div.), Pub. Relations Soc. Am. (mem. ednl. adv. council 1973—), D.A.R. (chpt. publicity dir. 1962-63), Internat. House, Internat. Platform Assn., Women in Communications (v.p. Southeastern Wis. chpt. 1973—), Kappa Delta Pi. Unitarian-Universalist (publicity dir. 1960-62). Mem. editorial bd. Quarto, 1950-51. Contbr. articles and short stories to publs. Home: PO Box 1094 621 Main St West Dennis MA 02670 Office: College of Journalism Marquette University 1135 W Kilbourn Av Milwaukee WI 53233

BRUNDAGE, MARJORIE UNDERWOOD (MRS. RICHARD K. BRUNDAGE), cons.; b. Bellefontaine, O., Feb. 5, 1940; d. James Madison and Louise (Mustaine) Underwood; B.S., Bowling Green State U., 1962; m. Richard K. Brundage, Dec. 20, 1967; children—Jennie Lee and Judith Lynn (twins). Systems engr. Internat. Bus. Machines, Toledo, 1962-63; with Kaiser Jeep Corp., Toledo, 1963-64; systems programmer Lazarus Dept. Store, Columbus, O., 1964-66; with Ohio State U., Columbus, 1966—, data processing cons. labor edn. div., 1973—. Violinist, Civic Orch., Columbus, 1966—, mem. planning com. 1972—. Mem. Bowling Green State U. Alumni Assn. Presbyn. Home: 328 Glenmont Av Columbus OH 43214 Office: Ohio State University 111 Page Hall Columbus OH 43210

BRUNDAGE, THELMA MARIE BROWNING (MRS. SAMUEL W. BRUNDAGE), realtor; b. Kansas City, Kan., Nov. 8, 1910; d. Charles M. and Mary Anna Marie (Kister) Browning; student U. Denver, 1948-49; m. Samuel W. Brundage, May 9, 1928; children—Ann (Mrs. Richard Lydenberg), Berton, Barbara Jo (Mrs. Norman Baston), Samuel Charles. Rep. Cal. Western States Life Ins. Co., Denver, 1948-51; with N.Y. Life Ins. Co., 1951-54, rep. Denver, 1951-53, Colorado Springs, Colo., 1953-54; with King Merritt and Co., Investments, 1954-61, El Paso, Tex., 1954-59, Phoenix, 1959-61; owner, dir. Thelma Brundage Real Estate Co., Phoenix, 1966—; v.p. Interstate Land Co., Phoenix, 1961. Vol. Heart Assn., 1959-64, United Fund, 1961-62. Mem. Am. Arbitration Assn., 1967—; mem. Service Corps of Ret. Execs. of Small Bus. Adminstrn., pres. 1968-70, counselor 1967—. Mem. Bus. and Profl. Women's Club, Navy League U.S., Am. Bus. Womens Assn. Mem. Ch. Christian Philosophy (bd. mem. 1968-73). Mem. Order Eastern Star. Home: 4325 Calle Feliz Phoenix AZ 85018 Office: 901 W McDowell Road Phoenix AZ 85007

BRUNDIGE, LINDA ANN, journalist, photographer; b. South Gate, Cal., Dec. 3, 1946; d. Ernest R. and Mary Elisabeth (James) Brundige; B.A. in Journalism, Cal. State U., Long Beach, 1969. Staff photographer Los Angeles Herald Examiner, 1972—. Instr. judo, Huntington Park, Cal., since 1970. First degree Black Belt Judo and jiujitsu expert. Mem. Women in Communications, Nat. Rifle Assn., Am. Ju Jitsu Inst., Nanka Kodokan Judo Yudanshakai, Amateur Athletic Assn., Alpha Phi Gamma. Office: 1111 S Broadway St Los Angeles CA 90015

BRUNER, LOUISE KATHERINE EISELE (MRS. RAYMOND A. BRUNER), journalist; b. Cleve., June 13, 1910; d. Charles and Martha Magdalene (Bashold) Eisele; B.A., Denison U., 1931; postgrad. U. Toledo, 1958-62, Mary Manse Coll., 1962-64, Bowling Green State U., 1968—; m. Raymond A. Bruner, Nov. 22, 1937 (dec. Sept. 1970); children—Madelin, Sylvia (Mrs. Jacques Navarro), Suzanne. Columnist, art critic Cleve. News, 1935-50; instr. Cleve. Coll., Case Western Reserve U., 1945-46; lectr. U. Fla., 1950-52; syndicated columnist, art editor Toledo Blade, 1953—; instr. U. Toledo, 1971—. Lectr. art Mus. Cin., J.B. Speed Mus. Art, Louisville, Toledo Mus. Art, U. Fla., Cleve. Inst. Art, 1969—. Trustee U. Toledo Library. Am. Fedn. Arts-Nat. Council Arts grantee, 1968; recipient Alumni citation, Denison U., 1971. First Prizes Critical writing Ohio Newspaper Women's Assn., 1955, 58-59, 61-62, 66-67, 69. Mem. Toledo Artists Club (trustee 1962—), Toledo Modern Art Group (trustee 1968—), Archaeol. Soc. (trustee Toledo chpt. 1960—), Art Interests, Inc. (trustee 1969—). Alpha Phi. Unitarian. Clubs: Detroit Press, Toledo Press. Contbr. to Am. Artist, Arts, Art News, Antiques; corr. The Art Gallery. Home: 2200 Scottwood St Toledo OH 43620 Office: Superior St Toledo OH 43604

BRUNGOT, HILDA CONSTANCE FREDERIKKA JOHNSON, real estate exec.; d. Hans Christian and Sara-Nora (Johan-Datter) Johnson; grad. high sch.; m. Sivert Brungot, Oct. 7, 1905 (dec. Sept. 1963); children—Constance Martin, Clarence Norman, Melvin, George, Nora (Mrs. Ven Revere Beasley). Owner real estate co., Berlin, N.H., 1950—. Justice of peace, Berlin, 1950—; notary public, Berlin, 1950—; rep. to Gen. Ct., Berlin, 1931—, sr. mem. judiciary com., 1937—; dean of Women Legislators in U.S.A., 1965—; chmn. Coos County delegation, 1953, 55, 57; chmn. Coos County Finance Com., 1949-71; del. N.H. Constl. Conv., 1930, 38, 48, 56, 64, 74. Named Outstanding Career Woman, No. N.H. Bus. and Profl. Women's Club, 1968. Mem. Order Women Legislators, V.F.W. Club, Women's Relief Corp., Am. Legion Aux., Grange, Skandinavian Frat. of Am. Lutheran. Club: LeChalet-Snowshoe (Berlin, N.H.). Address: 1285 Main St Berlin NH 03570

BRUNING, FRANCES LOUISE FRIDELL (MRS. VIRGIL LEE BRUNING), occupational therapist; b. Robinson, Kan., May 12, 1927; d. Ralph George and Maymie Opal (Gruver) Fridell; B.S. in Occupational Therapy, U. Kan., 1949; m. Virgil Lee Bruning, Sept. 2, 1950; children—Daniel Lee, Lynn Louise, Lee Ellen. Intern Cherokee (Ia.) State Hosp., 1948, Michael Reese Hosp., Chgo., 1949, Denver Children's Hosp., 1948, Robert Koch Sanitorium, St. Louis, 1948; initiator, supr. occupational therapy dept. Halstead Hosp.-Hertzler Clinic, Halstead, Kan., 1949-51, Menorah Med. Center, Kansas City, Mo., 1951-55, 60-61, George H. Nettleton Home, Kansas City, Mo., 1966-72, supr. occupational therapy Yuille Retirement Home, Kansas City, Mo., part-time, 1968-71, sec., treas., 1969—. Den mother Boy Scouts Am., Grandview, Mo., 1964-65; active P.T.A., Grandview, 1969—. Mem. Am. Occupational Therapy Assn. Republican. Mem. Christian Ch. Mem. Order Eastern Star. Home: 4704 E 139th St Grandview MO 64030

BRUNNER, LILLIAN SHOLTIS (MRS. MATHIAS J. BRUNNER), author, educator; b. Freeland, Pa.; d. Andrew J. and Anna (Tomasko) Sholtis; R.N., U. Pa. Sch. Nursing Hosp., 1940, B.S., 1945; M.S., Western Res. U., 1947; m. Mathias J. Brunner, Sept. 8, 1951; children—Janet Lillian, Carol Ann, Douglas Mathias. Head nurse gen. surgery U. Pa. Hosp., 1940-42, supr. operating rooms, 1942-45, head nursing arts dept. Sch. Nursing, 1945-46; surg. supr. Grace-New Haven Community Hosp., asst. prof. surg. nursing Yale Sch. Nursing, 1947-51; instr., lectr., cons. Bryn Mawr (Pa.) Sch. Nursing, 1955-66; mem. nursing adv. bd. Hosp. U. Pa. Sch. Nursing, 1956-72, Bryn Mawr Hosp. Sch. Nursing, 1958—, Presbyn.-U. Pa. Med. Center, 1973—; sec. Neighborhood League Nursing Service, Wayne, Pa., 1971-73. Member Am. Nurses Assn., Nat. League for Nursing, Assn. Operating Room Nurses, Am. Med. Writers Assn., Am. Assn. Critical Care Nurses, Nat. League Am. Pen Women, Pi Lambda Theta, Pi Gamma Mu, Sigma Theta Tau. Author: (with Eldridge L. Eliason and L. Kraeer Ferguson) Surgical Nursing, 9th edit., 1950, 10th edit., 1955; (with Jane S. Bragdon) Teaching Medical and Surgical Nursing, 1955; (with Ferguson) Eliason's Surgical Nursing, 11th edit., 1959; (with Bragdon) Art of Clinical Instruction, 1961; (with others) Textbook of Medical and Surgical Nursing, 1964, 2d edit., 1970; (with Frances Ginsburg and Vernita L. Cantlin) Manual of Operating Room Technology, 1966; (with Suddarth) Lippincott Manual of Nursing Practice, 1974. Guest editor Nursing Clinics of North America, Phila., 1968. Contbr. numerous articles to profl. jours. Home: 1247 Berwyn Paoli Rd Berwyn PA 19312

BRUNO, JOANNA, soprano. Former apprentice artist; made European debut in 1969 at Spoleto Festival as Monica in Menotti's The Medium, 1969, repeated role in 1970; made debut with Santa Fe Opera in 1970 as Anne Trulove in The Rake's Progress; made debut as Mimi in La Boheme with Netherlands Opera, 1970, engaged to appear with them again in 1971-72 season; sang world premiere performanced with N.Y.C. Opera of Menotti's The Most Important Man, 1971. Address: care Santa Fe Opera Taos Hwy Santa Fe NM 87501

BRUNO, MARIAN IONE HOPKINS (MRS. THOMAS R. BRUNO), occupational therapist; b. Van Buren, Ark., May 16, 1918; d. William Huskinson and Ione Marian (Roberts) Hopkins; B.A. in Sociology, Wichita U., 1941; Diploma in Occupational and Recreational Therapy, Washington U., St. Louis, 1943; m. Thomas R. Bruno, June 21, 1943; children—Gail Ann (Mrs. Carl Main), Linda Lee (Mrs. Ross Nye Giem). Occupational therapist Pinecrest Nursing Home, Manchester and Ballwin, Mo., 1943-45; with Malcolm Bliss Mental Health Center St. Louis, 1958—, dir. occupational and recreational therapy, 1960—. Cons., advisor on satellite clinics, 1970; asst. coordination Malcolm Bliss Mental Health Center Aux., 1963; mem. med. records com. Malcolm Bliss Mental Health Center, 1972.

Mem. Nat., Mo. occupational therapy assns., Nat. Parks and Recreation Assn., Mo. Parks and Recreation Assn. (sec. 1969), Liederkranz Singing Soc., Nat. Assn. Activity Therapy Rehab. Program Dirs. Presbyn. (chmn. women's circle 1950-52). Mem. Order Eastern Star. Home: 3256 California Av St Louis MO 63118 Office: 1420 Grattan St St Louis MO 63104

BRUNS, JUANITA ANN (MRS. WILLIAM GILMORE BRUNS), occupational therapist; b. Wapakoneta, O., Feb. 4, 1941; d. George Christian and Phyllis Juanita (Turner) Wehner; B.S., Mt. Mary Coll., Milw., 1963; m. William Gilmore Bruns, May 2, 1964; children—Edward William, Daniel Patrick. Occupational therapist VA Hosp., Danville, Ill., 1964-65; occupational therapist, dept. supr., organizer Ball Meml. Hosp., Muncie, Ind., 1965-67; occupational therapist, cons. Ind. regional med. program—stroke Ind. U., Indpls., 1969-72, Vis. Nurse Assn., Muncie, 1972, Blackford County Hosp., Hartford City, Ind., 1972—. Active, Meals on Wheels, 1971-73, Muncie Civic Theatre, Muncie Womens Symphony League, Ball Meml. Hosp. Aux., WIPB-TV Subscription Drive; capt. Mothers March, 1970. Com. chmn. Young Republicans, 1969. Bd. dirs. Hawthorne Woods Coop. Nursery Sch., 1971-72, v.p., 1974—. Mem. Am., Ind. occupational therapy assns., Ind. Lawyers Wives, Muncie Lawyers Wives Club (pres. 1968-69), Muncie Jr. C. of C. (1st v.p. 1970-71), St. Marys Womens Assn. Roman Catholic. Club: Halteman Village (v.p. Muncie). Home: 2003 W Purdue Rd Muncie IN 47304 Office: 503 E Van Cleve St Hartford City IN 47348

BRUNS, LINDA MARIE, librarian; b. Herrin, Ill., Apr. 22, 1946; d. Bernard Richard and Cora Marie (Blythe) Bruns; B.A., So. Ill. U., 1967; M.L.S., U. Ill., 1968. Librarian, Am. Oil Co., Whiting, Ind., 1968-69, staff librarian, 1969-70; staff librarian Standard Oil Co. (Ind.), Naperville, Ill., 1970—. Mem. Spl. Libraries Assn. (sec. petroleum div. 1971-72, div. chmn. 1975-76), Beta Phi Mu. Home: 1342 S Finley Rd Lombard IL 60148 Office: PO Box 400 Naperville IN 60540

BRUNSON, RUTH HUSKEY (MRS. JOHN HOWARD BRUNSON), educator, lawyer, law librarian; b. Prescott, Ark., June 22, 1916; d. Hampton Henry and Ollie Mae (Stewart) Huskey; A.A., Central Coll., Conway, Ark., 1935; grad. Draughons Sch. Bus., 1938; LL.B. with honors, U. Ark., 1941; m. John Howard Brunson, Oct. 2, 1943 (dec. Aug. 1959). Admitted to Ark. bar., 1941; practiced in Prescott, 1950-55; mem. firm Brunson & Brunson, 1950-55; with U.S. Engrs., Salzburg, Austria, 1955-61; law clk. to Ark. Supreme Ct. Justice, Little Rock, 1961-65; law librarian U. Ark., Little Rock, 1965—. Prof. legal bibliography, 1965—. Mem. Ark., Pulaski County Bar Assns., Ark. Law Rev. Bd., Ark. Assn. Women Lawyers, Am. Assn. Law Libraries (pres. S.W. chpt. 1972-74), Phi Alpha Delta, Kappa Beta Pi. Home: 6712 Greenwood Rd Little Rock AR 72207

BRUSILOFF, PHYLLIS HABER (MRS. EUGENE M. BRUSILOFF), psychotherapist, educator; b. N.Y.C., June 6, 1935; d. Benjamin and Belle (Simon) Haber; B.A., Bklyn. Coll., 1959; M.S., Yeshiva U., 1962; m. Eugene M. Brusiloff, Apr. 11, 1964; children—Paul, Amy. Dir. nursery sch., also ednl. therapist League Sch. for Seriously Disturbed Children, Bklyn., 1959-64; therapist Hudson Guild, N.Y.C., 1968-71; group therapist, also supr. Jewish Bd. Guardians, Child Devel. Center, N.Y.C., 1971—; adj. lectr. Coll. City of N.Y., 1973—. Cons. and lectr. to nursery schs., 1970—. Mem. Great Neck Econogical Com., 1969-71. Mem. Am. Orthopsychiat. Assn. Jewish religion. Author: Emerging Child, 1973. Home: 54 Berkshire Rd Great Neck NY 11023 Office: Child Development Center 120 W 57th St New York City NY 10019

BRUSON, VIRGINIA HABER (MRS. HERMAN A. BRUSON), civic worker; b. Cleve.; d. Jacob and Dollie (Weiner) Haber; B.A., Wellesley Coll., 1928; m. Herman A. Bruson, Mar. 30, 1929; children—Rita (Mrs. Joseph Peaslee), Dorothy (Mrs. John Govalia), Barbara (Mrs. Michael Burns). Vol., USCG, 1943-45, A.R.C. Motor Corp., 1945-52; chmn. Am. Cancer Soc., North Haven, 1953-59; bd. dirs. Am. Assn. U. Women, 1953-58, 65-67, 72-74, Women's Aux. New Haven Symphony, 1960-64; v.p. New Haven Nat. Council Jewish Women, 1960-64, pres., 1964-66, 68-69, bd. dirs., 1970-74, mem. nat. council, 1969-71, nat. pub. relations com., 1971-73, nat. campaign com., 1969-71; asst. dir. Women in Community Service, 1964-68; bd. dirs. Conn. Child Welfare Assn., 1964-70; pres. Brandeis U. Women's Com., New Haven, 1970-72; mem. League Women Voters, 1935—, bd. dirs., 1970—. Recipient plaque Pres. Harry S. Truman, 1947. Clubs: Woodbridge (Conn.) Country; Wellesley, Graduates (New Haven). Home: 98 Ansonia Rd Woodbridge CT 06525

BRUST, ELEANOR ADELAIDE ROTTACH (MRS. JOHN JACKSON BRUST), librarian; b. N.Y.C., July 23, 1918; d. Edwin William and Lillian Clara (Cornwall) Rottach; B.S., Fairleigh Dickinson U., 1965; M.L.S., Rutgers U., 1967; m. John Jackson Brust, Nov. 22, 1939; children—Kathryn Eleanor, John Jackson, Lillian Sharon, Lauretta Susanna. Report writer Dun & Bradstreet, Inc., N.Y.C., 1936-40; sr. librarian, adult dept. Bergenfield (N.J.) Library, 1955-61; reference librarian Fairleigh Dickinson U., Teaneck, 1962-66; head librarian media center Ft. Lee (N.J.) Bd. Edn., 1967—. N.J. Library Assn. scholar, 1965. Mem. Am., N.J., Bergen County library assns., Nat., N.J., Bergen County edn. assns., Ft. Lee Tchrs. Assn. (sec. 1969-70). Club: Zonta (Englewood-Tenafly, N.J.). Home: 38 N Lyle Av Tenafly NJ 07670 Office: Ft Lee Intermediate Sch 467 Stillwell Av Fort Lee NJ 07024

BRUUN, RUTH DOWLING (MRS. BERTEL BRUUN), psychiatrist; b. N.Y.C., Sept. 13, 1937; d. Robert Whittle and Alice Bevier (Hall) Dowling; grad. The Spence Sch., N.Y.C., 1955; A.B., Radcliffe Coll., 1959; M.D., Cornell U., 1968; m. Lawrence Walker Newman, June 19, 1958 (div. Feb. 1970); children—Timothy D., Isabel B., Thomas H.; m. 2d, Bertel Bruun, Dec. 19, 1970; 1 son, Christian B. Intern, N.Y. Infirmary, 1968-69; vis. fellow Neurol. Inst., N.Y., 1970; resident in psychiatry Payne-Whitney Clinic-N.Y. Hosp.-Cornell Med. Center, 1970-73; clin. instr. psychiatry Cornell U., 1973—; psychiatrist to outpatients Payne-Whitney Clinic, N.Y. Hosp., 1973—; asst. adj. psychiatrist Lenox Hill Hosp., 1973—. Psychiat. cons. to Harlem Drug Addiction Study Group. Bd. dirs. Spence-Chapin Services to Families and Children; trustee Dowling Coll., Oakdale, N.Y. Mem. Eastern Assn. Encephalographers, Am. Psychiat. Assn., N.Y. County Med. Soc., A.M.A., Soc. N.Y. Hosp. Clubs: Quantuck Beach (Westhampton, N.Y.); Radcliffe (N.Y.C.). Home and office: 52 E 73d St New York City NY 10021

BRYAN, CLEO STILES (MRS. LUTHER ODELL BRYAN), home economist, govt. extension service worker; b. Snyder, Okla., Mar. 3, 1917; d. James Lewis and Mary Elizabeth (Reed) Stiles; B.S., Central State Coll., Edmund, Okla., 1943; M.S., Okla. State U., 1959; m. Luther Odell Bryan, Feb. 22, 1953; children—Julia Karan (Mrs. William J. Tygart), Luther Kyle. Tchr. rural elementary and high schs., Okla., 1939-42; instr. Frederick (Okla.) Jr. Coll., 1942-43; with Okla. Extension Service, U.S. Dept. of Agr., Caddo County, 1943—, asst. home demonstration agt. Caddo County, 1943-44, home demonstration agt. Love County, 1944-46, Garvin County, 1946-61, extension home economist Cherokee County, 1961—, asst. for tng. fgn. vis. home economists, 1949, 53, extension service rep. study tour Austria, 1966. Bd. dirs. Okla. Mental Retardation Council. Recipient Nat. Distinguished Service award Extension Home Economists Assn. Chgo., 1958; Gold award Epsilon Sigma Phi, 1943; Outstanding Profl. Home Econs. award Okla. Home Econs. Assn., 1972; Cleo Bryan Recognition Day given by Cherokee County Extension Homemakers, 1972. Mem. Tahlequah C. of C., Nat. (rep. White House Youth Conf., 1963, mem. com. for tng. Mexican agts. joint project assn. and Ford Motor Co., 1963-64, nat. budget com. chmn. 1962-63, nat. treas. 1963-64), Okla. (dist. councilor southwest 1946-47, northeast 1964-65, v.p. 1960-61, pres. 1962-63) home demonstration agts. assns., Nat. Assn. Extension Home Economists (pres. 1972-73), Am. Home Economists Extension, Nat. Assn. Home Econs. (nat. chmn. profl. improvement 1960, nat. recruitment chmn. 1961, nat. research com. chmn. 1958), Okla. Home Econs. Assn. (rep. Internat. Home Econs. Conf., Bristol, Eng., home econs. study tour Norway, Ireland, Denmark, 1968), Epsilon Sigma Phi. Mem. Ch. of Christ (Sunday sch. tchr.). Home: Box 749 Tahlequah OK 74464 Office: Okla Extension Service PO Box 749 Tahlequah OK 74464

BRYAN, MARY PALMER, artist; b. Bklyn., July 22, 1926; d. Edward Lionel and Anna Margaret (Clyde) Palmer; grad. Pratt Inst., 1948; postgrad. Rutgers U., summer 1967; m. James Fearon Bryan, Dec. 9, 1950; children—Jeanne, James, Bruce, Christopher, Thomas, Susanna, Amy. Free lance illustrator, N.Y.C., 1948-52; exhibited paintings, U.S. and Europe, 1963—, including Nat. Acad. Design, N.Y.C.; tchr. St. Johns High Sch., West Islip, N.Y., 1973—, also pvt. adult classes; art dir. Awixa Pond Art Center, Bay Shore, N.Y., 1970. Mem. Nat. Assn. Women Artists. Illustrator: The Little Bee, 1955; When Children Speak, 1971. Address: 879 Gardiner Dr Bay Shore NY 11706

BRYAN, MILDRED GOTT (MRS. ERNEST ROWLETT BRYAN), lawyer; b. Washington; d. Howard Seymour and Cora Elizabeth (Norris) Gott; student Mount Holyoke Coll., 1924-26; A.B. magna cum laude, Trinity Coll., 1928; J.D., George Washington U., 1932; m. Ernest Rowlett Bryan, Sept. 15, 1932; 1 dau., Carolyn Norris (Mrs. Jack A. Veerman). Admitted to D.C. bar, 1932, since practiced in Washington; atty. real estate div. U.S. Dept. Def., Washington, 1942-46. Pres. Eastland Gardens, Inc., 1952—, Howard S. Gott Co., Inc., 1952-54, Municipal Realty Co., 1952-54, Mutual Devel. Co., 1952-55. Sec. Westmoreland Hills Citizen Assn., 1949; hon. field sec. World's Christian Endeavor Union, 1954-70. Trustee Allied Youth, 1952-68, Internat. Soc. of Christian Endeavor, 1952—. Mem. Am., D.C., Inter-Am., Internat. bar assns., Nat. Assn. Women Lawyers, World Peace Thru Law, English Speaking Union, Kappa Beta Pi. Club: Wesley Heights Spring Valley Garden (rec. sec. 1973—). Home: 4840 Quebec St Washington DC 20016 Office: 1028 Connecticut Av NW Washington DC 20036

BRYAN, MIRIAM GERTRUDE MAY (MRS. JAMES E. BRYAN), educator; b. P.E.I., Can., Feb. 1, 1908 (parents Am. citizens); d. George William and Emma (Lawless) May; B.S. in Edn., Bridgewater (Mass.) State Coll., 1929; postgrad. Boston U., 1929-30, Yale, 1935-36, U. Cal. at Los Angeles, 1937, U. Colo., 1938; M.A., N.Y.U., 1940, postgrad., 1941-61; m. James E. Bryan, Oct. 31, 1941. Tchr., Howard High Sch., West Bridgewater, Mass., 1929-35, Hamden (Conn.) High Sch., 1935-36, East Haven (Conn.) High Sch., 1936-40, Hastings on Hudson (N.Y.) High Sch., 1941-43; head adv. service Coop. Test Service, N.Y.C., 1943-45, adminstrv. asst., 1945-46, editor, 1947-48; editor-in-chief coop. test div. and nat. tchr. exams. Ednl. Testing Service, N.Y.C., 1948-49; asst. editor Silver Burdett Co., N.Y.C., 1949-55; test specialist Psychol. Corp., N.Y.C., 1955-56; asst. prof. edn. Rutgers U., New Brunswick, N.J., 1958-60, co-adjutant staff mem., 1956-58; sr. asso. in test devel. Ednl. Testing Service, Princeton, N.J., 1960-61; asso. dir. test devel., 1961-67, sr. editor, asso. dir. elementary and secondary sch. programs, 1967-68, cons., 1968-72, asso. dir. Atlanta office, 1972—; lectr. Mich. State U., summer 1970. Test editor, consultant Iowa testing programs State U. Ia., Iowa City, 1950-56; test cons. ednl. div. Reader's Digest Services, Inc., 1955-58; research cons. N.Y. State Dept. Edn., 1962-68; cons. N. H. Network, 1967-68, 70-71. Sec., West Bridgewater Republican Town Com., 1934-35. Mem. Am. Ednl. Research Assn., Internat. Reading Assn., Nat. Council Tchrs. of English, Nat. Council on Measurement in Edn., N.E.A., Am. Assn. U. Profs., Am. Assn. U. Women, N.Y.U., Bridgewater State Coll. (Nicholas Tillinghast award 1970) alumni assns., Am. Personnel and Guidance Assn., Assn. Measurement and Evaluation in Guidance, Kappa Delta Pi, Pi Lambda Theta (pres. Rho chpt. 1957-58, editor nat. publs. 1961-64, 71—, chmn. nat. fellowship awards com. 1961-64, nat. pres. 1965-69, cons. 1969-70). Author: (with others) Ability Grouping, 1970. Editorial asso., contbr. 4th Mental Measurements Yearbook, 1952-53, 5th, 1957-59, 6th, 1964, 7th, 1972. Contbr. numerous articles profl. publs. Author various tests. Home: 4978 Vernon Springs Dr Atlanta GA 30338 Office: Educational Testing Service 17 Executive Park Dr NE Atlanta GA 30329

BRYAN, NANCY MAE BONNEY (MRS. JAMES WALLACE BRYAN, JR.), computer systems analyst; b. Bridgeport, Conn., Apr. 6, 1943; d. Russell Norwood and Catharine (Yerkes) Bonney; B.A. in Math., U. Del., 1964; M.S. in Mgmt. Sci., Johns Hopkins, 1968; certificate in data processing Data Processing Mgmt. Assn., 1968; m. James Wallace Bryan, Jr., Feb. 3, 1968. Tech. asst. gen. engring. dept. Chesapeake & Potomac Telephone Co. of Md., Balt., 1964-66; cons. Benefacts, Inc., Balt., 1966-68; systems analyst Autotech Systems Corp., Wheaton, Md., 1968-69, Aries Corp., McLean, Va., 1969-71, Wolf Research & Devel. Corp., Riverdale, Md., 1971—. Mem. Assn. Computing Machinery, Assn. Computer Programmers and Analysts, Nat. Orgn. for Women (convener, 1st pres. No. Prince George County chpt.), Md. Women's Polit. Caucus. Home: Box 247 Greenbelt MD 20770 Office: Wolf Research & Devel Corp 6801 Kenilworth Av Riverdale MD 20840

BRYAN, SARAH ELIZABETH MILLER (MRS. BROOKE CECIL BRYAN), county ofcl.; b. Craig, Okla., Jan. 5, 1914; d. Edward Louis and Nell (Grimes) Miller; student Kan. U., 1931-32, LaSalle Extension U., 1960-63; m. Brooks Cecil Bryan, Oct. 2, 1932; children—Nella Ruth (Mrs. Jon Herbert Hartley), Linda Marie (Mrs. R.R. Yacconi), Paul Edward, Owner, Bryan Motor Co., 1946-59, Bryan Tractor & Implement Co., Howard, Kan., 1946-59; bus. mgr. Mathiason Bus. Service, Farmington, N.M., 1959-60, Leonard Olds, Farmington, N.M., 1960-62, Basin Motor Co., Farmington, N.M., 1962-64; treas. Elk County Howard, Kan., 1967—; bus. mgr. Thorobred Chevrolet, Inc., Wichita, 1973—. Auditor, Howard Nat. Bank, 1967-71. Active 4-H. Treas. Howard Sch. Dist., 1952-58; campaign mgr. Republican gubernatorial Candidate, Elk County, 1968. Recipient awards Ford Motor Co., 1956, 57, 58, 59, Gen. Motors Co., 1963. Mem. Howard C. of C., Bus. and Profl. Women's Club Howard, Elk County Rodeo Assn. Methodist (chmn. finance com. bldg. fund 1956). Mem. Order Eastern Star. Home: PO Box 613 Howard KS 67349 Office: Courthouse Howard KS 67349

BRYANT, BARBARA EVERITT, market research exec.; b. Ann Arbor, Mich., Apr. 5, 1926; d. William Littell and Dorothy Irwin (Wallace) Everitt; A.B., Cornell U., 1947; M.A., Mich. State U., 1967, Ph.D., 1970; m. John Harold Bryant, Aug. 14, 1948; children—Linda J., Randal E., Lois B. Art and Prodn. editor Chem. Engring. mag., 1947-48; editorial research U. Ill. at Urbana, 1948-49; freelance editor, writer, 1950-61; continuing edn. adminstrn. Oakland U., Rochester, Mich., 1961-66; grad. research asst. Mich. State U., 1966-70; with Market Opinion Research, Inc., Detroit, 1970—, v.p. social research, 1971—. Editor, dir. Mich. League Women Voters, 1959-61. Mem. council Cornell U., 1972—; bd. dirs. Cranbrook Schs., Bloomfield Hills, Mich., 1967—. Mem. Am. Assn. Pub. Opinion Research, Am. Marketing Assn. (dir. Detroit 1973—), Women in Communications (pres. Detroit chpt. 1974-75). Clubs: Detroit Press; Village Woman's (Bloomfield Hills). Author: High School Students Look at Their World, 1970; Young Adults Look at Vocational Education, 1973. Contbr. articles to profl. jours. Home: 1477 Lochridge Rd Bloomfield Hills MI 48013 Office: 28 W Adams St Detroit MI 48226

BRYANT, CELIA MAE SMALL, educator; b. Porum, Okla., Aug. 11, 1913; d. George Milton and Elsie (Sigmon) Small; Mus.B. in Piano, U. Okla., 1947, Mus.M., 1948; pvt. study Frank Mannheimer; m. William Cullen Bryant III, Oct. 3, 1932 (div. May 1945); children—Ann (Mrs. Robert L. Trent), Mary Carol (Mrs. Robert Fritchof Hansen), Culleen (Mrs. Ronald George Tobin). Mem. faculty U. Okla., Norman, 1948—, prof. music, 1967—; vis. prof. Interlochen U. div., summers, 1972-73. Appeared as pianist numerous recitals; music adjudicator, clinician; mem. Okla. State Commn., 1962-63; mem. adv. bd. Am. Music Scholarship Assn., 1972—. Mem. U.S. commn. for UNESCO, 1974—. Named one of Nine Outstanding Music Educators in Nation, Mu Phi Epsilon, 1962; recipient Nat. citation Phi Mu Alpha, 1972; Outstanding Okla. Musician award Gov. Okla., 1973; also nat. achievement awards numerous mus. tchr. assns.; commd. hon. col. Okla., 1973. Mem. Music Tchrs. Nat. Assn. (div. pres. 1956-58, nat. pres. 1969-73, life mem. 1973—), Okla. Music Tchrs. Assn. (life mem., pres. 1962-66), Nat. Music Council (dir. 1971—), U. Okla. Tchr. Edn. Council (chmn. 1958-62), Okla. Coll. Tchrs. Assn. (sec.-treas. 1963-64), Va. Tidewater Forum (life), Alpha Chi Omega Alumnae Assn. (state pres. 1950-51), Pi Kappa Lambda (chpt. pres. 1965-67). Club: Mac Dowell Allied Arts (pres. 1962-66). Editor piano pedagogy dept. Clavier Mag., 1961—, writer series Music Lesson, 1963—, rec. in Braille by Library of Congress. Contbr. articles to publs. Home: 614 E Okmulgee St Norman OK 73069

BRYANT, FRANCES JANE, editor; b. Cushing, Okla., Dec. 10, 1933; d. Edward Glahn and Dorothy (McLean) Bryant; A.A., Christian Coll. for Women, 1953; B.J., U. Mo., 1955. Reporter, Norman (Okla.) Transcript, 1955-57, wire editor, 1957-59, city editor, 1959-67, mag. editor, 1967—. Guest lectr. U. Okla. Journalism Sch., intermittently 1963—. Publicity chmn. Cleveland County Heart Assn., 1966-67. Bd. dirs. Norman Day Care Center for Handicapped Children, Cleveland County chpt. A.R.C. Named outstanding woman in communications Theta Sigma Phi, 1968; Bus. Woman of Year, Bus. and Profl. Women, 1969. Mem. Okla. Press Assn. (chmn. news com. 1968), Okla. Asso. Press Editors (pres. 1970-71), Sigma Delta Chi (dir.), Gamma Phi Beta. Democrat. Episcopalian. Club: Altrusa (pres.) (Norman). Home: 606 Sherwood Dr Norman OK 73069 Office: PO Drawer 1058 Norman OK 73069

BRYANT, HAZEL JOAN, theatrical producer, dir.; b. Zanesville, O., Sept. 8, 1939; d. Harrison James and Edith Drusilla (Holland) Bryant; student Peabody Conservatory Music, 1955-58, Oberlin Conservatory, 1958-62, Mozarteum, Salzburg, Austria, 1961-62, Columbia, 1970. Operatic performer in Europe and USSR; performer in Broadway and off-Broadway shows; concert and TV performer in U.S. and Can.; artistic dir. Afro-Am. Total Theatre, N.Y.C. Mem. N.Y.C. Mayor's Cultural Council; mem. performing arts panel N.Y. State Council on Arts; co-ordinator Lincoln Center St. Theatre Festival; founder, sec. Black Theatre Alliance. Recipient 1st ann. Audelco award, scholarship awards Rockefeller, Rockefeller Bros. Fund, Nat. Endowment for Arts, N.Y. State Council Arts, Nobel Found., N.Y. Found., Faberge Corp. Mem. A.M.E. Ch. Founder, exec. editor Muses art jour. Author original books for musical prodns. Home: 33 Riverside Dr New York City NY 10023 Office: Afro-American Total Theatre 49 W 32d St New York City NY 10001

BRYANT, JANE HILLES, occupational therapist; b. Phila., Sept. 7, 1922; d. Albert Letchworth and Edith Harvey (Walter) Hilles; student Harcum Jr. Coll., 1940-42, Phila. Sch. Occupational Therapy, 1942-44; B.S. in Edn., U. Pa., 1945; M.S., Russell Sage Coll., 1968; m. Clifford M. Bryant, Sept. 11, 1948; children—Clifford M., Barbara H., Laura H. Occupational therapist Germantown Hosp., Phila., 1945, Childrens Hosp. Cerebral Palsy unit, Hollywood, Cal., 1946-47, Childrens Rehab. Inst., Cockeysville, Md., 1947-48, Sunnyview Hosp., 1949; substitute occupational therapist United Cerebral Palsy of Schenectady, 1956-60, staff occupational therapist, 1969-72, home service dir., 1972—. Kindergarten tchr. aide Schenectady Pub. Schs., 1964, pre-kindergarten tchr., 1964-65; resource tchr. Niskayuna Pub. Schs., 1965-67, substitute tchr., kindergarten testing, 1967-69. Chmn. pre-sch. parents Niskayuna P.T.A., 1957; v.p. Hillside P.T.A., 1963-64; mem. Human Services Planning Council Task Force on Rehab. and Infant Stimulation and Child Devel., 1973—. Bd. dirs. Schenectady YWCA, 1964-70, Schenectady Child Guidance Center, 1969-72, Childrens Shelter, Family and Child Service, 1968-73. Mem. Panhellenic Assn. Schenectady (treas., scholarship chmn.), Kappa Kappa Gamma. Mem. Reformed Ch. Clubs: Edison, Glen Hills Swim, Ski Venture, Mountain View. Home: 1404 Myron St Schenectady NY 12309 Office: 124 Rosa Rd Schenectady NY 12308

BRYANT, JOAN, rehab. exec.; b. Newark, Aug. 5, 1934; d. William and Reba (Wright) Bryant; B.A., Upsala Coll., East Orange, N.J., 1956; M.A., Seton Hall U., 1965. Clk., Newark Pub. Library, 1950-56; social case worker Bur. Mental Deficiency, Trenton, N.J., 1956-59; instl. case worker N.J. Tng. Sch., 1959-60; rehab. counselor N.J. Rehab. Commn., 1960-63; exec. dir. Mt. Carmel Guild Tng. and Placement Service, Newark, 1963-70; dir. counseling, Hunterdon Occupational Tng. Center, Flemington, N.J., 1970-74; social worker N.J. Div. Youth and Family Services, 1974—. Vol., Salvation Army, 1954, St. Barnabas Hosp., 1956; part-time evaluator Youth Chance-Anti Poverty Program, 1965-67; mem. Cath. adv. council on spl. edn. Archdiocese Newark, 1968; mem. adv. council on spl. edn. N.J. Bd. Edn., 1968; mem. N.J. Developmental Disabilities Council, 1972—. Trustee N.J. Assn. Sheltered Workshops. Recipient certificate of recognition Work-Study Com. East Orange, Montclair, West Essex Pub. Sch., 1967. Mem. N.J. Rehab. Assn. (past v.p.), N.J. Assn. Sheltered Workshops (sec.-treas.), Am. Assn. Mental Deficiency, N.J. Personnel and Guidance Assn., Nat. Council Negro Women, Nat. Rehab. Counseling Assn., N.J. Assn. Retarded Children, Delta Sigma Theta. Baptist. Author: Mental Retardation-A Second Look at the Problem, 1968. Home: 752 S 16th St Newark NJ 07103 Office: 1100 Raymond Blvd Newark NJ 07103

BRYANT, JUNE CATES, youth counselor; b. Bradford, Tenn., Nov. 4, 1927; d. Lawrence J. and Unie L. (Waldrop) Cates; student U. Ark., 1965, U. Houston, 1966-67, Tex. Christian U., 1968, Ark. State U., 1969; children—Tommy, Jerry, Patricia, Braynt. Receptionist, sec. Drs. Price, Hayes, Wilson, Duckworth, Wynne, Ark., 1950-55; exec. sec. County Extension Office, Wynne, 1955-56; adminstrn. clk. Agr. Stblzn. County Com., Wynne, 1956-58; asst. mgr. Sears, Roebuck & Co., Wynne, 1958-67; distbr. Comml. Appeal, Memphis, 1963-68; mgr. Wynne C. of C., Wynne, 1966-70; corr. Ark. Gazette, Little

Rock, 1967-70, 1972—; propr. Chandolier Restaurant, Wynne, 1968-70; office mgr., bookkeeper East Ark. Regional Mental Health Center, Helena, 1970-71; youth counselor Neighborhood Youth Corps, Cross and St. Francis counties (Ark.), 1971—; asst. innkeeper, food and beverage mgr. Holiday Inn of Forrest City (Ark.) 1972-73. Named Woman of Year, Wynne Bus. and Profl. Womens Club, 1958 and 1972, Woman of Achievement, 1966, 67, 68. Mem. Bus. and Profl. Women's Club (pres. 1963), Cross County Aux., Cross County Devel. Council, Ark. Restaurant Assn., Wynne C. of C. (bd. dirs. 1959, 62, 64, 66). Baptist. Club: Women's Progressive (Wynne). Home: 1119 E Forrest Av Wynne AR 72396 Office: Cross County Court House Wynne AR 72396 also OEO Bldg 125 S Grant St Forest City AR 72335

BRYANT, MYNORA JOYCE (MRS. ERNEST DALTON BRYANT), coll. dean; b. Tarboro, N.C., Mar. 6, 1943; d. Ivery and Louella Verienne (Dickens) Johnson; B.A., Howard U., 1969, M.A., 1971; m. Ernest Dalton Bryant, Sept. 8, 1962; 1 dau., Laynee Verienne. Dental adminstr., children's counselor Dr. Stanley L. Fleming, Washington, 1968-73; tchr. dental assisting D.C. On the Job Tng. Program, 1969-71, Armstrong Adult Edn. Program, 1970-72; asso. dean students Md. Inst. Coll. Art, Balt., 1972—. Chmn., Sickle Cell Anemia Fund Raising drive, 1972. Asso. mem. Smithsonian Instn. Mem. Am., Md. personnel and guidance assns., Am., Md. coll. personnel assns., Kappa Delta Pi, Sigma Gamma Rho (campus adviser 1972—). Democrat. Baptist. Club: Howard University Alumni. Home: 2613 Oregon Av Landover MD 20785 Office: 1300 W Mt Royal Av Baltimore MD 21217

BRYANT, OLIVIA JANE CLOWER (MRS. JAMES LESLIE BRYANT), educator; b. Clarksdale, Miss., May 17, 1945; d. Harold Cottingham and Aline Elizabeth (Ragland) Clower; B.S., Blue Mountain Coll., 1967; M.Ed., U. So. Miss., 1970; postgrad. Northwestern State U., Natchitoches, La., 1969-70; m. James Leslie Bryant, May 30, 1970; 1 son, James Daniel Hunter. Tchr., R.H. Watkins High Sch., Laurel, Miss., 1967-68; instr., asst. U. So. Miss., Hattiesburg, 1968-69; inst. phys. edn. Centenary Coll., Shreveport, La., 1969-71, Upper Ia. Coll., Fayette, 1971—. Recreational dir. Petah Tiqva (Israel) Bapt. Village, summer 1969; instr. first aid and water safety A.R.C., Shreveport, La., 1969-71; instr. recreational activities YWCA, Shreveport, La., 1969-71. Mem. A.A.H.P.E.R. Home: 501 Mechanic St Fayette IA 52142 Office: Upper Ia Coll Fayette IA 52142

BRYANT, RIETTE SUE, librarian; b. Plaquemine, La., Oct. 29, 1944; d. Joseph Wilbert and Florence Mae (Lewins) Bryant; B.S., La. State U., 1966, M.S., 1969. Tchr. DeKalb County Bd. Edn., Decatur, Ga., 1966-67, East Baton Rouge Parish Bd. Edn., Baton Rouge, 1967-68; librarian Irma Dilg Nicholson Library, Walker Coll., Jasper, Ala., 1969—, head librarian, 1969—. Bd. dirs. Walker Coll. Civic Concert Series, Jasper, 1970—. Mem. Phi Mu, Beta Phi Mu. Roman Catholic. Home: 406 Court St Plaquemine LA 70764 also 906 Delaware Av Jasper AL 35501

BRYANT, TANYA MIFSUD (MRS. GLENDELL W. DOBBS), real estate exec.; b. Sliema, Island of Malta, May 15, 1920; d. Jose Louis and Vera (Jarmonkine) Mifsud; student pvt. schs.; m. Arthur J. W. Pitt, Nov. 17, 1937 (div. Feb. 1952); children—Natasha, Valerie (Mrs. Fino Calamaro), F. David, Micheline; m. 2d, William Cullen Bryant, Dec. 29, 1959 (div. June 1960); m. 3d, Jack F. Cutler, May 4, 1963 (div. Oct. 1968); m. 4th, Glendell W. Dobbs, Mar. 1969. Came to U.S., 1949, naturalized, 1957. Imported model Jacques Heim, Paris, France, 1949-50; Conover model all major fashion shows and TV shows U.S., 1950-52; sportswear buyer, exec. trainee Neiman Marcus, Dallas, 1952-54; mgr. ladies wear Broadway Dept. Store, Panorama City, Cal., 1954-56; owner, buyer Brides and Besides shops, Los Angeles, Bakersfield, Westwood, Cal., 1956-60; owner Tanya Bryant, realtor, San Jose, Cal., 1957—. Originator, dir. Pamper House, Rockefeller Center, 1952; staff asst. A.R.C., London, Eng., 1942-45; gray lady, Los Angeles, 1957-60. Mem. Women's Council Nat. Assn. Real Estate Bds. (chpt. pres. 1966, 69), San Fernando Valley Bd. Realtors (dir. 1966), Cal. Real Estate Assn. (dir. 1966-67, 69-72, chmn. pub. relations 1969, 70), San Jose Real Estate Bd. (dir. 1970-71, sec. 1970), Internat. Platform Assn., C. of C. (dir. 1966), Internat. Traders Club. Contbr. articles to profl. jours. Home: 9887 E Hwy 12 Lodi CA 95240 Office: 2072 The Alameda San Jose CA 95126

BRYMER, MARIAH BRADFORD, home economist; b. Elmore, Ala., May 11, 1926; d. George Washington and Easter (Duncan) Bradford; B.S., Tuskegee Inst., 1948, M.Ed., 1956; div. Cashier Peoples Coop., Tuskegee, Ala., 1951-53; instr. home econs. Russell County Tng. Sch., Hurtsboro, Ala., 1948-50, Saints Jr. Coll., Lexington, Miss., 1956-57, Sand Town High Sch., Millbrook, Ala., 1958-63; asso. county extension chmn. Auburn U. Extension Service, Rockford, Ala., 1963—. Sec., Family Child Care Com.; chmn. Coosa County vols. A.R.C. Mem. Nat., Ala. assns. extension home economists, Nat. Am., Internat. Am., Ala. home econs. assns. Home: PO Box 275 Rockford AL 35136 Office: County Activity Bldg Rockford AL 35136

BRYN, KATHERINE ROBINSON (MRS. KENNETH BRYN), editor; b. Chgo., Oct. 12, 1948; d. Michael Henry and Joanne (Loomis) Robinson; B.S. in Journalism 1970; m. Kenneth Bryn, Aug. 22, 1970. Editorial asst. Popular Mechanics Mag., N.Y.C., 1970; prodn. editor Sci. Digest Mag., N.Y.C., 1970-72, asst. editor, staff writer, 1972; asso. editor Coll. Bd. Rev., N.Y.C., 1972—, Coll. Bd. News, 1972—. Free lance writer, photographer, 1970—. Mem. Women in Communications, Kappa Tau Alpha, Phi Gamma Mu. Home: 39 BD Fox Hill Dr Dover NJ 07853

BRYSAC, SHAREEN BLAIR, audio-visual cons.; b. Denver, Jan. 15, 1939; s. Fred E. and Margaret (Whitely) Blair; student Juilliard Sch., 1957; B.A., Barnard, 1961; m. Peter Brysac, Dec. 13, 1969 (dec. Oct. 1971). Editor Harcourt Brace Jovanovich, N.Y.C., 1965-67; audio-visual coordinator Random House—Alfred Knopf, N.Y.C., 1969-73; cons. news and documentaries CBS, N.Y.C., 1973—. Solo dancer Merce Cunningham, Jose Limon, Paul Taylor, N.Y.C. Center Opera dance cos., 1960-64. Mem. publs. com. Barnard Coll., 1971—. Mem. Soc. Picture Profls. Home: 50 W 96th St New York City NY 10025 Office: CBS News 35 W 45th St New York City NY 10036

BRYSH, SISTER JANET FRANCES, coll. librarian; b. Meriden, Conn., July 12, 1931; d. Theodore Benjamin and Florence (Lynch) Brysh; B.A., Marymount Coll., 1958; M.A., Hunter Coll., 1964; M.L.S., Rosary Coll., 1968. Joined Sisters of Sacred Heart of Mary, 1951; tchr. Marymount Sch., N.Y.C., 1953-60; librarian, instr. Marymount Coll., Ste.-Foy Que., Can., 1960-67; librarian, tchr. Marymount Secondary Sch., Tarrytown, N.Y., 1967-68; chief librarian Marymount Manhattan Coll., N.Y.C., 1968—. Library cons. Marymount secondary schs., N.Y.C. and Rome, Italy, 1970-71. Mem. Am. Assn. U. Profs., A.L.A., N.Y. Library Assn. Home: 2465 Palisade Av Bronx NY 10463

BRYSON, VERENA LAMAR LEWIS (MRS. WILLIAM JEFFERSON BRYSON), pub. relations exec.; b. Brevard, N.C., Feb. 22, 1927; d. Lamar English and Margaret Louise (Erwin) Lewis; student U. N.C., Greensboro, 1944-46; B.A., U. S.C., 1948; B.S. in L.S., U. N.C. at Chapel Hill, 1949; m. William Jefferson Bryson, Feb. 18, 1951; children—William Jefferson, Verina Patton. Circulation and reference librarian Furman U., Greenville, S.C., 1949-50; librarian Army Air Support Center, Ft. Bragg, N.C., 1951; reference librarian Greenville (S.C.) County Library, 1952-53, 63-70, dir. community relations, 1970—; librarian Woman's Coll., Furman U., Greenville, 1953-55, Donaldson AFB, S.C., 1960-62. Recipient Outstanding Librarian award Mil. Air Transport Service, USAF, 1961, John Cotton Dana award A.L.A., 1961, 71. Mem. Southeastern, S.C. (mem. publicity com. 1974-75) library assns., Alpha Delta Pi. Episcopalian. Clubs: Woman's (dir. 1973-75), Thursday (1st v.p. 1972-74). Home: 127 Howell Circle Greenville SC 29607 Office: 300 College St Greenville SC 29601

BUBLITZ, DEBORAH KEIRSTEAD (MRS. CLARK BUBLITZ), pediatrician; b. Boston, Feb. 28, 1933; d. George and Dorothy (Kingsbury) Keirstead; B.S. cum laude, Bates Coll., 1955; M.D., Johns Hopkins, 1959; postgrad. Washington U., St. Louis, 1960; m. Clark Bublitz, June 1, 1958; children—Nancy, Susan, Philip, Caroline, Elizabeth. Intern, St. Louis Children's Hosp., 1959-60; resident neighborhood health program Denver Gen. Hosp., 1967-69; resident pediatrics Colo. Gen. Hosp., 1974; practice medicine, specializing in pediatrics, Denver, 1967—; pediatrician, dept. health and hosps. Neighborhood Health Program, Denver, 1967—; mem. staff Denver Gen. Hosp. Mem. A.M.A., Royal Soc. Health. Episcopalian. Home: 3222 S Florence Ct Denver CO 80231 Office: 1178 Mariposa St Denver CO 80204

BUCHANAN, CHRISTINE LUKENS (MRS. THOMAS STAVELY BUCHANAN), publisher; b. Beloit, Kan., Sept. 17, 1928; d. Lyle Milton and Lois (Tilton) Lukens; B.A., Sterling Coll., 1950; M.S., Kan. State U., 1962; postgrad. U. Minn., 1967; m. Thomas Stavely Buchanan, June 4, 1951; children—James Lee, Thomas Richard, Jean Anne, David Bruce, Beth Lynn. Publisher Bucklin (Kan.) Banner, 1956-59; pub. Washington (Kan.) County News, 1959—. Tchr. writing, journalism high schs.; instr. behavioral sci. writing Kan. State U., 1973. U.S. del. to Internat. Youth Conf., Wales, 1949. Pres. Washington P.T.A., Kan., 1966. Mem. Adv. Bd. North Central Kan. Vocational Tech. Sch., Beloit. Newspaper Fund fellow Wall St. Jour., 1967. Recipient numerous writing awards. Mem. Women in Communications, Kan. Press Women (pres. 1972-74), Nat. Fedn. Press Women (nat. bd.). Presbyn. Home: 119 West Second Washington KS 66968 Office: C St Washington KS 66968

BUCHANAN, CLARIBEL VALENTINE (MRS. WALLACE CLYDE BUCHANAN), realtor; b. Greenfield, Ill., Oct. 26, 1913; d. Luther Cameron and Etna (Linder) Valentine; ed. So. Ill. U.; m. Wallace Clyde Buchanan, July 10, 1932; children—Lynda (Mrs. Norman Schulz), Richard Clyde. Salesman, Harrison Agy., Alton, Ill., 1954-63, Russell Hale Agy., Alton, 1963-67; founder, prin. Buchanan Real Estate Agy., Alton, 1967-70, pres., 1970—. Mem. League Women Voters. Bd. dirs. Community Concert Assn., Alton. Mem. Ill., Alton-Wood River Area (bd. dirs.) bds. realtors, Alton C. of C. Presbyn. (elder, trustee). Clubs: Zonta, Literary (Alton). Home and office: 5323 Dover Dr Godfrey IL 62035

BUCHANAN, SUSAN TOWNSEND CARVER (MRS. J. ROBERT BUCHANAN), hosp. adminstr., physician; b. Bklyn., Aug. 6, 1930; d. William Van Ness and Marian Diller (Townsend) Carver; A.B., Swarthmore Coll., 1952; M.D., Columbia, 1956; m. J. Robert Buchanan, Oct. 27, 1962; children—Ross, Allyn. Intern N.Y. Hosp., 1956-57, asst. resident, 1957-60, chief resident, 1960-61, asso. dir., 1970—; practice medicine specializing in internal medicine and cardiology, N.Y.C.; instr. medicine Cornell U. Med. Coll., 1960-64, asst. prof. medicine, 1964—. Bd. dirs. Adoption and Children's Service Westchester, Chatfield Sch. Mem. Am., N.Y. (mem. adv. council 1971—) Heart Assns. Club: Cosmopolitan (N.Y.C.). Home: 10 Dellwood Circle Bronxville NY 10708 Office: 525 E 68th St New York City NY 10021

BUCHEN, CHARLOTTE, health service exec.; b. Canton, Ill. Jan. 11, 1927; d. Bert and Edith (Melgreen) Buchen; profl. journalism fellow Stanford U., 1966-67. Editor, house organ Cuneo Press, Inc., Chgo., 1949-51; mag. prodn. coordinator Internat. Harvester Co., Chgo., 1951-52; reporter, writer Canton (Ill.) Daily Ledger, 1953-56, The Arizona Republic, Phoenix, 1956-69; dir. urban affairs Nat. Housing Industries, Inc., Phoenix, 1969-72, dir. communications, 1971-73; asst. to pres. Samaritan Health Service, Phoenix, 1973—. Editorial cons. Ariz. Welfare Study, Ariz. State U., 1970; Mem. rate rev. com. Comprehensive Health Planning Council Maricopa County, 1972—. Bd. dirs. Phoenix Opportunities Indslzn. Center, 1970-71. Club: Phoenix Press (past dir.). Home: 1510 E Maryland Av Phoenix AZ 85014 Office: 1410 N 3d St Phoenix AZ 85004

BUCK, KATHRYN L(OUISE), librarian; b. McCammon, Ida.; d. Ralph Joseph and Mabel Louise (Hoerger) Buck; student Doane Coll., 1932-34; B.A., U. Neb., 1936; B.S. in L.S., U. Minn., 1939. Asst. librarian Neb. Library Commn., Lincoln, 1939-43; asst. librarian Chadron (Neb.) State Coll., 1943-48, head librarian, 1948-56; dir. library Doane Coll., Crete, Neb., 1956-69, asso. dir. library, 1969—. Recipient Doane Builder award, 1971. Mem. Am., Mountain Plains, Neb. library assns., Am. Assn. U. Profs., Neb. Hist. Soc., P.E.O., Delta Kappa Gamma. Republican. Mem. Order Eastern Star. Club: Faculty Women's. Home: 1205 Forest Av Crete NE 68333 Office: Perkins Library Doane College Crete NE 68333

BUCK, LOIS KIETERS, psychologist, educator; b. N.Y.C., Apr. 16, 1936; d. Samuel L. and Sadye (Rolfe) Kieters; B.S., N.Y. U., 1957; M.Ed., U. Houston, 1966, Ed.D., 1970. Psychometrist Allied Psychol. Services, Houston, Tex., 1969; supr. student tchrs. U. Houston, 1969-70; research psychologist and counselor Baylor U. Coll. of Medicine, Houston, 1968-69; chief diagnostician Harris County Dept. Edn., Houston, 1970-71; lectr. psychology Kingsbrough Community Coll., Bklyn., 1973—. Cons. to Tex. Edn. Agy., since 1970—; tchr. minimally brain injured Houston Ind. Sch. Dist., 1967-68. Fund raiser N.Y. U. Alumni Fund, 1973—; vol. Tex. Hosp. for Research and Rehab., 1966; rep. Contemporary Arts Mus., Houston, 1963—. Teaching fellow, 1969-70. Mem. Am. Psychol. Assn., N.Y. U. Alumni Assn. Office: Kingsborough College Oriental Blvd Brooklyn NY

BUCK, MARY SELLECK, educator; b. Bklyn., Nov. 24, 1927; d. Herbert Anthony and Winifred Julia (Platz) Selleck; B.S. in Elementary Edn., State U. N.Y. at Oneonta, 1959, M.S. in Sci. Edn., 1967; M.A. in Spl. Edn., Columbia, 1964, profl. diploma in Adminstrn. Spl. Programs, 1965; m. Carl E. Williams, Apr. 7, 1945; children—Mary (Mrs. Robert A. Freese), Carl, Nancy; m. 2d, David Louis Buck, Aug. 18, 1963. Tchr., Willowbrook (S.I.) State Sch., 1959-60, Sidney (N.Y.) Central Sch., 1960-61, Milford (N.Y.) Central Sch., 1961-64, Ramapo Central Sch., Suffern, N.Y., 1965—. Pvt. tutor, ednl. cons. exceptional children. Recipient Valley Forge Tchrs. medal. Mem. Am. Ednl. Research Assn., Am. Assn. Mental Deficiency, Assn. for Help Retarded Children, Council for Exceptional Children, Kappa Delta Pi. Home: Suffern NY 10901

BUCK, NATALIE SMITH (MRS. C.B. BUCK), state ofcl.; b. Carlsbad, N.M., Jan. 10, 1923; d. Milton R. and Rosa Adele (Binford) Smith; student William and Mary Coll., 1940-41; B.B.S., U. Colo., 1943; postgrad. U. Tex., 1945-46; m. C.B. Buck, Sept. 12, 1948; children—Warren Z., Barbara Anne. Chief clk. N.M. Senate, 1951-53; sec. of state State of N.M., Santa Fe, 1955-59; formerly supr. personnel N.M. Dept. Pub. Welfare; formerly chief personnel N.M. Health and Social Services Dept. Mem. Kappa Alpha Theta. Democrat. Home: 108 W Alicante Rd Santa Fe NM 87501 Office: PO Box 2183 Santa Fe NM 87501

BUCK, OLIVE MARGARET SIMPSON (MRS. CHARLES WILLIAM BUCK), journalist; b. Fowler, Colo., May 13, 1896; d. Joshua Clever and Cora Lee (Hughes) Simpson; B.A., U. Colo., 1919; m. Charles William Buck, May 27, 1923; children—Wilma (Mrs. Walter Dale Gager), Charles William. Head history dept. Cripple Creek (Colo.) High Sch., 1919-22; tchr. history Monte Vista (Colo.) High Sch., 1922-23; pub. Fowler (Colo.) Tribune, 1951-68, ret. Sec. Town Library Bd., Fowler, 1926-74; active Girl Scouts Am. Mem. D.A.R., Kappa Delta Pi. Baptist. Club: Woman's (Fowler). Home: 421 Main St Fowler CO 81039

BUCK, RUTH ELIZABETH, radiologist; b. Germantown, Pa., June 14, 1934; d. Frank and Laura Alice (Donovan) Buck; B.S., Wheaton (Ill.) Coll., 1961; M.D., Temple U., 1965. Intern Abington (Pa.) Meml. Hosp., 1965-66, resident radiology, 1966-70, asso. radiologist, 1970—. Diplomate Am. Bd. Radiology. Mem. Am. Coll. Radiology, A.M.A., Pa., Montgomery County, Christian med. socs., Pa. Radiol. Soc., Phila. Roentgen Ray Soc. Republican. Mem. Ch. of Open Door (Phila.) Home: 3625 W Moreland Rd Willow Grove PA 19090

BUCK, SALLY SYMMES (MRS. GEORGE THOMAS BUCK), banker; b. Cranbury, N.J., May 8, 1918; d. Charles Van Dyke and Ethel Louise (Cole) Symmes; student N.J. Coll. for Women, 1935-37; grad. Sch. Bank Mgmt., U. Va., 1963, Stonier Grad. Sch. Banking, Rutgers U., 1966; m. George Thomas Buck, July 11, 1947; children—Christine (Mrs. Kenneth L. Kirkland), Susan (Mrs. Robert T. Waters), Thomas C. With First Nat. Bank, Cranbury, N.J., 1939-47; with Citizens Trust Co., Portsmouth, Va., 1951—, sr. v.p., 1972—. Mem. adv. com. Coop. Office Edn. Portsmouth Schs., 1971-72. Bd. dirs. Tidewater Regional Health Planning Council, 1970-73, treas., 1972-73; bd. dirs. Child and Family Service, v.p., 1964-70, 72—; trustee Va.-Md. Banking Schs., 1964-67. Mem. Nat. Assn. Bank Women (regional v.p. 1970-71), Bank Adminstrv. Inst. (chpt. sec. 1970-71), Am. Inst. Banking (bd. govs. 1970-73), Portsmouth C. of C. (vice chmn. edn. com. 1970-71). Methodist (mem. adminstrv. bd. and finance com. 1968—). Home: 439 Riverside Dr Portsmouth VA 23707 Office: 355 Crawford St Portsmouth VA 23704

BUCKLAND, MARION MCIVER (MRS. CHARLES GARDNER BUCKLAND), home economist; b. Newport, Vt., Jan. 3, 1921; d. Leo Hazen and Carrie Edna (Davis) McIver; B.S., U. N.H., 1943; postgrad. Cornell U., summer 1955, Colo. State U., summers 1958, 70, U. Vt., 1961-64, 67, 70; m. Charles Gardner Buckland, Feb. 23, 1943; 1 dau., Janet Louise (Mrs. Earl P. Lucas). Asst. dietitian Boston City Hosp., 1943-44; extension agt. home econs. Orleans County, U. Vt. extension service, 1955-74; home econs. agt. Alachua County Extension, Gainesville, Fla., 1974—; tchr. Newport Community Coll., 1971. Bd. dirs. Orleans County Arts and Crafts Fair, 1957-73; trustee Northeast Kingdom Mental Health Service. Mem. Nat. (Distinguished Service award), New Eng. (past v.p.), Vt. (past pres., sec.) assns., extension home economists, Am., Vt. home economists assns., Memphremagog Grange, Orleans County Hist. Soc., Epsilon Sigma Phi (pres. Psi chpt. 1971-72), Mem. United Ch. Club: Newport Woman's. Home: 516 NW 101st Terrace Hamilton Heights Gainesville FL 32601 Office: Seagle Bldg Gainesville FL 32601

BUCKLEY, DOROTHY PATRICIA, educator; b. Hempstead, N.Y., Sept. 10, 1931; d. Thomas O. and Dorothy Phipps (Johnson) Shearman; B.S., Adelphi U., 1959; M.Ed., Miami U., 1960; m. Ronald L. Thron (dec.); children—Thomas, Billy; m. 2d, William Buckley, June 1964 (div.). Instr. nursing edn. Nassau Coll., Garden City, N.Y., 1963-64; asst. prof. nursing edn. State U. N.Y. at Farmingdale, 1965—; nurse adminstr., Hempstead, N.Y., 1974; instr. nursing edn. Adelphi U., Garden City, N.Y., 1974—. Vice pres. AMI Corp., N.Y.C., 1973—. Partner Med. Tng. Sch., Hempstead, N.Y., 1974—. Committeewoman Bethpage (N.Y.) Republican Com., 1966-67. Mem. Am. Assn. U. Women, U.S. Lawn and Tennis Assn., League Women Voters, Internat. Platform Assn. Clubs: West Side Tennis; Jockey (Fla.). Home: 413 Lopez Dr West Hempstead NY 11552

BUCKLEY, HELEN ANN, lawyer; b. San Francisco, June 12, 1926; d. Martin Joseph and Helen Bernice (Kuhl) Buckley; A.B., U. Cal., 1951, J.D. (Newhouse fellow), 1954. Admitted to Cal. bar, 1955, Colo. bar, 1956; asso. in law U. Cal., Berkeley, 1954-55; trial attorney, Tax Div., U.S. Dept. Justice, Washington, 1955-60; tax counsel Hunt Foods, Fullerton, Cal., 1961-63; mem. firm Pacht, Ross, Warne, Bernhard and Sears, Los Angeles, 1963-71; atty. Norton Simon, Inc., Los Angeles, 1971-74; instr. law U. So. Cal. Law Center, 1973; prof. law U. Ia. Coll. Law, Iowa City, 1974—. Bd. dirs. Young Audiences of Los Angeles, 1968—. Mem. Cal., Los Angeles, Beverly Hills bar assns., U.S. Dist. Court, D.C., Am. Civil Liberties Union, Japanese Am. Citizens League. Address: College of Law University of Iowa Iowa City IA 52240

BUCKLEY, MARY LORRAINE (MRS. JOSEPH PARRIOTT), artist, educator; b. New Haven; d. R. Riordan Buckley and Mary Buckley Thompson; student Keuka Coll., 1944-47, Yale, 1947-49, Bklyn. Mus. Art Sch., 1949-51, also pvt. tchrs.; m. Joseph Parriott, Feb. 14, 1970. Book editor Popular Sci. Pub. Co., N.Y.C., 1954-55; asst. prof. art Pratt Inst., Bklyn., 1958-67, asso. prof., 1967-71, prof. color and design, 1971—; color cons. Seagrams Bldg., N.Y.C., 1959, N.Y. State Bldg., 1964, N.Y. World's Fair; faculty People's Art Center, Mus. Modern Art, N.Y.C., 1961-62; pvt. tchr. art, Wis., N.Y.C., L.I., N.Y., 1960-68; partner, designer Mary Buckley Assos., color and design firm, Huntington, L.I., N.Y., designers for Brit. Pavillion, 1964 N.Y. Worlds Fair; color cons. Pubs. Clearinghouse, Port Washington, N.Y.; dir. Margaret Gate Inst., Huntington; color cons. to Philip Johnson, architect, 1959-60; executed sculptures and standards for N.Y. State Legislature Bldg., Albany, 1972-74; designer White Horse Mus., 1960, Seagrams Bldg., Paragon Inc., Farmingdale, L.I., also East Meadows. Exhibited at Marino Gallery, 1960, J. Walter Thompson, 1961, Pratt Inst., 1963, Caravan Gallery, 1968, N.Y.C., Pratt Inst., 1974; group shows Waverly Gallery, 1962, N.J. Argus Gallery, 1962, Nat. Acad., N.Y.C., 1961, 62, Heckscher Mus., Huntington, also in Me., Ill.; represented in permanent collection Pratt Inst., Erie Coll., many pvt. collections; murals executed Seagram Bldg., N.Y.C., Brasserie Restaurant, N.Y.C., Stadium Motel, N.Y.C., Dunwoodie Motel, N.Y.C. Macdowell Found. fellow, 1958—; N.Y. State Council on Arts grant, 1973-74. Mem. Indsl. Design Soc. Am., Nat. Assn. Women Artists, Nat. Art Edn. Assn., Eastern Arts Assn., Am. Assn. U. Profs., Huntington Twp. Art League (vice chmn., membership chmn. 1962-63). Illustrator: Silver Anthology of Light Verse. Contbg. editor Tech. Dictionary Art; editor Bibliography of Color Theory. Home: Bay Crest Huntington NY 11743 Office: Pratt Institute Brooklyn NY 11205

BUCKLEY, NANCY MARGARET, med. educator; b. Phila., Dec. 2, 1924; d. Thomas and Margaret Craig (Burns) Buckley; B.A., U. Pa., 1945, M.D., 1950. Intern Atlantic City Gen. Hosp., 1950-51; research asso. research medicine Ohio State U. Med. Center, 1951-52, asst. prof. physiology, 1952-55; asst. prof. physiology Albert Einstein Coll. Medicine, 1955-58, asso. prof., 1958-74, prof., 1974—. Mem. N.Y. Acad. Sci., A.A.A.S., Am. Physiol. Soc., Am., N.Y. State heart assns., Harvey Soc. Contbr. articles to physiol. jours. Home: 372 Central Park West New York City NY 10025

BUCKLEY, PRISCILLA LANGFORD, mag. exec.; b. N.Y.C., Oct. 17, 1921; d. William Frank and Aloise (Steiner) Buckley; B.A., Smith Coll., 1943. Copy girl, sports writer U.P., N.Y.C., 1944, radio rewriter, 1944-47; news editor sta. WACA, Camden, S.C., 1948-49; reports officer CIA, Washington, 1951-53; staff corr. U.P., Paris, France, 1953-56; with Nat. Rev. Mag., N.Y.C., 1956—, mng. editor, 1959—. Mem. St. Hubert's Soc. Republican. Roman Catholic. Club: Sharon (Conn.) Country. Home: Great Elm Sharon CT 06069 Office: 150 E 35th St New York City NY 10016

BUCKLEY, WINIFRED NELLIE (MRS. RALPH HOWARD BUCKLEY), editor, pub. relations exec.; b. Omaha, May 19, 1917; d. Frank Eugene and Millie Adeline (Brown) O'Brien; student Chaffey Coll., 1935-37; B.A. cum laude, U. So. Cal., 1939; m. Ralph Howard Buckley, Aug. 18, 1942; children—Linda (Mrs. Guy Lashlee), John Howard. Reporter San Bernardino (Cal.) Sun, 1940-42; reporter, photographer Progress Bull., Pomona, Cal., 1949-60, asst. city editor, 1960-66; reporter Star Bull., Honolulu, 1966; pub. relations asst. Hawaii Retarded Childrens Assn., Honolulu, 1966; photog. rep. Island Camera, Honolulu, 1966-70; editor Hawaii Employers Council, Honolulu, 1970—, also community relations coordinator. Recipient Photog. award A.P., 1952, Outstanding Service award State Tchrs. Assn., 1957, citation for Outstanding Reporting in Edn., State of Cal., 1957. Mem. Women in Communications (pres. Honolulu chpt. 1970-71), Hawaii Communicators Assn. Club: Honolulu Press. Address: 4191-3 Keanu St Honolulu HI 96816

BUCKNER, KATHRYN CURRENT (MRS. NEWT M. BUCKNER), educator; b. Chariton, Ia., June 18, 1926; d. Charles A. and Berniece (Cloe) Trimble; student Ball. State Tchrs. Coll., 1948-49, Ind. U., 1958-59; B.B.A., Ga. State U., 1961, M.B.A., 1965, D.Bus.Adminstn., 1971; m. James P. Current, Feb. 14, 1945 (dec. Feb. 1968); 1 son, James P.; m. 2d, Newt M. Buckner, May 29, 1971. Various secretarial positions, Pensacola, Fla., 1943-45, Santa Ana, Cal., 1945-46; accountant, office mgr. Thomas J. Marimon, auto sales and service, Valparaiso, Ind., 1950-55, Boney & Mellette Dodge Auto Sales and Service, Anaheim, Cal., 1955-56; accounting, jr. accountant Woodrow Hulme, C.P.A., Ardmore, Okla., 1957-58, Ralph M. Braswell, C.P.A., Atlanta, 1956-57, 59-61; accountant, auditor, asso. William T. Hankins, Jr., C.P.A., Atlanta, 1961, 62-66; asst. prof. accounting Ga. State U., Atlanta, 1966—. Mem. Pres.'s Council of Atlanta, 1964—. Recipient W.S. Kell award, 1961. Mem. Am. Soc. Women Accountants (1st v.p. 1963-64, pres. 1964-65), Ga., Am. Womans (nat. award com. 1966-68, tech. program chmn. joint ann. meeting with Am. Soc. Women Accountants 1973), socs. C.P.A.'s, Am. Accounting Assn., Am. Assn. U. Women, Nat. Assn. Accountants (chpt. dir., dir. edn. 1969-70, sec. 1971-72, treas. 1972-73, v.p., liaison officer 1973-75), Am. Inst. C.P.A's, Am. Assn. U. Profs., Phi Chi Theta (treas. 1960-61), Beta Alpha Psi (faculty v.p. 1970—), Delta Mu Delta (sec. 1960-61), Beta Gamma Sigma. Mem. editorial bd. The Woman C.P.A., 1973—. Home: Ono Rd Rt 1 Box 60 Palmetto GA 30268 Office: 33 Gilmer St SE Atlanta GA 30303

BUCKNER, LORAINE ANN SYRJALA (MRS. ROBERT EDWARD BUCKNER), city ofcl.; b. Watton, Mich., Aug. 12, 1941; d. William Isaac Kellogg Community Coll., 1966-67, 74; m. Robert Edward Buckner, Aug. 9, 1969; 1 son, Michael. Exec. sec. Wolverine Ins. Co., Battle Creek, Mich., 1961-68; city clk. City Battle Creek, Mich., 1968—. Mem. Mich. Clks. Assn., Internat. Inst. Municipal Clks., Altrusa. Methodist. Home: 35 Woodmer Lane Battle Creek MI 49017 Office: City Hall Div Av Battle Creek MI 49014

BUCKNER, RAMONA JOYCE, educator; b. Benton, Ark., Sept. 25, 1937; d. Waymond Floyd and Willie Evelyn (Wright) Pannell; B.A., Ouachita Baptist Coll., 1959; M.S.E., Henderson State Tchrs. Coll., 1964; Ph.D. (univ. scholar), North Tex. State U., 1970; children by previous marriage—Cheryl, John, Chris. Tchr. pub. sch. Ark., 1961-67; instr. North Tex. State U., Denton, 1967-70; asst. prof. edn. U. Tex. at Arlington, 1970—, acting chmn. edn. dept., 1973—. Ednl. and psychol. cons.; pvt. practice psychotherapy, since 1970—. Mem. Tex. Council Deans Edn., Am., Tex., Southwestern Psychol. assns., Tex. Assn. Coll. Tchrs., Arlington Club N. Tex. State U. Alumni (v.p. 1973-74). Home: 510D Av J E Grand Prairie TX 75050 Office: Education Dept University Texas Arlington TX 76019

BUDD, BEVERLY MAY MONCOL (MRS. THOMAS S. BUDD), psychometrist; b. Cleve., Feb. 3, 1942; d. William Emil and Dorothy Florence (Habel) Moncol; student Fenn Coll., 1962-63; B.S. in Edn., Ohio State U., 1965; M.Ed., Kent State U., 1970, Edn. Specialist, 1971; m. Thomas S. Budd, June 11, 1973. Tchr. sci. dept. Greenbriar Jr. High Sch., Parma, O., 1965-69; intern sch. psychologist Kent (O.) Pub. Schs., 1969-71; sch. psychologist Mt. Vernon (O.) City Schs., 1971-73; psychometrist on diagnostic reading van Washoe County Schs., Reno, Nev., 1973—. Guest tchr. clin. psychology Kenyon Coll., 1971-72; guest tech. psychology of mentally retarded Kent State U., 1970. Publicity chmn. Knox County Community Agys. Roundtable, 1972-73. Mem. Nat. Assn. Sch. Psychologists (mem. publs. com. 1971-73, profl. standards com. 1974). No. Nev. Psychol. Soc. Home: 2355 Sequoia Lane Reno NV 89502 Office: 425 E 9th St Reno NV 89502

BUDD, EDITH MARKS (MRS. ARTHUR EMERSON BUDD), ednl. and reading cons.; b. Huntington, N.Y., Nov. 11, 1913; d. Theodore A. and Greta (Boettiger) Marks; student Potsdam Coll., 1933-35, Oneonta State Tchrs. Coll., 1937, U. Vt., 1938, Columbia, 1942; B.S., N.Y. U., 1942, M.A., 1947; postgrad. U. Fla., 1948, Fla. State U., 1958-59, Fla. Atlantic U., 1968-69, 74; m. Arthur Emerson Budd, June 21, 1947. Tchr. schs., Finderne and Morris Plains, N.J., 1935-40, Roslyn, N.Y., 1944-45, Palm Beach, Fla., 1948-50; asst. N.Y. U. Reading Clinic, N.Y.C., 1940-47; reading specialist pub. schs., Point Pleasant Beach and Leonia, N.J., 1940-44, Manhasset, N.Y., 1945-47; founder, dir. Budd Ednl. Cons., West Palm Beach, Fla., 1950—. Mem. N.E.A. (life), Nat. Council Tchrs. English, Am. Assn. U. Women (br. pres.), Nat. Soc. Study Edn., Internat. Reading Assn., Internat. Oceanographic Soc., Menninger Found., Audubon Soc., Kappa Delta Pi. Democrat. Research detection and correction learning difficulties. Home: 3223 Parker Av West Palm Beach FL 33405 Office: 3227 Parker Av West Palm Beach FL 33405

BUDD, SISTER MARGARET MARY, hosp. adminstr.; b. New Bedford, Mass., May 11, 1914; d. Stanley Ward and Marguerite Harrison (Habicth) Budd; R.N., St. Mary's Sch. Nursing, 1935-38; student Coll. St. Catherine, 1962, St. Mary's Sch. Anesthesia, 1959, Cath. U. Am., 1966. Nursing supr. St. Joseph's Hosp., Superior, Wis., 1938-49, nurse anesthetist, 1959-61, adminstr., 1962-64; nursing supr. Holy Family Hosp., New Richmond, Wis., 1949-57, adminstr., 1967—, pres. bd. dirs., 1969—. Mem. Sisters of St. Joseph, 1930—. Mem. Am., Wis. nurses assns., Am. Assn. Nurse Anesthetists, Am. Acad. Med. Adminstrs. Address: 535 Hospital Rd New Richmond WI 54017

BUDDE, BERNADETTE ANN, assn. adminstr.; b. Beaver Dam, Wis., Apr. 13, 1947; d. Richard Arnold and Bernadine Lorraine (Becker) Budde; B.A. in Journalism, Marquette U., 1969; M.A. in Govt., U. Md., 1970. Research asst. Bus.-Industry Polit. Action Com., Washington, 1970-71, editorial dir., 1971-72, dir. polit. edn., 1972—. Mem. Am. Polit. Sci. Assn., Washington Jr. C. of C., Women in Communications. Roman Catholic. Home: 1330 Massachusetts Av NW Washington DC 20005 Office: 1747 Pennsylvania Av NW Washington DC 20006

BUDDE, JEANNE FRANCES, advt. exec.; b. Bklyn., Mar. 30, 1931; d. John Percy and Amy (Simonsen) Budde; diploma Packard Jr. Coll., N.Y.C., 1951; N.Y. Sch. Interior Design, N.Y.C., 1964; m. Joseph Malyniak, Jr., June 2, 1962; children—Susan Jeanne, Jeffrey Budde. Editor, Living for Young Homemakers mag. Street & Smith Publs., N.Y.C., 1951-61; mgr. home furnishings marketing communications fibers div. Am. Cyanamid Co., Wayne, N.J., 1961—. Fellow Nat. Home Fashions League (v.p. N.Y. chpt. 1971-73, treas. 1971, exec. v.p. 1972, pres. 1971-73). Home: 6 Peter Cooper Rd New York City NY 10010 Office: 630 Fifth Av New York City NY 10020 also Berdan Av Wayne NJ 07470

BUDER, RENEE VICKI (MRS. LEONARD BUDER), psychologist; b. N.Y.C., Mar. 1, 1925; d. Irving and Anne Mathilde (Dubinsky) Cantor; B.A., N.Y. U., 1945; M.S. in Edn., Coll. City N.Y., 1968; m. Leonard Buder, Dec. 6, 1953; children—Jon, Jane. Psychologist, Ethical Culture Schs., N.Y.C., 1971-73; sch. psychologist Bur. of Child Guidance, N.Y.C., 1973—. Mem. Am. Psychol. Assn., Kappa Delta Pi. Home: 2728 Henry Hudson Pkwy New York City NY 10463 Office: 362 Schermerhorn St Brooklyn NY 11217

BUDIC, CATHERINE MARY KASPER (MRS. ROBERT MARK BUDIC), occupational therapist; b. Marshfield, Wis., Feb. 26, 1945; d. Frank Walter and Catherine Margaret (Schnabel) Kasper; student Coll. St. Theresa, 1963-64; B.S. in Occupational Therapy, Mt. Mary Coll., 1967; m. Robert Mark Budic, Dec. 16, 1967; children—Patrick Robert, Thomas Francis. Staff therapist Milwaukee County Mental Health Instns., 1968; staff therapist Mt. Sinai Med. Center, Milw., 1969-70, chief occupational therapist, 1970-71; dir. occupational therapy Sacred Heart Rehab. Hosp., Milw., 1972; pvt. practice occupational therapy, Wauwatosa, Wis., 1973—. Cons., instr. Vols. for Stroke Program, Sacred Heart Rehab. Hosp., Milw., 1972; cons. U. Wis., Waukesha, 1972—. Mem. Am., Wis. occupational therapy assns. Home: 2353 Lefeber Av Wauwatosa WI 53213

BUDZAK, KATHRYN SUE (MRS. ARTHUR BUDZAK), physician; b. Racine, Wis., May 6, 1940; d. Raymond Philip and Emma Kathryn (Sorensen) Myer; student Stephens Coll., 1957-58, Luther Coll., 1958-59; B.S. with honors, U. Wis. at Milw., 1962; M.D., U. Wis., 1969; m. Arthur Budzak, Dec. 21, 1961; children—Ann Elizabeth, Lynn Marie. Intern, Madison (Wis.) Gen. Hosp., 1969-70; emergency physician, emergency suite St. Mary's Hosp., Madison, 1971—; with Emergency Physicians of Madison. Mem. Am. Coll. Emergency Physicians, A.M.A., Wis., Dane County med. socs., Am. Med. Women's Assn., Wis. Med. Alumni Assn., Sigma Sigma Sigma. Presbyn. Me. editorial bd. Wis. Med. Alumni Quar. Home: 6110 Davenport Dr Madison WI 53711 Office: 720 S Brooks St Madison WI 53715

BUDZINE, LEONA PEARL WILLIAMS, educator; b. Walker, Ia., Aug. 12, 1909; d. John Irvin and Nora Frances (Wylie) Williams; student Ia. State Tchrs. Coll., summers 1959-62, U. Wash., summer 1960, State U. Ia., 1964; B.A. cum laude, Upper Ia. U., 1965; grad. Newspaper Inst. Am., N.Y.C., 1967; m. Donald L. Budzine, Apr. 16, 1931; children—Barbara (Mrs. William Fenkner) and Marilyn (Mrs. Carl Buettemeier) (twins), Diana (Mrs. Robert Hildebrandt). Rural tchr.; tchr. jr. high schs. Winthrop and Walker, Ia.; tchr. pub. schs., Independence, Ia., 1959—. Mem. Am. Assn. U. Women (publicity chmn.), County Ednl. Assn. (pres.), Nat., Ia. edn. assns., Bus. and Profl. Women (pres., Mother-of-the-Year award 1959). Lutheran (tchr. Sunday sch.). Author: Clues. Contbr. poetry to mags. Pioneer, Pik-A-Blok lang. games. Home: 509 5th St SW Independence IA 50644 Office: PO Box 505 Independence IA 50644

BUEHL, ISABELLE ANN (MRS. ROBERT THEODORE BUEHL), physician; b. Ramsey, Ind., Sept. 2, 1934; d. Joseph Hobert and Daisy Leona (Thevenot) Davis; A.B., Ind. U., 1956, M.D., 1959; m. Robert Theodore Buehl, Sept. 14, 1957. Intern Methodist Hosp., Indpls., 1959-60; resident pathology Ind. U. Sch. Medicine, Indpls., 1960-64, asst. prof. pathology, 1964—; practice medicine, specializing in pathology, Indpls., 1964—; mem. staff St. Francis Hosp., Beech Grove, Ind., Univ. Heights Hosp., Indpls.; partner Med. Lab. of Drs. Thornton, Haymond, Costin & Buehl, Indpls., 1965—. Bd. dirs. Marion County Community Blood Bank. Am. Cancer Soc. fellow, 1963-64. Fellow Am. Coll. Pathologists; mem. Am. Soc. Clin. Pathologists, A.M.A., Ind., Marion County med. socs., Alpha Omega Alpha. Home: Rural Route 3 Box 229 Greenwood IN 46142 Office: 301 E 38th St Indianapolis IN 46205

BUEHRER, RUTH MARIE, ednl. adminstr.; b. Newark, Feb. 11, 1924; d. John Herman and Matilda Anne (Rose) Buehrer; B.S., Newark State Tchrs. Coll., 1944; M.A., Seton Hall U., 1949. Tchr., kindergarten pub. schs., Newark and South Orange, N.J., 1944-66; project coordinator—Title 1 Burnet State Sch., Newark, 1966-71; field coordinator Dept. Fed. Assistance, Newark, 1971; program adminstr. Primary Reading Center, Newark Bd. Edn., 1969-73; asso. prof. Newark State Coll. extension, 1950-52; instr. Operation Head Start, 1960-67. Bd. dirs. Rainbow Girls, 1960-74. Mem. N.E.A. (urban task force 1968-69), N.J. Edn. Assn. (chmn. profl. rights and responsibilities com.), Newark Tchrs. Assn. (pres. 1962-66), N.J. Assn. for Childhood Edn. (pres. 1958-60). Mem. Order Eastern Star. Home: 330 Mount Prospect Av Newark NJ 07104 Office: Bd Edn Newark NJ 07102

BUEKER, KATHLEEN ANN, sociol. cons.; b. Saginaw, Mich., May 10, 1930; d. John Wesley and Margaret (Hoff) Bueker; grad. St. Elizabeths Hosp. Sch. Nursing, 1951; B.S., Catholic U., 1957, M.A., 1962; Ph.D., Am. U., 1969. Clin. psychiat. nurse St. Elizabeths Hosp., Washington, 1951-57, instr., 1957-63, researcher, 1963-69; chief Vestermark Center, Nat. Inst. Mental Health, Rockville, Md., 1969—. Cons. in psychiat. services, 1970—. Mem. Am. Sociol. Assn. Contbr. articles to profl. jours. Home: 3835 N Chesterbrook Rd Arlington VA 22207 Office: 5600 Fischers Lane Rockville MD 20852

BUELL, KAYE MCCLURE, investment co. exec.; b. Cin.; d. William James and Virginia R. (Fuller) McClure; student U. Wash., Coll. Puget Sound, 1956-57, U. Cin., 1957-58, N.Y. Inst. Finance, 1962-63; Ph.D. (hon.), Colo. State Christian Coll., 1973; m. Bradley D. Buell, Aug. 1, 1959 (div. Sept. 1966); 1 son, Bradley E. With margin dept. Merrill Lynch Pierce Fenner & Beane, Cin., 1957-59, Seattle, 1959-62; sec.-treas. Aetna Investment, N.Am. Mortgage Co., Seattle, 1962-68; prodn. supr. for Gov. Wash., Seattle, 1968; pres., maj. stockholder Olympia Investment Corp., Seattle, 1969—; owner Central Lettershop and Answering Service, Seattle, 1973—. Active Seattle Symphony Orch., Seattle Opera. Recipient Top award Nat. Forensic League, 1956. Mem. Seattle C. of C. Republican. Home: 815 Hillside Dr E Seattle WA 98112 also Silver Skis Chalet 302 Crystal Mountain WA 98022 Office: 208 Central Bldg Seattle WA 98104

BUELL, NINA ORWICK, pharmacist, civic worker; b. Michigan Center, Mich., Apr. 21, 1909; d. Charles Prosser and Mary (Hague) Orwick; student Warner's Practical Inst. Pharmacy, 1927, Detroit Inst. Pharmacy, 1935; m. Harold Paul Buell, May 17, 1939 (dec. Sept. 1959); 1 dau., Ida (Mrs. Richard Frank Anderson). Owner, pharmacist Orwick's Drug Store, Inc., Lewiston, Mich., 1936-67. Pres. Mich. Winter Sports Council, 1953-54; mem. exec. com. East Mich. Tourist Assn., Bay City, 1967, also bd. dirs., pres., 1972-73, chmn. exec. com., 1973-74; mem. Lewiston Bd. Edn., 1952-61, pres., 1955-61; mem. Albert Twp. Bldg. Code Bd. Appeals, 1968-72; mem. board trustees Lewiston Civic Improvement Assn., 1968-73, v.p., 1970; membership chmn. Montmorency County Friends of Library, 1970-73; v.p. North Central Mich. Comprehensive Health Planning Council; mem. Au Sable River Task Force, 1971-73; mem. Northeast Mich. Planning and Devel. Commn. Recipient Bowl of Hygeia award A.H. Robins Co., Richmond, Va., 1966. Mem. Lewiston C. of C. (pres., 1961-62), Mich. Apothecaries for Polit. Action (exec. com.), North Eastern Mich. Pharmacists Assn. (past pres.), Mich. (exec. com., 1962-65), Am. pharm. assns. Republican. Conglist. (deaconess 1973—, trustee, past chmn.). Mem. Order Eastern Star. Clubs: Sheridan Valley Ski (sec.) (Lewiston), Lewiston Farm & Garden. Home: West Twin Lake Lewiston MI 49756 Office: PO Box 217 Lewiston MI 49756

BUERGER, ANNE FORTUNE (MRS. DAVID BERNARD BUERGER), civic worker; b. Pitts., Oct. 28, 1909; d. Joseph and Katharina (Ritter) Fortune; student U. Pitts., 1940, Duquesne U., 1968; m. David Bernard Buerger, June 30, 1946; 1 son, David Charles. Organizer, mem. Hampton Civic Assn., Allison Park, Pa., 1948—, pres., 1960-61, editor handbook, 1960, 64, 68, 72, treas., 1973-74; mem. Route 8 Civic Improvement Assn., Allegheny County, Pa., 1965—; mem. Pitts. Symphony Soc., 1948—; chmn. North Hills, 1962, chmn. Hampton Community Centers Allison Parks, 1962-1963; pres. Allegheny Acad., 1971-74. Bd. dirs. Divine Providence Aux., Pitts., Allegheny Gen. Hosp. Flower Cart Service, Pitts. Mem. Woman's Nat. Farm and Garden Assn. (nat. pres. 1968-70, nat. del. to Ireland 1965, Norway, 1971, chmn. various coms. 1954-72), Asso. Country Women of World (internat. council 1968-70). Roman Catholic (chmn. Easter com. 1962—, chmn. fashion show and luncheon 1963). Clubs: Hoe and Harvest Garden (organizer), Country Lane Garden (past pres.), Pittsburgh Garden Center, Federated Garden Clubs, Wildwood Golf (chmn. several ladies' coms. 1960-65). Home: 3000 McCully Rd Allison Park PA 15101

BUETTNER, EDNA SCHREIBER, realtor; b. Balt., Feb. 10, 1915; d. William and Rebecca (Dowling) Schreiber; student North Dade Jr. Coll.; m. Carl Buettner, Dec. 29, 1939 (dec. Dec. 1949); children—Carl R., Clifton V., Wilma (Mrs. Pacetti). Saleslady, Avon Products, 1949-52; stock car promoter Dorsey (Md.) Speedway, 1952-54; saleslady Stanley Home Products, 1954-57; realtor, Miami, Fla., 1957—. Mem. local draft bd. 177 SSS. Pres., Greater Miami Democratic Women's Club, 1966-67; mem. Dem. Exec. Com. 11th Congl. Dist., 1971—; pres. Dem. Women's Club Dade County, 1970-73; mem. credentials com. Dem. Exec. Com. Dade County. Mem. Miami Bd. Realtors, Fla. Assn. Realtors, Nat. Multiple Listing Service. Home: 1518 NW 101st St Miami FL 33147 Office: 10455 NW 7th Av Miami FL 33150

BUFFA, BETTE MEYER (MRS. HENRY ANDREW BUFFA), lawyer; b. St. Louis, Feb. 6, 1926; d. Elmer Raymond and Edith Mae (Kennedy) Meyer; B.S., Washington U., St. Louis, 1945, J.D., 1947; m. Henry Andrew Buffa, Dec. 6, 1947; children—Robert Matthew, Scott Kennedy, Allison Anne, Barbara Edith. Admitted to Mo. bar, 1947; practiced in St. Louis, 1946-48; mem. firm Neuhoff, Tremayne & Schaeffer; corporate atty. Am. Investment Co. Ill., St. Louis, 1949-54; corporate atty. Monsanto Co., St. Louis, 1966—. Chmn. St. Paul's Coop, Creve Coeur, Mo., 1970—. Mem. Am. (probation vol. 1972—), Mo., St. Louis Bar assns., St. Louis Women's Bar Assn. (pres. 1962-63), Parkway P.T.A., Order of Coif, Phi Beta Kappa, Alpha Chi Omega. Republican. Home: 143 Fiesta Circle Dr Creve Coeur MO 63141 Office: 800 N Lindbergh Blvd St Louis MO 63166

BUFFINGTON, HELEN ANNELLE TOLES, editor; b. Jamestown, Ala., Oct. 27, 1927; d. Thomas Taylor and Minnie Lea (Sentell) Toles; Asso., Young Harris Coll., 1946; m. Herman Buffington, Apr. 14, 1949; children—Michael Herman, Scott Lee. Reporter Rome (Ga.) News Tribune, 1946-47, feature writer, 1950-60; reporter Summerville (Ga.) News, 1947-50, mng. editor, 1960-65; editor Jackson Herald, Jefferson, Ga., 1965—; v.p. Jackson Herald, Inc., Jefferson, 1965—. Sec. Floyd County Mental Health Assn., 1956-58. Recipient TV Big Story award Pall Mall, 1956; first place award Ga. Conf. Social Welfare, 1957; first place award A.P., 1957; first place award Ga. Press Assn., 1968, 69; Freedoms Found. award, 1970; Blue Ribbon newspaper award, 1970-71. Mem. Women in Communications. Methodist. Home: Dry Pond Rd Jefferson GA 30549 Office: PO Box 37 Jefferson GA 30549

BUGBEE, ELAINE G., town ofcl.; b. Hartford, Conn., Jan. 5, 1932; d. Alfred Joseph and Beatrice Susan (Banks) Gordon; student Hillyer Coll., 1949-50, Town Clks. Sch. U. Conn., 1972, 73, 74; m. Howard Bugbee, Oct. 4, 1952; 1 dau., Sharon. Stenographer, Hartford Accident & Ins. Co. (Conn.), 1949-54; tax collector Town of Tolland (Conn.), 1965-69, town clk., 1971—. Sec., Republican town com., 1971-73, vice chmn., 1973—. Bd. dirs. Tolland High Sch. Scholarship Fund. Mem. Tolland Vol. Fire Dept. Aux. (pres. 1960-61), Tolland-Windham County Tax Assn. (sec. 1967-69). Conglist. Home: Mountain Spring Rd Tolland CT Office: Town Hall Tolland St Tolland CT 06084

BUGGEY, RUTH, librarian; b. Rivers, Man., Can., July 30, 1913; d. Francis Warren and Georgina Frances (Shannon) Buggey; B.A., U. Man., 1933; B.L.S., McGill U., 1934; M.A. in L.S., U. Mich., 1964. Asst. cataloguer, reference asst. Legislative Library, Province of Man., Winnipeg, 1934-46; head circulation and reference U. Man., Winnipeg, 1946-49, head circulation, 1964-65; head librarian Winnipeg Free Press, 1949-62, head librarian, 1967—; reader's adviser Kitchener (Ont.) Pub. Library, 1965-66; librarian Forest Research Lab. Library, Winnipeg, 1966-67. Home: 26-209 Furby St Winnipeg MB R3C 2A6 Canada Office: 300 Carlton St Winnipeg MB R3C 3C1 Canada

BUHRMAN, HAZEL MARGARET, nurse; b. Council Bluffs, Ia., Aug. 27, 1913; d. George and Sophie (Koester) Buhrman; R.N., Mercy Hosp. Sch. Nursing, Council Bluffs, 1935; B.S. in Nursing, Creighton U., 1952; M.A. in -Nursing, State U. Ia., 1960. Head nurse Mercy Hosp., 1935-37; staff nurse Knoxville (Ia.) VA Hosp., 1937-42; instr., 1954-60, asso. chief nursing service for edn., 1961-66; asst. prof. Coll. Nursing U. Ia., Iowa City, 1966-73; psychiat. nurse, clin. specialist VA Hosp., Omaha, 1973—; instr. St. Bernard's Hosp., Council Bluffs, 1950-54. Mem. Ia. Bd. Nurse Examiners, Des Moines,

1957-67, chmn., 1960-62, 65-67; mem. adv. com. on continuing edn. U. Ia. Coll. Nursing, Iowa City, 1960-61. Sec. Beta Sigma Phi State of Ia., Knoxville, 1940; mem. Council Bluffs City Council, 1953, treas., 1953. Served to lt., Navy Nurse Corps, 1943-46; PTO. Mem. Ia. League Nursing (Ia. treas. 1956-57, dir. 1958-59), Ia. Nurses Assn. (9th dist. treas. 1949-51, mem. Ia. legislative com. 1960-64). Bus. and Profl. Women's Assn. (achievement award 1965), Beta Sigma Phi (state sec. 1940; chpt. girl of year award 1964), Delta Kappa Gamma, Sigma Theta Tau. Mem. United Ch. of Christ (mem. council 1953-54). Home: 4428 Grover St Omaha NE 68105 Office: VA Hosp Omaha NE 68105

BUILER, DOROTHY MARION MUELLER (MRS. DONALD J. BUILER), sports shop exec.; b. Athens, Wis., Apr. 20, 1925; d. Edwin H. and Katherine M. (Dick) Mueller; student vocational courses; m. Donald J. Builer, May 24, 1947; 1 son, Thomas E. Partner, Builer's Sport Shop, Wausau, Wis., 1959—, Campers Haven, Heafford Junction, Wis., 1967—. Mem. Internat. Platform Assn., United Comml. Travelers, Bus. and Profl. Womens Club (pres. Northwood dist. 1973—, Marathon County 1968-69), Am. Legion Aux. (local unit pres. 1958-59, 8th dist. pres. 1963-64, state conv. chmn. 1964), Tomahawk, Wausau chambers of commerce. Home: 807 Brown St Wausau WI 54401 Office: 215 S 3d Av Wausau WI 54401

BUIST, JEAN MACKERLEY, veterinarian; b. Newton, N.J., Dec. 24, 1919; d. Ackerson Jacob and Mary Morris (Morford) Mackerley; D.V.M., Cornell U., 1942; m. Richardson Buist, Oct. 2, 1948; children—Peter Richardson, Jean Morford Buist Algatt, Mary Elizabeth (Mrs. Morrissey). Veterinarian, Summit (N.J.) Dog and Cat Hosp., 1942-48; pvt. practice vet. medicine, Sparta, N.J., 1948—. Mem. Sparta Twp. Bd. Health, 1962—, chmn., 1972—. Bd. dirs. N.J. Acad. Vet. Medicine and Surgery, 1972—. Recipient Gaines award Newton Kennel Club, 1970. Mem. Sussex County 4-H Horse Club Leaders Assn. (pres. 1970—). Home: 143 Old Stanhope Rd Sparta NJ 07871

BULGARELLA, ROSARIA GIANNETTO, psychologist; b. Bessemer, Mich.; d. Carmelo and Domenica (Compagna) Giannetto; B.A. with high honors, Ph.D., Mich. State U.; M.S., U. Wis. Research asso., project dir. Mich. State U., East Lansing, 1965-67, tchr. U. Extension, 1967-68, asst. prof., research coordinator U.S. Office Edn./Univ. Regional Instructional Materials Center, 1967-69; asst. research prof. and dir. Human Learning Center, Found. for Cal. State Coll. at San Bernardino, 1970-71; chief program evaluation and research San Bernardino County Dept. Mental Health, 1973—. Trustee scholar Mich. State U.; U.S. Office Edn. grantee, 1968. Mem. Am. Psychol. Assn., Alpha Lambda Delta, Phi Kappa Phi. Home: 3705 Osbun Rd San Bernardino CA 92404 Office: 700 E Gilbert St San Bernardino CA 92415

BULGRIN, LEILA BAMBER, judge; b. Riverside, Cal., Nov. 16, 1923; d. William Percy and Gladys (Purvis) Bamber; LL.B., U. So. Cal., 1947; m. Wayne Bulgrin, June 7, 1947 (div.). Admitted to Cal. bar, 1947; asst. U.S. atty., Los Angeles, 1947-60; judge Municipal Ct., Los Angeles Jud. Dist., 1960—. Mem. Los Angeles County Bar Assn., Phi Delta Delta. Club: Women Lawyers (Los Angeles). Home: Tujunga CA 91042 Office: New County Courthouse Los Angeles CA 90012

BULKELEY, CHRISTY CLAIRE, editor; b. Galesburg, Ill., Feb. 10, 1942; d. Gerald Clough and Patricia Ann (Pettingell) Bulkeley; B.J., U. Mo., 1964. Gen. assignment reporter Rochester (N.Y.) Times-Union, 1964-66, county govt. reporter, 1968-71, polit. reporter, 1971-72, editorial writer, 1973, editorial page editor, 1973-74; editor, pub. Saratogian, Saratoga Springs, N.Y., 1974—. Mem. Women in Communications (2d nat. v.p. 1972—, founder Rochester chpt. 1965, pres. 1965-68), Am. Soc. Pub. Adminstrn. (dir. Rochester chpt. 1968-69, v.p. 1969-70), Soc. Profl. Journalists, Sigma Delta Chi, Alpha Phi. Home: 163 5th Av Saratoga Springs NY 12866 Office: 22 Lake Av Saratoga Springs NY 12866

BULKLEY, BETTY LOU COMPTON (MRS. ROY LYMAN BULKLEY), occupational therapist; b. Lawrence, Kan., July 24, 1926; d. James Howard and Florence Mildred (Lemon) Compton; B.S. in Occupational Therapy, U. Kan., 1950; postgrad. U. Kan., 1969—; m. Roy Lyman Bulkley, Oct. 22, 1949; 1 son, Timothy Howard. Occupational therapist Topeka State Hosp., 1949-52, chief occupational therapy, 1961-69, dir. activity therapy dept., 1969—. Cons. Topeka Presbyn. Manor, 1970—; lectr. U. Kan. Occupational Therapy Evaluation Techniques, Lawrence, 1973. Sec., Shawnee County Republican Central Com., 1968. Mem. Am., Kan. (v.p. 1964) occupational therapy assns. Home: 3929 Dixie Ct Topeka KS 66614 Office: 2700 W 6th St Topeka KS 66606

BULL, FRANCES ELEANOR, physician; b. Ann Arbor, Mich.; d. Hempstead S. and Sarah E. (Carr) Bull; B.S., U. Mich., 1948, M.D., 1952, M.S., 1960. Intern Phila. Gen. Hosp., 1952-53; resident Mayo Found., Rochester, Minn., 1954-57; practice medicine specializing in internal medicine, Ann Arbor, 1957—; mem. staff U. Mich. Med. Center, Ann Arbor; mem. faculty U. Mich. Med. Sch., Ann Arbor, 1957—, asso. prof. internal medicine, 1968—. Office: 1405 E Ann St Ann Arbor MI 48104

BULLARD, HELEN (MRS. JOSEPH MARSHALL KRECHNIAK), sculptor; b. Elgin, Ill., Aug. 15, 1902; d. Charles Wickliffe and Minnie (Cook) Bullard; student U. Chgo., 1921-29; m. Lloyd Ernst Rohrke, June 11, 1924 (div. Feb. 1931); children—Ann Louise (Mrs. Ross DeWitt Netherton), Barbara Jane (Mrs. Valtyr Emil Gudmundson); m. 2d, Joseph Marshall Krechniak, Jan. 30, 1952 (dec. Feb. 1964); 1 dau., Mariana (Mrs. Epifanio Medina). With research dept. L.V. Estes, Inc., Chgo., 1920-22; operator Square D Co., Detroit, 1922-24; simple research Commerce and Adminstrn. Library, U. Chgo., 1924-25; dir. Crossville (Tenn.) Play Center, 1949-50; creator hand-carved dolls, 1949—, wood sculpture, 1959—; exhibited with Nat. Inst. Am. Doll Exhbns., Los Angeles, 1963, Cin., 1964, Washington, 1965, Chgo., 1966, Boston, 1967, New Orleans, 1969, Detroit, 1970, Los Angeles, 1971, Omaha, 1972, Louisville, 1973, Miami, Fla., 1974, also craftsmen's fairs, 1954-65, The Club, Birmingham, Ala., 1963, Oak Ridge Art Cen ter, 1965, Children's Mus., Nashville, 1967, McClung Mus., Knoxville, 1969. Campaign chmn. Cumberland County unit Am. Can cer Soc., 1947-52. Mem. So. Highland Handicraft Guild (dir. 1957-59), Nat. Inst. Am. Doll Artists (founder, pres. 1963-67, 69-71), United Fedn. Doll Clubs (2d v.p. 1967-69), Am. Craftsmen's Council, Tenn. Folklore Soc., Mensa. Democrat. Unitarian. Author: (with husband) Cumberland County's First Hundred Years, 1956; The American Doll Artist, 1965, Vol. II, 1974; A Bullard Family, 1966; Dorothy Heizer, the Artist and Her Dolls, 1972; Tennessee Craftsmen, 1975. Home: Ozone TN 37842

BULLARD, MARY KIMBERLEY (MRS. STANLEY COOLIDGE BULLARD), author, editor; b. Collins, Ia., Aug. 21, 1914; d. Charles Henry and Daisy Pearl (Nowning) Kimberley; student Simpson Coll., 1933-35; B.S., Ia. State U., 1938; m. Stanley Coolidge Bullard, Jan. 4, 1943; children—Charles S., Margaret (Mrs. Terrol Lewman), Virginia (Mrs. Darrel Millard). Home mgmt. supr. Farm Security Adminstrn., U.S. Dept. Agr., various counties, Ia., 1939-41; information adviser Farm Security Adminstrn., U.S. Dept. Agr., Indpls., 1941-42; census enumerator Bur. Census, Story County, Ia., 1950; free lance writer, 1945—; editorial asst. Information Service Ia. State U., Ames, 1958—. Mem. Women in Communication. Mem. Order Eastern Star. Contbr. numerous articles to popular mags. and newspapers. Home: 312 Maxwell St Maxwell IA 50161

BULLEN, IDA ANDRUS (MRS. ROBERT WHITEFIELD BULLEN), librarian; b. Opelousas, La.; d. Wade Hampton and Marie Areditte (Caron) Andrus; B.A., U. S.W. La., 1944; M.A., Emory U., 1950, postgrad., 1965-67; postgrad. U. Ga., 1966-68; m. Robert Whitefield Bullen, Dec. 22, 1951; children—Andrew, Anne. Asst. librarian, instr. Morris Harvey Coll., Charleston, W.Va., 1958-60; library cons. Cobb County Schs., Marietta, Ga., 1962-69; dir. Palatine (Ill.) Pub. Library, 1969-71; cons. DuPage Library System, Geneva, Ill., 1971—. Vis. prof. U. Ga., 1964, Emory U. Library Sch., 1967; cons. to schs. and pub. libraries. Recipient Britannic award, 1967. Mem. Am., Ill., library assns., Sigma Sigma Sigma, Sigma Delta Pi. Episcopalian. Home: 23 S Linden Av Palatine IL 60067 Office: 127 S First St Geneva IL 60134

BULLION, LYNDA CAROLE FERGUSON (MRS. DELBERT I. BULLION, JR.), occupational therapist; b. Huntington, W.Va., Nov. 5, 1938; d. Albert Carl and Olive Grace (Anderson) Ferguson; student Marshall U., 1956-58; B.A., U. Miami, 1960; Certificate in Occupational Therapy, Columbia, 1962; m. Delbert I. Bullion, Jr., July 21, 1967; children—Delbert Ishmael III, John Carl, Kimberly Michel. Dir. occupational therapy Huntington Orthopedic Hosp., 1962-63, Huntington State Hosp., 1963-66, Spencer (W.Va.) State Hosp., 1966-67; coordinator activity therapies Farmington (Mo.) State Hosp., 1967-70; staff therapist, dept. mental health St. Thomas U.S. V.I., 1970-73; staff therapist McLennan County Mental Health Assn., Waco, Tex., 1973—. Cons. nursing homes, 1968-70. Bd. dirs. Owens Clinic, Huntington, 1966-67; pres. New Corners Club, Farmington, Mo., 1967. Mem. Am., Tex. occupational therapy assns. Home: Box 31 Valley Mills TX 76689 Office: 905 N 18th St Waco TX 76707

BULLOCH, KATHLEEN LOUISE OATES (MRS. CLIFFORD ALLEN BULLOCH), speech pathologist; b. Teaneck, N.J., Feb. 20, 1949; d. Thomas Joseph and Daisy Loretta (Negretti) Oates; B.A., William Paterson Coll. N.J., 1971; M.A., Montclair State Coll., 1972; m. Clifford Allen Bulloch, June 17, 1972. Chief speech pathologist Barnert Meml. Hosp. Paterson, N.J., 1971-73; communications disorder tchr. Harbor Sch., Red Bank, 1973—; speech pathologist Monmouth County Orgn. for Social Service, Red Bank, 1973—; pvt. practice as speech pathologist, Matawan, N.J., 1973-74, Middletown, N.J., 1973—; prof. cons. N.J. Assn. for Children with Learning Disabilities, 1973—. Mem. Am., N.J. speech and hearing assns., Nat. Assn. Hearing and Speech Agys., N.J. Assn. Children with Learning Disabilities, Am. Legion Aux. Home: 9 Arlene Court Brick Town NJ 08723 Office: Harbor School 255 Harding Rd Red Bank NJ 07701

BULLOCK, BETTY JO, univ. adminstr.; b. Olney, Tex., Apr. 3, 1929; d. Orval Loyd and Mattie (Elliott) Bullock; B.B.A., Midwestern U., 1950, M.A., 1960; postgrad. Our Lady of Lake, 1952. Intelligence analyst U.S. Air Force Security Service, San Antonio, 1950-53; bookkeeper Wichita Falls (Tex.) C. of C., 1953-55; asst. registrar Midwestern U., Wichita Falls, 1955-58, registrar, 1958—. Sec. bd. dirs. Wichita Falls Southside Girls Club. Mem. Am., Tex. (treas. 1972-75) assns. collegiate registrars and admissions officers, Sigma Kappa. Democrat. Baptist. Club: Soroptimist (pres. 1959) (Wichita Falls, Tex.). Home: 2711 Devon Rd Wichita Falls TX 76308 Office: 3400 Taft Blvd Wichita Falls TX 76308

BULLOCK, MARIE LEONTINE GRAVES (MRS. HUGH BULLOCK), assn. exec.; b. Paris, France, June 30, 1911; d. William Leon and Florence Christmas (Eno) Graves; postgrad. Sorbonne, Paris, also Columbia, 1933-37, Juilliard Sch. Music, 1937; tchrs. astronomy course Hayden Planetarium, 1952-53; m. Hugh Bullock, Apr. 5, 1933; children—Florence Eno (Mrs. Allan Block), Fair Alice Seymour (Mrs. Peter H. McCormick). Dir. Calvin Bullock, Ltd. Founder Acad. Am. Poets, 1934, pres., 1939—; bd. dirs. MacDowell Colony; bd. dirs., exec. com. Theodore Roosevelt Assn.; ex-officio mem. pres. adv. com. on arts John F. Kennedy Center for Performing Arts, citizens adv. com., 1963; chmn. Belles Lettres committee Office Cultural Affairs, N.Y.C., 1964; mem. Philharmonic Symphony Soc.; vis. com. bd. overseers dept. astronomy Harvard. Decorated asso. officer St. John of Jerusalem; recipient King's medal service in cause of freedom, 1948; Gold medal Nat. Inst. Social Scis., 1961; award for distinguished service to arts Nat. Inst. Arts and Letters, 1963. Mem. Brit. Astron. Assn., Nat. Soc. Colonial Dames, Poetry Soc. Am. (exec. bd. 1938-39), Nat. Inst. Social Sci., Hroswitha Club, English-Speaking Union. Episcopalian. Clubs: Colony (gov. 1968—), River (N.Y.C.); Sulgrave (Washington). Address: 1030 Fifth Av New York City NY 10028

BULLWINKEL, IRMA NANCY (MRS. JOHN HENRY BULLWINKEL), real estate agt.; b. Lyndhurst, N.J., Oct. 22, 1920; d. Henry Edgar and Anna Weidner (Dubuy) Clay; student Tulsa U., 1951; A.A., Napa Coll.; postgrad. Realtor Inst. Cal., 1969; D.D. (hon.), Universal Life Ch., 1965; m. John Henry Bullwinkel, Nov. 1, 1941; children—John David, Douglas Kent. Sales analyst Prudential Ins. Co., Newark, 1937-41; teller Chase Nat. Bank, N.Y.C., 1942; real estate agt., Tulsa, 1950-62, Napa, Cal., 1962—. Vol. aide Napa Coll., 1968—; active A.R.C., 1942. Mem. Napa C. of C. (mem. law and order com., pub. com.), Napa County Bd. Realtors, Cal. Real Estate Assn., Nat. Inst. Realtors, Nat. Notary Assn. Presbyn. Club: Napa Women's (pres. Entre Nous sect. 1972-73). Contbr. poems to newspapers. Home: 2636 W Pueblo Av Napa CA 94558 Office: 1765 3rd St Napa CA 94558

BUMBRY, GRACE ANN, mezzo soprano; b. St. Louis, Jan. 4, 1937; d. Benjamin and Melzia (Walker) Bumbry; student Boston U., 1954-55, Music Acad. West, 1956-59; studied with Lotte Lehmann, Northwestern U., also fgn. countries; m. Andreas Jaeckel, July 5, 1963. Operatic debut Paris Opera, 1960; concert and operatic appearances in Europe, Japan, Bayreuth, Germany, U.S., also command performance The White House. Recipient John Hay Whitney award, 1959. Mem. Zeta Phi Beta. Home: via Motta Lugano Switzerland Office: care S Hurok Attractions 730 Fifth Av New York City NY 10019

BUMGARDNER, GEORGIA LOUISE BRADY (MRS. GEORGE HAAGEN BUMGARDNER, JR.), curator; b. Mt. Kisco, N.Y., Dec. 8, 1944; d. George Joseph and Elizabeth Louise (Kingsbury) Brady; B.A., Wellesley Coll., 1966; m. George Haagen Bumgardner, Jr., Aug. 27, 1966. Sec. to dean Davenport Coll., Yale U., New Haven, 1966-68; library asst. Am. Antiquarian Soc., Worcester, Mass., 1968-69, curator graphic arts, 1969—. Mem. Print Council Am. Author: American Broadsides, 1971. Office: 185 Salisbury St Worcester MA 01609

BUMGARDNER, GERTRUDE KELLER HENDERSON (MRS. SHERROD LEWIS BUMGARDNER), civic worker; b. Newport News, Va., Feb. 20, 1932; d. George W. and Gertrude (Keller) Henderson; student Vanderbilt U., 1949-50; B.A., Agnes Scott Coll., 1953; m. Sherrod Lewis Bumgardner, July 11, 1953; children—Sherrod Lewis, George Keller, Margaret Anne, Charles Gaither. Pres., Candytuft Garden Club, 1957-58; pres. Columbia (S.C.) Dental Aux., 1959-60; pres. Agnes Scott Alumnae Club, 1960-61; pres. League Women Voters, Columbia, 1963-65, pres. S.C., 1967-71, nat. dir., 1971—, trustee Edn. Fund, 1971—, Overseas Edn. Fund, 1971—; mem. Citizens Adv. Com. Adult Edn., 1964-65; mem. Citizens Design for Progress, 1964; v.p. President's Roundtable, 1964-65; bd. govs. Christian Action Council, 1968—; chmn. steering com. Gov.'s Coll. Leadership Conf., 1970; mem. Columbia Music Festival, S.C. Health Forum; vice chmn. Columbia-Richland County Study Commn., 1971-72; sec. S.C. Reorgn. Commn., 1971—; chmn. accountability study S.C. Commn. on Alcoholism, 1972—; trustee United Fund, 1969—; participant Am. Assembly, 1973; coordinator S.C. Coalition for Ratification Equal Rights Amendment, 1973—. Recipient Christian Action award, 1974. Mem. Mortar Bd. Baptist (tchr.). Home: 311 Spring Lake Rd Columbia SC 29206

BUMPERS, BETTY LOU FLANAGAN (MRS. DALE BUMPERS), wife gov. Ark.; m. Dale Bumpers, Sept. 4, 1949; children—Dale Brent, William Mark, Margaret Brooke. Address: Charleston AR 73933

BUNCE, ELIZABETH THOMPSON, oceanographer, marine geophysicist; b. Mineola, N.Y., Apr. 25, 1915; d. Russell and Elizabeth F. (Crawford) Bunce; A.B., Smith Coll., 1937; M.A., 1949, Sc. D. (hon.), 1971. Instr. physics Smith Coll., 1949-51; research asso., asso. scientist Woods Hole Oceanographic Instn., Woods Hole, Mass., 1951—. Fellow Geol. Soc. Am.; mem. Am. Geophys. Union, Soc. Exploration Geophysicists, Seismological Soc. Am., A.A.A.S., Sigma Xi. Contbr. articles to profl. jours. Home: Blacksmith Shop Rd West Falmouth MA 02574 Office: Woods Hole Oceanographic Instn Woods Hole MA 02543

BUNCH, ARLINE HAMMOND (MRS. ALFRED B. BUNCH), educator; b. Lowry City, Mo., Jan. 30, 1907; d. Hardin R. and Minnie (Slavens) Hammond; B.S., Springfield State Tchrs. Coll., 1928; m. Alfred B. Bunch, June 28, 1933; children—Bryan H., Robert Dale, Barbara (Mrs. Ernest B. Fields) (dec.). Tchr. St. Clair County (Mo.) rural schs., 1926-28, Springfield Draughon's Bus. Coll., 1928-30; mgr. Sarachon Hooley Secretarial Sch., St. Louis, 1930-35; tchr. advanced secretarial dept. Miss Hickey's Sch. for Secretaries, St. Louis, 1935-40; owner, mgr. Crescent Hall Secretarial Sch., Peoria, Ill., 1940-47; owner, exec. v.p. Midstate Coll., Peoria, 1966—. Bd. advisers Internat. Speedwriting Co., N.Y.C.; mem. adv. bd. Ill. State Pvt. Bus. and Vocational Schs., 1968—; commr. Accrediting Commn. for Bus. Schs., 1968-70. Trustee Barbara Fields Meml. Scholarship Fund, 1968—. Mem. Jubilee Bus. and Profl. Women's Assn. (pres. 1965), Peoria Advt. and Selling Club (dir. 1967—). Home: CMR 119 Byerly Hills East Peoria IL 61611 Office: 238 SW Jefferson St Peoria IL 61602

BUNCH, MARTHA LOUISE, assn. adminstr.; b. New Castle, Ind., Mar. 21, 1917; d. William Mahan and Clara Belle (Arnold) Bunch; B.S., Hanover Coll., 1939; postgrad. U. Cin., 1948-49, George Williams YMCA Coll., 1950. Tchr. phys. edn. Shields High Sch., Seymour, Ind., 1939-44; club dir. Am. Red Cross, E.T.O., 1944-46; women's and girls dir. Wade Br. YMCA, Covington, Ky, 1946—, asso. dir., 1969—. Mem. Am. Mgmt. Assn. (recipient certificate 1973), YMCA Assn. Profl. Dirs., Alpha Delta Pi. Republican. Club: No. Ky. Toastmistress (pres. 1959, regional coordinator 1963). Home: 325 Redwood St Fort Wright KY 41011 Office: 624 Madison Av Covington KY 41011

BUNCH, MARY ELIZABETH (MRS. JAMES HENDERSON LOVE), physician; b. Asheboro, N.C.; d. Walter Anderson and Pattie (Lowe) Bunch; student U. N.C., 1947; M.D., Bowman Gray Sch. Medicine, 1951; m. James Henderson Love, July 12, 1959; 1 son, James Henderson. Intern, N.C. Bapt. Hosp., Winston-Salem, N.C., 1951-52, asst. resident internal medicine, 1952-55; staff physician Western N.C. Sanitorium, Black Mountain, 1955-59; emergency room physician Meml. Mission Hosp., Asheville, N.C., 1969—. Served to 1st lt. Army Nurse Corps, 1943-46. Mem. Am. Med. Women's Assn., A.M.A., Am. Coll. Emergency Physicians (charter), N.C., Buncombe County med. socs., Am. Legion, V.F.W. Methodist. Home: 103 3d St Black Mountain NC 28711 Office: 509 Biltmore Av Asheville NC 28801

BUNCH, VERA FRANCES KENNEY (MRS. BILLY JOE BUNCH), editor; b. Platte City, Mo., Dec. 3, 1934; d. Marion Owen and Mary Alice (Tate) Kenney; student U. Mo., 1955; m. Billy Joe Bunch, Sept. 1, 1952; children—Cathy Jo, Ginger Lea, Billie Lou, Connie Frances. Typist clk. Fed. Res. Bank, Kansas City, Mo., 1952-53; dir. over copy Denton Yearbook Pubs., Kansas City, Mo., 1953-54; varitypist J.F. Pritchard & Co., Kansas City, Mo., 1954-55; co-editor Gladstone (Mo.) Gazette, 1960-62, Gladstone Press, 1962-65; pub., editor Gower (Mo.) Gazette, 1965-68, Democrat-Herald, Smithville, Mo., 1968—. Sec., Salvation Army, 1971-72; active Am. Cancer Soc., Heart Assn. Recipient awards Am. Cancer Soc., State Hwy. Patrol, Salvation Army. Mem. Mo., N.W. Mo. press assns., Bus. and Profl. Women (pres. 1971-72), C. of C. (treas. 1971-73), Beta Sigma Phi. Democrat. Home: 501 Highland Av Smithville MO 64089 Office: 112 S Bridge St Smithville MO 64089

BUNDA, BERTHA WALTERS (MRS. JOSEPH JOHN BUNDA), social worker; b. Greenwood, Miss., July 3, 1913; d. Leonard E. and Helen (McClain) Walters; A.B., Miss. State Coll. for Women, 1934; postgrad. Presbyn. Coll., 1941-42; M.S.W., U. Ill., 1957; m. Charles Heitzman, July 7, 1935 (dec. Mar. 1941); m. 2d, Joseph John Bunda, Oct. 27, 1944. Staff worker Hull House, Chgo., 1934-36; religious edn. dir. 4th Presbyn. Ch., Chgo., 1939-44; nat. trainer, community adviser Girl Scouts U.S.A., N.Y.C., 1944-53, Chgo. tng. coordinator, dist. adviser, 1953-55, dir. project for mentally and physically handicapped, 1961-64, dir. spl. services to Negroes in Disadvantaged Areas, 1964-66, staff supr., 1966-68; cons. Community Social Agys., Chgo., 1957-61; field instr. Jane Addams Grad. Sch. Social Work, U. Ill., 1961-68, recipient award for distinguished service in social welfare, 1966; dir. dept. social work Welfare Council Met. Chgo.; family counselor Family Service Assn., Jackson, Miss., 1970-73; dir. consultation Jackson Mental Health Center, 1973—. Mem. Ill. Gov's. Conf. for Service to Handicapped, 1963-64. Mem. Nat. Assn. Social Workers (chmn. group services council 1961-64, Chgo. del. nat. conf. 1964, Merit award for research in Miss. schs. 1971), Am. Camping Assn. Research projects: Integration of Mentally and Physically Handicapped Girl Scouts into Non-Handicapped Social Groups, 1961-64; Integration of Negro Girl Scouts from Low-Income and Middle-Income Groups, 1964-65. Home: 5153 Sun Valley Rd Jackson MS 39206 Office: Jackson Mental Health Center Jackson MS 39216

BUNKLEY, MARTHA BELLE GIBSON (MRS. FRANK K. BUNKLEY), civic worker; b. nr. Gilbertown, Ala.; d. Joseph D. and Annie (Savage) Gibson; student Livingston U., 1925-26; m. Frank K. Bunkley, Apr. 8, 1929; 1 son, Frank. Charter mem. Freedoms Found. at Valley Forge; mem. City of Mobile Beautification Bd., Mobile Legislation Council. Mem. Am. Legion Aux. (state dept. past pres.), U.D.C. (treas. Mobile chpt. 1955—, past pres.), V.F.W. Aux., Historic Mobile Preservation Soc. Methodist. Clubs: Forum, Womans, Mobile

Civic Round Table, Mobile Garden. Home: 217 Berwyn Dr Mobile AL 36608

BUNN, BEVERLY, lawyer; b. Sacramento, Sept. 2; d. Guy Alvis and Violet (Pelzel) Bunn; student Portland State Coll., 1950-51, U. Portland, 1952-54; J.D., Pepperdine U., 1969; m. D.L. Cramer (div.); 1 son, Jeffery Anthony. Stewardess, United Airlines, N.Y., Los Angeles, 1954-56, stewardess recruiter, 1956—; social service worker Cal. Dept. Social Welfare, Riverside County, 1965-68, Orange County, Santa Ana, 1970-71; registrar Sch. Law, Pepperdine U., Santa Ana, Cal., 1968-69; admitted to Cal. bar, 1971; individual practice law, Santa Ana, 1971—. Dir. Airline Hostess Tng. Sch., Riverside, Viva's Sch. Modeling, Riverside; lectr. U. Cal. at Irvine, 1973. Vice chmn. Orange County sect. Cal. Citizens Com. for Welfare Reform, 1971—. Legal counsel Anaheim Young Republicans, 1971—, sec. Orange County Young Republicans, 1972—; gen. counsel Cal. Young Republicans, 1972-73; candidate Orange County Rep. Central Com., 1972. Mem. Santa Ana C. of C., Am., Cal., Orange County bar assns., United Airlines stewardess Alumni Assn. (nat. recruitment chmn.; editor nat. mag. 1964-69), Iota Tau Tau (editor internat. mag. 1968-71). Club: Ambassador's (Santa Ana). Home: 1367 SE Sycamore St Tustin CA 92680 Office: Suite 315 615 Civic Center Dr W Santa Ana CA 92701

BUNTING, MARGARET ANNE (MRS. CLYDE E. BUNTING), state legislator; b. Brownsville, Pa., July 5, 1920; d. Charles Edward and Lillian Mae (Long) Rothrock; student George Washington U., 1943-44, Boise State Coll., 1954; m. Clyde E. Bunting, Nov. 16, 1945; children—Margaret Heidi Mae, Sally Anne. Sec., Hdqrs. Army Service Forces, Washington, 1943; adminstrv. sec. Exec. Office of Pres., Under Sec. of War, Washington, 1944-45; jour. clk. Ida. Ho. of Reps., 1967-70; mem. Ida. Ho. of Reps., 1973—. Corp. sec., dir. Bunting Tractor Co., Bunting Bldg. Corp. Chmn. Ida. Concert and Artist Series, 1952-53; chmn. Ida. Youth Concert, 1955; chmn. St. Lukes Hosp. Ball, 1964; chmn. Boise Philharmonic Assn., 1957; sec. bd. Boise Art Assn., 1960-63. Sec. Ida. Gov.'s House Heritage Com., 1968-69. Precinct com. woman Republican Party, 1967-72; dir. Ada County Rep., Central Com., 1970—; pres. Ada County Rep. Women's Club, 1972; pres. Ida. Fedn. Rep. Women, 1973. Pres., Ida. State Hist. Soc. Aux., 1967-68. Mem. Boise Jr. League, St. Luke's Hosp. Aux., Nat. Order Women Legislators. Episcopalian. Mem. Women of Rotary. Club: Hillcrest Country. Author: Historical Treasures from Idaho Kitchens, 1967. Home: 944 Lewis St Boise ID 83702

BUNTING, MARY INGRAHAM, univ. ofcl.; b. Bklyn., July 10, 1910; d. Henry A. and Mary T. (Shotwell) Ingraham; B.A., Vassar Coll., 1931; M.A., U. Wis., 1932, Ph.D., 1934; m. Henry Bunting, June 22, 1937 (dec.); children—Mary, Charles, William, John. Instr. biology Bennington Coll., 1936-37; instr. physiology and hygiene Goucher Coll., 1937-38; research asst. dept. bacteriology Yale 1938-40, 48-52, lectr., 1953-55; lectr. dept. botany Wellesley Coll., 1946-47; dean Douglass Coll., Rutgers U., 1955-59; pres. Radcliffe Coll., Cambridge, Mass., 1960-72; asst. to pres. Princeton (N.J.) U., 1972—. Commr., AEC, 1964-65. Mem. Am. Soc. Microbiologists, Phi Beta Kappa, Sigma Xi. Home: New Boston NH 03070

BUOY, JEAN LAURENE (MRS. LAWRENCE FORD BUOY), newspaper editor; b. Erie, Pa., Mar. 22, 1929; d. Walter Lawrence and Melitta Valeska (Iwig) Rosenstiel; student Heidelberg Coll., 1948-49; B.A., Mercyhurst Coll., 1952; m. Lawrence Ford Buoy, May 15, 1954. Asst. librarian, children's section Erie (Pa.) Pub. Library, 1952-55; with pub. relations William Morrow and Co., book pubs., N.Y.C., 1955-63; systems analyst Episcopal Ch. Pension Fund, N.Y.C., 1963-66; reporter Danbury (Conn.) News Times, 1967-70, editor family page, 1970—. Dir. pub. relations The Sherman (Conn.) Players, Inc., 1967-71. Home: Gaylord Rd Gaylordsville CT 06755 Office: 333 Main St Danbury CT 06810

BURACK, SYLVIA KAMERMAN (MRS. ABRAHAM S. BURACK), editor; b. Hartford, Conn., Dec. 16, 1916; d. Abraham and Augusta (Chermak) Kamerman; A.B., Smith Coll., 1938; m. Abraham S. Burack, Nov. 28, 1940; children—Janet Elizabeth (Mrs. Alan D. Biller), Susan Helen (Mrs. Chad A. Finer), Ellen J. (Mrs. Franklin Toker). Library asst. Hartford (Conn.) Pub. Library, 1938-39; sec. to dir. Assn. Jewish Philanthropies, Boston, 1940-41; asso. editor The Writer, Inc., also Plays, Inc., pubs. mags. and books, Boston, 1941—. Mem. Brookline (Mass.) Sch. Com., 1949-69; mem. Mass. Bd. Higher Edn., 1973—. Trustee Mass. State Coll. System, 1971—, vice chmn. bd., 1973—; trustee Max C. Rosenfeld Scholarship Fund; mem. Corp. Florence Crittenton League, Inc., Boston; mem. Ladies Com. Boston Museum Fine Arts, 1955-63, Girl Scouts Am., Boston, 1954-56, YWCA, Boston, 1950-53. Sylvia K. Burack Library at Brookline (Mass.) High Sch. named in her honor, 1971. Editor 6 anthologies plays for children. Home: 72 Penniman Rd Brookline MA 02146 Office: 8 Arlington St Boston MA 02116

BURBANCK, MADELINE PALMER (MRS. WILLIAM D. BURBANCK), research ecologist; b. Moorestown, N.J., Oct. 27, 1914; d. Edmond Winthrop and Margaret (Hopkins) Palmer; B.A., Wellesley Coll., 1935, M.A., 1938; Ph.D., U. Chgo., 1941; m. William D. Burbanck, Sept. 7, 1940; children—Melinda Ann (Mrs. John M. Miller), George Palmer. Instr., asst. prof. biology dept. Drury Coll., Springfield, Mo., 1944-50; Herbarium asst. biology dept. Emory U., Atlanta, 1956-65, research asso. in biology, 1961—. Mem. adv. conservation coms. Panola Mountain State Conservation Bank, vice-chmn. 1971—; chmn. Davidson-Arabia Mountain County Park, 1971—. Exec. com. Druid Hills Civic Assn. 1972—, editor, 1971—. Mem. A.A.A.S., Ecol. Soc. Am., Assn. Southeastern Biologists (archivist 1965—), So. Appalachian Bot. Club (pres. 1973-74), Ga. Bot. Soc., Sigma Xi (sec. 1973-75). Contbr. articles on plant cytology, ecology of estuarine isoped Cyathura, plant communities of granite outcrops in profl. jours. Home: 1164 Clifton Rd NE Atlanta GA 30307

BURBIDGE, ELEANOR MARGARET (MRS. GEOFFREY BURBIDGE), astronomer; b. Davenport, Eng.; d. Stanley John and Marjorie (Stott) Peachey; B.Sc., Ph.D., U. London; Sc.D. (hon.), Smith Coll., 1963, U. Sussex, 1970, U. Bristol, 1972, U. Leicester, 1972; m. Geoffrey Burbidge, Apr. 2, 1948; 1 dau., Sarah. Came to U.S., 1955. Mem. staff U. London Obs., 1948-51; research fellow Yerkes Obs., U. Chgo., 1951-53, Cal. Inst. Tech., Pasadena, 1955-57; Shirley Farr fellow Yerkes Obs., 1957-59, asso. prof., 1959-62; mem. Enrico Fermi Inst. for Nuclear Studies, 1957-62; prof. physics dept. physics U. Cal. at San Diego, 1964—; dir. Royal Greenwich Obs., 1972-73. Recipient (with husband) Warner prize in Astronomy, 1959; hon. fellow Girton Coll., Cambridge. Fellow Royal Soc., Royal Astron. Soc.; mem. Am. Acad. Arts and Scis., Am. Astron. Soc., Internat. Astron. Union (pres. commn. 28, 1970-73). Author: (with G. Burbidge) Quasi-Stellar Objects, 1967. Editor Observatory mag., 1948-51; editorial bd. Astronomy and Astrophysics, 1969—. Address: Dept Physics U Cal La Jolla CA 92037

BURBRIDGE, MARION HORTON (MRS. RUSSELL WEBB BURBRIDGE), nurse; b. Pompton Lakes, N.J., Apr. 19, 1913; d. J. Clarence and Susan Elizabeth (Roome) Horton; student N.J. Coll., 1931; R.N., Overlook Hosp. Sch. Nursing, 1935; postgrad. work, 1965, 70; m. Russell Webb Burbridge, Feb. 26, 1938; 1 dau., Marcellene, (Mrs. Donald Lester McCoy). With Passaic County Tb Sanitorium, Paterson, N.J., 1935-36; stewardess Am. Airlines, Chgo., 1936-38; dir. Egremont Schs., Inc., Encino, Cal., 1945-63; owner, dir. Burmar Sch., Encino, 1963-69; charge nurse, intensive care unit-coronary care unit Sherman Oaks Community Hosp., Van Nuys, Cal., 1969—. Mem. adv. bd. Salvation Army, Van Nuys, 1960-63. Named Woman of Year, Bus. and Profl. Women's Club, 1959, also Outstanding Club-woman, 1970. Mem. Nat. Kiwi Assn., D.A.R., Internat. Platform Assn., Am. Assn. Critical Care Nurses, Bus. and Profl. Women's Club (pres. Cal. fedn. 1970-71), Am. Heart Assn., Women's Equity Action League, Nat. Assn. Female Execs. Home: 22234 Victory Blvd Woodland Hills CA 91364 Office: Sherman Oaks Community Hosp 4929 Van Nuys Blvd Sherman Oaks CA 91405

BURCH, LILLIE MAE TERRY (MRS. JAMES AUSTIN BURCH), newspaper pub.; b. Auburn, Tex., Sept. 28, 1914; d. James Thomas and Love (Sisk) Terry; student Crosier Tech. Sch., Dallas, 1943-44; m. James Austin Burch, Apr. 11, 1936; 1 son, John Carl. Linotype instr. Tex.-Mexican Indsl. Inst., Kingsville, Tex., 1939; supr. backorder dept. H.W. Gossard Co., Dallas, 1942-45; clk. Ryan Howard Ins., Lampasas, Tex., 1958-59; editor, pub. Grandview (Tex.) Tribune, 1973—. Den mother Cub Scouts, 1957-60; local chmn. Am. Cancer Soc., 1971; vice chmn. Johnson County Hist. Survey Com., 1971-72. Mem. Tex. Ex-Students Assn. (local publicity dir. 1960-71), Wesleyan Service Guild (local sec. 1969-70). Methodist. Home: 304 E Pecan St Grandview TX 76050 Office: 106 E Criner St Grandview TX 76050

BURCHAM, GWENDOLYN FRANCES PARKER (MRS. RALPH JACK BURCHAM), home economist; b. Drakes Creek, Ark., June 11, 1932; d. Nolan Henry and Leta Clair (Drake) Parker; student John Brown U., 1949-51; B.S., U. Ark., 1953, M.S., 1957; postgrad., 1961-62; postgrad. Wichita State U., 1957-58; m. Ralph Jack Burcham, Apr. 9, 1955; 1 dau., Thresa Clair. Tchr. home econs., high schs. in Elkins, Ark., Decatur, Ark., Wichita, Kan., Mabelvale, Ark., 1953-61; extention home economist Pulaski County, Ark., 1961-62; dir. pub. relations Am. Dairy Assn., Ark., 1962-65; dir. Ark. Milk Promotion Com., Little Rock, 1965-66; exec. dir. Dairy Council Ark., Little Rock, 1966-68; state coordinator Dairy Council, Inc., Little Rock, 1968—. Hostess, Farm Roundup Show, KTHV-TV, Little Rock, 1961—. Recipient Outstanding Service award Ark. Extention Homemakers Council, 1968. Mem. Am. (recorder state pres. unit 1972, chmn. 1973-74, dir. 1973-74), Ark. (v.p. 1968-69, pres. 1971-72, membership chmn. 1967—) home econs. assns., Ark. Pub. Health Assn., Am. Bus. Womens Assn., Am., Ark. home economists in bus., Ark. Women's Com. on Pub. Affairs (past pres.), Ark. Interagy. Nutrition Com. (program com. 1969—, sec. 1971-72, Pulaski County 4-H Clubs (hon.), Ark. Genealogy Soc. Baptist. Clubs: Ark. Kennel (past sec. Little Rock), German Shepherd Dog of Little Rock (dir. 1972), Lakeside Country. Home: 3924 Base Line Rd Little Rock AR 72209 Office: 6423 Forbing Rd Little Rock AR 72209

BURCHETT, BETTY MARTELA, educator; b. Stambaugh, Ky., Nov. 16, 1934; d. Eddie and Beaunie (Van Hoose) Burchett; A.B. in Chemistry, Berea (Ky.) Coll., 1955; M.A. in Edn., Morehead (Ky.) U., 1963; M.A. in Natural Sci., Middle Tenn. State U., 1964; Ed.D. in Sci. Edn., Ind. U., 1971. Tchr. high sch. math. and sci. Paintsville (Ky.) City Schs., 1955-64; asst. prof. biology and chemistry Morehead State U., 1964-69; teaching asst. sci. edn. Ind. U., 1969-71; asst. prof. sci. edn. U. Mo. at Columbia, 1971—. Cons., leader in-service workshops Mo. Pub. Schs. Mem. Nat. Sci. Tchrs. Assn. (life), Am. Assn. U. Women (topic chmn. 1973—), Pi Lambda Theta (membership chmn. Alpha Chpt. 1972-73, faculty adviser 1973—), Delta Kappa Gamma, Zeta Tau Alpha. Home: 2309 W Broadway Columbia MO 65201 Office: Education Bldg U Mo Columbia MO 65201

BURCHWOOD, KATHARINE TYLER (MRS. LOUIS F. BURCHWOOD), writer, educator; b. Portland, Ore.; d. Lewis Morris and Ellen A. (Richmond) Tyler; A.B. in Edn., Art Inst. Chgo., 1916; Ph.B., U. Chgo., 1927, A.M., 1931; m. Louis F. Burchwood, Nov. 24, 1943. Asst. supr. pub. sch. art, Evanston, Ill.; head art dept., State Tchrs. Coll., Valley City, N.D., summer 1932; lectr. grad. sch. Syracuse (N.Y.) U., summer 1933; tchr., English, Art practice and history art Chgo. Bd. Edn., 1923-56. Mem. Nat. Soc. New Eng. Women Daus. Am. Colonists, Nat. Soc. Arts and Letters, D.A.R., Seabury Western Found., Ill. Soc. Mayflower Descs., Daus. Founders and Patriots Am., Colonial Dames 17th Century. Episcopalian. Republican. Co-author: (textbook) Art Then and Now, 1949; Origin and Legacy of Mexican Art, 1972; New Orleans Saga. Contbr. articles to mags. Home: 1305 Lincoln St Evanston IL 60201

BURDEN, JEAN, author, editor; b. Waukegan, Ill., Sept. 1, 1914; d. Harry Frederick and Miriam (Biddlecom) Prussing; B.A., U. Chgo., 1936; m. David Charles Burden, Aug. 31, 1941 (div. May, 1949). Sec. John Hancock Mutual Life Ins. Co., Chgo., 1937-39, Young & Rubicam Advt. Agy., Chgo., 1939-41; editor, copywriter Domestic Industries Inc., Chgo., 1941-45; office mgr. O'Brion Russell & Co., Los Angeles, 1948-55; adminstr. publs. Meals for Millions Found., Los Angeles, 1955-65; editor Stanford Research Inst., South Pasadena, Cal., 1965-66; owner Jean Burden & Assos., Altadena, Cal., 1966—. Supr. poetry workshop Pasadena (Cal.) City Coll., 1961-62, 65; lectr. poetry at numerous univs. and colls., 1960—. Recipient first prize Borestone Mountain Poetry Awards, 1963, Silver Anvil award Pub. Relations Soc. Am., 1969. MacDowell Colony fellow, 1973, 74. Mem. Bus. and Profl. Women, Mortar Bd. Democrat. Author: Naked as the Glass, 1963; Journey Toward Poetry, 1966; A Celebration of Cats, 1974; (under pseudonym Felicia Ames) The Dog You Care For, 1968, The Cat You Care For, 1968, The Bird You Care For, 1970, The Fish You Care For, 1971. Poetry editor Yankee Mag., 1955—. Contbr. to jours and mags. Home: 1129 Beverly Way Altadena CA 91001

BURDETTE, PATRICIA ANN (MRS. STANLEY WAYNE BURDETTE), city ofcl.; b. Huntington, W. Va., Aug. 27, 1931; d. Charles G. and Nellie (Young) Jones; grad. pub. high sch., 1949; m. Stanley Wayne Burdette; children—Charles Wayne, Sandra Lynn. Accountant, Rawlings & Amberger Motors, Point Pleasant, W. Va., 1949-51; sec. Mason County (W.Va.) Bd. Edn., 1962; accountant Two River Motor Co., Point Pleasant, 1964-66; sec. Mason County Clerk's Office, 1962-64, city clk., Point Pleasant, 1967—, city treas., 1967—. Vice pres. Pleasant Valley Hosp. Aux., 1963. Mem. Ordnance Sch. P.T.A. (treas. 1962, v.p. 1963), Mason County P.T.A. Council (pres. 1964—), Municipal Treasurers' Assn. Clubs: Mason County Republican Woman's (sec. 1968-69); Point Pleasant Woman's (sec. 1970-72). Home: 2602 Jefferson Av Point Pleasant WV 25550 Office: 400 Viand St Point Pleasant WV 25550

BURDICK, LOIS ANN (MRS. JOSEPH BURDICK), univ. adminstr., b. Brazil, Ind., Aug. 12, 1927; d. Leonard Emory and Mildred Jean (Edwards) Brown; B.S. in Social Sci. and Bus., Ind. State U., 1949, M.A. in Guidance, 1965; m. Joseph Burdick, June 11, 1953. Sec., Phila. Phillies Baseball Farm Club, Terre Haute, Ind., 1949-50; sec. extended services Ind. State U., Terre Haute, 1950-65, adminstrv. sec., 1965—, asst. dir. continuing edn. and extended services, 1965—. Mem. Nat. U. Extension Assn., Adult Edn. Assn. Ind., Assn. for Field Services in Tchr. Edn. (sec. treas. 1968—). Club: Ind. State U. Faculty Women's (membership chmn. 1973—). Home: Rural Route 2 Avian Oaks Brazil IN 47834 Office: Indiana State Univ Terre Haute IN 47809

BURFORD, GERAL DEAN (MRS. BLANTON WARD BURFORD), savs. and loan exec.; b. Sulphur Springs, Tex., June 13, 1918; d. Dean Edward and Anna Elizabeth (Robertson) Pulley; student Draughon's Bus. Coll., 1937; Am. Savings & Loan Inst., 1966; m. Blanton Ward Burford, July 18, 1970; 1 dau. by previous marriage—Carol (Mrs. Richard Currie Powers). Advt. dir. Baptist Book Store, Dallas, 1943-47; advt. staff Dallas Times Herald, 1947-50; dir. advt. Dallas Fed. Savs. & Loan Assn., 1951-69, v.p. marketing, 1969—. Chmn. pub. relations com. Am. Red Cross, Dallas, 1970-72; chmn. publicity operating fund drive Bishop Coll., 1972. Named Dallas Advt. Woman of Year, Dallas Advt. League, 1962. Mem. Dallas Advt. League (v.p. 1949-50, dir. 1948-53, named most valuable mem. 1955), Am. Advt. Fedn. (dir. S.W. 10th dist. 1949-51, Silver Medal award 1974), Savs. Insts. Marketing Soc. Am. (dir. 1969-72), Advt. Review Bd., Women in Communications, Press Club Dallas, Advt. Club Dallas, Better Bus. Bur., Theta Sigma Phi (Matrix award 1969), Gamma Alpha Chi. Methodist. Home: 6410 Vanderbilt St Dallas TX 75214 Office: 1505 Elm St Dallas TX 75201

BURGDORF, LOUISE TURNER (MRS. OLIN KARL BURGDORF), civic leader, clubwoman; b. Fort Lawn, S.C., Jan. 25, 1917; d. Claude Hyatt and Susie Cloud (Jones) Turner; student Columbia Hosp. Sch. Nursing, U. S.C., 1938-40; certificate landscape design U. S.C., 1966; summer study in garden design Pa. U.; m. Olin Karl Burgdorf, June 22, 1940; children—Carl, Augustus, Davie. Pres., Landscape Critics Council of S.C., 1969-71; state v.p. Keep S.C. Beautiful, 1971—; mem. Gov.'s Beautification and Community Improvement Bd., 1969—; mem. adv. com. U.S.C. Renovation Project, 1974—; bd. dirs. S.C. Heart Assn.; trustee S.C. Tb Assn. and Crippled Childrens Soc.; state rec. sec. D.A.R., 1967-70, state vice regent, 1970-73, state regent, 1973—, also mem. nat. officers club; state pres. Soc. Daus. Colonial Wars, 1971—, mem. nat. officers club; mem. Huguenot Soc., Dames Ct. of Honor, Daus. of 17th Century, Daus. Am. Colonists, Historic Columbia Found., Nat. Trust for Historic Preservation, S.C. Hist. Soc., S. Caroliniana Soc., Columbia Mus. Art, Nat. Audubon Soc. Democrat. Methodist. Clubs: South Carolina Palmetto Garden of Am. (life), State Garden (nat. council), S.C. Garden (flower show judge), Palmetto Officers, Nat. Soc. D.A.R. State Vice Regents. Home: Tivoli Plantation Springfield SC 29146

BURGER, AGNES LIN (MRS. JAMES MARK BURGER), educator; b. Chung-Ching, China, July 15, 1943; d. Tong and Kwei Cheng Lin; B.A. (coll. scholar), Marycrest Coll., 1964; M.Ed. (univ. fellow), Columbia, 1968, Ed.D. (univ. fellow), 1972; m. James Mark Burger, Sept. 3, 1966. Came to U.S., 1960, naturalized, 1970. Project asso. Columbia Research and Demonstration Center, 1968-70, research asso., part-time 1973—; intern Center for Multiply Handicapped, N.Y.C., 1970-71; asst. prof. ednl. psychology N.Y. U., N.Y.C., 1972—. Mem. Am. Psychol. Assn., Am. Ednl. Research Assn., Am. Assn. Mental Deficiency, Council for Exceptional Children. Contbr. articles to various jours. Cons. editor Am. Jour. Mental Deficiency, 1973—. Home: 2 Washington Square Village New York City NY 10012

BURGER, MARY LOU (MRS. JACKIE G. UNDERWOOD), editor; b. Pitts., May 31, 1944; d. Louis J. and Flora A. (Gaber) Burger; B.A., Duquesne U., 1966; m. Jackie G. Underwood, Apr. 19, 1973. Sales promotion mgr. Pitts. Outdoor Advt. Co., 1966; reporter New Castle News, New Castle, Pa., 1966-67; writer Pitts. Catholic, 1966-69; asso. editor U. Pitts., 1969—, instr., 1973—; cons. on journalism careers. Chairwoman, Chancelor's Adv. Council on Women's Opportunities, 1970-71. Recipient Golden Quill award Assn. W. Pa. Communications, 1970, 72; Best News Series award Pa. Newspaper Pubs. Assn. 1966. Mem. Women in Communications (v.p. 1969-70, ann. nat. meeting com. 1969), Arsenal Family and Children's Center Council, Pa. Women's Polit. Caucus. Home: 150 W Pike St Canonsburg PA 15317 Office: University Times 200 S Craig St Pittsburgh PA 15213

BURGESS, ANNETTE LOUISE CURNEN (MRS. ELISHA PAYNE JEWETT BURGESS), polit. worker; b. N.Y.C.; d. James Francis and Emma (Rick) Curnen; A.B., Barnard Coll., Columbia, 1917; m. Elisha Payne Jewett Burgess, Feb. 28, 1920 (dec. June 1955); 1 dau., Ruth Payne (Mrs. Emil Arndt). Mem. N.Y. County Republican Com., 17th Congl. Dist., N.Y.C., 1959-64; mem. Women's Republican Club Bronxville, 1964—. Mem. Nat. Trust for Historic Preservation of U.S., Hudson River Mus., Yonkers, N.Y. founder Burgess Family Collection and Papers, Columbia, N.Y.C., 1960—. Republican. Roman Catholic. Club: Barnard College. Home: 64 Sagamore Rd Bronxville NY 10708

BURGESS, CLARA SKIPWITH, sch. adminstr.; b. Newburgh, N.Y., Nov. 3, 1930; d. Luther Kerman and Clara Bell (Pickens) Skipwith; B.A., Hunter Coll., 1953, M.A., 1954; profl. diploma adminstrv. supervision (Ford Found. grant), Fordham U., 1970, postgrad., 1970—; m. Joseph Edward Burgess, May 14, 1966 (div. Sept. 1968). Early/Childhood instr. N.Y. Inst. for Blind, Bronx, 1953-54; tchr., kindergarten and early childhood tchr. trainer, exceptional edn. Pub. Sch. 43, Bronx, 1954-69; supr. Headstart, Dist. 7, Bronx, 1970, evaluator Headstart and Pre-Kindergarten Funding, 1970-71; dir. Morrisania Early Childhood Learning Center 3, Dist. 9, Bronx, 1971-72, prin., 1972—. Recreational counselor Pub. Sch. 43, Bronx, 1955-61; piano tchr. Pub. Sch. 18, Bronx, 1960-61, center dir., 1961, dance tchr., 1961-63; adj. instr. early childhood curriculum devel. City Coll. of City U. N.Y., 1972—. Bd. dirs. Wiltwyck Sch. for Boys, 1967—. Mem. Nat. Soc. for Study Edn., Nat. Soc. for Edn. Young Children, N.Y. Assn. Black Educators, Bronx Reading Council, Fordham Assn. Sch. Suprs. and Adminstrs., Alpha Kappa Alpha. Women's editor Community Jour. of Air, Radio Sta. WLIB, 1964-69. Home: 609 W 147th St New York City NY 10031 Office: 499 E 175 St Bronx NY 10457

BURGESS, ISABEL ANDREWS, govt. ofcl.; b. Cleve.; d. William Hayward and Alice (Ball) Andrews; student Mills Coll., 1930-31, Western Res. U., 1931-32; m. Richard Burgess, June 15, 1939 (div. Nov. 1967); children—Richard Ball, Susan Berry (Mrs. Allen Cordsen), Thomas Hayward. Mem. Ariz. Ho. of Reps., 1952-53, 56-57, 60-65; mem. Ariz. Senate, Phoenix, 1966-69, chmn. hwys. and transp. com.; mem. Nat. Transp. Safety Bd., Washington, 1969—; dir. Ball Co., Chgo. Pres. Heard Mus. Guild, 1959-60; sec. exec. com. Heard Mus.; mem. exec. bd. Western conf. Council State Govts., 1966-69. First vice chmn. Ariz. Republican Com., 1965-67. Clubs: Capitol Hill, 1925 F Street, Nat. Aviation, Aero (Washington). Home: 2500 Virginia Av NW Washington DC 20037 Office: 800 Independence Av SW Washington DC 20591

BURGESS, MYRTLE MARIE, lawyer; b. Brainerd, Minn., May 31, 1921; d. Charles Dana and Mary (Thayer) Burgess; B.A., San Francisco State U., 1947; J.D., Hastings Coll. Law, San Francisco, 1950. Admitted to Cal. bar, 1951; practiced in San Francisco, 1950-52, Reedley, Cal., 1952—; owner, lessor comml. and residential properties, 1956—. Sec., dir. Reedley Indsl. Sit-Devel. Found., 1970—. Dir., 2d v.p. Kings Cayon unit Cal. Republican Assembly, 1973-75. Past pres., bd. dirs. Sierra Community Concert Assn.; bd.

dirs. Reedley council Girl Scouts U.S.A., 1955-56. Mem. Am., Cal., Fresno County bar assns., Am. Trial Lawyers Assn., Bus. and Profl. Women (past chpt. pres.), Reedley C. of C. (past dir.; named Woman of Year 1971), Rep. Women Reedley (past pres.). Mem. Order Eastern Star. Home: 1076 N Kady St Reedley CA 93654 Office: 1107 G St Reedley CA 93654

BURGESS, VIRGINIA FROST (MRS. LEONARD RANDOLPH BURGESS), reading tchr.; b. Portland, Ore.; d. George Marquis and Jenny Gertrude (Elrod) Frost; B.S. (Pres.'s scholar 1947-56), Columbia, 1951, M.A., 1956; m. Leonard Randolph Burgess, May 26, 1946. Head repair sales dept. Taylor Instrument Co., San Francisco, 1941-43; hosp. staff aide A.R.C., overseas, 1944-46; research asst. writing project Tchrs. Coll., Columbia, N.Y.C., 1955-59; asst. to project dir. UNESCO Inst. of Edn., Hamburg, Germany, 1960-61; pvt. tutor in reading of emotionally disturbed children, 1956—. Chmn. steering com., exec. com. Brazos County Community Action Com., 1966—; mem. policy adv. com. Upward Bound Project, Brazos County, 1969-73. Co-chmn. Citizens for Eisenhower, Hastings-on-Hudson, N.Y., 1952, 56. Bd. dirs. Brazos Valley Community Action Program, 1972—. Mem. Am. Assn. U. Women, League Women Voters, Alpha Omicron Pi. Presbyn. Home: 302 Lorimer Dr Wyncote PA 19095

BURGGRAF, SHIRLEY PRUIT (MRS. RAY LOWELL BURGGRAF), educator; b. Covington, Ky., Dec. 20, 1938; d. Gobel B. and Alma (Whalin) Pruit; B.A. (Nat. Merit scholar), Muskingum Coll., 1961; M.A. (Nat. City Bank fellow), Case Western Res. U., 1965, Ph.D. (NDEA fellow), 1968; m. Ray Lowell Burggraf, Sept. 1, 1961. Instr. econs. Coll. Wooster (O.), 1967-68; lectr. econs. and statistics Cal. State Coll., Hayward, 1968-70; asst. prof. econs. Fla. A. and M.U., Tallahassee, 1970—. Mem. Am., Western, So. econs. assns. Home: 1507 Marion Av Tallahassee FL 32303 Office: Fla A and M Univ Tallahassee FL 32307

BURGMYER, PATRICIA LOTH (MRS. WARREN L. BURGMYER), elec. engr.; b. N.Y.C., Mar. 17, 1921; d. William R. and Josephine R. (Sgier) Loth; B.A., St. Joseph's Coll. for Women, 1942; M.S. in Physics, Poly. Inst. Bklyn., 1959; m. Warren L. Burgmyer, May 28, 1972. Jr. engr. standardization lab Western Electric Co., Kearny, N.J., 1942-43; jr. engr. test lab. Hazeltine Corp., Little Neck, N.Y., 1943-47, cons. engr., Green Lawn, N.Y., 1970—; devel. engr., Wheeler Labs., Inc., Great Neck, N.Y., 1947-70. Mem. I.E.E.E. Office: Research Laboratories Hazeltine Corp Greenlawn NY 11021

BURGOON, BEATRICE LOUISE MILLS (MRS. DAVID FLEGEAL BURGOON), govt. ofcl.; b. Phila.; d. James William and Bertha (Ridings) Mills; B.S., U. Pa., 1929, M.A., 1934; m. David Flegeal Burgoon, Dec. 24, 1935; children—Sandra Leigh (Mrs. Jules Jacob Schwartz), David Flegeal, Patricia Hargrave (Mrs. Michael David Wright). Asst. to bd. chmn. Regional War Labor Bd., Phila., 1944-45; disputes officer, div. chief, pub. mem. rev. and appeals com. Nat. Wage Stblzn. Bd., Washington, 1951-53; personnel cons. Health and Welfare Council, Washington, 1954-61; sr. staff analyst Presdl. R.R. Commn., Washington, 1961-62; indsl. relations specialist, asso. dir. longshore project U.S. Dept. Labor, Washington, 1962-65, chief div. labor-mgmt. policy devel., 1965-66, dir. Office Labor-Mgmt. Relations Services, 1966—. Mem. Indsl. Relations Research Assn., Am. Econ. Assn. Home: 1111 Army Navy Dr Arlington VA 22202 Office: US Dept Labor 14th and Constitution Av NW Washington DC 20210

BURGOYNE, SHIRLEY JEAN, lawyer; b. Saginaw, Mich., Oct. 25, 1932; d. Marshall Albert and Beatrice Viola (Clements) Cox; A.B., J.D., U. Mich., 1956; m. Bert Burgoyne, Apr. 22, 1955 (div.); children—Deborah Jeanne, David Edward, Douglas Jeffrey. Law clk. Ore. Supreme Ct., Salem, 1956-57; admitted to Ore. bar, 1957, Mich. bar, 1959; practiced in Roseburg, Ore., 1957-58, Lansing, Mich., 1959-63, Ann Arbor, Mich., 1963—; mem. firm Burgoyne & Burgoyne, Roseburg, 1957-58, Thomas C. Walsh, Lansing, 1959-63, Burgoyne & Morris, Ann Arbor, 1968-69. Debate coach Greenhills High Sch., Ann Arbor, 1969—; instr. bus. law Washtenaw Community Coll., Ypsilanti, Mich., 1973—; legal counsel Mich. Abortion Referendum Com., 1969-73. Mem. Mich. Women's Commn., 1971-72. Bd. dirs. Mich. Council for Study of Abortion, 1971-73. Mem. Am., Mich., Ore. bar assns., Am. Trial Lawyers Assn., Am. Judicature Soc., Am. Assn. U. Women, Kappa Beta Pi. Presbyn. Home: 746 Greenhills Dr Ann Arbor MI 48105 Office: 111 N Main St Ann Arbor MI 48108

BURK, BOBBIE JEAN MCBRIDE (MRS. JAMES MACK BURK), ednl. adminstr.; b. Dallas, May 13, 1930; d. Robert Edward and Thelma Edith (Grimes) McBride; B. Music, Oklahoma City U., 1952; M.Ed., U. Mo., 1969; m. James Mack Burk, June 12, 1954; 1 son, James Jeffrey. Tchr. music Oklahoma City pub. schs., 1952-54, 57-65, curriculum cons., 1965-67; tchr. Harrah (Okla.) pub. schs., 1954-55; instr. edn. U. Mo. at Columbia, 1967-70; dir. secondary edn. and music edn. Stephens Coll., Columbia, Mo., 1970—, dir. summer session, 1974—. Mem. Assn. for Tchr. Educators, Music Educators Nat. Conf., Am. Choral Dirs. Assn., Coll. Music Soc., Nat. Assn. for Humanities Edn., Sigma Alpha Iota (pres. Pi province 1968—), Pi Lambda Theta, Pi Kappa Lambda. Presbyn. Home: 3111 Crawford St Columbia MO 65201

BURKART, AUDREY CONSTANCE, nutritionist; b. Ridgefield, N.J., July 12, 1929; d. Frank Constance and Anna (Tepper) Burkart; B.S. cum laude, N.Y. U., 1953; M.A., Columbia, 1954. Tchr. home econs. Cliffside Park (N.J.) High Sch., 1954-56, Parsippany-Troy Hills (N.J.) High Sch., 1956-58, Ridgefield (N.J.) Meml. High Sch., 1958-64; asso. specialist foods and nutrition N.J. Coop. Extension Service, Rutgers U., New Brunswick, N.J., 1964—. Mem. liaison com. Am. Home Econs. Assn. and Am. Dietetics Assn., 1972—; state chmn. implementation of conf. goals White House Conf. Food Nutrition and Health, 1970-71. Recipient Distinguished Service award Epsilon Sigma Phi N.J. Coop. Extension Service, 1970. Mem. Am., N.J. (pub. relations chmn. 1971-72) dietetic assns., Am., N.J. (subject matter chmn. foods and nutrition 1971-72) home econs. assns., Kappa Delta Pi, Pi Lambda Theta, Omicron Nu. Home: 764 Broad Av Ridgefield NJ 07657 Office: Coop Extension Service Cook College Rutgers The State U New Brunswick NJ 08903

BURKE, BARBARA LEE (MRS. ROBERT EARL BURKE), lawyer; b. Richmond, Cal., Feb. 1, 1942; d. Charles Franklin and Evelyn Christine (Fox) Birch; A.B., U. Cal. at Los Angeles, 1963, J.D., 1966; m. Robert Earl Burke, Nov. 2, 1968. Admitted to Cal. bar, 1967; atty. Los Angeles County Office Pub. Defender, Pasadena, Cal. Mem. Glendale Council on Criminal Justice, State Bar Cal., Women's Lawyers' Club Los Angeles, Phi Delta Delta. Home: 1067 Pine Oak Lane Pasadena CA 91105 Office: 300 E Walnut St Pasadena CA 91101

BURKE, DOROTHY EVELYN (MRS. EDWARD H. BURKE), bank ofcl.; b. Youngstown, O., Sept. 23, 1912; d. Henry Jackson and Esther (Williams) Reapsummer; student Dana Sch. Music, Youngstown U., 1927-32; m. Edward H. Burke, June 12, 1938; 1 son, Edward Henry. Sec. to pres. Fitzsimmons Steel Co., Youngstown, 1940-45, Blanchard Bros. & Lane, Ashtabula, O., 1951-56; sec. to pres. Farmers Nat. Bank & Trust Co., Ashtabula, 1956-73, advt. and pub. relations dir., 1966-69, advt. and pub. relations officer, 1969—. Piano tchr., 1931—. Cellist, Youngstown Women's Symphony Orch., 1933-56. Mem. Music Tchrs. Nat. Assn., Ohio Music Tchrs. Assn., Nat. Guild Piano Tchrs., Nat. Secs. Internat. (charter mem.; v.p. 1956-57), Ashtabula Advt. Club (treas. 1972-73). Composer: Do You Remember. Home: 121 W Beech St Jefferson OH 44047 Office: 4641 Main St Ashtabula OH 44004

BURKE, EILEEN MARIE, educator; b. Perth Amboy, N.J., July 26, 1928; d. Thomas Patrick and Catherine (Shannon) Burke; B.S. in English, Seton Hall U., 1952; M.Edn., Rutgers U., 1957, Ed.D., 1963. Tchr. N.J. elementary schs., 1954-60; supr. Perth Amboy, also Woodbridge (N.J.) schs., 1961-63; asst. prof., coordinator of Instructional Materials Center, Rutgers Grad. Sch. Edn., New Brunswick, N.J., 1963-64; asso. prof. edn. Trenton (N.J.) State Coll., 1964-68, prof., 1968—, also supr. of M.Edn. program in elementary edn., 1966—. Recipient Dayley Seton award, 1952, Rutgers U. Distinguished Service award, 1969. Mem. Nat., N.J. edn. assns., N.J. Reading Tchrs. Assn. (pres. 1972-73), Am. Assn. U. Profs., Am. Assn. U. Women, Nat. Council Tchrs. English, Nat. Assn. Study Edn., Internat. Reading Assn., Am. Ednl. Research Assn., Kappa Delta Pi (pres.). Contbr. articles on teaching and ednl. research to profl. jours. Home: 48 Bayberry Rd Trenton NJ 08618 Office: Trenton State College Trenton NJ 08625

BURKE, ELLEN COOLIDGE, ret. librarian; b. Alexandria, Va., May 10, 1901; d. Henry Randolph and Rosella (Trist) Burke; B.A., Catholic U. Am., 1938, M.A., 1943. With Alexandria Library, 1939-70, successively cataloguer, reference, 1st asst., library dir., 1948-69, cons. dir., 1969-70. Mem. Alexandria Community Welfare Council, Project Friendship, Alexandria Council of Human Relations, Hopkins House Assn., Monticello Assn. Ellen Coolidge Burke Br. Library named in her honor. Mem. Va. Library Assn., Va. Council Human Relations, League Women Voters, Alexandria Hist. Found. (charter), Washington Urban League. Roman Catholic. Club: Zonta. Home: Washington House 5100 Fillmore Av Alexandria VA 22311

BURKE, JOSEPHINE MARY, educator; b. N.Y.C., July 21, 1914; d. Joseph T. and Maggie (Kloeti) Burke; B.A., Hunter Coll., 1936; M.A., Columbia, 1937. Temp. instr. Hunter Coll., City U. N.Y., 1936-38, tutor, 1938-42, instr., 1943-48, asst. prof., 1949-60, asso. prof. phys. edn., 1960-67, prof., 1967—, chmn. women's div. dept. phys. edn., 1961-68, chmn. dept. health, phys. edn., 1968-71. Mem. U.S. Olympic Volley Ball Sports Com. for XVIII Olympiad, 1961-64; mem. U.S. Pan-Am. Sports Com., 1962-63; organizer, operator, adminstr., supr. children's camp, 1951-62; staff mem. Nat. Red Cross Aquatic Sch., 1947-49, dean of women, staff mem., 1949; mem. nat. phys. edn. com. nat. YMCA, 1964—. Recipient gold medal Finnish League for Phys. Edn. of Women, 1962; Golden Eagle award Girl Scouts U.S.A., 1934; named to Volley Ball Hall of Fame, Los Angeles, 1956. Fellow A.A.H.P.E.R.; mem. U.S. Volley Ball Assn. (mem. at large on exec. bd. 1952—). Home: 5 Howard Rd Bayville NY 11709

BURKE, LILLIAN WALKER (MRS. RALPH L. BURKE), judge; b. Thomaston, Ga.; d. George P. and Ozelia (Daviston) Walker; B.S., Ohio State U., 1947; LL.B., Baldwin Wallace U., 1951, postgrad., 1964-65; m. Ralph L. Burke, June 8, 1948; 1 son, Rodney Bruce. Substitute tchr., Cleve., 1947-48; admitted to Ohio bar, 1951; practiced law, Cleve., 1951-62; asst. atty. gen. for trial lawyer workmen's compensation cases State of Ohio, Cleve., 1963-66; vice chmn. Ohio Indsl. Commn., Columbus, 1966-69; judge Cleve. Municipal Ct., 1969—. Mem. Ohio Gov.'s Com. on Status of Women, 1966-67, Cleve. Commn. on Status of Women; mem. adv. com. accreditation and instnl. eligibility Bur. Higher Edn., U.S. Dept. Health, Edn. and Welfare, 1972—. Ward leader Republican party, Cleve., 1958-66, precinct committeewoman, 1958-66; mem. exec. com. Cuyahoga County Rep. party, 1958-66, sec. central com., 1964-66. Recipient Merit award for outstanding community participation Parkwood Meth. Episcopal Ch. Mem. Nat., Ohio, Cleve., Cuyahoga bar assns., Am. Judicature Soc., Women Lawyers Assn., Am. Assn. U. Women, Nat. Council Negro Women (pres. Cleve br. 1955), John Harlan Law Club of Cleve., Alpha Kappa Alpha. Home: 829 East Blvd Cleveland OH 44108 Office: Cleveland Municipal Ct 601 Lakeside St NE Cleveland OH 44114

BURKE, SISTER MARGARET, coll. pres.; b. Morris, Minn.; grad. Duchesne Coll., Omaha; M.A. in Philosophy, Ph.D. in Psychology, Loyola U., Chgo.; postgrad. St. Louis U., Catholic U. Am. Mem. faculty Barat Coll., Lake Forest, Ill., 1941—, formerly chmn. dept. psychology, now pres. Trustee Lincoln Acad. Mem. Am. Philos. Assn., Am. Psychol. Assn. Address: Barat College Lake Forest IL 60045

BURKE, MARIANNE (MRS. HARRY GERDY), lawyer; b. Chgo., May 29, 1940; d. Walter James and Irene Georgia (Johnson) Burke; B.A., U. Ill., 1962; J.D., De Paul U., 1967; m. Harry Gerdy, Sept. 13, 1970. Admitted to Ill. bar, 1967; atty. Legal Aid Bur., Chgo., 1967-71; asst. pub. defender of Cook County, Chgo., 1971—. Mem. Chgo. Bar Assn. Democrat. Home: 5901 N Sheridan Rd Chicago IL 60660 Office: 2600 S California St Chicago IL 60608

BURKE, MARIE, journalist; b. Auburn, Pa.; d. Andrew F. and Dolores (Thayne) Burke; B.A., Albertus Magnus Coll., New Haven, 1941. Editorial asst. N.Y. Daily News, 1942-52, asst. to womans editor, asst. womans editor, 1952-69, womans editor, 1969—; fiction editor Chgo. Tribune-N.Y. News Syndicate, 1969-70. Office: 220 E 42d St New York City NY 10017

BURKE, YVONNE BRATHWAITE (MRS. WILLIAM A. BURKE), congresswoman; b. Los Angeles, Oct. 5, 1932; d. James T. and Lola (Moore) Watson; A.B. in Polit. Sci., U. Cal. at Los Angeles, 1953; J.D., U. So. Cal., 1956; m. William A. Burke, June 14, 1972; 1 dau., Autumn; 1 stepdau., Christine. Admitted to Cal. bar, 1956; practice in Los Angeles, 1956-66; mem. Cal. Assembly, 1966-71; mem. 93d congress from 37th Cal. dist. Dep. corp. commr. State of Cal., 1963-66; hearing officer Police Commn., Los Angeles, 1965; mem. staff McCone Commn., Los Angeles. Vice chmn. Democratic Nat. Conv., 1972, Dem. Charter Commn., 1972. Bd. dirs. U. Cal. at Los Angeles Alumni Found., Nat. Athletic Health Inst., United Negro Coll. Fund, West Los Angeles U. Sch. Law. Recipient Loren Miller award N.A.A.C.P.; Sojourner Truth award Negro Bus. and Profl. Women's Clubs; Profl. Achievement award U. Cal. at Los Angeles, 1974; named Future Leader Am. Time Mag., 1974; named Woman of Year, Iota Phi Lambda, 1972, Zeta Phi Beta, 1973, KNX Radio, 1974, named Chubb fellow Kennedy Sch. Politics Harvard U., 1972; numerous other citations and awards. Inst. Politics fellow, Harvard, 1972—. Mem. Media Women, Langston Law Club, Women's Nat. Polit. Caucus. Democrat. Address: House Office Bldg Washington DC 20515

BURKEN, JUDITH LUCILLE, journalist, educator; b. Des Moines, Aug. 6, 1939; d. Cletus Otto and Evelyn Elizabeth (Rea) Burken; A.A., Mount St. Clare Jr. Coll., 1960; B.A., U. Ia., 1962; M.A., Mich. State U., 1972. News reporter, photographer, feature writer Clinton (Ia.) Herald, 1962-65; state society editor Omaha World Herald, 1965; marketing promotion supr. Northwestern Bell Tel., Omaha, 1965-67; corporate pub. relations officer Gen. Learning Corp., Morristown, N.J., 1967-70; instr. journalism and Eng. Kellogg Community Coll., Battle Creek, Mich., 1971—. Cons. jr. coll. journalism; free lance writer. Mem. Women in Communications, Jr. Coll. Journalism Assn. (nat. pres. 1974-75), Mich. Journalism Edn. Assn. (state pres. 1973—), Ia. Press Women, Nat. Press Women, Assn. for Edn. in Journalism, Nat. Council Coll. Publ. Advisers (dir. for 2-year colls. 1973-74), Delta Psi Omega, Sigma Delta Chi, Gamma Alpha Chi. Roman Catholic (mem. women's service orgn. 1973—). Co-author History of Women's Job Corps, 1969. Home: 16 S Beckman St Battle Creek MI 49015 Office: 450 N Av Journalism Dept Battle Creek MI 49016

BURKES, ANN HUNTER (MRS. ROGER CLOWER BURKES), librarian; b. Philadelphia, Miss., Aug. 14, 1944; d. Homer Freeman and Ola (Carter) Hunter; A.A., E. Central Jr. Coll., 1963; student Delta State Coll., 1963; B.S., U. So. Miss., 1965, M.S., 1970; m. Roger Clower Burkes, Nov. 24, 1965. Librarian, tchr. English, Hickory (Miss.) High Sch., 1965-66; elementary librarian Meridian (Miss.) pub. schs., 1966-69; head librarian E. Central Jr. Coll., Decatur, Miss., 1969—. Mem. Miss. Edn. Assn., Miss. Library Assn. (sec. coll. and univ. sect. 1972-73), Miss. Jr. Coll. Faculty Assn. (sec. 1973—). Home: Box 391 Decatur MS 39327 Office: E Central Jr Coll Decatur MS 39827

BURKET, GAIL BROOK (MRS. WALTER CLEVELAND BURKET), author; b. Stronghurst, Ill., Nov. 1, 1905; d. John Cecil and Maud (Simonson) Brook; A.B., U. Ill., 1926; M.A. in English Lit., Northwestern U., 1929; m. Walter Cleveland Burket, June 22, 1929; children—Elaine (Mrs. William L. Harwood), Anne, Margaret (Mrs. James Boyce). Pres. woman's aux. Internat. Coll. Surgeons, 1950-54, now bd. dirs. Mus.; nat. vice chmn. Am. Heritage of D.A.R., 1971-74. Recipient Robert Ferguson Meml. award Friends of Lit., 1973. Mem. Nat. League Am. Pen Women (Ill. state pres. 1952-54, nat. v.p. 1958-60), Soc. Midland Authors, Poetry Soc. Am., Women in Communications, Am. Assn. U. Women (pres. N. Shore br. 1961-63), Daus. Am. Colonists (state v.p. 1973-75), Colonial Dames Am. (chpt. regent 1974—), Zonta, Phi Beta Kappa, Delta Zeta. Author: Courage Beloved, 1949; Manners Please, 1949; Blueprint for Peace, 1951; Let's Be Popular, 1951; You Can Write a Poem, 1954; Far Meadows, 1955; This is My Country, 1960; From the Prairies, 1968. Contbr. articles, poems to lit. publs. Address: 1020 Lake Shore Dr Evanston IL 60202

BURKETT, HELEN ROSE (MRS. CHARLES WILLIAM BURKETT, JR.), co. exec., club woman; b. Cleve., Dec. 22, 1903; d. Frederick Holland and Mary Chloe (Upson) Rose; B.A., Mt. Holyoke Coll., 1925; m. Charles William Burkett, Jr., Feb. 12, 1927; children—Charles William 3d, Diana Rose (Mrs. Hugh Cleland Brewer, Jr.), Helen Upson (Mrs. Gilbert H. Stevens). Sec., treas. Burkett Asso., 1951—. Chmn. communications Dept. Nat. Def., Harrison, N.Y., 1941-45, chief block leader service, 1943-45; mem. Harrison War Council, 1941-45, Service Corps A.R.C., 1945-47. Mem. Harrison Republican Town Com., 1946-47; mem. exec. com., Dade County, Fla., 1956-58. Mem. D.A.R. (Fla. chmn. radio and TV 1954-56, rec. sec. 1958-60, regent Biscayne chpt. 1956-58, regents' council, Miami 1956-60), Children Am. Revolution (sr. pres. Golden Sands soc. 1960-63, 70-74, sr. state v.p. 1972-74), Colonial Dames XVII Century (Fla. sec. 1957-59, treas. 1959-61, librarian gen. 1959-61, state 1st v.p. 1961-63, state pres. 1963-65, curator gen. 1965-67, pres. gen. 1967-69, hon. pres. gen. 1969), Colonial Dames Am. (chpt. scholarship com. 1959-61, chpt. dir. 1968-71), Cleveland Apt. Owners Assn., Nat. Assn. Parliamentarians, Daus. Am. Colonists (chpt. v.p. 1961-64), Women Descs. Ancient and Hon. Arty. Co., Daus. of 1812 (chpt. v.p. 1961-63), N.Y. Geneal. and Biog. Soc., N.E. Hist. and Geneal. Soc., Nat. Geneal. Soc., Ams. Royal Descent, Magna Charta Dames Fla. (corr. sec. 1960—). Clubs: Greenwich Country (Greenwich, Conn.); La Gorce Country, Surf, Indian Creek Country (Miami Beach, Fla.). Home: 5800 N Bay Rd Miami Beach FL 33140 Office: 8080 NE 2d Av Miami FL 33138

BURKETT, KATHERINE CLEVELAND, med. found. exec.; b. San Mateo, Cal., June 21, 1947; d. William Andrew and Juliet (Johnson) Burkett; student Pine Manor Jr. Coll., 1965-67, U. Cal., 1967-68; B.S., Briarcliff Coll., 1970. Asst. exec. dir. Inst. Med. Scis., Pacific Med. Center, San Francisco, 1971—; corp. asst. sec. med. research found., San Francisco, 1971—. Dir. Burkett Land Co.; mem. adv. bd. Security Nat. Bank of Monterey Co., 1961-66. Vol. Childrens Hosp., San Francisco, 1971—; vol., dir. Monterey Symphony Guild's Annual Domino Tournament, Pebble Beach, Cal., 1969—; vol. Monterey Peninsula Community Hosp., 1968-69. Trustee Nat. Hist. Found., 1970—. Mem. San Francisco Spinsters, Pine Manor Alumnae Club (co-chmn. San Francisco 1973), San Francisco Found., D.A.R., Monterey Co. Symphony Guild, St. Luke's Hosp. Jr. Aux., Briarcliff Coll. Alumnae Club of San Francisco, Common Cause, Kappa Alpha Theta. Clubs: Monterey Peninsula Golf and Country, Beach and Tennis (Pebble Beach, Cal.). Address: PO Box 726 Pebble Beach CA 93953

BURKHARDT, DOLORES ANN, librarian, educator; b. Meriden, Conn., July 28, 1932; d. Frederick Christian and Emily (Detels) Burkhardt; B.A., U. Conn., 1955, 6th year diploma, 1972; M.S., So. Conn. State Coll., 1960; postgrad. Central Wash. State Coll., 1962, Columbia, 1964—. Asst. librarian So. Conn. State Coll. Library, summers 1960, 62; sch. library tchr. Farmington High Sch., Unionville, Conn., 1955-66, North Haven High Sch., 1967-68; media specialist East Farms Demonstration Sch., Farmington, Conn., 1967-70; library coordinator Regional Dist. 13, 1970-72; library media coordinator Regional Dist. 10, Burlington-Harwinton, Conn., 1972—. Instr. So. Conn. State Coll., New Haven, 1967-68, Boston U. Media Inst., 1970-71. Spl. cons. Conn. Dept. Edn., 1965-68; chmn. Conn. Sch. Library Standards Com., 1968-70. Mem. Am. Assn. U. Women (sec. 1956-58, edn. chmn.), N.E.A., Conn. Edn. Assn., New Eng. (past pres.), Conn. (2d v.p. 1965-68) sch. library assns., Am. Assn. Sch. Librarians, New Eng. Sch. Devel. Council, Am. Soc. Curriculum Devel., Nat. Council Tchrs. English. Lutheran. Home: 812 Savage St Southington CT 06489 Office: Lewis E Mills Regional School Burlington CT 06085

BURKHART, ARDATH (MRS. JOHN BURKHART), civic worker; b. Vincennes, Ind., Sept. 2, 1905; d. Bert Hall and Fava (Tolbert) Yates; B.S. in Music, DePauw U., 1927; Litt.D., Tri-State Coll., 1974; m. John Burkhart, June 9, 1929; children—John (dec.), Gay (Mrs. A.Y. Brown, Jr.). Tchr., supr. music pub. schs., 1929-35. Mem. nat. devel. com. Girl Scouts U.S.A., 1951-55, mem. Region VII com., 1951-60, vice chmn. region VII, 1953-58, chmn. internat. work Region VII, 1958-60, Friends of Our Cabana Com. (Mexico), 1959-63, mem. bd. dirs., Hoosier Capital council, 1949-63, pres., 1951-54; v.p., mem. exec. com. Women's Affairs Com. of Civic Theatre, 1969-71; founder Women's Council for Ednl. TV Channel 20, 1970, pres., 1970-72; mem. Met. Planning Commn., 1963-65; chmn. women's div. United Fund campaign, 1957, bd. dirs., 1957—, mem. exec. com., 1958-69, 72—, mem. allocations com., 1958-69, mem. admission com., 1969—; chmn. women's div. Community Chest, 1950, 51, 56, bd. dirs., 1951-54; founder, pres. United Fund League, 1958-60, 64-65, chmn. selections com., 1961-63, mem. bd., 1958-67; mem. Bd. Sch. Commns., 1962-63; chmn. Charity

Solicitations Commns., 1955-65; bd. govs. Asso. Colls. Ind., 1968—, chmn., 1972—; bd. dirs. sec. Hoosier Art Salon, 1965—, v.p., 1972—; bd. dirs. 500 Festival, 1967-73, v.p., 1970-73; bd. dirs. Indpls. Day Nursery Assn., 1968-74, St. Mary's Child Center, 1968-71, Civic Theatre, 1970—, Jr. Achievement, 1970—; Marion County Pub. Library Found., 1972—; bd. dirs., pres. Met. Indpls. Television Assn., 1968-72, pres., 1972—, del. Pub. Broadcasting Service, 1972—; trustee Wenona Meml. Hosp., 1965—, DePauw U., 1955—, nat. alumni co-chmn. fund campaign, 1959-61; mem. Indpls. Sesquicentennial Commn., 1971, Greater Indpls. Progress Com., 1971—; mem. arrangements com. NATO Conf. on Cities, 1971; mem. Mayor's Task Force on Aging, 1972, Mayor's Task Force on Women, 1972—; mem. adv. com. Kennedy Center for Performing Arts; mem. pres.'s council Greater Indpls. Ch. Fedn., 1972—; pres. Porter Bus. Coll., 1972-74. Mem. nat. adv. com. Women for Nixon, 1972. Named Woman of Year, B'nai B'rith, 1958; recipient Adminstrv. Service award Girl Scouts U.S.A., 1963; TSP award Theta Sigma Phi, 1968, Woman of Year award, 1971; Distinguished Citizen award 11th dist. Am. Legion, 1970; Ind. Acad. Achievement award, 1973. Mem. Mid-Am. World Trade Assn., Inc. (charter), Nat. Friends Pub. TV, Alpha Chi Omega (past pres. Indpls. Alumni; chmn. Nat. Founders fellowship com. 1946-56, nat. conv. mgr. 1960, chmn. nat. nominating com. 1964, Nat. Achievement award for community service 1960). Methodist (bd. dirs.; chmn. congregational care commn.). Home: 4333 Sylvan Dr Indianapolis IN 46208

BURKHART, JEAN M. (MRS. GEORGE A. BURKHART), polit. party ofcl.; b. Parsons, Kan., Apr. 19, 1930; d. Clarence Harley and Lyda J. (Carter) Titus; grad. high sch.; m. George A. Burkhart, June 10, 1950; 1 dau., Monte Jean (Mrs. James F. Smith. Accountant, Speck, Elliuott, Saunders, Sanders & Veirs, tax attys., Oklahoma City, 1951-52, Nat. Gypsum Co., Parsons, Kan., 1952-70, Day & Zimmermann, Inc., ammunition plant, 1970-72; sec.-treas. HyGrade Constrn. & Materials Inc., 1972—. Precinct committeewoman Democratic Party, Lincoln Twp., Neosho County, Kan., 1964-72; pres. Neosho County Women's Democratic Club, 1966-68, v.p., 1968-72; sec. Neosho County Dem. Central Com., 1966-68, vice-chmn., 1968-70, chmn., 1970-72. Mem. bd. Graves Meml. Library, 1972—. Sec.-treas. St. Paul Comml. Club, 1966—, Osage Mission Hist. Soc., 1970—. Roman Catholic. Home: Box 35 St Paul KS 66771

BURKHEIMER, NANCY BROWN, state ofcl.; b. Colora, Md., Feb. 24, 1940; d. Joseph Jenny and Margaret Caroline (Clemens) Brown; B.S., U. Md., 1962, postgrad. Law Sch., 1962-64. Mem. planning staff Blair Asso., Washington, 1961; trainee Md. Dept. Motor Vehicles, Glen Burnie, 1962; tchr. Cecil County (Md.) Schs., 1963-67; real estate bus., 1963-70; polit. and pub. relations cons. R.C. Burkheimer & Assos., Elkton, Md., 1971-72; adminstrv. aide to Rep. Richard D. Mackie, 1970-73; adminstr. Md. Div. Labor and Industry, Balt., 1974—. Cons. Eagleton Inst. Politics Center for Am. Women and Politics. Mem. Cecil County Health Planning Com., 1969—, chmn., 1970; gen. chmn. Union Hosp. Fund Campaign, 1970. Commr. Md. Commn. on Status Women, 1968—; pres. Nat. Order Women Legislators, 1973; mem. Md. Ho. of Dels., 1962-70; chmn. Cecil County Tax Appeals Bd., 1972; v.p. Young Democrats Md., 1962-63; sec. Women Dem. Club, 1962. Bd. dirs. YMCA, 1966-72, v.p., 1973; bd. dirs. A.R.C., 1971-73, Cecil County Tng. Center for Handicapped, 1970-73; bd. dirs. Health Planning Council Eastern Shore, 1971—, v.p., 1973—; bd. dirs. Soc. Prevention Cruelty to Animals, 1968-72. Mem. Md. Order Women Legislators, Internat. Platform Assn., U. Md. Alumni Assn., Cecil County Hist. Soc., Women's Coll. Club (pres. 1966-68), Woman's Club (bd. mem. 1969-71), Pi Sigma Alpha. Home: Box 56 Colora MD 21917 Office: Div Labor and Industry 203 E Baltimore St Baltimore MD 21202

BURKMAN, CAROL LYNN VAN METER (MRS. REUBEN J. BURKMAN), educator, polit. worker; b. Ada, Kan., Feb. 21, 1930; d. Lee Spence and Doris Fern (Lambertson) Van Meter; B.S., Kan. State U., 1952; M.S., 1973; postgrad. Kan. U., 1951, Pittsburg State Coll., 1972; m. Reuben J. Burkman, Sept. 2, 1951 (div. June 1972); children—Ronald Lee, Jeanine H., Gary Linn. Tchr., John Fiske Sch., Kansas City, Kan., 1952-53, 54-55; home econs. adminstr., instr. Neosho Community Jr. Coll., Chanute, Kan., 1973—. Active Neosho County Hosp. Aux., 1958—. Co-chmn. Kan. Young Republicans, 1966-68; del. Rep. Nat. Conv., 1968; pres. Neosho County Rep. Women, 1971-74; dist. dir. 5th Dist. Rep. Women, 1974—; treas. 5th Dist. Reps., 1968—. Mem. Home Econs. Adminstrs. Kan., P.E.O. Presbyn. Elk. Club: Chanute Country. Home: 1608 S Malcolm St Chanute KS 66720

BURKS, SUSANNE MARTIN (MRS. WILLIAM F. BURKS), journalist; b. St. Louis, Mar. 11, 1930; d. Forrest L. and Madalyn (Ewing) Martin; student Lindenwood Coll., St. Charles, Mo., 1948-49; B.J., U. Mo., 1952; m. William F. Burks, Sept. 27, 1952; children—William Randolph, Julie Ann. Reporter-feature writer Nevada (Mo.) Daily Mail, 1947-51; asst. editor Torch, Beta Sigma Phi, Kansas City, Mo., 1952; civil service, secretarial work, 1953-61; editor South Suburbia, bi-weekly Byrneway Pub. Co., Toledo, 1962-64; reporter-feature writer News, Newspaper Printing Co., Albuquerque, 1966-70; information dir. Albuquerque C. of C., 1970; editor Messenger, weekly newspaper First Presbyn. Ch., 1965-72; food and home living editor Albuquerque Jour., 1971-72, edn. writer, editor, 1973—. Publicity, N.M. Arts and Crafts Fair, 1965; sec. House Corp., N.M. Alpha chpt. Pi Beta Phi, 1965-69. Recipient 1st place Albuquerque Press Club award for newswriting, 1966, 1st place award for analytical interpretive writing, 1969, 1st prize for newswriting, 1973; Guy Rader reporting award N.M. Med. Soc., 1967; 2d place for news story, weekly newspaper Nat. Fedn. Press Women, 1968, 2d place features, 1969; others. Mem. Am. Assn. U. Women, D.A.R., N.M. Press Women, Women in Communications, Pi Beta Phi Sigma Delta Chi (pres. N.M. profl. chpt.). Home: 6901 Seminole Rd NE Albuquerque NM 87110

BURLEIGH, JUDITH CUSHING, educator; b. Presque Isle, Me., Mar. 24, 1934; d. Parker Prescott and Mamie Arlene (Washburn) Burleigh; B.A., Wellesley Coll., 1956; M.Ed., Harvard, 1957; Ph.D., U. Conn., 1966; m. Erdmann Schmocker, Nov. 27, 1970. Tchr. 4th grad. Manchester, Mass., 1957-59, 60-61, Franklin Sch., Lexington, Mass., 1959-60; asst. prof. elementary edn., dir. elementary edn. program Am. Internat. Coll., Springfield, Mass., 1961-63; tchr. 3d grade Commonwealth Sch., Hato Rey, P.R., 1964-65; dir. elementary master of arts in teaching program Oberlin (O.) Coll., 1965-67; chmn. edn. dept. Colo. Coll., Colorado Springs, 1970-71, asst. prof., 1967-70, asso. prof., 1970-71; asso. prof. edn. Roosevelt U., Chgo., 1971—. Cons. Ohio Council Econ. Edn., 1965-67. Bd. dirs. Ruth Washburn Kindergrten and Nursery Sch., Colorado Springs, 1967-71; trustee Chase House, Chgo., 1974—. Colo. Coll. grant for observance of primary schs. Britian, 1969-70. Mem. Assn. Supervision and Curriculum Devel., Assn. for Childhood Edn. Internat., Internat. Council for Educating Tchrs. Nat. Council Social Studies, Pi Lambda Theta. Sch. observation in Mexico, England, Switzerland. Home: 3100 S Michigan Av No 301 Chicago IL 60616

BURLEIGH, MILDRED HAYNES, child psychologist; b. Oklahoma City, Oct. 17, 1913; d. James Sylvester and Hallie Bell (Ellsworth) Haynes; B.A., U. Pitts., 1935, M.Litt., 1938; Ed.D., U. Tulsa, 1966; m. William S. Burleigh, Dec. 25, 1934; 1 dau., Margery Elisabeth (Mrs. William Henson). Psychologist, Tulsa pub. schs., 1959-63, Kay Guidance Clinic, Ponca City, Okla., 1963-68; dir. pediatric psychology Bi-State Mental Health Found., Ponca City, 1968-70; pvt. practice, Tulsa, 1970-72; psychologist children and youth project Topeka-Shawnee County (Kan.) Health Dept., 1972—; adj. instr. U. Tulsa, 1970. Mem. Presbyn. Task Force on Status of Women, 1972—. Mem. Am., Southwestern, Clin. Child psychol. assns., Common Cause, Nat. Orgn. Women (convenor Tulsa 1971-72, pres. Topeka 1973—), Kappa Delta Pi, Delta Delta Delta. Democrat. Presbyn. Home: 3790 Park South Ct Topeka KS 66609 Office: 1615 W 8th St Topeka KS 66606

BURMEISTER, FLORENCE ESTELLE, librarian, educator; b. Cleve., Apr. 17, 1929; d. William Frederick and Josephine (Kostal) Burmeister; A.B., Western Res. U., 1956, M.S. in L.S., 1958. Library aide Cleve. Pub. Library, 1948-55, asst. childrens librarian E. 131st St. br., 1956-57, childrens librarian Miles Park br., 1958-60, Fleet br., 1960-61; childrens books reviewer Booklist and Subscription Books Bull., A.L.A., Chgo., 1962-63; head young peoples and childrens dept. Skokie (Ill.) Pub. Library, 1963—. Vis. lectr. Grad. Sch. Library Sci., Rosary Coll., River Forest, Ill., 1967—; instr. U.S. Office Edn. Inst. on Library Services for Gifted Children, Tex. Women's U., summer 1970; asst. prof. children's pub. library services U. Ill. Extension, 1971. Chmn. Children's Library Services Workshop for Bur Oak Library System, Joliet, 1968, 69, 70; mem. award jury Grolier Found., 1974—. Mem. Am. (past com. chmn., mem. and publicity chmn. Newbery and Caldecott awards com. 1969-70, chmn. Charles Scribner's Sons award com. 1971-72, Chgo. chmn. local arrangements com. Children's services div. 1972), Ill. (exec. bd., past sect. chmn., del. Ill. Commn. on Children, chmn. children's librarians sect. workshop for media selection 1970, 1st recipient Davis Cup award children's librarians sect. 1972) library assns., Library Adminstrs. Council No. Ill. (past sect. pres., chmn. children's reference services workshop 1969), Chgo. Library Club, Childrens Reading Round Table Chgo. (award com. 1968-74), Case Western Res. U. Sch. Library Sci., Flora Stone Mather Coll. alumni assns., Beta Phi Mu. Unitarian. Home: 201 E Walton St Chicago IL 60611 Office: 5215 Oakton St Skokie IL 60076

BURNELL, DIANA POTTER, educator, occupational therapist; b. Cambridge, Mass., May 9, 1931; d. Richard Montgomery Gilchrist and Harriet Keeney (Thompson) Potter; B.S. in Edn., Tufts U., 1954; Occupational Therapist, Boston Sch. Occupational Therapy, 1954; M.S. (Nat. Inst. Mental Health scholar), Cal. State U., 1969; M.A. in Psychology, Wright Inst., 1971, Ph.D., 1973; m. George M. Burnell, Dec. 22, 1956 (div. Mar. 1967); children—Cynthia Ann, David Montgomery. Staff therapist Pilgrim State Hosp., Brentwood, N.Y., 1954-55, N.Y. Psychiat. Inst., Columbia Med. Center, N.Y.C., 1955-57; sr. therapist Manhattan State Hosp., N.Y.C., 1957-58; staff therapist San Antonio State Hosp., 1958, coordinator rehab., 1959; cons. occupational therapy Terra Linda Valley Hosp., San Rafael, Cal., 1964; supr. occupational therapy Hope for Retarded Children and Adults, adult devel. center, San Jose, Cal., 1969-72; instr. dept. occupational therapy Cal. State U. at San Jose, 1972—. Mem. accreditation council for facilities for mentally retarded Joint Com. on Accreditation of Hosps., 1970. Mem. Human Relations Commn. of San Jose, 1971—. Dept. Health, Edn. and Welfare research grantee, 1971. Mem. Am., No. Cal. occupational therapy assns., Art Therapy Assn., Santa Clara Valley Watercolor Sch., Soc. Western Artists. Home: 3939 Altadena Lane San Jose CA 95127

BURNES, JUDITH CROOKS, ednl. research ofcl.; b. Evansville, Ind., Dec. 14, 1938; d. Harold E. and Irene (Petheram) Crooks; B.A., Ind. U., 1960; M.A. (fellow), U. Pa., 1962, Ph.D., 1966; m. Donald W. Burnes, Jan. 29, 1972. Asst. prof. dept. psychology Howard U., 1965-69; edn. program specialist follow through program U.S. Office Edn., Washington, 1969-72, also cons., 1967-69, 72-73; coordinator program analysis Bank St. Coll. Edn., N.Y.C., 1972—. NIH fellow, 1961-63. Mem. Am. Psychol. Assn., Am. Ednl. Research Assn., Phi Beta Kappa, Psi Chi. Author research reports. Home: 890 West End Av New York City NY 10025

BURNETT, ANNE PIPPIN (MRS. VIRGIL BURNETT), educator; b. Salt Lake City, Oct. 10, 1925; B.A., Swarthmore Coll., 1946; M.A., Columbia U., 1947; Ph.D. (Rosenberg fellow), U. Cal. at Berkeley, 1953; m. Virgil Burnett, 1960; 1 child. Instr. history U. Houston, summer 1953; instr. classics Vassar Coll., 1957-58; Am. Assn. U. Women traveling fellow Am. Sch. Classical Studies, Athens, Greece, 1956-57; fellow Am. Acad. Rome (Italy), 1958-59; Am. Philos. Soc. grantee, 1959-60, Am. Council Learned Socs. fellow, 1969-70; prof. classics U. Chgo. Author: Euripides Ion, 1969; Catastrope Survived, 1971. Contbr. articles to profl. jours. Research on Greek tragedy, poetry and epigraphy. Home: 51 Avon St Stratford ON Canada

BURNETT, CAROL, actress, comedienne, singer; b. San Antonio, Apr. 26, 1936; d. Jody and Louise (Creighton) Burnett; student U. Cal. at Los Angeles, 1953-55; m. Joe Hamilton, 1963; children—Carrie Louise, Jody Ann, Erin Kate. Introduced comedy song, I Made a Fool of Myself Over John Foster Dulles, 1957; Broadway debut in Once Upon a Mattress, 1959; regular performer Garry Moore TV show, 1959-62; appeared several CBS-TV Specials, 1962-63; appeared Broadway play/Fade Out-Fade In, 1964, play Plaza Suite, 1970, film Pete 'n' Tillie, 1972, musical play I Do! I Do!, 1973, film Front Page, 1974; club engagements Harrah's Club, The Sands, Caesar's Palace; now star Carol Burnett Show, CBS-TV Network. Recipient Outstanding Comedienne awards Am. Guild Variety Artists, 1959, 70, 71, 72, 73; outstanding variety performer Emmy award Acad. TV Arts and Scis., 1961, 62, 72; TV Guide award outstanding female performer, 1961, 62, 63; Peabody award, 1963; Golden Globe award for outstanding comedienne of year Fgn. Press Assn.; Woman of Year award Acad. Television Arts and Scis. Address: care Tom Corcoran Carol Burnett Show 7800 Beverly Blvd Los Angeles CA 90036

BURNETT, JEAN BULLARD (MRS. JAMES R. BURNETT), educator, biochemist; b. Flint, Mich., Feb. 19, 1924; d. Chester M. and Katheryn (Krasser) Bullard; B.S., Mich. State U., 1944, M.S., 1945, Ph.D. (Council fellow), 1952; m. James R. Burnett, June 8, 1947. Research asso. dept. zoology Mich. State U., East Lansing, 1954-59, dept. biochemistry, 1959-61, acting dir. research biochem. genetics, dept. biochemistry, 1961-62, asso. prof., asst. chmn. dept. biomechanics, 1973—; asso. biochemist Mass. Gen. Hosp., Boston, 1964-73; prin. research asso. dermatology Harvard, 1962-73, faculty medicine, 1964-73, also spl. lectr., cons., tutor Med. Sch. USPHS, NIH grantee, 1965-68; Gen. Research Support grantee Mass. Gen. Hosp., 1968-72; Ford Found. travel grantee, 1973; Am. Cancer Soc. grantee, 1974. Recipient Med. Found. award, 1970. Mem. A.A.A.S., Am. Chem. Soc., Am. Inst. Biol. Sci., Genetics Soc. Am., Soc. Investigative Dermatology, Sigma Xi (Research award 1971), Pi Kappa Delta, Kappa Delta Pi, Pi Mu Epsilon, Sigma Delta Epsilon. Home: 4480 Maumee Dr Okemos MI 48864 Office: Dept Biomechanics East Fee Hall Mich State U East Lansing MI 48824

BURNS, BARBARA JEAN, psychologist, health services adminstr.; b. Washington, Nov. 9, 1941; d. Robert and Bobbie (Robertson) Burns; student Am. U. Beirut, Lebanon, 1962; B.A., U. Ky., 1963; M.A., Columbia U., 1964; Ph.D. (teaching fellow), Boston Coll., 1972. Research fellow City U. N.Y., 1964; asst. dean students State U. N.Y., Cortland, 1964-67, acting dir. Coll. counseling services, 1967-68; psychologist Bunker Hill Health Center, Mass. Gen. Hosp., Boston, 1969-72, chief community mental health services, 1973—. Instr. Boston Coll., 1968—, Harvard Med. Sch., Cambridge, Mass., 1973. Vol. New Eng. Home for Little Wanders, Boston, 1968-71. Mem. Mass. Assn. for Mental Health (dir. Fanieul chpt. 1973), McLean Hosp. Aux., Mass. League Neighborhood Health Centers, Am., Mass. psychol. assns., New Eng. Ednl. Research Assn., Sigma Xi, Psi Chi. Editor: Mass. Psychol. Center Bull. Home: 251 Forest St Winchester MA 01890 Office: Bunker Hill Health Center Massachusetts General Hospital 73 High St Charlestown MA 02129

BURNS, BARBARA M., govt. ofcl.; b. Evanston, Ill., July 4, 1929; d. Martin Hughes and Miriam (Miller) Burns; B.A., Smith Coll., 1951; diploma U. London (Eng.), 1954, Evanston Bus. Coll., 1958. Researcher for dir. Presdl. Appointments Office, White House, Washington, 1959; personal sec. to Senator Jacob Javits, 1959-60; exec. asst. to asst. chmn. Republican Nat. Com., Washington, 1960-62; adminstrv. asst. to Hon. John Clifford Folger, Washington, 1962-63; spl. asst. to chmn. John F. Kennedy Center, spl. asst. to Pres. on Arts, White House, 1963-66; dir. confs. for corp. execs. Sch. Advanced Internat. Studies, Johns Hopkins, Washington, 1966-69; dep. asst. sec. for consumer services Dept. Health, Edn. and Welfare, Washington, 1969-73; asst. to Sec. Interior for internat. activities, 1973—. Mem. consumer council Am. Nat. Standards Inst., 1969-73; mem. nominating com. Am. Stock Exchange, 1972. Profl. chmn. vol. service bd. Washington Jr. League, 1965-66, profl. chmn. bd. dirs., 1966-67, mem. project research com. 1967-68, adv. planning com. 1968-69, mem. nominating com. 1969-70. Sustaining mem. Republican Nat. Com., mem. Nat. Fedn. Rep. Women, 1960-64, D.C. League Rep. Women, 1960-64; v.p., co-founder Georgetown Rep. Club, 1964. Mem. Smith Coll. Club Washington, Smithsonian Assos., Corcoran Gallery Art, Nat. Cathedral Assn. Club: 1925 F Street. Home: 6 Pomander Walk Washington DC 20007 Office: Dept Interior Washington DC 20240

BURNS, CHARLOTTE ANN (MRS. JAMES A. BURNS), ophthalmologist; b. Madison, Wis., Jan. 23, 1938; d. Robert E. and Charlotte J. (Calvert) Burns; B.A., U. Wis., 1959, M.D., 1962; M.S. (NIH fellow), U. Ia., 1969; m. James A. Burns, May 2, 1970; children—Edward James, Kathryn Ann. Intern U. Ia., Iowa City, 1962-63, resident, 1963-67; asst. prof. U. Ia., 1968-71; practiced medicine specializing in ophthalmology in Altus, Okla., 1971-73; med. missionary, fgn. countries, 1973—. Mem. A.M.A., Phi Beta Kappa, Phi Kappa Phi, Delta Delta Delta. Home: 109 N Roby Rd Madison WI 53705

BURNS, (DIANA) SUSAN CRAWFORD (MRS. ALTON FRANKLIN BURNS, JR.), advt., pub. relations exec.; b. Chgo., Aug. 7, 1935; d. Robert Brace Penn and Florence (Stiller) Crawford; A.B., U. Ga., 1957; m. Alton Franklin Burns, Jr., Dec. 28, 1957; children—Alton Franklin III, Robert Crawford. Asst. account exec. Grant Advt., Miami, Fla., 1958-59; account exec. Mason, Dow & Stone Advt., Jacksonville, 1959-60; with WFGA-TV, Jacksonville, Fla., 1960, WSFA-TV, Montgomery, Ala., 1960-62, Citizens & So. Nat. Bank of S.C., Columbia, 1966-67; asst. to dean journalism sch. U. S.C., Columbia, 1967-70; women's editor Brunswick (Ga.) News, 1970-72; feature writer Coastal Illustrated (bi-monthly), Sea Island, Ga., after 1972; now advt., pub. relations work. Bd. dirs. Brunswick Civic Ballet Co., Easter Seal Speech and Hearing Center, Brunswick, 1972-74, Glynn County A.R.C., 1973—; mem. St. Simon's Cotillion. Mem. Ladies Aux. Humane Soc. Glynn County, C. of C. Brunswick (mem. womens affairs com. 1971—), Glynn County Am. Cancer Soc. Mortar Bd., Kappa Alpha Theta, Theta Sigma Phi, Gamma Alpha Chi. Episcopalian. Club: Cassina Garden (v.p. program and publicity chmn. 1971-72) (St. Simons Island, Ga.). Home: 2400 Frederica Rd St Simons Island GA 31522 Office: First Associates 777 Gloucester St PO Box 1532 Brunswick GA 31520

BURNS, JUANITA WATERS (MRS. THOMAS L. BURNS), banker; b. Alta Vista, Ia., June 5, 1906; d. Harry A. and Edith L. (Arthur) Waters; student Hamilton Sch. Commerce, Mason City, Ia., 1925-26, 39-40; m. Thomas L. Burns, Aug. 7, 1942; children—Darlene (Mrs. Garfield E. Bieber), Roylene (dec.). With Clear Lake (Ia.) Bank & Trust Co., 1941—, asst. cashier, 1952-65, v.p., 1965—. Mem. Nat. Assn. Bank Women, Am. Legion Aux., Clear Lake C. of C., Beta Sigma Phi, Xi Mu. Republican. Club: Clear Lake Woman's. Home: 117 Fairway Dr Clear Lake IA 50428 Office: 322 Main Av Clear Lake IA 50428

BURNS, JULIA FOSTER (MRS. GROVER PRESTON BURNS), ednl. adminstr.; b. Bennettsville, S.C., Jan. 1, 1910; d. John Thomas and Gertrude C. (Lide) Foster; A.B., U. S.C., 1933, M.A., 1939; postgrad. Duke, summers 1940, 41; m. Grover Preston Burns, Nov. 3, 1941; children—Julia (Mrs. J.N. Jefferson), Grover Preston. Tchr. high sch., Rains, S.C., 1938-40, Brunson, S.C., 1940-41; instr. Miss. State Coll., 1943-44; dir. Burns Sch. of Dance, Fredericksburg, Va., 1952—. Sec., dir. Burns Enterprises, Inc., Fredericksburg, 1958—. Mem. D.A.R., Children Am. Revolution, Surgeon Lawrence Brooke Soc. (sr. pres. 1956-59), Kenmore Assn., Chi Omega. Club: Dahlgren Golf. Home: 600 Virginia Av Fredericksburg VA 22401

BURNS, KATHLEEN MARIE, publishing co. exec.; b. Chgo., Jan. 15, 1945; d. George Jerome and Eileen Isabel (O'Neill) Burns; B.A. in Eng., Clarke Coll., 1967; M.A. in Journalism (univ. fellow) U. Wis., 1970. Reporter Chgo. Tribune, 1968-73; writer, Chgo., 1973-74; dir. consumer affairs Montgomery Ward Inc., Chgo., 1973-74; chief Detroit bur. Fairchild Publs., 1974—. Instr. Broader Urban Involvement in Leadership Devel., Youth Center, Chgo., 1971-73. Mem. Council on Fgn. Relations, Chgo., 1971—. Adv. bd. dirs. Girl Scouts U.S.A., Chgo., 1972—. Recipient Outstanding Feature Story award Clarke Coll., 1967. Mem. Women in Communications (v.p. 1972-73), Soc. Profl. Journalists, Chgo. Women in Pub., Writers Internat., Pi Delta Phi. Club: Chicago Press. Office: 635 New Center Bldg Detroit MI 48202

BURNS, SUSAN SCHEBLE (MRS. ROBERT ROY BURNS), pub. relations exec.; b. Salt Lake City, Apr. 13, 1943; d. Max Carl and Winifred (Dillon) Scheble; B.A., U. Cal. at Berkeley, 1965; m. Robert Roy Burns, Mar. 31, 1973. Mgmt. trainee Kaufmann's Dept. Store, Pitts., 1965-66, asst. spl. events dir., 1966-67; home service coordinator Rubbermaid, Inc., Wooster, O., 1967-73, pub. relations supr., 1973—. Adviser Tri-Hi-Y, Wooster, YMCA, 1968-72. Publicity chmn. Wayne County Young Republicans, 1971. Mem. Elec. Women's Round Table, Women in Communications, Am. Women in Radio and TV, Pub. Relations Soc. Am., Sigma Kappa. Roman Catholic. Home: 460 Highland St Wooster OH 44691 Office: 1147 Akron Rd Wooster OH 44691

BURNS, VIRGINIA COMPTON (MRS. JOHN P. BURNS), pub. relations exec.; b. Detroit, June 20, 1927; d. John Martin and Claire Marie (LaFrance) Compton; Ph.B., U. Detroit, 1942; m. John P. Burns, Nov. 18, 1944 (dec.); children—Martina (Mrs. John M. Bertoni), Veronica Kelly. Asst. dir. pub. relations U. Detroit, 1966-69, Marygrove Coll., Detroit, 1969-72; dir. pub. relations Mercy Coll.,

Detroit, 1972—. Cons. to various non-profit charitable orgns. Mem. Am. Assn. U. Women, Women In Communications, Phi Gamma Nu. Club: Detroit Press. Home: 17556 Muirland Detroit MI 48221 Office: Mercy College of Detroit 8200 W Outer Dr Detroit MI 48221

BUROS, LUELLA GUBRUD (MRS. OSCAR KRISEN BUROS), artist, publisher; b. Canby, Minn.; d. Lauritz Martin and Anlaug (Ferguson) Gubrud; student Tchrs. Coll., Columbia, 1929-30, 33-34, Rutgers U., 1931-32, Ohio State U., 1934-35; m. Oscar Krisen Buros, Dec. 21, 1925. Pub., Gryphon Press, Highland Park, N.J., 1940—. Exhibited in group shows at Pa. Acad. Fine Arts, 1937, 40-41, 46-47, N.J. State Mus., 1938, 50-52, Corcoran Gallery Art, Washington, 1939-45, Golden Gate Internat. Expn., 1939, Art Inst. Chgo., 1940-43, N.A.D., 1941-42; 47, 49, 52-53, Met. Mus. Art, 1943, also others; represented in permanent collections Montclair Art Mus., Newark Art Mus., also pvt. collections. Sec., Buros Found., 1966—. Recipient awards Columbus Art League, 1935, Montclair Art Mus., 1938, 40, 41, Springfield (Mass.) Art League, 1941, Norfolk Mus. Arts and Scis., 1944, 45, 46, Washington Water Color Club, 1945, also others. Mem. Artists Equity Assn. (v.p. N.J. chpt. 1952-54), Asso. Artists N.J. (dir. 1958-60), Nat. Assn. Women Artists (medal of honor 1953), N.J. Water Color Soc., Art Council N.J. (v.p. 1951-55, awards 1949, 52), New Brunswick Art Center (dir. 1952-60), Phila. Water Color Club. Address: 220 Montgomery St Highland Park NJ 08904

BURR, BARBARA ANN, banker; b. Kalamazoo, Sept. 12, 1926; d. John Wainwright and Loie Sutherland (Simpson) Barton; student Parsons Bus. Coll., 1945; Stonier Grad. Sch. Banking, 1971. With Otsego State Savs. Bank (Mich.), 1950-52; with First Nat. Bank & Trust Co., Kalamazoo, 1952-54; cost accountant Frank Chevrolet Sales, Otsego, 1954-55; with Am. Nat. Bank & Trust Co. of Mich., Kalamazoo, 1955—, asst. v.p. systems and procedures, 1968-72, asst. v.p. pub. relations and bus. devel., 1973—; instr. Kalamazoo Am. Inst. Banking, 1965-70, Nat. Workshops of Bank Adminstrn. Inst., Park Ridge, Ill., 1968-69. Mem. Kalamazoo Inst. Arts, 1963—. Bd. dirs. Mich. Eye Collection Center, U. Mich. Hosp., 1965-72; trustee YWCA, 1972—. Recipient Jean Arnot Reid award, 1965, scholarship award, 1968, Nat. Assn. Bank Women. Mem. Am. Inst. Banking (chpt. pres. 1966-67, nat. committeeman 1967-68), Nat. Assn. Bank Women, Kalamazoo Symphony Soc. Episcopalian. Club: Altrusa of Kalamazoo (treas. 1962-64). Home: 431 Douglas Av Kalamazoo MI 49007 Office: 136 E Michigan Av Kalamazoo MI 49006

BURR, ELEANOR VIOLET (MRS. HARRY GIFFORD BURR, JR.), religious assn. dir.; b. English, Ind., Dec. 24, 1925; d. Albert Lloyd and Iva Vendetta (Sharp) Lechner; A.A., Spring Arbor Jr. Coll., 1948; student U. Toledo, 1952-53, Mich. State U. extension, 1953-54, U. Mich., 1953-54; m. Harry Gifford Burr, Jr., Apr. 16, 1949; 1 adopted dau., Cindy Lee. Statis. typist Kaiser Frazer Co., Ypsilanti, Mich., 1948-49; teller, bookkeeper Monroe State Savs. Bank, Temperance, Mich., 1949-53; tchr. kindergarten Erie Schs., Erie, Mich., 1953-55; publs. dir., editor OMS Internat., Greenwood, Ind., 1963—. Active Heart Fund, March of Dimes, Hemophilia drives, Los Angeles, 1964-65, Temperence, 1953, Greenwood, Ind., 1969-72; organized club for underprivileged girls, Temperance, 1954-56. Mem. Evang. Press Assn. (sec. 1967-68). Methodist. Editor: Harbor of Hope (Florence Munroe), 1962-63; Men Plus God (B.H. Pearson), 1967, Mission Accomplished (Ed Erny), 1967-68; For Me to Live (Florence Munroe), 1967; Motivated Men (D. Ferguson), 1971; Action, mag. Man for Missions Internat., 1959—; Pals, mag., 1963-67; OMS Outreach, 1963—. Home: 952 Erny Dr Greenwood IN 46142 Office: Box A Greenwood IN 46142

BURR, GUODA MARIJA (MRS. MICHAEL R. BURR), financial writer; b. Bludenz, Austria, July 25, 1945 (came to U.S., 1946, naturalized, 1953); d. Vytautas Alfonse and Aleksandra (Fledzinskis) Kasuba; B.S., Coll. City N.Y., 1967; m. Michael R. Burr, Dec. 23, 1966; children—Jonah Antony, Noah Simon. Securities analyst Value Line Investment Survey, N.Y.C., 1967-69; free lance financial writer, editor Anametrics Findings & Forecasts, N.Y.C., 1970—. Home: 170 Waukena Av Oceanside NY 11572

BURR, HELEN TURNER (MRS. JAMES J. BURR), social worker; b. N.Y.C., July 4, 1910; d. Samuel and Frances (Rosenthal) Fein; B.A., Hunter Coll., 1931; M.S., Columbia, 1944; m. H. Franklin Turner, Oct. 26, 1946 (dec. Feb. 1966); m. James J. Burr, 1968. Asst. to cons. on Services for the Aged, N.Y. State Dept. Mental Hygiene, Queens Village, 1956-67; research asso. Council Jewish Fedn. and Welfare Funds Project Mental Impairment of Aged, N.Y.C., 1964-68; cons. mental health services br. Nat. Inst. Mental Health, 1968-69; research asso. to unit on aging Fed. Protestant Welfare Agy. N.Y., 1968-70; research asso. Vis. Nurse Service N.Y., 1969-72; instr. social work N.Y. Sch. Psychiatry, 1960-67; vis. lectr. U. So. Cal. Inst. Gerontology, 1969, 70, 71, 73; spl. cons. D.C. Office on Aging, 1968-71; cons. nat. orgns. Nat. Council on Aging, 1972-73; project dir. tng. program Nat. Assn. Social Workers, 1973-74; cons. Gerontological Treatment Center, Washington Psychiat. Inst., 1974—. Mem. Pres.'s Task Force on Aging, 1967-68. Recipient fellowships, N.Y. Sch. Social Work, 1935, N.Y.C. Dept. Welfare at N.Y. Sch. Social Work, 1943-44, Nat. Pub. Health Service, 1955-56. Fellow Soc. Applied Anthropology; mem. Nat. Assn. Social Workers, Acad. Certified Social Workers, Am. Gerontol. Soc., Nat. Council on Aging. Author: Psychological Functioning of Other People, 3d edit., 1971. Contbr. articles to profl. jours. Home: 700 New Hampshire Av NW Washington DC 20037

BURRELL, MARY ELIZABETH GRANGER (MRS. CRAIG D. BURRELL), physician; b. Pontypridd, Wales, May 19, 1933; d. Walter and Hannah (Morgan) Granger; M.B., Ch.B., Welsh Nat. Sch. Medicine, 1957; m. Craig D. Burrell, May 19, 1960; children—Catherine, Sarah, Craig, Walter, David. Came to U.S., 1960, naturalized, 1968. Intern, resident Cardiff (Wales) Royal Infirmary, 1957-59, resident-fellow in neurology, 1959-60; fellow in neurology Cornell div. Bellevue Hosp., N.Y.C., 1960-61; practice medicine specializing in neurology. Presbyn. (elder). Contbr. med. articles to profl. jours. Home: 56 Grandview Pl North Caldwell NJ 07006

BURROUGHS, POLLY PAGE (MRS. RICHARD HANSFORD BURROUGHS, JR.), author; b. Waterbury, Conn., Jan. 8, 1925; d. Donald and Florence (Wilcox) Page; grad. high sch.; m. Richard Hansford Burroughs, Jr., July 14, 1945 (dec. July 8, 1946); 1 son, Richard Hansford III. Club: Edgartown (Mass.) Yacht. Author: The Honey Boat (Jr. Lit. Guild award 1968), 1968; The Great Ice Ship Bear, 1970; Zeb, A Celebrated Schooner Life, 1972; Exploring Martha's Vineyard, 1973; Nantucket, 1974; Thomas Hart Benton: An Island Portrait, 1975. Home: Egartown MA 02539

BURROUGHS, RUTH REUBEN, pediatrician; b. Omaha, Aug. 11, 1913; d. Harry and Susie (Green) Reuben; B.S., U. Neb., 1934, M.D., 1937; M.P.H., U. N.C., 1968; 1 dau., Barbara (Mrs. J. Lawrence Wilson III). Intern, Neb. Meth. Hosp., Omaha, 1937-38; resident Children's Meml. Hosp. and Montreal Children's Hosp., Montreal, Que., Can., 1938-40; asso. dir. Hinds County Health Dept., Jackson, Miss., 1942-44; practice medicine specializing in pediatrics, Jackson, 1944-64; pediatric cons. Miss. Bd. Health, 1965-67; pediatric cons. N.C. Bd. Health, Raleigh, 1968-69, chief crippled children's sect., 1969-72; adminstr. for med. services N.C. div. Vocational Rehab., 1972—. Cons. Regional Med. Program, Durham, N.C., 1971—. Diplomate Am. Bd. Preventive Medicine. Mem. A.M.A., Am. Pub. Health Assn., Am. Acad. Preventive Medicine, N.C. Pediatric Soc., Am. Rehab. Assn., Alpha Omega Alpha. Home: 4500 Yadkin Dr Raleigh NC 27609 Office: 620 Northwest St Raleigh NC 27611

BURROWS, JULIA LOWE (MRS. WILLIAM RICHARD BURROWS), occupational therapist, educator; b. Watertown, N.Y., Sept. 22, 1936; d. William Ralph and Muriel Ione (Carson) Lowe; B.S., U. N.H., 1959; postgrad. State U. N.Y., 1968; m. William Richard Burrows, Dec. 21, 1968; children—William Richard, Julia Ann. Occupational therapist N.H. Hosp., Concord, 1960-66, mem. adv. bd. assistants curriculum, 1968-71; instr. U. N.H., Durham, 1966—, also mem. univ. senate, 1967-68, sec. div. Biol. Scis., 1968-69. Mem. Sch. of Health Studies Acad. Policies Com., 1969-70. Vocational Rehab. Adminstrn. grantee, 1966. Mem. Am. (alternate del. 1963-64, del. 1966-70, com. basic profl. edn. 1965), No. New Eng. (exec. bd. 1962-73, v.p. 1962-64, pres. 1964-66, program chmn. 1970-71, placement chmn. 1961-73) occupational therapy assns., N.H. League Arts and Crafts. Clubs: Strafford Women's, Tops Barrington. Home: Canaan Rd Barrington NH 03825

BURROWS, RUTH ELIZABETH, physician; b. Alton, Ill., Sept. 13, 1916; d. Joseph and Ruth (Cummings) Burrows; student Cornell Coll., Mt. Vernon, Ia., 1934-35; R.N., Presbyn. Hosp. Sch. Nursing, Chgo., 1944; B.S., Elmhurst (Ill.) Coll., 1971; M.D., Woman's Med. Coll. Pa., 1951. Intern, St. Lukes Hosp., Chgo., 1951-52, resident internal medicine, 1952-54; resident internal medicine Joslin Clinic and New Eng. Deaconess Hosp., Boston, 1954-55; practice medicine, specializing in internal medicine, Evanston, Ill., 1957-61, Aurora, Ill., 1961-62; staff physician, diabetes cons. Northwestern U. Student Health Service, 1956-62, clin. instr. medicine Sch. Medicine, 1960-62; mem. staff Evanston Hosp. Assn., 1960-62, St. Joseph Mercy Hosp., Copley Meml. Hosp., Aurora, 1961-62; cons. physician, Chgo., 1962—; physician in residence Sacred Heart Convent, Lisle, Ill., 1971—. Asst. exec. dir. Ednl. Council for Fgn. Med. Grads., 1958-61. Mem. A.M.A., Ill., Chgo. med. socs., Am. Diabetes Assn., Diabetes Assn. Greater Chgo., Am., Chgo. heart assns. Contbr. articles to profl. med. jours. Address: 1910 Maple Av Lisle IL 60532

BURSON, MRS. PHYLLIS S., librarian; b. Seattle, Mar. 31, 1914; d. Harry and Theodosia (Porter) Sheidler; B.A., U. Wash., 1938, B.A. in Librarianship, 1939; postgrad. U. Ida. Coll. Law, 1939-45; m. G. Kent Burson, Dec. 24, 1942 (div. July 1952); children—Theo Lynne, Marilyn Kay. Asst. univ. libraries, 1934-40; head librarian U. Ida. Coll. Law, Moscow, 1940-45; asst. librarian Del Mar Coll., Corpus Christi, Tex., 1951-53; asst. librarian La Retama Pub. Library, Corpus Christi, 1953-56, head librarian, 1956-70, dir. libraries, 1970—. Library bldg. cons., 1966, 68-70; mem. adv. bd. Tex. Library Systems Act, 1971—; mem. exec. com. Southwestern Library Interstate Coop. Endeavor Council, 1971-72; mem. steering com. Gov.'s Conf. on Tex. Libraries 1974. Bd. dirs. Purple Sage council Girl Scouts U.S.A., 1963-65, mem. nominating com., 1964, bd. dirs. Paisano council, 1964-70; mem. Nueces County Hist. Survey Com., 1962—. Named Corpus Christi Woman of Year, Bus. and Profl. Women's Clubs, 1963. Mem. Am. (pub. libraries activities com. 1967-69, mem. council 1972-74), Coastal Bend (sec. 1952), Pacific N.W. (legislative chmn. 1941-42), Tex. (pub. libraries div. chmn. 1960-61; exec. bd., mem.-at-large 1962-65, 69-72, conf. chmn. 1965, Librarian of Year 1966, pres. 1970-71), Southwestern (chmn. pub. libraries sect. 1974—, mem. continuing edn. for library staffs adv. com. 1974) library assns., Am. Assn. U. Women. Episcopalian. Home: 3102 Santa Fe St Apt 37 Corpus Christi TX 78404 Office: 505 N Mesquite St Corpus Christi TX 78401

BURSTEIN, BEATRICE S. (MRS. HERBERT BURSTEIN), state justice; b. Bklyn., May 18, 1915; d. Joseph and Tillie (Starr) Sobel; student N.Y. U.; LL.B., St. John's U.; m. Herbert Burstein, June 17, 1937; children—Karen, Ellen, Patricia, Jessica, John, Judd. Admitted to N.Y. bar, 1940, U.S. Supreme Ct. bar, 1957; practiced in N.Y.C., 1940-62; asso. mem. firm Zelby & Burstein; partner Burstein & Agata, 1958-62; judge Dist. Ct. Nassau County 1962-68, Family Ct. Nassau County, 1969-73; justice N.Y. State Supreme Ct., 1973—. Commr. N.Y. State Commn. Correction, 1955-61; spl. adviser youth problems, Nassau County; former instr. L.I. U.; guest lectr. Moran Inst. Crime and Delinquency, St. Lawrence U., Columbia, Hofstra U., C.W. Post Coll., U. Philippines. Active numerous civic orgns. Bd. dirs. LeMoyne-Owens Coll., Am. Jewish Com., Am. Jewish Congress, Ct. Counseling Service Nassau County, Legal Aid Soc. Nassau County, Levittown Involvement Teens, Mental Health Assn., Nassau Council Girl Scouts, Inc., Nat. Conf. Christians and Jews, Nat. Cystic Fibrosis Research Found., others; mem. adv. bd. Adelphi U. Sch. Social Work, N.Y. State Coll. of Human Ecology, Cornell U. Recipient numerous awards civic and profl. orgns. Mem. Am., N.Y., Nassau County Women's bar assn. Am. Judicature Soc. Assn. Judges Family Ct. of N.Y. State, Internat. Fedn. Woman Lawyers (past v.p. U.S., del convs.), Nat. Assn. Woman Lawyers, Nat. Conf. State Trial Judges, Nat. Council Juvenile Ct. Judges, Nat. Legal Aid and Defender Assn., Bus. and Profl. Women's of Nassau County (past pres.), Am. Trial Lawyers Assn., Delta Kappa Gamma (hon.), Iota Tau Tau. Contbr. articles to profl. jours. Home: 62 Causeway Lawrence NY 11559 Office: Family Court Nassau County 1200 Old Country Rd Westbury NY 11590

BURSUK, LAURA ZELMAN (MRS. SAMUEL S. BURSUK), educator; b. N.Y.C., Mar. 1, 1926; d. Aaron and Jennie (Warshaw) Zelman; B.A., Hunter Coll., 1946; M.A. Coll. City N.Y., 1950; Ph.D., N.Y. U., 1969; m. Samuel S. Bursuk, Aug. 13, 1955; children—Barbara Jan, Lois Ilene. Tchr. early childhood edn., N.Y.C. Bd. Edn., 1947-56; reading cons. and specialist Lawrence High Sch., Cedarhurst, N.Y., 1964-69; asst. prof. edn. York Coll. of City U., Jamaica, N.Y., 1969—. Cons. research in edn. N.Y. U., and City U. of N.Y.; adj. asst. prof. ednl. psychology and reading N.Y. U., 1968-72. Mem. Manhattan Reading Council (pres., 1969-70), Am. Psychol. Assn., Internat. Reading Assn., Am. Ednl. Research Assn., Nat. Council on Measurement in Edn., Phi Beta Kappa, Kappa Delta Pi, Phi Lambda Theta (dissertation proposal award 1968). Home: 11 Harbor Lane Glen Head NY 11545 Office: 150-14 Jamaica Av Queens NY 11432

BURT, BEVERLY THERESA, ednl. adminstr.; b. Escanaba, Mich., Apr. 5, 1928; d. George D. and Margaret M. (LaPlante) Burt; student No. Mich. U., 1946-49; B.S., Mich. U., 1950; M.S. in Health Edn. and Psychology, Ore. State U. Tchr., Gladstone (Mich.) High Sch., 1950-51, Silverton (Ore.) Union High Sch., 1951-66; health educator Ore. Bd. Edn., Portland, 1967-73; tchr. Talmadge Jr. High Sch., Independence, Ore., 1967—, dist. health edn. coordinator, 1967—. Bd. dirs. Am. Cancer Soc. Mem. Ore. Assn. Health Edn., Ore., Am. assns. health, phys. edn. and recreation, Ore. Acad. Health Educators (pres. 1969—), Ore. Assn. Health Edn. Coordinators, Am. Assn. Univ. Women, Nat. (life mem.), Ore. (life) edn. assns. Contbr. articles to profl. jours. Home: 405 Madrona Av SE Salem OR 97302 Office: 16th St Independence OR 97351

BURT, MARY LOU DUMBAULD, univ. counselor; b. Columbus, O., June 9, 1926; d. Kiser E. and Gladys O. (Kavanagh) D.; B.A. summa cum laude, Ohio State U., 1947, M.A., 1966; Ph.D. in Counseling Psychology, 1968; m. James H. Niple, Mar. 19, 1948 (div. 1970); children—John C., Edward R., Thomas K., Craig K; m. 2d, Olan P. Burt, Nov. 27, 1970. Asst. to editor Jour. Counseling Psychology, 1966-67; teaching asst. psychology Ohio State U., Columbus, 1967-68, counselor Counseling Center, 1968, asst. dir., 1969—, coordinator tng., 1973—. Personnel cons. Measurex Corp., 1971—. Mem. Upper Arlington (O.) Bd. Edn., 1956-63, pres., 1960-62. Mem. Am., Ohio psychol. assns., Am. Group Psychotherapy Assn., Am. Personnel and Guidance Assn., Am. Coll. Personnel Assn., Assn. Women Psychology, Phi Beta Kappa, Mortar Bd., Alpha Lambda Delta, Kappa Kappa Gamma. Home: 1580 London Dr Upper Arlington OH 43221 Office: 154 W 12th Av Columbus OH 43210

BURTON, IRENE ANDERSON, univ. adminstr.; b. S.D., May 26, 1909; d. J. Alfred and Selma E. (Hoyer) Anderson; A.B., U. S.D., 1930, A.M., 1933; children—Eleanor J. Fabricius, Dorothy A. (Mrs. Thomas G. Lemonds). Tchr., Watertown (S.D.) Pub. Schs., 1931-32; asst. sec. Alumni Assn. U. S.D., 1941-46; asst. registrar U. S.D., Vermillion, 1946-65, registrar, 1965—. Mem. Am. Assn. U. Women, Alpha Gamma Delta. Methodist. Home: 1000 E Main St Vermillion SD 57069

BURTON, MARY JOAN, ednl. adminstr.; b. Hamilton County, Ind., July 1, 1918; d. William Nelson and Sybil Anna (Inman) Smith; primary certificate Ball State Tchrs. Coll., Muncie, Ind., 1938; B.S. in Edn., Ind. U., 1942, M.S. in Edn., 1960; m. Robert Ermer Burton, May 26, 1940; children—Ann E. (Mrs. J. Stephen Grimes), John E., Nancy E. (Mrs. Luis A. Morales), William L., James A. Tchr., Union Twp. Schs., Howard County, Ind., 1938-39, Westfield (Ind.) Schs., 1939-40; tchr. grade sch. Broadview Sch., Bloomington, Ind., 1956-63, tchr. educable retarded, 1963-65; tchr. trainable retarded Headley Sch., Bloomington, 1965-68; dir. Stone Belt Center for Retarded Children, Bloomington, 1968—. Sec., Monroe County Health Planning Council, 1972-73, Owen-Monroe County Health Planning Council, 1973—, Regional 10 Health Planning Council, 1973—. Mem. Council for Exceptional Children (pres. S. Central Ind. 1966, 72-73), Am. Assn. Mental Deficiency, N.E.A., Ind. State Tchrs. Assn., Altrusa, Delta Kappa Gamma (pres. Beta Lambda chpt. 1966, corr. sec. Alpha-Epsilon state 1969-71), Pi Lambda Theta (dir. Iota chpt. 1971). Methodist. Home: 501 S Swain Av Bloomington IN 47401 Office: 2815 E 10th St Bloomington IN 47401

BURTON, MARY REBECCA DAVIS (MRS. RUDY GRAY BURTON), elec. co. exec., civic worker; b. Perry, N.Y.; d. Albert E. and Rebecca Ann (Miller) Davis; student Rochester Bus. Inst., Am. Inst. Banking, 1938, Woodbury Coll., 1944, U. Cal. at Los Angeles, 1945; m. Richard Harned Bates, Oct. 4, 1940 (div. Sept. 1947); m. 2d, Floyd Burget Bigelow, 1948 (div. May 1952); 1 dau., Judith Lynne (Mrs. Daniel McMullen); m. 3d, Rudy Gray Burton, Nov. 17, 1962. Various positions, 1931-36; banking, 1936-41, advt., oil bus., 1944-50; sec.-treas. Emerald Bay Community Assn., Laguna Beach, Cal., 1950-52, Tel-I-Clear Systems, Inc., Laguna Beach, 1952-54; owner, operator Bigelow Bus. Services, Laguna Beach, 1954—; co-owner, mgr. Burton Electric, Laguna Beach, 1963—. Bd. dirs. Laguna Moulton Playhouse 1st Nighters, 1974—; asst., bd. dirs. Three Arch Bay Dist., South Laguna, 1957-73; com. mem. Opera League Laguna Beach, 1968—; mem. U. Cal. at Irvine Friends of Library, U. Cal. at Irvine Interfaith Found. Bd. dirs. Joe Thurston Found., 1957-64. Recipient various civic awards; named leading lady in bus. Laguna News-Post, 1971. Mem. Nat. Soc. Pub. Accountants, Soc. Cal. Accountants, Balboa, Dana Point power squadrons, Dolphinettes, World Affairs Council Los Angeles and Orange County. Laguna Beach C. of C. Mermaids (information chmn. Festival of Arts 1966, 67, 68), Nat. Assn. Tax Consultants, Cal. Women in Chambers Commerce (congresswoman). Clubs: Altrusa Internat. (Laguna Beach) (treas., dir.), West Coast Yacht, Executive Dinner, Opera league Riviera. Home and office: 697 Catalina St Laguna Beach CA 92651

BURTON, MARYANN (MRS. CHESTER GEORGE BURTON), city ofcl.; b. Berkley, Mich., Oct. 24, 1932; d. Fredrick Horace and Florence Emily (Miller) Fairbrother; student Mich. Jr. Christian Coll., 1965, Walsh Inst., 1971; m. Charles Raymond Nicolai, Feb. 25, 1955; children—Loretta Ann, Carol Anne; m. 2d, Chester George Burton, Aug. 6, 1971. Billing clk. City of Birmingham (Mich.), 1952-55; bookkeeper Internat. Sales, Detroit, 1957-60; cashier City of Berkley (Mich.), 1961-62, asst. city treas., 1962-67, dep. city clk., 1967-68, city clk., 1968—. Sec. civil trial bd. City of Berkley, 1968—, chmn. election commn., 1968—, sec. bd. canvassers, 1968—, sec. bd. appeals, 1968—. Mem. Berkley-Huntington Woods Youth Assistance Com., 1973—. Mem. Internt., Mich., Oakland County (treas. 1973) municipal clks. assns., Municipal Finance Officers Assn. Home: 1445 Wiltshire St Berkley MI 48072 Office: 3338 Coolidge St Berkley MI 48072

BURTON, PEGGY, advt. agy. exec.; b. N.Y.C., Sept. 1, 1936; d. Frank and Rose (Gatis) Delman; B.S. in Bus. Adminstrn., N.Y. U., 1957; certificate in Marketing, Advt. Inst. N.Y., 1970. Free lance television producer, N.Y.C., 1964-67; television producer Young & Rubicam, N.Y.C., 1967-69; sr. account exec. Daniel & Charles, N.Y.C., 1969-74; partner, v.p. Bruderer-Hartnett Advt. Agy., N.Y.C., 1974—. Mem. Advt. Women N.Y. Home: 220 Central Park S New York City NY 10019 Office: 485 Madison Av New York City NY 10017

BURTON, RUTH CECIL, psychiatrist; b. N.Y.C., June 2, 1912; d. Joseph and Lina (Marks) Burton; B.A., N.Y. U., 1932; certificat in Fr. lit. La Sorbonne, 1933; postgrad. N.Y. U., 1933-34; M.D., U. Buffalo, 1939; m. Peter Lewis Brandes, Aug. 29, 1936. Intern, Phila. Gen. Hosp., 1939-41; resident Triboro Hosp., N.Y.C., 1941-42; asst. resident Bellevue Hosp., 1942; practice medicine, specializing in internal medicine, N.Y.C., 1943, Binghamton, N.Y., 1944-54; resident psychiatry Binghamton and Marcy State hosps., 1960-63; practice medicine, specializing in community and forensic psychiatry, Syracuse, N.Y., 1965-71; dir. psychiat. services Syracuse U. Health Service, 1971—; adj. asso. prof. dept. psychology Syracuse U., 1973—; asst. clin. prof. psychiatry Upstate Med. Center, Syracuse, 1970—; asst. attending physician Univ. Hosp., Syracuse; attending physician Crouse Irving Meml. Hosp., Syracuse; dir. psychiat. services Elmcrest Children's Center, 1967-68; cons. Hutchings Psychiat. Center. Diplomate Am. Bd. Psychiatry and Neurology. Mem. A.M.A., Am. Psychiat. Assn., Acad. Psychosomatic Medicine, Assn. for Adolescent Psychiatry, Am. Ontoanalytic Assn., N.Y. State Med. Soc., Onondaga County Med. Soc., Am. Group Therapy Assn., Phi Beta Kappa. Presbyn. Home: 770 James St Syracuse NY 13203 Office: 804 University Av Syracuse NY 13210

BURTON, SHIRLEY, communications ofcl.; b. Lincoln, Neb., May 5, 1927; d. Jack Burton and Verle Marie (Cowin) Burton Morris; B.A., Union Coll., Lincoln, 1949; M.S., So. Ore. Coll., Ashland, 1959; postgrad. Portland State Coll., (Wall St. Jour. fellow) U. Ore. Tchr., English, speech, journalism Oak Park Acad., Nevada, Ia., 1949-52, dean girls, 1954-55; sec. Neb. Conf. Seventh-day Adventists, Lincoln, 1952-54; dean girls Milo (Ore.) Acad., 1955-56; tchr. English, speech, journalism Laurelwood Acad., Gaston, Ore., 1956-63; dir. pub. relations Ore. Conf. Seventh-day Adventists, Portland, also tchr. Walla Walla Coll. Extension, 1963-69; dir. dept. communication Pacific Union Conf. Seventh-day Adventists, Glendale, Cal., 1969—. Pub. relations cons. Union Coll., also hosps. in Cal., Ariz.; adv. bd. dept. communication World Ch. Hdqrs., Washington. Journalist, Young Democrats and Republicans, Seattle, 1966. Bd. dirs. KANG Radio, Angwin, Cal., Family Life Inst., Simi Valley, Cal., Voice of Prophecy Broadcast, Glendale, Adventist TV Center, Thousand Oaks, Cal., Quiet Hour Broadcast, Redlands, Cal. Mem. Religious Pub. Relations Council, Nat. Council Tchrs. English and Journalism, Nat. Assn. Religious Broadcasters. Editor: Pacific Union Recorder, weekly ch. paper; editorial staff Rev. & Herald. Contbr. articles to religious jours. Home: 9436 Carlynn Pl Tujunga CA 91042 Office: PO Box 146 Glendale CA 91209

BURTS, BETTY HUNT, librarian; b. Savannah, Ga., Oct. 16, 1912; d. George Wellington and Julia Reese (Moorhead) Hunt; A.B., Wesleyan Coll., 1933; B.L.S., Emory U., 1934; A.M. in L.S., Fla. State U., 1971; m. Albert Willard Burts, June 6, 1936; children—Julie (Mrs. Alex Reynolds, Jr.), Inez (Mrs. John Spear Colley). Librarian Norman Jr. Coll., Norman Park, Ga., 1934-35; library supr. WPA, Macon, Ga., 1936; children's librarian Macon Pub. Library, 1937; librarian Savanigh Sch., 1935-36, 42-46, Comml. High Sch., 1951-56, Jenkins High Sch., 1956—. Instr. library sci. U. Ga. extension at Armstrong, part time, 1965-70; tchr. French, Richard Arnold Jr. High Sch., Savannah. Hon. life mem. Ga. Congress Parents and Tchrs. Mary Calder scholar, 1967; Delta Kappa Gamma scholar, 1967. Mem. So. Assn. Evaluating Coms., Ga. Edn. Assn., N.E.A., Ga., Southeastern library assns., Ga. Assn. Educators (exec. com. library dept. 1972-74), Delta Kappa Gamma. Lutheran. Home: 2018 Speir St Savannah GA 31406 Office: 1800 E Derenne Av Savannah GA 31404

BURTSCHER, MARGARET CLAIRE FORSYTH (MRS. ALBERT WILLIAM BURTSCHER), educator, realtor, artist; b. Lamar, Colo., Oct. 9, 1917; d. Valoris Lawrence and Marguerite (Myers) Forsyth; student Williams Inst. Embalming, 1936, diploma Wichita Bus. Prep. Coll., 1937; B.S., Ft. Hays State Coll., 1958, M.S., 1968; postgrad. Kan. U., 1969-70; m. Albert William Burtscher, Dec. 20, 1950 (dec. Sept. 23, 1972); 1 dau., Valerie Ring. Formerly with Standard Oil Service, Wichita, Kan., Internal Revenue Service; office mgr. A.W. Burtscher Pub. Accountant, Hays, Kan., 1942-53; exec. sec. Anschutz Drilling Co. and Oil Promoter, Hays, 1949-53; owner Burtscher Books, Hays, 1960-69; tchr. Art and English Ellis (S.C.), High Sch., 1969-70; real estate asso., Hays, 1974—. Exhibited fabric and silversmithing in local shows, also Springfield, Mo., and Las Vegas (Nev.) art shows; exhibited watercolors in various shows, Wichita; nationally accredited flower show judge Nat. Council State Garden Clubs. Vol. tchr. Nat. Youth Corps, Hadley Regional Mental Health Hosp.; active Hays Arts Council, Russell County art shows. Pres. Ellis County Republican Women's Club, 1954; del. state Rep. Conv., 1954. Recipient various awards in flower shows. Mem. Phi Kappa Phi, Kappa Pi. Home: 414 18th St Hays KS 67601

BURTSCHI, MARY PAULINE, historian; b. Vandalia, Ill., Feb. 22, 1911; d. Joseph Charles and Olivia Pauline (Yoos) Burstchi; student St. Mary of Woods Coll., 1929-30; B.A., St. Louis U., 1933; M.A., U. Ill., 1954. Tchr. high sch., Carlyle, Ill., 1936-39, Effingham, Ill., 1939-70; cons. research historian Vandalia Hist. Soc.; mem. state history com. Ill. Sesquicentennial Commn., 1968. Recipient bronze medallion for hist. research for Ill. Sesquicentennial, 1968, award for teaching in student teaching program Eastern Ill. U., Charleston, 1970. Mem. Ill. (dir. 1965-68, v.p. 1968—, chmn. Diamond Jubilee com. 1973-74), Vandalia (pres. 1962-65, v.p., 1972—), Effingham Regional (dir. 1962-64) hist. socs., Coll. Edn. of U. Ill. Alumni Assn. (dir. 1970-72, sec.-treas. 1972—), Friends of Old Vandalia Statehouse. Roman Catholic (pres. Sir Thomas More Soc. 1971-72). Club: Vandalia Women's (v.p. 1974—). Author: Vandalia: Wilderness Capital of Lincoln's Land, 1963; various hist. soc. publs. Home: 307 N 6th St Vandalia IL 62471

BURWELL, SHIRLEY FAYE (MRS. VERLIN GALE BURWELL), banker; b. Texarkana, Tex., Feb. 6, 1943; d. James Truett and Loretta Faye (Roden) Hall; grad. high sch.; m. Verlin Gale Burwell, May 12, 1962. Note teller First Nat. Bank, Bay City, Tex., 1961-62; note teller First Freeport (Tex.) Nat. Bank, 1962-63, paying and receiving teller, 1963-65, exec. sec., 1965-69, dir. women's personal service, 1969-72, asst. v.p. consumer loan dept., 1973—; chmn. adv. bd. women's personal service, 1971—. Bd. dirs. Jr. Achievement, 1971—, Brazoria County Court Vols., 1971—. Mem. Brazosport C. of C. (membership and polit. edn. com. 1971—), Bay Area Heart Assn. (v.p. 1971-72, sec. 1969-71), Nat. Assn. Bank Women. Mem. Ch. of God of Prophecy (youth choir dir. 1970—). Clubs: Brazosport Bus. & Profl. (pres. 1971-72), Soroptimist (treas. 1971-72) (Freeport, Tex.). Home: 121 Mifflin St Clute TX 77531 Office: PO Drawer H Freeport TX 77541

BURY, KATHERINE DIANE, physician; b. Edmonton, Alta., Can., June 16, 1937; d. Joseph and Veronica (Majewski) Bury; B.A., St. Michael's Coll., U. Toronto, 1958; M.D., U. Toronto, 1962; M.S., Brown U., 1971. Intern Montreal (Que.) Gen. Hosp., 1962-63, resident, 1963-64; resident surgery U. Toronto, 1964-67, Toronto Gen. Hosp., 1964-66, Wellesley Hosp., Toronto, 1966-67; fellow surg. research R. I. Hosp. and Brown U., Providence, 1969-71, Yale-Yale New Haven Hosp., 1971; attending surgeon Wellesley Hosp., Toronto, 1971—; asst. prof. dept. surgery U. Toronto, 1971—; Michael Starr Meml. fellowship at Victoria U., Toronto, 1971-72. Med. Research Council Can. scholar, 1973. Fellow Royal Coll. Physicians and Surgeons Can., A.C.S.; mem. Assn. for Acad. Surgery, Am. Fedn. Clin. Research, Ont. Med. Assn., Acad. Medicine Toronto, Alpha Omega Alpha. Roman Catholic. Liberal. Home: 181 South Kingsway Toronto 3 ON Canada Office: 160 Wellesley St E Toronto M4Y 1J3 ON Canada

BUSBEE, BETTY ANN ANDERSON (MRS. BUSBEE), social worker; b. Anna, Ill., Apr. 29, 1933; d. Frank Walter and Mary Helen (Dallis) Anderson; B.S., Fla. So. Coll., 1953; postgrad. U. S.Fla., 1968-69, 1970; m. Walter Ray Busbee, May 12, 1957 (dec.); children—Donald Ray, Frank Anderson, William Rod, Bruce Philip. Reporter, Lakeland (Fla.) Ledger, 1952-53; tchr. Lake Wales (Fla.) High Sch., 1953-54; soc. editor Lake Wales Newspaper, 1954-58, 61; social worker Fla. Dept. Pub. Welfare, Highlands County, 1958-60; tchr., counselor Polk County Juvenile Detention Home, Bartow, Fla., 1960-61; social worker Fla. Dept. Pub. Welfare, Pensacola and Ft. Myers, 1962-63; with Fla. Div. Retardation, Ft. Myers, 1963—, community services coordinator, 1969-72, community field rep., 1972-73, social service dir., 1973—. Cons. mental retardation to various community groups; adviser various county mental retardation adv. coms., 1970—. Sec., Polk County Little Theatre Group, 1955-58; active Boy Scouts Am., P.T.A., Little League. Recipient Outstanding Journalism award Fla. So. Coll., 1953; various awards Fla. Press Assn. Mem. Fla. Women's Press Assn. (sec. 1956, membership chmn. 1971-72), Am. Assn. Mental Deficiency (regional membership chmn. 1972—), Nat., Fla. and Lee County assns. for retarded children, Council for Exceptional Children. Club: Quota (Lake Wales); Junior Woman's. Author: Handbook for Foster Parents, 1970. Contbr. articles to various publs. Home: 1635 Ricardo Av Fort Myers FL 33901 Office: PO Box 2369 Fort Myers FL 33902

BUSBEE, ELIZABETH DIVERS (MRS. CHARLES MANLEY BUSBEE), county ofcl.; b. Roanoke, Va., May 15, 1912; d. Alfred and Mary Bessie (Ramsey) Divers; student Martha Washington Coll., 1928, Milligan (Tenn.) Coll., 1928-29; B.S., Radford (Va.) Coll., 1934; postgrad. U. N.C., 1944-45, U. Va., 1945-46, Coll. William and Mary, 1946; m. Charles M. Busbee, July 3, 1957. Tchr., coach West Jefferson (N.C.) High Sch., 1935-37, Gretna (Va.) High Sch., 1937-38; social worker Franklin County Dept. Pub. Welfare, Rocky Mount, Va., 1938-42, supt., 1942—. Bd. dirs. S.W. Soc. for Crippled Children, 1944-50; treas. Franklin County chpt. Nat. Found., 1938—; pres. Va. League Local Welfare Execs., 1956-58; rep. from 5th Congl. Dist. Va. on League Local Welfare Execs., 1950-54, 63-65. Organizer Woman's Club of Rocky Mount, 1945, pres., 1950-52, 71—, organizer Jr. Woman's Club, 1949; pres. U.D.C., 1956—. Home: 114 Taliaferro Av Rocky Mount VA 24151 Office: Franklin County Dept Pub Welfare Rocky Mount VA 24151

BUSBEY, SYLVIA SPITZ, savs. and loan co. exec.; b. Mattoon, Ill., Nov. 7, 1933; d. Joseph Edward and Ruth Elizabeth (Reed) Spitz; grad. high sch. With Mattoon Fed. Savs. & Loan Co., 1951—, sec., 1971-72, v.p., 1972—. Mem. Am. Bus. Women's Assn., Controllers Soc. for Savs. Insts., Epsilon Sigma Alpha. Roman Catholic, (treas. Library Bd., Mattoon, 1970—). Home: 416 Crescent Dr Mattoon IL 61938 Office: 1520 Charleston St Mattoon IL 61938

BUSCH, VERLA MAXINE, extension home economist; b. Easton, Ill., Aug. 28, 1922; d. Chance Hardin and Nina Pearl (Brent) Stone; B.S., U. Ill., 1944, postgrad., summer 1945; m. Louis Busch, Jr., Dec. 28, 1946; 1 dau., Niceene (Mrs. Gary Connolly). Tchr. high sch. Tolono, Ill., 1944, Eldorado, Ill., 1944-47, Astoria, Ill., 1947-48; substitute tchr. pub. schs. Havana, Ill., 1951-69; extension adviser home econs. Mason County, Havana, 1969—. Leader 4-H Club, 1946-69, Girl Scouts, 1956-63. Bd. dirs. Mason County Health Improvement Assn., 1968-71. Mem. Ill., Nat. assns. extension home economists, Ill., Am. home econs. assns., Am. Assn. U. Women, Bus. and Profl. Womens Club, Am. Legion Aux., Beta Sigma Phi. Home: 613 N High St Havana IL 62644 Office: 133 S High St Havana IL 62644

BUSCHING, MARY LOUISE, librarian; b. Ranger, Tex., July 9, 1925; d. Homer and Iva Lorena (Hampton) Wood; student U. Ia., 1944, Hardin-Simmons U., Abilene, Tex., 1946-47, Cisco Jr. Coll., 1968; m. William Dale Busching, Nov. 27, 1949; 1 dau., Deborah Sarada. With Western Union, Springfield, Mo., 1944-45, Kerrvilee, Tex., 1945, Gatesville, Tex., 1945, Hobbs, N.M., 1945, San Angelo, Tex., 1947; with Golden Oak Milling Co., Gorman, Tex., 1948; sec. weigher, DeLeon, Tex., 1948-50; now librarian Gorman Pub. High Sch. Asst. band dir. Cisco High Sch., 1941, Gorman Pub. High Sch., 1942. Mem. Ch. of Jesus Christ of Latter-day Saints. Author: Castle of Dreams, 1952; Rivers Bend, 1964. Editor: Iowa Federated Womens Senior Club Book. Home: Route 1 Gorman TX 76545

BUSH, DOROTHY VREDENBURGH (MRS. JOHN W. BUSH), sec. Democratic Nat. Com.; b. Baldwyn, Miss., Dec. 8, 1916; d. Will Lee and Lany (Holland) McElroy; B.S., Miss. State Coll. for Women, 1937; postgrad. George Washington U.; m. Peter Vredenburgh III, Dec. 27, 1940 (dec.); m. 2d, John W. Bush, Jan. 13, 1962. Dir. Coastal Caribbean Oils & Minerals, Ltd., Pancoastal, Inc. Nat. committeewoman Ala. Young Dems., 1941-50; v.p. Young Dems. of Am., 1943-48; sec. Dem. Nat. Com., 1944— (first woman to hold this position); acting pres. Young Dems. of Am., 1944; sec. Dem. Nat. Conv., 1944, 48, 52, 56, 60, 64, 68, 72. Mem. Beta Sigma Phi. Home: The Towers 4201 Cathedral Av NW Apt 1115-E Washington DC 20016

BUSH, GLORIA K., psychologist; b. Huntington Park, Cal.; d. P. and S. (Moraga) Kemerer; A.B., U. So. Cal., Los Angeles, 1937, M.A., 1941, Ph.D., 1974; m. William R. Eckles, Oct. 27, 1953 (dec. Sept. 1970). Asst. chief statis. unit A.R.C., San Francisco, 1942-43, asst. chief nat. hdqrs. statis. unit, Washington, 1943-44; personnel mgr. Bullocks, Los Angeles, 1944; psychologist Juvenile Hall Hosp., Los Angeles, 1948-52; vocational rehab. worker Dept. Pub. Welfare Los Angeles, 1952-55; domestic relations officer Superior Ct. Los Angeles County, 1955-60; psychologist Meyers Clinic, Los Angeles, 1960-61; psychologist, Van Nuys, Cal., 1961—. Cons., Cal. Sch. of Profl. Psychology, 1973-74. Mem. Am. Psychol. Assn., Internat. Transactional Analysis Assn. Home: PO Box 3175 Van Nuys CA 91407 Office: 7430 Balboa Van Nuys CA 91406

BUSH, HELMA NITZSCHE (MRS. GEORGE FRANKLIN BUSH), artist, writer, camp dir.; b. Phila., June 18, 1910; d. George Erasmus and Elsa (Koenig) Nitzsche; B.F.A. in Edn., U. Pa., 1933, postgrad., 1934-36; postgrad. U. Geneva (Switzerland), 1936-37, U. Heidelberg (Germany), 1931-32; m. George Franklin Bush, June 12, 1938; children—Helma Dierdre (Mrs. Cristos Cupas), Penelope (Mrs. Andreas Graeser), Susan Polyelsa (dec.), George Christopher. Co-dir., owner French speaking girls camp Les Chalets Francais, Deer Isle, Me., 1937—; watercolor artist; solo dancer Phila. Civic Symphony, 1937-38, La Scala Opera Co., Milan, Italy, 1937-38; tchr. Friends Select Sch., Phila., 1936-37; tchr., librarian Miss Zara's Sch., Chestnut Hill, Pa., 1937-38; dir. 3d Grade Dramatic Group of Princeton (N.J.) Community Players, 1950-60; pub. relations chmn. Princeton council Girl Scouts U.S.A., 1950-58. Bd. dirs. Princeton Group Arts Soc., 1960-61. Mem. Writers Group Princeton (chmn. 1950-60), Kappa Kappa Gamma (pres. alumni chpt. Princeton 1962). Club: College of Princeton (chmn. entertainment com. 1949-50, 1965—). Author numerous children's plays and short stories. Home: 391 Nassau St Princeton NJ 08540 Office: Les Chalets Francais Deer Isle ME 04627 also Sapphire Bay A-17 St Thomas VI 00801

BUSH, JEANETTE SANDLIN (MRS. HARLEY W. BUSH), lawyer; b. Lebanon, Ind., May 8, 1903; d. Larkin Monroe and Bessie Bell (Threewits) Sandlin; B.S. in Edn., Butler U., 1945; J.D., Ind. U., 1956; m. Harley W. Bush, June 13, 1942; 1 son, Gerald L. Tchr., Boone County, Ind., 1929-31; dep. sheriff Boone County, 1929-31; technician, shipping clk. Ladoga Canning Co., Lebanon, Ind., 1931-39; tchr. Hopewell, Boone County, Ind., 1939-42, Met. Dist. Pike Twp., Marion County, Ind., 1942-69; admitted to Ind. bar, 1958, U.S. Supreme Ct., 1969; mem. firm Hutchinson & Bush, Lebanon, Ind., part-time 1959-69, full time 1969—. Sec., dir. Sheridan Chem. Corp. (Ind.), 1963—. Legal cons., dir. Boone County Humane Soc., 1972—. Sec. Central Sch. Pike Twp. P.T.A., 1962. Recipient Distinguished Service award Ind. State Tchrs. Assn., 1969; certificate of appreciation Nat. Police Officers Assn., 1973. Mem. Ind., Indpls., Boone County bar assns., Women Lawyers Assn., Bus. and Profl. Womens Club, Delta Kappa Gamma. Contbr. articles to profl. jours. Home: 2344 W 67th St Indianapolis IN 46260 Office: 319 N West St Lebanon IN 46052

BUSH, LOUISE FULTON (MRS. MAURICE S. BUSH), assn. adminstr., zoologist; b. Wichita, Kan., Feb. 7, 1907; d. Louis R. and Cora A. (Culver) Fulton; A.B., Friends U., 1928; M.A. (Zoology fellow), U. Kan., 1931; Ph.D., U. Minn., 1938; m. Maurice S. Bush, Jan. 1, 1936; children—Lois (Mrs. David Monson), John. Biol. artist, Mpls., 1931-43, Chgo., 1943-46, N.Y.C., 1946-57; asst. prof. zoology Drew U., Madison, N.J., 1959-63, asso. prof., 1963-67, prof., 1968-72, prof. emeritus, 1972—; exec. sec., treas. Beta Beta Beta, Nat. Hon. Biol. Soc., Madison, 1967—. Zool. artist U. Minn., St. Paul, 1936-37; instr. Apsola Coll., East Orange, N.J., 1956-57. U.S. Inst. Sci. fellow, 1963-64. Mem. N.J. Acad. Sci. (treas. 1958-64), A.A.A.S., Am. Soc. Zoologists, Sigma Xi. Unitarian (trustee 1969-71). Contbr. articles to profl. jours. Home: 269 Woodland Av Summit NJ 07901 Office: Drew University Madison NJ 07940

BUSHART, ANNE KONKOL, govt. ofcl., recreational therapist; b. Graceton, Pa., Apr. 19, 1916; d. Joseph and Anna Ilona (Maslonka) Konkol; B.S., Baldwin-Wallace Coll., 1939; m. Roland E. Kellum (dec. 1944); m. Roy Ralston Bushart, Oct. 1, 1955. Tchr. Cleve. bd. edn., 1939-42; lab. aide chem. analysis NACA, Cleve., 1942-45; hosp. recreation worker A.R.C., Eastern area 1945-52; asst. chief spl. services St. Elizabeth's Hosp., Dept. Health, Edn. and Welfare, Washington, 1952-57, chief recreational therapy, 1957—. Vis. instr. therapeutic recreation U. Wis., 1967, instr., 1968; spl. instr. therapeutic recreation U. Md., 1968-71; mem. Nat. Recreation Edn. Accreditation Project Com.; panel mem. recreation exam. U.S. Civil Service Bd. Examiners, 1962—; sec. Delinquency and Crime Control Conf., Health and Welfare Council, 1963, 64. Bd. dirs. Albert Deutch Center. Recipient Superior Work Performance award St. Elizabeth Hosp., 1957; Distinguished Service award Nat. Therapeutic Recreation Soc., 1970; fellowship award D.C. Recreation and Park Soc., 1970. Mem. Nat. Assn. Music Therapy, Am. Art Therapy Assn., Am. Guitar Found., D.C. Mental Health Assn. (rehab. com.), Nat. Therapeutic Recreation Soc. (dir. Fellowship v.p. 1968-69), D.C. Recreation and Park Assn. (pres. 1962). Nat. Assn. Recreational Therapists (pres. 1966-67), Unitarian. Contbr. articles profl. jours. Home: 7406 Ridgewood Av Chevy Chase MD 20015 Office: St Elizabeths Hosp Washington DC 20032

BUSHORE, LUCY ELLEN HATMAKER, broadcasting exec., ballet co. exec.; b. Knoxville, Tenn., Oct. 5, 1936; d. Raymond Leon and Mable Glen (Crass) Hatmaker; B.A., U. Tenn., 1962, M.A., 1968; m. Robert David Proffitt, Oct. 5, 1956 (div. 1974); children—Robert David, Karen Lelia, Stephen Keith, Kevin Scott; m. 2d, Arthur William Bushore, Sept. 10, 1974. Instr. speech/theatre dept. Maryville (Tenn.) Coll., 1966-72. Dir. children's theatre prodns., Maryville, 1966-67; actress in numerous summer playhouses with leads in Dark Moon, Lion in Winter, South Pacific; producer, host Homemaker Show sta. WATE-TV, Knoxville, 1970; co. mgr. Maryville-Alcoa (Tenn.) Civic Ballet, 1971—; producer, host Arts Around 2 TV Show, Knoxville, 1973—. Costume designer for dance cons. and theatre design cons. 1970—. Chmn. County (Tenn.) Council for the Arts, 1973—; mem. project future steering com. Blount County, 1972—; panel mem. Tenn. Arts Commn., Nashville, 1972—; treas. Knox Area Children's Internat. Village, 1973-74. Mem. bd. trust Sam Houston Meml. Assn. 1971-74, research dir., 1971-74; mem. bd. trust Child and Family Services, 1971-73, Maryville-Alcoa Civic Ballet, 1972—. Recipient N.Y. Poetry Forum award, 1972; Tenn. Women's Poetry award, 1968. Mem. Am. Assn. Dance Companies, Tenn. Assn. Dance, Tenn. Theatre Assn., Tenn. Arts Commn., Pi Beta Phi, Tau Kappa Alpha, Pi Kappa Delta. Club: Chilhowee (Maryville). Address: Crown Colony House #32 Colony 3 Kingsport TN

BUSK, PATRICIA LYNN JULIA (MRS. MICHAEL C. BUSK), statistician; b. Southampton, N.Y., Nov. 25, 1944; d. Andrew Stanley and Julia (Maziarz) Zuczek; B.A., Trenton State Coll., 1966; M.A., (NIH fellow), Catholic U. Am., 1969; m. Michael C. Busk, June 7, 1969. Summer intern NASA, Washington, 1969; statistician, project dir. Childrens Meml. Hosp., Chgo., 1969—. Mem. Am. Statis. Assn., Am. Ednl. Research Assn. Home: 115 S Bassett St Madison WI 53703 Office: 2300 Children's Plaza Chicago IL 60614

BUSOT, ADRIANA BERTA PINO (MRS. ALDO J. BUSOT), educator; b. Santa Clara, L.V., Cuba, Jan. 18, 1929; d. Adriano C. and Edelmira (Gomez) Pino; B.A., Inst. Santa Clara, Cuba, 1947; Doctor en Filosofia y Letras, Havana U., 1954; m. Aldo J. Busot, Sept. 21, 1951; children—Adriana C., Maria Victoria, Aldo G., Jorge A. Came to U.S., 1961, naturalized, 1969. Tchr. world history Hermanas Cuesta Sch., 1952-54; asst. prof. Inst. Santa Clara, 1954-59, U. Las Villas, 1959-61; Spanish tchr. Cedar Falls Community Sch. System, 1962-63; instr. U. No. Ia., 1963-64; tchr. Spanish, Waterloo Community Sch. System, 1964-65; mem. faculty Wis. State U., Whitewater, 1965—, asso. prof. fgn. langs., 1965—. Mem. Am. Assn. U. Profs., Modern Lang. Assn., N.E.A., Am. Assn. Tchrs. Spanish and Portuguese. Translator to Spanish: Wittgenstein Language and Philosophy (Warren Shibles), 1974. Office: Dept Fgn Langs U Wis Whitewater WI 53190

BUTCHER, HELEN ASTRID HENDRICKSON (MRS. OWEN JOHN BUTCHER), realtor; b. Newcastle, Wash.; d. Andrew and Selma (Sars) Hendrickson; grad. high sch.; m. Owen John Butcher, Apr. 3, 1942 (dec. July 1957); children—Merle Imogene (Mrs. Paul Pearson), Ann Christine (Mrs. Caedmon Liburd), Michael Owen. Treas., Spenard Utilities, Inc., 1961-65; sec., Turnagain Investments, Inc., 1960-73, M & G Corp., 1960-71, Trans-Am. Equity, Inc., 1962-67, Great No. Developers, Inc., 1964-70, 73-74, Ocean View Manor, Inc., 1964-70, 73-74, Heather Meadows Park, Inc., 1965-70, 73-74; pres. Consol. Services, 1968-71; broker Aurora Realty, Anchorage, 1970—; dir. Alaskan Constrn. and Investment, Inc. Mem. bd. Turnagain Rainbow Assembly, 1959-65; past officer Girl Scouts U.S.A. Recipient Nat. Bull. Excellence award Am. Fedn. Mineral. Socs., 1969. Mem. Multiple Listing Service, Nat., Alaska, Anchorage assns. real estate bds., Anchorage Bd. Realtors (sec. 1973, 2d v.p. 1974), Alaska Assn. Realtors (dir. 1974—, editor Realtor Reporter 1973—), Chugach Gem and Mineral Soc. (bd. mem. 1966-71, pres. 1969). Mem. Order Eastern Star, Pioneer Women Aux. Home: 2400 Douglas Dr Anchorage AK 99503 Office: 225 E Fireweed Lane Anchorage AK 99503

BUTCHER, SUZANNE AMELIA, physician; b. Lakeland, Fla., Feb. 19, 1940; d. Raymond Hamilton and Ruby Mae (Fennell) Ralston; B.A., Coll. Wooster (O.), 1961; M.D., Duke, 1965; m. Gene A. Butcher, Sept. 2, 1961; children—Suzanne, Mary Grace, Sarah. Intern Duke, 1965-66, resident, 1966-68; resident Youngstown (O.) Hosp. Assn., 1968-69; asso. pathologist Trumbull Meml. Hosp., Warren, O., 1969—, dir. Sch. Med. Tech., 1971—. Fellow Coll. Am. Pathologists, Am. Soc. Clin. Pathologists. Home: 11 Norwick Dr Youngstown OH 44505 Office: Trumbull Meml Hosp E Market St Warren OH 44482

BUTCHER, VADA EASTER (MRS. JAMES W. BUTCHER), coll. dean; b. St. Louis, Dec. 6, 1923; d. Joseph Henry and Benne (Parks) Easter; B.A., Fisk U., 1942; Mus.M., Chgo. Mus. Coll., 1946, D.F.A. (Rosenwald fellow), 1950; m. James W. Butcher, June 17, 1964. Instr., prof. music Howard U., Washington, 1946-72, dean Coll. Fine Arts, 1972—. Cons. Ford Found., Coll. Entrance Exam. Bd., Nat. Assn. Schs. Music; lectr. in African and Afro-Am. music in secondary schs., colls. and community instns. Trustee, Stockbridge (Mass.) Sch. Recipient Ford Found. grant, 1955, U.S. Office Edn. grant, 1968, Nat. Endowment for Humanities grant, 1972, Outsanding Educator award Alpha Kappa Alpha, 1972. Mem. Coll. Music Soc., Alliance for Arts in Edn., Internat. Conf. Fine Arts Deans, Soc. for Ethnomusicology,

Pi Kappa Lambda, Alpha Kappa Alpha. Author: Materials in African and Afro-American Music for the General Student, 1970; Materials in African and Afro-American Music for the Music Major, 1972. Home: 610 Quackenbos St NW Washington DC 20001

BUTEAU, MAGDELHAYNE FLORENCE, educator; b. Montreal, Que., Can., Oct. 31, 1916; d. Onesime and Angelina (Payette) Buteau; B.A., Marie-Anne Coll. (Can.), 1936; B.Ed., Mariancpolis Coll., 1938; Licenciate in Pedagogy, St. George Pedagogical Inst. (Can.), 1947; M.A., U. Montreal, 1943; Ph.D., McGill U., 1970. With Montreal Cath. Sch. Bd., 1936-55; prof. St. Joseph Tchrs. Coll., Montreal, 1955-70, head French dept., 1962-70; prof. applied linguistics McGill U., Montreal, 1970—, head edn. in 2d langs., 1972—; asso. dir. Inst. Translation, U. Montreal, 1958-66. Sec. Provincial Vocational Guidance Com., 1952-64; bd. Cath. High Sch. Ofcl. Exams., Que., 1950-64; mem. com. evaluation of teaching French, Protestant Sch. Bd. Greater Montreal, 1970-71; mem. provincial adv. coms. on secondary and elementary schs., 1971—, adult edn., 1972—; mem. Provincial Mission Six, 1973—, France-Que. Mission on Tchr. Tng., 1973. Trustee Fondation Edouard Montpetit, 1945-72. Decorated chevalier Ordre du Bon Parler Français; Order of Sch. Merit, Province Que. Mem. Superior Council Edn. (mem. adv. commn. secondary edn. 1964-72, U. Women, Corp. Guidance Counselors Que., Translators Soc. (charter), Canadian Assn. Applied Linguistics, Canadian Ednl. Researchers Assn., Canadian Coll. Tchrs. Author: The Teaching of French in Elementary School, Grade 1, 1961, Grade 2 and 3 1963. Contbr. articles to profl. jours. Home: 8449 Lajeunesse Montreal PQ H2P 2E7 Canada

BUTKUS, ELIZABETH HAAS, motel exec.; b. Kearny, N.J., Feb. 10, 1931; d. Otto Carl and Elizabeth Rose (Mugenhofer) Haas; grad. high sch.; m. Richard Butkus, Sept. 30, 1965; children—Sharon, Donna, Richard. Pres., owner, partner Ramapo Lodge Motel, Oakland, N.J., 1966—, Gallery Holiday Motel, Iselin, N.J., 1969—, Village Motel, Rahway, N.J., 1969—, Flagpost Motor Lodge, 1969—; v.p. B & S Enterprises, B & S Realty, Oakland, N.J., 1970—. Mem. Oakland C. of C. (sec. 1971-72). Home: 1 Eagle Crest Pl Oakland NJ 07436 Office: 13 Route 202 Oakland NJ 07436

BUTLER, ANNA MABEL LAND (MRS. FLOYD BUTLER), author; b. Phila.; d. John Weaver and Edith Frances (Jones) Land; student Trenton State Tchrs. Coll., 1920-22, 36, Temple U., 1953, U. Md., 1942-45; m. Maurice Alexander Hayes, June 1925 (div.); 1 son, Maurice Alexander (dec. 1943); m. 2d, Floyd Butler, Mar. 10, 1935. Tchr. pub. schs., Atlantic City, 1922-64; newspaper corr. Pitts. Courier, 1936-65; Atlantic City reporter Phila. Tribune, 1965—. Mem. edn. council Human Resources Atlantic County Anti-Poverty Program, 1965—. Pres. Seaboard Council Heritage House, 1954—, Atlantic City Study Center, 1959—; rec. sec. Episcopal Women, Diocese of N.J.; chmn. Christian social relations Atlantic dist. Episcopal Diocese N.J.; head tchr. for ednl. tng. Community Day Care Center. Mem. N.J. Fedn. Colored Women's Clubs (South Jersey state chmn. pub. relations dept.), Northside Bus. and Profl. Women's Club (pres. 1961-65, v.p. 1960-61, trustee 1971), N.J. Orgn. Tchrs. (v.p. 1960—), Nat. Assn. Negro Bus. and Profl. Women, Heritage House and Cotillion Soc. (dir. 1956—), Catholic Poetry Soc., Am. Poets Fellowship Soc., Atlantic City Tchrs. Assn. (life, exec. bd. 1962-64), Nat. Links, Inc. (nat. chmn. creative writing 1972, pres. Atlantic City chpt. 1971—), Atlantic City C. of C. (chmn. judges boardwalk div., planning com. ann. children's parade), Internat. Biog. Assn., Phi Delta Kappa. Episcopalian (v.p. women, vice chmn. stewardship com.). Author: Album of Love Letters—Unsent, 1952; Touchstone, 1962; High Noon, 1970; poems pub. in various anthologies. Editor: Responsibility, 1955-59, asso. editor 1953—; Eastern area editor Nat. Links Jours., 1968—. Initiator 1st Black history news scrapbook contest for jr. high sch. students, also Butler poetry contest, 1970. Home: 410 N Kentucky Av Atlantic City NJ 08401

BUTLER, BARBARA ANN ANDERSON (MRS. MELVIN BUTLER), coll. adminstr.; b. Madisonville, Tenn., Aug. 25, 1938; d. Charles Earl and Janie Mae (McDaniel) Anderson; certificate Nat. Bus. Coll., 1957; m. Melvin Butler, Feb. 2, 1958; children—Garry, Barry, Tammy, Terry. Sec. to acad. dean Hiwassee Coll., Madisonville, Tenn., 1958-69, registrar, 1969—. Address: Hiwassee Coll Madisonville TN 37354

BUTLER, CLEO (MRS. ELLIS NEAL BUTLER), nurse, polit. worker; b. Laurel, Mont., Jan. 21, 1927; d. Rush Floyd and Laura (Cornette) Bishop; student Long Beach City Coll., 1956-57; B.S. in Nursing, Mont. State U., 1971, M.N. in Nursing, 1973; m. Ellis Neal Butler, Feb. 8, 1951; children—Laura, Cherie, Irma, Montana Ellis. Clin. specialist psychiat.-mental health Butte (Mont.) Mental Hygiene Clinic, 1973—; faculty psychiat.-mental health nursing Mont. State U., 1973—. Organizer, Democratic Discussion Group, Gallatin County, Mont., 1955—; pub. monthly Dem. newspaper, Bozeman, Mont., 1955—; mem. nat. com. Young Democrats, Mont. dir. women's activities, 1955-62; del. Dem. Nat. Conv., 1956, alternate del., 1960; chmn. Citizens for Kennedy, 1960; chmn. Gallatin County Dem. Central Com., 1965—; sec. treas. Dem. Women's Club, 1957—. Mem. Council Advanced Practitioners Psych. and Mental Health Nursing, Am. Assn. U. Profs. Club: Fort Ellis Home Demonstration (Bozeman). Home: Route 1 Box 345 Bozeman MT 59715 Office: Butte Mental Hygiene Clinic 225 S Idaho St Butte MT 59701

BUTLER, COULA P. (MRS. LEON L. BUTLER), lawyer; b. Chgo., May 18, 1911; d. Stelios and Mary (Markas) Psaras; student Crane Jr. Coll., 1928, Northwestern U., 1929-32; J.D., John Marshall Law Sch., 1936; m. Leon L. Butler, Feb. 6, 1942; children—Sandra Lee (Mrs. T. Londos), Carla Penelope. Admitted to Ill. bar, 1936, since practiced in Chgo.; partner firm Endler, Harris & Butler, 1946—. Republican candidate for judge Chgo. Municipal Ct., 1950, 52. Trustee Edward T. Lee Found. 1944—; John Marshall Law Sch. Mem. Nat. Assn. Women Lawyers (del. from Ill., 1945-47, rec. sec. 1962-63), Chgo. bar Assn., Women's Bar Assn. Ill. (pres. 1948-49), Central Bus. and Profl. Women's Club, Hon. Order John Marshall, Kappa Beta Pi. Home: 480 North Shore Dr Crystal Lake IL 60014 Office: 33 N LaSalle St Chicago IL 60602

BUTLER, DORIS LANE, mus. adminstr.; b. Aurora, Ill., Nov. 23, 1904; d. Wilfred Emory and Stella (Cooper) Lane; student Sch. of Art Inst., Chgo., 1922-23, U. Ill., 1924-26; m. Eugene Kincaid Butler II, May 28, 1927 (dec. Sept. 1959); children—Shirley Turnbull, Eugene Kincaid, Dana (Mrs. Thomas Carey Strobel). Art critic Chgo. Daily News, 1957-59; Chgo. corr. Art in Am., 1958-65; dir. pub. relations Mus. Contemporary Art, Chgo., 1967—, sec. bd. trustees, 1964—; artist and critic. Mem. adv. com. Ill. Arts Council, 1966—. Mem. woman's bd. Internat. Visitors Center, Chgo., 1965—. Mem. Delta Gamma. Club: Arts of Chicago (dir.). Home: 1255 N Sandburg Terrace Chicago IL 60610 Office: 237 E Ontario St Chicago IL 60611

BUTLER, MRS. EDWARD H., newspaper exec.; b. Atlanta; d. Augustus Marcellus and Jennie (Maddux) Robinson; student Gunston Hall and France; m. Edward Hubert Butler, Feb. 2, 1909; 1 dau., Kate Robinson (Mrs. Bruce E. Wallis). Dir. Buffalo Evening News, Inc., 1951—, pres., 1956—, pub., 1971—; v.p. WBEN, Inc., 1956-67, pres., 1967—. Hon. mem. council U. Buffalo; mem. corp. Am. Hosp. Paris (France). Mem. Buffalo Fine Arts Acad., Colonial Dames Am. Republican. Presbyn. Clubs: Buffalo, Buffalo Country, Garret, Saturn, Adirondack League (Old Forge, N.Y.). Home: 672 Delaware Av Buffalo NY 14209 Office: Buffalo Evening News Buffalo NY 14240

BUTLER, ELAINE RUTH MARJORIE MALLORY (MRS. HAROLD ARTHUR BUTLER), civic worker; b. North Bergen, N.J., July 2, 1911; d. Eugene Lester and Adele May (Reeder) Mallory; A.B., Barnard Coll., 1930; postgrad. Montclair Coll., 1932; M.S., N.Y. Sch. Social Work, 1935; postgrad. Seton Hall U., 1939, 53; M.S., Newark State Coll., 1959; postgrad. San German U., P.R., 1959; m. Harold Arthur Butler, Feb. 17, 1928; 1 dau., Dellamay Dorothy (Mrs. Seibold). Tchr., Horace Mann Sch., Tchrs. Coll., N.Y.C., 1926; statistician, confidential sec. Boy Scouts Am., N.Y.C., 1927-30; investigator Tenement Housing Authority for N.Y. Assembly, 1927; tchr. elementary and secondary schs., coll., N.J., 1932-37; social worker N.J. Dept. Instns. and Agys., Trenton, 1937-48; adminstrv. sec. N.J. Heart Assn., Newark, 1948-51; tchr. specialist Montclair Pub. Schs., 1953-64; free-lance writer, artist, 1964— (paints under name Le Boutiliere). Worker, Gompers Rehab. Inst., Phoenix, 1966; mem. aux. Goodwill Industries, Phoenix, 1968—, Scottsdale Triangles YWCA, 1972—; chmn. Fun for Funds and Bridge Builders, Phoenix, 1966—; active Community Orgn. for Drug Abuse Control, Phoenix, 1969—, Juvenile Detention Homes for Boys and Girls, 1972—, Half-Way House for Ex-Felons, Phoenix. Sec., New Brunswick (N.J.) Democratic Club, 1939; campaign mgr. South Orange Village Council, 1955. Bd. dirs. 7th Step Found., 1974—, sec., 1974—. Fellow Intercontinental Biog. Assn.; mem. Am. Assn. U. Women, Nat. Assn. Ret. Fed. Employees (sec. Phoenix 1965-69, sec. treas. Ariz. Fedn. 1969-71, charter mem. Scottsdale 1972—, sec.-treas. 1972-73), Seven Coll. Conf., Nat. N.J. Montclair edn. assns., Scottsdale, Valley artists leagues, Franklin Mint Soc. (charter), Friends for Terros Aux. (charter), Phoenix Art Mus., Friends Mexican Art, Internat. Platform Assn. Republican. Presbyn. (fellowship chmn. 1965-66, coordinator for Involvement in Action 1966-68). Clubs: Orange Lawn Tennis (South Orange, N.J.), College of Oranges (West Orange, N.J.); Scottsdale College. Home: 4015 E Sierra Vista Dr Scottsdale AZ 85253

BUTLER, ELIZABETH HELEN, journalist; b. Salmon, Ida., Dec. 24, 1921; d. Walter Glen and Helen (Daniels) Bloomsburg; B.A., U. Mont., 1942; m. Donald William Butler, July 25, 1943; children—Erin Elizabeth, Michael Walter. Reporter, Great Falls (Mont.) Tribune, 1942, Spokesman Rev. Spokane, Wash., 1942-46, 52; stringer for several papers, Plummer, Ida. and Salmon, 1948-53; news asst., pub. relations dept. Mont. U., 1946-48; state corr. Spokesman Rev., Mont., 1958-59; news reporter Aberdeen (Wash.) Daily World, 1965—; tchr. Ocosta High Sch., Westport, Wash., 1961-64, Grays Harbor Coll., evening sch., 1965-70; free-lance writer. Mem. Com. on Drug Abuse and the Media, Aberdeen, 1969-71. Mem. Pacific Northwest Writers Assn., Wash. Press Women, Theta Sigma Phi. Episcopalian. Home: S Forrest St Westport WA 98595 Office: Daily World Aberdeen WA 98520

BUTLER, GLORIA LEE HUNT (MRS. BENJAMIN E. BUTLER), transp. co. exec.; b. Omaha, Jan. 19, 1933; d. Lewis Seth and Beulah Adele (Kemper) Hunt; A.A., Stephens Coll., 1952; m. Benjamin E. Butler, Nov. 7, 1953; children—Matt Lewis, John William. Appeared on daily program WOW-TV, Omaha, 1952-53; writer, supr. radio and TV advt. Dillon Supermarkets, Hutchinson, Kan., 1953-54; part owner, dir. Hunt Transp., Inc., Omaha, 1957-61, exec. v.p., 1961—. Mem. Omaha Symphony Guild, 1964-69. Mem. Daus. of Nile, Sigma Gamma Gamma. Republican. Home: 1617 S 109th St Omaha NE 68144 Office: 10770 I St Omaha NE 68144

BUTLER, KATHARINE GORRELL (MRS. JOSEPH FRANKLIN BUTLER), educator; b. Harvey, Ill., Mar. 15, 1925; d. Talbot John Howe and Katharine (Parmenter) Gorrell; B.A., Western Mich. U., 1950, M.A., 1953, Ed.S., 1961; Ph.D., Mich. State U., 1967; m. Joseph Franklin Butler, Sept. 1, 1944; children—Katharine Marie (Mrs. Clyde Nunes), Andrew Carlton, Paul Dean. Sch. speech clinician, Portage and Vicksburg, Mich., 1950-52, Kalamazoo, 1954-58; asso. dir. Soc. for Better Hearing, Kalamazoo, 1953-54; pvt. practice speech pathology, Kalamazoo, 1953-64; asst. prof. psychology Western Mich., U., Kalamazoo, 1962-64; asst. prof. Cal. State U. at San Jose, 1964-68, asso. prof., 1968-69, prof., 1969—, dir. speech and hearing center, 1969—, chmn. dept. spl. edn., 1969-74, asso. dean Sch. Edn., 1974—. Chmn. speech pathology and audiology examining com. Cal. Bd. Med. Examiners, 1973—; cons. to VA Hosp., Palo Alto, Cal., 1969—, Dept. Health, Edn. and Welfare, Office of Edn., Bur. Edn. Handicapped. Bd. dirs. Eastfield Center for Emotionally Disturbed, 1964-66. Recipient Distinguished Alumnae award Mich. State U. Coll. Communication, 1973. Fellow Am. Speech and Hearing Assn. (chmn. sci. and profl. meetings bd. 1974, chmn. conv. 1974, councilor from Cal. 1969—); mem. Cal. Speech and Hearing Assn. (pres. 1970-71), Am. Psychol. Assn., Cal. Assn. Profs. Spl. Edn. (pres. 1974-75). Author: (with C. VanRiper) Speech in the Elementary Classroom, 1955. Contbr. articles to profl. jours., chpts. to books. Address: Speech and Hearing Center California State University at San Jose San Jose CA 95109

BUTLER, LAVONNE RUTH GRASLIE (MRS. WARREN ELMER BUTLER), newspaper pub.; b. Faith, S.D., Aug. 22, 1922; d. Ludwig Martin and Lilly Regina (Ness) Graslie; first grade certificate Spearfish Normal Sch., 1942; m. Warren Elmer Butler, Dec. 29, 1942; children—Richard, James. Tchr., Cherry Creek Dist. 2, Ziebach County, S.C., 1943-45; sec. to supt. schs., Faith, 1966-68; editor, pub. Faith Independent, 1969—. Pres. P.T.A., 1953-54. Mem. Rep. State Central Com., 1970—. Mem. Nat. Newspaper Assn., S.D. Press Assn., C. of C. (v.p. 1970—), Beta Sigma Phi. Methodist. Mem. Order Eastern Star. Co-editor Faith Country Book, 1960. Home: Faith SD 57626 Office: Faith Independent Faith SD 57626

BUTLER, MARGARET KAMPSCHAEFER, mathematician; b. Evansville, Ind., Mar. 7, 1924; d. Otto Louis and Lou Etta (Rehsteiner) Kampschaefer; A.B., Ind. U., 1944; postgrad. U.S. Dept. Agr. Grad. Sch., 1945, U. Chgo., 1949, U. Minn., 1950; m. James W. Butler, Sept. 30, 1951; 1 son, Jay. Statistician, U.S. Bur. Labor Statistics, Washington, 1945-46, U.S. Air Forces in Europe, Erlangen and Wiesbaden, Germany, 1946-48; mathematician Argonne Nat. Lab., Lemont, Ill., 1948-49; statistician U.S. Bur. Labor Statistics, St. Paul, 1949-51; mathematician Argonne (Ill.) Nat. Lab., 1951-60, dir. Argonne Code Center, AEC Computer Program Exchange, 1960—. Cons., AMF Corp., 1956-57, OECD, 1964, Poole Bros., 1967. Treas., Timberlake Civic Assn., 1958; rep., mem. nominating com. Hinsdale (Ill.) Caucus; coordinator dist. 6 Equal Rights Amendment. Fellow Am. Nuclear Soc. (mem. publs. com. 1965-71, chmn. math. and computation div. 1966-67, reviewer for publs.); mem. Assn. for Computing Machinery (exec. com., sec. Chgo. chpg. 1963-65, publs. chmn. nat. conf. 1968, reviewer for publs.). Editor: Reactor Physics, 1969—. Contbr. chpt. to The Application of Digital Computers to Problems in Reactor Physics, 1968; also articles to profl. pubs. Home: 17W139 Hillside Lane Hinsdale IL 60521 Office: 9700 S Cass Av Argonne IL 60439

BUTLER, MILDRED, banker; b. White Plains, N.Y., Apr. 19, 1913; d. George W. and Maude Mary (Cuatt) Butler; certificate Am. Inst. Banking, 1938. With The Home Savs. Bank, White Plains, N.Y., 1933—, asst. sec., 1955—, asst. v.p., 1965—, v.p., 1970—. Mem. Savs. Bank Women of N.Y. (pres. 1967-68, membership sec. 1963-64), Nat. Assn. of Bank Women (chmn. 1970-71). Club: Soroptimist (pres. 1965-67, dir. 1967-70) (Central Westchester, N.Y.). Home: 9 Eastview Av White Plains NY 10601 Office: 1 Mamaroneck Av White Plains NY 10601

BUTLER, NATALIE STURGES (MRS. BENJAMIN BUTLER), writer; b. Melrose, Mass., July 13, 1908; d. Dwight Case and Clare (Vaughan) Sturges; student Vesper George Art Sch., 1926-28 M.A. (hon.), U. Me. at Farmington, 1972; m. Benjamin Butler, May 23, 1932; children—Diane-Clare (Mrs. Carl Alexander Brinkman), Benjamin Sturges. Librarian, decorator Irving & Casson-A.H. Davenport Co., Boston, 1928-31; pres. Sturdia Corp., Farmington, Me., 1955—. County chmn. Me. Sesquicentennial Com., 1970; sec. Me. Citizens for Historic Preservation, 1971, Red Schoolhouse Com., 1970—. Trustee, Farmington Pub. Library Assn., 1950—, treas., 1958—; trustee Franklin County Meml. Hosp., 1963-70; trustee Me. League Hist. Socs. and Museums, 1973—. Recipient (with Ben Butler) Outstanding Service award Me. Historic Preservation Commn., 1973. Mem. Me. Soc. Mayflower Descs., Me. Hist. Soc., New Eng. Historic and Geneal. Soc., John Howland Soc., Delta Kappa Gamma (hon.). Republican. Conglist. (deaconess 1963-68). Author: (with Ben Butler) History of Old South Church Farmington, 5 Historical Farmington Pilgrimage Books (certificate of commendation Am. Assn. for State and Local History 1970), Little Red Schoolhouse Museum, 1971. Contbr. to newspapers and mags. Home: 93 Main St Farmington ME 04938

BUTLER, SUSAN LEWIS (MRS. DIXON MATLOCK), journalist; b. Richmond, Va., Sept. 10, 1949; d. Sydney and Frances (Aaronson) Lewis; B.S., Boston U., 1971; student Northwestern U., 1967-69; m. Dixon Matlock, Aug. 24, 1969; 1 son, William Lewis. Reporter Quincy (Mass.) Patriot Ledger, 1969-71; fine arts reporter Houston Chronicle, 1971—. Corr. New Times mag., N.Y.C., 1974; bus. mgr. Houston Journalism Rev. Chairwoman Credit Task Force, Houston chpt., Nat. Orgn. Women. Bd. dirs. Sydney and Frances Lewis Found. Mem. Women in Communications. Home: 2712 Barbara Houston TX 77005 Office: Houston Chronicle Houston TX 77002

BUTLER-PAISLEY, MATILDA LOU, psychologist, educator; b. Oklahoma City, Feb. 5, 1942; d. Edward Ainsworth and Flossie Jewel (Calderhead) Butler; student U. Okla., 1960-62; B.S. magna cum laude, Boston U., 1964; M.A., Stanford, 1966; Ph.D., Northwestern U., 1970; m. William John Paisley, Oct. 16, 1970; children—Kenneth Earl, Edward Ainsworth. Research asso. psychology dept. Stanford, 1970, lectr., research asso. Inst. for Communication Research, 1971—; research asso. U. Cal. at Berkeley Grad. Sch. Pub. Policy, 1971. Prin., Paisley-Mick Assos.; cons. Coll. Bds., Lockheed-Technicon Information Systems, Palo Alto Unified Sch. Dist., Battelle Inst. Nat. Inst. Mental Health trainee. Mem. Am. Psychol. Assn., Am. Assn. Pub. Opinion Research (program chmn. Pacific chpt. 1972), Assn. for Edn. in Journalism, Internat. Communication Assn. Home: 717 Charleston Ct Palo Alto CA 94303 Office: Stanford U Stanford CA 94305

BUTMAN, BEVERLY ANN, newspaper reporter; b. Merkel, Tex., July 27, 1946; d. Louis S. and Pauline (Blackaby) Butman; A.A., York (Neb.) Coll., 1966; B.A. in Journalism, Pepperdine Coll., Los Angeles, 1968. Reporter, Pasadena (Cal.) Star-News, 1968-70, Boulder (Colo.) Daily Camera, 1970—. Mem. Women in Communications, Colo. Press Women, Nat. Assn. Press Women, Nat. Orgn. Women, Am. Civil Liberties Union (v.p. Boulder chpt. 1973—). Democrat. Mem. Ch. of Christ. Home: Box 1806 Boulder CO 80302 Office: Boulder Daily Camera Boulder CO 80302

BUTT, LILLIAN STUART, former educator; b. nr. Abingdon, Va., Nov. 25, 1901; d. Charles Henry and Josephine (Bailey) Butt; student Martha Washington Coll., 1919-20, Va. Intermont Coll., 1920-21; B.S., U. Va., 1929, M.S., 1936; summer study U. Wash., 1939. Tchr., Abingdon, Va., 1921-36, Charlottesville, Va., 1936-68, supervising tchr. dept. edn. U. Va., 1950-68, now ret.; chmn. social studies dept. Lane High Sch., 1953-64. Sponsor Jr. Red Cross, 1940-59; mem. youth in govt. com. Va. dist. YMCA. Recipient Valley Forge Classroom Tchrs. medal, 1959; Jeweled Tri-Hi-Y pin, 1951, YMCA plaque for service to youth, 1956, 66. Mem. Am. Assn. U. Women, D.A.R., U.D.C., Washington County, Albermarle hist. socs., Va., Charlottesville (pres. 1955-57) edn. assns., Va. Council for Social Studies (exec. bd. mem.), English-Speaking Union, Johnston Meml. Hosp. Aux., Wesleyan Service Guild, Nat. Retired Tchrs. Assn., Booklover's Club, Delta Kappa Gamma. Democrat. Methodist. Home: 363 Bradley St Abingdon VA 24210

BUTTERFIELD, RUTH VIRGINIA LANE (MRS. SIDNEY BUTTERFIELD), retail co. dir.; b. Lincoln, Neb.; d. John Monroe and Dora (Alta) Lane; ed. pub. schs.; m. Sidney Butterfield, Sept. 10, 1924; children—Ruth (Mrs. Alton Thomas), William S., Mary. Vice pres. Smith & Butterfield, Evansville, Ind., 1930-50, dir., 1930—. Bd. dirs. Vis. Nurses Assn., Evansville. Mem. Evansville Jr. League (charter). Clubs: Evansville Petroleum, Evansville Kennel, Evansville Country; Petosky (Mich.)-Bay View Country; Highland Park (Lake Wales, Fla.). Address: 600 Cullen Av Apt 107 Evansville IN 47715

BUTTERWORTH, MARY ELIZABETH LYONS (MRS. HERBERT H. BUTTERWORTH), physician; b. Boston, Mar. 23, 1927; d. John J. and Mary Agnes (McLaughlin) Lyons; A.B., Emmanuel Coll., 1948; M.S., Boston Coll., 1950; M.D., Tufts U., 1959; m. Herbert Hartley Butterworth, June 9, 1959; children—Betsy, Herbert, Anne, Carolyn, Michael, Patricia. Intern, St. Vincent's Hosp., Worcester, Mass., 1959-60; practice medicine, specializing in pub. health and preventive medicine, Boston, 1963—. Trustee Greater Brocton Cath. Charitable Bur. Mem. Mass. Med. Soc. Club: Junior Guild Infant Saviour (Boston). Home: 99 Pine Tree Dr Hanover MA 02339

BUTTERWORTH, MIRIAM FORD BROOKS (MRS. OLIVER BUTTERWORTH), educator; b. Hartford, Conn., Apr. 14, 1918; d. John Lee and Genevieve (Ford) Brooks; B.A., Conn. Coll. for Women, 1940; M.A., Wesleyan U., 1959; m. Olive Butterworth, June 30, 1940; children—Michael, Timothy, Dan, Kate (Mrs. Fernando Valdez). Tchr. history Ethel Walker Sch., Simsbury, Conn., 1960-62, Chaffee and Loomis Sch., Windsor, Conn., 1962-68. Mem. Conn. Dem. State Central Com., West Hartford, Conn., 1968-70; chairwoman Caucus Conn. Democrats, 1973—. Bd. trustees Conn. Coll. for Women, 1950-55; bd. dirs. Roots, Inc., Hartford, Conn., 1970-74. Author: The Mind and Heart of George Sorel, 1959. Home: 81 Sunset Farm Rd West Hartford CT 06107

BUTTIFANT, LOIS IRENE, ednl. adminstr.; b. Buffalo, July 11, 1929; d. Herbert Callow and Zella Theresa (Taylor) Buttifant; B.A., Houghton Coll., 1950; M.S. in L.S., Syracuse U., 1951; postgrad. St. Bonaventure U., 1968-70, State U. N.Y. at Fredonia, 1969, at Geneseo, 1970, at Syracuse, 1967-69. Librarian, Panama (N.Y.)

Central Sch., 1951-54, Jefferson Jr. High Sch., Jamestown, N.Y., 1954-67; head library dept. Jamestown Pub. Schs., 1967—. Librarian, interloan and summer bookmobile So. Tier Library System, Corning, N.Y., 1960-70. Mem. A.L.A., N.Y. Library Assn., Chautauqua County Sch. Librarians Assn., D.A.R., Delta Kappa Gamma. Republican. Baptist. Home: 63 Summit Av Jamestown NY 14701 Office: 200 E 4th St Jamestown NY 14701

BUTTON, HELEN LOUISE, physician; b. Scranton, Pa.; d. Alvin W. and Bertha (Gray) Button; B.S., U. Pa.; M.D., Loyola U. Chgo., 1931; m. Isadore Goldstein, July 9, 1939 (dec.); children—Morris Button, Alvin Button. Intern Walther Meml. Hosp.; resident Cook County Hosp., Chgo.; surg. resident Am. Hosp.; practice medicine specializing in surgery, Chgo.; mem. staffs, faculty, Norwegian Am., Am. hosp., Chgo.; Gynecol. Cook County Outpatient Clinic, 1940-52; mem. surg. faculty Chgo. Med. Sch. Co-founder Ladies in Blue Hosp. Aux., 1950—; named v.p. U. Vienna (Austria), 1962—; surgeon Luth. Mission Hosp., Eket, Nigeria, 1963. Diplomate Internat. Coll. Surgeons, Am. Soc. Abdominal Surgeons. Mem. A.M.A., Ill. (founding), State St. (charter) bus. and profl. women's clubs, Ill. Med. Soc., Am., Internat. med. women's assns., Am. Med. Soc. Vienna. Home: 206 N Pine Av Chicago IL 60644 Office: 108 N State St Chicago IL 60602

BUTTS, DOROTHY WORTHINGTON (MRS. RANDOLPH E. BROWN), poet, playwright; b. San Francisco, June 30, 1897; d. Freeman Worthington and Susan Margaret (Phillips) Butts; grad. Smith Coll., 1921; m. Glen H. Gardner, May 13, 1922 (div. 1928); Harvey Cushman; m. 2d, Bradford C. Durfee (dec. June 1964); m. 3d, Randolph E. Brown, Feb. 21, 1969. Dir., Playbox Theatre, Newfane, Vt., 1936-40; writer, pub. Poetry, a Mag. of Verse, 1921; playwright (under name Dorothy Gardner) Eastward in Eden, produced on Broadway, 1947-48, pub. Burns Montle 10 Best Plays, 1947-48, Brooks Atkinson's 10 Best, N.Y. Times, John Chapman's 10 Best, pub. Longman's Green, 1949, also produced London, Iron Curtain countries; libretist operas. Recipient Frances Frost prize for best lyrics, Vt., 1941. Mem. Dramatists Guild, Authors League. Republican. Club: Harvard (N.Y.C.). Author: Yankee Spirit, Green Mountain Verse. Instrumental in restoring original village of South Egremont, Mass., 1957-72. Home: 5 The Glen Tenafly NJ 07670

BUXER, CONSTANCE GERTRUDE, clin. psychologist; b. N.Y.C., Oct. 5, 1923; d. Charles and Eva (Tucker) Buxer; B.A. in English magna cum laude, Hunter Coll, 1944; M.A. in Psychology, Yeshiva U., 1973, Ph.D. in Clin. Psychology, 1974; m. Seymour D. Feinberg, Feb. 18, 1951; children—Andrew, Kenneth. Intern in psychology Bellevue Hosp., N.Y.C., 1969-70; psychologist VA Hosp., Bklyn. 1970-71; instr. psychology Bklyn. Coll., 1970-71; psychologist, clin. instr. Downstate Med. Center, State U. N.Y. at Bklyn., 1973-74; asst. prof. Baruch Coll. City U. N.Y., 1974—. Mem. Am. Psychol. Assn., LADO, Phi Beta Kappa. Home: 341 W 24th St New York City NY 10011 Office: 363 W 23d St New York City NY 10011

BUXTON, LUELLA SKILBRED (MRS. WILLIAM C. BUXTON), author; b. Berlin, Wis., July 13, 1934; d. Lawrence G. and Hattie (Becker) Skilbred; student Ripon Coll., 1952-54; B.S. in English and Edn., Marian Coll., 1956; B.S. in Journalism, Marquette U., 1958; m. William C. Buxton, May 8, 1964; 1 son, William Charles II. Asst. women's news editor Fond du Lac (Wis.) Commonwealth Reporter, 1958-59; women's news editor Oneonta (N.Y.) Daily Star, 1959-60, feature writer Oshkosh (Wis.) Northwestern, 1962-63; fashion copywriter Gimbel Bros., Milw., 1963-66; free lance writer periodicals and mags. Mem. Theta Sigma Phi. Author: The Old Testament for Beginners, 1960; We Love the Place, O God, 1961; The New Testament for Beginners, 1964; A Song of Saints, 1966; When the Church Was Young, 1966; Christian News-Herald, 1968; Letters to Young Christians, 1972. Home: 122 E Forest Av Neenah WI 54956

BUZBY, BARBARA JACQUELINE, editor; b. Columbus, O., Nov. 26, 1927; d. Arch and Gertrude (Offenburger) Miller; grad. high sch.; m. Richard Buzby, Feb. 14, 1948; children—Brian Lee, Nancy Ellen, Jeanine Rae. With Columbus Dispatch, 1961—, women's editor, 1972—. Mem. Women in Communications, Inc., Ohio Newspaper Women's Assn. (recipient writing awards), Press Club Ohio. Lutheran. Home: 443 Scott Ct Grove City OH 43123 Office: 34 S 3d St Columbus OH 43216

BUZICK, PHYLLIS E. HOLDEN, occupational therapist; m. Robert Dole, June 12, 1948 (div.); 1 dau., Robin; m. 2d, Lon M. Buzick, Nov. 24, 1973. Registered occupational therapist, 1947. Mem. Pres.' Task Force for Mentally Handicapped, 1970; now mem. staff VA Hosp., Topeka. Club: Congressional (v.p.). Home: Sylvan Grove KS 67481

BUZZI, RUTH ANN (MRS. BASIL KEKO), actress; b. Westerly, R.I., July 24, 1936; d. Angelo Peter and Rena Pauline (Macchi) Buzzi; student Pasadena Playhouse, 1954-57; pvt. study dance, drama, voice; m. Basil Keko, Nov. 28, 1965. Appeared on Broadway in Sweet Charity; appeared in N.Y. theater prodns. including Babes in the Wood, A Man's A Man, Misguided Tour; network TV appearances include That Girl, Steve Allen Comedy Hour, The Entertainers, Mike Douglas Show, Martin and Rowan Laugh-In, The Monkees, Carol Burnett Show, Garry Moore Show; featured comedienne in mus. revues; filmed TV commls. for various sponsors. Hon. mem. D.A.R. Home: 310 W 55th St New York City NY 10019

BYARS, ILA PEARL, orgn. exec., civic worker; b. Travis, Tex., June 25, 1908; d. William Lafayette and Sibyl Allen (Massey) Byars; student pub. schs. With Mid-west States Telephone Co., Blanco, 1924-53; with Bigden Ins. and Real Estate, Tex., 1953-55; pvt. kindergarten tchr., Blanco, 1955-56; waitress various restaurants, 1956-62, 63-65; with Wall Furniture, also Wall Funeral Home, Bianco, 1952-53, 65-66; staff food dept. Blanco Mill Nursing Home, 1966—. County chmn. Am. Heart Assn., 1957-72, meml. and campaign mgr., 1957-72. Bd. dirs. Blanco County unit Am. Cancer Soc., 1959-72, unit sec., 1971-74, pres., 1974—; trustee Blanco Library, 1950-53, librarian, 1952-53; bd. dirs. Blanco County Tb Assn., 1951-53. Recipient Achievement citations Am. Heart Assn., 1970, 71, 73, Am. Cancer Soc., 1971. Mem. Blanco C. of C. (sec. 1967-72, dir. 1967-71), Daus. of Nile, Wesleyan Service Guild (co-founder 1952, pres. 1968—). Methodist. (dir. Vacation Bible Sch. 1968—, Sunday Sch. tchr. 1949—, now mem. pastoral com.). Mem. Order Eastern Star. Home: PO Box 256 Blanco TX 78606

BYARS, NOELENE ELVA (MRS. DAVID CARLOS BYARS), biochemist; b. Melbourne, Australia, Jan. 5, 1943; d. Raymond Burnett and Laurel Myra (Tiller) Lobb; B.S., U. Melbourne, 1964, M.S., 1970; m. David Carlos Byars, July 6, 1968. Research asst. Baker Research Inst., Melbourne, Australia, 1965-67; biologist Syntex Corp., pharm. research, Palo Alto, Cal., 1967—. Recipient grant Asthma Found., Victoria, Australia, 1965-66. Contbr. articles to profl. jours. Home: 1091 Syracuse Dr Sunnyvale CA 94087 Office: 3401 Hillview St Palo Alto CA 94304

BYBEE, EMMA WILSON (MRS. JOHN CARLOS BYBEE), home economist; b. Se Ree, Ky., July 14, 1921; d. Granville and Lula (Kessinger) Wilson; B.S., Western State U., 1951; M.S., U. Wis., 1956; m. John Carlos Bybee, Feb. 23, 1953. Shipping clk., personnel dept. Ft. Knox, Ky., 1940-42; tchr. rural sch., Breckenridge, Ky., 1942, 46-47; with Evansville (Ind.) Ordnance Plant, 1942-43; faculty Western State Coll., Bowling Green, Ky., 1948-51; home demonstration agt., Barren County, Ky., 1951-56; supr. home agts., 4-H field agt. U. Ky., Lexington, 1957-61; home service adviser Farmers Rural Electric, Glasgow, Ky., 1961—. Commr., Barren County Bicentennial, 1974—. Served with WAVES, 1944-45. Recipient Felloww fellowship, 1956; Woman of Achievement award Bus. and Profl. Women, 1968. Mem. Am., Ky. (consumer interest chmn. 1961-62) home econs. assns., Elec. Illuminating Engrs. Assn. (asso.), Elec. Women of Ky. (chpt. pres. 1970-71), Elec. Women's Roundtable (nat. dir. 1972—), Ky. Mem. Services Assn. (pres. '971-72), Bus. and Profl. Women's Club (Glasgow pres. 1956, Ky. Nat. Bus. and Profl. Women Week chmn. 1968). Mem. Order Eastern Star. Home: 109 Cedar St Glasgow KY 42141 Office: 504 S Broadway Glasgow KY 42141

BYERS, DORIS VIRGINIA, lawyer; b. Newark, Mo., Oct. 13, 1922; d. Walter Rutherford and Hallie Emaline (Vaden) Byers; B.S., Northwest Mo. Coll., 1943; J.D., U. Mo., 1967. Admitted to Kan. bar, 1967, Mo. bar., 1971, sec. Gustin-Bacon Mfg. Co., Kansas City, Mo., 1943-45, Internat. Harvester Co., Kan. City, 1945-47; sec. Kansas City Transit, Inc., 1947-56, adminstrv. asst., 1957-64, corp. sec., 1959-62, dir. pub. relations, 1960-64; pvt. practice law, Shawnee Mission, Kan., 1967-70; mem. firm Gage, Tucker, Hodges, Kreamer, Kelly & Varner, Kansas City, Mo., 1970—, now jr. partner. Bd. dirs. Kansas City Area Safety Council, 1960-64. Mem. Mo. Safety Council (bd. dirs. 1960-64), Women's C. of C. (bd. dirs. 1962-64), Mo., Kan., Kansas City bar assns., Kappa Beta Pi. Republican. Mem. Christian Ch. Home: Route 1 Shawnee KS 66217 Office: 1000 Bryant Bldg Kansas City MO 64106

BYERS, FRANCES REES, ednl. research asso.; b. Phila., Oct. 14, 1940; d. Joseph Arthur and Frances Rees (Hollihan) Byers; B.A., Rosemont Coll., 1962; postgrad. (U.S. Office Edn. fellow, U. Pa. Dissertation Year fellow) U. Pa., 1966—. Computer programmer Bell Telephone Co. Pa., Phila., 1962-64; statis. asst. U. Pa. Office Admissions, Phila., 1964-66, teaching asst. Grad. Sch. Edn., 1970; research asst. Office Research and Evaluation Sch. Dist. Phila., 1970-71, research asso., 1971—. Mem. Nat. Council on Measurement in Edn., Am. Ednl. Research Assn. (rep. on student com. 1971-73, research tng. com. 1971-73), Psychometric Assn., Biometric Assn., Franklin Inst., Pi Lambda Theta. Democrat. Roman Catholic. Home: 4409 Baltimore Av Philadelphia PA 19104 Office: Sch Dist Philadelphia Office Research and Evaluation 21st St and Ben Franklin Pkwy Philadelphia PA 19103

BYHAM, GLADYS EDGINGTON (MRS. STEVEN H. BYHAM), librarian; b. Alamogordo, N.M., Feb. 4, 1906; d. John Edward and Helen Harriot (Johnson) Edgington; student Park Coll., 1927-29; B.S., U. Mo., 1955; M.S., Kan. State Tchrs. Coll.; m. Steven H. Byham, Apr. 24, 1930; 1 dau., Florence May (Mrs. Kurt Weinberg). Tchr. schs., Otero County, N.M., 1926-27, 29-30, 31-32, 37-41, Catron County, N.M., 1930-31; clk.-typist U.S. Army Air Force, 1942-44; elementary tchr., Viola, Ark., 1946-50; clk.-typist Internal Revenue Service, 1951-53; librarian Highland (Kan.) Jr. Coll., 1954-64, Crowder Coll., Neosho, Mo., 1964-74. Mem. Am., Mo. library assns., Mo. Assn. Jr. Colls. Presbyn. (deacon 1968-72). Mem. Order Eastern Star. Home: PO Box 186 Route 3 Anderson MO 64831

BYLANDER, PATRICIA LOUISE BATES (MRS. JAMES ROBERT BYLANDER), writer; b. Cin., Apr. 27, 1949; d. Patrick James and Lois Ethelda (Walker) Bates; B.A. in Journalism, U. Wis., 1971; certificat D'Etudes Francaise, Institut D'Etudes De Touraine Tours, 1966; m. James Robert Bylander, June 19, 1971. Tchr. St. Charles High Sch., St. Charles, Ill, 1971-72; pub. relations writer pub. affairs dept. Mt. Sinai Hosp. Med. Center, Chgo., 1973-74. Mem. women's aux. Central Du Page Hosp., Winfield, Ill., 1971-74; leader Brownies, Carol Stream, Ill., 1972-73. Mem. Women in Communications, Am. Contract Bridge League, U. Wis. Alumni Assn. Republican. Methodist. Club: Newcomers (Wheaton, Ill.). Home: 465 Dorland Ct Maplewood MN 55119 Office: Mt Sinai Hosp Med Center 15th St at California Av Chicago IL 60608

BYLLESBY, JOYCE ELAINE, physician; b. Sioux Falls, S.D., Apr. 2, 1933; d. Harold Rodney and Emily Josephine (Ross) Byllesby; B.A., Augustana Coll., 1957; B.S., U. S.D., 1960; M.D., Kan. U., 1962. Intern, Ia. Meth. Hosp., Des Moines, 1962-63; resident pathology Neb. Meth. Hosp., Omaha, 1963-67; asso. pathologist Patterson and Coleman Labs., Tampa, Fla., 1967-68; pathologist, dir. lab. Montgomery County Culver Union Hosp., Crawfordsville, Ind., 1968-69; dir. Radiology and Pathology Labs., Inc., Crawfordsville, 1969—; clin. asst. prof. pathology Ind. U. Med. Center, Indpls., 1968—. Diplomate Am. Bd. Pathology. Mem. Assn. Am. Physicians and Surgeons, Am. Soc. Clin. Pathologists, Coll. Am. Pathologists, Am., Ind. med. assns., Montgomery County Med. Soc. Methodist (bd. trustees 1970—). Home: 804 East Pike St Crawfordsville IN 47933 Office: PO Box 111 Crawfordsville IN 47933

BYMERS, GWEN J., educator; b. Turton, S.D., June 19, 1915; d. Cornelius and Nellie (Kerr) Bymers; B.S., U.N.D., 1948; M.A., U. Cal. at Los Angeles, 1950, Ph.D. (John Randolph-Dora Haynes fellow), 1958. Lectr. family econs. U. Cal. at Los Angeles, 1950-53; economist U.S. Dept. Labor, Washington, 1955; asst. prof. dept. home econs. and mgmt. Cornell U., Ithaca, N.Y., 1956-59, prof., 1964—, chmn. dept. consumer econs. and pub. policy, 1969—. Mem. adv. com. standard budgets Bur. Labor Statistics, 1961-63; mem. consumers' union Nat. Edn. Adv. Council, 1969—; mem. N.Y. State Women's Council, 1970—. Served with WACS, 1943-45. Mem. Am. Econs. Assn., Am. Home Econs. Assn., Am. Marketing Assn., Am. Council Consumer Interests, Am. Assn. U. Profs., Nat. Council Women, Omicron Nu, Pi Gamma Mu, Beta Gamma Sigma. Democrat. Unitarian. Contbr. articles to profl. jours. Home: 409 Linn St Ithaca NY 14850

BYRD, FLOSSIE MARIAN, univ. dean; b. Sarasota, Fla., Aug. 8, 1927; d. John and Lizzie (Smith) Byrd; B.S., Fla. A. and M. U., 1948; M.Ed., Pa. State U., 1954; Ph.D. (Anna Cora Smith scholar), Cornell U., 1962. Homemaking tchr. Quinn High Sch., Apalachicola, Fla., 1948-51, Douglas High Sch., Live Oak, Fla., 1951-53; tchr. educator Fla. A. and M. U., 1954-59; research asst. home econs. div. N.Y. State Coll. Home Econs., Cornell U., 1959-61; tchr. educator Prairie View (Tex.) A. and M. U., 1962-64, prof., dean Coll. Home Econs., 1964—. Dir. Nat. Def. Edn. Act Inst. for Home Econs. Tchrs. of Disadvantaged Youth, summer 1967; distinguished vis. prof. Ore. State U., 1970; dir. Inst. Family Planning/Home Econs., summer 1973; cons. Nat. Vocational and Tech. Edn. Seminar, Chgo., 1968, Workshop in Ednl. Media and Teaching Strategies for Disadvantaged, Murray (Ky.) State U., 1971, So. Assn. Schs. Accreditation Visitation Team, Miller High Sch., Corpus Christi, Tex., 1972. Recipient Distinguished Alumni award Fla. A. and M. U., 1968. Prentice Hall fellow for research Am. Home Econs. Assn., 1961-62; Summer Research fellow Cornell U., 1962; Am. Home Econs. Assn. Found. Inner City fellow, 1968. Mem. Am. Assn. U. Profs., Am. (chmn. nominating com. 1972—, adv. bd. Internat. Family Planning Project 1972, Council for Profl. Devel.), Tex. home econs. assns., Am. Vocational Assn., Assn. Adminstrs. Home Econs. in State Univs. and Land Grant Colls. (chmn. nominating com. 1972—), Nat. Alliance for Family Life, Nat. Council Adminstrs. Home Econs. (pres. 1972—), Southwestern, Rural sociol. socs., Tex. Council on Family Relations, Tex. Vocational Tech. Assn., Vocational Homemaking Tchrs. Tex., Tex. Consumer Assn. (regional v.p. 1965-69), Alpha Kappa Mu, Pi Lambda Theta, Kappa Omicron Phi. Contbr. articles to profl. jours. Home: 120 Oak St Prairie View TX 77445

BYRD, VEDA ENGLAND WOMACK (MRS. JUSTIN S. BYRD), sch. adminstr.; b. Ramsey, Ill., Oct. 16, 1911; d. Andrew and Edith (Cline) England; B.S., U. Tampa, 1949; M.A., U. Fla., 1952; m. Justin S. Byrd, Dec. 22, 1945. Elementary tchr., Ramsey, Ill., 1930-35, 44-46, Bayle City, Ill., 1935-41, Vandalia, Ill., 1941-44, Ediston Sch., Tampa, Fla., 1946-51, Bayside Sch., Tampa, 1951-56; prin. Henderson, Tampa, 1956-57, LaVoy Sch., 1957—. Tchr. evening div. U. Tampa, 1956-65; mem. bd. dirs. speech and hearing clinic, 1964-70; cons., research div. MacDonald Tng. Center Found., 1964. Recipient Dr. Thomas Dooley brotherhood award St. Patricks Day Assn., 1962. Mem. Am. Assn. U. Women, Fla. Council Exceptional Children (pres. 1961), Hillsborough Assn. Retarded Children (v.p. 1960), Hillsborough County Fedn. Women's Club (2d v.p. 1964-65), Hillsborough County Edn. Assn. (dir. 1954-65). Democrat. Methodist. Home: 113 Cedar Av Tampa FL 33606 Office: 4410 Main St Tampa FL 33607

BYRN, MARILYN KAY, occupational therapist; b. Weslaco, Tex., Oct. 8, 1946; d. James Sheldon and Wyndle Mae (Moore) Byrn; B.S., Tex. Womans U., 1969; postgrad. Lamar U., 1972-73. Dir. occupational therapy dept. Thomas Hughen Rehab. Center and Sch. for Crippled Children, Port Arthur, Tex., 1969—. Cons. pub. schs. Leader physically handicapped teenagers Girl Scouts U.S.A., 1969—. Recipient VA award for invention writing device for visual handicapped, 1968. Mem. Am. Occupational Therapy Assn., World Fedn. Occupational Therapists, Am. Personnel and Guidance Assn., Am. Rehab. Counseling Assn., Easter Seal Soc., Beta Sigma Phi. Methodist. Home: 814 N 21st St Harlingen TX 78550 Office: 3620 28th St Port Arthur TX 77640

BYRNE, IRENE HART (MRS. TOMMIE C. BYRNE), city ofcl.; b. Brookhaven, Miss., Sept. 8, 1917; d. Judge L. and Ethel Belle (Roberts) Hart; A.A., Copiah Lincoln Jr. Coll., 1938; student Whitworth Coll., 1968-69; postgrad. Miss. State U.; m. Tommie C. Byrne, Sept. 23, 1939; children—Patricia (Mrs. Frank Emerson), Tim, Kathy. Tchr., basketball coach Fair Oak-Springs Sch., Brookhaven, 1938-39; bookkeeper Office of County Supt. Edn., Brookhaven, 1949-52; dep. chancery clk. Lincoln County, Brookhaven, 1952-68; with Office of Sheriff, Brookhaven, 1968, First Fed. Savs. & Loan Assn., Brookhaven, 1968-69; city clk. City of Brookhaven, 1969—. Mem. Internat. City Clks. Assn., Miss. Municipal City Clks., Tax Assessors and Tax Collectors Assn., Brookhaven Bus. and Profl. Womens Club, Beta Sigma Phi. Club: Camellia (Brookhaven). Home: 1051 S Church St Brookhaven MS 39601 Office: PO Box 560 Brookhaven MS 39601

BYRNE, MARGERY ELEANOR LITTLE (MRS. THOMAS E. BYRNE), banker; b. N.Y.C., Feb. 28, 1918; d. George Packer and Dorothy (Beard) Little; grad. Elmira Bus. Inst., 1938; m. Thomas E. Byrne, Nov. 8, 1953; 1 dau., Melody Anne. With Marine Midland Bank-So. (formerly Elmire Bank & Trust Co.), Elmira, N.Y., 1938-41, 46—, sec., 1962—, v.p., 1973—; with Citizens Bank & Trust Co., White Plains, N.Y., 1941-43, Netherlands Information Bur., N.Y.C., 1943-45, George P. Little Co., Cleve., 1945-46. Pres. Elmira Little Theatre, 1951. Mem. Nat. Secs. Assn. (chpt. pres. 1967; Sec. of Year 1966), Beta Sigma Phi. Presbyn. (trustee). Home: 1448 W Water St Elmira NY 14905 Office: 150 Lake St Elmira NY 14902

BYRNES, HAZEL WEBSTER, ednl. adminstr.; b. Charles City, Ia., July 29, 1886; d. Abel Blinn and Susannah (Haines) Webster; B.A., Ia. State Tchrs. Coll., 1910; postgrad. U. Ia., 1925; M.A., Columbia, 1935; m. Frank Lloyd Byrnes, Jan. 1, 1912. Tchr., State Tchrs. Coll., Peru, Neb., 1910-12, State Tchrs. Coll., Cedar Falls, Ia., 1917-19; librarian, instr. library sci. State Tchrs. Coll., Mayville, N.D., 1924-48; dir. State Library Commn., N.D., 1948-65; instr. U. Nev., summer 1958; asst. dean, librarian Inst. of Lifetime Learning, Long Beach, Cal., 1965-68. Mem. adv. com. N.Y. World's Fair, 1938-39. Winner first prize index essay contest N.Y. Times, 1934; designated woman of year in edn. for N.D., by Adminstrv. Women in Edn., 1943; named Bismarck Woman of the Year, 1959; distinguished citation Mayville Tchrs. Coll. Mem. A.L.A. (council 1931-62, coordinator, mem. joint com. with N.E.A., 1953-58), Adult Edn. Assn. U.S., Nat. League Am. Pen Women (state pres. 1938-40, nat. historian 1952-53), Am. Assn. U. Women, P.E.O., D.A.R., Delta Kappa Gamma (state pres. 1951-59). Methodist. Mem. Order Eastern Star, Zonta Internat. (area dir. 1959-64). Editor: Library Bull. N.D., 1948-56. Contbr. articles to Nat. Ency., Collier Ency. Yearbook, also articles in profl. jours. Home: Mayville ND 58257

BYRON, CHERYL ANN (MRS. WILLIAM DUNCAN BYRON), psychiatrist; b. Evanston, Ill., Jan. 20, 1944; d. Robert Blane and Martha H. (Hirt) Maxwell; B.S.M., Northwestern U., 1966, M.D., 1968; m. William Duncan Byron, Mar. 23, 1968. Rotating intern Evanston (Ill.) Hosp., 1968-69; resident psychiatry Ill. State Psychiat. Inst., Chgo., 1969-71; fellow child psychiatry Michael Reese Hosp., Chgo., 1971-73; pvt. practice medicine specializing in psychiatry, Evanston, Ill., 1973—; psychiat. cons. Dysfunctioning Child Center, Michael Reese Med. Center, Chgo., 1973—. Mem. edn. com. Edgewater Clergy-Rabbi Assn. and Edgewater Community Council, 1970-72. Baptist.

BYRON, DORA LOUISE, educator; b. Pomona Park, Fla., Oct. 15, 1912; d. Edgar and Frances (Patterson) Byron; B.S., Fla. State U., 1932; M.A., Emory U., 1950, M.L.S., 1967. Instr. journalism Fla. State U., 1946-48; news editor Emory U., 1949-60, asso. dir. community edn., 1961-68; asst. prof. journalism and English West Ga. Coll., 1969—. Served with WAC, 1943-46. Recipient citation of Merit in Edn., Ga. Gerontology Soc., 1967, award of Merit, Theta Sigma Phi, 1970. Mem. Women in Communication. Author: The Bishop of Heard County, 1955. Contbr. articles to nat. mags. Home: 119 Griffin Dr Carrollton GA 30117

BYRON, GLORIA BLUM (MRS. STUART DAVID BYRON), pub. relations counselor; b. N.Y.C., June 10, 1937; d. Joseph and Theresa (Philip) Blum; student Bernard M. Baruch Sch. Bus. and Pub. Adminstrn., 1955-57, Fashion Inst. Tech., 1957-58; m. Stuart David Byron, Nov. 20, 1971; children—Linda Beth, Lisa Joan. Asst. fashion dir. Leather Industries Am., N.Y.C., 1958-62; account exec. Robert S. Taplinger Assos., Inc., N.Y.C., 1962-64; account exec. Daniel J. Edelman, Inc., N.Y.C., 1964-68, v.p., 1968-71; v.p. Rowland Co., Inc., N.Y.C., 1972-73; ind. pub. relations counselor, free lance writer, N.Y.C., 1973—. Lectr. on career opportunities in pub. relations for various groups; aided in publicizing U-Thant fellowship Adlai Stevenson Inst. Fgn. Affairs, 1971; mem. com. for starting exchange fashion program with Scandinavian countries Fashion Group-U.S. State Dept., 1969. Worker John V. Lindsay mayoralty campaign, 1965. Mem. membership, pub. relations coms. Knickerbocker League for Children's Asthma Research Inst. and Hosp., Denver, 1963-64.

Mem. Pub. Relations Soc. Am., Fashion Group, Inc. Home and office: 324 E 41st St New York City NY 10017

BYRON, RITA ELLEN COONEY (MRS. CARL J. BYRON, JR.), travel exec., real estate agt., civic leader; b. Cleve., July 28, 1928; d. Harry James and Marie (Hakey) Cooney; student Cleve. Coll., 1949-50, Western Res. U., 1950-51, John Carroll U., 1956; m. Carl James Byron, Jr., Nov. 27, 1954; children—Carey Lewis, Carl James III, Bradford William. Mgr. European immigration dept. U.S. S.S. Lines, Cleve., 1953-56; real estate agt. W.I. White Realtors, Inc., Shaker Heights, O., 1962-67, J.P. Malone Realtors, Inc., Shaker Heights, 1968-70, Thomas Murray and Assos., 1971—; dir. Am. Carved Crystal Corp. Cons. Allen Travel Service, Cleve., 1952; dir., cons. Travelworld, Cleve., 1969—; originator Invitational Tours, Shaker Heights, 1961—; v.p. Travel Center, 1972—; social dir. Shaker Traveler's Club, 1972—, Better Living League, 1972; travel dir. Brandywine Travel Agy., Northfield, O., 1973—. Vol., Univ. Hosps., 1953-57; vol. social worker Family Services, Red Feather Agy., 1957-63; benefit vol. Soc. for Blind, 1958; vol. Am. Cancer Soc., 1958-59; benefit vol. Cleve. Hearing and Speech Center, 1963; mem. Wightman Cup Women's Com., 1965—; vol., mem. Am. zone Davis Cup Finals Women's Com., 1965-69; benefit vol. Soc. for Crippled Children, 1966; mem. steering com. Cleve. Philharmonic Orch. Guild, 1966; benefit chmn. Cleve. Philharmonic Orch. Women's Com., 1967-68; adminstrv. asst. Cleve. Philharmonic Orch., 1968, bd. dirs., 1968-69; benefit vol., mem. women's com. Inst. Music, 1968—; U.S. Figure Skating Assn., 1960—; co-chmn. Cleve. Invitational Figure Skating Competition, 1972—; mem. unit spl. events English Speaking Union, 1968—; mem. vol. women's com. Cleve. Play House, 1968-69; mem. women's com. Cleve. Mus. Art, 1969—, Mus. Natural Sci., 1969—; patron, co-chmn. benefit Candlelight Theatre, 1968; benefit chmn. Pan Am. Cultural Soc., 1968; vol. Gt. Lakes Shakespeare Festival, 1970, benefit chmn., 1971; mem. women's council WVJZ-TV, 1973—; mem. Shaker Lakes Regional Nature Center, 1972; vol. Cleve. Mental Health Assn., 1972-73, Cleve. Music Sch. Settlement, 1972; mem. Ohio City Community Devel. Assn., 1972—, Friends Karamu Theatre, 1972-73; patroness N.Y. Debutante Assembly, 1973-74. Co-chmn. Heights Republican Hdqrs., 1962. Recipient Outstanding Women's Com. of Year award WJW Radio St., Cleve., 1968. Mem. Cleve. Real Estate Bd., Western Res. Hist. Soc., Garden Center of Greater Cleve., Friends of Cleve. Pub. Library, UN Assn. of U.S.A., Cleve. Council on World Affiars. Clubs: Broadmoor World Arena F.S.; Cleveland Skating. Home: 18513 Van Aken Blvd Shaker Heights OH 44122 also Es Turo Edificio Kontiki Majorica Balearic Islands Spain Office: Invitational Tours Travelworld 57 E Aurora Rd Northfield OH 44167

BYSIEWICZ, SHIRLEY RAISSI (MRS. STANLEY J. BYSIEWICZ), lawyer, educator; b. Enfield, Conn.; d. Kyriakos and Anna D. (Gavala) Raissi; B.A., U. Conn., also J.D.; m. Stanley J. Bysiewicz, July 18, 1959; children—Susan, Walter, Karen, Gail. Admitted to Conn. bar, 1954; mem. firm Raissi & Raissi, Enfield, Conn., 1954—. Asst. prof. law U. Conn., West Hartford, 1956-62, asso. prof., 1962-64, prof. law, 1965—, also law librarian. Mem. Am. Bar Assn., Bar Assn. Conn. (presider com. status women), Nat. Assn. Women Lawyers, Hartford County Bar Assn. (exec. com.), Am. Assn. Law Schs. (co-presider sect. on status of women, co-presider sect. legal research), Am. Assn. Law Librarians (law library jour. com.), U. Conn. Law Sch. Alumni Assn. (exec. sec. 1958-68), New Eng. Law Librarians (pres.), Women's Equity Action League, Delta Zeta. Mem. Greek Orthodox Ch. (choir). Author: (with Max R. White) Forms of Town Government in Connecticut, 1954; Survey of County Law Libraries in Connecticut, 1967; co-author Selected Annotated Bibliography on Education for Professional Responsibility, 1968. Bus. mgr. Law Library Jour., 1968-72; co-editor Materials on Estate Planning, 1969. Contbr. articles to law jours. Home: South Plumb Rd Middletown CT 06457 Office: 1800 Asylum Av West Hartford CT 06117

BYSTRYN, SARA WOLSKI (MRS. ISER BYSTRYN), importer; b. Brest Litovsk, Russia; d. Charles and Louba (Prilouk) Wolski; student Sorbonne, Paris, France, 1930-33; m. Iser Bystryn, Dec. 23, 1930; children—Denise (Mrs. Eric Kandel), Jean-Claude. Came to U.S., 1949, naturalized, 1954. Owner, pres. Ibis Export Import Co., N.Y.C., 1951—. Active mem. French Resistance, 1942-44. Home: 800 West End Av New York City NY 10025 Office: 250 W 57th St New York City NY 10019

BYXBEE, KATHLEEN DOWLING, educator; b. Harrison, N.Y., Nov. 13, 1946; d. Thomas Edward and Marion Frances (Burke) B.; B.A., Conn. Coll., 1968; M.Ed., U. Mass., 1972; m. William E. Byxbee, Dec. 16, 1967; children—Colin, Megan, Valley. Psychiat. social worker Norwich (Conn.) Hosp., 1968-69; research parprofl. deployment U. Mass., 1970-71, mem. staff K-12 Alternative Sch., 1971-72; dir. M.A. program in human devel., faculty edn. St. Mary's Coll., Winona, Minn., 1973—; cons. in field. Mem. Phi Beta Kappa. Home: N Briar Wood Winona MN 55987

CABALLE, MONSERRAT, soprano. N.Y.C. debut in Donizetti's Lucrezia Borgia, with Am. Opera Soc., 1965; also appeared with La Scala Opera, Milan, Vienna Staatsoper, Glydebourne Festival, Met. Opera; rec. RCA Victor; performed in works of Richard Strauss, Mozart, Falla, Luigi Nono. Home: Avenida Infanta Carlota 46 Barcelona Spain Office: care Columbia Artists Mgmt Inc 165 W 57th St New York City NY 10019*

CABALLERO, VELMA LOIS (MRS. JOE J. CABALLERO), health service adminstr.; b. nr. Crockett, Tex., Aug. 1, 1921; d. James William and Annie Elizabeth (Lindsey) Marks; grad. high sch.; m. Joe J. Caballero, Oct. 10, 1938; children—Jo Ann (Mrs. Donald Lambright), Lynda (Mrs. James Kapapski). Courtesy booth mgr. J. Weingarten, Inc., Texas City, Tex., 1952-56; bookkeeper Dayton (Tex.) Meml. Hosp., 1958-62, adminstr., 1962—. Mem. Am. Bus. Women's Assn. Roman Catholic. Home: Route 1 Box 389 Dayton TX 77535 Office: 702 N Winfree St Dayton TX 77535

CABLE, MYRL STEPHENSON (MRS. KENNETH BERYLE CABLE), educator; b. Okemah, Okla., June 8, 1919; d. John Logan and Lena (Dodd) Stephenson; A.A., Lindenwood Coll. for Women, 1936; B.A., U. Tulsa, 1938, postgrad., 1939, 40; postgrad. West Tex. Coll., 1947, 49, Eastern Ore. Coll., 1954, 57, Odessa Coll., 1956, 67; m. Kenneth Beryle Cable, Nov. 5, 1942. Tchr., Davenport, Okla., 1938-40, Muskogee, Okla., 1940-43; exec. sec. Braden Winch Co., Tulsa, 1943-45, Hopson-Roper Adjusting Service Br., Pampa, Tex., 1945-46; tchr., Pampa, 1946-52, Noble, Okla., 1952-53, Ontario, Ore., 1953-54, 56-58; tchr. Ector County Ind. Sch. Dist., Odessa, Tex., 1954-56, 58—. Patron mem. Permian Playhouse, Odessa, 1965—; mem. women's aux. Med. Center Hosp., Odessa, 1959—. Bd. dirs. Odessa Area chpt. Muscular Dystrophy Assn. Am. Mem. N.E.A., Tex. (pres. 6th grade level for dist. IV, co-chmn. 1970—), Ector County tchrs. assns., Tex., Ector County classroom tchrs. assns., Am. Assn. U. Women, Lindenwood Alumnae Assn., U. Tulsa Alumni Assn., Odessa C. of C., Kappa Kappa Iota (v.p. Tex. 1967-68, nat. exec. bd. 1967-68, pres. Tex. 1969-70, parliamentarian Tex. 1973—, nat. rec. sec. 1969-70; nat. pres. 1972-73, nat. dir. 1973—). Democrat. Baptist. Mem. Order Eastern Star. Home: 3304 Mercury St Rt 3 Box 163 Odessa TX 79763 Office: PO Box 3912 Odessa TX 79760

CABLE, RACHAEL GERTRUDE (MRS. GEORGE W. CABLE), educator; b. Marysville, Cal.; d. Peter James and Sarah (McElroy) Finnegan; grad. San Jose Normal Coll., 1909; B.Ed., Chico State Coll., 1954; m. George W. Cable, May 16, 1916 (dec. Sept. 1933); children—Kenneth, Elizabeth Jane (Mrs. Morris L. Quick, Jr.), Devore. Prin., adminstr. Arboga Elementary Sch., Marysville, Cal., 1923-62. Mem. Yuba County Bd. Edn., 1940-55; chmn. schs. and edn. Yuba County Grand Jury, 1968. Pres., Yuba County Tb and Health Assn., 1954-56; first aid chmn. Yuba County chpt. A.R.C., 1942-61; leader Yuba County 4-H, 30 years. Mem. Am. Assn. of U. Women (dir. Marysville-Yuba City br.), Yuba County Rural Tchrs. Assn. (past pres.), Yuba County Adminstrs. Assn. (past pres.), Sutter-Yuba Ret. Tchrs. Assn. (past pres.), Cal. Fedn. Women's Club (pres. 1964-66; dist. edn. chmn.), Notre Dame Alumnae (past pres. Marysville chpt.; past pres., treas. Cal. chpt.; past pres. internat. fedn.), Yuba County Tchrs. Assn. (past pres.), Daus. Golden West (past pres.), Delta Kappa Gamma (chpt. pres.), Phi Sigma Alpha. Club: Marysville (Cal.) Art (pres. 1964-66). Author: Three Summers with pop, 1939; Mama Came to California, 1971. Retired. Address: 611 E St Marysville CA 95901

CACACE, MAXINE BROWN (MRS. BARON AMEDEO CACACE), educator; b. Oakland, Cal., Apr. 20, 1925; d. Sidney Walker and Fern Grace (Brundage) Brown; B.A., U. Cal. at Berkeley, 1947; M. Sacred Scis. cum laude, Pontifical Inst. Regina Mundi, Rome, Italy, 1967; M. Sacred Scis., St. Mary's Coll., 1967; m. Baron Amedeo Cacace, Dec. 27, 1950; 1 son, Stephen. Tchr., Santa Cataline Sch., Monterey, Cal., 1969-70; prof. philosophy and history Hartnell Community Coll., Salinas, Cal., 1970—. Roman Catholic. Home: PO Box 356 Pebble Beach CA 93953 Office: Hartnell Community Coll Salinas CA 93901

CACCESE, MILDRED YOLANDA (MRS. WILLIAM D. CACCESE), pub.; b. Newfield, N.J., Sept. 15, 1913; d. Louis and Grace Marie (Gallo) Musto; grad. Clayton High Sch., 1931; m. William D. Caccese, Nov. 17, 1932; children—Louis W., Valerie F. Vice pres. Franklin Printing Co., Inc., Franklinville, N.J., 1971-74; pub. Franklin Twp. Sentinel, Franklinville, 1971—. Mem. Moose Aux. Home: Box 158 Franklinville NJ 08322 Office: Franklin Printing Co S Delsea Dr Franklinville NJ 08322

CACIOPPO, MARY (MRS. KENNETH MYRON KOLLER), lawyer; b. Akron, O., May 21, 1923; d. Charles and Josephine (Saladino) Cacioppo; J.D., U. Akron, 1945; B.A., Kent State U., 1946; m. Kenneth Myron Koller, July 18, 1959; 1 dau. by previous marriage, Charlotte (Mrs. David Wayne Fisher). Admitted to Ohio bar, 1945, since practiced in Akron; asst. law dir. City of Akron, 1954-57; mem. Akron Zoning Bd., 1957-62; trial counsel in land appropriations City of Akron, 1962-63; police prosecutor, Akron, 1963-64; domestic relations referee Summit County, O., 1974—. Instr. evening coll. Akron U., 1951-58. Mem. Akron Symphony Women's Com., 1970—. Bd. dirs. Summit County Home for Aged, 1965-68, Sr. Citizens Work Action Program, 1969-71; trustee East Akron Community House, 1957-60. Mem. Ohio, Akron (v.p. 1946-48) bar assns., Akron Law Library Assn., Akron Bus. and Profl. Women's Club. Democrat. Club: Akron Soroptimist (pres. 1954). Home: 217 Tyler St Cuyohoga Falls OH 44221 Office: 219 Ohio Bldg Akron OH 44308

CADBURY, JANE BALDERSTON (MRS. BRUCE KNIGHT SYMONDS), physician; b. Canton, China, May 30, 1918; d. William Warder and Catharine Balderston (Jones) Cadbury; B.A., Wellesley Coll., 1940; M.D., Yale, 1943; m. Bruce Knight Symonds, June 15, 1950; children—William Cadbury, Ann Fisk, Robert Bruce. Intern, N.C. Baptist Hosp., Winston-Salem, 1944,; resident Phila. Children's Hosp., 1944-45, Mass. Gen. Hosp., Boston, 1945-46, Hitchcock Clinic, Hanover, N.H., 1946-47; practice medicine specializing in pediatrics, Manchester, N.H., 1947-52; dir. maternal and child health St. Louis County Health Dept., Clayton, Mo., 1957-58, dist. health officer, 1958-68, dir. maternal and infant care project, 1966-68; health service physician Mankato State Coll., Mankato, Minn., 1969—; mem. staff Immanuel St. Joseph's Hosp.; chmn. health com. Mo. Assn. Social Welfare, St. Louis div., 1963-67. Bd. dirs. Mankato Symphony Orchestra, dir. publicity, 1969—. Mem. Am., Minn. med. assns., Blue Earth County Med. Soc. Club: Katonian Dance (Mankato, Minn.). Home: 221 Crestwood Dr Mankato MN 56001 Office: Mankato State College Health Service Mankato MN 56001

CADDELL, JOAN LOUISE, physician; b. N.Y.C., Jan. 16, 1927; d. Alfred Matthew and Anna Emily (Mielke) Caddell; B.A., U. Pa., 1948; M.D., U. Pa., 1953. Intern, Phila. Gen. Hosp., 1953; resident pediatrics Childrens Hosp., Phila., 1954-56, asst. chief resident, 1956-57, endocrine fellow, 1957-58, cardiology fellow, 1958-59; cardiology fellow Yale U., 1959-61, instr., 1961-62; Rockefeller Found. fellow Makerere U., Uganda, 1962-63; Rockefeller Found. fellow U. Ibadan, Ibadan, Nigeria, 1963-65; research fellow George Washington U., 1966-67; asst. prof. pediatrics St. Louis U., 1968—; NIH research fellow Chiang Mai, Thailand, and Anemia and Malnutrition Research Center St. Louis U., 1969-71, research investigator NIH, 1971—; physician Soc. to Protect Children from Cruelty, Phila., 1957-58. Am. Heart Assn. 1958-61. Diplomate Nat. Bd. Med. Examiners, Am. Bd. Pediatrics, Am. Bd. Pediatric Cardiology, Pan Am. Med. Assn. Fellow Am. Acad. Pediatrics, Am. Coll. Cardiology, Am. Coll. Nutrition. Contbr. articles to profl. pubs. Author text book chpts. Heart Disease in Infants, Children and Adolescents (Williams and Wilkins), 1968, Pediatric Cardiology (Lloyd Luke), 1968, Diseases of Childhood in the Subtropics and Tropics (London, Arnold,), 1971, McGraw Hill Yearbook of Science and Tech., 1971. Home: 1401 S Grand Blvd St Louis MO 63104 Office: St Louis U Sch Medicine 1402 S Grand Blvd St Louis MO 63104

CADE, BARBARA JANE (MRS. KYLE RICHARD CADE), library adminstr.; b. Miami, Fla., July 10, 1928; d. Rufus Lester and Ruby (Stapleton) Cox; A.A., Armstrong Coll., 1947; B.S. in Edn., Ga. Coll., 1949; M.S. in Librarianship, Emory U., 1953; Ed.S. in Library Edn., U. Ga., 1968; m. Kyle Richard Cade, Dec. 23, 1951. Asst. librarian Ga. Coll., Milledgeville, 1949-50; librarian Atlanta pub. schs., 1950—, Northside High Sch., 1950-56, West Fulton High Sch., 1956-65, Therrell High Sch., 1965-66, library supr., area IV office, 1966—. Mem. Am., Southeastern, Ga. library assns., Ga., Atlanta assns. educators, Assn. for Ednl. Communications and Tech., Assn. for Supervision and Curriculum Devel., N.E.A., Delta Kappa Gamma, Phi Kappa Phi, Kappa Delta Pi. Democrat. Presbyn. Home: 1820 Hurt Rd SW Marietta GA 30060 Office: 225 Chestnut St NW Atlanta GA 30314

CADENA, DOLORES PAREDES (MRS. ARNOLDO MELCHOR CADENA), bank ofcl.; b. Laredo, Tex., July 14, 1929; d. Enricue Herrera and Herminia (Solis) Paredes; grad. Am. Inst. Banking, 1968; m. Arnoldo Melchor Cadena, Feb. 15, 1953; children—Patricia Veronica, Arnoldo Melchor, Priscilla Yvonne, Armando Efrain. Credit clk. Montgomery Ward, Laredo, 1947; credit clk. Sears Roebuck & Co., Laredo, 1949-50; with note dept. Union Nat. Bank, Laredo, 1950-53, note teller, 1957-66; note teller Frost Nat. Bank, San Antonio, 1953-55; instn. auditor Bank of Commerce of Laredo, 1966-68, installment loan exec., 1968—. Bd. dirs. C.L. Milton P.T.A., 1970-71. Mem. Nat. Assn. Banking Women, Mary Help of Christians (treas. 1960-61). Home: 1318 Kearney St Laredo TX 78040 Office: PO Box 1359 Laredo TX 78040

CADEZ, PATRICIA POWELL (MRS. JOHN E. CADEZ), occupational therapist, state ofcl.; b. Reno, July 5, 1940; d. Alma C. and Dorothy Emma (Pope) Powell; student Tex. Woman's U., 1958-59; B.S., Colo. State U., 1966; m. John E. Cadez, Dec. 29, 1968; 1 dau., Tracy Lynn. Psychiat. occupational therapist Bethesda Psychiat. Hosp., Denver, 1967, VA Hosp., Denver, 1968; staff occupational therapy State Home and Tng. Sch., Grand Junction, Colo., 1968—, supr. occupational therapy dept., 1972—, instr. instl. in-service tng. program, 1969—. Cons. instr. for registered nurses and licensed practical nurses, dormitory personnel. Mem. P.T.A., 1970-72, Intermountain regional med. planning com., 1970-71. Easter Seal Found. scholar, 1964, 1965; Hilltop Guild grantee, 1965. Mem. Am., Colo. (finance chmn. 1969) occupational therapy assns., Mesa County Assn. for Retarded Children, Western Slope Rehab. Assn. (v.p. 1970). Mem. Order Eastern Star. Home: 2231 S Regent Circle Grand Junction CO 81501 Office: PO Box 2568 Grand Junction CO 81501

CADLEY, ALICE KILEY, educator; b. Milton, Mass., June 20, 1912; d. Cornelius and Margaret Mary (Smith) Kiley; B.S., Boston U., 1935, Ed.M., 1955, Ed.D., 1957; m. George Humphrey Nicholson, Feb. 22, 1941 (dec.); m. 2d, Edward Bernard Cadley, June 4, 1966. Tchr. remedial reading pub. schs., Hudson, N.H., 1935-36; tchr. kindergarten and remedial reading pub. schs., Milton, 1936-41; prin. Post Sch., March AFB, Cal., 1946-47; tchr., prin. Am. Dependents Schs., Germany, 1947-52; tchr. Escuela Bella Vista, Maracaibo, Venezuela, 1952-53; teaching fellow Boston U., 1954-55, instr. to asso. prof., 1955-66, Headstart tng. dir., 1965; asso. prof. St. Johns U., Jamaica, N.Y., 1966-73; ret., 1973. Mem. Am. Psychol. Assn., Assn. for Childhood Edn. Internat., Am. Ednl. Research Assn., Nat. Conf. for Research in English, Pi Lambda Theta. Home: 1270 NW 45th Ct Pompano Beach FL 33064

CADWELL, FRANKIE MARGARET, advt. agy. exec.; b. N.Y.C., Apr. 28, 1938; d. William E. and Margaret Mary (Rauston) Cadwell; B.S., Cornell U., 1959. Pres., Cadwell Davis, 1964-70; pres. Cadwell Compton, N.Y.C., 1971—. Mem. Fashion Group, Inc. (bd. dirs.). Office: 625 Madison Av New York City NY 10021

CADZOW, DOROTHY FORREST (MRS. RANDOLPH H. HOKANSON), musician, composer; b. Edmonton, Alta., Can., Aug. 9, 1916; d. Thomas Forrest and Gertrude (Weisman) Cadzow; B.A., U. Wash., 1940; postgrad. Juilliard Grad. Sch., 1942-45; m. Randolph H. Hokanson, Jan. 18, 1952. Music dir., Tacoma Pub. Schs., 1940-42; free-lance composer and arranger, N.Y.C., 1945-49; mem. faculty music U. Wash., 1949-52; free-lance composer, arranger, pvt. music tchr., Seattle, 1952—. Mem. Phi Beta Kappa, Mu Phi Epsilon, Pi Lambda Theta. Episcopalian. Club: Ladies Musical (Seattle). Composer: Northwestern Sketches, orchestral suite, 1945, Piano Sonata, 1952, Undine, opera, 1958, Dialogues for Violin and Piano, 1967. Contbr. articles to music mags. Home: 2636 11th Av E Seattle WA 98102

CAEDO, ROSE ELAINE SANGALANG, physician; b. Manila, Philippines, Nov. 27, 1941; d. Marcial T. and Juana F. (Sangalang) Caedo; student St. Paul's Coll., 1947-51, St. Theresa's Coll., 1957; A.A., U. Santo Tomas, 1959, M.D. benemeritus, 1964. Came to U.S., 1965. With North Gen. Hosp., Philippines, 1965; intern Misericordia Hosp., Phila., 1965-66, med. resident, 1966-69; resident nephrology Crozer Chester Med. Center, Chester, Pa., 1969—. Home: Crozer Chester Medical Center Chester PA 19013

CAENAHAN, WANDA EDWINA, labor union ofc.; b. Ellsinore, Mo., July 26, 1929; d. William Thomas and Ora Mae (Berry) Roark; grad. high sch.; m. Ernest Bryan Carnahan, Jan. 29, 1949; children—Ronald, Donald. Pres. local 410 Internat. Ladies Garment Workers Union, 1968-71, chairlady, 1971-74, chmn. COPE com., 1968-74, mem. exec. bd. Mo.-Ark. Dist. Council, 1971—. Sec.-treas. Ellsinore P.T.A., 1972-73; sec.-treas., mem. bd. East Carter County Ambulance Assn., 1973-74. Vice chmn. Mo. Democratic Central Com., 1963-70, mem. platform com., 1970-71, del. conv., 1968-72; auditor 10th Dist. Dem. Women's Fedn., 1970-71, 4th v.p., 1973-74; pres. Carter County Women's Dem. Club, 1969-72; sec.-treas. Carter County Dem. Club, 1970-72. Address: Ellsinore MO 63937

CAFFREY, CHARLOTTE EVERSTINE, editor; b. Greenville, Pa., July 16, 1925; d. Allen Perry and Charlotte Nycum (Skyles) Everstine; student Carnegie Inst. Tech., 1942-45, Art Students League, 1945-46; m. Frank L. Woodruff, Mar. 16, 1947 (div. June 1949); 1 son, Perry Skyles; m. 2d, Robert C. Caffrey, Dec. 21, 1949 (dec.). Advt. mgr. Hal Lewis, Inc., 1951-53; spl. supplement editor Pitts. Suburban Weekly Newspapers, 1953-59, Pompano Beach Town News, 1959-61; feature writer, reporter Miami Beach (Fla.) Daily Sun, 1961-65, Nightbeat sect. editor, 1968-69; news bur. chief Ft. Pierce News Tribune, Vero Beach, Fla., 1965-66; mng. editor Linen Supply News, Miami Beach, 1969—. Exhibited in watercolor show Ft. Pierce Civic Art Gallery, 1973. Recipient 2d place news citation Fla. Women's Press Assn., 1966, 1st place critical rev. citation, 1969, 2d place excellence citation Fla. Mag. Assn., 1972, 2d place feature citation, 1973. Home: 1542 Jefferson Av Miami Beach FL 33139 Office: 975 Arthur Godfrey Rd Miami Beach FL 33140

CAHILL, EDNA, editor; b. Los Angeles, Oct. 2, 1930; d. Kenneth L. and Roxanne (Smith) C.; B.A., U. Cal. at Los Angeles, 1952; M.A. in Bus. Adminstrn., Columbia, 1956. Asst. to editor World-Wide Publs., Inc., N.Y.C., 1952-55; publs. asst. IBM, N.Y.C., 1956-60; asst. prof. English, Coe Coll., 1960-64; asst. editor Smith Electronics Co., 1964-69, editor, 1969—. Mem. Indsl. Editors Assn. Am., Pi Kappa Delta. Presbyn. Address: 2727 Karen Lane Glenview IL 60025

CAHILL, JOAN FRANCES, physician; b. Halifax, N.S., Can., Mar. 14, 1933; d. Francis Dennis and Nora Evelyn (Mullane) C.; B.Sc., Dalhousie U., 1953, M.Sc. in Pharmacology (Women's Alumni scholar), 1955, M.D., 1963. Research dept. pharmacology Dalhousie U., Halifax, 1953-56; research pharmacology firm Ayerst, McKenna & Harrison Ltd., Montreal, Que., Can., 1956-59; intern Victoria Gen. Hosp., Halifax, 1962-63; practice medicine specializing in family medicine, Halifax, 1963-67, individual practice, Halifax, 1967-69; mem. Coburg Med. Group, Halifax, 1969—; instr. pharmacology Dalhousie U., 1966-70. Bd. govs. Dalhousie U., 1972—. NRC grantee, 1953-56; Eddy research fellow, 1954. Recipient Anatomy prize, 1959, Univ. prize, 1961; Upjohn Study award, 1975. Mem. Canadian Med. Assn., N.S., Halifax med. socs., Coll. Family Physicians Can., Alpha Omega Alpha. Progressive Conservative. Roman Catholic. Contbr. articles to med. jours. Home: 1170 Belmont-on-the-Arm Halifax NS B3H 1J3 Canada Office: 6287 Coburr Rd Halifax NS B3H 2A3 Canada

CAHILL, MARY FRAN, photojournalist; b. Milw.; d. Morgan Joseph and Claire Catherine (Warnimont) Cahill; B.A., Marquette U., 1962, M.A., 1963. Tchr., Grafton (Wis.) High Sch., 1964-65; photojournalist Cedarburg (Wis.) News Graphic, 1965-67, Milw.

Jour., 1967—. Mem. Nat. Press Photographers Assn., Wis. News Photographers Assn. (sec. 1973—), Women in Communications, Milw. Press Club, Zool. Soc. Milw. County, Wis. Emergency Med. Technicians Assn., Sigma Delta Chi, Phi Mu, Phi Alpha Theta, Pi Gamma Mu. Roman Catholic. Home: 3318 N 53d St Milwaukee WI 53216 Office: 333 W State St Milwaukee WI 53201

CAHILL, MARY-CAROL, psychologist, educator; b. N.Y.C.; d. Harold Daniel and Mildred Eva (Gessler) Cahill; A.B. (N.Y. State Regents fellow), Coll. New Rochelle; A.M., Fordham U., Ph.D., 1967. Engr. human factors life scis. div. Grumman Aerospace Corp., Bethpage, N.Y., 1967-70; asst. prof. dept. psychology Rensselaer Polytech. Inst., Troy, N.Y., 1970-74; asst. prof. psychology Fordham U., N.Y.C., 1974—. Cons. in human factors engring. and psychol. research. NSF fellow. Mem. Am., Eastern psychol. assns., A.A.A.S., Assn. Women in Sci., Am. Assn. U. Profs., Am. Assn. U. Women, Human Factors Soc., Soc. Information Display, N.Y. Zool. Soc., Am. Mus. Nat. History, Sierra Club, Wilderness Soc., Nat. Audubon Soc., Women's Equity Action League, Nat. Orgn. Women, Environmental Planning Lobby, Friends of Earth, Sigma Xi. Contbr. articles to profl. jours. Home: 60 Stratford Rd Scarsdale NY 10583 Office: Dept Psychology Fordham Univ New York City NY 10458

CAHN, JEAN CAMPER (MRS. EDGAR STUART CAHN), lawyer, coll. dean; b. Balt., May 26, 1935; d. John Emory-Toussaint and Florine (Thompson) Camper; B.S., Swarthmore Coll., 1957; postgrad. Newnham Coll., Cambridge, Eng., 1958-59; LL.B., Yale, 1961; m. Edgar Stuart Cahn, Mar. 22, 1957; children—Jonathan, Reuben. Admitted to D.C. bar, 1965; practiced in Washington, 1966-68; founder legal services program Office Econ. Opportunity, Washington, 1965-68; founder Antioch Sch. Law, Yellow Springs, O., 1971, dir. Urban Law Inst., 1971—, dean, 1972—; dir. urban law inst. George Washington U., Nat. Law Center, 1968-71, vis. prof., 1968-71; adj. prof. Howard U., 1967-68. Bd. dirs. Washington Center Met. Studies, 1972-74, Nat. Inst. Consumer Justice, 1971-74, Reginald Heber Smith Fellowship Program, 1968-74. Bd. dirs. Yale Law Sch. Assn., 1968-74, mem. univ. council, 1968-74. Mem. Am. Bar Assn. Home: 5500 39th St NW Washington DC 20015 Office: 1634 Crescent Pl NW Washington DC 20009

CAHOON, SISTER MARY ODILE, physiologist, educator; b. Houghton, Mich., July 21, 1929; d. William James and Ruth Thurston (Smothers) Cahoon; student Coll. St. Scholastica, 1947-50; B.S., DePaul U., 1954, M.S., 1958; Ph.D., U. Toronto, 1961. Instr., Coll. of St. Scholastica, Duluth, Minn., 1954-56, asso. prof., 1961-63, acad. dean, 1963-67, prof. biology, 1967—, chmn. natural sci. div., 1972—; research asso. DePaul U., summers 1962-64; vis. scientist Argonne (Ill.) Nat. Lab., 1970-73; research asso. Antarctic Research Program, 1973—. NSF faculty fellow, 1958-59; NSF Faculty Research Participation grantee, 1968-69. Mem. N.Y. Acad. Scis., Am. Soc. Microbiology, Am. Soc. Zoologists, Am. Inst. Biol. Scis. Mem. Order St. Benedict. Address: Coll of St Scholastica Duluth MN 55811

CAIN, ELIZABETH D. MCCALL (MRS. WALKER O. CAIN), civic worker; b. Florence, S.C., Feb. 25, 1919; d. Arthur M. and Julia H. (Lachicotte) McCall; B.S., Converse Coll., 1940; m. Arthur A. Houghton, Jr., Jan. 15, 1944; 1 dau., Hollister Douglas (Mrs. William D. Haggard III); m. 2d, Walker O. Cain, July 27, 1973. Mem. Women's Council N.Y. Pub. Library, 1950, chmn. women's council, 1964-70, exec. com. of com. for dance, 1957, trustee Poetry Soc. Am., 1960-65; sec.-treas. Keats-Shelley Assn. Am., Inc., 1961-73, dir., 1961—; trustee Converse Coll., Spartanburg, S.C., 1958—, exec. com., 1965—; trustee Wye Inst., Inc., Centreville, Md., 1964-72, v.p., 1964-72; trustee Inst. Internat. Edn. N.Y., mem. exec. com., 1968—; mem. altar guild St. James Ch., N.Y.C.; mem. bd. Hammond-Harwood House, Annapolis, Md., 1964-68; bd. mgrs. Hosp. for Spl. Surgery, 1968—; bd. dirs. Am.-Italy Soc., 1969—. Republican. Episcopalian. Clubs: Colony, Cosmopolitan (N.Y.C.). Home: 3 Beekman Pl New York City NY 10022

CAIN, JOAN TERESE, educator; b. Chgo., Nov. 2, 1929; d. Cornelius Rice and Anna (Lynch) Cain; B.A., Rosary Coll., 1951; M.A., U. Wis., 1959, Ph.D. (Fulbright scholar 1962-63), 1964. Tchr. fgn. lang. secondary schs., Wis., 1952-61; prof. Spanish, Rosary Coll., River Forest, Ill., 1964-66; prof. Spanish, U. Southwestern La., Lafayette, 1966—, adviser to Spanish majors, 1971—, chmn. communications com., 1973—, mem. curriculum com., 1972—. Named Distinguished Prof., U. Southwestern La., 1973. Mem. Am. Assn. U. Women (corr. sec. 1970-72), Lafayette Assn. Retarded Children, Modern Lang. Assn. (regional del. 1973—), Common Cause, La. Consumers League, Am. Assn. Tchrs. Spanish and Portuguese, Am. Council Teaching Fgn. Langs., La. Fgn. Lang. Tchrs. Assn., South Central Modern Lang. Assn., Kappa Gamma Pi, Sigma Delta Pi (chpt. adviser 1968—), Pi Delta Phi, Phi Kappa Phi. Home: 1013 Bonnie Dr Lafayette LA 70501

CAIN, RACHEL KING (MRS. STEPHEN P. CAIN), newspaper editor; b. Williamstown, W.Va., Dec. 8, 1914; d. O'Dale and Gertrude (Kennard) King; grad. Utica Sch. Commerce, 1932; m. Stephen P. Cain, Apr. 5, 1943. Mem. editorial staff Buffalo Evening News, 1936—, columnist The Social Mirror, 1952-58, soc. editor, 1958—. Founder troop Girl Scouts U.S.A., Oswego, N.Y., 1926; tchr. deaf scouts Sch. for Deaf, Rome, N.Y., 1928-31. Recipient Golden Eaglet, Girl Scouts U.S.A., 1932, commendation Volta Rev., 1931. Mem. Soc. Am. Social Scribes (charter), Sigma Delta Chi. Methodist. Home: 33 Winspear Av Buffalo NY 14214 Office: One News Plaza Buffalo NY 14240

CAIN, RUTH EDSTROM (MRS. CHARLES C. CAIN, III), pub. relations writer; b. Detroit, June 3, 1924; d. Emil Walter and Lydia Esther (Sanquist) Edstrom; B.A., Wayne State U., 1945; m. Charles C. Cain, III, Aug. 26, 1946; children—Nancy, Charles, Bradford, Christopher, Carol, Laura, Janice. Reporter Detroit bur. Asso. Press, 1945-46; writer Detroit bur. Business Week mag., 1946-48; copywriter promotion dept. Detroit Free Press, 1966-68; staff writer pub. relations Mich. Blue Shield, Detroit, 1968—. Program chmn. St. Brendan Moms and Dads Club, Detroit, 1971-74. Mem. Women in Communications (chmn. hospitality com. Detroit chpt. 1972-74). Club: Women's Economic (Detroit). Home: 10800 Balfour St Detroit MI 48224 Office: 600 Lafayette St E Detroit MI 48226

CAIN, RUTH RODNEY, polit. party ofcl.; b. Austin, Minn., May 17, 1935; d. Charles Frank and Ruth May (Woolery) Chambers; student U. Minn.; m. Richard R. Cain, Dec. 14, 1957; children—Jennifer Lee, Anna Rachel, Joseph Alexander. Service rep. N.W. Bell Telephone Co., Mpls., also Kansas City, Mo., 1956-58; case worker Buchanon County (Mo.), St. Joseph, 1958-59; office mgr. 4th Congl. Dist. Democratic Farmer Labor Com., White Bear Lake, Minn., 1970-72, asso. chairperson Minn. Democratic Farmer Labor Com., Mpls., 1972—. Home: 3554 Holes St Minneapolis MN 55408 Office: 730 E 38th St Minneapolis MN 55407

CAIRNS, SISTER MARIE LAURINE, educator; b. Midway, Okla., Nov. 2, 1914; d. James Joseph and Catherine Veronica (McManus) Cairns; Mus.B., Siena Heights Coll., 1944; Mus.M., Mich. State U., 1953; M.S. (Higher Edn. Act fellow 1969-72), Fla. State U., 1969, A.M.D., 1970, Ph.D., 1972. Joined Sisters of St. Dominic, 1930; tchr. elementary and secondary schs. Mich., Ill., and Fla., 1935-63; asst. librarian secondary sch., Miami Beach, Fla., 1964-66; head librarian secondary sch., Tampa, Fla., 1966-69; asst. prof. Sch. Library Sci., La. State U., Baton Rouge, 1972—, asst. dean, 1973—; mem. summer faculty, Siena Heights Coll., 1957, Barry Coll., Miami, Fla., 1960-61. Mem. Am., Cath. library assns., Beta Phi Mu, Phi Kappa Phi. Home: 220 Oklahoma St Apt 117 Baton Rouge LA 70802

CALDER, KATHLEEN MARIE, journalist, educator; b. New Orleans, Aug. 12, 1946; d. Harold James and Lucie Marie (Dalier) Calder; B.A. in English, Southeastern La. U., 1968; M.A. in Theatre, La. State U. at New Orleans, 1970. Tchr. speech and English, Holy Cross High Sch., New Orleans, 1970-71; tchr. journalism and English, Immaculata High Sch., Marrero, La., 1971—, also head dept. English, 1973—, publs. adviser yearbook, 1971—. Newspaper Fund fellow, 1973. Mem. Am. Legion Aux., Am. Theatre Assn., Journalism Edn. Assn., Nat. Council Tchrs. English, Nat. Collegiate Players, Quill and Scroll, Alpha Sigma Tau. Democrat. Roman Catholic (mem. parish liturgy com. 1973—). Home: 544 Rosa Av Metairie LA 70005 Office: Immaculata High Sch 6th St and Av D Marrero LA 70072

CALDERONE, MARY STEICHEN (MRS. FRANK A. CALDERONE), physician; b. N.Y.C., July 1, 1904; d. Edward J. and Clara (Smith) Steichen; grad. Brearley Sch., 1922; A.B., Vassar Coll., 1925; M.D., U. Rochester, 1939; M.P.H., Columbia, 1942; D.Med. Sci. (hon.), Women's Med. Coll., 1967; D. Sc., Adelphi U., 1971; L.H.D., Newark State Coll., 1971; LL.D., Kenyon Coll., 1972; m. Frank A. Calderone, Nov. 27, 1941; children—Linda Martin (Mrs. Stuart Hodes), Francesca (Mrs. J. Thomas Stuart II), Maria. Intern Bellevue Hosp., N.Y.C., 1939-40; fellow N.Y.C. Dept. Health, 1940-42; item constructor Profl. Exam. Service, Am. Pub. Health Assn., 1942-43; sch. physician Great Neck (N.Y.) Pub. Schs., 1949-53; med. dir. Planned Parenthood Fedn. Am., 1953-64; exec. dir. SIECUS (Sex Information and Edn. Council of U.S.), 1964—. Recipient 4th award for service to humanity, Women's Aux. Einstein Med. Center, Phila., 1966; Woman of Conscience award Nat. Council Women, 1968; Haven Emerson award Pub. Health Assn. N.Y.C., 1970. Fellow Am. Pub. Health Assn.; mem. A.M.A., Am. Med. Women's Assn., Soc. Sci. Study of Sex, Nat. Council Family Relations, Am. Assn. Marriage Counselors (affiliate). Mem. Soc. of Friends. Author: First and Second Picture Books, 1930; Release from Sexual Tensions, 1960; also articles profl. jours. Editor: Abortion in the U.S., 1958; Manual of Family Planning and Contraceptive Practice, 1964, 2d edit., 1970. Home: 55 Hoagland's Lane Old Brookville Glen Head NY 11545 Office: 1855 Broadway New York City NY 10023

CALDERWOOD, FRANCES NELLE, coll. dean; b. Sterling, Kan., Sept. 27, 1932; d. Robert Orr and Nellie May (Lindsay) Calderwood; B.A., Sterling Coll., 1954; M.R.E., Pitts. Theol. Sem., 1958; postgrad. Presbyn. Sch. Christian Edn., 1962, Calvin Coll., 1971, Regent Coll., 1973. Tchr. English, Hudson (Kan.) High Sch., 1954-56; dir. Christian Edn., Coll. Hill Presbyn. Ch., Dayton, O., 1958-59, First Presbyn. Ch., Hutchinson, Kan., 1959-60; prof. Christian edn. Sterling (Kan.) Coll., 1960—, dean women, 1972-74. Bd. dirs. Rice County Community Concert Assn. Mem. Am. Assn. U. Women (pres. local br. 1971-73), Nat. Assn. Women Deans and Counselors, Am. Assn. U. Profs., Delta Kappa Gamma. Presbyn. (elder 1969). Home: 409 N Pine Rd Sterling KS 67579

CALDWELL, ARLINE CLAIRE (MRS. EDWARD LOWELL PINNEY, JR.), physician; b. Princeton, N.J., Jan. 31, 1924; d. Leslie Godfrey and Arline (Graham) Caldwell; A.B., Coll. of Wooster, 1945; M.D., U. Mich., 1949; m. Dr. Edward Lowell Pinney, Jr., Aug. 2, 1957; children—David, Diane, Michael. Rotating intern Met. Hosp., N.Y.C., 1949-50, resident in dermatology, 1950-51; resident psychiatry Bronx VA Hosp., 1951-52, Hillside Hosp., 1952-53, Manhattan State Hosp., 1953-54; practice medicine specializing in psychiatry, N.Y.C., 1954—; tng. N.Y. Psychoanalytic Inst., 1956-59; attending physician, adolescent therapy Roosevelt Hosp., N.Y.C.; asst. in clin. psychiatry Columbia, 1973—. Diplomate Am. Bd. Psychiatry and Neurology. Mem. A.M.A., N.Y. County Med. Soc., Am. Psychiat. Assn., N.Y. Soc. for Clin. Psychiatrists, Psychiat. Inst. Alumni Assn., Assn. Psychoanalytic Physicians, Hillside Hosp. Alumni Assn. (v.p. 1955-59), A.A.A.S. Address: 148 E 78th St New York City NY 10021

CALDWELL, CHARLEEN CLAIRE, univ. counselor; b. Oklahoma City; d. Charles Luther and Ethleen (Doyle) Caldwell; B.S. in Edn., U. Okla. at Norman, 1953, M.S., 1955, postgrad., 1971—. Dir. union activities U. Okla., Norman, 1954-60; tchr. elementary sch., San Leandro, Cal., 1960-61; program and counseling dir. U. Ill. Med. Center at Chgo., 1961-68, admissions counselor, 1969-71; program devel. dir. YWCA Met. Chgo., 1968-69. Vol. program coordinator Erie Neighborhood House, Chgo., 1962-65. Named One of Outstanding Young Women of Am., 1967. Mem. Nat. Assn. Deans and Counselors, Assn. Personnel Guidance Counselors, Nat. Assn. Student Personnel Adminstrs., Ill. Personnel and Guidance Assn., Assn. Coll. Unions-Internat. (profl. devel. com. 1967-68), Chgo. Assn. Student Personnel Adminstrs., Chgo. Council Fgn. Relations, Ill. Assn. Women's Deans and Counselors, Am. Assn. U. Women, League Women Voters. Presbyn. (exec. council Northminster fellowship 1963-64). Clubs: Canyon, University Women's. Home: 825 Oakbrook Dr Norman OK 73069

CALDWELL, DOROTHY JOHNSON (MRS. JOSEPH C. CALDWELL), curator; b. Pawnee, Okla.; d. Ralph Waldo and Lula Alice (Bailey) Johnson; B.S., N.E. Mo. State Tchrs. Coll., 1926; B.F.A., U. Mo., 1930, B.J., 1949, M.A., 1954; m. Joseph C. Caldwell, Dec. 23, 1950; children—Sara (Mrs. William E. Rau), Helen (Mrs. James T. Seabaugh), Mary (Mrs. Donald Webb). Grad. asst. U. Mo. Sch. Journalism, Columbia, 1948-49; dir. Christian Rural Overseas Program, 1950-51; free lance writer, 1951-53; research asso. State Hist. Soc. Mo., Columbia, 1954-57, dir. state hist. sites survey, 1957-62; asso. editor Mo. Hist. Rev., Columbia, 1963-72; curator Friends of Rocheport (Mo.) Mus., 1972—. Chmn. Rocheport Planning and Zoning Commn., 1974-75. Mem. Women in Communications (pres. 1961-62), Mo. Writers Guild (pres. 1965-66), Mo. Press Women (1st Pl. awards 1957, 63), Mu Phi Epsilon. Author: Missouri Historic Sites Catalogue, 1963. Contbr. articles to trade jours. Home: 2d and Lewic Sts Rocheport MO 65279 Office: 111 Moniteau St Rocheport MO 65279

CALDWELL, ESEDRA EDA, real estate broker; b. Florence, Italy, June 24, 1921; d. Alvaro and Margherita (Pistelli) Gambassi; came to U.S., 1947, naturalized, 1949; student City Coll. San Francisco, 1958; m. Howard S. Caldwell, Aug. 25, 1946 (div. Oct. 1962); children—Sandra (Mrs. Thomas Dawson), Oliver. Salesman real estate George Alvers Real Estate Co., San Francisco, 1950; with West Coast Properties, 1958; salesman Sins & Goodwin Co., San Francisco, 1961-63; real estate broker, 1969—; with E. Caldwell Realtor, 1965-68, Davis Realty, 1970-72, Care Realty, 1971, Golden State Realty, 1972-74. Mem. San Francisco Real Estate Bd., 1958—. Mem. Nat. Assn. Realtors. Democrat. Home: 354 Douglass St San Francisco CA 94114 Office: 207 Clement St San Francisco CA 94118

CALDWELL, FRANCES THORNBURG (MRS. ALFRED BAKER CALDWELL II), librarian; b. Detroit; d. James Harvey and Della (Drummond) Thornburg; B.A., Wayne State U., 1938, M.Ed., 1964; m. Alfred Baker Caldwell II, Dec. 19, 1944 (dec. Dec. 1968); children—Alfred Baker III, Harvey Thornburg, Charles Husband. Vice pres. Alfred B. Caldwell, Inc., Detroit, 1944-69; archivist Wayne State U. Library Sci. Alumni, 1970-71, mem. book selection com. Detroit pub. schs., 1966, 70, 71. Treas., sec. Bushnell Child Study Club Nursery Sch., 1953-54; mem. Olivet Coll. Com., 1972-74. Recipient Kiwanis Internat. Service to Youth award, 1970. Mem. A.L.A., Am. Assn. Sch. Libraries, Am., Detroit fedns. tchrs., Wayne State U., Coll. Edn. Wayne State U. Library Sci. (dir. 1973—) alumni assns., Sigma Kappa. Republican. Conglist. (mem. library, social action com., pub. relations exec.). Clubs: Bushnell Child Study Club (life; pres. 1958-59, 1st v.p. 1957-58, chmn. library com. 1965-66), Detroit Athletic. Home: 16700 Shaftsbury Rd Detroit MI 48219

CALDWELL, JEAN ARLENE MESSECAR (MRS. ROBERT EARL CALDWELL), lawyer; b. Owosso, Mich., July 20, 1927; d. Forest Earl and Myrtle Jane (Kissane) Messecar; A.B., Alma Coll., 1949; postgrad. U. Detroit, 1950-52; J.D., U. Tulsa, 1953; m. Robert Earl Caldwell, Nov. 12, 1953; children—Catherine, Kevin, David, Ann, Mary Kay, Matthew. Admitted to Okla. bar, 1953; practiced in Tulsa, 1953—; asso. W.E. Green, Atty., Tulsa, 1953; mem. firm Green & Feldman, Tulsa, 1953-54; asst. county atty., Tulsa County, Okla., 1954. Supr. Madalene Pre-Sch., 1966-71. Mem. Okla., Tulsa County, Tulsa County Jr. bar assns., Phi Delta Delta, Phi Alpha Delta, Phi Mu. Republican. Roman Catholic. Club: Women's (Tulsa). Address: 3214 S Louisville Av Tulsa OK 74135

CALDWELL, JEAN GENELLE, educator; b. Parr Shoals, S.C., Oct. 20, 1915; d. Joel Blackwell and Daisy (Culbertson) Caldwell; B.A., Coll. William and Mary, 1935, M.A., 1950; postgrad. Universite de Laval, 1941, 45, Universite de Poitiers, 1947, La. State U., 1959, Alliance Francaise, 1961, Ind. U., summer 1966, Internat. U., Satillo, Mexico. Tchr., French and Latin, Shenandoah County Pub. Schs., Va., 1935-40; supervising tchr. French, Williamsburg, James City Pub. Schs. and Coll. of William and Mary, 1940-63; Fulbright tchr. Brest, France, 1961-62; instr. methods of teaching fgn. langs. Coll. William and Mary, 1962-63; asst. supr. fgn. langs. Va. Dept. Edn., 1963-64; supr. fgn. lang. edn. Del. Dept. Pub. Instrn., Dover, 1964-71; coordinator fgn. langs. Henrico County pub. schs., Highland Springs, Va., 1971—. Former mem. bd. Delaware/Panama Partners of Alliance under Alliance for Progress, also past pres.; del. Inter-am. Partners of the Alliance, Lima, Peru, Salt Lake City Costa Rica. Recipient French Cultural Agy. award, Fulbright teaching scholar, 1961. Mem. Nat., Va. edn. assns., Am. Council on Teaching Fgn. Langs., Am. Assn. Tchrs. French, Va. Classical Assn., Va. Modern Language Assn., Nat. Council State Suprs. of Fgn. Langs., Am. Assn. U. Women, Delta Kappa Gamma (past pres.), Kappa Delta Pi. Contbr. articles to profl. jours. Home: 124 Matoaka Ct Williamsburg VA 23185 Office: Henrico Edn Dept Highland Springs VA 23075

CALDWELL, JESSIE CROMBIE BROWN (MRS. ROBERT PAUL CALDWELL), govt. ofcl.; b. Philpstoun, Scotland, Mar. 30, 1917; d. George Gardner and Mary Wilson (Crombie) Brown; grad. high sch.; m. Robert Paul Caldwell, June 27, 1936 (dec. 1971); children—Robert Bruce, Ronald George. Came to U.S., 1923, naturalized, 1928. With Air Force Insp. and Safety Center, Directorate Data Automation, Norton AFB, Cal., 1951—, tabulating machine operator, 1951-53, sect. supr., 1953-55, shift supr., 1955-58, br. supr. data automation, 1958-63, data analyst, 1963-68, chief flight records mgmt., 1968—. Recipient Superior Performance award Air Force Logistics Command, 1962; Superior Performance award Safety Center, 1967, Outstanding Performance award, 1970. Mem. Am. Bus. Women's Assn. (chpt. pres. 1971-72), Federally Employed Women (v.p. 1973-74). Mem. Order Eastern Star. Club: Emblem (San Bernardino, Cal.). Home: 5784 Elmwood Rd San Bernardino CA 92404 Office: Air Force Insp and Safety Center Norton AFB CA 92409

CALDWELL, JUDITH ANN, educator; b. Birmingham, Ala., June 20, 1946; d. Arnold Eugene and Wynelle (Gunnells) Caldwell; B.A., U. Ala., 1968; M.Ed., U. Ark., 1970. Field sec. Phi Mu frat., Memphis, 1968-69; instr. English, Keystone Jr. Coll., LaPlume, Pa., 1970-71, asst. dean for residence halls, 1971-72, asst. dean students, 1972—. Music dir. Tunkhannock (Pa.) Community Theater, 1969-70; accompanist Scranton (Pa.) Catholic Choral Club, 1971—. Mem. Nat. Assn. Women Deans, Adminstrs. and Counselors, Am. Assn. U. Profs., Scranton Jr. League, Phi Mu (nat. standards chmn. 1970-72). Address: Keystone Jr Coll LaPlume PA 18440

CALDWELL, LEONA IOLA WILL (MRS. OLIVER CROMWELL CALDWELL), clergyman; b. Sabina, O., Apr. 13, 1903; d. Silas Joseph and Luella Marie (Reed) Will; B.S., Ohio State U., 1925; M.A., Columbia, 1933; D.H.L., Capitol Coll., 1965; m. Oliver Cromwell Caldwell, June 20, 1938. Ordained to ministry Methodist Ch., 1954; lectr. Swarthmore (Pa.) Chautauqua, 1925-29; tchr. speech Sabina High Sch., 1930-34; minister, Franklin Square (O.) Meth. Ch., 1957-58; minister, Leetonia, O., 1959—; spiritual dir. Hospitality House, Tampa, Fla., 1959-61. County v.p. A.R.C., Lisbon, O., 1940-44; vol. St. Stephens (Wyo.) Indian Sch., Wind River Indian Reservation, 1972—. Bd. dirs. County Health, Lisbon, 1943-47. Mem. Internat. Platform Assn. (life; bd. govs. 1950-65, 68-69), Am. Assn. Women Ministers, Nat. League Am. Pen Women (pres. br., state chaplain), Internat. Poetry Assn., Am. Poetry League, London Poetry Soc., Versewriters Guild Ohio, Epsilon Sigma Alpha. Methodist. Mem. Order Eastern Star. Address: 11 Terrace Gardens Lakeland FL 33801

CALDWELL, LOIS WILLIAMSON, psychologist; b. Denver, May 7, 1920; d. Glenn Foster and Maud Edna (Williams) Williamson; A.B., Colo. State Coll. Edn., 1941; M.B.A., U. Denver, 1949, M.A., 1952; postgrad. U. Minn., 1952-54, Fresno State Coll., 1964-69, U. Cal. at Santa Barbara, 1968-71, U. Denver, 1974; m. Cleon Carthue Caldwell, Dec. 26, 1953 (div. Oct. 1971); 1 dau., Susan Lenore. Elementary tchr. Denver pub. schs., 1941-43; head residence counselor U. Minn., Mpls., 1952-54; sch. psychologist Kern County Schs., Bakersfield, Cal., 1966—. Bd. dirs. YWCA, Lewiston, Ida., 1958-63. Served to capt. WAC, 1943-47. Mem. Nat. Assn. Sch. Psychologists (charter mem.), Cal., Kern County assns. sch. psychologists and psychometrists, Cal. Assn. Women Adminstrs. and Counselors, Am. Psychol. Assn. (asso.), Cal. Tchrs. Assn., Alpha Delta Kappa. Home: 4731A Columbus St Bakersfield CA 93306 Office: 1600 26th St Bakersfield CA 93301

CALDWELL, NORMA LEE DARBY (MRS. CHARLES THEDREN CALDWELL), city ofcl.; b. St. Louis, Mar. 12, 1930; d. Roy Samuel and Ethel Viola (Dains) Darby; certificate in accounting Sanford-Brown Coll., 1947-48; m. Charles Thedren Caldwell, Oct. 6, 1951; children—David Charles, Richard Darby, Linda Lee. Advt. mgr. C.C. Spink & Son, St. Louis, 1949-51; city clk. City of Hazelwood (Mo.), 1970—. Leader, cons. Girl Scouts U.S.A., 1966—; sec.-treas. council Hazelwood P.T.A., 1970-72. Mem. Mo. (dir. 1972-74), Met. St. Louis (sec.-treas. 1972-73) clks. and finance officers assns. Mem. United Ch. of Christ (chmn. Christian edn. 1968—).

Club: Soroptimist (charter pres. 1973). Home: 2150 Collier Dr Florissant MO 63031 Office: 9150 Pershall Hazelwood MO 63042

CALDWELL, PATRICIA ANNE, respiratory technologist; b. Halifax, N.S., Can., Oct. 21, 1950; d. Glen Russell and Mary Cora (MacRae) Caldwell; grad. Sch. Respiratory Tech., Victoria Gen. Hosp. (Can.), 1971. Staff respiratory technologist Victoria Gen. Hosp., Halifax, N.S., 1971-72; asst. supr. respiratory tech. dept. St. Martha's Hosp., Antigonish, N.S., 1972—. Recipient Mead Johnson award N.S. div. Nat. Respiratory Tech. Soc., 1971. Roman Catholic. Office: St Martha's Hosp Bay St Antigonish NS B0H 1B0 Canada

CALDWELL, RUTH (MRS. HUBERT A. CALDWELL), civic worker; b. Ely, Nev., Apr. 12, 1909; d. Henry Clay and Estelle (Davis) Herrick; A.B., U. Cal. at Berkeley, 1930, gen. secondary tchrs. certificate, 1931; m. Hubert A. Caldwell, Aug. 5, 1933; 1 dau., Ruth Anne (Mrs. Bert Geary). Tchr. pub. schs., Oakland, Cal., 1941-69; trustee Oakland Pub. Library and Museums, 1957-63, commr., 1963—, chmn. library commn., 1964-66, 68-69. Mem. Oakland Jr. League, Children's Foster Care Services, Cal. Atty. Gen.'s Vol. Adv. Council; women's bd. Oakland Mus. Assn., Oakland Community Betterment and Cultural Com., Mayors Cultural Affairs Com., 1957-60. Mem. Am. Library Trustees Assn. (Cal. membership chmn. 1959-61; nat. membership chmn. 1959-61, speakers bur. 1963—, exhibits chmn. 1963; chmn. legislative com. 1969-71, chmn., 1968-69), Cal. Library Assn. (legislative com. 1967—), Cal. League Cities (library adv. com.), Delta Kappa Gamma, Alpha Omicron Pi. Republican. Home: 23 Greenbank Av Piedmont CA 94611 Office: care Oakland Pub Library Oakland CA 94611

CALDWELL, SARAH, opera producer, condr.; b. Maryville, Mo.; student violin New Eng. Conservatory. Mem. faculty Tanglewood (Mass.) Sch. Music; created dept. music theatre at Boston U. and conducted Am. premiere of Hindemith's Mathis der Maler; founder, artist dir. Opera Co. of Boston which has produced 45 operas including Schoenberg's Moses and Aaron, 1966, Stravinsky's Rakes Progress, 1967; organized Am. Nat. Opera touring co., 1967, presenting Falstaff, Tosca and Berg's Lulu in San Francisco, Chgo., Dallas and N.Y.C. Address: 46 Fenway Boston MA 02215

CALHOON, WANDA COOKE (MRS. G. WILSON CALHOON), ednl. adminstr.; b. Norfolk, Va., Jan. 22, 1921; d. George Harris and Frances Marguerite (Williams) Cooke; B.A., William and Mary Coll., 1942; M.A. in Elementary Edn., State U. N.Y. at Brockport, 1965; postgrad. U. N.C., 1966-74; m. George W. Arend, Jan. 25, 1946 (div. Sept. 1965); children—Wanda C. (Mrs. Glenn I. Lazzar), Georgia Ann; m. 2d, G. Wilson Calhoon, Nov. 15, 1965. Tchr. elementary schs., Webster Central Schs., Webster, N.Y., 1963-65, Rochester (N.Y.) city schs., 1963-65, Irondequoit Central Schs., Rochester, 1963-65; asst. to registrar Rochester Meml. Art Gallery, 1965, asst. to curator, William Hayes Ackland Meml. Art Center U. N.C. at Chapel Hill, 1966—, registrar, 1966—. Mem. Southeastern Museums Conf., 1968-74. Mem. Steering Com., Univ. Women for Affirmative Action, U. N.C., 1973—; Girl Scout leader, Webster, N.Y., 1955-62; class agt. William and Mary Fund, Williamsburg, Va., 1973. Mem. Coll. Art Assn., Am. Assn. Museums, Am. Assn. U. Women (fellowship chmn. 1971). Republican. Mem. United Ch. of Christ (bd. deacons 1956-59, trustee 1960-63). Club: Chapel Hill Bird. Home: 712 Williams Circle Chapel Hill NC 27514 Office: William Hayes Ackland Art Center Univ North Carolina Chapel Hill NC 27514

CALHOUN, EDITH AUGUSTINE, educator; b. Augusta, Ga., Aug. 9, 1935; d. Robert Clinton and Virginia Carolyn (Latimer) Calhoun; B.A., Talladega Coll., 1955; M.S.W., Adelphi Coll., 1957. Psychiat. social worker Kings County Hosp., N.Y.C., 1957-59; instr. N.Y. Med. Coll., 1961-64; research scientist N.Y. U., N.Y.C., 1964—. Cons. ednl. programs and instns. U.S. Bd. dirs. Billy Martin Child Devel. Center, Bklyn. Home: 365 Clinton Av Brooklyn NY 11238 Office: 239 Greene St New York City NY 10003

CALHOUN, HAZEL RANDOLPH, univ. adminstr.; b. Cin., Oct. 1, 1928; d. Solomon Elbert and Clara Hollins (Griffin) Randolph; B.S., Hampton (Va.) Inst., 1948; M.S.W. (Dean's fellow), Wayne State U., 1960. Caseworker, Family Service of Oakland County, Mich., 1960-62; psychiat. social worker Wayne County Gen. Hosp. and Consultation Center, Eloise, Mich., 1962-65; dir. social services State of Mich., 1965-72; Ombudsperson, U. Mich. at Ann Arbor, 1972—. Tchr., Wayne County Community Coll. Recipient Mayor's award for pub. service, Detroit, 1967, Nat. Inst. for Mental Health grantee, 1958. Mem. Chums, Inc. (co-founder Detroit chpt.), Am. Assn. Marriage Counselors, Nat. Assn. Social Workers, Acad. Certified Social Workers, Conf. for Advancement Pvt. Practice, Grace Episcopal Ch. Altar Guild, Delta Sigma Theta. Clubs: Zonta International, Faculty Women's U Mich., University. Home: 1048 Greenhills Dr Ann Arbor MI 48105

CALHOUN, JOANNE PRINDLE (MRS. JOSEPH WILLIAM CALHOUN), psychologist; b. Honolulu, Feb. 26, 1931; d. Hoyt Leroy and Christine Montieth (Beatty) Prindle; B.A., U. Neb., 1967; Ph.D., U. N.M., 1971; m. Joseph William Calhoun, June 4, 1950; children—Christine, Colleen, Cathleen, Joseph William. Research asso. Albuquerque pub. schs., 1969-71; psychologist Child Guidance Clinic, Def. Dept. Schs., Clark Air Base, P.I., 1971—. Nat. Inst. Mental Health grantee, 1967-71. Mem. Am. Psychol. Assn., Overseas Ednl. Assn., Psi Chi. Episcopalian. Home: PSC 1 Box 398 APO San Francisco CA 96286 Office: Child Guidance Clinic DOD Schools APO San Francisco CA 96274

CALHOUN, LILLIAN SCOTT (MRS. HAROLD WILLIAM CALHOUN), editor; b. Savannah, Ga.; d. Walter Sanford and Laura (McDowell) Scott; B.A., Ohio State U., 1944; m. Harold William Calhoun, Sept. 20, 1950; children—Laura, Harold, Walter, Karen. N.Y. corr. Chgo. Defender newspapers, 1945-50; asso. editor Jet mag., Chgo., 1961, Ebony, Chgo., 1961-63; feature editor, columnist Chgo. Daily Defender, 1963-65; reporter, feature writer Chgo. Sun-Times, 1965-68; mng. editor Integrated Edn., Chgo., 1968-71; pub. information officer, region V Dept Labor, Chgo., 1971-73, acting regional information dir., 1972-73; co-editor Chgo. Reporter, 1973—. Columnist Chgo. Journalism Rev., 1969-74; moderator Black Forum, radio interview program, WLS, 1969-74. Mem. Ill. Commn. on Human Relations, 1973. Bd. dirs. Hyde Park Coop. Soc., 1962-64, Erikson Inst. for Early Edn., 1972—. Recipient 2d prize, feature writing Ill. A.P. Competition, 1967, 68. Mem. Soc. Midland Authors, Am. Civil Liberties Union (dir. Ill. div. 1968-71), Chgo. Urban League (dir. woman's bd. 1964-68). Clubs: Chicago Press, Publicity (Chgo.). Home: 601 Melrose Av Kenilworth IL 60043 Office: 111 N Wabash Av Chicago IL 60602

CALHOUN, RITA LORIE CONNER (MRS. LLOYD D. MILLS), career counselor; b. Sheridan, Ore., May 31, 1900; d. George W. and Zina (Syron) Conner; B.S., Sch. Home Econs., Ore. State U., 1923; m. Lewis Calhoun, Jan. 19, 1929 (dec. 1938); 1 dau., Nancy (Mrs. David Fisher); m. 2d, Lloyd D. Mills, Aug. 14, 1954. Lunchroom mgr. Boise (Ida.) YWCA, 1923-25; mem. home service staff Portland (Ore.) Gas & Coke Co., 1926-28, home service dir., 1938-58; home service staff Mont. Power Co. Gas div., 1931-32; sr. home economist Mary Cullens Cottage, Ore. Jour., Portland, 1933-38; partner Gen. Ins. Agy., Portland, 1958-72; vol. career counselor Portland High Sch. Active Waif adoption div. Internat. Social Service, 1960—. Mem. Am. Home Econs. Assn., Ore. Home Econs. Assn. (named Home Economist of Achievement 1958), Portland Home Economists in Bus. (past chmn.), Ore. Hist. Soc., Sons and Daus. of Ore. Pioneers, World Affairs Council Ore., Altrusa Internat. (past pres. Portland, chmn. internat. relations com.), Original Portland Woman's Forum (Woman of Distinction 1963), Theta Sigma Phi (Woman of Achievement 1957). Home: 7150 SW 8th Av Portland OR 97219

CALHOUN, SCOTIA ETTA THOMAS (MRS. GEORGE CALHOUN), sch. psychologist; b. Meridian, Miss., Nov. 11, 1909; d. Simon and Mary Lou (Fielder) Thomas; student Ill. U., 1946-47, St. Louis U., 1947-55; B.A., So. Ill. U., 1963, M.S., 1965; m. George Calhoun, Dec. 29, 1934. Owner, mgr. Scotia's Sch. Beauty Culture, East St. Louis, Ill., 1936—, Scotia's Fine Food Shops, East St. Louis, 1946—; sch. psychologist Sch. Dist. 189, East St. Louis, 1969—. Mem. pupil personnel services adv. bd., office of supt. pub. instrn. State of Ill., 1973—. Recipient Woman of Yr. award Pro-Eight Social Civic Club, East St. Louis, 1960, Outstanding Bus. Woman award Alpha Upsilon Sigma chpt. Sigma Gamma Rho, 1973, 74. Mem. N.A.A.C.P. (local pres. 1957), C. of C. (mem. park com. 1966-68, mem. jr. coll. feasibility com. 1967), Sigma Gamma Rho. Home: 7701 Lake Dr East St Louis IL 62203 Office: 10th and Gaty Sts East St Louis IL 62201

CALHOUN, WANDA JUNE, librarian; b. Mayfield, Ky., Jan. 23, 1932; d. Thomas Lewis and Lucile Elizabeth (Hamlet) Calhoun; B.S., Murray State U., 1953; M.A. in Library Sci., U. Mich., 1955. Div. librarian U. Mich., Ann Arbor, 1955-58; head librarian Heidelberg Coll., Tiffin, O., 1958-63, Eckerd Coll., St. Petersburg, Fla., 1963—. Vis. specialist in library sci. United Bd. for Christian Higher Edn. in Asia. Mem. Fla. Library Assn., Am. Assn. U. Women, Am. Assn. U. Profs. Presbyn. Home: 4822 D Coquina Key Dr SE St Petersburg FL 33705 Office: Eckerd College St Petersburg FL 33733

CALIFF, MARILYN ISKIWITZ (MRS. LEON HERMAN CALIFF), artist, designer; b. Memphis, Apr. 27, 1932; d. Leonard and Esther (Walberg) Iskiwitz; student U. Miami (Fla.), 1950-51; B.F.A., Memphis Acad. Arts, 1970; m. Leon Herman Califf, Mar. 8, 1951; children—Randy, Regina. Exhibited one-woman shows at Seabrook's Gallery, Memphis, 1965, Memphis Athletic Club, 1965, Carnegie Pub. Library, Clarksdale, Miss., 1966, The Gallery Upstairs, Nashville, Tenn., 1970, Mid-South Fair and Exposition, Memphis, 1970; exhibited in group shows Brooks Meml. Art Gallery, Memphis, 1962-65, 68-73, Juried Arts Nat. Exhbn., Tyler, Tex., 1962, 66, 2d Nat. Art Competition of B'nai B'rith Women, Washington, 1964, Atlanta Drawing Soc. Exhbn., 1965, Delta Painting Exhbn., Ark. Art Center, Little Rock, 1965-68, 70, Crafts Exhbn., 1970-73, Winston-Salem (N.C.) Gallery Fine Arts, 1965-66, Golden Isles Ann. Art Exhbn., Jekyll Island, Ga., 1965, All Tennesseans Exhbn., Nashville, 1968, 70, Ball State U., Muncie, Ind., 1971, Tenn. Artist-Craftsman's Assn. Crafts Fair, Nashville, 1972, 73, Miss. River Craft Exhbn., Brooks Meml. Art Gallery, Memphis, 1973, Lambuth Coll., Jackson, Tenn., 1972; represented in pub. collections at Brooks Meml. Art Gallery; executed glass mosaic murals at Baron Hirsch Synagogue, Memphis, 1964, Memphis Jewish Community Center, 1968, Memphis Hebrew Acad. Day Sch., 1962. Owner, operator Contemporary Quilts, Memphis, 1971—, Inside Out Pub. Co., Memphis. Vol. for Suicide and Crisis Intervention Service, Memphis, 1970—. Recipient Honorable Mention award B'nai B'rith Women, 1964, First prize in oil painting Brooks Meml. Art Gallery, 1968. Mem. Am. Crafts Council, Tenn. (purchase prize 1973), Memphis artist-craftsman assns., Hadassah. Author: Your First Quilt, 1973. Address: 5305 Denwood Av Memphis TN 38117

CALISHER, HORTENSE, author; b. N.Y.C., Dec. 20, 1911; d. Joseph Henry and Hedvig (Lichtstern) Calisher; A.B., Barnard Coll., 1932; m. Curtis Harnack, Mar. 23, 1959; children by previous marriage—Bennet Hughes, Peter Heffelfinger. Adj. prof. English, Barnard Coll., N.Y.C., 1956-57; prof. Columbia U. Sch. Art, 1968-70; vis. lectr. State U. Ia., 1957, 59-60, Sarah Lawrence Coll., Bronxville, N.Y., 1962, U. Pa.; vis. prof. English, State U. N.Y. at Purchase, 1971-72; adj. prof. Columbia, 1973. Guggenheim fellow, 1952, 55; Dept. of State Am. Specialist's grantee to visit S.E. Asia, 1958. Author: In the Absence of Angels (short stories), 1951; False Entry, 1961; Tale for the Mirror (novella, short stories), 1962; Textures of Life (novel), 1963; Extreme Magic (novella and stories), 1964; Journal from Ellipsia (novel), 1965; The Railway Police and The Last Trolleyride (2 Novellas), 1966; The New Yorkers (novel), 1969; Queenie (novel), 1971; Herself, 1972; Standard Dreaming, 1972; Eagle-Eye (novel), 1973. Contbr. short stories, articles, revs. to N.Y. Times, Harper's Bazaar, Mademoiselle, Reporter, The Nation, The Am. Scholar, Evergreen Rev., Kenyon Rev., Tex. Quar., also anthologies. Recipient award for lit. Nat. Inst. Arts and Letters, 1967; award for lit. Nat. Council Arts, 1967. Mem. P.E.N. Address: care Candida Donadio-Robert Lantz 111 W 57th St New York City NY 10019

CALKINS, (ALPHA) JEAN (MRS. TRACY J. CALKINS), mag. editor; b. Dansville, N.Y., Mar. 12, 1933; d. Roy Oakley and Freda Irene (Burns) Wyant; grad. high sch.; m. Tracy Jay Calkins, Mar. 14, 1951; children—Cheryl, Stephen, Vivian, Yvonne, Debra. Stenographer, F.A. Owen Pub. Co., Dansville, 1950; dental asst., Dansville, 1950-51; various secretarial positions, 1952-60; postal clk. Kanona, N.Y., 1962-67; founder, operator J & C Transcripts, Kanona, 1963—; founder, editor, pub. Jean's Jour., 1963—, Haiku Highlights, 1965-73; pub. various mags. including Haiku West, Orphic Lute, Sunburst, Dragon fly, The Rufus, also prose, poetry and ednl. materials. Mem. United Poetry Soc. Am. (life), Bus. and Profl. Women (woman of year, 1970), Western World Haiku Soc., World Poetry Soc. Intercontinental (liasion mem. 1969), Galley Slaves Ink. Republican. Methodist. Author: (poetry) Dawn of Promise, 1967; (prose) Some People Never Learn, 1974. Address: Box 15 Kanona NY 14856

CALL, HELEN LLOYD, journalist; b. St. Louis, Oct. 2, 1917; d. Allen Henry and Hazel Medora (Collins) Lloyd; B.A. in Journalism, U. Wash., 1941; m. Donald M. Call, Dec. 24, 1940 (div. 1944). Pub. relations writer Boeing Aircraft Co., Seattle, 1941-46; staff editor Better Homes and Gardens mag., Des Moines, 1948-54; interior decorating editor Capper Publs., Topeka, 1954-56; reporter Fresno (Cal.) Bee, 1962-71; staff writer San Diego Union, also syndicated writer Copley News Ser., 1971—. Mem. Women in Communications, Press Women (award 1972, 73), Newspaper Guild, Sigma Delta Chi. Democrat. Roman Catholic. Home: 610 Chalcedony San Diego CA 92109 Office: 350 Camino De La Reina San Diego CA 92112

CALL, MARGARET FLEMING (MRS. ASA V. CALL), civic worker; b. Los Angeles; d. Thomas J. and Ella (Thompson) Fleming; student pub. schs.; m. Asa V. Call, May 23, 1917; children—Thomas Fleming, Richard William, Janet Call (Mrs. William Burby, Jr.). Sponsor, Thomas J. Fleming Poison Information Center Children's Hosp. Vice pres., bd. dirs. Children's Hosp., Los Angeles; bd. dirs. Girls Collegiate, Ely Ct. Sch. for Girls. Recipient Outstanding Achievement award for exceptional service to safety Nat. Safety Council, 1966; Pro Ecelesia medal Pope John XXII. Mem. Town and Gown Soc. U. So. Cal. Home: Beverly Wilshire Apt 10-A 9500 Wilshire Blvd Beverly Hills CA 90212

CALLAHAN, CHERYL MANN (MRS. THOMAS MICHAEL CALLAHAN), educator; b. Greenville, S.C., Mar. 9, 1949; d. Joseph Griffin and Alice (Capell) Mann; B.A. with honors, U. N.C., 1971, M.Ed., 1972; m. Thomas Michael Callahan, July 15, 1972. Counselor, Del. State Coll., Dover, 1972—, also coordinator tutorial program, 1972—. Tchr. human communication workshops U.S. Air Force Dept., 1972—; counselor N.C. Girls State, summers 1971-74. Vol. worker Big Bros./Big Sisters of State of Del., 1973; alumni officer U. N.C., Greensboro, 1971—. Mem. Am. Personnel and Guidance Assn., Am. Coll. Personnel Assn., Nat. Assn. Women Deans, Adminstrs. and Counselors, Nat. Orientation Dirs. Assn. Democrat. Presbyn.

CALLAHAN, DOROTHY LOUISE, ednl. adminstr.; b. Sharon, Mass., Jan. 6, 1920; d. John Philip and Blanche (Morrill) Olson; B.S. in Edn., State Tchrs. Coll., Framingham, Mass., 1941; m. John David Callahan, Apr. 12, 1944; children—John David, Stephen Ambrose, Terence Edward. Am. Dietetic Assn. internship N.Y. Hosp., N.Y.C., 1941-42; clinic dietitian Mass. Gen. Hosp., 1942-43; nutritionist Boston Vis. Nurse Assn., 1943-44; research dietitian Mass. Gen. Hosp., 1948-53, editor diet manual, 1950-54; dir. cafeterias Milton (Mass.) pub. schs., 1953-69; foods tchr., 1960-69, dir. home econs., 1963-69; sch. lunch cons. Mass. Dept. Edn., 1965-69, sr. supr. edn., 1969-71, project dir. nutrition edn., 1971—. Dietary cons. nursing homes. Sec. Mass. Food Service Ednl. Council, 1969-70, v.p., 1970-71, pres., 1971-72; nutrition instr. Civil Def. Agy., Quincy; chmn. Mass. Council on Food, Nutrition and Health, 1972-73. Mem. Am., Mass. home econs. assns., Am., Mass. dietetic assns., Am., Mass. (mem. exec. bd. 1955—, pres. 1961-62) sch. food service assns., Mass. Tchrs. Assn., Club Altrusa (vice pres. Quincy). Author: (with Alma Smith Payne) The Low Sodium Cook Book, 1953, The Great Nutrition Puzzle, 1956. The Low Sodium, Fat-Controlled Cook Book, 1960, revision Young America's Cook Book, The Fat and Sodium Control Cook Book, 1966. Editor: Newsletter, Mass. Sch. Food Service Assn., 1962-65. Home: 97 Standish Av Wollaston MA 02170 Office: State Dept Edn 182 Tremont St Boston MA 02111

CALLAHAN, GERALDINE ANN, librarian; b. Saratoga Springs, N.Y., Sept. 17, 1925; d. Paul Daniel and Genevieve Marie (Crooks) Callahan; A.B., State U. N.Y. at Albany, 1947, M.L.S., 1953; postgrad. U. Colo., summers 1960-61, Temple U., summer 1965. Asst. librarian Metal & Thermit Corp., Rahway, N.J., 1948-49; research librarian Am. Smelting & Refining Co., Barber, N.J., 1949-52; high sch. librarian, Port Jervis, N.Y., 1952-65; sr. bus. librarian Newark Pub. Library, 1965—. Mem. Spl. Libraries Assn. Home: 339 Grafton Av Newark NJ 07104 Office: 34 Commerce St Newark NJ 07102

CALLAHAN, MARGARET THERESA, marketing research co. exec.; b. N.Y.C., May 6, 1929; d. John J. and Nora F. (O'Keefe) Callahan; student N.Y. U., 1964-65, New Sch. Social Research, 1966-67. Tabulating mgr. Stewart Dougall & Assos., N.Y.C., 1950-53; mgr. prodn. and cost estimates Crossley Surveys, Inc., N.Y.C. (merger Stewart Dougall & Assos. and Crossley Surveys, Inc.), 1954-58, estimating and research asso., 1959-63, sr. asso., 1964-68, v.p., 1969—. Mem. Am. Marketing Assn., Advt. Women N.Y. Home: 40 Sutton Pl New York City NY 10022 Office: 909 3d Av New York City NY 10022

CALLAHAN, THELMA, music tchr.; b. Sweetwater, Tenn., Feb. 2, 1908; d. Alvin S. and Ressa E. (Collins) Callahan; student Peabody Conservatory of Music, Balt., Eastman Sch. Music, Sherwood Music Sch., Chgo., N.Y.U.; studied with LaSalle Spier, Austin Conradi, James Friskin, Harold Bauer. Broadcast piano program, Washington radio stas. WRC, WJSV, WOL, WMAL, 1924-36; pvt. piano studio, Washington, 1924—. D.C. chmn., adjudicator Nat. Piano Playing Auditions, 1948—; adjudicator broadcasting cos.; mem. extension faculty Sherwood Music Sch., 1936. Mem. Washington Piano Tchrs. Forum (past pres.), Nat., D.C. (past pres.) fedns. music clubs, Nat. Guild Piano Tchrs., Washington Music Tchrs. Assn., Chevy Chase Citizens Assn. Methodist. Address: 3803 Ihgomar St NW Washington DC 20015

CALLAN, JOANNE ELIZABETH BURKES (MRS. JAMES RUUD CALLAN), psychologist, univ. adminstr.; b. Ft. Smith, Ark., Dec. 23, 1936; d. Hubbert and Virginia Dare (Atkins) Burkes; B.A. (Harriet Rutherford Johnstone scholar, Alumni Devel. Fund scholar, Panhellenic scholar), U. Okla., 1958, M.Ed. in Counseling, 1962; Ph.D. (Okla. Med. Research Found. fellow, Hogg Found. fellow), U. Tex., 1970; m. James Ruud Callan, Sept. 8, 1968; 1 dau., Megan Elizabeth. Tchr. dancing Casady Schs., Oklahoma City, 1960-62; gen. counselor, coordinator student activities U. Okla., Norman, 1962-63, 64-65, tng. coordinator, multipurpose tng. center, Austin, Tex., 1967-68, chief psychologist inpatient unit Univ. Hosp., Oklahoma City, 1970-73, dir., 1972, chief psychologist, dir. clin. psychology tng. dept. psychiatry Univ. Hosp. and Health Scis. Center, 1973—, asst. prof. med. psychology, 1970—; counselor Kaiserlautern, (Germany) Am. High Sch., Germany, 1963-64; dir. community action program S.W. Okla. Community Action Group, Inc., Altus, Okla., 1965-66. Cons. to FAA, VA, Okla. Coll. Continuing Edn., U. Tex. Leadership Bd.; sec. Okla. Bd. Examiners in Psychology, 1972—. Bd. dirs. Okla. Family Growth Center. Nat. Inst. Mental Health grantee, 1973-74. Mem. Am., Southwestern, Okla. psychol. assns., Am. (inst. com.), S.W. (research chmn.) group psychotherapy assn., Phi Kappa Phi, Kappa Delta Pi, Psi Chi, Pi Beta Phi. Episcopalian. Contbr. articles to profl. jours. Home: 615 NW 38th St Oklahoma City OK 73118 Office: PO Box 26901 Oklahoma City OK 73190

CALLAN, KATHLEEN MARIE CALLANAN, city ofcl.; b. Buffalo, May 29, 1913; d. Michael Aloysius and Elizabeth Antonio (Harrington) Callanan; student Mercyhurst Coll., Erie, Pa., 1932-34, U. Detroit, 1934-36; municipal clk. certificate Syracuse U., 1970; m. Thomas J. Callan, Dec. 16, 1939 (dec. Aug. 1973); children—Thomas J., John P., Diane (Mrs. Timothy Fekete). Librarian, Zimmer-Keller Co., 1936-39; sec. to pres. Gorman & Thomas, 1940-44; free-lance fashion coordinator and commentator, 1944-56; city clk. City of Oak Park (Mich.), 1962—. Cons. Thomas J. Callan Assos., 1959-73. Mem. Internat. Inst. Municipal Clks. (vice chmn. edn. com.), Municipal Clks. Assn. Mich. (pres.), Mich. Municipal League (chmn. elections com.), U. Detroit Alumnae Assn. (past pres.), Internat. Fedn. Cath. Alumnae (past gov.), League Catholic Women. Office: 13600 Oak Park Blvd Oak Park MI 48237

CALLAS, MARIA, soprano; b. N.Y.C., Dec. 2, 1923; d. George and Evangelia (Demitriadu) Callas; ed. pub. schs., N.Y.C., and Conservatoire d'Athene et National. Dramatic coloratura soprano in operas at La Scala, Milan, Italy, Met., N.Y.C., Covent Garden, London, Eng., State Opera House of Vienna, Austria, Opera House of Paris, France; appeared in operas at Lyric Theatre, Chgo., 1954, 55, Dallas Opera, 1957-59; also Amphitheatres of Verona Epidaures, Acropolis, Athens, Greece, Buenos Aires and Rio De Janeiro opera houses; starred in film Medea, 1969; concert tour, U.S. and Europe, 1973—; tchr. master classes Juilliard Sch. Music, N.Y.C. Made hon. citizen Mexico; recipient numerous medals, including commendatore of Italy. Address: 36 Av George Mandel Paris France

CALLAWAY, RHEA EVA HALL (MRS. ROBERT L. GLENN), journalist; b. Thomson, Ga., July 14, 1919; d. Nathan and Eva Jennie (Hawes) Hall; pvt. studies in music, 1928-39; student Coll. City N.Y., 1941-44, Pohs Inst., 1958-59; certificate pub. relations and journalism New Sch. Social Research, 1960, George Washington U.; m. Robert L. Glenn, Mar. 20, 1971; 1 dau., Sharon (Mrs. James (McCall). Owner, Miss R. Hall, N.Y.C., 1937-46; with Peerless Advt. Corp., N.Y.C., 1946-51; women's editor N.Y. Age, N.Y.C., 1958-59, ch. editor, 1973—; women's editor N.Y. Citizen Call, N.Y.C., 1960-61; with N.Y. Amsterdam News, N.Y.C., Bklyn., 1963-73. Dir. pub. relations Mt. Morris Park Hosp., N.Y.C., 1959-60; cons. pub. relations Camp Minisink, N.Y.C., 1957-63. Mem. adv. council Medgar Evers Coll., Bklyn.; mem. adv. bd. Harlem Inst. Fashion, N.Y.C. Exec. dir. Glendale Women's Guild, N.Y.C., 1971—, Recipient various honors, citations. Mem. Nat. Assn. Media Women, Nat. Council Negro Women (pres. Manhattan sect. 1968-70), Nat. Assn. Negro Bus. and Profl. Women (chmn. pub. relations 1957-60), Internat. Platform Assn., Nat. Assn. Media Women (founder 1965, pres. 1965-67), Iota Phi Lambda (chpt. pres.), Lambda Kappa Mu. Baptist (trustee). Mng. editor Women's Interfaith Reporter, 1973—. Home: 10 W 135th St New York City NY 10037

CALLERY, MARY, sculptor; b. N.Y.C., June 19, 1903; d. James Dawson and Julia (Welch) Callery; student Art students League, 1924-28; m. Frederic R. Coudert, Jr., June 1923; 1 dau., Caroline C. (Mrs. Don Porter) (dec.); m. 2d, Carlo Frua de Angeli, May 7, 1934. One-man shows Curt Valentin Gallery, 1944, 47, 50, 55, Arts Club, Chgo., 1945, Galerie Mai, Paris, 1949, Margaret Brown Gallery, 1951, Galerie Cahiers d'Art, Paris, 1954; exhbn. Knoedler & Co., 1957, 61, 62; commns. Laughlin Children's Center, Sewickley, Pa., Internat. Expn., Brussels, 1958; pub. commn. include 3 hanging birds aluminum co., Pitts.; also portrait heads Mellon Bank, Pitts.; also grille in pub. sch., N.Y.C.; work represented in Mus. Modern Art, Mus. Fine Arts of Toledo, Mus. Fine Arts of Cin., Mus. Fine Arts of San Francisco, Addison Gallery (Andover), Atheneum (Hartford), Mus. of Fine Arts (Richmond, Va.), Lincoln Center Opera, Exxon Bldg., N.Y.C., also numerous pvt. collections. Address: 168 E 68th St New York City NY 10021

CALLIS, BENNIE GREYE LEWIS, real estate broker; b. Samson, Ala., July 17, 1917; d. Benjamin Jefferson and Mary Coleman (Jordan) Lewis; A.B., U. S.C., 1936; secondary edn. certificate Coll. William and Mary, 1952; postgrad. U. Va., 1962, U. Fla., 1973; m. Gerald Powell Callis, Apr. 21, 1948 (dec.); 1 son, Gerald Powell. Various positions, 1938-52; agt. Callis Ins. Agy., Surry, Va., 1952-61, owner, 1961-64; real estate investor, 1965-68; condominium specialist, Key Biscayne, Fla., 1968-73; real estate broker, Coral Gables, Fla., 1974—. Chmn., Surry County Jr. Red Cross, 1952-56; publicity chmn. Surry County chpt. A.R.C., 1952-61, fund drive chmn., 1962; chmn. Surry County chpt. March of Dimes, 1959-64, Surry County Heart Fund, 1961-64. Mem. Nat., Va. edn. assns., Sigma Kappa. Democrat. Baptist. Clubs: Surry Cotillion, Key Biscayne Yacht, Coral Gables Woman's, Gableites. Home: 2523 Alhambra Circle Coral Gables FL 33134

CALLISON, CAROLINE HOLLINGSWORTH, physician; b. Charleston, S.C., Aug. 20, 1914; d. Henry Grady and Ethel Lorraine (Jagar) Callison; B.S., Coker Coll., 1936; M.D., Med. Coll. S.C., 1939; M.P.H., Columbia, 1947. Intern Crawford W. Long Meml. Hosp., 1939-41; health officer Washington, Coosa, Clarke, St. Clair counties, Ala., 1941-45, McCormick and Greenwood counties, S.C., 1945-46; asst. health officer Charleston County, S.C., 1947-48; county health officer Marlboro, Chesterfield, Abbeville, McCormick counties, S.C., 1948-52; Md. dept. health officer Queen Anne's County, Md., 1952-61; health dir. Sampson and Bladen counties, N.C., 1961—. Mem. Am. Coll. Preventive Medicine, Am. Assn. Pub. Health Physicians, N.C. Med. Assn., A.M.A., Am., N.C. pub. health assns., Sampson County Med. Soc. Episcopalian. Home: 406 Parker Dr Clinton NC 28328 Office: County Health Dept Clinton NC 28328

CALLOMON, JANE LEE (MRS. LEON ANTHONY ARKUS), advt. exec.; b. Pitts., Mar. 29, 1929; d. Verner B. and Florence (Schoenthal) Callomon; B.A., Vassar Coll., 1950; m. Leon Anthony Arkus, Dec. 19, 1971. Copywriter, Lando-Bishopric Inc., Pitts., 1951-53, dir. radio and TV, 1953-59, sr. v.p., creative dir., 1959—. Dir. Pitts. Playhouse, 1957-67, sec., 1964-66; dir. Women's Assn. Pitts. Symphony Soc., 1956—, Pitts. Plan for Art, 1965-69, Pitts. Council for Internat. Vistors, 1967-70, women's com. Mus. Art, Carnegie Inst., Pitts., 1969—. Named Advt. Woman of Year, Pitts. Advt. Club, 1966; awards for radio commls. in Hollywood Internat. Broadcasting competition, 1961, 63; comml. writing awards Brewer's Assn. of Am. ann. competition, 1963, 65, 68, 69; Clio award TV comml. Am. TV Festival, 1969. Mem. Women in Communications. Clubs: Pittsburgh Vassar, Pitts. Advertising. Home: 420 Coventry Rd Pittsburgh PA 15213 Office: US Steel Bldg Pittsburgh PA 15219

CALLON, RUTH ANN DOUB (MRS. GEORGE F. CALLON), educator; b. Greenwood, Ind., May 29, 1930; d. Harry W. and Martha (Bagby) Doub; B.A., Franklin Coll. of Ind., 1952; M.S. in Edn., Butler U., 1956; postgrad. Ind. U., 1966-70; m. George F. Callon, June 14, 1953; children—George Daniel, Catherine Anne. Tchr. math., phys. edn. Whiteland (Ind.) High Sch., 1952-55; home bound tchr. Whiteland Sch. System, 1956-62; mem. faculty Franklin Coll. of Ind., 1962—, asso. prof. phys. edn., 1966—, chmn. women's phys. edn. dept., 1970—. Chmn. Ind. div. Girls and Women's Sports, 1971-73; commr. Ind. Women's Intercollegiate Sports Orgn., 1973-75, sec. commrs., 1973-74. Asst. dir. Girl's Club, Franklin, Ind., 1950-52; leader, trainer Girl Scouts U.S.A., Whiteland, Ind., 1956-61; parliamentarian P.T.A., Whiteland, 1967—. Bd. dirs. Johnson County Assn. Retarded Citizens, 1973—; mem. alumni council Franklin Coll., 1973—. Mem. Am., Ind. (vice-chmn. S.E. dist.), Midwest (chmn. girls and womens sports sect. 1975) assns. health, phys. edn. and recreation, Nat. Assn. Phys. Educators of Coll. Women, Ind. High Sch. Athletic Assn. (mem. adv. bd.), Delta Zeta (named to Hall of Fame 1969). Mem. Christian Ch. (supt., tchr. jr. dept., 1956—). Home: Rural Route 1 Whiteland IN 46184

CALLOWAY, ANNA BELLE DANTZLER, mental health adminstr.; b. Carbon Hill, Ala., June 8, 1920; d. Henry L. and Willie M. (Foster) Dantzler; B.A., Livingstone Coll., Wilberforce U., 1947; M.S.W., U. Pitts., 1958; m. Jerome Thomas Calloway, June 28, 1952 (div. 1969); children—David Thomas, Barbara Anne. Co-owner, mgr. Tip Top Inn, 1951-55; caseworker to psychiat. social worker Torrance (Pa.) State Hosp., 1955-60; dir. extension office Somerset State Hosp., Uniontown, Pa., 1960-69, dir. social service dept., 1965-69; clinic adminstr. Fayette County Mental Health Mental Retardation Clinic, Uniontown, 1970—; Dir. Fayette County Mental Health Retardation Bd., 1967-69; cons. County Schs. Mental Health Program; mem. casework adv. com. U. Pitts. Sch. Social Work, field instr. Grad. Sch. Pub. Health, 1969-70; field instr. Grad. Sch. Social Work W.Va. U., Mongantown. chmn. recruiting social workers Fayette County. Dir. Fayette County Mental Health Assn., 1961—; bd. dirs. exec. Com. Pa. Mental Health, Inc., 1967—, del. nat. mental health conf., 1970, sec., 1972, chmn. community mental health-mental retardation group, 1971-72, chmn. Western region, 1972-73; sec. Uniontown Human Relations Commn., 1964-65; v.p., 1965-66, pres., 1968-70; sec. Fayette County Bd. Assistance; chmn. mental health com. Uniontown Area Council P.T.A., 1962—; sec. Fayette County Community Action Agy., 1965-69, chmn. steering com., 1968-69; mem. Western Pa. Comprehensive Health Planning Agy., 1970—. Bd. dirs. Sigmund A. Miller Meml. Fund, Community Services Pa. Mem. Nat. Council Community Mental Health Centers (asso.), Nat. Assn. Social Workers, Nat. Assn. Mental Health Adminstrs. (adv. com. on continuing edn., dir. research and edn. fund), Acad. Certified Social Workers, Nat. Conf. on Social Welfare, N.A.A.C.P., Assn. Retarded Children, Am. Trauma Soc. (dir. Pa. div.), Uniontown Area C. of C. (urban affairs council), U. Pitts. Alumni Council, Alpha Kappa Mu, Zeta Sigma Pi. Mem. A.M.E. Ch. Club: Uniontown College. 86 Coolspring St Uniontown PA 15401 Office: 410 Fayette Bank Bldg Uniontown PA 15401

CALOGGERO, CONSTANCE MARIA CATAUDELLA (MRS. SAMUEL F. CALOGGERO), hosp. adminstr.; b. Lawrence, Mass., Aug. 28, 1927; d. Sebastian and Josephine (Novello) Cataudella; student Boston U.; m. Samuel F. Caloggero, Apr. 24, 1949; 1 dau., Susan C. Adminstrv. asst. to gen. mgr. Am. Optical Co., 1954-56; adminstrv. asst. Chelsea Meml. Hosp., 1957-61, acting adminstr., 1961-63, adminstr., 1963—. Mem. Govt. Center Area Bd. for Mental Health; mem. Region 6 Health Planning Council. Mem. Am., Mass., N.E. hosp. assns., Greater Boston Hosp. Council, Mass. Mental Health Assn., Am., Mass. pub. health assns., Am., Mass. socs. hosp. personnel dirs., Interagy. Council. Home: 33 Winford Way Medford MA 02155 Office: 100 Bellingham St Chelsea MA 02150

CALVERT, MAUDE RICHMAN (MRS. GEORGE E. CALVERT), home economist, civic worker; b. Effingham, Kan.; d. Samuel Arthur and Mary Adda (Lookabaugh) Richman; B.S., Okla. A. and M. Coll., 1916; M.S., Okla. U., 1920; student Tchrs. Coll. Columbia, 1920-21, U. Chgo., summer 1924; m. George E. Calvert, Oct. 31, 1923 (dec. May 1959); children—Mary Ann (Mrs. John Price McCullough), Betty Lou (Mrs. Arthur B. Williams), Maude Richman (dec.). Tchr. pub. schs., Okla. until 1915, colls., univs., 1916-20; state supr. home econs., 1921-25. Originator Mothercraft Classes, Okla., 1921. Dir. Okla. Council Child Devel. and Parent Edn.; v.p. State Safety Council; chmn. state com. Care and Treatment Mentally Ill, 1946; vice chmn. State Bd. Affairs, 1943-47; mem. State Nutrition Com., 1942; mem. State Adv. Com for Child Care Facilities, 1962. Del. White House Conf., 1930; mem. Conf. Home Planning and Home Bldg., 1931, White House Conf. Children in Democracy, 1940; del. Nat. Conf. Family Life, Washington, 1947, White House Conf., 1950; chmn. meml. com. Okla. Heart Assn.; del. Golden Anniversary White House Conf. for Children and Youth, 1960, White House Conf. for Children, 1970; mem. Gov.'s Com. for Children and Youth, 1960—; mem. Okla. com. employment handicapped White House Conf. on Aging, 1961. Mem. state bd. Okla. Congress P.T.A., 1926-33, pres. Oklahoma City council, 1934-36, state pres., 1935-40, chmn. nat. chmns. conf. Nat. Congress, chmn. state pres. conf., 1938-39, chmn. home and family life, Nat. Congress, 1940-46, state chmn. character and spiritual edn., 1958—; mem. state bd. Okla. Soc. Crippled Children, 1923—, mem. exec. com., mem. care and treatment coms., 1958-74); cons. Okla. Commn. Health, Edn., Welfare, 1960—; mem. Christian social actions commn. Okla. Council Chs., 1962—; trustee Oklahoma Family Life Inst., 1935—; pres. Kindergarten Fedn. Oklahoma City, 1933-34; chmn. Okla. Day Care Com.; cons. Okla. Children's Adv. Com. Chmn. Oklahoma County Consumer's Council, 1934-35; chmn. woman's div. Civic Center Project, Oklahoma City, 1935; mem. Mayor's Com. on Employment of the Handicapped. Chmn. home econ. tng. Gen. Fedn. Women's Clubs, 1932-35. Selected one of the 24 women of achievement in Okla., 1934; most useful citizen of Oklahoma City, 1935; one of ten outstanding women, Okla., 1935; named Okla.'s most outstanding woman Theta Sigma Phi, 1946; recipient Okla. Gov.'s Distinguished award for over 50 years outstanding work with handicapped children and adults. Mem. Am. Home Econ. Assn., Nat. League Am. Pen Women (pres. Okla. br. 1930-31; nat. v.p. 1931-33), Gen. Fedn. Women's Clubs (pres. Oklahoma City 1957-60, program chmn. 1960-62, Okla. legislative chmn. 1960-62, local historian 1970-71), Okla. Hist Soc. (life mem.), Oklahoma State Better Homes Com. (vice chmn.), Am. Legion Aux., Okieland Reviewers (pres. 1971-72), Delta Kappa Gamma (life), Kappa Delta, Omicron Nu, Pi Kappa Sigma, Alpha Xi. Democrat. Mem. Christian Disciples Ch. (life deaconess; dir. study Womens Fellowship). Mem. Order Eastern Star. Clubs: New Century (parliamentarian), Red Bud Women's (an organizer, hon. life mem.), Monday Book Review (pres. 1970-71), Altrusa (hon. life mem.). Author: First Course in Home Making, 1924; Everyday Living for Boys and Girls, 1925; Home Making Students Note Book, 1927; The New First Course in Home Making, 1932; (with Leila Bunce Smith) Advanced Course in Home Making, 1938. Asso. editor Junior Home, 1934-38; state editor Oklahoma Parent-Teacher, 1940-58. Contbr. articles to jours. Home: 235 NW 34th St Oklahoma City OK 73118

CAMARA, DOROTHY, psychologist, health service adminstr.; b. Fall River, Mass., Apr. 16, 1927; d. Raul and Mary Lucy (Arruda) Camara; B.A. cum laude, U. Conn., 1956, M.A., 1958; Ph.D., U. Pitts., 1962. Clin. psychology intern Norwich (Conn.) State Hosp., 1955-56; clin. psychologist Beaver County Mental Health Clinic, Rochester, Pa., 1961-62; staff psychologist St. Elizabeth's Hosp., Washington, 1962-64, supervisory psychologist, 1964-71, clin. adminstr., 1971—. Mem. Assn. for Women in Psychology (corr. 1970—), Nat. Orgn. for Women (sec. treas. so. region 1971, treas. Montgomery county chpt. 1971, pres. Washington chpt. 1973—). Home: 7012 Western Av Chevy Chase MD 20015 Office: Saint Elizabeths Hospital O'Malley Division Washington DC 20032

CAMBER, ALICE ELIZABETH, occupational therapist; b. Shelby, Mich., May 20, 1948; d. Benjamin James and Ada Bell (Ossman) Camber; student U. Mich., 1966-67, postgrad., 1972—; B.S., Eastern Mich. U., 1970. Occupational therapist Washtenaw Intermediate Sch. Dist.-Day Tng. Center, Ann Arbor, Mich., 1971—. Supr. sr. and affiliate occupational therapy students Eastern Mich. U., Ypsilanti, 1973—. U. Mich. Regents scholar, 1966-67; Mich. Higher Edn. Assistance Authority scholar, 1966-70. Mem. Am. Occupational Therapy Assn. Home: 309 Maple St Ypsilanti MI 48197 Office: PO Box 1406 Ann Arbor MI 48106

CAMBER, MARY ELIZABETH, hosp. adminstr.; b. Eng., Apr. 3, 1925; d. John William and Lily Esther (Hudson) Butters; ed. Montreal (Que., Can.) Sch. Nursing Assts., 1949-50, U. Sask., 1971-72; m. Hugh Daniel Camber (div. 1974); children by previous marriage—Lily Anna (Mrs. Peter Hope), Linda Violet Madsen, Carolyn Joan Madsen; adopted children—Cecil Raymond Camber, William Hugh Camber. Mem. staff Cecil Butters Meml. Hosp., Austin, Que., 1950-55, adminstr., 1961—, former vice chmn., now sec. bd. dirs. Mem. Que. Assn. Nurses, Magog-Orford C. of C. Liberal Party. Mem. United Ch. Can. Address: Cecil Butters Memorial Hospital Austin PQ J0B 1B0 Canada

CAMERON, ALICE MANDERS, museum curator; b. Aberfeldy, Ont., Can., Jan. 13, 1909; d. Robert John and Mary Margaret (Camplin) Bailey; student pub. schs.; m. Malcolm Kenneth Cameron, June 5, 1935 (dec. 1967); children—Ralph, Lois, Donald. Asst. curator Oil Museum of Can., Oil Springs, Ont., 1965—. Local pres. Lambton County (Ont.) Folk Sch., 1958-60; leader 4-H Club, 1956-60. Mem. Rural Woman's Inst. (local pres. 1959-60, dist. pres. 1962-64). Mem. Order Eastern Star (past matron). Home: Rural Route 3 Oil Springs ON N0N 1P0 Canada Office: Oil Museum of Canada Rural Route 2 Oil Springs ON Canada

CAMERON, DOROTHY BLANDENIA SIMMONS (MRS. ARCHIE NAPOLEON CAMERON), educator; b. Spartansburg, S.C., Jan. 12, 1927; d. William O. and Ola (Noland) Simmons; B.S., Agrl. and Tech. Coll., Greensboro, 1948; M.Ed., U. N.C., 1964; m. Archie Napoleon Cameron, Dec. 25, 1949; children—Toni L. (Mrs. Stahle B. Vincent), Archie André. Sec., N.C. Agrl. Extension Service, Greensboro, 1951-56; with N.C. Agrl. and Tech. State U., Greensboro, 1948-50, 56-57, 60—, asst. prof. bus. edn., 1971—. Mem. Am. Assn. U. Profs., Nat. Collegiate Assn. Sec., N.C. Agrl. and Tech. State U. Alumni Assn., U. N.C. at Greensboro Alumni Assn., Delta Pi Epsilon, Alpha Kappa Mu. Baptist. Home: 1002 Julian St Greensboro NC 27406

CAMERON, ELSA SUE, art mus. adminstr.; b. San Francisco, Nov. 19, 1939; d. L. Don and Betty J. (Jelinsky) Cameron; B.A., San Francisco State Coll., 1961, M.A. magna cum laude, 1965. Tchr., San Francisco State Coll., 1961; art cons. Los Angeles Youth Services, 1962-63; tchr. San Francisco Unified Sch. Dist., 1963-64; asst. curator arts and crafts Josephine Randall Jr. Mus., San Francisco, 1964-66; curator-in charge Art Sch., Fine Arts Museums San Francisco, 1966—. Staff, Council on Mus. and Edn. in Visual Arts, 1973-74; mem. Mus. Intercultural Exchange Adv. Bd., San Francisco Mus. Art., 1972. Mus. Profl. fellow, 1973. Mem. Cal. Art Assn. Home: 15 Douglass St San Francisco CA 94114 Office: de Young Mus Golden Gate Park San Francisco CA 94118

CAMERON, MARGARET HARTLEY (MRS. COLIN CAMPBELL CAMERON), civic worker; b. Hilo, Hawaii, Sept. 4, 1928; d. Eric Ridgard and Jean Smith (McConn) Hartley; A.B., Pomona Coll., 1950; certificate San Francisco State Coll., 1951; postgrad Harvard, 1951-52; m. Colin Campbell Cameron, Aug. 25, 1951; children—Douglas Baldwin, Richard Hartley, Margaret Alexander, Frances Elizabeth. Dir., Haleakala Ranch, Kahului, Maui, Hawaii, 1973—, Haleakala Dairy, Kahului, 1973—. Pres. Maui Easter Seal Soc., 1960-71, dir. pub. relations, 1971—; sec. J. Walter Cameron Center, Wailuku, Hawaii, 1969—, also dir. Pres. Maui League Republican Women, 1954-59; v.p. State Fedn. Republican Women, 1961-63. Bd. dirs. Hawaii chpt. Nat. Soc. Crippled Children and Adults, 1964-70, Hawaii Youth Symphony, 1969-71; trustee Seabury Hall, Makawao, Maui, 1974—. Mem. Maui Philharmonic Soc. (dir. 1969-71, pres. 1969-71, 74—, bus. mgr. 1971-74, co-chmn. artist selection com. 1969—, co-chmn. hospitality com. 1973-74), Hui Noeau, Acad. Arts in Honolulu, Bishop Mus., Honolulu Symphony Soc., San Francisco Opera Soc., Maui Hist. Soc., Humane Soc., Outdoor Circle Hawaii, Japanese cultural Soc., Pomona Coll. Assos., Episcopal (vestryman, dir. diocese Hawaii 1970—, chmn. Diocesan program, Com. 1973—, supt. ch. sch. 1970-74, mem. stewardship com. 1974—). Club: Maui Country. Home: Stable Rd Spreckelsville Maui HI 96779 Office: PO Box C Paia Maui HI 96779

CAMERON, ROSALINE BRISKIN, educator, music therapist; b. Cleve.; d. Louis and Anna (Brisker) Briskin; diploma piano Juilliard Sch. Music, 1945; B.M. in Piano, Cleve. Inst. of Music, 1962; M.A. in Ednl. Psychology, Case Western Res. U., 1968; m. Harry Cameron, Apr. 28, 1946; children—Sharon L., David K. Tchr. piano Cleve. Inst. of Music, 1962—. Mem. Council for Exceptional Children; chmn. com. for older women Nat. Orgn. Women. Mem. Urban Fedn. Music Therapists (certified; chmn. certification com.), Am. Assn. on Mental Deficiency, Mu Phi Epsilon, Phi Delta Gamma. Home: 3339 Meadowbrook Blvd Cleveland Heights OH 44118 Office: 11021 E Blvd Cleveland OH 44106

CAMERON, SALLY FREEMAN, pub. relations exec.; b. Grosse Point, Mich., June 21, 1930; d. Frederick James and Clora Harriett (Riggs) Freeman; B.A., U. Ga., 1952; div.; 1 dau., Barbara Glenn. Staff writer Atlanta Jour., 1952-54; soc. editor Columbus (Ga.) Ledger, 1954-60; woman's editor Miami (Fla.) Herald, 1960-62; owner Image, Inc., Ft. Lauderdale, Fla., 1964—; partner Cameron-Friedlander, Inc., Ft. Lauderdale, 1971—. Pub. relations dir. Broward County Republican Com., 1968—; asst. to chmn. Fla. Rep. Com., 1969-71. Mem. Women in Communications, Fla. Pub. Relations Assn., Pub. Relations Soc. Am., Ft. Lauderdale C. of C. (chmn. leadership com. 1973—), Kappa Alpha Theta. Home: 6279 Bay CLub Dr Fort Lauderdale FL 33308 Office: 2455 E Sunrise Blvd Fort Lauderdale FL 33304

CAMERON, WINIFRED JEAN SAWTELL (MRS. ROBERT CURRY CAMERON), astronomer; b. Oak Park, Ill., Dec. 3, 1918; d. Amos Alexander and Mildred (Shields) Sawtell; B.E., No. Ill. U., 1940; M.A., Ind. U., 1952; postgrad. Georgetown U., 1954-56, 67-68; m. Robert Curry Cameron, Oct. 17, 1953 (dec. Dec. 1972); children—Selene Jean, Sheri Carina. Research asst., mgr. lab. Weather Forecasts, Inc., Chgo., 1942-46; teaching asst. Ind. U., Bloomington, 1946-49; instr. astronomy Mount Holyoke Coll., South Hadley, Mass., 1950-51; research astronomer U.S. Naval Obs., Washington, 1951-58, NASA Goddard Space Flight Center, Greenbelt, Md., 1959—. Recipient Spl. Act award NASA-Goddard Space Flight Center, 1966, Apollo Achievement award, 1970, Exceptional Contbns. to Edn. award, 1971; Distinguished Alumnus award No. Ill. U., 1968, Quality Increase award, 1974. Mem. Internat. Astron. Union, Am. Astron. Soc., Am. Geophys. Union, Internat. Platform Assn., Internat. Assn. Planetology, Assn. Lunar and Planetary Observers (lunar recorder for lunar transient phenomena), Sigma Pi Sigma, Burnham Astron. Soc. (sec. 1943-46). Contbr. articles to profl. jours. Home: 708 Schindler Dr Silver Spring MD 20903 Office: Goddard Space Flight Center Greenbelt MD 20771

CAMP, BERT ELLEN (MRS. JACK W. CAMP), librarian; b. Oklahoma City; d. James Elbert and Mary Brevard (Dunson) Weir; B.A., U. So. Cal., 1938; M.A., Sul Ross State Coll., Alpine, Tex., 1958; M.A. in Library Sci., U. Denver, 1961; m. Jack W. Camp, June 4, 1941; 1 son, John D. Tchr. rural sch., Monument, N.M., 1932-33; tchr. Hobbs (N.M.) Jr. High Sch., 1933-41; librarian N.M. Mil. Inst., Roswell, 1962—. Mem. Delta Kappa Gamma, Zeta Tau Alpha. Mem. Order Eastern Star (past matron). Home: 2505 Gaye Dr Roswell NM 88201

CAMP, MARGARET WHITTLESEY PERKINS (MRS. MORTIMER HART CAMP), ret. lawyer; b. New Britain, Conn., Nov. 27, 1897; d. John Russell and Mary Whittlesey (Brown) Perkins; A.B., Radcliffe Coll., 1919; J.D., U. Chgo., 1924; m. Mortimer Hart Camp, June 2, 1928. Tchr., La Veta (Colo.) High Sch., 1919-21; admitted to Conn. bar, 1925; practiced in New Britain, 1925-30; partner firm Camp, Williams & Richardson, 1930-66. Mem. cello sect. New Britain Symphony Orch., 1930-62. Dir. New Britain C. of C., 1949-51; trustee New Britain Inst., 1949—; corporator New Britain Gen. Hosp., 1942—. Mem. Am., Hartford County, New Britain bar assns., D.A.R., Order of Coif, Phi Beta Kappa. Republican. Methodist. Clubs: New Britain Musical, Woman's (pres. 1943-45), Shuttlemeadow Country. Home: 37 Russell St New Britain CT 06052 Office: 130 W Main St New Britain CT 06050

CAMP, ROSEMARY ANNE, pub. relations dir.; b. Mpls., Mar. 29, 1947; d. Robert Douglas and Ruth (Rosengren) Camp; B.A. (WCCO-TV Journalism scholar), U. Minn., 1971. Dir. pub. information Minn. Assn. for Retarded Children, Mpls., 1969-70; asst. mgr. employee communications Pillsbury Co., Mpls., 1971-73; dir. pub. information Mount Sinai Hosp., Mpls., 1973-74, editor, writer hosp. newsletter, 1973-74; editor Internat. Dairy Queen, 1974—. Vol. Amicus program working with inmates Shakopee State Prison for Women, 1972—. Mem. Nat. Pub. Relations Council of Health and Welfare Services, Am. Hosp. Assn. Pub. Relations Council, Twin City Council for Hosp. Pub. Relations, Women In Communications. Club: Press (Mpls.). Home: 4522-16th Av S Minneapolis MN 55408 Office: 5701 Green Valley Rd Minneapolis MN 55435

CAMPA, JUSTA CARMEN, guidance counselor; b. Bridgeport, Tex., July 16, 1915; d. Canuto and Justa (Zamora) Campa; B.A., Bapt. Missionary Tng. Sch., 1946; M.A., Berkeley Bapt. Div. Sch., 1951; postgrad. U. Miami, summer 1969. Community worker Bd. Nat. Missions, U.P. Ch., 1952-72, Bd. Nat. Missions, United Meth. Ch., Laredo, Tex., 1972—. Youth guidance counselor, tchr. religion and psychology Holding Inst., Laredo, 1972-75, counselor, 1975—. Mem. Nat. Assn. Women Deans Adminstrs. and Counselors, Nat. Assn. Health, Welfare and Edn. of U.P. Ch. Home: 419 W Delz St Houston TX 77018 Office: Holding Inst Box 269 Laredo TX 78040

CAMPBELL, AGNES KNIGHT (MRS. JOHN FRANKLIN CAMPBELL), social agy. exec.; b. Boom, Tenn.; d. George Allen and Nora (Clark) Knight; B.S., Tenn. Tech. U., 1934; postgrad. Vanderbilt U., 1935, U. Chgo. Sch. Social Service Adminstrn., 1942, 46; M.S., U. Tenn. Sch. Social Work, 1953; m. John Franklin Campbell, June 20, 1942. Regional dir. Tenn. Dept. Pub. Welfare, Nashville, 1942-55; social worker Youth Service, Child and Family Service, Knoxville, Tenn., 1955-58; exec. dir. Knoxville Travelers Aid Soc., 1958—. Bd. dirs. planning council United Community Services Greater Knoxville; pres. Profl. Exec.'s Council Knoxville, 1967-68; bd. dirs. Knoxville Legal Aid Soc. Mem. Nat. Assn. Social Workers (chmn. pub. relations commn.; pres. 1951-53, sec. 1966-67; editor Knoxville area Newsletter 1971-73), Tenn. Conf. of Social Work (state sec. 1955), Nat. Travelers Aid Assn. Club: Social Service of Knoxville. Author script: Some of Those We Help, 1962; play: Trouble Away From Home, 1964. Home: 6515 Sherwood Dr Knoxville TN 37919 Office: 100 Magnolia Av Knoxville TN 37917

CAMPBELL, ANNE (MRS. GEORGE W. STARK), writer; b. Lynn, Mich., June 19, 1888; d. Hugh J. and Mina (Atkinson) Campbell; ed. high sch.; Dr. of Arts (hon.), Wayne U., 1949; m. George W. Stark, Aug. 28, 1915; children—George Winter, Alison Jean (Mrs. Allan F. Wilson), Richard Campbell. Writer verse for Detroit News, 1927-71. Named Mich. Mother of Year, 1952. Author: Companionship and Other Poems; Back Home (collection of farm verse); The Heart of Home; Jesus and His Twelve Apostles; Four Songs from the Lord's Prayer; Songs from the Beatitudes (with Ward-Stephens); The House That Love Built; Two Heads are Better. Named Mich. Mother, Goodwill Woman of the Year. Contbr. poems to mags. Home: 2067 W Boston Blvd Detroit MI

CAMPBELL, ANNE RHODELLE JOHNSON (MRS. CHARLES ELWOOD CAMPBELL), broadcasting co. exec.; b. Phila., Jan. 8, 1920; d. Charles Henry and Anna (Schmidt) Johnson; student U. Pa., 1964-65; m. Charles Elwood Campbell, Aug. 25, 1942. With Lichtman Theatres, Washington, 1941-46; exec. sec. CBS, Inc., N.Y.C., 1948-62, television producer WCAU-TV, Phila., 1962-72, personnel dir. WCAU-TV, Phila., 1972—. Cons. secretarial conf. Sarah Lawrence Coll., N.Y. Urban League, 1959. Mem. Citizen's Fire Prevention Com., Phila., 1970—. Recipient Recruitment award U.S. Army, 1966; Brotherhood award East Trenton Civic Center, 1968; Outstanding Service awards Phila. Fire Dept., 1968, Def. Supply Agy., 1970; Pub. Service award Phila. Grand Opera Co., 1973. Mem. Am. Women in Radio and TV, Phila. Personnel Women's Group, Phila. Urban League, C. of C. (mem. com. 1970-73), Nat. Orgn. Girl Friends. Episcopalian (mem. alter guild 1969—). Home: Toledo 12-U Towers of Windsor Park Cherry Hill NJ 08034 Office: City Line Av Philadelphia PA 19131

CAMPBELL, CATHERINE F. GRAY (MRS. WALLACE ARNOLD CAMPBELL), writer; b. Balt.; d. Ernest Guy and Catherine (Daly) Gray; B.S., Md. Coll., 1941; M.S., Johns Hopkins, 1944; postgrad. Columbia, 1947-49, C.W. Post U., 1960-62; m. Wallace Arnold Campbell, July 22, 1945; 1 dau., Catherine Frances. Tchr. pub. schs., Balt., 1941-44, N.Y.C., 1945-49; writer various newspapers, L.I., N.Y., 1955-65, Los Angeles, 1966-69; writer for travel mags., 1960—; writer for Balt. City ednl. system, vol. groups, guides; lectr. world travel, various travel clubs, women's clubs, tchr. groups, 1958—. Chmn. vol. groups Glen Cove (N.Y.) Community Hosp., 1958-65; group chmn. Salvation Army, 1960-62; vice chmn. YMCA, Glen Cove, 1958-65; vol. Greenwich Hosp., 1971-74, Meals-on-Wheels, 1971-74. Mem. Am. Assn. U. Women, Nat. Writers Club, Kappa Delta Pi, Pi Delta Gamma, Pi Lambda Theta. Clubs: Garden (pres. 1965, chmn. horticulture com.) (Sea Cliff, N.Y.); American Women's (London, Eng.). Editor, pub. Newsletter monthly Woman's Club of Greenwich, Inc., 1970—. Home: Rockwood Lane Greenwich CT 06830

CAMPBELL, CUBA BELLE (MRS. RALPH ELBERT CAMPBELL), ednl. adminstr.; b. Wheeler, Ark., Nov. 9, 1910; d. Daniel Cosby and Nora Alice (Robbins) Thurman; student Dallas Sch. Fine and Applied Arts, 1932-33; B.S. in Edn., U. Ark., 1933; M.A., Okla. State U., 1942; diplomas in Spl. Edn., Ida. State U., 1959, E.Central State Coll., 1957; postgrad. Southeastern State Coll., Durant, Okla., 1941-43; m. Ralph Elbert Campbell, Dec. 1, 1933; 1 son, Charles N. Tchr. pub. schs., Ark., 1933-37; head art dept. Bacone Coll., Muskogee, Okla., 1949-53; dir. spl. edn. dept. Eastern Okla. State Tb. Sanatarium, Talihina, 1954-65; dir. Sequoyah County Spl. Edn. Project, 1966—; writer pilot project, mem. adv. bd. Northeastern Okla. Regional Media Services Center, Sallisaw, 1968-71. Co-founder 4-H House, U. Ark., 1930; Sequoyah County coordinator Okla. Lung Assn., 1971-73; mem. Sequoyah-Adair-Cherokee County Mental Health Com., 1973-74; pres. P.T.A., 1957-59. Mem. Muskogee League Women Democrats, Le Flore County Dem. League. Sec. bd. dirs. Murrow Indian Orphanage; mem. ednl. adv. bd. Eastern Okla. Tb. Assn.; patron, mem. Sequoyah County Arts and Humanities Council. Recipient citation Okla. Dept. Edn., 1940-41, St. Christopher cross for outstanding ednl. work Eastern Okla. State Sanatarium, 1965. Rockefeller Found. fellow, 1950-52. Mem. N.E.A., Okla., Sequoyah County edn. assns., Okla., Sequoyah County tchrs. assns., Am. Assn. U. Women, Internat. Council Exceptional Children, Internat. Council Children with Learning Disabilities, Alpha Delta Kappa (internat. state historian 1950-54, state pres. 1968-72, internat. publicity com. 1965-68), Epsilon Sigma Alpha, Kappa Kappa Gamma. Methodist. Mem. Order Eastern Star. Clubs: Business and Professional Women's, Pilot. Contbr. articles profl. jours. Home: 316 Mockingbird Lane Sallisaw OK 74955 Office: PO Box 511 Sallisaw OK 74955

CAMPBELL, ELLEN LOUISE, former educator; b. Ashland, O., June 20, 1902; d. Charles Orlo and Minnie Mae (Clark) Campbell; B.A. cum laude, Coll. Wooster (O.), 1924; M.A., Columbia, 1942; Litt.D., Ashland Coll., 1957. Tchr. English, prin. Nova (O.), 1924-26; tchr. English Coshocton (O.) High Sch., 1926-37; tchr., head dept. English, Ashland High Sch., 1937-63; prof. English, Ashland Coll., 1963-73. Trustee Ashland Pub. Library, 1963-70, pres., 1966; bd. dirs. Ashland Coll. Hist. Edn. Center. Named Tchr. of Year, Ashland C. of C., 1959, Outstanding Educator Am., 1971. Mem. Little Traverse Regional, Ashland hist. socs., Delta Kappa Gamma. Club: Esoteric (Ashland). Home: 203 Samaritan Av Ashland OH 44805

CAMPBELL, ENID HOBART (MRS. BYRON A. CAMPBELL), psychologist, educator; b. Toronto, Ont., Can., June 17, 1927; d. John Henry and Enid Rachael (Jones) Hobart; came to U.S., 1944, naturalized, 1955; A.B., Swarthmore Coll., 1948; M.A., Bryn Mawr Coll., 1951; Ph.D., Yale, 1957; m. Byron A. Campbell, June 19, 1954; children—Andrea Adams, Ian Hobart. Research psychologist Boston U., 1955-56; asst. prof. psychology Trenton (N.J.) State Coll., 1959-62, asso. prof., 1962-65, prof., 1965—, chairperson dept. of psychology, 1971—. Trustee Univ. League Nursery Sch., Princeton, 1968—. Mem. Am. Psychol. Assn., Phi Beta Kappa, Sigma Xi. Contbr. articles on psychology to profl. jours. Home: 111 Maclean Circle Princeton NJ 08540 Office: Dept of Psychology Trenton State College Trenton NJ 08625

CAMPBELL, FRANCES DENISE, librarian; b. Cape Girardeau, Mo., June 11, 1937; d. Galen Monroe and Frances Margaret Campbell; B.A., U. Colo., 1960, M.S., 1962, J.D., 1969. Librarian, Denver Pub. Library, 1962-64; law librarian Colo. Supreme Ct. Library, Denver, 1963—; admitted to Colo. bar, 1969; practice law, Denver, 1969—. Mem. Colo., Denver bar assns., Am. Assn. Law Librarians, Spl. Libraries Assn., Kappa Beta Pi. Home: 1390 Emerso St Denver CO 80203 Office: 220 State Capital Bldg Denver CO 80203

CAMPBELL, GRACE JONES POLLOCK, librarian; b. Old Kilpatrick, Scotland, July 8, 1908; d. Samuel and Margaret (White) Campbell; B.A., Acadia U., 1931; B. Library Sci., McGill U., 1950. Librarian, P.E.I. Libraries, Charlottetown, 1933-49, 52-55; gen. librarian North Central Sask. Regional Library, Prince Albert, Sask., 1950-52, regional librarian, 1955-73. Mem. Canadian, Sask. (pres. 1957) library assns., A.L.A. Club: University Womens. Home: 2102 647 Michigan St Victoria BC V84 1S9 Canada

CAMPBELL, HELEN ALEXANDER, writer; b. Phila.; d. Lucien Hugh and Mazie (Just) Alexander; student Barnard Coll., 1913-14, Bryn Mawr Coll., 1914-15; m. William Thomas Campbell, Jan. 30, 1943 (dec. 1969). Journalist, mem. editorial staff various newspapers; writer feature stories for numerous newspapers and mags., including N.Y. Sun, N.Y. Herald Tribune, Christian Sci. Monitor, San Francisco Chronicle, El Paso Times, Miles City Montanan, Travel, Cunarder mag., Sea Stories. Vol. worker A.R.C., N.Y.C. and France, Seamen's Ch. Inst., N.Y.C., Greenwich House, N.Y.C. Served with USNR, 1917-18. Mem. Overseas Press Club Am., Women's Overseas Service League. Home: The Roost PO Box 1064 Ojai CA 93023

CAMPBELL, HELEN WOERNER (MRS. THOMAS B. CAMPBELL), librarian; b. Indpls., Oct. 17, 1918; d. Clarence Julius and Gertrude Elizabeth (Colley) Woerner; student Ind. U., 1935-38; B.S., Butler U., 1967; postgrad. Ind. U. Grad. Library Sch., 1962-65; m. Thomas B. Campbell, Jan. 17, 1942; 1 dau., Martha (Mrs. L. Kurt Adamson). Asst. order librarian Ind. U., Bloomington, 1937-42; librarian Ind. U. Sch. Dentistry, Indpls., 1942-46, cataloger, part-time, 1960-65, asst. librarian, 1965-66, librarian, 1966—. Mem. Am. Assn. Dental Schs., Med. Library Assn., Spl. Libraries Assn. (chpt. pres. 1972-73). Home: 1865 Norfolk St Indianapolis IN 46224 Office: 1121 W Michigan St Indianapolis IN 46202

CAMPBELL, ILA GREEN (MRS. FRED YOUNG CAMPBELL), religious orgn. exec.; b. nr. Waynesville, N.C., June 6, 1912; d. James Isaac and Florence (Cates) Green; high sch. grad.; m. Fred Young Campbell, Jan. 27, 1939. Bookkeeper Unagusta Mfg. Corp., Hazelwood, N.C., 1934-50; with Lake Junaluska (N.C.) Assembly, Inc., Meth. assembly grounds, 1951—, asst. to supt., 1951-67, asst. treas., bus. mgr., 1967—. Mem. N.C. Bd. Cons. Devel., 1960-64; dir. Waynesville Centennial Com., 1971—. Vice-pres. county exec. com. Democratic party, 1946-60; pres. Haywood (N.C.) County Dem. Women's Club, 1962-64. Trustee, mem. adv. com. Haywood Tech. Inst. Recipient Outstanding Community Service award, Waynesville United Fund, 1968, 69, 70, 71, 72, 73. Mem. V.F.W. Aux. (pres. 1948-49), Am. Legion Aux. (pres. 1949-50), First Dist. Fed. (dist. dir. 1968-69), Waynesville (pres. 1965-67), N.C. Fedn. (rec. sec.) bus. and profl. women's clubs. Methodist (past steward, treas. Interpreters' Ho. 1967—, treas. Internat. Prayer Fellowship 1968-73, mem. Western N.C. Conf. Commn. Ecumenical Affairs 1968—). Mem. Order Eastern Star. Home: Route 1 Maggie NC 28786 Office: Lake Junaluska Assembly Inc Box 67 Lake Junaluska NC 28751

CAMPBELL, IRENE SMITH (MRS. G. MURRAY CAMPBELL), club woman; b. Somerville, Mass., Feb. 10, 1898; d. Frederick Glazier and Mabel (Johnson) Smith; A.B., Smith Coll., 1919; m. George Murray Campbell, June 17, 1922; children—Frederick Hollister, Edward Carleton, Anna May (Mrs. Roger Leon Conarty). Vice regent Ill. orgn. D.A.R., 1960-62, nat. chmn. Jr. Am. citizens com., 1962-65, nat. chmn. Americanism, manual citizenship com., 1965-68, Vt. historian, 1968-69, regent, 1969-71; v.p. gen., 1971-74; pres. Evanston colony Nat. Soc. New Eng. Women, 1961-62; mem. Woman's Aux. Goodwill Industries, Chgo., treas., 1958-60. Dir. Women's Nat. Republican Club Chgo., 1955-61. Bd. dirs. Tamassee (S.C.) D.A.R. Sch., 1970-73. Conglist. Home: West Rd Box 717 Manchester VT 05254

CAMPBELL, ISOBEL AGNES BRYDON (MRS. WENDELL CHESLEY CAMPBELL), nursing adminstr.; b. Fergus, Ont., Can., Dec. 15, 1912; d. Donald Harvey and Margaret May (McIntosh) Brydon; grad. Guelph (Ont.) Coll. Vocational Inst., 1925-30; R.N., Hamilton (Ont.) Civic Hosp. Sch. Nursing, 1931-34; m. Wendell Chesley Campbell, Aug. 30, 1952. Pvt. duty nurse, Hamilton, 1934-39; gen. staff nurse Hamilton Civic Hosps., 1939-41, asst. nurse, 1941-44, head nurse, 1944-58, supr., 1958—. Exec. sec. Central Service Assn., Province Ont., 1968—. Mem. Alumni Assn. (pres. 1969-72). Home: 347 Arlington Rd Hamilton ON L8K 3K6 Canada Office: 237 Barton St E Hamilton ON Canada

CAMPBELL, JUNE COLLYER PETERS (MRS. LEROY M. CAMPBELL), social worker; b. Pitts., June 18, 1929; d. Nathaniel R. and Cleo (Minor) Peters; B.A., Howard U., 1951, M.S.W., 1964; M.A., Am. U., 1959; m. Leroy M. Campbell, Aug. 22, 1952; 1 dau., Sharon. With Prince George's County Dept. Social Services, Hyattsville, Md., 1957—, caseworker, 1957-64, supr., 1964-66, asst. dir., 1967-71, dep. dir., 1971—. Mem. task force treatment of emotionally disturbed youth Md. Gov.'s Conf. Crime and Delinquency, 1968—; adv. com. Office for Coordination Services to Handicapped. Mem. Nat. Conf. Social Welfare, Council Local Adminstrs. Social Services, Child Welfare League Am., Nat. Assn. Social Workers, Am. Pub. Welfare Assn., Alpha Kappa Alpha. Home: 8019 16th St NW Washington DC 20012 Office: Prince Georges County Dept Social Services 6525 Belcrest Rd Hyattsville MD 20782

CAMPBELL, LILA JEAN, constrn. co. exec.; b. Blairsville, Ga., May 19, 1942; d. William Buren and Phoebe Iowa (Hood) Hunter; grad. high sch.; m. Knox Campbell, Jr. June 14, 1963; (div. Jan. 1973); children—Jeffrey, Tonia, Angela. Mgr., Hunter Outlet, Hiawassee, Ga., 1968-69, Blairsville Discount, 1969-70; bookkeeper Hunter Constrn. Co., Inc., Blairsville, 1970—, sec.-treas., 1972—. Home: PO Box 63 Blairsville GA 03512 Office: PO Box 457 Blairsville GA 30512

CAMPBELL, MAGDA PIJUKOVIC (MRS. FRANCIS P. CAMPBELL), physician; b. Subotica, Yugoslavia, Jan. 22, 1928; d. Bela and Marija (Lipozencic) Pijukovic; M.D., U. Belgrade (Yugoslavia), 1953; m. Francis P. Campbell, July 2, 1961; children—Maria D., John Francis. Came to U.S. 1957, naturalized 1962. Resident, Univ. Neuro-Psychiat. Hosp., U. Belgrade, 1953-56; resident psychiat. div. Bellevue Hosp., N.Y.C., 1958-59, 60-62, resident child psychiatry, 1961-62, NIH fellow child psychiatry, 1962-63; asst. prof. psychiatry N.Y. U. Sch. Medicine, 1969-72, asso. prof., 1972—, dir. children's psychopharmacology unit, 1969—. Diplomate in psychiatry and child psychiatry Am. Bd. Psychiatry and Neurology. Fellow Am. Psychiat. Assn.; mem. A.A.A.S., A.M.A., Am. Acad. Child Psychiatry, N.Y. Soc. Clin. Psychiatry, Med. Soc. County N.Y. Asso. editor Jour. Autism and Childhood Schizophrenia. Home: 333 E 30th St New York City NY 10016 Office: Dept Psychiatry NYU Med Center New York City NY 10016

CAMPBELL, MARGARET ANNE (MRS. LEONARD E. CAMPBELL), ednl. adminstr.; b. Denver, Nov. 13, 1917; d. Earl O. and Vera E. (Mallon) Linger; A.B., U. No. Colo., 1938; M.S., Wayne State Coll., 1959; Ed.D., U. Neb., 1969; hon. degrees Central Mo. Coll., Fayetteville, 1972, Midland Lutheran Coll., 1974; m. Leonard E. Campbell, July 4, 1938; children—Margilie (Mrs. John Sauer), Beverly, Marilyn (Mrs. Lonnie E. Waak). Tchr. schs. Erie, Colo., Framont and Battle Creek, Neb., 1938-55; county supt. schs., Madison County, Neb., 1955-63; dir. profl. relations Neb. State Edn. Assn., Lincoln, 1963-65; adminstrv. asst. govtl. relations Lincoln Pub. Schs., 1965-72; dir. pub. affairs, asso. prof. ednl. adminstrn. U. Neb. System, Lincoln, 1972—. Vice pres. Edutek, Inc., Lincoln, 1971—. Mem. Gov.'s Commn. on Status Women, 1964-71, chmn., 1966-69; chmn. Neb. Profl. Practices Com., 1968-70. Trustee Doane Coll., 1972—. Recipient Distinguished Service award Wayne State Coll., 1962; named Woman of Yr., Bus. and Profl. Womens Club, Lincoln, 1965, Neb. Woman of Achievement, 1974; named Omaha World-Herald Midlands mag., 1973; Cardinal Key Sorority, 1972. Mem. Am. Assn. U. Women (pres. Neb. div. 1952-54, regional v.p. 1963-71, pres. 1971—), N.E.A., Neb. Edn. Assn., Am. Assn. Sch. Adminstrs. (resolution com. 1970-72), Bus. and Profl. Womens Club, P.E.O., Mortar Bd. (hon.), Pi Lambda Theta, Phi Delta Gamma, Delta Kappa Gamma. Republican. Presbyn. Mem. Order Eastern Star. Home: 7500 South St Lincoln NE 68520

CAMPBELL, MARGARET GEORGESON, librarian; b. Dayton, O., Apr. 22, 1913; d. Andrew Gilbertson and Jessie (Taylor) Campbell; B.A., Ohio Wesleyan U., 1935; Med. Technologist, Mt. Sinai Hosp. Sch. Med. Tech., 1936; postgrad. music dept. U. S.C., 1940-45; M.S. in L.S., Western Res. U., 1952. Head serology lab. Mt. Sinai Hosp., Cleve., 1936-39; serologist S.C. Bd. Health, Columbia, 1939-45; club dir. recreational program A.R.C., Eng., Germany, 1945-46, Korea, 1947; club dir. recreation program U.S. Army Spl. Services, Korea, 1948-49, Ft. Sill, Okla., 1950, Ft. Benning, Ga., 1950-51, library sect., France, Berlin, West Germany, 1952-54, interviewer for recruiting service, Washington, 1956—; reference librarian, Shaker Heights (O.) Pub. Library, 1955-60, br. librarian, 1960-69, dir., 1969—. Mem. Women's Overseas Service League, Am. Overseas Assn., English Speaking Union, Shaker Hist. Soc., A.L.A., Delta Zeta. Methodist. Home: 2540 N Moreland Blvd Shaker Heights OH 44120 Office: 3450 Lee Rd Shaker Heights OH 44120

CAMPBELL, MARGUERITE DEXTER, editor; b. Fourth Crossing, Cal., June 14, 1912; d. John Lorenzo and Katrina Ross (Bund) Dexter; student Redlands U., 1930-31; m. Dale K. Campbell, Jan. 7, 1933 (dec. 1961); children—Dalmar John, Linda Kay (Mrs. Ken Melton), Dexter Joseph. Owner, editor Mariposa (Cal.) Gazette, 1932-36, editor, 1952—; owner Marguerite's Dress Shop, Mariposa, 1938-42; owner Ore. Cattle Ranch, Redmond, 1948-50. Life mem. P.T.A.; active 4H, Girl Scouts Am. Mem. Mariposa County C. of C., Native Daus. Golden West, Order Eastern Star, Soroptimists (charter). Home: 8th and Jones Mariposa CA 95338 Office: 9th and Jones Mariposa CA 95338

CAMPBELL, MARIA BOUCHELLE, lawyer; b. Mullins, S.C., Jan. 23, 1944; d. Colin Reid and Margaret Minor (Perry) Campbell; student Agnes Scott Coll., 1961-63; A.B., U. Ga., 1965, LL.B., 1967. Admitted to Ga. bar, 1967, Fla. bar, 1968, Ala. bar, 1969; practiced in Birmingham, Ala., 1968—; law clk. U.S. Circuit Ct. of Appeals, Miami, Fla., 1967-68; asso. firm, Cabaniss, Johnston and Gardner, Birmingham, 1968-73; sec., counsel Ala. Bancorp., Birmingham, 1973—. Cons. to various charitable orgns. Bd. dirs. Children's Aid Soc., Birmingham, 1970—, St. Anne's Home, Birmingham, 1969-74, chancellor, 1969—. Mem. State Bar of Ga., Fla. Bar, Am., Ala., Birmingham bar assns. Episcopalian (trustee 1971-72, 74—, mem. canonical revision com. Ala. Diocese 1973—). Exec. editor Ga. Law Rev., 1966-67. Home: 141 Camellia Circle Birmingham AL 35213 Office: PO Box 11007 Birmingham AL 35288

CAMPBELL, MARIANNE BOGGS (MRS. BILL C. CAMPBELL), communications cons.; b. Pitts., July 28, 1926; d. William Orville and Guida Arista (Harrington) Boggs; A.B., Pa. Coll. Women, 1948; m. Bill C. Campbell, Oct. 21, 1950. Gen. mgr. radio sta. WJEH, Gallipolis, O., 1950-67; dir. community affairs AVCO Broadcasting Corp., Cin., 1967-72; v.p. Holzer Med. Center, Gallipolis, 1972-73, communications cons., 1973—. Bd. dirs. Internat. Radio and TV Fedn., 1973-75; chmn. bd. trustees Ednl. Found. Am. Women in Radio and TV, 1972-74; trustee Ohio div. Am. Cancer Soc., 1973—. Mem. Ohio Assn. Broadcasters (pres. 1964), Ohio Fedn. Bus. and Profl. Women (pres. 1968-69), Assn. for Profl. Broadcasting Edn. (pres. 1969-70), Am. Women in Radio and TV (pres. 1971-72), VFW Aux. (recipient Outstanding Achievement award 1971). Home: Willowview Farm Lower River Rd Gallipolis OH 45631 Office: PO Box 264 Gallipolis OH 45631

CAMPBELL, MILDRED FLORENCE, ret. educator; b. Logansport, Ind., Apr. 5, 1906; d. Samuel Gilbert and Lottie Edith (Behmer) Campbell; A.B., Butler U., 1928; M.A., Woods Hole Marine, U. Mich. biol. stas., 1936; postgrad. Albion Coll., 1942, in Ecology, U. Ill., 1928-68. Tchr. nat. sci. Shortridge High Sch., Indpls., 1928-68; nature counsellor, field trip guide various civic orgns., summers, 1928-68; supplier bird nesting records Cornell U. N.Am. Nest Record Card Program; lectr. conservation, ecology, dress and dolls of fgn. countries to various children's and civic groups, 1941-68. Leader, counsellor, nature guide Campfire Girls, Girl Scouts U.S.A., chs. Mem. Nat. Audubon Soc. (took Christmas Count local plants and animals 1940-73), Ind. Audubon Soc. (past editor Yearbook), Irvington Hist. Soc. (mem. children's edn. commn. on hist. research 1962—, sci. editor 1966 Checklist Abstract, leader foot tours), Guild of Community Hosp., Cranbrook Inst., N.E.A., Ind. Tchrs. Assn., Nat. Biology Tchrs. Assn., Am. Inst. Biology, Soc. Central Math. and Sci., Am. Ornithol. Union, Wilson Ornithology Soc., Ind. Acad. Sci.

Republican. Presbyn. (tchr. ch. sch.). Contbr. chpts. to biology texts, articles to profl. jours. Home: 29 N Hawthorne Lane Indianapolis IN 46219

CAMPBELL, MILDRED WARD (MRS. FRANCIS MILLER CAMPBELL), mobile home co. exec.; b. Big Sandy, W.Va., July 1, 1920; d. William G. And Beulah M. (Stone) Ward; student Nat. Bus. Coll.; m. Francis Miller Campbell, Aug. 5, 1941; 1 dau., F. Camer (Mrs. David J. Guarino). Accounting clk. Harris Hardwood Co., 1947-60; office mgr. Ward Mobilehome Sales, Inc., Salem, Va., 1960-64, treas., 1964—. Baptist (ch. clk. 1940-44). Club: Quota (pres. 1949-50) (Roanoke, Va.). Office: 1231 E Main St Salem VA 24153

CAMPBELL, PAULINE BROWN (MRS. WILLIAM KENNETH CAMPBELL), librarian; b. Troy, Mo., Sept. 14, 1917; d. Raymond Edward and Gussie Pauline (Carwell) Brown; B.S., Washington U., St. Louis, 1951, M.A., 1958; m. William Kenneth Campbell, Aug. 5, 1939; 1 dau., Sandra Kay (Mrs. Ronald Joe Zappe). Tchr. elementary schs., Lincoln County, Mo., 1935-50; librarian Buchanan High Sch., Troy, Mo., 1950—. Mem. N.E.A. (life), Mo., Community tchrs. assns., Mo. Library Assn., Mo. Assn. Sch. Librarians (pres. 1955-56), Lincoln County Hist. Soc., Delta Kappa Gamma, Kappa Delta Pi. Democrat. Baptist. Club: Mark Twain Literary (Troy, Mo.). Home: 1055 Main St Troy MO 63379 Office: Buchanan High Sch Library Troy MO 63379

CAMPBELL, PHYLLIS CLARE ANDERSON (MRS. JOHN JASPER CAMPBELL), occupational therapist; b. Springfield, Ill., Sept. 27, 1924; d. Spencer Tyron and Eunice Pauline (Sellers) Anderson; B.S., U. Ill., 1946; postgrad. U. Ill., 1971-73, Milliken U., Ill. State U., 1972-73, Eastern Ill. U., 1970-73; m. John Jasper Campbell, Sept. 20, 1947; children—Ellyn Clare, Kevin John. Dir. occupational therapy dept. Cook County Childrens Hosp., Chgo., 1946-47; occupational therapy grad. asst. U. Ill., Urbana, 1947-49; occupational therapist Stuart Sch. Crippled Children, Springfield, 1949-50, Niles (Mich.) Sch. for Exceptional Children, 1954-56; dir. Macon County Easter Seal Center, Decatur, Ill., 1960-68; occupational therapist supr. Decatur Pub. Sch. System Spl. Edn., 1969—. Cons. occupational therapy, Decatur, 1972-73, United Cerbral Palsy of Macon County; sec. Decatur Power Squadron Aux., 1968-69. Bd. dirs. United Cerebral Palsy of Macon County, Macon County Rehab. Facilities. Mem. Am., Ill., Kickapoo Dist. occupational therapy assns., Council for Exceptional Children (pres. Decatur chpt. 1973-74), U. Ill. Alumni Assn., Pi Beta Phi. Home: 38 Larry Dr Decatur IL 62526 Office: William Harris Sch 600 E Garfield Decatur IL 62526

CAMPBELL, RUTH FRANCES WILLIAMS (MRS. JAMES GRAYSON CAMPBELL), physician, educator; b. Back Bay, Va., Dec. 14, 1932; d. Linus Alonzo and Edna (Halstead) Williams; B.S., Mary Washington Coll., 1953; M.D., Med. Coll. Va., 1957; m. James Grayson Campbell, June 29, 1963; children—John Randolph, Elizabeth Duke. Intern De Paul Hosp., Norfolk, Va., 1957-58; resident in pediatrics Med. Coll. Va., Richmond, 1958-60, instr. pediatrics, asst. dir. pediatric outpatient dept., 1962-65, asst. prof. pediatrics, 1965—, acting dir. pediatric outpatient dept., 1967-69; practice medicine specializing in pediatrics, Richmond, 1960-61; chief maternal and child health Richmond City Health Dept., 1961-62. Coordinator multiple handicaps program Bur. Crippled Children, Va. Health Dept., 1965-69. Mem. Richmond Area Safety Council, 1961-62. Fellow Am. Acad. Pediatrics; mem. Va., Richmond (sec., treas. 1966-67; pres. 1967-68) pediatric socs., Richmond Acad. Medicine, Am. Acad. Pediatrics, Med. Coll. Va., Mary Washington Coll. alumni assns. Episcopalian. Home: 7435 Riverside Dr Richmond VA 23225

CAMPBELL, SUSAN ANN MIKULA (MRS. COLIN A. CAMPBELL), congl. press aide; b. North Tonawanda, N.Y., Oct. 6, 1946; d. John Andrew and Pearl Marceline (Mongold) Mikula; B.A. cum laude, St. Bonaventure U., 1968; m. Colin A. Campbell, Oct. 18, 1969; 1 son, Colin Alexander III. Reporter Niagara Falls (N.Y.) Gazette, 1965-67; reporter, editor edn. and spelling bee Syracuse (N.Y.) Herald Jour., 1968-73; press aide Congressman Henry P. Smith III from N.Y., Washington, 1973—. Recipient Nat. Assn. Advancement Ednl. Writing award, 1973. Newspaper Fund scholar, 1966. Mem. Delta Epsilon Sigma, Pi Delta Epsilon. Roman Catholic. Home: 6600 Elk Park Ct Alexandria VA 22310 Office: 2331 Rayburn House Office Bldg Washington DC 22515

CAMPBELL, VERONICA MARY LEE, city ofcl.; b. Balt., May 10, 1917; d. Bernard J. and Sarah (Bailey) Lee; student Balt. Bus. Sch., 1937; m. John William Campbell, Mar. 17, 1943; children—Pat (Mrs. Olin), John William, Kevin, Brian. Local supr. Robinson Directories, Hillsdale, Mich., 1970; clk. municipal council City of St. Mary's (O.), 1972—; reporter Lima (O.) News, 1972—. Mem. Auglaize County Dem. Com., 1963—, exec. sec., 1972—. Mem. Am. Legion Aux., Eagle Aux. Roman Catholic. Home: 323 N Perry St St Marys OH 45885 Office: 101 E Spring St St Marys OH 45885

CAMPBELL, VY MCBRIAN (MRS. RAYMOND ROOSEVELT CAMPBELL), educator; b. Cadillac, Mich., 1918; d. Robert Albert and Rebecca (Kerr) McBrian; A.B., Eastern Mich. U., 1953; M.A., Mich. State U., 1958; m. Raymond Roosevelt Campbell, June 13, 1939; 1 son, Brian Raymond. Tchr., Lansing (Mich.) Pub. Schs., 1939-40, Ann Arbor, Mich., 1940-42, Chattanooga, 1942-43, Washington, 1943-45, Detroit, 1945-48; prin. Northwestern, Lansing, 1949-52, Pleasant Grove, Lansing, 1952-58, Pleasant View, 1958-71, Scottsdale, Ariz., 1971—. Mem. Nat., Lansing (pres.) assns. elementary prins., Am. Assn. U. Women, Ingham County Bar Aux., Lawyer Wives of Mich., Nat., Mich. edn. assns., Delta Kappa Gamma. Clubs: Lansing Country, City of Lansing. Home: 5330 E Calle Del Norte Phoenix AZ 65018 Office: 4243 N Brown Av Scottsdale AZ 85251

CAMPBELL, WINONA GOULD, physician; b. Danby, Vt., Oct. 11, 1910; d. Jay and Mary (Hart) Gould; R.N., Elliott Hosp. Nurses Tng. Sch., Manchester, N.H., 1931; B.S., Tufts Coll., 1935; M.D., Columbia Coll. Phys. and Surg., 1940; m. Frank C. Campbell, Sept. 3, 1938; 1 dau., Suzanne; adopted children—James, Jill, Lawrence. Intern Kings Park State Hosp., N.Y., 1940-41, M. I. Bassett Hosp., Cooperstown, N.Y., 1941-42; resident in pediatrics Babies Hosp., N.Y.C., 1942-44; practice medicine, Miami, Fla., 1944; asst. prof. pediatrics U. Colo. Sch. Medicine, 1946-57, sr. fellow in pediatric allergy, 1958-60, asst. clin. prof. pediatrics, 1961-65, asso. prof. clin. pediatrics, 1965—; practice medicine specializing in pediatric allergy, 1960—. Mem. Colo., Denver County (past. mem.) coms. on poliomyelitis, Denver Accident Prevention Com. Mem. Am. Acad. Pediatrics, Rocky Mountain Pediatrics Soc., Phi Beta Kappa, Alpha Omega Alpha, Alpha Omicron Pi. Clubs: Am. Alpine, Colo. Mountain, Explorationes de Mexico, Mountain of Uganda, East Africa. Author articles in field. Address: 684 Downing St Denver CO 80218

CAMPEAS, ROSELYN HALPERIN (MRS. HYMAN CAMPEAS), librarian; b. Bklyn., Aug. 11, 1928; d. Solomon and Sylvia (Blinder) Halperin; B.A. magna cum laude, Bklyn. Coll., 1965; M.L.S., Pratt Inst., 1967; tchrs. certificate Herzliah Hebrew Tchrs. Acad., 1949; m. Hyman Campeas, Aug. 21, 1948; children—Hedvah (Mrs. Kenneth S. Cohen), Raphael, David. Tchr., Hebrew Sch., Bklyn., 1950-67; head librarian, 1967—. Mem. United Fedn. Tchrs. (mem. media com.), Phi Beta Kappa, Sigma Lamdba Phi, Beta Phi Mu. Home: 72-65 Yellowstone Blvd Forest Hills NY 11375 Office: 800 Van Siclen Av Brooklyn NY 11207

CAMPION, EILEEN, lawyer; b. Great River, N.Y.; d. Patrick and Mary (Gaughan) Campion; J.D., U. Miami, Fla., 1961. Admitted to Fla. bar, 1962; pvt. practice law, Miami, Fla., 1962-64; law editor Lawyers Co-op. Pub. Co., Rochester, N.Y., 1964-65; atty. U.S. Treasury Dept., Miami, 1965—. Founding pres. Womens Com. of One Hundred, Miami, 1970-73; mem. fed. exec. bd. Miami Consumers Com., 1972—, chmn., 1974—; mem. Metro Dade County Water and Sewer Bd, 1973—; city rep. Bd. Legal Services Greater Miami, 1974—. Recipient Outstanding Service award Fed. Bar Assn., 1968, 69; award for untiring efforts for community betterment Womens Com. of One Hundred, 1973. Mem. Am., Dade County (Outstanding Service award 1971) bar assns., Fla. Bar, Am. Assn. U. Women, League Women Voters, Am. Arbitration Assn. (panel arbitrators), Bus. and Profl. Womens Club. Home: 453 Brickell Av Miami FL 33131 Office: 51 SW 1st Av Miami FL 33130

CAMPION, EILEEN MARIE, columnist; b. Yonkers, N.Y., Feb. 26, 1916; d. James Joseph and May Elizabeth (McDonough) Campion; B.A., Coll. Mt. St. Vincent, 1937. With Yonkers (N.Y.) Herald Statesman, 1937—, suburban reporter, society editor, reporter, 1943-68, city editor, 1968-70, editorial page editor, 1970-72, columnist, 1972—. Tchr. English, Mt. St. Vincent Coll., 1938; conf. speaker N.Y. State Edn. Dept., 1968. Mem. Yonkers Tercentennial Com., 1946; mem. Yonkers Centennial Com., 1972; mem. Yonkers Coordinating Com. on Arts, 1972; sec. Westchester Cath. Edn. Council, 1967-68; 3d v.p. United Way Yonkers. Bd. dirs. Yonkers A.R.C., 1943-44, Mt. St. Vincent Alumnae Assn., 1963-66. Recipient citation for distinguished reporting Nat. Edn. Writers Assn., 1959; named 1 of 10 best dressed working girls in U.S., Mayfair Mag., 1947. Mem. Yonkers Bus. and Profl. Women's Club, Yonkers Soroptimist Club, Yonkers C. of C. (publs. chmn. 1972—, dir., U.S. Bicentennial com. 1974—), Sigma Delta Chi (treas. chpt. 1972-73). Editor: Mt. St. Vincent Alumnae Rec., 1963-67. Home: Glenwood Gardens Yonkers NY 10701 Office: Larkin Plaza Yonkers NY 10702

CAMPIONI, SISTER HELEN FRANCES, hosp. adminstr.; b. Hancock, Mich., Jan. 13, 1911; d. Guido and Mabel (Lavorini) Campioni; R.N., St. Joseph's Hosp. Sch. Nursing, Hancock, 1934; postgrad., Mich. Coll. Sci. and Tech., 1943; B.S., Mt. St. Mary's Coll., 1944; postgrad., Seattle U., 1947; M.Ed., U. Ariz., 1957; certificate in Hosp. Exec. Devel., St. Louis U., 1969. Joined Order Sisters of St. Joseph of Carondelet, Los Angeles province, 1944; orthopedic-surg. nurse, Hancock, 1934-38; staff nurse Tb, St. Mary's Hosp., Tucson, 1938-41, sci. instr., 1941-44, pvt. duty nurse summer, 1940, 45, asst. dir. nurses, 1946, dir. nursing, 1947-57; supr. pediatrics and orthopedics St. Joseph's Hosp., Lewiston, Ida., 1957-58, dir. nursing service, 1958-66; adminstr, St. Joseph's Convent and Hosp., Lewiston, 1966—, supr., 1966-72, pres. governing bd., 1966—, organized St. Joseph's Hosp. Aux., 1970. State chmn. nursing edn. facilities No. Ida., 1958-65; now mem. regional adv. council and exec. com. Intermountain Regional Med. Program; mem. Statewide Emergency Med. Services Adv. Council, 1974. Bd. dirs. Blue Cross Ida., Ida. Ednl. Trust and Research Found. Instr. nurses aides A.R.C., World War II, mem. 2d Res., 1945—; instr. med. self-help Civil Def., 1963-64. Mem. Am. Coll. Hosp. Adminstrs., Am., Ida. (dir. 1965-67, organizer jr. vol. group Josettes, 1959, recipient citation for leadership in promoting, aiding, and opening Lewis Clark's Normal Sch. program 1966) nurses assns., Am. Pub. Health Assn., Ida. Conf. Cath. Hosps. (pres. 1958-60), Ida. League Nursing (chmn. nursing services 1958-65), North Ida. Hosp. Council (pres. 1967), Ida. Hosp. Assn. (trustee 1970—, moderator Safety Inst., chmn. conv. program 1971, pres. 1972-73), Nez Perce County Mental Health Assn. (sec. 1969), Lewis-Clark Coronary Care Adv. Council (sec. 1969), Lewis-Clark Comprehensive Health Planning Council (organizer, sec. 1969), C. of C. (Lewis-Clark Normal Sch. com.), North Central Areawide Comprehensive Health Planning (organizer 1969, pres. 1970), Practical Nursing Adv. Council (chmn. 1962), Greater Lewiston C. of C. (dir. 1973), Am. Acad. Med. Adminstrs., N.W. Hosps. Edn. and Research Alliance (dir. 1971-74). Office: 415 6th St Lewiston ID 83501

CAMPIS, CARMEN S., univ. ofcl.; b. Mayaquez, P.R., Nov. 26, 1937; d. Miguel and Hipolita (López) Campis; B.B.A., U. P.R., 1965; M.B.A., InterAm. U., 1969. Asst. to dir. cultural activities U. P.R., Rio Piedras, 1961-65, dir. information and pub. relations adminstrn. regional colls., 1970—; instr. secretarial sci. InterAm. U., San Germán, 1965-69. Mem. Am. Assn. Bus. Women, Am. Assn. U. Profs., Assn. Pub. Relations Officers P.R., Tau Delta Sigma, Alpha Delta Kappa. Home: Gallardo Apts K-3-A Rio Piedras PR Office: Box 21850 U PR Sta Rio Piedras PR 00931

CAMPUS, NANCY RUTH, psychologist, educator; b. N.Y.C., May 27, 1945; d. Hans and Berta (Lump) Salomon; B.A., U. Colo., 1965; Ph.D., N.Y. U., 1970; m. Steven Campus, Mar. 7, 1965; 1 dau., Tanya Deanne. Asst. prof. psychology Queens Coll. of City U. N.Y., 1970—. Cons. in evaluation of govt. sponsored projects. Nat. Def. Edn. Act fellow, 1966-68. Mem. Am. Psychol. Assn., Phi Beta Kappa, Sigma Xi. Home: 106 Brambach Rd Scarsdale NY 10583 Office: Dept Psychology Queens College Flushing NY 11367

CANADA, MARY WHITFIELD, librarian; b. Richmond, Va., June 13, 1919; d. Waverly Thomas and Ruth Bradshaw (Smith) Canada; B.A., magna cum laude, Emory and Henry Coll., 1940; M.A. in English, Duke, 1942; B.S.L.S., U. N.C., Chapel Hill, 1956. Asst. circulation dept. Duke U. Library, 1942-45, undergrad. librarian, 1946-55, reference librarian, 1956—, asst. head reference dept., 1967—. Mem. Am. (life), Southeastern (sec. coll. and univ. sect., chmn. nominating com. reference services div.), N.C. (chmn. nominating com., chmn. newspaper com., chmn. coll. and univ. sect.) library assns., Alumni Assn. Sch. Library Sci. U. N.C. (pres.), Am. Assn. U. Profs., Va. Hist. Soc. (life), Va. Geneal. Soc., D.A.R., Trinity Coll. Hist. Soc. Methodist. Mem. Historic Richmond Found., Beta Phi Mu, Tau Kappa Alpha, Alpha Psi Omega, Delta Kappa Gamma. Contbr. to profl. publs. Home: 1312 Lancaster St Durham NC 27701

CANADAY, MARTHA HELEN, educator; b. Malvern, Ark., June 13, 1918; d. Henry Newton and Martha (Adkins) Canaday; student Ouachita Bapt. Coll., 1936-39; B.S. H.E., Tex. Women's U., 1940; M.S., La. State U., 1945; D.Ed., Pa. State U., 1966. Tchr. pub. schs., Ark., 1940-44; asst. prof. home econ., dir. nursery sch. State Coll. Ark. at Conway, 1945-47, dean women, asso. prof., 1947-56; instr. Pa. State U., University Park, 1956-58; asso. prof. U. N.C., Greensboro, from 1958, now prof., 1972—, also dir. nursery sch., 1960—. Ednl. cons. Head Start program, Office Econ. Opportunity, Region II, 1964-68, United Day-Care Services, Greensboro, 1965—, also bd. dirs.; bd. dirs. Home Econs. Center for Research. Mem. Am., N.C., Guilford County (pres. 1966-67) home econs. assns., So. N.C. assns. children under six, Omicron Nu, Phi Epsilon Omicron, Pi Lambda Theta. Home: 2503 Overbrook Dr Greensboro NC 27408

CANALE, VIRGINIA CLARE, pediatrician; b. Bklyn., Sept. 20, 1936; d. Mario Gregory and Olga Irene (Poggi) Canale; B.S. magna cum laude, Marymount Coll., 1957; M.D., Women's Med. Coll. Pa., 1961. Rotating intern St. Vincent's Hosp., N.Y.C., 1961-62, resident in pediatrics, 1962-63; resident in pediatrics, teaching asst. Bellvue Hosp., 1963-64; NIH fellow in pediatrics, hematology and teaching asst. N.Y. Hosp.-Cornell Med. Center, 1964-67, instr. pediatrics, 1967-69, asst. prof., 1969-73, asso. prof., 1973—, dir. pediatric transfusion clinic, 1970—; pediatric hematology cons. St. John's Riverside Hosp., Yonkers, N.Y. Diplomate Am. Bd. Pediatrics. Mem. Am. Med. Women's Assn., Am. Soc. Hematology, Harvey Soc., Am. Soc. Clin. Research, Soc. Study Blood of N.Y.C. Home: 30 Sherman Av Dobbs Ferry NY 10522 Office: NY Hosp-Cornell Med Center 525 E 68th St New York City NY 10021

CANAVAN, ROBERTA NOLAN (MRS. RICHARD CANAVAN), educator; b. Elizabeth, N.J.; d. John James and Florence (O'Brien) Nolan; B.A., Caldwell Coll., 1964; M.L.S., Rutgers U., 1968; postgrad. Seton Hall U., 1964, U. Ottawa, 1970-71, Newark State Coll., 1973; m. Richard Canavan, Aug. 21, 1965; 1 son, Colin Michael. Tchr. English Linden (N.J.) High Sch., 1964-65; sch. librarian, Linden, N.J., 1965-70, 71-73; asst. dir. Linden Adult Sch., 1974, dir., 1975—. Vis. lectr. U. Ottawa Library Sch., 1970-71; adj. instr. library sci. Newark State Coll., Kean, 1972. Mem. Linden (N.J.) Cultural Affairs Com., 1972—; pub. relations chmn. Linden Bicentennial Celebration. Mem. committeewoman Democratic party, 1973—, sec., 1974—. Mem. N.E.A., N.J., Union County, Linden edn. assns., League Women Voters, Pi Delta Epsilon, Delta Epsilon Sigma, Sigma Tau Delta. Home: 1217 N Stiles St Linden NJ 07036

CANCIO, RITA MARIA, scholar; b. Havana, Cuba, July 25, 1925; d. Leopold and Carmen R. (Capote) Cancio; B.A., Maryville Coll. Sacred Heart, 1947; M.A., U. Ky., 1948; Ph.D., U. Madrid, 1952, St. Louis U., 1955; research scholar of Spanish Fgn. Dept., 1950-53, fellow Oriental Inst. Arias Montano, 1950-51; fellow Faculty Philosophy and Letters U. Madrid, 1950-53. Joined Third Order St. Francis, 1945, Discalced Carmelite Third Secular Order, 1958, Benedictine 3d Order, 1960; asso. prof. history and lit., U. Villanueva, Cuba, 1955, prof. ancient and Midieval history, 1955-59, asst. prof. modern lang. St. Francis Coll., Loretto, Pa., 1956-58; asso. prof. Duchesne Coll., Omaha, 1960—; asso. prof. Spanish and classical Latin, State Coll. Ia., 1960-62; asso. prof. Spanish U. Dayton, 1962-63. Margaret Voorhies Haggin Research scholar U. Ky., 1947-49; fellow Germanistics, U. Innsbruck (Austria), 1949-50; fellow Oriental Inst. Arias Montano for Classical Hebrew and Nr. Eastern studies, 1950-52. Mem. Am. Assn. Tchrs. Spanish and Portuguese, Instituto Cubano De Genealogia y Heraldica, Academia Cubana de Ciencias Genealogicas, Phi Sigma Iota. Author: Maria Cristina de Austria Reina de Espana, 1952; Jose Toniolo, 1956; Maria Christina of Austria's Regency, 1957; Las Ordenes Terceras Seculares Palestras de Santidad, 1960; Europe Eternal, 1969; The New Mass: From Holy Sacrifice to Popular Assembly, 1970; The Autodemolition of the Church, 1973; The Mystery of Iniquity, 1974; also numerous articles in field. Home: 931 Gainsborough Rd Dayton OH 45419

CANDEA, LELLA (HENRIETTA STEWART), journalist; b. Abington, Pa., Apr. 11, 1935; d. James Stewart and Frances (Heacock) Smith; B.A., Goucher Coll., 1956; postgrad. Santiniketan U., West Bengal, India, 1959, Oxford (Eng.) U., 1965; m. Randall Stewart Candea, Aug. 11, 1973. Librarian, UN, N.Y.C., 1956-57; editorial asst. New Yorker Mag., N.Y.C., 1957-59; adminstrv. asst. Am. Friends Service Com., Phila., 1960-61; nat. fundraiser Womens Internat. League for Peace and Freedom, Phila., 1962-65; program cons. D.C. Commrs. Council on Human Relations, Washington, 1965-66; program analysis officer Community Relations Service, Dept. Justice, Washington, 1967-72; journalist, 1972—. Cons. Am. Friends Service Com., African Am. Inst., Washington. Mem. exec. bd. Race Relations Com., Phila. Yearly Meeting of Friends, 1964-66; mem. Am. Friends Service Com. Corp., 1961-62. Mem. Planners for Equal Opportunity, Womens Internat. League for Peace and Freedom (nat. dir. 1966-69, nat. exec. bd. 1968-69), Nat. Assn. Inter-group Relations Ofcls. Mem. Soc. of Friends. Author: New Minority Enterprises, 1969. Home: 510 Sunset Santa Fe NM 87501

CANDELARIA, ANGIE DALLABETTA, educator; b. Durango, Colo., July 13, 1939; d. Angelo and Lucia M (Matteri) Dallabetta; B.A., Ft. Lewis Coll., 1965; postgrad. U. No. Colo., 1966; m. David Candelaria, Sept. 24, 1958 (div. Mar. 1963); children—David, Craig. Tchr. elementary pub. schs., Loveland, Colo., 1967-68; tchr. spl. edn. Dist. 9R, Durango, Colo., 1968—. Recipient hon. mention Colo. Tchr. of the Year Colo. Dept. Edn., 1970. Colo. Dept. Spl. Edn. grantee, 1966, Cross-Cultural Inst. grantee, 1972-74. Mem. Council for Exceptional Children, Am. Assn. for Mental Deficiency, Nat., Colo., Durango edn. assns. Republican. Roman Catholic. Home: 601 East 4th Av Durango CO 81301 Office: 12th St and 3rd Av Durango CO 81301

CANDY, ARDIS JEAN (MRS. GRANDON E. TOLSTEDT), physician; b. Milw., Dec. 29, 1924; d. Walter C. and Bertha (Johnson) Candy; B.S., Beloit Coll., 1946; M.S., U. Wis., 1948, M.D., 1950; m. Grandon E. Tolstedt, June 13, 1949; children—Margaret Ellen, Betsy Elaine, Mark Andrew, Anthony Ross. Intern Wesley Meml. Hosp., Chgo., 1950-51; staff physician Municipal Tb Sanitarium, Chgo., 1952-53, Firland Tb Sanitarium, Seattle, 1953-54; resident psychiatry Seattle VA Hosp., U. Wash., Seattle, 1954-57; attending physician psychiatry Seattle VA Hosp., 1957, cons. psychiatry, 1957-59, ward psychiatrist, 1959-60, attending in psychiatry, 1960-63; fellow, asst. dept. psychiatry King County Hosp., Seattle, 1957-59; part-time practice medicine specializing in gen. psychiatry Quain & Ramstad Clinic, Bismarck, N.D., 1963—; mem. staff Bismarck Hosp., Bismarck; mem. psychiat. staff St. Alexius Hosp., Bismarck, N.D., 1963—, chief, 1967, 71; clin. instr. psychiatry U. Wash., 1954-63. Bd. dirs. Charles L. Hall Youth Service, 1964—, chmn., 1964-67. Recipient Distinguished Service award Beloit Coll., 1971. Mem. A.M.A., Sixth Dist. N.D. Med. Soc., Am. Psychiat. Assn. (dist. sec. 1969-72, pres. elect 1971-72, pres. 1973—), Phi Beta Kappa. Home: 1257 E Highland Acres Bismarck ND 58501 Office: 221 N 5th St Bismarck ND 58501

CANE, ENA MARA MONK (MRS. ROGER DAVIES CANE), librarian; b. Boston, Feb. 26, 1909; d. Ernest George and Ena Yvonne (Hoag) Monk; ed. privately; m. Roger Davies Cane, May 26, 1935. Employee relations exec. R.H. Macy's, N.Y.C., 1934-42; tng. dir. Forbes & Wallace, Springfield, Mass., 1942-43; employment interviewer, job description writer U.S. Employment Service, Springfield, 1943-45; with S. White Dickinson Meml. Library, Whately, Mass., 1952—, chief librarian, 1953—; head circulation U. Mass. Library, Amherst, 1961-63; head cataloger Jones Library, Amherst, 1965—. Sec. exec. council Western Mass. Pub. Library System, 1962-66. Mem. Conn. Valley, Western Mass. library assns. Mem. Ch. of Eng. Author: Whately 1771-1971: A New England Portrait, 1972. Home: Chestnut Plain Rd Whately MA 01093 Office: Jones Library Amity St Amherst MA 01002 also S White Dickinson Meml Library Whately MA 01093

CANEDY, BRENDA HARAM (MRS. NORMAN WIGTON CANEDY), educator; b. Marion, Ind., Nov. 13, 1932; d. Benjamin Lewis and Margaret (Weesner) Haram; A.B., Radcliffe Coll., 1954; postgrad. Ind. U., 1954-55, Coll. St. Catherine, St. Paul, 1969-71; M.S., U. Minn., 1974; m. Norman Wigton Canedy, Sept. 15, 1956. Mem. faculty Lower Sch., Tudor Hall, Indpls., 1955-56, Lower Sch., Nightingale-Bamford Sch., N.Y.C., 1956-59; asst. to dir. Schlesinger Library, Radcliffe Coll., Cambridge, Mass., 1960; mem. faculty Lower Sch., Summit Sch., St. Paul, 1962-64, dir., 1964-67; instr. Sch. Nursing, coordinator community services Univ. Hosps., U. Minn., 1973—. Del., Council Community Councils, 1969—; mem. mayor's com. urban environment Task Force on Historic Preservation, Mpls., 1969—; commr. historic preservation, Mpls., 1972—. Bd. dirs. Kenwood Isles Area Assn., 1967—. Mem. Soc. Indiana Pioneers, Soc. Genealogists, D.A.R., Nat. Soc. Colonial Dames XVII Century (nat. roster chmn. 1960-64), Nat. Soc. Magna Charta Dames, P.E.O., Pi Lambda Theta, Sigma Theta Tau. Presbyn. Clubs: Radcliffe (pres. 1968-72), Woman's (Mpls.). Home: 1932 Kenwood Pkwy Minneapolis MN 55405

CANFIELD, JANE WHITE, sculptor; b. Syracuse, N.Y., Apr. 29, 1897; d. Ernest Ingersol and Katharine Curtin (Sage) White; student N.Y. Art Students League, 1918-20, Borglum Sch., 1920-22; m. Charles F. Fuller, Sept. 9, 1922; children—Jane Sage (Mrs. John Cowles, Jr.), Isabel W. (Mrs. Joseph M. Fox), Blair F. Exhibited one-artist shows Am.-Brit. Art Gallery, N.Y.C., 1951, County Art Gallery, Westbury, L.I., N.Y., 1960, FAR Gallery, N.Y.C., 1965, 74; exhibited World's Fair, 1939, Archtl. League, Knoedler Gallery, Am. Acad.; executed figure for ch., Locust Valley, N.Y., figures for Miss Porters Sch., Farmington, Conn. Chmn. bd. dirs. Bedford-Rippowam Sch., 1933-38; bd. dirs. A.R.C. Arts and Skills, Washington, 1942-45, Planned Parenthood, 1945-55, Internat. Planned Parenthood, 1955-65, Margaret Sanger Bur., 1965—, Huxley Inst. Biosocial Research, 1971—. Author: The Frog Prince, 1970. Address: Guard Hill Rd Bedford NY 10506

CANISIA, SISTER MARY, hosp. adminstr.; b. Sindersfeld, Germany, Aug. 29, 1914; d. Joseph and Maria Anna (Balzer) Gerlach; came to U.S. 1935, naturalized 1941; R.N., St. Francis Hosp., Peoria, Ill., 1940, certificate anesthesia, 1941; B.S., Creighton U., 1951; M.A. in Hosp. Adminstrn., St. Louis U., 1960. Joined Order of St. Francis, 1935; floor supr. St. Joseph's Hosp., Keokuk, Ia., 1940-43; staff St. Francis Hosp., Peoria, 1945—, instr. Sch. Nursing, 1946-48, Sch. Anesthesia, 1944, 51-54, dir. Sch. Anesthesia, 1954-58, adminstr. hosp., 1960—; pres. St. Francis Community Clinic, Peoria, 1967—. Mem. nursing service com. Central Ill. A.R.C.; mem. health occupations adv. council Ill. Central Coll., East Peoria, Ill. Fellow Am. Coll. Hosp. Administrs.; mem. Am., Ill., Catholic hosp. assns., Ill. Conf. Cath. Hosps. (sec. 1967-68). Address: St Francis Hosp 530 NE Glen Oak St Peoria IL 61603

CANN, MARJORIE MITCHELL, educator; b. Moncton, N.B., Can.; d. Douglas Robert and Maude (Dunham) Mitchell; B.S., Acadia U., N.S., 1940; M.A., Mich. State U., 1953; Ph.D., U. Mich., 1957. Tchr. prin. pub. elementary schs., N.S., Ont., Can., 1936-48; tchr. secondary schs., N.S., Que., Can. and East Lansing, Mich., 1950-56; instr. math. Acadia U., 1957-61; dir. math. Delta Coll., Bay City, Mich., 1961-63; adminstrv. head Greater Cleve. Math. Program, 1963-64; asso. prof. math.-edn. and research U. Akron (O.), 1964-67; prof. edn., head behavioral scis. Pensacola (Fla.) Jr. Coll., 1967—. Ednl. adviser Pensacola Cerebral Palsy Center, 1967-71; bd. dirs. N.W. Fla. Center, 1971—, chmn. professional adv. com., 1971—; pres. Mitchell-Meriwether Corp., 1969—. Mem. Nat. Council Tchrs. Math., Math. Assn. Am., Nat., Fla., Pensacola assns. supervision and curriculum devel., N.E.A., Canadian Edn. Assn., Nat. Soc. Programmed Instrn., Pensacola C. of C. (com. on edn. 1972-74). Author: (with other) A Synthesis of Teaching Methods, 1964; author, editor An Introduction to Education, 1972. Contbr. articles to profl. jours. Home: 4740 Peacock Dr Pensacola FL 32504

CANN, MRS. WILLIAM N. (RUTH CANN), club woman; b. Camden, N.J.; d. John A. and Martha (Williams) Miller; student Normal Sch., Camden, 1918; m. William N. Cann, June 26, 1920; children—Ruth Evelyn (Mrs. J. Donald Martone), Miriam Dorothy (Mrs. Robert Owen Lane), William N. Chief div. women's div. Del. Dept. Civil Def., hon. permanent chmn. govs. adv. council; vice pres. Del. Safety Council; rep. to VA com. Vets. Hosp. from Women's Clubs; vice chmn. Del. CARE com.; mem. Mayor's Christmas com.; mem. adv. council U.S.O. and dir. coordinating com.; chmn. Mother's March Polio; mem. Govs. Edn. Com.; bd. dirs. Del. Blood Bank Assn., Del. Humane Assn., Greater Wilmington Com., Nat. Found.; trustee Wesley Jr. Coll., Dover, Del., Nat. Soc. Crippled Children; pres. Fed. Services Com., Del. Soc. Crippled Children; dir. Needlework Guild, Cancer Soc.; treas. Del. Festival of the Arts; parliamentarian jr. bd. Wilmington Gen. Hosp.; v.p. Muscular Dystrophy Assn.; chmn. vol. service Mental Health Assn.; active A.R.C.; sec. Salvation Army, Women's Joint Legislative Com.; chmn. Mother of the Year Com.; mem. nat. bd. Japan Internat. Christian U.; pres. Wilmington Opera Guild, Del. Symphony Women's Aux. Mem. C. of C. (edn. com.), UN Am. Assn. (chmn. speakers bur.) Am. Legion Aux. (nat. v.p. 1942), City Fedn. Women's Clubs and Allied Organs. (pres.), League Women Voters (past pres.), City (pres. past officers club), State (radio chmn., pres.), Gen. (mem. nat. legislation com.) fedns. women's clubs, Nat. Fedn. Music Clubs. Clubs: Wilmington New Century (pres.); Washington Heights Century (pres.). Home: 2401 Pennsylvania Av Wilmington DE 19806

CANNAVA, DIANE FRANCES, educator; b. Boston, Apr. 1, 1947; d. John Anthony and Frances Marie (Lena) Cannava; B.A., St. Joseph's Coll., 1969; postgrad. Boston Coll., 1970—. Presch. tchr. Mystic Valley Assn. for Retarded Children, Lexington, Mass., 1969-70; tchr. Lexington Community Clin. Nursery, Mass. Dept. Mental Health, 1970—. Tchr. Lexington Summer Program for Presch. Retarded Children, summers 1970, 71; asst. tchr. Day Care for Retarded Children, Mystic Valley, summer 1972; mem. clin. team Mystic Valley Mental Health Clinic for Children, Lexington, 1970—; cons. to spl. edn. staff Lexington Pub. Schs., 1970—. Mem. Am. Assn. Mental Deficiency, Council for Exceptional Children, Mystic Valley Assn. for Retarded Children, Nat., Mass. assns. for retarded children, Mystic Valley, Central Middlesex mental health assns. Home: 130 Goldsmith St Littleton MA 01460 Office: 1997 Massachusetts Av Lexington MA 02173

CANNON, ELAINE WINIFRED ANDERSON, mag. editor; b. Salt Lake City, Apr. 9, 1922; d. Aldon Joseph and Minnie (Egan) Anderson; B.S., U. Utah, 1943; m. Donald James Cannon, Mar. 25, 1943; children—James Quayle, Carla, Christine (Mrs. Heber Jacobsen), Su (Mrs. Bryant McOmber), Holly (Mrs. Richard Metcalf), Anthony Joseph. With Deseret News, Salt Lake City, 1943-69, feature writer, columnist, 1944-47, editor teen dept., 1947-69; asso. editor New Era mag., Salt Lake City, 1970—; asso. editor Era of Youth mag., 1960-70; moderator It's a Date, Sta. KSL-TV, Salt Lake City, 1952-55, Focus on Youth, Sta. KUTV, 1961-65, 67-69, Public Pulse for Youth, Sta. KSL, 1966-67. Instr. continuing edn. U. Utah, Salt Lake City, 1964, Brigham Young U., Provo, Utah, 1958, Utah State U., Logan, 1968-70. Del. White House Conf. on Children and Youth, 1950-51; mem. adv. bd. Juvenile Ct., Salt Lake City, 1970-71, Boy's Ranch Utah, Salt Lake City, 1966—; mem. spl. program com. Am. Cancer Soc., Salt Lake City, 1965-66. Bd. dirs. Women Unlimited Conv. Program Bur., Salt Lake City. Recipient 1st prize writing youth div. Nat. Press Women Assn., 1958, service to youth citation Seventeen mag., 1955; named Woman Year, Ricks Coll., 1965, Weber State Coll., 1971, Ida. State U., 1972. Mem. Author's Club, Am. Press Women Assn., Mortar Bd., Alpha Lambda Delta, Chi Omega. Republican. Mem. Ch. Jesus Christ Latter-day Saints (All-Ch. Honored Woman 1967). Author: Time of Your Life, 1954; Corner on Youth, 1963; Teens and Their Times, 1964; How Glorious is Youth, 1969; A Time for Living; After the Manner of Happiness; It's A Great Idea; Home: 1283 E South Temple Salt Lake City UT 84102

CANNON, JEAN WARD (MRS. WILBUR J. CANNON), pub.; b. Bowling Green, Ky., July 19, 1926; d. Herbert A. and Ora B. (Clark) Ward; A.B., Western Ky. U., 1947; m. Wilbur J. Cannon, May 9, 1947; children—Lawrence W., Patrick Terence, Clark Robert. Feature writer, editor Jacksonville (Ark.) News, 1957-58; editor Weekly Herald, Universal City, Tex., 1970-71; co-publisher Allen County News, Scottsville, Ky., 1971—. Recipient awards column Ky. Weekly Newspaper Assn., 1972, 73. Mem. Ky., Western Ky. press assns., Nat., Weekly newspaper assns., C. of C. Home: 307 N 4th Scottsville KY 42164 Office: 101 N 1st Scottsville KY 42164

CANNON, MARILYN LUCILLE (MRS. CARL JOHN GUZZO), pediatrician; b. Newark, Aug. 6, 1926; d. George Dewey and Helen Gould (Haines) Cannon; B.S., U. Md., 1948; M.D., Woman's Med. Coll. Pa., 1952; m. Carl John Guzzo, June 6, 1960; 1 son, Carl John. Intern, Martland Med. Center, Newark, 1952-53; resident, St. Michael's Hosp., Newark, 1953-56; practice medicine specializing in pediatrics Spring Lake, N.J.; asst. chief pediatrics Jersey Shore Med. Center. Mem. State N.J. Crippled Children's Commn., 1956-72. Pres. P.T.A. H. W. Mountz Sch., Spring Lake, N.J., 1971-73. Diplomate Am. Bd. Pediatrics. Fellow Am. Acad. Pediatrics; mem. A.M.A., N.J. Med. Soc. Address: 20 Worthington St Spring Lake NJ 07762

CANNON, MARTHA RUTH SHELTON, city ofcl.; b. Los Angeles, Oct. 27, 1914; d. William Cortez and Ruth (Zimmerman) Shelton; student Scripps Coll., 1932-34; B.A., Pomona Coll., 1936; teaching certificate Claremont Grad. Sch., 1941; m. William J. Cannon, Dec. 31, 1941; children—Martha (Mrs. Bill Douglas Arnold), William Shelton. Tchr. phys. edn., 1938-41; mem. Library Bd., Burbank, Cal., 1954-58; mem. Planning Commn., Town of Los Gatos, Cal., 1968-70, mem. Town Council, 1970—, mayor, 1972-73. Trustee Good Samaritan Hosp. of Santa Clara County. Pres., Los Gatos High Sch. P.T.A., 1958-60, 62-64. Pres., West Valley Republican Women. Recipient hon. service award P.T.A., 1958. Mem. Am. Assn. U. Women (fellowships award 1968), Phi Lambda Theta. Home: 18400 Overlook Rd Los Gatos CA 95030 Office: 110 E Main St Los Gatos CA 95030

CANNON, MILDRED SOUTHERN (MRS. RUFUS R. CANNON), statistician; b. Washington, Sept. 29, 1935; d. Albert and Mildred Marian (Rivers) Southern; B.A., Howard U., 1957; M.P.H., U. N.C., 1974; m. Rufus R. Cannon, Apr. 7, 1958; children—Rufus R., Carole Lynne. Survey statistician U.S. Dept. Health, Edn. and Welfare, Washington, 1962-68; survey statistician, biometry br. Nat. Inst. Mental Health, Rockville, Md., 1968—. Mem. Am. Pub. Health Assn. Home: 5144 8th St NE Washington DC 20011 Office: 5600 Fishers Lane Rockville MD 20852

CANOVA, JUDY, actress; b. Starke, Fla., Nov. 20, 1916; d. Joseph Francis and Henriette (Perry) Canova; student pub. schs.; children—Julieta (Mrs. Gene Maurel), Diana Canova Rivero. Former star Judy Canova Show, NBC Radio; actress various motion pictures including Scatterbrain, Honey Chile, Sis Hopkins; state fairs N.Y., Ariz., Ky.; records; TV guest appearances include Alfred Hitchcock; on tour with No, No, Nanette, 1971-73. Home: PO Box 36261 Los Angeles CA 90036

CANTON, SHELLY TERMAN (MRS. IRVING D. CANTON), artist; b. Chgo., Apr. 16, 1930; d. Mandel A. and Gean (Vitkin) Terman; student U. Ia., 1948; m. Irving D. Canton, Sept. 28, 1958; 1 dau., Diana. One-man shows at Studio 47 East, N.Y., Gilman's and Feingartens galleries, Chgo.; exhibited in group shows at Art Inst. Chgo., N.Y. Downtown Gallery, Carlbach Gallery, N.Y.C., Chgo. Pub. Library, Gilman's Gallery, Chgo., others; represented in permanent collections at Art Inst. Chgo.; also pvt. collections; illustrator popular mags. including Seventeen, Harpers Bazaar, Todays Health, Playboy. Recipient Pauline Palmer prize Art Inst. Chgo., 1958. Home: 4141 Grove St Skokie IL 60076

CANTOR, LAURA MANUS LEWINN, lawyer, state ofcl.; b. Phila., Apr. 10, 1945; d. Emanuel Sigmund and Claire Charlotte (Rynes) Le Winn; B.A., Wellesley Coll., 1967; J.D., N.Y. U., 1970; m. Norman L. Cantor, Dec. 13, 1968. Admitted to N.J. bar, 1970, Fed. bar, 1970; asst. dep. pub. defender Appellate Sect., Office of the Pub. Defender, Newark, 1970-72; asst. dep. pub. defender Office of the Pub. Defender, Union County Trial Region, Elizabeth, N.J., 1972-74; dep. dir. N.J. State Dept. Mental Health Advocacy, Trenton, 1974—. Mem. Am. Civil Liberties Union, Nat. Lawyers Guild. N.J. State Bar Assn., Nat. Orgn. Women. Home: 40 Washington St Apt K4 East Orange NJ 07017 Office: Dept Mental Health Advocacy 214 S Broad St Trenton NJ 08608

CANTOS, IRENE RITA (MRS. EARL JAMES CANTOS), broker, mezzo soprano; b. N.Y.C., Aug. 25, 1922; d. Angelo and Mabel (Flamentov) Trifiatis; Mus.B., Southwestern Coll. and Coll. of Music, Memphis, 1944; m. Earl James Cantos, Jan. 26, 1947; children—Rita, Earl J., Roxanne, William. Mezzo soprano with San Diego Civic Light Opera, 1947—; mezzo soprano soloist with San Diego Philharmonic Orch., 1951, 56. numerous performances in concert, stage, TV and radio, 1940—; pres. Cantos Realty, San Diego, 1971—. Pres., Marvin Elementary Sch. P.T.A., 1956-57; adviser Com. for Beautification Downtown San Diego, 1960; mem. San Diego Symphony Aux., 1969—, San Diego Bar Aux., 1953—, Women's Aux. Salk Inst., 1969—. Named Citizen of the Year, San Diego Masonic Club, 1962. Republican. Mem. Greek Orthodox Ch. (trustee 1972). Home: 5249 Marlborough Dr San Diego CA 92116 Office: 4178 Adams Av San Diego CA 92116

CAPARN, RHYS (MRS. HERBERT JOHANNES STEEL), sculptor; b. Onteora Park, N.Y., July 28, 1909; d. Harold ap Rhys and Clara (Jones) Caparn; student Brearly Sch., N.Y.C., 1918-27, Bryn Mawr Coll., 1927-29, Ecole Artistique des Animaux, Paris, 1929-30, Archipenko Sch. Art, 1931-33; m. Herbert Johannes Steel, Sept. 9, 1935. Instr. sculpture, Dalton Sch., 1946-55, 60-72. Exhibited one-man shows Riverside Mus. Am., 1961, Delphic Studios, N.Y.C., 1933-35, Archtl. League, N.Y.C., 1941, Whitney Anns., 1941, 53, 54, 56, 60, N.Y. Zool. Park, 1942, Wildenstein & Co., 1944, 47, Dartmouth Coll., 1949, 55, John Heller Gallery, 1953, Art Colony Gallery, Cleve. 1955, Meltzer Gallery, N.Y.C., 1956, 59, 60, La Boetie Gallery, N.Y.C., 1970, New Bertha Schaefer Gallery, 1973; represented in permanent collections City Art Mus., St. Louis Morton May collection, Colorado Springs Fine Arts Center, Dartmouth Coll., Fogg Mus., Whitney Mus. Am. Art, Corcoran Gallery of Art, Barnard Coll. Library, Bryn Mawr Coll., Norfolk Mus., Va., Mus. City N.Y., Riverside Museum Collection at Brandeis U., Elrehjem Art Center U. Wis. at Madison, also represented in exhbn. Am. Painters and Sculptors, touring Asia and Europe under auspices Dept. State, 1957. Mem. N.Y. Mayor's Com. for Beautification N.Y.C., 1963-64; founder, mem. Harlem Cultural Council. Recipient 2d prize for Am. sculpture Met. Mus. Art, 1951; medal of honor, Nat. Assn. Women Artists, 1960, 61. One of eleven Am. sculptors representing U.S. in competition Unknown Political Prisoner, Tate Gallery, London, 1953. Fellow Internat. Inst. Arts and Letters; mem. Sculptors Guild, Am. Abstract Artists. Biog. material in library Syracuse U., Archives Am. Art. Address: Route 1 Taunton Hill Rd Newtown CT 06470

CAPECELATRO, ANN JOSEPHINE (MRS. JOSEPH V. LEVENDUSKI), optometrist; b. West Haven, Conn., Jan. 11, 1925; d. Gennaro and Frances Mary (Cuzzocreo) Capecelatro; O.D., Pa. Coll. Optometry, 1946; m. Joseph V. Levenduski, June 12, 1954; children—David Joseph, Kathryn Frances. Practice optometry, New Haven, 1947—. Trustee Cheshire Acad., v.p. bd. dirs. Parents Assn. Mem. Conn., New Haven County optometric socs., Optometric Extension Program Found., New Eng. Council Optometrists, Am. Assn. U. Women. Home: 451 Prudden Lane Orange CT 06477 Office: 646 George St New Haven CT 06511

CAPEHART, HARRIET JANE HOLMES (MRS. HOMER EARL CAPEHART, JR.), educator, civic worker; b. Springfield, Ill.; d. Walter Creager and Mary Gladys (Copeland) Holmes; A.B., Vassar Coll., 1938; A.M., Radcliffe Coll., 1945; Ph.D., Harvard, 1948; m. Homer Earl Capehart, Jr., June 17, 1950; children—Craig Earl, Caroline Mary, John Homer. Statistician, P.R. Mallory & Co., Inc., Indpls., 1942-43; instr. econs. Wheaton Coll., Norton, Mass., 1945-46, Wellesley (Mass.) Coll., 1947-48; asso. prof., head econs. dept. Western Coll. for Women, Oxford, O., 1948-50; lectr. econs. Butler U., summers 1948-50, asso. prof., 1950-51. Treas., Indpls. Day Nursery Jr. Aux., 1940-41, chmn. spl. project com., 1968—, mem. bldg. fund drive com., 1969-70; treas. Children's Mus. Guild, 1953-54, dir., 1972—; chmn. spl. projects com. women's com. Ind. State Symphony Soc., 1967-69, patrons chmn. Symphony Ball, also Stardust Over Indiana, 1957, capt. maintenance fund drives, 1961-68; pres. P.T.A., 1965-66; scholarship chmn. Indpls. Council P.T.A., 1959-60; active United Fund. Trustee Ind. Central Coll., Indpls., 1969—, mem. adv. com. for continuing edn. for women, 1969—, instr. course, 1972. Mem. D.A.R., Colonial Dames Am. (dir. Ind. 1973—), Phi Beta Kappa (mem. Ind. Bd. 1964—, v.p. 1972-73, pres. 1973—), Kappa Alpha Theta (v.p. 1955-56). Republican. Clubs: Vassar (Ind. pres. 1954-55, 73—, prospective student chmn. 1969—), Radcliffe (Ind. pres. 1964-66, mem. bd. Indpls. 1968—), Contemporary (dir.), Portfolio. Home: 445 Pine Dr Indianapolis IN 46260

CAPERS, CHARLOTTE, state ofcl.; b. Columbia, Tenn.; d. Walter B. and Louise (Woldridge) Capers; student Millsaps Coll., 1930-32, U. Colo., 1932; B.A., U. Miss., 1934. With Miss. Dept. Archives and History, 1938—, successively sec., research and editorial asst., asst. dir., 1938-55, dir., 1955-69, dir. spl. projects, 1969-74, dir. information and edn., 1974—; asst. editor Jour. Miss. History, 1942-43, asso. editor, 1943-55, editor-in-chief, 1956-69; columnist Jackson Daily News, 1944-55, State Times, 1955, Dixie Roto Mag., 1957; book reviews N.Y. Times Book Rev., various hist. jours. Recipient 1st Fed. award for outstanding service to Miss. Chmn. Miss. Hist. Commn., 1955-69. Bd. dirs. Miss. Arts Festival, 1969-74. Fellow Soc. Am. Archivists; mem. Jr. League of Jackson, Miss. State Hist. Soc. (sec.-treas. 1956-69, pres. 1974-75), Am., So. hist. assns., Am. Assn. Museums. Episcopalian (vestry). Editor: (with William D. McCain) Papers of the Washington County Historical Society, 1954. Editorial dir. Mississippi in the Confederacy, 1961; adv. editorial bd. Jefferson Davis Papers, Rice U., 1964—; contbg. editor Delta Rev., 1966-70. Home: 4020 Berkeley Dr Jackson MS 39211 Office: Archives and History Bldg Jackson MS 39205

CAPOZZI, MARIAN RITA, librarian; b. Balt.; d. Daniel Michael and Frances Jane (Ziolkowski) Capozzi; B.S., U. Md., 1949; M.S. in L.S., Catholic U. Am., 1967. Tchr. Baltimore County Schs., Md., 1950-55; librarian, tchr., adviser U.S. Dependent Schs., Stuttgart, Germany, also Rochefort, France, 1955-57; librarian Baltimore County Schs., 1957-61; librarian Westchester (N.Y.) County Schs., 1962-65; supr. library services Bd. Edn. of Baltimore County, Towson, 1966—. Mem. A.L.A., Md. Library Assn., Assn. for Edn. Communication Tech., Ednl. Media Assn. Md., Internat. Platform Assn., Beta Phi Mu, Delta Delta Delta. Soroptimist. Home: 6802 Dunhill Rd Baltimore MD 21222 Office: 6901 N Charles St Towson MD 21204

CAPP, CAROL CLAPP (MRS. GLENN RICHARD CAPP, JR.), educator; b. New Orleans, Mar. 13, 1944; d. Joseph Carlos and Brownie Marie (West) Clapp; student William Jewell Coll., 1962-64; B.A., U. Tex., 1966; M.A., Baylor U., 1968; postgrad. U. Mo., 1969; m. Glenn Richard Capp, Jr., Mar. 8, 1968; 1 dau., Catherine Elizabeth. Asst. instr. U. Mo., 1968-69; lectr. Humboldt State Coll., Arcata, Cal., 1969-70, Ft. Steilacoom Community Coll., Tacoma, Wash., 1970-71, St. Martin's Coll., Olympia, Wash., 1971, U. Puget Sound, 1971-72, Pacific Luth. U., Tacoma, Wash., 1970-74. Mem. Speech Communicationa Assn., Childbirth Edn. Assn., Speaker's Bur. (chmn. 1973-74), Alpha Gamma Delta. Baptist. Home: 12120 47th Av E Tacoma WA 98446

CAPP, THELMA ROBUCK (MRS. GLENN RICHARD CAPP, SR.), educator; b. Fort Worth, June 3, 1910; d. Milton Otway and Sarah Ethel (Myrick) Robuck; B.A., Mary Hardin Baylor Coll., 1935; M.A., Northwestern U., 1941; m. Glenn Richard Capp, May 25, 1940; 1 son, Glenn Richard. Dir. forensics, instr. speech Mary Hardin Baylor Coll., 1935-40; prof. oral communication Baylor U., Waco, Tex., 1946—. Past pres., Council Social Welfare, Waco; pres. P.T.A., 1951. Mem. Nat., So., Tex. speech communications assns., Baylor Round Table, Pi Kappa Delta, Alpha Psi Omega, Zeta Phi Eta. Methodist (mem. adminstrv. bd. 1968-73). Democrat. Club: Current Events (Waco). Author: (with Glenn R. Capp) Principles of Argumentation and Debate, 1965, Workbook for Principles of Argumentation and Debate, 1965. Home: 3000 Cumberland St Waco TX 76707

CAPPONE, MARGARET KATHLEEN, psychologist; b. Arnold, Pa., Feb. 26, 1940; d. Theodore T. and Josephine (Lilli) Cappone; B.A., Marymount Coll., 1961; M.A., Fordham U., 1963, Ph.D., 1967. Vocational counselor Cath. Charities, N.Y.C., 1963, 66-67; instr. psychology Marymount Coll., 1964-66; research asso. N.Y. Med. Coll., 1967-68; asso. prof., chmn. dept. psychology Saginaw (Mich.) Valley Coll., 1968—. Instr. psychology Pace Coll., also Queens Coll., 1966-68; exec. dir. Chrysallis Center for Devel. Human Resources; pvt. cons. psychologist. Pres., bd. dirs. Affiliated Research and Cons. Specialists, Inc.; mem. Saginaw Polit. Action Com., 1974. Mem. Am. Psychol. Assn., A.A.A.S., Sigma Xi. Contbr. articles to profl. jours. Home: 7880 Fishlake Rd Holly MI 48442 Office: 2250 Pierce Rd University Center MI 48710

CAPRIOLI, TERESA MARIA DI SALVO (MRS. CARLO CAPRIOLI), microbiologist; province ofcl.; b. Palermo, Italy (came to Can. 1953, naturalized 1959); d. Giacomo and Maria (Scholz) di

Salvo; Ph.D. in Natural Scis., U. Palermo, 1939; m. Carlo Caprioli, Sept. 25, 1940; 1 dau., Giacometta C. Vittoria. Asst. prof. Inst. Zoology, U. Palermo, 1938-39; prof. natural scis. and chemistry Liceo F. Crispi, Tirana, Albania, 1940-42; biochemist Biochem. Lab., Naples, Italy, 1946-52; in charge quality control lab. M. Loney Lab., Montreal, Que., Can., 1953-61; asso. chief Lab. Chemistry and Sanitation, Div. Labs., Provincial Ministry Health, Montreal, 1961-68, charge san. bacteriology, chief food microbiology, 1968—. Home: 179A Blvd Prairies Laval des Rapides Quebec Canada Office: Ministry Social Affairs 560 Blvd Cartier Laval PQ Canada

CAPRITTA, DIANNE MARY, librarian; b. Schenectady, Aug. 24, 1942; d. Joseph Michael and Claire Jeanette (MacLaury) Capritta; student Smith Coll., 1960-63; B.S., U. Ill., 1965; M.S. in L.S., Syracuse U., 1967. Asst. librarian F. Franklin Moon Library, State U. N.Y. Coll. Environmental Sci. and Forestry, Syracuse, 1967-73, acquisitions librarian, 1968—, asso. librarian, 1973—, Sec.-treas. Forestry chpt. Senate Profl. Assn., 1972—. Mem. Human Assn. Central N.Y., 1972—. Mem. Am., N.Y. library assns., Spl. Libraries Assn., State U. N.Y. Librarians Assn. (del. exec. council 1968—, asst. editor Newsletter 1970-72, sec. 1973—). Home: 225 Crawford Av Syracuse NY 13224

CAPRONI, JOANNA SLESINGER (MRS. LEO F. CAPRONI, JR.), marketing specialist; b. Chgo., Dec. 1, 1933; d. Donald and Dorothy Eaton (Avery) Slesinger; B.A., Brown U., 1954; postgrad. New Sch. for Social Research, 1955-60; m. Leo F. Caproni, Jr., Aug. 31, 1960. Research asst., project dir. Batten, Barton, Durstine & Osborne, N.Y.C., 1956-60; research mgr., print media buyer Luckie & Forney Advt. Co., Birmingham, Ala., 1960-61; broadcast specialist Doremus & Co., N.Y.C., 1961; research asso. Life Mag., N.Y.C., 1962-69; sr. research asso., marketing account mgr. Sports Illustrated, N.Y.C., 1969—. Mem. Travel Research Assn. (exec. bd. 1972—), Am. Marketing Assn., Am. Assn. Pub. Opinion Research. Clubs: Pamet Harbor Yacht and Tennis (Truro, Mass.); Windermere Island (Eleuthera, Bahamas). Home: 370 E 76th St New York City NY 10021 also N Pamet Rd Truro MA 02666 Office: 1271 Av of America New York City NY 10020

CAPUA, SARAJEAN MCARTHUR, educator, author; b. Balt., Aug. 1, 1943; d. Joseph Rodolph and Sara Jeanette (Bennett) McA.; A.A., Broward Community Coll., 1963; student U. South Fla., 1963-65; B.A., Fla. Atlantic U., 1966; m. Demetrio Joseph Capua, Feb. 18, 1965. Tchr. Headstart program, Palm Beach County, Fla., summer 1966; tchr. Margate Elementary Sch., Borward County, Fla., 1966-67, Pompano Beach (Fla.) Elementary Sch., 1967-68; tchr. Am. Learning Services, 1970-72; tchr. 1st grade Bayshore Elementary Sch., Lee County, Fla., 1973-74, tchr. reading, 1974—. Co-author: Art Continuum Techniques, 1969; Stitchery; Creative Crayon Techniques; Printing Without a Press; Jewelry Anyone Can Make; Holiday Ideas; Ends and Odds to Art, 1970. Asso. editor: Fla. Art Edn. Assn. mag., 1967. Contbr. articles to children's mags. Home: 1912 SE 36th Terrace Cape Coral FL 33904 Office: Box 601 Williams Rd North Fort Myers FL 33903

CAPUTO, ROSE A., lawyer; b. Bklyn., Mar. 12, 1926; d. Giacomo and Grace (Caputo) Caputo; B.A., Adelphi U., 1947; J.D., St. Johns U., 1950; M.L., N.Y. U., 1959. Admitted to N.Y. bar, 1951; practiced in N.Y.C., 1951—. Part-time tchr. law Interboro Inst., N.Y.C., 1969—; small claims arbitrator Civil Ct. N.Y., 1963—; hearing examiner Parking Violations Bur., N.Y.C., 1972—. Mem. Am. Bar Assn., Queens Womens Bar Assn., Assn. Arbitrators, Am. Judges Assn. Office: 229 Park Av South New York City NY 10003

CARACCIOLI, KATHERINE FRANCES, marketing research exec.; b. N.Y.C.; d. Louis N. and Catherine Josephine (Gargan) Caracccioli; A.B., N.Y. U., 1951, M.A., 1956. Sr. market analyst Sudler & Hennessey, N.Y.C., 1967-69; dir. marketing intelligence Deltakos div. J. Walker Thompson Co., N.Y.C., 1969—, v.p., 1972—, dir. subsidiary Diagenes Marketing Research, Inc., 1973—. Mem. Am. Marketing Assn., Advt. Women of N.Y., Eastern Pharm. Market Research Group, Pharm. Advt. Club N.Y. Home: 205 E 66th St New York City NY 10021 Office: 420 Lexington Av New York City NY 10021

CARAWAY, EDNA BUSBY (MRS. GLENN FRANKLIN CARAWAY), librarian; b. Greenville, Tex., Jan. 18, 1913; d. Samuel Edward and Irma Mae (Farmer) Busby; B.S., E. Tex. State U., 1962, M.S., 1963; m. Glenn Franklin Caraway, Nov. 29, 1933; children—Robert Edward, Glynda Sue (Mrs. Miller Wesley Harwell), William James. Sec., to atty., Greenville, 1930-33; asst. librarian Greenville (Tex.) Pub. Library, 1961-62; tchr. trainee Greenville (Tex.) Pub. Sch. System, 1962; librarian, Wilkinson Jr. High Sch., Mesquite (Tex.) Pub. Sch. System, 1962—. Pres., Houston Elementary Sch. P.T.A., 1948-49, Jr. High Sch. P.T.A., 1949-50; v.p. Sr. High Sch. P.T.A., Greenville City Council P.T.A., 1950-51; com. chmn. Am. Heart Assn., 1955-56, Am. Cancer Soc., Hunt County, Tex., 1957-58. Mem. Am. Assn. U. Women, Tex. State Tchrs. Assn., Tex. Library Assn., S.W. Library Assn., Dallas County Library Assn., Tex. Assn. Sch. Libraries, Teen-Age Library Assn. Tex., Mesquite Edn. Assn. (chmn. yearbook constn. and by-laws 1969-70), Hunt County League Women Voters. Democrat. Baptist (dir. orgn. ch. library 1973-74, tchr.). Clubs: Eclecta Study (pres. 1955-56), Loraine Art (pres. 1957-58) (Greenville). Home: 3605 Briscoe St Greenville TX 75401 Office: 2100 Crest Park Mesquite TX 75149

CARAWAY, LINDA DARNELLE, musician; b. San Antonio, Dec. 18, 1947; d. Bennie Thomas and May Delle (Dukes) Cherry; B.A. in Music Edn., Tex. Agrl. and Indsl. U. 1970; certificate occupational therapy, St. Phillips Jr. Coll., 1974; m. Clarence Caraway, June 13, 1970; children—Angela Adele, Anthony André, Michael Christopher. Asst. minister music New Union Baptist Ch., San Antonio, 1972—; pvt. tchr. elementary grade music, 1971—; dir.-musician Bicentennial Negro Baptist Celebration and Mus. Am., 1973. Past Mem. Symphony Orch. (youth), San Antonio. Mem. Tex. A. and I. Civic Symphony, Poetry Soc. Tex., Zeta Phi Beta. Author poems, mus. works. Address: 719 Richland Dr San Antonio TX 78219

CARBAUGH, BARBARA (MRS. DANIEL C. CARBAUGH), economist, educator; b. N.Y.C., June 23, 1929; d. Harold Goodwin and Hazel (Ground) Vick; B.B.A., U. Mo. at Kansas City, 1966, M.A. in Econs. (grad. fellow), 1969; postgrad. fellow Washington U., St. Louis, 1967-68; m. Daniel C. Carbaugh, Oct. 18, 1965; children from previous marriage—Barbara Moore, Harold Moore, Victoria Moore, Alexandra Moore. Economist, Fed. Res. Bank St. Louis, 1968; lectr. So. Ill. U. at Edwardsville, 1968-69; lectr. Ind. U. N.W., Gary, 1970-71. Small bus. cons., 1969—. Mem. Am. Econs. Assn., Beta Gamma Sigma. Home: 3020 Oak Circle Columbus GA 31907

CARBINE, PATRICIA THERESA, editor; b. Villanova, Pa., Jan. 31, 1931; d. James T. and Margaret (Dèe) Carbine; Mater Misericordiae Acad., 1936-48; B.A. in English, Rosemont Coll., 1952. Editorial researcher Look mag., N.Y.C., 1953-55, asst. editor, 1955-57, asst. mng. editor 1959-66, mng. editor, 1966-69, then exec. editor, 1969-70, sr. editor, after 1957; editor McCall's mag., N.Y.C., 1970-72; editor-in-chief Ms, N.Y.C., 1972—. Trustee Rosemont Coll. Home: 399 E 72d St New York City NY 10021 Office: 370 Lexington Av New York City NY 10017

CARBONE, ETHEL GENEROSA CARDONI, clothing co. exec; b. Jessup, Pa., Apr. 20, 1918; d. Cesare and Carmela (Meletti) Cardoni; grad. high sch.; m. Harry Roani, Oct. 9, 1943; 1 son, Richard Roani. Mgr., Town Mfg. Co., Olyphant, Pa., 1952-60, Joess Blouse Co., Scranton, Pa., 1960-64; sec., treas. Bar-Bee, Inc., 1968—; pres. Sonny Styles, Inc., Scranton, 1970—, Majer Styles, Inc., Scranton, 1968—; v.p. New Reisner Dress, Inc., 1972—. Home: MB 2 Donny Dr Scranton PA 18505 Office: 2010 Pittston Av Scranton PA 18505 also 420 Walsh St Scranton PA 18505

CARD, CLAUDIA FALCONER, educator; b. Madison, Wis., Sept. 30, 1940; d. Walter Munro and Achsah Susan (Falconer) Card; B.A., U. Wis., 1962; M.A., Harvard, 1964, Ph.D., 1969. Prof. dept. philosophy U. Wis., Madison, 1966—. Woodrow Wilson fellow, 1962, 65, Harvard U. fellow, 1963-64, 64-65. Mem. Phi Beta Kappa, Phi Kappa Phi. Home: 534 W Washington Av Madison WI 53703 Office: 600 N Park St Madison WI 53706

CARDILLO, SISTER FRANCES MARIE, educator; b. Rome, N.Y., Apr. 19, 1932; d. Dominick and Mary C. (Greco) Cardillo; B.S., Coll. of St. Rose, 1953, M.A., 1961; Ph.D., St. Bonaventure U., 1967. Sci. tchr. St. Paul High Sch., St. Petersburg, Fla., 1954-62; instr. St. Bonaventure U., Olean, N.Y., 1963-66, Immaculate Conception Jr. Coll., Kingston, Jamaica, W.I., 1966-67; asst. prof. botany Quincy (Ill.) Coll., 1969-72; asso. prof. Georgian Court Coll., Lakewood, N.J., 1972-73; asst. prof. Ladycliff Coll., Highland Falls, N.Y., 1967-69, asso. prof. botany, 1973—. Recipient NSF Research grant, 1969-72. Mem. Am. Inst. Biol. Scis., A.A.A.S., Am. Fern Soc., Bot. Soc. Am., N.Y. Acad. Sci., Assn. Women Sci. Address: Dept Biology Ladycliff College Highland Falls NY 10928

CARDONA, MARIA ELENE ARGUELLO (MRS. FRANCISCO J. CARDONA), librarian; b. Managua, Nicaragua, Jan. 18, 1925; d. Victorino and Rosa (Solorzano) Arguello; student Barnard Coll., 1945-46; B.A. magna cum laude, U. P.R., 1958; M.L.S., Pratt Inst., 1962; m. Francisco J. Cardona, Jan. 26, 1946; children—Francisco Victorino, Rosa Maria, Lidle Beatriz. Librarian, indsl. devel. lab. Indsl. Devel. Co., Hato Rey, P.R., 1955-57; with N.Y. Pub. Library, 1958-65, head Latin Am. bibliographic projects, 1962-64; Latin Am. cataloger U. Fla. at Gainesville, 1966-67; bibliographer, research asst. Inst. Caribbean Studies U. P.R., Rio Piedras, 1968-70; dir. Caribbean Regional Library, Hato Rey, 1970—. Cons. Latin Am. bibliography Bowker Co. N.Y.C., 1962-65; editor cataloging Fichero Bibliografico Hispanoamericano, 1962-64. Mem. A.L.A., Sociedad de Bibliotecarios de P.R., Assn. Caribbean U. and Research Libraries (exec. council, 1971-74, pres. elect 1974-75), Seminars on Acquisition of Latin Am. Library Materials. Compiler, author index vols. 1-28 Handbook of Latin American Studies, 1968. Home: 2208 Park Blvd Santurce PR 00913 Office: 452 Ponce de Leon Av Hato Rey PR 00919

CARDOZO, MARY BUXTON-HOLMES, speech pathologist; b. Paterson, N.J., Oct. 28, 1917; d. John Henry and Marjorie Smith (Begg) Buxton-Holmes; B.A., Bklyn. Coll., 1940; M.A., Columbia, 1941; postgrad. in edn. Harvard; m. Robert Lopes Cardozo, Dec. 26, 1941; children—Robert, Sarah, David, Peter. Lectr. speech pathology Bklyn. Coll., 1941-44; dir. speech and lang. pathology clinic Montreal (Que., Can.) Children's Hosp., 1944—; lectr. Sch. Human Communications Disorders, McGill U. Bd. dirs. Lethbridge Rehab. Center, Montreal Rehab. Inst., Montreal Oral Sch. Recipient outstanding achievement award Bklyn. Coll., 1955. Mem. Speech and Hearing Soc. Que. (founder, past pres.), Canadian Speech and Hearing Assn. (past pres.). Home: 635 Grosvenor Av Westmount PQ Canada Office: Montreal Children's Hosp 2300 Tupper St Montreal PQ Canada

CARDWELL, BILLIE JO, counseling psychologist; b. Angelina County, Tex., Jan. 12, 1931; d. Andrew Jackson and Rosa America (Murphy) Jumper; B.B.A., Stephen F. Austin State U., 1958, M.Ed., 1964; Ed.D., E. Tex. State U., 1971; m. Horace Milton Cardwell, Sept. 14, 1957. Asst. supt. Angelina County schs., Lufkin, 1959-62, counselor-supr., 1962-67; counselor E. Tex. Center Ednl. Services, Nacogdoches, 1967-69; spl. ednl. counselor Region VII Ednl. Service Center, Kilgore, Tex., 1971-73; counseling psychologist, Lufkin, 1971—. Seminar leader Okla.-Tex. Tng. Tchrs. of Tchrs. project. Mem. Am., Tex. personnel and guidance assns., Am., Tex. psychol. assns. Home: Route 5 Box 217X Lufkin TX 75901 Office: 1121 Ellis Av Lufkin TX 75901

CARDWELL, MARJORIE NELLE HYDER, ednl. adminstr.; b. Elizabethton, Tenn., Jan. 31, 1927; d. J. Hampton and Gladys Rhea Hyder; B.A., Tusculum Coll., Greeneville, Tenn., 1948; M.A., E. Tenn. State U., Johnson City, 1963, postgrad. in ednl. adminstrn., 1969—; m. Robert Ernest Cardwell, Jr., Oct. 23, 1948; children—Robert Ernest III, Jon Hampton, Jennifer Lynn. Dir. lang. clinic E. Tenn. State U., 1963-64; speech pathologist Elizabethton City Schs., 1964-69; dir. human devel. Greene Valley Hosp. and Sch., Greeneville, 1969-73; asst. supt. Greene Valley Developmental Center, Greeneville, 1973—. Mem. ancillary faculty Tusculum Coll.; adv. bd. Walters State Community Coll., Morristown, Tenn. Pres., Woman's Civic Club. Mem. Nat., Tenn. (dir.), Carter County (pres.) assns. for retarded children and adults, Am. Assn. Mental Deficiency, Council for Exceptional Children, D.A.R. (regent). Baptist (adult tchr.). Home: Dejarnette St Extension Elizabethton TN 37643 Office: PO Box 3087 Greene Valley Developmental Center Greeneville TN 37743

CARDWELL, MARY NADINE BOOTH (MRS. DONALD FRANCIS CARDWELL), ret. machinery mfg. co. exec.; b. Marshfield, Mo., Sept. 5, 1915; d. Arch Hodgin and Georgia Mae (Mitchell) Booth; student Draughons Bus. Coll., 1932-33; m. Donald Francis Cardwell, Mar. 15, 1941; 1 son, Donald Francis. Sec. to div. auditor accounting dept. Mo. Electric Power Co., Marshfield, 1933-41; sec. purchasing dept. Truscon Labs., Caniff at G.T. Ry., Detroit, 1941-42; with Star Cutter Co., Farmington, Mich., sec.-treas., 1963-73; ret., 1973; sec.-treas. subsidiaries Star Cutter Co., Kneeland Industries, Inc., West Br. Industries, Inc., Grayling Industries, Inc., North Star Specialities, Farmington Devel. Co., Oc-Oc Tree Farms, Star Cut Sales, Inc. Bd. dirs. YMCA, Lawton Found., Bus. and Profl. Women's Found. Named Woman of Year, Bus. and Profl. Women's Club, 1959. Mem. Soroptimist Fedn. Ams. (dist. dir. 1972-74). Club: Soroptimist (pres. 1968-70) (Farmington). Home: Box 128 239 Blair St Marshfield MO 65706

CARESS, DAISY FARRAN (MRS. EMMET HAROLD CARESS), social worker; b. Parsons, Kan., Oct. 22, 1918; d. Lorenzo Dow and Mary Ellen (Johnson) Farran; B.S., Kan. State Coll., 1960; M.S., U. Mo., 1965; m. Emmet Harold Caress, Feb. 12, 1954; 1 dau., Charlotte Ellen (Mrs. James Gordon Wolf). Social worker Labette County Welfare Dept., Parsons, 1947-50; asst. supt. Wichita (Kan.) Children's Home, 1950-51; with Parsons State Hosp. and Tng. Center, 1951—, dir. social service dept., 1967—. Exchange social worker cons. in mental retardation Gogarburn Hosp., Edinburgh, Scotland, 1968 also various other hosps; mem. S.E. Kan. regional planning com. White House Conf. on Children and Youth, 1970. Mem. Nat. Assn. Social Workers, Am. Assn. on Mental Deficiency, Am. Soc. for Hosp. Social Work Dirs., Kan. Council for Children and Youth, Kan. Assn. for Retarded Children, Acad. Certified Social Workers, Kan. Conf. Social Work, S.E. Dist. Assn. Social Workers. Republican. Methodist. Mem. Order Eastern Star. Home: 1326 Appleton St Parsons KS 67357 Office: 2601 Gabriel St Parsons KS 67357

CAREWE, SYLVIA, painter, tapestry artist; b. N.Y.C.; d. Louis and Esther (Oghstal) Carewe; student Columbia, Atelier 17; pupil Hans Hoffman, Kunyoshi; 1 son, John. One-man shows (paintings) A.C.A. Gallery, N.Y.C., 1948, 51, 53, 54, 56, 58, Three Arts, Poughkeepsie, N.Y., 1947, 52, 54, 58, 61, Barnett Aden Gallery, Washington, 1950, Art. Assn. Richmond, Ind., 1955, U. Ind., 1955, Ball State Tchrs. Coll., 1955, Terza Karlis Gallery, 1955, N.C. U., 1958, Decatur Art Center, 1955, Butler Art Inst., 1955, W.Va. U., 1956, Butler Inst. Am. Art (tapestry), 1960, Galerie Katia Granoff, Paris, 1957, Exhbn. '22 X 28" etchings Wittenborn Gallery, N.Y.C.; received sponsorship of French cultural ambassador, 1959; 1st Am. artist creating tapestries executed by Ambusson; one-man shows of tapestry at Butler Inst. Am. Art, 1960, ACA Gallery, N.Y.C., 1961, French & Co., N.Y.C., 1960, 62, show of tapestries and banners Fordham U., 1970; exhbn. Paintings for Tapestry Donnell Art Library, N.Y.C., 1968; N.C. Mus. Show, 1972; created headdresses for Aristophanes; play The Birds; exhibited group shows Whitney Mus. Am. Art, Mus. of Modern Art N.Y., Boston Museum of Fine Arts, Audubon Soc., Bklyn. Museum Phila. Print Club, Vassar Coll., Smith Mus. Springfield, Mass., Bruge Mus., Belgium, Staadliche Mus., Holland, many others, represented in permanent collections Whitney Museum Am. Art, Muse de l'Art Modern, Paris, Musee Nationale de Jakarta, Indonesia, Brandeis U., Butler Art Inst., Howard U., Art. Assn. Richmond, Tel Aviv Mus., Norfolk Mus., many pvt. collections, including Joseph H. Highborn, Julius Fleischman, others; lectr. on tapestry Columbia; poetry readings sta. WNEW, 1969; 100 signed posters distributed by State Dept., 1972. Recipient 1947 ann. A.C.A. Gallery competition for 1st one-man show. Contbr. works and articles to numerous jours. and mags. Address: 500 E 83d St New York NY 10028

CAREY, BARBARA BRICE (MRS. MELVIN DONALD CAREY), occupational therapist; b. Manchester, N.H., Oct. 23, 1924; d. Fred Mansfield and Irene (Kelly) Brice; B.S., U. N.H., 1945; m. Melvin Donald Carey, Aug. 3, 1946; children—Judith (Mrs. Richard Davidson), Martha Louise, Patience Ann. Occupational therapist N.H. State Hosp., Concord, 1945-46, Kings County Hosp., Bklyn., 1946-48, VA Hosp., Albany, N.Y., 1963—. Mem. Am., Capital Dist. (pub. relations chmn. 1971-73) occupational therapy assns., Am. Assn. U. Women (v.p. 1961-62, sec. 1958, 72). Office: 113 Holland Av Albany NY 12008

CAREY, CLAIRE LAMB, sch. psychologist; b. Lake Placid, N.Y., Mar. 11, 1927; d. Joseph Vernon and Mary Elsie (Tracy) Lamb; student Bennett Jr. Coll., 1946-47, Syracuse U., 1947-48; B.A., Keuka Coll., 1952; M.S., Plattsburg State U., 1963; m. Chester Elwood Carey, June 17, 1950; children—Dawn J., Sara J. (Mrs. Ronald Gordon LaHart). Tchr., Wilmington Village Sch., 1959-61; sch. psychologist Lake Placid Central Sch., 1961—, Westport Central Sch., 1961-69, Ausable Forks Central Sch., 1961-64, Elizabethtown Central Sch., 1964-69, Tupper Lake Central Sch., 1969—. Dir. Lamb Lumber Co., Inc. Mem. Regional Mental Health Planning Com., 1963. Bd. dirs. Essex County Mental Health Assn. Mem. Nat. Assn. Sch. Psychologists, Delta Kappa Gamma (chmn. com. on profl. affairs 1973). Republican. Episcopalian. Elk. Home: 22 Sentinel Rd Lake Placid NY 12946 Office: Lake Placid Central School Lake Placid NY 12946

CAREY, EILEEN FRANCES SCHUMANN (MRS. JOHN THOMAS CAREY), librarian; b. Burlington, Wis., Dec. 5, 1924; d. George Francis and Veronica Elizabeth (Prasch) Schumann; student Mt. Mary Coll., 1944-46; B.S., U. Wis., 1948, postgrad., 1954-55; postgrad. Bowling Green State U., 1955; M.A., No. Ill. U., 1964; m. John Thomas Carey, Sept. 23, 1947; children—Thomas George, Michael John. Research analyst Battelle Meml. Research Inst., Columbus, O., 1952-54; librarian, Sch. Dist., North Baltimore, O., 1954-56; librarian, tchr. Waterman (Ill.) High Sch., 1957-58; sch. dist. librarian Burlington-Central, Kane County, Ill., 1958-65; librarian, DeKalb (Ill.) High Sch., 1961-66; librarian Boone High Sch., Orlando, Fla., 1966-67; librarian, Pensacola (Fla.) Jr. Coll., 1967—. Vis. library dir. World Campus Afloat, div. Internat. Edn. Chapman Coll., Orange, Cal., 1973. Mem. Community Coll. Assn. Instrn. and Tech., Am. Assn. U. Profs., Fla. Assn. Media in Edn., West Fla. Library Assn. (pres. 1974-75), U. West Fla. Faculty Wives (pres. 1968-69), Nat. Faculty Assn. Pensacola Jr. Coll. (sec.-treas. 1969-70). Home: 2320 Risen Dr Cantonment FL 32533 Office: 1000 College Blvd Pensacola FL 32504

CAREY, FAYE VIVIAN KINGSBURY (MRS. RAYMOND G. CAREY), librarian; b. Belknap, Ill., Jan. 15, 1917; d. Emory S. and Vera (Gibbons) Kingsbury; A.B., U. Evansville, 1937; M.A., Northwestern U., 1940; M.A. in L.S., U. Denver, 1962; m. Raymond G. Carey, June 20, 1942; children—Raymond G., Cynthia. Tchr. Bosse High Sch., Evansville, Ind., 1938-41, Shimer Coll., Mt. Carroll, Ill., 1941-42, Kent Sch., Englewood, Colo., 1953-60; reference librarian Colo. Women's Coll., Denver, 1962—, fgn. student adviser, 1973—. Acting, tech. worker Evansville (Ind.) Community Theatre, Le Petit Theatre du Vieux Carre, New Orleans, Bonfils Meml. Theatre, Denver, Denver Post Opera, 1938-64. Mem. Allied Arts, A.L.A. (exec. dir. Colo. Nat. Library Week 1966, regional chmn. membership 1968-69), Colo. (membership com. 1967-68), Mountain Plains library assns., English-Speaking Union, Am. Assn. U. Profs. (sec. Colo. Women's Coll. chpt. 1973-74), Alumni Assn. U. Denver Grad. Sch. Librarianship (treas. 1968-69; sec. Rocky Mountain chpt. 1972-73). Mem. United Ch. of Christ. Club: Womens Faculty. Reference librarian U.S. World's Fair, N.Y.C., 1965. Home: 1590 S Monroe St Denver CO 80210 Office: 7055 E 18th Av Denver CO 80220

CAREY, MARGARET NELL WRIGHT (MRS. RODERICK PATRICK CAREY), ednl. adminstr.; b. Swastika, N.Y., Dec. 28, 1928; d. Edward Ernest and Della Rebecca (Eells) Wright; B.S., State U. N.Y., 1970, M.S., 1972, certificate advanced study, 1973; m. Roderick Patrick Carey, Sept. 6, 1947; children—Jeanne Margaret (Mrs. Leonard P. Prevo), Rod Eric. Sec. to prin. Au Sable Forks (N.Y.) Central Sch., 1946-57, dist. clk., 1957-68, purchasing agt., 1964-68; asst. to pres. Clinton Community Coll., Plattsburgh, N.Y., 1970, asso. dean for adminstrn., 1970—, sec. to bd. trustees, 1970—. Dist. tax collector Au Sable Forks, 1955-57. Mem. Republican Women Essex County, N.Y. Mem. Plattsburgh Alumni Assn., Ladies of Elks, N.Y. State Community Coll. Bus. Officers Assn. (sec. 1972-73, 74-75), N.Y. State Assn. Sch. Bus. Ofcls., Northeastern Sch. Bus. Ofcls. Assn. (sec., treas. 1972-74), N.Y. State Assn. Jr. Colls., Northeastern N.Y. Personnel and Guidance Assn. Roman Catholic. Home: Box 207 Au Sable Forks NY 12912 Office: Box 399 Plattsburgh NY 12901

CAREY, MARGARETTA ADELAIDE, educator; b. Harrisburg, Pa., July 28, 1921; d. John C. and Margaretta Anna (Fickes) Carey; B.S., Lebanon Valley Coll., Annville, Pa., 1943; M.Mus., U. Rochester,

1949; D.Ed., Pa. State U., 1958. Music tchr. Harrisburg (Pa.) City Sch., 1944-49; instr. So. Ill. U., Carbondale, Ill., 1949-56; asst. prof. No. Ill. U., DeKalb, 1956-59; asst. prof. Ball State Tchrs. Coll., Muncie, Ind., 1959-60; coordinator fine arts, Dept. of Pub. Instrn., Commonwealth of Pa., Harrisburg, Pa., 1960-64; chmn. dept. music edn. Coll. of Music, Temple U., 1964-68; chmn. dept. music edn. Sch. Music, West Chester (Pa.) State Coll., 1968—. Mem. Music Educators Nat. Conf., Pa. Music Educators, Nat., Pa. edn. assns., Mu Phi Epsilon, Pi Lambda Theta. Contbr. articles in field to profl. jours. Home: 310 Maple St Downingtown PA 19335 Office: West Chester State Coll West Chester PA 19380

CAREY, SISTER MARY CECILIA, coll. pres.; b. Casselton, N.D.; d. Thomas J. and Elizabeth (Mahon) Carey; B.S. in Edn., Edgewood Coll., 1946; M.A., U. Wis., 1952; Ph.D., U. Wis., 1959. Joined Order of Dominican Sisters, 1940; tchr. elementary and secondary schs., Omaha, Freeport and River Forest, Ill., Milw, Wis.; prof. English, Edgewood Coll., Madison, Wis., 1955-63, chmn. dept. English, div. lang. and lit., 1956, pres., 1968—, also trustee; chmn. dept. langs., adminstr. Inst. Santo Domingo, Cochabamba, Bolivia, 1963-68. Sec., Wis. Found. Ind. Colls., 1970—. Mem. Nat. Council Tchrs. English, Cath. Renascence Soc., Modern Lang. Assn., Delta Epsilon Sigma. Contbr. articles to profl. publs. Address: 855 Woodrow St Madison WI 53711

CARIKER, KOREN KEEVER (MRS. JOE WILLIAM CARIKER), docent; b. Kemp, Tex., May 23, 1922; d. George Leroy and Lochie Ella (Byrd) Keever; student Tex. State Coll. for Women, 1938-39; certificate Duke Sch. Med. Tech., 1943; B.A., U. Tex., 1947; m. Joe William Cariker, Oct. 29, 1949; children—Deborah Kay, William Bruce, Leigh Charles. Med. technologist Tex. State Health Dept., Austin, 1943-44, Dallas, 1944-45, San Benito, 1945-46; diagnostic bacteriologist Dr. S.W. Bohls Labs., Austin, 1947-49; Colo. Gen. Hosp., Denver, 1949-52; docent Varner-Hogg State Park, West Columbia, Tex., 1962—. Mem. Am. Soc. Med. Technologists, Women's Inst. Houston, First Capitol Study Club. Address: PO Box 696 West Columbia TX 77486

CARITHERS, CORNELIA MORSE (MRS. HUGH A. CARITHERS), physician; b. Winsted, Conn., Mar. 15, 1913; d. Charles M. and Susanna (Davis) Morse; A.B., Cornell U., 1934, M.D., 1938; m. Dr. Hugh A. Carithers, July 27, 1942; children—Susan (Mrs. John Callender), Hugh A., Starr (Mrs. Roy Waddell). Intern Bellevue Hosp., N.Y.C., 1938-40, resident, 1940-42; pvt. practice medicine specializing in pediatrics, Jacksonville, Fla., 1942—; pediatrician King Edward Indsl. Nursery; asso. in pediatrics St. Vincent's, Bapt. Meml., Hope Haven hosps., Univ. Hosp. of Jacksonville; asst. clin. prof. pediatrics U. Fla. Sch. Medicine; cons. pediatrics City Bd. Health. Dir. Nat. Found., 1945-61. Mem. Am. Acad. Pediatrics (com. on juvenile delinquency), A.M.A., Fla., Duval County med. socs., Pan-Am., Am. med. women's assns., Fla. Pediatric Soc., Duval County Tb Assn. (dir. 1946-52), Mental Health Assn. (dir. 1948-50), Am. Cancer Soc. (dir. 1953), Jacksonville Pan-Hellenic Assn., Mortar Bd., Phi Beta Kappa, Kappa Alpha Theta, Alpha Omicron Alpha. Clubs: Woman's, Bougainvillea Garden Circle. Home: 3010 St Johns Av Jacksonville FL 32205 Office: 1661 Riverside Av Jacksonville FL 32204

CARITHERS, POLLY HALL, pub. relations ofcl.; b. Burkburnett, Tex., July 31, 1921; d. James Neal and Lillie May (Clifton) Hall; student U. Tex. Sch. Journalism, 1940-41; m. Arthur D. Carithers, Mar. 15, 1941 (div. Oct. 1972); children—John, Mark, Andrew. Reporter, San Antonio Express, 1941, 46; pub. relations writer Cal. Shipbldg. Corp., Wilmington, 1943-44; publicity writer M-G-M Studios, Culver City, Cal., 1945; dir. pub. information Oakland Schs., Pontiac, Mich., 1961—. Pub. relations cons. to sch. dists. and community colls. Mem. Nat., Mich. (pres. 1970-71) sch. pub. relations assns., Pub. Relations Soc. Am. Author: How to Conduct Low Cost Surveys, 1973. Home: 4113 Telegraph St Bloomfield Hills MI 48013 Office: 2100 Pontiac Lake Rd Pontiac MI 48054

CARL, CHARLENNE WILDER (MRS. RICHARD M. CARL), advt. co. exec.; b. Seattle, July 21, 1945; d. William Raymond and Marie T. (King) Wilder; student LaGrange Coll., 1962-64; A.B. in Journalism, U. Ga., 1966; m. Richard M. Carl, May 1, 1971. Media buyer Burton, Campbell & Kelly Co., Atlanta, 1966-69; media dir. Gerald Rafshoon Advt., Inc., Atlanta, 1969—, v.p., 1973—. Mem. Atlanta Media Planners Assn. (sec. 1969, pres. 1972), Atlanta Broadcasting Execs. Club (sec. 1971). Democrat. Methodist. Clubs: Progressive, Standard. Home: 3004 Vinings Ferry Dr Atlanta GA 30339 Office: 1422 W Peachtree St Atlanta GA 30309

CARL, DIANA FOSTER (MRS. DAVID A. CARL), psychologist; b. Taylor, Tex., Oct. 6, 1940; d. Lloyd Vance and Ray Beth (Peterson) Foster; B.A., U. Tex., 1962; M.A., So. Meth. U., 1967; m. David A. Carl, July 30, 1966; children—Dana Lynne, David Foster. Instr. dept. pediatrics Baylor U. Coll. Medicine, Houston, 1969-70; sch. psychologist Houston Ind. Sch. Dist., 1967-69; research coordinator Dallas State Adult Mental Health Clinic, 1966; psychol. cons. Region IV Ednl. Service Center, Houston, 1971—. Mem. Am. Psychol. Assn., Delta Delta Delta. Contbr. articles to profl. jours. Home: 12634 Westella St Houston TX 77077

CARL, LAHOMA ATKINSON (MRS. JAMES FLEMING CARL), coll. dean; b. Otterville, Mo., Apr. 4, 1911; d. Joseph Byrd and Anna Lee (Dorsey) Atkinson; B.A., San Francisco State Coll., 1933; postgrad. U. Cal., Berkeley, summers 1940-41; m. Roscoe Dickey, Jr., Aug. 9, 1941 (dec. Jan. 1950); children—Janet (Mrs. John Pringle), Timothy Everett; m. 2d, James Fleming Carl, June 22, 1952. Tchr., Outside Creek Sch., Farmersville, Cal., 1933-35; tchr., prin. Linwood Sch., Visalia, Cal., 1935-38; tchr., Bakersfield, Cal., 1938-39; speech therapist Kern County Sch. Office, 1940-42; dean women Baptist Bible Coll., Clark Summit, Pa., 1965-73. Pres., Freshman Class, San Francisco State Coll., 1928, Jr. Women's Club, Exeter, Cal., 1936. Baptist. Home: 3225 Millcreek Dr Visalia CA 93277

CARLETON, WINNIE DAVIS SNELL, club woman; b. Hamilton, Tex.; d. William Davis and Eldora (Carter) Snell; grad. Draughon's Bus. Coll., 1920; studied tax law with Carleton & Neblett, Attys., Houston, 1945-47; m. Alfred Townes Carleton, June 28, 1923 (dec. Aug. 1959); children—Carolyn Jane (Mrs. Roy H. Reynolds, Jr.), Alfred Townes. With Fed. Land Bank of Houston, 1921-22; owner Winnie D. Carleton Internal Revenue Service, Houston, 1945—; mem. Tex. Fedn. Women's Clubs, 1928—, mem. information com. 1942-45, chmn. dept. edn., 1945-47, Pan-Am. relations div., 1947-49, industry, 1951-53, forums, 1951-53, program, 1953-56, life membership com., 1956-58, nominating com., 1958-60, hostess fgn. dels. conv., Houston, 1951, pres. local club, 1940-42, pres. 4th dist., 1949-51, dean dist. presidents, 1949-51, 3rd v.p., 1956-58, 2d v.p., 1958-60, 1st v.p., 1960-62, pres., 1962-64; pres. City Fedn. Women's Clubs, Houston, 1943-45, 69-71, chmn. year book, 1960-62, pub. affairs, 1958-60; internat. hostess Gen. Fedn. Women's Clubs, co-chmn. conv., San Antonio, 1970, mem. structure com. 1972—; mem. Houston Breakfast Club, 1954—, chmn. pub. affairs, 1956-58; mem. Sorosis Club, 1950—, mem. fedn. com., 1962-70. Mem. family and welfare com. Community Chest, Houston, 1948-52, edn. com., 1950-54; mem. Allied Arts Council Bd. Harris County, Tex., 1958-62, sec., 1960-62; mem. Salvation Army Adv. Bd., Houston, 1945-56, founder Salvation Army Women's Aux., 1954, pres., 1954-56; exec. com. Urban Library Council, 1970—; mem. Mayor's Com. on Jobs for Vets., 1971—; mem. bd. March of Dimes, 1971—. Pres. Houston Democratic Woman's Club, 1946-48. Pres. Houston Pub. Library Bd., 1967—; trustee Water Pollution Found., 1967-69, 71—. Selected Outstanding Clubwoman, Houston Press, 1962. Mem. M.B.L.S. Episcopalian. Home: 1826 Branard St Houston TX 77006

CARLEY, CLARA ELIZABETH GETMAN (MRS. HAROLD EDISON CARLEY), librarian; b. Ilion, N.Y., Oct. 19, 1918; d. George Burrill and Bertha Ella (Myers) Getman; student Mt. Holyoke Coll., 1936-38; student State U. N.Y. at Geneseo, 1939, 40; B.A. cum laude, St. Lawrence U., 1940; M.A. in L.S., U. Wis., 1966; m. Harold Edison Carley, June 21, 1941; children—Harold Edwin, David George. Tchr. English, librarian Onondaga Central Sch., Nedrow, N.Y., 1940-41; asst. librarian Cannon Free Library, Delhi, N.Y., 1952-54, head librarian, 1954-59; cataloguer Cornell U. Library, 1959-60; librarian elementary sch., Groton, N.Y., 1962; gen. services librarian Finger Lakes Library System, Ithaca, N.Y., 1962-65, bookmobile librarian, 1965-67, reference services specialist, 1967-73. Asst. tchr. U. Wis.-Madison, summer 1964. Mem. Interlibrary Loan Com., South Central Research Library Council, 1968-73. Mem. Am., N.Y. library assns., Finger Lakes Bottle Assn., Beta Phi Mu. Republican. Mem. Community Ch. (mem. council 1960-71, supt. Sunday sch. 1966-71). Home: 569 Ellis Hollow Creek Rd Ithaca NY 14850

CARLIN, ELECTRA MARSHALL (MRS. HOWARD LEE CARLIN), art gallery owner; b. Fort Worth, Sept. 28, 1912; d. Bert and Frances Ella (Peers) Marshall; student U. Okla., 1930-31, Beaver Coll., 1931-32; B.A., George Washington U., 1935; m. Howard Lee Carlin, Aug. 20, 1935; (dec. Sept. 1952); 1 son, Michael Lee. (dec.). Owner, dir., Carlin Galleries, Fort Worth, 1959—. Mem. City of Fort Worth Art Commn. Bd., 1963—. Mem. Fort Worth, Dallas Mus. art assns., Pi Beta Phi. Presbyn. Club: Jewel Charity Ball (Fort Worth). Home: 2401 Warner Rd Fort Worth TX 76110 Office: 710 Montgomery St Fort Worth TX 76107

CARLIN, JEAN EFFAL, psychiatrist; b. Hibbing, Minn., July 24, 1930; d. Earl William and Effal Octavia (Anderson) Carlin; B.A., U. Minn., 1950, B.S., 1952, M.A., 1953, M.D., 1954, Ph.D., 1959. Intern U. Minn. Hosp., 1954-55, resident psychiatry, 1955-56; resident psychiatry U. Cal. at Irving Hosp., 1967-69; mem. faculty student health counseling North Park Coll., Chgo., 1956-58, Long Beach (Cal.) State Coll., 1959-60; individual practice, Long Beach, 1961-67, Costa Mesa, 1974—; staff psychiatrist Orange County (Cal.) Hosp., 1969-71; asso. clin. prof. psychiatry Coll. Medicine, U. Cal. at Irvine, 1969—, exec. asso. dean, 1974—; chief profl. edn. Fairview (Cal.) State Hosp., 1971—; vol. physician for Vietnam, 1969, 71. Mem. Am., Cal. med. assns., Christian Med. Soc., Am. Women's Med. Assn. (local pres. 1965). Contbr. articles to profl. jours. Address: U Cal Coll Medicine Irvine CA 92664

CARLING, ANNE LOUISE, newspaperwoman; b. Easton, Pa., May 12, 1940; d. George Seem and Kathryn (Lehr) Carling; B.A., Stetson U., 1962. Gen. news reporter St. Augustine (Fla.) Record, 1962-64, 66-68, women's editor, 1968—; with Gen. Electric Co., Daytona Beach, Fla., 1964; publicity dir. St. Augustine C. of C., 1964-66. Sec. U.S.O. Council, St. Augustine, 1964—; mem. bd. Fla.'s Cross and Sword, 1970—; mem. Flagler Hosp. Aux., 1973—. Bd. dirs. Community Chest-United Fund, 1971—, A.R.C., 1969—, Am. Cancer Soc., 1965—. Decorated Bronze Tourism medal (Spain); recipient various awards for pub. service. Club: Pilot (1st v.p. 1968-69) (St. Augustine, Fla.). Home: 76 Willow Dr St Augustine FL 32084 Office: PO Box 1630 St Augustine FL 32084

CARLISLE, LILIAN MATAROSE BAKER (MRS. E. GRAFTON CARLISLE, JR.), author, lectr.; b. Meridian, Miss., Jan. 1, 1912; d. Joseph and Lilian (Flournoy) Baker; student Dickinson Coll., 1929-30, Pierce Coll. Bus. Adminstrn., 1930-31; m. E. Grafton Carlisle, Jr., Jan. 9, 1933; children—Mrs. E. S. Schwerdtle, Mrs. Leroy Meshel. Legal sec. A. W. Sanson, Phila., 1931-35; adminstrv. sec. Royal Air Force Ferry Command, Montreal, Que., Can., 1942-43; vol. stenographer A.R.C. Missing Persons Enquiring Bur., Montreal, 1944-45; vol. sec. McGill U. Sch. Social Work, Montreal, 1945-46; legal sec. Frederick P. Smith, Burlington, Vt., 1948-50; exec. staff mem. in charge collections, research Shelburne (Vt.) Mus., 1951-61; exec. sec. Burlington Area Community Health Study, 1963, coordinator, 1964; asst. coordinator Vt. Mental Retardation Planning Project, 1965; project dir. 4-county Champlain Valley Medicare Alert, 1966; dir. pub relations Champlain Valley Agrl. Fair, 1968—. Registrar Girl Scouts Am. Council, 1951-52, chmn. cookie sale, 1952; sec. Burlington P.T.A., 1948, v.p., 1947-49, pres., 1949-51, dist. radio chmn., 1948-51, state corr. sec., 1951-53, chmn. summer workshop, 1951; treas. Burlington Community Council for Social Welfare, 1951, v.p., 1956-58, pres., 59-61, 71-73; lay mem. Gov's. Conf. on Problems of Aging for White House Conf., 1960. Mem. Vt. Ho. of Reps., 1968-70. Mem. Vt. (trustee, chmn. mus. com. 1967), N.Y. (faculty seminar), Chittendon (pres. 1969-72), Nat. hist. socs., Vt. Old Cemetery Assn., Vt. Folklore Soc., League Vt. Writers (dir. 1962; v.p., pres. 1967-69). Am. Pen Women, Order Women Legislators (pres. Vt. br. 1972—), Chi Omega. Conglist. (clk.). Club: Zonta (pres. 1964-65). Contbr. articles to profl. jours. Co-author: The Story of the Shelburne Museum, 1955; Profile of the Community, 1964; Environmental and Personal Health of the Community, 1964; Vermont Clock and Watchmakers, Silversmiths and Jewelers, 1970; also numerous catalogs on collections at Shelburne Mus. Editor: Look Around Burlington, Vermont, 1972; Look Around Jericho, Underhill and Westford, Vermont, 1972; Look Around Winooski, Vermont, 1972; Look Around Essex and Williston, Vermont, 1973; Look Around Hinesburg and Charlotte, Vermont, 1973; editorial cons. Burlington Social Survey, 1967. Home: 117 Lakeview Terrace Burlington VT 05401

CARLISLE, SANDRA WALLS (MRS. LILBURN W. CARLISLE), realtor; b. Camden, Ark., Apr. 11, 1939; d. Joseph Edward and Mary Armorial (Gravette) Walls; student Ouachita Bapt. U., 1957-58, Ark. Poly. Coll., 1959; m. Lilburn Wayne Carlisle, June 7, 1958. Sec., Franke's Cafeteria, Little Rock, 1956-57, firm Parker & Mobley, Russellville, Ark., 1959-60; sec. Thomas Real Estate & Ins., Benton, Ark., 1960—, real estate broker, 1965—, corp. sec., 1965—. Corp. sec., Misty Meadows, Inc., Benton, 1969—. Vice pres. Young Democrats Saline County, 1961-62. Bd. dirs. Saline County Community Fund, 1969-70. Mem. Ark. Real Estate Assn., Nat. Assn. Real Estate Bds., Benton Bus. and Profl. Women's Club, Beta Sigma Phi. Dem. Baptist. Home: 300 E Conway St Beton AR 72015 Office: 114 E Conway St Benton AR 72015

CARLON, PATRICIA ALBINA HONSA (MRS. JOHN ALLAN CARLON), lawyer; b. Chgo., Oct. 20, 1938; d. Erwin John and Albina Marie (Urbancek) Honsa; B.S. in Edn., Ill. State U., 1960; LL.B., U. Ill., 1964; m. John Allan Carlon, June 6, 1959; children—Mark Allan, James Andrew. Admitted to Ill. bar, 1964; partner Carlon & Carlon, Normal, 1965—. Instr. bus. law Ill. State U., Normal, 1972—. Mem. adv. council Mennonite Hosp., Bloomington, Ill., 1972—. Mem. McLean County Bar Assn., McLean County Assn. Commerce and Industry, Normal C. of C., Kappa Beta Pi. Home: 1110 E Emerson St Bloomington IL 61701 Office: 4 Citizens Square Normal IL 61761

CARLSEN, RUTH CHRISTOFFER (MRS. G. ROBERT CARLSEN), author; b. Milw., Feb. 21, 1918; d. Carl Severin and Lydia Emilie (Diefenthaeler) Christoffer; B.A., U., Minn., 1939; m. G. Robert Carlsen, Apr. 5, 1941; children—Christopher Robert, Kristin (Mrs. R. William Rowley), Peter Severin, Jane Emilie. Trustee Lake Macbride Cottage Res. Corp., mem. Pen Women Am., Authors League, Authors Guild, Theta Sigma Phi. Unitarian. Clubs: Athens History Circle, Author: Mr. Pudgins, 1951; Henrietta Goes West, 1966; Hildy and the Cuckoo Clock, 1966; Monty and the Tree House, 1967; Sam Bottleby, 1968; Ride A Wild Horse, 1970; Sometimes It's Up, 1971; Half Past Tomorrow, 1973. Asst. editor McGraw Hill Lit. Series Themes and Writers, 1967; co-editor Auto Stories for Scholastic, 1965. Address: Lake Macbride Route 3 Solon IA 52333

CARLSON, ALICE NENA SALIBA (MRS. JOHN D. CARLSON), social worker; b. Blytheville, Ark., Apr. 16, 1921; d. Joseph A. and Akabir (Saliba) Saliba; student Ark. State Coll., 1939-40; B.A., La. State U., 1943; postgrad. U. Ark., 1949-50, Hosp. Recreation Inst., 1950; m. John D. Carlson. Asst. dir. U.S.O., Blytheville, 1943-45; acting exec., program dir. YMCA, Blytheville, 1945-48; women and girls' dir. YM-YWCA, Streator, Ill., 1951-54; recreational dir. Children's Convalescent Center, Jacksonville, Ark., 1948-51; women and girls' dir. Harvey (Ill.) Meml. YMCA, 1954-59; exec. dir. Roseville extension YM-YWCA, Newark, 1959-63, dir. adult program dept., bus. sch., downtown br., 1963-71; dir. adult and family program Montclair (N.J.) YMCA, 1971—. 2d v.p. sect. on work with adults Nat. YMCA 1969-70, 2d v.p. assn. profl. dirs. program sect., 1970-73, mem. bd. certification, 1959-69, adv. com. work with women and girls, 1959-67; mem. state conf. planning com. N.J. Commn. on Women, 1972. Mem. Bus. and Profl. Women's Club of Oranges (pres. 1968-70), Nat. (1st v.p. 1973-76), Mideast Regional assns. profl. YMCA dirs. (bd. dirs.), N.J. Fedn. Bus. and Profl. Women's Clubs (state civic participitation chmn. 1971-72). Presbyn. Home: 22 Hamilton Dr E North Caldwell NJ 07006 Office: Montclair YMCA 25 Park St Montclair NJ 07042

CARLSON, ALMA JANE, educator; b. Dobbs Ferry, N.Y., July 12, 1937; d. Gustav Leonard and Christine Mildred (Cushman) Carlson; B.A. cum laude, Marymount Coll., 1959; M.S., Hunter Coll., 1962; postgrad. William Paterson Coll. N.J., 1969-73. Tchr. elementary schs., Ossining, N.Y., 1959-65, Oakland, N.J., 1965—. Mem. Ossining Schs. In-Service Steering Com., 1962-65, Com. Reading Curriculum Revision, Oakland, 1970—; mem. Instructional Council Oakland, 1970-71. Mem. Nat., N.J. edn. assns., Oakland Tchrs. Assn. (rep. council 1971—), Curian Honor Soc., Nat. Soc. Study Edn., Alpha Delta Kappa (charter mem. chpt.). Home: 81 Manito Av Oakland NJ 07436 Office: Heights Sch Seminole Av Oakland NJ 07436

CARLSON, BARBARA LOUISE CLAUSSEN (MRS. JAMES G. CARLSON), civic worker; b. Fremont, Neb., Mar. 30, 1933; d. John Riemer and Frances Helen (Lass) Claussen; student Midland Coll., 1951-54, U. Omaha, 1956, U. Neb., 1960; B.S., Yankton Coll., 1971; m. James G. Carlson, Aug. 10, 1952; children—Marla, Jay, Colleen, Troy, Hollis. Tchr. rural schs., Blair, also Fremont, Valley (all Neb.), 1952-54, Mountview Elementary Sch., Omaha, 1956-58; substitute tchr., Omaha, 1958-59, Verdigre, Neb., 1961-72, Lincoln, Neb., 1959-60; bookkeeper Verdigre Pharmacy, Inc., James G. Carlson, M.D., Verdigre, 1961-73. Mem. Verdigre Park and Recreation Bd., 1970-74; mem. Verdigre Planning Com., 1971-72; pres. Verdigre Improvement Council, 1971-74. Mem. Women's Aux. to Neb. Med. Assn. (pres. 1972), Women's Aux. to Madison Six County Med. Assn. (pres. 1965). Republican. Methodist (ch. sch. supt. 1970). Club: Extension (pres. Verdigre 1963). Home: Box C Verdigre NE 68783

CARLSON, BEVERLY BELKNAP (MRS. BURTON OLIVER CARLSON, SR.), former bank ofcl.; b. Salamanca, N.Y., Apr. 17, 1916; d. Leo Ashton and Alma Mae (Handshaw) Belknap; grad. Jamestown (N.Y.) Bus. Coll., 1936; student Am. Inst. Banking, 1962-68; m. Burton Oliver Carlson, Sr., July 22, 1936; children—Burton Oliver, Bonita Belknap. Intermittently with Automatic Voting Machine Corp., Jamestown, 1937-59; stenographic and secretarial positions Harris Trust & Savs. Bank, Chgo., 1942-45; sec. Consol. Jr.-Sr. High Sch., also central treas. club activities Bemus Point (N.Y.) Central Sch. Dist., 1957-58; sec. to head adminstrv. div. trust dept. First Nat. Bank Ft. Lauderdale (Fla.), 1961-65, adminstrv. asst. to head trust dept., 1965-66; adminstrv. asst. Broward Nat. Bank, Ft. Lauderdale, 1966-69, asst. trust investment officer, 1969-71, trust investment officer, 1971-74. Lay leader Fluvanna (N.Y.) Pre-sch. Group, 1953-54; Brownie troop leader Chautauqua County council Girl Scouts U.S., 1955-56; pres. Fluvanna P.T.A., 1957-58; v.p. East Side Elementary Sch. P.T.A., 1960-62; mem. endowment com. U. Miami (Fla.), 1969—. Mem. Am. Bus. Women's Assn., Alpha Iota. Republican. Presbyn. Club: Zonta of Fort Lauderdale (dir., finance chmn. 1971-72). Home: 1228 SE 1st St Fort Lauderdale FL 33301

CARLSON, CONSTANCE HEDIN, univ. dean; b. Lewiston, Me., Sept. 11, 1915; d. Carl Johan and Julia Long (Lowell) Hedin; A.B., Vassar Coll., 1937; M.A., U. Me., 1945; Ph.D., Brown U., 1971; m. Carl Lennart Carlson, Sept. 8, 1948 (dec. June 1959); 1 dau., Julia Lowell. Instr., U. Me., Brunswick, 1946-48; guidance dir. Burrillville (R.I.) High Sch., 1957-59; lectr. R.I. Coll., Providence, 1959-60; asso. prof. dept. English, U. Me., Orono, 1962-72, dean instrn. Bangor, 1972—, asso. dir. experienced tchr. fellowship program, 1969-70, chairperson task force on spl. ednl. needs of women, 1972. Cons. U.S. Office Edn., 1965-66. Project English grantee U.S. Office Edn., 1964-66. Named Distinguished Faculty Mem. of Year, U. Me., 1972. Mem. Modern Lang. Assn., Nat. Council Tchrs. English, Bangor Hist. Soc., Penobscot Heritage Assn., Am. Assn. U. Women. (corporate del.), Phi Kappa Phi. Republican. Home: 5 Chapel Rd Orono ME 04473 Office: Auburn Hall Bangor ME 04401

CARLSON, DALE ELISSA BICK, author; b. N.Y.C., May 24, 1935; d. Edgar M. and Estelle (Cohen) Bick; grad. Riverdale Country Sch., 1953; B.A., Wellesley Coll., 1957; m. Albert W.D. Carlson, Jr., Nov. 24, 1962; children—Daniel Bick, Hannah Bick. Author childrens books, N.Y.C., 1961—, writings include Perkins the Brain, 1964; The House of Perkins, 1965; Miss Maloo, 1966; The Brainstormers; 1966; Frankenstein, 1968; Counting is Easy, 1969; Your Country, 1969; Arithmetic 1, 2, 3, 1969; The Electronic Teabowl, 1969; Warlord of the Genji, 1970; The Beggar King of China, 1971; The Mountain of Truth (Spring Festival Honor book), 1972; Good Morning Danny, 1972; Good Morning, Hannah, 1972; The Human Apes, 1973; Girls Are Equal Too, 1973; Baby Needs Shoes, 1974. Vice pres. Parents League of N.Y., editor-in-chief Parents League Bull., 1967—. Mem. Authors League Am., Authors Guild. Address: 116 E 63rd St New York City NY 10021

CARLSON, DARLA JEAN (MRS. DONALD ALLEN CARLSON), newspaper editor; b. Odessa, Tex., Nov. 5, 1932; d. Bolton Plato and Ruby Leona (Jones) Mead; B.A., San Diego State U., 1971; m. Donald Allen Carlson, Jan. 30, 1963. Pub. relations officer Project Concern, Inc., San Diego, 1971-72; news editor Valley Grove News, Lemon Grove, Cal., 1973, editor, 1973; editor La Mesa

(Cal.) Scout, 1973—. Pub. relations asst. United Way, San Diego, 1970-71; mem. Citizens Adv. Council, Lemon Grove, Cal., 1973; mem. human relations com. Monte Vista High Sch., Spring Valley, Cal., 1973. Mem. Women In Communications, La Mesa C. of C., Sigma Delta Chi. Republican. Methodist. Club: Press (San Diego). Home: 7310 LeConte St San Diego CA 92114 Office: 8242 La Mesa Blvd La Mesa CA 92041

CARLSON, JEAN BURKE, psychologist, educator; b. Chgo., Jan. 21, 1922; d. Vincent M. and Lilliam E. (Earle) Burke; B.A., U. Ill., 1943; M.A., Northwestern U., 1954, Ph.D., 1961; m. William H. Carlson, Dec. 3, 1949; children—James B., Andrew B. Instr. Kendall Coll., Evanston, Ill., 1961-71; prof. ednl. psychology Northeastern Ill. U., Chgo., 1971—. Mem. Evanston Mental Health Bd., 1969-72, 73-76. Served to lt. (j.g.), USNR, 1943-46. Mem. Am. Psychol. Assn., Am. Assn. Ednl. Research. Research in kinesthetic aftereffects. Home: 2716 Lincolnwood Evanston IL 60201 Office: Northeastern Ill U Chicago IL 60625

CARLSON, JOANN (MRS. JEROME GAYLORD CARLSON), educator; b. Corsicana, Tex., Nov. 27, 1945; d. Clifton Herbert and Jueldine (Heifner) McLin; B.A. cum laude, Pepperdine Coll., 1968, M.A., 1970; m. Jerome Gaylord Carlson, Aug. 9, 1960. Grad. asst. journalism, asst. dir. student publs. Pepperdine Coll., Los Angeles, 1968-70, instr. journalism, asso. dir. student publs., 1970-73; asst. prof., dir. of student publs. Pepperdine U., Malibu, Cal., 1973—. Mem. Am. Assn. U. Women, Women in Communications (faculty adviser 1969), Profl. Women of Pepperdine (pres. 1971-73), Pepperdine U. Alumni Assn., Zeta Kappa. Clubs: Century Press (Pepperdine U.). Home: 23926 D DeVille Way Malibu CA 90265

CARLSON, JUDITH HOLADAY (MRS. JACK R. CARLSON), govt. ofcl.; b. Springfield, Ill., Apr. 2, 1928; d. Kenneth M. and Frances E. (Kilts) Holaday; B.A., Oberlin Coll., 1949; postgrad. Washington U., 1949-50; M.S.W., U. Minn., 1952; m. Jack R. Carlson, Aug. 20, 1957; children—Michael Pine, Daniel Kilts, Thomas Holaday. Caseworker, State of Mo., Cape Girardeau, 1950-51, Family Service Assn., St. Paul, 1952-53, Ramsey County (Minn.) Dept. Welfare, St. Paul, 1953-56; supr. Yellowstone County, Dept. Welfare, Billings, Mont., 1956-58; marriage counsellor, Great Falls, Mont., 1962-64; exec. dir. Rocky Mt. Devel. Council, Helena, Mont., 1965-68; model city dir., Helena, 1968-73; coordinator Gov's. Office, Helena, 1973—. Mem. Mont. League Women Voters (v.p. state bd. 1964-65). Episcopalian (mem. exec. council 1970—). Home: 1823 Flowerree St Helena MT 59601 Office: State Capitol Helena MT 59601

CARLSON, LYNNE BECKER (MRS. JAMES A. CARLSON), vet. surgeon; b. Buffalo, N.Y., June 20, 1943; d. John Louis and Jeanne Lee (Rutland) Becker; B.S., Mich. State U., 1965, D.V.M., 1967; m. James A. Carlson, Nov. 29, 1969; 1 dau., Kymm Jeanne. Asso. vet. Glenview (Ill.) Animal Hosp., 1967-69, vet. surgeon, 1971—; staff vet. surgeon Niles (Ill.) Animal Hosp., 1969-71. Mem. Am., Chgo. Vet. medicine assns. Contbr. articles to profl. jours. Home: 6033 N Sheridan Rd Chicago IL 60660 Office: 2400 Waukegan Rd Glenview IL 60025

CARLSON, MARJORIE GWYNNE (MRS. ROBERT K. CARLSON), recreation dir.; b. Chgo., Jan. 5, 1924; d. George Henry and Florence (Simpson) Norman; student Wright Jr. Coll., Chgo., 1941-42, Arlington State Coll., 1960-63; B.S. in Journalism, Tex. Woman's U., 1971; m. Robert K. Carlson, Dec. 3, 1954; children—Kevin Bingham, Kimberly Georgianne. Credit clk. Bookhouse for Children, Chgo., 1942-45; stewardess C & S Delta Airlines, 1945-46; personnel interviewer Capital United Airlines, Chgo., 1946-47; advt. sales sect., co-editor house organ. Am. Colortype, Chgo., 1947-49; exec. sec., editor Tex. Women's U. Alumnae Assn., Denton, 1968-74; recreation dir. Decatur Convalescent Center and Golden Years Haven (Tex.), 1974—. Freelance reporter Denton Record Chronicle, 1969-71. Publicity chmn. Dallas Hunter and Jumper Club Horse Show, 1970; seminar leader 4-H Club reporters, Wise County, Tex., 1971; reporter Decatur Woman's Club, 1971-72; chmn. Am. Alumni Council Dist. IV, Dallas, 1973. Mem. Am. Assn. U. Women, Women in Communication, Alpha Chi, Sigma Tau Delta. Episcopalian (liturgical chmn. 1972, vestrywoman 1973—). Home: Route 3 Box 32AA Decatur TX 76234

CARLSON, MARTHA MARIE, freight co. exec.; b. Vancouver, Wash., Feb. 2, 1926; d. Charles Henry and Martha Matilda (Mason) Carlson; grad. higher accountancy LaSalle Extension U., 1953. With Exley Express, Inc., Portland, Ore., 1951—, sec.-treas., 1966—. Home: 1855 SE Reedway Portland OR 97202 Office: 2610 SE 8th Av Portland OR 97202

CARLSON, MAXINE MARY (MRS. JOHN R. CARLSON), newspaperwoman; b. Erie, Pa., Sept. 13, 1928; d. Max Richard and Frances Mary (Sechrist) Eichler; grad. high sch.; m. John R. Carlson, Mar. 5, 1949; children—Deborah, Lynnanne, Louise, Lea, Denise. With The Erie Dispatch, 1947-51, Derrick Newspaper, Oil City, Pa., 1960, Erie (Pa.) Times News, 1961-71; women's editor New Castle (Pa.) News, 1971—. Mem. Pa. Women's Press Assn. (chmn. N.W. sect.), Lutheran Ch. Women, Fedn. Jrs. New Castle Home: 3013 Pinehurst Dr New Castle PA 16105 Office: 27 N Mercer St New Castle PA 16101

CARLSON, RUTH HENRIETTA MCRAE (MRS. MARTIN EMILIUS CARLSON), educator; b. Central City, Neb.; d. John Alexander and Ellen (Dell) McRae; B.S., U. Md., M.Ed., 1943; postgrad. Pa. State U., 1947, Columbia, 1951; m. Martin Emilius Carlson, Oct. 22, 1947. Asst. prin., dean of girls Central High Sch., Washington, 1944-50, prin. Sch. Congl. Pages, Washington 1951-54; dir. home econs. Washington Pub. Schs., 1954-60; instr. U. Md., College Park, 1964; dir. D.C. YWCA, 1960-63; pres. Sumner Garden Club, 1966; chmn. hospitality Sumner Citizens Assn., 1966; chmn. scholarship fund Panhellenic D.C., 1969—. Precinct chmn. Democratic Party, Sumner, Md., 1965-67. Recipient Merit Alumnae certificate U. Md. Coll. Home Econs.; Distinguished Alumni certificate Central High Sch., 1950. Mem. Regional Assn. Deans of Women (pres. 1952-54), Am. (chmn. elementary, secondary and adult sect. 1956-58; consumer interest com., legislative com. 1962-64), D.C. (pres. 1956-58; certificate distinction 1971) home econs. assns., Panhellenic Assn. (pres. 1971-72), Zonta, Phi Kappa Phi, Delta Kappa Gamma (chmn. program com. Epsilon chpt. 1968—), Kappa Delta, Omicron Nu. Episcopalian. Clubs: Washington (asst. chmn. internat. com., 1969-70, gov. 1972—); Capital Speaker (Washington). Supervisory editor meats edit. Favorite Recipes of Am. Home Econs. Tchrs., 1960—, bd. adv. editors editions on salads, vegetables, desserts, casseroles, 2d edit. meats, 1969. Home: 5121 Westpath Way Sumner PO Washington DC 20016

CARLSON, RUTH KEARNEY (MRS. OSCAR E. CARLSON, JR.), educator; b. Ramona, Cal., June 2, 1911; d. Mark C. and Jessie C. (Martin) Kearney; A.B., U. Cal. at Berkeley, 1932, M.A., 1944, Ph.D., 1959; m. Oscar E. Carlson, Jr., July 20, 1945. Tchr., Ramona (Cal.) Elementary Sch., 1933-36, Valencia (Cal.) High Sch., 1936-39, Fullerton (Cal.) High Sch., 1939-40, Nevada City (Cal.) High Sch., 1940-41, San Diego City Schs., 1941-45, Richmond Elementary Schs., 1949-53; typist, asst. personnel dir. Pearl Harbor Naval Shipyard, Hawaii, 1945-48; cons. Contra Costa County Schs., 1953-59; faculty Cal. State U., Hayward, 1959—, now prof. edn. Cons., collaborator Coronet Films, Chgo.; cons. Scholastic and Readers Digest learning materials, Harcourt Brace & Jovanovitch; tchr. N.S. Summer Sch., Halifax, 1963-74, workshops at U. Las Vegas, Nev., 1970-74; speaker various orgns., assns. Mem. Nat., Central Cal. (Spl. award 1970) councils tchrs. of English, Internat. Reading Assn. (conf. chmn.), Assn. Childhood Edn. Internat. (chmn. publs. com.), Nat. Soc. for Study Edn., Cal. Assn. Tchrs. English, Am., Western folklore socs., U. Cal. Edn. Alumni Assn. (pres., dir.), Cal. Writers Club, Woman's Nat. Book Assn., Alpha Delta Kappa, Pi Lambda Theta. Mem. Order Eastern Star. Author: Language Sparklers for the Intermediate Grades, 1968; Poetry for Today's Child, 1968; Writing Aids Through the Grades, 1970; Literature for Children: Enrichment Ideas, 1970; Emerging Humanity, Multiethnic Literature for Children and Adolescents, 1972; Sparkling Words: Two Hundred Practical and Creative Writing Ideas, rev. edit., 1973. Editor, contbr. Folklore and Folktales Around the World, 1972. Contbr. articles to profl. jours. Home: 1718 LeRoy Av Berkeley CA 94709 Office: 25800 Hillary St Hayward CA 94542

CARLSON, SUZANNE OLIVE, architect; b. Worcester, Mass., Aug. 20, 1939; d. Sigfrid and Helga (Larson) Carlson; B.S., R.I. Sch. Design, 1963. Jr. partner Dingman-Fauteux & Partners, Worcester, Mass., 1969-70; partner firm Richard Lamoureux Asso., Worcester, 1970—; guest lectr. Holy Cross Coll., 1969-70. Mem. Worcester Art Museum, Worcester Craft Center. Recipient European Honors Program grant, Rome, Italy, 1961-62; recipient A.I.A. Sch. medal for excellence, 1963. Mem. Worcester Heritage Soc., A.I.A. (Central Mass. exec. bd. 1969-71, v.p. 1971-72, pres. 1973-74), Mass. State Assn. Architects (exec. bd. 1973, 74), New Eng. Regional Assn. Architects (exec. bd. 1972-74). Home: Old Turnpike Rd Oakham MA 01068 Office: 14 E Worcester St Worcester MA 01604

CARLSON, THEODORA ELIZABETH, govt. ofcl.; b. Great Falls, Mont., Nov. 28, 1909; d. Christopher Theodore and Klara Louise (Blomquist) Carlson; A.B., Wayne (Neb.) State Tchrs. Coll., 1930; postgrad. U. Neb., 1934-36, Columbia Sch. Library Service, 1941-43, Am. U., 1944-47, George Washington U., 1948-49, 54-55. Tchr. high sch., Concord, Neb., 1930-36, Wayne, Neb., 1936-42; tchr., librarian Rhinebeck (N.Y.) High Sch., 1942-43; editor U.S. Tariff Commn., 1943-48, commodity specialist, 1948-49; editor Fgn. Agrl. Service, Dept. Agr., 1949-55; editor Sch. Life and Am. Edn., Office Edn., 1955-65, chief periodicals sect., 1956-65, specialist fed.-state relations, 1965-67, dep. asso. commr. for fed.-state relations, 1970-73, spl. asst. to dep. asst. sec. edn., 1973—; mem. publns. com. Grad. Sch., Dept. Agr., 1953—. Fellow communications Ford Fund Adult Edn., 1959. Mem. Fed. Editors Assn. (pres. 1957-58), Am. Assn. Sch. Adminstrs., Am. Soc. Pub. Adminstrn., Nat. Council Adminstrv. Women in Edn. (pres. D.C. council 1971-72), Horace Mann League, N.E.A., Sigma Tau Delta, Phi Delta Gamma (pres. D.C. alumnae chpt. 1970-71). Lutheran. Club: Internat. (Washington). Home: 2206 Windsor Rd Alexandria VA 22307 Office: 400 Maryland Av SW Washington DC 20202

CARLTON, CATHERINE KENNEY (MRS. ELBERT PEARSON CARLTON), osteo. physician; b. Laredo, Tex., Oct. 20, 1915; d. Charles Francis and Helene (Larmoyeux) Kenney; student Incarnate Word Coll., 1933-34, U. Tex., Arlington, 1934; D.O., Kirksville Coll. Osteo. Medicine, 1938; m. Elbert Pearson Carlton, June 11, 1941 (dec. Dec. 1972); children—Cathy (Mrs. Steven F. Landon), Helen (Mrs. James Hattan), Jane (Mrs. Paul Lenau). Practice of osteo. medicine, Fort Worth, 1938—; mem. staff Ft. Worth Osteo. Hosp.; clin. prof., chmn. dept. osteo. theory and technique Tex. Coll. Osteo. Medicine, Ft. Worth, 1970—. Camp Fire leader, 10 yrs. Charter mem. Women's br. Ft. Worth br. Nat. Conf. Christians and Jews, also mem. bd. West Tex. 1966—. Recipient Outstanding Service award Kirksville Coll. Osteo. Medicine, 1959. Diplomate Bd. Gen. Practice Osteo. Medicine and Surgery. Fellow Am. Acad. Osteopathy (trustee 1972—); mem. Ft. Worth C. of C. (charter mem. women's div.), Tex. Acad. Osteopathy (pres. 1964), Kirksville Osteo. Alumni Assn. (pres. Tex. chpt. 1964-65), Ft. Worth Soc. Crippled Children and Adults (dir.), Tex. Acad. Applied Osteopathy (sec.-treas.), Am., Tex., Tarrant County (past pres.) assns. osteo. physicians and surgeons, Tarrant County Day Care Assn. (dir.), Kirksville Coll. Osteo. Medicine Alumni (sec.-treas. Tex. br. 1961-62), Internat. Fedn. Catholic Alumnae (chpt. v.p. 1970-71). Roman Catholic (pres. Ft. Worth Deanry Nat. Council Cath. Women 1962-63, mem. parish council, also research editor for parish anniversary book 1968, pres. St. Mary's Altar Soc. 1973—). Clubs: Zonta (pres. Ft. Worth 1956), Women of Rotary (rec. sec. 1965-66, dir. 1968-70). Home: 2505 Ryan Place Dr Fort Worth TX 76110 Office: 815 W Magnolia Av Fort Worth TX 76104

CARLTON, LOWIS BOWERS (MRS. CLAUD A. CARLTON), journalist; b. Barnesville, Ga., Mar. 28, 1920; d. Joe Worley and Connie Mamie (Martin) Bowers; A.B. magna cum laude, U. Miami, 1968, M.A., 1969; m. Claud A. Carlton, May 15, 1955. Publicity asst. to v.p. pub. relations Fla. Power & Light Co., Miami, 1949-60; food editor Miami Herald, 1961-63, columnist, 1973—; nat. columnist Fla. Dept. Agr., 1964-69; tchr. Hialeah (Fla.) High Sch., 1969-70; food editor Palm Beach Life, 1967-73; faculty U. Miami, 1968-69. Mem. Fla. Pub. Relations Assn., Women in Communications, Nat. Assn. Real Estate Bds., C. of C. (dir. women's div. 1958-60), Phi Lambda Pi, Phi Kappa Phi. Club: Miami Executive (pres. women's div. 1957-58). Author: Famous Florida Recipes, 1973. Home: 7600 SW 81st Av Miami FL 33143

CARLTON, SARA BOEHLKE (MRS. MASON GANT CARLTON), occupational therapist; b. Black River Falls, Wis., July 1, 1937; d. Ralph William and Hazel Olive (Drecktrah) Boehlke; B.S., U. Wis., 1959; m. Mason Gant Carlton, Sept. 9, 1961; children—Holly Gant, John Frederick. Occupational therapist VA Hosp., Lyons, N.J., 1960-65; occupational therapist Hunterdon Med. Center, Flemington, N.J., 1968-71, dir. occupational therapy, 1971-73, dir. infant stimulation program, 1973—. Mem. Bd. Edn. Holland Twp., Hunterdon County, N.J., 1972—, v.p., 1974—. Trustee Hunterdon Occupational Tng. Center, Flemington, 1972—. Mem. Am., N.J. occupational therapy assns. Presbyn. (mem. bd. Christian edn. 1972-73). Club: Woman's (exec. bd. 1971-72) (Milford, N.J.). Home: Route 1 Box 130 Milford NJ 08848 Office: Hunterdon Med Center Flemington NJ 08822

CARMEAN, MARIAN SMITH (MRS. JAMES L. CARMEAN), banker; b. Huntington, Ark., July 10, 1926; d. Walter Lauren and Agatha Bell (White) Smith; student Am. Inst. Banking, 1959-60; m. James Liggett Carmean, Apr. 16, 1949 (dec. Jan. 1968); 1 son, James Liggett. Sec. to dist. mgr. Nat. Cylinder Gas Co., Dallas, 1943-51; office clk. Vandergriff Chevrolet Co., Irving, Tex., 1952-53; exec. sec., v.p., asst. trust officer Irving Bank & Trust Co., 1953—. Bd. dirs., v.p. Community Concert Assn. Mem. Nat. Assn. Bank Women, Am. Inst. Banking. Methodist (mem. ofcl. ch. bd. 1969—). Club: Altrusa of Irving (treas., sec., dir. 1964—, pres. 1973-74). Home: 1632 Glen Valley St Irving TX 75061 Office: Irving Bank and Trust Co Main St and Irving Blvd Irving TX 75061

CARMEL, HILDA ANNE SCHAFFLE (MRS. JOSEPH P. CARMEL), artist; b. N.Y.C.; d. Joseph and Matilda (Katz) Schaffle; student Coll. City N.Y., 1930-31, N.Y.U., 1931-32, Art Students League, 1953; m. Joseph P. Carmel, June 7, 1930; children—Mona (Mrs. Alfred W. Guibord), Pola (Mrs. Leonard A. Perlman). Exhibited in one man shows at Miami Beach (Fla.) Library, 1956; Chgo. Womens Aid, 1960, Gallery 84, Inc., 1963-65, Awixa Pond Art Center, Bay Shore, L.I., N.Y., 1964, East Side Gallery, N.Y.C., 1964; exhibited in group shows at Lever House, N.Y.C., 1966, 68, 72, N.Y.U., 1966, 68, Loeb Center, N.Y.C., 1966, 68, L.I. U., 1965, Nat. Design Center, N.Y.C., 1965, 68, Union Carbide, 1972-73, Bronx Mus., 1972-73; represented in permanent collections at Jewish Mus., N.Y.C., Evansville (Ind.) Mus. Arts and Scis., Safad (Israel) Mus., Bat Yam (Israel) Mus., Awixa Pond Art Center, L.I. U., Zeckendorfer Campus, Bklyn.; owner, dir. Hilda Carmel Gallery, N.Y.C., 1959-63; founder Gallery 84, Inc., N.Y.C., 1963, treas., 1963—. Bd. dirs. League Present Day Artists, 1965—, pres., 1970—. Mem. Artists Equity Assn. N.Y. (dir. 1967-70, corr. sec. 1970—). Centro Studi E Scambi Internazionali (Roma, Italy), Gallery 84 (hon. mem.), Composers, Authors, Artists of Am., Bronx Council on Arts (visual arts chmn., dir. 1973—), Art Studio Club, Painters and Sculptors N.J., Yonkers Art Assn. Address 3210 Fairfield Av Riverdale New York City NY 10463

CARMICHAEL, ADELE FRANCES BOATWRIGHT, educator, clergyman; b. Granger, Ia.; d. David Elmo and Cora Ann (Cain) Boatwright; student Central (Mo.) Bible Coll.; B.A., San Jose State Coll., 1949, M.A., 1959; postgrad. U. Hawaii, 1963; m. Richard R. Carmichael, Nov. 9, 1923 (dec. Jan. 1960); children—Ralph R., Ruthadele (Mrs. Edward Dow Martin). Ordained to ministry Assembly of God Ch., 1918; evangelist-tchr., Quincy, Ill., 1925-35, Fargo, N.D., 1935-39, San Jose, Cal., 1939-49, Ventura, Cal., 1950-58; tchr. Ventura High Sch., 1957; tchr. mission sch., Honolulu, 1964-66; dean women Evangel Coll., Springfield, Mo., 1966-69. Mem. Am. Assn. Women Deans and Counselors, Mo. Assn. Tchrs. English, Am. Assn. U. Women, Internat. Platform Assn., Club: Christian Women's (Pasadena, Cal.). Home: 1340 E Broadway Glendale CA 91205

CARMICHAEL, CAROL ELIZABETH ROGERS, realtor; b. Boston, June 15, 1934; d. Lemuel James and Dorothy Hawthorne (Sewell) Rogers; student Fisher Jr. Coll., 1952-54; student U. Mass., 1964-68. Asso., D.H. Jones Real Estate Agy., Amherst, Mass., 1968—. Co-chmn. drive UNICEF, 1967; mem. Amherst Task Force on Growth and Housing. Mem. Nat. Inst. Real Estate Brokers, Nat., Mass. assns. real estate bds., UN Assn., Hampshire County Bd. Realtors, Hampshire County Mental Health Assn. (treas. 1967-68), Leverett Artists and Craftsmen Assn. (co-chmn. spring show and sale 1968). Home: Wendell Rd Shutesbury MA 01072 Office: 200 Triangle St Amherst MA 01002

CARMICHAEL, CAROLYN WILSON (MRS. JOHN HECTOR CARMICHAEL), educator; b. Flushing, N.Y., Jan. 30; d. Walter Pyle and Frances (Peschl) Wilson; B.S., The King's Coll., 1958; M.A., Ball State U., 1966; Ph.D., Mich. State U., 1971; m. John Hector Carmichael, June 15, 1963; children—Elizabeth Carolyn, Kimberly Janette. Tchr. religious edn. Fauquier and Loudoun Counties, Va., 1958-63; tchr. elementary sch., Bergen County, N.J., 1963-64, Holt, Mich., 1966-67; tchr. elementary sch., Hartford City, Ind., 1964-65, remedial reading tchr., 1966; instr. Mich. State U., East Lansing, 1966-68; asso. prof. Kean Coll. N.J., Union, 1971—. Ednl. cons. Dell Pub. Co. Mem. A.L.A. (mem. nat. planning com. for spl. collections), Nat. (asso. chmn. com. on lit. experiences for the presch. child), N.J. councils tchrs. English, Assn. for Supervision and Curriculum Devel., Internat., Coll. reading assns., Nat. Soc. for Study Edn., N.J. Reading Tchrs. Assn., The King's Coll. Alumni Assn. (mem. exec. com.), Pi Lambda Theta. Contbr. articles to profl. jours. Home: 46 Bristol Ct Berkeley Heights NJ 07922 Office: Kean College of New Jersey Union NJ 07083

CARMICHAEL, ELEANOR JOHNSON (MRS. CHARLES WESLEY CARMICHAEL), librarian; b. Mooresville, Ind., Aug. 31, 1916; d. Howard Vinson and Cora Alta (Newman) Johnson; B.A., Earlham Coll., 1938; B.L.S., Columbia, 1941; M.L.S., Ind. U., 1970; m. Charles Wesley Carmichael, July 2, 1948; 1 dau., Ann Bromley (Mrs. George H. Biada, Jr.). Librarian, Coll. Architecture, Cornell U., Ithaca, N.Y., 1942-46; librarian dept. physics Purdue U., Lafayette, Ind., 1946-49; librarian Indpls. Mus. Art, 1956-60; catalog librarian Roy O. West Library, DePauw U., Greencastle, Ind., 1960—. Mem. project task force Coop. Bibliographic Center for Ind. Libraries, 1972-74. Mem. Am. Assn. Univ. Women, D.A.R., Am., Ind. library assns., Ohio Valley Group Tech. Service Librarians (sec. 1962-63), Beta Phi Mu, Alpha Phi, Tri Kappa. Author: (with K. Lark-Horowitz) A Chronology of Scientific Development, 1848-1948, 1948. Home: 702 Highwood Av Greencastle IN 46135

CARMICHAEL, JAE (JANE GRANT GIDDINGS), artist; b. Hollywood, Cal., Aug. 22, 1925; d. Paul Hollingsworth and Harriett (Grant) Giddings; student Mills Coll., 1942-44; B.F.A., U. So. Cal., 1951; Ph.D., 1969; M.F.A., Claremont Grad. Sch., 1955. Instr. art Pasadena (Cal.) Art Museum, 1953-60, dir., 1969—; instr. art Pasadena Sch. Fine Arts, 1957-63, Upper Sch. Westridge Sch. Girls, 1957-58, Fullerton extension, Jr. Art Workshop Pasadena Art Museum, 1960, La Canada Youth House, 1963; guest lectr. art and film dept. cinema U. Cal., 1965-68, dept. drama U. So. Cal., 1966-68. co-owner, dir. Wooden Horse Gallery, Laguna Beach; owner, dir. Pasadena Sch. Fine Arts; instr. Jr. League Women, Farmers Market, Los Angeles, 1960; one man shows Dixie Hall Gallery, Laguna Beach, Cal., Pasadena Art Mus., Catalina Mus., Sidewalk Gallery, Manhattan Galleries, Pasadena, 1961, Paul Rivas Gallery, Los Angeles, 1962, others; exhibited in group shows at Palos Verdes Art Gallery, Nat. Acad., N.Y.C., Phila. Mus., Bodley Gallery, N.Y.C., Los Angeles Art Assn., Mount San Antonio Coll., others; represented in permanent collections Mills College, Frye Mus., Seattle, Scripps Coll., Long Beach Mus.; pvt. collections. Recipient Laguna Beach Art Festival award, 1957, 60, 61, 62, Pasadena Soc. Artists award, 1956, 60, 61, 62, Julia Ellsworth Ford award, 1956, Prix de Paris, 1958, Los Angeles County Art Mus., Nat. Arts Club award, 1960; many others. Mem. Art. Alliance of Pasadena Art Mus., Los Angeles County Rep. Central Com., 1948-49. Mem. Pasadena Soc. Artists (dir. 1959-60, 62-63, pres. 1971-72), Am. Cal. State sec. 1960) watercolor socs., Women Painters West, Laguna Beach Art Assn., Huntington Meml. Clinic Auxiliary, Westridge Sch. Alumni Assn., Mills Coll. Alumni Assn., D.A.R., Pasadent Pioneer Assn., Pasadena Soc., First Century Families of Los Angeles, Alpha Phi. Republican. Clubs: Valley Hunt, Balboa Bay. Home and studio: 985 San Pasqual St Pasadena CA 91106

CARMICHAEL, MARY DARGAN (MRS. ROBERT STEWART CARMICHAEL), librarian; b. Port Washington, N.Y., Sept. 20, 1919; d. John Cornell and Anna Blanche (Pierce) Dargan; B.A., Adelphi U., 1942; M.L.S., Columbia, 1947; postgrad. L.I. U., 1961, Rutgers U., 1964; m. Robert Stewart Carmichael, Feb. 5, 1949; children—John Harvey, Peter Stewart, Laurice. Asst. librarian Brookhaven Nat. Lab. Research Library, Upton, N.Y., 1947-48; chief librarian Naval Training Equipment Center, Orlando, Fla., 1948-50, 57—. Served with USCGR, 1943-46. Mem. Spl. Libraries Assn.

(sec.-treas. mil. librarians div. 1970-71), Council Navy Sci. and Tech. Librarians East (chmn. 1965-66), Orlando Fed. Women's Assn. (program chmn. 1972-73), Cath. Daus. Am., Kappa Kappa Gamma. Democrat. Roman Catholic. Club: Altrusa (corr. sec.) (Winter Park, Fla. 1973-74). Home: 151 N Orlando Av Winter Park FL 32789 Office: Naval Training Equipment Center Tech Library Orlando FL 32813

CARMIGNANI, KATHRYN LOUISE, city govt. ofcl.; b. Bakersfield, Cal., Mar. 14, 1926; d. Karl August and Maymie Ethel (Moon) Shaefer; grad. high sch.; m. Amato Carmignani, Aug. 23, 1942; children—Duane Karl, Ronald Lloyd. With Sears, Roebuck & Co., Oakland, Cal., 1949-65; mem. San Pablo (Cal.) City Planning Commn., 1961-70; councilwoman San Pablo City Council, 1974—. Pres. San Pablo Beautification Com., 1966-69, Brookside Hosp. Service League, 1973-74, Manzanillo-San Pablo Sister City Com., 1969-72; chmn. roadside devel. civic beautification and environmental improvement program Bay Bridges dist. Cal. Garden Clubs, 1973-75. Bd. dirs. San Pablo C. of C., Cal. Roadside Council, U.S./Mexico Sister Cities Assn., San Pablo Garden Club, San Pablo Hist. Soc. Named Woman of Year, Exchange Club San Pablo, 1968. Mem. Native Daus. Golden West (3d v.p.), Cal. Elected Women Edn. and Research, Assn. Western Hosps. (chmn. aux. div. 1975—), Soroptimist Internat. Mem. Order Eastern Star, Women of Moose. Address: 5601 Glenn Av San Pablo CA 94806

CARMINATI, ELINOR PERLEY (MRS. DOMINICK J. CARMINATI), psychologist; b. San Francisco, Aug. 28, 1907; d. Albion Edward and Ella (Lagoni) Perley; A.B. in History, U. Cal. at Berkeley, 1928; M.A. in Clin. Psychology, N.Y. U., 1950; m. Dominick J. Carminati, Oct. 16, 1946; 1 son, Paul. Psychologist Ednl. Inst. for Learning and Research, N.Y.C., 1950-67; psychol. cons. city and county schs., N.Y.C., 1964-67; clin. psychologist Orange County Community Mental Health Clinic, Goshen, N.Y., 1968—. Psychotherapist, N.Y.C., Monroe, N.Y., 1960—; cons. childhood disorders, 1964—; cons. Day Care Centers, Orange County, 1971—. Mem. Am., Orange County, Sullivan County psychol. assns. Home: Rural Delivery 2 Box 156 D Monroe NY 10950 Office: #2 Lake St Monroe NY 10950

CARNER, REBECCA LYNNE, educator; b. Ruston, La., Oct. 23, 1939; d. Elbert S. and Annie Jewell (Phillips) Brewer; B.A., La. Poly. Inst., 1961, M.A., 1962; Ed.D., U. Miami (Fla.), 1971; m. Richard L. Carner, Oct. 22, 1967; 1 dau., Anne Kathryn. Tchr. mentally retarded children Children's House, Ruston, 1961-62; tchr. emotionally disturbed children La. Evaluation Center, New Orleans, 1962-63; spl. edn. cons. New Orleans Regional Mental Health Center, 1963-65; grad. asst. in reading clinic U. Miami, 1965-67, tchr. grad. course reading and spl. edn., 1966-73; evaluation dir. McGlannan Sch., Miami, 1967-70, asst. dir. sch., 1970—. Cons., Alexander Montessori Sch., 1967—; conductor workshops on learning disabilities. Program chmn. Dade Reading Found., 1970, pres., 1973—. Mem. Internat. Reading Assn., Am. Psychol. Assn., Assn. Children Learning Disabilities, Eta Tau. Home: 11075 SW 90th Av Miami FL 33156 Office: 10770 SW 84th St Miami FL 33156

CARNEVALE, JESSIE BEVERLY (MRS. ANTHONY DANIEL CARNEVALE), educator; b. Wilkes Barre, Pa., Aug. 18, 1923; d. John and Annella (Kyfroe) Williams; B.A. in Psychology, U. Ariz., 1958, M.A. in Sociology, 1961, J.D., 1968; m. Anthony Daniel Carnevale, June 26, 1943; 1 son, Nicholas Theodore. Admitted to Ariz. bar, 1969; probate registrar Pima County, 1965-73; asst. prof. U. Ariz., 1968-73; pvt. practice law, Tucson, 1969-73; asso. prof. U. Nev., Las Vegas, 1973—; lawyer-referee Pima County Juvenile Ct., 1972. Counsellor, Tucson Lawyers for Housing; prof. criminal law and juvenile justice Police Acad., Puma County Juvenile Ct., 1969-71; invitational panelist 3d World Congress on Med. Laws under patronage of King and Queen of Belgium, 1973. Atty.-adviser Tucson Girls Club, 1972-73. Campaign mgr. Pima County Gubernatorial candidate, 1968. Mem. nat. adv. bd. Am. Security Council. Fellow Roscoe Pound Found., Internat. Acad. Law and Sci.; mem. Assn. Am. Trial Lawyers (treas. So. Ariz. chpt.), Fed., Ariz., Pima County bar assns., Am. Judicature Soc., Am. Criminal Justice Assn., Bus. and Profl. Women of Nev., Tucson Lawyers Club, Am. Assn. U. Profs., Am. Correctional Soc., Phi Beta Kappa, Phi Kappa Phi, Pi Lambda Theta, Psi Chi, Alpha Delta Delta (past pres.). Author: No-Fault Insurance, 1972; The Legal Right to a Healthful Environment, 1973; Legal Defenses to Medicial Malpractice Claims, 1973; Reconciling the Conflicting Roles of the Educator and the Criminal Justice Administrator, 1973; The Role of Industry in Environmental Law, 1973. Home: 1356 Elizabeth Av Las Vegas NV 89109 Office: Law Enforcement Dept Humanities Bldg U Nev 4505 Maryland Pkwy Las Vegas NV 89145

CARNINE, MARGARET LEE, editor; b. Madison, Ind., Oct. 4, 1925; d. Raymond McKinley and Eva Lena (Cole) Carnine; Registered Nurse, Bethesda Hosp. Sch. Nursing, 1946. Head nurse men's surg. ward Bethesda Hosp., Cin., 1946-50; supr. indsl. nursing Trailmobile, Inc., Cin., 1950-67; editor Charles B. Slack, Inc., Thorofare, N.J., 1968—. Mem. Am. Assn. Indsl. Nurses. Editor Occupational Health Nursing, 1968—. Home: 522 Crafton Av Pitman NJ 08071 Office: 6900 Grove Rd Thorofare NJ 08086

CARNWATH, NANCY L., lawyer; b. Muskoka, Ont., Can., Jan. 24, 1930; B.A., U. Toronto; legal degree Osgood Hall, Toronto. Admitted to Ont. bar, 1957, since practiced in Toronto; with firm McMillian, Binch, Berry, Dunn, Corrigan & Howland. Mem. Canadian Bar Assn. Office: McMillian Binch Berry Dunn Corrigan & Howland 20 King St W Toronto 1 ON Canada

CAROLA (CAROLA MUELLER), photographer, lectr.; b. Potsdam, Germany; d. Carl and Martha (Kaergel) Thimm; student Berlin U., 1937-38; m. Dr. Mueller. Interpreter Am. Occupation Army, Germany, 1945-46; dir. camera factory, Munich, 1946; photographer internat. fashion shows, France and Italy, also Internat. Film Festival, Cannes, 1951-54; photog. assignments include Caribbean Islands, European fashion shows, 1956; fashion shows, Fla., Italy and Germany, 1957, 59, South Africa, 1960, Italy and France, 1960, Berlin and Italy, 1961; travels to Mexico, 1958, safari through S.W. Africa, Bechuanaland, 1960, Spain and Mallorca, 1961, Cal. and Hawaiian Islands, 1962, Internat. Air Races Women, 1963; Hawaii, Samoa, Fiji, Tahiti, New Zealand, Australia, 1963; appeared on TV U.S., Europe, Australia; fgn. corr. Praline, 1964; Internat. Film Festival, Taormina, Sicily, 1965; Hawaii, Japan, Malayan Fedn. Afghanistan-Ceylon, 1966, Himalaya to Hunzaland, 1967, Greece, 1968, Panama, Columbia, San Blas Islands, Leeward Islands 1969, USSR, So. France, 1970, Pic du Midi-Spain-Ibiza, Stonehenge, 1971, Greece and Greek Islands, 1972, total solar eclipse, 1973; lectr., interviewer, throughout U.S.A., Europe, 1959-72. Recipient 2d prize color photography Internat. Exhbn. Photography, 1954; 1st prize for best travel-inspiring picture, 1956, award Internat. Salon Photography, Munich, 1968. Mem. Internat. Platform Assn. Theta Sigma Phi (hon.). Address: 901 N Birch Rd Fort Lauderdale FL 33304

CAROUSSO, DOROTHEE HUGHES, author; b. Winthrop, Mass., Oct. 4, 1909; d. Patrick Lawrence and Luella (Nowell) Hughes; student pub. schs., St. Agnes Acad., College Point, N.Y., Kurt's Bus. Sch., Los Angeles; L.H.D.; Combs College of Music, Phila., 1968; m. Georges Carousso, Dec. 31, 1930; 1 dau., Dorothee Nowell (Mrs. George Neil McKinnon). Author: Open Then the Door, 1942; Sports Afield, 1960; (TV plays) Climax, Studio One; also fiction, verse in Collier's, Household, All-Story mags., American, Woman's Home Companion, Canadian Home Jour.; contbr. articles to Pa. Geneal. Mag., Nat. Geneal. Quarterly, Geneal. Mag. N.J., New Eng. H & G Register, Md. and Del. Genealogist. Book critic Brooklyn Eagle. Mem. Geneal. Soc. Pa. (vice pres.), Hist. Soc. Pa., Chester County, Montgomery County hist. socs., Nat. Soc. Colonial Dames, D.A.R., Bucks County (Pa.) Writers Guild, Soc. Descs. Colonial Clergy, Colonial Daus. 17th Century. Address: 1072 Frederick Rd Meadowbrook PA 19046

CARPENTER, AGNES PROFFITT (MRS. WILLIAM OTIS CARPENTER), psychologist; b. Takoma Park, Md., Feb. 26, 1924; d. Max Jay and Agnes Charruaud (Healy) Proffitt; B.A. with distinction, DePauw U., 1945; M.A., George Washington U., 1952; postgrad., 1967-68; postgrad. U. Va., 1969-73; m. William Otis Carpenter, Sept. 24, 1949; 1 son, William Geoffrey. Personnel asst. Capital Transit Co., Washington, 1945-49; tchr., Overlee Presch. Coop. Assn., Arlington, Va., 1959-67; sch. psychologist Pub. Schs. D.C., Washington, 1967-70, clin. psychologist, 1970—. Mem. N. Arlington Parish Council, Arlington, Va., 1969-71; chmn. protective services com. Child Welfare Study Com., 1965. Named Woman of Year, Williamsburg Woman's Club of Arlington, 1960. Mem. Am. Assn. U. Women (v.p. 1960-62), Am. Psychol. Assn. (asso.), Council Exceptional Children, Nat. Assn. Sch. Psychologists (state del. 1973-75), No. Va. Fedn. Coop. Tchrs. (pres. 1965-66), Psi Chi, Pi Beta Phi. Conglist (mem. ch. council 1969-71). Club: Williamsburg Woman's (Arlington, Va.). Home: 5613 N 34th St Arlington VA 22207 Office: 3242-A Pennsylvania Av SE Washington DC 20020

CARPENTER, BETTE MARIE (MRS. HERBERT LARSON CARPENTER), realtor; b. Hemet, Cal., Mar. 8, 1927; d. Scott William and Eugenia LeProhon (de Beaufert) Carl; student Oceanside Jr. Coll., 1943-45, U. Cal. at Los Angeles, 1946-47; m. Herbert Larson Carpenter, May 6, 1944; 1 dau., Carolyn Lee (Mrs. Kenneth Ray Dabbs). Propr., Bette M. Carpenter, Realtors, Carlsbad and Riverside, Cal., 1954-60; pres. Interstate Equities Corp., Oceanside, Cal., 1960—; v.p., sec. LanInCo Corp. Nev., Las Vegas, 1964—; v.p. marketing Parkside Devel. Co., Santa Ana, Cal. Mem. Carlsbad Bd. Realtors (charter mem.), Cal. Real Estate Assn., Nat. Assn. Real Estate Bds., Nat. Inst. Real Estate Brokers, Urban Land Inst., Women Council Realtors. Carlsbad C. of C. Republican. Home: PO Box 254 Carlsbad CA 92008 Office: 804 3d St Oceanside CA 92054

CARPENTER, CECILE LORETTA, librarian; b. Seattle, Nov. 23, 1938; d. Cecil Vernon and Helen Jane (Roberts) Carpenter; student Wash. State U., 1957-58; B.A. in English, U. Wash., 1961, M.Librarianship, 1964. Jr. librarian lit. and history dept. Library Assn. Portland (Ore.), 1964-66, sr. librarian, 1966-72, head Gregory Heights br., 1972, asst. head social sci. and sci. dept., 1972-74, head dept. gen. information, 1974—. Mem. Pacific N.W. Library Assn. (sec. pub. libraries div. 1969-71), Portland Area Spl. Librarians (pres. 1972-73). Editor Ore. sect. Who's Who Among Pacific Northwest Authors, 1970. Home: 7900 SW Brentwood St Portland OR 97225 Office: 801 SW 10th St Portland OR 97205

CARPENTER, CORINNE TAYLOR (MRS. AARON CLARENCE CARPENTER), educator; b. Vicksburg, Miss., Oct. 4, 1916; d. Pink and Albertia (Brooks) Taylor; B.S., Tenn. State U., 1938; M.S., Ind. U., 1955, Ed.D., 1970; m. Aaron Clarence Carpenter, Aug. 8, 1953; 1 dau., Ivel Adair. Sec., Cannon Cosmetic Co., Atlanta, 1938; tchr. McIntyre Jr. High Sch., Vicksburg, 1938-39; tchr., matron, sec. Gailor Indsl. Sch., Mason, Tenn., 1939-40; sec., bursar Alcorn (Miss.) Coll. Alcorn, Miss., 1940-43, bus. mgr., 1943-50, asst. prof. bus., 1950-60; asso. prof. bus. Grambling (La.) Coll., 1960-70, prof., 1970—. Notary pub. Warren County, Miss., 1950-60, Lincoln Parish, La., 1962—. Parliamentarian, Monroe chpt. Links, Inc., Monroe, La., 1973—. Recipient Distinguished Prof. award Grambling Coll., 1973. Mem. La. Edn. Assn. (chmn. sectarial dept. 1972—), Nat., So. bus. edn. assns., La. Vocational Assn., Am. Assn. Univ. Profs., Nat. Assn. Bus. and Office Tchr. Edn., Am. Bus. Communication Assn. (mem. nat. membership com. 1972—), Delta Pi Epsilon, Alpha Kappa Mu, Pi Lambda Theta, Alpha Kappa Alpha. Baptist. Author: College Typewriting, 1960. Contbr. articles to profl. jours. Home: 214 Carver St Grambling LA 71245 Office: PO Box 387 Grambling LA 71245

CARPENTER, ELIZABETH SUTHERLAND (MRS. LESLIE CARPENTER), pub. relations exec., author, lectr.; b. Salado, Tex., Sept. 1, 1920; d. Thomas Shelton and Mary Elizabeth (Robertson) Sutherland; B.J., U. Tex., 1942; m. Leslie Carpenter, June 17, 1944; children—Scott, Christy. Reporter, U.P.I., Phila., 1944-45, News Bur., Washington, 1945-51; Washington corr. Carpenter News Bur., 1951-60; exec. asst. to Vice Pres. Lyndon B. Johnson, 1961-63; press sec., staff dir. to Mrs. Lyndon B. Johnson, 1963-69; now lectr., journalist; v.p. Hill and Knowlton, Inc., Washington; adv. bd. Nat. Bank Washington. Mem. adv. council Women's Nat. Polit. Caucus, 1971—. Adv. bd. Mt. Vernon Coll., Washington, Coll. V.I. Mem. Theta Sigma Phi (Nat. Headliner award 1962). Club: Washington Press (pres. Washington 1954-55). Author: Ruffles and Flourishes, 1970. Home: 4701 Woodway Lane Washington DC 20016 Office: One McPherson Sq Washington DC 20005

CARPENTER, HELEN MCCRACKEN, educator; b. Norwalk, O., July 31, 1909; d. Irving and Myrtle (McCracken) Carpenter; B.A., Ohio Wesleyan U., 1931; M.A., Columbia, 1934, Ed.D. (Grace Dodge fellow 1938-39), 1942; student Ohio U., summers 1931, 35, 36. Tchr. high sch., Crestline, O., 1931-33, Norwalk, O., 1934-36; mem. faculty Ohio Wesleyan U., 1936-38, Columbia Tchrs. Coll., 1940-42, Wilson Tchrs. Coll., 1942-43, R.I. State U., 1943-44; prof. history Trenton (N.J.) State Coll., 1944—; summer tchr. Columbia Tchrs. Coll., Syracuse U., Northwestern U., U. Wyo., La. State U. Dir. Nat. Council for Social Studies, 1951, 52, 57-59, 2d v.p., 1954, 1st v.p., 1955, pres., 1956; sec. Commn. Econs. in Tchr. Edn., 1952-54; ednl. cons. U.S. Stell Corp., 1954-66; ednl. cons. for publs. Am. Sch. Library Assn., Audio-Visual Assn., Assn. Supervision and Curriculum Devel.; field reader U.S. Office of Edn., 1965-70; cons. social studies sch. systems on curriculum revision. Mem. Nat. Council Social Studies, Am. Trenton hist. assns., Nat., N.J. edn. assns. Am. Assn. Supervision and Curriculum Devel., League Women Voters (dir. N.J. 1951-52), Middle States, N.J. councils social studies, Phi Beta Kappa, Delta Sigma Rho, Kappa Delta Pi, Pi Lambda Theta, Delta Kappa Gamma. Club: Zonta. Author: Gateways to American History, 1942; Leads to Listening, 1952-70. Co-author: Scribner Social Studies Series for Schools, 1948-62. Editor: Skills in Social Studies, 1953; Skill Development in Social Studies, 1963. Contbr. to profl. jours. Home: 301 W State St Trenton NJ 08618

CARPENTER, JUDITH LEE, govt. ofcl.; b. Washington, Feb. 17, 1940; d. Chester Jewett and Hazelle Irene (Friess) Carpenter; B.S. in Pub. Adminstrn., U. Mo., 1961; postgrad. Harvard, 1967-68. Budget analyst USPHS, Dept. Health, Edn. and Welfare, Washington, 1961-64, budget officer NIH, 1964-70, program analysis officer Nat. Center for Family Planning Services, 1970-72, sr. health policy implementation officer Dept. Health, Edn. and Welfare, 1972-73, sr. mgmt. analysis officer, 1973—. Nat. Inst. Pub. Affairs fellow, 1967-68. Mem. Am. Soc. for Pub. Adminstrn., Pi Sigma Alpha, Beta Gamma Sigma. Home: 3920 Tynewick Dr Silver Spring MD 20906 Office: 5600 Fishers Lane Rockville MD 20852

CARPENTER, LEONORE MELNICOFF, pub. health ofcl.; b. Phila., Aug. 20, 1924; d. Albert Richard and Ethel (Londa) Melnicoff; student U. Pa., 1945; B.S., U. Louisville, 1967; postgrad. Eastern Ky. U., 1973-74; children—Dean K., Sherry L. Occupational therapist State Hosp., Trenton, N.J., 1945-49; dir. occupational therapy dept. Rivercrest Sanitarium, L.I., N.Y., 1949-51; dir. occupational therapy dept. Rehab. Center, Louisville, 1962-65; health planner regional mental health Ky. Dept. Mental Health, Louisville, 1967-68; pub. health rep., devel. specialist Ky. Dept. Human Resources, Frankfort, 1973—. Precinct capt. Democratic party, Louisville, 1968-71. Mem. Am., Ky. occupational therapy assns. Home: 2098 Regency Rd Lexington KY 40503 Office: 275 E Main St Frankfort KY 40601

CARPENTER, MARGARET HALEY, author, editor; b. Frederick Hall, Va.; d. Charles R. and Nan (Cooke) Carpenter; B.A., U. Richmond. Reviewer poetry Chgo. Tribune Mag. Books, 1962-63; reviewer books Athens (Ga.) Daily News, 1973-74; adv. editor The Lyric, Va., 1973-74. Recipient Arthur D. Ficke award Poetry Soc. Am., 1956; Greenwood prize Poetry Soc. London (Eng.), 1957; Leitch Meml. award Poetry Soc. Va., 1974; numerous others. Mem. Va. Humanities Found. (v.p. 1970-74), Poetry socs. Am., Va. (adv. bd.). Author: Sara Teasdale: A Biography, 1960; illustrator: A Gift for the Princess of Springtime, 1964. Editor: Poems by Marion Cummings, 1957; Journey into Time by David Morton, 1958; (with William S. Braithwaite) Anthology of Magazine Verse for 1958, 1959. Home: 1032 Cambridge Crescent Norfolk VA 23508

CARPENTER, MARY ELIZABETH (MRS. LAWRENCE REID CARPENTER), librarian; b. Atlanta; d. William Matthew and Mary Georgie (Johnson) Morgan; B.S., Samford U., 1959; M.A., U. Ala., 1962; postgrad. U. Tenn., 1968; m. Lawrence Reid Carpenter, 1 dau., Mary Elizabeth (Mrs. Henry Albert Threlfall). Tchr., Jefferson County, Ala., 1952-57; librarian Samford U., 1958; asst. librarian Shades Valley High Sch., Birmingham, Ala., 1959-61; head librarian Berry High Sch., 1962—. Instr. Jacksonville State U., summer, 1967, U. Ala., Birmingham, summers, 1968-69. Pres., Belview Central Park Council of Clubs, Birmingham; div. leader United Appeal. Mem. Am., Southeastern, Ala. (pres. sch. librarians 1960-61) library assns., Foster Friends Alumni U. Ala. (pres. 1968—), Jefferson County Library Assn. (pres. 1961-63), Alpha Beta Alpha, Kappa Delta Epsilon, Alpha Lambda Alpha. Baptist (tchr., youth worker). Clubs: Cleophas Literary (pres.), Mountain Laurel Garden (pres. 1954-57), Shades Crest Civic (Birmingham, Ala.). Home: 537 Park Av Birmingham AL 35226 Office: 2826 Columbiana Rd Birmingham AL 35216

CARPENTER, MILDRED BAILEY, artist, educator; b. St. Louis; d. William Thomas and Lyle Ellen (Lockwood) Bailey; student St. Louis Sch. Fine Arts, Washington U., 1911-15, U. Madrid, 1955; m. Fred Green Carpenter, July 15, 1914 (dec. Mar. 1965); 1 son, David B. Exhibited in one-man shows St. Louis Artists Guild, Milw. Art Inst., Monday Club St. Louis, Springfield (Ill.) Art Assn., various galleries U.S.; exhibited in group shows Internat. Traveling Watercolor Shows, Nat. Assn. Women Artists, Europe, N.Y., 1956-65, Acad. Design, St. Louis Artists Guild, St. Louis Art Mus., Chgo. Art Inst., Kansas City Art Inst. Instr. figure-drawing, portraiture Washington U., 1950-70. Portrait painter convalescent service-men Army and Navy Hosps., 1945-49. Recipient Bronze medal for watercolors Kansas City Art Inst. (Mo.), 1924; numerous cash awards St. Louis Artists Guild, 1916-71; named St. Louis Woman of Achievement in Art, 1947. Mem. Nat. Assn. Women Artists, St. Louis Artists Guild (v.p. 1964-70, recipient Dr. Carlo Somino portrait prize 1969; Myrtle Dalton Portrait prize 1971), St. Louis Women's Advt. Club, Friends City Art Mus., Friends St. Louis Acad. Sci., Children's Art Bazaar, Women's Soc. Washington U., Woman's Club Washington U. Executed murals for St. Louis schs., Gatesworth Manor. Home: 416 Woodlawn Av Webster Groves MO 63119

CARPENTER, MYRTLE LUCILE, librarian; b. Lancaster, Wis., Sept. 22, 1914; d. William John and Esther Elizabeth (Hales) Cox; B.S., U. Minn., 1935; M.S.L.S., U. Wis.-Madison, 1965; postgrad. in English, U. Wis.-Platteville, 1971—; m. Glenn J. Carpenter, Sept. 11, 1946. Circulation asst. U. Ia., 1935-40; reference librarian Wausau (Wis.) Pub. Library, 1940-42; sch. librarian Madison Pub. Library System, 1942-44; librarian U.S. Dept. Navy, Olathe, Kan. and Great Lakes, Ill., 1945-46; young peoples librarian San Diego Pub. Library, 1947-48; high sch. librarian Lancaster Community Schs., 1956-64; supervising librarian S.W. Wis. Pub. Library Service Center, Fennimore, 1964-65; librarian fine arts div. U. Wis.-Platteville, 1965—. Trustee Lancaster Pub. Library, 1965—. Mem. Wis., S.W. Wis. library assns., S.W. Wis. Edn. Assn., Wis. Library Tchrs. Assn., Am. Assn. U. Women, Am. Fedn. Women's Clubs (past pres. Lancaster chpt.), Beta Phi Mu, Lambda Iota Tau. Mem. Order Eastern Star. Editor: Masters Theses and Seminar Papers of the Former Wisconsin State Universities, 1935—. Home: 128 S Taylor St Lancaster WI 53813 Office: Karrmann Library U Wis Platteville WI 53818

CARPENTER, NAN COOKE, educator; b. Frederick's Hall, Va., July 29, 1912; d. Charles Richard and Nan R. (Cooke) Carpenter; B.Music, Hollins Coll., 1934; M.A., U. N.C., 1941; M.A., Yale, 1945, Ph.D., 1948. Asst. prof. U. Montana, Missoula, 1948-52, asso. prof., 1952-56, prof. English, 1956-64; vis. prof. So. Ill. U., Carbondale, 1964-65; vis. prof. Syracuse (N.Y.) U., 1965-66; prof. English and comparative lit. U. Ga., Athens, 1967—, chmn. dept. comparative lit., 1974—. Dir. Athens Humane Soc., Recording for the Blind. Founder Va. Humanities Found., pres. 1970—. Ford Found. fellow, 1954; Am. Council Learned Socs. fellow, 1958. Mem. Modern Lang. Assn., Am. Musicol. Soc., Phi Beta Kappa. Author: Rabelais and Music, 1954; Music in the Medieval and Renaissance Universities, 1958; John Skelton, 1968. Home: Georgetown Apts 350 S Pope St Athens GA 30601

CARPENTER, PATRICIA HUMPHREY (MRS. WARREN CARPENTER), psychologist; b. Detroit, May 16, 1920; d. William Henry and Kathryn (Dix) Humphrey; A.B., Oberlin Coll., 1941; B.S. in L.S., Western Res. U., 1943; M.A., Wayne State U., 1958, Ph.D., 1961; m. Warren Carpenter, Mar. 29, 1958. Librarian, U.A.W.-CIO, Detroit Pub. Library, 1943-56; psychologist, research asso. Wayne State U., 1957-58; psychol. intern Lafayette Clinic, 1958-59; psychologist I, II, III Clinic for Child Study, Wayne County Juvenile Ct. Detroit, 1959-63, psychologist IV, chief psychologist, 1963-70, dir. psychol. services, 1970—. Diplomate Am. Bd. Examiners in Profl. Clin. Psychology. Mem. Am. Psychol. Assn., Sigma Xi, Psi Chi. Home: 3875 W Coon Lake Rd Route 2 Howell MI 48843 Office: 1025 E Forest Detroit MI 48207

CARPENTIER, BERTHA MAE POSEY (MRS. CHARLES NELSON CARPENTIER), real estate broker; b. Hillsboro, Tex., Apr. 2, 1919; d. Homer H. and Itylene (Moore) Posey; A.A., Hillsboro

Jr. Coll., 1939; postgrad. U. Cal. at Los Angeles, 1951-53; m. Charles Nelson Carpentier, Nov. 14, 1953; children—Carla, Nelson. Dept. head Air Assos., Dallas, 1940-43, Los Angeles, 1943-45; personnel mgr. North Am. Aviation Co., Los Angeles, 1947-50; dir. clerical personnel dept. Hughes Aircraft Co., Culver City, Cal., 1951-57; sales asso. Bert Elser Realty, Malibu, Cal., 1957-62, A.J. Pierson Realty, 1963-67, Malibu Sierra Realty, 1967-68; realtor, propr. Posey Carpentier Realty, Inc., Malibu, 1968-75. Bd. dirs. Malibu Bd. Realtors, 1971-75, pres., 1972-73; faculty Santa Monica (Cal.) Coll. Pres. P.T.A., Webster Sch., Malibu, Cal., 1968-69, pres. P.T.A., Malibu Park Jr. High Sch., 1971-72; historian Santa Monica P.T.A. Council, 1972-73. Bd. dirs. South Bay area Drug Abuse Council, 1971-73, Malibu Drug Action Bd., chmn., 1971-73. Mem. Cal. Assn. Realtors (mem. coms., dist. rep. property mgmt. div.), Malibu C. of C. Contbr. articles to profl. publs. Democrat. Home: 3868 Rambla Orienta Malibu CA 90265 Office: 21361 Pacific Coast Hwy Malibu CA 90265

CARPER, ANNA MARY, librarian; b. Palmyra, Pa.; d. Frank S. and Ella (Ebersole) Carper; A.B. cum laude, Elizabethtown Coll., 1941; M.S., Columbia U. Sch. Library Service, 1951. Tchr., librarian Fredericksburg (Pa.) High Sch., 1941-47; tchr. South Lebanon Schs., Lebanon, Pa., 1947-50; head cataloger U. Md., College Park, 1951-60; head librarian Elizabethtown (Pa.) Coll., 1960—, also dir. Mem. Am., Pa., Lancaster County library assns., Am. Assn. U. Women, Delta Kappa Gamma (Beta Theta chpt.). Mem. Ch. of Brethren. Home: 306 1/2 E High St Elizabethtown PA 17022 Office: Zug Meml Library Elizabethtown Coll Elizabethtown PA 17022

CARPY, MATHILDE PAULINE (MRS. JOSEPH CONOLLY), physician; b. San Francisco, Oct. 8, 1924; d. Albert Charles and Louise (Fortin) Carpy; B.S., Dominican Coll., 1947; M.D., Creighton U., 1951; m. Dr. Joseph F. Conolly, May 2, 1953; children—Morgan, Paula, Esther M., Colette U., Craig. Intern, St. Lukes Hosp., San Francisco, 1951-52, surg. resident, 1952-53, staff 1959—; practice medicine specializing in internal medicine and cardiology, 1959—; mem. active staff St. Helena (Cal.) Hosp. and Health Center. Mem. A.M.A., Am. Soc. Clin. Hypnosis, Acad. Psychomatic Medicine, Epsilon Iota, Gamma Pi Epsilon. Home: 1700 Doris Av Saint Helena CA 94574 Office: 1222 Pine St Saint Helena CA 94574

CARR, ANNE ELIZABETH, communications cons.; b. Ithaca, N.Y., May 24, 1939; d. John Franklin and Helen Louise (Ziegler) Carr; B.A., U. Rochester, 1960; M.A. in English Lit., U. Edinburgh (Scotland), 1962. Continuity dir. radio sta. WWCO, Waterbury, Conn., 1962-63; jr. copywriter Dancer, Fitzgerald, Sample, 1963-64; copy chief Weber & Heilbroner, 1964; asst. to pres. for pub. relations Communicorp, Inc., 1964-65; freelance writer, 1965-66; copy chief Takaro Advt., 1965-66; asst. to feature editor Design News, 1966-67; asso., dir. advt. and pub. relations PR-N.Y., Inc., 1967-71; mng. editor newsletter Cons. News, 1970-71; pres. Carr & Co., 1971—. Guest lectr. U. Waterloo (Ont., Can.). Communications chmn. Graham Home For Children Aux. Mem. Internat. Radio and TV Soc., Am. Bus. Press, Pub. Relations Soc. Am., Publicity Club N.Y., Internat. Platform Assn., Mensa. Address: 80 East End Av New York City NY 10028

CARR, BETTY BAKER (MRS. ELWOOD JAMES CARR), librarian; b. Tunkhannock, Pa., Jan. 13, 1923; d. Howard William and Helen Irene (Ball) Baker; B.S., Mansfield State Coll., 1943; postgrad. Pa. State U., 1945, 71, Elmira Coll., 1960, summers 1965, 67; m. Elwood James Carr, June 14, 1946; children—Barbara (Mrs. Jeffrey Kistler), Marilyn (Mrs. James Parks), Wendy, James, Rosalie. English tchr. Nicholson (Pa.) High Sch., 1943-45; social studies tchr. LeRaysville (Pa.) High Sch., 1945-47; English and reading tchr. Northeast Bradford High Sch., Rome, Pa., 1957-67, librarian 1967—. Mem. No. Tier Librarians Assn. (pres. 1971-72), Nat., Pa., Northeast (mem. negotiations com. 1971-72, chmn. pub. relations com. 1972-74) edn. assns., Friends of Bradford Wyoming County Libraries (sec. 1970-72). Home: Box 37 LeRaysville PA 18829 Office: Northeast Bradford High School Rural Delivery 1 Rome PA 18837

CARR, CAROLYN KINDER (MRS. NORMAN STEWART CARR), journalist; b. Providence, Feb. 23, 1939; d. Harold and Mildred (Fearney) Kinder; B.A., Smith Coll., 1961; M.A., Oberlin Coll., 1965; postgrad. Case Western Res. U., 1972; m. Norman Stewart Carr, July 6, 1961; children—Christopher Kinder, Courtney Elizabeth. Mem. art history faculty Kent (O.) State U., 1963-65, 66-68; art critic Beacon Jour., Akron, O., 1969—. Mem. Coll. Art Assn. Home: 2166 Tinkham Rd Akron OH 44313

CARR, DONNIE CRONIN (MRS. LEON CLEMENT CARR), journalist; b. Mpls.; d. Ralph Walter and Claire W. (Nehotte) Cronin; B.A. in Journalism, U. Minn., 1968; m. Leon Clement Carr, May 19, 1956; 1 son, John Patrick. Newspaper wire editor Pontiac (Ill.) Daily Leader, 1951-52; mag. editor Am. Collectors Assn., Mpls., 1952-56; pub. information specialist Tb and Respiratory Disease Assn. Hennepin County, Mpls., 1956-63; women's editor Mpls. Suburban Newspapers (Sun Newspapers), 1963-64; reporter St. Paul Suburban Newspapers, 1964-68, Dispatch, St. Paul, 1968-73; mgr., reporter, photographer Dakota County Tribune, Farmington, Minn., 1973—. Sec., Mpls. Mayor's Commn. on Employment Handicapped, 1960-61. Recipient numerous writing awards. Mem. Minn. Press Women (pres. 1973—), Nat. Fedn. Press Women, Internat. Assn. Bus. Communicators (pres. 1958), Internat. Council Indsl. Editors (dir. 1958), U. Minn. Sch. Journalism Alumni Assn. (sec. 1959), Women in Communications (pres. Twin Cities chpt. 1955-56), Soc. Profl. Journalists, Sigma Delta Chi. Home: 21 E Logan Av West St Paul MN 55118 Office: 420 3d St Farmington MN 55024

CARR, DOROTHY KELLEY (MRS. HARLAN B. CARR), city ofcl., educator; b. Syracuse, N.Y., Oct. 30, 1906; d. James J. and Margaret (McAuliffe) Kelley; B.A. magna cum laude, Syracuse U., 1928, M.Communications, 1972; m. Harlan B. Carr, Nov. 24, 1932; children—Nancy (Mrs. Robert Shepard), Bradley, Margo (Mrs. Robert Miller). Founder, dir. Syracuse U. Children's Theatre, 1930-40, Children's Theatre of Syracuse, 1940-57; exec. sec. Syracuse Radio and TV Council, 1945-49; hostess TV program Your Town, 1952-53; tchr. English, radio and TV, Vocational High Sch., Syracuse, 1954-62; tchr. drama and speech Corcoran High Sch., 1962, Manlius High Sch., Fayetteville, N.Y., 1965—. Women's dir. N.Y. State Fair, 1954-59; mem. Syracuse Recreation Commn., 1945—, vice chmn., 1949-50; recreation commr. WBFL Radio, Syracuse, 1928-43. Radio-TV writer and dir. for local Democratic campaigns, 1930—; mem. N.Y. State Dem. Com., 1950-55. Mem. Women of Press, Syracuse U. Alumnae Club, Beta Sigma Phi, Kappa Alpha Theta. Clubs: Syracuse Press, Corinthian. Home: 7911 Salt Springs Rd Fayetteville NY 13066

CARR, ELIZABETH ESTHER, ednl. adminstr.; b. Los Angeles, Oct. 14, 1947; d. Morris Louis and Theresa Rose (Mika) Carr; A.B. in History, U. So. Cal., 1969, M.S. in Counselor Edn., 1973; student Cambridge (Eng.) U., 1968. Asst. adminstrv. services officer Cal. State Colls. and Univs., Los Angeles, 1969-71; asst. dir. residential life U. So. Cal., 1971—. Mem. Nat. Assn. Student Personnel Adminstrs., Nat. Assn. Women Deans and Counselors, Cal. Assn. Woman Adminstrs. and Counselors, Kappa Kappa Gamma, Pi Delta Phi. Home: 1974 Palmerston Pl Los Angeles CA 90027

CARR, GWEN BRIDEN, educator, psychologist; b. Crookston, Minn., Feb. 6, 1924; d. Joseph E. and Constance G. (Evje) Briden; A.B., San Diego State Coll., 1951; M.A. in Clin. Psychology, George Washington U., 1955; children—Jeffrey T., William I., David R., John M. Tchr., Hobart (Wash.) Pub. Schs., 1944-45, Orange County (Cal.) Schs., 1945-46, Oceanside (Cal.) Pub. Sch., 1949-50; play therapist Speech Clinic, San Diego State U., also extension instr., 1955-57; instr. adult edn. program Carlsbad (Cal.) Coll., 1957-58; tchr. Arlington (Va.) High Sch., 1959-60; prof. psychology San Diego Mesa Coll., 1963—, also mem. adv. bd. Child Devel. Center, 1971—. Mem. vocational edn. adv. com. San Diego Community Colls., 1973. Asso. mem. Am. Psychol. Assn.; mem. Western Psychol. Assn., Psi Chi. Author: Marriage and Family in a Decade of Change, 1971; Growing People: Introduction to Child Development, 1975. Home: 1278 La Sulla Pancho Rd La Jolla CA 92037 Office: 7250 Mesa College Way San Diego CA 92111

CARR, KATHLEEN DOROTHY TANNER, sch. psychologist; b. Rome, N.Y., Nov. 24, 1909; d. Charles and Isabella Anna (Murphy) Tanner; B.S., Teacher's Coll. Columbia, 1954, M.A., 1958, profl. diploma, 1960; m. James Bryan Carr, June 29, 1929 (div. Apr. 1974); children—James B., David V., Mary Elizabeth (Mrs. Vahe Melkonian). Tchr. pub. schs. Laredo, Tex., 1942-43, Tenafly, N.J., 1943-46, Teaneck, N.J., 1946-60; sch. psychologist Cape May County (N.J.), 1960-62, Lakeland Central Schs., Westchester, N.Y., 1962-64, Bd. Coop. Ednl. Services Number 2, Spencerport, N.Y., 1964-65, Greece Central Schs., Rochester, N.Y., 1965—. Mem. Am. (asso.) Genesee Valley psychol. assns., Sch. Psychologists Upstate N.Y., N.E.A., N.Y. State United Tchrs. Roman Catholic. Home: 118 Dellwood Circle Rochester NY 14616 Office: 1790 Latta Rd Rochester NY 14612

CARR, LOIS IRBY ROGERS (MRS. RALPH WILLETT CARR), civic worker; b. Knoxville, Tenn., Apr. 25, 1915; d. James Harrison and Jane Rachel (Bolinger) Rogers; grad. Harriet Gregg's Pvt. Bus. Sch., 1940; m. Ralph Willett Carr, June 25, 1936; 1 dau., Sylvia Sue (Mrs. George Richard Gettys). Sec., TVA, Knoxville, 1938-63. Pres., Fountain City Grammar Sch. P.T.A., Knoxville, 1946-48, Chi-Omega Mothers Club, U. Tenn., Knoxville, 1957-58, Dixie Hwy. Garden Club, Knoxville, 1952-54, 65-67; state historian Tenn. Fedn. Garden Clubs, 1951-53, rec. sec., 1969-71, dist. membership chmn., 1971—, ways and means chmn.; mem. exec. com. Knox County Council, 1971-72; pres. Clionian Club, Lenoir City, Tenn., 1969-70; mem. women's com. Dulin Gallery Art, Knoxville, 1969—; chmn. all area chmn. East Tenn., 1964, membership chmn., Lenoir City, 1965-69; chmn. Dogwood Arts Festival and Auction, Knoxville, 1970-71, Hist. Zoning Com., Knoxville, 1973-74; treas. Knoxville chpt. Assn. for Preservation Tenn. Antiquities, 1966-68, membership co-chmn., 1969-70, dir., pres., 1972-74; mem. Blount Mansion Assn., Knoxville, 1965—, Nat. Trust for Historic Preservation, 1972—; mem. Women's Guild Knoxville Symphony Soc., 1955—, area chmn. women's guild, 1966-67; area chmn. for Lenoir City for Met. Opera Co. and John F. Kennedy Performing Arts, 1967. Asst. Teen Bd. Knoxville from Lenoir City, 1965—. Club: Tuesday (Knoxville). Editor: Economic and Technical Analysis of Fertilizer Innovations and Resource Uses. Address: "Aquarell" Beals Chapel Rd Lenoir City TN 37771

CARR, MARIE BERNICE, educator; b. Aberdeen, S.D., Oct. 13, 1917; d. James Michael and Minnie (Harder) Carr; B.A., San Jose State Coll., 1939; M.A., Stanford, 1942, Ph.D., 1957. Asst., instr. speech and drama dept. San Jose (Cal.) State Coll., 1939-43; rep. 12th region U.S. Civil Service, 1943-46; instr. dept. speech communication San Jose (Cal.) State U., 1946-47, asst. prof., 1947-51, asso. prof., 1951-57, prof., 1957—, chmn. dept. grad. com., 1960—. Reviewer Holbrook Press, 1967-71, Allyn & Bacon, 1965-67. Recipient Certificate of Achievement, All Women's Council, San Jose State U., 1970. Mem. Speech Communication Assn., Western Speech Communication Assn. Mem. Ch. of Jesus Christ of Latter-day Saints (stake and regional drama dir. 1958-63). Club: Women's Faculty (pres. 1969) (San Jose, Cal.). Home: 400 Halsey Av San Jose CA 95128

CARR, MARION GRUDIER, educator; b. Mansfield, O., Feb. 7, 1912; d. Lyman and Helen (Brinkerhoff) Grudier; A.B., Western Res. U., 1934; M.A., Syracuse U., 1938, postgrad., 1938-42; m. Arthur Japheth Carr, Dec. 27, 1941 (div. May 1963); children—Jennifer Marion (Mrs. John McGee), Alice Lockwood (Mrs. Jan Abram Van den Broek), Adam Fyfe, Daniel Arthur. Instr., U. Ill., 1944-47; faculty Eastern Mich. U., 1958-63, asst. prof. English, 1963-66; asst. prof. English State U. N.Y. Coll. at Buffalo, 1966-69, asso. prof., 1971—, chmn. dept. children's lit., 1971—. asso. prof. Central Mich. U., 1969-71. Exec. bd. Ann Arbor Washtenaw br. Am. Civil Liberties Union, 1963-66, mem. state bd., 1964-66; mem. Ann Arbor Human Relations Commn., 1957-60, chmn. housing com., 1957-59, edn. com., 1959-60. Mem. Democratic city com., Ann Arbor, 1950-54, vice chmn., 1953-54. Recipient Human Relations award Ann Arbor Jr. C. of C., 1959. Mem. Faculty Assn. State U. N.Y., Am. Assn. U. Profs., Nat. Council Tchrs. English, Modern Lang. Assn., N.E.A. Contbr. articles to profl. jours. Home: 122 Pickford Av Kenmore NY 14223 Office: 311 Butler Library State U NY 1300 Elmwood Av Buffalo NY 14222

CARR, MARY ANN (MRS. RICHARD LINES CARR), mfg. co. exec.; b. Akron, O., May 17, 1934; d. Frank and Elizabeth (Mahr) Hofbauer; student Albion Coll., 1952-53; B.S., Western Mich. U., 1957; m. Richard Lines Carr, Mar. 9, 1957; children—Richard Lines, Frank Stephen, Cynthia Ann, Daniel Edward. Elementary sch. tchr., Flint, Mich., 1957, Defiance, O., 1958; dir. Mohawk Tools, Inc., Montpelier, O., 1956—, also bd. reporter. Leader Jr. Great Book program, Dayton, 1968—, charge Jr. Great Book tng. session, 1969. Mem. Dayton Soc. Natural History (supporting), Dayton Engrs. Club (woman's bd.), Delta Zeta. Episcopalian (pres. ch. women's assn. 1971-72, treas. United Thank Offering 1973-74). Courtesy mem. Antioch Temple. Dir. state-wide husband-and-wife golf tournament, Bedford, Ind., 1965. Home: 7535 Yankee St Dayton OH 45459 Office: 910-14 E Main St Montpelier OH 43543

CARR, MELINDA MANNING, editor; b. Covington, Ky., Mar. 10, 1945; d. Arnol and Edith (Robinson) Manning; student U. Ky., 1962-65; B.A., Fla. State U., 1966; m. Slade L. Carr, Jr., Dec. 21, 1964. Elementary tchr., Quincy, Fla., 1966-67; asst. dir. research and information Fla. State Treas.'s Office, Tallahassee, 1967-71; writer, editor Fla. Dept. Commerce, Tallahassee, 1971-73; travel writer, coordinator nat. unit U.S. Travel Service, Washington, 1973—. Mem. Women in Communications, Fla. Pub. Relations Assn. (Image awards 1967-73, chpt. sect. 1969), Fla. Mag. Assn. Club: Sierra (Fla. chpt.). Home: 6079-12 Major's Lane Columbia MD 21045 Office: US Travel Service Room 1525 Dept Commerce Washington DC 20230

CARR, MILDRED LEE REFO (MRS. EBERLE WILLIAM CARR), librarian; b. Norfolk, Va., Feb. 10, 1915; d. Miles P. and Mildred Lee (Francis) Refo; B.A., Coll. William and Mary, 1934; B.S. in L.S., Columbia, 1939; m. Eberle William Carr, 1940; children—Lee Carr Finney, William Burch. Circulation asst. Enoch Pratt Free Library, Balt., 1936-38, first asst. lit. dept., readers adviser, 1939-42; reference librarian Md. State Tchrs. Coll., Towson, 1951-52; asst. circulation librarian U. N.C. at Greensboro, 1958-70, head circulation librarian, 1970—. Organizer Cockeysville Library, 1947, Patient Library, Moses Cone Hosp., Greensboro, N.C., 1954-56. Mem. Am., Southeastern, N.C. library assns., Democrat. Roman Catholic. Home: 202 Meadowbrook Terrace Greensboro NC 27408

CARR, SALLY SWAN (MRS. RAY DE LA MONTANYE CARR), sculptor; b. Minong, Wis.; d. Otto Olson and Anna Marie (Taft) Swan; student sculpture, N.Y.U., 1956; m. Ray de la Montanye Carr, Jan. 4, 1941. One man shows at Florence Gallery (N.Y.C.), Crespi; exhibited in group shows at N.Y. Burr Gallery, Thompson Galleries, Barzanski Gallery, Capricorn Gallery, So. Vt. Art Center (Manchester), U.S. Embassy (Bangui, Africa), many others; represented in permanent collections including Waldorf Astoria, Marco Polo Club, U.S. Embassy (Morocco), Capricorn Gallery, (Bethesda, Md.), Catharine Lorillard Wolfe Art Club, Inc., Cayuga Museum Art and Sci., Numis. Soc. N.Y.C., Basketball Hall of Fame, Springfield, Mass., also pvt. collections. Vol. worker Bellevue Hosp., 1952-59. Recipient Silver Medal, Albert Schweitzer Soc., 1967, also bronze medal, Gunsbach of Albert Schweitzer Circle. Mem. Composers, Authors and Artists Am. (historian; dir.), N.A.D., Smithsonian Instn. Clubs: Architectural League, Catharine Lorillard Wolfe Art (pres. 1971-74), Nat. Arts (Sherman Drake award), Pen and Brush (past dir., Founders prize 1969), Burr Artists (past v.p.). Home: 530 E 23d St New York City NY 10010 Studio: 30 E 20th St New York City NY 10003

CARRERA, ANA ESTRADA (MRS. GUILLERMO M. CARRERA), physician, pathologist; b. Rio Piedras, P.R., Apr. 16, 1921; d. Manuel and Josefina (Marquez) Estrada; student Stanford, 1945, Newcomb Coll., 1945-47; M.D., Tulane U., 1951; m. Guillermo M. Carrera, Sept. 5, 1945; children—Guillermo F., Carlos J. Am. Cancer Soc. research fellow Tulane U., New Orleans, 1951-53, research asso., instr. medicine, 1957-62, asst. prof. medicine, 1962-68, asso. prof. medicine, 1968-73, clin. prof., 1973—; clin. pathologist Ochsner Clinic, Ochsner Found. Hosp., New Orleans, 1958—, active staff clin. pathologist, 1961—. Mem. Am., Pan Am. med. assns., Am. Med. Women Assn., Coll. Am. Pathologists, Am. Soc. Clin. Pathologists, Am. Soc. Hematology, Alpha Omega Alpha, Sigma Xi. Contbr. articles to med. jours. Home: 3118 Jena St New Orleans LA 70125 Office: 1514 Jefferson Hwy New Orleans LA 70121

CARRIER, CONSTANCE VIRGINIA, poet; b. New Britain, Conn., July 29, 1908; d. Lucius Alonzo and Lillian M. (Jost) Carrier; B.A., Smith Coll., 1929; M.A., Trinity Coll., 1940. Tchr. Latin, English and French pub. schs., New Britain and West Hartford, Conn., 1930-70; instr. classics workshop Tufts U., Medford, Mass., 1967—. Mem. adv. bd. Reader/Writer Conf., Suffield (Conn.) Acad., 1970—. MacDowell Colony fellow, 1955-68. Recipient Lamont Prize for first book Am. Acad. Poets, 1955. Author: The Middle Voice (poetry), 1955; The Poems of Propertius, 1963; The Poems of Tibullus, 1968; The Angled Road (poetry), 1973. Home: 225 W Main St New Britain CT 06052

CARRIER, ESTHER JANE, librarian; b. Punxsutawney, Pa., June 22, 1925; d. Gerald Burton and Mabel E. (Lines) Carrier; student Bob Jones Coll., 1942-44; A.B., Geneva Coll., 1946; B.S. in L.S., Carnegie Library Sch., 1947; M.A., Pa. State U., 1950; M.A. in L.S., U. Mich., 1958, Ph.D., 1960. Circulation asst., reference asst. Pa. State U., 1947-50; head librarian Houghton Coll., 1950—. Mem. Am. Library Assn., Beta Phi Mu. Author: Fiction in Public Libraries, 1876-1900, 1965. Home: 410 Highland Av Punxsutawney PA 15767 Office: Houghton Coll Houghton NY 14744

CARRIGAN, HELEN LEOVY, civic worker; b. New Orleans, Oct. 12, 1903; d. Frank Adair and Augusta (Glenny) Leovy; student Spence Sch., N.Y.C., 1918-22; m. Harris Carrigan, Dec. 21, 1951 (dec. Dec. 1958). Pres. Jr. League, Pitts., 1929-31, Assn. Jr. Leagues Am., 1938-40; mem. Jr. League New Orleans, Jr. League N.Y.C.; sec. Nat. Social Welfare Assembly, 1941-44; mem. Allegheny County Bd. of Assistance, 1944-48; bd. dirs. San Francisco Assn. for Mental Health, 1958—, Californians for Juvenile Justice, Center Point; trustee Marin Gen. Hosp. Mem. Marin Mental Health Assn. (dir.). Clubs: St. Francis Yacht (San Francisco), Capitol Hill, Pass Christian Yacht. Republican. Episcopalian. Home: 651 E Scenic Dr Pass Christian MS 39571

CARRIGAN, JOANN, educator; b. Washington, Ark., Sept. 10, 1933; d. Gray Eugene and Lucile (Monroe) Carrigan; B.A., Henderson State Coll., 1953; M.A., La. State U., 1956, Ph.D. (Gottlieb scholar 1960-61), 1961; Andrew Mellon postdoctoral fellow U. Pitts., 1961-62. Tchr. Sheridan (Ark). High Sch., 1953-54; instr. social scis. Henderson State Coll., Arkadelphia, Ark., 1959, Nicholls State Coll., Thibodaux, La., summer 1962; mem. faculty La. State U., Baton Rouge, 1962-69, asst. prof., history, 1964-67, asso. prof., 1967-69; asso. prof. U. Neb. at Omaha, 1970-71, prof., 1971—; prof. med. history U. Neb. Med. Center, 1973—. Vis. prof. U. Ala., Tuscaloosa, summer 1967. Mem. Am. Civil Liberties Union, 1956—. Research grantee Am. Philos. Soc., 1965. Mem. Am., So., La. hist. assns., Orgn. Am. Historians, Phi Alpha Theta. Democrat. Editor La. History, 1963-69. Editor: History of Louisiana (Alcee Fortier), 1966. Contbr. profl. jours. med. and pub. health history. Home: 1633 Country Club Av Omaha NE 68104 Office: Dept History U Neb Omaha NE 68101

CARRINGTON, ELSIE REID, physician; b. Phila., Sept. 19, 1911; A.B., Wheaton (Ill.) Coll., 1933; M.D., Temple U., 1941, M.Sc., 1949; postgrad. Cornell Med. Sch., 1952, U. Buffalo, 1958. Intern Temple U. Hosp., Phila., 1941-43, resident in obstetrics and gynecology, 1943-45, 48-49, instr. in obstetrics and gynecology, 1949-51, asst. prof., 1951-58, asso. prof., 1958-61; mem. staff Jane Lamb Meml. Hosp., Clinton, Ia., 1945-48, Mercy Hosp., Clinton, 1945-48; asso. chief obstetrics and gynecology Phila. Gen. Hosp., 1953-58; mem. attending staff gynecology St. Christopher's Hosp. for Children, 1951-62; attending gynecologist VA Hosp., Phila., 1966-71, cons., 1971—; chief Women's Med. Coll. div. Phila. Gen. Hosp., 1961-66; research prof. obstetrics and gynecology Women's Med. Coll. Pa., Phila., 1961-65, prof. obstetrics and gynecology, 1965-67, chmn., 1967—; cons. in field. Recipient Four Freedoms award, 1964, Christopher R. and Mary S. Lindback award, 1968. Diplomate Am. Bd. Obstetrics and Gynecology. Mem. A.M.A., Am. Fertility Soc., Assn. Profs. Gynecology and Obstetrics, Coll. Physicians Phila., Am. Assn. Obstetricians and Gynecologists, Am. Coll. Obstetricians and Gynecologists, Internat. Fertility Assn., N.Y. Acad. Scis., Pa., Phila. med. socs., Internat. Soc. Research Biology Reprodn., Alpha Omega Alpha. Editorial bd. Obstetrics and Gynecology, 1972—. Address: Women's Medical Coll Philadelphia PA 19129

CARRINGTON, FRANCES KATHLEEN (MRS. ROYLE P. CARRINGTON III), pub. relations exec.; b. Abilene, Tex., June 20, 1943; d. Jefferson Davis and Martha Kathleen (Linton) Darden; B.S., Hardin-Simmons U., 1965; postgrad., Baylor U., 1965-68; m. Royle P. Carrington III, Nov. 20, 1971. Information specialist Baptist Gen. Conv. of Tex., Dallas, 1967; news services coordinator Baylor U., Waco, Tex., 1968-71, dir., 1971—. Lectr. pub. relations, journalism high sch. and coll. classes, 1968—; cons. pub. relations; free lance writer, 1965—. Volunteer A.R.C., 1961—. Named Outstanding Woman Journalist Baylor U., 1966. Mem. Women in Communications, Am. Coll. Pub. Relations Assn., Am. Assn. U. Women, Baptist, Tex. Baptist pub. relations assns., Sigma Delta Chi. Club: Baylor Law Wives, Air Force Wives Assn. Editor Baylor Report, 1971—; editor Guide to Things to Do in and around Waco, 1973. Home: 1721 S 9th St Waco TX 76706 Office: PO Box 6337 Waco TX 76706

CARRINGTON, HARRIETTE JEANETTE CASS (MRS. CHARLES TINSLEY CARRINGTON), state ofcl.; b. Chgo., Apr. 9, 1912; d. Harry Stewart and Jeanette (Reed) Cass; student Chgo. Normal Coll., 1929-30; m. Charles Tinsley Carrington, Nov. 14, 1948; children—Janet Virginia (Mrs. Norris Brock Johnson), Leon Henry. Sales and buyer asst. S. Center Dept. Store, Chgo., 1941; gen. clk. Ill. State Employment Service, Chgo., 1941-43, employment interviewer, unit supr., 1943-67, human relations rep., coordinator profl., sales, clerical office and Chgo. area office, 1967—. Mem. tech. adv. com. Opportunities Industrialization Centers, Chgo. Organizer, coordinator Career Fair and Job Fair, Berean Ch. Service League, 1967, 68. Mem. Internat. Assn. Personnel in Employment Security (dir., program chmn. Ill. chpt. 1971-73). Baptist (dir. Berean credit union 1969-73). Home: 5440 Indiana Av Chicago IL 60615 Office: 40 W Adams St Chicago IL 60603

CARRINGTON, WILLIE RAYNES, librarian; b. Louisville; d. William Henry and Virginia Beatrice (Suter) Raynes; A.B., Ind. U., 1930, M.A., 1936; M.S., Columbia, 1960; m. William E. Carrington, June 24, 1934; children—William E., Esther Virginia. Tchr., Dunbar High Sch., Lexington, Ky., 1930-31, Central High Sch., Louisville, 1931-34; tchr. English and French, Livingstone Coll., Salisbury, N.C., 1934-37; librarian New Rochelle (N.Y.) Pub. Library, 1960—. Mem. Am., N.Y. State library assns., Assn. Afro-Am. History, N.A.A.C.P., Phi Beta Kappa. Mem. A.M.E. Ch. (pres. ch. club, head ch. library com.). Home: 1 Clove Rd New Rochelle NY 10801 Office: New Rochelle Public Library New Rochelle NY 10805

CARRISON, MURIEL PASKIN (MRS. DONALD ALLEN CARRISON), educator; b. N.Y.C., Apr. 27, 1928; d. Jacob Michelin and Hattie Katz (Ganeles) Paskin; B.A., Hunter Coll., 1948; M.A., Cal. State U. at Long Beach, 1964; Ed.D. (Nat. Defense Edn. scholar, Educare scholar), U. So. Cal., 1968; m. N. Lombrozo, Feb. 1, 1948 (div. 1968); children—Michael, Amy, Peter, David; m. 2d, Donald Allen Carrison, Aug. 7, 1969. Tchr. elementary and secondary schs., N.Y.C., 1948-51, Long Beach, Cal., 1952-63, curriculum cons., 1963—; vis. asst. prof. social founds. edn. U. So. Cal., Los Angeles, 1964-68, Cal. State U., Long Beach, 1967-69, Cal. State U., Fullerton, 1969, Rio Hondo Jr. Coll., Whittier, Cal., 1969; asso. prof. edn. Cal. State Coll., Dominguez Hill, 1969—. Interim dir. Tchr. Corps, 1973; co-dir. Preparation of Samoan and Bi-Lingual Ednl. Aides, 1969; vice chmn. Acad. Senate Cal. State Coll., 1973. Mem. Fair-Housing Found. of Long Beach, Cal., Common Cause, Camp Fire Girls; co-leader YMCA Indian Guides; v.p. P.T.A. Vice pres. Acad. Advisers to Cal. Democratic Com. Mem. N.E.A., Am. Psychol. Assn., Am. Sociol. Assn., Am. Assn. Univ. Profs., Internat. Cent. for Edn. of Tchrs. Mem. Phi Lambda Theta (evaluator edn. book list). Contbr. to various publs. Home: 4130 Chestnut Av Long Beach CA 90807 Office: California State College 1000E Victoria Dominguez Hills CA 90747

CARROLL, ANN ELIZABETH, newspaper editor; b. Pocahontas, Ark., Aug. 29, 1922; d. Warrenn Lee and Thelma (Martin) Blankenship; student U. Ark., 1939-40, Capital City Bus. Coll., Little Rock, 1940-41; m. William Duard Carroll, Feb. 11, 1942; children—Carol Ann, William Neal, Patrick Warren. Sec., Ark. Workmen's Compensation Co., Little Rock, 1941; tchr. Pocahontas high schs., 1944-45, 53-54; with Pocohontas Star Herald, 1957—, editor, 1963—. Vice pres. Randolph County Democratic Central Com., 1964—. Finalist, Golden Quill contest; named to Golden Dozen group Internat. Conf. Weekly Newspaper Editors, 1969; recipient 5 1st pl. awards in Ark., 1970. Mem. Nat., Ark. woman's press assns., Ark. Press Assn., Nat. Newspaper Assn., U. Ark. Alumni Assn., Am. Legion Aux., Internat. Platform Assn. Methodist (bd. stewards). Home: 905 Black St Pocohontas AR 72455 Office: Box 608 Pocohontas AR 72455

CARROLL, ANNE WELCH (MRS. OWEN T. CARROLL), b. Lincoln, Ill., Dec. 15, 1939; d. Frank and Hannah Welch; B.A., U. Denver, 1957, M.A., 1958, Ph.D., 1965; m. Owen T. Carroll, May 29, 1965. Organizer Saturday Speech and Hearing Clinic, Limon, Colo., 1957-64; adminstrv. asst. in spl. edn. Adams County (Colo.) Sch. Dist., 1958-64; instr. Colo. State U., summer 1966; asso. prof. edn. U. Denver, 1967-72, coordinator spl. edn., prof. edn., 1972—, asst. dean Coll. Arts and Scis., 1974—. Cons. to Colo. Dept. Edn., 1964-67, U.S. Office Edn. bur. for edn. handicapped, 1966-71, Regional Mobile Lab. in Learning Disorders, 1966—, Nat. Speech and Hearing Prevalence Study, 1966—. Fellow Am. Speech and Hearing Assn. (regional chmn. comprehensive planning com., asso. editor clin. and ednl. materials jour.); mem. Colo. Speech and Hearing Assn., (chmn. comprehensive planning com.), Assn. for Children with Learning Disabilities, Colo. Council Tchr. Educators in Spl. Edn., Am., Colo. psychol. assns., Am. Assn. Mental Deficiency, Internat. Assn. for Logopedics and Phoniatrics, Zonta Internat., Phi Beta Kappa, Zeta Phi Eta, Alpha Gamma Delta, Mortar Bd. Contbr. numerous articles to profl. jours. Cons. editor Acad. Therapy, Teaching Exceptional Children. Home: 3941 S Clermont Englewood CO 80110 Office: Special Education Univ Denver Denver CO 80210

CARROLL, BILLY PRICE HOSMER (MRS. DAVID DONALD CARROLL), artist; b. Memphis, Nov. 27, 1920; d. Robert Ray and Olive (Thomas) Price; grad. Miss Hutchinson's Sch., 1939; student Memphis Acad. Arts, 1939-40, Farnsworth Sch. Painting, 1949, 1950-51, (fellow) Jay Hambridge Found., 1954, (fellow) Huntington Hartford Found., 1958, Accademia Delle Belle Arte, Florence, Italy, 1959; pvt. studies with PiHan C.K. Chang, H.C. Chao, KeiSzeto, Shou-Kwan Lui, Hong Kong; m. Robert Ray Hosmer, May 3, 1941 (div. Aug. 1948); 1 dau., Nadia Jan; m. 2d, David Donald Carroll, Dec. 25, 1964. Exhibited in one-man shows at Fine Arts Mus., Little Rock, 1953, McCaughen and Burr Gallery, St. Louis, 1954, 64, Brooks Meml. Art Gallery, Memphis, 1956, Greenville Art Assn., 1963, Hong Kong, 1968, Taiwan Nat. Art Center, 1969, others; exhibited in group shows at Fla. Artists Group, 1952-53, 57-58, Brooks Meml. Art Gallery, Memphis, 1953, 61, 66, 67, Painting of Year Exhbn., Atlanta, 1955, 1st Hunter Ann., Chattanooga, 1960; guest artist Mpls. Aquatennial Festival, 1970; represented in permanent collections Ct. Appeals, Jackson, Tenn., U. Tenn., Memphis, Memphis State U., Supreme Ct. and Circuits Cts., United Chinese Bank, Hong Kong, Taiwan Nat. Art Center, Taipei, also in pvt. collections. Recipient numerous art awards. Mem. Brooks Art Gallery League, Penwomen Am. Home: 1940 Carr Av Memphis TN 38104 Studio 1956 Central St Memphis TN 38104

CARROLL, CONSTANCE MARIE, coll. adminstr.; b. Balt., Sept. 12, 1945; d. James Lee and Rebecca Agnes (Evans) Carroll; B.A., Duquesne U., 1966; certificate Knubly U., Athens, Greece, 1967; M.A., U. Pitts., 1969. Dir. freshman advising U. Pitts., 1969-72; asst. dean, asst. prof. classics U. Me., Portland, 1972—. Asso. dir. U.S. Office Edn. Inst., 1972. Mem. Nat. Council Negro Women (nat. co-chmn. commn. on higher edn. 1972—), Am. Philol. Assn., Am. Assn. Univ. Profs., Nat. Assn. Women Deans and Counselors, Vergilian Soc., Pa., Me. women's polit. caucuses. Office: U Me Portland ME 04103

CARROLL, DIAHANN, singer, actress; b. N.Y.C.; d. John and Mabel (Faulk) Johnson; grad. Music and Arts High Sch.; student N.Y. U.; married; 1 dau., Suzanne Ottilee. Debut as vocalist, Latin Quarter, N.Y.C.; since has appeared as nightclub entertainer throughout U.S.; guest artist on leading TV shows, U.S. and Eng.; starring in TV series Julia, from 1968; appeared in Broadway musicals House of Flowers, 1954, No Strings; starred in motion picture Paris Blues; rec. artist for RCA Victor, Vik, United Artists. Address: care Merrick-Shefrin Co Inc 18 E 48th St New York City NY 10013

CARROLL, ELIZABETH, ballerina; b. Paris, Jan. 19, 1937; d. Jean and Suzanne (Beneyton) Pfister; ed. Ecole Elementaire de Filles, 1942-47, Coll. de Jeunes Filles, 1948-51; m. Felix Smith, July 18, 1957; 1 dau., Ariane Smith. Soloist, Monte Carlo Opera Ballet, Monte Carlo, 1952-54; 1st soloist Am. Ballet Theatre, 1954-61; prin. dancer Robert Joffrey Co., 1961-63, Harkness Ballet, 1964-70, also guest ballet tchr. Recipient hon. award Dance Masters Am., 1969. Home: RD 2 Box 296 Stockton NJ 08559 Office: 4 E 75th St New York City NY 10021

CARROLL, FRANCES BURLE (MRS. JIMMY LEE CARROLL), assn. ofcl.; b. Corsicana, Tex., Oct. 30, 1925; d. Henry Grady and Ruth Price (Starnes) Gibson; student U. Tex., 1942-44; m. Jimmy Lee Carroll, Nov. 8, 1944; children—Mary Annette (Mrs. Charles W. King), Paul Douglas, Dorothy Kathleen. Mem. staff S.W. Star-Builder newspaper, Sulphur, La., 1965-67, editor, 1966-67; editor West-Cal News, Lake Charles, La., 1967-68; corr. for La. edit. Beaumont (Tex.) Enterprise newspaper, 1968—; mgr. West Calcasieu Assn. Commerce, Sulphur, 1968—. Recipient numerous state and nat. writing awards. Mem. La. Press Women, Nat. Fedn. Press Women. Democrat. Baptist. Home: 323 Rio Hondo St Maplewood LA 70663 Office: PO Box 1054 Sulphur LA 70663

CARROLL, FRANCES LAVERNE, educator; b. Scammon, Kan., Dec. 6, 1925; d. Robert Allen and Truda Hilda (Flanagan) Carroll; B.S., Kan. State Tchrs. Coll., 1948; M.A., U. Denver, 1956; postgrad. Western Res. U., 1957; Ph.D., U. Okla., 1970. Bank bookkeeper Baxter Springs (Kan.) Bank, 1944; high sch. tchr., Caney, Kan., 1947-49; tchr. English and journalism, librarian Field Kindley Meml. High Sch., Coffeyville, Kan., 1949-54; librarian Coffeyville (Kan.) Jr. Coll., 1954-62, supr. elementary sch. libraries, 1957-62; asst. prof. library sci. U. Okla., Norman, 1962-67, asso. prof., 1971—, acting dir. sch. library sci., 1974—. Guest lectr. Drexel Inst. Tech., Phila., 1964, U. London, 1972; dir. U.S. Office Edn. Inst., 1966, 67, 69. Recipient grant U.S. Office Edn., 1969. Mem. Am. Assn. Univ. Women, Am. Assn. Univ. Profs., Internat. Assn. Sch. Librarians (chmn. membership 1970—), Internat. Relations Round Table, Internat. Fedn. Library Assns. (chmn. planning group on sch. libraries 1973), Am., Southwestern, Okla. library assns., Delta Kappa Gamma, Phi Delta Kappa, Beta Phi Mu. Contbr. articles to profl. jours. Office: 401 W Brooks St Norman OK 73069

CARROLL, HARLEAN MARIE, lawyer; b. Hollywood, Cal., June 8, 1937; d. William T. and Dolly M. (Allen) Carroll; A.B. in Polit. Sci. magna cum laude, U. So. Cal., 1959, LL.B., 1962. Admitted to Cal. bar, 1963; practice law with Voney F. Morin Law Offices, Hollywood, 1963—. Lectr. in field. Mem. State Bar Cal., Los Angeles County Bar, Hollywood C. of C., Soroptimists (past pres. Hollywood, also past v.p., sec., com. chmn.), Velada Bus. and Profl. Women, Town Hall Cal., Phi Beta Kappa, Phi Delta Delta (sec. 1960, treas. 1960-61, pres. 1961-62), Phi Kappa Phi, Pi Sigma Alpha, Alpha Mu Gamma. Office: 1341 N Cahuenga Blvd Los Angeles CA 90028

CARROLL, JANE ROBERTS CONNER (MRS. HERBERT BEELER CARROLL), county ofcl.; b. Newport News, Va., Oct. 26, 1930; d. Alexander McPhee and Angie (Lake) Conner; A.B., U. N.C., 1951; m. Herbert Beeler Carroll, Dec. 27, 1957; children—Sherilyn Jane, William Alexander. Tchr. pub. schs., Hampton, Va., 1951-57, Ft. Lauderdale, Fla., 1957-60; supr. elections Broward County, Ft. Lauderdale, 1968—. Mem. Broward County Republican Exec. Com., 1964—, 1st vice chmn., 1965-67; sec. Plantation Rep. Club, 1967-69; v.p. Broward County Womens Rep. Club, 1969-72; dir. Broward County Rep. Club, 1968-71; mem. Nat., Fla. fedns. Rep. women. Mem. League Women Voters, Fla. State Assn. Suprs. of Elections (dir. 1973-75), Am. Assn. U. Women Childrens Home Soc. Aux., Museum of Arts. Presbyn. Clubs: Womens Civic, Zonta. Home: 4847 NW 7th Ct Plantation FL 33317 Office: 201 SE 6th St Fort Lauderdale FL 33301

CARROLL, JEAN GAYTON (MRS. WALTER WILLIAM CARROLL), orgn. exec.; b. Chgo., Oct. 13, 1925; d. Loran DeLancey and Margaret (Hassett) Gayton; B.A., U. Chgo., 1943, M.A., 1951, Ph.D., 1967; m. Walter William Carroll, June 13, 1947; children—Michael Gayton, Christopher James. Research asst. J. Walter Thompson, Chgo., 1947-50; research asso. Commn. on Accreditation of Rehab. Facilities, Chgo., 1967-68, dep. program dir., 1969-70; dir. research Joint Commn. on Accreditation of Hosps., Chgo., 1970—. Cons. evaluation Am. Newspaper Pubs. Assn., Assn. Am. Med. Colls., Northwestern U. Med. Sch. Mem. women's bd. Ill. div. Am. Cancer Soc., 1951-59; mem. women's bd. Nat. Conf. Christians and Jews, 1951-59. Mem. Am. Psychol. Assn., Chgo. Hist. Soc. (life governing mem.), English-Speaking Union, Art Inst. Chgo. Club: Saddle and Cycle. Home: 230 E Delaware Pl Chicago IL 60611 Office: 875 N Michigan Av Chicago IL 60611

CARROLL, JENNIE ELIZABETH, mus. curator; b. Afton, Okla., Oct. 20, 1897; d. Jesse Ulysses and Emma A. (Reid) Carroll; grad. Ore. Coll. Edn., 1921; B.S., U. Ore., 1946; postgrad. U. Wash., 1954, 57, Chico State Coll., 1951, U. Cal., 1926. City librarian Lakeview, Ore.; sec. to county supt. schs.; tchr. Butte (Ore.) Rural Sch., 1917-20, primary grades, Prineville, Ore., 1921-24; tchr., librarian, prin. Lakeview City Schs., 1924-62, high sch. librarian, 1957-62; curator Schminck Meml. Mus., Lakeview, 1962—. Organizer, Sr. Citizen Group, 1972-73, now pres.; mem. com. for planning retirement home and center, 1974. Named Ore. Ret. Tchr. of Year, 1972; Outstanding Woman of County, 1973. Mem. Lake County Ret. Tchrs. Assn. (unit pres.), N.E.A. (del.), Ore. Edn. Assn. (pres. Lake County), D.A.R., Am. Assn. Ret. Persons (pres. Goose Lake Valley chpt. 1974). Methodist (trustee). Mem. Order Eastern Star, Rebecca Lodge. Club: Soroptimist. Address: 128 S E St Lakeview OR 97630

CARROLL, LARANDA, editor; b. Summerville, Ga., July 8, 1949; d. Edward and Betty Jane (Chitwood) Carroll; student Northeast State Jr. Coll., 1967-68; B.A., U. Ala., 1971. Reporter The Sand Mountain Reporter, Albertville, Ala., 1971-72; news editor The Leader Dispatch, Boaz, Ala., 1973—. Mem. steering com. Ala. Women's Polit. Caucus, 1971-73. Bd. dirs. Am. Cancer Soc., 1972-74. Mem. Women in Communications, Marshall County Assn. Retarded Children, Albertville Bus. and Profl. Women's Club (sec. 1972-73). Democrat. Baptist. Home: 202 1/2 Burns St Albertville AL 35950 Office: 101 N Church St Boaz AL 35957

CARROLL, LILLIAN REBECCA, guidance counselor; b. Nashua, N.H., Oct. 4, 1912; d. Richard Dunstan and Alice (Cotton) Fletcher; B.S., Boston U., 1965, M.Ed., 1967; postgrad. Fla. State U., 1969-73; m. Richard Parker Carroll, Jan. 27, 1961. Nurse, Baker Meml. Hosp., 1935-38; stewardess Am. Airlines, 1938-42; supr., asst. pub. relations dir. N.E. Airlines, 1942-48; founder, dir. airline course Ward Sch. Airline Tng., 1949-52; dir. airline course Mt. Ida Jr. Coll., Newton Centre, Mass., 1952-64, hygiene instr., 1955-62, head clinic nurse, 1963-67; dir. guidance blind dept. Fla. Sch. for Deaf and Blind, St. Augustine, 1967—, coordinator placement services, follow-up studies program, 1974—. Aviation lectr., cons., 1939-53. Coordinator, troop cons. Girl Scouts; blind dept. rep. St. Johns County Com. Drug Abuse, 1971-74. Mem. Assn. for Edn. Visually Handicapped, Assn. Classroom Tchrs., Tri-counties Counselors Assn., Congress Parents and Tchrs. (sec. campus chpt. 1971-73), Nat. Rehab. Assn., Nat. Wildlife Assn., Nat. Park Coll., Boston U. alumnae assns., Internat. Platform Assn. (life), Nat. Kiwi Club (chmn. chpt. formation 1954-58, founder, officer Boston chpt. 1952-67, conv. chmn. 1966), Pi Lambda Theta. Author stewardess manuals. Home: 7 Surf Dr St Augustine By-the-Sea FL 32084 Office: PO Box 1209 San Marco Av St Augustine FL 32084

CARROLL, MARGARET ELLEN, journalist; b. Chgo., Mar. 21, 1936; d. James Joseph and Agnes (Whelan) Carroll; B.S., Marquette U., 1958. Reporter, Economist Newspapers, Chgo., 1958-59, 60-61; copywriter Pub. Relations, Inc., Tucson, 1959-60; tchr. St. John Fisher Sch., Chgo., 1961-63; publicity dir. St. Xavier Coll., Chgo., 1963-65; soc. rep. Chgo. Am., 1966-67, soc. editor, 1967-68; soc. editor Chgo. Today, 1968—. Mem. Soc. Am. Social Scribes (treas. 1973-74). Home: 10346 S Sacramento Av Chicago IL 60655 Office: 441 N Michigan Av Chicago IL 60611

CARROLL, MARGUERITE RUTH, educator; b. Medford, Mass., June 25, 1926; d. Harry Anthony and Rose (Melanson) Carroll; B.S., Boston U., 1947; M.Ed., Boston Coll., 1954; Ed.D., St. John's U., 1974. Tchr. Great Mills (Md.) High Sch., 1947-51; dir. guidance Ware (Mass.) High Sch., 1953-54; sch. counselor North Jr. High Sch., Waltham, Mass., 1954-58, Darien (Conn.) High Sch., 1958-64; dir. guidance Weston (Conn.) Pub. Schs., 1964-68; asst. prof. Fairfield (Conn.) U. Grad. Sch. Edn., 1969—, dept. chmn. div. counseling and sch. psychology, 1972—. Mem. Am. (treas. 1969-70, nat. cons. task force group procedures 1969-71), Conn. (pres. 1967-68) sch. counselor assns., Am. Psychol. Assn., Am. (chmn. bd. jour. editors), Conn., Fairfield County (pres. 1962-63) personnel and guidance assns., New Eng. Guidance Conf. (exec. com. 1968-70), Assn. Counselor Edn. and Supervision. Asso. editor The School Counselor, 1971-72, editor, 1972—. Home: 9 Longview Dr Ridgefield CT 06877 Office: Fairfield U Fairfield CT 06430

CARROLL, MARY JOE (MRS. H.B. CARROLL), lawyer; b. Wichita Falls, Tex., June 25, 1914; d. Joe H. and Mary (Douglass) Durning; student Tex. State Coll. for Women, 1931-32; B.A., U. Tex., 1934, M.A., 1935, LL.B., 1955; m. H. Bailey Carroll, June 3, 1935 (dec.); 1 son, Joe Speed. Research asso. Tex. State Hist. Assn., Austin, 1945-52; editorial asst. The Handbook of Tex., 1952; research asso. U. Tex. Law Sch., 1952-55; partner law firm Clark, Thomas, Denius, Winters & Shapiro, 1955—. Parliamentarian 60th legislature Tex. Senate, 1967; chmn. Travis County Hist. Survey Com., 1967-68. Mem. Am., Travis County bar assns., State Bar Tex., Order of Coif, Philos. Soc. Tex., Zeta Tau Alpha, Kappa Beta Pi. Mem. bd., contbr. articles to Tex. Law Rev. Episcopalian. Home: 3203-A Pecos St Austin TX 78703 Office: Capital Nat Bank Bldg Austin TX 78701

CARROLL, SHIRLEY (MRS. NORMAN CARROLL O'CONNOR), advt., pub. relations co. exec.; b. Cleve., Oct. 13, 1917; d. Max and Fannie (Weisberg) Horn; Los Angeles City Coll., 1938, U. Cal. at Los Angeles, 1966; m. Norman Carroll O'Connor, Feb. 6, 1945 (dec.); 1 son, Kevin Carroll. Partner, Carrolls Agy., Los Angeles, 1945—, pres., 1967—. Cons. pub. relations com. Claremont (Cal.) Coll. Sch. Theology, 1972—. Mem. Save the Hollywood Sign Com., 1973. Recipient Spl. Service award Los Angelinas, 1972, Mexican Am. Center of Creative Arts, 1973. Mem. Nat. Fedn. Press Women (1st pl. nat. award 1960), Am. Women in Radio and TV (dir.), Women in Communications, Am. Advt. Fedn., Los Angeles Advt. Women (Lulu Merit award for Ringling Bros. publicity campaign 1968, Spl. Service award 1972; pres. 1971-72), Cal. Press Women, Pioneer Broadcasters Assn., Los Angelinas, So. Cal. Symphony Assn. (profl. com. 1970-73), C. of C. Address: 2001 N Curson Av Los Angeles CA 90046

CARROLL, VINNETTE JUSTINE, dir., actress; b. N.Y.C.; d. Edgar Edgerton and Florence (Morris) Carroll; B.A., L.I. U., 1944; M.A., N.Y.U., 1946; postgrad. New Sch. Social Research, 1948-50. Appeared in numerous plays including Caesar and Cleopatra, 1955, Small War on Murray Hill, 1956, Jolly's Progress, 1959, Member of the Wedding, 1960, Moon on a Rainbow Shawl, London, 1959, N.Y.C., 1962; dir. Dark of the Moon, 1960, Ondine, 1961, The Disenchanted, 1962, Black Nativity, N.Y.C., 1962, Spoleto Festival of Two Worlds, 1963, The Prodigal Son, 1965, The Flies, 1966, Los Angeles, 1967; Slow Dance on the Killing Ground, Don't Bother Me I Can't Cope, Los Angeles, Step Lively, Boy, 1973, Croesus and The Witch, 1973, The Flies, 1974, All the King's Men, Desire Under the Elms, Chgo., 1974; appeared on TV shows Jubilation, CBS, 1964, We the Women, 1974; movies include One Potato Two Potato, Up The Down Staircase, Alice's Restaurant; tchr. drama to srs. High Sch. Performing Arts; cons. in urban corps, former dir. ghetto arts programs N.Y.; former cons. N.Y. State Council Arts; now artistic dir. Urban Arts Corps. Mem. Dirs. Unit Actors Studio; asso. dir. Inner City Repertory Theatre. Recipient Emmy award for conception, supervision Beyond The Blues, 1964, Obie award for distinguished performance, 1962. Office: 26 W 20th St New York City NY 10011

CARROLL, VIRGINIA I. (MRS. MAURICE CARROLL JR.), counselor; b. Greenville, Tex., Jan. 1, 1925; d. Thomas F. and Ruth (Dial) Vines; B.S., U. Okla., 1947; M.A., Eastern N.M. U., 1964, postgrad., 1962—; m. Maurice W. Carroll, Jr., June 29, 1947; children—Maurice III, Richard Thomas, Randolph Lynn. Tchr. elementary sch. Hobbs (N.M.) Municipal Schs., 1955-56, secondary sch., 1960-62, counselor secondary sch., 1962-65, counselor coordinator elementary schs., 1965—. Mem. N.E.A., N.M. Edn. Assn., Hobbs Tchrs. Assn., Am. Sch. Counselors Assn., Am., N.M. Elementary Sch. Counselors Assn. (pres. 1970-72), N.M. (pres. elect 1972-73, pres. 1973-74), Southeastern N.M. (sec. 1962-63) personnel and guidance assns., Lea County Reading Assn. (v.p. 1968-69, pres. 1969-70). Democrat. Presbyn. Club: Altrusa (sec. Hobbs 1968-70; pres. 1971-72). Home: 226 W Silver St Hobbs NM 88240 Office: PO Box 1040 Hobbs NM 88240

CARRY, PATRICIA JANE, found. ofcl.; b. Bklyn., May 19, 1928; d. William J. and Eleanor (Murphy) Carry; student U. Paris, 1948-49; B.A., Cornell U., 1950. Fgn. corr. Irving Trust Co., N.Y.C., 1950-51; with Janeway Research Co., N.Y.C., 1951-60, sec., treas., 1955-60; dir. Galt Malleable Iron Ltd., 1958-60; with Buckner & Co., N.Y.C., 1961-71, partner, 1962-71; pres., treas. Knight, Carry, Bliss & Co., Inc., N.Y.C., 1971-73; pres., treas. G. Tsai & Co., Inc., 1973; v.p. Edna McConnell Clark Found. Inc., 1974—; dir. Trans World Airlines, F.W. Woolworth Co. Allied mem. N.Y. Stock Exchange, 1962-73;

vice chmn., dir. Investor Responsibility Research Center. Trustee Cornell U., vice chmn. investment com., mem. exec. com.; vis. com. Grad. Sch. Bus., Harvard, adv. com. Inst. Ednl. Mgmt.; bd. advisers Baruch Coll.; trustee N.Y. State 4-H Found.; mem. Virginia Gildersleeve Internat. Fund for Univ. Women Inc. Mem. Women's Bond Club, Pi Beta Phi. Clubs: Altrusa, Cornell, Cornell Women's, Cosmopolitan, Delray Dunes Golf and Country (Delray Beach, Fla.). Home: 215 E 66th St New York City NY 10021 Office: 250 Park Av New York City NY 10017

CARSON, DOROTHY VENDELA MYERS (MRS. ROY CARSON), judge, lawyer; b. Ogden, Utah, Nov. 18, 1924; d. Chester J. and Vendela (Brandt) Myers; student U. So. Cal., 1943-44; B.S., Utah State U., 1945; J.D., Stanford, 1948; m. Roy Carson, Nov. 29, 1952; children—Scott Roy, Dee Louise. Admitted to Cal. bar, 1949, Utah bar, 1949, Ariz. bar, 1960, U.S. Supreme Ct. bar, 1971; asst. editor Los Angeles Daily Jour., 1949-50; with legal div. Fed. Nat. Mortgage Assn., 1950-54; asso. firm Theodore Wiseman, Los Angeles, 1954; practiced in Garden Grove, Cal., 1954-57, Phoenix, 1960-64, 66-70; mem. firm Tupper, Skeens & Rapp, 1964-66; Judge City Ct. of Phoenix, 1970—. Mem. bd., parliamentarian YWCA, 1965-68; active Camp Fire Girls; past pres. P.T.A.; chmn. profl. div. Am. Cancer Crusade, Maricopa County, 1968; mem. legacy com. Salvation Army, legal adviser Ariz. Commn. Status Women, 1966, 70; del. to Interclub Council, 1961—; chmn. subcom. Phoenix Goals Com., 1969; mem. Phoenix Park Bd., 1969-70; mem. adv. bd. Turning Point Home for Women Alcoholics, 1970—; charter pres. Alexander Home for Girls Aux., 1973-74. Mem. Jud. and Ct. Adminstrs. com. Ariz. State U., 1974. Mem. Am., Maricopa County bar assns., Bankruptcy Bar Assn. (pres. 1968-69), Bus. and Profl. Women (Woman of Achievement award 1968, 73, dir. Ariz. 1973—), Am. Assn. U. Women (Ariz. dir. 1965—, pres. Phoenix br. 1967-69), Civic Plaza Bus. Assn. (charter), Soroptimist Internat. Am. Judges Assn., Am. Judicature Soc., Ariz. Municipal Judges Assn. (treas. 1971, sec. 1972, v.p. 1973, pres. 1974), Alpha Chi Omega, Phi Delta Delta, Pi Gamma Mu, Theta Alpha Phi. Mem. Ch. of Jesus Christ of Latter-day Saints (Sunday sch. tchr.). Home: 1916 W Cambridge St Phoenix AZ 85009 Office: 12 N 4th Av Phoenix AZ 85003

CARSON, MARY E., heating and air conditioning co. exec.; b. Anson, Tex., June 10, 1907; d. Xylander and Louise (Hamrich) Carson; ed. U. Tex., Austin, Dallas Coll. of So. Meth. U. Sec.-treas. Sam. P. Wallace Co., Inc., Dallas, Wallace Internat. Ltd., Sam P. Wallace & Co. of P.R., Inc., other subsidiaries. Methodist. Home: 5016 Milam St Dallas TX 75206 Office: PO Box 36256 Dallas TX 75235

CARSON, MARY WATSON, coll. dean; b. Maryville, Mo., Mar. 3, 1937; d. Robert Harvey and Elvira (Ward) Watson; B.A. magna cum laude, Wichita State U., 1959, M.A., 1961; postgrad. U. Kan., 1960-63; m. James W. Carson. Grad. teaching fellow Wichita State U., 1959-60; grad. teaching asst., asst. dir. resident hall U. Kan., 1960-62, resident hall dir., 1962-63, asst. dean of women, 1963-65; dean of women, asst. prof. polit. sci. Kan. State Coll. at Pittsburg, 1965-68; dean of women Dickinson Coll., Carlisle, Pa., 1968-73, asso. dean ednl. services, 1973—, also George Metzger chair. Speaker to various student groups. Bd. dirs. Cumberland County chpt. A.R.C. Mem. Nat. (mem. membership com. 1965—), Kan. (state membership chmn. 1965-67), Pa. assns. women deans and counselors, Am. Assn. U. Women (mem. edn. com. 1966—), Am. Coll. Personnel Assn., Am. Personnel and Guidance Assn., Nat., Pa., Kan. assns. student personnel adminstrs., Carlisle League Women Voters, Wichita State U., U. Kan. alumni assns., Am. Legion Aux., Mortar Bd. Alumnae, Delta Delta Delta Alumnae, Cwens. Home: 544 D St Carlisle PA 17013

CARSON, PAMELA RAYMOND, pub. relations ofcl.; b. Cleve., Apr. 27, 1947; d. Raymond Joseph and Mary Jane (Pancher) Carson; student St. Mary of the Springs Coll., Columbus, O., 1965-66; B.S. in Journalism, Kent (O.) State U., 1969. Asst. to pub. relations dir. Mt. Sinai Hosp., Cleve., 1969; pub. relations dir. Ohio div. Am. Cancer Soc., 1971-73; pub. relations dir. Schwab Rehab. Hosp., Chgo., 1973—. Instr. journalism Collinwood Inner-City Community Center, Cleve., 1971-72. Vol. worker presdl. campaign, Cleve., 1972. Mem. Women in Communications (v.p. Cleve. 1972-73). Home: 2801 N Sheridan Rd Chicago IL 60657 Office: Schwab Rehab Hosp 1401 S California St Chicago IL 60608

CARSON, RUBY LEACH, journalist; b. Joplin, Mo., June 9, 1894; d. John Milton and Minnie (Robinson) Leach; A.B., U. Miami; M.A., U. Fla.; m. James Milton Carson, Jan. 3, 1926 (dec.); children—Carol (Mrs. Thomas A. Stanford), Jackson C. Reporter, Miami (Fla.) Metropolis (now Miami News), 1916-22; v.p. South Dade Pub. Co., Homestead, Fla., 1923-27; instr. Fla. history U. Miami, 1939-41; co-founder Homestead (Fla.) Leader, 1923; free lance writer, 1924—. Mem. Hist. Assn. So. Fla. (dir.), Fla. Hist. Soc. (past dir.), Nat. League Am. Penwomen, Sigma Alpha Iota (patroness). Author: Fabulous Florida, 1942; Florida Story for Children of the U.S.A., 1946; (with others) The East Coast of Florida, 1961; (with Dr. C.W. Tebeau) Florida-From Indian Trail to Space Age, 1965; also articles in hist. jours. Home: 3373 SW 7th St Miami FL 33135

CARSON, SUSAN FLOY (MRS. JOHN HOWARD CARSON), educator; b. Omaha, Apr. 4, 1940; d. Henry Cameron and Lois Floy (Himes) Lucas; B.S. in Journalism, Northwestern U., 1962; m. John Howard Carson, June 23, 1962; children—Michael John, Jeffrey Cameron, Rebecca Susan. Tchr. English, Fairplain and Benton Harbor (Mich.) pub. schs., 1962-63, Benton Harbor, 1964-65; reporter, asst. woman's editor News Palladium, Benton Harbor, 1963-64, copy editor, 1965-66; tchr. pub. schs., Westlake, O., 1966-67; tutor pub. schs., Bay Village, O., 1968-69, tchr. Middle Sch., 1970—; columnist, reporter West Life, Westlake, 1968-69; tchr. English, Lake Michigan Jr. Coll., Benton Harbor, 1970. Mem. Alumni Admissions Council Northwestern U. Mem. Women in Communications, Mich. Women's Press Assn. Unitarian. Club: Bay Village Jr. Women's (v.p. 1973-74). Home: 277 Dover Center Rd Bay Village OH 44140 Office: 27725 Wolf Rd Bay Village OH 44140

CARSTEN, ARLENE DESMET, orgn. exec.; b. Paterson, N.J., Dec. 5, 1937; d. Albert F. and Ann (Greutert) Desmet; student Alfred U., 1955-56; m. Alfred John Carsten, Feb. 11, 1956; children—Christopher Dale, Jonathan Glenn. Dir. music and arts evening program Devereaux Sch., Santa Barbara, Cal., 1960; piano tchr., 1964-71; exec. dir. Inst. for Burn Medicine, San Diego, 1972—. Organizer, mem. numerous community groups; chmn. San Diego County Mental Health Adv. Bd., 1972-74, mem., 1971—; pres. La Jolla br. Women's Internat. League for Peace and Freedom, 1970-72; chmn. community relations subcom., mem. exec. com. Emergency Med. Services Com., San Diego, Riverside and Imperial Counties, 1973-74. Mem. Cal. Democratic Central Com., 1968-74, exec. com., 1971-72, 73-74; treas. San Diego Dem. County Central Com., 1972-74; chmn. edn. for legislation com. women's div. So. Cal. Dem. Com., 1972; dir. Muskie for Pres. Campaign, San Diego, 1972; organizer, dir. numerous local campaigns. Bd. dirs. San Dieguito Family Service Assn., 1969-71, San Dieguito Dem. Club, 1965-71. Recipient Key Woman award Dem. Party, 1968, 72. Home: 1415 Via Alta Del Mar CA 92014 Office: Cal Heritage Bank Bldg 3737 Fifth Av San Diego CA 92103

CARSTEN, MARY E., biochemist, physiologist; b. Berlin, Germany (came to U.S. 1940, naturalized, 1946); d. Paul and Frida (Born) Carsten; A.B., N.Y.U., 1946, M.S., 1948, Ph.D., 1951; m. Don Marlin. Fellow in chemistry N.Y.U., 1947-52, instr., 1952-53; research asso., dept. microbiology Columbia U. Coll. Phys. and Surg., 1953-55; asst. research biochemist U. Cal. Med. Sch., Los Angeles, 1956-61, asso. research biochemist, 1961-63, asso. prof. physiology, obstetrics and gynecology, 1963-70, prof. obstetrics and gynecology, 1970—. Participant, 5th Internat. Congress Biochemistry, Moscow, 1961, and Colloquium on Protides of Biol. Fluids, Bruges, Belgium, 1963, 66, 23d Internat. Congress Physiol. Scis., Tokyo, 1965, 24th congress, Washington, D.C., 1968, Symposium on Uterine Physiology and Pharmacology, Cornell U. Med. Sch., 1968, Brook Lodge symposium, Augusta, Mich., 1972, Gordon Research Conf. on Smooth Muscle, 1973; established investigator of Los Angeles County Heart Assn., 1961-64; mem. com. vis. scholars Internat. Student Center, 1960-63. Recipient Career Devel. award USPHS, 1964, 69; awards for investigations on cardiovascular system Los Angeles County Heart Assn., 1963, 64, 65. Fellow Nat. Found. Infantile Paralysis, 1954-55, Am. Cancer Soc., 1955-57. Mem. Am. Soc. Biol. Chemists, Am. Chem. Soc., N.Y. Acad. Scis., Am. Soc. for Microbiology, Am. Assn. U. Women, Am. Physiol. Soc., Sigma Xi. Research and publs. on ion exchange chromatography, amino acids, protein chemistry, hormones, immunochemistry, skeletal, heart and smooth muscle proteins, ion transport in skeletal, heart and uterine muscle, myometrial physiology, prosta glandins. Home: 624 N Highland Av Los Angeles CA 90036

CARSWELL, CATHERINE IDELLA FORBES, state senator; b. Brighton, Mass., Dec. 7, 1922; d. John Russell and Gertrude Nora (Stack) Forbes; student U. Me., 1969-70; m. Charles Gordon Carswell, Apr. 5, 1963. Pvt. sec. to dist. sales mgr. Nationwide Ins. Co., Portland, Me., 1961-63; instr. Golden Sch. Beauty Culture, Portland, 1963—; owner Suburban Beauty Shop, Portland, 1963-69; mem. Me. Ho. of Reps., 1957-69; mem. Me. Senate, 1971—. Recipient Me. Hwy. Safety award, 1957, award Mil. Order Purple Heart, 1965, Pres.'s Com. on Employment Handicapped, 1967; D.A.V. award, 1971. Mem. Me. Frat. Assn. for Blind (hon. life), Me. Cosmetologists Assn., Nat. Order Women Legislators, League Women Voters, Pineland Parents and Friends Assn. Democrat. Roman Catholic. Home: 26 Panoramic View Dr Portland ME 04103

CARTAN, GLORIA HARRISON (MRS. FRED O. CARTAN), govt. ofcl.; b. Helena, Mont., Sept. 9, 1931; d. Henry Thomas and Eva Hazel (Milliron) Harrison; B.S. in Chemistry, Mont. State U., 1952; m. Fred O. Cartan, July 9, 1955; children—John F., Joan K. Chemist, VA Hosp., Ft. Harrison, Mont., 1952-53, Phillips Petroleum Co., Idaho Falls, 1953-55; faculty Mont. State U., Bozeman, 1955-58; adminstr. State of Ida., Idaho Falls, 1972—. Mem. Ida. Traffic Safety Commn., 1970—, Gov.'s Council of Criminal Justice, 1973—; gov.'s rep. to Nat. Assn. Women Hwy. Safety Leaders. Vice chmn. Ida. Democratic Com., 1972; precinct committeeman, 1966-72. Mem. League Women Voters, Am. Chem. Soc., Am. Assn. U. Women (chmn. 1965). Address: 787 Sonja Av Idaho Falls ID 83401

CARTER, ADA BELLE (MRS. HOWARD GARLAND CARTER), city ofcl.; b. Brecksville, O., Aug. 7, 1916; d. Harvey George and Anna May (Chaffee) Bratton; B.B.A., Western Res. U., 1938; m. Howard Garland Carter, Aug. 30, 1940; children—Nancy (Mrs. J. Thomas Trantum), Anita (Mrs. Stuart Kutler), Lorna (Mrs. Arist D'Atri), Donna. Sec., Pres.'s Office, Western Res. U., 1938-42; dep. clk. City of Brecksville, O., 1944-45, clk., 1946-55, clk.-treas., 1956-57, finance dir.-clk. of Council, 1958—. Mem. Municipal Finance Officers Assn. Mem. United Ch. of Christ. Home: 6903 Daisy Av Brecksville OH 44141 Office: 9069 Brecksville Rd Brecksville OH 44141

CARTER, ANNA CURRY (MRS. E. KEMPER CARTER), civic worker; b. Kansas City, Mo.; d. William Adams and Susan Maud (Machette) Curry; B.S., U. Mo., 1918; M.A., Columbia, 1930; postgrad. Oxford U., (Eng.), 1935; m. E. Kemper Carter, Feb. 22, 1936 (dec. Dec. 1951); 1 son, E. Emper (dec.). Tchr., research Kansas City pub. schs., 1919-21; dir. speech and dramatics Westport Jr. High Sch., Kansas City, 1921-26; head speech dept. S.W. High Sch., Kansas City, 1926-36. Bd. govs. Kansas City Mus. History and Sci., 1960-66; parliamentarian women's div. Kansas City Philharmonic Assn., 1954—; mem. exec. bd., mem. at large Community Children's Theatre, 1955—. Trustee Kansas City Art Inst. and Sch. of Design, Conservatory of Music, U. Mo. at Kansas City, Kansas City Philharmonic Assn. Sponsor Winston Churchill Meml.; donar Lenox Hill-Skawhegan Art Projects, N.Y.C. Hon. fellow Harry S. Truman Library Inst.; Soc. fellows William Rockhill Nelson Gallery Art. Mem. Am. Assn. U. Women, Alliance Francaise, English Speaking Union, Pres. and Past Pres. Gen. Assembly, Sci. Pioneers, Am. Inst. Parliamentarians, Am. Nat. Theatre and Acad., Speech Assn. Am., Alpha Phi. Democrat. Baptist. Clubs: College, Woman's City, Carriage, Mission Hills Country, River, Kansas City, Rockhill Tennis. Home: Wornall Plaza 310 W 49th St Kansas City MO 64112

CARTER, ANNE C. (MRS. WILLIAM B. HELLER), physician; b. N.Y.C., Nov. 27, 1919; d. Arthur J. and Nellie (Zuckerman) Cohen; student Dana Hall, 1937; B.A., Wellesley Coll., 1941; M.D., Cornell U., 1944; m. William B. Heller, Nov. 4, 1947; children—James A., Susan K. Research fellow Bellevue Hosp., N.Y.C., 1944-45; asst. in medicine Cornell U. Med. Coll., N.Y.C., 1945-56, instr., 1946-52, asst. prof. 1952-55; research fellow Russell Sage Inst. Pathology, N.Y.C., 1951-55; asst. physician outpatient dept. N.Y. Hosp., 1945-47, attending physician, 1947-55; asst. attending physician, 1954-55; asst. prof. medicine State U. N.Y. Coll. Medicine N.Y.C., 1955-58, asso. prof., 1958-68, prof., 1968—; attending physician State U. Hosp., Bklyn., 1967—; asst. vis. physician Kings County Hosp., Bklyn., 1955-59, vis. physician, 1959—; vis. scientist, Bronx VA Hosp., 1963-64; cons. Nat. Cancer Inst., 1962-69, mem. clin. cancer tng. com., 1971. Trustee Wellesley Coll. Diplomate Am. Bd. Internal Medicine. Fellow N.Y. Acad. Medicine; mem. Soc. Exptl. Biology and Medicine, Endocrine Soc., Harvey Soc., Am. Diabetes Assn., Soc. Internal Medicine, Am. Med. Women's Assn., Sigma Xi. Club: Cosmopolitan (N.Y.C.). Mem. editorial bd. Endocrinology, 1953-55; abstractor Metabolism, 1955-62. Author numerous articles in field. Home: 33 E 70th St New York City NY 10021 Office: 450 Clarkson Av Brooklyn NY 11203

CARTER, (BARBARA) CORNELIA, educator; b. Lawrenceville, Ill., Aug. 20, 1911; d. Charles Duane and Clara (Vaught) Carter; student DePauw U., 1929, 30, East Stroudsburg State Tchrs. Coll., 1931-32; A.B., So. Meth. U., 1934; M.S., Ind. U., 1954; postgrad. Denver U. Tchr. pub. schs., Colo., 1934-35, Tex., 1935-37, Ill., 1937-47; dean women, asso. prof. English, Vincennes U., 1947-54, dean of students, asso. prof. English and edn., 1954-65, asso. prof. edn. and English, 1965—, dean of women, 1965-68, asst. to pres., cons. on women's affairs, 1968—. Mem. Lawrence County (Ill.) Hist. Soc. (sec. 1961-63), Vincennes Hist. and Antiquarian Soc. (charter), Ind. Pioneer Soc., Ind. Tchrs. Assn., N.W. Ter. Art Guild, Alpha Phi. Republican. Author: Free-Hand Paper Cutting, 1944. Contbr. articles to publs. Home: 710 Jefferson St Lawrenceville IL 62439 Office: Vincennes U Vincennes IN 47591

CARTER, BARBARA ELLEN, writer; b. Detroit, Aug. 7, 1925; d. John Maynard and Nell Luise (Dougan) Carter; B.A., U. Mich.; postgrad. Oxford U., 1949. Staff writer The Reporter Mag., N.Y.C., 1955-63; v.p. Free Lance Assos., Yonkers, N.Y., 1963—. Recipient Nat. Sch. Bell award N.E.A., 1963. Mem. Soc. Mag. Writers. Author: (with Gloria Dapper) A Guide for School Board Members, 1966; The Road to City Hall: How John V. Lindsay Became Mayor, 1967; Pickets, Parents and Power, 1971; (with Gloria Dapper) School Volunteers: What They Do, How They Do It, 1972; (with Gloria Dapper) Organizing School Volunteer Programs, 1974. Address: 8 Garmany Pl Yonkers NY 10710

CARTER, DENNIE HOUGHTON, communications co. exec.; b. Bklyn., Dec. 3, 1924; d. Owen Edward and Helen Hasbrouck (Reeve) Houghton; A.B., Allegheny Coll., 1945; postgrad. Columbia, 1955, Adelphi Coll., 1972; m. Richard Dalton Carter, Feb. 12, 1955; children—Kimberly Ann, Tracey Alden. Copy girl, cub reporter Bklyn. Eagle, also research editor Collier's mag., 1946-47; asso. editor, then editor Fawcett Publs., 1947-50; dir. pub. relations and edn. Conso Products, 1952-66; editor, pub., then v.p. Conso Pub. Co. div. Consol. Foods Corp., 1966-73; pres. Carter Communications, Jacksonville, Fla., 1973—. Pres. Woman's Drapery and Curtain Club, 1954-56. Recipient certificate of award Graphic Arts Assn., 1967. Mem. Am. Inst. Interior Designers, Nat. Soc. Interior Designers, Nat. Home Fashions League. Clubs: Huntington (N.Y.) Country; The Deerwood (Fla.). Author: All About Decorating, 1971; (with others) Homemaker's Handbook, 1969. Address: 8150 Hunters Grove Rd Jacksonville FL 32216

CARTER, MRS. ELLA MARGARETTE, real estate ofcl., club woman; b. Denton, Md.; d. John Tilghman and Elizabeth (DeWeese) Carter; Tchrs. Certificate in Music, Md. Coll. for Women, 1917; m. 1926 (div. 1936). Instr. music, Denton, Md., 1917-26; co-owner, mgr. John T. Carter Agy., (real estate mgmt.) Denton, 1937—, pres. Denton Improvement Corp., Shopping Center, 1961—. Active in civic affairs, fund campaigns. Mem. Womens Democratic Club. Bd. dirs. Meml. Hosp., Easton, Md. Mem. D.A.R., Meml. Hosp. Assn. (mem.-at-large), Md. Federated Garden Clubs (sec. dist. 1), Caroline County Hist. Soc. (dir. 1956-57), Delta Epsilon, Sigma Sigma. Methodist. Mem. Order Eastern Star. Clubs: Rehoboth Beach (Del.) Country, Rehoboth Art League; Caroline Country (Md.); The Harbor. Home: 201 Carter Av Denton MD 21629 Office: 309 S 3d St Denton MD 21629

CARTER, ETHEL ELIZABETH GIROIR (MRS. ROBERT EUGENE CARTER), real estate exec.; b. New Orleans, Oct. 3, 1928; d. Philip Louis and Ethyl Elizabeth (Bourg) Giroir; grad. high sch., New Orleans; m. Robert Eugene Carter, Oct. 1, 1946; children—Laurence, Susan, Catherine, Julie. With Roberts Bros., Inc., Mobile, Ala., 1960—, residential sales mgr., 1972—, v.p., 1972—. Mem. League Women Voters, Nat. Assn. Realtors (chpt. charter pres. 1971), Ala. Women's Council (state pres. 1972), Mobile County Bd. Realtors (pres. 1973—), Chickasaw Bus. and Profl. Women's Club. Clubs: Racquet, Bienville (Mobile). Home: 4205 Lantern Ct Mobile AL 36609 Office: PO Box 6217 Mobile AL 36606

CARTER, FAIRIE LYN, chemist; b. Biloxi, Miss., Oct. 1, 1926; d. William Raymond and Velma (Carter) Carter; B.S., Miss. State Coll. Women, 1948; M.A., U. N.C., 1950. Asst. curator limnology, chemist Acad. Natural Scis., Phila., 1950-54; chemist, Eastern Regional Research Lab., U.S. Dept. Agr., Phila., 1955-57, research chemist So. Regional Research Lab., New Orleans, 1957-65, prin. chemist Wood Products Insect Lab., Forest Service, Gulfport, Miss., 1965—. Mem. Am. Chem. Soc., Am. Oil Chemists Soc., Sci. Research Soc. Am., Entomol. Soc. Am., Audubon Soc., Mortar Board, Gamma Sigma Epsilon, Beta Beta Beta, Kappa Mu Epsilon. Baptist. Mem. Order Eastern Star. Home: 525 E Water St PO Box 495 Biloxi MS 39533 Office: PO Box 2008 Evergreen Sta Gulfport MS 39501

CARTER, FRANCES TUNNELL (MRS. JOHN T. CARTER), educator; b. Springville, Miss., May 21, 1922; d. David Atmond and Mary Annie (McCutcheon) Tunnell; A.A., Wood Jr. Coll., 1942; student Blue Mountain Coll., 1942; B.S., U. So. Miss., 1946; M.S., U. Tenn., 1948; Ed.D., U. Ill., 1954; postgrad. Ursuline Coll., 1961, Dayton U., 1963, Fla. State U., 1970; m. John T. Carter, Mar. 16, 1946; children—John Wayne, Frankye Nell. Elementary sch. tchr. Thaxton (Miss.) Sch., 1942-43, Cumberland (Miss.) Elementary Sch., 1943-44, home econs. Randolph (Miss.) High Sch., 1944-45, Maben (Miss.) High Sch., 1946-47, Wood Jr. Coll., 1948; head dept. home econs. East Central Jr. Coll., 1948-49, Clarke Meml. Coll., 1950-56; mem. faculty Samford U., Birmingham, Ala., 1956—, asst. prof., 1956-57, asso. prof., 1957-63, prof., 1963—. Vis. prof. Hong Kong Bapt. Coll., 1965-66; dir., also cons. workshops for tchrs., summers, 1962—; supervisory panel mem. Tri-State Project in Early Childhood Edn. Mem. Gov.'s Com. on Status of Women, 1964-68, adv. bd. Nat. Dairy Council Greater Birmingham, 1966—; organizer, former leader troop Girl Scouts U.S.A., 1963—. Recipient Spl. Service award A.R.C., 1962. Mem. Internat. Council on Edn. for Teaching, Ala. Acad. Sci., Nat. Assn. for Edn. Young Children, Nat. Aerospace Edn. Assn., Civil Air Patrol (maj.), Assn. for Childhood Edn. (adviser Samford U. br. 1963—, state 1st v.p. 1968-70, pres. 1970-72), Nat. Soc. D.A.R., Internat. Council Women, Ala. Writers Conclave, Internat. Reading Assn., Ala. Poetry Soc., So., Ala. assns. children under six, Birmingham Story League, Nat. League Am. Penwomen (pres. Birmingham br. 1968, state exec. bd.), Ala. Assn. Tchr. Educators, Kappa Delta Epsilon (nat. v.p. 1966-70), Alpha Delta Kappa, Kappa Delta Pi (co-sponsor 1970—), Kappa Omicron Phi, Pi Gamma Mu. Baptist. Author: Sammy in the Country, 1960; Teachers Guide for Mission Books, 1969; 'Tween-age Ambassadors, 1970; co-author Sharing Times Seven, 1971. Contbr. articles profl. and religious jours. Home: 2561 Rocky Ridge Rd Birmingham AL 35243

CARTER, GANN A., airline exec.; b. Dodge City, Kan., Jan. 1, 1923; d. Virgal A. and Estey (Beals) Carter; student Colo. Women's Coll., 1940-42; A.A., Eastman Sch. Music, 1943. Staff, USO Camp Shows, 1942-46; freelance radio-TV advt. promotion, 1946-53; dir. pub. relations, agy. and interline sales Aloha Airlines, 1953-58; mgr. convs., also spl. group sales Travel-World, Inc., Los Angeles, 1958-60; mgr. conv. dept. Toluca Lake Travel, 1960-62; owner Sherman Oaks Travel (Cal.), 1962-69; mgr. meetings, also conv. marketing Western Airlines, Honolulu, 1969-73, Los Angeles, 1973—. Hon. sheriff Redondo Beach, Cal., also Dodge City. Mem. Nat. Fedn. Bus. and Profl. Women (past pres. Los Angeles Sunset dist.), Waikiki Bus. and Profl. Women (past v.p.), Hawaii Profl. Songwriters Soc. Office: 6150 W Century Blvd Los Angeles CA 90009

CARTER, GLADYS (MRS. RICHARD CARTER), editor; b. N.Y.C., Aug. 17, 1923; d. Marcus Louis and Dorothy (Prokesch) Chasins; student Coll. City N.Y., 1940-44; m. Richard Carter, Oct. 20, 1945; children—Nancy, John. Asst. music editor Billboard Mag., N.Y.C., 1942-43; fgn. editor Federated Press, N.Y.C., 1944-48; free lance writer, 1952-59; free lance producer modern lang. materials Ednl. Audio Visual, Inc., Pleasantville, N.Y., 1960-63, catalog editor, 1963-64, editor-in-chief, 1965—, v.p., 1972—. Exec. sec. UN Housing

Co-op., 1953-55; housing chmn. Ossining N.A.A.C.P., 1967-71. Home: 165 Pinesbridge Rd Ossining NY 10562 Office: Educational Audio Visual Inc Pleasantville NY 10570

CARTER, GWENDOLEN MARGARET, educator, author; b. Hamilton, Ont., Can., July 17, 1906 (came to U.S. 1935; naturalized 1948); d. Charles and Nora (Ambrose) Carter; B.A., U. Toronto, 1929; M.A., Oxford U. (Eng.), 1936; Ph.D., Radcliffe Coll., 1938; Litt.D., Wheaton Coll., 1962, Russell Sage Coll., 1963, Goucher Coll., 1964; LL.D., Western Coll. for Women, 1963, Carleton U., 1965, McMaster U., 1966, U. Toronto, 1970; D.Litt., Boston U., 1966. Instr. McMaster U., Hamilton, 1932-35, Wellesley Coll., 1938-41; research asso. Harvard Bur. Internat. Affairs, 1941-42; instr. Tufts Coll., 1942-43; asst. prof. Smith Coll., 1943-47, asso. prof., 1947-52, prof., 1952-61, Sophia Smith prof., 1961-64; Melville J. Herskovits prof. African affairs, dir. African studies program Northwestern U., Evanston, Ill., 1964—. Mem. grant-in-aid com. Social Sci. Research Council, 1957. Mem. selection com. Ford Found. Tng. program (Africa), 1959-60; adv. council Africa Bur., Dept. State, 1962-67; mem. bd. Chgo. Council Fgn. Relations, 1967—. Recipient George V medal for pub. service, 1935; Achievement award Am. Assn. U. Women, 1962; Distinguished Achievement award grad. chpt. Radcliffe Coll., 1962. Fellow Am. Acad. of Arts and Scis.; mem. Am. (council mem. 1954-56; sec. 1959; v.p. 1963-64; nominating com. 1965-67; chmn. Woodrow Wilson Book award com. 1971-72), N.E. (pres. 1959-60), Internat. polit. sci. assns., Canadian Hist. and Polit. Sci. Assn., African Studies Assn. (pres. 1958-59; chmn. com. on langs. and linguistics 1959-63; policy and plans com., 1963-65; v.p. 1957-58), African-Am. Inst. (trustee 1964—), Am. Assn. U. Women (internat. relations com. 1951-57; bd. area rep. for world problems 1967-69). Author: British Commonwealth, International Security, 1947; (with John H. Herz) Major Foreign Powers, 1949, 52, 57, 62, 67, 72; The Politics of Inequality: South Africa since 1948, 1958, 59; Independence for Africa, 1960; (with John H. Herz) Government and Politics in the 20th Century, 1961, 66, 72, German, Arabic edit., 1963, Spanish, Bengali, Portuguese edit., 1964; (with Thomas Karis, Newell Stultz) South Africa's Transkei: The Politics of Domestic Colonialism, 1967, The Government of the United Kingdom, 1964, 3d edit., 1972; The Government of the Soviet Union, 1964, 3d edit., 1972; The Government of France, 1968, 2d edit., 1972; (with Thomas Karis) From Protest to Challenge, A Documentary History of African Politics in South Africa, 1884-1964, Vol. I, 1884-1934, 1972, Vol. II, 1935-1952, 1973. Editor: Transition in Africa: Problems of Political Adaptation, 1958; African One-Party States, 1962; Five African States: Responses to Diversity, 1963; (with Alan Westin) Politics in Europe, 1965; National Unity and Regionalism in Nine African States, 1966; Politics in Africa, 1966; Cornell U. Pres. Series Africa in the Modern World, 1968—. Home: 190 W Fern Dr Orange City FL 32763

CARTER, HELEN LOUISE STRICKLER (MRS. MITCHEL M. CARTER), law librarian; b. Hobart, Okla., June 20, 1926; d. Charles William and Ruth Esther (Long) Strickler; student, Stephens Coll., 1943-44, U. Okla., 1944-45, Kiowa County Jr. Coll., 1945; B.A., U.N.M., 1947; postgrad. George Washington U., 1948; J.D., U. Utah, 1951; m. Mitchel M. Carter, Jan. 21, 1949; children—Neville Ruth (dec.), Shannan Louise, Joseph William. Admitted to D.C. bar, 1951, N.M. bar, 1954; atty. on staff Senator Clinton P. Anderson, U.S. Senate Subcom. on Indian Affairs, Washington, 1951-52; pvt. law practice, Albuquerque, 1954-66; with U. N.M. Sch. Law, Albuquerque, 1966—, asso. in law, 1970—, instr. environmental law, 1971. Legal cons. City of Albuquerque, Ad-Hoc Com. for Environmental Concerns, Subcom. on Inter-Govt., 1970-71. Organizer, sponsor Tri-Hi-Y, YMCA, Albuquerque, 1969-71. Mem. State Bar N.M., Am. Bar Assn., Am. Assn. Law Libraries, N.M. Library Assn., U. N.M. Alumni Assn., Am. Civil Liberties Union (legal research cons. 1967—), Republican. Presbyn. Home: 2320 Ada Ct NE Albuquerque NM 87106 Office: U NM Sch Law 1117 Stanford NE Albuquerque NM 87131

CARTER, JOAN COOLEY, computer co. exec.; b. Jersey City, Nov. 16, 1931; d. Charles Buke and Olive (Simmons) Cooley; student San Diego State Coll., 1959-60, U. Hawaii, 1960-63; B.A. in Math., Am. U., 1966; m. Earl L. Carter, June 2, 1951 (dec. Apr. 1971); children—Earl, Jr., Eric, Pamela Joan. Lead programmer Inst. Astronomy, U. Hawaii, Honolulu, 1966-69; mgr. lunar seismology digital lab. Lamont Doherty Geol. Obs., Columbia, N.Y.C., 1969-72; pres. Cartronics, Inc., Franklin Lakes, N.J., 1972—. Mem. Oakland (N.J.) Human Relations Council, 1969—; mem. nat. adv. group Hampshire Coll., Amherst, Mass., 1970—. Mem. Am. Math. Soc., Am. Mgmt. Assn., Operations Research Soc. Am., Assn. Computer Programmers and Analysts. Home: 36 Tuscarora Dr Oakland NJ 07436 Office: PO Box 296 Franklin Lakes NJ 07417

CARTER, JOAN LEVERS, educator; b. Yonkers, N.Y., May 30, 1923; d. William A. and Mignon (Levers) Carter; B.A., Coll. New Rochelle, 1944; M.A., Columbia, 1952; postgrad. (Fulbright scholar 1956-57) U. Copenhagen, Denmark. Curator Children's Mus., Pasadena, Cal., 1947-50; program adviser scouting for handicapped, nat. hdqrs. Girl Scouts U.S.A., 1950-54, mem. nat. field staff, 1956-62; now instructional materials cons. spl. edn. div. Los Angeles City Schs. U.S. rep. Conf. of Handicapped, Finland, 1952; mem. U.S. com. Internat. Soc. Rehab. of Disabled, 1956—; exec. com. Conf. World Orgns. Interested in Handicapped, 1952-54. Mem. Cal. Assn. Neurol. Handicapped Children (adv. bd.), Jr. League Pasadena, Women in Edn., Am. Assn. U. Women, Pi Lambda Theta. Club: Nat. Arts (bd. govs. 1953-55) (N.Y.C.). Home: 985 San Pasqual Pasadena CA 91106 also (summer) 856 Cliff Dr Laguna Beach CA 92651 Office: Los Angeles Bd Edn Spl Edn Div 450 N Grand Av Los Angeles CA 90012

CARTER, LENORA (MRS. JULIUS CARTER), pub. co. exec.; b. Corrigan, Tex., Mar. 12, 1941; d. J.V. and Dessie Mae (Pervis) McQueen; student Ariz. State U., 1959-61; S. Tex. Jr. Coll., 1970-72; m. Julius Carter, May 25, 1967 (dec. Jan. 1971); children—Constance Y., Karen Y. With Forward Times Pub. Co., Houston, 1961—, publisher, 1971—. Bd. dirs. Riverside Gen. Hosp., 1970—, Eliza Johnson Home for the Aged, 1969—, A.R.C., 1967-72, Soc. for Performing Arts, 1968-72. Recipient Nat. Assn. Market Developers Emphasis award, 1971; Recognition award Houston Med. Forum, 1971; Outstanding Citizenship award State of Mich., 1972. Mem. Nat. Assn. Market Developers (chpt. v.p. 1972-74), Nat. Newspaper Pubs. Assn. (sec. 1971—), Amalgamated Pubs. (dir. 1973—), Eta Phi Beta, Gamma Phi Delta. Baptist. Home: 2925 Wuthering Heights Houston TX 77045 Office: 4411 Almeda Houston TX 77004

CARTER, MARGARET A., pathologist; b. Carthage, Mo., 1912; M.D., Washington U., St. Louis, 1938. Intern Albany (N.Y.) Hosp., 1938-39, Maternity Hosp., St. Louis, 1939-41; asst. resident pathology Washington U. Hosp., 1949-50, resident, 1950-51; asst. clin. pathologist Barnes Hosp., St. Louis, 1951-52, resident surg. pathology, 1952-53, asst. pathologist, surg. pathologist, 1953-54; pathologist Meml. Hosp., Houston, 1954-60; instr. dept. pathology Washington U., 1950-54, Baylor U., 1954—. Diplomate Am. Bd. Pathology. Address: 1835 Albans Rd Houston TX 77005

CARTER, MARIAN ELIZABETH, county ofcl.; b. Great Bend, Kan., June 14, 1935; d. Clarence John and Ella Joanne (Bartel) Glantz; B.A., U. Colo., 1957; postgrad. Colo. State U., 1958-59; m. J. Braxton Carter, Dec. 26, 1957; children—J. Braxton II, David Brian, Caorl Elizabeth. Pub. trustee EL Paso County, Colo., 1969—. Nat. committeewoman Young Republican League Colo., 1969-71, chmn., Colo., 1971-73; sec. Colo. Rep. central com., 1973—. Mem. Colo. Pub. Trustees Assn., Altrusa, Kappa Delta. Mem. Order Eastern Star. Home: 2521 N Chelton Rd Colorado Springs CO 80909

CARTER, MARY EDDIE, govt. ofcl.; b. Americus, Ga., Mar. 14, 1925; d. Walker G. and Esther (Stewart) Carter; B.A., LaGrange Coll., 1946; M.S., U. Fla., 1949; Ph.D., U. Edinburgh, Scotland, 1956; Microscopist Callaway Mills, Lagrange, Ga., 1947-48; textile chemist, microscopist So. Research Inst., Birmingham, Ala., 1949-51; chemist West Point-Pepperel, West Point, Ga., 1951-53; research asso. FMC Corp. div. Am. Viscose Corp., Phila., 1956-71; lab. chief textiles and clothing lab. U.S. Dept. Agr., Knoxville, Tenn., 1971-73; dir. So. Regional Research Center U.S. Dept. Agr., New Orleans, 1973—. Instr. Lagrange Coll. (Ga.), 1946-47; prof. chemistry grad. faculty U. Tenn., Knoxville, 1971-73. Mem. Am. Chem. Soc., Am. Assn. Textile Chemists and Colorists, Fiber Soc., Inter-Color Soc., Inst. Food Tech., Sigma Xi. Author: Essential Fiber Chemistry, 1971. Office: PO Box 19687 New Orleans LA 70179

CARTER, MILDRED GIBSON (MRS. WILLIAM AMOS CARTER), coll. adminstr.; b. Columbus, Kan., Nov. 22, 1924; d. Ralph A. and Clara Mabel (Johnson) Gibson; A.A., Northeastern Okla. A. and M. Coll., 1948; m. William Amos Carter, Mar. 1, 1957. Sec. County Engrs. office, Columbus, 1941-45; sec. to senator Kan. State Senate, Topeka, 1945; payroll clk. B.F. Goodrich, Miami, Okla., 1945-46; clk. bus. office Northeastern Okla. A. and M. Coll., Miami, 1946-60, bus. mgr., 1960—. Mem. Okla. Edn. Assn., Higher Edn. Alumni Assn., Okla. Assn. Coll. and Univ. Bus. Officers. Home: 512 Wea Dr Miami OK 74354

CARTER, RINTHA MARY, social worker; b. Mt. Vernon, Mo., Nov. 26, 1915; d. Harry McDan and Nola Fay (Mullins) Carter; student Springfield (Mo.) Draughon Bus. U., 1934-36; A.B., U. Cal. at Berkeley, 1948, postgrad., 1949; M.S.W., U. Mo., 1950. Treas., Soil Conservation Service, A.A.A., Mt. Vernon, 1936-39; sec. Social Security Adminstrn., St. Joseph, Mo., 1940; asst. cashier, sec. VA Hosp., North Little Rock, Ark., 1940-43; social worker Los Angeles County Hosp., Los Angeles, 1950-52, U.S. Naval Hosp., Great Lakes, Ill., 1952-53, VA Regional Office, Little Rock, 1953-55, St. Elizabeths Hosp., Washington, 1955-58, NIH, USPHS, Bethesda, Md., 1958-64, VA Hosp., Los Angeles, 1964—, USNR, Encino, Cal., 1955—. Del., White House Conf. on Children and Youth, 1960, 11th Internat. Conf. Social Work, Brazil, 1962, 13th Internat. Conf. Social Work, Washington, 1966. Served with USNR, 1943-45. Recipient USPHS medals, 1961-64, Cross Mil. Service, U.D.C., 1961. Mem. Nat. Assn. Social Workers, Acad. Certified Social Workers, Cal. Social Workers and Marriage Counselors, Marquis Biog. Library Soc., Am. Acad. Human Services. Baptist. Author: An Analogy for Living, 1969; I Paid $2,275 to be Satisfied, 1970. Home: 3631 S Sepulveda Blvd Los Angeles CA 90034 Office: Wadsworth Hosp Center Los Angeles CA 90073

CARTER, ROSA ROBERTO (MRS. LEE D. CARTER), ednl. adminstr.; b. Agana, Guam, Aug. 29, 1929; d. Jose D. and Antonia G. Roberto; B.A., No. State Coll., 1953; Diploma in Edn., U. Sydney, Australia, 1957; M.A. in Edn., No. Colo. U., 1962; m. Lee D. Carter, Feb. 20, 1970. Tchr., Adelup Sch., Guam, 1954-56; asst. prin. Wettengel Sch., Guam, 1958-59; asst. prof. Coll. Guam, Agana, 1959-61; asst. prof. U. Guam, Agana, 1962-65, registrar, 1965-70, part-time instr., dir. admissions and records, 1970—. Sec., Guam Girl Scouts, 1973—; sec. Guam TB Assn., 1969-71; mem., sec. Guam Beauty Pagent, 1969—; mem. retirement fund Govt. Guam, 1969—. Fulbright scholar, 1956-57. Mem. Am. Assn. U. Women (pres., sec. 1965-71). Home: Box 322 Agana GU 96910 Office: Univ Guam Box EK Agana GU 96910

CARTER, RUTH B. (MRS. JOSEPH C. CARTER), assn. exec.; b. Charlotte, Vt.; d. Ira E. and Sadie M. (Congdon) Burroughs; Ph.B., U. Vt., 1931; m. Joseph C. Carter, June 28, 1935. Prin., Newton Acad., Shoreham, Vt., 1931-35; substitute tchr. Spaulding High Sch., Barre, Vt., also Woodbury (Vt.) High Sch., 1935-36; tchr. Craftsbury Acad., Craftsbury Common, Vt., 1936-38; sales mgr., buyer Vt. Music Co., Barre, 1939-44; statistician Syracuse U., 1944-46; instr. English, Temple U., Phila., 1946-47; records clk. sec., 1947-56; tchr. English, Central High Sch., Phila., 1957, Springfield Twp. Sr. High Sch., Montgomery County, Pa., 1964-65; sec. Women's Univ. Club, Phila., 1961-64, treas., 1965-67. Exec. dir. White-Williams Found., 1966—. Mem. Am. Assn. U. Women (admissions chmn.; treas.; rec. sec. Phila. br.), D.A.R. (treas., historian, com. chmn., budget dir. Germantown chpt.), New Eng. Historic Geneal. Soc., Geneal. Soc. Vt., Soc. Mayflower Descs. Republican. Methodist. Clubs: Temple University Faculty Women's (pres. Center City group), Temple University Women's. Author: (with Joseph C. Carter) Anchors Aweigh Around the World with Ernest Vail Burroughs, 1960. Home: D-4 Glenside House Glenside PA 19038 Office: The Pkwy at 21st St Philadelphia PA 19103

CARTER, SELINA JEWELL ALEXANDER (MRS. BUFORD WILLIAM CARTER, JR.), librarian; b. Birmingham, Ala., Jan. 3, 1928; d. Houston Forrest and Edna (McGaughy) Alexander; student Judson Coll., Ala., 1945-46; B.S., Howard Coll., 1962; M.A., U. Denver, 1963; m. Buford William Carter, Jr., Aug. 25, 1967; stepchildren—Donald Howell, Buford William III. Comml. dept. service rep. So. Bell Tel. & Tel. Co., Birmingham, 1946-51; ordnance property clk. U.S. Govt., Fort Hood, Tex., 1951, ordnance dist. file clk., publs. librarian, Birmingham, 1951-53, office clk. Fort Richardson Alaska Hdqrs., 1953, internal revenue service, Birmingham, processing clk., 1954, ordnance dist. records mgmt. officer and procurement asst., Birmingham, 1954-62; operator Bapt. Book Store Denver, U. Denver, part-time, 1962-63; head tech. service Samford U. Library, 1963-66, head reader services, asst. librarian, 1966-68; reader services librarian U. Ala. Coll. Gen. Studies Library, Birmingham, 1968-71; circulation-reference librarian Golden Gate Bapt. Theol. Sem., Mill Valley, Cal., 1971—. Cons., field worker Ch. Library Dept., Sunday Sch. Bd. So. Bapt. Conv., 1963—. Mem. Ala. (handbook, recruitment coms. 1970-71), Southeastern library assns., Birmingham Library Club (v.p., pres. elect. 1970-71), Soc. Am. Archivists, Am. Bus. Women's Assn., Birmingham Bapt. Assn. Exec. Council, Associational Ch. Library Orgn. (pres. 1966-71), Birmingham Womens Jr. C. of C. (chaplain 1967-68; dir. 1969-70; historian 1969-71; 2d v.p. 1970-71), Am. Bus. Women's Assn., Redwood Empire Bapt. Assn., Kappa Delta Pi. Baptist. Home: 22 Platt Ct Mill Valley CA 94941

CARTER, THERESA HOWARD (MRS. EDWARD C. CARTER II), archaeologist; b. Millbrook, N.Y., May 15, 1929; d. Clarence K. and Ann (Warren) Howard; A.B., Syracuse U., 1950; M.A., U. Pa., 1954; Ph.D. in Classical and Near Eastern Archaeology, Bryn Mawr Coll., 1962; m. Edward C. Carter, II, Mar. 24, 1951; 1 dau., Laura Coffin. With reprodns. dept. Univ. Mus., Phila., 1950-52, student asst. ethnology dept., 1953-55, research asst. Mediterranean sect., 1960-62, research asso., 1962-64, dir. Iraq excavations, sect. Bibl. archaeology, 1964—, field dir. Sybaris project, 1968; teaching asst. Bryn Mawr Coll., 1961-62, deptl. asst., 1962-63; ann. prof. Am. Sch. Oriental Research, Baghdad, 1965-66; vis. lectr. Near Eastern studies Johns Hopkins, Balt., 1969-70, asst. prof., 1970—. Mem. staff U. Pa. Gordion Expdn., Polatli, Turkey, 1955, 57; dir. U. Pa. Phoenician excavations, Lepcis Magna, Homs, Libya, 1960, 61; dir. Cyrenaican Coastal Survey, U. Pa., 1962; participated Bryn Mawr Coll. excavations Kara Tash, Elmali, Turkey, 1963; co-dir. Tell al-Rimah Expdn., No. Iraq, 1964-66; collaborator for Univ. Mus. with Soprentendenza alle Antichita di Napoli at Pithecusa, Lacco Ameno, Ischia, 1965; dir. Johns Hopkins Expdn. to Arab-Iranian Gulf, 1972-74, to Euphrates River, Syria, 1972-74. Bd. dirs. Theatre of Living Arts, Phila., 1964—, chmn. women's com., 1964-65. Fellow Middle East Studies Assn.; mem. Archaeol. Inst. Am., Am. Oriental Soc., Middle East Inst., Soc. for Iranian Studies. Contbr. to profl. jours. Home: 2620 Quebec St NW Washington DC 20008 Office: Dept Near Eastern Studies Johns Hopkins Baltimore MD 21218

CARTER, VIRGINIA LESUEUR, coll. ofcl.; b. Bristol, Va.; Nov. 15, 1932; d. Homer C. and Jennie (Phillips) LeSueur; B.A., Westhampton Coll., U. Richmond, 1953; postgrad. Columbia, 1953-54; m. William J. Carter, Aug. 28, 1954 (separated); children—Jennie LeSueur, Laura Ann. Information officer Va. Dept. Agr., Richmond, 1954-55, 61-62; publs. editor Va.-Carolina Chem. Co., Richmond, 1955-57; information dir. Roanoke County Red Cross, Roanoke, Va., 1958-59; dir. information and publs. Hollins Coll., Roanoke, 1960-61, 65-72; dir. publs. U. Richmond (Va.), 1972-73; univ. publs. editor U. Md., College Park, 1973—. Mem. Am. Coll. Pub. Relations Assn. (trustee, awards 1967-73), Am. Alumni Council (awards 1967-73, communications com. 1971-73), League Women Voters Va. Westhampton Coll. Alumnae Assn., Mortar Bd., Phi Beta Kappa, Pi Delta Epsilon. Home: 907 Brantford Av Silver Spring MD 20904 Office: 241 Center of Adult Edn U Md College Park MD 20742

CARTER, VIRGINIA MADELON (MRS. DEAN WILLIAM CARTER), pub. relations ofcl.; b. Pitts., Aug. 10, 1919; d. Kosto and Josephine (Polic) Unkovic; B.S. in Bus. Adminstrn., Duquesne U., 1941, postgrad., 1942; postgrad. U. Mich., 1960; m. Dean William Carter, Jan. 17, 1953; 1 son, Dean William. Asst. to bursar Pa. Coll. for Women (now Chatham Coll.), Pitts., 1942-50; dir. spl. services U.S. Army, Wis. and Germany, 1950-53; community relations dir. St. Mary's Hosp., Saginaw, Mich., 1956—. Bd. dirs. Saginaw County unit Am. Cancer Soc., 1970—, mem. pub. relations com. Mich. unit, 1973—. Fellow Acad. Hosp. Pub. Relations (dir., sec. 1971); mem. Am. Soc. Hosp. Pub. Relations Dirs. (Mich. area rep.), Mich. Hosp. Pub. Relations Assn. (pres. 1968), Mich. Hosp. Assn. (pub. relations bd. 1973), Saginaw Valley Press Club, Epsilon Eta Phi. Home: 4333 Dirker Rd Saginaw MI 48603 Office: 830 S Jefferson St Saginaw MI 48601

CARTER, YVONNE BREAUX (MRS. WALTER R. CARTER), govt. ofcl.; b. Crowley, La., Aug. 3, 1922; d. Valentine Desire and Annie Helena (Oertling) Breaux; B.S., U. S.W. La., 1943; B.S. in L.S., George Peabody Coll. for Tchrs., M.A. in L.S., 1960, Edn. Specialist, 1966; m. Walter R. Carter, Apr. 24, 1943 (dec. Sept. 1958). Math.-history tchr., Sulphur, La., 1942-44; sch. prin., Sardis, Tenn., 1944-45; sch. librarian, Gueydan (La.) High Sch., 1945-64, 65-66; asst. prof. Northwestern State U., Natchitoches, La., 1964-65; asst. prof. U. So. La., Lafayette, 1966-67; ednl. specialist Bur. Postsecondary Edn., Div. Library Programs, U.S. Office Edn., Washington, 1967—. Sec. P.T.A., 1948-49. Mem. N.E.A., Am. Assn. Univ. Women (parlimentarian Lafayette br. 1965-66), Am. Assn. Sch. Librarians, A.L.A., La. Sch. Librarians (pres. 1966-67), Les Dames de Gueydan (pres. 1952-53), N.W. La., Attakapas (dir. 1965-67) hist. assns., Alpha Beta Alpha, Beta Phi Mu, Kappa Delta Pi, Delta Kappa Gamma (pres. Alpha chpt. Washington, 1972-74, corr. sec., Nu State D.C. 1973—), Kappa Kappa Iota. Roman Catholic. Home: 301 G St Washington DC 20024 Office: 400 Maryland Av Washington DC 20202

CARTMELL, HELEN (MRS. NEAL E. CARTMELL), ednl. media designer, artist; b. Bridgeport, Conn., Jan. 6, 1923; d. Thomas and Panayiota (Rassias) Theodore; student Detroit Soc. Arts and Crafts, 1941-42, Wayne State U., 1944-45, 70-72; m. Neal E. Cartmell, July 28, 1945; children—Thomas N., Nancy E. (Mrs. E. Neumann). Plant layout draftsman Fleetwood div. Gen. Motors Corp., Detroit, 1943-46; designer J.L. Hudson Co., Detroit, 1950-52; art dir. design services for ednl. media Wayne State U., Detroit, 1967—; one-woman shows at Arwin Galleries, Detroit, 1971; exhibited in group shows at Arwin Gallery, Founders Rental Program Detroit Inst. Art, Grand Rapids (Mich.) Art Mus., Detroit Artists Market, Grace B. Dow Library Invitational, Midlands, Mich., Grand Valley Delta Coll., Saginaw, Mich., Kresge Art Center Lansing, Mich., others; represented in permanent collections at Chrysler Corp., Wayne State U., Internat. Nickel Co., Art in Embassies program Dept. State, Detroit Bank and Trust Co., and pvt. collections. Recipient of prizes from Macomb County Artists, Thumb Area Art Exhbn., 1962, 63, 64, 66. Mem. Mich. Acad. Sci., Arts and Letters (prizes 1964, 69), Detroit Soc. Women Painters and Sculptors (prizes 1969, 70, 74), Nat. Assn. Ednl. Broadcasters. Home: 21700 Winshall Rd St Clair Shores MI 48081 Office: 5035 Woodward Detroit MI 48202

CARULLO, MARIA ELENA GARCIA (MRS. DOMINIC JOSEPH CARULLO), educator; b. N.Y.C., Oct. 13, 1934; d. Laureano Benito and Maria Elena (Alvarez) Garcia; B.A., Coll. of New Rochelle, 1956; M.A., Columbia, 1962; student Middle Tenn. State Coll., summer 1958; m. Dominic Joseph Carullo, June 9, 1956. Tchr. St. Rose of Lima Sch., Murfreesboro, Tenn., 1957-58, Haverstraw (N.Y.) Elementary Sch., 1958-59, New Rochelle (N.Y.) High Sch., 1959-65; head fgn. lang. dept. Ardsley (N.Y.) High Sch., 1965—. Cons. N.Y. State Edn. Dept., 1964—; tchr. Spanish, New Rochelle (N.Y.) Summer High Sch., 1960-61. Mem. Am. Assn. Tchrs. of Spanish and Portuguese (chpt. pres. 1963-68), N.Y. State Assn. Fgn. Lang. Tchrs. (dir. 1967-70), N.Y. State Tchrs. Assn., Spanish Inst., Am. Assn. Tchrs. of French, Am. Classical League, Classical Assn. of Empire State, Am. Council on Teaching of Fgn. Langs., Council of Fgn. Lang. Suprs. of Westchester, N.E.A., Ardsley Tchrs. Assn. (pres. 1971-72), Am. Assn. Tchrs. Italian, League Women Voters, Alpha Delta Kappa (chpt. v.p. 1968-70, chpt. pres. 1970-72). Contbr. articles in field to profl. jours. Home: 61 White Oak St New Rochelle NY 10801 Office: 300 Farm Rd Ardsley NY 10502

CARUSO, ANGELINE PAULINE, asso. supt. schs.; b. Chgo., Oct. 9, 1922; d. Peter John and Pauline (Papathanasiou) Caruso; B.E., Chgo. Tchrs. Coll., 1944; M.A. in English, Northwestern U., 1950; certificate advanced study (Kellogg Found. fellow) Harvard, 1960, Ed.D., 1962; L.H.D., DePaul U., 1974. Elementary sch. tchr., Chgo., 1944-53, high sch. tchr., 1953-59; prin. McDade Sch., Chgo., 1960-65; supt. schs. Dist. 25, Chgo., 1965-72, asso. supt. city sch. system, 1972—. Chmn. Chgo. Pub. Schs. com. to develop programs for non-English-speaking children, 1970-72. Active Chgo. council Girl Scouts U.S.A., 1943-50; pres. bd. edn. Koraes Sch. Sts. Constantine and Helen Ch., 1966—. Bd. dirs. Midwest Boys Club, 1966-70, Hellenic Edn. council, 1971. Recipient ann. award Helenic Cultural Circle, 1965. Mem. Am. Assn. Sch. Adminstrs., Adminstrv. Women in Edn. (pres. Chgo. chpt. 1970-72, award Chgo. Council 1972), Chgo. Area Reading Assn. (dir. 1966—), Chgo. State U. Alumni Assn. (dir.), Kappa Delta Pi (Educator of Year award Chgo. Alumni chpt. 1971). Mem. Byzantine Fellowship. Home: 1240 N Lake Shore Dr Chicago IL 60613 Office: Office of Area C Chgo Pub Schs 5025 N Laramie Chicago IL 60630

CARUSO, MARIE A., coll. counselor; b. Elizabeth, N.J., July 3, 1941; d. Dominick and Mary (Simeone) Caruso; B.A., Trinity Coll., 1963; M.A., Tchrs. Coll. Columbia, 1967. Registrar, Assn. of Bar of City N.Y., N.Y.C., 1964-65; dir. guidance Union Cath. High Sch., Scotch Plains, N.J., 1965-68; counselor Counseling Center, St. Peter's Coll., Jersey City, 1968-70; counselor Rockland Community Coll., Suffern, N.Y., 1970—. Vol., Millburn chpt. A.R.C., 1967—; mem. Aux. Childrens Home Soc., 1968-69. Mem. Am., N.J., Union County (sec. 1967-68) personnel and guidance assns., Nat. Vocational Guidance Assn., Am. Sch. Counselor Assn., N.J. Psychol. Assn., Nat. Assn. Women Deans and Counselors, Nat. Assn. Student Personnel Adminstrs. Home: Tall Oaks Suffern NY 10901 Office: Rockland Community Coll Suffern NY 10901

CARVER, CHARLOTTE MAHR, educator; b. Cleve., Feb. 17, 1925; d. Harry S. and Anna (Luntz) Mahr; student Case Inst. Tech., 1942-43, U. Dayton, 1943-45, Ohio State U., 1946-48; B.S. in Edn., Kent State U., 1964, M.Ed., 1966; Ph.D., U. Sarasota, 1972; div.; 1 son, Christopher James. Staff U.S. Govt. Signal Corps, Dayton, O., 1942-46, civilian in charge identification and correlation unit, 1945-46; tchr. St. Barnabas Sch., Northfield, O., 1959-61; head math. dept. Woodridge High Sch., Peninsula, O., 1962-66; elementary guidance counselor North Royalton (O.) Schs., 1966-67; dir. guidance Brecksville (O.) City Schs., 1967-74; asst. dean arts, scis. and profl. edn. Rio Grande (O.) Coll., 1974—. Reporter Cleve. Press, part-time 1956-59; grad. instr. St. John Coll., Cleve., part-time 1970-74; spl. lectr. Ursuline Coll., Cleve., 1969; mem. nat. adv. com. Coll. Admission Center, Chgo., 1969-71; hon. admissions counselor U.S. Naval Acad., Annapolis, Md., 1968; ednl. evaluator North Central Accreditation Assn., 1969—, Ohio Dept. Edn., 1971; mem. Midwest and nat. adv. coms. Am. Coll. Testing Program, 1971-72; mem. Cleve. Commn. Higher Edn., 1971-74, Task Force on Higher Edn., 1974—. Recipient certificate recognition U.S. Signal Corps, 1944, USAF, 1945, 70, DECA Clubs Am., 1968; named Hon. Citizen, Lexington, Ky., 1969. Mem. Cuyahoga County Coll. Counselors (handbook com. 1969—), Am., Northeastern Ohio Personnel and guidance assns., Nat., Am. vocational guidance assns., Am., Ohio (planning com. 1970), sch. counselors assns., Ohio Vocational Assn., Nat. (state rep. 1969-72), Ohio (exec. com., editor quar. 1971-72, counselor conferees 1970—) assns. coll. admissions counselors, Assn. on Measurement and Evaluation in Guidance, Nat., Ohio, Northeastern Ohio, Brecksville (state and dist. rep. 1970-72) edn. assns., Nat. Council on Measurement in Edn., Assn. Counselor Educators and Suprs., Am. Assn. U. Profs., Am. Assn. Community and Jr. Colls., Am. Assn. Higher Edn. (regional conf. 1973), Cleve. Assn. for Children with Learning Disabilities, Kappa Delta Pi, Delta Kappa Gamma. (rep. to Cleve. Commn. Higher Edn. 1971—). Founder, editor Voice of Hills community newspaper 1956-59, Brecksville Sr. High Schs. Guidance Newsline, 1967-74. Patentee automated scheduler. Address: Rio Grande College Rio Grande OH 45674

CARVER, DOROTHY LEE ESKEW (MRS. JOHN JAMES CARVER), educator; b. Brady, Tex., July 10, 1926; d. Clyde Albert and A. Maurine (Meadows) Eskew; student So. Ore. Coll., 1942-43, Coll. Eastern Utah, 1965-67; B.A., U. Utah, 1968; M.A., Cal. State Coll. at Hayward, 1970; postgrad. Mills Coll., 1971; m. John James Carver, Feb. 26, 1944; children—John James, Sheila (Mrs. Joseph English), Chuck, David. Instr., Rutherford Bus. Coll., Dallas, 1944-45; sec. Adolph Coors Co., Golden, Colo., 1945-47; instr. English, Coll. Eastern Utah, Price, 1968-69; instr. speech Modesto (Cal.) Jr. Coll., 1970-71; instr. personal devel. men and women Heald Bus. Coll., Oakland, Cal., 1972-74, dean curriculum, Walnut Creek, Cal., 1974—. Communications cons. Oakland Army Base, 1973. Mem. Gov.'s. Conf. on Higher Edn. in Utah, 1968; mem. finance com. Coll. Eastern Utah, 1967-69; active various community drives. Judge election Republican party, 1960, 64. Bd. dirs. Opportunity Center, 1965-66. Mem. Am. Assn. Univ. Women. Episcopalian (supt. Sunday Sch. 1967-69). Mem. Order Eastern Star. Clubs: Toastmistress (1st vice chmn. council 4, Diablo Valley); Square Wheelers Square Dance (membership chmn. Walnut Creek 1972-73). Home: 20 Coronado Ct Walnut Creek CA 94596 Office: 2085 N Broadway Walnut Creek CA 94596

CARVER, LUCILLE AVIS YOUNG (MRS. ROY JAMES CARVER, SR.), rubber mfg. co. exec.; b. Muscatine, Ia., July 27, 1917; d. Merle Archie and Marie Anna (Kollman) Young; student U. Ia.; m. Roy James Carver Sr., Aug. 22, 1942; children—Roy James, John Alexander, Clayton Charles, Martin Gregory. With Carver Pump Co., Muscatine, sec., treas., 1938—, dir., 1938—; with Bandag, Inc., Muscatine, 1957—, treas. 1957—, dir., 1957—; with Carver Foundry Products, Inc. Muscatine, sec., treas. 1954—, dir., 1954—; sec. Carver Tropical Products, Inc., Muscatine, 1968—. Bd. dirs. President's Club, U. Ia. Recipient Distinguished Service award U. Ia., 1972. Mem. Laura Musser Mus. Elk. Club: Geneva Golf and Country (Muscatine). Home: 2236 Mulberry Av Muscatine IA 52761 Office: 1056 Hershey Av Muscatine IA 52761

CARVER, MARGARET ANNE, physician; b. Hanover, Pa., May 3, 1921; d. Earnest Frederick and Viola May (Little) Carver; B.S., Carnegie Mellon U., 1943; M.D., U. Pitts., 1950. Intern, Harrisburg (Pa.) Hosp., 1950-52; resident obstetrics and gynecology Millard Fillmore Hosp., Buffalo, 1959-61; practice medicine, specializing in gen. practice, Uniontown, Pa., 1952-58; practice medicine specializing in obstetrics and gynecology, Uniontown, 1962—; chief dept. obstetrics and gynecology, Uniontown Hosp.; clinician State Family Planning Clinic; dir. Diversified Operations Corp. Diplomate Am. Bd. Obstetrics and Gynecology. Fellow Am. Coll. Obstetricians and Gynecologists, Royal Soc. Health; mem. A.M.A., Sigma Xi, Phi Kappa Phi, Alpha Omega Alpha, Delta Gamma. Republican. Lutheran. Club: Soroptimist Internat. Home: 448 W Berkeley St Uniontown PA 15401 Office: 30 Delaware Av Uniontown PA 15401

CARVER, PATRICIA NAIR, psychologist; b. New Britain, Conn., Apr. 11, 1933; d. Israel and Fritzie (Stoumen) Nair; A.B., Wellesley Coll., 1955; certificate U. Geneva, 1956; postgrad. U. Cal. 1956-57; M.A., Clark U., 1958, Ph.D., 1961; m. David H. Carver, Aug. 3, 1963; children—Randolph, Rebecca, Leslie. Staff psychologist Children's Hosp., Boston, 1961-63; research fellow Center for Cognitive Studies, Harvard, 1962-63; staff psychologist Montefiore Hosp., Bronx, N.Y., 1965-66; psychology cons. Inner City Community Mental Health Program, Balt., 1970—; clin. instr. psychiatry U. Md. Med. Sch., 1970—. Mem. Am., Eastern, Md. psychol. assns., Balt. Wellesley Club. Jewish religion. Home: 3404 Terrapin Rd Baltimore MD 21208 Office: 25 S Calvert St Baltimore MD 21202

CARY, LOSIE JOE PIERCE (MRS. CHARLES LEROY CARY), occupational therapist, health service adminstr.; b. South Charleston, W.Va., Dec. 11, 1930; d. John Benjamin Holmes and Irene Dorsey (Smith) Pierce; student Va. Intermont Coll., 1948-50; B.A. in Art, Berea Coll., 1952; B.S. in Occupational Therapy, Eastern Mich. U., 1957; m. Charles LeRoy Cary, June 30, 1960; children—James LeRoy, Charles Matthew, Zina Dorsey, Benjamin Ponton, Kirk Chenoweth. Tchr., Ky. Tng. Home for Retarded, Frankfort, Ky., 1952-54; staff therapist McGuire VA Hosp., Richmond, Va., 1958-65; staff therapist Med. Coll. Va., Richmond, 1965-72, supr., 1972—. Mem. Amelia County P.T.A., 1961—. Mem. Am. Occupational Therapy Assn., Am. Burn Assn. Episcopalian (Sunday sch. tchr. 1965—). Home: Route 1 Box 193 Amelia VA 23002 Office: Box 846 Medical College Virginia Hospital Commonweal U Richmond VA 23298

CARY, SYLVIA GRACE, microbiologist; b. Enid, Okla.; d. Boyd Balford and Margaret (McLaughlin) Cary; B.S., U. Md., 1947, M.S., 1958. Microbiologist div. communicable diseases and immunology Walter Reed Army Inst. Research, Walter Reed Army Med. Center, Washington, 1947-63, chief determinative bacteriology sect., 1963-71; microbiologist FDA, Washington, 1971—. Mem. subcom. on Moraxella and allied bacteria 10th Internat. Congress for Microbiology. Recipient Superior Performance award Dept. Army, 1959-60, certificate achievement, 1971. Mem. Soc. for Exptl. Biology and Medicine, Am. Soc. for Microbiology, N.Y. Acad. Sci., Phi Delta Gamma. Home: 2445 Lyttonsville Rd Silver Spring MD 20910

CARY, VERONICA FRANCES, librarian; b. N.Y.C.; d. James Jay and Wanda (Plawska) Cary; A.B., Douglass Coll., 1933; B.S. in L.S., Columbia, 1945. Librarian, Trenton (N.J.) Pub. Library. Bd. dirs. Trenton YWCA, Trent House Commn. Mem. Old Barracks Assn., Trenton Hist. Soc., Am., N.J. (pres. 1965-66) library assns., Delta Kappa Gamma. Club: Trenton College (past pres.). Home: 230 Garfield Av Trenton NJ 08629 Office: 120 Academy St Trenton NJ 08608

CASADESUS, GABY L'HOTE (MRS. ROBERT CASADESUS), pianist; b. Marseille, France, Aug. 9, 1901; d. Jules and Therese (Raynaud) Lhote; ed. Paris Conservatory; m. Robert Casadesus, July 16, 1921 (dec. Sept. 1972); children—Jean, Guy, Therese (Mrs. David W. Rawson). Appeared as soloist with maj. Philharmonics of Europe, North and South Am.; tchr. Am. Conservatory, Fontainebleau, 1937-48, 73-74, Acad. Maurice Ravel, 1973—. Jury mem. Faure Competion and Paris Conservatory. Recipient 1st prize Paris Conservatory, 1918, Pages prize, 1922. Home: 54 Rue Vaneau Paris France

CASADY, LILLIAN JENNY LIODAS, nursing adminstr.; b. Los Angeles; d. Nicholas and Mary (Marina) Liodas; R.N., Queen of Angels Hosp., 1936; B.S., pub. health nurse U. Cal. at Los Angeles, 1951, M.A., 1961; m. Donald G. Casady, Aug. 15, 1936 (dec.). Pvt. duty nurse, Los Angeles, 1937-40; asst. exec. sec. Dist. V, Cal. Nurses Assn., 1940-49; sch. nurse Los Angeles Sch. Dist., 1952-65; dir. Dist. Nursing Services, Los Angeles City Unified Sch. Dist., 1965—. Lectr. Cal. State Coll. at Los Angeles, 1970—; guest lectr. Cal. Assn. Health, Phys. Edn. and Recreation, 1965-67, Cal. Sch. Health Assn., 1965, 66, 68, Cal. Sch. Nurses Orgn., 1969, 70, 71. Mem. nursing com. A.R.C., 1965—; med. aux. U. Cal. at Los Angeles, 1971—. Chmn. adv. bd. SEARCH: A Link to Services, 1971—. Mem. Cal. Republican Com., 1968—. Served with Nurse Corps, AUS, 1945-46. Am. Sch. Health Assn. fellow, 1968. Mem. N.E.A. (pres. dept. sch. nurses 1972—), Cal. Sch. Nurses Orgn. (pres. 1966-68), Am. Sch. Health Assn. (governing council 1968-71), Cal. Sch. Health Assn. (dir. 1958-60), Am. Nurses Assn., Town Hall of Cal., Delta Kappa Gamma. Author: (with others) The School Nurse Services Program, 1971; Guidelines for School Nurse Evaluation, 1972. Asso. editor: Nursing Digest, 1972. Home: 205 Dochan Circle Montebello CA 90640 Office: 450 N Grand Av Los Angeles CA 90051

CASAS, LILLIAN, librarian; b. Cayey, P.R., Oct. 31, 1924; d. Guillermo and Maria (Lelras) Casas; B.A., U. P.R., 1951; M.S. in L.S., Syracuse U., 1958; M.Health Edn., U. P.R. Sch. Pub. Health, 1973. Tchr. dept. edn. Jacinto Martinez Sch., Dorado, P.R., 1950; asst. librarian U. P.R. Sch. Medicine, San Juan, 1951-57, head cataloger, 1959-60, librarian, 1961-65, dir. Med. Scis. Campus Library, 1966—. Mem. Med. Library Assn., P.R. Library Assn. (pres. 1964).

CASAVANT, LYDIA M., educator; b. Natick, Mass.; d. P. Victor and Margaret (MacGath) Casavant; B.A., Newton Coll. of Sacred Heart, 1950; M.S., Boston U., 1955. Adminstr., Girl Scouts of Am., Mass., Conn., and Heidelberg, Germany, 1952-62; dir. admissions and pub. relations Boston-Bouve Coll., Tufts U., Medford, Mass., 1962-65; asst. dir. admissions Northeastern U., Boston, 1964-67; dean of students Cardinal Cushing Coll., Brookline, Mass., 1967-71; exec. dir. Bay Path Colonial chpt. Girl Scouts U.S.A., Newton Upper Falls, Mass., 1971—. Lectr., Northeastern U., Boston. Mem. nat. com. Girl Scouts of U.S.A., 1966-70. Mem. Mass. Women Deans Assn. (mem. exec. bd. 1968-70, editor Newsletter 1968-70), Nat. Assn. Women Deans and Counselors, Nat. Assn. Girl Scout Profl. Workers. Home: 22 Ash St Cambridge MA 02138

CASCARIO, ELIZABETH FRINZI, psychologist; b. Easton, Pa., Nov. 11, 1919; d. John and Liboria (Scaduta) Frinzi; B.S., E. Stroudsburg State Coll., 1968; M.Ed., Lehigh U., 1969, Ed.D., 1972; m. Matthew Cascario, Sept. 14, 1940; children—Nicholas (dec.), Carole. Part-time elementary guidance counselor Penn Argyl (Pa.) Area Sch. Dist., 1969-72, part-time psychologist, 1972—; pvt. practice, 1972—. Mem. Am. Soc. Clin. Hypnosis, Am. Lehigh Valley psychol. assns. Roman Catholic. Home: RD 3 Box 285 Bangor PA 18013 Office: Box 92 RR 1 Pen Argyl PA 18072

CASCIANO-SAVIGNANO, CARMELA JENNIE, educator; b. Clifton Heights, Pa., Nov. 6, 1924; d. Domenic Pasquale and Filomena (Lalli) Casciano; B.S. in Commerce, Drexel U., 1947; M.S. in Edn., U. Pa., 1951, D.Ed., 1965; m. Anthony Philip Savignano, July 21, 1946. Tchr. North Coventry High Sch., Pottstown, Pa., 1947-50, Banks Bus. Coll., Phila., 1950-51; instr. bus. edn. Cedar Crest Coll., Allentown, Pa., 1951-56; asst. prof. bus. Immaculata Coll., 1956-59; evening coll. div. part-time instr. St. Joseph's Coll., Phila., 1959-60; research asst. U. Pa., 1965-66; asso. prof. Villanova (Pa.) U., 1966—. Mem. Assn. for Supervision and Curriculum Devel., Internat., Pa., Am. ednl. research assns., Pi Lambda Theta. Author: Guidelines in Educational Research; Guidelines to Curriculum Improvement. Contbr. articles to profl. jours.; also booklet. Home: 102 W North Lane Apt A-7 Conshohocken PA 19428 Office: Villanova Univ Villanova PA 19085

CASCIO, FRANCES ANTOINETTE, radiol. technologist; b. N.Y.C., June 13, 1928; d. Blaise Anthony and Frances Cecilia (Campione) Cascio; B.A., St. Joseph Coll., 1950; grad. course nuclear med. tech. Coney Island Hosp., Bklyn., 1967. Mem. staff Victory Meml. Hosp., Bklyn., 1961—, adminstr. radiology dept., 1973—. Mem. Am. Soc. Radiologic Technologists, Soc. Nuclear Med. Technologists, Radiologic Technologists Soc. N.Y. State (1st prize sci. film exhibit on arthrography of knee 1971; sec. 1970-72, pres. 1973-74), Kings, Richmond and Queens Soc. Radiologic Technologists (sec. 1969-72, pres. 1972-74), Women's Internat. Bowling League. Home: 41 Marine Av Brooklyn NY 11209 Office: 9036 7th Av Brooklyn NY 11228

CASE, ADELLE CAROLINE, realtor; b. Toledo, Mar. 25, 1916; d. Frank V. and Sophia (Wawro) Siemienkowski; certificate Western Res. U., 1965; m. Norman Case, Nov. 9, 1940 (dec. Aug. 1954); children—Ronna Lee (Mrs. James DelTorto), Susan Louise Case (Mrs. David Iofredo). Sec. Oldsmobile div. General Motors, Terminal Tower, Cleve., 1939-41; sec., receptionist, prodn. scheduling Jack & Heintz, Cleve., 1943-46; realtor, 1959—. Mem. adv. com. Cuyahoga County Coll. real estate program, 1972. Mem. Brecksville Little Theatre. Mem. Nat., Ohio, Cleve. real estate bds., Cleve. Area Bd. Realtors (trustee 1972-74), Nat. Assn. Real Estate Bds. Women's Council Real Estate (pres. Cleve. chpt. 1970, sec. Ohio 1972), Nat. Inst. Real Estate Brokers, Nat. Inst. Farm and Land Brokers. Home: 20619 Amherst Rd Warrensville Heights OH 44122

CASE, RUTH M. SMITH (MRS. CLIFFORD CASE), wife of U.S. senator; m. Clifford P. Case, July 13, 1928; children—Mary Jane (Mrs. William M. Weaver), Ann (Mrs. John C. Holt), Clifford P. III. Home: 191 W Milton Av Rahway NJ 07065

CASEI, NEDDA, mezzo-soprano; b. Balt., Sept. 9, 1934; d. Howard Thomas and Lyda Marie (Graupman) Casey; grad. high sch., Scarsdale, N.Y.; grad. Mozarteum, Salzburg, 1959; studied voice with William P. Herman, N.Y.C., 1950-58, Vittorio Piccinini, Milano, Italy, 1959—; also student piano, langs., ballet; m. John A. Wiles, Jr., Dec. 26, 1971. Operatic debut at Theatre Royal de la Monnaie, Brussels, Belgium, Dec. 1960; operatic performances at Basel (Switzerland) Stadttheater, Gran. Liceo, Barcelona, Spain, Pitts. Opera, Teatro Carlo Fenice, Genova, Italy, Vancouver (Can.) Opera, Teatro San Carlo, Naples, Italy, Chgo. Lyric, Met. Opera, N.Y.C., 1964—, also Phila. Grand Opera, Ulster Festival Ireland, Opera-Cape Town Opera, San Remo Opera, Hartford Opera, Toledo Opera, Miami Opera, Dayton Opera, Mobile Opera, San Diego Opera, Houston Opera, Prague Opera, Brno Opera, Ostrava Opera, Strasbourg, Opera Boston; appeared with many symphony orchs.; gave command performance at White House for Emperor Haile Selassie; performances in various mus. festivals and tours in Europe, S. Africa, Can. and U.S.; performed on radio and TV in Holland, Brussels, Italy, East Germany, U.S.A.; also made various recs. Recipient New Orleans Opera award, 1959, Rockefeller Found. award, 1962, 64. Mem. Actors Equity, Am. Guild Mus. Artists (gov.). Home: 15 W 72d St New York City NY 10023 Office: care Hurok Concerts 1370 Av of Americas New York City NY 10019 also Met Opera Lincoln Center Plaza New York City NY 10023

CASELLAS, ELIZABETH REED (BRANNON), library adminstr., educator; b. New Orleans, Jan. 7, 1925; d. Dallie Reed and Elizabeth (Robinson) Brannon; B.M., Chgo. Mus. Coll., 1948; M.A., Columbia U., 1949, Profl. Diploma, 1950; student U. Paris (Sorbonne), 1953-54; M.S., Columbia U. Sch. Library Service, 1964; m. Joaquin Casellas, Mar. 16, 1954. Instr., Valparaiso U., 1946-47; asst. librarian J. M. Mathes, Inc., N.Y.C., 1955-57; librarian Communications Counselors, Inc., N.Y.C., 1957-59; head librarian, mgmt. cons. Cresap, McCormick & Paget, Inc., N.Y.C., 1959-60; head librarian, marketing mgmt. cons. Stewart, Dougall & Assos., N.Y.C., 1960-65; asst. prof. Grad. Sch. Library Studies, bibliographer in bus. U. Hawaii, Honolulu, 1965-66; head bus., sci. and tech. dept. Orlando (Fla.) Pub. Library, 1966-69; asso. prof., dir. library Grad. Sch. Bus. Adminstn., Tulane U., New Orleans, 1969—. Recipient Composition award for Piano Sonata, No. 2, Phi Mu Gamma, 1948. Mem. Spl. Libraries Assn. (pres. La. chpt. 1974—, founder Fla. chpt. 1968, past lectr. N.Y. group Advt. div., rep. McKinsey Found. mgmt. book awards com.), A.L.A., La., S.W. library assns., Am. Assn. U. Women, Beta Gamma Sigma, Kappa Delta Pi, Phi Mu Gamma. Republican. Episcopalian. Author: Guide to Basic Information Sources in Business Administration, 1974. Contbr. articles on bus. librarianship and classification to profl. jours. Home: 5121 Clara St New Orleans LA 70118

CASEY, ALICE FRANCES, ednl. adminstr.; b. Boston, Aug. 9, 1917; d. Francis Augustine and Mary Frances (Callahan) Casey; B.S., Tchrs. Coll. City Boston, 1938, Ed.M., 1944; postgrad. Trinity Coll. Dublin (Ireland), 1951; Ed.M., Harvard, 1953; D.Ed., Boston Coll., 1964. Tchr. high sch. English, Boston Pub. Schs., 1940-50; guidance counselor Roslindale High Sch., also Jamaica Plain High Sch., Boston, 1951-57; guidance counselor Burke High Sch., Roxbury, Mass., 1957-64; head master Girls' High Sch., Roxbury, Mass., 1964-66; asst. supt. Boston Pub. Schs., 1966-70, asso. supt. for spl. services, 1970—. Vis. lectr. Newton Coll. Sacred Heart, Newton, Mass., 1957-64. Mem. Tufts Mental Health Area Bd., 1965-67; pres. S. Boston Neighborhood Council, 1966. Bd. dirs. Action for Boston Community Devel., 1968-70. Served with WAVES, 1944-46. Mem. Am. Assn. Sch. Supts., Am. Personnel and Guidance Assn., Pi Lambda Theta. Office: 15 Beacon St Boston MA 02108

CASEY, CORA MAE, bank ofcl.; b. Trinity, Tex., Dec. 24, 1930; d. William F. and Bessie B. (Pipes) Boyce; grad. high sch.; student Am. Inst. Banking, 1964; m. Billy George Casey, June 3, 1949; 1 dau., Donna Ann (Mrs. Kenneth K. Conger). With First Nat. Bank, Baytown, Tex., 1957—, asst. cashier, 1963-70, cashier, 1970-71, asst. v.p., 1971—, auditor, 1972—. Asst. bank examiner State Tex., 1973—. Mem. Nat. Assn. Bank Women. Home: 5032 Hillring St # 119 Fort Worth TX 76132

CASEY, DONNABELLE ANNE, coll. adminstr.; b. Cedar Falls, Ia., June 26, 1924; d. John Francis and Ruth Erma (Livingston) Casey. Registered Nurse, Kahler Hosps. Sch. Nursing, 1946; B.S., Marquette U., 1950; certificate occupational therapy U. So. Cal., 1954; M.S., U. Cal. at San Francisco, 1965. Staff nurse VA Hosp., Los Angeles, 1950-52; occupational therapist Cal. Elks Major Project for Cerebral Palsied Children, Palm Springs, 1954-59; instr. dept. nursing Palomar Coll., San Marcos, Cal., 1967-72, chmn. dept. nursing, 1972—. cons. USN Nurse Corps, 1973—; tchr. Native Am. Inst., Pala Indian Reservation, 1973. Served with Nurse Corps, USNR, 1959-64. St. Louis U. Sch. Nursing fellow, 1948-49; Elks Assn. scholar 1952-54; research grantee Cal. Elks. Assn., 1957. Mem. Am. Nurses Assn., Nat. League Nursing, Am., So. Cal. (pres. 1957) occupational therapy assns., Sigma Theta Tau. Home: 142 11th St Del Mar CA 92014 Office: Palomar Coll San Marcos CA 92069

CASEY, ELIZABETH TEMPLE, museum ofcl.; b. Providence, Sept. 24, 1901; d. Edward Norton and Elizabeth Case (Temple) Casey; student Brown U., 1920-21. Museum asst. Museum of Art, R.I. Sch. of Design, Providence, 1926-35, head of edn., 1928-43, curator of textiles, 1935-43, curator Aldrich collection, 1950—, curator Oriental art, 1956—. Mem. R.I., Cranston hist. socs., Providence Preservation Soc. Club: Pottery and Porcelain (Providence). Home: 89 Ingleside St Cranston RI 02905 Office: 224 Benefit Av Providence RI 02903

CASEY, ETHEL LAUGHLIN (MRS. WILLIS ROBERT CASEY), concert singer; b. Tarboro, N.C., Jan. 14, 1926; d. Maurice Lee and Mary Irene (Williams) Laughlin; student Va. Intermont Coll., 1944-45; B.A., Greensboro Coll., 1946-47; postgrad. U. N.C., 1948, Meredith Coll., 1949, Northwestern U., 1961, U.N.C., 1962; D.Mus., Hamilton State U., 1972, Ph.D., 1973; m. Willis Robert Casey, May 23, 1946; children—Willis Robert, Walker Laughlin. N.Y. debut, Town Hall, 1961; concert singer performing at Carnegie Hall all-Debussy concert, 1961, Tribute to Galli-Curci, 1965, Composer's

Showcase, N.Y., 1965, Electronic Concert, Ann Arbor, Mich., 1966, Webern World Premieres Internat. Webern Festivals, Seattle, Buffalo, 1962-66, World Premieres of Graphic Music, 1965, command performance Greek Royal Princess, 1966, New Vistas, World Premieres of Am. Music, 1968, Philomel electronic concert, 1968, Governor's concerts, 1969, Judson Hall, N.Y., 1970, Nat. Congress, Constitution Hall, Washington, 1970, world premieres, Webern and Earls music Carnegie Hall, 1971, world premieres own music and Webern, Lincoln Center, N.Y.C., 1971, Internat. Platform Assn., Washington, 1972; TV and radio performer, 1936—; performed at numerous festivals, 1960—, also opera world premieres; oratorio soloist; convention and mus. comedy performer. Founder concert series N.C. State Art Mus. Named Alumna of Year, Va. Intermont Coll., 1967, Singer of Year, Nat. Assn. Tchrs. Singing, 1963. Mem. N.C. State Music Soc. (founder). Author: Claude de France, 1962. Composer: Christmas Night, 1971; America Will Endure, 1972; U.S.A., 1972. Home: 1605 Park Dr Raleigh NC 27605

CASEY, MARTHA TANYA, biochemist; b. Gaffney, S.C., June 15, 1942; d. Eugene Perry and Beulah Martha (Meyer) Link; A.B., Bryn Mawr Coll., 1964; Ph.D., Mass. Inst. Tech., 1968; m. Charles Philip Casey, July 20, 1968. Research asso. chemistry U. Wis.-Madison, 1968—. NIH predoctoral fellow, 1965-68. Mem. Am. Chem. Soc., A.A.A.S., Sigma Xi. Research antibiotics. Home: 14 Farley Av Madison WI 53705

CASEY, MARY FRANCES YODER (MRS. TIMOTHY DENNIS CASEY), actress; b. South Bend, Ind., Nov. 14, 1944; foster dau. Gladys Pearl Yoder; grad. with honors (Greenleaf scholar) Interlochen (Mich.) Nat. Music Camp; B.S., Western Mich. U., 1967; M.A., S.W. Mo. State U., 1971; m. Timothy Dennis Casey, Sept. 16, 1972. Profl. actress appearing as Marifran Casey; appeared in Harvey, Kansas City; nat. tour as Ado Annie in Oklahoma; appeared in Music Man, South Pacific, Damn Yankees, Sunday in New York; participant USO tour to Orient, 1968. Tchr. music Northside Jr. High Sch., Elkhart, Ind., 1967-68; publicity, box office theatre mgr. S.W. Mo. State U., 1969-71; with Alley Theatre Co., Houston, 1971; women's editor, entertainment editor, reviewer Naples (Fla.) Daily News, 1972-73. Mem. fine arts com. Edison Community Coll., Ft. Myers, Fla., 1972-73. Mem. Actors' Equity Assn., Theta Alpha Phi, Alpha Psi Omega. Methodist. Home: 1002 S Orange Av Sarasota FL 33579

CASEY, MURIEL ZIMMERMAN (MRS. WILLIAM MALLAN CASEY, JR.), assn. exec.; b. N.Y.C., July 16, 1932; d. Lonnie Woodside and Ruth Bernadine (Carleton) Zimmerman; B.A., Randolph-Macon Woman's Coll., 1953; M.Ed., U. Va., 1969; postgrad. Lynchburg Coll., 1970; m. William Mallan Casey, Jr., Aug. 29, 1953; children—Carleton A., William W., David DeW. Tchr. English Seven Hills Sch., Lynchburg, Va., 1963-72, counselor, 1968-72, asst. headmistress, 1969-72; dir. Alumnae Assn. Randolph-Macon Woman's Coll., Lynchburg, 1972—. Mem. adv. com. on investigations involving human subjects Va. Dept. Mental Hygiene and Hosps., 1972—. Bd. dirs. Lynchburg Mental Health Assn. Mem. Am. Alumni Council, D.A.R., Delta Kappa Gamma, Kappa Delta. Episcopalian (mem. diocese dept. edn. 1970-72). Clubs: Lynchburg Junior Woman's (v.p. 1970-72), Woman's (Lynchburg), Garden (pres. 1957-58, garden fedn. parliamentarian); Ragged Robin Garden, Altrusa. Home: 3010 Sedgewick Dr Lynchburg VA 24503

CASEY, SISTER NATALIE, coll. pres.; b. Cleve., Oct. 12, 1916; d. Bernard T. and Phoebe (Cornell) Casey; B.A., Manhattan Coll., 1951; M.S. in Edn., Fordham U., 1955; M.S. in Chemistry, Syracuse U., 1963; postgrad. Columbia, 1964-70. Tchr., Holy Cross Sch., N.Y.C., 1938-42, St. Paul's High Sch., Daytona Beach, Fla., 1942-49, St. Pius Sch., Bronx, N.Y., 1949-55; asst. prin. Acad. Our Lady of the Blessed Sacrament, Goshen, N.Y., 1955-65; instr. Dominican Coll., Blauvelt, N.Y., 1965-66, pres., 1966—. Mem. com. evaluating secondary schs. Archdiocese of N.Y., 1963-65. Trustee Dominican Coll. NSF grantee in physics, 1958, in biology, 1959. Mem. Am. Assn. U. Women, Dominican, Nat. Cath. edn. assns., Am. Assn. Higher Edn., Pi Lambda Theta. Home: Western Hwy Blauvelt NY 10913

CASEY, NORINE THERESE, ednl. adminstr.; b. Arlington, Mass., Sept. 29, 1928; d. John Joseph and Norine Gertrude (Doyle) Casey; A.B., Wellesley Coll., 1949; M.A. in Teaching, Radcliffe Coll., 1951; postgrad. Stanford, 1956, U. Cal. at Berkeley, 1960, Tufts U., 1963, U. Vienna (Austria), 1959, U. Oslo (Norway), 1958, U. Sophia (Japan), 1966, U. Paris (France), 1962. Tchr., Bartlett Pvt. Elementary Sch., Arlington, 1950-53, dir., 1954—; research and teaching asst. Wellesley (Mass.) Coll., 1953-54; religious edn. tchr., 1966—. Lectr., Newton Coll. Sacred Heart (Mass.), 1958-59. Adviser to Tom Dooley Youth League, 1964—; pres. Friends of Robbins Library, 1972-73; Mem. town meeting, 1974. Trustee An Lac Orphanage, Saigon, Vietnam. Named Woman of Week Boston Herald Traveler, 1960. Club: Boston Wellesley College (pres. 1955-57, chmn. coll. reunion 1964). Home: 34 Bartlett Av Arlington MA 02174 Office: 36 Bartlett Av Arlington MA 02174

CASEY, SARAH ANN COUGHENOUR (MRS. RICHARD FIELDING CASEY), journalist; b. Pitts., July 7, 1946; d. Jesse William and Mary Ellen (Wilt) Coughenour; B. in Journalism, U. Mo., 1968; m. Richard Fielding Casey, Feb. 14, 1970. Asst. fashion editor, feature writer Phila. Inquirer, 1968-72, columnist, feature writer, copy editor, 1972-73; freelance fashion stylist, writer, copy editor Phila. Bull., 1973—; freelance writer Discover mag., 1973—, Met. mag., 1973—. Ballet dancer Phila. Civic Ballet, Phila., 1973-74. Mem. Women in Communications, Pa. Press Women's Assn., Phila. Press Assn., Fashion Group Phila., D.A.R., Pa., Phila. ballet assns., Spiritual Frontiers Fellowship. Republican. Methodist. Home: 71 Princess Ct Turnersville NJ 08012 Office: Phila Bull 30th and Market Sts Philadelphia PA 19101

CASEY, SUE (SUZANNE MARGUERITE PHILIPS), actress; b. Los Angeles, Apr. 8, 1926; d. Burke Dewey and Mildred Louise (Hansen) Philips; grad. high sch.; m. Harold Charles Eilen, Dec. 6, 1965; children (by previous marriage)—Colleen (Mrs. Bernard O'Shaughnessy), John Joseph Durant III, Christopher Kent Durant, Diane Marie Durant. Appeared in motion pictures, including Camelot, 1967, Paint Your Wagon, 1969, Never Steal Anything Wet, 1965, Surf Terror, 1964, Goldwyn Girl, 1945; TV appearances include Family Affair, Lucy, Farmers Daughter, Red Skelton, Bob Hope, Colgate Comedy Hour; appeared in numerous TV commls., including pub. service commls. Ball chmn. Footlighters, Inc., 1971-72, press chmn., 1972-73. Mem. Screen Actors Guild, A.F.T.R.A., Actors Equity.

CASGRAIN, CHARLOTTE ARDOIN, educator; b. Washington, Apr. 24, 1940; d. Ardoin Edmund and Mildred C. (Davis) Casgrain; A.B., Pembroke Coll., Brown U., 1962; M.S., U. Bridgeport, 1966; postgrad. Universite de Poiters, Universite de Aix Marseille. Asst. to dir., head counsellor tng. program Les Chalets Francais, Deer Isle, Me., 1958—; French specialist Greenwich (Conn.) Bd. Edn., 1962—. Recipient Danforth Found. citizenship award, 1955; Lucy Brownback award in French, 1955; French Govt. award for excellence in French, 1956; Fulbright award for travel-study in France, 1964; Alliance Francaise de N.Y. scholarship for study in France, 1969-70. Mem. Am. Assn. Tchrs. French, Nat., Conn., Greenwich edn. assns., Am. Assn. U. Women, Conn. Tchrs. of Lang., Pembroke Coll. Alumnae, Georgetown Visitation Alumnae. Home: La Chaumine 30 River Rd Cos Cob CT 06807 summer Pres du Port Stonington ME 04681

CASH, DORIS CAROLYN (MRS. FRANK E. PRUITT), educator; b. Atlanta, Aug. 20, 1937; d. Cenate Monroe and Louise (Buckner) Cash; B.B.A., Ga. State U., 1961, M.B.A., 1963, D.B.A. (Adele Hager Stamp Meml. scholar 1963-64), 1965; m. Frank E. Pruitt. Various office positions, 1955-61; with Tenn. Coal and Iron div. U.S. Steel Corp., Atlanta, 1961-62; research asst. econs. dept. Ga. State Coll., Atlanta, 1962-63, grad. teaching asst., 1963-65; mem. faculty W. Ga. Coll., Carrollton, 1965—, asst. prof. econs., 1968—; asso. prof. Oglethorpe Coll., 1968-72; coordinator bus. adminstrn. and econs., asso. prof. Clayton Jr. Coll., Morrow, Ga., 1972—; vis. asst. prof. econs., spl. lectr. Mercer U., Macon, summer, 1964, Mercer U., Atlanta, 1971, 72; research cons. econ. research service U.S. Dept. Agr., 1968—, mem. Joint Com. on Econ. Edn. Mem. Southeastern region Pres.'s Com. on Consumer Interest, 1964—. Recipient Alpha Lambda Delta Nat. Found. fellowship, 1963-64. Mem. Am. Assn. U. Women, So., Am. econ. assns., So. Finance Assn., Am. Inst. Urban and Regional Affairs, Southeastern Conf. Latin Am. Studies, Mortar Bd., Phi Chi Theta, Beta Gamma Sigma, Alpha Lambda Delta, Zeta Tau Alpha. Home: 1570 Buckner Rd SE Mableton GA 30059 Office: Clayton Jr Coll Morrow GA 30260

CASHMAN, SISTER MARY ELEANOR, coll. adminstr.; b. Coggon, Ia., Mar. 7, 1907; d. Thomas Francis and Elizabeth (Reilly) Cashman; B.A., Loras Coll., 1939; M.A., St. Louis U., 1941. Joined Sisters of Mercy, 1924; tchr. elementary sch. Archdiocese of Dubuque, Ia., 1926-38; prin. St. Matthew's Sch., Cedar Rapids, Ia., 1931-36; high sch. tchr. St. Wenceslaus High Sch. Cedar Rapids, 1938-40; dean of students Mt. Mercy Coll., Cedar Rapids, 1941-56, dean of coll., 1941-47, registrar, 1941-65, 71—. Mem. council Sisters of Mercy, Cedar Rapids, 1947-59, maj. superior, 1965-71. Mem. Am. Assn. Collegiate Registrars and Admissions Officers. Address: 1330 Elmhurst Dr NE Cedar Rapids IA 52402

CASKEY, SALLY ANNE, educator; b. Cleve., June 17, 1935; d. Harry B. and Carrie W. Caskey; B.S., Bowling Green, State U., 1957; M.A., Case Western Res. U., 1961. Tchr. math. and phys. edn. Cleve. Pub. Schs., 1957-60, chmn. phys. edn. dept., 1960-64; dir. women's phys. edn. program Case Western Res. U., Cleve., 1964—. Mem. Am. Alliance Phys. Edn. and Recreation, Ohio Assn. Health, Phys. Edn. and Recreation (past chmn. internat. relations N.E. Ohio), Cleve. Women's Phys. Edn. and Recreation Assn. (past pres., v.p., treas.), Kappa Delta Pi, Delta Psi Kappa. Home: 13701 Wainstead Av Cleveland OH 44111

CASON, CLEO STARGEL (MRS. CHARLES MONROE CASON, JR.), librarian; b. Dahlonega, Ga., June 24, 1910; d. John Jones and Georgia (Jones) Stargel; student N. Ga. Coll., 1926-28; LL.B., Am. Sch. Law, 1949; postgrad. U. Ala., 1951-53, U. Chgo., 1954-55; m. Charles Monroe Cason, Jr., May 8, 1930; 1 son, Charles Monroe III. Adminstrv. asst. to comdr. Redstone Arsenal, Ala., 1944-47, chief office service br., 1947-49, tech. librarian, 1949—. Recipient Meritorious Civilian award Dept. Army, 1970, Citation of Merit for outstanding service Madison County Ala., 1971. Mem. Spl. Libraries Assn. (pres. Ala. chpt. 1955-56), Southeastern, Ala. (pres. coll., univ. and spl. libraries div. 1959-60) library assns., Bus. and Profl. Women's Club (chpt. pres. 1950-51). Club: Aladdin (pres. 1958, 67) (Huntsville, Ala.). Home: 700 Watts Dr SE Huntsville AL 35801 Office: Redstone Sci Information Center Redstone Arsenal AL 35809

CASON, M. LOUISE, physician; b. Lakeland, Fla., Mar. 26, 1923; d. L. Oscar and Mossie (Turner) Cason; B.S., Fla. State U., 1945; M.D., U. Chgo., 1950. Intern in pediatrics Duke U. Hosp., 1950-51; resident pediatrics Jewish Hosp. of Bklyn., 1951-53; practice medicine specializing in pediatrics, Miami, 1953—; clin. asso. prof. pediatrics U. Miami Sch. of Medicine, 1961—; chief dept. pediatrics Variety Children's Hosp., 1958-71, pres. med. bd., 1971—; attending pediatrician Jackson Meml. Hosp., Variety Children's Hosp.; cons. pediatrician to Children's Service Bur., Cath. Welfare Bur. Mem. Am., So., Fla., Dade County med. assns., Miami Pediatric Soc., Fla. Pediatric Soc. Diplomate Am. Bd. Pediatrics. Fellow Am. Acad. Pediatrics. Episcopalian. Office: 3041 Grand Av Miami FL 33133

CASON, MARILYNN JEAN, lawyer; b. Denver, May 18, 1943; d. Eugene Martin and Evelyn Lucille (Clark) Cason; B.A., Stanford, 1965; J.D., U. Mich., 1969. Admitted to Colo. bar, 1969, Ill. bar, 1973; legal asst. Office Econ. Opportunity, Office of Inspection, Washington, summers 1967, 68; community counselor Urban League Colo., Denver, 1966; asso. firm Dawson, Nagel, Sherman & Howard, Denver, 1969-73; atty. law dept. Kraftco Corp., 1973—. Mem. Am., Ill., Chgo. bar assns., Stanford Alumni Assn. (dir.). Club: Chgo. Stanford (dir. 1973—). Home: 1702 Dempster St Evanston IL 60202 Office: Kraftco Ct Glenview IL 60025

CASPER, DOROTHY ANNE (MRS. KARL RAYMOND CASPER), realtor; b. Bridger, Mont., Apr. 7, 1916; d. George Allen and Dora (Kaiser) Huffman; grad. pub. high sch.; m. Roy Ernest Mulherin, Jan. 1934 (div. Oct. 1941); m. 2d, Raymond Arthur Sunkes, Feb. 1948 (div. June 1962); m. 3d, Karl Raymond Casper, Sept. 22, 1967; 1 dau., Barbara (Mrs. Gerald Wayne Baker). Cost accountant Myers Bros. Gen. Contractors, Los Angeles, 1940-50; partner Gradex Inc., Glendale, Cal., 1956-61; broker firm Jack Holt Realty, Glendale, 1962-72; broker firm Maurice C. Walters, 1972—; mem. Glendale Co-ordinating Council, 1970—, pres.'s adv. council all orgns., 1970—, Women's Civic League Glendale, 1970—, Glendale Beautiful Com., 1970—; chmn. Glendale Casa Adobe deSan Rafael Historic Landmark Com., 1972—; mem. Hear Found., Glendale, Meml. Hosp. Guild. Mem. Glendale Bd. Realtors, Nat. Assn. Real Estate Bds. (pres. Glendale women's council), Glendale Bus. and Profl. Women's Assn. (financial sec. 1971-72, 2d v.p. 1973—). Republican. Methodist. Moose. Home: 1225 Dorothy Dr Glendale CA 91202 Office: 1115 N Brand Blvd Glendale CA 91202

CASS, PHYLLIS JEAN, editor; b. Houston, Dec. 18, 1920; d. Neff Smith and Audrey Mae (Dayger) Cass; B.A., U. Tulsa, 1942. Army insp. ordnance Dickson Gun Plant, Houston, 1941-45; mfg. chemist Crowe Labs., Tulsa, 1946-47; chemist Midwest Rubber Reclaiming Co., East St. Louis, Ill., 1948-68, chief chemist Paramount (Cal.) plant, 1954-68; staff chemist Materials R & D, Inc., Oakland, Cal., 1968-73, tech. editor, 1969-73; editor Rubber Formulary, El Cerrito, Cal., 1973—. Compounding cons.; rubber-testing technician; cons., tech. writer, illustrator. Bd. dirs. Heart Assn., Downey, Cal., 1965. Recipient commendation meritorious civilian service War Dept., 1945. Mem. Am. Chem. Soc., A.A.A.S., No. Cal. Rubber Group (dir. 1973, sec. 1974), Cal. Fedn. Chaparral Poets, Cal. Writers (asso.). Home: 2729 Arlington Blvd El Cerrito CA 94530 Office: PO Box 570 El Cerrito CA 94530

CASS, ROSEMARY HIGGINS (MRS. PETER JOHN CASS), lawyer, sociologist; b. Orange, N.J., May 4, 1929; d. Michael Harold and Rose (Adrian) Higgins; student Trinity Coll., 1946-48; A.B., Coll. St. Elizabeth, 1950; LL.B., Columbia, 1953; Ph.D., Fordham U., 1964; m. Peter John Cass, June 12, 1954; children—Colleen Mary, John Michael. Case worker Cath. Charities N.Y.C., 1953-54; admitted to N.Y. bar, 1954, N.J., 1955; law clk., then asso. Joyce & Brown, Bloomfield, N.J., 1954-56; guidance dir. Mt. Saint Dominic Acad., Caldwell, N.J., 1956-58; practice law, N.Y.C. and Bloomfield, N.J., 1956—; mem. Cass & Cass. Dir. Liboak Realty Co., Marr Realty Co., Marr Agy., bd. mgrs. Bloomfield Savs. Bank, 1971—. Adj. prof. Seton Hall U., 1966-71; lectr. in law Katherine Gibbs Sch., 1966-69. Adv. com. internat. orgns. U.S. State Dept., 1972—; mem. legislative com. N.Y. State Commn. on Rights Women, 1972—. Active A.R.C.; bd. dirs. Jr. League, 1956-57; mem.-at-large Nat. Social Welfare Assembly, 1964-68; mem. Gov.'s Divorce Com., 1968-70; bd. dirs. League for Family Service of Bloomfield and Glen Ridge, 1961—, pres., 1970-72; bd. dirs., sec. Nat. Assembly for Social Policy and Devel., 1968-69, pres., 1971-74; bd. dirs. Mountainside Hosp., 1974—, Nat. Center Vol. Action, 1974—; trustee Nat. Council on Philanthropy, 1973—. Recipient Marian award Caldwell College, 1961, Mother Xavier award Coll. St. Elizabeth, 1968. Mem. Internat. Fedn. Cath. Alumnae (nat. chmn. internat. relations com. 1958, N.J. chmn. edn. dept. 1958-61), World Fedn. Cath. Youth (cons. to ECOSOC, 1957-59, chief cons. 1959—, U.S. rep. to exec. com., v.p.), Newark Archdiocesan Council Cath. Women (parliamentarian 1957-62). Am. Bar Assn., Am., Am. Cath. sociol. assns., Alumnae Assn. Coll. St. Elizabeth, N.J. State Bar Assn. (chmn. internat. law sect. 1965-68, chmn. world peace through law com. 1968—, chmn. women's rights com. 1972—). Roman Catholic (mem. archdiocesan pastoral council, Newark 1969-73). Home and office: 53 Park Pl Bloomfield NJ 07003 Office: 200 Park Av New York City NY 10017

CASS, RUTH CLAIRE MARX (MRS. MILLARD CASS), artist; b. Norfolk, Va., Sept. 1, 1923; d. Edward and Augusta (Ehrlich) Marx; student (DuPont Art Study scholar) Art Students League N.Y., 1941, student monitorship, 1942; pupil George Bridgman, 1941-42, Robert Brackman, 1941-42, William McNulty, 1942; m. Millard Cass, July 19, 1943; children—Sandra (Mrs. Jeffrey A. Burt), Ronald Andrew, Pamela Celeste. Exhibited in one man shows at Chevy Chase (Md.) Library, 1964, 65, 66, Roth's Theatre, Silver Spring, Md., others; exhibited in group shows at Norfolk Art Center, Norfolk Mus. Arts, Showcase of Art, Silver Spring, Rockville (Md.) Civic Center, Rockville Art League Gallery; represented in permanent collections; instr. Abbott Art Sch., Washington, 1944-45; instr. Golden Age Art Classes, Chevy Chase, also Washington, 1964—; Affiliated with Town Center Gallery, Rockville, Md., Island Art Gallery, Manteo, N.C. tchr. pvt. art students, 1963—; judge art exhibits, 1968—. Mem. art study group, curriculum study com. Montgomery County Schs., Md., 1960-61; mem. community adv. com. conf. Montgomery Jr. Coll., steering com. Montgomery County Arts Council, 1968. Mem. exec. com. P.T.A., Silver Spring, 1958-61; leader, chmn. troop com. Girl Scouts Am., Silver Spring, 1962-64. Recipient numerous prizes art shows, Montgomery County. Mem. Montgomery County Art Assn. (award 1966; pres. 1966-68, exec. com. 1968—), Rockville Art League, Art Students League N.Y., Artists Equity Assn. Home: 2103 Plyers Mill RD Silver Spring MD 20902

CASSADY, JANET CLAIRE (MRS. CLAUDE F. CASSADY), educator, statistician; b. Cin., Mar. 13, 1924; d. Cyril Otis and Ethel Andrews (Ahrendts) Pancoast; A.B., Fla. State U., 1945; postgrad. Nat. Inst. Pub. Affairs, 1945-46, N.M. State U., 1955-57; M.S., Cornell U., 1962; m. Claude F. Cassady, June 21, 1948 (dec. 1963); children—Sheila (Mrs. Roger E. Hollenbaugh), Justine (Mrs. Steven B. Binion). With U. Miami (Fla.) Sch. Medicine, 1963—, asst. prof., 1973—. Bd. dirs. Fla. Lung Assn.; bd. dirs. Dade-Monroe Lung Assn., 1969—, sec., 1973—. Mem. Am., Fla. pub. health assns., Biometric Soc., Phi Beta Kappa. Office: PO Box 875 Biscayne Annex Miami FL 33152

CASSARA, BEVERLY BENNER (MRS. ERNEST CASSARA), educator; b. Hanover, Mass., Aug. 2, 1922; d. Guy Percy and Julia Caroline (Whitney) Benner; A.B., Colby Coll., 1947; M.Ed., Bridgewater State Coll., 1954; postgrad. Cambridge (Eng.) U., 1962-63; Ed.D., Boston U., 1970; m. Ernest Cassara, Feb. 7, 1949; children—Shirley, Catherine, Nicholas. News editor WBET radio, Brockton, Mass., 1947-48; coordinator Billings lectureship, Unitarian Universalist Assn., Boston, 1964-66; dir. adult edn. Goddard Coll., Plainfield, Vt., 1966-70; asso. prof. adult edn. Federal City Coll., Washington, 1970—, acting dean Grad. Sch., 1973—, acting dir. Inst. Continuing Edn. Women, 1972—. Chmn., Vt. Commn. Status of Women, 1969-70; cons. Center Continuing Edn. U. Va., 1971-73. Pres., S.E. Fairfax Civic Assn., 1974—. Recipient Distinctive Service award Vt. Council Social Studies, 1968; featured TV program A Woman Is. Mem. Am. Soc. Tng. and Devel., Greater Washington Adult Edn. Assn. Nat. Commn. Profs. Adult Edn. (exec. com. 1973—), Women's Equity Action League, Adult Edn. Assn. Va. (regional coordinator 1972-73), Nat. Assn. Black Adult Educators, Adult Edn. Assn. U.S. (chmn. commn. status of women in adult edn., 1971-73, chmn. publs. com. 1973—). Editor: American Women—The Changing Image, 1962. Contbr. book revs. to mags. Home: 10421 Courthouse Dr Fairfax VA 22030 Office: Grad Sch Federal City College 724 9th St NW Washington DC 20001

CASSEDY, JANE, city ofcl.; b. Washington, Mar.9, 1916; d. John Irvin and Stephana (Prager) Cassedy; B.A., Mills Coll., 1937, M.A., 1948; Dr. Criminology, U. Cal. at Berkeley, 1970. Clin. psychologist San Francisco Juvenile Ct., 1950-54, probation officer, 1954-60, supervising clin. psychologist, 1960-63, asst. chief probation officer, 1963—. Bd. dirs. Central YMCA, San Francisco, Chinatown Youth Service Center, Child Abuse Council, San Francisco. Served to lt., USNR, 1943-47. Mem. Am. Psychol. Assn., Nat. Council on Crime and Delinquency, Mental Health Assn., Ret. Officers Assn., San Francisco Mills Coll. Club (pres. 1972-73). Democrat. Episcopalian. Home: 243 Molimo Dr San Francisco CA 94127 Office: 375 Woodside Av San Francisco CA 94127

CASSELBERRY, MARGARET JANE (MRS. LEONARD CASSELBERRY), newspaper editor; b. Winter Park, Fla., Feb. 12, 1925; d. Harvey Shannon and Bertha May (Williams) Williams; student Rollins Coll., 1943-44; m. Leonard Casselberry, June 9, 1944; children—Daniel Leonard, Richard Shannon, Melenda (Mrs. Patrick Edmiston), Catherine Lee. Reporter, photographer Sanford (Fla.) Herald, 1961-69, editor county and church, 1969—. Vol. Youth Programs, Inc. Bd. dirs. Outlook, Longwood, Fla., 1971-72. Republican. Methodist. Home: Box 355 Casselberry FL 32707 Office: 300 N French Av Sanford FL 32771

CASSELL, JEANNE TAYLOR (MRS. WILLIAM C. CASSELL), coll. adminstr.; b. Salinas, Cal., June 21, 1932; d. George Harvey and Hazel Henrietta (Osborn) Taylor; B.A., Pomona Coll., 1954; M.A. (Rosenberg fellow), Stanford, 1965; m. William C. Cassell, Dec. 27, 1955; children—Paul, Susan, David. Tchr. English, Upland (Cal.) High Sch., 1955-56; program asst. Claremont Coll. Center for Continuing Edn., 1965-66; asst. coordinator student activities, lectr. English and behavioral studies, asst. dir. admissions and records Arapahoe Community Coll., Littleton, Colo., 1971-74. Coordinator, Womens Resource Center, Colo. Commn. on Status Women. Mem. Am. Assn. U. Women (pres. Claremont br. 1964-65), Nat. Assn. Women Deans and Counselors, Arapahoe County League Women Voters, Mortar Bd., Phi Beta Kappa. Presbyn.

CASSELL, MARGUERITE ELLEN FLETCHER (MRS. FRANK H. CASSELL), civic worker; b. Crawfordsville, Ind., Apr. 18, 1918; d. Russell and Marguerite (Watts) Fletcher; student Butler U., 1936-39, Ind. U., 1942-43, Am. U., 1967-68, Mundelein Coll., 1973-74; m. Frank H. Cassell, Mar. 24, 1940; children—Frank Allan, Thomas Watts, Christopher. Social worker Welfare Dept., Montgomery County, Ind. Mem. Nat. Democratic Womens' Club. Mem. Nat. Council Negro Women (life), United World Federalists, League Women Voters, Northwestern U. Circle (pres. 1974-75). Conglist. Home: 128 Church St Winnetka IL 60093

CASSELL, SYLVIA, author, child clin. psychologist; b. Evanston, Ill., Apr. 29, 1924; d. Martin L. and Sylvia (Schafer) Cassell; B.A., Wellesley Coll., 1946; M.S., U. Wis., 1948; M.A., Northwestern U., 1961, Ph.D., 1963. Recreation leader Winnetka Community House, also phys. edn. instr. Winnetka Pub. Schs., 1946-47; condr. The Craft Shop with Sue Cassell, WBKB-TV, 1948; exec. dir. Winnetka Girl Scout Council, 1949-51; dir. field staff, research dept. Young & Rubicam, 1951-53; reporter and feature writer Chgo. Tribune, 1953-57; child clinic psychologist Children's Meml. Hosp., 1961-64; instr. dept. pediatric medicine U. Ill. Coll. Medicine, 1964-65, Northwestern U. Med. Sch., 1966—; research psychologist VA Research Hosp., Chgo., 1966-70; clin. asso. Chgo. Med. Sch., 1970—; practice psychology, 1970—. Mem. Am., Midwestern, Ill. psychol. assns., Soc. Midland Authors, Theta Sigma Phi, Pi Lambda Theta, Delta Gamma. Clubs: The Arts of Chicago, The Chicago Wellesley. Author: Fun with Puppets, 1956; Nature Games and Activities, 1956; Backyard Games and Activities, 1958; Fun Together, 1958; Indoor Games and Activities, 1960. Home: 1350 Lake Shore Dr Chicago IL 60610 Office: 185 N Wabash Av Chicago IL 60610

CASSEY, MARTHA MAE FOWLER (MRS. PHILIP THOMPSON CASSEY), realtor; b. Smithland, Ky., Mar. 3, 1902; d. Christopher and Luella (Parker) Fowler; student Bell's Bus. Coll., 1918, Burchett Beauty Coll., 1924, U. Mich. Extension, 1949, 50, 63; m. Philip Thompson Cassey, June 26, 1939. Sec. to Dr. Charles Isabell, Paducah, Ky., 1918, to Atty. Egelster, Paducah, 1919; beauty operator, Detroit, 1924-42; co-owner, mgr., saleswomen Phil-Marth Realty Co., Detroit, 1946—. Founder, pres. Mich. Women Civic Council, Detroit, 1951; vol. Torch Drive, 1954-69. Del., county Democratic conv., 1948. Bd. mgrs. Phyllis Wheatley Home, Detroit, 1954-65. Recipient United Found. Torch Drive award, 1969. Mem. Nat. Assn. Real Estate Bds. (women's council), Detroit Real Estate Bd., Detroit Real Estate Brokers (chmn. membership, 1962-64), NAACP. Episcopalian. Home: 3081 Oakman Blvd Detroit MI 48238 Office: 10332 Woodward Av Detroit MI 48202

CASSIDY, ESTHER BROOKE CHRISTMAS (MRS. BERTRAND J. CASSIDY), physicist; b. Washington, Aug. 5, 1933; d. Donelson and Esther Hill (Brooke) Christmas; B.A. (Mother Dammann scholar 1951-55), Manhattanville Coll., 1955; postgrad. U. Md., U. Toronto, RCA Inst.; m. Bertrand J. Cassidy, Sept. 8, 1956; children—William Keeling, Eleanor Carroll, Daniel Clark. Physicist, Nat. Bur. Standards, U.S. Dept. Commerce, Washington, 1955—, with high voltage lab., electricity div., 1966—; pres. Folas Enterprises, Inc., 1963-67. Nat. Bur. Standards rep. Fed. Women's Program Com., 1970-72. Commerce-Sci. fellow, 1973-74. Mem. I.E.E.E. (sr.), Am. Phys. Soc., Electrostatics Soc. Am., Pilgrims of St. Marys, Nat. Soc. Colonial Dames Am. Contbr. articles to profl. jours. Patentee in field. Home: 3 E Kirke St Chevy Chase MD 20015 Office: Nat Bur Standards Washington DC 20234

CASSIDY, JUANITA NEWTON HARRIS (MRS. LEWIS C. CASSIDY), lawyer; b. Newtonville, S.C.; d. Giles Preston and Jessie Lee (Moore) Newton; student Wingate Coll., 1913-15, Ph.D. (hon.), 1960; student Duke, 1915-16; J.D., George Washington U., 1941; m. Everett Grant Harris, Apr. 14, 1918 (dec.); children—Everett Grant, Charles Giles, Newton Nolen (dec.); m. 2d, Lewis Cochran Cassidy, July 8, 1943 (dec. Feb. 1949). Admitted to Mont. bar, 1941; atty., counsellor Supreme Ct. of Mont., 1941—, U.S. Supreme Ct., 1952—. Gray lady A.R.C. Recipient Certificate of Alumni Achievement, Wingate Coll., 1960. Mem. Gold Star Wives Am. (past nat. parliamentarian), U.D.C. (past state and chpt. historian), Mont. Bar Assn., D.A.R., Am. Legion Aux., Gen. Fedn. Women's Clubs, Mont. State Soc., Ia. State Soc., Va. Hist. Soc., D.C. Hist. Soc., Soc. Magna Charta Dames, English-Speaking Union, U.S. Capitol Hist. Soc. (hon. life), Daus. Brit. Empire, George Washington University Club (charter mem.), Ams. Royal Descent, Colonial Order of Crown, Internat. Platform Assn., Newton Reunion Assn., Order Eastern Star, Kappa Beta Pi (life). Clubs: Woman's (past co-chmn. bridge, chaplain Lyon Village), Fort Meyer Officers (Arlington, Va.); Naval Officers (Bethesda, Md.). Home: 3137 Key Blvd Arlington VA 22201

CASSIDY, MARY BARBARA (MARIBEE) (MRS. GEORGE R. CASSIDY), journalist; b. Leadville, Colo., Aug. 22, 1914; d. Nicholas and Barbara (Rogina) Frankovich; diploma in stenotypy and bus. English, La Salle Extension U., 1942; m. Joseph George Bost, Sept. 26, 1933 (dec. Oct. 1939); children—Barbara M., Joseph A.; m. 2d, George R. Cassidy, June 4, 1947. Clk., reporter Lake County Ct., 1941-43; railroad cashier, steno-clk., reporter for railroad mag. Green Light, 1943—. Columnist Leadville Herald Democrat, 1958-68, feature writer, 1958—; owner personal mus. of Leadville artifacts, 1964—, theatre based on Leadville history with old-fashioned ice cream parlor, 1970—; established summer theatre to portray Leadville history; tchr. machine shorthand Colo. Mountain Coll., 1971—. Reporter, Lake County Democratic Central Com., 1968—, sec., 1967-69. Mem. Lake County Arts and Humanities (asso.), Smithsonian Instn., Internat. Platform Assn., Am. Hist. Soc. Leadville C. of C. (corr. sec. 1970—). Clubs: Jane Jefferson (sec.), Railroad Veterans (sec.). Author: St. Joseph's Church and Parish, 1973. Home: 129 W 4th St Box 911 Leadville CO 80461

CASSIDY, SISTER MARY BRIGH, hosp. adminstn. cons.; b. Eyota, Minn., 1906; d. Timothy M. and Brigid (Maroney) Cassidy; B.S. in Nursing, Coll. St. Teresa Winona, Minn., 1940; M.S. in Nursing Edn., Cath. U. Am., 1942; M.B.A. in Hosp. Adminstrn., U. Chgo., 1949. R.N., St. Mary's Sch. Nursing, Rochester, Minn., 1928. Experience in private duty, staff nursing, supervision, Rochester, Minn., and Chgo., 1928-38; entered Sisters of St. Francis, Rochester, 1938; instr. St. Mary's Sch. Nursing, Rochester, 1939-45; personnel dir. St. Mary's Hosp., Rochester, 1945-47, adminstr. hosp., 1949-71, cons., 1971—. Chmn. Bldg. Commns. for a 7,000,000 and 6,000,000 hosp. bldg. project, Rochester, 1954—. Active various coms. Rochester Community Fund, 1960-65. Bd. dirs. Coll. St. Teresa, Winona, Minn., 1955—; mem. gen. counsel Sisters of 3d Order Regular of St. Francis, 1955-70. Recipient Teresa of Avila award Coll. St. Teresa, 1965. Fellow Am. Coll. Hosp. Adminstrs.; mem. Am. Hosp. Assn. (mem. council on profl. practice 1960-63, council on adminstrn. 1955-58, del. 1971—), Minn. (v.p. 1965; pres. 1969), Cath. (treas. 1960-64; pres. 1967-68) hosp. assns. Home: Saint Mary's Hosp Rochester MN 55901

CASSIN, BARBARA MACSWAIN JONES, civic worker; b. San Francisco, Dec. 17, 1919; d. Herbert C. and Elizabeth Anne (MacSwain) Jones; A.B., San Jose State U., 1941; children—Colleen M., Craig A. Med. lab. technician San Francisco City and County Pub. Health Dept. Labs., 1942-45, San Jose (Cal.) Clin. Labs., 1946-47; tchr. watercolor painting San Jose Met. Adult Edn. Program, 1960-66. Sec., Jr. League San Jose, Inc., 1950-51; sec. San Jose Art League, 1956-57; founding pres. Fine Arts Gallery Assn. San Jose, 1968-70; mem. exec. com. Citizen's Community Improvement Com., 1970—; founding pres. Council Arts, Greater San Jose area, 1971—; mem. San Jose Bicentennial Commn., 1973—; mem. Model Cities of San Jose, Inc., 1972-74. Bd. dirs. Sempervirens Fund. Mem. P.E.O., Alpha Phi. Democrat. Conglist. Home: 2367 Newhall St San Jose CA 95128

CASSTEVENS, MARILYN TERESE, psychologist, ednl. adminstr.; b. San Diego, Dec. 4, 1927; d. Francis and Florence Ruth (Carl) Casstevens; A.A., Sacramento City Coll., 1946; B.A. with honors, Cal. State U. at San Jose, 1948; M.A., Cal. State U. at Sacramento, 1962; Ph.D., Ariz. State U., 1969. Dept. chmn. girls' phys. edn. Turlock (Cal.) High Sch., 1948-57; high sch. counseling dept. chmn. San Juan Unified Sch. Dist., Carmichael, Cal., 1957-63, dist. counseling program specialist, 1963-68, dir. pupil personnel services, 1968-71, psychologist, 1971—. Pvt. practice as psychologist, marriage, family and child counseling, Sacramento, Cal., 1972—. Bd. dirs. Sacramento (Cal.) Tchrs. Credit Union, 1965-66. Mem. Am. Psychol. Assn., Cal. Tchrs. Assn., N.E.A., Sacramento Area Personnel and Guidance Assn. (pres. 1967-68). Home: 4161 Garden Hwy Sacramento CA 95834 Office: 3738 Walnut Av Carmichael CA 95608

CASTLE, EVA SKYTTE (MRS. TONY BRITTON), sculptor; b. Aarhus, Denmark, Dec. 6, 1922; d. Knud Skytte and Olga (Johnsen) Birkefeldt; Bealeksamen, Marselisborg Sch., Aarhus, 1940; student Royal Acad. Fine Arts, Copenhagen, 1945-47, Slade Sch. Art, London, 1947-49; m. Tony Britton, May 28, 1962; 1 son, Jasper Leslie. One-man show Peter Hyde Gallery, London, 1968; exhibited in group shows Royal Acad., 1951—, Royal Inst., Nat. Soc., Contemporary Arts Soc., Royal Watercolor Soc., Guild Hall, Festival Hall, St. James's Palace. Fellow Royal Brit. Soc. Sculptors, Soc. Portrait Sculptors (founding); mem. Soc. Women Artists, Chelsea Arts Club. Address: 39 Limerston St London SW 10 England

CASTLE, GLORIA FARTHING (MRS. RICHARD BRISTER CASTLE), pediatrician; b. Los Angeles, Mar. 10, 1931; d. James Edgar and Amy Leona (Huffman) Farthing; student Pacific Union Coll., 1947-50; A.B. in Chemistry, U. Pacific, 1951; M.D., U. So. Cal., 1958; m. Richard Brister Castle, Sept. 13, 1959; children—Gregory, Kelly Alison, John Richard. Lab. asst. Dow Chem. Co., Pittsburg, Cal., 1951-53; intern Childrens Hosp. Los Angeles, 1958-59, resident in pediatrics, 1959-60, fellow in adolescent medicine, 1967-69, attending physician, also dir. ambulatory care, div. adolescent medicine, 1970—; sch. physician Montebello (Cal.) Unified Sch. Dist., 1960-67, 70—. Bloomfield Sch. Dist., Hawaiian Gardens, Cal., 1960-67, Alhambra (Cal.) City Schs., 1964-65; mem. staff Adolescent Clinic, Telfair P.T.A. Clinic, Pacoima, Cal., 1968—; instr. adolescent medicine and pediatrics U. So. Cal. Sch. Medicine, 1969—. Mem. adv. council for early childhood edn. Glendale Unified Sch. Dist. Fellow Royal Soc. Health; mem. Los Angeles Pediatric Soc., Soc. for Adolescent Medicine (editor newsletter 1973—), Los Angeles Opera Assos., Gamma Phi Beta (pres. Glendale alumnae chpt. 1964-65). Home: 1411 Thurlene Rd Glendale CA 91206 Office: Childrens Hosp of Los Angeles Div Adolescent Medicine 4650 Sunset Blvd Los Angeles CA 90027

CASTLES, VIRGINIA MARY, counseling psychologist, educator; b. Lowell, Mass., July 26, 1932; d. Frederick Stephen and Amelia (Pond) Castles; B.S. in Edn., Lowell State Coll., 1954; M.Ed., Boston Coll., 1959, certificate Advanced Ednl. Specialization, 1970. Tchr. pub. schs., Chelmsford, Mass., 1954-60, Woburn, Mass., 1960-62, Salisbury, Mass., 1963, Andover, Mass., 1968; dir. admissions St. John Coll., Cleve., 1963-65; counselor women, instr. psychology Quinsigamond Community Coll., Worcester, Mass., 1965-66; elementary sch. guidance counselor, Haverhill, Mass., 1966-68; social worker Head Start Program, Haverhill, summer 1967; guidance cons. St. Bernard's Sch., West Newton, Mass., 1969-71; dir. student guidance St. Elizabeth's Hosp. Sch. Nursing, Brighton, Mass., 1970—. Mem. Newton Youth Commn. Mem. Am., Mass. psychol. assns., Am., Nat., Mass., Greater Boston personnel and guidance assns., Nat. Vocational Guidance Assn., Am., Mass. sch. counselors assns., N.E.A., Mass. Tchrs. Assn., Newton Mental Health Assn. (dir.; mem. exec. com.). Democrat. Home: Apt 4 280 Grove St Newton MA 02166 Office: 235 Washington St Brighton MA 02135

CASTOR, JANE COLKETT (MRS. CECIL DANIEL CASTOR), psychiat. social worker; b. Raymond, Wash., May 26, 1913; d. Emery Engle and Orletta (Yoho) Colkett; B.A., U. Wash., 1939; M.S.W., U. Cal. at Berkeley, 1950; m. Cecil Daniel Castor, Nov. 18, 1933. Social worker U.S. Mcht. Marine, 1943-47, Jewish Refugees, Shanghai, China, 1948-51; USPHS cons. San Francisco County Health Dept., 1951-53; social worker Cerebral Palsy Research Project, U. Cal. Med. Center at San Francisco, 1955-60, Langley Porter Neuropsychiat. Inst., 1960—, lectr. psychiat. social work dept. psychiatry, 1967—. Mem. Am. Civil Liberties Union, Acad. Certified Social Workers, Nat. Assn. Social Workers, Sierra Club, Phi Beta Phi. Democrat. Contbr. articles to profl. jours. Home: 2081 Eunice St Berkeley CA 94709 Office: 401 Parnassus Av San Francisco CA 94122

CASTRO, THERESA MARIE BARABAS (MRS. BERNARD CASTRO), bus. exec., civic worker; b. Pitts., Feb. 15, 1917; d. Andrew and Terez (Koronich) Barabas; grad. high sch.; H.H.D., Fla. Inst. Tech., 1973; m. Bernard Castro, Feb. 14, 1942; children—Bernadette (Mrs. David Frederick Austin), Bernard. Exec. v.p., sec. Castro Convertibles, New Hyde Park, L.I., N.Y., 1948—; v.p. Castro Realty Corp., Ocala, Fla., 1951—, Nostra Mfg. Corp., New Hyde Park, 1957—; exec. v.p. Teleradio Corp., N.Y.C., 1964—; dir. Nat. Life Fla. Co., Jacksonville, Central Sci. Mag., Ocala; founder, dir. Fort Lauderdale Pictorial Life Mag. Founder, Royal Dames Nova, 1969, Snowflake Ball, 1961, Derby Ball, 1966; organizer 1st ann. Marymount Coll. Charity Horse Show, Boca Raton, Fla., 1966; grand chmn., constructor non-sectarian chapel on campus Fla. Sch. for Deaf and Blind, 1969; introducer Big Hearts for New Hope, 1968, grand chmn., 1967-68; mem., dir. Oral Sch. Aux., Fort Lauderdale, Fla., 1961—; mem. Holy Cross Hosp. Women's Aux., Fort Lauderdale, 1956; mem. Lauderdale Beach Hosp. Aux., 1960; dir., benefactor Fort Lauderdale Symphony Soc., 1956; mem., benefactor Ft. Lauderdale Opera Guild, 1963; organizer Ocala Ann. Debutante Ball, 1970. Trustee Fla. Sch. for Deaf and Blind, St. Augustine; founder, pres., chmn. bd. Golden Hills Acad., Ocala, Fla., 1964; founder, chmn. bd. Montessori Sch. Golden Hills, Ocala, 1969. Recipient Appreciation awards Fla. Newspaper Advt. Execs. Assn., 1968, U.S. C.E., 1963, State of Fla., Council of 100, 1961, Humanitarian Women of Year award, 1971, Nat. Heart Fund Outstanding Achievement award, 1972. Mem. Ladies of Charity Cath. Diocese in N.Y., Equestrian Order of Holy Sepulchre of Jerusalem. Clubs: Golden Hills Turf and Country (founder 1964 Ocala); Coral Ridge Country, Le Club Internationale (founder Ft. Lauderdale 1968), Coral Ridge Yacht (Fort Lauderdale); Surf Jockey, Palm Bay (Miami, Fla.); New York Athletic (N.Y.C.); Huntington (N.Y.) Yacht; Boca Raton (Fla.); Sedgefield Country (Greenville, N.C.). Home: 296 Southdown Rd Huntington NY 11743 also 2300 N Atlantic Blvd Fort Lauderdale FL 33305 also Box 188 Route 3 Ocala FL 32670 Office: Castro Convertibles 1990 Jericho Turnpike New Hyde Park Long Island NY 11040

CASWELL, DORIS HELEN RAYBURN (MRS. DWIGHT ALLAN CASWELL), artist, writer; b. Long Beach, Cal., Mar. 16, 1923; d. Odis Claude and Helen Marian (Kepner) Rayburn; student U. Ore., 1940-42; m. Dwight Allan Caswell, Dec. 27, 1942; children—Dwight Allan, Philip, Mary (Mrs. Matthew Walsh), Christopher, John. Exhibited art in one-man shows including Gallery Americana, Carmel, Cal., Parks Gallery, San Jose, Cal., Austin Gallery, Santa Barbara, Cal., Gallery Two, Tucson, Galerie de Tours, San Francisco; exhibited in group shows at DeYoung Mus., San Francisco, Soc. Western Artists; represented in pvt. collections; painter portraits; pvt. tchr. Recipient James D. Phelan award for narrative poetry, 1958; award for dramatic monologue San Francisco Browning Soc., 1964. Mem. Soc. Western Artists. Author: Jesus, My Son, 1962; A Wind On the Road, 1964; Shadows from the Singing House, 1968; A New Song for Christmas, 1966; You Are More Wonderful, 1970; Thank You for Being You, 1972, Never Wed An Old Man, 1975. Address: 15095 Fruitvale Av Saratoga CA 95070

CATALANO, KATHLEEN JAMEA FERRARI (MRS. LOUIS W. CATALANO, JR.), pediatrician; b. Jeannette, Pa., Aug. 2, 1938; d. Louis and Lucy Catherine (Vezzetti) Ferrari; B.A. cum laude, Seton Hill Coll., 1959; M.D., Med. Coll. Pa., 1964; m. Louis W. Catalano, Jr., Oct. 1, 1966; children—Louis W. III, Jamea Elizabeth. Intern, Children's Hosp. of Pitts., 1964-65, resident, 1965-66; resident Presbyn.-St. Luke's Hosp., Chgo.; practice medicine specializing in pediatrics, Englewood and Paramus, N.J., 1971—; mem. staff Englewood Hosp.; pediatric cons. Montgomery County Health Dept., Rockville, Md., 1966-68; asst. in pediatrics Babies Hosp., N.Y.C., 1968—, also tchr. Diplomate Am. Bd. Pediatrics. Mem. Am. Acad. Pediatrics, Latrobe Acad. Medicine, Westmoreland County Med. Soc. Home: 314 Debra Dr Latrobe PA 15650 Office: 1100 Ligonier St Latrobe PA 15650

CATALDO, GLORIA MARY, fashion and design cons.; b. New Rochelle, N.Y.; d. Frank A. and Philomena (Creaturo) Cataldo; student Pratt Inst., 1941-42, Grand Central Art Sch., 1942-45. Artist, illustrator combat film detachment U.S. Army Air Force, N.Y.C., 1943-45; free-lance artist, studio mgr. Thompson Assos., 1945-48; fashion stylist Sterling Advt., N.Y.C., 1948-52, fashion coordinator, head photography dept., 1952-58; asso. fashion dir. Doyle-Dane-Bernbach Advt., Agy., Inc., N.Y.C., 1958-64, fashion adminstr., 1964-65, fashion dir., 1965-69, account exec., 1969-71; fashion, design cons., White Plains, N.Y., 1971—. Critic, lectr. Parsons Sch. Design, N.Y.C., 1962—. Mem. Fashion Group Inc., Ursuline Sch. Alumnae Assn. (past pres.), Ladies of Charity. Address: 90 Bryant Av White Plains NY 10605

CATANESE, GEORGIA EDJUENIA CANNON (MRS. FRANK SALVATORE CATANESE), lingerie firm exec.; b. Estelene, Tex., Mar. 3, 1933; d. Hugh Arch and Dorothy L. (Stroud) Cannon; student Sawyer Bus. Coll., 1953; m. Olen Bodine, July 17, 1948 (dec. July 1950); children—Brandy Lynn, Richard H.; m. 2d, Ramon L. Converse, Jan. 21, 1951 (div. Nov. 1953); children—Barbara Karen, Thomas Gene; m. 3d, Frank Salvatore Catanese, Sept. 20, 1958; children—Edmond Dantes, Frank Salvatore. With Fischers Welding & Engring. Co., Venice, Cal., 1953-54, Realty Mart, Culver City, 1955-66; v.p., dir. Conturessa Co., Huntington Beach, 1966—. Active Assn. for Retarded Children. Patentee in field. Home: 10011 Stonybrook Dr Huntington Beach CA 92646 Office: Conturessa Co PO Box 1667 Costa Mesa CA 92626

CATANIA, NANCY (MRS. WILLIAM A. MCDERMOTT), physician; b. Omaha, Apr. 8, 1903; d. Filadelfo and Nell Sebastiana (Garrotto) Catania; B.S., U. Omaha, 1925; M.D., U. Neb., 1926; m. William A. McDermott, Aug. 30, 1958. Intern Lincoln (Neb.) Gen. Hosp., 1926-27, asst. in gross anatomy and gynecology Creighton U. Sch. Medicine, 1928-30, instr. anatomy, asst. in gynecology, 1930-33, instr. anatomy and gynecology, 1933-38, asst. prof. anatomy, instr. gynecology, 1938-42, asst. in phys. diagnosis 1939, asst. in surgery 1949-53, mem. faculty 1953—; practice medicine, Omaha, 1927-72; staff mem. Saint Joseph's Hosp., 1929—, Children's Meml. Hosp., 1948—; med. dir. Supreme Forest Woodmen Circle, 1951-52. Cons. Nat. Lexicographic Bd., Ltd., 1953-58. Mem. A.M.A., Am. Acad. Family Practice, Nat., Omaha (pres. 1952-54) women's med. assns., Am. Assn. U. Women, Omaha C. of C., Neb., Omaha-Douglas County med. socs., Women's Interclub Council, Ak-Sar-Ben, Nu Sigma Phi, Phi Delta Gamma. Home: 401 N 61st St Omaha NE 68132 Office: Med Arts Bldg Omaha NE 68102

CATCHI, CATHERINE CHILDS, artist; b. Phila., Aug. 27, 1920; d. William Henry Harrison and Catherine Stuart (Oeland) Childs; student Briarcliff Jr. Coll., 1937, Comml. Illustration Studios, 1938-39, Paul Wood Studio, 1949-55; studied with Leon Kroll, Harry Sternberg, Hans Hoffman, also in Positano, Italy; m. Charles Everett Willis, Jr., Dec. 23, 1940 (div. Feb. 1958); children—Diane Willis Neuse, Heather Willis Sargent, Charles Everett Willis III, Jeffrey Childs Willis (dec.); m. 2d, Walter Donald Twomey, Nov. 21, 1964 (div. Oct. 1968). Exhibited in group shows at A.C.A. Gallery. Allied Artists, Lever House, Contemporary Arts, Springfield (Mass.) Mus., Royal Birmingham Soc. Artists Galleries, Eng., Conn. Acad. Fine Arts, Knickerbocker Artists, Queens Coll., Arts U.S.A., Royal Acad. Galleries, Edinburgh, Scotland, and others; one-man shows Heckscher Mus., Country Art Gallery, Locust Valley, N.Y., Hofstra U., Alfredo Valente Gallery, N.Y.C., Pepsi Cola Show, Universalist Gallery, Atlanta. Congl. exhbn., Rayburn Hall, Washington, 1968, Spinetti Gallery, Florence, Italy, 1973; represented in many pvt. collections. Mem. art adv. council Port Washington (N.Y.) Library, pres., 1974—. Recipient 1st prizes L.I. Regional Show, Guild Hall, East Hampton, Ligoa Duncan Gallery, 1962, Nat. Assn. Women Artists, 1962; Grumbacher award, 1963; 1st prize L.I. Open and Manhasset Art Assn., 1964, Internat. Platform Assn., 1973, Ligoa Duncan Gallery; Lillian Cotton Meml. award and Medal of Honor Nat. Assn. Women Artists, Irene Sickle Feist Meml. prize, 1971, 2d prize Riverside Mus. others. Mem. Nat. Assn. Women Artists (v.p.), Audubon Artists (treas., dir.), N.Y. Soc. Women Artists (v.p.), Manhasset Art Assn. (pres. 1962-64), Internat. Platform Assn. (art com.), Exec. and Profl. Hall of Fame. Contbr. articles to profl. publs. Address: 2 Grist Mill Rd Plandome Mills Manhasset NY 11030

CATER, KATHARINE C., educator; b. Macon, Ga., Sept. 1, 1914; d. Thomas J. and Maybelle (Moore) Cater; A.B. magna cum laude, Limestone Coll., 1935, Litt.D. (hon.), 1958; M.A., Mercer U., 1938; M.S., Syracuse U., 1942, postgrad., 1945-46. Tchr., Boiling Springs High Sch., Spartanburg, S.C., 1935-37; instr. English and French, Limestone Coll., Gaffney, S.C., 1937-40; dir. student personnel Furman U., Greenville, S.C., 1942-45; dean of women Auburn U., Ala., 1946—. Trustee Auburn Community Chest, 1955-57, Limestone Coll., Gaffney, S.C., 1970—. Mem. Ala. Assn. Women Deans and Advisers (pres. 1947-49), Ala. Edn. Assn., Ala. Guidance Assn. (v.p. 1954-56; treas. 1957-58), Am., So. coll. personnel assns., Am. Personnel and Guidance Assn., Am. Assn. U. Women (br. pres. 1947-49, div. pres. 1954-56), Nat. Assn. Women Deans and Counselors, Assn. Coll. and Univ. Concert Mgrs. (life; mem. exec. bd. 1963-66), Assn. Coll. Honor Socs. (exec. com. 1972-74), Mortar Bd., League Women Voters (state dir. 1965-69), Cwens, P.E.O., Pi Lambda Theta, Kappa Delta Pi, Alpha Lambda Delta (nat. pres. 1970—), Delta Kappa Gamma (chpt. v.p. 1960-62), Phi Kappa Phi (chpt. pres. 1963-64). Democrat. Baptist. Clubs: Garden of Alabama (life), Saugahatchee Country, Alabama Federation Womens, Auburn Campus, Auburn Faculty, Auburn Women's, Auburn Study, Garden Ala. (life). Home: Social Center Auburn U Auburn AL 36830

CATES, FLORINE CRUSE, writer, lectr., composer; b. Alex, Okla., Feb. 10, 1915; d. Joseph Emmitt and Gertrude (Ramsey) Cruse; spl. student Denver U., 1951-52, Columbia, 1957-58, U. Cal. at Los Angeles, 1961-62; m. Herman Garner Cates, Oct. 24, 1931 (div. Jan. 1965); 1 dau., Kay (Mrs. Joseph W. Stevens, Jr.). Pres., owner, art dir. Cates First Av., Exclusive Splty. Shop for Women, Denver, 1954-69, exec. dir., 1965-69; restored historic Chateau Cruse, Ojai, Cal., 1967-70, opened Chateau Cruse hist. tours and ecology center, 1970. Writer, dir., producer art and ednl. films, Seventh Italian High Fashion Show in Florence, 1952, Children of Russia, 1958, Tree of Man Allegory, 1965. Co-founder Internat. House, Denver, 1958, dir., 1958-65, hon. v.p., 1965—. Mem. Los Angeles Fashion Group. Author: (under pen name Regina Cruse-Cates) Daisies do Tell (poetry), 1972; (folk songs) My Soliloquy, 1974. Home: Morningbird care Irene 5910 Torreon Dr Albuquerque NM 87109

CATHCART, MILDRED DOOLEY (MRS. JOHN CARL CATHCART), educator; b. Jerome, Ia., June 28, 1915; d. Ernest Lee and Edith V. (Hughes) Dooley; grad. valedictorian Centerville Jr. Coll., 1933; student Ia. Wesleyan Coll., 1935; B.S. in Edn., Drake U., 1968; m. John Carl Cathcart, Aug. 10, 1940; children—Kerry Lee, Jean Marie. Tchr. elementary sch. Jerome Sch., Jerome, Ia., 1933-41; jr. high tchr. Seymour (Ia.) Community Sch., 1951—. Mem. Gov.'s. Commn. Health and Recreation, 1946-50; co-chmn. Ia. Federated Clubs, 1951-52. Bd. dirs. Appanoose County chpt. A.R.C., 1946-50. Recipient Luke Mallory award for poetry, 1956; named Merit Mother of Ia., 1969. Mem. Internat. Platform Assn., Nat. League Am. Penwomen (state pres. 1958-60), Delta Kappa Gamma. Author: Come Into Our Garden, 1955; Let Us Be Glad, 1955; A King in Bethlehem, 1955; Remember Thy Creator (1st prize in Nat. League Am. Penwomen contest), 1956; Let's Have a Party, 1958; Blessed is our Nation, 1959; God's Gifts, 1960; Life of Jesus, 1960; Year Round Fun, 1960; The Flower of Christmas, 1960. Club: Y.W. Study (pres. 1970, v.p. 1972). Address: Route 3 Centerville IA 52544

CATOE, BEATRICE HAWKINS (MRS. WALTER TRAVIS CATOE), ins. co. exec.; b. Cordell, Okla., Jan. 13, 1920; d. Joseph Ernest and Ella May (Hollingsworth) Hawkins; student St. Louis U., 1941-42; m. Walter Travis Catoe, Mar. 4, 1949; children—Wilton, Betty, Jackie (Mrs. Alford C. Johnson), Carol (Mrs. Cecil V. Elliott). Insp. radar mounts, gun sights Dept. Defense (Navy), Mission Mfg. Co., Houston, 1941-43; sec. personal affairs office Ellington AFB, Houston, 1943-46; legal sec., Houston, 1946; sec. to supt. agys. Am. Nat. Ins. Co., Galveston, Tex., 1947-54, sec. of agys., 1954-69, asst. v.p., sec. agys., 1969—. C.L.U. Mem. Galveston C. of C., Am. Soc. Chartered Life Underwriters. Republican. Baptist (former supt. intermediate dept.). Home: 2611 Av O Galveston TX 77550 Office: 1 Moody Plaza Galveston TX 77550

CATRON, MAY PADGETT (MRS. ROBERT T. CATRON), realtor; b. Atlanta, Mar. 27, 1909; d. Benjamin Robert and Mary Higdon (Andrews) Padgett; grad. high sch.; m. Robert T. Catron, Oct. 14, 1933; children—Mary Jane (Mrs. Tom McGouirk), Elizabeth Elaine (Mrs. Ronald Norton), Joanne (Mrs. Harold Johnson), Robert Tinsley, Benjamin Thomas. Owner, mgr. Catron Realty Co., Decatur, Ga., 1948-69; v.p. Thibadeau Co., realtors, Decatur, 1969—. Pres., DeKalb Grand Jurors Assn., 1974—; chmn. Hist. Com. Avondale Estates, Ga., 1971-73. Mem. DeKalb Bd. Realtors (charter, chmn. hist. com., 1971-72). Baptist. Clubs: Avondale Estates Garden; Pilot (charter, past pres. Decatur). Home: 1501 Clairmont Rd Decatur GA 30033 Office: 1240 Clairmont Av Decatur GA 30030

CATRON, PATRICIA ANNE D'ARCY (MRS. ROBERT F. CATRON), art center adminstr.; b. Memphis, Oct. 19, 1920; d. John Jeremiah and Kathryn (Blalack) D'Arcy; student Memphis Art Acad., 1938, Wittenberg U.; m. Robert F. Catron, June 1, 1946; children—Kathryn Valerie, Anne D'Arcy. Office mgr. Family Service Agy., Springfield, O., 1965-70; mng. dir. Springfield Art Center, 1970-73, dir., 1973—. Pres., Women's Assn. Springfield Symphony, 1957-59, trustee, 1957-60; del. Nat. Symphony Orch. Conv., 1957. Mem. Springfield Art Assn., D.A.R. (vice regent 1972-74, regent 1974-76), Altar Guild. Roman Catholic. Toastmistresses. Home: 2001 Fountain Blvd Springfield OH 45504 Office: 107 Cliff Park Rd PO Box 34 Springfield OH 45501

CATTANACH, NORMA (MRS. GEORGE S. CATTANACH), educator; b. N.Y.C.; d. John and Anne (Hanke) Harvester; A.B., Hunter Coll., 1937; A.M., N.Y.U., 1945, Ph.D., 1948; m. George S. Cattanach, 1972. Tchr., Drew Sem. for Young Women, 1938-43, Islip (N.Y.) High Sch., 1943-45; teaching fellow N.Y. U., 1945-48; instr. Hunter Coll., N.Y.C., 1948-56; prof. philosophy dept. edn. Adelphi U., Garden City, N.Y., 1956—, travel award as supr. fgn. study program, summer 1967, actress Summer Theatre Workshop. Author: Revolt Against Nature, Issues in Modern Art, 1972. Contbr. articles to profl. jours. Home: 200 E 66th St New York City NY 10021 Office: Dept Edn Adelphi U Garden City NY 11530

CATTANI, MARYELLEN BILLETTE, lawyer; b. Bakersfield, Cal., Dec. 1, 1943; d. Arnold Theodore and Corinne Marilyn (Kovacevich) Cattani; A.B., Vassar Coll., 1965; J.D., U. Cal. at Berkeley, 1968. Admitted to N.Y. bar, 1969, Cal. bar, 1969; asso. firm Davis Polk & Wardwell, N.Y.C., 1968-69, Orrick, Herrington, Rowley & Sutcliffe, San Francisco, 1970—. Adj. prof. Cal. Pub. Interest Law Center, Lone Mountain Coll., San Francisco, 1973—, also mem. legal analysis program bd. Mem. State Bar Cal., Bar Assn. San Francisco, San Francisco Barristers Club (com. on sex discrimination). Home: 1769 Spruce St Berkeley CA 94709 Office: 600 Montgomery St San Francisco CA 94104

CATTERTON, MARIANNE ROSE MAAS (MRS. ROBERT LEE CATTERTON), occupational therapist; b. St. Paul, Feb. 3, 1922; d. Melvin Joseph (dec.) and Catherine Marian (Bole) Maas; student Carleton Coll., 1939-41, U. Md., 1941-42; B.A., U. Wis., 1944; certificate occupational therapy Phila. Sch. Occupational Therapy, 1946; m. Robert Lee Catterton, Nov. 20, 1951; children—Jenifer Ann, Cynthia Lea. Occupational therapist VA, N.Y.C., 1946-50; cons. occupational therapist Fondo del Seguro del Estado, P.R., 1950-51; dir. rehab. therapies Spring Grove State Hosp., Catonsville, Md., 1953-56; editor Am. Jour. Occupational Therapy, Annapolis, Md., 1962-67; occupational therapist Anne Arundel County Health Dept., Annapolis, 1967—. Instr. tech. writing Anne Arundel Community Coll., Arnold, Md., 1974—. Chmn., Anne Arundel Gov.'s Com. Employment Handicapped, Annapolis, 1959-65. Bd. dirs. Anne Arundel chpt. Nat. Found., 1961-68. Mem. Am. (chmn. com. 1958-61), Md. occupational therapy assns., Delta Delta Delta. Unitarian (mem. com. 1962). Clubs: Severn (treas. 1965), International (Annapolis). Home: Kirkley Rd Annapolis MD 21401 Office: 3 Broadcreek Pkwy Annapolis MD 21401

CATTS, ANN BARBARA, physician; b. Elizabeth, N.J., Aug. 9, 1931; d. Elmer Paul and Helen (Gleason) Catts; B.A., U. Del., 1952; M.D., Woman's Med. Coll. Pa., 1956. Intern, Queens Hosp., Honolulu, 1956-57, resident pathology, 1958-61, 61-62, asst. pathologist, 1962-64, acting dir. labs., 1964-65, asso. pathologist, 1965—; resident Wilmington (Del.) Gen. Hosp., 1957-58; resident pediatric pathology St. Christopher's Hosp. for Children, Phila., 1961; practice medicine specializing in pathology, Honolulu, 1962—; mem. staff Queens Med. Center, Honolulu. Mem. A.M.A., Coll. Am. Pathologists, Am. Soc. Clin. Pathologists, Hawaii Med. Assn., Internat. Acad. Pathology, Am. Cytology Soc., Honolulu County Med. Soc. (treas.), Hawaii Soc. Pathologists (past pres.). Republican. Presbyn. Home: 920 Ward Av Honolulu HI 96814 Office: Queens Med Center Honolulu HI 98613

CAUGHMAN, MARGUERITE WHITE (MRS. FRANCIS WILFRED CAUGHMAN), mfg. co. exec.; b. Columbia, S.C., Sept. 1, 1933; d. Chester Arthur and Mary Ella (Bone) White; grad. high sch.; m. Francis Wilfred Caughman, Aug. 25, 1951; children—Francis Wilfred, Ronald Alan, Alacia Lynn. Co-owner, bookkeeper Caughman's Meat Plant, Inc., Lexington, S.C., 1954-67; sec., dir. Lexington Frozen Foods, 1967—, gen. mgr., 1967—; bookkeeper C-Bar-D Farms, Inc., Abbeville, S.C., 1971-73; bookkeeper, co-owner Bilmar Farms, Lexington and Salley, S.C., 1964—. Mem. Am. Assn. Meat Processors, S.C. Frozen Food Lockers Assn. (v.p. 1970-71, dir. 1968-71), Nat. Frozen Food Handling Com. (S.C. rep., 1971—). Democrat. Lutheran. Home: Route 5 Box 17 Lexington SC 29072 Office: 147 Columbia Av Lexington SC 29072

CAUL, JEAN FRANCES, food scientist, educator; b. Cleve., Aug. 19, 1915; d. Philip M. and Viola (Weil) Caul; A.B., Lake Erie Coll., 1937; M.A., Ohio State U., 1938, Ph.D., 1942. Chemist biology and chemistry research div. The Borden Co., Bainbridge, N.Y., 1942-44; sr. project leader food and flavor sect. Arthur D. Little, Inc., Cambridge, Mass., 1944-67; distinguished prof. foods Kan. State U., Manhattan, 1967-70, prof. dept. foods and nutrition Coll. Home Econs., 1970—. Guest lectr. Inst. Nutrition Liebig U., Giessen, Germany, 1960. Mem. Am. Chem. Soc., Inst. Food Technologists (chmn. northeast sect. 1954), N.Y. Acad. Scis., Common Cause, Sigma Xi, Gamma Sigma Delta, Omicron Nu, Phi Tau Sigma. Contbr. articles on consumer product testing and flavor to tech. jours. and chpts. in books. Office: Justin Hall Kansas State University Manhattan KS 66506

CAUSEY, NELL B. (MRS. DAVID CAUSEY), zoologist; b. Trenton, Tenn., Dec. 8, 1910; d. Harvey M. and Nettie (Hester) Bevel; B.S., Coll. of Ozarks, 1931; M.A., U. Ark., 1937; Ph.D., Duke, 1940; m. David Causey, Aug. 2, 1938. Tchr. high sch., Alma and Van Buren, Ark., 1931-36; biologist Marine Lab., Duke, 1944; instr. zoology U. Ark., 1943, 45-48; ind. investigator, 1948-64; asst. prof. zoology La. State U., 1964-66, asso. prof. zoology, 1966-70, prof. zoology, 1970—. Mem. Soc. Study Evolution, Soc. Systematic Zoology, Phi Beta Kappa, Sigma Xi. Author numerous articles profl. jours. Editor: Proc. of La. Acad. Scis., 1965-70. Research in taxonomy of the Diplopoda. Home: 1110 Magnolia Woods Dr Baton Rouge LA 70808

CAUVEL, MARTHA JANE, educator; b. Spokane, Wash., Jan. 25, 1930; d. S.T. and Martha (Baskett) Cauvel; B.A., Wash. State U., 1951; M.A., U. Hawaii, 1953; Ph.D., Bryn Mawr Coll., 1962. Prof. philosophy Agnes Scott Coll., 1959-60; prof. philosophy Colo. Coll., Colorado Springs, 1960—, chmn. dept., 1969—. Fulbright-Hays fellow 1965. Mem. Am. Philos. Assn., Soc. for Asian, and Comparative Philosophy, Am. Assn. U. Profs., Am. Soc. Aesthetics. Office: Colo Coll Colorado Springs CO 80903

CAVALLARI, ELFRIEDA LASMANE (MRS. FORD D. CAVALLARI), librarian; b. Talsi, Latvia, Sept. 9, 1928; d. Jakobs and Milda Marija (Upnere) Lasmanis; came to U.S., 1949, naturalized, 1956; A.B., Clark U., 1954; M.S., Simmons Coll., 1963; m. Ford D. Cavallari, May 28, 1955; 1 son, Ford Dominic. Librarian/statistician Tex. Eastern Corp., Shreveport, La., 1956-57; documentation engr. Itek Corp., Lexington, Mass., 1963-64; supervisory librarian Air Force Cambridge Research Labs. Library, Bedford, Mass., 1964—. Mem. Am. Assn. Univ. Women, Spl. Libraries Assn. (chmn. recruitment com. Boston chpt. 1967-69). Lutheran. Home: 18 Lantern Lane Chelmsford MA 01824 Office: LG Hanscom AFB Bedford MA 01730

CAVANAH, FRANCES, author; b. Princeton, Ind., Sept. 26, 1899; d. Rufus Oscar and Luella (Neale) Cavanah; A.B., DePauw U., 1920. Editorial staff Child Life Mag., Rand McNally & Co., Chgo., 1923-29, asso. editor, 1930-38; contbg. writer Western Printing Co., Row, Peterson & Co., Evanston, Ill., 1939-42; biography editor 1947 revision World Book Ency., Field Enterprises, Chgo., 1943-46, anthology editor 1949 revision Childcraft, 1947-48; dir. biography Real People series Row, Peterson & Co., 1948-52; free lance author, 1953—. Recipient Headliner award Theta Sigma Phi, 1942; citation for Meritorious Achievement DePauw U., 1952. Mem. Soc. Midland Authors, Authors League Am., Washington Children's Book Guild, Women In Communication, Mortar Bd., Delta Delta Delta. Democrat. Club: Am. Newspaper Women's. Author numerous books, including Our Country's Story, 1945; We Came to America, 1954; Abe Lincoln Gets His Chance (recipient Ind. U. Writers Conf. citation for Most Distinguished Children's book by Hoosier author 1960), 1959; Adventure in Courage, the Story of Theodore Roosevelt, 1961; Meet the Presidents, 1962; Triumphant Adventure, the Story of Franklin D. Roosevelt, 1964; Our Country's Freedom, 1966; Holiday Roundup, 1968; Freedom Ency., American Liberties in the Making, 1968; Jenny Lind's America (Christian Herald Family Bookshelf selection), 1969; Jenny Lind and Her Listening Cat, 1970; When Americans Came to New Orleans, 1970; We Wanted to Be Free, 1971; Marta and the Nazis, 1974. Contbr. to sch. readers, anthologies, encys. Home: 2501 E 104th Av Denver CO 80233

CAVANAUGH, SISTER JANET MARIE, coll. adminstr.; b. Schenectady, Nov. 11, 1942; d. George Washington and Miriam Frances (Mark) Cavanaugh; B.S. cum laude in Bus. and Econs., Coll. St. Rose; M.S., State U. N.Y., 1973. Joined Order Sisters of St. Joseph of Carondelet, 1960; tchr. bus. courses Cardinal McCloskey High Sch., Albany, N.Y., 1965-69; registrar Coll. St. Rose, Albany, 1969—. Sec. Albany County Right-to-Life, 1972—; mem. polit. edn. com. Albany Diocese Sisters Council, 1972-73; del. Sisters Rep. Assembly, 1973—. Mem. Am., Middle States assns. collegiate registrars and adminstr. officers. Home: 380 Western Av Albany NY 12203 Office: 432 Western Av Albany NY 12203

CAVANAUGH, JEAN, educator, counselor; b. Lake City, Ia., June 27, 1924; d. Orrin Ellsworth and Golda May (Howard) Van Horn; student U. Minn., Grinnell Coll.; B.S. in Bus. Edn. and Bus. Adminstrn., Ft. Hays (Kan.) State Coll., 1970, M.S., in Counseling, 1971, Edn. Specialist, 1974; m. Clair Joseph Cavanaugh, Mar. 21, 1947; children—Thomas, Kathleen, Michael, Terrence, James. With FBI, Washington, 1942-44; career counselor, substitute tchr., Great Bend, Kan.; med. sec. Central Kan. Med. Center; interviewer Response Analysis, Princeton, N.J. Past leader Girl Scouts; past den mother Cub Scouts. Bd. dirs. Youth Care. Mem. Am., Kan. personnel and guidance assns., Kan. A.M.A. Aux. (past chmn. edn. and research, v.p.), Barton County Aux. (past pres., sec.), Meml. Loan Fund (2d v.p.), Athenian, Cosmopolitan (v.p., program chmn.) study clubs, N.W. Home Demonstration Unit, Nat. Bus. Edn. Assn., Pi Omega Pi. Home: 1320 Cleveland St Great Bend KS 67530

CAVASINA, MARY MAGDALENE, physician; b. Canonsburg, Pa., Dec. 26, 1927; d. Joseph Edward and Rose Marie (Staffen) Cavasina; B.S., U. Pitts., 1948; M.D., Women's Med. Coll. Pa., 1952. Intern, Mercy Hosp., Pitts., 1952-53, resident in gen. surgery, 1953-57; practice medicine specializing in surgery, Canonsburg, 1957—; teaching fellow gen. surgery U. Pitts., 1953-57; mem. sr. surg. staff Canonsburg Gen. Hosp., 1957—, chief surgery, 1962; cons. gen. surgery Western State Sch. and Hosp., Canonsburg, 1957—. Mem., attending surgeon Canonsburg Vol. Fire Dept., 1960—; dir. emergency med. services council Washington County br. Am. Cancer Soc. mem. adv. bd. ambulance service V.F.W. Mem. Cath. Daus. Am., Bus. and Profl. Women's Club. Republican. Roman Catholic. Home: 123 S Jefferson Av Canonsburg PA 15317 Office: 160 W Pike St Canonsburg PA 15317

CAVER, KATY LOU FRANKLIN (MRS. WILLIAM RALPH CAVER), museum ofcl.; b. Dallas, Mar. 3, 1942; d. George Edward and Laura Eliza (Wilson) Franklin; B.A. (scholar), So. Meth. U., 1964; postgrad. N. Tex. State U., 1970-71, U. Poitiers (France), 1962-63, U. Guanajuato (Mexico), summers, 1965-68, U. Barcelona (Spain), 1969-70; m. William Ralph Caver, Aug. 3, 1962; 1 dau., Catherine Laura. Tchr. history Richardson (Tex.) Ind. Sch. Dist., 1965-66; tchr. Dallas Ind. Sch. Dist., 1964-65, Texarkana (Tex.) Ind. Sch., 1966-68; owner Casa del Bosque, imports, Texarkana, 1968-70; dir. Texarkana Hist. Museum, 1971—. Mem. Downtown Redevel. Plan, Texarkana, 1972-73; mem. social services sub-com. Model City Citizens Com., Texarkana, 1973; chmn. cultural devel. and recreation com. Texarkana Metro Plan, 1973. Mem. Am. Assn. Museums, Am. Assn. State and Local History, Tex. Museums Assn., Tex. Archeol. Soc., Texarkana Anti-Pollution Soc., Alpha Delta Pi, Delta Kappa Gamma. Democrat. Episcopalian. Club: Soroptimist (Texarkana). Home: Route 6 Box 453 Texarkana TX 75501 Office: 219 State Line Av PO Box 2343 Texarkana TX 75501

CAVIN, PATTY (MRS. F. EDWARD CAVIN), writer, commentator; b. Portland, Ore., Aug. 5, 1925; d. L. Bernard and Lela (Hatfield) Burwell; student U. Wash., 1943-45; B.A., Stanford, 1947; m. F. Edward Cavin, June 5, 1948 (dec. Feb. 1970); children—Chandler, Brooks. Fashion beauty editor the Times-Herald, Washington, 1949-54; beauty editor, spl. feature editor Washington Post & Times Herald, 1954; radio commentator NBC, Washington, 1954-62; mgr. news and information RCA Corp., Washington, 1962-70; exec. dir. Com. Single Taxpayers, Inc., 1971—; dir. marketing and communications Overly Mfg. Co., 1973—; Washington v.p. Fields & Silverman Architects, Beverly Hills, Cal., 1973—. Bd. dirs. Mt. Vernon Coll. Recipient 1st Individual Achievement award Army Times Pub. Co., 1956, Hamilton Time award, 1956, Mem. Am. Women in Radio and TV. Episcopalian. Clubs: Stanford of Washington, Washington Press (past pres.), Am. Newspaper Women's, Annapolis Yacht, Georgetown, Columbia Country, University (Washington). Home: 1628 21st St NW Washington DC 20009

CAWEIN, KATHRIN (MRS. SEABORY CONE MASTICK), artist; b. New London, Conn., May 9, 1895; d. Henry and Barbara (Franz) Cawein; M.A. (hon.), Oberlin Coll., 1966; student Art Students League; m. Seabury Cone Mastick, Apr. 3, 1964. Music roll editor, music interpreter with various musicians, 1911-32; tchr. County Center Work Shop, 1935-36; owner studio for children, 1950-55; one man shows at County Center, White Plains, N.Y., 1935, Village Art Center, N.Y.C., 1945, Town Hall, N.Y.C., 1950, 8th St. Playhouse, N.Y.C., 1953, Sarasota, Fla., 1973, U. Tampa, Tampa, Fla., 1973; exhibited group shows U.S., Eng., France, Italy, Ecuador, including Century of Progress, 1934, Tex. Centennial, 1937, World's Fair, 1939; represented in permanent collections at Met. Mus., Nat. Mus., Washington, Pa. State U., Tampa U., Oberlin (O.) Coll.; illuminated books St. Marks Ch., Van Nuys, Cal., St. Andrew Ch., Sarasota, Fla., Congl. Ch., Colorado Springs. Recipient Frank Talcott Non-Mem. prize Soc. Am. Etchers, 1936, prize for lithography Village Art Center, 1944, prize for etching Nat. Assn. Women Artists, 1947, price for dry point Pleasantville Woman's Club, 1950, prize for etching, 1952, prize for dry point Westchester Fedn. Women's Clubs, 1951, others. Mem. Nat. Assn. Women Artists, Art Students League (life), Chgo. Soc. Etchers, Soc. Graphic Artists. Home: 35 Mountain Rd Pleasantville NY 10570

CAWLEY, ELIZABETH HOON (MRS. ROBERT RALSTON CAWLEY), educator; b. Clay City, Ill., Feb. 12, 1906; d. Clarence Earl and Fannie Ruth (Waitman) Hoon; B.A., Northwestern U., 1926; M.A., Yale, 1930; Ph.D., U. London, Eng., 1934; m. Robert Ralston Cawley, Sept. 18, 1937; 1 dau., Margaret Elizabeth (Mrs. Kernighan). Tchr. history Sandwich (Ill.) High Sch., 1926-28; asso. prof. history Lewis and Clark Coll., 1930-31; dean Mary Baldwin Coll., 1936-37; vis. adj. prof. Rider Coll., Lawrenceville, N.J., 1963—. Pres., mem. Princeton Borough Bd. Edn., 1951-55; past mem. Princeton Council Community Services; sec., mem. exec. bd. Princeton U. League; mem. exec. bd. Princeton High Sch. and Elementary Sch. P.T.A.'s. Yardley Found. fellow 1933-34; Julia C.G. Piatt fellow Am. Assn. U. Women, 1934-35; Am. Philos. Soc. grantee, 1949, 70. Mem. Conf. Brit. Studies, League Women Voters, Women's Assn. Presbyn. Ch. (v.p.). Democrat. Author: The Organization of the English Customs System, 1696-1786, 1938. Editor: The American Diaries of Richard Cobden, 1952. Contbr. to Collier's Ency. Social Sci. Home: 228 Western Way Princeton NJ 08540 Office: Fine Arts Rider Coll Lawrenceville NJ 08648

CAWS, MARY-ANN RORISON (MRS. PETER JAMES CAWS), educator, lit. critic; b. Wilmington, N.C., Sept. 10, 1933; d. Harmon Chadbourn and Margaret Devereux (Lippitt) Rorison; student Nat. Cathedral, 1949-50; B.A. cum laude, Bryn Mawr Coll., 1954; M.A., Yale, 1956; Ph.D., U. Kan., 1962; m. Peter James Caws, June 2, 1956; children—Hilary Brooke, Matthew Rorison. Lectr., Barnard Coll. Columbia U., 1962-63; vis. asst. prof. U. Kan., Lawrence, 1963; faculty Sarah Lawrence Coll., Bronxville, N.Y., 1965; asst. prof. Hunter Coll. City U. N.Y., 1966-69, asso. prof. Romance langs., 1970-74, prof., 1974—, also mem. doctoral faculty City U. N.Y. Grad. Center, 1970—. City U. N.Y. research fellow, 1968, 70; Guggenheim fellow, 1972-73; sr. Fulbright-Hays research fellow, 1972-73. Mem. Assn. for Study Dada and Surrealism (treas. 1966-68, pres. 1971—), Modern Lang. Assn. (regional del. 1971-73, exec. council 1974—), Am. Assn. Tchrs. French. Author: Surrealism and the Literary Imagination, 1966; The Poetry of Dada and Surrealism, 1970; Andre Breton, 1971; The Inner Theatre of Recent French Poetry, 1972. Translator, editor: Tristan Tzara: Approximate Man and Other Writings, 1973; Editor: Dada/Surrealism, 1972—; Text and Theory, 1974; Le Siècle Eclaté, 1974; Michel Deguy, 1974; asst. editor French Rev., 1970—. Home: 140 E 81st St New York City NY 10028

CAWTHON, ELENORA ALBRECHT (MRS. JOHN ARDIS CAWTHON), coll. adminstr.; b. nr. Victoria, Tex., Dec. 6, 1917; d. Otto H. and Lillie (Lassmann) Albrecht; A.A., Victoria Jr. Coll., 1936; B.S., U. Tex., 1938, M.S., 1939, Ed.D., 1948; m. John Ardis Cawthon, May 30, 1948; 1 dau., Elisabeth Albrecht. Tchr. pub. schs., Bandera, Tex., 1938-40, Woodsboro, Tex., 1940-46; asst. depts. govt., elementary edn., curriculum and instrn. U. Tex. at Austin, 1936-38, summers 1943-46, 46-48; dir. tchr. edn. Ark. Polytech. Coll., Russellville, 1948-54; dir. dept. placement and service La. Polytech. Inst., Ruston, 1955—, sec. faculty senate, 1966-67, senate mem. 1967-68. Trustee Coll. Placement Council Found., 1967-68; chmn. visitation teams Coll. Placement Services, Inc., 1967-68; bd. dirs. Bus. and Profl. Womens Found., 1956-57; scholarship com. Delta Kappa Gamma Soc., Epsilon State Orgn., 1961—. Mem. Bus. and Profl. Womens Club (pres. Ark. fedn. 1954-55), La. Fedn. Womens Clubs, Coll. Placement Council (1st v.p. 1971-72, pres. 1972-73), S.W. Placement Assn. (pres. 1959-61), La. Council Coll. Placement Officers (pres. 1967-68), La. Tchrs. Assn., Am. Personnel and Guidance Assn., Am. Coll. Personnel Assn., Am. Assn. U. Women, Delta Kappa Gamma, Pi Sigma Alpha, Pi Lambda Theta, Alpha Tau Delta, Phi Kappa Phi. Club: Pierian. Contbr. articles to profl. jours. Home: 815 Wilaford St Ruston LA 71270 Office: Box 6245 Tech Sta Ruston LA 71270

CAWTHON, JUNE BRICE (MRS. JESSE MARVIN CAWTHON), educator; b. Knoxfork, Ky., Apr. 10, 1923; d. Hiram Lee and Ida McKinley (Brown) Brice; A.B., Berea Coll., 1945; M.L.S., Emory U., 1951; postgrad. Union Coll., 1946; m. Jesse Marvin Cawthon, June 16, 1956. Librarian, Black Star High Sch., Alva, Ky., 1945-47, Pineville (Ky.) High Sch., 1947-48, Jefferson Jr. High Sch., Oak Ridge, 1948-50; library supr. Elberton (Ga.) City Schs., 1951-53; library cons. Athens (Ga.) Regional Library, 1953-65; asst. prof. dept. library edn. U. Ga., Athens, 1965—. Mem. Library Devel. Subcom. to Study State Cataloging Service, 1969; mem. faculty Library Inst., 1969; mem. program com. Ga. Children's Book award, 1970, 71; mem. Ga. State Library Media Edn. Com., 1973. Mem. Southeastern, Ga. (mem. scholarship com. 1971-73, chmn. com. librarianship as a career 1973-75) library assns. Methodist. Clubs: Entre Nous (pres. 1960-61), Pilot (com. chmn. 1954-56) (Athens). Home: 240 Pine Needle Rd Athens GA 30601

CAYLOR, MARIE LOUISE, pub. relations exec.; b. Kansas City, Mo., Jan. 31, 1906; d. Joseph Valentine and Marie Anna (Weth) Straub; journalism certificate St. Teresa Coll., 1926; student U. Ill., 1927, U. Berlin, 1928-29; m. Harry Ernest Caylor, June 10, 1933; children—Mary (Mrs. Walter Altmayer), Sarah Ann Jestadt. Mgr., TELAD, 1931-32; account exec., co-pub. relations counsel Am. Osteo. Assn., 1937-45; probate genealogist W.C. Cox & Co., 1945—; pub. relations Nat. WCTU, 1944—, Chgo. Symphony Orch., 1946-52, Ill. Congress P.T.A., 1948-53, Am. Fedn. Tchrs., 1953-65, Nat. Congress P.T.A., 1948-53, Chgo. Tchrs. Union, 1965-67; editor Am. Tchr. Publs., 1955-65, World Forum, 1971—; owner pub. relations firm Harry E. Caylor Orgn. Mem. legislative com. edn. AFL-CIO, 1960; mem. Ill. Citizens Edn. Commn.; exec. bd. Crusade of Mercy, 1972; mem. Mt. Prospect (Ill.) Village Plan Commn.; mem. Mt. Prospect Bd. Trustees, 1974—. Exec. bd. Wheeling Twp. Republican Orgn. Mem. Indsl. Research Assn., Am. Fedn. Tchrs., N.W. Suburban Council Assns. (chmn.), Mt. Prospect C. of C. (dir.), Euclid Lake Assn. (past pres., editor), Chgo. lNewspaper Guild (past v.p., treas. credit union 1969-72), Internat. Labor Press Assn. (past v.p.), Chgo. Labor Editors Round Table (founder, 1st pres.), Union Tchr. Press Assn. (founder, 1st pres.). Address: 1308 Pima Lane Mount Prospect IL 60056

CAZALAS, MARY REBECCA WILLIAMS, lawyer; b. Atlanta, Nov. 11, 1927; d. George Edgar and Mary Annie (Slappey) Williams; R.N., St. Joseph's Infirmary Sch. Nursing, 1948; postgrad. Vanderbilt U., 1950-51, U. Ga., 1951-52; B.S., Ogelthorpe U., 1954; M.S., Emory U., 1960; J.D., Loyola U., 1967; m. Albert Joseph Cazalas. Gen. duty nurse St. Joseph's Infirmary, Atlanta, 1948-50, Vanderbilt U. Hosp., Nashville, Tenn., 1950-51, Johns Hopkins Hosp., Balt., 1953; instr. maternity nursing St. Joseph's Infirmary Sch. Nursing, Atlanta, 1954-59; med. researcher urology Tulane U. Sch. Medicine, New Orleans, 1961-65; legal researcher Fourth Circuit Ct. Appeals, New Orleans, 1965-71; admitted to La. bar, 1967, practiced in New Orleans, 1967-71; asst. U.S. atty., New Orleans, 1971—. Recipient awards Am. Jurisprudence, 1963, Loyola Law Rev., 1967; 1st place for oil painting Fed. Bus. Assn., 1973. Mem. D.A.R., Fed. Bus. Assn.. (dir. 1972—), Fed. (dir. New Orleans chpt. 1972—, v.p. 1973, pres. 1974), Am., La. State, New Orleans bar assns., Nat. Assn. Women Lawyers, Am. Judicature, Cardinal Key, Leconte, Phi Sigma, Alpha Epsilon, Phi Delta Delta, Phi Alpha Delta (vice justice New Orleans 1974). Democrat. Roman Catholic. Contbr. articles to profl. jours. Home: 1116 City Park Av New Orleans LA 70119 Office: 500 St Louis St New Orleans LA 70130

CAZAN, SYLVIA MARIE BUDAY (MRS. MATTHEW JOHN CAZAN), realtor; b. Youngstown, O., Nov. 17, 1915; d. John J. and Sylvia (Grama) Buday; student U. Bucharest, (Rumania), 1933-35, Youngstown Coll., 1936-38, Georgetown U. Inst. Langs. and Linguistics, 1950; m. Matthew John Cazan, July 14, 1935; 1 son, Matthew John G. Adminstrv. asst. statistics U.S. Dept. Def., 1941-52; spl. employee Dept. Justice, 1956-58; mgr. James L. Dixon & Co. Realtors, Falls Church, Va., 1959-70; mgr. Lewis &Silverman Inc., Chevy Chase, Md., 1970—. Mem. bd. Examiners Georgetown U., 1950. Bd. dirs. Magnolia Internat. Debutante Ball. Recipient Commendation and Meritorious award Dept. Justice, 1958. Mem. Gen. Fedn. Women's Clubs (pres. 1955-56), Interscholastic Debating Soc., Washington, No. Va. real estate bds. Mem. Rumanian Orthodox Ch. Home: 6369 Lakeview Dr Lake Barcroft Estates Falls Church VA 22041 Office: 8401 Connecticut Av Chevy Chase MD 20015

CAZERS, JANA SCARLETT, physician; b. Riga, Latvia, Jan. 13, 1943; d. Robert and Zenta Johanna (Ormanis) Cazers; came to U.S., 1949, naturalized, 1956; B.A., Western Mich. U., 1964; M.D., Wayne State U., 1968; m. Shaukat A. Khan, Aug. 4, 1972. Intern, Henry Ford Hosp., Detroit, 1968-69, resident in dermatology, 1969-72. Mem. Am. Women's Med. Assn., Imeria, Beta Beta Beta, Kappa Rho Sigma. Home: 1309 Southern Av Kalamazoo MI 49001

CECIL, ADELE AMMAR (MRS. EUGENE MOSS CECIL), retail trade exec.; b. Williamson, W.Va., Dec. 9, 1928; d. Keleel Abraham and Lydia Radwan Ammar; student Bluefield Coll., 1946, U. Ky., 1945-49; m. Eugene Moss Cecil, June 12, 1949; children—David Eugene, Diana Lydia. Mgr., Ammar Bros. Style Center, Grundy, Va., 1960-68; sec.-treas., bookkeeper, buyer Pobst & Tiller Dept. Stores, Inc., Clintwood, also Lebanon, Va., 1970—, Gene's, Inc., Grundy, Va., 1970—. Woman's dist. adviser Nat. Found. Infantile Paralysis, 1951-53; pres. P.T.A., 1958; dist. officer Va. Fedn. Women's Clubs, 1955-57; mem. Gov.'s Hwy. Safety Commn., 1956-57. Mem. Delta Zeta. Republican. Presbyn. Mem. Order Eastern Star. Club: Junior Woman's (mem. com. on devel. swimming pool community projects 1958-60 Grundy). Home: 104 Hill St Grundy VA 24614 Office: PO Box 991 Main St Grundy VA 24614

CEDERQUIST, ELEANOR NICHOLAS (MRS. STANLEY G. CEDERQUIST), civic worker; b. Toledo, Aug. 24, 1918; d. Ralph Forest and Marguerite (Wright) Nicholas; A.B., Ind. U., 1941; m. Stanley G. Cederquist, May 10, 1942; children—Eric Stanley, Robert Alan. Sec. The Nicholas Co., Inc., 1953—. Indpls. exec. chmn. Met. Opera Nat. Co., 1966, mem. nat. council, 1966-67; mem. nat. bd. Am. Nat. Opera Co., 1967; mem. Ind. U. Friends of Music Patron, 1965—, Friends of Kennedy Center, 1966—, Ind. Symphony Soc. Women's Com., 1953—, Salvation Army Aux., 1965—, Indpls. Mus. of Art Alliance, 1961—, St. Margaret's Hosp. Guild, 1960—, Boys Club Aux., 1960—; pres. Clowes Hall Women's Com., 1965-66, 66-67; residential chmn. Marion County (Ind.)-Am. Cancer Soc. Crusade, 1970—; bd. dirs. Women's Com. Ind. Symphony Soc., 1972—, Indpls. Council World Affairs, 1972—. Mem. Nat. Trust Historic Preservation, Kappa Kappa Kappa (past chpt. pres.). Home: 240 Williams Dr Indianapolis IN 46260

CELKE, HELEN E., broadcasting co. exec.; b. Cleve.; d. William and Wanda (Jassman) Celke; student Ohio U., 1940-41; B.A., Denison U., 1944. Systems analyst Standard Register Co., Dayton, O., 1945-49; program coordinator Empire Coil Co., Cleve., 1950-54; prodn. coordinator Storer Broadcasting Co., WJW-TV, Cleve., 1954-72, adminstr. broadcast standards, 1972—. Mem. Am. Women in Radio and T.V. Democrat. Lutheran. Club: Columbia Hills Country. Home: 2709 Clark Av Cleveland OH 44109 Office: 1630 Euclid Av Cleveland OH 44115

CELLA, ELISA, mgmt. cons. firm exec.; b. Paterson, N.J., May 23, 1938; d. Alexander and Frances (Biggio) Cella; B.S., Fairleigh Dickinson U., 1960, postgrad., 1960-62; postgrad. N.Y.U., 1965-67. Controller, Rogers, Slade & Hill, Inc., cons. to mgmt., N.Y.C., 1962-72; sec., controller Pipeco Steel Corp., 1969-72; controller, treas., asst. sec. Golightly & Co. Internat. Inc., cons. to mgmt., N.Y.C., 1972—. Home: 412 Pompton Av Cedar Grove NJ 07009 Office: 1 Rockefeller Plaza New York City NY 10020

CENDANA, CARMELITA ANGCO, physician; b. Manila, Philippines, Dec. 5, 1938; d. Dominador Ignacio and Rosario Crisologo (Angco) Cendaña; came to U.S., 1964, naturalized, 1974; A.A., U. Santo Tomas, Manila, 1958, M.D., 1963. Intern Evang. Deaconess Hosp., Detroit, 1964; resident in internal medicine Mercy Hosp., Balt., also VA Hosp., New Orleans, DVA Hosp., Winipeg, Man., Can.; practice medicine specializing in internal medicine, Clinton, Ia., 1972—; mem. staffs Mercy Hosp., Jane Lamb Meml. Hosp., Bluff Med. Center (all Clinton). Fellow Royal Coll. Physicians and Surgeons of Can. (diplomate internal medicine); mem. A.C.P. Home: 1219 Chateau Knoll Bettendorf IA 52722

CENSOR, THERESE ECKSTEIN (MRS. CHARLES CENSOR), sculptor; b. Antwerp, Belgium, Nov. 1908; d. Louis and Bessie (Schiff) Eckstein; student Mus. Modern Art, 1953-54, Art Life Craft Studios, 1955-65, New Sch. Social Research, 1965-66; m. Charles Censor, Dec. 18, 1928; children—Cecile Brunswick, John Z. Tchr., Art Life Craft Studios, N.Y.C., 1963-65; shows at Environment Gallery, N.Y.C.; exhibited in group shows at Lever House, Union Carbide, N.Y. Community Center, Princeton, Mus. Art, La Jolla, Cal., Smithsonian Instn., Washington; represented in permanent collections at Mus. Art, LaJolla, USIA Traveling Sculpture Exhibition, Smithsonian Instn., Charlotte & Louis Bergman Coll., Israel Mus.; also pvt. collections. Mem. Artists Equity N.Y., Artist Craftsmen N.Y., Yonkers Art Assn., Nat. Assn. Women Artists, Audubon Artists, Inc., N.Y. Soc. Women Artists. Office: 2231 Broadway New York City NY 10024

CENTERS, LOUISE VAN CORE DONAHUE, clin. phychologist; b. Los Angeles; d. Michael and Cathleen (Van Core) Donahue; student U. Copenhagen, 1951-52; B.A., U. So. Cal., 1953, Ph.D., 1958. Jr. research psychologist U. Cal. at Los Angeles, 1958-59, instr., 1958-59, supervising psychologist Clinic Sch., 1959-60, instr., 1960-61; staff psychologist Child Guidance Clinic, Hollywood Presbyn. Hosp., 1960-62, St. John's Hosp., Santa Monica, Cal., 1962-64; individual practice as clin. psychologist, 1960—; staff psychologist Langley Porter Inst., San Francisco, 1964-68; asst. clin. prof. med. psychology U. Cal. at San Francisco, 1964-68; psychology cons. St. Francis Hosp. Psychiat. Clinic, 1967-68; asst. chief preventive services, sr. psychologist Genesee County Community Mental Health Services, Flint, Mich., 1968-69; chief psychologist Sinai Hosp., Detroit, 1970—; asst. clin. prof. psychiatry Mich. State Coll. Human Medicine, 1970—; adj. clin. supr. dept. psychology U. Detroit, 1970—; adj. asst. prof. psychology dept. psychiatry Sch. Medicine, Wayne State U., 1974—. Mem. Am., Mich. psychol. assns., S.C. Bay Area Alumni Assn. (scholarship chmn. San Francisco 1968), Mich. Soc. Cons. Psychologists (membership chmn. 1970-72), Kappa Delta (treas. Mich. alumni assn. 1972—). Clubs: Women's City (Detroit). Contbr. articles to profl. jours. Office: Sinai Hosp 6767 W Outer Dr Detroit MI 48235

CERESOLI, PATRICIA GREGORY (MRS. RAYMOND A. CERESOLI), occupational therapist; b. Rock Hill, S.C., May 2, 1940; d. James Harvey and Margaret Ann (Skinner) Gregory; student U. S.C., 1958-61; B.S. in Occupational Therapy, Washington U., St. Louis, 1963; m. Raymond A. Ceresoli, Apr. 27, 1968. Staff therapist, S.C. State Hosp., Columbia, 1963-65; supervising therapist Methodist Hosp., Peoria, Ill., 1965-68; dir. activity therapy service Zeller Zone Center, Peoria, 1968-72; cons. occupational therapist to nursing homes, 1972—. Lectr., Ill. Central Coll., East Peoria, 1973. Mem. Comprehensive Mental Health Bd.-Mental Retardation Devel. Disabilities Commn., Woodford County, Ill., 1973—, Tri-County Comprehensive Health Planning Agy., Peoria, Tazewell, and Woodford Counties, Ill., 1970—. Mem. Am., Ill. (dir. 1968-72, chmn. Peoria dist. 1970-72) occupational therapy assns., Roanoke (Ill.) Art League, Peoria Ski Club. Lutheran. Address: 506 W Broad St Roanoke IL 61561

CERJANEC, RUTH LILIAN WADE, educator; b. Central Falls, R.I., 1913; d. John Thomas and Susanna (McDowell) Wade; A.B. magna cum laude (Overton scholar 1929-30), Pembroke Coll., 1933; postgrad. Brown U. Grad. Sch., 1934-35, R.I. Coll., 1932-55, Providence Coll., 1941, U. R.I., 1964, U. Wash., 1965, U. Colo., 1968, Western Mich. State U., 1969, Kent State U., 1970-72; M.S., Simmons Grad. Sch. Library Sci., 1960, postgrad., 1963; m. Earl Franklin Cerjanec, July 7, 1945 (dec. Mar. 1967); children—Nicholas Wade, Derek McDowell. Tchr., librarian high sch., Central Falls, R.I., 1933-43; head librarian U.S. Naval Air Facilities, R.I., 1943-47; part time tchr., R.I., Mass., 1947-52; dir. nursery sch., Central Falls, R.I., 1952-57; tchr. high sch., Barrington, R.I., 1957-59; librarian Dighton-Rehoboth Regional High Sch., Mass., 1960-66; cons. sch. media centers, coordinator Title II R.I. Dept. Edn., Providence, 1966-72; dir. library media services Cranston (R.I.) Sch. Dept., 1972-73; cons. continuing edn. for women U. R.I., 1973—. Adv. bd. U. R.I. Grad. Sch. Library Sci.; sec. Pembroke Coll. Class of 1933, 1957—, chmn. class secs. 1962-63, chmn. nomination com. 1965-66. R.I. Sch. Design scholar, 1924-26; sec. women's com. R.I. Bicentennial Commn., 1973—. Mem. A.L.A. (chmn. young adults services dir. nomination com. 1972-73), Am. Assn. Sch. Librarians, R.I. (chmn. library edn. 1970-71), New Eng. library assns. (chmn. pub. relations 1969-70) New Eng. Sch. Library Assn., R.I. Women Educators (sec. 1972—), R.I. Assn. Supervision and Curriculum Devel., Mass., Central Falls (v.p. 1938-43), Bristol County (coordinator library sect. 1961, 63) tchrs. assns., Am. Fedn. Tchrs., Phi Beta Kappa. Editor Media News, 1966—, Newsline for Women Educators, 1972—. Contbr. articles to profl. jours. Home: 22 Binford St Central Falls RI 02863 Office: U RI Promenade St Providence RI 02908

CERTAINE, EVELYN REBECCA, social work adminstr.; b. Phila.; d. Lawrence and Sadie (Hall) Certaine; B.S. in Edn., Temple U., 1938, postgrad., 1960-63; M.S.W., U. Pa., 1965, postgrad., 1968. With Pa. Dept. Pub. Assistance, 1940—, now adminstrv. asst. Vol., Big Sisters, 1932-38, Armstrong Assn. (Urban League), 1932-36, A.R.C., United Service Orgn., 1942-67, Hawthorne Neighborhood Council, 1960-63; fund raiser for alumni Sch. Social Work, 1968-69; active YWCA, various other community groups. Recipient Hon. citation for vol. work Chapel Four Chaplains, 1965; also plaques, awards, certificates United Service Orgns., Red Cross, Dept. Army, Air Force. Mem. Nat. Assn. Social Workers, Alpha Kappa Alpha (sec. 1942-43, reporter 1945-46). Republican. Episcopalian.

CERVENA, SONA, opera singer; b. Prague, Czechoslovakia, Sept. 9, 1925; d. Jiri and Sophie (Berger) Cerveny; ed. Gymnasium and Acad. Musik, Prague, 1945. Actress, Prague, 1948-52; singer Opera, Brno, 1952-58, East Berlin, 1958-61, West Berlin, 1962-64, Frankfurt, Germany, 1964—; appeared in festivals of music, Salzburg, Bayreuth, Glyndebourne, Edinburgh, San Francisco Opera, Chgo. Opera. Named Kammersangerin, State Opera, Berlin, 1960. Home: 8330 Lookout Mountain Av Los Angeles CA 90046

CESARONE, LUCILLE HILLMAN (MRS. WILLIAM J. CESARONE, JR.), pub. relations exec.; b. Glen Falls, N.Y., Mar. 1, 1942; d. Albert R. and Martha A. (Hoag) Hillman; B.A., Chatham Coll., Pitts., 1964; m. William J. Cesarone, Jr., Aug. 29, 1970. Staff asst. United Fund of Allegheny County, Pitts., 1966-68; dir. Alumnae Fund, Chatham Coll., 1968-70; dir. devel. and pub. relations Finch Coll., N.Y.C., 1971-73; WAIF dir. children's div. of Travelers Aid Internat. Social Service, N.Y.C., 1973—. Mem. D.A.R., Nat. Soc. Fund Raisers. Home: 309 1st Av New York City NY 10003 Office: 345 E 45th St New York City NY 10017

CESTNIK, SANDRA KAY COPELAND (MRS. TERI JACOB CESTNIK), librarian; b. Oklahoma City, Mar. 26, 1944; d. Donald Eugene and Marjorie Lucile (Groves) Copeland; B.A., Grinnell Coll., 1966; postgrad. Tulane U., 1966-67; M.S., La. State U., 1969; m. Teri Jacob Cestnik, Aug. 21, 1971. Asst. reference librarian U. Mont. Library, Missoula, 1969-73, asst. humanities librarian, 1973—, also asst. prof., 1973—. Mem. Am. Assn. U. Profs., Mont. Library Assn., Phi Kappa Phi, Beta Phi Mu. Home: 145 Strand St Missoula MT 59801

CHACEY, ELLA RAY BRADSHER, ednl. adminstr.; b. Wilson, N.C., Oct. 28, 1917; d. Jacob Thompson and Mary Emily (Jones) Bradsher; student Flora MacDonald Coll., 1935-36; B.S. in Commerce, U. Miss., 1956; M.Ed., U. N.C., 1964, postgrad., 1964-69; m. Lester P. Chacey, 1944 (div. 1951); 1 son, Franklin Bradsher. Tchr. bus. edn. Northwest Miss. Jr. Coll., Senatobia, 1956-57, Central High Sch., Sanford, N.C., 1957-62; counselor, dir. guidance Davidson County Schs., Lexington, N.C., 1962-64; dir. guidance Chatham County Schs., Pittsboro, N.C., 1964-68; evening counselor, coll. day rep. Tech. Inst. Alamance, Burlington, N.C., 1968—. Mem. Carolinas Assn. Collegiate Registrars and Admissions Officers, Am. Edn. Research Assn., Am., N.C. (mem. exec. council 1973—) personnel and guidance assns., Am., N.C. vocational assns., N.C. Assn. Educators, Delta Kappa Gamma.

CHADBOURN, ERIKA MARIANNE (MRS. JAMES HARMON CHADBOURN), curator of archives; b. Nuremberg, Germany, Jan. 21, 1915; d. Georg and Luise (Rabus) Sammeth; came to U.S., 1934, naturalized, 1943; B.A., U. Del., 1936; B.S. in L.S., Drexel Inst. Tech., 1937; m. James Harmon Chadbourn, Aug. 16, 1940; children—Marianne (Mrs. A.J. O'Leary), Leslie (Mrs. Donald West), James Harmon. Cataloger, Middlebury (Vt.) Coll., 1937-38; asst. librarian Hunterdon County Library, Flemington, N.J., 1938-39; cataloger Temple U., Library, Phila., 1939-40; curator of manuscripts and archives Harvard Law Sch. Library, Cambridge, Mass., 1966—. Mem. Soc. Am. Archivists, Assn. Am. Law Libraries, Oral History Assn., Internat. Council Archives, New Eng. Archivists, New Eng. Law Librarians. Home: 988 Memorial Dr Cambridge MA 02138 Office: Harvard Law School Library Langdell Hall Cambridge MA 02138

CHADWELL, BARBARA JEAN (MRS. LAVELLE WINFIELD CHADWELL), banker; b. Chelsea, Okla., Dec. 28, 1927; d. Tim Russel and Pearl (Evans) Sharp; grad. Bank Adminstrn. Inst., 1971; m. Lavelle Winfield Chadwell, Feb. 12, 1948. Bookkeeper, First Nat. Bank, Claremore, Okla., 1946-48; with Peoples State Bank, Tulsa, 1948—, auditor, 1969—, v.p., 1971—. Mem. Nat. Assn. Bank Women (chmn. Eastern Okla. group 1967-68, mem. edn. and tng. com. 1972—), Am. Inst. Banking, Adminstrv. Mgmt. Soc. (chmn. budget com. 1968-69, chmn. membership retention 1970—, chmn. audit com. 1972-73), Nat. Alumni Assn. Sch. for Bank Adminstrn. (hotel reservation chmn. So. regional conv. 1972), Bank Adminstrn. Inst. (dir. eastern Okla. chpt. 1972-73). Home: 10620 E Admiral Pl Tulsa OK 74116 Office: 2408 E Admiral Blvd Tulsa OK 74150

CHADWELL, EMMA FRANCES BARBE, guidance counselor; b. Williamson, W.Va., May 21, 1914; d. Abraham Wharton and Mathilda (Evans) Barbe; student Union Coll., Ky., 1930-32; A.B., Eastern Ky. U., 1934; M.Ed., U. Cin., 1960; m. Wallace Arringdale Chadwell, Dec. 11, 1936 (div. Nov. 1957); children—Lynn Frances (Mrs. William R. Harmon), John Jeffrey, Maribeth, Suzanne. Elementary tchr., Deer Park (O.) Sch., 1955-65, reading diagnostician, 1963-65; adult edn. developer, tchr. Deer Park Community Evening Program, 1958-65; counselor, dorm supr. Fla. Presbyn. Coll., 1965-68; job devel. specialist Va. Dept. Vocational Rehab., 1968-69; spl. counselor for culturally deprived youth Woodrow Wilson Comprehensive Rehab. Center, Fishersville, Va., from 1969; counselor Wenonoh Sch., Waynesboro, Va., 1971-72; elementary counselor Springhead Sch., Plant City, Fla., 1972—. Troop leader Cin. council Girl Scouts U.S.A., 1963-65, mem. council, 1957-63. Mem. Nat. Assn. Humanistic Psychologists. Democrat. Mem. Ch. of Christ. Home: 1803 W Oak Av Plant City FL 33566

CHADWICK, JUDITH SPOFFORD, govt. ofcl.; b. Pittsfield, Mass., Mar. 26, 1936; d. David Keith and Lida (Cameron) Spofford; B.A., McGill U., 1958; certificate Radcliffe program bus. adminstrn., Harvard, 1959, M.B.A., 1965; m. Geoffrey Allan Chadwick, June 18, 1960 (div. Jan. 1964). Asst. to gen. mgr. Campbell & Hall, Inc., Boston, 1959-61; personnel mgr. Houghton Mifflin Co., Burlington, Mass., 1961-62; asst. to pres. Elise Farar, Inc., Pittsfield, 1962-64; adminstrv. asst. to dean Harvard Grad. Sch. Bus. Adminstrn., Boston, 1965-66; mgr., asst. to sr. exec. v.p. Moore McCormack Lines, N.Y.C., 1966-69; exec. asst. to asst. sec. Commerce Dept., Washington, 1969-71, dep. asst. sec. for adminstrv. mgmt. Domestic and Internat. Bus. Adminstrv. 1971—; pres. J.B.L. Realty Co., Lenox, Mass., 1969—; v.p. Elise Farar, Inc., Lenox, 1959—. Edith Stedman fellow Harvard Bus. Sch., 1954. Mem. Kappa Kappa Gamma. Clubs: Harvard Bus. Sch. Club (bd. dirs. 1969-71, chmn. coll. relations 1969-71) (N.Y.C.); Harvard Business School (sec. 1970-71) (Washington). Home: 2501 Calvert St NW Washington DC 20008 Office: Department of Commerce Washington DC 20230

CHADWICK, LILLIAN FRANCES RODRIQUEZ (MRS. RONALD SPEARS CHADWICK), civic worker, educator; b. Denver; d. Rene Alvarez and Justine (Sarkisian) Rodriquez; student U. Geneva (Switzerland), 1955-56, (Fulbright-Govt. grantee) U. Andes, Bogota, Colombia, S.Am., 1959-60; B.A., U. Denver, 1959; m. Ronald Spears Chadwick, Dec. 28, 1962; children—Kevin Spears, Alison Renee. Sales rep. El Fondo Crecinco, 1960; tchr. English, Colegio Santa Maria de los Angeles, 1961; tchr. French, Colegio Nueva Granada, Bogota, Columbia, S.Am., 1960-61; tchr. French and Spanish, Jefferson County Pub. Sch., Lakewood, Colo., 1961-62; tchr. Spanish, art Sylvan Sch. Dist., Modesto, Cal., 1963-64; resource tchr. Santa Ana (Cal.) Pub. Sch. System, 1966-68. Mem. bd., chmn. Spanish, Parents Fgn. Lang. Sch., Tustin, Cal., 1966-68; tchr. Spanish League Women Voters, Modesto, 1963-65. Mem. Tacoma Art Mus., 1970-74, Tacoma Symphony, 1971-74, Allied Arts, 1969-74; mem. library com. Interfaith Center U. Cal. at Irvine, 1966-68; mem. Orange County Soc. Crippled Children and Adults, 1966-68, Symphony Assn. Orange County, 1966-68, U. Cal. at Irvine Gallery Assos., 1966-68, Denver Art Mus., 1961-62; area chmn. United Fund, 1961-62; block worker heart, cancer funds, 1965-74; area chmn. cancer fund, 1972, 73, 74; mem. World Affairs Council Orange County, 1967-68; pres. Idlewild Presch., 1970-71. Mem. Women of Rotary (corr. sec. 1973-74), Newcomers (program chmn. 1970), Jr. Ebell, Am. Assn. U. Women, Delta Gamma, Phi Sigma Iota. Mem. Baha'i (rec. sec. 1969-70, pub. information rep. 1969-74). Clubs: Lakewood Racquet (ladies bd. 1969) (Tacoma), Sudden Valley Country, Sandy Point (Bellingham, Wash.); Encore. Address: 10711 Hill Terrace Dr Tacoma WA 98498

CHAFFEE, HOLLY M. (MRS. FREDERIC H. CHAFFEE), museum curator; b. Bristol, Va., Dec. 27, 1940; d. Charles J. and Irene M. (Millard) Lowry; B.A. in Anthropology and English, U. Ariz., 1971, M.A. in Anthropology, 1974; m. Frederic H. Chaffee, Nov. 15, 1969; 1 son, Jack G. McReynolds, Jr. Asst. curator of collections Ariz. State Mus., Tucson, 1971-72, curator of collections, 1973—. Mem. Am. Assn. of Museums, Am. Anthrop. Assn., Phi Beta Kappa, Phi Kappa Phi. Office: Arizona State Museum Univ of Arizona Tucson AZ 85721

CHAFFIN, LILLIE D. (MRS. THOMAS CHAFFIN), librarian, author; b. Varney, Ky.; d. Kenis R. and Fairy Belle (Kelley) Dorton; B.S., Pikeville Coll., 1958; student Akron University, 1953-54; M.A., Eastern Ky. U., 1971; m. Thomas Chaffin; 1 son, Thomas Randall. Tchr. elementary schs., Loyal Oaks, O., 1953-54, Johns Creek, Ky., 1954-56; tchr. Johns Creek Sch., Pikeville, Ky., 1956-68; librarian Kimper Sch., 1968—, Johns Creek High Sch., 1970-73; writer in residence Pikeville Coll., 1973—; asso. poet laureate Ky., 1974—. Recipient Alice Lloyd meml. prize for poetry, 1968; named hon. Ky. Col., 1968. Mem. Am. Pen Women, Am. Poetry League (poetry analyst 1963; dir. 1964-70), League Children's Poets, Am. Poetry Fellowship Soc. (state dir., chmn. bd. 1963-66), Catholic, Ky. poetry socs. Club: Golden Quill. Author numerous poems, stories, articles pub. in Jack and Jill, Child Life, New Frontier, The Husk, others; also, edn. articles pub. in profl. jours.; also, juvenile poetry books Our Backyard, 1961; A Garden Is Good, 1963; Tommy's Big Problem, 1965; I Have a Tree, 1969 (1st prize Nat. League Am. Pen Women), Bear Weather, 1969; Lines and Points (adult poetry), 1966; A Stone For Sisyphus (adult poetry; won internat. poetry prize), 1967; America's First Ladies, 2 vols., 1968; First Notes (adult poetry), 1969; A World of Books (autobiography), 1970; John Henry McCoy (Child Study Assn. award 1971); Freeman (fiction), 1972; 8th Day 13th Moon (adult poetry), 1974; Coal: Energy and Crisis, 1974. Fiction editor The Pen Woman, 1970-72. Home: Box 46 Meta KY 41501

CHAFIZADEH, PATRICIA ANN SULLIVAN (MRS. MOHSEN CHAFIZADEH), pediatrician; b. Yonkers, N.Y., Apr. 14, 1936; d. Patrick Joseph and Elizabeth (Colgan) Sullivan; A.B., Manhattanville Coll. of Sacred Heart, 1958; M.D., Seton Hall Coll. Medicine, 1962; m. Mohsen Chafizadeh, June 16, 1962; children—Edward, Christopher, Darius. Intern, Jersey City Med. Center, 1963; resident Montefiore Hosp., N.Y.C., 1964-66; practice medicine, specializing in pediatrics, N.Y.C., 1966—; attending pediatrician Cath. Med. Center of Bklyn. and Queens, 1966-70; cons. pediatrician St. Charles Hosp., N.Y.C., 1968—. Diplomate Am. Bd. Pediatrics. Mem. Am. Med. Women's Assn. Address: 10 Old Forge Lane Tarrytown NY 10591

CHAFKIN, RITA MELNICK (MRS. SAMUEL CHAFKIN), dermatologist; b. Bklyn., Apr. 11, 1929; d. Joseph and Dora (Winslow) Melnick; B.A., N.Y. U., 1949, M.D., 1953, postgrad. in dermatology, 1955-56; m. Samuel Chafkin, June 29, 1952; children—Elise, Marc. Intern, Kings County Hosp., Bklyn., 1953-54; resident Bellevue Hosp., N.Y.C., 1954-55; research fellow dermatology div. N.Y. U. Postgrad. Hosp., also preceptee, 1956-57; practice medicine specializing in dermatology and allergies, Modesto, Cal., 1958—; mem. staff Scenic Gen. Hosp., Modesto, pres., 1967, chmn. dermatology instrn. dept., 1958—; mem. cons. staffs Doctors' Hosp., Meml. Hosp.; pres., treas. Rita M. Chafkin M.D., Inc., 1971—. Sec., dir. Modesto Mgmt. Corp., sec., 1963—, Profl. Enterprises Corp., Modesto, 1963—. Mem. A.M.A., Stanislaus County Med. Soc., Cal., Pan Am. med. assns., Pacific Dermatol. Assn., San Francisco Dermatol. Soc., Phi Beta Kappa, Mu Chi Sigma. Home: 2042 La Villa Rose Ct Modesto CA 95350 Office: 803 Coffee Rd Modesto CA 95350

CHAIT, HELEN SPORN (MRS. FREDERICK CHAIT), lawyer; b. N.Y.C., Jan. 6, 1914; d. Jacob S. and Bertha (Lax) Sporn; B.A., Barnard Coll., 1933; J.D., Columbia, 1938; m. Frederick Chait, Sept. 22, 1938. Admitted to N.Y. bar, 1938, Pa. bar, 1953; research asst. Am. Law Inst., 1938-41; rev. atty. N.Y. State Labor Relations Bd., 1941-42; atty. Office of Gen. Counsel U.S. Bd. Econ. Warfare, 1942-43; asso. Root, Clark, Buckner & Ballantine, 1943-46, Cleary, Gottlieb, Friendly & Hamilton, 1946-51; house counsel N.W. Levin, 1951-53; chief counsellor, dep. city solicitor Law Dept. of Phila., 1953-59; chmn. Phila. Tax Review Bd., 1960-65; partner Goodis, Greenfield, Narin & Mann, Phila., 1966-70, Narin & Chait, Phila., 1971—. Trustee, sec. bd. trustees Phila. Gen. Hosp. Research Fund; trustee, mem. ednl. policy com. exec. com. and senate liaison com. Phila. Coll. Art. Mem. Am., Phila. bar assns. Home: 250 S 17th St Philadelphia PA 19103 Office: 1521 Locust St Philadelphia PA 19102

CHALEF, RITA MENDELSON (MRS. MORTON N. CHALEF), child psychiatrist; b. N.Y.C., July 7, 1925; d. Samuel A. and Beatrice (Berman) Mendelson; B.A., N.Y.U., 1946; postgrad. Bklyn. Coll., 1946; M.D., Woman's Med. Coll. Pa., 1950; m. Morton N. Chalef, Feb. 11, 1950; children—Emily, Michael, Steven. Intern, Alexandria (Va.) Hosp., 1950-51; resident St. Elizabeth's Hosp., Washington, 1951-52, Perry Point (Md.) VA Hosp., 1952-53, VA Hosp., Bklyn., 1953-54; fellow child psychiatry Mt. Sinai Hosp., N.Y.C., 1955-56; practice medicine, specializing in child and adolescent psychiatry, Forest Hills, N.Y., 1955-59, Manhasset Hills, N.Y., 1959—; mem. staff Hillside Hosp., L.I. Jewish Hosp., Deepdale Hosp.; asso. prof. psychiatry Adelphi U., 1958-59; cons. Merrick Sch. Dist., 1957-63; supr. psychiat. fellows Hillside Hosp., 1968—. Program chmn. Citizen's Com. for Better Schs., 1959-62. Mem. Am. Psychiat. Assn., N.Y. State, Nassau med. socs., Nassau Psychiat. Soc., Beta Lambda Sigma. Address: 212 Robby Lane Manhasset Hills NY 11040

CHALIFOUX, ALICE ELLEN (MRS. JOHN GORDON RIDEOUT), harpist, educator; b. Birmingham, Ala., Jan. 22, 1908; d. Oliver Joseph and Alice (Halle) Chalifoux; B.Mus., Curtis Inst. Music, Phila., 1932; m. John Gordon Rideout, Apr. 24, 1937 (dec. May 1951); 1 dau., Alyce Gordon (Mrs. John David Reilly). First harpist Cleve. Orch., 1931—, also soloist; head harp dept. Cleve. Inst. Music, 1931-71; head harp dept. Oberlin (O.) Conservatory of Music, 1971—. Dir., tchr. Summer Harp Colony Am., Camden, Me., 1961—. Home: 115 South Lane Chagrin Falls OH 44022 Office: 11001 Euclid Av Cleveland OH 44106

CHALL, JEANNE S., psychologist, educator; b. Shendishov, Poland, Jan. 1, 1921; d. Hyman and Eva (Kreinik) Sternlicht; B.B.A. cum laude, Coll. City N.Y., 1941; M.A., Ohio State U., 1947, Ph.D., 1952; M.A. (hon.), Harvard, 1965; H.L.D., Lesley Coll., 1972; m. Leo P. Chall, June 8, 1946 (div. 1964). Research asst. Ohio State U., 1945-47, research asso., instr., 1947-49; instr. Coll. City N.Y., 1950-54, asst. prof., 1954-62, asso. prof., 1962-65, prof., 1965; vis. asso. prof. Harvard Grad. Sch. Edn., 1963, prof., 1965—; mem. faculty summer sessions Tchrs. Coll., Columbia, 1958, 60, 61; readability cons., 1950—. Mem. Nat. Com. on Dyslexia and Related Reading Disorders, 1968-69; mem. steering com. Project Literacy, U.S. Office Edn. Mem. Nat. Conf. on Research in English, 1950, sec.-treas., 1962, v.p., 1964-65, pres., 1965. Fellow Am. Psychol. Assn.; mem. Am. Ednl. Research Assn., Nat. Soc. for Study Edn. (dir. 1972-74), Internat. Reading Assn. (dir. 1961-65, chmn. pre-conf. inst. 1959-61, mem. membership com. 1958-60), Am. Assn. U. Profs., Nat. Assn. Remedial Teaching (chmn. program com. 1955), Nat. Reading Council, Pi Lambda Theta, Beta Gamma Sigma, Phi Delta Kappa (hon.). Author: (with Edgar Dale) A Formula for Predicting Readability, 1948; (with Florence G. Roswell) Roswell-Chall Diagnostic Reading Test of Word Analysis Skills, 1956; Readability: An Appraisal of Research and Application, 1958; Learning to Read: The Great Debate, 1967. Contbr. articles to profl. jours. Home: 1558 Massachusetts Av Cambridge MA 02138

CHALLMAN, JEAN CARSON (MRS. ROBERT CHESTER CHALLMAN), librarian; b. Oakland, Cal., Jan. 5, 1912; d. Francis Leveridge and Armor Jean (Deamer) Carson; B.A., Stanford, 1933; M.A., Ohio State U., 1936; M.A., U. Minn., 1962; postgrad. U. Cal. at Berkeley, 1934, Vassar Coll., 1945; m. Robert Chester Challman, Dec. 20, 1932; children—Jerome Alan, Martha Carson (Mrs. Gary Keith Mayer). Caseworker Fed. Emergency Relief Adminstrn., San Francisco, 1934; parole officer Conn. State Reformatory for Women, Niantic, 1944; bookmobile librarian Anoka County Library, Spring Lake Park, Minn., 1962-65; librarian, Met. Community Coll., Mpls., 1965—. Aide, Norwich (Conn.) State Hosp., 1944, Topeka State Hosp., 1949-50, Anoka (Minn.) State Hosp., 1957-59. Mem. Am. Assn. U. Women (pres. Norwich, Conn., 1944-46), League Women Voters (pres. Topeka 1949-50), Am. Civil Liberties Union, Am., Minn. library assns., Pi Beta Phi. Unitarian. Home: 3915 Beard Av S Minneapolis MN 55410 Office: 50 Willow St Minneapolis MN 55403

CHALMERS, CAROL BLOOM (MRS. JOHN CHALMERS), civic worker; b. Boston, Feb. 15, 1916; d. Albert Eugene and Ruth Hazel (Paddock) Bloom; B.A., Middlebury Coll., 1937; m. John Chalmers, July 13, 1940; children—James Anderson, Carolyn (Mrs. Eric Steven Janus), Virginia. Tchr. high sch., Sunapee, N.H., 1937-39; tchr. English Ithaca Coll., 1941. Mem. League of Women Voters, 1950—, pres. League of Broome County, Binghamton, N.Y., 1957-59, mem. N.Y. State Bd., 1959-61, mem. bd., Laramie, Wyo., 1962, Manhattan, Kan., 1964-66, mem. Kan. State Bd., 1967-71, pres., Kan., 1971—. Bd. dirs. Human Relations Bd., Manhattan, Kan., 1967-70, Guidance Center Bd., Manhattan, 1969—, United Campus Christian Fellowship at Kan. State U., 1967-70, Commn. United Ministries in Higher Edn., 1967-69. Recipient Theta Sigma Phi Community Service award, 1970. Mem. Pi Beta Phi. Presbyn. Home: 1009 Karla Lane Manhattan KS 66502

CHALMERS, GEORGIA ANN STRICKLER (MRS. LEE NELSON CHALMERS), mag. editor; b. Tulsa, Dec. 23, 1924; d. Hugh Carl and Minnie (Bivens) Strickler; B.A., Okla. State U., 1945; m. Lee Nelson Chalmers, June 20, 1948; children—Carla Ann, Mark Nelson. Editor, mgr. advt. Harper County Jour., Buffalo, Okla., 1945-46; editorial asst. The Liner, Tulsa, 1946-53; sec. U. Tulsa Sch. Nursing, 1968-70; pub. information rep., editor The Torch mag. St. Francis Hosp., Tulsa, 1970-72; asst. dir. pub. relations, editor The Pulse mag. St. John's Hosp., Tulsa, 1972—. Free-lance writer, 1966-70. Chmn. Tulsa residential drive Cancer Crusade, 1967; mem. bd. Am. Cancer Soc., Tulsa, 1967-69; vol. Southeast Tulsa Service League, 1967; publicity chmn. Tulsa Little Theater, 1967-68. Mem. Women in Communications (v.p. 1966-69), Internat. Assn. Bus. Communicators (bd. dirs. Tulsa chpt. 1974), Tulsa Hosp. Council (sec. pub. relations sect. 1971—). Mem. Christian Ch. Home: 5239 S Joplin St Tulsa OK 74135 Office: 1923 S Utica St Tulsa OK 74104

CHALMERS, WILMA GRAND (MRS. LAMONTE FRANKLIN CHALMERS), journalist; b. Toledo, Ore., Aug. 7, 1926; d. Reinold and Klara Emma (Denau) Grand; B.S. with honors, Ore. State U., 1969; m. LaMonte Franklin Chalmers, Aug. 8, 1945; children—Charla Rae Rodger, Larry Steven. News and feature corr. Ore. Statesman, Salem, 1963-69; feature writer, corr. Oregonian, Portland, 1963—; free-lance writer and photojournalist, 1969—. Recipient award of merit Sigma Delta Chi, 1969. Mem. Women in Communications, Phi Kappa Phi. Home: 620 Arthur St McMinnville OR 97128

CHAMBERLAIN, ELINOR WILSON (MRS. STUART HAY CHAMBERLAIN), journalist; b. York, Pa., Jan. 11, 1914; d. Thomas Huston and Bertha Elinor (Keet) Wilson; A.B., Coll. of Wooster, 1935; m. Stuart Hay Chamberlain, May 30, 1942; children—Stuart Hay, Thomas Wilson, Mary Elinor (Mrs. Daniel C. Postellon). Editorial asst. Columbia U. Press, N.Y.C., 1935-42; writer of news and features Dept. Pub. Information, Pa. State U., State College, 1952—. Bd. dirs. Schlow Meml. Library, State Coll., Pa., sec., 1955-70. Mem. Am. Assn. U. Women, Women in Communications. Republican. Episcopalian (sec. of vestry 1961). Home: 346 Ridge Av State College PA 16801 Office: 312 Old Main University Park PA 16802

CHAMBERLAIN, JOAN, educator; b. Boston, Aug. 10, 1946; d. G. Arthur and Mabel G. (Greene) Chamberlain; B.S., Wheaton Coll., 1968; M.A., U. No. Colo., 1973. Instr., Barrington (R.I.) Coll., 1968—, asst. prof. phys. edn., 1973—. Mem. N.E.A., Am., R.I. assns. health, phys. edn. and recreation. Home: 700 Metacom Av #232 Warren RI 02885 Office: Barrington Coll Barrington RI 02806

CHAMBERLAIN, NARCISSE, writer, editor; b. Paris, France, June 17, 1924; d. Samuel V. and Narcissa (Gellatly) Chamberlain; B.A., Bennington Coll., 1945. Researcher, Time mag., N.Y., 1950-52; researcher, reporter Newsweek mag., Paris, 1952-53; asst. editor Gourmet mag., N.Y., 1954-56; editor Hastings House Pubs., N.Y.C., 1956-60; editor Barrows & Co., N.Y.C., 1960-68; sr. editor William Morrow & Co., 1968—. Co-author: The Chamberlain Calendar of French Cooking, 1957-63; The Chamberlain Calendar of American Cooking, 1958-61; The Flavor of France, Vol. I, 1960, Vol. II, 1964; The Chamberlain Sampler of American Cooking, 1961; The Chamberlain Calendar of Italian Cooking, 1962-65; The Chamberlain Calendar of French Menus, 1965-68; The Flavor of Italy, 1965; French Menus for Parties, 1968; The Chamberlain Selection of New England Rooms, 1972. Home: 300 E 33d St New York City NY 10016 Office: 105 Madison Av New York City NY 10016

CHAMBERLIN, HOPE, journalist; b. Portland, Ore., Dec. 2, 1919; d. Willard Joseph and Frieda (Jones) Chamberlin; B.A., Ore. State U., 1938; M.S., Northwestern U., 1939. Reporter-photographer Portland Oregonian, 1939-41; regional pub. relations dir. USO, Chgo., 1942-45; information and editorial specialist U.S. Mil. Govt. for Bavaria, Munich, Germany, 1945-47; information specialist U.S. Army Hdqrs., Zone Command Austria, Salzburg, 1947-50; dir. pub. relations, asst. prof. English, Montclair (N.J.) State Coll., 1951-58; dir. pub. relations NBC-TV Continental Classroom, N.Y.C., 1958-61, Land-Grant Coll. and U. Centennial Washington, 1961; editor The Nat. Pub. Accountant, Washington, 1964-65; writer-editor pub. information division Internal Revenue Service, Washington, 1965-67; free-lance writer, editor, researcher, 1968—. Cons. journalism Prince George's Community Coll., 1962-65. Mem. Am. Assn. UN, Am. Assn. U. Women, Am. Women in Radio and Television, League Women Voters, Women in Communications, Gamma Phi Beta. Club: Overseas Press (N.Y.C.). Author: A Minority of Members: Women in the U.S. Congress, 1973. Home: 1884 Columbia Rd NW Washington DC 20009

CHAMBERS, CODA RUTH LANGLEY (MRS. ARTHUR RAY CHAMBERS), nurse; b. Greensboro, N.C., Apr. 14, 1909; d. Zimry Causey and Elizabeth (Spoon) Langley; diploma Mt. Sinai Hosp., 1934; student U. N.C. Sch. Pub. Health, 1952-56, Inst. for Physicians, Medicine and Rehab., 1958; m. Arthur Ray Chambers, Apr. 14, 1935; children—Tina Rae (Mrs. Fred Perry Hendrix, Jr.), Betty Jane (Mrs. Richard E. Walz), Billie Lee (Mrs. William H. Whisnant). Staff nurse, DePue Hosp., Spencer, W.Va., 1934-38; charge nurse Wesley Long Hosp., Greensboro, N.C., 1939-42; staff nurse, 1946-52; pvt. duty nurse Greensboro, 1946-52; pub. health nurse dist. 8, Guilford County Health Dept., 1953—; rehab. cons., 1958—. Recipient Dr. Benjamin Lipschutz's surg. nursing award, 1934. Mem. Am., N.C. nurses assns., N.C. Pub. Health Assn. Home: 1315 W Florida St Greensboro NC 27403 Office: 300 N Northwood St Greensboro NC 27403

CHAMBERS, MARJORIE BACHELER, coll. dean; b. Summit, N.J., May 16, 1922; d. Otis Dean and Margaret Josephine (Terry) Bacheler; B.A., Drew U., 1954; B.D., Drew Theol. Sem., 1957; M.A., Yale, 1959, Ph.D., 1962; m. Richard Netherton Chambers, Oct. 22, 1949 (dec. Dec. 1950). Prof. religion, philosophy Mary Baldwin Coll., Staunton, Va., 1962—, acad. dean, 1971—. Mem. Am. Philos. Assn., Am. Acad. Religion. Home: 687 E Beverley Staunton VA 24401

CHAMBLISS, MADELON ELAINE AHERNE, bus. exec., artist, poet; b. Buffalo, Apr. 14, 1912; d. Charles Patrick and Emilie (Beaumont) Aherne; student U. Buffalo; grad. Bryant and Stratton Coll., Buffalo; m. Willard Eugene Wagner (dec.); 1 dau., Dolores (Mrs. Colin Rose, Jr.); m. 2d, Phiroze Nazir, Mar. 16, 1963 (div. 1970); m. 3d, William Campbell Chambliss, 1971. Sales rep. Coldwell, Banker & Co., Beverly Hills, Cal., 1957-59; partner Madelon Sheron-Wadsworth Real Estate Devel. Co., 1961-63; with Colwell Co., Los Angeles, 1963-64, Century City Alcoa, 1965, Internat. Tower, Long Beach, Cal., 1966; realtor, Los Angeles, 1967-69; broker Coldwell, Banker & Co., Securities Beverly Hills, 1969—; poet; painter, sculptor, works exhibited Ambassador Hotel, Dippell Art Gallery, Mascagni d'Italia. Pres., co-founder Sisters and Servants of Mary Guild, 1960-62; co-founder Mary Health of the Sick Hosp. Guild; dir. Ladies of Charity, 1963-64; bd. dirs. Colonia Pan Americana, 1966-67, Internat. Orphans. Mem. Hancock Park Art Council (co-founder), Women's Div. Los Angeles C. of C., So. Cal. Symphony Assn., Valley Artists Guild, Am. Composers and Condrs. Assn. (nat. adv. bd. 1957-58, 61), Navy Belles, Navy League, Assistance League. Republican. Club: Ebell (Los Angeles). Author: Moods and Musings, 1970. Home: 8645 Wakefield Av Panorama City CA 91402

CHAMPION, LUCILLE MARIE KELLMER, physician; b. Cleve., May 28, 1917; d. Early Boynton and Kate (Hebbard) Kellmer; student Pacific U., 1936-38; B.A., Reed Coll., 1942; M.D., U. Ore., 1946; m. Walton Thomas Champion, Feb. 15, 1952 (div. Oct. 1962); children—William Thomas, Charles Earl, James Robert, Betty Jo. Intern, New Eng. Hosp. for Women and Children, Boston, 1946; resident Children's Hosp., San Francisco, 1947, Mt. Zion Hosp., San Francisco, 1948, U. Ark. Med. Center, Little Rock, 1949-52; gen. practice medicine, Stuttgart, Ark., 1952-69; maternal and child health clinician Ark. County Pub. Health Dept., 1952-69, venereal disease clinician, 1960-69; clin. asst. U. Ark. Med. Center, 1952-69; staff physician VA Hosp., North Little Rock, Ark. Active in Cub Scouts Am., P.T.A. Mem. A.M.A., Am. Med. Women's Assn., Am. Acad. Family Practice, Ark. Pub. Health Assn., Ark. County Tb Assn., Stuttgart Civic Music Assn., Ark. Orch. Soc. Symphony. Methodist (ch. bd.). Club: Brush and Palette of Ark. County. Home: 3113 Donaghey Dr North Little Rock AR 72116 Office: VA Hosp North Little Rock AR 72114

CHAN, SAU UNG LOO, lawyer; b. Honolulu; d. Joe and Ah Bin (Choy) Loo; student, U. So. Cal., 1923; B.A., U. Hawaii, 1926; LL.B., Yale, 1928; postgrad., U. Hong Kong, 1932-34; 1 dau., Janice Sheung Mun (Mrs. Lindesay Marc Parrott, Jr.). Head pub. relations, Sang Hop Constrn. Co., Hong Kong, 1933-40; asst. legal counsel William Hunt & Co., Hong Kong, 1937-40; spl. investigator Immigration and Naturalization Service, Dept. Justice, Washington, also N.Y.C., 1940-41; admitted to Hawaii bar, 1943; since practiced in Honolulu; estate and guardianship atty. 1st Circuit Ct., Honolulu, 1944—. Bd. dirs. Internat. Inst. Hawaii, Honolulu, 1955-61. Mem. Am., Fed. bar assns., Bar Assn. Hawaii (mem. model probate code com. 1959-61, mem. com. on TV legal ednl. programs, 1971-72), Estate Planning Council Hawaii (mem. exec. bd. 1966-68), Am. Assn. U. Women, Legal Aid Soc., Chinese Am. Women's U. Assn., Chinese Am. Women's Assn., Chinese C. of C., Kappa Beta Pi. Clubs: Yale, Zonta (Honolulu). Home: 2730 Terrace Dr Honolulu HI 96822 Office: First Circuit Court Judiciary Bldg Honolulu HI 96813 Mailing Address: PO Box 3315 Honolulu HI 96801

CHANCE, ELIZABETH MARGARET WINANS (MRS. R. ROBINSON CHANCE, JR.), civic worker; b. Linden, N.J., Apr. 7, 1926; d. Raymond Wood and Cora (Spillinger) Winans; B.A. in Econs., Tufts U., 1948; m. R. Robinson Chance, Jr., June 11, 1955; children—Elizabeth Margaret, Raymond Robinson III, Lawrence Winans. With prodn. expdn. dept. Weston Electric Co., Elizabeth, N.J., 1948-49; tchr. Vaile Deane Sch., 1949-50, Short Hills (N.J.) Country Day Sch., 1950-57; v.p. dir. Robinson Chance Enterprises, Inc., Ocean City, N.J., 1958—. Founder Ocean City (N.J.) Christmas Tour of Homes, 1962, chmn., 1962-69; co-founder Ocean City Cultural Arts Center, 1963, entertainment chmn., 1963-69; mem. Meth. Women's Soc. Christian Service; active community drives; chmn. Wheeling Country Day Antique Show, 1971, 72. Trustee Ocean City Vis. Homemaker-Home Health Aide Service, Wheeling Country Day Sch.; bd. dirs. Wheeling Salvation Army Women's Aux., Florence Crittenton Home, Wheeling. Mem. Cape May County Art League, Friends of Ocean City Hist. Mus., Cape May County Hist. and Geneal. Soc., Sigma Kappa. Republican. Clubs: Wheeling

Country, Oglebay Inst. Garden. Home: Shawnee Hills Wheeling WV 26003 Summer 2536 Wesley Av Ocean City NJ 08226

CHANCE, JEAN CARVER (MRS. CHESTER B. CHANCE), educator; b. Gainesville, Fla., Sept. 4, 1938; d. William G. and Mary T. (Hull) Carver; B.S., U. Fla., 1960, M.A., 1969; m. Chester B. Chance, Dec. 17, 1964; children—Mark, Jennifer. Reporter, Miami (Fla.) Herald, 1960-61, Sarasota (Fla.) Herald-Tribune, 1961-63, Gainesville (Fla.) Sun, 1963-64, Tampa (Fla.) Tribune, 1965-67; interim instr. journalism U. Fla., Gainesville, 1968-69, instr., 1969-72, asst. prof., 1972—. Sec.-treas. Fla. Communications Cons., Inc., Gainesville, 1971—. Treas., Alachua County Exec. Com., Gainesville, 1972—. Mem. Assn. for Edn. in Journalism (minority affairs com. 1972—), League Women Voters, U. Fla. Alumni Assn. (county publicity chmn. 1972—), Sigma Delta Chi. Methodist. Home: Rural Route 3 Box 191 V-2 Gainesville FL 32601

CHANCE, JUNE ELIZABETH (MRS. ALVIN GEORGE GOLDSTEIN), psychologist, educator; b. Gambrills, Md., June 18, 1926; d. Grover C. and Georgianna E. (Tucker) Chance; B.A., U. Md., 1947, M.A., 1949; Ph.D. (USPHS fellow), Ohio State U., 1952; m. Alvin George Goldstein, Mar. 6, 1964. Research psychologist Columbus (O.) Receiving Hosp., 1952-53; asst. prof. psychology U. N.C. at Chapel Hill, 1953-59; asst. prof. psychology U. Mo. at Columbia, 1959-60, asso. prof., 1960-67, prof., 1967—. USPHS grantee, 1960-66. Fellow Am. Psychol. Assn.; mem. Midwestern Psychol. Assn., Soc. for Research in Child Devel., A.A.A.S., Sigma Xi. Author: (with J.B. Rotter and E.J. Phares) Applications of Social Learning Theory to Personality, 1972. Home: 2909 Crawford St Columbia MO 65201 Office: 209 McAlester Hall University of Missouri Columbia MO 65201

CHANCE, LUCILLE EDWARDS (MRS. ALBION S. CHANCE), lawyer; b. Georgetown, Brit. Guiana, Dec. 8, 1899; d. Fitz Benjamin and Julia Matilda (Jordan) Edwards; came to U.S., 1921, naturalized, 1928; student Hunter Coll., 1929; LL.B., N.Y. U., 1932; m. Edmund A. Rohlehr, Jan. 9, 1920 (dec. Apr. 1931); 1 son, John A.; m. 2d, Albion S. Chance June, 1932. Sec. Fisher Albach Employment Agy., N.Y.C., 1921-22; founder Edward Bowen Employment Agy., N.Y.C., 1922, also mgr., 1922-25; real estate broker Edwards Sisters Realty Assos., N.Y.C., 1925-31; fee appraiser Home Owners Loan Corp., N.Y.C., 1933-34; admitted to N.Y. bar, 1933; practiced in N.Y.C., 1933—; successively mem. firms Chance & Grey, Chance, Grey & Rohlehr, Chance & White; atty., pres. Harlem Property Owners and Taxpayers Assn., 1948-68. Dir. Freedom Nat. Bank, N.Y.C., 1966-71. Pres. Inner City Housing and Devel. Council, N.Y.C., 1972—. Mem. N.Y. State Electoral Coll., 1968. Mem. Nat. Assn. Negro and Profl. Womens Clubs (past mem. state com.). Address: 740 St Nicholas Av New York City NY 10031

CHANDLER, BARBARA SUSAN, mus. ofcl.; b. Green Bay, Wis., Sept. 22, 1948; d. Roger and Ruth W. (Chandler) Gormican; student Ripon Coll., 1966-68. Asst. to curator extension exhbns. dept. Cleve. Mus. Art, 1968-70; registrar Peabody Mus., Harvard Cambridge, Mass., 1970-73, Phila. Mus. Art, 1973—. Faculty seminar Am. Assn. Museums, 1974. Seminar on Legal Problems Mus. Adminstrn. grantee 1973. Mem. Am. Assn. Museums (mem. com. 1969—, vis. com. mus. accreditation). Club: Print (Phila.). Home: 210 Locust St Apt 15D Philadelphia PA 19106 Office: Phila Mus Art 26th and Pkwy Philadelphia PA 19101

CHANDLER, BERTHA KRONE (MRS. CHARLES P. CHANDLER), librarian; b. Pittsfield, Mass., Apr. 13, 1913; d. Ward Eugene and Anna Eleanor (Heath) Krone; B.S., Simmons Coll., 1934; postgrad. Gorham State Coll., 1962, 70; M.Ed., Boston U., 1970; postgrad. U. N.Y., 1966; m. Charles P. Chandler, Sept. 1, 1941; children—Charles Peleg, Bertha A. Librarian, Monson (Mass.) Pub. Library, 1935-36; acquisition librarian Baker Library, Harvard Grad. Sch. Bus. Adminstrn., 1936-37; asst. librarian Ferguson Library, Stamford, Conn., 1937-39; asst. librarian Patchogue (N.Y.) Pub. Library, 1939-41; med. librarian Pineland Hosp., Pownal, Me., 1959-61; circulation supr. Bates Coll., Lewiston, Me., 1961-62; librarian Gray-New Gloucester High Sch., Gray, Me., 1962—, media supr., 1970—. Library trustee New Gloucester High Sch., 1943-55. Mem. Am. Forestry Assn., Audubon Assn., A.L.A., N.E. (chmn. personnel com. 1971—), Me. (treas. 1965-69) sch. librarians assns., Me. Audio-Visual Assn., Simmons Coll. Alumnae Assn., Alumnae Assn. Simmons Coll. Library Sch. Home: Sunset View Apt 4 Gray ME Office: Gray-New Gloucester High Sch Gray ME 04039

CHANDLER, DOROTHY B(UFFUM) (MRS. NORMAN CHANDLER), publishing co. exec.; b. Lafayette, Ill.; d. Charles Abel and Fern (Smith) Buffum; student Stanford U., 1919-22; L.H.D., U. Judaism; LL.D. Mt. Mary Coll., Occidental Coll.; D.F.A. (hon.), U. Portland, Pepperdine Coll.; D.Arts (hon.), Otis Art Inst.; L.H.D., U. Redlands, U. Cal.; m. Norman Chandler, Aug. 30, 1922 (dec. Oct. 1973); children—Camilla (Mrs. Chandler Spear), Otis. Dir., asst. to the chmn. The Times Mirror Co. Hon. life chmn. Soc. Cal. Symphony Assn.-Hollywood Bowl Assn.; chmn. bd. govs. Performing Arts Council of Music Center of Los Angeles; past regent U. Cal.; hon. life trustee Occidental Coll. Home: 455 S Lorraine Blvd Los Angeles CA 90020 Office: Times Mirror Sq Los Angeles CA 90053

CHANDLER, DOROTHY MARTELL (MRS. FLOYD LEON CHANDLER), printing co. exec.; b. Ithaca, N.Y., July 10, 1925; d. William Lloyd and Dorothy May (Martell) Rust; grad. high sch.; m. Floyd Leon Chandler, Nov. 23, 1946; children—Daryl Wayne, Douglas Alan, Steven Lee, Scott Martell. Dir. A.E. Martell Co., Keene, N.H., 1947—, pres., 1970—. Active Boy Scouts Am., Girl Scouts U.S., P.T.A., Girls Club. Mem. Broome County (N.Y.) Doll Club. Home: Neal Rd Endicott NY 13760 Office: A E Martell Co Congress St Keene NH 03431

CHANDLER, EDITH SAVELY (MRS. WILLIAM H. CHANDLER), chem. co. exec.; b. Cleve., June 8, 1907; d. John J. and Elizabeth (Weiss) Hansen; student Dyke Sch. Bus., 1925-26, Western Res. U., 1952, John Carroll U., 1973; m. William H. Chandler, Mar. 1, 1958; 1 dau. from previous marriage, Marilyn J. Savely (Mrs. W.A. Fotheringham). Sec. to div. traffic supt. Am. Tel.&Tel., Cleve., 1926-32; asst. to exec. Mountain States Tel.&Tel., Denver, 1929; exec.-tech. tng. staff Lubrizol Corp., Wickliffe, O., 1946-58; pres. Chandler Chem. Co., Cleve., 1973—. Mem. Cleve. Health Mus. and Edn. Center, Cleve. Sr. Council. Mem. Garden Center Greater Cleve. Presbyn. Mem. Order Eastern Star. Clubs: Shaker Heights (O.) Country; Inter-Colony Book Club; Hermit (Cleve.); Coral Ridge Yacht (Ft. Lauderdale, Fla.). Home: 20201 Shelburne Rd Shaker Heights OH 44118 Office: 1965 E 66th St Cleveland OH 44103

CHANDLER, EDNA LOUISE WALKER (MRS. JOSEPH ORTMAN CHANDLER), author; b. Macksville, Kan., Nov. 16, 1908; d. Clarence Sheldon and Mamie Wilhelmina (Johnson) Walker; student Friends U., 1925-27; B.Ed., Sacramento State Coll., 1958; m. Joseph Ortman Chandler, June 8, 1930; children—Ted Joseph, Donald Ortman, Robert Blaine, Ruby Louise (Mrs. Jay Nolan), Nancy Kristen (Mrs. Robert Kaniatobe). Tchr. Redmound Rural Sch., nr. Lewis, Kan., 1927-28, elementary sch., Kinsley, Kan., 1928-30, various schs. San Juan Unified Sch. Dist., Cal., 1946-63; parole advisor, Sacramento, 1971-73. Active in Campaign to elect Dr. Wilson Riles as State Supt. Edn., Placerville, Cal., 1968-69. Mem. Cal. Writers, Am. Assn. U. Women, Delta Kappa Gamma. Author numerous books including Charley Brave, 1962; Tom Logan series, 1966—; Five Cent, Five Cent, 1967; With Books On Her Head, 1967; Will You Carry Me, 1967; Popcorn Patch, 1969; Almost Brothers, 1967; Women in Prison, 1973.

CHANDLER, ELISABETH GORDON (MRS. R.K. CHANDLER), sculptor, harpist; b. St. Louis, June 10, 1913; d. Henry Brace and Sara Ellen (Sallee) Gordon; grad. The Lenox School, 1931; pvt. study sculpture and harp; m. Robert Kirtland Chandler, May 27, 1946 (dec.). Exhibited sculptures N.A.D., National Sculpture Soc., Allied Artists Am., Nat. Arts Club, Pen and Brush, Lyme Art Assn., Mattatuck Museum, Catherine Lorillard Wolfe Art Club, Am. Artists Profl. League, Hudson Valley Art Assn.; represented in permanent collections Aircraft Carrier USS Forrestal, Gov. Dummer Acad., James Forrestal Research Center of Princeton U., Lenox Sch., James L. Collins Parochial Sch., Tex., Storm King Art Center, Columbia U., Forrestal Meml. Medal, Timoshenko Medal for Applied Mechanics, Benjamin Franklin Medal, Albert A. Michelson medal, Woodrow Wilson Sch. of Princeton U., Georgia Pacific Bldg., Portland, Ore.; also represented in pvt. collections; performed as concert harpist on stage, radio, TV, 1933-45; mem. Mildred Dilling Harp Ensemble, 1934-46. 1942-45. Dir. Abbott Coin Counter Co., Inc., 1941-55. Chmn. Asso. Taxpayers Old Lyme, 1969-72. Trustee The Lenox Sch., 1953-55. Served with mus. therapy div. Am. Theatre Wing. Recipient 1st prize Bklyn. War Meml. competition, 1945; 1st prize sculpture Catherine Lorillard Wolfe Art Club, 1951, 58, 63; Founders prize Pen and Brush, 1954, Gold medal, 1957, 61, 63, Gold medal sculpture, 1969, Am. Heritage award, 1968, Solo Show award, 1969; Thomas R. Proctor prize N.A.D., 1956, Dessie Greer prize, 1960; sculpture prize Nat. Arts Club, 1959, 60, 62, Gold medal, 1971; Gold medal Am. Artists Profl. League, 1960, 73, Harriet Mayer Meml. prize, 1961, sculpture prize, 1969; Gold medal Hudson Valley Art Assn., 1956, 69, Anna Hyatt Huntington award, 1970; Lindsey Morris Meml. prize Allied Artists Am., 1973. Fellow Nat. Sculpture Soc., Am. Artists Profl. League, Internat. Inst. Arts and Letters; mem. Nat. Arts Club, Allied Artists of Am., Pen and Brush, Catherine Lorillard Wolfe Art Club, Lyme Art Assn. Council Am. Artist Socs. (dir.), Am. Artists Profl. League (dir.), N.A.D. (asso.). Home: Mill Pond Lane Old Lyme CT 06371

CHANDLER, NANCY ANN, Democratic nat. committeewoman; b. Stoneham, Mass., Aug. 30, 1933; d. George Albert and Evangeline Gray (Lister) Ransdell; A.B., R.N., Bates Coll., 1957; m. Bruce Warwick Chandler, Dec. 26, 1954; children—Brooks, Kimberly, Kristin. Instr. maternal and child health Washington Hosp. Center, 1957-60; coordinator rehab. nursing Thayer Hosp., Wakeville, Me., 1961-63; instr. rehab. nursing U. Me., 1962. Mem. Me. Gov.'s Adv. Com. Mental Health. Mem. Me. Democratic state com., 1968-72; mem. Dem. Nat. Com. from Me., 1972—; del. Dem. nat. conv., 1972; co-chmn. McGovern campaign Me., 1972. Mem. Am. Assn. U. Women, Nat. Women's Polit. Caucus. Address: Strawberry Meadows South China ME 04355

CHANDLER, VIRGINIA LOU GOODMAN (MRS. ROBERT JOSEPH CHANDLER), occupational therapist; b. Evanston, Ill., Jan. 10, 1930; d. Daniel Guy and Helen (Schneider) Goodman; B.A. in Art and Psychology, So. Methodist U., 1951; postgrad. in occupational therapy Tex. Women's U., 1953; m. Robert Joseph Chandler, Dec. 22, 1952; children—Ron Lee, Chuck Lee. Occupational therapist Beverly Hills Sanitarium, Dallas, 1953-55; dir. occupational therapy Baylor U. Med. Center, Dallas, 1956-60, 68—; dir. occupational therapy Fla. Sanitarium and Hosp., Orlando, 1962-65; staff therapist Parkland Meml. Hosp., Dallas, 1965-68. Cons. Goodwill Industries, 1957, United Cerebral Palsy, 1957-58, Arthritis Found., 1974; dir. clin. edn. internship program univs. Kan., Ind., Pudget Sound, Va., Ark., Colo., N.Y., 1972—. Mem. Am. Occupational Therapy Assn. (del. Fla., 1964), Am. Heart Assn., Chi Omega. Club: Boomerang (dir. 1971—). Home: 11106 Shortmeadow Dallas TX 75218 Office: Baylor Univ Medical Center 3500 Gaston Av Dallas TX 75246

CHANDOR, MARY MCDONALD (MRS. JEFFREY F. CHANDOR), museum curator; b. Winnipeg, Man., Can., Nov. 10, 1941; d. David Scott Dick and Virginia Frances (Pelletier) McDonald; student Mt. Allison U., 1959-61; B.F.A., Syracuse U., 1963; M.Art Edn., U. Ga., 1966; m. Jeffrey Frazer Chandor, July 20, 1968; children—Heather Jean, Jeffrey McDonald. Came to U.S., 1963. Travelling sec., counselor Sigma Kappa Sorority, Indpls., 1963-65; asst. curator edn. Nat. Gallery of Can., Ottawa, 1966-68; art curator Morris Museum Arts and Scis., Morristown, N.J., 1968—. Mem. Morris Area Arts Council, 1973—. Mem. Morris County Urban League (sec. fine arts project bd. 1968-69), Phi Kappa Phi, Sigma Kappa. Home: 9 Sunnybrook Rd Basking Ridge NJ 07920 Office: PO Box 125 Convent NJ 07961

CHANEY, DORETA WHITE, fund raiser; b. Oakland, Cal., Feb. 9, 1920; d. Charleston I. and Georgia R. (Savage) White; student Cal. Coll. Arts and Crafts, 1937-38; B.A., Cal. State U. at Hayward, 1970; postgrad. communications Cal. State U. at San Francisco, 1970—; m. Leonard Menke Chaney, Sept. 28, 1940; 1 son, Gary White. Exec. sec. Oakland Museum Assn., 1957-61, campaign mgr. gen. bond issue, 1961; pub. relations dir. R.T. Nahas Co., Oakland, 1961-64; asst. to pres. Coll. Holy Names, Oakland, 1964-67; asst. community relations Merritt Coll., Peralta Community Coll. Dist., Oakland, 1967-70; devel. specialist East Bay Regional Park Dist., Oakland, 1970—. Cons. Nat. Parks and Recreation Assn., Washington, 1973. Pres. Jr. Alliance, 1945; v.p. Lincoln Child Center, 1949; del. white House Conf. Children and Youth, 1960; pres. Oakland-Fukuoka Sister Cities Assn. Bd. dirs. Council Social Planning Alameda County, Cal. Health and Welfare Assn., Young Peoples Symphony Orch. Assn., Oakland Civic Music Assn., Alameda County United Crusade, United Bay Area Crusade, Oakland Mus. Assn. Mem. Pub. Relations Soc. Am., Nat. Soc. Fund Raisers (dir. No. Cal. chpt.). Clubs: Women's Athletic (Oakland), Cotillion of East Bay. Office: 11500 Skyline Blvd Oakland CA 94619

CHANEY, EARLYNE CANTRELL (MRS. ROBERT GALEN CHANEY), clergywoman; b. Dallas, Dec. 1, 1916; d. Edgar Earl and Mae E. (Wilson) Cantrell; student Indpls. Coll. Divine Word, Moser Bus. Coll. (Chgo.); m. Robert Galen Chaney, Oct. 4, 1947; 1 dau., Sita Earlyne. Dramatic actress and singer, 1940-46; ordained to ministry, co-founder, co-dir., minister Astara, Inc., Los Angeles, 1951—. Mem. Order Eastern Star. Author: Remembering (autobiography), 1974. Address: 261 S Mariposa Av Los Angeles CA 90004

CHANEY, ISABELLE CAROLINE (MRS. LAWRENCE H. CHANEY), county ofcl.; b. Cadiz, O.; d. William Grant and Margaret Belle (Gaines) Kent; student Geneva Coll., 1953; m. George F. Stevens, July 20, 1929 (dec. Nov. 1947); 1 dau. Naomi Jeanne (Mrs. Harold Root); m. 2d, Lawrence H. Chaney, Feb. 13, 1954. Staff law office, 1923-29; dep. clk. probate and juvenile cts. Harrison County, O., 1929-54, 55-65; sec. to pros. atty., 1965-69; mem. Harrison County Election Bd., Cadiz, 1972—. Mem. Republican State Central Com., 1966-72; Rep. committeeman, Harrison County, 1968. Mem. Civic Club Ohio Fedn. Women's Club (pres. dist. 1964-66, chmn. dist. 1958-62, Ohio chmn. Legislation, Citizenship and Pub. Affairs Com. 1962-64, 66-68), Daughters Union Vets. (pres. Ohio dept. 1971), Am. Legion Aux. (pres. local chpt. 1967), Cadiz Bus. and Profl. Women (pres. 1952), Women's Missionary Soc. (pres. 1932-54). Methodist (mem. adminstrv. bd., chmn. pastor-parish relations com. 1971-75, del. annual conf. 1970, 71, 74). Home and office: PO Box 244 Cadiz OH 43907

CHANG, CHARITY HEADRICK (MRS. JOHN CLEMENT CHANG), librarian; b. Maryville, Tenn., Dec. 30, 1916; d. Hugh Edward and Cora (Cummings) Headrick; student E. Tenn. State Coll., 1935-37; B.S., Austin Peay State Coll., 1949; M.A., U. Tenn., 1956; M.S. in L.S., U. Ill., 1959; postgrad. Baylor U., 1963-64, U. Neb., 1965-67; m. Samuel W. Greene, July 23, 1941 (dec. Mar. 1964); 1 dau., Vivian Jo (Mrs. Harold J. Pierce); m. 2d, John Clement Chang, Sept. 29, 1967. Tchr. pub. schs., Tenn., Fla., 1937-54; asst. acquisitions dept. Library U. Tenn., Knoxville, 1954-56; grad. asst. catalog dept. Library U. Ill., Urbana, 1958-59; head circulation dept. Morris Library, So. Ill. U., Carbondale, 1959-62; chief bibliographer acquisitions dept. Wilbur Cross Library, U. Conn., Storrs, 1962, head serials dept., 1967—; asst. librarian for pub. services Library Baylor U., Waco, Tex., 1962-64; asst. dir. libraries for humanities Love Library, U. Neb., Lincoln, 1964-67; library cons. Children's Lit. Assn., Jour. Children's Lit.: The Great Excluded. Mem. Lincoln Community Playhouse Backstage Club and Ladies Guild, 1965-68, Lincoln Theatre, 1966—; sec. Lincoln Toastmistress Club, 1965-66. Mem. Neb. Assn. Community Theatres (chmn. 1966-67), Am. Assn. U. Women (chmn. program devel. 1967—, legislative chmn. Storrs-Willimantic br. 1969-70), Am. Assn. U. Profs., Nat., Neb. library assns., Ia. Assn. Community Theatres, Am. Ednl. Theatre Assn., A.L.A., Internat. Platform Assn., Beta Phi Mu. Home: PO Box 42 Centre St Mansfield Center CT 06250 Office: Wilbur Cross Library U Conn Storrs CT 06268

CHANG, CHRISTINE, occupational therapist; b. San Fernando, Cal., Aug. 28, 1946; d. Tennyson Po-Hsun and Anna May (Ing) Chang; B.S., U. Wis.-Madison, 1968; postgrad. pub. health U. Mich., 1973—. Staff occupational therapist children's psychiat. unit U. Mich. Hosp., 1969-72, supr. occupational therapy, 1972—. Cons. Ann Arbor (Mich.) Pub. Elementary Schs., 1970—. Clin. rep. Mich. Council Edn. Occupational Therapy, program chmn., 1973; mem. Bryant Neighborhoods Steering Com., 1973—. Mem. Am., Mich., Ann Arbor occupational therapy assns., Kappa Kappa Gamma. Home: 535 Longshore Ann Arbor MI 48105 Office: Children's Psychiat Hosp U Mich Hosp Ann Arbor MI 48105

CHANG, DIANA TAN (MRS. TE-WEN CHANG), radiologist; b. Hankow, China, Feb. 24, 1924; d. Joseph and May (Low) Tan; A.B., Nat. Central U., 1945, M.D., Nanking, 1948; m. Te-Wen Chang, June 28, 1952; children—Lynn, Frank, Joseph, Janet, Catherine. Came to U.S., 1949, naturalized, 1960. Resident, Meth. Hosp., Phila., 1949-50, Deaconess Hosp., Cin., 1950-51, Lynn (Mass.) Hosp., 1951-52; resident radiology Mass. Meml. Hosp., Boston, 1953-56; asst. radiologist R.I. Hosp., Providence, 1958-59; radiologist St. John's Hosp., Lowell, Mass., 1960—. Fellow Am. Roentgen Soc., N.Am. Roentgen Soc.; mem. A.M.A., Mass. Med. Soc., Mass. X-Ray Soc., Suffolk Med. Soc., Charles River Med. Soc. Home: 122 Bellevue St Newton MA 02158 Office: St John's Hosp Lowell MA 01852

CHANG, JACQUELINE WAN-CHIN SUN, anesthesiologist; b. Ningpo, China, Dec. 21, 1919; d. Poo and Shau (Yin) Sun; came to U.S., 1949, naturalized, 1960; M.D., Aurora U.; m. Han Min Wong, May 1, 1947 (dec. Dec. 1972). Intern, N.Y. Hosp. for Women, N.Y.C., 1950-51; resident French Hosp., N.Y.C., 1951-52, Med. Center N.J., Jersey City, 1952-53; resident anesthesiologist, Bellview Hosp., N.Y.C., 1953-55; practice medicine specializing in anesthesiology, N.Y.C., 1953—; anesthesiologist Hempstead Hosp., N.Y.C., 1957-61; staff Syosett (N.Y.) Hosp., 1962—, dir. anesthesiology, 1963—. Mem. N.Y. State Soc. Anesthesiologists. Roman Catholic. Home: Split Rock Rd PO Box F Syosset NY 11791 Office: 225 Jericho Turnpike Syosset NY 11791

CHANG, KAREN KWEI-LENG (MRS. HENRY KWONG TAN), textile craftsman; b. Hilo, Hawaii, Apr. 4, 1940; d. Mun Leon and Mew Keam (Chock) Chang; B.A., U. Cal. at Berkeley, 1963, M.A., 1965; m. Henry Kwong Tan, Sept. 4, 1965. One-man show at Mus. Contemporary Crafts, N.Y.C.; exhibited in group shows at First West Coast Craft Competition, Seattle, Richmond Art Center, Norfolk Mus. Arts and Scis., Mus. Contemporary Crafts, N.Y.C., Mus. West, San Francisco, E.B. Crocker Gallery, Sacramento, Bloomfield (Mich.) Art Assn., Henry Gallery, Seattle, Md. Art Inst., Craft House, Washington, Media Galleries, Los Angeles; represented in permanent collections at Mus. Contemporary Crafts, N.Y.C., Honolulu Acad. Art, State of Hawaii Art Collection. Mem. Am. Craftsmen's Council, Phi Beta Kappa. Democrat. Address: 6412 Bradley Blvd Bethesda MD 20034

CHANG, LITA WOU (MRS. ALBERT C. CHANG), banking exec.; b. Tienstsin, China (came to U.S. 1947, naturalized 1956); d. K.N. and Tsin Yun (Chu) Wou; B.A., St. John's U., Shanghai, China, 1946; student Grad. Sch. Bus. Columbia, 1947-49; m. Albert C. Chang, June 17, 1950; 1 dau., Laura Lynne. Asst. investment counselor Bank N.Y., N.Y.C., 1953-60, investment counselor, 1961-65, asst. investment officer, 1965, investment officer, 1967, v.p., 1968—. Trustee nat. bd. YWCA. Mem. Beta Gamma Sigma. Mem. Community Ch. Home: 26 Johnstone Rd Great Neck NY 11021 Office: 48 Wall St New York City NY 10015

CHANG, MABEL LI (MRS. T. TIMOTHY CHANG), educator; b. Hong Kong; d. Hung Chan and Yan Chi (Chung) Li; came to U.S., 1946, naturalized, 1962; B.A., Nat. Central U., China, 1945, Manhattanville Coll. Sacred Heart, 1948; M.A., N.Y. U., 1948, Ph.D., 1956; m. T. Timothy Chang, Nov. 23, 1957; 1 son, Robert T. Tchr., English exec. staff Yu Fung Mills, Inc., Chungking, China 1944-45; asst. to chief accountant Chungking and Shanghai offices United China Relief, 1945-46; head Claver Index project Cath. Interracial Council N.Y., Inc., N.Y.C., 1948-60; lectr. Bernard Baruch Sch. Bus. Adminstrn., Coll. City N.Y., 1960-65; instr. econs. Bronx Community Coll., City U. N.Y., 1962-65, asst. prof. 1966-68, asso. prof., 1969-72, prof., 1972—. Recipient Founders Day award N.Y. U., 1957. United Bd. for Christian Colls in China fellow, 1955-56. Mem. Am. Assn. U. Profs., Am., Met. econ. assns., Assn. for Comparative Econs., Econometric Soc. Home: 501 W 123d St New York City NY Office: 181st St and University Av Bronx NY 10453

CHANG, ROSIE KIM (MRS. JOHN W.F. CHANG), health adminstr.; b. Honolulu, March 29, 1919; d. Chung Chip and Mary (Park) Kim; B.S., U. Hawaii, 1947; M.Litt., U. Pitts., 1950; m. John W.F. Chang, Feb. 21, 1942; 1 son, John W.K. Head nurse Queen's Hosp., Honolulu, 1942-43, supr. 1943-45, clin. instr., 1945-47, asst. dir. nursing, 1950-51, ednl. dir., 1951-54; lectr. nursing U. Hawaii, 1951-52; dir. nursing Hawaii State Hosp., Kaneohe, 1954-69, asst. dep. dir. Regional Med. Program Hawaii, 1969—; liquor commr., Honolulu, 1973—. Mem. ednl. TV panel, Challenge for Women, U. Hawaii Div. Continuing Edn., 1970. Mem. Honolulu Acad. Arts (docent), Spalding House, YWCA, Korean Cultural Com.; pres.

Hawaii chpt. Campfire Girls, Inc., 1971, mem. nat. council, 1972—; mem. Mayor's Health Adv. Com., 1961; mem. Hawaii Bd. Nursing, 1951-56, sec., 1952-56; mem. Ethics Commn. City and County Honolulu, 1970-73, Hawaii State Bd. Hearing Aid Dealers and Fitters, 1969-73; trustee Hawaii Heart Assn., 1953-56, chmn. nursing edn. committee, 1969-72; vice chmn. Gov.'s Commn. Status Women, 1964-66, mem. Citizens Ethics Com., 1965, 66, U.S. Army Pacific Korean Friendship Mission, 1966; dir. Hosp. Inservice Tng. Program, 1964-66. Mem. Citizens Com. on Establishing Sensitivity Tng. Center Hawaii, 1968; mem. Citizens Com. on Constitutional Conv., Hawaii, 1968. Recipient Oahu Career Woman of Yr. award Bus. and Profl. Woman's Club, 1967. Mem. Am. Nurses Assn., Hawaii Nurses Assn. (acting counsellor 1952, 1st v.p. 1963-65, pres. Oahu Dist. 1945-47, 53-55, 60), Nat. League for Nurses, Hawaii League for Nursing (dir. 1947, chmn. publicity com. 1963-64), Am. Soc. Pub. Adminstrs., Hawaii Dance Assn. (sec. 1962), Manoa Kai Bus. and Profl. Women's Club (pres. 1972-73), Friends of East-West Center (sec. 1973—), Sigma Theta Tau. Clubs: Zonta (dir. 1962-64, chmn com. on status women 1969-71), Chinese Women's (sec. 1963, 1st v.p. 1964, pres. 1972), American Chinese (pres. 1963), Korean University (pres. 1963). Contbr. various articles to profl. jours. Home: 4141 Kaimanahila St Honolulu HI 96816 Office: 770 Kapiolani Blvd Honolulu HI 96813

CHANG, SOPHIA HO-YING (MRS. CHARLES CHI CHANG), physician; b. Shanghai, China, Mar. 21, 1923 (came to U.S. 1948, naturalized 1960); d. Zia Pieu and Hsu Jean (Li) Zien; B.S., St. John's U., Shanghai, 1945, M.D., 1948; certificate Harvard Med. Sch. postgrad. course in Pediatrics, 1950; m. Charles Chi Chang, Dec. 16, 1950; children—Betty, Nancy. Rotating intern Washington County Hosp., Hagerstown, Md., 1948-49; asst. resident pediatrics New Eng. Hosp. for Women and Children, 1949-50; chief resident pediatrics St. Paul's Hosp., Dallas, 1951-52; pediatric resident contagion Willard Parker Hosp., N.Y.C., 1952-54; instr. pediatrics, research fellow virology N.Y. U.-Bellevue Med. Center, 1955-56; practice medicine specializing in pediatrics and pediatric allergy, Bklyn., 1957—; asso. attending pediatrician Coney Island Hosp., 1957-68, vis. attending pediatrician, 1968—; asst. attending pediatrician Maimonides Med. Center, 1968-71, asso. attending pediatrician, 1972—; clin. instr. pediatrics Downstate Med. Sch., Bklyn., 1961-69, clin. asst. prof. pediatrics, 1969—; clin. asst. attending pediatrician Kings County Hosp., 1961-69, asst. vis. pediatrician, 1969—; supervising physician Dept. Health, Bur. Child Health, 1966—. Am. Assn. U. Women internat. scholar, 1949-50. Diplomate Am. Bd. Pediatrics. Mem. Kings County Med. Soc., Am., Bklyn. acads. pediatrics, Am. Chinese Med. Soc. Home: 2436 National Dr Brooklyn NY 11234 Office: 1755 E 55th St Brooklyn NY 11234

CHANNING, ROSE MARIE (MRS. JAMES GORDON CHANNING), coll. dean; b. Adrian, Pa., Sept. 12, 1920; d. Paul A. and Josephine (Bugala) Manger; diploma Jersey City Hosp. Sch. Nursing, 1949; B.S., N.Y. U., 1954; M.A., Columbia, 1961, M.Ed., 1971, Ed.D., 1973; m. James Gordon Channing, Jan. 24, 1954 (dec.); children—Rose Marie (Mrs. David Buhrman), Lorraine. Staff nurse, asst. supr. Pub. Health Nursing Service, Jersey City, 1949-55; dir. health and recreation, clin. coordinator, asso. dir. nursing edn. Charles E. Gregory Sch. Nursing, Perth Amboy (N.J.) Gen. hosp., 1958-66; chmn. dept. nurse edn., dir. health techs., dean div. health techs. Middlesex County Coll., Edison, N.J., 1966—. Mem. Middlesex County Comprehensive Health Planning Council, 1973—, N.Y. Com. Regents External Degree in Nursing, 1972—, Council on Continuing Edn. for Allied Health Personnel, N.J. Regional Med. Program, 1968-71; vice-chmn. N.J. Health Professions Edn. Adv. Council, N.J. Dept. Higher Edn., 1972—; mem. health careers com. J.F. Kennedy Hosp., 1972—. Recipient award for excellence in Tb nursing Jersey City Hosp. Sch. Nursing, 1954; Am. Nurses Assn. pin N.J. Nurses Assn., 1973. Mem. Am. Nurses Assn., Nat. League for Nursing, Jersey City Sch. Nursing, N.Y. U., Tchrs. Coll. Columbia alumni assns., Kappa Delta Pi. Contbr. articles to profl. jours. Home: 234 Amherst Av Colonia NJ 07067 Office: Middlesex County Coll Edison NJ 08817

CHANTI, ANTONINA ARLENE, metal mfg. exec.; b. Louisville, Dec. 8, 1937; d. Anthony Joseph and Sidney Arlene (Sherman) Castiglia; children—Patricia Ann, Robert Anthony. Pres., Coren Metalcrafts Co., Inc., Burlington, N.J. Home: 527 Cherry St Roebling NJ 08554 Office: Route 130 S 580 High St Burlington NJ 08016

CHAPIN, ANITA HENRY (MRS. NOEL RAY CHAPIN), wholesale trade co. exec.; b. Rising Star, Tex.; d. Walter Scott and Nettie Rivers (Cooper) Henry; student McMurry Acad., 1923-25, McMurry Coll., 1925-27; pvt. art instrn. Hardin-Simmons U., 1927-29; m. Noel Ray Chapin, Sept. 30, 1950. Instr. art, illustrator Tyler and Troup, Tex., 1930-34; designer, cons. purchasing Mid Tex. Lumber Co., Tyler, 1934-40; owner Mid-Tex. Art Co., Tyler, 1940-50; designer, cons. purchasing Noel R. Chapin Co., Dallas, 1950-60, v.p., 1960—. Instr., cons. art. Republican. Methodist. Home: 5716 Willow Lane Dallas TX 75230 Office: 1201 S Ervay St Dallas TX 75215

CHAPIN, CATHERINE MAYFIELD WISWELL (MRS. TROY ALBERTUS CHAPIN, JR.), civic worker; b. Jacksonville, Ill., Sept. 10, 1916; d. Earl Burr and Clara (Mayfield) Wiswell; A.B., MacMurray Coll., 1937; M.S., U. Colo., 1945; m. Troy Albertus Chapin, Jr., May 15, 1950; children—Catherine Virginia, Louise Tunison. Tchr., Mt. Pulaski (Ill.) High Sch., 1937-38, Lincoln (Ill.) High Sch., 1938-43, U. Colo., Boulder, 1943-44; office mgr., comptroller Conf. Am. Small Bus. Orgns., Chgo., 1945-46; exec. sec. Northwestern U., Chgo. and Evanston, Ill., 1946-50. Pres. Evanston Aux. Cradle Soc., 1961-62; mem. bd. Citizens Alert Youth Program, Tampa, Fla., 1968-70; mem. Nat. Com. for Support Pub. Schs., Washington, 1968—, Fla. Courses of Study Council, 1971—, Fla. Career Services Commn., 1973—; mem. bd. Hillsborough County Council Parent-Tchrs. Assn., Tampa, 1965—; pres. P.T.A., Tampa, 1967-68, pres.-elect Fla. Congress, 1972-74, pres., 1974—; mem. bd. Community Concert Assn., 1966-69. Mem. Evanston Bd. Edn., 1964-65. Bd. dirs. Mental Health Assn. Hillsborough County. Recipient Alumna of Year award MacMurray Coll., 1965. Mem. Bus. Profl. Women Chgo. (pres. 1951-52), D.A.R. (first vice regent 1963-64), Mayflower Soc., Nat. Soc. Daus. Founders and Patriots Am., Nat. Soc. New Eng. Women, Am. Assn. U. Women, P.E.O. (chpt. pres. 1961-63), Krewe of Venus. Presbyn. Clubs: Tampa Woman's, Palma Ceia Golf and Country, Tower (Tampa); Tides Bath and Tennis (Redington Beach, Fla.). Address: 4524 Brookwood Dr Tampa FL 33609

CHAPIN, CORNELIA VAN A., sculptor; b. Waterford, Conn.; d. Lindley Hoffman and Cornelia Garrison (Van Auken) Chapin; ed. pvt. schs.; studied with Mateo Hernandez, Paris. Exhibited Works, 1930—, including Internat. Expn. Art and Technique, Paris, 1937 (won 2d Grand Prize, class stone sculpture), World's Fair, N.Y., 1939-40, San Francisco Golden Gate Internat. Expn., 1939, Bklyn. Mus., Modern Museum, Washington, Art Centre, Oganquit, Me., Salon des Tuiteries. Salon d'Automne, Paris, Fairmont Park Art Assn., Internat. Sculpture Show, Phila. Museum, Pa. Acad., Phila., San Francisco Art Museum, Montclair (N.J.) Mus., Springfield Art Museum; represented in pvt. collections--Paris, London, N.Y., Phila., Washington; Christ the King, high altar of Cathedral St. John the Divine, N.Y. City; Giant Frog, Rittenhouse Square, Phila. Mem. sculpture jury Contemporary Art Exhibit N.Y. World's Fair, 1939; sculpture chmn. N.Y. Met. Area, Nat. Art Week, 1941; work invited for 3d Internat. Exhbn. of Sculpture, Phila., 1949; sculptor mem. N.Y.C. Art Commn., 1951-53. Works in leading mus. and nat. parks. Fellow Nat. Sculpture Soc. (sec. 1942-45; chmn. library and research com. of council); academician Nat. Acad. Design; mem. Soc. Salon d'Autmore, Paris, 1936, Allied Artists Am., Artists for Victory (Sculpture chmn., 1942). Dir. Kips Bay Boys' Club, N.Y.C. Lectures widely on Carving Direct from Life, Some Tales and Tools. Clubs: Cosmopolitan, National Arts, Architectural League of New York. Home: Wells Hill Rd Lakeville CT 06039

CHAPIN, JOAN LOUISE BEGGS, curator, entomologist; b. St. Louis, Feb. 8, 1929; d. Thomas Putnam and Myra Barbara (Huntington) Beggs; B.S., Kan. State U., 1950; M.S., La. State U., 1959, Ph.D., 1971; m. Bobie T. Chapin, Dec. 23, 1949 (div. Mar. 1971); children—Larry T., Mark Roger, Martha H. Research asst. dept. entomology La. State U., Baton Rouge, 1958-61, asso. dept. entomology curator insect collection, 1961-73, asst. prof., 1973—. Mem. Entomol. Soc. Am., La. Entomol. Soc. (sec.-treas. 1966-68, 73-74), La. Acad. Scis., Bus. and Profl. Woman's Club, Sigma Xi, Gamma Sigma Delta. Club: Bonaire Garden (publicity chmn., historian 1970-71). Home: 3702 Forrest Dr Baton Rouge LA 70809 Office: Dept Entomology Life Scis Bldg La State U Baton Rouge LA 70803

CHAPIN, JUNE ROEDIGER (MRS. NED CHAPIN), educator; b. Chgo., May 19, 1931; d. Henry W. and Stephania (Palke) Roediger; B.A., U. Chgo., 1952, M.A., 1954; Ed.D., Stanford, 1963; m. Ned Chapin, June 12, 1954; children—Suzanne, Elaine. Asst. prof. San Francisco State Coll., 1962-64, U. Santa Clara, Cal., 1965-67; dir. ednl. devel., asso. prof. Coll. Notre Dame, Cal., 1967—; co-dir. Prospective Tchrs. Math., U.S. Office Edn., 1966-67; dir. Computer-Assisted Instrn. Inst. for Coll. Faculty, U.S. Office Edn., summer 1967; cons. Nat. Assessment Project, 1966-67; dir. NSF Sociology Project, summers 1969-71. Distinguished scholar Title III Higher Edn. Act, 1967-68. Mem. Am. Sociol. Assn., Am. Ednl. Research Assn., Nat. Council for Social Studies, Pi Lambda Theta. Co-author: Quest for Liberty: Investigating U.S. History, 1971; Voices of the Nation: A Sourcebook for American History, 1972; Teaching Social Studies Skills, 1973; Women: The Majority-Minority, 1973; Social Studies Dissertations, 1969-1973, 1974. Contbr. articles to profl. jours. Home: 1190 Bellair Way Menlo Park CA 94025 Office: College of Notre Dame Belmont CA 94002

CHAPIN, SUZANNE PHILLIPS, psychologist; b. Syracuse, N.Y., Aug. 9, 1930; d. Harold Bridge and Charlotte (Warner) Phillips; A.B., Syracuse U., 1952; M.A., Columbia, 1965; m. Richard Hilton Chapin, June 13, 1953 (div. June 1964); children—Bruce Phillips, Linda Jean. Psychology examiner Stamford (Conn.) Bd. Edn., 1965-68; psychologist Southbury (Conn.) Tng. Sch., 1968-74; ednl. specialist Onondaga County Assn. Retarded Children, Syracuse, 1974—. Instr. Mattatuck Community Coll., Waterbury, Conn., 1972-73; cons. Head Start Program, 1967-68. Mem. Am. Psychol. Assn., Am. Assn. Mental Deficiency. Home: 4211 Regulus Course Liverpool NY 13088 Office: 600 S Wilbur Av Syracuse NY 13204

CHAPLIN, MAUD HAZELTINE (MRS. ANSEL BURT CHAPLIN), educator, coll. dean; b. N.Y.C., June 27, 1935; d. L. Alan and Elizabeth (Barrett) Hazeltine; B.A., Wellesley Coll., 1956; M.A., Brandeis U., 1958, Ph.D., 1967; m. Ansel Burt Chaplin, Feb. 14, 1959; children—Rawson Alan, Margaret Maud, Jane Dunbar. Lectr. history Wellesley (Mass.) Coll., 1963-64, dean of sophomores, 1967-68, also asst. prof. history, dean of jrs., 1968-69, asst. dean students, 1969-70, dean of studies, 1971—. Radcliffe fellow, 1974. Home: 126 Great Plain Av Wellesley MA 02181

CHAPMAN, AMANDA MARGARITA GONZALEZ (MRS. KENNETH E.M. CHAPMAN), physician; b. Juarez, Mexico, Apr. 17, 1923; d. Herlindo and Guadalupe (Fierro) Gonzalez; student Los Angeles City Coll., 1942-44, U. Cal. at Los Angeles, 1944-45, U. Guadalajara, 1941-42; D.O., Coll. Osteo. Physicians and Surgeons, 1949; M.D., U. Cal. at Irvine, 1962; m. Kenneth E.M. Chapman, May 31, 1947 (div. Jan. 1974); 1 son, Kenneth Luis. Came to U.S., 1930, naturalized, 1943. Intern, Los Angeles County Hosp., 1949-50, resident, 1950-51; staff Cancer Detection Center, Los Angeles, 1962-68; sch. physician Pasadena and Alhambra, Cal., 1964-70; gen. practice medicine, Wilmington, Cal., 1969—, Pasadena, Cal., 1969—; coll. physician Los Angeles Community Coll., 1972—; staff physician Cal. State U. at Los Angeles, also Foothill Free Clinic. Mem. Am., Cal., Los Angeles County med. assns., Am. Acad. Gen. Practice. Democrat. Home: 1175 S Oak Knoll Av Pasadena CA 91106 Office: 1111 S Figueroa Pl Wilmington CA 90744

CHAPMAN, BEATRICE MURRAY, pub. relations cons.; b. Portland, Me., July 14, 1908; d. Melvin and Ellie J. (Libby) Goff; grad. Gorham Normal Sch., 1927; m. John W. Chapman, Oct. 25, 1958 (dec. 1967); 4 stepchildren. Dir. World Affairs Council, World Peace Found., Boston, 1944-51; dir. pub. relations Peter Bent Brigham Hosp., Boston, 1951-61; with Me. Dept. Health and Welfare, Augusta, 1962—, dir. info. and edn., 1963-74, ret., 1974; pub. relations cons., Peaks Island, Me., 1974—. Project dir. Casco Bay Islands Devel. Assn.; pres. Peaks Island Conf. Center; past pres. Me. Press-Radio-TV Women; 1st del. from Me. to Nat. Security Forum, Air War Coll., 1970, Harvard Summer Inst. Non-Profit Mgmt. Mem. Nat. Assn. Human Services Pub. Information Officers (v.p.). Founder, editor Concern quar. newspaper. Home and office: Peaks Island ME 04108

CHAPMAN, CAROLYN, county ofcl.; b. Chgo., Jan. 26, 1924; d. Edward Samuel and Mildred Mary (McNeill) Nelson; student U. Chgo., 1942-44; m. Robert Arthur Chapman, Dec. 16, 1944; children—Diana (Mrs. David G. Miller), Victoria (Mrs. Lawrence K. Forness). Clk., Ill. Bell Telephone Co., Chgo., 1941-42, Allstate Ins. Co., Chgo., 1942, Chgo. Symphony, 1942-45; tchr. swimming Belleville (Ill.) Swimming Pool, 1954-59; pres. Belleville Med. Aux., 1959-60, Belleville League Women Voters, 1961-63, Ill. Coordinated Child Care Com., 1970-72, Tri-County Health and Welfare Council, 1973-74; chmn. St. Clair County Mental Health Bd., 1970—. Organizer, operator vol. poll watching programs, East St. Louis, Ill., 1970-74. Named Outstanding St. Clair County Citizen, St. Clair Health and Welfare Council, 1971; recipient Oscar G. Thalinger verse play award, 1971. Mem. Ill. Assn. Community Mental Health Bds. (pres. 1973-74), St. Louis Poetry Center, Nat. League Am. Pen Women, Archaeol. Inst. Am. Democrat. Home: 5927 Memory Lane Belleville IL 62223 Office: 7 N High St Belleville IL 62220

CHAPMAN, CARRIE ETHELYN, physician; b. Manchester, N.H., Dec. 17, 1906; d. John Wilbert and Carrie Ethelyn (Crawford) Chapman; B.S., Fla. State U., 1928; M.D., Tufts U., 1934. Intern, Mass. State Infirmary, Tewksbury, 1934-35; resident anesthesiology Mass. Gen. Hosp., 1937-38, Faulkner Hosp., 1938-41; fellow anesthesiology Mayo Clinic and Found., 1946, fellow phys. medicine and rehab., 1946-49; practice medicine, specializing in phys. medicine, rehab., anesthesiology, Oakland, Cal., 1951-63, Los Angeles, 1963—; asst. surgeon USPHS, 1944-51; lt. comdr., then comdr. U.S. Navy, 1950—, chief phys. medicine, rehab. service Oakland Naval Hosp., 1951-53, cons., 1955-63; clin. instr. anesthesiology Postgrad. Med. Sch. Harvard, 1938-41; cons. dept. occupational therapy San Jose (Cal.) State Coll., 1960-63; asst. clin. prof. phys. medicine and rehab. U. So. Cal. Med. Sch., 1964-70, asso. prof., 1970—; chief phys. medicine, rehab. VA Hosp., Oakland, 1954-63; cons. San Joaquin Gen. and County Hosp., Stockton, Cal., 1962-63; asso. dir. adj. staff Ben R. Meyer Rehab. Center Cedars of Lebanon Hosp., Cedar Sinai Med. Center, 1963, asso. attending, 1964—; cons. VA Hosp., Long Beach, Cal., 1964-65; attending staff Los Angeles County Gen. Hosp., 1964—. Liaison officer Am. Acad. Phys. Medicine and Rehab. to A.M.A. Nat. Congress Vol. Health Agys. Chmn. Alameda County chpt. Muscular Dystrophy Assn., 1954-56; mem. Pres.'s Com. Employment Handicapped, 1963—, Cal. Gov.'s Com. Employment Handicapped, 1971; vice chmn. So. Cal. chpt. Multiple Sclerosis Soc., 1966—, chmn. med. adv. bd., 1968-70; mem. adv. bd. East Bay Rehab. Center; mem. med. adv. bd. Diablo Therapy Center, Pleasant Hill, Cal., 1954-63. Chmn. Beverly Hills (Cal.) Com. to Employ the Handicapped, 1972-73. Founder, pres. Am. Found. for Treatment Burn Injuries, 1970. Recipient award of merit Dept. Cal. Mil. Order Purple Heart, 1958; D.A.V. Nat. citation for distinguished service, 1961; certificate of merit A.C.S., 1963; named Cal. Physician of Year, 1969; award for meritorious contbns. to rehab. Am. Assn. Med. Dirs.-Am. Assn. Rehab. Therapists, 1973. Diplomate Am. Bd. Phys. Medicine and Rehab. Fellow Am. Acad. Phys. Medicine and Rehab., Am. Geriatrics Soc.; mem. A.M.A. (certificate of merit 1964), Cal. (asst. sec. sect. phys. medicine 1958, 71; chmn. 1960, 73), Alameda-Contra-Costa (chmn. rehab. com. 1962-63), Pan Am. med. assns., Am. Congress Phys. Medicine and Rehab. (Bronze medal 1962, sec. Western sect.), Cal., Peruvian (hon.) socs. phys. medicine and rehab., Am. Inst. Ultrasonics in Medicine (pres. 1963-64, plaque for outstanding contbns. as pres. 9th ann. meeting 1964), Am. Med. Womens Assn. (life), Cal. (chmn. 1970), So. Cal. (pres. 1970-71; exec. bd. 1969—) socs. phys. medicine, Am. Assn. Electromyography and Electrodiagnosis, Assn. for Rehab. Centers, Assn. Mil. Surgeons U.S., Assn. Med. Rehab. Dirs. and Coordinators (past chmn. med. certification bd.), Tufts Med., Mayo Grad. Sch. Medicine (life), Mass. Gen. Hosp. alumni assns., Nat. Rehab. Assn. (pres. So. Cal. chpt. 1970), Nat. Assn. Sheltered Workshops and Homebound Programs, Pan Am. Med. Womens Alliance, Soc. for History Medicine, Internat. Soc. for Burn Injuries (Edinburg, Scotland), N.Am. Acad. Manipulative Medicine (v.p. 1969-71, pres. elect 1971, pres. 1972), Cal. Phys. Med. Soc. (v.p. So. Cal. 1969, pres. 1970). Contbr. articles to profl. jours. Home: 165 N Swall Dr Beverly Hills CA 90211 Office: Brentwood VA Hosp Wilshire and Sawtelle Blvds Los Angeles CA 90073

CHAPMAN, DOROTHY HURD (MRS. WILLIAM JACKSON CHAPMAN, SR.), b. Bessemer, Ala., Aug. 11, 1915; d. Clarence Spencer and Tressie Mae (Heffner) Hurd; B.S. (art scholar), Huntingdon Coll., 1938; occupational therapist, Milw.-Downer Coll., 1946; postgrad. U. S.C., 1968-69; certified ceramics instr. Heron Sch. Art, Ind. U., 1969; m. William Jackson Chapman, Jan. 4, 1947; children—William Jackson, Mark Spencer Horace. With Paragon Press, Montgomery, Ala., 1939-42; statistician, cadet hdqrs. U.S. Army, Maxwell Field Air Base, Ala., 1942-45; occupational therapist Lawson Gen. Hosp., Atlanta, 1945, Kennedy VA Hosp., Memphis, 1946; sec. Meth. Bd. Edn., Spartanburg, S.C., 1948-50; teller, installment loan dept. First Nat. Bank, Orangeburg, S.C., 1955; arts and crafts, ceramics instr. S.C. Sch. for Deaf, Spartanburg, 1965-71. Den mother Boy Scouts Am., Spartanburg, 1961-66; active fund drives March of Dimes, Heart Fund, 1962-64. Surgeon Gen.'s Dept. grantee for occupational therapy, 1945-46. Recipient 1st prize, art exhibit, Spartanburg, 1952, 70, 2d prize, 1970; 1st prize, Orangeburg, 1953. Mem. Am. Occupational Therapy Assn. Home: 117 Oakleaf Dr Spartanburg SC 29301

CHAPMAN, DOROTHY RADCLIFFE TUTHILL, editor; b. N.Y.C.; d. Daniel Stuart and Lillian (Radcliffe) Tuthill; student Phoenix Jr. Coll., 1940, Ariz. State Coll., 1942; div.; children—Deborah (Mrs. Peter Joseph Synder), Rosemary, Amy (Mrs. Robert Thomas Elliot, Jr.). Continuity dir. radio sta. KPHO, Phoenix, 1942-45; mem. staff radio sta. KOY; advt. mgr. Porters, Phoenix; engaged in pub. relations, advt. Chapman Enterprises, Phoenix; editorial dept. Sentinel Star Co., Orlando, Fla., 1960-68, women's editor, 1967-71, food editor, 1971—. Mem. Gov.'s Commn. on Status of Women, 1968-73. Mem. Council for Continuing Edn. Women, Inc. (dir.), Fla. Press Club (pres.), Kappa Delta Pi, Alpha Psi Omega. Presbyn. Home: 1220 S Eola Dr Orlando FL 32806 Office: 633 N Orange Av Orlando FL 32802

CHAPMAN, ERNA MARTA RIEDEL (MRS. RAY F. CHAPMAN), educator; b. Dresden, Germany, May 20, 1909 (brought to U.S. 1914, naturalized 1923); d. Joseph and Elsa (Mueller) Riedel; B.S., U. Md., 1934, M.S., 1936; postgrad. Ind. U., D.C. Tchrs. Coll., U. Md.; m. Ray F. Chapman, Sept. 5, 1942. Sales, acting asst. buyer The Hecht Co., Washington, 1928-30; card punch operator Census Bur., 1930-31; grad. asst. U. Md. Coll. Home Econs., College Park, 1934-36; corr. editor Social Security Bd., Balt., 1936-38; vocational home econs. tchr. D.C. pub. schs., Washington, 1938-56, state supr. home econs. edn., 1960-65; asst. prin. Roosevelt High Sch., Washington, 1956-60; state supr., supervising dir. home econs. edn. D.C. Pub. Schs., Washington, 1967—; acting dean U. Md., College Park, 1965-67; mem. nat. adv. com. J.C. Penney Co., Inc. Family life cons. Teamwork Found.; mem. Gov.'s com. State of Md., Status of Women in Higher Edn., 1965-67. Mem. N.E.A., Am. Vocational Assn., Am. Home Econs. Assn., Am. Assn. U. Women, Nat. Council Adminstrs. of Home Econs., Assn. Home Econs. Adminstrs., Nat. Assn. State Univs. and Land Grant Colls., Md. Home Econs. Assn., Omicron Nu, Phi Kappa Phi, Phi Delta Gamma. Club: Research (D.C.). Contbr. articles in field to profl. jours. Home: Route 1 Box 388 Gambrills MD 21054 Office: Presdl Bldg 415 12th St NW Washington DC 20004

CHAPMAN, EUGENIA SHELDON, state legislator; b. Fairhope, Ala., Jan. 10, 1923; d. Chauncey Bailey and Rose (Donner) Sheldon; B.Ed., Chgo. State U., 1944; m. Gerald M. Chapman, Nov. 24, 1948; children—George, John, Katherine, Andrew. Tchr. pub. schs., Cicero, Ill., 1944-47, Chgo., 1947-51; mem. Ill. Ho. of Reps., 1964—. Mem. Dist. 214 Bd. Edn., Cook County, Ill., 1961-64, sec., 1962-64; mem. exec. com. Tri-County div. Ill. Assn. Sch. Bds., 1964. Recipient Best Freshman and Best Legislator awards Ind. Voters Ill.; Golden award Ill. League Conservation Voters, 1974; Spl. award United Auto Workers, 1973; Presdl. citation Ill. Assn. Sch. Adminstrs., 1974. Mem. League Women Voters (pres. Arlington Heights 1957-59). Democrat. Address: 16 S Princeton Ct Arlington Heights IL 60005

CHAPMAN, FRANCES ELIZABETH CLAUSEN (MRS. WILLIAM JAMES CHAPMAN), civic worker; b. Atchison, Kan., Feb. 27, 1920; d. Erwin W. and Helen (Hackney) Clausen; B.A., Wellesley Coll., 1941; m. W. MacLean Johnson, Aug. 31, 1940 (dec. Nov. 1965); children—Stuart MacLean, Duncan Scott, Douglas Hamilton; m. 2d, William James Chapman, Dec. 5, 1970. Project dir. Women in Community Service, Inc., St. Louis, 1965-66; pres. Nursery Found., St. Louis, 1956-58, dir., 1953-59, 65-68; adv. com. Mo. State Children's Day Care, 1963—; chmn. day care com. Mo. Council Children and Youth, 1961, chmn. foster care sect., 1961-63; spl. asst. to the pres. Webster Coll., 1966-68. Bd. mem. New City Sch.,

1967-69, Mid-County YMCA, 1967-70; mem. steering com. Mo. Council on Children and Youth, 1967—. Trustee Jr. Coll. Dist., St. Louis-St. Louis County, pres. bd. trustees, 1971-73; trustee John Burroughs Sch., 1973—; bd. dirs. Assn. Governing Bds. Univs. and Colls., 1970—; bd. commrs. Nat. Commn. on Accrediting, 1971—. Mem. Nat. Soc. Arts and Letters, Wellesley Coll. Alumnae Assn. (sec. dir. 1958-61). Club: Wellesley College (pres. 1965-67). Home: 10 Overbrook Dr St Louis MO 63124

CHAPMAN, GLORIA KATHERINE ORTNER, psychologist; b. Buffalo; d. Charles Franklin and Laura (Hollister) Ortner; B.A., U. Buffalo, 1943, Ed.D., 1954; M.B.A., U. Chgo., 1945; m. Norman Chapman, Oct. 12, 1955 (div. 1962). Personnel research technician Curtis Wright Corp., Buffalo, 1944-45; tchr. Kenmore (N.Y.) Sr. High Sch., 1945-46; psychologist U. Buffalo, 1946-48, chief counselor women, 1949-55; tng. dir. Goodwill Industries, Buffalo, 1948-49; counselor, instr. Rochester Inst. Tech., 1955-56; tchr. remedial reading and guidance San Mateo (Cal.) Schs., 1956-59; sr. counselor, remedial reading specialist Stanford, 1959-61; asst. dir. guidance services Coll. Entrance Exam. Bd., Ednl. Testing Service, Princeton, N.J., 1961-63; sr. psychologist N.Y.U. Testing and Advisement Center, N.Y.C., 1963-70; testing cons. tng. N.Y. State Employment Service, 1970-71, employment counselor, 1971-73, cons. test research, 1973—. asst. prof. Bank St. Coll. Edn., 1969-70. Bd. dirs. Assn. Neighborhood Community Councils, 1967-70. Bd. visitors Central Islip State Hosp. Mem. Am. Psychol. Assn., Am. Personnel and Guidance Assn., Nat. Vocational Guidance Assn. Unitarian (chmn. community affairs 1966-68, chmn. worship 1970-72). Club: Women's City (mem. youth and community com. 1967-73). Home: 145 E 27th St New York City NY 10016

CHAPMAN, HELEN LOUISE BUSCH (MRS. THEODORE STILLMAN CHAPMAN), civic worker, club woman; b. Coldwater, Mich., Apr. 20, 1904; d. Francis X. and Jeannette Frances (Morrison) Busch; B.A., U. Wis., 1925; M.A., U. Chgo., 1936; LL.D., Blackburn U., 1955; m. Theodore Stillman Chapman, June 28, 1939 (dec. June 1943). Formerly taught history, econs., English Chgo. high schs., Crane Jr. Coll., Chgo.; tchr. history Monticello Coll., Godfrey, Ill. Held many offices including pres. Beverly Hills Woman's Club (Chgo.), other local clubs; jr. chmn., 3rd dist. Ill. Fedn. Women's Clubs, 1st v.p., pres. 20th dist., pres. Ill. fedn., 1945-47; edn. chmn. Gen. Fedn. Women's Clubs, 1947-50, 2d v.p., 1950-52, 1st v.p., 1952-54, pres., 1954-56, hon. pres.; pres. Chautauqua (N.Y.) Woman's Club, 1946-53. Past. mem. correctional services adv. bd. Ill. Youth Commn.; dir. Boys Town of Ill., Grafton, 1943-63; Ill. Citizens Edn. Com. dir. Am. Council to Improve Our Neighborhoods, 1954-59; bd. dirs. Care, Inc., Am. Heritage Found., 1954-56; trustee inst. internat. Edn., 1952-56; mem. nat. women's adv. com. FCDA, 1954-56; mem. nat. citizens com. United Community Campaigns Am., 1954-56; dir. Freedom's Found. at Valley Forge, 1955-62; mem. nat. adv. bd. FDA, 1954-56; nat. adv. food and drug council FDA, 1964-68; trustee, vice chmn. Allied Youth, Inc., pub. adv. com. Nat. Arts Found., 1954-60; nat. com. Am. Mus. of Immigration, 1955—; nat. adv. council Keep Am. Beautiful, Inc., 1954-56; coordinator for consumers, 50th Anniversary Com. Assn. Food and Drug Ofcls. U.S., 1956; dir. Citizens for Hoover Report; mem. laymen's com. Religion in Am. Life, 1954-56; mem. gen. sponsoring com. Christian Children's Fund; mem. consumer com. Ill. Status Women Commn.; mem. Ill. Citizens Edn. Council; mem. adv. bd. Berea in Korea; mem. sponsoring com. UN Assn.; past mem. Nat. Health Council. Trustee Monticello Coll., 1943-66, Mary Thompson Hosp., Chgo., 1961-65, Blackburn U.; mem. nat. bd. Woman's Med. Coll. Pa.; bd. dirs. Am. Heritage Found., 1954-56. Program asst. Nat. Presbyn. Center, 1967-73. Mem. Sch. Bd., Jersey County, Ill., 1950-54; mem. nat. com. citizens for Eisenhower-Nixon, 1956. Decorated by King Paul (Greece), 1956; recipient Distinguished Service award Monticello Coll., 1955, citation pub. service U. Chgo., 1955, Centennial award Berea Coll., 1955, Freedoms Found. at Valley Forge award, 1955. Mem. Am. Assn. U. Women, Am. Assn. Ret. Persons (pres. Fontana chpt.), D.A.R., P.E.O., Nat. Assn. Parliamentarians, Delta Kappa Gamma, Alpha Gamma Delta. Presbyn. Home: Country Fairway Estates Fontana WI 53125

CHAPMAN, HOPE VIETTA (MRS. RALPH CHAPMAN), ednl. adminstr.; b. Spokane, Wash., Oct. 27, 1923; d. George Henry and Leila May (Parsons) Severance; B.S., Milw.-Downer Coll., 1945, diploma in occupational therapy, 1946; postgrad. Keene State Coll., 1969-74; M.Ed., 1974 m. Ralph Chapman, Aug. 5, 1951; children—Ralph Severance, Christopher George, Jonathan William. Dir. occupational therapy Brattleboro (Vt.) Retreat, 1947-54, Hicks Sch.-Retarded, 1956-65; dir. Head Start, Brattleboro, 1965-69; coordinator pre-sch. screening Windham S.E. Supervisory Union, 1970-73; developmental disabilities specialist Windham County Dept. Mental Health Service, 1974—; houseparent Am. Youth Hostels, 1955-65. Cons., Windham County Mental Retardation Service, 1970—. Vice pres. Vt. Childrens Aid Soc., Better Housing, Inc.; treas. Green Mountain Camp, Windham County 4-C, Brattleboro Child Devel., Dental Health Com.; bd. dirs. Community House. Mem. Am. Assn. U. Women (sec., v.p., dir. 1954—), Am., No. New Eng. Occupational Therapy Assns. Episcopalian. Home: Route 1 Box 31 Brattleboro VT 05301

CHAPMAN, JANE ROBERTS, labor economist; b. Holdenville, Okla., Apr. 8, 1937; d. Vernon Edmund and Grace Lillian (Enos) Roberts; student U. Okla., 1955-57, M.A., 1963; B.A., Stanford, 1959; m. Gordon Chapman, June 25, 1959; children—Kristin, Patrick. Asst. mng. editor Monthly Labor Rev., U.S. Dept. Labor, Washington, 1961-63, manpower specialist, 1963-67; cons. labor economist, 1970-72; Co-dir. Center for Women Policy Studies, 1972—. Mem. Employment Task Force Leadership Conf. on Civil Rights, 1971—. Mem. Am. Econ. Assn., Nat. Orgn. Women (Nat. compliance com. 1971—), Assn. Feminist Cons. Address: 4136 Leland St Chevy Chase MD 20015

CHAPMAN, LORNA T., librarian; b. Glen Lyon, Pa., Apr. 26, 1933; d. Stanley and Helen Zubris; B.A., Western Mich. U., 1961, M.S., 1973; student Wayne State U., 1951-52; div.; children—Cathy (Mrs. David Hostetler), Linda, Bradley, Michael. Library asst. Chrysler Guided Missile Tech. Library, Centerline, Mich., 1951; asst. librarian Comstock Twp. (Mich.) Library, 1957-60; bookmobile librarian Kalamazoo Pub. Library, 1960-63; head librarian East Br. Library, 1964—. Cons., New Designs for Environmental Living, 1973—; exec. dir. Nat. Library Week program in Mich. Bd. dirs. Kalamazoo Community Action Program, Inc. Mem. Mich. Library Assn. (chmn. recruitment com. 1970, chmn. pub. relations and nat. library week com. 1972-73). Author: Directory of Community Resources of Kalamazoo County, 1973, supplement, 1974. Contbr. articles to profl. jours. Home: 2244 Oakland Dr Kalamazoo MI 49008 Office: 1719 E Main St Kalamazoo MI 49001

CHAPMAN, MARY LUCILE, educator; b. Louisa, Ky.; d. Napoleon Bonaperte and Ida Belle (Porter) Chapman; A.B., U. Ky., 1929, M.A., 1937, Ph.D., 1945. Tchr. pub. schs., Ashland, Ky., 1921-40, supr., 1940-56; asst. prof. history Marshall Coll., Huntington, W.Va., 1946-48; asso. prof. history East Tenn. State Coll., Johnson City, 1948-55; prof. social studies Jr. Coll., 1955-57; prof. history Ashland Center U. Ky., 1957-59; head dept. history Piedmont Coll., Demorest, Ga., 1959-62, chmn. div. social studies, 1959-62; asso. prof. history Jacksonville State U. (formerly Jacksonville State Coll.), 1962-65, prof. history, 1965—. Mem. Ala. Coalition for Better Schs., Women's Civil Def. Council Ala. Named Community Leader Am., 1968, 70, 72. Mem. Nat. Council Social Studies, Am., So., Ala., Calhoun County hist. assns., Am. Assn. U. Women (mem. Ala. bd.; pres. Anniston br. 1967-69), Nat., Ky., Ala. edn. assns., Internat. Fedn. U. Women, Am. Acad. Social and Polit. Scis., U.D.C., D.A.R. (bicentennial research com.), Ga. Hist. Soc., Acad. Polit. Sci., So. Polit. Sci. Assn., Internat. Platform Assn., Assn. Am. Historians, Am. Assn. U. Profs., Nat. Hist. Soc. (founding asso.), North Atlantic Council U.S., Council So. Mountains, Inc., Friends of the Library, InterContinental Biog. Assn., Marquis Biog. Soc., Kappa Delta Pi, Phi Kappa Theta. Democrat. Methodist. Clubs: Piedmont Woman's Faculty (chmn.), Demorest Woman's, Jacksonville College Faculty. Home: 703 12th Av Jacksonville AL 36265

CHAPMAN, MURIEL E., educator; B.S. in Nursing Edn., U. Walla Walla, 1947; M.Nursing, Emory U., 1956; Ed.D., Columbia, 1969. Prof., chmn. dept. nursing Berea Coll., 1968—. Address: Dept of Nursing Berea College Berea KY 40403

CHAPMAN, RUBY BAKER (MRS. BENJAMIN BURTON CHAPMAN), elec. mfg. co. exec.; b. Darlington Heights, Va., May 29, 1914; d. Walter Henry and Lula Sarah (Driskill) Baker; degree Chgo. Sch. Interior Decoration, 1961; m. Benjamin Burton Chapman, Apr. 17, 1933. Sec.-treas. Burton Chapman, Inc., Ashland, Va., 1954—. Mem. Greater Ashland C. of C. (rec. sec. 1970-71), Extension Home Makers Club Va. (county pres. 1962-63, dist. pres. 1971-73), U.D.C. Democrat. Methodist (life mem. Women's Soc. Christian Service). Mem. Order Eastern Star (past worthy matron). Clubs: Henry Clay Woman's (treas. 1960-63), Henry Clay Home Demonstration (pres. 1961-62); Hanover County, Elmont Club 20 (all Ashland). Home: 113 Cubs Lane Ashland VA 23005 Office: PO Box 467 112 England St Ashland VA 23005

CHAPMAN, RUTH BRINDLEY (MRS. HAROLD E. CHAPMAN, JR.), editor; b. Bloomington, Ill., May 16, 1918; d. Emmett Brown and Lottie Vliet (Webster) Brindley; student Northwestern U., Sch. Journalism, 1936-39; m. Harold E. Chapman, Jr. May 25, 1940; children—Cynthia (Mrs. Larry LaFollette), David Brindley. Reporter, Lombard (Ill.) Spectator, 1939-40; reporter News-Jour., Pensacola, Fla., 1943-46, legislative reporter, Tallahassee, Fla., 1947-49; women's editor Tallahassee Democrat, 1954-61; cons., editor Fla. Schs. mag. Fla. Dept. Edn., Tallahassee, 1965—. Pres. Leon County Council of P.T.A., 1962-64; co-chmn. Com. to Survey Need for Jr. Coll., 1961-64; sec. Friends of Leon County Pub. Library, 1954-55. Bd. dirs. Tallahassee Jr. Mus., 1956-59, YMCA, 1958-59; mem. adv. bd. Leon County Pub. Library, 1967-72; trustee Tallahassee Community Coll., 1964-67. Recipient Distinguished Achievement award Ednl. Press Assn. Am., 1971, 72, 73, award for Distinction in Ednl. Communication Nat. Sch. Pub. Relations Assn., 1970, 71, 73. Mem. League Women Voters, Delta Kappa Gamma (sec. Alpha Lambda chpt. 1974—). Democrat. Episcopalian. Home: 1025 Alachua Tallahassee FL 32303 Office: Florida Dept of Education Tallahassee FL 32304

CHAPNICK, MARILYN JANICE, food co. exec.; b. St. Louis, Mar. 1, 1937; d. Jack and Betty (Schwartz) Chapnick; student U. Wis., 1955-56; B.S. in Bus. Adminstrn., Washington U., St. Louis, 1959; postgrad. Harvard-Radcliffe, 1960; m. Roberto Schwartzman, May 25, 1969 (div.). Personnel mgr. Mayfair Lennox Hotel, 1960-61; dir. marketing Lawrence and Marilyn Foods, St. Louis, 1961-67; merchandising mgr. Lawry's Foods, Inc., Los Angeles, 1967-69; founder Marilyn Foods, Inc., St. Louis; pres. Chapnick's Buffets, 1970—; mgr. Marilyn and Lawrence Foods. Lectr. restaurant mgmt. St. Louis Jr. Coll. Mem. Playgoers. Mem. Nat. (award 1963), Mo. (dir.) restaurant assns., St. Louis Art Mus., Mo. Bot. Gardens, Bus. and Profl. Women, Arts and Ednl. Council Craft Alliance, Zonta. Mem. B'nai B'rith (chmn. edn. 1968, guarantor Library Forum). Club: Women in Advertising (St. Louis); Gridiron Cast. Home: 4400 Lindell Blvd St Louis MO 63108 Office: 101 Weldon Pkwy Maryland Heights MO 63043

CHAPPELLE, YVONNE JUANITA REED (MRS. WILLIAM D. CHAPPELLE, III), govt. ofcl.; b. Washington, Dec. 20, 1937; d. George Raymond and Beatrice (Murray) Reed; B.A. cum laude, Allegheny Coll., 1959; M.A. (Woodrow Wilson fellow), Am. U., 1960; Ph.D., Union Grad. Sch., 1974; m. William D. Chappelle, III, Oct. 12, 1966; children—Felicia Yvonne, William Reed Sedar, David Khari Webber. Engaged as bi-lingual sec. African-Am. Inst., Washington, 1960-61; exec. sec. High Commn. for Inga Dam Project, Republic of Zaire, 1961-63; French tchr. Fgn. Lang. in Elementary Schs., Washington Pub. Schs., 1963-64; fgn. affairs officer Dept. of State, Washington, 1965-67; placement dir. Wilberforce (O.) U., 1967-68, coordinator student life programs, 1968-70; dir. Black Cultural Resources Center, Wright State (O.) U., 1970-73; mem. staff D.C. com. U.S. Ho. of Reps., 1973—. Mem. U.S. delegation UNESCO, Paris, 1966; mem. Nat. Fedn. of Blind. Mem. African Heritage Studies Assn., Black World Found., Phi Beta Kappa, Pi Gamma Mu, Pi Sigma Alpha. Democrat. Home: 1808 Grace Church Rd Silver Spring MD 20910

CHARACHE, PATRICIA (MRS. SAMUEL CHARACHE), scientist, med. educator; b. Newark, Dec. 26, 1929; d. Harold Solomon and Carye-Belle (Henle) Connamacher; student Oberlin Coll., 1948-51; B.A., Hunter Coll., 1952; M.D., N.Y. U., 1957; m. Samuel Charache, June 11, 1951; 1 dau. Barbara. Intern, Balt. City Hosps., 1957-58; research asso. Harvard, 1962-64; instr. medicine Johns Hopkins Sch. Medicine, 1964-67, asst. prof. medicine, 1969-73, asso. prof. medicine, 1973—, asso. prof. lab. medicine in pathology, 1973—, asst. prof. microbiology, 1969—, dir. microbiology labs. Johns Hopkins Hosp., 1973—. USPHS fellow, 1958-59, 60-62; Robert Robinson Porter fellow, 1959-60; recipient research career devel. award USPHS-Nat. Inst. Allergy and Infectious Diseases, 1969-73. Mem. A.A.A.S., Reticuloendothelial Soc., Infectious Diseases Soc. Am., Am. Soc. Microbiology, Am. Fedn. Clinical Research. Home: 2006 Sulgrave Av Baltimore MD 21209 Office: John Hopkins Hospital Baltimore MD 21205

CHARGAR, ELEANORE LIPKIN (MRS. ALBERT CHARGAR), retail trade exec.; b. Bklyn., June 5, 1919; d. Samuel and Ida (Marks) Lipkin; student Bklyn. Coll., 1935-37, N.Y. U., 1937-39; m. Albert Chargar, Feb. 8, 1941; children—John, Richard. Buyer pilot store Charles Stores, Inc., N.Y.C., 1940-42; asst. infantswear buyer Hecht Co., Washington, 1942-43; resident buyer adminstrv. Karl J. Marx Co., N.Y.C., 1957-68; merchandise mgr. all soft goods Bonanza Stores, Inc., Renton, Wash., 1968—. Mem. B'nai B'rith, Hadassah. Home: 416 101st St SE Bellevue WA 98004 Office: 705 SW 7th St Renton WA 98055

CHARGOIS, DEBORAH MAJEAU (MRS. ASHTON JOSEPH CHARGOIS), neurophysiologist, educator; b. New Orleans, Nov. 8, 1940; d. John Ashton and Marie Antoinette (Barbot) Majeau; B.A., St. Mary's Coll., 1963; M.S. (NIH fellow), La. State U., 1967, Ph.D. (Bio-space Tech. Tng. Program fellow), 1969; m. Ashton Joseph Chargois, Sept. 6, 1969. Instr., La. State U. Med. Center, New Orleans, 1968-69; asst. prof. physiology, 1969-71, clin. asst. prof., 1971—. Cons., lectr. Marshall Space Flight Center Miss. Test Facility, 1969-71. Recipient First award for Sci. Merit, Am. Speech and Hearing Assn., 1970. NIH fellow in tropical medicine, 1973; Deafness Research Found. grantee, 1970-71. Mem. A.A.A.S., Am. Inst. Biol. Sci., Am. Physiol. Soc., Soc. Neurosci., USCG Aux., Sigma Xi. Home: 2339 Palmer Av New Orleans LA 70118 Office: Dept Physiology La State U Med Center 1542 Tulane Av New Orleans LA 70112

CHARLES, CAROLYN HEATH STOWELL, counselor educator; b. Derby, Conn., Aug. 14, 1921; d. Austin Leavitt and Doris (Hillery) Stowell; B.A., Fla. State U., 1943; M.R.E., Presbyn. Sch. Christian Edn., Richmond, Va., 1946; M.A., U., Ala., 1970, Ph.D., 1973; m. Douglas E. Charles, May 20, 1947 (div.); children—Elizabeth Stowell (Mrs. Wadislau Martins Gomes), Kathryn Doris (Mrs. James Marcus Calton). Tchr., evang. ednl. missionary, Brazil, 1948-65; counselor U. Hosp. Sch. Nursing, Birmingham, Ala., 1965-67; counselor New Careers, Birmingham, 1967-69; counselor Lawson State Community Coll., Birmingham, 1969-70; teaching fellow, instr. U. Ala., 1971-72; asso. prof. counseling and guidance U. North Ala., Florence, 1972—. Mem. Am., Ala. personnel and guidance assns., Am., Ala. coll. personnel assns., Am. Assn for Higher Edn., Nat. Vocational Guidance Assn., Am., Ala. (exec. com.) assns. counselor edn. and supervision, Delta Kappa Gamma, Chi Delta Phi, Kappa Delta Pi, Alpha Chi Omega, Mortar Bd. Republican. Baptist. Translator: Um Avivamento Entre Missionarios Na Coreia, 1961. Home: 4-A Doris Lane Florence AL 35630 Office: Coll Edn U North Ala Florence AL 35630

CHARLES, SISTER ISABEL, educator; b. Bklyn., Mar. 10, 1926; d. James Patrick and Isabel (Roney) Charles; B.A., Manhattan Coll., 1954; M.A., U. Notre Dame, 1960, Ph.D., 1965; postgrad. U. Mich., 1968-69. Chmn. dept. English, Bishop Watterson High Sch., Columbus, O., 1954-59, St. Mary of The Springs Acad., Columbus, 1959-62; asst. prof. English, Ohio Dominican Coll., Columbus, 1965-68, acad. dean, exec. v.p., 1969-73; asst. dean Coll. Arts and Letters, U. Notre Dame, 1973—. Mem. Modern Lang. Assn., Am. Assn. Acad. Deans, Am. Assn. Higher Edn. Contbr. articles to profl. jours. Home: Apt D 1609 N Riverside Dr South Bend IN 46616 Office: Coll Arts and Letters Univ Notre Dame Notre Dame IN 46556

CHARLIER, PATRICIA MARY SIMONET (MRS. ROGER HENRI L.C.L. CHARLIER), educator; b. Enderlin, N.D., July 12, 1923; d. John Jerome and Sophia Cecelia (Krueger) Simonet; student Coll. of St. Scholastica, 1941-43; B.S., U. Minn., 1944, M.A., 1958; Ph.D. (Pi Lambda Theta scholar), 1960; postgrad. U. Aix-Marseilles (France), summer 1958, U. Paris (France), 1958-59, U. Bordeaux (France), 1971-73; m. Roger Henri L.C.L. Charlier, June 17, 1958; children—Constance Cecelia-Paula, Jean-Armand Leonard. Tchr., Buffalo (Minn.) High Sch., 1944-47; librarian, tchr. Delano (Minn.) High Sch., 1947-49, prin., 1949-56; instr. U. Minn., 1956-57, 57-58, adminstrv. fellow Office Admissions and Records 1959-60; asst. prin. U. Minn. High Sch., 1957-58; asso. prof. ednl. psychology, chmn. secondary edn. dept. Parsons Coll., Fairfield, Ia., 1960-61; asso. prof. psychology Chgo. State U., 1961-64; asso. prof. edn. and psychology U. Ill., Chgo., 1965—, head div. curriculum, instrn. and evaluation, 1973—. Asso. dir. div. ednl. travel U. Travel Hdqrs., Inc., Chgo., 1962-69; dir. Edn. Travel Projects, 1954—; vis. prof., asso. dir. Edn. Travel Programs Western N.M. U., 1963-66; vis. lectr. psychology Loyola U., Chgo., 1964-65; cons. div. ednl. travel Vacations, Internat., Chgo., 1964-67, ednl. travel div. N.E.A., 1962-65; vis. prof. U. Autonoma de Baja Cal. (Mexico), 1967; spl. cons. to supr. pub. instrn. Ill., 1969-71; exchange scientist Internat. Research Exchange Commn., 1969-70; vis. prof. Romanian Superior Council on Sci. Research, 1970; co-dir. Sea-Camp '70 Project, 1970; vis. prof. psychology U. Bordeaux, 1971-73; French Ministry Fgn. Affairs cultural exchange scholar, 1973-74; USIA lectr., Asia, Africa and Europe, 1971-74. Recipient Silver medal arts, letters and scis., France, 1972, chevalier Ordre des Palmes Academiques, 1973. Mem. Nat. Council Tchrs. English, Comparative Edn. Soc., Am. Assn. U. Profs., N.E.A. (cons. div. ednl. travel), Chgo. Psychol. Assn., Assn. for Higher Edn., Assn. for Student Teaching, Assn. Francophone pour l'Education Comparée, Pi Lambda Theta. Contbr. articles on edn. psychology, sci. teaching, comp. edn. and statistics to profl. jours. Home: 4055 N Keystone Av Chicago IL 60641

CHARLOTTE, GRAND DUCHESS OF LUXEMBOURG, b. Chateau de Berg, Luxembourg, Jan. 23, 1896; d. Guillaume, Grand Duke of Luxembourg and Marie-Anne of Braganca; m. Felix, Prince of Bourbon-Parma, Nov. 6, 1919; children—Jean, Elizabeth, Adelaide, Gabrielle, Charles, Alix. Succeeded to throne (after abdication of elder sister), Jan. 15, 1919; left country after German invasion, 1940, spent years, 1940-43 in U.S. and Can., returning after liberation of Grand Duchy by U.S. Army; abdicated in favor of son, Jean, 1964. Address: Grand Ducal Palace Luxembourg

CHARLTON, BARBARA ANN, librarian; b. Rochester, Minn., Jan. 7, 1926; d. Walter Cyril and Ethel Rose (Mercier) Kos; B.S., Coll. St. Catherine, St. Paul, 1947; m. Charles L. Charlton, 1949; children—Mark, Cheryl, Christine. Librarian chemistry library Washington U., St. Louis, 1947-52; librarian, head sci. and tech. reference dept. Cal. State U., Sacramento, 1961—. Home: 6150 Parkoaks Dr Citrus Heights CA 95610 Office: 6000 Jay St Sacramento CA 95819

CHARRON, DONNA SUE (MRS. WILLIAM C. CHARRON), research co. exec.; b. Flint, Mich., Sept. 2, 1938; d. Donald Alton and Rita B. (Eagan) Card; B.A. in Philosophy, U. Detroit, 1962; M.A. in Philosophy, U. Kan., 1968; m. William C. Charron, Sept. 1, 1962. Pub. relations cons., dir. opinion research Fleishman-Hillard, Inc., St. Louis, 1968-71; exec. dir. St. Louis Inst. of Music, 1971-72; pres. Research and Information, Inc., St. Louis, 1972—. Chmn. Bd. News Rev., Inc., St. Louis, 1973—. Communications cons. candidate campaigns for office. Pub. information chmn. Am. Civil Liberties Union, Eastern Mo., 1973—. Trustee St. Louis Inst. Music. Recipient John C. Vismara Philosophy award, 1962. Mem. Women in Communications (legislative chmn. St. Louis chpt. 1973—), Pub. Relations Soc. Am., Am. Assn. for Pub. Opinion Research, Atchison (Kan.) Art Assn. (founder 1966). Publisher: Mo. Pub. Opinion Report, 1973—. Home: 339 North Gore Av St Louis MO 63119 Office: 111 South Bemiston Suite 524 St Louis MO 63105

CHASAN, ROSLYN PEARL, lawyer; b. Wilkes Barre, Pa., Sept. 22, 1932; d. Harry Herman and Esther (Newman) Lefkowitz; A.A., Los Angeles City Coll., 1951; J.D., Southwestern U., 1967; m. Fred Chasan, Jan. 3, 1954; children—Mark Stephen, Jeffrey Alan, Paul Elliott. Admitted to Cal. bar, 1967, since practiced in Torrance. Guest lectr. Marymount Coll., U. Cal. at Los Angeles, Miraleste High Sch. Mem. Cal. Trial Lawyers Assn. (chmn. woman's rights com. 1972, chmn. family law sect. seminar 1973), Cal. State Bar, Woman Lawyers Assn., Los Angeles County Bar Assn., Torrance C. of C., League Women Voters, ORT, Hadassah, S.W. Jewish Council (dir.). Democrat. Jewish religion. Home: 2012 Paseo del Mar Palos Verdes Estates CA 90274 Office: Union Bank Tower 21515 Hawthorne Blvd Torrance CA 90503

CHASE, BETTY ADELLE, investment rep.; b. Ames, Ia., Sept. 19, 1926; d. Francis Chapin and Nellie Josephine (Shaw) Chase; student Evangel Coll., 1958-70. Sec., Ia. State U., 1944-50; sec. Gospel Broadcasters, Inc., Waterloo, Ia., 1950-52; editorial asst. Assemblies of God Internat. Hdqrs., Springfield, Mo., 1952-58; dir. information service Evangel Coll., Springfield, 1958-72; registered rep. Waddell & Reed, Inc., 1972—. Mem. Springfield Citizens Com. Municipal Revenue, 1966. Mem. Springfield Press Club (v.p. 1968, 69, 71), Mo. Press Women, Pub. Relations Soc. Am., Bus. and Profl. Women's Club, Pi Delta Epsilon. Mem. Assembly of God Ch. Home: 1530 N Waverly Springfield MO 65803 Office: 1835 S Stewart St Springfield MO 65804

CHASE, DORIS TOTTEN, sculptor, artist, film-maker; b. Seattle, Wash., 1923; d. William Phelps and Helen (Feeney) Totten; student U. Wash., 1941-43; m. Elmo Chase, Oct. 20, 1943; children—Gregary Totten, Randall Jarvis Totten. Artist, exhibited in one-man shows Seligman Gallery, Seattle, 1959, 61, Gallery Numero (Florence), 1961, Internat. Gallery (Italy), 1962, Hall Coleman Gallery, Seattle, 1962, Formes Gallery (Tokyo), 1963, 70, Bangkok Center Mus. (Thailand), 1963, Bolles Gallery (San Francisco), 1964, Suffolk Mus. (N.Y.), 1965, Smolin Gallery, N.Y.C., 1965, Gallery Numero (Rome), 1962, 66, Collectors Gallery, Seattle, 1964, 66, 69, Tacoma Art Mus., 1967, Ruth White Gallery (N.Y.), 1967, 69, 70, Fountain Gallery, Portland, Ore., 1970, U. Wash. Henry Gallery, 1971, Wadsworth Atheneum, Hartford, 1973; circulating exhibit Western Museum Assn., 1970-71; represented in permanent collections Finch Coll. Mus., N.Y., Seattle Art Mus., Ashai Shimbum (Tokyo), Battelle Inst., Mus. Fine Arts, Boston, Milw. Art Inst., Art Inst. Chgo., Mus. Fine Arts, Houston, Frye Art Mus., Seattle, Nat. Collection Fine Arts, Smithsonian Instn., Washington, Wadsworth Atheneum, Hartford, Conn., N.C. Museum Art, Raleigh, Mus. Modern Art, Kobe, Japan, Pa. Acad. Art, Phila., Portland Art Museum, Vancouver (B.C.) Art Gallery, Met. Mus. Art, N.Y.C., Mus. Fine Art, Montgomery, Ala., Hudson River Mus., N.Y.C., Mus. Performing Arts Lincoln Center, N.Y.C.; works reproduced in various art mags. and books; executed monumental Kinetic sculpture Kerry Park, Seattle, Expo '70, Osaka, Japan, Sculpture Park, Atlanta, Met. Mus. Art, N.Y.C., Mus. Fine Art, Montgomery; multi-media sculpture for 4 ballets Opera Assn., Seattle; included in Sculpture in Park program, N.Y.C., Playground of Tomorrow ABC-TV, Los Angeles; films Circles I, Circles II, Moon Gates, Rocking Orange, Squares, Blue Arches; work with TV Exptl. Lab., Nat. Edn. TV, N.Y.C. Address: 222 W 23d St New York City NY 10011

CHASE, ELIZABETH WAGNER (MRS. HAROLD F. CHASE), librarian; b. Susquehanna, Pa., Aug. 14, 1917; d. Charles Tingley and Marion Elizabeth (Dimock) Wagner; B.S., Phila. Coll. Pharmacy and Sci., 1939; M.S. in Library Sci., Drexel Inst., 1950; m. Elof Fritiof Johnson, Nov. 23, 1939 (dec. Sept. 16, 1962); m. 2d, Harold F. Chase, Sept. 2, 1966. Librarian Phila. Coll. Pharmacy and Sci., 1946-63, 64—, acting dean women, 1946-62; acquisition librarian Drexel Library Sch., Phila., 1963-64, instr. library sci., 1959-62. Mem. Med. Library Assn., Spl. Libraries Assn., Am. Documentation Inst., Am. Chem. Soc., Lambda Kappa Sigma. Republican. Episcopalian. Home: 1732 Old Gulph Rd Villanova PA 19085 Office: Joseph W England Library 42d St and Woodland Av Philadelphia PA 19104

CHASE, HELEN CHRISTINA MATULIC (MRS. DONALD F. CHASE, JR.), biostatistician; b. N.Y.C., Mar. 21, 1917; d. Joseph and Kristina (Gerwich) Matulic; A.B., Hunter Coll., 1938; M.Sc., Columbia, 1951; Dr.P.H., U. Cal. at Berkeley, 1961; m. Donald F. Chase, Jr., Nov. 5, 1942. With div. placement and unemployment ins. N.Y. State Dept. Labor, 1939-48; statistician to asso. statistician N.Y. State Dept. Health, 1948-57, prin. biostatistician, 1957-63; health statistician Nat. Center for Health Statistics, U.S. Dept. Health, Edn. and Welfare, 1963-69; dir. research Assn. Sch. Allied Health Professions, Washington, 1969-71; staff asso. Inst. Medicine Nat. Acad. Scis., 1971-72; statistician Social Security Adminstrn., U.S. Dept. Health, Edn. and Welfare, 1973—. Cons. USPHS, 1961-62, White House Conf. Food, Nutrition, and Health, 1969, Nat. Acad. Scis., 1970-71, Maternal and Child Health project George Washington U., 1970-73, Maternal and Child Health project Minn. Systems Research Inc., 1974—; mem. radiation bio-effects and epidemiology adv. com. Food and Drug Adminstrn., 1972—. Lectr. Grad. Sch. Nursing, Cath. U., Washington, 1966—. Fellow Am. Pub. Health Assn. (sec. statistics sect. 1965-68, vice chmn. 1968-70, chmn. 1970-72; mem. governing council 1965-70, 72—, exec. bd. 1972—), A.A.A.S., Am. Statis. Assn., Population Assn. Am., Delta Omega. Home: 6417 15th St Alexandria VA 22307 Office: 1875 Connecticut Av NW Washington DC 20009

CHASE, JOAN BARBARA, univ. adminstr.; b. N.Y.C., June 11, 1936; d. Noah and Anne (Witkin) Chase; B.S., City Coll. N.Y., 1959; postgrad. Northwestern U., 1959, Hunter Coll., 1961-62, N.J. State Tchrs. Coll., 1959-63, N.Y.U., 1959-61; Ed.D., Rutgers U., 1968. Edn. counselor N.J. Commn. for the Blind, Newark, 1959-65; asst. prof., psychologist Jersey City State Coll., 1966-67; asst. prof. spl. edn. Hunter Coll., City U.N.Y., N.Y.C., 1967-71; dir. spl. edn., asso. prof. dept. psychiatry Rutgers Med. Sch., New Brunswick, 1971—. Cons., specialist field reader Bur. Edn. for the Handicapped, U.S. Office Edn., Washington, 1967—; cons. psychologist Cerebral Palsy Rehab. Inst., Orange, N.J., 1968—. Projects for Psychologists for Social Action, N.Y.C., 1970; mem. adv. bd. Highland Community and Sch., Paradox, 1967—. Recipient Teaching fellowship Rutgers Grad. Sch. Edn., 1965-66, Tremaine Scholarship, City Coll. N.Y., 1957. Mem. Am. Civil Liberties Union (state dir. 1969—), Council for Exceptional Children, Am. Psychol. Assn., Assn. for Edn. Visually Handicapped (chmn. nominations com. 1970-72), Kappa Delta Pi. Author: Retrolental Fibroplusia and Autistic Symptomatology, 1972. Cons. editor Exceptional Children Jour., 1969—. Home: RD 1 Whitehouse Station NJ 08889 Office: Dept Psychiatry Coll Medicine and Dentistry Rutgers Med Sch Box 101 Piscataway NJ 08854

CHASE, JUDITH WRAGG (MRS. RICHARD CHASE), mus. curator; b. Augusta, Ga., Feb. 18, 1907; d. Samuel Alston and Emma Louise (Sparks) Wragg; student William Smith Coll., 1923-24, Cooper Union Art Sch., 1924-27; B.A., Syracuse U., 1960; m. Richard Chase, July 18, 1931; children—Richard Conant, Alston Sparks, Pamela Wragg (Mrs. Peter Murray Hain). On profl. stage, N.Y.C., 1927-28; advt. artist Barron Collier, Inc., N.Y.C., 1928-30; profl. artist, illustrator, 1927-47; free lance advt. artist, Panama, C.Z., 1931-33; art dir. Ft. Benning (Ga.) Childrens Sch., 1930-31; leading lady No. Dramatic Co. (radio), Washington, 1934-35; owner pvt. art sch., tchr. high sch. art Charlottesville, Va., 1944-47; housemother Pine Manor Jr. Coll., 1954-55; tour dir. Chase Teen Tours to Europe from Manlius, N.Y., summers 1958-60; guidance counselor Lancaster (Mass.) Sch. for Delinquent Girls, 1956-57; art dir. Manlius (N.Y.) Mil. Sch., 1957-60; mus. curator, ednl. dir. Old Slave Mart Mus., Charleston, S.C., 1960—; profl. photographer, 1968—. Lectr. Negro history and art, to clubs, schs., church groups; teacher Negro history; rep. 1st World Festival Negro Arts, Dakar, Senegal, Africa, 1966. Mem. Charleston Bi-Centennial Black History Com. Sec. bd. trustees Miriam B. Wilson Found., Charleston, 1963—. Recipient Silver medal of excellence Cooper Union Art Sch., numerous awards in exhibitions including Asbury Park Soc. Fine Arts, Ga. Artists, So. States Art League, Va. Artists; Community Service award Alpha Phi Alpha, 1973. Mem. Carolina Art Assn., Charleston Library Soc., S.C. Council on Human Rights, Authors Guild, Authors League Am., Internat. Speakers Network, So. Assn. Africanists, Assn. for Study of Afro-Am. Life and History, Am. Assn. State and Local History, S.C. Hist. Soc. Democrat. Author: Books to Build World Friendship, 1964; Afro-American Art and Craft, 1972. Address: Box 446 Sullivan's Island SC 29482 (summer) Box 335 Squirrel Island ME 04570

CHASE, LOUISE TECLA HOGLE (MRS. LLOYD RAYMOND CHASE), pathologist; b. Manila, Phillippines, Sept. 23, 1919; d. Warren Gordon and Maximina (Quiner) Hogle; B.S., U. Philippines, 1943; M.D., Union U., 1947; m. Lloyd Raymond Chase, Nov. 27, 1952; children—Mary Anita, Raymond, Michael, Robert. Intern, Woman's Hosp. of Phila., 1947-48; resident Glenridge Hosp., Schenectady, 1948-49, Albany (N.Y.) Hosp., 1949-50, N.Y. State Dept. Health, Albany, 1950-51, Meml. Hosp., N.Y.C., 1951-52; dir. labs. St. Mary's Hosp., Troy, N.Y., 1952-57; sr. pathologist Albany VA Hosp., 1957-62; dir. labs. St. Clare's Hosp., Schenectady, 1962—, chief nuclear medicine, 1965—; asso. prof. pathology and bacteriology Albany Med. Coll., 1952-57. Leader 4-H, 1962-64; den mother Fort Orange council Boy Scouts Am., 1963-64; mem. exec. com. St. Clare's Hosp., 1963—. N.Y. State Dept. Health fellow in pathology, 1950-52. Mem. A.M.A., Coll. Am. Pathologists, Am. Soc. Microbiology, Am. Soc. Clin. Pathologists, Am. Soc. Nuclear Medicine, Schenectady County Soc. Medicine. Home: 16 N Gate Dr Albany NY 12203 Office: 600 McClellan St Schenectady NY 12304

CHASE, LUCIA, ballet dancer; b. Waterbury, Conn., Mar. 24, 1907; d. Irving Hall and Elizabeth Hosmer (Kellogg) Chase; student St. Margaret's Sch., Waterbury, Theatre Guild Sch., N.Y.C.; m. Thomas Ewing, Jr., Dec. 28, 1926; children—Thomas III, Alexander Cochran. Ballerina Mordkin Ballet, 1937-39; ballerina The Ballet Theatre, N.Y.C., 1940-60, co-dir., 1945—. Home: 720 Park Av New York City NY 10021 Office: Am Ballet Theatre 888 7th Av New York City NY 10019

CHASEN, MIGNON CHARNEY, physician; b. Moscow, Russia, Jan 5, 1911 (came to U.S. 1938, naturalized 1942); d. Daniel and Anna (Kissin) Charney; student U. Leipzig and Berlin, Germany, 1929-33; M.D., Royal U., Palermo, Italy, 1935; m. William H. Chasen, Apr. 10, 1942; children—Barbara Z., Laura R. Intern, Maimonides Hosp., Bklyn., 1940-42; sch. physician, physician in charge Child Health Sta., N.Y.C., N.Y. Health Dept., 1944-46; asst. physician Boston State Hosp., 1946-49, asst. psychiatrist, 1949-54; sr. resident in psychiatry Boston VA Hosp., 1954-55; asst. then asst. attending asst. in psychiatry Mass. Gen. Hosp., Boston, McLean Hosp., Waverly, Mass., 1956—; asst. in psychiatry Harvard Med. Sch., 1957—; attending psychiatrist Brockton VA Hosp., 1958-62, cons. psychiatrist, 1962—; cons. Boston State Hosp., 1961—, Boston VA Clinic, 1962—, Mental Hygiene Clinic Boston Vets. Hosp.; psychoanalysis, 1952-56; asst. psychiatry Tufts Med. Sch., 1962, now clin. instr.; cons. Met. State Hosp., 1972—, St. Elizabeth's Hosp., Boston, 1973—. Diplomate in psychiatry, Am. Bd. Psychiatry and Neurology. Fellow Am. Psychiat. Assn. (dist. councilor); mem. Am. Group Psychotherapy Assn., A.M.A., Mass. Psychiat. Assn., Soc. Research in Psychiatry. Contbr. articles in field. Home: 111 Cedar St Newton Center MA 02159

CHASIN, DORIS HOROWITZ (MRS. MILTON JACK CHASIN), ednl. adminstr.; b. Bklyn., Nov. 29, 1928; d. Leon and Shirley (Greenberg) Horowitz; student N.Y. U., 1945-49; B.A., Cal. State U. at Los Angeles, 1960; M.Ed. (Ford Found. grantee 1963), U. Cal. at Los Angeles, 1963, Ed.D. (Francis L. Bacon fellow 1965), 1969; m. Milton Jack Chasin, Apr. 28, 1949; children—Gilbert Edwin, Barbara Iris (Mrs. Mark B. Ginsburg). Acad. counselor AID Africa Contracts U. Cal. at Los Angeles, 1963-66, instr. African edn., extension, 1966-71, acad. dean, dir. continuing edn. Marymount Coll. Los Angeles, 1970-73; asst. to acad. v.p., dir. continuing edn. for women, asso. prof. edn. Loyola Marymount U., Los Angeles, 1973-74, West Coast regional dir. Inst. Internat. Edn., 1974—; mem. faculty Loyola U., Los Angeles, 1968—, vis. lectr. comparative edn., 1968-70; vis. lectr. Cal. State U. at Northridge, 1970. Mem. Community Anti-Narcotics Program, Los Angeles, 1967-73; bd. commrs. Camp Hess Kramer, Malibu, Cal., 1970-74; nat. v.p. Assn. Women's Active Return to Edn., Los Angeles, 1971-74; mem. budget com. United Way, Western region Los Angeles, 1972-74. Mellon Found. grantee Am. Council Edn., 1972. Mem. Comparative and Internat. Edn. Soc., Am. Assn. U. Profs., African Studies Assn., Am. Ednl. Studies Assn., Am. Ednl. Research Assn., Am. Assn. U. Women, Am. Assn. Higher Edn., Pi Lambda Theta (chpt. pres. 1967-69). Home: 10441 Ashton Av Los Angeles CA 90024

CHASTAIN, PAULINE HELEN (MRS. ROBERT EVRETT CHASTAIN), constrn. co. exec.; b. Vanita, Okla., July 27, 1918; d. Ohmer B. and Beulah (Shull) Pebley; grad. Ann Bishop's Beauty Coll., 1937; m. Robert Evrett Chastain, Oct. 11, 1935; 1 son, Ronald Eugene. Office mgr., part owner Chastain Paving Co., McAllen, Tex., 1948—; former owner beauty shops, Decatur, Ill. and Texarkana, Tex. Pres. exec. bd. Tex. A. and M. U., 1960-61. Democrat. Baptist. Mem. Order Eastern Star. Address: PO Box 580 McAllen TX 78501

CHATFIELD, RUTH, artist; b. Bklyn., Nov. 2, 1918; d. Henry and Sonia (Zigberman) Chatfield; grad. N.Y. Sch. Applied Design for Women, 1938; student Art Students League N.Y., 1939, 40, J. Albert Cavanaugh Art Sch., 1939, Manhattan Sch. Music, 1940-44. Artist, McFadden Publs., N.Y.C., 1939-41; art dir. Fawcett Publs., N.Y.C., 1941-44; art dir. Doe-Anderson Advt. Agy., Louisville, 1944-48; violinist Louisville Symphony Orch., 1944-48; free-lance graphic artist, San Francisco, 1948-65; one-man shows at Winblad Galleries, San Francisco, Maxwell Galleries, San Francisco, Pacific Grove (Cal.) Mus., Fine Arts Gallery San Francisco, Garden Cafe Gallery Burlingame, Cal., 1968, St. Mary's Coll. Gallery, Moraga, Cal., 1969, Morgan Knott Gallery, San Francisco, 1970-72, Longview (Tex.) Mus. and Art Center, 1974, others; exhibited in group shows Frye Mus., Seattle, DeYoung Mus., San Francisco, Palace of Fine Arts, San Francisco, Oakland (Cal.) Art Mus., Crocker Mus., Sacramento, Butler Inst. Am. Art, Youngstown, O., others; represented in numerous permanent collections U.S., Eng., Japan. Mem. Marin Symphony Orch., Cal., 1963—. Recipient numerous awards, prizes at art shows. Mem. Artists Equity Assn., Musicians Union Local 6. Democrat. Home: 458 Joost Av San Francisco CA 94127

CHATHAM, LOIS ALBRO (MRS. GEORGE NORTON CHATHAM), govt. ofcl.; b. Groveland, Ill., July 28, 1928; d. Arthur Francis and Daisy Delilah (Roth) Albro; A.B. magna cum laude, Houghton Coll., 1951; M.A., So. Methodist U., 1954; Ph.D., U. Houston, 1960; m. George Norton Chatham, Mar. 14, 1959; 1 son, Bruce, Psychol. adviser Nat. Health Surveys, Nat. Center Health Statistics, Dept. Health, Edn. and Welfare, Washington, 1963-67; asst. div. dir. for research narcotic addiction and drug abuse Nat. Inst. Mental Health, Dept. Health, Edn. and Welfare, Washington, 1967-69, chief narcotic addict rehab. br. Nat. Inst. Mental Health, Rockville, Md., 1969-74; dep. dir. div. of resource devel. Nat. Inst. Drug Abuse, Dept. Health, Edn. and Welfare, Rockville, 1974—. Recipient Superior Performance award Nat. Inst. Mental Health, 1969, Fed. Women's award, 1972, Outstanding Service award Dept. Social Services, P.R., 1971. Mem. Am. Psychol. Assn., Antique Aircraft Assn., Aircraft Owner-Pilots Assn. Office: 11400 Rockville Pike Rockville MD 20852

CHAUVIN, JOAN ELAINE, lawyer; b. New Orleans, Apr. 7, 1932; d. Irving August Chauvin and Mary Ann Sarah McQuilling; B.B.A., Loyola U. of South, 1952, J.D., 1959; postgrad. Northwestern U. Sch. Law, 1963; 1 son, Ernest Anthony Schiro, Jr. Admitted to La. bar, practiced in New Orleans area, 1959-67; mem. firm Hassinger and Chauvin, 1959-62; asst. dist. atty., Parish of Orleans, La., 1962-67; individual practice, 1962-67; asst. U.S. atty. eastern dist. La., 1967—. Recipient Henry L. Sarpy award, 1959, Spl. Achievement award Dept. Justice, 1973. Mem. Fed., La. bar assns., Nat. Assn. Women Lawyers, New Orleans Geneal. Research Soc., Nat. Rifle Assn., Phi Alpha Delta. Presbyn. Mem. Order Eastern Star (chaplain 1962). Club: Delta Rifle and Pistol. Office: 500 St Louis St New Orleans LA 70130

CHEADLE, HELEN KAUPER (MRS. DAVID WARD CHEADLE), pub. relations exec.; b. Newport News, Va., Sept. 5, 1918; d. William Patrick and Ruth Eleanor (Hutton) Kauper; B.A. cum laude, Lawrence U., 1940; m. David Ward Cheadle, Nov. 26, 1949; children—David Christopher, Lisa Maria, William Kauper. Copywriter, fashion asst. Gimbel Bros. Co., Milw., 1939-41; copywriter, asst. to promotion dir. Marshall Field & Co., Chgo., 1941-44; fashion publicity dir. Saks Fifth Av. N.Y.C., 1944-49; free lance pub. relations Manila, Philippines, 1950, Melbourne, Australia, 1950-54; radio commentator, producer sta. WHOA, San Juan, P.R., 1958-61; asst. pub. relations dir. Mountainside Hosp., Montclair, N.J., 1965-66, dir. pub. relations, 1966—. Trustee St. John's Preparatory Sch., 1959-62, adminstr., 1963-64; hon. life trustee Children's Hosp., Melbourne. Mem. Am. Soc. Hosp. Pub. Relations, N.J. Hosp. Pub. Relations Assn. (v.p. 1970-72), Am. Assn. Univ. Women, Acad. Hosp. Pub. Relations, Nat. Fedn. Press Women. Home: 561 Highland Av Upper Montclair NJ 07043 Office: Mountainside Hospital Bay Av & Highland Av Montclair NJ 07042

CHEATHAM, LONIE LEE NELMS (MRS. GOODE RUTLEDGE CHEATHAM), clubwoman; b. Louisburg, N.C.; d. David Nicholas and Mattie Lee (Conn) Nelms; grad. Sarah Elizabeth Hosp., 1923; grad. study N.Y.C. Children's Hosp., 1924; m. Goode Rutledge Cheatham, Aug. 17, 1927 (dec.); children—Goode Rutledge, James William (dec.). Sch. nurse Dept. Pub. Health, Durham, N.C., 1925-26; supr. Dept. Hosps., N.Y.C., 1926-27. Active A.R.C., Community Chest; v.p. Girls Club; mem. Broome County Mental Health Bd.; mem. N.Y. State Citizens Council consumers adv. com. to the Gov. of N.Y.; chmn. Broome County Mental Health Bd. Mem. Women's Aux. A.M.A., Inner Wheel Internat., English-Speaking Union N.Y., Harmony Circle, C. S. Wilson Meml. Hosp. Aux., N.C. Nurses Assn. (past v.p.), Gen. (treas. 1966-68, chmn. finance and budget com. 1968-70, dir. advt. 1970-72), N.Y. State (county chmn., 1940-42, state dir., 1950-52, state treas. 1952-54, pres. 1954-56, sec., chmn. finance 1968-72), fedns. women's clubs, Nat. Assn. Parliamentarians. Clubs: Sorosis Inc., Chautauqua Woman's, Monday Afternoon, Endicott Civic, Binghamton Westside Literary. Named to Broome County Hall of Fame, for outstanding service to the Community, State and Nation, 1943. Presbyn. Republican. Home: 618 High Av Endicott NY 13760

CHEBUHAR, TERESA MARIE, journalist; b. Seattle, Dec. 7, 1946; d. Charles Joseph and Eleanor Irene (Follme) Chebuhar; B.S., No. Ill. U., 1968; M.A. (Alfred P. Sloan fellow), U. Mo., 1971. Feature writer, reporter Decatur (Ill.) Herald, 1968-69; tchr. Oak Lawn (Ill.) High Sch., 1970-71; sr. med. writer Abbott Labs., North Chicago, 1972-73; mgr. regulatory affairs Medtronic, Mpls., 1973—; free lance writer, 1970—. Cons. pub. relations Kidney Found. of Ill., 1972—. Recipient Award for Excellence in Med. Journalism, U. Mo., 1970. Mem. Women in Communications, Young Friends of the Arts, No. Ill. Univ. Alumni Assn. (dir. 1972—, editorial adv. bd. 1972—). Contbr. articles on medicine to Buffalo Evening News. Office: 3055 Old Hwy Eight Minneapolis MN 55418

CHEEK, MARIAN WHEELIN (MRS. JOSEPH D. CHEEK, JR.), coll. ofcl.; b. Preston, Ida., May 21, 1942; d. Thomas Joseph and Claudia Jean (Kesler) Wheelin; B.A. in Journalism U. Ga., 1964; m. Joseph D. Cheek, Jr., July 9, 1966; children—Joseph Scott, Bradford Kesler. Gen. assignment reporter Augusta (Ga.) Herald, 1964-66; edn. reporter 1966-69; coordinator information and pub. relations Augusta Coll., 1969—. Mem. Elks Aux., 1970-73. Mem. Am. Coll. Pub. Relations Assn., Beta Sigma Phi. Roman Catholic. Club: Forest Estates Garden. Home: 3301 Forest Estates Dr Augusta GA 30904

CHEESEMAN, ELIZABETH MARGARET, librarian; b. Muncie, Ind.; d. Arthur Clinton and Eunice May (Hollingsworth) Cheeseman; B.S., Northwestern U., 1953; M.A., U. Chgo., 1960. Tchr., librarian Mt. Morris (Mich.) High Sch., 1953-55; teller Citizens Bank, Flint, Mich., 1955-56, Continental Bank & Trust Co., Chgo., 1956-58; asst. librarian U. Chgo. Lab. Sch., 1957-58; bookmobile librarian Grace A. Dow Meml. Library, Midland, Mich., 1958-60; head librarian Lakeview High Sch., Battle Creek, Mich., 1960-66; sch. library cons. Mich. State Library 1966-68; cons. library service in instns., coordinator library service to handicapped Pa. State Library, Bur. Library Devel., Harrisburg, 1968—. Recipient Schuman award for composition Northwestern U., 1952. Mem. A.L.A., Am. Correctional Assn., Pa. Library Assn., Med. Library Assn., U. Chgo., Northwestern U. alumni assns. Contbr. articles to profl. jours. Home: RD 2 Mechanicsburg PA 17055 Office: Pa State Library Box 1601 Harrisburg PA 17126

CHEKENIAN, IRIS, assn. exec.; b. N.Y.C., Sept. 10, 1930; d. Aram and Rose (Merchikian) Chekenian; A.B., Adelphi U., 1949; A.M., Duke, 1951. Asst. editor Argosy mag., N.Y.C., 1951-54; reporter Sports Illustrated mag., N.Y.C., 1955-56; articles editor Am. Girl, N.Y.C., 1958-60; asso. editor Savs. Bank Jour., N.Y.C., 1963-68; story editor motion pictures, Hollywood, Cal., 1956-57, 61-63; mgr. advt. and pub. relations Chem. Constrn. Corp., N.Y.C., 1968-73; asst. dir. information Nat. Assn. Mut. Savs. Banks, N.Y.C., 1973—. Pres., Chem. Advertisers Group of N.Y., 1970-71. Mem. Savs. Bank Women of N.Y., Duke Met. Alumni Assn. (v.p. 1969-72). Home: 136 E 55th St New York City NY 10022 Office: 200 Park Av New York City NY 10017

CHELF, THELMA SKAGGS (MRS. FRED BIVEN CHELF), govt. ofcl.; b. Buffalo, Ky., Apr. 21, 1915; d. Henry Blaine and Viola (Ferrill) Skaggs; student Western State U., 1932-33, Campbellsville Baptist Jr. Coll., 1935; m.(Fred Biven Chelf, Mar. 4, 1955. Tchr. pub. elementary sch., La Rue County, Hodgenville, Ky., 1933-42; with Ky. Bur. Pub. Assistance, Elizabethtown, 1946—, social service supr., 1963-69, field office adminstr., 1969—. Partner realty firm Chelf Real Estate Co., Elizabethtown, 1959—. Mem. Human Resources Com., Elizabethtown, 1970—. Mem. Am. Pub. Welfare Assn., Ky. Welfare Assn. (dist. pres.), Elizabethtown Bus. and Profl. Women's Club (pres. recipient Bus. Woman Year award 1968). Republican. Baptist (chmn. finance com. 1962-67). Home: 108 Sounset Dr Elizabethtown KY 42701 Office: 229 N Miles St Elizabethtown KY 42701

CHELLAND, ORPHIA CYNTHIA, ednl. adminstr.; b. Old Forge, Pa.; d. Michael and Clementine (Comita) Chelland; B.S., Marywood Coll., 1944; M.Ed., Temple U., 1959; postgrad. Columbia, 1960, Temple U., 1961-66, 69; Ph.D., Head U., 1973. Tchr., Bensalem Jr.-Sr. High Sch., Cornwell Heights, Pa., 1945-55, guidance counselor, 1956-66, psychometrist, summers 1962-64; dir. pupil services Chichester Schs., Boothwyn, Pa., 1966—; psychologist, dir. Chichester Home Sch. Guidance Center, 1966—. Mem. scholarship com. Bensalem P.T.A., 1961-66; mem. adv. council Title 111, Delaware County Schs., 1968-70, adv. council title 1, Chichester Schs., 1969-70. Mem. Council for Exceptional Children, Pa. Edn. Assn., N.E.A., Am. Personnel and Guidance Assn., Nat. Pupil Personnel (charter, dir. 1966), Nat. Assn. Sch. Psychologists (charter), Bucks County and Delware County Counselors Assn., Pa. Psiphalogical Assn., Internat. Platform Assn., Alpha Delta Kappa. Home: 210 E Jefferson St Media PA 19063 Office: 3333 Chichester Av Boothwyn PA 19061

CHELLAS, MERRY MOREHOUSE (MRS. BRIAN FARRELL CHELLAS), writer; b. N.Y.C., Dec. 21, 1940; d. David Wilmot and Elisabeth Pauline (Chevalier) Morehouse; B.A., Fla. State U., 1962; M.A., Stanford, 1968; m. Brian Farrell Chellas, Dec. 30, 1962; 1 dau., Anne Morehouse. Editorial positions Per Se Mag., Stanford, Cal., 1965-68; reporter Palo Alto (Cal.) Times, 1965-68; freelance writer, 1968—; editorial asso. Nursing, 1972; contbg. editor Met. mag., Phila., 1971-74; writer news bur. U. Pa., 1974—. Mem. U. Pa. Faculty Tea Club (pres. 1973-74, coordinator Resources for Women Project 1971—). Home: 2523 South St Philadelphia PA 19146 Office: 521 Franklin Bldg U Pa Philadelphia PA 19174

CHELSTROM, MARILYN ANN, ednl. inst. exec.; b. Mpls., Dec. 5; d. Arthur Rudolph and Signe (Johnson) Chelstrom; B.A., U. Minn., 1950. Staff asst. Mpls. Citizens Com. Pub. Edn., 1950-57; coordinator, policies and procedures Lithium Corp. Am., Inc., Mpls., N.Y.C., 1957-62; exec. dir. The Robert A. Taft Inst. Govt., N.Y.C., 1962—. Active League Women Voters, Mpls., 1950-60; charter mem. Citizens League Greater Mpls., 1952-60; del. White House Conf. on Edn., 1955. Vice chmn. Minn. Women for Humphrey, 1954. Recipient Certificate of Recognition for Service to Mpls. Pub. Schs., Mpls. Citizens Com., 1957; named Town Topper, Mpls. Star, 1958. Mem. Am. Polit. Assn., Minn. Alumni Assn. (gov. N.Y. 1963—, pres. 1971—; nat. dir. 1971—). Lutheran (treas. councilman). Clubs: Marco Polo (N.Y.C.); Minn. Alumni (Mpls.). Home: 155 E 38th St New York City NY 10016 Office: The Robert A Taft Inst Govt 420 Lexington Av New York City NY 10017

CHEN, CONCORDIA CHAO, mathematician; b. Peiping, China (came to U.S. 1955, naturalized 1969); d. Chun-fu and Kwie Hwa (Wong) Chao; B.A. in Bus. Adminstrn., Nat. Taiwan U., 1954; M.S. in Math., Marquette U., 1958; postgrad. Purdue U., 1958-60, Mass. Inst. Tech., 1961-62; m. Chin Chen, July 2, 1960; children—Marie Hui-mei, Albert Chao. Teaching asst. Purdue U., Lafayette, Ind., 1958-60; system analysis engr. electronic data processing div., Mpls.-Honeywell, Newton Highlands, Mass., 1960-63; mgmt. planning asst. Lederle Labs., Am. Cyanamid Co., Pearl River, N.Y., 1964-68, computer applications specialist, 1967, operations analyst, 1967-68; staff programmer IBM, Mahwah, N.J., 1968—. Mem. Am. Math. Soc., Soc. Indsl. Applied Maths. Home: Mountain Pass Box 107 RD 6 Hopewell Junction NY 12533 Office: IBM PO Box 950 Poughkeepsie NY 12602

CHEN, EDITH T., educator; b. China; d. Kui Chong and Po (Lim) Chen; B.S., Syracuse U., 1922; M.A., Columbia, 1923; M.A., U. N.C., 1950. Came to U.S., 1948, naturalized, 1955. Instr., Amoy U., China, 1923-36; asso. prof. Fukien Christian U., China, 1938-40, prof., 1940-47; research asso. U. Pitts. Grad. Sch. Pub. Health, 1955-61, 65-67, Sch. Medicine, Tufts U., 1961-64. Trustee Yong Cheng Sch. for Girls, Changchow, China. Mem. A.A.A.S., Am. Psychol. Assn., Am. Pub. Health Assn., Am. Acad. Polit. and Social Sci., Wayne County Hist. Soc., Theta Beta Phi. Author publs. in Chinese, including Dictionary of Educational and Psychological Terms, 1945. Contbr. articles to English lang. profl. jours. Address: 67 College Hills Portage Rd Wooster OH 44691

CHEN, ELLEN MARIE CHANG (MRS. VINCENT CHEN), educator; b. Shanghai, China, Mar. 25, 1933; d. Chih Han and Wen-Hsiu (Han) Chang; came to U.S., 1955, naturalized, 1965; Ph.D., Fordham U., 1966; m. Vincent Chen, June 11, 1960; children—Lucian, Michele. Teaching fellow Columbia, 1963-64; asst. prof. philosophy St. John's U., N.Y.C., 1964-73, asso. prof., 1973—; vis. asso. prof. philosophy Nat. Taiwan U., spring 1971. Home: 88-30 195th St Hollis NY 11423 Office: St John's U Jamaica NY 11432

CHEN, KATHLEEN CHAN, educator, psychologist; b. Rangoon, Burma, June 14, 1929; d. Hum Gyan and May (Aw) Chan; came to U.S., 1953, naturalized, 1969; B.A. summa cum laude, U. Rangoon, 1951; M.A., Bryn Mawr Coll., 1955; Ph.D., Pa. State U., 1957; m. Mou-Ta Chen, June 13, 1964; children—Denise Lynn, Donna Ann. Research dir. psychol. testing U. Rangoon, 1957-60; asst. prof. psychology Muskingum (O.) Coll., 1960-65, Rochester (N.Y.) Inst. Tech., 1971—. Cons., Genesee Ecumenical Ministries, 1972-73. Burma Govt. scholar, 1953-57; NSF fellow, 1963, summer instl. research grantee, 1972. Mem. Am., Eastern psychol. assns., Sigma Xi. Contbr. papers in field to profl. publs. Constructed, adapted psychol. tests for Burmese population, 1957-60. Home: 15 Lancet Way Brockport NY 14420 Office: 1 Lomb Meml Dr Rochester NY 14623

CHEN, LILY WAN-JOH LEE (MRS. PAUL P. CHEN), social worker; b. China, May 27, 1936 (came to U.S. 1959, naturalized 1968); d. Yao-Lin and Shu-Chin (Chang) Lee; student Chung-Hsing U., 1954-59; B.A., San Francisco State Coll., 1960; M.S. in Social Work, U. Wash., Seattle, 1964; m. Paul P. Chen, Apr. 17, 1960; children—Arthur K., Helen K. Dir., Voice of Am. program Am. Today, China, 1957-59, U.S. West coast reporter, 1959-67; dir. med. social service dept. El Cerrito County Hosp., Long Beach, Cal., 1967-70; head Asian program Los Angeles County Dept. Pub. Social Services, 1970-72, dir. planning dept., 1972—; reporter, commentator Tv sta. KTTV, 1972—. Med. social worker Long Beach Med. Aid Dist., 1965-66; field work supr. social welfare students Cal. State Coll., Long Beach, 1969—. Mem. Acad. Certified Social Workers, Nat. Assn. Social Workers, So. Cal. Pub. Health Assn. Home: 179 Barranca Dr Monterey Park CA 91754 Office: 4900 Triggs St Commerce CA 90022

CHEN, VIVIAN (MRS. STEPHEN H. YANG), ophthalmologist; b. N.Y.C., May 25, 1937; d. Forman M. and Phoebe (Pong) Chen; B.A. cum laude, N.Y.U., 1959, M.D., 1962; m. Stephen H. Yang, Oct. 28, 1961; children—Preston Harvey, Kenneth Edward. Intern, Kings County Hosp., Bklyn., 1962-63; resident, Met. Hosp.-N.Y. Med. Coll., 1963-66; practice medicine, specializing in ophthalmology, East Brunswick, N.J., 1966—; asst. attending in ophthalmology Middlesex Gen. Hosp., New Brunswick, 1966—; asst. attending ophthalmologist St. Peter's Gen. Hosp., New Brunswick. Diplomate Am. Bd. Ophthalmology. Fellow A.C.S., Am. Acad. Ophthalmology and Otolaryngology; mem. Phi Beta Kappa. Address: 2 Hillwood Rd East Brunswick NJ 08816

CHENEY, FRANCES NEEL (MRS. BRAINARD CHENEY), educator; b. Washington, Aug. 19, 1906; d. Thomas Meeks and Carrie (Tucker) Neel; B.A., Vanderbilt U., 1928; B.S. in Library Sci., Peabody Library Sch., 1934; M.S., Columbia, 1940; Litt.D. (hon.), Marquette U., 1966; m. Brainard Cheney, June 21, 1928. Librarian, chemistry library Vanderbilt U., 1928-29, circulation asst., 1929-30, reference librarian, 1930-37; reference librarian Joint U. Libraries, 1937-43, head reference dept., 1945-46; asst. to chair of poetry Library of Congress, 1943-44, bibliographer gen. reference div., 1944-45; asst. prof. Peabody Library Sch., 1946-49, asso. prof., 1949-50, 52-67, prof., 1967—, also asso. dir.; vis. faculty Japan Library Sch., Tokyo, Japan, 1951-52. Recipient Beta Phi Mu award for outstanding teaching, 1959; also Mudge award for reference service, 1962. Mem. Am. (exec. bd.), S.E. (pres. 1960-62), Tenn. (past pres.) library assns., Tenn. Hist. Assn., Tenn. Folklore Soc., Bibliog. Soc. Am., Assn. Am. Library Schs. (past pres.), Delta Delta Delta. Home: 112 Oak St Smyrna TN 37167 Office: Peabody Library Sch Nashville TN 37203

CHENEY, LOIS ANN, educator; b. Cleve., May 2, 1931; d. Clark W. and Lillian M. (Burton) Cheney; B.A., Muckingum Coll., 1954; M.A., Kent State U., 1957; Ph.D., Mich. State U., 1961. Tchr., speech and English, Kent (O.) Roosevelt High Sch., 1954-56; faculty, speech dept. Tarkio (Mo.) Coll., 1956-59, 61-63; faculty, speech dept. Bowling Green (O.) State U., 1963—, prof., 1964—. Mem. Ohio, Central States speech assns., Speech Communications Assn. Am. Presbyn. Author: God is No Fool, 1969. Home: 8 Springhill Dr Bowling Green OH 43402

CHENEY, NANCY ADELE (MRS. JOHN DOUGLAS LOW), pediatrician; b. San Jose, Cal., Aug. 20, 1933; d. Adelbert and Fay (Tower) Logan; B.A., Occidental Coll., 1955; M.D., Northwestern U., 1959; m. John Douglas Low, June 20, 1970 (dec. Mar. 1972); children—David Raymond, Stephen James. Intern, Mt. Auburn Hosp., Cambridge, Mass., 1959-60; resident in pediatrics Children's Meml. Hosp., Chgo., 1960-62; pediatrician Nat. Inst. Neurol. Diseases and Blindness project Boston Lying-In Hosp., 1962-63; practice medicine, specializing in pediatrics, San Jose, Cal., 1964-69, Anaheim, Cal., 1971-73; fellow neonatology Orange County Med. Center, 1973—; staff pediatrician San Mateo County Hosp., 1969-70; clin. instr. U. Cal. at Irvine Med. Sch., 1971—. Fellow Am. Acad. Pediatrics; mem. Los Angeles County Pediatric Soc., Zonta. Home: 11831 Colony Dr Santa Ana CA 92705 Office: 101 City Dr S Orange CA 92668

CHENG, BARBARA DAVIS (MRS. GUY CHENG), psychologist, educator; b. Hartland, Vt., Apr. 3, 1924; d. Elbridge Nathanial and Eudora Cleora (Sykes) Davis; student U. Mass., 1942-44; A.B., Smith Coll., 1946; Ph.D. (research fellow), U. Vt., 1972; m. Burton A. Sisco, June 19, 1947 (div. Feb. 1968); children—Burton R., David B., Tod K., Elizabeth A.; m. 2d, Guy Cheng, Sept. 12, 1970. Social worker State of Vt., Burlington, 1947-54; tchr. pub. elementary schs., Shelburne, Vt., 1961-63; grad. research asst. U. Vt., Burlington, 1967-70, research asso., 1970-71; asst. prof. psychology Trinity Coll., Burlington, 1971—. Cons., Countermeasures Relating to Alchol and Hwy. Safety (CRASH) project, Waterbury, Vt., 1970-73. Mem. Am. Psychol. Assn., Am. Assn. Univ. Profs., A.A.A.S. Mem. United Ch. of Christ. Home: Hill's Point Charlotte VT 05445 Office: Trinity College Burlington VT 05401

CHENG, SYLVIA FAN (MRS. JOHNSON CHU), physician; b. Shangtung, China, June 26, 1918 (came to U.S. 1948, naturalized 1957); d. Stanley C. and Flora C. (Chu) Cheng; B.S., U. Shanghai, 1938; M.D., Woman's Christian Med. Coll., Shanghai, 1942; postgrad. N.Y.U., 1948, Columbia, 1955; m. Johnson Chu, June 11, 1949; children—Stephen Cheng, Timothy Cheng. Rotating intern Margaret Williamson Hosp., 1942-43; resident in medicine, surgery, obstetrics and gynecology St. Luke's and St. Elizabeth Hosp., St. John's U. Hosp., 1943-47; practice medicine specializing in chest diseases, Shanghai, 1947-48, psychiatry and gen. practice, Logansport, Ind., 1956—; chief female service, dir. Tb unit Weston (W.Va.) State Hosp., 1955; chief female service, admission and intensive service, unit dir. Logansport (Ind.) State Hosp., 1956—; cons. physician White County Meml. Hosp., Monticello, Ind., Cass County Meml., St. Joseph hosps., Logansport, Ind., Southeastern Med. Center, Walton, Ind. Recipient award A.R.C., 1959. Fellow Am. Coll. Chest Physicians, Am. Psychiat. Assn.; mem. A.M.A., Am. Thoracic Soc., Mental Health Assn., Cass County Med. Soc., Am. Acad. Gen. Practice, Ind. State Med. Assn. Baptist (deaconess 1956-69). Home: E 36 Lake Shafer Monticello IN 47960 Office: Logansport State Hosp Logansport IN 46947 also Southeastern Med Center Walton IN 46994

CHENG, VIRGINIA WAI, pediatrician; b. Nanking, China, Jan. 1, 1944; d. Shu-Chun and Min-Fong (Liu) Cheng; B.A., Concordia Coll., 1965; B.S. in Medicine, U. N.D., 1967; M.D., Northwestern U., 1969. Came to U.S., 1961. Intern, Los Angeles County U. So. Cal. Med. Center, Los Angeles, 1969-70, resident in pediatrics, 1970—, mem. staff, 1970—. Home: 4631 Los Feliz Blvd Los Angeles CA 90027 Office: 1539 W Garvey Blvd West Covina CA 91790

CHENNAULT, ANNA CHAN (MRS. CLAIRE LEE CHENNAULT), airlines exec., author; b. Peking, China, June 23, 1925; d. Y. W. and Bessie (Joung) Chan; B.A., Ling Nan U., Hong Kong, 1944; Litt.D., Changang U., Seoul, Korea, 1967; LL.D., Lincoln U., 1970; H.H.D., Manahath Ednl. Center, 1970; m. Claire Lee Chennault, Dec. 21, 1947 (dec. July 1958); children—Claire Anna, Cynthia Louise. Came to U.S., 1948, naturalized, 1950. War corr. Central News Agy. (then located in Kunming, China and Shanghai, China), 1944-48, spl. Washington corr., 1965—; feature writer Hsin Ming Daily News, Shanghai, 1944-49; with Civil Air Transport, Taipei, Formosa, 1946-57, editor bull., 1946-57, pub. relations officer, 1947-57; chief Chinese sect. Machine Translation Research Georgetown U., 1958-63; broadcaster Voice of Am. USIA, Washington, 1963-66; U.S. corr. Hsin Shen Daily News, Washington, 1958—; v.p. Flying Tiger Line, Inc., Washington, 1968—; dir. D.C. Nat. Bank; lectr., writer, fashion designer, U.S. and Asia. Mem. Pres.'s Adv. Com. on Arts, John F. Kennedy Center for Performing Arts; mem. U.S. Nat. Commn. for UNESCO; spl. rep. of Pres. to Philippine Aviation Week celebrations, 1973; spl. asst. to chmn. Asian-Pacific council Am. C. of C.; mem. women's adv. com. on aviation Dept. Transp. Pres. Chinese Refugee Relief, Washington, 1962—; pres. Gen. Claire Lee Chennault Found., Washington, 1961—; bd. govs. Am. Acad. Achievement, Dallas; trustee Center for Study of Presidency, Library Presdl. Papers. Committeewoman Washington Republican Party, 1960—, mem. Nat. Rep. Finance Com.; cons. heritage groups, nationalities div. on Asian affairs Rep. Nat. Com.; co-chmn. Finance Com. to Re-elect Pres., 1972; co-chmn. Nat. Rep. Heritage Groups Council, 1972; chmn. U.S. Citizens in Asia to Re-elect Pres., 1972; del. Rep. Nat. Conv., 1972. Recipient Woman of Distinction award Tex. Tech. Coll., Lubbock, 1966; Freedom award Order of Lafayette, Washington, 1966; Freedom award Free China Assn., Taipei, 1966, Golden Plate award Champion Democracy and Freedom Am. Acad. Achievement, 1967. Mem. Overseas Press Club N.Y.C., Nat. League Am. Pen Women, Writers Assn., Free China Writers Assn., 14th Air Force Assn. (chmn. awards), U.S. Air Force Wives Club, Flying Tiger Assn., Internat. Platform Assn., Am. Newspaper Women's Club Washington, Theta Sigma Phi. Clubs: Internat., F Street, Capitol Hill (Washington). Author: Chennault and the Flying Tigers; Way of a Fighter, 1949, translated into Chinese, 1955; A Thousand Springs, 1962; numerous books in Chinese including Song of Yesterday, 1961, M.E.E., 1963, My Two Worlds, 1965, The Other Half, 1966, Letters from U.S.A., 1967; author Chinese-English dictionaries. Home: 2510 Virginia Av NW Washington DC 20037 Office: 1511 K St NW Washington DC 20005

CHENNAULT, MADELYN JOANNE, educator; b. Atlanta, July 15, 1932; d. Benjamin Q. and Othello Ann Chennault; B.S., Morris Brown Coll., 1957; M.A., U. Mich., 1961, postgrad., 1971-72; Ed. Spl. Edn. (Dept. Health, Edn. and Welfare fellow), Ind. U., 1965, Ed.D., 1966; Tchr., R.L. Craddock Sch., Compton, Cal., L.C. Perry Sch., Ypsilanti, Mich., 1961-62; asst. prof. psychology Albany (Ga.) State Coll., 1962-64; grad. research asst. mental retardation Ind. U., Bloomington, 1964-66; research prof. edn. Atlanta U., 1966-67; prod. ednl. psychology Fort Valley (Ga.) State Coll., 1967—; vis. lectr. Mercer U., Macon, Ga., 1970-71, U. Ga., 1968-71; cons. Heart of Ga. Pre-Sch. Program, 1970-72. Mem. Am. Assn. U. Profs., Am. Assn. Mental Deficiency, Council Exceptional Children, Assn. Instnl. Research, Assn. Black Psychologists, Am. Psychol. Assn., Alpha Kappa Alpha. Home: 76 Howard Rd NW Atlanta GA 30314

CHENOWETH, ALICE DREW, physician; b. Albany, Mo., Feb. 21, 1903; d. John William and Ruby (Wheatley) Chenoweth; A.A., Palmer Coll., 1922; B.S., Northwestern U., 1924, M.A., 1926; M.D., Vanderbilt U. Sch. Medicine, 1932; m. John Ralston Pate, Feb. 12, 1942; 1 son, John Ralston. Instr. history Huntingdon Coll., Montgomery, Ala., 1926-28; intern Strong Meml. Hosp., Rochester, N.Y., 1932-33, Johns Hopkins Hosp., 1933-34; asst. chief resident Children's Hosp., Phila., 1934-36; research fellow Phila. Pediatric Soc. at U. Pa., 1936-38; pvt. practice medicine, specializing in pediatrics, Rosemont, Pa., 1938-42; dir. div. maternal and child health Ky. Dept. Health, 1942-49; research pediatrician Children's Bur., Dept. Health, Edn. and Welfare, Washington, 1949-52; med. tng. cons., 1952-54, pediatric cons., 1954-58, chief program service br. div. health services Maternal and Child Health Service, Health Services and Mental Health Adminstrn., 1958-73. Recipient Superior Service award Dept. Health, Edn. and Welfare; Outstanding Career Woman award Bus. and Profl. Women's Club, Arlington, Va., 1970; Blackwell award Am. Med. Women's Assn., 1973. Diplomate Am. Bd. Pediatrics. Fellow Am. Acad. Pediatrics, Am. Pub. Health Assn. (sec. maternal and child health sect. 1959-62), Am. Sch. Health Assn. (chmn. legis. com. 1969—); mem. Am. Med. Women's Assn. (pres. 1968), Med. Women's Internat. Assn., Pan Am. Med. Women's Alliance, Ambulatory Pediatric Assn., A.M.A., Women's Med. Soc. D.C. (rec. sec., 1960-62), A.A.A.S., Am. Assn. Maternal and Infant Health, Alpha Omega Alpha, Phi Beta Kappa. Episcopalian. Contbg. editor Jour. Sch. Health, 1969—. Home and office: 1503 N Jefferson St Arlington VA 22205

CHENOWETH, PRISCILLA CAROLYN READ (MRS. DONALD READ CHENOWETH), lawyer, editor; b. Bklyn., June 7, 1930; d. Burton Lester and Gerda Carolyn (Rosenquist) Read; student Oberlin Coll., 1948-50, U. Chgo., 1950-51; J.D., Rutgers U., 1968; m. Donald Read Chenoweth, June 24, 1951; children—Karin Read, Lesley Read, Eric Donald Read. Admitted to N.J. bar, 1968, U.S. Supreme Ct. bar, 1972; atty. Middlesex County Legal Services Corp., New Brunswick, N.J., 1968-69; dep. atty. gen. of N.J., Trenton, 1969-70; asso. Sills, Garretson, Levine & Goceljack, Perth Amboy, N.J., 1970-71; pvt. practice, Metuchen, N.J., 1971-74; mng. editor N.J. Law Jour., Newark, 1974—. Instr. constl. law Middlesex County Coll., Edison, N.J., 1972-73. Vice chmn. Middlesex County Congress Racial Equality, Metuchen, 1962-65; chmn., vice chmn. Middlesex County Econ. Opportunities Corp., New Brunswick, 1964-68. Trustee United Community Services, 1971—, mem. exec. com. 1971-73. Mem. Am., N.J., Middlesex County bar assns., N.J. Trial Lawyers Assn. Democrat. Home: 31 Graham Av Metuchen NJ 08840 Office: 240 Mulberry St Newark NJ 07101

CHERMAK, MARIANNE WALLENBERG, physician; b. Danzig, Germany; d. Adolf and Helene (Levitus) Wallenberg; M.D., U. Heidelberg (Germany), 1930; postgrad. student U. Clinics Vienna (Austria), 1933-38, Muensingen (Switzerland), 1938; m. Frank Chermak, Jan. 19, 1949. Intern Peoria (Ill.) State Hosp., 1939-40; resident Manteno (Ill.) State Hosp. 1940-41, clinic dir. 1942-59; staff mem. St. Joseph's Hosp., Joliet, 1959—. Cons. psychiatrist Ill. Dept. Corrections, Joliet 1960—; mem. county med. adv. com. Ill. Pub. Aid Commn. Diplomate Am. Bd. Psychiatry and Neurology. Mem. A.M.A., Am. Psychiat. Assn., Ill. Med. Soc. Author articles profl. jours. Home: 1122 Plainfield Rd Joliet IL 60435 Office: Box 702 McDonough St Joliet IL 60436

CHERN, NONA ELINORE ZIFFERBLATT (MRS. DAVID S. CHERN), educator; b. Phila.; d. Louis M. and Elizabeth (Burrison) Zifferblatt; B.S. in Edn., Temple U., 1943, postgrad., 1968-74; M.S. in Edn., U. Pa., 1963; postgrad. U. Chgo., 1965-67; m. David S. Chern, Aug. 26, 1945; children—Michael J., Katherine J. Tchr. elementary edn., Phila., 1943-47, Glenolden, Pa., 1957-60; tchr. reading Upland, (Pa.) Schs., 1960-63; coordinator reading Rose Tree Media Sch. Dist., Media, Pa., 1963-68; asso. prof. edn. West Chester (Pa.) State Coll., 1968—. Cons. reading Lancaster County Schs., Pa., 1967-69. Recipient citation Dept. Pub. Instrn., Media, Pa., 1964. Mem. Nat., Pa. edn. assns., Delaware County, Keystone State, Internat. reading assns., Am. Assn. U. Profs., Iota Alpha Pi, Pi Lambda Theta. Home: 1518 Manley Rd West Chester PA 19380

CHERNESKEY, MARY BODNARCHUK, educator; b. Winnipeg, Man., Can., July 27, 1929; d. Peter and Ewdokia (Kajda) Bodnarchuk; B.Sc., U. Man., 1950, diploma edn., 1951, B.Ed., 1961; postgrad. U. Sask., 1971-75; m. Morris Thomas Cherneskey, July 7, 1956; children—Annemarie, Paula, Christina. Interpreter, Teaton Co., Winnipeg, 1947-50; tchr. jr. high home econs., Winnipeg, 1951-56; research asst. chemistry dept. U. Sask. (Can.), 1956-58, lectr. psychology, supr. student teaching Coll. Edn., Saskatoon, 1971—; tchr. sr. high home econs., librarian, Saskatoon, Sask., 1968-69. Resource person Consumers Assn. Can., Saskatoon br., 1959-68; active publicity and edn. North Sask. UNICEF, 1969-72. Mem. Sch. Bd. Com. on Continuing Edn., 1969-71. Bd. dirs. St. Joseph Old Folks Home, Saskatoon, Sask., Can., 1967, Sask. Eparchy Mus. Culture. Mem. Canadian Fedn. U. Women (mem. standing com. on edn. 1973-76), Council Exceptional Children, Sask. Home Econs. Assn., Ukranian Cath. Women's League. Club: Saskatoon University Women's. Home: 1405 Park Av Saskatoon SK S7H 2N7 Canada

CHERNOCK, BEATRICE KRAVITSKY (MRS. MORRIS CHERNOCK), city ofcl.; b. Phila., May 30, 1909; d. Joseph and Faga Duba (Gulka) Kravitsky; B.S., Temple U., M.A.; diploma Phila. Normal Sch., 1926; m. Morris Chernock, June 23, 1933; children—Deborah (Mrs. Arnold Block), Joel. Tchr. elementary and secondary pub. schs. Phila., 1929-50, social studies collaborator, 1950-53, tchr. social studies WHYY-TV, 1958, prin. C.W. Henry Sch., 1958-72; mem. City Council, Phila., 1972—. Cons. Elementary State Commn., Harrisburg, Pa., 1949-50. Bd. mgrs. Greene St. YMCA; bd. dirs. Phila. Tribune Charities, 1966-68, A.R.C., 1968-70. Recipient West Mount Airy Neighbors Ann. award, 1961, Man of

Year award YMCA, 1967, Nat. Freedom Educators medal Freedom Found. Valley Forge, 1968, Outstanding Alumnus award W. Phila. High Sch., 1972; citation Chapel of Four Chaplains, 1960; Woman of Yr. award B'nai B'rith Educators Lodge, 1973. Jewish religion. Home: 1820 Wynnewood Rd Philadelphia PA 19151 Office: City Hall Philadelphia PA 19107

CHERNUCHIN, ELAYNE LINK (MRS. PAUL CHERNUCHIN), mgmt. cons. co. exec.; b. N.Y.C., Oct. 8, 1928; d. Sydney and Lillian (Kalish) Link; B.A., Bklyn. Coll., 1950, M.A., 1952; Ph.D., U. London, Eng., 1957; m. Paul Chernuchin, Sept. 12, 1952; children—Michael Scott, Cindy Jo. Tchr. math., N.Y.C. Pub. Sch. System, 1950-52; math. analyst Nat. Security Agy., 1952-54; instr. math. USAF, 1955-57; officer Chernuchin Assos., N.Y.C., 1965—. Mem. Am. Statis. Assn., Assn. Computing Machinery, Operational Research Soc. Research in applications specific statis. problems to high speed electronic equipment, comparative course in geometry for high school. Home: 108-19 67th Rd Forest Hills NY 11375

CHERNUCK, DOROTHY, theatre dir. and producer; b. N.Y.C.; d. William and Alice (Mulligan) Chernuck; B.A., Coll. of Mt. St. Vincent (N.Y.C.); M.A., Catholic U. of Am.; student Columbia U. Artistic dir., producer Arena Theatre, Rochester, N.Y., 1950-56; dir., free lance Inst. for Advanced Studies in Theatre Arts, Houston, N.J., Conn., N.Y.C., 1956-66; artistic dir. Theatre East, Rochester, N.Y., 1966-67; producer, dir. Corning (N.Y.) Summer Theatre, 1953—; co-producer Kennebunkport (Me.) Playhouse; free lance dir., Balt., N.H., off-Broadway, Corning, N.Y., 1968-73; dir. Plays for Living. Former instr. Trinity Coll., Washington; former asst. prof. Skidmore Coll., Saratoga Springs, N.Y., acting chmn. drama dept.; lectr. Hunter Coll., N.Y.C., 1965-66; summer workshop in acting State U. N.Y. Coll. at Geneseo. Mem. governing bd., past pres. Theatre Festival Assn. of N.Y. State, 1960—. Mem. Soc. Stage Directors and Choreographers, Actors Equity, Am. Theatre Assn., Speech Assn. of Am., Eastern States Theatre Assn.; Speech Assn. Eastern States, Inst. for Advanced Studies in Theatre Arts, Kappa Gamma Pi. Home: 220 E 52d St New York City NY 10022 Office: Box 51 Corning NY 14830

CHERRY, FLORA FINCH (MRS. WILLIAM A. CHERRY), physician, educator; b. McComb, Miss.; d. Thomas J. and Virginia Ann (Martin) Finch; B.S., Miss. Coll., 1944; M.D., Tulane U., 1948, M.P.H. in Pub. Health and Tropical Medicine, 1966; m. William A. Cherry, June 9, 1949; children—William Neal, Darrell Keith, Philip Allan, Susan Elisabeth. Intern Phila. Gen. Hosp., 1948-50; house physician Sacred Heart Hosp., Norristown, Pa., 1950-51; sch. physician Phila. Bd. Edn., 1952-53; practice medicine specializing in pediatrics, New Orleans, 1953-55, New Iberia, La., 1957-63; instr. pediatrics Tulane U., 1955-57, 63-65, asst. prof. dept. maternal and child health Sch. Pub. Health, 1965-70, asso. prof. maternal and child health 1970—, acting coordinator, 1974—. Isador Dyer Medal scholar, 1948. Diplomate Am. Bd. Pediatrics. Fellow Am. Acad. Pediatrics; mem. So. Soc. Pediatric Research, Am. Pub. Health Assn., Alpha Omega Alpha, Delta Omega. Home: 4828 St Charles Av New Orleans LA 70115 Office: 150 S Roman St New Orleans LA 70112

CHERRY, GWENDOLYN SAWYER BARNETT (MRS. JAMES LERON CHERRY), state legislator; b. Miami, Fla., Aug. 27, 1923; d. William Benjamin and Alberta (Cobb) Sawyer; B.A., Fla. A. and M. U., 1946, J.D. cum laude, 1965; M.A., N.Y. U., 1950; m. James Leron Cherry, June 3, 1960; children—William Barnett, Mary Elizabeth Barnett. Tchr., Bd. Pub. Instrn. Dade County Schs., Miami, Fla., 1948-65; admitted to Fla. bar, 1965; mem. firm Abramson & Butter, 1967-68; legal services atty. Office Econ. Opportunity, Dade County, 1966-68; prof. law Fla. A. and M. U Coll. Law, Tallahassee, 1968-69; mem. Fla. Ho. of Reps., 1970—. Mem. exec. com. Day Care and Child Devel. Council Am., 1971—; mem. Black Legislative Clearinghouse, Chgo., 1970—. NSF fellow, 1958-61. Mem. Nat. Assos. of Black Women Attys. (treas. 1972-74), Nat. Assn. State Legislators, Nat. Orgn. Women (Fla. pres. 1973), Hist. Assn. So. Fla., League Women Voters. Democrat. Conglist. Author: (with Ruby Rayford) Portraits in Color—Colorful Negro Women, 1961. Asst. editor Aurora, Sigma Gamma Rho, 1961-72. Home: 2545 NW 46th St Miami FL 33142 Office: 636 NW 2d Av Miami FL 33136

CHERRY, JANET ELLIS (MRS. ARTHUR CHERRY), health service adminstr., statistician; b. Camden, N.J., Oct. 12, 1937; d. Zellie and Dorothy (Vernekoff) Ellis; B.S. in Econs., U. Pa., 1959, M.A., 1972; m. Arthur Cherry, Feb. 25, 1967; children—Deborah, Alisha. Statistician Phila. Dept. Pub. Health, 1959-64; asst. study dir. Nat. Analysts, Phila., 1964; sales analyst Phila. Electric Co., 1964-65; research analyst Delaware Valley Regional Planning Commn., Phila., 1965-67; statis. analyst Greater Delaware Valley Regional Med. Program, Phila., 1967-68; mgr. systems Comprehensive Health Services Program, Phila., 1968-69, statis. cons., 1969-72, mgr. research and evaluation, 1973—. Cons., Research for Better Schs. Pres., Young Adult Council, Camden Jewish Community Center, 1961-63; treas. Soc. Hill Synagogue Sisterhood, 1973. Bd. dirs. N.J. State Council Young Adults, 1963. Mem. Am. Pub. Health Assn., Regional Sci. Assn., Am. Statis. Assn. (sec.-treas. Phila. chpt. 1964-66, pres. 1972-74), Phila. Area Econ. Research Soc. (sec. treas. 1964-65). Home: 2227 Panama St Philadelphia PA 19103 Office: 3701 N Broad St Philadelphia PA 19140

CHERRY, MARY ISABELLE LENZ (MRS. GEORGE THOMAS CHERRY), graphoanalyst; b. Washington; d. William Christopher and Mary (Schafer) Lenz; student U. Cal. at Los Angeles, 1935; m. George Thomas Cherry, Nov. 2, 1934; children—Donald Fred, Anne. Faculty, Internat. Graphoanalysis Congress, Chgo., 1964-69, Internat. U. for Young Presidents, Phoenix, 1966; resident tng. in graphoanalysis, 1963-69; cons. to psychologists, drs., bus. leaders, bus. and psychol. instns. Active local youth activities. Recipient excellence of performance award Internat. Graphoanalysis Soc., 1967, Co-op. award, 1967; named Graphoanalyst of Yr., 1971. Mem. Internat. Platform Assn., Internat. Graphoanalysis Soc. Address: 1876 San Pablo Dr Lake San Marcos CA 92069

CHERRY, SUSAN ELIZABETH, mus. curator; b. Detroit, Mar. 1, 1945; d. Donald George and Leah Ellen (Shefferly) Cherry; B.A., U. Mich., 1967; postgrad., Wayne State U., 1968. Tchr. Detroit Bd. Edn., 1969; mgr. money mus. Nat. Bank of Detroit, 1969—. Recipient Exhibit Merit award Mich. State Numis. Soc., 1972. Mem. Mich. Hist. Soc., Detroit Art Inst. Founders Soc., First Soc. Detroit, Mich. Museums Assn. (treas. 1973—), Am. Numis. Soc., Token and Medal Soc., Am. Numis. Assn. Club: Detroit Coin. Home: 480 Neff Grosse Pointe MI 48230 Office: 611 Woodward St Detroit MI 48232

CHERTOW, DORIS SALTZMAN (MRS. BERNARD CHERTOW), editor, educator; b. N.Y.C., Apr. 23, 1925; d. Jacob and Ella (Salzman) Saltzman; B.A., Hunter Coll., 1945; M.A., Radcliffe Coll., 1947; Ph.D. (Office Econ. Opportunity grantee 1967), Syracuse U., 1968; m. Bernard Chertow, Feb 2, 1947; children—Andrew, Richard, Marian, Douglas, David. Tchr. Central City Bus. Inst., Syracuse, N.Y., 1962; asst. to dir. Inter-Univ. Case Program, Syracuse U., 1963, tchr. grad. div. Syracuse U. (N.Y.), 1964-66, research asso., 1967, editor-dir. publs. continuing edn., 1968—. Instr. Syracuse U. Extended Campus, 1973—, Onondaga Community Coll., Syracuse, 1967-68. Mem. N.Y. Democratic com., 1968—. Mem. UN Assn. Central N.Y. (bd. dirs. 1973—), Adult Edn. Assn., Assn. Continuing Edn., Temple Soc. Concord. Editor: (with J. Whipple): The University and Community Service: Perspectives for the Seventies, 1970; (with M. Reagen) The Challenge of Modern Church-Public Relations, 1972. Adv. bd. newsletter N.Y. Assn. Continuing Edn. Home: 139 Sunnyside Park Rd Syracuse NY 13214

CHERVIN, RONDA DESOLA (MRS. MARTIN CHERVIN), educator; b. N.Y.C., Apr. 24, 1937; d. Ralph and Helen (Rosenson) DeS.; student Coll. City N.Y., 1953-55, U. Rochester, 1955-57; M.A., Fordham U., 1960, Ph.D., 1967; m. Martin Chervin, July 9, 1962; children—Carla, Diana, Charles. Asst. prof. evening Fordham U., 1967-68; lectr. U. Cal. at Irvine, 1969—; guest lectr. Chapman Coll., 1969; asst. prof. St. Joseph's Coll., 1969; asso. prof. dept. philosophy Loyola Marymount U., Los Angeles, 1969—. Woodrow Wilson fellow, 1957-58; Fulbright-Danforth grantee, 1966-67. Mem. Am. Philos. Assn., Phi Beta Kappa. Author: The Church of Love; Choice. Home: 7612 Cowan Av Los Angeles CA 90045 Office: Dept Philosophy Loyola U Box 353 Los Angeles CA 90045

CHESELDINE, ANNE MILLIGAN (MRS. RICHARD J. CHESELDINE), realtor; b. Cin., Aug. 16, 1914; d. William John and Anna (Brand) Milligan; grad. high sch., Cin.; m. Richard J. Cheseldine, Oct. 16, 1937; 1 son, Richard J. Saleswoman, Lind Davis Real Estate Co., Montgomery, Ala., 1962-64, owner, 1964—, sec.-treas., 1972—, also mng. broker. Recipient Million Dollar award, 1967. Mem. Montgomery Real Estate Bd. (dir. 1968-71), Ala., Nat. assns. real estate bds. Roman Catholic. Club: Woodley Country. Home: 2859 McGehee Rd Montgomery AL 36111 Office: PO Box 2627 Montgomery AL 36105

CHESEN, DORIS SCHIMMEL, couture buyer; b. Lincoln, Neb., Mar. 10, 1932; d. A. Q. and Marion (Fantle) Schimmel; student Goucher Coll., 1949-51; m. Irwin Somberg Chesen, Dec. 12, 1951; children—Catherine Sue, William Schimmel, Carrie Lynn. With Hovland-Swanson, women's specialty store, Lincoln, 1964—, couture buyer, 1969—; profl. organist, 1959-64. Mem. Neb. Arts Council, 1968-71; pres. Lincoln Symphony, 1969-71. Bd. dirs. local Girl Scouts, Child Guidance, Rotary Ann, P.T.A., S. St. Temple Sisterhood, Lincoln Gen. Hosp. Guild. Clubs: Hillcrest Country, Lincoln University, Neb. Home: 1350 Aldrich Rd Lincoln NE 68510 Office: 1230 O St Lincoln NE 68508

CHESHIRE, MAXINE (MRS. HERBERT W. CHESHIRE), columnist; b. Harlan, Ky., Apr. 5, 1930; d. M.F. and Sylvia (Cornett) Hall; student Union Coll., Barbourville, Ky., 1951-52, U. Ky., 1949-50; m. Herbert W. Cheshire, Apr. 25, 1954; children—Marc, Hall, Paden, Leigh. Reporter, Knoxville (Tenn.) News-Sentinel, 1951-54; reporter Washington Post, 1954-65, columnist, 1965—. Contbr. articles to popular mags. Home: 2011 White Oaks Dr Alexandria VA 22306 Office: 1515 L St NW Washington DC 20005

CHESNEY, BARBARA HAACK (MRS. ALAN PARKER CHESNEY), psychologist; b. Milw., Aug. 4, 1944; d. Donald Herman and Leila Gertrude (McNitt) Haack; B.A. cum laude (Coll. scholar), Lake Erie Coll., 1966; M.A., Case Western Res. U., 1968, Ph.D. (Nat. Def. Edn. Act fellow), 1970; m. Alan Parker Chesney, Aug. 10, 1968. Research cons. ednl. psychology, Oklahoma City, 1972-73; ednl. psychologist Learning Resources Center U. Okla. Med. Sch., Oklahoma City, 1973—, cons. dept. dental hygiene, 1973. Cons. Coll. Sagrado Corazon, San Juan, P.R., 1972, State of Okla. Dept. Instns., Social and Rehabilitative Services, 1973, U. Saigon (South Vietnam) Med. Sch., Repub. Vietnam Nat. Inst. Pub. Health, 1973. Mem. Am. Psychol. Assn., Assn. Am. Med. Colls., Alpha Lambda Delta. Office: PO Box 26901 Oklahoma City OK 73190

CHESS, STELLA (MRS. ALEXANDER THOMAS), psychiatrist; b. N.Y.C., Mar. 1, 1914; d. Benjamin and Clara (Schwartzman) Chess; B.A., Smith Coll., 1935; M.D., N.Y.U., 1939; postgrad. in Psychoanalysis, N.Y. Med. Coll., 1946-49; m. Alexander Thomas, June 28, 1938; children—Joan, Richard, Leonard, Kenneth. Extern children's psychiat. ward Bellevue Hosp., N.Y.C., 1939-40; intern Montefiore Hosp., 1940-41; resident in psychiatry Grasslands Hosp., 1941, Pleasantville Cottage Sch., 1941-45, Riverdale Children's Assn., 1942-54; practice medicine specializing in child psychiatry, N.Y.C., 1943—; psychiatrist Northside Center Child Devel., N.Y.C., 1946-47, chief co-ordinating psychiatrist, 1947-58; attending psychiatrist Met. Hosp. N.Y.C., 1958-60, dir. child psychiat. clinic, 1960-66; mem. postgrad. faculty N.Y. Med. Coll., N.Y.C., 1949-66; dir. child psychiatry, 1960-66, prof. psychiatry, 1954; prof. child psychiatry N.Y. U. Sch. Medicine; asso. attending in psychiatry N.Y. U. Med. Center; vis. psychiatrist Bird S. Coler Hosp., 1958-66, Bellevue Hosp., N.Y.C., 1966—. Fellow Am. Psychiat. Assn., Am. Orthopsychiat. Assn., Am. Acad. Child Psychiatry (charter); mem. Am. Women's Med. Assn., N.Y. Soc. Clin. Psychiatry, Soc. Research Child Devel. Author: An Introduction to Child Psychiatry, 1959, 2d edit., 1969; Behavioral Individuality in Early Childhood, 1963; (with Thomas and Birch) Your Child is a Person, 1965; (with Thomas and Birch) Temperament and Behavior Disorders in Children, 1968; (with Fernandez and Korn) Psychiatric Disorders in Children with Congenital Rubella; Annual Progress in Child Psychiatry and Child Development, 1968, 69, 70, 71, 72, 73, 74. Editor: Jour. Autism and Childhood Schizophrenia, 1972-73. Contbr. to profl. publs. Research on longitudinal study individual behavioral characteristics of children, behavioral study of mentally retarded children, of children with congenital rubella. Home: 10 Mitchell Pl New York City NY 10017 Office: 333 E 49th St New York City NY 10017

CHESSON, REVA JONES (MRS. JOHN BRENT CHESSON), educator, library adminstr.; b. Fenton, La., Aug. 20, 1927; d. Dave John and Mary Francis (Sorbet) Jones; B.A. in Edn., U. S.W. La., 1948; B.S. in L.S., La. State U., 1951; M.Ed., McNeese State U., 1971; m. John Brent Chesson, Nov. 12, 1948; children—John Brent, Aline. Asst. librarian Calcasieu Parish Library, Lake Charles, La., 1948-54, br. supr., 1954-56; asst. prof. library sci. McNeese State U., Lake Charles, 1960-67; supr. sch. libraries Calcasieu Parish Sch. Bd., 1967—. Mem. Am. (com. chmn. 1973—), La. (pres. 1971-72), Calcasieu, Southwestern Regional (sec. 1968-70) library assns., La. Tchrs. Assn., La. Assn. Sch. Librarians, Delta Kappa Gamma. Democrat. Methodist. Home: 1040 Holly Lake Charles LA 70601 Office: 626 Kirkman Lake Charles LA 70601

CHESTER, CHARLOTTE WANETTA, artist; b. Columbus, O., Oct. 27, 1921; d. Charles William and Edna May (Casteel) Harper; student Capitol U., 1953-54, Okla. City U., 1958-59, Pa. Acad. Fine Arts, 1968-69, Phila. Coll. Art, 1971, many workshops, 1968-69; m. David Murel Chester, Sept. 27, 1939; children—Carol (Mrs. Verne Landt), Janet (Mrs. Ronald Cocklereece), David Murel. With U.S. Govt., 1955-71; propr. Char's Studio and Gallery, Ventnor, N.J., 1968-69; tchr. advanced painting Atlantic Community Coll., N.J., Fed. Art Assn. N.J., 1968-69, chmn. So. sect., 1971; co-owner gallery Art is the Key, W. Orange, N.J., 1972-73; paintings in permanent collections Nat. Air and Space Mus., Smithsonian Instn., Frankfort, Germany, Yearbook Ocean City, Kerr Mus. Recipient honorable mention A.C. Art Center, Atlantic City, 1965, 70, merit award Atlantic City C. of C., 1970, honorable mention Cultural Art Center, Ocean City, 1973. Mem. League S. Jersey Artists (pres. 1968), Nat. Polit. Caucus, Nat. Orgn. Women. Unitarian-Universalist (program chmn. 1973). Address: 7 S Wyoming Av Ventnor City NJ 08406

CHEVALIER, CHARLOTTE BERGERSEN (MRS. JACQUES E. CHEVALIER), pianist, educator; b. Chgo., Sept. 14, 1926; d. Earl Olaf and Myrtle Lillian (Winingstad) Bergersen; B.Mus., Am. Conservatory of Music, 1949, M.Mus., 1952; student Northwestern U., 1945, U. Chgo., 1946-48; B. Music Theory, Am. Conservatory Music, 1969, B. Music Composition, 1972; m. Jacques E. Chevalier, Sept. 7, 1949; children—Nicole, Marc. Tchr. Am. Conservatory of Music, Chgo., 1949—, dir. children's dept., 1968—; pianist and accompanist. Mem. Soc. Am. Musicians, Musicians Club of Women, Sigma Alpha Iota. Club: Highland Park (Ill.) Music (v.p. 1963-66). Home: 606 Burton Av Highland Park IL 60035 Office: Am Conservatory of Music 410 S Michigan Av Chicago IL 60605

CHEVALIER, ELIZABETH PICKETT, author; b. Chgo., Mar. 25, 1896; d. Montgomery and Alma (Osborne) Pickett; A.B., Wellesley Coll., 1918; Litt.D., Transylvania Coll., 1943, Occidental Coll., 1966; m. Stuart Chevalier, Oct. 17, 1936. Publicity dir. A.R.C. Nursing Service, Washington, 1918-19; hist. research, writing, 1919-23; author, dir. scenics and short subjects Fox Studios, N.Y.C., 1923-24, Hollywood, Cal., 1925-28; scenarist, writer original stories Fox West Coast Studios, 1926-28; author, scenarist, asso. producer first Am. full length color motion picture Redskin, starring Richard Dix, released by Paramount, 1928. Mem. bd. incorporators A.R.C., 1944-47 (dissolution), mem. nominating com. for 1947 A.R.C. Nat. Conv., mem. adv. com. on orgn., 1946; mem.-at-large bd. govs., 1947-52, woman mem. bd. gov.'s com. nat. blood program, 1947-51. Mem. Cal. Welfare Study Commn., 1961-63. Trustee Southwest Mus., Los Angeles, Occidental Coll., Los Angeles; pub. advisor U.S. Mission 15th World Health Assembly. Recipient Culture Series award So. Editors Assn., Holland, 1950; Pasedena (Cal.) Women's Civic League Recognition award, 1959. Mem. Nat. Soc. Colonial Dames Am. (chmn. patriotic services com.), P.E.N. Democrat. Presbyn. Clubs: Sulgrave (Washington, D.C.); Cosmopolitan, Pen and Brush (N.Y.C.); Town (Pasadena, Cal.). Author: Official History of American Red Cross Nursing Service, 1921; The American Red Cross: Its Origin, Purposes and Service, 1922; Redskin, 1928; (novel) Drivin' Woman, 1942. Home: 401 N Bowling Green Way Los Angeles CA 90049

CHEVERS, WILDA ANITA YARDE (MRS. KENNETH CHEVERS), probation officer; b. N.Y.C.; d. Wilsey Ivan and Herbertlee (Perry) Yarde; B.A., Hunter Coll., 1947; M.S.W., Columbia, 1959; m. Kenneth Chevers, May 14, 1950; 1 dau., Pamela Anita. Probation officer, 1947-55; supr. probation officer, 1955-65; br. chief Office Probation for Cts. N.Y.C., 1965-72, asst. dir. probation, 1972—. Sec. Susan E. Wagner Adv. Bd., 1966-70. Sec., bd. dirs. Allen Community Day Care Center, 1971—. Mem. Nat. Council on Crime and Delinquency, Nat. Assn. Social Workers, Acad. Certified Social Workers. Queensboro Council for Social Welfare (dir. 1965-70, chmn. com. alcoholism 1969-70), Middle Atlantic States Conf. Correction, Alumni Assn. Columbia Sch. Social Work, N.Y. State Probation and Parole Assn., Probation and Parole Assn. Greater N.Y., N.A.A.C.P., Counseliers, Delta Sigma Theta. Club: Hansel and Gretel (pres. 1967-69) (Queens, N.Y.). Home: 105-62 132d St Richmond Hill New York City NY 11419 Office: NYC Dept Probation 66 Court St Brooklyn NY 11201

CHEWNING, ELLEN GREEN HUNT (MRS. THOMAS OREN CHEWNING), ednl. adminstr.; b. nr. Wake Forest, N.C., Apr. 23, 1925; d. Edwin C. and Nellie (Fuller) Hunt; student U. N.C., Greensboro, 1941-43; A.B., Wake Forest U., 1944; M.Ed., U. Va., 1960; m. Thomas Oren Chewning, June 6, 1943; children—Thomas Oren, Barbara Sue. Tchr. social studies Fairfield Jr. High Sch., Henrico County, Va., 1958-59; counselor John Marshall High Sch., Richmond, Va., 1960-69, guidance coordinator, 1969-70; guidance coordinator Maggie L. Walker High Sch., Richmond, 1970-73; supr. guidance services Richmond Pub. Schs., 1973—. Vice chmn. Henrico County Sch. Bd., 1959; mem. Gov.'s Ednl. Facilities Commn., Va., 1957-59; chmn. Citizens Com. on Status of Women in Va., 1966-68; v.p. Va. Congress Parents and Tchrs., 1959-61; mem. Gov.'s Com. Employment Handicapped, 1971-73. Mem. Henrico County Democratic Com., 1962—, vice chmn., 1971-73, chmn., 1973—. Bd. dirs. J. Sargeant Reynolds Community Coll., 1972—. Mem. N.E.A., Va. Edn. Assn. (v.p. 1969-71), Va. Council Social Welfare (dir.), Family and Children's Service Soc. (bd. dirs.), Am. Va. (pres. 1971-72), Richmond (pres. 1964-65) personnel and guidance assns., Nat. Vocational Guidance Assn., Am. Sch. Counselors Assn., Delta Kappa Gamma. Baptist. Home: 7506 S Pinehill Dr Richmond VA 23228

CHEWNING, PHYLLIS WISTING (MRS. WALTER L. CHEWNING), hosp. communications co. exec.; b. Seattle, Dec. 25, 1924; d. George Henry and Mabel Elizabeth (Lofstrom) Wisting; student U. Ore., 1942-44; m. Walter L. Chewning, Jan. 1, 1967; 1 stepson, Jeffrey L. Owner, operator Hosp. Television Co., 1948-60; asst. to v.p. Wells Nat. Services Corp. (now a subsidiary Am. Hosp. Supply Corp.), N.Y.C., 1961-63, mgr. hosp. div., 1963-68, v.p. 1968—. Mem. Alpha Phi. Home: 523 Oenoke Ridge Rd New Canaan CT 06840 Office: Pan Am Bldg New York City NY 10017

CHI, LOIS WONG (MRS. HENRY CHI), educator; b. Fuchow, China (came to U.S. 1941, naturalized 1954); d. Leland and Ada (Pang) Wang; B.S., Wheaton (Ill.) Coll., 1945; M.S., U. So. Cal., 1948, Ph.D., 1953; m. Henry Chi, Jan. 14, 1956; children—Lanie, David, Joyce-lyn. Research asso., instr. Loma Linda (Cal.) U., Sch. Medicine, 1952-55; instr. to asso. prof. Immaculate Heart Coll., Los Angeles, 1957-66, chmn. biology dept., 1963-65; asso. prof. Cal. State Coll., Dominquez Hills, 1966-70, prof., 1970—, chmn. dept. biol. scis., 1970-72. Bd. dirs. NSF grant for biology dept., 1962-64; mem. nat. adv. allergy and infectious diseases council NIH, 1974. NIH grantee, 1957—. Mem. N.Y. Acad. Sci., Am. Soc. Tropical Medicine and Hygiene, Am. Soc. Parasitology, Am. Micros. Soc. Contbr. articles to profl. jours. Home: 2839 El Oeste Dr Hermosa Beach CA 90254

CHIANG CHING, cultural adminstr.; b. about 1913; m. Tang Na, 1934 (div. 1937); m. 2d, Mao Tse-tung, 1940; children—Hsiao Li, Mao Mao. Stage, film actress, Shanghai; appeared in A Doll's House; appeared in films, including The Sons and Daughters of China; joined China Alliance Film Enterprise, Shanghai, 1936, also, Shanghai Practical Amateur Dramatic Theatre, with Central Film Studio of the Propaganda Bur. of Kuomintang Govt.; mem. Motion Picture Guidance Council Communist Party of China, 1950—; dir. Shachiaping, Peking, 1963, The Taking of the Bandit Stronghold, 1964, The Red Detachment of Women, The White Haired Girl, 1963-64, The Red Lantern, 1964; producer films A Great Wall Along the South Coast, Sentinels under Neon Lights, 1964; dep. to N.P.C., 1964—; 1st dep. head Cultural Revolution Group, Central Com. of Chinese Communist Party, 1966—, head sub-group responsible for directing art and lit., 1967—; adviser to People's Liberation Army on Cultural Work, 1966—; mem. Politburo, 1969—. Office: Central Committee of the Communist Party of China Peking People's Republic of China*

CHICAGO, JUDY, artist; b. Chgo., July 20, 1939; d. Arthur M. and May (Levenson) Cohen; B.A., U. Cal. at Los Angeles, 1962, M.A., 1964; m. Lloyd Hamrol, June 28, 1969. An organizer Feminist Studio Workshop Inc., Los Angeles, Cal., 1970—; exhibited numerous one artist exhbns., numerous group shows; represented in permanent collections. Recipient Mademoiselle Woman of Year award, 1973. Mem. Phi Beta Kappa. Author: Through the Flower, 1975. Address: 1651B 18th St Santa Monica CA 90404

CHICK, JOYCE MURRIEL, psychologist, educator; b. Titusville, Fla., Mar. 22, 1930; d. Joseph M. and Thelma G. (Gray) Chick; B.S., Fla. State U., 1951, M.S., 1952; Ph.D., Mich. State U., 1963. Dir. guidance Melbourne (Fla.) High Sch., 1952-54; asst. personnel office and security div. Radiation Inc., Melbourne, summer, 1954; counselor Hialeah (Fla.) Sr. High Sch., 1954-56; dean of girls, chmn. guidance Henry H. Filer Jr. High Sch., Hialeah, 1956-58; asso. dir. counseling and personnel services Sch. Edn., Fla. State U., Tallahassee, 1958-60; asst. prof. counselor edn. Western Mich. U., Kalamazoo, summer, 1961; asst. instr. guidance and counseling Mich. State U., East Lansing, 1960-62; asst. prof. counselor edn. Fla. State U., Tallahassee, 1962-67, asso. prof., 1967-71, acting dept. head, counselor edn., 1969-70, dept. head counselor edn., 1970-71, prof. counselor edn., 1972—, dir. div. profl. and clin. programs, 1972—. Vocational cons. Social Security Adminstrn., Washington, 1964—, various law offices and sch. bds. Named Outstanding Educator of Am., Fla. State U., 1973. Mem. Am., Fla. personnel and guidance assns., Nat. Vocational Guidance Assn. (com. mem. 1967-69, chmn. profl. mem. com. 1969-72), Fla. Assn. Counselor Educators And Suprs. (pres. 1972-73, mem. commn. on women 1971-72), Dade County Deans and Counselors Assn. (pres. 1957-58), Big Bend Guidance Assn., Am. Psychol. Assn. Contbr. numerous articles on vocational counseling and guidance to profl. jours. and publs. Home: 1245 Halifax Court Tallahassee FL 32303 Office: 213 Education Florida State Univ Tallahassee FL 32306

CHIESA, DANETA DANIEL (MRS. RUDOLPH MATTHEW CHIESA), educator; b. Shreveport, La., July 24, 1940; d. Claude L. and Freta (Sullivan) Daniel; B.A., La. Tech. U., 1961, M.A., 1963; postgrad. Northwestern State U. La., 1964; Syracuse U., 1965; Ed.D. in Spl. Edn., George Peabody Coll. for Tchrs., 1974; 1 dau. by previous marriage, Mary Denise Barton; m. Rudolph Matthew Chiesa, July 5, 1969; 1 dau., Antonia Elisabetta. Tchr. mentally retarded Caddo Parish Sch. Bd., Shreveport, 1961-67; student tchr. supr. George Peabody Coll., Nashville, 1968; in-service co-coordinator Clover Bottom Hosp. and Sch., Nashville, 1968-69; asst. prof. La. Tech. U., Ruston, 1969—. Del., Internat. Conv. Council for Exceptional Children, 1971. Mem. Am. Assn. Mental Deficiency, Am. Assn. U. Profs., Nat. Orgn. for Women, La. Tchrs. Assn. (pres. spl edn. sect. 1974—), Am. Assn. U. Women, Council for Exceptional Children, Delta Zeta. Democrat. Unitarian. Home: Cedar Creek Park Al Ruston LA 71270

CHIHUARIA, ERNESTINE ELIZABETH RIEDEL (MRS. VICTOR CHIHUARIA), violinist; b. Oakland, Cal.; d. Fred and Francisca Lena (Cheli) Riedel; student San Francisco Conservatory of Music, 1953-55, Salzburg (Austria) Mozarteum, 1960-61; m. Victor Chihuaria. Violinist, San Francisco Symphony Orch., 1964—, soloist, 1966-67; soloist BBC, Eng., 1966, Radio Orch., Holland, 1964, San Francisco Symphony Orch., 1967; recitals in Nurnberg, Freidrickshafen, Munich, Stuttgart, Hamburg, Kiel, Cologne, Germany, Salzburg, Vienna, Austria, Wels, Austria, 1963, Mexico, 1967; radio, TV broadcasts, Mexico, 1971—. Mem. San Francisco Symphony Orch. Assn. Office: San Francisco Symphony Orch Opera House Civic Center San Francisco CA 94102

CHILD, JULIA MCWILLIAMS (MRS. PAUL CHILD), cooking tchr.; b. Pasadena, Cal., Aug. 15, 1912; d. John and Julia Carolyn (Weston) McWilliams; B.A., Smith Coll., 1934; m. Paul Child, Sept. 1, 1945. With advt. dept. W. & J. Sloane, N.Y.C., 1939-40; with OSS, Washington, also Ceylon, China, 1941-45; condr. program The French Chef, WGBH-TV, Boston, 1962—, 2d series on Pub. Broadcasting Service, 1970—, 3d series, 1971-72. Decorated Ordre de Merite Agricole, 1969; recipient Peabody Broadcasting award, 1965; Emmy award, 1966. Author: (with Simone Beck and Louisette Bertholle) Mastering the Art of French Cooking, 1961, Vol. II (with Simone Beck), 1970; The French Chef Cookbook, 1968, 71. Office: WGBH-TV 125 Western Av Boston MA 02134

CHILD, LEILA AVERELL (TONI), editor; b. Milw., Mar. 24, 1926; d. Frank Moore and Leonora Averell (Cowdrey) Child; student U. Ga., 1943-44; A.B., U. S.C., 1947. Editor, U.S. Army Intelligence, Manila, Philippines, 1947-48; editor lit. and cultural events, news reporter Columbia (S.C.) Record, 1949-55; pub. information dir., dir. personnel City of Columbia, 1955-61, dir. pub. information, 1961-65; editor, designer, pub. all books, booklets, tchrs. guides and publs. S.C. Dept. Edn., Columbia, 1965—. Mem. pub. relations com. United Fund, 1971-72; mem. League Women Voters, 1950-55; sec. Shandon Neighborhood Council, 1972-73; chmn. publicity Town Theatre, 1950-57; v.p. Drama Club, 1971, pres., 1972-73; v.p. Players Club, 1968. Bd. dirs. U.S.O., 1953-55, Assoc. Social Agys., 1972-74. Recipient awards for excellence of publs. design, Nat. Sch. Pub. Relations Assn., Sch. Mgmt. Mag., 1968-72. Mem. Alpha Delta Pi, Alpha Kappa Gamma (life). Roman Catholic. Home: 3000 Wilmot Av Columbia SC 29205 Office: 1429 Senate St Columbia SC 29201

CHILD, WINIFRED LINDSEY, real estate cons.; b. Burlington, Kan.; d. Fred H. and Burneice (Duryea) Hahn; m. John F. Child, Jr.; children—Carole Lee, William Jay. Sec. John Child & Co., Honolulu, 1961-65; sec., treas. Childoo Internat., Inc., Honolulu, 1965-70, pres., 1970—; exec. v.p. Child's Marine, Ltd.; v.p. Child & Waters, Inc. Mem. Bd. Realtors Honolulu. Mem. Internat. Union Travel Orgns., Delta Theta Tau (chpt. pres. 1959). Club: Waikiki Yacht (Honolulu). Home: 295 Ainahou St Honolulu HI 96825 Office: 821 Alakea St Honolulu HI 96813

CHILDERS, MARIE ELLEN TURNIPSEED, ednl. adminstr.; b. Newton, Ill., July 17, 1940; d. David A. and Christine (Westford) Turnipseed; B.A., So. Ill. U., 1962, M.S., 1964; postgrad. State U. N.Y. at Buffalo, 1964-65; div.; 1 dau., Lisa Christine. Asst. supr. small group housing So. Ill. U., 1962-64; activities coordinator, counselor State U. N.Y. at Buffalo, 1964-68; dean of women U. Evansville (Ind.), 1968-70, dean student affairs, 1970—. Mem. Mayor's Task Force on Human Resources. Bd. dirs. Planned Parenthood of Evansville, 1969-74, v.p., 1969-71, 73-74. Mem. Nat. (mem. continuing edn. com. 1971-73), Ind. (exec. bd. 1971—) assns. women deans, adminstrs. and counselors, Nat. Assn. Student Personnel Adminstrs. (mem. commns. publ. bd. 1971-72), Am. (mem. commn. orgn. adminstrn. and devel. of student personnel services 1973—), Ind. (v.p. 1970-71) coll. personnel assns., Jr. League Evansville (chmn. profls. com. 1974), Am. Assn. U. Women (br. program v.p. 1971-73), Alpha Lambda Delta (hon.), Delta Kappa Gamma. Methodist (com. on continuing edn. for ministers). Home: 520 S Spring St Evansville IN 47714

CHILDRESS, ANNE MATTHEWS, journalist; b. Balt., July 27, 1939; d. William Bernard and Louisa (Bowen) Matthews; B.A. magna cum laude, Washington Coll., Chestertown, Md., 1960; m. Richard W. Childress, Apr. 6, 1963 (div. 1971). Copy girl Balt. News Am., 1960, feature writer, 1961, asst. music critic, 1962-63, asst. movie and drama critic, 1963-65, motion picture editor, 1965-72, women's editor, 1972—; writer Hearst Headline Service, 1970-72. Sec., Dickeyville Improvement Assn., 1970. Democrat. Episcopalian. Home: 5107 Wetheredsville Rd Baltimore MD 21207 Office: News Am Baltimore MD 21203

CHILDRESS, EVELYN MAE TUTT (MRS. JOHN WESLEY CHILDRESS), educator; b. Joplin, Mo., Feb. 8, 1926; d. Augustus Garvin and Fannie (Waite) Tutt; B.S. cum laude, Lincoln U., 1947; M.S., U. Mich., 1948 and 1956; postgrad. U. Wash., 1954; Ph.D., Stanford U., 1967; m. John Wesley Childress, Dec. 23, 1967. Tchr. Fla. A. and M. U., Tallahassee, 1948-49; asst. prof. biology Lincoln U., Jefferson City, Mo., 1949-52, 54-55, 56-63; tchr. Fullerton (Cal.) Jr. Coll., 1967-69; asso. prof. biology Cal. State Coll. at Dominguez Hills, 1969—; NSF fellow 1963-65. Mem. Am. Assn. U. Profs., Am. Assn. U. Women, Am. Soc. Microbiology, A.A.A.S., Cal. Tchrs. Assn., Crenshaw Neighbors, Sigma Xi, Alpha Kappa Alpha, Phi Sigma, Beta Kappa Chi, Delta Kappa Gamma. Home: 4623 Don Miguel Dr Los Angeles CA 90008 Office: 1000 E Victoria St Dominguez Hills CA 90747

CHILDS, LOUISE SNYDER, physician; b. Brookville, Pa., Jan. 4, 1910; d. Wayne Lawson and Ruth (Luther) Snyder; grad. The Baldwin Schs., 1927; A.B., Bryn Mawr Coll., 1931; M.D., Johns Hopkins U., 1935; postgrad. U. Pa., 1952; M.P.H., U. Cal. at Berkeley, 1966; m. Edgar S. Childs, June 19, 1936; children—Diane (Mrs. H. Russel Holland), William Alexander Keola, Robert Edgar Kuiani. Intern pediatrics, Johns Hopkins Hosp., 1935-36, Bellevue Hosp., N.Y.C., 1936-37; resident pediatrics Sea View Hosp., S.I., N.Y., 1937-38; practice medicine, specializing in pediatrics, Honolulu, 1939-65; chief maternal and child health br. Hawaii State Dept. Health, 1966—; asso. clin. prof. pub. health U. Hawaii Sch. Pub. Health, 1968—; acting dir. Bur. Maternal & Infant Hygiene, Territorial Bd. Health, 1940-41; lectr. home econs. (child care), pub. health nursing U. Hawaii, 1942-45; instr., clin. asst. in pediatrics Jefferson Med. Coll., Phila., 1952-54. Diplomate Am. Bd. Pediatrics, Nat. Bd. Med. Examiners. Fellow Am. Acad. Pediatrics, Am. Pub. Health Assn.; mem. Honolulu Pediatric Soc., A.A.A.S. Home: 222 Wailupe Circle Honolulu HI 96821

CHILDS, MARJORIE MAY VICTORIA, judge; b. N.Y.C., July 13, 1918; d. Charles William and Eva May (Tarrant) Childs; student Hunter Coll., 1942-46; B.A., U. Cal. at Berkeley, 1948; postgrad. Hastings Coll. Law, 1948-49; J.D., U. San Francisco, 1956; LL.D., Ia. Wesleyan Coll., 1973. Econ. research analyst Fgn. Service U.S. State Dept., Paris, France, 1949-50, Frankfurt, Germany, 1950-51; legal asst. Dept. Navy, San Francisco, 1956-60; admitted to Cal. bar, 1957; practiced in San Francisco, 1962-64; asst. county counsel Humboldt County, Eureka, Cal., 1960-62; mem. firm Berry, Childs & Berry, San Francisco, 1962-64; referee, judge Juvenile Ct. San Francisco, 1964—. Mem. Mayor's Com. on Status of Women, 1969—; chmn. subcom. on city govt. San Francisco, 1971—. Trustee Maria Kip Orphanage Fund. Recipient James Harlan award Ia. Wesleyan Coll., 1969. Mem. Cal. State Bar (com on juvenile justice 1969—, chmn. 1970-72, adviser 1972-75), Internat., Am., Fed. bar assns., Nat. Assn. Women Lawyers (pres. 1974-75), Queen's Bench (pres. 1967-68), Am. Assn. U. Women (pres. San Francisco br. 1970-72), Bar Assn. San Francisco. Club: Metropolitan. Contbr. articles to profl. jours. Home: 64 Turquoise Way San Francisco CA 94131 Office: 375 Woodside Av San Francisco CA 94127

CHILES, MARGARET VIOLA (MRS. MELVIN F. CHILES), county ofcl.; b. Central City, Colo., June 29, 1907; d. Charles William and Lila (Hosking) Light; student Barnes Comml. Sch., 1924; m. Melvin F. Chiles, Oct. 30, 1926; children—Melvin F., Doris J. (Mrs. Roy C. Huner), Robert L., Donald H. Typist Gates Rubber Co., Denver, 1925; gen. office work Denver Sch. Adminstrn., 1925; dictation, gen. office work Kansas City Life Ins. Co., Denver, 1925; dep. Gelpin County Clks. Office, Central City, Colo., 1926; dep. Clear Creek County Office, Georgetown, Colo., 1956-68, county clk, 1968—, recorder, 1970—. Mem. Republican club, 1956-73; cons. Rep. party, 1956—. Mem. Navy Mothers Club (sec. 1960-70). Episcopalian. Home: 2030 Virginia St Idaho Springs CO 80452 Office: 5th and Argentine Georgetown CO 80444

CHILES, MARGUERITE MOORE, univ. dean; b. Simpsonville, S.C., Oct. 22, 1916; d. Robert Lee and Martha (Moore) Chiles; B.A., Furman U., 1940; M.A. in Guidance, Columbia, 1944. Sec. to dean of Woman's Coll., Furman U., Greenville, S.C., 1940-43, dir. student personnel for women Furman U., 1945-65, dean women, 1965-73, asst. v.p. student affairs, 1973—; resident hall counselor Woman's Coll., U. N.C., Greensboro, 1944-45. Chmn. personnel com. YWCA, 1959, bd. dirs., 1965; mem. Greenville County Family Planning Council. Recipient Mary Mildred Sullivan award as outstanding alumna Furman U., 1953, Alumna Service award, 1972. Mem. S.C. Assn. Women Deans, So. Personnel and Guidance Assn., C. of C., Nat., S.C. (pres. 1968) assns. women deans and counselors, S.C. Student Personnel Assn. Democrat. Baptist. Home: 219 Randall St Greenville SC 29609

CHILMAN, CATHERINE EARLES STREET (MRS. C. WILLIAM CHILMAN), educator; b. Cleve., Sept. 20, 1914; d. Elwood Vickers and Augusta (Jewitt) Street; A.B., Oberlin Coll., 1935; M.A., U. Chgo., 1938; Ph.D., U. Syracuse, 1958; m. C. William Chilman, Sept. 7, 1936; children—Margaret (Mrs. John Carpenter) Jeanne (Mrs. Alden Klovdahl), Catherine (Mrs. Richard Brown). Caseworker United Charities, Chgo., 1937-39, Family Services, Roanoke, Va., 1939-40; psychiat. cons. A.R.C., Syracuse, N.Y., 1943-44; lectr. dept. child devel., family relations Syracuse U., 1947-49, instr., 1949-57, asst. prof., 1957-61; sr. social worker N.Y. State Mental Health Research Unit, Syracuse, 1955-57; parent edn. specialist Children's Bur., U.S. Dept. Health, Edn. and Welfare, Washington, 1961-64, research dir. sect. U.S. Welfare Adminstrn., 1964-69; dean faculty Hood Coll., Frederick, Md., 1969-71; sr. research asso. U. Mich., Ann Arbor, 1971-72; prof. U. Wis., Milw., 1972—. Speaker, cons. on research, family life, population planning, poverty to univs. and profl. orgns., internat. groups. U.S. Office Edn. grantee, 1960-62. Mem. Nat. Council on Family Relations (exec. com.), Am. Social Health Assn. (exec. com. 1965-69), Sex Information and Edn. Council U.S. (exec. com. 1965-69), Am. Psychol. Assn. Asso. asst. editor Jour. of Marriage and the Family, 1963-69. Author: Your Child: Six to Twelve; Moving Into Adolescence; Growing Up Poor; (with others) Mental Health Crises and the Nation's Children. Contbr. to profl. jours., books. Home: 4424 N Frederick St Milwaukee WI 53211

CHILTON, ALICE PLEASANCE HUNTER (MRS. ST. JOHN POINDEXTER CHILTON), state ofcl., vocational counselor; b. Boyce, La., Apr. 16, 1911; d. Albert Eugene and Maggie (Texada) Hunter; B.A., La. Coll., 1931; M.S., La. State U., 1934, Guidance Counselor certificate, 1954; m. St. John Poindexter Chilton, Mar. 2, 1935. Tchr. secondary sch., Glenmora, La., 1931-35; with La. Div. Employment Security and USES, Baton Rouge, 1937-74, employment interviewer and supr., 1937-43, personnel officer, 1943-46, operations analyst, 1946-55, supr. counseling and tech. services, 1955-74. Vice pres., dir. LaPlace Enterprises, Inc., Belle Pointe Enterprises, Inc. Mem. curriculum study com. East Baton Rouge, Parish Sch. Bd., 1968—; rec. sec. Quota Internat., 1961-62, 2d v.p., 1963-64. Bd. dirs. YWCA. Recipient certificate of merit La. Acad. Sci., 1960; certificate-35 years meritorious service La. Div. Employment Security, 1972. Mem. Am. Personnel and Guidance Assn., Nat. Vocational Guidance Assn., Am. Sch. Counselor Assn., Assn. for Counselor Edn. and Supervision, Nat. Employment Counselors Assn., La. Guidance Assn., Internat. Assn. Personnel in Employment Security, Nat. Trust Historic Preservation, La. Geneal. and Hist. Soc. (pres. 1957), La. Landmarks Soc., Found. for Hist. La. Clubs: Campus Louisiana State University (Faculty Wives). Methodist. Home: 3617 Hyacinth Av Baton Rouge LA 70808 Office: Life Sciences Bldg La State U Baton Rouge LA 70803

CHILTON, SHIRLEY RAY SHAFER (MRS. FREDERICK R. CHILTON), securities co. exec.; b. Vancouver, Wash., Apr. 3, 1923; d. Shannon Brice and Helen Corrine (Bishop) Shafer; student U. Wash., 1941-43; Grad. Sch. Mgmt. U. Cal. at Los Angeles, 1965-66; M.B.A., Pepperdine U., 1969; m. Frederick Roy Chilton, Nov. 21, 1952; children—Raymond Ewell, Richard Ward, Robert Scott. Operations mgr. Daniel Reeves & Co., Sherman Oaks, Cal., 1955-59, mng. partner, pres., Los Angeles, 1972—; v.p., personnel exec. Hayden Stone, Inc., Palos Verdes, Estates, Cal., 1959-69; asst. to pres. William O'Neil & Co., Inc., Los Angeles, 1969-71. Cons. in econs. to Dept. Health, Edn. and Welfare, Menominee, Wis., 1970-71; internat. lectr. money markets and balance of payments. Founder Industry-Edn. Council, So. Los Angeles, 1969, explorer scout post in bus. mgmt. and finance Palos Verdes Estates council Boy Scouts Am., 1967. Bd. mgrs. YMCA, San Pedro, Cal., 1968; mem. dean's council Grad. Sch. Mgmt., Pepperdine U. Recipient George Washington medal, 1967, Freedoms Found. award, 1967, 69. Mem. Soroptimists, Palos Verdes C. of C. (pres., 1962), Alpha Chi Omega, Beta Sigma Phi. Christian Scientist. Author: Economics in Action—The Rainbow Truck Company, 1967; Economics for Young People—Everyone Has Important Jobs to Do, 1970; How We Learned To Move About, 1970; Where Things We Use Come From, 1970; How Things We Use Are Made, 1970. Home: 3801 Via Palomino Palos Verdes Estages CA 90274 Office: 10960 Wilshire Blvd Los Angeles CA 90024

CHING, GERRY WONG, educator; b. Paia, Maui, Hawaii, Jan. 5, 1935; d. Ahoon Hugh and Fannie Beatrice (Tong) Wong; B.A., Mills Coll., 1957; M.A., Stanford, 1958; m. Philip Hoo Ching, Aug. 9, 1958; children—Melissa Ann, Debbie Marie, Donna Lee, Christina Gayle. Tchr., Hawaii Dept. Edn., 1958-59; admissions evaluator East West Center, U. Hawaii, Honolulu, 1972—; coordinator community relations Japan-Am. Inst. Mgmt. Sci., Honolulu, 1973—. Bd. dirs. Kindergarten and Children's Aid Assn., 1968-70; bd. dirs. Women's Assn. Honolulu Symphony, 1966-68, Honolulu Jr. League, 1969-71, Friends of East West Center, 1971—. Conglist. Home: 1700 Palaau St Honolulu HI 96821 Office: 6660 Hawaii Kai Dr Honolulu HI 96825

CHINICH, BESSIE (MRS. HARRY FEDERBUSH), lawyer; b. Newark; d. Barnet and Nettie (Chinich) Chinich; J.D., Rutgers U., 1930; m. Harry Federbush, May 28, 1933; children—Paul Gerard, Roberta Dianne. Admitted to N.J. bar, 1930; practice law, Newark, 1931-44, 48-51; conferee salary stblzn. unit Dept. Treasury, N.Y.C., 1944-46; investigator Civilian Prodn. Authority, N.Y.C., 1946-47; claims examiner Nat. Prodn. Authority, Dept. Commerce, Newark, 1951-53; contract specialist N.Y. ordnance dist. Dept. Def., N.Y.C., 1953-65; adminstrv. contracting officer Def. Supply Agy., Springfield, N.J., 1965—. Atty. Newark Commn. Neighborhood Conservation and Rehab., 1962. Active local service, charity projects. Recipient awards N.Y. Ordnance Dist., 1953, 65. Mem. Nat. Council Juvenile Ct. Judges, Essex County Bar Assn., Rutgers Alumni Assn., Internat. Platform Assn., Am. Judicature Soc., Nat. Assn. Women Lawyers. Home: 815 S 11th St Newark NJ 07108 Office: Def Supply Agy 240 Route 22 Springfield NJ 07801

CHINITZ, DOROTHY (MRS. DAVID W. WEINER), artist; b. N.Y.C.; d. Morris and Helen (Saypol) Chinitz; grad. Pratt Inst., 1937; m. David W. Weiner, May 7, 1947; 1 dau., Melissa Ellen. Fashion staff artist Gimbel Bros., N.Y.C., 1937-39, R. H. Macy's, N.Y.C., 1939-40, Franklin Simons, N.Y.C., 1940-41; free lance artist for companies including Saks 5th Av., N.Y.C., B. Altman & Co., N.Y.C., L. Bamberger & Co., Newark, John Wanamaker, Phila., Simplicity Pattern Co., N.Y.C., W.T. Grant Co., N.Y.C., J.C. Penny & Co., N.Y.C., Franklin Stores Corp., N.Y.C., Sterns, Paramus, N.J., E.J. Korvette Inc., N.Y.C., Belk Stores Services Inc., N.Y.C., Lord & Taylor, N.Y.C., Good Housekeeping mag., Sears Roebuck and Montgomery Ward catalogues, Allied Graphic Art, Inc., N.Y.C. 1942—. Mem. scholarship com. Englewood (N.J.) Jewish Community Center, 1963—, Englewood Hosp. Assn., 1964—. Selected to show at America's Best Comml. Art, Art Dirs. Club N.Y., 1951. Mem. Pratt Inst. Alumni, Mus. Modern Art. Jewish religion. Illustrated all children's sect. J. J. Newberry and R. H. Macy Christmas books, 1967; contbr. illustrations mags. Address: 263 Arch Rd Englewood NJ 07631

CHIPOURAS, JACALYN GRIGGS (MRS. PHILIP S. CHIPOURAS), occupational therapist, educator; b. Paterson, N.J., Sept. 14, 1947; d. Nelson Steven and Arvilla Dolores (Leidal) Griggs; B.S., Colo. State U., 1970; postgrad. U. No. Colo., 1973—; m. Philip S. Chipouras, Dec. 5, 1970. Occupational therapist United Cerebral Palsy Treatment and Rehab. Center, Roosevelt, N.Y., 1971-73; instr. Colo. State U., Ft. Collins, 1974—. Mem. Am., Colo. Occupational Therpy assns. Home: 500 Remington St Fort Collins CO 80521

CHISHOLM, MARGARET ELIZABETH BERGMAN (MRS. ROBERT L. CHISHOLM), educator; b. Grey Eagle, Minn., July 25, 1921; d. Henry D. and Alice (Thomas) Bergman; A.A., St. Cloud State U., 1940; B.A., U. Wash., 1957, M.L., 1958, Ph.D., 1966; m. John Lane, June 7, 1943 (div. Aug. 1960); children—Nancy Diane, Janice Marie; m. 2d, Robert L. Chisholm, Dec. 30, 1966. Librarian Community Coll., Everett, Wash., 1960-63; asso. prof. U. Ore., Eugene, 1963-66; dir. libraries and instructional materials Seattle Pub. Schs., 1966-67; asso. prof. U. N.M., Albuquerque, 1967-69; dean Coll. Library and Information Services U. Md., College Park, 1969—. Cons. on media programs, tech. and information retrieval to sch. dists., state depts. edn. and colls.; cons. to Library Congress on bibliographic control media. Recipient Ruth Worden award U. Wash., 1958. Mem. N.E.A., Assn. Supervision and Curriculum Devel., A.L.A., Am. Soc. Information Sci., Assn. for Ednl. Communication and Tech., Assn. Am. Library Schs., Am. Assn. Sch. Librarians, Pi Lambda Theta. Contbr. articles in field to edn. and library jours. Home: 3888 N 30th St Arlington VA 22207 Office: Undergraduate Library Bldg U Md College Park MD 20740

CHISHOLM, SHIRLEY ANITA ST. HILL, educator, congresswoman; b. Bklyn., Nov. 30, 1924; d. Charles Christopher and Ruby (Seale) St. Hill; B.A. cum laude, Bklyn. Coll.; M.A., Columbia; hon. doctorates Talladega Coll., Hampton U., N.C. Central Coll., Wilmington Coll., LaSalle Coll., William Patterson Coll., Capitol U., U. Me., Coppin State Coll., Pratt Inst.; m. Conrad Chisholm, Oct. 8, 1949. Former nursery sch. tchr., and dir. nursery sch.; ednl. cons. Div. Day Care, Bur. Child Welfare; mem. N.Y. State Assembly, 1964-68; mem. 91st-92d Congress from 12th Dist. N.Y. Candidate primary elections Democratic nominee Pres. U.S., 1972. Named Alumna of

Year, Bklyn. Coll. Alumni Bull., 1957; recipient award for outstanding work in field of child welfare Women's Council of Bklyn., 1957; key woman of year award, 1963; woman of achievement award Key Women, Inc., 1965; Humanitarian award of family counselling Youth in Action, 1969; Achievement award women's div. Albert Einstein Coll. Medicine, 1969; Woman of Year, Soc. Afro Am. Postal Workers, 1969; Deborah Gannett award Nat. Media Women, 1969; Golden Doughnut award Salvation Army, 1969; Dr. Martin Luther King award Bottle and Cork Sales Club, 1970; hon. life mem. Women's Com. of 1000, 1969; hon. citizen City of Kansas, 1970. Mem. Nat. Assn. Coll. Women, Bklyn. Coll. Alumni, League Women Voters. Methodist. Home: 1355 President St Brooklyn NY 11213 Office: US House of Representatives Washington DC 20515

CHISOLM, ELISE T., newspaper editor; b. L.I., N.Y., Mar. 7, 1924; d. Charles and Lily M. (West) Townsend; student The Baldwin Sch., Bryn Mawr, Pa., 1940; student West Tex. State U.; m. Apr. 23, 1943; children—Sally (Mrs. Lyle Buck), Guy, Susan, Richard. Formerly columnist Amarillo (Tex.) Globe News; women's page editor Amarillo Citizen; feature editor Ann Arundel (Md.) Star; now soc. editor, humor columnist. Balt. Evening Sun. Bd. dirs. U.S.O., Jr. League, League Women Voters, YWCA. Contbr. articles to mags. Office: Baltimore Sun 501 N Calvert St Baltimore MD 21203

CHITWOOD, SARAH ELIZABETH ROBERTS (MRS. EDMUND M. CHITWOOD), physician; b. Newport News, Va., Oct. 14, 1922; d. Russell Watson and Virginia (Akers) Roberts; B.S., U. W.Va., 1943; M.D., U. Va., 1948; m. Edmund Madison Chitwood, June 14, 1948; children—Bryan Roberts, Deborah, Susan, Edmund Madison III, Howard Lee. Intern U. Va. Hosp. at Charlottesville; 1948-49; civilian surgeon U.S. Army, Germany, 1949-50; resident in pediatrics U. Louisville, 1951-52; practice medicine specializing in pediatrics, pub. health, Pulaski, Va., Roanoke, Va., Radford, Va.; mem. staff Pulaski (Va.) Gen. Hosp., 1953—. Mem. A.M.A., Va., S.W. Va. med. socs., Va. Pediatric Soc. Home: Route 1 Draper VA 24324 Office: Pulaski Hosp Clinic Pulaski VA 24301

CHLAN, FANNIE ANGELOS (MRS. CHARLES EDWARD CHLAN), lawyer; b. Karpathos, Greece, Mar. 19, 1927; d. John G. and Frances (Melissanos) Angelos; came to U.S., 1928, naturalized, 1948; A.A., U. Balt. 1949, LL.B., 1951; m. Charles Edward Chlan, Nov. 14, 1953; children—Frances, Charles E.G., John C.M. Admitted to Md. bar, U.S. Supreme Ct. bar; practiced law, Balt. and Towson, Md.; atty. Senate Investigating Com., Washington, 1947-49; supr. IBM, Balt., 1949-52; mem. firm Chlan & Chlan, Towson. Dir. Crossroads Realty, Towson; treas. Danaker Clock Co., Fallston, Md., 1973—. Mem. Women's Bar Assn., U. Balt. Alumni, Karpathian Ednl. Assn., Baltimore County Bar Assn., Balt. Mus. Art, Balt. Opera Soc., Dulaney Valley Symphony, Philoptohos Soc., Iota Tau Tau (past pres.). Democrat. Mem. Greek Orthodox Ch. Club: Hillendale Country. Home: 540 Wyngate Rd Timonium MD 21093 Office: Loyola Federal Bldg Towson MD 21004

CHO, KIYOKO TAKEDA (MRS. YUKIO CHO), religious educator; b. Japan, 1917; student Kobe Coll., Japan, Olivet Coll., Union Theol. Sem.; m. Yukio Cho, 1953; 1 son, Kohei. Worked for YWCA, Japan, 1947-53; mem. faculty Internat. Christian U., 1953—, now prof. history, dean grad. sch., 1970-74, dir. Inst. Asian Cultural Studies. Mem. presidium World Council Chs., Geneva, Switzerland. Mem. United Ch. Christ in Japan. Author: Conflict in the Concept of Man in Modern Japan; The Emperor System and Educational Thought; Indigenization and Apostasy: Traditional Ethos and Christianity, others. Editor: volume on comparative modernization theories. Contbr. essays national newspaper of Japan. Translator works of Reinhold Niebuhr into Japanese. Office: World Council Churches 150 Route de Ferney 1211 Geneva 20 Switzerland

CHOATE, BELLE TURNER, lawyer; b. Harrisburg, Ill., Aug. 18, 1944; d. OL and Bernice (McCormack) Turner; student Baylor U., 1962; B.A., So. Ill. U., 1966, M.A., 1966; J.D., Ind. U., 1971; m. Daniel Choate, Mar. 16, 1968 (div. June 1973). Instr. speech and English, Oakland City (Ind.) Coll., 1968-69; tchr. English, Park Tudor Sch., Indpls., 1969-71; admitted to Ind. bar, 1971, since practiced in Indpls.; asso. firm Allison and Barnhart, Indpls., 1971-73; partner Choate, Maguire & Olsen, Indpls., 1973—. Mem. Am., Ind., Indpls. bar assns., Am., Ind. (legal panel 1971—). civil liberties unions. Home: 2245 Rome Dr Indianapolis IN 46208 Office: 6302 Rucker Rd Indianapolis IN 46205

CHOPEK, ANNA, lawyer; b. Kozowa, Ukraine, Sept. 16, 1912; d. Elias and Mary (Olijnyk) Chopek; J.D. magna cum laude, New Eng. Sch. Law, 1935. Came to U.S., 1914, naturalized, 1926. Admitted to Mass. bar, 1936; atty. Mass. Bonding & Ins. Co., Boston, 1935-44; atty. Civil Service Commn., Washington, 1945-47; investigator Civil Service Commn., N.Y.C., 1944-45; asso. Albert G. Tierney, Boston; asst. atty. gen. Commonwealth of Mass., 1961-62. Mem. New Eng. Fraternal Congress (pres. 1970-71), Ukrainian Nat. Assn. (supreme adviser 1954—), Mass. Assn. Women Lawyers (v.p. 1964-70, treas. 1961-62), Mass. Bar Assn., Mass. Trial Lawyers Assn., Mass. Conveyancers Assn. Home: 117 Greenfield Rd Mattapan MA 02126 Office: 40 Court St Boston MA

CHOPER, FRANCES STEEBLE (MRS. WAYNE SHELDON CHOPER), physician; b. Bridgeton, N.J., July 29, 1932; d. Harry Edward and Evelyn (Jacobson) Steeble; B.S., Douglass Coll., 1955; M.D., N.Y. Med. Coll., 1959; m. Wayne Sheldon Choper, Dec. 19, 1954; children—Jessica, Ethan. Intern Mary Fletcher Hosp., Burlington, Vt., 1959-60; resident Met. Hosp., N.Y.C., 1960-61; resident pathology Montefiore Hosp., N.Y.C., 1961-62, resident medicine, 1962-63; practice medicine specializing in internal medicine, Highland Park, N.J., 1964—; sr. med. attending Middlesex Gen. Hosp., St. Peters Gen. Hosp.; clin. asst. prof. N.J. Coll. Medicine and Dentistry, Rutgers U. Med. Sch. Diplomate Am. Bd. Internal Medicine. Mem. A.M.A., N.Y. Acad. Scis., N.J. Med. Soc. Address: 729 Raritan Av Highland Park NJ 08904

CHOREN, BERNADINE GABRIELLA, occupational therapist; b. Milw., May 14, 1926; d. John and Mary Elizabeth (Pavlis) Choren; B.S. in Occupational Therapy, Mt. Mary Coll., 1948; M.S. in Occupational Therapy, U. So. Cal., 1958. Commd. 2d lt. U.S. Army, 1949, advanced through grades to lt. comdr., 1972; occupational therapist, 1949-56; dir. occupational and recreational therapy Wis. Diagnostic Center, Madison, 1956-57; asso. in occupational therapy U. San Francisco, 1958-61, asst. prof. occupational therapy U. So. Cal., Los Angeles, 1961-67; ednl. coordinator occupational therapy Letterman Gen. Hosp., San Francisco, 1967-71; chief occupational therapy sect. Walter Reed Army Med. Center, Washington, 1971-74, Brooke Army Med. Center, San Antonio, 1974—. Mem. Am., D.C., Md. Occupational Therapy assns., Mt. Mary Coll. Alumnae Assn. Office: Occupational Therapy Sect Brooke Medical Center San Antonio TX 78234

CHORLEY, SARA SANDRA FALCONER (MRS. JOHN ELLIOTT CHORLEY), shopping center adminstr.; b. Johnstown, Pa., Dec. 13, 1933; d. John Alexander and Myrtle Mae (Hershelman) Falconer; R.N., Presbyn. Hosp. Sch. Nursing, 1954; student U. Brandon, 1970-72; grad. hosp. orgn. and mgmt. Canadian Hosp. Assn., 1974; m. John Elliott Chorley, July 28, 1954; children—Jeffrey Todd, Kimberly Ann, Kelly Lynn. Staff nurse Springfield (Mass.) Meml. Hosp., 1955; staff nurse, pvt. duty nurse Gen. Hosp., Deer Lodge Hosp., Victoria, Man., Can., 1956-65; adminstr., dir. nursing Central Park Lodge, Brandon, Man., 1967-73; dir. profl. services Yordale Shopping Centre, Toronto, Ont., 1974—. Pres., Red Cross, Brandon, 1971-72; v.p. Southwestern Nursing Home Assn., 1971. Dist. commr. Nat. Pony, 1968-71. Mem. Order Eastern Star. Club: Soroptomist (v.p. Brandon). Home: Ste 1002 2645 Kipling Toronto ON Canada Office: Ste 203 Yordale Shopping Centre Toronto ON M6A 2T9 Canada

CHOU, CHARISSA JAR-RONG (MRS. BILLY JAR-RAY CHOU), statistician; b. Kweichow, China, Feb. 24, 1944; d. Si Ying and Yi (Drang) Kao; B.S. in Accounting, Nat. Taiwan U., 1966; Ph.D. in Statistics, Kan. State U., 1972; m. Billy Jar-ray Chou, May 31, 1970. Came to U.S., 1968, naturalized, 1970. Teaching asst. Nat. Taiwan U., Taipei, 1966-68; grad. research asst. Kan. State U., Manhattan, 1968-72, research asso., 1973; now with accounting dept. Villanova U. Mem. Am. Statis. Assn., Inst. Math. Statistics, Sigma Xi. Home: La Maison Apt H-302 219 Sugartown Rd Wayne PA 19087 Office: Accounting Dept Villanova U Villanova PA 19085

CHOW, YI CHANG (MRS. YUAN SHIH CHOW), computer scientist; b. Peking, China, Aug. 7, 1931; d. Chung Fu and Shan Fin (Chen) Chang; brought to U.S., 1947, naturalized, 1962; B.A. in Math., Oberlin Coll., 1953; M.S., U. Ill., 1958; postgrad. in Computer Sci., Purdue U., 1963-65; m. Yuan Shih Chow, June 8, 1963; children—Patrick, Grace, Nelson. Asst. prof. math. Cleve. State U., 1958-61; staff mem. div. sponsored research Mass. Inst. Tech., Cambridge, 1961-63; staff programmer IBM Corp., Morris Plains, N.J., 1968—. Vis. prof. Tamkang Coll., Taipei, Taiwan, 1971. Mem. Math. Assn. Am., Pi Mu Epsilon. Home: 24 Beach Dr Morris Plains NJ 07950 Office: 202 Johnson Rd Morris Plains NJ 07950

CHREKJIAN, RUTH YOUNG (MRS. GEORGE P. CHREKJIAN), ednl. adminstr.; b. Hackensack, N.J., June 4, 1920; d. James Simpson and Elsie (Distel) Young; B.A., Barnard Coll. Columbia U., 1942; M.A., William Paterson Coll., 1968; postgrad. Columbia Tchrs. Coll., 1942—; m. George P. Chrekjian, July 24, 1941; children—Jane, Georgann. Classroom tchr. West Milford (N.J.) Twp. Schs., 1955-65, remedial reading tchr., 1965-67, supr. elementary edn., West Milford, 1967—. Dir. West Milford Twp. Environmental Edn. Com., 1971—; mem. exec. bd. Ringwood Manor Assn. for Arts, 1967—. Bd. dirs., cons. Operation Headstart, Ringwood, N.J.; bd. dirs. Ringwood Library Assn. Recipient Educator of Year award West Milford Twp., 1973. Mem. Am. Assn. Sch. Adminstrs., Internat. Reading Tchrs. Assn., N.E.A., N.J. Edn. Assn. Home: 15 Skyview Rd Ringwood R D Wanaque NJ 07465 Office: Board of Education Bldg Route 23 West Milford NJ 07435

CHRISMAN, ANN RAE, state ofcl., lawyer; b. Sutton, W. Va., May 12, 1945; d. C.F. and Juanita (Engel) Chrisman; B.S., B.A. in Accounting, W. Va. U., 1967, J.D., 1970. Admitted to W.Va. bar, 1970; with State Tax Dept. W. Va., Charleston, 1970—, tax analyst II, 1972—. Mem. W. Va. State Bar Assn. Home: 7 Abney Circle Charleston WV 25314 Office: State Tax Dept Charleston WV 25305

CHRISTENSEN, ANNA MAE PARKER (MRS. EDGAR W. CHRISTENSEN), pianist, composer; b. Alexandria, Va., Apr. 15, 1899; d. Charles William and Evelyn Virginia (Henry) Parker; student pub. schs., Washington, Md., Ind., Neb.; student Inst. Mus. Art, N.Y.C., 1924; m. Edgar W. Christensen, May 31, 1928. Pvt. piano tchr., Omaha, 1921-73. Performer, composer piano solos for elementary grades, Slumber Song, Mazurka, Dream Castles, Birthday Candles, Snow Fairy, Yankee Shuffle, Silver Ship, Swedish Dance, Loneliness, Chinese Tinkle Glass, Persian Chant, Tyrolian Holiday. Mem. P.E.O., Neb. Music Tchrs. Assn., Nat. Fedn. Music Clubs. Conglist. Address: 5635 Emile St Omaha NE 68106

CHRISTENSEN, JOYCE LORRAINE (MRS. HARRY RUSSELL CHRISTENSEN), newspaperwoman; b. San Pedro, Cal., Jan. 23, 1927; d. Wilder Wellington and Laura Mae (Clarke) Hartley; grad. high sch.; m. Harry Russell Christensen, Aug. 20, 1965; children by previous marriage—Robert Earl Kent (dec.), Keith Alan Kent. Society editor San Pedro News-Pilot, 1945-48; staff writer Long Beach Independent Press Telegram, 1955-58, club editor, 1960-69, asst. women's editor, 1958-69, life style editor, 1969—. Bd. dirs. Long Beach chpt. March of Dimes. Recipient 1st place award for best women's sect. in newspapers of 100,000 circulation Cal. Press Women, 1969, 70, 71, 1st place award best women's page Nat. Newspaper Assn., 1970, merit award Cal. Newspaper Pubs. Assn., 1970. Mem. Nat. Press Women, Cal. Press Women, Pacific Coast Press Club (2d v.p. Long Beach 1970-71, treas. 1973-74, Bill Hunter meml. award 1973), Long Beach C. of C. (dir. womens council 1971—, chmn. 1972-74). Club: Soroptimist (pres. found. Long Beach 1968-69). Home: 417 Marble Cove Way Seal Beach CA 90740 Office: 604 Pine Av Long Beach CA 90801

CHRISTENSEN, JUDY SIKES (MRS. H.L. CHRISTENSEN), personnel exec.; b. Abbott, N.M., Apr. 8, 1919; d. William Henry and Grayce Irene (Pursley) Sikes; A.A., U. N.M., 1941; B.S. in Psychology, Loyola U., 1952, M.S. in Indsl. Relations, 1953; m. C.J. Ricker, Apr. 18, 1947 (div. May 1952); 1 son, Charles J. III; m. 2d, H.L. Christensen, Dec. 28, 1972. Cashier, Walgreen Drug Co., Albuquerque, 1940-43, personnel asst., Chgo., 1947-48; personnel asst. Mpls.-Honeywell Co., Chgo., 1953-55; asst. personnel mgr. Needham, Louis & Brorby., Chgo., (name changed to Needham, Harper & Steers Advt., Inc.), 1955-65, personnel mgr., 1969—. Lectr., Am. Mgmt. Assn., 1970-71. Mem. five years program com. YMCA. Mem. Speakers Bur. Young Republicans, 1952. Bd. dirs. Loyola Bus. Seminar Program, Chgo., 1962-63. Served to 2d lt. WAC, 1943-46; PTO. Mem. Internat. Assn. Personnel Women (newsletter editor Women in Personnel of Chgo., 1971-72), Indsl. Relations Assn. Chgo. (dir. 1970-74, pres. 1973-74), WAC Vets. Assn. (pres. Chgo. chpt. 1953). Home: 925 Marshall Dr Des Plaines IL 60016 Office: 401 N Michigan Av Chicago IL 60611

CHRISTENSEN, MARGUERITE ALICE, librarian; b. Trout Lake, Wis., Aug. 24, 1917; d. Peter Carl and Alice (Cady) Christensen; B.A., U. Wis., 1938, B.L.S., 1939. Librarian, high sch. and Pub. Library, Bloomer, Wis., 1939-41; asst. librarian Wis. State U., Superior, 1941-43, Carroll Coll., Waukesha, Wis., 1943-45; asst. reference librarian U. Wis.-Madison, 1945-66, head gen. reference dept., 1967—. Mem. A.L.A., Assn. Coll. and Research Libraries. Home: 4469 Hillcrest Dr Madison WI 53705

CHRISTENSEN, RUTH ELLEN, physician; b. Terre Haute, Ind., Feb. 18, 1928; d. Leo Martin and Eva Inez (Patterson) Christensen; B.A. in English and Zoology, U. Neb., 1950, M.D., 1954. Intern, Touro Infirmary, New Orleans, 1954-55, resident internal medicine, 1955-58, chief resident, 1957-58; physician on staff Central Colo. Med. Center, Colorado Springs, 1959-60; physician on staff Vets Hosp., Wadsworth, Kan., 1961, practice medicine specializing in internal medicine, Miller, Neb., 1962—. Co-organizer Citizens Against the Dam, Miller, 1971; mem. Miller Womens Improvement Club, 1963—. Mem. A.M.A., Neb. State, Buffalo County med. socs. Methodist. Home and office: Miller NE 68858

CHRISTIAN, BERA LAKE, scenic designer; b. Fresno, Cal., Apr. 15, 1946; d. David Allen and Mildred Nellie (King) Christian; B.A., Cal. State U. at Fresno, 1968, M.A., 1974; postgrad. U. Cal. at Los Angeles, 1970, U.S. Inst. Tech. Theatre, 1972. Scenic designer, Fresno, 1969—. Scenic designer for The Effect of Gamma-Rays of Man-in-the-Moon Marigoals, Cal. State U. at Fresno, 1973, Antony and Cleopatra, U.S. Inst. Tech. Theatre Internat. Design Contest, 1972; art works exhibited Fresno Arts Center, 1969-72, Dist. Fair Art Show, 1970, 72, U.S. Inst. Tech. Theatre Masters Classes, 1971-73; owner small horse breeding operation; pvt. speech and theatre tchr. to contestants in beauty pageants. Mem. Fresno Arts Center, Am. Theatre Assn., Am. Assn. U. Women, U.S. Inst. Tech. Theatre, Am. Quarter Horse Assn., Appaloosa Horse Club, Pi Epsilon Delta, Pi Kappa Delta. Democrat. Baptist. Address: 4225 E Harvard Av Fresno CA 93703

CHRISTIAN, CONNIE JO, city ofcl.; b. Colorado Springs, Colo., Feb. 15, 1935; d. Edward Lyle and Evelyn Louise (Davis) Alsbury; student Colo. Coll., Am. Sch. Corr.; m. May 3, 1974; children—Rod L., Steven L., Greg A. Opthalmic asst., Colorado Springs, 1969-71; clk., recorder, treas. City of Dillon, (Colo.), 1971-74; accounting clk. jud. dept. City of Colorado Springs, 1974—, County of El Paso, 1974—. Pres., Longfellow Sch. P.T.A., 1963-64. Mem. Colo. Clks. Assn. (v.p. 1972-73), Internat. Inst. Clks. Home: 2728 Flintridge Dr Colorado Springs CO 80904 Office: City Hall Colorado Springs CO

CHRISTIAN, MARILYN JEAN, nurse, educator; b. Trenton, N.J., Jan. 20, 1933; d. Rolland Jay and Marion (Darrell) Christian; B.S., Columbia Union Coll., Takoma Park, Md., 1954; M.S., Catholic U. Am., 1957; Ed.D., U. So. Cal., 1974. Asst. prof. pub. health nursing Columbia Union Coll., 1954-61, nursing dir. Student Health Services, 1954-57, asst. dean Sch. Nursing, 1958-61; nursing supr., Tb nursing cons. Richmond (Va.) Health Dept., 1961-63; asst. prof. nursing, chmn. dept. pub. health nursing Loma Linda (Cal.) U., 1963-65, asso. prof. nursing, 1965-67, adminstrv. coordinator home care dept. Med. Center, 1966-68, asso. prof. nursing, 1967-68, dean Sch. Nursing, 1969—, prof. pub. health nursing, 1969—. Mem. Western Interstate Commn. Higher Edn. in Nursing, Cal. Commn. Nursing. Fellow Am. Pub. Health Assn.; mem. Am. Assn. Colls. of Nursing, Nat. League Nursing, Am. Cal. (dir. region 4) nurses assns., Royal Soc. Health (London), Am. Assn. U. Women. Assn. Seventh Day Adventist Nurses (nat. pres.). Office: Sch Nursing Loma Linda U Loma Linda CA 92354

CHRISTIAN, VIRGINIA DAVISON (MRS. WILLIAM M. CHRISTIAN, JR.), physicist; b. Washington, Oct. 29, 1929; d. Archie R. and Marie (Burke) Davison; B.S. in Physics, Howard U., 1951; postgrad. U. Conn., 1951-52; m. William M. Christian, Jr., 1952; children—William M. III, David G., Marie F. Scientist, mathematician Gen. Dynamics Corp./Electric Boat div., Groton, Conn., 1956-57, 59-63, nuclear project engr., 1965—. Mem. Conn. Joint Fedn. Engrs., 1972—. Mem. Gov.'s Council for Human Rights and Opportunities, Gov.'s Council for Youth Opportunity; mem. United Negro Coll. Fund Com., 1971—; mem. econ. devel. coordinating com. Norwich Community Devel. Corp.; mem. West Side Community Action Com., 1966—. Mem. Conn. Bd. Edn., 1967-73; mem. Norwich (Conn.) City Council, 1965-67, sec. Citizens Conf. on Gen. Assembly, 1968-70; mem. adv. council Thames Valley Regional Tech. Coll., 1973—; mem. Norwich Sch. Bd., 1973—. Trustee Thames Valley Council for Community Action, 1955-71, A.R.C., Norwich, 1967-69, State Tech. Colls., 1967-73, Easter Seal Rehab. Center S.E. Conn., 1970—; adv. council Mohegan Community Coll. Mem. Nat. Council of Women, Norwich Area C. of C., Nat. Soc. Women Engrs. (pub. relations chmn. 1971-73), N.A.A.C.P. (pub. relations chmn. br.). Soc. Founders Norwich, Nat. Mgmt. Assn. (dir. Electric Boat div. 1974—). Presbyn. Home: 118 McKinley Av Norwich CT 06360

CHRISTIANSEN, MARJORIE MINER (MRS. THEODORE LEO CHRISTIANSEN), educator; b. Canton, Ill., Feb. 28, 1922; d. John Earnest and Margaret Ellen (Wilson) Miner; student Joliet (Ill.) Jr. Coll., 1939-41, Ia. State U., 1941-42; B.S., U. N.M., 1949, M.A., 1955; Ph.D. (Research Council fellow), Utah State U., 1967; m. Theodore Leo Christiansen, Aug. 10, 1951; 1 dau., Karen Lee (Mrs. James Vythoulkas). Instr. sci. and nutrition Regina Sch. Nursing, Albuquerque, 1950-64, project dir., 1966-69; project dir., adj. prof. U. Albuquerque, 1969; prof. home econs. Madison Coll., Harrisonburg, Va., 1969—. Nutrition cons. Mental Devel. Center, Albuquerque, 1968-69; leader Summer Workshops in Nutrition, Utah State U., 1968-69; project dir. Renal Dietary Mgmt. Seminars, USPHS, 1974. Mem. adv. com. on spl. edn. Harrisonburg Pub. Schs., 1972—. Corn Products Co. grantee, 1965, Nurse Tng. Act, USPHS grantee, 1966-69; Mem. Am., Va. (pres. elect) dietetic assns., Am. Home Econs. Assn., Soc. for Nutrition Edn., Sigma Xi, Phi Kappa Phi, Kappa Omicron Phi, Phi Upsilon Omicron, Pi Lambda Theta. Home: 94 Laurel St Harrisonburg VA 22801

CHRISTIANSON, MARY FAUBION (MRS. BRUCE WILTON CHRISTIANSON), child psychiatrist; b. Freeport, Tex., Apr. 13, 1927; d. Roy Arthur and Nantilee (Donathan) Faubion; B.A., U. Tex., 1948; M.D., U. Tex. at Galveston, 1953; postgrad. in psychiatry Mayo Clinic, 1954-56; m. Bruce Wilton Christianson, Dec. 10, 1955; children—Jeffrey B., James A. Intern, Emergency Hosp., Washington, 1953-54; resident in psychiatry U. Cal. at Los Angeles, 1957-58, asst. clin. prof. child psychiatry, 1965—; asst. clin. prof. child psychiatry Harbor Gen. Hosp., Torrance, Cal., 1967—. Mem. Am. Psychiat. Assn., Los Angeles Soc. Child Psychiatry. Home: 3915 Deervale Dr Sherman Oaks CA 91403

CHRISTIE, AGATHA MARY CLARISSA, author; b. Torquay; d. Frederick Alvah Miller; m. Col. Archibald Christie, 1914 (div. 1928); 1 dau.; m. 2d, Max Edgar Lucien Mallowan, 1930. Decorated dame comdr. Order Brit. Empire. Fellow Royal Soc. Lit. Author 33 books including: Thirteen at Dinner, 1933; Murder of Roger Ackroyd, 1926; Death Comes as the End, 1944; The Hollow, 1946; A Murder Is Announced, 1950; They Came to Baghdad, 1951; Mrs. McGinty's Dead, 1952; Murder With Mirrors, 1952; Funerals are Fatal; A Pocketful of Rye, 1954; So Many Steps to Death, 1955; Hickory Dickory Death, 1955; Dead Man's Folly, 1956; What Mrs. McGillicuddy Saw, 1957; The Pale Horse, 1962; Hallowe'en Party, 1969; Passenger to Frankfurt, 1970; Nemesis, 1971; Elephants Can Remember, 1972; Postern of Fate, 1973; also plays including The Mouse Trap, Witness for the Prosecution, The Spider's Web, Towards Zero, The Unexpected Guest, Fiddlers Three. Address: Greenway House Churston Ferrers S Devon England

CHRISTIE, JULIE FRANCES, actress; b. Assam Province, India, Apr. 14, 1940; d. Frank St. John and Rosemary (Pamsden) Christie; student Brighton (Eng.) Tech. Coll., 1957-58, Central Sch. Speech and Drama, London, Eng., 1958-61. Asso. with Birmingham (Eng.) Repertory, 1960, Royal Shakespeare Theatre, Stratford-upon-Avon, 1963; appeared in motion pictures Crooks Anonymous, 1962, The Fast Lady, 1962-63, Billy Liar, 1963, Darling, 1964, Young Cassidy, 1964, Dr. Zhivago, 1965, Gahrenheit 451, 1966, Far From the

Madding Crowd, 1966, Petulia, 1967; In Search of Gregory, 1968; also TV performances including A For Andromeda, 1962, Dangerous Corner, 1963, The Saint, 1963. Recipient Best Actress of Year award Brit. Film Acad., 1966, Oscar award, 1966. Address: care Olive Harding London Internat Park House Park St London W I England

CHRISTIE, MARILYN ELEANOR, library adminstr.; b. Berkeley, Cal., Oct. 25, 1922; d. Darwin Russell and Jeannette (Markham) Smith; A.B., U. Cal. at Berkeley, 1944; teaching certificate U. Wash., 1958; M.L.S., U. Wash., 1965; m. Sept. 27, 1945; children—Lynne (Mrs. Randall A. Benton), Richard Holt, Forrest Manning. Tchr., Lake Washington Sch. Dist., 1958-61, librarian, 1961-63; librarian Bellevue Sch. Dist., 1963-64; library cons. King County Schs. Office, 1964-66; supr. library services Seattle Sch. Dist., 1966—. Treas., Clyde Hill Town Council, 1956. Mem. Nat., Wash. edn. assns., Wash. Assn. Sch. Librarians, Wash. Assn. Ednl. Communications and Tech. (sec. 1972-74), Am. Assn. Ednl. Communications and Tech., Seattle Schs. Mgmt. Assn. (treas. 1970-72), Adminstrv. Service Center League Seattle Sch. Dist. (sec. 1967-68), Pi Beta Phi (past pres. Cal. Beta). Republican. Christian Scientist. Home: 3012 92d Pl NE Bellevue WA 98004 Office: 815 4th Av N Seattle WA 98109

CHRISTIE, MARY LOU BRANDON, educator; b. Waverly, Ia., Nov. 7, 1917; d. William Lewis and Mary Wilson (Cooke) Brandon; A.B., John B. Stetson U., 1942; M.S., Fla. State U., 1969, postgrad., 1968-69; m. William Traugott Christie, Jr., May 2, 1942 (div. Oct. 1970), remarried May 18, 1974; children—Mary Elizabeth, Lewis Traugott, Terris Jean. Tchr., Orange City (Fla.) Elementary Sch., 1939-43; tchr., dir. girls phys. edn. Leon High Sch., Tallahassee, 1943-45; owner, mgr. Christie's Kiddie Kottage-Juvenile Retail Store, Tallahasse, 1948-61; tchr. Fed. Correctional Instn., Tallahassee, 1966-67; counselor Leon County Juvenile Ct., Tallahassee, 1969-70, supr. tng., 1970-71; dir. tng., youth counselor supr. Bur. Field Services, Fla. Div. Youth Services, Tallahassee, 1971—, dist. coordinator vol. programs, 1972—; tchr. piano, Tallahassee, 1934-48, 62—; guest lectr. Fla. State U., also Fla. A. and M. U., 1967-71. Mem. Leon County Sch. Bd., 1965-69, chmn. bd., 1968. Chmn. adv. com. Sunland Hosp., Tallahassee, 1969-70; sec., dir. Leon Assn. for Retarded Children, 1969-70; mem. Leon County Assn. Community Services. Bd. dirs. Easter Seal Rehab. Center, 1953—, sec., 1955-65; bd. dirs. Vol. Action Center of Leon County; adv. bd. Supplementary Assistance Center Leon County, Fla. Assn. Health and Social Services, Inc. Mem. Fla. Employees Assn., Tallahassee Music Tchrs. Assn., D.A.R. (regent 1959-61), Fla. Council on Crime and Delinquency, Lamba Alpha Epsilon. Baptist. Club: Tallahassee Womans. Author: A Model for the Training of Interns in Juvenile Corrections, 1974. Home: 1437 Chowkeebin Nene Tallahassee FL 32301 Office: 2425 Torreya Dr Tallahassee FL 32303

CHRISTIE, ROBERTA, educator; b. Oak Park, Ill., May 19, 1915; d. Edwin Paul and Clara (Herman) Christie; B.A., Mundelein Coll., 1937; M.A., Columbia U., 1946, Ed.D., 1948. Dist. dir. Mpls. Girl Scouts, 1937-41; program cons. N.Y. Girl Scouts, N.Y.C., 1941-43; overseas club dir. A.R.C., Eng., 1943-45; group work cons. N.Y.C. Youth Bd., 1948; instr. Bklyn. Coll., 1949; asso. prof. psychology Stephens Coll., 1949-51; asso. dean students, prof. psychology Sacramento State Coll., 1951-60; prof. psychology Mt. St. Mary's Coll., Los Angeles, 1961-62; asso. prof. edn., 1962-69, prof. guidance and counseling, 1969—, dir. student personnel work in higher edn. Loyola U., Chgo., 1962—. Bd. dirs. Sacramento YWCA, 1953-55, council Girl Scouts U.S.A., Sacramento, 1955-60; bd. dirs. Sacramento Community Welfare Council, 1955-60, sec., 1959-60; dir. Nat. Def. Edn. Act. Inst., 1967. Mem. Am. Assn. U. Profs., Am. Assn. for Higher Edn., Am., Ill. Psychol. Assn., Am., Ill. (pres. 1968-70) coll. personnel assns., Assn. for Counselor Edn. and Supervision, Assn. for Measurement and Evaluation in Guidance, Am. Assn. U. Women, Nat., Cal. (hon. life) assns. women deans and counselors, Am. Personnel and Guidance Assn., Ill. Guidance and Personnel Assn. (exec. bd. 1967-72, senator 1972-73), Council Student Personnel Assn., Ill. Assn. Women Deans and Counselors, Ill. Counselor Educators and Suprs., Nat. Vocational Guidance Assn., Nat. Assn. Student Personnel Adminstrs., Internat. Platform Assn., Kappa Delta Pi, Lumen Vitae, Sigma Delta Upsilon, Psi Chi. Office: 820 N Michigan Av Chicago IL 60611

CHRISTIN, VIOLET MARGUERITE, banker; b. Chgo., Oct. 4, 1903; d. Charles A. and Eva M. (Bosse) Christin; student Northwestern U., 1936-37, Am. Inst. Banking, 1955—. With Nat. Bank of Austin, 1922—, asst. sec., 1953-57, sec., 1957-65, now sec., asst. v.p., vice chmn. marketing com., 1969—. Mem. Am. Inst. Banking, Ill. Bankers Assn. (50 year club), Assn. Chgo. Bank Women, Nat. Assn. Bank Women, Bank Marketing Assn., Chgo. Financial Advertisers (treas. 1964-65, 69—, dir. 1973—), Land Trust Council Ill. Clubs: Chicago Press, Chicago Advertising. Home: 805 North Grove Av Oak Park IL 60302 Office: 5645 W Lake St Chicago IL 60644

CHRISTOPHER, MAURINE BROOKS (MRS. MILBOURNE CHRISTOPHER), editor; b. Three Springs, Tenn.; d. John Davis and Zula (Pangle) Brooks; B.A., Tusculum Coll., 1941; m. Milbourne Christopher, June 25, 1949. Reporter, Kingsport (Tenn.) Times, 1941-43, Balt. Sun, 1943-45; free-lance mag. writer, U.S.A., Eng., 1945—; TV-radio editor Advt. Age, N.Y.C., 1947—; moderator radio show Adbeat, WHN, N.Y.C. Mem. Am. Women in Radio and TV (pres. N.Y.C. chpt.), Assn. for Study Afro-Am. Life and History. Author: America's Black Congressmen. Home: 333 Central Park W New York City NY 10025 Office: 708 3d Av New York City NY 10016

CHRISTOPHERSON, KATHRYN KENDALL DONLEY (MRS. WILLIAM MARTIN CHRISTOPHERSON), civic worker; b. Hiram, O., July 8, 1921; d. Gerard Vernon and Rosa (Kendall) Donley; A.B., Hiram Coll., 1941; m. William Martin Christopherson, July 24, 1943; 1 son, George Walter II. Mem. adv. com. Gov.'s Conf. Ky.'s Stake in World Trade, 1962; mem. Gov.'s Adv. Com. Campaign Financing, 1965-66; mem. Louisville Health and Welfare Council, 1961-66; mem. housing com. Louisville Commn. on Human Relations, until 1966; vice chmn. Ky. Geriatrics Found. Inc.; dir. Nat. Com. U.S.-China Relations, 1971-73, sec., 1973—; mem. Louisville Urban League; commr. Jefferson County (Ky.) Community Improvement Dist., 1970-72; mem. Gen. Hosp. Aux., Friends Ky. Opera, Friends Ky. Libraries, Jewish Hosp. Women's Guild, Ky. Conservation Council, Women's Assn. Louisville Orch. Bd. dirs. Citizen's Met. Planning Council, 1959-61, Louisville Fund, 1964-73, Ky. Govt. Council, 1961-69, Louisville Heart Assn., 1964-67, Citizens Advocate Center, 1968—, Overseas Devel. Council, 1968—. Recipient Ottenheimer Spl. award for outstanding community service Jewish Community Center, 1962. Mem. League Women Voters (dir. Louisville 1950-51, 53-58, dir. Ky. 1957-58, 63-64, nat. dir., 1964-66, v.p. 1966-74, pres. Louisville br. 1958-60, pres. Ky. 1960-62, sec. edn. fund 1964-66, trustee 1964—, trustee overseas edn. fund 1964—, dir. 1969-70, pres. 1970—), Jefferson County Med. Soc. Aux., English-Speaking Union, Urban League, N.A.A.C.P., United World Federalists. Unitarian. Club: Woman's (U. Louisville). Address: 2211 Cherokee Pkwy Louisville KY 40204

CHRISTOPLOS, FLORENCE WOLLMAN (MRS. GEORGE CHRISTOPLOS), educator; b. N.Y.C., Oct. 29, 1928; d. Isidore and Tille (Green) Wollman; B.A., Hunter Coll., 1951; M.A., U. Md., 1965, Ph.D., 1968; m. George Christoplos, Nov. 10, 1947; children—Laura, Ian Keith. Tchr. pub. schs., Washington, 1960-61, Prince Georges County, Md., 1961-64; instr. spl. edn. U. Md., College Park, 1966-67; asso. prof. spl. edn. Coppin State Coll., Balt., 1968-71, prof., 1971-72; prof. Grad. Sch., Bowie (Md.) State Coll., 1972—; dir. edn. programs Kennedy Inst., Johns Hopkins, 1968-69, asst. prof. pediatrics, 1969—; research dir. model cities research project Dept. Vocational Rehab., Balt., 1969-72. Cons. various depts. Md. Dept. Edn., 1969-73, bur. handicapped U.S. Office Edn., 1971-73, Calverton Sch., Huntington, Md., 1971—; mem. adv. bd. Acad. Ednl. Disciplines, Richmond Hill, N.Y., 1971—; mem. evaluation teams tchr. tng. colls. and univs. Md., 1970-73; mem. Md. Standards Revision Com. for Emotionally Handicapped, 1969-70; chmn. Md. Council on Programming for Institutionalized Youth, 1971-72. Mem. Am. Assn. Mental Deficiency, Council Exceptional Children, Assn. Children with Learning Disabilities, Assn. Childhood Edn. Internat., Am. Ednl. Research Assn., Nat. Assn. for Edn. Young Children, Phi Kappa Phi. Contbr. profl. jours. Home: 6410 Sandy St Laurel MD 20810 Office: Bowie State College Bowie MD 20715

CHRISTRUP, HELEN JEANNE, psychologist; b. St. Louis, July 29, 1927; d. George and Velma (DuBray) Christrup; B.A., Mo. U., 1949; B.S., Washington U., 1951; M.A., George Washington U., 1958. Occupational therapist U.S. Army hosps., 1951-55; chief indsl. therapist St. Elizabeth's Hosp., Washington, 1956-58, asst. chief occupational therapist, 1959-61, employee devel. and research specialist, office of personnel, 1962-68; personnel psychologist Gen. Services Administrn., 1968-73; research psychologist U.S. Civil Service Commn., 1973-74, asso. dir. Personnel Research & Devel. Center, 1974—. Pvt. edn. and vocational guidance, 1958—. Mem. Hunters Valley Civic Assn., Wildlife Mgmt. Inst., Am., D.C. psychol. assns., Internat. Personnel Mgmt. Assn., Am. Sociol. Assn., Psi Chi. Contbr. articles to profl. jours. Home: 2505 Leeds Rd Oakton VA 22124 Office: Civil Service Commn Washington DC 20415

CHRISTY, MARIAN, fashion editor; b. Ridgefield, Conn., Nov. 9, 1932; d. Peter and Anna (Saba) Christy; student Sch. Journalism, Boston U. Formerly reporter Women's Wear Daily, Boston bur.; fashion, lifestyle editor Boston Globe-United Features Syndicate, N.Y.C., 1965—, columns syndicated through United Feature Syndicate. Numerous TV appearances, Boston, N.Y.C. and Chgo. Recipient citations Men's Fashion Assn. N.Y., 1965-68, 70-72; citations Am. Footwear Assn., 1966-72, including Golden Slipper awards; J.C. Penney-U. Mo. journalism awards for fashion stories, 1966, 68, 70; Fashion Reporter's award of N.Y., 1967; Prestige award France, 1969; 2d prize internat. competition Italian Fashion Press award, 1970; Humor prize for story U.P.I., 1972; named Woman of Achievement, Mass. Bus. and Profl. Women's Club, 1965; First Lady of Fashion, Mass. chpt. Nat. Assn. Cystic Fibrosis, 1972; Woman of Year, New Woman Mag., 1973. Decorated cavaliere Al Merito della Repubblica Italiana. Address: 135 Morrissey Blvd Boston MA 02107

CHRYSOSTOM, SISTER MARY, educator; b. Berlin, N.H.; d. Carl and Anna (Pirsch) Truka; B.A., Marygrove Coll., 1933; M.A., U. Detroit, 1936; Licence es Lettres, U. Montreal, 1966; student Sorbonne, summer 1962, Laval U., summer 1958; Ph.D., Wayne State U., 1973. Tchr., elementary parochial schs., Mich. 1936-38, parochial high schs., Mich., Ohio, 1938-49, St. Mary Acad., Monroe, Mich., 1949-53; instr. Marygrove Coll., Detroit, 1953-56, asst. prof., 1956-61, asso. prof., 1962-73, chmn. French dept., 1958-64 (leave of absence to study 1964-66), founder French Inst., 1961; tchr. St. Mary Acad., 1973—. Mem. Am. Council Tchrs. Fgn. Langs., Am. Assn. Tchrs. French, Mich. Fgn. Lang. Assn., Am. Assn. Tchrs. Spanish. Home: 502 W Elm Av Monroe MI 48161

CHRYSSAFOPOULOS, HANKA WANDA SOBCZAK (MRS. NICHOLAS CHRYSSAFOPOULOS), civil engr.; b. Porto Alegre, Brazil; d. Stefan and Estacia (Wilkoszynska) Sobczak; C.E., U. Rio Grande do Sul, 1951, Elec.-Mech. Engr., 1952; M.S. in C.E., U. Ill., 1954, Ph.D., 1963; m. Nicholas Chryssafopoulos, Sept. 6, 1956. Engr. in charge research, head soils lab. Soil Mechanics and Found. Engring. Sect., Tech. Inst. of Rio Grande do Sul, 1952-53, 54-55; research asst. U. Ill., 1955-59; research asst. Ill. State Geol. Survey, Urbana, 1959-60; research engr. Woodward, Clyde, Sherard & Assos., soil and found. cons., Kansas City, Mo., 1964-65; asst. prof. civil engring. Cal. State Coll. at Long Beach, 1965-67; now engaged in pvt. research. Fulbright fellow, 1953. Registered profl. engr. Brazil. Mem. Am. Soc. C.E., Conselho Regional de Engenharia e Arquitetura. Internat. Soc. Soil Mechanics and Found. Engring., Soc. Women Engrs., Geol. Soc. Am., Sigma Xi. Contbr. articles on soil mechanics and engring. geology to profl. jours. Research in connection with differentiation of young glacial tills and their engring. properties. Home: 5 Horizon Rd Fort Lee NJ 07024

CHU, ESTHER BRINEY (MRS. H. T. CHU), educator, civic worker; b. Bluff City, Ill.; d. John and Charlotte (Shaw) Briney; student Ill. Coll.; B.A., U. Ill., then M.A.; Ph.D. (Univ. fellow), Northwestern U.; m. H.T. Chu; children—David S. C., Edna S. C., George S. T. Instr. history Hunter Coll., N.Y.C., 1943, lectr., 1955-58; faculty Jersey City State Coll., 1960—, asso. prof. 1964-68, prof. history, 1968—, chmn. Day Council, 1967-68, senate com. on acad. standards, 1969-71, senator, 1971—, mem. exec. com., 1971-73. Mem. bd., com. chmn. Mt. Vernon (N.Y.) P.T.A., 1951-60; com. chmn., Westchester rep. UN Women's Guild, Westchester, 1951-60. Chmn., Young Peoples Democratic Club Schuyler County, Ill., 1932-33. Past pres. bd. dirs. Mt. Vernon YWCA. Mem. Jersey City State Coll. Faculty Assn. (pres. 1963-64), League Women Voters (mem. bd., fgn. policy chmn. Jersey City 1970-73), Am. Hist. Assn. (life), Am. Assn. U. Profs. (chpt. pres. 1970-72; mem. N.J. exec. com., com. status women 1971-73, nat. com. 1973—), N.J. Commn. Women (edn. com. 1973—), Am. Assn. U. Women. Episcopalian. Pioneer of Ill. Agrl. Adjustment Act, 1933. Home: 846 Scripps Dr Claremont CA 91711 Office: Jersey City State Coll Jersey City NJ 07305

CHU, FLORENCE C. (MRS. PERCY TUNG), radiologist; b. Shanghai, China, May 20, 1918 (came to U.S. 1947, naturalized 1955); d. Kung Shu and Quang Shu (Loh) C.; M.D., Nat. Coll. Shanghai, 1942; m. Percy Tung, Feb. 20, 1943; children—Shirley, William (dec.), Allan. Intern, China, 1941-42; resident in radiology Teaching Hosp. Nat. Med. Coll., Shanghai, 1942-45; asst. in radiology Shanghai San., 1945-47, Cambridge Hosp., Shanghai, 1945-47, Nayang Hosp., Shanghai, 1945-47; fellow, resident in diagnostic roentgenology N.Y.C. Hosp., 1947-49; fellow in radiology, clin. asst. radiation therapist Meml. Hosp., N.Y.C., 1949-55, asst. attending radiation therapist, 1955-65, asso. attending radiation therapist, 1965-69, attending radiation therapist, 1969—; instr. radiology Cornell Med. Sch., N.Y.C., 1951-55, asst. prof., 1955-69, asso. prof., 1969-73, clin. prof. radiology, 1973—. Diplomate Am. Bd. Radiology. Fellow Am. Coll. Radiology; mem. Am. Roentgen Ray Soc., N.Y. Roentgen Soc., A.M.A., N.Y. Cancer Soc., Am. Radium Soc., Am. Coll. Radiology, Radiol. Soc. N.Am., Am. Assn. Cancer Research, Am. Soc. Therapeutic Radiologists, Med. Soc. State N.Y., Am. Chinese Med. Soc., Radiol. Soc. State N.Y., N.Y. County Med. Soc. Home: 1500 Palisade Av Fort Lee NJ 07024 Office: Meml Hosp 1275 York Av New York City NY 10021

CHU, JOSEPHINE SHOU-CHEN, pediatrician; b. Shaoshing, China, Jan. 20, 1921 (came to U.S. 1954, naturalized 1969); d. Shih Tong and Chi Zen (Yao) C.; M.D., Nat. Cung Cheng Med. Coll., 1945. Intern Kangsi Provincial Hosp., Tai Hoo Kangsi, China, 1944-45; resident in pediatrics Henrietta Egleston Hosp. for Children, Atlanta, 1954-55, T.C. Thompson Children's Hosp., Chattanooga, 1955-56, Phila. Gen. Hosp., 1956-57, 57-58; staff children's Tb Jefferson Davis Hosp., Houston, 1958-59; mem. attending staff Vancouver Gen. Hosp., 1960-62; research fellow Mt. Sinai Hosp., Cleve., 1962-64, mem. teaching staff, 1964—; practice medicine specializing in pediatrics, North Olmsted, O., 1964-66; in-patient dir. Broadview Center for Mentally Retarded, 1966-68; vis. pediatrician Cleve. Met. Hosp., 1964-66, 1968—; sr. clin. instr. Case-Western Reserve U. Diplomate Am. Bd. Pediatrics. Fellow Am. Acad. Pediatrics; mem. Ohio Med. Assn., Cleve. Acad. Medicine, Cleve. Med. Women's Assn. Home: 6902 Glenella Dr Seven Hills OH 44131 Office: 1465 E 55th St Cleveland OH 44103

CHU, MAY KOO (MRS. JOHN CHU), psychologist; b. Nanking, China, Jan. 8, 1932; d. Shao Cheng and Sauchun C. (Chan) Koo; B.A. (scholar), Chinese U., Hong Kong, 1955; M.A. (scholar), Mich. State U., 1959, Ph.D., 1962; m. John Chu, June 10, 1962; children—Alan, Olivia. Came to U.S., 1958, naturalized, 1966. Instr. psychology dept. Wittenberg U., Springfield, O., 1961-66, asst. prof., 1966-70; psychologist Clark County Comprehensive Mental Health Center, Springfield, 1970-73; chief psychologist Muskingum County Comprehensive Mental Health Center, Zanesville, O., 1973—. Cons. Head Start Program, Springfield, 1971-73. Mem. adv. bd. child care dept. Clark County Tech. Coll. Mem. Am., Ohio psychol. assns. Author: The Growing Years, 1955; Hasty Journey, 1957. Home: Route 1 Nashport OH 43830 Office: 2845 Bell St Zanesville OH 43701

CHUA, MAUREEN YU, obstetrician and gynecologist; b. Manila, Philippines, Jan. 10; d. Tian Han and Giok Toan (Yu) Chua; B.A., U. of East, Manila, 1962, M.D., 1967. Rotating intern St. Elizabeth's Hosp., Elizabeth, N.J., 1967-68; resident in obstetrics and gynecology Washington Hosp. Center, 1968-72, fellow in obstetrics and gynecology, 1972-73. Fellow Am. Fertility Soc., Am. Soc. Abdominal Surgeons, Am. Coll. Obstetrics and Gynecology (jr.); mem. D.C. Med. Soc. Home: 3617 Gallatin St Apt 1023 Hyattsville MD 20782 Office: 106 Irving St NW Washington DC 20010

CHUN, DAISY LOOK (MRS. PETER J. CHUN), realtor; b. Honolulu, Sept. 12, 1924; d. Kwock Fong and Yuk Kang (Wong) Look; diploma Honolulu Bus. Coll., 1945; m. Peter J. Chun, Oct. 20, 1945; children—Derelyn Sandrea, Deborah Gayle, Coralie Ann, Corinne Julie. Pres., mgr. Daisy Chun Realty, Honolulu, 1967—. Vice pres. Regal Properties, Inc., 1970—. Mem. Honolulu Bd. Realtors. Vice pres. Hawaiian Chinese Civic Assn., 1968—; v.p. Freedoms Found. at Valley Forge, 1967—; edn. chmn. Hawaii Opera Theatre; mem. Honolulu Symphony Soc. Bd. dirs. Hawaii Big Sisters, Inc. Mem. Nat. Assn. of Real Estate Bds. Club: Chinese Women's of Hawaii. Home: 3838 Poka St Honolulu HI 96816 Office: 1441 Kapiolani Blvd Honolulu HI 96814

CHUN, THERESA WON CHOON, physician; b. Sung Chon, Korea, Feb. 28, 1929; s. Soon Woo and Si Sul (Chun) Chun; M.D., Seoul Women's Med. Coll., 1955. Came to U.S., 1956, naturalized, 1972. Intern, St. Luke's Hosp., Chgo., 1957-58; resident Children's Meml. Hosp., Chgo., 1958-59, Univ. Hosp., Cleve., 1959-60; hematology research fellow in pediatrics Downstate Med. Center, Bklyn., 1961-62; chief pediatrics Miller Bay Hosp., Prince Rupert, B.C., Can., 1965-67; pediatrician Pineland Hosp., Pownal, Me., 1967-68; practice medicine, specializing in pediatrics, Newark, N.Y., 1969—; chief pediatric service Newark State Sch., 1969—; pediatric cons. Wayne County Mental Health Service, Newark, 1970—; clin. instr. pediatrics U. Rochester (N.Y.) Sch. Medicine, 1969—; pub. health physician N.Y. State Dept. Health, Syracuse, 1972—. Fellow Am. Acad. Pediatrics; mem. A.M.A. Address: 677 S Salina St Syracuse NY 13202

CHURCH, JEAN JANE (MRS. HAROLD MELVAN CHURCH), occupational therapist; b. Milw., Jan. 25, 1929; d. Charles Robert and Adella Rose (Henkel) Schmiel; B.S., Mt. Mary Coll., 1951; m. Harold Melvan Church, Nov. 29, 1952; children—Janell (Mrs. Dennis Andwew Garrison), Charles, Stuart. Head occupational therapy dept. St. Joseph Hosp., Bloomington, Ill., 1952; occupational therapist Genesee Meml. Hosp., Flint, Mich., 1953; head occupational therapy dept. Hurley Hosp., Flint, 1961-65, 67—. Mem. Am. Occupational Therapy Assn. Home: 615 E 2d St Flint MI 48503 Office: 6th and Begole Sts Flint MI 48502

CHURCH, MARGARET, educator; b. Boston, Apr. 8, 1920; d. Joseph W. and Sophy (Phillips) Church; A.B., Radcliffe Coll., 1941; Ph.D., 1944; M.A., Columbia, 1942. Instr. English, Temple U., 1944-46, Duke, 1946-53; asst. prof. English, Purdue U., Lafayette, Ind., 1953-61, asso. prof. English, 1961-65, prof. English, 1965—, also chmn. comparative lit. Mem. Comparative Lit. Assn., Ind. Coll. English Assn., Modern Lang. Assn. Am.; Phi Beta Kappa (hon.). Episcopalian. Author: Time and Reality: Studies in Contemporary Literature, 1963; Don Quixote: The Knight of La Mancha, 1971; also articles in field. Editorial, bd. Modern Fiction Studies, 1968, co-editor, 1971—. Home: 808 N Rd 400W West West Lafayette IN 47906

CHURCH, MARTHA ELEANOR, educator; b. Pitts., Nov. 17, 1930; d. Walter Seward and Eleanor (Boyer) Church; B.A., Wellesley Coll., 1952; M.A., U. Pitts., 1954; Ph.D., U. Chgo., 1960. Lectr. geography Mt. Mercy Coll., Pitts., 1953; instr. geology and geography Mt. Holyoke Coll., South Hadley, Mass., 1953-57; lectr. geography Ind. U. Gary Center, 1958; instr., then asst. prof. geography, Wellesley Coll., 1960-65; dean coll., prof. geography Wilson Coll., 1965-71; asso. exec. sec. Commn. Higher Edn., Middle States Assn. Colls and Secondary Schs., 1971—. Cons. for Choice: Books for College Libraries. Recipient Christian R. and Mary F. Lindback Found. Distinguished Teaching award Wilson Coll., 1971. Mem. Assn. Am. Geographers, Am. Assn. U. Women, Am. Conf. Acad. Deans (sec., editor 1969-71), Council Protestant Colls. and Univs. (dir. 1969-71), Am. Schs. Oriental Research, Nat. Assn. for Women Deans, Adminstrs. and Counselors, Sigma Delta Epsilon. Author: The Spatial Organization of Electric Power Territories in Massachusetts, 1960. Co-editor: A Basic Geographical Library: A Selected and Annotated Book List for Am. Colls., 1966. Home: 25 Hickory Pl Apt A-26 Chatham NJ 07928

CHURCH, PEARL DEE (MRS. DONALD EISENBREY CHURCH), artist; b. N.Y.C., Nov. 16, 1907; d. Harry and Mollie (Miller) Friedman; B.A., Barnard Coll., 1928; postgrad. U. Mich., 1936, Am. U., 1956; M.A., Ohio U., 1938; m. Donald E. Church, June 16, 1929; 1 son, Russell M. Advt. research Churchill-Hall, N.Y.C., 1928-30; vocational counselor USES, 1936-38; dir. Athens (O.) Guidance Bur., 1938-41; occupational research Office Def. Moblzn., 1942-43; profl. artist, 1955—; originator stone collage and mazdalith techniques; one man shows Madison Gallery, N.Y.C., 1961,

Collectors Gallery, Washington, 1958, 62, Bridge Gallery, N.Y.C., 1964, 66, Massillon (O.) Museum Arts, 1967, Internat. Gem Show, 1969, Town East Gallery, 1970, Goldman Fine Arts Gallery, 1972; one-man traveling shows at Arlington and Alexandria (Va.) pub. libraries, 1966, also tour at 10 Southwest museums, 1972-73; works permanently exhibited Nat. Petroleum Council, Smithsonian Instn., Nev. Mus. Art (Reno), Wellfleet Art Gallery, Aden Gallery, Massillon Mus. Art, Am. Mus. Immigration, Randolph Macon, Houston Mus. Sci. Asst. dir. tng. Am. Women's Voluntary Services 1941-42; vol. work neurospsychiat. wards at White Plains (N.Y.) Mental Hosp., USN Med. Center, St. Elizabeth's Hosp. (Washington); dir. Workshop Center of the Arts. Mem. adv. com. Nat. Acad. Scis. Recipient First prize S. E. Regional Art Exhibit, 1956, 60, Am. Pen Women's Art Exhibit, 1958, 61. Mem. Nat. League Am. Pen Women (nat. art chmn.; pres. Capital br.), Internat. Platform Assn. (bd. govs.; best in show 1967), Artists Equity. Home: Harbour Sq 560 N St SW Washington DC 20024 Studio: 510 N St SW Washington DC 20024

CHURCH, ROBERTA, govt. ofcl.; d.; Robert R. Jr. and Sara (Johnson) Church; A.B., Northwestern U., 1935, M.A., 1937. Social worker Family and Child Welfare div. Chgo. Welfare Adminstrn., 1940-43, adoption div. Ill. Children's Home and Aid Soc., Chgo., 1943-53; cons. for minority groups U.S. Dept. Labor, 1953-61; cons. Rehab. Services Adminstrn., Dept. Health, Edn. and Welfare, Washington, D.C., 1961—. Mem. Pres.'s Nat. Adv. Council on Adult Edn., 1970—. Mem. Rep. State Exec. Com. Tenn., 1952-53. Recipient Certificate of Merit, Alpha Phi Alpha, 1956. Mem. Am. Assn. U. Women, Nat. Assn. Social Workers, Delta Sigma Theta. Republican. Episcopalian. Home: 1629 Columbia Rd NW Washington DC 20009 Office: US Dept Health Edn and Welfare Independence Av Washington DC 20201

CHURCH, RUTH ESTELLA, physician; b. Walworth, Wis., Aug. 8, 1905; d. Wells D. and Effie (Dake) Church; B.S. in Nursing, Milw.-Downer Coll., 1929; grad. Presbyn. Hosp. Sch. Nursing, Chgo., 1929; M.S., U. Wis., 1935, M.D., 1937; M.S. in Pub. Health, Columbia, 1941. Staff nurse Chgo. Vis. Nurses Assn., 1929-32; maternal and child health physician with Wis. Bd. Health, 1938-40; med. dir. Washington County (Ia.) Health Unit, 1941-45; dist. health officer, Ill. Dept. Pub. Health, 1945-50, cons. in field studies, 1953-54, chief bur. communicable disease control, 1954-57, dept. dir. charge div. hosps. and chronic diseases, 1957-61; med. dir. Waukesha County Health Dept., 1961-67; cons. in community health services, 1967—; participated in research studies on poliomyelitis vaccine prepared with ultra-violet radiation technique. Served as maj. M.C., AUS; with div. preventive medicine Office Surgeon Gen., 1950-53. Mem. Am. Assn. U. Women, Am. (past pres. Middle States br.; gov.), Wis. pub. health assns., A.M.A., Phi Beta Kappa. Conglist. Contbr. articles to profl. jours. Home: 435 Starin Rd Whitewater WI 53190

CHURCHILL, CONSTANCE LOUISE, educator; b. Los Angeles, May 10, 1941; d. Alfred Brooks and Mary Louise (Errett) Churchill; B.S., Baylor U., 1963, Ph.D., 1969. Chemistry technician Aerojet Gen. Corp., Azusa, Cal., 1961-62; teaching and research asst. Baylor U., 1963-68; asst. prof. Dakota State Coll., Madison, S.D., 1968-69, asso. prof., 1969-72, prof. chemistry, 1972—. Trustee, N.Am. Baptist Sem., Sioux Falls, S.D. Mem. Am. Assn. U. Women (sec. Madison br. 1969-71, 1st v.p. charge programs 1971-72), P.E.O. Baptist. Home: 621 N Lee St Madison SD 57042

CHURCHILL, DOROTHY HELEN KING (MRS. WALTER AUGUSTUS CHURCHILL, SR.), food co. exec.; b. Evansport, O., Nov. 24, 1906; s. Edward Nicholas and Olide (Spangler) King; student Defiance Coll., 1924-25; m. Walter Augustus Churchill, June 9, 1928; children—Walter Augustus, Carolyn Ann (Mrs. Lynn Albert Colwell). Sec.-treas. Churchill's Super Markets, Inc., Toledo, 1953—, Certified Leasing Co., Inc., Toledo, 1967—. Republican. Republican. Mem. Order Eastern Star. Home: 3003 Cheltenham Rd Toledo OH 43606 Office: 2845 W Central St Toledo OH 43606

CHURCHILL, JOAN RUSSELL (MRS. FREDERICK DEANE CHURCHILL), pub. relations co. exec.; b. Greenfield, Mass., Dec. 9, 1931; d. Rolfe Spaulding and Hilda (Belknap) Russell; B.A., U. Vt., 1953; m. Frederick Deane Churchill, May 1, 1954; children—Rolfe Russell, Katherine Deane, Lucius Bradford. Newspaper reporter, editor Vt. Jour., Windsor, 1952; advt. rep. Rutland (Vt.) Herald, 1953-55; editor Carrier Internat. News, Carrier Corp., N.Y.C., 1955-57, Builders Pub. Co., Mt. Vernon, N.Y., 1956-59; pub. relations dir. Knudsen-Moore Inc., Stamford, Conn., 1959-66; pres. Churchill Co., Pub. Relations, Windsor, Vt., 1966—; pres. Vt. Sports & Hobby, Windsor, 1973—; v.p., clk., broker Hilda B. Russell Realty, Inc., Windsor, 1970—; asso. Stevens & Kirwan, Hanover, N.H., 1973—. Vice pres. Jr. League of Pelham, 1968-70. Bd. dirs. United Fund, Pelham, 1967-70; bd. dirs., trustee Historic Windsor, Inc. Home: 24 N Main St Windsor VT 05089 Office: 149 S Main St Windsor VT 05089

CHURCHMAN, CAROLYN MARGARET HAUGHT (MRS. RAY E. CHURCHMAN), broadcaster; b. Indpls., June 9, 1927; d. Edgar L. and Lillian (Ilg) Haught; student Jordan Coll. Music, 1941-43, Ohio State U., 1944-46; m. Ray E. Churchman, Mar. 6, 1954. Musician, sta. WCOL, Columbus, O., 1944; woman's dir. sta. WBNS, Columbus, 1946-48; announcer WFBM-TV, Indpls., 1956; free lance radio and TV commls., N.Y.C., 1956; hostess daily interview program WTTV, Indpls., 1957-60; interview radio sta. WFBM, Indpls., 1961-73; free lance writer, producer radio and TV commls., 1950—; hostess daily radio program Carolyn Churchman Show, women's dir., broadcaster WXLW, 1973—. Account exec. Bill Henke Advt. Agy., Indpls., 1961-73. Mem. Mayor's Task Force on Aging; chmn. fund raising dr. Am. Cancer Soc., 1967; chmn. campaign Cystic Fibrosis, 1965-66, now regional pres.; chmn. campaign Retarded Olympics, 1969, Easter Seal campaign, 1970. Bd. dirs. Indpls. Sr. Citizens Center. Recipient Ind. Boys Sch. award, 1967, Sr. Citizens Center award Indpls. Sr. Citizen Center, 1966, Community Blood Bank award, 1966, 67, Am. Cancer Soc. award for leadership in campaign, 1967, Casper award Community Service Council, 1967; Ind. Health Assn. award, 1969. Mem. Indpls. Community Service Council, Am. Women in Radio and TV, Indpls. Advt. Club, Chi Omega. Home: 4888 Kesslerview Dr Indianapolis IN 46220 Office: WXLW Stas 3003 Kessler Blvd Indianapolis IN 46222

CIANCIOLO, PATRICIA JEAN, educator; b. Chgo., Oct. 24, 1929; d. Michael C. and Lottie Cianciolo; Ph.B. cum laude, Cardinal Stritch Coll., 1949; M.Ed., U. Wis., 1954; Ph.D., Ohio State U., 1963. Tchr. elementary grades Milw. pub. schs., 1949-58; instr. Marquette U., Milw., 1958-60, asst. prof. elementary edn., 1962-64; prof. elementary edn., Mich. State U., East Lansing, 1964—; instr. Ohio State U., Columbus, 1960-62, U. Hawaii, summer 1967, U. Nev. at Las Vegas, summer 1971, 74. Recipient Delta Kappa Gamma Spl. scholarship award, 1960; Centennial award Ohio State U., 1970. Mem. Assn. for Supervision and Curriculum Devel., Assn. Higher Edn., Nat. Council Tchrs. English (com. children's lit. 1961-64, com. children's responses to lit. 1965—, com. on authors-illustrators 1965—, com. on elementary booklist 1965—), Assn. for Childhood Edn. Internat. (county pres. 1963-64), Nat. Soc. for Study of Edn., A.L.A. (Newberry-Caldecott award com. 1972-73, Batchelder award com. 1973—), Phi Delta Kappa, Delta Kappa Gamma, Delta Epsilon Sigma (chpt. pres. 1954-56, 62-64). Author publs. in field. Home: 4206 Wabaningo Okemos MI 48864

CIARAMELLI, LETIZIA CARMELA, physician; b. N.Y.C.; d. Anthony and Jeanne (Roy) Ciaramelli; A.B., Hunter Coll., 1934; M.D., N.Y. Med. Coll., 1942; M.S. in Medicine, U. Minn., 1947. Intern, Met. Hosp., Welfare Island, 1942-43; fellow Mayo Clinic, 1943-47; instr. N.Y. Med. Coll., N.Y.C., 1947-51; practice medicine specializing in internal medicine, N.Y.C., 1947-51; physician internal medicine Ross Loos Med. Group, Los Angeles, 1951-58; psychiat. resident VA Hosp., Brentwood, Cal., 1958-61; psychiatrist VA Hosps., Lexington, Ky., 1961-63, Brentwood, 1963-66; dir. inpatient services Olive View (Cal.) Hosp., 1966—; dir. Los Angeles Remedial Services, Culver City, 1966—. Instr., U. Cal. at Los Angeles, 1964-66; cons. Peace Corps, 1964-66, Convent of Good Shepherd, Los Angeles, 1960-66. Diplomate Am. Bd. Psychiatry and Neurology. Mem. Am., Cal., Los Angeles med. assns., Am., So. Cal. psychiat. assns., Los Angeles County Soc. Neurologists and Psychiatrists. Office: 9708 Venice Blvd Culver City CA 90230

CIARICO, SISTER BARBARA JEAN, coll. adminstr.; b. Albion, N.Y., May 27, 1930; d. Patrick William and Anna Catherine (Ross) Ciarico; B.A., Niagara U., 1961; M.S., Canisius Coll., 1968. Tchr. elementary schs. Diocese of Buffalo, 1951-69; dir. remedial reading program Sisters of Mercy, Buffalo, 1962-66; asst. prin. St. Martin Sch., Buffalo, 1968-69; registrar Trocaire Coll., Buffalo, 1969—. Mem. N.Y. State Curriculum Com., 1970-73; chmn. adv. bd. Sisters of Mercy, Buffalo Diocese, 1972—, mem. Sister's Assembly, 1972—; asso. superior Mt. Mercy Convent, Buffalo, 1970—. Mem. human rights council City of Buffalo, 1973—. Mem. Am., Middle States assns. collegiate registrars and admissions officers, Am. Hist. Assn., Western N.Y. Personnel and Guidance Assn., Western N.Y. Consortium Registrars and Admissions Officers. Home: 625 Abbott Rd Buffalo NY 14220 Office: 110 Red Jacket Pkwy Buffalo NY 14220

CIBILICH, SLAVKA MARY, social worker; b. Oakland, Cal., Mar. 31, 1925; d. Joseph and Katherine (Splivalo) Cibilich; B.A., U. Cal. at Berkeley, 1946, M.S.W., 1949. Sr. psychiat. social worker Sonoma State Hosp. Cal. State Dept. Mental Hygiene, Eldridge, 1949-53, 55-61; with San Mateo County (Cal.) Welfare Dept., 1954-55; child welfare worker Marin County (Cal.) Welfare Dept., San Rafael, 1961-63; child welfare supr. San Francisco Dept. Pub. Social Services, 1963-65; med. social worker San Francisco Gen. Hosp., 1966; counselor Regional Center Mentally Retarded Children's Hosp. Los Angeles, 1967-71; med. social work supr. Los Angeles County Community Health Services, 1972—. Mem. Nat. Assn. Social Workers, Assn. Licensed Clin. Social Worker, Am. Assn. Mental Deficiency, U. Cal. Alumni Assn., Delta Zeta. Prytanean. Home: 5414 1/4 Franklin St Los Angeles CA 90027 Office: 1522 E 102d St Los Angeles CA 90001

CIBOCH, LORRAINE, librarian; b. Cicero, Ill.; d. Frank Michael and Anna (Sobolik) Ciboch; grad. Morton Jr. Coll., 1941; B.S., U. Ill., 1944; B.S. in L.S., 1947. Jr. chemist Gen. Foods Corp., 1944; chemist Libby, McNeill & Libby, 1945-46; reference librarian, editor Gas Abstracts, also instr. gas lit. Inst. Gas Tech., 1947-51; librarian Am. Can Co., 1951-60, Charles Bruning Co., Inc., Mt. Prospect, Ill., 1960-61, chief librarian Fansteel Metall. Corp., North Chgo., Ill., 1962-63; research librarian Teletype Corp., Skokie, Ill., 1964-65; librarian research and devel. div., bus. equipment group Bell & Howell Co., Chicago, 1965-69; systems librarian Library Health Scis., U. Ill. Med. Center, Chgo., 1969—. Mem. adv. council librarians U. Ill. Grad. Sch. Library Sci., 1964-67. Gray Lady, A.R.C., 1952-55. Mem. Spl. Libraries Assn. (dir. 1959-62; pres. Ill. chpt. 1962-63; chmn. documentation div. 1973), Med. Library Assn., Am. Soc. Information Sci. (sec. Chgo. chpt. 1962-63), League Women Voters. Presbyn. Home: 1827 S Harlem Av Berwyn IL 60402 Office: 1853 W Polk St Chicago IL 60612

CICKELLI, HANNAH MARY ZIEGLER (MRS. FRANK A. CICKELLI), city ofcl.; b. Niles, O., Aug. 16, 1910; d. John Henry and Christine (Schuler) Ziegler; student Warren Bus. Coll., 1930, 31; m. Frank A. Cickelli, Aug. 17, 1937; 1 son, James A. Chief dep. recorder Trumbull County, Warren, O., 1949-58, chief cashier for county treas., 1959-72; city auditor City of Warren, 1972—. Sec., Federated Democratic Club Trumbull County, 1948-52; mem. Federated Dem. Women Ohio, Jefferson Dem. Club Trumbull County. Mem. Nat. Fedn. Bus. and Profl. Women's Clubs, Trumbull Bus. and Profl. Women, Am. Legion Aux. Roman Catholic. Home: 1689 Norwood St NW Warren OH 44485 Office: City Hall 391 Mahoning NW Warren OH 44483

CIGARROA, MARGARET GILLER (MRS. LEONIDES GONZALES CIGARROA), physician; b. Chgo., Oct. 24, 1925; d. George Byron and Ruth (Moore) Giller; B.A., U. Ill. at Urbana, 1944; M.D., U. Ill. Med. Sch. at Chgo., 1948; m. Leonides Gonzales Cigarroa, Oct. 14, 1950; children—Mary Margaret, Joaquin III, Jane Elizabeth, Leonides Gonzales, Ruth Ann, Martha Louise. Intern Cook County Hosp., Chgo., 1948-50; gen. practice medicine, Laredo, Tex., 1951—; city health officer, 1964—; chief of obstetrics Mercy Hosp., Laredo. Sec. Bi-nat. Council Pub. Health, Laredo, Tex., Laredo, Mexico, 1964—. Mem. Webb County Med. Soc. (pres. 1968—). Home: 2320 Fremont St Laredo TX 78040 Office: 1502 Logan St Laredo TX 78040

CIMONS, MARLENE FRANCES, journalist; b. Yonkers, N.Y., Mar. 13, 1945; d. Bernard and Clara (Bromberg) Cimons; B.A., Syracuse U., 1967. Reporter, Syracuse (N.Y.) Post-Standard, 1967-68, Newsday, Garden City, N.Y. 1968-69, Washington bur. Los Angeles Times, 1969—. Free-lance writer for mags. Recipient Hearst writing award, 1967. Mem. Women's Legal Def. Fund, Journalists for Profl. Equality (founder), Nat. Orgn. Women, Nat. Women's Polit. Caucus, Sigma Delta Chi, Theta Sigma Phi. Club: Washington Press. Home: 1100 6th St SW Washington DC 20024 Office: 1700 Pennsylvania Av NW Washington DC 20006

CIOLLI, ANTOINETTE, librarian; b. N.Y.C., Aug. 20, 1915; d. Pietro and Mary (Palumbo) Ciolli; A.B., Bklyn. Coll., 1937, M.A., 1940; B.S. in L.S., Columbia, 1943. Tchr. history and civics Bklyn. high schs., 1943-44; circulation librarian Bklyn. Coll. Library, 1944-46; instr. history Sch. Gen. Studies, Bklyn. Coll., 1944-50, asst. prof. library dept., 1965-72, asso. prof., 1973—; reference librarian Bklyn. Coll. Library, 1947-59, chief sci. librarian, 1959-70, chief spl. collections div., 1970—. Mem. A.L.A., Am. Hist. Assn., Am. Assn. U. Profs., Spl. Libraries Assn. (museum group chpt. sec. 1950-51, 52-54), N.Y. Library Club, Beta Phi Mu. Author: (with Alexander S. Preminger and Lillian Lester) Urban Educator: Harry D. Gideonse, Brooklyn College and the City University of New York, 1970. Contbr. articles to profl. jours. Home: 1129 Bay Ridge Pkwy Brooklyn NY 11228

CION, JUDITH ANN SCHNEIDER, lawyer; b. N.Y.C., June 27, 1943; d. Peter and Ruth Jeannette (Levy) Schneider; student Smith Coll., 1961-63; A.B., Pomona Coll., 1965; LL.B., Harvard Law Sch., 1968; m. Richard M. Cion, Mar. 30, 1968 (div.). Admitted to N.Y. bar, 1968; asso. Poletti, Freidin, Prashker, Feldman & Gartner, N.Y.C., 1968-71, Lovejoy, Wasson, Lundgren & Ashton, N.Y.C., 1971—. Dir, sec., treas. Light Opera Manhattan, Inc., N.Y.C., 1973—. Mem. Am., N.Y. bar assns., Assn. Bar City N.Y. Home: 1175 York Av New York City NY 10021 Office: 250 Park Av New York City NY 10017

CIORDIA, ELSIE (MRS. JOSE E. GONZALEZ), hosp. adminstr.; b. Vega Baja, P.R., Apr. 13, 1929; d. Angel Juan and Ramona (Robles) Ciordia; bus. adminstrn. Spencer Inst. Bus. Coll., 1950; hosp. adminstrn. Workshop Columbia U., 1963-64; m. Jose E. Gonzalez, Aug. 29, 1966. Asst. adminstr. Nine East Ninety-First St. Hosp., N.Y.C., 1960-64, adminstr., 1964—. Home: 2400 Johnson Av Riverdale NY 10463 Office: 9 East 91st St New York City NY 10028

CIPRIANI, HARRIET EMILY STICKELS (MRS. ALFRED BERNE CIPRIANI), polit. party ofcl.; b. N.Y.C., Aug. 20, 1915; d. Floyd and Emily (Gaethke) Stickels; student Art Students League, 1945-46, Craft Students League, 1947-49; m. Alfred Berne Cipriani, Feb. 10, 1945. Accounting positions Singer Sewing Machine Co., N.Y.C., 1935-42, Brewster Aero. Corp., N.Y.C., 1942-45; vol. activities, 1946-68; dep. vice chmn., dept. dir. women's activities Democratic Nat. Com., Washington, 1968-71, dir. women's activities, 1971—. Exec. dir. Humphrey for Pres. Com., Washington, 1959-60; sec. Washington Dem. Central Com., 1960-64, vice chmn., 1964-67; mem. Citizens Adv. Council, Washington, 1962-67; alternate Dem. Nat. committeewoman, 1964-67, Nat. committeewoman, 1967-68; chmn. vol. participation Presdl. Inaugural Comm., 1965; nat. coordinator Women for Humphrey-Muskie, 1968; treas. Woman's Nat. Dem. Club, Washington, 1963-65; co-founder D.C. Dem. Women's Club, 1966. Mem. League Women Voters, Nat. Ballet Soc., Common Cause, Smithsonian Assos. Home: 1761 Harvard St NW Washington DC 20009 Office: 1625 Massachusetts Av NW Washington DC 20036

CIRUTI, JOAN ESTELLE, educator; b. Ponchatoula, La., Aug. 8, 1930; d. Joseph Aloysius and Olga (Jordan) Ciruti; B.A., Southeastern La. Coll., 1950; M.A., U. Okla., 1954; Ph.D., Tulane U., 1959. Instr. modern langs. U. Okla., Norman, 1957-59, asst. prof., 1959-63; research asst. U.S. Office Edn., Washington, 1959-60; asst. prof. Spanish, Mt. Holyoke Coll., South Hadley, Mass., 1963-66, asso. prof., 1966-71 chmn. dept. Spanish, 1965-71, prof., 1971—, dean of studies, 1971-74. Cons. Ednl. Testing Service, 1968—. Named Distinguished Alumnus, Southeastern La. Coll., 1973. Mem. Am. Council on Teaching of Fgn. Langs., Modern Lang. Assn. (nominating, adv. com. 1962-64), Latin Am. Studies Assn. (mem. steering com. consortium Latin Am. studies programs 1969-72, com. on women 1973-74), New Eng. Modern Lang. Assn., Am. Assn. Tchrs. Spanish and Portuguese, Am. Assn. U. Profs., Am. Assn. U. Women, Phi Sigma Iota, Sigma Delta Pi. Co-author: Modern Spanish, 2d edit., 1966; Continuing Spanish, 1967. Contbg. editor: Handbook of Latin-American Studies, vol. 28, 1966, vol. 30, 1968, vol. 32, 1970. Home: 21 Jewett Lane South Hadley MA 01075

CISNEY, MARCELLA (MRS. ROBERT C. SCHNITZER), theatre dir., adminstr.; b. Altoona, Pa.; d. Moses J. and Anne (Epstein) Abels; ed. Am. Acad. Dramatic Arts, Bennington Sch. Arts, Neighborhood Playhouse Dir.'s Seminar, N.Y. U. Radio-TV Workshop; m. Robert C. Schnitzer, June 7, 1953. Featured on Broadway in Girls in Uniform, Lady Precious Stream; dir. Off-Broadway and summer theatres; exec. dir. Jacksonville (Fla.) Civic Theatre, 1942-45; producer-dir. Pasadena Playhouse, 1946-48, Laguna Playhouse, Las Palmas Theatre, Hollywood, 1948-49; head coach Warner Bros. Studio, 1948; network dir. for CBS-TV, N.Y., 1950-54; lectr. advanced theatre direction Columbia U., 1955; adminstr. Rockefeller Found. project for refugee artists, 1956; dir. N.Y.C. Opera, 1957-58; U.S. asso. coordinator performing arts Brussels Fair, 1957-58; directed all-star Skin of Our Teeth for Theatre Guild-State Dept. world tour, Latin Am. tour of Glass Menagerie, 1959-60; co-founder, artistic dir. Profl. Theatre Program, U. Mich., Ann Arbor, 1961-73, directed premieres Child Buyer, 1963, An Evening's Frost, 1964, Wedding Band, 1965, Ivory Tower, 1966, Amazing Grace, 1967, The Castle, 1968, The Conjurer, 1969; dir. nat. tour An Evening's Frost, 1966, ACT West Coast premiere, 1968; producer Siamese Connections, 1971, Lost Respects, 1972. Mem. hon. council Am. Acad. Dramatic Arts; bd. govs. Am. Playwrights Theatre. Recipient Bronze medal Israeli minister of culture; Gold medal for Brussels Fair Program; Spl. Pres.'s Citation U. Mich., 1972. Mem. Am. Theatre Assn., Actors Equity Assn., Univ. Resident Theatre Assn. Home: 6 Woods End Lane Westport CT 06880

CISZ, JOAN VERONICA, educator; b. Johnstown, Pa., Apr. 20, 1941; d. Joseph Francis and Mary (Mucheska) Cisz; A.B., Wilson Coll., 1963; M.Ed., Temple U., 1965; Ph.D., U. Pitts., 1973. Tchr., Phila. Pub. Schs., 1963-66; field rep. Spl. Edn. Inst. Materials Center, Austin, Tex., 1968; inst. materials specialist Ashtabula County (O.) Schs., 1969; asst. dir. U. Pa. Spl. Edn. Regional Resource Center, Pitts., 1969-72, univ. inst., 1969-70; supr. supplementary edn. Montgomery County pub. schs., Rockville, Md., 1973—. Cons. in field. Mem. Assn. Supervision and Curriculum and Devel., Council Exceptional Children, Wilson Coll. Alumnae Assn., Pi Lambda Theta. Home: 446 N Summit St Gaithersburg MD 20760 Office: Area 2 Adminstrv Office 12518 Greenly Dr Silver Spring MD 20906

CITRIN, JOSEPHINE LAZAROWICS (MRS. KERRY A. CITRIN), lawyer; b. Chgo., Jan. 31, 1948; d. Julius Henry and Gertrud (Smoli) Schwaier; B.A., Temple U., 1968, postgrad., 1968-70; J.D., U. Me., 1971; m. Kerry A. Citrin, Mar. 29, 1969; 1 dau., Sarah Rebecca. Admitted to Me. bar, 1971; practiced in Portland, 1972—; lawyer VISTA, Pine Tree Legal Assistance, Inc., Portland, Me., 1971-72. Instr. continuing edn. div. dept. criminal justice U. Me., Portland, 1972-74. Family advocate Community Counseling Center, Portland, 1973-74. Bd. dirs. Combat, Inc., 1973—. Mem. Me., Cumberland County bar assns. Jewish religion. Home and office: 18 Cobbert Rd Portland ME 04102

CITRON, SYLVIA (MRS. RUBIN CITRON), advt. co. exec.; b. N.Y.C., Nov. 12, 1917; d. Jacob and Frieda (Meth) Feuer; student Queens Coll., 1966-68; m. Rubin Citron, June 10, 1939; 1 dau., Felice. Sec., Lewis Bros. Co., N.Y.C., 1934-39; adminstrv. and exec. sec. Century Factors Co., N.Y.C., 1939-43; exec. sec. Jebtowne Corp., N.Y.C., 1943-46; adminstrv. and exec. sec. Ralph Stark, Inc., N.Y.C., 1953-67; adminstrv. asst., controller, personnel dir. Franklin & Joseph, Inc., N.Y.C., 1968—, v.p., 1973—. Group finance sec. Sunnyside Council Girl Scouts Am., 1953-55. Home: 4100-43 Av Long Island NY 11104 Office: 641 Lexington Av New York City NY 10022

CLADIS, PATRICIA ELIZABETH RUTH (MRS. GEORGE H. CLADIS), physicist; b. Shanghai, China, July 13, 1937; d. Frank Moule and Ellen Diana (Kawaguchi) Grossmith; came to U.S., 1962, naturalized, 1967; B.A. with honors in Math. and Physics, U. B.C., Can., 1959; Ph.D., U. Rochester, 1968; m. George H. Cladis, Dec. 29, 1962; children—Harrison Moule, Franklyn Paul. Chargée de Recherche, Physique des Solides, U. Paris-South, Orsay, France, 1969-72; research physicist tech. staff Bell Labs., Murray Hill, N.J., 1972—. Mem. Am. Phys. Soc. Contbr. articles on physics to sci. jours. Home: 27 Beacon Rd Summit NJ 07901 Office: 600 Mountain Av Murray Hill NJ 07970

CLAFFORD, PATRICIA MARY WISE (MRS. JEAN HERBERT CLAFFORD), lectr., writer; b. Gridley, Ill., Aug. 6, 1907; d. Daniel Wellesley and Mary-Constance (Bateman) Wise; student Northwestern U. Medill Sch. Journalism, 1945-48; m. Jean Herbert Clafford, June 8, 1925 (dec. Apr. 1970); children—Kenneth Wellesley, Arthur Herbert. Critique staff Northwestern U., 1946-48; program cons. radio sta. WBBM, Chgo., 1958-60; contbr. poetry and fiction to Chgo. Daily News, Hearst Syndicate, Chgo. Tribune, Curtis Publs., Reader's Digest, Good Housekeeping, various mags., newspapers, jours., 1933—; lectr. personality power, 1948—; poetry editor and weekly writer Hinton (Okla.) Record; feature writer various publs., 1962—. Recipient award for sonnet Ill. Fedn. Women's Clubs, 1948, for poem, 1948, Iota Sigma Epsilon award of merit, 1966, 68, 69. Mem. Nat. Soc. Arts and Letters (v.p. Chgo. 1948-49, 62-63; lit. chmn. 1958-59; TV-radio chmn. 1961-62, 64-65; drama chmn., lit. chmn. Evanston chpt. 1968-69; now poet laureate Evanston chpt.), Nat. League Am. Pen Women (v.p. Chgo. 1948-49; chmn. short story, poetry and lecture divs. 1951-54; award for Even the Wind, 1950, award for poem nat. orgn. 1948), Women's Lit. Soc. Chgo. (hon.), Internat. Platform Assn., Pegasus Writers Forum (co-founder 1946; pres. 1948-49), Iota Sigma Epsilon (awards of merit 1952, 54, 56, 60, 62, 64, 67-73), Women in Communications. Episcopalian. Author: (poetry) Even the Wind, 1949. Home: 6158 N Hamilton Av Chicago IL 60659

CLAIRE, COLLEEN MARION (MRS. GUY KING CLAIRE), lawyer; b. Tucson, Nov. 18, 1931; d. Fred William and M. Marion (Pennington) Koerner; B.S., U. So. Cal., 1952, LL.B., 1955; m. Guy King Claire, July 15, 1955. Admitted to Cal. bar, 1957; mem. firms Lawler, Felix & Hall, Los Angeles, 1957-65, Rutan & Tucker, Santa Ana, Cal., 1965—. Lectr. probate adminstrn. and inheritance tax Cal. Continuing Edn. of Bar, 1969—; mem. Cal. Atty. Gen.'s vol. adv. com., 1971—. Named Better Bus. Girl, U. So. Cal. Sch. Commerce, 1952. Mem. Am., Orange County (dir., chmn. probate and trust law com. 1969, 71, 72, 73) bar assns., Cal. State Bar (com. on probate and trust law), Beta Gamma Sigma. Clubs: Big Canyon Country, Irvine Coast Country, Balboa Bay (Newport Beach, Cal.). Home: 1907 Sabrina Terrace Corona del Mar CA 92625 Office: 401 Civic Center Dr W Santa Ana CA 92702

CLAIRMONTE, GLENN (MRS. HAROLD SPENCER CLAIRMONTE), author; b. S.I., N.Y., May 14, 1896; d. Herman Adolph and Nina (Lambert) Gerbaulet; A.B. with honors, U. Cal. at Berkeley, 1923; m. Harold Spencer Clairmonte, Aug. 3, 1932 (dec.); 1 son, Stephen (dec.). Columnist, S.I. World, 1911-13; mem. staff N.Y. Mail, 1915-17; feature writer San Francisco Examiner, 1919-20; asst. editor Overland Monthly, San Francisco, 1923-24; free lance advt. writer, 1926-34; feature writer, book columnist Carmel (Cal.) Pine Cone, also creative writing tchr., 1945-51; free lance copy editor, N.Y.C., 1951-59; creative writing tchr. N.Y.C. Coll., 1958-59; in charge English dept. Williams Coll., Santa Fe, 1970—. Lectr. current lit. Downey, Cal., 1960—. Served with U.S. Naval Aviation, 1917-19; France. Recipient Gold Plaque for cultural contbn. Downey Adult Sch., 1971, Gold Plaque for Library Citizen of Year, Downey City Council, 1972, prizes for poetry U. Cal. Ann., 1923. Mem. Assn. Research and Enlightenment, Acad. Parapsychology and Medicine, Assn. Humanistic Psychology, Spiritual Frontiers Fellowship, Parapsychology Found., Am. Civil Liberties Union, U. Cal. Alumni Assn. (life). Author: John Sutter of California, 1953; Calamity Was the Name for Jane, 1959; (poetry) Carcassonne, 1923, Contours, 1931, enlarged edit., 1975; contbr. articles and poetry to popular mags. Home: 8109 3d St Downey CA 90241

CLAMAN, LEONI CAMILLE NEUMANN (MRS. IRVING CLAMAN), physician; b. N.Y.C., Oct. 5, 1901; d. Ignac and Flora (Vogel) Neumann; B.S., Columbia, 1922, M.D., 1924; m. Irving Claman, July 19, 1925; children—Stephanie Sigal, Henry N., Bettina Magnus, Victor N. Intern, Bellevue Hosp., 1924-25; researcher, Vienna, Austria, 1925, Berlin, Germany, 1926; practice medicine specializing in allergy, N.Y.C., 1934—; attending physician allergy N.Y. Infirmary, 1937—, cons. pediatric allergy, 1967—, organizer comprehensive care unit for asthmatic children, 1963, organizer phys. fitness program for asthmatic children, 1969; asso. attending physician allergy Roosevelt Hosp., 1942—. Chmn. com. pub. edn., Allergy Found. Am., 1963—, chmn. bd., 1974—. Active Met. Mus. Art, Mus. Modern Art, N.Y. Bot. Garden, N.Y. County Milk Commn. Recipient citation com. on Resettlement of Fgn. Physicians, 1951. Fellow A.M.A., N.Y. State Med. Soc., N.Y. Acad. Medicine, Am. Acad. Allergy; mem. Am. Med. Women's Assn., Women's Med. Assn. N.Y.C. (pres. 1950-54), N.Y. Allergy Soc. (pres. 1957-58), Am. Forestry Assn., Nat. Wildlife Assn., Hort. Soc. N.Y., Alumni Assn. Columbia P. & S. (century club). Home: 40 E 88th St New York City NY 10028 Office: 19 E 80th St New York City NY 10021

CLAPP, ELLEN RICHARDSON (MRS. CLYDE ALVIN CLAPP), social and civic worker; b. Chgo., July 2, 1897; d. Charles Fremont and Marcia (Stevens) Richardson; B.A., Wellesley Coll., 1919; M.A., Johns Hopkins U., 1926; m. Clyde Alvin Clapp, Aug. 7, 1928; stepsons—Roger A., Clyde M. Substitute tchr. High Sch., Evansville, Ind., 1920-21; with research-investment dept. Merc. Trust, St. Louis, summer 1922-23; resident social work South End House, Boston, 1923; Latin tchr. John Burroughs Sch., St. Louis, 1923-24; med. social worker Johns Hopkins Hosp., 1926-28; dir. nat. bd. YWCA, N.Y.C., 1949-61, mem. world service council, 1961—. Exec. com. chmn. Md. State for Wellesley Coll. Alumnae Fund; mem. pres.'s resources council Wellesley Coll., 1973—; chmn. Balt. U.S.O. Council, 1942-43; bd. dirs. Balt. Symphony Orch. Assn.; trustee Balt. Community Chest; chmn. schs. com. Balt. Civic Opera Co., Inc.; Women's Aux., Johns Hopkins Hosp. Bd. mgrs. Bryn Mawr Sch.; mem. Wellesley Coll. Alumni Council. Mem. YWCA (dir.), Women's Civic League Balt. (dir.), Md. Hist. Soc., Md. Acad. Sci. Presbyn. (ruling elder V.P. Ch. U.S.A.) Clubs: Johns Hopkins Faculty Gibson Island, Hamilton Street. Home: 100 W University Pkwy Baltimore MD 21210

CLAPP, MAUD MILLICENT (MRS. EUGENE H. CLAPP 2D), artist, bus. exec.; b. Kealakekua, Hawaii, Feb. 13, 1916; d. William H. and Maud (Johnstone) Greenwell; B.A. Stanford, 1936; student Cal. Sch. Fine Arts; m. Eugene H. Clapp II, Apr. 10, 1943; children—Eugene H. III, Candace M. Paintings exhibited in San Francisco, Monterey, Cal., Marblehead, Boston, Nantucket Wellesley and Springfield, Mass., Mus. Fine Arts, Boston, Hawaii, elsewhere. Vice pres., asst. clk., asst. sec.-treas. Penobscot Capitol Investment Co., also dir., trustee, v.p., sec. Pine Tree Co., trustee v.p. King Spruce Co.; past-pres., dir. Ind. Investors Co. Corp. Mem. Childrens Hosp., Boston; bd. dirs. Robert B. Brigham Hosp. Mem. Wellesley Soc. Artists (asst. treas., dir.). Address: 78 Arnold Rd Wellesly Hills MA 02181

CLAPS, ALBINA ANGELA (MRS. MICHAEL A. PAGLIA), pediatrician; b. N.Y.C., Sept. 13, 1922; d. Vincent Marie and Marie Louise (Claps) Claps; B.A., Hunter Coll., 1943; M.D., N.Y. Med. Coll., 1951; m. Michael A. Paglia, May 5, 1956; children—Anne Marie, Susan, Arnold. Intern, Lenox Hill Hosp., 1951-52; resident Charles Chapen Hosp., 1952, Lenox Hill Hosp., 1952-54; fellow in pediatric cardiology N.Y.U.-Bellevue Med. Center, 1954-56; practice medicine, specializing in pediatric cardiology, S.I., N.Y.; dir. pediatrics St. Vincent's Med. Center, S.I., 1956—; cons. pediatrics-cardiologist N.Y.C. Dept. Health, 1958—; asso. prof. clin. pediatrics N.Y.U. Med. Sch. Fellow Am. Acad. Pediatrics. Home: 47 Eddy St Staten Island NY 10301 Office: 355 Bard Av Staten Island NY 10310

CLARIDGE, JUNIETTA CHILDERS (MRS. ALLEN HUGH CLARIDGE), educator, asso. exec.; b. Safford, Ariz., Jan. 16, 1947; d. Rollie Thomas and Marjorie Ann (Cole) Childers; A.A. with honors, Eastern Ariz. Coll., 1967; B.S. with honors, No. Ariz. U., 1970; m. Allen Hugh Claridge, July 29, 1966; children—Thomas Hugh, Delbert Allen. Tchr. elementary sch., Thatcher, Ariz., 1972—; mem. Eastern Ariz. Museum and Hist. Soc., 1971—, pres., 1972—. Dir. Christmas lighting contest Pima C. of C., 1971, 72. Mem. Ariz. Hist. Soc., Brigham Young U. Archaeol. Soc. Mem. Ch. of Jesus Christ of Latter-day Saints. Home: 124 W Center St Pima AZ 85543 Office: 2 N Main St Pima AZ 85543

CLARK, ADELE JEANNE ADAIR (MRS. JACK W. CLARK), lawyer; b. Alhambra, Cal., Nov. 15, 1935; d. Harvey Bruce and Margaret (Mulholland) Adair; LL.B. cum laude, Western State U., 1971; m. Jack W. Clark, June 19, 1953; children—Bruce W., Kimberly Ann. Admitted to Cal. bar, 1972; co-founder, dir. tchr. Write-Way Bar Rev., Anaheim, 1971—; individual practice law, Newport Beach, 1972-73; partner Clark & Hamilton, Anaheim, 1973—. Mem. Am., Orange County bar assns., State Bar Cal. Home: 1739 Tradewinds Lane Newport Beach CA 92660 Office: 1681 W Broadway Suite V Anaheim CA 92802

CLARK, ALFRIEDA SORRELS (MRS. M.C. CLARK), librarian; b. Gloster, Miss., Dec. 5, 1935; d. Iddo Lyle and Ernestine Evelyn (Poole) Sorrels; A.A., S.W. Miss. Jr. Coll., 1955; B.S., U. So. Miss., 1957; m. M.C. Clark, Mar. 8, 1963. Asst. circulation librarian U. So. Miss., 1957-58; librarian, Jefferson Mil. Coll., Washington, Miss., 1958-59; circulation librarian Hinds Jr. Coll., Raymond, Miss., 1961; cataloger Research Center Library, Waterways Expt. Sta., Vicksburg, Miss., 1961, cataloger library br. 1962-64, head cataloging dept., 1964-73, chief tech. processing sect. library br. Tech. Information Center, 1973—; librarian, Jefferson High Sch., Fayette, Miss., 1961-62. Mem. Fed. Women's Program Com., 1971—. Recipient Quality Increase award U.S. Army Engr. Waterways Expt. Sta., 1970. Mem. Am. Bus. Women's Assn., D.A.R., Miss. Library Assn. Baptist. Home: 206 Enchanted Dr Vicksburg MS 39180 Office: PO Box 631 Vicksburg MS 39180

CLARK, ALICE THOMPSON, educator; b. Oneida Station, Ida., Mar. 2, 1926; d. Melvin Billings and Hazel Kirk (Justesen) Thompson; B.S., U. Utah, 1947; M.S., Brigham Young U., 1960, Ph.D., 1965; m. Selby Gamette Clark, Mar. 21, 1947 (div. July 1962); children—Frederick Selby, Sherrie Ellen, Gordon Thomas, Terrence Andrew, Laurie Anne, Riley Gamette. Tchr., McKinley Sch., Salt Lake City, 1947-48, Arsonal Sch., New Brighton, Minn., 1948-49; asso. prof. U. N.D., Grand Forks, 1965—, chmn. psychology dept., 1974—. Psychol. cons. Mental Retardation Center for Adults, Grand Forks, 1965—. Mem. Am., N.D. (state pres. 1973-74), Midwest psychol. assns., Council for Advancement Psychol. Professions and Scis. (N.D. chmn.), Am. Assn. U. Profs., Am. Assn. U. Women, Valley Mental Health Assn., Phi Kappa Phi, Psi Chi, Pi Lambda Theta, Alpha Phi (dir. 1972—). Home: 622 23d Av S Grand Forks ND 58201

CLARK, ALMA BETH, educator; b. Lecompte, La., June 3, 1923; d. Eddie C. and Lily (Earnest) Clark; B.S., La. State U., 1944; M.S., U. Tenn., 1947; Ph.D., Cornell U., 1961. Tchr. Dutchtown (La.) High Sch., 1944-45; instr., asst. prof. home econs. La. State U., Baton Rouge, La., 1947-59; with The Ford Found., Karachi, Pakistan, 1954-56; adviser Coll. of Home Econs. Karachi, also Okla. State U., 1961-63; asso. prof. La. State U., Baton Rouge, La., 1963-64; prof., dir. Sch. Home Econs., La. State U., 1964—. Mem. Family Ct. adv. com., Baton Rouge, 1968-69. Mem. Am. Home Econs. Assn. (vice chmn. Family Econs.-Home Mgmt. sect. 1967-69; mem. resolutions com. 1966-68; chmn. nominating com. 1970), La. Home Econs. Assn. (pres. 1971-72), So. Regional Research Adminstrn. of Home Econs. (chmn. 1967-69), Conf. La. Colls. and Univs. (chmn. home econs. sect. 1967-68), Nat. Assn. Extension Home Economists (adv. council 1972-74), Nat. Assn. State Univs. and Land Grant Colls. (commn. home econs. 1971-73), Phi Upsilon Omicron, Omicron Nu, Phi Kappa Phi, Pi Lambda Theta, Gamma Sigma Delta. Club: Pilot of Baton Rouge (pres. 1971-72).

CLARK, ANN LIVEZEY (MRS. MARSHALL F. CLARK), educator; b. Bel Air, Md., Nov. 27, 1913; d. Jacob O. and Florence L. (Everitt) Livezey; diploma, Md. Gen. Hosp. Sch. Nursing, 1935; B.S., Seton Hall U., 1953; M.A., N.Y. U., 1957; m. Marshall F. Clark, May 25, 1937. Supr. Mountainside Hosp., Montclair, N.J., 1939-54; supr. obstetric nursing Margaret Haque Maternity Hosp., Jersey City, 1954-55; faculty Rutgers U., Newark, 1955-70, prof., chmn. dept. maternal child nursing, 1955-70; prof. nursing U. Hawaii, Honolulu, 1970-73. Pres., Bd. of Nursing, State of N.J., 1969-70. Mem. Nat. League of Nursing, Am. Nurses Assn. (vice chmn. maternal child health div. practice 1972—), Sigma Theta Tau. Author: Leadership Technique in Expectant Parent Education, 1962, 2d edit., 1973; (with others) Patient Studies in Maternal and Child Nursing, 1966. Contbr. articles to profl. jours. Home: Apt 1536 1777 Ala Moana Honolulu HI 96815

CLARK, ANNA LUCILLE (MRS. GEORGE WILLIAM CLARK), clergywomen, educator; b. Chgo., Aug. 29, 1914; d. Ralph Sellon and Catherine Veronica (Ryan) Van Valkenburgh; certificate Central Bible Coll., 1938; B.S., Bethany Bible Coll., 1969; M.S. in Guidance and Counseling, Southwestern Mo. State U., 1973; m. George William Clark, Dec. 14, 1930 (dec. Apr. 1966); children—Georganne (Mrs. Robert Heslen), Carol (Mrs. John D. Compton), David William. Ordained to ministry Assemblies of God, 1945; co-pastor chs. Elgin, Ill., Blue Island, Ill., Des Plaines, Ill., Galesburg, Ill., Rock Island, Ill., 1938-66; fgn. missionary St. Anna, El Salvador, also Guatemala City, Guatemala, Brit. Honduras, 1945-52; dean women Bethany Bible Coll., Santa Cruz, Cal., 1967-69; dean women Evangel Coll., Springfield, Mo., 1969-73, counselor, coordinator ednl. devel. lab., 1973—. Vol., Fed. Med. Prison, 1972—. Mem. Mo. Guidance Assn., Nat. Assn. Women Deans and Counselors. Home: 302B N Burton Springfield MO 65802

CLARK, BARBARA CAMPBELL (MRS. AMOS OLIVIA CLARK), library adminstr.; b. Elizabethtown, N.C., May 10, 1933; d. Norman Alexander and Eva Lillian (Gooden) Campbell; B.S., U. N.C., 1955; M.A. in Edn., East Carolina U., 1969, M.L.S., 1973; postgrad. N.C. State U., 1973—; m. Amos Olivia Clark, Oct, 21, 1955; children—Lisa Olivia, Kevin Amos, David Campbell. Asst. home demonstration agt. Craven County, N.C., 1955-58; asst. mgr. Gilbert Addams Cafeteria, Duke U. dining halls, Durham, N.C., 1960-61; teaching fellow Library Sci. dept. East Carolina U., Greenville, N.C., 1968-69, guest lectr., 1969-73; head librarian Pitt. Tech. Inst., Greenville, 1969-70, library dir., 1970-72, dir. library resources, 1972—. Mem. Am., N.C. Southeastern library assns., N.C. Community Coll. Assn., Learning Resources N.C. Community Coll. Adult Edn. Assn., N.C. Assn. Educators, N.C., Am. vocational assns., Kappa Delta Pi. Home: 2007 Sherwood Dr Greenville NC 27834 Office: Box 7007 Pitt Technical Institute Greenville NC 27834

CLARK, BETTIE ILEANA GRAVES (MRS. ROSS JAMES CLARK), pediatrician; b. Mt. Holly, N.J., Feb. 12, 1927; d. Norman Norwood and Edna (Stanley) Graves; B.S., Morgan State Coll., 1949; M.D., Howard U., 1954; M.P.H., Johns Hopkins, 1973; m. Ross James Clark, Sept. 4, 1953; children—Ross James, Patricia Leigh, Robyn Marie. Intern, D.C. Gen. Hosp., 1954-55, resident in pediatrics, 1955-57, vis. staff, 1957-60; Pediatric med. officer D.C. Dept. Pub. Health, Washington, 1960—; asst. clin. prof. pediatrics Howard U., Washington; mem. staff Freedmen's Hosp., Washington. Diplomate Am. Bd. Pediatrics. Fellow Am. Acad. Pediatrics; mem. Med. Soc. D.C., Pan Am. Med. Assn., Alpha Kappa Alpha. Contbr. articles to med. jours. Address: 5045 Millwood Lane NW Washington DC 20016

CLARK, BETTINA, purchasing exec.; b. S.I., N.Y., Sept. 26, 1941; d. John B. and Teresa B. (Baker) Clark; B.A., Cedar Crest Coll., 1963. Asst. buyer Peck & Peck, N.Y.C., 1963-66; asst. buyer J.C. Penney Co., N.Y.C., 1966-72, buyer, 1972—. Home: 610 Victory Blvd Staten Island NY 10301 Office: 1301 Av of Americas New York City NY 10019

CLARK, BEVERLY BENZ, county ofcl.; b. Syracuse, N.Y., Sept. 23, 1919; d. Charles J. and Maryann (Schrader) Benz; student Syracuse U., 1937-38; B.S., Cornell U., 1944; M.Ed., U. Md., 1965; m. Duane W. Clark, Sept. 14, 1941 (div. 1968); children—Duane W. II, Christopher Gleason. Pres.-dir. Community Nursery Sch., Silver Spring, Md., 1949-51; dir. ednl. Information Service, Silver Spring, 1951-55; counselor low-achieving students Counseling Center, U. Md., College Park, Md., 1963-65, coordinator criminal justice programs, curriculum adviser U. Coll., 1969-73; personnel and mgmt. analyst U.S. AEC, Washington, 1965-67; edn. and tng. coordinator div. personnel, 1965-66; dean women Washington Coll., Chestertown, Md., 1967-69; exec. dir. Commn. for Women Prince George's County, Md., 1973—. Mem. steering com. Md. Gov.'s Commn. on Law Enforcement; chmn. World Day Prayer, Silver Spring Council Chs., 1949; liaison to Women's League, Chestertown, Md., 1967-69; mem. Montgomery and Prince George's Counties Status of Women Com., 1971-72; active various other community activities. Mem. Am. Assn. U. Profs., Nat., Regional assns., women deans and counselors, Am. (senator), Md. (citation for meritorious service 1969), personnel and guidance assns., Am., Md. (v.p. 1968-69, pres. elect 1969, pres. 1970—) coll. personnel assns., Am. Assn. U. Women (corp. del. 1967-69). Producer radio program Designed for Women sta. WGTS-FM. Clubs: Chestertown Yacht and Country; Argyle Country; Cornell Women's (pres. 1952-54); Cornell (dir. 1954-58 Washington); Embassy Wives (v.p. Buenos Aires). Home: 10649 Weymouth St Bethesda MD 20014 Office: Commn Women Courthouse Upper Marlboro MD 20870

CLARK, CLARA ANN (MRS. GEORGE MERLE CLARK), real estate broker; b. Muskegon, Mich., Apr. 3, 1918; d. Ernest and Ella Jane (Waybill) Crooks; student Pasadena City Coll., 1953-54; m. George Merle Clark, Sept. 23, 1939; 1 son, Craig. Clk., Mich. Consol. Gas Co., Detroit, 1936-39, Ford & Lincoln Mercury dealers, Detroit, and City Lincoln Mercury, Pasadena, Cal., 1946-49; with Beach-Flaaten Realty, 1954-62; owner Clara Clark Realty, Pasadena and Sierra Madre, Cal., 1962—. Mem. Pasadena (dir. 1969-70), Arcadia bds. realtors and multiple listing service, Delta Theta Chi. Mem. Christian and Missionary Alliance Ch. Home: 1165 Pine Bluff Dr Pasadena CA 91107 Office: 373 W Sierra Madre Blvd Sierra Madre CA 91024 also 3820 E Colorado Blvd Pasadena CA 91107

CLARK, DORIS V., chem. co. exec.; b. Sherman, Ky., Jan. 11, 1912; d. Thomas Webb and Clara Belle (Vest) Clark; A.B., Randolph-Macon Woman's Coll., 1931; M.S., Washington U., St. Louis, 1932; postgrad. U. Cin., 1933-35. Chief chemist Indo Vin, Inc., Cin., 1936-37, Century Chemists, Williamstown, Ky., 1937-41; chemist DuBois Co., Cin., 1941-42, indsl. sales promotion, 1946-50, dir. research, 1950-65, asst. v.p., dir. research DuBois div. W. R. Grace & Co., Inc., 1965-67, v.p. devel., 1967-71; v.p. bus. devel. DuBois div. Chemed Corp. subsidiary W.R. Grace & Co., 1971—. Active A.R.C. Bd. dirs. Grant County Hosp. Served to capt. WAC, 1942-46. Mem. Am. Legion, Am. Chem. Soc., Soc. Am. Mgmt., Soap and Detergent Assn., Chem. Specialties Mfg. Assn. (chem. exec. bd. detergent and cleaning compound div., bd. govs.), Gamma Phi Beta, Sigma Xi. Clubs: Altrusa, Woman's. Home: N Main St Williamstown KY 41097

CLARK, EDITH CUMMIN (MRS. JOE HALLER CLARK), sch. bd. pres.; b. Jackson, Mich., May 17, 1916; d. Gaylord Church and Hazel Edith (Carr) Cummin; B.A., Vassar Coll., 1939; M.A., Columbia, 1947; m. Joe Haller Clark, Sept. 13, 1947; children—William C., James G., G. Thomas. Tchr., Belmont (Mass.) Day Sch., 1940-43, Greenwich Pub. Schs., 1943-44, Temple Nursery Sch., Westwood, N.J., 1957-58; mem. Woodcliff Lake (N.J.) Bd. Edn., 1968—, pres., 1973—. Charter mem. Youth Guidance Council, Woodcliff Lake, 1968—. Active League Women Voters, Woodcliff Lake Democratic Club. Served to lt. (j.g.) USNR, 1944-46. Home: 25 Clinton Pl Woodcliff Lake NJ 07675

CLARK, ELIZABETH ALICE, radiologist; b. Auburn, Ind. Feb. 6, 1916; d. George Leroy and Jessie Katherine (Aber) Clark; B.A. DePauw U., 1937; M.D., U. Mich., 1940 ; m. John Jerrard Halbert, Nov. 14, 1948; children—Susan, Judith, Charles. Intern Wis. Gen. Hosp., Madison, 1940-42, resident, 1942-45; instr. radiology U. Wis. Med. Sch. at Madison, 1945-47, asst. prof., 1947-48; radiologist, Duluth, Minn., 1949—; cons. radiologist Moose Lake (Minn.) State Hosp., 1966-71; mem. staff Miller-Owan Hosp., Duluth. Founder Duluth City Mental Health Com., 1955, pres., 1959-61; mem. Arrowhead Regional Planning Council for Health Facilities and Services, 1967-73. Bd. dirs. Duluth Welfare Council, 1964-70, Arrowhead Regional Planning Council for Health Facilities and Services, 1967—, United Way Greater Duluth, 1971—, Human Resources Planning Coalition, 1972—. Diplomate Am. Bd. Radiology. Mem. A.M.A., Am. Coll. Radiology, Radiol. Soc. N. Am., Sigma XI, Alpha Omega Alpha. Presbyn. Home and Office: 408 Leicester Av Duluth MN 55803

CLARK, ELSIE MARIE KUNKEL (MRS. CHARLIE C. CLARK), county agt.; b. Kress, Tex., Feb. 17, 1921; d. Oscar Theodore and Mary Sophina (Buhrkuhl) Kunkel; B.S., N.M. State U., 1942; M.Home Econs., Ore. State U., 1971; m. Charlie C. Clark, July 27, 1944; children—Cheryl (Mrs. Roger Hockett), Betty Anne (Mrs. Byron Ness). Tchr. home econs., Grenville, N.M., 1942-43; county extension agt., Carlsbad, N.M., 1943-44, 53-60, Dallas, Ore., 1960—. Recipient Rural Service award Office Econ. Opportunity, 1967; Service award U.S. Dept. Agr., 1972. Mem. Am. Home Econs. Assn., Am. Bus. Women's Assn., Nat. (recipient Distinguished Service award 1968, Florence Hall award 1966), Ore. (pres. 1966-68) assns. extension home economists, Omicron Nu. Home: 1214 Clay St Dallas OR 97338 Office: Box 469 Dallas OR 97338

CLARK, ESTHER FRANCES (MRS. JOHN H. CLARK, JR.), lawyer; b. Phila., Aug. 29, 1929; d. John and Lucy (Scapula) Giaccio; B.A., Temple U., 1950; J.D., Rutgers U., 1955; m. John H. Clark, Jr.,

June 12, 1954; 1 dau., Jacqueline. Admitted to Pa. bar, 1956, since practiced in Chester. Lectr., Pa. Bar Inst., 1973—. Mem. S.E. Pa. regional council Gov.'s Justice Commn., 1973—; mem. adv. com., adminstrn. justice div. Nat. Urban League, 1973—. Solicitor, County Council Democratic Com. of Delaware County, Pa., 1973—. Mem. adv. bd. Project Prepare, Widener Coll., 1972—. Recipient Citizenship award Chester N.A.A.C.P., 1973. Mem. Am., Pa. (chmn. com. on youth edn. 1973), Delaware County bar assns., Am. Trial Lawyers Assn., Delaware County Legal Assistance Assn. (dir. 1972—, pres. bd. dirs. 1974—), Delaware County Black Policeman's Assn. (solicitor 1972-74), Soroptimists. Roman Catholic. Asso. editor Rutgers U. Law Rev., 1954-55. Home: 207 Knoll Rd Wallingford PA 19086 Office: Fidelity-Chester Bldg Chester PA 19013

CLARK, EUGENIE, marine biologist, ichthyologist; b. N.Y.C., May 4, 1922; B.A., Hunter Coll., 1942; M.S., N.Y.U., 1946, Ph.D. in Zoology (Pacific Sci. Bd. fellow), 1950; m. Hideo Umaki, 1942; m. 2d, Illas Konstantinu, 1951; children—Hera, Aya, Tak, Niki; m. 3d, Chandler Brossard, 1966; m. 4th, Igor Klatzo, 1969. Research asst. ichthyology Scripps Inst. Oceanography, 1946-47, N.Y. Zool. Soc., 1947-48; animal behavior Am. Mus. Natural History, 1948-49, research asso., 1950—; instr. Hunter Coll., 1954; exec. dir. marine biology Cape Haze Marine Lab., Sarasota, Fla., 1955-67; research asso., mem. bd. dirs. Mote Marine Lab., 1967—; asso. prof. City U. N.Y., 1967-68; asso. prof. dept. zoology U. Md., 1968-73, prof., 1973—; cons. shark research panel Am. Inst. Biol. Scis., 1960-70; research asso. New Eng. Inst. Med. Research, 1956-72; panel mem. oceanography and earth sci. sect. NSF; vis. scholar Coll. Center of Finger Lakes, 1966. Recipient Alumna award Hunter Coll., 1952, named to Hall of Fame, 1972; recipient Nogi award Underwater Soc. Am., 1965; Golden Plate award Am. Acad. Achievement in Sci., 1966; AEC fellow, 1950; Fulbright scholar, Egypt, 1951; Saxton fellow, 1952; Breadloaf Writer's fellow, 1952. Mem. Am. Soc. Ichthyologists and Herpetologists (life), Soc. Women Geographers, Acad. Underwater Arts and Scis. (hon.), Am. Littoral Soc. (Dugan award 1969, v.p.), Internat. Assn. Profl. Diving Scientists (life), Gesellschaft fur Biologisches Aquarien und Terrarienkunde (hon.). Author: Lady With a Spear, 1953; The Lady and the Sharks, 1969. Research in Red Sea fishes, reproductive behavior of fishes, morphology and taxonomy of plectognath fishes, isolating mechanisms of poeciliid fishes, shark and garden eel behavior. Home: 7817 Hampden Lane Bethesda MD 20014 Office: Dept Zoology U Md College Park MD 20742

CLARK, EVELYN GAEBEL, editor; b. San Francisco, Aug. 22, 1907; d. Arthur Henry and Maud (Mason) Gaebel; student Louis Chalif Ballet Sch., 1920-24, Hunter Coll. Art Sch., 1946-47; children—Judith (Mrs. Richard N. McVity), Jacqueline (Mrs. James Gilmour Hill). Receptionist, sec. Walker & Gillete, architects, N.Y.C., 1927-31; owner Evelyn Clark Creations, toys, Larchmont, N.Y., 1942-46; editor Med. Soc. N.Y. State, Lake Success, 1947-74. Co-owner, v.p., dir. Arthur H. Gaebel, Inc., Syracuse, N.Y., 1946—. Republican vol. worker Larchmont Town Com., 1960-63. Episcopalian. Club: Twenty-Five Year of Medical Society State of N.Y. Home: 12 Ervilla Dr Larchmont NY 10538 Office: 420 Lakeville Rd Lake Success NY 11040

CLARK, FRANCES DYE (MRS. EDWARD S. CLARK), librarian; b. Spartanburg, S.C., July 23, 1922; d. William Ernest and Lucile (Shippey) Dye; B.A., Converse Coll., 1945; M.S. in L.S., State U. N.Y., 1960, postgrad., 1965; m. Edward S. Clark, Jan. 14, 1942; children—Edward Stephen, Randolph Shippey. English tchr., Cornwall (N.Y.) High Sch., 1945-47; librarian, Cornwall (N.Y.) Central High Sch., 1952-66; dir. sch. libraries Cornwall Central Sch. Dist., 1966—; audio visual coordinator Cornwall Central Sch. Dist., 1969—. Trustee Cornwall Pub. Library, 1963-70. Recipient fellowship Nat. Defense Edn. Act, 1965. Mem. N.E.A., Am., N.Y. (v.p. sch. libraries media sect. 19—), Orange County library assns., Sch. Librarians Southeastern N.Y. (pres. 1972-73), N.Y. State United Tchrs., N.Y. State Ednl. Communications Assn. Clubs: Book, Garden, Bridge (Cornwall). Home: 58 Laurel Av Cornwall NY 12518 Office: 122 Main St Cornwall NY 12518

CLARK, GEORGETTE ANTOINETTE HARPIN (MRS. JOHN L. CLARK), town ofcl.; b. New Bedford, Mass., Sept. 26, 1912; d. Oscar and Josephine (Guillette) Harpin; student pub. schs., New Bedford; m. John L. Clark, Oct. 11, 1947; Order clk. Colonial Candle Co., Hyannis, Mass., 1940-45; sr. clk. Wakefield (Mass.) Bd. Registrars, 1951-61; asst. town clk. Town of Wakefield, 1962-67, town clk., 1968—. Troop leader Girl Scouts U.S.A., Wakefield, 1948-51; driver Cape Cod chpt. A.R.C., Hyannis, 1942-45. Mem. Wakefield Profl. and Bus. Women's Club. Home: 276 Albion St Apt 22 Wakefield MA 01880 Office: 1 Lafayette St Wakefield MA 01880

CLARK, GERTRUDE JOSEPHINE, ry. equipment mfg. co. exec.; b. Chgo.; d. George W. and Helen (Cooper) Clark; grad. Moser Bus. Coll., 1937, Boulevard Modeling Sch., 1949; student Northwestern U., 1948-69, Central YMCA Coll., Chgo., 1969. Sec. Cardwell Westinghouse Co., Chgo., 1941-63, dir. advt., pub. relations, 1964—; also subsidiaries. Feature writer articles Chgo. Tribune, 1957—, Chgo. Daily News, 1969—, Greek Press, Chgo., 1962—. Mem. dialogue Recorded Mag. for Blind, Berwyn, Ill., 1969—. Bd. dirs. Friends of Lit., Chgo., 1969—. Recipient 2d pl. award Medill Sch. Journalism, Northwestern U. ann. short story contest, 1962. Mem. Nat. Secs. Assn. Chgo., Met. Bus. and Profl. Women's Club, Women's Advt. Club Chgo. (mem. membership com. 1968-69, chmn. scholarship com. 1970-71), Ill. Women's Press Assn., Women in Communications, Iota Sigma Epsilon (pres. 1967-68). Methodist (mem. adminstrv. bd., finance com.). Clubs: Zonta (dir. 1966-67); Chgo. Press (Chgo.); Toastmistress.

CLARK, HELEN EDITH, researcher, educator; b. Edam, Sask., Can., Feb. 4, 1912; d. Charles A. and Rhoda M. (Balfour) Clark; B.H. Sci., U. Sask., 1939; postgrad. Wash. State U., 1942-43; M.S., Ia. State U., 1945, Ph.D. in Nutrition, 1950. Came to U.S., 1942, naturalized, 1951. Tchr. home econs. high sch., B.C., 1939-42; teaching fellow Wash. State U., Pullman, 1942-43; research asst. Ia. State U., 1943-45, research asso., 1945-50; asst. prof., asso. prof. Kan. State U., 1950-54; asso. prof. foods and nutrition dept. Purdue U., Lafayette, Ind., 1954-59, prof., 1959—. Recipient Borden award Am. Home Econs. Assn., 1968; Centennial award Coll. Home Econs., Ia. State U., 1971; H.B. Schleman gold medallion Mortar Board, 1972; named Outstanding Educator Am., 1970. Fellow A.A.A.S.; mem. Am. (sect. chmn.), Ind. (div. chmn.) home econs. assns., Am. Dietetic Assn., Ind. Nutrition Council (chmn.), Am. Inst. Nutrition, Am. Bd. Nutrition, N.Y. Acad. Scis., Sigma Xi, Omicron Nu, Sigma Delta Epsilon, Iota Sigma Pi, Phi Kappa Phi. Presbyn. Contbr. articles profl. jours. Research on protein and amino acid requirements of man. Home: Apt A 414 Vine St West Lafayette IN 47906 Office: Foods and Nutrition Dept Purdue U Lafayette IN 47907

CLARK, JOAN ROBINSON, physicist; b. Madison, Wis., Jan. 22, 1920; d. Daniel Sommer and Oma (Glasburn) Robinson; student Ind. U., 1935-36, U. Pa., 1942-43; B.A. magna cum laude, Barnard Coll., 1945; Ph.D., Johns Hopkins, 1958; m. Charles Richard Clark, Oct. 7, 1939 (dec. July 1960); 1 son, Dennis Rayleigh (dec.). Research aide Eastern Regional Research lab. Dept. Agr., Phila., 1943; math. asst. Carbide & Carbon Chems. Corp., N.Y.C., 1945; project engr. Brown Instruments div. Mpls.-Honeywell Regulator Co., Phila., 1946-49; research asso. Inst. Cancer Research, Phila., 1949-53; physicist U.S. Geol. Survey, Washington, 1953-72, phys. scientist, dep. chief for geochemistry, 1972—. co-investigator Apollo lunar minerals, 1969-72. Fulbright research grantee Sch. Chemistry. U. Sydney (Australia), 1962. Fellow Mineral. Soc. Am. (sec. 1972—), Washington Acad. Scis., Geol. Soc. Am.; mem. A.A.A.S., Mineral. Assn. Can., Geochem. Soc., Am. Crystallographic Assn., Am. Phys. Soc., Geol. Soc. Washington, Am. Geophys. Union, Phi Beta Kappa, Pi Beta Phi. Contbr. articles on crystal structures and crystal chemistry to sci. jours. Home: 2401 H St NW Washington DC 20037 Office: Nat Center Stop 906 Reston VA 22092

CLARK, LAVERNE HARRELL (MRS. L.D. CLARK), author, photographer; b. Smithville, Tex., June 6, 1929; d. James Boyce and Isabella Ocie (Bunte) Herrell; B.A. Tex. Women's U., Denton, 1950; postgrad. Columbia U., 1951-54; M.A., U. Ariz., 1962; m. L.D. Clark, Sept. 15, 1951. Newspaper reporter, librarian Ft. Worth (Tex.) Press, 1950; staff sales-advt. dept. Columbia U. Press, N.Y.C., 1951-53; asst. promotion dept. Bulletin mag., Episcopal Diocese N.Y., N.Y.C., 1958-59; dir. poetry center U. Ariz., 1962-66. Speaking tour in Ariz. Indian schs. sponsored by Bur. Indian Affairs and Ariz. Commn. Arts, 1972; cons. Indian lore Conv. Nat. Council Tchrs. English, 1971. Represented in photographic studies U. Tex. Humanities Research Center, 1964, 70. Recipient 1st place folklore prize U. Chgo., 1967; Non-fiction award Nat. League Am. Pen Women, 1968, Fiction award, 1972, Best Informational Mag. Article award, 1974, Slide Lecture award, 1974; Distinguished Alumna award Tex. Woman's U., 1973. Am. Philos. Soc. research grantee, 1967, 69. Mem. Nat. League Am. Pen Women, Western Writers Am., Am. Folklore Soc., Soc. Southwestern Authors, Women in Communications (v.p. Alpha Pi chpt. 1950), Kappa Alpha Mu. Democrat. Episcopalian. Author: They Sang for Horses, 1966, paperback, 1971. Contbr. articles and reviews: Arizona and the West, Ariz. Quarterly, Ariz. English Bull., Am. Scandinavian Review, Bits and Pieces, Round-Up, Western Am. Lit. Photographs pub. in numerous mags., anthologies. Address: 4690 N Campbell Av Tucson AZ 85718

CLARK, LEE (SHARYLEE BRISCOE), TV exec.; b. Billings, Mont., Apr. 10, 1938; d. Glen Harold and Esther Emelia (Fatland) Van Schoyck; B.F.A., Tulsa U., 1971; m. Joe T. Briscoe, May 28, 1971; 1 son, Steve M. Clark. Producer, newscaster Midday Report, KOTV-TV, Tulsa, Okla., 1971-74; producer evening news, newscaster noon news KHOU-TV, Houston, 1974—. Mem. Nat. Orgn. for Women. Office: 1945 Allen Pkwy Houston TX 77019

CLARK, LILLIE REBECCA BROOME, furniture co. exec.; b. Greenville, S.C., Dec. 25, 1938; d. Claudis Lavester and Mae Jewell (Alexander) Broome; M.S., Extra Sensory Perception Lab., Los Angeles, 1971; grad. Famous Writers Sch., Westport, Conn., 1971; grad. LaForest Sch. Design, New Orleans, 1956; children—Sandra Ann, Mike Anthony. Exec. sec. Dumas Milner Corp., Jackson, Miss., 1959-62; mem. Miss. Bd. Water Commrs., 1962-64; advt. dir. Gravely Furniture Co., Ridgeway, Va., 1965—. Publicity dir. United Fund, 1968-69. Recipient Citizenship award C. of C., 1969. Mem. Assn. Research and Enlightenment. Home: 937 Colborn Rd Lee's Summit MO 64063 Office: Unity School of Christianity Unity Village MO 64063

CLARK, LINDA MARIE, statistician, mathematician; b. Chgo., June 9, 1940; d. Harold Dean and Edith Mathilda (Nystrom) Clark; B.S., U. Mich., 1962; M.B.A., U. Chgo., 1969. Analyst biol. scis. computation center Billings Hosp., U. Chgo., 1962-65; dir. math., statis. services Armour & Co., Chgo., 1965-68; pres. LMC Cons. Co., Flossmoor, Ill., 1969—. Dir. Internat. Computer Edn. Corp. Mem. Am. Statis. Assn. (pres. Chgo. chpt. 1972-73, dir. 1971-74), A.A.A.S., Chgo. Assn. Commerce and Industry (dir.), Optical Soc. Am., U. Chgo. Alumni Council, P.E.O., Alpha Chi Omega. Home: 1127 Dartmouth Rd Flossmoor IL 60422

CLARK, LORRAINE HOWARD (MRS. BANKS WORTH CLARK), educator; b. Knoxville, Tenn., Dec. 1, 1924; d. Thomas Oliver and Mary Agnes (Smith) Howard; B.A., Duke, 1948; M.S., E. Tex. State U., 1966, Ph.D. (Teaching fellow), 1969; m. Banks Worth Clark, Sept. 4, 1942; children—Banks Jefferson, Roderick Howard, Victoria Jean. Adminstrv. dir. Bur. Testing and Guidance, Duke, 1948-50; girl's Work sec. Cone Meml. YMCA, Greensobo, N.C., 1950-52; adj. prof. edn. research, lit. E. Tex. State U., Dallas, 1968—. Cons. adult edn., 1967—, preretirement edn., 1969—. Pres., W.E. Truax Scholarship Found., 1971, 74. Mem. Am., Tex. personnel and guidance assns., Adult Edn. Assn., Am. Psychol. Assn., Gerontological Soc., Tex. (lobbyist 1972—), Nat. (asst. regional rep. 1972—) ret. tchrs. assns., Am. Assn. Ret. Persons, Dallas Zonta. Research in life-styles ret. tchrs., needs older Ams., psychophysiol. aspects of empathy. Home: 5338 Drane Dallas TX 75209

CLARK, M. CORINNE, educator; b. Ottawa, Ill., Sept. 28, 1923; d. Roger H. and Marcia (Brown) Clark; B.S., Ill. State U., 1947; M.A., Columbia Tchrs. Coll., 1950; Dr. Phys. Edn., Ind. U., 1968. Tchr. phys. edn. secondary sch., East Peoria, Ill., 1947-49, West Aurora High Sch., Aurora, Ill., 1950-51; supr. student tchrs. elementary and secondary sch., Kan. State Tchrs. Coll., Pittsburg, 1951-54; dept. chmn. Maine Twp. High Schs., Des Plaines and Park Ridge, Ill., 1954-66; coordinator phys. edn. for women U. Wis., Whitewater, 1966-69, prof. phys. edn., chmn. dept. health phys. edn. and recreation-women, 1969—. Served with WAVES, 1943-46. Mem. Nat., Wis. edn. assns., Am., Midwest (sec.-treas. 1967-72; pres. 1973-74), Ill. (dist. pres.), Wis. (div. v.p. 1969-70), Midwest assns. health phys. edn. and recreation, Sch. Health Assn., Nat., Midwest assns., phys. edn. for coll. women, Pi Lambda Theta, Tri-Sigma. Contbr. articles to profl. jours. Home: Route 3 Whitewater WI 53190

CLARK, MAMIE PHIPPS (MRS. KENNETH B. CLARK), child guidance specialist; b. Hot Springs, Ark., Oct. 18, 1917; d. Harold H. and Katie (Smith) Phipps; B.S. magna cum laude, Howard U., 1938, M.S., 1939; Ph.D. (Rosenwald fellow), Columbia, 1944; m. Kenneth Bancroft Clark, Apr. 14, 1938; children—Kate Miriam, Hilton Bancroft. Research psychologist Am. Pub. Health Assn., N.Y.C., 1944-45, U.S. Armed Forces Inst., N.Y.C., 1945-46; exec. dir. Northside Center for Child Devel., N.Y.C., 1946—; dir. Am. Broadcasting Co. Cons. Operation Headstart, Office Econ. Opportunity. Bd. dirs. Mus. Modern Art, N.Y.C. Mission Soc., N.Y. Pub. Library; bd. dirs. Tchrs. Coll., Columbia U., Phelps Stokes Fund. Mem. Am. Psychol. Assn., Am. Assn. Orthpsychiatry, Phi Beta Kappa. Research and pubs. related to devel. of consciousness of self in Negro children. Home: 17 Pinecrest Dr Hastings-on-Hudson NY 10706 Office: 31 Central Park New York City NY 10026

CLARK, MARGARET ANN (MRS. EDGAR MCCLAIN NEPTUNE, JR.), govt. ofcl.; b. Akron, O., Jan. 30, 1923; d. Darwin Frank and Bessie (Brown) Clark; A.B., Syracuse U., 1945, M.D., 1949; m. Edgar McClain Neptune, Jr., Nov. 26, 1948; children—Darby Ann, Melissa. Intern, Woman's Coll. Hosp., Phila., 1949-50; resident Mass. Meml. Hosp., Boston, also Samuel Merritt Hosp., Oakland, Cal., 1950-53; practice medicine, specializing in anesthesiology, nr. Washington, 1953-63; with FDA, Rockville, Md., 1968—, div dir. Bur. Drugs, 1973—. Mem. Internat. Anesthesia Research Soc., Am. Soc. Anesthesiology, Alpha Epsilon Iota, Phi Mu. Home: 11921 Goya Dr Potomac MD 20854 Office: 5600 Fishers Lane Rockville MD

CLARK, MARGARET GOFF (MRS. CHARLES ROBERT CLARK), author; b. Oklahoma City, Mar. 7, 1913; d. Raymond Finla and Fanny Lorena (Church) Goff; B.S. in Edn., Buffalo State Tchrs. Coll., 1936; student Columbia, 1934; m. Charles Robert Clark, Sept. 2, 1937; children—Robert Allen, Marcia Almeda (Mrs. Stanford Noel). Adult edn. tchr., Niagara Falls N.Y., 1961-63; pub. sch. tchr., N.Y., 1933-39. Writer predominantly children's short stories, plays, poetry, books; lectr. schs., civic groups on writing, 1960—. Adopted by Seneca Indians, Akron, N.Y., 1962. Mem. Mystery Writers Am., Nat. League Am. Pen Women, Western N.Y. Assn. Profl. Women Writers, Alpha Delta Kappa, Delta Kappa Gamma (hon.). Author: The Mystery of Seneca Hill, 1961; The Mystery of the Buried Indian Mask, 1962; Mystery of the Marble Zoo, 1964; Mystery at Star Lake, 1965; Adirondack Mountain Mystery, 1966; Mystery of the Missing Stamps, 1967; Danger at Niagara, 1968; Freedom Crossing, 1969; Benjamin Banneker, 1971; Mystery Horse, 1972; Their Eyes on the Stars: Four Black Writers, 1973; John Muir, 1974. Home: 5621 Lockport Rd Niagara Falls NY 14305

CLARK, MARGARET THERESE (MRS. JOHN J. CLARK), educator; b. N.Y.C., July 28, 1925; d. James S. and Theresa C. (Gardella) Norton; B.A., Manhattanville, 1948; M.A., Columbia, 1953; Ph.D., N.Y. U., 1963; m. John J. Clark, July 1, 1965. Financial analyst Columbia Gas System, N.Y.C., 1952-62; economist Mobil Oil Corp., N.Y.C., 1962-68; lectr. Queens Coll., Flushing, N.Y., 1965-66; lectr. City Coll.-Baruch, N.Y.C., 1966-68; asso. prof. Pace Coll., N.Y.C., 1968-69; asso. prof. finance Villanova (Pa.) U., 1969—. Mem. Financial Mgmt. Assn. (exec. sec.). Contbr. articles to various publs. Home: 1704 Brigantine Av Brigantine NJ 08203 Office: Villanova University Villanova PA 19085

CLARK, MARGERY MARSTON, librarian; b. Manhattan, Kan., Oct. 30, 1926; d. Henry White and Helen Chase (Fisher) Marston; B.A., U. Del., 1948; M.S. in L.S., Catholic U. Am., 1962; div.; 1 dau., Shelley Marston. Interlibrary loan librarian Applied Physics Lab., Johns Hopkins, Balt., 1958-62; with Nat. Housing Center Library, Washington, 1962—, asso. librarian, 1966—. Mem. Spl. Libraries Assn. (past chmn. urban affairs sect. social scis. div.). Episcopalian. Home: 4523 Everett St Kensington MD 20795 Office: 15th and M Sts NW Washington DC 20005

CLARK, MARIA LOUISA GUIDISH, educator; b. Munhall, Pa., Dec. 22, 1926; d. Frank J. and Mary D. (Farkas) Guidish; B.S., U. Pitts., 1948, M.S., 1950; M.S., Carnegie Inst. Tech., 1964; postgrad. Ind. State U., 1962-63, U. Me., summer 1962, N.M. State U., summer 1964, San Diego (Cal.) State Coll., summer 1965, Carnegie-Mellon U., 1970; m. Daniel J. Clark, June 8, 1950 (dec.); children—Mary Sherry (dec.), Heather Anne, Danny, Erin. Owner, operator children's summer camp, 1959-62; instr. chemistry, biology Ogontz Jr. Coll., Phila., 1949-50; dir. research U. Ill., 1950-51; sci. tchr. Valley Sch. of Ligonier (Pa.), 1954-57; tchr. chemistry, physics, head sci. dept. Ligonier Valley Sr. High Sch., 1959-67; faculty sci. curriculum devel. Learning Research Devel. Center, Sch. Edn. and Dept. Devel. and Pub. Affairs, U. Pitts., 1967—; edn. cons. Pa. State U., 1966—; sci. edn. cons. U. Akron (O.), 1968—; cons. AEC, Washington, Learning Research Asso., N.Y., 1969—, D.C. Health Dept., 1961—, Pa. State Edn. Assn., 1971—, others. Leader, Girl Scouts U.S.A., 1953-58. Bd. dirs. Buhl Found. NSF fellow, 1964-66. Recipient award A.A.A.S., 1963, Medal of Honor Centro Studie Scambi Internationali, Rome. Mem. Am. Assn. Physics Tchrs., Nat. Sci. Tchrs. Assn., Pa. Sci. Tchrs. Assn., Ligonier Valley Tchrs. Assn. (pres. 1960), Internat. Platform Assn., Pi Lambda Theta. Democrat. Author: The Effects of Adrenalis Injections, 1949; The Hermatoencephalic Barrier, 1950; The True Book of Dinosaurs, 1955; You and How the World Began, 1957; Long, Long Ago, 1958; My Easy to Read Book of Dinosaurs, 1959; The Cat God, 1959; The True Encyclopedia of Science, 1963; Measuring the Wave Length of Light, 1964; You and Relativity, 1965; You and Electronics, 1966; Nutmeg, 1966; Fission and Fusion, 1969. Contbr. short stories and sci. articles to popular mags., trade and profl. jours. Address: 5564 Forbes Av Pittsburgh PA 15217

CLARK, MARJORIE AGNES RIGLER (MRS. JAMES A.G. CLARK), writer; b. Poole, Dorset, Eng., July 15, 1911; d. Albert Walter and Agnes Emma (Eyers) Rigler; student Multnomah Sch. of Bible, 1937-38; m. James A.G. Clark, Dec. 29, 1943 (dec. 1966); 1 son, James Douglas. With Royal Bank of Can., 1930-37; missionary, clk. consular office, Portuguese West Africa, 1939-44; writer Moody Inst. of Sci., West Los Angeles, 1956-65, Academy Films, Hollywood, 1960-61; writer Success with Youth, Tempe, Ariz., 1960—. Author: African Holiday, 1954; Seaview Adventures, 1956; The Link, 1956; Water Chase, 1956; The Silent Search, 1972; Captive on the Ho Chi Minh Trail, 1974. Contbr. articles, short stories, serials to various publs. Home: Astra Rd Rural Route 1 Comox BC Canada

CLARK, MARJORIE JUSTUS (MRS. ROYCE JACKSON CLARK), coll. librarian; b. Tallulah Falls, Ga., Jan. 19, 1929; d. Hugh Mandeville and Ruth Marie (Atkins) Justus; A.B., Piedmont Coll., 1948; M.L.S., Emory U., 1966; postgrad. U. Ga., summer 1950, Rutgers U., 1970, Kent State U., 1972; m. Royce Jackson Clark, June 3, 1948; 1 son, Stephen Scott. Tchr. pub. schs., Hall, Gwinnett, Atlanta, Ga., 1948-66; head librarian Gainesville (Ga.) Jr. Coll., 1966-73; head librarian, asst. prof. library sci. N. Ga. Coll., Dahlonega, 1973—. Chmn. acad. com. libraries U. System Ga., 1972-74. Mem. Southeastern, Ga. (sec. coll. and univ. sect. 1971-73) library assns., Ga. Assn. Educators, Am. Assn. U. Profs. Methodist. Home: Route 6 Box 271 Big Oak Farm Gainesville GA 30501 Office: North Ga Coll Dahlonega GA 30533

CLARK, MARTHA SPRINGER (MRS. WILLIAM J. CLARK), psychologist; b. Evanston, Ill., Feb. 16, 1910; d. George Ward and Klahr (Mead) Springer; B.Ed. (scholar), Nat. Coll. Edn., 1931; M.A. (scholar), Columbia, 1935; postgrad. U. Wis., 1960-70; m. William J. Clark, June 30, 1948; children—Peter Michael, Martha Danielle. Instr. Northrop Collegiate Sch., Mpls., 1931-33, Garden City (N.Y.) Schs., 1933-35, Cranbrook Schs., Bloomfield Hills, Mich., 1935-38; dir.-instr. U. Wis.-Oshkosh, 1938-39, Nat. Coll. Edn., Evanston, Ill., 1939-48; psychologist Mequon-Thiensville Schs., Mequon, Wis., 1960—. Dir. Shuttle Studio, Milw., 1948—. Mem. Nat. Assn. Sch. Psychologists, Wis. Sch. Psychologists Assn., Suburban Psychologists Assn. (sec. 1968-70). Home: 7930 N Lake Dr Milwaukee WI 53217 Office: Steffen Dr Mequon WI 53092

CLARK, MARY ROMAYNE SCHROEDER (MRS. DONALD ARTHUR CLARK), civic worker; b. Fergus Falls, Minn., Aug. 9, 1922; d. Christian Frederick and Dorothy Genevieve (Miller) Schroeder; B.A., Coll. St. Teresa, 1944; diploma fine arts Conservatory St. Cecelia, 1944; m. Donald Arthur Clark, Aug. 24, 1946; children—Donald Arthur, Anne Elizabeth, Christopher John. Instr., Ottumwa (Ia.) Heights Coll., 1944-46; instr. U. N.D., Grand Forks, 1946-48, Marquette U., Milw., 1948-52, Milw. Area Tech. Coll., 1962-66. Mem. com. on edn. U.S. Cath. Conf., Washington, 1971—; state vol. adviser Nat. Found., 1971—; mem. adv. bd. Sickle

Cell Disease Center, Deaconess Hosp., Milw., 1970-73; mem. nat. alumnae bd. Coll. St. Teresa, Winona, Minn., 1970—; mem. bd. edn. Archdiocese Milw., 1965-71, pres., 1967-71. Named Wis. Woman of Year, Wis. Cath. War Vets., 1963, Alumna of Year, Coll. St. Teresa, 1969. Mem. Archdiocesan Confraternity Christian Mothers (pres. 1961-63), Archdiocesan League Cath. Home and Sch. Assns. (pres. 1963-65), Archdiocesan Council Cath. Women (dist. pres. 1965-67), Internat. Fedn. Cath. Alumnae, Am. Assn. Univ. Women, Marquette U. Faculty Wives (pres. 1959). Home: 317 N Story Pkwy Milwaukee WI 53208

CLARK, SISTER MARY TWIBILL, educator; b. Phila.; d. Francis S. and Regina Holland (Twibill) Clark; B.A., Manhattanville Coll., 1939; M.A., Fordham U., 1952, Ph.D., 1955. Joined Soc. Sacred Heart, 1939; tchr., supr. studies secondary schs. Acad. Sacred Heart, Albany, Rochester, N.Y., N.Y.C., 1941-51; instr. Manhattanville Coll., Purchase, N.Y., 1951-53, asst. prof., 1953-57, asso. prof., 1957-61, prof. philosophy, 1961—. Cons. N.J. Dept. Edn., 1970-72; tchr. summer sch. U. San Francisco, 1971-74; adviser Social Action Secretariat, 1959-65. Postdoctoral fellow Yale, 1968-69. Mem. Internat. Metaphys. Soc., Am. Philos. Assn., Am. Cath. Philos. Assn. (mem. exec. council 1971—), Am. Assn. U. Profs., Religious Edn. Assn. Democrat. Roman Catholic. Author: Augustine, Philosopher of Freedom, 1959; Logic, 1963; Discrimination Today, 1966, Augustinian Personalism, 1970; An Aquinas Reader, 1972; The Problem of Freedom, 1973. Contbr. articles to profl. jours. Address: Manhattanville Coll Purchase NY 10577

CLARK, MAUREEN MORTON (MRS. BRUCE GUYTON CLARK), broadcasting exec.; b. McComb, Miss., Aug. 20, 1936; d. Bayless E. and Mary (Lewis) Morton; grad. high sch.; m. Bruce Guyton Clark, July 5, 1955; children—Cynthia, Bill, Caryl Ann. With Broadcast Service, Inc., McComb, Miss., 1954—, asst. mgr., 1970—. Pres. Otken P.T.A., McComb, 1970, McComb P.T.A. Council, 1973-74. Mem. McComb C. of C. (publicity chmn. 1972-73). Republican. Home: 601 Hart Rd McComb MS 39648 Office: PO Drawer E McComb MS 39648

CLARK, MAYBELLE, health services ofcl.; b. East Africa, Oct. 10, 1918; d. William Charles and Jessie Bell (Goodsmith) Terril; B.S., Northwestern U., 1938; R.N., Frances Payne Bolton Sch. Nursing, 1947; M.Nursing, Case Western Res. U., 1947; m. Robert C. Clark, Nov. 23, 1961. Nurse, VA hosps., Hines and Chgo., 1947-58; asst. dir. nursing Kaiser Hosp., Honolulu, 1958-65; exec. sec. health profl. bds., Honolulu, 1966—. Mem. Am. Nurses Assn., Nat. League Nursing, Northwestern U., Case Western Res. U. alumni assns. P.E.O. Methodist. Home: 1381-3 Hunakai Honolulu HI 96816 Office: PO Box 3469 Honolulu HI 96801

CLARK, MEREDITH KAYE PLIER (MRS. PHILIP C. CLARK), Republican nat. committeewoman; b. Oconto Falls, Wis., Jan. 14, 1927; d. Arnold W. and Hersa (Boyce) Plier; B.A., Lawrence Coll., 1948; student N.Y. Sch. Social Work, 1949; m. Philip C. Clark, June 24, 1950; children—James William, Meriweather Kaye. Dept. head stock Saks 5th Av., N.Y.C., 1948-49; psyciat. social worker Bklyn. State Hosp., 1949-50; clk. U.S. Govt., Washington, 1951-53; clk.-typist V.I. Telephone Co., St. Croix, 1956; receptionist, sec. V.I. law and ins. firm; v.p. Pentheny Ltd., 1973—. Mem. task force V.I. Comprehensive Health Planning Council, 1969; mem. St. Croix Bd. Appeals for Med. Assistance, 1972—. Treas. St. Croix br. Rep. Com. V.I., 1963-65; mem. Rep. Territorial Com. V.I., 1964—, sec., 1964-68; mem. V.I. Inauguration Com. for Pres. Nixon, V.I., Washington, 1969; Rep. committeewoman from V.I., publicity chmn. Rep. Women's Conf., 1968-72; adviser inaugural com. First Elected Gov. V.I., 1971; mem. arrangements com. Rep. Nat. Conv., 1972; mem. V.I. Finance Com. for Re-election Pres. Nixon, 1972; pres. St. Croix br. V.I. Rep. Party, 1974. Mem. Bus. and Profl. Women's Club (legislative chmn. Christiansted 1971-72, 73-74), Navy League U.S., Island Center of St. Croix, St. Croix Arts Council, St. Croix Diving Assn., League of Women Voters, Kappa Delta. Methodist. Club: Tennis (St. Croix). Home: Estate The Sight Box 788 Christiansted St Croix VI 00820

CLARK, PATSY SUE (MRS. JOHN DANDRIDGE CLARK), pub. relations exec.; b. Vernon, Tex., Aug. 6, 1934; d. Henry Devrick and Christine Beulah (Barrett) Hays; B.A., Baylor U., 1955; m. John Danridge Clark, June 12, 1954; children—Russell Devrick, Susan Patricia. Chmn. pub. information com. Dallas Health and Sci. Mus., 1965-67; copywriter Alexander McKensie Advt. Co., Dallas, 1967-68; writer, prodn. coordinator Vic Lundberg, Inc., Grand Rapids, Mich., 1968-70; dir. pub. information Williams & Work, Inc., Grand Rapids, 1970—. Mem. Environmental Writers Assn. Am. (dir.), Soc. Technican Communications (dir. St. Joseph Valley chpt.), Pub. Relations Soc. Am. (officer Western Mich. chpt. 1973—), Cons. Engrs. Council Mich. (mem. engring. excellence awards competition com. 1971—). Contbr. articles to newspapers, mags. Home: 4243 Greenbrier Court SE Grand Rapids MI 49506 Office: 611 Cascade West Parkway Grand Rapids MI 49506

CLARK, PEGGY (MRS. LLOYD R. KELLEY), theatrical lighting designer; b. Balt., Sept. 30, 1915; d. Eliot Round (M.D.) and Eleanor (Linton) Clark; A.B. cum laude, Smith Coll., 1935; M.F.A., Yale, 1938; m. Lloyd R. Kelley, Jan. 28, 1960. Designer theatrical costumes, 1938—; designer settings and lighting Gabrielle, 1941, High Ground, 1951, Curtain Going Up, 1952, Agnes de Mille Dance Theatre, 1953-54; designer stage lighting numerous plays, including Beggar's Holiday, 1946, Song of Norway, 1952, Peter Pan, 1954, Will Success Spoil Rock Hunter, 1955, Kiss Me Kate, 1955, No Time for Sergeants, 1956; designer decor Stage Door Canteen; tech. dir. Lunchtime Follies, Am. Theatre Wing; lighting and tech. dir. other plays including Connecticut Yankee, 1942, Brigadoon, 1946, High Button Shoes, 1947, Along Fifth Avenue, 1948, Gentlemen Prefer Blondes, 1949, Pal Joey, 1951, Mr. Wonderful, Auntie Mame, Bells Are Ringing, 1956, N.Y.C. Center Musical Revivals, 1956, 57, 58, 63-67, Say Darling, 1957; prodns. of Carousel, Susannah, Wonderful Town, at Brussels Internat. Expn., 1958; lighting tech. supr. Flower Drum Song, Juno, Goodbye Charlie, 1959, Bye Bye Birdie, Unsinkable Molly Brown, Under the Yum Yum Tree, 1960, Show Girl, Mary Mary, 1961, Sail Away, 1961, Romulus, 1962, The Girl who Came to Supper, 1963, Around the World in 80 Days, Jones Beach, 1964, Bajour, Poor Richard, 1965, Rose Tattoo, 1966, Darling of The Day, 1967; lighting designer South Pacific, Jones Beach, 1968, 69, Sound of Music, Jones Beach, 1970, 1971, Los Angeles Civic Light Opera, 1969, Jimmy, 1969, Last of the Red Hot Lovers, 1970, How the Other Half Loves, 1971, Candide, 1971, The King and I, Jones Beach, 1972, Carousel, Jones Beach, 1973, others. Mem. bd. counselors Smith Coll., 1961-69, lectr. lighting design, 1967, 69; instr. lighting design Lester Polakov Studio, Forum Stage Design, 1965—; vis. critic lighting design Yale Drama Sch., 1969-70. Mem. United Scenic Artists (rec. sec. 1942-47, trustee 1948-51, 53-55, pres. 1968-69), U.S. Inst. Theatre Tech. (dir. 1969-72), Yale Drama Alumni Assn. (v.p. 1970—), Illuminating Engring. Soc. Clubs: Brooklyn Smith (dir.), New York Smith, French Bulldog of America (dir., v.p. 1968-72, pres. 1972—), Woods Hole Yacht. Home: 36 Cranberry St Brooklyn NY 11201

CLARK, PETULA (MRS. CLAUDE WOLFF), actress, pop singer; b. Eng., 1935; m. Claude Wolff; children. Singer, child entertainer, Eng., World War II; singer night clubs, concert stage, TV, Europe, U.S.; recording artist including Downtown, My Love, A Sign of the Times; starring role in film Finian's Rainbow, 1968, Goodbye, Mr. Chips, 1969. Address: care NHD International Service PO Box 498 Quakerstown PA 19851

CLARK, PHYLLIS B. WILSON (MRS. BRUCE E. CLARK), educator, artist; b. Elgin, Man., Can.; d. Alvin Eldred and Mary Jane (Bryans) Wilson; student Regina Coll., 1925; B.Ed., Marjorie Webster Jr. Coll., 1929; m. Perry O. Huff, May 28, 1932 (dec. 1942); m. 2d, Bruce E. Clark, Dec. 18, 1943 (dec. Aug. 1959); 1 dau., Gretchen Huff Clark (Mrs. William Matthews Hobby III). Came to U.S., 1926, naturalized, 1941. Tchr. dept. speech Marjorie Webster Jr. Coll., Washington, 1929-34, 42-43; co-owner Lucker-Huff Studio, Washington, 1934-39; tchr. Beauvoir Sch. Nat. Cathedral Found., Washington, 1946-66, summer dir., 1965-67; asst. to prin. Sheridan Sch., Washington, 1967-68. Program writer, producer, performer Lady Next Door, Radio Sta. WMAL, Washington, 1930-33. Auditor, League Republican Women, Washington, 1969-73, program chmn., 1973—. Treas., Crittenton Circle, Florence Crittenton Home, 1968-70, pres., 1974—. Mem. Internat. Platform Assn., English Speaking Union, Delta Psi Omega. Clubs: Chevy Chase (Md.); Washington (bd. govs. 1967-73, treas. 1967-70, pres. 1970-72); Am. Newspaper Women's. Home: 2219 California St Washington DC 20008

CLARK, RUTH ANN (MRS. PAUL LUTHER CLARK), mus. adminstr.; b. Flatwoods, Ky., Oct. 26, 1919; d. Clyde and Margaret Katherine (Jones) Callihan; student Santa Monica Jr. Coll., 1944; m. Paul Luther Clark, June 7, 1941; children—Paula Renee (Mrs. Robert Alison Sparrow), Steven Christ, Kathy Marie. Entertainer radio sta. WCMI, Ashland, Ky. and Ironton, O., 1938-39; country-western singer Paramount Movie Studios, Hollywood, Cal., 1943-44; tour condr. Warner Bros. Movie Studios, Hollywood, 1943-44, 20th. Century Fox, Hollywood, 1943-44; charge tours Oregon (O.) Jerusalem Hist. Mus., 1964—, dir., 1967—. Served with WAF, 1944-45. Mem. Smithsonian Assos., Archaeol. Soc. Ohio, Oregon Jerusalem Hist. Soc., Am. Inst. Antiques. Methodist (sch. tchr. 1960-67). Home: 3464 Starr Av Oregon OH 43616 Office: 3320 Starr Av Oregon OH 43616

CLARK, RUTH HOLLINGSHEAD (MRS. HAROLD D. CLARK), state legislator; b. Newark, Sept. 7, 1916; d. George Given and Ethelwyn Alward (Pell) Hollingshead; B.A., Conn. Coll., 1938; m. Harold Deming Clark, Jr., Oct. 7, 1939; children—Leslie (Mrs. John A. Goulet), Jonathan D., Jeffrey C. Grand juror, Branford, Conn., 1949-51; mem. Branford Bd. Edn., 1951-59; rep. Branford Town Meeting, 1959-61; mem. Branford Commn. on Services to Elderly, 1966-70, chmn., 1970; mem. Conn. Ho. of Reps., 1971—, vice chmn. human rights and opportunities com., 1973—, clk. edn. com., 1973—. Pres. Branford Vis. Nurse Assn., 1962-64; exec. sec. United Fund Branford, 1963-64; pres. Homemaker-Home Health Aide Service Branford Area, 1967-70. Mem. League Women Voters. Home: 50 Little Bay Lane Branford CT 06405

CLARK, RUTH MARIE, psychologist; b. Union, Ore.; d. Roger Adams and Mary (Wittman) Clark; student Barnard Coll., 1929-32; B.S., Columbia, 1933; M.A., N.Y.U., 1950, Ph.D., 1957. Asst. adminstr. Nat. Hosp. for Speech Disorders, N.Y.C., 1936-48, re-ednl. dir., 1948-58, editor Talk Mag., 1936-54; dir. spl. services Community Sch., Tenafly, N.J., 1959-65; Pvt. practice psychology, Union, N.J., 1959-65, Portland, Ore., 1965—. Cons. Nat. Hosp. for Speech Disorders, N.Y.C., 1959-65; research cons. Good Samaritan Hosp., Portland, Ore., 1969; cons. Speech Rehab. Inst., N.Y.C., 1968—. Mem. Am. Speech and Hearing Assn., Am., N.Y. psychol. assns. Home: 316 SE 157th Av Portland OR 97233

CLARK, RUTH MILLER (MRS. JAMES WILLIAM CLARK), bank ofcl.; b. Decatur, Ill., Oct. 3, 1914; d. John Henry and Dora Etta (Kelley) Miller; student Knoxville Bus. Coll., 1935; m. James William Clark, Apr. 29, 1945. With Home Beneficial Life Ins. Co., Knoxville, Tenn., 1936-43; with Bank of Knoxville, 1943—, asst. cashier, 1952-71, asst. v.p., 1971—. Mem. Nat. Assn. Bank Women, Credit Women Internat. (pres. Knoxville 1959-60). Methodist (ch. treas. 1963-70). Home: 3425 Feather St Knoxville TN 37920 Office: 625 Market St Knoxville TN 37902

CLARK, SANDRA HELEN BECKER (MRS. ALLEN LEROY CLARK), geologist; b. Kansas City, Mo., July 27, 1938; d. LuVern John and Mildred (File) Becker; student Ia. State U., 1956-60; B.S., U. Ida., 1963, M.S., 1964, Ph.D., 1968; m. Allen LeRoy Clark, Nov. 10, 1955; children—Ken Allen (dec.), Brett Harlan, Holly Lin. Field asst. Ida. Bur. Mines and Geology, Moscow, 1963, 64, Bear Creek Mining Co., Spokane, Wash., 1965; teaching asst. U. Ida., Coll. of Mines, Moscow, 1964-66; geologist Cominco Am., Inc., Spokane, 1966-67, Alaskan Mineral Resources br. U.S. Geol. Survey, Menlo Park, Cal., 1967-72, Office Mineral Resources, U.S. Geol. Survey, 1972—. NSF grad. fellow, 1963-64; NSF summer fellow, 1966. Mem. Geol. Soc. Am., A.A.A.S., Peninsula Geol. Soc., Sigma Xi, Sigma Gamma Epsilon, Phi Kappa Phi. Contbr. articles to profl. jours. Home: 12124 Quorn Lane Reston VA 22091 Office: US Geol Survey Nat Center Reston VA 22092

CLARK, SANDRA JEAN, coll. dean; b. Binghamton, N.Y., Jan. 4, 1938; d. James R. and Marylou (Ivison) Clark; B.A., U. Pacific, 1960; M.A., San Jose State Coll., 1962; Ed.D., U. Cal. Los Angeles, 1969. Resident counselor U. Pacific, 1959-60; asst. dir. summer camp Camp Fire Girls, Silver Lake, Cal., 1960; head resident counselor San Jose State Coll., 1960-63; dean women Hiram (O.) Coll., 1963-66; senior residence adviser U. Cal. at Los Angeles, 1966-69, spl. asst. to vice chancellor student and campus affairs, 1970-72; dean of student services Fla. Internat. U., 1972—. Adviser, Asso. Women Students group, 1960—; mem. Dade County Planning Adv. Bd.; cons. Nat. Action Com. for Drug Edn. Named Outstanding Young Woman of Am. for Fla., 1973. Office Edn. fellow, 1969-70. Mem. Am. Assn. U. Women, Nat. Assn. Women Deans and Counselors (chmn. research com. 1972—), Nat. Vocational Guidance Assn., Am. Coll. Personnel Assn., N.E.A., Am. Assn. Higher Edn., Fla. Assn. Community Colls., Pi Lambda Theta, Alpha Chi Omega. Home: 4915 Riviera Dr Coral Gables FL 33146 Office: Fla Internat U Tamiami Trail Miami FL 33144

CLARK, VIRGINIA LEE, educator; b. Milw., July 13, 1945; d. James LeRoy and Harriet Elizabeth (Janda) Clark; certificate in arts Monticello Coll., 1966; B.A., Culver-Stockton Coll., 1969. Spl. edn. tchr. Seymour Grade Sch., Payson, Ill., 1969—. Mem. Council for Exceptional Children, Nat., Ill., Payson (bldg. rep. 1971-73, 74—) edn. assns., Am. Assn. Spl. Educators, Am. Assn. Mental Deficiency, Assn. for Study Perception, Mental Health Assn., Found. Exceptional Children, Friends of Mentally Retarded, Am. Assn. U. Women, Alpha Xi Delta, Delta Psi Omega, Theta Alpha Phi. Methodist. Home: 430 S 14th St Quincy IL 62301 Office: 404 State St Payson IL 62360

CLARKE, ANGELA WEBB (MRS. HANS F. HOLZAPFEL), physician; b. Balt., Nov. 4; d. Luke Eulysses and Cora (Mayfield) Webb; B.S., summa cum laude, Morgan State Coll., 1957; M.D., U. Md., 1961; m. Hans F. Holzapfel; children-Wuan Angelo, Indranee Khurisingh, Tarita Khurlsingh. Intern, Sacramento Hosp., 1961-62; practice medicine, Los Angeles, 1963—; mem. staff Culver City Meml., Queen of Angels, Century City hosps.; asso. prof. U. Cal. at Los Angeles; physician So. Cal. Permanente Med. Group, Los Angeles, 1962-63. Served with USAAF, 1951-53. Diplomate Am. Bd. Family Practice. Fellow Royal Soc. Health; mem. N.A.A.C.P. (life), World Med. Assn., Am. Med. Womens Assn., Am. Acad. Gen. Practice, Cal. Physicians Service. Office: 2080 Century Park E Los Angeles CA 90067

CLARKE, ELVIRA FARENTHEA WIERMAA (MRS. WILLIAM O. CLARKE), educator; b. Aurora, Minn.; d. John and Elizabeth (Wiermaa) Wiermaa; B.S., U. Minn., 1937, M.A. 1948; m. William O. Clarke, Nov. 27, 1935 (dec. June 1946). Tchr. pub. schs., Mpls., 1935-39, prin., 1939-40, tchr., St. Paul, 1951-57, counselor, 1957—; dean women Central Mo. State Coll., 1948-51. Pres. Palo Real Estate, Inc., 1971—. Mem. Am. Personnel and Guidance Assn., Am. Sch. Counselors Assn., Am. Coll. Personnel Assn., Minn. Counselors Assn., Minn. Assn. High Sch. Counselors and Coll. Admissions Officers (sec.-treas. 1971—), Am. Fedn. Tchrs., N.E.A., Minn. Edn. Assn., Nat. (chmn. credentials com. 1969 nat. conv.), Twin City (pres. 1969-70) vocational guidance assns., Am. Assn. U. Women, Internat. Platform Assn. Mem. Order Eastern Star. Home: 1254 Raymond Av St Paul MN 55108

CLARKE, FRANCES MARGUERITE, psychologist; b. Lorain County, O., Nov. 11, 1905; d. Carl Thomson and Miriam E. (Price) Clarke; A.B., Barnard Coll., 1924; A.M., Columbia, 1925, Ph.D., 1928; postgrad. Yale, 1931-33; grad. U. Balt. Law Sch., 1953. Practice psychology, New London, Conn., 1931-36, Towson, Md., 1950-60; faculty U. Md. overseas and Western Md. Coll., Westminster; admitted to Md. bar, 1953. Fellow Am. Psychol. Assn.; mem. Conn., Md. psychol. assns., Internat. Applied Psychotherapists, Soc. Mayflower Descendants in Conn., Md. Bar Assn., Women's Bar Assn. Md. Club: Zonta International of Frederick County. Home: 506 Locksley Rd Towson MD 21204

CLARKE, HELEN HOPKINS (MRS. DONALD WALLACE CLARKE), wholesale trade co. exec.; b. Aliquippa, Pa., Aug. 18, 1911; d. Thomas Richard and Edna Ellen (Bradford) Hopkins; A.B. cum laude, Allegheny Coll., Pa., 1933; m. Donald Wallace Clarke, Oct. 12, 1935; children—Holly (Mrs. Robert J. MacKinnon), Douglas Wallace. Tchr. French and English, Aliquippa (Pa.) High Sch., 1933-35; dir., v.p. Clarke Oil Co., Hastings, Neb., 1945—; dir., sec. D.W. Clarke, Inc., Hastings. Mem. Hastings Civil Service Commn., 1936-38, Hastings Bd. Edn., 1950-62, pres. 1960-61. Chmn. Adams County (Neb.) Zoning Commn., 1957-58; founder, pres. Adams County Republican Women, 1958-60; del. to Rep. Nat. Conv., 1968; mem. Adams County Central Com., 1958-72, vice chmn., 1958-61; mem. Neb. state Central Com., 1964-68, state exec. com., 1968-72; vice chmn. 3d congl. dist., 1968-72. Bd. dirs. Adams County Red Cross, 1942-58, sec., 1944-58. Mem. Hastings (pres. 1936-38), Neb. (v.p. 1937-39) leagues of women voters, P.E.O., Phi Beta Kappa, Phi Sigma Iota, Alpha Chi Omega. Mem. Presbyn. Ch. Club: George Eliot. Address: 1124 N Lincoln Hastings NE 68901

CLARKE, JUNO-ANN KROHN, educator; b. Detroit, Mar. 3, 1935; d. Bernhard and Bertha (VanSchellen) Krohn; B.S. (Hinman scholar), Mich. State U., 1956; M.S. (Mead Johnson fellow), U. Cal. at Berkeley, 1960, Ph.D. (Mary Rose Schwartz fellow), 1969. Faculty, San Francisco State U., 1960—, asso. prof. nutrition, 1969—. Cons. nutrition and nutrition edn. U.S. AID, Liberia, 1969, Med. Assistance Programs, Afghanistan, 1970; nutrition cons. Am. Tech. Assistance Corp., Pakistan, 1970, INDECO, Mexico, 1973. Recipient Am. Assn. U. Women fellowship, 1970-71; Outstanding Service award Bay Area Dietetic Assn., 1973. Mem. Am. Dietetic Assn., Am. Home Econs. Assn., Am. Pub. Health Assn., Sigma Xi, Iota Sigma Pi, Omicron Nu, Pi Lambda Theta. Home: Box 155 Oakland CA 94604 Office: San Francisco State University 1600 Holloway San Francisco CA 94132

CLARKE, L(ULA) BEATRICE FLEMING (MRS. ALLEN CLARENCE CLARKE), educator; b. Jacksonville, Fla., Oct. 1, 1910; d. Lucius Samuel and Eva (Jackson) Fleming; B.S., Fla. A. and M. Coll., 1931; M.A., U. Mich., 1933, postgrad summer, 1951; postgrad. summers U. Chgo., 1938, (fellow) Brown U., 1945, (NSF fellow) U. Kan., 1958, 59, Tufts U., 1968; m. Allen Clarence Clarke, Nov. 21, 1942; 1 dau., Karen Eileen. Tchr. sci. Howard Acad., Ocala, Fla., 1931-32; tchr. high sch. math. Edward Waters Coll., Jacksonville, 1933-34; instr. English and math. Fla. and A. and M. Coll., 1934-40, asst. prof., 1940-45, asst. prof. math., 1947-49, asso. prof., 1949—, dir. 13 coll. curriculum program, 1969—, acting chmn. dept. math., 1949-62; substitute tchr. pub. schs., Bridgeport, Conn., 1946. Active Jack and Jill Club Am., 1952-65. Bd. dirs. Leon Interfaith Child Care, Inc., 1969-73, v.p., 1969-70. Named Tchr. of Year, Fla. A. and M. Coll., 1954. Mem. Math. Assn. Am., Delta Sigma Theta, Alpha Kappa Mu, Beta Kappa Chi. Presbyn. (elder). Author: (with others) College Algebra, 1956; College Algebra and Basic Set Theory, 1962. Home: 1442 Coleman St Tallahassee FL 32304

CLARKE, MARY GILL, psychologist; b. Laurinburg, N.C., May 17, 1918; d. Thomas Jeffries and Mamie (Massey) Gill; A.B., Woman's Coll., U. N.C., 1940; M.A., U. Minn., 1943; Ph.D., Duke, 1954; m. Jack H. Lively, Apr. 5, 1938 (dec. July 1939); m. 2d, Joseph I. C. Clarke, Feb. 10, 1952 (dec. Feb. 1955). Psychologist Worcester (Mass.) State Hosp., 1942-44; chief psychologist Med. Coll. Va. Hosp., Richmond, 1944-47; clin. psychologist Richmond VA Mental Hygiene Clinic, 1947-50; VA clin. psychology trainee, 1950-53; research asst., bur. testing and guidance Duke, 1953-54; clin. psychologist VA Hosp., Durham, N.C., 1954-56; asst. prof. psychology, depts. psychiatry and psychology U. N.C., 1956-59, asso. prof., now prof.; chief psychologist In-Patient Service, N.C. Meml. Hosp., Chapel Hill, 1956-63, dir. psychol. services, 1963-72, dir. psychology tng., 1970—. Mem. Va. Exam. Bd. for Certification Clin. Psychologists, 1945-50; mem. N.C. Bd. Examiners Practicing Psychologists, 1967-70, chmn., 1967-70. Diplomate in clin. psychology Am. Bd. Profl. Psychology. Mem. Am., Southeastern, N.C. psychol. assns., A.A.A.S., Phi Beta Kappa. Home: Timberlake Estates Route 5 Chapel Hill NC 27514 Office: Psychol Services NC Meml Hosp Chapel Hill NC 27514

CLARKE, MARY RUSSELL STETSON (MRS. EDWIN LEAVITT CLARKE), author; b. Melrose, Mass., Dec. 27, 1911; d. Horace and Mabel Pitts (Russell) Stetson; A.B., Boston U., 1933; postgrad. Columbia, 1937-38; m. Edwin Leavitt Clarke, June 8, 1937; children—Edwin Stetson, Susan (Mrs. Spence W. Perry), Joyce (Mrs. David M. Hockman). Copywriter Christian Sci. Monitor, 1933-37; tchr. creative writing Boston Center Adult Edn., 1960-61. Bd. dirs. Melrose Council Expt. in Internat. Living, 1959-65, Melrose Community Council, 1963-68, First Iron Works Assn., 1968-69, Middlesex Canal Assn.; trustee Melrose Pub. Library; mem. Melrose Conservation Commn., 1967-69. Mem. Soc. for Preservation New Eng. Antiquities, Boston Authors Club (dir. 1967-68). Author: Petticoat Rebel, 1964; The Iron Peacock, 1966; The Limner's

Daughter, 1967; Pioneer Iron Works, 1968; The Glass Phoenix, 1969; Piper to the Clan, 1970; Guide to the Middlesex Canal, 1971; Bloomers and Ballots, 1972; Immigration in Colonial Times, 1973; History of Women's Rights in the United States, 1974; The Old Middlesex Canal, 1974; A Visit to the Iron Works, 1974. Address: 333 W Emerson St Melrose MA 02176

CLARKE, RUTH ELLIOTT JOHNSON (MRS. ERIC GEORGE CLARKE), oriental art cons., business exec.; b. Wai-Hsien-Shantung Province, North China, Apr. 2, 1890; d. Charles Fletcher and Agnes (Elliott) Johnson (parents Am. citizens); B.A., Wilson Coll., 1912; m. Eric George Clarke, June 21, 1916 (dec. June 1963). Tchr. primary dept. Miss Jewell's Sch., Shanghai, China, 1912-13; office work Am. Bible Soc., Shanghai, 1913-14; founder The Peking (North China) Am. Sch., 1915-16; mem. bd. Sch. for Blind, Shanghai, 1935-36; charter mem. Peking Inst. Fine Arts, 1915; an asst. organizer Peking Choral Soc., 1915, Shanghai Choral Soc., 1932; v.p., gen. sales mgr. Eric G. Clarke & Co., Portland, Ore., 1950—; jade cons. Zell Bros., jewelers, Portland, 1956—. Lectr. on experiences during half-century in China, jade and its place in Chinese culture, Chinese decorative art and art symbols; exhibited jade, other art objects from her pvt. collection at Arden Galleries, N.Y.C., 1939. Mem. YWCA, Women's League Lewis and Clark Coll. (pres. 1953), Women's Advt. Club Portland (past dir.), Zonta Internat. (pres. Portland 1953-54), Portland Art Mus., English Speaking Union, Ore. Hist. Soc., Friends of Mus. U. Ore. Republican. Presbyn. Mem. Mystic Order of Rose. Clubs: Corriente, Knife and Fork (Portland). Home and office: Ione Plaza 1717 SW Park Av Portland OR 97201

CLARKE, URANA, musician, writer; b. Wickliffe-on-the-Lake, O., Sept. 8, 1902; d. Graham Warren and Grace Urana (Olsaver) Clarke; artists and tchrs., diploma Mannes Music Sch., N.Y.C., 1925; Dalcroze certificate Sch. Music, N.Y.C., 1950; passed navigators exam. U.S. Power squadron, 1943; student Pembroke Coll., Brown U.; B.S., Mont. State U., 1967, M.S., 1970. Mem. faculty Mannes Music Sch., 1922-49, Dalcroze Sch. Music, 1949-54; adv. editor in music The Book of Knowledge, 1949-61; v.p., dir. Saugatuck Circle Housing Devel., 1964—; with daily radio astronomy show, 1964—, weekly radio Birds of Big Sky Country, 1972—; writing monthly astron. forecast; instr. continuing edn. Mont. State U. Guest lectr. celestial navigation, nautical astronomy, Hayden Planetarium, 1945; guest lectr. Roger Williams Planetarium, Providence, 1959-63. Adv. com. Nat. Rivers and Harbors Congresses, 1947-58; co-chmn. Barrington Town Blood Assurance Program, 1960-64; chmn. Park County chpt. A.R.C., 1965—, co-chmn. blood program, 1965—, 1st aid instr., 1941—, Red Cross first aid instructor, trainer, 1969—. Rep. town meeting Westport, Conn., 1955. Mem. Am. Acad. Polit. Sci., Am. Musical. Soc., Music Library Assn., Royal Astron. Soc. Can., Inst. Nav., Maria Mitchell Soc. Nantucket, N.A. Yacht Racing Union, A.A.A.S., R.I. Meteor Research Orgn. (dir.), Internat. Soc. Mus. Research, Big Sky Astron. Soc. (dir.), Renaissance Soc., Internat. Musicological Soc., Mont. Wilderness Soc., Am. Guild of Organists, Am. Assn. U. Women. Conglist. Club: Cedar Point Yacht. Author: The Heavens Art Telling (astronomy), 1951; Skies Over the Big Sky Country, 1965. Contbns. to mags. on music, nav. and astronomy. Publ. music elementary two-pinao pieces. Inventor, builder of Clarke Adjustable Piano Stool. Address: 9th St Island Livingston MT 59047

CLARY, SONJA-LOU LINNEA BARK (MRS. ROBERT CLARY), ednl. adminstr., cons.; b. Chgo., June 21, 1943; d. Eric Gustav and June Mathilda (Rosenkilde) Bark; B.A., Purdue U., 1965, M.S., 1968; m. Robert Clary, June 21, 1969. Learning disability tchr. Lake Forest (Ill.) Country Day Sch., 1965-66; instr. spl. edn. dept. Purdue U., West Lafayette, Ind., 1966-68; dir. student teaching for spl. edn. Ind. U., Bloomington, 1968; cons. program devel., handicapped div. State Ill. Office Supt. Pub. Instrn., Chgo., 1969-70; cons. program devel. N.W. Suburban Spl. Edn., Arlington Heights, Ill., 1970-71; learning disability tchr. Rolling Meadows (Ill.) High Sch., 1971-72; dir. Achievement Center for Children with Learning Disabilities, Deerfield, Ill., 1971—; faculty Nat. Coll. Edn., Evanston, Ill., 1972—, extension center coordinator, 1973—. Ednl. cons. Larkin Home for Children, 1972—, Joseph P. Kennedy Sch. for Exceptional Children, 1972-73. Mem. Council Exceptional Children, Am. Assn. Mental Deficiency, Ill. Adminstrs. Spl. Edn., Assn. for Children with Learning Disabilites, Purdue Mus. Orgns., Alpha Phi. Club: Swedish Glee Aux. (Chgo.). Home: 2411 Brandenberry Ct Arlington Heights IL 60004 Office: 400 County Line Rd Deerfield IL 60015

CLAUDEL, ALICE MOSER (MRS. CALVIN ANDRE CLAUDEL), poet, educator; b. New Orleans, Apr. 5, 1918; d. Herbert Mayberry and Jeannette McLeod (Hayes) Moser; student summers U. N.C., 1958, Georgetown U., 1961; B.A., Tulane U., 1963; M.A., 1968; m. Enrique Rivera Baz, June 5, 1935 (div. Mar., 1941); 1 son, William McLeod; m. 2d, Calvin Andre Claudel, Feb. 23, 1943. Tchr., Delacroix Elementary Sch., Delacroix, La., 1957-64; instr. English, W.Va. Wesleyan Coll., Buckhannon, 1966-69; lectr. English and creative writing Eastern Shore Community Coll. Gen. chmn. Greater New Orleans Area Acadian Bicentennial Celebration, 1955; mem. La. adv. bd. Acadian Bicentennial Celebration, 1955; lectr. English, Am. poetry, 1943—; poet-in-the-schs. Worcester and Somerset Counties (Md.), chmn., lower eastern shore Md. Com. for Arts; mem. Gov's adv. bd. Com. for Devel. French in La. St. Bernard Parish rep. La. Council Tchrs. English, 1961—. Mem. La. Poetry Soc. (pres. 1958; poetry workshop chmn.), English-Speaking Union, La. Fgn. Lang. Teachers Assn. (program chmn. 1957), St. Bernard Parish Tchrs. Assn. (publicity chmn. 1959-60), L'Athenee Louisianais, Order of Bookfellows, Nat. League Am. Pen Women, Am. Assn. U. Women, Nat. Bus. and Profl. Women's Clubs (del. state conv. 1965), Am. Studies Assn. (publicity chmn. ann. meeting Lower Miss. Valley 1965), Alpha Sigma Lambda. Episcopalian. Poetry editor New Laurel Rev. Contbr. articles and poetry to various publs. Address: Eastern Shore Community Coll Melfa VA 23418

CLAUS, KAREN EMILY, educator, psychologist; b. McMinneville, Ore., Oct. 29, 1941; d. John Nicholas and Grace Flavyh (Moriarty) Shellabarger; B.A., Stanford, 1963, Ph.D. (grad. fellow), 1968; M.A., San Jose (Cal.) State U., 1966; m. Robert James Claus, Feb. 4, 1963; children—Christian Conrad, James Joshua. Fgn. lang. cons. Alum Rock Sch. Dist., San Jose, 1963-64, tchr., 1964-66; asst. prof. Grad. Sch. Edn., Cal. State U. at San Jose, 1966-68; research psychologist, lectr. Sch. Nursing, U. Cal. at San Francisco, 1968—; cons. in field. Mem. Am. Psychol. Assn., Am. Mgmt. Assn., A.A.A.S., Am. Edn. Research Assn., Nat. League Nursing, Assn. Devel. Instructional Systems, Internat. Soc. Study Symbols. Author: Psychological Considerations of Lettering for Identification, 1971; The Visual Environment, 1971; An Experiment in Nursing Curriculums at a University, 1971; Signs: Legal Rights and Aesthetic Considerations, 1972; Visual Communication through Signage: Vol. I Perception of the Message, 1974; Decision Making in Nursing: Tools for Change, 1975. Home: 3093 Ross Rd Palo Alto CA 94303 Office: N-511N Sch Nursing Univ Cal San Francisco CA 94143

CLAUS, KATHERINE ROY (MRS. BODO CLAUS), architect; b. Baton Rouge, Apr. 16, 1939; d. Victor Leander and Margaret (Ewing) Roy; B.Arch., La. State U., 1962; m. Bodo Claus, Dec. 17, 1960; children—Heidi Katherine, Laura Elizabeth, Michael Stallmann. Draftsman, A. Hays Town, architect, Baton Rouge 1958-61; architect Wilson & Coleman, architects, Baton Rouge, 1961-66; partner Claus & Claus, architects, Baton Rouge, 1966—. Mem. A.I.A. (honor award 1968, 70, 1st honor award 1969), Jr. League Baton Rouge, Kappa Delta. Episcopalian. Prin. works include Coastal Studies Inst. Labs. and Office, 1967, Jefferson Plaza Shopping Center, 1968, Arlington Townhouse Apts., 1968, Patiohouse Apts., 1969, Varsityhouse Apts., 1970, all Baton Rouge. Home: 5050 Bluebell Dr Baton Rouge LA 70808 Office: 5225 Capital Heights Baton Rouge LA 70806

CLAUSON, ALBERTA LILLIAN AYER (MRS. BRUCE KENMORE CLAUSON), librarian; b. Deer River, Minn., May 5, 1913; d. Charles Edward and Inez Mildred (Randall) Ayer; B.E., St. Cloud State Coll., 1935, postgrad., 1936; postgrad. Moorhead State Coll., 1953-55, U. Minn., 1956-57, Columbia, 1958, Mont. State U., 1960, Brigham Young U., 1967; m. Bruce Kenmore Clauson, Dec. 31, 1938; children—Bruce Edward, Kay Renee (Mrs. Burkhard Siedhoff), Christopher Charles. Grade sch. tchr., Ashby (Minn.) Pub. Schs., 1935-38; prin. jr. high sch., math. and English instr. Gaylord Pub. Sch., 1938; treas. sch. bd. rural sch., St. Olaf Twp.-Ottertail County, Minn., 1939-46; tchr. English, Alexandria Jr. High Sch., 1946-51; tchr. English, librarian Underwood High Sch., 1952-55, Hoffman High Sch., 1955-56; tchr. English, Elbow Lake Jr. High Sch., 1957-58; librarian, Henning High Sch., 1958-62, Fergus Falls Elementary Sch., 1962-66; librarian Media Center, Fergus Falls (Minn.) Jr. High Sch., 1965—. Tapes programs for radio program, Minn. State Service for Blind, 1968—. Active P.T.A., 4-H; mem. Otter Tail County Hist. Mus. Mem. N.E.A., Minn., Fergus Falls (treas. 1963-64) edn. assns., Am., Minn. (chmn. western div. 1969-70) assns. sch. librarians, A.L.A., Kappa Delta Pi, Delta Kappa Gamma. Lutheran (Sunday sch. supt. 1949-51, tchr.). Mem. Job's Daus., Order Eastern Star. Home: Route 1 Ashby MN 36309 Office: Jr High Sch Media Center Office Fergus MN 36337

CLAUSS, JANE WEST, architect; b. Mpls., Sept. 23, 1907; B.A. in Interior Architecture, U. Minn., 1929. Instr. interior architecture dept. art Beaver Coll., 1946-64, Museum Coll. Art, Phila., 1956-57; asso. firm Clauss & Nolan, Trenton, N.J., 1956—. Mem. A.I.A., Tau Sigma Delta. Prin. works include Schwerdle residence, Vineland, N.J., 1962, Phillipsburg Convent, N.J., 1966, N.J. State Health and Agr. Bldg., 1966, N.J. Transp. Dept. Office Bldg., 1969. Home: 314 Copples Lane Wallingford PA 19086 Office: Clauss & Nolan 114 W State St Trenton NJ 08608

CLAUSSEN, CONSTANCE JOAN, educator; b. Omaha, Apr. 20, 1939; d. Erwin J.D. and Sylvia M. (Anderson) Claussen; B.S., Omaha U., 1961; M.A., Adams State Coll., 1963. Phys. edn. tchr. Lindbergh Jr. High Sch., Long Beach, Cal., 1961-62; grad. asst. Adams State Coll., 1962-63; instr. U. Neb., Omaha, 1963—, chmn. women's phys. edn., 1964-73, women's athletic dir., 1973—, asso. prof., 1972—. Co-chmn. Women's Coll. World Series of Softball, 1969—. Recipient Recognition award Amateur Softball Assn., 1970. Mem. Am. (membership chmn. 1965), Neb. (newsletter editor 1963) assns. health, phys. edn. and recreation, Central Assn. Phys. Edn. Coll. Women, Neb. Women's Intercollegiate Sports Council (treas. 1971-74), Nat. Assn. Girls and Women's Sports (membership chmn. 1974-75), Chi Omega. Editor Div. Girls and Women's Sports Softball Guide, 1972-74. Home: 2716 N 60th Av Omaha NE 68104 Office: 60th and Dodge Sts Omaha NE 68101

CLAWSON, CAROL ANN, newspaper corr.; b. N.Y.C., Nov. 13, 1946; d. Lester Peter and Helen (Nathan) David; B.A., Ohio Wesleyan U., 1967; m. Ken W. Clawson, Mar. 16, 1969; stepchildren—Karen, David, Geoffrey. Reporter, Toledo Blade, 1967-68; staff writer Congl. Quar., Washington, 1968-69; Washington corr. Newhouse News Service, 1969—. Mem. White House Corrs. Assn., Alpha Delta Pi, Sigma Delta Rho. Clubs: Washington Press; Langley (dir. 1973-74) (McLean). Home: 850 Merriewood Lane McLean VA 22101 Office: 1750 Pennsylvania Av NW Washington DC 20006

CLAY, JOYCE L., newspaper pub.; b. Farmington, Minn., Sept. 2, 1927; d. Humphrey A. and Margaret M. (Cannon) Case; student pub. schs.; m. Roger Clay (dec. 1971); children—Diana (Mrs. Edward Sievers), Joseph, Daniel, Cynthia (Mrs. Bernard Travis). Pres., pub. Dakota County Tribune, Farmington, 1971—. Recipient 1st pl. awards for excellence Minn. Newspaper Assn., 1973. Mem. Farmington C. of C. (dir.). Home: 421 Ash St Farmington MN 55024 Office: 420 3d St Farmington MN 55024

CLAY, MARGARET LEONE, psychologist; b. St. Joseph, Mo., Oct. 23, 1923; d. William H. and Carol (McConnell) Clay; B.S., U. Mich., 1956, M.S., 1958, Ph.D., 1962; student U. Wis., 1962, Rutgers U., 1963. Teaching fellow, research asst. dept. psychology U. Mich., Ann Arbor, 1957-59, asst. research psychologist, 1959-62, asso. research psychologist, lectr. psychology, 1962—, asso. research psychologist Mental Health Research Inst., 1963—, asst. dir. mental health research inst., 1965-68, group workshop cons. sch. pub. health, 1969—; alcoholism cons. Mich. Office Highway Safety Planning, 1968—. Research cons. Mich. Dept. Pub. Health Alcoholism Program, 1964—; planning cons. Rutgers Center Alcohol Studies, 1971; evaluation cons. Heartline Inc., Detroit, 1971; mem. faculty alcohol studies insts. Chmn. Washtenaw County Council Alcoholism, 1965-67; chmn. Mich. Dept. Edn. Curriculum Com. on Alcohol, Drugs, and Edn.; mem. exec. com. Mich. Inst. Alcoholism Programs, 1964-67; mem. Mich. Alcohol Studies Assn., 1963-67; mem. exec. com. Mich. Alcohol and Addiction Assn., 1967—; mem. Gov.'s Task Force on Drinking Driver, 1970—. Mem. Am. Psychol. Assn., Am. Assn. U. Profs., N.Am. Assn. Alcoholism Programs, Alcohol and Drug Problems Assn. N. Am. (chmn. research sect. 1971-72) Soc. for Study of Social Problems, Am., Mich. (chmn. mental health div., dir. 1969-72), Am. pub. health assns. Research on causative factors in alcoholism, interpersonal dynamics of social change. Cons. editor Jour. Biol. Psychology and Quarterly Jour. Studies on Alcohol. Home: Box 251 Hillman MI 49746 Office: Mental Health Research Inst U Mich Ann Arbor MI 48104

CLAYBROOK, DOROTHY ANDREWS (MRS. JAMES WELDON CLAYBROOK), educator; b. Latham, Tenn., July 13, 1927; d. James Henry and Anna Rebecca (Latham) Andrews; B.A., Lane Coll., 1949; postgrad. Fisk U., 1954, U. Tenn., 1960; M.A., Memphis State U., 1971; m. James Weldon Claybrook, Mar. 12, 1950. Tchr. Gibson County Bd. Edn., Trenton, Tenn., 1949-66, supr. instructions, 1966—. Mem. City Civil Club, Humboldt, Tenn., 1952-74; mem. Beautification of County Club, Humboldt, 1952-74. Trustee Gibson Pub. Day Care Center, 1960-71. Mem. N.A.A.C.P., Am. Assn. U. Women, Nat., Tenn., Gibson County, Aerospace edn. assns., Tenn. Assn. for Children Under Six, Tenn. Assn. Supervision and Curriculum Devel., Sigma Gamma Rho. Baptist. Elk. Club: Vogue (Humboldt). Home: 913 12th Av Humboldt TN 38343 Office: 410 Trenton TN 38382

CLAYTON, CYNTHIA LAUREL CARLSON (MRS. WILLIAM FRANK CLAYTON), pediatrician; b. Boston, Feb. 25, 1943; d. Harry Louis and Anita (Pearl) Carlson; B.A., Smith Coll., 1963; M.D., N.Y.U., 1967; m. William Frank Clayton, July 4, 1965; children—W. Justin Albert, Austin Buck. Intern, Buffalo Children's Hosp., 1967-68, sr. resident, 1968-69, asst. chief resident, 1970-71; pediatric hematology fellow, 1969-70; practice medicine specializing in pediatrics, Buffalo, 1971—; mem. staff Buffalo Children's Hosp., E.J. Meyer Meml. Hosp., Sisters of Charity Hosp.; asst. prof. pediatrics State U. N.Y., Buffalo, 1971—. Mem. N.Y. State, Erie County med. socs., Nat. Orgn. of Women. Home: 87 Highland Av Buffalo NY 14222 Office: 462 Grider Buffalo NY 14215

CLAYTON, ELIZABETH MYERS, educator; b. Pueblo, Colo., May 8, 1931; d. Lafe and Edna (Daugherty) Myers; B.A., U. Wash., 1953, M.A., 1966, Ph.D. (Ford Found. dissertation fellow), 1968; m. James W. D. Clayton, Mar. 19, 1955 (div. Apr. 1964); 1 dau., Alexandra. Asst. prof. U. Mo. at St. Louis, 1968-71, asso. prof. econs., 1971—. Mem. Am. Econ. Assn., Am. Assn. Advancement Slavic Studies, Assn. for Comparative Econ. Systems, Phi Beta Kappa. Contbr. articles to econ. jours. Home: Clayton MO Office: Dept of Economics University of Missouri St Louis MO 63121

CLAYTON, LAURA BLAND (MRS. CHARLES LINDSAY CLAYTON), educator; b. Winston-Salem, N.C.; d. Joseph Franklin and Mozella (Dugan) Bland; A.B., Salem Coll., 1938; M.A., U. N.C., 1939, Ph.D., 1950; diploma Am. Acad. Rome, 1950; m. Charles Lindsay Clayton, May 25, 1958; Piano, organ instr. Bland Piano Co., Winston-Salem, 1938-50, cons., partner, 1940-58; instr. Latin, Salem Acad., Winston-Salem, 1948-50; asso. prof. English, journalism, dramatics, speech Lees-McRae Coll., Banner Elk, N.C., 1950-53; asst. prof. English, Latin, Lenoir Rhyne Coll., Hickory, N.C., 1963-65, asso. prof., 1966-67, prof., 1969—, also chmn. humanities div. Mem. S. Atlantic Modern Lang. Assn., N.C. Edn. Assn., N.E.A., Am. Classical League, Classical Assn. Middle West and South, Vergilian Soc., Am. Assn. U. Women, Am. Assn. U. Profs., Nat. Council Tchrs. English, Am. Assn. Higher Edn., Nat. Assn. Music Mchts., Modern Lang. Assn., N.C. Classical Assn. (pres.), Am. Translators Soc., Internat. Platform Assn., Mu Sigma Epsilon. Clubs: Lake Hickory Country; Lenoir (N.C.) Country (Lenoir), Blowing Rock Country (N.C.) Home: 327 2d St NE Hickory NC 28601

CLAYTON, MARGARET BELLE MCCAULEY (MRS. OVERTON WILSON CLAYTON), photojournalist; b. Balt., Nov. 26, 1914; d. John William and Malinda Pearl (Piper) McCauley; student Goucher Coll., 1931-33; B.A., U. N.C., 1935; m. Overton Wilson Clayton, Sept. 25, 1937; children—Carol (Mrs. Earl Norris), Margaret (Mrs. Bruce Gebhardt), Patricia (Mrs. Bob Giddings), Virginia M. Tchr., Leaksville (N.C.) High Sch., Berry Hill High Sch., Charlotte, N.C., 1935-37; profl. writer, photojournalist, 1957—. Tchr. course Writing to Sell, Charlotte, 1965—. Active P.T.A., 1947-72; leader Girl Scouts U.S.A., 1961-64. Mem. Asso. Bus. Writers Am., Charlotte Writers Club (pres. 1972-74), Am. Assn. U. Women (past scholarships chmn.), Legal Aux. (past sec.), Opti-Mrs. (past sec.), Women in Communications, Phi Beta Kappa, Chi Omega. Lutheran. Contbr. numerous articles to mags., newspapers. Address: 6500 Burlwood Rd Charlotte NC 28211

CLAYTON, PAULA JEAN, physician; b. St. Louis, Dec. 1, 1934; d. Oscar George and Dorothea (Pflasterer) Limberg; B.S., U. Mich., 1956; M.D., Wash. U., 1960; m. Charles Clayton, July 12, 1958; children—Clarissa, Matthew, Andrew. Intern, St. Lukes Hosp., St. Louis, 1960-61; resident Renard Hosp., 1961-64, chief resident, 1964-65; instr. psychiatry Wash. U., St. Louis, 1965-67, asst. prof. psychiatry, 1967-72, asso. prof. psychiatry, 1972—. Mem. Am. Psychiat. Assn., Psychiat. Research Soc., Assn. for Research in Nervous and Mental Disease, Am. Psychopathol. Assn., Soc. Biol. Psychiatry, Eastern Mo. Psychiat. Assn., Sigma Xi, Alpha Omega Alpha. Contbr. articles in field to med. jours. Home: 7 Rio Vista St Louis MO 63124 Office: 4940 Audubon St Louis MO 63110

CLAYTON, SHERYL ANNE HOWARD (MRS. GEORGE CLAYTON), librarian; b. Kansas City, Mo., May 17, 1929; d. Maurice Lawrence and Gladys Benton (Garvin) Howard; B.S., Prairie View A. & M. Coll., 1948; M.S. in Library Sci., U. Ill., 1958; postgrad. Simmons Coll., 1966, Webster Coll., 1971, So. Ill. U., 1969-71, U. Mo., 1973; m. George Clayton, Sept. 19, 1953; children—Ruth (Mrs. Wendall A. Robbins, Jr.), Wynne, Elbert, Edgar. Tchr., librarian Sch. Dist. 188, East St. Louis, Ill., 1948-58, Sch. Dist. 189, 1958-70. librarian, State Community Coll., East St. Louis, Ill., 1970—. Mem. Golden Garden Com., East St. Louis, Ill., 1965. Sch. bd. sec. Sch. Dist. 184, East St. Louis, Ill., 1962-65; Ill. state chmn. Subsidies to Increase Black Adoptions, 1971-74. Named Woman of Year, Chick Finney Assos., 1973; recipient Friend of Children award Child Care Assn. Ill., 1974. Mem. N.A.A.C.P., Ill., St. Louis library assns., Alpha Kappa Alpha. Democrat. Christian Scientist. Club: Friday Night Bridge (East St. Louis). Editor: Metro-East Guide to Black Churches, 1973. Home: 519 S Jefferson St East St Louis IL 62205 Office: 417 Missouri Av East St Louis IL 62201

CLAYTON, VERNA ANN LEWIS (MRS. FRANK RODGERS CLAYTON, JR.), city ofcl.; b. Hamden, O., Feb. 28, d. Matthews L. and Yoil K. (Miller) Lewis; Okla. State U., 1954-55; m. Frank Rodgers Clayton, Jr., Feb. 4, 1956, children—Valerie Suzanne, Barry Lewis. Sec. Okla. Gas & Electric Co., Oklahoma City, 1955-56; cashier Denver Amarilla Express, Oklahoma City, 1956-57; sec. to asso. dean arts and scis. U. Okla., 1957-58; sec. Torklson Assos., Indpls., 1968-69; salesperson Avon, Buffalo Grove, Ill., 1969-71; village clk., Buffalo Grove, 1971—, village collector, 1972—, office mgr., 1972—. Inter club council chmn. YWCA, Winston-Salem, N.C., 1961, Y-Teen adviser, 1961. Precinct chmn. Republican party, 1965. Mem. Internat. Inst. Municipal Clks., Municipal Clks. Ill., Municipal Clks. North and N.W. Suburbs Cook County, Municipal Clks. Lake County (legislative chmn. 1973—), Strathmore Homeowners Assn. (schs. com. chmn. 1969), Women's Soc. Christian Service (pres. 1963), Delta Zeta. Methodist (mem. edn. commn. 1972). Home: 911 Twisted Oak Lane Buffalo Grove IL 60090 Office: 50 Raupp Blvd Buffalo Grove IL 60090

CLEARE, JULIE ANNE, psychologist, educator; b. Fall River, Mass., Jan. 20, 1937; d. William M. and Mary A. (Lomax) Cleare; B.A. magna cum laude, Seton Hill Coll., 1961; M.A., Fordham U., 1963, Ph.D., 1968. Intern in clin. psychology Columbia Presbyn. Med. Center, N.Y.C., 1965-67; staff psychologist Montefiore Med. Center, Bronx, N.Y., 1967-69; instr. psychology The Med. Center, Phila., 1969-70; asst. prof. psychology Southeastern Mass. U., North Dartmouth, Mass., 1971—. Individual practice Psychology, Portsmouth, R.I., 1970—; cons. psychology pub. schs., Fall River, Mass., 1971—, fed. programs, 1971—, various social service agys., 1971—. Bd. dirs. Big Bros. of Greater Fall River, sec. 1972-73. Mem. Am., Mass., R.I. psychol. assns., Mass., Fall River (dir. 1971—, sec. 1972-74) assn. for mental health, Phi Beta Kappa, Sigma Xi. Home: 50 Cliff Av Portsmouth RI 02871 Office: Southeastern Mass North Dartmouth MA 02747

CLEARWATER, FRANCES NEOMIA, city ofcl.; b. Paris, Ill., Apr. 4, 1924; d. John R. and Iva (Flickner) Blair; student extension bus. adminstrn. Ind. State U.; m. Clarence Eldon Clearwater, Apr. 18, 1942; children—Sandra (Mrs. Ray A. Clark), Johnnie Joe, Carolyn (Mrs. Robert Cash, Jr.), Robert. Legal sec., 1951-56; area radio and TV news corr. WPRS, Paris, 1956-63, accountant, 1957-61; pvt. investigator Paris Credit Bur., 1962-63; accountant City of Paris, 1963-66, city clk., 1966—. Exec. sec. Edgar County Cancer Soc.,

1956-63; team capt. New Paris Community Hosp. Fund Dr., 1970-71; mem. tng. inst. bds. U. Ill., 1972—. Mem. Ill. Municipal League (fed. revenue sharing panels and seminars), Municipal Clks. Ill. (state bd., 4th jud. rep. 1969-71, state treas. 1971-73, v.p. 1973—), Edgar County Legal Secs. Assn. (charter), Ill. P.T.A. (life), Paris Bus. and Profl. Women's Club (legislation chmn.). Methodist (membership chmn.). Home: 502 Clinton Av Paris IL 61944 Office: 123 S Central Av Paris IL 61944

CLEARY, BEVERLY ATLEE (MRS. CLARENCE T. CLEARY), author; b. McMinnville, Ore.; d. Chester Lloyd and Mable (Atlee) Bunn; B.A., U. Cal., 1938; B.A. in Librarianship, U. Wash., 1939; m. Clarence T. Cleary, Oct. 6, 1940; children—Marianne Elisabeth, Malcolm James. Children's librarian, Yakima, Wash., 1939-40; post librarian Regional Hosp., Oakland, Cal., 1942-45. Mem. Authors Guild of Authors League Am. Author: Henry Huggins, 1950; Ellen Tebbits, 1951; Henry and Beezus, 1952; Otis Spofford, 1953; Henry and Ribsy, 1954; Beezus and Ramona, 1955; Fifteen, 1956; Henry and the Paper Route, 1957; The Luckiest Girl, 1958; Jean and Johnny, 1959; The Real Hole, 1960; Hullabaloo ABC, 1960; Two Dog Biscuits, 1961; Emily's Runaway Imagination, 1961; Henry and the Clubhouse, 1962; Sister of the Bride, 1963; Ribsy, 1964; The Mouse and the Motorcycle, 1965; Mitch and Amy, 1967; Ramona the Pest, 1968; Runaway Ralph, 1970; Socks, 1973. Recipient Young Reader's Choice award Pacific N.W. Lbrary Assn., 1957, 60, 68, 71; Dorothy Canfield Fisher Children's book award Vt. Congress of Parents and Tchrs., 1958, 66; Nene award Hawaii Assn. Sch. Librarians and Hawaii Library Assn., 1968, 69, 71, 72; William Allen White award Kan. Assn. Sch. Librarians and Kan. Tchrs. Assn., 1968; Youth award South Central Ia. Assn. Classroom Tchrs., 1968; Ga. Children's Book award U. Ga., 1970; Sequoyah Children's Book award Okla. Library Assn., 1971; Simon award Ark. Elementary Sch. Council, 1973. Address: care William Morrow & Co 105 Madison Av New York City NY 10016

CLEARY, CATHERINE BLANCHARD, trust co. exec.; b. Madison, Wis., Dec. 19, 1916; d. Michael J. and Bonnie (Blanchard) Cleary; A.B., U. Chgo. 1937; LL.B., U. Wis., 1943; LL.D., Ripon Coll., 1955, Alverno Coll., 1970, Marquette U., 1972, Smith Coll., 1973. Pres., dir. First Wisconsin Trust Co., Milw.; trustee, mem. exec. com. Northwestern Mut. Life Ins. Co.; dir. Am. Tel. & Tel. Co., Kraftco Corp., First Wis. Bankshares Corp., Gen. Motors Corp., asst. treas. U.S., 1953; asst. to Sec. of Treasury, 1954. Pres. Milw. Children's Hosp., 1957-61. Mem. Nat. Assn. Bank Women (pres. 1952-53). Home: 929 N Astor St Milwaukee WI 53202 Office: 777 E Wisconsin St Milwaukee WI 53202

CLEARY, MARGUERITE ANN, coll. adminstr.; b. Oak Park, Ill., Jan. 27, 1925; d. Edmund Thomas and Elizabeth Mary (Green) Cleary; B.A. in Chemistry, Barat Coll., Lake Forest, Ill., 1953; M.A. in History, Lone Mountain Coll., 1965; M.Ed. in Counseling, Boston Coll., 1973; postgrad. U. Wis., Northwestern U., No. Ill. U. Joined Soc. Scared Heart, 1953; tchr. Acad. Sacred Heart, Chgo., also Woodlands Acad., Lake Forest, 1948-65, Christ the King Sch., Kalisizo, Uganda, East Africa, 1965-68; dir. studies Woodlands Acad., 1968-70, faculty supr. secondary sch. tchrs. edn. dept., 1970-72; dir. continuing edn. Barat Coll., 1973—. Counselor, Lake County Jail, 1971-72. Address: Barat College Lake Forest IL 60045

CLEARY, THERESA ANNE, educator; b. Shanghai, China, Dec. 12, 1935 (parents Am. citizens); d. Frank C. and Janet Elizabeth (Sweeney) Cleary; B.S., Marquette U., 1958; M.A., U. Minn., 1960; Ph.D., U. Ill., 1964. Research asst., statistician Ednl. Testing Service, Princeton, N.J., 1960-62, asso. research psychologist, 1964-65, research psychologist, 1965-66; mem. faculty U. Wis., Madison, 1966-72, asso. prof. dept. ednl. psychology, 1969-72; exec. dir. exams. Coll. Entrance Exam. Bd., N.Y.C., 1971-72, chief program services div., 1972-74, v.p. program planning and research, 1974—. Mem. Psychometric Soc. (trustee 1971-74), Am. Psychol. Assn., Am. Ednl. Research Assn., Am. Assn. U. Profs., Nat. Council Measurement in Edn., Am. Statis. Assn. Contbr. articles to profl. jours. Home: 25 W 68th St New York City NY 10023 Office: College Entrance Exam Bd 888 7th Av New York City NY 10019

CLEAVER, MARY JO, lawyer; b. Omaha, Oct. 7, 1930; d. Joseph J. and Mary (Kastan) Connell; B.S., Creighton U., 1952, J.D., 1954, M.A., 1955; m. Wayne C. Cleaver, Oct. 4, 1969. Admitted to Neb. bar, 1955; atty. U.S. Army Engrs. Dist., Omaha, 1955—, asst. dist counsel, 1965—. Mem. Am., Fed., Neb. bar assns. Republican. Roman Catholic. Home: 4766 Bedford Omaha NE 68104 Office: 6014 US Post Office and Courthouse Omaha NE 68102

CLEGG, RUBY FRANCES, educator; b. nr. Rotan, Tex., Aug. 10, 1939; d. Joseph Frank and Narcissia Clementine (Poteet) Clegg; B.S., Bethany Nazarene Coll., 1962; M.S., Okla. State U., 1964; Ph.D., 1973; postgrad. Southwestern State Coll., 1965-66. Instr. Southwestern State Coll., 1964-66; teaching asst. Okla. State U., 1963-64, 66; research asso. dept. obstetrics and gynecology Vanderbilt U., 1970-71; prof. sci., chmn. div. sci. and math. Western Tex. Coll., 1971—. NSF fellow, 1962-63; NIH pre-doctoral fellow, 1967-70. Mem. A.A.A.S., Am. Assn. U. Profs., Soc. Study Reprodn. (charter), Am. Soc. Zoologists, Southwestern Assn. Naturalists. Contbr. articles to profl. jours. Home: Box 863 407 N Garfield St Rotan TX 79546 Office: Western Tex Coll Snyder TX 75949

CLEGG, SUE WALL ROBERSON (MRS. CHARLES MYRON CLEGG), realtor, civic worker; b. Franklinton, N.C., June 4, 1904;; d. John Sachel and Florence (Tomlinson) Roberson; A.B., U. N.C., 1926; postgrad. Georgetown U. Grad. Sch. Govt., 1954-56; m. Charles Myron Clegg, Sept. 17, 1943; stepchildren—Charles Myron, Myles Standish, Eleanor Standish (Mrs. John Ennis Holloway). Realtor, Sandoz, Inc., Md., also D.C., 1972—. Sec. Georgetown Citizens Assn., del Fedn. Citizens Assns., Washington; mem. Zoning and Planning Com., chmn. Home Beautification Com.; mem. Nat. Trust for Historic Preservation. Publicity chmn. League Republican Women Washington, 1950's. Mem. Washington Bd. Realtors (asso.), UN Assn., U.S.A., Georgetown U. Alumni Assn., Nat. Wildlife Fedn. Home: 2800 Woodley Rd NW Washington DC 20008 Office: Sandoz Inc 4836 Mac Arthur Blvd Washington DC 20007

CLEMENGER, FLORENCE DIECKMANN, educator; b. Cin., Nov. 26; d. William and Frances (Jeckel) Dieckmann; A.B., U. Cin., 1942; M.W.S., U. Cal. at Berkeley, 1951; D.S.W., U. So. Cal., 1965; m. James William Clemenger, Aug. 7, 1943 (div. Aug. 1949). Program dir. various YWCAs, 1940-48; asst. exec. dir., Sunny Hills Children's Home, San Anselmo, Cal., 1951-52; exec. dir. YWCA, Richmond, Cal., 1952-55; mem. field staff Nat. YWCA, N.Y.C., 1955-56; lectr., field work cons. Sch. Social Welfare, U. Cal. at Berkeley, 1956-62, 64-65; asso. prof. Portland (Ore.) State Coll. Sch. Social Work, 1965-67; prof. dept. social work edn. San Francisco State Coll., 1967-68; prof. Grad. Sch. Social Work, U. Houston, 1968—. Cons. YWCA, Sch. Social Work, U. Hawaii, VA Hosp., Houston, social work staff Cath. Charities Houston. Mem. Berkeley Sr. Citizens Housing Assn., 1960-65; active YWCA. Mem. Nat. Assn. Social Workers, Nat. Conf. on Social Welfare, Acad. Certified Social Workers, Council on Social Work Edn., Internat. Conf. Social Welfare. Contbr. articles to profl. jours. Home: 725 International Blvd Houston TX 77024

CLEMENT, ANNIE, educator; b. Duluth, Minn., Feb. 13, 1937; d. Charles J. and Irene (Walsh) Clement; B.S. cum laude, U. Minn., 1959, M.A., 1964; Ph.D., U. Ia., 1966. Tchr., Hibbing (Minn.) High Sch., 1959-62; instr. phys. edn. U. Ia., Iowa City, 1962-66; asst. prof. phys. edn. U. Minn., Duluth, 1966-67, Ohio State U., Columbus, 1967-69; asso. prof. phys. edn., chmn. phys. edn. and recreation dept. Bowling Green (O.) State U., 1969-73, coordinator acad. program devel., 1973—. Mem. A.A.H.P.E.R. (chmn. coll. commn. 1970—), Ohio Coll. Assn.-Women's Phys. Edn., Ohio Assn. Health, Phys. Edn. and Recreation (mem. com. 1970-72), Nat., Midwest (mem. internat. relations com. 1971-72) assns. phys. edn. for coll. women, Internat. Acad. Aquatic Art. Editor: Ohio Secondary Curriculum Guide 1968-71. Contbr. articles to profl. jours. Home: 10835 Oak St Portage OH 43451

CLEMENT, BETTY KING, advt. co. exec.; b. Dallas, Sept. 17, 1938; d. Henry Grady and Annette (Clayton) King; B.A., So. Methodist U., 1961; m. John L. Clement, Dec. 20, 1967 (dec. Dec. 1969). Pub. relations asst. Dallas C. of C., 1960-65; advt. copywriter Lone Star Gas Co., Dallas, 1965-68; pub. relations account exec. Rominger Advt. Agy., Dallas, 1968-69, advt. account exec., 1969—, also v.p. recruitment advt. div., 1971—, corporate sec., 1972—. Mem. Gamma Alpha Chi. Methodist. Home: 3329 Prescott Av Dallas TX 75219 Office: 2900 Turtle Creek Plaza Dallas TX 75219

CLEMENT, EVELYN GEER, educator; b. Springfield, Mass., Sept. 1, 1926; d. Elihu and Helen Dorothy (Schenck) Geer; student Okla. Coll. Women, 1944-46; B.A. with honors, Tulsa U., 1965; M.L.S., U. Okla., 1966; postgrad. (U.S. Office Edn. doctoral fellow), Ind. U., 1968-72; m. J. Randall Clement, Sept. 9, 1946 (div. Apr. 1971); children—James Randall, Timothy, Susan (Mrs. Robin Henson), Marc, Audrey. Bookmobile librarian, reference librarian, readers adviser Tulsa City-County Library, 1961-66; learning resources librarian Oral Roberts U., Tulsa, 1966-68; spl. instr. U. Okla., Norman, 1966-70; dir. U.S. Office Edn. Inst., 1968, asst. dir., 1969-70; asso. prof., chmn. dept. library sci. Memphis State U., 1972—. Mem. Baker and Taylor Nonprint Media Adv. Task Force, 1972-73. Mem. Am. Soc. Information Sci., Assn. Ednl. Communications and Tech., Am. Assn. U. Profs., Am., Southeastern, Tenn., West Tenn. library assns., West Tenn. Edn. Assn., Memphis Library Council, Pi Gamma Mu, Phi Alpha Theta, Beta Phi Mu, Pi Lambda Theta. Home: 585 S Goodlett St Memphis TN 38111

CLEMENT, IDA KRAUSE (MRS. FRITZ CLEMENT), editor; B. Java, S.D., June 9, 1906; d. Israel R. and Anna Mary (Diegel) Krause; grad. high sch.; m. Fritz Clement, Feb. 21, 1926; children—Bruce, Germaine (Mrs. Wendel G. Mead). Telephone operator N.W. Bell Telephone Co., Java, S.D., 1924-34; postal clk., Java, 1924-34; Editor Java Herald, 1926—, news writer, 1924—, bookkeeper, 1924—, columnist, 1945—; with Selby (S.D.) Record, 1945—, editor, columnist, bookkeeper, 1945—. Named Woman of Year Selby Jr. C. of C., 1965. Mem. S.D. Press Women (treas. 1950-54), Selby Woman's Club (pres. 1952-53; treas., 1967—), Sigma Delta Chi. Methodist. Mem. Order Eastern Star (matron 1934-35). Home: Box 343 Selby SD 57472 Office: 4911 Main St Selby SD 57472

CLEMENT, MARY EDNA BROWN, artist, poet; b. Bowie, Tex.; d. James Houston and Ruth (Roark) Brown; student pub. schs., Gainesville, Tex.; m. J. T. Clement, Oct. 31, 1937 (div. Apr. 1956); children—Joan (Mrs. Don Danyko), Richard Bruce, Jane Barbara. Exhibited in group shows at Art League Spring Round Up, 1966, Dula Center, 1966, Artists and Craftsmen's Guild Show, 1967, Jr. C. of C. Community Fair, 1967, (First prize), 1969, Sands Hotel Conv. Center, 1967 (all Las Vegas, Nev.), Clark County Sch. Bldg., 1966, Moapa Valley Festival, Overton, Nev., 1966, 69, 70, 71, North Las Vegas Art Festival, 1966, Boulevard Mall, 1969, 70, Hanging Tree Art Gallery, 1970, Studio Art Gallery, 1972, Western Art Show, Las Vegas, 1966-71. Auditor, So. Nev. Hist. Soc., 1965—. Recipient Honorable Mention awards Jaycee Nev. State Fair, 1970, 71. Mem. Nat. League Am. Pen Women (past nat. insignia chmn., Las Vegas br. pres., past state pres., v.p., treas), D.A.R. (past chpt. sec., registrar, librarian), Royal Neighbors, Gallery Guild (past historian), Archaeol. Nev. Soc. (historian), Artists and Craftsmens Guild Las Vegas (sec. 1971) So. Nev. Hist. Soc. (treas.), Allied Arts Council (v.p., pres.), Las Vegas Stamp Club. Unitarian. Author: (poems) Black and Silver, 1944. Home: 2402 Marlin Av Las Vegas NV 89101

CLEMENTS, GERALDINE RUTH, nurse; b. Perth, N.B., Can., June 5, 1921; d. Hugh Francis and Catherine Rose (Larlee) Smith; grad. St. John Gen. Sch. Nurses, 1944; student Mt. Allison U.; B.Nursing, Dalhousie U., 1968; m. Cedric Stead Clements, Apr. 11, 1970. Dr.'s office nurse, 1944-45; nurse Victoria Pub. Hosp., Fredericton, N.B., 1945-46; obstet. supr. Sackville (N.B.) Meml. Hosp., 1946-57, dir. nursing, 1957-70; dir. nursing Oromocto (N.B.) Pub. Hosp., 1971—. Mem. Interim Commn. on Alcoholism, 1973—. Home: 245 Parkhurst Dr Fredericton NB Canada

CLEMENTS, JOY, soprano; b. Dayton, O.; d. Verne Brent and Lulu Frances (Day) Albrecht; student Acad. Vocal Arts, Phila., 1951, U. Miami (Fla.), 1954-56; m. L. D. Clements, Dec. 29, 1957; children—Lori Elena, Matthew David, Debut in La Boheme, Opera Guild Miami, 1956; mem. N.Y.C. Opera, 1959-62, Met. Opera Assn., 1963—; leading soprano Copland's The Tender Land, N.Y. Philharmonic, 1965; rec. artist for Columbia Records; solo appearances with Israel Philharmonic, Tel Aviv, N.Y., Cleve. Symphony, also operas in Cin., Duluth, Minn., Houston and Tulsa; guest artist with Pitts., Chgo. orchs., Central City, Colo., Miami opera cos.; guest soloist Hawaii Opera, 1973, Memphis Opera, Boston Symphony, Balt. Opera, San Francisco Symphony, San Diego Opera; guest appearance at White House, 1967; appeared as Gretel in Hansel and Gretel at Met. Opera, 1967-68; created role of Mary Warren in opera The Crucible; appearances N.Y.C. Opera, 1972, Lake Erie (Cleve.) Opera, 1969, Vancouver (B.C.) Opera, 1969, Ft. Worth Opera, 1970, Balt. Civic Opera, 1970; appeared in Gilda, Orlando, Fla., Ft. Worth, 1972, Barber of Seville, San Diego Opera, 1972, others. Home: Lake Shore Dr West Lake Tamarack Stockholm NJ 07460 Office: Lustig-Florian Artists Mgmt 111 W 57th St New York City NY 10019

CLEMMONS, FRANCES ANNE MANSELL (MRS. SLATON CLEMMONS), govt. ofcl.; b. Camden, Miss., Dec. 21, 1915; d. Otho Franklin and Pearl (Dunlap) Mansell; B.S., Belhaven Coll., 1937, Mus.B., 1937; m. Rowe Sanders Crowder, Dec. 17, 1938 (div. Mar. 1954); children—Rowe Sanders, Frances Elizabeth; m. 2d, Slaton Clemmons, Nov. 21, 1965. Owner, operator Crowder Art Gallery, Jackson, Miss., 1946-50; dept. mgr., buyer Valley Dry Goods Co., Vicksburg, 1954-56; with Social Security Adminstrn., 1956—, asst. dist. mgr., Rome, Ga., 1962—. Mem. Internat. Platform Assn., Rome Community Concert Assn. Democrat. Presbyn. Club: Quota Internat. (pres. 1974) (Rome, Ga.). Home: 412 E 3d Av Rome GA 30161 Office: Federal Bldg Rome GA 30161

CLEMONS, ELIZABETH CAMERON (MRS. NELSON T. NOWELL), author; b. Berkeley, Cal.; d. Alfred George and Edith (Catton) Cameron; A.B. San Jose State Coll., 1928; M.A., Stanford U. 1937; m. Wood Clemons, Dec. 22, 1946 (div. Dec. 1958); m. 2d, Arthur G. Robinson, May 27, 1961 (dec. Jan. 1967); m. 3d, Nelson T. Nowell, Feb. 15, 1969 (dec. Sept. 1973). With edn. dept. San Jose State Coll., 1928-39, in service tng. U. Cal. Extension Div., 1939-42; elementary editor The John C. Winston Co., 1942-43, Silver Burdett Co. 1943-44, D. C. Heath, 1944-46; instr. English dept. U. Minn., 1947; writing, editing publs. services Gen. Mills, 1947-50; free-lance writer 1950—; reading cons. Monterey City Sch., 1959-62, asso. editor Cal. edit. Am. Home Mag., 1965-70. Mem. Peninsula Community Hosp. Aux. Mem. Nat. League Am. Pen Women, Authors Guild, League Women Voters, Kappa Alpha Theta, Pi Lambda Theta, Delta Phi Upsilon, Kappa Delta Pi, Delta Kappa Gamma. Republican. Episcopalian. Clubs: Women's City, Carmel Valley Golf and Country, Monterey Peninsula Country, Soroptimist. Author: The Pixie Dictionary, 1953; the Catholic Child's First Dictionary, 1954; The Winston Dictionary for Canadian School Children, 1955; Away I Go., 1956; All About Baby, 1956; I Live on A Farm, 1956; A Wish for Billy, 1956; Wings, Wheels, and Motors, 1957; The Big Book of Real Fire Engines, 1958; The Big Book of Real Trains, 1958; The Big Book of Real Trucks, 1958; Rodeo Days, 1960; Shells Are Where You Find Them, 1960; Rocks and The World Around You, 1960; Big and Little, 1961; Tide Pools and Beaches, 1964; Tides, Waves, and Currents, 1967; Here and There Stories; Now and Then Stories; Near and Far Stories; A Source Book for the Teaching of Literature for Children (all 1967); The Seven Seas, 1971; The Friendly Frog, 1971; What I Like, 1971; also feature articles in nat. mags. Home: Box 686 Carmel CA 93921

CLEMONS, FRAN VANCE (MRS. PERRY REESE CLEMONS), charitable instn. adminstr.; b. Plumtree, N.C., Dec. 11, 1925; d. Ivor Charles and Daisy (Edwards) Vance; B.A., Woman's Coll., U. N.C., 1945; m. Perry Reese Clemons, Nov. 21, 1951; children—Vanessa Leigh, Risa Lynn, Kay Frances. Dir. drama dept. Callaway Mills Co., LaGrange, Ga., 1948-54; radio program dir. sta. WTRP, LaGrange, 1956-59; field adviser, pub. relations dir. Girl Scouts, Albany, Ga., 1960-62; pub. relations dir. United Fund, Albany, Ga., 1962-66; exec. dir. United Way, Marion County, Ocala, Fla., 1966—. Pres. Marion County Social Service Council, 1974; mem. Task Force for Local Missions, Ocala, Marion County Adv. Com. on Crime Prevention. Bd. dirs. Ocala Civic Theatre, treas., 1970—; bd. dirs. Marion County Comprehensive Health Planning Council, 1973—. Mem. United Way Execs. Fla. (treas. 1966-69, sec. 1972). Republican. Presbyn. Office: 120 SE Broadway Ocala FL 32670

CLEMONS, LULAMAE, univ. adminstr.; b. Widener, Ark., Dec. 17; d. Will and Mamie (Moore) Clemons; B.S., Lincoln U., 1945; M.A., Tchrs. Coll. Columbia, 1951; postgrad. U. So. Cal., 1964; m. Frank Clay McClanahan Jr.; 1 son, Frank Clay III. Dir. student health services Lincoln U., Jefferson City, Mo., 1945-46; cons. health edn. Office County Supt. Schs., Riverside, Cal., 1956-70; dir. intergroup edn. health, counseling and pupil personnel unit U. Cal. at Riverside, 1970—, lectr., 1970—; adminstr. fed. project Title IV (sch. desegregation tech. assistance), Riverside. Instr. multi-cultural edn. Cal. State Coll. at Fullerton, 1969-70. Chmn. Riverside City Community Relations Commn., 1965—; pres. N.A.A.C.P., Riverside, 1958-60; vol. dir. Headstart, 1966—. Bd. dirs. United Fund, 1966—, Heart Assn., 1957-62, Health and Tb Assn., 1960-70, Girl Scouts U.S.A., 1967—. Recipient Bronze award Heart Assn., 1971. Intercultural scholar, 1960—. Mem. N.E.A. (life), Am. Assn. U. Women, EDUCARE, Alpha Kappa Alpha (Woman of Year 1967). Author: (with Gardiner and Hollitz) The American Negro, 1965. Home: 5837 Walter St Riverside CA 92504

CLESCERI, LENORE STANKE, educator; b. Chgo., Aug. 9, 1935; d. Walter C. and Elinor C. (Schuster) Stanke; B.S., Loyola U., Chgo., 1958; M.S., Marquette U., 1959; Ph.D., U. Wis.-Madison, 1963; postgrad. Eidgenossichen Technischen Hochschule, Zurich, 1965; m. Nicholas L. Clesceri, Aug. 31, 1957; children—Pamela, Kristine, Craig, Erika, Jeffery. Instr. U. Wis., 1957-59, research asst. 1959-63; Eidgenossichen Technischen Hochschule 1963-65; research fellow Rensselaer Poly. Inst., 1966-70, research fellow asst. prof. microbial biochemistry, 1970-74, asso. prof., 1974—; cons. in field. Active local Girl Scouts U.S.A., Confrat. Christian Doctrine. grantee USPHS 1963-65, NIH, 1972-74, NSF, 1971-74, Environmental Protection Agy., 1966-70. Mem. Am. Chem. Soc., Soc., Internat. Limnologiae, Am. Soc. Microbiology, Sigma Xi (pres. regional chpt. 1971-73). Contbr. profl. jours. Home: Lake Shore Dr Bolton Landing NY 12814 Office: Dept Biology Rensselaer Poly Inst Troy NY 12181

CLESS, ELIZABETH LAWRENCE (MRS. HOWARD L. CLESS); educator; b. Akron, O., Jan. 28, 1916; d. James Cooper and Ruth Elizabeth (Williamson) Lawrence; student U. Florence (Italy), 1933-34; B.A. cum laude, Radcliffe Coll., 1938; postgrad. museum adminstrn. Harvard Grad. Sch. Arts and Scis., 1937-38, Oriental Inst. U. Hawaii, 1938-39; m. C. Irving Clark, 1939 (div. 1953); children—Peter Irving Clark, Julia (Mrs. Cornelius Lansing Fair); m. 2d, Howard Louis Cless, June 1, 1956. Lectr. Honolulu Acad. Arts, 1938-39; asst. dir. for community services Walker Art Center, Mpls., 1939-40, tchr., 1939-41; library dir. research Ames Library of South Asia, St. Paul, 1940-43, 46-48; asst. chief Indic sect. Div. Orientalia, Library of Congress, Washington, 1944; coordinator South Asian desk Div. Cultural Cooperation Dept. of State, Washington, 1944-45; fashion dir. Field-Schlick, Inc., St. Paul, 1953-54; program cons. Nolte Center for Continuing Edn. U. Minn., 1954-59, lectr. gen. extension div., 1954-59, asst. prof., 1959-62, asst. to dean liberal arts programs, 1957-66, asso. prof., 1962-66; dir. spl. acad. programs Claremont Colls. (Cal.), 1966—, dir. Office Continuing Edn., 1966—, prof. grad. sch., 1966—; tchr. U. Cal. brs. extension div., 1966—, Claremont Grad. Sch., Pomona Coll., Claremont Men's Coll., Pitzer Coll., Scripps Coll., 1966—; cons. in field. Mem. council Blaisdell Inst. Advanced Study in World Cultures and Religions, Claremont, 1969—; initiator St. Paul Council Arts and Sci., 1947-52. Trustee Radcliffe Coll.; bd. dirs. Nat. Coalition for Research on Womens Edn. and Devel., pres., 1972—. Named Nat. Woman of Year, Am. Women's Active Return to Edn., 1967; recipient Radcliffe Coll. Alumnae Recognition award, 1970, Los Angeles Times Woman of Year award, 1970. Rockfeller-Carnegie grantee Brit.-Am. meeting on woman's edn., Bellagio, Italy, 1964. Mem. Am. Oriental Soc., Am. Adult Edn. Assn., Jr. League (pres. St. Paul 1950-52), Colonial Dames Am., Nat. U. Extension Assn. (arts and humanities com. 1954-66), Am. Assn. U. Women, Radcliffe Coll. Alumnae Assn. (pres. Minn. chpt. 1947-49), Women's Equity Action League. Contbr. articles to profl. jours., anthologies. Home: 626 W 9th St Claremont CA 91711

CLEVELAND, HATTYE MAE JOHNSON (MRS. JOHN MARION CLEVELAND, JR.), occupational therapist; b. Laurens, S.C., Sept. 22, 1912; d. William Guy and Rosa Lee (Fuller) Johnson; B.S., Shaw U., 1935; certificate occupational therapy N.Y. U., 1956; m. John Marion Cleveland, Jr., Aug. 29, 1936. Sci. tchr. head sci. dept. UpChurch High Sch., Raeford, N.C., 1935-37; staff therapist Willobrook State Sch., Staten Island, N.Y., 1956-60; sr. occupational therapist Beth Abraham Home, Bronx, N.Y., 1960-65; chief occupational therapist Montefiore-Morrisania Affiliation, Bronx, N.Y., 1965-72, supr., 1972—. Reporter News Election Service, Mt.

Vernon, N.Y., 1970-73. Recipient Certificate of Honor and Loyalty, Shaw U. Alumni Assn., 1965, Service awards Montefiore Hosp. and Med. Center, 1970, Beth Abraham Home, 1964. Certificate of Recognition, Grace Bapt. Ch., 1968, Certificate of Merit, United Missionary Bapt. Assn., 1964. Mem. Nat. Council Negro Women, Inc. (pres. Westchester County sect. 1971-74), League Women Voters, Am., N.Y. State (dir. N.Y. dist. 1960-62, 65-67, chmn. legislative com. 1967-70) occupational therapy assns., Nat. Assn. Study-Life History. Baptist (asst. gen. supt. ch. sch. 1969-74). Club: Shaw University Alumni (chaplain 1960-73) (N.Y.C.). Home: 22 Union Av Mount Vernon NY 10550 Office: Gerard Av and 168th St Bronx NY 10452

CLEVER, ELAINE COX, librarian; b. N.Y.C.; d. Russell Scarlott and Estelle Ruth (Gilliland) Cox; B.A., Pa. State U., 1944; M.S., Drexel U., 1961; m. Fred E. Clever, Feb. 18, 1944; 1 son, Eric Conrad. Reading tchr. Avon Sch., Barrington, N.J., 1954-59; librarian Woodland Sch., Barrington, 1959-63, Haddon (N.J.) High Sch., 1963-64; univ. librarian Temple U., Phila., 1964—, head circulation div. Mem. Fedn. Internat. de Documentation, Nat. Information Retrieval Colloquium (exec. com. Phila. 1973), Am. Assn. U. Profs. (exec. com., treas. Temple U. chpt. 1973—), Am. Soc. Information Sci., Am. Civil Liberties Union, N.J. Women's Coalition, Engrs. Club Phila., Theta Sigma Phi, Beta Phi Mu. Author: Faculty Use of Library Reference Facilities for Citation and Data Information, 1970. Home: Sherry Way-Hunt Tract Cherry Hill NJ 08034 Office: Paley Library Temple U Philadelphia PA 19122

CLEVIDENCE, MARY-JUELL ANNE (MRS. ARTHUR CARL CLEVIDENCE), educator; b. Cleve., Apr. 26, 1929; d. John Thomas and Julia Anne (Florence) Cooper; B.S., Duquesne U., 1950; postgrad. (Martha Holden Tennings grant), Akron U., 1968-70; m. Arthur Carl Clevidence, Apr. 18, 1953; children—Mary Kathleen, John, Patrick William. Tchr. primary schs., Seville, O., 1951-53; tchr. jr. high sch., Lodi, O., 1953-62, Seville, 1966—. Chmn. Cancer Drive, 1970—; area chmn. A.R.C., 1968—. Chmn. Rep. Com., 1969—. Bd. dirs. Heart Fund, Medina County O. Mem. Ohio Edn. Assn, N.E. Ohio Tchrs. Assn., N.E.A. Address: 94 Liberty St Seville OH 44273

CLEWELL, FLORENCE EVELYN, ednl. adminstr.; b. Buffalo, Kan., Mar. 27, 1905; d. Harry E. and Bertha Mae (Pratt) Clewell; student Hardin-Simmons U., 1923-24, Baylor U., 1926-27; B.A., U. Okla., 1929; postgrad. Tex. Tech U., 1930. Asst. dir. Meth. Ednl. Hdqrs., Waco, Tex., 1925-26; asst. registrar Tex. Tech U., Lubbock, 1929-64, coordinator of space, 1964-67, dir. instnl. research, 1968-73, cons., supr. compilation Univ. Facts Book, 1973—. Mem. Tex. Coordinating Bd. Com. on Univ. Facilities Survey, 1965-70; mem. com. on doctoral granting univs. So. Regional Ednl. Bd., 1969-72. Bd. dirs. YWCA, Lubbock, 1961-62. Mem. Am. Assn. Collegiate Registrars and Admissions Officers, Tex. Assn. Collegiate Registrars, Assn. Instnl. Research (charter), Lubbock C. of C., Theta Sigma Phi, Alpha Kappa Gamma, Delta Gamma. Club: Pilot (pres. 1953-54, dist. treas. 1954-55). Home: 1605 55th St Lubbock TX 79412 Office: Box 4380 Texas Tech University Lubbock TX 79409

CLIFF, MAY MURPHY, physician; b. Houston, Oct. 20, 1938; d. Ivan Spaulding and Mary Lynn (Stevenson) Cliff; B.A., U. Rochester, 1959; M.D., U. Ill. at Chgo., 1962. Intern Phila. Gen. Hosp., 1962-63; resident in radiology Temple U. Hosp., Phila., 1963-66, NIH cardiovascular fellow, 1966-67, staff radiologist, 1967—; instr. Temple Med. Sch., 1967-68, asst. prof. radiology, 1968-71, asso. prof., 1971-72; asso. prof. U. Colo. Med. Sch., 1972—. Mem. Colo. Commn. on Status Women. Mem. Women's Am. Med. Assn., Rocky Mountain Radiol. Soc., Colo., Denver med. socs., U. Ill. Alumni Assn., Am. Coll. Radiology, Colo. Radiol. Soc., Radiol. Soc. N.Am., Assn. Univ. Radiologists, A.M.A., Colonial Dames Blockley Soc. (sec., 1962-63), Colo. Drs. Ski Patrol Assn., Nat. Commn. Single Taxpayers, Am. Assn. Higher Edn., Denver Resource Center for Women (charter), Common Cause, Phi Beta Kappa. Home: 860 Clermont St Denver CO 80220 Office: U Colo Med Center Dept Radiology 4200 E 9th Av Denver CO 80220

CLIFFORD, MRS. DONALD K. (MARGERY M. CLIFFORD), corp. ofcl.; b. Malone, N.Y., Aug. 20, 1900; d. Ferris J. and Louise (Lawrence) Meigs; B.A., Vassar Coll., 1923; LL.D. (hon.), Bethune-Cookman Coll., Daytona Beach, Fla., 1973; m. Donald K. Clifford, June 15, 1929; children—Louise M. (Mrs. Andrew D. Hart, Jr.), Donald Knight, Margery Meigs (Mrs. John B. Henneman, Jr.). Began as field secretary N.Y. Child Labor Com., 1923-27. Mem. bd. dirs. Lawrence Investing Co., Hotel Gramatan, Bronxville, N.Y., Brooklands Corp., Bronxville. Mem. Bronxville Sch. Bd., 1950-56. Mem. Rep. Town Com., Bronxville, 1947-50. Bd. govs. Lawrence Hosp., Bronxville; trustee Bethune-Cookman Coll. Club: Vassar (pres. 1953-55) (Westchester, N.Y.). Home: 42 Prescott Av Bronxville NY 10708

CLIFFORD, GERALDINE MARIE JONCICH (MRS. WILLIAM F. CLIFFORD), educator; b. San Pedro, Cal., Apr. 17, 1931; d. Marion and Geraldine (Mustacich) Joncich; A.B., U. Cal. at Los Angeles, 1954, M.Ed., 1957; Ed.D., Columbia, 1961; m. William F. Clifford, July 12, 1969. Tchr., San Lorenzo, Cal., 1954-56, Maracaibo, Venezuela, 1957-58; researcher Inst. Lang. Arts, Tchrs. Coll., Columbia, 1958-61; asst. prof. edn. U. Cal. at Berkeley, 1962-67, asso. prof., 1967—. Macmillan fellow, 1958-59, Guggenheim fellow, 1965-66. Mem. Am. Hist. Assn., History Edn. Soc., Am. Ednl. Studies Assn., Am. Studies Assn., Phi Beta Kappa, Pi Lambda Theta. Author: The Sane Positivist: A Biography of Edward L. Thorndike, 1968. Home: 2428 Prince St Berkeley CA 94705

CLIFFORD, MARGARET CORT, author; b. Cin., Sept. 20, 1929; d. George Edward and Margaret Barrington (Mackoy) Clifford; grad. Chatham Hall Prep. Sch.; B.A., Chatham Coll., 1951. Freelance writer, Pitts. and N.Y.C., 1951-53; mng. editor Aspen (Colo.) Times, 1956-59, columnist, 1960—; editor Aspen Flyer, 1954-59; editor Jr. Reviewers mag., 1958-59. Cons. Patricia Moore Art Gallery, Aspen, 1965—. Recipient Parkhurst Community Service award (with Aspen Times) Colo. Press Assn., 1958. Author: Elliott, 1967; The Gnu and the Guru Go Behind the Beyond, 1970; Aspen: Dreams and Dilemmas, 1970. Contbr. numerous articles to mags. Writer documentary films for Pub. Broadcasting Service, 1972—; writer series of documentaries on Am. environments and search for community, 1972-74. Home: 214 Lake Av Aspen CO 81611 Office: Box 371 Aspen CO 81611

CLIFT, MARY MAGDALENE, physician; b. Cin.; d. James A. and Mary J. (Hagemeyer) Clift; A.B., U. Cin., 1946, M.D., 1950; postgrad. U. Pa., 1955-56. Intern Md. Gen. Hosp., Balt., 1950-51; surg. resident Good Samaritan Hosp., Cin., 1951-54, Cin. Gen. Hosp., 1954-55; staff mem. Providence, Good Samaritan, Christ, Deaconess hosps. (all Cin.); pvt. practice gen. surgery and gynecology, Cin., 1956—. Mem. profl. edn. com. Am. Cancer Soc. Diplomate Am. Bd. Surgery, Pan Am. Med. Assn. Fellow A.C.S.; mem. A.M.A., Am. Med. Women's Assn., Acad. Medicine Cin., Ohio Med. Assn., Cin. Surg. Soc., Mont Reid Surg. Soc., Iota Sigma Pi. Home: 446 Wood Av Cincinnati OH 45220 Office: Carew Tower Cincinnati OH 45202

CLIFT, ULYSSINE GWENDOLYN GIBSON (MRS. JOSEPH WILLIAM CLIFT), social worker; b. Port Arthur, Tex., Aug. 12, 1937; d. Ulysses Grant and Matilda Louise (McShann) Gibson; B.A., Fisk U., 1958; M.A., U. Chgo., 1960; m. Joseph William Clift, Aug. 10, 1963. Med. social worker social service dept. U. Tex. Med. Br., Galveston, 1960-65; caseworker Family Service, Berkeley, Cal., 1965-67; dist. dir. Family and Childrens Service Assn., Dayton, O., 1967-69; caseworker, field work supr. Family Service, Berkeley, Cal., 1969-72; field work supr. U. Cal., Berkeley, 1969-72; pvt. practice, 1972—. Mem. Nat. Assn. Social Workers, Acad. Certified Social Workers, Alpha Kappa Delta, Alpha Kappa Alpha. Home: 14030 Broadway Terrace Oakland CA 94611 Office: 3023 Summit St Oakland CA 94609

CLIFTON, ALMA CHRISTINA DEBRULER (MRS. JOHN ROBERTSON CLIFTON), city ofcl.; b. Indpls., Feb. 8, 1925; d. Henson Raymond and Alma (Sellers) DeBruler; student U. Cal. at Los Angeles, 1943, U. So. Cal., 1944, Los Angeles Harbor Coll., 1961-63; m. John Robertson Clifton, Nov. 3, 1945; children—John Robertson, Christina Alma. Engring. draftsman Northrop Corp., Hawthorne, Cal., 1943-47; city clk. pro tem City of Rolling Hills Estates, Cal., 1957-58, councilwoman, 1957-64, vice mayor, 1960-62, mayor, 1963-64, city mgr., 1964—; dep. sheriff Los Angeles County, 1958—. Mem. Mayors' Com. Los Angeles County. Sec.-treas. Am. Mgmt. Corp. Sec.-treas. Home Owners Assn., Rolling Hills Estates, 1952-55; treas. P.T.A., Rolling Hills Estates, 1953, safety chmn., 1955-56; mem. Needlework Guild, Rolling Hills Estates, 1956-66; mem. Peninsula Com. Los Angeles Philharmonic Orch., 1959-65; mem. adv. bd. Los Angeles Harbor Coll., 1962-64; area chmn. Community Chest, Rolling Hills Estates, 1959—. Bd. dirs. Los Angeles County Sanitation Dist., 1957-60, 63-64. Recipient hon. life membership Cal. Congress Parents and Tchrs., 1960, award Palos-Verdes-Rolling Hills Assn. U. Women, Beautiful Activist award So. Cal., 1973. Mem. South Bay Mgrs. Assn. (v.p.). Methodist (communion steward, mem. parsonage com., bldg. com., trustee). Home: 32 Strawberry Lane Rolling Hills Estates CA 90274 Office: 2 Portuguese Bend Rd Rolling Hills CA 90274

CLIFTON, NANCY LYNN, univ. adminstr.; b. Greensburg, Ind., Jan. 20, 1946; d. Max T. and Carol N. (Howe) Clifton; B.S., Ball State U., 1968; M.S., State U. N.Y., 1969. Asst. residence hall dir. State U. N.Y., Albany, 1968-69; head resident Cal. State U., Fullerton, 1969-70; dir. women's residence halls Ball State U., Muncie, Ind., 1970—, also now instr. Edn. Sch. Mem. Am. Personnel and Guidance Assn., Am. Coll. Personnel Assn. (mem. nat. program planning com. 1974 mem. nat. women's task force 1974—), Nat. Assn. Women Deans, Adminstrs. and Counselors, Ind. Nat. Women Deans, P.E.O. (chaplain 1972), Sigma Kappa, Tri Kappa. Republican. Home: 1403 Maddox Dr Muncie IN 47304

CLIFTON, RAMONA PORTER (MRS. FARRIS WILLIAM CLIFTON), optometrist; b. Central City, Ky., Mar. 14, 1925; d. Edgar Deboe and Molly (Roby) Porter; student U. Louisville, 1942-44; D. Optometry, So. Coll. Optometry, 1946; m. Farris William Clifton, Oct. 25, 1957; 1 son, David Lee. Individual practice optometry, Bardstoun, Ky., 1947—. Mem. Ky. Bd. Optometric Examiners, 1952-60; cons. Kentuckiana Center Edn., Health and Research; mem. optometric tech. adv. com. Ky. Med. Assistance. Mem. Ky. White House Conf. on Children and Youth, 1960. Mem. Am. Sch. Health Assn., Nat. Eye Research Found., D.A.R., Am. (com. career guidance 1973—), Ky. (pres. 1970-71, trustee at large) optometric assns., Ky. Pub. Health Assn. (named Outstanding Ky. Optometrist of Year 1965), Ky. Hist. Soc., Bardstown C. of C. (sec. 1955-56), Chi Omega. Mem. Disciples of Christ (deaconess 1962, chmn. congregation 1974—). Club: Stephen Foster Music (pres. 1969-70). Home: 313 N 3d St Bardstown KY 40004 Office: 311 N 3d St Bardstown KY 40004

CLINE, CATHERINE ANN, historian; b. West Springfield, Mass., July 27, 1927; d. Daniel Edward and Agnes (Howard) Cline; A.B. cum laude, Smith Coll., 1948; M.A., Columbia, 1950; Ph.D., Bryn Mawr Coll., 1957. Asst. history dept. Smith Coll., Northampton, Mass., 1952-53; instr. St. Mary's Coll., South Bend, Ind., 1953-54; asst. prof. Notre Dame Coll., S.I., 1954-68, asso. prof., 1954-57, prof., 1957-68; asso. prof. Catholic U. Am., 1968-73, prof., 1973—. Am. Philos. Assn. grantee, 1960. Mem. Am. Hist. Assn., Am. Cath. Hist. Assn., Conf. British Studies. Author: Recruits to Labour: The British Labour Party, 1914-31, 1963. Contbr. articles to profl. jours. Home: 3801 Connecticut Av NW Washington DC 20008 Office: History Dept Catholic Univ America Washington DC 20017

CLINE, DOROTHY MAY STAMMERJOHN (MRS. EDWARD WILBURN CLINE), educator; b. Boonville, Mo., Oct. 19, 1915; d. Benjamin Franklin and Lottie (Walther) Stammerjohn; grad. nurse U. Mo., 1937. B.S. in Edn., 1939, postgrad., 1966-67; M.S., Ark. State Coll., 1964; m. Edward Wilburn Cline, Aug. 16, 1938 (dec. May 1962); children—Margaret Ann (Mrs. Rodger Orville Bell), Susan Elizabeth (Mrs. Gary Lee Burns), Dorothy Jean. Dir. Christian Coll. Infirmary, Columbia, Mo., 1936-37; asst. chief, nursing service U.S. VA Hosp., Poplar Bluff, Mo., 1950-58; tchr.-in-charge Tng. Center No. 4, Poplar Bluff, 1959-66, State Sch. No. 53, Boonville, 1967—; part-time instr. U. Mo., 1973—. Mem. Boonslick Assn. for Retarded Children, 1966— (v.p. 1970). Mem. Am. Assn. U. Women (v.p. Boonville 1969—), Mo. Writers Guild, N.E.A., Mo. Tchrs. Assn., Am. Assn. Mental Deficiency (sec.-treas. Mo. chpt.), Council for Exceptional Children, U. Mo. Alumni Assn., Bus. and Profl. Women's Club, Internat. Platform Assn., Creative Writer's Group, Eastern Center Poetry Soc., Laura Speed Elliott High Sch. Alumni Assn., Ark. State U. Alumni Assn., Boonslick Hist. Soc., Alpha Delta Kappa. Mem. Christian Ch. Home: 603 E High St Boonville MO 65233

CLINEDINST, KATHERINE PARSONS (MRS. WENDEL WATERS CLINEDINST), artist; b. Stamford, Conn., July 13, 1903; d. Harold Ashton and Mary Brookfield (Paxson) Parsons; student Pratt Inst., 1923, China Inst., 1958-61; m. Wendel Waters Clinedinst, Oct. 24, 1925; 1 son, Richard Wendel Parsons. Asst. mgr. Boston Soc. Arts and Crafts 1923-24; exhibited in one-man show at First Nat. Bank of Westchester, Mamaroneck, N.Y., 1957, Bronxville (N.Y.) Library, 1962, Engring. Womans Club, N.Y.C., 1963; exhibited in numerous group shows in U.S., and fgn. countries, represented in permanent collections at Bronxville Library. Co-founder Larchmont (N.Y.) Outdoor Art Show, 1958. Recipient numerous art awards. Mem. Nat. League Am. Pen Women (organizer, dir. Westchester br. 1954, pres. 1958-60), Am. Artists Profl. League, D.A.R., Acad. Artists, Meridan Arts and Crafts, Kent Art Assn., Miniature Soc., Hudson Valley Art Assn. (dir. 1958-66). Home and studio: 951 A Argyll Circle Lakewood NJ 08701

CLINTON, HARRIET PETTIBONE (MRS. FRED DAVIDSON CLINTON), assn. exec.; b. Burlington, Ia., Dec. 29, 1896; d. John Holland and Margaret Cornelia (Danner) P.; B.A., U. Wis., 1919; postgrad. Columbia, 1923-24, U. Queensland, Australia, 1943; m. Fred Davidson Clinton, Apr. 30, 1925. With Milw. Jour., 1920-21, Milw. Sentinel, 1921-23, Milw. Leader, 1926-32; with pub. information dept., div. for children and youth Wis. Dept. Pub. Welfare, Madison, 1949-53; pub. relations cons. Internat. Inst., Milw., 1953—, Holiday Folk Fair, 1953—. Dir. women's and profl. div. WPA, Milw. County, 1934-40, Eastern Wis., 1940-42; club dir. A.R.C., Australia, 1943-45; work relief specialist UNRRA, China, 1946-47; mem. Wis. Bd. Mental Hygiene, 1938-39; mem. Mayor's com. for Observance UN Day, 1962-63; sec. Gov.'s Conf. on Children and Youth, 1952-53. Mem. Women In Communications, English Speaking Union of Wis. (dir. 1964—). Club: Milw. Press. Home: 1825 N Oakland Av Milwaukee WI 53202 Office: 2810 W Highland Blvd Milwaukee WI 53208

CLINTON, MARY JANE, editor; b. San Mateo, Cal., Dec. 7, 1934; d. John Hart and Helen A. (Amphlett) Clinton; A.B. cum laude, Stanford, 1955; m. Raymond Otto Zirkel, Jan. 4, 1974. Women's news asst. The Times, San Mateo, 1955-57, women's news editor, 1957—. Home: 2311 Carlmont Dr Belmont CA 94002 Office: Box 5400 San Mateo CA 94002

CLODFELTER, YUBA LENORA SHAW (MRS. DONAL D. CLODFELTER), clubwoman; b. Trenton, Mo., May 17, 1923; d. Bart S. and Otie E. (Shearrow) Shaw; grad. high sch.; m. Donal D. Clodfelter, Apr. 3, 1949; 1 dau., Connie Lenora. Employee, Bemis Bag Co., St. Louis, 1941, Kansas City, Mo., 1947, Emerson Electric, St. Louis, 1942, Aluminum Co., Kansas City, Mo., 1944. Local treas. Ladies Aux. V.F.W., 1956-66; nat. treas. Women's Aux. Mil. Order of Cootie, 1965—. Address: 4521 Llama Lane St Joseph MO 64506

CLOKE, WILMA JEAN NEWSOM (MRS. ARTHUR L. CLOKE), educator; b. Breckenridge, Tex., Dec. 1, 1928; d. Clarence William and Mary Anita (Taylor) Newsom; B.S., (univ. scholar 1946) Tex. Christian U., 1950; M.A. (scholar), U. Redlands, 1964; postgrad. U. Tex., 1950, U. Dayton, 1960-61, Pepperdine Coll., 1961-62, Los Angeles State Coll., 1961, La Salle Sch. Law, 1962-64, Claremont Grad. Sch.; Ph.D. (hon.), Colo. State Christian Coll., 1973; m. Arthur L. Cloke, June 5, 1948; children—Linda Cheryl (Mrs. John Andrew Kreutzer, Jr.), Victoria Lynn. Tchr. various schs., Tex., 1949-53, 57-59, Ohio, 1959-61, Inglewood (Cal.) pub. schs., 1961-62, Highland (Cal.) Jr. High Sch., 1962-71, Serrano Jr. High Sch., Highland, 1971—. Owner, dir. Camp Sugar Cone, 1967-71; mem. White House Conf. Edn., 1960. Mem. adv. bd. mother adviser San Bernardino assembly 78, Mountain Shadows assembly 254 Order Rainbow for Girls, 1965—. Mem. Am. Assn. U. Women, Tex. Christian U. Women's Execs., Graduation Task Force, Secondary Curriculum Council (exec. bd. combined curriculum councils), N.E.A., Cal., San Bernardino (mem. personnel policy com. 1965—) tchrs. assns., Marquis Biog. Library Soc. (dir.), Internat. Platform Assn., Alpha Delta Kappa. Mem. Disciples of Christ. Mem. Order Eastern Star (Grand Cross Color). Club: Officers' Wives (Norton AFB). Home: 25760 Holly Vista St San Bernardino CA 92404 Office: Serrano Jr High Sch 3131 E Peidmont Dr Highland CA 92364

CLOPTON, CARTER BELLE MUNT (MRS. JULIAN CAMPBELL CLOPTON), govt. agy. exec.; b. Petersburg, Va., July 18; d. Irving Christian and Louisa (Claiborne) Munt; B.S. in Edn., Longwood Coll.; m. Julian Campbell Clopton, Apr. 20, 1946 (dec. Nov. 1957); 1 dau., Elizabeth Randolph. Former tchr. high schs. Cyprus Chapel, Va., Petersburg; asst. gen. clk. Tex. Senate, 1962; co-ordinator Gov. (Tex.) Office Aging Services, 1965; exec. dir. Gov. (Tex.) Com. Aging, 1965—; cons. Tex. agys. on aging, 1965—. Vice-pres. Austin (Tex.) Planned Parenthood Assn., 1954-58, Foster Grandparent Project, Austin, 1967; mem. adv. council Denton (Tex.) and Austin state schs., 1967—; mem. state adv. com. Green Thumb. Past bd. dirs. Austin Cerebral Palsy, Austin Jr. League, Austin Adult Services Council, vol. council Austin State Hosp. Mem. D.A.R., mem. Nat. Council Aging, Tex., Austin-Travis social welfare assns., Tex. Soc. Aging. Nat. Assn. State Units Aging, Sigma Sigma Sigma. Democrat. Episcopalian (dir. sr. center 1958-61, mem. bd. 1954-57). Club: Austin Lawyers' Wives. Home: 1501 Elton Lane Austin TX 78703 Office: Govs Com Aging PO Box 12786 Capitol Sta Austin TX 78711

CLOS, MARJORIE CATHERINE BALLING, psychologist, health service adminstr.; b. Louisville, June 21, 1926; d. Walter A. and Irene Catherine (Meyer) Balling; B.S., U. Louisville, 1948, M.A., 1950; M.P.H., U. Minn., 1958; Ph.D., So. Ill. U., 1963; m. Jean Henri Clos, May 3, 1952 (div. Jan. 1962); children—Laura Catherine, Carla Florence. Health educator Ky. Dept. Pub. Health, Louisville, 1950-52; dir. health edn. Louisville Jefferson County Dept. Pub. Health, 1954-57; chief mental health educator Ky. Dept. Mental Health, 1960-63; dir. research Central State Hosp., Louisville, 1963-65; with Mich. Dept. Mental Health, Lansing, 1967-68, dir. programs Caro Regional Center, 1968—; practice psychology, Bay City, Mich., 1971—. Tchr. psychology U. Louisville, 1954-56, Merrill Palmer Inst., Detroit, 1966-67, Delta Coll., University City, Mich., 1970-73, Saginaw Valley Coll., University City, 1973—. Del., Mid Century White House Conf. on Children and Youth, 1950. Bd. dirs. Helpline. Mem. Am. Assn. Mental Deficiency, Am., Mich. (standards and ethics com. 1973—), Mid Mich. psychol. assns., Mich. Soc. Clin. Psychologists. Address: Lock Box A Caro MI 48723

CLOSE, ELIZABETH SCHEU (MRS. WINSTON A. CLOSE), architect; b. Vienna, Austria, June 4, 1912 (came to U.S. 1932, naturalized 1938); d. Gustav and Helene (Riesz) C.; student Technische Hochschule, Vienna, 1931-32; B.Arch., Mass. Inst. Tech., 1934, M.Arch., 1935; m. Winston A. Close, Apr. 11, 1938; children—Anne Miriam (Mrs. Milton Ulmer), Roy Michel, Robert Arthur. Draftsman Oscar Stonorov, Architect, Phila., 1935-36; designer Magney & Tusler, Mpls., 1936-38; partner, architect Close & Scheu (name changed to Close Assos., Inc., 1969), Mpls., 1938—; instr. Mpls. Sch. Art, 1936-37; instr. design U. Minn. Sch. Arch., 1938-39. Mem. Gov.'s Commn. on Minn.'s Future. Bd. dirs. Civic Orch. Mpls., 1951-68; bd. dirs. Minn. Opera Co.; pres. New Friends Chamber Music, 1973-74. Recipient Honor award Pub. Housing Adminstrn., 1964; hon. mention F.D. Roosevelt Meml. competition, 1960. Fellow A.I.A. (dir. Mpls. chpt., 1964-69); mem. Minn. Soc. Architects. Prin. works include Garden City Devel., Brooklyn Center, Minn., 1957; Duff House, Wayzata, Minn., 1959; variety structures Met. Med. Center Complex, 1960—, Golden Age Homes, 1960, both Mpls.; Peavey Tech. Center, Chaska, Minn., 1970; Freshwater Biological Institute, 1973. Home: 1588 Fulham St St Paul MN 55108 Office: Close Assos Inc 3101 E Franklin Av Minneapolis MN 55406

CLOSE, MARJORIE PERRY (MRS. FRANK M. CLOSE), artist; b. Chloride, Ariz., Nov. 11, 1899; d. Victor Elmo and Martha Annette (Quade) Perry; student U. Cal. at Berkeley, 1918-20; m. Frank M. Close, Aug. 13, 1920; children—Perry, Marjorie (Mrs. Robert Francis Elliott. Free-lance comml. artist, Chgo., 1920-23, San Francisco, 1923-26; advt. mgr. Robert Walker Furrier, San Francisco, 1924-28; exhibited in one man shows Frye Museum, Seattle, 1973, Rosicrucian Mus., San Jose, Cal., 1967-73; exhibited in group shows at DeYoung Mus., San Francisco, Hammond Mus. North Salem, N.Y., Nat. Acad. Design, N.Y.C., Palace Fine arts, San Francisco, San Francisco Mus. Art, Haggin Galleries, Stockton, Cal.; represented in permanent collection Charles and Emma Frye Art Mus., Seattle; lectr. on color to clubs and San Francisco pub. schs.; art judge throughout Cal. Recipient Grand Prix in still life, 23d Internat. Exhibit, Deauville, France, 1972, many other awards and prizes. Fellow Am. Artists Profl. League; mem. Nat. Assn. women Artists, Soc. Western Artists (pres. 1968-69, dir. 1960-73, exhbns. dir. 1970-74), Palace Fine Arts

League, Acad. Artists Assn. Springfield (Mass.). Clubs: Catherine Lorillard Wolfe Art (N.Y.C.); Women's Big Ten University (San Francisco). Home: 50 Beachmont Dr San Francisco CA 94132

CLOSSER, EVELYNE VINCENT BOND (MRS. LEWIS EDMUND CLOSSER), real estate broker; b. East Aurora, N.Y., Dec. 10, 1891; d. George Addy and Alma Harriet (Goulton) Bond; student Ohio Wesleyan U., 1910-11; m. Lewis Edmund Closser, Apr. 6, 1915 (dec. 1922); children—Evelyne Louise (dec.), Lewis Bond. Tchr. pub. schs., Petersburg, N.Y., 1912-13, Angelica, N.Y., 1913-14; with auditing dept. N.Y. State Rwys., Rochester, 1924-25; owner, operator restaurant, Rochester, 1925-29; office worker Meth. Home for Children, Buffalo, 1930-40; receptionist Harvard Club, Boston, 1940-46; realtor Closser Realty, North Hollywood, Cal., 1946-74; realtor, notary pub., Rosemead, Cal., 1974—. Mem. San Fernando Valley Bd. Realtors, Am. Legion Aux., Ohio Wesleyan Alumni Assn. Methodist. Mem. Order Eastern Star. Address: 3225 N Del Mar Av Rosemead CA 91770

CLOTHIER, FLORENCE (MRS. GEORGE B. WISLOCKI), psychiatrist; b. Wynnewood, Pa., Nov, 1, 1903; d. Walter and Edith (Ball) Clothier; A.B., Vassar Coll., 1926; M.D., Johns Hopkins, 1931; m. George B. Wislocki, Feb. 13, 1931; children—Louis Clothier, Johanna, George Stanislau, Edith Ball. Intern Phila. Gen. Hosp., 1930; child guidance clinic Mass. Gen. Hosp., 1932-35, Beth Israel Hosp., 1941-46; staff psychiatrist N.E. Home for Little Wanders, 1934-57; individual practice, 1934-57; instr. Harvard Med. Sch., 1948-51; psychiat. cons. Eliot-Pearson Sch. Nursery Edn., Tufts U., 1949-57; vis. psychiatrist Cushing VA Hosp., 1947-50; chief psychiatrist Fall River Community Mental Health Center, 1969—. Dir. James Jackson Putnam Children's Center, 1945-55; mem. Milton Bd. Pub. Welfare, 1943-57, N.Y. State Hudson River Regional Mental Health Planning Com., 1962-65; dir. Duchess County Community Chest, 1960-66; trustee Vassar Coll., 1945-53, pres. Alumni Assn., 1954-57, asst. pres. Coll., 1957-69; mem. exec. com. Coll. Research Center, 1959-69; pres. Fall River Family Planning Com., 1971—. Served WAC, induction bd., 1942-44. Diplomate Am. Bd. Psychiatry and Neurology. Fellow Am. Psychiat. Assn. (com. on manpower), Am. Orthopsychiat. Assn., Am. Psychoanalytic Assn., Mass. Med. Soc., Mass. Planned Parenthood League (dir. 1942-57, 72—), N.E. Grenfell Assn. (dir.) 1945-57, Euthanasia Soc. Am. (v.p. 1968—), Planned Parenthood Fedn. Am. (med. adv. com. 1961-65). Contbr. articles on child psychiatry to med. jours. Home: Little Compton RI 02837 Office: Fall River Community Mental Health Center Fall River MA 02722

CLOUGH, MARY EVALYN, librarian; b. Kansas City, Mo., July 10, 1930; d. Arthur M. and Candace M. (White) Clough; student Kan. U., 1947-50; B.A., U. Cal. at Los Angeles, 1952; M.S., Columbia, 1956; advanced certificate U. Pitts. Grad. Sch. Library and Information Sci., 1967. Med. library cataloger Columbia, N.Y.C., 1954-56; 1st asst. catalog dept. N.Y. Acad. Medicine Library, N.Y.C., 1956-58; sr. tech. librarian, tech. library, Rep. Aviation Corp., Farmingdale, L.I., N.Y., 1958-64; head librarian PPG Industries, Inc., Glass Research Center, Pitts., 1964—. Mem. A.L.A., Spl. Library Assn. (chmn. engring. div. 1973-74), Am. Soc. Information Sci., Sigma Alpha Iota, Phi Delta Gamma. Home: 6813 Penn Av Pittsburgh PA 15208 Office: PO Box 11472 Pittsburgh PA 15238

CLOUSE, DELORIS RAE, educator; b. Colon, Neb., Dec. 3, 1931; d. Clarence Dillard and Henrietta Agatha (Dolezal) Clouse; B.F.A. (Wood scholar), U. Neb., 1953; M.S., 1968. Visual communications specialist, asso. prof. dept. information U. Neb. at Lincoln, 1953—. Cons. Kan. State U., Manhattan, 1970-71. Mem. Neb. Coop. Extension Assn. (state sec. 1967), Am. Assn. Agrl. Coll. Editors, Am., Neb. (dir. 1972-74) home econs. assns., Soc. Tech. Communicators, Omicron Nu. Home: 5322 Cleveland St Lincoln NE 68504

CLOUSE, MILDRED DELORIS (MRS. CLAREN M. CLOUSE), photographer; b. Toledo, Aug. 28, 1909; d. Arthur Marion and Lelah Estelle (Kenyon) Eidson; grad. Cygnat High Sch., 1927; student Sch. of Modern Photography, N.Y., 1949-50; m. Claren M. Clouse, May 8, 1930. Photographer, propr. The Clouse Studio, Miami, Fla., 1952—. Mem. Profl. Photographers of Am., Profl. Photographers of Fla., Profl. Photographers Guild of Greater Miami, Zonta Internat. Contbr. photographs and various articles on photography to mags. Address: 15020 SW 89th Ct Miami FL 33158

CLOUSE, RUTH GILBERT, editor; b. New Haven, Mar. 25, 1909; d. Jacob Franklin and Augusta Marie (Schneider) Clouse; B.A. cum laude, Mt. Holyoke Coll., 1929. With New Haven Register, 1933-43, 46—, soc. editor, 1946—. Mem. New Haven County Nat. Found. Bd., 1969-71; mem. Mental Health Bd., Greater New Haven, 1960-62. Mem. Mt. Holyoke Alumnae Quar. Bd., 1955-58, mem. promotion com. Alumnae Fund, 1969-71. Active Girl Scouts U.S.A. Served to lt. (j.g.) USCG Women's Res., 1943-46. Recipient Americanism award Stanley Fishman Post Aux. Jewish War Vets., 1959; Most Distinguished award Am. Legion Aux. Dept. Conn., 1970; named Woman of Year, Bus. and Profl. Womens Club, 1965. Mem. Am. Assn. U. Women (pres. New Haven br. 1967-69), Grad. Club Assn. New Haven (mem. bd. 1972—), Alpha Iota (hon.), Gamma Sigma Sigma (hon.). Republican. Episcopalian (vestryman 1968-71). Home: 54 Woodlawn St Hamden CT 06517 Office: 367 Orange St New Haven CT 07503

CLOW, MARTHA DE MEY (MRS. JOHN WARNER CLOW), author; b. Columbus, O., Nov. 16, 1932; d. Charles Frederic and Amelia Webster (Smith) de Mey; student (Kinsmen Trust scholar) Reodean Sch. for Girls, Brighton, Eng., 1949-50; B.A., Smith Coll., 1954; m. John Warner Clow, Apr. 10, 1956; children—John Frederic de Mey, Gregory Vincent, Amelia Bayley, Guy Rowan, Louise Crankshaw. Prodn. asst. advt. Macy's Cal., San Francisco, 1954-56; artist adv. Joseph Magnin Co., San Francisco, 1956-57; free lance artist and writer, 1957—. Art cons. and dir. Marin County (Cal.) Dist Atty. election, Presidential election 1964, Municipal ct. judge election: ofcl. artist Marin Republican Sponsors. Mem. Mill Valley Outdoor Art Club, Marin County Smith Club (pres. 1960-63), Seven Coll. Conf. (pres. 1961-63). Author: Starbreed, 1970. Home: Box 934 Ross CA 94957

CLOW, MAURINE, educator; b. Grafton, N.D., Sept. 30, 1908; d. Chester W. and Ellen C. (Terrill) Clow; student U. N.D., 1926, 28-30, B.A., Stanford, 1934, M.A., 1936, Ph.D., 1946; summer study Columbia, 1942. Counselor, English tchr. Sarah Dix Hamlin Sch., San Francisco, 1935-36; resident asst. to dean of women Stanford, 1936-38; dean women Whitman Coll., Walla Walla, Wash., 1938-46; asso. dean of students prof. psychology U. Mont., Missoula, 1946-73, prof., asso. dean emeritus, 1973—. Recipient Distinguished Woman award Matrix Table, 1971. Mem. Am., N.W. (life) Coll. personnel assns., Nat. Assn. Women Deans and Counselors (citation 1972), Am. Assn. U. Women (pres. Walla Walla br., Wash. ednl. chmn. 1943-44), P.E.O., Mortar Bd., Sigma Xi, Pi Lambda Theta, Psi Chi, Delta Gamma (Shield award 1972), Delta Kappa Gamma. Republican. Presbyn. (co-chmn. canvass program 1960, elder 1960—). Mem. Order Eastern Star. Home: Lynnwood 951 Ronald Av Missoula MT 59801

CLOYD, HELEN MARY (MRS. CHESTER L. CLOYD), educator, accountant; b. Austria-Hungary, 1918;; d. Valentine and Elizabeth (Kretschmar von Kienbusch) Yuhasz; came to U.S. 1922, naturalized, 1928; B.S., Eastern Mich. U., 1953; M.A., Wayne State U., 1956; Ph.D., Mich State U., 1963; m. George S. Smith, Mar. 4, 1939; children—George, Nora; m. Chester L. Cloyd, Apr. 16, 1960. Pub. accounting Haskins & Sells, Detroit, 1945-53; tchr. Marine City (Mich.) High Sch., 1954-59; instr. accounting Central Mich. U., Mt. Pleasant, 1959-60; asst. prof. Wayne State U., Detroit, 1960-61; tchr. Grosse Pointe (Mich.) High Sch., 1961-64; asso. prof. accounting Ball State U., Muncie, Ind., 1964-71; prof. Shepherd Coll., Sheperdstown, W.Va., 1971—. Recipient McClintock Writing award. C.P.A., Mich., Ind., W.Va. Mem. Am. Inst. C.P.A.'s, Am. Accounting Assn., Am. Econs. Assn., A.A.A.S., Assn. Sch. Bus. Ofcls., Delta Pi Epsilon, Pi Omega Pi, Pi Gamma Mu. Mem. Order Eastern Star, White Shrine. Contbr. numerous articles to publs. Home: Box 186 Inwood WV 25428 Office: Shepherd College Shepherdstown WV 25443

CLYATT, EMILY GWENDOLYNE JONES, home economist; b. Eastland, Tex., Sept. 23, 1915; d. Thomas A. and Ora Bell (Duffer) Jones; B.S., N. Tex. U., 1938; postgrad. Ia. State Coll., 1943, Cornell U., 1955; M.S., U. Houston, 1962; 1 dau., Sally. Extension county home demonstration agt., Hamilton County, 1939-43; extension home economist, Ia., 1944; extension foods specialist, Tex., 1945-47; food economist U. Md., 1954-56; consumer marketing information specialist Tex. Agrl. Extension Service, Houston, 1956—. Bd. dirs. Bluebell chpt. Order Rainbow Girls, 1963-67. Recipient Grand Cross Color Internat. Order Rainbow for Girls, 1965. Mem. Am. (consumer interest com.), Tex. (1st v.p. 1963-64), Houston Area (pres. 1963, named Outstanding Profl. Home Economist 1963), home econs. assns., Epsilon Sigma Phi. Editor Tex. Tattler, 1960—. Home: 3400 Timmons St Houston TX 77027 Office: 3815 Montrose Houston TX 77006

CLYDE, CAROL GRANT, librarian; b. Houston, Feb. 13, 1943; d. Viller Ging and Margaret Helen (Grant) Clyde; B.A., U. Tex. at Austin, 1965; M.L.S., U. Okla. at Norman, 1967. Bookmobile librarian Houston Pub. Library, 1965-66; asst. librarian S. Tex. Jr. Coll., Houston, 1967-71; librarian Tex. State Tech. Inst., Rio Grande Campus, Harlingen, 1971—. Mem. Baha'i Faith. Home: 2531 Erie McAllen TX 78501 Office: Texas State Tech Inst Rio Grande Campus Harlingen TX 78550

CLYMA, GAIL DOUGLAS, pub. co. exec.; b. N.Y.C., Sept. 2, 1935; d. E. Ramon and Cecil Scott (Chase) Clyma; B.S. in Journalism, Syracuse U., 1957. Sec. Ted Bates Advt. Co., N.Y.C., 1958-59; sec. Fortune Mag., N.Y.C., 1959-61, asso. dir. market research, 1966-70, dir. market research, 1970—. Mem. Eastside Young Republican Club, N.Y.C. Mem. Am. Marketing Assn., Media Research Dirs. Assn. Office: Fortune Mag Time and Life Bldg New York City NY 10020

COADY, MARY LUZ, physician; b. Dallas, June 5, 1933; d. Leo Dean and Marie (Guillen) Coady; M.D., Women's Med. Coll. Pa., 1962; m. Joseph Harlan Calhoun, Sept. 24, 1963; children—Julia Luz, Lia Ann. Rotating intern Hosp. of U. Pa., Phila., 1962-63; resident Children's Hosp., Phila., 1963, Children's Hosp., San Francisco, 1965-66; resident St. Christopher's Hosp. for Children, Phila., 1966-67, physician outpatient dept., 1967—; physician outpatient dept. Bryn Mawr (Pa.) Hosp., 1967—. Bd. dirs. Phila. Child Guidance Clinic of Children's Hosp. Phila., 1974—. Diplomate Am. Bd. Pediatrics. Mem. Alpha Omega Alpha. Office: 1330 Montgomery Av Rosemont PA 19010

COAKLEY, MARY LEWIS (MRS. WILLIAM DRUMMOND COAKLEY), author; b. Balt., Dec. 8, 1907; d. Charles Edward and Rose Athalia (Kerchner) Lewis; student Dominican Coll., 1925-27, U. San Francisco, 1927-28; m. William Drummond Coakley, Dec. 25, 1939; 1 son, Joseph. Author, contbr. to newspapers and mags. Pres., Rep. Neighbors, Phila. Winner first prize in article writing Nat. League of Am. Pen Women, 1968; first prize in lecture category, 1970. Author: Fitting God into the Picture, 1950, rev. as A Woman's Way 1968; Our Child—God's Child, 1953; Mister Music Maker, 1958; Never Date Women, 1964; also 4 booklets Know Your Bible Series, 1960-61. Home: 110 Hewett Rd Wyncote PA 19095

COARI, ELAINE JENKINS, ednl. ofcl.; b. Chgo., Sept. 16, 1925; d. Jules Edward and Shirley Elaine (Florence) Jenkins; B.S., Mundelein Coll., 1947; postgrad. Northwestern U., 1946, U. Wis., 1946; m. Frances Paul Coari, Oct. 4, 1947 (div. June 1968); children—Mark, Ronald, Noel, Paul. Sec. to admissions Tulane U. Sch. of Medicine, New Orleans, 1966-67; dir. vol. services Hotel Dieu Hosp., New Orleans, 1967; dir. vol. services and child recruitment Head Start, New Orleans, 1967-68; dir. Sch. Vol. Services, New Orleans Pub. Schs., 1968—. La. State coordinator Pub. Sch. Vol. Programs, 1973-74; appeared on NBC Today Show, 1970; treas. Nat. Sch. Vol. Program, 1970-71. Mem. Pub. Relations Soc. Am., Women in Communications (treas. 1973-74), Nat. Assn. for Industry-Edn. Cooperation (mem. program com. 1973—, exec. bd. dirs. 1974). Office: 1 Shell Sq New Orleans LA 70139

COATES, ELEANOR MCNEILL (MRS. FREDERICK FLETCHER COATES), writer; b. Yarmouth, N.S., Can.; d. Hubert C. and Isabelle S. (Shipley) McNeill; student N.Y. U., U. Paris (France); m. Frederick Fletcher Coates, July 17, 1937; children—Jacqueline (Mrs. David Spinney), Virginia (Mrs. R.D. Busiek), Susanne (Mrs. John Alcock). Naturalized, Am. citizen, 1953. Writer fiction published in Cosmopolitan Mag., McCalls, Good Housekeeping (Eng.), Wife and Home (Eng.), Chatelaine (Can.), Canadian Home Jour., Montreal Standard, Toronto Star Weekly, Macleans, Weekend mag.; writer travel articles Atlantic Advocate; writer various radio plays produced in Hollywood for Canadian Govt. fund raising. Home: 468 Riverside Dr New York City NY 10027

COATES, PAMELA ZIMMER, antique dealer, author; b. Bronx, N.Y., Aug. 2, 1941; d. Charles John and Helene (Lapinski) Zimmer; student econs. Westchester Community Coll., Valhalla, N.Y., eves. 1959-61; m. John Joseph Coates, Jr., June 6, 1966; 1 dau., Candace Noel. With Children's Village, Dobbs Ferry, N.Y., 1959-60, Urban Renewal, Hastings-on-Hudson, N.Y., 1960-61, Albert Trostel & Sons, Co., Hastings-on-Hudson, 1961-62, Bankers Trust Co., N.Y.C., 1962-63, Promotional Imports, N.Y.C., 1963-65, Condor Chem. Co., N.Y.C., 1965-66; propr. Pamela Coates Antiques, Indpls., 1967—. Founder, pres. Burlington County (N.J.) Antique Dealers Assn., 1972-73. Mem. Nat. Assn. Dealers in Antiques. Author: (pottery) The Real McCoy, 1971, Vol. II, 1975; (Pottery) Hull, 1974; also articles, columns. Address: 5121 S Harlan St Indianapolis IN 46227

COAXUM, CALLIE VIRGINIA BUTLER (MRS. LYMON ANDREW COAXUM), ednl. adminstr.; b. Clinton, N.C., June 7, 1930; d. William Curtis and Virginia Elizabeth (Williamson) Butler; B.A. cum laude, Johnson C. Smith U., 1949; M.S., S.C. State Coll., 1960; postgrad. Va. State Coll., 1963, Ind. U., 1964, U. S.C., 1969; m. Lymon Andrew Coaxum, Jan. 25, 1952; children—Donald, Ronald, Kelvin. Prin., Porter Elementary Sch., Burton, S.C., 1951-52; tchr., counselor St. Helena High Sch., Frogmore, S.C., 1955-69; dir. coll. counseling, asst. dean students Benedict Coll., Columbia, S.C., 1970-72, dean student affairs, 1972—. Informal cons. leadership devel. program Ford Found., 1973. Pres., Beaufort County Planned Parenthood, 1967; mem. adv. com. Home Health Services, 1967. Pres., Lady's Island Democratic Precinct, 1968. Summer fellow Va. State Coll., 1963. Mem. S.C. Coll. Personnel Assn., Am. Legion, Alpha Kappa Alpha. Contbr. articles to ednl. mag., publs. Home: 1610 Oak St Columbia SC 29204

COBANE, EDITH MAE, educator; b. Utica, N.Y., Dec. 8, 1922; d. Harold Sutton and Eva (Baker) Cobane; B.S., State U. N.Y., 1943; M.A., St. Lawrence U., 1949; Ed.D., Syracuse U., 1959. Tchr. phys. edn. Waterville (N.Y.) Central Sch., 1943-45, Watertown (N.Y.) High Sch., 1945-48; grad. asst. Syracuse (N.Y.) U., 1949-51, 52-53, instr. 1953-59, asst. prof., 1959-65; instr. State Tchrs. Coll., Oswego, 1951-52; prof. phys. edn., chmn. State U. N.Y., Albany, 1965—. Mem. A.A.H.P.E.R. (chmn. officiating sect. Eastern dist. div. girls and womens sports 1971-73), Assn. Women in Phys. Edn. in N.Y. State (pres. 1959, chmn. adv. council 1968-70), Nat., Eastern (pres. 1963) assns. phys. edn. coll. women, N.Y. State Assn. Health, Phys. Edn. and Recreation (pres. 1973-74), Am. Assn. U. Profs., Capital Dist. Bd. Women Ofcls. Contbr. articles to publs. Home: Aspen Heights Slingerlands NY 12159 Office: 1400 Washington Av Albany NY 12222

COBB, ALVA STARLING, educator; b. Benton, Miss., Sept. 5, 1939; d. John Wesley and Betha (Wilburn) Starling; B.S., Tenn. State U., 1962, M.S., 1965; postgrad. Sonoma (Cal.) State Coll., 1967, Mich. State U., 1968-69, N.Y. U. (fellow), 1972—. Sec., Tenn. A & I State U. Health Center, Nashville, 1964-65; social worker Solano County Welfare Dept., Vallejo, Cal., 1965-66; substitute tchr., Fairfield, Cal., 1966; tchr.-counselor Golden West Intermediate Sch., Travis Unified Sch. Dist., Fairfield, 1966-68; grad. resident adviser Mich. State U., 1968-69, occupational information librarian Counseling Center, 1968; coordinator spl. projects Oakland U., 1969-70; dean women Alcorn A. and M. Coll., Lorman, Miss., 1970-72. Mem. Am. Assn. Higher Edn., Am. Coll. Personnel Assn., Urban League, N.A.A.C.P., Alpha Kappa Alpha. Home: 88 Hillcrest Av Trenton NJ 08618

COBB, FAITH MALTBY, psychologist; b. Buffalo, Feb. 12, 1930; d. George Frederick and Olive Elizabeth (Todd) Maltby; B.A., Syracuse U., 1951, M.A., 1966, Ph.D., 1973; divorced; children—Robert Alan, Deborah Lynn. Psychologist, Counseling Center, Syracuse U., 1965-66, Syracuse Cerebral Palsy Center, 1966; sch. psychologist Fayetteville-Manlius (N.Y.) schs., 1966—. Cons. in field. Mem. Am. Psychol. Assn., Sch. Psychologists Upstate N.Y., Sch. Psychologists Onon County, Mensa, Assn. Children with Learning Disabilities, Alpha Gamma Delta. Home: 100 Radcliffe Rd Dewitt NY 13214 Office: Special Help Center Seneca Turnpike Manlius NY 13104

COBB, HELEN R., utility exec., former city ofcl.; b. Wichita, Kan., Aug. 23, 1922;; d. Pleasant Albert and Lydia (Waters) Smith; grad. high sch.; m. Marvin Earl Cobb, June 29, 1941 (div. 1967); children—Marvin Earl, Mary Kathleen. Profl. accountant; now pub. affairs rep. San Diego Gas & Electric Co.; mem. San Diego City Council, 1961-71. Dep. mayor San Diego. Pres., San Diego County div. League of Cal. Cities. Active March of Dimes, women's aux. Salk Inst. Mem. Bus. and Profl. Women. Home: 3411 Ray St San Diego CA 92104

COBB, JERRIE M., aviator; b. Norman, Okla., Mar. 5, 1931; d. William Harvey and Helena Butler (Stone) Cobb. Profl. pilot, 1949—; chief pilot South Am. Fleetway, Inc., FAA adv. com., 1964; former cons. to NASA, FAA, aviation/aerospace cons. in pvt. practice; now operates Amazonia (S. Am.) airlift service, working with missionaries, anthropologists, etc. for welfare of Amazon Indian Tribes, work funded by Jerrie Cobb Found., Inc., Coral Gables, Fla. Named 1 of 9 women selected in the 100 most important in U.S., 1962; first woman to pass astronaut tests, 1960; holder 4 world aviation records; recipient Gold Wings Fedn. Aeronautique Internationale; recipient Harmon Internat. trophy for world's outstanding aviatrix, 1973; named Woman of Year in Aviation, Women's Nat. Aero. Assn., Capt. of Achievement, Internat. Acad. Achievement; hon. pilot Colombian Air Force, 1964; honored for pioneering new air route over Andes and into jungle by Govt. Ecuador. Mem. Am. Rocket Soc., Am. Astronautical Soc., Aerospace Medicine Assn., Nat. Aero. Assn., 99's (Amelia Earhart Gold medal), Nat. Pilots Assn. (Pilot of Year 1959), Women's Nat. Aero. Assn. Club: Whirlygirls. Author: (with Jane Rieker) Woman Into Space: The Jerrie Cobb Story, 1963. Home: 4057 Malaga St Miami FL 33133

COBB, JOSEPHINE, cons., ret. librarian; b. Portland, Me.; d. Allen H. and Nellie (Lochhead) Cobb; B.S., Simmons Library Sch., 1931; M.A., Boston U., 1935; postgrad. Am. U., 1940—. In charge of Rare Book Room, Boston Pub. Library, 1932-35; asst. State Archives of Mass., 1935-36; with photog. records br. Nat. Archives, 1936-73, specialist in iconography, 1960-73, staff tchr. for trainees for the 5 Presdl. Libraries, 1969-71; cons. in Am. art history. Mem. adv. bd. Civil War Centennial Commn.; hon. mem. Abraham Lincoln Sesquicentennial Commn.; mem. com. selection Photography's Hall of Fame, Am. Mus. Photography, 1965; adv. mem. Nat. Capital Landmarks Commn.; mem. Fairfax Hist. Preservation Commn., Arlington Beautification Group, Cape Elizabeth Bd. Historic Preservation Advisers; adviser to com. on bibliography of U.S. Capitol Bldg., Capitol Hist. Soc., 1970. Recipient Nat. Abraham Lincoln award, Lincoln Group D.C., 1966, Abraham Lincoln award Phila. Lincoln-Civil War Round Table, 1969. Mem. Spl. Libraries Assn. (chmn. Washington group picture div. 1966-70), Columbia Hist. Soc. (curator prints and photographs 1956-71), Abraham Lincoln Group of Washington (pres. 1970-71), Atlanta and N.Y.C. Civil War Round Tables, Am. Assn. State and Local History, U.S. Capitol Hist. Assn. (charter mem.), George Eastman House Mus. Photography, Royal Photog. Soc. Gt. Britain, Me. Hist. Soc. (dir. 1974—), Me. Old Cemeteries Assn., Me. League Hist. Socs., Cape Elizabeth Hist. Soc. Episcopalian. Author articles on lives early Am. photographers including M.B. Brady and Alex Gardner, and American artists prior to 1880 including the Washington Art Assn., 1856-60; American Historical Prints of the 19th Century. Home: 6 Hunt's Point Cape Elizabeth ME 04107

COBB, NANCY LOU (MRS. DOYLE COBB), librarian; b. Wagoner, Okla., Oct. 24, 1936; d. Euel Ray and Jessie Mae (Hamm) Lancaster; B.S., Okla. Coll. for Women, 1958; M.L.S., U. Okla., 1959; postgrad. Eastern N.M. U., 1960; m. Doyle Cobb, Jan. 26, 1963; children—Timothy Doyle, Mark Caleb. Sec., Searcy-Lancaster Ins. Agy., Wagoner, 1951-54, summers 1954-58; serials and pub. services librarian Eastern N.M. U., Portales, 1959-61; asst. librarian East Central State Coll., Ada, Okla., 1961-63; librarian First Bapt. Ch., Ada. 1961—. Mem. N.E.A., A.L.A., Okla., N.M., Southwestern library assns., Okla. Edn. Assn. Democrat. Baptist. Home: 2100 E 18th St Ada OK 74820 Office: 15th St and Broadway Ada OK 74820

COBB, RUTH (MRS. LAWRENCE KUPFERMAN), artist; b. Boston, Feb. 20, 1914; d. Charles E. and Bessie (Cohen) Cobb; diploma Mass. Coll. Art, 1935; m. Lawrence Kupferman, Apr. 29, 1937; children—Nancy Rose, David. One man shows Shore Galleries, Boston, 1954, 58, 60, 63, 65, Provincetown, Mass., 1957, 59, 60, De Cordova Mus., Lincoln, Mass., 1955, Art Unltd. Gallery, San Francisco, 1961, Cober Gallery, N.Y.C., 1962, 65, 67, Marion

Koogler McNay Mus., San Antonio, 1962-63, 65-66, Phila. Art Alliance, 1962, Shore Gallery, 1968, 72, Galerie Moos, Montreal, 1969; exhibited in group exhbns. Ruth Cobb and Lawrence Kupfermen, Fitchburg Art Mus., Mass., 1953, Va. Mus. Fine Arts, Richmond, 1962-64, Witte Mus., San Antonio, 1967; exhibited nat. exhbns. Phila. Watercolor Soc., 1949, Chgo. Art Inst., 1949, Am. Watercolor exhibit Met. Mus. Art, N.Y.C., 1952, Hallmark award Traveling Exhibit, 1952, Ill. Wesleyan U. Purchase Exhbn., Bloomington, 1965, Allied Artists Am., N.Y.C., 1966, Audubon Artists 25th Ann. Exhbn., N.Y.C., 1967, Pa. Acad. Fine Arts, Phila., 1967. Recipient prizes and awards including Hallmark Art Award, N.Y.C., 1952, Hatfield award, Boston Soc. Watercolor Painters, 1957, first prize watercolors Portland (Me.) Mus. Fine Arts, 1957, first prize Edwin T. Webster award, Boston Soc. Watercolor Painters, 1958, First Sponsors Show, Copley Soc., 1961; The Barbara Vassillieff award Allied Artists N.Y.C., 1966, The George Walter Dawson award Pa. Acad. Fine Arts, 1967, Lehmann award Am. Watercolor Soc. Ann., 1968, Council Purchase prize of the N.A.D., 1968. Represented in permanent collections Boston Mus. Fine Arts, Brandeis U., Waltham, Mass., Fitchburg (Mass.) Art Mus., Butler (Pa.) Inst. Am. Art, Munson-Williams-Proctor Inst., N.Y.C., Addison Gallery of Am. Art Andover, Mass., De Cordova Mus., Lincoln, Mass., Va. Mus. Fine Arts, Richmond, Wheaton Coll., Norton, Mass., U. Mass., Amherst, Tufts U., Medford, (Mass.). Juror for San Antonio Watercolor Soc., 1969, Audubon Artists, 1974. Mem. Am. Watercolor Soc. (Lena Newcastle award 1970). Address: 38 Devon Rd Newton MA 02159

COBBE, MARGARET JANELLE HAMMETT (MRS. JEROME FRANCIS COBBE), polit. party ofcl.; b. Gaffney, S.C., Aug. 3, 1920; d. Davis Eugene and Era Ava (Barrett) Hammett; grad. Strayer Coll., 1938; m. Jerome Francis Cobbe, Nov. 23, 1943; children—Jerome Francis, Sheila (Mrs. Walter Tobin), Michael Timothy, Luane Carol. Govt. sec. Bur. Old Age and Survivors Ins., Washington, 1940-43; sec. to pres. Glenn E. McCormick Co., Inc., St. Petersburg, Fla., 1955-59. Sec., Gulfport Area Democratic Club, 1961-62; sec. Pinellas County Dem. Exec. Com., 1962-65, vice chmn., 1965-69; legislative chmn. St. Petersburg Dem. Women's Club, 1967-68, 1st v.p., 1968-70, pres., 1971; alternate del. Dem. Nat. Conv., 1968; state pres. Dem. Women's Club Fla., 1971-73; St. Petersburg mgr. Askew for Gov. campaign, 1970; dir. women's activities Dem. Nat. Conv., 1972; spl. asst. to state Dem. party chmn., 1973—. Mem. Gov.'s Commn. on Status Women, 1973—, Gov.'s Adv. Com., 1970—, Gov.'s Fuel Allocation and Conservation Council, 1973—. Served with WAC, 1943-45. Recipient Jeffersonian award St. Petersburg Dem. Club, 1972; All-Am. City award City St. Petersburg, 1973; named Outstanding Dem. Woman of Fla., Dem. Women's Club Fla., 1968. Mem. Suncoast Consumers' League (co-founder, v.p. 1969—). Baptist. Address: 901 62d St S Gulfport FL 33707

COBBS, SUSIE ANN HARDISON (MRS. THERION ELLIS COBBS), educator; b. Toledo, Feb. 8, 1924; d. Oscar Vergus and Rosa Paulene (Robinson) Hardison; student U. Toledo, 1944; B.S., Central State Coll., O., 1948; M.S., U. Kan., 1965; m. Therion Ellis Cobbs, July 21, 1946; children—Therior Ellis, Therman Vergus, Jonathan Lawrence. Recreation dir. Recreation Dept., Los Angeles, 1948-49; tchr. pub. sch. systems, San Diego, Cal., 1951-54, Kansas City, Mo., 1959-64; asso. prof. phys. edn. Fisk U., Nashville, 1964—. Water safety and first aid instr. A.R.C., 1964—. Recipient Spl. award for service Nat. A.R.C., 1972. Mem. Am., Tenn. assns. health, phys. edn. and recreation, Tenn. Coll. Women's Sports Fedn., Am. Assn. Coll. Women, Alpha Kappa Alpha. Club: Women's progressive (Nashville). Home: 617 Malta Dr Nashville TN 37207

COBLE, HELEN BROWN (MRS. PAUL W. COBLE), ednl. adminstr.; b. Bridgeport, Conn., Sept. 29, 1913; d. Albert Fisher and Anna (Sachs) Brown; grad. Senn High Sch., 1929; m. Paul W. Coble, June 8, 1937; children—Barbara (Mrs. A. Guenther), Katherine (Mrs. Richard B. Barker), Alicia Sharon. Newspaper reporter DeLand (Fla.) Sun News, 1948-57, 59-70, columnist, editorial writer, 1959-70; reporter Daytona Beach (Fla.) News Jour., 1957-59; activities dir., yearbook adviser DeLand High Sch., 1970—. Chmn. Volusia County (Fla.) Traffic and Safety Commn., 1969-70, vice-chmn., 1973-74. Recipient 1st place awards Fla. Women's Press Club, 1953, 56, 58, award of merit Fla. Bar, 1957, citation Fla. Civil Def., 1960. Mem. Fla. Women's Press Club (pres. 1969-71), Fla. Press Club. Club: Pilot of DeLand (pres. 1972-73). Home: 1502 West Stevens Av DeLand FL 32720 Office: DeLand High School DeLand FL 32720

COBLENTZ, JEAN BERLIN (MRS. WILLIAM COBLENTZ), interior designer; b. N.Y.C., Mar. 11, 1926; d. Alexander and Miriam (Greenspan) Berlin; B.A., Conn. Coll. Sch. Architecture, 1948; postgrad. Columbia U., 1948-49; m. William Coblentz, Nov. 26, 1952; children—Wendy, Andy. With Leon & Lionel Levy, architects, N.Y.C., 1949-50, Ninette Mulvany, designer, N.Y.C., 1950-51, Eugene Schoen & Sons, N.Y.C., 1951-53, John Carl Warnecke & Assos., architects, San Francisco, 1958—. Mem. San Francisco Art Commn., 1967-71. Mem. Am. Inst. Interior Designers. Home: 10 5th Av San Francisco CA 94118

COBLER, LOIS BEULAH, ret. educator; b. Garrett, Ind., June 1, 1899; d. Thomas C. and Ida M. (Van Zile) Cobler; grad. Tri State Coll., 1923; B.S., Ind. U., 1937; postgrad. Manchester Coll., Clark U., Western Mich. U., Ball State U., Ind. U., 1938-58. Tchr. pub. schs., Garrett-DeKalb County, Ind., 1918-66, tchr. Garrett Jr. High Sch. 1927-28; librarian J.E. Ober Elementary Sch., Garrett, 1956-66. Vol. worker Garrett Hosp.; team capt. New Garrett Community Hosp. Fund Raising Campaign, 1967; sec., publicity chmn. DeKalb County Women's Internat. Christian Leadership Prayer Breakfast, 1972-73. Bd. dirs., parliamentarian Garrett Women's Hosp. Aux., 1968—, chmn. radio and pub. relations, 1969—, hosp. vol., 1971—; mem. Garrett Community Hosp. Aid Found. Recipient Alumni Distinguished Service award Tri State Coll. and Alumni Orgn., 1969. Mem. Garrett Hosp. Assn., Ind. Sch. Librarians Assn. (dir. 1965—), Ind. State Tchrs. Assn., Bus. and Profl. Women's Club (pres. 1932-34, 65-66; Woman of Year 1966, chaplain 1972, hon. mem. 1971), Nat. Ret. Tchrs. Assn., Ind. Ret. Tchrs., DeKalb County Tchrs. Assn., A.L.A., Delta Kappa Gamma (publicity com.), Kappa Kappa Kappa (chpt. v.p. 1972—). Mem. Ch. of Christ (sec. women's council 1968—, librarian 1968—, organist 1968—, program chmn. women's soc. 1972) Clubs: Roadside Garden (historian 1969-70, sec. 1972—), Northeast Indiana Garden (parliamentarian 1972—). Author: History of Garrett First Church of Christ, 1971. Contbr. articles profl. jours. Home: 301 W King St Garrett IN 46738

COBURN, BETTE LEE DOBRY (MRS. MARVIN COBURN), artist; b. Chgo., July 31, 1921; d. Dudley A. and Mary (Goldfelt) Dobry; student art Grinnell Coll., 1938-40, Evanston Art Center, 1954, Art. Inst. Chgo., 1954-56, U. N.C., summer 1963; m. Marvin Coburn, Dec. 21, 1947; children—Mark Emil, Randy Sue. One-man shows Asheville (N.C.) Mus. Art, 1960, Greenville (S.C.) Mus. Art., 1961, Skyland Hotel, Hendersonville, N.C., 1960; permanent exhibit Donaldson AFB, 1960-62, Silo Theatre, Black Mountain, N.C., 1961, Peoples Nat. Bank, S.C., 1961, 62, Columbia (S.C.) Mus. Art, 1962, Atlanta Decorative Arts Center, 1964, Greenville-Spartanburg Jet-Port, 1964, Furman U., 1968; exhibited group shows including Evanston Art Center, 1955, Guild S.C. Artists, 1959—, Greenville Mus. Art, 1959—, Gibbes Art Gallery, Charleston, S.C., 1959—, Carolina Art Assn., 1961—, Hunter Art Ann., Chattanooga, 1961, Spring Art Ann., 1961-63, Clemson Coll., 1962, Columbia (S.C.) Coll., 1962, Columbia Mus. Art, 1962-63, Nat. Traveling Exhibit Oils, 1970—, Nat. Traveling Exhibit Drawings, 1970—, Contemporary Artists S.C. Tricentennial Exhbn., 1970, Greenville County Mus. Art, Gibbes Gallery, Charleston, represented in permanent collections including Greenville Mus. Art, First Fed. Bank Hendersonville, Spartanburg Art Guild, U.S. Air Corps Savannah Base, Saco Lowell Corp. of Me. and S.C., Canal Ins. Co., Greenville, Christ Ch., Louisville, Swirl of N.Y., also numerous pvt. collections. Color cons., stylist Swirl of N.Y., 1959-60, Stayon Products, Easley, S.C., 1960—; designer program covers and brochures; art instr. Greenville County Mus. Art, Furman U. Bd. dirs. Phyllis Wheatley Community Center. Recipient awards Guild South Carolina Artists, 1959, 62, 64, S.C. Art Ann., 1961, 62, 63, Greenville Art Assn., 1958, 60-63; Grand award Advt. Club Greenville's Sidewalk Art Show, 1962, 63; Bank award Asheville Mus. Art, 1961; Top award S.C. Artists, 1967; Graphics Purchase award, 1967; named Piedmont's Outstanding Woman of Year in Art, Greenville News-Piedmont Newspaper, 1962. Mem. Art Assn. Greenville (dir., 1962-64), Greenville Museum of Art (chmn. creative artists 1963-64, dir. 1962-65), Nat. League Am. Pen Women (v.p. Piedmont br. 1962-63), Guild S.C. Artists (dir. 1961-62), Artists Equity, Advt. Club Greenville (dir. 1962-64, chmn. sidewalk art show 1963-64, sec. 1964). Club: Soroptomist. Home: 101 Lake Fairfield Dr Greenville SC 29607

COCHRAN, ALICE HOLMES, librarian; b. Newton, Miss., Mar. 20, 1923; d. Oliver Wendell and Rena Belle (Logan) Holmes; student E. Central Jr. Coll., Miss., 1940-41, Augusta Coll., Ga., 1941-42; B.A., Converse Coll., S.C., 1963; M.L.S., Emory U., 1971; m. William Norman Cochran, Feb. 24, 1943; children—William Norman (dec.), Linda (Mrs. William Russell Tyler), John Oliver, Alice Dinsmore. Bookmobile asst. Spartanburg (S.C.) Pub. Library, 1946-48, clerical asst., 1961-62; asst. librarian Converse Coll., 1962-65, order and acting reference librarian Wofford Coll., Spartanburg, 1965-66, acquisitions librarian, 1966—. Chmn., Jr. League Thrift Shop, 1952-55, Spartanburg Speech and Hearing Clinic, 1958-61; pres. Spartanburg County Med. Aux., 1958-59; corr. sec. S.C. Med. Aux., 1959-60. Mem. S.C., Southeastern library assns., Beta Phi Mu. Clubs: Book Reporters (past pres.), Garden (past pres.), Assembly (dir. 1972-73) (Spartanburg). Presbyn. Contbr. articles to profl. jours. Home: 18 Woodburn Rd Spartanburg SC 29302

COCHRAN, GLORIA GRIMES (MRS. WINSTON EARLE COCHRAN), physician; b. Washington; d. Paul DeWitt and Muriel (Quackenbush) Grimes; B.S., Duke, 1945, M.D., 1949; summer study Guys Hosp., London, Eng., 1948; m. Winston Earle Cochran, June 10, 1950; children—Edith Ann, Winston Earle, Donald Lee, Robert Edward. Intern pathology Children's Med. Center, Boston, 1949-50, jr. asst. resident in pediatrics, 1950-51, research tumor therapy, 1953-54; pediatric resident Charlotte (N.C.) Meml. Hosp., 1952-53; fellow pediatric habilitation St. Christophers Hosp. for Children, Phila., 1965-66; instr. health Mt. Vernon Jr. Coll., Washington, 1963-64; sch. med. advisor Montgomery County, Md., 1956-65; asst. prof. pediatrics Baylor U. Coll. Medicine, 1966-72, asso. dir. child devel. Clinic. Tex. Childrens Hosp., Houston, 1966-72; pediatric cons. Bur. Child Health, Va. Dept. Health, 1972—; dir. No. Va. Child Devel. Field Services, 1972—. Diplomate Am. Bd. Pediatrics. Fellow Am. Acad. Pediatrics; mem. Am. Med. Womens Assn. (local br. pres. 1964-65, br. 42, 1970-72), Am. Assn. Mental Deficiency, Phi Beta Kappa. Home: 5708 Bradley Blvd Bethesda MD 20014

COCHRAN, JACQUELINE (MRS. FLOYD B. ODLUM), aviatrix; b. Pensacola, Fla.; orphaned in infancy; reared in Columbus, Ga.; LL.D., Elmira Coll.; D.Sc., Notre Dame Coll.; L.H.D., Russell Sage Coll.; D.Sc., Northland Coll.; m. Floyd B. Odlum, May 11, 1936. Left school at early age to work; connected with cosmetics industry since age 14; owner cosmetic co., 1935-63; received pilot's license at Roosevelt Field, L.I., 1932; additional training in Cal. for 1 yr., equal to U.S. Navy course in groundwork and flight; has flown comml., transport and army fighter planes and bombers; only Am. Woman entrant in McRobertson London-Melbourne race, 1934; 1st woman to fly in Bendix transcontinental race, 1934; winner 1st place in women's div. and 3d place against field of men in Bendix race, 1937; winner of Bendix race, 1938, 2d place, 1946, 3d place, 1948, first woman to pass sonic barrier and exceed speed of sound in Sabre Jet F-86, 1953; piloted bombing plane across the North Atlantic, June 1941; took group of Am. women pilots to Eng., Mar. 1942, for service with Brit. Air Transport Aux., in which she held rank of flight capt.; apptd. dir. Women Pilots, USAAF, 1942-1944, after having headed Woman Pilot Tng. Program, Army Air Forces for several months; commd. lt. col. USAFR, 1948, col., 1968-70, ret., 1970; corporate officer Cochran-Odlum Ranch, Indio, Cal. Dir. Northeast Airlines. Cons. NASA. Bd. dirs. Air Force Acad. Found.; trustee George Washington U. Holder nat., transcontinental and internat. speed records including 9 in Northrop jet trainer, 1961, numerous in Jet Star, 1962, and 2 in the Lockheed 104 Starfighter, 1963, 3 in 1964; Clifford Burke Harmon trophy Internat. League of Aviators, 1937, 38, 39, 46, 50 (for years 1940-49), 53, 62; Air Force Assn. Award for Distinguished Civilian Service, 1948; Mitchell award for gen. aerial achievements 1937; McGough Meml., 1940; decorated D.F.C. with 2 oak leaf clusters, Legion of Merit, D.S.M.; Legion of Honor, Air medal (France); recipient Gold medal Fedn. Aeronautique Internationale, 1953; Zonta Achievement award, 1957; 1st living women to be named to Aviation Hall Fame, 1971. Hon. fellow Soc. Exptl. Test Pilots; pres. Ninety-Nines (orgn. of women pilots), 1942-43; sr. v.p. Fedn. Aeronautique Internationale, 1956-57, pres., 1959-63; mem. Nat. Aero. Assn. (pres. 1961, chmn. 1962). Author: The Stars at Noon, 1954. Home: Cochran-Odlum Ranch Indio CA 92201

COCKER, BARBARA JOAN (MRS. JOHN T. COCKER), painter, interior decorator; b. Uxbridge, Mass., Oct. 16, 1923; d. Frank Blessing and Mary (Anderson) Cassidy; A.A., Becker Jr. Coll., 1943; student Mt. St. Mary Coll., 1944-45, Clark U., summer 1945, N.Y. Sch. Interior Design, 1965-67; m. John T. Cocker, June 26, 1948; children—David John, Neil Joseph. Owner, operator Barbara J. Cocker, Interior Design, Rumson, N.J., 1966—, Barbara J. Cocker Marines, Nantucket, Mass., 1975—; tchr. adult edn. courses in interior design, 1965-68; painter and tchr. marine art; exhibited one-man shows marine paintings Little Gallery, Barbizon, N.Y., 1971, Old Mill Assn., 1971, Pacem en Terris Gallery, N.Y.C., 1972, Monmouth County (N.J.) Library, 1973, Central Jersey Bank & Trust Co., Rumson, 1971, 72, 74, Little Gallery, Nantucket Art Assn., 1975, Caravan House Galleries, N.Y.C., 1975; exhibited group shows including Burr Artists N.Y., Guild Creative Art, Composers, Authors and Artists Am. biennial conv., Shrewsbury, N.J., N.A.D., Zonta Internat. Conv., Boston, Salmagundi Club N.Y.C., Red Bank Arts Festival, Caravan House Galleries, N.Y.C., Monmouth Festival of Arts. Mem. Burr Artists, N.Y. Guild Creative Arts, Nat. Soc. Lit. and Arts, Nantucket Art Assn., Mass., Monmouth arts founds., Old Mill Art Assn., Zonta Internat. Address: 3 Rumson Rd Rumson NJ 07760

COCKRELL, LILA MAY BANKS (MRS. SIDNEY EARL COCKRELL, JR.), civic worker; b. Fort Worth, Jan. 19, 1922; d. Robert Bruce and Velma (Tompkins) Banks; student Ward-Belmont Jr. Coll., 1938-39; B.A., So. Meth. U., 1942; m. Sidney Earl Cockrell, Jr., June 20, 1942; children—Carol Ann (Mrs. Arch G. Adams, Jr.), Cathy Lynn. Chmn. women's div. A.R.C. Fund Campaign, Dallas, 1955; sec. Council Internat. Relations, San Antonio, 1961-64, San Antonio P.T.A. Council, 1960-61; mem. urban beautification com. Nat. League of Cities, 1965-66, mem. community devel. com., 1967-68; pres. region 7 Tex. Municipal League, 1965-66; exec. com. Alamo Area Council Governments, 1970, vice-chmn., 1971; co-ordinator vol. services San Antonio State Chest Hosp., 1970-73. Vice-chmn. Gov.'s Commn. Status Women, 1970-72, sec. charter revision com., San Antonio, 1971, City councilwoman, San Antonio, 1963-70, 73—, mayor-protem, 1969; exec. com. Alamo Area Council Govts., 1969—, vice-chmn., 1971, chmn., 1974—. Trustee McAllister Scholarship Fund, 1962-63, Ecumenical Center Religion and Health; bd. dirs. Alamo area Tb and Respiratory Disease Assn., 1972-73. Served as ensign WAVES, 1943-44. Recipient Headliner of Year award Theta Sigma Phi, 1964; Woman of Achievement award So. Meth. U., 1967; Woman of Achievement award San Antonio Bus. and Profl. Women's Club, 1969, Woman of Year-Ch. Leader San Antonio Express News, Lulac Council, 1972. Mem. Tex. Congress Parents and Tchrs. (life), Ch. Women United Tex. (hon.), San Antonio League Women Voters (pres. 1959-63), Tex. Municipal League (state 2d v.p. 1974), San Antonio Garden Center (hon. life), Beautify San Antonio Assn. (hon. v.p.), Nat. League Cities (mem. coms.), Am. Assn. Vol. Services Coordinators, Delta Delta Delta. Home: 4107 Sylvanoaks St San Antonio TX 78229 Office: City Hall Military Plaza San Antonio TX 78205

COCKRILL, EDITH HERRING, lawyer, business exec.; b. Covington, Tenn., Mar. 11, 1914; d. Lucian and Martha (McLennan) Cockrill; student So. Meth. U., 1936-37; A.B., U. Tenn., 1936, LL.B., 1940. Admitted to Tenn. bar, 1940; govt. atty., 1943-44; pvt. practice law Washington, 1944-49; juvenile Ct. judge, Washington, 1949-57; hearing examiner ICC, Washington, 1960-72, adminstrv. law judge, 1972—. Trustee United Community Services D.C.; bd. dirs. Soc. for Prevention of Blindness D.C., D.C. Rehab. Service White House Conf., 1950; adv. council D.C. Mental Health Assn.; D.C. Heart Assn. vol. Crippled Children's Hosp. Mem. Nat. Council Juvenile Ct. Judges (treas. 1952-54, exec. com. 1953-55), Profl. Panhellenic Assn., D.C., Fed. Women's bar assns., Fed. Trial Examiners Conf., Kappa Delta, Phi Kappa Phi, Phi Delta Delta, Mortar Bd. Presbyn. Clubs: Altrusa, Am. Newspaper; Farmington Country. Home: 3016 Tilden St Washington DC 20008 Office: ICC Washington DC 20423

COCKS, ANNA PEARL RHODES (MRS. RICHARD E. COCKS), librarian; b. Moscow, Mich., July 18, 1918; d. Wilfred G. and Florence (Moulton) Rhodes; B.A. in Chemistry, Western Mich. U., 1940; B.S. in L.S., George Peabody Coll. for Tchrs., 1941; m. Richard E. Cocks, June 20, 1943; children—Valerie Ann, Margaret Ann. Asst. librarian Agr. Library, Pa. State U., State College, 1941-42; librarian Lincoln Sch. br. pub. library, Kalamazoo, 1942-43; tech. processing librarian Miles Labs., Inc., Elkhart, Ind., 1957—. Pres. P.T.A., 1955; active Concert Club, 1955-56, YMCA membership drs., 1956-57. Mem. Am. Assn. U. Women, Am. Chem. Soc., Spl. Libraries Assn., Med. Library Assn., A.L.A., A.A.A.S., Am. Soc. Information Scis., Phi Sigma Alpha. Episcopalian (sec. bd. Women of Ch. 1957). Mem. Order Eastern Star. Contbr. to COPNIP List, 1958-71, editor-in-chief, 1964-65. Home: 1622 Victoria Dr Elkhart IN 46514 Office: 1127 Myrtle St Elkhart IN 46514

CODD, JOAN MARIE KLEFFNER (MRS. DENNIS M. CODD), ednl. adminstr.; b. Lewiston, Ida., June 4, 1946; d. Frank Gregory and Dorothy Rita (Roy) Kleffner; B.A. in History, Ida. State U., 1968, M.Ed. in Student Personnel Work and Counseling, 1969; postgrad. Gonzaga U., 1970-73; m. Dennis M. Codd, May 29, 1971. Coordinator student curriculum advising program Ida. State U., Pocatello, 1968-69; asst. dean students Gonzaga U., Spokane, Wash., 1969-70, asso. dean student life, 1970—, instr. edn., 1972—, counselor counseling center, 1970—, coordinator life style workshops. Mem. tutorial adv. bd. A.R.C., Spokane, 1971—. Named Outstanding Young Woman of Am., 1971, 72. Mem. Am. (Peace Commn. 1972—), Wash., N.W. personnel and guidance assns., Am. Coll. Personnel Assn., Jesuit Assn. Student Personnel Workers, Alpha Chi Omega. Home: West 233-22d St Spokane WA 99203

CODDINGTON, DOROTHY TERESA WESTON (MRS. ALBERT H. CODDINGTON), editor; b. N.Y.C., Aug. 12, 1912; d. Hugh Francis and Mary Regina (McKenna) Weston; student Manhattanville Coll. Sacred Heart, 1928-29, Fordham U., 1929-31, Columbia Sch. Journalism, 1931-32; m. Albert H. Coddington, Dec. 29, 1933; children—Christopher, Joan, Cecily, Ann (dec.). Editor Cath. Worker, 1933-36; free-lance editor med. and edn. publs., 1936-52; with Time mag., 1942-44; editor McGraw-Hill Book Co., 1952-55, mgr. editing dept. Blakiston div., 1955-58; editor, cons. med. edn. WHO, Geneva, Switzerland, 1961-64; editor Ency. World Art, McGraw-Hill, Rome, Italy, 1958-61, 64-66, sr. editor, 1966-67; editor Health Services Research, Am. Hosp. Assn., Chgo., 1968—. Bd. dirs. Manhattanville Nursery, N.Y.C., 1941-45, Newport (R.I.) Community Center, 1947-50. Author: (juvenile) Glory to God, 1951. Home: 718 W Waveland St Chicago IL 60613

CODER, WANDA BANKS (MRS. ANDREW W. CODER), county ofcl.; b. Wamego, Kan., Aug. 11, 1926; d. Gilbert R. and Selma Rose (Birk) Banks; student Clark Sch. Bus., 1943-44; m. Andrew W. Coder, Mar. 8, 1946; children—Lawrence Ray, Jane Kathleen, LeAnne. Sec. Kan. State U., Manhattan, 1946-50; dep. county clerk Riley County, Manhattan, 1960-68, county clk., 1968—. Mem. Manhattan C. of C., Bus. and Profl. Women's Assn. Republican. Clubs: Pilot (Manhattan). Home: 1604 Beechwood St Manhattan KS 66502 Office: Riley County Court House Manhattan KS 66502

CODERE, HELEN FRANCES, educator, anthropologist; b. Winnipeg, Man., Can., Sept. 10, 1917 (came to U.S. 1919, naturalized 1924); d. Charles Francis and Mabelle (Prosser) Codere; B.A. summa cum laude, U. Minn., 1939; Ph.D., Columbia, 1950. Instr., Vassar Coll., 1946-50, asst. prof., 1951-53; vis. lectr. anthropology U. B.C., 1954-55; asso. prof. Vassar Coll. 1955-57, prof., 1958-63; vis. lectr. Northwestern U., winter 1963; mem. faculty Bennington (Vt.) Coll., 1963-64; prof. anthropology Brandeis U., Waltham, Mass., 1964—; anthrop. fieldwork Kwakiutl Indians of B.C., 1951-55, Rwanda, Africa, 1959-60. Faculty fellow Vassar Coll., 1956; Social Sci. Research Council fellow, 1956, 62-63; Guggenheim fellow, 1959-60. Fellow Am. Anthrop. Assn. (exec. council. 1966—), A.A.A.S., African Studies Assn., N.Y. Acad. Scis., Phi Beta Kappa. Author: Fighting with Property: a study of Kwakiutl Potlatching and Warfare, 1927-1930, 1950. Contbr. articles to profl. jours. Office: Dept Anthropology Brandeis U Waltham MA 02154

COE, MINNA NEMEROVSKY PELZ (MRS. WILLARD COE), singer, educator, author; b. N.Y.C., Feb. 12, 1896; d. David and Nahoma (Swartz) Nemerovsky; certificate U. Ore. Normal Sch., 1915; studied voice with Yeatman-Griffith, N.Y.C., Ely Cohen, Paris; m. Mischa Pelz, June 25, 1916 (div. 1924); 1 son, Mischa; m. 2d, Willard Coe, Nov. 20, 1931. Leading soprano roles Portland (Ore.) Opera Assn., 1918-39; leading soprano, mus. dir. Temple Beth Israel, Portland, 1920-37, Temple Emmanuel, Beverly Hills, Cal., 1940-44; head voice dept. Ellison-White Conservatory Music, Reed Coll., Portland, 1920-37; voice tchr. profl. artists, 1918—; producer opera Kwan-Yen, Portland, 1930; condr. Portland Symphony Orch. and

Melodians, Minna Pelz Singers, 1919-29; mus. dir. Police Glee Club, 50-50 Club, Portland, 1920-29, Rose Festival, Portland, 1928-36; soloist, master of ceremonies Santa Barbara Fiesta, 1932-44; chmn., Los Angeles, Ojai Music Festival, 1949; chmn. Los Angeles Internat. Music Olympiad, 1951; founder, pres. Inst. Music for China, 1944-49; pres. 8 o'clock Concerts, Beverly Hills, 1952-54; chmn. Fine Arts Community Concerts, U. Cal. Los Angeles, 1958-61; sponsor, chmn. Friends Westwood Musical Artists, U. Cal., 1959-61; founder Internat. Congress Strings, Los Angeles, 1960—; TV panelist, CBS, NBC, KCET, Los Angeles, 1962-66; star of documentary film Story of a Patroness, 1963, The Imposters, 1966; chmn. Young Audiences, Inc., Cal., 1958-61. Hon. dir., charter mem. adv. bd. Ind. Radio Sta. KPFK, Los Angeles, 1957-61; adv. bd. Shakespeare Festivals, 1961-62, Theatre Unlimited, 1960, Hollywood-Wilshire Symphony Assn., 1965-67; bd. dirs. Everywoman's Village, Van Nuys, Cal., 1973—; v.p. bd. dirs. Friends of Charles W. Coe Meml. Library of Mt. St. Mary's Coll.; bd. dirs. Women's Council KCET Ednl. TV, 1964—, Assn. Women's Return to Edn., 1965-70, Friends Music, U. So. Cal., 1965-70, Brentwood-Westwood Symphony Orch. Assn., 1968—; mem. bd. Beverly Hills Symphony, 1960-65; hon. mem. bd. Braille Inst. Am., 1970—; hon. mem. Brentwood Symphony Women's Guild, 1967—; trustee Cal. Fund for Music, 1965; mem. exec. com. Mayor's Council Internat. Visitors and Sister Cities, Los Angeles, 1965-73; mem. exec. bd. Mayor's Adv. Com., 1966-73; chmn. bd. fine arts Cal. State U. at Los Angeles, 1973; mem. adminstrs. adv. bd. Am. Fedn. Musicians, 1967—; sponsor, chmn. Hollywood Theatre Arts Workshop, Los Angeles City Schs., 1964-65; adv. bd. Try Found., Los Angeles, 1973—; 1st v.p., chmn. bd. Am. Acad. Arts in Europe, 1973—; mem. Women's finance com. Los Angeles Beautiful, 1965-70; sponsor Teach Found., 1967-70; bd. dirs., chmn. communications Internat. Student Center, U. Cal. at Los Angeles, 1971—; adv. bd. Los Angeles Community Arts Alliance, 1972—, So. Cal. Opera Co., Van Nuys, Cal., 1974—, Victor Gruen Center for Environmental Planning, Los Angeles, 1974—. Mem. Nat. Assn. Am. Composers and Condrs. (v.p., founder-chmn., charter life mem. Los Angeles chpt.), Temianka Little Symphony (bd. mem. Los Angeles 1962—), Chamber Symphony Soc. Cal., Inc. (trustee 1962—, founder), Etude Music Club (hon.), Phi Beta (hon. patron 1970—). Author lyrics for symphonic songs, also narrator for world premier performance Royce Hall UCLA, 1969. Author: Born Enthusiastic (book of poetry), 1967; co-author: Brothers Arise (text of cantata by Richard Ralf), 1969. Address: 1650 N Amalfi Dr Pacific Palisades CA 90272

COE, MIRIAM, author, librarian; b. Liverpool, Eng., July 1, 1902;; d. David Avrom and Shaynah Froma (Lippsman) Cohen; honors diploma, Oulton Coll.; diploma, Skerry's Civil Service Coll.; student Liverpool U., Liverpool City Sch. Art, U. Rochester (N.Y.), Columbia, N.Y. Sch. Theatre, Carnegie Hall Studios, Sch. Chinese Brushwork, L.I. U., George Peabody Coll. for Tchrs., Utah, Fla., La. State univs. Sec., J. Ogden Co., Shipbrokers, Eng., 1916-19; tchr. violin, 1924-29; article writer Liverpool Express, 1928; lectr. on psychology of music Sta. WHAM, Rochester; comml. artist, N.Y.C.; coach in English lang. to fgn. students, librarian, Baton Rouge; lectr. La. State U.; exhibitor paintings, N.Y., La. Recipient prizes for art work. Mem. A.L.A. (round table on library service to blind), La., Southeastern, Southwestern library assns., Am. Assn. Sch. Librarians, Alumni Palmer Grad. Sch. Library Sci., Am. Hist. Soc., Am. Assn. Natural History, Am. Sociol. Assn., Am. Acad. Polit. and Social Scis., Am. Judicature Soc., Am. Pub. Health Assn., La. Water Color Soc., Am. Soc. Photogrammetry, Poetry Soc. South and Southwest, Acad. Am. Poets, La. Art and Artists Guild, Am. Dickens League (hon. life) Friends La. State U. Library, Smithsonian Assos., Alpha Beta Alpha. Club: Rumplestillskits, Mystery (N.Y.). Author: Irish Fairy Tales, Children of Other Lands, Animal Story Book, Fruit and Vegetables, Poems for the Young, Haiku: Pictures and Poems, Miscellaneous Poems, School Librarian's Manual, Anthology of World Literature, Careers in Art, A Sociological Cyclopedia; Dictionary and Handbook of Photogrammetry and Related Terms; Pitrim Sorokin: His Life and Work; Librarianship as a Career Field; Development of Education in England; (songs) Our Land (nat. anthem), I'm Praying for Him. Developed original color system for teaching typewriting, spectrum color system for teaching music; inventor typeface, adjuncts for mechanism in constructing typewriters. Home: 839 Azalea Baton Rouge LA 70803 Office: 18184 University Sta Baton Rouge LA 70803

COE, PAMELA SUSAN, govt. ofcl.; b. N.Y.C., Dec. 15, 1942; d. Robert Allan and Ethel (Whichard) Coe; student St. Mary's Coll., 1962. Asst. account exec. Eleanor Lambert, Inc., N.Y.C., 1962-63; dir. continuity Sta. WITN-TV, Washington, 1963-64; dir. pub. service and community relations Sta. WFMY-TV, Greensboro, N.C., 1964-66; asst. producer Grey Advt. Co., N.Y.C., 1966-67; dir. radio and TV publicity J. Walter Thompson Co., N.Y.C., 1968-71; spl. asst. to sec. of Interior for broadcast and media, Washington, 1971-73, asst. to sec. Interior for arts, dir. cultural affairs, 1973—. Bd. dirs. Henry Street Settlement, N.Y.C., 1968-71, Ford's Theatre, Washington, 1973—. Named Outstanding Young Woman in Am., 1972. Mem. Am. Women in Radio-TV, Friends of Lincoln Center. Home: 2700 Virginia Av NW Washington DC 20037 Office: Office of Sec Dept of Interior Washington DC 20240

COE, PEARLE WINNIFRED HERSEY (MRS. HENRY SUTCLIFFE COE), civic worker; b. Bangor, Me., May 26, 1906; d. Justus Loren and Winnifred (Paige) Hersey; student drama Leland Powers, Jr., 1924; voice study scholar with Leda Gregory Jackson, San Jose, Cal., 1929-33; m. Henry Sutcliffe Coe, Oct. 9, 1928; children—Nancy Patricia, Winnifred Hannah (Mrs. Robert George Verbica). Vocal soloist, dramatist, 1911-28; bookkeeper, Nichols Co., Bangor, 1925-26; sales promotion Lufkins Candy Co., Bangor, 1927-28; pub. accountant San Jose, 1930-32; vocal soloist, dramatist No. Cal., 1932-33. Organizer, Evergreen Youth Center, San Jose, 1946; hon. life mem. Cal. Congress Parents and Tchrs., 1956—; patroness Valle Monte League, San Jose, Montalvo, Saratoga, Cal., San Jose Symphony Assn., Cal. Hist. Soc., San Francisco, Children's Home Soc., San Jose. Mem. Republican Nat. Com., 1968-70. Pres. bd. dirs. Evergreen Youth Center, 1946-56, hon. life mem. bd. dirs., 1956—. Mem. Music and Arts Found. Santa Clara, P.E.O. Sisterhood (pres. San Jose 1966-69), Performing Arts League, Tokalon, San Jose Opera Guild, Santa Clara County Cow Belles. Mem. Order Eastern Star. Clubs: Bonanza Investors (San Jose); San Jose Country; Capitol Hill (Washington). Home: Route 3 Box 440C San Jose CA 95121

COEN, RENA NEUMANN (MRS. EDWARD COEN), art historian, educator; b. N.Y.C., Feb. 22, 1925; d. Joshua Heschel and Tamar (Mohl) Neumann; B.A., Barnard Coll., 1946; M.A. (Jr. Sterling fellow), Yale, 1948; Ph.D. (Danforth Found. fellow), U. Minn., 1969; m. Edward Coen, June 26, 1949; children—Deborah, Joel, Ethan. Docent Jewish Mus., N.Y.C., 1948; research asst., lectr. Mpls. Inst. Art, 1961-66; asst. prof. art history St. Cloud State Coll., Minn., 1969-73, asso. prof., 1973—. Organizer bicentennial exhbn. of early Minn. art for 1976, U. Minn. Gallery. Fellow Soc. for Religion in Higher Edn.; mem. Minn. Hist. Soc., Coll. Art Assn., Am. Assn. U. Profs., League of Women Voters (chmn. 1963), Women's Equity Action League. Author: Kings and Queens in Art, 1965; American History in Art, 1967; Medicine in Art, 1970; The Black Man in Art, 1970; The Old Testament in Art, 1970; The Red Man in Art, 1972. Contbr. articles on Am. art to scholarly jours. Home: 1425 Flag Av S Minneapolis MN 55426 Office: Dept of Art St Cloud State College St Cloud MN 56301

COENRAAD, SHARON OLESON (MRS. DAVE COENRAAD), advt. exec.; b. Laurens, Ia., June 22, 1930; d. Guy Efford and Lura (Strickland) Oleson; spl. student Dana Inst. Music, 1948-49; bus. course Am. Inst. Bur., 1949-50; m. Dave Coenraad, Feb. 1971. With Fingerprint Identification div. FBI, Washington, 1951; with promotion and pub. relations dept. Hotel Ft. Des Moines, Des Moines, 1953-58; account group sec. Foote, Cone & Belding Advt., Los Angeles, 1959-62; adminstr. asst./exec. sec. Grey Advt., Inc., Beverly Hills, Cal., 1962-65; media dir., office mgr. Oppenheim, DeMarco & Westfall Advt., Inc., Honolulu, 1965; office mgr. Eisaman, Johns & Laws Advt., Hollywood, Cal., 1965-67; corporate sec.-treas., media dir., office mgr. Sol R. Shein Advt., Inc., Los Angeles, 1967—. Recipient 1st place award, menu design Nat. Restaurant Assn., 1957; outstanding service award Advt. Assn. West, 1965. Mem. Advt. Club Los Angeles (hon. life). Mem. Order Eastern Star, White Shrine of Jerusalem. Home: 3375 Manning Av Los Angeles CA 90064 Office: 3242 W 8th St Los Angeles CA 90005

COFER, ELOISE SNOWDEN, home economist; b. Pocahontas, Va., May 15, 1917; d. Richard Clyde and Laura (Gildersleeve) Cofer; B.A., Marshall U., 1937; M.S. (Borden fellow) Columbia, 1939; Ph.D. (U. fellow), U. Chgo., 1955. Research asst. Columbia, 1937-39; instr. Stephens Coll., Columbia, Mo., 1939-42; specialist foods and nutrition W.Va. Agrl. Extension Service, Morgantown, 1942-55; food economist Agrl. Research Service, U.S. Dept. Agr., Washington, 1955-63; asst. dir. N.C. Agrl. Extension Service, Raleigh, 1963—. Cons. Research Triangle Inst., 1967—, others. Bd. dirs. N.C. Council Women's Orgns., 1967—, pres., 1973—; bd. dirs. N.C. Council World Affairs, 1966-68. Mem. Am. Home Econs. Assn. (treas. 1964-66), Am. Dietetics Assn., Sigma Xi, Kappa Omicron Phi, Delta Kappa Gamma, Kappa Delta Pi. Club: Altrusa Internat. Home: 3203 Ruffin St Raleigh NC 27607 Office: Box 5097 NC State U Raleigh NC 27607

COFFEE, BERNICE FRENCH (MRS. R. CLIFFORD COFFEE), educator; b. Rector, Ark.; d. George H. and Gertrude (Toone) French; B.S., U. Kan., 1946, M.S., 1947; Ph.D. (Gregory fellow), U. Mo., 1956; m. R. Clifford Coffee, June 11, 1933. Prin., Clay County Sch., Ark., 1925-48; instr. English, U. Kan., 1946-47; dir. tchr. tng. Ark. State Coll., 1948; instr. English, U. Mo., 1949-53; prof., head dept. English, Shaw U., 1957-62; prof., acting head dept. English, Wis. State U., at Platteville, 1963—; dir. Writing Clinic; editor Masters and Doctors Thesis U. Mo.; mem. N.C. Adv. Council for Coll. Programs; mem. U. Wis. Adv. Council for Master Arts Program in English. Mem. Modern Lang. Assn., Midwestern Modern Lang. Assn., Nat. Council Tchrs. English, Shakespeare Soc., Southeastern, Midwestern Renaissance confs., Faculty Womens Assn., Am. Assn. U. Women (pres.), Assn. Wis. State U. Faculties, Wis. Coll. English Tchrs. Assn. (adviser student governing bd.), Delta Tau Kappa. Mem. Order Eastern Star. Home: 430 N 4th St Platteville WI 53818

COFFEE, KAREN ELAINE, ednl. adminstr.; b. Sturgis, Mich., May 9, 1947; d. Raymond Loren and Florence Irene (Hooley) Rheinheimer; Asso. degree Internat. Jr. Coll. Bus., 1967; m. Michael J. Coffee, May 20, 1972. Sec. to dean Internat. Jr. Coll. Bus., Ft. Wayne, Ind., 1966-68, sec. to pres., 1968, housing dir., 1968—, registrar, 1969—, financial aid dir., 1970—. Mem. Nat. Secs. Assn. (sec. Tawasi chpt. 1971-73), Phi Kappa Chi (sponsor). Home: 2444 Sandpoint Rd Fort Wayne IN 46809 Office: 120 W Jefferson St Fort Wayne IN 46802

COFFELT, ANITA JEAN (MRS. RICHARD EARLE COFFELT), mag. editor; b. Shenandoah, Ia., Dec. 21, 1930; d. Porter Leslie and June (Lawson) Alley; student Am. Inst. Bus., 1949-50, U. Cal. at Los Angeles, 1964; m. Richard Earle Coffelt, Oct. 4, 1963; 1 dau., Rhonda Kay. Employed in various secretarial positions, 1951-57; asst. to publicity dir. El Rancho Vegas, Las Vegas, 1957-58; exec. sec. 20th Century Fox, Los Angeles, 1958-60, 63; owner Anita Coffelt Typing Service, Springfield, Va., Bridgeville, Pa. and Arlington Heights, Ill., 1963—; editor, pub. Animal Lovers mag., Bridgeville, 1969—. Bd. dirs. Animal Care and Welfare, Inc., Pitts., 1970-71. Home: 85 Glenside Rd Murray Hill NJ 07974 Office: PO Box 16 Murray Hill NJ 07974

COFFILL, MARJORIE LOUISE (MRS. WILLIAM CHARLES COFFILL), club woman; b. Sonora, Cal., June 11, 1917; d. Eric J. and Pearl (Needham) Segerstrom; A.B. with distinction in Social Sci., Stanford, 1938; M.A. in Edn., 1941; m. William Charles Coffill, Jan. 25, 1948; children—William James, Eric John. Asst. mgr. Sonora Abstract & Title Co. (Cal.), 1938-39; mem. staff Dean of Women, Stanford, 1939-41; social dir. women's campus Pomona Coll., 1941-43, instr. in psychology, 1941-43; asst. to field dir. A.R.C., Le Moore AFB, Cal., 1944-46; partner Riverbank Water Co., Riberbank and Hughson, Cal., 1950-68; mem. Tuolumne County Mental Health Adv. Bd., 1963-69; mem. Central adv. council Supplementary Edn. Center, 1966-68; mem. Pres.' adv. bd. Columbia Jr. Coll., chmn. bd. dirs. found., 1973—; mem. Tuolumne County Bicentennial Com. Bd. dirs. Tuolumne County Tb Assn.; clk. bd. trustees Sonora Union High Sch., chmn. bd. trustees, 1969-71. Pres., Tuolumne County Republican Women; asso. mem. Cal. Rep. Central Com., 1950. Active P.T.A., A.R.C. Recipient Pi Lambda Theta award, 1940. Mem. Am. Assn. U. Women (charter mem. Tuolumne County br., pres. Sonora br. 1965-68). Episcopalian (sr. warden 1970-71, mem. vestry). Home: 376 E Summit Av Sonora CA 95370

COFFIN, LINDA LEE, govt. ofcl.; b. Hutchinson, Kan.; d. Ralph B. and Virginia (Richards) Coffin; B.A., U. Okla., 1964, M.A., 1965. Mgmt. intern U.S. AEC, Richland, Wash., 1965-67, adminstrv. asst., 1967-68, contract adminstrn. asst., 1968-69, contract adminstrn. specialist, 1969-72; contract negotiator, acting dept. chief Office Bus. Devel., Small Bus. Adminstrn., Boston, 1972—; cons. Richland Flying Service, 1971-72. Bd. dirs. Campfire Girls, Richland Civic Light Opera. Mem. Am. Polit. Sci. Assn., Am. Acad. Arts and Scis., Nat. Contract Mgmt. Assn. (bd. dirs.), Cal. Alumni Assn., Wash. Pilots Assn. (bd. dirs.), Pi Sigma Alpha, Phi Alpha Theta, Zeta Tau Alpha. Home: 1965 Burnside Rd Sebastopol CA 95472 Office: Small Bus Adminstrn John F Kennedy Fed Bldg Govt Center Boston MA 02203

COFFMAN, MARY ELOISE, editor; b. Cumberland, Md., May 22, 1943; d. William Eugene and Eloise Ethel (Clarke) Coffman; A.B. cum laude in French, Dickinson Coll., 1965. Editorial asst. McGraw-Hill, Inc., N.Y.C., 1965-66, asst. editor, 1966-68, asso. editor, 1968-71, editor, 1971—. Tutor adult edn. program, St. Louis, 1967-68. Recipient Printing Industries of Am. award for La France au Cours des Ages, 1973, Pensee et Litterature Francaises, 1971. Mem. Modern Lang. Assn., Am. Assn. Tchrs. French, Am. Council on Teaching Fgn. Langs., Pi Delta Phi. Author: Schaum's Outline of French Grammar, 1973. Editor: Passe Partout, 1968-69. Home: 155 W 95th St New York City NY 10020 Office: 1221 Av of the Americas New York City NY 10025

COFFMAN, SISTER MARY RUTH, educator; b. Memphis, Oct. 15, 1929; d. Runa David and Genevieve (Dickinson) Coffman; B.S., U. Ala., 1950; M.A., Cath. U. Am., 1962; M.L.S., George Peabody Library Sch., 1972. Joined Order Sacred Heart; English instr. Chilton County Pub. Schs., 1950-51; head dept. English John Carroll High Sch., Birmingham, Ala., 1954-65; prof. English, librarian Cullman (Ala.) Coll., 1964—. Mem. Kappa Delta Pi, Beta Phi Mu. Home: Sacred Heart Convent Cullman AL 35055

COFFMAN, PENELOPE DALTON (MRS. ALDINE J. COFFMAN, JR.), lawyer; b. Pulaski, Va., Apr. 16, 1938; d. Gomez and Hazel (Davis) Dalton; A.B., Randolph-Macon Womans Coll., 1958; J.D., Marshall-Wythe Sch., Coll. William and Mary, 1966; m. Aldine J. Coffman, Jr., Mar. 27, 1965; 1 dau., D'Maris Dalton. Research chemist, research biologist Arthur D. Little, Inc., Cambridge, Mass., 1958-63; admitted to Va. bar, 1966; law clk. Asso. Justice C. Vernon Spratley, Va. Supreme Ct. Appeals, Hampton, Va., 1966-67; practiced in Norfolk, Va., 1967-68, Virginia Beach, Va., 1968—; asst. commonwealth atty. City of Virginia Beach, 1971—; partner Coffman & Coffman, Virginia Beach. Mem. Gov.'s Council on Ednl. TV, 1971—. Mem. Va. State, Virginia Beach bar assns., Nat. Assn. Women Lawyers, William and Mary Alumni Assn., William and Mary Soc., Randolph-Macon Womans Coll. Alumni Assn., Zeta Tau Alpha. Home: 2861 River Rd Virginia Beach VA 23454

COFFMAN, RUTH ELIZABETH, univ. dean; b. Birmingham, Ala., Mar. 28, 1910; d. Charles Cannon and Gertrude Elizabeth (Hoit) Ellis; A.B., Samford U., 1931; M.A., U. Ala., 1963; postgrad. Northwestern U., 1962; m. Michael Rufus Coff, May 5, 1934 (div.); children—Marie (Mrs. T.E. Stull), Kay (Mrs. S. Flowers), Helen. Tchr. pub. schs. Midfield-Jefferson County, Ala., 1956-59, Mountain Brook (Ala.) Sch. System, 1959-68; dean of women U. Montevallo, Ala., 1968—. Supervising tchr. for student tchrs. from Auburn and Samford univs., 1965-68; adviser to Pan-Hellenic Council, U. Montevallo (Ala.), 1971—. P.T.A., Mountain Brook Ednl. Assn. grantee, 1962. Mem. Ala., Mountain (sec. 1965) ednl. assns., Am. Assn. U. Women (sec. 1968), Ala. Assn. Women Deans and Counselors (v.p. 1974), D.A.R. (civic regent), Alpha Lambda Delta. Delta Kappa Gamma, Phi Mu. Club: Faculty (v.p. 1969). Home: 105 Poinciana Dr Birmingham AL 35209 Office: Calkins Hall University Montevallo AL 35115

COGER, LESLIE IRENE, educator; b. Huntsville, Ark.; d. Ira M. and Minnie Lee (Presley) Coger; diploma Curry Sch. of Expression, Boston, 1932; B.A., Coll. of Ozarks, 1933; M.A., U. Ark., 1940; Ph.D., Northwestern U., 1952; studied profl. schs. acting, London, Eng., 1961-62. Tchr., Huntsville State Vocational Sch., 1934-38; head speech and phys. edn. depts. Central Coll., 1938-43; prof. speech S.W. Mo. State U., 1943—; grad. asst. Northwestern U., 1946-47; tchr. Queen's Coll., City U. N.Y., summer, 1966; condr. oral interpretation and readers theatre workshops, 1960, 62, 63, 65, 66, 69-71, 72, 73, research on acting methods, N.Y.C., 1958, London, Eng., 1962; research on kinesics U. So. Cal., 1967. Mem. bd. Springfield Little Theatre, participating acting roles, 1956, 57, 59, 62, 69, 73; dir. play Am. Ednl. Theatre, U.S.O., European tour, 1961, N.E. command, 1965, Pacific Command, 1968, European Command, 1972. Recipient Lew Sarrett Poetry Reading award Northwestern U., 1946; named Woman of Year in Edn., Springfield C. of C., 1962. Mem. Am. Assn. U. Women, Am. Ednl. Theatre Assn. (mem. U.S.O. touring com. 1966—, children's theatre workshop 1964), Speech Communication Assn. Am. (mem. interpretation com. 1953-55; sec. interpretation interest group 1963-65, chmn. interpretation div. 1972, editor interpretation div. newsletter, The Readers Theatre Handbook, 1967, rev. edit. 1973). Editor: Ark. Speech Jour., 1942-43; studies in Readers Theatre, 1961; cons. editor: Players mag., 1957-61. Cons. editor: The Speech Teacher, 1964-66. Contbr. to Stanislavsky and America, 1966; also articles to jours. and mags. Home: 941 S Weller St Springfield MO 65802

COGGINS, DEBORAH F. REED (MRS. WILMER JESSE COGGINS), physician; b. Tampa, Fla., Apr. 28, 1924; d. Ernest Victor and Ferne (Adams) Reed; student Fla. State U., 1940-42, B.S. U. Wash., 1944; M.D., Duke, 1951; m. Wilmer Jesse Coggins, Apr. 16, 1949; children—Pamela, Deborah, Wilmer J., III, Audrey Ann, Christopher Reed. Intern, Georgetown U. Hosp., 1951-52; resident St. Elizabeth Hosp., Washington, 1952-53; gen. practice medicine with husband, Fla., 1953-59; resident psychiatry Shands Teaching Hosp., U. Fla., Gainesville, 1959-61, asst. prof. psychiatry, 1966-69, chief in-patient unit Shands Teaching Hosp., 1967-69, clin. asso., 1969—; pvt. practice psychiatry, 1969—. Diplomate Am. Bd. Psychiatry and Neurology in Psychiatry. Fellow Am. Psychiat. Assn.; mem. Fla. Med. Assn., Alachva County Med. Soc., Fla. Psychiat. Soc. (sec. 1967-68). Home: 1608 SW 56th Pl Gainesville FL 32601 Office: 2306-807 SW 13th St Gainesville FL 32601

COGHLAN, ANNE EVELINE, educator; b. Boston, Mar. 29, 1927; d. William Henry and Alice E. (Blake) Coghlan; B.S., Simmons Coll., 1948; M.Ed., Boston U., 1953; M.S., U. Vt., 1957; Ph.D., U. R.I., 1965. Instr., faculty resident Colby Jr. Coll., New London, N.H., 1949-59; asso. prof. biology Simmons Coll., Boston, 1962-70, prof. biology, 1970—, chmn. dept., 1972—. Asso. dir. NSF Summer Inst. Microbiology, Simmons Coll., 1962, U. R.I., 1966-68. NSF Faculty fellow, 1959-61. Mem. A.A.A.S., Am. Soc. Microbiology (pres. N.E. br. 1972), Am. Soc. Cell Biology, Am. Assn. U. Profs., Sigma Xi. Home: 65 Belcher Circle Milton MA 02186 Office: 300 The Fenway Boston MA 02115

COGSWELL, DOROTHY MCINTOSH, educator; b. Plymouth, Mass., Nov. 13, 1909; d. Clarence H. and Ruth (McIntosh) Cogswell; B.F.A., Yale, 1933, M.F.A., 1939. Instr. Mt. Holyoke Coll., 1939-44, asst. prof., asso. prof., 1947-59, prof. 1959—, chmn. dept. art, 1960-69, dir. collections, 1970—. One man shows G.W.V. Smith Mus., Springfield, Albany Inst. of History and Art, U. Mass., Elmira Coll., Rutgers U.; exhibited group shows N.Y. World's Fair, N.Y. Watercolor Soc., Conn. Acad., New Haven Paint and Clay Club; works in permanent collection Springfield Mus. Fine Arts, Newport Assn., Wisteriahurst, Holyoke City Museum; murals Mt. Holyoke Coll. Recipient 1st watercolor prize Eastern States Exhibition, 1941; Fulbright award for lectureship in Nat. Art Sch., Sydney, Australia, 1957-58. Mem. Springfield Art League (pres. 1942-43), Am. Assn. Museums, Mt. Holyoke Friends of Art (chmn. 1947-60), Coll. Art Assn., South Hadley Hist. Soc. (charter), Nat. Trust for Historic Preservation, Soc. for Preservation New Eng. Antiquities. Conglist. Club: New Haven Paint and Clay. Home: 23 Jewett Lane South Hadley MA 01075

COGSWELL, MARGARET PRICE, museum ofcl.; b. Evanston, Ill., Sept. 15, 1925; d. Ralph John and Hazel (Price) Cogswell; B.A., Wellesley Coll., 1947; postgrad. Pratt Inst., 1951-52, Art Inst. Chgo., 1952, N.Y.U., 1955-56, Columbia U. Grad. Sch. Arts and Architecture, 1965-66. Program dir. Riverside Community House, N.Y.C., 1948-52; prodn. mgr. The House of J. Hayden Twiss, 1953-54; exhbn. asso. The American Fedn. of Arts, N.Y.C., 1955-58, head dept. publns., 1958-66; dep. chief Office Exhbns. Abroad, Nat. Collection of Fine Arts, Smithsonian Instn. Washington, 1966—. Chmn. 50 Books of the Year, Am. Inst. Graphic Arts, N.Y.C. 1964; organized mountain craftsmen exhbns., features in mags. Trustee The Ben and Abby Grey Found., St. Paul. Mem. Am. Assn. Museums, Museum Pubs. Assn. Author: The American Poster, 1968. Contbr. articles in field to profl. jours. Office: 9th and G St NW Washington DC 20560

COHAGEN, CYNTHIA, newspaper co. exec.; b. Boulder, Colo., Mar. 24, 1949; d. John H. and Virginia Case (Platts) Cohagen; B.A. magna cum laude, U. Wash., 1971. Pub. relations dir. A.M. Hunter & Assos., Boulder, 1971; account exec. Robert Dacey & Assos., Boulder, 1971-72; adminstrv. asst. Town & Country Review, Boulder, 1972—. Dir., pub. relations cons. Western Industries, Inc., 1971—. Cons. Boulder Day Nursery, 1970—. Mem. Jr. Guild of Boulder Philharmonic, 1971—. Mem. Women In Communications, Theta Sigma Phi, Phi Beta Kappa, Delta Gamma. Episcopalian. Home: 1106 Cascade Boulder CO 80302 Office: 5735 Arapahoe PO Box 4299 Boulder CO 80303

COHAN, CAROLE KRITZ (MRS. RONALD COHAN), broadcasting co. exec.; b. N.Y.C., Dec. 16, 1945; d. Martin and Tulsa B. (Rosenzweig) Kritz; m. Ronald Cohen, Apr. 23, 1967; 1 dau., Leslie. Vice pres., supr. prodn. Grey Advt. Inc.; exec. producer McCann Erickson; asso. producer sta. WABC-TV, N.Y.C., Sammy Davis Enterprises. Mem. Broadcast Advt. Producers Soc. Am. Home: 254 E 68th St New York City NY 10021 Office: 777 3d Av New York City NY 10017

COHAN, DIANA WOODWARD (MRS. JOHN MEADE COHAN), lawyer, state ofcl.; b. Oakland, Cal., Nov. 21, 1942; d. Richard Davis and Gladys Barbara (Stables) Woodward; A.B. in Polit. Sci., Stanford, 1964; J.D. (Mabel Wilson Richard scholar), U. Cal. at Los Angeles, 1969; m. John Meade Cohan, Aug. 7, 1971. Admitted to Cal. bar, 1969, since practiced in San Francisco. Dep. atty. Gen. Dept. Justice State of Cal., San Francisco, 1969—. Mem. State Bar Cal., San Francisco Bar Assn., Queen's Bench, Stanford Alumni Assn., U. Cal. Los Angeles Law Alumni Assn., Sierra Club. Home: 50 Baywood Av San Anselmo CA 94960 Office: 350 McAllister St San Francisco CA 94102

COHAN, ROWENA JOYCE KIMZEY, television exec.; b. Hot Spring County, Ark., Dec. 15, 1931; d. Joseph W. and Jalina Jane (Thomas) Kimzey; student Henderson State Tchrs. Coll., 1948; m. John Colley Cohan, Apr. 2, 1961 (dec. Jan. 1974); children—John Kimzey, Thomas Alan, Mark Randolph. Adminstrv. asst. to pres. Salinas Broadcasting Corp. (Cal.), 1951-59; gen. adminstr. Central Cal. Communications Corp., Salinas, 1961-69, dir., sec.-treas., 1967-70; pres. Ocean View CableVision, Inc., Seaside, 1970—, Hudson-Cohan Pub. Co., Salinas, 1970—. Treas. Salinas Valley Meml. Hosp. Aux., 1963-65. Mem. Monterey County Art and History Assn., Am. Mgmt. Assn. Club: Carmel Valley (Cal.) Racquet. Home: 20 Carmel Av Salinas CA 93901 Office: 1780A Fremont Blvd Seaside CA 93955

COHEN, ADELE RIEGER, artist; b. Buffalo; d. Theodore and Etta (Siegel) Rieger; student Parsons Sch., N.Y.C., N.Y. Art Inst. Buffalo, Albright Art Sch. of U. Buffalo; m. Paul Lenard Cohen, Sept. 21, 1943; children—Henry Joseph, Tina. Exhibited group shows Albright-Knox, Buffalo, Boston, Nat. Outdoor Festival, City Center Monthly Nat., N.Y.C., Chautaugua Nat., N.Y.C., Silvermine Nat., New Canaan, Conn., Nat. Assn. Women Artists, N.A.D., N.Y.C., N.Y. State Fair, Syracuse, N.Y., Ball State Coll., Muncie, Ind., 1959—. N.E. Regional Exhbn., Mus. for Contemporary Art, Boston, Art Across Am. N.E. Region, 1965; one-man shows Bodley Gallery, N.Y.C., 1960, 1963, Phoenix Gallery, N.Y.C., 1968, 71, traveling show, starting at New Gallery, Tel Aviv, Israel. Mem. Gallery of Albright-Knox, Buffalo, 1965; represented permanent collections Museum of Arts and Scis., Evansville, Ind., Lending Library Mus. Modern Art, N.Y.C., U. Mass., Amherst; reprodns. of works in Design mag., N.Y. Times Mag., Womans Day; participated Art in Embassy Program U.S. State Dept; represented in pvt. collections, Buffalo, Lakewood, N.J., Cleve., Atlanta, New Orleans, La., Denver, Colo., and Los Angeles. Recipient First prize City Center Nat., 1958; Hengerer award Western N.Y. Ann., 1960; drawing prize N.Y. State Expn., Syracuse, 1963; 1st prize Western N.Y. Ann., Albright-Knox Art Gallery, 1964; oil painting prize, W. N.Y. Ann., 1965, 69; Silvermine prize, 1966; Chautaugua prize, 1967. Mem. Buffalo Soc. Artists, Patteran Soc. Buffalo, Nat. Assn. Women Artists, B'nai B'rith Women. Home: 66 Burbank Dr Buffalo NY 14226

COHEN, ANITA JAYNE, state ofcl.; b. Los Angeles; d. David Robert and Delphine (Silberman) Cohen; student U. Cal. at Los Angeles, 1933-34, 36-37, U. Minn., 1937-38; A.B., U. Cal. at Berkeley, 1939; M.S. in Edn., U. So. Cal., 1970. With Cal. Employment Devel. Dept., 1941—, sr. interviewer, 1944-47, employment security officer II, supr. various offices, Los Angeles, 1947-63; supr. terminal student sch. program Los Angeles Youth and Student Office and Los Angeles Central Youth Opportunity Center, 1963-67; supervising employment counselor Los Angeles Central Youth Opportunity Center, 1967-69; supr. youth services and tng. Los Angeles Central Human Resources Devel. Center, 1970-73; occupational information cons. Office of Edn., 1973—; tng. liaison and labor market specialist Los Angeles Central Manpower Devel. Center, 1973—. Mem. U. Cal. at Los Angeles Alumni Scholarship Com. for Hollywood-Wilshire Area, 1969—. Recipient 25-Year Service award State of Cal., 1966, Merit award, State of Cal., 1959. Mem. Am., Cal. personnel and guidance assns., Nat., Cal. employment counselors assns., Nat., Cal. vocational guidance assns., Los Angeles Personnel and Guidance Assn. (pres. 1964-65), Nat. Rehab. Assn. So. Cal. (exec. bd. 1965-69). Home: 535 S Curson Av W Los Angeles CA 90036 Office: 161 W Venice Blvd Los Angeles CA 90015

COHEN, AUDREY COHEN (MRS. MARK I. COHEN), coll. pres.; b. Pitts.; d. Abe and Esther (Morgan) Cohen; B.A. magna cum laude, U. Pitts., 1953; grad. student George Washington U., 1957-58; m. Mark Ivan Cohen, Aug. 31, 1952; children—Dawn Jennifer, Winifred Alisa. Tchr. social scis., 1953-57; founder, pres. Part-Time Research Assos., Inc., social sci. research, N.Y.C., 1959-64; founder Gallery Passport Ltd., N.Y.C., 1960; founder, pres. Women's Talent Corps, N.Y.C., 1964-66, Coll. Human Services, N.Y.C., 1967—. Mem. Newman Com., task force on higher edn., 1970—; mem. policy adv. com. U.S. Office Edn. Accreditation and Instl. Eligibility, 1971—; bd. dirs. Higher Edn. Compact; mem. regents adv. com. on external degrees N.Y. State Bd. Regents; cons. commn. occupational status Nat. Vocational Guidance Assn.; mem. Pres. Manhattan Borough's Adv. Com. Health Careers for Disadvantaged; bd. dirs. Nat. Conf. Pub. Service Employment. Bd. visitors U. Pitts.; mem. N.Y. council Boston Symphony. Recipient Stanley M. Isaacs award Am. Jewish Com., 1969; George Champion award Chase Manhattan Bank, N.Y.C., 1970. Mem. Women's Polit. Caucus, Am. Polit. Sci. Assn., Profl. Women's Caucus, Nat. Orgn. Women. Contbr. articles to profl. jours., chpts. to books. Home: 37 E 67th St New York City NY 10021

COHEN, BARBARA SUE, psychologist; b. Urbana, Ill., Mar. 5, 1941; d. Ephraim Bernard and Lillian (Kay) Cohen; B.A. cum laude, Radcliffe Coll., 1963; Ph.D., N.Y. U., 1971; postdoctoral study psychotherapy and psychoanalysis Adelphi U., 1971—. Staff psychologist New Hope Guild Guidance Center, Bklyn., 1969-71, Huntington (N.Y.) Mental Health Clinic, 1971—; individual practice psychoanalysis and psychotherapy, Glen Cove, N.Y., 1973—. First oboist Great Neck (N.Y.) Symphony, 1973—. Mem. Am., Nassau County psychol. assns., Adelphi Soc. Psychoanalysis and Psychotherapy (treas.), Am. Civil Liberties Union. Democrat. Home: 24 Gaffney St Glen Cove NY 11542

COHEN, BESS, civic worker; b. Dallas, June 25, 1919; d. Ben and Rebecca (Golman) Coleman; grad. high sch.; m. Morris Cohen, July 26, 1942 (dec. Jan. 1972) children—Jan Michelle, Michael Ben. Mem. nat. bd. dirs. Israel Bonds, 1967—; bd. dirs. Julius Schapps Community Center, 1966—, B'nai B'irth, 1970—; bd. dirs. women's div. Jewish Welfare Fedn., 1969—, v.p., 1969-70; v.p. Mizrachi, 1971—, nat. women's com. Brandeis U., Dallas, 1972; pres. Shearith Israel Sisterhood, 1952-54, Council Jewish Women's Orgns., 1968-70; v.p. Dallas Save a Life, 1959-60; v.p. Women's Service Orgn., 1965-67; mem. nat. adv. bd. Am. Coll. in Jerusalem, 1971—; leader Girl Scouts, 1937-42, Camp Fire Girls, 1956-58; bd. dirs. Golden Acres, 1958-61, Jewish Family Service, 1958-60, Hadassah, 1955-57, S.W. Regional Bd. Jewish Women's League Sisterhoods, United Synagogue Am., 1967-69, Dir. Cohen Candy Co., Dallas, McCraw Candies, Farmersville, Tex. Mem. Community Relations Council, 1970-71. Named 1st Woman of Valor Tex., Israel Bonds, 1966, Man of Year, Zionist Orgn. Am., 1971, American of Week, 1971; recipient Israel Bond Tribute award, 1963; Leadership award Jewish Welfare Fedn., 1970. Editor Shearith Israel Newsletter, 1954—. Home: 6206 Joyce Way Dallas TX 75225 Office: 171 Howell St Dallas TX 75207

COHEN, CAROL ANN HOROWITZ (MRS. GEORGE COHEN), lawyer; b. Bronx, N.Y., Jan. 12, 1943; d. Abraham and Mona (Silverman) Horowitz; B.A., U. Md., 1963, J.D., 1969; m. George Cohen, July 14, 1962; children—Joseph, Susan, Linda. Admitted to N.J. bar, 1970, practiced in Plainfield, 1970-72; house counsel, corporate sec. Applied Data Research, Inc., Princeton, N.J., 1972—. Democratic county committeewoman, 1970-72; mem. steering com. Women's Polit. Caucus, State of N.J., 1972—. Mem. N.J. Bar Assn., Computer Lawyers Assn. Home: 34 Sherwood Lane Green Brook NJ 08812 Office: Route 206 Center Princeton NJ 08540

COHEN, CHARLOTTE JOAN HURWITZ (MRS. HAROLD ROBERT COHEN), physician; b. N.Y.C., Mar. 7, 1923; d. William and Sophie Olga (Schultz) Hurwitz; B.S., U. Ill., 1944, M.D., 1945; m. Harold Robert Cohen, July 10, 1943; children—Sandra, Gail, Marsha (Mrs. Richard Hagel), Vicki, Scott, Deborah. Intern, No. Permanente Found., Vancouver, Wash., 1945-46, resident, 1946-47, staff pediatrician, 1947; staff physician Dammasch State Hosp., Wilsonville, Ore., 1969—. Active Girl Scouts Am. Home: 16351 Phantom Bluff Lake Oswego OR 97034 Office: Dammasch State Hosp Wilsonville OR 97070

COHEN, EDNA NATALIE LIEBERMAN (MRS. HARRY COHEN), librarian; b. Boston, May 21, 1921; d. Edward Albert and Anne Ida (Andelman) Lieberman; B.L.S., Simmons Coll., 1942; m. Harry Cohen, Aug. 23, 1942; children—Karen Susan (Mrs. Michael Shapiro), Stephen Peter. Children's librarian Boston Pub. Library, 1942-43; librarian Post Library, Fort Ord, Cal., 1943-44; ordnance librarian Benicia Arsenal (Cal.), 1944-45; reference and interlibrary loan librarian Newton (Mass.) Free Library, 1959—, head staff assn., 1973—. Mem. New Eng., Mass. library assns., Young Adult Book Review Group. Home: 19 Chestnut Terrace Newton Centre MA 02159 Office: 414 Centre St Newton MA 02158

COHEN, ELAINE HELENA (MRS. MARVIN L. GALE), physician; b. Boston, Oct. 14, 1941; d. Samuel Clive and Lillian (Stocklan) Cohen; A.B., Conn. Coll., 1963; postgrad. Tufts U., 1963-64; M.D., Woman's Med. Coll. Pa., 1969; m. Marvin Leon Gale, May 7, 1972. Research technician div. molecular biology Mass. Inst. Tech., Cambridge, 1964-65; intern pediatrics Childrens Hosp. of Los Angeles, 1969-70, resident pediatrics, 1970-71; fellow in pediatric cardiology Center for the Health Scis., U. Cal., Los Angeles, 1971-72, Los Angeles County-U. So. Cal. Med. Center, Los Angeles, 1972-74. Recipient Paul Abel Schwartz Meml. prize for excellence in chemistry Conn. Coll., 1963. Home: 850 2d St Santa Monica CA 90403 Office: Pediatric Cardiology Los Angeles County-U Southern Cal Medical Center Los Angeles CA 90033

COHEN, ELAINE VICTORIA, psychologist; b. Laurelton, N.Y., Dec. 14, 1945; d. Abe and Anna (Samuels) Cohen; B.A. in Psychology, Adelphi U., 1967; Ph.D., 1972. Psychol. trainee South Oaks Psychiat. Hosp., Amityville, N.Y., 1967-72; postdoctoral intern Jewish Community Services, Smithtown, L.I., N.Y., 1972-73; staff psychologist Jewish Bd. Guardians, Hawthorne, N.Y., 1973—. Mem. Am., N.Y. State, Eastern psychol. assns., Psi Chi. Home: 142 West End Av New York City NY 10023

COHEN, ELINOR MARGOT, librarian; b. Long Island City, N.Y., Jan. 2, 1936; d. Harry M. and Doris (Altman) Cohen; B.A. cum laude, N.Y. U., 1956, M.L.S., Columbia, 1968. Chemist, Evans Research and Devel. Corp., N.Y.C., 1956-61; chemist, Gen. Foods Corp., White Plains, N.Y., 1961-65, librarian, 1966—, supr. information services, 1972—. Mem. Spl. Libraries Assn. (pres. Hudson Valley chpt.), A.A.A.S., Am. Soc. Information Sci. Home: 316 Woodland Hills Rd White Plains NY 10603 Office: Gen Foods Corp Tech Center White Plains NY 10625

COHEN, ESTELLE ATLAS (MRS. REUBEN COHEN), artist; b. Niagara Falls, N.Y.; d. Abram M. and Mary (Schwartz) Atlas; student Art Inst. Buffalo, 1949-50, U. Buffalo Art Sch., 1962-63, Rochester (N.Y.), Inst. Tech., 1964-65; m. Reuben Cohen, Jan. 2, 1926. Exhibited in group shows at Paul Kesler Gallery, Provincetown, Mass., N.Y. State Nat. Expns., 1950-51, State Fair, Invitational, Syracuse, 1960; Albright-Knox Art Gallery, Buffalo, Ball State Coll. Art Gallery, Muncie, Ind., 1964, Northeastern U.S. traveling exhbn. Inst. Contemporary Art, Boston, Pitts. Plan for Art, 1961-62, Roswell Park Meml. Inst., Buffalo, many others; represented in Members Gallery, rental and sales collection Albright-Knox Art Gallery, Buffalo, No. 1, M&T Plaza, Buffalo, Gallery West, Buffalo, Price-Waterhouse Collection, Buffalo, others. Active YWCA; Hadassah; bd. dirs. Art Inst. Buffalo, 1953-54. Recipient James J. Draper award for drawing Western N.Y. Ann., Albright-Knox Gallery, 1960; Isenberg Meml. award for water color Chautauqua Nat., N.Y., 1961; graphics award Religious Arts Festival, Buffalo, 1962. Mem. Buffalo Soc. Artists, Nat. League Am. Penwomen, World Hospitality Assn., Buffalo Craftsmen. Illustrated: Measure for Pleasure (a cook book). Address: 1 Windsor Av Buffalo NY 14209

COHEN, EVELYN AYEROFF (MRS. HARRY JOSEPH DONNERSTAG), psychiat. social worker; b. N.Y.C., Jan. 13, 1915; d. Aaron and Gussie (Hudoff) Ayeroff; B.S., U. So. Cal., 1937; M.S.W., U. Cal., Los Angeles, 1959; m. Jehudah M. Cohen, Feb. 28, 1943 (dec. 1966); children—Michael, Jonathan; m. Harry Joseph Donnerstag, Apr. 1974. Social work experience in group work, casework Pub. Housing and USO, 1937-46; psychiat. casework specialist Dept. Psychiatry Children's Hosp. of Los Angeles, 1959-64; psychiat. social worker, psychology clinic, psychology dept. Grad. div. U. Cal. at Los Angeles, 1964-70, field instr., psycho-therapist, psychology trainee supr. Sch. Social Welfare, 1967-72, field instr.; psychiat. social worker, mental health cons., group therapist Santa Monica-West region Los Angeles County Dept. Mental Health, 1970—; field supr. in marriage and family counselling, dept. sociology U. So. Cal., 1970—; social welfare cons. Kaswan-Love Research project; profl. adv. bd. Oak Hill Sch., Ziff Speech Devel. Found.; mental health cons. W. Los Angeles Coll., Pacific Palisades High Sch., Beethoven Day Care Center, others. Case conf. com. Westside Coordinating Council, 1964—. Mem. regional adv. bd. Anti Defamation League; mem. Mayor's Community Adv. Com., Los Angeles; mem. regional adv. bd. Kennedy Regional Center; mem. exec. bd. Santa Monica Community Services Council. Mem. Nat. Assn. Social Workers, Acad. Certified Social Workers, Cal. Assn. Marriage and Family Counselors, Am. Group Psycho-Therapy Assn. Assn. Psychiat. Social Workers of Los Angeles County, U. Cal. Los Angeles Social Welfare Alumni Assn., Nat. Conf. Social Welfare, B'nai B'rith Women (past legislative chmn. dist. 4). Home: 10501 Wilshire Blvd Los Angeles CA 90024

COHEN, FLOSSIE (MRS. HULING USSERY), physician, educator; b. Calcutta, Brit. India; d. Charles and Sarah (Wolf) Cohen; came to U.S., 1947, naturalized, 1955; I.Sc., Scottish Ch. Coll., Calcutta, 1943; M.B., Med. Coll., Calcutta, 1945; M.D., U. Buffalo, 1950; m. Huling Ussery, May 2, 1958; 1 dau., Xilla Tegan. Intern Jewish Hosp. Bklyn., resident Jewish Hosp. Bklyn., 1951-53; fellow in hematology Children's Hosp. Mich., 1953-56, asso. hematologist, 1956-58; research asso. Child Research Center Mich., Detroit, 1958-60, sr. research asso., 1960—; mem. faculty Wayne State U. Sch. Medicine, Detroit, 1958—, asso. prof. pediatrics, 1964-70, prof. pediatrics, 1970—; hosp. dir. clin. immunology, 1969—. Mem. Soc. Pediatric Research, Am. Soc. Hematology, Am. Soc. Human Genetics, Am., Mich. assns. blood banks, Am. Pediatric Soc., Am. Soc. Immunology, N.Y. Acad. Scis., Alpha Omega Alpha. Contbr. articles profl. publs. Home: 1270 Puritan St Birmingham MI 48009 Office: 3901 Beaubien Blvd Detroit MI 48201

COHEN, JEAN FREUDENTHAL (MRS. JULIUS BERNARD COHEN), civic worker; b. Highland Park, Ill., Dec. 26, 1935; d. James Hart and Margaret (Eisenstaedt) Freudenthal; B.A. cum laude U. So. Cal., 1957; m. Julius Bernard Cohen, Mar. 3, 1957; children—Katherine Lyn, Karen Gayle. Editor, publicist Westchester News-Advertiser, Los Angeles, 1957-59; human relations dir. Los Angeles League of Women Voters, 1968-72; spl. personnel trainer Los Angeles County Registrar of Voters, 1972—. Human relations ednl. cons., 1973—. Mem. edn. com. Los Angeles County Commn. on Human Relations, 1972—; mem. community adv. com. Office of Multi-Cultural Edn., Los Angeles City Schs., 1972—. Mem. Cal. Congress of Parents and Tchrs. (hon. service award 1972), Women In Communications, Los Angeles World Affairs Council, Alpha Epsilon Phi. Home: 3256 Corinth Av Los Angeles CA 90066 Office: 1134 S Crenshaw Blvd Los Angeles CA 90019

COHEN, JUDITH LOUISE CARTER (MRS. LESTER MARTIN COHEN), occupational therapist; b. Kingston, Pa., Mar. 20, 1940; d. Leslie George and Charlotte Greenwood (Lewis) Carter; B.A., Bucknell U., 1962; profl. certificate occupational therapist U. Pa., 1965; m. Lester Martin Cohen, Jan. 15, 1966; children—Susan Amy, Daniel Carter. Staff occupational therapist Hillside Hosp., Glen Oaks, N.Y., 1965-67; occupational therapy cons. Pa. Hosp., Phila., 1967-72; co-founder, co-owner, co-dir. Children's Workshop-Ednl. Treatment Center, San Diego, 1972—. Pres., Coop. Nursery Sch., San Diego, 1971-72. Mem. Am., So. Cal. occupational therapy assns., Cal. Assn. Neurologically Handicapped Children, Mortar Bd., Phi Beta Kappa. Home: 4721 Coronado Av San Diego CA 92107 Office: 248 Nutmeg Av San Diego CA 92103

COHEN, JULIA (MRS. DAVID H. COHEN), painter, graphic artist; b. Cairnbrook, Pa.; d. Michael and Nancy (Hawrylak) Elko; student (Albert H. Baldwin scholar, Julius Hallgarten scholar, William H. Fogg scholar) N.A.D.; 1968-73; m. David H. Cohen, June 8, 1957; 1 son, Richard N. Exhibited in 148th ann. N.A.D., 1973; exhibited in group show Upstairs Art Gallery, N.J.; dir. Markel Gallery, N.Y.C., 1970-71. Home: 142-01 41st Av Flushing NY 11355

COHEN, MARSHA NAN, lawyer; b. Paterson, N.J., Mar. 16, 1947; d. Samuel S. and Ida (Gelman) Cohen; B.A. cum laude, Smith Coll., 1968; J.D. cum laude, Harvard Law Sch., 1971; m. Robert Paul Feyer, Oct. 22, 1972. Admitted to Cal. bar, 1972, D.C. bar, 1972; research atty. Justice Raymond L. Sullivan, Supreme Ct. Cal., San Francisco, 1971-72; atty. Consumers Union U.S., Inc., Washington, 1972—. Vol. Presdl. Election Campaign, 1972. Bd. student advisers Harvard Law Sch., 1969-71. Mem. Bar Cal., D.C. Bar Assn., Common Cause, Nat. Orgn. Women. Democrat. Office: 1714 Massachusetts Av NW Washington DC 20036

COHEN, RAQUEL EIDELMAN (MRS. LAWRENCE COHEN), psychiatrist; b. Lima, Peru, Apr. 12, 1922; d. Samuel and Pola (Kozac) Eidelman; B.S., San Marcos U., Lima, 1943; M.P.H., Harvard, 1945, M.D., 1949; m. Lawrence Cohen, June 26, 1947; children—Myer, Sarita, Polita. Came to U.S., 1943, naturalized, 1948. Intern, Met. State Hosp., Waltham, Mass., 1950-55, resident in psychiatry Mass. Mental Health Center, Boston, 1956-59; chief Day Hosp., Mass. Mental Health Center, Boston, 1959-60; mem. faculty Harvard Med. Sch., 1960—, instr. psychiatry, 1960-67, asst. prof. psychiatry, 1969-72, asso. prof., 1972—, asso. dir. Lab. Community Psychiatry, 1967—, dir. clin. and tng. programs Erich Lindemann Mental Health Center, 1971-72; dir. psychiatry North Suffolk Mental Health Center, Boston, 1963-67; asso. psychiatrist Mass. Gen. Hosp., Boston, 1971—. Mem. psychiat. com. Cambridge (Mass.) Ct. Clinic, 1958-60, Northeastern U., Boston, 1962-63; cons. Big Sister Assn., Boston, 1965—, Day Care Centers, Inc., Boston, 1967—; mental health cons. Boston Sch. System, 1967; mem. Harvard Center Community Health and Med. Care, 1968-69; mem. Gov.'s Task Force for Spanish Speaking Affairs, 1969; mem. com. on continuous edn. Nat. Inst. Mental Health, 1968, cons. on mental health programs for Spanish-speaking populations, 1970. Mem. program adv. com. Overseas Edn. Fund Inst., Boston, 1969—. Bd. dirs. Sch. Vols. for Boston. Fellow Am. Psychiat. Assn. (chmn. psychiat. nursing com. No. N.E. dist. br., 1964-69, chmn. mental health council 1967-69, chmn. task force on mental health Spanish-speaking populations 1971, mem. council on emerging issues 1972); mem. Mass. Pub. Health Assn. (chmn. mental health sect., 1969—). Contbr. to American Handbook of Psychiatry, Vol. II, 1972; also numerous articles profl. jours. Home: 770 Boylston St PH-A Boston MA 02199 Office: 58 Fenwood Rd Boston MA 02115

COHEN, REBECCA SLUTSKY (MRS. MARTIN A. COHEN), educator, social service adminstr., psychotherapist; b. Chgo., Mar. 22, 1919; d. Simon and Mary (Zevin) Slutsky; B.A., U. Chgo., 1940, M.A., 1944; m. Martin A. Cohen, June 15, 1941; children—Daniel L., Miriam J. Intake supr. pediatric psychiatry U. Chgo. Clinics, 1941-47, research asso. Sch. Social Service Adminstrn., 1954-61, lectr., 1973—; dir. social work tng. dept. psychiatry Michael Reese Hosp., Chgo., 1961-63, chief social worker dept. psychiatry, 1963—. Clin. asso. prof. Smith Coll. Sch. for Social Work, 1973—. Fellow Am. Orthopsychiatric Assn., Ill. Clin. Social Work Soc., Phi Beta Kappa. Home: Apt 1412 4800 Chicago Beach Dr Chicago IL 60615 Office: 2959 Ellis Av Chicago IL 60616

COHEN, ROSALIE PALTER (MRS. JOSEPH COHEN), civic worker; b. New Orleans; d. Leon and Fannie (Brener) Palter; B.A., Tulane U., 1930; m. Joseph Cohen, July 7, 1929; children—Carmel

Jonathan, Sharon (Mrs. Albert J. Leviton). Mem. bd. New Orleans Jewish Fedn., 1941-69, v.p., 1954-58, pres., 1959-61, hon. mem. bd., 1972, chmn. casework study com., 1955-56, chmn. study com. on aged, 1956-58, chmn. gen. assembly com., 1957, chmn. social planning com., 1961-63; mem. exec. bd. New Orleans Jewish Welfare Bd., 1942-46, chmn. women's div. Jewish Welfare Fund campaign, 1945; mem. adv. bd. women's div. United Jewish Appeal, 1950—, nat. vice chmn. women's div., 1954-60; mem. founding bd. Nat. Found. Jewish Culture, 1960—; organizer Willow Wood, New Orleans Home for Jewish Aged, 1962, mem. bd., 1959-65; organizer Year-Round Women's div. Jewish Welfare Fedn. New Orleans, 1966, 67, hon. pres., 1967—; mem. bd. Pub. Welfare Dept. Orleans Parish, 1958-66, organizer citizens steering com., 1966; mem. citizens' com. Orleans Parish Juvenile Ct., 1963-66; mem. bd. Council Jewish Fedns. and Welfare Funds, 1961-69, v.p., 1963-66, sec., 1966-69, mem. overseas missions, 1964, 67, chmn. gen. assembly program com., 1964, 65, chmn. personnel for Jewish communal services com., 1965-69; mem. bd. Pub. Welfare Dept. City New Orleans, 1958-70; trustee, mem. bd. overseers Philip Lown Grad. Center Near Eastern and Judaic Studies, Brandeis U., 1966—; mem. bd. Fgn. Relations Assn., 1963, sec., 1966-67; trustee Jewish Publ. Soc. Am., 1967—; mem. bd. women's com. New Orleans Philharmonic Symphony Soc., 1954-62, chmn. parent-sch. com., 1954-55, co-chmn. Youth Concerts, 1955-57, 61-62; chmn. women's membership campaign Young Women's Hebrew Assn., 1945; pres. New Orleans Zionist Council, 1942-46; co-founder, pres. New Orleans chpt. Am. Friends of Hebrew U., 1950-54; chmn. women's div. Govt. Israel Bonds Campaign, 1952; founder sr. citizens club Jewish Community Center, 1957, organizer, chmn. Our Enduring Heritage Inst., 1964-69, hon. chmn., 1971—; mem. bd. United Israel Appeal, 1964-67; v.p. Am. Assn. Jewish Edn., 1965-69, mem. nat. governing council, 1969—; mem. World Conf. Human Welfare, Jerusalem, 1969; pres. New Orleans Hillel Corp. 1954-69; pres. Tulane Hillel Found. 1954-59, mem. exec. bd. 1959—; mem. regional bd. Anti-Defamation League, 1954-69; commr. at large B'nai B'rith Adult Jewish Edn. Commn. 1959-65; mem. bd. Inst. Jewish Life, 1972; chmn. UN Day, New Orleans, 1972. Recipient United Jewish Appeal Service award; Award of Honor Govt. Israel Bonds, 1954; citation Orleans Parish Bd. Welfare, 1966, City New Orleans Bd. Welfare, 1970; certificate merit Mayor New Orleans, 1971; certificate merit U.S. Office Censorship. Mem. P.T.A. (pres. Isidore Newman Sch. 1950-51). Mem. Hadassah (chpt. pres. 1932-36, 40-42, 46-47, hon. v.p. 1950—, chmn. regional edn. inst. 1956). Address: 241 Audubon Blvd New Orleans LA 70125

COHEN, SYLVIA ROSLYN SCHIFF (MRS. ALBERT L. COHEN), educator; b. Bklyn., July 27, 1931; d. Solomon and Clara (Wolberg) Schiff; B.A. cum laude, Upsala Coll., East Orange, N.J., 1969; M.A. in Social Sci., Montclair State Coll., 1973; m. Albert L. Cohen, Mar. 21, 1953; children—Lisa, David, Reva. Social sci. tchr. East Hanover Middle Sch. (N.J.), 1970—. Intern U.S. Senator Harrison Williams, 1974. Active League Women Voters, West Orange, N.J., 1961. Named Tchr. of Year, East Hanover Jaycees, 1972; recipient Valley Forge Tchrs. medal Freedoms Found., 1973. Nat. Conf. Christians and Jews scholar, 1962. Mem. N.E.A., N.J., East Hanover edn. assns., Ladies Aux. Jewish War Vets. (pres. chpt. 146, 1959, historian N.J. chpt. 1960), Phi Alpha Theta. Mem. B'nai B'rith (Americanism chmn. West Orange chpt. 1956). Home: 72 Warren Rd West Orange NJ 07052 Office: East Hanover Middle Sch 477 Ridgedale Av East Hanover NJ 07936

COHEN, WENDY ELLEN JOSEPH (MRS. NORMAN H. COHEN), neurologist; b. L.I., N.Y., Mar. 23, 1944; d. Rudolph and Mildred (Miner) Joseph; student Simmons Coll., 1962-63; B.A., N.Y. U., 1966; M.D., N.Y. Med. Coll., 1970; m. Norman H. Cohen, Apr. 18, 1970; 1 dau., Jessica Dara. Resident in neurology Flower Fifth Av. Hosp., Met. Hosp. Center, N.Y.C., 1970—. Home: 525 E 86th St New York City NY 10028

COHN, BARBARA NORFLEET (MRS. ALFRED B. COHN), photographer, educator, mus. curator; b. Lakewood, N.J., Feb. 18, 1926; d. Joseph Pugh and Henriette (Plangere) Norfleet; B.A., Swathmore Coll., 1947; M.A., Harvard, 1950, Ph.D., 1951; m. Alfred Bretauer Cohn, July 5, 1950; children—Stephen, Derry, Timothy. Mem. faculty in gen. edn. Harvard, 1961-70, mem. faculty in visual and environmental studies, 1970—, curator of photography, 1972—; exhbns. Mus. Modern Art. Bd. dirs. Cambridge Nursery Sch., 1958-70, Cambridge Community Services, 1970-73, others, Mass. Council on Arts and Humanities grantee, 1972-73. Mem. Am., New Eng., Mass. psychol. assns. Democrat. Author: Six Speak, 1968. Home: 79 Raymond St Cambridge MA 02140 Office: Carpenter Center 19 Prescott St Cambridge MA 02138

COHN, HILDE DOROTHEA, educator; b. Goerlitz, Germany; d. Ludwig and Meta (Klinkowstein) Cohn; came to U.S., 1938, naturalized, 1944; student U. Munich, 1929, U. Berlin, 1930; Ph.D., U. Heidelberg, 1933. Instr. Bryn Mawr Coll., 1938-48; faculty Swarthmore (Pa.) Coll., 1948—, prof. German, 1967—. Mem. Modern Lang. Assn. Am., Am. Assn. Tchrs. German, Internationaler Germanisten Verband. Writer essays. Home: 302 N Chester Rd Swarthmore PA 19081

COHN, SONDRA LEE ROSENTHAL (MRS. FREDERICK COHN), civic worker, educator; b. Chester, Pa., June 15, 1934; d. Simon M. and Cecelia (Savits) Rosenthal; B.A., Millersville State Coll., 1955; M.A., U. N.M., 1969; m. Frederick Cohn, July 16, 1954; children—Janice Marie, Lawrence Stephen, Robert Hirsch. Tchr., Media (Pa.) Elementary Sch., 1955-57. Mem. Albuquerque City Council, 1974—. Regional pres. B'nai B'rith, 1951-52; bd. dirs. Hadassah, San Francisco, 1958; pres. Foster Homes Council, Albuquerque, 1964-66; bd. dirs. Albuquerque YMCA, 1964-66; dir. League of Women Voters Albuquerque and N.M., 1964-69, N.M. pres., 1969-71, nat. sec., 1972-74; reading cons. San Mateo, Cal., 1962, Albuquerque, 1963; mem. gov.'s adv. bd. Human Rights Commn. in N.M., 1970—; mem. Albuquerque Charter Revision Commn., 1971, Gov.'s Comprehensive Health Planning Bd. N.M., 1971—; Gov.'s Council on Environmental Quality, 1971-74; mem. adv. com. on environmental concerns Albuquerque City Commn., 1972; mem. exec. com. Urban Coalition, Albuquerque; bd. dirs. Community Council Albuquerque, 1971—. Mem. Med. Aus., Symphony Assn. Jewish religion (bd. dirs. Sisterhood 1963-67). Home: 1428 Columbia Av NE Albuquerque NM 87106

COIT, ELISABETH, architect; b. Winchester, Mass.; d. Robert and Eliza Richmond (Atwood) Coit; student Radcliffe Coll., 1909-11, Boston Sch. Mus. Fine Arts, 1911-13; B.Arch., Mass. Inst. Tech., 1919; grad. study U. Paris, Sorbonne, 1923-24. Designer with Grosvenor Atterbury, architect, 1919-23; pvt. practice of architecture, N.Y.C., 1924-42; architect PHA, 1942-47; prin. project planner N.Y.C. Housing Authority 1947-62; cons. PHA, Washington, 1962-65; mem. N.Y.C. Landmarks Preservation Commn., 1970—; cons. N.Y.C. Office Mayor Office Aging, 1969—, Dept. Housing and Urban Devel., Washington; mem. Dept. Pub. Affairs Community Service Soc., N.Y.C., 1963—. Recipient citation Wilson Coll., 1969; citation N.Y. chpt. A.I.A., 1969. Fellow A.I.A.; mem. N.A.D. (asso.), Nat. Assn. Housing and Redevel. Ofcls. Citizens' Housing and Planning Council N.Y.C. Author: Report on Family Living in High Apartment Buildings, 1965. Editor: Required Reading N.Y. Archtl. Record, 1941-43; Public Housing Design, 1946. Contbr. articles profl. jours. Home: 330 W 72d St New York City NY 10023 also Thacher Rd Rockport MA 01966

COKENS, HARRIET JEAN (MRS. GEORGE COKENS), newspaper pub.; b. Burlington, Ia., Nov. 19, 1929; d. Harry Leslie and Ruth Marie (Ruedy) Waste; grad. high sch.; m. George Cokens, July 25, 1957; children—Fred, Gloria (Mrs. David Smith), Stephana Jean (Mrs. Dale Neuberger), Tamara Marie (Mrs. Bill Benjamin), George Anthony, Constance Kay, Harry Steven, Ruth Lynette. Employed with various newspapers, Ill., 1957-59, Parshall, N.D., 1960-61, Beulah, N.D., 1962-68; pub., editor Tripp (S.D.) Ledger, 1969—. Pres., P.T.A., Beulah, 1967-68. Chmn., Dist. Women N.D. Democrats, 1967, 68; vice chmn. Hutchinson County Democrats, 1972—. Mem. Am. Legion Aux. (sec. 1971-72). Methodist. Home: Box 0 Tripp SD 57376 Office: Tripp Ledger Tripp SD 57376

COLBRY, VERA L., govt. ofcl.; b. Seattle, Sept. 11, 1910; d. Ira R. and Lena M. (Guggin) Colbry; B.S. in Edn., Ore. State Coll., 1931; M.A. in Botany, George Washington U., 1956; m. Miles E. Drake (div.). Seed analyst, botanist Coop. Fed.-State Seed Lab., Ore. State Coll., Corvallis, 1931-35, Ransom Seed Lab., Los Angeles, 1935-38; seed analyst Fed. Seed Lab., Consumer and Marketing Service, U.S. Dept. Agr., Beltsville, Md., 1938-69, officer-in-charge Fed. Seed Lab., Agrl. Marketing Service, Sacramento, 1969—. Cons., tchr. seed testing methods and procedures in fed., state and comml. labs., 1942—. Recipient Superior Service award U.S. Dept. Agr., 1954, certificate of merit, 1967. Mem. Soc. Comml. Seed Technologists (hon.), Internat. Seed Testing Assn. (germination com. 1954—, del. internat. congresses 1956, 65, 68), Assn. Ofcl. Seed Analysts (ofcl. del. numerous convs. 1937—, merit award 1974), Sigma Xi. Contbr. numerous articles on seed testing to profl. publs. Home: 6102 Via Casitas Carmichael CA 95608 Office: Federal Seed Lab PO Box 1641 Sacramento CA 95808

COLBURG, DOLORES, state ofcl.; b. Big Timber, Mont., Apr. 3, 1932; d. Victor Jerome and Doris (Webb) Erickson; ed. Eastern Mont. Coll., 1961-62, U. Colo., 1962-63; B.A. with honors, U. Mont., 1964. Supt. pub. instrn. State of Mont., 1969—. Sec. Yellowstone County (Mont.) Democratic central com., 1956-57; v.p. Young Dems. U. Mont., 1963-64. Mem. Am. Assn. U. Women, Council Chief State Officers, N.E.A., Am. Assn. Sch. Adminstrs., U. Mont. Alumni Assn. Address: PO Box 992 Helena MT 59601*

COLBURN, MARJORIE DORIS (MRS. JOHN CARLTON), state ofcl.; b. Milford, N.H., June 26, 1924; d. Herbert George and Avis Mabel (Maxwell) Elliott; grad. pub. schs., New Boston, N.H.; m. John Carlton, Jan. 27, 1946; children—Edward, Mary Ellen (Mrs. Leland Vadney, Jr.), Christine. Rep. N.H. gen. court, 1965-66, 67-68, 71-72, 73—. Mem. New Boston Conservation Commn., 1969—. Del. N.H. Constl. Conv., 1964. Club: Emerson Bailey Clover. Home: 1 Woods Lane New Boston NH 03070

COLBURN, NORMA ELAINE WHEELER (MRS. JAMES AUSTIN COLBURN), city ofcl.; b. St. Johnsbury, Vt., June 26, 1933; d. Clayton Wallace and Ida Minerva (Lang) Wheeler; student Burdett Coll., 1951, Rutgers U., 1968; m. James Austin Colburn, Jan. 19, 1952; children—Candice Margaret, James Austin. Exec. sec. Oswald L. Sanborn C.P.A.'s, Ridgewood, N.J., 1952; exec. sec. archtl. div. Am. Brakeshoe Co., Mahwah, N.J., 1952; postal clk. U.S. P.O., Lyndon Center, Vt., 1956-60; partner Colburn's Store, Lyndon Center, Vt., 1956-60; corr., feature writer Burlington (Vt.) Free Press, 1959-60; dep. borough clk., ct. clk., Allendale, N.J., 1968-70, sec. planning bd., dep. water collector, 1969-70, borough clk., 1970—, borough adminstr., 1972—. Active Girl Scouts U.S.A., 1965-66. Recipient Time Mag. Current Events award, 1950, 51. Mem. Municipal Clk's Assn. N.J., Berge County Municipal Clk's. Assn. Mem. Order Eastern Star. Home: 310 Brookside Av Allendale NJ 07401 Office: Office City Clk City Hall Allendale NJ 07401

COLBY, JEAN POINDEXTER (MRS. FLETCHER H. COLBY), author; b. Pine Orchard, Conn.; d. Charles Edward and Lena L. (Steinhoff) Poindexter; grad. Wellesley Coll., 1928; m. Fletcher H. Colby, July 16, 1932; children—Antonia, Peter Fletcher, Jean P. Editor, Houghton, Mifflin Co., 1940-45, Farrar, Straus & Co., 1952-55, Hastings House Pub. Inc., N.Y.C., 1955-70. Author: Peter Paints the U.S.A.; Jim The Cat; Dixie of Dover; The New Wellesley; The Elegant Eleanor; Jenny, The Children's Book Field; Writing, Illustrating and Editing Children's Books; Jesus and the World; Tear Down to Build Up; (adult books) Mystic Seaport: The Age of Sail; Plimoth Plantation, Then and Now; Rebirth of an Ancient Area; Building Wrecking, The How and Why of a Booming Business; Lexington and Concord—What Really Happened. Address: 27 Chestnut St Brookline MA 02146

COLBY, RACHEL EDITH, hotel exec.; b. Bitterroot, Mont., Dec. 31, 1911; d. John Henry and Laura Carrie (Maynard) Holst; B.A., U. Md., 1932; m. Douglas S. Armstrong, Aug. 26, 1933 (dec. Oct. 1958); Barbara (Mrs. J.A. Jamieson), Robert, Judith (Mrs. F.M. Bear); m. 2d, John Stitt Colby, Apr. 19, 1961. Co-founder, propr., mgr. The Buccaneer, Inc., Hotel, Christiansted, St. Croix, V.I., 1948-64, dir., treas., 1964—. Chmn. St. Croix Hosp. Found., 1957-60; bd. dirs. St. Croix Hosp. Mus., 1950-52. Chmn. V.I. Adv. Council of Libraries, 1972—; mem. V.I. Bd. Edn., 1962-64; mem. V.I. Bicentennial Commn., 1973—. Mem. St. Croix Landmarks League (co-founder 1950), Delta Delta Delta. Republican. Mem. Anglican Ch. Research in the local history of St. Croix. Address: Box 218 Estate Shoys Christiansted St Croix VI 00820

COLE, A(NNA) RUTH, ret. educator; b. Eaton, O.; d. George Washington and Esther (Akel) Cole; B.S., Miami U., Oxford, O., 1939; M.A., Ohio State U., 1953; summer student U. Colo., 1937, Vassar Coll., 1963. Tchr. Morris Sch., Hamilton, O., 1921-23, 24-25, Edison Elementary Sch., Columbus, O., 1925-26, Robert Louis Stevenson Sch., Columbus, 1926-71. Mem. arithmetic textbook selection com. Grandview Heights Pub. Schs., 1967-68. Mem. Grandview Heights Tchrs. Assn. (dir. 1947-50, pres. 1954-56) (social chmn. 1969-70), Assn. for Childhood Internat. (v.p. 1956-58, pres. 1958-60), N.E.A. (life), Ohio Edn. Assn., Central Ohio Tchrs. Assn., Wesleyan Service Guild (pres. 1943-45, 62-64, 64-65, dist. sec. 1957-61; v.p. 1968-69), Grandview Heights P.T.A., Ohio Conservation and Outdoor Edn. Assn., Ohio State U. Alumni Assn., Nat., Ohio, Franklin County ret. tchrs. assns., Am. Assn. Ret. Persons, Nat. Fedn. Rep. Women, Franklin County Hist. Soc., Center Sci. and Industry, Kappa Phi (life), Phi Delta Gamma (pres. 1955-57), Delta Kappa Gamma (membership chmn. 1962-64, recruitment com. 1964-66, chmn. initiation com. 1973—. Life mem. Silhoutte Nat. Health Studios. Republican. Methodist (commn. on edn., youth counselor; sec. Wesleyan Service Guild 1971—, chmn. program resources 1973—, mission coordinator Christian global concerns 1974—). Home: 1314 W 7th Av Columbus OH 43212

COLE, BARBARA ANN (MRS. NORMAN WARD COLE), banker; b. Bate City, Mo., Feb. 5, 1933; d. Charles Maurice and Edith Lee (Bailey) Marcott; pre-standard certificate Am. Inst. Banking, 1965, gen. certificate, 1972; m. Norman Ward Cole, Apr. 18, 1964; children (of previous marriage)—Diana Rae (Mrs. James A. Glenn), David Richard Lawrence, Demma Mae Lies, Edith Catherine Lies, Charles Edward Lies. With Bourns Inc., Ames, Ia., 1958-59; billing and posting clerk, City of Fairbanks, Alaska, 1960-61; teller First Nat. Bank of Anchorage, Alaska, 1961-62; br. mgr., personnel officer Matanuska Valley Bank, Anchorage, 1963-72, asst. v.p., 1972—. Mem. Nat. Assn. Bank Women, Inc. (group chmn. 1970-71), group bd. dirs. 1971-72), Am. Inst. Banking (bd. dirs. 1968-71, council 1965—). Home: 4902 Lake Otis Pkwy Anchorage AK 99507 Office: Pouch 7012 Anchorage AK 99510

COLE, DOLLIE ANN, civic worker; b. Ft. Worth, May 13, 1930; d. George and Dorothea (Stegall) Feoliner; B.A., U. Tex., 1949; Ph.D., Miss. Valley State Coll.; m. Edward N. Cole, Dec. 11, 1963; children—William J., Anne Murray, Robert Michael, Edward. Active Am. Cancer Soc., Project Hope; bd. dirs. Mich. Humane Soc.; mem. animal adv. bd. Oakland County, Mich.; commr. Detroit Zool. Park. Fund raiser Republican party. Contbr. articles to mags. Address: 1371 Kirkway Bloomfield Hills MI 48013

COLE, DOROTHY HINCKLEY COLEMAN, occupational therapist; b. St. Louis, Dec. 3, 1933; d. Daniel Bernard and Dorothy Jessamine (Mumford) Coleman; student U. Mo., 1951-53; B.A. in Biology, Antioch Coll., 1957; certificate in occupational therapy Boston Sch. Occupational Therapy, 1958; postgrad. San Diego State Coll., 1967-71, Cal. State Coll., Los Angeles, 1967, U. Cal. Extension, 1969-71; Cal. secondary teaching credential, 1971; div.; 1 son, Franklin Topper. Staff occupational therapist Patton State Hosp., San Bernardino, Cal., 1958, Nev. State Hosp., Reno, 1959, Utah State Hosp., Provo, 1960-61, San Diego County Crippled Children Services, 1962-67; tchr. cerebral palsied Grossmont Union High Sch. Dist., La Mesa, Cal., 1967—, dept. chmn. cerebral palsy program, 1967-71. Mem. Am. Occupational Therapy Assn., Zeta Tau Alpha. Designer cutout desk for handicapped Home: 6315 Southern Rd La Mesa CA 92041 Office: PO Box 1043 La Mesa CA 92041

COLE, ELIZABETH STIRLING, psychotherapist; b. Washington, Aug. 28, 1936; d. William Calhoun and Marguerita (Tillman) Stirling; B.A., George Washington U., 1958, M.A., 1960, Ph.D., 1967; diploma Gestalt Inst., Cleve., 1972; m. Eugene T. Cole, Dec. 28, 1963 (dec. Mar. 1973). Supervisory psychologist St. Elizabeth's Hosp., Washington, 1966-70, chief psychol. forensic services, 1970-72, cons. Gestalt therapy, 1972—; pvt. practice individual, couples, family group psychotherapy, Washington, 1972—. Mem. Am., D.C. psychol. assns., Am. Acad. Psychotherapists, Soc. Personality Assessment, Gestalt Inst. Cleve., Am. Soc. Group Psychotherapy and Psychodrama. Sigma Xi, Psi Chi. Episcopalian. Contbr. articles to profl. publs. Address: 151 Kentucky Av SE Washington DC 20003

COLE, ELMA PHILLIPSON (MRS. JOHN STRICKLER COLE), social welfare exec.; b. Piqua, O., Aug. 9, 1909; d. Brice Leroy and Mabel (Gale) Phillipson; A.B., Berea Coll., 1930; M.A., U. Chgo., 1938; m. John Strickler Cole, Oct. 3., 1959. Various positions in social work, 1930-42; dir. social service dept. Children's Hosp. of D.C., 1942-49; cons. in pub. cooperation Midcentury White House Conf. on Children and Youth, 1949-51; exec. sec. Nat. Midcentury Com. for Children and Youth, 1951-53; cons. on recruitment Am. Assn. Med. Social Workers, 1953; asso. dir. Nat. Legal Aid and Defender Assn., 1953-56; exec. sec. Marshall Field Awards, Inc., 1956-57; dir. asso. orgns. Nat. Assembly Social Policy and Devel., 1957-73; asso. exec. dir. Nat. Assembly Nat. Vol. Health and Social Welfare Orgns., 1974—; cons. to nat. orgns. Golden Anniversary White House Conf. on Children and Youth, 1959-60; mem. adv. council on pub. service Nat. Assn. Life Underwriters and Inst. Life Ins.; mem. judges com. Louis I. Dublin Pub. Service awards, 1961—. Mem com. on pub. relations and fund raising Am. Found. for Blind Commn. on Accreditation, 1964-67; chmn. personnel and program com. Salvation Army Foster Care and Adoption Service, N.Y.C. Mem. Pub. Relations Soc. Am. (accredited), Nat. Assn. Social Workers (accredited), Nat. Conf. on Social Welfare (com. on pub. relations 1961-66, 69—; chmn. adminstrn. sect. 1966-67), Internat. Council Social Work, Jr. League Washington, Ohio Soc. N.Y., Pi Gamma Mu, Phi Kappa Phi. Clubs: N.Y. University Faculty, Women's of N.Y.; Advertising (N.Y.C.). Contbr. articles to profl. jours., encys. Home: 19 Washington Sq N New York City NY 10011 Office: 345 E 46th St New York City NY 10017

COLE, GLORIA GLASTON (MRS. ALAN Y. COLE), civic worker; b. Mt. Vernon, N.Y., Apr. 3, 1924; d. A. Lawrence and Hattie (Shinsky) Glaston; B.A., Barnard Coll.; m. Alan Y. Cole, Sept. 18, 1946; children—Charles Glaston, Robert Barry. Bd. dirs. League Women Voters Montgomery County, 1961-66, pres., 1966-69; pres. League Women Voters Md., Inc., 1969-73; sec. Citizens Com. on Md. Cts. and Justice, Inc., 1969-73, pres., 1973—; mem. Md. Commn. on Functions of Govt., 1972—; dir. Citizens Program for Chesapeake Bay, Inc., 1973—. Mem. Phi Beta Kappa. Home: 6808 Marbury Rd Bethesda MD 20034

COLE, HELEN CHAMPNEY, artist; b. Cleve., June 4, 1918; d. Thomas James and Bessie Coe (Champney) Cole; student Scripps Coll., 1936-38, Wellesley Coll., 1938-40, Cleve. Inst. Art, 1940-42. Diversional therapist Babies & Children's Hosp., Cleve., 1942-45; maker jigsaw puzzles Leni's, Cleve., 1958-73; one-man shows at Ten Thirty Gallery; exhibited in group shows at Cleve. May Show, Butler Show. Chmn. jr. council Cleve. Mus. Art, 1947-49. Bd. dirs. Jr. League, 1947-49. Home: 2701 Scarborough St Cleveland OH 44106

COLE, LOIS MARGARET ROBERTS (MRS. HARRY M. COLE), credit agy. exec.; b. Cleve., Apr. 30, 1921; d. Ralph G. and Estella Cora (Huselton) Roberts; student Ohio U., 1967-68, Bowling Green State U., 1969, U. Wis., 1970; m. Harry M. Cole, Nov. 3, 1939; children—Harry Melrose III, Carol Lynn (Mrs. John P. Williams). Mgr. Cleve. Crane & Engring. Co. Employees Credit Union, Wickliffe, O., 1965-71; treas., mgr. Ohio Rubber Co. Employees Credit Union, Inc., Willoughby, O., 1971—. Mem. Ohio Credit Union League (sec. exec. com. 1972-73, 2d v.p. 1974), Dirs. Credit Unions (dir. N.E. chpt. 1966-70). Club: Internat. Management (Lake County, O.). Home: 7276 Trotter Lane Mentor OH 44060 Office: Ben Hur Av Willoughby OH 44094

COLE, LORENE EDNER MARSH (MRS. MYRON C. COLE), govt. ofcl.; b. Placerville, Cal., July 31, 1915; d. Clyde Charles and Marvel (Edner) Marsh; student Sacramento State Coll., 1933-36; A.B., Cal. State Coll., 1957; m. Ernest E. Debs, Aug. 5, 1944 (div. July 1968); children—David Marsh, Catherine Claire; m. 2d, Myron C. Cole, Sept. 1, 1968. Mem. Cal. Women's Bd. of Terms and Paroles, 1966—. Chmn. adv. commn. Los Angeles County Dept. Adoptions, 1961-62; chmn. Family Service Agy. of Assistance League, 1963-64; mem. council Salvation Army Home and Hosp. for Unwed Mothers, 1957—. Vice chmn. women's div. United Crusade, Los Angeles, 1960—; mem. exec. com. Friends of Sta. KCET-TV. Mem. Democratic State Central Exec. Com., 1965-68. Bd. dirs. Assistance League So. Cal., 1963-66; bd. dirs. Los Angeles Council Chs., 1964—, chmn. pub. affairs commn., 1965—; bd. dirs. Protestant Community Services, Los Angeles, Los Angeles Child Guidance Clinic; mem. exec. bd. Cal. Christian Home. Recipient awards including Award of Merit Los Angeles County Heart Assn., 1966, Agy. Leadership award United Crusade, 1966, Outstanding Service award B.A.B.Y., Los

Angeles County award for contbn. to Mexican-U.S. relations. Mem. Cal. Peace Officers Assn., Cal. Parole and Probation Officers Assn., Women's Div. Hollywood C. of C. Mem. Christian Ch. (bd. dirs.). Clubs: Los Angeles Women's Breakfast; Women's of the Desert. Address: 102 Paseo Laredo N Cathedral City CA 92234 also Mokuleia Beach Colony Waialua HI

COLE, LOUISE (MRS. CLOYSE CHARLES COLE), editor, artist; b. Eagle City, Okla., Aug. 8, 1913; d. Francis Marion and Lucy Evelyn (Wright) Miller; B.A., Williams Coll., Boise, Ida., 1943; m. Cloyse Charles Cole, Feb. 23, 1940; children—Cheri Christine (Mrs. Ronald Walker Massey), Curtis Craig. Office mgr. Oklahoma City Postal Telegraph, 1934-40; owner, operator two sundries stores, 1945-60; gen. illustrator Tinker AFB, 1957-58; advt. artist, editor in-house publ. Okla. Press Assn., 1958-60, Mut. Fed. Savs. & Loan Assn., 1960-64; reading editor, in-house publ. editor Economy Co., 1964-66; with Learning Lab., Guthrie (Okla.) Job Corps Center, 1966-69; tchr. tng., artist, cons., in-house mag. editor Central Amids, govt. agy., Oklahoma City, 1969-73; artist, editor Finders Seekers mag., Oklahoma City, 1973—. Tchr. arts and crafts Mission Ch. Named Indsl. Editor of Year, 1964. Mem. Indsl. Editors Central Okla. (pres. 1960, Outstanding Achievement with Okla. Manpower Devel. and Tng. 1969), Art Dirs. Club Oklahoma City, Okla. Mus. Art (treas., pub. 1963), Theta Sigma Phi. Presbyn. Author: Meat Substitutes for Meatless Meals, 1973. Editor: Oklahoma Publisher, 1957-58, Oklahoma Nurse, 1960-65, Mutual-ly Speaking, 1960-64, Key Notes, 1964-66, Sooner Sashay, 1964-66, Oklahoma Oil Jobber, 1964-66, Admidsview, 1969-73. Home: 3900 NW 60th St Oklahoma City OK 73112 Office: 232 NW 63d St Oklahoma City OK 73112

COLE, MACEOLA LOUISE, pediatrician; b. Brentwood, Mo., June 18, 1934; d. Maceo Lexcy and Anna Clarabelle (Tibbs) Cole; B.S., St. Louis U., 1954, M.D., 1958. Intern Cardinal Glennon Meml. Hosp., St. Louis, 1958-59, resident, 1959-61, now mem. staff; practice medicine specializing in pediatrics, St. Louis, 1961—; also mem. staff Jewish Hosp.; instr. dept. pediatrics St. Louis U., 1961—. Mem. St. Louis Pediatric Soc. Home: 4466 W Pine St St Louis MO 63108 Office: 2715 N Union St St Louis MO 63113

COLE, MARGARET EVELYN, educator, biologist; b. Aberdeen, Miss., June 10, 1910; d. Stephen Wall and Effie Clifton (Jones) Cole; B.A., Miss. U. for Women, 1932; M.A., Duke, 1943; Ph.D., Vanderbilt U., 1966. Tchr. biology, chemistry and physics high schs. in Hatley and Plantersville, Miss., Alexander City and Ft. Payne, Ala., 1932-45; asst. prof. Greensboro (N.C.) Coll., 1945-57; teaching fellow Vanderbilt U., 1957-59; prof. biology Murray (Ky.) State U., 1960—. Mem. Am. Inst. Biol. Scis., Am. Soc. Zoologists, Soc. Systematic Zoology, Assn. Southeastern Biologists, Ky. Acad. Sci. Democrat. Baptist. Contbr. to profl. jours. Home: 1703 Ryan Av Murray KY 42071

COLE, MARGARET PAYNE, librarian; b. Astoria, N.Y.; d. George John and Margaret Jean (Aitken) Cole; student Mt. Holyoke Coll., 1927-28; A.B., Barnard Coll., 1931; B.S., Sch. Library Service, Columbia, 1932, M.S., 1953; postgrad. New Sch. for Social Research, 1945-47, N.Y. U., 1956-58. Children's librarian Queens Borough Pub. Library, Jamaica, N.Y., 1932-33, reference librarian, 1933-35, cataloger, 1935-48, supt. book selection, 1948-66; acquisitions librarian Hofstra U., Hempstead, N.Y., 1966—. Mem. A.L.A. (life), N.Y., Nassau County library assn., Women's Nat. Book Assn., Booksellers' League N.Y., Am. Assn. U. Profs., Am. Assn. U. Women, Library Assos. Hofstra U., Beta Phi Mu. Home: 36-36 31st St Long Island City NY 11106 Office: Hofstra Univ Hempstead NY 11550

COLE, MARILYN BUSH (MRS. CARL EDWARD COLE), occupational therapist; b. Flushing, N.Y., Jan. 29, 1945; d. George Lyman and Theis O. (Maurer) Bush; B.A., U. Conn., 1966; certificate occupational therapy (Nat. Health Profession scholar), U. Pa., 1968; postgrad. U. Mex., summer 1967; m. Carl Edward Cole, 1968; children—Charlot Evangeline, Bradley Eric. Staff therapist Eastern Pa. Psychiat. Inst., Phila., 1968-69; dir. occupational therapy, psychiat. unit Middlesex Meml. Hosp., Middletown, Conn., 1973—. Tchr., painter watercolors, 1971—; vis. artist Madison (Conn.) Elementary Schs., 1972, 73. Mem. Am., Conn. occupational therapy assns., Am. Assn. U. Women (chmn. cultural arts 1972-73), Guilford Art League, Clinton Art Soc. Episcopalian. Club: Madison Newcomers (membership chmn. 1973-74). Art editor Minute Woman, Air Force wives monthly mag., 1970-71. Home: 80 Flintlock Rd Madison CT 06443 Office: 28 Crescent St Middletown CT 06457

COLE, MARTHA FAIRBANKS, librarian; b. Boston, Mar. 15, 1921; d. George Ellsworth and Helen Mary (Healy) Cole; B.A., Manhattanville Coll., 1943; B.S. in L.S., Simmons Coll., 1947. Librarian, Harvard Coll. Library, 1948-58, Boston Coll. Library, 1958-59, Brandeis U. Library, 1959-62; med. librarian Beth Israel Hosp., Boston, 1963—. Mem. Spl. Libraries Assn. (past treas. Boston chpt.). Home: 383 Belmont St Belmont MA 02178 Office: 330 Brookline Av Boston MA 02215

COLE, MARY CAROLINE, architect; b. Tulsa, Nov. 13, 1912; A.B. (scholar), Smith Coll., 1934; postgrad. Okla. A. and M. Coll., 1936; B. Arch. (Paul Dickinson prize 1936-37, 2d Sch. medal 1941), Cornell U., 1941. Prin. Mary Caroline Cole, Tulsa, 1948—. Bd. dirs. YWCA, Tulsa, 1964-70. Chmn. Mayors Commn. on Archtl. Barriers, Mayor's Com. Employment Handicapped. Registered architect, Okla. Mem. A.I.A. (dir. Tulsa chpt. 1965). Prin. works include Phillips residence, Tulsa, 1950, 56, Tulsa City Fire Sta. 18, 1955, sta. 19, 1957, sta. 21, 1956, Long residence, Tulsa, 1963, Walco-Lorain Mfg. plant, Okmulgee, Okla., 1966, Worrell residence, Keystone Lake, Okla., 1969, William Slater residence, 1970, John Campbell residence, 1972, Smallwood residence, 1973. Address: 15 E 21st St Tulsa OK 74114*

COLE, NANCY D. (MRS. ROBERT EARL COLE), ins. agt., club woman; b. Cleve., Apr. 18, 1927; d. Frank Jerome and Elizabeth (Davis) Kutak; student Orlando Jr. Coll., 1951-52, U. Miami, 1957—; m. Dean Marlow Dolison, Oct. 1, 1949 (div.); children—Drew, Scot Marlow, Tina Lee, Penny Sue; m. 2d, Donald A. Mitchell, Nov. 13, 1965 (div. Apr. 1970); m. 3d, Robert D. Baynard, May 30, 1970 (div. Dec. 1973); m. 4th, Robert Earl Cole, May 18, 1974. Med. sec. Morton Levy, M.D., Orlando, Fla., 1951-52; spl. agt. Am. Bankers Life Assurance Co., Miami, Fla., 1959-64; cons. to Met. Life Ins. Co., 1964—; spl. agt. Voyager Life Ins. Co., Miami, 1970—; sales work So. Bell Tel. & Tel. Co., Coral Gables, Fla., 1971—; also agt. All Am. Ins. Agy., Miami. Dist. mgr. Franklin Life Ins. Co., 1965—; co-owner Sky Harbour Marina, Ltd., 1965—. Vice pres. Coral Gables Jr. C. of C. Aux., 1961—; welfare treas. Coral Gables Jr. Womens Club, 1958-59, parliamentarian, 1961—; capt. Am. Cancer Soc. Drives, 1958, 59, 61; vol. South Miami Hosp., 1961—, 2d v.p. aux., 1963, parliamentarian, 1961-62; publicity chmn. Dade County Med. Assn. Aux., 1958-59; chmn. Dade County Civil Def. Med. Alert Program, 1958-59; parliamentarian Snapper Creek Elementary P.T.A., 1964-65. Mem. Delphian Soc. (pres. 1958-59), Burdines Consumers Adv. Council. Lutheran. Clubs: Coral Gables Jr. Woman's (stage mgr. 1963-64), Coral Gables Woman's (chmn. mental health 1967-68), Dinner Key Cruising, Coconut Grove Sailing, Coral Gables Country. Home: 8501 SW 96th St Miami FL 33143 Office: Chase Fed Bank 7000 Kendall Dr Dadeland Miami FL 33143

COLE, NATALIE GALATZER (MRS. EARL B. COLE), artist; b. Chgo.; d. Barney and Adeline (Kaplan) Galatzer; B.A. in Art Edn., Sch. of Art Inst. Chgo., 1954; m. Earl B. Cole, Dec. 21, 1952; children—Peter, Judith. One-man show Ontario East Art Gallery, Chgo., 1965, U. Chgo., Covenant Club Ill., 1966; exhibited in group shows Devorah Sherman Gallery, Chgo., 1960, Old Orchard Art Festival, Skokie, Ill., 1962-65, New Horizons in Sculpture, Chgo., 1961, 62, Alice Nash Art Gallery, N.Y.C., 1964. Recipient Si Gordon Meml., De Woskin awards. Artist mem. U. Chgo. Renaissance Soc. Illustrator children's book Hooper the What-What Owl, 1963. Home: 235 E Ontario St Chicago IL 60611

COLE, NYLA JESSAMINE (MRS. A.H. KELSON), psychiatrist; b. Wasco, Cal., Dec. 5, 1925; d. R.T. and Emily E. (Moisling) Cole; A.A., U. Cal. at Berkeley, 1945, B.A., 1947; M.D., U. Rochester, 1951; m. Albert Hulbert Kelson, Dec. 14, 1955. Intern Salt Lake County Gen. Hosp., Salt Lake City, 1951-52; resident U. Utah Coll. Medicine at Salt Lake City, 1952-54, USPHS fellow psychiatry, 1955-56, research instr. psychiatry, 1956-60, asst. prof. psychiatry, 1960-68, asso. prof., 1968—, dir. outpatient sect. dept. psychiatry, 1956-62, adult sect., 1962-65, psychiat. screening clinic, 1965—; practice medicine specializing in psychiatry, Salt Lake City, 1955—; dir. Utah State Mental Hygiene Clinic, Salt Lake City, 1956-62; psychiat. cons. Hill AFB, Utah, 1967—. Lectr. dept. social work U. Utah, 1967—. Mem. Pres.'s Com. Mentally Handicapped, 1967—; mem. Gov.'s Com. Employment of Handicapped, chmn. med. subcom., Utah, 1968—. Mem. Am. (mem. com. psychotherapy 1959, Smith Kline & French com. 1961-62, com. relations with psychology 1962-68, com. rehab. 1968-73, chmn. 1969-73), Utah, Salt Lake City psychiat. assns., Am., Utah, Salt Lake County med. assns., Nat. Assn. Mental Health, Phi Beta Kappa. Home: 2574 Maywood Dr Salt Lake City UT 84109 Office: 50 N Medical Dr Salt Lake City UT 84112

COLEBERD, FRANCES AGATHA, editor, author; b. San Francisco; d. John Walter and Ada Blanche (Mountz) Coleberd; A.B., U. Cal. at Berkeley, 1941; postgrad. Stanford, 1950-52. Editorial asst., writer, photographer Sunset Mag., Menlo Park, Cal., 1952-58, travel news editor, writer, photographer, 1958-68; free lance writer and photographer, 1969—. Editor, writer, researcher Western Bus. Publs., San Francisco, 1971-73. Served to lt. (j.g.), WAVES, 1944-47. Recipient first prize in photography Nat. Presswomen's Assn., 1962. Mem. Women in Communications, Soc. of Photographers in Communications, Sierra Club. Author-photographer: Islands of the South Pacific, 1972; Japan, 1973; Australia, 1973. Contbr. numerous photographs to books on travel in U.S. and the Pacific. Address: 1273 Mills St Menlo Park CA 94025

COLELLA, JANE MAE PAULI (MRS. NICHOLAS E. COLELLA), horse breeder, trainer; b. Syracuse, N.Y., Mar. 31, 1915; d. William and Grace M. (Cornelius) Pauli; B.S., Syracuse U., 1941; m. Nicholas E. Colella, Dec. 1, 1947; 1 son, William S. Sec., Morris Berinstein Bern Furniture, Syracuse, 1941-45; co-owner Colella Racing Stables, 1956—, operator Valley Creek Farm, Chittenango, N.Y., 1957—. Mem. U.S., Central N.Y. trotting assns., Kappa Kappa Gamma. Club: Coriathian (Syracuse). Home: 1030 E Genesee St Syracuse NY 13210 also 8 Peterbow St Vernon NY 13476

COLEMAN, ALICE, ednl. adminstr.; b. Florence, S.C., Jan. 30, 1944; d. William Washington and Martha Elizabeth (Hightower) Coleman; student Meredith Coll., 1962-64; student, King's Coll., 1965. Sec. loan dept. First Union Nat. Bank, Charlotte, N.C., 1966-70; sec. bus. affairs Francis Marion Coll., Florence, S.C., 1970-71, personnel officer, 1971—. Mem. Coll. and Univ. Personnel Assn. Baptist. Home: PO Box 185 Pamplico SC 29583 Office: PO Box 7500 Florence SC 29501

COLEMAN, ANNA MARGARET, plastics mfg. co. exec.; b. New Concord, O., Jan. 5, 1913; d. John and Mary (Willson) Coleman; B.S. summa cum laude, Geneva Coll., 1933; M.S. in Chemistry (Univ. scholar), Pa., 1934; Ph.D., U. Pitts., 1959. Tchr., Monaca, Pa., 1934-42; mem. lab. research staff Mellon Inst., Pitts., 1942-50; mgr. tech. information service Dow Corning Corp., Midland, Mich., 1950—. Mem. Am. Chem. Soc., Research Soc. Am., Am. Assn. U. Women. Home: 1915 Eastlawn Drive Midland MI 48640 Office: Dow Corning Corp Midland MI 48640

COLEMAN, ANNIE WALTON, assn. editor; b. Washington, Mar. 20, 1898; d. Robert Cherry and Verdie (Catterton) Walton; grad. high sch.; m. George Melchiades Coleman, Sept. 26, 1921 (div.); children—Thomas J., Catherine V., George Melchiades, Robert F. Tchr. piano, 1930-34; with statis. div., bituminous coal div. NRA, Washington, 1934-35; clk. in charge statistics Pa. anthracite and lignite Bur. Mines, Interior Dept., 1939-43; statistician OPA, 1943-45; distbn. analyst synthetic rubber, sales div. RFC, Washington, 1945-55; editor Voice mag. AIDS Internat., Inc., Arlington, Va., 1967—. Composer popular music. Home: 6015 Chesterbrook Rd McLean VA 22101 Office: 1815 N Fort Myer Dr Arlington VA 22209

COLEMAN, BARBARA ANN NASH (MRS. JAMES H. COLEMAN), librarian; b. Lincolnton, Ga., Dec. 13, 1932; d. Harvey Morgan and Daisy (Murray) Nash; B.A., Spelman U., 1956; M.S., Atlanta U., 1962; m. James Henry Coleman, Mar. 5, 1949. Asst. librarian Donaldson AFB Library, Greenville, S.C., 1959-62, head librarian, 1962-63; head librarian Paine AFB, Everett, Wash., 1963-66, Hamilton AFB, Novato, Cal., 1966-73, Peterson Field, Colorado Springs, Colo., 1973—. Mem. Cal. Pub. Library Devel. Bd., 1969. Recipient Outstanding Performance award Hdqrs. Air Def. Command, USAF, 1965. Mem. Am., Cal. library assns. Home: 5235 S Carefree Circle Colorado Springs CO 80917 Office: Base Library Peterson Field CO 80912

COLEMAN, BEATRICE, apparel mfg. co. exec.; b. Jersey City, 1916; grad. Barnard Coll., 1938; m. Pres. Maidenform, Inc., N.Y.C. Office: 90 Park Av New York City NY 10016

COLEMAN, BEULAH LEHNHARD (MRS. ROBERT HUMPHRIES COLEMAN), museum curator; b. Paducah, Ky., Mar. 3, 1902; d. George Frederick Adolphus and Frances Lucinda (Hall) Lehnhard; grad. high sch.; m. Robert Humphries Coleman, Feb. 16, 1926; children—Robert Lehnhard, Clover Frances, Gordon Edward. Curator, Liberty Hall Museum, Frankfort, Ky., 1961—. Home: 277 Laurel St Frankfort KY 40601 Office: 218 Wilkinson St Frankfort KY 40601

COLEMAN, CATHERINE OFFLEY, headmistress; b. Burlington, Ia., Feb. 9, 1921; d. Francis A. and Catherine (Robertson) Coleman, Jr.; A.B. magna cum laude, Sweet Briar Coll., 1942; M.A., Mills Coll., 1946; postgrad. State U. of Ia., Ind. U., U. Va., Yale. Sec., math. tchr., asst. dean St. Katharine's Sch., Davenport, Ia., 1943-45; tchr. St. Anne's Sch., Charlottesville, Va., 1946-50; dormitory head, 1947-50, dean, 1950-56; headmistress, tchr. sacred studies Hannah More Acad., Reisterstown, Md., 1956-64; headmistress St. Paul's Sch., Walla Walla, Wash., 1964-66, St. John's Parish Sch., Olney, Md., 1966—; mem. N.E. regional panel secondary sch. cons. Coll. Entrance Exam. Bd., 1962-64. Mem. exec. com. Diocesan Schs. Assn., 1966—, chmn., 1971—; mem. Diocesan Council, 1970-72; mem. Diocesan Standing Com., 1973—; mem. Citizens Planning and Housing Assn., 1957-64. Mem. Assn. Chaplains and Tchrs. of Religion in Ch. Schs. (chmn. 1959-60), Episcopal Sch. Assn., (commn. on Old and New Testament curriculum, council 1960-66, 71—), Assn. Ind. Schs. Greater Washington (sec.-treas. 1973—) Nat. Assn. Prins. Schs. for Girls, Natural Bridge Conf. (vice chmn. 1952-56), Soc. Bibl. Lit. and Exegesis, Nat. Assn. Bibl. Instrs., Am. Schs. of Oriental Research, Cum Laude, Md. Hist. Soc., Religious Edn. Assn., Phi Beta Kappa. Contbr. articles to profl. jours. Home: 3008 Bel Pre Rd Apt 1-A Wheaton MD 20906

COLEMAN, DOROTHY IRENE HART (MRS. PATRICK COLEMAN), pub. relations exec.; b. Juneau, Alaska, Nov. 9, 1924; d. Julius Harold and Dorothy (Canfield) Hart; B.A., U. Wash., 1947, postgrad. 1947-50; postgrad. U. Cal. at Los Angeles, 1956-60; m. Patrick Coleman, Dec. 15, 1957; children—Mary Patricia and Anne Dorothy (twins). Asst. to dir. U. Wash. Sch. Journalism, Seattle, 1947-50; reporter Seattle Post-Intelligencer, 45-47, 1950-52; columnist Honolulu Star-Bull., 1952-53; women's editor Vancouver (B.C., Can.) News-Herald, 1953-54; pub. relations dir. U. B.C., Vancouver, 1954-55; news editor Wenatchee (Wash.) Daily World, 1955-56; feature writer Los Angeles Mirror, 1956-59, women's editor, 1959-62; asst. family sect. editor Los Angeles Times, 1962; women's editor Los Angeles Herald-Examiner, 1963-68; pub. relations dir. Hollywood Presbyn. Hosp., 1968-72; pres. Dorothy Coleman Pub. Relations, Los Angeles, 1972-73; dir. communications Braille Inst. Am., Inc., 1973—. Served to lt. comdr. USNR. Mem. Los Angeles, San Francisco, Honolulu, Wash. State, Canadian Womens press clubs, Am. Coll. Pub. Relations Assn., Women in Communications (chpt. pres. 1964), Pub. Relations Soc. Am., Los Angeles Advt. Women, Los Angeles Publicity Club, Gifted Children's Assn., Lawyers Wives of Los Angeles, Kappa Alpha Theta Alumnae, Home: 2054 Laughlin Park Dr Los Angeles CA 90027 Office: 741 N Vermont Av Los Angeles CA 90029

COLEMAN, GEORGIA FORBES (MRS. LLOYD O. COLEMAN), accountant; b. Statesboro, Ga.; d. John Walter and Piety Rachel (Lee) Forbes; student Jacksonville Sch. Bus., 1923-24; m. Lloyd O. Coleman, July 15, 1930 (dec. Apr. 1961); children—Georgia Leida (Mrs. Forney R. Yarbrough III), Mary Lloyd (Mrs. Roger Harrell Toler). Accountant, R.R. Rosborough & Bro., Inc., Jacksonville, Fla., 1924-70; pub. accountant, tax. cons. Milam's Accounting Service, Jacksonville, 1965—. Vocational guidance counselor Riverside Presbyn. Ch., 1960-64. Funds collector Community Chest, 1965, March of Dimes, 1974; mem. Duval County Safety Council; voting mem. Am. Security Council; sponsor Inst. Am. Strategy. Recipient 1st pl. award Div. Poetry Contest, 1974. Mem. Cummer Art Gallery, Columbia Theol. Sem. Friendship Circle, U.D.C. (3d v.p. Robert E. Lee chpt. 1951-52, 54-55, parliamentarian 1964, mag. chmn. 1965, registrar 1958-59, 1st v.p. 1960-61, pres. 1962-63, gen. com. sales of histories 1958, 59, state chmn. widows relief 1963, 64), Nat. Trust Historic Preservation, Bullock County, Jacksonville, Nat. hist. socs., Friday Musicale Jacksonville, Jacksonville Symphony Soc., Spirit of 1976 Soc., Smithsonian Assos. Presbyn. (pres. Sunday sch. 1969-70). Club: Jacksonville Woman's (safety rep. 1956-58, chmn. safety div., advt. mgr. 1974-75). Home: 3559 Riverside Av Jacksonville FL 32205

COLEMAN, JEAN MACMICKEN, lawyer; b. Rochester, N.Y., Dec. 2, 1907; d. Kenneth Bruce and Ada Louise (Chase) McMicken; B.A., U. Rochester, 1929; student Law Sch., Cornell U., 1929-32; m. John Edward Coleman, May 16, 1931; children—George Leidigh II, Chase (Mrs. Davies). Admitted to Ohio bar, 1932; practice law, Dayton, O., 1932—. Third v.p. YWCA, 1951-52, treas., 1952-56, 1st. v.p., 1959-62, pres., 1962-64; mem. steering com. United Health Found., 1965-67, bd. dirs., 1967—, v.p., 1967-68, chmn. budget panel, 1967-73, 1st v.p., 1972-74, pres., 1974—; bd. dirs. Community Welfare Council, 1951-67, 68—, chmn. group work div., 1959-61; trustee Dayton and Montgomery County Library, 1962—, pres. bd., 1968-71, 73—, v.p., 1971-73; mem. budget com. Community Chest, 1954-61, bd. dirs., 1960-69. Mem. Am., Ohio State, Dayton bar assns., Am. (program chmn. 1969-70, sec. 1971-72, regional rep. 1971-73, pres.-elect 1973—), Ohio (exec. com. 1966-72, pres. 1968-70) library trustee assns., Nat. Assn. Women Lawyers, Kappa Beta Pi. Recipient Trustee of Year award Ohio Library Assn., 1971. Club: Dayton Womans. Home: 191 Folsom Dr Dayton OH 45405 Office: Third National Bldg Dayton OH 45402

COLEMAN, MARGARET MARY MCKEON (MRS. JOHN F. COLEMAN), ednl. psychologist; b. N.Y.C., Apr. 15, 1932; d. Thomas P. and Margaret (Holahan) McKeon; A.B. in Psychology, Notre Dame Coll. of S.I., 1954; M.Ed., State U. Tchrs. Coll. N.Y., 1961; M.S.W., Cath. U. Am., 1965; m. John F. Coleman, Feb. 2, 1957. Elementary tchr. Kingston (N.Y.) Pub. Schs., 1957-59; elementary tchr., supr. student tchrs. Newton (Mass.) Pub. Schs., 1959-61; psychiat. social worker tchr.-therapist, cons., coordinator childrens psychiat. services, field supr. grad. students in social work Children's Services, Community Mental Health, San Diego, 1965-68; research social worker, clinician Child Devel. Lab., Mass. Gen. Hosp., Boston, 1968-69; elementary guidance counselor, psychologist, cons. schs. Belmont (Mass.) Pub. Schs., 1969—; instr. Boston U. Grad. Sch. Edn., 1971—; asst. prof. dept. edn. grad. studies div. Salem State Coll., 1974—. Served to lt. (j.g.) USNR, 1954-57. Mem. N.E.A., Nat. Assn. Social Workers (exec. council, chmn. psychiat. council 1967), Mass. Sch. Counselors Assn., Acad. Certified Social Workers. Home: 81 Marsh St Belmont MA 02178

COLEMAN, MARION MOORE (MRS. ARTHUR P. COLEMAN), author, pub.; b. Bklyn., Mar. 10, 1900; d. David Halsey and Elizabeth Shaw (Merrill) Moore; B.A., N.Y. State Coll., 1920; L.H.D., Alliance Coll., 1974; m. Arthur P. Coleman, July 1, 1922. Tchr. Latin, history Athens (N.Y.) High Sch., 1920-21, prin., 1921-22; tchr. history and sci. Fort Lee (N.J.) High Sch., 1922-23; tchr. English, The English Coll., Pargue, Czecho-Slovakia, 1923-24; tchr. pub. high schs. in Mich., 1925-26; lectr. comparative cultures Alliance Coll., Cambridge Springs, Pa., 1950-62; free lance writer, pub., partner Cherry Hill Books, 1963—. Vol., Pub. Library, Cheshire, Conn., 1964—. Recipient Chevalier decoration Polonia Restituta, 1962, Warsaw P.E.N. Club award, 1972, Medal of Honor, Kosciuszko Found., 1973. Author: Biography of Adam Mickiewicz, 1955; Bibliography of Polish Literature in English, 1963; (with Arthur P. Coleman) Wanderers Twain, 1964; Letters to Emilia, 1967; Fair Rosalind, 1969; The Man on the Moon, 1971; A Brigand, Two Queens and a Prankster, 1972; Vistula Voyage, 1973. Translator: Seven Years in Russia and Siberia (Roman Dyboski), 1971. Address: 202 Highland Av Cheshire CT 06410

COLEMAN, MARY CATHERINE, chemist; b. Cumberland, Md., Mar. 9, 1919; d. Joseph James and Teresa (Graebenstein) Coleman; A.B., Notre Dame, 1940; M.S., Georgetown U., 1955; postgrad. Johns Hopkins, 1955-56, W.Va. U., 1959-63, Am. U., 1965-68, George Washington Law Sch., 1969. Sr. bacteriologist U. Md., 1940-41; chemist Johns Hopkins U., 1941-42, Coca-Cola Co., Atlanta, 1942-56; tech. writer Hercules Alleghany Ballistics Lab., Rocket Center, W.Va., 1956-58, research chemist, 1958-61, research chemist mass spectros. nuclear magnetic resonance, 1961-63; chemist Bur. Drugs U.S. FDA, Rockville, Md., 1963—. Leader sr. troop Girl Scouts U.S.A., 1958—. Mem. A.A.A.S. (life), Am. Chem. Soc. (sec.

1958-63), Soc. Microbiol., Inst. Aeros. and Astronautics (sec. 1962-63), Soc. Tech. Writers and Editors, Albertus Magnus Guild, Internat. Platform Assn., Nat. Hist. Soc., Am. Pharm. Assn., Acad. Pharm. Sci., Am. Acad. Polit. and Social Sci., Beta Beta Beta, Beta Sigma Phi. Home: 5101 River Rd 1609 Chevy Chase MD 20016 Office: BD 325 Fisherlane Rockville MD 20852

COLEMAN, MARY JANE (MRS. NATHANIEL R. COLEMAN, JR.), assn. ofcl.; student Coll. William and Mary. Formerly in advt. Active Youth Builders Club Greeneville; founder, pres. Greeneville Arts Guild; Tenn. co-partner Partnership for the Arts; active Tenn. Arts Commn. 1968—, sec., 1972—, mem. exec. com., long range planning com., purchase com., adv. to Film Panel. Bd. dirs. Friends Carroll Reece Mus.; founder, dir. Sinking Creek Film Celebration, 1970—; mem. Tenn. arts com. Bicentennial Com.; adv. bd. Tenn. Cultural Center; chmn. film panel Tenn. Arts Commn. Home: Route 8 Creekside Farm Greeneville TN 37743

COLEMAN, MARY LEE, educator; b. Pine Bluff, Ark., Aug. 21, 1935; d. Lercy W. and Mildred O. (Petty) Coleman; B.S., Ark. A.M. and N. Coll., 1956; M.S., Chgo. State Coll., 1969; postgrad. Northwestern U., 1969-74. Sec. Opportunity Pub. Co., Chgo., 1956-58; tchr. spl. edn. Chgo. Bd. Edn., 1958—. Adult edn. tchr. evening schs., Chgo., 1958—. Y teen leader YWCA, Chgo., summer 1962; pre-sch. children program aide Ada S. McKinley House YWCA, Chgo., summer 1963. Research Study Socialist Edn. scholar, 1974. Mem. Nat., Ill. edn. assns., Council for Exceptional Children, Council for Children with Learning Disabilities, Nat. Council of Social Studies, League of Black Women, N.A.A.C.P., Chgo. State U. Ark. A.M. and N. alumni assns., Sigma Gamma Rho. Home: 9108 South Blackstone Chicago IL 60619 Office: 6145 South Ingleside Chicago IL 60637

COLEMAN, NELDA REYNOLDS (MRS. JAMES GRAHAM COLEMAN), former radio sta. exec.; b. Ruston, La., July 11, 1944; d. Miller Guy and Daisy Amanda (Mitcham) Reynolds; student North La. Vocational Tech. Sch., 1962; m. James Graham Coleman, June 6, 1964. Women's dir. Sta. KBCL AM and FM, Shreveport, La., 1968-74. Home: Route 1 Oak Haven Cuero TX 77954

COLEMAN, SYLVIA ETHEL (MRS. AL HERBERT BERNSTONE), microbiologist; b. Gainesville, Fla., Mar. 23, 1933; d. John Melton and Jessie Lee (Coleman) Coleman; B.S., U. Fla., 1955, M.S., 1956; Ph.D. (grad. fellow, Nat. Def. Edn. Act fellow), 1972; m. Al Herbert Bernstone, Dec. 21, 1967. Research microbiologist VA Center, Bay Pines, Fla., 1960-67, Gainesville, 1972—. Mem. Am., Southeastern Br. socs. for microbiology, Electron Microscopy Soc. Am., Southeastern Electron Microscopy Soc., Fla., N.Y. acads. scis., Sigma Xi (Best Research by Grad. Student, U. Fla. award, 1972). Contbr. articles in field to profl. jours. Home: 1408-38 SW 10th Terrace Gainesville FL 32601 Office: Research Service 151 VA Hosp Gainesville FL 32602

COLEMAN, WILLYE ALITA FORTENBERRY (MRS. JERRY H. COLEMAN, JR.), state ofcl.; b. McComb, Miss.; d. William and Ella (Smith) Fortenberry; A.B., U. Ill. at Urbana, 1933; M.A., U. Chgo., 1938; m. Jerry H. Coleman, Jr., Dec. 25, 1936; children—Alan Bruce, Janice Alita. With N.Y. Children's Aid Soc., 1940-41, Ill. Children's Home and Aid Soc., 1941-43, Greenleigh Study on Aid to Dependent Children in Cook County, Ill., 1960-61; supr. Cook County (Ill.) Dept. Pub. Aid, 1943-48; cons. instns. State of Tenn., 1948-49; supr. social work, coordinator adoption information Ill. Dept. Children and Family Services, Chgo., 1961-70, supr. licensing sect., 1970—. Pres. Woman's Aux. Cook County Physicians Assn., 1961-63, Meharry Alumni Assn. Aux., 1963-65. Recipient Radio salute WBBE, Chgo., 1963; 1st Pl. award Welfare Pub. Relations Forum, Chgo., 1966. Mem. Nat. Assn. Social Workers, Child Welfare League Am. Home: 7441 S Prairie Av Chicago IL 60619 Office: Ill Dept Children and Family Service 1026 S Damen Av Chicago IL 60612

COLETTI, JEANNETTE DICKERSON (MRS. VINCENT JOSEPH COLETTI), librarian; b. Dallas, Sept. 24, 1927; d. Emmett Wesley and Martha Lorena (Wright) Dickerson; B.A., Fla. State U., 1960; M.L.S., Pratt Inst., 1965; m. Vincent Joseph Coletti, Apr. 14, 1953; 1 son, David Vincent. Court reporter Dept. of Army, Japan, 1949-53; librarian Burdick Vocational High Sch., Washington, 1966-73, Nat. Endowment for Humanities, 1974—. Mem. A.L.A., Phi Beta Kappa, Phi Kappa Phi, Sigma Tau Delta. Republican. Home: 3619 Chesapeake St NW Washington DC 20008 Office: 806 15th St NW Washington DC 20506

COLFAX, JANE A., physician; b. Paterson, N.J., June 21, 1923; d. Richard S. and Elsye (Schoonmaker) Colfax; student U. Vt., 1941-42; R.N., Flower Fifth Av. Sch. Nursing, 1945; student Columbia, 1946-47; B.A., Hunter Coll., 1950; M.D., Woman's Med. Coll. Pa., 1955; m. Michael DeNike, 1962. Intern, Kings County Hosp., Bklyn., 1955-56; resident Woman's Hosp. div. St. Luke's Hosp., N.Y.C., 1956-60, mem. staff, 1960-66, asst. attending obstetrician and gynecologist Woman's Hosp. div., 1962; sr. attending obstetrics and gynecology St. Joseph Hosp., Paterson, 1966—; attending gynecologist Preakness Hosp., Wayne, N.J., 1962—; practice medicine specializing in obstetrics and gynecology, Wayne, 1960—; sr. attending physician St. Joseph's Hosp., Paterson, 1960—; attending gynecologist Preakness Hosp. Diplomate Am. Bd. Obstetrics and Gynecology, Nat. Bd. Med. Examiners. Fellow Am. Coll. Obstetricians and Gynecologists; mem. Internat., Am. med. women's assns., N.J., Passaic County med. socs., Woman's Med. Coll. Alumni Assn., N.J. Obstet. and Gynecol. Soc., N.Y. Acad. Scis., Zeta Phi. Home: 2343 Hamburg Turnpike Wayne NJ 14893 Office: No 4 2411 Hamburg Turnpike Wayne NJ 07470

COLGAN, MARY CRESWELL, museum curator; b. Augusta, Ga., Dec. 12, 1918; d. George Washington and Bennie George (Johnson) Summers; student Louisville Inst. Tech., 1937-40; m. Arthur Rudolf Colgan, July 6, 1953; 1 dau., Dorothy Anne. Adminstrv. asst., sec. to pres. S.D. Sch. Mines and Tech., Coll. of Engring. and Sci., 1949-54; exec. sec., office mgr. Dr. Joseph S. Knight, D.C., Hawthorne, Cal., 1970-73; partner ARCI Enterprises, Palos Verdes, Cal., 1969-73; mgr., artist MARCI originals for ARCI Assos., Edgemont, S.D., 1973—; sec.-treas. A.R. Colgan, Inc., Edgemont, 1964-73; dir., curator Colgan's Old Gen. Store Mus., Edgemont. Dist. chmn. Los Angeles County dist. 8, Am. Cancer Soc., 1965-66. Mem. Geneal. Soc. Pa. Republican. Episcopalian. Editor: St. Martha's By The Stove, edit. I, 1966, edit. II, 1967; Friendly Cookerie From Edgemont, 1968; Swedish Corner Cookbook, 1972. Home: 603 3d Av Edgemont SD 57735 Office: 411 2d Av Edgemont SD 57735

COLIGAN, SISTER MARY MELANIE, hosp. adminstr.; b. Morrisburg, Ont., Can., Aug. 27, 1912; d. Thomas and Margaret (Daley) Coligan; B.S. in Nursing, Ottawa U., 1944; M.S. in Nursing Edn., Catholic U. Am., 1951. Joined Sisters of Providence of St. Vincent de Paul, 1932; supr. operating room Providence Hosp., Moose Jaw, Sask., Can., 1935-39; nursing supr. obstet. and gynecol. dept. St. Francis Gen. Hosp., Smith Falls, Ont., Can., 1937-43; operating room supr. St. Vincent de Paul Hosp., Brockville, Ont., 1944; ednl. dir. Sch. of Nursing St. Mary's Hosp., Montreal, Que., Can., 1944-55, asst. exec. dir., 1955-58, exec. dir., 1958—. Cons. to Sisters of Providence, Kingston, Ont., 1951—; preceptor U. Montreal, 1959—, U. Ottawa, 1966—. Warden St. Kevins Parish, Montreal, 1972—; mem. St. Mary's Hosp. Found. Bd. dirs. St. Mary's Hosp. Center, Pillars Found. of Diocese of Montreal. Fellow Am. Coll. Hosp. Adminstrs., Royal Soc. Health; mem. Canadian Coll. Health Service Execs. (founder 1970), Montreal Joint Hosp. Inst. (dir.), Assn. Exec. Dirs. Que. Health and Social Services, Intercommunity Religious Assn. Montreal, Sigma Theta Tau. Contbr. articles on nursing to profl. publs. Address: 3830 Lacombe Montreal PQ H3T 1M5 Canada

COLINS, CHRISTINE MILLAR MAYNARD (MRS. CHRISTOPHER COLINS), social worker; b. Conway, S.C., Apr. 6, 1915; d. Thomas Sprugeon and Ione Myrtle (Lane) Maynard; B.S., U. N.C., 1938; postgrad. Nashville Sch. Social Work, 1948-49; M.S.W., Columbia Sch. Social Work, 1949; m. Christopher Colins, Aug. 3, 1953. Ballerina Miriam Winslow-Concert Co., Boston, 1938-41; exec. dir. A.R.C., Kinston and Tarboro, N.C., 1941-48; acting dir. Family and Childrens Services, Norfolk, Va., 1950-53; psychiatric social worker Mental Health Clinic, Roanoke, Va., 1953-54, Norristown, Pa., 1954-55, Westchester, Pa., 1955-60, Charlotte, N.C., 1960-68; supr. dept. social scis. Caswell Center, Kinston, N.C., 1970—. Grantee N.C. Dept. Mental Health, 1963. Fellow Am. Orthopsychiat. Assn.; mem. Nat. Assn. Social Workers, N.C. Social Services Assn. Home: 310 Sherwood Pl Kinston NC 28501 Office: Caswell Center Goldsboro Hwy Kinston NC 28501

COLL, HELEN FRYE (MRS. ROBERT FRANCIS COLL), bank exec.; b. nr. Lovettsville, Va., Dec. 2, 1921; d. Raymond C. and Minnie (Peters) Frye; grad. Wash. Sch. Secs., 1940, Sch. Financial Pub. Relations Northwestern U., 1963; grad. Stonier Grad. Sch. Banking Rutgers U., 1966; m. Lee Stanley Sherline, Sept. 1, 1942 (div. Feb. 1955); m. 2d, Robert Francis Coll, May 25, 1957. With Nat. Savs. & Trust Co., Washington, 1940—, sec. to pres., 1948-51, asst. sec., 1951-55, sec., 1955—, v.p., 1963—, v.p., sec. bd., 1966-72, sr. v.p., sec. bd., 1972—. Mem. Met. Bd. Trade, Nat. Assn. Bank Women, D.C. Bankers Assn., Bank Marketing Assn. Clubs: National Aviation, City Tavern (Washington). Home: 1310 29th St Washington DC 20005 Office: Nat Savings & Trust Co 15th St and New York Av Washington DC 20005

COLLETT, KAY GENTRY, govt. ofcl.; b. Fayetteville, Ark., Aug. 7, 1941; d. Kirby Benjamin and Susan Elizabeth (Sutton) Collett; B.A., U. Ark., 1963, M.A., 1966; Ph.D., W. Va. U., 1974. Instr., Westark Community Coll., Fort Smith, Ark., 1966-68; asst. prof. polit. sci. U. Ark., Fayetteville, 1966, 68, 69-72; chief legislative asst. to Congressman Ray Thornton, Washington, 1973—. Mem. Ark. Constl. Revision Study Commn., 1967; research asso. Ark. Constl. Conv., 1969. Coordinator Campaign for Fayetteville City Mgr. Govt., 1966, 70; del. state Democratic Conv., 1972. Bd. dirs. Ark. for a Revised Constn., 1968-70. Mem. Ark. League Women Voters (dir. 1965-68). Methodist. Author: (with Henry M. Alexander) The City Manager Plan in Arkansas, 1966; (with Walter H. Nunn) Constitutional Revision in Arkansas: A Study in Political Paradox, 1971. Home: 11 6th St SE Washington DC 20003 Office: 1109 Longworth Bldg Washington DC 20515

COLLETT, LOUISA BARRY, petroleum co. exec.; b. San Antonio, Aug. 31, 1931; d. Charles Drew and Louise Antoinette (Burton) Collett; B.A., Centenary Coll., 1953. Continuity dir. radio sta. KTBS, Shreveport, La., 1953-54; editorial asst. Ark. Fuel Oil Corp., Shreveport, 1954-60; with Cities Service Oil Co., 1960—, editor, N.Y.C., 1960-62, Tulsa, 1962-70, coordinator spl. services, pub. relations div., Tulsa, 1970-73; coordinator spl. services, pub. relations div. Cities Service Co., Tulsa, 1973—. Mem. Nat. Assn. Women Hwy. Safety Leaders (dir.), Am. Marketing Assn. (v.p. chpt.), Am. Women in Radio and TV, Women in Communications, Internat. Assn. Bus. Communicators, Okla. Petroleum Council, Am. Petroleum Inst. (mem. consumer affairs com.), Tulsa Safety Council. Home: 3903 Riverside Dr Tulsa OK 74105 Office: Cities Service Box 300 Tulsa OK 74102

COLLETT, NAOMI JEAN (MRS. HUGO R. PAGANELLI), advt. exec.; b. Cambridge, Mass., Nov. 12, 1923; d. Charles H. and Edith S. (Scamman) Collett; A.B., Colby Coll., 1945; m. Hugo R. Paganelli, May 31, 1947. Clk. information bur. N.Y. Daily News, N.Y.C., 1946; copywriter/designer Harper & Row pubs., N.Y.C., 1946-56, advt. and promotion mgr., 1956—. Home: 2 Horatio St New York City NY 10014 Office: 10 E 53d St New York City NY 10022

COLLEY, LOIS GRACE BARON, health service adminstr.; b. Scranton, Pa., July 31, 1923; d. Harry Everett and Selena Maud (Baron) Colley; B.S., U. Pitts., 1946; M.S., Marywood Coll., 1952; postgrad., U. Rome, Italy, 1968, Royal Soc. Medicine, London, Eng., 1970. Dir. nursing dept. Clark's Summit (Pa.) Hosp., 1943-55, Holidaysburg (Pa.) State Hosp., 1955-59; nursing cons. Dept. Welfare, Harrisburg, Pa., 1959-61; dir. dept. residential care Hamburg (Pa.) State Sch. and Hosp., 1961-72, adminstr. residential programs, 1972—. Mem. adv. com. Pa. State United Cerebral Palsy, 1964—, mem. long term care com., 1966—. Bd. dirs. United Cerebral Palsy of Berks County, Pa., 1968—, Threshold Inc., Reading, Pa., 1969—. Recipient citation United Cerebral Palsy Pa., 1968. Mem. Pa. (mem. exec. com. psychiat. conf. 1960—), Am. nurses assns., Assn. for Advancement of Psychiatry, Am. Assn. on Mental Deficiency, Order Eastern Star, Soroptomists. Home: Box 108 A RD 1 Allendale Rd Shoemakersville PA 19555 Office: Hamburg State School and Hospital Hamburg PA 19626

COLLIER, DOROTHY VIRGINIA, constrn. co. exec.; b. Klamath Falls, Ore., June 17, 1929; d. Alfred Douglas and Ethel Hannah (Foster) Collier; B.A., U. Ore., 1951; m. H. Buford Hargus, July 7, 1951 (div. June 1959). Corporate sec. Swan Lake Moulding Co., Klamath Falls, Ore., 1951—; v.p. All Type Roofing Co., 1973—. Staff aide chmn. Red Cross, Klamath Falls, 1963. Republican precinct committeewoman, Klamath Falls, 1953. Mem. Women's Aux. to Klamath County Med. Soc. (pres. 1957), Women's Aux. to Ore. State Med. Soc. (dir. 1959), Am. Assn. U. Women, Klamath County C. of C., Aircraft Owners and Pilots Assn., Pi Beta Phi. Episcopalian. Clubs: Klamath Art Assn. Home: 1930 Lowell St Klamath Falls OR 97601 Office: 3226 S 6th St Klamath Falls OR 97601

COLLIER, JUDY AUDREY GOBEN, bus. exec.; b. Indpls., Feb. 13, 1926; d. John and Myrtle (Long) Goben; student U. Louisville, 1946-52; m. Jack Collier, Dec. 24, 1943 (div. 1946). Bookkeeper, Bell & Koch, Inc., 1946-53; office mgr. Ry. Signal Equipment Co., 1953-54; bookkeeper Wetherton Tile Co., 1954-57; decorator Berndsen-Jones, Inc., 1957-59; decorator DeLaney Furniture Co., 1959-61; free lance decorator, 1961-62; sec.-bookkeeper Holiday Inn, 1962 (all Louisville); field rep. tng. Holiday Inn personnel Holiday Inns, Inc., Memphis, 1962-64; field rep. tng. Holiday Inn personnel Allen & O'Hara, Inc., Memphis, 1964-66; innkeeper Holiday Inn, Chicago Heights, Ill., 1966-73, Franklin, Tenn., 1973—. Mem. Am. Bus. and Profl. Womens Assn., Heritage Found., Hist. Soc. Episcopalian. Office: Route 7 Berry Chapel Rd Franklin TN 37064

COLLIER, LOLA GAMBLE (MRS. JOHN WAYNE COLLIER), owner clothing store; b. Stonegia, Va., Oct. 9, 1911; d. Waymond Walter and Mary Elizabeth (Maggard) Gamble; grad. high sch.; student U. Va. Extension, 1958; m. John Wayne Collier, June 11, 1937; children—Gale Annette (Mrs. Charles Lawrence Wright), Kenneth Wayne, John Chadriek. Dress maker, designer, Appalachia, Va., 1935; owner, propr. The Grill, Appalachia, 1936-47; owner, buyer, mgr. Collier's Style Shop, Appalachia, 1947—, St. Paul, Va., 1949—, Lexington, Ky., 1952—, Kingsport, Tenn., 1966-71. Coordinator Ky. div. Am. Cancer Soc.; active vol. Voluntary Workers in Reach for Recovery Program. Asst. in town politics regarding better civic conditions. Mem. Women's Soc. (leader 1937-47), Baptist. Clubs: Woman's (pres. 1954-58), Bridge. Home: 1001 Castleton Way Lexington KY 40502 Office: 201 Eastland Shopping Center Lexington KY 40505

COLLIER, MARILYN DEE, occupational therapist; b. Okmulgee, Okla., Sept. 18, 1948; d. James Leslie and Virginia Valentine (Spore) Collier; B.S. in Occupational Therapy, Tex. Woman's U., 1970; certificate Northwestern U., 1973. Occupational therapist Crippled Children's Soc. Easter Seal Sch., Charleston, S.C., 1970-71; sr. occupational therapist, student supr. Med. U. of S.C., Charleston, 1972-74; chief occupational therapist St. Francis Hosp., Tulsa, 1974; occupational therapy coordinator phys. disabilities Tulsa Rehab. Center, 1974—. Mem. Am. co-chairman Nat. Spl. Interest Group on Burn Treatment, 1973-74), S.C. occupational therapy assns. Methodist (Sunday sch. tchr. 1972-74). Home: 1347-B E 61st St Tulsa OK 74136

COLLIER, MAUDE DISEKER (MRS. WILLIAM HOOPER COLLIER, JR.), physician; b. Tallassee, Ala., July 17, 1929; d. Robert Arthur and Mary Fain (Lunsford) Diseker; A.B., Birmingham-So. Coll., 1950; M.D., Med. Coll. Ala., 1955; M.P.H., Johns Hopkins, 1961; m. William Hooper Collier, Jr., Jan. 19, 1963; children—John Bryant, Mary Martelle. Intern, U. Va. Hosp., Charlottesville, 1955-56; resident pediatrics U. Ala. Hosp., Birmingham, 1956-58; fellow maternal and child health Johns Hopkins, Balt., 1959-61; cons. pediatrics Jefferson County Health Dept., Birmingham, Ala., 1961—; cons. Head Start Program Jefferson County, 1968—; practice medicine specializing in pediatrics, Birmingham, 1967—; mem. staff Children's Hosp., Birmingham, U. Ala. Hosp., Birmingham; asso. clin. prof. pediatrics U. Ala., 1961—. Recipient fellowship USPHS, 1959-60, Nat. Found., 1960-61. Diplomate Am. Bd. Pediatrics. Mem. Am. Acad. Pediatrics, Mortar Bd., Alpha Omega Alpha, Pi Beta Phi. Home: 3236 Salisbury Rd Birmingham AL 35213

COLLIER, ROSE MAE MCMILLAN, club woman; b. Piedmont, Mo., May 15, 1900; d. Rev. Charles Milas and Katherine (Day) McMillan; student pub. schs., Kan.; m. James E. Collier, July 22, 1917; 1 dau., Phyllie Lee (Mrs. Robert Clarke Matchette). Accounting T. M. Deal Lumber Co., Dodge City, Kan., 1942-51; co-owner, mgr. Collier Grocery Mart, Dodge City, Kan., 1952-58. Worthy matron Order Eastern Star, 1932, worthy grand matron State of Kan., 1940-41, grand treas., 1942-71, grand treas. emeritus, 1971—; grand teller gen. grand chpt. 1952 Triennial session Order Eastern Star, Milw., mem. registration com. gen. grand chpt., 1955-58, worthy grand chaplain Gen. Grand chpt., 1967-70; mem. council of adminstrn. Grand chpt. Order Eastern Star, State of Kan., 1942—, chmn. chpt. bd. trustees, 1940—, chmn. exec. bd. Dodge City assembly Social Order of Beauceant, 1938—, local pres., 1927, supreme worthy pres., 1937-38, nat. chmn. K.T. Eye Found., Inc. for Supreme Assembly, 1951-60, adv. chmn., 1961—. Mem. Needlework Guild of Am., League Women Voters, Community Concert Assn., Dodge City C. of C. Presbyn. (officer Presbyterial 1961—, del. to nat. meeting 1961, deacon 1964—). Clubs: Knife and Fork, Sorosis Study (charter mem.), Dodge City Country (Dodge City, Kan.), Kansas Authors. Home: 1204 Central Av Dodge City KS 67801

COLLIER, SUSAN ELISABETH, librarian; b. Doty, Wash., Feb. 9, 1914; d. William Randolph and Ova (Roller) Collier; student Centralia (Wash.) Jr. Coll., 1935; B.A., Linfield Coll., 1940; spl. student Washington U., St. Louis. Geodetic computer U.S. Geol. Survey, 1946-50; with Mass. Inst. Tech. Operations Evaluation Group, Pentagon, Washington, 1958-60; information specialist Martin-Marietta Corp., Orlando, Fla., 1960-63; engring. librarian Ingersoll-Rand Co., Princeton, N.J., 1964—. Served to lt. comr. USNR, 1942-46, 50-58. Mem. Soc. Women Engrs., Spl. Libraries Assn., U.S. Naval Inst., Am. Congress Surveying and Mapping, Geosci. Information Soc. Mem. Order Eastern Star. Presbyn. Home: 26-A Bradford Lane Rossmoor Jamesburg NJ 08831 Office: Ingersoll-Rand Research Center Box 301 Princeton NJ 08540

COLLIER, SUSAN STARR, chemist; b. Washington, Nov. 5, 1939; d. Melville Chase and Dorothy Sorerhill (Atwood) Williams; A.B. in Chemistry, Cornell U., 1961; Ph.D. in Phys. Chemistry, U. Rochester, 1966; postdoctoral fellow photochemistry, Ohio State U., 1966-69. Sr. chemist, research labs. Eastman Kodak Co., Rochester, N.Y., 1969—. Mem. Am. Chem. Soc. (chmn. women chemists com. 1973—), Iota Sigma Phi. Author articles gas phase photochemistry, spectral sensitization silver lalile. Home: 7330 Selden Rd LeRoy NY 14482 Office: Research Labs Eastman Kodak Co Rochester NY 14650

COLLIER, VIRGINIA ROLLWAGE, music patroness, assn. exec.; b. Forrest City, Ark., July 5; d. Otto Benjamin and Virginia (Anderson) Rollwage; grad. Lenox Hall, St. Louis, Nat. Coll. Edn., Evanston; student Columbia, Geo. Washington U.; m. John Francis Collier (div.). Tchr. mathematics Comstock Sch. for Girls, N.Y.C., 2 yrs.; econ. analyst and internat. economist U.S. Dept. Commerce, Washington, 1943-53. Pres. Motion Picture and TV Council of D.C., 1952—; chmn. Embassy of Iran Benefit Ball for Blind, 1965; judge U.S. Navy Band Am. Youth Awards Concert, 1970. Mem. Partner's in Alliance com. Dept. State. Commd. Ark. Traveler, Ky. Col. Mem. Nat. Assn. Am. Composers and Condrs. (award for outstanding service to Am. music 1953, founder D.C. chpt. 1950, since pres.), Nat. League Am. Pen Women (gen. chmn. nat. biennial conv. 1960, nat. membership chmn. 1974—), Internat. Platform Assn., Nat. Soc. Arts and Letters (gen. chmn. Nat. 20th Anniversary conv. 1964, 1st v.p. 1964-66, program chmn. Washington chpt. 1974—), U.D.C. (trustee Confederate Meml. Hall, pres. Stonewall Jackson chpt. 1967-68), Nat. Council Women U.S. (lectr.), D.C. Soc. Dames Ct. of Honor (state treas. 1971-73), D.C. Fedn. Women's Clubs (chmn. dept. pub. affairs 1970-72, chmn. dept. performing arts 1972-74), Friends of Kennedy Center (founding mem.), Pan Am. Liaison Com. Women's Orgns. Club: Washington; D.C. State Officers (pres. 1974-76). Author govt. publs.; columnist nat. film weekly Boxoffice, 1961—. Home: 5112 Connecticut Av NW Washington DC 20008

COLLIER, VIRGINIA VALENTINE SPORE (MRS. JAMES LESLIE COLLIER), librarian; b. Dallas, Feb. 14, 1919; d. Claude Leroy and Woodie Dee (Black) Spore; B.A., U. Tex., 1940; B.S. in Library Sci., Emory U., 1941; m. James Leslie Collier, Dec. 9, 1945 (dec.); children—Dana Jane (Mrs. Charles W. Rooks), Douglas James, Marilyn Dee. County librarian Austin (Tex.) Pub. Library, 1941-43; asst. librarian McCloskey Army Hosp. Library, Temple, Tex., 1944; asst. br. librarian Lakeview br. Oakland (Cal.) Pub. Library, 1945; librarian Okmulgee (Okla.) Pub. Library, 1953-60; dir.

Bookmobile service Tulsa City-County Library, 1961-68; constrn. cons. Okla. Dept. Libraries, Oklahoma City, 1968—. Named Mother of Year Okmulgee County, 1959. Mem. Am. (membership chmn. 1964-70), Okla. (div. sec. 1955-56; div. chmn. 1956-57) library assns., Com. Gov's. Mansion Library (chmn. 1973-75), Southwestern Library Assn. (div. chmn. 1960-62), Am. Assn. U. Women. Home: 4316 NW 56th Terrace Oklahoma City OK 73112 Office: Oklahoma Dept Libraries 200 NE 18 Oklahoma City OK 71105

COLLINS, ALIDA MARIE WICKS (MRS. ARCHIBALD DAVID COLLINS), hosp. adminstr.; b. Amityville, L.I., N.Y., Mar. 9, 1944; d. William Elmer and Alida Marie (Drake) Wicks; R.N., Stamford Hosp. Sch. Nursing, 1964; m. Archibald David Collins, Mar. 5, 1964; children—Alida Marie, Archibald David, David Stanley. Staff nurse St. Anne Hosp., Arichat N.S., Can., 1965-66, adminstr., 1967—. Home: PO Box 361 West Arichat Richmond County NS Canada Office: PO Box 279 Arichat Richmond County NS Canada

COLLINS, ANN ELIZABETH AVERITT (MRS. GALEN FRANKLIN COLLINS), civic leader; b. Peru, Ind., July 28, 1934; d. Robert Chancellor and Cleo (Hite) Averitt; student Ind. U., 1952-55; Goshen Coll., 1958, East Tenn. State U., 1967-68; m. Galen Franklin Collins, Sept. 30, 1956; children—Galen Robert, Amelia Lynn, Scott Franklin, Daniel Chancellor. Co-soc. editor Elkhart (Ind.) Truth, 1955-56; mem. Elkhart Civic Theatre, 1957-60; mem. Chenango County Community Players, N.Y., 1960-63; co-founder Dogwood Playhouse, Bristol Va.-Tenn., 1964, bd. dirs., 1964-69; co-founder Collero Puppets, Bristol, 1967; writer, performer puppet shows, Miami, Fla., 1972—; free lance writer, 1972—. Mem. Puppeteers Am., Delta Zeta Alumni Assn. Presbyn. Musical compositions include Why Am I Old, 1969; Little Boy, My Dear Son, 1969; Color, 1969; Willows, 1969; Soldier Boy, 1969; Is That Your Voice I Hear?, 1969. Home: 10800 SW 69th Av Miami FL 33156

COLLINS, BEULAH STOWE (MRS. THOMAS HIGHTOWER COLLINS), columnist, editor; b. Ft. Dodge, Ia., Mar. 28, 1923; d. Herman Wilmer and Beulah Blanche (Blagden) Stowe; B.A. in Journalism, U. Ia., 1942; M.A. in Comparative Lit., U. N.C., 1967; m. Thomas Hightower Collins, Apr. 6, 1946; children—Kent Stowe, Paul Harlan, Todd Stowe. Editor Today's Chuckle, Los Angeles Times Syndicate, 1958—, also columnist weekly humor column Weekend Chuckles, 1955—. Served to ensign USNR, 1944-46. Mem. Women in Communications. Episcopalian (sec. of vestry 1971-73, diocesan officer 1967-73). Author: The Senior Forum, 1964; For Benefit of Clergy, 1966. Home: 15 Lake Shore Dr Chapel Hill NC 27514

COLLINS, CARDISS, congresswoman; b. St. Louis, Sept. 24, 1931; d. Finley and Rosia Mae (Robertson) Robertson; certificate bus. Northwestern U., 1966, diploma in profl. accounting, 1967; m. George Collins (dec.); 1 son, B. Kevin. Stenographer, then sec. employment service Ill. Dept. Labor, 1950-58; sec., then revenue auditor Ill. Dept. Revenue, 1958-72; mem. 93d congress from 7th Ill. Dist. Mem. Lawndale Youth Commn., Chgo. Committeewoman 24th Ward Regular Democratic Orgn., Chgo.; adv. bd. Ill. Dem. Central Com. Bd. dirs. Lawndale Conservation Com. Home: Chicago IL Office: 1123 Longworth House Office Bldg Washington DC 20515

COLLINS, CHARLOTTE ANNA HAHNE, ednl. adminstr.; b. Toledo, Dec. 31, 1935; d. Friedrich G. and Ilse K. (Schnippering) Hahne; B.S., Bowling Green State U., 1957; M.Mus., U. Mich., 1970, Ph.D., 1972; m. Verne E. Collins, June 30, 1957; children—Beth, Christopher. Tchr. pub. schs., Ohio and Ill., 1956-58; mem. faculty Shenandoah Conservatory Music, Winchester, Va., 1958—, chmn. faculty, 1971—. Mem. Alpha Kappa Lambda, Sigma Alpha Iota. Home: 182 Hawthorne Dr Winchester VA 22601

COLLINS, DORIS NUNES (MRS. RAYMOND C. COLLINS), physician; b. St. Andrew, Jamaica, B.W.I., Nov. 26, 1920; d. Theodore Alfred and Kathleen Florence (Gunter) Nunes; student U. Durham, Eng., 1938-39; M.D., C.M., McGill U., Montreal, 1944, M.Sc., 1949; m. Raymond Charles Collins, June 4, 1955. Came to U.S., 1950, naturalized, 1955. Intern Montreal Gen. Hosp., 1944-45, pathology intern, 1945-46; lectr. bacteriology McGill U., 1946-48; teaching fellow pathology Queens U., Kingston, Ont., 1949-50; pathology resident Cleve. City Hosp., 1950-51; dir. labs. Otsego County Labs., Cooperstown, N.Y., 1951-52; pathologist Mary Imogene Bassett Hosp., Cooperstown 1952-55; sr. pathologist div. labs. and research N.Y. State Dept. Health, 1955-56, asso. pathologist, 1956-66, prin. pathologist, 1966—; dir. pathology and cytology, 1968—. Licentiate Med. Coll. Can. Fellow Am. Coll. Pathologists; mem. Am. Soc. Clin. Pathologists, N.Y. Assn. Pub. Health Labs., Am. Soc. Cytology, N.Y. State Soc. Pathologists, N.Y. State Soc. Electron Microscopy, Internat. Acad. Pathology, Am. Orchid Soc. Home: Gardner Rd RD 2 Altamont NY 12009 Office: NY State Dept Health Div Labs New Scotland Av Albany NY 12201

COLLINS, DOROTHY JANE WALKER (MRS. WILLIAM HOWES COLLINS), civic worker; b. Portland, Ore., Aug. 30, 1911; d. Ralph Coffyn and Eugenie F. (Richet) Walker; A.B., Mills Coll., Oakland, Cal., 1932; m. William Howes Collins, Oct. 18, 1932; children—William Walker, Kent Howes, Derfla Jean. Sec., Intercontinental Assos., Inc., Essex, Conn., 1964—. Sec., Com. for N.J., 1933-36; scout leader Montclair (N.J.) council Girl Scouts U.S.A., 1934-37; bd. mgrs. 200 Club, Montclair, 1934-36; chmn. Mills Coll. Student Recommendation Com., N.J., N.Y., Conn., 1935-37; rep. Mills Coll. at 550th Anniversary Jubilee, Heidelberg, Germany, 1936, inauguration pres. convocation Carnegie Inst. Tech., 1948; organizer, chmn. Swarthmore br. Navy League Service, 1942-45; organizer Jr. Nells, Delaware County, Pa., 1943-45; pres. Shady Side Acad. Mothers Assn., Pitts., 1954-55; mem. Darien (Conn.) High Sch. Parents Adv. Com., 1962-65. Bd. dirs. Mt. Lebanon Lecture Soc. Recipient Meritorious Service bar, Silver bar Navy League Service; 1943, U.S. Treasury citation War Finance Program, 1944. Commd. lt. gen. Pa. Blue Star Brigade for conspicuous patriotic endeavor and outstanding accomplishment in sale war bonds, 1945. Mem. D.A.R., Essex Hist. Soc. Club: Essex Garden. Home: Kentwill Essex CT 06426

COLLINS, DOROTHY (MRS. AKIBA EMANUEL), advt. co. exec.; b. Salt Lake City; d. Joseph L. and Dorothy (Frey) Collins; A.B., U. Denver; m. Akiba Emanuel, Oct. 31, 1947; 1 dau., Lynn Collins. Woman's page editor Rocky Mountain News, Denver; fashion editor NBC, N.Y.C.; pub. relations dir. Woman's Home Companion, N.Y.C.; pub. relations mgr. Shwayder Bros., Denver; pub. relations account exec. Ellington & Co., N.Y.C.; v.p. Infoplan, N.Y.C.; now v.p., mgr. women's interest group Burson-Marsteller, N.Y.C. Former nat. dir. women's activities Nat. Jewish Hosp., Denver. Mem. Nat. Home Fashions League (v.p. 1973-74), Nat. Soc. Interior Designers, Asia House. Club: Denver Women's Press. Home: Hollis Lane Croton-on-Hudson NY 10520 Office: 866 3d Av New York City NY 10022

COLLINS, ELIZABETH HARPER, librarian; b. Centreville, Md., Dec. 23, 1915; d. John Frank and Mabel Price (Bryan) Harper; A.B., Goucher Coll., 1937; M.L.S., Rutgers U., 1957; m. Jackson Rosse Collins, Aug. 26, 1967; children—Elizabeth (Mrs. Henry R. Pupke), Susan (Mrs. A. Russum Orme), Sarah (Mrs. John W. Shepard). Desk asst. Enoch Pratt Free Library, Balt., 1940-41, 44-45, pre-profl. asst., 1953-54; library adminstr., dir. Queen Anne's County Free Library, Centreville, Md., 1954-59, Talbot County Free Library, Easton, Md., 1959-68; reference and acquisitions librarian Chesapeake Community Coll. Library, Wye Mills, Md., 1969—. Mem. Md. Gov.'s Commn. to Revise Pub. Library Laws, 1968-70. Active Meml. Hosp. Jr. Aux. Trustee Queen Anne's County Free Library, 1973—; bd. dirs. Queen Anne's County Hist. Soc., 1960-64, sec., 1968; bd. dirs. Queen Anne's County cancer Soc., 1970—, sec., 1972-73. Mem. Am., Md. (2d v.p. 1961-62) library assns., Pub. Library Adminstrs. Assn. (pres. Md. assn. 1965-66). Episcopalian (pres. ch. women 1973-74). Club: Harbor (Easton, Md.). Home: Spaniard's Point Centreville MD 21617 Office: Chesapeake Coll Library Wye Mills MD 21679

COLLINS, EVA MAE LOMERSON, ins. agt.; b. Lake Orion, Mich., July 10, 1930; d. J.M. and Thelma Marie (Kimmery) Lomerson; ed. U. Mich., Wayne State U.; m. John Armstrong Collins, Feb. 24, 1968. Dept. mgr. Sears Roebuck & Co., 1951-69; personal lines mgr. Bingham & Bingham, Inc., ins., 1970-73, comml. accounts mgr., resident ins. agt., 1973—. Mem. Nat. Assn. Ins. Women, Ins. Women Met. Detroit, D.A.R. (chpt. chmn. good citizens program, jr. mems., regent, vice regent, state chmn. pages and jr. mems. 1967-70, state outstanding jr. mem. 1966), Am. Bus. Women's Assn. (pres. Land-O-Oak chpt. 1964-65, woman of year 1965), Nat. Hist. Soc., Hist. Soc. Mich., Detroit Soc. Geneal. Research, U. Mich. Alumni Assn., Daus. Colonial Wars. Home: 1122 Mill Valley Rd Rochester MI 48063 Office: 101 Southfield Rd Birmingham MI 48009

COLLINS, GRETCHEN LANGE (MRS. WALTER EDES COLLINS), physician; b. Janesville, Wis., Jan. 9, 1938; d. Robert Echlin and Elizabeth Ann (Saunders) Lange; A.B. cum laude, Radcliffe, 1959; M.D., Harvard, 1965; m. Walter Edes Collins, May 23, 1967; children—Taylor David, Jason Michael. Intern, Med. Coll. Va., Richmond, 1965-66, resident surgery, 1966-67; resident pediatrics Childrens Hosp., Washington, 1967-69; practice medicine, specializing in pediatrics Community Group Health Found., Washington, 1969-73; mem. staffs Comprehensive Clinic of Children's Hosp., Washington, Freedmen's Hosp., Washington; clin. instr. pediatrics Howard Med. Sch., 1969—, George Washington U. Med. Sch., 1973—. Bd. dirs. Hopkins House, Alexandria, Va. Mem. Am. Pub. Health Assn., D.C. Med. Soc., D.C. Pub. Health Assn. Episcopalian. Home: 2319 Kimbro St Alexandria VA 22307 Office: 2125 13th St NW Washington DC 20009

COLLINS, HELEN CLARK (MRS. ARNOLD MILLER COLLINS), ednl. service co. exec.; b. Bklyn.; d. James Alexander and Alice (Van Velzor) Clark; B.S., Columbia, 1920, M.A., 1921, Ph.D., 1923; m. Arnold Miller Collins, June 28, 1924; 1 son, James Miller. Chem. technician Gen. Chem. Co., 1917-18; patent researcher E.I. duPont de Nemours & Co., Inc., 1928-30; tutor remedial reading, 1935-45; pres. Ednl. Service, Inc. diagnostic testing, reading cons. for learning disabilities, Wilmington, Del., 1945—, chmn. Ednl. Service Scholarship Found., 1965-72. Mem. com. Elementary Sch. Edn. Act Title I, 1965-67, mem. com. testing St. Paul's and St. Mary-St. Patrick's schs., 1974—. Dir. Kennett Consol. Sch. Bd., Kennett Square, Pa., 1955-70, chmn. pub. relations, 1966-70; dir. Beechwood Sch., 1970—; bd. mgrs. Friends Sch., Wilmington, 1935-55. Recipient outstanding service to children award Coordinating Council for Handicapped of Del., 1974. Mem. Internat. Reading Assn., Assn. Learning Disabilities, Am. Assn. U. Women, Orton Soc., Sigma Xi. Republican. Mem. Soc. of Friends. Author: We Discover Lights, 1935, 2d edit., 1950. Home: 1301 N Harrison St Wilmington DE 19806 Office: 1203 Gilpin Av Wilmington DE 19806

COLLINS, HELEN FLETCHER, writer, editor; b. La Monte, Mo., Jan. 10, 1894; d. James Harwood and Claudia Fields (O'Dell) Fletcher; A.A., Coll. of Redwoods, 1969; m. Kenneth L. Collins, Feb. 24, 1916 (dec. 1932); children;George Harwood (dec.), Adrian O'Dell (dec.), Thomas (dec.), Jessamine (Mrs. Dan A. Montelbetti), Kennth Claude, Carole Collins Kendall. Telegrapher, 1945-47; feature writer, soc. editor, reporter Holly Tribune, Lamar, Colo., 1947-52, Daily News, Daily Sun, Flagstaff, Ariz., 1952-56; contbr. column Arcata (Cal.) Union; mem. staff Am. Horologist and Jeweler mag., 1957—, also Diamond News, Kimberley, South Africa, Brit. Jeweller/Watch Buyer, Birmingham, Eng., Trade Post, Bombay, India. Pres., West High P.T.A., Denver, 1936-37. Dist. rep. Humboldt County (Cal.) Democratic Central Com., 1971—; state vice chmn. gubernatorial campaign, 1974. Mem. Am. Gem Soc. (hon. asso.), Am. Assn. Ret. Persons, Sr. Helpers Council, Eureka (Cal.) C. of C. (mem. image com. 1973—), N.Y. Poetry Forum, Nat. Fedn. State Poetry Socs., Nat. Fedn. Press Women (pres. Colo. 1958-59, founding pres. Ariz. 1954, organizer Utah 1955, regional dir. 1953-55, nat. historial 1958), Cal. Fedn. Chaparral Poets, Eureka Woman's Club, Soroptimists. Author (poetry) Prairie Wife, 1949; Pacific Symphony, 1972; The Wind Blows from the West. Home: 2214 Fairfield St Eureka CA 95501

COLLINS, JANICE ALMEDA BAKER (MRS. ROY F. COLLINS), real estate broker; b. Prague, Okla., Feb. 14, 1914; d. Harry Thomas and Myrtie Almeda (Wilmot) Baker; grad. Lumbleau Real Estate Sch., 1969; m. Roy F. Collins, Oct. 18, 1941; children—Galen Roy, Marlin Terry. Salesman Collins Real Estate, Woodland, Cal., 1962-70; real estate broker, Woodland, 1970—. Sec. Woodland div. Yolo County Bd. Realtors. Bd. dirs. YMCA Womens Club. Clubs: Square Dance, Beaux and Belles Square Dance (dir. 1968-69, 72). Address: 1130 McKinley Av Woodland CA 95695

COLLINS, JOYCE MARIE SLATKY (MRS. EDWARD D. COLLINS), educator; b. Kewaunee, Wis., Sept. 14, 1926; d. James J. and Carolyn A. (Andrele) Slatky; B.S., Mt. Mary Coll., 1948; m. Edward D. Collins, Nov. 25, 1950; children—Michael Sean, Maridaun, Patrick, Keyron, Kevin, Dan. Chief occupational therapist, coordinator Med. Coll. Ga., Augusta, 1961-64, 72—, instr. neurology, 1966-73, asst. prof. neurology, 1973—; cons. Hitchcock Rehab. Center, Aiken, S.C., 1964-66. Cons. developmental disabilities Med. Coll. Ga., Augusta, 1972—, instr. Sch. Occupational Therapy, 1972—, lectr. Sch. Phys. Therapy, 1973. Den Mother Cub Scouts Am., North Augusta, S.C., 1969—. Bd. dirs. United Cerebral Palsy, Augusta, 1962—; bd. dirs. Our Lady of Peace Sch., North Augusta, 1968—, pres., 1972; mem. utilization bd. Beverly Manor, Augusta, 1969-71. Named Therapist of Year, Ga. Occupational Therapy Assn., 1964. Mem. Am. Occupational Therapy Assn. (chmn. com. 1969), World Fedn. Occupational Therapists. Club: Crestland Garden (treas. 1973, pres. 1974) (North Augusta). Home: 1114 Seymour Dr North Augusta SC 29841 Office: Neurology Dept Med Coll Ga Augusta GA 30902

COLLINS, JUDY MARJORIE, singer; b. Seattle, May 1, 1939; d. Charles T. and Marjorie (Byrd) Collins; pvt. study piano, 1953-56; m. Peter A. Taylor, Apr. 1958 (div.); 1 son, Clark Collins. Made debut as profl. folk singer, Boulder, Colo., 1959, since has appeared in numerous clubs in U.S. and Can.; performer in concerts including Newport Folk Festival, Orch. Hall, Chgo., Carnegie Hall, N.Y.C., also appeared radio and TV; tours in Europe; producer, co-dir. documentary film Antonia: The Woman. Rec. artist Elektra albums A Maid of Constant Sorrow, Golden Apples of the Sun, Judy Collins 3, The Judy Collins Concert, Judy Collins 5, In My Life, Wildflowers, Who Knows Where The Time Goes, Recollections, Whales and Nightingales, Living, Colors of the Day, True Stories and Other Dreams. Author: Judy Collins Songbook. Home: care Rocky Mountain Prodns 1775 Broadway New York City NY 10019

COLLINS, LEALA MAE REAVES (MRS. JAMES BURNETT COLLINS), home economist; b. Webster, Fla., Dec. 25, 1928; d. Norman and Leala (Watkins) Reaves; A.A., Edward Waters Coll., 1948; B.S., Fla. A. and M. U., 1951; postgrad. Prairie View A. and M. Coll., 1954, 62; m. James Burnett Collins, July 10, 1961. Negro home demonstration agt. Fla. Agrl. Extension Service, U. Fla., Putnam County, Palatka, 1953-62; extension home econs. agt. Fla. by Fla. Coop. Extension Service, U. Fla., Orange County, Orlando, 1963—. Recipient Plaque for outstanding service Putnam County Homemaker's Council, 1961, Distinguished Service award Coop. Extension Service, 1965. Mem. Am. Home Econs. Assn., Nat. (exhibit chmn. 1962-63), Fla. State (v.p. 1962-64) assns. extension home economists, Outlook Central Fla. (2d v.p. 1972-73), Epsilon Sigma Phi, Gamma Phi Delta. Baptist. Mem. Order Eastern Star. Home: 355 Coleman Pl Orlando FL 32805 Office: 2350 E Michigan Av Orlando FL 32806

COLLINS, LENORA WASHINGTON, home economist; b. Fayette, Miss., Feb. 25, 1925; d. Jurel and Winnie (Hudson) Washington; B.S., Xavier U. of La., 1946; M.A., Governors State U., 1974; m. Joe H. Collins, Aug. 13, 1951; 1 son, Tracy A. With Cook County Dept. Pub. Aid, Chgo., 1955—, asst. chief bur. home econs., 1967—. Tchr. home econs. Chgo. Bd. Edn., 1948-54. Organizer, Wacker Neighborhood Assn., 1972, bd. dirs., 1972—, chmn. nominating com., 1972-73. Mem. Am. (life), Ill. (life) home econs. assns., Chgo. Home Econs. Assn. (pres. 1970-71), Chgo. Nutrition Assn., Am. Pub. Welfare Assn., Delta Sigma Theta. Home: 1055 W 98th St Chicago IL 60643 Office: 624 S Michigan Av Chicago IL 60605

COLLINS, LOIS COWAN (MRS. VINCENT PATRICK COLLINS), physician; b. McKeesport, Pa., July 1, 1914; d. Victor W. and Mabel (Cook) Cowan; B.S., U. Pitts., 1937, M.D., 1937; m. Vincent Patrick Collins, Dec. 26, 1942; children—Arthur Cowan, Vincent Ross, Christopher Ray. Intern McKeesport (Pa.) Hosp., 1937-38; resident in radiology Mass. Meml. Hosp., Boston, 1939-42; practice medicine specializing in radiology N.Y.C., 1942-52, Houston, 1952—; mem. faculty Columbia U. Coll. Physicians and Surgeons, 1942-52, Baylor U. Coll. Medicine, 1952-68; clin. asso. prof. radiology U. Tex. Postgrad. Sch. Med. and Biomed. Scis. at Houston, 1953—; asst. radiologist M.D. Anderson Hosp. and Tumor Inst., Houston, 1953-65; attending radiologist Meth. Hosp., 1962-65, Ben Taub Gen. Hosp., 1965-68, radiologist Rosewood Gen. Hosp., 1968— (all Houston). Fellow Am. Coll. Radiologists; mem. Am., Tex., Harris County med. assns., Radiol. Soc. N.Am., Am. Roentgen Ray Soc., Tex., Houston (pres. 1967-68) radiol. socs., Houston Gastroenterol. Soc. Co-author: (with C.W. Schwartz) The Skull and Brain Roentgenographically Considered, 1951; Radiological Diagnosis of Small Bowel Lesions, Cancer of the Gastro-Intestinal Tract, 1967; Diagnostic Radiology-The Digestive Tract, 1969. Home: 105 Shasta Dr Houston TX 77024 Office: 9200 Westheimer St Houston TX 77042

COLLINS, LORA SUZANNE, economist; b. Bklyn., Nov. 14, 1935; d. Warren E. and Marion (Farrell) Collins; B.A., Smith Coll., 1957; M.A. (Woodrow Wilson fellow 1959-60), Harvard, 1961, Ph.D., 1965. Economist Fed. Reserve Bank N.Y., N.Y.C., 1964-69, chief domestic research div., 1968-69; chief economist, editor Survey of Current Bus., Bur. Econ. Analysis, U.S. Dept. Commerce, Washington, 1969-74; v.p., economist Chase Manhattan Bank, N.Y.C., 1974—. Recipient Gold Medal award for distinguished service Dept. Commerce, 1973. Mem. Am. Econ. Assn., Am. Statis. Assn., Nat. Assn. Bus. Economists, Phi Beta Kappa. Home: 40 Fifth Av New York City NY 10011 Office: 1 Chase Manhattan Plaza New York City NY 10015

COLLINS, MARCIA LYNN (MRS. RUDOLF A. HOFMANN), obstetrician; b. Dayton, O., July 17, 1940; d. Harold Farrell and Clare Angela (Noble) Collins; B.A., Miami U., Oxford, O., 1962, M.A. (fellow), 1964; M.D., Med. Coll. Pa., 1968; m. Rudolf A. Hofmann, Sept. 5, 1969. Intern, Miami Valley Hosp., Dayton, O., 1968-69, resident in obstetrics, 1969-72; practice medicine, specializing in high risk obstetrics, Dayton, 1972—; mem. staff Miami Valley Hosp., dir. Adolescent Prenatal Clinic, sec., v.p. House Staff Council, 1969-70, dir. obstetrical intensive care unit, 1973, asso. dir. dept. obstetrics and gynecology, 1973; med. dir. Dayton Woman's Health Center, 1973; adj. asst. prof. Wright State U., 1973. Mem. coordinating com. Second Nat. House Staff Conf., 1971-72. Mem. A.A.A.S., Am. Med. Woman's Assn., Am. Fertility Soc., Am. Coll. Obstetricians and Gynecologists, Student A.M.A. (regional v.p. 1967-68), Jr. League. Republican. Clubs: Women's, Opera Guild (Dayton). Home: 335 Southview Rd Dayton OH 45419 Office: 26 Wyoming St Dayton OH 45409

COLLINS, MARIAN PATRICIA PRZYWARA (MRS. JOHN J. COLLINS), coll. adminstr.; b. Hartford, Conn., Oct. 4, 1944; d. Andrew A. and Stella D. (Zieminski) Przywara; B.S., Central Conn. State Coll., 1966; M.A., U. Conn., 1967; m. John J. Collins, Apr. 27, 1968. Counselor, U. Hartford (Conn.), 1967; tchr. math. Timothy Edwards Jr. High Sch. South Windsor, Conn., 1967-68, Big Springs (Tex.) High Sch., 1968-69; asst. to dean coll. Greater Hartford (Conn.) Community Coll., 1970-71, dir. financial aid and placement, 1971—. Mem. Nat., Eastern assns. student financial aid adminstrs., Am. Assn. Community Colls., New Eng. Assn. Jr. Colls. and Employers Assn., Conn. Dirs. Financial Aid. Clubs: Flying Yankee Officer's Wives, Socially Yours (v.p. 1971-75). Office: 61 Woodland St Hartford CT 06105

COLLINS, MARJEANNE (MRS. LUIS BLASCO), pediatrician; b. St. Louis, Dec. 8, 1935; d. Walter J. and Marjorie Kathleen (Rees) Collins; A.B., Bryn Mawr Coll., 1957; M.D., U. Pa., 1961; m. Luis Blasco, May 30, 1970. Intern Bryn Mawr (Pa.) Hosp., 1961-62; resident Hosp. of U. Pa., Phila., 1963-66; practice medicine specializing in pediatrics, Phila., 1966—; mem. staff Hosp. of U. Pa., Children's Hosp. of Phila.; pediatric coordinator children and youth program Children's Hosp., Phila., 1970-71; instr. pediatrics U. Pa. Med. Sch., 1966—. Fellow Am. Acad. Pediatrics; mem. Am. Civil Liberties Union, Ams. for Democratic Action, SANE, Phila. Pediatric Soc., Philadelphia County Med. Soc. Home: 26 University Mews Philadelphia PA 19104 Office: Garden Ct Apts 47th and Pine Sts Philadelphia PA 19143

COLLINS, MARY BETH (MRS. TABER LOREE COLLINS), assn. exec.; b. Detroit, Jan. 3, 1925; d. James Edward and Mildred Ina (Barding) Hughes; B.A., Manhattanville Coll. of Sacred Heart, 1947; M.A., Ariz. State U., 1970; m. Taber Loree Collins, Aug. 7, 1947; children—Louise (Mrs. Conwell O. Ponath), James, Suzanne (Mrs. Lance Giroux), Mary Beth, Mildred (Mrs. Richard Wilson), Marguerite, Miriam, Frank, Jesse, Kathleen, Martha. Case worker Maricopa County Welfare Dept., Phoenix, 1965-67; community services coordinator Alcohol and Drug Abuse div. Ariz. Health Dept., Phoenix, 1967-68, acting dir., 1968-70; coordinator City of Phoenix Drug Control, 1970-73; exec. dir. Drug Action Coalition, Montgomery County, Md., 1973-74; exec. dir. Community Orgn. for

Drug Abuse Control, 1974—. Cons. Sch. Alcohol Studies, U. Ariz., 1969, Drug Abuse Workshop, Ariz. State U. and Ariz. Western Coll., 1969, Ill. Health Dept., 1971, Neb. Sch. Alcohol Studies, 1972. Mem. regional and state task forces on alcohol, narcotics and drug abuse Ariz. Justice Planning, 1970-73, 74—. Pres. Ariz. Family, Inc., 1970-71; bd. dirs. Community Orgn. for Drug Abuse Control, 1969-73; mem. adv. bd. Good Samaritan Hosp., Mental Health Services; mem. ad hoc adv. bd. on drug abuse prevention Montgomery County Bd. Edn., 1973-74. Mem. Alcohol and Drug Problems Assn. N.Am., Internat. Council on Alcoholism and Addictions, Counselors on Alcoholism and Related Disorders, Ariz. Alumnae of Sacred Heart (founding pres. 1963-64), Pi Lambda Theta. Home: 6401 W Campbell Phoenix AZ 85033 Office: 760 E McDowell Phoenix AZ 85006

COLLINS, MARY FRANCES WHITE, home economist; b. Pine Mountain, Ga., May 3, 1939; d. O.E. and Mary (Davis) White; student Tift Coll., 1957-60; B.S., The Womens Coll. Ga., 1961; M.S. in Home Mgmt. (Ellen H. Richards fellow Am. Home Econs. Assn. 1965), U. Tenn., 1966; m. William Randolph Collins, Aug. 27, 1972. Asst. county extension home economist Coop. Extension Service, Cobb County, Marietta, Ga., 1961-62, county extension home economist, Monroe County, Forsyth, Ga., 1962-65, Clayton County, Jonesboro, Ga., 1966-67, extension home furnishings and art specialist U. Ga., Athens, 1968-70, extension home mgmt. specialist, 1970-72; substitute tchr. Cobb County Sch. System, 1972-73; mgr. div. domestics and gifts Davison's at Cumberland Mall, Atlanta, 1973—; Food coordinator Operation Buddy program VA Hosp. Mem. Ga. Home Econ. Assn. (state sec. 1968-70, chmn. 10th dist. 1971-72). Methodist (chmn. worship and social concern com.). Club: Pilot (corr. sec. 1971-72) (Athens). Home: 200 Fontaine Rd Mableton GA 30059

COLLINS, MURIEL MORSE (MRS. DENIS AUGUSTUS COLLINS), ret. found. exec.; b. Bklyn., Apr. 15, 1912; d. Frederick and Henrietta (Grasser) Morse; grad. high sch.; m. Denis Augustus Collins, Nov. 15, 1952. Dept. head Uniform Printing & Supply Co., Bklyn., 1935-45; sec., bookkeeper Borough Press, Inc., N.Y.C., 1945-52; pvt. sec. to service mgr. Atlantic Service Co., 1952-57; asst. sec., asst. treas., confidential sec. to chmn. bd. Shaker Mus. Found., Inc., Old Chatham, N.Y., 1957-68; sec. Greater Charlotte County C. of C., Port Charlotte, Fla., 1969-70; reporter Sarasota Jour., 1970-72. Mem. Old Chatham Improvement Assn., 1952—; past chaplain Old Chatham Grange; sec. Charlotte County Pageant Assn., 1969; charter mem. Tri-Village Fire Aux., pres., 1965-66. Mem. Am. Assn. Ret. Persons, Nat. Fedn. Bus. and Profl. Women's Clubs (charter pres. 1968), Am. Assn. Museums, N.Y. State Hist. Assn., Early Am. Industries Assn., N.E. Museums Conf., Port Charlotte Bus. and Profl. Women's Club, Animal Welfare League Charlotte County, Port Charlotte Civic Assn., Fla. Sheriff's Assn. (hon. mem.), Med. Center Aux. Punta Gorda, Intercontinental Biog. Assn. Clubs: Charlotte County Booster, Empire State (Charlotte County, Fla.); Alan Devoe Bird. Home: 3159 Windmill Village Punta Gorda FL 33950

COLLINS, PATRICIA ANN, educator; b. Madison, Wis., Sept. 9, 1931; d. Earl L. and Stella (Morelli) Collins; B.S., Wis. State U., 1953; M.S., U. Wis., 1960; Ph.D., U. Ia., 1968. Tchr. phys. edn. Wilson Jr. High Sch., Appleton, Wis., 1953-59; prof. phys. edn. Wis. State U., Platteville, 1960—. Mem. Nat., Wis. edn. assns., Am., Wis. (chmn. membership 1953-54, v.p. health 1968-69) assns. health, phys. edn. and recreation, Wis. Div. Girls and Women's Sports, Wis. Women's Interscholastic Athletic Assn. (chmn. 1972—), Delta Psi Kappa, Kappa Delta Pi, Pi Lambda Theta. Research in film analysis of overarm, side arm throw, 1962, a film analysis of selected swimming stroke kicks, 1968. Home: 995 7th Av Platteville WI 53818

COLLINS, WANDA PEARL, testing service exec.; b. Yuma, Ariz., June 26, 1932; d. William F. and Pearl (Edmundson) Collins; B.A., Eastern N.M. U., 1956; M.A., U. Colo., 1962. Counselor Cherry Creek High Sch., Englewood, Colo., 1956-60; dir. residence hall U. Colo., 1960-61, asst. dean women, 1961-64, asso. dean women, 1964-66; dir. counseling Colo. Woman's Coll., Denver, 1966-68; dean students Dominican Coll., San Rafael, Cal., 1968-70; asst. dir. operations Ednl. Testing Service, Berkeley, Cal., 1970—. Mem. adv. bd. Upward Bound, Colo. Woman's Coll., 1966-68; mem. Colo. Co-ordinating Council Women's Orgns., 1966-67. Named to Outstanding Young Women Am., 1966. Mem. San Rafael C. of C. (mem. community action com. 1969-70), Nat., Colo. (pres. 1966-67) assns. women deans and counselors, Cal. Assn. Women Deans and Vice Prins., Colo.-Wyo. Acad. Sci., Am. Personnel and Guidance Assn. (area exec. sec. 1958-59), Alpha Sigma Chi. Home: 4344 Fleming Av Oakland CA 94619 Office: 1947 Center St Berkeley CA 94704

COLLIS, LOUISE EDITH, author; b. Burma, Jan. 29, 1925; d. Maurice Stewart and Eleanor Louise (Bourke) Collis; B.A., Reading U. (Eng.), 1945. Author: Without A Voice, 1951; A Year Passed, 1952; The Angel's Name, 1955; After The Holiday, 1954; Seven in the Tower, 1958; The Great Flood, 1966; The Apprentice Saint, 1964; Soldier In Paradise, 1965; A Private View Of Stanley Spencer, 1972. Home: 65 Cornwall Gardens London SW7 England

COLLYER, MURIEL MATOTT (MRS. GEORGE C. COLLYER), home economist; b. Plattsburgh, N.Y., June 24, 1921; d. Milon Meader and Neila Mabel (Atwood) Matott; B.S., State U. N.Y. at Plattsburgh, 1942, permanent certificate, 1969; m. George C. Collyer, Dec. 17, 1948 (dec. Jan. 1965); children—Steven, Susan, Sally. Program leader home econs. Warren County Coop. Extension, Warrensburg, N.Y., 1966—. Co-chmn. Warren County Interagy. Council, 1970-72, mem., 1973—; chmn. eastern dist. Extension Home Economists, 1971. Mem. community services com. Adirondack Community Coll., 1971. Mem. Mayor's Com. Aging, 1973—, adv. com. Warren Hamilton Counties Office for Aging, 1974—. Bd. dirs. Warren Hamilton Counties Action Com. Econ. Opportunity, Inc., 1967—, mem. exec. com., 1967-71. Mem. Am. Home Econs. Assn., Nat. Assn. Extension Home Economists, Home Econs. Tchrs. Assn., Plattsburgh Alumni Assn. Home: 5 Carleton Ct Glens Falls NY 12801 Office: 17 Hudson St Warrensburg NY 12885

COLOMBO, ELDA A., librarian; b. Chgo., 1909; d. Luigi and Maria (Zordan) Colombe; B.S., U. Chgo., 1942, B.L.S., 1946. Reference librarian Chgo. Pub. Library, 1936-54, br. librarian, 1954-59, chief edn. dept., 1959-65, asst. librarian, central library, 1965—. Mem. A.L.A., N.E.A., Spl. Libraries Assn., Ill. Library Assn., Chgo. Library Club. Contbr. articles in field to profl. jours. Home: 12138 Princeton Av Chicago IL 60628 Office: 78 E Washington St Chicago IL 60602

COLONE, ANN LINDBERGH, TV personality, commentator; b. Fort Wayne, Ind.; d. Joseph and Mary (LaRosa) Colone; grad. high sch. Sec., traffic mgr. WKJG, Fort Wayne, 1947-50; traffic mgr. WGL. Ft. Wayne, 1950-58; woman's dir. WANE-TV, Fort Wayne, 1958—, also promotion dir., hostess Ann Colone Shows, 1958—. Narrator style shows; narrator Fort Wayne Philharmonic Orch.; appeared various prodns. in Festival Music. Adviser, A.R.C., 1957-59. Vice pres. Young Democrats Club, 1955-58. Bd. dirs. Limberlost council Girl Scouts U.S.A., 1950-53, Festival Music Theatre, 1951-61, Fine Arts Found., 1959-62; trustee Ind. grand lodge Order Sons Italy, 1953-56, Allen County Cancer Soc. Recipient TV Radio Mirror Mag. Gold medal award for Best TV Women's Interest Show for Mid-West, 1960, citations various civic and mil. orgns; Best Actress Gold Anthony award Ft. Wayne Civic Theatre, 1968-69; Gold medal Nat. Found.-March Dimes; Gold Plaque award for meritorious services Northeastern Ind. Kennel Club, 1972; Gold Parky award Ft. Wayne Park Bd. Theatre Workshop, 1972; Sterling Cup award TV Picture Life mag., 1974. Roman Catholic. Clubs: Orders Sons Italy Women's (pres. 1952-53); Fort Wayne Press (past v.p., dir., charter mem.), Fort Wayne Advertising. Home: 3207 Bellshire Way Fort Wayne IN 46805 Office: 2915 W State Blvd Fort Wayne IN 46808

COLORNI, EVELINA, educator; b. Milan, Italy; degrees in Music and Linguistics, U. Milan, Mozarteum, Salzburg, Austria; other mus. study Munich, Germany, London, Eng., also spl. study speech, voice therapy. Tchr. lyric diction langs., phonetics various schs. U.S., 1939—, including Mannes Coll. Music, N.Y.C., Finch Jr. Coll., N.Y.C., N.Y. Singing Tchrs. Assn., Music Acad. of West, Santa Barbara, Cal., Aspen (Colo.) Music Sch.; mem. faculty Juilliard Sch. Music, N.Y.C., 1952—; staff San Francisco Opera Merola program, 1960—; staff Juilliard Am. Opera Center, 1969—. Author: Singers' Italian, A Manual of Diction and Phonetics, 1970. Contbr. articles to profl. jours. Office: Juilliard School Lincoln Center Plaza New York City NY 10023

COLP, CHARLOTTE RAPPAPORT (MRS. RALPH COLP, JR.), physician; b. N.Y.C., Dec. 18, 1930; d. Israel and Regina (Stern) Rappaport; B.A. cum laude, Radcliffe, 1951; M.D., N.Y. U., 1955; m. Ralph Colp, Jr., Nov. 24, 1956; children—Ruth, Judith. Intern, Montefiore Hosp., Bronx, N.Y., 1955-56, resident, 1956-57; resident Beth Israel Hosp., Boston, 1957-59; practice medicine specializing in chest diseases, N.Y.C., 1960—; mem. staff Bronx Municipal Hosp.; clin. asso. prof. medicine, attending physician Albert Einstein Coll. Medicine, 1960—; adj. attending physician Montefiore Hosp.; chest cons. Beth Abraham Hosp. Fellow Am. Thoracic Soc., Am. Coll. Chest Physicians, mem. A.M.A., N.Y. County Med. Soc. Contbr. articles to profl. jours. Address: 350 Central Park W New York City NY 10025

COLSON, ELIZABETH FLORENCE, anthropologist; b. Hewitt, Minn., June 15, 1917; d. Louis H. and Metta (Damon) Colson; B.A., U. Minn., 1938, M.A., 1940; M.A., Radcliffe Coll., 1941, Ph.D. (Am. Assn. U. Women Travelling fellow 1942-43), 1945. Asst. social sci. analyst War Relocation Authority, 1942-43; research asst. Harvard, 1944-45; research officer Rhodes-Livingston Inst., 1946-47, dir., 1948-51; sr. lectr. Manchester U., 1951-53; asso. prof. Goucher Coll., 1954-55; research asso. African Research Program, Boston U., 1955-59, part-time 1959-63; prof. anthropology Brandeis U., 1959-63; prof. anthropology U. Cal. at Berkeley, 1964—. Fellow Center for Advanced Study in Behavioral Scis., Stanford, 1967-68. Fellow Am. Anthrop. Assn., African Studies Assn., Brit. Assn. Social Anthropologists, Royal Anthrop. Inst.; mem. Phi Beta Kappa. Author: The Makah, 1953; Marriage and the Family Among The Plateau Tonga, 1958; Social Organization of the Gwembe Tonga, 1960, The Plateau Tonga, 1962; The Social Consequences of Resettlement, 1971; Tradition and Contract, 1974. Sr. editor: Seven Tribes of British Central Africa, 1951. Office: Dept Anthropology U Cal Berkeley CA 94720

COLSON, ERNESTINE CELENDA STANFORD (MRS. JOHN EVERETTE COLSON), civic worker; b. Chgo., July 17, 1903; d. George Ernest and Celenda Alden (Pease) Stanford; student Augustana Coll., 1926-27; A.B., Denison U., 1929; registered occupational therapist Va. Commonwealth U., 1947; M.A., U. Ia., 1971; m. John Everette Colson, Dec. 24, 1955. Tchr. elementary schs., Rock Island and Marion, Ill., 1922-25; tchr. Week Day Sch. of Religion, Rock Island and Oak Park, 1929-32; tchr. Lotts Creek Community Sch., Hazard, Ky., 1935-38; therapist VA, Marion, Ill., 1947-53, Madison, Wis., 1953-54, Nat. Soc. for Crippled Children and Adults, Peoria, Ill., 1954-59, Galesburg, Ill., 1960-63; dir. occupational therapy Klein Meml. Hosp., Burlington, Ia., 1964-67; free-lance cons. occupational therapy, 1967-68; tchr. certified occupational therapy Kirkwood Community Coll., Cedar Rapids, Ia., 1969-70; dir. edn. Lead Poisoning Prevention Program, Burlington, 1973. Vol. craft worker Burlington Care Center, 1973—. Baptist (deacon 1968, ch. clk. 1971). Rebekah. Clubs: Pilot, Altrusa. Home: Sylvan Heights Route 2 Burlington IA 52601

COLSON, JUDITH KELLY, librarian; b. Syracuse, N.Y., Sept. 1, 1936; d. Clyde Logan and Myrtle (Fairfield) Kelly; B.A., Roberts Wesleyan Coll., 1958; M.S., in L.S., Syracuse U., 1960; m. Theodore Colson, Sept. 4, 1957; 1 dau., Amy. Readers adviser Syracuse Pub. Library, 1960-61; acquisitions librarian U. Mich., Ann Arbor, 1961-67; documents librarian U. N.B., Fredericton, 1967—. Mem. Am., Canadian library assns., Beta Phi Mu. Home: 230 Winslow St Fredericton NB E3B 2A1 Canada

COLT, JULIE GEORGE HEWITT (MRS. S. BARCLAY COLT), civic worker; b. Princeton, N.J.; d. Charles Albert and Mary Leslie (Guion) George; student Vassar Coll., 1921-23; m. Edward Cooper Hewitt, June 11, 1927 (dec. Aug. 1966); children—Mary Leslie Guion (Mrs. David Waddell Bird), Edward Cooper; m. 2d, S. Barclay Colt, Sept. 15, 1973. Social reporter, social editor Elizabeth (N.J.) Daily Jour., 1920-35, N.Y. Herald Tribune, 1925-37, Charm mag., Newark, 1928-33, Sportsman Mag., Summit, N.J., 1933-36, Newark Sunday Call, 1930-40, Newark Evening News, 1940-45; saleslady Morrell Studio Portraits, Plainfield, N.J., 1932-38. Pres., Jr. League, Elizabeth, 1941-43; pres., exec. com. N.J. Jr. Leagues, 1943-45. Trustee, Vail Deane Sch., Elizabeth, N.J., 1967—, chmn. centennial com., 1967-69. Episcopalian. Clubs: Elizabeth Town and Country, Vassar (Essex County chpt.), Baltusrol Golf, Bay Head Yacht, Elizabethtown Cotillion. Home: 50 Georgian Ct Elizabeth NJ 07208 also 634 East Av Bay Head NJ 08742

COLTHART, SHIRLEY MAE, psychiatrist, b. Waterford, Ont., Can., Feb. 24, 1915; d. Ernest Robert and Pearle (Lamont) Fitch; A.B., Denison U., 1937; M.D., U. Western Ont., 1942; m. John Marshall Colthart, Apr. 4, 1942; children—James Myron, Carol (Mrs. Robert M. Brock), Peggy (Mrs. Robert J. McCalla), Alice, Joan (Mrs. David Robertson). Intern, Toronto (Ont.) East Gen. Hosp., 1942-43; resident, asst. supt. Ont. Hosp., Toronto, 1943-46; practice medicine, specializing in psychiatry, Toronto, 1946-54; cons. Psychiatry Geriatric Study Centre, Toronto, 1954-65; dir. geriatric program J. Madden Mental Health Center, Chgo., 1967-69; clin. asst. prof. dept. psychiatry Loyola U. Stritch Med. Sch., Chgo., 1967-69; psychiatrist Community Mental Health Center, Rochester, N.Y., 1970—; asst. prof. U. Rochester Med. Sch., 1970—. Recipient alumni citation, Denison U., 1971. Mem. Ont. Med. Assn. (sec. geriatrics sect. 1963-65), Am. Psychiat. Assn., Am. Geriatrics Soc., Phi Beta Kappa, Alpha Omega Alpha, Alpha Phi. Presbyn. Contbr. articles in field to profl. jours. Home: 102 Panorama Trail Rochester NY 14625 Office: 260 Crittenden Blvd Rochester NY 14642

COLTON, HATTIE KAWAHARA, educator; b. Portland, Ore., Feb. 18, 1921; d. Ayao and Yoshino (Naito) Kawahara; student Reed Coll., 1939-42; B.A., Mt. Holyoke Coll., 1943, M.A., 1945; Ph.D., U. Minn., 1949; m. Kenneth Elmer Colton, June 15, 1954; children—Kendrew Hiram, Barbara Mary, David Everett. Grad. asst. Mt. Holyoke Coll., South Hadley, Mass., 1943-45, U. Minn., 1947-48, instr., 1948; instr., asst. prof. Wayne State U., 1948-55; Ford Found. fellow fgn. area tng., Tokyo, Japan, 1952-54; asst. prof. Internat. Christian U., 1955-58; prof., chmn., East Asia, area studies Fgn. Service Inst., Dept. State, Washington, 1961—. Mem. Am. Polit. Sci. Assn., Assn. for Asian Studies. Contbr. articles to profl. jours. Home: 4619 Hunt Ave Chevy Chase MD 20015 Office: Fgn Service Inst Dept of State Washington DC 20520

COLTON, HELEN (MRS. IRVIN E. GOOD), author; b. Newark, Jan. 4, 1918; d. Sander and Rose (Colton) Grossman; m. Martin Field, Nov. 19, 1942 (div. Mar. 1965); children—Mona, Corey; m. 2d, Irvin E. Good, Oct. 9, 1969. Free-lance writer mag. articles, 1940—; capital transactional analysis therapist Los Angeles, 1971—; lectr. numerous U.S. colls. Founder, moderator, lectr. Family Forum, Los Angeles, 1965—; mem. Western Regional Conf. Ombudsman, 1968—; mem. faculty Inst. Comprehensive Medicine. Mem. Los Angeles City Commn. Human Relations, 1968—. Hon. bd. dirs. Soc. Human Abortion. Mem. Nat. Conf. Family Relations, Am. Assn. Sex Educators and Counselors, Soc. Sci. Study Sex, Assn. Humanistic Psychology, Am. Soc. Psychosomatic Dentistry and Medicine, Internat. Acad. Forensic Psychology, Transactional Analysis Assn., Am. Humanist Assn., Harbor Soc. Clin. Hypnosis, A.F.T.R.A. Author: Adults Need Sex Education, Too, 1970; What's on Woman's Future Agenda?, 1967; Our Sexual Evolution, 1971; Sex after the Sexual Revolution, 1972. Address: 9735 Wilshire Blvd Beverly Hills CA 90212

COLUCCI, GENEVIEVE LUCY, therapist; b. Cornwall, Ont., Can., Dec. 12, 1934; d. James and Florence (Sullivan) Colucci; student St. Joseph's Sch. Nursing, 1957; postgrad. maternal and child care Margaret Hague Maternity Hosp., Jersey City, 1958; certificate nursing edn. and adminstrn. Ottawa U., 1967-68; postgrad. Harrisburg Sch. Enterostomal Therapists, 1973. Staff nurse delivery room Hotel Dieu Hosp., Cornwall, Ont., Can., 1957, head nurse obstetrics, 1958-63; missionary, Dominican Republic, 1963-64; clin. instr. obstetrics Hotel Dieu Hosp., Cornwall, Ont., Can., 1964-67, dir. in-service edn. dept., 1969—. Co-dir. Companions of St. Luke, 1973. Physicians Services Inc. Found. fellow, 1974. Home: 423 6th St E Cornwall ON K6H 2P2 Canada Office: Hotel Dieu Hosp 840 McConnell Av Room 522 Cornwall Ontario K6H 585 Canada

COLUMBRO, SISTER MARY ELECTA, educator; b. Aurora, O., Mar. 16, 1934; d. Nicola and Nancy (DeNicola) Columbro; B.A., Notre Dame Coll., 1956; M.A., Cath. U. Am., 1966; Ph.D. (Ranney Found. grantee), Case Western Res. U., 1974. Instr. various Ohio Sch., 1956-62; prof. music Notre Dame Coll., Cleve., 1963—, chmn. music dept., 1963—. Kulas Found. grantee, 1970; Newberry Library fellow, Chgo., 1973. Address: 4545 College Rd Cleveland OH 44121

COLVIN, EMSIE D., librarian; b. Letohatchee, Ala., Dec. 4, 1912; d. William Joseph and Malissa (Alexander) Davis; B.S., Ala. State U., 1941, M.Ed., 1950; M.S. in Library Sci., Case Western Res. U., 1956; m. Willie Graham Colvin, Sept. 20, 1946. Tchr. elementary schs., Butler and Lowndes counties, Ala., 1932-41; tchr. Chapman (Ala.) High Sch., 1941-43; tchr. Bapt. Hill High Sch., 1943-45, prin., 1945; tchr. Mt. Zion Elementary Sch., Greenville, Ala., 1945-47; with Fairfield (Ala.) Bd. of Edn., Birmingham Bd. of Edn., Ala., 1947-50; librarian Talladega County Schs., 1950-53; librarian Daniel Payne Coll., Birmingham, Ala., 1955—. Mem. Ala. Council on Human Relations, Birmingham, 1964—; active YWCA; mem. Ala. Christian Movement, 1964—. Recipient Human Relation award Pi Lambda Sigma, 1970. Mem. Am., Ala., Southeastern library assns., Ala. Media and Materials Assn., Nat., Ala., edn. assns., N.A.A.C.P., Alpha Chi Pi Omega. Clubs: Sojourner Truth Federate, Alert 12 Profl., City Federation of Women's. Baptist (Sunday sch. tchr.). Home: 726 Alabama Av Birmingham AL 35211 Office: Daniel Payne College Birmingham AL 35212

COLWELL, FRANCES IONE (MRS. DEWEY CARROLL COLWELL), city ofcl.; b. Collinsville, Tex., Nov. 17, 1924; d. James Roy and Vira Ione (Smith) Rudd; grad. Draughn's Bus. Coll., 1943; m. Dewey Carroll Colwell, Nov. 1, 1946; children—Charlotte Dawn (Mrs. Joel McCoy Barger), Karen Michelle (Mrs. Steven Craig Childers). Clk.-typist U.S. Govt., Camp Howze, Tex., 1943; sec., bookkeeper Coca-Cola Bottling Co., Gainesville, Tex., 1944-46; sec. B.F. Goodrich Rubber Co., Borger, Tex., 1946-48; sec. U.S. Rubber Co., Borger, 1948-50; bookkeeper Bill & Joe Automotive, Ft. Worth, 1957-61; city sec. City of White Settlement, Tex., 1961—. Mem. Assn. City Clks. and Secs. Tex., White Settlement C. of C., North Central Tex. City Secs. Assn., Bus. and Profl. Women's Club. Baptist (Sunday Sch. tchr. 1969—, ch. clk. 1974—). Home: 8500 Gibbs Dr White Settlement TX 76108 Office: 214 Meadow Park Dr White Settlement TX 76108

COLWELL, RITA ROSSI, educator, scientist; b. Beverly, Mass., Nov. 23, 1934; d. Louis and Louise (DiPalma) Rossi; B.S., Purdue U., 1956, M.S., 1958; Ph.D., U. Wash., 1961; m. Jack H. Colwell, May 31, 1956; children—Alison Eleanor Louise, Stacie Anne. Asst. research prof. U. Wash., 1961-63; guest scientist Nat. Research Council Can., 1963-64; vis. asst. prof. Georgetown U., 1963-64, asst. prof., then asso. prof., 1964-72; prof. microbiology U. Md., 1972—; cons. in field. Trustee Am. Type Culture Collection, 1970—. NSF grantee, 1963—, NIH grantee, 1969—, Environmental Protection Agy. grantee 1970—, Office Naval Research grantee, 1964—. Fellow A.A.A.S., Washington Acad. Sci., Am. Acad. Microbiology; mem. Am. Soc. Microbiology, Soc. Gen. Microbiology, Canadian Soc. Microbiologists, Am. Soc. Limnology and Oceanography, Severn Sailing Assn., Delta Gamma. Author: Effect of the Ocean Environment on Microbial Activities, 1974; Estuarine Microbial Ecology, 1973; Methods in Aquatic Microbiology, 1972; Lab. Manual for Estuarine and Marine Microbiology, 1975; also numerous articles, abstracts and chpt. in book. Editorial bd. Applied Microbiology; asso. editor Canadian Jour. Microbiology, Jour. Microbiol. Ecology. Home: 6313 Walhonding Rd Washington DC 20016 Office: Dept Microbiology Univ Md College Park MD 02742

COLYER, BERTHA MARIE VANZANDT (MRS. CURLEY COLYER), city ofcl.; b. Van Buren, Ark., Jan. 15, 1912; d. James and Gertrude E. (Morrison) VanZandt; student pub. schs., Piedmont, Kan.; m. Edwin F. Nicholas, Oct. 15, 1932 (dec. May 1939); 1 son, Edwin; m. 2d, Curley Colyer, Jan. 12, 1949; 1 dau., Pavela L. (Mrs. Richard W. James). Mayor, Grenville, N.M., 1971—, asst. postmaster, 1967—. Leader 4-H, 1950—; chmn. Union County Women's Extension Council, 1963-65, treas., 1961-62, 69-70; treas. Women's Soc. Christian Service, 1951—. Recipient award J.C. Penney Co., 1971. Methodist (treas. ch. 1964—). Democrat. Address: Box 205 Grenville NM 88424

COMASSAR, PERLA ANNE GRYMEK, sch. psychologist; b. Warsaw, Poland, May 13, 1926; d. Issie and Yetta (Vigoda) Grymek; came to U.S., 1946, naturalized, 1950; student Syracuse U., 1948, 50; A.B. with high honors, U. Cin., 1967, B.S. with high honors, 1969, M.Ed., 1970, postgrad., 1970—; postgrad. Miami U., 1971; m. Seymour Comassar, Oct. 10, 1946 (div. Oct. 1967); 1 dau., Gene Lesley. Sec. to dir. pub. health nursing Coll. Medicine, Syracuse (N.Y.) U., 1947-48; sec. to dir. pathology Mt. Sinai Hosp., Toronto, Ont., Can., 1953-54; elementary sch. sec. Cin. City Schs., 1957-66;

tchr., Burton Elementary Sch., Cin., 1967-68; asst. Project for Youth, U. Cin., 1969; grad. asst. U. Cin., 1969-70, grad. teaching asst., 1973-74, guest lectr., 1972; sch. psychologist intern Hamilton County Bd. Edn., Cin., 1970-71; learning disabilities cons., sch. psychologist Wilmington (O.) City and Clinton County (O.) Schs., 1971-73; psychoednl. cons. Toronto Bd. Edn., 1974-75. Mem. com. to formulate, refine and integrate ednl. screening instrument for tchr. use, 1971-73; cons. Hopewell Spl. Edn. Resource Center, Hillsboro, 1973. Vol., Jewish Hosp. Aux., Cin., 1967—; leader Cin.-Hamilton County Council Girl Scouts U.S.A., 1955-57; Faculty adviser gifted children, Wilmington, O., 1971-73; mem. steering com. to organize regional chpt. Council Exceptional Children, Hillsboro, O., 1972; active P.T.A. Served with Canadian Women's Army Corps, 1944-46. Mem. Assos. Smithsonian Instn., Women's Internat. Bowling Congress, Upper Grade Study Council, N.E.A., Assn. Children with Learning Disabilities, Council Exceptional Children, Nat., Ohio, Southwestern Ohio sch. psychologists assns., Ohio Edn. Assn., Cin. Tchrs. Assn., Hamilton County Assn. Slow Learners, Young Friends of the Arts, Alpha Sigma Lambda, Kappa Delta Pi, Psi Chi, Delta Tau Kappa, Alpha Kappa Delta, Phi Delta Kappa. Home: 7980 Stillwell Rd Cincinnati OH 45237 also 692 BriarHill Av Toronto ON M6B 1L3 Canada

COMBES, MOLLIE HART ALLENSWORTH, pediatrician, educator; b. San Antonio, July 24, 1927; d. George Taylor and Emelyn (Carnahan) Allensworth; student U. Tex. at Austin, 1944-45; A.B., Barnard Coll., 1948; M.D., Columbia, 1952; m. Burton Combes, June 3, 1948; children—Burton, Hilary Elizabeth, Rustin Bradley. Fellow Cornell U. Sch. Medicine, 1952-53; rotating intern St. Luke's Hosp., N.Y.C., 1953-54; resident in pediatrics Babies Hosp., Columbia-Presbyn. Med. Center, N.Y.C., 1954-56; postdoctoral research fellow Nat. Found., Hosp. for Sick Children, London, Eng., 1956-57; attending physician in charge Premature Nursery, Parkland Meml. Hosp., Dallas, 1957-62, also Premature Infant Follow-up Clinics; instr. pediatrics U. Tex. Med. Sch. at Dallas, 1957-62, clin. instr. pediatrics, 1962—; practice medicine specializing in pediatrics, Dallas, 1964—; mem. staffs Children's Med. Center, Dallas, Presbyn. Med. Hosp., Baylor U. Hosp. Med. Center; also mem. staffs clinics. Bd. dirs., med. cons. Dallas Soc. Prevention of Blindness, 1960-62. Diplomate Am. Bd. Pediatrics. Mem. A.M.A., Dallas County (health careers com. Women's Aux. 1971—, dir. 1973—, rep. to women's council 1973-74), Tex. med. socs., Dallas County, Tex. pediatric socs., So. Soc. Pediatric Research (charter, sec.-treas. 1963-65), Newborn Soc. (charter), Am. Fedn. Clin. Research, U. Tex. Faculty Wives (co-chmn. new members 1962-63, mem.-at-large Women's Council Dallas County 1971—, program chmn. 1972-73, dir.), U. Tex. Health Scis. Center Faculty Wives (coordinator benefit 1974), Chi Omega. Home: 3541 Greenbrier Dr Dallas TX 75225

COMBS, ADELE WESTGATE (MRS. RICHARD EARL COMBS), librarian; b. Mendota, Ill., Jan. 10, 1933; d. Walter Allen and Emma Lee (Moorhead) Westgate; A.B., Ind. U., 1956, M.A., 1961; m. Richard Earl Combs, Apr. 20, 1957. Children's librarian Indpls. Pub. Library, 1957; asst. documents librarian Ind. U. Library, Bloomington, 1957-64; reference librarian Columbia U. Library, N.Y.C., 1964-65; reference and circulation librarian East Asian Library, 1965-66; librarian, Vernon Ct. Jr. Coll., Newport, R.I., 1966-68; librarian, Newport Sch. for Girls, 1966-68; reference librarian Northwestern U. Library, Evanston, Ill., 1968-69, dep. asst. univ. librarian for pub. services, 1969—, acting asst. univ. librarian for pub. services, 1973—. Mem. Am., Ill. library assns., Beta Phi Mu. Home: 1927 Sherman Av Evanston IL 60201

COMBS, (DORIS) LORRAINE EVANS (MRS. WILLIAM LLOYD COMBS), assn. exec.; b. Linn Grove, Ia., Oct. 28, 1921; d. Everett John and Gladys Ellen (Fuller) Evans; B.A., U. Ia., 1943; postgrad. Morningside Coll., 1956; m. William Lloyd Combs, Aug. 20, 1943; children—Stephen, Diane (Mrs. Bruce Hanson), Christine, William, Charles. Exec. dir. YWCA, Spencer, Ia., 1956-66; program dir. YMCA, Mesa, Ariz., 1966—, valleywide coordinator YMCA Family Focus Program, 1973—. Del. Mesa Speaks, 1971-72; mem. Hot-Line Com., 1973-74; mem. Statewide Youth and Govt. Program, Citizens for Bikeways in Mesa Com., 1973—, Mesa Community Council Youth Agys. Com., 1973—, Mesa Citizens' Safety Com., 1974—, Tumbleweed Com., 1974—, Head Start Com., 1974—. Conglist. Club: Soroptimists (pres.-elect 1973—). Home: 1458 W 5th St Mesa AZ 85201 Office: 207 N Mesa Dr Mesa AZ 85201

COMBS, WILLA MAE RYAN (MRS. SYLVESTER COMBS), educator; b. Oklahoma City, Aug. 11, 1925; d. William and Lala (Lambeth) Ryan; B.S. cum laude, Langston U., 1947; M.S., Okla. State U., 1955, Ed.D. in Home Econs., 1974; m. Sylvester Combs, Apr. 10, 1947. Tchr. vocational and gen. home econs. Attucks High Sch., Vinita, Okla., 1947-49, L'Ouverture High Sch., Slick, Okla., 1949-57, Slick High Sch., 1957-60, 61-66; dir. home mgmt. So. U., Baton Rouge, 1960-61; extension human resource devel. specialist Okla. State U., Stillwater, 1966—. Cons. agt. dirs. and groups in devel. of human, social, cultural and econ. resources. Bd. dirs. Creek Farmers Fed. Credit Union, Bristow, Okla., 1950-60; mem. Creek County Guidance Com., Slick High Sch., 1965-66; treas., mem. exec. com. Okla. State U. Home Econs. Alumni Assn., Stillwater, 1967-71; mem. State Extension Conf. for Okla., 1967; mem. Pres.'s Equal Employment Opportunity Com., Okla. State U., 1968—; chmn. exhibits Okla. Homemakers Conf., 1968—; group leader Okla. Coalition for Clean Air, 1970. Recipient longevity awards 4-H, 1960, 65. Mem. Am., Okla. (chmn. family econs. and home mgmt. sect. 1968-71) home econs. assns., Okla. Edn. Assn., N.E.A., Langston U. Alumni Assn., Am. Assn. U. Women (implementation chmn. The Beleaguered Earth, Stillwater br. 1969—), Okla. State U. Alumni Assn., League Women Voters, YWCA, YMCA, Alpha Kappa Alpha, Phi Upsilon Omicron, Phi Delta Kappa. Baptist (Sunday Sch. supt. 1960-72). Mem. Order Eastern Star (chpt. matron 1955-60). Writer booklets in field. Home: 2136 W Sunset Dr Stillwater OK 74074

COMEAU, CATHERINE EVELYN, educator; b. Belmont, Mass., June 16, 1926; d. Alphonse J. and Zoe M. (Saulnier) Comeau; B.S., Sargent Coll. Boston U., 1948, Ed.D., 1966; M.A., Columbia Tchrs. Coll., 1952. Chmn. health and phys. edn. dept. Georgian Court Coll., Lakewood, N.J., 1948-52; asst. prof. State Coll. at Bridgewater (Mass.), 1952-62; asso. prof. Sargent Coll. Boston U., 1963-65; asso. prof., chmn. health and phys. edn. dept. Douglass Coll., Rutgers U., New Brunswick, N.J., 1966-70; prof., chmn. women's health and phys. edn. dept. Bridgewater (Mass.) State Coll., 1970—. Recreation leader Little House, Inc., Boston, summers 1944-46; counselor Camp Hanoum, Thelford, Vt., summer 1947; vis. instr. Sargent Coll. Camp, 1952-65, chmn. golf dept., 1959-65. Recipient Dudley Allen Sargent Service award Sargent Coll. Alumni Assn., 1961, Boston U. Sargent Alumni Centennial award, 1969. Mem. Am. Assn. U. Profs. (sec.-treas. Bridgewater chpt. 1956-57), Nat. Assn. Phys. Edn. for Coll. Women, Internat. Assn. Phys. Edn. and Sports for Girls and Women, A.A.H.P.E.R. (sec. Eastern dist. div. for girls and women's sports 1962-64, chmn. Mass. div. 1963, mem. constn. com. 1967, pres. Eastern dist. 1968-70, Eastern dist. Honor award 1971), Mass. Assn. for Health, Phys. Edn. and Recreation (v.p. health 1956-57, pres. 1963-65; honor award 1965) U.S. (mem. exec. com. 1956-58, ofcl. 1959-62, rules com. 1961-62), Boston (pres. 1956-58) field hockey assns., So. Mass. Bd. Women Ofcls. (chmn. 1954-56, nat. basketball judge 1954-61), Women's Nat. Ofcls. Rating Com. (nat. basketball ofcl. 1953—), Sargent Alumni Assn. (treas. 1955-58, pres. 1963-65, Twiness award 1965), Boston U. Alumni Assn. (v.p. 1965-67), Pi Lambda Theta. Home: 307 Beech St Belmont MA 02178 Office: Health and Phys Edn Dept Bridgewater State Coll Bridgewater MA 02324

COMER, ANNA MARIE HADLEY (MRS. ELDON A. COMER), ret. banker; b. Menlo, Ia., Aug. 22, 1911; d. James Garfield and Clara Amanda (Freese) Hadley; grad. high sch.; m. Eldon A. Comer, Oct. 12, 1937. Clk., med. dept. Bankers Life Co., Des Moines, 1928-38; typist Central Nat. Bank, Des Moines, 1938-40; sec. to supt. personnel KNWL, Fort Leonard Wood, Mo., 1940-42; sec. to chmn. bd. Central Nat. Bank, Des Moines, 1943-65, corporate sec., 1965-74, ret., 1974; corporate sec. Central Nat. Bankshares, Inc.; sec. bd. Central Nat. Bank. Mem. personnel com. YWCA. Mem. Nat. Assn. Bank Women (Ia. group chmn. 1959-60, dir. 1959-60), Nat. Secs. Assn., Am. Inst. Banking, Des Moines C. of C. (dir. women's div. 1972-74). Home: 1536 32d St Des Moines IA 50311 Office: Locust at 6th St Des Moines IA 50304

COMER, ELMA MARGARET, physician; b. South Plainfield, N.J.; d. Howard Mickle and Emma (Carman) Comer; student N.J. Coll. Women, 1934-37; M.D., L.I. Coll. Medicine, 1942; m. Dr. Sidney L. Tamarin, May 8, 1943. Gen. rotating internship Bklyn. Hosp., 1942-43; asst. resident Montefiore Hosp., Bronx, 1943-44; resident in psychiatry Psychiat. Inst. and Hosp., 1944-45; sr. psychiatrist Bklyn. State Hosp., 1945-50, Kings County Med., 1950-52; practice medicine specializing in psychiatry, Bklyn., 1952—; asst. clin. prof. psychiatry N.Y. State Coll. Medicine, Downstate Med. Center, 1955—; asst. attending neuropsychiatry St. John's Episcopal Hosp., Bklyn., 1955-59, cons., 1968—; asst. attending Meth. Hosp., Bklyn., 1959—. Tech. dir. movie Snake Pit, 1947. Sec., Sidney L. Green Found. for Adolescent and Child Psychiatry, 1966—; mem. Bklyn. Mus. Modern Art, Friends Art at Cornell. Diplomate Am. Bd. Psychiatry and Neurology. Fellow Am. Psychiat. Soc.; mem. Bklyn. Mental Hygiene Soc., Bklyn. Psychiat. Soc. (exec. council), Kings County Med. Soc. Address: 90 8th Av Brooklyn NY 11215

COMERFORD, RUTH BARBARA, publishing co. ofcl.; b. Boston, Sept. 18, 1926; d. Frank John and Barbara (McDonough) Comerford; student Bentley Coll., 1955-57. Asst. treas. Silton Co., advt., Boston, 1950-65; asst. to pres., dir. customer relations Warren, Gorham & Lamont, Inc., pub. Boston, 1969—. Notary pub. Club: Executives (Boston). Home: 6 Marlborough St Boston MA 02116 Office: 89 Beach St Boston MA 02111

COMES, MARCELLA (MRS. W. RANDOLPH WINSLOW), painter; b. Pitts.; d. John Theodore and Honora (Webber) Comes; ed. Carnegie Sch. Fine Arts, Phillips Gallery, pvt. European studies; m. W. Randolph Winslow, Oct. 5, 1934 (dec.); children—Mary Rodange (Mrs. John Poole, Jr.), John Randolph. Tchr. painting Cath. U., 1965-69; works exhibited Carnegie Inst., Pitts., Corcoran Gallery, Washington, Brooks Mus., Memphis, also Balt., Norfolk, Florence, Italy; 11 one man shows; rep. U.S. Navy Today in Marine Mus., Paris; muralist Homewood Library, Pitts., Stone Ridge Sch., Washington; represented in pvt. collections Mrs. Eugene Meyer, Lionberger Davis, Chauncey Stillman, Katherine Anne Porter, Francis Biddle, C.V. Whitney, Bryn Mawr Coll.; portrait painter, works include Robert Frost, Allen Tate, Ezra Pound, Eudora Welty, John Rothenstein, Mrs. Nicholas Longworth, Supt. at West Point; lectr. art; author art reviews. Mem. women's com. Corcoran Gallery Art, Asso. Artists Pitts., Washington Soc. Artists, Artists Equity Assn. (pres. D.C. chpt. 1969-72, nat. v.p. 1972-74), Artists Guild (pres. 1956-58). Home: 3106 P St NW Washington DC 20007

COMINS, ETHEL MAE, educator, author; b. Clayton, N.Y., May 16, 1901; d. Hayes H. and Alice H. (Burnham) Comins; grad. Plattsburgh Normal Sch., 1919; B.S. cum laude, Syracuse U., 1930; M.S. in Edn., N.Y. U., 1936. High sch. tchr., Margaretville, N.Y., 1919-20, Carthage, N.Y., 1920-22, Syracuse, N.Y., 1922-30, N.Y.C., 1930-61; sec. studies instr., mem. guidance council, chmn. orientation, Queens U., N.Y.C., 1958-61. Chmn. art show Jefferson County (N.Y.) Fair, 1964, 65; bd. dirs. Thousand Island Mus., 1966—, chmn. art show, 1965-67, art dir., 1971—. Recipient prizes and awards including 1st prizes Deep South Writers Conf., 3-act play, 1964, feature, 1967, column, 1970, Nat. League Am. Pen Women, one-act plays, 1956, 58. Mem. Nat. League Am. Pen Women (pres. Queens br. 1956-58, editor newsletter 1954-56, 58-60, state pres. 1960-62, nat. contest chmn. 1962-64, rec. sec. Central N.Y. br. 1965-67), Watertown (N.Y.) Artists Guild (dir. 1962-66), Jefferson County Hist. Soc., N.Y. Authors League, Thousand Island Mus. Asso. Artists (pres. 1971-72), Zonta, Delta Kappa Gamma (hon.). Author: Magic School House, 1964; Cloth of Dreams, 1967; Island Castle, 1968; Beyond the Night, 1969; Her Father's Daughter, 1970 (paperback edit. 1972); Black Jade Filly, 1971; Mystery Island, 1973; Moon Goddess, 1974. Contbr. hist. articles to various publs. Home: RFD 1 Steele's Point Clayton NY 13624

COMMINS, MARY JO, lawyer; b. Cuba City, Wis., July 22, 1942; d. Charles William and Theda Mae (Hillary) Curwen; B.S., U. Wis., 1964; J.D., U. Cal. at Los Angeles, 1971; m. Donald J. Commins, Oct. 19, 1974. Admitted to Cal. bar, 1972; atty. Cal. Dept. Social Welfare, Sacramento and Los Angeles, 1971-73; mem. firm Trygstad & Odell, Los Angeles, 1973—. Bd. dirs. Majority Club House Inc., 1973-74, pres., 1973-74. Mem. State Bar Cal., Los Angeles County Bar Assn. (arbitration com. 1973—), Women Lawyers Assn. Los Angeles, Delta Zeta, Omicron Nu. Democrat. Home: 9032 W 25th St Los Angeles CA 90034 Office: Suite 312 1730 W Olympic Blvd Los Angeles CA 90015

COMOLA, JUNE WILTSHIRE, clin. psychologist; b. Carrollton, Miss., June 1, 1931; d. Eli Eugene and Katherine Farr (Broome) Wiltshire; B.A. summa cum laude, Belmont Coll., 1960; M.A., George Peabody Coll., 1962, Ed.S., 1968; m. Constantine Douglas Comola, Feb. 13, 1970; 1 dau., Constance Jean. Staff clin. psychologist Met. Bordeaux Psychiat. Hosp., Nashville, 1962-64, co-dir. after-care clinic, 1964-67; psychol. cons. King's Daughter's Hosp. Sch., Columbia, Tenn., 1962-64; clin. psychologist, dir. sch. consultation Community Mental Health Center, Tupelo, Miss., 1968—. Lectr., U. Miss. State U. Mem. Am., Miss. psychol. assns., Council Exceptional Children, Miss. Mental Health Assn. (profl. adviser). Baptist. Club: Tupelo Altrusa. Spl. feature writer Tng. Union mag., So. Bapt. Conv., 1958-59. Home: 518 N Park St Tupelo MS 38801 Office: N Miss Med Center Mental Health Complex Tupelo MS 38801

COMPAIN, RITA, educator; b. N.Y.C., Dec. 4, 1926; d. Benjamin and Sarah B. (Modell) Romer; B.S., City U. N.Y., 1947; M.L.S., L.I. U., 1967; advanced degree Columbia, 1970; postgrad. St. John's U.; m. Ernest A. Compain, Apr. 17, 1948; children—Michael, Daniel, Andrew. Tchr., N.Y.C. Schs., 1956-59; library coordinator Oceanside (N.Y.) Pub. Schs., 1959-61; librarian Franklin Square (N.Y.) Pub. Schs., 1961-71, grade chmn., 1964-71; asst. prof. L.I. U., 1969—. Ednl. cons., guest speaker Nassau County Jail Pilot Library Project, 1970—. Youth group leader, Elmont, N.Y., 1959-61. Mem. Am., N.Y. (chmn. service standards com. 1960), Nassau-Suffolk Sch. (pres. 1970-71) library assns., L.I. Ednl. Communication Council. Author; Self-Educators Guide, 1974. Contbr. articles to profl. jours. Home: 12 Grace Ct W Great Neck NY 11021

COMPTON, ESTHER A., educator; b. Wabash, Ind., Mar. 28, 1908; d. Joseph John and Ida May (Kanower) Compton; A.B., Ind. U., 1930, A.M., 1933; postgrad. U. Ky., summers 1950-54, Kan. U., summer 1959, U. Tenn., evenings 1964-67; M.A.T., Mich. State U., 1963. Tchr., Butler Twp. High Sch., Peru, Ind., 1931-32, Wood Jr. Coll., Mathiston, Miss., 1935-41, Banquo High Sch., Huntington, Ind., 1941-44, Williamsport (Ind.) High Sch., 1944-46; mem. faculty Cumberland Coll., Williamsburg, Ky., 1947—, asst. prof. math., 1960-65, asso. prof., 1965—. Mem. Nat. Council Tchrs. Math., Math. Assn. Am., Am. Math. Soc. Baptist. Clubs: Williamsburg Woman's (pres.), Cumberland College Woman's (past pres.). Home: Box 153 Williamsburg KY 40769

COMPTON, MARY BEATRICE BROWN (MRS. RALPH THEODORE COMPTON), pub. relations exec., writer; b. Washington, May 25, 1923; d. Robert James and Abie Eliza (Stone) Brown; grad. Leland Powers Sch. Radio, TV, and Theatre, Boston, 1941-42; m. Ralph Theodore Compton, Mar. 18, 1961, step-children—Ralph Theodore, Patricia (Mrs. William R. Schnitzler). Radio program dir. Converse Co., Malden, Mass., 1942-45; head radio continuity dept. WAAB sta. Yankee Network, Worcester, Mass., 1945-46; asst. dir. radio Leland Powers Sch. Radio, TV, Theatre, Boston, 1946-49, dir., 1949-51; program asst. KNBH, Hollywood, Cal., 1951-52; v.p. Acorn Film Co., Boston, 1953-54; dir. women's communications, editor Program Notes, radio interviewer Nat. Assn. Mfrs., 1954-61; cons. on women's communications to N.Y. advt. agys., 1961—. Celebrities pub. relations Nat. Citizens for Nixon, 1968. Mem. Am. Women in Radio and TV, Soc. Old Plymouth Colony Descs., Magna Carta Dames. Clubs: Capitol Hill (com. chmn. women's div. 1962-67) (Washington); Congressional Country (Bethesda, Md.); Chesapeake Country (Lusby, Md.). Home: Box 181 Cove Point Beach Lusby MD 20657

COMPTON, MILDRED SARTOR (MRS. JOHN H. COMPTON), mus. adminstr.; b. Bicknell, Ind.; d. Noble P. and Dora (Mason) Sartor; B.S. in Chemistry, U. Mich., 1938; M.S., Tulane U., 1940; m. John H. Compton, Jan. 29, 1944; children—Sara, John. Teaching asst. Sophie Newcombe Coll., New Orleans, 1938-40; chemist Eli Lilly & Co., Indpls., 1940-46; exec. sec. Children's Mus. Indpls., 1961-64, dir., 1964—. Mem. Am. Assn. of Museums (nat. accreditation com. 1972—, v.p. 1972—), Assn. of Ind. Museums (pres. 1971-73), Ind. Hist. Soc., Soc. Ind. Pioneers, Children's Mus. Guild (pres. 1955-56), Am. Assn. for State and Local History, Ind. C. of C. (pres. women's council 1974—), D.A.R., Sigma Xi. Rotarian. Home: 5420 North Delaware St Indianapolis IN 46220 Office: 3010 North Meridian St Indianapolis IN 46208

COMPTON, NORMA HAYNES (MRS. WILLIAM RANDALL COMPTON), educator; b. Washington, Nov. 16, 1924; d. Thomas N. and Lillian (Laffin) Haynes; A.B., George Washington U., 1950; postgrad. Catholic U., 1954, Am. U., 1954-55, U. Tenn., 1958, Ia. State U., 1960; M.S., U. Md., 1957, Ph.D., 1962; m. William Randall Compton, Mar. 27, 1946; children—William Randall, Anne Elizabeth. Psychology extern St. Elizabeth's Hosp., Washington, 1962-63; researcher Julius Garfinckel & Co., Washington, 1955; tchr. Montgomery Blair High Sch., Silver Spring, Md., 1955-57; instr. home econs. U. Md., College Park, 1957-60, teaching and research fellow Inst. Child Study, 1960-61, asso. prof. home econs., 1962-63; asso. prof. Utah State U., 1963-64, prof., 1964-68, head dept. clothing and textiles, 1964-67, dir. Inst. for Research on Man and His Personal Environment, 1967-68; dean Sch. Home Econs., Auburn U. (Ala.), 1968-73; dean sch. home econs. Purdue U., 1973—. Mem. Am. Home Econs. Assn., Am. Assn. Univ. Adminstrs., Nat. Council of Adminstrs. of Home Econs. (chmn.), Assn. Adminstrs. Home Econs. in State Univs. and Land Grant Colls., Ind. Home Econs. Assn., Assn. Coll. Profs. of Textiles and Clothing, Am. Assn. Textile Chemists and Colorists, Nat. Council on Family Relations, Phi Beta Kappa, Sigma Xi, Phi Upsilon Omicron, Phi Kappa Phi, Omicron Nu, Psi Chi. Episcopalian. Author: (with Olive Hall) Foundations of Home Economics Research: A Human Ecology Approach. Contbr. articles to profl. jours. Address: Purdue U West Lafayette IN 47907

COMSTOCK, THEDA LEE ELBRADER (MRS. DARRELL M. COMSTOCK), broadcasting co. exec.; b. Great Falls, Mont., Sept. 3; d. Lee and Ruth (Miles) Elbrader; student U. Ore.; m. William Conley; 1 son; m. 2d, Darrell M. Comstock, Dec. 23, 1964. Passenger sales agt. Air Can., Seattle, 1951-54; hostess TV show 5 days week The Woman's Touch, Midnight Sun Broadcasters, KENI-TV, Anchorage, 1962—, TV weather forecaster, 1963—, promotion and TV continuity dir., 1963—. Consumer adviser to Gov. Alaska, 1970-71. Mem. Bus. and Profl. Women's Club. Club: Anchorage Woman's (asso.). Office: KENI-TV Box 1160 Anchorage AK 99501

COMVALIUS, NADIA HORTENSE, physician; b. Paramaribo, Surinam; d. Rudolf B. and Martha (James) Comvalius; M.D., U. Utrecht, Netherlands, 1949. Came to U.S., 1955, naturalized, 1962. Intern Grand Central Hosp., N.Y.C., 1961-62; asst. resident in obstetrics and gynecology Wyckoff Heights Hosp., Bklyn., 1961-62; resident obstetrics and gynecology Harlem Hosp., N.Y.C., 1956-57; resident gynecology, cancer research Hahnemann Med. Coll., Phila., 1959-61, fellow surg. research; mem. staff Moral Rearmament, Eng., Switzerland, 1951; sch. physician, sec. Leprosy bd., Pub. Health Dept. Paramaribo-Surinam, S.Am., 1952-55; practice medicine specializing in obstetrics and gynecology, N.Y.C., New Rochelle, N.Y., 1964—. Physician, Planned Parenthood Assn., New Rochelle, N.Y.C., 1965—, med. cons. So. Westchester Planned Parenthood. Diplomate Am. Bd. Obstetrics and Gynecology. Mem. Am. Med. Womens Assn., Royal Soc. Health, Westchester County, N.Y. State, Netherlands-Am. med. socs., A.M.A. Club: Zonta. Home: 50 Echo Bay Dr New Rochelle NY 10805 Office: 150 Lockwood Av New Rochelle NY 10801

COMYNS, JEAN EDMONSTON (MRS. RICHARD BENJAMIN COMYNS), occupational therapist; b. Asheville, N.C., Dec. 8, 1931; d. Ralph Tappan and Ollilu (Jackson) Edmonston; B.S. in Applied Scis., Va. Commonwealth U., 1954, certificate in occupational therapy, 1954; m. Richard Benjamin Comyns, Aug. 6, 1955; children—Caroline, Richard. Staff therapist Eastern State Hosp., Williamsburg, Va., 1954-55, U. Va. Hosp., Charlottesville, 1955-57, Central Ala. Rehab. Center, Montgomery, 1972—. Neighborhood chmn. Asheville (N.C.) Heart Assn., 1966; troop leader Girl Scouts U.S.A., 1967-69; mem. sch. bd. Fledgling Sch., Maxwell AFB, Ala., 1969, 70, chmn., 1971; Grey Lady, A.R.C., 1970-71. Mem. Am., Ala. occupational therapy assns. Home: 514 D Catalpa St Maxwell AFB AL 36113 Office: 2125 East South Blvd Montgomery AL 36111

CONAGHAN, DOROTHY DELL, state legislator; b. Oklahoma City, Okla., Sept. 24, 1930; d. John Joseph and Wilhelamina Elizabeth (Boyer) Miller; student U. Okla., 1949-51; m. Brian Francis Conaghan, June 10, 1951; (dec. Apr. 1973); children—Joseph Lee, Charles Alan, Roger Lloyd. Mem. Okla. Legislature, 1973—. Vice chmn. Kay County (Okla.) Republicans, 1961-64, 6th Congl. Dist. Rep. Party, 1967-69; del. Rep. Nat. Conv., 1968. Bd. dirs. United

Fund, 1966-69. Mem. Tonkawa C. of C., Am. Legion Aux., Orgn. Women Legislators, P.E.O. Mem. Christian Ch. Mem. Order Eastern Star. Clubs: Delphi Study, Tonkawa Rep. Women's. Home: 904 E Grand St Tonkawa OK 74653 Office: House of Representatives State Capitol Bldg Oklahoma City OK 74653

CONAHAN, KATHLEEN KAM OI, lawyer; b. Honolulu, Apr. 6, 1943; d. Henry Sung Yau and Helen (Chun) Kau; B.Ed., U. Hawaii, 1965; J.D., Harvard, 1968; m. James Patrick Conahan, Dec. 1966; children—Paul Koon Tim, Heather Kwai Lan. Admitted to Hawaii bar, 1968; law clk. Hawaii Supreme Ct., Honolulu, 1968-69; dep. corp. counsel Office of Corp. Counsel City and County of Honolulu, 1969-70; exec. dir. Hawaii State Ethics Commn., 1970-74; asso. firm Torkildson, Katz and Conahan, Honolulu, 1974—. Mem. Am., Hawaii bar assns., Phi Kappa Phi, Pi Lambda Theta. Home: 59-639 Ke Iki Rd Haleiwa HI 96712 Office: Suite 1512 700 Bishop St Honolulu HI 96813

CONANT, LUCY HOUGHTON, nurse, educator; b. Littleton, Mass., Oct. 13, 1926; d. Harold W. and Dorothy (Priest) Conant; B.A., Radcliffe Coll., 1947; M.Nursing, Yale, 1950; M.P.H., Harvard, 1957; Ph.D., Yale, 1964. Pub. health nurse, Mich., Eng., 1950-54; head nurse Grace-New Haven Hosp., 1954-56; asst. prof., research asso. Yale Sch. Nursing, 1957-68; prof., dean U. N.C. Sch. Nursing, Chapel Hill, 1968—. Mem. Am. Nurses Assn., Nat. League Nursing, Am. Pub. Health Assn., Am. Sociol. Assn. Home: 6 Davie Lane Chapel Hill NC 27514

CONANT, MIRIAM BERNHEIM (MRS. FRANCIS P. CONANT), educator; b. Paris, France, Aug. 4, 1931; d. Claude and Janine (Wertheimer) Bernheim; came to U.S., 1940; B.A. magna cum laude, Bryn Mawr Coll., 1951; M.A., Columbia, 1953, Ph.D., 1962; m. Francis P. Conant, Aug. 4, 1952; children—Oliver, Nora. Instr. Columbia, 1963-65, asst. prof. polit. theory, 1965-69; prof. polit. theory Sarah Lawrence Coll., 1969—; mem. acad. adminstrn. internship program Am. Council Edn., 1966-67. Mem. Am. Polit. Sci. Assn., Acad. Polit. and Social Sci. Home: 1261 Madison Av New York City NY 10028 Office: Sarah Lawrence Coll Bronxville NY 10708

CONARROE, CAROLYN JEANNETTE MORRIS, librarian, newspaper exec.; b. Springfield, O., June 30, 1927; d. Edward Tuttle and Catherine (Fissel) Morris; B.S., Ohio Wesleyan U., 1949; m. Percy A. Conarroe, July 15, 1950; children—David, Cynthia, Douglas. City editor, co-pub. Louisville (Colo.) Times, 1955—; dir. Louisville Pub. Library, 1970—. Mem. Kappa Alpha Theta, Theta Alpha Phi. Methodist (organist). Mem. Colo. Federated Women's Club. Home: 1131 Jefferson St Louisville CO 80027 Office: 916 Main St Louisville CO 80027 also 749 Main St Louisville CO 80027

CONCANNON, SISTER JOSEPHINA, educator; b. Lawrence, Mass.; d. Michael J. and Annie T. (McDermott) Concannon; B.S., Mt. St. Joseph Tchrs. Coll., Buffalo, 1942; M.Ed., Boston Coll., 1947, Ed.D., 1957; LL.D. (hon.), Regis Coll., 1965; postgrad. study Montessori, other ednl. systems, Europe, 1961-62, 69-70. Joined Congregation of St. Joseph, Roman Catholic Ch., 1925; tchr. elementary schs. Archdiocese Boston, 1927-40; supr. elementary schs., 1944-54; mem. faculty Boston Coll. Grad. Sch., 1948-70, instr. edn., 1948-51, asst. prof. supervision, adminstrn., elementary edn., 1951-57, asso. prof. edn., psychology, 1957-60, prof., 1960-70, organizer Montessori Lab. Sch., Coll. Edn., 1962, organizer, dir. Campion Children's Class, Montessori, 1962, mgr. insts. on supervision and edn. Grad. Sch., summers 1959-65; prof. State Coll., Worcester, Mass., 1970—; vis. lectr. Cath. U., Washington, Regis Coll., Weston, Mass., St. Joseph Coll. at Framingham, Mass. and Wyndham, Me., St. Mary Coll., Omaha, 1960—. Cons. Operation Headstart, Office Econ. Opportunity, Charlestown, Mass., 1965—; cons. childhood edn. Children's Mus., Jamaica Plain, Mass., 1964—; cons. curriculum changes Boston pub. schs., 1965—; dir. workshops for tchrs., suprs., adminstrs. Boston, Omaha, Portland, Me., 1957—; lectr. civic orgns., profl. assns., confs. tchrs. colls., ednl. confs., New Eng., nationally; guest speaker ednl. methodology ednl. TV, radio, 1961—. Mem. planning bd. classroom TV Channel 2, Boston, 1958-61; mem. Mass. Program Academically Talented; mem. Program Culturally Disadvantaged, U.S. Office Edn., 1964, research grantee, 1967; participant Conf. Disadvantaged Child, Nat. Inst. Mental Health, Boston, 1964; participant White House Conf. Edn., 1965. Recipient Alpha and Omega award Boston Coll. Sch. Edn., 1963; named Tchr. of Year, Boston Coll., 1969. NSF grantee, conf. behavioral sci., Austin, Tex., 1964. Mem. Am. Ednl. Research Assn. (speaker Headstart, annual meeting, 1966), Nat. Soc. Study Edn., Internat. (exec. bd. 1960—), New Eng. reading assns., Assn. Supervision and Curriculum Devel., Nat. Cath. Edn. Assn., Cath. Psychol. Assn., Nat. Council Tchrs. Arithmetic. Author: Mental Arithmetic Workbooks, 1955; (with others) Word Power Through Spelling, 1951; Spell Correctly, 1965. Contbr. articles to encys., profl. publs., book chpts., book revs. Cons. editor Doubleday and Co., 1959-63; ednl. dir. Rand-McNally Co., 1959-60. Home: 637 Cambridge St Brighton MA 02135 Office: State Coll Worcester MA 01602

CONDAS, JOANNE MARY DAVIES (MRS. MICHAEL CONDAS), lawyer; b. Salt Lake City, Dec. 18, 1932; d. Harry Joseph and Mary Caroline (Jaynes) Davies; B.A. magna cum laude, U. Utah, 1953; J.D., Hastings Coll. Law, 1966; m. Michael Condas, Sept. 13, 1954 (dec. Mar. 1966). Admitted to Cal. bar, 1966; practiced in San Francisco, 1966—; with Office Cal. Atty. Gen. Lectr., Hastings Coll. Law, 1971-72; coordinator Atty. Gen's. Adv. Com. Problems of Aging, 1973. Sponsor, San Francisco Opera Guild, 1972-73. Mem. State Bar Cal., Am., San Francisco (sect. chmn. 1971-73) bar assns., Bar U.S. Supreme Ct., San Francisco Mus. Soc., Cal. Acad. Scis., Am. Conservatory Theatre. Club: Commonwealth (San Francisco). Home: 21 Dalewood Way San Francisco CA 94127 Office: State Bldg San Francisco CA 94102

CONDIT, (ELEANOR) LOUISE, museum supr.; b. Balt., May 7, 1914; d. George Smith and Bessie Blaine (Madeira) Condit; A.B., Vassar Coll., 1935; Carnegie grantee student edn. in mus. Brit. Isles, Scandinavia, Germany, France, Netherlands, summer 1939; A.M., Columbia, 1941; m. Frederic G.M. Lange, Sept. 19, 1946. Supr. edn. Bklyn. Children's Mus., 1935-42; supr. jr. mus. Met. Mus. Art, 1943-61, asst. dean charge jr. mus., 1961-68, asso. charge jr. mus., 1968-72, head jr. museum, 1972—, dep. vice dir. ednl. affairs, 1974—. Arts adviser Bank St. Arts in Edn. Com., Boys Clubs Am., 1961-70; chmn. children's mus. sect. Am. Assn. Mus., 1946-47, 51-52, councillor 1957-63, v.p., 1960-63; chmn. com. profl. publs. Internat. Council Museums, 1947-50, mem. U.S. com. 1972—. Met. Mus. Travel grantee to study museums, Europe, summer 1961, 71. Mem. Mus. Council N.Y.C. (sec.-treas. 1960-64), Assn. Youth Mus. Dirs. (pres. 1972-74), Am. Assn. Museums (com. Internat. Council Museums), N.Y. Film Council, Phi Beta Kappa. Author articles in profl. jours. Home: 1203 Emerson Av Teaneck NJ 07666 Office: Met Museum Art Fifth Av at 82d St New York City NY 10028

CONDIT, MARTHA OLSON (MRS. MILTON ARMSTRONG CONDIT), ednl. cons.; b. East Orange, N.J., Sept. 8, 1913; d. Olof and Ida Christina (Johnson) Olson; certificate Pratt Inst., 1934; B.A., Rutgers U., 1953, M.L.S., 1958; supervisor's certificate Montclair State Coll., 1971; m. Milton Armstrong Condit, June 17, 1944. Children's librarian, pub. libraries, Nutley, N.J., 1936-43, Passaic, N.J., 1943-45, East Orange, N.J., 1945-56; sch. librarian Montclair, (N.J.) Pub. Schs., 1956-65, coordinator media services, 1965-72, cons. media services, 1973—. Mem. coadj. staff Sch. Edn., Rutgers U., 1961-62, Grad. Sch. Library Service, 1962-64; cons. Scholastic Book Services, 1963—, Elementary Sch. Library Collection, Mayor's Com., Montclair, N.J. Cable TV, 1973. Mem. A.L.A., Am. Assn. Sch. Librarians, Essex County N.J. Sch. Librarians (pres. 1961). Presbyn. Club: Operetta (Montclair, N.J.). Contbr. articles to profl. jours. Home and office: 65 Hathaway Lane Essex Falls NJ 07021

CONE, BONNIE ETHEL, ret. univ. chancellor; b. Lodge, S.C.; d. Charles Jefferson and Addie (Harter) Cone; B.S., Coker Coll., 1928, D.Litt., 1961; A.M., Duke, 1941; H.H.D., Queens Coll., 1969; LL.D., Davidson Coll., 1961, Belmont Abbey Coll., 1962. Tchr. math. various high schs., N.C. and S.C., 1928-43, 46-47; instr. math. Duke U., 1943-45; statis. work with Naval Ordinance Lab., Washington, 1945-46; instr. math. Charlotte Coll., 1946-47, dir., 1947-61, pres., 1961-65; acting chancellor U. N.C., Charlotte, 1965-66, vice chancellor student affairs and community relations, 1966-73, vice chancellor emeritus devel. U. N.C. at Charlotte Found., 1973—. Pres. N.C. Coll. Conf., 1955-56, So. Assn. Jr. Colls., 1958-59; mem. Gov.'s Commn. on Status of Women, 1964-65; chmn. residential campaign United Appeal, 1968; mem. poverty study com. United Community Service, 1968-69; chmn. panel cons. Charlotte-Mecklenburg Citizens Com. on Urban Living, 1969—; mem. citizens rev. com. Charlotte Mecklenburg Charter Commn., 1969—; mem. N.C. Community Coll. Adv. Council, 1963—; mem. accreditation screening com. N.C. Community Colls., 1970—; mem. Mecklenburg Mental Retardation Planning Council, 1967-69, N.C. Small Bus. Adv. Council, 1967-69; mem. planning com. for curriculum project So. Regional Edn. Bd.'s Commn. Higher Ednl. Opportunity in South, 1968; mem. program activities com. Mecklenburg-Union Tb and Respiratory Disease Assn., Inc., 1967-68; chmn. Christmas Seal, 1966; mem. Mecklenburg Mental Health adv. bd., 1971—, Mecklenburg County Water Pollution Control adv. com., 1973—. Trustee Charlotte Children's Nature Mus., 1963-65, Coker Coll., Hartsville, S.C., 1954-72, Sacred Heart Coll., Belmont, N.C., 1970-73; hon. bd. dirs. Central Lions Ednl. Found., Inc., 1973—. Recipient awards including Distinguished Citizenship award N.C. dist. Civitan Internat., 1965, Liberty Bell award 26th Jud. Dist. Bar Assn., 1966. Mem. So. Assn. Colls. and Schs. (trustee 1969-70), Am. Assn. U. Women, Charlotte Sales and Marketing Execs. Inc. (hon.), Historic Properties Commn. (project com. 1973—), Com. of 100 for a Greater Charlotte. Baptist (mem. bd. missions 1967-68, mem. exec. com., pulpit com. 1967-68, chmn. stewardship promotion 1973). Club: Altrusa (Charlotte). Chmn. editorial bd. Jr. Coll. Jour., 1958-61; editorial bd. Community Coll. Rev., 1972—. Home: 9234 Sandburg Av Charlotte NC 28213

CONE, GERTRUDE ELLEN MARY, historian, librarian; b. Syracuse, N.Y.; d. William Horton and Persis (Mather) Cone; A.B., U. Rochester, 1931; M.A., U. Vt., 1945; postgrad. Fordham U. Grad. Sch. Edn., 1960-61, Sch. Social Service, 1964, Canisius Coll., 1963-64, State U. Coll., Geneseo, N.Y., summers 1931-33, 35. Tchr., librarian Moira (N.Y.) High Sch., 1931-34, Ft. Edward (N.Y.) High Sch., 1934-35, Sr. High Sch., Bristol, Conn., 1939-42; librarian Jr.-Sr. High Sch., Plattsburgh, N.Y., 1942-44; asst. coll. librarian State U. N.Y. Coll. at Plattsburgh, 1945-61, asst. librarian emeritus, 1966—; tchr., librarian Nardin Acad., Buffalo, 1961—. Active A.R.C. Mem. Am., N.Y., Catholic library assns., Western N.Y. Catholic Libraries Conf. (sec. 1963-64), N.Y. State Tchrs. Assn., NEA, Am. Assn. U. Women, Theta Alpha Epsilon. Democrat. Roman Catholic. Author: Selective Bibliography of Publications on the Champlain Valley, 1959. Asso. editor York State Tradition, 1948—. Contbr. articles on Champlain Valley to hist. jours. Home: 135 Cleveland Av Buffalo NY 14222

CONE, HELEN BESS FINCH, interior designer; b. Champaign, Ill.; d. James Hugh and Helen M. (Trevett) Finch; B.S., U. Ill., 1929; m. Russell A. Cone, Feb. 22, 1930 (div. June 1968); children—Carol Finch (Mrs. Thomas O. Rose), Linda R. (Mrs. John W. Allen), Helen Claire (Mrs. Edward L. Robertson III). Interior designer The Rose Shop, Champaign, 1934-43; owner, operator Helen Bess Cone Interiors, Champaign, 1947—; dir. Bank of Ill., Champaign. Pres., Champaign-Urbana Jr. Service League, 1941-43; chmn. Well Baby Clinic, 1946, 1st chmn., 1953; chmn. Service League Follies, 1958-61. Mem. Am. Inst. Interior Designers (chpt. pres. 1968-71, nat. bd. govs. 1969-73, chmn. bd. Ill. chpt. 1970-72, dist. bd. govs. 1967-73), Am. Inst. Design, Jr. League, Kappa Alpha Theta. Club: Champaign-Urbana Art. Home: 909 W University Av Champaign IL 61820

CONE, JANE HARRISON, mus. ofcl.; b. Sussex, Eng., Oct. 1, 1939; d. R. Howard and Mary Cohen (Zamora) Harrison; student Sorbonne, Paris, 1957-58, Central Sch. Speech and Drama, London, 1958-59, Ecole du Louvre, Paris, 1959-60; M.A. in Fine Arts, Harvard, 1966; m. Richard A. Cone, Aug. 26, 1966; 1 dau., Tania. Came to U.S., 1963, naturalized, 1974. Asst. on catalog Mellon collection English paintings, 1961-62; critic Arts Rev., 1961-62; London corr. Arts Mag., 1962-63, contbg. editor, 1963-66; contbg. editor Art Forum, 1967-69; curator painting and sculpture Balt. Mus. Art, 1971—. Mem. congl. campaign staff, 1970. N.E.A. fellow for mus. profls., 1973. Compiler David Smith Catalog, 1967. Home: 225 W Lafayette Av Baltimore MD 21217 Office: Baltimore Museum of Art Art Museum Dr Baltimore MD 21218

CONE, MOLLY ZELDA, author; b. Tacoma, Oct. 3, 1918; d. Arthur and Frances (Sussman) Lamken; student U. Wash., 1936-39; m. Gerald J. Cone, Sept. 9, 1939; children—Susan (Mrs. Gary Dale), Gary, Ellen. Author: Only Jane, 1960; Too Many Girls, 1960; The Trouble with Toby, 1961; Mishmash, 1962; Stories of Jewish Symbols, 1963; (with Margaret Pitcairn Strachen) Batch of Trouble, 1963; Reeney, 1963; Mishmash and the Substitute Teacher, 1963; The Real Dream, 1964; A Promise is a Promise, 1964; Who Knows Ten, 1965; Mishmash and the Sauerkraut Mystery, 1965; The Jewish Sabbath, 1966; The Jewish New Year, 1966; Crazy Mary, 1966; Hurry Henrietta, 1966; Purim, 1967; The Other Side of the Fence, 1967; The House in the Tree, 1968; Mishmash and Uncle Looey, 1968; The Green Green Sea, 1968; Annie Annie, 1969; Leonard Bernstein, 1970; Simon, 1970; The Ringling Brothers, 1971; You Can't Make Me If I Don't Want To, 1971; Hear, O Israel, 4 story books, 1971, 72; Number Four, 1972; Dance Around the Fire, 1974. Recipient certificate of recognition Wash. Gov.'s Festival of Arts, 1966, 70, Myrtle Wreath Achievement award Seattle chpt. Hadassah, 1967, Women of Achievement award Theta Sigma Phi, 1968, Lit. Creativity citation Music and Art Found. Seattle, 1968, 1st pl. award Wash. Press Women, 1969, 70, 2d pl. award, 1971, Sugar Plum award, 1972, Neveh Shalom Centennial award for lit. contbn. toward edn. Jewish children, 1970, 1st pl. award Nat. Fedn. Press Women, 1970, Shirley Kravitz Children's Book award Assn. Jewish Libraries, 1973. Mem. Authors Guild, Wash. Press Women, Seattle Free Lances.

CONE, PATRICIA CLAPP (MRS. EDWARD DELLA TORRE CONE), author; b. Boston, June 9, 1912; d. Howard and Elizabeth (Blachford) Clapp; grad. Kimberly Sch., 1930; student Columbia Sch. Journalism, 1930-32; m. Edward della Torre Cone, Mar. 3, 1933; children—Christopher, Patricia (Mrs. John Shelter), Pamela (Mrs. William Wakefield). Playwright, 1954—; juvenile author, 1968—. Bd. mgrs., bd. dirs., life mem. Studio Players Essex County. Author: (plays) The Honeysuckle Hedge, 1959; Edie-Across-the-Street, 1959; Red Heels and Roses, 1960; Never Keep Him Waiting, 1961; The Friendship Bracelet, 1963; The Invisible Dragon, 1970, others; (novels) Constance, 1968 (runnerup children's div. Nat. Book Award 1969, recipient Lewis Carroll Shelf award Wis. Book Conf. 1969); Jane-Emily, 1969; Dr. Elizabeth, 1974; King of the Dollhouse, 1974. Contbr. to Ency. Brit. Ednl. Corp. Lang. Experiences in Reading, 1972. Home: 83 Beverley Rd Upper Montclair NJ 07043

CONE, VIRGIE HORNE HYMAN (MRS. EDWARD E. CONE), ret. educator; b. Brooksville, Fla.; d. George G. and Virgie (Horne) Hyman; B.S., Fla. State Coll. Women, 1945; M.Ed., U. Fla., 1956; m. Edward Elbert Cone, Dec. 20, 1930 (dec. Feb. 1962); children—Molly (Mrs. Cernl), Edward Elbert. Tchr., Meml. Jr. High Sch., Hillsborough County, 1929-31; tchr. Duval County Robert E. Lee Sr. High Sch., Jacksonville, Fla., 1943-55, dean, 1955-70; prin. Lee High Sch. (1st woman secondary sch. prin. in county), 1971-74; owner Cone's Antiques. Chmn., A.R.C. night vols. St. Vincents Hosp., 1969-71; mem. task force Mayor's Community Planning Council, 1969. Mem. Fla. Council Tchrs. Math. (curriculum chmn. 1952, sec. 1949), Am. Assn. U. Women (Jacksonville v.p. 1953), Duval Tchrs. Assn. (chmn. profl. rights and responsibilities com. 1965-66), Jacksonville Panhellenic Assn. (pres. 1959-60, mem. scholarship com. 1963-68), Duval Personnel and Guidance Assn. (organizing chmn. 1966-69), Nat., Fla. assns. secondary prins., Delta Kappa Gamma (chpt. pres. 1959-61), Sigma Kappa (nat. scholarship chmn. 1963—). Club: Pilot of Jacksonville. Home: NW 3d St Jasper FL 32052

CONFORTH, ELIZABETH LOIS, physician, pathologist; b. Rockford, Minn., 1908; M.D., U. Minn., 1933. Intern Children's Hosp. for Women and Children, San Francisco, 1932-33; resident in pathology St. Vincent's Hosp., Los Angeles, 1938-40; practice medicine, specializing in pathology, Los Angeles and San Diego, 1940-73; instr. pathology Women's Med. Sch., 1940-41, U. Ark., 1941-42; asst. prof. U. Ark., 1942-46. Diplomate Am. Bd. Pathology. Fellow Coll. Am. Pathologists; mem. A.M.A., Am. Med. Women Assn., Am. Soc. Clin. Pathologists. Address: 4444 W Point Loma Blvd San Diego CA 92107

CONGDON, HELEN ELIZABETH CORNELL (MRS. PAUL E. CONGDON), clubwoman; b. Montpelier, Vt., Dec. 31, 1909; d. William Oliver and Ethel Maude (Roberts) Cornell; grad. high sch.; m. Paul E. Congdon, Aug. 27, 1938. Pres. East Springfield Women's Club, Western Mass. Women's Club, 14th Dist. Pres.' Club; clk. Mass. State Fedn. Women's Clubs, then v.p., now pres.; chmn. vet.'s service, treas., editor Fedn. Topics. Mem. D.A.R., Pres.' Club Mass., Past Chmn.'s Club, Council Club Mass., Dir.'s Club. Episcopalian (active local and diocesan offices). Home: 1372 Page Blvd Springfield MA 01104

CONGER, LUCINDA DICKINSON (MRS. BRUCE CALDWELL CONGER), librarian; b. Fort Bragg, N.C., June 11, 1941; d. Meredith Moore and Ann Oliver (Mumford) Dickinson; B.A. cum laude, Radcliffe Coll., 1963; M.L.S., Rutgers, 1964; m. Bruce Caldwell Conger, June 25, 1966. Reference librarian U. Cal. at Davis, 1964-65; cataloger Library of Congress, 1965, reference librarian, 1966; annex librarian Princeton, 1966-70; dir. reclassification Albion Coll., 1970-71, serials and documents librarian, 1971-73, tchr. library research course, 1970-73; sr. reference and data archive librarian Social Sci. Library Yale, 1973—. Mem. A.L.A., Am. Civil Liberties Union. Democrat. Episcopalian. Contbr. articles to profl. jours. Office: Social Science Library Box 1958 New Haven CT 06520

CONGLETON, ANN, educator; b. Dayton, O., Aug. 26, 1936; d. Ray Thomas and Jane (Helper) Congleton; B.A., Wellesley Coll., 1958; Ph.D., Yale, 1962; m. Francis Gilman Hutchins, July 8, 1972. Systems programmer mech. translation group Mass. Inst. Tech., 1962-64; asso. prof. philosophy Wellesley (Mass.) Coll., 1964—. Mem. Am. Philos. Assn., Am. Assn. U. Profs. Author: Two Kinds of Lawlessness: Plato's Crito, Political Theory, 1974. Home: 38 Cedar Lane Way Boston MA 02108 Office: Dept Philosophy Wellesley College Wellesley MA 02181

CONKLIN, EVELYN GRACE, museum curator; b. San Diego, Mar. 29, 1927; d. Percy Frank and Edith Kent (Ziny) Conklin; grad. high sch. Established mus. San Dimas (Cal.) Park, 1951, nature specialist, 1951-59; established nature program Los Angeles County Park and Recreation Dept., 1951, nature specialist, 1951-59; established Hi-Desert Nature Mus., Yucca Valley, Cal., 1964, naturalist, curator, 1964—. Recipient award in appreciation of services Yucca Valley C. of C. Mem. Yucca Valley Art Assn. (hon. life), Soroptimists, Yucca Valley Camera Club (co-founder 1965). Home: Box 473 Pipes Rd Yucca Valley CA 92284 Office: 57117 29 Palms Hwy Yucca Valley CA 92284

CONKLIN, FRANCES PHILLIPS (MRS. J. WALLACE CONKLIN), physician; b. Port Jervis, N.Y., July 8, 1924; d. Robert Conkling and Marion (Rice) Phillips; B.A., U. Wis., 1945; Registered Phys. Therapist, Harvard Med. Sch., 1946; M.D. cum laude, U. Vt., 1951; m. J. Wallace Conklin, July 31, 1949; children—Jonathan, Jennifer, Elizabeth, Suzanne. Intern, Santa Barbara (Cal.) Cottage Hosp., 1951-52; resident U. Minn. Hosps., 1952-55; practice medicine specializing in radiation therapy, Providence, 1958—; mem. staff R.I. Hosp., Miriam Hosp., VA Hosp. Mem. Service and profl. edn. commn. R.I. div. Am. Cancer Soc., 1969-72. Diplomate Am. Bd. Radiology. Mem. New Eng. Cancer Soc., R.I. (pres. 1965), N.Am. radiolog. socs., New Eng. Soc. Radiation Oncology. Author: (with Paul Olfelt) Manual of Radiation Therapy, 1958. Home: 54 Hybrid Dr Cranston RI 02920 Office: 1 Randall Sq Providence RI 02904

CONKLIN, GLADYS (MRS. IRVING CONKLIN), author; b. Harpster, Ida., May 30, 1903; d. Oliver Levi and Hettie May (Myers) Plemon; B.S., U. Wash., 1926; m. Irving Conklin, Apr. 9, 1934. Children's librarian Ventura (Cal.) Pub. Library, 1926-28; N.Y.C. Pub. Library, 1929-31, Los Angeles Pub. Library, 1934-42; supr. children's work Hayward (Cal.) Pub. Library, 1950-65; writer of childrens books, 1958—. Pres., Ohlone Audubon Soc., Hayward, 1965. Mem. Assn. Children's Librarians (pres. 1953), Cal. Library Assn. (pres. childrens sect. 1963), Women's Nat. Book Assn. Author: I Like Caterpillars, 1958; If I Were A Bird, 1964; How Insects Grow, 1969; Little Apes, 1970; Tarantula, The Giant Spider, 1972; Fairy Rings and Other Mushrooms, 1973. Address: 16582 Kent Av San Lorenzo CA 94580

CONKLIN, SHIRLEY LORRAINE, coll. dean; b. Santa Barbara, Cal., Feb. 27, 1925; d. Harold Stock and Mary (Morrelli) Conklin; diploma Knapp Coll. Nursing, 1946; B.S., U. San Francisco, 1950; M.A., Columbia, 1964. Staff nurse, Santa Barbara Cottage Hosp., 1946, So. Pacific Hosp., 1947-48, Stanford U. Hosp., 1946-47, St. Mary's Hosp., San Frnacisco, 1948-50; instr. fundamentals of nursing St. Mary's Coll. of Nursing, San Francisco, 1950-55; instr. fundamentals of nursing Knapp Coll. Nursing, Santa Barbara, 1958-60, dir., 1960-63; coordinator registered nursing program Coll.

of Marin, Kentfield, Cal., 1964-70; asst. dean health occupations Santa Barbara City Coll., 1970—. Cons., U.S. Dept. Health, Edn. and Welfare; mem. adv. panel on nursing A.M.A., 1972—. Bd. dirs. Comprehensive Health Planning, 1972-73, Regional Med. Planning, 1973-74. Mem. Am. Nurses Assn., Nat. League for Nursing (past vice chmn. exec. com. Asso. Degree Council, now mem. accreditation bd. rev.), alumnae assns. Knapp Coll. Nursing, U. San Francisco, Tchrs. Coll. Columbia U., Kappa Delta Phi, Pi Lambda Theta. Home: 6155 La Goleta Rd Goleta CA 93017 Office: 721 Cliff Dr Santa Barbara CA 93109

CONKLIN, WILLA CHARLENE DEWITT (MRS. DWIGHT EMERSON CONKLIN), former state senator; b. Griswold, Ia., July 10, 1929; d. Charles Willard and Viola Gertrude (Turner) DeWitt; B.A., Ia. State Tchrs. Coll., 1950; M.A., State U. Ia., 1953; m. Dwight Emerson Conklin, June 7, 1952; children—Beth Ann, Ralph Willard, Robert Charles, Barbara Jeanne-Anne, James Dwight. High sch. tchr., Massena, Ia., 1950-52; speech therapist Univ. Hosp. Sch. for Handicapped Children, State U. Ia., Iowa City, 1953-54; mem. Ia. Ho. of Reps., 1967-69, Ia. Senate, 1969-73. Pvt. speech therapist, 1954—. Curator state Hist. Soc. Ia. Active Girl Scouts U.S.A.; chmn. Black Hawk County Cancer Crusade, 1968. Mem. Waterloo-Black Hawk County YWCA, Easter Seal Soc. Black Hawk County, Old Capitol Commn., Terrace Hill Commn. Dir. Black Hawk County Republican Women, 1965—, auditor, 1967—. Bd. dirs. Ia. Soc. Historic Landmarks, 1969—. Mem. N.E.A., Am. Assn. U. Women, Nat. Soc. State Legislators, Nat. Order Women Legislators, Ladies Legislative League, Women's Aux. Black Hawk County Med. Soc. (pres. 1967-68, mem. state med. aux. bd. 1967-68), Ia. (curator 1973—), Cass County, Cedar Falls, Cedar Valley (pres.) hist. socs., D.A.R. (chpt. regent 1969-70, state chmn. 1965-68, state officer 1970-71), Children Am. Revolution (organizing pres. Red Cedar River Soc. 1965-68, state sr. pres.), P.E.O., Alpha Gamma Delta, Kappa Delta Pi. Presbyn. Home: 141 Woodlawn Rd Waterloo IA 50701

CONLAN, SISTER MARY SAMUEL (PATRICIA EDITH), coll. pres.; b. San Francisco, Mar. 10, 1927; d. Samuel Leo and Gertrude Margaret (O'Brien) Conlan; B.A., Dominican Coll. San Rafael, 1948; M.A., Cath. U. Am., 1957; Ph.D., Stanford, 1963. Joined Congregation Dominican Sisters San Rafael, 1949; tchr. elementary grades St. Raphaels Sch., San Rafael, 1951-52; tchr. high sch. Dominican Sch., San Rafael, 1952-57; mem. faculty Dominican Coll. San Rafael, 1957—, dean students, 1963-67, acad. dean, 1967-68, trustee, 1968—, pres., 1968—. Bd. dirs. Ind. Colls. No. Cal., Inc. Mem. Assn. Ind. Cal. Colls. and Univs. (trustee). Address: Dominican College San Rafael CA 94901

CONLEY, LOIS SPARKMAN (MRS. EDWARD W. CONLEY), clubwoman; b. Hamilton, Tex., Sept. 8, 1900; d. James Sumner and Ida May (Spears) Sparkman; student St. Mary's U., Trinity U.; m. Edward W. Conley. Organizing regent, chaplain Rose Window of San Jose chpt., state chmn. Golden Acorns com., state treas. Tex. soc. Daus. Am. Colonists; founding pres. San Antonio Geneal. and Hist. Soc., 1959-63, also bd. dirs., hon. pres., life mem.; past registrar, chmn. genealogy com. De Bexar chpt. D.A.R.; past registrar Gov. Richard Preston chpt. Colonial Dames 17th Century; past v.p., pres., registrar Capt. Augustus Jones chpt., v.p., historian Tex. soc., treas. state officers club Tex., nat. soc. U.S. Daus. of 1812; mem. many geneal. and hist. socs., including Magna Charta Dames (past state treas.), Sovereign Colonial Soc. Ams. of Royal Descent, Colonial Order of Crown, Soc. Descs. of Knights of Most Noble Order of Garter, Tex. Hist. Found., Council of Pres., San Antonio Conservation Soc., Witte Meml. Mus., Nat. Geneal. Soc. (Distinguished Service award), Am. Genealogist, Local History and Geneal. Soc., Dallas, Soc. Genealogists, London, Eng. Hon. guest speaker, also recipient hon. citizens certificate State Geneal. Soc. Conv., Ft. Worth, 1963; named Woman of Week, San Antonio Express-News, 1961. Mem. Ch. of Christ (hosp. visitation com., Wednesday's Ladies Bible Class). Club: Jasmine Garden (tri-color award for flower arrangement 1960, past v.p.). Address: 165 Treasure Way San Antonio TX 78209

CONLIN, ROXANNE BARTON, lawyer; b. Huron, S.D., June 30, 1944; d. Marion William and Alyce Muraine (Madden) Barton; B.A., Drake U., 1964, J.D., 1966; m. James Clyde Conlin, Mar. 21, 1964; children—Jacalyn Rae, James Barton. Admitted to Ia. bar, 1966; asso. Davis, Huebner, Johnson & Burt, Des Moines, 1966-67; dep. indsl. commr. State of Ia., Des Moines, 1967-68, asst. atty. gen., 1969—. Mem. Ia. Commn. on the Status of Women, 1972—. State chmn. Ia. Women's Polit. Caucus, Des Moines, 1973—, del. nat. steering com. 1973—; nat. committeewoman Ia. Young Dems., pres. Polk County Young Dems., 1965-66; del. State Presdl. Conv., 1972. Recipient Fischer Found. scholarship 1965-66, Readers Digest scholarship, 1963-64. Mem. Am. (mem. individual rights and responsibilities com. 1971—), Ia. (mem. career day panel 1971—, mem. bar review com. 1972-73) bar assns., Women's Equity Action League, Nat. Organ. for Women (dir. 1969), Phi Beta Kappa, Alpha Lambda Delta, Chi Omega (social service award). Home: 1623 SW Evans Des Moines IA 50315 Office: State Capitol Bldg Des Moines IA 50319

CONLON, SARA FRANCES SMITH (MRS. WILLIAM F. CONLON), lectr.; b. Waco, Tex., Aug. 15, 1901; d. John E. and Sara (Robertson) Smith; A.B., Manchester Coll., 1923; postgrad. U. Wis., 1924-25, Northwestern U., 1930-31; spl. student U. London (Eng.), 1926-27, U. Geneva (Switzerland), 1926; m. William F. Conlon, Sept. 1, 1928; 1 dau., Ellen Augusta (Mrs. Robert K. Adams). Lectr. ancient methods spinning textile fibres, 1931—; tchr., mus. cons. ancient methods and equipment spinning textile fibres. Sec. Alliance Francaise de Chgo., mem. Magna Charta Dames, Antiquarian Soc., D.A.R. Republican. Club: Womans Athletic. Address: 1509 W Jackson Blvd Chicago IL 60607

CONLY, PATRICIA WALLACE (MRS. PATRICK E. CONLY), educator, pediatrician; b. Monterey Park, Cal., Nov. 4, 1934; d. Herschel Everett and Emma Helene (Novak) Wallace; B.S., U. So. Cal., 1956; M.D., Med. Coll. Pa., 1960; m. Patrick E. Conly, May 13, 1961 (div. 1973); children—Susan Anne, Diane Carroll. Intern Meadowbrook Hosp., East Meadow, N.Y., 1960-61; resident in pediatrics Bellevue Hosp., N.Y.C., 1961-62, Jackson Meml. Hosp., Miami, Fla., 1962-63; fellow in pediatric endocrinology U. Miami, 1963-66; asst. prof. U. Miami Sch. Medicine, 1966-74. Fellow Am. Acad. Pediatrics; mem. Endocrine Soc., Fla. Diabetes Assn., So. Soc. Pediatric Research. Office: 2435 N Grand Av Santa Ana CA 92701

CONN, JOAN ANN, mathematician; b. Flushing, N.Y., May 24, 1932; d. Edward Daniel and Leonore (Biales) Jacobs; A.B., Barnard Coll., 1953; M.S., Adelphi U., 1958; Ph.D., N.Y. U., 1964. Statistician, Psychol. Corp., N.Y.C., 1952; stress analyst Rep. Aviation Corp., Farmingdale, N.Y., 1953-54, sr. dynamics engr., 1955-57; dynamics engr. Martin Co., Balt., 1954-55; research asst. math. N.Y.U. Courant Inst. Math., N.Y.C., 1958-62; asst. prof. math. St. John's U., Bklyn., 1962, Cooper Union, N.Y.C., 1963-64; math. analyst-engr. Sperry Gyroscope Co., Great Neck, N.Y., 1962-63; sr. analyst Computer Applications, Inc., Inst. Space Studies, N.Y.C., 1965-70; math. and statis. cons., N.Y.C., 1970—. Mem. Inst. Math. Statistics. Research in differential equations, elasticity, fluid-dynamics, queueing theory, statistics and stochastic processes. Home: 136-39 41st Av Flushing NY 11355

CONNATSER, BILLIE CAMPBELL (MRS. LEMUEL HORACE CONNATSER), educator; b. Baileyton, Tenn., Feb. 16, 1903; d. Looney Peck and Mae (Kidwell) Campbell; student East Tenn. State U., 1922, Md. U., summer 1924, Bethel Coll., 1926; B.S., U. Tenn., 1941; m. Lemuel Horace Connatser, Aug. 22, 1941. Tchr., Greene County Schs., Greeneville, Tenn., 1922-25, Holston Orphanage, Greeneville, 1925-27, Hellier (Ky.) High Sch., 1927-29, Clinton (Tenn.), Elementary Sch., 1929-37; tchr. art Knoxville (Tenn.) City Schs., 1937-47, art cons., 1949-56, supr. art edn., 1956-69, critic, demonstration tchr. U. Tenn., 1943-47. Mem. arts adv. com. Dulin Gallery of Art, 1966-68. Mem. youth com. A.R.C., 1966-71. Mem. Internat. Sch. Art Program, Nat., Tenn., East Tenn. (chmn. art dept. 1953-55) edn. assns., Southeastern Arts Assn., Nat. Art Edn. Assn., Internat. Soc. for Edn. through Art, Internat. Platform Assn., Pi Lambda Theta, Delta Kappa Gamma. Methodist. Home: 911 Eagle Bend Rd Clinton TN 37716

CONNAWAY, INA LEE WALLACE (MRS. CHARLES EARL CONNAWAY), artist; b. Cleburne, Tex., Dec. 27, 1929; d. Lee O. and Edith (Slaughter) Wallace; student Baylor U., 1947-48, Famous Artists Sch., 1954-57, U. Alaska, 1964-65; B.A. in Fine Art, George Washington U., 1968; student Corcoran Sch. Art, 1965-68; m. Charles Earl Connaway, Dec. 1, 1948; children—Richard Earl, Robert Wallace. One-man shows at Anchor Gallery, Anchorage, Alaska, 1963, Hotel Baranof, Juneau, Alaska, 1963, Officers Wives Club, Ft. Richardson, Alaska, 1964, Anchorage Westward Hotel, 1965, Lynn Kottler Galleries, N.Y.C., 1966, 68-71, Lasting Americana, U.S. Mil. Acad., 1970-71, Army and Navy Chpt. D.A.R., Washington, 1971; exhibited in group shows at Alaska Fur Rendevous, Anchorage, 1964, Fairfax County Cultural Assn. Va. Area Art Show, 1965, Episcopal Ch. Area Art Show, Fredericksburg, Va., 1966, Austrian Exposition, State Dept., Washington, 1967, Internat. Platform Assn. Art Show, Washington, 1967, 68, 69, 70, Christ Church Art Show, Alexandria, Va., 1967, Empire Chpt. show Nat. Soc. Arts and Letters, N.Y.C., 1969, numerous others. Recipient Honorable Mention award Alaska Fur Rendevous, 1963, Artist award Ann. Beaux Arts Ball, 1963, Artist of Month award Alaska Artist Guild, 1963, award Am. Art Week, 1963, 1st place Alaska State Fair, 1964, Popular Vote award Officers Club Art Show, 1965, Gold medal Accademia Interzionale Leonardo da Vinci Science, Lettere-Art, Rome, Italy, 1972-73. Fellow Am. Artist Profl. League; mem. Internat. Platform Assn., Nat. Soc. Arts and Letters, Am. Assn. Museums. Address: PO Box 1111 St Augustine FL 32084

CONNEELY, MARGARET AGNES, ednl. adminstr.; b. Providence, Dec. 16, 1907; d. Thomas Francis and Delia Maria (Healy) Conneely; A.B., Brown U., 1930, A.M., 1935; postgrad. Harvard, 1934, Providence Coll., 1936-39, Boston Coll., 1962-68. Student tchr. Gilbert Stuart Jr. High Sch., Providence Pub. Schs., 1931-32, math. tchr. Oliver Hazard Perry Jr. High Sch., 1932-33, Hope High Sch., 1933-38, Mt. Pleasant High Sch., 1938-67, head math. dept., 1952-67; coordinator Title III Elementary and Secondary Edn. Act Math. Project, 1967-70; supr. math. Providence Pub. Schs., 1970—. Instr. math. Roger Williams Jr. Coll., 1953-63; NSF research asst. Brown U., 1956; cons. Jr. High Sch. Math. Curriculum Com., 1965-66; tchr. in-service math. Jr. High Sch. tchrs. math., 1964. Mem. Com. on Children and Youth, 1949-71. Mem. Am. Assn. U. Women (asst. treas. Providence Plantations br. 1971-73, treas. 1973), Nat. Council Tchrs. Math., Assn. Tchrs. Math. in New Eng., R.I. Math. Tchrs. Assn. (pres. 1970—), N.E.A., Assn. Supervision and Curriculum Devel., R.I. Edn. Assn., Pembroke Alumnae Assn., Internat. Fedn. Cath. Alumnae. Club: Catholic Woman's (Providence). Home: 1 Mayfair Dr Rumford RI 02916 Office: 211 Veazie St Providence RI 02904

CONNELL, ELIZABETH BISHOP (MRS. JOHN T. CONNELL), physician; b. Springfield, Mass., Oct. 17, 1925; d. Homer G. and Margaret (Kincaid) Bishop; A.B., U. Pa., 1947, M.D., 1951; m. John T. Connell, June 11, 1949; children—Robert, Thomas, Richard, David, James, Patricia. Intern, Lankenau Hosp., Phila., 1951-52, resident pathology and anesthesia, 1952-53; resident gynecology Grad. Hosp U. Pa., 1958-60; resident obstetrics Mt. Sinai Hosp., N.Y.C., 1960-61; individual practice and anesthetist, Blue Hill, Me., 1953-58; asso. prof. obstetrics and gynecology N.Y. Med. Coll., 1962-69, dir. Family Planning Center, 1964-69; asso. prof. obstetrics and gynecology Coll. Phys. and Surg. Columbia, 1970-73, dir. research and devel. Family Life Services, Internat. Inst. Study Human Reprodn., 1970-73; asso. dir. health scis. Rockefeller Found., N.Y.C., 1973—. Mem. med. adv. bd. Planned Parenthood, N.Y.C., 1964, nat. adv. council Center Family Planning Program Devel., 1968; mem. exec. com. Am. Assn. Planned Parenthood Physicians, 1968; mem. obstetrics and gynecology adv. com. FDA, 1970; cons. family planning N.Y.C. Dept. Health, Family Planning Project Human Resources Adminstrn.; mem. com. med. and pub. health Assn. Vol. Sterilizations, Inc. Diplomate Am. Bd. Obstetrics and Gynecology. Mem. A.M.A., Am. Coll. Obstetricians and Gynecologists, A.C.S., Am. Pub. Health Assn., Am. Fertility Soc., Am. Med. Women's Assn. Inc., Med. Women's Internat. Assn., Pub. Health Assn. N.Y.C., Soc. Sci. Study Sex Inc., N.Y. Gynecol. Soc. Inc., N.Y. Acad. Scis., Med. Soc. State N.Y., Population Crisis Com., Royal Soc. Health. Home: 101 Hudson Terrace Yonkers NY 10701 Office: 111 W 50th St New York City NY 10020

CONNELL, LOUISE FOX, author; b. Bayonne, N.J.; d. Hugh Francis and Virginia (Herrick) Fox; A.B., Barnard Coll., 1914; m. Richard Connell, Nov. 8, 1919 (dec.). Advt. writer J. Walter Thompson Co., 1915-20; asso. editor Delineator mag., 1920-23; asso., then mng. editor Charm, Newark, 1923-25; West Coast editor You, 1936-41; contract writer Conde Nast, 1941-43; free-lance writer 1943—. Vol. Lenox Hill Hosp., N.Y.C., 1953-54; mem. exec. com. community adv. bd. Fordham Hosp., N.Y.C., 1954-72. Mem. staff U.S. Food Adminstrn., World War I. Ghost writer, Cal., World War II. Mem. League Women Voters, Civil Liberties Union, So. Christian Leadership Conf., N.A.A.C.P., Am. Assn. UN, Nat. Council Women U.S., Inc., Interfaith Neighbors, Citizens Union, SANE. Democrat. Unitarian (deacon). Club: Query (N.Y.C.). Co-author: (play) The Queen Bee, 1929. Contbr. articles to mags. including Reader's Digest, Parents Mag., Woman's Day. Home: 240 E 82d St Apt 21D New York City NY 10028 Office: care Brandt & Brandt 101 Park Av New York City NY 10017

CONNELL, SUZANNE (SPARKS) MCLAURIN, librarian; b. Bennettsville, S.C., Sept. 12, 1917; d. John Bethea and Aleine (McLeod) McLaurin; A.B., Woman's Coll. of U. N.C., 1938; A.B. in L.S., U. N.C., 1940; 1 son, John Alexander (dec.). Library asst. Mt. Pleasant br. D.C. Pub. Library, Washington, 1940-41; post librarian Camp Sutton, N.C., 1943-44; post librarian McGuire Gen. Hosp., Richmond, Va., 1945-46, chief librarian McGuire VA Hosp., 1946-52, 59-62; chief librarian VA Hosp., Lake City, Fla., 1952-56; cataloger, chief circulation, asst. chief documents acquisitions Air U. Library, Maxwell AFB, Ala., 1956-59; head extension, head circulation Greensboro (N.C.) Pub. Library, 1962-63; reference librarian asst. and acting base librarian Marine Corps Base, Camp Lejeune, N.C., 1963-66; part time cataloger Wilmington (N.C.) Pub. Library, 1967—. Mem. A.L.A. (pres. assn. hosp. and instn. libraries 1955-56), N.C., Southeastern library assns., Am. Bus. Women's Assn., Phi Beta Kappa. Contbr. articles to Brit. and Am. periodicals. Home: 502 Brunswick St Southport NC 28461

CONNELLY, FRANCES, coll. ofcl.; b. Boston, Aug. 18, 1922; d. John Joseph and Isobel Clare (Furlong) Connelly; A.S. in Accounting, Bentley Coll., 1957; B.S. in Bus. Adminstrn., Suffolk U., 1963; M.Ed., Boston State Coll., 1968. Asst. in bus. adminstrn. Mass. Dept. Edn., 1945-62, asst. supr. Mass. Div. State Colls., 1962-64, supr., dir. grad. and continuing studies, 1964-69; registrar Newton Coll. Sacred Heart, 1969—. Mem. Am., New Eng. assns. collegiate registrars, Delta Kappa Gamma. Home: 51 Mellen St Dorchester MA 02124 Office: Newton Coll 885 Centre St Newton MA 02159

CONNELLY, MARGARET BARBARA, ednl. adminstr.; b. N.Y.C., Feb. 9, 1946; d. Thomas Francis and Margaret Helen (West) Connelly; B.S., in Edn. summa cum laude (Regents scholar), St. Thomas Aquinas Coll., Sparkill, N.Y., 1967; M.S. in Edn. and Sch. Psychology, St. John's U., 1973, postgrad., 1973—. Tchr., St. Agnes Home and Sch., Sparkill, 1965-67, 68-70, E.S.E.A. Title I coordinator, 1968-72, prin., 1970-72; tchr. St. Christopher Sch., Red Hook, N.Y., 1967-68; dir. student personnel services, lectr. psychology St. Thomas Aquinas Coll., 1972-73. E.S.E.A. Title I evaluator Research Found. City N.Y., 1972-73. Mem. Nat. Assn. Sch. Psychologists, Am. Personnel and Guidance Assn., Council Exceptional Children, Rockland Westchester Student Personnel Assn. Mem. Dominican Congregation of Our Lady of Rosary, Sparkill, mem. congl. chpt., 1972-73, mem. community council, 1973—, mem. financial, fund raising, govt., child care coms. Address: Dominican Congregation Route 340 Sparkhill NY 10976

CONNER, BETTY OGDEN (MRS. CLARENCE E. CONNER), art curator; b. Utica, N.Y., July 7, 1921; d. Myron L. and Mildred (Cole) Ogden; student Russell Sage Coll., 1939-40; m. Elmer W. Knapp, Dec. 28, 1940 (dec. Dec. 1957); children—E. William, Robert Ogden; m. 2d, Clarence E. Conner, Apr. 23, 1965. Art librarian Munson-Williams-Proctor Inst., Utica, 1956-63; art curator dept. fine arts Colgate U., Hamilton, N.Y., 1965—. Mem. Daus. of Nile. Home: Box 276 Waterville NY 13480 Office: Dept Fine Arts Colgate U Hamilton NY 13346

CONNER, LOLA PHYLLIS (MRS. MERLIN L. CONNER), dept. store exec.; b. Grand Rapids, Mich., Feb. 5, 1930; d. Wesley Louis and Effie Mabel (Stephens) Crips; grad. Felt & Tarrant Comptometer Sch., 1950; m. Merlin L. Conner, Aug. 13, 1948; children—Kristi Louise, Robert Lee, Mary Lyn. Payroll clk. Keeler Brass, Grand Rapids, 1947-55; dept. mgr., buyer Rogers Dept. Store, Wyoming, Mich., 1957—, store auditor 1960—. Campfire, Bluebird leader, dist. chmn., 1955-65; mag. chmn. Grand Rapids P.T.A., 1958-59, mother v.p., 1960-61; conducts style shows for charitable orgns., 1968—. Bd. dirs. fashions Davenport Coll.; bd. dirs. Kent Skill Center Retail Marketing. Home: 2000 Melvin St Wyoming MI 49509 Office: 959 28th St SW Wyoming MI 49509

CONNER, SHIRLEY ROBERTS (MRS. JAMES W. CONNER), journalist; b. Lockport, N.Y., Jan. 13, 1923; d. George K. and Marian (Thompson) Roberts; B.S., State U. N.Y. Coll. at Buffalo, 1943, postgrad., 1953-60; m. James W. Conner, Apr. 7, 1944; children—Coleen M., Janine S. Tchr., Kendall Central Sch., Orleans County, N.Y., 1943-45, Barker Central Sch., Niagara County, N.Y., 1945-47, Starpoint Central Sch., Niagara County, 1953-60; feature writer, corr. Tonawanda News, Buffalo Evening News, Niagara Falls Gazette and Union-Sun and Jour., 1959-62; edn., gen. assignment writer Tonawanda News, North Tonawanda, N.Y., 1963—; regular corr. Edn. News, 1967-68. Organizer, Com. for Superintendency Starpoint Sch. Dist., 1959-60, vol. writer dist. newspaper Spartana, 1962—; corr. sec. Starpoint Citizens Com., 1950-53; participant White House Conf. on Edn., 1955. Recipient Am. Newspaper Guild-Buffalo Page One writing award, 1967, 72, Excellence in Sci. Writing award Cornell Labs., Cornell U., 1967, 68; award Am. Edn. Writers', 1970, first prize for community service N.Y. State Pubs. Assn., 1970. Mem. Edn. Writers Assn., N.Y. State P.T.A. (life), Am. Newspaper Guild (unit chmn., exec. com. 1971-73), Nat. Congress Parents and Tchrs., Internat. Platform Assn., Zonta Internat. Republican. Mem. United Ch. of Christ. Home: 4933 Mapleton Rd Lockport NY 14094 Office: 435 River Rd North Tonawanda NY 14120

CONNOLLY, MARGARETE AGNES MALONE (MRS. WILL CONNOLLY), assn. exec.; b. Portland, Ore., Nov. 27, 1910; d. Martin James and Theresa Elizabeth (O'Rourke) Malone; A.B., Holy Names Coll., 1934; certificate social work U. Cal. at Berkeley, 1963; m. Will Connolly, July 15, 1939; children—Paul Martin, William Philip, Anne Mary. Exec. sec. Los Angeles Catholic Theatre Guild, 1937-39; exec. dir. San Francisco Aid Retarded Children, 1951—. Am. del. World Congress on Rehab., Dublin, 1969; cons. mental retardation project rev. com. Dept. Health Edn. and Welfare, 1969-71; vice-chmn. Cal. Adv. Council, Dept. Rehab., 1950; mem. adv. com. mental retardation Cal. Dept. Pub. Health, 1967-68. Bd. dirs. Nat. Assn. Retarded Children, 1954-56, Nat. Rehab. Assn., 1962-64, Internat. Assn. Rehab., 1965-67. Recipient Koshland award, 1972, Golden Rule award Cal. Assn. for Retarded, 1968, Gold Medallion award for distinguished service Phoebe Apperson Hearst, 1963. Mem. N.A.A.C.P., Am. Assn. U. Women, League Women Voters. Home: 375 Pacheco St San Francisco CA 94116 Office: 1362 9th Av San Francisco CA 94122

CONNOLLY, MARY KENNEDY (MRS. FRANCIS X. CONNOLLY), ednl. adminstr.; b. N.Y.C., Aug. 3, 1913; d. Henry Lawrence and Cicely Agatha (Murphy) Kennedy; A.B. cum laude, Coll. Mount St. Vincent, 1933; M.A., Tchrs. Coll., Columbia, 1957, postgrad., 1969-73; m. Francis X. Connolly, Sept. 7, 1940; children—Katharine (Mrs. E. Menze), Lisa (Mrs. M. Leser), Joseph. Office mgr. prodn. dept. NBC, Radio City, N.Y.C., 1934-41; ednl. dir. Nueces County Tb Assn., Corpus Christi, Tex., 1943-45; tchr. elementary sch. Holy Family Sch., New Rochelle, N.Y., 1956-63; coordinator cooperative program between Manhattan Coll. and Coll. of Mt. St. Vincent, N.Y.C., 1970—. Asst. prof. econs. Coll. Mt. St. Vincent, N.Y.C., 1966-70; coordinator for non-pub. elementary schs. in New Rochelle, N.Y., 1965—. Bd. dirs. Westchester Catholic Edn. Conf., 1961-67. Mem. Am. Assn. U. Women, Am. Assn. Higher Edn., Kappa Gamma Pi, Kappa Delta Pi. Roman Catholic. Club: Larchmont Shore. Home: 1255 North Av New Rochelle NY 10804 Office: College of Mount St Vincent Riverdale NY 10471

CONNOLLY, VIRGINIA STRAUGHAN (MRS. JAMES C. CONNOLLY), state legislator, epidemiologist; b. Manchester, Conn., June 25, 1914; d. Wayland Kemper and Ruth Elizabeth (Wright) Straughan; R.N., Hartford Hosp. Sch. Nursing, 1934; B.S., St. Joseph Coll., 1951; postgrad. Boston U., 1951-53, Harvard extension, 1951-54, Nat. Communicable Disease Center Dept. Health, Edn. and Welfare, 1968-69; m. James Cyril Connolly, Aug. 10, 1935; children—Pamela (Mrs. David Bartlett IV), James Patrick. Adminstr., Simsbury (Conn.) Vis. Nursing Assn., 1950-65; interim exec. dir. Am. Cancer Soc., Hartford, 1966; head epidemiology services St. Francis Hosp., Simsbury, 1968—; mem. Conn. Gen. Assembly, 1970—, Ho. chmn. pub. health and safety com. Dir. Simsbury Bank and Trust Co. Sec. welfare Salvation Army, 1955—; chmn. Simsbury Voluntary

Social Service Dept., 1960-65; mem. legislative com. Conn. Hosp. Assn., 1970—; chmn. Simsbury Com. on Aging; sec., Simsbury Housing Authority, 1967-71. Bd. dirs. Simsbury Hist. Soc. Mem. Hartford Hosp., St. Joseph Coll. alumane assns. Fellow Royal Soc. Health (London). Contbr. articles to profl. jours. Home: 91 Old Farms Rd West Simsbury CT 06092

CONNOR, DONNA JANE AYER (MRS. FRANCIS A. CONNOR), univ. adminstr.; b. Rawlins, Wyo., Jan. 1, 1932; d. Walter Dewey and Lula (McCargar) Ayer; B.A., U. Wyo., 1954, M.Ed., 1969; m. Francis A. Connor, June 9, 1958. Bus. tchr. Evanston (Wyo.) High Sch., 1954-55, Rawlins (Wyo.) High Sch., 1955-58; Carbon County Supt. Schs., Rawlins, 1959-69; instr., field coordinator U. Wyo., Rawlins and Rock Springs, 1969—. Trustee Harry Hougard Student Loan Fund. Mem. Am. Assn. U. Women (pres. Wyo. div. 1963-65, v.p. Rocky Mountain region 1971—), Kappa Delta, Delta Kappa Gamma. Soroptimist (pres. 1965-66). Home: 121 E Maple St Rawlins WY 82301

CONNOR, MARJORIE ALICE WELLS (MRS. HARRY BLAKE CONNOR), psychologist; b. Pitts.; d. Harry Burton and Jean Carolyn (Wilbright) Wells; B.S., Webster Coll., 1936; M.S., St. Johns U., 1959; Ph.D. in Ednl. Psychology, U. Cin., 1968; m. Harry Blake Connor, Nov. 28, 1936; children—George Wells, Matthew Blake, Christopher Sean. Clin. psychologist trainee Longview State Hosp., Cin. 1959-61; sch. psychologist Cin. Pub. Schs., 1961-62; tchr. math. guidance McAuley High Sch., Cin., 1962-63; chief psychologist Norwood (O.) Pub. Schs., 1963-65; sch. psychologist Hamilton County Bd. of Edn. Cin. 1965-69; chief psychologist Indian Hill Village Exempted Bd. Edn., Cin., 1969-72; individual practice psychology, counseling child devel., 1970—; mem. firm Pediatric Assos. Inc., 1971—. Pres. scholarship com. Port Washington Community Chest, 1957-59, social worker, 1956-59. Bd. dirs. Littig House, Port Washington. Mem. Am., Ohio psychol. assns., A.A.A.S., Am. Assn. Sch. Psychologists, Ohio Sch. Psychologists, Am. Assn. U. Women. Research on retardation, drug abuse, reading disabilities, effect of parent pathology upon learning disabilities, child devel., hyperactivity Contbr. articles to profl. jours. Home: 6555 Ridge Rd Cincinnati OH 45213

CONNORS, ARLENE DORIS PACHESNEY (MRS. DOUGLAS R. CONNORS), lawyer; b. Milw., Feb. 6, 1929; d. John Jacob and Ann Christine (Kuczkowski) Pachesney; B.S., Marquette U., 1951; J.D., U. Wis., 1957; m. Douglas R. Connors, June 15, 1955; children—Kathleen, Scott, Laurie, Douglas, James. Admitted to Wis. bar, 1957; practiced in Milw., 1957-74; dep. registrar in probate Milwaukee County, Wis., 1974—. Mem. Women's Ct. and Civic Conf., Milw., 1971—, mem. Southside Scholarship Found. Chmn. schs. com. Milw. Safety Commn. Mem. Milw. Sch. Bd., 1973—, vice chmn. pub. relations com. 1973—. Mem. Wis. Bar Assn., Bayview Bus. Assn., Latin Council of Wis., League of Women Voters, Phi Delta Gamma. Democrat. Club: South Side Women's. Home: 1907 East Morgan Av Milwaukee WI 53207 Office 901 N 9th St Milwaukee WI 53233

CONNORS, DORSEY (MRS. JOHN E. FORBES), TV and radio commentator, newspaper columnist; b. Chgo.; d. William J. and Sara (MacLean) Connors; ed. Marywood Sch. for Girls, U. Ill.; m. John E. Forbes; 1 dau., Stephanie (Mrs. Edward J. Lyng). Appeared on Personality Profiles, WGN-TV, Chgo., 1948, Dorsey Connors Show, WMAQ-TV, Chgo., 1949-58, 61-63, Armchair Travels, WMAQ-TV, 1952-55, Home show, NBC, 1954-57, Haute Couture Fashion Openings, NBC, Paris, France, 1954, 58, Dorsey Connors program, WGN, 1958-61, Tempo Nine, WGN-TV, 1961, Society in Chgo., WMAQ-TV, 1964; writer column Hi! I'm Dorsey Connors, Chgo. Sun Times. Founder Ill. Epilepsy League; mem. exec. bd. Chgo. Beautiful Com.; mem. woman's bd. Ill. Children's Home and Aid Soc. Mem. A.F.T.R.A., Screen Actor's Guild, Nat. Acad. TV Arts and Scis., Fashion Group Guild of Chgo. Hist. Soc., Chi Omega. Author: Gadgets Galore, 1953; Save Time, Save Money, Save Yourself, 1972. Address: care Chgo Sun Times 401 N Wabash Chicago IL 60611

CONNORS, EDANA MARIE, educator; b. Milw., Aug. 21, 1906; d. Edward Bernard and Louise (Hofert) Connors; B.A., Coll. St. Teresa, 1928; M.Ed., U. Minn., 1938; postgrad. (N.E.A. fellow), U. Mexico, 1947. Tchr., Albert Lea, Minn., 1931-32, Austin, Minn., 1931-32, Mpls., 1933-73. Mem. Alumni Bd. Coll. St. Teresa, 1967-73. Mem. N.E.A. (life), Minn. City Mpls. edn. assns., Minn. Tchrs. Speech, Nat. Forensic League (Mpls. com. chmn., numerous awards). Home: 203 W Diamond Lake Rd Minneapolis MN 55419

CONNORS, MARGARET MARY, clin. psychologist; b. Bklyn., June 2, 1936; d. Patrick Gregory and Mary Margaret (Sullivan) Connors; B.A., St. Jospeh's Coll., 1958; M.S., L.I. U., 1960; Ph.D., St. John's U., 1973. Clin. psychologist Angel Guardian Home, Bklyn., 1959—. Cons. psychologist St. Mary of the Angels Home, Syosset, N.Y., 1962-71, St. Christopher's Home, Sea Cliff, N.Y., 1968-69, Mercy Home for Children, Bklyn., 1963-66, Cleft Palate Rehab. Clinic, Meth. Hosp., Bklyn., 1973—; clin. instr. dept. pediatrics Downstate Med. Center, State U. N.Y., Bklyn., 1969—; adj. asst. prof. St. John's U., Jamaica, N.Y., 1973—. Mem. Am. Psychol. Assn. Research on relationship of electrophysiol. brain maturation and test intelligence. Office: 6301 12th Av Brooklyn NY 11219

CONNORS, MARY ANN, pub. relations exec.; b. Hartford, Conn., Oct. 18, 1930; d. Richard Thomas and Mary Prudence (Gaghan) Connors; B.S., St. Joseph Coll., 1952; postgrad. Georgetown U., 1953-57, U. Hartford, 1966—. Campaign sec., office mgr. Washington and Conn. offices U.S. Senator William A. Purtell, 1953-59; asst. to pub. relations dir. Conn. Rep. State Hdqrs., Hartford, 1959-61; advt. rep. Farmington Valley Herald, Simsbury, Conn., 1961-62; dir. music and art information U. Hartford, 1962-73; dir. pub. relations and marketing Hartford Symphony Orch., 1973—. Sec., Greater Hartford coordinating Council for Arts, 1964-67, v.p., 1968. Mem. nat. com. Young Republicans, 1962-63; state co-chmn. Conn. Young Reps., 1963-64; pres. Hartford Women's Rep. Club, 1966-67. Adv. bd. Hartt Opera-Theater Guild. Mem. Women in Communications, Am. Assn. U. Women, Am. Symphony Orch. League. Editor: New Eng. region newsletter Am. Coll. Pub. Relations Assn., 1972-73. Contbr. articles to profl. jours. and mags. Home: 249 Lowrey Pl Newington CT 06111 Office: Hartford Symphony Orch 15 Lewis St Hartford CT 06103

CONOLEY, COLLEEN ADELE WYATT (MRS. MERTON GILBERT CONOLEY), educator; b. Beaumont, Tex., Nov. 15, 1922; d. Collie Roy and Nola (Straughan) Wyatt; student Southwestern U., 1939-41; B.A., U. Ark., 1943; M.A., U. Tex., 1959, Ph.D., 1966; m. Merton Gilbert Conoley, June 13, 1943; children—Jill Lauren, Collie Wyatt, Catherine Ellen. Tchr., Taylor (Tex.) Ind. Sch. Dist., 1948-49; advt. mgr. Williamson County Sun, Georgetown, Tex., 1953-57; tchr. Leander (Tex.) Ind. Sch. Dist., 1957-58; multi-sch. librarian Williamson County, Georgetown, Tex., 1958-59; instr. ednl. psychology U. Tex. at Austin, 1961; counselor, dir. guidance service Williamson County Sch., Georgetown, Tex., 1962-66; vis. faculty Pa. State U., University Park, 1966; asso. prof. edn., psychology S.W. Tex. State U., San Marcos, 1966-72. Group leader Tex. Ednl. Desegregation Tech. Assistance, 1969-70. Chmn., Vol. Child and Family Guidance Orgn., 1968—; cons. San Marcos Youth Council, 1970. Nat. Def. Edn. Act fellow, 1961-62. Mem. Am. Assn. U. Profs., Am., Tex., S.W. psychol. assns., Am., Tex. personnel and guidance assns., Am. Ednl. Research Assn., Delta Delta. Presbyn. Contbr. articles in field to profl. jours. Home: 105 E Mimosa Circle San Marcos TX 78666

CONRAD, AGNES CATHERINE, archivist; b. Pasadena, Cal., Sept. 7, 1917; d. Albert and Catherine (McElroy) Conrad; B.A., Coll. of Holy Names, 1939; certificate U. Cal. Sch. Library Sci., 1940. Rare book cataloger Henry E. Huntington Library, San Marino, Cal., 1941-42; librarian USAAF, Victorville, Cal., 1942-45; cataloger U. Cal. at Los Angeles, 1946-50; dept. head U. Hawaii Library, Honolulu, 1950-55; state archivist Hawaii, Honolulu, 1955—. Chmn. Territorial Commn. Historic Sites, 1956-59; pres. Conservation Council for Hawaii, 1966; mem. Mayor's Historic Bldgs. Task Force, Honolulu. Trustee Hawaii Found. for History and Humanities, 1972—, Friends of Iolani Palace, 1971-76. Fellow Soc. Am. Archivists; mem. Am., Hawaii (v.p., pres.) library assns., Hawaiian Hist. Soc. (trustee, pres. 1967-69), Internat. Council on Archives, Cath. Library Soc. Hawaii, Am. Soc. State and Local History, Nat. Trust for Historic Preservation, Hawaii Museums Assn. (pres. 1970), Kappa Gamma Pi. Club: Soroptimist (dist. dir. Hawaii 1972-74, pres. Honolulu). Editor: Proceedings of the Constitutional Convention of Hawaii, 1950, 1960; Don Francisco de Paula Marin, Letters and Jours., 1973. Home: 1634 Makiki St Honolulu HI 96822 Office: State Archives Iolani Palace Grounds Honolulu HI 96813

CONRAD, EVA TALITHA ELDRED, editor; b. Los Angeles, Dec. 9, 1919; d. Elisha and Eva Louise (Baur) Eldred; grad. high sch.; m. Lloyd Ray Conrad, Nov. 26, 1948; children—Bowen Eldred, John William. With radio sta. KFI, Los Angeles, 1942-48, publicity dir., 1943-48; owner, editor, pub. Apple Valley (Cal.) News, 1952—. Mem. San Bernardino County Airport Commn., 1973—. Republican. Episcopalian. Home: 21874 Waalew Rd Apple Valley CA 92307 Office: 21825 Hwy 18 Apple Valley CA 92307

CONRAD, JOYCE LEE (MRS. CHARLES O. CONRAD), journalist; b. Devils Lake, N.D., Apr. 27, 1926; d. Carl and Lillian Alice (Erickson) Lee; B.A., U. N.D., 1947; m. Charles O. Conrad, July 23, 1949; children—Kari, Marcia, Peter. With Morning Pioneer, Bismarck, N.D., 1963—, editor, 1969—. Mem. adv. com. N.D. Park Service, 1961-70; mem. N.D. Health Council, 1968-70, 73—, sec., 1966-68, chmn., 1968-70, v.p., 1973—; chmn. Gov.'s Inauguration Com., 1961; mem. task force N.D. Combined Law Enforcement Council. Mem. Am. Assn. U. Women (chpt. pres. 1956-58), UN Assn. U.S. (state pres. 1960-62). Unitarian (local pres. 1962-64). Home: 1110 W Highland Acres Rd Bismarck ND 58501 Office: Box 310 Bismarck ND 58501

CONRAD, MARCIA HART (MRS. D. IRVING CONRAD), coll. dean; b. Albion, N.Y., July 2, 1939; d. Elizur Kirke and Marcia (Brown) Hart; A.A., Briarcliff Coll., 1959; B.S., Springfield Coll., 1961, M.S., 1962, Profl. certificate, 1963; m. Donald Irving Conrad, June 20, 1964. Dir. women's residence hall Springfield (Mass.) Coll., 1962-63; dir. student activities Bay Path Jr. Coll., Longmeadow, Mass., 1963-64, dean of students, 1965—; asst. dean students State U. N.Y. at Plattsburg, 1964-65. Chmn. Coll. Scholarship Clearing House, Springfield, 1968—. Mem. Longmeadow Drug Action Commn., 1970—. Bd. dirs. Springfield chpt. A.R.C. Mem. Am., Mass. personnel and guidance assns., Nat. Assn. Women Deans and Counselors. Address: 588 Longmeadow St Longmeadow MA 01106

CONRAD, PRISCILLA PAULETTE, paralegal adminstr.; b. Scottsbluff, Neb., Aug. 10, 1932; d. Carl John and Jacqueline (Gullett) Greisen; student U. Pa., 1957-59; m. Louis N. Conrad, Feb. 25, 1963; children—Randyl Jenise, Louis N. III. Asst. buyer May D&F Dept. Store, Denver, 1962-63; state campaign coordinator Cystic Fibrosis Research Found., Denver; paralegal adminstrv. non-support div. Denver Dist. Atty.'s Office, 1973—. Sustaining mem. Greater Parkhill, Inc., exec. bd., governing bd., 1968-70; regional adv. com. Centennial-Bicentennial Commn.; charter mem. Virginia Blue Center for Women, Colo. Women's Coll. Committeewoman, Denver Democratic party, 1964-66, co-capt., 1966-68, vice chmn., 1968-73; co-founder Colo. Dem. Women's Caucus, 1972, Denver Dem. Women's Caucus, 1972. Mem. Nat. Orgn. Women. Home: 2870 Magnolia St Denver CO 80207 Office: 1460 Kalamath St Denver CO 80204

CONREY, LUCILE ELIZABETH, lawyer; b. Cascade, Mont., Jan. 9, 1901; d. Justus Andrew and Clara Matilda (Kerr) Conrey; A.B., U. So. Cal., 1921, J.D., 1931. Tchr., San Bernardino, Cal., 1921-22, Woodlake (Cal.) High Sch., 1923-25, Whittier (Cal.) High Sch., 1925-28; admitted to Cal. bar, 1931; practiced in Los Angeles, 1931-42; atty. USDA, Washington, 1943-47; codification officer Div. Adminstrv. Procedure, Cal. Dept. Profl. and Vocational Standards, Sacramento, 1948-52; asst. adminstrv. adviser Cal. Dept. Edn., Sacramento, 1952-57, asso. counsel, 1957-70. Mem. Cal. Bar Assn., Cal. Writers Club, Phi Alpha Delta, Phi Kappa Phi. Democrat. Methodist. Home: 7508 Cerrito Rojo Cucamonga CA 91730

CONROY, SISTER GERMAINE, hosp. adminstr.; b. Fairmont, W.Va., Mar. 31, 1938; d. Charles Herbert and Evelyn Marie (DeVan) Conroy; B.A., St. Mary of the Springs Coll., 1961; M.H.A., St. Louis U., 1966. Joined Dominican Sisters of St. Mary of the Springs, now gen. councillor, 1974—; tchr., Seven Sorrows Sch., Middletown, Pa., 1960-61; tchr. high sch. sci. St. Francis de Sch., McKees Rocks, Pa., 1961-63; asst. adminstr. St. George Hosp., Cin., 1963-64, adminstr., 1966-74, cons. spl. projects, trustee, 1974—; adminstrv. resident Carney Hosp., Boston, 1965-66. Trustee Ohio Dominican Coll., 1973—, Albertus Magnus Coll., New Haven, Conn., 1971—, Dominican Acad., N.Y.C., 1974—, Mary Immaculate High Sch., Ossining, N.Y., 1974—, St. Mary's High Sch., New Haven, 1974—. Mem. Am. Coll. Hosp. Adminstrs., Am. Mgmt. Assn., Am., Ohio (sec. S.W. dist. 1968-71, mem. manpower and edn. com. 1971—), Cath. (mem. council on hosp. orgn. and adminstrn. 1971-73, mem. awards com. 1973-74) hosp. assns. Home: 3650 Glenmore Av Cincinnati OH 45211 Office: 3156 Glenmore Av Cincinnati OH 45211

CONSAGRA, SOPHIE CHANDLER, state ofcl.; b. Radnor, Pa., Apr. 28, 1927; d. Alfred D. and Carol (Ramsay) Chandler; grad. Ethel Walker Sch., Simsbury, Conn., 1945; B.A., Smith Coll., 1949; M.A., Cambridge (Eng.) U., 1952; divorced; children—Maria, Pierluigi, Francesca, George. Historic site surveyor State of Del., 1971; exec. dir. Del. Arts Council, 1972—; cons. visual arts. Mem. accessions and exhbn. coms. Del. Art Mus. Home: 2325 W 16th St Wilmington DE 19806 Office: 1105 N Market St Wilmington Tower Wilmington DE 19801

CONSTANTINE, ELIZABETH G. FREDERICK (MRS. FRANK HAMILTON CONSTANTINE), physician; b. N.Y.C., Oct. 21, 1910; d. Charles Louis and Catharine (Anderson) Frederick; A.B., Vassar Coll., 1931; M.D., Johns Hopkins, 1937; m. Frank Hamilton Constantine, Jan. 2, 1937; 1 dau., Barbara Byrd. Intern, Johns Hopkins Hosp., Balt., 1937-38; Mellon fellow Johns Hopkins U., 1938-39; practice medicine, specializing in ophthalmology, N.Y.C., 1939—; mem. staff N.Y. Hosp., Manhattan Eye, Ear and Throat Hosp.; instr. ophthalmology Cornell U. Med. Coll., 1949-72, asst. clin. prof., 1972—. Diplomate Am. Bd. Ophthalmology. Mem. A.M.A., Pan-Am. Assn. Ophthalmology, Am. Acad. Ophthalmology and Otolaryngology. Contbr. articles in field to profl. jours. Home: 270 Next Day Hill Ct Englewood NJ 07631 Office: 215 E 64th St New York City NY 10021

CONVERSE, BEULAH BELL, extension home economist; b. Leetonia, O., June 10, 1912; d. Ernest Kimsey and Blanche E. (Galbreath) Bell; B.Sc., Ohio State U., 1936; m. Curney Converse, May 28, 1938; children—Philip, Patricia (Mrs. William Settlemyre), Jean (Mrs. Don Rapp), James, Linda (Mrs. Ramon Hahn), Sally (Mrs. Russell Moran), Judith, Roger. Tchr. home econs. pub. schs. Dola, O., 1936-38; Mahoning County extension agt. Cooperative Extension Service Ohio State U., Canfield, 1959-70, home economist, 9-county area, Canfield, 1970—. Mem. Fairfield-Waterford Sch. Dist. Sch. Bd., 1957-69, pres., 1965-66. Recipient Diamond Anniversary award Ohio State U. Sch. Home Econs., 1971, Distinguished Service award Nat. Assn. Extension Home Economists, 1970. Mem. Nat., Ohio (chmn., 1966) assns. extension home economists, Ohio Coop. Extension Agts. Assn., Epsilon Sigma Phi. Methodist. Home: RD 2 Leetonia OH 44431 Office: 430 Lisbon St Canfield OH 44406

CONVERSE, MARY MASON (MRS. MELVILLE CONVERSE), former editor; b. Richmond, Va., June 14, 1938; d. Sam Anthony and Venita (Fowler) Mason; B.A., Smith Coll., 1960; m. Melville B. Converse, May 4, 1963; 1 dau. Mary Tabb. Advt. copywriter Miller & Rhoads, Inc., Richmond, 1960-61; staff dir. pub. relations A.R.C., Richmond, 1962-64, bd. dirs. Loudon County 1972-73; editor Colonial Williamsburg (Va.) News, 1965-68, coordinator employee tng. Colonial Williamsburg, 1968-69, editor Craft House Catalogue, 1969-70. Bd. dirs. 20th Century Art Gallery, Williamsburg, 1966-68, Williamsburg Pre-Sch. for Spl. Children, 1966-68; treas. Loudoun County chpt. Va. Mus. Fine Arts, 1972—; mem. Jr. League Richmond, 1963-65, Jr. League Hampton Rds., 1965-70, Washington, 1970—. Mem. Asso. Bus. Editors Va. (sec. 1962-64), Leesburg Garden Club. Home: 37 W Cornwall St Leesburg VA 22075

CONVERY, SUSANNAH JOHNSON (MRS. JOHN HENRY CONVERY), lawyer; b. Bklyn., Aug. 25, 1926; d. Frank Willard and Katherine (Dow) Johnson; B.A., Conn. Coll. for Women, 1947; LL.B., U. Cal. at San Francisco, 1960; m. Harold W. Walters, Feb. 15, 1947 (div. Apr. 1957); children—David, Katherine Byrd, Susannah Scott; m. 2d, John Henry Convery, Apr. 4, 1964. Admitted to Cal. bar, 1961; research atty. Cal. Supreme Ct., San Francisco, 1960-62; dep. dist. atty. Santa Clara County (Cal.) Dist. Atty.'s Office, 1962-74. Del. to Cal. Democratic Conv., 1956, precinct chmn. Orinda, Cal., 1954-56. Mem. Am., Santa Clara City bar assns., U. Cal. Alumnae Assn., Am. Assn. U. Women (organizer Orinda br. 1956). Editor Hastings Law Jour., 1959-60. Home: 36 Waverly Court Alamo CA 94507 Office: 2 N 2nd St Suite 1475 San Jose CA 95113

CONWAY, ANNE ELIZABETH (MRS. HARRY P. CONWAY), educator; b. Jessup, Pa., Oct. 7, 1911; d. James F. and Margaret (O'Brien) Sweeney; A.B., Marywood Coll., 1932, M.A., 1936; m. Harry P. Conway, June 26, 1945; children—Patrick, Margaret Mary. Math. tchr. Jessup High Sch., 1932-46, 50-58, guidance counselor, math. tchr., 1958-68, dir. guidance, 1968-70; dir. elementary guidance Valley View Sch. Dist., 1970—. Sch. chmn. March of Dimes Campaign, 1952—. Mem. Pa., Nat., Valley View edn. assns., Jessup Tchr. Assn., Am., N.E. Pa. personnel and guidance assns., Sch. Counselor Assn., Pa. Assn. Guidance Counselors, Pa. Assn. Womens Deans and Counselors, Nat. Assn. Vocational Counselors, Testing and Evaluation Assn. Home: 324 Church St Jessup PA 18434

CONWAY, DORRIS GARRETT, social worker; b. Dallas, Dec. 8, 1914; d. Claude Manning and Eva Lazetta (Pierson) Garrett; student Hardin-Simmons U., 1932-35; B.S., Tex. Woman's U., 1936; M.S. in Social Work, U. Tex., 1968; m. Walter C. Conway, June 15, 1937; children—W. Philip, Robert W., John R. Newspaper reporter, Denton, Tex., 1935-37; freelance writer articles, fiction for Ladies Home Jour., other mags., newspapers, 1937-62; psychiat. social worker Counseling Center, U. Tex., Austin, 1968—, instr., 1972—. Co-founder, bd. dirs. Orange County (N.Y.) Mental Health Assn., 1957-58; bd. dirs. Austin Mental Health Assn., 1968-70. Mem. Am. Assn. Marriage and Family Counselors (chmn. paraprofl. com. 1972-73), Nat. Council on Family Relations, Am. Assn. Sex Educators and Counselors, Internat. Transactional Analysis Assn., Nat. Assn. Social Workers, Acad. Certified Social Workers, Internat. Conf. on Social Welfare. Home: 3611-A Las Colinas Dr Austin TX 78731 Office: Counseling-Psychol Services Center U Tex Austin TX 78712

CONWAY, ELIZABETH PEASE, orgn. exec.; b. Chgo., June 18, 1919; d. John Henry and Jessie Carmen (Pease) Conway; grad. pvt. schs.; Sec., asst. pub. relations Inst. Scrap Iron and Steel, Washington, 1954—, dir. membership services, 1970—, editor, program chmn. Monthly Newsletter, 1970. Mem. Chevy Chase Bus. and Profl. Women's Club. Home: 3702 34th St NW Washington DC 20008 Office: 1729 H St NW Washington DC 20006

CONWAY, FLORRIE JEWELL, librarian; b. Floydada, Tex., Jan. 10, 1920; d. Ollie Mitchell and Blanche Griffith (Price) Conway; A.A., Wayland Baptist Coll., 1940; B.A., Baylor U., 1942; M.L.S., U. Tex., 1953. Sec. to pastor 1st Bapt. Ch., Plainview, Tex., 1943-52; librarian Wayland Bapt. Coll., Plainview, 1953—. Mem. Tex. Library Assn. (memberships chmn. 1957). Bapt. Home: 901 Utica St Plainview TX 79072 Office: Van Howeling Meml Library Wayland Baptist Coll Plainview TX 79072

CONWAY, GRACE MARIE, graphic arts co. exec., comml. artist; b. Leonard, Tex., Mar. 30, 1919; d. Lacy Cecil and Myrtle G. (Clemmons) Conway; student Aunspaugh Sch. Art, 1928-40; m. B.R. Hudson (div. 1969). Comml. artist Stevens Studios, Dallas, 1937-38; art dir. Superior Decal Co., Dallas, 1938-53; v.p. DeCals Inc., Dallas, 1953-60; estimator Tech Mark Inc., Dallas, 1960-65; co-ordinator and comptroller Superior Marking Systems, Dallas, 1965-67; v.p. Fleetmark Inc., Dallas, 1968—. Republican. Methodist.

CONWELL, MILDRED HEBGEN, real estate broker; b. San Francisco, Aug. 3, 1918; d. Adolph Gustav and Mildred Emma (Newbury) Hebgen; student U. Md., 1938, 41-42, U. Cal., 1940-41; A.A. Coll. San Mateo (Cal.), 1940; div.; 1 dau., Gail (Mrs. William J. Cusack). Real estate broker, Menlo Park, Cal., 1945-47; real estate broker with John Wickett, Atherton, Cal., 1947-53; credit mgr. San Francisco Glass Co., Mountain View, Cal., 1953-58; real estate broker with Linne Wyckoff, Palo Alto, Cal., 1960-63; real estate broker, Menlo Park, 1964—. Active Motor Corps, A.R.C., San Francisco and Palo Alto, 1941-44; mgr. Peninsula Vols. Properties, Inc., 1959, treas., 1960; active Woodside-Atherton Aux. to Childrens Hosp. Stanford. Mem. Nat. Assn. Realtors, Cal. Real Estate Assn., Menlo Park-Atherton Bd. Realtors (dir. 1972-74), Nat. Soc. Colonial Dames Am., Delta Delta Delta. Clubs: Alpine Hills Swimming and Tennis, Palo Alto Hills Golf and Country (exec. mem.). Home: 1025 Cascade Dr Menlo Park CA 94025 Office: 661 Live Oak Av Menlo Park CA 94025 Address: Box K Station A Menlo Park CA 94025

CONZELMAN, DOROTHY ROSTRON (MRS. WALID BURHANI), physician; b. Waukegan, Ill., Sept. 13, 1930; d. John Wilson and Dorothy (Rostron) Conzelman; B.A., Lake Forest Coll., 1952; M.D., Woman's Med. Coll. Pa., 1956; m. Walid Burhani, Dec. 26, 1958; children—Mary Jamila, John Zeki. Intern Presbyn. St. Luke's Hosp., Chgo., 1956-57, resident pediatrics, 1957-58; resident pediatrics Children's Meml. Hosp., Chgo., 1958-59, hematology fellowship, 1959-60; practice medicine specializing in pediatrics, Kenosha, Wis., 1961—; mem. staffs Kenosha Meml. Hosp., St. Catherine's Hosp. Mem. Alpha Epsilon Iota. Episcopalian. Home: 200 68th St Kenosha WI 53140 Office: 6530 Sheridan Rd Kenosha WI 53140

COOGAN, IRENE HENRY (MRS. JAMES ADARE COOGAN), educator, ednl. adminstr.; b. nr. Fairmount, Mo., Jan. 4, 1905; d. Elijah Lee and Orpha Ardella (Bailey) Henry; B.S., Kirksville (Mo.) State Tchrs. Coll., 1926; A.M., U. Mo., 1930; postgrad. U. Ill., 1960, Ill. State U., 1970; m. James Adare Coogan, May 28, 1938; children—Margaret (Mrs. Frederick Blanford), David Lee. Demonstration tchr., supr. lab. jr. high sch., Kirksville State Tchrs. Coll., 1926-38; tchr. Lincoln (Ill.) Coll., 1941-43; tchr., supr. mentally retarded Lincoln State Sch., 1952—. Mem. N.E.A., Am. Assn. U. Women (pres. 1931), Am. Assn. Mental Deficiency, Internat. Council for Exceptional Children. Home: 208 11th St Lincoln IL 62656 Office: 861 S State St Lincoln IL 62656

COOK, ARLENE ETHEL, author; b. Escondido, Cal., July 1, 1936; d. Oscar Emil and Leona Lucy (Wells) Knappe; B.A. in Elementary Edn., San Diego State Coll., 1958; m. Richard H. Cook, Dec. 23, 1964; children—Alan Jason, Alyse Jennifer, Jon Andrew. Home tchr., substitute tchr. elementary grades, Escondido, 1961-62; tchr. Poway (Cal.) Unified Sch. Dist., 1962-67; founder, adviser 8 ladies stock investment clubs in Escondido, 1970. Mem. Mayor Escondico 1st Blue Ribbon Com., 1973—. Mem. Cal. Fedn. Chapparral Poets, Nat. League Am. Pen Women (pres. Escondido 1970-72), Nat. Assn. Investment Clubs (v.p. San Diego 1970-73), Nat. Writers Club, Soc. Children's Book Writers, So. Cal. Writers Guild, Scribblers. Republican. Lutheran. Author: (under pen name Cannon Cole) From the Ashes of Hell, 1973; (with others) The World of Long Ago, 1971. Contbr. to nat. mags., 1966—. Home: 371 Cypress Point Terrace Escondido CA 92025 Office: PO Box 184 Escondido CA 92025

COOK, BARBARA IVY WOOD (MRS. SALEM FRANCIS COOK), educator; b Memphis, Dec. 8, 1929; d. Karl and Thelma (Champagne) Wood; B.A., U. Ark., 1951; M.A., Syracuse U., 1954; Ph.D., Purdue U., 1967; m. Salem Francis Cook, Aug. 20, 1955 (dec. July 1956). Asst. to dean women U. Ark., Fayetteville, 1951-52, asst. dean of women, 1954-55; dir. placement service for women Purdue U., Lafayette, Ind., 1956-66, asso. dean women, 1966—, tchr. counseling and guidance Dept. Edn. 1970—. Mem. Ind. Assn. Women Deans, Adminstrs. and Counselors (exec. bd. 1973-74), Nat. Assn. Women Deans, Adminstrs. and Counselors (dir. univ. sect.; exec. bd. 1969-71, pres. elect 1974—), Nat. Orgn. for Women, Am. Assn. U. Women, Women's Equity Action League, Alpha Kappa Delta, Pi Lambda Theta, Mortar Bd. (2d v.p. 1970-73). Democrat. Home: 1808 Summit Dr West Lafayette IN 47906 Office: Office Dean of Women Purdue U Lafayette IN 47907

COOK, BLANCHE HELEN MCLANE, artist; b. Moulton, Ia., July 1, 1901; d. Alva Randolph and Eva (Wynn) McLane; honor grad., Phila. Sch. Design for Women, now known as Moore Coll. Arts, 1928, postgrad (fellow), 1929; student Temple U., 1929; B.A., Central Wash. State Coll., Ellensburg, 1959, M.A., 1965; m. Harry Christian Cook, Feb. 19, 1938. Tchr., Phila. Sch. Design, and Baldwin Sch., 1927-29; irrigation dep., Yakima County Treas. office, 1930-34, chief dep., treas., 1934-40; pvt. instr. art, 1930—; 1st art instr. Yakima Valley Jr. Coll. 1933-48, 57-58; free-lance comml. artist, 1928—; portrait painter, 1928—; art instr., counselor Moxee Elementary Sch., dist. 90, 1959-60; art instr. Wilson Jr. High Sch., Sch. Dist. 7, Yakima, Wash., 1961-66, chmn. art dept., 1962-66; works exhibited in various galleries and museums, including Frederick & Nelson Little Gallery, 1948—, Larson Gallery, Yakima, Washington, 1954-63, Seattle Art Mus., Woessner Gallery, Studio Gallery (all Seattle), Palace Legion of Honor, San Francisco, Spokane Art Gallery, U. Ore., Salem, 1971, 72; represented several pub. and pvt. collections. Recipient 2d popular vote N.W. Ann., 1947; 2d Traditional award, Spokane, 1954. Mem. Seattle Art Mus., Women Painters of Wash., Internat. League Am. Pen Women (founder, past pres. Yakima Valley chpt.), Larson Gallery Guild (co-founder), Wash. Art Assn., Yakima Allied Arts Council, Yakima Valley Art Assn. (co-founder), Yakima Valley Soc. Artists (charter), Nat. Ret. Tchrs. Assn., Moore Coll Arts (life), Alumnus Central Wash. State Coll. (life), Am. Assn. U. Women, P.E.O., Delta Kappa Gamma, Alpha Sigma. Mem. Order Eastern Star. Club: Woman's Century (Yakima). Address: 915 Pleasant Av Yakima WA 98902

COOK, CONSTANCE KNOWLES EBERHARDT, lawyer, state legislator; b. Cleve., Aug. 17, 1919; d. Walter R. and Catherine (Sellmann) Eberhardt; B.A., Cornell U., 1941, LL.B., 1943; postgrad. Columbia, (Fulbright grantee) U. Oslo (Norway), 1953, The Hague (Netherlands) Acad. Internat. Law; m. Alfred P. Cook, June 24, 1955; children—Catherine P., John K. Admitted to N.Y. State bar, 1944; asso. firm Shearman & Sterling, N.Y.C., 1944-49; confidential law asst. to Gov. Thomas E. Dewey, 1949-51; legal cons. Div. Municipal Affairs, Dept. Audit and Control, N.Y.C., research counsel Law Revision Commn., N.Y.C., asst. counsel Temporary State Commn. Fire Laws; counsel to Joint Legislative Com. on Unemployment Ins.; practiced in Ithaca, N.Y., 1953—; mem. N.Y. Assembly, Tompkins County, 1962-65, Tompkins and Tioga Counties, 1966—, chmn. standing com. on edn., mem. coms. on ways and means, health. Trustee Cornell U. Named Republican Woman of Year for N.Y. State, 1969. Mem. N.Y. Republican Women of Legislature, Am., N.Y., Tompkins County bar assns. Assn. of Bar City N.Y., Am. Assn. U. Women, Bus. and Profl. Women's Club, Zonta Internat., Delta Kappa Gamma. Episcopalian. Address: Coy Glen Rd Ithaca NY 14850

COOK, GLADYS EMERSON, animal artist; b. Haverhill, Mass.; d. George Ward and Hattie Burson (Emerson) Cook; B.S., Skidmore Coll., 1921; M.S., U. Wis., 1923. One man exhbns. Heads and Horns Mus., Bronx Zool. Park, 1941, Soc. Illustrators, 1944; work exhibited at Black, Starr and Gorham, Brentano's, Scribner's, Harlow and Co., Kennedy and Co., Grand Central Art Gallery; works in many pvt. collections; drawings have appeared in N.Y. Times, Boston Herald, Christian Sci. Monitor, Boston Transcript; ten originals reproduced in Ringling Brothers circus programs, 1943; exhbn. clown painting at Ringling Bros. Circus; lectr. on drawing the cat Met. Mus., 1943; illustrator animal calendars for Am. Soc. Prevention Cruelty to Animals, 1943-44, Christmas cards for Am. Artist Group, 1940—; illustrator for motion pictures The Yearling and Bob, Son of Battle; draws cats for Carter's Ink advt., on television for Puss 'n Boots Cat Food; did portraits of President Nixon's 3 dogs; one-man exhibit of horse paintings Nat. Horse Show, Madison Sq. Garden, 1954. Tchr. art in pub. schs., N.Y.C. Lithographs in permanent collections Met. Mus., Congl. Library, Cin. Mus. Chosen Artist of the Year by Albany Print Club. Demonstration talk to Humane Soc. U.S.A. Fellow Royal Soc. Arts Eng.; mem. Soc. Illustrators, Met. Mus. Art, Soc. Am. Etchers, Am. Assn. U. Women, English-Speaking Union, U. Wis. Alumni, Panhellenic Soc., Soc. Am. Graphic Artists, Audubon Soc., Asia House, Artists Guild, Mu Phi. Club: Skidmore College. Illustrator several cat and dog books and publs. among latest The Siamese Cat; Sketching Wild Life; Cat Stories (James Mason); wrote and illustrated Personal Acquaintances, a cat book; Big Book of Cats; Portfolio of Cats; How to Draw Cats; Drawing Horses; Circus Clowns on Parade; How to Draw Dogs; Portfolio of Dogs; My Dog; Champion Dogs of the World; Drawing Wildlife. Home: Hotel Wolcott 4 W 31st St New York City NY 10001 Studio: 32 Union Sq New York City NY 10003

COOK, GLADYS MAY, author; b. Columbia, Ia., Apr. 8, 1907; d. Elmer Homer and Bertha Ellen (Miller) Moon; student Des Moines U., 1925-27, Northwestern U.; B.A. in Communication Arts, Columbia Coll., Chgo., 1967; m. Robert Neil Cook, May 5, 1928 (dec. 1956); 1 son, Bruce Alexander. With A.C. McClurg & Co., wholesalers; bookkeeper Russel Seeds, Advt.; charge of books Perrin & Assos., Advt., 1954-70. Past mem. conf. Wesleyan Service Guild, United Methodist Ch. Recipient award for excellence in writing Columbia Coll., 1967. Mem. Poets of Chgo. (past pres.), Poets and Patrons (treas., past workshop chmn., Best of the Best award ann. contest 1972), Soc. Midland Authors, Nat. League Am. Pen Women, Iota Sigma Epsilon. Author: Escape; Vashti, Girl of India, 1975. Contbr. poetry to mags. Home: 1628 W Touhy Av Chicago IL 60626

COOK, GLORIA HOUSTON (MRS. JAMES THOMAS COOK, JR.), civic worker; b. Portland, Me., Aug. 22, 1933; d. Ellwyn Kenelm and May Elvera (Delay) Houston; student U. Fla. Sch. Journalism; m. James Thomas Cook, Jr., Jan. 28, 1952; children—Victoria Ann, Sheryl Ann. Del., White House Conf. on Food, Nutrition and Health, 1969, Fla. Conf. on Food, Nutrition and Health, 1970; mem. Pres.'s Com. on Employment Handicapped, 1963—; Gray lady A.R.C., 1964—; mem. Welsh Area planning com. State Div. Vocational Rehab., 1971-73; chmn. Christmas Cotillion, 1971—; bd. dirs. Volusia County Personnel, 1974—, P.T.A., 1958—; active campaign worker for various local civic orgns. Bd. dirs. Nat. Easter Seal Soc., 1967-70, ho. of dels. 1965—, vice-chmn., 1971—, also mem. coms.; bd. dirs. Fla. Easter Seal Soc., 1962—, sec. 1964-66, 1st v.p. 1970-72, pres., 1973-74; bd. dirs. Volusia County Easter Seal Soc., 1960—, sec. 1962-64, pres. 1965-67, ho. of Fla. dels., 1966—; bd. dirs. Jr. Service League Daytona Beach, 1956-73, v.p., 1966, pres. 1967-68, other offices, 1968-74, chmn. future policies com. 1968-74; bd. mem. Jr. Service League Orthopedic Center, 1957-66, v.p., 1967; bd. mem. Volusia County Cancer Soc., sec., 1969, v.p., 1970-71; bd. dirs. Fla. Internat. Festivals, Inc., sec. trustee bd. 1967—. Named Woman of Year, Halifax Area, 1965, Woman of Year, Palmetto Jr. Woman's Club, 1957. Mem. Nat., Fla. rehab. assns., Palmetto Jr. Woman's Club (dir., officer 1953-58). Mem. United Ch. (trustee pub. relations dir. 1974—). Clubs: Hibiscus Garden (bd. mem., v.p., sec. 1958-62), Oceanside Country. Home: 825 John Anderson Dr Ormond Beach FL 32074

COOK, HELEN TILLMAN ENNIS (MRS. WESLEY H. COOK), educator; b. Milledgeville, Ga., Sept. 29, 1913; d. Howard Bert and Kathleen (Alsbrook) Ennis; A.B., Ga. State Coll. for Women, 1934; M.Ed., Emory U., 1957; Ed.D., U. Ga., 1964; m. Wesley H. Cook, Apr. 18, 1935; children—Helen Kathleen (Mrs. William N. Postell, Jr.), Elizabeth Harper, Carol Susan (Mrs. Gene Nardin, Jr.). Caseworker Fed. Emergency Relief Agy., Atlanta, 1934-35; supr. WPA, Atlanta, 1935-36; caseworker Fulton County (Ga.) Pub. Welfare, Atlanta, 1941-43; interviewer USES, Atlanta, 1943-46; editor Write mag., 1950-51; counselor Atlanta Pub. Schs., 1952-67, dir. central placement service, 1952-67, dir. Gen. Edn. Devel. Testing Center, 1952-67, dir. occupational information, 1967-71, dir. comprehensive career edn. model project, 1971—. Chmn. personnel adv. com. Fulton County Dept. Family and Children's services, 1966-67, 69-70: state chmn. Nat. Vocational Guidance Week, 1966-67; mem. Gov.'s Comm. on Edn., 1967, Gov.'s Com. on Illegitimacy and Adoption, 1965-66. Mem. Am., Ga. (pres. 1962-63, treas. 1971-72) personnel and guidance assns., Nat. Vocational Guidance Assn., Ga., Atlanta assns. educators, Ga. Assn. Sch. Counselors, So. Assn. Counselor Educators and Suprs., Am. Vocational Assn., Pi Gamma Mu, Kappa Delta Pi. Methodist. Club: Johnson Estates Garden (pres. 1949-50) (Atlanta). Home: 1745 Meadowdale Av NE Atlanta GA 30306 Office: 2930 Forrest Hill Dr SW Atlanta GA 30315

COOK, JEANNINE SALVO (MRS. DONALD CARTER COOK), librarian; b. N.Y.C., Apr. 11, 1929; d. Ernest August and Edith Agatha (Lombardo) Salvo; A.B., Hunter Coll., 1951; M.L.S., Columbia, 1958, advanced library degree, 1973; m. Donald Carter Cook, June 9, 1962; 1 son, Carter Steven. Chemist, Charles Pfizer & Co., Inc., Bklyn., 1951-56; lit. chemist, 1956-58; central med. librarian Am. Cyanamid Co., N.Y.C., 1958-60; sr. profl. adminstr. Columbia U. Engring. and Phys. Scis. Library, N.Y.C., 1960-62; asso. librarian State U. N.Y., Stony Brook, 1962-63; dir. Emma S. Clark Meml. Library, Setauket, N.Y., 1967—. Co-chmn. ednl. com. Assn. Community/Univ. Coop., 1973-74. Mem. Spl. Libraries Assn., Med. Library Assn., Am. Chem. Soc., League Women Voters, Suffolk County Library Assn. Methodist (trustee 1971-73). Home: 40 Seabrook Lane Stony Brook NY 11790 Office: 120 Main St Setauket NY 11733

COOK, JUANITA WHITNEY, speech pathologist; b. Jamestown, N.Y., Dec. 16, 1936; d. Leo Edwin and Helen Elnora (Fleming) Whitney; B.A., U. Buffalo, 1959; M.S., U. Vt., 1967; divorced; 1 son, Daryl Whitney. Speech pathologist Binghamton (N.Y.) City Sch. Dist., 1959-60; Brandon (Vt.) Tng. Sch., 1961-72, Bennington (Vt.) City Sch. Dist., 1972—; individual practice speech pathology, 1960—. Mem. Commr.'s Adv. Council on Spl. Edn., State of Vt., 1972—. Sch. dir. Town of Clarendon, Vt., 1970-71. Bd. dirs. Rutland Community Concerts, Inc., 1968-69. U.S. Dept. Health, Edn. and Welfare grantee, 1964-65. Mem. Am. Assn. on Mental Retardation, Council on Exceptional Children, Vt. (sec. 1962-65), Am. speech and hearing assns. Home: RD 1 Pownal VT 05261 Office: 604 Main St Bennington VT 05201

COOK, MARIAN ALICE, educator; b. Louisville, Aug. 4, 1928; d. Clarence Frederick and Aline (Swisher) Cook; B.Mus., Ohio Wesleyan U., 1950; M.Ed., Miami U., Oxford, O., 1955. Music tchr. Hamilton (O.) Bd. Edn., 1951-58; cons. Clearwater (Fla.) Bd. Pub. Instrn., 1959-71, music specialist, 1971—. Chmn. textbook evaluation and recommendations Fla. Com. on Facilities; cons. workshops, supr. student tchrs. Recipient recognition awards W. Coast Profl. Pan-Hellenic, St. Petersburg Boychoir. Mem. Am. Recorder Soc., Pinellas County Music Educators Assn. (sec.-treas. 1963-71, pres.-elect 1973-74), Music Educators Nat. Conf., Delta Kappa Gamma (pres. Beta Iota chpt. 1972-74, chmn. Tri-county coordinating council 1974—), Mu Phi Epsilon (sec. St. Petersburg alumnae chpt. 1967), Alpha Delta Kappa (sec. 1964). Methodist (music com.). Home: 4210 24th Av N St Petersburg FL 33713

COOK, MARY ELEANOR, metal products mfg. co. exec.; b. Scottville, Mich., June 5, 1933; d. Hiram Stuart and Bernice Marie (Robinson) Martin; grad. high sch.; children—Kathy (Mrs. William V. Lavin, Jr.), Diane, Mary Ann, Debra. Bookkeeper, Rocco Bono Constrn. Co., Sharon, Pa., 1956-66; gen. office work Shenango Metalcraft Co., West Middlesex, Pa., 1966-67, gen. mgr., 1967—. Mem. adv. council Nat. Fedn. Ind. Bus. Mem. Nat. Assn. Nameplate Mfrs., Shenango Valley C. of C. (dir.). Home: 1740 Ashton Av Sharpsville PA 16150 Office: Shenango Metalcraft Co Main St West Middlesex PA 16159

COOK, MYRTLE MAY (MRS. VINCENT D. COOK), banker; b. Edgerton, O., Apr. 25, 1922; d. William Franklin and Alma Olivia (Klinksick) Knecht; B.S. summa cum laude, Defiance Coll., 1969; postgrad. Toledo U., 1971; M.S. with honors, St. Francis Coll., 1974; m. Vincent D. Cook, Sept. 2, 1943; 1 son, Tad Lee. With Nat. Bank of Montpelier, O., 1939—, asst. v.p., 1971—, also dir., 1968—. Part time faculty art dept. Defiance (O.) Coll., 1970—. Sec. Montpelier Recreation Bd., 1958-64; mem. Montpelier Beautification com., 1970-72; treas. Williams County Heart Assn., 1956-60; treas. Williams County Red Cross Drive, 1962-63; pres. P.T.A., Montpelier, 1956. Recipient Art awards, hon. mention in oils Ann. Fine Arts Exhibit, Montpelier, 1963, 72, hon. mention in ceramics Toledo Area Artists Show, 1964, third place in crafts 3d Ann. Festival Religious Art, Defiance, 1965, hon. mention acrylics Van Wert County Art Show, 1973, Women in Art Show Defiance Coll., 1973. Mem. Defiance Coll. Women's Commn., Nat. Art Edn. Assn., Am. Crafts Council. Republican. Lutheran (treas. 1970, mem. bd. parish edn. 1966). Clubs: Toledo Art; Lima Art; Montpelier Art and Craft (pres. 1963), Twice-Ten Study (pres. 1947) (Montpelier). Illustrator: The Heart Is A Gypsy (J.R. LeMaster), 1967. Home: 114 E Lawrence St Montpelier OH 43543 Office: Main and Empire Sts Montpelier OH 43543

COOK, SHIRLEY GEDDES (MRS. FARRELL EUGENE COOK), lawyer; b. Tacoma, Wash., Nov. 14, 1920; d. Thomas William and Frances (Frazier) Geddes; B.S., U. Wash., 1949, J.D., 1950; m. Farrell Eugene Cook, May 9, 1953. Admitted to Wash. bar, 1950; practiced in Port Townsend, 1950-53, Bremerton, 1955—; dep. pros. atty. Jefferson County (Wash.), 1950-53; city atty. Port Townsend, Wash., 1952-53; dep. pros. atty. Kitsap County, Bremerton, 1955-59; mem. firm Cook and Cook, Bremerton, 1959—. Served to 1st lt. WAC, 1942-46. Mem. Wash., Kitsap County bar assns., Am. Assn. U. Women. Home: 1736 Shorewood Dr Bremerton WA 98310 Office: 307 Dietz Bldg Bremerton WA 98310

COOK, THELMA CAROLINE, pub. relations cons.; b. Spokane, Wash., June 22, 1912; d. Albert Peter and Florence Mae (Eagle) Ness; student U. Ore., 1930-32; m. Donald H. Wilson, Dec. 18, 1948 (dec. Aug. 1965); children—Donald H., David P.; m. 2d, Miles Gordon Cook, Mar. 23, 1974. Asst. pub. affairs dir. Columbia Aircraft Industries, Portland, Ore., 1942-46; dir. pub. relations KGW, Portland, 1946-48; publicity dir. March of Dimes, Portland, 1954-58; free-lance writer Ore. Jour., Portland, 1948-61; writer Oregonian, Portland, 1948-61; editor Imprint, office pub. affairs U. Ore. Med. Sch., Portland, 1961—. Mem. Human Relations Commn. Met. Portland, 1969-73. Bd. dirs. Met. chpt. Mental Health Assn. Ore. Mem. Ore. Newspaper Pubs. Assn., Pub. Relations Roundtable Portland, Women in Communications. Author: Men and Milestones in Medicine, 1961. Contbr. to various mags., including McCall's mag., Parent's mag., also med. jours. Home: 5101 SW Richardson Dr Portland OR 97201 Office: 3181 SW Jackson Rd Portland OR 97201

COOK, TRUDY CLARE MOSS (MRS. DAVID LEROY COOK), educator; b. Meshoppen, Pa., Nov. 12, 1949; d. William Elmer and Jessie Mae (Grose) Moss; B.S., East Stroudsburg State Coll., 1971; m. David Leroy Cook, July 3, 1971. Instr., Bapt. Bible Coll. Pa., Clarks-Summit, 1971—, also intramural dir., women's basketball coach, 1971—. Home: RD 5 Tunkhannock PA 18657 Office: 538 Venard Rd Clarks-Summit PA 18411

COOK, VESPER WILKINSON, mus. ofcl.; b. Peru, Ind., June 21, 1917; d. John Elmer and Mary B. (Stickel) Wilkinson; grad. high sch.; m. Horace Dean Cook, June 27, 1965. Research worker Ind. Hist. Soc., 1952-53; curator Miami County Hist. Mus., Puterbaugh Mus., Peru, 1961—. Mem. Ind., Miami County, Circus hist. socs., Midwest Museums Conf., Am. Numis. Assn., Circus Fans Am., Miami County (sec.), N. Central Ind. (sec.) geneal. socs., Bus. and Profl. Women. Republican. Methodist. Club: Monday Night Literary. Contbr. to Furniture Makers of Indiana 1793-1850, 1972; also articles to newspaper. Research on homes built in Miami County before 1860. Home: 327 E 6th St Peru IN 46970

COOK, WILDA JOSEPHINE, county ofcl.; b. Pitts.; d. Charles Isaac and Sarah (Scott) Cook; B.S. in Social Sci., Carnegie Mellon U., 1943. Asst. field dir. A.R.C., 1943-46; med. social worker VA, Pass-A-Grille, Fla., 1946; supr. elections County of Pinellas, Clearwater, Fla., 1952-73. Chmn. campaign activities com. Women's Republican Club, St. Petersburg, 1965—, mem. bd., 1951. Recipient Angus D. Smith Meml. award for outstanding pub. service Gulf Beaches Republican Club, 1955; citation WLCY Radio, WDAE Radio, 1965. Mem. Fla. Assn. Suprs. Elections (mem. legislative com. 1963, chmn. manual com. 1963, pres. 1967). Methodist. Clubs: St. Petersburg Woman's, Bath. Home: 221 Osceola Av N Clearwater FL 33515

COOKE, ANN MARIE, purchasing exec.; b. Newark, Aug. 25, 1936; d. Frank J. and Mary D. (Donegan) Cooke; student Seton Hall U., 1955-56; student exec. mgmt. Drake Coll., 1955. Purchasing agt. Robert McKeown Co., Livingston, N.J., 1958-64; asst. purchasing agt. Charms Co., Bloomfield, N.J., 1964, purchasing agt., 1968-73, dir. purchases, 1973—. Roman Catholic. Club: Plainfield Ski (dir. 1970-71, 73-74) (Clark, N.J.). Home: 28 Freneau Dr Morganville NJ 07751 Office: Halls Mill Rd Freehold NJ 07728

COOKE, CYNTHIA WENTWORTH, physician; b. Needham, Mass., May 4, 1939; d. Milton Ellery and Marjorie Oakford (Wood) Cooke; A.B., Douglass Coll., 1961; M.S. (NSF fellow), U. Wis., 1963, M.D., 1967. Intern, Hosp. U. Pa., Phila., 1967-68, resident obstetrics and gynecology, 1968-72; dir. family planning and adolescent obstetric and gynecology services Phila. Gen. Hosp., 1971—; cons. pediatric gynecology Children's Hosp. Phila., 1973—; med. dir. Phila. Dance Co., 1970—. Mem. FDA study panel. Jr. fellow Am. Coll. Obstetrics and Gynecology; mem. Am. Fertility Soc., Am. Med. Women's Assn., Nat. Orgn. of Women, Pan-Am. Med. Women's Alliance, Med. Women's Internat. Assn., Women's Equity Action League, Phi Beta Kappa, Alpha Omega Alpha. Contbr. articles to profl. jours. Home: 275 Bryn Mawr Av Bryn Mawr PA 19010 Office: Dept Adolescent Obstetric and Gynecology Services Phila Gen Hosp Philadelphia PA 19104

COOKE, EILEEN DELORES, librarian, assn. exec.; b. Mpls., Dec. 7, 1928; d. Walter William and Mary Frances Cooke; B.S. in L.S., Coll. St. Catherine, 1952; extension courses U. Minn. Bookmobile librarian Mpls. Pub. Library, 1952-57; br. asst. Queensborough Pub. Library, 1957-58; br. asst., hosp. librarian, pub. relations specialist Mpls. Pub. Library, 1958-63; asst. dir. Washington office A.L.A., 1964-68, asso. dir., 1968-69, dep. dir., 1969-72, dir., 1972—. Lectr., Drexel U., U. Mich., Ann Arbor; cons. to fed. relations commn. Am. Council on Edn.; mem. adv. council nat. orgns. Corp. Pub. Broadcasting. Mem. Minn., D.C., Am. library assns., Women's Joint Congl. Com., Coalition Adult Edn. Orgns. (sec.-treas.). Higher Edn. Group

Washington. Contbr. articles to profl. jours. Office: 110 Maryland Av NE Washington DC 20002

COOKE, EVELYN KATHLEEN CHATMAN, educator; b. Jackson, Tenn.; d. Charles Elijah and Josie (Bond) Chatman; B.A. cum laude, Lane Coll., 1955; m. James T. Cooke, Apr. 21, 1954 (div. Aug. 1970); 1 dau., Madelyn LaRene. Tchr. pub. schs., Chattanooga, 1957-67, Cin., 1967—. Sec. Harriet Tubman's Black Women's Democratic Club. Mem. Nat. Fellowship Meth. Musicians, N.A.A.C.P., Council for Co-op Action, Am., Ohio, Cin. fedns. tchrs., Sigma Gamma Rho, Gamma Theta Sigma, Sigma Rho Sigma. Methodist (dir. music ch.). Home: 6748 Elwynne Dr Cincinnati OH 45236

COOKE, HELEN HEMLIN, editor, writer; b. N.Y.C.; d. Valentine and Katherine (Fischer) Hemlin; student U. N.M., 1925-26, Columbia, 1927-29; m. Charles Cooke, Jan. 29, 1931 (div. Sept. 1955); 1 son, Harris Craig. Mem. staff writers Lowell Thomas, 1929-33; reporter New Yorker Mag., N.Y.C., 1933-35; publicity dir. Douglas Leigh, Inc., N.Y.C., 1938-45; publicity dir. Monroe Dreher Advt. Agy., N.Y.C., 1941-45; free-lance editor, writer, Washington, 1948—; asst. to exec. v.p. Aerospace Med. Assn., Washington, 1960-61. Mem. Am. Newspaper Womens Club. Author: (with Evelyn D. Boyer) Distinguished Women of Washington, 1964. Contbr. articles to various newspapers, mags. including Washington Star Sunday mag., Balt. Sun, Aerospace Medicine, Cue mag., others. Patentee in field toys. Home: 2244 N Nottingham St Arlington VA 22205

COOKE, JANE KLUTTZ (MRS. CHARLES L. COOKE), educator, clin. psychologist; b. Charlotte, N.C., May 1, 1937; d. Lex W. and Beverly (Neale) Kluttz; A.B., Queens Coll., Charlotte, 1959; M.A., Ph.D., U. N.C., 1964; m. Charles L. Cooke, Sept. 3, 1960; children—David Lee, Stephen Marshall. Instr. dept. psychology U. N.C. Med. Sch., 1964-65; instr. dept. psychiatry Med. Coll. Va., Richmond, 1963-65, asst. clin. prof., 1967—. Cons. clin. psychology N. Tex. Mental Health Center, 1965-67; dir. psychology Va. Treatment Center for Children, 1967-69, cons., 1969—; pvt. practice clin. psychology, Richmond, 1969—; cons. Westbrook Psychiat. Hosp. Mem. Am., Va., Richmond (pres. 1960) psychol. assns. Presbyn. (mem. council Sunday sch.). Contbr. articles to profl. jours. Home: 4512 W Grace St Richmond VA 23230 Office: 2702 Grove Av Richmond VA 23220

COOKE, JULIA FITCHETT, lawyer; b. Flushing, L.I., N.Y., Nov. 13, 1929; d. Beverly Tucker and Olivia DeHaseltine (Davis) Fitchett; student Asheville-Biltomore Jr. Coll., 1947-48; Western Carolina Tchrs. Coll., 1948-50; J.D., Stetson U., 1968. Rate clk. Tenn.-Carolina Transp. Co., Asheville, N.C., 1958-60; salesman Fgn. Car Center, Asheville, 1959-60; sec., Asheville, 1960-61, Daytona Beach, Fla., 1961-64; sec. Law Center Found., Stetson Coll. Law, St. Petersburg, Fla., 1965-66, asst. Law Library, 1967-68, admissions counselor, 1969; law clk. and sec., St. Petersburg, 1968; admitted to Fla. bar, 1968, practiced in St. Petersburg, 1968-69, 72—; v.p., trust officer Central Plaza Bank & Trust Co., St. Petersburg, 1970-71; research asst. Edn. Funding Research Council, Washington, 1971-72. Worker in McCarthy campaign, St. Petersburg, 1968. Home: 1709-A 56th Terrace South St Petersburg FL 33705 Office: 1427 22d St South St Petersburg FL

COOKE, LORRAINE DAY (MRS. RICHARD A. COOKE), sch. adminstr.; b. Los Angeles, Oct. 21, 1919; d. Loring Allen and Dorothy Emily (Merriell) Day; student U. So. Cal., 1938-42; m. Richard Alexander Cooke, Feb. 19, 1953; 1 dau., Cynthia Loring; children by previous marriage—Brian Day Farquharson, Marcia (Mrs. Richard Duff). Founder Hawaii Sch. for Girls, Honolulu, 1961, chmn. bd., 1961—. Founder, pres. Grasshoppers Inc., 1967—. Bd. dirs. Honolulu Community Theater. Mem. Honolulu Garden Club (v.p. 1966—). Clubs: Oahu Country, Outrigger Canoe (Honolulu). Home: 2345 Makiki Heights Dr Honolulu HI 96822

COOKE, MARY SALISBURY, journalist; b. Redlands, Cal., May 3, 1917; d. Frank Melvin and Mary (Benton) Salisbury; grad. Punahou Sch., Honolulu, 1934; divorced; children—Alexandra (Mrs. John M. Webster III), Stephen Montague. Staff reporter, feature writer Garden Island Newspaper, Lihue, Kauai, Hawaii, 1936-37; mem. staff pub. relations dept. Matson Nav. Co., Honolulu, 1956; staff reporter, feature writer Honolulu Advertiser, 1956—. Bd. dirs. Honolulu Community Theatre, 1951-56, div. promotion, publicity and pub. relations, 1952-54, v.p., 1953. Recipient Aline Bernstein playwriting award YM and YWHA, N.Y.C., 1957; award Honolulu Press Club, 1959, 63. Author: (novel) To Raise a Nation, 1970. Home: 21 Craigside Pl Honolulu HI 96817 Office: PO Box 3110 Honolulu HI 96802

COOKE, PHYLISS (MRS. THOMAS LEE COOKE), psychologist; b. Cleve., Sept. 6, 1933; d. Reuben and Margaret (Oldach) Swanson; B.A., Baldwin Wallace Coll., 1969; M.A., Cleve. State U., 1971; Ph.D., Kent State U., 1974; m. Thomas Lee Cooke, Apr. 19, 1952; 1 son, Thomas Lee II. Instr. Patricia Stevens Modeling Agy., Cleve., 1962-68, instr., 1964-66; free lance profl. model, 1962-68; sch. psychologist pub. schs., Cleve., 1970—. Instr. Grad. Edn., Kent (O.) State U., 1973—; cons. to Assn. of Humanistic Edn. Mem. Am., Ohio, Cleve. psychol. assns., Am. Personnel and Guidance Assn., North Central Assn. for Counselor Educators, Nat. Assn. Sch. Psychologists, Ohio Sch. Psychologists, Cleve. Area, Kent-Akron Area sch. psychologists assns., Am. Assn. U. Profs. Home: 200 Granger Rd No 15 Medina OH 44256 Office: University School Kent State Univ Kent OH

COOKSEY, WANDA JEAN MOSLEY (MRS. ROBERT C. COOKSEY), educator; b. Indpls., Oct. 28, 1934; d. Virgil and Margie (Lowe) Mosley; B.S., Western Ky. U., 1956, M.A., 1962; postgrad. U. Minn., U. Alaska, Alaska Meth. U., Central Wash. State Coll., East Carolina Coll.; m. Robert C. Cooksey, Mar. 13, 1957; 1 dau., Sandi Jean. Classroom tchr., Ky., N.C., 1956-61; sch. counselor, Fairbanks, Alaska, 1961-66; sect. chief guidance services Alaska Dept. Edn., Juneau, 1967—. Mem. Am., Alaska personnel and guidance assns., Nat., Alaska edn. assns., Am. Vocational Assn. Mem. Order Eastern Star. Home: Box 52 Douglas AK 99824 Office: Pouch F Alaska Office Bldg Juneau AK 99801

COOKSON, LUIDA WENDELL (MRS. JOHN ALFRED COOKSON), editor; b. Maquoketa, Ia., Dec. 18, 1910; d. George Milton and Bess Antoinette (Hinman) Wendell; B.A., Grinnell Coll., 1932; m. John Alfred Cookson, May 7, 1947; children—Miranda Jane, John Wendell. Reporter, editor Maquoketa (Ia.) Community Press, 1932-35; editor Scott Foresman Pubs., Chgo., 1935-46; reports officer OSS, Washington and Cairo, Egypt, 1943-46; mem. editorial staff Royal Inst. Internat. Affairs, London, 1947; with Am. Geol. Inst., Washington, editor Internat. Geology Rev., 1964—. Mem. Women in Communications, Assn. of Earth Sci. Editors, English-Speaking Union. Episcopalian. Home: 3262 Worthington St NW Washington DC 20015 Office: 2201 M St NW Washington DC 20037

COOLEY, DORIS EVONNE, advt. exec.; b. Keysor, Colo., Jan. 18, 1931; d. Daniel Walter and Velda Charlotte (Radefeld) Leyerle; student Parks Sch. Commerce, 1948-50, San Bernardino Valley Coll., 1962-63; m. Robert E. Cooley, Nov. 8, 1963. With E.J. Scarry Co., Denver, 1953-61, office mgr., 1958-60, gen. mgr., 1960-61; with 4th St Rock Crusher, San Bernardino, 1962-68, head bookkeeper, 1965-68; with Bryan (Tex.) Eagle, 1969—, planning coordinator, 1971, classified advt. mgr., office mgr., 1971-74, comptroller, 1974—. Home: 3701 Parkway Terrace Bryan TX 77801 Office: 124 E 26th St Bryan TX 77801

COOLEY, ELEANOR NEWCOMB, editor; b. Melba Ida., Nov. 30, 1915; d. Lewis Elmer and Helen Alice (Prisk) Newcomb; student Coll. of Ida., 1934-35, U. Colo., 1935-37, Ariz. State U., 1960; m. Robert Miller Cooley, July 1, 1937; 1 son, Richard Lewis. Co-pub., soc. editor, office mgr. Mountain Home (Ida.) News, 1946-53; soc. editor Ariz. Daily Sun, Flagstaff, 1966-67; editor Pine alumni mag. No. Ariz. U., Flagstaff, 1971—. Co-chmn. publicity Coconino unit Am. Cancer Soc., 1971-73. Mem. Sigma Delta Chi, Theta Sigma Phi, Chi Omega, Beta Sigma Phi, Daus. of Nile. Republican. Episcopalian. Home: 518 Charles Rd Flagstaff AZ 86001 Office: Box 4101 Flagstaff AZ 86001

COOLEY, FLORENCE DECAMP, ret. pub. relations cons.; b. Spokane, Wash.; d. Wellington S. and Sarah (Foster) DeCamp; student Northwestern U., 1933-34; grad. Kinman U., 1936; m. Welland B. Cooley, Oct. 4, 1918 (div. Oct. 1936); 1 son, Richard B. Sec., Hon. Compton I. White, 1936-43; adminstrv. asst. Hon. James H. Morrison, 1943-67; pub. relations cons., law firm James H. Morrison, Washington, 1967-70. Democrat. Clubs: Top Side Aviation (1st pres. 1956-59), Congressional Staff, Washington Athletic. Home: 801 Pine St Seattle WA 98101

COOLEY, MARGUERITE BOWERS, librarian; b. Wellington, Kan., Sept. 6, 1909; d. Albert Eugene and Jennie V. (McManis) Bowers; A.B., U. Kan., 1931; M.A. in L.S., George Peabody Coll., 1951; m. Gerald A. Cooley, June 30, 1931 (div. 1950). Asst. librarian Pub. Library, Medford, Okla., 1933-38; clk. med. library VA Hosp., McKinney, Tex., 1948-50; asst. at reference George Peabody Coll. Library, 1951; librarian Dept. of Library and Archives, Phoenix, 1952-61, dir. dept., 1961—. Reader, Rec. for Blind, Phoenix. Mem. Ariz. Library Assn. (pres. 1962-63), Am. Assn. U. Women, Am. Library Assn., Altrusa Internat. (rec. sec. Phoenix 1963-64, treas. 1965-66), Gamma Phi Beta. Episcopalian. Home: 922 W Monterosa Phoenix AZ 85013 Office: State Capitol Phoenix AZ 85007

COOLIDGE, MRS. JAMES H. III, club woman; b. Atlanta, May 16, 1915; d. William Olin and Lucia A. (Cromer) Mashburn; student U. Cin., 1933-35; m. James Henry Coolidge III, Feb. 20, 1948; children—Carlton Cromer, James Henry IV, William Mashburn. Dir. Coca-Cola Bottling Works Co. div. Coca-Cola Corp., Cin., 1972—. Sec. Garden Center, Cleve., 1959—; mem. women's com. MacDonald House, U. Hosps., Cleve., 1953—; mem., past pres. Friends of Univ. Hosps.; bd. Soc. of Blind; pres. women's com. Fenn Coll. Bd. dirs. Cuyahoga unit Am. Cancer Soc.; trustee Met. Opera, N.Y. Mem. Cleve. Zool. Soc. (trustee, chmn. women's com.), Kappa Kappa Gamma. Clubs: Intown (dir. 1958—), Sundial Garden (past pres.), Kirtland Country, Union (Cleve.); Rolling Rock (Ligonier, Pa.); Gulfstream (Del Ray Beach, Fla.); Farmington Country (Charlottesville, Va.); Bath and Tennis, Little (Delray, Fla.). Home: 18100 S Park Blvd Cleveland OH 44120

COOMBE, PATRICIA JEFFRIES, govt. ofcl.; b. Washington, Feb. 26, 1932; d. George Neville and Lois Katherine (Pettit) Jeffries; 1 son, Stephen Coombe. Exec. secretarial positions Istituto Mobiliare Italiano, Washington, 1951-58, Raub Electronics Corp., Washington, 1958-60; staff asst. to mem. congress U.S. Ho. of Reps., Washington, 1960—. Home: 8715 1st Av Apt 722-C Silver Spring MD 20910 Office: 2243 Rayburn House Office Bldg Washington DC 20515

COOMBS, ALICE C'CEAL PHELPS (MRS. BRUCE AVERY COOMBS), air co. exec., civic worker; b. nr. Portland, Ore.; d. Perry Edwin and Flora (Gowey) Phelps; B.S., U. Ida., 1929; student Wash. State Coll., 1941; m. Bruce Avery Coombs, Nov. 28, 1929; children—Keith Avery, Glinda C'Ceal (Mrs. Nick E. Mason). Tchr. pub. schs., Ida., 1929-30; adminstrv. asst. Coombs West-Air Co. and Coombs Flying C Ranches, Yakima, Wash., 1945—; lobbyist for civic activities Wash. Ho. of Reps., 1947—; notary pub., 1960—. Del. White House Conf. on Children and Youth, 1960, Wash. State White House Conf. on Edn., 1955; mem. Wash. Citizens Council, Nat. Council on Crime and Delinquency, 1956—, chmn. Washington council, 1971—; mem. Allied Sch. Council Wash. 1951-53; mem. Western regional scholarship com. Ford Found., 1955-57; chmn. regional dist. Wash. Cities Legislation, 1960; chmn. Yakima County Sch. Bd., 1957-59; mem. Yakima County Health Dept., 1959-60; city councilwoman Yakima, 1959-61, asst. mayor, 1960; mem. Wash. Library Commn., 1960, 64-68, 72—, vice chmn., 1965—; mem. bd. Nat. Book Com., New York, 1969—. Trustee Wash. 4-H Found., 1960—, chmn., 1969—. Mem. Am. Library Trustee Assn. (regional dir. 1962—, pres. 1967-68), Pacific N.W. Library Assn., C. of C., Wash., Ida., Mont., Cal. hist. socs., Fort Simcoe Restoration Soc. (life), Am. (internat. trustee citation 1966, mem. bd. 1972—, council 1967-68, 71-72), Pacific N.W. (chmn. trustee sect. 1962-63), Wash. (chmn. 1960, trustee award 1967) library assns., League Women Voters, Allied Arts Council, Broadway Theatre League, Nat., Am., Aviation Assn., P.E.O., Federated Women, Colonial Dames, Altrusa Address: 908 S 25th Av Yakima WA 98902

COOMBS, HOPE CHANDLER BENTON (MRS. CHARLES EDWARD COOMBS, JR.), civic leader; b. Seattle, Mar. 30, 1910; d. Paul Amasa and Ruth (Chandler) Benton; B.S. in Textiles, U. Wash., 1932; m. Charles Edward Coombs, Jr., Apr. 14, 1934; children—Charles Paul, Marcia Joan (Mrs. John Tadlock Howe). Vol. St. Luke's Hosp. Aux., San Francisco, 1955-66; mem. Mother's Milk Bank, Inc., 1948—, aux. bd., 1956, 69; club photographer Century Club of Cal., 1962; mem. bd. dirs., docent council M.H. de Young Museum, San Francisco, 1966-68; mem. San Francisco Garden Club, 1948—, historian, 1966-68, photographer, 1965—, bd. dirs., 1954-56, 66-68; mem. D.A.R., Cal., 1954—, bd. dirs., 1958-68, regent, 1964-65. Mem. U. Wash. Alumni Assn., Cal. Geneal. Soc., Photog. Soc. Am., Soc. Asian Art, M.H. de Young Mus. Soc., Nat. Soc. Magna Charta Dames, Soc. Mayflower Descs., Nat. Soc. Daus. of Founders and Patriots Am., Sovereign Colonial Soc. Ams. Royal Descent, Order of Washington, Alpha Chi Omega. Club: Photochrome (San Francisco).

COOMBS, VIRGINIA RUTH HILL, home economist; b. Punta Gorda, Fla., Feb. 1, 1931; d. David Sylvester and Lillian Violet (Peile) Hill; B.S. in Home Econs. Edn., Fla. State U., 1952; m. Richard John Coombs, July 22, 1961 (dec. Apr. 1964). Vocational home econs. tchr., Highlands County, Fla., 1952-54; extension home econs. agt. Fla. Coop. Extension Service, Hillsborough County, Fla., 1954—. Sec., Hillsborough County Nutrition Com., 1963, chmn., 1964. Mem. West Coast Dist. Home Econs. Assn. (sec.-treas. 1957-58, vice chmn. 1958-59), Nat., Fla. (sec. 1964) assns. extension home economists, Am., Fla. home econs. assn., Nat. Assn. Extension 4-H Agts. Home: 220 6th Av SW Ruskin FL 33570 Office: 101 14th Av SE Ruskin FL 33570

COON, GERALDINE ALMA, educator; b. North Stonington, Conn., Sept. 13, 1913; d. Frank Eugene and Melissa (Greene) Coon; B.A., Conn. Coll., 1935; M.S., Brown U., 1937; Ph.D., U. Rochester, 1950. Instr. shop math. Scovill Mfg. Co., Waterbury, Conn., 1939-44; research mathematician Taylor Instrument Cos., Rochester, N.Y., 1944-58; asst. prof. U. Conn., 1958-61, asso. prof., 1961-64; mem. Courant Inst., N.Y.U., 1959-60; prof. Goucher Coll., 1964—. Vis. prof. Brown U., 1967-68. Mem. Am. Math. Soc., Math. Assn. Am., Soc. Indsl. and Applied Math., Assn. for Computing Machinery, Phi Beta Kappa, Sigma Xi. Author (with W. I. Caldwell and L. Zoss) Frequency Response for Process Control, 1959. Home: 5 Fellowship Ct Towson MD 21204

COON, JEAN RUSSELLA MCCOY (MRS. ROGER L. COON, JR.), lawyer, state ofcl.; b. Norristown, Pa., July 29, 1930; d. Kenneth Argue and Mary (Supplee) McCoy; B.A. cum laude, Syracuse U., 1951, LL.B. magna cum laude, 1953; m. Roger L. Coon, Jr., June 4, 1960; children—Sherry Marie, Beth Anne. Admitted to N.Y. State bar, 1953; legal cons. municipal affairs N.Y. State Dept. Audit and Control, Albany, 1953-54; atty., dep. clerk Onondaga County Childrens Ct., Syracuse, N.Y., 1955-56; research cons. N.Y. State Assembly, Albany, 1956-57; asst. atty. gen. State of N.Y., Albany, 1957-71, asst. solicitor gen., 1971—. Pres., Saratoga County Womens Republican Club, 1969-71; mem. council Fedn. Women's Rep. Clubs N.Y. State, 1971—.Mem. N.Y. State, Saratoga County bar assns. Club: Zonta (pres. 1968-70, lt. gov. Dist. II 1969-72, gov. 1972—). Home: 65 E Grove St Ballston Spa NY 12020 Office: Dept of Law Albany NY 12224

COONEY, DOROTHY FRANCINE, radiologist; b. Hermiston, Ore., 1929; M.D., U. Ore., 1958. Intern U. Ore. Hosp., 1958-59; resident U. Chgo. Hosp., 1959-62; chmn. radiology Mercy Med. Center, Chgo., 1964-69; mem. staff St. Bernard's Hosp., Chgo., Christ Community Hosp., Oaklawn, Ill., Provident Hosp., Chgo. Diplomate Am. Bd. Radiology. Address: 2600 S Michigan Av Chicago IL 60616

COONEY, JOAN GANZ (MRS. TIMOTHY J. COONEY), television exec.; b. Phoenix, Nov. 30, 1929; d. Sylvan C. and Pauline (Reardan) Ganz; B.A., U. Ariz., 1951; D.Sc.Ed. (hon.), Boston Coll., 1970; L.H.D. (hon.), Hofstra U., Oberlin Coll., Ohio Wesleyan U., 1971, Princeton, 1973; m. Timothy J. Cooney, Feb. 22, 1964. Reporter, Ariz. Republic, Phoenix, 1953-54; publicist NBC, N.Y.C., 1954-55; tv publicist U.S. Steel Corp., N.Y.C., 1955-62; producer Channel 13, WNET, N.Y.C., 1962-67; TV cons. Carnegie Corp., N.Y.C., 1967-68; exec. dir. Childrens TV Workshop, producers Sesame St. and Electric Co., N.Y.C., 1968-70, pres., trustee, 1970—. Bd. dirs. First Pa. Corp., City Center Cinematheque, 1971; trustee Channel 13 Ednl. Broadcasting Corp., Am. Film Inst., 1971—, Mayo Found., 1973—. Mem. Pres.'s Commn. on Marijuana and Drug Abuse, 1971-73; mem. com. Pub. Understanding of Sci., 1972—; pub. mem. Nat. News Council, 1973—. Recipient Emmy award for Poverty, Anti-Poverty and the Poor, 1966; Distinguished Service medal Columbia U. Tchrs. Coll., 1971; award Soc. for Family of Man, 1971; Gold medal Nat. Inst. Social Scis., 1971; Frederick Douglass award N.Y. Urban League, 1972, Quest medal, 1973, numerous others for Sesame St., Electric Co. Mem. Acad. TV Arts and Scis., Internat. Radio and TV Soc., Am. Women in Radio and TV (Silver Satellite award 1972), Nat. Orgn. for Women, Nat. Inst. Social Scis., Council on Fgn. Relations. Home: 201 E 21st St New York City NY 10010 Office: 1 Lincoln Plaza New York City NY 10023

COONEY, MARY ELLEN, physician; b. N.Y.C., June 21, 1936; d. Vincent T. and Margaret (Burgett) Cooney; B.A., Cornell U., 1958; M.D., N.Y. Med. Coll., 1962; m. Alan Theodore Bowes, June 15, 1962; 1 son, Theodore Vincent. Intern Lenox Hill Hosp., N.Y.C., 1962-63; resident asst. anesthesiologist, then anesthesiologist N.Y. Hosp., 1963-65; instr. anesthesiology Cornell U. Med. Coll., N.Y.C., 1963-65; anesthesiologist Overlook Hosp., Summit, N.J., 1965-73, personnel health physician, 1973—; instr. coronary care nursing program Rutgers U., 1966-70. Diplomate Am. Bd. Anesthesiology. Fellow Am. Coll. Anesthesiologists; mem. A.M.A., N.J., Essex County med. socs., Am. Occupational Med. Assn., Pi Beta Phi. Home: 1455 Woodacres Dr Mountainside NJ 07092

COONEY, SISTER MIRIAM PATRICK, educator; b. South Bend, Ind., May 6, 1925; d. Walter James and Catherine Rose (McGuinness) Cooney; B.S., St. Mary's Coll., 1951; M.S., U. Notre Dame, 1953; S.M., U. Chgo., 1963, Ph.D., 1969. Entered Cong. Sisters of Holy Cross, 1942; tchr. Acad., Morris, Ill., 1946-50; mem. faculty St. Mary's Coll., Notre Dame, Ind., 1950—, prof. math. Liberal Arts Coll., 1971—, v.p., 1958-61. Tchr. U. Notre Dame, 1971-72; cons. East Africa, Ethiopia, summer 1971. Trustee Dunbarton Coll., Washington. Mem. Am. Math. Soc., Math. Assn. Am., Nat. Council Tchrs. Math. Contbr. articles to profl. jours. Address: St Mary's Coll Notre Dame IN 46556

COONROD, DORIS ANNETTE, judge; b. Carrollton, Tex., June 6, 1930; d. Noble Saxon and Helen Lois (Padgett) Coonrod; B.S., Tex. U. for Women, 1952; J.D., John Marshall Sch. Law, 1958. Admitted to Ill. bar, 1958, Wash. bar, 1967, U.S. Supreme Ct. bar, 1971; practiced in Chgo., 1958-66; claims examiner Wash. Dept. Social and Health Services, Olympia, Wash., 1967-68, hearing examiner, 1968-71; adminstrv. law judge Bur. Hearings and Appeals, Social Security Adminstrn., U.S. Dept. Health, Edn. and Welfare, Seattle, 1971—. Mem. Fed. Adminstrv. Law Judges Conf. Mem. Am., Wash. State bar assns., Adminstrv. Law Judges Assn. Health Edn. and Welfare. Clubs: Edmonds Yacht, Swedish. Home: 9320 31st Av NW Seattle WA 98117 Office: Jones Bldg 1331 3rd Av A Seattle WA 98101

COOPER, AGNES PEARSON (MRS. DAVID ACRON COOPER), educator; b. Bonner Springs, Kan., Oct. 18, 1910; d. James P. and May B. (Luther) Pearson; B.S., Kan. State Tchrs. Coll., 1932; M.S., U. Denver, 1938; postgrad. Harvard, 1939, 40; m. David Acron Cooper, Oct. 15, 1941; 1 son, David Acron. Tchr. high schs., Kan., Mo., 1929-37; tchr. Wyandotte High Sch., Kansas City, Kan., 1937-39; instr. secretarial sci. Alfred U., 1939-41; instr. U. Tenn., 1941-42; dir. edn. and placement Knoxville (Tenn.) Bus. Coll., 1942-48; dir. edn., treas. Cooper Inst., Inc., Knoxville 1948—. Mem. Knox County adv. com. Tenn. Welfare Dept., Knoxville, 1955—, chmn., 1959; mem. East Tenn. Community Improvement Central Com., 1952—, vice chmn., 1954, pres. 1968; hostess spl. luncheons Tenn. Valley Agrl. and Indsl. Fair, 1956—, dir. spelling match, 1972—. Mem. nat. bd. Women's Med. Coll., Philadelphia. Mem. East Tenn. Edn. Assn. (chmn. bus. sect. 1958, sec. 1957), Nat. Office Mgrs. Assn., Am. Assn. U. Women, Am. Bus. Women's Assn., Better Bus. Bur., Internat. Platform Assn. Baptist. Club: Quota (1st v.p. 1963-64, 2d v.p. 1961-63, gov. 23d dist. 1956-57, gov. 8th dist. 1949-51, trustee ednl. revolving fund Knoxville 1962-63, internat. pres. 1965-66). Home: 720 N 5th Av NE Knoxville TN 37917

COOPER, BARBARA ANN ACHESON (MRS. WILLIAM GILL COOPER), physiotherapist; b. Havana, Cuba, Mar. 1, 1935; d. Archibald Alexander and Freda Margaret (Butcher) Acheson; student therapy U. Toronto, 1953-56; postgrad. McMaster U., 1973; m. William Gill Cooper, June 9, 1956; children—Liane Louise, James Gill. Staff physiotherapist Henderson Gen. Hosp., Hamilton, Ont., Can., 1956-58, Clinic, 68 Charlton Av. West Hamilton, 1958-60; staff therapist McGregor Clinic, Hamilton, 1961—; head therapist Dr. Rygiel's Home for Children, Hamilton. Cons. physiotherapy as related to mental retardation and multi-handicapped children,

1970-74; tchr. nurses aides, univ. phys. edn. students physiotherapy in mental retardation, 1970-74. Establisher art classes for multi-handicapped Chedoke Hosp., 1973. Bd. dirs. Jr. League, Hamilton, 1964-66, Victorian Order Nurses, 1971-73; bd. govs. Dundas Valley Sch. Art. Mem. Canadian Physiotherapy Assn. (v.p. Hamilton br. 1959-60), Delta Gamma. Mem. Anglican Ch. Address: 87 Auchmar Rd Hamilton ON L9C 1C6 Canada

COOPER, BETTY MARGUERITE, anesthesiologist; b. San Angelo, Tex., May 9, 1915; d. Charles Thomas and Patty McClellan (Griffin) Cooper; student San Angelo Jr. Coll., 1933-34; B.A., U. Tex., 1937, M.D., 1944. Intern, Hosp. of Women's Med. Coll., Phila., 1945-46; resident Tb Sanitarium, Sanitarium, Tex., 1944-45, resident chest diseases Herman Keifer Hosp., Detroit, 1946-47, resident anesthesia U. Tex. Med. Br., Galveston, 1947-49, instr. anesthesia, 1949-51; sr. scientist Oak Ridge Inst. Nuclear Studies, 1951-59; practice medicine specializing in anesthesiology, Oak Ridge, 1959-66, Amarillo, Tex., 1966—; mem. staff Northwest Tex. Hosp., Amarillo, chief dept. of anesthesia, 1971—. Address: 6706 Dreyfuss Rd Amarillo TX 79106

COOPER, BEVERLY MARIE, furniture exec.; b. Conrad, Ia., June 5, 1932; d. John Robert and Arsula Marie (Spencer) Morse; grad. high sch.; m. Elmer Ray Cooper, Feb. 4, 1972; children by previous marriage—Terry Lee and John Frederick Caldemeyer. With Holland Dairies, Inc. (Ind.), 1958-73; partner Mary's Furniture, Tell City, Ind., 1973—. Precinct committeewoman Republican Party, 1968-70. Club: Tell City Country. Home: Rural Route 3 Box 222 Tell City IN 47586 Office: 135 13th St Tell City IN 47586

COOPER, DANIELLE CHAVY, educator; b. Paris, France, Dec. 11, 1921; d. Henri Paul and Jeanne (Vasselin) Chavy; student City of London (Eng.) Coll., 1937; B.A., U. Paris, 1939, M.A., 1941, D.E.S., 1942; postgrad. Sorbonne (France), 1941-42, Bryn Mawr Coll., 1946-47; Ph.D., U. So. Cal., 1963; m. Wilmer A. Cooper, Sept. 23, 1947 (dec. Mar. 1965); 1 dau., Laurel Martine. Came to U.S., 1946, naturalized, 1954. Instr. French, U. Alta., Banff, Can., 1948, 60; editor Topanga News, Malibu, Cal., 1953-54; columnist, reporter Topanga (Cal.) Jour., 1954-55; instr. U. So. Cal., Los Angeles, 1958; lang. coordinator Isabelle Buckley Schs., Beverly Hills, Cal., 1955-56; instr., pub. relations chmn. French Found. Cal., Los Angeles, 1956-59; asst. prof. French, German, Immaculate Heart Coll., Los Angeles, 1957-63; vis. lectr. U. Colo., Boulder, 1963-65; asso. prof. French, Keuka Coll., Keuka Park, N.Y., 1965-68, prof. 1968-70, chmn. dept. modern langs., 1965-70; prof. French, head French program Monterey Inst. of Fgn. Studies, Monterey, Cal., 1970—, chmn. div. langs. and civilizations, 1971-73. Reporter, Le Californien, French newspaper, San Francisco, 1972—. Decorated medaille du Combattant Volontaire de la Resistance, Croix du Combattant, medaille de la France Liberse, Palmes Académiques. Mem. Am. Assn. Tchrs. French (pres. U. So. Cal. chpt. 1958-59), Am. Assn. U. Profs., Am. Assn. U. Women, Am. Name Soc., Am. Council on Teaching Fgn. Langs., Modern Lang. Assn. Am., Modern Lang. Assn. So. Cal. (exec. council 1958-59), Fgn. Lang. Assn. No. Cal., Nat. Assn. Lang. Lab. Dirs., Alliance Francaise, (pres. Monterey Peninsula chpt. 1972—), Societe des Professeurs de Francais en Amerique, Les Amis de la Varende, Vergilian Soc., Am. Name Soc., Pi Delta Phi, Phi Sigma Iota, Alpha Mu Gamma (nat. exec. bd., nat. scholarship chmn. 1967-73, nat. pres. 1973-75). Roman Catholic. Author: Les Suites Romanesques de Jean de La Varende (microfilm), 1963. Contbr. articles to profl. jours. Address: Monterey Inst Foreign Studies Monterey CA 93940

COOPER, DONNA LAURE, physician; b. Phila., Apr. 3, 1942; d. Donald Treat and Virginia Mason (Clement) Cooper; B.A., Oberlin Coll., 1965; M.D., Jefferson Med. Coll., Phila., 1969 M.P.H., U. Cal. at Los Angeles, 1973; m. James Winter, Dec. 19, 1972. Intern U. Wis. Hosp., 1969-70; physician Family Planning Clinic, Women's Hosp., Los Angeles County/U. So. Cal. Med. Center, 1970-73; dir., 1973—, instr. obstetrics and gynecology, 1971—. Diplomate Nat. Bd. Med. Examiners. Mem. Am. Assn. Planned Parenthood Physicians, Planned Parenthood-World Population, Population Assn. Am., Am. Pub. Health Assn. Home: 1440 Veteran Av Apt #456 Los Angeles CA 90024 Office: Women's Hosp Los Angeles County U/So Cal Med Center Los Angeles CA 90033

COOPER, DOTTIE DEE SCARBOROUGH (MRS. FRED LITTON COOPER), civic worker; b. Spanish Lake, La., July 1, 1902; d. Robert Lee and Minnie Lucretia (Smith) Scarborough; student Lake Charles Bus. Coll., 1925; m. Fred Litton Cooper, Mar. 28, 1926; children—Norman Otto, Margaret Sue (Mrs. Aubrey R. Barnette), John Thomas (dec.). Bookkeeper, Lay's Ice Cream Co., Natchitoches, La., 1922-23; tchr. one room sch., Commack, La., 1923-24; tchr. pvt. sch., Haynesville, La., 1924-25; bookkeeper Jordan's Pharmacy, Mansfield, La., 1927; co-owner, clk. bookkeeper, buyer Cooper's Pharmacy, Robeline, La., 1928-71. Pres. Natchitoches Parish Hosp. Guild Soc., 1972-74. Alderman, Village of Robeline, 1970—. Trustee Library Bd. Control, Natchitoches Parish Library. Recipient certificate of appreciation Pres. of U.S., 1942, recognition award A.R.C., 1945, certificate of recognition Gov. of La., 1943, certificate of recognition Agrl. Extension Service, 1958, certificate appreciation La. Baptist Children's Home, Monroe, La., 1972. Mem. Am., La. library assns., D.A.R. (state chaplain 1969-71), Colonial Dames of XVII Century, Women for the Preservation of Historic Natchitoches, La. Outdoor Drama Assn., La. Moral and Civic Found., Los Adais Hist. Found. (life). Baptist (tchr., ch. clk.). Address: PO Box 188 Robeline LA 71469

COOPER, EDITH CHRISTENSEN, investment co. exec.; b. Jersey City, Dec. 4, 1905; d. Knud and Laura (Christensen) Christensen; A.B., Cornell U., 1928; postgrad. Sch. Bus. Adminstrn., N.Y.U., 1944-49, Exec. Devel. Clinic, Columbia, 1951; m. Ronald Cooper, Mar. 24, 1934 (dec. June 1943); children—Ronald Leslie, Martha Laura (Mrs. Isaac V. Young, III). Sec. to pres. Becton, Dickinson & Co., Rutherford, N.J., 1931-43; asst. to orgn. planning supr. Fed. Shipbldg. & Drydock Co., 1943-46; confidential exec. sec. to financial v.p. Am. Machine & Foundry Co., N.Y.C., 1946-49; exec. asst. to pres. Lincoln Savs. Bank, Bklyn., 1950-56; sec. corp. Midland Bank, Paramus, N.J., 1957-60; investment adviser, registered rep., account exec. A.W. Benkert & Co., Inc., N.Y.C., 1961-71; portfolio mgr., asst. corporate sec. Fundamental Advisors, Inc., N.Y.C., 1972—; sec., asst. treas., dir. Cleve-Walt Holding Co., Inc., Bklyn., 1950-56. Pub. relations cons. to financial instns., 1959-60. Mem. Zonta Internat., Mortar Bd., Delta Delta Delta. Clubs: Cornell of New York, Cornell Women's of N.Y. Presbyn. Home: 286 Wood-Ridge St Wood-Ridge NJ 07075 Office: Fundamental Advisors Inc 30 Broad St New York City NY 10004

COOPER, ERLYNE ELMIRA STROLL (MRS. LEONARD COOPER), social worker; b. Montreal, Que., Can., Jan. 12, 1931; d. William and Edna (Druyen) Stroll; A.A., Los Angeles City Coll., 1950; B.A. in Psychology, U. Cal. at Los Angeles, 1952; M.S.W. (Nat. Inst. Mental Health fellow), U. So. Cal. Sch. Social Work, 1959, postgrad. 1955-66; m. Leonard Cooper, Sept. 1, 1957; 1 son, Ward Ross. Came to U.S., 1946, naturalized, 1952. Remedial tchr. Clin. Sch., U. Cal. at Los Angeles, 1952; spl. edn. tchr. Los Angeles Bd. Edn., 1953; social worker Los Angeles County Bur. Pub. Assistance, 1954; med. social worker Los Angeles County Hosp., 1956, 57; child welfare worker Los Angeles County Bur. Adoptions, 1957-58; student social worker Bur. Social Work, Los Angeles, 1959; casework specialist Psychiat. Clinic, cons., psychiat. social worker Rehab. Center, Children's Hosp., Los Angeles, 1960-65; casework specialist Blind Childrens Center, Los Angeles, 1965, dir. casework, spl. services, 1966-67, exec. dir., 1968-70; coordinator services Marianne Frostig Center Ednl. Therapy, Los Angeles, 1970-71; dir. casework Los Angeles Child Guidance Clinic, 1971-73; clin. social worker U. Colo. Med. Center, Denver, 1973-74, coordinator student social work tng., 1974—. Mem. profl. adv. bd. Park Century Sch., West Los Angeles; social work cons. to narcotics officer edn. Certinella Valley Union High Sch. Dist. Mem. Nat. Assn. Social Workers, Am. Assn. Workers for Blind, Assn. Edn. Visually Handicapped, Acad. Certified Social Workers, Colo. Clin. Social Work Soc. Research in study on children born with bladders on the outside of their bodies, multiply handicapped, emotionally disturbed children. Home: 13180 E Iliff Bldg 2 Apt 413 Denver CO 80232 Office: 4200 E 9th Av Denver CO 80220

COOPER, GRACE ROGERS (MRS. SANFORD LEE COOPER), museum curator; b. Sharon, Pa., Nov. 22, 1924; d. Byron Alonzo and Wilda Emily (Boyer) Rogers; student Maryville (Tenn.) Coll., 1942-44; B.S., U. Md., 1946; m. Sanford Lee Cooper, Dec. 15, 1961. Asst. curator textiles U.S. Nat. Mus., Smithsonian Instn., 1948-56, asso. curator, 1956-61, curator, 1961—; cons. in field, 1948—; sr. tech. editor textiles Ency. Brit., 1959—. Mem. Internat. Inst. Conservation Historic and Artistic Works, Internat. Center Study Ancient Textiles, Am. Assn. Museums. Lutheran. Author: The Invention of the Sewing Machine, 1968; The Copp Family Textiles, 1971; 13 Star Flags: Keys to Identification, 1973. Home: 3114 Wisconsin Av NW Washington DC 20016 Office: Div Textile Nat Museum History and Tech Smithsonian Inst Washington DC 20560

COOPER, ISABEL HOFFMANN (MRS. MILTON H. COOPER), found. exec.; b. Pitts.; d. Alvin Anthony and Fannie (McCormick) Hoffmann; student voice diction and piano, pvt. tutors, 1914-35; student voice Cin. Conservatory Music, 1921; student God's Bible Coll., 1920, Missionary Tng. Inst., 1922 (Organ scholar) Pa. Coll. for Women (now named Chatham Coll.), 1924, Ft. Lauderdale U., 1971; m. Milton H. Cooper, Sept. 15, 1928 (dec. July 1946); children—Paul Milton, Ethel (Mrs. Henry William Kurtz, Jr.), Ruth (Mrs. James Huber). Profl. soprano soloist radio stas. KDKA, 1926-28, also 1/2 hour program WCAE, summer 1928; numerous concert appearances include Boston Symphony Orch., harpist, 1927, Little Symphony Orch., Pitts., 1939, also soprano soloist Christ Meth. Ch., Pitts., 1940-46, First Presbyn. Ch., 1946-53; with YMCA, Pitts., 1926-28, Maison Frederick Sch. Beauty Culture, Pitts., 1938, Labor Standards Assn., Pitts., 1939-42, USO, 1942-46; sec. to v.p. Hickman, Williams & Co., Pitts., 1947-50; controlled materials sec. Dravo Corp., Pitts., 1950-52; asst. to dir. Pitts. Found., 1952-67; sec.-bookkeeper Pitcairn-Crabbe Found., Pitts., also sec. to cons. Howard Heinz Endowment, Pitts., 1952-67; adminstr. theater parties Pitts. Playhouse, 1968; adminstrv. exec. World Center Liturgical Studies, Inc. Boynton, Fla. 1969; adminstrv. asst. Frank Martens & Asso., Ft. Lauderdale, 1970—. Corr. sec., mem. exec. com., chmn. promotions com. Opera Workshop, Chatham Coll., 1959, judge competitive auditions of singers 1963-68; historian The Opera Workshop. Mem. Hist. Soc. Western Pa., Chatham Coll. Alumnae Assn. Episcopalian. Club: Women's City of Pittsburgh (music com. 1962-64). Address: The Westwinds Apt 2A-East 740 Tuckahoe Rd Yonkers NY 10710

COOPER, JOANNE BECKMAN (MRS. HAROLD COOPER), artist; b. Columbus, O., Apr. 14, 1930; d. Theodore N. and Esther (Baker) Beckman; student Northwestern U., 1948-49, Ohio State U., 1950-51, Art Students League of N.Y., 1962-65, Mus. Modern Art (N.Y.), 1961; m. Harold Cooper, Mar. 27, 1954; children—Robert Neil, Elisa Mara. Exhibited paintings in one man shows Coll. City N.Y., 1967, Panoras Gallery, N.Y.C., 1966; two man shows at Verzyl Gallery, L.I., 1967, Iona Coll., New Rochelle, N.Y., 1967; exhibited in nat. competitions Allied Artists Am., N.A.D., Purdue U., Indpls., Ind., 1966, Newport (R.I.) Festival of Arts, 1966; represented in permanent collections; tchr. art Ethical Culture Childrens Assembly, Riverdale, N.Y., 1966. Recipient 1st prize Riverdale Art Show, 1966, 2d prize 1965; 2d prize Westchester (N.Y.) Art Show, 1965, 66, 67, Festival of Irish Culture, Hunter Coll., N.Y.C., 1966, Westchester Art Soc., 1973; hon. mention Benedictine Art Awards, 1971; 1st prize Riverdale Neighborhood House, 1973. Mem. Silvermine Guild of Artists, Westchester Art Soc., Yonkers Art Assn., Nat. Soc. Painters in Casein, Am. Soc. Contemporary Artists, Artists Equity Assn. N.Y. Address: 4483 Douglas Av Riverdale NY 10471

COOPER, JOY MCCORMICK RHODES (MRS. ROBERT L. COOPER), educator; b. Chgo., July 10, 1927; d. Willard and Lillian (Hansen) Rhodes; B.S., Columbia, 1949; M.A., Columbia, 1951; m. Robert L. Cooper, Apr. 9, 1959; children—Lawrence Michael, Patricia Jane. Materials specialist Bur. Indian Affairs Dept. Interior, Brigham City, Utah, 1951-54; materials specialist Puerto Rican study Ford Found. N.Y.C. Bd. Edn., 1954-55; program specialist Girl Scouts Am., N.Y.C., 1955-59; ind. edn. cons., 1965—. Bd. dirs. Overseas Edn. Fund League Women Voters, 1971—; bd. trustees Bancroft Sch., 1972—. Mem. Civil Air Patrol, Aircraft Owners and Pilots Assn., Air Force Assn., Navy League, Nat. Oceanography Assn., Internat. Oceanographic Found., Oceanic Soc., Club: Croton Dam Yacht (commodore) (Ossining, N.Y.). Author: series spl. vocational textbooks, 1951-54. Home: 9 Taconic Rd Ossining NY 10562

COOPER, JOYCE, educator; b. Raleigh, N.C.; d. William Alexander and Lula (Joyce) Cooper; A.B., U.N.C., 1928; M.A., U. N.C. at Chapel Hill, 1941; Ed.D., Columbia, 1950. Tchr. Raleigh Pub. Schs., 1928-41; asst. prof. U. N.C. at Greensboro, 1941-46; asst. supt. pub. instrn. State Wash., 1948-57; prof. edn. U. Fla., Gainesville, 1957—. Mem. Study Commn. of Chief State Sch. Officers, 1952-57; adviser tchr. edn. Korean minister edn., 1960-61; dir. Nat. Def. Edn. Act Insts. for Tchrs. of Disadvantaged Children, 1965-67, EPDA Inst. for In-Service Suprs., 1969-71. Mem. exec. com. Gainesville YMCA, 1966-71. Mem. Assn. supervision and Curriculum Devel. (exec. com. 1968-72), N.E.A., Assn. Childhood Edn., Nat. Soc. for Study Edn., John Dewey Soc. Club: Soroptimist International (Gainesville pres. 1967-68). Home: 3468 NW 11th Av Gainesville FL 32601

COOPER, JULIA PERRY, lawyer; b. Fayetteville, N.C., July 17, 1920; d. Dallas L. and Emily (McKay) Perry; B.S., Hampton Inst., 1940; LL.B., Howard U., 1951; m. Jerry S. Cooper, July 30, 1943; 1 dau., Cheryl; m. 2d, Clifford S. Mack, Nov. 21, 1957. Admitted to D.C. bar, 1952; legal cons. OPS, Washington, 1952-53; atty.-advisor office gen. counsel Gen. Services Adminstrn., 1953-54; trial appellate atty. criminal div. Dept. Justice, 1954-68; civil rights atty. Office Gen. Counsel, Equal Employment Opportunity Commn., Washington, 1968—. Mem. Am., Fed., Washington, Nat. bar assns. Home: 1610 Varnum St NW Washington DC 20011 Office: Equal Employment Opportunity Commn Washington DC 20506

COOPER, LORRAINE ARNOLD ROWAN (MRS. JOHN SHERMAN COOPER), civic worker; b. Pasadena, Cal., Dec. 18, 1906; d. Robert Arnold and Laura Madeline (Schwarz) Rowan; ed. pvt. schs., Pasadena, Stevenson, Md., Florence, Italy; formerly married to Robert McAdoo (dec.), Thomas Shevlin; m. John Sherman Cooper (U.S. Senator from Ky.), Mar. 17, 1955. Vol. worker Inter-Am. Affairs Council, N.Y.C., 1943-46; vol. worker, observer First UN Conf., San Francisco, 1945; pres. Republican Congl. Wives Club, 1960-62; mem. com. Restoration Blair House; chmn. Opera Ball for Opera Soc. Washington, 1965; active as speaker, columnist in Ky. newspapers. Dir. R.A. Rowan & Co., Los Angeles. Bd. dirs. Asia Found., San Francisco, Frontier Nursing Service, Ky.; past dir. Asia Soc., N.Y. Mem. Am. Newspaper Women's Club, Homemakers of Am., Nat. Soc. Arts and Letters, Internat. Good Neighbors Club. Episcopalian. Home: 2900 N St Washington DC 20007

COOPER, MARGARET KATHRYN HUNT, secondary sch. tchr.; b. Hugo, Okla., June 23, 1929; d. Jodie and Josephine (Henry) Hunt; B.A., Langston (Okla.) U., 1951; M.L.S., U. Okla., 1957; Ph.D. candidate, U. Cal. at Berkeley, 1970—; m. Reginald D. Cooper, May 31, 1952; 1 son, Rupert McLloyd. Tchr., librarian schs. in Okla., 1951-56; asst. circulation librarian, asst. sci. librarian U. Neb., 1957-62; head librarian Fremont Jr. High Sch., Stockton, Cal., 1962-69; reading and math. project dir. Marshall Jr. High Sch., Stockton, 1970-71; tchr. Webster Jr. High Sch., Stockton, 1972—; coordinator instructional media services Stockton Unified Sch. Dist., 1974—; cons. in field. Mem. N.E.A., Cal., Stockton (v.p. 1967-68) tchrs. assns., Black Tchrs. Alliance, Nat. Assn. U. Women, N.A.A.C.P., Links, Delta Kappa Gamma (chpt. v.p. 1968-70), Pi Lambda Theta, Alpha Kappa Alpha. Democrat. Roman Cath. Contbr. profl. jours. Home: 44 E Pine St Stockton CA 95204 Office: 2725 Michigan Av Stockton CA 95204

COOPER, MARY GENEVIEVE, lawyer; b. Wilkes-Barre, Pa., May 31, 1938; d. Samuel and Genevieve (McNelis) Cooper; B.A. in Econs., U. Pa., 1960; LL.B., Dickinson Sch. Law, 1963; LL.M., N.Y. U., 1967. Admitted to Pa. bar, 1964; since practiced in Hazleton; asso. firm Bigelow, Gillispie, LaRocca, Hazleton, 1964-71, partner, 1971—. Asst. dist. atty. Luzerne County, Pa., 1971; asst. city solicitor Hazleton, Pa., 1972-74; law clk. to judge Luzerne Ct., Wilkes-Barre, Pa., 1972—, pres. Meri-Dan, Inc., Hazleton, 1968—. Instr. bus. law Pa. State U., 1968—. Second v.p. Easter Seal Soc. of Hazleton and Carbon Counties, 1971—. Mem. State com. Pa. Young Republicans, 1968-70; mem. Hazleton Zoning Hearing Bd., 1964, chmn., 1965-70; vice chmn. exec. com. 116th legislative dist. Rep. Com., 1971—. Bd. dirs. Vis. Nurses Assn., 1964-70; asst. treas., 1966-68, 2nd. v.p., 1968-70; bd. dirs. United Rehab. Services, Inc., 1970—, treas., 1974—. Mem. Am., Pa., Lower Luzerne County (sec. 1965—) bar assns., Wilkes-Barre Law and Library Assn., Greater Hazleton C. of C. (dir. 1974—). Club: Soroptimist (pres. 1971-73). Home: 74 Coxe St Hazleton PA 18201 Office: 1100 Northeastern Bldg Hazleton PA 18201

COOPER, MARY GREEN (MRS. MILTON LEROY COOPER), educator; b. Norfolk, Va., Oct. 29, 1938; d. George Herbert and Lillian Louise (Vaughn) Green; student Norfolk State Coll., 1955-57; B.S., Howard U., 1959; postgrad. N.Y. U., 1960; M.Ed., So. U., 1962; postgrad. Ind. U., 1963, U. Ill., 1964, Temple U., 1968, U. Del., 1973; m. Milton Leroy Cooper, June 4, 1961. Health and phys. edn. tchr. Newport News (Va.) City Schs., 1959-61, East Baton Rouge Parrish, 1962-63; instr. health and phys. edn. Dillard U., New Orleans, 1963-65; asst. prof. health and phys. edn. Del. State Coll., Dover, 1967-70, asst. prof., acting chmn. health and phys. edn., 1970—. Recipient award Dover YMCA, 1968, Plaque Phys. Edn. Major's Club, 1970-73, grant, DuPont Co., 1973. Mem. Am. (mem. nat. com. 1969-71), Del. (mem. scholarship com. 1970) assns. health, phys. edn. and recreation, Nat., Eastern assns. health, phys. edn. and recreation, Delta Sigma Theta. Democrat. Roman Catholic. Clubs: Delicadoes (Norfolk); Racquet, Indoor Tennis (Dover). Home: 600 Carriage Lane RD 1 Dover DE 19901

COOPER, MARY JANE, pub. relations exec.; b. Joplin, Mo., Sept. 21, 1942; d. Ethelbert Jackson and Pauline Nannie (Harmon) Cooper; B.S., U. Omaha, 1964. Asst. dir. pub. relations A.R.C., Omaha, 1964; editorial asst., editor univ. relations dept. Washington U., St. Louis, 1964-69; publs. editor Citizens Gas & Coke Utility, Indpls., 1969-71; freelance writer and photographer, Mpls., 1972; pub. information rep. No. States Power Co., Mpls., 1972—. Mem. Women in Communications (historian 1972-73, fund-raising chmn. 1973-74, pres. 1974-75). Home: 7330 Gallagher Dr Edina MN 55435 Office: 414 Nicollet Mall Minneapolis MN 55401

COOPER, MARY WARMBIER (MRS. JOHN R. COOPER), educator; b. Meriden, Conn., Aug. 15, 1905; d. Henry A. and Clara (Slade) Warmbier; B.S magna cum laude, Tufts Coll., 1926; M.S., U. Pitts., 1928, Ed.D., 1972, postgrad., summers 1929-36, Boston U., summers 1954-60, Harvard, 1968-72; m. John R. Cooper, June 25, 1942; 1 dau., Sarah Anne (Mrs. Richard Leslie Hendrickson). Grad. instr. U. Pitts., 1926-28; tchr. sci. Gloucester (Mass.) High Sch., 1928-29; tchr. sci. Swampscott (Mass.) High Sch., 1929-39, sch. psychologist, 1940-70, dir. guidance, 1951-70; ednl. cons. adolescent unit Children's Med. Center, Boston, 1958—; cons. U.S. Dept. Health, Edn. and Welfare, 1970—; dir. Lynn Mental Health Clinic; dir. Washington Sq. House, 1971; asst. dir. North Shore Guidance Clinic, 1971—; instr. summer sch. Harvard Research com. Mass. Dept. Edn. Mem. North Shore and Essex County Guidance Dirs. Assn. (pres. 1963-64), Mass. Deans Assn., Nat. Assn. Women Deans and Counselors, Am. Psychol. Assn., Mass. Sch. Counselors Assn., Mass. Sch. Psychologists Assn., Am. Personnel and Guidance Assn., New Eng. Guidance Assn., Nat. Vocational Guidance Assn., Nat. Deans Assn., Phi Beta Kappa, Delta Kappa Gamma, Sigma Xi. Author: Guidance in a Changing World, Elementary Guidance Programs; Guidance in Secondary Schools, 1968; Planning for College; Vocational Education in the 70's. Contbr. articles to profl. jours. Home: 107 Aspen Rd Swampscott MA 01907

COOPER, MARY WEIS (MRS. LEON COOPER), operations research scientist; b. St. Louis, Aug. 10, 1942; d. Arthur John and Anita Olivia (Landy) Weis; B.A., Washington U., 1961, M.S., 1968, D.Sc., 1970; m. Leon Cooper, June 3, 1968; 1 son, Matthew Leon. Sci. programmer Monsanto Co., St. Louis, 1961-62, McDonnell Corp., St. Louis, 1963-65; research scientist Advanced Tech. Center, Dallas, 1971-72, cons., 1972; vis. asst. prof. operations research So. Meth. U., 1974. Cons., Degolyer, Macnaughton, Inc., 1970-71. Mem. Operations Research Soc. Am. (prize 1972), Pi Mu Epsilon, Eta Sigma Phi. Home: 8118 Inwood Rd Dallas TX 75209

COOPER, MILDRED PIVETZ (MRS. FRANKLIN D. COOPER), ednl. adminstr.; b. Paterson, N.J., Feb. 11, 1921; d. Louis Patrick and Mary Anna (Pallay) Pivetz; B.A., Alfred U., 1942; Ed.M., U. Buffalo, 1960; Ed.D., State U. N.Y. at Buffalo, 1962, Ednl. Adminstrn. Specialist degree, 1963; m. Franklin D. Cooper, Nov. 17, 1962; children—Carol Ellen, Reid Franklin. Secondary sch. math. tchr., N.Y., 1942-45; dist. and exec. dir. Girl Scout Councils, Buffalo and Lockport, N.Y., 1946-58, research asst., research asso., 1958-59; asst. exec. sec. Western N.Y. Sch. Study Council, 1960-63; instr. ednl. adminstrn. Sch. Edn., U. Buffalo, 1961-62; asst. for research, budget and legislation Pub. Sch. District Columbia, 1964-70, asst. supt. for research and evaluation, 1970—; cons. in research and evaluation. Active Girl Scouts, Boy Scouts Am. Mem. Soc. Ednl. Adminstrs., Am. Assn. Sch. Adminstrs., Am. Ednl. Research Assn., Am. Soc.

Information Specialists, Am. Personnel and Guidance Assn., Nat. Council Adminstrv. Women in Edn., Pi Lambda Theta. Office: 415 12th St NW Washington DC 20004

COOPER, NANCY MARGARET MAYS (MRS. ANDREW COOPER), educator; b. San Francisco; d. Charles Edgar and Nancy (Martin) Mays; B.A., Stanford, 1952, Ph.D., 1961; postgrad. (Fulbright scholar) U. London, 1954-55; m. Andrew Cooper, June 14, 1945; children—Andrew Kenneth, Georgia Cassandra. Tchr., head dept. English, curriculum asso. Palo Alto (Cal.) Sr. High Sch., 1954-63; lectr. Stanford, 1963; asst. prof. English, Cal. State U., San Jose, 1963-70, asso. prof. English, supr. student tchrs., 1970—. Chief planner for lit. Hawaii English Project, Honolulu, 1972-74. Vol. tchr. Project Head Start, 1966. Mem. Modern Lang. Assn., Nat. Council Tchrs. English, Am. Assn. U. Profs., N.E.A., Cal. Tchrs. Assn. Home: 14440 Manuella Av Los Altos Hills CA 94022 Office: Cal State U San Jose CA 95192

COOPER, PATRICE O'HEGARTY COBB, business exec.; b. Collooney, Sligo, Ireland, July 5, 1909; d. Timothy and Honorah E. (Scanlon) O'Hegarty; came to U.S., 1922, naturalized, 1943; student Bay State Inst. Commerce, 1926, St. Mary's Coll., 1927-29, Rutgers U. Sch. Bus. Adminstrn., 1944-45, Berkeley Secretarial Sch., 1951; m. Francis Cutter Cobb, Oct. 30, 1943 (dec. Jan. 1965); 1 dau., Patricia (Mrs. Dean Parker Oliver); m. 2d, J. Gilbert Cooper, Feb. 20, 1971. Fashion and beauty exec. Best and Co., N.Y.C., 1935-43; personnel mgmt. Heil Co., N.J., 1945-49; staff Lord and Taylor, 1950; fashion coordinator and commentator, Fla., 1957-69; fashion writer, soc. writer Pompano Beach (Fla.) Town News, Sun Sentinel, Pompano and Palm Beach Post Times, 1960-68; travel cons. Boca Raton (Fla.) Travel Agy., 1961—; pres., owner Irish Imports Galore, Ltd., Boca Raton, 1967—; co-owner Personnally Yours, pub. relations, 1962-64; writer radio commls. Chmn., Community Concerts Assn., Short Hills, N.J., 1952-55; com. head Project Hope, Palm Beach and Broward Counties, 1961-62; mem. adv. bd. Ft. Lauderdale Forum, 1963—; chmn. art exhibit Boca Raton Art Guild, 1967; life mem. North Broward and Ft. Lauderdale Symphony Soc., Debbie Rand Service League, charter mem. Fla. Atlantic Music Guild, Civic Ballet Ft. Lauderdale, Round Table Palm Beach; chmn. Le Premier Bal A Boca Raton, 1970, El Segundo Baile de Boca Raton, 1971; chmn. Symphony Ball, 1973, mem. com., 1974; chmn. Heart and Harness at Pompano Park, Heart Fund, 1972, mem. com., 1973; reservations chmn. Tiara Ball, Royal Dames, 1972; royal dame Nova U. Mem. Soc. of Ireland in Fla. (founder). Clubs: La Coquille (Palm Beach); Boca Raton; Royal Palm Yacht. Home: 1200 S Ocean Blvd Boca Raton FL 33432 Office: 403 Golf View Dr Boca Raton FL 33432

COOPER, PATRICIA E. PENNINGTON (MRS. ROBERT H. COOPER), microbiologist, educator; b. Wilmington, Del., Nov. 2, 1937; d. Joseph Cass and Evelyn (Hayes) Pennington; B.S., U. Del., 1959; m. Robert Harwin Cooper, Jan. 9, 1965. Microbiologist, Del. Hosp., Wilmington, 1959-60; virology research E.I. duPont de Nemours, Inc., Wilmington, 1960-63; microbiologist, supr. sch. med. tech., serologist Wilmington Gen. Hosp., 1963-66; cons. Elkton Hosp., 1963-66; microbiologist St. Francis Hosp., Colorado Springs, Colo., 1966-67, Wilmington Med. Center, 1967-68; virologist, microbiologist First U.S. Army Med. Lab., Ft. George G. Meade, Md., 1968-69; head dept. microbiology Crozer-Chester Med. Center, Chester, Pa., 1969-70; microbiologist New Orleans Clinic, 1970-71; microbiologist Profl. Clin. Labs., Wilmington, 1971—. Recipient Specialist Microbiologist award, Registered Microbiologist award, 1971. Mem. A.A.A.S., Am. Inst. Biol. Scis., Am., Pa. socs. for microbiology, Research Soc. Del., Am. Acad. Microbiology, Am. Soc. Clin. Pathologists (asso.), Am. Mus. Natural History, Mental Health Soc., Internat. Platform Assn. Methodist. Home: 1905 Fairfield Rd Wilmington DE 19810

COOPER, PAULETTE MARCIA, author; b. Antwep, Belgium; d. Theodore S. and Stella Rose (Toepfer) Cooper; came to U.S., 1948, naturalized, 1950; B.A. with honors, Brandeis U., 1964; M.A., City U. of N.Y., 1968. Writer, analyst Schwerin Research Corp., N.Y.C., 1965-66; copywriter Batten Barton Durstine & Osborn, N.Y.C., 1966-67; copywriter Norman Craig & Kummel Co., N.Y.C., 1967-68; free lance writer, 1968—. Mem. Soc. Mag. Writers, Author's League, Am. Med. Writers Assn., Mystery Writers Am. Author: The Medical Detectives, 1973; Growing Up Puerto Rican, 1972; The Scandal of Scientology, 1971; Halloween, 1972. Contbr. numerous articles to periodicals. Address: 300 E 40th St New York City NY 10016

COOPER, PHYLLIS NORTON (MRS. GRANT BURR COOPER), lawyer; b. Coalinga, Cal.; d. Hugh Russell and Albine (Power) Norton; B.A. magna cum laude, U. So. Cal., 1935, J.D., 1938; m. Grant Burr Cooper, Apr. 3, 1935; children—Natalie Caroline (Mrs. Rollin David Wallace), Judith Ann (Mrs. Charles David Hunt), Meredith Jane (Mrs. Robert Knox Worrell), Grant Burr, John Norton. Admitted to Cal. bar 1938; Supreme Ct. U.S.; practiced in Los Angeles, 1938—; pvt. practice, 1938-56; mem. firm Cooper & Nelson, 1956-71; practice with Grant B. Cooper, 1971—. Co-ordinator, chmn. youth activities Assistance League Jrs. 1951; mem. Nine O'clock Players Childrens Theatre Guild, 1954—, Muses of State Mus. Sci. and Industry, 1964—; nat. chmn. Ann. Giving U. So. Cal., 1966-67. Pres., bd. dirs. Las Benevolas; sec., bd. dirs. YWCA; bd. dirs. Municipal Art Commn. Los Angeles, Assistance League So. Cal., Jr. Aux. Assistance League, Jr. Philharmonic Com. So. Cal. Symphony Assn., Las Floristas; trustee U. So. Cal., 1967-70. Recipient Dr. Von Kleinsmid medal, 1935; alumni service award U. So. Cal., 1970. Mem. Am., Cal., Los Angeles County bar assns., Women Lawyers Assn. Los Angeles, U. So. Cal. Law Alumni (bd. dirs., past pres.), Los Angeles C. of C. (bd. dirs. womens div.), Gen. Alumni Assn. U. So. Cal. (pres., bd. dirs.), Lawyers Wives Los Angeles, Trojan League, Legion Lex, Pres.'s Circle, Phi Beta Kappa, Phi Delta Delta, Delta Sigma Rho, Zeta Phi Eta, Alpha Chi Omega. Home: 3447 Wrightview Dr North Hollywood CA 91604 Office: 1880 Century Park East Los Angeles CA 90067

COOPER, ROSALIE BAKER, lawyer; b. N.Y.C., June 22, 1931; s. Samuel and Jennie (Baker) Cooper; B.A., N.J. Coll. Women, 1952; LL.B., Rutgers U., 1953, J.D. (hon.), 1970; m. Dwight N. Halpern, Aug. 23, 1953; children—Brian, Nancy, Lisa. Admitted to N.J. bar, 1953; asso. firm McCarter, English & Studer, Newark, 1953-55; land aquisition counsel Twp. Lakewood, N.J., 1964—; asst. prosecutor Ocean County, N.J., 1971—. Realtor, 1964—. Republican committeewoman, 1970. Mem. N.J., Ocean County bar assns., Nat. Dist. Attys. Assn., N.J. Prosecutors Assn., Lakewood Citizens Action Com., League Women Voters. Jewish religion (mem. bd. temple sisterhood). Mem. bd. editors Rutgers U. Law Rev., 1953. Home: 1290 14th St Lakewood NJ 08701 Office: Municipal Bldg Lakewood NJ 08701

COOPER, ROSE MARIE (MRS. WILLIAM H. JORDAN), composer; b. Cairo, Ill., Feb. 21, 1937; d. Allen Britten and Janie May (Lawrence) Cooper; B. Music, Okla. Bapt. U., 1959; M.A., Columbia, 1960; postgrad. U. N.C.; m. William H. Jordan, Oct. 29, 1960; children—James Bailey, Elizabeth Talley. Working composer Concordia, Broadman, Shawnee Press, Gordon V. Thompson, Ltd., Harold Flammer, Belwin, Brodt; v.p. Julian Assos., Cape Girardeau, Mo. and Greensboro, N.C.; contbr. to basic music series Prentice Hall, McGraw-Hill. Named Outstanding Young Woman of N.C., Mem. A.S.C.A.P. (recipient awards 1966-74), Nat. Fed. Music Clubs, Mortarboard, Sigma Alpha Iota. Home: 607 W Greenway St Greensboro NC 27403

COOPER, ROSEMARY PATSY GARRETT (MRS. CHRISTIAN EDWIN COOPER, JR.), realtor; b. Phenix City, Ala., Jan. 8, 1916; d. Harry Lee and Rosaline Henrietta (Blau) Garrett; grad. Weaver Sch. Real Estate, 1961; grad. Ga. Realtors Inst., 1971; m. Christian Edwin Cooper, Jr., July 5, 1933. Sales mgr., broker Holly Realty Co., Columbus, Ga., 1960-61; owner-broker Patsy Cooper Realty, Columbus, 1961—. Kindergarten tchr. Muscogee County (Ga.) Sch. System, 1956-57; tchr. ednl. courses Columbus Bd. Realtors, 1963-64, tchr. adult edn. for mil. men Columbus Coll., 1966. Mem. Historic Planning Review Bd., City of Columbus, 1971—, co-chmn., 1972. Asso. mem. Soc. Real Estate Appraisers (dir. 1962-63); mem. Ga. Assn. Real Estate Bds. (dir. 1971-72), Ga. Assn. Realtors (regional v.p. 1974), Bd. Realtors (pres. Columbus 1966, v.p. 1967). Methodist. Club: Quota (dir. 1973) (Columbus). Home: 1010 Lockwood Av Columbus GA 31906 Office: 1355 13th Av Columbus GA 31906

COOPER, SHARON ABELS, lawyer; b. Baton Rouge, July 24, 1944; d. Raymond Randolph and Lila Dale (Mixon) Abels; B.S., La. State U., 1966, M.S., 1967, J.D., 1971; m. Robert Sibley Cooper, Jr., June 28, 1969. Admitted to La. bar, 1971; grad. asst. Law Library, La. State U., 1966-69, research asst. La. State Law Inst., 1971-72, coordinator research, 1972—. Partner firm Cooper & Cooper, Baton Rouge, 1974—. Mem. Phi Kappa Phi, Mu Sigma Rho, Phi Delta Delta (pres. Alpha Omega chpt. 1972). Democrat. Roman Catholic. Home: 3027 E Lakeshore Dr Baton Rouge LA 70808 Office: PO Box 2382 Baton Rouge LA 70821

COOPER, SIGNE S., nursing educator; b. Maquoketa, Ia., Jan. 29, 1921; d. Hans Edward and Clara (Steen) Skott; B.S., U. Wis., 1948; postgrad. Tchrs. Coll., Columbia, summers 1948-51; M.Ed., U. Minn., 1955. Staff nurse Army Nurse Corps, Ft. Belvoir, Va., also CBI; 1943-46; head nurse Wis. Gen. Hosp. Madison, 1946-48; instr. U. Wis. Sch. Nursing 1948-54, prof., chmn. dept. nursing extension div., Madison, 1955—. Mem. Madison Community Welfare Council, 1949-51; adv. com. Madison Gen. Hosp. Sch. Nursing, 1960—. Mem. Am., Wis. (pres. 1958-60) nurses assns., Nat. League Nursing (Linda Richards award for pioneering efforts in continuing edn. in nursing 1967), Wis. Edn. Assn., Adult Edn. Assn. U.S., Wis. Hist. Soc., Pi Lambda Theta. Author: Contemporary Nursing Practice, 1970. Editorial bd. R.N. mag., 1959-69, Nursing Forum, Jour. Continuing Edn. in Nursing. Contbr. articles to profl. publs. Home: 7207 University Av Middleton WI 53562 Office: 610 Langdon St Madison WI 53706

COOPER, VALDA MARGARET (MRS. DAVID H. COOPER), newspaperwoman; b. Melbourne, Australia, Nov. 15, 1915; d. Hugh F. and May (Pinsent) Cypher; came to U.S., 1916; student Amarillo Bus. Coll., 1933-34; m. David H. Cooper, Feb. 24, 1945; children—Valda Kay (Mrs. McKinney), David Cypher. Gen. reporter Borger (Tex.) News-Herald, 1934-43; continuity writer radio sta. KGNC, Amarillo, Tex., 1943-44; night editor Capital bur. Asso. Press, Santa Fe 1944-45; city editor Farmington (N.M.) Daily Times, 1954-66, mng. editor, 1966—. Regional dir. Nat. Fedn. Press Women, 1963-65. Bd. dirs. San Juan Coll. Found., 1973—. Recipient citation Am. Petroleum Inst., 1957; Zia award N.M. Press Women's Assn., 1958; N.M. Press Woman of Achievement, 1964; N.M. Med. Soc. award for outstanding reporting in field of medicine, 1964; N.M. Petroleum Industries Com. award, 1966. Mem. N.M. Press Women (pres. 1960-62), N.M. A.P. Mng. Editors Assn. (pres. 1967-68), N.M. Press Assn. (dir. 1969-72, Shaffer award 1946), Beta Sigma Phi. Home: 1809 Chaco St Farmington NM 87401 Office: 201 N Allen St Farmington NM 87401

COOPERMAN, SHIRLEY ROSENFELD (MRS. ROBERT COOPERMAN), educator; b. Jamaica, N.Y., May 12, 1928; d. Samuel and Esther (Kleinberg) Rosenfeld; B.A., Queens Coll., 1949; M.A., N.Y. U., 1961; postgrad. Hofstra U., French Fashion Acad., 1973-74; m. Robert Cooperman, Feb. 6, 1949; 1 son, Mitchell Arlen. Tchr. home econs. N.Y.C. schs., 1950-51, 53-55, Syosset (N.Y.) High Sch., 1955—; chmn. home econs. Syosset Pub. Schs., 1955—. Mem. Am., N.Y. State, Nassau County home econs. assns., N.Y. State, Nassau County home econs. tchrs. assns., Queens Coll. Home Econs. Alumni Assn., Omicron Nu, Pi Lambda Theta. Home: 17 Alden Av Syosset NY 11791 Office: Syosset High Sch South Woods Rd Syosset NY 11791

COPE, ABIGAIL JOHNSON (MRS. WILLIAM COPE JR.), librarian; b. Pueblo, Colo., Sept. 20, 1915; d. Clarence Horace and Bessie Elnora (Lane) Johnson; B.S. cum laude, Tenn. A. and I. State U., 1939; M.A., East Tenn. State U., summers 1956, 57, 58; m. William Cope, Jr., Oct. 22, 1943; children—William III, Ronald Clarence. Elementary tchr. McReynolds High Sch., South Pittsburg, Tenn., 1936-39, tchr. math., English, 1940-46; tchr. math., English Douglass High Sch., Elizabethon, Tenn., 1952-54; tchr. Dunbar Elementary Sch., Johnson City, Tenn., 1954-56; tchr. English, math. L.B. Landry Jr.-Sr. High Sch., New Orleans, 1957-62; asso. prof. English So. U., New Orleans, 1962-63; copy editor Prentice-Hall, Inc., Englewood Cliffs, N.J., 1964; librarian Englewood (N.J.) Sch. Library, 1965—. Lay mem. Program Council, bd. Christian Edn. No. N.J. Conf. United Methodist Ch., 1970-72, program materials sec. United Meth. Women. Mem. Nat. Tchrs. English (chpt. pres. 1961-62), Jack and Jill of Am., Inc. (chpt. v.p. elect 1963), Bus. and Profl. Women's Club, N.E.A., Phi Beta Tau, Delta Sigma Theta. Methodist (chmn. commn. on edn. 1966—). Home: 59 Garden St Teaneck NJ 07666 Office: 11 Engle St Englewood NJ 07631

COPE, CORRINE SNYDER, educator; b. Lewisburg, O., Dec. 6, 1912; d. Roscoe Portland and Agnes (Schlotterbeck) Snyder; A.B. summa cum laude, Ohio U., 1938; M.S. in Social Adminstrn., Western Res. U., 1940; Ph.D. in Psychology, Ohio State U., 1968; m. Elmer F. Cope, Jan. 13, 1940 (dec.); children—Jon Michael, Suzanne (Mrs. William R. Acton. Case worker Children's Service Bur., Cleve., 1938-42; tchr. Lewisburg High Sch., 1956-58; teaching asso. Ohio State U., Columbus, 1964-68; asst. prof. psychology U. Mo., Columbia, 1968-71, asso. prof., 1971—, research asso. Regional Rehab. Research Inst., 1968-73, counseling psychologist, 1968—. Bd. dirs. Woodhaven-Boone County Extended Employment Workshop, 1971—. Mem. Am. Psychol. Assn., Am. Personnel and Guidance Assn., Am. Rehab. Counselors Assn., A.A.A.S., Nat. Rehab. Assn., Phi Beta Kappa, Mortar Bd. Author: The Badge of Poverty: The St. Louis Study (Nat. Research award Am. Rehab. Counselors Assn.), 1972. Co-editor: Rehabilitation and the Culturally Disadvantaged, 1969. Contbr. numerous articles to profl. publs. Home: 1617 Stanford Dr Columbia MO 65201

COPE, JOHNNYE LOUISE, librarian; b. Eden, Tex., Dec. 15, 1923; d. John Findley and Georgia (Curry) Cope; B.A., N. Tex. State U., 1945; M.A. in English, Ohio State U., 1950; M.A. in L.S., U. Mich., 1954. Tchr. lab. sch. N. Tex. State U., Denton, 1945-49, humanities librarian, 1966—; reference asst. El Paso (Tex.) Pub. Library, 1954-55, Trinity U., San Antonio, Tex., 1956-66. Mem. Tex. Library Assn. Democrat. Methodist. Home: 1315 Greenbrier St Denton TX 76201

COPE, MAXINE JULUSON, coll. dean; b. Hoytsville, Utah, Nov. 2, 1913; d. John Martin and Florence (Wilkinson) Juluson; B.S., U. Utah, 1948, M.S., 1957, Ed.D., 1967; m. Richard L. Cope, Apr. 13, 1940. Head nurse Latter-day Saints Hosp., Salt Lake City, 1938-40, supr., 1940-46; ednl. dir. U. Utah, 1950-55; dir. nursing Salt Lake Trade and Tech. Inst., 1958-64; dir. med.-surg. nursing grad. program U. Utah, 1965-70; dean Coll. Nursing, Brigham Young U., Provo, Utah, 1970—. Mem. Women's State Legislative Council Utah, 1967—. Mem. Nat. (dir. 1963-67), Utah (pres. 1954-56) leagues nursing, Am., Utah (v.p. 1972—) nurses assns., Phi Kappa Phi. Home: 3320 Cherokee Lane Provo UT 84601 Office: Brigham Young U Provo UT 84602

COPE, RUTH WARNER (MRS. WILLIAM S. COPE), realtor; b. Evanston, Ill., Mar. 31, 1916; d. Raymond Heald and Bertha Louisa (Hammond) Lindman; student Santa Ana Jr. Coll., 1934-36, U. Cal. at Berkeley, 1936-39; m. William Samuel Cope, Nov. 26, 1941; children—Lindy (Mrs. Melvin T. Cobb, Jr.), Candace (Mrs. Edward Jarecki). Sales rep. Strachan Realty, Fresno, Cal., 1959-63; pres. Ruth Cope Realtors, Inc., Fresno, 1963—. Mem. Madera County Selective Service Bd., 1971-73. Mem. Community Theatre, 1960—. Mem. Am. Assn. U. Women, C. of C., Cal. Real Estate Assn. (dir. 1969-72), Fresno Bd. Realtors (pres. women's div. 1968), Multiple Listing Service (chmn. Fresno, 1971), Alpha Delta Pi. Republican. Conglist. Club: Women's League. Home: 7439 N Feland Fresno CA 93705 Office: 5492 N Palm St Fresno CA 93704

COPELAND, EMILY AMERICA, orgn. exec.; b. Tifton, Ga.; d. Jerry and America (Vaughn) Copeland; A.B., Spelman Coll., 1937; B.S. in L.S. (Carnegie grantee), Atlanta U., 1942; M.S., Columbia, 1948, postgrad., 1959-60; postgrad. N.Y. U., 1949-50. Tchr., Tift County Indsl. High Sch., Tifton, 1937-38; librarian Finley High Sch., Chester, S.C., 1938-41; library asst. Atlanta U. Library, summers 1938-40, 42; head librarian Gammon Theol. Sem., Atlanta, 1942-44; acquisitions librarian Atlanta U., 1944-46; reference, sch. work asst. N.Y. Pub. Library, N.Y.C., 1945-46; head dept. library sci. S.C. State Coll., 1946-51; formerly head dept. library service Fla. A. and M. U., Tallahassee, chmn. dept. library service; guest prof. No. Mich. U., summer 1967; founder, pres. Black Research Information Coordinating Services, Inc., 1972—; host TV show WFSU Ednl. TV. Mem. S.C. Library Devel. Com., 1947-51, S.C. Library Edn. Planning Com., 1948-51; participant Inst. for Tng. Information Sci. Faculty, U. So. Cal., 1969. Recipient Honor Merit award Spelman Coll., Atlanta, 1968, certificate hist. research and archival mgmt. Ohio Hist. Soc., 1973. Mem. Am. (mem. library adminstrn. div. com. representing Fla. 1957—), Southeastern, Fla. State (pres. 1953-56) library assns., Am. Assn. U. Profs. (exec. bd. Fla. conf. 1972—), Alpha Beta Alpha. Author: A Handbook for the Guidance of Students in School Library Internship, 1964; Combes, 1973: A Guide to Minority Resources. Contbr. articles to profl. jours., World Book Ency. Home: 614 Howard Av Tallahassee FL 32304 also 1212 Peachtree St Tifton GA 31794 Office: JNT Inc Office Bldg 540 W Brevard St Tallahassee FL 32307

COPELAND, HELEN MASSON, author; b. Rochester, Minn., Apr. 23, 1920; d. James Carruthers and Alice Marion (Knowles) Masson; A.B., Wheaton Coll., 1942; postgrad. Brown U., 1943, Queen's Evening Coll., 1958-62; m. Herbert Jones Copeland, June 2, 1945 (div. 1958); children—Howard Carlisle, Marion Knowles, Herbert William, James Masson. Author children's books, novels. Named Mother of the Year, Charlotte (N.C.) Downtown Assn., 1963. Mem. Women in Communication (pres. Charlotte chpt. 1974—). Author: Meet Miki Takino, 1963; Duncan's World, 1967; This Snake is Good, 1968; Festival in the Park, 1970. Home: 1850 Maryland Av Charlotte NC 28209

COPELAND, HOPE ABRAMSON, real estate broker; b. Cleve., June 29, 1929; d. Ralph Donald and Jeannette Julyan (Stern) Abramson; grad. Tobe Coburn Sch. Fashion Careers, 1947; m. Mark E. Coplin, Apr. 16, 1950 (div. July 1952). Advt. mgr. May Co. Wilshire, 1948-49, Mode O Day, 1952-54; real estate salesman Ken Kremith Co., Philip Norton, Inc., 1954-55, Wilds Realty, 1955-60, Harleigh Sandler Co., 1960 (all Los Angeles); owner Hope Copeland Real Estate, Los Angeles, 1964—. Chmn. dept. U. Cal. at Los Angeles Art Council Thieves Market, 1972—. Editor Brentwood Dem. Club News, 1964-65. Recipient award for advt. Nat. Retail Dry Goods Assn., 1949, Telegraph Advt. award Painesville (O.) Telegraph, 1960, 61, 62, 63, award for best newspaper in state Cal. Dem. Council, 1964. Mem. Am. Fedn. Radio and TV Artists, Nat. Acad. TV Arts and Scis., Screen Actors Guild, Nat. Assn. Real Estate Bds., Cal. Real Estate Assn., Los Angeles, Santa Monica realty bds. Office: 1211 Stoner Av Los Angeles CA 90025

COPELAND, JUDITH MAY JAMES (MRS. T.P. LINDSAY COPELAND), advt. exec.; b. Tucson, Apr. 12, 1949; s. Hubert Roe and Ruby May (Buehrer) James; B.A. with honors and distinction, U. Ariz., 1970; m. T.P. Lindsay Copeland, Sept. 19, 1970. Columnist, Tucson Newspapers, Inc., 1970; copywriter Broadway-Hale, Inc., retail store, Los Angeles, 1970-71; copy dir. Diamond's retail store, Phoenix, Las Vegas and Tulsa, 1971-73; writer, broadcast producer Robt. A. Mullen Advt., Phoenix, 1973—. Mem. Women in Communications (v.p. 1973-74), Nat. Acad. TV Arts and Scis., U. Ariz. Alumnae (dir. Los Angeles 1971), Mortar Bd. Alumnae, Alpha Omicron Pi Alumnae, Sigma Delta Chi. Home: 9039 N Concho Lane Phoenix AZ 85028 Office: 4144 N 49th St Phoenix AZ 85018

COPELAND, LOIS JACQUELINE (MRS. RICHARD A. SPERLING), physician; b. Malden, Mass., Sept. 16, 1943; d. Arnold Alan and Ann (Goldfarb) Copeland; B.A. magna cum laude, Cornell U., 1964, M.D., 1968; m. Dr. Richard A. Sperling, June 7, 1970. Intern N.Y. Hosp., N.Y.C., 1968-69, resident, 1969-70; resident Bellevue Hosp., N.Y.U. Med. Center, 1970-71; teaching asst. internal medicine, N.Y.U. Med. Center, 1971—. Mem. Phi Beta Kappa, Phi Kappa Phi, Alpha Lambda Delta. Home: 25 Sparrowbush Rd Upper Saddle River NJ 07456 Office: 315 W 57th St New York City NY 10019

COPELAND, LORRAINE FRANCES HILE (MRS. SAM H. COPELAND), occupational therapist; b. Ithaca, N.Y., Nov. 7, 1923; d. Edwin M. and Mary A. (O'Connor) Hile; B.S., Cornell U., 1945; Occupational Therapist, Registered, U. Pa., 1946; postgrad. E. Carolina U.; m. Sam H. Copeland, Apr. 11, 1946; children—Leonard, Mary Sue (Mrs. F. Curtis Barry), Larry. Occupational therapist VA hosps., Cal., Tex., 1946-48; sr. case worker Tompkins County Welfare Dept., Ithaca, 1953-60; occupational therapist Tompkins County Hosp., Ithaca, 1960-63; sr. occupational therapist Willard (N.Y.) State Hosp., 1963-69; supr. occupational therapy Sampson State Sch., Willard, 1969-71; asst. prof. occupational therapy dept. E. Carolina U., Greenville, N.C., 1971-72; dir. occupational therapy Edgecombe-Nash Mental Health Center, Rocky Mount, N.C., 1972-74; unit coordinator for partial hospitalization Neuse Clinic, New Bern, N.C., 1974—. Cons. to nursing homes. Mem. Democratic Com. Town of Ithaca, 1965-71, vice chmn., 1968-69. Active Girl Scouts U.S.A. Mem. Am., N.C. occupational therapy assns., Alpha

Omicron Pi. Roman Catholic. Home: Shady Acres Route 8 Greenville NC 27834 Office: Neuse Clinic PO Box 2535 New Bern NC 28560

COPELAND, MARY ELIZABETH, state ofcl.; b. Union City, Ga., Dec. 31, 1911; d. Millard Newton and Jennie Belle (Hyde) Copeland; grad. Meml. Mission Hosp. Sch. Nursing, 1938; certificate pub. health nursing Richmond Profl. Inst., 1941; B.S., U.N.C., 1949; M.S. (USPHS scholar), Tchrs. Coll. N.Y.C., 1953. Operating room supr. Haywood County Hosp., Waynesville, N.C., 1938; pub. health nurse City Health Dept., Asheville, N.C., 1939-42; staff nurse, supr. Muscogee County Health Dept., Columbus, Ga., 1946-52; dir. nursing City Hosp., Columbus, Ga., 1953-54; asso. prof. pub. health nursing Emory U., Atlanta, 1954-56; cons. pub. health nursing N.C. State Bd. Health, Asheville, 1956-64; dir. nursing Ariz. State Dept. Health, Phoenix, 1964—. Served to capt., Nurses Corps, 1942-46. Fellow Am. Pub. Health Assn.; mem. Am. Jour. Nursing Co. (v.p. 1971-72), Am. (dir. 1966-70), Ariz. State nurses assns., Bus. and Profl. Women's Club. Mem. Christian Ch. Home: 4490 E Belleview St Phoenix AZ 85008 Office: 1740 W Adams St Phoenix AZ 85007

COPLEY, DONNA TUTTLE, sch. adminstr.; b. Wichita, Kan., Nov. 11, 1923; d. Clyde E. and Ola E. (Fuller) Tuttle; B.A., U. Mich., 1944; M.Ed., Wichita State U., 1965; Ed.D., U. No. Colo., 1972; student U. Wichita, 1940-42; m. Wallace Lester Copley, Nov. 17, 1945 (div. Sept. 1969); children—James, John, Sarah. Edn. sec. U. Mich., Ann Arbor, 1942-44; med. sec. Dr. J.W. Shaw, Wichita, Kan., 1944-53; tchr. Robinson Jr. High Sch., Wichita, 1961-69, Wichita State U., 1967-70, Heights High Sch., Wichita, 1969-73; asst. prin. Truesdell Jr. High Sch., Wichita, 1973-74; prin. Brooks Jr. High Sch., Wichita, 1974—; coordinator preparation univ. studies Wichita State U., 1967-70; bus. mgr. Cowtown Repetory Co., 1960-62. Pres. Wichita Council English, 1966-69; v.p. Community Theatre Guild, 1959. Exec. com. Wichita State U. Coll. Edn. Alumni Fund, 1973-74. U. No. Colo. Dept. Ednl. Adminstrn. fellow, 1971-72. Mem. Sedgwick County Med. Assts. (pres. 1953), Wichita Council Tchrs. English, Nat. Council Tchrs. English (state rep. nat. cons. 1967-68), Nat. Council Adminstrn. Women Edn., Wichita Ednl. Adminstrs. Assn. Episcopalian. Home: 1011 N Armour Wichita KS 67206 Office: 3802 E 27th N Wichita KS 67220

COPPEDGE, JOSEPHINE MORRISON, nursing sch. adminstr.; b. Man Hall Park, Mich., Jan. 31, 1919; d. James Eaton and Elizabeth (Easton) Morrison; R.N., Sch. Nursing D.C. Gen. Hosp., 1939; B.A. in Nursing and Edn., San Jose State Coll., 1953; M.S. in Nursing Service Adminstrn., U. Colo., 1956; postgrad. U. Cal., U. Hawaii, Holy Names Coll.; m. William Harold Coppedge, Nov. 11, 1945 (div. Aug. 13, 1963). Asst. head nurse, head nurse, supr. D.C. Gen. Hosp., 1939-42; head nurse, supr. Firland's Sanatorium, Seattle, 1948; staff Waldo Gen. Hosp., Seattle, 1946-48, Alum Rock Sanatorium, San Jose, 1949-50; asst. dir. nursing edn. Sch. Nursing San Jose Hosp., 1953-55; teaching fellow, Sch. Nursing U. Colo., 1955-56; asso. dir. edn. Kaiser Found. Sch. Nursing, Oakland, Cal., 1956-57, dir., 1957—, v.p., 1973—; dir. tng. Kaiser Found. Internat., 1973—; nursing cons. Kaiser Found. Internat., Ghana, Nigeria, 1971, Tacoma Sch. Nursing; mem. nurse faculty, adviser Trainex Corp., Garden Grove, Cal. Asst. co-ordinator statewide ednl. confs. nursing U. Colo., 1955-56; mem. U.S. Govt. Rev. Com. Nurse Tng. Act 1964; mem. med. adv. bd. Ednl. Films Prodn.; mem. Bay Area Regional Planning for Clin. Facilities Com., Hosp. Adminstrs. and Dirs. Com. 3-Year Diploma Programs No. Cal.; past adviser to divisional pres. Student Nurses' Assn. Cal.; past mem. task force continuing edn. and licensure Cal. Bd. Nursing Edn. and Nurse Registration; mem. adv. bd. Alameda County Dept. Mental Hygiene, Kaiser Found. Research; edn. adv. com. Coll. of Alameda. Served from instr., M.C. students to asst. chief adminstrv. nurse, Nurses Corps, AUS, 1942-46; NATOUSA. Decorated African, Italian campaign ribbons; recipient Air Force Commendation award; named hon. citizen Boys' Town, Omaha. Mem. Med. Entities Mgmt. Assn. (Achievement award Kaiser Found. 1962), Nat. (past mem. steering com., past accreditation visitor, mem. Western regional conf. com. 1968, mem. council agy. membership, baccalaureate and higher degree programs, bd. review diploma programs), Cal. leagues for nursing, Am., Cal. (dir. Alameda County br.) nurses assns., Dirs. Diploma Schs. Nursing No. Cal., Am. Assn. U. Women, Am. Mgmt. Assn., Am. Hosp. Assn. (mem. diploma programs sect.), Exec. Information Guild (asso.), Nat. Fedn. Bus. and Profl. Women's Clubs (named woman of achievement Oakland 1973-74), Am. Assn. Higher Edn., Smithsonian Instn., Am. Security Council, Kaiser Employees Club, Cal. Acad. Sci., Kappa Delta Pi. Author: (with others) Cardiac Nursing Cases, 1956. Contbr. profl. publs. Home: 3750 Harrison St Oakland CA 94611 Office: Sch Nursing Kaiser Found 3451 Piedmont Av Oakland CA 94611

COPPOLA, SISTER MARY CARMINA, coll. pres.; b. Buffalo, Mar. 1, 1919; d. Ralph A. and Josephine A. (Casilla) Coppola; B.A., Canisius Coll., 1952, M.A., 1957; Ed.D., U. Sarasota, 1972. Tchr. St. Thomas Aquinas Sch., Buffalo, 1952-66; adminstr. St. Teresa's Sch., Buffalo, 1966-67; prof. ednl. psychology Trocaire Coll., Buffalo, 1965-68, pres., 1970—. Trustee Trocaire Coll., 1970-74, U. Sarasota, 1971-74, Western N.Y. Consortium Colls. and Univs., 1971—. Contbr. articles to profl. jours. Home: Marian Hall 360 Choate Av Buffalo NY 14220 Office: 110 Red Jacket Pkwy Buffalo NY 14220

CORAM, HELEN FERGUSON, newspaper editor; b. Starkville, Miss., Sept. 26, 1938; d. Thomas Lee and Earlene (Simmons) Ferguson; B.A., Miss. State Coll. for Women, 1959; M.A., State U. Ia., 1961. With Miami (Fla.) Herald, 1961—, asso. editor Living Today, 1972—. Mem. Fla. Press Club (v.p. 1974-75), Sigma Delta Chi. Home: 2343 Tigertail Av Coconut Grove FL 33133 Office: 1 Herald Plaza Miami FL 33101

CORAY, CARLA WINN (MRS. MAX CORAY), Republican state com. chmn.; b. Smithfield, Utah, Aug. 25, 1925; d. William Frank and Lavon (Cragun) W.; B.S., Utah State U.; postgrad. Brigham Young U., U. Hawaii, 1966-67; m. Max S. Coray, Aug. 21, 1946; children—Craig Winn, Lisa Nalani. Pres. Star Valley League Rep. Women, Wyo., 1956-57; pres. Kona League Rep. Women, 1961-64; West Hawaii rep. Rep. State Women's Adv. Council, 1963-64; del. Rep. Nat. Conv., 1964, 72, chmn. rule 29 com., 1972; Rep. campaign chmn., West Hawaii, 1964; 1st v.p. Hawaii State Fedn. Rep. Women, 1967-68; editor newsletter Oahu League Rep. Women, 1967-68; sec. Hawaii Rep. Exec. Com., 1967-68, chmn., 1969, 71—, vice chmn., 1969-71. Pres. Kona Community Theatre, 1964-65, resident dir., 1964-65. Bd. dirs. Rocky Mountain Theater Conf., 1955-57; bd. dirs., publicity chmn. Honolulu Theatre for Youth, 1968. Mem. Am. Assn. U. Women (drama co-chmn. 1968), Am. Ednl. Theater Assn., Nat. Children's Theater Conf. Assn., Western Speech Assn., Maunalua Triangle Community Assn., Theta Alpha Phi, Lambda Rho, Alpha Sigma Nu. Member Ch. of Jesus Christ of Latter-day Saints. Clubs: Kona Civic, Kona Yacht. Address: 83 Lunalilo Home Rd Honolulu HI 96825

CORBETT, ALICE CATHERINE, mem. Democratic Nat. Com.; b. Seattle, July 17, 1929; d. Marshall Richard and Carolyn (Bauer) Reckard; student Reed Coll., 1944, Mills Coll., summer 1944; B.S. in Edn., U. Ore. 1947; postgrad. Marylhurst Coll., 1949; m. J. James Corbett, Jan. 17, 1948. Tchr., Portland, Ore. 1948-52; sec. Dem. Party of Ore., 1955-58. Mem. Ore. Senate, 1959—, mem. interim com on welfare, 1959-60, interim com. on taxation, 1959-60; chmn. Senate Financial Affairs Com., mem. Nat. Com. for Mills, 1964-67. Pres. Young Democrats Multnomah County, 1954-55, nat. committeewoman, 1954-58; vice chmn. Multnomah County Dem. Central Com., 1957-58; mem. Dem. Nat. Com. for Ore., 1960—. Named one of ten outstanding women grads. U. Ore. Mem. N.A.A.C.P., Am. Assn. U. Women, Portland Women's Forum, Ore. Prison Assn., Urban League, Willamette Soc. (v.p. 1966—), Portland Women's Investment Group (v.p. 1969). Club: Jane Jefferson (pres.). Home: 3562 SE Harrison Portland OR 97214 Office: 2222 NE Schuyler St Portland OR 97212 also State Capitol Salem OR 97302

CORBETT, JANICE MARGARET, religious ednl. dir.; b. Avoca, N.Y., June 3, 1935; d. Orlo C. and Margaret (Owen) Corbett; B.A., Eastern Coll., 1957, M.R.E., 1959; M.S., Temple U., 1974. Editor youth publs. Am. Bapt. Bd. Edn. and Publ., Valley Forge, Pa., 1959-62, editor Action, 1966-72, dir. resource devel., 1973—; asst. in pub. relations Jack T. Holmes & Assos., Fort Worth, 1962-64; dir. religious edn. First Bapt. Ch., Brockton, Mass., 1964-66. Pres. New Sch. Coop., New Sch., Wayne, Pa., 1971-73, treas., 1973; mem. Middle Atlantic Film Bd. Mem. Conf. Editors of Ch. Mags., Nat. Com. for Support of Pub. Schs. Author: It's Happening with Youth, 1972. Editor: Respond II, 1973; Explore, 1974. Home: 500 Wayne Dr King of Prussia PA 19406 Office: Am Bapt Bd Edn Min Valley Forge PA 19481

CORBETT, JOAN DUFNER (MRS. JERRY CORBETT), realtor; b. St. Louis, Feb. 4, 1928; d. Arthur Edmund and Cecilia (Higgins) Dufner; B.S. in Biology and Dietetics, Webster Coll., 1950; m. Jerry G. Corbett, Feb. 13, 1955; children—Kelly Ann, Duff. Vice pres. Dufner-Corbett, Inc., Hermann, Mo., 1960—; owner, broker J.J. Corbett Real Estate, Hardin, Ill., 1967—. Pub. guardian and conservator Calhoun County, Ill., 1960-68. Chmn. Democratic County Com., 1960—. Bd. dirs. Ill. state chpt. Am. Cancer Soc., 1963-72, chmn. Calhoun County Unit, 1958—. Club: Illinois Federation Women's (pres. 20th dist. 1968-70, state chmn. conservation 1970-72), Hardin Woman's (pres. 1963-67). Home: French and County Rd Hardin IL 62047 Office: French St Hardin IL 62047

CORBETT, (MARTHA) LINDA STALTER (MRS. DAVID DANFORTH CORBETT), journalist; b. Council Groves, Kan., Jan. 1, 1941; d. Stanley Atwood and Mary Ellen (Burns) Stalter; B.S. in Journalism, Medill Sch. Journalism, Northwestern U., 1962, M.S. in Journalism, 1963; m. David Danforth Corbett, Apr. 27, 1968; 1 adopted son, David Christian. Information writer Kan Hwy. Commn., summers 1959-62; editorial asst. Look mag., N.Y.C., 1963-65; asst. editor Today's Sec. mag., McGraw-Hill, N.Y.C., 1965-68; reporter Irvington (N.J.) Herald, 1969-72; editor the Experiencer Citizen, Whippany, N.J., 1972; reporter Andover (Mass.) Townsman, 1973—; also free lance writer. Mem. Alumni Admissions Council Northwestern U. Mem. Women in Communications. Democrat. Disciple of Christ. Home: 100 Abbot St Andover MA 01810 Office: 15 Central St Andover MA 01810

CORBETT, MARY ELLEN MOHR (MRS. HAROLD THOMAS CORBETT), journalist; b. Eagle River, Wis., Mar. 20, 1941; d. Myron George and Lila (Besaw) Mohr; student Compton Coll., 1962-63; m. Edward L. Perry, June 7, 1958 (div. 1966); 1 son, Edward L.; m. 2d, Harold Thomas Corbett, Oct. 28, 1967. With Abingdon (Ill.) Argus, 1958-59; asst. to pub. Galesburg (Ill.) Post Pub. Co., 1959-60; state editor Galesburg Register Mail, 1960-62; feature writer Herald Am. Newspapers, Compton, Cal., 1962-63; sr. editor Homebuyers Mag., Redondo Beach, Cal., 1963-64; with Cal. Girl Mag. and Am. Aviation Publs., 1964-65; account exec. Fred Kline Agy., Inc., Los Angeles, 1965; staff writer South Bay Daily Breeze, Torrance, Cal., 1966-68; owner, editor newspaper, Wailuku, Hawaii, 1968-69; editor and pub. Valley Grove News, Spring Valley, Cal., 1969-73; free lance journalist, 1973—. In charge publicity Powder Puff Derby Air Race, 1967. Recipient 1st place Mate E. Palmer award Ill. Women's Press Assn., 1960, 2d place, 1960; Ring of Truth award Copley Newspapers, 1966, 67; Merit citation for best series articles in weekly Cal. Newspaper Pubs. Assn., 1971, 72; nominee Pulitzer prize, 1973. Mem. Nat. Fedn. Press Women, Cal. Press Women, Nat. Orgn. for Women (publicity dir. Greenwich, Conn. br.), Pacific Coast Press Club (Merit award 1967), Women in Communications, Inc. (Matrix award 1973, nat. award 1973), Sigma Delta Chi (awards 1971, 72). Home: Brook Dr Greenwich CT 06830

CORBETT, SISTER THOMAS ALBERT, educator; b. Columbus, O., Feb. 9, 1914; d. John William and Elizabeth (Sweeney) Corbett; B.A., Coll. St. Mary of the Springs, 1935; M.A., Ohio State U., 1936; Ph.D., Cath. U. Am., 1950. Joined Dominican Order, 1939; research asst. Nat. Youth Adminstrn., Columbus, 1936-39; instr. sociology, polit. sci. Coll. St. Mary of the Springs (name later changed to Ohio Dominican Coll.), Columbus, 1941-44, 49-52, dir. instl. research, 1962—; asst. prof. polit. sci. Cath. U. Am., Washington, 1952-53; asst. prof. polit. sci. Albertus Magnus Coll., New Haven, 1953-56, acad. dean, 1956-62. Mem. staff workshop social scis. in Cath. coll. curriculum Cath. U. Am., 1953, cons. com. affiliation, 1963; dir. project Upward Bound, Columbus, 1968-73. Treas. Cath. Interracial Council, Columbus, 1965-68, v.p., 1968—; exec. com. Adult Edn. Council, Columbus, 1968-70; mem. Columbus Diocesan Bd. Edn., 1968-71; trustee Albertus Magnus Coll. Mem. Am. Polit. Sci. Assn., Cath. Assn. Internat. Peace (v.p. 1954-57), Assn. Instl. Research, Soc. Coll. and U. Planning, Am. Cath. Sociol. Soc. (chmn. com. teaching 1953), Pi Gamma Mu. Author: People or Masses: A Comparative Study in Political Theory, 1950. Contbr. articles to New Cath. Ency., 1967. Home: care Ohio Dominican Coll 1216 Sunbury Rd Columbus OH 43219

CORBIT, MARY LOU (MRS. JOHN F. CORBIT), supt. schs.; b. Lakeville, Ind., Aug. 13, 1935; d. Leonard Aloysius and Ruth Eloise (Truitt) Carrico; teaching certificate, Cass County Normal Coll., 1953-54; B.S. cum laude, Western Mich. U., 1963, M.A., 1967, postgrad. (Elmer H. Wild scholar), 1968; m. John F. Corbit, Nov. 25, 1954; children—John Jeffrey, Carmel Marie, Christel Ann, Merry Piper, Shane Francis, Heidi Jeanne. Tchr., Mechanicsburg Sch., Cassopolis, Mich., 1954-55, Bklyn. Sch., Cassopolis, 1955-58, Cassopolis Pub. Schs., 1958-65; asst. to supt. Cassopolis Pub. Schs., 1965-69; supt. Lewis Cass Intermediate Sch. Dist., Cassopolis, 1969—. Mem. St. Joseph River Valley Health Clinic Bd., 1969-71; commr. Cass County Planning Commn., 1972—. Mem. Am., Mich. assns. sch. adminstrs., Mich. Assn. Sch. Bds., Mich. Assn. Intermediate Sch. Adminstrs., Western Mich. Alumni Found., Cassopolis Edn. Assn. (pres. 1958-66), St. Ann's Altar and Rosary Soc. (pres. 1955-57), D.A.R. Home: Rural Route 1 Happy Dr Cassopolis MI 49031 Office: Lewis Cass Intermediate Schools Rural Route 1 Lake LaGrange Cassopolis MI 49031

CORBITT, PHYLLIS JEAN DAVIDSON (MRS. DUVON CORBITT, JR.), med. missionary; b. Mechanicstown, O., Jan. 16, 1924; d. Harrison and Mary A. (Love) Davidson; B.A. cum laude, Asbury Coll., 1946; M.D., Vanderbilt U., 1952; Diplome en Medecine Tropicale (with distinction), Institut Medecine Tropicale, Antwerp, Belgium, 1964; m. Duvon Clough Corbitt, Jr., Sept. 18, 1947; children—Janine Marilyn, Duvon Clough, III, Douglas Davidson. Intern, Vanderbilt Hosp., 1952-53; resident St. Joseph Hosp., Lexington, Ky., 1953-55; dir. nursing edn., chief med. and pediatric services Piper Meml. Hosp., Kapanga, Katanga, Congo, 1957-60, 64-67, established rural treatment centers; lectr. in Chs., colls. and womans' orgns., 1960-63, 67—; spl. assignment for Methodist Mission Bd., Clinica Americana, La Paz, Bolivia, summer, 1969; establishing Med. Sch. in Congo, also dir. program health edn. for women Congo; gen. practice medicine, Wilmore, Ky., 1970—. Active P.T.A.; mem. exec. com. So. Congo Conf. United Methodist Ch., 1957-60; mem. Jessamine County Bd. Health. Bd. dirs. Jessamine County Assn. for Mentally Retarded, Found. for United Methodists, Asbury Theol. Sem. Recipient (with husband) award for distinguished service Asbury Alumni Assn., 1965. Mem. A.M.A., Christian Med. Soc., Ky. Med. Assn., Asbury Coll. Alumni Assn. (mem. bd.), Internat. Platform Assn. Methodist. Home: 200 E Main St Wilmore KY 40390

CORBRIDGE, MAURINE WALKER SOWERS (MRS. MAURICE H. CORBRIDGE), social worker; b. Rushville, Ill., Dec. 21, 1917; d. Howard B. and Irma Nell (Corbridge) Walker; B.S., Western Ill. U., 1953; M.A., Bradley U., 1968; m. Marvin W. Sowers, June 1936 (dec. Nov. 1963); m. 2d, Maurice H. Corbridge, June 27, 1968; stepchildren—Kyra Corbridge-Dremann, Margaret (Mrs. Bruce Keegan). Tchr. elementary sch., McDonough County, Ill., 1939-42; supt. Schuyler County Dept. Pub. Aid, Rushville, 1942-56; caseworker Peoria County Dept. Pub. Aid, 1956-57, casework supr., 1957-60, asst. supt., 1960-61, county supt., 1961—. Mem. Peoria Mayor's War on Poverty Bd., 1966—. Bd. dirs. Greater Peoria Legal Aid Soc., 1961-71, sec., 1962-71; bd. dirs. Peoria Area Council on Alcoholism, 1964-72, Central Ill. Council on Aging, 1972—, Sr. Community Service Aides Project of Nat. Ret. Tchrs. Assn.-Am. Assn. Ret. Persons, 1972—. Mem. Ill. Welfare Assn., Am. Pub. Welfare Assn., Nat. Assn. Social Workers, Peoria Jubilee Bus. and Profl. Women's Club (chpt. pres. 1967-68). Republican. Methodist. Club: Willow Knolls Country. Home: 301 W Clara Av Peoria IL 61614 Office: 607 NE Jefferson St Peoria IL 61601

CORCORAN, EBBA KNUDSON, orgn. exec.; b. N.Y.C., Feb. 18, 1925; d. George and Sophie (Bengtsson) Knudsen; B.A., Hunter Coll., 1950; M.A., N.Y. U., 1961; m. John J. Corcoran, June 27, 1948. Exec. sec. Carnegie Corp., N.Y.C., 1947-62; corporate sec. Edn. and World Affairs, N.Y.C., 1963-70; corporate sec. adminstrv. officer Internat. Council Ednl. Devel., N.Y.C., 1970—. Mem. N.Y. U., Hunter Coll. alumni assns., Vols. of the Shelters, N.Y. Personnel and Mgmt. Assn. Home: 404 E 66th St New York City NY 10021 Office: 680 Fifth Av New York City NY 10019

CORCORAN, GERTRUDE BEATTY (MRS. JAMES T. CORCORAN), educator; b. Torrington, Wyo., Sept. 19, 1922; d. Frank S. and Jessie M. (Macdonald) Beatty; A.A., Colo. Woman's Coll., 1941; B.A. magna cum laude, San Jose (Cal.) State Coll., 1950, M.A., 1952; Ed.D., Stanford, 1960; m. James T. Corcoran, July 1, 1952. Tchr., College Park Elementary Sch., San Jose, 1950-54, Peter Burnett Jr. High Sch., 1954-55; faculty San Jose State U., 1955—, asso. prof. edn., 1960-65, prof., 1965—, coordinator tchr.-licensing implementation program, 1971-73. Tchr., KNTV, KTEH; active lang. arts and creative writing workshops No. Cal., also cons.; cons. Campbell Union Sch. Dist. Trainer, Girl Scouts U.S.A., Santa Clara Valley, 1960. Faculty Research grantee 1965-66. Mem. Cal. Tchrs. Assn., Nat. Council Tchrs. English, Nat. Council for Social Studies, Assn. for Student Teaching, Cal. State Employers Assn., Assn. for State Coll. Profs., Am. Assn. U. Profs., Assn. for Supervision and Curriculum Devel., N.E.A., Kappa Delta Pi, Pi Lambda Theta. Presbyn. Author: Language Arts in the Elementary School—A Modern Linguistic Approach, 1970. Home: 16025 Greenridge Terrace Los Gatos CA 95030 Office: San Jose State Univ San Jose CA 95114

CORCORAN, JUDITH KATHRYN FARRELL (MRS. CHARLES ADAMS CORCORAN), journalist; b. St. Louis, Feb. 18, 1944; d. Francis Wayne and Mary Kathryn (Kinman) Farrell; B.S. cum laude in Journalism, U. Kan., 1966; m. Charles Adams Corcoran, Apr. 8, 1967. Reporter Topeka (Kan.) Capital-Jour., 1966—, asst. state editor, 1967, religion editor, 1966-67, edn. editor, 1967-70; reporter, edn. editor Hannibal (Mo.) Courier-Post, 1970-73, women's editor, 1973, editorial asst., publs. editor Ia. Credit Union League, 1973—. Bd. dirs. Hannibal YMCA, 1973; communications adv. bd. Ia. Lutheran Hosp., Des Moines, 1974—. Recipient award for best feature story and best young people's page Mo. Better Newspaper Contest, 1971. Home: 712 10th St West Des Moines IA 50313

CORCORAN, MARY RITZEL (MRS. WILLIAM S. CORCORAN), educator; b. Los Angeles, July 3, 1928; d. Joseph Peter and Annie Rebecca (Burnett) Ritzel; B.A., U. Cal. at Los Angeles, 1953, Ph.D., 1959; m. William S. Corcoran, July 6, 1957; children—Richard, Patrick. Jr. research chemist U. Cal. at Los Angeles, 1959-62; asst. prof. biology Cal. State U., Northridge, 1962-66, asso. prof., 1966-71, prof., 1971—. NSF grantee, 1963-68. Mem. A.A.A.S., Am. Soc. Plant Physiologists, Bot. Soc. Am., Cal. Bot. Soc., Sigma Xi. Home: 11038 Lindley Av Granada Hills CA 91344 Office: 18111 Nordhoff St Northridge CA 91324

CORDELL, DEWITT BYNUM CROMER (MRS. ALFRED ROBERT CORDELL), civic worker; b. Winston-Salem, N.C., Feb. 27, 1930; d. Clarence Franklin and Grace (Bynum) Cromer; A.B., Duke, 1950; postgrad. U. Buffalo, 1956-57; m. Alfred Robert Cordell, June 4, 1955; children—Alfred Robert, Franklin Cromer, Carl Dewitt, Mark Bynum. Pres., Winston-Salem Jr. League, 1963-64; dir. region XIII Assn. Jr. Leagues Am., 1965-67, 2d v.p., 1967-68; treas., 1st v.p., pres., bd. dirs. YWCA, 1962-68; pres., v.p., bd. dirs. Forsyth-Stokes County Med. Aux., 1967-69; asst. sec., pres., bd. dirs. Nature-Sci. Center, 1965-73; v.p. Civic Music Assn., 1964-68; pres. Forsyth County Heart Assn., 1969-70, Amos Cottage Guild, 1969-70; 1st v.p. N.C. Council Crime and Delinquency, 1970-73; v.p., project rev. chmn. Piedmont Triad Comprehensive Health Planning Council, 1971-74, pres., 1974-75; v.p., chmn. health services com. Forsyth Health Planning Council; 1st v.p. Expt. in Self Reliance, 1970-72; mem. Mayor's Com. on Status Women, 1972—. Bd. dirs. United Fund. Mem. Winston-Salem Symphony Guild, Bowman Gray Guild, Alpha Delta Pi. Home: 349 Arbor Rd Winston-Salem NC 27104

CORDELL, FRANCES WRIGHT, editor; b. Savannah, Ga.; d. Robert Vaughan Montague and Anna Cope (Harmon) Cordell; A.B., Goucher Coll., 1930. With News-Times Pub. Co., El Dorado, Ark., 1930—, various editorial and reportorial positions, 1930-33, women's editor, 1933—; corr. Ark. Gazette, Little Rock, 1962. Mem. Nat., Ark. fedns. press women, D.A.R., Delta Delta Delta. Home: 2001 N Madison Av El Dorado AR 71730 Office: 111 N Madison Av El Dorado AR 71730

CORDES, MARY KENRICK, psychologist; b. Flint, Mich., Aug. 6, 1933; d. Charles Fay and Margaret Lydia (Mitchell) Kenrick; B.A., Denison U., 1955; M.A., Oakland U., 1968; postgrad. Mich. State U., 1968-69, also Wayne State U.; m. John Cordes, July 30, 1955 (div. 1968); children—James Charles, Mari Kenrick. Research asst. Lafayette Clinic, Detroit, 1968; sch. psychologist, Roseville, Mich., 1968—. Asso., Psychol. and Ednl. Assos., Inc., Pontiac, Mich.,

1969—. Recipient award vol. work Oakland County Dept. Social Services, 1966. Mem. Am., Mich., Macomb County (pres. 1971) psychol. assns., Mich. Assn. Sch. Psychologists (regional dir. 1973—), Mortar Bd., Psi Chi, Chi Omega. Republican. Episcopalian. Home: 2452 Blockton St Rochester MI 48063 Office: 18175 E 11 Mile Rd Roseville MI 48066

CORDO, WENDY ANNE, librarian; b. Oceanside, N.Y., Nov. 20, 1945; d. Joseph James and Kelma Elizabeth (Weatherlow) Cordo; B.A., St. Joseph Coll., 1967; M.L.S., N. Tex. State U., 1969. Young adult librarian Bklyn. Pub. Library, 1969-70; librarian Ogilvy & Mather Advt., Inc., N.Y.C., 1970—. Mem. Phi Alpha Theta, Alpha Lambda Sigma. Office: Ogilvy & Mather Inc 2 E 48th St New York City NY 10017

CORDRAY, ANNA RUTH BLASBERG (MRS. ROBERT MATTHEW CORDRAY), clergywoman; b. Owensboro, Ky., Nov. 28, 1922; d. Daniel A. and Anna (Greiner) Blasberg; A.A., Stephens Coll., 1941; B.S., Western Mich. U., 1945; postgrad. Union Theol. Sem., N.Y.C., 1948; B.D., Eden Theol. Sem., 1949; S.T.M., Yale, 1955; postgrad. U. Mich., 1945, George Williams Coll., 1946, McCormick Theol. Sem., 1946; m. Robert Matthew Cordray, Apr. 6, 1958; 1 dau., Sue Ann. Tchr. art and art histroy Oak Grove Sch., Vassalboro, Me., 1943-45; girl's program sec. YMCA, Chgo., 1945-46; minister to students U. Wis., 1948-51; ordained to ministry United Ch. of Christ, 1949; regional sec. Student Christian Movement in Middle Atlantic Region, 1951-55; asso. minister Bethany Ch., Cuyahoge Falls, O., 1955-58; pastor St. Peter's Pikeland United Ch. Christ, Chester Springs, Pa., 1958-63; asso. pastor, minister Christian edn. Plymouth Congl. Ch., Miami, Fla., 1963-69; pvt. practice personal, marriage and family counseling, 1969—; minister Christian edn. Pinecrest Presbyn. Ch., Miami, 1969-71; asso. minister Coral Gables Congl. Ch., Miami, 1971-73; exec. dir. Mental Health Assn. Dade County, 1971—, also mem. staff council. Rep., United Ch. at World Student Christian Fedn. Work Camp. Bievres, France, 1958; nat. field work staff Bd. Christian Edn., United Ch. Christ, 1958; dir. Plymouth Presch., 1963-67; dir. youth tour seminars for young people United Ch. Fla., 1963-66; chmn. edn. com. S.E. Coast Assn. Christian United Ch. Christ, 1964-65; bd. dirs. Greater Miami Council Chs., 1965-67, chmn. dept. Christian edn., 1965-67; dean First Community Sch. Religion, Miami, 1966; chmn. Fla. State Conf. Com. on Christian Edn., 1966-68; chmn. Lab. Tng. Sch. for Ch. Sch. Tchrs., Fla., 1966; adviser Coconut Grove Ecumenical Youth Council, 1968. Bd. dirs. Family Camp, Little Switzerland, N.C. Mem. Nat. Council Chs. (chmn. dirs. sect., dept. Christian edn. 1958), Christian Edn. Fellowship United Ch. Christ, United Ch. Christ Ministerium, Greater Miami Ministeral Assn., Internat. Platform Assn. Home: 4780 SW 86th Terrace Miami FL 33143 Office: 800 Brickell Plaza Miami FL 33131

CORDWELL, MIRIAM, hair stylist; b. Bklyn., Jan. 6, 1908; d. Thomas J. and Sarah Ellen (Lynch) Bradley; grad. Baur's Beaty Acad., 1933; m. Richard Cordwell, Apr. 17, 1926; children—Miriam Ann (Mrs. Richard Kurisko), Dorothy Lorraine (Mrs. Robert Yarsinsky). Owner, operator beauty shop, 1934—; mem. faculty Inst. Cosmetology, U. Md., summers, 1950-59; tchr. cosmetology inst. Ohio State U., summers 1960-62, State U. N.Y., Alfred Tech., summers 1962-64; tchr. U. Ark., Fayetteville, 1964; tchr. hair design, fashion, coordinator speech and platform devel. Sec. Hairdressers Bd. Trade, N.Y., 1940-48, chmn. styles com., 1949-50; adv. bd. cosmetology Ednl. Commn. Vocational and Extension Edn., N.Y.C. Named Woman of Distinction, Soroptimist Fedn. Ams. North Atlantic region, 1962, Woman of Yr., Bus. and Profl. Women's Club, 1965; recipient Charles award Nat. Hairdressers and Cosmetologists Assn. Nat. Hairdressers and Cosmetologists Assn. (past styles dir., past chmn. ofcl. hair fashion com.). Rockland County Mental Health, Catholic Big Sisters, New City Fireman's Aux., Bus. and Profl. Women's Club. Club: Soroptimist, Author: (with Marion Rudoy) Hair Design and Fashion, 1956, 5th rev. edit., 1970; The Complete Book of Hair Styles, Beauty and Fashion, 1971; The Complete Book of Men's Hairstyles and Hair Care, 1974. Home: 254 N Main St New City NY 10956

CORELL, ANN MUIR, newspaper editor; b. Grand Rapids, Mich., Feb. 21, 1937; d. Horace George and Janet Rockwell (Muir) Corell; grad. Grand Rapids Jr. Coll. Gen. reporter, then asst. women's editor, women's editor Grand Rapids Press. Home: 2444 Gilmour SE Grand Rapids MI 49502 Office: Press Plaza VandenBerg Center Grand Rapids MI 49502

COREY, ELSIE LUCILLE (MRS. VIRGIL E. COREY), librarian; b. Epworth, Ia., Mar. 7, 1918; d. George Dale and Kathryn (Tischhauser) Gaide; B.A., Cornell Coll., Mt. Vernon, Ia., 1939; M.A., U. Ia., 1967; m. Virgil E. Corey, May 2, 1941; children—Leroy, Virgil E., Carolyn, John. Tchr. high sch., Nemaha, Ia., 1939-40, Little Rock, Ia., 1941-42; tchr., librarian pub. schs., Yarmouth, Ia., 1957-60, Mediapolis, Ia., 1960-68; librarian Louisa Muscatine Community Sch., Letts, Ia., 1968—. Mem. Farm Bur., Federated Clubs, Ia. Sch. Library Assn., Woman's Soc. Christian Service (dist. officer 1952-57). Methodist. Mem. Order Eastern Star. Home: Rural Route 2 Morning Sun IA 52640 Office: Rural Route 2 Letts IA 52754

COREY, JANET CURTIS (MRS. BRUCE L. COREY), editor; b. Winona, Minn., Feb. 7, 1906; d. Julius Edward and Harriet (Townsend) Curtis; tchrs. certificate Winona State Coll., 1925; postgrad. Wichita State U., 1952; m. Bruce Lincoln Corey, Mar. 6, 1926; 1 dau., Barbara (Mrs. Robert E. Mallonee). Tchr. jr. high sch., Winona, 1925-26; registrar East High Sch., Wichita, Kan., 1953-56; pub. relations dir. Internat. Flying Farmers, Wichita, 1956-61, exec. sec., mng. editor, advt. mgr., 1961—. Mem. C. of C., Internat. Bus. Communicators (sec.-treas., 1965-66). Club: Zonta Internat. Home: 19 Laurel Dr Wichita KS 67206 Office: Mid-Continent Airport Wichita KS 67209

COREY, JO, television personality; b. Charleston, W.Va.; d. George N. and Behia (Jorge) Corey; student Morris Harvey Coll., Charleston, Ohio U., 1963-64, Dayton U., 1968-69, Wright State U., Dayton, 1972. Television and radio commls. WCHS-TV, Charleston, 1960-63; childrens tv program WTVN-TV, Columbus, O., 1964-65; childrens programs, women's program, news show, weather forecaster, WKEF-TV, Dayton, O., 1965-73; asso. producer, co-host monthly documentaries WKEF-TV, Dayton, 1970-71; co-anchor news and weathercaster, news coordinator WBBH-TV, Ft. Myers, Fla., 1974—. Featured in TV Radio Mirror, 1967, 71. Home: Forum Apt Bldg Carrell Rd and Central Av Fort Myers FL 33901 Office: 3719 Central Av Fort Myers FL 33901

COREY, KATHRYNE ELDER COOKSEY DIMMITT (MRS. JAMES E. COREY), artist; b. Washington, May 8, 1910; d. Claude Bonifant and Bessie (Suite) Cooksey; A.B., Conn. Coll., 1932; m. E. Hewitt Dimmitt, July 11, 1939 (dec. Aug. 1957); m. 2d, James E. Corey, Jan. 19, 1971. Illustrator, mus. preparator artist Nat. Park Service, Dept. Interior, Washington, and Yorktown, Va., 1934-35, illustrator Bur. Reclamation, Washington, 1935-38, 40-45, 60-65; diorama artist Office of Exhibits, N.Y. World's Fair, 1938-40. Exhibited in group shows at Smithsonian Instn., 1946-63, Corcoran Gallery of Art, 1944-46, Arts Club Washington, 1962-74, Acad. Arts, Easton, Md., 1963-74. Recipient 1st prize Mid-Atlantic Regional Art Exhibit, 1955; 1st prize landscape Nat. League Am. Pen Women, 1948, 55, 63, best oil in show, 1963; Superior Performance award Dept. Interior, 1961. Mem. Nat. League Am. Pen Women (nat. art bd. 1956-66), Miniature Painters, Sculptors and Gravers Soc. Washington (v.p. 1964-66, pres. 1970-72), Arts Club Washington (exhibits chmn. 1968-70), Conn. Coll. Alumnae Assn. (chpt. pres. 1943-44), P.E.O. (chpt. pres. 1953-55). Home: 5801 Massachusetts Av Washington DC 20016

COREY, MARGARET DUDLEY TERRY (MRS. HENRY G. COREY, JR.), educator; b. Chgo.; d. Zebulon Alexander and M. Lucile (Jones) Terry; B.A., Stanford, 1943, M.A., 1944; m. Henry G. Corey, Jr., Feb. 2, 1946; children—Phair, Anne Victoria. Program dir. Nat. League Women Voters, 1943-47; asst. dir. Jr. A.R.C., 1948-49; parent edn. specialist Los Angeles City Bd. Edn., 1951-56; cons. Tex. Episcopal Schs., 1957-65; dir. testing and counselling div. Ednl. Records Bur. N.Y., N.Y.C., 1966-72, dir. field testing Ednl. Testing Service, 1972—. Vice pres. San Jacinto council Girl Scouts U.S.A., 1963-65, mem. personnel com. nat. bd., 1966-69; pub. relations rep. for World Assn. Girl Guides and Girl Scouts to UN, 1970—; active P.T.A., Am. Field Service. Recipient Girl Scouts statuette for exceptional service, 1965. Mem. Am. Personnel and Guidance Assn., Assn. Measurement and Evaluation in Guidance, Child Study Assn. Am. (mem. book review com. 1966—), Cap and Gown Soc., Phi Beta Kappa, Pi Beta Phi, Pi Beta Phi. Home: 5231 Arlington Av Riverdale NY 10471 Office: 3 E 80th St New York City NY 10021

COREY, MARGARET JEAN, med. adminstr.; b. Nackawic, N.B., Can., Jan. 11, 1939; d. Clifford George and Evelyn Flora (MacDonald) Corey; B.A., U. N.B., 1959; M.S., U. Me., 1961; Ph.D., McGill U., 1965. Research fellow pediatrics U. B.C., 1964-66, research asso., 1966-67, asst. prof. med. genetics, 1967-69; asst. prof. pediatrics Dalhousie U., 1969-70; dir. dept. genetics Douglas Hosp., Children's Services, Verdun, Que., Can., 1971-74; asst. prof. pediatrics McGill U., Montreal, 1972—; asst. dept. med. genetics Montreal Children's Hosp., 1973—, coordinator services and facilities for retarded children, 1974—. Vice pres. Corey Rentals, Ltd., Nackawic, N.B., 1968—; dir. Southampton Contractors, Ltd. Bd. dirs. Montreal Assn. Mentally Retarded, Lakeshore Assn. Retarded Citizens. Med. Research Council Can. scholar, 1967-69, grantee, 1965-70. Mem. Tissue Culture Assn., Am. Soc. Human Genetics, Genetics Soc. Can. A.A.A.S., Environmental Mutagen Soc., N.Y. Acad. Sci., Sigma Xi, Phi Kappa Phi. Contbr. articles to profl. jours. Home: 121 Irvine Av Montreal H3Z 2K3 Canada Office: 2300 Tupper Montreal PQ H3H 1P3 Canada

CORFMAN, EUNICE LUCCOCK (MRS. PHILIP A. CORFMAN), author; b. Oak Park, Ill., June 23, 1928; d. Emory W. and Lois M. (Maddock) Luccock; B.A. cum laude, Oberlin Coll., 1950; M.A., Radcliffe Coll., 1951; M.A., U. Md., 1970; m. Philip A. Corfman, Jan. 29, 1950; children—Stanley, Caris, Tim, Mark. Short story writer, Harper's 1967, McCall's, 1968, Tex. Quar. 1967, Hudson Rev., 1972; journalist Washington Post, 1971-72, Washington Monthly, 1972, The Washingtonian, 1972; cons. Urban Inst. Author: The Roaring Shock Test, 1968; (with Peter Brown) An Historical Analysis of Some Moral Political Values as these Bear on Population Control and Distribution, 1972. Home: 5417 Linden Ct Bethesda MD 20014

CORGAN, VIRGINIA EILEEN ROBINSON (MRS. MICHAEL H. CORGAN), educator; b. Alma, Mich., Aug. 18, 1918; d. Dwight W. and Eathel L. (Bennett) Robinson; diploma Acme Bus. Coll., 1937; B.S. with honor, U. Wyo., 1961, M.S., 1962; Ph.D., U. Neb., 1966; m. Michael H. Corgan, Aug. 26, 1939; children—Sharon (Mrs. Donald Leeber), Sheila (Mrs. T.J. Tierney), Shannon. Sec. to pres. Lobdell-Emory Mfg. Co., Alma, 1937-40; teaching asst. U. Wyo., 1961-62; mem. faculty U. Neb. at Lincoln, 1962—, asso. prof. bus. tchr. edn., vice chmn. dept., 1971—. Chmn. 1st ann. Give A Dress drive, Petoskey, Mich., 1950-51. Recipient Sr. Secretarial Sci. award U. Wyo., 1961; named Outstanding Jr. Woman Student, Coll. Commerce U. Wyo., 1960. Mem. Nat., Mountain-Plains bus. edn. assn., Neb. Council Occupational Tchr. Edn. (dir. 1972—), Delta Pi Epsilon, Beta Gamma Sigma (sec.-treas. 1965-71, nat. ritual com.), Pi Lambda Theta, Phi Kappa Phi, Phi Gamma Nu. Club: University of Neb. Faculty (dir. 1971-73). Contbr. to profl. jours. Home: 3820 S 39th St Lincoln NE 68506 Office: 302 Teachers College Univ Neb Lincoln NE 68508

CORITA, SISTER MARY, artist, educator; b. Ft. Dodge, Ia., Nov. 20, 1918; d. Robert Vincent and Edith (Sanders) Kent; B.A., Immaculate Heart Coll., 1941; M.A., U. So. Cal., 1951. Entered community of Immaculate Heart Sisters, 1936; now prof. art Immaculate Heart Coll., Los Angeles. Artist specializing in serigraphy; exhibited numerous one-man shows in museums, galleries, univs. in U.S., Can. and Spain, including Cin. Art Mus., Munson Williams Proctor Inst., Brooks Meml. Art Gallery, Cal. Palace Legion of Honor, Balt. Mus., Morris Gallery, The Contemporaries, Mus. N.M., Sala Gaspar, Barcelona; represented in collections of instns. including Met. Mus., Mus. Modern Art, Library of Congress, Rosenwald Collection at Nat. Gallery, Cin., Mus., Cal. Palace Legion of Honor, Los Angeles County Mus., Phila. Mus., N.Y. Pub. Library, Art Inst. Chgo., Victoria and Albert Mus., London, Bibliothaque Nationale, Paris; complete collection of prints in Willis Garbriel collection; executed commns. for internat. Graphic Arts Soc., Mus. Modern Art., Container Corp. Am., Los Angeles County Mus., Nelman-Marcus, Reynolds Aluminim. Address: 5515 Franklin Av Los Angeles CA 90028

CORKERY, L. ELIZABETH KNAUF (MRS. CHARLES DENNIS CORKERY), ins. agy. exec.; b. Chgo., Sept. 21, 1923; d. John Stanley and Elizabeth M. (Jansen) Knauf; ed. U. Cal. at Berkeley, 1942-43, Wash. State U., 1946-47, Northwestern U. Sch. Bank Pub. Relations and Marketing, 1967-68, Am. Inst. Banking, Chgo., 1967-68; m. Charles Dennis Corkery, Nov. 24, 1945; children—Craig Dennis, Bruce Charles, Robert Thomas, Brian Donald, Charles David. Asst. advt. mgr. Harper-Wyman Mfg. Co., 1943-46, 48-55; advt. mgr., office mgr., property mgr. Chicken Unltd. Franchises, 1961-66; advt. officer, mgr. marketing Pullman Banking Group, 1966-68; asst. cashier, dir. marketing Union Nat. Bank, Chgo., 1968-69; asst. v.p., dir. marketing Louis Joliet Bank (Ill.), 1969-71; dir. pub. relations, mem. pres.'s council Lewis Coll., Lockport, Ill., 1971-72; mng. officer customer account and teller depts. Matteson-Richton Bank, Matteson, Ill., 1972-74; office mgr. Koenning Ins. Agy., Beecher, Ill., 1974—. Mem. Nat. Assn. Bank Women (membership com. Ill. group), Ill. Bankers Assn. (nat. membership devel. com. 1971), Bank Marketing Assn. (Presdl. award), Chicago South C. of C. (treas., dir. pub. relations 1968-69), Chgo. Financial Advertisers, Advt. Club Chgo.. Bank Adminstrn. Inst., Am. Inst. Banking, Am. Bankers Assn., Chgo. Real Estate Bd., Joliet Region Pub. Relations Soc., Joliet Region C. of C. (pub. relations com.). Connecticut Hills Homeowners Assn. (pres.), Sigma Kappa Pi (pres. Chgo. council 1968-72; chpt. pres.). Roman Catholic. Contbr. to Ill. Bankers Mag., Bank Marketing Jour. Home: 21626 Richton Rd Matteson IL 60443 Office: 618 Gould St Beecher IL 60401

CORKEY, ELIZABETH MOON CONARD (MRS. WILLIAM BARNET HAROLD CORKEY), physician; b. Phila., May 2, 1903; d. Henry Shoemaker and Elizabeth Laetitia (Moon) Conard; A.B., Grinnell Coll., 1925; M.D., U. Mich., 1929; M.P.H., U.N.C., 1954; m. William Barnet Harold Corkey, Aug. 24, 1935; children—Caroline Louise, David Conard. Intern Phila. Gen. Hosp., 1929-31; resident St. Louis Maternity Hosp., 1931-32; asso. prof. obstetrics Women's Christian Med. Coll., Shanghai, China, 1932-35; physician mission hosps., Manchuria, North China, 1935-46; asst. health dir., Wayne and Greene Counties, N.C., 1946-55; asst. health dir., Mecklenburg County, N.C., 1955-68; med. dir. Community Health Assn., Charlotte, N.C., 1968—. Mem. Charlotte-Mecklenburg Charter Commn., 1968-70; mem. Charlotte-Mecklenburg Community Relations Com., 1965—; mem. adv. bd. Charlotte-Mecklenburg Mental Health, 1968—. Bd. dirs. Nevins Vocational Tng. Center; bd. dirs., pres. Charlotte YWCA, 1968-69. Named Woman of Year Goldsboro Bus. and Profl. Women, 1955, Charlotte, 1960, Downtown Charlotte Assn., 1966. Fellow Am. Pub. Health Assn.; mem. A.M.A., Friends Med. Soc., N.C., Mecklenburg County med. assns., Bus. and Profl. Women's Club, Phi Beta Kappa, Alpha Omega Alpha. Contbr. articles to profl. jours. Address: 519 Hermitage Ct Charlotte NC 28207

CORLETTE, SUZANNE, museum curator; b. Schenectady, Oct. 4, 1934; d. Lyle Horace and Edith Mary (McCulley) Corlette; B.A., Smith Coll., 1956; M.A., U. Pa., 1965. Lab. technician Wyeth Labs., Radnor, Pa., 1958-61; tchr. chemistry Rosemary Hall, Greenwich, Conn., 1962-63; curator N.J. State Museum, Trenton, 1968—. Office: 205 W State St Trenton NJ 08625

CORLEY, LILLIAN MYERS (MRS. GALE COSART CORLEY), constrn. co. exec.; b. Logansport, Ind., Jan. 12, 1916; d. Leon Goodbrake and Rose (Kent) Myers; student home econs. U. Ill., 1934-37; m. Gale Cosart Corley, Sept. 12, 1937; children—Sue Ann (Mrs. John David Peyton), Ellen. Partner, Corley Real Estate, Valparaiso, Ind., 1939-41; corporate sec. Nat. Constrn. Corp., Valparaiso, 1955-73, pres., 1973—; interior decorator, 1952-71; dir. Davidson Manors, Inc., Neighborhood Utilities, Inc., Rental Homes, Inc. Active Red Cross, 1943-44; leader 4-H, 1935-39, Girl Scouts, 1938-60; pres. Valparaiso council Girl Scouts U.S.A., 1952-54, East Lake-Porter Counties council, 1957-58. Mem. Community Concert Assn. (dir. 1954-66), P.E.O. (state pres. 1969-70, mem. nat. study com. 1970-73, mem. bd. trustees for continuing edn. 1973—), Alpha Lambda Delta. Presbyn. (pres. women's assn. 1950-52). Clubs: Mathesis (Valparaiso). Home: 1207 Beech St Valparaiso IN 46383 Office: National Construction Corp 2401 Campbell St Valparaiso IN 46383

CORLEY, NORA TERESA, librarian; b. Montreal, Que., Can., Feb. 18, 1929; d. John Kevin and Anna Sara (Magnusdottir) Corley; B.A. with honors in Geography McGill U., Montreal, 1951, B.L.S., 1952, M.A. in Geography, 1961; m. John T. Murchison, 1972. Asst. librarian Law Library, McGill U., 1952-54; librarian-in-charge Arctic Inst. N.Am., Montreal, 1954-72, fellow, 1972—. Mem. Que. Library Assn. (English sec. 1958-59, editor Bull. 1963-64), Spl. Libraries Assn. (editor Montreal 1961-62, pres. Montreal chpt. 1964-65, chmn. geography and map div. 1969-70), Corp. Profl. Librarian of Province of Que., A.L.A., Canadian Assn. for Information Sci., Canadian Assn. Geographers. Contbr. articles, book revs. to geog. and library jours. Home: 185 Kamloops Av Ottawa ON K1V 7E1 Canada

CORLEY, ONETA GARVIN (MRS. OLAN G. CORLEY), educator; b. Caney, Okla., Mar. 16, 1922; d. Willard O. and Minnie A. (Provence) Garvin; B.S. in Edn., Southwestern State Coll., 1944; M.S. in Bus. Edn., Okla. State U., 1954; m. Olan G. Corley, Aug. 17, 1946; children—Robert Olan, Ted Leroy. Sec. to registrar Registrar's Office, Southwestern State Coll., 1941-44; clk.-typist Q.M. U.S. Army, 1942-43; tchr., Beaver, Okla., 1944-45, 48-50; asst. registrar Southwestern State Coll., 1945-47; tchr. secondary schs., Okla., 1947-57, Ariz., 1957-64; asst. prof. bus. adminstrn. Grand Canyon Coll., Phoenix, 1964—, acting dean women, 1967-68; dean women and prof. Dept. Bus. Adminstrn., 1968—. Mem. Nat. Bus. Edn. Assn. N.E.A., Ariz. Coll. Assn., Okla., Ariz. edn. assns. Home: 10539 Calle Del Sol Phoenix AZ 85039 Office: 3300 W Camelback Phoenix AZ 85017

CORMANEY, PATRICIA JOHNSON (PATTY JOHNSON), journalist; b. Cedar Falls, Ia., Nov. 3, 1921; d. Vivian Wells and Bernice Maurine (McClain) Johnson; B.A., U. Ia., 1943; m. Elmer E. Cormaney, Aug. 29, 1957. Women's editor Waterloo (Ia.) Daily Courier, 1944-57, columnist, 1954—, feature editor, 1965-72; columnist Family Weekly, 1954-69; free-lance writer, 1944—. Recipient Jane Arden award Theta Sigma Phi, 1958; award Nat. Fedn. Press Women, 1955; Sweepstakes award A.P., 1960. Mem. P.E.O., Kappa Kappa Gamma. Presbyn. Author: I Was Just Thinking, 1962. Home: 2217 Rownd St Cedar Falls IA 50613

CORMIER, RAMONA THERESA, educator; b. Breaux Bridge, La., Jan. 21, 1923; d. Arthur Joseph and Florence (Breaux) Cormier; B.A., U. Southwestern La., 1943; M.A., U. So. Cal., 1948; Ph.D., Tulane U., 1960. Music tchr., St. Martin Parish, La., 1948-49; vocal music tchr., Ouachita Parish High Sch., Monroe, La., 1949-58; instr. philosophy Newcomb Coll., New Orleans, 1960-61; instr. philosophy U. Tenn., Knoxville, 1961-63, asst. prof., 1963-65; asst. prof. philosophy Bowling Green (O.) State U., 1965-68, asso. prof., 1969-72, prof., 1972—, asso. dir. Philosophy Documentation Center, 1967-73, v.p. Philosophy Information Center, 1967-73. Served as ensign USNR, 1943-46. Mem. Am. Philos. Assn., Am. Soc. Aesthetics, So. Soc. Philosophy and Psychology, Ohio Philos. Assn. (program chmn. 1971-72, pres. 1973—), A.A.A.S., Delta Kappa Gamma. Author: (with Pallister) Waiting for Death, 1974. Asso. editor: The Philosopher's Index; An International Index to Philosophical Periodicals, 1967-73. Co-editor: International Directory of Philosophy and Philosophers, 1971. Editor: (with Lineback and Chinn) Encounter: An Introduction to Philosophy, 1970. Home: 149 Baldwin Av Bowling Green OH 43402

CORN, PAULINE PIERCE (MRS. ERNEST CORN), journalist; b. Austell, Ga., Dec. 6, 1896; d. Wilds Lovick and Zula (Lewis) Pierce; A.B., Wesleyan Coll., 1918; m. Ernest Corn, July 3, 1918; children—Ann (Mrs. George Felton), Lovick Pierce, Thomas Lewis, Susan (Mrs. James Conway), Charles Philip. Feature writer Macon (Ga.) Telegraph and News, 1967-73. Mem. Macon Beautification Commn., 1962-64, Macon Arts Commn., 1970—. Wesleyan Coll. alumnae trustee, 1969-72. Mem. D.A.R., Bibb County Med. Soc. Aux., A.M.A. Aux. (local pres. 1932-33). Republican. Methodist (pres. altar guild 1960-62). Clubs: Macon Writers; Garden of Ga. (exec. bd. 1943-66). Home: 607 College St Macon GA 31208

CORNELIUS, DOROTHY A., nurse exec.; b. Johnstown, Pa., Mar. 9, 1918; d. Ray N. and Cleo (Horton) Cornelius; nursing diploma Conemaugh Valley Meml. Hosp., Johnstown, Pa., 1939; B.S., U. Pitts., 1942, postgrad., 1948-50. Dir. out-patient dept. Tb League Hosp., Pitts., 1942-45; pub. health nurse Vis. Nurse Assn., Johnstown, Pa., 1947-48; chief nurse Johnstown Regional Blood Center, 1950-52; asst. dir., chief nurse Cleve. Regional Blood Center, 1952-57; exec. dir. Ohio State Nurses Assn., Columbus, O., 1957—; treas. Am. Jour. of

Nursing Co., 1964-66, pres., 1967-68; chmn. Civil Service Commn., Reynoldsburg, 1964—; mem. Health Ins. Benefits Adv. Council, 1965-67. Chmn. com. Girls' Indsl. Sch., 1958-60; mem. Gov.'s Commn. Aging, 1959-60; mem. nat. adv. com. SSS, 1960—; mem. Pres. com. Traffic Safety, 1958-59; mem. O. Citizens Council Health and Welfare; chmn. Ohio Women's Civil Def. Council, 1962-64; sec. Ohio Cancer Coordinating Com., 1963-64; mem. Gov.'s Commn. on Status of Women. Served as lt. (j.g.) Nurses Corps, USN, 1945-46. Mem. Am. Nurses Assn. (vice-chmn. nat. sect. 1960-64, 1st v.p. 1964-68, pres. 1968-70), Nat. League Nursing, Internat. Council Nurses (pres. 1973—). Editor: Ohio Nurses Review jour. Ohio State Nurses Assn., 1957—. Home: 1128 Briarcliff Rd Reynoldsburg OH 43068 Office: 4000 E Main St Columbus OH 43213

CORNELL, JEAN SPRINGER (MRS. C. DAVID CORNELL), educator; b. Chgo., Apr. 5, 1919; d. James Earl and Daisy (Fickes) Springer; student Md. Coll. for Women, 1936-37; B.A., Ohio Wesleyan U., 1940; M.S. in Journalism, Northwestern U., 1943; M.A., U. Ariz., 1965; m. C. David Cornell, Nov. 4, 1966. Classified advt. saleswoman Akron (O.) Beacon Jour., 1940-41; asst. to mgr. classified advt. Chgo. Tribune, 1941-43; dir. suburban promotion, asst. dir. spl. events Marshall Field & Co., Chgo., 1943-48; co-owner, designer, promotion dir. Ariz. Originals, Tucson, 1956-63; instr. U. Ariz., Tucson, 1963-65; asst. dir. devel., pub. relations and publs., lectr. speech and drama Scripps Coll., Claremont, Cal., 1965-69; coordinator editorial services Am. Coll. Testing Program, Iowa City, 1969-71; asst. prof. speech Davidson (N.C.) Coll., 1971—. Publicity dir. women's bd. Chgo. Hort. Soc., 1951-56; vol. Elgin (Ill.) Community Hosp., 1954-56; vol. Chgo. Maternity Center, 1954-56, chmn. fund drive Barrington area, 1955; vol. Chgo. Infant Welfare, 1948-56. Bd. dirs. area council Girl Scouts U.S.A., Barrington, Ill., 1950-54. Bd. dirs. Tucson Assistance League, 1958-64. Mem. So. Speech Assn., Fashion Group, Inc., Speech Communication Assn., Women in Communication, Delta Gamma, Delta Sigma Rho-Tau Kappa Alpha. Co-editor Assessment of Colleges and Universities. Home: 544 Concord Rd Davidson NC 28036

CORNELL, JOANN COPE, nurse; b. Martins Ferry, O., Mar. 20, 1938; d. Ellis Pratt and Elisabeth (Kithcart) Cope; grad. Charity Hosp. Sch. Nursing, New Orleans, 1959; m. Paul J. Cornell, Dec. 26, 1958; children—Michael, Elisabeth, Mark. Obstet. nurse Charity Hosp., 1959-60; pvt. duty and obstet. nurse St. Vincent Infirmary, Little Rock, 1960; night supr. pvt. clinic and hosps., El Paso, Tex., 1962; part time office nurse, Little Rock, 1969—. Active Pulaski P.T.A. Mem. Woman's Aux. Pulaski County (pres. 1974-75), Woman's Aux. Ark. med. socs., St. Vincent, Bapt. hosp. auxs., U. Ark. Med. Center Aux., Women's Aux. A.M.A., Nurses Assn. Am. Coll. Obstetricians and Gynecologists, Ark. Orch. Soc. Guild, Greater Little Rock Fedn. Womens Clubs. Clubs: U. Ark. Faculty Women's, Little Rock Pistol, Little Rock Racquet. Home: 7400 Rockwood St Little Rock AR 72207

CORNESKY, AGNES THERESA KULCYK (MRS. ANDREW CORNESKY), physician; b. Zanesville, O.; d. Jacob and Anelia (Bartos) Kulcyk; B.S., Geneva Coll., 1956; M.D., Woman's Med. Coll. Pa., 1960; m. Andrew Cornesky, June 26, 1937; 1 son Robert Andrew. Jr. chemist Koppers Co., Inc., 1943-53; intern Allegheny Gen. Hosp., Pitts., 1960-61; gen. practice medicine, Sewickley, Pa., 1961—; mem. staff Sewickley Valley Hosp., Allegheny Gen. Hosp., Pitts., med. dir. family planning. Med. adviser Am. Cancer Soc., Beaver County (Pa.), 1962—. Recipient Am. Cancer Soc. award, 1964. Diplomate Am. Bd. Family Practice. Mem. A.M.A., Am. Acad. Family Practice, Allegheny County Med. Soc., Am. Med. Women's Assn., Am. Heart Assn. Inc., Alumnae Assn. Women's Med. Coll., Zeta Phi. Home: 1437 Beaver Rd Sewickley PA 15143 Office: Locust Pl Sewickley PA 15143

CORNING, MARY ELIZABETH, govt. sci. adminstr; b. Norwich Conn.; d. Horace Francis and Mary (Sullivan) Corning; B.A., Conn. Coll. for Women, 1947; M.A., Mt. Holyoke Coll., 1949. Phys. chemist Nat. Bur. Standards, Washington, 1949-58; phys. sci. adminstr., spl. asst. to sci. adviser U.S., sec. of state, 1958-60; project dir., planning group, asso. dir. edn. and internat. activities NSF, 1960-61, spl. asst. to head Office Internat. Sci. Activities, 1961-62, asso. program dir. coop. internat. sci. activities, 1962-64, head sci. publs. and translations div. Nat. Library Medicine, 1964-66, spl. asst. to dep. dir., 1966-67, spl. asst. to dir. for internat. programs, 1967-72, asst. dir. for internat. programs, 1972—. Expert examiner Civil Service Commn.; mem. chemistry panel Bd. U.S. Civil Service Examiners, 1953—; tech. editor, writer Navy Dept. Bd. Civil Service Examiners, 1958-60; U.S. nat. liaison officer OECD, 1962—. Bd. dirs., mem. exec. com., sec. Gorgas Meml. Inst. Tropical and Preventive Medicine. Recipient Silver medal Dept. Health, Edn. and Welfare, 1971. Fellow Optical Soc. Am. (sec. Capitol sect. 1964-65); mem. Nat. Acad. Scis., Internat. Commn. for Optics (U.S. nat. com.), Internat. Fedn. Documentation, Am. Chem. Soc., A.A.A.S., Med. Library Assn., Phi Beta Kappa. Asst. editor Jour. Optical Soc. Am., 1950-60; mem. staff Capital Chemist Publ. 1957-67. Contbr. articles to profl. jours. Home: 4501 Connecticut Av NW Washington DC 20008 Office: 8600 Rockville Pike Bethesda MD 20014

CORONA, MINNIE (CARMELA) CORINNE ROSE (MRS. VINCENT MICHAEL CORONA), city ofcl.; b. Williamsport, Pa., Mar. 17, 1913; d. Thomas and Delecata (De Santis) Sarandrea; student Central City Bus. Sch., 1930-31, Internat. Corr. Schs., 1932-33; m. Vincent Michael Corona, June 24, 1939; children—Corinne (Mrs. J. Piccione), Helene (Mrs. J. Wallace). Clk. Canastota Fruit Co. (N.Y.), 1931-33; bookkeeper, sec. Caruso, Rinella, Battaglia Co., Inc., Canastota, 1933-35; inspector O & S Bearing Co., Detroit, 1935-37; bookkeeper, sec. Frank Curulla Produce Co., Oneida, N.Y., 1937-58; village clk., treas. Village of Canastota, 1958-74, police matron, 1958-74, sec. Zoning Bd. Appeals, 1974—. Treas. Greater Lenox Ambulance Service, Canastota, 1972-74. Sec. Village Planning Bd., Canastota, 1967-73. Bd. dirs. March of Dimes. Home: 322 NE Canal St Canastota NY 13032 Office: 126 East Center St Canastota NY 13032

CORRADINI, MARGARET MCMULLEN (MRS. PAUL ROBERT CORRADINI), congl. press sec.; b. Providence, Apr. 11, 1944; d. Horace Martin and Marie Louise (Strehlau) McMullen; student Drew U., 1961-63; B.S., U. Utah, 1965, M.S., 1967; m. Paul Robert Corradini, June 13, 1965; children—Andrew Stafford, Andrea Marie. Adminstrv. asst. for pub. information State Office Rehab. Services, Salt Lake City, 1967-69; pub. relations cons. Utah Dept. Community Affairs, Salt Lake City, 1971-72; media coordinator, press sec. for congressional campaign, 1972; press sec. U.S. Rep. Wayne Owens of Utah, Washington, 1973—. Del. to county and state Democratic convs., Utah, 1968; mem. Dem. com. for Chemung County N.Y., 1969-71. Recipient awards for publs. Rehab. Services Adminstrn., 1968, U.S. Dept. Health, Edn. and Welfare, 1968, Intermountain Assn. Indsl. Editors, 1968. Mem. Pub. Relations Soc. Am., Jr. League. Democrat. Mem. United Ch. of Christ. Home: 3312 Ardley Ct Falls Church VA 22041 Office: 222 Cannon Office Bldg Washington DC 20515

CORRIGAN, ANNE MARIE WOODWARD, govt. ofcl., writer; b. Corvallis, Ore., Mar. 16, 1926; d. Horace McParlin and Harriet (Swart) Woodward; B.A., Trinity Coll., 1946; M.A., Cath. U., 1968; postgrad., U. Coll. London Sch. Econs. (Eng.), 1969-70; m. Edward Corrigan, Feb. 12, 1949 (div. Feb. 1961); children—Francis Patrick II, John Beatty Woodward, Blaise, Edward IV. Researcher, Time mag., N.Y.C., 1948; reporter N.Y. Herald Tribune, N.Y.C., 1948-49; free-lance writer, fashion coordinator TV, Cleve., 1949-58; dir. Fashion Career Coll., Cleve., 1958-61, John Robert Powers Sch., Washington, 1961-63; writer-editor Office of Sec. U.S. Dept. of Labor, Washington, 1963-71; spl. asst. to U.S. Senator Adlai Stevenson III, Washington, 1971-72; spl. legislative asst. to Congressman Joseph M. McDade, 1972-74; information officer, asst. to dep. dir. Center Econ. and Social Information, UN, N.Y.C., 1974—. Recipient Fed. Career Service award for study European New towns Sec. Labor, 1969. Mem. Town and Country Planning Assn. (Eng.), Am. Anthrop. Assn., Am. Inst. Planners, Washington Press Club, Nat. Press Club, Fashion Group, Nat. Trust for Historic Preservation. Author: Learning from British New Towns (honorable mention Govt. Publs. annual awards 1972). Contbr. to books, mags., daily jours. Home: 2709 O St NW Washington DC 20007 Office: 1048 UN Secretariat New York City NY 10017

CORRIGAN, DOROTHY DANIELS (MRS. RICHARD F. CORRIGAN), lectr., assn. exec.; b. Rockford, Ill.; d. Lee G. and Louise (Nelson) Daniels; student U. Ala., 1939-40, Brown Bus. Coll., 1940-41, Rockford Coll., 1960-64; m. Richard F. Corrigan, Sept. 17, 1949; children—Alan, Carolyn, Lucy. Library cons. Kieth Country Day Sch., 1964-65, Bradley & Bradley Architects, 1964-66; trustee cons. Ill. State Library, 1966—; producer Semi-Educational Entertainment Prodns., 1962—; pres. S.E.E. Prodns., 1973—; producer, performer TV series Let's Look at Books, WREX-TV, 1961 (all Rockford) writer Sci. Research Assos., 1965-66; lectr. Internat. Programs, Inc., 1968—; also writer ednl. scripts for TV; producer slide show Where the People Are--The Library Goes, 1970; lectr. univs., educators and various groups throughout U.S. Pres., Am. Library Trustee Assn., 1965-66, chmn. spl. com. on library service to disadvantaged, 1969—; pres. Rockford Pub. Library Bd., 1956-68; vice-chmn. Ill. Library Trustee Assn., 1965-67, chmn., 1967-69, recipient Distinguished Service Citation for Trustees, 1965; mem. nat. bd. Nat. Book Com., 1966—. Author: (play) The Drama of Prayer, 1963; Children of Europe, 1966; Seasons and Holidays, 1967; Workbook for a Successful Workshop, 1967; The Story of Nancy and The Story of Jimmy, 1968. Trustee editor column Across the Board, Library Jour., 1966-67; book rev. editor Armed Forces Mgmt. Mag., 1955-57; asso. editor Ill. Libraries, 1967-68; editor Ill. Library Trustee Newsheet, 1968-69. Contbr. articles and revs. to mags., jours. Address: 1931 Old Orchard Ct Rockford IL 61107

CORRY, ANNE IRROVIA, lab. and x-ray tech.; b. Siloam, Ga.; d. William R. and Harriot (Delvin) C.; B.A., Maryville Coll., 1920; M.A., U. Ga., 1929. Tchr., Abbyville (Kan.) Rural High Sch., 1920-24, Burns (Kan.) High Sch., 1924-25, Glasco (Kan.) High Sch., 1925-26, Jerome (Ariz.) High Sch., 1926-35; tng. for lab. and x-ray registry Miller Hosp., St. Paul, 1935-37; lab. and x-ray technician Bapt. Hosp., Little Rock, 1937-39, St. Vincents Infirmary, Little Rock, 1939-50; supr. lab. and x-ray dept. M. G. Boswell Meml. Hosp., Greensboro, Ga., 1950—. Mem. Ark. Soc. Med. Technologists (pres. 1942-45), Ark. Soc. X-ray Technologists (past pres., past sec.), P.E.O. (past chaplain). Home: Nurses Home Greensboro GA 30642 Office: M G Boswell Meml Hosp Greensboro GA 30642

CORSA, HELEN STORM, educator; b. Amherst, Mass., Sept. 27, 1915; d. John and Mary (Thomas) Corsa; B.A., Mt. Holyoke Coll., 1938; M.A., Bryn Mawr Coll., 1939, Ph.D., 1942. Instr. English, Hartwick Coll., Oneonta, N.Y., 1942-43; instr., asst. prof. English, Russell Sage Coll., Troy, N.Y., 1943-48; instr., asst. prof., asso. prof. Martha Hale Shackford prof. English, Wellesley (Mass.) Coll., 1948—. Roman Catholic. Author: Chaucer; Poet of Mirth and Morality, 1964. Home: 6 Richland Rd Wellesley MA 02181

CORSE, WAHNETA ZEYSING (MRS. JOHN CORSE), banker; b. Wellington, Mo., Sept. 22, 1914; d. William L. and Martha K. (Shafer) Zeysing; student Central Mo. State Coll., 1933; m. John Corse, Sept. 7, 1933; children—Kay (Mrs. G.L. Emery), Sandra (Mrs. Herbert Soendker, Jr.). With Wellington Bank, 1950—, exec. v.p., 1969—. Treas. Wellington-Napoleon Schs., 1966-70; treas. Wellington-Napoleon Spl. Road Dist., 1966—. Vice chmn. Lafayette County Central Dem. com., 1970-72. Mem. Sigma Sigma Sigma. Methodist (treas. 1971-72). Home: Tanyard Dr Wellington MO 64097 Office: Box 116 Wellington MO 64097

CORSON, JOAN STIFEL (MRS. LOUIS DAMARIN CORSON), civic worker; b. Wheeling, W.Va., June 1, 1917; d. Arthur C. and Adelaide E. (Flaccus) Stifel; A.A., Briarcliffe Jr. Coll., 1936; m. Louis Damarin Corson, June 17, 1947; children—Linda Diane, Joan Adelaide. Mem. Motor Corps and blood bank A.R.C., World War II; vol. nurses aide Ashford Gen. Hosp., White Sulphur Springs, W.Va., 1945; sustaining mem. Jr. League Wheeling. Bd. dirs. Peterson Hosp. Gift Shop, Poplar Twig Ohio Valley Gen. Hosp.; bd. lady mgrs. House Friendship. Mem. Nat. Audubon Soc., Nature Conservancy, Am. Hort. Soc., Nat. Trust Historic Preservation, Aircraft Owners and Pilots Assn., Silver Wings. Episcopalian. Home: 155 Meadow Lane Wheeling WV 26003

CORSON, ROSALIE P., marketing cons.; b. Elkhart, Ind., Jan. 4, 1938; d. Carl Woodard and Charlotte Louise (Keyser) Corson; student Butler U., 1955-56, Ind. U., 1957; B.A., Purdue U., 1960. Asst. editor Tool and Mfg. Engr., Am. Soc. Tool and Mfg. Engrs., Detroit, 1960-62; social investigator Wayne County Dept. Social Welfare, Detroit, 1963-64; exec. dir. Camp Fire Girls, Inc., Adrian, Mich., 1964-66; asst. v.p. Coachmen Industries, Middlebury, Ind., 1966-71; founder, pres. Corson Pub. Co., Middlebury, Ind., 1970-74; editor, pub. Progressive Woman News Mag., 1971-73, The Middlebury Independent, 1971-74; marketing cons. to several firms. Mem. Nat. Orgn. for Women, Ind. Women's Polit. Caucus, Women's Press Club. Home and office: PO Box 62 Middlebury IN 46540

CORTELL, RUTH ELEANOR (MRS. MYER M. MEDINE), physician; b. Portland, Me., June 25, 1914; d. Edward S. and Ethel (Segal) Cortell; B.A., Wellesley Coll., 1935; Ph.D., U. Chgo., 1939; M.D., Yale, 1948; m. Myer M. Medine, Apr. 1, 1951; children—David S., Emily S. Intern Mt. Sinai Hosp., N.Y.C., 1948-49, resident 1951; resident Montefiore Hosp., N.Y.C., 1949-50; practice medicine specializing in internal medicine, N.Y.C., 1951—; staff physician Met. Life Ins. Co., 1962-67, asst. med. dir., 1967-71, asso. med. dir., 1971—; mem. staff Bellevue Hosp., 1963—; asst. prof. clin. medicine, N.Y. U. Sch. Medicine, 1971—. Diplomate Am. Bd. Internal Medicine. Mem. A.M.A., Indsl. Med. Assn., Med. Soc. N.Y. County, N.Y. State Med. Soc. Home: 431 E 20th St New York City NY 10010 Office: 1 Madison Av New York City NY 10010

CORTLANDT, LYN, artist; b. N.Y.C.; d. Graf Karl von Lublénski and Elinor Ernestine (Thiel) Cortlandt; student Chouinard Art Inst., Jepson Art Inst., Los Angeles; student Art Students League of N.Y., Art Sch. of Pratt Inst., Columbia, U. Sch. Painting and Sculpture, Hans Hofmann Sch. Fine Arts, China Inst. Am., N.Y.C.; also pvt. instrn. Solo exhbns. in U.S. and abroad; represented in nat. exhbns. U.S.A., including Pa. Acad. Fine Arts, Bklyn. Mus., N.A.D.; exhibited internationally including France, Netherlands, Belgium, Switzerland, Greece, Italy, Portugal, Brazil, Argentina, Japan, India; works in permanent collections Met. Mus. Art, Musée National d'Art Moderne, Paris, France, Stedelijk Mus., Amsterdam, Netherlands, Mus. Fine Arts, Boston, Fogg Mus. Art, Boston Pub. Library, Bklyn. Mus., Balt. Mus. Art, Springfield (Mass.) Mus. Fine Arts, N.Y. Pub. Library, Cin. Art Mus., other important pub. and pvt. collections. Recipient citation for humanitarian service Nephrosis Found of N.Y.; spl. service award N.Y. Heart Assn., C.S.S.I. medal of honor; Knight of Mark Twain. Fellow Royal Soc. Arts (London), Internat. Inst. Arts and Letters (Germany); mem. Marquis Library Soc. (adv.), Comitato Internazionale Centro Studi e Scambi Internazionali, Acad. Polit. Sci., Nat. Trust for Historic Preservation, UN Assn., Center for Study Democratic Instns., N.Y. Zool. Soc., Accademia Internazionale Leonardo da Vinci, Comitato Internazionale, Centro Studi E Scambi Internazionali, Allied Artists of America, also Painters and Sculptors Soc. N.J., Internat. Platform Assn., Am. Acad. Polit. and Social Sci., Am. Judicature Soc. Clubs: Pen and Brush, Philadelphia Water Color, Le Cercle d'Or. Radio moderator panel forums on art. Home: 1070 Park Av New York City NY 10028

CORTY, SUSANNE PISKO (MRS. CLAUDE CORTY), journalist; b. Vienna, Austria, Apr. 19, 1925; d. Ernest Sigmund and Risa (Fried) Pisko; B.A. cum laude, Radcliffe Coll., 1946; M.A., Yale, 1947; m. Claude Corty, June 15, 1948; children—Andrew P., Eric W. Research asst. U. Mich. Law Sch., Ann Arbor, 1948-51; pub. relations coordinator Mt. Pleasant Sch. Dist., Wilmington, Del., 1960-67; editorial asst. News-Jour., Wilmington, 1967-69, editorial writer, 1969—. Recipient 2d prize, editorial writing Md.-Del.-D.C. Press Assn., 1970. Mem. Nat. Conf. Editorial Writers, League Women Voters (Wilmington dir. 1953-57, Del. dir. 1957-60). Home: 1511 Emory Rd Wilmington DE 19803 Office: 831 Orange St Wilmington DE 19899

CORWELL, MARION, pub. relations exec.; b. Hinsdale, Ill., July 1, 1926; d. Andrew Preston and Ellen (Knudson) Petersen; student Andrews U., 1944-46, U. Cal., 1951-52; B.A., Mich. State U., 1953, M.A., 1954; m. William Shertzer; 1 dau., Ann. Actress radio shows on Armed Forces radio network in Japan, 1950-51; prodn. asst. WKAR-TV, East Lansing, Mich., 1952-54; asst. film dir. WJBK, Detroit, 1953; mgr. ednl. TV, Henry Ford Mus. and Greenfield Village, Dearborn, 1954-62; dir. sch. relations Dearborn Pub. Schs., Dearborn Bd. Edn., 1962-66; instr. speech Henry Ford Community Coll., 1963-66; ednl. affairs rep. pub. relations staff Ford Motor Co., 1966-70, consumer affairs rep., pub. relations, 1970-72, pub. relations Lincoln-Mercury, 1973, corporate tech. and product information staff, 1973—; TV producer-writer-broadcaster, appeared on several nationally syndicated TV series, 1954-62. Mem. gen. com. WTVS, 1957-62; vice chmn. operations com. Detroit Ednl. TV Found., 1959-60; mem. Mich. Women's Commn. Recipient award for outstanding contbns. to ednl. TV, Detroit Adv. Council, 1958; award for TV program Window to the Past, Ohio State U., Five-to-Watch award Detroit chpt. Am. Women in Radio and TV, 1964; Nat. Headliner award Theta Sigma Phi, 1969; Distinguished Alumni award Mich. State U., 1972, named one of 10 Outstanding Mich. Women Bus. and Profl. Women's Club, 1973. Mem. Am. Women in Radio and TV (pres. Detroit chpt. 1959-61, v.p. East Central area 1961-64, nat. pres. 1969-70; bd. trustees ednl. found. 1961-63, 68-72; program chmn. nat. conv. 1966), Pub. Relations Soc. Am. (mem. nat. edn. com. 1972-73, Detroit bd. 1973—), Nat. Assn. Ednl. Broadcasters (chmn. pub. relations com. 1962-66). Met Detroit Sch. Pub Relations Assn. (pres. 1964-66), Women in Communications (chmn. Book Fair 1965), Gamma Alpha Phi (hon. v.p.), Alpha Epsilon Rho (past sec. local chpt.). Clubs: Detroit Press; Trenton Music (pres. 1971—). Contbr. articles in field to profl. jours. Home: 28911 W Huron River Dr Flat Rock MI 48134 Office: World Hdqrs Ford Motor Co American Rd Dearborn MI 48121

CORWIN, JOYCE ELIZABETH STEDMAN, constn. co. exec.; b. Chgo.; d. Cresswell Edward and Elizabeth Josephine (Kimbell) Stedman; student Fla. State U., U. Miami; m. William Corwin, May 1, 1965; children—Robert Edmund Newman, Jillanne Elizabeth Newman. Investment rep. A.M. Kidder & Co., N.Y.C., 1954-56; pres. Am. Properties, Inc., Miami, Fla., 1966-72; v.p. Stedman Constrn. Co., Miami, 1971—. Gray lady A.R.C., 1969-70; guidance worker Youth Hall, 1969-70; sponsor Para Med. Group of Coral Park High Sch., 1969-70. Hostess, Republican presdl. campaign, 1968; aide Rep. Nat. Conv., 1972. Mem. Dade County Med. Aux. (chmn. directory com. 1970), Fla. Psychiat. Soc. Aux., Vizcayans, Fla. Morgan Horse Assn. Clubs: Coral Gables Junior Women's (chmn. casework com. 1959-63), Riviera Country, Palm Bay, Coral Gables Country, Coral Reef Yacht, Royal Palm Tennis, Jockey. Home: 3929 Granada Blvd Coral Gables FL 33134

CORWIN, SOPHIA M. (MRS. JOHN W. CORWIN), artist; b. N.Y.C.; d. Isadore and Mary (Plovnik) Miller; BA., N.Y. U., 1941, M.A., 1962; student N.A.D., 1930-33, Art Students League, 1933, Archipenko Sch., Woodstock, 1944, Phillips Meml. Gallery, Washington, 1944-48, Hoffman Sch., Provincetown, 1954; m. John W. Corwin, Mar. 30, 1940; children—Lauren Anita, Alexandra Jeanne (Mrs. John Hankin). One-man shows Capricorn Gallery, N.Y.C., 1967-70, Colony Gallery, Washington, 1952, Creative Arts Gallery, N.Y.C., 1954; exhibited in group shows Balt. Mus., Nat. Collection Fine Arts, Corcoran Gallery Art, Phillips Meml. Galleries, Washington Silvermine Guild, Conn. N.Y. U. Loeb Center, Lehigh U., Columbia U. Club Gallery; represented in pvt. collections; asst. instr. Painting N.Y. U., 1961-62; tchr. painting and drawing, dir. studio workshop Bronx House Community Center, 1962-73; lectr. art history Coop. Coll. Center Westchester, State U. N.Y., Purchase, 1971-72. Juror art show N.Y. State Council Arts, 1970. Recipient scholarship Philips Meml. Art Sch., 1944-48, Nat. Competition award Creative Arts Gallery, N.Y.C., 1954; a winner nat. sculpture competition for decorating pub. bldgs. Dept. Housing and Urban Devel., 1973. Mem. Nat. Soc. Women Artists, Am. Soc. Contemporary Artists, League Present Day Artists, Coll. Art Assn., Nat. Com. on Art Edn., Sculptors League, Artists Equity, Soc. Washington Artists, Yonkers Art Assn. Address: 79 Franklin Av Yonkers NY 10705

CORYLLOS, ELIZABETH VASILIKI DESPINA (MRS. PAUL F. LARDI), physician; b. N.Y.C., July 3, 1929; d. Polivious Nicholas and Lois (Ralli) Coryllos; grad. Spence Sch., N.Y.C., 1946; A.B. cum laude Barnard Coll., 1949; M.D., Cornell Med. Sch., 1953; M.S. surgery N.Y.U., 1959; m. Paul F. Lardi, Nov. 30, 1963; children—Lisa, Paul, Janice, Gordon. Served internship at Bellevue Hospital, N.Y.C., 1953-54, asst. resident in surgery, 1954-56, research fellow N.Y. Heart Assn., 1956-57, sr. resident in surgery, 1957-59; resident-in-chief, dept. surgery Hosp. for Sick Children, Toronto, Ont., Can., 1959-60; instr. surgery U. Toronto, 1959-60; asso. surgery N.Y. Med. Coll., 1960-61, asst. prof. surgery, 1961-63; clin. instr. surgery Cornell U. Med. Coll., 1972—; asso. prof. clin. surgery State U. N.Y. at Stony Brook, 1973—; chief in pediatric surgery Flower Fifth Av., Met. hosps., 1960-63; asst. surgeon Flower Fifth Av. Hosp., 1960-63; asst. vis. surgeon Met. Hosp., 1960-63, asso. vis. surgeon in charge pediatric surgery Elmhurst Gen. Hosp., 1961-64; attending surgeon French Hosp., 1963-69; asst. adj. surgery Lenox Hill Hosp., 1963-67; asst. vis. surgeon Morrisania div. Montefiore Hosp., 1963-68, Queens Gen. div. L.I. Jewish Hosp., 1964-68, Booth Meml. Hosp., 1963-68, Meadowbrook Hosp., 1964—, sect. chief, pediatric surgery 1966-74; cons. in pediatric surgery Hosp. for Bone and Joint Diseases, 1964—; chief pediatric surgery Mercy Hosp., 1974—; active surg. staff South Nassau Communities, 1963—, Mercy Hosp., 1963—, Community Hosp., Glen Cove, 1966—, Central Gen. Hosp., Franklin Gen. Hosp., 1966-71, Hempstead Gen. Hosp., 1966-72, Nassau Hosp., 1966—, Syosset Hosp., 1968—, Long Beach, 1963-68, Deepdale Hosp., 1963-67, Wykoff Heights Hosp., 1964-68, Madison Av Hosp., 1963-66, Midtown Hosp., 1963-66, Freeport Hosp., 1966-72, others; courtesy staff Central Gen. Hosp., Plainview, Hempstead Gen. Hosp., Mid-Island Hosp., Bethpage, Syosset Hosp., St. Francis Hosp., Roslyn (all N.Y.). Diplomate Nat. Bd. Med. Examiners, Am. Bd. Surgery. Fellow Royal Coll. Physicians and Surgeons of Can., Am. Acad. Pediatrics, A.C.S., N.Y. Acad. Medicine, Am. Coll. Chest Physicians, Nassau Acad. Medicine, N.Y. Cardiol. Soc.; mem. Am. Trauma Soc. (charter), Nassau County, N.Y. State med. socs., A.M.A., Nat Resuscitation Soc., N.Y. State Soc. Med. Research, Hellenic Med. Soc. (pres. 1965), Soc. Med. Judisprudence, N.Y. Pediatric Soc. (pres. 1970-72), Am. Women's Med. Assn. (v.p. 1972—), Nassau Acad. Medicine, Am. Thoracic Soc., N.Y. Thoracic Surgery Soc., Nassau Pediatric Soc., N.Y. Soc. for Pediatric Surgery (founder 1965, pres. 1970-72), N.Y. Acad. Scis., Pan Am. Med. Assn. (sec. pediatric sect. 1963), Nassau Surg. Soc., N.Y. State Women's Med. Soc. (v.p. 1969—, in charge sci. programs 1971), Am. Pediatric Surg. Assn. (charter). Contbr. articles to profl. jours. Address: 8 Jaegger Dr Old Brookville Glen Head NY 11545

COSGROVE, GRACE REGINA, advt. exec.; b. N.Y.C., Dec. 7, 1915; d. John and Margaret (Corrigan) Cosgrove; B.A., Hunter Coll., 1938. Sales promoter, editor Baker & Taylor Co., 1939-50; advt. mgr. Barnes & Noble, Inc., 1950-70; advt. mgr. Littlefield, Adams & Co., Totowa, N.J., 1971—. Mem. Booksellers League N.Y. (rec. sec. 1966-69). Co-editor The Bookwoman (Womens Nat. Book Assn.), 1973-74. Home: 65 Montclair Av Montclair NJ 07042 Office: 81 Adams Dr Totowa NJ 07512

COSGROVE, ZOE LEIGHTON (MRS. DONALD W. COSGROVE), librarian; b. St. Paul, Feb. 19, 1932; d. Hartwell Harvell Winfield and Zoe Margaret (Johnston) Wilkerson; student Radcliffe Coll., 1949-50; B.A. summa cum laude, U. Minn., 1952, M.A., 1953, postgrad., 1954-56; m. Donald W. Cosgrove, May 31, 1963. Jr. librarian St. Paul Pub. Library, 1956-57, Donnell Reference Center, N.Y.C., 1958; reference asst. James Jerome Hill Reference Library, St. Paul, 1958-63; reference librarian Minn. Mining & Mfg. Co., 1963-68, Tape Div. Library, 1968—. Mem. A.L.A., Minn. Library Assn., Spl. Libraries Assn. (chpt. pres. 1968-69, dir. 1971-73, chmn. adv. council 1972-73), Phi Beta Kappa. Unitarian. Home: 111 E Kellogg Blvd Apt 3001 St Paul MN 55101 Office: 3M Co Tape Div Library 3M Center 230-1-13 St Paul MN 55101

COSSEY, HAZEL BELLE, coll. ofcl.; b. Wetumka, Okla., Dec. 14, 1918; d. John Henry and Pearl May (Sims) Banta; student Tulsa U., Okla. Bapt. U., St. Gregory's Coll., U. Mont.; m. Ernest Orlendo Cossey, Oct. 8, 1937; children—Nona (Mrs. Adrian L. Jones), Ernest Orlendo. With U. Tulsa, 1940-43, Okla. Bapt. U., 1961-66; registrar, admissions officer St. Gregory's Coll., Shawnee, Okla., 1967—. Mem. Am., Okla. assns. collegiate registrars and admissions officers, Beta Sigma Phi, Altrusa. Home: 222 W Midland St Shawnee OK 74801

COSSOTTO, FIORENZA (MRS. IVO VINCO), mezzo soprano; b. Crescentino, Italy, Apr. 22, 1938; d. Ettore and Marina (Ferrero) Cossotto; Diploma, Conservatorio di Musica G. Verdi, Turin, Italy, 1956; m. Ivo Vinco, June 14, 1958; 1 son, Roberto. Permanent singer LaScala, Milan, Italy, 1957—; appearances in opera houses of Milan, Rome, Naples, Florence, Venice, Vienna, London, Paris, Barcelona, Met. Opera, also at Edinburgh Festival and in USSR. Address: Via Ezlo Biondi 1 Milan Italy

COSTA, MAZEPPA KING, pub. relations specialist; b. Memphis, Oct. 24, 1927; d. Robert Morris and Mary St. Aubert (Tucker) King; student U. Miss., 1945-46; A.A., George Washington U., 1947, B.A., 1949; M.A., U. Hawaii, 1951; m. Robert Oliver Costa, Sept. 16, 1949; children—Mazeppa Montague, Anthony Blair, Montgomery Page. With Maury Realty, Honolulu, 1951-53; office mgr., pub. relations dir. Honolulu Community Theatre, 1953-59; propr. Mazeppa Costa Pub. Relations, Honolulu, 1959—. Dance, drama critic Honolulu Advertiser, 1956-60; columnist, feature writer Paradise of Pacific mag., 1958-60; corporate sec. Kokohala Pub. Co., Inc., 1962-67. Appointment sec. Hawaii gubernatorial campaign, 1959. Bd. dirs. Hawaiian Music Found. Mem. Bishop Mus. Assn. (charter), Hawaii Found. on Culture and Arts (charter), Hawaii C. of C., Friends of Iolani Palace, Friends of Library of Hawaii, Hawaii Heart Assn., Honolulu Acad. Arts, Aloha Week Hawaii, Delta Gamma, Alpha Lambda Delta. Episcopalian. Contbg. editor, co-founder Beacon mag., 1961-68. Home: 325 Puamamane St Honolulu HI 96821 Office: PO Box 7024 Honolulu HI 96821

COSTA, NORA B. (MRS. MORRIS F. COSTA), banker; b. Pitts., Feb. 14, 1924; d. Noah and Alvina (Klins) Sheppard; student Pasadena Jr. Coll., 1942, U. Cal., Los Angeles, Nat. Trust Sch., 1961; m. Morris Frank Costa, Mar. 21, 1972; children (of previous marriage)—Susan (Mrs. Paul Becher), Christine Diane Birdsall. With trust dept. First Western Bank, Pasadena, Cal., 1942-47, exec. sec., mgr. trust dept., 1955-63, asst. sec., 1963-64, asst. trust officer, 1964, trust officer, 1965—, also asst. v.p., 1973—; instr. trust services Am. Inst. Banking, 1970. Sec., Rosemary Cottage, 1969. Bd. dirs. Pasadena Child Health Found., 1972, treas., 1973-74. Mem. Nat. Assn. Bank Women, Inc. (group sec., treas. 1965), Am. Inst. Banking (bd. dirs. 1943). Clubs: First Western Bank President's Sales (pres. 1971-73); Girls of Pasadena (pres. 1972), Women's City of Pasadena (treas. 1971—). Home: 447 N Sunnyslope St Pasadena CA 91107 Office: PO Box 439 Pasadena CA 91102

COSTANTINO, JOSEPHINE MARIE, editor; b. Dunkirk, N.Y.; d. Charles F. and Margaret (Gerage) Costantino; B.S., Buffalo State Tchrs. Coll., 1936; M.A., Cornell U., 1940; postgrad. S.E. Jr. Coll., Chgo., 1957-59, Columbia Coll., Chgo. Editorial asst. Am. Council Edn., Washington, 1947-49; editor Center for Intergroup Edn., U. Chgo., 1949-50, Field Enterprises, Chgo., 1950-51, Nat. Congress Parents and Tchrs., Chgo., 1951-56; editor U. Chgo. Press, 1957—, asst. editor Elementary Sch. Jour., 1957-70, mng. editor, 1970—. Home: 5716 Kimbark Av Chicago IL 60637 Office: 5835 Kimbark Av Chicago IL 60637

COSTANZA, MARGARET, Democratic nat. committeewoman; b. LeRoy, N.Y., Nov. 28, 1932; d. Philip Joseph and Concetta (Granata) Costanza; grad. high sch. Exec. sec., adminstrv. asst. John J. Petrossi Real Estate Devel. Co., Rochester, N.Y., 1954—; mgr. Powers Bldg., Rochester. Exec. Democratic committeewoman 22d ward, Rochester, 1959-64; mgr. Robert F. Kennedy Senatorial campaign, Monroe County, N.Y., 1964; vice chmn. Monroe County Dem. Com., 1966-70, mem., 1966—; mem. N.Y. Dem. Com., 1967—; mem. Dem. Nat. Com., 1972—; mem. Women's Polit. Caucus, 1972—; mem. Rochester City Council, 1974—, vice mayor, 1974—. Bd. dirs. Rochester Community Chest, Inc. Mem. Hudson Av. Businessmen's Assn., Italian Civil Rights League, Sons of Italy, Italian Women's Civic Club, Rochester C. of C. (mem. women's council). Roman Catholic. Office: 105 Powers Bldg Rochester NY 14614

COSTELLO, MARIE CATHERINE HUGHES (MRS. EDWARD HUGH COSTELLO), nursing educator; b. Chgo.; d. John and Mary (Hayden) Hughes; student St. Joseph Hosp. Sch. Nursing, Chgo., 1936-38; B.S., De Paul U., 1948, M.A., 1952; m. Edward Hugh Costello, Feb. 16, 1944 (dec. Nov. 1944). Staff nurse St. Joseph Hosp., Chgo., 1938-40, head nurse, 1940-42, clin. instr. sch. nursing, 1946-52; instr. De Paul U. Chgo., 1952-54, asst. prof., 1954-61, asso. prof. nursing 1961-67; instr. VA Hosp., Downey, Ill., 1967-68, asso. chief nursing service for edn., 1969-71; coordinator asso. degree nursing program Coll. of Lake County, Grayslake, Ill., 1971—. Served from 2d lt. to capt., Army Nurse Corps, 1942-45. Mem. Am. Nurses Assn., Nat., Chgo., Northeastern leagues nursing, Am. Assn. U. Profs. Home: PO Box 547 Lake Forest IL 60045 Office: Nursing Program College of Lake County Grayslake IL 60030

COSTELLO, MARY, writer; b. Lawrence, Mass., Aug. 1, 1942; d. John A. and Mary C. (Howard) Costello; B.A. with honors, Trinity Coll., Washington, 1964; M.A., U. Pa., 1965, student Annenberg Sch. Communications, 1967-68. Writer books on Latin Am. Inst. Comparative Study Polit. Systems, Washington, 1966; free-lance writer in Greece, 1966-67; tchr. high sch. history and social scis., Lawrence, 1968-69; writer editorial research reports, Washington, 1969—. Mem. Am. Press Inst. (seminar editorial writers 1974). Club: Washington Press. Home: 916 E Capitol St NE Washington DC 20003 Office: 1414 22d St NW Washington DC 20037

COSTELLO, VIRGINIA GERTRUDE SMITH (MRS. VIRGINIA COSTELLO), librarian; b. Santa Fe, May 12, 1916; d. Leonidas Ward and Corrina Gertrude (Hanes) Smith; student Washburn U., 1933-34, St. Mary's Hall, 1934-36, McGill U., summer 1938; B.A., U. Neb., 1938; B.S. in L.S., Columbia, 1940; M.A., Colo. State Coll., 1948; m. Franklin Albert Costello, Feb. 16, 1952; (div. Aug. 1953); 1 dau., Gertrude Virginia. Reference and young people's librarian N.Y. Pub. Library, N.Y.C., 1940-42; faculty and library staff mem. Colo. State Coll., Greeley, 1942-71, reference librarian and asso. prof. library sci., 1966-71, head reference librarian and asso. prof. U. No. Colo., 1971-72, prof. library sci., asst. dir. for collections devel., 1972—. Organizer, adviser Friends of U. No. Colo. Libraries, 1972—. Appointee Bd. Examiners Civil Service Personnel Colo., 1967—, mem. profl. growth and devel. com., 1967-69; past pres. Faculty Assn. Colo. State Coll. Recipient French Govt. prizes for excellence in coll. French lang. and lit., 1934, 38; univ. library rep. on Presdl. Selection Com., 1971. Mem. A.L.A., Assn. Coll. and Research Libraries, Colo., Mountain-Plains library assns., State Hist. Soc. Colo., Am. Assn. U. Women, Soroptimists, Pi Lambda Theta, Kappa Delta Pi, Delta Kappa Gamma, Phi Sigma Iota, Pi Beta Phi. Home: 2646 15th Av Ct Greeley CO 80631

COSTEN, SYLVIA ANN, journalist; b. Charlottesville, Va., Dec. 13, 1920; d. Rufus Joseph and Mary Elizabeth (Carter) Costen; A.B., Randolph-Macon Woman's Coll., 1941; M.S., Columbia Sch. Journalism, 1946. Instr. journalism Richmond (Va.) Profl. Inst. Evening Coll., 1948-60; woman's editor Richmond News Leader, 1947—. Mem. Va. Press Women, Club, Va. Writers Club, Nat. Fedn. Press Women. Mem. council Va. Mus. Fine Arts. Clubs: Hermitage Country; Washington Press; Nat. Press. Home: 7005 Park Av Richmond VA 23226 Office: 333 E Grace St Richmond VA 23291

COSTER, DORIS BAYER (MRS. DOUGLAS W. COSTER), coll. dean; b. Bklyn., Aug. 22, 1920; d. George H. and Clara C. (Rebscher) Bayer; A.B. (George Welwood Murray fellow), Barnard Coll., 1942; M.A., Columbia, 1949; m. Douglas W. Coster, Apr. 4, 1944 (dec.); children—Wendy, Peter, Michael, Rebecca. With U.S. govt., 1942-45; lectr. Am. govt., later dean students Mt. Vernon Coll., Washington, 1963-68; dean students Coll. of Wooster (O.), 1968—. Mem. Nat., Ohio assns. student personnel adminstrs., Nat., Ohio assns. women deans and counselors, Am. Assn. U. Women, Am. Assn. Higher Edn., Phi Beta Kappa. Home: 1452 Beall Av Wooster OH 44691

COTE, ALINE G., city ofcl.; b. Champlain, N.Y., Jan. 28, 1933; d. Gabriel A. and Christine (Bisaillon) C.; grad. high sch. From jr. typist to dep. city clk. City of Plattsburgh (N.Y.), 1951-72, clk., 1972—, dep. registrar vital records, 1965-72, registrar vital records, 1972—. Address: City Hall Plattsburgh NY 12901

COTE, MARY LOUISE, pediatrician; b. Springfield, Mass., 1929; M.D., Woman's Med. Coll. Pa., 1959. Intern Episcopal Hosp., Phila., 1959-60, dep. dir. pediatrics, 1964—; resident in pediatric pathology St. Christopher's Hosp. for Children, Phila., 1960-61, resident in pediatrics, 1961-63, chief resident, 1963-64, asst. attending pediatrician, 1964—; instr. pediatrics Women's Med. Coll., 1964-66, U. Cin., 1967-68; instr., then asst. prof. pediatrics Temple U., 1968—. Diplomate Am. Bd. Pediatrics. Address: 2600 N Lawrence St Philadelphia PA 19133

COTHERMAN, AUDREY CATHERINE MATHEWS, civic worker; b. St. Paul, 1930; d. Anthony Joseph and Nina (Harmon) Mathews; B.A., Hamline U., 1952; M.A., U. Wyo., 1974; m. Richard L. Cotherman, Dec. 30, 1950 (div.); children—Steven Robert, Michael Mathews, Bruce Richard, Gen Elizabeth. Dir. News Bur. Hamline U., St. Paul, 1952-53; dir. community club awards KTWO-Radio-TV, Casper, Wyo., 1967-69; communications coordinator Casper-Midwest Sch. Dist., 1969-70; exec. dir. United Fund Natrona County, 1971-72; exec. sec. Wyo. Council for Humanities, 1972—. Dir. League Women Voters St. Paul, 1956-57, pres., 1959; pres. Casper League Women Voters, 1965-67; pres. Wyo. League Women Voters, 1967-70; pres. P.T.A., 1957, 60, 62, 63, 65; pres. Natrona County Mental Health Assn., 1967-69; mem. Wyo. Gov.'s Edn. Council, 1967-70; mem. State Sch. Code Adv. Com., 1967-68. Precinct chmn., ward chmn., Republican party, del. state conv., 1958. Bd. dirs. Community Recreation Bd. Casper. Methodist. Home: 875 N 15th St Laramie WY 82070

COTSWORTH, DORCAS DUTROW (MRS. JOHN L. COTSWORTH), steel co. exec.; b. Phila., Oct. 13, 1917; d. Charles E. and Isabel W. (Wasbers) Dutrow; drama student Erskine Jr. Coll., 1936-38; m. John G. Berry, Feb. 8, 1941 (dec.); children—John Gaines, Dorcas Ann (Mrs. Calvin Comfort Beatty), C. Bruce, Hollace; m. 2d, John L. Cotsworth, June 24, 1964. Vice pres. Berry Steel Corp., Edison, N.J., 1960-62, chmn. bd., 1962—. Founder, pres. Dorcas, Inc., Bayhead, N.J., 1964; founder House Check Service, Short Hills and Bay Head, N.J.; dir. Ardmore Textured Metals. Mem. Jr. League. Clubs: Baltusrol Golf (Springfield, N.J.); Short Hills; Bay Head Yacht. Office: PO Box 327 Edison NJ 08817

COTTER, KATHARINE CECILIA, educator; b. New Bedford, Mass., Dec. 2, 1921; d. John James and Mary (Carlson) Cotter; B.S., Hyannis State Tchrs. Coll., 1943; M.Ed., Fordham U., 1945; Ph.D., 1951. English, social sci. tchr., Milford, Conn., 1943-44; asst. prin., Sagamore, Mass., 1945-48; faculty Fordham U., 1948-52; faculty Boston Coll., Chestnut Hill, Mass., 1952—, prof. elementary edn., 1967—, coordinator elementary edn., 1954-62, coordinator spl. edn., 1959-65, dir. div. curriculum and instrn., 1968-73. Geographic field study, Guadalajara, Mexico, 1969. Phi Delta Kappa internat. edn. research grantee, 1967. Mem. Assn. for Supervision and Curriculum Devel., Nat. Soc. Study Edn., Am. Ednl. Research Assn., Internat. Council Edn. Tchrs., Nat. Council for Social Studies, Mass. Council for Social Studies, Nat. Council Geog. Edn., Boston Coll. Faculty Assn. (pres. 1959-60). Contbr. articles to pubs., also monograph. Home: Osterville MA 02655 Office: Boston Coll Chestnut Hill MA 02167

COTTLE, BETTY LOWELL, anesthesiologist; b. St. Louis, 1925; M.D., N.Y.U., 1949. Intern Methodist Hosp., Bklyn., 1949-50, resident, 1950-51; resident Bklyn. VA Hosp., 1953-55; practice medicine, specializing in anesthesiology, Bklyn., 1955-71, Hollidaysburg, Pa., 1971—; dir. attending anethesiologist Peck Meml. Hosp., Bklyn., until 1971; asso. attending anesthesiologist Bklyn. Hosp., until 1971 dir. dept. anesthesiology Victory Meml. Hosp., Bklyn., until 1971; anesthesiologist Mercy Hosp., Altoona, Pa., 1971—, also dir. respiratory therapy, 1973—. Diplomate Am. Bd. Anesthesiology. Mem. Am. Soc. Anesthesiologists, Pa. (del. 1972), Blair County (sec. 1972—) med. socs. Address: 25 Sylvan Dr Hollidaysburg PA 16648

COTTLE, ELEANOR CRAY (MRS. EDGAR WILLIS COTTLE), lumber co. exec.; b. Quincy, Mass., Oct. 13, 1891; d. John D. and Mary Ann (Sullivan) Moriarty; student Boston U.; m. Edgar Willis Cottle, Jan. 17, 1929. Credit mgr. Quincy Lumber Co., 1924-28, pres., treas., 1944—; pres., treas. Rhines Lumber Co., Weymouth, Mass. Trustee Edgar W. Cottle Found., Boston. Home: The Crossways Harvard MA 01451 Office: 809 Massachusetts Av Boston MA 02118

COTTON, DOROTHY M., radio-TV exec.; b. Balt., July 9, 1920; d. Lawrence R. and Minnie (Gusdorff) Cotton; student U. Balt., 1937-39. Dir. women's programs sta. WIOD, Miami, Fla., 1942-44, Sta. WBAL, Balt. 1945-47; fashion copy chief Stewart & Co., Balt. 1949-53, Schliesner Co., Balt., 1953-54; dir. women's programs Sta. WHEC, Rochester, N.Y., 1954—, dir. publicity and promotion, 1956-65, asst. program mgr., 1966-68, writer, producer TV morning show, 1969—; vis. lectr. Coll. Bus., Rochester Inst. Tech., 1968—. Nutrition com. Rochester and Monroe County, 1958; bd. dirs. Family Service Rochester. Mem. Fashion Group, Inc., Rochester Community Players, Women's Advt. Club of Balt., Am. Women in Radio and Television (pres. Central N.Y. chpt. 1956-58, N.E. area v.p. 1964-66; trustee Ednl. Found. 1973—), Advt. Council Rochester, Women in Communications (Rochester Matrix award 1971). Club: Altrusa (pres. 1958-60, vocational information chmn. 2d dist. 1960-62) Home: 16 Sibley Pl Rochester NY 14607 Office: 191 East Av Rochester NY 14604

COTTON, F. JANE, charitable orgn. exec.; b. Jackson, Mich., May 28, 1928; d. Lee Roy and Hal (Wright) Cotton; A.A., Jackson Jr. Coll., 1946; B.A., Hofstra U., 1954; M.Ed., Springfield (Mass.) Coll., 1964. Enlisted as pvt. USAF, 1949, advanced through grades to lt. col., 1968, ret., 1970; guest lectr. psychology U. Philippines, 1958; tchr. English to Japanese profls. in Japan, 1968; youth dir. A.R.C., Washington, 1970—. Decorated Meritorious Service medal, Air Force Commendation medal. Mem. Nat. Council Children and Youth, Am. Assn. Secondary Sch. Prins., N.E.A. Unitarian. Office: 18th Between D and E Sts NW Washington DC 20006

COTY, EVA MARIE, savs. and loan exec.; b. Torrington, Conn., Feb. 3, 1907; d. Eugene and Georgianna (Gengras) Coty; student Bay Path Inst., 1925-26. Asst. sec.-asst. treas. Comml. Securities Corp., Torrington, 1941-45; mgr. First Fed. Savs. & Loan Assn., Torrington, 1945—, pres., 1968—, also dir. Corporator Charlotte Hungerford Hosp., 1969-73; mem. adv. council Cath. Family Services, 1973, Lark Industries, 1969-72; chmn. Torrington Beautification Com., 1969-73; mem. Mayor's Bldg. Com. for Civic Center, 1973. Bd. dirs. Community Chest, Girl Scouts U.S., Easter Seals - Crippled Children and Adults. Named Woman of Year, Quota Club, 1966. Club: Quota (Torrington). Home: 56 Orchard Rd Torrington CT 06790

COUCH, JANET ANN KORREY (MRS. MICHAEL ALLEN COUCH), occupational therapist; b. Sterling, Colo., Nov. 18, 1948; d. George and Minnie Emma (Abood) Korrey; student Northeastern Jr. Coll., 1966-67; B.S., Colo. State U., 1970; postgrad. U. Neb., 1970-71; m. Michael Allen Couch, Dec. 14, 1969. Staff occupational therapist C. Louis Meyers Children's Rehab. Inst., Omaha, 1970-71; dir. occupational therapy Immanuel Med. Center Phys. Medicine and Rehab., Omaha, 1971—. Asst. instr. dept. pediatrics U. Neb. Med. Sch., Omaha, 1970-71. Mem. Am. (task force to devel. standards of practice in phys. disabilities 1973-74), Neb. (sec. 1971-72) occupational therapy assns. Club: Creighton Dental Wives. Home: 814 Elwood Sterling CO 80751 Office: 1406 S 6th Av Sterling CO 80751

COUCH, SUSAN KULP (MRS. ANDREW GERARD COUCH), sales exec., TV sta. exec.; b. Pottstown, Pa., May 5, 1938; d. Harry Monroe and Bess Lurline (Weaver) Kulp; B.A., Wilson Coll., 1960; m. Andrew Gerard Couch, Oct. 13, 1962. Merchandising coordinator WCAU-TV, 1962-64; sales promotion mgr. WPIX, Inc., 1964-67; advt. mgr. WCBS-TV, 1967-69; dir. retail sales CBS TV Stas., 1969-71; v.p. broadcast advt. R. H. Macy, N.Y.C., 1971-73; gen. sales mgr. WXLO-FM, N.Y.C., 1973—. Mem. Nat. Retail Mchts. Assn., Radio Advt. Bur., Am. Women in Radio and TV, Internat. Radio and TV Soc., TV Bur. Adv. (Sales promotion steering com. 1969-71), Wilson Coll. Alumni Assn. (pres. N.Y./Conn. chpt. 1969-71). Home: 1 Forest Ct Larchmont NY 10538 Office: 1440 Broadway New York City NY 10018

COUDERT, JO, author; b. Williamsport, Pa., Mar. 14, 1923; d. John and Jane (Krouse) Coudert; student Smith Coll., 1940-43; m. Eugene H. Clay, Sept. 15, 1942 (div. Apr. 1948). Mng. editor Internat. Jour. of Group Psychotherapy, N.Y.C., 1960—. Author: I Never Cooked Before Cookbook, 1963; Advice From a Failure, 1965; The Alcoholic in Your Life, 1972; GoWell, 1974. Home: 372 Bleecker St New York City NY 10014 Office: Box 349 Rural Route 2 Califon NJ 07830

COUGHLIN, BETTY MARIE, librarian; b. Davenport, Ia.; d. Thomas A. and Monica Ann (Kerrigan) Coughlin; B.S., Marycrest Coll., 1944; M.S., Western Res. U., 1952. Head extension dept. Davenport Pub. Library, 1947-54, asst. reference librarian, 1954-58, head reference dept., 1958—. Active Mercy Hosp. Aux. Mem. A.L.A. (councilor 1970-72), Ia. Library Assn. (sec. 1960-62), Beta Phi Mu. Home: 20 McClellan Blvd Davenport IA 52803 Office: 321 Main St Davenport IA 52801

COUGHLIN, VIOLET LOUISE, ednl. adminstr.; b. Montreal, Que., Can.; d. Sydney and May Elizabeth (Gregory) Hulin; B.Sc., McGill U., 1928, B.L.S., 1938; M.A., Columbia, 1958, D.L.S., 1966; m. Errol Bernard Coughlin, June 27, 1936; 1 son, Robert. Tchr. chemistry high sch., Montreal, 1929-36; technician Royal Victoria Hosp., Montreal, 1928-29; cataloguer Redpath Library McGill U., Montreal, 1941; librarian Royal Victoria Coll., McGill U., 1941-51, mem. faculty Grad. Sch. Library Sci., 1951—, prof., 1969—, dir., 1971-72; vis. prof. library sci. U. Pitts., 1966-67, U. Hawaii, summers 1968, 70. Canada Council fellow, 1958-59; Miriam Tompkins scholar,

Columbia, 1958-59. Mem. Am. Assn. Library Schs. (sec.-treas. 1970—), A.L.A. (past sec. bd. library edn. div.), Canadian Library Assn., Que. Library Assn. (pres. 1954-55), Beta Phi Mu. Home: 3800 Wilson Av Montreal 260 PQ H4A 2T8 Canada

COUKOS, PATRICIA B., educator; b. Weirton, W.Va.; d. Angelo and Mary (Karnis) Bakos; student Duke, summer 1941; B.A., West Liberty State Coll., 1943; M.S. in Edn., U. Richmond, 1966; postgrad Mary Baldwin Coll., 1948; certificate Advanced Studies, Coll. William and Mary, 1973; m. John L. Coukos, Feb. 6, 1944; children—Luke J., Louise Marie. Tchr., Weirton Elementary Sch., 1940-45, supr., 1942-43, Hancock County Schs., Weirton, Richmond, Va., 1956-64; elementary sch. counselor William Fox Elementary Sch., Richmond, 1966-68; coordinator elementary guidance Richmond Pub. Schs., 1968-72, specialist in developmental guidance, 1973—, instr. parent effectiveness tng., 1973—; vis. lectr. elementary guidance U. Richmond, summer 1969-70. Sec., Greek Ladies Philoptohos Soc., 1952-56, v.p., 1957-64. Recipient medal for Unselfish Service, 1938; Danforth Found. award, 1940. Mem. Am. Assn. U. Women (edn. co-chmn. 1966, area br. rep. in edn. 1971-73), Nat., Va., Richmond edn. assns., Am. Sch. Counselor Assn., Am., Va. (com. on by-laws 1969—, ethics chmn. on exec. bd. 1971-72, Career Service award 1972, (pres. Richmond 1973-74) personnel and guidance assns., Commn. on Elementary Guidance Study, Friends Library, Assn. Suprs. and Dirs., Va. Mus. Fine Arts, Assn. Counselor Edn. and Supervision, Nat., Va. vocational guidance assns., Va. Elementary Sch. Counselors Assn., Alpha Delta Kappa, Kappa Delta Pi. Club: Willow Oaks Country (Richmond). Mem. Greek Orthodox Ch. (supt. Sunday sch. 1950—). Home: 2820 Westchester Rd Richmond VA 23225 Office: 312 N 9th St Richmond VA 23219

COULIHAN, LUCILLE GENEVIEVE ZIENER (MRS. JAMES JOSEPH COULIHAN), social worker; b. Rockford, Ill., Aug. 19, 1914; d. Nicholas and Louise Marie (Schoknecht) Ziener; A.B. (Univ. scholar), Rosary Coll., 1936; postgrad. Nat. Cath. Sch. Social Work, 1941; m. James Joseph Coulihan, Dec. 29, 1951 (dec. 1972); 1 dau., Kathleen Louise. With USO Nat. Catholic Community Service, Rockford, Ill., 1941-43, St. John's, Nfld., 1943-44, St. Lucia, B.W.I., 1944-45, Guyana, S. Am., 1945-46; with Alma Savage Lecture Platform, N.Y.C., 1952-53; tng. dir. Girl Scout Council of Greater N.Y., N.Y.C., 1952-53, 63-69, mem. wider opportunities com., 1972-74; Cath. Youth Orgn.-Girl Scouts supr. Cath. Charities Diocese of Bklyn., 1969—. Named Woman of the Year, Avon Products Inc., 1957, 58, 59; scholarship N.Y. Sch. Social Work, 1952-53. Mem. Nat. Council Cath. Women (family affairs chmn. 1972-74, pres.), Nat. Council of Christians and Jews (mem. Dolls for Democracy program 1972-74), Kappa Gamma Pi. Roman Catholic (mem. parish council 1972-74). Home: 51-01 39th Av Long Island City NY 11104 Office: 191 Joralemon St Brooklyn NY 11201

COULSON, ZOE ELIZABETH, mag. editor; b. Sullivan, Ind., Sept. 22, 1932; d. M. Allan and Mary (Thompson) Coulson; B.S., Purdue U., 1954. Asso. dir. home econs. Am. Meat Inst., Chgo., 1954-57; account rep. pub. relations dept. J. Walter Thompson Co., Chgo., 1957-60; dir. home econs. Leo Burnett Co., advt. Chgo., 1960-64; editorial dir. What's New In Home Econs., N.Y.C., 1964-68; food editor Good Housekeeping mag., N.Y.C., 1968—; editor Good Housekeeping Cookbook, 1973. Recipient Distinguished Alumni award Purdue U. Sch. Home Econs., 1971, named Old Master, 1972. Mem. Am. Home Econs. Assn., Kappa Alpha Theta, Theta Sigma Phi. Republican. Presbyn. Home: 315 E 72d St New York City NY 10021 Office: 959 8th Av New York City NY 10019

COULTAS, ELIZABETH L. (MRS. E.C. STOCKMAN), physician; b. Madison, N.J., May 7, 1922; d. Aldo Bliss and Annabelle (Miller) Coultas; A.B., Goucher Coll., 1944; M.D., U. Md., 1947; m. John C. Stockman, Sept. 15, 1953 (div.); children—John, Peter, Ann. Intern Woman's Med. Coll. Hosp., Phila., 1947-48; resident N.Y. Infirmary, N.Y.C., Aultman Hosp. Canton, 1948-51; practice medicine specializing in obstetrics and gynecology; mem. staff Morristown Meml. Hosp. Mem. Harding Township Bd. Edn. Diplomate Am. Bd. Obstetrics and Gynecology. Mem. Bus. and Profl. Women, D.A.R. Home: Tempe Wick Rd Morristown NJ 07960 Office: 151 Madison Av Morristown NJ 07960

COULTER, ELIZABETH JACKSON (MRS. N. A. COULTER, JR.), biostatistician, economist; b. Balt., Nov. 2, 1919; d. Waddie Pennington and Bessie (Gills) Jackson; A.B., Swarthmore Coll., 1941; A.M., Radcliffe Coll., 1946, Ph.D., 1948; m. Norman Arthur Coulter, Jr., June 23, 1951; 1 son, Robert Jackson. Asst. dir. health study Bur. Labor Statistics, San Juan, P.R., 1946; research asst. Milbank Meml. Fund, N.Y.C., 1948-51; economist Office Def. Prodn., 1951-52; research analyst Children's Bur., U.S. Dept. Health, Edn. and Welfare, 1952-53; statistician Ohio Dept. Health, 1954-55, chief statistician, 1955-65; asst. clin. prof. biostatistics U. Pitts., Grad. Sch. Pub. Health 1958-62; lectr. econs. Ohio State U., 1954-55, clin. asst. prof. preventive medicine, 1963-65; asso. prof. biostatistics Sch. Pub. Health, U. N.C. at Chapel Hill, 1965-72, prof. biostatistics, 1972—, also asso. prof. econs. U. N.C., 1965—; adj. asso. prof. hosp. adminstrn. Duke U., 1972—. Fellow Am. Pub. Health Assn. (mem. governing council 1970-72); mem. Am. Statis. Assn., Am. Acad. Polit. Social Sci., Am. Econ. Assn., Biometric Soc., A.A.A.S., Am. Sociol. Assn., Delta Omega. Methodist. Author, co-author book revs., profl. articles. Home: 1825 N Lake Shore Dr Chapel Hill NC 27514

COUNCILMAN, ELIZABETH (MRS. HOWARD W. ROGERS), physician; b. Marion, Mass., Aug. 25, 1899; d. William Thomas and Isabella (Coolidge) Councilman; student Radcliffe Coll., 1920-22; M.D., Columbia, 1930; m. Howard W. Rogers, Feb. 10, 1933; children—Henry H., William C. Intern, Presbyn. Hosp., N.Y.C., 1931-33; practice medicine, specializing in family practice, Newburyport, Mass., 1934—; mem. staff Anna Jacques Hosp.; sch. physician Town of Newbury, Mass., 1940—, Town of West Newbury, 1959-73, Town of Salisbury, 1949-72. Mem. Newburyport Sch. Bd., 1940-42. Club: Oldtown Country (Newbury). Address: 83 High St Newburyport MA 01950

COUNTEE, SANDRA FLOWERS, occupational therapist; b. Oklahoma City, Okla., Feb. 15, 1943; d. LeRoy and Minnie Ola (Hawthorn) Flowers; B.S. in Occupational Therapy, U. Kan., 1965; postgrad. Columbia Sch. Social Work, 1972—; div. Staff occupational therapist D.C. Gen. Hosp-Community Mental Health Center, Washington, 1965-68; supr. occupational therapy Harlem Hosp. Center, N.Y.C., 1968—. Mem. Am. Occupational Therapy Assn., Am. Pub. Health Assn. Contbr. articles to profl. jours. Home: 2420 Sedgwick Av Bronx NY 10468 Office: Harlem Hosp Center 135th at Lenox Av New York City NY 10037

COUNTER, MARJORIE LOIS LITTLE (MRS. BENJAMIN COUNTER), librarian; b. Clarks, Neb., July 6, 1911; d. Lowell and Daisy (Harger) Little; B.A., Colo. State U., 1933, postgrad., 1960; postgrad. U. No. Colo., 1958-59, Kan. State U., 1963, Denver U., 1963-65, West State Coll., Gunnison, Colo., 1966, 68, U. Wyo., 1970-72; m. Benjamin Frink Counter, June 24, 1934; children—Ann Marguerite (Mrs. Bradner Allen Tate), Benjamin Tucker, James Dana, Karna Kristine Wells. Tchr. Ft. Lupton (Colo.) High Sch., 1959—, librarian Media Center, 1961—, head ednl. materials center, 1961—. Mem. N.E.A., Colo. Edn. Assn., Colo. Assn. Sch. Libraries, Colo. Assn. Audio-Visual, P.E.O. Sisterhood (pres. 1951-52), Ft. Lupton Edn. Assn. (pres. 1962), Delta Delta Delta (life), Upsilon Delta Omicron (life). Home: 208 Fort Lupton CO 80621 Office: 201 S McKinley St Fort Lupton CO 80621

COUPER, MILDRED COOPER, composer; b. Buenos Aires, Argentina; d. Reginald and Harriet (Hathaway) Couper; student Williams Conservatory Music, Buenos Aires, 1900-02, Karlsruhe Conservatory Music, Germany, 1902-06; m. Richard Hamilton Couper, Aug. 27, 1910 (dec. 1918); children—Clive R.H., Rosalind (Mrs. Ernest Nordli). Tchr. piano Mannes Music Sch., N.Y.C., 1918-27; co-founder Music Acad. West, Santa Barbara, Cal., 1946, tchr. theory, harmony, piano. Composer: We Are Seven, 1926; Seven More, 1942, Dirge in 1/4 tones, 1937; Variations on the Irish Washerwoman, 1945; Barnyard Cogitations, 1939; Fur and Feathers, 1940; Sea-Drift Cycle, 1965, Intro. and Scherzo for String Quartet, 1967; The Nine Muses, piano suite, 1968. Address: 3010 Foothill Rd Santa Barbara CA 93105

COUPLIN, MARIE CORRINE FRANKLYN (MRS. JAMES R. COUPLIN), hotel exec.; b. Chgo.; d. Ralph K. and Rose K. (Rood) Franklyn; student U. Ill., 1928-30; m. James R. Couplin, Aug. 3, 1936. Chief billing dept. Glasco Products, Inc., Chgo., 1944-60; partner, mgr. Hotel Douglas, Elgin, Ill., 1960-74, sec., dir. Douglas Tap Corp., 1960-74. Mem. Elgin Assn. Commerce, Geneal. Soc. N.J., Nat. Geneal. Soc., Conn. Soc. Genealogists, Am., Ill. motel assns., Animal Welfare Inst. N.Y., Humane Soc. North Central Ill., Am. Legion Aux., Humane Soc. U.S. Republican. Unitarian. Home: 1170 Dundee Av Elgin IL 60120 Office: PO Box 345 Elgin IL 60120

COURAIN, MARGARET EILEEN, pharm. co. exec.; b. Bayonne, N.J., Nov. 23, 1927; d. Joseph F. and Ellen M. (Murphy) Courain; B.S., Douglass Coll., 1948; M.S., Columbia, 1955. Research asst. Douglass Coll., New Brunswick, N.J., 1946-48; research records coordinator Merck Sharp & Dohme Research Labs., Rahway, N.J., 1948-53, supr. research information, 1953-61, sect. head research information, 1961-66, mgr. research information, 1966-70, mgr. research information systems, 1970—. Resource lectr. information sci. Pratt Inst., 1969-72, curriculum cons., 1973. Mem. Landscape Design Appraisers Council N.J., 1963—. Mem. Drug Information Assn. (dir. 1972-75, v.p. Am. Soc. Information Sci. (sec. 1960-63, rep. nat. council 1964-65), Phi Beta Mu. Clubs: Maplewood (N.J.) Garden; Westfield (N.J.) Tennis; Short Hills Ski (Springfield, N.J.); Watchung Tennis (Chatham, N.J.). Contbr. articles to profl. jours. Home: 420 Harding Dr South Orange NJ 07079 Office: Merck Sharp & Dohme Research Labs div Merck & Co Inc Rahway NJ 07065

COURTNER, DEBORAH JO, editor; b. Topeka, Kan., Apr. 4, 1949; d. Forest and Eva Louise (Grigsby) Courtner; B.S. in Journalism magna cum laude, Kan. State U., 1971. Newspaper intern Topeka (Kan.) Capital Jour., 1970, Garden City (Kan.) Telegram, 1971; editor KPL Service Mag., Kan. Power & Light Co., Topeka, 1971-73; editor Telephone Times, Southwestern Bell Telephone Co., Topeka, 1973—. Violinist Topeka Civic Symphony, 1971-73. Mem. Topeka (pres. 1973-74), Kan. (writing contest awards 1971, 73) press women Nat. Fedn. Press Women, Women in Communications (conf. planning chmn. region 7 1973). Home: Apt 105 2318 Briarwood Plaza S Topeka KS 66611 Office: 220 E 6th St Topeka KS 66603

COUSSENS, NADINE ALICE SCHORMANN (MRS. GEORGE FRANK COUSSENS), home economist; b. Effingham, Ill., Sept. 16, 1944; d. Arthur John and Mathilda Pauline (Zimdars) Schormann; B.S., Eastern Ill. U., 1966; m. George Frank Coussens, May 18, 1969; 1 dau., Sheila Ruth. Asst. extension adviser, Whiteside County, 1966-68, asso. extension adviser, 1968-70; extension adviser Fulton County, Lewistown, Ill., 1970—. Mem. Am., Ill. home econs. assns., Nat., Ill. assns. extension home economists, Gamma Sigma Delta. Home: Route 1 Ellisville IL 61431 Office: Box 68 Lewistown IL 61542

COVAL, NAOMI MILLER, orthodontist; b. Bayonne, N.J.; d. Jacob Paul and Bertha (Blumstein) Miller; student U. Chgo., 1931-35; B.A., N.Y.U., 1939; D.D.S., Columbia U., 1943. Children—Ilya Sandra, Payson Rodney, Mark Lawrence. Private practice dentistry, specializing in orthodontics, N.Y.C., 1943-44, Bklyn., 1944-59, Lawrence, N.Y., 1959—. Postgrad. lectr. Pam-Am. Med. Assn., 1960; lectr. to profl. groups throughout world, 1947—; mem. staff Peninsula Gen. Hosp., Queens, N.Y.; attending dentist N.Y. Infirmary, N.Y.C., 1946-50, Peninsula Hosp. Center, 1967—; instr. N.Y.U., N.Y.C., 1948-49; vis. lectr. orthodontics, various S. Am., European, Asian and Australian univs., 1969—. Chairlady L.I. Com. for Fluoridation Water; del. Oral Hygiene Com., 1948-51; lectr. to Women's Clubs on Worldwide anthrop. and archaeol. tours. Active P.T.A., 1948—, pres. Lawrence High Sch. P.T.A., 1966-67; leader Girl Scouts U.S.A., 1950-58; group leader Jane Addams' Hull House, Chgo., 1933—; charter patron, sponsor Island Concert Hall; pres. Five Towns Aux. Penninsula Gen. Hosp., 1964-66; v.p. B'nai B'rith, Nat. Council Jewish Women; pres. Pulse of Women, 1971. Bd. dirs. Am. Cancer Soc., Lawrence (chmn. art show); chpt. pres. Am. Jewish Congress, 1968-72, del. nat. conv., 1970. Fellow Soc. for Oral Physiology and Occlusion; mem. Fedn. Dentaire Internat. (lectr. Rome 1957, Tel Aviv 1966, Australia 1973), Acad. Dental Medicine, Internat. Acad. Orthodontics (v.p. 62-66, sec.), Fedn. Am. Orthodontists (charter), A.A.A.S., Am. Acad. Oral Medicine, Internat. Platform Assn. (charter), UN Assn. U.S.A., Fellowship Reconciliation, Nat. Geog. Soc., Am. Mus. Natural History, Am. Dental Assn., Tenth Dist., Rockaway dental socs., Nassau-Suffolk Acad. Dentistry, Am., Brit. socs. for study orthodontics, Pan-Am. Med. Assn., Nat. Assn. Women Dentists, William Jarvie Soc. for Dental Research, N.Y. Assn. Women Dentists (editor Dentistae 1948, v.p. 1962-66), Am. Assn. Dental Editors (only woman dentist elected to assn.), N.Y. State Assn. for Professions (charter), Am. Soc. for Preventive Dentistry, Columbia Dental Alumni Assn., Nat. Women's Polit. Caucus (charter; mem. bd.), Nat. Orgn. Women, Am. Assn. for Study Psychoanalysis, Am. Red Mogen David Soc., Met. Opera Guild, Lawrence Assn., Rapa-Nui Soc. for Easter Islanders, Wildlife Soc. Kenya, Am. Field Service, Club: Wayfarers. Editor, Internat. Jour. Orthodontics, 1962-66, Internat. Acad. Orthodontics, 1961. First women dentist invited to lecture in Bucharest, 1971; 1st woman elected by organized dentistry to be on TV, 1964. Developed technique for repositioning the mandible; research on thyroidectomies in rat; designed and exhibited original gold jewelry executed from dental materials. Contbr. articles to dental jours. Address: 30 Westover Pl Lawrence NY 11559

COVEL, BETSEY BORDEN, librarian; b. Boston, Aug. 4, 1942; d. Peter and Sally Severence (Scudder) Covel; A.B., Hood Coll., 1964; postgrad. No. Ariz. U., spring, 1965, 66, U. Ariz., summer 1965, U. Cal. at Los Angeles, summer 1966, U. Cal. at Riverside, 1965, 70; M.S. in L.S., Cath. U. Am., 1972. Tchr. English and reading, pub. schs., Tuba City, Ariz., 1964-66; tchr. English and reading, librarian pub. schs., Thermal, Cal., 1966-70; asst. librarian Med. Library, Children's Hosp., Washington, 1970—. Leader, DeAnza council Girl Scouts U.S.A., 1968-70. Mem. N.E.A., A.L.A., Spl. Libraries Assn., Cal. Assn. Sch. Librarians. Home: 9260 Piney Branch Rd 201 Silver Spring MD 20903 Office: Children's Hospital Washington DC 20009

COVER, MARY LEYMAN (MRS. JOHN H. COVER), artist; b. nr. Makow, Poland, July 25, 1906; d. Wojciech and Jozefa (Roszkiewicz) Lejmanski; student Corcoran Sch. Art, Cleve. Sch. Art; m. John H. Cover, Dec. 16, 1938. With East Asiatic Co. of Copenhagen in Warsaw, 1923-25; stenographer, translator Am. Consulate Gen., Warsaw, 1925-28; sec. with Flint Structural Steel Co., 1928-29, W.S. Tyler Co., Cleve., 1929-31; asst. to comml. counsellor Polish embassy, Washington, 1931-35; personnel officer econ. research project U. Chgo., 1936-37; co-founder Artist Mart, Washington, 1951-68; exhibited one man shows Artists Mart Gallery, 1960, 67; exhibited in group shows at Cleve. Art Inst., Potter & Mellen, Ten Thirty Gallery, Cleve., Corcoran Gallery, Mus. Natural History, Nat. Collection Fine Arts, Artists Coop., Washington, Antioch Theatre, Oten Gallery, Yellow Springs, O., Springfield (O.) Art Center; paintings, sculpture pvt. collections. Recipient 1st hon. mention, 2d prize in sculpture Corcoran Sch. Art, 1950, 51, 2d prize in sculpture Soc. Washington Artists, 1959. Mem. Soc. Washington Artists (corr. sec. 1958, v.p. 1959, pres. 1960, chmn. bd. 1961). Address: 211 Fairfield Pike Yellow Springs OH 45387

COVET, SYLVIA SOPHIA, editor; b. Superior, Wis.; d. Oscar and Sarah (Lewenstein) Covet; B.A., U. Wis., 1938. Patent agt. Universal Oil Products Co., Chgo., 1939-44; continuity writer radio sta. WEBC, Duluth, Minn., 1945-46; exec. editor Postgrad. Medicine, Mpls., 1946-71; editorial dir. Modern Medicine Publs., 1971-72; now nat. editor Med. Opinion, Mpls. Mem. Mpls. Art Inst., Walker Art Center, Mpls. Recipient Neal award Am. Bus. Press Assn., N.Y.C., 1969. Fellow Am. Med. Writers Assn. (dir. 1966-68); mem. Council Biol. Editors, Women in Communications, Nat. Assn. Sci. Writers (dir. 1967-68). Clubs: Minnesota Press University. Office: care Med Opinion Suite 209 5050 Excelsior Blvd Minneapolis MN 55416

COVEY, CAROL BETH, banker; b. Lubbock, Tex., Apr. 1, 1939; d. Foy Wallace and Letha Beatrice (Dumas) Covey; B.B.A., Tex. Technol. Coll., 1960. With Lubbock Nat. Bank, 1960—, v.p., 1974—; asst. v.p. W. Central Investment Corp., Lubbock, 1974—. Flight instr. Wes-Tex Aircraft Comml. Inst. Mem. Nat. Assn. Bank Women, Ninety-Nines. Democrat. Mem. Ch. of Christ. Home: Rural Route 2 Box 315 Lubbock TX 79415 Office: 916 Main St Lubbock TX 79401

COVEY, SUSAN COWLES (MRS. STEPHEN GOULD COVEY), broadcasting exec.; b. Watsonville, Cal., Nov. 30, 1947; d. Omar Horace and Betty Lou (Sauer) Cowles; B.A., U. Cal. at Santa Barbara, 1969; m. Stephen Gould Covey, June 17, 1972. Media dir., publicity dir. Braverman-Mirisch, Inc., advt., Los Angeles, 1970-72; media dir. Patrick Andrews Advt., San Jose, 1972-73; sales systems coordinator/analyst KLOK Radio, San Jose, 1973; operations mgr. KPEN-FM Radio, Los Altos, Cal., 1973—. Home: 1062 Morse St San Jose CA 95126 Office: 2550 El Camino Real Mountain View CA

COVINGTON, CONSTANCE JOAN (MRS. WILLIAM C. DALLMANN), physician; b. Miles City, Mont., Aug. 13, 1936; d. Elbert Gorton and Juliana Clara (Richter) Covington; student Chico State Coll., 1953-54; A.B., U. Cal. at Berkeley, 1957; M.D., U. Cal. at San Francisco, 1960; m. William C. Dallmann, June 12, 1960; children—Shane Morgan Alan Nathanael, Lara Catherine. Intern, U. Cal.-Children's Hosp., San Francisco, 1960-61, resident pediatrics, 1961-63; asst. dir. pediatric outpatient clinic San Francisco Presbyn. Hosp., 1963-64; asst. dir. Valparaiso (Ind.) U. Student Health Service, 1964-72; practice medicine, specializing in pediatrics, Valparaiso, Ind., 1970—; mem. staff Porter Meml. Hosp., Valparaiso. Bd. dirs. Porter County Guidance Clinic, 1971-72. Mem. Porter County Med. Soc. Lutheran. Home: 1905 Rock Castle Park Dr Valparaiso IN 46383 Office: 1101 E Glendale St Valparaiso IN 46383

COVINO, SYLVIA ANGELA DE FINE (MRS. CHARLES P. COVINO), indsl. engring. and research co. exec.; b. Bklyn., July 19, 1922; d. Joseph D. and Teresa (Renna) De Fine; B.A., St. Joseph's Coll. for Women, 1944; M.A., Columbia, 1946; m. Charles P. Covino, Dec. 28, 1947; 1 dau., Candida Marie. Asst. prof. psychology Bard Coll., Annondale-on-the-Hudson, Hudson, N.Y., 1946-48, inaugurator in-tng. program Nursery Sch., 1946-48; tchr. N.Y.C. Pub. Sch. System, 1945-46, N.J. Pub. Schs., 1949-58; sr. partner Gen. Magnaplate Corp., Linden, N.J., 1957-59, v.p., treas., 1959—; v.p. Tufram, Inc., 1964—; v.p., dir. Magna-Cook Corp. Am., 1964—; sec.-treas. Exec. Air Charter, Montclair, also Linden, N.J. Singer local charity affairs, also directing shows. Mem. Womens Aux. Columbus Hosp., Newark; troop leader Brownie Scouts, Upper Montclair, N.J.; dir. Montclair (N.J.) Pre-Sch. P.T.A., 1955-57; mem. Overseas Neighbors, Montclair. Vice pres. Theoretical Research Inst. Advanced Design. Lyric-soprano scholar Met. N.Y. Studios, 1943-46. Mem. St. Joseph's Coll. Alumnae Assn. Club: Cosmopolitan (Montclair). Address: 31 Woodmont Rd Upper Montclair NJ 07043

COWAN, CHARITY ALLENE, educator; b. Lancaster, Ky., Oct. 1, 1924; d. John Theo and Julia Mae (Stevens) Cowan; B.S., Eastern Ky. U., 1946; M.A., U. Ky., 1952; postgrad. U. Ky., 1959-60. Grade Sch. tchr. Locust Street Sch., Erlanger, Ky., 1946-58; gen. supr. Erlanger-Elsmere Bd. Edn., 1958—. Mem. Assn. Childhood Edn. (state sec. 1956-58, chpt. pres. 1968-70), N.E.A. (life mem., br. pres. 1967-68), Eastern State U. Alumni Assn. (life), U. Ky. Alumni Assn. (life), Ky. Edn. Assn., Assn. for Childhood Edn. (life), Ky. Assn. for Ednl. Suprs., Assn. for Supervision and Curriculum, Am. Assn. U. Women (v.p. 1964-66; program chmn. 1964-66), Ky. P.T.A. (life), Ind. Order Foresters, Ky. Assn. Sch. Adminstrs., Kappa Delta Pi, Delta Kappa Gamma (pres. Zeta chpt. 1974—). Baptist (sec. chmn. kindergarten 1964—). Home: 440 B Graves Av Erlanger KY 41018 Office: 39 Erlanger Rd Erlanger KY 41018

COWAN, HAZEL WITHERELL DAMON (MRS. ROBERT G. COWAN), civic worker; b. Rockland, Mass.; d. Everett Stanwood and Mabel (Hobart) Damon; A.B., Jackson Coll. of Tufts U., 1926; m. Robert G. Cowan, May 29, 1930. Mem. exec. com. The Woman's Assn. Morristown Meml. Hosp., 1946—, pres., 1950-54, trustee hosp., 1946—, mem. com. of mgrs., 1955-70; mem. Jr. League Morristown, pres., 1943-45. Club: Garden (pres. 1958-60) (Somerset Hills). Home: Boxwood Hollow Bernardsville NJ 07924

COWAN, LOIS L. GOLDMAN (MRS. MARVIN S. COWAN), educator; b. Miami, Fla., Jan. 7, 1924; d. Nathan and Ida (Fine) Goldman; B.A., Wesleyan Coll., Macon, Ga., 1945; M.A., Columbia Tchrs. Coll., 1946, postgrad., 1950-51; postgrad. U. Fla., 1946, Harvard, 1948; m. Marvin S. Cowan, Nov. 24, 1949; children—Hillery Dee, Beryl Ann, Candiss Lynn. Mem. deans' staff Fla. State U., Tallahassee, 1946, instr. sociology and psychology, 1946-49; asst. dean students Bronx campus Hunter Coll. City of N.Y., 1950-52. Vice pres. Edgemont Scholarship Council, 1973-74. Mem. Edgemont Sch. Dist. Bd. Edn., Scarsdale, N.Y., 1967-73, v.p., 1970, 71, pres., 1972-73. Bd. dirs. Edgemont Community Com. on Edn., 1961-67, chmn., 1965-67; bd. dirs. Internat. Student Exchange Club, Edgemont, 1970—, co-pres., 1974-75; bd. dirs. Greensburgh Narcotics Guidance Council, 1974—, Mental Health Assn. Westchester County. Mem. Nat. Assn. Women Deans and Counselors, League Women Voters, Alpha Kappa Delta. Club: Scarsdale Woman's Home: 4 Leone Close Scarsdale NY 10583

COWAN, PAULINE MADELONE SPIEGEL (MRS. LOUIS G. COWAN), civic leader; b. Chgo., Apr. 10, 1913; d. Modie J. and Lena (Straus) Spiegel; B.A., Sarah Lawrence Coll., 1936; m. Louis G. Cowan, Aug. 7, 1939; children—Paul, Geoff, Holly, Liza. Producer radio program Conversation, 1954-57, radio program Of Many Things, 1956; creator, producer TV show Down You Go, 1950-56; book club rep. Contemporary Affairs Soc., 1962-64, Co-chmn. WMCA; Call for Action, Nat. Council Negro Women, 1963-65, chmn. Wednesday in Miss., 1964-67, chmn. Workshops in Miss., 1967—, mem. exec. bd. orgns., 1965—; mem. exec. bd. Citizens Com. for Children of N.Y., 1966-70. Bd. overseers Brandeis U. Center for Study Violence, 1967-73; mem. adv. com. Eagleton Inst. Women in Politics, chmn., 1971—; v.p. Cowan Found., 1952—. Recipient George Peabody Broadcasting award, Kappa Mu award. Mem. Delta Sigma Theta (hon.). Home: Hotel Westbury Madison Av at 69th St New York City NY 10021 Office: 147 E 81st St New York City NY 10028

COWAN, PERSIS HAMILTON, educator; b. Mt. Home, Ida., Sept. 22, 1909; d. Dean Stuart and Pearl (Lucas) Hamilton; B.A., U. Redlands, 1931; M.A., U. So. Cal., 1941; Ed.D., Stanford, 1956; m. A. William Cowan, June 14, 1942 (div. June 1956). Teaching prin. Bardsdale Elementary Sch., Fillmore, Cal., 1931-37; tchr. Ventura (Cal.) Jr. High Sch., 1937-38; supr., dir. rural edn. Ventura County (Cal.), 1938-41; curriculum cons. Los Angeles County (Cal.), 1941-44; primary supr., San Mateo (Cal.) City Schs., 1944-45; asst. curriculum dir. Alameda County (Cal.), 1945-48; chmn. edn. dept. Mills Coll., 1948-52; dir. curriculum Marin County Schs., 1952-54; fellow Stanford, 1954-56; asst. prof. edn. Los Angeles State Coll., 1956-59, asso. prof. edn., 1959-65; prof. edn. Cal. State U. at Los Angeles, 1956-74, asso. coordinator child devel. program, 1970-74; edn. adminstr. Center for Early Edn., Los Angeles, 1974—. Pres. Cal. Coll. and U. Assn., 1965-67. Mem. Pasadena Community Planning Council-Health, 1967—; chmn. edn. com., trustee Center for Early Edn., Coll. and Children's Sch., 1968—. Mem. Am. Assn. U. Women (v.p. Pasadena br., 1963-64, pres. Pasadena br. 1964-66, area rep. edn. Cal. div. 1965-66), Assn. Childhood Edn. (adviser student br. Cal. State Coll., Los Angeles 1959-65), Internat. Assn. for Childhood Edn. (tchr. edn. com. 1963-65, internat. cons. kindergarten edn. 1967-69), N.E.A., Cal. Tchrs. Assn., Los Angeles State Coll. Faculty Women (pres. 1962-63), Council Women's Clubs (mem. bd.), P.E.O. (pres. San Marino-South Pasadena reciprocity 1973-74), Delta Kappa Gamma (pres. Cal. 1950-53), Delta Phi Upsilon (nat. pres. 1960-66, adviser Kappa chpt. 1962-66), Pi Lambda Theta. Club: Women's City of Pasadena (v.p. for program 1971—). Office: 563 N Alfred St Los Angeles CA 90048

COWAN, TRUDI BERGER (MRS. GEORGE COWAN), newspaper editor; b. N.Y.C., May 29, 1925; d. William and Ida S. (Kaufman) Berger; student Art Students League N.Y., 1943-44, Columbia, 1944-45; m. George Cowan, June 10, 1950; children—Stephen Scott, Jill Ellen. Staff art dept. N.Y. Times, 1943-50, free-lance writer feature articles, art illustrator, 1950—; editor, editorial cartoonist weekly newspaper, Bellmore (N.Y.) Life, 1964—. Mem. North Bellmore Library Bd., 1963-66; pres. Friends of North Bellmore Library, 1961-62; chmn. Bellmore-Merrick Adult Edn. Adv. Com., 1963—; hon. chmn. Cancer Care Fund Drive, Bellmore, 1972-73; mem. nominating com., chmn. fund drive Girl Scouts U.S.A., Bellmore, 1972-74. Life mem. N.Y. State P.T.A., Another Mother for Peace. Recipient 1st prize for cartoon of yr. N.Y. State Press Assn., 1970. 1st prize for service to edn., 1967; award N.Y. State Bar Assn., 1972. Mem. Bellmores Hist. Soc. (pres. 1974). Home: 16 Silver Birch Rd Merrick NY 11566 Office: 2717 Grand Av Bellmore NY 11710

COWART, MAROLYN MAURINE (MRS. WILLIAM RUSSELL), physician; b. Alma, Ark., Feb. 17, 1926; d. William Troy and Lucille (Milligan) Cowart; student Jefferson Davis Hosp. Sch. Nursing, 1944-46, U. Houston, 1948-52; M.D., U. Tex., 1956; m. William Ogburn Russell, Dec. 23, 1959; children—Lucy, Ellen Lark, William Ogburn III. Intern Jefferson Davis Hosp., Houston, 1956-57; attending staff Rosewood Gen. Hosp., Houston, 1966—, dir. gen. practice sect., 1967-73; courtesy staff Hermann, Meml. Bapt., Meth., Spring Br. Meml., St. Joseph's, St. Luke's Episcopal, Tex. Children's hosps.; lectr. in medicine U. Tex. Grad. Sch. Biomed. Scis. Houston, 1970; dir. family practice residency program Baylor Coll., Medicine, 1973—. Cons. cancer detection in gen. practice U. Tex. M.D. Anderson Hosp. and Tumor Inst., 1968—, Dept. Health, Edn. and Welfare, others. Mem. med. adv. bd. Kidney Found. Houston and Greater Gulf Coast, 1969—. Bd. dirs. St. Francis Episcopal Day Sch. Diplomate Am. Bd. Family Practice. Mem. Harris County Med. Soc. (editorial com. 1966-68), Tex. Med. Assn. (com. on nursing 1970—), A.M.A., Am. (pub. relations com. 1974), Tex. (phys. edn. com.), Harris County (chmn. edn. and program com. 1961-68; treas. 1964) acads. family physicians, Spring Branch Meml. C. of C. (dir. 1963-64, sec. bd. dirs. 1964), Osler Soc., Tex. Med. Assn. (mem. joint practice commn. Tex. Nurses Assn.), Alpha Epsilon Iota, Mu Delta. Episcopalian. Home: 25 E Broad Oaks Houston TX 77027 Office: 9100 Westheimer Houston TX 77042

COWDEN, JULIANAN, steel co. exec., craftsman; b. Midland, Tex.; d. Robert Edwin and Jett (Baker) Cowden; student Hackaday Jr. Coll., 1940-41; B.A., U. Tex., 1944. Rancher, oil investments JAL Co., Alvarado, Tex., 1950—, chmn. bd., 1970—; treas. J & M Steel Co., Inc., Fort Worth, 1971—. Instr. jewelry and silversmith Ft. Worth Art Center, 1963-66; exhibited jewelry and sculpture in one-man shows at Simpson Gallery, Amarillo, 1969, Sq. House Mus., Panhandle, 1971; exhibited in group shows at Ft. Worth Art Center, Carlin Gallery, Mus. Internat. Folk Art, Santa Fe, Wichita Falls (Tex.) Art Mus., Tech. Mus., Lubbock, Artist's Jamboree, San Antonio. Mem. exec. com. Tex. State Sch. Bd. Assn.; sec.-treas. Alvarado Community Hosp., 1967—; pres. Alvarado Ind. Sch. Dist. Bd., 1966—. Alternate del. Democratic Nat. Conv., 1964, del., mem. rules com., 1968, del., mem. credentials com., 1972, del. Dem. nat. mini-conv., 1974; mem. Tex. Dem. Exec. Com., 1960-68; sec. Tex. Dem. party, 1972—; mem. Nat. Fedn. Dem. Women; co-chmn. Briscoe gubernatorial campaign, 1972; Dem. precinct chmn., Alvarado, 1970—. Trustee Hockaday Sch., 1971-73. Mem. Tex. Designer Craftsmen, Tex. Artists Craftsmen Guild (pres. 1970-72), Zeta Tau Alpha. Episcopalian. Clubs: Amarillo; Texas Executive (Houston). Home: PO Box 305-308 JAL Ranch Alvarado TX 76009

COWELL, CATHERINE ROSE CUNNINGHAM (MRS. F. WESLEY COWELL), educator; b. Davis, Okla., Oct. 9, 1922; d. Clell Ivor and Nancy Agnes (Clapp) Cunningham; B.A., U. Denver, 1966, M.A., 1967, Ph.D., 1971; m. Harlan Harry Mendenhall, Sept. 6, 1941 (div. 1946); 1 son, Harlan Vincent; m. 2d, F. Wesley Cowell, June 22, 1952 (div. 1969). Teaching asst. U. Denver, 1967-68, 68-69; summer guest faculty No. Colo. U., Greeley, 1968; asst. prof. speech Angelo State U., San Angelo, Tex., 1969—. Pres. Elmwood Sch. P.T.A., Denver, 1953-56; reader Denver Unit Recording for Blind, 1958-66. Bd. dirs. Littleton (Colo.) Sch. Dist. Six, 1958-63, treas. 1961-63. Mem. Speech Communication Assn., Internat. Soc. Communication, Am. Assn. Univ. Profs. (chpt. pres. 1973—), So. Speech Communication Assn., Littleton League Women Voters (v.p. 1957-59), Pi Kappa Delta. Club: Denver Woman's Press (pres. 1958-59). Home: 3755 Arden Rd Apt 1-C San Angelo TX 76901

COWEN, DOROTHY RITA, lawyer; b. Ponchatoula, La., Jan. 13, 1923; d. Everett Paul and Eugenia A. (Yokum) Cowen; B.S., Southeastern La. U., 1942; M.A., Columbia, 1946; J.D., Loyola U., 1959. Stenographer F.B.I., New Orleans, 1950-54; sec. Judge J. Skelly Wright, U.S. Dist. Ct., New Orleans, 1954-59; admitted to La. bar, 1959, since practiced in New Orleans; mem. firm Cohen & Cowen, New Orleans. Mem. Fed., La. bar assns. Home: 4425 S Johnson St New Orleans LA 70125 Office: 822 Perdido St New Orleans LA 70100

COWGER, MARILYN LOUISE, research pediatrician; b. Douglas, Neb., June 7, 1931; d. Telferd Evan and Marian Elithe (Meek) Cowger; B.A. in Biology summa cum laude, U. Omaha, 1953; M.D., U. Neb., 1956. Intern, Bryan Meml. Hosp., Lincoln, Neb., 1956-57; fellow in pediatrics Mayo Clinic, Rochester, Minn., 1957-60; asst. dept. pediatrics U. Wash., Seattle, 1960-62, instr. pediatrics, 1962-64, asst. prof., 1964-69, asso. prof., 1969-70; asso. prof. pediatrics Albany Med. Coll. of Union U., Albany, 1970—; adj. prof. dept. chemistry State U. N.Y. at Albany, 1970—; attending pediatrician Albany Med. Center Hosp., 1970—. NIH research trainee, 1960-63, career devel. award, 1965-74; Am. Heart Assn. advanced research fellow, 1963-65. Mem. Soc. Pediatric Research, Am. Acad. Pediatrics, Western Soc. Pediatric Research, Am. Assn. U. Profs., Alpha Omega Alpha. Contbr. to Pediatrics, The Biology of Brain Dysfunction, Metabolic and Endocrine Disorders of Children; also research articles to profl. pubis. Home: 867 Hereford Way Schenectady NY 12309 Office: Dept Pediatrics Albany Med Coll Albany NY 12208

COWIN, HAZEL LOUISE MEACHAM (MRS. JOSEPH GORDON COWIN), educator; b. Fulton, Ky., Aug. 17, 1926; d. John Wayne and Nancy Jane (Hopkins) Meacham; B.S., Murray State Coll., 1947; M.A., U. Ky., 1957; postgrad. So. Ill. U., 1960; M.A., U. Ill., 1965; postgrad. Murray State U., 1967, 70, Vanderbilt U., 1971; m. Joseph Gordon Cowin, Nov. 21, 1945; children—Nancy (Mrs. Sammy Knight), Carolyn (Mrs. William Collura. Tchr., Lafayette Jr. High Sch., Lexington, Ky., 1954-57, Murray Tng. Sch. Murray (Ky.) State Coll., 1957-59; prof. math. Murray (Ky.) State U., 1960—. Recipient NSF Stipend, 1961-65, 67, 71. Mem. Math. Assn. Am., Assn. Women in Math., Am. Assn. U. Profs., Murray State U. Women's Soc., Nat. Council Tchrs. Math. Methodist. Home: 1508 Story St Murray KY 42071

COWING, JEAN FRANCES LAURENCE, journalist; b. Woodland, Cal., Dec. 3, 1912; d. Jesse Francis and Estelle (Packer) Laurence; A.A., Sacramento City Coll., 1931; m. Ralph H. Cowing, May 12, 1934 (dec. 1952); children—Janice Laurence (Mrs. Donald Bruce Geer), Ralph Jeffrey, Eric Cavell, Robert Devlin; m. 2d, James H. Oakley, May 14, 1969 (dec. July 1970). Owner toy shop, Woodland 1957-66; womens editor Daily Democrat, Woodland, 1966-69. Sec., Reclamation Bd., 1952-69; treas. Jr. League, 1942, editor of paper, 1943, radio chmn., editor of mag., 1944. Treas., bd. dirs. Kingsley Art Club, Sacramento, Woodland P.T.A.; bd. dirs. Sacramento Symphony, Sacramento Opera Guild, 1969-70, Sacramento World Affairs Council, 1970—. Mem. Cal. Press Women. Republican. Episcopalian. Home: 4100 Folsom Blvd Sacramento CA 95819

COWLES, FLEUR FENTON, artist; b. N.Y.C.; d. Matthew M. and Eleanor (Pearl) Fenton; student Columbia Sch. Applied Art, Pratt Inst.; LL.D., Elmira (N.Y.) U., 1955; m. Atherton Pettingell, Feb. 13, 1942; m. 2d, Gardner Cowles, Dec. 27, 1946 (div. 1955); m. 3d, Tom Montague Meyer, Nov. 18, 1955. Newspaper columnist N.Y. World Telegram, 1935-36; exec. v.p. Dorland Internat., Pettingell & Fenton Advt. Agy., 1936-45; spl. con. Famine Emergency Com., White House, Washington, 1946; asso. editor, dir. spl. editorial depts. Look mag., 1947; asso. editor Quick mag., 1949; editor Flair mag., 1950-51, Flair Annual, 1952; fgn. Corr. Look mag., 1946-55; bd. dirs. Cowles Mags., Inc. Cons. to chief of staff Hdqrs. USAF, 1950. Spl. rep. Pres. Eisenhower (with rank of spl. ambassador) at coronation of Queen Elizabeth II of Eng., 1952; mem. Lord Mayor's Adv. Com., Mermaid Theatre Trust, London; mem. council for Am. Museum, Bath, Eng. Mem. Commn. to Study Potentials of Aging, 1953-54. Trustee Soc. Rehab. Facially Disfigured, N.Y.C.; mem. nat. adv. com. on women's participation Fed. Civil Def. Adminstrn., 1953-55. Decorated chevalier Legion Honor (France), 1951; cavailer Order So. Cross 1953, comdr. 1973 (Brazil); Queen's medal (Eng.), 1953; comdr. Order Bienfasence (Greece), 1955. Mem. Order Les Compagnons de Rabalais. Women's Nat. Press Club, Overseas Press Club, Royal Soc. Arts, Theta Sigma Phi. Author: Bloody Precedent, 1952; The Case of Salvador Dali, 1959; Hidden Journey to the Hadhramontt, 1962; Tiger Flower, 1968, Lion and Blue, 1974. Exhibited painting Jeffress Gallery, London, 1959, 63, L'Obelisco Gallery, Rome. 1961, Hammer Galleries, N.Y.C., 1962, 64, 67, 69, 73, Andre Weil Gallery, Paris, 1962, 8th Biennale, Sao Paulo, 1965, Museu de Arte Moderno, Rio de Janeiro, Athens Gallery, 1966, Rex Evans Gallery, Los Angeles, Galeria Kreisler, Madrid (all 1967), Galeria Bonino, Rio de Janeiro, 1968, Seattle Art Mus., 1970, Dallas, 1971, Museu do Arte Moderna, Sao Paulo, Brazil, 1972, Herbert Hoover Gallery, San Francisco. Home: A5 Albany Piccadilly W 1 London England

COWLES, MILLY, educator; b. Ramer, Ala., May 29, 1932; d. Russell Fail and Sara (Mills) Cowles; B.S., Troy State U., 1952; M.A., U. Ala., 1958, Ph.D. (grad. fellow), 1962. Tchr. pub. schs., Montgomery, Ala., 1952-59; asst. then asso. prof. Grad. Sch. Edn., Rutgers U., 1962-66; asso. prof. U. Ga., 1966-67; prof., dir. early childhood devel. and edn. Sch. Edn., U. S.C., Columbia, 1967-73; asso. dean, prof. Sch. Edn., U. Ala., Birmingham, 1973—. Dir. Williamsburg County Schs. Career Opportunity Program, 1970-73; cons. So. Edn. Found., Atlanta, Ga. Inst. Higher Edn. U. Ga., also numerous sch systems throughout Northeast and South. Pres. bd. dirs. 2d Reformed Ch. Nursery Sch., New Brunswick, N.J., 1963-66; bd. dirs. S.C. Assn. on Children Under Six, 1969-73. Mem. Am. Ednl. Research Assn., Soc. for Research Child Devel., A.A.A.S., Am. Assn. U. Profs., Nat. Council Tchrs. English, Internat. Reading Assn., Assn. for Supervision and Curriculum Devel. (mem. council on early childhood edn. 1969—), Nat. Assn. for Edn. Young Children, Assn. for Childhood Devel. Internat., N.Y. Acad. Scis., Kappa Delta Pi (chpt. treas. 1964-66), Delta Kappa Gamma. Editor, contbg. author: Perspectives in the Education of Disadvantaged Children, 1967. Research and publs. on psycholinguistic behaviors of rural children. Home: 1022 Essex Rd Birmingham AL 35222

COWLEY, RUBY DIXON (MRS. ANGUS WAYNE COWLEY), educator; b. Provo, Utah, July 26, 1912; d. Charles Owen and Virginia Elizabeth (Beckstead) Dixon; B.S., Brigham Young U., 1951, M.Ed., 1969; postgrad. U. Wash., 1960; m. Angus Wayne Cowley, Aug. 25, 1937; children—Wayne Dixon, Shirl Curtis. Tchr. remedial reading Parker Sch., Provo, Utah, 1934; prin. Hanna Sch., Duchesne County, Utah, 1935-36; tchr. Altonah Sch., Duchesne County, 1936-37, Grandview Sch., Provo, 1951-53; tchr. Timpanogos Sch., Provo Sch. Dist., 1953—. Dist. chmn. Democratic party, 1962—. Mem. Am. Childhood Edn. Assn. Internat. (pres. Provo br. 1969-71, publ. chmn. 1971—), N.E.A. (conv. rep. 1968), Am. Assn. U. Women (historian, art study leader 1951-57), Utah Edn. Assn. (chmn. edn. and profl. standards com. 1966-70), Utah Art Educators Assn., Xi Beta, Delta Kappa Gamma (program com. 1960—). Mem. Ch. of Jesus Christ of Latter-day Saints. Home: 1430 N 380 W Provo UT 84601

COX, ABBE ROSE (MRS. HAROLD F. CRAVEN), artist; b. Houston; d. Benjamin Franklin and Carolyn (Horn) Cox; B.S., Columbia U. Tchrs. Coll., 1944, M.A. in Fine Arts, 1946; student Art Students League, Am. Art Sch., Taubes-Pierce Sch. Art, Chgo. Art Inst.; m. Harold F. Craven, on December 18, 1946 (deceased September 21st, 1968); 1 son (by previous marriage), Howard. Pvt. tchr. fine arts, 1935—; instr. mech. drawing Fair Lawn (N.J.) High Sch., 1945-47; instr., dir. adminstrn. Ridgewood (N.J.) Sch. Art, 1961-64; tchr. at Glade Valley, nr. Sparta, N.C., during summers; tchr. art history and painting Surry Community Coll., Dobson, N.C., 1967-73. Exhibited at shows of numerous cultural, lit. and art socs. in N.Y.C. and N.J.; represented in collection Fine Arts Mus., Montgomery, Ala., Arts and Sci. Mus., Statesville, N.C.; designed stained glass window for Archer Meml. Meth. Ch., Allendale, N.J., 1966. Recipient numerous awards including Ford Motor Co. award, 1956, purchase award Bergen Mall Show, Paramus, N.J., 1958, Silver medal for landscape painting Am. Artist Profl. League Nat. Show, 1963. Life fellow Royal Soc. Arts (Gt. Britain); mem. Catherine Lorillard Wolfe Art Club, Phi Lambda Theta. Home: Gen Delivery Roaring Gap NC 28668

COX, BERTHA MAE HILL (MRS. WILLIS L. COX), educator; b. Kosse, Tex., Mar. 10, 1901; d. Marshall Victor and Ollie Evelyn (Phifer) Hill; student Southwest Tex. U., 1922, Baylor U., 1923, So. Meth. U.; B.S., North Tex. State U., 1935, M.S., 1950; m. Willis L. Cox, June 8, 1924. Prin. rural sch., Harmony, Tex., 1918; acting postmaster, Kosse, Tex., 1919-21; tchr. pub. schs., Kosse, 1922-24, Dallas County, 1925-29; prin. Dallas City Schs., 1930-33, tchr., 1934-64; tchr. Dallas Ind. Sch. Dist., 1964—; founder, now emeritus dir. Kessler Park United Meth. Ch. Day Sch., Dallas. Named tchr. of the year Dallas Times Herald, 1950. Mem. Dallas Assn. Childhood Edn. (pres. 1938, state sec.-treas., 1940), Speech Arts Tchrs., (pres. 1954), N.E.A., (life), Tex. Tchrs. Assn. (life), Tex. Parents and Tchrs. Assn. (hon. life), Wesleyan Service Guild (hon. life), Kappa Delta Pi, Delta Kappa Gamma. Democrat. Methodist. Author: True Tales of Texas, 1949; Susan's Happy Year, 1957; Let's Read about Texas, 1963; Our Texas, 1964; also ch. sch. materials for Meth. Ch. Editor: Tell Us about Texas, 1947; The Texans! Texas to Today, 1972. Contbr., adviser Ideas Readers Series, 1973; contbr. articles to profl. jours. Home: 1130 N Winnetka St Dallas TX 75208

COX, BETTY PACK, newspaper editor; b. Paintsville, Ky., Oct. 4, 1934; d. William Martin and Mary (Lester) Pack; student Eastern Ky. U., 1952-56, 61; m. James Macklin Cox, May 29, 1955; children—Teresa Lee, James Macklin. Substitute tchr., 1967-69; founder Madison County Newsweek, Richmond, Ky., 1970, editor, mng. editor, 1970—. Charge students internship in journalism Eastern Ky. U., 1971-73; condr. radio program Let's Talk, WEKY; adv. bd. Distributive Edn., 1972-73. Mem. Ky. Homecoming Commn., 1965; county fund-raising chmn. Cerebral Palsy, 1958-59; mem. Ad Hoc Com. for Ky. Jud. Improvement, 1973. County chmn. Democratic gubernatorial election, 1968. Named Mrs. Ky., 1964; recipient editorial-news story awards Ky. Press Assn., 1971. Mem. Ky. Weekly Newspaper Assn., Pattie A. Clay Hosp. Aux. Mem. Christian Ch. Clubs: Garden (past sec., treas., 1st and 2d v.p.), Junior Woman's (past sec., treas., 1st v.p.). Home: 17 Lancaster Woods Richmond KY 40475 Office: Box 732 Richmond KY 40475

COX, BEVERLEY LENORE, animal physiologist, educator; b. Huntingdon, Pa., Jan. 11, 1929; d. Elwood Beck and Orlee Arcola (Davis) Cox; B.S., Pa. State U., 1951, M.S., 1953; Ph.D., U. Okla. at Norman, 1960, postgrad. isotope and nuclear reactor tech. and cardiovascular physiology summer insts., 1963, 65, 66. Instr. U. Okla. at Norman, 1959-60, vis. asso. prof. zoology dept., 1967, 68, 69; research asso., postdoctoral fellow U. Ore., Eugene, 1960-61; asst. prof. Central State U., Edmond, Okla., 1961-65, asso. prof., 1965-69, prof., 1969—; participant neuroendocrinology inst. U. Cal. at Berkeley, summer 1970. AEC grantee, 1963-66, NSF grantee, 1965-67. Mem. A.A.A.S., Am. Assn. Univ. Profs., Am. Soc. Zoologists, Am. Inst. Biol. Sci., Sigma Xi, Phi Sigma. Contbr. articles in field to profl. jours. Home: Route 1 Box 184 Oklahoma City OK 73111 Office: Biology Dept Central State University Edmond OK 73034

COX, BEVERLY JEAN (MRS. HENRI WEIBE), physician; b. Yuba City, Cal., Feb. 6, 1936; d. John Hilton and Christine Doris (Lassen) Cox; B.A., Pacific Union Coll., 1957; M.D., Loma Linda U., 1961; m. Henri Wiebe, Oct. 20, 1971; 1 dau., Alexandra. Intern, Glendale (Cal.) Adventist Hosp., 1961-62, resident, 1962-64, Los Angeles County Gen. Hosp., 1967-68; physician, Thailand, 1966; vol. physician Ty. Papua and New Guinea, New Britain, 1967; mem. attending staff Aquadilla Dist. Hosp., P.R., 1969; practice medicine specializing in internal medicine, Mayaguez, P.R., 1970—; mem. staff Bella Vista Adventist Hosp., Mayaquez, P.R.; tchr. interns and residents Aquadilla Dist. Hosp., 1969—, externs Bella Vista Hosp., 1971—. Seventh-Day Adventist (ch. pianist 1971). Home: Box 1750 Mayaguez PR 00708 Office: 35 Mendez Vigo Oeste Mayaguez PR 00708

COX, CLAIRE (MRS. MAX L. LOWENTHAL, JR.), publicist, author; b. St. Louis, Dec. 11, 1919; d. Raymond J. and Klaire (Hasgall) Cox; B.A., U. Cal at Los Angeles, 1941; M.S., Columbia, 1942; m. Max L. Lowenthal, Jr., July 2, 1951. Reporter Daily News, Ft. Lauderdale, Fla., 1942, Balt. Sun, 1942-44; reporter, writer, feature writer, columnist United Press Internat., Chgo., 1944-47, N.Y.C., 1947-62; eastern pub. relations dir. Combined Ins. Co. Am., N.Y.C., 1962-69; pres. Claire Cox Assos., Inc., pub. relations, 1969—. Mem. adv. bd. Walter Hoving Home. Bd. dirs. Am. Found. Religion and Psychiatry, 1969-72; bd. dirs., mem. exec. com. Citizens Scholarship Found. Am.; mem. bd., sec., mem. exec. com. Laymen's Nat. Bible Com.; trustee Southeast Museum, Brewster, N.Y. Recipient ann. award for writing Newspaper Women's Club, N.Y., 1956. Mem. Religion Newswriters Assn., Authors Guild Am., Pub. Relations Soc. Am. (accredited, chmn. task force on vol. action). Author: The New-Time Religion, 1961; The Upbeat Generation, 1962, How Women Can Make Up to 1,000 A Week in Direct Selling, 1963; Rainy Day Fun for Kids, 1963; How To Beat the High Cost of College, 1965, rev., 1971; (with David Wilkerson) Parents On Trial, 1967; (with Charles DiSalvo) Faces People Wear, 1968; The Fourth R, 1969; (with Billy B. Sharp) Choose Success-How To Set and Achieve All Your Goals, 1970; (with Sondra Gorney) The Second Forty, 1972. Contbr. to various mags. including Ladies Home Jour., Good Housekeeping, Seventeen, Pageant, Success Unlimited; columnist Copley News Service. Home and Office: Towners Rd RD 6 Brewster NY 10509

COX, CONSTANCE CHARLOTTE (MRS. NORMAN COX), writer; b. Sutton, Surrey, Eng., Oct. 25, 1915; d. John Frederick and Anne Elizabeth (Vince) Shaw; grad. high sch.; m. Norman Cox, June 7, 1936. Writer classic serials BBC-TV, 1955-69; adaptor (with others) The Forsyte Saga, 1967, War and Peace, 1970, The Herries Chronicle, 1971, The Barchester Chronicles, 1973; writer plays including Vanity Fair, 1948; Spring at Marino, 1950; Lord Arthur Savile's Crime, 1952; Pride and Prejudice, 1971; Nightmare, 1973; Wuthering Heights, 1974; writer libretto of Two Cities 1968, Vanity Fair 1970, Smiling Through, 1972. Recipient awards for adaption of classic serials News Chronicle award best TV serial, 1956, TV and Screen Writers' award,

1965, 67. Clubs: Sussex Playwrights'; West Sussex Writers. Home: 2 Princes Av Hove Sussex Bn34GD England

COX, ELEANOR, sculptor and illustrator; b. Montrose, Colo., Apr. 12, 1914; d. Henry Aubrey and Mary Elizabeth (Moore) Cox; student Abbott Sch. Fine and Comml. Art, Washington, 1933-35, Corcoran Sch. Fine Art, 1934-37, Yard Sch. Fine Art, 1937-38, Temple U. Art Sch., 1940-41. One-man sculpture exhibits Central High Sch., Washington, 1939, Nat. League Am. Pen Women, 1947, Woman's City Club of Washington, 1948, Silver Spring (Md.) Gallery, 1954; exhibited in group shows at Corcoran Art Gallery, Nat. Mus. Art Gallery, Statler Hotel, Internat. Galleries, Central Br. Pub. Library and Arts Club, Pa. Acad. Fine Arts and others; sculptures on permanent display Nat. Red Cross Hdqrs. Bldg., Washington, MacFarland Jr. High Sch., Washington, West Point Mil. Acad., Bur. of Yards and Docks, U.S. Navy Bldg., Episcopal Eye, Ear and Throat Hosp., Washington, U.S. Dist. Ct. for D.C., Fed. Bar Bldg., D.C. Chief heraldic sect., awards br. Dept of Air Force, 1957-63; sci. illustrator tech. illustrations br. U.S. Geol. Survey, 1963-74. Designed Air Force Commendation medal and Air Force cross. Mem. Soc. Washington Artists, Soc. Miniature Painters, Sculptor and Gravers of Washington (sec. 1956-59), Nat. League Pen Women, D.A.R. Baptist. Club: Zonta. Home: 4411 Fairfax Rd McLean VA 22101 Office: US Geol Survey Blair Bldg Silver Spring MD 20910

COX, GAYLE NANCY, journalist; b. Rochester, N.Y., Mar. 5, 1937; d. Clarence E. and Marion Barbara (Fischer) Krompart; B.S., Marquette U., 1959; m. Thomas Claud Cox, Sept. 1, 1962; children—Christopher Quin, T. Cameron. Copywriter Sanger's Dept. Store, Dallas, 1959-61; fashion editor Tex. Fashion Mag., Dallas, 1961-63, Fashion Trend Mag., Dallas, 1963-64; free lance writer Women's Wear Daily, Dallas, 1965, Dallas Times Herald, 1967-68, Fashion Week, Dallas, 1966-67; copy editor Tex. Fashion's Mag., Dallas, 1970-72; fashion writer J.C. Penney Regional Advt., Dallas office, 1972—. Mem. Women in Communications. Home: 1441 San Rafael Dr Dallas TX 75218 Office: J C Penney Regional Sales Office 5217 Ross Av Dallas TX 75206

COX, JOSIE MAE WARD (MRS. THOMAS NELSON COX), artist, craftsman; b. Moxley, South Staffs, Eng., Apr. 7, 1926; d. Joseph and Gwendoline V. (Butler) Ward; came to U.S., 1946, naturalized, 1956; student Wolverhampton Municipal Sch. Art, 1940-43, Wolverhampton Coll. Art, 1943-45; m. Thomas Nelson Cox, Nov. 11, 1945 (dec. Feb. 1969); 1 dau., Colleen Fae. Artist, craftsman specializing in hand carved crosses, with straw overlay; engaged in restoration ancient Am. Indian pottery Arrowsmith-Fenn Galleries; one-man shows Botts Meml. Hall, Albuquerque, 1965, Jonson Gallery, U. N.M., 1970; paintings exhibited in group shows Smithsonian Instn., 1958, N.M. State Fair, 1959, 67, 68, Pasadena Mus. Art, 1972-73; crosses exhibited in group shows U.S. Dept. State, 1966-68, U. N.M., 1965, 67, Art Mus. Santa Fe, 1965, 66, 67, 68, Visual Arts Contemporary Craft Mus., N.Y.C., 1967, New West Gallery, Albuquerque, 1970, Pasadena Cal. Exhbn., 1972-73; represented in permanent collections, including Mus. of N.M., Jonson Gallery. Recipient scholarships Staffordshire Edn. Com., 1940-43. Recipient awards including award of honor Nat. League Am. Pen Women, 1958, U. N.M. Award, 1965, hon. mention Fuller Lodge Competition and Exhbn., 1970, 1st prize N.M. State Fair, 1967, 68, Purchase award Biennial Internat. Folk Art Mus., 1972. Home: 300 Homeland Rd NW Albuquerque NM 87114 Office: PO Box 10120 Alameda NM 87114

COX, LOIS VIRGINIA, ret. ednl. adminstr.; b. Norfolk, Va., Mar. 20, 1911; d. Robert Llewellyn and Eula (Jester) Cox; B.S. Longwood Coll., 1933; M.Ed., Boston U., 1959. Tchr., Md. Sch. for Blind, Balt., 1933-52, prin., 1956-73; teenage dir. YWCA, Balt., 1952-53; supervising tchr. dept. blind, S.C. Sch. for Deaf and Blind, 1953-56. Speaker convs., in-service tng. sessions, 1950—; supr. tchr. tng. Salisbury State Coll., Towson State Coll., U. Md., 1956—; dir. summer programs for multi-handicapped blind pre-sch. children Md. Sch. for Blind, 1968-71; 69; mem. suburban regional task force com. Gov's. Study Group on Vocational Rehab., 1968. Y-Teen Club adviser, 1934-52; chmn. teenage activities com. YWCA, 1950, chmn. com. on adminstrn. central br., 1951, sec. bd. dirs., Balt., 1952, del. nat. conv. Chgo., 1952. Bd. dirs. Am. Found. Blind, 1960-62. Recipient Pres's. plaque Am. Assn. Instrs. Blind, 1962, Centennial citation for work with blind children Wilson Coll., 1969. Mem. Council for Exceptional Children (exec. bd. Md. state fedn. 1966-68), Assn. for Edn. Visually Handicapped (dir. 1954-64, pres. 1960-62), Longwood Alumnae, Pi Gamma Mu, Sigma Pi Rho, Alpha Phi Sigma, Delta Kappa Gamma. Episcopalian. Asst. editor Internat. Jour. for Edn. of Blind, 1954-58. Home: 8401 Atlantic Av Virginia Beach VA 23451

COX, LOVE WORRELL (MRS. ALVIN COX JR.), educator, social worker; b. Sylvatus, Va.; d. Aaron Perry and Bertha (Cooley) Worrell; student Radford Coll., Va., 1932-34, B.S., 1962; m. Alvin Cox, Jr., June 19, 1946; children—Larry Herbert, Richard Alvin, Julia Kate. Tchr., Carroll County Schs., Carroll County Sch. Bd., Hillsville, Va., 1934-42, Hillsville Elementary Sch., 1948-70; insp. Lukas Harold Corp., Indpls., 1942-44; social worker Carroll County Dept. Welfare, Hillsville, Va., 1944-46, supt., 1970—; corr. Times, 1960-65; reporter Carroll News, Hillsville, 1955—. Active Boy Scouts Am., Cub Scouts; mem. citizen's adv. bd. Mt. Rogers Mental Health Services; mem. adv. council sr. citizens programs Mt. Rogers Planning Dist. Commn. Mem. bd. sponsors Children's Home Soc. Va., 1960—; bd. dirs. Childrens Home Abingdon Presbytery, Carroll, Grayson Galax Assn. Retarded Children. Mem. Nat. (pub. relations local contact chmn.), Va., Carroll edn. assns., Dist. M Classroom Tchrs. (pres.), Va. League Social Service Execs. Va. Council Social Welfare, Delta Kappa Gamma (pres. 1968-70), D.A.R. (regent) 1959-61, state chmn. membership com. Va., 1965—), Ladies Aux. V.F.W., John Carroll Soc., Children Am. Revolution (sr. pres. 1967—). Home: PO Box 31 Hillsville VA 24343 Office: Carroll County Welfare Dept Hillsville VA 24343

COX, MARGARET LILLIAN, physician; b. Lenoir, N.C., Jan. 26, 1932; d. Henry Herschel and Margaret (Powledge) Cox; student Vanderbilt U., 1953-56; M.D., U. Tenn., 1960. Intern U. Ala. at Birmingham, 1960-61; resident in medicine Charity Hosp., La. State U. at New Orleans, 1961-62; resident in medicine VA Hosp., Memphis, 1962-64, mem. staff, 1965—; tng. fellow endocrinology VA Hosp., U. Tenn. at Memphis, 1964-65; practice internal medicine, Memphis, 1965—; asst. prof. internal medicine U. Tenn., 1966—. Recipient Govt. pin for 10 years service in WAC and Memphis VA Hosp., 1969. Diplomate Am. Bd. Internal Medicine. Mem. A.C.P., Memphis Acad. Internal Medicine, Am., So. med. assns. Author: Leukoerythoblastosis in the Adult, 1965; Acinic Cell Carcinoma of the Parotid with Ectopic Production of Adrenocorticotrophic Hormone, 1970. Contbr. articles in field to profl. jours. Home: 1528 Linden St Memphis TN 38104 Office: 1020 Jefferson St Memphis TN 38104

COX, MARGARET STORKE (MRS. EXUM MORRIS COX), civic worker; b. Santa Barbara, Cal., Apr. 15, 1908; d. Thomas More and Elsie (Smith) Storke; A.B., Scripps Coll., 1931; m. Exum Morris Cox, Sept. 6, 1934; children—Cynthia (Mrs. Huntting), Susan More (Mrs. James T. Fousekis), Thomas Storke. Dir. Santa Barbara News Press Pub. Co. 1957-64. Mem. women's bd. San Francisco Mus. of Art, pres., 1962-64; bd. dirs. San Francisco Players Guild, 1960-64; San Francisco Planning and Urban Renewal, 1964-66, Stern Grove Festival Assn. Com. 1965—, Music Acad. of West, Santa Barbara, 1962-64; trustee Scripps Coll., 1971—. Clubs: Social, Town and Country. Home: 2361 Broadway San Francisco CA 94115

COX, MARTHA ANN, educator; b. Brantley, Ala., July 26, 1939; d. Hezz Malone and Suaylor (Wyatt) Cox; B.S., Samford U., 1960; postgrad. Jacksonville State U., 1960; M.A., U. Ala., 1963, advanced profl. degree in counseling and guidance, 1964. Student counselor Samford U., Birmingham, Ala., 1958-60, instr. Coll. Edn., 1966—, dir. women's programs, 1969—; counselor, asst. dir. Girl's Aux. Camps, Ala. Women's Missionary Union, summers 1960-65; pub. sch. tchr. Munford (Ala.) High Sch., 1960-62; resident counselor U. Ala., University, 1962-64, freshman counselor, summer counseling, 1963; dir. guidance, student activities Sch. Nursing, Birmingham Bapt. Hosp., 1964-66, asso. dean for student affairs, 1966-69. Curriculum writer So. Bapt. Sunday Sch. Bd., Nashville, 1969—; mem. Pres.'s Com. Employment Handicapped, Ala. Gov.'s Com. on Employment Handicapped, gen. chmn. Birmingham Area Com. on Employment Handicapped, 1972—; mem. women's com. Spain Rehab. Center, mem. Mayor's Youth Council, 1972—. Mem. Am., So. Ala. coll. personnel assns., Nat. Vocational Guidance Assn., Am. Sch. Counselors Assn., Assn. for Measurement and Evaluation in Guidance, Ala. Edn. Assn., Nat., (sec. 1967-71, pres. 1972—), Ala. assns. women deans and counselors, Am., Ala. personnel and guidance assns., Am. Assn. U. Women, Hypathia Honor Soc., Delta Kappa Gamma, Kappa Delta Pi. Baptist. Home: 800 Lakeshore Dr Birmingham AL 35209

COX, MARTHA JANE MCCORMICK (MRS. JAMES MORGAN COX), librarian; b. Lisbon, O., July 2, 1928; d. Alvy George and Mary Catherine (Crawford) McCormick; student Coll. Wooster, 1948; B.A. (fellow), Carnegie Inst. Tech., 1951; M.A. (fellow), Kent State U., 1962; m. James Morgan Cox, Aug. 29, 1948; children—Ariel Sibylla, Shannon Elise, Claudia Renee. Library asst., acting bookmobile librarian Lepper Library, Lisbon, O., 1946-48; library asst. Coll. Wooster, 1946-48, Carnegie Inst. Tech., 1948-51; head librarian Malone Coll., Canton, O., 1962—, prof. children's lit., 1965—. Mem. A.L.A., Ohio Library Assn., Am. Assn. U. Women, Stark County Librarians Assn. (pres. 1966), Kent State Library Sch. Alumni (pres. 1967), Beta Phi Mu, Delta Kappa Gamma. Presbyn. (elder). Home: 151 33d St NW Canton OH 44709

COX, MARTHA WILLIAMS, radio and TV producer; b. Charlottesville, Va., May 22, 1928; d. John William II and Louise Gray (Anderson) Williams; student U. Va., 1954-55; m. Richard McDonald Cox, Mar. 16, 1957; 1 dau., Gray (Mrs. Ralph A. Dowell). Tchr., Danville (Va.) pub. schs., 1953-54; model, producer, film editor sta. WBTM-TV, Danville, Va., 1954-55; with sta. WRC-Radio and WRC-TV, Washington, 1960—, exec. producer, 1973—; tchr. communications Am. U., 1966—. Recipient numerous awards of appreciation for civic work. Mem. Am. Women of Radio and TV, Internat. Platform Assn. Methodist. Club: Farmington Country (Charlottesville). Author: TV Tips, 1965. Home: 2221 Gt Falls St Falls Church VA 22046 Office: 4001 Nebraska Av Washington DC 20016

COX, MARY CLAIRE OLIVER (MRS. HENRY MIOT COX), educator; b. nr. Grayson, Ga., Dec. 17, 1911; d. Hoyt Pinckney and Mamie Alma (Langley) Oliver; student Agnes Scott Coll., 1928-31; B.S., U. Neb., 1952; m. Henry Miot Cox, June 8, 1935; 1 dau., Mary Miot (Mrs. John McKee Hale). Tchr. elementary schs., DeKalb County (Ga.), 1931-35; tchr. Elliott Elementary Sch., Lincoln, Neb., 1952-61; tchr. Eastridge Multi-unit Elementary Sch., Lincoln, 1961—, unit leader, 1972—. Sustaining mem. Lincoln YWCA, 1961—; mem. Lincoln Symphony Guild, 1959—; pres. St. Paul Woman's Soc. Christian Service, Lincoln, 1942-44; sec. Christian Social Relations, promotion sec., v.p. Neb. Conf. Woman's Soc. Christian Service, 1944-52; chmn. Altar Guild com. St. Paul Methodist Ch., Lincoln, 1951-73, steward 1955-65, rep. to Meth. City Evangelistic Union, 1960-68; mem. women's planning com. Japan Internat. Christian U. Found., 1967—. Recipient award as Tchr. of Year 1968 in Am. Heritage, Daus. Colonial Wars. Mem. Am. Assn. U. Women (fellowship chmn. 1968-72), Neb. Art Assn., Neb. P.T.A. (life), Nat. (life) Neb., Lincoln edn. assns., Nat. Council for Tchrs. Social Studies. Council for Exceptional Children, Assn. for Gifted, Assn. for Childhood Edn. Internat., Nat. Sci. Tchrs. Assn., Nat. Council for Tchrs. Math., D.A.R. (Neb. program chmn. 1962-64, chmn. schs. com. 1960-64, chmn. flag of U.S.A. 1969-72), Am. Assn. for UN, Daus. Am. Colonists (state chmn. nat. def.), Nat., Neb. councils tchrs. social studies, Friends of Chamber Music (charter mem.). Democrat. Clubs: Lincoln Garden, University of Neb. Faculty Wives, Willeva Dinner, Mothers (Lincoln). Home: 1145 N 44th St Lincoln NE 68503 Office: Eastridge Multi-Unit Elementary Sch Lincoln NE 68510

COX, MELVA GRACE ECKERT, city ofcl.; b. South Haven, Kan., May 3, 1912; d. Lawrence Edward and Gladys Faye (Jeffries) Eckert; student Northcentral Coll., 1930-32; m. Charles William Cox, Feb. 16, 1936 (div. 1941); 1 dau., Janice Sue (Mrs. J.V. Seay). Bookkeeper and sec. Hyten & Packard Motor Co., Wellington, Kan., 1932-39; accountant Boeing Airplane Co., Wichita, Kan., 1941-45; sec. City of Wellington, Kan., 1945-48, asst. city clk., also city treas. 1948-58, city clk., 1958—. Mem. adv. com. Meals on Wheels Program, Wellington, Kan., 1972—. Mem. Internat. Inst. of Municipal Clks., Municipal Finance Officers of U.S. and Can., City Clk.'s Assn. of Kan. (com. 1964-65), City Clks. and Municipal Officers Assn. Kan. (v.p. 1974-75), Wellington C. of C. (chmn. women's div. 1972-74), Bus. and Profl. Women's Club, Sumner County Hist. Soc., Mem. First Christian Ch. Club: Soroptimist (pres. 1972-73). Home: 119 East 21st St Wellington KS 67152 Office: City Hall Wellington KS

COX, PATRICIA LEGAN, nursing adminstr.; b. Dallas, Dec. 26, 1921; d. Cloyd Hutchins and Lee Belle (James) Legan; R.N., U. Tex. Sch. Nursing, 1942; student in nursing Tex. Woman's U., 1963; m. William Murris Cox, Sept. 26, 1942 (dec. Jan. 1969); children—Sally Lee (Mrs. John O. McGraw), Martha Joy (Mrs. William Robert Hammond, Jr.). With City of Galveston Health Dept., 1942-43, City of Houston, 1949-68; dir. nursing service Richmond State Sch., Tex. Dept. Mental Health and Mental Retardation, 1968—. Mem. Am. Nurses Assn., Am. Assn. Mental Deficiency, Tex. Pub. Employees Assn. Democrat. Roman Catholic. Home: 8464 Leawood Blvd Houston TX 77072 Office: 2100 Preston St Richmond TX 77469

COX, VERGIE LEE FRANCIS (MRS. ALBERT LEE COX, JR.), ednl. media cons.; b. Crumpler, N.C., Mar. 29, 1924; d. Coy Roscoe and Lanie Zelphia (Wiles) Francis; student Lees McRae Coll., 1941-43; B.S. magna cum laude, Appalachian State U., 1953, M.A., 1956; postgrad. East Tenn. State U., 1965; m. Albert Lee Cox, Jr., May 17, 1946 (dec.); 1 dau., Nancy Lee (Mrs. Charles David Bowers). Cryptanalytic aide U.S. Govt., Washington, 1941-43; tchr. Ashe (N.C.) County Schs., 1950-61, librarian, 1961-66; asso. sch. library supr. N.C. Dept. Pub. Instrn., Raleigh, 1966-67, state supr. learning resources and textbooks, 1967-69, chief cons. materials evaluation, 1969—. Mem. Am., N.C., Southeastern library assns., Am., N.C. assns. sch. librarians, Assn. Ednl. Communications and Tech., N.C. Assn. Educators, Delta Kappa Gamma. Home: 821 Sans Souci Dr Raleigh NC 27609 Office: Materials Evaluation State Dept Pub Instruction Raleigh NC 27602

COXE, MRS. THOMAS CHATTERTON (EMILY BADHAM COXE), civic worker; b. Edenton, N.C., May 3, 1910; d. Richard Paxton and Emily Wood (Fagan) Badham; grad. St. Mary's Jr. Coll., 1929; m. Thomas Chatterton Coxe, Jr., Nov. 6, 1929; children—Thomas Chatterton III, Emily Wood (Mrs. William Alfred Winburn III), Patricia Barringer (Mrs. Marshall Taylor Ware), Charlotte Victoria (Mrs. Charles E. Commander III), Richard Badham. Darlington County chmn. S.C. Council Common Good, 1958—; pres. Darlington County unit S.C. div. Am. Cancer Soc., mem. state bd.; mem. S.C. Ednl. TV Commn., 1973—. Bd. dirs. Darlington County Tb Assn., 1956—; trustee St. Mary's Jr. Coll. Mem. Darlington County Hist. Soc., Nat. Soc. Colonial Dames Am. Episcopalian. Author: (with Frances Warfield) Mother of the Maid, 1960. Home: Skufful Farm Darlington SC 29532

COYNE, LOLAFAYE, statistician; b. Topeka, Dec. 10, 1926; d. Lester Theodore and Faye (Rush) Coyne; A.B. in Math., Washburn U., 1948; M.A., U. Kan., 1949, Ph.D., Kan. State U., 1972. Dir. statis. lab. research dept. Menninger Found., Topeka, 1949—, asst. dir. hosp. research, 1974—. Statis. cons. Social Systems Research project Osawatomie State Hosp., rehab. living unit research project Kan. State U., comprehensive health services for children and youth Topeka-Shawnee County Health Dept., LSD and psychotherapy research Topeka VA Hosp. Mem. com. on program evaluation and biometrics Div. Instn. Mgmt. and Community Health Services, State Dept. Social Welfare, 1964. Clarinetist, Topeka Civic Symphony, 1945—; solo clarinet Topeka Santa Fe Band, 1955—. Mem. Am. Statis. Assn., Psychometric Soc., Topeka Psychol. Assn., Sigma Alpha Iota. Contbr. articles to sci. jours. Home: 1830 Lane Topeka KS 66604 Office: Box 829 Topeka KS 66601

COYNE, MARY JEANNE, lawyer; b. Mpls., Dec. 7, 1926; d. Vincent Mathias and Mae Lucille (Steinmetz) Coyne; B.S.L., U. Minn., 1955, J.D., 1957. Admitted to Minn. bar, 1957, U.S. Supreme Ct., 1964; law clerk for Justice Leroy E. Matson, Minn. Supreme Ct., St. Paul, 1956-57; partner Meagher, Geer, Markham, Anderson, Adamson, Flaskamp & Brennan, Mpls., 1957—. Instr. appellate advocacy U. Minn. Law Sch., 1964-68; mem. nat. panel arbitrators Am. Arbitration Assn., 1967—; mem. bd. arbitration Archdiocese St. Paul and Mpls., 1973—. Trustee Hennepin County Law Library. Mem. U. Minn. Law Alumni Assn. (sec. 1966-72, dir. 1971—), Am., Minn., Hennepin County bar assns., Nat. Assn. Women Lawyers (rec. sec. 1968-69, assembly del. 1969-71, treas. 1972—), Order of Coif, Beta Sigma Phi. Clubs: Minneapolis Golf. Editor: Women Lawyer Jour., 1971-72. Home: 5405 York Av S Edina MN 55410 Office: 2250 IDS Center Minneapolis MN 55402

COYNE, NADENE, physician; b. O'Neill, Neb., Sept. 6, 1920; d. Hugh Eugene and Anna Marie (Dwyer) Coyne; student Coll. St. Teresa, 1938-40, U. Neb., 1940-41; certificate in phys. therapy Northwestern U., 1942; B.S. in Medicine, U. Ill., 1948, M.D., 1950 Intern, Phila. Gen. Hosp., 1950-51; resident, fellow phys. medicine and rehab. U. Kan., 1952, N.Y. U., 1953-54; dir. phys. medicine and rehab. Cleve. City Hosp., 1955-59; dir. edn., med. dir. Respiratory Center, N.Y. U.-Bellevue Med. Center, 1959-62; dir. phys. medicine and rehab. Cleve. Met. Gen. Hosp., 1963—. Asso. prof. medicine (phys. medicine and rehab.) Case Western Res. U. Sch. Medicine, 1963—; chmn. exec. med. staff Health Hill Hosp. for Children, Cleve., 1968-72; med. adv. bd. Thoreau Park Sch. for Crippled Children, Soc. for Crippled Children, Ohio State Crippled Children's Services, Multiple Sclerosis Soc., North East Ohio Muscular Dystrophy Assn. Am. Diplomate Am. Bd. Phys. Medicine and Rehab., Nat. Bd. Med. Examiners. Mem. Am. Acad. Phys. Medicine and Rehab., Am. Congress Rehab. Medicine, Am. Phys. Therapy Assn., A.M.A., Acad. Medicine Cleve., Ohio State Med. Soc., Assn. Acad. Psychiatrists (pres. 1971-72), Am. Assn. Electromyography and Electrodiagnosis, Ohio Soc. Phys . Medicine and Rehab. (pres. 1970-72), Am. Rheumatism Assn. Roman Catholic. Contbg. author: (text book) Rehabilitation Medicine, 1971; (chpt.) to Restorative Medicine in Geriatrics, 1964. Contbr. articles to med. jours. Home: 15025 Shore Acres Dr Cleveland OH 44110 Office: 3395 Scranton Rd Cleveland OH 44109

COYNER, MARTHA JANE (MRS. RALPH NUTTER), physician; b. Buckhannan, W.Va., June 8, 1921; d. Erric Christian and Martha J. (Tallman) Coyner; B.S. in Med. Sci., U. W.Va., 1950; M.D., U. Pitts., 1952; m. Ralph Nutter, June 4, 1966; children—Beth Ann, Erric Christian; 1 stepson, Steven Ross. Intern Ohio Valley Hosp., Wheeling, W. Va., 1952-53; practice medicine in Harrisville, W.Va., 1953—; mem. staff St. Joseph's Hosp., Parkersburg, W.Va., Camden Clarke Hosp., Parkersburg; clin. prof. family practice W.Va. U. Sch. Medicine. Pres., Ritchie County P.T.A. Bd. dirs. Ritchie County Emergency Ambulance Service, W.Va. Cancer Soc., W.Va. Heart Assn. Mem. Am. Assn. Gen. Practitioners (pres. W.Va. chpt. 1967), Am. Acad. Gen. Practice, A.M.A. (adv. council to Sears Found. 1965-69, mem. rural health council 1965—), W.Va. Med. Soc. (chmn. med scholarships com., rural health com.), Parkersburg Acad. Medicine, Alpha Omega Alpha, Phi Epsilon Omicron. Address: 505 W High St Harrisville WV 26362

CRABTREE, CLARA OPAL JENKINS (MRS. BRUCE WILSON CRABTREE), librarian; b. Durham, N.C., Apr. 24, 1928; d. Clarence Levoy and Lillian Gray (Smith) Jenkins; B.S., E. Carolina U., 1951; M.Ed., U. N.C., 1966; m. Bruce Wilson Crabtree, June 30, 1967. Tchr., Brentwood Sch., High Point, N.C., 1951-52; tchr. Glenn Sch., Durham, N.C., 1952-59, librarian, 1959-64; library supr. Durham (N.C.) County Schs., 1964—. Mem. Internat. Reading Assn., Assn. Childhood Edn. Internat., N.E.A., A.L.A., Southeastern Library Assn., N.C. Library Assns., N.C. Assn. Educators, Ednl. Media Assn., Delta Kappa Gamma. Home: Route 1 Box 347A Bahama NC 27503 Office: 102 E Seminary St Durham NC 27702

CRACCHIOLO, EDITH ELEANOR, psychologist, educator; b. Detroit, Mar. 27, 1929; d. William Blewett and Margaret Lillian (Matthews) Hosking; B.A., Cal. State U. at Long Beach, 1962, M.A., 1964; children—Raphelle Celeste, Salvator William II. Prof. psychology Cerritos Coll., Norwalk, Cal., 1964—. Mem. Am. Psychol. Assn., A.A.A.S., So. Cal. Acad. Sci., Cal. Higher Edn. Assn., Cal. Tchrs. Assn. Research on brain temperature changes accompanying motivation. Home: 16231 Eucalyptus Av Bellflower CA 90706 Office: 11110 E Alondra Blvd Norwalk CA 90650

CRAFT, MARJORIE-LEE (MRS. JOHN EDGAR CRAFT), real estate broker; b. Cin., Mar. 21, 1924; d. Leon Frederick and Gertrude May (Wyatt) Hammond; student Whittier Coll., 1943-44, U. So. Cal., 1947-48, Shasta Coll., 1966-67; m. John Edgar Craft, July 21, 1956; children—Eric Steven, Merrie (Mrs. Daniel Cochran Sears), David W. Dist. mgr. Beauty Counselors, Inc., Anderson, Cal., 1961-65; owner Lee Craft Realtors, Anderson, 1971—. Served with WAC, 1944-47. Mem. Nat. Assn. Realtors, Cal. Real Estate Assn., Bus. and Profl. Women's Club, Epsilon Sigma Alpha. Republican. Presbyn.

Home: PO Box 262 Anderson CA 96007 Office: 4352 Hwy 99 Anderson CA 96007

CRAFT, NANCY MAE RUNYAN, librarian; b. Kansas City, Mo., Nov. 2, 1932; d. George Harold and Dorothy Lee (Carpenter) Runyan; B.B.A., Sul Ross State Coll., 1958; M.L.S., Syracuse U., 1965. Exec. sec. Crucible Steel Corp., Syracuse, N.Y., 1958-62; with Meml. Library, State U. N.Y. Coll. at Cortland, 1963-69; head George A. Barry Meml. Library, Tompkins-Cortland Community Coll., Groton, N.Y., 1969—. Mem. N.Y. Library Assn., Am. Assn. U. Profs., N.Y. State Assn. Jr. Colls., Beta Phi Mu. Club: Zonta. Home: 77 James St Homer NY 13077 Office: Main St Groton NY 13077

CRAFT, PEARL SARAH SERBUS, newspaper editor; b. Riverdale, Ill.; d. Emil Edwin and Pearl (Kaiser) Dieck; m. Gerald Serbus, Jan. 26, 1946 (dec. Aug. 1969); children—Allan Lester, Bruce Alan, Curt Lyle; m. 2d, James E. Craft, Jan. 16, 1974. Mem. home econs. staff writer, Chgo. Herald Examiner, 1934-39; operator test kitchen Household Sci. Inst., Mdse. Mart, Chgo., 1940-45; free-lance writer grocery chains, Chgo., 1945-49; Riv.-Dolton corr. Calumet Index, Chgo., 1953-58, editorial asst., 1958-60, asst. editor, 1960-68, editor, 1968—; with Suburban Index, Chgo., 1959—, editor, 1960—; mng. editor Index Publs., 1972-74; free lance writer, 1974—. Pub. relations vol. New Hope Sch., 1959-67. Recipient Distinguished Service Mem. scroll, P.T.A., 1959, Sch. Bell award Ill. Edn. Assn., 1965, Outstanding Citizen award Chgo. South C. of C., 1972. Named Outstanding Civic Leader Am. Bd. dirs. United Fund of Riverdale, Roseland Mental Health Assn., Thornton chpt. Am. Field Service. Mem. Ill. Woman's Press Assn. (past pres. Woman of Distinction 1968, recipient 44 state awards, 3 nat. awards), Riverdale (v.p. 1966-68), Chgo. South (v.p., dir.) chambers commerce. Home: 111 W 144th St Riverdale IL 60627 Office: 160 W 144th St Riverdale IL 60627

CRAIG, BARBARA MARY, educator; b. Ottawa, Ont., Can., Feb. 24, 1914; d. William Woodham and Edith Mary (Silcock) Craig; B.A., Queen's U., Kingston, Ont., 1937, M.A., 1939; Ph.D. (fellow), Bryn Mawr Coll., 1949. Came to U.S., 1939, naturalized, 1954. Tchr. Mt. Royal Coll., Calgary, Alta., Can., 1943-46; instr. French and Italian, U. Kan., Lawrence, 1947-49, asst. prof., 1949-59, asso. prof., 1959-64, prof., 1964—. Recipient Outstanding Tchr. award Standard Oil Co. Ind. Found., 1973. Sr. fellow Canadian Fedn. U. Women. Author articles, revs., critical edits. of mediaeval French plays. Home: 2707 W 24th St Terrace Lawrence KS 66044

CRAIG, CATHERINE ROSE KOEHNE, librarian; b. Alton, Ill., Aug. 1, 1944; d. James Earl and Catherine Rose (Howard) Koehne; B.S., Western Ill. U., 1966; postgrad. Middle Tenn. State U., summer 1969. Librarian, Cambridge (Ill.) pub. schs., 1966-68, tchr. art, 1968-69; librarian Palmer Jr. Coll., Davenport, Ia., 1969—, Palmer Coll. Chiropractic, Davenport, 1970—. Mem. Ill. Edn. Assn., Ill. Art Edn. Assn., Ia. Library Assn., Ia. Coll. and Jr. Coll. Librarian's Assn., Beta Sigma Phi. Club: Junior Women's (Cambridge). Home: 3326 E 46 St Davenport IA 52807 Office: 1000 Brady St Davenport IA 52803

CRAIG, ELEANOR DUGUID (MRS. ALAN DANIEL CRAIG), educator; b. Bklyn., July 16, 1938; d. Raymond Brighton and Jeannette (Weightman) Duguid; B.A. (with honors), Swarthmore Coll., 1960; M.A., U. Pa., 1961; m. Alan Daniel Craig, June 25, 1960; children—Robert Russell, Bruce Alan, Jeffrey Brighton, Jeannette Rankin. Lectr. econs. Rutgers U., Camden, N.J., 1961-62, U. Del., 1962-65; instr. in econs. U. Del., 1965-72, asst. prof., 1972—. Econ. adviser to U.S. Congressman P.S. DuPont IV, 1970—. Mem. Del. Gov.'s Council Women, 1970-73. Recipient 3d place award for Coll. econs. teaching Kazangian Found., 1973. Research grantee Ford Found., 1959; grantee U. Del., 1971, 72. Mem. Jr. League of Wilmington (dir. 1969-73, mem. exec. com. and treas. 1969-71), Pi Gamma Mu, Omicron Delta Epsilon, Am. Econs. Assn. Clubs: Wilmington (Del.) Country. Home: 808 Greenwood Rd Wilmington DE 19807 Office: Dept of Economics University of Delaware Newark DE 19711

CRAIG, MARJORIE LOUISE, ednl. cons.; b. Ridgewood, N.J., Apr. 25, 1913; d. James Douglas and Nellie (Scott) Craig; B.A., Smith Coll., 1934; M.A., Tchrs. Coll. Columbia, 1935; postgrad. pub. health Coll. Phys. & Surgeons; m. Colin Gray-Lewis. Tchr. Smith Coll. Nursery Sch., 1935-36; mem. staff sch. health bur., health and welfare div. Met. Life Ins. Co., 1937-47, dir. sch. health bur., health and welfare div., 1947-64, program coordinator, 1964-68, ret., 1968; ednl. cons., 1968—. Fellow Am. Pub. Health Assn., Am. Sch. Health Assn.; mem. Am. Assn. for Gifted Children (sec., dir.), Am. Assn. Sch. Adminstrs., Assn. for Childhood Edn., Nat. Assn. for Edn. Young Children, Internat. Orgn. Early Childhood Edn., Council for Exceptional Children. Address: RD 5 Hammonton NJ 08037

CRAIG, MARJORIE REED (MRS. JOHN THOMAS CROWLEY), phys. therapist, author; b. Bangor, Me., Mar. 9, 1912; d. Warren Everet and Harriet (Humphrey) Craig; B.S. in Phys. Edn., Arnold Coll., 1932; postgrad. in phys. therapy Columbia, 1932-33; m. John Thomas Crowley, Sept. 9, 1935. Instr., Neurol. Inst., Columbia-Presbyn. Med. Center, 1935-42; supr. exercise Richard Hudnut Salon, N.Y.C., 1942-52, Elizabeth Arden Salon, N.Y.C., 1952—; pres. Crocraig Corp. Author: Miss Craig's 21-Day Shape-Up Program; Miss Craig's Face-Saving Exercises; Miss Craig's Growing Up Exercise, 1973. Home: Old Post Rd Bedford Village NY 10506 Office: care Random House 201 E 50th St New York City NY 10022

CRAIG, MARY FRANCIS SHURA (MRS. RAYMOND CRAIG), author; b. Pratt, Kan., Feb. 27, 1923; d. Jack Fant Young and Mary Francis (Milstead) Y.; student Maryville State Coll., 1941-44; m. Daniel C. Shura, Oct. 24, 1943 (dec. June 1959); children—Marianne Francis (Mrs. William Webb Sprague), Daniel C.; m. 2d, Raymond Craig, Dec. 8, 1961; children—Alice Barrett, Mary Forsha. Creative writing tchr. summer conf. U. Kan., Lawrence, 1961, adult edn. Coll. St. Teresa's, Kan. City, Mo., 1960-61. Recipient 3d prize in poetry, Writer's Digest, 1965. Mem. Young Brother's Cattle Corp. (v.p., dir. 1950—), Author's Guild, Inc., Author's League Am., Inc., Theta Sigma Pi. Club: Belvedere Tennis (dir.). Author: Simple Spigott (on 100 Best list World Book Ency. 1960), 1960; Garrett of Greta McGraw, 1967; Mary's Marvelous Mouse, 1962; Nearsighted Knight (on 77 Best list, N.Y. Times 1963), 1963; Run Away Home, 1964; Backwards for Luck, 1968; Shoeful of Shamrock, 1965; A Tale of Middle Length, 1967; Pornada, 1969; The Valley of the Frost Giants, 1971; Topcat of Tam, 1972; The Shop on Threnody Street, 1972; The Seven Stone, 1972; A Candle for the Dragon, 1973; Ten Thousand Several Doors, 1973; The Cranes of Ibycus, 1974. Contbr. fiction to popular mags., 1959—, poetry, 1960—; weekly column Scrapbook from Shuranuff Farm, 1960-64. Address: 33 Ash Av Corte Madera CA 94925

CRAIG, MILDRED CAROLYN, educator; b. Lawrenceville, Ga.; d. Henry Rochelle and Beatrice (Hambrick) Craig; B.S., Woman's Coll. of Ga., 1939; M.S., U. Ga., 1956. Tchr. primary grades Gwinnett County, 1936-38; tchr. home econs., sci. and biology Gordon County, 1939-46; asst. supr. sch. lunch program Ga. Dept. Edn., 1946—. Mem. N.E.A., Am. Home Econs. Assn., Am. Sch. Food Service Assn., Assn. Sch. Bus. Ofcls., Ga. Assn. for Supervision and Curriculum Devel., Ga. Nutrition Council. Democrat. Presbyn. Home: 183 Hardin Dr Athens GA 30601 Office: Box 969 Athens GA 30601

CRAIG, NANCY RYAN (MRS. WILLIAM JOSEPH CRAIG), physician; b. Norman, Okla., June 24, 1924; d. Henry Grady and Anna (Butler) Ryan; B.S., U. Okla., 1946; M.D., U. Okla., 1949; m. William Joseph Craig, Apr. 25, 1946; children—John Joseph, Christopher Patrick, Mary Elizabeth, Kathleen Frances. Intern, U. Okla. Hosps., 1949-50; residency anesthesiology, 1955-57; dir. health service, 1951-53; mil. dependent in Alaska, 1953-54; pvt. practice anesthesiology, 1957—; mem. staffs Presbyn., St. Anthony, Bapt. Meml., Mercy Okla., City Gen., U. Okla. hosps.; asst. attending anesthesiologist Mt. Sinai Hospital, New York City, summer 1968; now asst. clin. prof. U. Okla. Sch. Medicine. Mem. Okla. Art Center, Oklahoma City Symphony Soc., Oklahoma City Ballet Soc. (charter), YWCA. Diplomate Am. Bd. Anesthesiology. Mem. Am., Pan. Am., Okla., Oklahoma County med. assns., So. Med. Soc., Am., Okla. (pres. 1974—) socs. anesthesiologists, N.Y. Acad. Scis., Oklahoma City Clin. Soc., Internat. Anesthesia Research Soc., Phi Beta Kappa, Alpha Lambda Delta, Alpha Epsilon Delta, Phi Sigma, Alpha Epsilon Iota. Republican. Roman Catholic. Club: Oklahoma Medical Faculty. Home: 525 NW 39th St Oklahoma City OK 73118 Office: 525 NW 11th St Oklahoma City OK 73103

CRAIG, SUESETTA ELIZABETH TALBERT, educator; b. Detroit, May 5, 1931; d. Henry Payne and Dora Adeline (Russell) Talbert; B.S., Wayne State U., 1954; M.A., N.Y. U., 1962; m. Herbert Craig, Nov. 24, 1962 (div. 1964); 1 son, Geoffrey Levi. Research asso. occupational therapy Wayne State U., Detroit, 1955-58, asst. prof., 1967—; supr. occupational therapy Rehab. Inst., Detroit, 1958-67. Cons. Mich. Dept. Vocational Rehab., 1973—; mem. adv. com. occupational therapy asst. program Wayne County Community Coll., Detroit, 1972-73; activities program cons. LaSalle Nursing Home, David Nursing Home, Detroit, 1966-67; mem. adv. and planning com. to implement program for handicapped adults, 1973—; mem. adv. bd. Schoolcraft Community Coll., 1974—. Mem. Founders' Soc. Detroit Inst. Arts, 1963—; mem. pres.'s council Marygrove Coll., Detroit, 1973—. Sec. bd. dirs. Delta Home for Girls, Detroit, 1958-61. Nat. Recreation Assn. grantee N.Y.C., 1961-62; Rehab. Inst. grantee, Detroit, 1961-62. Mem. Am., Mich. (bull. editor 1956-58) occupational therapy assns., Wayne State U. Occupational Therapy Alumni Assn. (organizer), Detroit Occupational Therapy Assn., Jack and Jill of Am. (sec. 1972-74), Delta Sigma Theta, Pi Lambda Theta. Clubs: Detroit Study (pres. 1970-72); Flair, Carrousels, Kaleidoscope. Home: 3265 W Outer Dr Detroit MI 48221

CRAIG, THELMA MAE RUSSELL (MRS. DOUGLAS EVANS CRAIG), hosp. adminstr.; b. North Vancouver, B.C., Can., Feb. 1, 1913; d. George Washington Frederick and Minnie Lucinda (Edgett) Russell; grad. St. John Gen. Hosp. Sch. Nursing, 1935; postgrad. Kahler Corp. Hosps., 1938; m. Douglas Evans Craig, Dec. 10, 1949. Nurse operating room Jewish Hosp., Bklyn., 1939; supr. operating room Chipmer Meml. Hosp., St. Stephen, N.B., Can., 1939-42, St. John Gen. Hosp., Perth, N.B., 1935-38, 42-45, 50-52; supr. operating room and emergency room Hotel Dieu Hosp., Perth, 1952—. Mem. N.B. Assn. R.N.s, Round Table Lit. Club. Anglican. Home: Main St Perth NB E0J 1O0 Canada Office: Hotel Dieu St Joseph Hosp Perth NB E0J 1O0 Canada

CRAIK, MARY BERNICE WILHITE (MRS. JAMES S. CRAIK, JR.), psychologist, educator; b. Louisville, May 26, 1924; d. Huse and Grace Elizabeth (Meredith) Wilhite; B.A., U. Tex., 1960, M.Ed., 1963; Ph.D., U. Ia., 1968; m. James S. Craik Jr., Nov. 29, 1946; children—Richard, Stephen, Juliet. Tchr. art Bowie High Sch., El Paso, Tex., 1960-62; instr. U. Tex., El Paso, 1962-65, Western N.M. U., Silver City, 1965; from instr. to prof. psychology St. Cloud (Minn.) State Coll., 1968—. Mem. Minn. Bd. Examiners of Psychologists, 1973—. Mem. Am. Psychol. Assn., Am. Ednl. Research Assn., Am. Assn. U. Profs., Women's Equity Action League. Contbr. articles on ednl. psychology to profl. jours. Home: Route 2 St Cloud MN 56301

CRAM, ELSIE MAY (MRS. WILLARD W. CRAM), journalist; b. Vickery, O., May 22, 1920; d. Grover Cleveland and Glenna Irene (Hughes) McKay; B.A., Ohio State U., 1942; m. Willard Winston Cram, Oct. 22, 1949 (dec. Nov. 1965). Journalist Fremont (O.) News Messenger, 1942-43; journalist Toledo Blade, 1943-72, asst. city editor, 1972—. Mem. Newspaper Guild, Toledo Press Club, Ohio Newspaper Womens Assn., Women in Communications. Lutheran. Home: 2640 Overbrook Dr Toledo OH 43614 Office: 541 Superior St Toledo OH 43604

CRAMER, ANN MARIE JOAN (MRS. HUGH BERNARD MICHAEL CRAMER), real estate exec., nat. Democratic committeewoman; b. Buffalo, Nov. 1, 1925; d. Lawrence Nicholas and Barbara Marie (Herman) Bowman; student Rollins Coll., 1959; m. Hugh Bernard Michael Cramer, May 30, 1941; children—Annmarie (Mrs. Robert Wayne Baxley), Mary E. (Mrs. I. Nat. Giuliano), Cathleen Bridget, Hugh Skiffington and Lawrence Robert (twins). Real estate broker Ann M. Cramer Real Estate, Hollywood, Fla., 1957—. Vice chmn. Democratic exec. com. of Fla., 1962-69, 70—, chmn., 1970; Dem. state committeewoman, 1958—; del. Dem. Nat. Conv., 1960, 64, 68, 72, mem. credentials com., 1964, mem. platform com., 1964; mem. Dem. Nat. Com., 1972—. Mem. Pres.'s Commn. on Voting and Registration, 1963; mem. U.S. adv. council World's Fair, Toronto, Ont., Can., 1967. Named Fla. Dem. Woman of Year, Dem. Nat. Com., 1960. Mem. West Hollywood C. of C. (dir. 1963, 64), Womens C. of C. (dir. 1964, 65), Women of Moose, Am. Legion Aux., West Broward Lions Aux., League Women Voters. Club: Catholic (v.p.). Office: 6011 Rodman St Hollywood FL 33023 also PO Box 1758 Tallahassee FL 32304 and 6249 SW 7th St Miramar FL 33023

CRAMER, BELLE (MRS. WILLIAM CRAMER), artist; b. N.Y.C., Aug. 11, 1883; d. David and Eliza (Shottick) Klauber; student Tchrs.' Coll., Columbia U., 1903-05, Barnard Coll., 1905-06, Edinburgh (Scotland) Coll. Art, 1910-13; m. William Cramer, July 31, 1906; children—Ian D.W., Michael U. Represented in permanent collections St. Louis Art Mus., Washington U., St. Louis, Denison U., Lindenwood Coll., St. Charles, Mo., Webster Coll., St. Louis, Mary Inst., St. Louis, also in pvt. collections, U.S. and Eng.; tchr. art YMCA, St. Louis, early 1950's. Recipient 22 prizes St. Louis Artists Guild, 1941-72, 2d prize St. Louis Art Mus. Mem. St. Louis Artists Guild, Acad. Profl. Artists St. Louis, Nat. Soc. Women Artists. Home: 5354 Delmar St Louis MO 63112

CRAMER, DOROTHY JANE FEITLER (MRS. ALLEN CRAMER), recreation exec.; b. N.Y.C., Apr. 25, 1922; d. Richard and Sophie (Greenwald) Feitler; B.S., Temple U., 1942, M.S., 1948; m. Allen Cramer, Oct. 25, 1942; 1 dau., Carol Lynn (Mrs. Larry Kemelgor). Instr. health and phys. edn. Phila. Pub. Schs., 1942-44, Deveraux Schs., Paoli, Pa., 1942; dir. Camp Vacamas Assn., N.Y.C., 1946-49; exec. dir. Camp Poyntelle, N.Y.C., 1949-52; owner, dir. Camp Somerset, Oakland, Me., 1952—, Camp Cobbossee, Winthrop, Me., 1962—. Instr. blind Lighthouse, N.Y.C., 1968—; mem. social services bd. Harlem Hosp., 1954-59; active YMHA. Mem. Am. Camping Assn., Camp Vacamas Assn. Home: 180 E End Av New York City NY 10028 Office: 225 E 57th St New York City NY 10022

CRAMER, ESTHER RIDGWAY (MRS. STANLEY E. CRAMER), writer; b. La Habra, Cal., Jan. 17, 1927; d. Claude Arthur and Ida Alma (Leutwiler) Ridgway; B.A., Pomona Coll., 1948; postgrad. U. So. Cal., 1949, Cal. State Coll., 1960-67; m. Stanley E. Cramer, June 17, 1948; children—Cynthia Ann, Melinda, Janet. Supr. phys. edn. Fullerton (Cal.) Schs., 1948-51; writer, historian, pub. relations adminstr. Alpha Beta Co., La Habra, Cal., 1973—. Sec. Nixon Law Office Preservation Trust, 1973; adviser Orange County Hist. Commn., 1973—; mem. Orange County Bicentennial Com., 1969; chmn. La Habra City Anniversary and Am. Bicentennial Com., 1973—. Vice pres. bd. govs. Patrons of Library, Cal. State U., Fullerton, 1971—. Mem. Cal., Orange County (pres. 1971-72) hist. socs., Cal. Conf. Hist. Socs., La Habra Old Settlers' Hist. soc. (dir. 1973, historian 1973—), Phi Beta Kappa, Mortar Bd. Author: La Habra: The Pass through the Hills (award Am. Assn. for State and Local History 1970, U. Cal. at Irvine outstanding author award 1970), 1969; The Alpha Beta Story, 1973. Home: 600 Linden Lane La Habra CA 90631

CRAMER, JEAN ABEL (MRS. HARRY CALVIN CRAMER), physician; b. Elizabeth, N.J., Apr. 2, 1928; d. Henri E. and Alice (Gibb) Abel; B.A., Barnard Coll,, 1947; M.D., Cornell U., 1950; m. Harry Calvin Cramer, Apr. 16, 1947; children—John Stearns, Paul, Peter, Anne. Intern, Bellevue Hosp., N.Y.C., 1950-51; resident dermatology N.Y. Hosp., 1951-54; practice medicine, specializing in dermatology, Elizabeth, N.J., 1954—; attending in dermatology Elizabeth Gen. Hosp.; instr. dermatology Cornell Med. Sch., N.Y.C., 1954-68, asst. prof. dermatology, 1968—. Bd. dirs. Elizabeth Planned Parenthood. Diplomate Am. Bd. Dermatology and Syphilology. Mem. A.M.A., Union County Med. Soc., N.J. Dermatologic Soc. (past pres.). Home: 625 Union Av Elizabeth NJ 07208 Office: 360 Elmora Av Elizabeth NJ 07208

CRAMER, LAURA SCHWARZ (MRS. ROBERT R. CRAMER), coll. dean; b. St. Louis, Aug. 13, 1925; d. Frederick William and Gertrude Margaret (Kipp) Schwarz; A.B., Duke, 1947; M.A. (Jesse M. Barr fellow), Washington U., St. Louis, 1948; m. Robert R. Cramer, Oct. 29, 1949; children—Anne (Mrs. Geoffrey N. Coleman), Carol, Laura. Model, John Robert Powers Agy., N.Y.C., 1946; grad. asst. dept. psychology Washington U., St. Louis, 1947-48, instr., 1948-49; psychometrist Clayton (Mo.) Pub. Schs., 1961; dir. testing Columbia Sch., Rochester, N.Y., 1964-71; asst. registrar, counselor women students St. John Fisher Coll., Rochester, 1971-72, registrar, dean of women, 1972—. Chmn. bd. dirs. Inst. of St. Louis, 1960; bd. dirs. St. Louis Community Music Sch., 1959-61, Vol. Service Bur., St. Louis, 1960-61, Jr. League St. Louis, 1957-61, Jr. League Rochester, 1963-65, Monroe County Hosp. Aux., 1974—. Mem. Phi Beta Kappa, Sigma Xi. Home: 542 Allens Creek Rd Rochester NY 14618

CRAMER, MARGERYFAY REESER (MRS. ROBERT ELI CRAMER), social worker; b. Paris, Ill., Jan. 13, 1920; d. William Charles and Grace Zimmerly (Moffett) Reeser; A.B., Ohio U., 1941; M.Psychiat. Social Work, Washington U., St. Louis, 1945; m. Robert Eli Cramer, Dec. 31, 1941; children—Judith Fay, Barbara Elaine, Timothy Robert. Caseworker, student supr. social service dept. Jewish Hosp., St. Louis, 1945-47; caseworker U. Chgo. Clinics, 1947-49; caseworker, student supr. A.R.C., Washington, 1951-54, caseworker, supr. Memphis, 1949-51; instr. E. Carolina U., Greenville, N.C., 1963-69; social work supr., coordinator staff devel. Caswell Center, Kinston, N.C., 1969—. Mem. Council Social Work Edn., Nat. Assn. Social Workers, Acad. Certified Social Workers, Am. Assn. Mental Deficiency. Club: East Carolina University Faculty Wives. Home: 1408 Evergreen Dr Greenville NC 27834 Office: Caswell Center Kinston NC 28501

CRAMER, PATRICIA ANN JOHNSTON (MRS. PHILIP W. CRAMER), television sta. exec.; b. Louisville, Sept. 3, 1942; d. William H. and Mary Allene (Watson) Johnston; B.S., Ind. U., 1964; postgrad. Pa. State U., 1964-65; m. Philip W. Cramer, July 3, 1965; 1 dau., Carrie Lynn. Field rep. Phi Mu Frat., Memphis, 1964, extension dir.; polit. analyst Indonesian embassy, Washington, 1965-66; adminstrv. asst. to congressman, Washington, 1966-68; pub. affairs dir. WTVN-TV Columbus, O., 1969—. Instr. speech Columbus Tech. Inst., evenings, 1972. Bd. govs. Nat. Acad. Television Arts and Scis. Home: 5418 Aspen Rd Columbus OH 43229 Office: 753 Harmon Av Columbus OH 43223

CRAMER, POLLY (MRS. DOUGLAS S. CRAMER), journalist; b. Garfield, Ky., Oct. 14, 1903; d. Paul and Elizabeth Macy) Compton; student Va. Coll. for Girls, 1921-22; m. Douglas S. Cramer, Nov. 2, 1929 (dec. Oct. 1956);children—Douglas S., Paul, Peyton. Columnist interior decorating Cin. Post Times Star, 1940-71, household hints Newspaper Enterprise Assn., N.Y.C., 1963—. Edit. scout various home furnishing mags., 1950's. Mem. Am. Inst. Interior Designers. Author: Polly's Pointers, 1965. Home: 2370 Madison Rd Cincinnati OH 45208 Office: Newspaper Enterprise Assn 230 Park Av New York NY 10017

CRAMPTON, MARION WRIGHT, occupational therapist; b. Boston, Aug. 17, 1914; d. Arthur William and Bertha Claire (McIntyre) Crampton; A.B., Wellesley Coll., 1935; certificate Boston Sch. Occupational Therapy, 1937. Occupational therapist hosps. in N.Y., Mass. and Hawaii, 1937-52; supr. occupational therapy Mass. Dept. Mental Health, Boston, 1952—; cons. psychiat. occupational therapy Boston Sch. Occupational Therapy, 1951-54, 57-59. Bd. dirs. Am. Occupational Therapy Found., 1966-74, sec., 1965-74; pres. Occupational Therapy Assn. Hawaii, 1941. Dept. Health Edn. and Welfare grantee, 1965-69. Mem. Am. (award merit 1972), Mass. (treas. 1959-52, 61-63, v.p. 1964-65) occupational therapy assns., World Fedn. Occupational Therapists, League Women Voters, Arlington Hist. Soc., Zonta Internat. Republican. Conglist. Co-editor: Changing Concepts and Practice in Psychiatric Occupational Therapy, 1959. Home: 109 Bartlett Av Arlington MA 02174 Office: 190 Portland St Boston MA 02114

CRANDALL, MARDEL ASBURY MCCLURE (MRS. PHILIP G. CRANDALL), editor; b. Washington, Apr. 15, 1948; d. Harold LeRoy and Lois Eloise (Keller) McClure; B.S. in Home Econs., Kan. State U., 1970; M.S. in Family Life Edn., Purdue U., 1972; m. Philip G. Crandall, Dec. 21, 1969. Asst. editor Kan. Coop. Extension Service, Kan. State U., Manhattan, 1970; information specialist Ind. Cooperative Extension Service, Purdue U., West Lafayette, Ind., 1970—. Mem. Mortar Bd. (sec. 1969-70), Am. Assn. Agrl. Coll. Editors, Women in Communications, Alpha of Clovia, Omicron Nu, Phi Upsilon Omicron, Theta Sigma Phi, Phi Kappa Phi. Republican. Methodist. Home: 127 Woodland Terrace West Lafayette IN 47906 Office: 206 AGAD Bldg Purdue U West Lafayette IN 47906

CRANDALL, NORMA, writer, editor; b. Brooklyn Heights, N.Y., Nov. 20, 1907; d. Edward H. and Marie Vanderveer (Hall) Crandall; student Barnard Coll., 1926-27; m. Wilson Chamberlain McCarty, Sept. 15, 1933 (dec.). Contbr. book reviews to New Republic, The Nation, N.Am. Rev., N.Y. Times, Saturday Rev., New Leader, Humanist, Chgo. Rev., book reviews and essays to Trace, Am. Book Collector, articles to Collier's, Pageant, English Digest, Poetry to Town and Country Rev.; adv. editor Harcourt Brace & Co., 1939; free lance editor to individual writers, 1939—; author biography Emily

Bronte, 1957, 70; presented dramatic reading An Evening with the Brontes, 1968-69, 73. Mem. Poetry Soc. Am., Author's Guild, Acad. Am. Poets (patron), Bronte Soc. Home: 44 E 63d St New York City NY 10021

CRANDALL, VICTORIA FRANZEN (MRS. G. BURR CRANDALL), performing arts adminstr.; b. Cleve., Apr. 13, 1908; d. Victor A. and Anna K. (Olson) Franzen; Mus.B., Eastman Sch. of Music, 1931; B.Mus., U. Rochester, 1931; m. G. Burr Crandall, May, 1936. Concert pianist Columbia Artists, 1932-41; pianist Broadway shows, N.Y.C., 1942-51; producer Brit. Colonial Playhouse, Nassau, Bahamas, 1956-59; pres., producer Brunswick (Me.) Music Theatre, Inc., 1959—. Mem. Bath-Brunswick Regional Arts Council, 1971—. Bd. dirs. Stowe House, Brunswick, 1970—. Served with USO, World War II; ETO. Recipient plaque for benefit concerts Pine Tree Soc. Crippled Children, 1970, 71. Mem. Theatre of Me. Assn., Am. Assn. U. Women, Brunswick C. of C., Sigma Alpha Iota. Home: Clark's Point Wiscasset ME 04578 Office: 185 Park Row Brunswick ME 04011

CRANDALL, VIRGINIA CAROL, psychologist, educator; b. Pinconning, Mich., Aug. 20, 1922; d. John R. and Fern B. (Harris) Fotheringham; student U. Mich., 1940-42, Mich. State U., 1942-43; B.A., Tex. Christian U., 1944; postgrad. U. Cal. at Berkeley, 1959-60; M.A. in Psychology, Ohio State U., 1961; m. Vaughn J. Crandall, June 20, 1942 (dec. Oct. 1963); children—Grant, Joel, Neal. Psychiat. intake interviewer U. Mich. Hosp., Ann Arbor, 1945; research asst. Fels Research Inst., Yellow Springs, O., 1960-61, research asso., 1963, dir. of achievement devel. project, 1963—, sr. investigator, 1963-71, sr. scientist, 1971—. Instr. psychology Antioch Coll., Yellow Springs, 1961-67, asst. prof. psychology, 1967, asso. prof., 1968—. Nat. Inst. Mental Health grantee, 1963—. Mem. Am. Psychol. Assn. (mem. div. 7 exec. com. 1972—), A.A.A.S., Internat. Soc. for Study Behavioral Devel., Soc. for Research in Child Devel., League Women Voters (pres. 1958-60). Cons. editor Psychol. Bull., 1969—; editorial bd. Developmental Psychology and Child Development, 1969—. Contbr. articles on child development to profl. jours. Home: 1318 Spillan Yellow Springs OH 45387 Office: Fels Research Institute Yellow Springs OH 45387

CRANE, BARBARA COHEN (MRS. STUART G. CRANE), publisher, author; b. Trenton, N.J., June 2, 1934; d. Herman and Elizabeth (Stein) Cohen; B.A., Vassar Coll., 1956; m. Stuart G. Crane, Aug. 27, 1956; children—Susan Jill, Patricia Lynne. Tchr., Trenton Pub. Schs., 1956-58; prin. Little People's Reading Sch., Yardley, Pa., 1964-66; reading cons. Newtown (Pa.) Friends Sch., 1967-68; pres. Motivational Learning Programs, Inc., Trenton, N.J., 1968—. reading cons. Trenton State Coll., 1968-69, dir. Demonstration Sch. for Center City Five Year Olds; lectr. linguistics, reading, child psychology. Trenton State Coll. grantee, 1968-69. Mem. Internat. Platform Assn., Pi Beta Alpha. Author Categorical Sound System (structured prereading and beginning reading program), 1964-73. Home: 1909 Yardley Rd Yardley PA 19067

CRANE, KATHARINE ELIZABETH, editor, writer; b. Kenton, O.; d. George Edward and Kate (Rhodes) Crane; A.B., Smith Coll., 1916; Ph.D., U. Chgo., 1930. Tchr., St. Katherine's Sch., Davenport, Ia., 1916-17, Shippen Sch., Lancaster, Pa., 1920-22, Women's Coll., U. N.C., 1925-26; asst. editor Ency. Social Scis., 1929-30; asst. editor Dictionary Am. Biography, 1930-36, Social Studies and Social Edn., 1936-39; state supr., state guide, Va. Hist. Survey. Library Services, 1940-43; officer Dept. State, 1943-50; historian Mil. Air Transport Service, 1950-60; free-lance writer, 1960—. Author: Status of Countries in Relation to the War, 1944; Blair House, 1946; Mr. Carr of State, 1960. Contbr. articles to profl. jours. Home: 500 North Main St Kenton OH 43326

CRANE, LILLY EDNA HAMLET (MRS. GEORGE L. CRANE), librarian; b. Hackensack, N.J., Sept. 2, 1937; d. Felix Max and Annemarie Elizabeth (Korting) Hamlet; B.A., Ind. U., 1959; M.L.S., U. Mich., 1967; m. George L. Crane, Jan. 24, 1959; children—James Thomas, Michael Joseph. Asst. edn. and psychology reference librarian Morris Library, So. Ill. U., Carbondale, 1967-69, serials cataloger, 1969-74, head computerized cataloging, 1974—. Book reviewer Library Jour., 1968-70. Precinct committeewoman Jackson County Democratic Com., 1969-72, sec., 1974—; precinct committeewoman Makanda Dem. Com., 1974—. Mem. Am. Motorcycle Assn., Phi Alpha Theta. Home: Route 1 Cedar Creek Rd Makanda IL 62958 Office: Catalog Dept Morris Library So Ill U Carbondale IL 62901

CRANE, MARGERY ANN HALE, editor; b. Akron, O., June 6, 1921; d. Laurence Henry and Hilda (Schmidt) Hale; A.B., Am. U., 1942, postgrad., 1943-44; div. asst. book review editor Am. Statis. Assn., Washington, 1944-46; editorial asst. Changing Times, Kiplinger Mag., Washington, 1946-55, research editor, 1955-64, asso. editor, 1965—. Sponsor, Youth Gardens, Washington. Clubs: Washington Press (treas. 1957-58), Am. Newspaper Women's (pres. 1965-66), International (Washington). Home: 4706 Windom Pl NW Washington DC 20016 Office: 1729 H St NW Washington DC 20006

CRANE, MARILYN JOYCE, paleontologist; b. Grand Rapids, Mich., May 10, 1931; d. H.D. and Dorris (Northrup) Crane; B.S., Mich. State U., 1953, M.S., 1955. Geologist, Ind. Geol. Survey, Bloomington, 1955-56; paleontologist Exxon Corp. U.S.A., 1956—. Mem. Nat. Audubon Soc. (charter Houston, sec. 1971), Am. Assn. Petroleum Geologists, Soc. Econ. Mineralogists, and Paleontologists, Houston Geol. Soc., Gulf Coast Soc. Econ. Mineralogists and Paleontologists, Conservation Arts of Houston, Houston Outdoor Club, Corpus Christie Outdoor Club (sec. 1965, chmn. Christmas bd. count 1967), Ornithology Group (chmn. 1972-73). Contbr. articles to profl. jours. Home: 3601 Alley Pkwy Houston TX 77019 Office: PO Box 2180 Houston TX 77001

CRANGLE, EVA A., educator; b. Ogden, Utah, Oct. 9, 1925; d. Dinsmore C. and Mary (Rowse) Crangle; B.S., Neb. U., 1947; M.A., Columbia, 1953; postgrad. (Shell Merit fellow), Stanford, 1956; Ed.D., U. Utah, 1971. Tchr. math. Bryant Jr. High Sch., Salt Lake City, 1947-54, West and Highland Sr. High Schs., Salt Lake City, 1954-62; math. specialist Salt Lake City Schs., 1962—; vis. faculty mem. Utah State U., 1964. Mem. Utah Curriculum and Textbook Com., Math., 1962—. NSF fellow, 1959, 63. Mem. Nat. Council Tchrs. Math., N.E.A., Nat. Council Suprs. Math., Math. Assn. Am., Utah Edn. Assn., Salt Lake City Schs. Adminstrs. Assn., P.E.O., Pi Lambda Theta. Methodist. Mem. Order Eastern Star (worthy matron 1967-68). Club: Ladies' Literary. Contbr. articles to profl. jours. Home: 3650 Carolyn St Salt Lake City UT 84106 Office: 440 E 1st St S Salt Lake City UT 84111

CRANSTON, GENEVA MCMATH (MRS. ALAN CRANSTON), wife of U.S. senator; b. Berkeley, Cal., 1912; d. Edgar Harold and May (Amend) McMath; B.A., Pomona Coll., 1934; m. Alan Cranston, Nov. 6, 1940; children—Robin MacGregor, Kim MacGregor. Case worker, Los Angeles, 1934-40; legislative rep. Common Council for Am. Unity, Washington, 1942-43; legislative rep. Pearl Buck's Com. to Repeal Chinese Exclusion, Washington, 1943-44; writer for Orson Welles, N.Y.C., 1944-45. Mem. Women's Nat. Democratic Club. Club: Senate Wives. Home: 2700 Virginia Av NW S-112 Washington DC 20037

CRASE, DRUCIE (MRS. J.C. CRASE), lectr.; b. Jackson, Cal., Aug. 14, 1893; d. Henry Holman and Annie (Provis) Hicks; A.B., San Francisco State Coll., 1934; adminstrv. credential Cal. State Schs., 1932; m. James Crase, June 21, 1916; 1 dau., Corena (Mrs. Harold Green). Tchr., Nevard County, Cal., 1913-15, Alameda County, 1918-20; tchr. Berkeley (Cal.) schs., 1920-28; adminstr. Oakland (Cal.) schs., 1931-37, formerly Vallejo (Cal.) Unified Sch. Dist.; now lectr. on Meeting the Needs of the Gifted. Chmn. local chpt. A.R.C., 1954-55, mem. Pacific area adv. council, also bd. dirs.; Hawaii state chmn. vols. A.R.C., now rep., bd. dirs. Rossmoor; bd. dirs. Campfire Girls, Inc., Honolulu dist. organizer; bd. dirs. Community Concerts Assn., Santa Rosa Jr. Coll. Sch. Nursing. Founder, chmn. Petaluma Town Meeting. Mem. Nat., Cal. (rep. Internat. Conv. Educators, Oxford, Eng. 1935) tchrs. assn., Vallejo Sch. Adminstrs. Assn. (pres. 1948). Am. Assn. U. Women (v.p.; chmn. edn. Honolulu br.; Hawaii chmn. community problems). Methodist. Clubs: Zonta, Woman's (pres. Petaluma 1939-41); Women's Athletic (Oakland). Author: A Practical Plan for Meeting the Needs of Gifted Children. Founder wartime Hospitality House; originator visual aids program for gifted children. Home: 2956 Tice Creek Dr Rossmoor Walnut Creek CA 94595

CRASS, GWENDOLYN, ret. physician; b. Ada, Okla.; d. Newton Zollie and Mamie (Perry) Crass; B.A., So. Meth. U., 1934; M.D., U. Tex., 1944. Intern, Balt. City Hosp., 1944-45; resident pathology Baylor Hosp., Dallas, 1945-49; fellow pathology, then asst. prof. pathology U. Tex. Med. Br., Galveston, 1951-59; asso. pathologist Baylor Hosp., 1959-74, dir. Sch. Med. Tech., 1969-74; ret., 1974. Mem. A.M.A., Internat. Soc. Hematology, Am. Coll. Pathology, Am. Soc. Clin. Pathology, Internat. Acad. Pathology, Am. Soc. Cytology. Home: 6520 Linden Lane Dallas TX 75230

CRATON, JEAN, physician; b. Chgo., Sept. 1, 1926; d. Hugh George and Bessie (Linn) Craton; student Park Coll., Parkville, Mo., 1945-47, Ind. U., 1947-49; A.B. in Chemistry, Ind. U., 1949, M.D., 1953; postgrad. psychiatry Menninger Found. Sch. Psychiatry, 1955-58; m. Donald A. Neher, Mar. 28, 1954 (div. Aug. 1961); 1 son, Jonathan. Intern, Detroit Receiving Hosp., 1953-54; practice medicine, Pittsburg, Cal., 1954-55; psychiat. resident Menninger Found. Sch. Psychiatry, Topeka, 1955-58; staff psychiatrist Topeka State Hosp., 1959, Menninger Found., Topeka, 1959-62, San Mateo County Mental Health Services (Cal.), 1962-69; pvt. practice medicine specializing in psychiatry, Menlo Park, Cal., 1969—, Redwood City, Cal., 1963-69; Mental health cons. social agys., 1964-71; clin. instr. dept. psychiatry Stanford U. Med. Sch., 1964-69, clin. asst. prof., 1969—. Mem. Am., No. Cal. (task force on confidentiality), Mid-Peninsula psychiat. assns., A.M.A., Cal. Med. Assn., San Mateo County Med. Soc. (mental health com. 1971-74), Nat. Orgn. Women, Am. Med. Women's Assn., Common Cause, Sierra Club, Menninger Found. Alumni Assn., League Women Voters, Am. Civil Liberties Union. Home: 675 Maybell Av Palo Alto CA 94306 Office: 560 Oxford Av Palo Alto CA 94306

CRAUGH, CAROLYN, travel cons.; b. Dallas, May 3, 1929; d. John McAdams and Sara (Thompson) Craugh; B.A. in Psychology, Skidmore Coll., 1950; postgrad. Cornell U., 1951, So. Meth. U., 1954. Travel cons. Sargent Travel Agy., Inc., Rochester, N.Y., 1961—; adminstrv. asst. to pres. Travel Cons., Washington, 1967; spl. assignments Travel-Time Advisors, Dallas, 1969-70, Travelguide, Inc., Hollywood, Cal., 1970-71. Leader, Mayor's Rochester-Sister City tour to Europe, State Dept. People to People Program, 1971, 72. Bd. dirs. Bicentennial Congress Monroe County, Civic Music Assn., Meml. Art Gallery, Rochester Mus. and Sci. Center, Crystal Charity Ball Found., Dallas, Girls Club Dallas, Cystic Fibrosis Found., Dallas. Mem. Jr. League Dallas, Landmark Soc. Western N.Y., Nat. Honor Soc. Clubs: City, Tennis, Oak Hill Country (Rochester). Home: 1132 East Av Rochester NY 14607 Office: Sargent Travel Agy Inc Midtown Plaza Rochester NY 14604

CRAVEN, ELIZABETH (MRS. WALES CRAVEN), physician; b. Camden, N.J., Mar. 9, 1936; d. Charles R. and Anne E. (Singley) Muffett; B.A., Douglass Coll., 1957; M.D., N.Y. Med. Coll., 1961; m. Wales Craven, May 29, 1965; 1 son, Rodrick Patten. Intern, Bryn Mawr (Pa.) Hosp., 1961-62; resident St. Christopher's Hosp. for Children, 1962-64; fellow in pediatric habilitation, Phila., 1964-65; pediatrician Elwyn (Pa.) Inst., 1965-69; dir. pediatric clinics Wilmington (Del.) Med. Center, 1970—; asst. prof. Jefferson Med. Coll., Phila., 1970 cons. in pediatric neurology Chester County Mental Health Center, West Chester, Pa., 1967-69. Diplomate Am. Bd. Pediatrics. Fellow Am. Acad. Pediatrics; mem. A.M.A., Phila. Pediatric Soc., Alpha Epsilon Iota. Contbr. articles to profl. jours. Home: 8 Gen Wayne Dr Media PA 19063 Office: Wilmington Med Center 501 W 14th St Wilmington DE 19899

CRAVEN, REBECCA JAYNE, librarian; b. Chattanooga, Nov. 8, 1931; d. Roy Curtis and Edna (Morris) Craven; B.Mus., U. Chattanooga, 1953; M.A. in L.S., George Peabody Coll., 1954. Spl. services librarian U.S. Army Dept., Germany, 1954-56; with Pub. Library Cin. and Hamilton County, 1957—, 1st asst. fine arts dept., 1962-64, head films and recs. center, 1964-74, head fine arts dept., 1974—. Violist, Chattanooga Symphony Orch., 1951-53, Nashville Symphony Orch., 1954, Cin. Community Orch., 1957-64. Mem. Ohio Library Assn. (chmn. audiovisual roundtable 1970), Common Cause (telephone coordinator), Matinee Musicale, Euterpe Music Clubs. Club: Contemporary. Democrat. Unitarian. Home: 1802 Walker St Cincinnati OH 45210 Office: 800 Vine St Cincinnati OH 45202

CRAVENS, MARGARET EVELYN JOHNSON (MRS. DENNIS CARL CRAVENS), motel exec.; b. nr. Versailles, Ky.; d. Denny Johnson and Bethel (Goodpaster) Johnson Cox; student Draughn Bus. Coll., Springfield, Mo., 1943, U. Ky., 1951, Sch. Civil Def., 1959, mgmt. course U. Mich., 1968, Quality Inns, Inc. Motel Mgmt. Sch., 1969; m. Dennis Carl Cravens, Aug. 7, 1937; children—Dennis Wayne, Glenn Allen, Margaret Gayle. Bookkeeper Cravens & Cravens, Inc., Lexington, Ky., 1946-50; mgr. Quality Inn, N.W. Lexington, 1968—; pres., dir. Motel Developers, Inc.; treas., dir. Dea-Mar Enterprises, Inc.; chmn. region 9 Quality Inns Internat. Operators Council. Vice chmn. Lexington-Fayette County Recreational, Tourism and Conv. Commn. Bd. dirs., sec. Lexington Center, Inc.; trustee Ky. Travel Council. Chmn. commn. on missions, mem. bd. stewards Epworth Methodist Ch., 1961-65, sponsor, counselor World Friendship Group of Girls, 1953-57. Bd. dirs. Nathanael Methodist Mission in slum area Lexington. Mem. Greater Lexington C. of C. (chmn. hotel-motel div.), Am., Ky. (dir., membership chmn.) hotel-motel assns. Home: 423 Clinton Rd Lexington KY 40502 Office: Quality Inn NW 1050 Newtown Pike Lexington KY 40505

CRAVER, MARY ADELAIDE AUSTELL (MRS. RICHARD DAVIDSON CRAVER), banker; b. Charlotte, N.C., July 1, 1942; d. Charles Benjamin and Mary Adelaide (Roberts) Austell; A.B., Duke, 1964; J.D., U. N.C., 1967; m. Richard Davidson Craver, Apr. 29, 1972. Admitted to N.C. bar, 1967; trust adminstr. First Union Nat. Bank N.C., Charlotte, 1967-69, trust officer, 1969—, asst. v.p., 1972—. Chmn. finance com. YWCA, Charlotte, 1973-74, treas., 1974-75; also bd. dirs; group chmn. United Way campaign, 1973; active various community drives. Mem. Am., Mecklenburg, N.C. bar assns., N.C. State Bar, Mecklenburg Legal Aux. Democrat. Baptist. Home: 4106-C Providence Rd Charlotte NC 28211 Office: 301 S Tyron St Charlotte NC 28202

CRAWFORD, ALEXANDRA MAGDOLNA STEFANIA, architect; b. Budapest, Hungary, Apr. 21, 1935; diploma architecture Kingston-upon-Thames, Surrey, Eng., 1964. With firm Masiello & Assos., 1967-69; partner A & R Crawford, Architects, Planners and Landscape Architects, Crofton, Md., 1969—. Archtl. asst. W.S. Atkins & Partners Architects Dept., London, Eng., 1957-59; tech. asst. London County Council Architecture, 1959-60. Mem. panel arbitrators Am. Arbitration Assn. Registered architect, Md., Eng. Prin. works include Merc. Bank Hdqrs., Kuala Lumpur, Malaya, 1961, Community Center, Terendak Camp, Malacca, Malaya, 1962-63, Swimming Pool Complex, Malacca, 1963, New Carrollton (Md.) Library, 1968-69. Project architect proposed Springfield (Mass.) Regional Center for Mentally Retarded. Mem. A.I.A., Royal Inst. Brit. Architects. Address: 1503 Crofton Pkwy Crofton MD 21113*

CRAWFORD, ANN FEARS, educator, author; b. Beaumont, Tex., Aug. 26, 1932; d. Thaddeus Alvin and Dorothy (Huey) Fears; B.F.A., U. Tex., 1953; M.A., Los Angeles State Coll., 1954; postgrad. U. Tex., 1970-72; 1 son, Kevin Brooks. Editor, Steck Vaughn Pub. Co., Austin, Tex., 1960-65; research asso. Inst. Texan Cultures, San Antonio, 1967-68; tchr. English, McCallum High Sch., Austin, 1970-72; free lance writer, journalist, 1973—; editor Austin People Today mag., 1974—. Active Austin Environmental Council, Action Coalition of Tex. Bd. dirs. O'Henry Mus. Mem. Tex. Hist. Assn., Austin Heritage Soc., Tex. Women's Polit. Caucus, Tex. Press Women, Women in Communications. Author: A Boy Like You, 1966; The Eagle, 1968; Texas, 1972; John Connally: Portrait in Power, 1973; Viva: The Mexican Americans, 1974. Contbr. articles to mags. Home: 2104 Indian Trail Austin TX 78703

CRAWFORD, ANNE CHRISTINE KESTING (MRS. VERNON SLOVER CRAWFORD), antiques dealer; b. Balt., Sept. 13, 1907; d. Charles Adolph and Anna Henrietta (von Schueler) Kesting; high sch. diploma YWCA Comml. Coll., 1928; m. Vernon Slover Crawford, Feb. 10, 1951; 1 son, Vernon Slover. Accountant, officer mgr. Redding Radio, Balt., 1929-33; cost accountant Rice's Bakers, Balt., 1933-36; accountant, office mgr. Howard E. Jones & Co., Balt., 1936-50; owner Crawfords Corner, Voorhees, N.J., 1961—. Pres., Aux. to Montgomery County Assn. for Physically Handicapped Children, Norristown, Pa., 1959-61. Lutheran. Mem. Order Eastern Star, Lion's Aux. (pres. 1962-64). Address: PO Box 86 Arbor Meadows Sicklerville NJ 08081

CRAWFORD, CHERYL, theatrical producer; b. Akron, O., Sept. 24, 1902; d. Robert K. and Luella Elizabeth (Parker) Crawford; student Buchtel Coll., 1 year; A.B. cum laude, Smith Coll., 1925. Dr. Arts. Produced plays while at Smith Coll.; casting dir. Theatre Guild, N.Y.C., 1926-30; founder and dir. Group Theatre, 1930-37 (produced Men in White by Sidney Kingsley; Awake and Sing by Clifford Odets); produced (independently) Family Portrait with Judith Anderson; also produced Porgy and Bess by Gershwin and a musical, One Touch of Venus, Shakespeare's The Tempest, Brigadoon, Love Life, Regina, The Rose Tattoo, Good as Gold, Comes a Day, Shadow of a Gunman, Rivalry, Sweet Bird of Youth, Period of Adjustment, Andorra-Mother Courage, Colette; a founder and dir. Actors Studio with Kazan & Strasberg. Named Woman of the Year, N.Y.C. Am. Assn. U. Women, 1959. Home: 400 E 52d St New York City NY 10022 Office: 400 E 52d St New York City NY 10022

CRAWFORD, CLARE WOOTTEN, journalist; b. Durham, N.C., July 22, 1936; d. Charles Thomas and Clare (Erly) Wootten; B.A., U. Md., 1958; children—Victor Lawrence Jr., Charlene Elizabeth. Copy girl Washington Post, 1958-60; dictationist Washington Evening Star, 1960-61; reporter, columnist, soc. editor Washington Daily News, 1961-72; columnist Washington Star News, 1972-74; Washington corr. People mag., 1974—; free-lance articles N.Y. Daily News-Chgo. Tribune Syndicate, Washingtonian mag., Features and News Syndicate, 1969—. Reporter, Producer Sta. WRC-NBC-TV, Washington, 1969—. Bd. dirs. D.C. Assn. Retarded Children. Recipient Bill Pryor Meml. award, 1st prize Washington Newspaper Guild, 1966; Distinguished Pub. Affairs Reporting award Am. Polit. Sci. Assn., 1967; award for broadcast investigative reporting Am. Assn. U. Women, 1972; award for media contbn. to pub. edn. D.C. Citizens for Better Pub. Edn., 1972; two Emmy awards Nat. Acad. TV Arts and Scis., 1972; Nat. Assn. Broadcasters award, 1971; award for investigative reporting Chesapeake Press Assn., 1971; Douglas Southall Freeman award for pub. service Va. Assn. Press Broadcasters, 1972. Mem. Am. Newspaper Guild (daily news chmn. 1965), A.F.R.T.A., Alpha Delta Pi. Democrat. Roman Catholic. Clubs: Washington Press, Am. Newspaper Women's (Washington). Home: 1116 Nora Dr Silver Spring MD 20904 Office: Washington Evening Star Washington DC 20005 also WRC-TV 4001 Nebraska Av NW Washington DC 20016

CRAWFORD, GAY JOHNSTON (MRS. ROY P. CRAWFORD), publicist; b. N.Y.C., Dec. 1, 1943; d. William Dickson and Jessianna Louise (Holmes) Johnston; A.A., Bradford Jr. Coll., 1963; B.A., U. Cal. at Berkeley, 1965; m. Roy P. Crawford, June 11, 1966; children—David William, Katharine. Reporter, fashion editor Berkeley (Cal.) Daily Gazette, 1965; spl. assignment editor, reporter, Christmas edit. Oakland Tribune, 1965; prodn. asst. San Diego Mag., 1965-66; writer pub. affairs-publs. U. Cal. at San Diego, 1966-68; free-lance publicist, editor Santa Clara County, 1968—. Mem. Women in Communications. Republican. Episcopalian. Editor: Discovering Santa Clara Valley, 1973; Tailoring for Women, Step by Step, 1974. Home: 14711 Aloha Av Saratoga CA 95070

CRAWFORD, HELEN, librarian; b. Sentinel Butte, N.D., July 19, 1906; d. Lewis Ferandus and Cora (Hazlett) Crawford; B.A., U. N.D., 1928; B.S., Simmons Coll., 1931; postgrad. U. Chgo., 1944-45. Classifier, Ia. State U. Library, Ames, 1931-44; asso. prof., librarian Med. Sch. Library, U. Wis., 1945-71, cons. 1971—; resident cons. Tex. Tech. U. Sch. Medicine, 1971-72. Cons. bldg. planning, history medicine. Recipient presdl. citation State Med. Soc. Wis., 1961. Mem. Med. Library Assn. (exec. bd., pres. 1972-73), Am., Wis. library assns., Phi Beta Kappa, Kappa Alpha Theta. Club: Zonta (pres. 1958-59) (Madison, Wis.). Contbr. Med. Library Assn. bull. Wis. Med. Jour., Handbook Med. Library Practice. Home: 1305 Chandler St Madison WI 53715 Office: Middleton Medical Library Univ Wisconsin 1305 Linden Dr Madison WI 53706

CRAWFORD, HELEN MARY BAILEY (MRS. R. E. JACK CRAWFORD), librarian; b. Vardaman, Miss., Aug. 2, 1934; d. Elisha Allen and Mary Ann (Smith) Bailey; A.A., Wood Jr. Coll., 1953; B.S., Delta State Coll., 1955; M.L.S., U. Miss., 1964, postgrad. 1969—; m. R.E. Jack Crawford, May 29, 1960; 1 son, Ray Ed. Tchr. music and choral Okolona Pub. Schs., 1955-58; tchr. English Brunswick (Ga.) Pub. Schs., 1958-59; librarian, choral dir. Hernando (Miss.) High Sch., 1959-62; asso. law librarian Sch. Law, U. Miss., University, 1962—. Rep. A.R.C., Oxford, Miss., 1972. Recipient Outstanding Tchr.

award, Hernando High Sch., 1962. Mem. Miss. Library Assn., Am. Assn. Law Librarians. Methodist (council on ministries 1971—, children's coordinator 1955-58). Home: 305 Phillip Rd Oxford MS 38655 Office: Sch Law Library U Miss University MS 38677

CRAWFORD, JEAN VEGHTE, educator, chemist; b. Buffalo, Mar. 13, 1919; d. William J., Jr. and Mildred C. (Veghte) Crawford; A.B., Mt. Holyoke Coll., 1940; A.M., Oberlin Coll., 1942; Ph.D., U. Ill., 1950. Instr., Mt. Holyoke Coll., 1942-45; chemist Eastman Kodak Co., 1945-47; adj. prof. Randolph-Macon Woman's Coll., 1950-51; mem. faculty Wellesley Coll., 1951—, prof. chemistry, 1963—, chmn. dept., 1961-64, dean students, 1966-68. Mem. Am. Chem. Soc., Am. Assn. U. Profs., Phi Beta Kappa, Sigma Xi, Iota Sigma Pi, Sigma Delta Epsilon. Home: 3 Hallowell House Wellesley MA 02181

CRAWFORD, JEANNE BROZMAN, ednl. adminstr.; b. Buffalo, July 28; d. Nathan Hyman and Carrie Birdie (Harris) Brozman; B.A., Bucknell U.; children—Candace (Mrs. Michael Andrews), Melton L. Former owner-editor Kodiak (Alaska) Mirror; former editor Yakima (Wash.) Sun; former exec. sec. Allied Arts Council of Yakima Valley, Inc.; arts in edn. coordinator Yakima Intermediate Sch. Dist. 105, 1974—. Mem. Yakima Citizens Com. for Sch. Spl. Levy, Yakima Citizens Com. To Study Studio Study Center; mem. central steering com. Conv. Center Bond Issue, Yakima; mem. Wash. State exec. com. Alliance for Arts Edn. Served with WAC, Recipient award for outstanding service Allied Arts Council, 1963. Mem. Yakima Little Theatre Group, Altrusa. Author: As the Valley Was, 1968; Wheels Led the Way, 1973. Home: 2 N 44th Av Yakima WA 98902 Office: Courthouse Yakima WA 98901

CRAWFORD, JOAN, actress; b. San Antonio, Mar. 23, 1908; student schs. of Kansas City and Stephens Coll., Columbia, Mo.; m. Douglas Fairbanks, Jr., June 3, 1929 (div.); m. 2d, Franchot Tone, Oct. 11, 1935 (div.); m. 3d, Phillip Terry, July 21, 1942 (div.); m. 4th, Alfred Nu Steele, May 10, 1955 (dec.); adopted children-Christina, Christopher, Cynthia, Cathy. Appeared on stage (dancing) as Lucille Le Sueur; entered movies 1926; starred in following films: Dancing Daughters; Blushing Brides; Untamed; Modern Maidens; Paid; Laughing Sinners; Possessed; Rain; Grand Hotel; Dancing Lady; The Georgeous Hussy; The Bride Wore Red; Mannequin; Forsaking All Others; No More Ladies; The Last of Mrs. Cheyney; Ice Follies of 1939; The Shining Hour; The Women; A Woman's Face; They All Kissed the Bride; Above Suspicion; Reunion in France; Hollywood Canteen; Mildred Pierce (Acad. Award 1945); Humoresque; Daisy Kenyon; Flamingo Road; The Damned Don't Cry; Harriet Craig; Goodbye, My Fancy; This Woman Is Dangerous; Sudden Fear; Torch Song; Johnny Guitar; Female on the Beach; Queen Bee; Autumn Leaves; The Story of Esther Costello; The Best of Everything; What Ever Happened to Baby Jane; The Caretakers; Strait-Jacket; I Saw What You Did, 1965; Berserk, 1967, Trog, 1970; exec. Pepsi-Cola Co. Author: A Portrait of Joan, 1962; My Way of Life, 1971. Home: 8008 W Norton Av Los Angeles CA 90046

CRAWFORD, JOYCE CATHERINE HOLMES, sch. psychologist; b. Kansas City, Mo., May 30, 1918; d. Morton Henry and Lillian Catharine (Burton) Holmes; student Kansas City Jr. Coll., 1934-36; B.S. in Edn., U. Mo., 1938; M.A. in Guidance and Counseling, No. Ariz. U., 1957; postgrad. Ariz. State U., 1969—; m. Merle Eugene Crawford, Dec. 18, 1938; children—Hal Wayne, Kent Holmes. Tchr., Cottonwood, Ariz., 1952-69; sch. psychologist, child study cons., Phoenix, 1971—. Ranger-naturalist Tuzigoot Nat. Monument, U.S. Park Service, summers 1959-66. Mem. Ariz. Gov.'s Adv. Com. on Mental Health, 1964-65, Ariz. Hosp. Survey and Constrn. Adv. Council, 1965-68; head start chmn. Cottonwood Neighborhood Council, 1967-69; sec. Yavapai County Head Start Policy Adv. Com., 1968-71. Bd. dirs. Ariz. Assn. Mental Health, 1955-67, sec., 1961-64, founder Verde Valley chpt., 1956, pres., 1959-61; incorporating com. Verde Valley Community Guidance Clinic, 1965, bd. dirs., 1965-70; bd. dirs. No. Ariz. Comprehensive Guidance Center, 1967-69; bd. dirs., recreation chmn. Ariz. Congress Parents and Tchrs., 1954-55. Mem. Nat., Ariz. assns. sch. psychologists, Am., Ariz. psychol. assns., Ariz. Edn. Assn. (mental health and spl. edn. com. 1961-66, chmn. 1964-65), Ariz. Assn. Retarded Children, Am. Assn. UN, Am. Civil Liberties Union. Democrat. Home: Box 95 616 N 161st Av Goodyear AZ 85338 Office: 1141 E Rose Lane Phoenix AZ 85014

CRAWFORD, MARGO ARNOLD (MRS. ROBERT CRAWFORD), historian, educator; b. Chgo., Feb. 6, 1942; d. William and Thelma (Butler) Arnold; M.Ed., Northeastern Ill. U., 1970; postgrad. Northwestern U.; m. Robert Crawford, Sept. 5, 1965; children—Romi, Robert, Syeeda, Margo, Seitu, Malcolm. Asst. prof. history Northeastern Ill. U., Chgo., 1972-74; prof. Afro-Am. history Barat Coll., Lake Forest, Ill., 1970, Loyola U., Chgo., 1971—. Home: 1451 E 55th St Chicago IL 60615

CRAWFORD, MARY NEWELL (MRS. PEARSON C. CUMMIN, JR.), physician, educator; b. Phila., Apr. 12, 1923; d. Alan and Dorothy (Hurd) Crawford; A.B., Vassar Coll., 1945; M.D., U. Pa., 1949; m. Pearson C. Cummin, Jr., Sept. 16, 1961. Intern, Allentown (Pa.) Gen. Hosp., 1949-50; fellow U. Pa. Hosp., 1950-51; resident, then asst. chief resident Children's Hosp. 1951-53; practice virology, 1953-57, blood banking, 1957— (all Phila.); asst. prof. pediatrics Sch. Medicine, U. Pa., 1962-64; asso. prof. medicine Sch. Medicine, Temple U., Phila., 1964-71, research asso. prof. medicine, 1971—; asso. clin. prof. clin. pathology Med. Coll. Pa., 1970—; asso. dir. Phila. Blood Center, 1964-74. Diplomate Am. Bd. Pediatrics. Mem. Am. Assn. Blood Banks, Phi Beta Kappa. Home and office: 125 Ashwood Rd Villanova PA 19085

CRAWFORD, OLGA ELVERA ANDERSON (MRS. WILLIAM JOHN CRAWFORD), publishing co. exec.; b. Boston, Apr. 13, 1909; d. Carl Axel and Elsa Maria (Dahlgren) Anderson; grad. high sch.; m. William John Crawford, June 15, 1929; children—James Clarke, William John. Sec., Frost & Adams Co., Boston, 1926-30; sec. to v.p. Spaulding-Moss Co., Boston, 1931-32, supr. tech. typing dept., 1932-42; with Addison-Wesley Pub. Co., Reading, Mass., 1942—, supr. copy-editing, 1942-64, corporate sec., clk., 1947—, v.p., 1949-65, sr. v.p., 1965—, also dir.; corporate sec., dir. Cummings Pub. Co., Menlo Park, Cal.; corporate sec. Benjamin Pub. Co., Menlo Park, Cal., Fondo Educativo Interamericano, S.Am., Panama; dir. Crawford Marine Electronics, Gloucester, Mass. Republican. Conglist. Club: Rockport Golf. Home: 83 Phillips Av Rockport MA 01966 Office: Addison-Wesley Pub Co Reading MA 01867

CRAWFORD, SARA E. TWIGG (MRS. HOMER CRAWFORD), vol. services exec.; b. Long Beach, Cal., Jan. 29, 1928; d. William C. and Emma (Fitzgerald) Twigg; student Immaculate Coll., 1950-52; m. Homer Crawford, May 3, 1952; children—Georgiana, William Twigg. Asst. media dir. Needham & Grohmann Advt., N.Y.C., 1948-54; acting dir. vol. services N.Y. Hosp.-Cornell Med. Center, N.Y.C., 1967-69, dir. vol. services, 1968—. Bd. dirs. Speedwell Services for Children, 1957—, sec. bd., 1960-64, v.p. bd., 1964-73, pres. bd., 1973—; mem. Am. Soc. Dirs. Vol. Services, N.Y. Assn. Dirs. Vol. in Hosps. (dir.), Fedn. Protestant Welfare Agys. (del. 1964—). Republican. Roman Catholic. Home: 1170 Fifth Av New York City NY 10029 Office: 525 E 68th St New York City NY 10029

CRAWFORD, SUSAN N. YOUNG (MRS. JAMES W. CRAWFORD), librarian, educator; b. Vancouver, B.C., Can.; d. James Y. and S. (Chow) Young; B.A., U. B.C., 1948; M.A., U. Toronto, 1950; M.A., U. Chgo., 1954, Ph.D., 1970; m. James Weldon Crawford, July 5, 1955; 1 son, Robert James. Came to U.S., 1952, naturalized, 1955. With bur. library and indexing service Am. Dental Assn., 1954-56; with office exec. v.p. A.M.A., Chgo., 1956-60, dir. archive-library dept., 1960—; asso. prof. Sch. Library Sci. Columbia U., N.Y.C., 1972—. Bd. regents Nat. Library Medicine, NIH, 1971—. Mem. A.L.A., Med. Library Assn., A.A.A.S., Am. Soc. Information Sci. Author 2 books, also articles in profl. jours. Home: 2418 Lincoln St Evanston IL 60201 Office: 535 N Dearborn St Chicago IL 60610

CRAWFORD, TWILA JEAN VON FANGE (MRS. H. STANLEY CRAWFORD), journalist; b. Sylvan Grove, Kan., Feb. 15, 1939; d. Walter William and Irma Louise (Ziegenbalg) V.; B.A., Kan. State U., 1967, M.S. (Grad. Teaching asst.), 1971; m. H. Stanley Crawford, June 18, 1960; children—Rachel Shelle, Curtis Stanley. Free lance writer, 1964—; news dir. KMAN Radio, Manhattan, Kan., 1964-69; news corr. Topeka Daily Capital, 1964-69; extension editor Kan. State U., Manhattan, 1971—. Vice pres. Manhattan Jr. High Sch., P.T.A., 1973-74. Bd. dirs. Luth. Hosp. Assn., Manhattan. Recipient A.P. Radio News awards, 1964-69; Concordia Coll. grantee, 1957-58. Mem. C. of C., League Women Voters, Manhattan Cultural Arts Council, Riley County Hist. Assn., Women in Communications (treas. 1969-71, chpt. pres. 1971-72, legislative chmn. 1973-74), Kan. Press Women radio, newspaper, mag. awards 1964-69, scholarship chmn. 1967-68), Nat. Fedn. Press Women (radio, newspaper, mag. awards 1964-69), Am. Assn. U. Women, Am. Assn. Agrl. Coll. Editors (blue ribbons 1972-73), Kan. Fedn. Rep. Women, Sigma Delta Chi. Lutheran (librarian 1970-74). Home: Route 4 High Meadow Manhattan KS 66502 Office: Umberger Hall Kan State U Manhattan KS 66506

CREA, MARIA ANTOINETTE, pediatrician; b. Struthers, O., Jan. 5, 1928; d. Joseph and Rose (Toriello) Crea; A.B., Western Res. U., 1949; M.D., Johns Hopkins, 1953; m. Edward L. Smith, May 15, 1961; children—Joseph, Edward. Intern, Cleve. City Hosp., 1953-54; resident, Cleve. City Hosp. and Children's Hosp., Cleve.; practice medicine, specializing in pediatrics, Niagara Falls, N.Y., 1958—; chief pediatrics Niagara Falls Meml. Med. Center. Active Youth Bd., Center for Young Parents, Heart Assn., United Givers Fund. Mem. Niagara County Med. Soc. (pres. elect 1971-72, pres. 1972-73), Bus. and Profl. Women's Club. Moose. Home: 5252 Lewiston Rd Lewiston NY 14092 Office: 706 9th St Niagara Falls NY 14301

CREAGHE, NORMA STANTON (MRS. JOHN ST. GEORGE CREAGHE), librarian; b. Colorado Springs, Colo., July 30, 1925; d. James Elmo and Esther Theresa (Perkins) Stanton; B.A., U. Colo., 1947; M.L.S., Tex. Woman's U., 1969; m. John St. George Creaghe, Aug. 24, 1947; 1 son, Colin Stanton. Asst. librarian Geisel Library, St. Anselm's Coll., Manchester, N.H., 1969-70, acting librarian, 1970-71, librarian, 1971—. Mem. exec. com. New Eng. Library Information Network. Bd. dirs. N.H. Adv. Council on Libraries, 1973—. Mem. Am., New Eng. (chmn. publicity com. 1974—), N.H. library assns., Acad. Librarians of N.H. (pres. 1973-74), N.H. Coll. and Univ. Council (chmn. library com. 1971-72), N.H. Library Council (v.p. 1974—), New Eng. Council on Library Resources in Nursing, Delta Delta Delta, Beta Phi Mu. Episcopalian. Club: Hopkinton (N.H.) Woman's. Home: Dolly Rd Route 1 Concord NH 03301 Office: Geisel Library St Anselm's College Manchester NH 03102

CREAMER, ALICE DUBOIS, artist; b. Roadstown, N.J., Apr. 16, 1915; d. Lester Maul and Eva Amy (James) duBois; m. Malcom Kenneth Creamer, Jan. 30, 1934; children—Malcom Kenneth, Alice Virginia (Mrs. Gary Stansell). One man show Bridgeton Art Gallery, 1973; exhibited sculpture and copper enameling, Chgo. and Dallas, 1966; numerous commd. sculpture portraits. Leader, 4-H Clubs, 1945-55. Mem. Bridgeton Antiquarian League (art gallery com., curator hist. mus. instruments), Cumberland County Hist. Soc. (curator hist. mus. instruments), Christian Art Assos. (charter), Soc. Internat. Harpsichord Builders, Am. Recorder Soc., Viola da Gamba Soc. Am. Home: RD 5 Finley Station Rd Bridgeton NJ 08302

CREAMER, DELENA, librarian; b. Chipley, Fla., Sept. 21, 1923; d. Arthur Wade and Zora Lee (Baxley) McDaniel; A.A., Chipola Jr. Coll., Marianna, Fla., 1942; m. Apr. 1, 1944; children—Norma (Mrs. Philip Reginald Miner), Toni (Mrs. Tommy Hugh New). Med. sec. Mobile (Ala.) Infirmary, 1951-53, St. Vincent's Hosp., Jacksonville, Fla., 1953-57, Brunswick (Ga.) Hosp., 1960-62; dir. med. records Jackson Hosp., Marianna, 1962—. Cons. in field; teaching staff med. terminology and introduction to med. records Chipola Jr. Coll. Mem. Panhandle Med. Soc. (exec. sec.). Home: Route 1 Box 34 Chipley FL 32428

CREAMER, GERALDINE MARGARET, librarian; b. Sayreville, N.J., June 23, 1914; d. Thomas Aloysious and Ann Marie (Johnson) Creamer; student Drakes Bus. Coll., 1930-31. Sample girl, Dupont Photo Products, Parlin, N.J., 1932-34; salesgirl Daylight Bakery, South Amboy, N.J., 1935-40, Berkley Bake Shop, New Brunswick, N.J., 1945-46. Bd. dirs. Sayreville Free Pub. Library, 1946—. Mem. Am., N.J. (co-chmn. room arrangements com. 1972-73) Cath. library assns. Home: 7 S Minnisink Av Sayreville NJ 08872 Office: Washington Rd Parlin NJ 08859

CREAMER, LUCILLE MARIE (MRS. KEVIN DANIEL CREAMER), savs. and loan exec.; b. Monterey, Cal., July 18, 1927; d. Lawrence George and Adele (Fea) Gavazza; LL.D., U. San Francisco, 1974; m. Kevin Daniel Creamer, Aug. 25, 1951. With Bay View Fed. Savs., San Francisco, 1946—, sr. v.p., 1972—. Mem. master city planning com. City of South San Francisco, 1966-70. Mem. Am. Savs. and Loan Inst. (pres. 1965-66), Cal. Savs. and Loan League (chmn. adminstrn. savs. accounts com. 1972-74). Home: 529 Eucalyptus Av South San Francisco CA 94080 Office: 2601 Mission St San Francisco CA 94110

CREASMAN, CATHRYN PAULINE, assn. exec.; b. Asheville, N.C., Aug. 26, 1921; d. Henry Clay and Gussie (Cordell) Creasman; B.S., Western Carolina U., 1942; M.A., U. N.C., 1948; postgrad. U. Ill., 1953, U. Ga., 1969, Furman U., 1973. Tchr. N.C. High Schs., 1942-53; exec. dir. Central Carolina Girl Scout Council, Sanford, N.C., 1953-61; dir. field services Coastal Carolina Girl Scout Council, Goldsboro, N.C., 1961-65; exec. dir. Old Ninety Six Council, Greenville, S.C., 1965—. Mem. orgn. com. Furman U. Collegiate Service Corps, 1966—. Recipient Distinguished Service award Western Carolina U., 1942; Thanks badge award Girl Scouts Am., 1957, 68. Mem. Nat., N.C. (pres. 1947) edn. assns., Assn. Girl Scout Profl. Workers (mem. nat. resource com. 1973-76), Bus. and Profl. Womens Club (v.p. 1950-53), Woodmen of World, Alpha Phi Sigma. Club: Zonta (v.p. 1970) (Greenville). Home: 33 Sevier Greenville SC 29605 Office: 8 Sevier Greenville SC 29604

CRECCA, LUCILLE, lawyer; b. Newark, Nov. 22, 1914; d. Joseph and Vincenza (Mombrea) Crecca; LL.B., Rutgers U., 1937, A.B., 1963, J.D., 1970. Admitted to N.J. bar, 1939; atty. War Dept. Q.M.C., 1941-43; adjudicator VA, 1943-47; claims examiner, claims authorizor Social Security Adminstrn., Dept. Health, Edn. and Welfare, part time legal practice, Irvington, 1971—; now arbitrator Better Bus. Bur., Newark. Club: Union County Hiking. Address: 16 Marshall St Irvington NJ 07111

CREECY, AUDREY ELLEN BENNEWITZ, TV hostess and producer; b. St. Cloud, Minn., Mar. 14, 1935; d. Leo William and Anna (Mathiasen) Bennewitz; student St. Cloud State Tchrs. Coll., 1953; m. James Loran Creecy, Oct. 1, 1960 (div. June 1969); children—Bruce James, Rebecca Sue. Community Club awards dir. KFBB Radio, Great Falls, Mont., 1964-66; hostess, producer It's A Woman's World (named changed to Audrey, 1970), KFBB-TV, Great Falls, 1966—. Seminar speaker Connie Craney Radio TV Seminar, Mont. State Coll., Bozeman, 1970—, State of Mont. Council on Human Resources, 1970—, Mont. Atty. Gens. Law Enforcement Conf. Council mem. Community Concert Assn., 1967-71, Great Falls Symphony, 1969-71; mem. community adv. com. Precision Teaching for Children with Learning Deficiencies; producer, dir. documentary on summer theatre in Mont.; hon. Mont. chmn. Heart Found., 1974. Bd. dirs. Golden Skyliners Drum and Bugle Corp., Mont. Epilepsy Found. Recipient award of merit Advt. Club, 1970, hon. mention Greater Mont. Found. Awards, 1968, 69, award Am. Music. Assn., 1968, 69, 70, 71. Mem. Am. Women in Radio and Television (pres. chpt. 1969-71, nat. vice chmn. seminars Ednl. Found. 1969, seminar chmn. of chpt. 1968, co-chmn. western area conf. 1970, nat. chmn. seminars 1973-74, summer theatre showcase 1973), Great Falls Advt. Club (dir.), Marquis Biog. Library Assn. (adv. mem. 1973), Great Falls Press Club, Zonta, Theatre Guild, Presbyn. Mem. Order Eastern Star. Home: 421 Riverview Dr NE Great Falls MT 59401 Office: KFBB-TV Box 1139 Great Falls MT 59401

CREEKMORE, BETSEY BEELER (MRS. FRANK B. CREEKMORE), author; b. Knoxville, Tenn., May 23, 1915; d. Ulysses D. and Bessie (Hoskins) Beeler; A.B., Vassar Coll., 1935; postgrad., U. Tenn.; m. Frank B. Creekmore, Nov. 10, 1938; children—David D., Betsey B. 1st chmn. Knoxville Ann. Dogwood Trails, 1957-60, permanent adviser. Mem. Jr. League Knoxville (pres. 1937-39), Downtown Knoxville Assn. (dir. 1957-67), Authors Guild, Phi Beta Kappa. Presbyn. Club: Knoxville Garden (pres. 1954-56). Author: Knoxville, 1958; Arrows to Atoms, 1959; Dark and Bloody Ground, 1967; Traditional American Crafts, 1968; Gifts from Oddments and Outdoor Materials, 1970. Zone editor Garden Club Am. Bull., 1956-59. Home: 4734 Sylvan Lane Knoxville TN 37919

CREGGER, MILDRED RODGERS (MRS. MORRIS MCCLURE CREGGER), assn. adminstr.; b. Forest, Va., Jan. 7, 1922; d. Martel Oliver and Bessie Lee (Owen) Rodgers; student Roanoke Coll., 1942; student N.Y. U., 1945, Va. Poly. Inst., 1949; m. Morris McClure Cregger, June 27, 1939; 1 son, Morris McClure Cregger. Advt. and pub. relations Sports Service Co., Buffalo, 1941-46; activities co-ordinator YWCA Roanoke Valley, Roanoke, Va., 1953-56, adult dir., 1956-57, dir. health, phys. edn., recreation dept., 1957—. Chmn. Gray Ladies Corp., 1950. Mem. Motor Service A.R.C., Roanoke Valley Safety Council. Mem. Nat., Internat. wildlife assns., Nat. Recreation Assn., Wilderness Soc., Am. Camping Assn., Roanoke Valley C. of C., Bus. and Profl. Women (pres. 1964). Methodist (Sunday sch. tchr. 1944-54). Club: Recreation, Ideals and Friendship (pres. 1945). Editor: Gray Tattler, 1948-49. Home: 4509 Northwood Dr NW Roanoke VA 24017 Office: 605 First St SW Roanoke VA 24011

CREIGH, DOROTHY WEYER (MRS. THOMAS CREIGH, JR.), educator, writer; b. Hastings, Neb., Dec. 4, 1921; d. Frank E. and Mabelle (Carey) Weyer; A.B., Hastings Coll., 1942; M.S., Columbia, 1945; m. Thomas Creigh, Jr., July 17, 1948; children—Mary Elizabeth, Thomas III, John Weyer, James Carey. Society editor Hastings Daily Tribune, 1941-42; tchr. Central City (Neb.) High Sch., 1942-43; editor weekly newspaper Naval Ammunition Depot, Hastings, 1943-44; news and radio AP, Richmond, Va., 1945-46; with UNRRA, Hankow and Shanghai, China, 1946-48; tchr. Hastings Coll., 1952, 61-68; garden editor Hastings Daily Tribune, 1960; editor Stringing Along music quar., 1967, Adams County Hist. quar., 1968—. Mem. Neb. Bd. Edn., 1974—. Dir. Community Devel. Commn., 1966-67, Adams County Centennial Commn., 1970-72; bd. dirs. Hastings Civic Symphony, 1950-60, City Library Campaign, 1961, Neb. Hist. Soc. Found., 1971—. Mem. Gov.'s Conf. Edn., 1963. Mem. Adams County Hist. Soc. (dir.), Neb. Arts Council (dir.), P.E.O. Presbyn. Clubs: Meadowbrook, Lochland Golf. Editor: Hastings Coll. Alumni Quar., 1949-51. Author: (with C. Brock) Journalism for Nebraska High Schools, 1943; (with F.E. Weyer) Hastings College, 75 Years, 1958; Bellevue College, 1962; Tales from the Prairie, Vol. I, 1970, Vol. II, 1973; Adams County History: The People, 1971; Adams County: A Story of the Great Plains (Merit award Am. Assn. for State Local History), 1972; The First Hundred Years (Presbyn. history), 1973; Where in The World Have We Been?, 1973. Author cassettes for Exec. Inst., 1973. Contbr. to mags. and newspapers. Address: 1650 N Elm St Hastings NE 68901

CREIGHTON, HARRIET BALDWIN, educator; b. Delavan, Ill., June 27, 1909; d. Cyrus Murray and Bertha (Baldwin) Creighton; B.A., Wellesley Coll., 1929; Ph.D., Cornell U., 1933. Lab. asst. botany Cornell U., 1929-33, instr., 1933-34; instr. botany Conn. Coll., 1934-39, asst. prof., 1939-40; asso. prof. botany Wellesley Coll., 1940-52, prof., 1952-74, prof. emeritus, 1974; Fulbright lectr. genetics Australia, 1952-53, Peru, 1959-60; NSF cons. Summer Insts., India, 1968, 69. Served as lt. comdr. USNR, 1943-46. Fellow A.A.A.S. (sec. sect. G 1960-63, v.p. 1964); mem. Am. Soc. Cell Biology, Bot. Soc. Am. (pres. 1956), Soc. Am. Naturalists, Genetics Soc. Am., Soc. for Devel. Biology, Am. Genetic Assn., Am. Soc. Plant Physiologists, Phi Beta Kappa, Sigma Xi, Phi Kappa Phi. Contbr. articles to profl. jours. Office: Wellesley Coll Wellesley MA 02181

CREIM, MARJORIE ROSANOFF, lawyer; b. L.I., N.Y., Apr. 12, 1914; d. Aaron J. and Isabel Jean (Ross) Rosanoff; A.A., Pasadena (Cal.) Jr. Coll., 1931; J.D., U. So. Cal. at Los Angeles, 1938; m. Conrad Creim, Aug. 8, 1942 (dec. Oct. 1966); 1 son, William B. Admitted to Cal. bar, 1938, Wash. State bar, 1946; practiced in Los Angeles, 1939-42, Seattle, 1946-47, Pasadena, 1960—; mem. firm Creim, Cohn & Jacobs, Seattle, 1946-47, Potter, Creim, Ridenour & Rogers, Pasadena, 1960—. Sec. treas. Bow Lake Engring. Co., Seattle, 1946-47. Pres. Hastings Ranch Nursery Sch., 1958-59. Mem. Los Angeles County Democratic Central Com., 1972-74. Bd. dirs. Pasadena Mental Health Assn., 1962-65. Mem. Cal., Pasadena, Washington State bar assns., Los Angeles Trial Lawyers Club, Common Cause, Order of the Coif. Home: 3365 Grayburn Rd Pasadena CA 91107 Office: 3852 East Colorado Blvd Pasadena CA 91107

CREMINS, SISTER MARIA RENATA, coll. dean; b. Boston, Apr. 16, 1937; d. Patrick J. and Mary G. (Coady) Cremins; student Emmanuel Coll., 1954-58, Oxford U., 1959-60; M.Ed., Boston U., 1973, doctoral fellow, 1973. Tchr., Acton-Boxborough Regional High Sch., 1958; asst. prin. St. Marys High Sch., Melrose, Mass., 1966-68; asst. headmistress Sch. of Holy Child, Old Westbury, N.Y., 1968-70, headmistress, 1970-72; dean students Salve Regina Coll., Newport, R.I., 1972—. Recipient Alliance Francaise grant to study at Sorbonne, Paris, 1972. Mem. Nat. Assn. Women Deans and Counselors. Office: Salve Regina Coll Ochre Point Av Newport RI 02840

CRENSHAW, JAN CAROL, librarian; b. Odessa, Tex., May 1, 1945; d. J.B. and Willie Sue (Stanhiser) Crenshaw; B.A., Tex. Woman's U., 1967, M.L.S., 1968; student Brite Div. Sch., Tex. Christian U., 1968-69. Librarian, Lon Morris Coll., Jacksonville, Tex., 1969-74, guest lects. art history, 1971-73; librarian Brazosport Coll., Lake Jackson, Tex., 1974—. Mem. Jacksonville (Tex.) Civic Chorus, 1969-72, librarian, 1970-72. Mem. Southwest, Tex. (v.p., pres. elect arts round table 1974—) library assns., Tex. Jr. Coll. Tchrs. Assn. (mem. exec. bd. library sect. 1973), Am. Assn. U. Women, Beta Phi Mu. Mem. Christian Ch. Home: 132 Greenlawn St San Antonio TX 78201 Office: Brazosport Coll Lake Jackson TX 77566

CRENSHAW, JENE MABEL, publisher; b. Huntington Park, Cal., June 23, 1924; d. Leslie M. and Ethel Iona (Wilson) Crenshaw; student pub. schs. Editor, Masonic News, Huntington Park, 1946-52; pub. Summit Mag., Big Bear Lake, Cal., 1955—. Served with USCGR, World War II. Mem. Seventh-Day Adventist Ch. Mem. Sierra Club. Home: 44 Mill Creek Rd Big Bear Lake CA 92315 Office: PO Box 1889 Big Bear Lake CA 92315

CRENSHAW, TENA LULA, librarian; b. Coleman, Fla., Dec. 15, 1930; d. Herbert Joseph and Nellie Jackson (Wicker) Crenshaw; B.S., Fla. So. Coll., 1951; postgrad. U. Fla., 1952-55; M.L.S. (Univ. scholar), U. Okla., 1960. Tchr. pub. schs., Coleman, Fla., 1952-55, St. Petersburg, Fla., 1955-57, Houston, 1957-59; tech. librarian Army Rocket & Guided Missile Agy., Redstone Arsenal, Huntsville, Ala., 1960-61; acquisitions librarian Martin Marietta Corp., Orlando, Fla., 1961-64; reader services librarian John F. Kennedy Space Center, NASA, Fla., 1964-66; research information analyst, specialist, Lockheed Missiles and Space Co., Palo Alto, Cal., 1966-68; head services to pub. A. W. Calhoun Med. Library, Emory U., Atlanta, 1969—. Mem. High Mus. Art, Spl. Libraries Assn. (treas. S. Atlantic chpt. 1970-72, chmn. membership com. 1973, v.p. 1973-74, pres. 1974—), Med. Library Assn. (mem. conf. planning com. 1973-74), Southeastern (mem. new directions com. 1972—), Ga. (careers in librarianship com. 1974—) library assns., Alpha Delta Pi, Kappa Delta Pi. Democrat. Episcopalian. Author: Lasers: An Annotated Bibliography, Vol. I, 1966, Vol. II, 1967. Home: 2284 La Vista Rd NE Atlanta GA 30329 Office: A W Calhoun Med Library Emory U Atlanta GA 30322

CRESPIN, REGINE (MRS. LOU BRUDER), soprano; b. Marseilles, France; d. Henri and Margherite (DiMerione) Crespin; student Lycee Francais, Conservatoire de Paris; m. Lou Bruder, Apr. 16, 1960. Appeared in numerous operas including Lohengrin, Mulhouse, France, 1950, Paris, 1951, N.Y.C., 1964, Tosca, Il Trovatore, Otello, Die Walkuere, Oberon, Fidelio, Der Rosenkavalier, Marseilles, Le Nozze di Figaro, Paris, 1956, Dialogues of the Carmelites, 1957, Parsifal, 1958, Ballo in Maschera, 1958, Fedra, Milan, Italy, 1959, Die Walkuere, Vienna, 1959, Der Rosenkavalier, Berlin, 1960, as the Marshallin, London, 1961, Les Troyens, Paris, 1961, Penelope, Buenos Aires, 1961, Otello, Ballo in Maschera, Die Walkuere, Der Rosenkavalier, Vienna, also Rosenkavalier, N.Y.C., 1962, Flying Dutchman, N.Y.C., 1962, Ballo in Maschera, N.Y.C., 1962, La Vestale, N.Y.C., 1962, Herodiade, N.Y.C., 1963, Fidelio, Ballo in Maschera, Tannhauser, Fidelio, Chgo., 1963, Brunhilde-Die Walkuere, Met. Opera, 1971; soloist N.Y. Philharmonic, 1964-65; appeared in recital Hunter Coll., 1965, Carnegie Hall, 1969. Office: care Herbert H Breslin 119 W 57th St New York City NY 10019

CRESS, LOIS ROBERTA, journalist; b. Low Point, Ill., July 7, 1916; d. Floyd Henry and Alma Elizabeth (Prenevost) Cress; B.A., U. Denver, 1940. Tchr. art Glenwood Springs (Colo.) Pub. Schs., 1940-45; asst. editor Brighton (Colo.) Blade, 1946-55; staff writer, columnist Denver Post, 1956-68, women's editor, 1968-73, sr. staff writer, 1973—. Pres. Glenwood Springs Community Edn. Assn., 1943-44. Recipient 1st place award for news writing Colo. Press. Women, 1950, 52, 1st place award for editorial writing, 1948, 50, 55; Human Relations award Colo. Fedn. Women's Clubs, 1960, 62, 68. Mem. Soc. Profl. Journalists, P.E.O., Sigma Delta Chi, Kappa Delta Pi, Alpha Lambda Delta, Sigma Phi Alpha. Club: Altrusa (hon. mem.) (Denver). Home: 167 S 12th Av Brighton CO 80601 Office: 650 15th St Denver CO 80201

CRETAN, GLADYS YESSAYAN (MRS. CLARENCE A. CRETAN), author; b. Reedley, Cal., Nov., 1921; d. Vahan Hodge and Annig (Keleshian) Y.; student U. Cal. at Berkeley, 3 yrs.; m. Clarence A. Cretan, Aug. 18, 1943; children—Clifford, Lawrence. Exec. dir. San Mateo Found., 1970—. Author: A Gift from the Bride, 1964; All Except Sammy (selected by Jr. Lit. Guild), 1966; Runaway Habeeb!, 1968; Me, Myself and I, 1969; Lobo, 1969; Because I Promised, 1970; Lobo and Brewster, 1971; Messy Sally, 1972; A Hole, A Box and A Stick, 1972; Sunday for Sona, 1973; others. Address: 717 Barneson Av San Mateo CA 94402

CREWS, D'ANNE MCADAMS (MRS. JAMES EDWARD CREWS, JR.), merc. co. exec.; b. Huntsville, Tex., Nov. 1, 1934; d. W. D. and Annette A. (Turner) McAdams; B.B.A. with high honors, So. Meth. U., 1954; M.A., Sam Houston State U., 1967; m. James Edward Crews, Jr., June 1, 1957; children—Kay Allison, Kelly Anne. Sec. to dir. Tex. Dept. Corrections, Huntsville, 1954-57; certification clerk for univ., sec. to dir. edn. dept. Sam Houston State U., Huntsville, 1961-66; partner McAdams Co., Huntsville, 1966—. Dir., sec. Walker County Tchrs. Fed. Credit Union, 1964-66. Chmn. Mayor's Commn. on Status of Women, Huntsville, 1970-72; pres. Huntsville P.T.A., 1969-70; chmn. cookie sales, Girl Scouts U.S.A., Huntsville, 1970-71; active Huntsville Enrichment Activities Program, 1969—. Del. State Democratic Conv., Dallas, 1970; worker local, state and nat. elections, 1966—. Bd. dirs. Walker County unit Am. Cancer Soc., sec., treas. 1970—. Named Girl of Year, Beta Sigma Phi, 1958, 62, 65, Outstanding Young Woman of Am., 1970. Mem. Walker County (Tex.) Geneal. Soc., D.A.R. (librarian 1972-74, curator 1974—), Daus. Am. Colonists (1st vice regent 1971-73, regent 1973—, state microfilm chmn. 1971-73, state rec. sec. 1973—), Daus. Republic of Tex. (v.p. 1973—), Huguenot Soc. of Founders Manakin in Colony Va., U.D.C., Huntsville Meml. Hosp. Aux. (pres. 1972-73), Sam Houston State U. Alumni Assn. (life; dir., treas. 1972—), Zeta Tau Alpha Alumnae (v.p. 1973—). Methodist. Clubs: Huntsville Book Review, Huntsville Study (pres. 1972-73). Home: 253 Royal Oaks Huntsville TX 77340 Office: 1215 Sam Houston Av Huntsville TX 77340

CREWS, EDNA HEBNER (MRS. ARTHUR K. CREWS), artist; b. Woodinville, Wash., May 6, 1915; d. George H. and Ethel (Provan) Hebner; B.S., Wash. State U., 1936; postgrad. U. Wash., 1960-61, Phoenix (Ariz.) Art Center, 1938-40, Spokane (Wash.) Art Center, 1940-42; m. Arthur K. Crews, June 20, 1936; children—Carolyn, Sharon (Mrs. Howard David Hobart), Diane. One-man shows Hanforth Gallery at Tacoma (Wash.) Pub. Library, 1956, Eastern Wash. Coll., Cheney, 1958, Grays Harbor Coll., Aberdeen, Wash., 1960, Am. Assn. U. Women Ann. Show, Raymond, Wash., 1956; exhibited in group shows including U.S. Nat. Mus., Smithsonian Instn., Seattle Art Mus., Woessner Gallery, Seattle, State Capitol Mus., Olympia, Wash., Western Wash. Art Show, Tacoma, Am. Assn. U. Women State Art Show, Wenatchee, Wash. Frye Art Mus., Seattle; art tchr. Lake Washington Sch. Dist., Redmond, Wash., 1955-57, Aux. pres. YMCA, Aberdeen, 1954, bd. dirs., 1954-56. Mem. Nat. League Am. Pen Women, Spokane, Aberdeen art Leagues, Omicron Nu, Phi Kappa Phi. Home: 434 Hanna Av Aberdeen WA 98520 Office: 405 W Wishkah St Aberdeen WA 98520

CREWS, EMMA KATHERINE, educator; b. Copperhill, Tenn., Sept. 20, 1921; d. Robert Harvey and Della (Mason) C.; B.A., Maryville Coll., 1943; M.A., Eastman sch. Music, U. Rochester, 1950; postgrad. Columbia, 1955; Ed.D., Fla. State U., 1961. Music instr. Morristown (Tenn.) Jr. High Sch., 1945-48; violist Knoxville (Tenn.) Symphony Orch., 1947-48, 50-62, Knoxville Choral Soc., 1952-62, Middle Tenn. State U. Symphony, 1973—; asso. prof. music edn. Maryville (Tenn.) Coll., 1950-62, Ohio U., Athens, 1962-65, Eastman Sch. Music, 1965-71; music tchr., asst. to dirs. implementing elementary music improvement E.S.E.A. Title III project McDowell Sch., Columbia, Tenn., 1971-74; asso. prof. music edn. U. So. Miss., Hattiesburg, 1974—. Cons. elementary music, dir. pub. sch. music workshops, Tenn., Ohio, N.D., N.Y., 1945—; condr. fifth grade chorus Ontario County Elementary Music Festival, Naples, N.Y., 1967; dir. Youth Orch. First Meth. Ch., Morristown, 1947-48. Tenn. scholar Delta Kappa Gamma, 1957; grad. fellow under Frederick Fennell, Eastman Sch. Music, 1949. Mem. E. Tenn. Hist. Soc. (life), Music Educators Nat. Conf. (life; Eastern div. chmn. student mems. 1968-71), Am. String Tchrs. Assn. (life), Am. Assn. U. Women, Am. Orff-Schulwerk Assn., Tenn. Music Educators Assn., Tenn. Audio Visual Assn., Am. Assn. Elementary-Kindergarten-Nursery Educators, Delta Kappa Gamma, Sigma Alpha Iota (life), Pi Kappa Lambda. Author: Music and Perceptual Motor Development, 1974. Contbr. articles to profl. jours. Office: Fine Arts Bldg Univ So Miss Hattiesburg MS 39401

CRICKENBERGER, MARGARET ELIZABETH, educator; b. Staunton, Va., Oct. 22, 1924; d. Leon Samuel and Lorena Elizabeth (Davis) Crickenberger; B.S., Mary Washington Coll. of U. Va., 1947; M.S., La. State U., 1951; Ed.D., U. Fla., 1970. Tchr., Washington Lee High Sch., Arlington, Va., 1947-48, So. Sem. and Jr. Coll., Buena Vista, Va., 1948-49; teaching asst., then instr. La. State U., 1949-51; instr. Purdue U., 1951-54; asst. prof. U. Fla., 1954-61; asst. prof. phys. edn., tchr. edn. U. So. Fla., Tampa, 1961-65, asso. prof., 1965-72, prof., 1972—. Fellow A.A.H.P.E.R.; mem. Assn. Supervision and Curriculum Devel., Nat., So., Fla. (past pres.) assns. phys. edn. coll. women, Fla. Assn. Health, Phys. Edn. and Recreation, Phi Kappa Phi. Home: 639 Riverhills Dr Temple Terrace FL 33617 Office: Univ South Fla N Fowler St Tampa FL 33620

CRIDER, JOAN LENORE, educator; b. Berkeley, Cal., Feb. 12, 1932; d. Ralph Albert and Dorothy Christine (Wuhrman) Potter; student San Jose State Coll., 1949-51; B.S., U. So. Cal., 1954; m. Byron Wayne Crider, Jan. 28, 1956; children—Susan Lynne, Gayle Leann. Occupational therapist intern U. So. Cal., 1954-55; occupational therapist State Hosp., Camarillo, Cal., 1955-56; occupational therapist for handicapped children Harlan Shoemaker Sch., San Pedro, Cal., 1956-57; tchr. Norwalk (Cal.) Sch. Dist., 1957-59; tchr. educationally handicapped Tustin (Cal.) Sch. Dist., 1966-68; tchr. Garden Grove Unified Sch. Dist., Westminster, Cal., 1968—. Free lance artist. Active P.T.A. Cal. Elks scholar, 1952-53; Ford Found. grantee, 1957-58. Mem. Cal. Tchrs. Assn., Garden Grove Edn. Assn., Anaheim Art Assn. Republican. Methodist. Office: Post Sch 14641 Ward St Westminster CA 92642

CRIDER, KATHERINE LOIS THERRELL (MRS. CHESTER H. CRIDER), newspaper editor; b. State College, Miss., Mar. 28, 1945; d. James Solon and Rebekah Lois (O'Kelly) Therrell; B.S., U. Tenn., 1966; m. Chester Hobart Crider, Jr., June 4, 1966. Women's staff writer Huntsville (Ala.) Times, 1967-69, food editor, 1967—. Mem. Heritage Jr. Woman's Club, 1969—, awards chmn., 1970. Bd. dirs. Nat. Multiple Sclerosis Soc., 1969-71. Named Distinguished Young Woman in Huntsville, Heritage Club, 1971. Baptist. Author: (with Eva B. Purefoy) History of the Purefoy Hotel, 1971. Editor, co-author The Purefoy Hotel Cook Book, 1971. Home: 7102 Jones Valley Dr Huntsville AL 35802 Office: 2317 Memorial Pkwy Huntsville AL 35807

CRILLY, BETSY J. GOODER (MRS. EDGAR CRILLY), civic worker; b. Chgo., Dec. 1, 1925; d. Seth M. and Jean (McMullen) Gooder; grad. Roycemore Sch., 1944; m. Edgar D. Crilly, Aug. 22, 1947; children—Marilyn Joan (Mrs. Michael Wetterauer), Jeanne Claire (Mrs. Thomas Dardis). Asst. to pres. Gooder-Henrichsen Co., Inc., civil engrs., Chgo., 1945-49, dir., sec., 1955—; sec., treas. Triple R., Inc., 1965—; dir. pub. affairs radio stas. KSJB-KSJM AM-FM, Jamestown, N.D., WQTC-AM-FM, Two Rivers, Wis., 1970—. Mem. women's bd. Northside Chgo. Heart Assn., 1950-53; chmn. Deerfield (Ill.) Heart Fund, 1955-58; pres. Chgo. Service Club, 1958, dir. benefit, 1957, 62, 65, adv. bd., dir., 1957-66; pres. Deerfield div. Arden Shore, 1961; chmn. Roycemore Sch. Benefit, 1965; mem. women's aux. bd. Jamestown Hosp., 1967-69; pres. Stutsman County chpt. Am. Cancer Soc., 1969. Pres., Deerfield Twp. Women's Republican Club, 1958-59. Recipient Service award Am. Heart Assn.; Spl. Service award Service Club Chgo. Mem. Ill. Opera Guild. Episcopalian. Club: Jamestown Country. Home: 817 Elmwood Pl Jamestown ND 58401

CRINER, BEATRICE HALL, editor; b. Hamilton, Ill., Nov. 25, 1915; d. Henry Nelson and Nellie (Hyer) Hall; A.B., Monmouth Coll., 1937; postgrad. Northwestern U., 1942, Lake Forest Coll., 1942, Harvard, 1943; m. Calvin L. Criner, Dec. 18, 1953. Sec., Stowe Thread Co., Belmont, N.C., 1945-51; asso. dir. spl. study religion Am. Council Edn., Washington, 1951-53; bus. mgr. Lees McRae Coll., 1953-56; registrar, 1956-62, tchr., 1956-61; chief examiner admissions office U. N.C., Chapel Hill, 1963-66; editor N.C. Dept. Edn., Raleigh, N.C., 1966—; mng. editor Longview Jour., Raleigh, 1967-70. Mem. Am. Assn. U. Women, Longview Writers, Delta Kappa Gamma, Kappa Delta. Author with Calvin L. Criner: Jobs in Public Service, 1974; Jobs in Personal Service, 1974; also books for juveniles. Address: PO Box 26403 Raleigh NC 27611

CRINER, HELEN CLARE, coll. adminstr.; b. Point Marion, Pa., Sept. 18, 1916; d. Francis and Anna Josephine (O'Hare) Criner; B.S., W.Va. U., 1937; M.Letters, U. Pitts., 1941; postgrad. State Tchrs. Coll., Indiana, Pa., 1940-41. Tchr. English, social studies Summersville (W.Va.) High Sch., 1937-39; tchr. secretarial studies Keyser (W.Va.) High Sch., 1941-45; asst. admissions officer, resident counsellor Western Coll. for Women, Oxford, O., 1945-46; asso. prof. commerce Potomac State Coll., Keyser, 1946-65, 72—, asst. registrar, 1946-65, registrar, 1965—, dir. admissions, 1964-72. Mem. Am. Assn. Collegiate Registrars and Admissions Officers, Am. Assn. U. Women (local pres. 1944-45, 51-52, state chmn com. on higher edn. 1960-61), W.Va. Edn. Assn., Delta Kappa Gamma (chpt. chmn. com. on profl. affairs 1971—). Club: Catholic Women's. Home: 70 E Piedmont St Keyser WV 26726

CRINO, MARJANNE HELEN, physician; b. Rochester, N.Y., Aug. 18, 1933; d. Michael Jay and Helen Barbara (Kennedy) Crino; B.S., Coll. St. Teresa, 1955; M.D., Marquette U., 1959; m. Michael Anthony LaIuppa, Nov. 12, 1960; children—James Michael, Barbara Anne, John Christopher. Intern, Genessee Hosp., Rochester, 1959-60, resident obstetrics and gynecology, 1960-61; research in perinatal mortality U. Miami (Fla.) Sch. Medicine, 1961-63, resident anesthesiology, 1964-65, instr. anesthesiology, 1966-67; practice medicine, specializing in anesthesiology, Miami, Fla., 1966-67, Rochester, 1968—; anesthesiologist Genesee, Rochester Gen., Highland hosps.; mem. attending staff anesthesiology F.F. Thompson Hosp., Canandaigua, N.Y.; cons. anesthesia Rochester State Hosp. Mem. A.M.A., N.Y. State Med. Soc., Med. Soc. County Monroe, Am., N.Y. State (sec.-treas. dist. VI) socs. anesthesiologists, Rochester Acad. Medicine, Rochester Pathol. Soc., St. Mary's Hosp. Aux., St. Thomas More Adult Choir. Roman Catholic. Address 330 Kilbourn Rd Rochester NY 14618

CRIPPEN, BETTY BOWMAN, univ. ofcl.; b. New Orleans, Dec. 25, 1928; d. David Wesley and Emma (Leonard) Bowman; student U. Fla. (Gainesville), Marymount Coll., Boca Raton, Fla.; B.A. summa cum laude, Fla. Atlantic U., 1967; postgrad. U. W. Fla.; M.Ed. in Counseling, U. Ga., 1971. With registrar's office U. Fla., 1953-60, with fgn. aid program, Karachi, Pakistan, 1960-62; adminstrv. asst. to registrar Fla. Atlantic U., Boca Raton, 1963-66, asst. dir. admissions, 1967-68; dir. records, registrar U. W. Fla., Pensacola, 1968-70; registrar U. N. Fla., Jacksonville, 1971—. Mem. Am. (panel mem.), So. (panel chmn.), Fla. (past sec.-treas., constn., awards coms.) assns. collegiate registrars and admissions officers. Presbyn. (deacon, com. mem.). Home: 1732 El Camino Rd Jacksonville FL 32216

CRISCI, PAT EVA, ednl. adminstr.; b. Bklyn., Oct. 29, 1931; d. Victor Anthony and Christine Mary (Capobianco) DeVita; B.A., Bklyn. Coll., 1952; M.A., John Carroll U., Cleve., 1968; Ph.D., Kent (O.) State U., 1974; m. S. George Crisci, Jan. 10, 1954; children—Debra, George, Wayne, Lorraine. Tchr. intern, then tchr. Mayfield City Sch. System, Mayfield Heights, O., 1966-67; sch. psychologist Cleveland Heights-University Heights (O.) City Sch. System, 1967-71, supr. spl. edn., 1971-72, dir. edn.-pupil personnel services and spl. edn., 1972-74; supt. schs. Tallmadge City Schs., 1974—; guest lectr. in field. Mem. President's Com. Mental Retardation, 1971; profl. adv. bd. Fedn. Community Planning, 1973-74; mem. Nat. Project on Classification of Exceptional Children, 1974; sch. adv. council edn. dept. John Carroll U., 1974—; adv. bd. Position Edn. Program, 1973-74; adv. bd., exec. bd. Cuyahoga East Program Spl. Edn., 1972-74; exec. bd. Cuyahoga Regional Resource Center, 1974; adv. com. licensing exam. Ohio Bd. Psychology. Mem. Nat. Assn. Sch. Psychologists, Am. Personnel and Guidance Assn., Council Exceptional Children, Nat. Orgn. Legal Problems of Edn., Assn. Children with Learning Disabilities, Am. Assn. Sch. Adminstrs., Ohio Sch. Psychologists Assn. (past com. person), Cleve. Assn. Sch. Psychologists (past pres.), Coalition Edn. Handicapped, Assn. Supervision and Curriculum Devel., Ohio Assn. Gifted Children, Ohio Assn. Pupil Personnel Adminstrs., Ohio Assn. Adminstrs. Spl. Edn., Buckeye Assn. Sch. Adminstrs., Phi Delta Kappa, Alpha Delta Pi. Contbr. articles in field. Home: 586 Fairwood Dr Tallmadge OH 44278 Office: 486 East Av Tallmadge OH 44278

CRISP, EDNA LUCILLE MYERS, editor; b. Morley, Colo., Aug. 3, 1913; d. James Bard and Elizabeth Frances (Dunbar) Myers; tchrs. certificate Highlands U., Las Vegas, N.M., 1931; m. Archer Crisp, Jan. 7, 1935; children—James Wayland, David Archer. Soc. editor Huerfano World (formerly Walsenburg (Colo.) World Independent), 1954-65, editor, 1965—; columnist Crisp Comments, 1966—; former feature writer, corr. Pueblo (Colo.) Chieftain. Vice chmn. Huerfano County Republican Central Com. Mem. Colo. Press Women, Huerfano County Cowbelles (charter mem., past sec.), Order Eastern Star. Home: Cucharas Dam Ranch Box 104 Walsenburg CO 81089 Office: Huerfano World PO Box 191 Walsenburg CO 81089

CRISP, ELIZABETH AMANDA, obstetrician, gynecologist; b. Uvalde, Tex., Dec. 17, 1922; d. David Hardee and Mary Gazelle (Poynor) Crisp; B.S., Tex. Women's U., 1943; certificate Charity Hosp. La. Sch. Med. Tech., 1946; M.D., La. State U. Sch. Medicine, 1950. Intern Garfield Meml. Hosp., Washington, 1950-51; resident in gen. surgery Seaside Meml. Hosp., Long Beach, Cal., 1954-55, resident in obstetrics and gynecology, 1955-56; resident in obstetrics and gynecology Columbia Hosp. for Women, Washington, 1957-60; practice medicine specializing in obstetrics and gynecology, Washington, 1960—; surgeon Long Beach Naval Shipyard, 1956, Examinig Clinic and Surgery Clinic Dept. Health Edn. and Welfare, Washington, 1956-57; chief gynecology service Columbia Hosp. for Women, Washington, 1971; asst. clin. prof. obstetics and gynecology George Washington U. Sch. Medicine, Washington, 1960—. Served to lt. M.C. USNR, 1950-54. Diplomate Am. Bd. Obstetrics and Gynecology. Fellow A.C.S., Am. Coll. Obstetrics and Gynecology; mem. Am. Fertility and Sterility Soc., Washington Gynecologic Soc., D.C. Med. Soc., A.M.A., Am. Med. Women's Assn. Office: 730 24th St NW Washington DC 20037

CRISP, HELEN EYSTER, psychologist; b. Sunbury, Pa., July 27, 1925; d. William Henry and Elmira (Snyder) Eyster; B.A., U. N.C., 1946; M.S., N.C. State U., 1960, Ph.D., 1974; m. William T. Crisp, June 25, 1946 (div. Nov. 1973); children—Donna, Cynthia, Shelley (Mrs. William Rathbun), Rebekah, Priscilla. Sch. psychologist Raleigh (N.C.) Pub. Schs., 1961; staff psychologist Dorothea Dix Hosp., Raleigh, 1962-72; instr. psychology dept. continuing edn. N.C. State U., 1958-68; staff mem. Pisgah Workshop Lab., N.C. Dept. Mental Health, 1972-73; pvt. practice, Raleigh. Pres., Raleigh Children's Theatre, 1955. Bd. dirs. Raleigh Little Theatre, 1960-61, 63-64, 72-73, N.C. Mental Health Assn., 1958-60; bd. dirs., pub. relations Stage 74, 1974. Mem. Am., N.C. psychol. assns., N.C. Women in Psychology (chmn. 1974, editor newsletter 1968), N.C. Group Behavior Soc., Otto Ranic Soc., League Women Voters (finance chmn. 1964-65), Alpha Lambda Chi, Phi Kappa Phi, Common Cause. Chmn. health and family welfare com. N.C. Commn. on Status of Women, 1963-64. Home: 2700 Rosedale Av Raleigh NC 27607

CRISP, MARJORIE, educator; b. Grover, N.C., May 18, 1912; d. S.A. and Lucy (Fellers) Crisp; B.S., Appalachian State U., 1934; postgrad. George Peabody U., 1944. Head dept. phys. edn., womens athletics Gardner Webb Coll., Boiling Springs, N.J., 1935-41, Louisburg (N.C.) Coll., 1941-47; head women's program, Wake Forest U., Winston Salem, N.C., 1947—, asst. prof., 1955—. Club: Old Town (chmn. womens golf 1960) (Winston-Salem). Author: Physical Education Syllabas, 1965. Home; Box 7334 Reynolda St Winston-Salem NC 27109 Office: Room 302 Reynolda Gym Winston-Salem NC 27109

CRISPIN, MILDRED SWIFT (MRS. FREDERICK EATON CRISPIN), civic worker; b. Branson, Mo.; d. Albert Duane and Anna (Harlan) Swift; student Galloway Woman's Coll., 1922-24; m. Herbert William Kochs, Dec. 1, 1928 (div. Mar. 1955); children—Susan Kochs Judevine (dec.), Herbert William, Judith Ann (Mrs. Nelson Shaw); m. 2d, George Walter King Snyder, Oct. 6, 1962 (dec. 1969); m. 3d, Frederick Eaton Crispin, May 20, 1972. Bd. dirs. Travelers Aid Soc., Chgo., 1936-68, nat. dir., 1948-71; bd. dirs. U.S.O., Chgo., 1944-65, nat. dir., 1951-57; bd. dirs. John Howard Assn., 1958-67, Community Fund Chgo., 1950-56, Welfare Council Met. Chgo., 1950-56; chmn. woman's div. Crusade of Mercy, Chgo., 1964. Mem. U.S. Women's Curling Assn. (co-founder 1947, pres. 1950, founder Winnetka, Ill. club 1945, chmn. 1945-46), D.A.R. Republican. Methodist. Clubs: Woman's Athletic, Saddle and Cycle, Town and Country Arts (pres. 1957-58) (Chgo.); Everglades, Beach (Palm Beach, Fla.); Venice (Fla.)

Yacht; Coral Ridge Country, Coral Ridge Yacht (Ft. Lauderdale, Fla.). Home: 151 Bay Colony Dr Fort Lauderdale FL 33308 also 100 The Esplanade Venice FL 33595

CRISSMAN, CAROL GRACE, lawyer, accountant; b. Cedar Rapids, Ia., Dec. 9, 1937; d. William W. and Thelma (Bain Crissman; student U. Colo., summers 1956, 57; B.S., Ind. U., 1958; M.B.A., U. Denver, 1959; J.D., U. Ia., 1964; m. Ben Vincent, Nov. 27, 1963 (div. Feb. 1968); 1 dau., Catherine Diane. Admitted to Ia. bar, 1964, No. dist. Ia. U.S. Dist. Ct., 1965, So. dist., 1966, U.S. Supreme Ct. bar, 1970, Ill. bar, 1970; mem. staff Peat, Marwick, Mitchell & Co., C.P.A.'s, Cedar Rapids, 1961-62; partner firm Willie & Willie, Eagle Grove, Ia. 1964-66; practiced in Davenport, Ia., 1967-69; with firm Adler, Anderson & Merker, Bloomington, Ill., 1969—; atty. Gen. Counsel's staff Ill. Agrl. Assn., 1969—. Committeewoman, Republican Com., 1964-67; asst. county atty. Scott County, Ia., 1967-68; chief probation officer Scott County, 1968-69. C.P.A., Colo. Mem. Am., Ia. bar assns., Am. Inst. C.P.A.'s, Colo. Soc. C.P.A.'s, Am. Assn. Atty. C.P.A.'s, P.E.O., Kappa Beta Pi, Beta Alpha Psi. Home: 219 Eisenhower Dr Bloomington IL 61701 Office: 1701 Towanda Av Bloomington IL 61701

CRIST, GERTRUDE H. (MRS. HOWARD G. CRIST, JR.), civic worker; b. Barnard, S.D.; d. Jacob H. and Lillian Belle (Freeman) Hartman; student S.D. State Coll., 1936-38; m. Howard Grafton Crist, Jr., Nov. 2, 1940; children—Howard Grafton III, Douglas Freeman. Dir. Columbia Bank & Trust Co. Chmn., Westmoreland County chpt. A.R.C., 1946—, sec., 1943-45, chmn. vol. spl. services, 1944-45; dist. chmn. Cancer drive Howard County; mem. Howard County Bd. Edn., 1953-70, pres., 1963-65; bd. dirs. Howard County Tb Assn.; adv. council Catonsville Community Coll.; chmn. Emergency Civil Def. Hosp. Howard County, 1961-62; sec. Community Action Council Howard County, 1965, dir., 1966; bd. dirs. Girl Scout Council Central Md., 1967-68. Owner, partner Farm and Home Service. Trustee Howard Community Coll., 1966-71, v.p., 1969-70; bd. dirs. Howard County chpt. A.R.C., 1973—. Mem. Md. Council Higher Edn., 1968—, State Bd. for Community Colls., 1968—, Md. Congress Parents and Tchrs. (life), Md. Assn. Bds. Edn. (pres. 1966, 67), Nat. Sch. Bds. Assn. (dir. 1968-71), W. Friendship P.T.A. (sec. 1949-51), League Women Voters (county sec. 1957-59, dir. 1960-62, pres. 1959), Nat. Congress Parents and Tchrs. (hon. life mem.), Delta Kappa Gamma (hon. Alpha Beta State and Lambda chpts.). Episcopalian (vestryman; chmn. parish day sch. bd. 1970-73). Club: Cattail River Garden. Home: Burnt Woods Rd nr Glenelg PO Sykesville MD 21784

CRIST, JUDITH, critic; b. N.Y.C., May 22, 1922; d. Solomon and Helen (Schoenberg) Klein; A.B., Hunter Coll., 1941; M.S., Columbia, 1945; m. William B. Crist, July 3, 1947; 1 son, Steven Gordon. Fellow State Coll. Wash., 1942-43; instr. USAF, 1943-44; reporter N.Y Herald Tribune, 1945-59, editor for the arts, 1960-63, film critic, asso. drama critic, 1963-66; film critic N.Y. World Jour. Tribune, 1966-67, TV Guide, 1966—; critic-at-large Ladies Home Jour., 1966-67; instr. journalism Hunter Coll., 1947, Sarah Lawrence Coll., 1958-59; asso. in journalism, grad. sch. Columbia, 1959-61, lectr., 1961-66; adj. prof., 1966—; film and drama commentator Today Show, NBC-TV, 1963-73; film critic New York mag., 1968—, The Washingtonian, 1970—, Los Angeles, 1971-72, Palm Springs Life, 1971—, Metro Hampton Roads, 1972—, Tex. Monthly, 1972—. Asso. trustee U. Pa.; mem. nat. bd. Women's Med. Coll.; trustee Eugene O'Neill Meml. Theater Center. Recipient George Polk award L.I. U., 1951; awards Edn. Writers Assn., Am. Newspaper Guild, N.Y. Newspaper Guild, N.Y. Newspaper Women's Club, 1955, 59, 63, 65, 67; Columbia Journalism 50th Anniversary Medallion, 1963; Centennial medal Hunter Coll., 1970; named to Hunter Coll. Alumni Hall Fame, 1973. Mem. A.F.T.R.A., N.Y. Film Critics Circle (chmn. 1967, 73), Am. Civil Liberties Union, Phi Sigma Mu, Sigma Tau Delta. Democrat. Author: The Private Eye, the Cowboy and the Very Naked Girl, 1968. Contbr. articles on film to Look, Vogue, Glamour and others. Office: 180 Riverside Dr New York City NY 10024

CRISWELL, ELEANOR CAMP, psychologist; b. Norfolk, Va., May 12, 1938; d. Norman Harold Camp and Eleanor (Talman) David; B.A., U. Ky., 1960, M.A., 1961; Ed.D., U. Fla., 1969. Asst. prof. edn. Cal. State Coll., Hayward, 1969; asso. prof. psychology Cal. State Coll., Sonoma, 1969—; faculty adviser Humanistic Psychology Inst., San Francisco, 1970—. Cons. Venturi, Inc., Autogenic Systems, Inc. Bd. asso. dirs. Humanistic Psychology Inst., founder, 1970. Mem. Am. Psychol. Assn., Assn. for Humanistic Psychology, Aerospace Med. Assn., Assn. for Transpersonal Psychology. Patentee optokinetic perceptual learning device. Office: Psychology Dept Cal State Coll Sonoma CA also 1803 E Cotati Rohnert Park CA 94928

CRITTENDEN, JUDITH SULLIVAN (MRS. RICHARD JAMES CRITTENDEN), lawyer; b. Fayette, Ala., Apr. 27, 1945; d. Gilbert Franklin and Helen Pauline (Wiginton) Sullivan; A.B., Judson Coll., 1967; J.D., Samford U., 1970; m. Arthur Cherny Segal, June 3, 1967 (div. Jan. 1972); m. 2d, Richard James Crittenden, Jan. 25, 1974. Admitted to Ala. bar, 1970; staff atty. Legal Aid Soc., Birmingham, Ala., 1970-72; dep. dist. atty. Jefferson County, Birmingham, 1972—. Mem. youth com. A.R.C., Birmingham, 1973—; mem. speakers bur. Citizens for Equal Rights Amendment, 1972-73; mem. adv. bd. Narcotics Addiction Treatment Program, 1974—. Bd. dirs. Family Counseling Assn., 1973—. Mem. Am. Bar Assn., Ala. State Bar, Nat. Orgn. for Women, Am. Civil Liberties Union, Nat. Dist. Attys. Assn., Nat., Ala. (steering com., sec.) womens polit. caucuses, Phi Alpha Delta. Democrat. Home: 2930-D Columbiana Ct Birmingham AL 35216 Office PO Box 3747 Birmingham AL 35211

CRITTENDEN, REBECCA ELLEN SLOVER (MRS. JOHN BARRETT CRITTENDEN), educator; b. Lake City, Tenn., July 10, 1936; d. Henry Clay and Maude (Harrell) Slover; B.S., Georgetown Coll., 1958; M.A., U. N.C., 1962, Ph.D., 1963; m. John Barrett Crittenden, Aug. 7, 1966. Asst. prof. Georgetown (Ky.) Coll., 1963-64, Vanderbilt U., Nashville, 1966-67; asst. prof. Va. Poly. Inst., Blacksburg, 1964-70, asso. prof., 1970—. Woodrow Wilson fellow, 1958-59; Career Teaching fellow, U. N.C., 1959-60. Mem. Am. Math. Soc., Sigma Xi, Pi Mu Epsilon, Sigma Kappa. Home: 3010 Kent Rd Louisville KY 40205 Office: Math Dept Va Poly Inst Blacksburg VA 24061

CRITZ, NANCY JANE MCGREW (MRS. GUY BARRY CRITZ), home economist; b. Seminary, Miss., Oct. 28, 1932; d. Fred Wheeler and Pauline (Watts) McGrew; B.S., U. So. Miss., 1953; m. Guy Barry Critz, Aug. 30, 1959; children—Paula Jane, Barry Lee. Asst. extension home economist, Laurel, Miss., 1954-55; home economist, Quitman, Miss., 1955-56; asst. state 4-H Club leader, Starkville, Miss., 1956-59; area extension home economist, Starkville, 1968—. Bd. dirs. Emergency Food and Nutrition Service, Office Econ. Opportunity. Mem. Nat., Miss. assns. extension home economists, Nat., Miss. home econs. assns. 4-H All Stars, Epsilon Sigma Phi, Phi Kappa Phi. Methodist. Home: Route 2 Box 20 Starkville MS 39759 Office: Box 430 Starkville MS 39759

CROCKER, DIANE W. (MRS. BENJAMIN B. CROCKER), physician, pathologist; b. Cambridge, Mass.; d. M. Richard and Rose (Fisher) Winston; student pvt. schs., Boston and Switzerland; B.A., Wellesley Coll., 1947, M.Sc., Brown U., 1948; M.D., Boston U., 1952; m. Benjamin Ballard Crocker, Aug. 20, 1949; children—Deborah Bliss, Kimberly, Anne. Intern Mallory Inst. Pathology, 1952-53; asst. resident New Eng. Deaconess Hosp., Boston, 1953-54; resident, then research fellow Heart Assn. at Los Angeles Children's Hosp., 1955-56; resident, then Am. Cancer Soc. fellow Columbia-Presbyn. Med. Center, N.Y.C., 1956-58; asst. in pathology U. So. Cal., 1955-56, Columbia Coll. of Phys. and Surgs., N.Y.C., 1957-58; asso. pathologist Peter Bent Brigham Hosp., Boston, 1958-70, sr. asso. pathologist, 1970, chief cytology, 1969-70, attending staff, 1970-71, cons. computer and data processing in pathology, 1970-71; attending West Roxbury VA Hosp., Boston, 1960-70; instr. Harvard Med. Sch., 1958-65, asso. in pathology, 1965-68, asst. clin. prof., 1968-69, asst. prof., 1969-70; prof. pathology Temple U. Sch. Medicine, Phila., 1970-73; chief pathology service Temple U. Hosp., 1970-72; prof. pathology U. So. Cal. Sch. Medicine, 1973—; surg. pathologist, chief anatomic pathology data processing Los Angeles County Gen. Hosp., 1973—. Bus. mgr. Sci. Investment Research, 1966-70; securities broker and financial cons. Hogan-Harry & Co. Inc., 1967-70. Bd. dirs. Phila. div. Am. Cancer Soc., 1972-73, N.E. Los Angeles unit, 1973—. Diplomate Nat. Bd. Med. Examiners, Am. Bd. Pathology. Fellow Royal Soc. Medicine (London); mem. So. Cal. Soc. Pathologists, Am. Soc. Clin. Pathologists, Am. Assn. U. Profs., A.A.A.S., Am. Soc. Cytology, Am. Heart Assn. (council on kidney), Am. Soc. Nephrology, Internat. Acad. Pathology, Am. Assn. Pathologists and Bacteriologists, Los Angeles Soc. Pathologists, Soc. Computer Medicine, Phi Beta Kappa. Clubs: Phila. Medical, Phila. Country; Lake Placid (N.Y.). Editor: UP Report, 1967-73, New Sci. Investor, 1967-74; Computer PV Charts, 1969-74, Crocker Reports, 1973-74. Contbr. articles med. jours. Home: 1464 Ridge Way Pasadena CA 91106 Office: 1200 N State St LAC/USC Med Center Los Angeles CA 90033

CROCKER, GOLDIE, educator; b. Keene, N.H.; d. Harry and Julia (Teitelbaum) Crocker; R.N., Beth Israel Hosp. Sch. Nursing, 1947; B.S., Boston U., 1952, M.S., 1956, D.Ed., 1966. Night supr. Beth Israel Hosp., Boston, 1947-51; adminstrv. supr. Mass. Gen. Hosp., Boston, 1952-53; surg. clin. instrn., 1956-61; guidance counselor Boston Coll. Sch. Nursing, 1964-65; asso. prof. nursing Northeastern U., 1965-69; chmn. nursing dept. N.H. Tech. Inst., Concord, 1969—; med.-surg. cons. VA; planned and implemented 1st asso. degree nursing program in N.H.; vocational counselor underprivileged, 1966-68. Dir. nursing adv. com. Countway Library, 1968-69; mem. N.H. Bd. Nursing Edn. and Nurse Registration, 1970; mem. N.H. adv. bd. New Eng. Regional Kidney Program, 1972. Recipient outstanding student award, Boston Lying-In Hosp., 1946; Nat. League Nursing fellow, 1962. Mem. Am. Personnel and Guidance Assn., Nat. League Nursing (mem. bd. rev. for reasonable assurance of accreditation), Am., N.H. (dir. 1971—, com. on nursing edn. 1971—) nurses assns., New Eng. Council Higher Edn. in Nursing, United Community Services Careers, Sigma Theta Tau. Club: Quota (dir.). Contbr. articles to profl. jours., chpt. in book. Home: Summit Rd Keene NH 03431 Office: Fan Rd Concord NH 03301

CROCKER, HELEN MARIE (MRS. THOMAS SHETRORD HERSHEY), physician; b. Phila., Dec. 24, 1915; d. Walter James and Rosa Ernestine (Binder) Crocker; B.A., U. Pa., 1937; M.D., Temple U., 1941; m. Thomas Shetrord Hershey, June 14, 1941; children—Karen Therese (Mrs. J. Valentine), Gregory Thomas, Hope Therese. Intern, Allentown (Pa.) Gen. Hosp., 1941-42; tchr., sch. physician Edgewood Park Sch., Briarcliff Manor, N.Y., 1943-55; gen practice medicine, Briarcliff Manor, 1943—, Ossining, N.Y., 1943—; mem. staff Phelps Meml. Hosp., North Tarrytown, N.Y. Mem. A.M.A., Westchester County Med. Soc., Med. Soc. Notre Dame de Lourdes, Kappa Kappa Gamma. Roman Catholic. Home: Box 307 Scarborough Manor Scarborough NY 10510 Office: 100 S Highland Av Ossining NY 10562

CROCKER, JULIE SCHOEPF (MRS. AUGUSTUS THORNDIKE CROCKER), anesthesiologist; b. Detroit, Oct. 5, 1927; d. Albin Kesley and Virginia Joy (Goodbar) Schoepf; grad. Masters Sch., Dobbs Ferry, N.Y., 1944; A.B., Vassar Coll., 1948, M.A., Columbia, 1949; M.D., 1953; m. Augustus Thorndike Crocker, Dec. 20, 1952; children—Augustus T., Jonathan A., Christopher S. Intern Mary Hitchcock Hosp., Hanover, N.H., 1953-54; resident Mass. Gen. Hosp., Boston, 1954; resident Peter Bent Brigham Hosp., Boston, 1955, jr. asso. in surgery, 1957-58. asso. anesthesiologist, 1960-63; asso. anesthesiologist Free Hosp. for Women, Boston, 1958-60; anesthesiologist West Roxbury VA Hosp., Boston, 1960-63, Lahey Clinic Found., Boston, 1963-72, Boston Hosp. for Women, 1972—; clin. instr. Harvard, 1972—. Diplomate Am. Bd. Anesthesiology. Mem. A.M.A., Mass. Med. Soc., New Eng., Mass. socs. anesthesiology. Home: 18 Mill St Dover MA 02030 Office: 220 Longwood Av Boston MA 02115

CROCKER, MARY IDA REED (MRS. JAMES PETER CROCKER), educator; b. Lima, O., May 20, 1915; d. Joseph Emanual and Rhea Irene (Rodabaugh) Reed; B.S., Kent State U., 1957, M.S., 1959; Ed.D. (Nat. Def. Edn. Act fellow), U. Pitts., 1970; m. James Peter Crocker, June 9, 1933; children—Budd J., Laquita (Mrs. Jack McCarthy), Gaynol (Mrs. William Wapotich), Michael D. Spl. edn. adminstr. Ashtabula (O.) County Schs., 1968-71; elementary tchr. Gladwin County, Mich., 1946-50; spl. edn. supr. Willoughby (O.) Schs., 1950-67; sch. psychologist Geauga County, O., 1967-68; prof. spl. edn. Fla. Internat. U., Miami, 1972—. Spl. edn. cons. Am. Found. Overseas Blind, Republic of Phillippines, 1963-64; vis. prof. Kent (O.) State U., 1964-72, Lake Erie Coll., Painesville, O., 1964-72; psychologist Bur. Vocational Rehab., Cleve., 1962-63. Leader 4-H, Leatonville, Mich., 1946-48; chmn. pre-sch. activities for handicapped Soc. for Crippled Children; spl. edn. chmn. Ohio P.T.A., 1966-67. Bd. dirs. Epilepsy Clinic, Cleve., 1957-60; pres. bd. trustees Lake County Sheltered Industries, Mentor, O., 1954-57, 1954-57. Recipient Plaque of Appreciation, Republic of Phillippines, 1964, Nat. Pacesetter award Presidents Council on Supplementary Centers and Services, 1972. Mem. Council for Exceptional Children (chpt. pres. 1952-53, 64-65, del. to state governing bd. 1965-66, advisor student chpt. 1972). Rebekah. Home: 12941 SW 10th Terrace Miami FL 33144 Office: Tamiami Trail Miami FL 33144

CROCKETT, DOROTHY NELL FOUTS, educator, civic worker; b. Denton, Tex., Nov. 7, 1924; d. Theron Judson and Leslie Vann (Sams) Fouts; B.S., North Tex. U., 1944; student U. Colo., summer 1943, U. Tex., 1945-46; m. Leonard Frank Crockett, Aug. 20, 1946; children—Leslie Carol, Linda Irene, Leesa Kay. Tchr., Austin (Tex.) High Sch., 1947-48, Odessa (Tex.) High Sch., 1950-55; tchr. interior design, landscape design, adult edn. program Odessa Coll., 1968-72. Co-owner, dir. N.Am. Enterprises; owner Fancy Pants, Inc., Pandora's, Odessa; accredited flower show judge; landscape design critic. Bd. dirs. Community Chest, United Fund, 1961-63, Ector County Friends of Library, 1966-70, Odessa-Midland Symphony Assn., 1960-69; pres. Odessa Symphony Guild, 1958-59; dir. Odessa Beautiful Assn., 1959-71; state dir. Beautify Tex. Assn., 1968-74; dir. Permian Basin chpt. Arthritis Found., 1967-72, nat. dir., 1972-75, regional rep., 1972-74, chmn. state steering com., 1973—, bd. dirs. S. Tex. and Capital City, 1973—; dir. Presdl. Mus., 1962-72, Planned Parenthood Assn., 1966-70, Civic Concert Assn., 1958-72, Crystal Ball Found., 1960-62, Knife and Fork Assn., 1960-64, Broadway Theater League, 1962-64. Mem. Nat. Council State Garden Clubs, Landscape Design Critics Council Tex. (treas. 1971-73), Odessa Womens Forum (dir. 1950-70, pres. 1964-65), Alpha Delta Phi (pres. alumni assn. 1964-65). Baptist. Clubs: Odessa Contemporary Garden (dir. 1960-68), Texas Garden (state dir. 1961—), Highland Lakes Garden. Home: Route 3 Box 606 Marble Falls TX 78654

CROCKETT, HELEN MILLIRONS, univ. dean; b. Penokee, Kan., Nov. 20, 1918; d. Lilburn Patterson and Ola (Bell) Millirons; A.B. in Edn., Wichita State U., 1951, M.A., 1955; postgrad. U. Chgo., 1959, U. Colo., 1968; m. Albert G. Crockett, Aug. 7, 1940; 1 son, David G. Elementary tchr., Wichita, Kan., 1938-44; office mgr. F.L. Whan Assos., Wichita, 1944-49; with div. continuing edn. Wichita State U., 1949—, exec. sec., 1949-52, asst. to dean, 1952-60, dir., 1960-73, asso. dean div. continuing edn., 1973—. Del., 1st World Conf. on Adult Edn., Denmark, 1965; cons. Urban League Leadership Project. Bd. dirs. Wichita State U. Credit Union, 1962-71; bd. dirs. YWCA, 1957-63, mem. fgn. policy com., 1973—; mem. steering com. Wesley Hosp. Bldg. Fund, YWCA Bldg. Fund. Mem. Kan. Adult Edn. Assn. (pres. 1969), Mo. Valley Adult Edn. Assn. (v.p. 1968), Assn. Univ. Eve. Colls. (dir. 1971-74), Phi Kappa Phi (sec. 1970). Episcopalian. Home: 446 N Vassar St Wichita KS 67208

CROFT, AMY BALL, polit. worker; b. Columbia, S.C., June 9, 1888; d. George Jay and Lillie A. (Carpenter) Ball; student pub. schs., Los Angeles; m. John C. Croft, Apr. 12, 1904 (dec. June 1955); children—Walter A. (dec.), June (Mrs. Monroe L. Reuland, dec.), Dixie (Mrs. Carol Linsted), Kathryn (Mrs. Paul B. Kerston), Barbara (Mrs. James G. Searls). Agt., Pacific Coast Paper Co., Los Angeles, 1935; saleswoman Helen T. Reed, broker, Palm Desert, Cal., 1960-61; owner Ye Eating Home, Alhambra, Cal., 1922-25; ret. saleswoman Verda M. Covey, broker, Palm Desert. Active various community activities. Charter mem. Nat. Com. Dem. party, 1957—; mem. Cal. Central Com., 1954—, v.p. Riverside County Central Com., 1958-62, vice-chmn. Cal. Dem. Council, 1956-58, treas., 1958-60, trustee, mem. exec. com., 1962—, treas. Dem. Women 29th Congl. Dist., 1961—, dir. 4th Supervisoral Dist., 1961—; pres. Dem. Club, Desert Hot Springs; legislative chmn., treas. Riverside County Dem. Central Com.; pres. Cove Area Dem. Club; chmn. Coachella Valley Dem. Women. Mem. Internat. Platform Assn., Assn. U.S. Army, Rancho Mirage C. of C. (dir.; named Outstanding Citizen 1972). Home: 71835 Sahara Rd PO Box 22 Rancho Mirage CA 92270 Office: 73945 Hwy III Palm Desert CA 92260

CROFT, VIRGINIA JEANETTE, editor, public relations exec.; b. Altoona, Pa., Oct. 6, 1940; d. Walter Lavern and Mildred Lucille (Skyles) Croft; B.A. in Journalism, Pa. State U., 1962. Editorial asst. USPHS, Rockville, Md., 1962-63, Armed Forces Communications and Electronics Assn., . Washington, 1963-66; editor, dir. pub. information VICA mag. Vocational Indsl. Clubs Am., Falls Church, Va., 1966—. Mem. Ednl. Press Assn. Am. Home: 3000 Spout Run Pkwy Arlington VA 22201 Office: 105 N Virginia Av Falls Church VA 22046

CROMWELL, EVALYN TETSU-SEI, librarian; b. Mazon, Ill., Mar. 14, 1915; d. John Sebastian and Ann Marie (Dunlop) Cromwell; diploma, Wright Jr. Coll., 1938, library certificate, 1941; student Art Inst., evenings 1945-47; Ph.B., Northwestern U., 1961. With Chgo. Pub. Library, 1941—, jr. library asst. Taft High Sch. Library, 1941-42, Albany Park br. library, 1942-43, children's library asst. Norwood Park sub-br., 1943-54; adult service librarian Hild Library, 1954—. Instr. first aid A.R.C., 1961—, vol. first aid stas., 1961—. Recipient citation A.R.C., 1970. Mem. Am. Assn. U. Women (resolutions chmn., bd. dirs. Chgo. br.), Ill. Audubon Soc., A.L.A., Ill. Library Assn., Sierra Club, Art Inst. Chgo., UN Assn. U.S.A., Oceanic Soc. Mem. Northwestern Chorale (librarian 1955—). Clubs: Apollo Musical, Chicago Art, Chicago Library, (Chgo.); Evanston (Ill.) Bird. Address: 4816 N Talman Av Chicago IL 60625

CRON, ANNE MARIE, publishing co. exec.; b. Hempstead, L.I., May 31, 1929; d. Thomas Morgan and Dorothy Josephine (McNally) Bohen; A.A., Mount Ida Jr. Coll., 1947; m. John Bowes Cron, Apr. 15, 1950; children—Kevin J., Christopher J., Claudia Anne, Ian Morgan. Asst. sales service mgr. Columbia Broadcasting Co., N.Y.C., 1948-50; mgr. directory services, mgr. product information for schs. Mgmt. Publs., Greenwich, Conn., 1965-66; dir. marketing services, bus. mgr. and editor Conover-Mast Purchasing Indsl. Directory, Greenwich, 1966-73; asso. pub. U.S. Indsl. Directory, Cahners Pub. Co., 1974—. Republican. Roman Catholic. Club: Nat. Badminton Assn. Home: 32 Winthrop Dr Riverside CT 06878 Office: 1200 Summer St Stamford CT 06905

CRONEMEYER, CORA SISAM (MRS. GEORGE T. CRONEMEYER), editor; b. Champaign, Ill., Jan. 24, 1913; d. Charles Herschel and Cora Anna (Hutton) Sisam; A.B., U. Ill., 1934; M.A., Western Res. U., 1938; m. George T. Cronemeyer, May 6, 1942; 1 dau., Cora Sue. Economist, Bur. Lab. Statistics, Washington, 1946-50, Bur. Employment Security, Washington, 1950-69, Manpower Adminstrn., U.S. Dept. Labor, Washington, 1969—, editor mag. Rural Manpower Devels., Rural Manpower Service, 1960—. Mem. Internat. Assn. Personnel in Employment Security, Am. Fedn. Govt. Employees. Unitarian. Club: Town and Country. Home: 4346 Alton Pl NW Washington DC 20016 Office: 601 D St NW Washington DC 20023

CRONIN, DORA RUTH KIME (MRS. FRANK E. CRONIN), museum curator; b. Pyllman, Neb., Feb. 7, 1892; d. Charles Milton and Lillian Geneva (Bartley) Kime; student pub. sch.; m. Frank E. Cronin, Oct. 25, 1911 (dec. 1951); children—Leo, Lucille (Mrs. Jerry Rillahan), Lillian (Mrs. Ansel Wrage), John Milton. Tchr. rural schs., Neb., 1910, 11; practical nurse Sandhills Gen. Hosp., Valentine, Neb., 1944-70; curator mus. Cherry County Hist. Soc., Valentine, 1970—. Treas., Sch. Dist. 53, 1920-30. Mem. Cherry County Hist. Soc. (sec.-treas. 1962—), Bus. and Profl. Women. Roman Catholic (pres. Altar Soc. 1945-46). Home: 312 W 3d St Valentine NE 69201 Office: Hwy 20 and Main St Valentine NE 69201

CRONKRITE, VELMA VAN HORN (MRS. JOHN LLEWELYN CRONKRITE), librarian; b. Tulsa, Mar. 5, 1916; d. Fred Porter and Wilma Eda (Howell) Van Horn; B.S., Northeastern State U., 1938; postgrad. Houston U., 1951, Tex. Arts and Industries, 1956-57, Sul Ross State Coll., 1958; M.L.S., Tex. Woman's U., 1963; m. John Llewelyn Cronkrite, Mar. 27, 1970; 1 son, David Van Horn Spell. Classroom tchr. Vinita, Okla., 1938-40, Corpus Christi, Tex., 1949-50, Brownsville, Tex., 1950-53, Los Fresnos, Tex., 1953-59; Los Fresnos High Sch., 1959-65; library co-ordinator Los Fresnos Sch. Dist., 1965—. Mem. Tex. State Tchrs. Assn. (pres. 1968-69), Alpha Sigma Alpha, Delta Kappa Gamma, Kappa Kappa Iota. Mem. Order Eastern Star. Home: 1649 Sam Houston Dr Harlingen TX 78550 Office: Box 308 Los Fresnos TX 78566

CROOKE, PAULINE HILTY, TV reporter; b. Nampa, Ia., Aug 3, 1928; d. Louis T. and Martha (Detweiler) Hilty; student Wash. State Coll., 1945, N.W. Nazarene Coll., Nampa, Ida., 1946-48, U. Wis., 1948-49; B.A., Coll. of Ida., 1950; m. Richard W. Crooke, Dec. 28, 1951 (div. May 1959); 1 dau., Cheryl Elizabeth. Mem. advt. staff Ida. Free Press, Nampa, 1946-48, reporter, city editor, 1949-52; with

Madison (Wis.) Capitol Times, part time, 1948-49; successively dir. pub. information, coll. editor, dir. pub. relations Coll. of Ida., Caldwell, 1953-65, dir. information services, 1965-70; reporter KBOI-TV, Boise, Ida., 1970—. Chmn. com. for passage of new state civil rights bill Ida. Legislature, 1968; pres. Canyon County Young Republican Club, 1950-51; v.p. Ida. Young Rep. League, 1950-51. Bd. dirs. Caldwell chpt. A.R.C., 1962-68; legal chmn. Boise chpt. N.A.A.C.P., 1965-68. Mem. Am. Coll. Pub. Relations Assn., Am. Alumni Council, Am. Assn. U. Women, Ida. Press Women (dir., state scholarship chmn.), Boise Ad Club, Coll. of Ida. Alumni Assn. (exec. dir.), Faculty Women's Assn. (pres.), Coll. Clan (pres.). Presbyn. (deacon 1949-51). Editor: The Relator, 1968-69. Contbr. short stories and articles to nat. mags. Home: 960 S Curtis Rd Boise ID 83651

CROOKS, LOIS ANDERSON, psychologist; b. Waldo, O., May 2, 1911; d. Clayton Enlow and Laura (Markley) Anderson; B.S. in Commerce, Temple U., 1938, M.S. in Edn., 1950, postgrad., 1970—; m. Robert M. Crooks, June 8, 1940; children—William Clayton, Robert Anderson. Personnel asst. 1st Pa. Bank, Phila., 1937-48; adminstrv. asst. Edward N. May & Assos., Phila., 1946-48; asso. research psychologist Ednl. Testing Service, Princeton, N.J., 1962—. Cons. measures for job performance measurement. Mem. Am. Psychol. Assn., Am. Ednl. Research Assn., Smithsonian Instn., Beta Gamma Sigma, Theta Sigma Phi. Author: The In-Basket Study, 1971; The Criterion Study, 1971. Editor: An Investigation of Sources of Bias in the Prediction of Job Performance, 1972; Selection and Development of Job Performance Measures for Assessment Programs, 1974; Career Progress of MBAs, 1974. Home: 1101 Yardley Rd Morrisville PA 19067 Office: Ednl Testing Service Rosedale Rd Princeton NJ 08540

CROPPER, EVELYN TYLER GILLESPIE (MRS. CLARENCE CROPPER), librarian; b. Mayslick, Ky., Jan. 17, 1929; d. John Elwood and Mary (Burnaugh) Gillespie; A.B., U. Ky.; postgrad. Kent State U., Xavier U.; m. Clarence Cropper, Mar. 17, 1948; 1 dau., Mary Martha. Head children's dept. Brumback Library, Van Wert, O., 1951-54; librarian Van Wert High Sch., 1954-57, Delaware County (O.) Library, 1957-60, Lima (O.) Sr. High Sch., 1967-68, Clermont (O.) N.E. High Sch., 1968-70, Anderson Middle Sch., Cin., 1970—. Mem. Am. Assn. U. Women, Nat., Ohio edn. assns., Ohio Assn. Sch. Librarians, Ohio Library Assn. Episcopalian. Home: 8184 Northport Dr Cincinnati OH 45230 Office: Beechmont Av Cincinnati OH 45230

CROSBIE, LUCY BARTLETT (MRS. ARTHUR W. CROSBIE), newspaper pub.; b. Willimantic, Conn., May 24, 1929; d. G. Donald and Teresa K. (Shea) Bartlett; B.S., Boston U., 1951; m. Arthur W. Crosbie, July 16, 1952; children—Vincent, Kevin. Pres. Chronicle Printing Co., Willimantic, Conn., 1954—; pub. Willimantic Daily Chronicle, 1954—. Sec. Conn. Tb and Health Assn., 1967-69. Bd. dirs. Conn. Child Welfare Assn. Mem. Conn. Daily Newspaper Assn. (pres. 1969), Conn. Editorial Assn. (v.p. 1972—), United Press Internat. Newspapers of Conn. (pres. 1968), Delta Delta Delta. Home: 215 Church St Williamantic CT 06226 Office: Chronicle Rd Willimantic CT 06226

CROSBY, CYNTHIA GAIL CARSON, psychologist; b. Savannah, Ga., Nov. 28, 1945; d. Edwin Williams and Lillie Corene (Smith) Carson; A.B., Ga. So. Coll., 1967; M.S. in Psychology (fellow) Auburn U., 1969, Ph.D., 1971. Grad. instr. psychology Auburn (Ala.) U., 1968-71; unit dir. E. Central Ala. unit Bryce Hosp., Tuscaloosa, 1973—. Charter mem. health professions adv. com. Sch. Arts and Scis., Auburn U., 1973—. NSF trainee, 1967-71. Mem. Am., Southeastern, Ala. psychol. assns., Assn. Advancement Behavior Therapy, Southeastern Assn. Behavior Therapy. Address: ECA Unit Bryce Hosp Tuscaloosa AL 35401

CROSBY, JUNE KUHN (MRS. GEORGE ROBERT CROSBY), writer; b. Chgo., Feb. 27, 1919; d. Leroy Philip and Grace Christiane (Engles) Kuhn; student Sarah Lawrence Coll., 1937, U. Cal. at Los Angeles, 1952-59; m. Bob (George Robert) Crosby, Sept. 22, 1938; children—Cathleen D. (Mrs. Brian Harvey), Christopher D., George Robert, Stephen R., J. Malia. Columnist, Honolulu Star-Bull., 1962-64; pres. June Crosby's Rainbow Kitchen, Inc., Honolulu, 1963-64; columnist San Diego Union, 1965-69, Australian Women's Weekly, 1966, Elgin Daily Courier News, Elgin, Ill., 1967-69, Ill. State Jour., Springfield, 1967-69, Sacramento Union, 1966-68, Sarah Lawrence Alumnae Mag., 1967, Woman's Day mag., 1968, Western's World, 1970—, Carte Blanche mag., 1970-71; pres. Crosstown Publs., LaJolla, Cal., 1971—; dir. Women's Bank, San Diego. Hon. co-chmn. San Diego Am. Heart Assn., 1966-69, San Diego Mental Health Assn., 1971—; founder, pres. Belles for Mental Health, 1972; sec. exec. com. Combined Health Assn. Drive, 1973, 74. Bd. dirs. San Diego County Mental Health Assn., 1972-74. Mem. Am. Fedn. TV and Radio Artists, Nat. League Am. Pen Women, Women in Communications, D.A.R. Author: Serve It Cold!, 1969; San Diego Fare, 1972. Home: 939 Coast Blvd La Jolla CA 92037 Office: 7730 Herschel Av Suite G La Jolla CA 92037

CROSBY, KATHRYN GRANT, actress; m. Bing Crosby, Oct. 24, 1957; children—Harry Lillis III, Mary Frances, Nathaniel Patrick. Numerous appearances on stage and with stock companies. Home: 170 N Robertson Blvd Beverly Hills CA 90211

CROSBY, MURIEL, ednl. cons.; b. Washington, Mar. 1, 1908; d. George W. and Mary (Granville) Crosby; B.S., Wilson Tchrs. Coll., 1936; M.A., U. Md., 1942, D.Ed., 1951. Supr., tchr. pub. schs., Washington, 1928-47; asso. dir. research Curriculum div. Silver-Burdett Pub. Co., 1947-49; asso. prof. edn. Adelphi Coll., Garden City, N.Y., 1949-51; asst. supt. charge elementary edn. Wilmington (Del.) Bd. Edn., 1951-65, asst. supt. for ednl. programs, 1965-68, asso. supt., 1968; cons. on urban edn., 1968—; adv. bd. Grolier Pub. Co., 1968-69. Bd. dirs. Girls Club Am., 1966-67. Recipient Brotherhood award Nat. Conf. Christians and Jews, 1965, Human Relations award Nat. Sorority Phi Delta Kappa, 1962, award for Outstanding Del. Educator Bus. and Profl. Women's Club, 1966; Distinguished Service award Nat. Council Tchrs. English, 1969, Distinguished lectr., 1970. Mem. Nat. Council Tchrs. English (pres. 1966-67), Assn. for Supervision and Curriculum Devel. (pres. 1968-69), Phi Kappa Phi, Kappa Delta Pi. Author: Supervision as Cooperative Action, 1957; Curriculum Development for Elementary Schools in Changing Society, 1964; An Adventure in Human Relations, 1965. Editor: Reading Ladders for Human Relations, 1963; co-editor Language Programs For The Disadvantaged; gen. editor: The World of Language, 1974. Home: 1627 N Franklin St Wilmington DE 19806

CROSS, ANNA ELIZABETH, editor, publisher; b. Hopkins, Mo., Nov. 13, 1922; d. John Henry and Ellen Catherine (Ford) Campbell; student N.W. Mo. State U., 1940-41; m. Russell Lewis Cross, Dec. 31, 1941; children—Sharon (Mrs. John R. Shipley), Mary Ann. Co-editor, co-pub. Hopkins Jour., 1958—. Committeewoman, Hopkins Twp. Republican Com. Mem. Hopkins C. of C., P.E.O. (past chpt. pres.). Methodist. Editor: Hopkins Centennial History Book. Home: 302 S 2d St Hopkins MO 64461 Office: 113 N 3d St Hopkins MO 64461

CROSS, ANNE ESTELLE MONAGHAN (MRS. WILLIAM TIFFANY CROSS), civic worker; b. Canadaigua, N.Y.; d. John and Helen (O'Connor) Monaghan; B.A., D'Youville Coll., 1921; postgrad. Cornell U., summer 1922; m. William Tiffany Cross, June 30, 1923; children—Esther (dec.), William J., Linda (Mrs. Patrick FitzSimons), Anne Margot (Mrs. Robert J. Allen). Tchr., Bloomfield (N.Y.) Sch., 1921-23; substitute tchr., Canadaigua, 1942-48; social worker Ontario County Children's Ct. and Probation Dept., 1950-61; exec. dir. Ontario County Homemaker Service Inc., 1966-70. Active P.T.A., A.R.C., Cancer Funds. Bd. dirs. Wood Library, Canandaigua, 1969-72, Ontario County Homemaker Service, 1970-73. Recipient Dist. Capt. Community Chest awards, 1955, 56, 57. Roman Catholic (pres. Rosary Soc. 1964-65). Home: 3367 W Lake Rd Canandaigua NY 14424

CROSS, ANNE LOUISE, coll. dean; b. Coalingo, Cal., Oct. 16, 1939; d. Gordon Buford and Rubye Louise (Parker) Cross; B.S. in Secondary Edn., U. Tenn., 1969, M.Ed. in Sch. Adminstrn., 1972. Tchr. English, Hamilton County (Tenn.) Dept. Edn., 1969-72; dean women Limestone Coll., Gaffney, S.C., 1972—. Judge Am. Kennel Club, Inc. Active United Way. Mem. Am. Humane Soc., Am. Dog Owners Assn., Inc., Am. Assn. Higher Edn., Nat. Assn. Student Personnel Adminstrs., Nat., S.C. assns. women deans and counselors, Collie Club Am., Inc., Kappa Delta Pi, Alpha Xi Delta. Clubs: Spartanburg Kennel, Chattanooga Kennel (sec. 1963, pres. 1972). Contbr. articles to dog-oriented publs. Home: 637 Morrison Springs Rd Chattanooga TN 37416 Office: Office Student Affairs Limestone Coll Gaffney SC 29340

CROSS, GERTRUDE SARA ERHARD (MRS. ROBERT BLACK CROSS), physician; b. Pa., June 2, 1916; d. Elmer Sylvester and Lydia Mae (Park) Erhard; student Beaver Coll. Women, 1933-34; B.M., Grove City Coll., 1937; student Mansfield State Tchrs. Coll., 1938; D.O., Kirksville Coll. Osteopathy and Surgery, 1945; grad. student Kirksville Coll. Osteopathy, 1946, 62, Phila. Coll. Osteopathy, 1950-66; m. Dr. Robert Black Cross, Nov. 29, 1938. Intern, resident, Kirksville (Mo.) Osteo. Hosp.; gen. practice osteo. medicine, Columbus, O., 1946-70, ret.; vis. intern lectr. Doctors Hosp., Columbus, with dept. manipulation, physio-therapy and rehab., cons. manipulative therapy, 1966-68. Mem. sustaining bd. Boys Ranch. Diplomate Am. Bd. Gen. Practice. Fellow Am. Coll. Gen. Practice in Osteo. Medicine and Surgery (sec. and treas. Ohio chpt.; mem. Columbus Dist. Acad. Osteo. Medicine and Surgery, Ohio (sec.-treas. 1962-66), Nat. (component socs. com. 1965-68) acads. applied osteopathy, Nat. Coll. Gen. Practitioners (nominating com.), Kirksville Alumni Assn. (past pres. Ohio chpt.), Am., Ohio osteo. assns., Am. Assn. U. Women, D.A.R., Am. Osteo. Coll. Phys. Medicine and Rehab., Theta Alpha Phi, Theta Kappa (past pres.), Delta Omega (past pres., past nat. chpt. treas., nat. pres. 1964-66). Clubs: Zonta Internat. (past pres., past bd. dirs., past program chmn. Columbus Chpt.), Masquers. 750 (Kirksville Coll. Osteopathy and Surgery). Home: 5961 Emerald Harbor Dr Longboat Key Sarasota FL 33577

CROSS, JENNIE BELLE SCHOOLFIELD (MRS. ROBERT MONROE CROSS), librarian; b. Wichita Falls, Tex., Jan. 12, 1935; d. John Ralph and Bessie (Wythe) Schoolfield; B.A., Harding Coll., Searcy, Ark., 1959; A.M. in L.S., U. Mich., 1968; m. Robert Monroe Cross, Sept. 5, 1954; children—John Stephen, Charles Robert, Keven Lewis. Bookmobile librarian Tulsa Pub. Library, 1955-57; paleontol. library asst. Jersey Prodn. Research Corp., Tulsa, 1957-59; asst. librarian Tex. Eastern Gas Transmission Corp., Shreveport, 1961, Mich. Christian Jr. Coll., Rochester, 1962-67; documents librarian Oakland U., Rochester, 1967—. Adj. instr. Wayne State U. Bd. dirs. MSU Employees Credit Union; trustee Bottles for Bldg., Inc. Mem. A.L.A., Midwest Archives Conf., Mich. Archival Assn., Spl. Libraries Assn., U. Mich. Library Sch. Alumni, Hist. Soc. Mich. (trustee). Republican. Mem. of Christ. Ch. Home: 3942 Embarcadero Drayton Plains MI 48020 Office: Oakland U Rochester MI 48063

CROSS, JENNIFER MARY (MRS. ELLIS M. GANS), author; b. London, Eng., May 10, 1932; d. Thomas Reginald and Ruth Neil (Hodgson) Cross; B.A. with honors in History, Kings Coll. U. London, 1953; m. Ellis Myron Gans, July 12, 1965; 1 son, Jason David Mycroft. Sec. to book pub., London, 1953-56; personal asst. to editor Brit. Med. Jour., 1957-58; pub. relations Napper, Stinton, Woolley, London, 1958-63; free-lance writer, 1963—; contbr. to The Nation, The Times (London), Punch, Economist, Sunday Times (London), New Statesman; tchr. and lectr. on consumer affairs. Mem. Assn. Cal. Consumers, 1966-72, Consumer Fedn. Cal., 1972—; participant White House Conf. on Food, Nutrition and Health, 1969. Author: The Supermarket Trap, 1970; Justice Denied, A History of the Japanese in the United States (for Children), 1974. Home: 301 Surrey St San Francisco CA 94131

CROSS, KATHRYN PATRICIA, psychologist; b. Normal, Ill., Mar. 17, 1926; d. Clarence Le Roy and Katherine Delia (Dague) Cross; B.S., Ill. State U., 1948; A.M., U. Ill., 1951, Ph.D. (Nat. Inst. Mental Health fellow), 1958; LL.D., Ill. State U., 1970. Asst. dean of women U. Ill., Urbana, 1953-59; dean of women Cornell U., Ithaca, N.Y., 1959-60, dean of students, 1960-63; dir. coll. and univ. programs Ednl. Testing Service, Princeton, N.J., 1963-66, sr. research psychologist, Berkeley, Cal., 1966—; sr. research psychologist Center for Research and Devel. in Higher Edn., U. Cal., Berkeley, 1966—. Mem. adv. com. Russell Sage Found., N.Y.C., 1972—, Ednl. Policy Center, N.Y.C., 1970—, Danforth Found., St. Louis, 1970—. Bd. govs. Change, Inc., 1969—. Recipient research award Nat. Assn. Student Personnel Adminstrs., 1972, Medallion of Honor U. Ill., 1973. Mem. Am. Assn. Higher Edn. (pres. 1974-75). Author: The Junior College Student (Best Books award Pi Lambda Theta, 1968), Beyond the Open Door (Outstanding Book in Education award Sch. and Soc., 1971). Home: 904 Oxford St Berkeley CA 94707

CROSS, LAURA ELIZABETH, lawyer; b. Lathrop, Mo.; d. Pross T. and Nina (Peel) Cross; A.B., Lindenwood Coll., 1923; B.Litt., Columbia Sch. Journalism, 1925; J.D., George Washington U., 1939. Bibliog. research Library of Congress, Washington, 1931-42; admitted to D.C. bar, 1940; atty. Office Chief of Engrs., U.S. Army, 1942-73; practice in Washington, 1973—. Mem. Fed. Bar Assn., Kappa Beta Pi, Theta Sigma Phi. Home and office: 2500 Wisconsin Av Washington DC 20007

CROSS, LOUISE PORTLOCK, mfg. co. exec.; b. Norfolk, Va., Jan. 20, 1907; d. William Seth and Mary Louise (Fanshaw) Portlock; grad. high sch.; m. James Byron Cross, July 17, 1929; children—Blanche Louise (Mrs. Charles Louis Kerzanet). With J.B. Cross, Inc., Norfolk, 1952—, exec. pres., 1959-60, pres., chief exec. officer, 1960—. Mem. Phi Sigma Alpha (charter). Episcopalian. Club: Altrusa of Norfolk (co-chmn. internat. relations com. 1973—). Mem. Order Eastern Star (past matron), Ladies Oriental Shrine N.Am. Home: 1605 Mayflower Apts Virginia Beach VA 23451 Office: 3797 Progress Rd Norfolk VA 23502

CROSS, MARY CLEMSON (MRS. JOHN EMORY CROSS, JR.), biostatistician; b. Westminster, Md., July 7, 1919; d. Charles O. and Mary (Gray) Clemson; B.A., Western Md. Coll., 1939; postgrad. Johns Hopkins U., 1941, 43, 48, 56, 66—; m. John Emory Cross, Jr., June 20, 1942; children—Mary Laveille Holliday (Mrs. John Charles Heine), John Emory, III, Katherine Laws, David Dorsey, Charles Thomas, Sarah Emily Clemson. With Johns Hopkins U. Sch. Hygiene and Pub. Health, 1941-44, 1965—, biostatistician dept. population and family health, 1967—. Family life ednl. cons. Balt. City Pub. Sch. System 1967—. Mem. diocesan bd. Churchwomen of Episcopal Diocese of Md., 1953-56, 58-68, pub. relations chmn., editor Episcopal Churchwomen of Md., 1962-65; pres. Churchwomen of St. Thomas, Garrison Forest, 1951-52; v.p. Towson Convocation, 1965-68; area rep. Debutante Register, 1940; active Johns Hopkins Hosp. Women's Aux. Mem. Royal Soc. Health, Am. Pub. Health Assn., A.A.A.S., Johns Hopkins U. Alumni Assn., Western Md. Coll. Alumni Assn., Phi Alpha Mu Alumnae Assn. (organizing chmn., 1st pres. 1944). Democrat. Club: Hamilton Street (Balt.). Home: 314 Golf Course Rd Owings Mills MD 21117 Office: 615 N Wolfe St Baltimore MD 21205

CROSS, PEARL ALENE ACRES (MRS. HARRISON CROSS), librarian; b. Oneida, Tenn., July 22, 1917; d. Samuel and Bessie Minerva (Reynolds) Acres; B.S., U. Tenn., 1955, postgrad., 1957, 69, summer 1966; postgrad. Tenn. Tech. U., 1970-71; m. Harrison Cross, Sept. 4, 1937; children—Anita (Mrs. Joseph B. Cummins), Maudeane (Mrs. Linden Lee Shaw). Tchr. elementary schs. Scott County, Tenn., 1937-55; librarian Oneida High Sch., 1955—. Mem. N.E.A., Tenn., E. Tenn., Oneida edn. assns., Tenn., E. Tenn. library assns., Tenn. Audiovisual Assn., Internat. Reading Assn., Am. Assn. Univ. Women, Oneida Bus. and Profl. Women's Club, Delta Kappa Gamma (chpt. pres. 1968-70, Xi state chmn. personal growth and services com. 1973—). Mem. Order Eastern Star (sec. 1955-56). Home: Route 1 Box 190 Oneida TN 37841 Office: PO Box 439 Oneida TN 37841

CROSSLAND, KATHRYN MCALLISTER (MRS. ROBERT B. CROSSLAND), nursing educator; b. Spartanburg, S.C., Aug. 5, 1914; d. Abram Cammie and Eva (Setzler) McAllister; grad. Spartanburg Gen. Hosp., 1934; B.S., U. Ala., 1953, M.S., 1957; Ed.D., U. Fla., 1967; m. Robert Benton Crossland August 9, 1939 (deceased July 19, 1963). Engaged as nursing supervisor Morristown (N.J.) Meml. Hosp., 1936-38; pub. health nurse Met. Life Ins. Co., Miami, Fla., 1938-42, Birmingham, Ala., 1943-49; instr. Jefferson Hillman Hosp. Sch. Nursing, Birmingham, Ala., 1950-52; dir. nursing edn. and service U. Hosp. and Hillman Clinic, 1953-59; asso. dean Coll. Nursing, Tex. Woman's U., Houston, 1960-65; research asst. Coll. Edn., U. Fla., 1965-67; prof. nursing, dir. undergrad. studies Sch. Nursing Duke U., Durham, N.C., 1967-71; prof. nursing, dean Sch. Nursing U. Ala., Huntsville, 1971—. Pres. Ala. Bd. Nursing; mem. adv. com. Ala. Bd. Health; mem. Ala. Comprehensive Health Planning Agy. Mem. Am. Ednl. Research Assn., Assn. Supervision and Curriculum Devel., Nat. Soc. Study Edn., Am. (pres. Ala. 1952-56), Tex. (1st v.p. 1962-65) nurses assns., Nat. League Nursing, Pi Lambda Theta, Kappa Delta Pi. Methodist. Clubs: Pilot Internat., Valley Hill Country (Huntsville). Home: 7824 Haven St SE Huntsville AL 35802

CROSSLIN, HIAWATHA, ret. educator; b. Waco, Tex.; d. John Stephen and Mary Francis (Conger) Crosslin; A.B., Baylor U., 1923; B.S., U. Tex., 1928, M.Ed., 1929, Ed.D., 1943. Tutor, U. Tex., Austin, 1923-26; supr. phys. edn. Austin Pub. Schs., 1926-27; dean women and head women's phys. edn. Edinburg (Tex.) Coll., 1927-29; acting dir. women's phys. edn. Sam Houston State Tchrs. Coll., Huntsville, Tex., summer 1921, dir., 1930-32; dean women, head phys. edn. Carroll Coll., San Antonio, 1929-30; from asst. prof. to head dept., prof. Southwest Tex. State Tchrs. Coll., San Marcos, 1934-55; head men's and women's depts. phys. edn., asst. to dean of women San Angelo (Tex.) Coll., 1955-58; cons. in curriculum to pub. schs., 1959-60; cons. Kellogg Found. Project Stephen F. Austin Coll., 1947; dean women, dir. women's phys. edn. Ferrum (Va.) Jr. Coll., 1960-68, dean women, prof. edn., 1960-65, head div. women's phys. edn., varsity coach basketball, tennis, swimming, 1960-68; acting dir. women's phys. edn. program U. Tex., summers 1954-56, Tex. Woman's Coll., 1957. Chmn., dir. A.R.C. Tchr. edn. del. 2d Pan-Am. Congress Phys. Edn., Mexico City, 1946, 3d congress, Montevideo, Uruguay, 1950; del. Congress Internat. Affairs for Women in Health, Copenhagen, Denmark, 1949, Northampton, Mass., 1954; mem. Va. gov.'s com. to select young business woman of year, 1968; chairman women's guild Chapel-in-the Hills. Recipient citation So. Assn. Edn. for Coll. Women, 1958; Barbour award Ferrum Coll., 1968. Fellow Am. Sch. Health Assn.; mem. Royal Soc. Health (London), Am. Assn. U. Women, Wimberley Home Demonstration (pres.), A.A.H.P.E.R., Delta Psi Kappa, Delta Kappa Gamma (Woman of Year award 1958), Phi Lambda Theta, Pi Gamma Mu, Alpha Xi Delta (named one of 10 most successful). Club: Woman's of Rocky Mount (pres., chmn. fine arts dept.). Author articles in field. Home: PO Box 43 Wimberley TX 78676

CROSSMAN, MURIEL LOUISE COX (MRS. JOHN NORRIS CROSSMAN), librarian; b. Quincy, Mass., Jan. 22, 1913; d. G. William and Theresa Marie (Deans) Cox; student Pub. Schs., Quincy; m. John Norris Crossman, Dec. 7, 1935; children—John D., Peter F., David W. Br. librarian Thomas Crane Library, Quincy, 1931-35; garden writer Patriot Ledger, Quincy, 1958-62; librarian Mass. Hort. Soc., Boston, 1962-73, Power-Gifford Library, Ashland, Mass., 1973—. Mem. Mass., Royal, Am. hort. socs., Farm and Garden Assn., Garden Writers Assn. of Am. Club: Seaside Gardeners (Quincy). Home: 16 South St Ashland MA 01721 Office: 579 Chestnut St Ashland MA 01721

CROSSON, DOROTHY PATRICIA CRUICKSHANK (MRS. DAVID THOMAS CROSSON), occupational therapist; b. Detroit, Dec. 6, 1944; d. William Mellon and Dorothy Jane (Wager) Cruickshank; student Syracuse U., 1962-64; B.S. in Occupational Therapy, Wayne State U., 1968; m. David Thomas Crosson, Oct. 3, 1970; 1 dau., Jill Ellen. Staff occupational therapist Ridge State Home and Tng. Sch., Wheatridge, Colo., 1968-70; head occupational therapy Havern Center, Littleton, Colo., 1970—. Mem. Am. Occupational Therapy Assn. Home: PO Box 669 Indian Hills CO 80454 Office: 4000 S Wadsworth St Littleton CO 80120

CROTHERS, JESSIE FRANCES, puppeteer, bibliographer; b. Ravenna, O., June 24, 1913; d. William Jerome and Ethel Diadama (Soper) Hinds; B.A., Kent State U., 1935; M.A., Northwestern U., 1949; drama and art studies U. Hartford, Willimantic Sch. Art; m. Thomas Eben Crothers, June 4, 1938; 1 son, Jerome Thomas. With Otis Art Inst., Los Angeles, 1936; asst. dir. Parret Fine Art Research Library, Los Angeles, 1937-38; sch. art dir., So. Ohio, 1938-41; asst. to dir. Children's Theatre, Northwestern U., also dir. drama and puppetry Evanston (Ill.) Pub. Parks, 1943-44; dir., designer Cain Park Children's Theatre, Cleveland Heights, O., 1943-44; tchr. drama Evanston Pub. Sch., 1943-44, Gary (Ind.) Pub. Schs., 1944-46; speech specialist, Salem, O., 1946; owner puppet touring co., 1946-51; research and pub. speaking, New Eng., 1951-66; art and craft instr., Hartford, Conn., 1957-72. Head women's div. Civil Def., Washingtonville, O., 1941-43. Mem. Brit. Ednl. Puppetry Assn., French Puppetry and Marionette Assn., Nederlandse Vereniging voor het Poppenspel, Puppeteers of Am., Internat. Marionette Assn., Ont. Puppetry Assn., Alpha Gamma Delta, Phi Alpha Alpha, Alpha Psi Omega, Phi Beta, Lambda Chi. Author: Puppeteer's Library Guide, 6 vols., 1971—. Contbr. to America Singing Anthology, 1933-35. Home: 81 Flagg Rd West Hartford CT 06117

CROUCH, ANNA BELLE, educator; b. Springfield, Mo., Nov. 11, 1918; d. Joseph Earl and Iva Mae (Garoutte) Crouch; B.S., S.E. Mo. State U., 1942; M.R.E., So. Bapt. Theol. Sem., 1947; M.A., Columbia, 1967; postgrad. So. Bapt. Theol. Sem. Sch. Sacred Music, 1947-48, E. Carolina U., summers 1958, 69, 70, Union Theol. Sem., summers 1962, 64, Va. State Coll., 1968, Coll. William and Mary, 1970-71. Tchr. pub. schs. Barton and Newton Counties, Mo., 1938-40; asst. chief clk. Post Pubs., Fort Crowder, Mo., 1942-45; youth dir. First Bapt. Ch., Florence, Ala., summer 1947; young people's sec. Mo. Bapt. Woman's Missionary Union, Jefferson City, 1948-54; dir. music, edn. Rosemary Bapt. Ch., Roanoke Rapids, N.C., 1955-58; asst. dean women Chowan Coll., Murfreesboro, N.C., 1958-66, prof. women's phys. edn., 1958-60, prof. hygiene, 1960-63, prof. music, 1958-62, prof. religion, 1959-63, prof. personal devel., 1960-69, prof. speech, 1961—. Dir. music Murfreesboro (N.C.) Bapt. Ch., 1966-71, Branchville (Va.) Bapt. Ch., 1973-74; speech correctionist Southampton (Va.) Pub. Schs., 1970. Mem. Murfreesboro Hist. Assn., 1971—; Miss. flood vol. worker, Cape Girardeau, 1937; vol. youth dir., worker among service men and women, Neosho, Mo., 1942-45; field worker with women county jail and Waverly Sanitarium, Louisville, 1945-48; mem. Roanoke Rapids (N.C.) Hosp. Guild, 1956-58; modeling dir. Roanoke-Chowan Beauty Pageants, 1960-72; rep. Mo. Baptist Gen. Assn., Panama, 1952. Mem. N.C. Speech and Drama Assn., So. Speech Communication Assn., Speech Communication Assn. Am., Jr. Coll. Speech Assn., Chowan Community Concert Assn., Chowan Coll. Speakers Bur., N.C. Hist. Soc., Murfreesboro C. of C. (Chowan Coll. rep. to women's div. 1973—). Democrat. Baptist (youth leadership rep. Mo. Bapt. Inter-Racial Council, 1950-54). Clubs: Murfreesboro Federated Woman's, Chowan Coll. Women and Wives. Contbr. articles to profl. jours. Home: 211 College St Murfreesboro NC 27855

CROUCH, (NORA) JOSEPHINE, librarian; b. Hereford, Tex.; d. Joseph Evvy and Nora (Betts) Crouch; B.S., Ga. Coll., 1942; M.L.S., George Peabody Coll., 1950. Librarian, Boys' High Sch., Rome, Ga., 1942-44, Parker High Sch., Greenville, S.C., 1944-46; library supr. Bartow (Fla.) Sch. System 1946-47; librarian high sch., Aiken, S.C., 1950-53; chief librarian Aiken County Pub. Library, 1954-58; dir. Aiken-Bamberg-Barnwell-Edgefield Regional Library, 1958—. Apptd. dir. to establish 1st S.C. Regional Demonstration Library, 1958—; mem. Com. for Standards for S.C. Pub. Libraries, 1962-68. Sec. Dibble Meml. Library Bd., 1963—. Library rep. Gov.'s Conf. on bus., industry, edn., agr., 1960-67; mem. Gov.'s Hwy. Safety Conf., 1962, 63, mem. conf. state-wide traffic safety, 1961, Gov.'s Conf. on Pub. Libraries, 1965. Mem. Aiken County Hist. Soc., A.L.A. (fed. relations coordinator for S.C. Library Assn. 1963-65), Southeastern, S.C. (pres. 1966-67; mem. exec. com. 1956-58, 64-70, chmn. nominating com. 1968—) library assns., Am. Assn. U. Women (corr. sec. state div. 1964-65, parliamentarian state div. 1965-67, exec. bd. state div. 1964-67), Assn. Community Service Leaders Aiken County, S.C. Council for the Common Good (sec. 1968-70). Club: Pilot. Contbr. to profl. mags. and newspapers. Home: 823 Fermata Pl SW Aiken SC 29801 Office: Box 909 Aiken SC 29801

CROUP, MARGARET MARY (MRS. WILLIAM L. BRUDON), med. illustrator; b. Pitts., Feb. 1, 1920; d. Lawrence Edward and Elizabeth (Ellis) Croup; B.S., Ind. State Tchrs. Coll., 1940; certificat Mass. Gen. Hosp. Sch. Med. Illustration, 1949; m. William L. Brudon, 1971. Tchr., supr. art, Castle Shannon, Pa., 1940-44; tchr. art, McCandless Twp., Pa., 1944-46; free-lance med. illustrator, Pitts., 1949-51; med. illustrator, photographer St. Margaret Meml. Hosp., Pitts., 1951-54; med. illustrator VA Hosp., Pitts., 1951-58, Children's Hosp., Pitts., 1958-67; research asso. in med. illustration Cleft Palate Research Center, 1967-69; med. illustrator sci. illustration div. Armed Forces Inst. Pathology, Walter Reed Army Med. Center, Washington, 1969-71; asst. prof., med. illustrator U. Mich., Ann Arbor, 1971-73; free-lance med. illustrator, 1973—. Co-exhibitor Am. Coll. Physicians and Surgeons, Atlantic City, 1957. Recipient 1st prize for prodn. and design exhibit Surg. Anatomy of Temporal Bone (R.J. Caparosa), at Acad. Ophthalmology and Otolaryngology, 1965; Nephrons in Health and Disease (G.H. Fetterman), Am. Soc. Clin. Pathologists and Coll. Am. Pathologists, 1964; 2d prize hon. mention for effective use med. illustration in exhibit neonatal surgery, A.M.A., 1967. Mem. Advt. Artists Pitts. (rec. sec. 1956-62 trustee 1962-63), Assn. Med. Illustrators (rec. sec. 1961-64, gov. 1962-67, vice chmn. bd. 1965-66, chmn. bd. govs. 1966-67, v.p. 1968-69, pres. 1969-70, 2d pl. award exhbn. mems. work 1959). Illustrator; Oral Surgery (W.H. Archer), 1952, 56, 61, 66; Atlas of Roentgen Anatomy of the Skull (L.E. Etter), 1955; Muscle Relaxants in Anesthesiology (F.F. Foldes), 1957; Orthopedic Surgery in Infancy and Childhood (A.B. Ferguson), 1957; Narcotics and Narcotic Antagonists (F.F. Foldes), 1964; Roentgenography and and Roentgenology of the Middle Ear and Mastoid Process (L.E. Etter), 1965; co-illustrator (with B. Hulbert) Biology: The Human Approach (C.A. Villee), 1950, (with R.A. Barmettler) An Atlas of Congenital Heart Disease (F.E. Sherman), 1963; contbr. illustrations to Basic Physiology and Anatomy (E.E. Chaffee and E.M. Greisheimer), 1969. Home: 2104 Needham Rd Ann Arbor MI 48104

CROUT, ELEANOR MUECKE (MRS. G. STANLEY CROUT), civic worker; b. N.Y.C., Jan. 13, 1938; d. Berthold Muecke, Jr. and Eleanor B. Thalmann; B.A., Mt. Holyoke Coll., 1959; M.A., Columbia, 1960; m. G. Stanley Crout, May 14, 1960; children—Alexandra Lynn, Stephen Andrew, Charles Merrill. Tchr., Walnut Hill Sch., Natick, Mass., 1960; DeWitt Clinton High Sch., Bronx, N.Y.C., 1961-62. Mem. Jr. Welfare Assn., Santa Fe, 1962-68, program chmn., 1963-64, treas., 1964-65, pres., 1965-66, pub. relations chmn., 1967-68; chmn. Community Christmas Store, Santa Fe, 1965; co-chmn. ticket sales Heart Fund Benefit, 1969; active March of Dimes drive, 1964, Heart Fund, 1965, Am. Cancer Soc. Drive, 1969; mem. St. Vincent Hosp. Aux., 1967-68, chmn. com., benefit, 1965, 69; mem. Santa Fe Council Internat. Relations, 1968—; chmn. Girl Scout Expn., 1972. Bd. dirs. Jr. Welfare Assn., 1964-68, Girl's Club, 1965-66; bd. dirs., chmn. personnel services Sangre de Cristo council Girl Scouts U.S.A., 1972—. Mem. Mt. Holyoke Alumnae Assn., Sch. Am. Research, Friends of St. John's Coll., Delta Kappa Pi, Phi Lambda Theta. Club: Santa Fe Garden (co-chmn. house and garden tours 1972, sec. 1974, dir. 1972-74). Episcopalian. Address: Route 3 Box 32 Santa Fe NM 87501

CROUTHAMEL, ELLA KNIESNER (MRS. PAUL S. CROUTHAMEL), banker; b. Phila., Mar. 16, 1919; d. John and Katie S. (Sellers) Kniesner; pre-standard certificate Am. Inst. Banking, 1968; m. Paul S. Crouthamel, May 28, 1938; children—Thomas P., Allan W. Clerk First Nat. Bank, Perkasie, Pa., 1951-55; with Bucks County Bank & Trust Co., Perkasie, Pa., 1955—, branch mgr. and asst. v.p., 1971—. Mem. Pennridge C. of C. (sec.). Lutheran. Home: 1105 Old Post Rd Perkasie PA 18944 Office: Box 67 Perkasie PA 18944

CROVER, DIANA HOEFFDING (MRS. FRANK JOHN CROVER), psychologist; b. Parkgate, Great Britain, Sept. 13, 1918; d. Thomas Humfrey and Winifred Tysilio Castle (Thomas) Welsby; B.Sc. with honors in Econs., London (Eng.) Sch. Econs., London U., 1940; M.S., Cal. State U., Los Angeles, 1970; m. Oleg Hoeffding, Dec. 17, 1941 (div. Apr. 1970); children—Harald, Virginia; m. 2d, Frank John Crover, Dec. 30, 1970 (dec. July 1972). Came to U.S., 1946, naturalized, 1955; Research asst. Fgn. Office, Ministry Fgn. Affairs, London, 1940-42; social worker Family Service Agy., Santa Monica, Cal., 1965-68; counselor Alcoholic Rehab. Center, Los Angeles, 1970; counseling psychologist VA Los Angeles, 1970—. Asst. prof. Cal. State U., Los Angeles, 1971; child, family and marriage counselor, Cal., 1970—. Mem. Am. Psychol. Assn., Am. Personnel and Guidance Assn., Am. Rehab. Counseling Assn., Common Cause, Human Relations Soc., Sierra Club, U. Cal. Alumni Assn. Home: 505 S Barrington Av Los Angeles CA 90049 Office: 11000 Wilshire Blvd Los Angeles CA 90024

CROW, MARY LYNN COX (MRS. R. PHILLIP CROW), educator, psychologist; b. Denton, Tex., Aug. 30, 1934; d. Herman G. and Harriett (Copeland) Cox; student Monticello Jr. Coll., 1952-53; B.A. summa cum laude, Tex. Christian U., 1956, M.Ed., 1967; Ph.D., North Tex. State U., 1970; m. R. Phillip Crow, Feb. 4, 1965. Pub. sch tchr. Ft. Worth, Tyler, Tex., 1956-59; promotion and merchandising dir. KTVT-TV, Ft. Worth, 1960; Romper Room tchr., Dallas/Ft. Worth area Romper Room Internat. Television Kindergarten, 1961-67; pub. sch. guidance counselor, Hurst, Tex., 1967-68; play therapist Pupil Appraisal Center, Denton, Tex., 1968-69; part-time instr. North Tex. State U., Denton, 1969-70; instr. U. Tex., Arlington, 1969-70, asst. prof. edn., 1970-72, asso. prof. edn., 1973—, dir. faculty devel. resource center, 1973—. Actress, Ft. Worth, Tyler Community Theatre, 1956-61; creativity cons., guidance cons. Project Change, 1967-68; co-author, narrator Guidance Vistas, audio tapes, 1967—. Recipient Standard Oil Ann. Outstanding Tchr. award U. Tex. at Arlington, 1972. Mem. Am., Tex. (bd. dirs. 1971-72, exec. council 1971-72, chpt. coordinator 1971-73), North Central Tex. (pres. 1971-72) personnel and guidance assns., Am. Sch. Counselors Assn., Assn. for Counselor Edn. and Supervision, Tex. Sch. Counselors Div., Tex. Assn. Coll. Tchrs. (chpt. pres. 1973-74), Tex. Assn. Counselor Educators and Suprs., Am., Tex. psychol. assns., Alpha Delta Pi, Alpha Chi, Alpha Psi Omega, Phi Theta Kappa. Author: (with others) Guidance: Guidelines from Kindergarten Through College, 1969. Home: 5000 Fall River Dr Fort Worth TX 76103

CROWDER, RUBY JO SATTERWHITE (MRS. JAMES M. CROWDER), librarian; b. Sherman, Tex., Oct. 8, 1918; d. James Clyde and Willie Mae (King) Satterwhite; B.A. in L.S., Tex. Woman's U., 1940; postgrad. North Tex. State U., 1971, 72; m. James Maurice Crowder, Dec. 25, 1942; 1 dau., Karen Elizabeth. Librarian, Dickinson (Tex.) High Sch., 1940-43; govt. documents librarian Mont. State Coll. Library, Bozeman, 1944; children's librarian Sioux Falls (S.D.) Pub. Library, 1944-45; tech. div. librarian Mrs. Tucker's Foods, Sherman, 1949-51; records librarian Gaylord Mfg. Co., Dallas, 1952-53; librarian St. Michael Sch., Dallas, 1961—. Mem. A.L.A., Southwestern, Tex., Dallas County library assns., Dite-moi French Club. Republican. Mem. Ch. of Christ. Home: 3200 Amherst St Dallas TX 75225 Office: 8011 Douglas at Colgate St Dallas TX 75225

CROWE, ARLENE JOYCE MAXIMCHUK (MRS. NEIL BRUCE CROWE), clin. chemist; b. Wakaw, Sask., Can., Oct. 8, 1931; d. Michael Edward Alexander and Mary Verna (Worobetz) Maximchuk; B.S., U. Alta., 1950; M.S., McGill U., 1956, Ph.D., 1962; m. Neil Bruce Crowe, Oct. 8, 1966. Research asst. McGill U. Inst. Pathology, 1951-55, Hammersmith Hosp., 1956-57; chief tech. biochemistry Montreal (Que., Can.) Childrens Hosp., 1957-59; clin. chemist Hotel Dieu Hosp., Kingston, Ont., Can., 1962—, dir. Sch. Med. Tech., 1965—. Lectr. dept. biochemistry Queens U., 1963—. Mem. Canadian (council 1972-74), Ont. (pres. 1974-75), Am. socs. clin. chemists, N.Y. Acad. Scis., Sigma Xi. Home: PO Box 682 Kingston ON K7L 4X1 Canada Office: Dept Biochemistry Hotel Dieu Hosp Kingston ON K7L 3H6 Canada

CROWE, BETTINA LUM, author; b. Mpls., Apr. 27, 1911; d. Burt Francis and Bertha (Bull) Lum; ed. privately; m. Colin Crowe, May 21, 1938. Mem. Soc. Women Geographers. Author (under name Peter Lum) Stars in Our Heaven, 1948; Fabulous Beasts, 1953; Peking, 1950-53, 1958; The Purple Barrier, 1960; The Story of the Great Wall of China, 1960; Italian Fairy Tales, 1963; Fairy Tales From the Barbary Coast, 1967; The Holiday Moon, 1963; Fairy Tales of China, 1959; The Growth of Civilization in East Asia, 1969; Folk TAles from North America, 1973; Six Centuries in East Asia; China, Japan and Korea from the 14th Century to 1912, 1973. Address: Pigeon House Bibury Cirencester Gloucester England

CROWE, CATHERINE MARY F., social worker; b. Bklyn., Jan. 7; d. William J. and Hanora (Sullivan) Crowe; B.A., Notre Dame Coll., 1941; M.S. in Social Service, Fordham U., 1948; postgrad. U. P.R., 1958. Case aide family service Catholic Charities Diocese, Bklyn., 1944-46, caseworker with aged, family ct. rep., 1949-55, asst. supr., 1955, supr., 1955-63; case worker for unattached girls Cath. Guardian Soc., Bklyn., 1948-49; supt. N.Y. Founding Hosp., 1963-64, adminstrv. supr., 1964-65; adminstrv. supr. St. Cabrini Home, 1965-69, dir. city office, 1969-70; supr. Mission of Immaculate Virgin, 1970-71; adminstrv. supr. Catholic Home Bur., 1971—. Girl Scout leader, 1941-52, pres. S.I., 1947-49. Mem. Nat. Assn. Social Workers, N.Y. Welfare Conf., Nat. Assn. Cath. Charities, Acad. Certified Social Workers, Notre Dame Coll. Alumnae, Conf. Cath. Coll. Alumnae. Home: 22 Coddington Av Staten Island NY 10306 Office: 56 Bay St Staten Island NY 10301

CROWE, ELLENIA AUGUSTA BATES, artist, author; b. Dardanelle, Ark.; d. James Fillmore and Alice (Putnam) Bates; student Columbia, 1946; m. Theopholis Waldon Crowe; children—Blonnie Dell (Mrs. Eugene Lambert), Adrian Bates, Rodney Page Thomas, Doris Ellenia (Mrs. Shannon Townley). Sales, Macy's N.Y.C., 1946; one-man shows Little Rock Fine Arts Bldg.; exhibited in group shows at Philbrook, Tulsa, U. Ark., Ark. Arts Center, Verdigris Valley, Independence, Kan., Fort Smith Arts Center. Mem. D.A.R. (treas.), Friends of Library, League Women Voters, Fort Smith Asso. Artists, Ark. Hist. Assn., Internat. Platform Assn., Bus. and Profl. Women's Club, Zeta Phi Sigma Alpha. Methodist. Author: volume of poetry, 1954; (novel) Hilda's Miracle, 1955; Days of Passion, Nights of Love, 1964. Home: 718 N 16th St Fort Smith AR 72901

CROWE, LOIS RAY, mag. editor; b. Jackson, Tenn., Sept. 3, 1920; d. John J. and Mary Lee (Smith) Ray; student Murray State Coll., 1939-40; m . Charles David Crowe, Sr., Oct. 9, 1951 (div. Aug. 1959); children—Charles David, John Hunter. Staff writer Memphis Press-Scimitar, 1944-61; editor Holiday Inn mag., Memphis, 1961—; mng. editor Continental Trailways mag., Memphis, 1969—. Mem. Theta Sigma Phi. Home: 1836 Cherry Rd Memphis TN 38117 Office: 3791 Lamar Av Memphis TN 38118

CROWE, PATRICIA BARR (MRS. J. GODFREY CROWE), clin. psychologist; b. Paris, France, June 29, 1933; d. David Goodwin and Vivian Louise (Bell) Barr; came to U.S., 1933; A.A., Holton Arms Jr. Coll., 1953; A.B., George Washington U., 1962, M.A., 1967, Ph.D., 1972; m. J. Godfrey Crowe, Oct. 5, 1954; children—David Barr, Susan Godfrey, Patricia Bell, Karen Louise, Mary Teresa. Asst. psychologist Kingsbury Center, Washington, 1966; staff psychologist Arlington (Va.) Mental Health Center, 1966-69; psychology intern D.C. Dept. Health, Washington, 1969-70; staff psychologist Arlington Mental Health Center, 1970-71, chief child treatment service, chief psychologist, 1971—. Instr. psychology George Mason U., 1972—; asst. clin. prof. psychology George Washington U., 1973. Mem. Am., Va., D.C. psychol. assns., Va. Acad. Sci., Psi Chi. Clubs: Army-Navy Country (Arlington); George Washington U. (Washington). Home: 3000 N Military Rd Arlington VA 22207

CROWLEY, ANN MARIE CASSIDY (MRS. JOHN D. CROWLEY), nutritionist; b. Elkton, S.D., Mar. 20, 1923; d. Walter J. and Matilda (Harms) Cassidy; B.S., U. Minn., 1944; postgrad. U. Ind., 1945; M.S., U. Minn., 1957; m. John D. Crowley, Dec. 20, 1947; children—Patrick (dec.), Kathleen, Thomas Cassidy, Colleen, Michael, Kevin, William Shawn, John David. Dietetic intern Ind. Med. Center, Indpls., 1945-46; asst. adminstrv. dietitian Glen Lake San., Mpls., 1946-48; nutrition instr. Sch. Nursing, Hamline U., St. Paul, 1949-51; asst. adminstrv. dietitian Mt. Sinai Hosp., Mpls., 1950-51; clin. cons. dietitian Nicollet Clinic, Mpls., 1951-55; dir. dietetics Abbott Hosp., Mpls., 1955-65; dir. nutrition, asso. prof. U. Ia. Hosps., 1965—. Cons. dietitian instnl. div., and research dept. Pillsbury Co., Mpls., Dietene Co., Mpls., SAGA II, Palo Alto, Cal., ARA Hosp., Nutrition Council for Consumers; lectr. Sch. Hosp. Adminstrn., U. Minn.; mgmt. cons. dietary depts. St. Joseph Hosp., Minot, N.D., Women's Hosp. of Md., Balt., Mt. Sinai Hosp., Mpls., Chisago Lakes Hosp., Chisago City, Minn. Mem. Am. Mgmt. Assn., Am. Assn. U. Profs., Am., Minn. (chmn. food adminstrn. sect. 1961-62, pres. 1964-65), Twin City (chmn. career guidance 1959-60) dietetic assns., Soc. Advancement Food Service Research (chmn. constn. com. 1961-62, v.p. 1973-74), Home Econs. Assn., League Catholic Women, Cenacle League, Alpha Omicron Pi. Author syndicated column Our Daily Bread, Ann Crowley's Table Topics, Menu Plan With Ann. Contbr. articles to profl. publs. Home: 125 Mount Vernon Dr Iowa City IA 52240

CROWLEY, BILLIE BLALACK (MRS. H.W. CROWLEY), newspaper editor; b. Mt. Vernon, Ill., Mar. 25, 1930; d. William James and Mildred Alice (Barefield) Elliott; student Kilgore Coll., 1967-69, N. Tex. U., 1949-50, So. Meth. U., 1958-59; m. Joe Blalack, Aug. 30, 1950 (dec. Feb. 1966); children—John, Jack, James, Jay, Jill; m. 2d, H.W. Crowley, May 26, 1970. Owner, operator Blalack Oil Co., Longview, Tex., 1966—; founder, owner Am. Real Estate Co., Longview, 1968—; co-pub., editor Woman's World Weekly, newspaper, Longview, 1969—; syndicated columnist, 1972—; v.p. Longview Post, Inc.; co-owner Tri-W Publishing Co.; news commentator radio sta. KOCA, 1974—. Recipient 9 state awards in ann. honor award writer's contest Tex. Press Women, 1970, 9 awards, 1971, 16 awards, 1973; Nat. Journalism award Nat. Fedn. Press Women, 1970. Mem. Tex. Press Women (dist. v.p. 1972-74, state rec. sec. 1971-73, 2d v.p. 1973—, pres. dist. 1974-75), C. of C. (ambassador, mem. pub. relations and information com.). Presbyn. Home: 1803 Hughey Dr Longview TX 75601 Office: Box 3206 Longview TX 75601

CROWLEY, MARY ELIZABETH WEAVER (MRS. DAVID CROWLEY), interior designer; b. Slater, Mo., Apr. 1, 1915; d. Lennox Grove and Nell (Crain) Weaver; student U. Ark., 1931-32, So. Meth. U., 1940-41; m. Joseph H. Carter, Mar. 4, 1932 (div. June 1942); children—Donald J., Ruth (Mrs. Ralph Leon Shanahan); m. 2d, David Crowley, Apr. 17, 1948. Accountant, Republic Ins. Co., 1941-46, Purse Furniture Co., 1946-50; unit mgr. Stanley Home Products, Inc., 1950-54; sales mgr. World Gift Co., Dallas, 1954-55, v.p. charge sales, 1955-57; pres., sales mgr. Home Interiors and Gifts, Inc., Dallas, 1957—. Guest lectr. and speaker. Trustee, Dallas Bapt. Coll.; bd. dirs. Dallas unit Am. Cancer Soc. Recipient Oscar of Salesmanship, Am. Salesmasters Orgn., 1967, Mature Woman of Yr. award Altrusa Club, 1969; Knight of the Royal Way award Direct Selling Assn., 1973. Mem. Nat. Home Fashion League, Dallas C. of C. Baptist (mem. edn. commn. So. Bapt. Conv. 1966—). Author: Moments with Mary. Home: 6115 Aberdeen St Dallas TX 75230 Office: 4550 Spring Valley Dallas TX 75247

CROWLEY, PATRICIA CARON (MRS. PATRICK F. CROWLEY), civic worker, travel agy. exec.; b. Chgo.; d. O.J. and Marietta (Higman) Caron; A.B., Trinity Coll., 1936; student Sorbonne, Paris, France, 1935; Litt.D., St. Mary's Coll., 1961; m. Patrick F. Crowley Oct. 16, 1937; children—(Sister) Patrica, Mary Anne, Patrick, Catherine, Theresa. Pres., Space Inc., travel agy., Chgo. Co-pres. Internat. Confedn. of Christian Family Movements, 1949—; mem. bd. Chgo. Internat. Visitors Center, 1960-66, pres., 1973—; mem. women's bd. Catholic Interracial Council, 1961—; co-organizer Wilmette Human Relations Com., 1963; bd. dirs. Found. for Internat. Cooperation, 1960—. Nat. Conf. on Religion and Race, 1963, World Lay Congress, Rome, 1957, 67; mem. Spl. Commn. of Pope Paul VI to Study Population Problem. Mem. nat. bd. dirs. Women for McCarthy, 1968. Recipient Magnificat medal Mundelein Coll., 1962; co-recipient Laetare medal Notre Dame U., 1966. Contbr. articles to various publs. Home: 175 E Delaware Pl Chicago IL 60611 Office: Space Inc 875 N Michigan Av Chicago IL 60611

CROWN, CHARMAINE (MRS. HILLIARD CROWN), govt. ofcl.; b. Manila, Philippines, Nov. 10, 1928; d. Philip A. and Marguerite (Lecocq) Gaffney; came to U.S., 1936; student U. Cal. at Berkeley, 1949-50; m. Hilliard Crown, Aug. 29, 1953; 1 dau., Rebekah. Women's program dir. radio sta. KTRC, Santa Fe, N.M., 1956; dir. Consumer Protection div. Office of Atty. Gen., 1971—; adviser Am. Automobile Assn., Albuquerque, 1971—; v.p. Arbitration Bd., Better Bus. Bur. N.M., Albuquerque, 1971—. Chmn. UNICEF, Santa Fe, 1969—; mem. council St. Vincent Hosp., Santa Fe, 1971—. Mem. Democratic Nat. Com., 1971-72; publicity dir. Santa Fe County Dems., 1960-62; mem. N.M. Dem. Platform Com., 1968; Dem. candidate N.M. sec. state, 1970. Clubs: Albuquerque Press; Santa Fe Press. Home: PO Box 4758 Santa Fe NM 87501 Office: PO Box 2246 Santa Fe NM 87501

CROWNINGSHIELD, GLORIA ELAINE (MRS. JOHN F. CROWNINGSHIELD), real estate broker; b. Buffalo, Feb. 15, 1925; d. Harold Theodore and Lillian Edith (Grant) Jenkins; grad. high sch.; m. John F. Crowningshield, Oct. 3, 1967; 1 dau. by previous marriage, Janet Elaine Peart. Propr., Peninsula Realty, San Diego, Cal., since 1967. Lectr. on condominium and apt. conversions. Mem. Nat. Assn. Real Estate Bds., Cal. Real Estate Assn., Point Loma Ocean Beach Realty Assn. (dir. 1969-72, pres. 1973), Peninsula C. of C. (dir. 1968—), Sunset Cliffs Anti-Erosion Assn. Home: 1054 Devonshire Dr San Diego CA 92107 Office: 1352 Sunset Cliffs San Diego CA 92107

CROWTHER, ANNABELLE KOONCE (MRS. CHARLES EDWARD CROWTHER), librarian; b. Pass Christian, Miss., May 20, 1923; d. Riley Joseph and Alice Wilhelmina (Patenotte) Koonce; B.S., Miss. State Coll. for Women, 1944; B.S. in L.S., U. Ill., 1947; m. Charles Edward Crowther, July 7, 1956; children—Carol Alice, Edward Riley, Carl Koonce. Asst. librarian Miss. State Law Library, Jackson, 1944; reference librarian Army Med. Library, Washington, 1944-46; librarian Miss. Coll., Clinton, 1947-50; library supr. Miss. State Dept. Edn., 1950-56; librarian Carr Central Jr. High Sch. and High Sch., Vicksburg, Miss., 1956-59; library supr. Vicksburg Pub. Schs., 1966—. Pres., Citizens for Library Improvement, 1963; state exec. dir. Nat. Library Week, 1974. Mem. Miss., Vicksburg edn.

assns., Miss. Library Assn., Miss. Assn. Sch. Librarians (pres. 1969-70). Baptist. Contbr. articles to mags. Home: 104 Rialto St Vicksburg MS 39180 Office: Box 1058 Vicksburg MS 39180

CRUESS, SYLVIA ROBINSON (MRS. RICHARD LEIGH CRUESS), physician, educator; b. Cleve., Feb. 13, 1930; d. Alexander Cochrane and Marjory (Woods) Robinson; B.A., Vassar Coll., 1951; M.D., Columbia, 1955; m. Richard Leigh Cruess, May 30, 1953; children—Leigh Saunders, Andrew Cochrane. Came to Can., 1963, naturalized, 1972. Intern, Royal Victoria Hosp., Montreal, Que., Can., 1955-56, resident, 1956-57, now mem. staff; practice medicine specializing in endocrinology, Montreal, 1972—; lectr. medicine N.Y. U., N.Y.C., 1961-63; dir. Metabolic Day Center, The Royal Victoria Hosp., Montreal, Quebec, Can., 1966—; asst. prof. medicine McGill U., Montreal, 1972—. Chmn. Westmount Med. Adv. Council, 1973—. Vice pres. Westmount (Que.) Municipal Assn., 1972-74. Mem. Am., Canadian diabetic assns., Canadian Soc. Endocrinology and Metabolism, Quebec Med. Assn. Presbyn. Author: (with M.M. Hoffman, L.L. Kovacs) Current Concepts of Diagnosis and Treatment of Diabetes Mellitus, 1969. Home: 526 Mt Pleasant Av Montreal PQ H3Y 3H5 Canada Office: The Royal Victoria Hospital 687 Pine Av West Montreal PQ 112 H3A 1A1 Canada

CRUM, ELIZABETH BELL (MRS. CECIL CRUM), social worker; b. Asheville, N.C.; d. Wallie L. and Eula (Duckett) Bell; student Bennett Coll., 1944-46; A.B., Morris Coll., 1948; M.S.W., Atlanta U., 1952. High sch. tchr., Sumter, S.C., 1948-50; center dir. Salvation Army-Lincoln Community Center, N.Y.C., 1953-61; group work and recreation cons. N.Y.C. Youth Bd., 1961-67, area adminstr., 1967—. Pres. bd. Morrisania Day Care Center. Recipient certificate of appreciation Kiwanis Club of Parkchester, Bronx, N.Y., 1965, 67. Mem. Nat. Assn. Social Workers, N.Y. State Welfare Conf., Social Work Vocational Bur., Gothamettes Inc. (historian 1963—), Internat. Platform Assn., Sigma Gamma Rho. Democrat. Methodist. Home: 26-24 96th St Elmhurst NY 11369 Office: 144 W 125th St New York City NY

CRUM, STELLA BAIN, educator; b. Stuart, Va., May 25, 1921; d. Alonzo L. and Nancy Mallie (Draughon) Venable; student Guilford Coll., 1938-39; ed. Internat. Bus. Coll., Fort Wayne, 1950; B.S., Ind. U., 1956, M.S., 1961, Ed.D., 1966; m. James Joseph Bain (div. Mar. 1969); children—Nancy Mae (Mrs. Jack Daenell), James Edward; m. 2d, Russell Elbert Crum, May 22, 1970. Sec., Gen. Electric Co., Ft. Wayne, Ind., 1950-54; tchr. elementary schs. Fort Wayne, 1956-64; supr. tchr. Ind. U. Bloomington, 1964-66; asso. prof. edn. Ball State U., Muncie, Ind., 1966-71; asso. prof. edn. St. Francis Coll., Fort Wayne, 1971—, dir. student teaching, 1973—. Cons. Ellsworth Community Coll., Iowa Falls, Ia., various curriculum studies; v.p. Ind. sponsors council Ind. Student Edn. Assn. Instr. den mothers Boy Scouts, 1958—. Soc. of Friends scholar, 1938; Ind. U. Asso. Tchr. fellow, 1964. Mem. Assn. Tchr. Educators (regional membership chmn. 1971—, exec. sec. 1972—), Ind. U. Alumni Assn. (life), Assn. Supervision and Curriculum Devel., Am. Assn. U. Profs., Assn. Childhood Edn., Ind. Tchrs. Assn., Internat. Platform Assn., N.E.A. (life), Internat. Reading Assn., Pi Lambda Theta (life), Delta Kappa Gamma. Home: 1302 W Branning Av Fort Wayne IN 46807

CRUMBAKER, MARY KATHRYN (MRS. WILLIAM GOODMAN WILLIAMSON), coll. adminstr.; b. Great Falls, Mont.; d. Calvin and Kathryn Elizabeth (Harbaugh) Crumbaker; student U. Mont., 1939, Southwestern U. at Memphis, 1942-43, Whitman Coll., 1939-41; B.S., U. Ore., 1946; postgrad. Hochschule for Music, Vienna, Austria, 1947-48; M.Ed., Ore. State U., 1966; Ph.D., Nat. Christian U. Dallas, 1974; m. William Goodman Williamson, Dec. 17, 1941 (dec. Oct. 1970); children—James Calvin, Albert Jerome, Kathryn Erilda. Sec., exec. sec. Granada (Miss.) Elementary Sch., also U.S. C.E., 1941-44; substitute sec. U. Ore., 1944-46, lectr. music, 1946-48; head comml. studies Internat. Trade Coll., Chgo., 1948-51; tchr. Mich. Dept. Rehab., Am. Legion Tb Hosp., Battle Creek, 1952-53; tchr. Army Dept., Kokura, Japan, 1954-56; tchr. Clark Bus. Coll., Topeka, Kan., 1956-58; charm sch. dir., dir. training Eugene Bus. Coll. (Ore.), 1959-70, mgr., corp. sec.-treas., 1970—. Lectr., Am. econ. system and music Austro-Am. Soc., Vienna, 1946-48. Mem. exec. bd. S.W. Ore. Mus. Sci. and Industry, 1972—; den mother Ore. Trail council Boy Scouts Am., 1959-69. Precinct committeeman Republican party, 1960—; pres. Central Lane Rep. Women, 1970. Named Woman of Year, Bus. and Profl. Women's Club, 1967, Troup Mother of Year, Boy Scouts Am., 1971. Mem. Nat. Fedn. Bus. and Profl. Women's Clubs, Am. Mgmt. Soc., Pacific N.W. Personnel Mgr. Assn., Am. Bus. Women, Rubicon Soc., Eugene Bus. and Profl. Women's Club (pres. 1966), D.A.R., Daus. of Nile, P.E.O., Beta Gamma Sigma, Mu Phi Epsilon. Mem. Order Eastern Star. Clubs: City (life mem.), Zonta, Dial (pres. Eugene 1973—). Author: Typing with Less Than 2 Hands, 1962. Home: 1159 Mill St Eugene OR 97401 Office: 383 E 11th St Eugene OR 97401

CRUMP, ANITA HOOVER (MRS. LEROY CRUMP), ednl. adminstr.; b. New Orleans; d. Thomas and Lizzie (Boatner) Hoover; B.A., Xavier U., 1950, postgrad. 1950-51, 62, M.A. in Edn., 1955; postgrad. Tulane U., 1963, 64, adminstrv. intern, 1968-69; m. Leroy Crump, June 23, 1953. Sch. tchr., New Orleans, 1951-64; remedial reading tchr. McDonogh no. 41 Jr. High Sch., New Orleans, 1964-66; elementary guidance counselor in pilot program, New Orleans, 1966-67; asst. prin. J.S. Clark Sr. High Sch., 1968-71; prin. Thomas Edison Elementary Sch., 1971—. Lang. arts cons. Remedial Elementary Reading Program, 1967. Y-teen adv. YWCA, 1956-64; sponsor Jr. A.R.C., 1964-66, coordinator and program dir. P.T.A., 1957-64; chmn. Ebony Fashion Fair, Women's Aux. Flint Goodridge Hosp. Bd. dirs. St. John Berchman's House (all New Orleans). Named Teen Adviser of Year, YWCA, 1963; Tchr. of Year, Medard H. Nelson Sch., 1959; Outstanding Churchwoman of Year, Philips Meml. Meth. Ch., 1963; New Orleans Woman of Year, 1968. Mem. Am. Personnel and Guidance Assn., Assn. Childhood Edn. Internat., League Women Voters, Prins. Assn. Orleans Parish, La. Assn. Supervision and Curriculum Devel., N.A.A.C.P., Urban League, Nat. Assn. Elementary Sch. Prins., Nat. Reading Assn., Blue Rev. (nat. dir. 1963-65, chmn. finer womanhood scholarship 1963-64, chmn. study com. 1966—), Zeta Phi Beta (Outstanding Zeta So. region 1971, chpt. Woman of Year 1968, nat. 2d anti-basileus 1965-70, rep. to Nat. Pan-Hellenic Council 1970-72). Methodist (chmn. work area on edn. 1968—, rec. steward 1950—, ch. sch. tchr. 1945—, dist. dir. gen. ch. sch. work New Orleans dist. 1963—; mem. United Meth. Women). Home: 7321 Dalewood Rd New Orleans LA 70126 Office: 1339 Forstall St New Orleans LA 70117

CRUMP, MARJORIE VIRGINIA DODSON (MRS. STEPHEN HENRY CRUMP, JR.), univ. adminstr.; b. Smithville, Tex., Sept. 12, 1924; d. P. J. and Marjorie (Dietz) Dodson; B.A., Baylor U., 1946, M.A., 1962; m. Stephen Henry Crump, Jr., Oct. 24, 1947. Adminstrv. asst. to librarian Baylor U., Waco, Tex., 1946-60, research asst. devel. dept., 1960-61, asst. dean women, 1961-64, asst. dean students, 1964-72, asso. dean students, 1972—, chmn. univ. council, 1972—. Active McLennan County Democratic Women; mem. Women's council Waco Symphony Assn.; sec. exec. bd. Wesley Found. at Baylor U. Named Outstanding Alumna, Baylor U., 1966. Mem. Nat. (nominating com. 1971-72, com. on concerns for students 1972—), Tex. (membership chmn. 1963-65, sec. 1965-66, 2d v.p. 1967, program chmn., pres. 1969-71) assns. women deans and counselors, Am. Assn. U. Women (bull. editor Waco br. 1962-64, 1st v.p. Waco 1966-67, pres. 1967-68), Waco C. of C. (vice chmn. youth council 1972—), Friends Waco Pub. Library, Mortar Bd., Phi Gamma Nu, Alpha Lambda Delta. Methodist (mem. pastoral relations com. 1966-68; commn. on edn., trustee 1972—). Home: Route 10 Box 368 Waco TX 76708

CRUMP, MILDRED LEE (MRS. VERNER WALTER CRUMP), home economist; b. Roswell, N.M., Oct. 5, 1916; d. Richard Clarence and Georgia (Knight) Smith; B.S., Tex. Tech U., 1939; postgrad. Tex. A. and M. U., 1966, 68, 71, 72, Tex. Tech. U., 1968-69, Kan. State U., 1971, Tex. Tech U., 1973; m. Verner Walter Crump, Nov. 25, 1939; children—Richard, Nita (Mrs. Munger Burner II), Sandra (Mrs. Gary Mayfield), Pamela (Mrs. Ronald Hester). Dist. supr. sch. lunch programs WPA, Lubbock, Tex., 1939-42; child welfare worker, Dawson County and Lynn County Tex., 1963-66; home demonstration agt. Dawson County Extension Service, Lamesa, Tex., 1966-67, extension agt., 1973-74. Pres. local P.T.A.'s, 1956-62, v.p. dist. P.T.A., 1958-63; del. White House Conf. on Aging, Washington, 1971. Bd. dirs. Community Action Council, Non Profit Day Care Center, Sr. Citizen Assn. Recipient Florence Hall, 1971. Mem. Am. Assn. U. Women, Am., Tex. home econs. assns., Nat. Assn. Extension Home Economists, Lamesa C. of C., Alpha Zeta, Epsilon Sigma Phi. Home: 404 N 17th St Lamesa TX 79331 Office: Courthouse Lamesa TX 79331

CRUMP, WINNIE JO SOSEBEE (MRS. THOMAS CRUMP), physician; b. Anson, Tex., Mar. 8, 1929; d. Joseph M. and Jewel (Fish) Sosebee; B.S., Abilene Christian Coll., 1950; M.D., Southwestern Med. Sch., 1954; m. Thomas M. Crump, Oct. 23, 1954; children—Mark Allen, James Robert, Rebecca Lynn, Lee Thomas. Intern Houston VA Hosp., 1954-55; resident affiliated residency program Baylor U., Houston, 1955-57; asst. chief anesthesia VA Hosp., 1958-59; practice medicine specializing in anesthesiology, Houston, 1960—; pres. Drs. Crump, Ericsson & Assos., 1971—; chief anesthesia Med. Arts Hosp., Houston, 1962-65, Meml. Bapt. Hosp. S.W., Houston, 1965-68, chief surgery, 1969, 70. Leader, Girl Scouts U.S.A., 1969—. Diplomate Am. Bd. Anesthesiology. Fellow Am. Coll. Anesthesia; mem. Tex. Gulf Coast Anesthesia Soc. (sec.-treas. 1968-70, v.p. 1970-71, pres. 1971-72), Tex. Anesthesia Soc., Am. Soc. Anesthesiology, A.M.A., Internat. Anesthesia Research Soc. Home: 10203 Raritan St Houston TX 77043 Office: 6440 Hillcroft St Houston TX 77036

CRUNDEN, MARJORIE MORSE (MRS. ALLEN B. CRUNDEN), educator, b. Sulfu, Szechwan, West China, Feb. 24, 1913; d. William Reginald and Anna (Kinney) Morse; A.B., Wellesley Coll., 1934; M.Nursing, Yale, 1937; M.A., Columbia, 1940; (Am. Assn. U. Women scholar), Vassar Coll., 1943; m. Allan B. Crunden, Jr., July 10, 1937; children—Robert Morse, Joan Morse (Mrs. Lewis). Asst. in nursing edn. Tchrs. Coll., Columbia, 1939-40; dir. Central Sch. for Nurses, Temple U., 1937-38. Mem. Bd. Edn., Montclair, N.J., 1952-59; trustee Adult Sch. of Montclair, 1951-59. Mem. adv. health com. Montclair, 1961-64, sec., 1962-63; mem. adv. com. Montclair State Coll. Devel. Fund, 1962-64; chmn. arts and awards com., historian Overseas Neighbors, Montclair-Graz, 1960-74. Mem. Montclair Rep. Com., 1973-74. Mem. Assn. U. Women, Community Nursing Service (v.p. 1953-54), Jr. League Montclair (chmn. sustaining membership com. 1963-64), Soc. Mayflower Descs., Friends Montclair High Sch. Library (sec. 1962-65, chmn. 1966-68), Kappa Delta Pi, Alpha Phi. Republican. Episcopalian. Clubs: Montclair Golf, Glen Ridge Tennis, Montclair Music (pres. 1959-61, trustee 1970—), Montclair Garden (life), Montclair Women's (adv. council 1961-69; chmn. internat. affairs dept. 1970—); N.J. Wellesley (regional chmn., publicity chmn. Montclair); Cosmopolitan. Home: 30 Porter Pl Montclair NJ 07042 also Paradise Rural Route 1 Port Lorne NS Canada

CRUNK, DOROTHY ELIZABETH, educator; b. Priest River, Ida., June 7, 1918; d. James Frederick and Elizabeth (Caprai) Crunk; B.S., U. Ida., 1940, M.S. Edn., 1951; Ed.D., Ind. U., 1959. Tchr. high sch. Middleton, Ida., 1940-43, Moses Lake, Wash., 1943-50; instr. Eastern Wash. Coll., Cheney, 1950-53, Modesto (Cal.) Jr. Coll., 1954-56; mem. faculty Ball State U., Muncie, Ind., 1957-66, prof., 1966-67; guest editor South Western Publ. Co., Cin., 1966-67; prof. bus. edn. N. Tex. State U., Denton, 1967-72; chmn. dept. office adminstrn. Northeast La. U., Monroe, 1972—. Mem. Ind. Mental Health Assn., 1964-65. Bd. dirs. A.R.C., Muncie, 1962-66. Recipient Nat. award for research Delta Pi Epsilon, 1960. Mem. Tex. Bus. Tchr. Edn. Council (vice chmn. 1968-70, chmn. 1970-72), Nat. Bus. Edn. Assn. (chmn. membership 1967-72). Mem. Nat. Guidelines Com. for Preparation Tchrs. of Bus. Edn., 1968-71. Contbr. articles to profl. jours. Asso. editor Ball State Jour., 1958-66, Delta Pi Epsilon Jour., 1965-69, Bus. Studies, 1969-70; editor Delta Pi Epsilon, 1969—. Editor: Secretarial Procedures and Administration, 1967. Address: Northeast La Univ Monroe LA 71201

CRUSE, IRMA BELLE RUSSELL (MRS. JESSE CLYDE CRUSE), telephone co. exec.; b. Hackneyville, Ala., May 3, 1911; d. Charles Henry and Nellie Dunn (Ledbetter) Russell; student Birmingham-So. Coll., 1927-28; corr. student U. Ala., U. Chgo., U. Wis., U. Minn., intermittently 1958-68; m. Jesse Clyde Cruse, Dec. 22, 1931; children—Allan Baird, Howard Russell. With So. Bell and successor South Central Bell, Birmingham, Ala., 1928-44, 54—, pub. relations supr., 1965-68, rate supr., 1968—. Free lance writer, 1956—. Mem. bd. Festival of Arts, Birmingham, 1970—; v.p. Birmingham Council Clubs, 1973-74; pres. Jefferson County Radio and TV Council, 1971-72. Recipient numerous awards including Freedoms Found. award, 1967-69; Beautiful Activist, 1972; nominated Women of Year, Birmingham, 1971, 72, Woman of Achievement Met. Bus. and Profl. Women's Club, 1970-71. Mem. Birmingham Bus. Communicators, Ala. Writers' Conclave (pres. 1973-74), Birmingham Council Clubs (sec. 1973-74), Birmingham Bus. and Profl. Women (pres. 1970-71), Women in Communications (pres. 1970-71), Birmingham Bus. Communicators (pres. 1968-69), Telephone Pioneers Am. (editor newsletter 1970—), Ala. State Poetry Soc. (program chmn. 1972-74). Baptist. Contbr. articles to various publs. Home: 136 Memory Ct Birmingham AL 35213 Office: 600 N 19th St Birmingham AL 35203

CRUSE, VIRGINIA WOODLAND (MRS. CHARLES S. CRUSE), psychologist; b. Balt., Oct. 17, 1920; d. Eldridge Kurtz and Lola Virginia (Williams) Woodland; student U. Md., 1939-41; B.S., Loyola Coll., 1960, M.A., 1973; M.Ed., Johns Hopkins U., 1967; m. Charles S. Cruse, Dec. 21, 1941; children—Charles H., Linda W. (Mrs. James E. Waters), Susan L. (Mrs. John P. VonHagen), Bryant G., Donald R. Free lance med. illustrator, Balt., 1941-42; aircraft illustrator Glenn L. Martin Co., Balt., 1942-44; tchr. Balt. Pub. Schs., 1960-66; counselor for pregnant girls Edgar Allen Poe Sch., Balt., 1966-67; counselor, psychologist Harford County Schs., Harford County, Md., 1967-69; sch. psychologist Newark (Del.) Sch. Dist., 1969—. Cons psychologist Newark, Del., 1972—. Mem. N.E.A., Nat. Assn. Sch. Psychologists, Del. Psychol. Assn., Daus. Am. Colonists (chpt. regent 1968), Delta Kappa Gamma. Home: Box 228 North East MD 21901 Office: 83 E Main St Newark DE 19711

CRUSO, THALASSA, TV performer, author; b. London, Eng., Jan. 7, 1909; d. Antony Alford and Mildred S. (Robinson) Cruso; acad. diploma anthropology and archeology London Sch. Econs., 1932; m. Hugh O'Neill Hencken, Oct. 12, 1935; children—Ala Mary (Mrs. William S. Reid), Sophia (Mrs. David L. Stone), Thalassa (Mrs. Asghar Ali). Asst. keeper London Mus., 1933-35; dir. excavations Bredon Hill, Worcester, Eng., 1934-37; mem. staff Brit. Consulate, Boston, 1938-45; dir., author tv series Making Things Grow, Channel 2, Boston, 1967-69, Making Things Work, 1971-72, A Small City Garden, 1972, The Cape Cod Dunes, 1974. Trustee Chestnut Hill (Mass.) Sch., 1946-58, Beaver Country Day Sch., Chestnut Hill, 1950-58. Recipient Merit medal, 1969, Distinguished Service medal, 1970 (both Garden Club Am.); Distinguished Hort. Service citation Hort. Soc. N.Y., 1970. Fellow Soc. Antiquaries London; mem. Royal Archeol. Inst. Gt. Britain and Ireland (asst. sec. 1933-35), English Speaking Union (dir.), Mass. Hort. Soc. (trustee). Clubs: Chestnut Hill Gard (pres. 1956-58); Chilton (Boston). Author: Making Things Grow, 1969; Making Things Grow Outdoors, 1971; To Everything There Is a Season, 1973. Columnist, Boston Sunday Globe, 1968—; contbr. McCall's, 1970—, Country Jour., 1974—. Address: 329 Hammond St Chestnut Hill MA 02167

CRUSSELLE, MARION AUDREY (MRS. WILLIAM HARDY CRUSSELLE, JR.), driving cons.; b. Homestead, Fla., July 18, 1920; d. Frank Peguese and Effie Mae (Stephens) Cahoon; grad. Dale Carnegie Courses, Dorothy Carnegie Courses; m. William Hardy Crusselle, Jr., Aug. 3, 1947. Ch. sec., 1945-49; tng. supr. dept. store, cons. Met. Life Ins. Co.; cons. Prevention of Blindness; now cons. Defensive Driving Course, State of Ga., Atlanta. Recipient WSB Radio Eager Beaver award, 1971. Mem. Ga. Fedn. Bus. and Profl. Womens Clubs (past pres.), Womens C. of C. Methodist. Clubs: Quota; Women Sold on Safety; Business and Professional Womans. Home: 2883 Cravenridge Dr NE Atlanta GA 30319 Office: 2581 Piedmont Rd NE Atlanta GA 30324

CRUTCHER, ANNE NEILSON, newspaper editor; b. N.Y.C., Oct. 18, 1919; d. Henry Christian and Anna Henrietta (King) Neilson; A.B., Syracuse U., 1941; m. Leon Crutcher, May 10, 1941 (dec. 1968); children—Stephanie, Claudia (Mrs. Richard Winkler), Jennifer, (Mrs. Kenneth Wilkinson), Colette. Asso. editor Civic Edn. Service, Washington, 1942-47; speech writer Dept. Health, Edn. and Welfare, 1967-70; food and woman's editor Washington Daily News, 1969-72; dep. portfolio editor Washington Star-News, 1973—. Recipient Headliner award for best feature column Headliners Club, 1970. Home: 700 E Capitol St Washington DC 20003 Office: 225 Virginia Av SE Washington DC 20003

CRUTCHFIELD, VERNA MAE (MRS. JODY B. CRUTCHFIELD), educator; b. Clyde, Tex., July 9, 1915; d. Robert Lee and Myrtle (Ferguson) Edwards; B.A., Howard Payne Coll., 1941; M.A., Hardin-Simmons U., 1950; Ed.D., U. Denver, 1964; m. Jody B. Crutchfield, Apr. 16, 1933; 1 dau., Mary Frances (Mrs. Norman Ralph Handelsman). Tchr., Lampasas (Tex.) Jr. High Sch., 1941-43, San Saba (Tex.) Elementary Sch., 1943-45; home service worker A.R.C., Abilene, Tex., 1945-46; tchr., Breckenridge (Tex.) Jr. High Sch., 1946-51; speech therapist, Breckenridge, 1951-59, Graham, Tex., 1959-60; asst. prof. speech correction and spl. edn. Hardin-Simmons U., Abilene, 1960-66; asso. prof. edn. and psychology Angelo State College, San Angelo, Texas, 1966-69, prof. edn., 1969—, Piper prof., 1971. Comparative Edn. Soc. Seminar and Field Study of Eastern Europe, 1964, 70, of Far East, 1965; Study Schs. for retarded in Mexico, 1967; study in Hungary, Russia, 1971. Mem. Mental Health-Mental Retardation Board. Recipient of the Elks Nat. Found. scholar, Syracuse U., 1954; recipient Tchr. of Year award Rotary, 1959. Mem. Am., Tex. speech and hearing assns., Am. Hearing Soc., Nat. Epilepsy League, Tex. Assn. Retarded Children (edn. chmn. 1963-64), Tex. Assn. Coll. Tchrs. (exec. bd.), Tex. Council Exceptional Children (state sec. 1955-56, mem. chpt. council, pres. 1953-54), Bus. and Profl. Women. Baptist. Club: Altrusa. Mem. editorial staff Digest of Mentally Retarded Workshop in England and Scandinavia, 1968. Home: 241 Westwood Dr San Angelo TX 76901

CRUZ, MERCEDES ESPERANZA, physician; b. Mayaguez, P.R., May 7, 1932; d. Baltazar Augusto and Antonia (Vidal) Cruz; A.B., Radcliffe Coll., 1953; M.D., U. P.R., 1959. Intern, Kings County Hosp., Bklyn., 1959-60; asst. resident in medicine U. Hosp., San Juan, P.R., 1960-61, asso. resident in medicine, 1961-62, fellow in cardiovascular diseases, 1962-63; fellow in cardiovascular diseases Phila. Gen. Hosp., 1963-64; practice medicine, specializing in internal medicine and cardiology, Rio Piedras, P.R., 1969—; instr. biol. scis. U. P.R., Summers 1956, 57; instr. in medicine U. P.R. Sch. Medicine, 1964-65, asso. in medicine, 1965-69, asst. prof. medicine, 1969—; mem. courtesy staff San Jorge Hosp., Hosp. del Maestro, Hosp. Auxilio Mutuo; instr. biol. scis. Coll. Agr. and Mech. Arts, Mayaguez, 1953-55. Mem. Am., Pan Am., P.R. (pres. 1973-74) woman's med. assns., P.R. (sec. internal medicine sect. 1969-71, pres. council on public policy 1973-74, dir. 1973-74, sec. sect. cardiol. 1973-74), P.R. Eastern med. assns., Radcliffe Coll. Alumnae Assn., Alumnae Assn. Sch. Medicine U.P.R., Eta Gamma Delta. Home: 9-10 Malaga St Torrimar-Guaynabo PR 00619 Office: 400 Domenech Av Hato Rey PR 00918 also PO Box 21929 U PR Sta Rio Piedras PR 00931U

CRUZ, MIRIAM IRIS, city govt. ofcl.; b. San Juan, P.R., Sept. 21, 1940; d. Pedro and Venancia (Ramos) Cruz; B.A., Shelton Coll., Ringwood, N.J., 1961; postgrad. U. P.R., 1965-66. Came to U.S., 1966. High sch. tchr., P.R., 1962-66; exchange tchr. Operation Understanding, Phila., 1963-64; program dir. Met. YWCA, Chgo., 1966-68; dir. Spanish speaking areas Met. Chgo. Camp Fire Girls, 1968-73; adminstrv. asst. to mayor of Chgo. for Spanish speaking affairs, 1973—. Adv. mem. Nat. P.R. project Civil Rights Commn., 1969-71; sec. bd. P.R. Conf., 1967-71; adviser Spanish Speaking People of Lawndale, Chgo., 1970; mem. adv. com. TV program Oiga Amigo, 1970; pres. Nat. Conf. P.R. Women, Chgo., 1972, 1st v.p. nat. bd., 1973; chmn. bd. Spanish Christian Ch., 1970; organizer, dir. 1st P.R. Musical and Poetry Festival in Chgo., 1972. Mem. Com. Fgn. and Domestic Arts; a founder, past mem. bd. Aspira of Ill., 1968-69; del. mem. Chgo. Disciples Union; mem. validating com., Self Devel. of People, Chgo. Presbytery, 1972. Named to Order of Toa, Inst. P.R. Culture, 1973; recipient citation of merit Spanish Am. Businessmen Assn., 1973. Home: 1920 N Clark St Chicago IL 60614 Office: Room 507 City Hall Chicago IL 60602

CRYAN, MARJORIE ELAINE NIXON, editor; b. Easton, Pa., Dec. 17, 1922; d. Leroy and Elsie May (Long) Nixon; B.A., U. Pa., 1945; m. James Edward Cryan, Feb. 6, 1951 (dec. Mar. 1964); 1 son, James Nixon. Asst. women's editor The Trentonian, Trenton, N.J., 1948-50; editor Trenton Mag., 1964-70, Mercer County Messenger, Trenton, 1970—. Pub. relations dir. Morris Hall Rehabilitation Center, Lawrenceville, N.J. Mem. N.J. Press Assn., Nat. Newspaper Assn., U. Pa. Alumna Assn., Alpha Omicron Pi. Republican. Home: 17 Mountain View Rd Trenton NJ 08628 Office: 540 State Hwy 33 Trenton NJ 08619

CRYDER, HATTIE BINKLEY (MRS. RUSSELL M. CRYDER), club woman; b. Adelphi, O., Nov. 26, 1892; d. Cary L. and Joanna (Karshner) Binkley; student pub. schs., Adelphi; m. Russell M. Cryder, Oct. 20, 1912. Nurse aide Chillicothe (O.) Hosp., 1944-59;

matron Ross County Home, Chillicothe, 1941-59; horse breeder, Adelphi. Pres., Matrons of County Home group of Ohio Welfare Conf., 1950, sec., 1952. Pres., Allen Av. Garden Club, Chillicothe, 1958-60; presiding judge Chillicothe Election Bd., 1938-40, clk., 1936-38; treas. Pythian Sisters, Chillicothe, 1914-62, pres. Past Chief's Club, 1960-61, dist. dep., 1931-33, past Ohio dist. dep. grand chief. Presiding judge Republican precincts, 1933-76. Chmn. bd. trustees Pythian Bldg., Adelphi. Recipient certificates of service awards A.R.C., 1956-58. Mem. Chillicothe Bus. and Profl. Women's Club (mem. health and safety com. 1955-56, career advancement com. 1956-57, pub. affairs com. 1957-58, social com. 1958-59, scrapbook compiler 1960). Mem. M.E. Ch. (pres. circle 6 1944-45, sec. 1947-48). Home: Concord St Adelphi OH 43101

CSAKY, SUSAN DISCHKA (MRS. T. Z. CSAKY), librarian; b. Budapest, Hungary, July 25, 1926; d. Victor and Hertha (Willerstorfer) Dischka; came to U.S., 1948, naturalized, 1954; student Peter Pazmany U., Budapest, 1945-47; B.A., U. Ga., 1948; M.A. (Rotary fellow), Johns Hopkins, 1951; M.L.S., U. N.C., 1964; postgrad. U. Ky., 1970—; m. T.Z. Csaky, June 18, 1953; children—Catharina Maria, Karl Geza. Research asst. Johns Hopkins, Balt., 1949-53; librarian, lectr. U. N.C. Sch. Library Sci., Chapel Hill, 1960-61; bibliographer U. Ky., Lexington, 1962, cataloger Coll. Law, 1963-66, asst. law librarian, 1966-74, asso. law librarian, 1974—, adj. instr. Coll. Law, 1967—, lectr. Sch. Library Sci., 1970—. Mem. Am. Assn. Law Libraries (chpt. chmn. scholarship com. 1972—), Beta Phi Mu. Home: 1032 The Lane Lexington KY 40504

CUADRANTE, MINERVA R. (MRS. JOSE YOLANDO HERNANDEZ), physician; b. Naga, Phillippines, Oct. 20, 1937; d. Arsenio F. and Mercedes (Relunia) Cuadrante; A.A., U. Santo Tomas, 1956-58, M.D., 1962; m. Jose Yolando Hernandez, Dec. 17, 1966; children—Jay Yolando, Myra Jane, Maureen Juliet. Intern St. Clare's Hosp., Schenectady, 1964-65; resident internal medicine Springfield (Mass.) Hosp., 1965-66, pediatrics Trumbull Meml. Hosp., Warren, O., 1966-68, pathology Allentown (Pa.) Hosp., 1969-70; now staff physician Fla. State Hosp., Chattahoochee. Roman Catholic. Home: 321 N 9th St Quincy FL 32351

CUDE, SANDRA LATANE GRAHAM (MRS. JOHN HAROLD CUDE), interior decorator, modeling instr.; b. Memphis, Oct. 23, 1945; d. Herman A. and Latane (Jordan) Graham; student Memphis State U., 1963-64; B.A., U. Ala., 1968; m. John Harold Cude, Aug. 16, 1969. Asst. dir. pub. relations Neiman-Marcus, Dallas, 1968-69; publs. mgr. Chilton Corp., Dallas, 1969-70; publicity writer Tex. div. Salvation Army, Dallas, 1970; editor Southwest Furniture News, Dallas, 1970-72; instr. Barbizon Sch. of Modeling, Dallas, 1970—; asso. Eva Cude Office of Interiors, Dallas, 1973—. Mem. Childrens Asthma Research Inst. and Hosp., Dallas, 1969—, bd. dirs., 1970-71; bd. dirs. Dallas County Dental Aux., 1973—. Mem. Dallas Heritage Soc., Women in Communications, Gamma Phi Beta. Mem. Christian Ch. (youth counselor 1973—). Home and office: 2908 Amherst Dallas TX 75225

CULBERTSON, DONNA (MRS. ROBERT CULBERTSON, JR.), city ofcl.; b. Terre Haute, Ind., Sept. 29, 1924; d. Roy Clement and Jessie Arzalia (Lamb) Stableton; B.A. in Polit. Sci., Ariz. State U., 1969; m. Robert Culbertson, Jr., Sept. 8, 1945; children—William Kenneth, Donna Ann. Right of way agt. I, City of Phoenix, 1955-58, title examiner, 1963-64, right of way agt. II, 1964-66, spl. projects supr., 1966-69, city clk., 1969-73, city clk. dir., 1973—. Cons. for City of Tempe, Ariz., 1967—. Mem. Internat. Inst. Municipal Clks. (v.p. 1973), State of Ariz. City Clk.'s Assn., Nat. Microfilm Assn., Am. Records Mgmt. Assn., Am. Soc. for Pub. Adminstrn., Am. Right of Way Assn., Mexican C. of C. Soroptimist. Home: 3241 East Granada Phoenix AZ 85008 Office: 251 West Washington Phoenix AZ 85003

CULBERTSON, KATHERYN CAMPBELL, lawyer, state ofcl.; b. Tom's Creek, Va., Aug. 14, 1920; d. Robert Fugate and Mary E.V. Campbell (Leonard) Culbertson; B.S., E. Tenn. State U., 1940; B.S. in L.S., George Peabody Library Sch., 1942; J.D., YMCA Night Law Sch., 1968. Librarian, Bur. Ships Tech. Library, U.S. Navy Dept., Washington, 1945-49, 51-53; librarian Lincoln Elementary Sch., Kingsport, Tenn., 1949-50, 50-51; librarian Regional Library, Tenn. State Library and Archives, Johnson City, 1953-61; dir. extension services library Met. Govt. Nashville, and Davidson County (Tenn.), 1961-71; Tenn. state librarian and archivist, 1972—; admitted to Tenn. bar, 1969; since practiced in Nashville. Mem. library com. Pres.'s Com. Employment of the Handicapped, 1966-71; mem. library com. Nat. Bus. and Profl. Women's Found., 1968-70; pres. elect Tenn. Fedn. BPW Clubs, Inc., 1973-74. Mem. Am., Tenn. bar assns., Am., Southeastern, Tenn. library assns., D.A.R. Republican. Clubs: Zonta, Business and Professional Women's (pres. 1970-71) (Nashville). Contbr. to Ency. of Edn. Editor: YMCA Alumni Assn. bull. Home: 800 Glen Leven Dr Nashville TN 37204 Office: 403 7th Av N Nashville TN 37219

CULBRETH, JANE, civic worker; b. Fort Deposit, Ala.; d. William B. and Mary R. (White) Culbreth; tchrs. certificate State Tchrs. Coll., Troy, Ala., 1936-39; student U. Ala., 1939. Tchr. pub. schs., Red Level, Ala., 1939-41; accountant So. Bell Tel. & Tel. Co., Birmingham, Ala., 1941-42; with FBI, Washington, 1942-46, Dept. State, Washington, 1946-47; exec. sec. to pres. Moss-Thornton Co., Inc., Leeds, Ala., 1947-73, asst. corp. sec., 1956—. Councilwoman, City of Leeds, 1960-68, chmn. health, recreation and schs. Mem. Gov.'s Com. on Status of Women; mem. recreation com. Ala. League Municipalities, also mem. exec. com., 1963-65; dist. rep. on bd. dirs. Jefferson County A.R.C.; mem. Ala. adv. council for Comprehensive Health Planning, to 1970; pres. Ala. Joint Legislative Council, 1970-72; mem. Ala. Adv. Council for Comprehensive Health Planning, 1968-70; state legislative contact for A.L.A., 1969—; chmn. City Leeds Library Bd. Trustees, 1967—, Park Landscape Bd., 1960-68, Leeds Beautification Bd., 1960-70. Dir. Jefferson County Soc. Crippled Children and Adults, 1964-70, Jefferson County Am. Cancer Soc., 1968-70. Named Outstanding Woman, Leeds Bus. and Profl. Women's Club, 1962; hon. state trooper, hon. mem. Senate of Ala.; hon. lt. col. State Ala., on Gov.'s staff, hon. adminstr. State Neb., hon. citizen Huntsville, Ala., State Tenn., hon. Ark. Traveler. Mem. Nat. Fedn. Bus. and Profl. Women's Clubs (mem. legislation com. 1967-70, chmn. 1968-69; mem. exec. com., parliamentarian Ala. fedn. 1970-71, 3d v.p. 1972-73, 2d v.p. 1973-74), Nat. Secs. Assn. (Future Secs. Assn. chmn. Birmingham chpt. 1970-71; chmn. pub. and world affairs com.). Democrat. Methodist (chmn. commn. on Christian vocations 1968-69). Clubs: Zonta (pres. 1970-72, dist. treas. 1972-74) (Birmingham); Bus. and Profl. Women's (pres. Ala. fedn. 1966-67). Home: 504 Maplewood SW Leeds AL 35094 Office: PO Box 486 Leeds AL 35094

CULL, MILLIE ALEXANDER, librarian; b. Gatesville, Tex., June 16, 1943; d. Robert Lee and Lucile Frances (Simmons) Alexander; B.A. (Mary Hill Davis scholar), Mary Hardin-Baylor Coll., 1965; M.A. (fellow) U. Houston, 1967; postgrad. Tex. A. and M. U., 1968; m. Herbert Graham Cull, Jr., June 26, 1971. Instr. govt. Blinn Coll., Brenham, Tex., 1967-69; indsl. librarian Oceanonics, Inc., Houston, 1969-70; aquisitions asst., children's librarian Harris County Pub. Library, Houston, 1970—. Notary pub., 1970—. Precinct del. Republican Party, 1972, 74, dist. conv. del., 1974. Mem. Royal Academia Soc., Poetry Soc. Tex., Internat. Poetry Soc., Heather and Thistle Soc., Tex. State Guard Assn., Alpha Chi. Baptist. Club: German (Belton, Tex.). Home: 3815 Oberlin St Houston TX 77005 Office: 2301 Caroline St Houston TX 77004

CULLEN, HELEN FRANCES, educator; b. Boston, Jan. 4, 1919; d. James Francis and Letitia Ellen (Johnson) Cullen; A.B., Radcliffe Coll., 1940; M.A., U. Mich., 1944, Ph.D. (fellow), 1950. Asst. prof. math. U. Mass. at Amherst, 1949-56, asso. prof., 1956-71, prof., 1971—. Mem. Am. Math. Soc., Math. Assn. Am., Am. Assn. U. Profs., Sigma Xi. Author: Introduction to General Topology, 1968; also articles in profl. jours. Home: 92 Rocky Hill Rd Hadley MA 01035 Office: Dept Math U Mass Amherst MA 01002

CULLEN, IRIS JUANITA, resort owner, land devel. co. exec.; b. Brainerd, Minn., Apr. 10; d. Clyde Raymond and Anna Josephine (Hegland) Belden; student U. Wash.; 1 son, Harold Michael. Dir., office mgr. Norris, Beggs & Simpson, San Francisco, 1933-42; real estate-land acquisition asst. USN, Hawaii, 1942-46; v.p. Hawaiian Property Mgmt. Co., Honolulu, 1946-51; pres. Cullen's Ltd., property mgmt. and land devel. co., Honolulu, 1946—; pres., owner Cullen's Cooper Ranch Inn, Hauula, Hawaii, 1951—; past v.p., dir. King Kalakawa Super Market; sec., dir. Kalawa Land Co.; bus. mgr. Young Hawaii mag., Honolulu. Active Hiawaii Loa Coll. Bldg. Fund, Castle Meml. Hosp. Fund, Kahukuku Hosp. Fund; pub. information officer, capt. Civil Air Patrol. Republican county committeewoman, Honolulu, Rep. precinct worker. Recipient award of merit USN, 1946. Mem. Nat. Assn. Real Estate Bds., Honolulu Realty Bd., Hawaii C. of C. (chmn. edn. com.), Pub. Relations Women (membership chmn.), Hauula (past pres.), Punaluu, Kaneohe improvement assns., Zonta Internat., Beta Sigma Phi (exemplar mem.). Club: Outrigger Canoe. Contbr. numerous articles to profl. and popular publs. Home: Cullen's Cooper Ranch Inn Homestead Road Hauula HI 96717 also Woodside Lane Sacramento CA 95825 Office: Box 446 Hauula HI 96717

CULLEN, JOAN (MRS. THOMAS CULLEN), mus. ofcl.; b. N.Y.C., Jan. 30, 1929; d. Thomas Kenefick and Margaret (Swartwout) O'Brien; student Finch Coll., 1947-48; B.A., Marymount Coll., 1951; m. Thomas Cullen, Apr. 9, 1953. Real estate sales agt. C.S. McClellan & Co., Inc., Pelham, N.Y., 1969—; with Bartow-Pell Mansion Mus. and Garden, N.Y.C., 1968—, pres. Internat. Garden Club, 1971-74. Mem. Pelham, Westchester County realty bds., Jr. League of Pelham (pres. 1961-63), Jr. League of Am. (del. to annual assn. 1955-56, 61-62). Home: 914 Wynnewood Rd Pelham Manor NY 10803 Office: 215 Wolf's Lane Pelham NY 10803

CULLEN, MARY TERESA (MRS. CHESTER FRANCIS CULLEN), physician; b. Wilkes Barre, Pa., Sept. 26, 1928; d. James Edward and Agnes Marie (Knebels) Murphy; B.S. (cum laude), Coll. Misericordia, 1950; M.D., Womans Med. Coll. Pa., 1956; m. Chester Francis Cullen, June 9, 1956; children—Michael Hugh, Joseph Patrick. Med. technologist Hazelton (Pa.) State Hosp., 1950-52; intern Hartford (Conn.) Hosp., 1956-57; gen. practice medicine, Hartford, 1959—, Newington, Conn., 1968—; physician Hartford Health Dept., 1959—; sch. physician Newington Sch. System, 1968—. Mem. adv. bd. Holy Innocents Guild, Hartford, 1961-70. Mem. bd. assos. Gengras Center for Exceptional Children, St. Joseph's Coll., Hartford, Conn., 1965-70; pre-cana lectr. Archdiocese of Hartford, 1959-68; mem. archdiocesan exec. bd. Confraternity of Christian Doctrine, 1961-70. Bd. dirs. Hartford Assn. for Retarded Children, 1969-71, Community Health Services, Inc., Hartford, 1970-71. Mem. A.M.A., Am. Womens Med. Assn., Hartford County Med. Assn., Conn. Med. Soc., Kappa Gamma Pi. Home: 27 Fernwood Rd West Hartford CT 06119 Office: Burgdorff Health Center 80 Coventry St Hartford CT 06112

CULLER, ELIZABETH HARRELL, art mus. curator; b. Bluefield, W. Va., Feb. 27, 1943; d. Charles McDaniel and Elizabeth (McClaugherty) Harrell; B.A. with honors, Hollins Coll., 1965; postgrad. Oberlin Coll., 1965-66; m. Edward Olen Culler, Dec. 17, 1968 (div. Apr. 1972). Registrar, asst. curator Va. Mus. of Fine Arts, Richmond, 1966—. Mem. Am. Assn. Museums. Home: 801 E North Hamilton St Richmond VA 23221 Office: Virginia Museum Boulevard and Grove Av Richmond VA 23226

CULLERS, MARY ALICE MARQUES (MRS. JAMES B. CULLERS), librarian; b. Anciao, Portugal, Oct. 22, 1930; d. Albino and Maria Jose (Paulo) Marques; came to U.S., 1936, naturalized, 1946; A.B., Mt. Holyoke Coll., 1952; postgrad. U. Mass., 1959; m. Robert F. Denehy, Apr. 11, 1953 (dec. 1963); children—Robert F., Rosemary; m. 2d, James B. Cullers, May 2, 1964; 1 son, James B. Engring. librarian Monsanto Co., Springfield, Mass., 1959-64; research librarian Tecnifax Corp., Holyoke, Mass., 1965-67; librarian Tantasqua Regional High Sch., Sturbridge, Mass., 1967-68; asst. librarian engring dept. Combustion Engring. Inc., Windsor, Conn., 1968—. Mem. Spl. Libraries Assn. Clubs: Mt. Holyoke (sec. 1972—) (Springfield); Portuguese-Am. (Holyoke). Home: 133 Longmeadow St Longmeadow MA 01106 Office: Combustion Engring Inc Windsor CT 06095

CULLIGAN, GLENDY (MRS. WILLIAM R. PABST, JR.), writer, reviewer; b. Chgo., Oct. 26, 1915; d. Albert Francis and Marie (Sage) Culligan; B.A., Newcomb Coll., 1936; M.A., Am. U., 1968; m. Frank R. Dawedeit, February 1, 1950 (div. 1953); 1 dau., Nora Sage. Reporter, editor New Orleans Item, 1937-49; asst. woman's editor Washington Post, Washington, 1949-53, features editor, 1953-56, book editor, 1956-65; freelance writer and reviewer, 1965—; cons. editor Population Reference Bur., 1967; instr. Montgomery Coll., Rockville, Md., 1969-71. Mem. adv. awards com. Nat. Books Awards, 1961-66. Mem. Phi Beta Kappa, Phi Kappa Phi. Home: 3420 Quebec St NW Washington DC 20016

CULLINAN, IMOGENE HUDSON (MRS. HENRY MORTIMER CULLINAN), social worker; b. Atlanta, Nov. 20, 1909; d. Robert James and Imogene (Richardson) Hudson; student Randolph Macon Womans Coll., 1928-30; B.A., Agnes Scott Coll., 1932; M.S.W., Tulane U., 1940; m. Henry Mortimer Cullinan, Apr. 24, 1943; children—Mortimer James, Michael Patrick. Caseworker Spl. Relief Com., Atlanta, 1933-34, Fed. Emergency Relief Adminstrn., 1934-36, Fulton County (Ga.) Welfare Dept., Atlanta, 1936-38, Disaster Service, A.R.C., Louisville, 1937; med. social worker Cook County Hosp., Chgo., 1940-43; home service worker Craven County chpt. A.R.C., Newbern, N.C., 1943-44, Albany (Ga.) chpt. A.R.C., 1954-59; social worker VA Hosp., Augusta, Ga., 1959-72, Ga. Regional Hosp., Augusta, 1972—. Field instr. Fla. State U. Sch. Social Welfare Augusta, 1962-69. Mem. exec. bd. Friends of Library, Augusta, 1969—, v.p., 1970, pres., 1971. Mem. Nat. Assn. Social Workers, Acad. Certified Social Workers, Alpha Xi Delta. Presbyn. (circle chmn. women of ch., 1964-67). Home: 739 Oxford Rd Augusta GA 30904 Office: Ga Regional Hospital Augusta GA 30906

CULP, MARTHA EDWARDINE STREET (MRS. DELOS POE CULP), educator, civic worker; b. Gadsden, Ala., Nov. 4, 1915; d. Alonzo Cranford and Mattie (Miller) Street; student Jacksonville State Coll., 1932-34; B.S., Auburn U., 1940; postgrad. Columbia, 1948; m. Delos Poe Culp, Dec. 23, 1934; children—Martha Jean (Mrs. William McIver Flanigan), James David, John Stephen. Tchr. elementary grades, Ala. Schs., 1934-42; sec. to sch. supt. Chilton County, Ala., 1942-45; tchr. pub. kindergarten Tappan, N.Y., 1948-49; tchr. Marbury, Ala., 1950-51, Auburn, Ala., 1952-53; registrar Livingston U., 1957-63. Chmn. Washington County chpt. Easter Seal Soc.; mem. bd., budget com. United Fund Bd. Bd. dirs. Friends of Reese Mus., Johnson City Symphony Orch. Mem. D.A.R. (chpt. regent), U.D.C. (v.p.), Watauga Valley Art League, Nat. League Am. Pen Women, Community Concert Assn., Am. Hort. Soc., Am., East Tenn. (v.p.) Hemerocallis socs., Faculty Wives Club (past pres.), Johnson City C. of C. (pres. Women's div., Outstanding mem. award), Alpha Lambda Delta, Delta Kappa Gamma, Kappa Delta Pi. Clubs: Dogwood Acres, Tenn. Women, Press and Author, Pilot (hon.), Monday, Johnson City Garden. Contbr. articles to newspapers and mags.; exhibitor art work, needlepoint design. Home: Pres' Home East Tenn State U Johnson City TN 37602

CULPEPPER, BETTY MINERVA, librarian; b. Lynchburg, Va.; d. Roosevelt and Agnes Louise (Head) Culpepper; B.A., Howard U., 1963; M.A., Kent State U., 1966; M.L.S., Cath. U., 1969. Librarian, D.C. Pub. Library, 1964-67, Prince George's County Meml. Library, Hyattsville, Md., 1967-72, D.C. Pub. Library, Washington, 1972—. Md. Library Assn. scholar, 1965; Kent State U. fellow, 1963. Mem. A.L.A., D.C., Md. library assns. Home: 9770 Basket Ring Rd Columbia MD 21045 Office: Martin Luther King Memorial Library 901 G St NW Washington DC 20001

CULPEPPER, MARIAN MISH (MRS. JAMES HENRY CULPEPPER), pub. relations exec.; b. nr. Staunton, Va.; d. Robert Warren Howe and Ligia (Botts) Mish; student Mary Baldwin Coll., 1938; m. James Henry Culpepper, Dec. 1, 1969; children from previous marriage—Jay, Stuart Wentworth Ganong. Sec., office mgr. to alumni sec. Va. Mil. Inst. Alumni Assn., Lexington, 1937-39; sec. Van Strum & Towne, Inc., San Francisco, 1940-42; sales rep. Henry Fayette, Inc., Chgo., 1946-53; asso. John J. Greer A.I.D. & Assos., Georgetown, Washington, 1950-53; sales rep. Walter Lamb, Pebble Beach, Cal., 1953-54; mgr. campaign hdqrs. Teaque for Congress, Monterey, Cal., 1954; rancher, developer Edison A. Holt, Carmel Valley, Cal., 1953-54; social dir. preparatory to opening, Disneyland, Cal., 1955; account coordinator Hixon & Jorgensen Advt., Los Angeles, 1956-57; dir. contact div., speakers' bur. Knowland for Cal. Gov. campaign, Los Angeles, 1958; account exec., West Coast rep. Farson Huff & Northlich Advt. & Pub. Relations, Cin., 1958-59; dir. contact div. Bell-for-Congress campaign, Beverly Hills, Cal., 1960; pub. relations Frost & Shaffer Advt., Hollywood, Cal., 1959-61; pub. relations dir. Cal. Adoption Found., Holy Family Adoption Service, Los Angeles, 1961-62, Leo J. Shanahan Co., Tustin, Cal., 1962-64; pub. relations Blakiston Ranch, Inc., Chatsworth, Cal., 1965-68. Founding chmn. Orange County (Cal.) Women's chpt. Freedoms Found. Valley Forge. Founding dir., show chmn. Peacock Hill Nat. Horse Show to Benefit John Tracy Clinic, Tustin, 1964, 65; coordinator City of Hope Internat. Horse Show, 1968. Mem. Pub. Relations Soc. Am. Republican. Episcopalian. Editor, pub. The Orange Book, 1966-67. Home: Windy Cove Farm at High Chicky Mountain Millboro Springs VA 24460

CULVER, DORIS DAHLBERG (MRS. LESTER CULVER, JR.), social worker; b. New Iberia, La., Oct. 7, 1914; d. Young S. and Mable (Blanc) Dahlberg; B.A., Sophie Newcomb Coll., 1935; M.S.W., Tulane U., 1939; m. Lester Clayton Culver, Jr., June 17, 1937; 1 son, Lester Clayton, III. Med. social worker Charity Hosp., New Orleans, 1940-41, Fla., Parishes Charity Hosp., Independence, La., 1941-42, Monmouth Meml. Hosp., Long Branch, N.J., 1943-45; instr. Tulane U. Sch. Social Work, New Orleans, 1945-47; welfare case supr. Orleans Parish Welfare Dept., New Orleans, 1949-62, social analyst, 1962-63, dir., 1963-71, field rep. New Orleans area, 1971—. Tech. cons. Total Community Action, Inc. Mem. La. com. for White House Conf. on Children, 1970; mem. task force Regional Planning Commn.; consumer adv. com. Health Edn. Authority La.; home health services adv. bd. La. Dept. Health. Mem. Met. Area Council on Aging, Mayor's Task Force on Aging, New Orleans Met. Area Manpower Planning Council, Dist. Alcoholism Adv. Council. Mem. bd. Consumers Credit Counseling Service Greater New Orleans. Mem. Acad. Certified Social Workers, Nat. Assn. Social Work, Am. Pub. Welfare Assn., La. Conf. Social Welfare. Democrat. Episcopalian. Home: 1316 Harmony St New Orleans LA 70115 Office: 2601 Tulane Av Box 51870 New Orleans LA 70151

CULWELL, VERA CHRISTINE, film story editor; b. Avoca, Tex., Apr. 16, 1925; d. Charles Wesley and Mary Salena (Smithey) Culwell; B.A. in Journalism, Tex. Tech U., 1944; postgrad. U. So. Cal., 1954-66. With stenographic dept. Universal Pictures Co., Inc., Universal City, Cal., 1945-46, story dept. and office story editor, 1946-56, story analyst, 1957, story dept., 1959-65; story analyst Regal Films, Inc., Culver City, Cal., 1957-58, Desilu, 1958-59; asst. to story editor Westinghouse Desilu Playhouse, Hollywood, Cal., 1958-59; head story dept., asst. story editor Universal City Studios/MCA, Inc., Universal City, 1966—. Pvt. tchr. film writing, 1970—. Mem. Am. Assn. U. Women, United Methodist Women, Women in Communications. Democrat. Methodist. Home: 4027 Cartwright Av North Hollywood CA 91604 Office: Universal City Studios Universal City CA 91608

CUMBER, (VICTORIA) LILLIAN, theatrical agt.; b. San Antonio, Feb. 5, 1920; d. David H. and Lora Lillian (Johnson) Johnson; student Met. Bus. Sch., 1936-38; m. Bené Greene, Aug. 5, 1941 (div. Mar. 1945); m. 2d, Gerald Cumber, Apr. 5, 1945 (div. Mar. 1955); m. 3d, Edward I. Fisher, Nov. 30, 1956 (div. 1969). Publisher Sepia Hollywood mag., 1943-45, Bronz mag., Los Angeles, 1941-45; mgr. Herald Attractions Agy., Hollywood, Cal., 1949-55; theatrical agt. L.L. Cumber Attractions Agy., Hollywood, Cal., 1956—. Columnist Southwest Wave newspaper, Los Angeles, 1967—. Sec. Community Actions Com., Los Angeles, 1958-60. Recipient placque Bus. and Profl. Women's Club, 1967; named to Black Filmmaker's Hall of Fame, Oakland, Cal., 1974. Mem. N.A.A.C.P. (sec. Hollywood Beverly Hills br. 1972—). Democrat. Home: 6478 Ivarene Av Hollywood CA 90068 Office: 6515 Sunset Hollywood CA 90028

CUMMINGS, ALICE BEATRICE (MRS. EARL DEAN CUMMINGS), assn. exec.; b. Lancaster, Pa.; d. Ira Hipple and Mary Elizabeth (Tappany) Groff; B.S. in Edn., Millersville State Tchrs. Coll.; student Lancaster Bus. Coll.; M.A., Temple U.; m. Earl Dean Cummings; children—Marilyn (Mrs. David A. Collins), Julie D., Annabel L. Formerly continuity editor, women's program dir. radio sta. WGAL, Lancaster, Pa.; later exec. asst. Norwood Studios, Washington, then Nat. Civil Service League, Washington; spl. asst. adminstrn. and mgmt. N.E.A.-Assn. Classroom Tchrs., Washington, 1958—, staff contact for environmental edn., 1970-72, program devel. specialist for social issues, environmental edn., 1973—. Bd. dirs. Sch. Nurses Project on Drug Abuse and Venereal Disease Edn., also program devel. specialist for Social issues, 1973—. Mem. Phi Delta Gamma. Club: Soroptimist (charter). Home: 1417 Aiden Dr Woodbridge VA 22191 Office: 1201 16th St NW Washington DC 20036

CUMMINGS, LAURA, librarian; b. Toledo; d. Benjamin and Margaret (Fox) Cummings; A.B., Toledo U., 1936; A.B. in L.S., U. Mich., 1937; M.S. in L.S., Columbia, 1950. Cataloger Toledo Pub.

Library, 1936-46; catalog editor Pacific N.W. Bibliog. Center, Seattle, 1946-48; cataloger Columbia, N.Y.C., 1948-51, head serials cataloging sect., 1951-73, chief bibliog. control div., 1973—. Mem. N.Y. Library Club, N.Y. Tech. Services Librarians, A.L.A. Home: 615 W 113th St New York City NY 10025 Office: Bibliographic Control Div Library Columbia U New York City NY 10027

CUMMINGS, MARJORIE PLACE, orgn. exec.; b. Woonsocket, R.I., June 16, 1928; d. Albert Nelson and Marjorie May (Carnie) Place; student U. R.I., 1945-47; m. Robert Joseph Cummings, Oct. 4, 1947; children—William Joseph, Christopher Place. Asst. to housing dir. U. R.I., 1959-60; sec. to gen. mgr. WNHC-TV, New Haven, 1960-63; asst. to v.p. Puritan Aerosol Corp., Berkeley, R.I., 1963-66; head data processing dept. Am. Mathematical Soc., Providence, 1966—. Recipient community service award Radio Sta. WDEE, New Haven, 1962. Home: 69 Forestdale Dr Cumberland RI 02864 Office: American Mathematical Society PO Box 6248 Providence RI 02904

CUMMINGS, MILDRED HUBBARD, art center exec.; b. Middletown, Conn., Oct. 8, 1917; d. Elijah Kent and Helen Keep (Otis) Hubbard; B.A., Bennington Coll., 1940; m. Willard W. Cummings, Sept. 20, 1941 (div. Jan. 1962); children—Daphne DeKoven Hall, Williard Howe. Asst., Skowhegan (Me.) Sch. Painting and Sculpture, 1946-62; dir. Me. Coast Artists, Rockport, 1967—. Docent, Whitney Mus. Am. Arts. Bd. dirs. Katonah (N.Y.) Art Gallery, 1955-60. Democrat. Author: South Solon, The Story of a Meeting House, 1959. Contbr. articles to mags. Home: Main St Rockport ME 04856 Office: Box 22 Rockport ME 04856

CUMMINGS, MINNETTE HUNSIKER (MRS. H. KING CUMMINGS), state legislator; b. Washington; d. Harold Whiting and Florence M. (Lufkin) Hunsiker; B.A., Bennington Coll., 1940; m. H. King Cummings, Aug. 1, 1942; children—Stephen H., Wende (Mrs. Robert A. Richter), Lee L., Jennifer. Agt. Me. Sch. and Coll. Adv. Center, 1965—; mem. Me. Ho. of Reps., 1969-73, Me. Senate, 1973—. Mem. Fed. Water Bank Commn. Dir. Sch. Adminstrn. Dist. #48; bd. dirs. Me. State Ballet, Bangor Theol. Inst., Pa. Med. Coll. for Women; trustee Unity Coll., Newport (Me.) Pub. Library. Club: Newport Woman's. Address: 24 High St Newport ME 04953

CUMMINGS, MOZELLE BROWN (MRS. TRUMAN CUMMINGS), librarian; b. Oakman, Ala., Feb. 11, 1913; d. C.S. and Nannie (Taggart) Brown; A.B., Athens Coll., 1931; M.S., Auburn U., 1937; M.S., Peabody Library Sch., 1957; m. Truman Cummings, May 21, 1938; children—Nancy (Mrs. Robert L. Gonce), Stephen F. Tchr. secondary schs., Ala., Ga., S.C., 1931-50; sch. librarian, Ala., 1950-61; field rep. Ala. Pub. Library Service, Montgomery, summers 1958, 59, head field services, 1961-69, asst. dir., 1970—. Vis. prof. U. Ala. Sch. Librarianship, 1962, 65. Mem. gov.'s Com. on White House Conf. for Children, 1970; mem. Gov.'s Com. Ala. Devel. Orgn., 1963-72; mem. adv. bd. Library for Blind and Physically Handicapped, 1965-68, Project Libra, Knapp Found. Project Auburn U., 1971-72. Mem. Am. Assn. U. Women, A.L.A., Am. Assn. State Libraries, Southeastern (mem. planning com. 1971-72), Ala. (chmn. sch. library div. 1956-57) library assns., Alpha Delta Kappa. Home: 365 Polk St Montgomery AL 36107 Office: Adminstrv Bldg Montgomery AL 36104

CUMMINGS, PAMELA ROBERTA, photographer; b. Montague, Mass., Mar. 8, 1945; d. Henry David and Helen Margaret (Martin-Bragg) Cummings; grad. Cathedral High Sch., 1962; certificate N.Y. Inst. of Photography, 1965. Staff photographer Springfield (Mass.) Herald, 1965-67; free lance photographer Springfield Daily News, 1967-69; photographer, propr. Pecum Creative Photography, East Longmeadow, Mass., 1974—. Cons. Mini Gallery, East Longmeadow, 1974—; lectr. photography. Mem. Mass. Profl. Photographers (Blue Ribbon Awards 1972, 73), Profl. Photographers Am. (awards), N.Y. Photog. Hist. Soc., Profl. Photographers New Eng. (award 1973). Home: 26 Orlando St Springfield MA 01108 Office: 35 Maple St 3 Crane Av East Longmeadow MA 01028

CUMMINS, ELEANOR CATHERINE, editor; b. Indpls., Sept. 10, 1945; d. Laurence George and Evelyn Louise (Greer) Cummins; grad. Central Bus. Coll., Indpls., 1964; student Butler U., 1969. With Curtis Pub. Co. (formerly Review Pub. Co.), Indpls., 1965—, asso. editor Brownie Reader, 1969-70, mng. editor, 1970-73, asso. editor Child Life, 1969-71, mng. editor, 1972, editor, 1972—, asso. editor Children's Playmate, 1970—, editor Barbie Talk, 1972, asso. editor Jack and Jill, 1972—. Mem. Am. Bus. Women's Assn. (pub. relations dir. 500 chpt.). Home: 6061 Beachview Dr Indianapolis IN 46224 Office: 1100 Waterway Blvd Indianapolis IN 46202

CUNDIFF, JENNIFER ANN DOYLE, occupational therapist, nurse; b. London, Eng., July 22, 1943; d. John Anthony Felix and Audrey Frances (Reed) Doyle; brought to U.S., 1952, naturalized, 1963; B.S. in Occupational Therapy, San Jose (Cal.) State U., 1969; Asso. Sci. in Nursing with honors, Grossmont Coll., 1973; m. David Keith Cundiff, Aug. 17, 1968. Occupational therapist Univ. Hosp. of San Diego County, San Diego, 1970; registered nurse hematology unit Presbyn.-Univ. Hosp., Pitts., 1973-74; nurse oncology unit Magee-Women's Hosp., Pitts., 1974—. Mem. Am. Occupational Therapy Assn., Nat. Orgn. for Women, Nurses Now, Cal. Scholarship Fedn. (life), Animal Protection Inst., Nat. Orgn. for Non-Parents, Common Cause, Am. Civil Liberties Union, Med. Com. Human Rights. Home: 120 Ruskin Av Apt 612 Pittsburgh PA 15213 Office: Magee-Women's Hosp Pittsburgh PA 15213

CUNIN, BERTHA HOFFMAN (MRS. BERT CUNIN), educator, psychologist; b. Santo Domingo, Dominican Republic, July 12, 1943; came to U.S., 1948, naturalized, 1955; d. Markus and Rachela (Brande) Hoffman; B.A., Coll. City N.Y., 1965; M.A. (Nat. Inst. Mental Health fellow), U. Mont., 1969, Ph.D., 1973; m. Bert Cunin, Jan 30, 1965; 1 dau., Sharon Claire. Asst. prof. psychology Alfred (N.Y.) U., 1969-71, lectr. in psychology, 1971—, research asso. counseling Center, 1974—. Mem. Am. Psychol. Assn. (asso.), Phi Beta Kappa, Psi Chi. Home: Georgian II Glen St Alfred NY 14802

CUNKLE, ELISABETH CLARK, librarian; b. San Francisco; d. Charles Vincent and Henrietta Pauline (Hagen) Clark; A.B., U. Cal. at Berkeley, 1931; M.S., Columbia, 1932; children—Annette (Mrs. John W. Fuller III), Lorna, Wendy. Librarian, San Diego State Coll., 1948-61; humanities librarian Chico (Cal.) State Coll., 1962-68; coll. librarian San Francisco Art Inst., 1969—. Mem. acad. liaison com. Cal. State Colls., 1964-68; mem. San Francisco Museum Art, Fine Arts Museums San Francisco, Strybing Aboretum Soc., San Francisco Symphony Found. Mem. Spl. Libraries Assn., Found. for San Francisco's Archtl. Heritage, Soc. Archtl. Historians, Nat. Trust for Historic Preservation, Cal. Tomorrow, Cal. Heritage Council, Cal. Hist. Soc., Cal. Roadside Council, Audubon Soc., Nature Conservancy, English-Speaking Union, Spur, San Francisco Beautiful, World Affairs Council, U. Cal. Alumni Assn., Cal. Acad. Scis., Cal. Native Plant Soc., Sierra Club, League Women Voters. Democrat. Unitarian. Home: 900 Chestnut St San Francisco CA 94109 Office: 800 Chestnut St San Francisco CA 94133

CUNNINGHAM, ALMA WHITLEY, editor; b. Bell County, Tex., Oct. 4, 1912; d. George Cornelius and Julia (Matthews) Whitley; B.S., N. Tex. U., 1933; m. Bruce Cunningham, Dec. 27, 1933 (div. Feb. 1947); 1 son, Bruce Herbert. Editor, feature writer Dallas Morning News, Dallas, 1935-43; regional radio officer OWI, Dallas, 1944-46; dir. Fashion Center, Dallas, 1947-51; publicity dir. Johnston Inc., Dallas, N.Y.C., 1952-56; mdse. dir. Good Housekeeping Mag., N.Y.C., 1958-60; advt. dir. Simplicity Pattern Co., N.Y.C., 1960-63, editor in chief publs., 1963-73, dir. design, 1973-74, v.p. in charge design and publs., 1974—. Mem. Fashion Group Inc. (past dir.), Advt. Women N.Y. (past dir.). Home: 405 W 23d St New York City NY 10011 Office: 200 Madison Av New York City NY 10016

CUNNINGHAM, SISTER CATHARINE JULIE, coll. pres.; b. San Francisco, Oct. 22, 1910; d. John Francis and Mary Cecilia (McCarthy) Cunningham; B.A., U. Cal. at Berkeley, 1932; M.A., Catholic U. Am., 1954. Joined Sisters of Notre Dame de Namur, 1932; prin. Notre Dame High Sch., Alameda, Cal., 1942-45, 55-56, San Jose, Cal., 1945-47, Belmont, Cal., 1947-55; pres., Coll. of Notre Dame, Belmont, 1956—. Bd. dirs. Far West Lab. Ednl. Research and Devel. Mem. N.E.A., Nat. Cath. Ednl. Assn. (dir. S.W. region 1956-62), Ind. Colls. No. Cal. (dir. 1956—), Assn. Ind. Cal. Colls. and Univs. (trustee 1956—). Address: Coll of Notre Dame 1500 Ralston Av Belmont CA 94002

CUNNINGHAM, CORA ANNE BERLINER (MRS. RUSSELL EDWARD CUNNINGHAM), psychologist; b. Washington, June 29, 1922; d. Henry Adler and Josephine (Mitchell) Berliner; student Wellesley Coll., 1939-41; B.A., Am. U., 1965; M.A., George Washington U., 1968; m. Russell Edward Cunningham, May 2, 1945; children—Juliet Eyre, Anne Mithcell (Mrs. Richard Joel Leader), Margaret Darling, Russell Edward. Sec., Bd. Econ. Warfare, Washington, 1942-45; sch. psychologist D.C. Pub. Schs., 1969-74. Dir., sec.-treas. Sigma Systems, Inc., Washington, 1968—; dir. Outlook Engrng. Corp., Alexandria, Va.; sec.-treas. Check-A-Book Corp., Washington, 1971—. Trustee D.C. Inst. Mental Hygiene, Emile Berliner Found.; trustee Planned Parenthood Met. Washington, 1946-49, 57-63, chmn. of solicitors, 1959-61, campaign chmn., 1962. Mem. Am. Psychol. Assn. (asso.), Nat., D.C. assns. sch. psychologists, Psi Chi. Republican. Clubs: George Washington University (Washington); Henlopen Acres (Del.) Beach. Home: 4015 29th St NW Washington DC 20008

CUNNINGHAM, DOLORA G. GALLAGHER, educator; b. Sacramento, Sept. 4, 1920; d. Anthony James and Marie C. (Eymard) Gallagher; A.B., Stanford, 1944, M.A., 1946, Ph.D., 1953; m. James V. Cunningham, Mar. 26, 1945 (div. Nov. 1949). Instr. English, Reed Coll., 1952-54; asst. prof. English, Harpur Coll., State U. N.Y., 1954-59; asso. prof. English, San Francisco State Coll., 1959-68, prof., 1969—. Exec. dir. Inst. Renaissance Studies of Ore. Shakespeare Festival, 1963-72; vis. prof. U. Colo., 1969-70. Trustee, Shakespeare Assn. Am., 1972—. Folger Shakespeare Library research fellow, 1955, 69; Huntington Library research fellow, 1959. Mem. Modern Lang. Assn., Renaissance Soc. Am., Stanford Alumni Assn. Democrat. Roman Catholic. Research in Shakespeare and Renaissance English literature. Home: 137 Clifford Terrace San Francisco CA 94117

CUNNINGHAM, SISTER FRANCES CECELIA, educator; b. N.Y.C.; d. Joseph Louis and Blanche A. (Donnelly) Cunningham; B.A., Manhattanville Coll. of Sacred Heart, N.Y.C., 1930; M.S., Villanova Coll., Phila., 1950; Ph.D., Catholic U. Am., 1956. Sci. tchr., 1932-52; prof. biology Newton (Mass.) Coll. of Sacred Heart, 1952—, chmn. biology dept., 1966-69. Tchr. Coll. Bound Poverty Program, 1966-67. Asst. research specialist Sci. Resources Found., Watertown, Mass. 1965—; research specialist sci. SIAS Med. Research Lab., div. Lahey Clinic Found., Brooks Hosp., Brookline, Mass., 1973-74. Mem. Am. Cytology Soc., Am. Soc. Cell Biology, A.A.A.S. Contbr. articles to profl. jours. Address: Newton Coll of Sacred Heart 885 Centre St Newton MA 02159

CUNNINGHAM, MARIE (MRS. THOMAS CUNNINGHAM), mfg. co. exec.; b. Dover, N.J., Nov. 15, 1936; d. Joseph and Mina (Sutton) Romano; grad. high sch.; m. Thomas Cunningham, Feb. 12, 1966; children—Thomas III, Nancy Mina. With Precision Mfg. Co., Inc., Dover, 1954—, office mgr., 1960—, asst. to pres., 1965-70, v.p., comptroller, 1970—. Republican. Home: 6 Richards Av Succasunna NJ 07876 Office: 88 King St Dover NJ 07801

CUNNINGHAM, MARILYN ALICE ENEIX (MRS. MARCUS E. CUNNINGHAM), bus. and advt. exec.; b. Warren, Minn., Mar. 8, 1917; d. Frederick C. and Mary (Boman) Eneix; B.A., U. Mich., 1937; m. Marcus E. Cunningham, Oct. 1, 1966. Account supr. Grant Advt., Inc., Chgo., N.Y.C., 1945-60; v.p., dir. Brady Hill Co., Detroit, 1960-69; dir. advt. Cunningham-Limp Co., Detroit, 1960-69, v.p., dir., Birmingham, Mich., 1969-72; vice chmn. bd., v.p., dir. Cunningham-Limp Internat., 1971—; vice chmn. bd., dir. Cunningham-Limp Co., Birmingham, 1972—, Cunningham-Limp de Las Americas, 1972—, Cunningham-Limp Ltd., 1972—. Active in civic and philanthropic activities. Mem. Fine Arts Soc. Detroit (chmn. script com.), Smithsonian Assos., Internat. Platform Assn., Alpha Phi. Clubs: Bloomfield Hills Country; Oakland Hills Country (Birmingham); Recess (Detroit); Indian Creek Country (Bal Harbour, Fla.); Jockey (Miami Beach, Fla.). Republican. Presbyn. Author: The Right Plant on The Right Site for Maximum Profit, 1962; The Comprehensive Approach to Facility Expansion, 1967; Design and Engineering, 1970; Facility Planning Services, 1973. Author, publ. SCOPE mag. Contbr. articles to nat. mags., bus. publs., tech. periodicals. Home: 104 Brady Lane Bloomfield Hills MI 48013 also Ocean Blvd Golden Beach FL 33160 Office: 1400 N Woodward Av Birmingham MI 48011

CUNNINGHAM, MARY ELLEN (MRS. FRANK B. CUNNINGHAM), musician; b. Santa Rita, N.M., Aug. 20, 1904; d. Clarence and Irene (Richardson) Severns; student U. N.M., 1924-25, 27-30, 36-37; pvt. voice student Dr. Burton Thatcher; m. Frank B. Cunningham, Mar. 11, 1950. Soloist, lyric soprano, choir dir. Congl. Ch., Albuquerque, 1928-30; worked with numerous choral groups, N.M., Cal., 1928—; founder, dir. Bel Canto A Capella Choir, Albuquerque, 1938-41; dir. choirs First Meth. Ch., Albuquerque, 1949-52; soloist Temple Albert choir, 1940-44, soloist dir., 1946-53; soloist Albuquerque Civic Symphony, 1942, 45, 46, 52, 53; dir. choirs Community Meth. Ch., Fairfield, Cal., 1953-58, 1st Presbyn. Ch., Livermore, Cal., 1959-63; dir. Livermore Civic Chorus, 1963-69; dir. choral group Sandia Corp. Livermore Lab.; instr. voice and piano, Fairfield and Livermore. Bd. dirs. Fairfield Community Concert Assn., 1955-58, Livermore Valley Concert Assn., 1968-73, pres., 1972-73; chmn. Livermore Valley Festival Choirs, 1959. Pres. Albuquerque Choral Assn., 1946. Mem. Chi Omega, Sigma Alpha Iota (life). Presbyn. Club: Toastmistress (pres. 1958) (Fairfield, Cal.). Home: 1475 4th St Livermore CA 94550

CUNNINGHAM, MERCEDIER CASSANDRA TURNER (MRS. CALVIN M. CUNNINGHAM), univ. adminstr.; b. Forrest City, Ark., July 25, 1941; d. Colbert and Mattie Beatrice (Walker) Turner; B.A. magna cum laude, Philander Smith Coll., 1962; M.Ed., U. Ark., 1969; postgrad. U. Ia., summer 1970, Okla. State U., 1973—; m. Calvin M. Cunningham, Mar. 3, 1959; children—Calvin M., Theodore, Darwin. Recreational officer Camp Lejeune, N.C., 1964-65; tchr. Eudora (Ark.) Pub. Schs., 1965-72, guidance counselor, 1966-72; asst. dir. student activities Okla. State U., Stillwater, 1973—, asst. dean of student affairs, 1972-73. Co-chmn. Human Relations Planning Com., Eudora, Okla., 1971-72. Recipient scholarship Eudora Pub. Schs., summers 1966-68. Mem. Personnel and Guidance Assn., Am. Coll. Personnel Assn., U. Ark. Alumni Assn., Am. Civil Liberties Union, Alpha Kappa Alpha, Alpha Kappa Mu. Home: 3022 N Lincoln St Stillwater OK 74074

CUNNINGHAM, NANCY LYNN, constrn. co. exec., artist; b. Rockford, Ill., June 18, 1942; d. Lawrence E. and Evelyn (Swenson) Cunningham; B.S., U. So. Miss., 1965. Vice pres. Cunningham Bros., Inc., Beloit, Wis., 1965—; one-woman show Kinkeby Center Gallery, 1973. Recipient Nat. Interior Decorator award Burlington Industries, Inc., N.Y.C., 1972, paintings awarded 1st place Norton Art Gallery, 1966, 68. Mem. Delta Delta Delta. Winner 5-gaited 500 Stake, Lexington Jr. League, 1961, 3-gaited stake Madison Sq. Garden, 1962, 3-gaited stake Chgo. Internat., 1960. Home: 268 Reeves Av Beverly Hills CA 90212 Office: 520 W Grand Av Beloit WI 53511

CUNNINGHAM, NELL ELIZABETH, real estate broker; b. Ottumwa, Ia., June 6, 1910; d. Maurice William and Catherine (Cecil) Poling; student Ia. Wesleyan U., 1928-29, Grinnell Coll., 1929-30; B.Music Edn., Northwestern U., 1935; m. Edward Charles Cunningham, June 23, 1938; children—James William, Ann Catherine. Salesman, California City, land devel., Los Angeles, 1963; real estate salesman, broker Brentwood Investment Co. (Cal.), 1963-66, Kolleck Realty, Vista, Cal., 1969-71; owner Nell E. Cunningham, Realtor, Vista, 1972—. Mem. North County Exchangors, Vista, 1969—, sec., 1973—. Mem. Vista Beautiful, 1969—, chmn., 1972—; mem. Vista Ad-Hoc Com. to Plan Redevel. of Downtown Area, 1973. Mem. Nat. Assn. Realtors, Cal. Real Estate Assn., Vista Bd. Realtors, Kappa Delta. Home: PO Box 1662 Vista CA 92083 Office: 984 E Vista Way Vista CA 92083

CUNNINGHAM, PHYLLIS, educator; b. Martinsville, Ill., Aug. 16, 1923; d. William S. and Rachel (Bach) Cunningham; B.S., U. Ill., 1945; M.A., N.Y.U., 1949; Ph.D., U. Ia., 1964. Instr. phys. edn. Meredith Coll., Raleigh, N.C., 1945-55, Washington U., St. Louis, 1955-58, asst. prof., 1958-64, asso. prof., 1967-70; prof., chmn. dept. phys. edn. for women No. Ill. U., DeKalb, 1970—. Mem. Am., Ill. assns. health, phys. edn. and recreation, Nat., Midwest assns. phys. edn. coll. women, Nat. Found. Health, Phys. Edn. and Recreation, Assn. for Study Perception, Ill. Assn. Tchr. Educators, Pi Lambda Theta, Alpha Lambda Delta, Alpha Sigma Nu, Torch. Contbr. articles to profl. jours. Home: 1522 Mayflower Dr DeKalb IL 60115

CUNNINGHAM, SARAH JANE, lawyer, polit. ofcl.; b. Des Moines; d. Paul Harvey and Harriet (Plummer) Cunningham; A.B., Sterling Coll., 1944; LL.B., U. Neb., 1959; postgrad. U. Ia., 1947, U. Neb., 1948-49. Pub. sch. tchr. Kan., 1944-46, Neb., 1946-52; owner, mgr. McCook (Neb.) Bus. Service, 1952-56, Sally's Gift Shop, McCook, 1953-56; admitted to Neb. bar, 1959, since practiced in McCook. Mem. Neb. Gov.'s Commn. on Status of Women, 1962-71, chmn., 1962-64; mem. citizen's adv. council on status of women, 1969—; trustee McCook City Library, 1967—, chmn. bd., 1970-73; mem. legislative com. Neb. Heart Assn., 1966. Trustee Bus. and Profl. Women's Found., Washington, 1963-71, pres., 1966-67. Vice chmn. Red Willow County Republican central com., 1967-69. Trustee Sterling (Kan.) Coll., 1968—, Kearney (Neb.) State Coll. Found., 1970—. Named Woman of Achievement, Neb. Fedn. Bus. and Profl. Women's Clubs, 1964, Cal. Fedn. Bus. and Profl. Womens Clubs, 1966. Mem. McCook C. of C. (indsl. com. 1967), Nat. Assn. Parliamentarians, D.A.R., Internat. (v.p. 1968-71), Nat. (pres. 1966-67), Neb. (Neb. pres. 1957-59) fedns. bus. and profl. women's clubs, Am., Neb. bar assns., P.E.O. Conglist. (moderator 1960-62). Home: 201 Park Av McCook NE 69001 Office: Temple Bldg McCook NE 69001

CUNNINGHAM, SARAH MARTHA, editor; b. Girard, Ala., Aug. 25, 1925; d. Moses Marshall and Zula Ethel (Easterwood) C.; B.S., S.E. Mo. State Coll., 1947; M.A., Syracuse U., 1953; postgrad. Union Theol. Sem., 1959-60. Editor, Ch. Sch. Pubs., Cumberland Presbyn. Ch., 1953-57; asst. editor Youth Pub., Nat. Council Chs., 1961-63; asst. editor Concern, N.Y.C., 1963-64, editor, 1964—. Mem. Asso. Ch. Press (v.p. 1973—). Home: 606 W 116th St New York City NY 10027 Office: 475 Riverside Pl New York City NY 10027

CUNNINGHAM, TOM JOYCE (MRS. JAMES ROBERT CUNNINGHAM), home economist; b. Dublin, Tex., Aug. 14, 1916; d. W. Tom and Sallie (Powell) Easley; B.S., Mary Hardin Baylor Coll., 1938; M.S., Tex. Woman's U., 1964; postgrad. U. Wis., 1967; m. James Robert Cunningham, Nov. 30, 1939. Tchr. vocational home econs. Comanche (Tex.) High Sch., 1946-50; county home demonstration agt. Tex. Agrl. Extension Service, Stephens County, 1950-59, area home mgmt. specialist, 1959-61, dist. home demonstration agt., Denton, 1961-74; dist. extension agt. Tex. A. and M. U., 1974—. Mem. Profl. Agr. Workers Tex. (pres. 1974), Am., Tex. home econs. assns., County Home Demonstration Agts. Assn. (treas. bd. dirs. 1957-58), Alpha Chi, Zeta Phi Kappa, Epsilon Sigma Phi. Presbyn. Clubs: Dallas Agricultural; Denton Country. Home: 1102 Piping Rock Lane Denton TX 76201 Office: Box 43 Renner TX 75079

CUONO, DOROTHY BOSETTI, coll. dean; b. Union City, N.J., Jan. 30, 1918; d. Guy Charles and Marie Louise (Tagliabué) Bosetti; B.A., Manhattanville Coll., 1939; M.A., Columbia, 1940; m. Joseph D. Cuono, Aug. 16, 1941; children—Maryrose C. Head, Charles B., Noëlle D. Tchr., Fort Lee (N.J.) High Sch., 1940-42, pvt. schs., Caldwell, N.J., 1956-60, Orange, N.J., 1960-67; asst. prof. biol. scis. Tombrock Coll., West Paterson, N.J., 1967-70, chmn. dept., 1968-70, dean acad. affairs, 1970—. Trustee Mt. St. Dominic Acad., Caldwell, 1965. NSF fellow Fairleigh Dickinson U., 1966. Mem. Manhattanville Alumnae Assn. (class rep. 1965—). Office: 44 Rifle Camp Rd West Paterson NJ 07424

CUPIDO, RAFFAELLA ELIZABETH, social worker; b. Rochester, N.Y., Apr. 12, 1929; d. Salvatore and Elizabeth (Squilla) Cupido; B.A. in Sociology, U. Rochester, 1951; M.Social Service, U. Buffalo, 1954. Group worker Lewis St. Center, Rochester, 1951-53; with Baden St. Settlement House, Rochester, 1952-53; Council Social Agys., 1953, Neighborhood House, 1953-54 (both Buffalo); asst. dir. Neighborhood House, Auburn, N.Y., 1954-55; 1st group worker House of Providence, 1955-58, supr. group work Huntington Family Center, 1958-61 (both Syracuse, N.Y.); staff cons. recreation and group work R.I. Council Community Services, Inc., Providence, 1961-65; coordinator pub. and profl. edn. mental retardation Child Health and Devel. Center, faculty Brown U., Providence, 1965-66; exec. dir. Federal Hill House Assn., Providence, 1966-70, Smith Hill Center, Providence, 1970—. Field instr. Syracuse U. Sch. Social Work, 1958-61, Boston Coll., 1963-64, 71—, U. Conn., 1967. Mem. R.I. Gov.'s Com. on Youth Employment, 1962, Gov.'s Task Force on Youth Employment, 1963; mem. Attys. Gen.'s Youth Adv. Bd., 1967—, R.I. Youth Opportunity Council, 1968-70 (award 1964); treas. United Fund Execs., 1967-69, vice chmn., 1969-71; mem. Bd. Registration Social Workers, 1970—, sec. bd., 1971—; mem. capital funds com. United Way Southeastern New Eng., 1971—; v.p. Citizens for Preservation Waterman Lake, 1970-72, pres., 1972-73. Mem. Glocester Democratic Town Com., 1971-73. Mem. Nat. Assn. Social Workers (chmn. membership Syracuse chpt. 1958-61, editor newsletter R.I. chpt. 1967-70, sec. 1969-73, pres. 1973—), Acad. Certified Social Workers. Home: Waterman Lake Shore Dr Harmony RI 02829 Office: 110 Ruggles St Providence RI 02908

CURDA, DORIS ELLEN SWEET (MRS. VERNE CURDA), former advt. agy. exec., writer; b. Tacoma, Sept. 16, 1927; d. John Milton and Nores Ellen (Hutchinson) Sweet; B.S., U. Ore., 1949; m. Verne Curda, May 3, 1952. Advt. salesman Bend (Ore.) Bull., 1949-50, Astorian Budget, Astoria, 1950-52; copywriter Bon Marche, Tacoma, 1954-55, advt. mgr., 1955-57; promotion mgr. KTNT-TV and Radio, Tacoma, 1957-67; pub. relations writer Bozell & Jacobs, Tacoma, 1967-71; copy chief Ad/PR Group, Inc., Tacoma, 1971-73, 1st v.p., 1971-73; free lance writer, 1974—. Mem. Women in Communications, Alpha Gamma Delta, Gamma Alpha Chi.

CURIE, EVE, author, lectr.; b. Paris, France, Dec. 6, 1904; d. Pierre (Nobel prize winner for work in radium 1903) and Marie (Skiodowska) (Nobel prize winner in radio-active substances, 1903, in chemistry 1911) Curie; B.S., Ph.B., Sevigne Coll.; D.H.L. (hon.), Mills Coll., 1939, Russell Sage Coll., 1941; Litt.D. (hon.), U. Rochester, 1941; m. Henry Richardson Labouisse, Nov. 19, 1954. Took up study of music and gave her first concert as pianist, Paris, 1925; later gave concerts in France and Belgium; mus. critic for Candide (weekly jour.) for several years; also wrote articles on motion pictures and the theater; made first visit to U.S. with her mother, 1921; on 2d visit lectured in 10 U.S. cities (speaks English, French and Polish), 1939; witnessed the fall of France, 1940, went to London to work for cause of Free France; came to U.S., 1941, lectured on the war in France and Eng.; because of her pro-ally activities deprived of French citizenship by the Vichy Govt., 1941. Served in Europe with Fighting French as officer in Women's div. of army; one of pubs. of Paris Presse (daily), resigned to return to independent writing, 1949. Spl. adviser Sec. Gen., NATO, 1952-54. Decorated Chevalier Legion of Honor (France), 1939; Polonia Restituta (Poland), 1939; Croix de Guerre (France), 1944. Author: Madame Curie (selection of Lit. Guild, Jr. Guild, Book-of-the-Month Club, Scientific Book of the month; Nat. book award for non-fiction), 1937; Journey Among Warriors (Literary Guild Selection), 1943. Home: 1 Sutton Pl S New York City NY 10022

CURLEE, JOAN E., psychologist; b. Ft. Worth, Tex., Oct. 6, 1930; d. Urchel V. and Velma (Newman) Curlee; B.A., Baylor U., 1950; Ph.D., Vanderbilt U., 1957; Ph.D., U. Minn., 1968. Tchr., Am. Coll. for Girls, Istanbul, Turkey, 1957-59; mem. faculty Coll. of Emporia (Kan.), 1959-65; psychologist Hazelden Found., Garter City, Minn., 1966-68 Menninger Found., Topeka, 1968-70, VA Hosp., Indpls., 1970—. Mem. Am., Ind. psychol. assns. Democrat. Episcopalian. Author articles on alcoholism. Home: 6399 Clydes Rd Indianapolis IN 46268 Office: VA Hosp 1481 W 10th St Indianapolis IN 46202

CURNEN, MARY GODENNE MCCREA (MRS. EDWARD C. CURNEN, JR.), physician; b. Brussels, Belgium, Nov. 25, 1922; d. Pierre and Olive Dudley (Short) Godenne; M.D. magna cum laude, Louvain U., Belgium, 1948; D.T.M. summa cum laude, Inst. Tropical Medicine, Antwerp, Belgium, 1949; D. Pub. Health, Columbia U., 1973; m. John F. McCrea, July 23, 1955 (dec. Sept. 1967); children—Andrew, Pierre, Claire, John; m. 2d, Edward C. Curnen, Jr., Oct. 12, 1968; stepchildren—Sheila, Tim, Cotty. Intern pediatric dept. Louvain U., Belgium, 1947-48; resident Bellevue Med. Center, N.Y. U. Coll. Medicine, 1952-53; clin. research fellow pediatrics Yale Sch. Medicine, 1949-52, instr., 1953-56; sch. and child health clin. physician New Haven City Health Dept., 1959-64; exec. dir., pediatrician in charge New Haven Live Poliomyelitis Vaccine Trial, Yale, 1960; research asso. in pediatrics Yale, 1964-66, research asso. in medicine, 1967-69; practice medicine, specializing in pediatrics, New Haven, 1949—; asso. in medicine and pediatrics Yale-New Haven Hosp. Interpreter to sr. legal officer U.S. Army Hdqrs., Brussels, Belgium, 1944; asst. in operating room Neuro-Surgical Unit, Brit. Liberation Army, 1944; del. Belgian Ministry Health, UNICEF course in social pediatrics, 1949; bd. dirs. Bethany Pub. Health Agy., 1959-62. Fulbright Travel grantee, 1949; Mary Putnam Jacobi fellow Women's Med. Assn. City N.Y., 1949-50, Hon. Grad. fellow Belgian Am. Ednl. Found., 1949-50, Spl. Grad. fellow Belgian Am. Ednl. Found., 1950-51, James Hudson Brown Meml. Research fellow Yale, 1951-52. Mem. Belgian Soc. Pediatrics, Peruvian Pediatric Soc., Soc. for Epidemiology Research, Am. Pub. Health Assn., Sigma Xi. Club: Cosmo (N.Y.C.). Home: 103 Paulin Blvd Leonia NJ 07605 Office: 600 W 168th St New York City NY 10032

CURRAN, FRANCES ROSE (MRS. JEAN ALONZO CURRAN), civic worker; b. Alford, Mass., Apr. 14, 1898; d. Lansing Sheldon and Maude (Strivell) Rose; grad. Bklyn. Hosp. Sch. Nursing, 1919; m. Jean Alonzo Curran, Aug. 5, 1923; children—Jean Alonzo, William Sheldon, Robert Theodore. Served with husband, med. missionary, N. China, 1923-30; trustee Vis. Nurses Assn., Bklyn., 1935-57, pres., 1947-55, bd. dirs., Cambridge, Mass., 1959—, pres., 1966-69; dir., YWCA, Bklyn., 1935-57, v.p., 1947-57, Cambridge, 1966—; chmn. Bklyn. women's coordinating com. United Hosp. Fund; mem. ladies com. New Eng. Med. Center Hosps., Boston Mus. Fine Arts. Mem. League Women Voters (asst. to husband tour middle east, 1959, Egypt, Lebanon, Iran, Pakistan, S. Korea, 1961-62, to aid orgn. new Med. Center Yonsei U., Seoul, Korea, for China Med. Bd. N.Y. Inc.), Cambridge Mus. Soc. Conglist. Clubs: Women's Travel, College (Boston). Home: 985 Memorial Dr Cambridge MA 02138

CURRAN, HELEN, educator; b. Chgo., Aug. 6, 1916; d. Samuel Audley and Edna (Sandiford) Curran; student Lewis Inst. Tech., 1935-37; B.S., Ill. Inst. Tech., 1946; M.E. in Guidance and Counseling, U. Ill., 1952; postgrad. Internat. Inst. Edn., 1957, U. Me., 1962, U. London, 1963, No. Ill. U., 1964; Advanced certificate in ednl. adminstrn., U. Ill., 1966; m. William Zorn, 1937 (div.); 1dau., April; m. 2d, J.W. Fenner, May 10, 1972. Teacher public schs., Maywood, Ill., 1946-47, tchr., Fox Lake, Ill., 1947-49, guidance dir., dean girls, 1949-57; dean girls, Peoria Heights, Ill., 1957-59, dir. guidance, 1959-63, administrv. asst., dir. curriculum, McHenry (Ill.) Pub. Schs., 1963-66, asst. supt., 1966-71; asst. supt. instrn. Tech. Information Center, Charleston, S.C., 1972—. Instr., The Citadel, Charleston, summer 1973. Bd. dirs. Orphans of the Storm. Mem. Ill. Assn. Sch. Adminstrs., N.E.A., Ill. Edn. Assn., Am. Assn. Sch. Personal Adminstrs., Nat. Assn. Su ervision and Curriculum, Am. Legion Aux., Delta Kappa Gamma. Office: 64 Society St Charleston SC 29401

CURRAN, JUDITH STRANG, pub. relations ofcl.; b. Burlington, Wash., Sept. 17, 1942; d. Allan Gene and Roberta (Graham) Strang; student U. Vt., 1960-61; B.A. in Polit. Sci., U. Wash., 1964, postgrad., 1966-67; m. John William Curran, Dec. 11, 1971. Pub. information dir. Intermediate Sch. Dist. 110, Seattle, 1965—. Mem. Nat. Sch. Pub. Relations Assn. (past pres. Wash. chpt., N.W. v.p., dir.), Wash. Press Women, U. Wash. Alumnae Assn., Pi Beta Phi. Presbyn. Clubs: Seattle Tennis, Wash. Athletic. Home: 1861 McGilura Blvd E Seattle WA 98112 Office: 100 Crockett St Seattle WA 98112

CURRAN, KATHRYN, pub. relations exec.; b. N.Y.C., Oct. 7, 1939; d. George A. and Dorothy A. (Stillwell) Nickeon; B.A., N.Y. U., 1961; postgrad. Russian Inst. Fordham U.; m. William H. Curran, Oct. 1, 1962. Account exec., pub. relations B.B.D.O., 1969-71; v.p. pub. relations Wisser & Sanchez, Inc., N.Y.C., 1971—; cons. in field. Mem. Am. Women in Radio and TV. Republican. Club: Publicity (N.Y.C.). Office: 223 E 48th St New York City NY 10017

CURRAN, LOUISE CARRICO, mag. editor, publisher; b. Round Hill, Va., Dec. 13, 1925; d. Guy Frank and Myrtle Anne (Howell) Carrico; grad. high sch.; m. Mr. Curran, Dec. 30, 1946 (div.); children—Daniel, Sharon, Patricia, Constance. Columnist McLean (Va.) Providence Jour., 1962; editor, publisher The Art Scene, McLean, 1962—. Mem. McLean Bus. & Profl. Assn. (past sec., also dir.) Author: (with others) McLean Remembers, 1968. Home and Office: 1724 Rupert St McLean VA 22101

CURRAN, MARY LYNN COGAN (MRS. EUGENE GREGORY CURRAN), coll. adminstr.; b. Chgo., May 20, 1937; d. Edward Joseph and Evelyn Elizabeth (Amos) Cogan; B.A., St. Xavier Coll., 1960; m. Eugene Gregory Curran, Oct. 29, 1960; children—Scott, Stephen, Mary Lynn. Job. placement dir. St. Xavier Coll., Chgo., 1971—. Pres., Kolmar P.T.A., 1970-71. Mem. League Women Voters. Elk. Clubs: Lawn Aqua, Racquet (Oak Lawn, Ill.). Home: 10420 S Kildare St Oak Lawn IL 60453 Office: 103rd and Central Park Av Oak Lawn IL 60453

CURRAN, VA LENA, lawyer; b. Walla Walla, Wash., Aug. 25, 1933; d. Peter and Rose (Gallo) Scarpelli; student Holy Names Coll., Spokane, Wash., 1951-53; J.D., Gonzaga U., Spokane, 1959; m. J. Donald Curran, Aug. 26, 1961; children—Kevin, Kelly, Kerry. Admitted to Wash. bar, 1959; practiced in Spokane, 1959-61; atty. Support Enforcement Services, Dept. Social and Health Services, State of Wash., 1961—. Mem. Wash., Spokane County bar assns. Roman Catholic. Home: 4808 S Hogan St Spokane WA 99203 Office: 1801 N Monroe St Spokane WA 99205

CURRIE, CATHERINE LOUISE MOLEX (MRS. WILLIE CURRIE), univ. dean; b. Jackson, Miss., Dec. 23, 1932; d. Nelson and Lula (Hughes) Molex; B.S. (Univ. grantee), Jackson State Coll., 1959, M.S., 1970, postgrad., 1970—; m. Willie Currie, Jan. 10, 1959 (div. 1966); 1 son, Willie. Tchr. Bowman Elementary Sch., Vicksburg, Miss., 1959-63; high sch. counselor Rosa A. Temple Sch., Vicksburg, 1963-71; jr. high sch. counselor East Vicksburg Jr. High Sch., 1971-72; resident counselor Wilberforce (O.) U., 1972-73, acting dean of women, 1973, dean of women, 1973—. Worker Civil Def., Vicksburg, also Jackson, 1952-59. Named Outstanding Educator in Am., 1974-75. Mem. Vicksburg Tchrs. Assn. (pres. 1968-69), Jackson State Coll. Alumni Assn. (pres. 1967-68), N.A.A.C.P., League Women Voters, N.E.A., Am. Personnel Guidance Assn., Am. Coll. Personnel Assn., Nat. Assn. Women Deans, Adminstrs. and Counselors. Democrat. Baptist. Home: PO Box 28 Wilberforce OH 45384 Office: Dean of Women Office Wilberforce U Wilberforce OH 45384

CURRIE, JOANNE BREE, computer systems analyst; b. Chgo., Oct. 18, 1930; d. Leopold John and Margaret (Milbert) Bree; B.A., DePaul U., 1954; postgrad. San Diego State Coll., 1957-61, Pepperdine Coll. Law, 1969-70; m. George Van Currie, Jan. 12, 1968. Engring. aide Convair, San Diego, 1955-57; asso. engr. Ryan Aero., San Diego, 1957-60, Solar Aircraft, San Diego, 1960-61; digital programmer Aeronutronic, Newport Beach, Cal., 1961-64; computing engr. N.Am. Aviation Co., Downey, Cal., 1964-65; computer system analyst Astrodata, Inc., Anaheim, Cal., 1965-70, Hughes Aircraft Co., Fullerton, Cal., 1971-72, Planning Research Corp., Los Angeles, 1972—. Mem. Am. Inst. Aeros and Astronautics, Am. Astron. Soc., Simulation Councils Inc., Assn. for Computing Machinery (past industry rep., sec.), Aircraft Owners and Pilots Assn., Ninety-Nines. Home: 9936 Sage Circle Fountain Valley CA 92708

CURRIE, VIOLANTE EARLSCORT, physician; b. Chgo., Jan. 10, 1939; d. Clarence Clifton and Violante Earlscort (Robertson) Currie; M.D., U. Ill., 1967. Intern, R.I. Hosp., Providence, 1967-68, resident internal medicine, 1968-70; fellow in med. oncology Meml. Hosp. for Cancer and Allied Diseases, N.Y.C., 1970-71; research fellow Sloan Kettering Inst. Cancer Research, 1970-71; teaching fellow dept. medicine Cornell U. Coll. Medicine, 1970-71; Am. Cancer Soc. fellow, 1970-71; Nat. Cancer Inst. fellow in med. oncology Thomas Jefferson Coll. Medicine, Phila., 1971-72, attending physician dept. medicine, div. med. oncology, 1972-73; attending physician dept. medicine, div. med. oncology Meml. Hosp. for Cancer and Allied Diseases, N.Y.C., 1973—; research asso. Sloan Kettering Inst., N.Y.C., 1973—; instr. dept. medicine Cornell U. Coll. Medicine. Active Big Sister Assn. R.I. Mem. Am. Med. Women's Assn. Methodist. Home: 6049 S Champlain Av Chicago IL 60637

CURRIE, WINIFRED, educator; b. Pavilion, N.Y., Apr. 2, 1918; d. Samuel James and Agnes (Cogle) Currie; student Zion Bible Inst., 1937-39; B.A., Gordon Coll., 1945; postgrad. Gordon Divinity Sch., 1945-46, Ecole Coloniale, Brussels, Belgium, 1953; Ed.M., Boston U., 1959, Ed.D., 1963. Ordained to ministry Assembly of God, 1946; minister Akron (N.Y.) Full Gospel Tabernacle, 1939-43; asst. minister Maplewood Bapt. Ch., 1943-46; missionary educator Oriental Province, Belgian Congo, 1947-60; tchr. remedial reading, Westerly, R.I., 1960-61; instr., lectr. Boston U., 1961-63; asst. prof. edn. Gordon Coll., Wenham, Mass., 1962-63, asso. prof., 1963-69, prof. edn., 1969—, dir. reading center, 1963—. Cons. Title I remedial reading program Gloucester (Mass.) pub. schs., 1966-68; lectr. missions Congo chs. N.J., N.Y., 1952, 58; vis. asst. prof. Cal. State Coll., Hayward, summer 1969. Named Alumna of Year, 1963, Tchr. of Year, 1973 (both Gordon Coll.). Mem. Internat., New Eng., North Shore (adviser 1968—), reading assns., Mental Health Assn. (edn. com. 1967—), Assn. Children with Learning Disabilities (adviser, panelist chpt. 1968-69), Orton Soc., Cape Ann Sci., Lit. and Hist. Assn., Gen. Council Assemblies of God, Am. Assn. Higher Edn., Essex County Green Belt Assn., Internat. Platform Assn., Phi Alpha Chi, Pi Lambda Theta. Author: Creative Classroom Communications. Home: 98 Holly St Gloucester MA 01930 Office: Grapevine Rd Wenham MA 01984

CURRY, DONNA JAYNE, singer, educator; b. Los Angeles, Jan. 26, 1939; d. Escar Clio and Louise Evelyn (Williams) Curry; B.A., Whittier Coll., 1958; student lute and voice, Schola Cantorum Basiliensis, Basel, Switzerland, 1970, 73-74. Biochemist research technician U. Cal. at Los Angeles, 1959-61; pvt. instr. guitar and singing, 1960—; dir. Donna Curry's Music Sch., Los Angeles and Santa Monica, 1965-71; pvt. instr. lute, voice and guitar, 1965—; extension instr. lute U. Cal. at Los Angeles, 1969-70, Mt. St. Mary's Coll., 1970—, Stanford, summer 1973; instr. lute and ensemble music Lute Soc. summer sch., Cheltenham Eng., 1967-73; dir. summer sch. in lute Hidden Valley Music Seminars, Carmel Valley, Cal., 1973—; touring concert artist, U.S. and Europe, 1970—; owner Donna Curry's Music, supplies, 1968—; founder, dir. ann. summer sch. in lute, 1973; rec. of Renaissance lute songs. Mem. Lute Soc. Am. (sec., mem. bd. 1969-75, newsletter editor 1969-75), Lute Soc. Eng., Galpin Soc., Am. Musicol. Soc., Viola da Gamba Soc. Am., Am. Recorder Soc., Coll. Music Soc. Address: PO Box 194 Topanza CA 90290

CURRY, ELEANOR NEEL (MRS. THOMAS HARVEY CURRY), economist; b. Newberry, S.C., Oct. 3, 1921; d. William Edward and Mildred Vurton (Abrams) Neel; student St. Petersburg (Fla.) Jr. Coll., 1939-41; B.S., Fla. State Coll. for Women, 1944; postgrad. Antioch Coll., 1945; M.A., Ohio U., 1960; postgrad. Columbia, 1964-67; m. Thomas Harvey Curry, June 6, 1945; children—John, Emily, Neel. Microanalyst Tenn. Eastman Corp., Kingsport, 1945-46; instr. chemistry Antioch Coll., Yellow Springs, O., 1949-50; instr. econs. Ohio U., 1960-61, U. Me., Orono, 1961-67; economist regional econs. div., U.S. Dept. Commerce, Washington, 1969—. Mem. Am. Econ. Assn. Office: 1401 K St NW Washington DC 20230

CURRY, FLORENCE GRACE BURGES (MRS. CHARLES ERNEST CURRY), social worker; b. Jacksonville, Tex., Feb. 4, 1920; d. Austin Earle and Maggie (Grimes) Burges; B.A. (La Verne Noyes scholar), So. Methodist U., 1942; postgrad. U. Okla., 1945, U. So. Cal., 1946-47; M.S.W. (Women's Council Dallas County scholar), Our Lady of Lake Coll., 1965; m. Charles Ernest Curry, Sept. 25, 1948; children—Flora Ann (Mrs. Donald R. Sperry), Charles Austin, Linda Nell. Field worker, child welfare worker, sr. child welfare worker Tex. Dept. Pub. Welfare, 1943-48; family counselor Dallas Services for Blind Children, 1963-66; case supr. Dallas County Dept. Pub. Welfare, 1966-68; clin. social worker Dallas VA Hosp., 1968—. Recipient award in sociology Chi Omega, 1940; Mem. Nat. Assn. Social Workers, Acad. Certified Social Workers, Nat. Conf. on Social Welfare, Tex. United Community Services, Tex. Soc. for Clin. Social Work. Methodist (mem. council ministries). Home: 2308 Greenhill St Mesquite TX 75149 Office: 4500 S Lancaster Rd Dallas TX 75216

CURRY, LAURA JUNE, educator; b. Cin., Jan. 13, 1928; d. Willard Lyle and Laura Mabel (Hauck) Curry; B.S. in Edn., U. Ala., 1950; M.S. in Edn., U. Va., 1962; postgrad. U. Miami, 1966—. Tchr. English Cleburne County High Sch., Heflin, Ala., 1950-52; tchr. elementary sch. Graymont Sch., Birmingham, Ala., 1952-57, Sherwood Forest Sch., Norfolk, Va., 1957-61; tchr. reading Norfolk pub. schs., 1961-66, coordinator reading instrn. throughout system, 1968—. Instr. extension div. U. Va., 1963-66, 68—. Mem. Internat., Va. State (chmn. gen. conf. 1974, pres. 1974—) reading assns., Va. Assn. Children with Learning Disabilities (rec. sec. 1972-73, certificate 1973), N.E.A., Edn. Assn. Norfolk, Nat. Soc. Study Edn., Alpha Lambda Delta, Alpha Delta Kappa, Sigma Delta Pi, Kappa Delta Pi. Methodist (adminstrv. bd. 1970-73, commn. edn. 1970—, tchr. 1970—). Home: 8105 Deerfield Dr Norfolk VA 23518

CURRY, SISTER MARTHA MULROY, educator; b. Chgo., June 30, 1926; d. Harry Joseph and Franc Adele (Mulroy) Curry; B.A., Barat Coll., 1948; M.A., U. Chgo., 1950; Ph.D., Loyola U., Chgo., 1972. Joined Sisters of the Soc. of Sacred Heart, 1952; tchr., Lindblom High Sch., Chgo., 1950-51, Acad. Sacred Heart, Lake Forest, Ill., 1955-60, Acad. Sacred Heart, Cin., 1960-61, Omaha, 1961-65; lectr. English Duchesne Coll., Omaha, 1965-67; asst. prof. English, Barat Coll., Lake Forest, 1969—, acad. adviser, 1969—, coordinator transfer advisement, 1972—, dir. program of study at Oxford (Eng.) U., 1971. Mem. Modern Lang. Assn. (del. assembly 1971—). Author: The Writer's Book by Sherwood Anderson: A Critical Edition, 1975. Home: 700 Westleigh Rd Lake Forest IL 60045

CURRY, MARY EARLE LOWRY (MRS. PEDEN GENE CURRY), poet; b. Seneca, S.C., May 13, 1917; d. Ullin Sidney and Mary Sloan (Earle) Lowry; student Furman U., 1944-45; m. Peden Gene Curry, Dec. 25, 1941; children—Eugene Lowry, Mary Earle. Mem. Aux. Rotary, Charleston, S.C., 1972-74. Mem. Internat. Platform Assn., Centro Studie Scambi Internat. Roma, United Meth. Women. Methodist. Club: Meth. Ministers Wives (pres. 1973-74). Author: Looking Up, 1949; Looking Within, 1961; Hymn, 1973. Contbr. poems to lit. jours. and periodicals. Address: 118 Sharon Dr Walterboro SC 29488

CURTIN, PHYLLIS, soprano; b. Clarksburg, W.Va.; d. E. Vernon and Betty R. (Robinson) Smith; student Monticello Coll., 1939-41; B.A., Wellesley Coll., 1943; m. Eugene Cook, May 6, 1956; 1 dau., Claudia Madeleine. Recital debut Town Hall, N.Y.C., 1950, 53, 57; opera debut N.Y.C. Opera in U.S. premiere of The Trial, 1953; recitals throughout U.S. and fgn. countries; soprano soloist leading symphony orchs.; performer, tchr. Aspen Mus. Festival, 1953-57; appeared as Cressida in Troilus and Cressida in N.Y. premiere, 1955; title role in Susannah world premiere, Tallahassee, 1955; title role in Medea, U.S. premiere, Brandeis U., 1955; world premiere opera Wuthering Heights, 1958; leading soprano Vienna Staatsoper, 1960, 61; debut Met. Opera, 1961, leading soprano, 1961—; debut La Scala as Fiordiligi in Cosi Fan Tutte, 1962; world premiere The Passion of Jonathan Wade N.Y.C. Opera, 1963, Flower and Hawk: Testament of A Queen (Carlisle Floyd), Washington, 1972. U.S. premiere War Requiem Berkshire Music Festival, Tanglewood, Mass., 1963, Intermezzo, N.Y.C., 1964, Shostakovitch Symphony No. 14, Phila. Orch., 1971. Named Woman of Year for debut of year A.P. Home: 110 Riverside Dr New York City NY 10024 Office: care Columbia Artists 165 W 57th St New York City NY 10019

CURTIN, WYLMA R(OSE), educator; b. Williston, N.D., Dec. 6, 1914; d. William Stephen and Rose H. (Maguire) Kellar; A.B., Trinity Coll., Washington, 1936; A.M., Cath. U. Am., 1937, Ph.D., 1939; m. James Reddington Curtin, Jan. 23, 1946. Asso. prof. ednl. psychology Grad. Sch. Boston Coll., 1939-49, Cath. U. Am., 1949-54; prof. Loyola U. Grad. Sch., New Orleans, 1954-55; research statistician Dept. Commerce, 1955-57; prof. ednl. psychology Cath. U. Am. Grad. Sch., 1957—. Mem. Am. Psychol. Assn., Am. Cath. Psychol. Assn., Nat. Soc. Study Edn., Pi Gamma Mu. Author: Basic Statistics Programmed for the IBM 1620 Computer, 1965; Statistical Data Processing, 1972. Home: 9600 Culver St Kensington MD 20795 Office: Cath Univ Am Washington DC 20017

CURTIS, ALICE READY PARTLOW (MRS. HAL L. CURTIS), pub. relations exec.; b. Keystone, W.Va.; d. Ira Judson and Andrea B. (Martin) Partlow; A.B., Marshall Coll., 1928; postgrad. King's Coll., U. London (Eng.), 1932, Columbia U., 1933; m. Hal L. Curtis, Apr. 15, 1939 (dec.). Writer, Jam Handy Orgn., Detroit, 1941-43; newspaper editor Ft. Wayne Army Post, Ind., 1943-44; asst. pub. relations dir. Mich. Blue Cross, Detroit, 1944-50; pub. relations dir. YWCA Met. Detroit, 1950-66; pub. relations officer Merrill-Palmer Inst., Detroit, 1966-70; owner Alice Curtis Pub. Relations, Grosse Pointe, Mich., 1970—; pub. relations dir. Cottage Hosp., Grosse Pointe, 1972—. Recipient citation, journalism dept. Mich. State U., 1950; award Women's Advt. Club Detroit, 1950. Mem. Mich. Hosp. Pub. Relations Assn. (bd. mem. 1971), Pub. Relations Soc. Am. (mem. bd. 1966-68), Mich. Humane Soc., Founders Soc., Am. Soc. Hosp. Pub. Relations Dirs., Detroit Inst. Arts, Theta Sigma Phi. Democrat. Episcopalian. Clubs: Detroit Press. Author: Is Your Publicity Showing, 1949. Home: 16826 Cranford Lane Grosse Pointe MI 48230 Office: 159 Kercheval Av Grosse Pointe Farms MI 48236

CURTIS, CHARLOTTE MURRAY, editor; b. Chgo.; d. George Morris and Lucile (Atcherson) Curtis; B.A. in Am. History, Vassar Coll., 1950. Reporter, soc. editor Columbus (O.) Citizen, 1950-61; reporter N.Y. Times, 1961—, family/style editor, 1965-73, asso. editor, 1974—, editor Op-Ed page, 1974—. Free-lance writer, 1950—;

tchr. narrative and short story writing, Columbus YWCA, 1952-54; radio commentator, radio sta. WMNI, Columbus, 1959-60, WQXR, N.Y.C., 1970-71. Founder, pres. Young Assos. Columbus Symphony Orch.; chmn. edn. Columbus Jr. League, 1958-60; mem. N.Y. Jr. League 1964—; mem. Manhattan adv. bd. N.Y. Urban League. Recipient various awards for reporting, writing N.Y. Newspaper Women's Club, Ohio Newspaper Women's Assn.; Ohio Gov.'s award for journalism, 1973. Mem. Am. Newspaper Women's Club. Author: First Lady, 1963. Contbr. to The Soviet Union: The Fifty Years, 1967. Home: 40 E 10th St New York City NY 10003 Office: 229 W 43d St New York City NY 10036

CURTIS, CHAUNCIE CAROLINE (MRS. HOWARD CROSBY CURTIS), club woman; b. Laurel Hill, Tenn., Aug. 14, 1895; d. Thomas Jefferson and Mattie (McDonald) Smith; R.N., Peabody Coll.; m. Howard Crosby Curtis, Oct. 14, 1912; children—Howard Jefferson, Caroline Lark. Fellow Inst. Am. Genealogy; mem. English-Speaking Union, Dames Ct. Honor, Daus. Am. Colonists, D.A.R., U.D.C., Philippine-Am. Assn. Episcopalian. Clubs: Capitol Speakers, Welcome to Washington (chmn. internat. luncheon div. Washington), Country. Home: 4600 Connecticut Av NW Washington DC 20008 also 140 E 63d St New York City NY 10021

CURTIS, EDITH ROELKER, author; b. East Greenwich, R.I., July 29, 1893; d. William Greene and Eleanor (Jenckes) Roelker; student Miss Porter's Sch., 1909-12; spl. student Radcliffe Coll.; m. Charles Pelham Curtis, Jr., July 17, 1914; children—Sarah Cary (Mrs. Lewis Iselin, Jr.), Anita Deidaemia (Mrs. E. Curtis McClellan), Charles Pelham, William Roelker (dec.), Richard Cary (dec.). Occasional speaker on methods of research and biog. technique. Mem. Nat. League Am. Pen Women (past pres. Boston br., state pres. 1962-64), Authors Guild, M.B.L.S. Author: Anne Hutchinson, A Biography, 1930; Lady Sarah Lennox, An Irrepressible Stuart, 1946; Love's Random Dart, 1960; A Season in Utopia, the Story of Brook Farm, 1961 (1st award League of Am. Pen Women 1962); Mexican Romance, 1969 (2d prize biennial contest Nat. League Am. Pen Women 1970). Contbr. numerous articles to nat. mags. Papers preserved in archives Sophia Smith Coll. Library, Northampton, Mass. Home: Two Apple Trees Box 71 Dublin NH 03444

CURTIS, FRANCES JO (MRS. HENRY C. CURTIS), real estate broker-developer; b. Winnepeg, Man., Can., Oct. 17, 1923; d. William and Anna (Strelecki) Curnell; brought to U.S., 1925, naturalized, 1951; student U. Mich., 1941-42, U. Detroit, 1952-54; m. Henry C. Curtis, Oct. 18, 1952; children—Carol (Mrs. Bill Lowery), Dennis Curtis, Bradley. Founder, prin. Troy (Mich.) Realty, 1954—; pres. Champion Realty & Assos.; founder, pub. Tri-City Messenger, Troy, 1956-61. Sec. of incorporation City Troy, 1955; founding mem. Indsl. Com. Troy, 1957-62, Library Com., 1959-65, Sewer Com., 1958-62, Civic Center Com., 1960-65 (all Troy); mem. Crittenton Hosp. Com., Rochester, Mich., 1958-62. Mem. Troy C. of C. (founder 1959). Former editor Mich. Bus. and Profl. Women's Mag. Contbr. poetry jours. Home: 336 Greenwood St PO Box 475 Birmingham MI 48012 Office: 123 Big Beaver Rd Troy MI 48084

CURTIS, GENEVIEVE MAY (MRS. OCE CURTIS), clubwoman, civic worker; b. Lac qui Parle, Minn.; d. Angel and Celestia (Wilkinson) Barton; student Northwestern Conservatory, Mpls., U. Minn.; grad. Newspaper Inst. Am., 1966; m. Oce Curtis, Sept. 25, 1911 (dec. Sept. 1963). Parliamentary law cons., 1925-72; moderator radio program on prohibition, 1931-33; radio promotion cons. Hoskins Assos., Chgo., 1942-44; writer, moderator radio program on alcohol problem, 1949-50; columnist Women in Action for suburban papers, 1970-73. Vol., Asso. Charities, United Fund, 1922-71; head women's div. Salvation Army Financial Campaign, 1926-30; pres. Internat. Relations Club, 1926-46, Mpls. Housewives League, 1942-46, Soc. Citizenship, 1961-72, Law Observance League, 1961-72; sec. Voters Information Bur., 1928-31; radio, press chmn. United Temperance Movement Minn., 1949-50; chmn. Susan B. Anthony Meml. Fund, 1949-56; mem. Mpls. Council Americanization, 1952—, UN Com., 1961—, Minnegasco Consumer Bd., 1969-70; issued proclamation Susan B. Anthony Day, Feb. 15, 1974. Founder, pres. Minn. Democratic Club, 1921-23; treas. Hennepin County (Minn.) Dem. Com., 1920-22; del. Dem. Nat. Conv., 1922, 28; exec. sec. Woodrow Wilson Club Mpls., 1922—; chmn. 5th dist. Women's Congl. Com., 1923-24; sec. Minn. Central Dem. Com., 1926-28; Minn. radio chmn. women's div. Dem. Nat. Com., Washington, 1936-46, Roosevelt campaign, 1936, 44; hon. sec. Minn. Dem. Conv., 1944; sec. Roosevelt Ladies Dem. Club, 1944-46; corr. sec., radio-TV, press chmn. Minn. Dem. Farmer Labor Club, 1945—; precinct chmn. 6th ward Dem. Com., 1966-69; del. 7th ward Dem. Farmer Labor Conv., 1971. Mem. exec. bd. Minn. Allied Drys, 1925-28, Mpls. Com. for World Peace, 1926-31. Recipient essay award Gen. Fedn. Women's Clubs, 1952, award for article and slogan on pollution Fifth Dist., 1965, various others. Mem. Minn. State Sunshine Soc. (pres. Golden Glow Circle 1918-25), Lewis Parliamentary Law Assn. (pres. 1961-72), Pathfinder Club (pres. 1945-46), Council of Civic Clubs, Minn. Fedn. Women's Clubs (state, dist. chmn. Law Observance Div. 1926-31, chmn. internat. relations dept. 1926-34, publicity chmn. 1965-72, pres. Founders and Pioneers 1952-57, sec.-treas. 1959-72), Epsilon Sigma Omicron. Baptist. Home: 501 W Franklin St Apt 103 Minneapolis MN 55403

CURTIS, KATHRYN CHARITY, mental retardation vol.; b. Portland, Ore., Nov. 19, 1940; d. John Henry and Dorothy Marguerite (Hansen) Epperson; B.A. in Psychology, Portland State Coll., 1963; M.A. in Edn./Guidance, Mich. State U., 1967; m. Alan Merit Curtis, Aug. 14, 1965; children—Karen Elaine (dec.), Jenifer Ann, Emily Kathryn Jean. Activity worker, housemother Parry Center Emotionally Disturbed Children, Portland, 1963-64; grad. residence hall adviser Mich. State U., 1964-65; social worker Henderson (Ky.) Area Mental Health Center, 1965-66; adminstrv. asst. Evansville (Ind.) Mental Retardation Regional Adv. Com., 1968; bookkeeper Mt. Vernon (Ind.) Pharmacy, 1966—; author feature articles in field. Instigator, mem. Posey County Assn. Retarded Children, 1968—, treas., 1975; mem. Ind. Assn. Retarded Children, 1968—; mem. Ind. Mental Retardation Residential Services Planning Project, 1969-71; local membership chmn. Nat. Assn. Retarded Children, 1970-75; adv. council Ind. div. Mental Retardation and Other Devel. Disabilities, 1971—; vice chmn. patient renumeration bd. Ind. Dept. Mental Health, 1972-75; mem. Gov. Ind. Task Force Employment Handicapped, 1974—; dir. Girl Scout Day Camp, Mt. Vernon, 1967. Mem. Posey County Young Republican Club, Ind. Young Rep. Fedn. Mem. Am. Personnel and Guidance Assn., Am. Coll. Personnel Assn., Nat. Assn. Women Deans, Adminstrs. and Counselors, Epsilon Sigma Alpha (chpt. pres. 1969). Mem. United Ch. Christ (primary supt. Sunday sch. supt. 1967-68, pres. Dorcas Soc. 1975, sec. ch. bd. dirs. 1975—). Address: 805 Walnut St Mount Vernon IN 47620

CURTIS, MARCIA, univ. dean; b. Quincy, Mass., Aug. 8, 1931; d. Arthur Bicknell and Ethel Beatrice (Fraser) Curtis; A.B. in Biology, Colby Coll., 1954; M.Nursing, Yale, 1957; Ed.D., Boston U., 1969. Staff nurse surg. ward Grace-New Haven Hosp., 1957; instr. fundamentals of nursing Boston U. Sch. Nursing, 1959-61, instr. gen. nurse program, 1963-65; staff nurse Carney Hosp., Dorchester, Mass., 1961-62, Univ. Hosp., Boston, 1965; instr. Quincy City Hosp. Sch. Nursing, 1966; Human Relations Center teaching fellow in ednl. founds. Boston U. Sch. Edn., 1966-67; asso. dean Med. U. S.C. Sch. Nursing, Charleston, 1968-69, dean Coll., prof. nursing, 1969—. Cons. Quincy Hosp. Sch. Nursing, 1966, Jersey City Med. Center, 1967, S.C. Nurses Assn., 1969-71, S.C. Regional Med. Program, 1972; ednl. cons. Morris Coll., Sumter, S.C., 1973-74; participant numerous workshops; mem. adv. council for comprehensive health planning S.C. Bd. Health; mem. Charleston Area Comprehensive Health Planning Com., Statewide Master Planning Com. on Nursing Edn., State Task Force on Health Resources; mem. adminstrv. adv. group sub com. for cancer S.C. Regional Med. Program.; asso. Boston U. Human Relations Center. Served to lt. Nurse Corps, USNR, 1957-59. Mem. Am., S.C. (joint commn. on practice, speakers bur., council on edn.) nurses assns., Nat. League Nursing, Am. Assn. Colls. Nursing, Am. Pub. Health Assn., Am. Assn. Higher Edn., Am. Assn. U. Profs., Am. Acad. Polit. and Social Scis., Center for Study Democratic Instns., Soc. for Psychol. Study Social Issues, Nat. Wildlife Assn., Audubon Soc., Pi Lambda Theta. Home: 18 Charlestowne Ct Charleston SC 29401

CURTIS, MARTHA ANN CLAY (MRS. C.D. CURTIS), pub. relations exec.; b. Okemah, Okla., Dec. 30, 1943; d. Curtis Lee and Charlene (Crook) Clay; B.A., Wayland Coll., 1966; M.A., Ind. U., 1967; m. C.D. Curtis, Dec. 23, 1963; 1 dau., Kristin Mozelle. Profl. writer U. Okla., 1964-65; grad. asst. journalism dept. Ind. U., Bloomington, 1966-67; higher edn. reporter Norman (Okla.) Transcript, 1967-68; news coordinator, editor, chief media information asst., office media information U. Okla., Norman, 1968-71; writer, editor Ozark Nat. Forest, U.S. Forest Service, Russellville, Ark., 1972-73; dir. pub. relations Garland County Community Coll., Hot Springs, 1973—. Pub. relations cons., newsletter editor Oklahomans for Indian Opportunity, 1970-71; free-lance writer and pub. relations cons., 1971-72. Chmn. pub. relations task force Gov.'s Commn. on Status of Women, 1972—. Named Ark.'s Outstanding Young Women, 1972; recipient nat. and regional awards for news and feature stories Am. Coll. Pub. Relations Assn. Mem. Pub. Relations Soc. Am., Am. Assn. U. Women (state chmn. media study topic 1973—), Women in Communications, Sigma Tau Delta. Home: 102 St Francis Dr Hot Springs AR 71901 Office: First Federal Bldg Hot Springs AR 71901

CURTIS, MARY ALZOA, librarian; b. Trempealeau, Wis., May 25, 1914; d. Archie Robert and Kate Mae (Gibson) Curtis; B.A. in Gen. Lit., U. Wash., 1937, B.A. in Librarianship, 1938. Librarian, Puyallup (Wash.) Pub. Library, 1938-40, VA Hosp., Am. Lake, Tacoma, Wash., 1940—. Recipient Superior Accomplishment award VA, 1958. Mem. A.L.A., Med. Library Assn., Fed. Librarians Assn., Pacific N.W., Wash. library assns., Snohomish County Mus. Assn. (founder mem.). Presbyterian. Editor: History and Records of the Kidder Family, 1955. Home: 6412 Wildaire Rd SW Tacoma WA 98499 Office: VA Hosp American Lake Tacoma WA 98493

CURTIS, NANNIE BEATRICE PETERSON (MRS. WILLIAM DUBOIS CURTIS), psychologist; b. Jackson, Miss., June 5, 1916; d. Aaron and Josie Bell (Porter) Peterson; A.B., Tougaloo Coll., 1938; M.A., Fisk U., 1940; postgrad. Cath. U., 1964-65, D.C. Tchrs. Coll., summer 1955, 56-57, 66-67, 70-71, Am. U., summer 1963; m. William DuBois Curtis, Aug. 4, 1943; children—Donald Joseph, Linda Ruth (Mrs. Karleton Blaire Skipper, dec.). Girls group worker, co-dir. Bethlehem Community Center, Nashville, 1940-42; service club hostess War Dept., Camp Tyson, Tenn., 1942-43; exec. dir. S.W. Community House, D.C., 1947-48; attendance officer D.C. Pub. Schs., Washington, 1949-65, sch. psychologist 1965—, clin. psychologist Sharpe Health Sch. Learning Disabilities Center, summers 1969, 70. Tchr. cons., psychologist Program for Learning Studies, Children's Hosp., Washington, summer 1973; cons. psychologist Family Task Force, Council of Chs., Washington, 1972-73. Bd. dirs. Little Flower Meml. Trust Fund, Washington, 1972—; bd. dirs. Ionia R. Whipper Home, Inc., Washington, 1968-71, sec., 1970-71. Recipient Award for Ednl. Excellence, Council for Exceptional Children, 1970, faculty award Payne Elementary Sch., 1972. Licensed psychologist, D.C. Mem. D.C. (pres. 1972—), Nat. (charter, alternate delegate 1971-73, co-chmn. nat. membership com. 1974—), assns. sch. psychologists, D.C. Psychol. Assn., Council for Exceptional Children (sec. Fed. 524 1971-72), Fisk U. Alumni Assn., Ch. Women United, Attendance Officers Assn. (pres. 1952-54), Omega Wives, Alpha Kappa Alpha. Democrat. Baptist (chmn. audit com. 1953-63). Home: 1933 Shepherd St NE Washington DC 20018 Office: 3242A Pennsylvania Av SE Washington DC 20020

CURTISS, JULIANNE LADUE, librarian; b. New Haven, Dec. 16, 1926; d. Frank Russell and Eleanor Ward (King) Curtiss; A.A., Colby Coll. of N.H., 1946; B.S., So. Conn. State Coll., 1956. Editorial asst. Yale U. Sch. Alcohol Studies, New Haven, 1948-53; asst. librarian, cataloger West Haven (Conn.) Pub. Library, 1956-63; asso. librarian, head cataloger New Coll., Sarasota, Fla., 1963-66; media specialist Sarasota County Bd. Pub. Instruction, 1966—. Mem. Sarasota County Tchrs. Assn., Fla. Edn. Assn., Asolo Opera Guild Chorus, Am. Mensa Ltd., D.A.R. Republican. Conglist. Home: 2155 Wood St Apt B9 Sarasota FL 33577 Office: 1901 Webber St Sarasota FL 33579

CURTISS, URSULA REILLY (MRS. JOHN CURTISS, JR.), author; b. Yonkers, N.Y., Apr. 8, 1923; d. Paul and Helen (Kieran) Reilly; student pub. schs.; m. John Curtiss, Jr., May 24, 1947; children—Katherine, John, Paul, Kieran, Mary. Fashion copywriter Gimbels, N.Y.C., 1944, Macy's, 1944-45, Bates Fabrics, Inc., 1945-47. Recipient Zia award, 1963. Mem. Mystery Writers Am., Authors Guild, Crime Writers' Assn. Author: Voice Out of Darkness, 1948, The Second Sickle, 1950, The Noonday Devil, 1951, The Iron Cobweb, 1953, The Deadly Climate, 1954, The Stairway, 1955, Widow's Web, 1956, The Face of the Tiger, 1957, So Dies the Dreamer, 1960, Hours to Kill, 1961, The Forbidden Garden, 1962, The Wasp, 1963, Out of the Dark, 1964, Danger: Hospital Zone, 1966, Don't Open The Door!, 1968; Letter of Intent, 1971. Home: 8408 Rio Grande Blvd Albuquerque NM 87114

CURTIS-VERNA, MARY, opera and concert singer, soprano; b. Salem, Mass.; d. Charles Leverett and Josephine (Nason) Curtis; student Abbott Acad., Andover, Mass.; A.B., Hollins Coll.; m. Ettore Verna, Aug. 3, 1954 (dec. 1962). Debut in Otello, Milano, Italy, 1949; appeared La Scala, Milano, San Carlo, Naples, Opera Rome, Massino of Palermo, Opera Lyon, France, Gaity of Dublin, others; Am. debut Phila. Civic Opera Co., 1951, also San Francisco Opera Assn., Monterey, Mexico and Lima, Peru; N.Y. debut City Center Opera Co., 1954; debut Met. Opera, N.Y.C., 1957, appearing soprano roles, 1957—; concerts N.Am., Europe; prof. U. Wash., Seattle, 1969—. Mem. Sigma Alpha Iota (hon.). Home: 308 E 79th St New York City NY 10021 Office: care Ludwig Lustig Mgmt 111 W 57th St New York City NY 10019

CURZON, ELIZABETH JEANNETTE GORE, pub. accountant; b. Alton, Ill., Oct. 15, 1911; d. Forrest Bird and Annella (Denby) Gore; A.B., U. Ill., 1932, M.S., 1934, postgrad., 1950-54; m. George J. Curzon, Jan. 6, 1930 (div. Apr. 1946); 1 dau., Marjorie A. Grad. asst. U. Ill., 1932-34, library research asst. in animal nutrition, 1934-39; office mgr., accountant George J. Curzon, Champaign, Ill., 1940-46; accountant Curzon Parks Bookkeeping Service, Champaign, 1946-55; partner, Peer, Hunt & Curzon, C.P.A.'s, Champaign, 1955—; sec. Clark St. Bldg. Corp., Champaign, 1958-72. Treas., Champaign County Community Chest, 1954-55, pres., 1955-56, dir., 1950-56; sec. Com. on Elm Tree Disease, 1954-55; pres. Laymon Convalescent Home, Inc., 1950-63; treas. Champaign County Estate Planning Council, 1969-70, sec., 1970-71, vice chmn., 1971-72, chmn., 1972-73. Bd. dirs. Urban League Champaign County, 1960-66, McKinley YMCA, 1960-66, 68—. Mem. Ill. Soc. C.P.A.'s (chpt. chmn. 1961-62, chpt. treas. 1960-61, profl. devel. com. 1967-68, state taxation com. 1969-71, com. ann. tax conf. 1972—), Am. Inst. C.P.A.'s, Am. Forestry Assn., Nat. Audubon Soc., Am. Athletic Assn., Phi Beta Kappa, Phi Upsilon Omicron, Omicron Nu, Alpha Delta Pi. Baptist. Home: 617 W University St Champaign IL 61820 Office: 203 W Clark St Champaign IL 61820

CUSACK, BEVERLY MAY DOWNING (MRS. JAMES E. CUSACK), univ. dean; b. Voluntown, Conn., May 11, 1923; d. Charles Augustus and Veda Aurilla (Selway) Downing; B.S., R.I. State Coll., 1944; M.A., Columbia, 1948, Ed.D., 1962; m. James E. Cusack, Jan. 15, 1966. High sch. tchr. Spaulding High Sch., Barre, Vt., 1944, Griswold High Sch., Jewett City, Conn., 1944-47; instr. home econs. U. R.I., Kingston, 1948-50, asst. prof. home econs., 1950-56, asso. prof., 1956-62, prof., 1962—, dean home econs., 1962—. Mem. edn. and program com. Women's Council United Fund, 1968—. Mem. Assn. for Higher Edn., Nat. Council Adminstrs. Home Econs., Am. Home Econs. Assn., Phi Kappa Phi, Omicron Nu, Kappa Delta Pi, Delta Zeta, Phi Upsilon Omicron (nat. hom. mem.). Democrat. Roman Catholic. Home: 127 Oakwood Dr Peace Dale RI 02879 Office: Coll Home Econs U RI Kingston RI 02881

CUSACK, MARY JO, lawyer; b. Canton, O., Mar. 3, 1935; d. Edward Thomas and Mary (O'Meara) Cusack; A.B, Marquette U., 1957; J.D., Ohio State U., 1959. Admitted to Ohio bar, 1959, U.S. Supreme Ct. bar, 1962; mem. firm Cotruvo and Cusack, Columbus, O.; atty. for Indsl. Commn. Ohio, Columbus, 1960-61, Office Tax Commr., Columbus, 1961-65. Pres. E.T. Cusack, Inc., Canton, 1963-64, dir., 1960-64; spl. counsel to Atty. Gen. William J. Brown. Mem. Ohio (workmen's compensation com., sec.), Columbus (profl. ethics com., speakers bur.) bar assns., Women Lawyers Club Columbus (pres.), Ohio Acad. Trial Lawyers (workmen's compensation com.), Franklin County Trial Lawyers (trustee), Nat. Assn. Women Lawyers, Ohio Assn. Attys. Gen. (sec.), Am. Arbitration Assn. (nat. panel arbitrators), Kappa Beta Pi (internat. pres.), Theta Phi Alpha, Thomas More Soc. Club: Columbus Toastmistress (past pres.). Home: 3039 Stadium Dr Columbus OH 43202 Office: 50 W Broad St Columbus OH 43215

CUSHING, PATRICIA NASH (MRS. RAYMOND EMERY CUSHING), microbiologist; b. Bangor, Me., Sept. 19, 1930; d. Austin Walton and Carolyn Frances (Bartlett) Nash; B.A., U. Me., 1953; m. Raymond Emery Cushing, Aug. 10, 1952. Hematologist Providence Hosp., Washington, 1953-55; microbiologist St. Elizabeth's Hosp., Washington, 1955-63, U.S. FDA, Washington, 1963-67, U.S. Army Material Command, Washington, 1967-70; microbiologist, consumer safety officer FDA, Washington, 1970—. Recipient award Civil Service, 1970. Mem. Am. Soc. Microbiology, Soc. Indsl. Microbiology, Am. Soc. Clin. Pathology, Phi Beta Kappa. Editor: Microbiological Degradation of Materials - Research and Development, 1970. Home: 910 Lindsay Rd Oxon Hill MD 20021 Office: 5600 Fishers Lane Rockville, MD 20852

CUSHMAN, HELEN NEWBAUER (MRS. ELLIOTT L. CUSHMAN), civic worker; b. San Francisco, 1917; d. George Stephen and Selma Beatrice (Levi) Newbauer; grad. Dominican Convent, San Rafael, Cal.; m. Elliott L. Cushman, Jan. 27, 1940; 2 sons. Chmn., Heart Sunday, chmn. Salvation Army Bd., also co-founder Women's Aux.; past chmn. Jr. Charity League. Bd. dirs. Women's Assn. for Salk Inst., San Diego Heart Assn., San Diego Girls Club, Com. of 100, Soc. for Prevention Blindness, Fine Arts Philatelists, San Diego Hist. Soc., San Diego Library Commn. Mem. Brandeis U. (life), Womens Aux. Donald N. Sharp Hosp. (life), Starlight Opera Assn. (life), San Diego Symphony, Globe Guilders, Globe 400, Fine Arts Soc., U. San Diego Womens Aux., Braille Transcribers Guild. Home: 1001 Genter St La Jolla CA 92037 Office: 770 B St San Diego CA 92101

CUSHMAN, JUDITH, pub. relations exec.; b. N.Y.C., Nov. 22, 1942; d. David S. Cushman and Hannah (Einbinder) Cushman Kilroy; B.A., Barnard Coll., 1964; grad. student Boston U. Sch. Pub. Communications, 1964-66; m. Robert L. Quick, Aug. 1, 1971. Employee relations Mobil Oil Co., 1966-67; asst. editor Air Travel mag., 1967-68; pub. relations Lufthansa German Airlines, 1969-70; mem. pub. relations bd. Chgo. Service Exec., 1970-71; v.p. Marshall Cons., N.Y.C., 1971—; cons. newsletter Pub. Relations News, cons. Newtime, Inc. Mem. Pub. Relations Soc. Am. (chmn. com. youth N.Y.C. chpt. 1973—), Publicity Club N.Y.C. (dir., membership chairperson), N.Y. Bus. Press Editors, Am. Women in Radio and TV (resource person on career devel.). Office: 360 E 65th St New York City NY 10021

CUSHMAN, VIVIAN ELIZABETH, univ. dean; b. Seattle, Dec. 5, 1907; d. Andrew Alexander and Gustava Caroline (Johnson) Nelson; B.A., Walla Walla Coll., 1931; M.A., Pacific Union Coll., 1956; m. Elwyn Perry Smith, June 10, 1931; children— Mitzi (Mrs. Jerry Lee Wiggle), William Orville Thomas Smith; m. 2d, Lester Harvey Cushman, Dec. 12, 1967. Tchr. elementary schs., 1925-27, 31-44; secondary tchr. Lynwood (Cal.) Acad., 1944-62; dean women Loma Linda U., Riverside, Cal., 1962—. Mem. Nat. Assn. Women Deans, Adminstrs. and Counselors. Co-author: Witnesses for Jesus, 1952. Address: Loma Linda U Riverside CA 92505

CUSSLER, MARGARET THEKLA, sociologist, educator; b. Jersey City; d. Henry Charles and Margaret Allan (King) Cussler; M.A., Radcliffe Coll., 1941; Ph.D. (Whitney fellow), Radcliffe-Harvard, 1943. Asst. tech. adviser FSA, 1940-41, information specialist, 1941; asso. editor Eastman Kodak, 1944-45; partner Social Documentary Films, 1945-63; faculty U. Md., College Park, 1947—, asso. prof. sociology, 1962—. Chief evaluation Internat. Motion Picture Services, USIA, 1951-53; pres. Margaret Cussler Assos., College Park, 1963—; vis. asso. prof. Cornell U., Ithaca, N.Y., 1965-66, vis. lectr., 1967; editor Food Habit series McGrath Pub. Co. Grantee Nat. Fedn. Bus. and Profl. Womens Research Found., 1956, 57, 69, A.L.A., 1956, Gen. Research Bd., U. Md., 1960, Nat. Inst. Mental Health, 1961, USPHS, 1964, 65. Fellow Inter-U. Council Tng. Inst. in Social Gerontology, 1959. Mem. Am. Sociol. Assn., Sociologists for Women in Soc., Eastern (nominating com. 1966-67), So., D.C. (pres. 1966-67) sociol. socs., Internat. Inst. Sociology, D.A.R., Womens Equity Action League, Phi Beta Kappa, Alpha Kappa Delta. Author: Not By a Long Shot, 1951; Twixt the Cup and the Lip, Psychological and Socio-Cultural Factors Affecting Food Habits, 1952, rev. edit., 1972; The Woman Executive, 1958; Dentists, Patients and Auxiliaries, 1968. Contbr. to Sociology of Underdevelopment, 1970; also articles to publs. Home: 4704 Harvard Rd College Park MD 20740

CUSTER, CAROLE ANN ZIKE (MRS. ROGER ELZEA CUSTER), newscaster; b. Perry, Ia., Aug. 5, 1949; d. Victor Milton and Rosalene Annette (Corbus) Zike; B.S., Ia. State U., 1971; m.

Roger Elzea Custer, June 7, 1970. News reporter, newscaster KGLO-Radio-TV, Mason City, 1971—. Guest lectr. Ia. State U., 1972-73. Vol. worker Mason City United Fund, 1972-73; mem. MacNider Art Mus., Mason City. Mem. Am. Women in Radio and TV, Ia. News Broadcasters Assn., Women in Communication, League Women Voters, Ia. State U. Alumni Assn. (dir. N. Ia. 1973—), Cerro Gordo County Panhellenic Assn. (loan adviser 1973-74), Alpha Chi Omega. Republican. Methodist. Clubs: Mason City Women's, Mason City Junior Women's. Home: 60 Country Circle Mason City IA 50401 Office: 112 N Pennsylvania Av Mason City IA 50401

CUSTER, MARY MAXINE, food co. ofcl.; b. Konawa, Okla., Mar. 20, 1923; d. Earl Everett and Mary Lois (Alexander) Miller; student Hills Bus. Coll., Oklahoma City; m. Emerson De Leath Custer, Apr. 11, 1942; 1 son, Vaughn De Leath. With Star-Kist Foods, Inc., Terminal Island, Cal., 1952—, traffic mgr., 1967—. Office: 582 Tuna St Terminal Island CA 90731

CUTHBERT, EVELYN ALICE, orgn. exec.; b. Winslow, Ill., July 6, 1918; d. Benjamin Lewis and Edith Louella (Lied) Zipse; B. Music with honors, U. Wis.-Madison, 1941; postgrad. Columbia; M.A., Tex. Women's Coll., 1969; m. Kenneth Neil Cuthbert, June 1, 1941; children—Carolyn (Mrs. Jerry E. Tobias), Frederick Neil. Asst. music edn. dept. U. Wis.-Madison, 1936-41; dir. instrumental music Merrill (Wis.) pub. schs., also dir. Merrill City Band, 1942-43; tchr. Santa Rosa (Cal.) pub. schs., 1943-44; asst. to provost Columbia, 1945-47; tchr. flute and piano, 1941-58; prin. flutist Bloomington-Normal (Ill.) Symphony Orch.; instr. flute East Carolina U. Music Clinic, summers 1951-58; nat. chmn. music in schs. and colls. Nat. Fedn. Music Clubs, 1968—, nat. chmn. edn. dept., 1973—. Mem. Dallas Civic Ballet Soc., Dallas Civic Opera, Dallas Symphony Orch. League (v.p. 1971), U. Women North Tex. State U. (pres. 1966), Denton Benefit League, Tex. Fedn. Music Clubs (state student adviser 1968—), Denton Fine Arts League, P.E.O., Sigma Alpha Iota. Methodist. Mem. Order Eastern Star. Address: 1919 Mistywood Lane Denton TX 76201

CUTHBERT, VIRGINIA (MRS. PHILIP C. ELLIOTT), artist; b. West Newton, Pa., Aug. 27, 1908; d. Richard Bruce and Frances Irene (Cartwright) Cuthbert; B.F.A., Syracuse U., 1930; student Academie de la Grande Chaumiere, Academie Colarossi, Paris, 1930, Chelsea Poly. Inst., London, 1931; studied with George Luks, N.Y.C., 1932; student U. Pitts., 1933-34, Carnegie Inst. Tech., 1934-35; m. Philip Clarkson Elliott, June 8, 1935. Instr. painting Albright Art Sch., Buffalo, 1943-54, U. Buffalo, 1954—, State U. N.Y. at Buffalo, 1962-64; one-man shows Carnegie Inst., 1938, Butler Art Inst., 1938, Syracuse Mus. Fine Arts, 1939, Syracuse U., 1945, Contemporary Arts, N.Y. City, 1945, 1949, 1953, Rehn Gallery, N.Y.C., 1958, 66, N.Y. State Coll. Tchrs. Albany, 1959, Chautauqua (N.Y.) Art Assn., 1959, Albright-Knox Art Gallery, 1963, and many others throughout the U.S.; exhibitions include: Met. Mus. Art, Whitney Mus. Am. Art, Art Inst. Chgo., Pa. Acad. Fine Arts, Carnegie Internats., Ft. Worth Art Center, Butler Inst. Am. Art, Albright-Knox Art Gallery, retrospective exhbn. Burchfield Center, State U. Coll. N.Y. at Buffalo, 1971, others; represented in collections Albright-Knox Art Gallery, Hundred Friends of Pitts. Art, Syracuse Univ., Princeton Museum of Art, Phila. Mus. Art, pvt. collections. Awarded Augusta Hazard fellowship Syracuse U., 1930; prize Asso. Artists of Pitts. Ann., 1934, 1936-40. Butler Art Inst., 1940. Western N.Y. Exhbn., 1944, 46, 50, 52, 55, 58, 65, 66, Pepsi-Cola Ann., 1946-47, Nat. Inst. Arts and Letters, 1954; Chatauqua Prize, 1955; prize Sisti Exhbn., Buffalo, 1956, 57, Western N.Y. Exhbn. Albright Art Gallery, 1958. Cover of Fortune, 1956. Mem. Urban League Buffalo, Kappa Alpha Theta. Methodist. Home: 147 Bryant St Buffalo NY 14222

CUTHBERTSON, MRS. GEORGE RAYMOND, club woman; b. Liberty, Mo., Apr. 2, 1911; d. Edgar and Mary Jane (Anderson) Archer; student William Jewell Coll., 1929-31; m. George Raymond Cuthbertson, Sept. 3, 1931. Dist. capt., Mothers' March of Dimes, 1959-60; mem. Bergen County Panhellenic Council 1957-60. Mem. Mo. Hist. Soc., D.A.R., Huguenot Soc. S.C., S.C. Hist. Soc., Alpha Delta Pi. Baptist. Clubs: Saturday, Ladies Assn. of Oak Meadow Country. Home: 1106 Sycamore Dr Rolla MO 65401

CUTLER, CLAIRE MINTZ (MRS. MAX CUTLER), lawyer; b. N.Y.C., Jan. 19, 1919; d. Nathaniel I. and Jessie Beatrice (Guttentag) Mintz; B.A., Hunter Coll., 1939; J.D. cum laude, Bklyn. Law Sch., 1942; m. Max Cutler, Oct. 8, 1944; children—William Lewis, John Martin. Admitted to N.Y. bar, 1942; asso. firm William Weisman, N.Y.C., 1942-43, Davis & Gilbert, N.Y.C., 1943-44; partner Cutler & Cutler, N.Y.C., 1944—. Bd. dirs. Citizens Sch. League, Stamford, Conn., 1956-66; exec. bd. North Stamford Democratic Club, 1956-66; exec. bds. P.T.A. assns., N.Y.C., Stamford. Mem. Bklyn. Bar Assn., Hunter Coll., Bklyn. Law Sch. alumni assns., Bklyn. Law Rev. Assn., Pi Alpha Tau. Jewish religion (dir. young married guild 1944-56). Asst. editor Bklyn. Law Rev., 1941-42. Home: 1175 York Av New York City NY 10021 Office: 150 E 58th St New York City NY 10022

CUTLER, DOROTHY RUTH, librarian; b. Hood River, Ore., Nov. 5, 1917; d. Asa B. and Ruth (Hyndman) Cutler; B.A., Willamette U., 1940; B.A. in Librarianship, U. Wash., 1941; M.S., U. Ill., 1951. Library asst. Salem (Ore.) Pub. Library, 1941-43; librarian U.S. Army, Hawaii and Guam, 1944-46; reference librarian Contra Costa County Library, Martinez, Cal., 1946-50, U. Ill., Urbana, 1950-51; cons. Wash. State Library, Olympia, 1951-65, dir. library devel., 1965—. Mem. A.L.A., Pacific N.W., Wash. library assns., Am. Assn. U. Women. Home: 1618 Evergreen Park Lane Olympia WA 98502 Office: Washington State Library Olympia WA 98504

CUTLER, FELICE REINITZ (MRS. RICHARD B. CUTLER), lawyer; b. N.Y.C., Apr. 15, 1937; d. Nathan and Claire (Sacks) Reinitz; B.A. magna cum laude, Bklyn. Coll., 1957; LL.B., Yale, 1960; m. Richard B. Cutler, June 7, 1959; children—Stephen Marc, Laura Jane. Admitted to Cal. bar, 1961; dep. atty. gen. Office Atty. Gen. State of Cal., 1960-66; mem. firm Cutler & Cutler, P.C., Los Angeles, 1966—. Mem. vol. adv. council Atty. Gen. Cal., 1970—. Mem., treas. Los Angeles County Democratic Central Com., 1964-66; mem. Cal. State Dem. Central Com., 1964-66. Mem. Am., Los Angeles County bar assns., State Bar Cal., Phi Beta Kappa. Club: So. Cal. Yale (dir. 1971—, treas. 1972—). Author: (with James W. Moore) Moore's Federal Practice, Vol. 1, 1964. Home: 157 Delfern Dr Los Angeles CA 90024 Office: 700 S Flower St Los Angeles CA 90017

CUTLER, SUZANNE, economist; b. Hartford, Conn., Aug. 21, 1939; d. Samuel and Rivy (Rosenberg) Cutler; B.S., Boston U., 1961; M.B.A., U. Pa., 1963; Ph.D., N.Y.U., 1970. Economist Fed. Reserve Bank of N.Y., N.Y.C., 1970-73, spl. asst. to sr. v.p., 1973—. Dir. N.Y.U. Bus. Forum, 1971-72, treas., 1973-74, v.p., 1974—. Recipient Harold Stonier fellowship in banking Am. Bankers Assn., 1965-66. Mem. Am. Econ. Assn., Beta Gamma Sigma, Omicron Delta Epsilon. Office: 33 Liberty St New York City NY 10045

CUTNAW, MARY-FRANCES, educator, horse breeder; b. Dickinson, N.D., June 15; d. Delbert A. and Edith (Pritchard) Cutnaw; B.S., U. Wis. at Madison, 1953, M.S., 1957, Ph.D. candidate, 1959-60, 67-68. Tchr. Displaced Persons Vocational Sch., Stevens Point, Wis., 1951-52, Pulaski High Sch., Milw., 1953-55; teaching asst. dept. speech U. Wis.-Madison, 1956-57, spl. asst. Sch. Edn., summer 1957; instr. speech and English, U. Wis.-Stout, Menomonie, 1957-58, dean of women, 1958-59, asst. prof. speech, 1959-64, asso. prof., 1964—; hon. scholar, teaching asst. dept. speech U. Wis.-Madison, 1959-60, hon. scholar dept. speech, 1967-68. Organizer, past adviser Young Democratic Orgn., U. Wis.-Stout. Mem. Internat. Platform Assn., Am. Assn. U. Women, Am. Assn. U. Profs., U. Wis. Alumni Assn., Am. Quarter Horse Assn., Nat. Soc. Prevention Cruelty to Animals, Nat. Anti-Vivisection Soc., Nat., Wis. edn. assns., Center for Study Democratic Instns., Nat. Assn. Ednl. Broadcasters, Speech Communications Assn., Central States Speech Assn., Am. Civil Liberties Union, Common Cause, Nat. Orgn. Women, Phi Beta, Sigma Tau Delta, Pi Lambda Theta, Gamma Phi Beta. Roman Catholic. Contbr. articles to profl. jours. Research in speech proficiency and teaching success, curricular speech for spl. occupational groups, speech as guidance tool. Founder, Edith and Kent P. Cutnaw Scholarship, U. Wis.-Stevens Point. Home: 240 Elm Av W Golf View Acres Menomonie WI 54751 also Red Cedar Farm Box 282 Menomonie WI 54751

CUTTNER, JANET, physician; b. N.Y.C., Aug. 23, 1931; d. William Robert and Ida (Greenspan) Cuttner; B.A., N.Y.U., 1953; M.D., Woman's Med. Coll. Pa., 1957. Intern, King's County Hosp., Bklyn., 1957-58; resident internal medicine King's County Hosp., Bklyn., 1958-61; trainee hematology Mt. Sinai Hosp., N.Y.C., 1961-63, research asst. hematology, 1963-65, asso. attending hematology, 1972—; asso. prof. medicine Mt. Sinai Sch. Medicine, 1967—. Mem. A.M.A., Am. Soc. Hematology, N.Y. State, N.Y. County med. socs., Am. Soc. Clin. Oncology, N.Y. Acad. Scis., Am. Assn. U. Profs. Home: 73 Carlton Rd Monsey NY 10952 Office: 1176 Fifth Av New York City NY 10029

CYR, HELEN WHEELER (MRS. GORDON C. CYR), librarian; b. Oakland, Cal., Nov. 18, 1926; d. Edward Lawrence and Lilly (Zimmer) Wheeler; A.B., U. Cal., Berkeley, 1947, tchr. certificate, 1948, B.L.S., 1954; m. Gordon C. Cyr, Aug. 11, 1951. With Oakland (Cal.) pub. schs., 1949-71, dir. libraries, 1963-65, dir. instructional media, 1965-71; head audiovisual dept. Enoch Pratt Free Library, Balt., 1971—. Mem. A.L.A., Md. Library Assn., Cal. Assn. Sch. Librarians (pres. 1971), Md. Ednl. Communications and Tech. Assn., Assn. for Ednl. Communications and Tech., Am. Film Inst. Author: Evaluation Report: The Sobrante Park Multi-Media Services Project, 1970. Contbr. articles to profl. jours. Home: 110 Glen Argyle Rd Baltimore MD 21212 Office: 400 Cathedral St Baltimore MD 21201

CYRIL, RUTH, engraver, designer, graphic artist; student Greenwich House Art Sch., Sch. Contemporary Art, Art Students League, Hoffmann Sch. Art, Atelier 17, N.Y. U., New Sch. for Social Research, Sorbonne U. Art and Archeology, also thoughout Europe. One-man shows, 1961—, including La Guilde de la Gravure, Paris, Smithsonian Instn., Corning Glass Mus., New State Dept. Bldg., Washington, Bibliotheque Nationale, Paris, Library of Congress, Met. Mus. Art, N.Y.C., Victoria and Albert Mus., London, U. Me., N.Y. Pub. Library, Print Club, Phila., Fogg Mus., Harvard U., Delgado Mus., New Orleans, Dallas Mus. Fine Art, Addison Gallery Art, Andover, Mass., Asso. Am. Artists, N.Y.C., Rochester Inst. Tech., McMurray Coll., Beloit Coll., U. S.C., Furman U., Baylor U., La Guilde de la Gravure, Switzerland, Conn. Coll., Pistoia, Italy, St. John's Art Gallery, Wilmington, N.C., State U. N.Y. at Buffalo, Alaska Internat. Art Mus., Anchorage, Alaska Hist. and Fine Arts Mus., Anchorage, numerous others; exhibited in numerous group shows in U.S., France, Eng., Italy, Switzerland, Scandanavia; represented in numerous collections of museums and galleries in U.S. and Europe, including Art Inst. Chgo., Carnegie Mellon Library and Inst. Instr. graphic art and painting Adelphi U., 1963-66. b. N.Y.C.; Recipient numerous awards. Fulbright fellow. Mem. Guilde de la Gravure. Address: 800 West End Av New York City NY 10025

CYRUS, ADA STRONG, dietitian; b. Huntsville, Ala.; d. Willie Lee and Jannie Lee (Jefferson) Strong; B.S., Mt. Mercy Coll. (now Carlow Coll.), 1962; postgrad. Pa. State U. Tchr. home econs. Allegheny County Detention Home, Pitts., 1961-62; food prodn. and service mgr. Mount Mercy Coll., Pitts., 1958-62; relief dietitian Children's Hosp., Pitts., 1963; prodn. dietitian Presbyn U. Hosp., Pitts., 1965; pvt. dietitian Pa. Hosp., Phila., 1965-67; home econs. product home economist Foodservice, Heinz U.S.A. Co., Pitts., 1967-73, community relations coordinator, 1973—. Tchr. sewing and cooking Ozanam, 1972—. Sec. econ. devel. com. Forever Action Together, 1968—; mem. youth motivation task force Plans For Progress, 1967—. Bd. dirs. Martin Luther King Home, Inc.; bd. dirs., chairwoman publicity-pub. relations com. East Area YWCA, Pitts. Mem. Am. Home Econs. Assn., Pitts. Home Economists in Bus. (chmn. nutritional com. 1969-70, chairwoman ways and means com. 1970-71, historian 1971-72), Pa. (sect. chairwoman 1972—), Pitts. (co-chmn. nominating com. 1969-70, mem. publicity com. 1971-72, chmn. community nutrition com. 1972-73) dietetic assns. Home: 7945 Madiera St Pittsburgh PA 15221 Office: PO Box 57 Pittsburgh PA 15230

CZERWINSKI, ANN ELIZABETH LANGLEY (MRS. EDMUND M. CZERWINSKI), educator; b. Omaha, Mar. 29, 1914; d. John W. and Ann (Cunningham) Langley; B.A. magna cum laude, Creighton U., 1935, B.S. magna cum laude, 1948, M.S., 1951; Ph.D., U. Neb., 1967; m. Edmund M. Czerwinski, Aug. 31, 1937; 1 dau., Agnes Ann (Mrs. Wm. J. Riedmann). Prin., Ashton (Neb.) High Sch., 1935-37; registered pharmacist, Omaha, 1948—; instr. biol. scis. Sch. Pharmacy, Creighton U., Omaha, 1948-54, asst. prof., 1954-58, asso. prof., 1958-67, prof. biol. scis., 1967—, also chmn. com. on scholarships and grants-in-aid, pres. Faculty Council, 1969-71, acting dean Sch. Pharmacy, 1971-72, dir. profl. studies, 1972-73, prof. pharmacology Sch. Medicine, 1970—, mem. pres.'s adv. com., mem. exec. com. Health chmn. Douglas County Parochial Schs., 1961-63; chmn. Regional Med. Drug Information Com., 1970-72; dir. Omaha Drug Abuse Edn. and Information Center, 1970—; mem. Gov.'s Commn. on Drugs, 1971-73; chmn. Commn. on Materials Validation, State of Neb.; mem. Mayor's Commn. on Drugs, 1971—, chmn. edn. com. Recipient Distinguished Service award Creighton U., 1972. Mem. Am., Neb., Omaha pharm. assns., A.A.A.S., Neb. Acad. Scis., Gamma Pi Epsilon, Phi Delta Gamma, Rho Chi. Democrat. Roman Catholic. Contbr. articles to profl. jours. Home: 4530 Harrison St Omaha NE 68117

CZUFIN, MARGARET JOSTEDT, advt. agy. exec.; b. St. Louis, Feb. 20, 1925; d. Theodore Anthony and Catherine Gertrude (Egan) Jostedt; B.A., Webster Coll., 1947; postgrad. St. Louis U., 1947-48, Washington U., St. Louis, 1948-49. Ednl. dir. KWK-TV, St. Louis, 1949-56; v.p. Gardner Advt., St. Louis, 1956-69; sr. writer William Esty Advt., N.Y.C., 1969-73; sr. writer Erwin Wasy Advt., Los Angeles, 1973; v.p. Fred Czufin Assos., West Redding, Conn., 1974—. Vol. March of Dimes, N.Y.C., 1969-73. Bd. dirs. Webster Coll. Recipient 1st pl. comml. category Cannes Film Festival, 1968; named Advt. Woman of Year, St. Louis, Outstanding Young Woman St. Louis. Mem. Women's Advt. Club St. Louis (pres. 1960-61), Am. Women in Radio and TV (pres. Midwest chpt. 1962-63), Webster Coll. Alumni Assn. (pres. 1950-52), Common Cause. Address: Lonetown Rd RFD 2 West Redding CT 06896

DABBS, MIRIAM ADAIR (MRS. CHESTER NORWOOD DABBS), artist, journalist; b. Rialto, Cal., May 6, 1908; d. Watts McIntosh and Betty (Pearson) Adair; B.A., Miss. State Coll. for Women, 1930; m. Chester Norwood Dabbs, Dec. 24, 1933; 1 son, Willis Norwood. English instr., Jones County Jr. Coll., Ellisville, Miss., 1933-34, also Am. history Northwest Jr. Coll., Senatobia, Miss., 1935-36; soc. editor Clarksdale (Miss.) Daily Register, 1942-47; feature writer, corr. Clarion-Ledger, Jackson, Miss., 1964—, Jackson Daily News, 1968—, Memphis Press-Scimitar, 1969—. Exhibited in one-man shows at Galeries Raymond Duncan, Paris, France, 1970-71, Originals Only Gallery, Memphis, 1971, Ligoa Duncan Gallery, N.Y.C., 1971, Christ Only Mus., Eureka, Springs, Ark., Robinson-Carpenter Library, Cleveland, Miss., 1971, others. Missionary Soc., Bapt. Ch., 1952-53; mem. Clarksdale Beautification Commn., chmn., 1952-54, 56-63, sec., 1955, 68. Recipient Beautification Merit award, Miss. C. of C. community program at Clarksdale, 1961; recipient Art award Prix de Paris competition, 1970. Mem. Nat. League Am. Pen Women (award; editor Pen Drifts, 1957), Ulster-Scot Hist. Soc. (Belfast, Ireland), D.A.R. Clubs: Clarksdale Woman's (past pres.), Town and Country Garden (Clarksdale). Author: Idyls of the Delta: Coahoma, 1948; The Passing Storm; Sepaled Horns; Sonnets From India, 1962. Contbr. articles on founding families of Miss. to tech. lit. Research in genealogy. Home: 321 Maple St Clarksdale MS 38614 Office: Clarion Ledger Jackson MS 39205

DABBS, PHYLLIS SELBY, educator; b. Akron, O., Dec. 5, 1923; d. Warren Fowke and Phyllis Barbara (Sabin) Selby; B.A. (scholar in speech), U. Akron, 1944; M.S. in Edn., U. So. Cal., 1952, Ph.D. in Speech, 1961; m. Lowell Parker Dabbs, Dec. 21, 1956; 1 dau., Ellen Chafee. Tchr.-librarian Hawthorne (Cal.) High Sch., 1952; asst. activities officer Los Angeles State Coll. Applied Arts and Scis., 1953-54; mem. faculty Bakersfield (Cal.) Coll., 1954—, prof. speech, 1965—, chmn. dept., 1967-68, 74—. Active local coms. favoring sch. tax and bond elections, coms to elect sch. bd. mems. Grantee Knight Meml. Edn. Fund, 1941-42. Mem. Am. Assn. U. Profs. (pres. Bakersfield Coll. 1966-68; So. Cal. Collegiate Forensic Assn. (v.p. 1960-61), Cal. Jr. Coll. Speech Assn. (pres. 1964-65), League Women Voters (dir. Bakersfield 1963), Speech Assn. Am., Western Speech Assn., Faculty Assn. Cal. Community Colls., Cal. Fedn. Tchrs., Mortarboard, Phi Rho Pi (v.p. 1956-57), Pi Kappa Delta. Episcopalian. Contbr. articles to profl. jours. Home: 5200 Ojai Dr Bakersfield CA 93306

DABNEY, ELOISE WALNE, business exec.; b. Vicksburg, Miss., Apr. 3, 1906; d. James Hunt and Annie Groves (Barber) Walne; grad. All Saints Coll.; student Brenan Coll., 1925-26, La. State U., 1926-27; m. Frederic Yeamons Dabney, Dec. 16, 1927 (dec.); children—Mary Moncure (Mrs. Hugh Nicholls), Freddie (Mrs. Louis Hataway, Jr.), David Hunt, Eloise (Mrs. Yves Lautier); m. 2d, Clayton Harrington (div.). Mgr. The Dabney Co., 1954—. Pres. Frederic Yeaman Dabney Family Found.; dir. Vicksburg Little Theatre; bd. Am. Cancer Soc.; adv. bd. Salvation Army, 1965—; bd. dirs., membership chmn. Vicksburg-Warren Humane Soc. Vice chmn. Women's Rep. Party. Mem. Va., Vicksburg hist. socs., M.M.S., Alpha Delta Pi. Episcopalian. Clubs: Vicksburg Country, Magnolia Garden. Home: 1714 Cherry St Vicksburg MS 39180

DACUS, MELDONA DELIA BUMGARDNER WATERS (MRS. HENRY JUNIOR DACUS), ednl. adminstr.; b. Casar, N.C., Aug. 22, 1912; d. Louis Holden and Delia (Johnson) Bumgardner; grad. Wingate Jr. Coll., 1930; A.B., U. S.C., 1932, M.Ed., 1948, postgrad., 1948-54; postgrad. Furman U., summer 1940, Winthrop Coll., 1935, Clemson U., 1937; m. Frank Cullen Waters, Aug. 22, 1932; 1 dau., Thelma Delia (Mrs. James Nelson Addison); m. 2d, Henry Junior Dacus, Dec. 28, 1972. Tchr. elementary sch., Saluda, S.C., 1932-33, adult schs., Columbia, S.C., 1933-34, area supr., 1934-41; county mgr. Crescent Hill Meml. Gardens, 1941-43; Richland County sch. attendance supr., Columbia, 1943-66; attendance supr., social worker Richland County Sch. Dist. 1, Columbia, 1966-72, state supr. sch. attendance, 1972—. Mem. S.C. gov's. com. White House Conf. on Children and Youth 1950; treas. S.C. Com. on Children and Youth, 1950-52; v.p. Columbia Hearing and Speech Center, 1954-58. Recipient certificate of award as registrar Selective Service from Pres. of U.S., 1948. Mem. Internat. Assn. Pupil Personnel Workers (dir. 1971—, nominating com.), N.E.A., S.C. Attendance Suprs. Assn. (exec. bd. 1948—, state pres. 1970-72), S.C. Adult Edn. Assn. (pres. 1937), S.C. Ednl. Assn. (council of dels. 1947-49), Richland County Edn. Assn. (pres. 1947), Internat. Platform Assn. (bd. dirs.). Baptist (chmn. nominating com. 1967-68, chmn. ch. personnel com. 1968—). Home: 4506 Sandy Ridge Rd Columbia SC 29206 Office: State Dept of Edn 107 Wallaa Bldg Columbia SC 29201

DADE, AUDREY JACKSON (MRS. DENSLOW MOWBRAY DADE), former editor; b. Albany, N.Y., Aug. 3, 1907; d. Holmes C. and Mary A. (Read) Jackson; A.B. magna cum laude, Smith Coll., 1929; m. Denslow Mowbray Dade, Feb. 5, 1955. Asst. to head promotion dept. L. Bamberger and Co., Newark, 1930-34; asst. pub. relations dept. Princeton U., 1934-42; editorial asst. Reader's Digest, Pleasantville, N.Y., 1942-45, asso. editor, 1945-66, sr. editor, 1966-69, ret. Presbyn. Club: Womans of White Plains (asso. editor club mag.). Home: 210 Martine Av White Plains NY 10601 also 129 Corporation Rd Dennis MA 02638

DADE, ESTHER SMITH (MRS. WILLIAM A. DADE), banker; b. McFall, Ala., Aug. 9, 1911; d. John Floyd and Willie Emma (Parker) Smith; student Fla. State Coll. for Women, 1930-31, Am. Inst. Banking, 1950-60; m. William A. Dade, June 1, 1934; children—Robert William, John Thomas, Mary Elaine (Mrs. Larry Rule). Sec., Fla. Pub. Service Co., Orlando, Fla., 1928-30, Seminole Hotel, Winter Park, Fla., 1930-36; with Broward Nat. Bank, Ft. Lauderdale, 1950—, now v.p. Named Woman of Yr., Broward County chpt. Am. Inst. Banking, 1965; Distinguished Bus. Women of Yr., 1967. Mem. Am. Bus. Women's Assn. Ft. Lauderdale (pres. 1964-66), Pilot Club Ft. Lauderdale (pres. 1966-67, 70-71), Greater Ft. Lauderdale C. of C. (chmn. women's div. 1966-68), Jr. League Am. Home: 1630 SE 12th Ct Fort Lauderdale FL 33316 Office: 25 S Andrews Av Fort Lauderdale FL 33301

DADE, MARY JUDITH (MRS. MERRELL ELLIMAN DADE), librarian; b. Hebron, O., July 14, 1918; d. Charles Sumner and Judith Mary (Balcom) Bates; A.B., Hiram Coll., 1942; B.S. in L.S., Western Res. U., 1946; m. Merrell Elliman Dade, June 18, 1942. With, Cleve. Pub. Library, 1943-49; librarian George Fox Coll., Newberg, Ore., 1951-56; asst. librarian Seattle Pacific Coll., 1956-59; asst. librarian Pacific Power & Light Co., Portland, Ore., 1960—. Mem. Spl. Libraries Assn. Home: 9906 NW Leahy Rd Portland OR 97229 Office: Public Service Bldg Portland OR 97204

DADIGAN, ELEANOR MARTHA TAVLAN (MRS. STEVE DADIGAN), violinist; b. Reedley, Cal., July 30, 1921; d. Peter and Katherine (Koumarion) Tavlan; A.A., Reedley Coll., 1941; B.S., U. So. Cal., 1943, postgrad., 1943-44; m. Steve Dadigan, July 5, 1948; 1 dau., Donelle. Tchr., Los Angeles City Schs., 1943-53; violinist So. Cal. Chamber Symphony Orch., 1943-46, So. Cal. Symphony Orch., 1945-47; pvt. tchr. violin, Beverly Hills, Cal., 1959—. Pres. Parents Assn. Le Lycee Francais de Los Angeles, 1970-73. Decorated chevalier Order Merit Culture and Philanthropy (France), Grand Prix Humanitaire de France. Mem. Ebell of Los Angeles (dir. 1963-65, mem. 75th anniversary com. 1969, asst. curator art, travel, book chamber and Cal. history), Sigma Alpha Iota (life). Episcopalian. Home: 723 N Beverly Dr Beverly Hills CA 90210

DAEN, PHYLLIS HELENE (MRS. JEROME DAEN), psychologist, educator; b. N.Y.C., Feb. 22, 1931; d. Herbert M. and Esther (Suckalitsky) Deutsch; B.S., Queens Coll., 1950; Ph.D., Adelphi U., 1960; m. Jerome Daen, Dec. 25, 1952; children—Jonathan, Matthew, Meris. Chief psychologist Easton Children's Home, Easton, Pa., 1961-66, Lincoln Consultation Center, Bethlehem, Pa., 1962-66, South County Mental Health Center, Springfield, Va., 1967-72; dir. tng. and research Woodburn Center, Annandale, Va., 1972—. Asso. clin. prof. psychiatry/pediatrics Georgetown U., Washington, 1971; clin. asso. Catholic U., Washington, 1972—. Mem. Am. Psychol. Assn., A.A.A.S. Home: 11446 Orchard Lane Reston VA 22090 Office: 3340 Woodburn Rd Annandale VA 22003

DAETWEILER, LAVETA ARBIE (MRS. WALTER HARRY DAETWEILER), educator; b. McCurtain, Okla., Feb. 29, 1920; d. Alvin Norton and Carrie (Neal) Adams; A.A., Taft Jr. Coll., 1939; certificate in early childhood edn. Fullerton Coll., 1968; m. Walter Harry Daetweiler, Sept. 11, 1939; 1 dau., Melanie (Mrs. Michael Clayton Boone). Operator Kern Mut. Telephone Co., Taft, Cal., 1939-42; sec. to wire chief, 1942-45; med. asst. Drs. Babcock and Harmon, El Monte, Cal., 1962-64; tchr. Pilgrim Pre-Sch., Brea, Cal., 1964-69, asst. dir., tchr., 1969—. Pres. Brea (Cal.) Jr. High Sch. P.T.A., 1960-62; chmn. spectacular div. Brea Golden Jubilee, 1967. Commr. recreation and parks City of Brea, 1967—, vice chmn. commn., 1973-74, chmn., 1974—. Named Brea Citizen of Year, Brea C. of C., 1967; Brea Woman of Year Orange Dist. Fedn. Womens Clubs, 1968, Woman of Year Brea Woman's Club, 1968. Mem. Cal., Orange County assns. for edn. young children, Brea Hist. Soc. (founder, pres. of bd. dirs. 1970-72, sec., treas. of bd. dirs. 1973—), Delta Theta Tau. Conglist. (dir. children's choir 1964-67) Womens. Home: 415 S Poplar St Brea CA 92621 Office: 300 E Imperial Brea CA 92621

DAGGETT, AVALON FLORENCE, film co. exec.; b. Jennings, La., Mar. 30, 1907; d. Ephraim Nickerson and Sarah Francina (Powers) Daggett; student U. Cal. at Los Angeles, 1924-26; B.S., U. So. Cal., 1928, M.S., 1929. Tchr., Unified Secondary Sch., Compton, Cal., 1929-36; mgr. Metcalf Constrn. Co., Los Angeles, 1941-45; owner Avalon Daggett Prodns., Los Angeles, 1950-60, Baton Rouge, 1960—. Recipient nat., internat. numerous awards. Mem. Bus. and Profl. Womens Club, Women in Communications, N.E.A., Cal. A-V Assn., Cal. A-V Edn. Dealers Assn. Presbyn. Clubs: Womens, Univ. Womens (Baton Rouge); Friday Morning (Los Angeles). Address: PO Box 14656 Baton Rouge LA 70808

DAGIRMANJIAN, ROSE, educator; b. Whitinsville, Mass., July 4, 1930; d. Roupen and Esther (Arakelian) Dagirmanjian; B.A., Clark U., 1952; M.S., U. Rochester, 1954, Ph.D., 1960. Riker Internat. fellow Inst. Animal Physiology, Babraham, Cambridge, Eng., 1960-62; asst. prof. pharmacology Ohio State U., Columbus, 1963-69; asso. prof. pharmacology U. Louisville, 1969—. Cons. toxicology USPHS, 1972—. Mem. Am. Soc. Pharmacology and Exptl. Therapeutics, Soc. Toxicology, Soc. Exptl. Biology and Medicine, Sigma Xi. Home: 1935 Gardiner Lane Louisville KY 40205

D'AGNESE, HELEN JEAN (MRS. JOHN J. D'AGNESE), artist; b. N.Y.C., July 6, 1922; d. Leonardo and Rose (Redavid) De Santis; student City U. N.Y., 1940-42, Oakland Art Inst., 1954-56; m. John J. D'Agnese, Oct. 29, 1942; children—John, Linda, Diane, Michele, Helen, Gina, Paul. One-man shows Maude Sullivan Gallery, El Paso, 1964, John Wanamaker Gallery, Phila., 1966, U. N.M., 1967, Karo Manducci Gallery, San Francisco, 1968, Tuskegee Inst. Carver Mus., 1968, Lord & Taylor Gallery, N.Y.C., 1969, Harmon Gallery, Naples, Fla., 1970, Fountainbleau, Miami, 1970, Reflections Gallery, Atlanta, 1972, Williams Gallery, Atlanta, 1973, others; exhibited in group shows Musseo des Artes, Juarez, Mexico, 1968, Benedictine Art Show, N.Y.C., 1967, Southeast Contemporary Art Show, Atlanta, 1968, Atlanta U., 1969; represented in permanent collections Gov.'s Mansion, Atlanta, DeKalb Library, Atlanta, Mario Spada Gallery, Juarez; series of liturgical paintings exhibited at various churches, also at Mus. Contemporary Art at the Vatican, Rome, Italy. Judge art show Mt. Loretto Acad., El Paso, 1967; art demonstration and lectr. Margaret Harris Sch., Atlanta, 1970. Mem. Atlanta Lawn Tennis Assn. Clubs: Tennis, Fencing (Atlanta). Address: 1683 Knob Hill Ct NE Atlanta GA 30329

DAHL, ARLENE, actress, columnist, fashion designer; b. Mpls., Aug. 11, 1928; d. Rudolph and Idelle (Swan) Dahl; student (1st, 2d, 3d prizes for fashion designs) U. Minn., Minn. Inst. Art, Minn. Coll. Music, Minn. Bus. Coll.; m. Rounsevelle W. Schaum, 1969; 1 son, Rounsevelle Andreas; children by previous marriage—Lorenzo Lamas, Carole Christine Holmes. Broadway appearances include Mr. Strauss Goes to Boston, 1945, Cyrano de Bergerac, 1953, Applause, 1972; 28 motion pictures include My Wild Irish Rose, 1947, Three Little Words, 1950, Sangaree, 1953, Woman's World, 1954, Journey to the Center of the Earth, 1959, Kisses for My President, 1963, The Landgrabbers, 1969; syndicated beauty columnist, 1950-71; designer sleepwear A. N. Saab & Co., 1952-57; v.p., pres. woman's world div. Kenyon & Eckhardt, Inc., 1967-72; beauty dir. Sears, Roebuck & Co., 1970—; pres. Arlene Dahl Enterprises, 1970—. Hon. life mem. Father Flanagan's Boys Town; bd. dirs. Hollywood Museum. Named Woman of Yr. in Communications, N.Y. Advt. Club, 1969. Mem. Acad. Motion Picture Arts and Scis., Authors League Am. Author: Always Ask a Man, 1965; 12 Beautyscopes, 1968; Secrets of Hair Care and Secrets of Skin Care, 1970, 2d edit., 1973. Address: 730 Fifth Av New York City NY 10022

DAHL, PAM MAY MARGARET JOHNSON (MRS. JOHN A. DAHL), educator; b. Kansas City, Mo., Apr. 20, 1928; d. Roy and Margaret Bonner (Mosely) Johnson; B.A., U. Cal. at Los Angeles, 1950; M.S., Cal. State U., 1968; postgrad. Claremont Grad. Sch., 1962-63; m. Richard D. Wright, Aug. 6, 1950 (dec. May 1963); children—R. Douglas, Kimberley; m. 2d, John A. Dahl, Sept. 8, 1964. Elementary tchr. Ontario (Cal.) Schs., 1950-52; substitute tchr. Ontario, Pomona, Claremont and Alhambra (Cal.) Schs., 1953-63; sch. psychologist Pomona Unified Sch. Dist., 1966—. Bd. examiner Behavioral Scis. Commn., State of Cal., 1972-73. Mem. Pomona Valley chpt. Nat. Assistance League, 1952—; mem. Hosp. Aux. of Pomona Valley, 1952-60. Mem. Nat. Assn. Sch. Psychologists (Cal. del. 1974—), Cal. Assn. Sch. Psychologists and Psychometrists (mem. research com. 1968-72), S.E. Counties Sch. Psychologists Assn. (mem. exec. bd. 1968—), Lazy Susans Aux., Chi Omega. Home: 509 E Baseline Rd Claremont CA 91711 Office: 800 S Garey Av Pomona CA 91769

DAHL, (ROSE) MARGARET MASER (MRS. PHILIP O. DAHL), realtor; b. Lincoln, Neb.; d. George and Matilda (Brungardt) Maser, Jr.; grad. dental hygiene U. Minn., 1944; student U. Cal. at Los Angeles, 1965-68; m. Philip O. Dahl, Apr. 12, 1946; children—Jean Anne, Mary Anne. Dental hygienist, Los Angeles, 1945-64; real estate broker Coldwell, Banker Realty Co., Los Angeles, 1964—. Bd. dirs. Coronet Debutante Ball, 1971. Mem. Am. Dental Hygienists Assn., Cal. Real Estate Assn., Nat. Charity League (modelette chmn. 1964-66), Women's Aux. Los Angeles Dental Soc., Alpha Kappa Gamma (nat. pres. 1953-55), Sigma Phi Alpha. Club: Brentwood Bel-Air Women's (charter). Home: 2192 Banyan Dr Los Angeles CA 90049 Office: 13030 San Vicente Blvd Los Angeles CA 90049

DAHLBERG, JANE S., polit. scientist, educator; b. N.Y.C., Feb. 7, 1923; d. Sidney and Aimee (Rothschild) Silsdorf; B.A., Hunter Coll., 1944; M.S., Syracuse U., 1945; Ph.D., N.Y. U., 1964; m. Charles Clay Dahlberg, June 28, 1959; children—John Garrett, James Richard, Charles S. Mem. staff, James Felt & Co., 1945-46; tchr. polit. sci. Coll. City N.Y., 1945-65; asst. dean, asst. prof. govt. U. Coll. N.Y. U., 1965-68; asso. dean Sarah Lawrence Coll., 1968-69, tchr. polit. sci., 1969-70; prof. Empire State Coll., N.Y.C., 1971—, dean, 1972—. Research asso. William Alanson White Inst. Psychoanalysis in Polit. Psychology. Chmn. Manhattan Ind. Com. for Adlai Stevenson, 1956. Mem. Am. Polit. Sci. Assn., Am. Soc. Pub. Adminstrn., Phi Beta Kappa. Home: 516 E 87th St New York City NY 10028

DAHLIN, JEAN ELIZABETH (MRS. RONALD ALLEN DAHLIN), civic worker; b. Warren, O., Jan. 18, 1934; d. Wayne Alvin and Ruth Elizabeth (Swick) Deringer; B.S., U. Wis., 1956; M.A., San Diego State U., 1963; m. Ronald Allen Dahlin, Aug. 22, 1959; children—Michael, Kimberlee, Katherine, Kirsten. Past mem. Housing Adv. and Appeals Bd., Housing Adv. Bd., Regional Com. on Housing; adv. bd. Human Resource Devel. Center; now mem. policy adv. com. Regional Planning Orgn., San Diego Planning Commn., 1974—. Bd. dirs. League of Women Voters, also legislative v.p. Home: 5918 Sagebrush Rd La Jolla CA 92037

DAHLMAN, BETTY JO DUEPPEN (MRS. JOHN HENRY DAHLMAN, JR.), med. technologist; b. Madison, Wis., Feb. 11, 1943; d. James William and Lettie (Fisher) Dueppen; student Mt. Mary Coll., Milw., 1961-62, U. Wis., summers 1962, 63; B.S., Edgewood Coll., 1965; m. John Henry Dahlman, Jr., Jan. 8, 1966; children—Kathleen Marie, Joel Scott, Kevin James. Med. technologist St. Michael Hosp., Milw., 1965-66, S.M. Feld Med. Clin., Milw., 1966-68, Milw. Med. Clinic, 1967-70, St. Michael Hosp., Milw., 1970-72, St. Alphonsus Hosp., Port Washington, Wis., 1972-73. Mem. Nat. Profl. Panhellenic Assn. (mem.-at-large exec. com. 1971-73), Milw. Area Profl. Panhellenic Assn. (sec.-treas. 1969-71, pres. 1973—), Edgewood Coll. Alumnae Assn. (class corr. 1969-71), Alpha Delta Theta (nat. parliamentarian 1963-64, nat. pres. 1965-66, nat. publ. editor 1966-70, ofcl. rep. to Milw. Area Profl. Panhellenic Assn. 1967-69, 71-73, to Nat. Profl. Panhellenic Assn. 1970-72, dir. central office 1970—). Home: W66 N376 Kennedy Av Cedarburg WI 53012

DAHM, LIDA INGE SWAFFORD (MRS. KARL HEINZ DAHM), anesthesiologist; b. Norfolk, Va., Aug. 18, 1937; d. Chester Arthur and Lida T. (Inge) Swafford; B.A., Tulane U., 1959, M.D., 1962; m. Karl Heinz Dahm, Dec. 21, 1968; children—Lida Elizabeth, Karl Arthur. Intern U. Pa. Hosp., Phila., 1962-63; resident Columbia U. Coll. Physicians and Surgeons, 1963-65, vis. fellow, 1965-66; vis. fellow Presbyn. Hosp. Med. Center, N.Y.C., 1965-66; staff anesthesiologist Children's Meml. Hosp., Chgo., asso. dept. anesthesiology Northwestern U., 1965-68; asst. prof. dept. anesthesiology and pediatrics Baylor Coll. Medicine, Tex. Med. Center, Houston, 1969—; asst. anesthesiologist Ben Taub Gen. Hosp., Houston, 1969—, Jefferson Davis Hosp., Houston, 1969—; staff physician, anesthesiologist Tex. Inst. Rehab. and Research, Houston, 1971—; cons. staff St. Joseph's Hosp., Bryan, Tex., 1972. Diplomate Am. Bd. Anesthesiologists. Fellow Am. (sec. sect. anesthesiology 1972—, Tex. acads. pediatrics, Am. Coll. Anesthesiology; mem. Am. Soc. Anesthesiologists, Brazos-Robertson County Med. Soc., Tex. Pediatric Soc., Tex. Soc. Anesthesiologists, Alpha Omega Alpha. Episcopalian. Contbr. articles to profl. jours. Home: 1403 Skrivanek Ct College Station TX 77840 Office: 1200 Moursund Blvd Houston TX 77025

DAHMEN, GENE DAVIDSON (MRS. LLOYD C. DAHMEN), lawyer; b. Bedford, Va., June 12, 1941; d. Jesse Thornhill and Maxwell Phillips (Dudley) D.; A.B. magna cum laude, Randolph-Macon Woman's Coll., 1963; M.A.T., Johns Hopkins, 1964; LL.B., U. Va., 1967. Tchr. Edward J. Broome Jr. High Sch., Rockville, Md., 1964; admitted to Mass. bar, 1967; atty. John Hancock Mut. Life Ins. Co., Boston, 1967-69; asso. firm Choate, Hall & Stewart, Boston, 1970—. Mem. Mass. Commn. Status of Women, 1970-72; vol. atty. Cambridge (Mass.) and Somerville (Mass.) Legal Services, Inc., 1968-71. Bd. dirs. The Third Nail, drug center, Mass. Council Crime and Correction, Prisoners Rights Project, Women Concerned with Criminal Justice. Mem. Boston, Am. bar assns., Nat. Orgn. Women, League Women Voters, Phi Beta Kappa. Methodist. Home: 29 Denny Rd Chestnut Hill MA 02167 Office: 28 State St Boston MA 02109

DAIBER, OLGA (MRS. BRUCE HOWARD), physician; b. Otepaa, Estonia, Aug. 25, 1927; d. Georg W. and Helene (Chmielevski) Daiber; cand. med., Eberhard-Karls-Universitat Medizinische Fakultat, Tubingen, Germany, 1950; postgrad. Albert-Ludwigs-Universitat Medizinische Fakultat, Freiburg, Baden, Germany, 1950-51; M.D., U. Cal. at San Francisco, 1954; m. Bruce Godfrey Howard, July 7, 1958; children—Gordon, Mark, Linda. Came to U.S., 1951, naturalized, 1957. Rotating intern Kings County Hosp., Bklyn., 1954-55; resident in internal medicine Cottage Hosp., Santa Barbara, Cal., 1955-56, Harbor Gen. Hosp., Torrance, Cal., 1956-58; physician in geriatric rehab. Long Beach Gen. Hosp., 1961-63; practice medicine specializing in internal medicine, Santa Maria, Cal., 1963—; chief staff Santa Maria Hosp., Santa Maria, 1971; physician Santa Maria Alcoholic Detoxification Center, 1973—. Bd. dirs. Santa Barbara County Heart Assn., 1967-73, chmn. Santa Maria com., 1971-73. Am. Assn. U. Women (pres. Santa Maria br. 1970-71, dist. chmn. Central Coast dist. Cal. div. 1973-74). Home: 3536 Drake Dr Santa Maria CA 93454 Office: 1414 S Miller St Santa Maria CA 93454

DAIGLE, SISTER JEANNINE LOLITA, hosp. adminstr.; b. Ft. Kent, Me., July 27, 1931; d. Eddie J. and Helene (Daigle) Daigle; B.S., St. Joseph's Coll., 1968; M.B.A. in Health Care Adminstrn., George Washington U., 1971. Bookkeeper, Guy & Martin, Inc., Ft. Kent, Md., 1950-51; joined Little Franciscan Sisters of Mary, 1951; tchr. elementary sch., Auburn, Me., 1954-66; project dir., accounting Franciscan Sisters, Bais Saint Paul, Que., Can., 1966-67; asst. adminstr. St. Francis Home, Worcester, Mass., 1967-68; adminstrv. resident Thayer Hosp., Waterville, Me., 1970-71; exec. dir. No. Me. Med. Center, Ft. Kent, Me., 1971—; superior St. Louis Convent. Cons. St. Joseph Nursing Home, Frenchville, Md., No. Me. Security Home, Eagle Lake, Me., St. John Valley Nursing Home, Madawaska, Me., St. Francis Home, Worcester, Mass. Trustee St. John Valley Nursing Home, Am. Cancer Soc., Human Relations Services, St. Joseph Nursing Home, Aroostook Health Devel. Services. Mem. Am., Cath., Me. (trustee 1972-73) hosp. assns., Am. Coll. Hosp. Adminstrs. Home: 12 E Main St Fort Kent ME 04743 Office: 143 E Main St Fort Kent ME 04743

DAILEY, (CLARA) CHRISTINE (MRS. JAMES F. DAILEY), editor; b. Blackwell, Okla., Dec. 26, 1925; d. Fountain Emmett and Louisa Carolina (McGuire) Long; B.J., U. Mo., 1947; m. James F. Dailey, Dec. 14, 1953; 1 dau., Shawn Marie. State editor St. Joseph News-Press (Mo.), 1947-50; head bur. Fairchild Publs., Kansas City, Mo., 1950-54; editorial asst. ITT Cannon Electric Co., Los Angeles, 1954-56; editor Here & Now mag. Holmes & Narver Inc., Los Angeles, 1956-71; editor tech. publs. Ralph M. Parsons Co., Los Angeles, 1971-73, So. Pacific Pipe Lines, Inc., 1973—. Named Editor of Year, United Way, 1963. Mem. Assn. Nuclear Editors, Internat. Assn. Bus. Communicators (judge evaluation and awards 1969—), So. Cal. Indsl. Editors Assn., Theta Sigma Phi, Kappa Tau Alpha. Home: 1137 S Hoover St Los Angeles CA 90006 Office: 610 S Main St Los Angeles CA 90014

DAILEY, LAURA CHRISTENSEN (MRS. WILLIAM M. DAILEY), ednl. adminstr.; b. Urbana, Ill., Sept. 9, 1913; d. Nels Andrew and Verna Marguerite (Johnson) Christensen; B.S., Ia. State U., 1935; m. William M. Dailey, June 11, 1938; children—Susan Jane, William M., Christie Lynn. Woman's page editor Washington Times-Herald, 1935-38; instr. Ia. State U., Ames, 1938-40, proof reader, copy editor Ia. State U. Press, 1950-53, editor, adminstr. Ia. State U. Alumni Assn., 1953—. Mem. Am. Alumni Council, Women in Communication, Phi Kappa Phi, Phi Upsilon Omicron, Omicron Nu. Democrat. Methodist. Home: 1605 Burnett Ames IA 50010 Office: Room 223 Iowa State University Alumni Assn Memorial Union Ames IA 50010

DAILEY, MAE HILEMAN (MRS. EARL C. DAILEY), social worker; b. Mabel, Ore.; d. Richard and Martha (Trotter) Hileman; B.A., U. Ore., 1929; postgrad. U. Chgo. and Chgo. Theol. Sem., 1934-36; m. Earl C. Dailey, Nov. 8, 1944. Tchr. high sch., Langlois, Ore., 1930-31, Cove, Ore., 1931-34; prin. Smith River (Ore.) High Sch., Smith River-Reedsport, 1936-38; social worker West Oakland Children's Home, Oakland, Cal., 1938-39; social worker, asst. dir. Home of Benevolence, San Jose, Cal., 1939-44, exec. dir., 1949-56; exec. dir. Children's Receiving Home, Sacramento, 1944-49; owner, mgr. Mobile Home Park, Seaside, Cal., 1956-58; Mothers march dir. March of Dimes, San Jose, 1958-67; co-owner pvt. family camp, 1965—; also co-owner Pine Cone Drive-In. Pres. Children's Home League, 1972—, Ming Quong Bus. and Profl. Women's League, Children's home, 1972. Mem. License and Appeals Bd., City of San Jose, 1974—. Bd. dirs. YWCA, 1965-74, v.p., 1968, pres., 1971-72, 72-73; bd. dirs. Council of Child Care Agencies, 1952-54. Mem. Coordinating Council Women's Clubs (pres. 1952-53, 66-68, 73-74), Cal. Conf. Social Work (regional v.p. 1952-54), Community Welfare Council (sect. chmn. 1952-53), National Parks Assn., Am. Bus. Women's Assn. (pres. 1964-66), Assn. Exec. Dirs. Children's Home for No. Cal. and Nev. (pres. 1949-52), Community Social Workers Orgn. (pres. 1952-53). Clubs: Quota of San Jose (pres. 1951-53, dist. gov. 1968-69); Willow Glen Business and Professional Women's (v.p. 1967-68, pres. 1971-72). Home: 1127 Delynn Way San Jose CA 95125

DAILEY, WILDA JUNE, social worker; b. Janesville, Wis., June 17, 1917; d. Robert S. and Keitha (Wild) Dailey; B.A., Beloit Coll., 1937; M.A., U. Chgo., 1948. With Family Service Bur. of United Charities, Chgo., 1948—, dist. dir., 1953-69, dir. profl. edn., 1969—. Tchr. summer insts. U. Chgo. Sch. Social Service, 1957—. Mem. Am. Group Psychotherapy Assn., Nat. Assn. Social Workers (charter), Phi Beta Kappa, Phi Sigma Iota. Home: 1451 E 55th St Chicago IL 60615 Office: 64 E Jackson Chicago IL 60604

DAILY, EDWINA NOLAN (MRS. WALTER JONATHAN DAILY), author, business cons.; b. Mpls., Nov. 2, 1902; d. William I. and Hannah Matea (Solem) Nolan; student U. Minn., 1918-20; m. Walter Jonathan Daily, Apr. 26, 1941. Home service dir. No. States Power Co., Mpls., 1922-29; mng. dir. Elec. Refrigeration Instn., Gen. Elec. Co., Cleve., 1929-37, exec. dir. Consumers Inst., Bridgeport, Conn., 1939-41; exec. dir. Home Laundry Inst., Bendix Home Appliance, Inc., South Bend, Ind., 1944-47; cons. to pvt. industry, U.S. Govt., Bridgport, New Eng., 1942—. Mem. Conn. Nutrition Com., 1939-43; mem. women's library com. New Coll.; mem. bd. Women's Aux., chmn. dietary services Meml. Hosp., Sarasota, Fla., also chmn. aux. com. surgery reception room. Mem. Sarasota County (Fla.) Women's Rep. Club, publicity dir., 1960-61; vol. Woman's Exchange Sarasota. Mem. Ringling Mus., Woman's Library Assn., Allied Arts Council (gov.), Mental Health Assn. Sarasota, Nat. League Am. Pen Women (pres. Sarasota br. 1968-70, membership chmn.), Nat. Girls Clubs Am. (exec. bd. 1950-60), Nat. Assn. Pen Women. Clubs: Field, Stamford (Conn.) Girls (pres.1951-54). Author: The Art of Cookery, 1939; Food and Health, 1943; The Art of Electric Cooking, 1945; also instrn. books. Home: 5160 Jungle Plum Rd Sarasota FL 33581

DAILY, ELISABETH M., lawyer; b. Kiev, Ukraine, July 21, 1916; d. Gregory and Isabel Maranc; student U. Warsaw (Poland), 1934-35; LL.B. summa cum laude, Ind. U., 1966; m. John H. Daily, Sept. 4, 1946 (dec. Nov. 1962). Came to U.S., 1946, naturalized, 1948. Interpreter, document analyst War Crimes br. 12th Army Group, U.S. Army, Wiesbaden, Germany, 1945-46; admitted to Ind. bar, 1966; free-lance sci. and legal translator, Indpls., 1946-65; law clk. firm Henderson, Daily, Foxworthy & Van Winkle, Indps., 1965-66, asso., 1966-69, partner, 1970—. Mem. Am., Ind., Indpls. bar assns., Order of Coif, League of Women Voters (dir. Indpls. 1962-65, 67-72). Office: Henderson Daily Foxworthy & Van Winkle 1 Indiana Sq Suite 2450 Indianapolis IN 46204

DAILY, EVELYNNE BERNLOEHR (MRS. EDWARD R. DAILY), artist; b. Indpls., Jan. 8, 1903; d. John A. and Anna (Giezendanner) Bernloehr; student Butler U., 1920, Herron Sch. Art, Ind. U., 1920-24, Chgo. Art Inst., 1938, Ecole Des Beaux Arts, Fontainebleau, France, 1929, Bauhaus Sch. Design, Chgo., Wayman Adams Sch. Painting, N.Y.C.; m. George Joe Mess, Apr. 28, 1925 (dec. June 1962); m. 2d, Edward R. Daily, May 16, 1969 (dec. Feb. 11, 1974). One-man shows Brown County Art Gallery, Nashville, Ind., Indpls. Mus. Art, Swope Art Gallery, Fort Wayne Mus., Lieber Gallery, Purdue U., Ind. U., Indpls.; exhibited in group shows at Soc. Am. Etchrs, Nat. Arts Club, N.Y.C., 1933-35, 46, 47, Pa. Acad. Fine Arts, Phila., 1934, Phila. Soc. Etchers, Newman Gallery, 1935, Print Club Phila., 1946, 47, N.A.D., N.Y.C., 1949, Herron Mus., Indpls., 1928-59, 61, Lieber Gallery, Indpls., 1934-54, Hoosier Salon Gallery, Indpls., 1934—, Lafayette (Ind.) Art Center, 1966, Los Angeles Mus., 1931, 32, 34, 36, Seattle Art Mus., 1936, Ball State U. Sesquecentennial Exhbn., 1966; represented in permanent collections Herron Museum, Indpls., Library Congress, Washington, Central Art Studio-Gallery, Indpls., DePauw U., Art Assn. Gallery, Richmond, Ind., Ft. Wayne (Ind.) Art Mus.; art tchr. high schs., Indpls., Indpls. Art League, 1960-66, Summer Art Sch., Oxbow Acres, Brown County Ind., 1950—. Dir. Brown County Art Gallery, Nashville, Ind. Mem. Ind. Fedn. Art Clubs (pres. 1968-70), Indpls. Art League Found., Ind. Artists Club (past sec.-treas.), Ind. Printmakers (founder), Nat. Soc. Arts and Letters (past v.p. Ind. chpt.), 20 Ind. Artists (past sec.), Butler U., Indpls. Mus. Art, Ind. Artist-Craftsman, Herron Art Sch., Ecole des Beaux-Arts alumni assns. Address: Central Art Studio 6237 Central Av Indianapolis IN 46220

DAILY, VICTORIA LEE DEFORE (MRS. IVAN PARKS DAILY), educator; b. Fristoe, Mo., Mar. 11, 1914; d. James Harrison and Stella Viola (Pennington) DeFore; B.S., Kan. State Tchrs. Coll., 1939, M.S., 1950; Ed.D., Colo. State Coll., 1969; m. Ivan Parks Daily, July 11, 1936; children—Mary Leota (Mrs. David V. Pool), James Allen. Tchr. highs schs. Kan., 1942-62; prof. edn. Coll. of Emporia, Kan., 1962—. Gen. Electric Econ. Edn. fellow, 1960. Mem. Kan. Bus. Edn. Assn. (treas. 1963-65, pres. 1966), Am. Assn. U. Women (1st v.p. 1965-66), Delta Pi Epsilon, Delta Kappa Gamma (pres. chpt. 1972—). Home: 3 Lakeshore Dr Emporia KS 66801

DAINGERFIELD, MARJORIE JAY, sculptress, educator; b. N.Y.C.; d. Elliott and Anna (Grainger) Daingerfield; student Veltin Sch., N.Y.C., Sch. Am. Sculpture, Grand Central Sch. Art and several pvt. tutors; m. Oliver Ellsworth Holmes, Dec. 19, 1928 (dec. Dec. 1930); m. 2d, James Louis Lundean, Oct. 23, 1945 (dec. Oct. 24, 1961); m. 3d, Arthur E. Howlett, Oct. 9, 1965 (dec. May 1969). Former tchr. Grand Central Sch. Art, N.Y.C., Sch. Am. Sculpture, N.Y.C., Rollins Coll., Winter Park, Fla. Norton Gallery and Sch. Art, Palm Beach, Fla. Exhibited N.A.D., N.Y., Archtl. League, Pen and Brush, Norton Gallery, Nat. Sculpture Soc.; works in permanent exhbns. Govt. of P.R., St. Louis Mus., Georgetown U., Mus. City N.Y., Hobart Coll., Mint Mus., Charlotte, N.C., others; one man shows Duke, Mint Mus.; madonna dedicated St. Mary's of the Hills Ch., Blowing Rock, N.C., 1972. Recipient Anna Hyatt Huntington award Pen and Brush, 1956, Silver medal, 1963. Fellow Nat. Sculpture Soc.; mem. Pen and Brush, Blowing Rock Art Assn. (pres. 1957). Episcopalian. Club: Catherine Lorillard Wolfe. Author: The Fun and Fundamentals of Sculpture. Address: Hotel des Artises 1 W 67th St New York City NY 10023 also Daingerfield Blowing Rock NC 28605

DAKIN, KATHLEEN DOROTHY, nurse; b. New Ross, N.S., Can., July 2, 1918; d. Lincoln Hansen and Mary Berdette (Gates) Meister; grad. Halifax (N.S.) Children's Hosp. Sch. Nursing, 1941; m. Aubrey Porter Dakin, Apr. 10, 1941; children—Judith Ferne (Mrs. Keith Wendall Thompson), Aubrey Porter, Kenneth Robert. Staff nurse to dir. nursing services N.S. Sanatorium, Kentville, 1962—. Mem. N.S. Registered Nurses Assn. (3d v.p. 1969-70). Home: 1104 Commercial St New Minas NS Canada Office: Nova Scotia Sanatorium Kentville NS Canada

DAKIN, MARION JANET, physician; b. Chgo., Apr. 17, 1912; d. Walter and Genevieve Louise (Clarke) Dakin; student Monticello Coll., 1929-31; B.A. with honors, Wellesley Coll., 1933; postgrad. U. Wis., 1933-36; M.D., Washington U., St. Louis, 1938; m. John David Isherwood, May 4, 1950 (div. Dec. 1964); children—Pamela Joan, John Philip, Peter Brian, Janet Mary Ellen. Intern Barnes Hosp., St. Louis, 1938-40; asst. resident chest diseases Bellevue Hosp., N.Y.C., 1940; resident internal medicine Cottage Hosp., Santa Barbara, Cal., 1940-41, Los Angeles County Hosp., 1941-42; plant physician Lockheed Aircraft Plant, Burbank, Cal., 1942-45; fellow dept. neuropsychiatry U. Wis., Madison, 1945-46, student health cons., 1945-46; asst. in dept. gastro-enterology U. Chgo., 1946-48; practice medicine specializing in internal medicine, Los Angeles, 1948—; acting asst. dir. Student Health Services, U. Cal. at Los Angeles, 1952-53, student health physician, 1971—; asst. clin. prof. internal medicine, 1957—; active mem. med. staff U. Cal. at Los Angeles Med. Center, 1957—; active mem. sr. med. staff Santa Monica (Cal.) Hosp., 1948—. Asso. cons. internal medicine U. Cal. at Los Angeles Student Health, 1948—; adv. bd. Los Angeles Ileostomy Assn., 1964—. Diplomate Am. Bd. Internal Medicine. Mem. Am., Cal., Los Angeles County med. assns., Am. Heart Assn., Am. Geriatrics Soc., Kappa Alpha Theta. Home: 15643 Woodfield Pl Sherman Oaks CA 91403 Office: University of California at Los Angeles Center for the Health Sciences Los Angeles CA 90024

D'ALBERT, MARIA EMILIA (MRS. CHARLES MATYAS), rec. co. exec.; b. Gyor, Hungary; d. Julius and Maria T. (De Varga) D'Albert; operatic singer diploma Royal Liszt Acad. Music (Budapest), 1947; m. Charles Matyas, Nov. 21, 1970. Singer, Budapest State Operahouse, 1947; prof. singing Leinster Acad. and Municipal Sch. Music, Dublin, Ireland, 1950-54, Galway Univ. Coll., Eire, 1951-54, Coll. de l'Assomption (Que., Can.), 1956-58; voice faculty Chgo. Conservatory Coll., 1960—; pres. Hussar Rec. Co., Chgo., 1965-67, Rapsodia Rec. Co., Chgo., 1967—; concert soloist, Europe, Can., U.S., 1947—. Mem. Chgo. Artists Assn., Ill. State Music Tchrs., Music Tchrs. Nat. Assn., Internat. Soc. for Contemporary Music, Am. Assn. U. Profs., Phi Beta (hon.). Club: Chicago Woman Musical. Home: 4046 N Ashland Av Chicago IL 60613 Office: 410 S Michigan Av Chicago IL 60605

DALE, DORIS CRUGER, educator; b. Madison, Wis., July 22, 1927; d. Victor and Anna (Wipperfurth) Cruger; B.A., U. Wis.-Madison, 1950, M.A. in L.S., 1954; postgrad. U. Ill. Extension div., 1964-65; D.L.S., Columbia, 1968; m. Richard Dale, Aug. 18, 1967. Reference librarian Madison Pub. Library, 1954-57, br. librarian, 1957-58; circulation librarian Appleton (Wis.) Pub. Library, 1958-59; bus. and sci. librarian Rockford (Ill.) Pub. Library, 1959-62; reference librarian U. Wis.-Milw., 1962-64; bus. librarian No. Ill. U., De Kalb, 1964-66; teaching asst. Columbia, 1966-67; asst. prof. instructional materials So. Ill. U., Carbondale, 1969-73, asso. prof., 1973—. Recipient Jour. Library History Ann. award, 1972. So. Ill. U. Office Research and Projects grantee, 1969-72; Pres.'s Acad. Excellence program grantee, 1973-74. Mem. A.L.A. (subscription books com. 1965-69, Beta Phi Mu award com. 1973-75), Ill. Library Assn., Ill. Audiovisual Assn., Beta Phi Mu. Author: The United Nations Library: Its Origin and Development, 1970; also several bibliographies. Contbr. articles, book revs. to mags., profl. jours. Home: Union Hill Route 4 Carbondale IL 62901

DALE, EMILY GERTRUDE DUNN (MRS. STEVEN DALE), educator; b. Normal, Ill., Oct. 19, 1924; d. Richard Francis and Clara (Huxtable) Dunn; B.A., Western Res. U., 1946; M.S., Ill. State U., 1947; postgrad. U. Ill., 1948, 1963-64, U. Colo., 1961; Ph.D., Union Grad. Sch., 1972; m. John R. Scott, Aug. 22, 1947 (div. 1955); children—John, Elizabeth (Mrs. Steven Sceniak), Robert, Mary; m. 2d, Steven Dale, Jan. 27, 1962. With Am. Friends Service Commn., 1942-43; recreation dir. Fed. Housing Project, S. Side, Chgo., 1943; asst. dir. U. Settlement House, Cleve., 1945; instr. sociology Ill. Wesleyan U., Bloomington, 1959-61, asst. prof., 1961-72, asso. prof., 1973—, acting head, dept. anthropology and sociology, 1967-68. Cons., Lincoln Coll., Blackburn Coll., Am. Friends Service Regional Office on Coll. Program; Welfare cons. Regional Planning Commn., 1973; dir. seminar U. London, summer 1969. Mem. state bd. dirs. Ill. Citizens Commn. Freedom Residence, 1960—; pres. Bloomington-Normal Human Relations Com., 1955-60; pres. Metcalf, P.T.A., 1959-60; bd. dirs. McLean County Family Services Agy., 1962-70, v.p., 1966-67; bd. dirs. Mental Health Com., 1968-72; residential chmn. United Community Services, 1958-59; mem. priority planning com. United Way, 1972-74. Recipient Brotherhood award Anti-Defamation League, 1958-59, 60; award for Human Relations Women's Civic Improvement Assn., 1961; Pantagraph Letters award 1960-65, 67, 69, 70, 72, 73. NSF grantee in anthropology, 1961; Nat. Council on Social Work grantee to develop undergrad. program, 1966, 1967. Mem. Am., Midwest, Ill. (sec. 1968-70, exec. bd. 1971-72) sociol. assns., P.E.O., McLean County Archeol. Assn. (co-founder), Bloomington-Normal Soc. Friends (co-founder; clk. 1959-61), Urbana-Champaign Soc. Friends (co-founder), Alpha Kappa Delta, Phi Kappa Phi. Contbr. articles to profl. jours. Home: 304 W Virginia St Normal IL 61761 Office: Wesleyan U Bloomington IL 61701

DALE, MARCIA L. (MRS. WILLIAM G. DALE, JR.), nurse, educator; b. Ft. Dodge, Ia., Mar. 4, 1938; d. William Russell and Erma L. (Umland) Bradley; B.S. in Nursing, U. Wyo., 1960; M.N. in Nursing, U. Wash., 1961; m. William G. Dale, Jr., June 30, 1967; children—Dori Lyn, Devin Glenn. Staff nurse Meml. Hosp., Cheyenne, Wyo., summer 1961, Providence Hosp., Seattle, summer 1962; asso. prof. U. Wyo., Laramie, 1961—. Named Outstanding Young Woman of Am., 1969. Mem. Am. Assn. U. Women (sec. br. Cheyenne 1967-69; treas. 1969-70), Nat., Wyo. (pres. 1963-64) leagues for nursing, Am., Wyo. (mem. bd. 1964-66, sec. dist. 1972-74) nurses' assns., Alpha Delta Kappa (v.p. Wyo. Delta chpt. 1968-70), Sigma Theta Tau (counselor Alpha Pi chpt. 1965-70). Home: 827 Evergreen St Cheyenne WY 82001 Office: U Wyo Laramie WY 82070

DALE, MARTHA ERICSON (MRS. EDWARD C. DALE), educator, clin. psychologist; b. Chgo., Apr. 29, 1914; d. Ivar George and Caroline (Nelson) Ericson; B.S., Northwestern U., 1939; M.S., Ia. State U., 1941; Ph.D., U. Chgo., 1945; m. Edward C. Dale, June 25, 1949; children—Peter David and John Daniel (twins), Edward Charles. Grad. asst. Ia. State U., Ames, 1939-41; dir. Parker Nursery Sch., Chgo., 1941-42; research asst. U. Chgo., 1942-44; asso. prof. psychology Merrill Palmer Sch., Detroit, 1944-50; psychologist Grosse Pointe (Mich.) Pub. Schs., 1957-59; clin. psychologist Lansing (Mich.) Child Guidance Clinic, 1959-60; asst. prof. Mich. State U., East Lansing, 1961-68; asso. prof. psychology Lake Superior State Coll., Sault Ste. Marie, Mich., 1968-69; cons. psychology Eastern Upper Peninsula Mental Health Clinic, Sault Sainte Marie, 1969-71; dir. dept. psychol. services Newberry (Mich.) State Hosp., 1971—. Mem. Am. Psychol. Assn. Episcopalian. Home: 13410 108th Dr Sun City AZ 85351

D'ALESSIO, THERESA HILDA (TERRY, HILDA) (MRS. GREGORY D'ALESSIO), cartoonist; b. Newburyport, Mass., June 25, 1914; d. Charles Zacharia and Annie Toby (Aronson) Fellman; student Boston Trade Sch. for Girls, 1929, N.Y. Nat. Acad. Design, 1932-33, Art Students League, 1934-40, N.Y. U., 1968; m. Gregory D'Alessio, June 11, 1938. Creator, Carrots O'Hara, Am. Mag., 1939-40, Daisy, Saturday Evening Post, 1938-42, Teena, Internat. Syndicated King Features, 1941—; creator animation program Kansas City Royals Computered Scoreboard, Harry S. Truman Sports Complex, 1972—; creative designer Am. Information Corp., N.Y.C., 1968—. Instr. N.Y. Sch. Social Research, 1969, N.Y. Phoenix Sch. Art and Design, 1970-72. Bd. dirs. Prescott Neighborhood House. Recipient Wohelo award Campfire Girls, 1955. Mem. Nat. Cartoonists Soc. Author: Teena Comic Books, 1947; Originality in Art, 1953; Art and Cartoon, 1954. Asso. editor Art Collectors Almanac, 1965-67, N.Y. Arts Calendar, 1965-67. Inventor self-mail book cover, typewriter pen, lamp matrix ruler. Address: 8 Henderson Pl New York City NY 10028

DALEY, ELEANOR GUILFOYLE (MRS. RICHARD J. DALEY), wife of Chgo. mayor; m. Richard J. Daley, June 23, 1936; children—Patricia, Mary Carol, Eleanor, Richard, Michael, John, William. Address: 3536 Lowe Av Chicago IL 60609*

DALEY, ELIZABETH ROYLANCE (MRS. CECIL ALEXANDER DALEY), physician; b. N.Y.C., July 28, 1904; d. Frank Dean and Sallie (Gunter) Roylance; A.B., Vassar Coll., 1926; postgrad. Coll. City N.Y., 1927-29, N.Y. Sch. Social Work, 1927-29; M.D., Coll. Phys. and Surg., Columbia U., 1933; m. Cecil Alexander Daley, July 31, 1926; children—Sara E. (Mrs. Fredric de G. Schuh), Daniel R., Peter S., Richard A., Mary D. (Mrs. R. Haydn Silleck). Sales clk. R. H. Macy & Co., 1926; social case worker N.Y. Nursery and Child's Hosp., 1927-29; intern Englewood (N.J.) Hosp., 1933-35; gen. practice medicine, Bronxville, N.Y., 1934-67, practice medicine, specializing in treatment of arthritis, Bronxville, 1967-70, Charleston, S.C. and Cutchogue, N.Y., 1970—; clin. asst. in pediatrics Vanderbilt Clinic, Columbia-Presbyn. Med. Center, N.Y.C., 1938-41; clin. asst. in internal medicine Mt. Vernon (N.Y.) Hosp., 1947-67. Named Woman of Year, Eastchester Bus. and Profl. Women's Club, 1967. Mem. Med. Soc. County Westchester (pub. relations com. 1954), Westchester County Med. Women's Club (pres. 1942-43), N.Y. Acad. Scis., Phi Beta Kappa. Republican. Mem. Reformed Ch. Address: 2059 Lake Av Charleston SC 29407

DALEY, KATHERINE FAY, journalist; b. San Mateo, Cal., Sept. 9, 1926; d. John Peter and Minerva (Bosse) Daley; A.B., Stanford, 1948. Mem. editorial staff Pathfinder Mag., Washington, 1948-51; mem. publs. staff Stanford (Cal.) U. Alumni Assn., 1952—, asso. editor, 1970—. Mem. Cal. Republican State Central Com., 1962—; mem. Santa Clara County Rep. Central Com., 1962—, treas., 1964-65, chmn. county precinct com., 1965-69, pub. relations chmn., 1970—; mem. Rep. Alliance, 1969—, Cal. Fedn. Rep. Women; alternate del. Rep. Nat. Conv., 1972. Mem. Am. Assn. U. Women, Stanford Alumni Assn., Women in Communication. Methodist. Home: PO Box 387 Los Altos CA 94022 Office: Stanford Alumni Assn Bowman Alumni House Stanford CA 94305

DALEY, NANCY PHYLISS OLDFIELD (MRS. THOMAS JAMES DALEY), civic worker; b. Elyria, O., June 10, 1920; d. Robert Donald and Ellen Adler (Roberts) Oldfield; B.A., Ohio Wesleyan U., 1941; M.S., Northwestern U., 1943; m. Thomas James Daley, Jan. 10, 1948; children—Mary Ann (Mrs. Ronald William Harris), Patricia Ellen. Home town editor publicity dept. Ohio Wesleyan U., Delaware, O., 1940-41; credit mgr. Haynes Pub. Co., Cleve., 1941; editor Skokie (Ill.) News, 1942; display advt. rep. Ironwood Daily Globe (Mich.), 1942-43, Chronicle-Telegram, Elyria, O., 1943-47, Miami (Fla.) News, 1947-48; bookkeeper Regaline Mfg. Co., Miami, 1948-49, 1950-52; sec. Art Guild Boca Raton, Fla., 1971-72; substitute tchr. Coral Gables (Fla.) High Sch., 1952-65; instr. reading Miami-Dade Jr. Coll., 1965-68; guidance counselor Coral Park High Sch., Miami, 1968-69. Sec., U. Miami Woman's Cancer Assn., Coral Gables, 1963-64, treas., 1970-71. Mem. Am. Assn. U. Women, Boca Buckeyes (sec. 1970-71), Cambrian Fla. Welsh Soc., Phi Beta Kappa, Pi Delta Epsilon, Beta Sigma Phi, Theta Sigma Phi (chpt. pres. 1955-56, chpt. headliner 1967). Home: 670D High Point Blvd N Delray Beach FL 33444

DALIS, IRENE, mezzo-soprano; b. San Jose, Cal.; d. Peter A. and Mamie (Boitano) Dalis; A.B., San Jose State Coll., 1946, M.S. (hon.), 1957; M.A., Columbia Tchrs. Coll., 1947; studied voice with Edyth Walker, N.Y.C., 1947-50, Paul Althouse, 1950-51, Dr. Otto Mueller, Milano, Italy, 1952—; m. George Loinaz, July 16, 1957; 1 dau., Alida Mercedes. Operatic debut as dramatic mezzo-soprano Berlin Staedtische Opera, 1956; debut Met. Opera, N.Y.C., 1957, now leading mezzo-soprano. 1st Am.-born singer Kundry Bayreuth Festival, 1961; opened Bayreuth Festival in Parsifal, 1963 Commemorative Wagner 150th Birth Anniversary; opened 1963 Met. Opera Season in Aida. Recipient Fulbright award for study in Italy, 1951. Address: care Eric Semon Assos Inc 111 W 57th St New York City NY 10019

DALLAS, KATHARYN TICE (MRS. JOHN W. DALLAS), bus. exec.; b. Oshkosh, Wis., July 27, 1906; d. George Nelson and Etta J. (Ruddy) Tice; student Wis. State U., Oshkosh, 1925-28; B.S., Northwestern U., 1934, M.S., 1935; m. John W. Dallas, June 6, 1936 (dec. Mar. 1962); children—John W (dec.), Charles W. Tchr., West Allis, Wis., 1928-31, Orthogenic Sch., U. Chgo., summers 1929-31, Hinsdale, Ill., 1931-33; asst. in psychology Northwestern U., 1934-35; tchr. Boulder (Colo.) Pub. Schs., 1935-36, dir. spl. edn., 1935-36; spl. services Inst. for Juvenile Research, Chgo., 1933-35; partner Trader Jack's Pine Furniture, Denver, 1946—. Charter mem. Rocky Mountain Kidney Found.; chmn. bd. Adams County Youth Scholarship Fund. Mem. Am. Assn. U. Women, Pi Lambda Theta. Contbr. articles to profl. jours. Home: 3547 W 23d Av Denver CO 80211 Office: 6606 N Federal Denver CO 80221

DALLAS, MARY E. BOOTH (MRS. FRED R. DALLAS), physician; b. Sharpsville, Ind., Sept. 20, 1926; d. Vern and Clara Grace (Warner) Booth; student Lindenwood Coll. for Women, 1944-45; B.A., DePauw U., 1948; M.D., Ind. U., 1952; m. Fred R. Dallas, Jan. 2, 1954; children—Carol Lenore, Stephen Gregory. Fellow in anesthesia Lahey Clinic, Boston, 1953-54; resident in anesthesia Ind. U. Med. Center, Indpls., 1956-58, mem. faculty dept. anesthesiology, staff mem., 1958-65; now staff mem. Community Hosp., St. Francis Hosp. Bd. dirs. Vis. Nurses Assn., Indpls., 1966-74, pres., 1973. Diplomate Am. Bd. Anesthesiology. Fellow Am. Coll. Anesthesiologists; mem. A.M.A., Ind., Marion County med. socs., Am., Ind. socs. anesthesiologists. Home: 3649 E 71st St Indianapolis IN 46220

DALLIGAN, ALICE GRACE COOK, librarian; b. Detroit, Apr. 28, 1923; d. Floyd John and Grace Louise (Davis) Cook; B.A. in Edn., Wayne State U., 1945; M.A. in History, U. Mich., 1948, M.A. in L.S., 1950; m. Carl John Dalligan, Aug. 15, 1960. Tchr., Detroit, 1945-48; librarian Detroit Pub. Library, 1948-64, curator manuscripts Burton Hist. Collection, 1964-71, 1st asst., 1971-73, chief collection, 1973—. Mem. Soc. Am. Archivists, Detroit, Mich. hist. socs., Mich. Library Assn., Archivists Soc. Mich., Historic Memls. Soc. Detroit. Home: 2101 Fleetwood St Grosse Pointe Woods MI 48236 Office: 5201 Woodward Av Detroit MI 48202

DALLY, GRATIA DINSMORE (MRS. KENNETH H. DALLY), librarian; b. Owatonna, Minn., Feb. 4, 1908; d. John H. and Elizabeth P. (Plumb) Dinsmore; student Carlton Coll., 1928-29, Tex. Technol. Coll., 1943, West Tex. State Coll., 1945; B.S., U. Minn., 1955; m. Kenneth H. Dally, Aug. 6, 1930; 1 dau., Gratia (Mrs. William M. Felknor, Jr.). Asst. county librarian Hutchinson County, Borger, Tex., 1939-44; high sch. librarian, Borger, 1944-54; librarian Nursing Sch., St. Barnabas Hosp., Mpls., 1953-54, Nursing Sch., Swedish Hosp., Mpls., 1955-59, Nursing Sch., Fairview Hosp., Mpls., 1959—. Mem. A.L.A., Nat. League for Nursing, Minn. Assn. Hosp. and Instnl. Librarians, Mpls. Hosp. Med. Librarians, Twin City Nursing Sch. Librarians, Delta Kappa Gamma. Home: 6327 James Av S Minneapolis MN 55423 Office: 2312 S 6th St Minneapolis MN 55406

DALO, CHARLOTTE OWENS (MRS. MICHAEL DALO), lawyer; b. Pippapass, Ky., Feb. 8, 1922; d. Elisha H. and Frances (Reynolds) Owens; student Berea Coll., 1938-39; B.S., Eastern Ky. State Tchrs. Coll., 1942; LL.B., Ind. U., 1945; postgrad. U. Ky., 1942-43, Southwestern U. Sch. Law, 1945-46, U. Cal. at Los Angeles, 1959-60; m. Michael Dalo, Feb. 14, 1960; children—Denise Ann, Michael Owen. Admitted to Cal. bar, 1948; practiced in North Hollywood, Cal., 1948-49, Beverly Hills, Cal., 1949-60, Van Nuys, Cal., 1960—; mem. firm Barnett & Owens, Van Nuys, 1960-62. Mem. San Fernando Valley Bar Assn., Iota Tau Tau. Democrat. Home: 10133 Petit Av Granada Hills CA 91343 Office: 14411 Vanowen St Van Nuys CA 91405

DALTON, DOROTHY (MRS. LEROY EDWARD KUEHN), poet, editor; b. N.Y.C., Sept. 25, 1915; d. John Aloysious and Mary Agnes (Ferris) Dalton; B.A., U. Wis.; m. LeRoy Edward Kuehn, Jan. 12, 1946; children—Christine Claire, Stephanie Lenore. Editor, Poetry View, Sunday Mag. sect. Appleton (Wis.) Post Crescent, 1970—; poetry pub. in various nat. mags., including N.Y. Quar., Sat. Eve. Post, McCall's, Good Housekeeping, Wall St. Jour., Christian Sci. Monitor. Served with WAC, 1944-46. Mem. Poetry Soc. Am., Am. Legion (past 2d vice comdr. 1970). Author: Poems, 1967; Midnight, and Counting, 1973. Home: 1125 Valley Rd Menasha WI 54952

DALTON, FRANCES LOUISA, artist, educator; b. Amesbury, Mass., Dec. 28, 1906; d. Harry Clement and Mary (Bunting) Dalton; student Ecoles des Beaux Arts, Paris, France, 1932, Sch. of Mus. Fine Arts, Boston, 1923-30, Paige traveling fellowship Europe, 1930-33; summer courses, study with Robert Laurent. Portrait painter, specialized children's portraits throughout New Eng.; pvt. classes and portraits, Andover, 1936-44; tchr. creative arts Andover Jr. and Sr. High Sch., 1944-68, Pikes Pvt. Sch., 1950-51. Exhibited Whistler House, Boston Mus. Fine Art, Silvermine Guild Artists, Woodstock Art Gallery, Addison Gallery of Am. Art, Exhbn. 13 Artist-Tchrs., John-Esther Art Gallery, 1961; one-man show, 1962; group shows, Parker Gallery, Museum of Fine Arts, Boston; also others; portraits and landscapes Royal Hawaiian Hotel, pvt. collections. Chmn. Am. Art Week—Greater Lawrence Area. Recipient Richard Mitton Gold medal and award Jordan Marsh Exhbn., Boston; 1st prize painting Laurence Centennial Exhbn.; 2d prize in painting and 2d prize in graphics Unitarian-Universalist Art Exhbn., 1968, hon. mention, 1969. Mem. Andover's Artists Guild, Fine Arts Soc., Andover Artist Group, Boston Soc. Ind. Artists, Nat. Art Edn. Assn., Eastern Arts Assn., Mus. Sch. Alumni, Guild of Scholars. Episcopalian. Home: 70 Chestnut St Andover MA 01810

DALTON, GERMAINE, editor; b. Raberval, Que., Can., May 5, 1913; d. Arthur Joseph and Alida Marie (Tremblay) Fortin; Tchrs. Diploma in French, U. Ottawa (Ont., Can.), 1953; m. Joseph Samuel Dalton, Sept. 22, 1935 (dec. Sept. 1940); children—Arthur, Marcel, Albert. Tchr. French, Edmonton (Alta.) Sch. Bd., 1943-49; owner Dalton Gen. Store, 1949-54; with Beverly Page, Edmonton, 1953—, editor, publisher, 1953—; pres. Dalton Printing Co., Edmonton, 1972—. Mem. adv. bd. Brit. Commonwealth Games, Edmonton. Sec. Beverly Bus. Assn., 1965-66; chmn. civic affairs Edmonton Bus. Assn. 1971-72. Mem. Alta. Press Gallery, 1958—. Home: 11407 50th Edmonton AB T5W 385 Canada Office: 11405 50th St Edmonton AB T5W 385 Canada

DALTON, MARGARET (MRS. WALTER W. DALTON), civic worker, occupational therapist; b. St. Louis, Oct. 10, 1920; d. Norman Steigers and Margaret May (Kalbaugh) Brown; grad. Mt. Vernon Jr. Coll., 1941; B.S., Washington U., St. Louis, 1945; m. Walter W. Dalton, June 6, 1959. Chief occupational therapist St. Louis Children's Hosp., 1945-55; tchr. Edgewood Children's Center, Webster Groves, Mo., 1957-59; now substitute tchr. Ladue (Mo.) Sch. dist. Past vol. Ranken-Jordan Home for Convalescent Crippled Children, St. Louis; now vol. Scholar Shop; past v.p. St. Louis Soc. for Crippled Children, bd. dirs., 1959—; dir. Jr. League Lily Day Campaign, 1964, co-chmn. Junior League Junior Kindergarten, past v.p. Freedom's Found. Past bd. dirs. Bd. Religious Orgns., YWCA, Kidney Found. Conglist. (chmn. coffee hour). Clubs: Sowing Circle

Garden (pres. 1973), St. Louis Women's (past sec.). Home: 4 Wakefield Dr St Louis MO 63124

DALTON, RUTH MARGARET, physician; b. Chgo., Apr. 30, 1926; d. Maurice Jewett and Madeline (Murphy) Dalton; diploma, Thornton Jr. Coll., 1945; student DePaul U., 1946-48; B.S., M.D., U. Ill., 1953. Intern, Madison (Wis.) Gen. Hosp., 1953-54, resident in pathology, 1954-57; resident in pathology Phila. Gen. Hosp., 1957-58; asso. pathologist St. Francis Hosp., La Crosse, Wis., 1958—. Pres., Wis. Assn. Blood Banks, 1963, bd. dirs., 1962; chmn. exec. bd. regional blood com. Badger Red Cross Blood Center, 1966-68; bd. dirs. Am. Assn. Blood Banks, 1969-72, dist. chmn. inspection and accreditation program, 1968-73; sec.-treas. La Crosse chpt. Cath. Physicians Guild, 1963. Sr. planning bd. advisor Girl Scouts U.S.A., 1965-71; bd. dirs. La Crosse County chpt. A.R.C. Bd. advisers Viterbo Coll. Recipient Service award, A.R.C. Badger Regional Blood Center, 1969. Fellow Am. Soc. Clin. Pathologists; mem. A.A.A.S., A.M.A., State Med. Soc. Wis., La Crosse County Med. Soc. (sec.-treas. 1963-65), La Crosse Pediatric Soc. (sec.-treas. 1962-67), Wis. Soc. Pathologists, Wis. Assn. Blood Banks, Am. Assn. Blood Banks, U. Ill. Alumni Assn., Nat. Wildlife Assn., Am. Forestry Assn. Home: 1107 Nancy Ct La Crosse WI 54601 Office: 709 S 10th St La Crosse WI 54601

DALUGE, SUSAN MARY, medicinal chemist; b. Lancaster, Pa., Apr. 8, 1942; d. Robert Emmet and Mary Elizabeth (Stegner) Sisco; B.A., Macalester Coll., 1964; Ph.D. in Organic Chemistry, U. Minn., 1969. Postdoctoral fellow in medicinal chemistry U. Minn., Mpls., 1969—. NSF fellow, 1965-68. Mem. Am. Chem. Soc., Sigma Xi. Research on protein biosynthesis, design of molecules to probe areas of ribosome involved in peptide bond formation with emphasis on utilizing differences between ribosomes in study of cancer. Home: 2330 Jackson St NE Minneapolis MN 55418 Office: Dept Medicinal Chemistry U Minn Minneapolis MN 55455

DALY, BETTY MILLER (MRS. ROSWALD BERNARD DALY), poet; b. Winston-Salem, N.C., Sept. 25, 1926; d. Paul Felix and Florence Summers (Crews) Miller; student Winston-Salem Bus. Coll., 1943, Bowman Gray Sch. Medicine, 1945-46; m. Roswald Bernard Daly, Dec. 19, 1946; children—Mary Ann, Roswald Bernard, John Miller, Martha Elizabeth. Teletype printer operator Merrill, Lynch, Pierce, Fenner & Beane, Winston-Salem, 1943-45; pathology and neuropathology technician Bowman Gray Sch. Medicine and Yale U., New Haven, Conn., 1946; research technician Americal Oncologic Hosp., Phila., 1946-47; path. technician Phila. Gen. Hosp., 1947, Rex Hosp., Raleigh, 1947-48; med. asst. to husband, 1971-72. Mem. Am. Pen Women, Poetry Soc. Am., N.C. Poetry Soc. (pres. 1971-72), Lee County Med. Aux. (pres. 1970-71). Clubs: Waxhaw (N.C.) Womans' (pres. 1953-54); Woman's Club of Broadway (N.C.) (organizer, pres. 1966-68). Author: As A Woman Thinketh, 1957. Contbg. editor Fellowship in Prayer, 1969—. Home and office: Box 108 Broadway NC 27505

DALY, GEORGE ANNE PORTER (MRS. JOHN EDWARD DALY), ins. cons.; b. Kansas City, Kan., July 26, 1941; d. Howard Lomax and Geraldine Dorothy (Ramsey) Porter; B.A., U. Kan., 1963; M.A., U. Pa., 1965; m. John Edward Daly, Aug. 7, 1965. With INA Corp., Phila., 1965-74, dir., mgr. mus. and archives, 1970-74, cons., 1974—. Author: The Historical Collection of Insurance Company of North America, 1967; (with John J. Robrecht) An Illustrated Handbook of Fire Apparatus, 1972. Home: 1778 Old Chatham Rd Springfield IL 62704

DALY, MAGGIE DOROTHEA (MRS. ARTHUR BAZLEN), writer, lectr.; b. Castle Caufield, County Tyrone, Ireland, July 2; d. Joseph and Margaret (Kelly) Daly; m. Arthur Bazlen, Aug. 13, 1939 (dec. Dec. 1957); 1 dau., Brigid. Profl. model, Milw., Chgo., 1945-52; fashion co-ordinator Chez Paree Show, radio, 1952-54; feature writer Ladies Home Jour., 1954; appeared on Home Show, TV, 1954; hostess evening TV talk show sta. WFCD, Chgo., 1970-72; interviewer weekly radio show; now lectr. on fashions to women's and men's groups; columnist Chgo. Today. Bd. dirs. Chgo. U.S.O.; hon. chmn. Chgo. Mental Health Assn. Mem. Adult Edn. Assn., Fashion Group of Chgo. Author: Guide to Charm, 1955; Kate Brennan, 1957. Home: 1400 Lake Shore Dr Chicago IL 60610

DALY, MARSHA H., mag. editor; b. Akron, O., Sept. 16, 1941; d. Saul H. and Vera V. (Balber) Daly; B.A., N.Y.C., 1963. Am. instruction list writer Metro-Goldwyn, Mayer, N.Y.C., 1965-66; editor Ideal Pub. Corp., N.Y.C., 1968—. Office: 295 Madison Av New York NY 10017

DALY, MARY, educator, author; b. Schenectady, Oct. 16, 1928; d. Frank X. and Anna C. (Morse) Daly; B.A., Coll. St. Rose, 1950; M.A., Cath. U. Am., 1952; S.T.D., U. Fribourg, Switzerland, 1963, Ph.D., 1965. Tchr. theology, philosophy Cardinal Cushing Coll., Brookline, Mass., 1954-59, Fribourg, 1959-66; asst. prof. theology Boston Coll., 1966-69, asso. prof., 1969—. Mem. task force women and religion Women's Liberation Movement, 1966—. Author: The Church and the Second Sex, 1968; Beyond God the Father: Toward a Philosophy of Women's Liberation, 1973; contbr. Sisterhood is Powerful, 1970, Voices of the New Feminism, 1970, Radical Feminism, 1973, Religion For a New Generation, 1973. Home: 2018 Commonwealth Av Brighton MA 02135 Office: Dept Theology Boston College Chestnut Hill MA 02167

DALY, MARY ANN, pub. relations exec.; b. Erie, Pa., Dec. 29, 1943; d. Damian John and Letitia Mary (Lawson) Daly; student St. Vincent Nursing Sch., 1961-62; B.S., Mercyhurst Coll., 1966. With Mercyhurst Coll., Erie, 1966—, dir. found. research, 1966-67, adminstrv. asst. to asst. to pres., 1966-67, dir. pub. relations, 1967—. Cons. pub. relations Erie Consortium of Colls., 1970—, Sr. Citizen Adv. Office, 1972—. Mem. Arts Council, Erie; exec. bd. dirs. Muscular Dystrophy Assn. Am. (chmn. pub. health edn. com.). Mem. Am. Coll. Pub. Relations Assn., Am. Assn. for Higher Edn., Mercyhurst Coll. Alumni Assn. (pres. chpt.), Erie Advt. Club. Democrat. Roman Catholic. Club: Erie Press. Home: 718 St Clair Erie PA 16505 Office: Mercyhurst College 501 E 38th St Erie PA 16501

DALY, MAUREEN PATRICIA (MRS. WILLIAM PETER MCGIVERN), author; b. County Tyrone, No. Ireland, Mar. 15, 1927; d. Joseph Desmond and Margaret Dorothea (Kelly) Daly; came to U.S., 1930, naturalized, 1930; student St. Mary's Springs Acad., 1940-44; B.A., Rosary Coll., 1948; m. William Peter McGivern, Dec. 28, 1948. Reporter, columnist Chgo. Tribune and Syndicate, 1948-50; asso. editor, reporter, fgn. corr. Ladies Home Jour., Phila., 1948-54; spl. editor, cons. Saturday Evening Post, Phila., 1958-62. Recipient Freedom Found., 1952. Author: Seventeenth Summer, 1948; Spanish Roundabout, Moroccan Roundabout, Twelve Around the World, Sixteen and Other Stories; (with William McGivern) Mention My Name in Mombasa. Home: 73-305 Ironwood Dr Palm Desert CA 92260

DALY, MAXINE ELIZABETH FREDENBURG, govt. ofcl.; b. Springfield, Ore., Oct. 7, 1915; d. John A. and Hattie (McQuinn) Fredenburg; grad. Olympia (Wash.) High Sch. div.; children—Joanne (Mrs. Robert Fitzsimmons), Beverly (Mrs. Bratton), Nancy (Mrs. Laurel R. Alexander). Supr. budget, fiscal statistics Wash. Dept. Labor and Industries, Olympia, 1939-60, asst. dir. indsl. relations, 1965-66, asst. dir. indsl. ins., 1966; commr. Wash. Dept. Employment Security, 1966-71; regional dir. U.S. Dept. of Labor, Seattle, 1972-73; asst. dir. bus. and professions adminstrn. Wash. Dept. Motor Vehicles, 1973—; dir. indsl. relations Assn. Wash. Industries, 1960-65. Active various civic orgns. Home: 1215 W 6th St Olympia WA 98502 Office: Hwy-Licenses Bldg Olympia WA 98504

DALZELL, JEANNE ALEXANDER, artist, art center adminstr.; b. New Haven, Nov. 3, 1929; d. John Morrell and Winnifred (Keeler) Alexander; student U. Wis., 1968-70, Rockford Coll., 1971-72, Beloit Coll., 1974; m. David Rudolf Dalzell, Jr., Feb. 9, 1952 (div. Apr. 1972); children—David Paul, Jeffrey Alexander. Acting dir. Wright Art Center, Beloit (Wis.) Coll.; exhibited in group shows Madison Art Center, Beloit and Vicinity Anns., Rockford and Vicinity Ann., also several invitational exhbns.; work represented in several pvt. collections; represented by Earthwork Gallery, Rockton, Ill. Former mem. Jr. League, Pittsfield, Mass.; an organizer Berkshire Hist. Soc.; former mem. bd. Community Music Sch., Berkshire Mus., Berkshire Art Center, Pittsfield. Recipient Achievement in Art award, 1st place Two D Design, U. Wis., 1969. Nat. Endowment for Arts grantee Mpls. Inst. Art, 1972, curatorship program Asian Mus., San Francisco, 1975. Mem. Am. Assn. Museums. Episcopalian. Home: 1856 Northgate Dr 201C Beloit WI 53511 Office: Wright Art Center Beloit College Beloit WI 53511

D'AMBROSIO, LILLIAN MARIE, judge; b. Boston, Dec. 27, 1920; d. Michele Angelo and Rose Raffaele (Sammaria) D'Ambrosio; B.S. in Bus. Adminstrn., Boston U., 1946; J.D., 1950, LL.M., 1952. Admitted to Mass. bar, 1950; pvt. practice law, Boston, 1950-66; commr. Mass. Indsl. Accident Bd., 1966-73; mem. firm Parker, Coulter, Daley & White, 1973—; spl. justice Dist. Ct., Chelsea, Mass., 1973—. Adminstrv. sec. to Gov., 1957-58, adminstrv. sec., legal counsel, 1958-59; tax counsel Mass. Dept. Corps. and Taxation, Boston, 1959-66. Mem. women's council Don Orione Home, East Boston, 1973—; dir., clk. Social Service Credit Union, Boston, 1963—. Sec., Young Democrats, 1952-54. Bd. dirs. Christopher Columbus Community Center. Recipient Golden Lady award Amita, 1969-70; Circolo Lettario Italiano Soc. award, 1973. Mem. Mass., Boston bar assns., Justinian Law Soc. (sec. 1960—), Am. Justinian Soc., Nat., Mass. assns. women lawyers, Sons Italy in Am. (state chmn. charity drive for birth defects 1969-70), Profl. and Bus. Woman's Lodge (venerable 1972-74), Boston U. Law Sch. Alumni Assn. Roman Catholic. Club: Women Graduates Boston U. (dir. 1973-76). Home: 37 Union St Charlestown MA 02129 Office: 50 Congress St Boston MA 02109

DAMES, JOAN FOSTER (MRS. URBAN L. DAMES), editor; b. New Orleans, Sept. 29, 1934; d. Albert Steere and Lucia (Valdes) Foster; student St. Louis U., 1953-56; m. Urban Louis Dames, Feb. 10, 1959; children—Alice Catherine, Lucia Ann, Cecilia Mary, Madeline Sophie. Seismograph rec. librarian St. Louis U., 1954-55; feature writer St. Louis Globe Democrat, 1955-60; feature writer St. Louis Post-Dispatch, 1966-68, women's editor, 1968—, editor Everyday mag., 1972—, features editor, 1973—. Vice pres. St. Louis Bridal Bur., 1959—. Radio personality sta. KMOX-CBS, 1969—. Mem. Soc. Am. Social Scribes (dir. 1969-72), Theta Sigma Phi. Author: Prelude, 1956. Home: 7149 Lindell Av University MO 63130 Office: 1133 Dr Martin Luther King Dr St St Louis MO 63101

DAMIANI, JOAN DOROTHY, guidance counselor; b. Bklyn., Mar. 7, 1941; d. Emanuel and Lillian (Viccica) Damiani; B.A., Jersey City State Coll., 1962; M.A., N.Y. U., 1965; certification in guidance, State U. N.Y. at Albany, 1967. Art tchr. Rahway (N.J.) Pub. Schs., 1962-63, Bayonne (N.J.) Pub. Schs., 1963-67; guidance counselor Central Sch. Hillsdale, N.Y., 1967-71, Hudson (N.Y.) Pub. Schs., 1971—. Tchr. adult edn., Bayonne, 1963-64; exhibited paintings in group shows Jersey State Coll., 1961, 62, 63; founder Children's Art Expn., Bayonne, 1966. Mem. Assn. Women Dean's and Counselors, Columbia County Counselors Assn. (sec. 1967-70), Columbia County Agrl. Extension. Home: RD 2 Hillsdale NY 12529 Office: Hudson Middle Sch Harry Howard Av Hudson NY 12534

D'AMICO, LAURA CATHERINE DIGENNARO (MRS. CHARLES A. D'AMICO), personnel exec.; b. N.Y.C., Feb. 4, 1920; d. Neil and Catherine (Marigliano) DiGennaro; B.A., Hunter Coll., 1938; postgrad. Delahanty Inst., 1940-41, N.Y. Bus. Sch., 1941-42; m. Charles A. D'Amico, Aug. 4, 1942. Adminstrv. exec. sec., personnel sec. Am. Home Products, Inc. and subsidiary Ayerst, McKenna & Harrison, N.Y.C., 1948-51; office mgr. New Eng. Mutual Life Ins. Co., Lambert H. Huppler Agy., 1951-56; adminstrv. mgr. Nat. Soc. Crippled Children & Adults, Inc., N.Y.C., 1957-63; personnel and office mgr. S.B. Penick & Co., N.Y.C., 1964-67; personnel mgr. Geon Industries, Inc., Woodbury, N.Y., 1968-69, N.Y. Inst. Tech., Old Westbury, N.Y., 1969—. Mem. Adminstrv. Mgmt. Soc., Nat. Fedn. Bus. and Profl. Women's Clubs, Personnel Dirs. Council L.I. Republican. Home: 55 Roslyn Dr Glen Head NY 11545 Office: Wheatley Rd Old Westbury NY 11568

DAMM, CARYLNN ANN, educator; b. Elk Creek, Neb., Jan. 29, 1927; d. Albert J. and Salome (Durst) Damm; grad. Lincoln (Neb.) Gen. Hosp. Sch. Nursing, 1947; B.S., Neb. Wesleyan U., 1951; M.S. in Nursing, U. Cal. No. Br., 1961. Mem. nursing staff Lincoln Gen. Hosp., 1947-54, dir. nursing service, 1950-54; med. surg. supr. Peninsula Hosp., Burlingame, Cal., 1954-57; asso. dir. nursing service U. Tenn. Meml. Research Center and Hosp., Knoxville, 1957-59; ednl. coordinator Alta Bates Hosp., Berkeley, Cal., 1959-61; asst. prof. Sacramento State Coll., 1961-67; cons. USPHS, Sante Fe, 1966; instr. Palomar Coll., San Marcos, Cal., 1967-68; ednl. coordinator Ross (Cal.) Gen. Hosp., 1968-71, cons. Ross Med. Corp., 1969-71; asso. dir. nursing Sutter Community Hosps., Sacramento, 1971—. Mem. workshop planning com. Sacramento County Heart Assn., 1961; mem. seminar planning com. Cal. Council Hosp. Pharmacists and Cal. Nursing Assn., 1969; mem. task force Cal. Bd. Nursing Edn. and Nurse Registration Inst., 1969. Mem. Am., Cal. (nominating com. 1963, dist. 7 pres. 1964-67, dir. 1971—) nurses assns., Nat. League for Nursing, Psi Chi. Home: 11890 Cresthill Dr Elk Grove CA 95624 Office: 52-F S 6th St Sacramento CA 98519

DAMON, LINDA LEE (MRS. FRANKLIN LEE DAMON), psychologist; b. Springfield, O., July 12, 1942; d. Herbert M. and Ruth M. (Clinger) Foster; student (NSF fellow) Colo. Coll., 1960-62; B.A. cum laude, Conn. Coll., 1964; Ph.D. in Clin. Psychology (Nat. Inst. Mental Health research grantee), U. Cal. at Los Angeles, 1971; m. Franklin Lee Damon, Sept. 11, 1971. Chief psychologist Am. River Community Mental Health Center, Sacramento, 1971-73; clin. psychologist Fort Logan Mental Health Center, Denver, 1974—. Cons., lectr. London U., U. Tel Aviv, 1973. Nat. Def. Edn. Act fellow, 1964. Mem. Am., Colo. psychol. assns. Democrat. Home: 11635 Mayfield Los Angeles CA 90049

D'AMORIM, MARIA ALICE, psychologist, educator; b. Sao Paulo, Brazil, Apr. 16, 1928; d. Mario and Maria Luiza (Magahaes) D'Amorim; B.A. in Philosophy, Catholic U. Rio de Janeiro, 1950, B.A. in Psychology, 1962; M.A. in Social Psychology, State U. Ia., 1964-65; Ph.D., U. Louvain (Belgium), 1969. Asst. prof. Cath. U. Rio de Janeiro, 1962-64, asso. prof., 1965-66; prof. U. Que., Three Rivers, Can., 1969—. Fellow Sch. Medicine, U. N.C. at Chapel Hill, 1974—. Mem. Am., Canadian psychol. assns. Home: 3275 Rene Kimber St Three Rivers PQ Canada

DANA, MARGARET BLOXHAM (MRS. HENRY TRUMBULL DANA), consumer attitude researcher; b. Verona, N.J.; d. Charles Mason and Evelyn Lydia (Wilder) Bloxham; student Oberlin Coll.; m. Henry Trumbull Dana; children—Margaret, Cynthia. Ind. research, studies of many communities, adviser to industry, govt., consumers, 1937—. Dir. Underwriters' Lab.; lectr. to colls., univs., indsl. groups, consumer orgns. Mem. nat. adv. com. Flammable Fabrics Act, U.S. Consumer Product Safety Commn., Washington, 1967—. Bd. dirs. Better Bus. Bur. Eastern Pa. Recipient Distinguished Service award Nat. Alliance of TV and Electronic Service Assns., 1965, Am. Apparel Mfrs. Assn. for Better Customer Relations, 1968; certificate appreciation Am. Assn. for Textile Tech., 1973; award meritorious service field standardization Standards Engrs. Soc.-Am. Soc. Testing and Materials, 1974. Mem. Nat. Fire Protection Assn. (dir.), Am. Nat. Standards Inst., Am. Soc. for Testing and Materials (dir.). Author: Behind the Label, 1939. Writer syndicated consumer information columns Before You Buy also Consumer's Question-Box, 1965—. Contbr. articles to profl. jours. Home: Research Center Rural Route 1 Chalfont PA 18914

DANA-BASHIAN, PAULINE, lawyer; b. Boston, July 17, 1941; d. John and Helen (Paddock) Dana-Bashian; B.A., U. Wis., 1964; J.D., Suffolk U., 1971. Admitted to Mass. bar, 1971; research asst. Mass. Superior Court, Boston, 1968-71; atty. Eaton & Howard, Inc., Boston, 1971-72; atty., trust officer Mass. Co., Inc., Boston, 1973—. Mem. Mass., Boston bar assns., Democrat. Home: 85 Sutherland Rd Brookline MA 02146 Office: 100 Federal St Boston MA 02110

DANCE, JOY MARIE, endl. adminstr.; b. Clearwater, Fla., Aug. 10, 1945; d. Clifford Ferns and Ruby (Blackburn) Dance; B.S., Fla. State U., 1967; postgrad. U. South Fla., 1968-70; M.Ed., Ga. State U., 1974. Tchr. coach tennis Pinellas County pub. schs., St. Petersburg, Fla., 1967-71; dean women, instr. phys. edn. Atlanta Christian Coll., 1971—. Instr. water safety A.R.C., Nat. Aquatic Sch., Brevard, N.C., 1963—. Mem. Fla. Assn. Health, Phys. Edn. and Recreation (co-membership chmn. 1967-70; mem. internat. relations com. 1971), Pinellas County Phys. Edn. Assn., A.A.H.P.E.R., Fla. Edn. Assn., Ga. Assn. Dean and Women Counselors, Fla. State Alumni Assn., Phi Delta Pi. Home: 2605 Ben Hill Rd East Point GA 30344

DANDOY, MAXIMA ANTONIO (MRS. APOLINARIO M. DANDOY), educator; b. Santa Maria, Ilocos Sur, P.I.; d. Manuel and Isidra (Mendoza) Antonio; came to U.S., 1949, naturalized, 1951; teaching certificate Philippine Normal Coll., 1940; A.B., Nat. Tchrs. Coll., Manila, P.I., 1947; M.A., Arellano U., Manila, 1949; Ed.D. (John M. Switzer scholar, 1950, Newhouse Found. scholar, 1951), Stanford U., 1951, postgrad. (Cal. Fedn. Bus. and Profl. Women's Club scholar), 1952; m. Apolinario M. Dandoy, Mar. 14, 1947. Tchr. elementary sch., P.I., 1928-38; lab. sch. supervising tchr. Philippine Normal Coll., Manila, 1940-49; instr. Arellano U., Manila, 1947-49; lab. sch. prin. U. of East, Manila, 1952-53, asso. prof., 1952-55; prof. edn. Cal. State U. at Fresno, 1956—. Mem. com. for the selection social studies textbooks for state adoption, Cal., 1970-71; mem. gov.'s conf. on traffic safety for Cal., 1962; mem. scholarship award panel Bank of Am., 1968; mem. Cal. Gov.'s Conf. Delinquency Prevention, 1963. Named distinguished Woman of Year, Fresno Bus. and Profl. Women's Club, 1957, Woman of Achievement award, 1973. Mem. Nat. Council for Social Studies (chmn. sect. internat. understanding, nat. conv. 1966), Cal. Fedn. Bus. and Profl. Women's Club (state chmn. scholarships 1961-63), Cal. Tchrs. Assn., Am. Assn. U. Women (liaison Cal. State U. at Fresno 1970-71), People to People of Fresno, Soc. Profs. Edn., Filipino-Am. Women's Club (adv. 1969-74), Nat. Geographic Soc., Pi Lambda Theta, Kappa Delta Pi (counselor 1973—). Home: 1419 W Bullard Av Fresno CA 93705

DANELLIS, JOAN VERNIKOS, educator, pharmacologist; b. Alexandria, Egypt, May 9, 1934; d. Apostolos and Catherine (Manganari) Vernikos; B.Pharm., U. Alexandria, 1955; Ph.D., U. London (Eng.), 1960; m. Constantine Danellis, June 15, 1960 (dec. Apr. 1971); children—Eftihia, George. Came to U.S., 1960, naturalized, 1972. Asst. prof. Ohio State U. Med. Sch., Columbus, 1960—. NRC research asso. Ames Research Center, NASA, Moffett Field, Cal., 1964-66, research scientist, 1966—, chief human studies br., 1972—; lectr. Cal. State U. San Jose, 1968—; lectr. aeronautics and astronautics Stanford U., 1971—. Mem. Endocrine Soc., Am. Soc. Pharmacology and Exptl. Therapeutics, Am. Physiol. Soc., Internat. Brain Research Orgn. Republican. Mem. Greek Orthodox Ch. Editorial bd. Jour. Pharmacology and Exptl. Therapeutics, 1971—, Endocrinology, 1973—. Home: 21545 Monrovia St Cupertino CA 95014 Office: Human Studies Br Ames Research Center NASA Moffett Field CA 94035

DANENHOWER, ELOISE MARIE GARTON (MRS. WILLIAM HAUSEMAN DANENHOWER), assn. exec.; b. N.Y.C., Apr. 9, 1916; d. Cyril Sidney and Elsie Evelyn (Stapleton) Garton; student Taylor Bus. Coll., 1933-35; m. William Hauseman Danenhower, May 25, 1940; 1 dau., Diane Eloise (Mrs. John Paul Bonfiglio). Legal sec. Schnader & Lewis, Phila., 1935; Women's dir., asst. news dir. daily radio interview show Housewives Holiday, WCOJ, West Chester, Coatesville, Pa., 1952-55; pres. Chester County Soc. for Prevention Cruelty to Animals, West Chester, Pa., 1953-54, exec. sec., 1954-55; dir. pub. relations Pa. Soc. Prevention Cruelty to Animals, Phila., 1955—. Recipient Human-Animal Relationship award Inst. Human-Animal Relationship, 1966; Lassie Gold award Lassie Prodns., Inc., 1967; Pepper Pot award Pub. Relations Soc. Am., 1966-67. Mem. Am. Women in Radio and TV (trustee nat. ednl. found. 1967-68, dir. 1972-73, pres. chpt. 1966-67, v.p. mid-east area 1974—), Internat. Soc. to Protect Animals, Internat. Platform Assn., Chester County Soc. Prevention Cruelty to Animals, Phila. Art Alliance, Nat. Assn. Am. Pen Women, Nat. Dog Writers Assn. Writer, editor Animaldom, 1955—. Home: 620 W Ellet St Philadelphia PA 19119 Office: 350 E Erie Av Philadelphia PA 19134

DANER, REBA ENGLER, lawyer; b. Key West, Fla., June 21, 1911; d. Abram and Anna (Schechtman) Engler; student U. Fla., 1927; A.B., U. Miami, 1930, J.D., 1936; m. Leonard Epstein, 1930 (dec. 1943); m. 2d, Jack L. Daner, Feb. 1, 1948; children—Ann (Mrs. Anderson), Leonette E. Admitted to Fla. bar, 1936, since practiced in Miami. Chmn. bd. trustees Miami Beach Pub. Library, 1958-72; mem. Met. Dade County Library Bd. 1962-72, chmn. bd., 1966. Bd. dirs. Brandeis U. Women's Assn.; trustee Bass Mus. Art, Miami Beach. Mem. Fla. Bar, Am., Dade County (chmn. resolutions com. 1965-67, mem. library com. 1959-70) bar assns., A.L.A., Southeast Library Assn. (chmn. 1970-72), Am., Fla. (pres. 1959-60) library trustees assns., Nat. Assembly Library Trustees (Fla. rep. 1958), Hadassah (pres. Greater Miami chpt. 1936), Fla. Women's Golf Assn. (sec. 1948), Soc. Founders U. Miami. Jewish religion (pres. Sisterhood temple 1944-48). Clubs: Westview Country, Miami Woman's Fla. Women's Golf Assn. (sec. 1948); Lawyers (dir. 1969-71); Century. Home: 303 E San Marino Dr Miami Beach FL 33139 Office: Alfred I DuPont Bldg Miami FL 33131

DANEY, SHIRLEY JEWEL, psychologist; b. Franklin County, Kan., July 10, 1933; d. Harley Bryan and Nina Louisa (Beach) Finch; student Ottawa U., 1950-52; U. Cal. at Berkeley, 1955; B.A. with honors, U. Tulsa, 1966, M.A. with honors, 1967; m. Herschell Eugene Daney, June 1, 1952 (div. July 1967); children—Stephen Bryan, Gregory Eugene. Sch. psychologist Tulsa Pub. Schs., 1967—; psychologist Marriage & Family Growth Center, Tulsa, 1968—. Mem. Nat. Assn. Sch. Psychologists (local sch. psychology pres. 1968-70), Okla. Edn. Assn. (sch. psychology sect. pres. 1971). Home: 4746 E 7th St Tulsa OK 74112 Office: Edn Service Center PO Box 45208 Tulsa OK 74145

DANFORD, JULIA WEPFER (MRS. BART H. DANFORD), educator, psychologist; b. El Dorado, Ark., May 12, 1936; d. Joseph Gottlieb and Julia Witherspoon (Fletcher) Wepfer; B.S. in Bus. Adminstr., U. Ark., 1958, M.A. in Psychology, 1965; m. Bart H. Danford, Feb. 1, 1969; 1 dau., Holly Ames Metcalf. Market analyst Am. Investment Advisers, Little Rock, 1958; office mgr. to orthodontist, Little Rock, 1958-60, to physician, Little Rock, 1961-64; psychol. examiner dept. psychiatry U. Ark. Med. Center, Little Rock, 1966-67, teaching asst., 1967-69, instr. dept. psychiatry 1969—. Dir. Columbia Land & Timber Co., Beauregard Parish, La. Ark. coordinator Deaf-Blind Project, 1971-72. Mem. Ark. Bd. Examiners in Psychology, 1973-77. Mem. Am., Ark. psychol. assns., Southwestern, Am. group psychotherapy assns., Psi Chi, Chi Omega. Home: 13001 Ridgehaven Rd Little Rock AR 72205

DANFORTH, FRANCES MUELLER (MRS. WILLIAM PAUL DANFORTH), civic worker; b. Austin, Tex., Mar. 23, 1914; d. Rudolph George and Laura Emma (Von Boeckmann) Mueller; B.J., U. Tex., 1935, B.A., 1936; M.S., Columbia, 1938; m. William Paul Danforth, Aug. 16, 1942; children—William Paul, Douglas Mueller, Donald Lee. Grader dept. journalism U. Tex., Austin, 1934; asst. dir. Interscholastic League Press Bur., U. Tex., 1936-37; asst. editor Alcalde, monthly alumni mag., 1936-37, 38-42; editor Star Points, nat. papers Delta Delta Delta Chgo., 1968-70. Pres., Austin Symphony League, 1967-68; state v.p. Tex. Women's Assn. Symphony Orchs., 1970; pres. Austin Vol. Bur., 1966-68. Bd. dirs., sec. U.S.O., 1971-72; bd. dirs. Symphony Orch. Soc.; bd. dirs., sec. Cen-Tex. chpt. A.R.C., pres. Altenheim, 1961-62. Mem. Women in Communications, Mortar Board, Delta Delta Delta. Lutheran (pres. ch. women 1972-74). Clubs: Settlement, Lawyers Wives (mem. bd., sec. 1973-74), Woman's (sec. 1972-74) (all Austin). Home 1400 West Av Austin TX 78701

D'ANGELO, GIANNA, soprano; b. Hartford, Conn.; d. Stephen Howard and Dorothy (Holt) Angelovich; student Mt. Ida Jr. Coll., 1947-48, then Juilliard Conservatory; pupil of Hazel Porter Snow, Giuseppe de Luca, Toti dal Monte. Debut, Baths of Caracalla, 1954; appearances major opera houses Europe and U.S., 1954—; debut Met. Opera, 1961. Recipient Gold medal, Barcellona, Spain, 1958, Gold medal, Luxemburg, 1959. Office: Sch Music Indiana U Bloomington IN 47401

D'ANGELO, RITA YVONNE, psychologist; b. N.Y.C., Apr. 21, 1928; d. Anthony and Alice (Mignona) D'Angelo; B.A., Hunter Coll., 1948; M.A., Fordham U., 1950, Ph.D., 1961. Clin. psychologist Catholic Charities Psychiat. Clinic, N.Y.C., 1950-53, part-time 1953—; asst. prof. Marymount Coll., Tarrytown, N.Y., 1953-57; supervising clin. psychologist St. Germaine's Residential Treatment Center for Disturbed Delinquent Girls, Peekskill, N.Y., 1957-62; asst. prof. L.I. U., Bklyn., 1962-64; asst. prof. psychology Lehman Coll., Bronx, N.Y., 1964-70, asso. prof., 1971—. Dir. psychol. services Archdiocesan Summer Head Start, 1967-69; Am. Psychol. Assn. mental health cons. to Head Start region II, 1973—. Recipient Distinguished Tchr. award Lehman Coll., 1973. Mem. Am., N.Y. State (dir. 1971-74), Eastern psychol. assns., Psychologists Interested in Religious Issues (dir. 1970-73), N.Y. Acad. Scis., N.Y. Soc. Clin. Psychologists (asso. editor Profl. Digest 1965-70), Sigma Xi, Psi Chi, Alpha Gamma Delta. Home: Box 307 Scarborough NY 10510 Office: Lehman Coll Bronx NY 10468

DANGREMOND, LUCILLE MARTIN (MRS. HARLEY L. DANGREMOND), civic worker; b. St. Louis; d. George H. and Julia (Blattner) M.; B.A., Washington U., St. Louis, 1922; M.A., Tchrs. Coll., Columbia, 1940; m. Harley L. Dangremond, June 28, 1924; children—Jack M., Dorothy J. Tchr., Bogota (N.J.) High Sch., 1940-43; substitute tchr. Teaneck (N.J.) High Sch., 1943-60; tchr. Englewood (N.J.) High Sch., 1940-55; profl. mag. writer, 1946-48. Mem. adv. com. Sch. Edn., Rutgers U., 1957-59; former mem. adv. panel pub. health services Dept. Health, Edn. and Welfare; liaison officer Am. Mothers Com.; mem. Bergen County (N.J.) Easter Seal Com., 1971—. Recipient citation Nat. Police Officers Assn. Mem. N.J. State Fedn. Women's Clubs (pres. 1960-62), Gen. Fedn. Women's Clubs (chmn. religion 1962-64, dir. 1960-70, chmn. vets. div. 1968-70, State Jewel 1966; recipient award for leadership, 1964-66, for longest outstanding record leadership N.J. 1966), Am. Mothers Com., Inc. (regional dir. 1958-60), Middle Atlantic Conf. Gen. Fedn. Women's Clubs (pres. 1964-66, chmn. home life dept. 1964-66) P.E.O. (chpt. pres. 1967-69). Clubs: Past Presidents' (pres. 1949-51), Washington University Alumni, Teachers College Alumni. Home: 753 Larch Av Teaneck NJ 07666

DANIEL, ALICE, educator, lawyer; b. N.Y.C.; d. Edwin and Rose (Barnett) Glantz; A.B., Boston U., 1958; LL.B., Columbia, 1963; 1 son, John. Admitted to N.Y. bar, 1963, Cal. bar, 1971; asso. appellate counsel criminal appeals div. N.Y. Legal Aid Soc., N.Y.C., 1967-70; asso. counsel N.A.A.C.P. Legal Def. and Edn. Fund, San Francisco, 1970-72; asso. prof. law U. Cal. Hastings Coll. Law, San Francisco, 1972—. Bd. dirs. No. Cal. Service League. Mem. Am. Civil Liberties Union (dir. No. Cal.). Editorial adv. bd. Prison Law Reporter, 1973—. Office: 198 McAllister St San Francisco CA 94102

DANIEL, DONNA MARY, librarian; b. Galion, O., Oct. 19, 1932; d. Ambrose Louis and Gertrude (Daniel) Daniel; B.S., Ohio U., 1956; M.S. in L.S., Western Res. U., 1964. Librarian, Galion Jr. and Sr. High Schs., 1956-57; tchr. Northridge High Sch., Dayton, 1957-59; librarian Madison High Sch., Mansfield, 1959-66; asst. librarian Mansfield br. Ohio State U., 1966-67; librarian Shelby (O.) Jr. High School, 1967—. Chmn. exec. com. St. Joseph's Sch., Galion, 1969-71; mem. steering com. Right to Read. Mem. North Central Ohio Tchrs. Assn. Sch. Librarians (sec.-treas.), Ohio Assn. Sch. Librarians (regional dir.), Am., Ohio library assns., N.E.A., Richland County, Madison tchrs. assns., Ohio Edn. Assn., Ch. Music Assn. Am., Delta Kappa Gamma. Roman Catholic. Home: 406 Fairview Galion OH 44833

DANIEL, ELEANOR WILMA SAUER (MRS. JOHN C. DANIEL), economist; b. Bklyn., Feb. 8, 1917; d. Charles P. and Elsie (Dommer) Sauer; B.A. magna cum laude, Mt. Holyoke Coll., 1936; M.A., Columbia, 1937; m. William C. Bagley, Jr., June 11, 1937 (div. 1951); m. 2d, John Carl Daniel, Dec. 31, 1952; children—Victoria Ann, Charles Timothy. Research economist U.S. Steel Corp., 1938; lectr. econs. Bklyn. Coll., 1939-40; supr. research div. Mut. Life Ins. Co. N.Y., 1940-44, research asso., 1945-55, dir. econ. research, 1955-72, asst. v.p., sr. econ. adviser, 1972-74; economist Fed. Home Loan Bank N.Y., 1974—. Mem. joint subcom. on monetary and fiscal policy Life Ins. Assn. Am.-Am. Life Conv., 1962—, mem. life ins. investment research com., 1957-60, 64-67; mem. econ. growth com. bus. research adv. council U.S. Bur. Labor Statistics, 1966—; mem. various tech. coms. Nat. Bur. Econ. Research; research review panel Dept. Health, Edn. and Welfare; mem. coms. Project Econs.; mem. Pres.'s Task Force on Fed. Credit Programs, 1968-69; mem. econ. adv. bd. U.S. Dept. of Commerce, 1970-72. Mem. Downtown Economists (treas. 1962-64, chmn. 1964-66), Am. Finance Assn. (dir. 1957-59), Am. Statis. Assn. (mem. finance com. 1968—), Am. Econ. Assn., Acad. Polit. Sci., Nat. Assn. Bus. Economists, Forecasters Club N.Y. (sec.-treas. 1970-72), Nat. Planning Assn., Women's Bond Club (v.p. 1970-72, pres. 1972—), Atlantic Council, Phi Beta Kappa. Author: (with J.J. O'Leary and S. Foster) Our National Debt and Our Savings, 1949. Contbr. articles in field. Home: 34 N Drive East Brunswick NJ 08816 Office: 60 Broad St New York City NY 10004

DANIEL, GEORGIA LEE, city ofcl.; b. Pontotoc, Miss., May 15, 1925; d. George Lee and Ella Ardena (Caldwell) Reeder; grad. high sch.; m. William Curtis Daniel, Mar. 24, 1946; children—Glenda (Mrs. Paul B. Anderson, Jr.), Donna (Mrs. Clifford Austin Hughes). Bookkeeper Ala. Furniture Mfg. Co., Clanton, Ala., 1945-49, 52-54; billing clk. City Hall, Clanton, Ala., 1959-62, city clk., 1962—. Substitute tchr. New Harmony High Sch., Blue Springs, Miss., 1943-44, elementary schs., Clanton, 1957-58. Mem. City Planning Commn., 1968—. Mem. Ala. Assn. Municipal Clks. and Adminstrs. Baptist (mem. women's missionary union). Home: 905 5th Av N Clanton AL 35045 Office: PO Box 580 Clanton AL 35045

DANIEL, KATHRYN BARCHARD educator; b. Foley, Ala., Jan. 9, 1931; d. Frank Vernon and Myrtle (Morris) Barchard; B.S., U. Ala., 1952, M.A., 1961, Ph.D., 1963; m. James L. Daniel, 1954 (div. 1958); 1 dau., Pamela Kathryn. Tchr. pub. schs. Baldwin County, Foley, Ala., 1952-60; asst. prof. ednl. psychology Monmouth Coll., West Long Branch, N.J., 1963-64; asso. prof. ednl. psychology Newark State Coll., Union, N.J., 1964-66; asso. prof. U. S.C., Columbia, 1966-69, prof. ednl. psychology, 1969-73, chmn. ednl. psychology Coll. Edn., 1969-70, chmn. ednl. founds., 1971-73; prof., coordinator research and devel. Sch. Nursing, U. Ala., Birmingham, 1973—. Cons., Regional Ednl. Lab., pub. schs. N.C., S.C., Va., N.J., 1963-68. Nat. Def. Edn. Act fellow, 1960-63. Mem. Am. Psychol. Assn., Am. Personnel and Guidance Assn., Am. Ednl. Research Assn., Assn. for Supervision and Curriculum Devel., Soc. for Research in Child Devel., Am. Assn. U. Profs., Assn. for Student Tchrs., A.A.A.S. Contbr. articles to profl. jours., chpts. to books. Home: 1022 Essex Rd Birmingham AL 35222

DANIEL, LOUISE JANE, educator; b. Phila., Oct. 28, 1912; d. Frank W. and Mabel (Brensinger) Daniel; B.S., U. Pa., 1935; M.S., Pa. State U., 1936; Ph.D., Cornell U., 1945. Tchr. Penn Hall Jr. Coll., Chambersburg, Pa., 1936-42; research asso. Cornell U., 1945-48, asst. prof. biochemistry, 1948-51, asso. prof., 1951-58, prof. biochemistry and molecular biology, 1958-73, prof. emeritus, 1973—. Mem. A.A.A.S., Am. Chem. Soc., Am. Soc. Biol. Chemists, Am. Inst. Nutrition, Soc. Exptl. Biology and Medicine, N.Y. Acad. Scis., Sigma Xi, Phi Kappa Phi, Alpha Xi Delta. Home: 210 Highgate Rd Ithaca NY 14850

DANIEL-DREYFUS, SUSAN B. RUSSE (MRS. MARC ANDRE DANIEL-DREYFUS), civic worker; b. St. Louis, May 30, 1940; d. Frederick William and Suzanne (Mackay) Russe; student Smith Coll., 1958-60, Corcoran Sch. Fine Arts, 1960-61, Washington U. (St. Louis), 1961-62; m. Don B. Faerber, Nov. 27, 1962 (div. Nov. 1969); 1 dau., Suzanne Mackay; m. 2d, Marc Andre Daniel-Dreyfus, Aug. 9, 1969. Mem. St. Louis-St. Louis County White House Conf. on Edn., 1966-68; mem. Mo. 1st Gov.'s Conf. on Edn., 1966, 2d Conf., 1968. Bd. dirs. St. Louis Smith Coll.; hon. bd. dirs. New Music Circle; Woman's bd. dirs. Washington U., New Music Circle, 1963-67; Woman's bd. Mo. Hist. Soc.; bd. dirs. Non-Partisan Ct. Plan for Mo., Young Audiences Inc., 1967-69; bd. dirs. Childrens Art Bazaar, 1968-70; founder St. Louis Opera Theater; jr. bd. dirs. St. Louis Symphony, 1966-68; legislative chmn. bd. dirs. Boston League of Women Voters, 1969-72; mem. council Jr. League of Boston, 1970-72; chmn. Art. Mus. Bond Issue election St. Louis, 1966; bd. govs. Tunbridge Sch. Mem. Colonial Dames, Boston League Women Voters, Soc. Art Historians. Club: Women's City (dir.) (Boston). Home: 10 Otis Pl Boston MA 02108

DANIELLS, LORNA MCLEAN, librarian; b. Toledo; d. John E. and Mary (McLean) Daniells; B.A., Miami U., 1940; B.S., Columbia, 1941. Asst. catalog dept. Vassar Coll., 1941-43, serial cataloger, 1943-46; cataloger Harvard Bus. Sch., 1946-49, reference librarian, 1949-69, head reference dept., 1969—. Mem. Spl. Libraries Assn. (chmn. bus. and finance div. 1958-59; chmn. adv. council 1964-65; pres. Boston chpt. 1968-69; chmn. admissions com. 1968-69; chmn. nominating com. 1972-73). Author: Studies in Enterprise: a Selected Bibliography of American and Canadian Company Histories and Biographies of Businessmen, 1957, and ann. supplements appearing in Bus. History Rev. Compiler bibliographies Harvard Bus. Sch. Reference List Series. Contbr. to library and bus. jours. Home: 26 Concord Av Cambridge MA 02138 Office: Soldiers Field Rd Boston MA 02163

DANIELS, ARLENE KAPLAN (MRS. RICHARD RENE DANIELS), sociologist; b. N.Y.C., Dec. 10, 1930; d. Jacob and Elizabeth (Rathstone) Kaplan; A.B. with honors, U. Cal. at Berkeley, 1952, M.A., 1954, Ph.D., 1960; m. Richard Rene Daniels, June 9, 1956. Instr. dept. speech U. Cal. at Berkeley, 1959-61; research asso. Mental Research Inst., Palo Alto, Cal., 1961-66; asso. prof. dept. sociology San Francisco State Coll., 1966-70; research asso. Sci. Analysis Corp., San Francisco, 1970—, chief Center for Study of Women in Soc., 1971—. Cons. Nat. Inst. Mental Health, Washington, 1971-73. Nat. Inst. Mental Health fellow, 1965-66; Faculty Research fellow Soc. Sci. Research Council, 1970-71. Mem. Am., Pacific (adv. council, program chmn. 1972—) sociol. assns., A.A.A.S., Sociologists for Women in Soc. (v.p. 1971-73), Women's Equity Action League, Soc. for Study of Social Problems (dir., program chmn. 1972-73), Assn. Women in Sci., Nat. Orgn. for Women. Club: Commonwealth (San Francisco). Home: 3404 Lodge Dr Belmont CA 94002 Office: 4339 California St San Francisco CA 94118

DANIELS, BARBARA NEIL, social worker, educator; b. Tyler, Tex., Sept. 12, 1932; d. John Eugene and Lelda (Barnes) Daniels; B.S., Lamar State Coll. Tech., 1958; M.S.W., La. State U., 1960. Caseworker, Family Counseling Service, Port Arthur, Tex., 1960-62, Family Service Assn., Fort Worth, 1962-64; chief social worker Fort Worth State Adult Mental Health Clinic, 1964-65; supr. adoption service Edna Gladney Home, Fort Worth, 1965-69; field instr. U. Tex. Sch. Social Work, Arlington, 1968-69, asst. prof., 1969-70. Social work cons. Day Care Assn., Fort Worth and Tarrant County, 1969-73; dir. project outreach for Edna Gladney Home and U. Tex., 1969-70, project dir., placement supr., 1970-72, dir. services to unwed parents, 1972-75; exec. dir. Chaparral Home and Adoption Service, Albuquerque, 1975—. Program chmn. Fort Worth Community Theatre Guild, 1967-68. Mem. Nat. Assn. Social Workers (chpt. pres. 1964-66, mem. chpt. profl. accreditation com. 1967—). Acad. Certified Social Workers, Child Welfare League Am. (planning com. S.W. regional conf. 1968-70). Episcopalian. Home: 6312 Avenida La Costa Albuquerque NM 87109 Office: 323 10th St Albuquerque NM 87102

DANIELS, BERNICE VIOLA (MRS. EDWARD BERNARD DANIELS), librarian; b. Racine, Wis., Dec. 27, 1932; d. Alex Albert and Ida Elizabeth (Wilke) Emerich; B.S., U. Wis., 1954, M.S., 1958; m. Edward Bernard Daniels, May 17, 1971; children (by previous marriage)—Timothy Alan Cudd, Ann Elizabeth Cudd, Benjamin Kermit Cudd. Bookmobile librarian Rapid City (S.D.) Library, 1955-57; with Ohio State U. Libraries, 1958-67, asst. circulation librarian, 1958-59, cataloger, 1961-63, asst. head personnel and budget, 1966-67; head librarian Worthington (O.) Pub. Library, 1967—. Mem. Am., Ohio (chmn. recruitment 1968-69, intellectual freedom 1970-71) library assns., Beta Phi Mu. Unitarian. Home: Route 1 Gambler OH 43022 Office: 752 High St Worthington OH 43085

DANIELS, CHARLOTTE LOUISE (MRS. BERT FRANKLIN DANIELS), artist; b. Fostoria, O., Nov. 27, 1920; d. Alfred Henry and Edna (Roush) Shultz; student Grant Hosp. Sch. Nursing, 1939, Toledo Mus. Sch. Design, 1950-52, Art Instrn., Inc., 1951-52, U. Cin., 1966-69; pupil E. Burkhart, 1952-54; m. Bert Franklin Daniels, May 17, 1942; children—Larry Bert, Cheri Lynn, Neil Dana. Portrait demonstrator numerous galleries, colls., museums, TV, 1951-67; radio, TV appearances on art, 1952-72; exhibited in one man shows at Toledo Artists Club, 1954, So. Gallery, Columbus, O., 1955, Wilsons Restaurant, Columbus, 1955, Toledo Mus. Art, 1955, Black Kettle, Bucyrus, O., 1956, Youth Center, Columbus, 1957, Findlay Coll., 1957, Sugar 'N Spice, Cin., 1962, 63, Garrett Gallery, Cin., 1964, Town Club, Cin., 1968; exhibited in group shows including at Toledo Mus. Art, Midwest Landscape Art Exhibit, 1953, Montpelier Tri-State, 1950-52, Toledo Downtown Commerce Bank, 1953, Ohio State Fair, 1950-55, Cin. Zoo Festival, 1965; tchr. pvt. adult and youth art classes, 1950-56; dir. art Defiance Coll., 1956-57; art asst. Ohio State Fair, 1955; dir. art Ohio State Fair, 1956-57; dir. art Summer Ch. Camp, 1960-64; lectr. in liturgical art, 1966—. Leader, art cons. Girl Scouts Am., Boy Scouts Am., 1953-68, nat. art dir. for Sr. Girl Scout Round-up, Button Bay, Vt., 1962; del. State Conf. Child Conservation League, 1954—, Nat. Conf. Girl Scouts Am., 1960—; tchr. community free adult classes, 1962-66; art tchr. Project Upward at U. Cin., 1968; docent for Contemporary Arts Center, Cin., 1972-73. Recipient Scouters award Boy Scouts Am., 1957. Mem. Cin. Womans Art Club, Cin. Liturgical Art Group, Cincinnatians United for Good Schs., Ohio Watercolor Soc., Columbus Art League, Author, illustrator: Aiming in His Direction, 1970; team couple Marriage Encounter, 1972. Home: 2437 Madison Rd Cincinnati OH 45208

DANIELS, DIANNE SUSAN, state ofcl.; b. Pauls Valley, Okla., Nov. 16, 1940; d. Henry Winton and Gladys Susan (Richardson) D.; student U. Ark., 1960-61; B.B.A., U. Okla., 1964. Clk. First Nat. Bank & Trust Co., Oklahoma City, 1964-65; supr., credit woman Sunray DX Oil Co., Tulsa, 1965; asst. cashier Am. Exchange Bank & Trust Co., Norman, Okla., 1966-73, asst. v.p., 1973; bank examiner state of Okla., 1973—. Mem. United Daus. Confederacy, D.A.R. (outstanding jr. mem. Black Beaver chpt. 1968, 69). Baptist. Home: 820 W Eufaula St Norman OK 73069 Office: 4545 Lincoln Blvd Suite 12 Oklahoma City OK 73105

DANIELS, ELIZABETH ADAMS (MRS. JOHN LOTHROP DANIELS), educator; b. Westport, Conn., May 8, 1920; d. Thomas Davies and Minnie Mae (Sherwood) Adams; B.A., Vassar Coll., 1941; M.A., (Vassar fellow), U. Mich., 1942; Ph.D., N.Y.U., 1954; m. John Lothrop Daniels, Mar. 21, 1942; children—John L., Eleanor Bradford, Sherwood Adams, Ann Sheffield. Instr. to asst. prof. English, Vassar Coll., 1948-58, asso. prof. English, 1958-65, prof., 1965—, dean of freshmen, 1954-57, dean of studies, 1966-73. Named Outstanding Woman Grad. of Yr., N.Y.U., Alumni award medal, 1954. Mem. Am. Assn. U. Profs., Am. Assn. U. Women, Modern Lang. Assn., League Women Voters, Phi Beta Kappa. Clubs: Vassar, Tennis (Poughkeepsie). Home: 129 College Av Poughkeepsie NY 12603

DANIELS, HELEN SLOAN (MRS. FRANK CRAWFORD DANIELS), author; b. Durango, Colo., Dec. 21, 1899; d. Robert Henry and Ada (Maupin) Sloan; A.B., U. Colo., 1920; m. Frank Crawford Daniels, Oct. 26, 1921. Sec., Graden Merc. Co., Durango, 1948—. Mem. central com. Cultural Center, Fort Lewis Coll., Durango, 1964—. Trustee library, 1936-66, sec., 1940-62; mem. Nat. League Am. Pen Women (state pres. 1956-58), League Women Voters, P.E.O., D.A.R., Beta Sigma Phi (hon.), Alpha Chi Omega. Clubs: Garden, Reading (past pres.). Author: (with Editha Berry) Echoes from Navajo Land, 1934; Ute Indians of Southwestern Colorado, 1941; Los Rodriquez, 1942; Pictographs of Falls Creek, 1975. Home: 1131 3d Av Durango CO 81301 Office: 777 Main Av Durango CO 81301

DANIELS, MINA HAYES, librarian; b. Trenton, N.J., Apr. 23, 1927; d. George Michels and Ruth Bodine (Sexton) Hayes; B.A. (regional scholar), Coll. of Wooster, 1949; M.S. in L.S. (H.W. Wilson Co. fellow), U. N.C., 1965; postgrad. U. Tenn., 1973; m. Boyd Lee Daniels, June 13, 1949 (div. Aug. 1974); children—Diantha, Lee, Ellen, Gregory, Amy. Cataloger, Duke, 1965-66, head serials sect., 1966-67; catalog librarian U. Tenn. at Knoxville, 1968, asst. prof. Grad. Sch. Library and Information Sci., 1968-72, cons. Psychol. Clinic Library, 1971; sr. tech. librarian Central Research Library, Oak Ridge Nat. Lab., 1972-73, head circulation and reference, 1973-74; head cataloging dept. Morris Library So. Ill. U., 1974—. Cons., Cleveland (Tenn.) State Community Coll., 1972. Mem. A.L.A., Spl. Libraries Assn. (sec. Mid-Appalachian chpt. 1973-74), Phi Beta Kappa, Delta Phi Alpha, Phi Alpha Theta, Beta Phi Mu. Home: 604 S Oakland Av Apt 10 Carbondale IL 62901

DANIELS, MYRA JANCO (MRS. DRAPER DANIELS), advt. co. exec.; b. Gary, Ind., June 25, 1925; d. Elias and Cecelia (Remstein) Janco; B.S., Ind. State U., 1948, M.A., 1954; Ph.D., Ind. U., 1957; m. Draper Daniels, Aug. 19, 1967; Advt. dir. Meis Bros. Co., Terre Haute, Ind., 1944-50; v.p., account exec. Gregory & House Advt., Cleve., 1951-53; pres. Wabash Advt. Agy., Terre Haute, Ind., 1950-54; account exec. Kuttner & Kuttner, Chgo., 1954-62; v.p., Roche, Richerd & Cleary, Chgo., 1962-63; exec. v.p. Roche, Rickerd, Henri & Hurst, Chgo., 1963-65; pres. Draper Daniels, Inc., Chgo., 1965—. Recipient Distinguished Alumni award Ind. State U., 1966. Mem. Am. Advt. Fedn. (dir., mem. exec. com. 1967-69, Nat. Advt. Woman of Year award 1965), Am. Humane Assn., Am. Marketing Assn., Am. Assn. Advt. Agys., Am. Assn. U. Profs., Gamma Alphi Chi, Kappa Delta Pi, Pi Omega Pi, Lambda Theta, Delta Pi Epsilon, Tau Kappa Alpha, Theta Sigma Phi. Clubs: Women's Advertising, Altrusa, Sales Executive (Chgo.). Home: 990 Lake Shore Dr Chicago IL 60611 Office: 2501 John Hancock Center 875 N Michigan Av Chicago IL 60611

DANIELS, ROWENA VEATRICE COULTER (MRS. RUDOLPH A. DANIELS), assn. exec.; b. South Royalston, Mass.; d. James and Ella (White) Coulter; spl. student Yale, 1957, 58, Syracuse U. 1959-65; m. Rudolph A. Daniels, Sept. 21, 1941 (dec.). Credit mgr. Montgomery Ward & Co., 1932-51; mgr. Credit Bur., Claremont, N.H., 1952-57; pub. stenographer and secretarial service,

1951-55; exec. dir. Claremont C. of C., 1955—. Mem. Mayor's Community Action Com., 1964—; mem. Claremont City Council, 1966—, chmn. indsl. com., 1968—; apptd. mayor's Econ. Devel. Commn., 1969—, sec., 1969-72. Recipient Community Service awards Claremont Fire Dept., 1960, Distributive Edn. Club, 1960; Distinguished Service award Am. C. of C., 1963. Mem. Am. C. of C. Execs. Assn., N.H. Chamber Execs. Assn. (sec. 1968—), New Eng., N.H. chambers commerce assns., Nat. Credit Assn. Home: 20 Hartford St Claremont NH 03743 Office: 36 Tremont Sq Claremont NH 03743

DANIELS, TINA LUCY CARBONARO (MRS. JOSEPH JAMES DANIELS), realtor; b. Catania, Sicily, July 10, 1913; d. Vincent and Grace (Licciardello) Carbonaro; brought to U.S., 1914; student Boston U., 1932, Mt. San Antonio Coll., 1962-64; m. Joseph James Daniels, June 21, 1939. Buyers asst. Gilchrist's, Boston, 1932-42; prodn. control Boston Gear Works, Quincy, Mass., 1944-45; asst. campaign dir. Long Beach (Cal.) Community Chest, 1950-59; asso. broker A.L. Snell, Realtors, Covina, Cal., 1962-70, Tina Realty, Covina, 1970—. Day camp dir. Camp Fire Girls, Long Beach, Cal., 1948-49. Sec., Covina Valley Bd. of Realtors Credit Union, 1965-66, 69—, treas., 1967-68, pres., 1968—, activities vice chmn., 1969—; pres. Covina Coordinating Council, 1974-75. Bd. dirs. Verona Missionary League, 1969-70, v.p., 1970-71; sec. treas. bd. dirs. Lung Assn. San Gabriel Valley. Mem. real estate adv. com. Mt. San Antonio Coll. Recipient Grad. Realtors Inst. designation, 1966. Mem. Nat. Assn. Realtors (pres. Cal. Women's Council 1975) Cal. Real Estate Assn. (state dir. 1966-67, dist. chmn. bd. activities), Covina Valley Bd. Realtors (dir. 1966-67, sec. 1972, pub. relations chmn. 1966— pres. 1974-74), Verona Missionary League (pres. 1971-72), Covina C. of C. (dir.). Clubs: Whittier Riding (Cal.) (sec.-treas. 1957-59); Twin Lakes Womens Golf (El Monte, Cal.) (pres. 1960-61); Mt. Meadows Country (Pomona, Cal.) (sec. 1965); Altrusa (corr. sec. 1969-70, treas. 1970-71, pres. 1971-72). Home: 2117 E Cortez St West Covina CA 91790 Office: 532 D S Citrus Av Covina CA 91722

DANIELSON, DORIS ANDRESEN (MRS. PHILIP M. DANIELSON), pub. relations exec.; b. Chgo., Aug. 6, 1940; d. August Arnold and Lillian Mae (Rice) Andresen; B.A., Ill. Wesleyan U., 1961; postgrad. Roosevelt U., 1963-65; m. Philip M. Danielson, June 10, 1961. Editorial clk. Argonne (Ill.) Nat. Lab., 1961-62; asst. editor No. Trust Bank, Chgo., 1962-64, editor, 1964-66, supr. pub. relations, 1966-68, asst. mgr. advt. and pub. relations, 1968-73; dir. pub. relations Manpower, Inc., Milw., 1973—. Recipient Golden Trumpet awards Publicity Club Chgo., 1965, 66. Mem. Pub. Relations Soc. Am. Home: 6939 W Glenbrooke St Milwaukee WI 53223 Office: 5301 N Ironwood St Milwaukee WI 53201

DANIELSON, HARRIET ANN, educator; b. Jamestown, N.Y., June 25, 1922; d. Gordon C. and Mabel M. (Morse) Danielson; exec. secretarial diploma, Jamestown Bus. Coll., 1944; B.S., Alfred U., 1950; M.S., Syracuse U., 1951; Ed.D. (Nonservice grad. fellow 1954-56), Ind. U., 1959. Sec. Prudential Ins. Co., Jamestown, 1944-46, Jamestown Upholstery Corp., 1946-48; tchr. Irondequoit High Sch., Rochester, N.Y., 1951-52; teaching asst. Ind. U., Bloomington, 1952-54; prof. bus. edn. Kent (O.) State U., 1957—. Mem. Am. Assn. U. Profs., Am. Vocational Assn., Tri-State bus. edn. assns., Ohio, Cleve. Area bus. tchrs. assns., Beta Gamma Sigma, Delta Pi Epsilon, Delta Kappa Gamma, Pi Lambda Theta, Phi Gamma Nu, Pi Omega Pi, Gamma Phi Beta. Home: 1227 E Main St Kent OH 44240

DANILOVA, ALEXANDRA, ballet dancer; b. Peterhof, Russia (came to the U.S. 1934); d. Dionis and Claudia (Gotovtzeva) Danilova; ed. Theatrical Sch., Petrograd, curriculum comprising gen. and coll. edn. Mem. Russian State Ballet, Maryinsky Theatre, 1922-24; soloist, Diaghileff Ballet, 1925, ballerina, 1929; ballerina Monte Carlo Opera House, 1930-31; star Oswald Stoll's prodn. Waltzes from Vienna, Alhambra Theatre, London, 1932; ballerina Col. de Basil's Ballet Russe, 1933-38; prima ballerina Ballet Russe de Monte Carlo, 1938—; currently head own co. touring various countries, lecture tours on her life and art in U.S.A., Europe; guest star several ballets, including Royal Ballet, Covent Garden, 1946; star Song of Norway, 1944, Broadway musical Oh Captain, 1958; choreographer Met. Opera Co. Mem. faculty Sch. Am. Ballet. Adjudicator, Southeastern Ballet Conf., 1960. Recipient Capezio Dance award, 1958. Mem. Greek Orthodox Ch. Address: 100 W 57th St New York City NY 10019

DANKER, ANNA LUCILE, educator; b. Kahoka, Mo., Apr. 6, 1916; d. Martin Edward and Anna Charlotta (Zerull) Danker; student Kirksville State Coll., 1939, Culver-Stockton Coll., 1937; B. Music Edn., Mt. St. Scholastica Coll., 1945; M.Ed., Mo. U., 1950; postgrad. Denver U., 1957, U. Chgo., 1952. Tchr. elementary schs. Clark County, 1933-42, Quincy, Ill., 1950-52; supr. fine arts Knox and Marion Counties, Ill., 1942-44; supt. St. Patrick Schs., 1952-53; dir. placement Quincy Coll., 1953-63, asso. dean students, 1955-63, asso. prof. edn., 1953—, also lectr. in math. U. Chgo. grantee Youth Devel. Quincy, 1950-52. Mem. Am. Assn. U. Women, Am. Personnel and Guidance Assn., College Placement Orgn. Assn., Bus. and Profl. Women's Club (pres. 1962-63), Daus. of Isabella (regent 1944, 70), Delta Kappa Gamma. Club: Altrusa. Home: Rural Route 3 Kahoka MO 63445 Office: Dept Edn Quincy Coll Quincy IL 62301

DANNER, BLYTHE KATHARINE (MRS. BRUCE W. PALTROW), actress; b. Phila.; d. Harry Earl and Katharine Danner; B.A. in Drama, Bard Coll., N.Y.; m. Bruce W. Paltrow, Dec. 14, 1969. Appeared as Laura in Glass Menagerie, 1965; repertory at Theatre Co. Boston, The Knack and 7 new Am. plays, 1965-66; repertory in R.I., Trinity Sq. Playhouse, appearing as Helena in Midsummer Night's Dream, Irena in Three Sisters, 1967; off-Broadway shows include Collision Course, 1968, Up Eden, 1968, Someone's Comin Hungry, 1969; Lincoln Center Repertory Co. included Summertree, 1968, Cyrano de Bergerac, 1968, Elise in The Miser, 1969; appeared on Broadway as Jill Tanner in Butterflies Are Free (Tony award 1971); TV spls. include To Confuse the Angel (with Lee J. Cobb), George M (with Joel Grey), Doctor Cook's Garden (with Bing Crosby). Recipient Theatre World award, 1969. Home and office: 333 W 71st St New York City NY 10023

DANNER, CARMEL INEZ BIXBY (MRS. H. KENNETH DANNER), assn. exec.; b. McKeesport, Pa., Sept. 21, 1915; d. Kenneth Roberts and Ila (Mosher) Bixby; B.A., U. Ill., 1936; m. H. Kenneth Danner, Mar. 21, 1942; children—Cheri Lee (Mrs. John Gianitsis), Terry Allen. With Peterson Harned Von Maur Dept. Store, Davenport, Ia., 1936-39; part-owner Rocket Coal Co., Peoria, Ill., 1939-51; real estate broker, Sarasota, Fla., 1952-62; asst. mgr. conv. dept. Sarasota County C. of C., Sarasota, 1963-67, mgr. conv. dept., 1967-73, mgr. econ. devel. and conv. depts., 1973—. Bd. dirs. Sarasota div. Am. Cancer Soc., 1955—, sec. bd., 1962-67. Recipient citation for distinguished service Fla. div. Am. Cancer Soc., 1967. Mem. Internat., Fla. (sec.-treas. 1969, pres. 1971) assns. conv. burs., Am., Fla. socs. assn. execs., Hotel Sales Mgmt. Assn., Gen., Fla. fedns. womens clubs, Sarasota-Bradenton Sigma Kappa Alumnae (pres. 1953-55), Sarasota Panhellenic (pres. 1953-55), Sigma Kappa. Presbyn. Club: Golden City Womans (Sarasota, pres. 1962). Home: 1846 Tulip Dr Sarasota FL 33579 Office: PO Box 308 Sarasota FL 33578

DANNER, MARGARET ESSIE (MRS. OTTO CUNNINGHAM), poetess; b. Chgo., Jan. 12, 1915; d. Caleb and Naomi Danner student YMCA Coll., Roosevelt U.; studied under Karl Shapiro, Paul Engle; m. Cordell Strickland; m. 2d, Otto Cunningham; 1 dau., Naomi (Mrs. Sterling Montrose Washington). Editorial asst. Poetry mag., Chgo., 1951-55, asst. editor, 1956-57; poet-in-residence Wayne State U., Detroit, 1961-62; touring poet Baha'i Teaching Com., 1964-66; Whitney fellow in Senegal, Africa, Paris, France, 1966; poet-in-residence Va. Union U., Richmond, 1968-69. Recipient Poetry Workshop award Midwestern Writers' Conf., 1945, Women's Aux. Afro-Am. Interests grant, 1950, African Studies Assn. grant, 1950, Harriet Tubman award, 1956, John Hay Whitney Found. award, 1959, Am. Soc. African Culture grant, 1960, African Studies Assn. award, 1961, Poets in Concert award, 1968. Mem. Writers, Inc. (pres.), Nologonya African Cultural Orgn. Author poetry: Impressions of African Art Forms in the Poetry of Margaret Danner, 1960; To Flower: Poems, 1963; (with Dudley Randall) Poem Counterpoem, 1966, rev. edit., 1969; Iron Lace, 1968. Works included in several anthologies. Editor: Brass Horses, Regroup. Contbr. Negro Digest, Baha'i World Order, Poetry, Accent, Chgo. Rev. Mem. Baha'i religion. Home: 626 E 102d Pl Chicago IL 60628*

DANNER, PAT BERRER (MRS. LAVON E. DANNER), govt. ofcl.; b. Louisville, Jan. 13, 1934; d. Henry Joseph and Catherine M. (Shaheen) Berrer; B.A. cum laude, N.E. Mo. State U., 1973; m. Lavon E. Danner, Feb. 12, 1951; children—Stephen, Stephanie, Shane, Shavonne. Operator Danner-Maddy Tax Preparation, Macon, Mo., 1967-70; asst. to U.S. Congressman Jerry Litton, Kansas City, Mo., 1972—. Pres., Macon Neighborhood council Girl Scouts Am., 1968-70; sec., Macon County Tb Assn., 1963-66; mem. adv. bd. Park Coll., Parkville, Mo., 1973. Sec., Macon County Young Democrats, 1966-70; Macon County women's dir. Senator Stuart Symington, 1970; chmn. Macon County Dem. Com., 1970-72; vice-chmn. 9th Congl. Dist., 1970-72, committeewoman Hudson Twp., 1970-72; del. Dem. State Conv., 1972. Mem. Beta Sigma Phi. Roman Catholic. Home: 4242 NE Davidson Rd Kansas City MO 64116

DANNETT, SYLVIA GWENDOLYN LIEBOWITZ (MRS. EMANUEL DANNETT), author; b. N.Y.C., Dec. 25, 1909; d. Abraham Lionel and Hannah (Weinberg) Liebowitz; B.A., N.J. Coll. for Women, 1930; m. Emanuel Dannett, June 29, 1933; children—Kenneth, Wendy. Free lance advt., 1930-42; author, 1942—. Mem. Douglass Coll. Alumni Assn., Civil War Round Table of N.Y. (v.p. 1968-69; editor Dispatch), N.A.A.C.P., N.Y. Hist. Soc., Am. Jewish Hist. Soc., Civil War Centennial Commn. (mem. ladies com. 1962-63), Hadassah. Jewish religion (synagogue trustee). Clubs: Oversees Press (Am.), Woman Pays. Author books including: Mr. Bilge of the Aquarium, 1942; Defy the Tempest, 1944; Down Memory Lane, 1954; Noble Women of the North, 1959; She Rode With the Generals, 1960; Treasury of Civil War Humor, 1963; Profiles of Negro Womanhood 1619-65, I-II, 1964-65; The Door to the Tower, 1966; Confederate Surgeon, 1969; The Yankee Doodler, 1973; The Low Blood Sugar (Hypoglycemia) Gourmet Cookbook, 1974. Editorial staff Overseas Press Club Bull., 1972-73. Contbr. articles to various publs. Home: 9 Reimer Rd Scarsdale NY 10583

DANTA, ROSEMARIE JANE JOHNSON (MRS. JOHN EDWARD DANTA), co-owner motel; b. Detroit, Apr. 16, 1929; d. Stanley George and Ethel Matilda (Harris) Johnson; A.A., Stephens Coll., 1948; m. John Edward Danta, Dec. 31, 1954; children—Elizabeth Jane, John Stanley. Sec., bookkeeper John E. Danta Real Estate Exchange, St. Clair Shores, Mich., 1955-68; mgr. Shorian Motor Inn, St. Clair Shores, 1969—, co-owner, sec.-treas., 1968—. Bd. dirs. St. Clair Shore Symphony Orch., 1970-73, v.p., 1971-73. Mem. Am. Hotel and Motor Hotel Assn., Hotel Sales Mgmt. Assn., Greater Detroit Motel Assn., Hotel Greeters Am., S.E. Mich. Tourist and Travel Assn. (v.p. 1972-73, dir. 1970-73), St. Clair Shores C. of C. (v.p. 1972—). Home: 27300 Lane St Clair Shores MI 48041 Office: 20000 Nine Mile Rd St Clair Shores MI 48080

D'ANTUONO, ELEANOR, ballerina; b. Cambridge, Mass., Oct. 13, 1939; d. Louis and Marie (D'Antuono) Jacobs; student Am. Corr. Schs. Appeared with Ballet Russe De Monte Carlo, 1954-60, soloist, 1956-60; appeared with Robert Joffrey Ballet, 1960-61; soloist Am. Ballet Theatre, N.Y.C., 1961-63, prin. dancer, ballerina, 1963—. Address: care Am Ballet 1790 Broadway New York City NY 10019

DANTUONO, LOUISE M. (MRS. JOHN D. ANGELIDES), physician; b. N.Y.C., July 29, 1916; d. Anthony A. and Margaret (Cogliano) Dantuono; B.A. magna cum laude, Adelphi Coll., 1937; M.D., Womans Med. Coll. of Pa., 1942; m. John D. Angelides, May 28, 1955 (dec. June 1970); children—Helen Margaret, Elaine Marie. Asst. chemistry dept. Adelphi Coll., N.Y., 1937-38; interne Queens Gen. Hosp., Jamaica, N.Y., 1942-43; resident Bellevue Hosp., N.Y.C., 1943-46; practice medicine specializing in obstetrics and gynecology, N.Y.C., 1946—; mem. staff Bellevue, Columbus, Univ. hosps., N.Y. Infirmary; instr. obstetrics and gynecology N.Y.U., 1947-55, asst. clin. prof., 1955-60, asso. clin. prof., 1960—. Diplomate Am. Bd. Obstetrics and Gynecology. Fellow A.C.S.; mem. A.M.A., Med. Soc. County of N.Y., N.Y. Acad. Scis., Bellevue Obstet. and Gynecol. Soc., N.Y. Womans Med. Assn., Queens Gen. Hosp., N.Y. Infirmary, Womans Med. Coll. of Pa. alumni assns. Office: 35 E 35th St New York City NY 10016

DANTZIC, CYNTHIA MARIS (MRS. JERRY DANTZIC), artist, educator; b. Bklyn., Jan. 4, 1933; d. Howard Arthur and Sylvia (Wiener) Gross; student Bklyn. Mus. Art Sch., 1947-50, Bard Coll., 1950-52; B.F.A., Yale, 1955; M.F.A., Pratt Inst. (fellow), 1963; m. Jerry Dantzic, June 15, 1958; 1 son, Grayson Ross. Tchr. art Baldwin Sch., Bryn Mawr, Pa., 1955-58; head art dept. Bentley Sch., N.Y.C., 1958-63; instr. art City U. N.Y., 1963; mem. faculty L.I. U., Bklyn., 1964—, asst. prof. art, 1965-69, asso. prof., 1969—, chmn. faculty com. community relations, 1972-73. One-man modular paintings show E. Hampton Gallery, N.Y.C., 1966; two-man shows Brownstone Gallery, Bklyn., 1973, Bklyn. Mus. Art Sch. Gallery, 1973; exhibited in group shows including A.M. Sachs Gallery, N.Y.C., 1964, Phila. Art Alliance, 1957, Bklyn. Mus., 1968, La Jolla (Cal.) Mus. Art, 1969, Delgado Mus. Art, New Orleans, 1972; represented in permanent collections Springbok Editions, Inc., N.Y. Soc. Gen. Semantics, also pvt. collections. Art coordinator North Shore Community Arts Center, Roslyn, L.I., 1963-64; design cons. Bklyn. Children's Mus., 1969; art cons. Montessori Sch., Bklyn., 1973-74. Co-chmn. Bklyn. Mus. Art Festival for legal def. fund N.A.A.C.P., 1963; mem. adv. com. Community Gallery Bklyn. Mus., 1973-74. L.I. U. research grantee, 1967. Mem. Am. Assn. U. Profs., Coll. Art Assn., United Fedn. Coll. Tchrs. Author: Stop Dropping breAd crumBs on my yaCht: a silent ABC, 1974. Works include stained-glass windows Ch. of Resurrection, Lakeland, Fla., 1972. Home: 910 President St Brooklyn NY 11215

DANZIG, JOAN (MRS. JOSEPH KRASNER), editor; b. Elmira, N.Y.; d. George Hamilton and Estelle (Saqui) Danzig; student Elmira Coll.; m. Joseph Krasner, May 23, 1953; children—Susan, Karin. Reporter, Athens bur. Sayre (Pa.) Evening Times, 1948-50, soc. editor, 1950-52; women's editor, fashion editor Buffalo Evening News, 1952—. Mem. Buffalo Philharmonic Publicity Com. 1958-60; sec. Bradford County chpt. Pa. Cancer Soc., 1948-49, publicity work, 1949-50; mem. Athens (Pa.) Sch. Adv. Com., 1950; pub. information officer Civil Air Patrol, Tioga Point, 1951. Recipient feature writing award Pa. Women's Press Assn., 1949; headline writing (Page One) award Buffalo Newspaper Guild, 1957, Women's Page Writing award 1964. Mem. Am. Newspaper Guild, Bus. and Profl. Women's Club (Athens charter pres. 1948-50), Sigma Delta Chi. Office: One News Plaza Buffalo NY 14202

DAOUD, EVELYN TANOUS (MRS. A. JOSEPH DAOUD), bus. exec.; b. Bellaire, O.; d. Azeez Joseph and Nora (Yarbroudi) Tanous; student St. John's U., 1928-31; LL.B., U. Miami (Fla.), 1949; m. Joseph Daoud, Feb. 6, 1932 (dec. Dec. 1963); children—Joseph A. III, Patricia, Alex. Admitted to N.Y. bar, 1932; practice law, Lawrence, L.I., N.Y., 1932; exec. sec. Joseph Daoud & Sons, Atlantic City, 1933-39; v.p. Joseph Daoud Sons, Miami Beach, Fla., 1936-41; v.p. Joseph Daoud, Inc., Miami Beach, 1941—, also dir. pres., St. Patrick's P.T.A., Miami Beach, 1955-56, mem. bd., 1953-56; mem. bd. Barry Coll. Aux., 1954-56, 52-57; mem. bd. Community Chest Dade County (Fla.), 1951, 52-57, chief dir. fund drive, Miami Beach, 1950-60; mem. bd. Vis. Nurses Assn. Dade County, 1956; mem. St. Francis Hosp. Aux., Miami Beach, 1954-57; mem. Friends of Bethany Home for Dependent Teenage Girls, Miami, 1966—, also bd. dirs.; sec. Miami Beach Pub. Library, also bd. dirs.; mem. endowment com. St. Jude's Research Children's Hosp., Memphis, 1966—. Sec. Miami Beach Pub. Library, 1956-60; now trustee. Recipient awards Community Chest, Miami Beach, 1952-59; named Woman of the Year, Civic League Miami Beach, 1956. Mem. Am., N.Y. bar assns., Patrician Club (mem. bd. 1954-57), Syrian Lebanese Inst. Miami, U.S. C. of C., Iota Tau Tau, Kappa Beta Pi. Home: 1777 Michigan Av Miami Beach FL 33139 Office: 18180 Collins Av Miami Beach FL 33160

DARBY, FRANCES ADAH RUCKER, elec. equipment mfg. co. exec.; b. South Bend, Ark., Aug. 6, 1919; d. Eculid McHose and Lucy Kate (McGehee) Rucker; B.S., Tex. Woman's U., 1940; m. Joseph J. Darby, Jr., Nov. 17, 1940 (div. Sept. 1964); children—Joseph Jasper III, Michael Rucker. Co-owner Paragon Industries, Dallas, 1949-54, sec.-treas., 1954-64, pres., 1964—. Trustee Bishop Mason Retreat and Conf. Center, Episcopal Diocese Dallas. Mem. Nat. Assn. Ceramic Mfrs. (dir. 1966-71), Nat. Ceramic Assn., Nat. Assn. Mfrs., Better Bus. Bur. Met. Dallas, C. of C. Dallas. Episcopalian. Club: Dallas Athletic Country. Home: 3937 Purdue St Dallas TX 75225 Office: Box 10133 Dallas TX 75207

DARKEN, MARJORIE ALICE, editor; b. Bklyn.; d. William Henry and Gertrude (Stamper) Darken; B.S. cum laude, St. Lawrence U., 1936; M.A., U. Mich., 1937. Research technician U. Mich. Hosp., Ann Arbor, 1937-39; research asst. Inst. of Living, Hartford, Conn., 1939-41, chief labs., 1941-43; research microbiologist Am. Cyanamid Co., Princeton, N.J., 1943-55, sr. tech. writer, N.Y.C., 1955-56, sr. research scientist, Pearl River, N.Y., 1956-63, pharmacology editor, 1963-69, med. editor, 1969—. Fellow A.A.A.S.; mem. Am. Assn. U. Women, Am. Chem. Soc., Am. Soc. Microbiology, Phi Beta Kappa Sigma Xi. Editorial bd. Applied Microbiology, 1961-74; editorial reviewer Reinhold Pub. Co., 1966-74. Contbr. articles in field to profl. jours. Home: PO Box 645 Highland Lakes NJ 07422 Office: Pearl River NY 10965

DARKIS, MILDRED LEE MORRIS (MRS. FREDERICK RANDOLPH DARKIS), civic worker; b. nr. Salisbury, Md.; d. Elisha Purnell and Martha Florence (Bailey) Morris; A.B., U. Md, 1924; m. Frederick Randolph Darkis, Oct. 6, 1928; children—Frederick Randolph, Thomas Morris, Barbara Lee (Mrs. James Frederick Blake). Tchr. English and Am. history high sch., Pittsville, Md., 1924-25, Salisbury, 1925-28. Pres. Durram Parent-Tchr. Council, 1945-47, Hope Valley Garden Club, 1962-64; bd. dirs. Durham YWCA, 1946-48, v.p., 1948; bd. dirs. Durham Child Guidance Clinic, 1945-47, Girl Scout Council, 1944-48; chmn. woman's div. Community Chest, Durham, 1946-47. Mem. D.A.R. (N.C. chmn. nat. honor roll 1961-64, chpt. regent 1968-70), Phi Kappa Phi, Alpha Omicron Pi. Republican. Methodist (tchr. adult Bible class, v.p. Durham dist. Woman's Div. Christian Service 1957-59, steward 1960, bd. stewards 1972—). Club: Hope Valley Country. Address: 3010 Surrey Rd Durham NC 27707

DARLING, EMILY HOWLAND (MRS. C. EDWARD DARLING), librarian; b. Phila., Nov. 7, 1911; d. Arthur Charles and Emily W. (Berry) Howland; B.A., Swarthmore Coll., 1933; M.L.S., Drexel U., 1967; m. C. Edward Darling, Dec. 27, 1939; children—Arthur H., Roger W. Officermgr. Mgmt. Consultants Assos., Cleve., 1956-58; librarian Scott Paper Co., Phila., 1959—. Mem. Spl. Libraries Assn. (treas. advt. and marketing div. 1971-72), Beta Phi Mu. Office: Scott Paper Co Philadelphia PA 19113

DARLING, LOUISE, librarian; b. Los Angeles, Aug. 3, 1911; d. Andrew Francis and Irene (Matas) Darling; B.A., U. Cal. at Los Angeles, 1933; M.A., U. Cal. at Berkeley, 1935, certificate librarianship, 1936. Asst. librarian Giannini Found. Agrl. Econs. U. Cal. at Berkeley, 1936-39; librarian Acalanes Union High Sch., Lafayette, Cal. 1940-41; sci. reference librarian, U. Cal. at Los Angeles, 1941-44; army librarian Hawaii and the Philippines, 1944-47; librarian Biomed. Library, U. Cal. Med. Center, Los Angeles, 1947—; lectr. med. history U. Cal. at Los Angeles Sch. Medicine, 1958—, lectr. Grad. Sch. Library and Information Sci., 1961—, dir. Pacific Southwest Regional Med. Library Services, 1969—. Mem. Am., Cal., Med. (dir. 1961-65, pres. 1963-64, Marcia C. Noyes award 1974) library assns., Spl. Libraries Assn., Soc. for History of Med. Sci. (sec. 1950-60, v.p. 1960-62), Am. Assn. History Medicine (council mem. 1961-63, 69-71), A.A.A.S., Am. Soc. Information Sci., Med. Library Group So. Cal. (pres. 1950-51), Assn. Coll. and Research Libraries (vice chmn. agrl. and biol. scis. subsect. 1967-68, chmn. agrl. and biol. scis. subsect. 1968-69). Author articles in field. Home: 197 Beloit Av Los Angeles CA 90049

DARMSTADT, MARGARET ANN (MRS. ROBERT M. DARMSTADT), psychologist; b. Jersey City, July 24, 1926; d. William A. and Estelle M. (Palm) Dillman; B.A., Douglas Coll., 1963; M.Ed., Rutgers U., 1964, Ed.D., 1971; certificate in sch. psychology Columbia, 1965; m. Robert M. Darmstadt, June 6, 1944; children—Barbara (Mrs. David Taylor), Robert. Spl. tchr. Plainfield (N.J.) Schs., 1959-63; asst. to dir. Collegefields project Newark (N.J.) State Coll., 1964-65; sch. psychologist Hazlet (N.J.) Bd. Edn., 1965-69; sch. psychologist, coordinator child study Matawan (N.J.) Regional Sch. Dist., 1969—. Prof. psychology Brookdale Coll., Lincroft, N.J., 1974—. Mem. Monmouth County Mental Health Bd., 1970-73. Sec. Democratic Club, 1969-73. Mem. Am., N.J. psychol. assns., N.J. Sch. Psychology Assn., Soc. for Psychol. Study Social Issues, Am. Philos. Soc., Soc. for Ednl. Reconstruct, Am. Assn. Ednl. Research, Chi Psi, Kappa Delta Pi. Home: 22G Meadow Green Circle Englishtown NJ 07726 Office: Matawan Regional School Dist Broad St Matawan NJ

DARNELL, EDNA ERIE BURNLEY (MRS. WILLIE DARNELL), librarian; b. Kevil, Ky., Mar. 4, 1925; d. Willie Lee and Ora Mae (Casey) Burnley; B.S., Murray State U., 1960, M.A., 1967; Ed.S., George Peabody Coll., 1971; m. Willie Darnell, May 21, 1942; children—Willie Darnell, Daralina Ann. Tchr., librarian Hardin (Ky.) Elementary Sch., 1960-61; library cons. Ky. Dept. Libraries, 1961-64; asst. librarian Murray (Ky.) State U., 1964-66, grad. asst. library sci. dept., 1966-67, asst. prof., 1967-71, chmn. dept., 1971-72; reference librarian Three Rivers Community Coll., Poplar Bluff, Mo., 1973—. Mem. Curriculum Revision Com. Library Edn. Ky., 1971-72. Mem. N.E.A., Nat. Audio-Visual Assn., Mo. State Tchrs. Assn., Ky., First Dist. library assns., Ky., First Dist. edn. assns., Ky. Audio-Visual Assn., Kappa Delta Pi, Alpha Delta Kappa, Alpha Beta Alpha. Democrat. Baptist. Woodman of World. Club: Woman's (v.p. Alpha dept. Murray 1966-68). Home: 8808 Chicory Circle Knoxville TN 37919

DARR, CAROLE, television dir.; b. Santa Fe, Dec. 10, 1942; d. Aud F. and Emma (Coury) Darr; B.A., U. N.M., 1965; certificate Northwestern U., 1968. Writer, J. Walter Thompson, Chgo., 1965-66, McCann Erickson, Chgo., 1966-68; gen. writer for gov. State of Ill., Chgo., 1968-70; writer A. Eicoff & Co., Chgo., 1970—; owner Carole Darr, Inc., Chgo., 1970—; dealer, retailer Hoard House, Chgo., 1971—. Office: 520 N Michigan Av Chicago IL 60611

DARRAGH, HELEN ALICE, psychiat. social worker; b. Cedar Rapids, Ia., July 12, 1915; d. John William and Frances (Hurych) Darragh; B.A., U. Mo., 1938; M.Social Service, Smith Sch. Social Work, 1942; postgrad. U. Mich., 1943, Inst. Psychoanalysis, 1955. Therapist, Family Consultation Service, Wichita, Kan., 1938-64, Consultation Bur., Detroit, 1943-44, Family Service, Chgo., 1950-51, Chgo. Child Care Soc., 1951-52; therapist dept. psychiatry Jewish Hosp., St. Louis, 1956-64, chief psychiat. social worker, 1958-64; casework supr. Family Welfare Assn., Scranton, Pa., 1944-46; dist. sec. Children's Services, Cleve., 1946-48; dist. dir. United Charities Chgo., 1952-56; exec. dir. Met. Commn. on Aging, Chgo., 1956-59, also children's instl. cons. Social Planning and Welfare Council; dir. profl. services Family and Children's Service Greater St. Louis, 1964—; practicum instr. Wayne U., Detroit, 1943-44, U. Mich., Detroit, 1943-44, Smith Coll., Northampton, Mass., 1944-46, Western Reserve U., Cleve., 1946-48, 53-55, U. Chgo., 1948-56, Washington U., St. Louis, 1957; asst. prof. dept. psychiatry St. Louis U., 1968—; Ford Found. for Aging fellow; intern Eloise State Hosp., Detroit, 1941. Bd. dirs. Day Care Nursery, 1955, Housing Project, 1956. Fellow Am. Orthopsychiat. Assn.; mem. Nat. Assn. Social Workers, Council on Social Work Edn., Family Service Assn. Am., Council Family Relations, Mo. Assn. Social Welfare, Alpha Gamma Delta. Democrat. Clubs: University, St. Louis University Women's, Washington University Women's. Home: 1 Whitehall Ct Brentwood MO 63144 Office: 2650 Olive St St Louis MO 63103

DARRELL, EVELYN JUNE BOYDEN (MRS. THOMAS E. DARRELL), psychologist; b. Spring Lake, N.J., June 15, 1925; d. John and Ethel (Notis) Boyden; B.A., N.Y. U., 1959, M.A., 1961, postgrad., 1961-63; m. Thomas E. Darrell, Sept. 4, 1954; 1 dau., Michele Ann. With Western Electric Co., Kearny, N.J., 1944-45, Afro Am. Newspaper, Inc., Balt., part-time 1945-53, Office Dependence Benefits, War Dept., 1946-50, VA Regional Office: Newark, 1952-56; supt. typing unit Testing and Advisement Center, N.Y. U., 1956-60, psychometrist, 1960-61, supt. testing, 1960-63, asst. psychology dept. Grad. Sch. Edn., 1964-65, staff psychologist charge adolescent girls service, 1964—, research asso. charge testing, 1966—, clin. psychologist Med. Sch., 1967—, part-time teaching asst., dept. of psychiatry, 1971—; intern psychology Bellevue Psychiat. Hosp., 1963-64; instr. Newark State Tchrs. Coll., Union, N.J., 1969—. Mem. Nat. Assn. Black Psychologists, Am. Psychol. Assn. (asso.), N.A.A.C.P. (Newark br. sec. 1955-58, mem. exec. bd. 1955-58, br. centennial chmn. 1963), Iota Phi Lambda (chpt. pres. 1966—). Home: 36 Hawthorne Pl Montclair NJ 07042 Office: Bellevue Psychiat Hosp Ward PG-5 30th St and 1st Av New York City NY 10016

DARROW, HARRIET DRISKELL (MRS. NORMAN DARROW), coll. dean; b. Terre Haute, Ind., Jan. 6, 1921; d. Willis S. and Ina K. (Apple) Driskell; B.S., Ind. State U., 1955, M.S., 1957; Ed.D., Ind. U., 1961; m. Norman Darrow, Jan. 18, 1941; 1 son, Gregory. Mem. faculty Ind. State U., Terre Haute, 1954—, prof. edn., 1966—, dean summer sessions and acad. services, 1967—. Vice pres. Nat. Council for Edn. and Family Finance. Mem. Nat. Assn. Summer Sessions (pres. 1972-73), N.E.A., Assn. Higher Edn., Assn. Supervision and Curriculum Devel. (past pres. Ind. chpt.), North Central Conf. Summer Sessions (past pres.), Delta Kappa Gamma (past pres. Beta Eta chpt., past 2d v.p. state chpt.). Club: Altrusa. Home: 59 Lakeview Dr Terre Haute IN 47803

DARROW, HELEN FISHER, educator; b. Washington, Dec. 9, 1921; d. Thomas Tobias and Lena S. (Lewandoski) Fisher; m. Dean J. Darrow (div.); 1 son. Tobin. Tchr. Washington Pub. Schs., 1943-53; curriculum coordinator San Diego County Dept. Ed., 1955-61; asso. prof. San Fernando Valley State Coll., 1962-67; curriculum specialist Inst. for Devel. of Ednl. Activities, Los Angeles, 1967-69; mem. faculty Western Wash. State Coll., Bellingham, 1968—, prof. edn., 1968—. Vis. prof. San Francisco State Coll., 1958, Springfield (Mass.) Coll., 1959; cons. elementary edn. Kern County Dept. Edn., El Monte, Cal., Delano, Cal., Dairy Valley, Cal., Los Alamitos, Cal., Whittier, Cal., Mt. Diablo, Cal., Hanover, Cal., Baton Rouge, Ottawa Hills, O., State Dept. Edn., Phoenix, U. So. Cal., Los Angeles, Fresno (Cal.) State Coll., Bakersfield State Coll., Bakersfield Internat. Center Edn. Devel., Encino, Cal., Dominguez Hills State Coll., Los Angeles, others, 1962-72. Mem. Cal. (life), So. Cal. (pres. 1964-66) assos. childhood edn., Nat. Soc. Study Edn., Assn. Supervision and Curriculum Devel., Internat. Reading Assn., Nat. Council Tchrs. English, Wash. Edn. Assn., N.E.A. (life). Author: Approaches to Individualized Reading, 1961; Independent Activities for Creative Learning, 1962; Social Studies for Understanding, 1964. Editor: Reading and the Elementary Child, 1968. Home: 222 Hawthorne Rd Bellingham WA 98225

DARST, MARIE ROENA (MRS. HARRY WALTER DARST), civic worker; b. Davisville, Mo., Dec. 13, 1919; d. John Leonard and Allie (Wilkinson) Britton; student Central Bapt. Coll., 1953-54; pvt. music studies, 1962-63; m. Harry Walter Darst, May 21, 1938; 1 dau., Marilyn Ruth (Mrs. Roy G. Orr). Saleslady, Fine Bros. Matison Dept. Store, Hattiesburg, Miss., 1963, Belk-Whitney Dept. Store, Hattiesburg, 1964-65. Pres., Ala. Bapt. Women's Missionary Assn., 1960-61; pres. Miss. Bapt. Women's Missionary Assn., 1964-66, Mo. Bapt. Women's Missionary Assn., 1970-72; editor youth aux. page Golden Words, Bapt. Publs. Com., 1970—; nat. youth aux. dir. Bapt. Missionary Assn. Am., pres. womens missionary aux., 1969-71, corr. sec., 1973—. Home: 1169 Whispering Wind Dr Arnold MO 63010

DART, JANE O'BRIEN (MRS. JUSTIN DART), civic worker; b. Los Angeles, June 11, 1918; d. James Mathew and Irene (Murray) O'Brien; grad. high sch., Los Angeles; m. Justin Dart, Dec. 31, 1939; children—Guy Michael, Jane (Mrs. John Campbell), Stephen Murray. Actress under name Jane Bryan, Warner Bros., Los Angeles, 1936-39. Mem. Cal. Arts Commn., Los Angeles 1967-71, Commn. Fine Arts, Washington, 1971—. Trustee, also bd. govs. Found. Natural History Mus. of Los Angeles; trustee L.S.B. Leakey Found. Home: 444 N Faring Rd Los Angeles CA 90024

DASZEWSKI, CAROLINE JOICE, ednl. adminstr.; b. Grand Rapids, Mich., Apr. 30, 1924; d. Byron David and Caroline Gustina (Pape) Coats; student Mich. State U., 1941-43, State Tchrs. Coll., Albany, N.Y., 1959-60; B.A., St. Francis Coll., 1963, M.A., 1964; postgrad. Purdue U., 1966-67, Va. Poly. Inst., 1973-74; m. Edward Walter Daszewski, Dec. 11, 1943 (dec.); 1 dau., Carole Ann (Mrs. Carl Edward Jacquay). Instr. Crosier Monastery, Ft. Wayne, Ind., 1963, 67; tchr. Central Cath. High Sch., Ft. Wayne, 1964-66; faculty Purdue U., Ft. Wayne, 1966-67, Ind. U., Bloomington, 1967-68; coordinator career devel. activities Va. Highlands Community Coll., Abingdon, 1970—. Coordinator job placement and career devel. Girl Scouts Am., Schenectady, 1953-63; instr. home nursing Red Cross, Ft. Wayne and Abingdon, Va., 1965-66, 74—; mem. Holston Valley Arts and Crafts Coop., Abingdon, 1971-74. Bd. dirs. Offender Aid and Restoration, 1973—. Mem. Nat. Assn. Women Deans and Counselors, Va. Placement Assn., S.W. Va. Personnel and Guidance Assn., Cooperative Edn. Assn., Middle Atlantic Career Counselors Assn., Jr. Coll. Journalism Assn., Columbia Press Assn., Delta Epsilon Sigma. Club: Bristol Christian Women's (Abingdon, Va.). Home: PO Box 648 Abingdon VA 24210 Office: Virginia Highlands Community College PO Box 828 Abingdon VA 24210

DATCHE, RUTH, advt. exec.; b. St. Louis; d. John David and Letha Ditch; student Washington U. Fine Arts Sch., St. Louis; m. Maurice Falchero (div.); children—Mary R., Ruth Annalea. Formerly creative fashion artist Stix, Baer & Fuller; art dir. Scruggs, Vandervoort & Barney; established own art studio; pres. Datche Advt. and Pub. Relations, Inc., St. Louis, 1944—. Chmn. bd. St. Louis Bd. Parks and Recreation. Mem. Fashion Group of N.Y., A.I.M. (pres.'s council), Am. Women in Radio and TV. Home: 5125 Lindell Blvd St Louis MO 63108 Office: 4144 Lindell Blvd St Louis MO 63108

DATE, JANET SADAKO, cosmetologist; b. Waialua, Hawaii, Feb. 3, 1917; d. Jinhichi and Aki (Tanimoto) Kaya; grad. East Bay Sch. Beauty Culture, 1940; m. Henry Date, Jan. 3, 1959; 1 son, John Shigemichi. Owner, operator Lotus Beauty Center, Honolulu, 1941—. Mem. Hawaii Bd. of Cosmetology, 1955-66. Mem. Honolulu Hairdressers and Cosmeticians Assn. (pres. 1951-52, dir. 1948-50, 53-56), Am. Bus. Women's Assn. Methodist. Home: 3074 Kahewai Pl Honolulu HI 96822 Office: 2615 S King St Honolulu HI 96814

DATTA, LOIS-ELLIN GREENE (MRS. PADMA DATTA), psychologist; b. Paterson, N.J., June 12, 1932; d. Gerald G. and Martha (Cohen) Greene; B.A., W.Va. U., 1952, M.A., 1956; M.A., Bryn Mawr Coll., 1957, Ph.D., 1961; m. Padma Datta, Dec. 20, 1952; children—Tane Mohan, Eric Raman. Research psychologist Gen. Electric Co., Phila., 1961-63, Nat. Inst. Mental Health, Bethesda, Md., 1963-68; nat. coordinator Head Start evaluation, Washington, 1968-70; chief Office Child Devel. Evaluation, 1970-71; chief early childhood and evaluation Office Child Devel., 1971-72; dir. planning, research and evaluation, career edn. program Nat. Inst. Edn., Washington, 1972—. Mem. Am. Statis. Assn., Am. Psychol. Assn., Phi Beta Kappa, Sigma Xi, Sigma Delta Epsilon. Home: 8514 Whittier Blvd Bethesda MD 20034 Office: Nat Inst Edn 1200 19th St NW Washington DC 20208

DAUGERT, PATRICIA JEAN, educator; b. Cleve., Jan. 27, 1932; d. Frank Robert and Constance (Gaskey) Daugert; B.S., Bowling Green State U., 1954: M.A., U. Mich., 1957, Ph.D., 1966; tchr. phys. edn. Crary Jr. High Sch., Waterford Twp., Mich., 1954-55, Detroit Pub. Schs., 1956-57, Harper Woods (Mich.) High Sch., 1957-61; instr. phys. edn. U. Mich., Ann Arbor, 1961-67; prof. women's div. health, phys. edn. So. Conn. State Coll., New Haven, 1967—. Mem. Conn. Assn. Health, Phys. Edn. and Recreation, A.A.H.P.E.R., Delta Psi Kappa. Office: Southern Conn State Coll 501 Crescent St New Haven CT 06515

DAUGHDRILL, PATRICIA ANN, clothing mfg. co. exec.; b. Tyler, Tex., Apr. 3, 1936; d. Lloyd S. and Mary F. (Roe) Steverson; student Pearl River Jr. Coll., U. So. Miss.; m. Robert Kendall Daughdrill, Feb. 13, 1959; children—Kenny, Kevin. With New Hebron Mfg. Co., Inc. (Miss.), 1954—, sec., 1974—. Mem. League of Women. Baptist (tchr., mem. tng. union). Home: PO Box 65 New Hebron MS 39140 Office: PO Box 96 New Hebron MS 39140

DAUGHERTY, JANE BLANCHARD KERR, occupational therapist; b. Balt., May 15, 1920; d. Charles Phillips and Isabel Grant (Howell) Kerr; student Guilford Coll., 1938-39, Ia. State Tchrs. Coll., 1940-42; B.S. in Edn., Ohio State U., 1943; B.S., Phila. Sch. Occupational Therapy, 1945; m. Burton Perry Daugherty, Jr., Dec. 11, 1954 (dec. 1969); children—Ann Isabel, John Burton. Tchr. Post Sch., West Point, N.Y., 1943-45; occupational therapist VA Hosp., Palo Alto, Cal., 1946-47, Nat. Naval Med. Center, Bethesda, Md., 1947-54; occupational therapist, dir. Sparrow Hosp., Lansing, Mich., part-time, 1955-57. Mem. Am., Mich. occupational therapy assns., Ingham County Bar Aux. (sec. 1972-73), Coll. Women's Vol. Service. Episcopalian (tchr. 1948-54, 60-61). Clubs: Child Study, Ladies Figure Skating (treas. 1971-72) (East Lansing). Home: 1515 Columbine Dr E East Lansing MI 48823

DAUGHERTY, JEAN SANDERS (MRS. WILLIAM MASON DAUGHERTY), journalist; b. Superior, Neb., July 11, 1919; d. Morton Alonzo and Nellie (Head) Sanders; B.A., U. Neb. 1940; m. William Mason Daugherty, Mar. 21, 1942; 1 dau., Patricia Ann. Editor newspaper pub. relations com. Girl Scouts U.S.A., Franklin County, Columbus, 1953-54, sr. troop leader, Oklahoma City, 1958-59; chmn. pub. relations Jefferson Recreation Council, Gahanna, 1956-57; free-lance writer, Okla., Ariz., 1959—; pub. relations asso. World Neighbors, Inc., 1964-65; mem. editorial bd. Ambassador news sheet Bethany (Okla.) Children's Convalescent Hosp., 1959-66, bd. dirs., 1961-66; pub. information specialist Pub. Affairs Office Fort Huachuca, Ariz., 1969—. Recipient Outstanding Performance awards and commendation Ft. Huachuca, 1972-73. Mem. Nat. Fedn. Press Women, Ariz. Press Women, Ariz., Cochise County hist. socs., Women in Communications (nat. treas. 1959-65, regional v.p. 1971-73, Distinguished Service award 1972). Psi Chi, Alpha Omicron Pi. Episcopalian. Home: PO Box 1332 Sierra Vista AZ 85613 Office: Pub Affairs Office Fort Huachuca AZ 85635

DAUGHTREY, ANNE SCOTT (MRS. GREYSON DAUGHTREY), educator; b. Radford, Va., Jan. 12, 1920; d. Joppa Beebe and Minnie Virginia (Hutton) Scott; B.S., Radford Coll., Va. Poly. Inst., 1941; M.A., U. S.D., 1956, Ed.D., 1967; m. Greyson Daughtrey, Nov. 22, 1945. Sec. Roanoke (Va.) City Schs., 1937-38, The Harris Co., 1941, Barrett & Hilp Corp., Portsmouth, Va., 1942; part-time reporter Radford Times, 1941; adminstrv. asst. Camp Lynnhaven, Va., 1944-45, tchr. bus. edn., adult edn. pub. schs., South Norfolk, Va., 1941-46; tchr. bus. edn. Maury High Sch., Norfolk, Va., 1946-59, head bus. edn. dept. 1955-58, co-ordinator vocational office trng., 1948-59, tchr. adult edn., 1942-47; asst. prof. bus. edn. Coll. William and Mary, Norfolk, 1959-62; prof. bus. edn. Old Dominion U., Norfolk, 1962—. Co-chmn. Tidewater Va. Adv. Council Bus. and Edn., Norfolk, 1958. Recipient Outstanding Alumna award Radford Coll., 1969. Mem. Nat., So., Va. (pres. 1959), S. Norfolk (pres. 1944) edn. assns., Adminstrv. Mgmt. Soc., Nat. Office Mgmt. Assn. (v.p. 1956), Va. (v.p. 1959), Am. vocational edn. assns., Eastern Bus. Tchrs. Assn., Va. Council on Econ. Edn. (sec. 1970), Norfolk Soc. Arts, Norfolk Gen. Hosp. Aux., Women's Aux. Norfolk Symphony and Choral Assn., Tau Kappa Alpha, Kappa Delta Pi. Methodist. Author: Methods of Basic Business and Economic Education; (with DeBrum, Haines, Malsbury, Crabbe) Methods and Resources for General Business. Lectr., editorial cons.; contbr. articles profl. jours. Editorial adviser jour. Teaching, 1973. Home: 4816 Gosnold Av Norfolk VA 23508

DAUM, MARGUERITE MARY (PEGGY), newspaper editor; b. Milw., May 23, 1933; d. George Henry and Anne Marie (Manion) Daum; B.A., U. Ariz., 1954, M.A. Marquette U., 1963. Reporter women's dept. Ventura (Cal.) County Star-Free Press, 1954-55, Ariz. Daily Star, Tucson, 1955; reporter-copy editor women's dept. Milw. Jour., 1955-68, food editor, 1968—. Recipient Vesta award Am. Meat Inst., 1968, 69, 70, 73, Golden Carnation award, 1970, 71, Alma award Nat. Home Appliance Mfrs., 1969. Mem. Newspaper Food Editors and Writers Assn. (pres. 1974—), Milw. Press Club, Sigma Delta Chi (chpt. bd. dirs. 1974—). Roman Catholic (parish council, 1970-71). Clubs: Vagabond Ski, South Shore Indoor Racquet. Office: 333 W State St Milwaukee WI 53201

DAUME, DAPHNE MARIE, editor; b. Grand Rapids, Mich., June 17, 1924; d. Selden Bennett and Marie Elizabeth (Hixson) Daume; B.S. in Journalism, Northwestern U., 1945; M.A., Columbia, 1948. Reporter, Iroquois County Daily Times, Watseka, Ill., 1945-46; prodn. editor Ency. Brit., Chgo., 1948-60, asso. editor Book of Year, 1960-72, editor, 1972—. Mem. Women in Communications, Inc., Chgo. Council Fgn. Relations, Acad. Polit. Sci., League Women Voters (dir. Chgo.). Address: 7221 N Paulina Chicago IL 60626

DAUME, MARY ROSSITER, librarian; b. Detroit, July 10, 1913; d. Frederick and Anna Etta (McLaughlin) Rossiter; A.B., Wooster Coll., 1934; B.S. in L.S., Western Res. U., 1935; m. Karl W. Daume, Dec. 24, 1936; children—Kurt Frederick, John Emil. Librarian St. Mary's (O.) Pub. Library, 1936-38, Monroe (Mich.) County Library, 1947—; also library service cons.; instr. library sci. dept. Wayne State U., Sch. Library Sci., U. Mich. Chmn., Mich. State Bd. Libraries, 1962-64. Active Monroe County Council Service Agys., Monroe County Citizens' Com. Mental Health; pub. relations chmn. Monroe County United Fund, 1957; dep. dir. Monroe County Civil Def., 1957—; mem. Monroe City Charter Commn., 1955; active Monroe County Planning League; supt. sch. exhibits div. Monroe County Fair, 1952—; chmn. family service A.R.C. disaster com., 1956, chmn. registration com., 1957—; sec. adv. bd. Goodwill Industries of Southeastern Mich., Inc., 1966-70. Recipient citation Woman of Year, Monroe Rotary, 1954; Library Binding Inst. Silver Book award, 1963. Mem. Am. Library Trustees Assn., Am. (sec. audio-visual roundtable 1954-56, council 1956-57, bd. mem. exhibitor's roundtable 1957-60, 66-70), Mich. (dist. chmn. 1951, chmn. county libraries sect. 1956, legislative chmn. county and regional sect. 1958-59, chmn. pub. libraries div. 1968-69, chmn. audio-visual sect. 1969-70, pres. 1972-73) library assns., Monroe Bus. and Professional Women's Club (pres. 1952-53), Am. Assn. U. Women (pres. 1948-50), Monroe County Council Women's Orgns., (sec. 1954-59), Mich. Archeol. Soc., Assn. Ednl. and Communication Tech., Mich. Edn. Assn., Friends in Council, Mich. Assn. Media Edn., Monroe County Hist. Soc. (pres. 1971-72). Episcopalian. Clubs: Altrusa (bd. mem. 1956-57, 71-72, pres. 1962-64), Monroe Woman's. Home: 102 E Grove St Monroe MI 48161 Office: 3700 S Custer Rd Monroe MI 48161

DAUTRICH, MARY JANE WARD (MRS. PAUL H. DAUTRICH), librarian; b. Reading, Pa., Feb. 25, 1921; d. Oscar Clinton and Madeline (Hilzinger) Ward; A.B. cum laude, Albright Coll., 1942; postgrad. Middlebury Coll.; summer 1950; M.S. in L.S., Drexel U., 1954; m. Paul H. Dautrich, Dec. 9, 1972. Tchr. English, Spanish Borough High Sch., Wernersville, Pa., 1942-46; instr. Spanish and Latin Albright Coll., Reading, Pa., 1946-52, head circulation dept. coll. library, 1952-53; asst. circulation librarian Reading Pub. Library, 1953-57, head br. librarian, 1957-58; sch. librarian So. Jr. High Sch., Reading, 1958—. Mem. Fellowship House, Reading, YWCA, Reading. Mem. Am., Pa. assns. sch. librarians, Nat., Reading, Pa. edn. assns., Am., Pa. library assns., Albright Coll., Drexel Grad. Library Sch. alumni assns., Beta Phi Mu, Phi Kappa Phi, Pi Gamma Mu, Sigma Tau Delta, Phi Delta Sigma. Democrat. Lutheran (mem. Inner Mission Soc.). Home: 337 Miller St Reading PA 19602 Office: 10th and Chestnut Sts Reading PA 19602

DAVENPORT, ELLA SMITH (MRS. CHRISTIAN JEFFERSON DAVENPORT), educator; b. Lynchburg, Va.; b. Robert Nelson and Sylvia Roxie (Cox) Smith; student Va. Sem., 1922-23; B.S., Hampton Inst., 1947; postgrad. U. Va., 1954-55; M.A. in Speech Edn., N.Y. U., 1957; diploma Ch. Women's Leadership Sch., 1967; m. Christian Jefferson Davenport, Dec. 26, 1933; children—Gwendolyn (Mrs. Kenneth Singleton), Christian Jefferson. Tchr. English and speech Bedford (Va.) Tng. Sch., 1949-54, Susie G. Gibson High Sch., Bedford, 1955-62. Active numerous civic community fund drives, 1948-74. Mem. Nat. Ret. Tchrs. Assn., Va. Edn. Assn., Ministers Wives Alliance, Speech Assn. Am., Hampton U. Alumni Assn., N.Y. U. Alumni Assn. Baptist. Mem. Order Eastern Star; mem. Courts of Calanthe. Home: 2342 Garfield Av Lynchburg VA 24505

DAVENPORT, JOANNA, educator; b. Salem, Mass., Jan. 17, 1933; d. Carleton and Virginia (Price) Davenport; B.S., Skidmore Coll., 1954; M.S., Smith Coll., 1958; Ph.D., Ohio State U., 1966. Instr., Mt. Holyoke Coll., South Hadley, Mass., 1954-56, Flood Jr. High Sch., Englewood, Colo., 1956-57, Jack Jr. High Sch., Portland, Me., 1959, U. Vt. at Burlington, 1959-62, Colo. State U., Ft. Collins, 1962-63; grad. asst., instr. Ohio State U., Columbus, 1963-65; asst. prof., chmn. dept. women's phys. edn. U. Vt., Burlington, 1965-67; asso. prof. phys. edn. U. Ill. at Urbana, 1967—. Mem. A.A.H.P.E.R. (editor Tennis Guide, 1970-72; chmn. sports guides and ofcl. rules 1972-74), Midwest, Nat. (historian, archivist) assns. phys. edn. for coll. women. Home: 24 Harbor Av Marblehead MA 01945 Office: U Ill Urbana IL 61801

DAVERN, JEANNE MARGUERITE, archtl. writer, editorial cons.; b. Plattsburgh, N.Y.; d. Jeremiah William and Marguerite (Beaucaire) Davern; B.A., Wellesley Coll., 1944. Reporter, Plattsburgh Press-Republican, 1944-48; staff Archtl. Record, 1948-69, mng. editor, 1963-69; archtl. writer, editorial cons., 1969—. Mem. A.I.A. (hon.; asso. mem. N.Y. chpt.), Soc. Archtl. Historians, Municipal Art Soc., Nat. Trust for Historic Preservation, Nat. Council Arts and Govt. Address: 80 Park Av New York City NY 10016

DAVEY, MARY GENEVIEVE, coll. adminstr.; b. Providence, Feb. 14, 1921; d. John and Ellen T. (McDonough) Davey; Ed.B., R.I. Coll., 1941, Ed.M., 1951. Tchr., Warwick, R.I., 1941-45, Providence, 1945-54; dir. pub. relations and alumni affairs R.I. Coll., Providence, 1954—. Pres., R.I. Assn. Mental Health, 1965-67. Mem. Am. Assn. U. Women (pres. Providence plantations br. 1970-73), Providence Tchrs. Union (treas. 1951-53). Home: 84 Ravenswood Av Providence RI 02908

DAVID, ADELLE (MRS. FRANK V. SIEGLINGER), author; b. Lizton, Ind., Feb. 25, 1904; d. Charles Eugene and Harriet (McBroom) Davis; A.B., U. Cal. at Berkeley, 1927; M.S., U. So. Cal., 1939; D.S. (hon.), U. Plano, 1972; m. Frank V. Sieglinger, Apr. 23, 1960; children by previous marriage—George D. Leisey, Barbara A. Leisey. Supr. nutrition Yonkers (N.Y.) Pub. Schs., 1928-30; cons. nutritionist, Oakland, Cal., 1931-33; writer, lectr., cons. nutritionist, Los Angeles, 1934—. Dir. Insts. for Achievement of Human Potential. Recipient Brazilian Honor of Merit award Inst. for Achievement Human Potential, 1972, Raymond Dart award, 1973. Fellow Internat. Coll. of Applied Nutrition (hon.). Author: Let's Cook it Right, 1947, rev. edit. 1962; Let's Have Healthy Children, 1951, rev. edit. 1972; Let's Eat Right to Keep Fit, 1954, rev. edit. 1971; Let's Get Well, 1965. Home: 3625 Palos Verdes Dr N Palos Verdes Estates CA 90274

DAVID, ALMA AUGUSTA WILLIAMS (MRS. BEN EDWARD DAVID), educator; b. Thompson Station, Tenn., Apr. 27, 1916; d. William Townsend and Ola (Crawford) Williams; B.S., Middle Tenn. State Tchrs. Coll., 1934-38; M.A., Columbia Tchrs. Coll., 1947, Ed.D., 1956; m. Ben Edward David, Aug. 3, 1957. Tchr. elementary sch., Columbia, Tenn., 1938-42; tchr. nursery sch. Hamilton Sch., N.Y.C., 1946-47; dir. weekday kindergarten West End Meth. Ch., Nashville, 1947-51; instr. Columbia Tchrs. Coll., 1951-53; prof. elementary edn. U. Miami, Coral Gables, Fla., 1953—; vis. prof. Columbia Tchrs. Coll., George Peabody Coll., Richmond Profl. Inst., summers 1953—. Cons. Toy Guidance Council, N.Y.C., 1954-60; mem. supervisory panel Ala. Fla. Ga. Early Childhood Tng. Inst.; mem. Gov.'s Coordinating Council on Early Childhood Devel., 1974—. Mem. personnel com. Girl Scout council Trop., Fla., 1964—; acting chmn. day care adv. com. Fla. Div. Family Services, 1964—; mem. higher edn. com. Fla. Meth. Bd. Edn., 1964-72. Bd. dirs. St. Albans Day Nursery, 1961-71. Mem. Assn. for Childhood Edn. Internat., So. (exec. bd. 1954—, pres. 1969-70), Fla. (pres. 1959-61), assns. on children under six, Nat. Assn. for Edn. Young Children, Organisation Mondiale Pour l'Education Prescolaire. Clubs: University of Miami Women's, University of Miami Faculty. Home: 8505 SW 48th St Miami FL 33155 Office: U Miami Coral Gables FL 33124

DAVID, ELIZABETH LIKERT (MRS. MARTIN HEIDENHAIN DAVID), educator; b. N.Y.C.; d. Rensis and Jane (Gibson) Likert; A.B., Swarthmore Coll.; Ph.D., U. Mich., 1961; m. Martin Heidenhain David; children—Peter Rensis, Margaret Meigs, Andrew John Heidenhain. Faculty U. Wis., Madison, 1962, now research asso. Resource Econs. Inst. for Environmental Studies. Home: 207 Du Rose Terrace Madison WI 53705

DAVID, FLORENCE NIGHTINGALE, educator; b. Leominster, Hereford, U.K., Aug. 23, 1909; d. William Richard and Florence Maude (James) David; came to U.S., 1960; B.Sc., U. London, 1931, Ph.D., 1937, D.Sc., 1951. Mem. faculty U. London, 1935-39, 45-58, prof., 1961-67; with Ministry of Home Security, 1939-45; vis. faculty mem. U. Cal. at Berkeley, 1961-62, 64-65, also various summers; prof. statistics, U. Cal. at Riverside, 1967—, also head dept. Cons. Fed. Forestry Service, U.S. Dept. Agr., 1965—, Pacific State Hosp., Pomona, Cal., 1964—. Fellow Am. Statis. Assn., Inst. Math. Statistics, Royal Statis. Soc.; mem. Internat. Statis. Inst., Biometrics Soc. Author books including Games, Gods and Gambling, 1963; Combinatorial Chance, 1962; Probability Theory for Statistical Methods, 1948; Contbr. articles to publs. Home: 156 Highland Blvd Kensington CA 94708 Office: Statistics Dept U Cal Riverside CA 92502

DAVID, HEATHER MACKINNON (MRS. RICHARD STANLEY DAVID), journalist, author; b. Tokyo, Japan, Dec. 11, 1937; d. Joseph Ayer and Sylvia Jessamine (Clarke) MacKinnon; B.A., U. Md., 1959; came to U.S., 1940, naturalized, 1945; student U. Colo., 1955-56; B.A., U. Md., 1959; m. Richard Stanley David, May 14, 1960; 1 dau., Laurel Allyson. Editorial asst. Missiles and Rockets Mag., Washington, 1959-61; asso. editor, 1961-67; corr. Missile/Space Daily, Washington, 1963-67; Pentagon corr. Capitol Cities Radio and Fairchild Publs., Washington, 1967-70; chief Washington Bur., Electronic Design Mag., 1971-74; Capitol Hill corr. Energy Digest, 1972-74; account exec. Wagner and Barody, pub. relations, Washington, 1974—. Vice pres., sr. editor Nations Capital News Bur., Washington, 1973-74. Mem. Armed Forces Communications and Electronics Assn. Author: Wernher von Braun, 1963; Admiral Richover and the Nuclear Navy, 1969; Operation Rescue, 1971. Address: 2506 Eye St NW Washington DC 20037

DAVID, HILDA BLACK, educator; b. Thomasville, N.C., Aug. 7, 1927; d. John William and Mamie Elizabeth (Graham) Black; A.B. in English and French, Shaw U., 1947; M.A. in Speech and Phonetics, Cornell U., 1956; m. Lawrence Thomas David, Feb. 28, 1953; children—Lawrence Kenneth, LaDonna Malise, Lark Chappelle, Marc Charlton. With N.C. Pub. Schs., 1947-53, Ga. Pub. Schs., 1955-60, European div. U. Md., Heidelberg, Germany, 1961-64; asst. prof. English and speech Benedict Coll., Columbia, S.C., 1965—. Reading cons. Silver Burdett Pub. Co. Vol. tutor Columbia Pub. Schs.; mem. Columbia Literacy Council; pres. Logan Sch. P.T.A., 1973-74; active Sickle Cell Anemia Found.; mem. S.C. Textbook Adoption Com., S.C. Sch. Supts. Adv. Com. Mem. Internat. Reading Assn., Speech Communication Assn., Nat. Reading Conf., Coll. Lang. Assn., League Women Voters, Delta Sigma Theta. Baptist (Sunday sch. tchr.). Home: 2300 Adams St Columbia SC 29203

DAVIDOFF, DENISE TAFT (MRS. JERRY DAVIDOFF), advt. agy. exec.; b. N.Y.C., Mar. 11, 1932; d. Allen Robert and Bunnee Lola (Zuckerman) Taft; A.B., Vassar Coll., 1953; m. Jerry Davidoff, Oct. 2, 1955; children—Douglass, John. With C.A. Smith & Co., Westport, Conn., 1960-67, exec. v.p., 1966-67; pres. Shailer Davidoff Rogers, Inc., Fairfield, Conn., 1967—. Mem. Westport (Conn.) Democratic Town Com., 1964—; justice of the peace, Westport, 1969—. Trustee Westport Pub. Library, 1973—; bd. dirs. Unitarian-Universalist Womens Fedn., 1973—. Named Advt. Woman of the Year, Advt. Club of Fairfield, 1967. Home: 20 High Point Rd Westport CT 06880 Office: Heritage Sq Fairfield CT 06430

DAVIDOFF, IDA FISHER (MRS. LEO M. DAVIDOFF), educator, psychologist; b. Chelsea, Mass., Aug. 30, 1903; d. Jacob and Mamie (Lurensky) Fisher; B.S., Simmons Coll., 1924; M.A., Radcliffe Coll., 1925; Ed.D., Columbia, 1961; m. Leo M. Davidoff, Oct. 3, 1926; children—Helen (Mrs. Jules Hirsch), Leonore (Mrs. David Lockwood), Frank, Mary (Mrs. Peter Houts). Tchr. English, Wheelock Sch., Boston, 1924-26; practice psychology, New Canaan, Conn., 1955—; family counselor Jewish Family Service, N.Y.C., 1956-59, marriage and family counselor Family Mental Health Research Program, 1961-62; student counselor Albert Einstein Coll. Medicine, Bronx, N.Y., 1962-68, asst. prof. psychiatry, 1966-72, asso. prof., 1972-74, vis. lectr., 1974—; founder, dir. program to train women as psychiat. rehab. workers Dept. Psychiatry, Bronx Municipal Hosp. Center, 1963—. Vice chmn. New Canaan Bd. Edn., 1947-55. Bd. dirs. Nat. Bd. YWCA, 1956-62. Nat. Inst. Mental Health grantee, 1966-69. Mem. Nat. Cong. on Family Relations, Am. Orthopsychiat. Assn., Am. Assn. Marriage and Family Counselors (dir. 1973—, chpt. sec. 1965), Am. Psychol. Assn., Home: 73 Marshall Ridge Rd New Canaan CT 06840 Office: Albert Einstein College of Medicine Jacobi Hospital Dept of Psychiatry Pelham Parkway Bronx NY 10461

DAVIDOFF, JOANNE MARIE MALATESTA (MRS. IRA JOSEPH DAVIDOFF), educator; b. Canton, O., Mar. 2, 1930; d. John Rubano and Erma (Carpinelli) Malatesta; A.B., Chestnut Hill (Pa.) Coll., 1954; spl. teaching certificate Cath. U. Am., 1953; certificate Visually Handicapped Inst., 1958; Ed.M., Temple U., 1959; m. Ira Joseph Davidoff, Aug. 21, 1965; children—Cynthia Louise Marie, Michael John Elliott Patrick. Family visitor, asst. nursery sch. tchr. Upsal Day Sch. for Blind Children Phila., 1954-56, prin., 1956-68, dir., 1968—. Ednl. cons. Parents Assn. For Guidance and Edn. Visually Impaired Children, 1954—, Am. Assn. Workers For Blind, 1955-63, Pa. Fedn. For Blind, 1957—, Delawars Valley Assn. Nursery Sch. and Kindergarten Edn., 1960—, Am. Assn. Instrns. For Blind, 1963—; cons. Beacon Lodge Camp For Blind, 1958-59. Treas. Phila. Council Recreation For Handicapped, 1960-63; evaluation com. Nat. Accreditation Council for Agys. Serving Blind and Visually Handicapped, 1967—; trustee center for Blind, Phila. Recipient numerous awards for work with blind, 1950—; named Most Beautiful Blind Girl in Am., Mayor of Phila., 1952. Mem. Nat. Assn. Edn. for Young Children, Assn. for Childhood Edn. Internat., Parents Assn. For Guidance and Edn. Visually Impaired Children, Overbrook Sch. For Blind (bd. dirs.), Chestnut Hill Coll., Temple U. alumni assns., Cath. Guild For Blind, Internat. Platform Assn. Home: 7808 Pine Rd Wyndmoor PA 19118 Office: 220 W Upsal St Philadelphia PA 19119

DAVIDOW, KATHERINE LORAINE (MRS. JOEL DAVIDOW), lawyer; b. Berlin, Wis., Aug. 12, 1944; d. John Selby and Irene Elizabeth (Brooks) Barton; student Stanford U., 1962-64; A.B., George Washington U., 1966; J.D., Georgetown U., 1969; m. Joel Davidow, June 13, 1964; children—Elizabeth, Judith Loraine. Admitted to D.C. bar, 1971, Ill. bar, 1969, Va. bar, 1974; atty. Leva, Hawes, Symington, Martin & Oppenheimer, Washington, 1971-72; atty. Sonnenschein, Levinson, Carlin, Nath & Rosenthal, Chgo., 1969-70. Mem. Ill., Fed. Dist. Ct. No. Dist. Ill., D.C., Am., Va., bar assns. Home: 1637 Bentana Way Reston VA 22090

DAVIDSON, ANITA LORAIN, real estate broker; b. Rocky Comfort, Mo., Feb. 1, 1918; d. Roscoe and Esther Madosa (Cantrell) Davidson; student Filbin Beauty Coll., 1939, Lumbleau Real Estate, 1959-60, 63. Long distance operator Pacific Tel. & Tel., Florence, Ariz., 1943-46; owner/operator Anitas Beauty Shop, Whittier, Cal., 1947-51; clk. Safeway Stores, Inc., Los Angeles, 1951-59; saleswoman Ray Davenport Realtor, Whittier, 1960-64; real estate broker Anita Davidson Realtor, Whittier, 1964—. Home: 1431 Grissom Park Dr Fullerton CA 92633 Office: 12525 E Lambert Rd Whittier CA 90606

DAVIDSON, MRS. CHARLES (KATE S. DAVIDSON), educator, civic worker; b. Emporia, Va., May 13, 1910; d. John William and Ida Florence (Hill) Saunders; student Chowan Coll., 1926-27; A.A., Louisburg Coll., 1927-28; summer student Forest Coll., 1928, 29, Longwood Coll., 1932; m. Charles Reuber Davidson, July 1, 1933; 1 dau., Katharine Saunders (Mrs. John Byers Horner). Tchr., Emporia High Sch., 1930-33, 46-50, substitute tchr., 1950—. Gen. chmn., dir. Greenville Tb Assn.; bd. mem. Southside Tb and Health Assn.; bd. mem. Richmond Girl Scout Council; 2d v.p. Southside Girl Scout Area Council; bd. dirs. A.R.C. of Greenville, Greensville County Hosp. Aux., Southside Area Planning Bd.; sec. Emporia Band Boosters Club; mem. bd., dist. dir. Va. Tb and Respiratory Disease Assn.; mem. bd. Emporia Tb Assn.; mem. bd. Commonwealth Girl Scouts U.S.A., publicity chmn. Emporia; pres. Petersburg Dist. United Methodist Women, mem. exec. bd. Va. Conf., mem. dist. council ministries; del. conf. Meth. Ch. Women, 1st v.p. Va. Lung Assn. Recipient award Girl Scouts Am. Mem. P.T.A. (asst. dist. dir. Southside area, dir. Emporia, Va.), U.D.C. (pres. Greensville County, Va.) Butts Tavern Assn. (trustee), Federated Woman's Club (corr. sec.), Woman's Soc. Christian Service (promotion sec. corr., dist. zone leader, pres., dist. chmn. program materials), Greensville Meml. Hosp. Aux. (pres.), Va. Hist. Soc., Epsilon Sigma Omicron. Methodist (supt. Cradle Roll, mem. bd. edn., chmn. commn. on missions). Clubs: Emporia Ladies Golf Assn. (pres.); Riparian Garden (publicity chmn., hort. and flower arrangements chmn.), Woman's (past pres., parliamentarian), Riparian Woman's (v.p.), Va. Federated Garden. Home: 506 Ingleside Av Emporia VA 23847

DAVIDSON, DIANA LEE, advt. agy. exec.; b. Council Bluffs, Ia., May 1, 1934; d. Donald W. and Maxine (Aney) Gohlinghorst; student William Woods Coll., Fulton, Mo., 1952-54; grad. Twin Cities Advt. Inst., U. Minn., 1966; m. John Robert Davidson (div.); 1 son, Douglas L. Sec. advt. dept. McCulloch Motors Corp., Mpls., 1955-60; media buyer Clyne-Maxon Advt. Agy., Mpls., 1960-65; asst. media supr. Knox-Reeves Advt. Agy., Mpls., 1965-66; media dir. Martin-Williams Advt. Agy., Mpls., 1966-69; promotion dir. radio sta. KDWB, 1969-71; media dir. Barickman/Red Barron Advt., Inc., Mpls., 1971—. Bd. dirs. Better Bus. Bur. Minn., 1974-75. Mem. Am. Women in Radio and TV, Advt. Club Minn. (pres. 1974-75), Mpls. C. of C. Home: 1247 Brighton Sq New Brighton MN 55112 Office: 400 Baker Bldg Minneapolis MN 55402

DAVIDSON, DOROTHY HARRIET BURT (MRS. PAUL MOODY DAVIDSON), librarian, educator; b. Troy, N.Y., Oct. 2, 1909; d. William James and Grace Agnes (Hoyt) Burt; student Trinity U., 1927-28; B.A., Park Coll., 1931; M.A., Memphis State U., 1965; m. Paul Moody Davidson, Jan. 12, 1936; 1 dau., Ruth Grace (Mrs. James Edward Latham, Jr.). Tchr., Fortescue (Mo.) Consol. High Sch., 1931; family counselor United Charities, Dallas, 1932-35; missionary Evang. Union of South Am. Brazil, 1936-60; prof., librarian Mid South Bible Coll., Memphis, 1960—. Mem. Christian Librarians' Fellowship, Am., Tenn., West Tenn. library assns. Home: 3779 Cardinal Av Memphis TN 38111 Office: 2485 Union Av Memphis TN 38112

DAVIDSON, DOROTHY LOUISE (MRS. GEORGE WILLIAM DAVIDSON, JR.), librarian; b. Carmi, Ill., Apr. 22, 1919; d. Joseph Otto and Mary (Clifford) Henning; B.E., Ill. State U., 1940; M.S., Chgo. State U., 1964; M.A., Rosary Coll., 1967; m. George William Davidson, Jr., June 28, 1941; children—George William 3d, Deborah Jo. Tchr. Orland Park (Ill.) Sch., 1959-63; librarian Oak Lawn (Ill.) Community High Sch., 1963-66; dir. library media service, 1966—. Bd. dirs. Orland Park (Ill.) Pub. Library, 1963-65. Mem. Am., Ill. library assns., Assn. Chicagoland Sch. Librarians, Ill. Audiovisual Assn., Nat. Ednl. Assn., Ill. Edn. Assn., North Central Assn. (sch. evaluation cons. 1966-71), Beta Phi Mu, Kappa Delta Pi. Methodist. Home: 12120 S 76th Av Palos Heights IL 60463 Office: 94th and Southwest Hwy Oak Lawn IL 60453

DAVIDSON, JEAN DOLORES (MRS. ELMER HAYES DAVIDSON), psychologist; b. Greenville, N.C., May 31, 1930; d. Frank Clifton and Pauline (Fornes) Dail; B.A. magna cum laude (Nat. Methodist scholar), Greensboro Coll., 1957; M.S. (Research grantee), Pa. State U., 1963, now postgrad.; m. Elmer Hayes Davidson, Sept. 14, 1957; children—Brenda Joy, David Franklin. Sch. psychometrist Greensboro (N.C.) Pub. Schs., 1958-60; instr. Tex. Technol. U., Lubbock, 1965-66; dir. New World Sch., Oklahoma City, 1966-71; dir. psychol. services Southeastern Mental Health Center, Wilmington, N.C., 1971. Part time instr. Oklahoma City U., summer 1968; pvt. cons. sch. psychologist Va., Pa., 1960-65. Mem. Com. Early Childhood Degree programs State Dept. Edn., Okla., 1969-70. Bd. dirs. Head Start program, New Hanover County, Inc., Wilmington, N.C. Fellow Vanderbilt U., 1957, fellow Gen. Foods Co., 1963-65. Mem. Soc. Research in Child Devel., N.E.A., Nat. Assn. Ind. Schs., Omicron Nu. Home: 402 Lansdowne Rd Wilmington NC 28401 Office: 718 S 5th St Wilmington NC 28401

DAVIDSON, JOY ELAINE (MRS. ROBERT S. DAVIDSON JR.), mezzo soprano; b. Fort Collins, Colo., 1940; A.B., Occidental Coll.; also edn. Fla. State U.; m. Robertson S. Davidson Jr.; 1 son, 1 dau. Mezzo soprano with Miami Opera Guild, from 1964, Welsh Nat. Opera, from 1968, Met. Opera Nat. Co., 1965-66, 66-67, Bayerisch Staatsoper, Munich, Germany, 1968, La Scala Opera, 1970—, N.Y.C. Opera, San Francisco, 1971—, Vienna State Opera, 1973. Recipient 1st place Internat. Competition for Young Opera Singers, Sofia, Bulgaria, 1967. Mem. Zeta Tau Zeta, Sigma Alpha Iota. Democrat. Presbyn. Address: 5751 SW 74th Av South Miami FL 33143

DAVIDSON, KATHRYN LOUGHRAN (MRS. JOHN HOWARD DAVIDSON), advt. exec.; b. Peru, Ind., Apr. 5, 1916; d. Harry E. and Daisy May (Healy) Loughran; grad. high sch.; m. John Howard Davidson, Dec. 27, 1943; children—Michael Loughran, John Robert. Service rep. Ind. Bell Telephone Co., Peru, 1934-45; sec. to plant mgr. Square D Co., Peru, Ind., 1956-65; gen. advt. mgr. Peru Daily Tribune, 1969—. Mem. Bus. and Profl. Women's Club, Psi Iota Xi. Baptist (ch. clk. 1967-70). Mem. Order Eastern Star (past matron). Home: 12 Glenway Dr Peru IN 46970 Office: PO Box 87 Peru IN 46970

DAVIDSON, MARGARET RUTH ASHE (MRS. HARRY ARNOLD DAVIDSON), educator; b. Monroe, La., Jan. 18, 1929; d. Claude Harmon and Margaret Ruth (Berry) Ashe; B.A., Panhandle Agrl. and Mech. Coll., 1948; M.A., U. Tex., 1963, Ph.D., 1967; m. Harry Arnold Davidson, Sept. 1, 1948; children—Margaret Ellen, Harry Arnold, Thomas Joel, John Patrick. Tchr. territorial pub. schs., rural Alaska, 1951-62; research asst. U. Tex., 1963; tchr. elementary sch., Juneau, Alaska, 1963-64; instr. U. Tex., 1965-66, asst. prof. elementary edn., 1967-69; asso. prof. edn. Trinity U., 1969—. Coordinator, Curriculum Writing Conf., S.W. Ednl. Devel. Lab., summers 1967, 68, cons., 1967-68. Vol. worker Pan Am. Center, 1965-67. Trustee All Saints Episcopal Sch. Mem. Inst. Latin Am. Studies, Am. Assn. U. Profs., Nat. Council Social Studies, Am. Assn. U. Women, Assn. Childhood Edn. Internat., Phi Kappa Phi, Pi Lambda Theta, Psi Chi, Kappa Delta Pi. Episcopalian. Home: 623 Mandalay Dr E San Antonio TX 78212

DAVIDSON, NORMA LEWIS, violinist; b. Provo, Utah, Oct. 12, 1929; d. Arthur and Mary (Mortimer) Lewis; student Juilliard Sch. Music, 1949-50, Mannes Coll. Music, 1950-54, North Tex. State U., 1957-61, 62-64, So. Meth. U., 1968-70, Music Acad. West, summers 1950-54; m. Dec. 29, 1949; children—Kevin James, Nathanael Arthur. Concert tours Columbia Artists Community Concerts, 1949-55; soloist with orchs. in U.S., Mexico, Can.; weekly TV show NBC, N.Y.C., 1950-51; recs. for Columbia, Bell, Stax records; mem. faculty Mannes Coll. Music; artist-in-residence, Tex. Woman's U., Denton, former mem. faculty psychology dept.; clin. psychologist. Mem. Am. String Tchrs. Assn., Nat. Music Tchrs. Assn., Am., Tex. psychol. assns., Alpha Chi, Pi Kappa Lambda, Alpha Lambda Delta. Unitarian (trustee, bd. dirs.). Contbr. articles to jours. Home: 1810 Williamsburg St Denton TX 76201

DAVIDSON, PATRICIA WHITE (MRS. HAROLD DAVIDSON), artist; b. Newark, Sept. 12, 1924; d. Newton Heston and Marguerite Christie (Greene) White; A.A., Centenary Coll. for Women, 1944; m. Harold Davidson, Oct. 25, 1947; children—Cynthia Ann (Mrs. Glenn A. Millar), Glenn Randolph. Asst. to art dir. Keuffel & Esser, Hoboken, N.J., 1945; asst. sec. to dean Rutgers U. Sch. Law, Newark, 1946; free-lance designer packaging and gift paper, East Orange, N.J., 1945-46; artist Anthony Advt., Massillon, O., 1970-71; dir. Heritage Gallery, Canton, O., 1972-73; mgr. occupational therapy dept. Genesee Meml. Hosp., Batavia, N.Y., 1966-67; one-man shows at Siesta Key First Fed. Bank, Sarasota, Fla., Harter Bank and Downtowner Hotel, Canton, O.; exhibited in group shows at Grand Nat. Exhibit, Am. Artists Profl. League, N.Y.C., Heritage Gallery, Brookside Country, Club, Canton; represented in pvt. collections. Tchr. drawing, painting YMCA, Massillon, O., 1962-63. Mem. screening com. Ohio Soc. Prevention Blindness, Canton, 1971-72; Gray lady A.R.C., Vets. Hosp., Batavia, N.Y., 1965-66; mem. Little Gallery North Canton, Ringling Art Mus. Bd. dirs. Genesee Symphony Orch., 1966-67. Recipient Judges Choice award Little Gallery, 1973. Mem. Am. Artists Profl. League, Canal Fulton Art and Crafts Guild (rev. bd. 1973), Canton Art Inst. Pro Arts Club, Outdoor Workshop, Mini-Painters Ohio, Sarasota Art Assn. Methodist (mem. council ministries 1972-73). Home: 523 Beach Rd Sarasota FL 33581

DAVIDSON, RITA CHARMATZ (MRS. DAVID STERNHEIMER DAVIDSON), judge; b. Bklyn., Sept. 1, 1928; d. Michael and Eiga (Rokeach) Charmatz; B.A., Goucher Coll., 1948; LL.B., Yale, 1951; m. David Sternheimer Davidson, Aug. 27; children—Minna Konn, Leo Charmatz. Admitted to Supreme Ct., Md., D.C. bars, practiced in Washington, and Md.; mem. firm Leibik & Weyand, 1952-63; sec. Dept. Employment and Social Services, State of Md., Balt., 1970—; judge Ct. spl. Appeals State of Md., 1972—. Zoning examiner Montgomery County, 1967-70; commr. Md. Nat. Capital Park and Planning Commn., 1967. Mem. Md. Suburban Fair Housing Assn.; chmn. Md. Manpower Planning Council, Interstate Conf. Employment Security Agys.; pres. Youth Opportunities, Inc. Founding mem. Dem. Action Group, 1962-66. Mem. Am., Md., Montgomery County bar assns., Am. Judicature Soc., Am. Civil Liberties Union, Am. Pub. Welfare Assn., Nat. Assn. Social Workers, Am. Soc. Planning Ofcls. Home: 8814 Altimont Lane Chevy Chase MD 20015

DAVIDSON, RUTH NORMA (MRS. OSCAR CLAUS DAVIDSON), banker; b. Williston, N.D., Dec. 16, 1915; d. George Washington and Lillie May (Rearick) Pfeiffer; ed. Williston pub. schs.; m. Oscar Claus Davidson, Feb. 21, 1938; children—Jacquelin (Mrs. Richard Olness), Linda Kay (Mrs. Dale Isaacson). With Am. State Bank, Williston, 1956—, poster, 1956-60, head bookkeeper, 1960—, asst. cashier, 1972—. Active United Fund Way, Williston, 1973. Recipient award for work with high sch. students Williston C. of C., 1971. Mem. Bus. and Profl. Women's Club (state chmn. econ. conf. 1970-72; state chmn. Young Careerist 1973-74), Nat. Assn. Bank Women (pres. N.D. chpt. 1971-72, 73-74). Democrat. Lutheran. Mem. Order Eastern Star. Home: Box 381 Williston ND 58801 Office: Box 1446 Williston ND 58801

DAVIDSON, SARAH JEAN, educator, govt. ofcl.; b. North Little Rock, Nov. 26, 1947; d. Earnest Jefferson and Alice (Saunders) Davidson; B.A. in Sociology, Howard U., 1970; M.A. in Early Childhood Edn. (Urban Tchrs. Corps fellow) Catholic U., 1971. Pre-sch. tchr., Urban Tchr. Corps intern Garrison Elementary Sch., Washington, 1970-71; tchr. Janney Elementary Sch., Washington, 1971-72; research asst. Pres.'s Nat. Adv. Council on Edn. of Disadvantaged Children, Washington, 1972—. Chmn. North Little Rock Voter Registration Drive, 1965; vol. Juvenile Ct. Big Sister

Program, 1971; vol. Mayor's Youth Tng. Program, 1971. Named Outstanding Personality in Human Relations in North Little Rock, 1965. Mem. Nat. Assn. for Edn. of Young Children, Am. Ednl. Research Assn. Baptist. Club: Howard U. Alumni. Home: 732 Rittenhouse St NW Washington DC 20011 Office: 425 13th St NW Suite 1012 Washington DC 20004

DAVIE, ETHEL MARIE O'HARA (MRS. ROBERT PARK DAVIE), educator; b. Newark; d. Walter F. and Gertrude (Hancox) O'Hara; B.S. summa cum laude, W.Va. State Coll., 1961; B.A. summa cum laude, 1963; M.A., Columbia, 1964; postgrad. Sorbonne, 1963-66, Case Western Res. U., 1968-69; m. Robert Park Davie, Mar. 27, 1942; children—Robert S., Thomas H. Faculty, W.Va. State Coll., Institute, 1961—, asso. prof. French, 1969—. Mem. Am. Assn. Tchrs. French (chpt. pres. 1968-69, chpt. sec.-treas. 1969—), Am. Assn. Higher Edn., Am. Council Teaching Fgn. Langs., Am. Assn. U. Women, Internat. Council Edn. for Teaching, Pi Delta Phi, Lambda Iota Tau, Sigma Delta Phi, Alpha Kappa Mu. Contbr. revs. to various publs. Home: 2706 Knox Av St Albans WV 25177 Office: WVa State Coll Institute WV 25112

DAVIES, MRS. CHARLES P., (see Banning, Elizabeth).

DAVIES, ELIZABETH JANE, editor; b. Cleve.; B.A., Denison U., 1934; M.A., U. So. Cal., 1955. Commd. 2d lt. U.S. Army, 1945, advanced through grades to lt. col., 1959; dir. army phys. therapy course Med. Field Service Sch., Fort Sam Houston, Tex., 1960-62; asst. chief Army Med. Specialist Corps, Washington, 1962-66; ret., 1966; editor Phys. Therapy Jour., Am. Phys. Therapy Assn., Washington, 1970—. Decorated Legion of Merit. Mem. Am. Med. Writers Assn., Am. Phys. Therapy Assn. Home: 6624 Rannoch Rd Bethesda MD 20034 Office: 1156 15th St NW Washington DC 20005

DAVIES, HARRIET WILLARD (MRS. ROBERT VAN CLEVE DAVIES), ednl. adminstr.; b. Chgo.; d. Frederic Wilson and Maude Myrtle (Foote) Willard; B.A. cum laude, Mt. Holyoke Coll., 1934; postgrad. Traphagen Sch., N.Y.C., 1934-35, Stafford Hall Sch., Summit, N.J., 1955-56; m. Robert Van Cleve Davies, June 15, 1940; 1 dau., Christine (Mrs. Christopher Naranjo). Owner, operator dress designer bus., 1935-40; sec. to v.p. Kemper Ins., Summit, N.J., 1956-64; admissions counselor, placement dir. N.Y. sch. Berkeley Sch., East Orange, N.J., 1964-67; placement dir. Katharine Gibbs Sch., Montclair, N.J., 1967—. Bd. mem., asst. dir. sch. library P.T.A., 1948-55; nurses aid A.R.C., 1941-43; Brownie troop leader Girl Scout council Greater Essex County, 1951-53; chmn. sewing activities Sunshine Soc., Summit, 1954-56; active various community drives. Mem. Internat. Wedgwood Soc., Nat. Historic Trust, N.J. Personnel and Guidance Assn., N.Y. Personnel and Mgmt. Assn., Phi Beta Kappa. Democrat. Unitarian. Clubs: Fortnightly (Summit, N.J.); Mt. Holyoke of No. N.J. Home: 19 Myrtle Av Summit NJ 07901 Office: 33 Plymouth St Montclair NJ 07042

DAVIES, JANE BADGER, librarian; b. Amboy, Ill., Sept. 9, 1913; d. Henry Harold and Clara May (Heermans) Badger; B.A., Wellesley Coll., 1935; M.A., Columbia, 1942, B.S. in L.S. with high honors, 1944; postgrad. U. Mich., summer 1936, U. Wis., summers 1937, 38; m. Lyn Davies, July 18, 1942. Tchr. Monticello Prep. Sch., Godfrey, Ill., 1935-37; tchr. Kent Sch. Girls, Denver, 1937-41, Halsted Sch., Yonkers, N.Y., 1942-43; reference librarian Columbia Libraries, 1944-50, rare book cataloger, 1951—; cons. Nat. Trust Historic Preservation, 1965, Smithsonian Inst., 1967, Greensboro (N.C.) Preservation Soc., 1967-70, Historic Green Springs, 1970-73; lectr. in field. Am. Council Learned Socs. grantee, 1970, Am. Philos. Soc. grantee, 1970-71. Mem. Soc. Archtl. Historians (sec.-treas. N.Y. chpt. 1959-67), Victorian Soc. Am. (adv. com. 1966—), Nat. Trust Historic Preservation, Bridgeport (Conn.) Hist. Soc., Greensboro Preservation Soc. (hon.), Phi Beta Kappa, Beta Phi Mu. Presbyn. Author intro. reprint Rural Residences (Alexander J. Davis). Editorial asst. Jour. Soc. Archtl. Historians, 1964-65. Contbr. articles on archtl. history to mags. and jours. Home: 549 W 123d St New York City NY 10027 Office: 320 Butler Library Columbia New York City NY 10027

DAVIES, JENNIE ARLENE SAVAGE, accountant; b. Salt Lake City, Sept. 22, 1923; d. Edrick Alonzo and Jennie Katheryn (Rillston) Savage; student Henegers Bus. Coll., 1942-44, Internat. Corr. Sch. Accounting, 1959-61; m. Robert Binnell, Oct. 22, 1950; children—Bryan Ray, Diane Louise, Edyth Colleen, Denise Cathleen. Accountant Round Cal. Chain Co., South San Francisco, 1949-53, Swift & Co., South San Francisco, 1952-54; office mgr. Green Hills County Club, Millbrae, Cal., 1956-65, mgr., 1965-68; accounting officer Cal. Coll. Podiatric Medicine, San Francisco, 1969—. Pres. Young Womens Mut. Improvement Assn., Ch. of Jesus Christ of Latter-day Saints, 1956-58, 71-73. Recipient Service award Millbrae Lions Club, 1965. Mem. Nat., Western assns. coll. and univ. bus. officers, Nat. Notary Assn. Mem. Ch. of Jesus Christ of Latter-day Saints. Home: 247 Longford Dr South San Francisco CA 94080 Office: 1770 Eddy St San Francisco CA 94115

DAVIES, JOAN SCHINDELER, dermatoglyphic specialist; b. Scranton, Pa., Aug. 13, 1932; d. J. Nelson and Geraldine (Walser) Davies; Med. Technologist, Hahnemann Hosp., 1952; div.; children (adopted)—Susan, Curtis. Med. technologist, lab. dir. W. Side Hosp., Scranton, Pa., 1950-53; med. technologist Miami (Fla.) Med. Labs., 1953-54; artist, research asst. Communication Research Inst., Coconut Grove, Fla., 1963-65; artist, dermatoglyphic specialist Developmental Evaluation Clinic, Miami, 1965-70; tchr., artist, lectr. Mailman Center for Child Devel., Miami, 1970—. Sec., World Dolphin Found., Coconut Grove, Fla., 1973—. Mem. A.A.A.S., Am. Soc. Human Genetics, Am. Assn. on Mental Deficiency, Inst. Maya Studies, Environmental Mutagen Soc., Miami Art Center, Miami Philharmonic Soc. Author: Clinical Dermatoglyphs, 1971. Contbr. articles to profl. jours. Home: 9300 SW 82nd St Miami FL 33143 Office: 1201 NW 16th St Miami FL 33152

DAVIS, AGNES MARION, univ. librarian; b. San Antonio, Aug. 14, 1923; d. Charles William and Elma Agnes (Sarber) Davis; B.S., Lincoln Meml. U., 1951; M.A., George Peabody Coll. Tchrs., 1954. Asst. librarian Lincoln Meml. U., Harrogate, Tenn., 1951-53; reference librarian Va. Poly. Inst. and State U., Blacksburg, 1954—. Mem. Am., Southeastern, Va. library assns., Am. Assn. U. Women, Am. Assn. U. Profs., Kappa Delta Pi, Delta Kappa Gamma. Presbyn. (pres. Women of Ch. 1972-74). Home: Draper's Meadow NW Blacksburg VA 24060

DAVIS, ALICE ELIZA MORSE (MRS. GEORGE ARTHUR DAVIS), club woman; b. Milo, Me.; d. John Willis and Mabel (Martin) Morse; student U. Me., 1919-21; grad. Gilman Comml. Sch., Bangor, Me., 1936; m. Maynard Havey, Dec. 22, 1921 (dec. Dec. 1930); 1 dau., Gloria (Mrs. Lee Baker); m. 2d, George Arthur Davis, Aug. 18, 1947 (dec. Jan. 10, 1969). Tchr. pub. schs. Me., 1922-25; sec. Agrl. Marketing Service, USDA, Washington, 1936-46; mem. community adv. com. Me. Hwy. Safety Com., 1962-64; mem. adv. council Me. Civil War Centennial Commn., 1961-65; mem. nat. voter adv. bd. Am. Security Council, Washington, 1971—; Me. chmn. nat. def. com. D.A.R., 1958-65, resolutions com., 1958—, regent chpt., 1962-64, 72—, area rep. speakers staff com., 1968-74; nat. vice chmn. Northeastern div. Americanism and D.A.R. Manual for Citizenship Com., 1965-68; Me. pres. Daus. Colonial Wars, 1965-68, nat. vice chmn. program com. 1st div. states, 1968-71, mem. Nat. Officers Club, 1966—; nat. chmn. Am. def. and legislation, Nat. Soc. New Eng. Women, 1966-69, nat. vice chmn. resolutions com., 1966-69, v.p. Augusta Colony, Me., 1966-72; pres. 1972—; mem. Soc. Mayflower Descs.; charter mem. Mason (N.H.) Hist. Soc., 1969—. Mem. Order Eastern Star. Address: Twin Coves Southport ME 04569

DAVIS, ANN BRADFORD, actress; b. Schenectady, May 5, 1926; d. Cassius Miles and Marguerite (Stott) D.; B.A., U. Mich., 1948. Actress plays, Erie, Pa., 1948-49, Porterville, Cal., 1949-51, Yosemite, Cal., 1950-51, Monterey, Cal., 1952-53, Hollywood, Cal., 1954-55, summer stock and dinner theatres, 1958—; actress TV series The Bob Cummings Show, 1955-59, The Keefe Brasselle Show, 1963, The John Forsythe Show, 1965-66, The Brady Bunch, 1969—; actress Broadway play Once Upon a Mattress, 1960; toured with USO, Asia, S. Pacific, Korea; actress 2d nat. co. No No Nanette, 1972-73. Chmn. West Coast auditioning com. USO, 1969—, mem. Hollywood overseas com., 1969-70, nat. council, 1970, Cal. adv. com., 1971. Recipient Emmy award 1957, 58, 59, for Best Supporting Actress as Schultzie on The Bob Cummings Show. Mem. Girls Friday of Showbiz, Spotlighters. Home: 11725 Laurelwood Dr Studio City CA 91604*

DAVIS, ANNE LOGAN (MRS. WALTER ADAM WICHERN), educator, physician; b. Rahway, N.J., Dec. 2, 1924; d. Chester Morrison and Elisabeth (Logan) Davis; B.A., Wellesley Coll., 1945; M.D., Columbia 1949; m. Walter Adam Wichern, Mar. 24, 1956; children—Walter Adam III, Anne Logan. Intern, Bellevue Hosp., N.Y.C., 1949-50, resident, med. and chest services, 1952-54, 55-56, vis. physician, 1970—; Dazian Found. fellow Columbia Coll. Physicians and Surgeons, N.Y.C., 1954-55, instr. medicine, 1957-60, asso. medicine, 1960-64, asst. prof. medicine, 1964-68; asso. prof. clin. medicine, N.Y. U., 1968—. Physician, cons. dept. medicine VA Hosp., N.Y.C., 1972; spl. cons. Am. Coll. Chest Physicians, 1973. Trustee Nightingale-Bamford Sch., N.Y.C. Diplomate Am. Bd. Internal Medicine. Fellow N.Y. Acad. Medicine (chmn. com. on admissions 1965), A.C.P.; mem. Am. Thoracic Soc., N.Y. Lung Assn. (dir., v.p. 1973—), N.Y., N.Y. County med. socs., A.M.A., N.Y. Trudeau Soc. (pres. 1973—), Alpha Omega Alpha. Club: Cosmopolitan (N.Y.C.). Contbr. articles in field to profl. jours. Home: 1088 Park Av New York City NY 10028 Office: Chest Service Bellevue Hosp 462 1st Av New York City NY 10016

DAVIS, AUDREY BLYMAN (MRS. MILES DAVIS), instn. curator; b. Hicksville, N.Y., Nov. 9, 1934; d. George William and Helen Rosalie (Usewack) Blyman; B.S., Adelphi U., 1956; Ph.D. (NIH fellow), Johns Hopkins, 1969; m. Miles Davis, Aug. 6, 1960; children—Laura Helen, Allan Watson. Tchr. biology and chemistry Sewanhaka High Sch., Floral Park, N.Y., 1956-59, Saugus (Mass.) High Sch., 1960-61, Winsor Sch., Boston, 1961-62; cons. Sci. Service, Washington, 1965-67; curator med. scis. Smithsonian Instn., Washington, 1967—; lectr. U. Md., 1970, 73-74. NSF fellow Harvard, 1959-60; Commonwealth Found. fellow, 1972-73; recipient Smithsonian Research Found. award, 1971-72; Houston Endowment Research award, 1974-75. Mem. A.A.A.S., Am. Hist. Assn., History of Sci. Soc., Am. Assn. History of Medicine. Author: Circulation Physiology and Medical Chemistry in England 1650-1680, 1973; Bibliography on Women: with Special Emphasis on their Roles in Science and Society, 1974. Contbr. articles to profl. jours. Home: 1214 Bolton St Baltimore MD 21217 Office: Smithsonian Instn Div Med Scis Washington DC 20560

DAVIS, BARBARA ELLEN, librarian; b. McKeesport, Pa., May 14, 1925; d. George Thomas and Ethel Sarah (Todd) Davis; student Robert Morris Sch. Bus., 1942-43; B.S. with honors, Carnegie Inst. Tech., 1950, M.L.S., 1951; B.Mus., U. Wis., 1958. Clk., Carnegie Steel Co., Duquesne, Pa., 1943-47; librarian circulation dept. Madison (Wis.) Free Library, 1951-55; asst. music library U. Wis. Sch. Music, Madison, 1956-58, U. Ill. Library, Urbana, 1958-60; head readers service Cal. State U., Fullerton, 1960—. Chmn. Placentia (Cal.) Fine Arts Commn., 1967. Mem. Cal., Music, Orange County library assns., Sigma Alpha Iota. Episcopalian. Home: 439 Melody Lane Placentia CA 92670 Office: Library California State University Fullerton CA 92634

DAVIS, BARBARA GRACE, occupational therapist; b. Detroit, Feb. 10, 1932; d. Martin Adelbert and Marie Theresa (Rheiner) Mix.; student Highland Park Jr. Coll., 1950-51; B.S. in Occupational Therapy, Eastern Mich. U., 1954, certificate elementary edn., 1954; m. Jerry Darrell Davis, Dec. 28, 1958; children—Mark Allen, William Martin, Charles Vincent, Scott Rheiner, Robin Lee. Occupational therapist Henry Ford Hosp., Detroit, 1954-58, dir., 1968-69; chief occupational therapist Allenwood (N.J.) Hosp., 1959; occupational therapist Phys. Therapy Assos., Detroit, 1964; dir. occupational therapy St. John Hosp., Detroit, 1969-73; occupational therapist Northeastern Mich. Mental Health Center, Alpena, 1973—. Mem. Am., Mich., Detroit occupational therapy assns., Sigma Nu Phi. Home: Route #1 Box 526 Hubbard Lake MI 49747 Office: 1521 W Chisholm St Alpena MI 49707

DAVIS, BARBARA M(AE), librarian; b. Cranston, R.I., Dec. 23, 1926; d. Harrie S. and Marguerite M. (Cameron) Davis; Sc.B. in Chemistry, Brown U., 1948; M.S. in L.S., Simmons Coll., 1956. Asst. research librarian research and devel. dept. Cabot Corp., Cambridge, Mass., 1948-57, research librarian, 1957-61, research librarian Billerica (Mass.) Research Center, 1961-68, head tech. information services, 1968—. Dir. Cabot Boston Credit Union, 1956-59, 61-64, 72—, clk., 1961-64, 72—. Chmn. research com. Greater Boston Young Republican Club, 1959-61. Mem. Am. Chem. Soc. (sec. div. chem. lit. 1961-65), Spl. Libraries Assn. (chmn. Boston chpt. 1965-66, chmn. chemistry div. 1971-72), Simmons Coll. Library Sch. Alumni (v.p. 1965-66). Home: 65 St Mary's St Apt 1 Brookline MA 02215 Office: Cabot Corp Concord Rd Billerica MA 01821

DAVIS, BERNICE H. SPIES (MRS. ARTHUR LAIRD DAVIS), civic worker; b. Irvington, N.J.; d. Rudolph George and Emma (Hornich) Spies; A.A., Centenary Coll. for Women, 1931; student Columbia, 1931-32, N.Y.U., 1932-33, 36-37, 38-39; m. Arthur Laird Davis, Nov. 16, 1934; children—Arden Laird (Mrs. David M. Melick), Douglas Spies. Tchr. music Irvington Pub. Schs., 1931-46, 68-73. Pres., N.J. Congress Parents and Tchrs., 1962-65, legislation chmn., 1965-70; pres. Essex County council P.T.A., 1956-58, hon. pres., 1973, high sch. service chmn., mem. exec. com. Nat. P.T.A., 1967-69; mem. Essex County Vocational Sch. Bd., 1969-71, pres., 1971-74; v.p. Essex County Asso. Bds. Edn., 1972-74, pres., 1974—; mem. Gov.'s Com. Safety, 1962-65; mem. Citizen's Com. Higher Edn., 1965, N.J. Nat. Library Com., 1966, Nat. Com. Sch. Support, 1965-71, Gov.'s Task Force on Basic Skills, 1972-74; sec. Irvington council Girl Scouts, 1946-47; chmn. Chmn.'s Conf. Recipient Nat. P.T.A. award, 1967-68. Essex County Edn. Assn. award for service to edn., 1963. Mem. Nat. Congress Parents and Tchrs. (life), N.J. Fedn. Women's Clubs (chmn. 8th dist. music and civics 1947-49), Suburban Woman's Club (pres.). Methodist. Republican. Home: 17 N Crescent Maplewood NJ 07040

DAVIS, BETTE (RUTH ELIZABETH), actress; b. Lowell, Mass., Apr. 5, 1908; d. Harlow Morrell and Ruth (Favor) Davis; ed. Cushing Acad., Ashburnham, Mass.; m. Harmon Oscar Nelson, Jr., Aug. 18, 1932 (div.); m. 2d, Arthur Farnsworth, Dec. 1940 (died Aug. 1943); m. 3d, William Grant Sherry, Nov. 30, 1945; 1 dau., Barbara Davis; m. 4th, Gary Merrill, Aug. 1950 (div.); adopted children—Margot, Michael. Began as moving picture actress, 1931; leading pictures are: Of Human Bondage, Bordertown, Dangerous, The Petrified Forest, Jezebel, Dark Victory, Juarez, The Old Maid, The Private Lives of Elizabeth and Essex, The Great Lie, The Bride Came C.O.D.; All About Eve, 1950; Payment on Demand, 1951; Phone Call from a Stranger, 1952; The Star, 1953; The Virgin Queen, 1955; Storm Center, The Catered Affair, 1956; John Paul Jones, 1959; Scapegoat, 1959; Whatever Happened to Baby Jane?, 1962; The Anniversary, 1967; Connecting Rooms, 1969; Bunny O'Hare, 1970; Madam Sin, 1971; The Scientific Card Game, 1972; (play) The Night of the Iguana. Received award of Motion Picture Acad. Arts and Scis. as best woman actress of year, 1935 (in picture Dangerous), 1938 (in picture Jezebel). Author: (autobiography) The Lonely Life. Address: care Gottlieb Schiff Fabricant & Sternklar 555 Fifth Av New York City NY 10017

DAVIS, BOBBIE LEE (MRS. GARLAND THOMAS DAVIS), med. record librarian; b. Mercedes, Tex., Oct. 25, 1928; d. Robert L. and Teatsy (Keene) Harrison; student Southwestern Union Coll., 1947, Pan-Am. Coll., 1964, Am. Assn. Med. Record Library Corr. Sch., 1967; m. Garland Thomas Davis, June 15, 1947; children—Teatsy (Mrs. William S. Nichols Jr.), Kathleen K., Tomi Jayne, David Allen. Med. record librarian McAllen Gen. Hosp., McAllen, Tex., 1965—. Cons. med. records to nursing homes, 1969—. Pres. Firemen Aux., Pharr, Tex., 1968. Mem. Hidalgo-Starr County Med. Soc. (exec. sec. 1968—). Seventh-day Adventist (jr. div. leader 1968—). Home: 701 W Kelly Pharr TX 78577 Office: 701 S Main McAllen TX

DAVIS, BONNIE JEAN DILLEHAY (MRS. THURMAN M. DAVIS), educator; b. Jacksonville, Tex., Jan. 24, 1926; d. Joseph Henry and Annie Laurie (Whitehead) Dillehay; student Okla. Coll. for Women, 1943, U. Houston, 1947-48, 54-55; B.S., U. So. Miss., 1964, M.S., 1966, Ph.D. (Doctoral fellow 1966-68), 1968; m. Thurman Davis, May 16, 1942 (dec. 1962); children—Charles Thurman, James Stephen, Bonnie Jean. Exec. legal sec. Vinson, Elkins, Weems & Sears, Attys., Houston, 1947-49, Baker, Botts, Andrews & Sheppard, Attys., Houston, 1952-55, Hercules Powder Co., Houston, 1956-60; worked for psychologist Huntsville State Prison Houston, 1955-56; research sec. MM Roberts, Attys., Hattiesburg, Miss., 1962-68; tchr. Central Forest Sch., Hattiesburg, Miss., 1964-65; mem. faculty U. So. Miss., Hattiesburg, 1968—, prof. guidance, 1968—. Mem. Am., Miss. personnel and guidance assns., Kappa Delta Pi, Delta Kappa Gamma. Home: Rt 4 Hattiesburg MS 39401 Office: U So Miss Box 215 So Station Hattiesburg MS 39401

DAVIS, CAROLYNE ALICE KAHLE (MRS. OTT HOWARD DAVIS, JR.), nursing educator; b. Penn Yan, N.Y., Jan. 31, 1932; d. Paul F. and Alice Edgerton (Cargill) Kahle; student Dickinson Coll., 1949-51; B.S. in Nursing, Johns Hopkins, 1954; M.S., Syracuse U., 1965, Ph.D., 1972; m. Ott Howard Davis, Jr., June 28, 1953; 1 son, Richard Ott. Evening supr. Lankenau Hosp., Phila., 1954-55; instr. med.-surg. nursing Mercer Hosp. Sch. Nursing, Trenton, N.J., 1957-60; lectr. pediatric nursing Syracuse (N.Y.) U. Sch. Nursing, 1964-65, instr. med.-surg. nursing, 1965-66, asst. prof., 1967-71, asso. prof., 1971-73, asst. chmn. baccalaureate program, 1967-68, acting chmn., 1968-69, chmn., 1969-73; dean U. Mich. Sch. Nursing, Ann Arbor, 1973—. Chmn. nursing edn. com. Upstate Heart Assn., 1968-71; mem. Upstate N.Y. bd. dirs. Am. Heart Assn., 1967-73, v.p. bd., 1972-73; bd. govs. Univ. Hosp., U. Mich., 1973, Am. Assn. Colls. Nursing, 1973; chmn. Heart Teaching Day for Nurses, 1967, 68; mem. Mott Rd. Home and Sch. Assn., 1967-73; mem. Fayetteville-Manlius Sch. Bd., 1971-73. Mem. Am., Mich. (mem. council baccalaureate and higher degree programs resolutions com. 1973, pub. relations com.) nurses assns., Am. Assn. Higher Edn., Nat. League for Nursing, Mich. Lung Assn. (profl. edn. com.), Mich. Heart Assn. (profl. nursing edn. com.), Assn. of Acad. Affairs Adminstrs. (chpt. sec. 1967-68, mem. N.E. regional council 1967-68), Zonta Internat., Pi Beta Phi. Home: 631 Oxford Rd Ann Arbor MI 48104 Office: 1355 Catherine St Ann Arbor MI 48104

DAVIS, CORNELIA HAVEN CASEY (MRS. FRANK V. DAVIS), club woman, ret. business exec.; b. Greenville, Ill., Sept. 17, 1909; d. George Farnum and Cornelia (Ravold) Casey; A.B., Millikin U., 1931; m. Frank V. Davis, May 9, 1936; children—James Casey, Thomas Wait (dec.), Andrew Waggoner. Bond County statistician Ill. Emergency Relief Commn., 1934-36; sec.-treas., dir. E.H. Paul Co., Hookdale, Ill., 1957-67, Davis & Royer, Inc., Greenville, 1967-73. Pres. Greenville P.T.A., 1944-45; charter mem. Utlaut Meml. Hosp. Found., 1957; historian Utlaut Meml. Hosp. Aux., 1958-59, pres., 1966-67; pres. Greenville Garden Club, 1954-56; chmn. Bond County chpt. A.R.C., 1962-64, Ill. fund vice chmn., 1966, territorial fund chmn., 1967-68, nat. resolutions com., 1968, sec. Bond County chpt., 1970-74; 1st v.p. Heritage Trail Tb and Respiratory Disease Assn., 1970; chmn. Greenville and Bond County Bicentennial Commn., 1974. Bd. dirs. Bond County Tb Assn., 2d v.p., 1965-68, pres., 1969-71; bd. dirs. Greenville Sesquicentennial, 1965; bd. dirs., sec. Bond County Art and Cultural Assn. Recipient various citations for service, Good Citizenship medal S.A.R., 1962. Mem. Audubon Soc., Nat. Trust for Historic Preservation, Ill. (life mem.), Bond County (charter, sec. 1955-73, pres. 1973, dir.) hist. socs., Bond County Fair Assn. (life), D.A.R. (regent Benjamin Mills chpt. 1952-54, 68-70, registrar 1964-66, rec. sec. 1974—, dir. 6th Ill. div. 1955-56, Ill. corr. sec., 1956-58, nat. def. com. state chmn. 1963-65, Ill. chmn. girl homemakers com. 1935-36, Ill. chmn. program com. 1953-55, Ill. chmn. honor roll com. 1959-60), Children Am. Revolution (sr. state pres. 1960-63, nat. life promoter, nat. officers club, now hon. life sr. state pres.), U.S. Daus. War of 1812 (pres. Kaskaskia chpt. 1963-66, Ill. 2d v.p. 1963-66, 1st v.p. 1966-70, state pres. 1970-73, hon. life state pres. 1973; nat. chmn. nat. def. com. 1970-73), Ill. Ct. Women Descs. Ancient and Hon. Arty. Co. (Ill. librarian 1963-64, nat. def. chmn. 1965-66, nat. chmn. nat. def. com. 1969-71), Daus. Am. Colonists (state chmn. colonial heritage com. 1973—), Col. Daus. 17th Century (charter Ill. chpt., treas.-registrar 1961-66, pres. 1966-70, nat. chmn. nat. def. and resolutions com. 1967—, corr. sec. gen. 1970-73, 2d v.p. gen. 1973—), Magna Charta Dames, Colonial Dames Am. (rec. sec. chpt. 1969-71, 1st v.p. 1974—), Soc. Descs. Colonial Clergy, Ill. Geneal. Soc., Sons and Daus. Pilgrims (Okla. chpt.), S. Central Ill. Woman's Golf Assn. (chmn. 1953, 66, 71), Delta Delta Delta. Republican. Episcopalian (chmn. region IV Episcopal Churchwomen Diocese of Springfield 1966-68). Address: Rural Route 2 Greenville IL 62246

DAVIS, DOLORES IRENE BIDLACK (MRS. DONALD C. DAVIS), craftsman, artist; b. Oakwood, O., June 30, 1907; d. John W. and Elsa (Brillhart) Bidlack; grad. high sch.; m. Donald C. Davis, July 15, 1931; 1 dau., Nancy Mae (Mrs. Eugene Daniel Zbrezny). Exhibited in group shows at Canton (O.) Inst. Art, Massillon (O.) Mus., Butler Inst. Am. Art, Youngstown, O., Beaux Arts, Columbus Gallery Fine Arts, Columbus, O.; tchr. (craft) Adult Edn. Inst., Lorain, O., 1952-58, (glass lamination) YWCA, Elyria, O., 1957—, (enameling) Vermilion (O.) Art Crafters, 1957—, (pottery) Vermilion Clay Barrel, Lorain, 61, (pottery, enameling) O. Clay Barrel, 1950-60; (crafts) Art League Lorain County, Inc., intermittently 1948—. Mem. White House Task Force on Retirement Roles and Activities for Aging, 1971. Recipient numerous awards including Best of Show, Art League Lorain County, 1961, Lorain Mud Hens, 1959; best in crafts Ann. Firelands Exhibit, Huron, O., 1962. Chmn. art shows YWCA, 1965-67. Mem. Nat. League Am. Pen Women (treas. 1966-68), Art League Lorain County, Inc (treas.), Ohio Designers Craftsman, Am. Craftsman Council. Republican. Mem. Order Eastern Star. Club: Lakeland Women's (hospitality chmn. 1966-68). Home: 1141 10th St Lorain OH 44052

DAVIS, DORIS ANN, mayor; b. Chgo., Nov. 5, 1935; d. Cornelius and Ruby Pearl (Brown) Collins; B.A., U. Ill., 1955; M.A., Northwestern U., 1957; M.A., U. Chgo., 1959; postgrad. U. Cal. at Los Angeles, 1959-64. Tchr. elementary sch., Chgo., 1955-59, Los Angeles City Sch., 1959-67; city clk. City of Compton (Cal.), 1965-73, mayor, 1973—; owner, pres. Dee Employment Agy., Compton, 1969—. Pres. Daisy Found., Compton, 1969-74. Mem. policy council Nat. Democratic Com., 1970-72; mem. joint com. on the revision of the election code State of Cal., 1971-73. Mem. N.A.A.C.P., Urban League, Conf. Negro Elected Ofcls., Links Internat., League Women Voters, So. Cal. Clks. Assn., Welfare Information Service, Nat. Council Negro Women. Home: 409 W Palmer Compton CA 90224 Office: 600 N Alameda Compton CA 90224

DAVIS, EDITH F. (MRS. GEORGE P. DAVIS), club woman; b. Waltham, Mass., Sept. 17, 1893; d. John Lamar and Elizabeth (Bates) Totten; student Lasell Sem.; m. George P. Davis, June 12, 1917; children—Priscilla (Mrs. Robert G. Hoye), Lydia (Mrs. Hugh J. Scarborough). Lectr., collector Chinese Export Porcelain. Pres. China Students' Club, Boston, 1945-47, Watertown (Mass.) Antiques Club, 1943; bd. dirs. Leland Home, Waltham, 1934—. Mem. Golden Ball Tavern, Weston, Centerville, Waltham hist. socs., Gore Place Soc., Kappa Phi. Republican. Conglist. Club: Weston (Mass.) Golf. Home: 85 Robin Rd Weston MA 02193

DAVIS, EDITH LUCKETT (MRS. LOYAL DAVIS), civic worker; b. Petersburg, Va.; d. Charles and Sarah Frances (Whitlock) Luckett; m. Loyal Davis, May 21, 1929; children—Nancy (Mrs. Ronald Reagan), Richard A. 1st. chmn. women's div. Chgo. Community Fund, 1938-63; mem. women's bd. Passavant Meml. Hosp., Chgo., 1931—; founder, 1st pres. Sarah Siddons Soc. Bd. dirs. Ariz. div. Am. Cancer Soc. Address: 24 Arizona Biltmore Estates Phoenix AZ 85016

DAVIS, EDITH MARY, educator; b. Cleve., Jan. 23, 1910; d. William E. and Edith (Gade) Davis; A.B. summa cum laude, Alma Coll., 1934; postgrad. U. Mich., 1937-41; M.S.W., U. Denver, 1950; D.Social Work, U. So. Cal., 1962. Supr. intake Bur. Old Age Assistance, Detroit, 1937-39; supr. information and adjustment service WPA, Wayne County, Mich., 1939-42; research asst. Los Angeles County Mental Health Survey, 1958-59, Los Angeles County Probation Dept., 1959-60; faculty U. Denver Grad. Sch. Social Work, 1947-58, 62—, prof. social work, 1962—; research dir. studies various social agys., Denver, 1950—. Mem. Colo. State Child Welfare Adv. Com., 1950-53, Mayor's Com. of 500, Denver, 1963. Served to lt. col. WAC, 1942-46. Decorated Legion of Merit (U.S.); Order of Brit. Empire (Eng.); recipient Distinguished Teaching award U. Denver, 1969. Mem. Acad. Certified Social Workers, Nat. Assn. Social Workers (chpt. publs. chmn. 1965-66), Nat., Colo. (editor newsletter 1956-58) confs. social welfare. Home: Apt 2 2085 S Josephine St Denver CO 80210

DAVIS, EDNA ELEANOR, ednl. adminstr.; b. Ramsey County, N.D., Jan. 10, 1891;; d. George W. H. and Margaret Ann (Buttery) Davis; B.S., Hamline U., 1915; Diploma, Central Inst. for Deaf, St. Louis, 1918; spl. courses Wash. State Coll., Eastern Wash. Coll. Edn. Tchr. schs. for deaf, 1915-22; tchr., then head tchr., prin. Edna E. Davis Sch., Spokane, 1922-57, prin. emeritus, 1956—. Named Woman of Achievement, Spokane br. Quota Club, 1954; recipient Woman of Merit award Spokane Fedn. Women's Orgns., 1957. Mem. Am. Assn. U. Women, Alexander Graham Bell Assn. for Deaf. Methodist. Club: Quota. Home: E 2903 25th Av Spokane WA 99203

DAVIS, EDNA LOUISE, educator; b. Sumter, S.C., Jan. 27, 1921; d. Thomas Benjamin and Edna Leonora (Lowery) Davis; Mus.B., Oberlin Conservatory Music, 1943, Mus. M., 1950; Dr. Musical Arts, Boston U., 1964. Instr. music Jackson (Miss.) Coll., 1943-47, 48-54, chmn. dept. creative and recreative arts, 1951-54; mem. faculty Elizabeth City (N.C.) State U., 1954—, prof. music edn., 1964—, chmn. music dept., 1965—. Cons. Pasquotank County and Albemarle Area Arts Council, 1970—. Mem. Mus. of the Albemarle, Elizabeth City, Norfolk (Va.) Symphony Orchestra Assn. Mem. N.A.A.C.P., Nat. Assn. Schs. of Music, Am. Assn. U. Profs., Music Educators Nat. Conf., N.C. Music Educators Assn. (chmn. state student chpts. 1969-73), N.C. Assn. Educators, Delta Sigma Theta, Pi Kappa Lambda, Kappa Delta Pi. Presbyn. Clubs: Harmonia Music (pianist 1943-54) (Jackson); Faculty Womens and Wives (pres. 1956-58) (Elizabeth City). Home: Apt 1J Hugh Cale Hall Elizabeth City State University Elizabeth City NC 27909

DAVIS, EDNA ROBERTA CONNOLLY (MRS. OLIVER C. DAVIS), librarian; b. June 25, 1919; d. Edward Robert and Mary F. (Palmatary) Connolly; A.B. with honors, U. Cal. at Los Angeles, 1942; certificate Sch. Librarianship, U. Cal. at Berkeley, 1943; m. Oliver C. Davis, Apr. 2, 1943; 1 dau., Laurel Lynn. Reference-acquisitions librarian William Andrews Clark Meml. Library, U. Cal. at Los Angeles, 1943-69, asst. librarian, 1969-73, asso. librarian, 1973—. Mem. A.L.A., Cal. Library Assn., Cal. State Employees Assn., Augustan Reprint Soc. (corr. sec. 1949—). Home: 5933 Le Doux Rd Los Angeles CA 90056 Office: 2520 Cimarron St Los Angeles CA 90018

DAVIS, ELDRED DENNIS, educator; b. Macon, Ga., Apr. 26, 1922; d. Everett D. and Pearl (Grant) Dennis; student Fort Valley (Ga.) State Coll., 1939-40, Ga. State Coll., 1946-48; B.S., 1948; A.M., U. Mich., 1954, A.M. in L.S., 1960; Ed.D., U. Tenn., 1968; m. Walter C. Davis, Nov. 23, 1940 (div. May 1953). English tchr. Ballard-Hudson Sr. High Sch., Macon, Ga., 1949-55; faculty Knoxville Coll., 1955—, asso. prof., 1961-68, prof. edn., 1968—. Vis. prof. Miss. Valley State Coll., Itta Bena, Miss., 1968. Active Girl Scouts U.S.A., 1944-48. Named Woman of Year, Pi chpt. Zeta Phi Beta, 1969. Mem. N.E.A., N.A.A.C.P., Am. Assn. U. Women, So. Coll. Personnel Assn. (sec. 1964-66), Nat. Soc. Study Edn., Pi Lambda Theta. Home: 3338 Lansing Av Knoxville TN 37914 Office: Knoxville Coll Knoxville TN 37921

DAVIS, ELISE MILLER (MRS. JAY ALBERT DAVIS), author; b. Corsicana, Tex., Oct. 12, 1915; d. Moses Myre and Rachelle (Daniels) Miller; student U. Tex., 1930-31; m. Jay Albert Davis, June 27, 1937 (dec. June 1973); 1 dau., Rayna Miller (Mrs. Michael Edwin Loeb). Freelance writer, Amarillo, Tex., 1945—; buyer and dir. Jay Davis, Inc., Amarillo, Tex., 1956-73. Mem. Soc. Mag. Writers. Author: The Answer Is God, 1955. Contbr. articles to periodicals including Reader's Digest, Woman's Day, Nation's Business, others. Home: 1512 Austin Amarillo TX 79102

DAVIS, ELIZABETH B., psychiatrist; b. Pitts., 1920; M.D., Columbia, 1949, postgrad. psychoanalytic clinic, 1950-55. Intern Harlem Hosp., N.Y.C., 1949-50, resident N.Y. Psychiat. Inst., 1950-52, out patient dept. Columbia U. Psychoanalytic Clinic, 1952-53; now prof. clin. psychiatry Coll. Phys. and Surg., Columbia; dir. dept. psychiatry Harlem Hosp. Diplomate Am. Bd. Psychiatry and Neurology. Mem. Am. Psychiat. Assn., Am. Psychoanalytic Assn., Assn. Psychoanalytic Medicine. Office: Dept Psychiatry Harlem Hosp Lenox Av at 136th St New York City NY 10037

DAVIS, ELIZABETH HUSTEAD, educator; b. Clarksburg, W.Va., Dec. 31, 1916; d. Delbert L. and Bessie Mae (Hammond) Hustead; B.S., Salem Coll., 1937; M.Ed., Edinboro Coll., 1966; children—Judith (Mrs. Jerry Johnson), Eugene D. Home econs. tchr. Ft. LeBoeuf High Sch., Waterford, Pa., 1947-65, Westminster Jr. High Sch., Erie, Pa., 1965-66; guidance counselor James S. Wilson Jr. High Sch., Erie, 1965-73, Millcreek Intermediate High Sch., Erie, 1973—. Mem. fund raising com. Erie Philharmonic, 1967-68; pres., program chmn. P.T.A., 1960-61; mem. Erie County fund raising com. Cerebral Palsy, 1972-73; active Girl Scouts Am., Boy Scouts Am. Mem. Nat. Assn. Women Deans and Counselors (mem. coordinating com. 1973-74), Am., Pa. personnel and guidance assns., Erie County Counselors Assn. (sec. 1969-70, 72-73), Delta Kappa Gamma (past state officer, past pres. Alpha Omega chpt.). Mem. Order Eastern Star (worthy matron 1964-65). Home: 5044 Lexington St Erie PA 16509 Office: 3320 Caughey Rd Erie PA 16506

DAVIS, ELIZABETH MARDRE (MRS. HARTWELL DAVIS), civic worker, educator; b. Lumpkin, Ga.; d. Wilson Little and Sarah (Bivins) Mardre; student U. Cal. at Berkeley, 1927; B.S., Auburn U., 1929; m. Hartwell Davis, Feb. 24, 1933; children—Hartwell, Letitia D. Hamill. Tchr. English Clift High Sch., Opelika, Ala., 1929-33, Lanier High Sch., Montgomery, Ala., 1934-36, 39, Robert E. Lee High Sch., Montgomery, Ala., 1962-68, Jefferson Davis High Sch., Montgomery, 1968-69; adminstrv. clk. Bur. Census, Ala. 2d Congl. Dist. Office, 1960. Mem. Ala. Citizens Adv. Ednl. Council, Ala. Com. for Better Schs., Inc.; pres. Montgomery Know-Your-Schs. Com., 1951-52. Trustee Carnegie Library Assn. Mem. Montgomery County Rep. exec. com., 1956-66, 71-73; vice chmn. Ala. Rep. Exec. Com., 1961-62, mem., 1956-66. Mem. United Ch. Women (pres. Montgomery 1951-53, pres. Ala. 1955-57, mem. adminstrv. and exec. coms. gen. dept. 1957-58), Republican Women of Montgomery (pres. 1971-73), League Women Voters (exec. bd. Montgomery 1952-54), D.A.R., Daus. Am. Colonists, Colonial Dames 17th Century, Auburn Alumni Assn. (v.p. 1946-48), Kappa Delta, Phi Kappa Phi, Kappa Delta Pi. Methodist. (exec. com., sec. promotion Ala.-W. Fla. Woman's soc. 1952-58, mem. exec. com. 1960-64; mem. Ala.-West Fla. Conf. Bd. Missions 1952-56). Clubs: 20th Century Literary (pres. 1944-45, 72-73), Hypatia Literary (pres. 1944-45), Panjandrum Literary (pres. 1948-49). Home: 2216 Allendale Pl Montgomery AL 36111

DAVIS, ELIZABETH YOUNG (MRS. FRANK BELL DAVIS), educator; b. Ft. Collins, Colo., Apr. 23, 1920; d. Clyde Wells and Imogene (Nesbitt) Young; B.S., Colo. State U., 1941; M.S., Auburn U., 1957, Ph.D., 9164; m. Frank Bell Davis, Aug. 30, 1941; children—Sue Carol, Kim Elaine, John Roy. Instr., Auburn (Ala.) U., 1957-60, research asst., research asso., 1961-64, prof. nutrition and foods, 1966—, coordinator home econs. research, 1968—; asso. prof. nutrition research Tuskegee (Ala.) Inst., 1964-66; asst. to adminstr. for home econs. Cooperative State Research Service, U.S., Dept. Agr., Washington, 1973-74. Mem. panel to rev. applications for internat. fellowships appointments Internat. Fedn. U. Women, Geneva, Switzerland, 1973—; mem. Ala. Edn. Study Commn., Montgomery, 1967-69. Mem. Am. Chem. Soc., Am. Home Econs. Assn., Am. Pub. Health Assn., Am. Dietetic Assn. (pres. Ala. 1971-72), Am. Assn. U. Women (pres. Ala. 1966-68), Inst. Food Technologists, N.Y. Acad. Sci., Soc. Nutrition Edn., P.E.O., Sigma Xi, Delta Kappa Gamma, Gamma Sigma Delta, Phi Kappa Phi, Omicron Nu, Gamma Phi Beta. Home: 907 6th St SW 916-C Washington DC 20024 Office: Co-op State Research Service US Dept Agr Washington DC 20250 also Dept Nutrition and Foods Auburn U Auburn AL 36830

DAVIS, EMMA JO LEVEY (MRS. ANDREW JACKSON DAVIS, JR.), mus. curator; b. Greensboro, N.C., June 5, 1932; d. Harry Nelson and Alma (Snellen) Levey; student Mary Washington Coll., 1949-51; A.B., U. N.C., 1953; M.Ed., Coll. William and Mary, 1969; m. Andrew Jackson Davis, Jr., July 3, 1957; children—Catherine Hart, Anne Stone, Kelsie Lee. Editorial asst. Woman's Day, N.Y.C., 1953-54; prodn. asst. William Byrd Press, Richmond, Va., 1954-56; research asst. U. N.C. at Chapel Hill, 1957-59, history tchr., 1959-61; tech. researcher, writer, editor U.S. Army, Ft. Eustis, Va., 1961-64; curator U.S. Army Transp. Mus., historian, U.S. Army Transp. Center, Fort Eustis, 1964—. Instr. mil. history U.S. Army Transp. Sch., 1967—. Community ambassador City of Richmond, 1954. Bd. dirs., sec. Transp. Corps. Mus. Found. Mem. D.A.R., Am. Assn. State and Local History, Nat. Assn. Regular Army Sgts., Assn. Am. Museums, Bicentennial Action Team, New Eng. Historic and Geneal. Soc., Va. History Fedn., Alpha Gamma Delta. Episcopalian. Home: 115 Villa Rd Newport News VA 23601 Office: US Army Transp Mus Fort Eustis VA 23604

DAVIS, EUNICE ANDERSON (MRS. GORDON DAVIS), physician; b. Sturgeon Lake, Minn., Apr. 29, 1929; d. Emil and Rose (Balme) Anderson; B.A., U. Minn., 1950, M.D., 1954; m. Gordon L. Davis, Oct. 8, 1955; children—Craig Steven, Cynthia Marie, Bryce Carroll. Rotating intern Mpls. Gen. Hosp., 1954-55; resident pediatrics, pediatric fellow U. Minn., 1955-57; pediatric cons. Minn. Dept. Health, 1957-63; med. dir. Four-County Project for Retarded Children 1957-63; clin. asst. pediatrics U. Minn., 1962-64, clin. instr., 1967—; chief med. services Minn. Residential Treatment Center, 1963-64; coordinator Mental Retardation Planning, N.D. State Dept. Health, 1965-67; dir. child devel. sect. St. Paul Ramsey Hosp., St. Paul, 1967—. Mem. Devel. Disabilities Adv. Council of Minn. Mem. A.M.A., Northwestern Pediatrics Soc., Am. Assn. Mental Deficiency (chmn. region VIII, 1974—). Episcopalian. Contbr. articles profl. jours. Home: 436 Transit Av Roseville MN 55113 Office: Dept Pediatrics St Paul Ramsey Hosp St Paul MN 55101

DAVIS, EVELYN LEOTA, realty exec.; b. Kalkaska, Mich., Oct. 31, 1908; d. Ralph H. and Sarah (Fields) Patterson; grad. Baker Bus. U., 1928; m. Ward A. Parks, July 31, 1928 (div. Mar. 1955); m. 2d, John W. Davis, Nov. 3, 1970; step-children--John W., Robert, Anne (Mrs. Bruce Wilcox). Partner Davis Realty Co., Flint, 1939-73, Atlas Investment Co., Flint, 1947-71, Flint Appraisal and Consulting Co., 1955-73; sec. treas. Davis Realty Corp., 1967-73; founder, exec. v.p. Charlotte Shores Apt. Corp., Fort Myers, Fla., 1967-70. Mem. Flint (pres.), Mich. (treas.) women's councils real estate bds., Nat. Real Estate Bd. (mem. ethics com.), Fedn. Women's Clubs, U. Mich. Club Flint, Flint, Pine Island chambers commerce. Mem. Order Eastern Star (Mich. grand treas. emeritus). Clubs: Zonta (Flint); Tropic (Ft. Myers, Fla.). Home: 1620 Flint Lane RR 8 Fort Myers FL 33901

DAVIS, EVELYN LOUISE (MRS. CALVIN C. DAVIS), mfg. co. exec.; b. Belleville, N.J., June 23, 1931; d. Clarence F. and Evelyn V. (Zanes) McDermott; grad. Eagan Sch. Bus., 1949-51; m. Calvin C. Davis, Sept. 8, 1951; children—Gary C., James M. Purchasing asst. Lapine Scientific, Norwood, N.J., 1966-68; buyer Dynelec Systems, Inc., Montvale, N.J., 1968-69; purchasing agt. Timeplex, Inc., Norwood, 1969-71; with Datascope Corp., Paramus, N.J., 1971—, dir. purchasing, 1973—. Mem. Nat. Assn. Purchasing Mgrs., Purchasing Mgrs. Assn. No. N.J. Mem. Order Eastern Star. Home: 574 Forest Dr River Vale NJ 07675 Office: 580 Winters Av Paramus NJ 07652

DAVIS, FRANCES MAIRANDA LOUISE FREEMAN (MRS. CLARENCE BROWN DAVIS), librarian; b. Atlanta, Aug. 18, 1924; d. James Henry and Bessie (Scott) Freeman; B.S. in Home Econs., Clark Coll., 1950; M.S. in Library Sci., Atlanta U. Sch. Library Sci., 1966; m. Clarence Brown Davis, Dec. 25, 1944; children—Gizelle, Claryce (Mrs. Marvin Taylor), Alyce (Mrs. John Howell), Dwight. With Tuskegee Inst., Hollis Burke Frissell Library, Tuskegee Inst. Ala., 1955-62, circulation library asst., 1962-65, res. librarian, 1965-66, engring., vet. med. librarian, 1966-69, nursing/vet. med. librarian, 1966-69, engring. architecture librarian, 1969—, instr. sch. Edn., 1972-73; vis. staff U. Cal. Los Alamos Sci. Lab. Library, 1973-75. Mem. Ala. State Adv. Council Libraries, Ala. Pub. Library Service State Exec. Bd. Mem. Ala. Library Assn. (v.p. 1972-73, pres. 1973-74), Am. Assn. U. Profs., Am. Assn. U. Women, Am. Soc. Engring. Edn., Spl. Libraries Assn., Southeastern Libraries Assn., Alpha Kappa Alpha. Home: 1912 Washington St Tuskegee Institute AL 36088 Office: Sch Engring Tuskegee Institute AL 36088

DAVIS, GERTRUDE ELIZABETH CODDINGTON (MRS. WILLIAM L. DAVIS), librarian; b. Roanoke, Va., June 7, 1915; d. Harry Wilbur and Ruth (Todd) Coddington; student Coll. William and Mary, 1932-33; student Roanoke Coll., Berea Coll.; B.A. in English Lit., Oberlin Coll., 1936; B.S. in L.S., U. N.C., 1942; postgrad. George Washington U., U. Va., Drexel Inst. Tech. Grad. Sch. L.S.; M.S., Columbia, 1969; m. William L. Davis, May 16, 1942 (dec. May 1962); children—Dorothy Scott (Mrs. Douglas S. Fielder), William Shannon. Sec., Assn. Am. Railroads, Washington, 1936-39; children's asst. N.Y. Pub. Library, N.Y.C., 1941-42; librarian Staunton (Va.) Mil. Acad., 1955-57, Mary Baldwin Coll. Library, Staunton, 1957—. Mem. Am., Southeastern, Va. library assns., Archeol. Soc. Va., Augusta County Hist. Soc. (charter), D.A.R., Am. Assn. U. Women, Staunton Fine Arts Assn., Delta Kappa Gamma, Beta Phi Mu. Methodist. Club: Augusta Country. Home: 315 Vine St Staunton VA 24401

DAVIS, HELEN LEE (MRS. JOHN RICHELIEU DAVIS), polygraph examiner; b. Mobile, Ala.; d. James Homer and Frances Esther (Johnson) Lee; B.S., U. Ala., 1946; A.B., Lake Forest Coll., 1956; M.S., Loyola U., Chgo., 1967; m. John Richelieu Davis, Mar. 7, 1947; children—Jennifer Lee, Susan, Helen K., John Richelieu, Thomas Ruff. Singer, Jimmy Dorsey, Tex Beneke, Les Brown, NBC-TV, N.Y.C., CBS Radio and TV, Chgo., 1940-59; polygraph examiner, 1958—; v.p., dir. testing John R. Davis Assos., Inc., Lincolnwood, Ill., 1959—. Tchr., guidance counselor pub. schs., Ill., Ala., 1966-70. Mem. Vol. Bur. Winnetka-Northfield Area, 1973-74. Mem. exec. com. Evanston (Ill.) Caucus. Fellow Am. Acad. Forensic Scis., Am. Assn. Polygraph Examiners; mem. Am. Personnel and Guidance Assn., Am. Sch. Counselors Assn., Nat. Assn. Parliamentarians, Am. Assn. U. Women (v.p.), U. Ala. Alumni Assn. (pres.). Club: Woman's (dir.) (Evanston). Home: 71 Coventry Rd Northfield IL 60093 Office: 7101 N Cicero Av Lincolnwood IL 60646 also 135 S LaSalle St Chicago IL

DAVIS, HELEN NANCY MATSON (MRS. CHAUNCEY D. DAVIS), real estate broker, civic worker; b. Zanesville, O., Nov. 18, 1905; d. Austin F. and Georgianna (Hale) Matson; grad. high sch.; m. Chauncey D. Davis, May 1, 1924; children—James Harvey, Robert Lee. Real estate broker, South Bend, Wash., 1964—. Exec. sec. Pacific County Tb League, 1936-62; chmn. Park Bd., South Bend, 1955—; trustee Pacific County Hist. Soc. Named Woman of Yr. Pacific County C. of C., 1949, 61. Mem. Propaelaeum Study Club, Grange, Chinook Indian Tribe (hon.), Wash. Fedn. Music Clubs, Delta Kappa Gamma. Republican. Methodist. Rebekah. Club: Garden (South Bend). Composer: Washington, My Home (ofcl. state song Wash.), 1959; Eliza and the Lumberjack (mus. play). Home: 606 W 2d St South Bend WA 98586 Office: 705 Robert Bush Dr South Bend WA 98586

DAVIS, HELEN SUSIE (MRS. CHARLES DAVIS), former banker; b. Indianola, Ill., Apr. 1, 1918; d. Homer Oscar and Collistia Jane (Tuggle) Allen; student La Salle Extension U., 1969-70; m. Charles W. Davis, Dec. 6, 1941; children—Carolyn (Mrs. Dale Liggett), Charles Alan. Payroll clk. Rec. Statis. Corp., Danville, Ill., 1940-41; state Sec. Ill. Rural Letters Carriers Ladies Aux., 1953-55; with First Nat. Bank of Ogden (Ill.), 1955-72, asst. cashier, 1971-72, operations officer, 1970-72. Gray Lady VA, Danville, 1942-43; block chmn. March of Dimes, 1947-48. Recipient Good Citizenship award Indianola Community High Sch., 1936. Mem. Riverview Women's Golf Assn. Mem. Order Eastern Star. Club: Ogden Woman's. Home: 9616 Glen Oaks Circle Sun City AZ 85351

DAVIS, HOLLY ANNE, therapist; b. Cleve., Nov. 26, 1947; d. Frank Eugene and Doris Elizabeth (Salzman) Davis; student U. Rome, summer 1965, U. Grenoble, summer 1967; B.A., Hillsdale Coll., 1969; postgrad. Arica Inst. Am. With South Hills Area YMCA, Pitts., 1969-71, Good Earth Natural Food, Pitts., 1972; coordinator growth center and teen hot-line Chartiers Mental Health/Mental Retardation, Pitts., 1973—. Mem. Pi Beta Phi. Home: 2209 Spruce St Philadelphia PA 19103 Office: 11 East Mall Plaza Carnegie PA 15106

DAVIS, IRIS ANNE (MRS. ROYCE LEE DAVIS), univ. librarian; b. Garland, Tex., Jan. 21, 1931; d. Thomas Shelton and Alice Mae (Ragsdale) Anderson; B.S., E. Tex. State U., 1952; M.S., Tex. Woman's U., 1959; m. Royce Lee Davis, May 9, 1953. High sch. librarian Winnsboro (Tex.) Sch. Dist., 1952-53, Stinnett (Tex.) Ind. Sch. Dist., 1954-59; cataloger W. Tex. State U., Canyon, 1959-66; serials cataloger N. Tex. State U., Denton, 1966—. Mem. Am., Tex., Southwestern library assns. Home: 311 Jagoe Denton TX 76201

DAVIS, JACQUELINE MARIE VINCENT (MRS. LOUIS REID DAVIS), educator; b. Birmingham, Ala.; d. Jud Fred and Marie (Yates) Vincent; A.B. cum laude, Birmingham-So. Coll., 1943; M.A., Columbia, 1950; M.S., U. Ala., 1958, Ed.D., 1961; postgrad. U. Va., George Washington U.; m. Louis Reid Davis, July 17, 1943. Tchr., Fork Union (Va.) Mil. Acad., 1943-46, Ft. Belvoir, Va., 1946-48; tchr., adminstrv. asst., supr. Quantico (Va.) Post schs., 1950-52; instr., prof. dept. child devel. and family life U. Ala. Sch. Home Econs., 1952-57, asso. prof., 1957-67, prof. child devel., dir. Child Devel. Center, 1967—, mem. grad. council, adminstr. head start tng. program. Dir. Ala. Presch. Inst., 1964—; mem. NASA scholarship selection bd. U. Ala., 1966; mem. Gov.'s Adv. Com. on Day Care, 1963-66; mem. State Adv. Com. on Children and Youth, 1960—; coordinator Head Start supplementary tng. programs State of Ala. Adviser, mem. selection com. Tombigbee council Girl Scouts U.S.A., 1961-66; cons. Tuscaloosa Community Action Program, 1965-66. Mem. Nat. Assn. for Edn. of Young Children (mem. planning bd. 1963-64), U.S. Nat. Com. for Early Childhood Edn., World Orgn. for Early Childhood Edn., Southeastern Council Family Relations, So. (pres. 1961, mem. exec. bd. 1961—, chmn. 19th ann. conf.), Ala. (pres. 1963-64) assns.

children under six, Ala. Home Econs. Assn. (chmn. professional section family life and child devel., 1963—, v.p., mem. governing bd. 1969-70), Comparative Edn. Soc., N.E.A., Am. Home Econs. Assn., Phi Beta Kappa, Kappa Delta Pi, Kappa Delta Epsilon. Methodist. Contbr. articles to profl. jours. Home: 47 Guilds Wood Tuscaloosa AL 35401 Office: PO Box 1211 University AL 35486

DAVIS, JANIS GOVER, physician; b. Fayetteville, W.Va., Feb. 28, 1925; d. Robb and Nell (Hamilton) Gover; B.A., W.Va. U., 1945, B.S., Sch. Medicine, 1948; M.D., Med. Coll. Ga., 1950; m. Albert J. Davis, May 8, 1948 (div. Dec. 1973); children—Daniel Robb, Susan (dec.). Gen. med. officer U.S. Army Hosp., Okinawa, 1950-52; intern Bapt. Meml. Hosp., San Antonio, 1952-53, resident, 1953-54; resident anesthesia Louisville Gen. Hosp., 1954-56; practice medicine specializing in anesthesiology, St. Petersburg, Fla., 1956-72, specializing in structural integration, 1972—; mem. staff All Children's Hosp., St. Anthony's Hosp.; instr., mem. staff Bay Front Med. Center, St. Petersburg, 1956—. Mem. Am., Fla. med. socs., Fla. Soc. Anesthesiologists, Am. Coll. Anesthesiology. Home and office: 386 26th Av SE St Petersburg FL 33705

DAVIS, JEAN PATRICIA, physician; b. Chgo.; d. David I. and Elizabeth (Nelson) Davis; A.B., Smith Coll., 1939; M.D., Yale, 1943; postgrad. Nat. Hosp. Neurol. Disease, London, 1953-54. Lectr. pharmacology, instr. pediatrics and psychiatry (neurology) U. Utah, 1948-52, asst. prof. pediatrics and psychiatry (neurology) 1952-53; asso. neurology Columbia U., 1954-56, asst. prof. neurology, 1956; asst. attending neurologist Presbyn. Hosp., N.Y.C., 1954-56; dir. Variety Club Epilepsy Center, Mt. Sinai Hosp., Milw., 1956-62; asst. clin. prof. neurology div. medicine, asst. clin. prof. neurology in pediatrics Marquette U., 1967—; pvt. practice specializing in child neurology, neurology, electroencephalography, Milw., 1956—; mem. staff Mt. Sinai, Milw. Children's, Columbia, St. Joseph's hosps. (all Milw.), Trinity Meml. Hosp., Cudahy, Wis. Mem. governing staff Milw. Children's Hosp., 1968-71. Recipient Woman of Achievement award, Quota Club Milw., 1962. Mem. Milw. Neuropsychiat. Soc. (pres. 1965-66), Epilepsy Assn. Am. (profl. adv. bd. 1965-68), Wis. Epilepsy League (pres. 1961-67), Wis. Med. Soc. (com. nervous and mental diseases 1960-72), Milw. County Med. Soc., A.M.A., Am. Acad. Pediatrics, Eastern EEG Soc., Am. EEG Soc., Am. Acad. Neurology (asso.), Milw. Acad. Medicine, Assn. for Research in Nervous and Mental Diseases. Home: 733 E Beaumont Av Milwaukee WI 53217 Office: 3003 W Good Hope Rd Milwaukee WI 53209

DAVIS, JEAN REYNOLDS (MRS. WARREN HIRST DAVIS, JR.), author, composer; b. Cumberland, Md., Nov. 1, 1927; d. Foster Ray and Wilhelmina Ferguson (Barrick) Reynolds; Mus. B., U. Pa., 1949; m. Warren Hirst Davis, Jr., Dec. 9, 1949; children—Mark Reynolds, Stephen Scott. Editorial cons. Music Pubs. Holding Corp., N.Y.C., 1960-65; self employed as author and composer, 1965—. Recipient Cultural Olympics award of merit, U. Pa., 1953. Mem. A.S.C.A.P (grantee 1961). Episcopalian. Author: A Hat On The Hall Table, 1967; To God With Love, 1968; Parish Picnic, 1970. Composer: Doors Into Music, 1966; Slick Tricks, 1962; Tricks and Treats, 1963; Yankee Doodle Doodles, 1960. Contbr. articles to profl. jours. Address: 226 Righters Mill Rd Gladwyne PA 19035

DAVIS, JEANNE FRANCES WEST (MRS. WAYNE PITMAN DAVIS), newspaper editor; b. Chariton, Ia., Oct. 3, 1922; d. Thomas Francis and Maude (Baxter) West; B.A., Drake U., 1944; m. Wayne Pitman Davis, May 28, 1944; children—Kenneth Wayne, Polly Jeanne. Editor, co-pub. Seymour (Ia.) Herald, 1947—. County pres. Wayne County Republican Women's Club, 1957-59; co-chmn. Wayne County Rep. Central Com., 1970—. Named Ia. master editor-pub., Ia. Press Assn., 1971. Mem. Wayne County Federated Women's Clubs (county pres. 1949-50), Bus. and Profl. Women's Club (pres. 1952-53, 56-57), Mortar Bd., Nat. TTT Soc. (chpt. pres. 1966-68), P.E.D. Home: Seymour IA 52590 Office: 114 N 4th St Seymour IA 52590

DAVIS, JESSICA G. (MRS. ANDREW P. DAVIS), pediatrician; b. N.Y.C., Apr. 3, 1934; d. Nathan S. and Sylvia (Teplitz) Grosof; B.A. (Wellesley scholar) Wellesley Coll., 1955; M.D., Coll. Physicians and Surgeons, 1959; m. Andrew P. Davis, June 12, 1956; children—Jennifer, Margot, David. Intern St. Luke's Hosp., N.Y.C., 1960-61; NIH fellow med. genetics and pediatrics Albert Einstein Coll. Medicine, Bronx Municipal Med. Center, 1962-68; practice medicine specializing in pediatrics and genetic counselling, N.Y.C., 1968—; mem. attending staff Jacobi Hosp., Lincoln Hosp., Albert Einstein Coll. Hosp.; asst. prof. pediatrics Albert Einstein Coll. Medicine, N.Y.C., 1968—; asso. prof. pediatrics Cornell U. Med. Coll., N.Y.C., 1973—; dir. Child Devel. Center, North Shore Hosp., 1973—. Contbr. articles to profl. jours. Home: 333 West End Av New York City NY 10023

DAVIS, JOAN PATRICIA, librarian; b. Columbus, O., Nov. 4, 1927; d. Emmerson G. and Kathryn Cecilia (Naughton) Davis; B.S., Ohio State U., 1950; M.A., U. Mich., 1961. Staff librarian Columbus (O.) Pub. Library, 1950-51; med. records librarian St. Francis Hosp., Columbus, 1951-54; med. research librarian Ross Labs., Columbus, 1954-60; asst. reference librarian Grandview Heights Pub. Library, Columbus, 1957-60; br. head Huber Heights br. Dayton and Montgomery County Pub. Library, Dayton, 1961-65; med. reference and research librarian Northwestern U. Med. Sch., Chgo., 1965—. Recipient Soroptimist scholarship, 1960. Mem. Alpha Delta Pi, Sigma Alpha Sigma. Home: 6150 N Kenmore Av Chicago IL 60660 Office: 320 E Superior St Chicago IL 60610

DAVIS, JOYCE ELAINE STRIPLING (MRS. PHIL DAVIS), physician; educator; b. Big Spring, Tex., Feb. 18, 1924; d. Leslie Dayton and Alta (Hull) Stripling; B.S., Baylor U., 1945, M.D., 1947; m. Phil Davis, Mar. 27, 1946; children—Roger, Diane, Mark Owen, Phillip Scott. Intern Washington U. Hosps., St. Louis, 1947-48; resident Meth. Hosp., Dallas, 1949; practice medicine, Mt. Vernon, Tex., 1950-51; pathology resident physician Baylor Hosp., Dallas, 1952-53; resident pathology Baylor U. Coll. Medicine, Houston, 1954-57, instr. pathology, 1957-60, asst. prof. pathology, 1960-65, asso. prof. pathology, 1965—; mem. staffs VA, Ben Taub Gen. hosps., Houston. Diplomate Am. Bd. Pathologists. Mem. Am., Houston (pres. 1969-70) socs. clin. pathologists, Alpha Omega Alpha. Baptist. Home: 4314 Cheena Dr Houston TX 77035

DAVIS, JUDITH LEE (MRS. DONALD DEWITT DAVIS), writer; b. Chadron, Neb., July 7, 1936; d. John Warren and Mabel Viola (Sturgeon) Moxon; student, Seattle U., 1954-55, Coll. San Mateo, 1967; m. Donald DeWitt Davis, July 12, 1955; children—John Kerr, AnnAlise. Free lance writer of short stories and articles to various mags. including True, Man's Mag., Westways, Lady's Circle, Home Life, Teen and Light and Life Evangel, 1966—. Speaker on profl. writing and selling to various classes and clubs. Mem. Nat. League of Am. Penwomen, Cal. Writers Club (v.p.), Soc. of Confession Writers. Home and office: 905 Ivy St Carson City NV 89701

DAVIS, JULIA (MRS. WILLIAM M. ADAMS), author; b. Clarksburg, W.Va.; d. John W. and Julia (McDonald) Davis; student Wellesley Coll., 1918-21; B.A., Barnard Coll., 1922; m. Charles P. Healy, June 18, 1951; m. 2d, William M. Adams, Mar. 30, 1974. Author: Swords of the Vikings, 1929; Vaino, 1930; Mountains are Free, 1931; Stonewall Jackson, 1932; Remember and Forget, 1933; No other White Men, 1937; Peter Hale, 1939; The Sun Climbs Slow, 1942; The Shenandoah, 1945; Cloud on the Land, 1951; The Devils Church, 1951; Cruise with Death, 1952; Bridle the Wind, 1953, Eagle on the Sun, 1956; Legacy of Love, 1962; Ride with the Eagle, 1963; A Valley and a Song, 1963; Mount Up, 1967; also play The Anvil, 1963. Mem. Child Adoption Service. Authors League, Author's Guild, Mystery Writers Am. Club: Cosmopolitan. Home: 115 Brookstone Dr Princeton NJ 08540

DAVIS, KATHERINE MCPHERSON, realtor; b. Grand Rapids, Mich., Dec. 14, 1907; d. Melville B. and Nellie (Newland) McPherson; B.A., Mich. State U., 1933, postgrad., 1938-42; Real Estate certificate with acad. distinction, U. Mich., 1969, grad. Real Estate Inst., 1970; m. Russell J. Davis, Feb. 15, 1927; children—Barbara (Mrs. Russell Van Houten), Margaret (Mrs. Frank Wulff). Sec., Mich. Tax Comm., Lansing, 1934-42; asso. realtor Edward G. Hacker Co., Lansing, 1962-64, realtor, 1965—. Pres. Sparrows, Edward W. Sparrow Hosp., Lansing, 1964-65, also life mem. Women's Hosp. Assn.; pres. Coll. Women's Volunteer Service, 1971-72; chmn. women's div. Community Chest, Lansing, 1950-52, Harvest Fest. for Rehab. Center, Lansing, 1965; active fund drs. various divs. YWCA, YMCA. Del. State Republican Conv., County Conv. Recipient sercvice award YMCA, 1964, Edward W. Sparrow Hosp., 1967. Mem. Nat. Inst. Farm and Land Brokers (v.p. Mich. chpt., chpt. chmn. profl. standards of practice com.), Mich. Real Estate Assn. (taxation com.), Nat. Assn. Real Estate Bds. (mem. legislative com.), Spartan Alumni Assn., Mich. Assn. Hosp. Auxs. (legislative chmn. 1969-70, 72—, past pres. S.W. dist.). Methodist. Mem. Order Eastern Star (life). Club: Faculty Folk (Mich. State U.), East Lansing Womens; Entre Nous Literary (pres. 1970-71) (Lansing). Address: 1053 Parnell Av NE Lowell MI 49331

DAVIS, KATHERINE SUE EDWARDS (MRS. KING F. DAVIS), pub. relations exec.; b. St. Louis, Aug. 27, 1948; d. Ninian Murry and Mary Catherine (McKeown) Edwards; B.J., U. Mo., 1971; m. King F. Davis, Feb. 7, 1970; 1 dau., Kellie Marie. Reporter, feature editor, news dir. Radio Sta. WJNC, Jacksonville, N.C., 1971; coordinator community relations Kirkwood (Mo.) R-7 Sch. Dist., St. Louis County, 1972-73. Interviewer for candidates Am. Abroad program Am. Field Service, Kirkwood, 1972; swimming instr. Good Shepherd Sch., St. Louis, 1972; pres. Mil. Wives Who Wait, St. Louis, 1972; vol. swimming instr. A.R.C., 1966-74. Mem. Women in Communications, Kappa Epsilon Alpha, Sigma Rho Sigma, Kappa Alpha Theta. Club: Marine Officers Wives (Oahu, Hawaii). Home: 363 Hornet Av NAS Barbers Point (Hawaii) FPO San Francisco CA 96611

DAVIS, KATHLEEN L., educator; b. Bklyn.; d. James C. and Hilde (Arndt) Davis; B.S., U. S.C., 1961; M.Ed., U. Ga., 1964, Ed.D., 1967; postgrad. U. Va., summer 1965. Math. and sci. tchr. Beaufort (S.C.) Jr. High Sch., 1961-63; Nat. Def. Edn. Act fellow, 1963-64; counselor Princess Ann High Sch., Virginia Beach, Va., 1964-65; teaching asst. U. Ga., Athens, 1965-67, counseling psychologist div. mental health, 1967-73, asst. prof. edn., 1967-73, adviser Mortar Bd., 1968-71; asso. prof. ednl. psychology and guidance U. Tenn., Knoxville, 1974—. Active Am. Cancer Soc., 1968. Mem. Am. Psychol. Assn., Am. Personnel and Guidance Assn., Assn. for Counselor Edn. and Supervision, Phi Kappa Phi, Zeta Tau Alpha (alumnae sec. 1970; pres. 1970-72). Office: University of Tenn Knoxville TN 37916

DAVIS, L. CLARICE, art historian, library; b. Akron, O., Jan. 30, 1929; d. Kenneth F. and Ethel (Locken) Davis; student N.M. State Coll., 1950, Akron Art Inst., 1950, 57, Richmond Profl. Inst., 1951-54, Applied Art Acad., 1955; B.A. (Howard Cambell scholar), U. Akron, 1955; M.L.S. (Deborah King scholar), U. Cal. at Los Angeles, 1961, M.A., 1968, postgrad. (Samuel Kress fellow), 1971. Free lance artist, 1950—; library asst. Richmond (Va.) Pub. Library, 1952-54; tchr. art Cuyahoga Falls (O.) Bd. Edn., 1956-57; prin. library asst. art library U. Cal. at Los Angeles, 1957-60; art librarian San Fernando Valley State Coll., Northridge, Cal., 1961-63, asst. prof. art, 1961-63, cons. librarian, 1963-64, asst. prof. art, 1968—; head art research library Los Angeles County Mus. Art, 1963-68; lectr., originator course bibliography and research methods in history of art U. Cal. Extension, Los Angeles, 1966—; West Coast contbg. editor and cons. Worldwide Books, Inc., N.Y., 1968-69; lectr. Otis Art Inst., Los Angeles, 1969-70; asso. librarian Art Library, U. Cal. at Los Angeles, 1973—. One-man show Wingfoot Theatre Gallery, Akron, O., 1956; exhibited in group shows at Akron Art Inst., 1954-57, Akron Area Artists Annual, 1955-57, Dayton (O.) Art Inst., 1956-57, Falls Civic Center (Cuyahoga Falls), 1956-57; owner, mgr. L. Clarice Davis, mail order art books, 1971—; lectr., cons. art history art libraries, 1965—. Treas. So. Cal. chpt. Nat. Orgn. for Women, 1967. Recipient award outstanding woman painter of year graduating from coll. in Ohio, Women's Art League, 1955, Fedn. Women's Clubs, 1955. Mem. Coll. Art Assn., Assn. Archtl. Historians, Art Historians So. Cal., Am. Assn. Mus., Am. Assn. U. Profs. Address: PO Box 3057 Santa Monica CA 90403

DAVIS, LINDA JANE, occupational therapist; b. Oakland, Cal., Oct. 26, 1939; d. Stanley Spencer and Martha Madeline (Kerwin) Davis; B.A., Mills Coll., 1960; M.P.H., U. Mich., 1970, Ph.D., 1974. Commd. ensign USN, 1960, advanced through grades to lt. comdr., 1969, Res., 1969—; trainee Adminstrn. on Aging, Ann Arbor, Mich., 1969-70, Nat. Center for Health Services Research and Devel., Ann Arbor, 1970-73; research sci., asst. prof. U. Mich., Ann Arbor, 1973—. Mem. Nat. Hist. Soc. (founder), Am. Pub. Health Assn., Am. Occupational Therapy Assn. Home: 2150 Pauline Blvd Ann Arbor MI 48103 Office: 543 Church St Ann Arbor MI 48104

DAVIS, M. JOAN, educator; b. Mt. Kisco, N.Y., Jan. 30, 1934; d. Harvey Corey and Margaret Ada (Haynor) Davis; B.S., Russell Sage Coll., 1956; M.S., Columbia U., 1965, Ed.D., 1972. Recreator, Goldwater Hosp., N.Y.C., 1963-64; researcher Comeback, Inc., N.Y.C., 1965-67; faculty Northeastern U., Boston, 1968-69, Fresno State Coll., 1969-70; asst. prof. recreation and leisure State U. N.Y., Brockport, 1973—. Cons., N.Y. State Rehab. Hosp., 1968, Internat. Soc. Rehab. Disabled, 1968-69. USPHS fellow, 1967-68; Vocational Rehab. Adminstrn. trainee, 1964-65. Mem. Nat. Recreation and Park Assn., Nat. Therapeutic Recreation Soc., Les Amis du Ven. Home: 41 Chappell St Apt 4 Brockport NY 14420

DAVIS, MAMIE MYRTIS, educator; b. Bessemer, Ala., Oct. 16, 1918; d. Samuel Walker and Maude Myrtis (Braswell) Davis; A.B., Birmingham-So. Coll., 1939; A.M., La. State U., 1948, postgrad., 1949. Tchr. Bayview Elementary Sch., Jefferson County, Ala., 1939-43; math. tchr. Fairfield (Ala.) High Sch., 1943-46; asst. math. dept. La. State U., 1947-48; asst. prof. math. dept. Southeastern La. Coll., Hammond, 1948-49; instr. math. dept. Miss. So. Coll., 1949-50; instr. Francis T. Nicholls Jr. Coll., La. State U., Thibodaux, 1950-53, asst. prof., 1953-54; asso. prof. math. Wesleyan Coll., Macon, Ga., 1954-62, acting head math. dept., 1955-56; asso. prof. math. Greensboro (N.C.) Coll., 1961-62, prof. math., 1962—, chmn. dept. math. and sci., 1971—. Recipient 1st Faculty award Greensboro Coll. Alumni Assn., 1974. NSF grantee to summer inst. U. Kan., 1957. Mem. N.C. Acad. Scis., Bus. and Profl. Women, Math. Assn. Am., Nat. Council Tchrs. Math., Am. Assn. U. Women, Alpha Delta Kappa, Pi Mu Epsilon. Methodist. Club: Soroptimist. Home: 1309 Cardinal Pl Greensboro NC 27408

DAVIS, MARGARET, govt. ofcl.; b. Wichita, Kan., May 31, 1916; d. H. Dale and Elanora (Burch) Davis; A.B., George Washington U., 1937, M.A., 1941; student Harvard, summer 1935, Nat. U. of Mex., summer 1936, Middlebury Coll., summer 1949, Am. U., 1946-47, Georgetown U., 1953. Library asst., editorial asst., reporter Washington Post, 1938-46; spl. writer, asst. dir. George Washington U., 1946-52, asso. dir. pub. relations, 1952-68; pub. information specialist Econ. Devel. Adminstrn. U.S. Dept. Commerce, 1968-69, writer-editor, 1969-73; writer-editor VA, Washington, 1973—. Mem. Progressive Citizens Assn. Georgetown (now Georgetown Citizens), 1958—, sec., 1960-62; mem. exec. com. Prevention Blindness Soc. of Met. Washington, 1965-69. Mem. women's bd. George Washington U. Hosp., Calvert County (Md.) Hosp. Recipient Distinctive Merit Time-Life award Am. Alumni Council, 1965; Golden Lamp award Ednl. Press Assn., 1967; Alumni Service award George Washington U., 1967. Mem. Am. Newspaper Women's Club (pres. 1962-63), Women's Nat. Press Club (treas. 1949-50), Ednl. Press Assn., Am. Assn. U. Women, George Washington U. Gen. Alumni Assn., George Washington U. Faculty Women (pres. 1957-58), George Washington U. Columbian Women (pres. 1961-63), Soc. Women Geographers (nat. exec. council 1969-72), Assn. Preservation Va. Antiquities, Women in Communications, Pi Delta Epsilon, Phi Delta Gamma. Democrat. Episcopalian. Clubs: George Washington University; Scientists Cliffs Assn. and Garden (Calvert County, Md.); Chesapeake Country, Washington, Zonta (dir. 1974—), Washington Forum (sec. 1972-73). Editor, George Washington U. Federalist, 1954-64; George Washington U. Alumni Rev., 1952-63; founder, editor George Washington U. Mag., 1964-68. Home: 1657 31st St NW Washington DC 20007 Office: VA Central office Washington DC 20420

DAVIS, MARGARET ELOISE MORTON (MRS. MELVIN WILSON DAVIS), library supr.; b. Nashville, May 7, 1917; d. Howard Tillman and Margaret Althea (Lassiter) Morton; student Middle Tenn. State Tchrs. Coll., 1934-37; B.S., George Peabody Coll., 1938, B.S. in Library Sci., 1939; postgrad. Troy State Tchrs. Coll., 1948, Tex. Woman's U., 1966; m. Melvin Wilson Davis, Dec. 21, 1940; children—Margaret Ann (Mrs. Norman Richard Carlson), Charles Wilson, Barbara Joyce, Carol Elaine. Librarian, Carthage (Tenn.) High Sch., 1939-40; librarian circulation and res. dept. Peabody Coll. and Joint U. Library, Vanderbilt Sch. Religion Library, 1940-41; tchr. elementary and high sch., Crenshaw County, Ala., 1947-54; chem. and engring. librarian U. Ala., 1954-56; tchr., librarian, Bolivar County, 1962-68; elementary library supr. Bolivar County Dist. IV, Cleveland, Miss., 1968—. Nat. Def. Edn. Act Inst. grantee, Tex. Womans U., 1966. Mem. Kappa Delta Pi, Pi Gamma Mu. Methodist. Club: Faculty Wives, Delta State Coll. (pres. 1960-61). Home: 1203 Maple St Cleveland MS 38732

DAVIS, MARIANA, ednl. counselor; b. Knoxville, Tenn., Mar. 9, 1938; d. Wendell W. and Anna Will (McClain) Davis; B.S., U. Tenn., 1960, M.S., 1963, Ed.S., 1970. Social and recreation work Dale Av. Settlement House, Knoxville, 1957-60; tchr. Knox County schs., 1960-63; tchr., counselor Knoxville City Schs., 1963—, counselor Rule High Sch., 1968—; part time faculty St. Mary's Meml. Hosp. Sch. Nursing, 1970—. Vis. lectr. U. Tenn., 1967—; ednl. inservice cons., Athens, Tenn., 1967, Mountain City, Tenn., Cooke County, Tenn., 1969; Big Stone Gap, Va., 1970; cons. high risk edn. Meth. Hosp. Sch. Nursing, 1973-74, Southeastern Tenn. Ednl. Coop., 1974; mem. adv. bd. Knox County Juvenile Ct. Named Counselor of Year, East Tenn., 1969-70; Outstanding Young Educator, West Knoxville Jaycees, 1973. Mem. Am. Sch. Counselors Assn., Tenn. Edn. Assn., Am. (presenter nat. conv. 1970, 72, 74), Tenn. (Outstanding Contbn. award 1974) personnel and guidance assns., Am. Psychol. Assn., Pi Lambda Theta. Contbr. articles to profl. jours. Research on affective learning, high risk edn. in nursing. Home: 1930 Gilbert Lane Knoxville TN 37920

DAVIS, MARIE AGATHA, library adminstr.; b. Pitts., June 29, 1918; d. Frances R. and Agatha (Fischerkeller) Davis; B.S. in Social Sci., Carnegie Mellon U., 1941; B.L.S., Carnegie Library Sch., 1945. Pub. affairs librarian Carnegie Library Pitts., 1945-47, pub. relations dir., 1947-56; coordinator adult and young adult services Free Library Phila., 1956-70, asso. dir., 1970—; lectr. to various library schs.; cons. to demonstration interrelating library and basic edn. services for disadvantaged adults in Appalachian region. Bd. dirs. Adult Basic Edn. Acad. Recipient certificate of Merit Pa. Library Assn., 1962, Distinguished Service award, 1971; Merit award Carnegie Mellon U., 1971. Mem. Am. (pres. adult services div. 1967-68, councillor 1968-72), Pa. (pres. 1962-63) library assns., Middle Atlantic Regional Fedn. (conf. chmn. 1967, sec.-treas. 1968-72), Pa. Acad. Fine Arts (Peale Club). Roman Catholic Address: 7900 C Stenton Av Philadelphia PA 19118

DAVIS, MARJORIE FRY, civic worker; b. Natchez, Miss., Aug. 1, 1918; d. Louis and Regina G. Fry; student Newcomb Coll., 1936-40; m. Walter Davis, June 15, 1939; children—Patricia, Rodney, Walter III. Exhibits pvt. collection art to benefit small communities. Mem. Mayor's Com. of Cultural Resources. Bd. dirs. Womens Com., New Orleans Symphony, New Orleans Womens Opera Guild, Davis Family Fund, Touro Womens Aux. Bd., New Orleans Speech and Hearing Clinic; trustee New Orleans Mus. of Art; mem. exec. bd. Council of Arts for Children, La. Arts Council. Clubs: Plimsoll, International House. Home: 1819 Octavia St New Orleans LA 70115 Office: PO Box 6099 New Orleans LA 70174

DAVIS, MARJORIE SMITH CONZELMAN (MRS. DEANE CHANDLER DAVIS), civic worker; b. Warren, N.H., July 18, 1904; d. Arthur Leroy and Lena Olin (Merrill) Smith; A.B., Skidmore Coll., 1926; m. Clair McKinley Conzelman, Oct. 8, 1927; children—Peter Smith, Patricia Jane (Mrs. Sidney F. Greeley, Jr.); m. 2d, Deane Chandler Davis, July 5, 1952. Tchr., Corregidor (Philippines) Sch., 1929-30; adminstrv. asst. Vt. Civilian Def., 1942-45; exec. sec. New Eng. br. Am. Camping Assn., Boston, 1946-52. Lectr. on Far East, 1942-46; one-man show Wood Art Gallery, Montpelier, Vt., 1968, Chittenden Bank, Burlington, Vt., 1970, Howard Bank, Burlington, 1974; represented in pvt. collections. Active Vt. women's anti-crime vol. action program; state chmn. Gov.'s Com. on Child Care, 1944-45; mem. organizing com. Vt. br. UN Assn., 1944. Vt. del. Republican Fgn. Policy Conv., N.Y.C., 1944. Bd. dirs. Vt. YWCA, v.p., finance chmn., 1968-72; trustee Skidmore Coll., 1962-66, Thomas Waterman Wood Art Gallery, Montpelier, 1962-73; trustee, v.p. Vt. Arthritis and Rheumatism Found., 1965-73. Named Hon. Vt. Mother of Year, 1971. Mem. Am. Assn. U. Women (Vt. chmn. for world problems 1970-71, for community problems 1971-72), Nat. League Am. Pen Women (v.p. 1970-72, state pres. 1974—), League Women Voters, No. Vt. Artists Assn., D.A.R. Republican. Methodist. Mem. Order Eastern Star. Club: Womans. Home: 5 Dyer Av Montpelier VT 05602

DAVIS, MARTHA VIVIAN MCCLELLAN (MRS. JOHN FRANCIS DAVIS, JR.), nurse adminstr.; b. Leesburg, Fla., June 26, 1923; d. Samuel Jeff and Ethel (Cooksey) McClellan; R.N., So. Baptist Hosp., 1944; certificate pub. health nursing George Peabody Coll. for Tchrs., 1945, B.S. in Nursing Edn., 1947; M.A. in Adminstrn.,

Columbia, 1951; m. John Francis Davis, Jr., May 12, 1948 (dec. May 1958); 1 son, John Francis III. Mem. staff Vanderbilt U. Hosp., Nashville, 1944-46; staff pub. health nurse Baton Rouge Health Dept., 1947; organizer La. State Sch. for Spastic Children, 1948, asso. supt., 1948-50; organizer nursing service, dir. of nurses Lake Charles Meml. Hosp., 1952; nurse adminstr. Bapt. Hosp. S.E. Tex., Beaumont, 1952—, organizer Bapt. Hosp. Sch. Profl. Nursing, 1954. Mem. health sect. Community Council, Beaumont, 1964—; mem. Tex. Bd. Nurse Examiners, 1963—, pres., 1965-69; mem. adv. com. on nursing edn. Coordinating Bd. Tex. Coll. and U. System, 1966; vice chairman-Regents Devel. Council Lamar U. Goals for Greatness Faculty, Com. on Faculty Relationships, 1969—. Mem. Jefferson County Council Alcoholism. Mem. Am. Nurses Assn., Nat. League for Nursing, Am. Cancer Soc. (bd. mem. 1966—; pres. local unit 1970—), Tex. Hosp. Assn. (council hosp. nursing 1964—), M.B.S. Club: Soroptimist (Beaumont, Woman of Distinction award 1970). Home: 290 Canterbury Dr Beaumont TX 77707 Office: PO Box 1591 Beaumont TX 77704

DAVIS, MARY ALICE WHITE (MRS. ROBERT C. DAVIS), city ofcl.; b. Tuscola, Tex., Jan. 28, 1936; d. Hill V. and Evelyn Elizabeth (Hafner) White; grad. high sch.; m. Robert C. Davis, Dec. 11, 1954. Gen. ledger bookkeeper City of Abilene (Tex.), 1956-64, asst. chief accountant, 1964-68, chief accountant/treas., 1968—. Sec.-treas. Abilene Firemen's Relief and Retirement Bd., 1968—. Mem. Nat. Accounting Assn. (sec. chpt. 1971—). Home: 626 Gill St Abilene TX 79601 Office: 501 Walnut St Abilene TX 79601

DAVIS, MARY WRIGHT, govt. ofcl.; b. Washington, Dec. 18, 1918; d. Calvin Crawford and Irene Josephine (Douglass) Davis; grad. Notre Dame Bus. Coll., 1937. Sec. to atty., Washington, 1937-38; mem. staff various mems. of Congress, 1939—; adminstrv. asst. to congressman, Washington, 1952—. Home: 3505 Inverness Dr Chevy Chase MD 20015 Office: 2453 Rayburn Office Bldg Washington DC 20515

DAVIS, MATILDA LEVERNE, physician; b. Elizabeth, N.J., Sept. 23, 1926; d. James Taylor and Martha (Hilton) Davis; B.S., Howard U., 1947, M.D., 1951; postdoctorate Karen Horney Clinic, 1967-71; m. Robert M. Cunningham, Aug. 19, 1950; children—Dellena, Robert, William. Intern Harlem Hosp., N.Y.C., 1951-52; practice gen. medicine, Elizabeth, 1953—; mem. staff Alexian Bros., St. Elizabeth, Elizabeth Gen. hosps. (all Elizabeth); sch. dr. Bd. Edn., Elizabeth, 1965—; examining physician Planned Parenthood Assn., Newark, 1971—. Pres. North End Tennis Club scholarship orgn. Recipient Matilda L. Davis award Howard U., 1953. Mem. A.M.A., Nat. Med. Assn., Am. Acad. Psychosomatic Medicine, N.A.A.C.P. (life), Jack and Jill of Am. Club: Finesse (Elizabeth). Home: 27 Dayton St Elizabeth NJ 07202 Office: 230 W Jersey St Elizabeth NJ 07202

DAVIS, NANCY DAVIS (MRS. JOSEPH RAY DAVIS), psychologist, educator; b. South Bend, Ind., Mar. 13, 1945; d. James Fredrick and Nina Agnes (Macomber) Davis; B.S. in Elementary Edn., U. Ala., 1965, M.A., 1967; Ph.D., U. Md., 1972; m. Joseph Ray Davis, Aug. 21, 1965; 1 son, Eric Joseph. Psychologist II psychology dept. Bryce State Hosp., Tuscaloosa, Ala., 1965-66, counselor-evaluator, 1967-68; rehab. counselor-psychologist Rehab. Inst., Kansas City, Mo., 1968-69; instr. rehab. U. Md., College Park, Md., 1971-72; asst. prof. psychology Towson State Coll., Balt., 1972—. Cons. Md. State Adv. Council on Vocational Edn.; supr. workshop Crownsville State Hosp., Annapolis, Md., 1973. Rehab. Services Adminstrn. grantee, 1966, 72. Mem. Am. Psychol. Assn., Nat. Rehab. Assn., Am. Personnel and Guidance Assn. Home: 6768 Bison St Springfield VA 22150 Office: Psychology Dept Towson State College Baltimore MD 21204

DAVIS, NINA MILLER MOSELEY, educator, civic worker; b. N.Y.C., Sept. 21, 1932; d. J. Malcolm and Kathryn (Wilenzick) Miller; A.B., Vassar, 1954; M.A., U. Va., 1956; postgrad. Sorbonne, Columbia; m. Charles Guy Moseley, Aug. 28, 1954 (dec.); children—Kathryn Drew, Charles Edward Keeble; m. 2d, Mr. Bancroft G. Davis, Dec. 31, 1971. Exec. asso. Part Time Research Assos., 1961-63; founder, pres. Adventures Abroad, Ltd., 1964-71, also asst. to dir. profl. examinations div. Psychol. Corp., N.Y.C., 1968-71; program officer Internat. Inst. Ednl. Planning UNESCO, Paris, France, 1971-72; program adminstr. French lang. teaching asst. program Inst. Internat. Edn., N.Y.C., 1973—. Founder, dir. Women's Talent Corps, 1965-67; mem. N.Y. Jr. League. Dir. Masters Nursery and Children's Center, 1962—; trustee, chmn. nominating com. Dobbs Sch., 1968-71. Mem. Delta Delta Delta. Republican. Episcopalian. Author: U.S. Citizenship Today, 1963. Contbr. articles to periodicals. Home: 380 Stanwich Rd Greenwich CT 06830 also Villa Candide Veules-les-Roses S-M France Office: Inst of Internat Education 809 UN Plaza New York City NY 10017

DAVIS, OLIVIA ANNE CARR (MRS. TOM LUCIAN DAVIS), author; b. Leeds, Eng., Dec. 4, 1922; d. Henry Marvell and Olive Frances Kate (Rumble) Carr; grad. high sch.; m. Tom Lucian Davis, Oct. 13, 1943; children—Sebastian, Miranda, Penelope (Mrs. Daniel Howell). Came to U.S., 1951, naturalized, 1956. Sec., Mil. Intelligence, War Office, London and Oxford, Eng., 1941-44. Recipient Emily Clark Balch award Va. Quar. Rev., 1969. Mem. Authors Guild, Inc., Nat. Trust for Historic Preservation. Author: The Last of the Greeks, 1968; The Steps of the Sun, 1972; The Scent of Apples, 1973. Contbr. short stories to lit. quars. U.S. and abroad. Address: 6828 Floyd Av Springfield VA 22150

DAVIS, PEARL WALDMAN (MRS. LAWRENCE A. DAVIS), polit. scientist; b. Cambridge, Mass., June 5, 1918; d. Samuel and Sarah (Pearlman) Waldman; B.S., Simmons Coll., 1940; M.A., U. Louisville, 1965; m. Lawrence A. Davis, Aug. 13, 1943; children—Richard, James. Asst. chief Netherlands sect. Fgn. Econ. Adminstrn., Washington, 1943-45; cons. Urban Studies Center, U. Louisville, 1967; office dir. Ky. Civil Liberties Union, Louisville, 1968-69; sec. New Democratic Coalition Ky., 1968—. Vice pres. Children's Hosp. Aux., Louisville, 1961-63. Pres. New Democratic Club of 32d Legislative Dist., 1968-69; Ky. liaison New Dem. Coalition, 1968-69; del. to Ky. Dem. Conv., 1968; mem. Gov.'s Conf. Constl. Revision, 1961. Recipient Am. Assn. U. Women scholarship, 1963. Mem. League Women Voters Louisville (treas. 1958-63, mem. bd.), Ky. Civil Liberties Union (sec. bd. dirs. 1969-71, vice chairperson 1972). Home: 28 Pawnee Trail Louisville KY 40207

DAVIS, RUTH DILLARD JOHNSTON (MRS. DOUGLAS J. DAVIS), librarian; b. Wilson, N.C., June 29, 1915; d. Hugh Bolden and Ruth (Thomas) Johnston; A.B., Converse Coll., 1936; B.S. in Library Sci., U. N.C., 1942; postgrad. East Carolina U., 1967; m. Douglas Jones Davis, Jan. 19, 1947. Librarian, Snow Hill (N.C.) Schs., also supr. Greene County Pub. Library, 1940-44; librarian N.Y.C. Pub. Library, summers 1943-45; supr. Hyconeechee Regional Library, Roxboro, N.C., 1948-52; librarian Wilson (N.C.) City Schs., 1944-47, Greensboro (N.C.) City Schs., 1952-54, Raleigh County Schs., Beckley, W. Va., 1954-56, Elm City (N.C.) Graded Schs., 1956—. Bd. dirs. Wilson County Mental Health Assn., Wilson County Crippled Children's Assn., Wilson Community Concert Assn., 1960—. Mem. U.D.C. (pres. chpt. 1966-68, dir. dist. 8 N.C. div. 1972—), D.A.R., Nat., N.C. (pres. Elm City 1957-59, 64-67) edn. assns., Am., N.C. library assns., Delta Kappa Gamma (sec. chpt. 1964-66). Democrat. Presbyn. (mem. choir, circle Bible leader). Club: Elm City Garden (pres. 1960-62, 66-68). Home: Main St Elm City NC 27822 Office: PO Box 244 Elm City NC 27822

DAVIS, RUTH ELEANOR JONES (MRS. JAMES JOSEPH DAVIS), town ofcl.; b. Northbridge, Mass., Oct. 17, 1920; d. Arthur Willis and Catherine Irene (Fitzgerald) Jones; student pub. schs., Uxbridge, Mass.; m. James Joseph Davis, Oct. 7, 1942; children—J. Michael, John J., P. Timothy. Store clk. Cooper's Cut Rate Store, Northbridge, 1960-64, Lynch's Pharmacy, Uxbridge, 1964-68; clk. Uxbridge Tax Collector's Office, 1968-71; town clk. Town of Uxbridge, 1971—. Sec., mem. Uxbridge Sch. Bldg. Com., 1950-56. Mem. Uxbridge Democratic Town Com., 1940—, sec., 1955-72. Mem. Town and City, Mass. clks. assns., Am. Legion Aux. Roman Catholic. Club: Uxbridge Women's. Home: 14 Veterans' Pkwy Uxbridge MA 01569 Office: Office of City Clk City Hall S Main St Uxbridge MA 01569

DAVIS, RUTH LENORE, coll. pres.; b. Toledo; d. Thurber Phillips and Ila Lenore (Andrews) Davis; student Ohio Wesleyan U., 1928-30; B.S. in Bus. Adminstrn., U. Ariz., 1934; postgrad. U. Mich., 1941-42. Sec. Davis Jr. Coll., Toledo, 1934-35, exec. v.p., 1941-55, pres., 1956—; sec. to supt. schs., Tucson; tchr. Tucson Sr. High Sch., 1935-41; sr., then supervising accountant Willys-Jeep Corp., 1943-46. Mem. Adminstrn. Mgmt. Soc. (pres. 1973; Diamond award 1973), Internat. Assn. Personnel Women, (pres. 1974), Ohio Bus. Schs. Assn. (pres. 1964-67), Phi Theta Pi (Outstanding Bus. Educator award 1973). Club: Zonta (pres. 1948) (Toledo). Home: 2720 Inwood Dr Toledo OH 43606 Office: 502 Adams St Toledo OH 43603

DAVIS, RUTH MARGARET (MRS. BENJAMIN FRANKLIN LOHR), govt. ofcl.; b. Sharpsville, Pa., Oct. 19, 1928; d. W. George and Mary Anna (Ackermann) Davis; B.A., Am. U., 1950; M.A., U. Md., 1952, Ph.D. 1955; m. Benjamin F. Lohr, Apr. 29, 1961. Statistician, FAO, UN, Washington, 1946-49, mathematician Nat. Bur. Standards, 1950-51, head operations research div. David Taylor Model Basin, 1955-61, staff asst. office dir. def. research and engring. Dept. Def., 1961-67; asso. dir. research and Devel. Nat. Library Medicine, 1967-68, dir. Lister Hill Nat. Center for Biomed. Communications, 1968-70; dir. Inst. for Computer Scis. and Tech. Nat. Bur. Standards, 1970—; lectr. U. Md., 1955-57, Am. U. 1957-58; vis. prof. computer sci. U. Pitts., 1969-73. Cons. Republic China, Office Naval Research, Washington, 1957-58. Mem. Md. Gov.'s Sci. Adv. Council. Fellow Soc. for Information Display; mem. A.A.A.S. (dir., Am. Math. Soc., Math. Asso. Am., Washington Philos. Soc., Operations Research Soc. Am., Phi Kappa Phi, Sigma Pi Sigma. Author articles to profl. jours. Home: 12720 Eldrid Pl Silver Spring MD 20904

DAVIS, SALLY ANN, librarian; b. Chgo., Feb. 28, 1929; d. Joseph T. and Mabel (Billett) Davis; B.A., Carroll Coll., Waukesha, Wis., 1951; M.A., U. Wis., 1954. Tchr., librarian Edgar (Wis.) Pub. Schs., 1951-53; librarian Winnetka (Ill.) Pub. Schs., 1954-58; librarian Oconomowoc (Wis.) Pub. Schs., 1958-60, dir. sch. libraries, 1960—. Mem. Nat., Wis., Oconomowoc edn. assns., A.L.A., Wis. (pres. 1969-70), Waukesha County library assns., Metropolitan Sch. Librarians Assn., Am. Assn. U. Women. Methodist. Home: 1140 Daisy Lane Oconomowoc WI 53066 Office: 641 Forest St Oconomowoc WI 53066

DAVIS, SUSAN HAMM (MRS. PAUL ARNOLD DAVIS), pub. relations exec.; b. Prosperity, S.C., Oct. 16, 1948; d. Daniel Hezekiah and Harriett (Clarkson) Hamm; B.A., U. S.C., 1969; m. Paul Arnold Davis, July 26, 1968. Copy writer Bradley, Graham & Hamby Advt. Agy., Columbia, 1969-70; travel writer S.C. Dept. Parks, Recreation and Tourism, Columbia, 1970-72; pub. relations dir. Charles Towne Landing Expn. Park, Charleston, 1972-73; pub. relations dir. Charleston County Park, Recreation and Tourist Commn., Charleston, 1973—. Sec. North Pinepoint Civic Assn., 1973—. Mem. Women in Communication, Gamma Alpha Chi, Epsilon Sigma Alpha (sec.). Contbr. articles to various mags. Home: 1547 N Pinebark Lane Charleston SC 29407 Office: 186 Concord St Charleston SC 29402

DAVIS, SUSAN SCOTT (MRS. GAYLORD DAVIS), civic worker; b. Kearney, Neb.; d. Thomas Jefferson and Mary Estelle (Grant) Scott; A.B., U. Neb., 1918, Neb. State Tchrs. Coll., 1919; M.A., Columbia, 1935; m. Gaylord Davis, July 4, 1925; 1 dau., Susanne (Mrs. Daniel Oliver Newberry). Dir. tng. sch., dept. kindergarten Neb. State Tchrs. Coll., 1914-16; mem. casts plays in N.Y. theatres, 1921-23. Mem. Council Juvenile Planning Group, Asheville and Buncombe County, N.C., 1956-59; sec. exec. com. Buncombe County Com. 1960 White House Conf. Children and Youth; dir. Children's Welfare League, Asheville, N.C., 1949, 52, 60, pres., 1955-57; dir. Family and Children's Service Agy., 1948-55; dir. Asheville Day Nursery, 1960-62, v.p., 1963-64, pres., 1964-66, dir., 1967-73; mem. permanent conf. Buncombe County Planning Council, 1964-67, exec. com., 1965-67, mem. day care council Family and Children's Services div., 1969-71. Dir. United Social Services, 1955-60, Candelight Concerts, Inc., (exec. com. 1959-62). Mem. nat. council Women's Rep. Club, 1963-74, membership com., 1969-74; mem. Women's Nat., Buncombe County rep. clubs. Mem. bd. dirs. Asheville Community Concerts Assn., 1972—. Mem. English-Speaking Union, The Duetters (founder), Pi Beta Phi. Republican. Christian Scientist. Clubs: Biltmore Forest Country; University (N.Y.C.). Home: 12 Fairway Pl Biltmore Forest Asheville NC 28803

DAVIS, VERA JINKS (MRS. ALLEN D. DAVIS), state ofcl.; b. Hickory, Okla., Mar. 19, 1909; d. John M. and Viola (Bradley) Jinks; B.S., East Central State Coll., Ada, Okla., 1930; M.S.W., U. Okla., 1959; m. Allen D. Davis, Sept. 4, 1926. Tchr. pub. schs., Okla., 1928-46; with Okla. Dept. Pub. Welfare, 1949—, dir. Pittsburg County, Mcalester, 1950-53, Osage County, Pawhuspa, 1949, Tulsa County, Tulsa, 1954-58, asst. supr. div. family services, Oklahoma City, 1958-66, supr. assistance payments Social and Rehab. Services, 1966—, supr. field services, from 1969, now supr. div. assistance payments Adult Med. Social and Rehab. Service. Vis. lectr. Tulsa U., 1954-58. Cons., bd. dirs. Council Social Agys., Tulsa, 1954-56; bd. dirs. Tulsa Juvenile Ct., 1956-58; mem. adv. bd. Youth Opportunities Unltd., Oklahoma City, 1966—. Fellow Acad. Certified Social Workers; mem. Okla. (dir.), Am. (dir.) pub. welfare assns., Nat. Assn. Social Workers, Bus. and Profl. Women's Club. Home: 1600 NW 34th St Oklahoma City OK 73118 Office: Sequoyah Bldg Capitol Complex Oklahoma City OK 63105

DAVIS, WANZA YELTON (MRS. ISIAH CORNELIUS DAVIS), ednl. adminstr.; b. Kings Mountain, N.C., Jan. 9, 1926; d. Joseph Henry and Jennie Lou (Sanders) Yelton; student Western Carolina U., 1944-45; m. Isiah Cornelius Davis, Aug. 25, 1946; 1 dau., Jean Ellen (Mrs. John Edward Taylor). With materials dept. So. Bell Tel. & Tel., Charlotte, N.C., 1945-47; cost control clk. Burlington Industries, Cramerton, N.C., 1947-52; treas. Kings Mountain City Schs., 1952—. Instr., Cleve. Tech. Inst., 1971—. Grand dep. Order Rainbow for Girls, 1965-68. Mem. N.E.A., Nat. Assn. Ednl. Secs. (life mem., dir. 1973—, chmn. nat. conf. and inst. 1971), N.C. Assn. Ednl. Secs. (state pres. 1957-59), N.C. Assn. Educators (dist. pres. 1955-57). Republican. Mem. Order Eastern Star (matron 1964-65). Home: 210 E Parker St Kings Mountain NC 28086 Office: Kings Mountain Schs Box 192 Kings Mountain NC 28086

DAVIS-CLARK, BERTHA M. (MRS. RANDOLPH LEE CLARK), anesthesiologist; b. Asheville, N.C., Jan. 16, 1908; d. Leander E. and Jennie (Parker) Davis; student Carson Newman Coll., 1925-27, U. N.C., 1927-28; M.D., Med. Coll. Va., 1932; postgrad. U. Paris, 1934, U. Minn. and Mayo Clinic, 1935-40; m. Randolph Lee Clark, June 11, 1932; children—Randolph Lee III, JoLynn (Mrs. Ray Pamulo). Intern, Garfield Meml. Hosp., Washington, 1933, Hosp. Tarnier, Am. Hosp., Paris, France, 1934; fellow gynecology, anesthesiology Mayo Clinic, Rochester, Minn., 1935-38, jr. staff anesthesiology, 1938-40; practice medicine specializing in anesthesiology Miss. Baptist Hosp., Jackson, 1940-43, Hermann Hosp., Houston, 1946—. Cons. anesthesiology U. Tex., 1947—, M.D. Anderson Hosp. and Tumor Inst., Houston, 1947—. Mem. Am. Soc. Anesthiology. Home: 1600 Holcombe Blvd Houston TX 77025 Office: Hermann Hosp Houston TX 77007

DAVISON, JEAN MARGARET, educator; b. Glens Falls, N.Y., Apr. 19, 1922; d. Aldace Henry and Ruth Alice (Wilder) Davison; A.B., U. Vt., 1944; A.M., Yale U., 1950, Ph.D., 1957; Diploma in Etruscology and Italic Antiquities, Universita per Stranieri, Perugia, Italy, 1960. Cryptanalyst, U.S. War Dept., 1944-45; fgn. service clk. Dept. State, Athens, Greece, Vienna, Austria, 1945-49; Am. Numismatic Soc. summer grantee, 1952; Fulbright scholar Am. Sch. Classical Studies, Athens, 1954-55, vis. prof., 1974-75; instr. dept. classics U. Vt., Burlington, 1955-57, asst. prof., 1957-63, asso. prof., 1963-69, prof., 1969—, Roberts prof. classical langs. and lit., 1972—, also prof. ancient history. Mem. mng. com. Am. Sch. Classical Studies, 1965—, mem. exec. com., 1973—; mem. screening com. N.E. div. Fulbright-Hays awards for study in Italy, Spain, Portugal and Greece, Inst. Internat. Edn., 1971—. Am. Philos. Soc. research grantee, 1967-68. Mem. Archaeol. Inst. Am., Am. Schs. Oriental Research, Vergilian Soc. Am., Classical Assn. New Eng., Am. Assn. U. Profs., Phi Beta Kappa. Club: Champlain Valley Skating. Author: Attic Geometric Workshops, 1961; Seven Italic Tomb-Groups From Narce, 1972. Made summer expdns. to Petra, Jordan, 1961, Hagios Stephanos, Greece, 1963, Hebron, Jordan, 1965, Palace of Diocletian, Split, Yugoslavia, 1969. Home: 125 Buell St Burlington VT 05401

DAVISON, LOUISE ROGERS DAVIS (MRS. WILLIAM CHANDLER WATSON DAVISON), educator; b. Macon, Ga.; d. William Chisholm and Sarah (Clark) Davis; A.B., Worthen Coll., 1907; diploma Curry Coll., 1909; postgrad. Wesleyan Coll., 1908, U. Cal., 1925; m. William Chandler Watson Davison, July 31, 1912 (dec. Sept. 1959); children—William Hall, Sarah Louise (Mrs. Howard Barrett), Jaquelin Clark. Tchr., U. for Women, Florence, Ala., 1909-11, Liberty Coll. Glasgow, Ky., 1911-12; founder, dir. Davison Sch., Inc., 1928-70, pres., 1963—, chmn. bd. trustees, 1963—; founder 1st free speech correction clinic in U.S., Central Presbyn. Baby Clinic, 1929, (now Atlanta Speech Sch., Inc.). Recipient Wesleyan Coll. Alumnae award for distinguished achievement, 1951. Fellow Am. Speech and Hearing Assn.; mem. So. (past pres.; Distinguished award 1954-55), Ga. (charter, past pres.) speech assns., Speech Assn. Am., Ga. Fedn. Council for Exceptional Children (charter, past pres. Atlanta area chpt.; CEC Spl. award 1968), Ga. Speech and Hearing Assn. (charter), Atlanta Art Assn., League Women Voters, Internat. Council for Exceptional Children, Cerebral Palsy Soc. Ga., Ga. Assn. for Mentally Retarded Children, Zeta Phi Eta (past v.p., Zeta of Year 1965), Delta Kappa Gamma (past pres.). Contbr. articles to profl. jours. Home: 3750 Peachtree Rd NE Atlanta GA 30319

DAVISON, MARIAN MARGARET BIGELOW (MRS. HUGH M. DAVISON), youth orgn. adminstr.; b. Malone, N.Y., Jan. 18, 1917; d. Henry Jay and Eva (Elliott) Bigelow; A.B., Syracuse U., 1938; Ed.M., Harvard, 1941; Ed.D., Pa. State U., 1964; m. Hugh M. Davison, July 1, 1939 (dec. Jan. 1969); children—John B., Janet E., Anne M. Tchr. English, sch. librarian, Hammondsport, N.Y., 1938-39; county commr. Centre County, Bellefonte, Pa., 1958-60; asst. dean women Pa. State U., University Park, 1960-64, asso. dean women, 1964-68, asso. dean students, 1968-73; exec. dir. Girl Scouts Genesee Valley, Inc., Rochester, N.Y., 1973—. Bd. dirs. Asso. Charities, State College, Pa., 1952-56; pres. State College League Women Voters, 1955-57; mem. central region plannınc council Pa. Gov.s Justice Commn., 1969—, chmn., 1971-73; mem. State Coll. Borough Planning Commn., 1970-73; vice chmn. Day Care/child Devel. Council Central Pa., 1971-72, chmn., 1972-73. Mem. Am. Assn. U. Women (pres. 1967-69), State College Bus. and Profl. Women (v.p. 1962-63), Am. Personnel and Guidance Assn., Am. Coll. Personnel Assn., Nat. Assn. Women Deans and Counselors, Phi Kappa Phi, Pi Lambda Theta, Alpha Xi Delta. Methodist. Home: 210 Suburban Rochester NY 14620 Office: 550 E Main St Rochester NY 14606

DAVISSON, VIRGINIA, security analyst; b. Lafayette, Ind., July 11, 1927; d. William McKinley and Avanelle (Carter) Davisson; B.S., Purdue U., 1949. Registered rep. Harris, Upham & Co., Inc., San Francisco, 1957-63, sr. security analyst, N.Y.C., 1966-73; security analyst Eurofinance, Paris, France, 1963; with Standard & Poor's Corp., N.Y.C., 1964-66; sr. security analyst Wood, Walker & Co., Inc., N.Y.C., 1974—. Mem. N.Y. Soc. Security Analysts, Machinery Analysts of N.Y., Environmental Control Analysts N.Y. (pres. 1971). Home: 215 W 13th St New York City NY 10011 Office: 63 Wall St New York City NY 10005

DAVISSON, ZITA (MRS. EDGAR STERN), painter; b. N.Y.C., Apr. 15, 1928; d. John P.V. and Luella M. (Stohn) Heinmuller; art student Belmont Acad., St. Moritz, Switzerland, 1948-49, Nat. Acad. and Art Student League, 1950-53; m. Edgar Stern, June 15, 1972; children by previous marriage—Lacy Davisson, Darcy Davisson. Tchr. fine and graphic art Carnigie Chambers, N.Y.C., 1955-60, Soc. Illustrators, N.Y.C., 1965-68; exhibited one-man shows including Gugenheim Gallery, London, 1970, Gallerie Michel-Ange, Monte Carlo, 1971, Nenas Choice Gallery, N.Y.C., 1970—; exhibited group shows Portraits Inc., N.Y.C., 1963-73, Carroll Reece Mus., Tenn., 1968, Parish Mus., L.I., 1968, 70, 72; represented in permanent collections Portraits Inc. Mem. Soc. Illustrators. Address: 815 Park Av New York City NY 10021

DAWES, THELMA ELIZABETH, educator; b. Auburn, Ky., Jan. 5, 1908; d. William M. and Bertha A. (Hunt) Dawes; student Ind. U., 1925-26; A.B., Stanford, 1942, M.A., 1947. Tchr., Franklin Sch., Washington County, Ind., 1926-28; asst. nurse Tulare County, Cal., 1928-29; tchr., prin. Tulare County schs., 1929-51; supr., dir. testing and evaluation, tchr. psychometrist Taft (Cal.) City Schs., 1951-73, sch. psychologist, 1969-70, ret., 1973; vendor psychol. services State of Cal., 1973—. Chmn. Westside Assn. for Retarded Children, 1951-64. Mem. Am. Assn. U. Women (chmn. local edn. com. 1962-63), Assn. for Childhood Edn. (pres. Tulare County br. 1949-50), Internat. Assn. for Childhood Edn. (Westside rep. Kern County br. 1956-63), N.E.A., Cal. Tchrs. Assn., Cal. Psychol. Assn., Cal. Assn. Sch. Psychologists and Psychometrists, Kern County Psychol. Assn. (sec. 1960-62), Ind. U. Alumni Assn., Stanford Alumni Assn., Bus. and Profl. Women's Club (woman of year Taft 1965), Pi Lambda Theta, Delta Kappa Gamma. Baptist. Club: Taft Teachers. Address: 635 W Harold St Visalia CA 93277

DAWKINS, LOLA B. BEASLEY (MRS. NATHANIEL T. DAWKINS), educator; b. Ft. Worth, Dec. 29, 1913; d. James Bridges and Drudie (Rowe) Beasley; student Tex. Christian U., 1931-32; A.A., Odessa Coll., 1954; B.B.A., U. Tex., El Paso, 1954; M.B.A., Austin, 1956, Ph.D., 1962; Ford Found. fellow U. Cal., Los Angeles, 1961; m. Nathaniel T. Dawkins, July 17, 1934. Certifying officer Tex. Relief Commn., Odessa, 1933-36; asst. sec. City Odessa, 1936-46; exec. sec. First Bapt. Ch., Odessa, 1948-51; bookkeeper John Williams Ins., El Paso, 1954; spl. instr. U. Tex., Austin, 1955-58; asst. prof. Ariz. State U., Tempe, 1959-64, asso. prof., 1964-65; asso. prof. bus. U. Tex., El Paso, 1965-68, prof. mgmt., 1968—, chmn. dept. bus., 1973—, instr. in-service tng. programs Center for Continuing Edn., 1965—. Mem. Am. Bus. Communication Assn. (life mem.), Southwestern Social Sci. Assn. (sec.-treas. bus. communication sect. 1970), Acad. Mgmt., Nat., Tex. (dist. rep. 1968-71, v.p. 1971-72, pres. 1972-73, chmn. nominating com. 1973-74), Mountain Plains bus. edn. assns., Am. Assn. U. Women (br. treas., circulation mgr. Ariz. bull. 1964-65), Soc. Tech. Communication (chmn. student activities 1968—, v.p. 1971), Soc. for Advancement Mgmt. (sec.), Pi Omega Pi (historian), Beta Gamma Sigma (sec.), Sigma Iota Epsilon (sec.), Delta Pi Epsilon (del. 1969), Alpha Pi Epsilon (faculty sponsor), Phi Kappa Phi. Democrat. Baptist. Author: Readings in Office Management, 1967. Contbr. articles to profl. jours. Home: 3500 Sun Bowl Dr El Paso TX 79902

DAWSON, ALEXANDRA DEGHIZE (MRS. JAMES A. DAWSON), lawyer; b. Balt., May 4, 1931; d. Alef and Eleanor May (Jencks) DeGhize; B.A. summa cum laude, Barnard Coll., 1953; J.D., Harvard, 1966; m. James A. Dawson Jr., Aug. 13, 1955; children—Rachel, Alexander, Adam. Admitted to Mass. bar, 1966; asso. firm Nutter, McClennen & Fish, Boston, 1966-67, McCormack & Zimble, Boston, 1967-73; atty. Conservation Law Found. of New Eng., Boston, 1973—. Asso. mem. Town of Weston (Mass.) Conservation Commn., 1973—. Mem. Mass., Boston bar assns. Club: Sierra (mem. exec. com. New Eng. chpt. 1969-71). Office: Statler Office Bldg Boston MA 02116

DAWSON, ALICE MARIE (VONBERGEN), psychologist; b. Gordon, Neb., Mar. 25, 1894; d. John F. and Anna L. (Schulz) von Bergen; B.A., U. Neb., 1919, M.A., 1959, Ph.D., 1962; m. Fredrick Thomas Dawson, May 27, 1944 (dec. Aug. 1965); 1 adopted son, Jack Thomas. Dir. employee tng. Roberts Dairy Co., Omaha, 1919-32, br. mgr., Lincoln, Neb., 1932-42, direct sales and advt., 1942-54, corp. sec., 1922-70; instr. psychology U. Omaha, 1955-57; cons. in psychology, 1957—. Chmn. Home Safety Com., Omaha Safety Council, 1943; pres. Omaha br. Am. Assn. Ret. Persons, 1965-66. Recipient Distinguished Service award U. Neb., 1942. Mem. Am., Neb. psychol. assns., Neb. Hist. Soc., Joslyn Liberal Arts Soc., Lincoln C. of C. (pres. women's div. 1941-42), U. Neb. Alumni Assn. (pres. Omaha br. 1946), Phi Beta Kappa, Phi Delta Gamma. Republican. Presbyn. Author: A Pioneer Family, 1973. Address: 10317 Broadmoor Court Omaha NE 68114

DAWSON, BESS AMANDA PHIPPS (MRS. DAVID ALLEN DAWSON), artist; b. Tchula, Miss.; d. James Glyn and Mary (Holliday) Phipps; student Belhaven Coll., 1931-33, S.W. Miss. Jr. Coll., 1951-53, Allison's Art Colony, 1953-63, Miss. Art Colony, 1963-67; m. David Allen Dawson, Feb. 5, 1933; children—Sally Amanda (Mrs. Don Hook Stone), David Allen. One-man shows including 331 Gallery, New Orleans, 1966-68, Municipal Gallery, Jackson, Miss., 1967, Mary Chilton Gallery, Memphis, 1966; three-man shows including Internat. Trade Mart, New Orleans, Miss. Art Assn. Municipal Gallery, Jackson, La Font Gallery, Pascagoula, Holiday Inn Gallery, McComb, Miss. State Coll. for Women, Columbus, 331 Gallery, New Orleans; exhibited group shows including Municipal Art Gallery, Jackson, Ark. Fine Arts Center, Little Rock, La. Commn. Galleries, Baton Rouge, High Mus., Atlanta, Hunter Gallery of Art, Chattanooga, U. Ala., Tuscaloosa; represented in permanent collections; executed murals First Nat. Bank, McComb, Miss., Hankins Container Corp., Magnolia, Delta Electric, Greenwood. Tchr. art classes, 1955—; art supr. McComb (Miss.) Pub. Schs., 1968-72; co-owner, dir. Gulf South Galleries, McComb, Greenville, 1971—. Recipient awards including First awards Miss. Art Colony, 1964, 66, 70, Contemporary So., 1965, 66. Mem. Miss., S.W. Miss. (sec. 1966—) art assns., Miss., Allisons art colonies. Home: PO Box 32 Summit MS 39666 Office: Gulf South Galleries 211 Llewellyn Av McComb MS 39648

DAWSON, CHARLOTTE MAY, librarian; b. Beaver Falls, Pa., May 11, 1932; d. Charles Courtney and Gladys May (Hall) Dawson; B.S. in Edn., Geneva Coll., 1966; M.L.S., U. Pitts., 1967; postgrad. Pa. State U., 1972-73. Sec., Pitts. and Lake Erie R.R., Pitts., 1952-55; exec. sec. Investors Diversified Services, Inc., Beaver Falls, 1955-59, H.H. Robertson Co., Pitts., 1959-64; asst. librarian Geneva Coll., Beaver Falls, 1965-66; elementary librarian Northeastern Beaver County Sch. Dist., 1966-71; children's librarian Carnegie Library, Pitts., 1971-72; elementary library coordinator Beaver Area Sch. Dist., 1972—. Mem. Am. Assn. U. Women, Nat., Pa., Beaver Area edn. assns., Pa. Library Assn., Pa. Sch. Librarians Assn., U. Pitts. Alumni Assn., Pitts. Symphony Soc., Archaeol. Inst. Am., Geneva Coll. Alumni Assn., Beta Phi Mu. Presbyn. (bd. deacons). Club: Century (Beaver). Home: 110 Bradmore St Beaver Falls PA 15010 Office: Dravo and Jefferson Sts Beaver PA 15009

DAWSON, ELSIE HALSTROM (MRS. EDWARD DAWSON), cons.; b. Reedley, Cal., Feb. 4, 1913; d. Albin and Mary Cecelia (Ahlstrom) Halstrom; B.A., U. Cal. at Berkeley, 1933, M.A., 1935; m. Edward Dawson, Sept. 14, 1936; 1 son, Edward Douglas. Asst. food analyst U. Cal. at Berkeley, 1933-35; instr. chemistry of foods Syracuse U., 1935-40; instr. exptl. foods Cornell U., 1940-41; research on food U.S. Dept. Agr., Beltsville, Md., 1941-71; food cons., 1971—. Recipient Superior Service award U.S. Dept. Agr., 1951. Mem. Inst. Food Technologists, Am., Cal. home econs. assns., Am. Assn. U. Women, Navy League. Contbr. articles to research jours. Address: 6121 Terryhill Dr La Jolla CA 92037

DAWSON, FRANCES LEDLIE (MRS. HORACE DAWSON), former state legislator; b. Des Moines, Dec. 23, 1903; d. James Douglas and Lydia (Sheriff) Ledlie; A.B., Simpson Coll., 1925; M.A., Northwestern U., 1928; LL.D., Simpson Coll., 1968; m. Horace Dawson, June 26, 1929; children—Jeannette (Mrs. Richard Kahlenberg), Margaret (Mrs. James L. Alkire). High sch. tchr., Knoxville, Ia., 1925-27; asst. prof. history Simpson Coll., Indianola, Ia., 1928-29. Mem. Ill. Ho. of Reps., 1956-70, chmn. edn. com., 1968-70. Mem. Evanston Plan Commn., 1945-50, Evanston High Sch. Bd. Edn., 1952-57, Evanston United Fund Bd., 1950-57; bd. dirs. Chgo. A.R.C., 1961-67; mem. Sch. Problems Commn., 1962-70; women's div. Nat. Safety Council, 1960—, v.p. for women, 1966-68; mem. Ill. Commn. Status Women, 1967-71; gen. council Chgo. Presbytery, 1971-74. Mem. adv. council Comprehensive State Health Planning Agy., 1971—. Trustee Simpson Coll. Recipient Simpson Coll. achievement award, 1958; Northwestern U. Alumni award, 1960, Sch. Bell award Ill. Edn. Assn., 1971. Mem. Am. Assn. U. Women, C. of C., Ill. (v.p. 1951-53), Evanston (pres. 1943-45) league women voters, Bus. and Profl. Women's Club, P.E.O., Delta Delta Delta, Delta Kappa Gamma. Republican. Presbyn. (pres. women's orgn. 1950-52, elder 1965-68). Clubs: Zonta, Women's Republican, Evanston Woman's (pres. 1953-55). Home: 2609 Lincoln St Evanston IL 60201

DAWSON, FRANCES TRIGG (MRS. CARL H. DAWSON), author, lectr.; b. Chesterfield County, S.C., Oct. 31, 1901; d. John Wilson and Frances (Harris) Warr; B.A., Western Res. U., 1947; M.S., N.C. U., 1957; Ed.D., N.C. State U., 1969; m. Harry E. Trigg, June 18, 1918 (dec. Nov. 1929); children—Margaret Alice (Mrs. Margaret Sanderson), Harry Edward, Virginia Mae (Mrs. J.P. Ellington); m. 2d, Carl Horn Dawson, Apr. 6, 1946. Social worker Colo. Emergency Relief Adminstrn., Denver, 1929-30, asst. state supr., 1930-32; asst. dir. edn. Dept. Vocational Edn., Denver, 1932-37; supr. Vocational and Adult Edn., Wilmington, N.C., 1937-43; spl. rep. U.S. Office Edn., Washington, 1943-45; chief personnel counselor Office Indsl. Relations Dept. Navy, Washington, 1945-47; dir., supr. Vocational and Adult Edn., Burlington, N.C., 1947-67. State treas. League Women Voters N.C., 1967-69, state pres., 1969-73; mem. Gov.'s Com. on State Govt. Reorgn., 1970-72; mem. curriculum study com. State Dept. Pub. Instrn. N.C., 1969-73; mem. N.C. Adv. Com. on Pub. Edn., 1970—, also mem. exec. com. Named Mother-of-Yr., 1958. Mem. Am. Assn. U. Women (br. pres. 1952-54, 63-64), N.C. Vocational Assn. (sec. 1938-40), N.C. Ednl. Assn. (pres. Burlington unit 1948-49), Am. Acad. Polit. and Social Sci., Bus. and Profl. Womens Club (pres. Burlington 1952-54), Altrusa Internat. (dist. gov., mem. internat. bd. dirs. 1958-62). Methodist (supt. young peoples div. Sunday sch. 1949-53). Author: (with Earl M. Bowler) Counseling Employees, 1945; More Efficient Use Of Women In Industry, 1943; The Job Of The Counselor, 1943; Training Counselors, 1944; also pamphlets, brochures. Home: PO Box 505 Elon Coll NC 27244

DAWSON, GLADYS QUINTY (MRS. DONALD EMERSON DAWSON), educator; b. Trenton, N.J., Sept. 3, 1924; d. Joseph Leo and Stella May (Ritter) Quinty; student Albright Coll., 1942-44; B.S., U. Ill., 1946, Ph.D., 1951; m. Donald Emerson Dawson, Jan. 21, 1952; 1 son, Timothy. Research chemist Battelle Meml. Inst., 1951-52; instr. Pa. State U., 1952-58; sr. patent chemist E.I. duPont de Nemours & Co., Inc., 1958-63; asso. prof. Mich. Tech. U., Houghton, 1964—. Patent liaison, cons. Calumet & Hecla Co., 1966-69. Trustee Portage Twp. Library. Mem. Am. Chem. Soc., Sigma Xi, Iota Sigma Pi, Phi Kappa Phi. Home: Royalewood Addition Box 39 Houghton MI 49931

DAWSON, MARY RUTH, mus. curator; b. Highland Park, Mich., Feb. 27, 1931; d. John E. and Olga J. (Down) Dawson; B.S., Mich. State Coll., 1952; Ph.D. (NSF fellow 1954-56), U. Kan., 1957. Instr., Smith Coll., Northampton, Mass., 1958-61; asst. program dir. NSF, Washington, 1961-62; research asso. sect. vertebrate fossils Carnegie Mus., Pitts., 1962-63, asst. curator, 1963-65, asso. curator, 1965-69, acting curator, 1970, curator, 1970—, chmn. earth sci. div., 1973—. Adj. asso. prof. U. Pitts., 1970—. Nat. fellow Am. Assn. U. Women, 1957-58, NSF research grantee, 1961-62, 63—. Fellow Geol. Soc. Am.; mem. Paleontol. Soc., Palaontologische Gesellschaft, Soc. Vertebrate Paleontology (pres. 1973-74). Home: RD 2 Logan Rd Valencia PA 16059 Office: 4400 Forbes Av Pittsburgh PA 15213

DAWSON, SALLY JO, banker; b. El Paso, Tex., Dec. 29, 1930; d. Allen and Agnes (Carnes) Dawson; student U. Tex., 1948-50; grad. Sarachon-Hooley Bus. Sch., Kansas City, 1951. With TV dept. CBS, N.Y.C., from 1951, Stork Club TV Show; relief sec, comml. loan dept. First Nat. Bank, Amarillo, from 1965, now bank officer in charge comml. loan collateral. Bd. dirs. Amarillo Little Theatre. Mem. Nat. Assn. Bank Women, Inc., Kappa Kappa Gamma. Presbyn. Home: 1300 S Jackson St Amarillo TX 79101 Office: Box 1331 Amarillo TX 79105

DAWSON, VIRGINIA SUE MORGAN (MRS. NEIL S. DAWSON), editor; b. Concordia, Kan., June 6, 1940; d. John Edwards and Wilma Aileen (Thompson) Morgan; B.S., Kan. State U., 1962; m. Neil S. Dawson, Nov. 28, 1964; children—Shelley, Lori, Christy. Home econs. editor Coop. Extension Service, Ohio State U., 1962-64; home editor Ohio Farmer, Columbus, 1964—. Mem. Home Economists in Bus. (pres. Columbus chpt. 1967), Am., Ohio, Franklin County home econs. assns., Theta Sigma Phi. Home: 2097 Springhill Dr Columbus OH 43221 Office: 1350 W 5th Av Columbus OH 43212

DAY, BETH FEAGLES, author; b. Ft. Wayne, Ind., May 25, 1924; d. Ralph L. and Mary (West) Feagles; B.A., U. Okla., 1945. Free-lance writer, 1949—; short stories, articles pub. in various mags., including Readers' Digest, Ladies Home Jour., McCalls. Tchr. profl. writing, adult sch., Chappaqua, N.Y., 1956. Mem. Soc. Mag. Writers, Authors League, Authors Guild Am., Am. Civil Liberties Union. Democrat. Presbyn. Author: The Little Professor of Piney Woods, 1955; Grizzlies in Their Back Yard, 1956; Glacier Pilot, 1957; No Hiding Place, 1957; A shirttail to Hang To, 1959; This Was Hollywood, 1960; Passage Perilous, 1962; (with Helen Klaben) Hey, I'm Alive, 1964; (with Tom Pyle) Pocantico, 1964; (with Frank Wilson) Special Agent, 1965; (with Margaret Liley) Modern Motherhood, 1967; I'm Done Crying, 1969; (with Jacqui Schiff) All My Children, 1970; Sexual Life Between Blacks and Whites, 1972; The Philippines: Shattered Showcase of Democracy, 1974; author juvenile books: (with Donald Day) Will Rogers, Boy Roper, 1950; Joshua Slocum, Sailor, 1952; Gene Rhodes, Cowboy, 1954; America's First Cowgirl, 1955; (pub. under name Elizabeth Feagles) Talk Like A Cowboy, 1955; The World of the Grizzlies, 1969; The Secret World of the Baby, 1968; Life on A Lost Continent: A Natural History of New Zealand, 1971. Address: 35 E 38th St New York City NY 10016

DAY, BILLEE RUTH (MRS. JOHN PAUL DAY), librarian; b. Duncan, Okla., Apr. 5, 1925; d. Harold Leland and Ruth June (Tyer) Masden; B.A., Tex. Woman's U., 1946; m. John Paul Day, Sept. 6, 1947; children—Paul Lauren, Philip Courtney, Priscilla Ruth, Peter Masden. Asst. to librarian Okla. State U., Stillwater, 1946, librarian Sch. Tech. Tng., Okmulgee, 1946-47, reference librarian, Stillwater, 1947-48; bookmobile librarian Chickasaw Library System, Ardmore, Okla., 1960-62, extension librarian, 1962-64, dir., 1964—; instr. library sci. Southeastern State Coll., Durant, Okla., 1968-69. Trustee Chickasaw Hist. Soc.; mem. Library Services and Constrn. Act adv. bd. Okla. Dept. Libraries. Mem. Am., Southwestern, Okla. library assns. Methodist. Editor: Oklahoma Librarian, 1969-71. Home: 1615 W Broadway Ardmore OK 73401 Office: 22 Broadlawn Village Ardmore OK 73401

DAY, DONNA JOYCE, occupational therapist, mil. officer; b. Walnut Creek, Cal., July 25, 1931; d. Harry John and Muriel Lucy (Treadway) Day; B.A., San Jose State Coll., 1953; M.A., N.Y. U., 1968. Commd. 2d lt. U.S. Army, 1953, advanced through grades to lt. col., 1974; clin. affiliation coordinator Brooke Army Med. Center, Fort Sam Houston, Tex., 1968-71; chief occupational therapy sect. U.S. Army Med. Center, Ft. Gordon, Ga., 1974—. Decorated Meritorious Service medal, Commendation medal. Mem. Am. Occupational Therapy Assn. Home: 3311 Old Church Rd Augusta GA 30907 Office: US Army Med Center Fort Gordon GA 30905

DAY, DORIS, actress; b. Cin., Apr. 3, 1924; d. Frederick Wilhelm and Alma Sophia von Kappelhoff; student pub. schs., Cin.; m. Al Jorden, Mar. 1941 (div. 1943); 1 son, Terry; m. 2d, George Weidler, 1946 (div. 1949); m. 3rd, Marty Melcher, Apr. 3, 1951. Made profl. dancing appearances Doherty & Kappelhoff, Glendale, Cal.; was singer Karlin's Karnival, radio sta. WCPO; singer with bands, Barney Rapp, Bob Crosby, Fred Waring, Les Brown; singer, leading lady Bob Hope NBC radio show, 1948-50, Doris Day CBS show, 1952-53; singer Columbia Records, 1950—; star Warner Bros. Studio motion pictures include Romance on the High Seas, 1948, My Dream is Yours, 1949, Young Man With a Horn, Tea for Two, West Point Story, 1950, Lullaby of Broadway, On Moonlight Bay, I'll See You in My Dreams, 1951, April in Paris, 1952, By the Light of the Silvery Moon, 1953, Lucky Me, Yankee Doodle Girl, 1954, Love Me or Leave Me (selected as 1 of 10 best films by N.Y. Herald Tribune), 1955, Pajama Game, 1957, Teacher's Pet, Tunnel of Love, 1958, It Happened to Jane, 1959; Pillow Talk, 1959, Midnight Lace, 1960. Winner 1st prize (with Jerry Doherty) as best dance team in Cin.; Laurel award as leading new female personality in motion picture industry, 1950. Christian Scientist. Office: Warner Brothers Studios Burbank CA 91505

DAY, FRANCES STATTER, civic worker; b. Sioux City, Ia., Apr. 16, 1911; d. Humphrey and Estella (Stackeri) Statter; B.A. cum laude, Radcliffe Coll., 1933; m. Fairfield Pope Day, June 28, 1932 (div. Feb. 1956); children—Fairfield Pope, Estella Pope. Bus. mgr. Radcliffe Daily newspaper, 1930; editor Short Hills (N.J.) Jr. Service League mag., 1938-40; editor Observer mag. N.Y.C. Jr. League, 1950-52; mem. sr. adv. bd. B. Altman & Co., 1962; pres. White Collar, Inc., N.Y.C., 1964—; vice chmn. Republican Com.; bd. dirs. A.R.C., Millburn, N.J., 1954—; chmn. Millburn-Short Hills chpt. A.R.C., 1958-61; dir. Essex County chpt. Am. Heart Assn., 1952—, N.J. div. Am. Heart Assn. 1957—; mem. women's com. Judson Health Center, N.Y.C., 1954—; mem. admissions com. N.Y.C. Jr. League, 1957—; mem. mgmt. com. YWCA, N.Y.C., 1938-58; mem. women's com. Salvation Army, N.Y.C., 1955-58; chmn. patrons Overlook Hosp., Summit, N.J., 1954-57; chmn. Community div. St. Barnabas Hospital; mem. women's aux. N.Y. Infirmary N.Y.C., 1956—; chmn. Essex County (N.J.) Heart Fund Dr., 1953-56; active Planned Parenthood Assn., Am. Cancer Soc. Episcopalian. Club: Home Garden (pres. 1958—) (Short Hills, N.J.). Address: 51 Forest Dr Springfield NJ 07081

DAY, IMOGENE (MRS. RALPH LESLIE DAY), educator; b. Sherman, Tex., Apr. 24, 1918; d. Edmund Beall and Annie Almetta (Bondurant) Grinnell; student Austin Coll., 1934-36; B.S., Tex. Womens U., 1938; m. Ralph Leslie Day, May 19, 1946; 1 dau., Leslie Ann. Tchr. Guthrie (Okla.) Pub. Schs., 1938-40; camp counselor, program dir. Camp Mystic for Girls, Hunt, Tex., summers 1939, 40, 41; tchr. high sch. health and phys. edn. Sherman (Tex.) Pub. Sch., 1940-42; hosp. recreation dir. A.R.C., Camp Bowie, Brownwood, Tex., ETO, 1942-46; faculty Austin Coll., Sherman, 1947-49, 51—, prof. phys. edn., 1951—; exec. Camp Fire Girls, Inc., Sherman, Tex., 1949-51. Group leader Camp Fire Girls, Sherman, 1957-67; pres. Sherman Parents' League, 1964-65. Trustee Sherman Ind. Sch. Dist., 1965-71; bd. dirs. Sherman Youth Center, 1967-68, Sherman Tutorial and Edn. Program, 1966-70, Sherman Girls Club of Am., 1971-72. Named First Lady of Sherman Beta Sigma Phi, 1957. Mem. Am. Camping Assn. (dist. bd. mem. 1969), Am., Tex. assns. health, phys. edn. and recreation, Sherman Tennis Assn. (founder, pres. 1967-69, dir. 1969—), Womens Soc. Christian Service. Methodist (mem. ofcl. bd. 1960). Club: Austin Coll. Campus (Sherman), Home: Rural Route #3 Sherman TX 75090

DAY, JUDITH OLGA JOHNSON (MRS. BRUCE F. DAY), Republican nat. committee woman; b. Watts, Cal., Mar. 16, 1926; d. Carl Ragnar and Dorothy Florence (Rivenburg) Johnson; B.A., teaching certificate, U. Cal. at Los Angeles, 1948; m. Bruce Frederick Day, Aug. 1, 1948; children—Michael Bruce, Jonathan Ragnar. Tchr. pub. schs., Los Angeles, 1947-48, Wilmington, Del., 1949-50. Election dist. committeewoman Republican Party, 1950-69, com. chmn., 1952-55, 64-68, vice chmn. rep. dist., 1968-69, vice chmn. New Castle County, 1969-71, nat. committeewoman, 1971—. Bd. mem. Del. League for Planned Parenthood. Mem. Kappa Delta. Home: 35 Indian Field Rd Wilmington DE 19810 Office: 2007 Pennsylvania Av Wilmington DE 19806

DAY, KATHLEEN MARY, assn. exec.; b. Hartford, Conn., May 1, 1944; d. John Michael and Mary Catherine (Hurley) Day; B.A., U. San Diego, 1963. On-air talent KPHO-TV, Phoenix, 1949-55; asst. dir. radio-TV, Republican Congl. Com., 1964-66; reporter Washington News Bur., Metromedia Radio, 1966-68; reporter-editor Straus Broadcast Group, Washington, 1969-71; asst. exec. v.p. Nat. Assn. Broadcasters, Washington, 1971—; free lance reporter. Mem. Am. Women in Radio and TV (pres. Washington chpt. 1973-74). Clubs: Nat. Press, Washington Press. Home: 3040 Idaho Av NW Washington DC 20016 Office: 1771 St NW Washington DC 20036

DAY, MARIAN MCDONAGH, realtor; b. Saginaw, Mich., Nov. 27, 1907; d. Thomas Blakely and Eleanor (Hill) McDonagh; B.S. in Home Econ., Mich. State U., 1931; m. John Edward Day, Aug. 25, 1934; children—Thomas, Patricia, John E. II, Marilyn J. Partner John Day Constrn. Co., Saginaw, 1947-65; founder, partner John Day Realty, Saginaw, 1955-74; dir., sec. treas. John Day Co., Saginaw, 1966-74, Brokers Investment Inc., Saginaw, 1968-73; dir., v.p. Saginaw Leasing Corp., 1967-72. Chmn. edn. com., bd. dirs. Women's Nat. Farm and Garden Assn., Saginaw, 1963-67; co-developer real estate curriculum Delta Coll., Bay City, Mich., 1970, mem. edn. com. real estate, 1964-74. Named Realtor of Year, Saginaw Bd. Realtors, 1967. Mem. Mich. Real Estate Assn. (chmn. edn. com.), Saginaw Bd. Realtors (v.p. 1971), D.A.R. (bd. dirs. 1959-62), Home Econ. Alumni Assn. Mich. State U. (bd. dirs. 1959-65), Real Estate Alumni U. Mich. (bd. dirs. 1966-72). Roman Catholic. Club: Saginaw Culture. Home: 1591 Short Rd Saginaw MI 48603 Office: 6225 Gatiot Rd Saginaw MI 48603

DAY, MARJORIE HELEN STARR (MRS. WILLIAM ALVIN DAY), univ. dean; b. Los Angeles, Apr. 25, 1922; s. Elmer Martin and Helen Christina (Erskine) S.; A.A., Santa Monica City Coll., 1959; A.B., U. Cal. at Los Angeles, 1961, M.A., 1966, Ph.D., 1970; m. William Alvin Day, May 5, 1946; 1 son, Dennis William. Elementary tchr. Santa Monica (Cal.) Unified Schs., 1961-65; teaching asst. spl. edn. Grad. Sch. Edn., U. Cal. at Los Angeles, 1966-68, adminstrv. analyst Grad. Sch. Edn., 1968-72, instr. spl. edn. edn. extension, 1967—, asst. dean program and planning Grad. Sch. Edn., 1972—, lectr. counseling Grad. Sch. Edn., 1972—. Mem. Council for Exceptional Children (state fedn. sec. 1969), Phi Beta Kappa, Pi Lambda Theta, Delta Kappa Gamma. Home: 20462 Pacific Coast Hwy Malibu CA 90265 Office: 405 Hilgard Av Los Angeles CA 90024

DAY, MARY WINIFRED GARVEY (MRS. GEORGE EARL DAY), pub. relations agy. exec.; b. Chgo., May 5, 1932; d. William and Mary Patricia (Kennedy) Garvey; student U. Tex., 1971, Richland Coll., 1972-73; m. George Earl Day, Jan. 15, 1955; children—Patricia Ann, Shawn Michael, Kathleen Mary. Asso. editor Bell Telephone Labs., White Sands Missile Range, N.M., 1961-67; city editor Richardson (Tex.) Daily News, 1968; dir. pub. relations Drs. Hosp. Found., Dallas, 1969-72; owner Mary Day/Media Design, Richardson, 1972—. Recipient Key to City Corpus Christi (Tex.), 1971. Mem. Nat. Fedn. Press Women (dir. 1970-71), Women in

Communications (dir. 1973-74), Am., Tex. socs. hosp. pub. relations dirs., Profl. Photographers Am., Tex. Press Women (dir. 1966-73), Tex. Pub. Relations Assn., Dallas Hosp. Council (mem. pub. relations com. 1969-72). Roman Catholic (bd. dirs. ch. 1974—). Clubs: Canyon Creek Country (Richardson); Press (Dallas). Address: 512 Copper Ridge Richardson TX 75080

DAY, MARYLOUISE MULDOON (MRS. RICHARD DAYTON DAY), appraiser; b. St. Louis; d. Joseph A. and Dorothy (Lang) Muldoon; A.B., Washington U., St. Louis, 1940; postgrad. Air U., 1958, George Washington U., 1963-64; grad. Real Estate Inst. Md., 1972; m. Richard Dayton Day, Aug. 15, 1959. Intelligence specialist U.S. Air Force, Washington, 1947-60; asst. dir. radio and TV dept., pub. relations George Washington U., Washington, 1963-64; asst. to information dir. Mfg. Chemists Assn., 1964-65; program officer, spl. asst. to dir. project devel. VISTA, Office Econ. Opportunity, 1965-67; free lance writer, 1967-69; v.p. Culpeper Corp., Wilmington, Del., 1955—; pub. relations cons., 1966-69; with Joint Intelligence Bur., London, Eng., 1953; appraiser, cons. on antiques, fine arts, 1969—. Chmn. publicity com. Seton Guild. Recipient citation U.S. Air Force, 1960. Mem. Am. Women in Radio and TV, Am. Soc. Appraisers, Irish Georgian Soc., Zonta Internat. (pres. Silver Spring chpt. 1973-74), Delta Gamma. Club: Kenwood Golf and Country (Washington). Home: 4928 Sentinel Dr Sumner MD 20016

DAY, MRS. R. ERVEN (STELLA H. DAY), civic worker; b. Fillmore, Utah; d. G. Riley and Hannah (Hanson) Huntsman; tchrs. certificate U. Utah, 1909, student Brigham Young U., Utah State U., Northwestern U.; m. Richard Erven Day, Aug. 4, 1909; children—Erven Vance, Glade Riley, Belva, Daila (Mrs. Wendell Pixton Paxton). Tchr. jr. high sch., Utah. Chmn. A.R.C., Millard County, Utah, 1918-28; pres. East Millard Cancer Assn., 1935-46; sec. Fillmore (Utah) Latter-day Saints Hosp., 1950—; chmn. Civic Improvement. Named Club Woman of Yr. Utah, 1960; Dist. Mother Yr., 1961; awards Utah State U., 1967, 69, 70-71, 72, 73, Utah Nurserymen's Assn., 1968, 1st place for environmental improvement in state and Rocky Mountain region, 1973. Mem. Utah Asso. Garden Clubs (pres. 1957-58, dir. 1945—), Nat. Council State Garden Clubs (dir. 1957—, 1st nat. accredited flower show judge in Utah), E. Millard Fine Arts Guild (pres. 1954-55), Nat. Assn. Daus. of Pioneers (v.p. 1948-72, historian 1958—), Gen. Fedn. Women's Clubs, Am. Rose Soc. (accredited judge), Am. Iris Soc. (judge), Civic Improvement Soc. (v.p.), Utah Hist. Soc., Utah Beautification Soc. Mem. Ch. of Jesus Christ of Latter-day Saints. Compiler: Milestones of Millard History of Millard County. Author: Everything Is Relative, 1970. Contbr. articles to profl. jours.; also weekly column for newspaper. Home: 95 E Center St Fillmore UT 84631

DAY, SAVANNAH SEGRAVES (MRS. ROYAL P. DAY), educator, home econs.; b. nr. Roaring River, N.C., Jan. 26, 1927; d. Robert Clay and Alma (Sparks) Segraves; B.S. cum laude, Appalachian State U., 1951; M.S. in Home Econs., U. N.C., 1953; Ph.D. (Am. Home Econs. Assn. fellow), Fla. State U., 1968; m. Royal Palmer Day, Nov. 22, 1945; children—Patricia Faye (Mrs. Gayle Michael Poplin), Robert Clay, Melinda Alma-Etta. Tchr. home econs. Ronda (N.C.) High Sch., 1947-48; tchr. Collettsville (N.C.) Elementary Sch., 1951; research asst. U. N.C., Greensboro, 1953-54, research instr., 1954-61, asst. research prof., 1961-66, asso. prof., 1968-69; asso. prof. Fla. State U., Tallahassee, Fla., 1969—; supr. research projects agrl. expt. sta. N.C. State U., 1959-66. Chmn., So. Region Housing Research Tech. Com. 1962, 64; housing commr. Tallahassee Housing Authority. Mem. Am., N.C. (chmn. research com. 1964-66), Fla. home econs. assn., Am. Assn. Housing Educators, Interior Design Educators Council, Internat. Assn. for Housing Sci., Am. Assn. U. Profs., Nat. Trust Hist. Preservation, Nat. Home Fashions League, Fla., Tallahassee realtors, Delta Kappa Gamma, Omicron Nu (chpt. pres. 1967-68). Contbr. articles to profl. jours., tech. bulls., chpts. in books. Home: 2105 Great Oak Dr Tallahassee FL 32303

DAY, SUSAN JANE, educator; b. Oak Park, Ill., Feb. 23, 1931; d. Herman Samuel and Myrtilla (Stewart) Day; B.S., Wis. State U., 1952; M.S., Winona (Minn.) State Coll., 1957; certificate advanced study No. Ill. U., 1969, postgrad., 1969—. Tchr. health and phys. edn. Winona pub. schs., 1952-57; instr. Winona State Coll. 1957-68, asst. prof., 1968-70, asso. prof., 1970—, dir. health and phys. edn. for women, 1967—, head dept., 1970—. Mem. Civil Def. Communications, Winona, 1967—; adv. com. phys. dir. YMCA Winona, 1965—; mem. Minn. Gov.'s Com. on Phys. Fitness for Youth, 1959-60; mem. adv. com. Minn. supr. for Health, Phys. Edn. and Recreation, 1959—. Mem. Nat. Found. Health, Phys. Edn. and Recreation, Am., Minn. assns. for health, phys. edn. and recreation, Nat., Central assns. phys. edn. for coll. women, Delta Psi Kappa. Home: 1566 Heights Blvd Winona MN 55987

DAY, WORDEN, sculptor, graphic artist; b. Columbus, O.; d. Daniel E. and Amelia (Worden) Day; M.A., N.Y. U.; student Art Students League; studied with Maurice Sterne, Vytlacil, Hofmann, and Hayter. Instr., Stephens Coll., U. Louisville, U. Wyo., State U. Ia., Pratt Inst., New Sch., Art Students League N.Y.; solo exhbns. Peris Gallery, Bertha Schaefer Gallery; N.Y.C., Smithsonian Instn., Krasner Gallery, U. Minn., Cin., Norfolk and Balt. museums art, Phila. Art Alliance, Grand Central Moderns, N.Y., Sculpture Center, N.Y.; represented in permanent collections Mus. Modern Art; N.Y.C., Bklyn. Mus., Library of Congress, Phila. Mus. Art, Met. Mus. Art, N.Y.C., many others. J. Rosenwald fellow, 1942-44, John Simon Guggenheim fellow, 1952-53, 61-62. Mem. Sculptors Guild, Fedn. Modern Painters and Sculptors. Address: 285 Claremont Av Montclair NJ 07042

DAYHOFF, MARGARET OAKLEY, biomed. researcher; b. Phila., Mar. 11, 1925; d. Kenneth Wilson and Ruth Prettyman (Clark) Oakley; B.A., N.Y. U., 1945; M.A., Columbia, 1946, Ph.D., 1948; m. Edward Samuel Dayhoff, May 29, 1948; children—Ruth Elizabeth, Judith Elaine. Head dept. chem. biology Nat. Biomed. Research Found., Georgetown U., Washington, 1960—, asso. dir. research, 1962—, asso. prof. Med. Sch., 1970—. Prin. investigator NIH, Nat. Biomed. Research Found., 1962—, NASA, 1965—. Mem. Biophys. Soc. (sec.). Editor-in-chief Atlas Protein Sequence and Structure. Home: 1618 Tilton Dr Silver Spring MD 20902 Office: 3900 Reservoir Rd Washington DC 20007

DAYTON, FRANCES BERNETTA KAP (MRS. CHARLES A. DAYTON), physician; b. Westboro, Wis., Sept. 23, 1909; d. Victor and Bernetta (Kalisz) Kapusinski; student Crane Coll., Chgo., 1927-29, Lewis Inst. Tech., 1929-31; M.D., Chgo. Med. Sch., 1935; m. Charles A. Dayton, May 27, 1952. Intern Childrens Meml. Hosp., Montreal, Que., Can., 1935-36, St. Joseph's Gen. Hosp., Port Arthur, Ont., Can., 1936-37, resident, 1936-37; resident Port Arthur Gen. Hosp., 1937-38; practice medicine specializing in pediatrics, Chgo., 1939-45, Galesburg, Ill., 1946—; chief med. examiner Polish Womens Alliance, Chgo., 1939-43; asso. physician Lumbermans Mut. Casualty, Chgo., 1942-45; mem. staff Galesburg Cottage Hosp., tchr. nurses, 1955—; St. Mary's Hosp. staff Mem. A.M.A., Ill., Knox County (mem. pub. sch. com.) med. socs. Home: 1987 N Broad St Galesburg IL 61401 Office: Bank of Galesburg Galesburg IL 61401

DAYTON, LINDA LEIGH REZAC (MRS. JOHN W. DAYTON), ednl. adminstr.; b. Topeka, June 5, 1940; d. James Elmer and Evelyn Marie (Fauerbach) Rezac; B.S., Kan. State Tchrs. Coll., 1961, M.S., 1965; m. John W. Dayton, May 29, 1965; children—Ellen Marie, James Wade. Tchr. bus. Wenatchee (Wash.) High Sch., 1963-64; tchr. bus. Highland Park High Sch., Topeka, 1961-63, counselor, 1965-70; dir. admissions Johnson County Community Coll., Overland Park, Kan., 1970—. Nat. Def. Edn. Act grantee, 1967. Mem. Nat. Council Adminstrv. Women in Edn., Am., Kan. (sec. 1973-74) assns. collegiate registrars and admissions officers, Am. Assn. Women Deans and Counselors, Kan. Assn. Student Personnel Adminstrs. Mem. Order Eastern Star. Home: 9227 England St Overland Park KS 66212 Office: Johnson County Community Coll 111th and Quivira Rd Overland Park KS 66210

DCAMP, LUAN JEANETTE, psychologist; b. Fairfield, Ia.; d. Glenn Franklin and Nina (Larson) Dcamp; R.N., St. Francis Hosp. Sch. Nursing; B.S., U. Ill.; M.A. (Ruth Kirk scholar), U. Chgo. Formerly nurse, St. Francis Hosp., Peoria, Ill., A.R.C. Disaster Service, Peoria, nurse Augustana Hosp., Chgo., 1957-59, Grant Hosp., Chgo., 1959-61; with Ill. Dept. Mental Health, Chgo., 1955-68; dir. psychol. services Grant Hosp., 1963-70; gen. basic sci. staff Luth. Gen. Hosp., Park Ridge, Ill., 1966—; mng. dir. Incentives, Des Plaines, Ill., 1967—; individual practice psychology, Chgo., 1963—. Instr. psychology, biology Crane Jr. Coll., Chgo., 1961-69. Mem. Am., Ill. psychol. assns., Am. Group Psychotherapy Assn., Ill. Group Psychotherapy Soc., Psychologists Interested in Advancement Psychotherapy, Assn. Women Psychologists. Contbr. articles to profl. lit. Office: 2424 Dempster Des Plaines IL 60016

DEACH, DOROTHY FRANCES, univ. athletic adminstr.; b. Moweaqua, Ill., Nov. 5, 1909; d. Arthur Wood and Carrie Mae (Dufur) Deach; B.S., U. Ill., 1931, M.S., 1932; Ph.D., U. Mich., 1951. Supr., chmn. women's phys. edn. Lindenwood Coll., 1941-47, Allegheny Coll., Meadville, Pa., 1942-45, U. Md., 1947-61; asso. dean Coll. Health, Phys. Edn. and Recreation, Tex. Woman's U., 1961-67; prof., chmn. women's phys. edn. Ariz. State U., Tempe, 1967—. Mem. Am. Acad. Phys. Edn., Am. Coll. Sports Medicine, Nat. Assn. Phys. Edn. for Coll. Women, A.A.H.P.E.R. Address: Arizona State University Tempe AZ 85282

DEADERICK, LUCILE, librarian; b. Knoxville, Tenn., June 22, 1914; d. Paul Stuart and Josephine Lee (Galyon) Deaderick; B.A., U. Tenn., 1934; B.S. in L.S., U. Ill., 1937. With Lawson McGhee Library, Knoxville, 1934-41; editor A.L.A., Chgo., 1941-47; librarian Ft. Loudoun Regional Library, Lenoir City, Tenn., 1947-51, Knox County schs., Knoxville, 1951-68; asst. prof. library service U. Tenn., 1968-69; dir. Knoxville-Knox County Pub. Library, 1970—. Mem. Am., Southeastern, Tenn. library assns., Assn. Preservation Tenn. Antiquities, East Tenn. Hist. Soc. (pres.), Tenn. Farm Bur. Democrat. Roman Catholic. Home: Route 17 Knoxville TN 37921 Office: 500 W Church Av Knoxville TN 37902

DEAL, BABS HODGES (MRS. BORDEN DEAL), author; b. Scottsboro, Ala., June 23, 1929; d. Hilburn Tyson and Evelyn Hudson (Coffey) Hodges; B.A., U. Ala., 1952; m. Borden Deal, June 6, 1952; children—Ashley, Brett H., Shane. Recipient Edgar Allan Poe Spl. award Mystery Writers Am., 1966, Literary award Ala. Library Assn., 1969, Oppie award for best suspense novel Evelyn Oppenheimer, 1969. Mem. P.E.N., Author's Guild, Mystery Writers Am. Author: Acres of Afternoon, 1959; It's Always Three O'Clock, 1961; Night Story, 1962; The Grail, 1963; Fancy's Knell, 1966; The Walls Came Tumbling Down, 1968; High Lonesome World, 1969; Summer Games, 1972; The Crystal Mouse, 1973; The Reason for Roses, 1974. Contbr. articles to profl. jours., short stories to mags. Home: 4740 Ocean Blvd Sarasota FL 33581

DEAL, ELEANOR HASSON (MRS. CHARLES H. DEAL), physician; b. Rushville, Ind., Mar 17, 1907; d. Alfred and Mary Elizabeth (Snyder) Blackledge; student Butler U., 1925-27; B.S., Ind. U., 1929, M.D., 1934; m. Charles H. Deal, Dec. 26, 1936 (dec. Dec. 1957); children—Mary Elizabeth (Mrs. Robert J. Wicker), Charles, James, Thomas, Michael. Intern Indpls. City Hosp., 1934-35; resident Madison State Hosp., 1935-37; practice gen. medicine, Indpls., 1938, Speedway, Ind., 1939—; mem. staffs St. Vincent Hosp., Indpls., Meth. Hosp., Indpls., Univ. Heights Hosp., Indpls., Winona Hosp., Indpls.; physician Ind. Girls Schs., 1943—. Roman Catholic. Home: 3510 W Michigan St Indianapolis IN 46222 Office: 4917 W 15th St Speedway IN 46224

DEAL, ELISABETH EARLE, educator; b. Dighton, Mass., Oct. 13, 1903; d. Ralph and E. Anna (Mann) Earle; A.B., Eastern Nazarene Coll., 1931; R.N., Newport Hosp. Sch. Nursing, 1934; m. Noah F. Deal, Apr. 12, 1944 (dec. Mar. 1961). Sch. nurse Mt. Hermon Sch., Darjeeling, India, 1936-40; nurse Internment Camp Hosp., Manila, Philippines, 1942-43; case worker Gloucester County Dept. Pub. Welfare, Gloucester, Va., 1956-58; supt. King and Queen County (Va.) Dept. Pub. Welfare, 1958-69; tchr. All Tribes Indian Mission Sch., Bernalillo, New Mexico, 1969—. Chmn. district III of Va. Council Social Welfare, 1963-65; v.p. Tidewater Tb and Respiratory Disease Assn., 1963-68; mem. County Tech. Action Panel. Mem. Am. Pub. Welfare Assn., Nat. Rehab. Assn., King and Queen County Hist. Soc., Phi Delta Lambda. Presbyn. Clubs: King and Queen Woman's, King and Queen Christ (Pres.). Address: All Tribes Indian Mission Sch Box 207 Bernalillo NM 87004

DEAN, ALICE ROGERS, physician; b. Clearfield, Pa.; d. Charles Calvin and Minerva (Dunlap) Rogers; student Western Res. 1956-62; M.D., Case-Western Reserve U., 1962; m. Robert Stanley Dean, Sept. 3, 1956 (div. Dec. 1967); children—Alice Kathryn, Lisa Carol. Research, child devel. Case-Western Res. U., Cleve., 1962-65; intern Milw. Children's Hosp., 1965-66; resident adult psychiatry Marquette U., Milw., 1966-68; resident child psychiatry Milw. County Gen. Hosp., Wauwatosa, Wis., 1968-70, dir. adolescent girls div., dept. psychiatry, 1970-71; pvt. practice, 1971—; cons. Milw. County Children's Ct., 1970—. Mem. A.M.A., Am., Wis. psychiat. assns. Home: 5426 N Lake Dr Milwaukee WI 53217 Office: 2040 W Wisconsin Av Milwaukee WI 53233

DEAN, JANET E. VAUGHN, ednl. adminstr.; b. Baldwin City, Kan., Jan. 5, 1934; d. Earl William and Waneta (Sowers) Vaughn; B.A., Baker U., 1955; M.S., Barry Coll., 1963; L.H.D., London Inst. Applied Research; m. Wendell Hungtington Dean, May 21, 1957 (div. Sept. 1961). Tchr. speech, counselor Carol City Jr. High Sch., Miami, Fla., 1958-66; pres. Dade County Classroom Tchrs. Assn. Inc., Miami, 1966-70; asst. prin. for curriculum Miami Northwestern Sr. High Sch., 1970—. Mem. exec. com. Miami Emergency Planning Commn. on Human Relations, 1968—. Bd. dirs. P.T.A., Dade County, Fla. Mem. Democratic Exec. Com., Dist. 7, Dade County, 1966-68. Recipient award N.E.A., 1967; named Woman of Year, 1973. Mem. Fla. Edn. Assn. (chmn. urban com. 1967-68), Nat. Com. Educators for Human Rights, Nat. (pres. 1968-69), Fla. (pres. 1967-68) council urban edn. assns., Am. Assn. U. Women, Nat. Assn. Supervision and Curriculum Devel., League Women Voters, Alpha Chi Omega. Home: 367 NW 153 St Miami FL 33169 Office: 7007 NW 12th Av Miami FL 33150

DEAN, LYDIA MARGARET CARTER (MRS. HALSEY ALBERT DEAN), food and nutrition cons.; b. Bedford, Va., July 11, 1919; d. Christopher C. and Hettie (Gross) Carter; grad. Averett Coll.; B.S., Madison Coll., 1941; M.S., Va. Poly. Inst. and State U., 1951; postgrad. U. Va.; m. Halsey Albert Dean, Dec. 24, 1941; children—Halsey Albert, John Carter, Lydia Margerae. Dietetic intern, therapeutic dietitian St. Vincent de Paul Hosp., Norfolk, 1942, physicist, U.S.N. Naval Operating Base, Norfolk, Va., 1943-45; clin. dietitian, instr. Roanoke Meml. Hosps., 1946-51; asso. prof. nutrition Va. Poly. Inst. and State U., 1951-53; community nutritionist and supr. sch. lunch program Roanoke (Va.) Pub. Schs., 1953-60; dir. dept. dietetics and nutrition Southwestern Med. Center, Roanoke, Va., 1960-67; food and nutrition cons. Nat. Hdqrs. A.R.C., Washington, 1967-73; nutrition cons. U.S. Dept. Agr., Dept. Army, Washington, A.R.C., 1973—. Cons. Am. Dietetic Assn., 1969—; mem. task force White House Conf. Food and Nutrition, 1969—; chmn. fed. com. Interagy. Com. on Nutrition Edn., 1970-71; now tech. rep. to AID; chmn. Crusade for Nutrition Edn., Washington, 1970—; food cons. internat. tng. Dept. Agr., 1973; cons., participant U.S. Senatorial Nat. Nutrition Policy Conf., 1974. Fellow Am. Pub. Health Assn.; mem. Am. Dietetic Assn., Bus. and Profl. Women's Clubs (cons. 1970—), Am. Home Econs. Assn. (rep. and treas. Joint Congl. Com.), Am. Assn. U. Women, Food Service Execs. Assn., Inst. Food Technologists, Soc. for Nutrition Edn., Soc. for Nutrition Today (charter). Author: (with Virginia McMasters) Community Emergency Feeding, 1972; (with Stanton and Hatfield) Help! My Child Won't Eat Right, 1973. Contbr. articles to profl. jours. Home: 7816 Birnam Wood Dr McLean VA 22101

DEAN, MARIAN HAZEL THOMSON (MRS. JOSEPH J. DEAN), occupational therapist; b. Ferndale, Mich., May 21, 1931; d. Roderick Fraser and Anne Grace (Cooper) Thomson; student U. Mich., 1949-51; B.S., Eastern Mich. U., 1953; m. Joseph J. Dean, Sept. 29, 1956; children—Jay Fraser, Ellen Louise, Richard Arthur. Staff therapist Detroit Orthopaedic Clinic, 1953-56; sr. staff therapist Ga. Retardation Center, Atlanta, 1970-72; dir. devel. program for multihandicapped child United Cerebral Palsy, Atlanta, 1973; programs dir. United Cerebral Palsy Ind., Indpls., 1973—. Den mother Atlanta area Boy Scouts Am., 1972-73; pres. Fontainbleau Swim and Diving Team Booster Club, 1973. Mem. Gamma Phi Beta. Home: 677 Holliday Lane Indianapolis IN 46260 Office: 445 N Pennsylvania Av Indianapolis IN 46204

DEAN, PATRICIA KAY, broadcasting exec.; b. Chgo., Oct. 3, 1946; d. William Henry and Muriel Josephine (Fleser) Dean; B.S., Ia. State U., 1968. News reporter Paddock Publs., Arlington Heights, Ill., 1967; TV reporter-writer WOI-TV, Ames, Ia., 1967-68; news writer/producer NBC, Chgo., 1968—, producer 10 P.M. news, 1973—. Mem. Chgo. Council Fgn. Relations, Women in Communications. Home: 300 N State St Apt 3033 Chicago IL 60610 Office: Merchandise Mart Chicago IL 60654

DEAN, RUTH ALDEN DEAN (MRS. EDWIN WENDELL DEAN), pub. co. exec.; b. Elburn, Ill., Mar. 8, 1909; d. Harry Adelbert and Eva Elizabeth (Riplits) Dean; B.S., Ia. State U., 1930, postgrad., 1931; m. Edwin Wendell Dean, June 9, 1931; children—Edwin Wendell, Dennis Richard. Tchr., Barrington (Ill.) High Sch., 1930-32; asso. pub., co-owner Seymour (Ia.) Herald, 1932-34; asso. pub., co-owner Marengo (Ill.) Republican News, 1934-46; asso. pub., co-owner Inglewood (Cal.) Daily News, 1946—; sec.-treas. Modern Housing, Inc., Culver City, Cal., 1969—; sec.-treas. Pen and Sword, Inc., Culver City, 1969—, Dean Newspapers, Inc., Culver City, 1970—. Chmn. women's service div. Centinela (Hosp.) Citizens Council, 1966-67; mem. adv. bd. Centinela Valley Community Hosp., 1973—; mem. City of Inglewood Library Bd., 1974. Bd. govs. Otis Art Inst. Los Angeles County, Cal. Named Inglewood Woman of Year, Am. Legion Post 188, 1962. Compiler booklets travel news stories. Home: 806 S Myrtle Av Inglewood CA 90301 Office: 4043 Irving Pl Culver City CA 90230

DEANE, LYDIA GERTRUDE GIBERSON (MRS. JACQUES GREGORY DEANE), physician, civic worker; b. Bath, N.B., Can.; d. Alfred and Annie (Nason) Giberson; student U. Alta., 1921-25; M.D., McGill U., 1928; postgrad. Neurol. Inst. N.Y.C., 1929; m. Jacques Gregory Deane, Mar. 4, 1933 (dec. Jan. 1964). Came to U.S., 1928, naturalized, 1951. Intern, Buffalo City Hosp., 1928-29, Nuerol. Inst. N.Y.C., 1929-30, Butler Hosp., Providence, 1930-31; resident Bradley Hosp., East Providence, R.I., 1931-32; practice medicine specializing in neurology and psychiatry, N.Y.C., with Met. Life Ins. Co. Med. Office, N.Y.C., 1932-61, v.p., 1958-61; 2d v.p., bd. dirs. Saddleback Community Hosp., Laguna Hills, Cal. Bd. dirs. Lung Assn. Orange County, Mental Health Assn. Orange County, Laguna Hills, Cal. Named Profl. Woman of Year N.Y. State Bus. and Profl. Women, 1960. Fellow Am. Psychiat. Assn., Am. Pub. Health Assn., Indsl. Med. Assn. Contbr. articles to profl. jours. Home: 908-N Ronda Sevilla Laguna Hills CA 92653

DEANE, MARJORIE SCHLESINGER (MRS. DISQUE D. DEANE), fashion merchandising exec.; b. N.Y.C., Apr. 18, 1923; d. Walter C.B. and Marjorie (Walsh) Schlesinger; grad. with distinction Tobe Coburn, 1943; m. Disque D. Deane, May 20, 1952; children—Marjorie Gregg, Kathryn Morgan, Disque D., Walter L. With Franklin Simon, N.Y.C., 1943-45; jr. editor Tobé Fashion Report, N.Y.C., 1945-47; accessories stylist Macy's, N.Y.C., 1947-56; with Tobé Assos., N.Y.C., 1956—, chmn. bd., 1963—. Mem. fashion com. Smithsonian Instn., 1973—. Adv. bd. Tobe Coburn Sch., 1971—, chmn. exec. com., 1973-74; pres. bd. trustees Lenox Sch., N.Y.C., 1968—; v.p. bd. trustees Kips Bay Boys Club, N.Y.C., 1971—. Mem. Fashion Group (pres. 1970-71). Home: 16 E 76th St New York City NY 10021 Office: 11 W 42d St New York City NY 10036

DEANE, NANCY HILTS (MRS. ROBERT HENRY DEANE), univ. adminstr.; b. Detroit, Dec. 27, 1939; d. Roy Ellis and Helen Amanda (Ludwig) Hilts; B.A. (Ford Motor Co. Fund scholar), Albion Coll., 1962; M.A. (House fellow), U. Wis., 1964; m. Robert Henry Deane, Aug. 1, 1964. Sr. English tchr. Portage (Wis.) Sr. High Sch., 1964-66; instr. English dept. U. N.H., Durham, 1966-69; asst. prof. English, dir. freshman English program, 1969-71, asst. dean Coll. Liberal Arts, lectr. English, 1972-74, dir. affirmative action, 1974—. Am. Assn. Univ. Profs., Nat. Council Tchrs. English, Coll. Composition and Communication, Mortar Board, Phi Beta Kappa. Author: Teaching with a Purpose: Instructor's Guide and Resource Book, 1971; Teaching with a Purpose, 1972; also instrs. rhetorical guide for Voices of Revelation, 1970. Home: Box 15 Nottingham NH 03290 Office: Affirmative Action U NH Durham NH 03824

DEARMIN, JENNIE TARASCOU (MRS. GEORGE GARDNER DEARMIN, JR.), educator; b. Upland, Cal., Feb. 23, 1924; d. John B. and Trini (Gallardo) Tarascou; B.A., U. Cal. at Santa Barbara, 1946; M.A., Stanford, 1957; m. George Gardner Dearmin, Jr., Aug. 31, 1947. Tchr., Fontana (Cal.) Elementary Schs., 1946-50; tchr. Santa Barbara city schs., 1950-60, asst. prin., 1965-66; project dir. compensatory edn. 1966—; acting asst. prof., supr. tchr. edn. U. Cal. at Santa Barbara, Goleta, 1960-65; Spanish cons. Cal. Dept. Edn., 1962-65. Mem. N.E.A., Cal. Tchrs. Assn., Nat. Congress Parents and Tchrs. (unit welfare chmn.), Cal. Assn. Supervision and Curriculum Devel., Modern Lang. Assn. So. Cal. (bd. mem. 1961, 65), Am. Assn.

U. Women, Cal. Assn. Women Deans and Vice Prins. (mem. bd. 1965-66), Assn. Cal. Adminstrs. Compensatory Edn., Phi Sigma Alpha, Delta Kappa Gamma (sec. 1958-60, pres. 1968-70 treas. 1960-62), Chi Omega (pres. alumnae chpt. 1959, financial adviser 1959-66, personnel ad·ser 1966—, pres. corp. bd. 1972—). Club: City Teachers (treas. 1956). Author: Japan, Home of the Sun, 1963; The Smiling Dragon, 1963; Peru, Land of Treasure, 1965. Home: 1030 Arbolado Rd Santa Barbara CA 93103 Office: 720 Santa Barbara St Santa Barbara CA 93101

DEARNLEY, MARION FRANCES, coll. adminstr.; b. N.Y.C., Sept. 1, 1938; d. George Butler and Marion (Bloom) Dearnley; B.A., U. Rochester, 1960, M.Ed., 1965. Dist. adviser Rochester-Genesee (N.Y.) Girl Scout Council, 1960-62; asst. dir. student activities U. Rochester (N.Y.), 1962-63, asso. dir. student life, 1963-64, dir. student activities, 1964-65; asst. to the dean of women State U. N.Y. at Potsdam, 1965-66, dir. housing, 1966—. Bd. dirs. 1000 Islands Girl Scout Council, 1973-74, mem. selections com. 1970—. Recipient Innovative Teaching and Counseling award State U. N.Y. Faculty Senate, 1972. Mem. Nat. Assn. Women Deans, Adminstrs. and Counselors, Am. Personnel and Guidance Assn., Am. Coll. Personnel Assn., Assn. Coll. Unions. Home: Box 423 Potsdam NY 13676

DEATHERAGE, MARTHA MARTIN, musician, educator; b. Parsons, Kan.; d. Maxwell Metier and Helen Louise (Ott) Martin; student Stephens Coll., 1951; B.Mus. with honors, U. Tex., 1952, Mus.M., 1953; m. Bruce H. Deatherage, July 1953 (div. Nov. 1972); children—Alison Ann, Laura Ellen. Soprano soloist St. Louis Symphony, St. Louis Philharmonic, St. Louis Municipal Opera; soloist Rockefeller Meml. Chapel, U. Chgo., 1958; soloist numerous oratorio and symphonic concerts in Midwest, 1954-61; concertized throughout Midwest, 1956-61; various radio and TV appearances, Los Angeles, 1959-61; instr. voice U. Tex., Austin, 1961-67, asso. prof., 1967—. Recipient Nat. Young Artist award Nat. Fedn. Music Clubs, 1957. Mem. Nat. Assn. Tchrs. Singing (regional lt. gov. 1973), Sigma Alpha Iota, Pi Kappa Lambda. Office: Music Dept U Tex Austin TX 78705

DEATON, BERTHA LILLIAN, ret. chemist; b. Pocahontas, Va.; d. John William and Sarah Frances (Jones) Deaton; student Longwood Coll., 1910-11; diploma, normal sch. Concord Coll., 1914; student U. Va., 1920, Columbia U., 1920. Tchr., prin. elementary sch., Boissevain, Va., 1911-12; prin. elementary sch, Marytown, W.Va., 1914-15; tchr. consolidated schs., Gary, W.Va., 1916-21; chemist Pocahontas Fuel Co., 1921-45; partner Mademoiselle Shop, Bluefield, W.Va., 1947-58, owner, 1958-60. Mem. D.A.R., Daus. of Colonial Wars, United Daus. Confederacy. Methodist. Home: 501 Albemarle St Bluefield WV 24701

DEAVER, JEANNETTE, social worker; b. Macon, Ga., Jan. 9, 1919; d. Bascom Sine and Emily (Cook) Deaver; B.A., Wesleyan Coll., Macon, 1938; postgrad. Mills Coll., 1938-39, Boston U., 1946-47; M.S.W., Wayne State U., 1949. Asst. girls dir. Sunny Hills, San Anselmo, Cal., 1939-41; field dir. Girl Scouts U.S.A., Waterbury, Conn., 1941-43, dir. program and tng., Boston, 1943-47, exec. dir., South Oakland County, Mich., 1950-56, exec. dir., Oakland, Cal., 1956-60, mem. nat. field staff, Region XII, 1960-63, dir. field service San Francisco Bay Area, 1963-68; psychiat. social worker alcoholism and drug abuse program Mendocino State Hosp., Talmage, Cal., 1968-72; social worker therapist Mendocino County Mental Health Services, 1972—; group worker Detroit Orthopaedic Clinic, 1947, Merrill-Palmer Inst., Detroit, 1948-50; field work supr. Wayne State U. Sch. Social Work, Detroit, 1949-56, U. Cal. Sch. Social Welfare, 1958; part-time instr. Wayne State U. Sch. Edn., 1950. Chmn. membership policy com. United Community Services, Detroit, 1955-56; div. chmn. United Bay Area Crusade, Oakland, 1956-57; chmn. youth sect. Mental Health Conf. No. Cal., 1957-59; mem. steering com. for formation dist. community councils Oakland Area Council Social Planning, 1957-60, mem. program policy com., 1963—, bd. dirs., chmn. group work and recreation services com., Alameda County, 1965-67. Mem. Nat. Assn. Girl Scouts Exec. (New Eng. pres. 1945-47), Am. Assn. Group Workers (Detroit pres. 1952-55), Assn. Girl Scout Profl. Workers (membership chmn., mem. bd. sect. 12 1958-63, nat. bd. dirs. 1961-64, publs. editor 1961-64), Acad. Certified Social Workers, Am. Camping Assn., Nat. Conf. Social Work, Cal. Health and Welfare Assn., Nat. Assn. Social Workers, Mills Coll. Alumnae Assn., Wayne State U. Sch. Social Work Alumni Assn. Club: Altrusa. Home: PO Box 1221 Fort Bragg CA 95437 Office: Mendocino County Mental Health Services 960-A Bush St Ukiah CA 95482

DEBARROS, THERESA SHAMES, ophthalmologist; b. San Francisco, Apr. 10, 1941; d. Paul and Lillian (Creisler) Shames; A.B., Mills Coll., 1962; postgrad. Sorbonne U. Paris, 1960-61; M.D., U. Chgo., 1967; m. Rene de Barros, July 11, 1964; children—Regis, Maissa, Colette and Nadine (twins). Intern Michael Reese Hosp., Chgo., 1967-68; resident U. Chgo. Hosps., 1968-71; ophthalmologist Blue Island (Ill.) Med. Center, 1971—; mem. staff St. Francis Hosp., Blue Island. USPHS trainee, 1968-71. Home: 823 Hutchison St Flossmoor IL 60422 Office: 13000 S Maple Av Blue Island IL 60406

DE BLOIS, ELIZABETH, physician; b. Ipswich, Mass.; d. George Lewis and Mary (Brooks) De Blois; A.B., Vassar Coll., 1925; postgrad. Columbia Coll. Phys. and Surg., 1925-26; M.D., Tufts U., 1930. Intern, New Eng. Hosp. for Women and Children, Roxbury, Mass., 1930-31; practice medicine, specializing in ear, nose and throat, Boston, 1932—; hon. asst. surgeon Mass. Eye and Ear Infirmary, Boston, 1971—; med. staff Hahnemann Hosp., 1969—; asso. staff Faulkner Hosp., Jamaica Plain, Mass., Benjamin Stickney Cable Meml. Hosp., Ipswich, Mass.; clin. instr. otolaryngology Tufts U. Med. Sch., 1959-65. Mem. Tufts U. Med. Alumni Council, 1952-60, Tufts U. Alumni Council, 1957-60. Fellow Am. Acad. Otolaryngology; mem. A.M.A., New Eng. Otolaryn. Soc., Mass., Suffolk Dist. med. socs., Nat. Soc. Colonial Dames. Episcopalian. Clubs: Chilton, College. Home: 62 Chestnut St Boston MA 02108 Office: 412 Beacon St Boston MA 92115

DEBOER, BARBARA JEAN GREGORY (MRS. EUGENE CALVIN DEBOER), pub. relations exec.; b. Sandborn, Ind., Mar. 23, 1924; d. John Lewis and Ella Christina (Hole) G.; student Purdue U., 1942-44; Asso. Sci., Vincennes U., 1954; postgrad. U. Evansville, 1972-73; m. Eugene Calvin DeBoer, Jan. 23, 1944; children—Karen (Mrs. Richard L. Martin), John David, Steven Eugene. Greetings Lady, Family Services, Inc., Vincennes, 1955-63; asst. to v.p. I & S Motor Express, Vincennes, 1962-63; tchr. English, Central Catholic High Sch., and St. Rose Acad., Vincennes, 1963-66; dir. news bur., dir. pub. relations Vincennes U., 1967—. Sec., Community Council, Vincennes, 1948-50; leader Girl Scouts Am., Vincennes, 1952-62; 4-H leader, Vincennes, 1954-64. Mem. Ind. Coll. Pub. Relations Assn., Vincennes U. Alumni Assn. (mem. exec. com. 1952—), Alpha Xi Delta, Psi Iota Xi. Mem. Christian Ch. (sec. ofcl. bd. 1971-73). Mem. Order Eastern Star. Club: Vincennes (Ind.) Fortnightly. Home: 1215 Oak St Vincennes IN 47591

DEBOER, RUTH MAE, farmer; b. Chicago Heights, Ill., June 4, 1942; d. Simon and Alice (Oostman) DeBoer; A.B., Hope Coll., 1964; M.A., Bowling Green State U., 1965; postgrad. U. Denver, 1968, Programming Inst. Denver, 1969-70. Grad. asst. speech Bowling Green (O.) State U., 1964-65; instr. speech communication U. No. Colo., Greeley, 1965-72; vis. instr. speech Hiram Scott Coll., Scottsbluff, Neb., 1967; farmer De Boer Farms, Chicago Heights, Ill., 1973—; with U.S. Post Office, 1974—; customer relations rep. Rosalee Lincoln Corp., 1974—. Theatre apprentice Huron Playhouse (O.), 1965; dir. Readers Theatre Troupe, U. No. Colo., 1967-72; substitute tchr. Illiana Christian, 1973. Recipient 4-H award Danforth Found. Mem. Am. Theatre Assn., Speech Communication Assn., Interpretation Theatre Alliance (Colo. rep. 1967-72), Central States Speech Assn., Pi Epsilon Delta, Pi Kappa Delta, Alpha Gamma Phi. Democrat. Christian Reformed. Address: Rural Route 2 Box 391 Chicago Heights IL 60411

DE BORHEGYI, SUZANNE SIMS (MRS. STEPHAN FRANCIS DE BORHEGYI), mus. ofcl., author; b. Pitts.; d. Clarence E. and Corinne (Landgraf) Sims; B.A., Ohio State U., 1948; postgrad. U. Ariz., San Carlos U. of Guatemala; M.S., U. Wis. at Milw., 1973; m. Stephen Francis de Borhegyi, July 5, 1949; children—Ilona Marie, Stephan Ernest, Carl Robert, Christopher Francis. Archaeol. and hist. research, 1949; tchr. world history and anthropology Univ. Sch. Milw., 1966-73; coordinator continuing edn. Alverno Coll., 1973; dir. Mus. of Albuquerque, 1974—. Recipient hon. mention Clara Ingram Judson Meml. award, 1962; Ohioana book award, 1962. Mem. Soc. Midland Authors. Author: Ships, Shoals and Amphoras, 1961; Museums: a Book to Begin On, 1962; The Secret of the Sacred Lake, 1967. Home: 300 Dorado Pl SE Apt K005 Albuquerque NM 87123

DE BRULER, OLIVE CLEO, media specialist; b. nr. Jasper, Ind.; d. Edgar Ambrose and Vinnie Lemmon (Alexander) De Bruler; A.B., Ind. U., 1935; B.S. in L.S., U. Ill., 1944, postgrad., 1958-62; M.A. in L.S., U. Chgo., 1954. Chmn. libraries and audiovisual service Joliet (Ill.) Twp. High Sch. and Joliet Jr. Coll., 1943-58; instr. library sci. U. Ill., Urbana, 1958-62; supervising dir. Sch. Library Media Centers, D.C. Pub. Schs., 1962—. Mem. action com. D.C. Sch. Libraries, 1962-67; mem. Friends of Washington Ednl. TV Assn., 1972—, life mem. D.C. Congress Parents and Tchrs. Helen R. Messenger fellow, 1959-60. mem. A.L.A., N.E.A., Am., Internat. assns. sch. librarians, Assn. Ednl. and Curriculum Tech., Assn. Supervision and Curriculum Devel., Nat., D.C. (pres. 1972) council adminstrv. women in edn., Delta Kappa Gamma, Beta Phi Mu. Home: 4201 Massachusetts Av NW Washington DC 20016 Office: 801 7th St SW Washington DC 20024

DEBRUN, ELSA (NUALA), artist; b. Stockholm, Sweden, Oct. 11, 1896 (came to U.S. 1916, citizen by marriage 1917); d. Gustav and Charlotte (Boettcher) Dahn; student Anna Sandstrom Sch., Stockholm, 1916; m. Olav J. deBrun, June 9, 1917 (div. Aug. 1936); children—John B., Patricia (Mrs. Douglas Leigh) (dec.), Guy. One-man shows Carroll Carstairs Gallery, 1947, Kleeman, 1949, Passedoit, Feingarten Galleries, 1961, Seattle Art Mus., 1957, Lyman Allen Mus., 1957, Conn. Coll., 1957, U. Ore., 1958, Pacem In Terris Library, N.Y., 1967, Betty Parsons Gallery, N.Y.C., 1970, 71; exhibited in group shows at Whitney Mus., Am. Acad. Arts and Letters, Am. Fedn. Arts, Bklyn. Mus., Union Theol. Sem., Rose Fried, N.Y. World's Fair, Smithsonian Instn., Soc. Advancement Sci., Dallas, 1968-69, Iconography in Art-House of El Dieff, N.Y.C., 1970, Organic Vision exbhn. Hobart and William Smith Colls., 1972, Copenhagen, Denmark, 1973, others; represented in permanent collections U. Tex., Carnegie Endowment for Peace Bldg., N.Y., Glenstol Benedictine Abbey, Limerick Ireland, Carnegie Hall, N.Y.C., Kierkegaard Library, St. Olaf Coll., Northfield, Minn. Active A.R.C. Mem. James Joyce Soc. Democrat. Address: 161 E 81st St New York City NY 10028

DEBUSK, EDITH M., lawyer; b. Waco, Tex., April 12, 1912; d. Otto Clifton and Margaret (Hatcher) Mann; LL.B., Dallas Sch. Law, 1941; Certificate, So. Meth. U. Sch. Law, 1941; m. Manuel C. DeBusk, June 13, 1941. Atty., Regional Atty.'s Office, O.P.A., Dallas, 1942; asso. atty. Office of Karl F. Steinmann, Balt., 1945-46, partner DeBusk & DeBusk, 1946—. Vice pres. Killeen Savs. & Loan Assn., The Teeling Mortgage Co., Inc.; dir. DeBusk Corp., Lincoln Housing Corp., Texas Mortgage Liquidation Corp.; officer East Town Osteo. Hosp. Corp. Former mem. Gov.'s Com. on Aging; dir. Dallas Citizens Commn. on Action for Aging, Inc., del. to White House Conf. Children and Youth 1960, Conf. on Aging, 1961; former dir. Dallas United Cerebral Palsy Assn., Tex. Soc. Aging, Dallas County Community Action Com., Inc., Crossroads Community Center; mem. adv. council Sr. Citizens Found., Inc.; former mem. div. aging Council of Social Agys., Citizen's Traffic Commn. Former sec., legal adviser Tex. Fedn. Bus. and Profl. Women's Clubs. Bd. visitors Freedoms Found. at Valley Forge. Named Woman of Month, Dallas Mag., 1948; Woman of Week, Balt., 1945; recipient George Washington honor medal Freedoms Found. Fellow Tex. Bar Found.; mem. State Bar Tex., Am. (vice chmn. com. real estate financing 1974—), Dallas bar assns., Women's C. of C., Dallas Council on World Affairs, Women's Council of Dallas County, Bus. and Profl. Women's Club Dallas (past pres.), Kappa Beta Pi (past dean province IV). Presbyn. Clubs: Altrusa (past pres. Dallas; pres. internat. 1963-65). Home: 7365 Elmridge Dr Dallas TX 75240 Office: First Nat Bank Bldg Dallas TX 75202

DE CAMP, CATHERINE CROOK (MRS. LYON SPRAGUE DE CAMP), writer; b. N.Y.C., Nov. 6, 1907; d. Samuel and Mary Eliza (Beekman) Crook; A.B. magna cum laude, Barnard Coll., 1933; postgrad. Columbia, 1936, 38-39, Temple U., 1948-49; m. Lyon Sprague de Camp, Aug. 12, 1939; children—Lyman Sprague, Gerard Beekman. Tchr. English and history Oxford Sch., Hartford, Conn., 1934-35, Laurel Sch., Shaker Heights, O., 1935-37, Calhoun Sch., N.Y.C., 1937-39; instr. Temple U., Phila., 1949-50; free-lance writer, 1950—. Fellow, Fellows in Am. Studies; mem. Cum Laude Soc., Authors League Am., Acad. Natural Scis., Hist. Soc. Pa., U. Pa. University Museum, Phi Beta Kappa. Episcopalian. Club: Barnard (Phila.) (pres. 1956-59). Author (with L. Sprague de Camp) Ancient Ruins and Archaeology (retitled Citadels of Mystery), 1964, Spirits, Stars and Spells, 1966; The Story of Science in America, 1967; The Day of the Dinosaur, 1968, Darwin and His Great Discovery, 1972, 3,000 Years of Fantasy and Science Fiction, 1972; The Money Tree, 1972; Tales Beyond Time, 1973; Teach Your Child To Manage Money, 1974. Address: Villanova PA 19085

DECAMP, ROSEMARY, actress; m. John A. Shidler; 4 daus. Motion pictures include Cheers for Miss Bishop, Hold Back the Dawn, Jungle Book, Yankee Doodle Dandy, Eyes in the Night, Pride of the Marines, Look for the Silver Lining, Story of Seabiscuit, Big Hangover, Scandal Sheet, On Moonlight Bay, Treasure of Lost Canyon, By the Light of the Silvery Moon, Main Street to Broadway, The Life of Riley, So This Is Love, Many Rivers To Cross, Strategic Air Command; appeared on TV in Robert Cummings Show, That Girl, Partridge Family. Guest columnist Los Angeles Daily Jour.; copper enamelist. Mem. Screen Actors' Guild (bd. dirs. 12 years, v.p. 3 terms). Author: (juvenile) Here Duke. Address: care Lew Sherrell Chan Gross Agy Ltd 7060 Hollywood Blvd Los Angeles CA 90028*

DE CESARE, RUTH, educator; b. N.Y.C., July 2, 1923; d. Milton and Ida (Rosenblum) Konigsberg; A.B. magna cum laude, Hunter Coll. City U. N.Y., 1943; M.S., Queens Coll. City U. N.Y., 1960; Ph.D., N.Y. U. Sch. Edn., 1972; m. Sam J. De Cesare, Apr. 1943 (div. Apr. 1969); children—Nina, Marc. Tchr. music Long Beach (L.I.) Pub. Schs., 1943; broadcaster, writer radio sta WPDQ, Jacksonville, 1944-45; instr. piano Jacksonville (Fla.) Coll. Music, 1944-45, Bklyn. Music Sch., Turtle Bay Music Sch., N.Y.C., 1947-48, Music Sch. Settlement, N.Y.C., 1948-50; pvt. studio piano, group piano, theory, 1951-60; children's editor Listen mag., N.Y.C., 1959-60; record editor Bowmar Records, Glendale, Cal., 1959-62; tchr. music, Levittown, N.Y., 1962-65, State U. N.Y. at Buffalo, summer 1963, Adelphi U., 1964-65; asso. prof. music Ind. U. Pa., 1969—; dir. workshops N.Y.C. Music Tchrs. Assn., N.Y., Pa., Conn. music educators assns., 1959—. Cravath fellow Juilliard Sch. Music, 1942. Mem. Music Educators Nat. Conf., Pa. Music Educators Assn., Phi Beta Kappa. Composer collections folksongs French, German, Italian, Spanish, Russian; also choral arrangements, piano pieces, children's songs. Contbr. articles to profl. jours. Home: 545 Grandview Av Indiana PA 15701

DE CHABON, ADA LEIBOVICH (MRS. IRWIN DE CHABON), physician; b. Buenos Aires, Argentina; d. Aser David and Rosario (Garcia) Leibovich; B.A., Liceo de Senoritas No. 3, 1950; M.D., U. Buenos Aires, 1956; m. Irwin de Chabon, Dec. 6, 1958; children—Brenda, Arthur David. Intern, Grasslands Hosp., Valhalla, N.Y., 1957-58; resident Beth-El Hosp., Bklyn., Flower-Fifth Av. Hosp., N.Y.C., 1958-61; instr. pathology N.Y. Med. Coll.-Flower-Fifth Av. Hosps., 1961-64, asst. prof. pathology, 1964-70, asso. pathologist, 1964-70; asst. clin. prof. pathology dept. Coll. Phys. and Surgs. Columbia, 1971—; dir. labs. Knickerbocker Hosp., N.Y.C., 1970-73; cons. Dept. Health, N.Y.C., 1972-73; asso. attending pathologist, asso. dir. dept. pathology (anatomic pathology) Beth Israel Med. Center, N.Y.C., 1973—. Diplomate Am. Bd. Pathology. Fellow Am. Soc. Clin. Pathology; mem. N.Y. Acad. Medicine, Pathologists Club N.Y., Coll. Am. Pathologists, Assn. Am. Med. Colls. Research in lymph node reactivity in certain disease entities breast cancer, intrauterine devices. Office: Dept Pathology Beth Israel Med Center 10 Nathan D Perlman Pl New York City NY 10003

DE CHAMPLAIN, PATRICIA ANN, real estate broker, educator; b. Sacramento, May 1, 1930; d. Frederic Edwin and Gladyce Cathy (Wilson) de Champlain; B.A. with honors in French, U. Cal. at Berkeley, 1951, postgrad., 1966; postgrad. Universite de Paris, 1951-53; M.A., Middlebury Coll., 1953. Fgn. lang. specialist Martinez (Cal.) Unified Sch. Dist., 1963-66, Adult Sch., Berkeley (Cal.) Unified Sch. dist., 1965—; pres. de Champlain Translators and Interpreters, Berkeley and Piedmont, Cal., 1953-63; pres., broker-owner Crocker Highlands Real Estate and Investment Co., Piedmont, 1969—. Instr. fgn. langs. A.R.C., Berkeley, 1965—. Fulbright scholar, 1951. Mem. Oakland Real Estate Bd., Nat. Assn. Real Estate Bds., D.A.R., Pi Delta Phi, Phi Beta Kappa. Clubs: Art Collectors' Guild, Sculpture Collectors' Guild (N.Y.C.). Address: 622 Highlands Av Piedmont CA 94611

DECHARMS, DESIREE, librarian; b. Abington, Pa., Mar. 25, 1925; d. Richard and Carita (Pendleton) de Charms; Mus.B., Eastman Sch. Music, 1947; M.L.S., U. Chgo., 1954; Mus.M., U. Ill., 1972. Student asst. Sibley Music Library, Rochester, N.Y., 1944-47; tchr. music theory David Hochstein Meml. Sch. Music, 1946-47; tchr. classroom music lower sch. Locust Valley Friends Sch., L.I., N.Y., 1947-48, pre-profl. cataloger U. Pa., Phila., 1948-51; music librarian, audio-visual dir. Roosevelt U., 1951-55; reference asst. music and drama dept. Detroit Pub. Library, 1955-61; asst. music librarian U. Ill., Urbana, 1961-65; music and humanities librarian Oakland U., Rochester, Mich., 1965-67; music librarian, asst. prof. Kent (O.) State U. Music Library, 1967—. Mem. Am. Musicol. Soc., Music Library Assn., Mensa. Author: Songs in Collections: An Index, 1966. Home: 140 Ernest Dr Tallmadge OH 44278 Office: Music and Speech Bldg Kent State U Kent OH 44242

DECKER, ALMEDA ANN ALLEN, osteopathic physician; b. Wilson, Kan., July 2, 1925; d. Lloyd and Rose E. (Padlasek) Allen; R.N., West Suburban Hosp. Sch. Nursing, Oak Park, Ill., 1946; B.Biol. Scis., Loyola U., Chgo.; D.O., Chgo. Coll. Osteopathic Medicine, 1953; m. William James Decker, June 25, 1949; children—William James, Charles R., Robert A., Rosemarie. Intern Chgo. Osteopathic Hosp., 1953-54; mem. faculty Chgo. Osteopathic Coll. Medicine, 1954—; pvt. practice family medicine, Chgo., 1954—. Mem. Beverly Bus. and Profl. Women's Club (charter), Beverly Area Planning Assn., Delta Omega. Home: 10335 Longwood Av Chicago IL 60643 Office: 9858 S Vincennes Av Chicago IL 60643

DECKER, BEATRICE MADELINE SCHIRM (MRS. ROBERT A. DECKER), religious social service orgn. ofcl.; b. Pitts., June 14, 1919; d. John Charles and Beatrice (Levy) Schirm; grad. high sch.; m. Robert Arthur Decker, Apr. 28, 1945 (dec. July 1961); children—Beatrice (Mrs. Richard F. Vuocolo), Mary Louise, Roberta. Founder, Theo, Inc., orgn. to assist widows, widowers and their families, Pitts., 1962, pres., 1962—; dir. THEOS Found., Lakeview, Ore. Mem. Internat. Platform Assn. Co-author: After the Flowers Have Gone, 1973. Contbr. articles to religious publs. Address: 125 Veronica Dr Pittsburgh PA 15235

DECKER, HERMINE DUTHIE, writer, photographer; b. Pullman, Wash., Sept. 15, 1908; d. John Purvis and Idabelle (Gibson) Duthie; B.A., Wash. State Coll., 1930; M.Ed., U. Portland, 1952; postgrad. Reed Coll., 1953, U. Ore., 1953, 54, 57; m. A. Thomas Decker, Aug. 16, 1932 (div. 1950); children—Aletha Hermine, Tamara Maureen. Coll. instr., radio drama dir. and speech instr., 1928-33; faculty mem. Clark Coll., Vancouver, Wash., 1950-71; free-lance writer plays, 1930—; pres. Old Slocum House Theatre Company; radio series for children, 1945; short series KPOJ, 1948. Recipient Dramatists Alliance award, 1946; 2d prize Portland Civic Theatre, 1956; 1st prize Kanawaha Players; 1st prize for playwriting Sacramento State Coll., 1968; Northwest Writers Conf., 1968. Mem. Nat. Collegiate Players, Jr. Collegiate Players, Women in Communications, Pi Gamma Mu, Kappa Alpha Theta, Club: Soroptimist. Author: Stars Over Hollywood, 1951; (play) Esther Short Heroic Pioneer Mother, 1972; also articles in field. Home: 801 W 45th St Vancouver WA 98660

DECKER, MARY ELIZABETH NISBET (MRS. EDWARD ALBERT DECKER), educator; b. Portland, Ore., Mar. 17, 1928; d. Oliver Martin and Lois (Mangus) Nisbet; B.S., Northwestern U., 1950; M.A., Stanford U., 1961; m. Richard Adrian Duryea, 1950 (dec. 1958); 1 dau., Maria; m. 2d, Edward Albert Decker, Jan. 28, 1967. Began career as social worker City of Austin, Tex., 1950-51; dir. social service Brackenridge City Hosp., 1951-54; med. social worker County of Monterey, Cal., 1955-57; instr. San Jose City Coll., San Jose, 1961-62; dean students staff Stanford U., 1962-65; dean student Scripps Coll., Claremont, Cal., 1965-69; asst. vice chancellor student affairs U. Cal., San Diego, LaJolla, 1969—. Vice pres. United Way San Diego, 1974—. Bd. dirs. Vol. Bur. of San Diego, Inc., 1969—, pres. 1973-74. Mem. Nat. Assn. Student Personnel Adminstrs., Western Deans' Assn., Coll. Student Personnel Inst. Home: 1659 Torrey Pines Rd La Jolla CA 92037

DECOITE, ARLENE CLARICE, banker; b. Chicago Heights, Ill., Jan. 30, 1931; d. Owen Henry and Helen Mary (Otis) Boughton; student Fairleigh Dickinson U., 1962-63, Am. Inst. Banking, 1959-61,

64-69, Dale Carnegie, 1965, Dorothy Carnegie, 1965, Stonier Grad. Sch. Banking, Rutgers U., 1974; m. Manuel J. DeCoite, 1952 (div. 1959); children—Michael, Patricia, Ernest, Michele. Clk. typist Continental Ill. Nat. Bank & Trust Co., Chgo., 1948-49, Seattle First Nat. Bank, 1949-52, First Nat. Bank, Juneau, Alaska, 1952; clk. Bank of Am., Oakland, Cal., 1953; comml. loans and data processing supr. People's Trust, Hackensack, N.J., 1958-64; v.p., office mgr. Edgewater Nat. Bank (N.J.), 1965—. Mem. Am. Inst. Banking (women's chmn. Bergen County 1971-72), Bergen County Bankers Assn. (com. chmn.). Club: Soroptimist. Home: 12 Columbia Terrace Edgewater NJ 07020 Office: Edgewater Nat Bank 28 Dempsey Av Edgewater NJ 07020

DE CORDOVA, DIANE JANE, librarian; b. N.Y.C., Feb. 15, 1934; d. Douglas and Runa (Patterson) Stevens; B.S., Trenton State Coll., 1956; M.L.S., Rutgers U., 1969; M.A. in Edn., Seton Hall U., 1974; m. Donald W. de Cordova, June 24, 1956 (div. July 1971). Tchr.-librarian Arlington (Va.) Bd. Edn., 1956-58; media specialist elementary schs. libraries River Edge (N.J.) Bd. Edn., 1958—. Lectr.-instr. children's lit. Alphonsus Coll., Woodcliff Lake, N.J., 1969-72; field service cons. N.J. Dept. Edn., 1969—; cons. New Books Preview, Baker & Taylor Co., 1972—. Active Girl Scouts U.S.A. Mem. A.L.A., Am. Assn. Sch. Librarians (mem. com. on instrnl. media 1971—), N.J. Sch. Media Assn. (state chmn. recruitment 1968-69, state chmn. hospitality 1972-73, state chmn. county liaison 1973-74), Bergen County Sch. Libraries Assn. (pres. 1966-68), River Edge Tchrs. Assn. (pres. 1964-66). Episcopalian (lay reader 1973—). Home: 8 Patton Place Dumont NJ 07628 Office: 410 Bogert Rd River Edge NJ 07661

DE CORDOVA, FRANCES MONNA, educator; b. Gordonville, Tex., June 14, 1919; d. Richard and Artie B. (Franklin) Myers; B.A., Tex. Woman's U., 1941, M.L.S., 1951; m. Jack M. deCordova, Aug. 16, 1941; 1 son, Richard M. Tchr. Gordonville pub. schs., 1939-41; librarian Waco (Tex.) Pub. Library, 1942-46; librarian demonstration sch. Tex. Woman's U., Denton, 1946-59, prof. library sci., 1959—; dir. Higher Edn. Act Inst. Programs Academically Gifted Child, Denton, 1970, Nat. Def. Edn. Act Insts., Denton, summer 1965, 66; lectr. in field. Mem. A.L.A., Tex. Library Assn. (exec. bd. 1966-69, rep. at large), Tex. Assn. Sch. Librarians, Am. Assn. Library Schs., Tex. Assn. Coll. Tchrs., Delta Kappa Gamma (corr. sec. 1973-74). Contbr. to Ency. Library and Information Sci., 1970. Home: 1214 Emerson St Denton TX 76201

DECOSTER, BARBARA LOU GRAY (MRS. DON THEODORE DECOSTER), librarian; b. Salt Lake City, Dec. 22, 1932; d. Frederic Knowles and Lucille (Campbell) Gray; student Mass. Inst. Tech., 1950-51, W.Tex. State U., 1951-53, U. Tex., 1957-58, Ariz. State U., 1959-61; B.A., U. Wash., 1965, M.L.S., 1967; m. Don Theodore DeCoster, Aug. 29, 1952; children—Don Theodore, Carol Ann (Mrs. John Allen), Catherine Alene. Clk., C.E., U.S. Army, 1951-52, U.S. Bur. Mines, 1953-54, Bur. Internal Revenue Service, 1959; enumerator Bur. Census, 1960; cons. audio-visual dept. U. Wash., 1967, teaching asst., 1966-67; tech. processes librarian Bellevue (Wash.) Community Coll., 1967—. Cons. Research-Advt. Agy., 1970. Mem. Am., Pacific N.W., Wash. library assns., D.A.R., Bellevue Community Coll. Profl. Assn. (mem. exec. bd. 1970-73), Beta Phi Mu. Presbyn. Club: University Wash. Faculty Wives (Seattle). Home: 6343 NE 156th St Bothell WA 98011 Office: 3000 145th Pl SE Bellevue WA 98007

DECOURSEY, EILEEN MARIE, pharm. co. exec.; b. N.J., Sept. 20, 1932; d. Andrew A. and Mildred H. (Shields) DeCoursey; B.S. in Speech and Edn., N.J. State Coll., 1954. Personnel supr. Warner-Lambert, 1956-59; account exec. Johnson & Higgins, 1960-64; supr. benefits Time Inc., N.Y.C., 1964-66; mgr. benefits Bristol Myers Co., N.Y.C., 1966-71; v.p. and exec. asst. to pres. Squibb Corp., 1971—. Mem. Am. Compensation Assn., Am. Pension Conf., Am. Sec. Personnel Adminstrs. (dir., exec. com.). Office: 40 W 57th St New York City NY 10019

DECOURSEY, JEAN, assn. exec.; b. Springfield, Tenn.; d. Archie Ernest and Lillie (Christian) DeCoursey; B.S., Carson Newman Coll., 1953; postgrad. U. Tenn., 1963. Tchr., Columbia High Sch., Lake City, Fla., 1953-55; asst. dir. women and girls program YMCA, Covington, Ky., 1955-59; dir. women and girls program YMCA, Longview, Tex., 1959-60, Cleveland, Tenn., 1960-64; program dir. YMCA, Louisville, 1964-68; exec. dir. Clark County Family Br. YMCA, Jeffersonville, Ind., 1968—. Mem. Assn. Profl. Dirs. (regional sec. 1969). Baptist. Club: Pilot (dist. chmn. 1970, corr. sec. 1971, dir. 1971, 1st v.p. 1972, pres. 1973). Home: 816 Wellington Ct Clarksville IN 47130 Office: Marlow At Tennyson PO Box 715 Jeffersonville IN 47130

DECOUX, JANET, sculptor; b. Niles, Mich.; ed. Carnegie Inst., N.Y. Sch. Indsl. Design, R.I. Sch. Design. Exhibited in one-man shows Carnegie Inst., Pitts. Arts and Crafts Center; works represented in permanent collections Coll. New Rochelle, St. Mary's Ch., Manhasset, N.Y., Sacred Heart Sch., Pitts., Liturgical Art Soc., St. Vincent's Coll., Latrobe, Pa., St. Scholastica, Aspinwall, Pa., Crucixion Group, Lafayette, N.J., numerous others. Recipient Widener Gold medal, Lindsay Meml. Prize, others. Guggenheim fellow. Mem. N.A.D., Nat. Sculpture Soc., Pitts. Asso. Artists. Address: Gibsonia PA 15044

DECTER, MIDGE ROSENTHAL (MRS. NORMAN PODHORETZ), author, editor; b. St. Paul, July 25, 1927; d. Harry and Rose (Calmenson) Rosenthal; student U. Minn., 1945-46, Jewish Theol. Sem., 1946-48; m. Moshe Decter (div.); m. 2d, Norman Podhoretz, Oct. 21, 1956; children—Rachel, Naomi, Ruth, John. Mem. staff Midstream Mag., Commentary Mag.; editor Hudson Inst., CBS Legacy Books; exec. editor Harper's Mag.; lit. editor Saturday Rev./World; freelance writer, critic, and social commentator gen. mags., 1954—. Author: The Liberated Woman and Other Americans, 1971; The New Chastity, 1972. Home: 924 West End Av New York City NY 10025 Office: 488 Madison Av New York City NY 10016

DEDE, BONNIE AILEEN, librarian; b. Racine, Wis., Mar. 21, 1942; d. Edward Charles and Gracebelle Roeber; B.A., U. Mich., 1963, M.A., 1966, A.M. in L.S., 1968; certificate U. Ill., 1970; m. Metin Dede, Sept. 24, 1966; 1 dau., Suzan Aylin. Bibliographer U. Mich. at Ann Arbor, 1968, asst. librarian, Slavic and East European div., 1968-70, asso. librarian, 1970-72, asso. librarian, head book purchasing and receiving sect., 1972-73, sr. asso. librarian rare books and spl. collections cataloging div., 1973—. U.S. Office Edn. Title II grantee, 1970. Mem. Am. Assn. Advancement Slavic Studies, Alpha Lambda Delta, Beta Phi Mu. Home: 957 Greenwood St Ann Arbor MI 48104 Office: Harlan Hatcher Grad Library U Mich Ann Arbor MI 48104

DEDIEMAR, DONNA JEAN, telephone co. exec.; b. Chula Vista, Cal., June 18, 1948; d. Jerry Lane and Takouhi Helen (Adzigian) DeDiemar; A.B. cum laude, U. So. Cal., 1970. Accounting office supr. Pacific Tel. & Tel. Co., San Francisco, 1970-71, accounting staff asst., 1971-73, regional staff asst., 1973—. Writer, Nat. Med. Enterprises, 1971-72. Pres. policy adv. com. Stanislaus County Family Planning, 1972-73; vol. Stanislaus County Legal Assistance, 1971-74. Mem. Common Cause, Women in Communications. Home: 205 S I St Madera CA 93637 Office: Bur Indian Affairs Tng Center 19500 Rd 28 1/2 Madera CA 93637

DEDOMENIC, LILLIAN KAY (MRS. DOM L. DEDOMENIC, JR.), ednl. adminstr.; b. Albuquerque, Sept. 14, 1944; d. Charles Howard and Naomi Pearl (Graham) Davis; Asso. Sci. in Journalism and Communications, Point Park Coll., 1964; m. Dom L. DeDomenic, Jr., Dec. 14, 1973. Paste-up and lay-out artist Gateway Press, Inc., Monroeville, Pa., 1964-65; mng. editor Radio-TV News, Monroeville, 1965-67; gen. reporter Progress, Penn Hills, Pa., 1967-68, women's editor, 1968-69; editor Green Tab, Penn Hill, 1969-70; asst. dir. pub. information Duquesne U., Pitts., 1970—. Mem. Women in Communications, Women's Press Assn. Pa., Duquesne U. Faculty Club (soc. sec. 1972-73, v.p. 1973-74), Beta Phi Gamma. Office: Public Information Office Administration Bldg Duquesne University Pittsburgh PA 15219

DEE, ELAINE EVANS (MRS. LEO J. DEE), curator; b. Cleve., Jan. 11, 1924; d. Charles Glenn and Grace Leona (Hillock) Evans; B.A., Oberlin Coll., 1945; M.A., Radcliffe Coll., 1951; m. Leo J. Dee, Nov. 30, 1962; 1 son, Jeffrey E. Asst. curator drawings and Oriental art Fogg Art Mus., Harvard U., 1945-51, 52-53; asst. curator drawings Cleve. Art Mus., 1951-52; asst. curator drawings and prints Pierpont Morgan Library, N.Y.C., 1961-68; curator drawings and prints Cooper-Hewitt Mus., N.Y.C., 1968—. Mem. Am. Fedn. Arts (nat. exhbns. com. 1968—), Print Council Am., Drawing Soc. (nat. com.). Author numerous exhbns. catalogues including Views of Florence and Tuscany by Giuseppe Zocchi, 1968; The Two Sicilies, 1970; Master Printmakers, 1970. Home: 38 Ridgewood Terrace Maplewood NJ 07040 Office: Cooper-Hewitt Mus 9 E 90th St New York City NY 10028

DEE, RUBY, actress; b. Cleve., Oct. 27; d. Marshall Edward and Emma (Benson) Wallace; B.A., Hunter Coll., 1945; m. Ossie Davis; 3 children. Apprentice Am. Negro Theatre, 1941-44; stage appearances include Jeb, 1946, Raisin in the Sun, 1959, Purlie Victorious, 1961; appeared off-Broadway in Boesman and Lena, 1970 motion pictures include The Jackie Robinson Story, Take a Giant Step, St. Louis Blues, Raisin in the Sun, Purile Victorious; also appeared in Wedding Band, stage and TV. Recipient (with husband) Frederick Douglass award N.Y. Urban League, 1970. Mem. N.A.A.C.P., CORE, Student Non-Violent Coordinating Com., So. Christian Leadership Conf. Address: 15 Cooly Pl Mount Vernon NY 10550

DEEN, EDITH ALDERMAN (MRS. EDGAR DEEN), author; b. Weatherford, Tex., Feb. 28, 1905; d. James Harris and Sara Provine (Scheuber) Alderman; student U. Tex., 1922-23, Tex. Christian U., 1923-24, Columbia, 1926; B.A., Tex. Woman's U., 1953, LL.D. (hon.), 1959, M.A., 1960; LL.D. (hon.), Tex. Christian U., 1972; m. France Ernest Guedry, Mar. 1, 1930, (dec. Oct. 1932); m. Frank Edgar Deen, Dec. 30, 1945 (dec. May 1967). Women's editor, daily columnist Fort Worth Press. 1925-54; radio, TV commentator, 1949-54. Mem. council City of Fort Worth, 1965-67. Bd. regents Tex. Woman's U., 1951-63. Recipient citation Nat. Conf. Christians and Jews, 1960; named Altrusa First Lady, Fort Worth, 1949. Mem. Tex. Inst. Letters, Authors League Am., Women in Communications (Nat. Headliner award 1963). Democrat. Mem. Christian Ch. (elder 1972—). Clubs: Woman's Ridglea, Colonial Country (Fort Worth). Author: All of the Women of the bible, 1955; Great Women of the Christian Faith, 1959; Family Living in the Bible, 1963; The Bible's Legacy for Womanhood, 1970; All of the Bible's Men of Hope, 1974. Address: 2420 Refugio St Fort Worth TX 76106

DEEN, FRANCES MAY MAHONEY, educator; b. St. Charles, Mich.; d. Stephen Phillip and Mary Fleming (Wright) Mahoney; Mus. B., Stetson U., 1925; M.A., Columbia U., 1940; m. George Deen, Dec. 26, 1940 (dec. 1959). Head music edn. dept. Stetson U., 1928-31; dir. choral music Edison Sr. High Sch., Miami, Fla., 1931-58, dean of girls, 1962-63, guidance counselor, 1963-71; acting supr. music Dade County, Fla., 1958-59; head fine arts dept. Miami-Dade Jr. Coll., 1960-62. Sec. recording for blind unit, Miami chpt. Zonta Internat., 1963-64; music chmn. Dade County Fedn. Women's Clubs, 1962-64; chmn. scholarship com. Miami Woman's Club, 1949-52, vice chmn. Am. citizenship dept. 1968-69, chmn. edn. dept., 1973-75. Mem. Coll., (sec.-treas. 1962-64), Fla. (pres. 1955-57) music educators assns., Music Educators Nat. Conf. (life), Fla. Vocal Assn. (pres. 1951-53), Miami Music Club (pres. 1970-73), Philharmonic Women's Guild, Fairchild Tropical Garden Assn., Nat. League Am. Pen Women, Fla. Fedn. Music Clubs (rec. sec. 1973-75), Zonta Internat. (pres. Miami 1972-73), Sigma Kappa, Phi Beta, Delta Kappa Gamma (chpt. pres. 1970-72). Club: Coral Gables Country. Home: 1011 Cotorro Av Coral Gables FL 33146

DEER, E. DOROTHY, occupational therapist; b. Pitts., Apr. 1, 1920; d. Lewis Hutchinson and Martha (Caughey) Deer; certificate in occupational therapy Richmond Profl. Inst., 1945; B.S., San Jose State Coll., 1964, M.S., 1966. Dir. music and recreation N.H. State Hosp., Concord, 1946-47; asst. to exec. dir. Am. Occupational Therapy Assn., N.Y.C., 1947-48; asst. dir. occupational therapy Eastern State Hosp., Williamsburg, Va., 1948-50; therapist VA Hosp., Vancouver, Wash., 1950-54; dir. occupational therapy U. Okla. Med. Center, Oklahoma City, 1954-57; dir. occupational therapy Central State Hosp., Norman, Okla., 1957-59; indsl. therapist Agnews State Hosp., San Jose, Cal., 1964-67; counselor Santa Clara County Welfare Dept., San Jose, 1967-68, Clay County Health Dept., Liberty, Mo., 1968-70; vocational rehab. counselor Kansas City (Kan.) Dist. Office, 1970-72; work evaluator Indsl. Rehab. Center, Merriam, Kan., 1972-74; supr. evaluation Jewish Vocational Services, Kansas City, Mo., 1974—. Cons. Juvenile Ct., Clay County, 1968-70, Clay County Rural Schs., 1968-70. Mem. exec. bd. Clay-Platte Health and Welfare Council, Clay County, 1968-71, Mental Health Services Corp., Clay County, 1968-72. Mem. Am. Assn. U. Women, Nat. Rehab. Assn., Am. (del. ho. of dels. 1955-58, sec. 1957-58), Kan. occupational therapy assns., Nat., Kan. assns. rehab. counselors, N.E. Kan. Assn. Rehab., Kan. Rehab. Assn. (membership sec. 1971-72). Home: 700 E 8th St Apt 208 Kansas City MO 64106 Office: 1516 Grand Av Kansas City MO 64108

DEERING, ELLEN LORAINE, univ. registrar; b. Orland Cal., Dec. 10, 1898; d. Clarence Ernest and Mary Elizabeth (Read) Deering; student Chico State Normal, 1915-18. Sec. and registrar Chico (Cal.) State Normal, 1918-26; asst. registrar Coll. of Pacific (name changed to U. of Pacific 1961), 1926-37, asso. registrar, 1937-46, registrar, 1948-69, organizer, dir. summer workshops in admissions and records, 1948-70. Recipient Order of Pacific award U. Pacific, 1969; commendation for community leadership Cal. Legislature, 1971. Mem. Pacific (charter mem. 1926, pres. 1940-41, hon. mem. 1969, historian 1973—), Am. (v.p. 1954-55, hon. mem. 1969) assns. collegiate registrars and admissions officers, Cal. Acad. Sci., League Women Voters, Nat. League Am. Pen Women (pres. No. Cal. 1952-54), Am. Acad. Polit. and Social Scis., Western Folklore Soc., Cal. Conf. Hist. Socs., Mortar Board, Mu Phi Epsilon (patroness), Delta Delta Delta, Delta Upsilon (patroness). Methodist. Editor career bull. Am. Assn. Coll. Registrars; collaborating editor career bull. Cal. Dept. Edn. Home: 208 W Knoles Way Stockton CA 04952

DEERSON, ADELE SHAPIRO, lawyer; b. Bklyn., July 14, 1924; d. Samuel and Marion (Pastreich) Shapiro; B.A., Hunter Coll., 1944; LL.B. magna cum laude, Bklyn. Law Sch., 1946, J.S.D. magna cum laude, 1949; m. Nathan Deerson, Sept. 8, 1946; children—Bruce, Jayne. Admitted to N.Y. bar, 1946; practiced in N.Y.C., 1949—; trial counsel Cosmopolitan Mut. Ins. Co., 1957—. Mem. faculty N.Y. Inst. Tech., 1967-70, asso. prof., 1970—, mem. faculty senate, 1969-72, pres. campus council, 1972—. Mem. Queens County Bar Assn., Queens County Women's Bar Assn., N.Y.-Bronx Retail Meat and Food Dealers Assn. Aux. (pres. 1950), N.Y. Family Ct. Lawyers Assn. (trustee), Philonomic Council, Delta Mu Delta, Upsilon Phi. Mem. B'nai B'rith (chpt. v.p. 1954-55). Home: 76-12 176th St New York City NY 11366 Office: 163-18 Jamaica Av New York City NY 11432

DEES, HELEN MARIE (MRS. JIMMY LOYE DEES), clothing co. exec.; b. Tellico Plains, Tenn., June 18, 1944; d. Billy Larnzy and Verna Lee (Graves) Nichols; grad. high sch.; m. Jimmy Loye Dees, Mar. 30, 1962. With Royals, Inc., Belle Glade, Fla., 1971—, buyer childrens wear, 1971—. Home: Belle Glade FL 33430 Office: 324 S W 16th St Belle Glade FL 33430

DEES, MARGARET NYHUS (MRS. DENZIL ELLIS DEES), librarian; b. Dupree, S.D., Mar. 5, 1917; d. Olaf A. and Rena (Johnson) Nyhus; B.S., U. Ill., 1939, M.A., 1950, M.S., 1957; m. Denzil Ellis Dees, May 23, 1941; children—Kristin Susanna (Mrs. Daugherty), Robert Laughlin. Tchr. pub. schs., Ill., 1939-44; communications officer WAVES, 1944-46; tchr. elementary sch., Redlands, Cal., 1948-49; supr. student tchrs. U. Ill., 1950-52; tchr. elementary sch., Miami Shores, Fla., 1952-53; librarian Champaign (Ill.) Sr. High Sch., 1957-58; dir. libraries Urbana (Ill.) Sch. Dist. 116, 1958—; tchr. Library Inst., N.E. La. State Coll., Monroe, La., summer 1969, 70. Cons. Ill. Supt. Pub. Instruction, 1965-66. Mem. Am., Ill. (pres. 1967-68) assns. sch. librarians, Nat., Ill., Urbana (pres. 1963-64) edn. assns., Am., Ill. (pres. 1973-74), library assns., Champaign County Assn. for Childhood Edn. (pres. 1964-65), Ill. Audio Visual Assn., Nat. Council Tchrs. English, Delta Kappa Gamma (chpt. pres. 1970-72), Kappa Delta Pi (treas. 1969—). Contbr. articles to profl. jours. Home: 2016 Boudreau Dr Urbana IL 61801 Office: 1201 S Vine St Urbana IL 61801

DEETZ, MARY JEANETTE TAGGART (MRS. S. WILLIAM DEETZ), realtor; b. Wooster, O., May 12, 1918; d. Frank and Ruth Isabelle (Davis) Taggart; B.S., Ohio State U., 1939; postgrad. West Valley Coll., Saratoga, Cal., 1968; m. S. William Deetz, Aug. 10, 1940; children—Robert William, Tom Richard, Gary Edward. Real estate saleslady Fred Duerr Realty, San Mate, Cal., 1953-64, real estate saleslady, broker, Saratoga, Cal., 1964-70; real estate broker asso. Burke Realty, Saratoga, Cal., 1970—. Precinct worker Republican party, 1968-72. Mem. Los Gatos-Saratoga Bd. Realtors, San Jose Real Estate Bd., Am. Assn. U. Women, Burke Realty Million Dollar Club, Sigma Kappa. Home: 12293 Saratoga Creek Dr Saratoga CA 95070 Office: 12300 S Saratoga/Sunnyvale Rd Saratoga CA 95070

DEEVEY, GEORGIANA BAXTER (MRS. EDWARD SMITH DEEVEY, JR.), zoologist, mus. curator; b. Branford, Conn., Feb. 24, 1914; d. Charles Newcomb and Iva Georgiana (Bishop) Baxter; A.B., Radcliffe Coll., 1934; Ph.D. in Zoology, Yale, 1939; m. Edward Smith Deevey, Jr., Dec. 24, 1938; children—Ruth (Mrs. Gerd Lehmann), Edward Brian, David Kevin. Research asst. Woods Hole (Mass.) Oceanographic Instn., 1945-47, Bingham Oceanographic Lab., Yale, New Haven, Conn., 1947-60; research asso., Yale, 1960-67; research asso. Bermuda Biol. Sta., St. George's West, Bermuda, 1967-71; curator Biol. Oceanography, Fla. State Mus., Gainesville, 1971—. NSF grantee, 1964-74. Mem. Marine Biol. Assn. U.K., Biol. Soc. Washington, Bermuda Biol. Sta. Research Inc. Contbr. articles to profl. jours. Home: 1702 S W 35th Place Gainesville FL 32608 Office: Florida State Museum University of Florida Gainesville FL 32601

DE FIGUEROA, DOLORES, mfg. co. exec.; b. Bklyn., May 21, 1937; d. Stephen and Elsie (Capone) deFigueroa; grad. high sch. Prodn. asst. Pan Am. Broadcasting Co., N.Y.C., 1957-59; adminstrv. asst. Art Found. Press, N.Y.C., 1959-60; sales and promotion mgr. Blaisdell Pub. Div., Random House, Inc., N.Y.C., 1960-63; exec. asst. All-State Properties, Inc., N.Y.C., 1963-64; prodn. asst. Dolphin Prodns., N.Y.C., 1964-65; corporate sec. Dynamic Classics, Ltd., N.Y.C., 1965—. Active Republican polit. campaigns. Home: 32 Gramercy Park S New York City NY 10003 Office: 307 Fifth Av New York City NY 10016

DEFLEUR, LOIS BEGITSKE (MRS. MELVIN L. DEFLEUR), educator; b. Aurora, Ill., June 25, 1936; d. Ralph E. and Isabel (Cornils) Begitske; A.B., Blackburn Coll., 1958; M.A., Ind. U., 1961; Ph.D., U. Ill., 1965; m. Melvin L. DeFleur, Dec. 5, 1961. Research asso. Cordoba (Argentina) Nat. U., 1962; asst. prof., then asso. prof. Transylvania Coll., Lexington, Ky., 1963-67; asst. prof. sociology Wash. State U. at Pullman, 1967-70, asso. prof., 1970—. Mem. Am., Pacific (v.p. 1973-74) sociol. assns., Soc. for Study Social Problems, Law and Soc. Assn., Internat. Inst. Sociology. Author: Delinquency in Argentina, 1970; (with M. DeFleur and W. D'Antonio) Sociology: Human Society, 1971, 73. Dep. editor Am. Sociol. Rev., 1971-74. Contbr. numerous articles to profl. jours. Home: SW 1045 Viento Dr Pullman WA 99163

DEFORD, SARA WHITCRAFT, educator; b. Youngstown, O., Nov. 9, 1916; d. Union Corwin and Grace (Whitcraft) deFord; A.B., Mt. Holyoke Coll., 1936, M.A., 1938; Ph.D., Yale, 1942. Instr. English, Barnard Coll., 1942-46; asst. prof. Goucher Coll., 1946-50, asso. prof., 1950-57, prof. English, 1957—. Lit. instr. NDEA Inst., U. Del., summer 1966; prof. Tsuda Coll., Japan, 1969-70. Nurses aide A.R.C., 1950-71. Eugene F. Saxton Meml. fellow, 1948, Fulbright lectr., Japan, 1954-55, 61-62. Mem. Medieval Acad. Am., Coll. English Assn., Am. Assn. U. Profs., Am. Assn. U. Women. Mem. Soc. of Friends. Home: 921 Dulaney Valley Ct Towson MD 21204

DE FOREST, AGNES BATTELLE BONELL (MRS. LIONEL THEODORE DE FOREST), club woman; b. Manitou, Colo., 1908; d. Benjamin Walter and Agnes (Bailey) Bonell; student U. Hawaii, St. Mary's Coll., Dallas, Manaolu Coll., Hawaii, Sam Houston State U., Tex.; m. Lionel Theodore De Forest, 1929; children—Alice Battelle (Mrs. Emil Henry Klatt, Jr.), Amber (Mrs. James Calvin Sharp, Jr.). Pres. United Ch. Women, Beaumont, Tex.; regent George Washington chpt. D.A.R., Galveston, Tex., 1963-65, state chmn. D.A.R. Mag., 1964-67, Good Citizens, 1967—; v.p. Episcopal Churchwomen Diocese Tex., 1966-68; instr. yoga exercises. Mem. D.A.R., Descs. of Signers Declaration of Independence (pres.-gen. 1972—), Mayflower Descs., Pilgrim John Howland Soc., Women Descs. Ancient and Honorable Arty. Co., Colonial Dames XVII Century. Republican. Episcopalian. Address: Star Route 1 Box 121A Beaufort SC 29902

DE FOREST, JULIE MORROW, artist, poet; b. N.Y.C.; d. Cornelius W. and Rosalie Caroline (Morrow); A.B., Wellesley Coll.; M.A., Columbia; pupil Jonas Lie, Charles W. Hawthorne, John Carlsen; m. Cornelius Wortendyke De Forest, Mar. 9, 1929. Painter in oil; six one-woman shows, N.Y.C., annually Loring Andrews Gallery, Cin., others; exhibited N.A.D., N.Y. World's Fair, Cin. Art. Mus., Pa. Acad., Corcoran Gallery, Allied Artists Am., Nat. Arts

Club, Profl. Artists Cin., Cin. Mac Dowell Soc., Bklyn. Mus., several others; represented in permanent collections Wellesley Coll., Cin. Art Mus., U. Cin., Aurora, Ind. Hist. Found., numerous others. Recipient Purchase prize painting, Federated Women's Clubs, 1936; two medals for patriotic service Women's Theodore Roosevelt Meml. Assn.; two regional poetry awards Coll. Club Cin.; citation for attainment in art, lit., patriotic service, 1963. Fellow Royal Soc. Arts (life); mem. D.A.R., Minute Women, Allied Artists Am., Cin. Art. Mus. Assn., Theodore Roosevelt Assn. (2 citations for patriotic service for cooperation in nat. centennial celebration), Cin. MacDowell Soc., Internat. Platform Assn. Conglist. Clubs: Nat. Arts, Women's University (N.Y.C.); Welleseley, Cincinnati Country, Town (Cin.). Author: Belfry Chimes and Other Rimes, 1974. Address: Vernon Manor Hotel Oak St and Burnet Av Cincinnati OH 45219

DEFRANCESCO, JOSEPHINE CATHERINE, physician; b. Phila., June 26, 1923; d. Nicholas A. and Santa (Vitullo) DeFrancesco; B.A., Temple U., 1944, M.D., 1948; m. Hernando Trujillo, June 30, 1962 (div. May 1968); 1 son, Hernando. Intern, Albert Einstein Med. Center No. Div., Phila., 1948-50; resident Presbyn. Columbia Med. Center, N.Y.C., 1951-53; practice medicine specializing in anesthesiology, 1953—; anesthesiologist St. Christopher's Hosp., Phila., 1953-54, Chester (Pa.) and Crozer hosps., 1954-64, also Taylor Hosp., Ridley Park, Pa., Sacred Heart Hosp., Chester; anesthesiologist St. Francis Hosp., Trenton, N.J., 1965—. Diplomate Am. Bd. Anesthesiology. Fellow Am. Coll. Anesthesiology; mem. A.M.A., Pa., N.J., med. socs., Pa., N.J., N.Y. socs. anesthesiologists. Republican. Roman Catholic. Home: 368 Green Valley Rd Langhorne PA 19047 Office: 2667 Nottingham Way Trenton NJ 08619

DEFRANCIS, PATRICIA DIANNE PRESTON (MRS. ROBERT DEFRANCIS), radio broadcasting co. exec.; b. Bridgeport, W.Va., June 24, 1947; d. Basil Homer and Martha Agnes (Smell) Preston; B.S. in Journalism, W.Va. U., 1969; m. Robert DeFrancis, Oct. 4, 1969. News announcer, city reporter 1430 Corp. Weirton, W.Va., 1969—; with WEIR-Radio, Weirton, 1969-70, news dir., 1970-72, adminstrv. asst., 1973-74; tchr., 1970-72; with Wheeling Intelligencer, Steubenville, O., 1974—. Named Outstanding Woman in Journalism, Weirton Civic Club, 1973. Mem. Women in Communciations. Home: 420 Marland Heights Rd Weirton WV 26062 Office: Sinclair Bldg Steubenville OH 43952

DEFRANK, CLAIRE MARIE, educator; b. Chgo., Feb. 9, 1951; d. Carlo and Clara (Cottone) DeFranco; Mus.B., Roosevelt U., 1973. Tchr., Elementary Schs. Instrumental Music Program, Chgo., 1973—; pvt. instrumental tchr.; tchr. vocal, gen. music Gen. Pershing Sch., Berwyn, Ill., 1974—. Recipient D.A.R. Good Citizenship award, 1968. Ill. State grantee, 1968; Mayor Daley Youth Found. scholar, 1968, Gregorian Assn. scholar, 1968, Roosevelt Competitive Music scholar. Mem. Women Band Dirs. Assn., Am. Theater Assn., Joint Civic Com. of Italian Ams. Youth Group. Home: 2109 W Race Av Chicago IL 60612

DEFRANZ, CAROLINA HENRIETTA VON ATZINGEN (MRS. REINHARDT JOSEPH DEFRANZ), archtl. firm exec.; b. North Haledon, N.J., July 24, 1925; d. Mark Nicholas and Lina (Brustlin) Von Atzingen; student Rutgers U., 1966, 71; N.J. Municipal Clks. Assn. scholar, Syracuse U., 1972; m. Reinhardt Joseph Defranz, Aug. 17, 1946; 1 dau., Carol Renee. Stenographer, sec. R.G. Buser, Paterson, N.J., 1943-44, Kurt Schmitz, Paterson, 1945-46; dep. borough clk. Borough of North Haledon (N.J.), 1963-66, dep. welfare dir., 1963-66, borough clk., 1966-73, welfare dir., 1966-71, assessment search officer, 1966-73; adminstrv. asst. Gar Chew Lai, architect/engr., North Haledon, N.J., 1973—. Cons. North Haledon (N.J.) Borough Clk., 1973. Mem. Welfare Assistance Bd., 1971-73; asst. tax search officer, North Haledon, 1967-73; active Girl Scouts Am.; active various community drives. Mem. Nat. Secs. Assn. (pres. Paterson chpt. 1971-72), Passaic County Municipal Clks. Assn. (pres. 1972-73). Home: 204 North Haledon Av North Haledon NJ 07508 Office: 154 Saw Mill Rd North Haledon NJ 07508

DE FREES, MADELINE (FORMERLY SISTER MARY GILBERT), educator, author; b. Ontario, Ore., Nov. 18, 1919; d. Clarence C. and Mary (McCoy) De Frees; B.A., Marylhurst Coll., 1948; M.A., U. Ore., 1951; Litt.D. (hon.), Gonzaga U., 1959. Mem. Sisters Holy Names Jesus and Mary, Roman Catholic Ch., 1936-73; tchr. elementary schs., Ore., 1938-42, high schs., 1942-49; asso. prof. English, Ft. Wright Coll., Spokane, from 1950; vis. asso. prof. dept. English, U. Mont., Missoula, 1967-70, asso. prof. English, 1970-72, prof., 1972—; vis. lectr., writer-in-residence Seattle U., 1965-66; instr. Roethke courses in verse writing and poetry U. Wash., Seattle, summer 1970; vis. lectr. U. Victoria (B.C., Can.), 1974. Mem. Am. Assn. U. Profs. Author: Springs of Silence, 1953; Later Thoughts from the Springs of Silence, 1962; (poems) From the Darkroom, 1964. Home: 135 E Central Av Missoula MT 59801

DEFRIES, ZIRA (MRS. AARON KELLNER), physician; b. N.Y.C.; d. Benjamin and Grace (Abelson) DeFries; B.A., Hunter Coll., 1938; M.D., N.Y. Med. Coll., 1942; m. Aaron Kellner, May 4, 1942; children—David Paul, William DeFries, Charles Horn. Intern Lincoln Hosp., N.Y.C., 1942-43; resident Columbia Presbyn. Med. Center, N.Y.C., 1946-48; practice medicine specializing in psychiatry and psychoanalysis, N.Y.C., 1948—; acting dir. Epilepsy Center, 1949-51; mem. staff Seizure Clinic, Presbyn. Hosp., 1951-55; med. dir. Leake and Watts Children's Home, 1950-58, West Chester Children's Assn., 1958-64; cons. psychiatrist Barnard Coll., Columbia U., 1964—; supervising psychiatrist N.Y. State Psychiat. Inst., 1967—; asst. clin. prof. psychiatry Coll. Physicians and Surgeons, N.Y.C., 1970—. Mem. bd. dirs. N.Y. Council on Child Psychiatry, 1965-67; profl. adv. com. United Epilepsy Assn., 1955—, Met. Coll. Mental Health Assn., 1969—. Diplomate Am. Bd. Psychiatry and Neurology. Fellow Am. Psychiat. Assn.; mem. Assn. for Research in Nervous and Mental Diseases, Am. Acad. Psychoanalysis. Mem. editorial bd. Contemporary Psychoanalysis, 1960—. Home: 40 E 83d St New York City NY 10028 Office: 35 E 85th St New York City NY 10028

DEGANI, EDITH SCHUMACHER (MRS. MEIR DEGANI), librarian; b. N.Y.C., Apr. 12, 1922; d. William and Ida (Weiss) Schumacher; B.A., Queens Coll., 1942; B.L.S. with honors, Pratt Inst., 1943; m. Meier Degani, Dec. 23, 1948; children—Vivian, Lynne. Cataloger, N.Y. Pub. Library, 1943-44; head cataloger Pratt Inst., N.Y.C., 1944-47; head tech. services State U. N.Y. at Bronx, 1947-49, Yeshiva U., N.Y.C., 1956-58; librarian Carl H. Prorzheimer Library, N.Y.C., 1959-66; adminstrv. librarian Jewish Theol. Sem., N.Y.C., 1966—. Mem. Assn. Jewish Libraries, Spl. Libraries Assn., N.Y. Library Club (sec. 1947-48), Pratt Inst. Library Sch. Alumni Assn. (sec. 1944-45, v.p. 1947-48). Home: Fort Schuyler Bronx NY 10465 Office: 3080 Broadway New York City NY 10027

DEGENHART, PEARL C., artist, educator; b. Phillipsburg, Mont., Feb. 25; d. L.C. and Ellen (O'Neill) Degenhart; A.B., U. Mont., 1923; A.M., Columbia, 1928. Instr. art Arcata (Cal.) Union High Sch., 1928—; one-man shows Stafford Inn, Scotia, Cal., 1954, Humboldt State Coll., 1951; exhibited group shows San Francisco Art Assn., 1932, 37, 40; Contemporary Arts Gallery, N.Y.C., 1939; Denver, 1938; Humboldt State Coll., 1935, 45, 54; Spokane Wash., 1948; Oakland Art Gallery, 1948; Humboldt Fed. Gallery, 1966; Eureka Courthouse, 1968. Mem. Bus. and Profl. Women's Club, Nat. League Am. Pen Women, Alpha Xi Delta, Delta Phi Delta. Contbr. to art, juvenile mags. Address: Box 142 Trinidad CA 95570

DEGNAN, JUNE OPPEN, publisher; b. N.Y.C., June 7, 1918; d. George August and Seville (Shainwald) Oppen; U. Cal. at Berkeley, Sorbonne U., Paris, France, U. San Francisco Law Sch.; 1 dau., Aubrey (Mrs. Orly Lindgren). Pub., San Francisco Rev., N.Y.C., San Francisco, 1959—, Oceans Mag. Cons. Internat. Learning Inst., San Francisco, 1969; pres. Internat. Child Art Center, San Francisco, 1971-72; v.p. Infonet Systems, Inc., San Francisco. Mem. finance com. Cal. State Democratic Central Com., 1956—; nat. finance co-chmn. Sen. Eugene McCarthy's presdl. campaign, 1967-68; nat. vice chmn. Sen. George McGovern presdl. campaign, 1972. Mem. San Francisco City and County Adv. Com. for Adult Detention Facilities, 1974. Bd. dirs. Norman Thomas Endowment Fund, New Sch. Social Research, 1968, E.W. Found., San Francisco, 1968. Mem. Ams. for Dem. Action (nat. dir. 1962—), Cons. Assn. Lit. Mags., Oceanic Soc. San Francisco. Clubs: Commonwealth, Metropolitan (San Francisco). Address: 1000 Mason St San Francisco CA 94108

DE GONZALEZ, JULIA M. MERCADO (MRS. CARLOS P. DE GONZALEZ), educator; b. Juana Diaz, P.R., Oct. 15, 1903; d. Isaias and Juliana (Negron) Mercado; student U. P.R., 1964-66; B.A., Inter-Am. U., 1968; m. Carlos P. de Gonzalez, May 3, 1923; children—Della E. (Mrs. Humberto Palmierl), Elsie E. (Mrs. Erasmo L. Bernier), Carlos J., Caleb, Julia A. (Mrs. William R. Culpepper), Miriam (Mrs. James J. Zabawa, Jr.), Ruth D. (Mrs. Elmer Barkel), Eunice (Mrs. Carter Nowak), Jose B. Dir., Head Start Center, Naguabo, P.R., 1965-67, Catano, P.R., 1968, Roosevelt, P.R., 1969—. Hon. pres., adviser Assn. Evang. Women P.R. Council Chs. Named Puerto Rican Mother of Year, 1974. Mem. Govs. Com. of Geriatrics, 1962-68. Author: Violatos, 1938. Home: PO Box 692 San Juan PR 00936 Office: 516 J Carbonell Roosevelt PR 00936

DEGRACE, MARGARET MARIE MARRIA (MRS. WILLIAM JAMES DEGRACE), pub. relations exec.; b. Detroit, June 12, 1930; d. Matthew Edward and Margaret Rose (Mahew) Marria; B.A., Marygrove Coll., 1952; postgrad. U. Mich., 1952-53; m. William James DeGrace, Oct. 6, 1956. Print, radio, TV copywriter Grant Advt., Inc., 1952-56; asst. to account exec. N.W. Ayer & Son, Inc., 1956-61; partner, W.J. DeGrace Co., 1961-63; press relations officer Detroit Inst. Arts, 1963—. Recipient Fellowship, U. Mich., 1952-53. Mem. Women in Communications. Home: 2113 Yorkshire Rd Birmingham MI 48008 Office: 5200 Woodward Av Detroit MI 48202

DE GRAFFENRIED, VELDA MAE CAMP (MRS. THOMAS P. DEGRAFFENRIED), clin. lab. exec.; b. Kirwin, Kan.; d. George Robert and Laura (Woodward) Camp; student No. Ill. U., 1959-60; m. Thomas P. deGraffenried, May 23, 1942; children—Donna Rae (Mrs. Kenneth George Pigott), Albert Lawrence II, Nicholas Thomas. With deGraffenried & Fisher Clin. Labs., DeKalb, Ill., 1957—, office mgr., 1957-64, exec. sec., 1964—. Vice-pres. Haish Sch. P.T.A., DeKalb, 1958-59; den mother cub scouts Chief Shabbona council Boy Scouts Am., 1957-60; supr. Teen Age Club, Louisville, 1949-50; county crusade chmn. Am. Cancer Soc., 1965, exec. bd. DeKalb County, 1964—, dir. pub. affairs, 1970—, chmn. bd., 1970—; sec. DeKalb County Soc., 1969—. Recipient commendations Am. Cancer Soc., 1965, Boy Scouts Am., 1955. Mem. DeKalb County Med. Soc. Aux. (sec. 1959-60, pres.-elect 1973), DeKalb Hosp. Aux. Methodist. Home: 1208 Sunnymeade Trail DeKalb IL 60115

DE HAVILLAND, OLIVIA MARY, actress; b. Tokyo, Japan, July 1, 1916 (naturalized Am. citizen 1941); d. Walter Augustus and Lilian Augusta (Ruse) de Havilland; ed. in schools and convent in Cal.; awarded scholarship Mills Coll.; m. Marcus Goodrich, Aug. 26, 1946 (div.); 1 son, Benjamin Briggs Goodrich; m. 2d, Pierre Galante, Apr. 2, 1955; 1 dau., Gisele. Made stage debut as Hermia in Midsummer Night's Dream (Max Reinhardt prodn.), Hollywood Bowl, 1934; 1st motion picture in same role, 1935; starred in pictures, including: Captain Blood, Anthony Adverse, Robin Hood, Gone With the Wind (nominated for Acad. award), Strawberry Blonde, Hold Back the Dawn (nominated for Acad. award), Princess O'Rourke, To Each His Own (recipient Acad. award for best actress performance 1946), Dark Mirror, Snake Pit (nominated for Acad. award; recipient N.Y. Critics award; Laurel award, best performance 1948-53), The Heiress (recipient 2d Acad. award for best actress performance 1949, N.Y. Critics award), My Cousin Rachel, 1952, Not As A Stranger, 1954, Ambassador's Daughter, 1955 (Belgian Critics Prix Femina), Proud Rebel, 1957, Libel, 1959; Light in the Piazza, 1961, Lady in A Cage (British Films and Filming Award), 1963, Hush Hush Sweet Charlotte, 1965, also The Adventurers, 1969; starred in play A Gift of Time, 1962; TV appearances in Neon Wine, 1966, The Screaming Woman, 1972; summer stock appearances include What Every Woman Knows (Westport, Conn., and Easthampton, N.Y.) 1946; Candida, 1951, 245 performances Trans-continental Tour, 1951-52; 100 performances Juliet, 1951; lectr., U.S., 1971, 72, 73, 74. Toured Army and Navy hosps. in U.S., Alaska, Aleutians, South Pacific, 1943-44; toured U.S. Mil. Hosps. in Europe, 1956-60. Recipient Women's Nat. Press Club award, presented by Pres. Truman, 1950. Pres. jury Cannes Film Festival, 1965. Mem. Screen Actors Guild, Acad. of Motion Picture Arts and Scis. Democrat. Episcopalian. Author: Every Frenchman Has One, 1962. Address: BP 156-16 75763 Paris Cedex France

DEHNEL, MARGARET ANNE LEWIS, psychologist; b. Ottawa County, O., Apr. 24, 1915; d. Charles Edward and Lulu Anne (Kamke) Lewis; B.Ed., U. Toledo, 1939, M.Ed., 1960; postgrad. George Washington U., U. Mich., Wayne State U.; m. John E.E. Dehnel (div.). Instr. U. Toledo, 1945-47; chief sch. psychologist Bedford Pub. Schs., Temperance, Mich., 1960-67; chief psychol. services Project PUPIL, Fremont, O., 1967-70; dir. Child Study Auglaize County (O.) Schs., Wapakoneta, 1970—. Individual practice as psychologist, Temperance, also Toledo, 1965-70; U.S. del. Internat. Assn. Spl. Edn., London, Eng., 1966. Bd. dirs. Regional Spl. Edn. Center. Served with USNR, 1943-45. Mem. Nat. (charter), Ohio sch. psychologists assns., Council on Mental Retardation (charter), Council on Children with Learning Disorders (charter), Council Adminstrs. Spl. Edn., Toledo Mus. Art, Phi Kappa Phi, Kappa Delta. Conglist. Home: 326 Stinebaugh Dr Apt 1 Wapakoneta OH 45895 Office: Courthouse Wapakoneta OH 45895

DEHNER, DOROTHY, sculptor; b. Cleve.; d. Edward Pius and Louise (Uphof) Dehner; student U. Cal. at Los Angeles, Art Students League, 1927-31, B.S., Skidmore Coll., 1952; m. David Smith, Dec. 24, 1927 (div. Dec. 24, 1952); m. 2d, Ferdinand Mann, Sept. 8, 1955; stepchildren—Irwin Mann, Abigail Mann (Mrs. Stephan Thernstrom). Numerous one-man shows, 1942—, latest being Chgo. Art Inst., 1955, Rose Fried Gallery, N.Y.C., 1952, Willard Gallery, N.Y.C., 1957, 59, 60, 63, 66, 70, 73, Gres Gallery, Washington, 1959, Phila. Art Alliance, 1962, (retrospective) Jewish Mus., N.Y.C., 1965, Baruch Coll., N.Y.C., 1970, J. Walter Thompson Gallery, N.Y.C., 1970; two-man shows, Cummer Gallery Art, Jacksonville, Fla., 1965; one man retrospective Hyde Mus., Glens Falls, N.Y.C., 1967; exhibited in numerous group shows, 1940—, including Albert Knox-Gallery, Buffalo, 1960, Balt. Mus. Art, 1965, Bklyn. Mus., 1955, St. Louis City Art Mus., 1960, Dallas Mus. Contemporary Art, 1960, Los Angeles County Mus., 1955, 60, Met. Mus. Art, 1953, Mus. Modern Art, N.Y.C., 1953-71, Mus. Fine Arts, Boston, 1955, 60, Pa. Acad., Phila., 1963, Guggenheim Mus., N.Y.C., 1963, Wadsworth Atheneum, Hartford, Conn., 1964, Whitney Mus. Am. Art, N.Y.C., 1949-62, Nat. Inst. Arts and Letters, 1970, also in fgn. countries; important works include Low Landscape, 1959, River Landscape, 1959, Arcanorum, 1960, Watcher No. 1 and Watcher No. 2, 1966, North Country, 1967; represented in permanent collections Seattle Art Mus., Birla Acad. Art, Calcutta, India, 1st Nat. Bank, Chgo., Great S.W. Indsl. Park, Atlanta, Columbus (O.) Gallery Fine Art, U. Wis., Skidmore Coll., Union Camp Corp., Wayne, N.J., Free Library Phila., Mus. Modern Art, N.Y. Pub. Library, Met. Mus. Art, Columbia U., Jewett Arts Center, Wellesley Coll., Cummer Gallery Art, Dept. State, Munson Williams Proctor Inst., Utica N.Y., U. N.C., Am. Tel and Tel. Co., Chgo., N.Y. Med. Coll., Valhalla, N.Y., Barnat Bank, Winter Haven, Fla., Bear-Stearns, Bankers Trust, B. F. Hutton & Co., Rockefeller Plaza (all N.Y.C.), Cleve. Mus. Art, Mus. of Palm Beaches (Fla.), Hirshhorn Found., Washington, also pvt. collections. Recipient award Audubon Artists, 1946, Art U.S.A., 1959, 1st prize for sculpture Kane Meml. Exhbn., Providence, 1963; fellow Tamarind Lithography Workshop, 1970. Mem. Sculptors Guild (dir.), Fedn. Modern Painters and Sculptors. Contbr. articles to publ. in field. Home: 33 Fifth Av New York City NY 10003 Studio: 41 Union Sq New York City NY 10003

DEIBLER, BARBARA ELLEN, librarian; b. Pottsville, Pa., Aug. 11, 1943; d. Samuel Elwood and Miriam Elizabeth (Houser) Deibler; B.A., Pa. State U., 1965; M.S., Drexel U., 1966. Cataloger, State Library Pa., Harrisburg, 1966—, head cataloger, 1972—. Librarian, Hist. Soc. Schuylkill County, 1971—. Mem. Am. Acad. Polit. and Social Scis., Acad. Polit. Sci. Baptist. Club: Pilot of Pottsville (rec. sec. 1974-75). Home: 2285 W Norwegian St Pottsville PA 17901 Office: Box 1601 Harrisburg PA 17126

DEITCH, ARLINE DOUGLIS (MRS. WALTER DEITCH), educator; b. N.Y.C., Mar. 12, 1922; d. Charles Oscar and Sylvia Dorothea (Aaronson) Douglis; B.A. cum laude, Bklyn. Coll., 1944; M.A., Columbia, 1946, Ph.D., 1954; m. Walter Deitch, Sept. 6, 1942. USPHS fellow surgery Columbia Coll. Phys. and Surg., N.Y.C., 1955-56, research asso., 1956-62, asst. prof., 1962-73, asso. prof. exptl. pathology, 1973—. Mem. Histochem. Soc. (councillor 1964-68, program chmn. 1961-63), Am. Soc. Cell Biology, Tissue Culture Assn., Sigma Xi. Contbr. articles to profl. jours. Home: 37 Perry St New York City NY 10014

DEITER, FRANCES CORA WOODS (MRS. CHARLES DEITER), former journalist; b. Omaha, May 19, 1909; d. Francis Lyman and Cora Belle (Gay) Woods; student N.W. Mo. Coll., 1927-29; m. Charles Deiter, May 24, 1930; children—Daniel Woods, Molly (Mrs. Joe D. Holt). Tchr. rural schs. N.W. Mo., 1927-30; proof room and bindery Ovid Bell Press, Fulton, Mo., 1931-39; co-editor, pub. Wellsville (Mo.) Optic-News, 1944-70. Leader, Girl Scouts U.S.A., 1954-59; pres. Montgomery County P.T.A., 1960. Active 9th Congl. Dist. Republican Women, 1944-60; mem. Montgomery County Rep. Women, 1944—. Mem. Mo. Press Assn. (sec. 1965-66), P.E.O. Methodist (tchr. Sunday Sch.). Mem. Order Eastern Star, White Shrine. Home: 111 Bates St Wellsville MO 63384

DE JEU, CAROLE ANN SCHMITZER, newspaper editor; b. Pitts., Nov. 3, 1934; d. Bernard Louis and Ella Mae (Hudgen) Schmitzer; B.A., Pa. State U., 1956; m. Paul De Jeu, June 16, 1956 (div. June 1973); children—Mark D., Suzanne A., John B. Free-lance writer, editor, 1956-68; editor Sylvania (O.) Sentinel, 1968—. Talk show host, dir. community affairs WXEZ-FM, Toledo, 1972—. Bd. dirs. Sylvania Area Community Improvement Corp. Mem. Ohio Newspaper Women's Assn., Sylvania Area C. of C. (v.p. 1974, dir.), Alpha Chi Omega. Home: 6013 Indian Trail Sylvania OH 43560 Office: 5716 Summit St Sylvania OH 43560

DEJONG, LINDA CLARK, charitable orgn. exec.; b. Cleve., Apr. 20, 1938; d. Kenneth Crocco and Elizabeth Louise (Basler) Clark; B.A. cum laude, Mich. State U., 1960; m. William Frank DeJong, Jan. 3, 1964 (div. Oct. 1970). Copywriter, television prodn. asst. Axelband & Brown & Assos., Cleve., 1960; promotion and pub. relations sec. Wood & Wood-TV, Time-Life Broadcast, Inc., Grand Rapids, Mich., 1961-63, exec. producer audio/visual prodn. div. Time-Life 8 Prodns., 1963-69, account exec., 1969-70; account exec. audio/visual prodn. div. Prodn. 13, West Mich. Telecasters, Inc., WZZM-TV, Grand Rapids, 1970-71; pres. Heritage Hill Found., Grand Rapids, 1971, exec. dir., 1972—. Pres., Heritage Hill Assn., 1968-71. Bd. dirs. Western div. Mich. chpt. Arthritis Found., 1970-72. Recipient award of merit Hist. Soc. Mich., 1970. Mem. Grand Rapids Mus. Assn., Nat. Trust for Historic Preservation, Kent County Council for Historic Preservation, Press Club Grand Rapids, Smithsonian Assos. Club: Womens City. Author: (with Barbara L. Roelofs) Heritage Hill Hstoric Home Tour Guide, 1969. Contbr. articles to mags. Home: 21 Union Av SE Grand Rapids MI 49503 Office: 300 E Fulton St Grand Rapids MI 49502

DEJONG, MADGE ANNA BROOK (MRS. RUSSELL N. DEJONG), civic worker; b. Grandville, Mich., Dec. 31, 1907; d. Jacob Daniel and Mary (Vander Velde) Brook; A.B., U. Mich., 1929, postgrad., 1929-31; m. Russell Nelson DeJong, Apr. 23, 1938; children—Mary Cynthia, Constance Jacqueline, (Mrs. Gary C. Armitage), Russell Nelson. Bibliographer, dept. engring. research U. Mich., 1929-31; abstractor French and German metall. articles Metals And Alloys, 1931-40; sec. U. Mich. Dental Sch., 1931-40. Mem. Woman's Aux. Washtenaw County Med. Soc., 1938—, pres., 1957-58, exec. bd., 1955-73, sec., 1952-53, historian, 1955-57; liaison, organizer, adviser U. Mich. chpt. Women's Aux. Student A.M.A., 1957-73; dist. dir. Woman's Aux. Mich. State Med. Soc., 1962-64, financial sec., 1967; charter mem. Woman's Aux. Am. Acad. Neurology, 1949—, newsletter editor, 1953-55, sec., 1955-57, pres., 1961-63, exec. bd., 1951-65, 69—; bd. dirs. Ann Arbor br. Woman's Nat. Farm and Garden Assn., 1968—, 1st v.p., program chmn., 1968-70, exec. bd., 1973—; charter mem. Ann Arbor Women's City Club, 1951—, bd. dirs., 1969-72, 1st v.p., pres.-elect, 1969-71, pres., 1971-72, personnel chmn. Camp Takona com. YM-YWCA Ann Arbor, 1954-58; mem. Thrift Shop Assn. Ann Arbor, 1950—, bd. dirs., 1963-66, 67-70, pres., 1967, sec., 1969; bd. govs. U. Mich. League, 1959-71, chmn. bd., 1963-65, sec. bd., 1959-63, 65-67, mem. joint conf. com., 1965-71, chmn. com., 1966, 70. Mem. Republican Women's Club. Mem. U. Mich. Faculty Women's Club, League Women Voters, U. Mich. Alumnae Assn., Sara Brown Smith Group, Kappa Kappa Gamma (sec. bd. dirs. Beta Delta Assn. 1956—). Club: Ann Arbor Golf and Outing. Home: 1526 Harding Rd Ann Arbor MI 48104

DE JOVE, JOSEFINA COLON (MRS. FEDERICO JOVÉ), occupational therapist; b. Coamo, P.R., Mar. 18, 1925; d. Rufo Antonio and Carmen Colon; B.A., Western Mich. U., 1950; B.S., U. P.R., 1965; m. Federico Jové, Oct. 5, 1947; children—Vivian Josefina, Heriberto Gabriel, Carlos Federico. Occupational therapist Arecibo dist. (P.R.) Hosp., 1951—; dir. occupational therapy University Hosp., Rio Piedros, P.R., 1954-59. Cons. occupational therapy Crippled Children Services, Santurce, P.R., 1960-75. Mem. Occupational

Therapy Assn. (pres. P.R. 1962-63, del. conv. 1965, 69-74). Home: 463 Bustamante Hato Rey PR 00918 Office: 1409 Ponce de Leon Santurce PR

DE KOONING, ELAINE MARIE FRIED, painter; b. N.Y.C., Mar. 12, 1920; student Leonardo da Vinci Art Sch., 1937, Am. Artists Sch., 1938, with Willem de Kooning, 1938-43; Dr. Fine Arts Western Coll., Oxford, O., 1964; m. Willem de Kooning, Dec. 7, 1943. Tchr. at U. N.M., 1957-58, Pa. State U., 1960, U. Cal. at Davis, 1963-64; Andrew Mellon prof. art Carnegie-Mellon U., 1969-70; prof. Fine Art U. Pa., 1970—; tchr. Drew U. Art Seminar, 1968—; asso. prof. contemporary arts, Houston, 1962; prof. Yale, 1967. One-man shows at Stable Gallery, 1954, 56, Tibor de Nagy Gallery, 1957, U. N.M., 1958, Tanager Gallery, N.Y.C., 1960, Graham Gallery, 1960, 61, 64, 65, De Aenile Gallery, N.Y.C., 1961, Washington Gallery Art, also Pa. Acad. Fine Arts, Kansas City Art Inst., 1965; retrospective exhn. New London, 1959; exhibited in group shows at Kootz Gallery, 1950, Internat. Biennial Exhbn. Paintings, Tokyo, Japan, Carnegie, 1956, Jewish Mus., N.Y.C., 1957, Walker, 1956, 60, Mus. Modern Art (circulating), 1957-59, Am. Fedn. Arts, 1957; portraits of John F. Kennedy painted 1962-63 exhibited Washington Gallery Modern Art, Pa. Acad. Fine Arts, Graham Gallery, Kansas City Art Mus.; in collections Truman Library, J.F. Kennedy Library, Kennedy Family, Montclair Art Mus., Benson Gallery, Bridgehampton, N.Y. Recipient Hallmark Art award, 1960. Contbr. articles to art jours. Home: 51 Raynor St Freeport NY 11520 Office: Graham Gallery 1014 Madison Av New York City NY 10021

DE LA BURDE, BRIGITTE ELISABETH (MRS. ROGER Z. DE LA BURDE), physician; b. Frankfurt am Main, Germany, June 12, 1928; d. Hans Lorenz and Emma (Krause) Stoltenberg; M.D., Philipps U. (Marburg, Germany), 1953; m. Roger Zigmund de la Burde, June 7, 1958; children—Colette, Corinna. Came to U.S., 1958, naturalized, 1963. Intern Millard Fillmore Hosp., Buffalo, 1958-59; resident Michael Reese Hosp., Chgo., 1960-62; practice medicine, specializing in pediatrics, Richmond, Va.; mem. staff Va. Commonwealth U., Med. Coll. Va.; instr. pediatrics, pediatric coordinator child devel study Va. Commonwealth U., 1963-65, asst. prof., dir. child devel. study, 1965—. Dir. Consol. Indsls., Inc., Powhatan, Va. Fellow Am. Acad. Pediatrics; mem. Richmond Pediatric Soc., Richmond Acad. Medicine, Assn. Childhood Edn. Home: Box 168 Rte 2 Powhatan VA 23139 Office: Box 24 MCV Sta Richmond VA 23298

DE LA CASA, MARIA LUISA GARZON (MRS. DE LA TORRE DE SAN BRAULIO), author, educator; b. Madrid, Spain; d. Luis M. and Jeronima (Garrido) Garzon; student (scholar) Sophia Newcomb Coll., 1939-40; B.S. (scholar), Tex. State Coll. for Women, 1941; postgrad. U. Tex., 1941-42, Tex. U. N.M., 1942-43, U. Cal. at Los Angeles, 1944-45, Columbia, 1947-48, U. N.M., U. Cal. at Berkeley; Ph.D., U. Ind., 1957; m. de la Torre de San Braulio, Aug. 26, 1945. Faculty, Maryhurst Coll., Portland, Ore., 1943-45, U. Cal., Berkeley, 1945-46, Mills Coll., Oakland, 1946-47; lectr. modern langs. and lit. U. Utah, Salt Lake City, 1947—. Pub., editor Revista Iberica, 1954—. Decorated Lady of Mil. Order of Knights of St.-John, Dame of Honor and Sovereign Devotion Mil. Order of Malta. Mem. Humane Soc. Am. Author: Nuevas Magias en Pasiones Eternas, 1958; Si y no Entre Rimas, 1959; (with husband) Cenas do Setrao, 1951, Rasgueos y Traveses, 1957. Home: 2602 Walker Lane Salt Lake City UT 84117

DE LAGUNA, FREDERICA ANNIS, anthropologist; b. Ann Arbor, Mich., Oct. 3, 1906; d. Theodore and Grace (Andrus) de Laguna; A.B., Bryn Mawr Coll., 1927; Ph.D. in Anthropology, Columbia, 1933. Asst. Am. sect. U. Pa. Mus., 1930-35; asso. soil conservationist U.S. Dept. Agr., 1935-36; with Bryn Mawr (Pa.) Coll., 1938—, successively lectr., asst. prof., asso. prof., prof., chmn. dept. anthropology, now prof., 1972—. Leader archaeol. and ethnol. expdns. to Alaska, 1930, 31, 32, 1935, 1949, 1950, 1952, 1954, 1958, 1960, 1968, also to Ariz., 1941; co-leader for the Danish Nat. Mus., Alaska expdn. 1933. Served from lt. (j.g.) to lt. comdr. USNR, 1942-45. NRC fellow 1936; Rockefeller post-war fellow, 1945, Wenner-Gren fellow, 1949; Social Sci. Council Faculty Research fellow, 1962-63. Fellow Am. Anthrop. Assn. (exec. bd. 1956-59, pres. 1966-67), Arctic Inst. N.Am., Soc. Am. Archaeology, A.A.A.S.; mem. Soc. Pa. Archaeology, Phila. Anthrop. Soc., Am. Ethnol. Soc., Sigma Xi. Home: 221 Roberts Rd Bryn Mawr PA 19010

DELAHANTY, MARY THERESA, ret. educator; b. Bronx, N.Y.; d. John C. and Mary A. (Lavin) Delahanty; Ph.B., Marygrove Coll., 1943; M.A., Columbia, 1945; Ph.D., Fordham U., 1949. Instr. Regis Coll., Weston, Mass., 1947-56, asst. prof., 1956; asso. prof. Marymount Manhattan Coll., N.Y.C., 1956-60, prof. history, 1960-73; ret., 1973. Mem. Am. Polit. Sci. Assn., Am. Assn. U. Profs. Author: The Integralist Philosophy of James Wilson, 1969. Home: 3151 Perry Av Bronx NY 10467

DELAIN, ELOISE V., physician; b. N.Y.C., May 5, 1938; d. Joseph and Eleanor (Chittick) DeLain; certificate proficiency in Spanish, U. Madrid, Spain, 1958; B.A., Hunter Coll., 1959; M.D., Howard U., 1963; M.P.H., Mich. Sch. Pub. Health, 1971. Intern Kings County Hosp., Bklyn., 1963-64; U.S.-Mexican Govt. grantee for study tropical diseases Inst. Enfermedades Tropicales, Mexico City, 1966-67; physician in charge Bushwick Tropical Disease Clinic, N.Y.C. Dept. Health, 1967-71, tchr. tropical diseases to student nurses, 1968-71; resident in occupational medicine U. Mich., 1970-71; resident rehab. medicine Rusk Inst., N.Y.C., 1971-72; practice medicine specializing in tropical diseases, Queens, N.Y., 1964—; mem. staffs Terrace Heights Hosp., Hollis, N.Y., Elmhurst div. Mt. Sinai Hosp., Queens, Interfaith Hosp. Queens, Univ. Hosp., Ann Arbor, Mich., 1970, Vasser Bros. Hosp., N.Y., 1971-72; guest lectr. tropical diseases U. Coahuila, Torreon, Mexico, Howard U., 1968; med. dir. AVCO Econ. Systems Corp., Moses Lake, Washington, 1969-70; occupational physician N.Y.C. Met. Transit Authority, 1974—. Owner of Pan Euro-Carib Tours Bx, N.Y.C., 1959—. Instr. 1st aid, swimming, small crafts Bklyn.-Queens, A.R.C., 1958-62; leader Mariner troop Girl Scouts U.S.A., City Island, N.Y., 1956-60; active Am. Youth Hostels, N.Y.C., 1960—. USPHS fellow in occupational medicine, 1970. Diplomate Nat. Bd. Med. Examiners. Mem. Royal Society of Health (England), National Med. Association, Queens Clin. Soc., Am. Med. Women's Assn., Am. Profl. Practice Assn., Indsl. Med. Assn. Clubs: McBurney's Sq. Dance, Social Argentino, Centra Mexicano, Howard U. Alumni (N.Y.C.). Translator booklet into English Mal de Pinto (Dr. Sanchez-Castro), 1967. Address: 36 Ganung Dr Ossining NY 10562

DELANEY, ELEANOR CECILIA COUGHLIN, educator; b. Elizabeth, N.J.; d. John C. and Eleanor C. (Fadde) Coughlin; B.S., Sch. Edn. Rutgers U., 1930, M.A., 1939; Ph.D., Columbia, 1954; 1 son, John. Tchr. pub. schs., Elizabeth, N.J., 1927; prin. Woodrow Wilson Sch., Elizabeth, 1941-55; prof. Grad. Sch. Edn. Rutgers U., N.B., N.J., 1955—, chmn. dept. ednl. adminstrn. and supplementation, 1974—; vis. prof. William and Mary Coll., U. N.M., Columbia. Ednl. cons. to sch. systems, N.J., N.Y. Va., 1950—. Mem. Elizabeth Charter Commn., 1960-61; chmn. Mayor's Adv. Commn. on Urban Devel., 1962-64, Elizabeth Human Relations Commn., 1968—; mem. Elizabeth Bd. Edn., 1972—, pres., 1973—. Mem. Am. Assn. Univ. Women, Nat., N.J. edn. assns., Dept. Elementary Sch. Prins., Am. Assn. Univ. Profs., A.A.A.S., Am. Ednl. Research Assn., Kappa Delta Pi, Pi Lambda Theta, Phi Delta Kappa. Author: Spanish Gold, Lands of Middle America, Our Friends in South America, Science-Life Series, Book 4. Contbr. articles to profl. mags. Home: 220 W Jersey St Elizabeth NJ 07202 Office: 10 Seminary Pl New Brunswick NJ 08901

DELANEY, ELLA MAE (MRS. PAUL DELANEY), lumber co. exec.; b. Gregory, S.D., Dec. 26, 1908; d. Wilhelm Frederick and Elvina (Romm) Steppat; Teaching Certificate, Black Hill Tchrs. Coll., 1928; m. Paul Delaney, June 10, 1929; children—Donald LeRoy, Robert Lynn. Tchr. in S.D., 1927-29; partner Hill City Feed Store (S.D.), 1936-44; v.p. Mont. Lumber Sales, Inc., Missoula, 1953-61, chmn. of bd., 1962—; sec.-treas. Mont. Pacific Internat., 1973—; dir. Lolo Hot Springs Resort, Missoula, 1964-68. Chmn. Mont. Women's affairs Am. Forest Products Industry, Missoula, 1965-69; mem. Yellow Bay Conservation Workshop, 1964-69. Mem. Missoula Bus. Profl. Women's Club (pres. 1967-68), Missoula C. of C. (mem. consumer edn. com. 1971). Presbyn. (deacon 1973—). Clubs: Soroptomist (Missoula), Missoula Home Extension. Office: 1701 Stephens Av Missoula MT 59801 Address: 111 Mary Av Missoula MT 59801

DELANEY, MARIE GENEVIEVE O'CONNOR, librarian; b. Auburn, N.Y., May 16, 1926; d. Michael F. and Mary (Kennedy) O'Connor; B.S., State U. N.Y., Geneseo, 1949; M.S., Syracuse U., 1959; 1 dau., Mary Margaret Damron. Tchr. Port Byron (N.Y.) Central Sch., 1949-50, librarian, 1950-51, 62-65; librarian U.S. Dept. of Army, Europe, 1951-53; tchr., Alexandria (Va.) Pub. Schs., 1953-54, 55-56, librarian, 1956-57; librarian Waterloo (N.Y.) Pub. Schs., 1957-58; serials librarian Wells Coll., Aurora, 1959-62, head librarian, 1965—. Mem. N.Y. State Library Assn., Beta Phi Mu, Kappa Delta Pi. Home: Main St Aurora NY 13026 Office: Wells Coll Library Aurora NY 13026

DELANEY, SHIRLEY MARIE (MRS. DON WAYNE DELANEY), banker; b. Longview, Tex., Dec. 31, 1934; d. Arvid Samuel and Ruby Pearl (Bassham) Hutchings; student Howard County Jr. Coll., 1965-72; m. Don Wayne DeLaney, Nov. 25, 1954; children—Richard Neal, Cara Lee. Bookkeeper, City Nat. Bank, Colorado City, Tex., 1951-52, 1957—, head bookkeeper, 1963-70, asst. cashier, supr., asst. to exec. officers, 1970-73, asst. v.p., 1973—; bookkeeper Ft. Worth Nat. Bank, 1953. Bd. dirs. county unit Am. Cancer Soc., 1967—, sec., 1966—. Named Woman of Year, Colorado City Bus. and Profl. Women's Club, 1971. Mem. C. of C. (dir. 1974—). Episcopalian (tchr. Sunday sch., treas.). Home: 617 E 9th St Colorado City TX 79512 Office: PO Box 1031 Colorado City TX 79512

DELANEY, WILLIE JOHN DUNKLIN (MRS. OLEN DELANEY), civic worker; b. nr. Rosebud, Tex.; d. Thomas Wathen and Parthenia (Jones) Dunklin; grad. Met. Bus. Coll., Dallas, 1918; student Okla. City U., 1943; m. Olen Delaney, Sept. 5, 1926; 1 son, Patrick Owen. Dist. office mgr. Sunmaid Raisin Growers, Dallas, 1923-28; partner Olen Delaney Co., food brokerage, Oklahoma City, 1932-62. Mem. com. Keep Okla. Beautiful, 1964-70; dir. Oklahoma City Beautiful, 1963—; dir. devel. William Freemont Harn Gardens, Oklahoma City, 1967—; com. on civic and capitol area beautification N.E. C. of C., Oklahoma City, 1964-67. Bd. dirs. Oklahoma County chpt. Am. Cancer Soc., Oklahoma County chpt. Arthritis Found., Nat. Hall of Fame for Am. Indians. Recipient Freedoms Found. George Washington award, 1966. Mem. Okla. Hist. Soc., Okla. Geneal. Soc., D.A.R. (regent chpt. 1954-56, state regent 1966-68), U.D.C. (v.p. chpt. 1963-65), Huguenot Soc. Founders of Manakin in Colony of Va. (state pres. 1971-73), Daus. Am. Colonists (state chaplain 1961-64), Nat. Soc. Colonial Dames of XVII Century (pres. gen. 1971-73, pres. Okla. 1960-62, organizing pres. chpt. 1958-60, Outstanding Woman of Year 1968), Nat. Gavel Club, Smithsonian Assn., Daus. Colonial Wars, Okla. Heritage Assn., Nat. Soc. Magna Charta Dames (state regent 1974—). Presbyn. (pres. Ch. Women 1945-46). Mem. Order Eastern Star (worthy grand matron Okla. 1953, gen. grand chpt. officer 1961-64). Clubs: Tau Nu Study, Apogan Iris Flower (Oklahoma City). Home: 1921 NW 21st St Oklahoma City OK 73106

DELATOUR, MARGERY D. (MRS. HUNTER LABATUT DELATOUR), artist; b. Bklyn., Sept. 20, 1891; d. John A. and Clara A. (Alexander) Dohrman; student Smith Coll., 1908-12, Chateau Brillantmont, Lausanne, Switzerland, 1912-13; m. Hunter Labatut Delatour, June 1, 1915; children—Hunter Labatut, Robert J. Exhibited Nassau County Art League, Nat. Art League, Albany Inst. Arts, Woodstock Art Assn., Manhasset Art Assn., Nat. Arts Club, Twilight Park Artists, Catherine Lorillard Wolfe Art Club, Pen and Brush, Locust Valley Art Show; exhibited one-man show Suffolk Mus., Stony Brook, L.I., N.Y. Mem., sec. Gt. Neck, L.I. Bd. Park Commnrs., 1934-40. Recipient numerous medals and awards Nat. Art League, Nassau Art League, Twilight Park Artists; 1st prize Pen and Brush Water Color Show, 1963; 2d prize Nat. Art League, 1963. Mem. Smith Coll. Club L.I. Home: 5 Buckingham Pl Great Neck NY 11022

DELAURENTIS, LOUISE BUDDE (MRS. MARIANO A. DELAURENTIS), author, editor; b. Stafford, Kan., Oct. 5, 1920; d. Louis and Mary (Lichte) Budde; B.A., Ottawa U., 1942; m. Mariano A. DeLaurentis, Mar. 26, 1948; 1 son, Delbert Louis. Air traffic control operator U.S. Govt., 1943-55. Treas., Tompkins County Liberal Party, 1964-67, chmn., 1969-72; mem. N.Y. State Liberal Com., 1972—. Mem. League Women Voters, Women's Polit. Caucus, Nat. Orgn. Women, Nat. Writer's Club, Writers Assn. Ithaca Area (pres. 1964-65). Author: Etta Chipmunk, 1962. Editor (with M.H. Brown and Eunice deChazeau) Torn Out of Time, 1967; Gentle Sorcery (Bessie Jeffery), 1972. Contbr. poems and stories to profl. jours. Home: 983 Cayuga Heights Rd Ithaca NY 14850

DE LA VEGA, DIANNE WINIFRED DE MARINIS (MRS. JORGE DE LA VEGA), univ. adminstr.; b. Cleve.; d. Gerald M. and Dorothy (Phlip) DeMarinis; student Case Western Res. U., 1948-50; B.A., U. of Am., 1953; M.A., Western Res. U., 1969; m. Jorge Alejandro de la Vega, July 19, 1952; children—Constance, Francisco Javier, Alexandra. Faculty, Western Res. U., Cleve., 1961-62; tchr. Instituto Mexicano-Norteamericano de Relaciones Culturales Mexico, 1967; supr. fgn. press Mexican Olympic Organizing Com., Mexico, 1968; asst. to producer Producciones Ojo, Canal 8 TV, Mexico, 1969; exec. asst. Internat. Exec. Service Corps, Mexico City, 1969-70; asst. to dir. U.S. Internat. U. Mexico, Mexico City, 1970—. Chmn. puppet's Jr. League, Mexico City, Mexico, 1967, chmn. ways and means, 1968; sec. Tlaxcala-Okla. Partner's of Alliance for Progress, 1967—. Bd. dirs. Hot Line of Mexico City. Mem. Am. Benevolent Soc. Mex., Am. Soc. Mexico, Jr. League Mexico City, Pro Salud Maternal. Club: Foreign Correspondents (Mexico City, Mex.). Home: Alcazar de Toledo 202 Mexico City 10 Mexico Office: Km 16 Carretera Toluca apdo post 10-881 Mexico

DELAY, DOROTHY (MRS. EDWARD NEWHOUSE), violinist, educator; b. Medicine Lodge, Kans., Mar. 31, 1917; d. Glenn Adney and Cecile (Osborn) DeLay; student Oberlin Coll., 1933-34; B.A., Mich. State U., 1937; Artists diploma, Juilliard Grad. Sch. Music, 1941; m. Edward Newhouse, Mar. 5, 1941; children—Jeffrey H., Alison O. Solo, chamber music performances in U.S., Can., S.Am., 1937—; violinist, founder Stuyvesant Trio, 1940-42; mem. faculty Juilliard Sch. Music, N.Y.C., 1947—, Sarah Lawrence Coll., 1948—, Meadowmount Summer Sch. Music, Westport, N.Y., 1948-70, Aspen Music Sch., 1971—; Dorothy Starling prof. violin studies U. Cin., 1974—. Mem. Juilliard Alumni Assn. (v.p. 1961-64), Mu Phi Epsilon. Contbr. articles on violins, violinists to various encys. Home: 349 N Broadway Upper Nyack NY 10960 Office: Julliard Sch Lincoln Center Plaza New York City NY 10023

DEL BENE, JANET ELAINE, educator; b. Youngstown, O., June 3, 1939; d. Anthony Joseph and Elizabeth Josephine (Pastier) Del B.; B.S., Youngstown State U., 1963, A.B., 1965; Ph.D., U. Cin., 1968. NIH fellow Theoretical Chemistry Inst., U. Wis., Madison, 1968-69; NIH fellow Mellon Inst., Pitts., 1969-70; asst. prof. chemistry Youngstown (O.) State U., 1970-73, asso. prof., 1973—. NSF fellow, 1966, recipient Agnes Fay Morgan research award Iota Sigma Pi, 1972; Am. Chem. Soc. research grantee, 1971-74. Mem. Am. Chem. Soc., Am. Inst. Physics, Am. Assn. U. Profs., N.Y. Acad. Sci., Sigma Xi, Phi Kappa Phi, Iota Sigma Pi. Contbr. articles to profl. jours. Home: 871 N Ward Av Girard OH 44420 Office: Dept Chemistry Youngstown State U Youngstown OH 44503

DEL DUCA, BETTY SPAHR, chemist; b. Warren, O., Nov. 12, 1930; d. Sullivan F. and Elizabeth R. (St. Clair) Spahr; A.B., Case Western Res. U., 1952, M.S., 1954, Ph.D. (USPHS fellow), 1957, M.S. in Mgmt., 1973; children—Gretchen (Mrs. John Elmore), Carolyn E. Research scientist Lewis Research Center, NASA, Cleve., 1957-72; sr. planning asso. spl. projects Standard Oil of Ohio, Cleve., 1973—. Chmn. Fedn. Women's Program for Fed. Exec. Bd., Cleve., 1971, 72; sci. adviser Sci. Frontiers for Gifted Children, 1967-69. Bd. dirs. P.T.A., 1968-69, Trinity Cathedral Day Care Center, 1970-74. Named Woman of Achievement, Inter Club Council, Cleve., 1967. Mem. Electrochem. Soc., Spectrographic Soc., Sigma Xi, Iota Sigma Pi. Conglist. (mem. bd. 1969-71, chmn. Christian edn. com. 1970-71). Club: Altrusa (pres. Cleve. 1969-70, vice gov. dist. 1968-69). Contbr. articles to profl. jours. Home: 2816 Tonawanda Dr Rocky River OH 44116 Office: 1424 Midland Bldg Cleveland OH 44115

DEL DUCA, FRANCES HORAN (MRS. LOUIS F. DEL DUCA), lawyer; b. Phila., Aug. 4, 1928; d. Thomas and Ellen (Kilgallon) Horan; B.A., Chestnut Hill Coll., 1950; M.A., U. Pa., 1952; J.D., Dickinson Sch. Law, 1966; m. Louis F. Del Duca, Jan. 28, 1956; children—Patrick, Maureen, Kevin. Fgn. service res. officer Dept. State, Washington, 1954-56; Y-Teen dir. YWCA, Carlisle, Pa., 1956-57; admitted to Pa. bar, 1967; mem. firm George B. Faller, Carlisle, Pa., 1967—. Research cons. on taxation of mobile homes for local govt. commn., 1972; solicitor Mt. Holly Planning Commn., 1970, Mt. Holly Zoning Hearing Bd., 1970, Dickinson Twp. Planning Commn., 1971. Mem. Gov.'s Commn. to Study Capital Punishment, 1973. Bd. dirs. Carlisle Area Sch. Bd. Mem. Am. (co-editor Jud. Highlights Bull. 1971, specializing com. gen. practice sect. 1973—), Pa. pub. records com. 1972—, Cumberland County (law day chmn. 1971) bar assns., Nat. Assn. Women Lawyers, League Women Voters (pres. 1957). Home: 506 S College St Carlisle PA 17013 Office: 10 W High St Carlisle PA 17013

DELEEUW, ADELE LOUISE, author, lectr.; b. Hamilton, O., Aug. 12, 1899; d. Adolph Lodewyk and Katherine (Bender) DeLeeuw; grad. Hartridge Sch. for Girls. Mem. Author's League Am., Plainfield Art Assn. (past pres.), Pen and Brush (past mem. governing bd.). Clubs: Words and Music (pres. 1967-68), Listentome (Orange, N.J.) (pres., 1964-65). Author: The Flavor of Holland; Rika; Island Adventure; Year of Promise; A Place for Herself; Anim Runs Away; Doll Cottage; Dina and Betsy; Berries of the Bittersweet; Life Invited Me; Career for Jennifer; Gay Design; Linda Marsh; Doctor Ellen; With a High Heart; Future for Sale; The Patchwork Quilt; Nobody's Doll; Title to Happiness; Clay Fingers; Curtain Call; Blue Ribbons for Meg; It's Fun to Cook; The Barred Road; The Story of Amelia Earhart; The Rugged Dozen; Hawthorne House; Donny; The Goat Who Ate Flowers; A Heart for Business, others; (with Marjorie Paradis) The Golden Shadow, Dear Stepmother; (with Cateau De Leeuw) Mickey the Monkey, 1951, Make Your Habits Work for You, 1952, Hideaway House, 1953, The Expandable Browns, 1955, Showboat's Coming., 1956, Breakneck Betty, 1957, The Caboose Club, 1957, Strange Garden, 1958, Apron Strings, 1959, Where Valor Lies, 1959, Love Is The Beginning, 1960, (also with Cateau deLeeuw), Nurses Who Led the Way, 1961; (with Margaret Dudley) The Rugged Dozen Abroad, 1960, Indonesian Folk Tales and Legends, 1961, Legends and Folk Tales of Holland, 1963, Richard E. Byrd, 1963, James Cook, 1963, Sir Walter Raleigh, 1964, The Salty Skinners, 1964, The Story of the Girl Scouts, 1965, Miss Fix-It, 1966; John Henry, 1966, Who Can Kill The Lion?, 1966; George Rogers Clark, 1967; Paul Bunyan's Blue Ox, 1968; Old Stormalong, 1967; Edith Cavell, 1968; Behold This Dream, 1968; Lindbergh Lone Eagle; 1969; Paul Bunyan Finds a Wife, 1969; Marie Curie, 1970; Peter Stuyvesant, 1970; Maria Tallchief, 1971; Uncle Davy Lane, 1970, Boy with Wings, 1971, Casey Jones Drives an Ice Cream Train, 1971; Civil War Nurse: Mary Ann Bickerdyke, 1973. Address: 1763 Sleepy Hollow Lane Plainfield NJ 07060

DELEEUW, CATEAU WILHELMINA (KAY HAMILTON, JESSICA LYON), writer, lectr., painter, illustrator; b. Hamilton, O., Sept. 22, 1903; d. Adolph Lodewyk and Katherine Caroline (Bender) DeLeeuw; student Met. Art Sch., Art Students League, Academie de la Grande Chaumiere, Paris. Addresses numerous women's clubs, art assns., schs.; one-man shows various eastern states; illustrator of 16 books, travel and juvenile mags. Mem. Pen and Brush, Am. Artists Profl. League, Plainfield (N.J.) Art. Assn. (hon.) Listentome, Words and Music. Recipient Martha Kinney Cooper Ohioana Library Citation (with Adele de Leeuw), 1958. Author: Dutch East Indies and the Phillippines, 1943; Hurricane Heart, 1943; A Day to Come, 1944; The Doctor on Elm Street, 1946; Love is Where You Find It, 1947; Betty Loring—Illustrator, 1948; Young Doctor Glenn, 1948; The Gentle Heart, 1949; For a Whole Lifetime, 1949; Doctor Alice's Daughter, 1950; From This Day Forward, 1951; Portrait By Kathie, 1951; This My Desire, 1952; Bright Gold, 1953; To Have and Not Hold, 1954; The Loves of Holly Bennett, 1953; William Tyndale, 1955; Not for One Alone, 1955; The Proud Air, 1956; The Given Heart, 1957; One Week of Danger, 1959; Give Me Your Hand, 1960; Fear in the Forest, 1960; A Home for Doctor T., 1960; (with sister Adele de Leeuw) Mickey the Monkey, 1952, Make Your Habits Work for You, 1952, Hideaway House, 1953, The Expandable Browns, 1955, Showboat's Coming, 1956, Breakneck Betty, 1957, The Caboose Club, 1957, The Strange Garden, 1958, Apron Strings, 1959, Where Valor Lies, 1959, Love Is The Beginning, 1960; Nurses Who Led the Way, 1961; The Turn in the Road, 1961; Against All Others, 1961; The Proving Years 1962; Determined to be Free, 1963; (with Adele De Leeuw) The Salty Skinners, 1964; Truth to Tell, 1965; Roald Amundsen, 1965; Benedict Arnold, 1970. Contbr. serials, short stories Am. and fgn. mags. Unitarian. Republican. Home 1763 Sleepy Hollow Lane Plainfield NJ 07060

DELEMARRE, HELEN BURKE (MRS. JOHN B. DELEMARRE), town ofcl.; b. Middletown, Conn., Jan. 18, 1910; d. John Patrick and Ann Louise (Potter) Burke; grad. high sch.; m. John B. Delemarre, Aug. 19, 1944; 1 dau., Ann (Mrs. Bruce Rogol). Clk., Travelers Ins. Co., Hartford, Conn., 1929-44; Republican registrar voters Town of Newington, Conn., 1954-66. Tax collector Newington, 1966—. Mem. Hartford County (pres. 1971-73), Conn. (legislative com. 1971-73) tax collectors assns., Newington Hist. Soc. (pres. 1971-74). Club: Woman's (Newington). Home: 16 Lawton Av Newington CT 06111 Office: 131 Cedar St Newington CT 06111

DELEMOS, ANITA, govt. ofcl.; b. Dominican Republic; ed. pvt. sch., Hamburg, Germany; grad. U. Frankfurt au Maim (Germany), Med. Sch. U. Sorbonne, Paris, France. Intern, German Univ. Clinic, Prague, Czechoslovakia.; owner, operator rooming houses, East Orange, N.J. and N.Y.C., 1943-51; export mgr. Phila. Ampoule Lab., 1951-61; export mgr. Walter Ritter, Hamburg, Germany, 1961-62; with Import-Export Office, N.Y.C., 1962-63; owner, mgr. health spa, So. Md., 1963-66; with Profl. Placement Service, Washington, 1966-70; research and investigation of investments in Dominican Republic, from 1972; rep. Attys. of Jurisdiction from Santa Domingo, 1972—. Cons., mem. nat. adv. research resources council NIH, 1972—; mem. Pan Am. Liaison Com. of Womens Orgns., Washington; pres. exec. chpt. Greater Washington Area, City of Hope. Chmn. Profl. Women for Nixon Campaign, Washington, 1968; supr. election bd., N.Y.C., 1954-60. Mem. Alianza Inter-Americana (dir. 1948-58), League Republican Women, Nat. Fedn. Rep. Women, Nat. Fedn. Bus. and Profl. Women's Clubs (chmn. 1958). Republican. Address: 4450 S Park Av Chevy Chase Washington DC 20015

DELENE, LINDA MAE, ednl. adminstr.; b. Negaunee, Mich., June 23, 1939; d. Clovis Edward and Eleanora F. (Miller) Delene; B.A., U. Mich., 1964; M.B.A., U. Hawaii, 1968; Ph.D., U. Toledo, 1974. Information specialist U.S. Dept. Def., Washington and Tokyo, 1964-68; systems analyst U. Mich. at Ann Arbor, 1968-69; asst. to pres. Marygrove Coll., Detroit, 1969-72; dir. instl. research and planning Oberlin (O.) Coll., 1972-73; dep. dir. Coll. Osteo. Medicine, Mich. State U., East Lansing, 1973—. Cons. on finance and planning Carlow Coll., 1970-71, Earlham Coll., 1972-73, Kalamazoo Coll., 1972-74, Heartline, Inc., Detroit, 1969-72. Served with USMC, 1957-60. Earhart Found. fellow, 1971-73. Mem. Am. Assn. U. Profs., Am. Assn. Higher Edn., Am. Assn. U. Profs., Am. Assn. U. Adminstrs., Common Cause. Roman Catholic. Club: Weimaraner Club of Am. (Detroit). Home: 45201 Mayo Dr Northville MI 48167 Office: East Fee Hall College Osteopathic Medicine Michigan State University East Lansing MI 48823

DELEON, ROSEMARY ESPINO (MRS. ARTURO J. DELEON), physician, civic worker; b. Manila, Philippines, July 5, 1939; d. Jose Cancio and Dolores M. (Farrales) Espino; came to U.S., 1963; B.A., Far Eastern U., 1956, M.D., 1961; m. Arturo J. deLeon, Aug. 22, 1963; children—Arthur Ariel, Avelita, Roselia, Perlita, Arthur Joel. Intern, Far Eastern U., Philippines, 1960-61, Edgewater Hosp., Chgo., 1963-64; resident anesthesia U. Ill., Chgo., 1965-67, clin. instr., 1967-68; preceptorship anesthesia Rex Hosp., Raleigh, N.C., 1968-71. Pres. Tyrrell Elementary Sch. P.T.A., Columbia, N.C., 1972-73; chmn. fund raising Heart Fund, 1973—; instl. chmn. Boy Scouts Am., Columbia, 1973—; chmn. health com. Tyrrell Elementary Sch. P.T.A., Columbia, 1973—. Recipient Vanguard award Tyrrell County Pub. Schs. System. Mem. Am., N.C. socs. anesthesiologists. Home: 5337 Edington Lane Foxcroft Sect Raleigh NC 27604

DELEON, SHIRLEY ANN FELTMANN (MRS. CANDIDO A. DELEON), editor; b. Washington, Mo., July 4, 1935; d. John Henry and Josephine E. (Patke) Feltmann; B.A., Marquette U., 1957; postgrad. New Sch. Social Research, 1962-65, 72-73; m. Candido A. DeLeon, Sept. 14, 1961; children—Mark, Sarah, Paul, Carl. Mem. staff Kalamazoo Gazette, 1958-59; writer, Jubilee Mag., N.Y.C., 1959-60; asso. editor Children's House Mag., N.Y.C., 1968—; asso. editor Parents' Mag., 1974—. Mem. Riverdale Community Council, 1972-73. Philip M. Stern Family Fund grantee, 1965. Mem. Women in Communications. Roman Catholic. Author: The Puerto Ricans in America, 1974. Home: 434 W 260th St New York City NY 10471

DE LESSEPS, TAUNI, artist; b. Paris, France, Mar. 10, 1920; d. Jacques and Grace (Mackenzie) de Lesseps; student pvt. schs.; 1 son, Guy Michael. Came to U.S., 1945, naturalized, 1946. Owner pearl fishing co., Mexico, 1937-38; fashion editor N.Y. Jour. Am., 1945-47; fashion coordinator Ellington Advt., 1952-54; one man shows Coopers Gallery, Amsterdam, Netherlands, Palm Beach (Fla.) Galleries; exhibited group shows Nat. Art Mus. Sport, N.Y.C., Lyford Cay Gallery, Nassau; represented in permanent collections White House, Washington, Joseph H. Hirshhorn Mus. and Garden, Washington, also U.S. and fgn. museums, pvt. collections. Cons., Nat. Art Mus. Sport, N.Y.C., 1959—. Co-founder Soc. Rehab. Disfigured, 1952; active various charitable orgns. Mem. Soc. Illustrators, Order Knights of Malta. Club: River (N.Y.C.). Home: 535 E 86th St New York City NY 10028 Office: Studio Marbella Spain

DELFINADO, MERCEDES DELFINO, entomologist, state ofcl.; b. Cabuyao, Philippines, Jan. 16, 1933; d. Jose Alcarez and Herminia (Delfino) Delfinado; B.S. in Agr., U. P.I., 1955; M.S., Cornell U., 1960; Ph.D., U. Hawaii, 1966. Research entomologist Dept. of Health, Manila, Philippines, 1956-62; entomologist Smithsonian Instn., Washington, 1965-67; asst. entomologist, asst. prof. entomology, U. Hawaii, Honolulu, 1967-73; asso. scientist N.Y. State Mus. and Sci. Service, Albany, 1973—. John Simon Guggenheim fellow, 1963, NIH Bishop Mus. fellow, 1964, AID Philippine Nat. Research Council fellow, 1958, Research asso. Bishop Mus. 1969, Nat. Acad. Sci. travel grantee, 1967, Sigma Delta Epsilon grant in aid, 1966, NSF grantee, 1972. Mem. Entmol. Soc. Am., Hawaiian Entomol. Soc., Sigma Xi. Author: Culicine Mosquitoes of the Philippines, 1966. Editor: Catalog of the Diptera of the Oriental Region, vols. 1-3, 1972. Contbr. sci. articles to profl. jours. Home: 422 San Creek Rd Albany NY 12205

DELGADO, STELLA, realtor; b. Oxnard, Cal., Apr. 22, 1930; d. Julio G. and Carmen (Vasquez) Delgado; student Ventura Coll., 1956-62, U. Cal. Los Angeles Extension, 1961-62. Supr., Pacific Missile Range, Pt. Mugu, Cal., Oxnard AFB, Constrn. Bn. Center, Port Heuneme, Cal., 1950-63; real estate salesman, income tax cons. Covarrubias Realty, Oxnard, Cal., 1964-65; real estate salesman, income tax and immigration cons. Chaney Real Estate, Oxnard, 1965-66; realtor, income tax and immigration cons. Stella Delgado, Oxnard, 1966-73, Mission Realty, Oxnard, 1973—. Recipient awards Pacific Missile Range, 1961-63. Mem. Oxnard Harbor Bd. Realtors, Oxnard Multiple Listing Service, Oxnard C. of C. Roman Catholic. Home: 260 S G St Oxnard CA 93030 Office: 305 S C St Oxnard CA 93030

DELLENBACK, MARY JANE (MRS. JOHN R. DELLENBACK), civic worker; b. Covington, Ky., Sept. 17, 1928; d. Paul C. and Marian (Ostrom) Benedict; student U. So. Cal., 1945-48, George Washington U.; m. John R. Dellenback, Sept. 10, 1948; children—Richard Ludlow, David Albright, Barbara Clare. Legislative sec. Ore. State Legislature, 1959-64. Active United Fund, Am. Cancer Soc., Am. Heart Assn. Mem. 90th Congress Wives (pres. 1967), Republican Congl. Wives (sec. 1974—), Civic Music Assn., P.E.O., Tudor Guild (dir.), Kappa Alpha Theta. Presbyn. Home: 131 C St SE Washington DC 20003

DELLINGER, SUSAN ELAIN (MRS. ROBERT D. DELLINGER), educator; b. Elwood, Ind., Dec. 30, 1942; d. Norwood Everett and Mary Evelyn (Roush) Allen; student Northwestern U., 1961-63; B.S., Ind. U., 1965; M.S., U. Fla., 1970; Ph.D., U. Colo., 1973; m. Robert D. Dellinger, Aug. 22, 1964; 1 son, Jade Roush. Tchr. English, speech and theatre Broad Ripple High Sch., Indpls., 1964-65, Leto High Sch., Tampa, Fla., 1965-67, Chofu High Sch., Tokyo, Japan, 1967-68; teaching asso. U. Colo., Boulder, 1970-73; asst. prof. speech communication U. Ore., Eugene, 1973—. Communication cons. to various businesses and industries, 1971—. Bd. dir. Tampa (Fla.) Civic Ballet, 1967, Tims Meml. Presbyn. Players Theatrical Co., 1965-67. Mem. Am. Assn. U. Women, Ore. Speech Communication, Assn., Speech Communication Assn., N.E.A., Alpha Chi Omega, Tri Kappa. Home: 3745 Petter Eugene OR 97405

DELLIS, ARLENE BATCHKER, designer, art adminstr.; b. Bklyn., Apr. 12, 1927; d. Jospeh L. and Ida (Freedman) Batchker; B.A., U. N.C., 1949. Head audio-visual aids and lending services Bklyn. Mus., 1949-55; head circulating exhibitions Soloman R. Guggenheim Mus., N.Y.C., 1955-60, registrar, 1960-63; registrar, Gallery of Modern Art, N.Y.C., 1964; registrar Marlborough-Gerson Gallery, N.Y.C., 1964-67; registrar and editor Inst. Contemporary Art, Boston, 1967-68; registrar, editor-designer Bernard Danenberg Galleries, N.Y.C., 1969-72, also dir. circulating exhibitions, 1971-72; asst. to dir., editor, designer La Boetie, Inc., N.Y.C., 1972—. Mem. Am. Assn. Museums, Am. Fedn. Arts. Editor exhibition catalogues: Young Italians, 1968; Archipenko: The American Years, 1923-63, 1970; The Rediscovered Years-Leon Kroll, 1970; Sculpture by William Zorach, 1970; Max Weber: Early Works on Paper, 1971; Max Weber: Drawings, 1972; Kurt Seligmann: His Graphic Works, 1973. Home: 320 Central Park West New York City NY 10025 Office: La Boetie 9 East 82 St New York City NY 10028

DELO, AUDREY MAE, mfg. co. exec.; b. McKeesport, Pa., July 18, 1929; d. Charles A. and Bertha A. (Wisser) Delo; student Pa. State U., 1961-68. Office clk. Potter McCune Co., McKeesport, 1948-51; sec., treas. Nat. Carbide Die Co., McKeesport, 1951-70; v.p., treas. Compacting Tooling, Inc., McKeesport, 1970—. Sec., treas. Wid Corp., McKeesport, 1968—. Bd. dirs. Thomas A. Wilson Found. Mem. jr. com. McKeesport Hosp., 1972—. Mem. Nat. Secs. Assn., Mon Yough C. of C. Club: Youghiogheny Country (McKeesport). Home: 803 Golfview Dr McKeesport PA 15135 Office: 403 Wide Dr McKeesport PA 15135

DELOACH, ROSEMARY (MRS. DUANE DELOACH), educator; b. Marquette, Mich., Apr. 18, 1923; d. Joseph Oliver and Edna Sophia (Bjork) Leonard; B.S., No. Mich. U., 1944; M.A., U. Mich., 1957, Ph.D. (Univ. fellow), 1968; m. Guy Eugene Cummins, July 5, 1946 (dec. Oct. 1948); 1 dau., Jean (Mrs. James McLean); m. 2d, Duane DeLoach, May 7, 1966. Bookkeeper-mgr. bus. office No. Mich. U., Marquette, 1949-53, asso. prof. bus. edn. 1957-65; tchr. bus. high sch., Escanaba, Mich., 1953-57; prof. Eastern Mich. U., Ypsilanti, 1967—. Served with WAVES, 1944-46. Mem. Nat. Mich bus. edn. assns., Am. Bus. Communications Assn., Am. Vocational Assn., Mich. Occupational Edn. Assn., Assn. Tchr. Edn., Phi Kappa Phi, Kappa Delta Pi, Pi Lambda Theta, Delta Pi Epsilon. Co-author: College Typewriting, 1961. Home: 9220 Gorman Rd Apt 2 Blissfield MI 49228 Office: Dept Bus Edn Eastern Mich U Ypsilanti MI 48197

DELONG, ERIKA VENTA (MRS. MARK E. DELONG), psychiatrist, neurologist; b. Riga, Latvia, Oct. 14, 1925; d. Janis and Zinaida (Weseler) Cielens; cand. Med., U. Göttingen, Germany, 1953; M.D., U. Vienna (Austria), 1957; m. Mark Eldridge DeLong, Apr. 12, 1952; 1 dau., Ruth Ellen. Came to U.S., 1949, naturalized, 1955. Practice medicine specializing in psychiatry and neurology; mem. staffs Fairview Gen. Hosp., Ridgecliff Hosp., Woodruff Meml. Hosp., Evang. Deaconess Hosp. Diplomate Am. Bd. Psychiatry and Neurology. Mem. A.M.A., Ohio Med. Assn., Neuropsychiat. Soc. of Cleve. Republican. Clubs: West Valley Riding; North Ridge Racquet. Home: 4495 Valley Forge Dr Fairview Park OH 44126 Office: 5500 Ridge Rd Parma OH 44129 also 20800 Westgate Plaza Fairview Park OH 44126

DE LOS ANGELES, VICTORIA, concert and opera singer; b. Barcelona, Spain, Nov. 1, 1924; d. Bernardo and Victoria (Garcia) Lopez; student Conservatorio de Liceo, Barcelona; m. Enrique Margina Mir, Nov. 20, 1948; two children. Concert debut as soprano, 1944, Carnegie Hall debut, 1950, Met. Opera debut in Faust, 1951; performed opera La Scala, Covent Garden Theatre, Staats Oper, Vienna, Grand Opera, Paris, Colon Buenos Aires, Royal Opera, Stockholm, Brussells, Copenhagen, Liceo, Barcelona, others; concerts in U.S., Can., Australia, South and Central Am., South Africa, festivals in Europe. Recipient Conservatorio Liceo Gold medal Barcelona, 1943; 1st prize Internat. Contest, Geneva, Switzerland, 1947; Ofelia Nieto, Spain, 1946; 1st Critics prize Buenos Aires, 1951, 53; decorated cross Lazo de Dama de la Orden de Isabel la Catolica (Spain), 1957; Decoration with the Gold medal of Barcelona, 1958, Silver medal, 1959; cravate du commandeur Education Civique (France); Banda de la Orden Civil de Alfonso X. Home: Avenido de la Victoria 57 Barcelona-17 Spain Office: care Enrique Magrina Paseode Gracia 87 7 E Barcelona Spain

DELOUGHERY, GRACE LEONA (MRS. HENRY O. DELOUGHERY), coll. dean; b. Allison, Ia., Jan. 17, 1933; d. Ed F. and Alma K. (Kampman) Meinen; B.S., U. Minn., 1955, M.P.H., 1960; Ph.D., Claremont Grad. Sch., 1963-66; diploma completion-computer programming Market Tech. Inst., 1967; m. Henry O. Deloughery, Nov. 30, 1966; children—Paul E.; stepchildren—Michael, Kathleen. Staff pub. health nurse City of Mpls., 1955-59; research fellow dept. epidemiology U. Minn. Sch. Pub. Health, Mpls., 1960-63; community coordinator, nurse Riverside (Cal.) County Supt. Schs., 1966; computer programmer U. N.D., Grand Forks, 1967, asso. prof. Coll. Nursing, 1967-68; asst. prof. in residence U. Cal. at Los Angeles Sch. of Nursing, 1968-72; dean Intercollegiate Center for Nursing Edn., Spokane, Wash., 1972—. Regional asso. Nat. Commn. for Nursing and Nursing Edn., Spokane, 1970-73; mem. Grand Forks Community Planning Com., 1967-68. Recipient award Cal. Research and Guidance Assn. Fellow Am. Pub. Health Assn., Am. Assn. for Social Psychiatry (treas. 1973—); mem. Nat. League for Nursing, Internat. Platform Assn., World Fedn. Mental Health, Am. Nurses Assn., Am. Assn. U. Profs., Council Nurse Researchers, Assn. Colls. of Nursing, Spokane C. of C., Pi Lambda Theta. Home: 911 W 33d St Spokane WA 99203

DEL PIZZO, DIANE, coll. dean; b. Trenton, Mo., Mar. 19, 1937; d. Ferdinand and Allalie (Wilson) Del Pizzo; B.S., U. Mo., 1959; M.A., Mich. State U., 1965. Elementary tchr., Columbia, Mo., 1959-60, St. Louis County, Mo., 1960-64; women's adviser Western Mich. U., Kalamazoô, 1965-67, asst. dean of students, 1967-71; dean of students Queens Coll., Charlotte, N.C., 1971—. Bd. dirs. Hornets Nest council Girl Scouts U.S.A., Charlotte. Mem. Nat. Assn. Women Deans, Adminstrs. and Counselors, N.C. Assn. Women Deans, N.C. Student Personnel Assn., Chi Omega Alumnae, P.E.O., Zonta Internat. (v.p. Charlotte 1972-74, pres. 1974—). Home: 2115 Selwyn Av Charlotte NC 28207

DEL ROSARIO, MARIA LUISA TAN GATUE (MRS. DAVID R. DEL ROSARIO), physician; b. Manila, Philippines, Aug. 25, 1926; d. Pablo de Jesus Tan Gatue and Josefa Navarro Gan; A.A., U. Philippines, 1947; M.D., U. Santo Tomas (Philippines), 1952; m. David R. del Rosario, Oct. 11, 1959; children—David, Jocelissa, Bernard, Andrew. Came to U.S., 1963, naturalized, 1969. Intern, Norwegian Lutheran Hosp., Deaconess Home and Hosp., 1954-55; resident Balt. City Hosps., 1955-58, Lawrence and Meml. Hosps., 1958-59; practice medicine specializing in obstetrics and gynecology, La Platta, Md., also Indian Head, Md., Waldorf, Md.; mem. staff Physicians Meml. Hosp., La Plata. Meml. Charles County Med. Soc., A.M.A., Am. Cancer Soc. Home: 1123 Howard Dr Port Tobacco MD 20677 Office: 114 La Grange Av La Plata MD 20646 also 1201 Strauss Av Indian Head MD 20646 also Waldorf Clinic Waldorf MD 20601

DELUCIANO, MARIA CADSAWAN (MRS. RUDOLPH DELUCIANO), physician; b. Pakil, Laguna, Philippines, Jan. 1, 1917; d. Stevan and Eufemia (Martinez) Cadsawan; A.A., U. Philippines, 1933, B.S., M.D., 1939; certificate U. Cornell, 1959; m. Rudolph DeLuciano, Dec. 3, 1960. Came to U.S., 1954, naturalized, 1965. Rotating intern, Philippine Gen. Hosp., Manila, 1939; resident obstetrics and gynecology, 1954-63; gen. practice medicine, Philippines, 1940-41, 45-54; practice medicine, 1963-67; staff physician Woodrow Wilson Rehab. Center, Va., 1967-68; sr. physician VA Hosp., Downey, Ill., 1968-69; med. dir. U.S. Navy Ordnance Sta., Forest Park, Ill., 1969-70; with FAA Dept. Transp., Washington, 1970—, chief med. clinic, 1970—. Mem. Iloilo (Philippines) Charity Womens League, 1939-54; v.p. Iloilo City Tennis Assn., 1940-50; mem. Citizenship Council Met. Chgo., 1961—. Vice pres. Am. Democratic Club, Chgo., 1965-70. Bd. dirs. Iloilo City YWCA, 1940-54; mem. bd. dirs. Royal Opera Co., 1965-69, 20th Century Opera Co., 1965-69. Served with M.C. U.S. Armed Forces, 1941-45; guerilla forces Philippines. Recipient Citation and Medal of Honor, D.A.R., 1965; Medal of Honor award for woman of achievement Bus. and Profl. Womans Club, 1966. Fellow Am. Geriatric Soc.; mem. Internat. Med. Womens Assn., Internat. Acad. Geriatrics, Nat. Veterans Assn., Am., Ill. (asso.), Philippine, World, Canadian med. assns., No. Va. (pres. 1973-74), Va. acads. family physicians, Am. Acad. Gen. Practice, Council Fed. Med. Dirs. Occupational Health, Lake County, Iloilo, Manila med. socs., Philippine Med. Assn. of Chgo., Philippine Med. Womens Assn., Am. Assn. U. Women, Internat. Assn. U. Women, Bus. and Profl. Womens Club, U. Philippines Alumni Assn. (dir. 1940-54). Served to 1st lt. M.C., AUS, 1941-45. Home: 2611 S Grant St Arlington VA 22202 Office: Dept Transp FAA 800 Independence Av SW Washington DC 20590

DELUISE, HELEN MARGUERITE, bank exec.; b. N.Y.C.; d. Michele and Immacoltae (Martinetti) De Luise; A.B., St. John's U., 1955; grad. Bankers Sch. Pub. Relations, 1950, Sch. Financial Pub. Relations, Northwestern U., 1958. With East River Savs. Bank, N.Y.C., 1932—, v.p. pub. relations and advt. 1966-72, cons., 1972—. Chmn. fgn. exhibits First Nat. Thrift Congress, Washington, 1961. Mem. Nat. Assn. Bank Women (organizer real estate forum 1951, chmn. publicity and pub. relations), Savs. Bank Women N.Y., N.Y. Financial Advertisers Assn., Pub. Relations Forum (exec. com.), Savs. Bank Assn. (mem. com. on pub. information), Advt. Women (N.Y.) (membership com.), Savs. Instns. Marketing Soc. Am. (charter), Cath. Inst. Press, Bank Pub. Relations and Marketing Assn., Legion of Mary (1st U.S. viator to Latin Am., 1971—), Pub. Relations Soc. Am. Club: Women's University (mem., treas. com. of women in pub. relations) (N.Y.C.). Home: 8801 Shore Rd Fort Hamilton NY 11209 Office: East River Savs Bank 26 Cortlandt St New York City NY 10007

DELUSSA, SALLY-JO ANNE (MRS. J. BRUCE DELUSSA), pub. relations cons.; b. Vineland, N.J., Dec. 15, 1943; d. Kermit Roosevelt and Marie Theresa (Figarole) Delph; B.A. in English and Library Sci., Glassboro (N.J.) State Coll., 1965, M.A. in English and Pub. Relations, 1967; m. J. Bruce DeLussa, Nov. 24, 1967; children—Heather Anne, Marnie Jill. Tchr. Bridgeton (N.J.) High Sch., 1965-66; grad. asst. Glassboro State Coll., 1966-67; coordinator pub. information Cumberland Community Coll., Vineland, N.J., 1967-70, prof. English, 1967-70; asst. dir. for publs. N.J. Edn. Assn., Trenton, 1970-71. Pub. relations cons. numerous area hosps.; pub. relations staff Johnson-Kosygin Summit Conf.-Holly Bush, Glassboro, 1970. Coordinator N.J. Bond Issue campaign Cumberland County, 1968; pub. relations com. Newcomb Hosp. Bldg. campaign Vineland, 1970; pres. Greater Vineland Health and Welfare Council, 1974. Recipient medallion of excellence writing Glassboro State Coll., 1965; medal for outstanding contbn. to collegiate journalism Pi Delta Epsilon, 1965. Mem. Nat., N.J. edn. assns., Nat. Assn. Tchrs. English, Nat. Sch. Pub. Relations Assn. (sec. South Jersey chpt. 1968-69, v.p. 1969-70), Am. Assn. U. Profs., Cumberland County Coll. Faculty Assn. (sec. 1968-69), Cumberland County League Women Voters, Am. Assn. U. Women (pres.-elect Cumberland County chpt. 1970). Home: 32 DeShibe Terrace Vineland NJ 08360

DEL VALLE, MICHELLE MARY, coll. adminstr.; b. N.Y.C., Oct. 7, 1949; d. Louis Anthony and Louise Theresa (Landolfo) Del Valle; B.S., Ohio U., 1971, M.Ed. (Leona Hughes scholar 1971-72), 1974. Coordinator sorority affairs, resident dir. of dormitory Ohio Wesleyan U., Delaware, 1972-73; female guidance counselor, Upward Bound Project, Ohio U., Athens, summer 1972. Telephone hot-line trainer, counselor Care Line, Athens, 1971-72, drug edn. program, 1971-72, telephone hot-line trainer We Care, Inc., Packersburg, W. Va., 1972. Mem. Nat. Assn. Women Deans, Adminstrs. and Counselors, Am. Personnel and Guidance Assn., Am. Coll. Personnel Assn., Cardinal Key, Phi Mu. Home: 3981 St Mary Court Whitehall OH 43213

DELWORTH, URSULA MARIE, assn. exec., psychologist; b. San Diego, Oct. 22, 1934; d. Lee J. and Gertrude (Roberts) Delworth; B.A., Cal. State U. at Long Beach, 1956; M.A., U. Cal. at Los Angeles, 1962; Ph.D., U. Ore., 1969. Asso. prof. psychology Colo. State U., Ft. Collins; program dir. Western Interstate Commn. Higher Edn., Boulder, 1973—. Author: Student Paraprofessionals: A Working Model for Higher Education, 1974. Editor: Crisis Center/Hot Line, 1972. Home: 3830 Paseo del Prado Boulder CO 80301

DEMARCE, VIRGINIA EASLEY (MRS. JAMES LYLE DEMARCE), educator; b. Columbia, Mo., Nov. 28, 1940; d. William Henry and Margaret (Jongebloed) Easley; B.A., U. Mo., 1961; postgrad. Friedrich-Alexander U., Erlangen, Germany, 1961-62; M.A., Stanford, 1963, Ph.D., 1967; m. James Lyle DeMarce, Aug. 25, 1962; children—Karl August William, John Baptiste. Asso. prof. history and humanities N.W. Mo. State Coll., Maryville, 1965-72, acting chmn. dept., 1970-72; state convener Women's Equity Action League, 1972; asst. prof. history George Mason U., Fairfax, Va., 1973—. Mem. Am. Assn. U. Women, Am. Assn. U. Profs., Am., Am. Cath. hist. assns., Am. Soc. for Reformation Research, Renaissance Soc. Am., Am. Soc. for Ch. History, Luther-Gesellschaft, Phi Beta Kappa. Home: 2508 N Kenilworth St Arlington VA 22207

DEMARÉ, MARY BONNIE CURRAN (MRS. B. LEO DEMARÉ), mathematician; d. John George and Mary (McCrystle) Curran; student Peabody Conservatory Music, Balt., 1936-38; B.S. in Math., Johns Hopkins, 1940, postgrad., 1940-42; m. B. Leo DeMaré,

Feb. 14, 1947; children—Mary Bonnie, John George, Frank Xavier. Mathematician ballistics research labs. Aberdeen Proving Ground, Md., 1942-48, mathematician, devel. and proof services, 1962—. Mem. Am. Math. Soc. Home: 627 W Belair Av Aberdeen MD 21001 Office: Devel and Proof Services Aberdeen Proving Ground MD 21001

DEMAREST, ANNE SHANNON, composer; b. Waldron, Ark., Nov. 26, 1919; d. Leonard Claude and Maude Almeda (Farnsworth) Shannon; student Okla. Coll. Women, 1937-38, Ballard Sch., 1938-39, N.Y. U., 1940-41, Hunter Coll., 1942-43, Denver U., 1946-47; m. Stephen Robertson Demarest, Nov. 20, 1944; children—Richard Shannon, Claudia Dianne. Asst. editor children's publs. Friendship Press, N.Y.C., 1938-43; composer, piano tchr., Denver and Arvada, Colo., 1951—; dir. Arvada Recorder Consort. Served with WAVES, 1944-45. Recipient Spl. Individual award Nat. Fedn. Music Clubs, 1971-73. Mem. Soc. Colo. Composers, Musicians Soc. Denver, Nat., Colo. music tchrs. assns., Am. Recorder Soc., Delta Omicron. Co-author (8 book piano course) Bobbie Lee's Keys, 1969. Composer: (piano suite) Banff Panorama, 1971; children's piano pieces, 1973, 74; Banff Panorama Symphonic Suite, 1973 (1st Colo. woman composer for full orch.). Inventor Dial-A-Key, piano teaching device. Address: 10821 W 68th Pl Arvada CO 80004

DEMAREST, ROSEMARY REGINA, librarian; b. N.Y.C., Jan. 20, 1915; d. William Gustavus and Rosemary Ann (MacElhinny) Demarest; B.A., Sarah Lawrence Coll., 1936. Asst. librarian The Hanover Bank, N.Y.C., 1940-44, librarian, 1945-53; research asst. OSS, London, Eng., 1944-45; chief librarian Price Waterhouse & Co., N.Y.C., 1953—. Mem. Spl. Libraries Assn. (pres. N.Y. chpt. 1955-56, chmn. bus. and finance div. 1961-62, dir. 1968-71), Royal Soc. Lit. (London), N.Y. Jr. League. Author: Accounting Information Sources, 1970. Home: 430 E 86th St New York City NY 10028 Office: 1251 Av of Americas New York City NY 10020

DEMARIA, CAROLYN MARIE (MRS. FRANK DEMARIA, JR.), physician; b. Paterson, N.J., Dec. 15, 1935; d. Michael and Linetta (Mariconda) DeMattia; B.S., Marymount Coll., 1957; M.D., Seton Hall Coll. Medicine, 1961; m. Frank DeMaria, Jr., June 20, 1959; children—Frank III, Edythe Ann. Intern Jersey City Med. Center, 1961-62, resident, 1962-64, instr., 1966-67, clin. asst. prof. pediatrics, 1967—; pediatrician Port Mugu (Cal.) Naval Air Sta., 1964-66; practice medicine specializing in pediatrics, Hawthorne, N.J., 1967—; mem. staff Newark City, Paterson (N.J.), Gen. hosps. Diplomate Am. Bd. Pediatrics. Fellow Am. Acad. Pediatrics; mem. N.J., Passaic County med. socs. Home: 175 Arlington Av Hawthorne NJ 07506 Office: 344 Lafayette Av Hawthorne NJ 07506

DEMARKO, SHARON KINN, newspaperwoman; b. Spearfish, S.D., Aug. 19, 1945; d. James and Margaret (White) Kinn; student Long Beach State Coll., 1963-64, U. Ariz., 1964-67, Ariz. State U., 1967-68. Staff writer Pensacola (Fla.) News-Jour., 1969-70, editor Image, 1970, editor living sect., 1971-72, arts editor, 1973—; editorial cons. Title I edn. project, NOW! Mag. Guest film reviewer WSRE-TV, 1972—. Community adv. mem. Peruvian-Andean com. U. West Fla., 1971—; mem. task force Action 76, 1971—; adv. bd. Pensacola Symphony Orch. Bd. dirs. Div. Family Services Vol. Program, 1971—. Clubs: Fla. Press, Pensacola Press. Home: 2007 E Gadsden St Pensacola FL 32507 Office: 101 E Romana St Pensacola FL 32501

DEMASTERS, CAROL RAE, newspaper editor; b. Kansas City, Mo., Mar. 4, 1947; d. Robert S. and Evelyn Carol (Listrom) DeMasters; student U. Kan., 1965-66, William Jewell Coll., summers 1966, 67; B.J., U. Mo., 1969. Student asst. to editor The Columbia Missourian, 1968-69; women's news editor Green Bay (Wis.) Press-Gazette, 1969-71; food editor Milw. Sentinel, 1971—. Mem. Wis. Heart Assn., 1970-71. Recipient Service award Wis. Heart Assn., 1971, Vesta award excellence food page news, 1973, Golden Carnation award nutrition news, 1973. Mem. Newspaper Food Editors and Writers Assn. (treas. 1974), P.E.O. (corr. sec. 1974), Sigma Delta Chi. Presbyn. Club: Milwaukee Press. Home: 1029 N Jackson St 602 Milwaukee WI 53202 Office: 918 N 4th St Milwaukee WI 53201

DE MAZIA, VIOLETTE, educator, found. exec.; b. Paris, France; d. Jean Jules S. and Fanny (Franquet) de Mazia; student Ecole Supérieure de la Rue Des Marais, Brussels, Belgium, Priory House Sch., St. John's Wood, Eng., Swiss Cottage Conservatoire, Hampstead, Eng., Barnes Found., 1926-27; D.F.A. (hon.), St. Joseph's Coll., Phila., 1970; L.H.D., Lincoln U., 1969. Came to U.S., 1926, naturalized, 1934. Tchr. Barnes Found., Merion Station, Pa., 1927—, dir. edn., 1935—, v.p. bd. trustees, 1966—. Decorated Knight Order of Arts and Letters, French Ministry of Cultural Affairs, 1973; recipient Legion of Honor. Chapel of Four Chaplains, Phila. Author: (with A.C. Barnes) Art and Education, 1929, rev. edit., 1947, 54; The Art of Henry-Matisse, 1933; The French Primitives and Their Forms, 1931; The Art of Renoir, 1935, The Art of Cézanne, 1939. Editor: Barnes Found. Jour., 1970—. Contbr. articles to various French Am. mags. Home: 242 Derwen Rd Merion Station PA 19066 Office: 300 Latch's Lane Merion Station PA 19066

DEMBITZ, NANETTE (MRS. ALFRED BERMAN), judge; b. Washington; d. A. Lincoln and Sara (West) Dembitz; B.A., U. Mich., 1932; LL.B., Columbia, 1937, LL.M., 1946; m. Alfred Berman, Feb. 11, 1939; 1 son, Jonathan Dembitz. Admitted to N.Y. State bar, 1938; practiced in N.Y.C., 1938-39, 45-67, Washington, 1939-45; judge Family Ct., N.Y.C., 1967—. Former mem. Columbia Law Sch. Alumni Assn. Com. to Abolish Capital Punishment. Bd. dirs. United Neighborhood Houses, Am. Jewish Congress. Contbr. articles to profl. jours. Office: 135 E 22d St New York City NY 10010

DEMING, LOUISE MACPHERSON (MRS. OLCOTT HAWTHORNE DEMING), civic worker; b. Evanston, Ill., July 8, 1916; d. C. Rust and Helen (Bennett) Macpherson; B.A., Rollins Coll., 1937; postgrad. Am. U., 1955-57, George Washington U., 1960-62; m. Olcott Hawthorne Deming, June 2, 1937; children—Rust Macpherson, John Hawthorne, Rosamond Bennett. Tchr., Fairfield Country Day Sch., 1937-40; mgmt. planning OWI, 1940-41; vis. prof. history Am. lit. Chulalongkom U., Bangkok, Thailand, 1949-51. Fgn. policy chmn. Montgomery County (Md.) League Women Voters, 1946; grey lady A.R.C.-Tokyo Army Hosp., 1951-53, Bethesda Naval Hosp., 1955-57; founding mem., bd. dirs. Fgn. Service Council, 1957-72; pres. Okinawa Internat. Women's Club, 1957; founder Okinawa chpt. Ikebana Internat. Club, 1958; organizer Folkcraft exhibit Smithsonian Inst., 1959; curator William Meads Prince Collection, Ackland Mus., Chapel Hill, N.C., 1967. Mem. Am. Assn. Fgn. Service Women (pres. 1962), Kappa Alpha Theta. Club: Cosmopolitan (N.Y.C.). Episcopalian. Author: The History of Uganda Museum, 1964. Editor: Letters of Sophia Peabody Hawthorne, 1964. Home: 1510 Dumbarton Rock Ct Washington DC 20007

DEMIT, PATRICIA ANN (MRS. MELVIN EVERETT DEMIT), assn. exec.; b. Lynn, Mass., Aug. 15, 1943; d. John Patrick and Sarah Bernadette (Cole) Flynn; student pub. schs.; m. Melvin Everett Demit, Apr. 24, 1965; children—Paul Edward, Laurie Ann, Amy Elizabeth. Sec. to asst. dir. Mass. Bur. Library Extension, Boston, 1961-65; exec. sec. Mass. Library Assn., 1968—. Democrat. Roman Catholic. Home: 4 White Way Nahant MA 01908 Office: Box 7 Nahant MA 01908

DEMOPOULOS, RITA IOVINE (MRS. HARRY BYRON DEMOPOULOS), pathologist; b. N.Y.C., Oct. 28, 1931; d. Gennaro and Rose (DiMeglio) Iovine; B.A. magna cum laude, Hunter Coll., 1952; M.D., N.Y.U., 1956; m. Harry Byron Demopoulos, July 24, 1955; children—Thomas, Laura, Richard, Byron. Intern med. service King's County Hosp., N.Y.C., 1956-57; resident pathology N.Y.U. Sch. Medicine, 1957-61; asst. pathologist Washington Sanitarium Hosp., Silver Spring, Md., 1961-63; USPHS research fellow pathology Los Angeles County Hosp., 1965-67; asst. prof. pathology, dir. tumor registry and analysis center N.Y.U. Sch. Medicine, N.Y.C., 1967—. NIH grantee, 1964. Mem. N.Y. Acad. Sci., Pathologists' Club. Contbr. articles to profl. jours. Home: 24 Syucamore Rd Scarsdale NY 10583 Office: 550 1st Av New York City NY 10016

DEMORY, HELEN JEFFRIES (MRS. MYRL WESLEY DEMORY, JR.), pub. relations and advt. agy. exec.; b. Washington, Oct. 14, 1926; d. Albert Carmie and Agnes May (Reed) Jeffries; student Am. U., 1945-46; m. Myrl Wesley Demory, Jr., June 21, 1946; children—Anita Lee, Jeanne Marie, Myrl Wesley III. Staff mem. various congressmen, 1953-63; adminstrv. asst. Town Mgr., Spl. asst. to Mayors Pub. Information Officer, Town of Vienna (Va.), 1964-68; pub. information officer City of Fairfax (Va.), 1968-70; partner Reamy & Demory, pub. relations, Vienna, Va., 1966-68; pres. Demory Assos., Advt. and Pub. Relations Agy., Vienna, 1968—. Mem. No. Va. Builders Assn., Va. Hosp. Pub. Relations Assn., No. Va. News Assn. (pres. 1970-71), Fairfax County, Fairfax City, Vienna chambers commerce. Home: 122 Cherry Circle SW Vienna VA 22180 Office: 160 Maple Av E Vienna VA 22180

DEMPSEY, DOLORES VIVIAN, mfg. co. exec.; b. Culver City, Cal., Jan. 30, 1924; d. Stephen and Thelma Dolores (Reeve) Dempsey; grad. Exec. Program, U. Cal. at Los Angeles, 1963. Systems engr. IBM, Los Angeles, 1942-55, instr. data processing, 1961-72, mgr. data processing regional instrn., 1972—. Tchr. devel. Los Angeles City Coll. Mem. Mayor's Adv. Com. Status of Women, Mayor's Adv. Com. Labor and Mgmt. Bd. dirs. IBM Credit Union; mem. adv. council women's exec. program U. Cal. at Los Angeles. Mem. Los Angeles C. of C. (dir. women's div.), Com. Profl. Women, (dir.), Assn. Women Execs. (past pres.), Am. Soc. Tng. Dirs. Republican.

DEMPSEY, HANNAH CAROLINE (MRS. FRANK AMARAL DEMPSEY), real estate exec.; b. Richlands, N.C., Nov. 5, 1924; d. Johnny Franklin and Bessie June (Huffman) Huffman; grad. high sch.; m. Frank Amaral Dempsey, Apr. 18, 1947; 1 son, Jeffrey Amaral. Head bookkeeper First National Bank, Waterloo, N.Y., 1952-57, Nat. Bank of Sarasota (Fla.), 1958-60; realtor, 1964—; pres. Dempsey Real Estate Inc., Sarasota, 1970—. Mem. deed restriction com. South Gate Assn., 1972-73; mem. vol. talent pool Sarasota High Sch., 1971-72. Recipient Woman of Year award Sarasota chpt. Women's Council, 1969; Certificate of Appreciation, Sarasota Bd. Realtors, 1969. Mem. Sarasota Bd. Realtors (sec. 1969-70), Women's Council (pres. Sarasota chpt. 1973). Home: 2717 Grove St Sarasota FL 33579

DEMPSEY, SISTER MARY GREGORY, librarian; b. Bklyn., Jan. 14, 1925; d. Maurice Francis and Mary (O'Driscoll) Dempsey; B.A., Manhattan Coll., 1955; M.L.S., St. John's U., 1963. Joined Sisters of Saint Joseph, 1942; tchr. Roman Cath. Diocese Bklyn., 1944-65; librarian St. John's Hosp. Sch. Nursing (now part Cath. Med. Center Bklyn. and Queens), 1965—. Mem. Am., Cath. library assns. Home: 90-02 Queen's Blvd Elmhurst NY 11373 Office: 23-18 44th Dr Long Island City NY 11101

DEMUNCK, AUDREY PHYLLIS, sch. psychologist; b. Cedarburg, Wis., Nov. 2, 1932; d. Gilbert Claire and Emma Maybelle (Raymond) Fellows; student LaCrosse State U., 1950-52; B.S., U. Wis.-Milw., 1957; M.Ed., Marquette U., 1962, Ed.D., 1970; m. Robert L. Lagerman, Aug. 4, 1951 (div. 1972); children—Robert Ray, Richard Lee; m. 2d, John Heath DeMunck, Aug. 18, 1973. Tchr. elementary grades pub. schs., Shorewood, Wis., 1958-73, psychologist, 1974—. Mem. Am., Wis. psychol. assn., Nat., Wis., Shorewood edn. assns., Kappa Delta Pi (chpt. pres. 1958). Home: 2313 E Menlo Blvd Shorewood WI 53211 Office: 1600 E Lake Bluff Shorewood WI 53211

DEMUTH, AUDREY ALLYNE HARRIS (MRS. WINSTON DEMUTH), newspaper editor; b. Washington, Jan. 29, 1928; d. Allyn and Reba (Donaghey) Harris; B.A., U. Dubuque, 1950; m. Winston DeMuth, June 10, 1950; children—Joan, James, Donna. Mng. editor Sun Colony Mag., Ft. Lauderdale, Fla., 1951-52; asst. editor Home Life Mag., Chgo., 1952-54; editor Crete (Ill.) Record, 1963-73; Peotone (Ill.) Vedette, 1973—, seven newspapers East Will County (Ill.), 1973—; mng. editor Russell Printing Co., Peotone, 1973—. Home: 616 1st St Crete IL 60417 Office: 111 1st St Peotone IL 60468

DE NAGY, EVA (MRS. PAUL STUART), artist; b. Ercsi, Hungary; d. Erno and Jolan (Erendits) de Nagy; student Acad. Royal Des Beaux Arts De Bruxelles (Belgium), 1927-31; m. Paul Stuart, Apr. 15, 1943; 1 son, Peter Paul. Came to U.S., 1932, naturalized, 1939. One-man shows, Park Lane Galleries, Princeton Theol. Sem., Perth Amboy (N.J.) Pub. Library, Trenton Presbyn. Ch., Ridgewood (N.J.) Presbyn. Ch.; exhibited in group shows Park Lane Galleries, Montclair Art Mus., Nat. Acad. Gallery, Nat. Arts Club Gallery, Jersey City Mus., Nat. Acad. Gallery, Nat. Arts Jersey City Mus., many others; represented in permanent collections at Princeton Theol. Sem., Robert E. Speer Library, Build Slide Library of Ch. Archtl. Guild of Am.; owner, dir. Eva De Nagy Gallery, Provincetown, Mass., 1960—. Bd. dirs. Am. Hungarian Studies Found., Rutgers U., 1960-64; mem. arts com. Trenton State Mus., 1960-62. Recipient 1st prize N.J. State Med. Assn., 1958; N.J. State Fedn. Woman's Clubs, 1954; Morris County Art Assn., 1951; others. Mem. World Fedn. Hungarian Artists (v.p. 1964—), Am. Hungarian Art Assn. (v.p. 1964—). Mem. Provincetown Art Assn. (life), Cape Cod Art Assn., Am. Artists Profl. League, Painters and Sculptors Soc. N.J., Fedn. Ex-Club, Woman's Aux. Med. Staff Elizabeth Gen. Hosp., A.M.A. Woman's Aux. Middlesex County Med. Soc. Woman's Aux. Presbyn. Home: 462 Commercial Princeton MA 02657 Office: 244 Commercial St Provincetown MA 02657

DENARD, RUTH COLEMAN (MRS. SAMUEL E. DENARD, SR.), occupational therapist; b. Muskogee, Okla., Aug. 2, 1906; d. Walter and Mary (Lyons) Coleman, Sr.; B.S., Tuskegee Inst., 1934; certificate occupational therapy, Columbia, 1946; m. Samuel E. Denard, Sr., June 14, 1947; 1 son, Samuel E. Instr. home econs., Fargo, Ark., 1934-35; home demonstration agt. U.S. Dept. Agr., Greensboro, Ala., 1935-40, Ala. 4-H Club agt., Tuskegee Inst., 1940-45; occupational therapist VA Hosp., Tuskegee, Ala., 1946-73, supervisory occupational therapist, 1957—. Mem. Am., Ala., Miss. Occupational Therapy assns., World Fedn. Occupational Therapists, N.A.A.C.P., Needle Art Club, Zeta Phi Beta. Baptist. Home: PO Box 184 Tuskegee Institute AL 36088 Office: VA Hospital Tuskegee AL 36083

DENCKLA, MARTHA SYLVIA BRIDGE (MRS. WILLIAM DONNER DENCKLA), neurologist; b. N.Y.C., Dec. 19, 1937; d. Frederick David and Rebecca Leah (Hochmeyer) Bridge; B.A. summa cum laude, Bryn Mawr Coll., 1958; M.D. cum laude, Harvard, 1962; m. William Donner, Aug. 26, 1962; children—Matthew Rodgers, Derek Anthony, Benjamin Frederick. Intern, Beth Israel Hosp., Boston, 1962-63, resident, 1963-64; resident Boston VA Hosp., 1964-66, Georgetown U. Hosp., Washington, 1967; asst. neurology Columbia Coll. Physicians and Surgeons, N.Y.C., 1968-70, asso. neurology, 1971—; practice medicine specializing in neurology, Tenafly, N.J., 1970—; mem. staffs Neurol. Inst., Columbia-Presbyn., N.Y.C. Vis. Lectr. Columbia Tchrs. Coll., 1971-73. Alumni dir. Bryn Mawr (Pa.), Coll., 1973—. Recipient research grant Robinson Opthalnic and Dyslexia Fund, 1972—. Mem. A.M.A., N.J., Bergen County med. assns., Acad. Neurology, Acad. Aphasia, Internat. Neuropsychology Soc., Alpha Omega Alpha. Contbr. articles to profl. jours. Address: 91 Knickerbocker Rd Tenafly NJ 07670

DENEBRINK, JOYCE, journalist; b. Long Beach, Cal., July 28, 1936; d. Francis Compton and Fanny (McCook) Denebrink; B.A. in Modern European Lit., Stanford, 1958; divorced. Guest mng. editor Madamoiselle mag., coll. issue, N.Y.C., Aug. 1958, asst. feature editor, 1962-64, fashion and beauty copywriter, 1964; asst. to v.p. advt. promotion and publicity Simon and Schuster, 1966; asst. editor Family Circle Books, 1968; researcher-writer Talent Assos., TV prodn., N.Y.C., 1969; crafts editor Christmas issue Family Circle mag., 1970, 71; researcher WNET-TV, ednl. TV, 1971-72; writer KETC-TV, ednl. TV, 1972; editor Free-Time Ency., 1973-74. Compiler, editor: Barbed Wires, 1965. Contbr. articles to mags. Home: 25 W 10th St New York City NY 10011

DENES, AGNES CECILIA, conceptual artist; b. Budapest, Hungary; ed. Coll. City N.Y., New Sch. Social Research, Columbia (M.L. Robinson scholar), 1964-65; married; 1 son. One-woman shows include Columbia, 1965, Granite Gallery, N.Y.C., 1966, New Masters Gallery, N.Y.C., 1967, Ruth White Gallery, 1968, 69, Corcoran Gallery, Washington, 1974, A.I.R. Gallery, 1972, 74, Ohio State U., 1974, others; group shows include Whitney Mus. Art, Smithsonian Instn., Nat. Acad. Gallery, Jewish Mus., N.Y.C., Mus. Modern Art, Buenos Aires, Argentina, Kent (O.) State U., N.Y. U., Galleries Raymond Duncan, Paris, France, Wallraf-Richartz Mus., Cologne, Germany, Mus. Fine Arts, Santiago de Chile, N.Y. Cultural Center, Inst. Contemporary Art, Lima, Peru, Mus. Modern Art, N.Y.C., Finch Coll. Mus., Suffolk (N.Y.) Mus., Bklyn. Mus., Allen Meml. Art Mus., Oberlin Coll., Museo Emilio A. Caraffa, Cordoba, Spain, Kunsthalle, Cologne, Germany, others; participated in traveling show C. 7500, 1973-74; represented in permanent collections Mus. Modern Art, Whitney Mus., Smithsonian Instn., Nat. Collection Art, Washington, Finch Coll., Roy R. Neuberger Mus., Purchase, N.Y., Chase Manhattan Art Collection, Israel Mus., Syracuse Mus., others; guest lectr. N.Y. U., 1971, City U. N.Y., 1972, Guilford Coll., 1972, Syracuse U., Oberlin Coll., N.Y. Inst. Tech., Corcoran Sch. Art, Washington, 1973, Moore Coll. Art, 1974, U. Mass., 1974, Pratt Inst., 1974, Nova Scotia Sch. Art and Design, 1974, Nat. Endowment Arts Fellowship, 1974-75. Recipient John J. Myers Art Sch. award, 1959-63, Alfred P. Cohen Art Sch. awards, 1961, 62, others. Address: 93 Crosby St New York City NY 10012

DENES-RADOMISLI, MAGDA (MRS. MICHEL RADOMISLI), psychologist, educator; b. Budapest, Hungary, Aug. 2, 1934; d. Gyula and Margaret (Indig) Denes; came to U.S., 1950, naturalized, 1955; B.A., Coll. City N.Y., 1956; M.A., Boston U., 1958; Ph.D., Yeshiva U., 1961; grad. N.Y. U., 1967; m. Michel Radomisli, May 4, 1963; children—Gregory John, Timothy Evan. Psychotherapist, New Hope Guild Guidance Center, Bklyn., 1959-60; lectr. Bklyn. Coll., 1959-62; adj. asst. prof. N.Y. U., N.Y.C., 1963, asso. vis. prof., psychotherapy supr., 1972—; psychol. counselor Columbia, 1965; psychotherapist, N.Y.C., 1959—; asso. clin. prof., psychotherapy supr. Inst. Advanced Psychol. Studies, Adelphi U., Garden City, L.I., N.Y., 1969—. Cons. VA Hosp. Bd. dirs. N.Y. Inst. for Gestalt Therapy, mem. faculty, 1970—. Mem. Am. Eastern, N.Y. Clin. (com.) psychologists assns., Assn. Applied Psychoanalysis (sec. 1960-61), N.Y. State Psychol. Assn. (chmn. com. consumer protection 1974, mem. ethics com. 1972—), Nat. Inst. for Psychotherapies (faculty, mem. bd. 1971—). Home: 1049 Park Av New York City NY 10028 Office: 125 E 87th St New York City NY 10028

DENGEL, GISELA ANNEMARIE (MRS. OTTMAR H. DENGEL), physician; b. Muensterberg, Germany, Aug. 3, 1936; d. Walter Hermann and Charlotte Anna (Nass) Harder; Physicum, U. Cologne (Germany), 1958; postgrad. U. Hamburg (Germany), 1958; M.D., U. Munich (Germany), 1960; m. Ottmar Hubert Dengel, June 1, 1962; children—Tobias Alexander, Florian Kristoffer. Came to U.S., 1965. Resident pediatrics D.C. Gen. Hosp., Washington, 1966-69; chief med. officer pediatrics Southwest Neighborhood Health Center, Washington, 1969-73; practice medicine specializing in pediatrics, Front Royal, Va., 1973—; mem. staff Warren Meml. Hosp., Front Royal. Fellow Am. Acad. Pediatrics; mem. A.M.A., Am. Med. Women's Assn., Med. Soc. Va., Northern Va. Clubs: Appalachian Trail (Washington); German Alpine (Kempten, Germany). Address: Route 1 Box 155-A Browntown Rd Front Royal VA 22630

DENHAM, ALICE, author, educator; b. Jacksonville, Fla., Jan. 21, 1933; d. Thompson Brooks Simkins and Leila (Meggs) Denham; student Mary Washington Coll., 1949-50, U. Tenn., 1950-51; B.A., U. N.C., 1953; M.A., U. Rochester, 1954; m. Lee Kutz, Aug. 4, 1954 (div. Dec. 1955). Free-lance author; asso. prof. English, John Jay Coll., City U. N.Y., N.Y.C., 1970—. Lectr. various colls., workshops, and orgns. MacDowell Colony fellow, 1969, 70, 71. Mem. Nat. Orgn. for Women, MacDowell Colony Fellows, Authors' Guild, P.E.N., Phi Beta Kappa. Author: My Darling From the Lions, 1968; The Ghost and Mrs. Muir, 1968; Coming Together, 1969, 70; Adios Sabata, 1971; Amo, 1974. Contbr. articles and stories to profl. publs. and mags. including Playboy, Cosmopolitan, N.Y. Times Book Rev. Home: 96 Grove St New York City NY 10014

DENHOF, MIKI, graphic designer; b. Triste, Italy, Jan. 1, 1912; d. Bernard and Olga (Krieger) Bardach; ed. Vienna, Austria, also Reiman Sch. Art. Berlin, Germany; m. Hans Denhof, Aug. 27, 1933 (div.). Came to U.S., 1938, naturalized, 1944. Asst. to art dir. Esquire mag., 1940-44; art dir. J. Walter Thompson, advt., 1944-45; promotion art dir. Conde Nast Publs., 1945-55; art editor Glamour mag., 1955-60, art dir., 1960-70; asso. editor House and Garden mag., 1970—; work represented in Art. Dirs. shows, also permanent graphic arts file Mus. Modern Art. Recipient awards Am. Graphic Arts Soc. Mem. Met. Mus. Art, Mus. Modern Art, Met. Opera Guild. Home: 227 Central Park W New York City NY 10024 also 17 Barns Lane Easthampton NY 11937 Office: Conde Nast Publs Inc 350 Madison Av New York City NY 10017

DENISON, BARBARA, librarian; b. Cleve., Dec. 12, 1926; d. Adam Benjamin and Ruth Ray (McConnell) Denison; A.B., Radcliffe Coll., 1948; M.A., Western Res. U., 1949, M.S. in L.S., 1965; student Katharine Gibbs Sch., 1950. Sec. U.S. Govt., Washington, 1950-53; sec. to dean, Sch. of Bus., Case Western Res. U., 1953-55, sec. to dean

Sch. Library Sci., 1955-56, research asso., 1956-60, adminstrv. asst., 1960-65, research asst., 1965-68, mgr. edn. research activities, 1968-70. Asst. curator Spl. Libraries Assn. loan collection, 1956-63, dir. spl. classifications center, 1963-66; mng. editor Ency. of Librarianship, 1961-66; exec. sec. Tng. Program in Med. Librarianship, 1967-70; music librarian Cleve. Pub. Library, 1970-74, music cataloger, 1974—. Mem. Cleve. Orch. Chorus; asst. minister music Plymouth Ch., Shaker Heights, O., 1973—. Fiscal officer Hope Inc., 1967-68. Mem. Archeol. Inst. Am., English-Speaking Union (dir. Cleve. chpt. 1961-66, sec. 1969-73), Musart Soc., Nat. Geog. Soc., Nat. Trust Historic Preservation. Author: (with Bertha R. Barden) two specialized bibliographies; also book and articles in journals; Co-author articles ency. Home: 12700 Shaker Blvd Cleveland OH 44120 Office: Cleveland Public Library 325 Superior Av Cleveland OH 44114

DENISON, MARY ELIZABETH, savs. and loan exec.; b. Bridgeport, Ill., May 13, 1921; d. Floyd Braxton and Ruth (Siegle) Denison; student Sanford Brown Bus. Coll., 1939. Bookkeeper Gen. Telephone Co., Olney, Ill., 1939-41; bookkeeper Lawrenceville (Ill.) Nat. Bank & Trust Co., 1941-46; v.p., mng. officer Lawrenceville Fed. Savs. & Loan Assn., 1946—. Mem. Lawrence County C. of C. (dir. 1971). Presbyn. (deacon 1967). Mem. Order Eastern Star, Women of the Moose. Home: 2113 Maple St Lawrenceville IL 62439 Office: 619 12th St Lawrenceville IL 62439

DENKHOFF, ELIZABETH, farm equipment co. exec.; b. Madelia, Minn., Oct. 12, 1914; d. Theodore Francis and Anna Maria (Meis) Denkhoff; student St. Louis Conservatory Mus., 1929-30, Brown's Bus. Coll., Davenport, Ia., 1934-35. Instr. secretarial sci. Brown's Bus. Coll., 1935-37; supr. office staff Motor Club Ia., Davenport, 1937-44; exec. sec. to pres. Deere & Co., 1944-64, exec. sec. to chmn. bd. and chief exec. officer, 1964-71, corporate sec., 1971—. Mem. Am. Soc. Corporate Secs., Nat. Secs. Assn. Democrat. Roman Catholic. Home: 2648 12th St Moline IL 61265 Office: John Deere Rd Moline IL 61265

DENMAN, MARY ELIZABETH WILLIAMS (MRS. RICHARD HASTINGS DENMAN), cosmetic co. exec.; b. Power, W.Va., June 28, 1922; d. Thomas Joseph and Rose Anna (Care) Williams; B.S. in Edn., Miami U., 1943; m. Richard Hastings Denman, Jan. 29, 1944; children—Daryl Ann Cates, Deborah, Richard Thomas. Free lance broadcaster, Corpus Christi, Tex., 1951-65; hostess, producer Our Town KENS-TV, San Antonio, 1966-73, news producer, broadcaster, 1973-74; v.p. Lorraine Basche, Inc., 1974—. Mem. Def. Adv. Com. Women in Services, 1972, chmn. sub-com. community relations, 1973—, vice chmn., 1974; chmn. San Antonio Cystic Fibrosis Fund, 1967-71; bd. mem. San Antonio Assn. for Blind, 1970—, Morningside Manor, San Antonio, 1972—, San Antonio chpt. Am. Heart Assn., 1972—; pres. Arts Council San Antonio, 1974—; bd. mem. San Antonio Little Theatre, 1972-73, Little Theatre, Corpus Christi, Tex., 1955-57. Recipient Nat. Cystic Fibrosis Research Found. award, 1972. Mem. Am. Women Radio and TV (chpt. pres. 1967-68, nat. v.p. 1969-72, Nat. TV Broadcaster of Year 1973), Women in Communications, Alpha Omicron Pi. Methodist. Home and office: 701 Strings Dr San Antonio TX 78216

DENNARD, LILLIAN MAURINE WHEELER (MRS. MACK WILLIAM DENNARD, SR.), secretarial service exec.; b. Dodd City, Tex., Feb. 25, 1929; d. Mitchell Gail and Florence Lillian (Glover) Wheeler; grad. high sch.; m. Mack William Dennard, Sr., Sept. 22, 1973; children by previous marriage—Danny Gail Campbell, Dorita Jean Campbell (Mrs. Ronnie Henderson), Mark Weldon Campbell. Owner, mgr. Sherman Telephone Answering & Secretarial Service (Tex.) 1962—; bldg. mgr. Sherman Exchange Office Bldg., 1968—; mgr. Woodland Terrace Apts., Sherman, 1972-73. Named Boss of Year, 1968-69. Methodist. Club: Soroptimist. Home: Route 1 Box A482 Pottsboro TX 75076 Office: 2007 Hwy 75 N Sherman TX 75090

DENNEY, ANNIE LORENE (MRS. ERNEST E. DENNEY), educator; b. Franklin, Ga., Feb. 24, 1932; d. Gordon and Annie Clem (Miller) Allen; student Berry Coll., 1948-50, N.E. La. State Coll., 1956-57; B.J. with honors, U. Tex., 1965; m. Ernest E. Denney, June 17, 1951; children—Deborah, Teresa, Pamela, Leisa. Relief woman's editor Winkler County News, Kermit, Tex., 1960-62; tchr. Austin (Tex.) Ind. Sch. Dist., 1967; tchr. journalism Reagan High Sch., Austin, 1971—. Neighborhood chmn. March of Dimes, 1973. Mem. Women in Communication, Austin Women's Tennis Assn. Baptist. Home: 6612 Argentia Rd Austin TX 78731 Office: 7104 Berkman St Austin TX 78752

DENNEY, FRANCES ETHEL MORRIS (MRS. FRANK C. DENNEY), realtor; b. Kansas City, May 5, 1899; d. William and Florence Eva (Shoup) Morris; student Kansas City Jr. Coll., 1917-18; m. Frank C. Denney, June 1, 1922; children—Frank Mike Carroll, Evalyn (Mrs. Maury Tuckerman Stadler), William George. Real estate broker Frances Denney, Realtor, Belton, Mo., 1952-70, asso., 1970—. Sec., treas. City of Belton Planning Comm., 1963, 64. Mem. Midwest Mo. Bd. Realtors (sec. 1953, 56, 57, 58, 59, 60, pres. 1964), Midwest, Mo. real estate bds., Mo. Real Estate Assn. Unitarian. Club: Kansas City (Mo.) Musical. Home: 711 Belton Av Belton MO 64012 Office: Scott St Belton MO 64012

DENNIN, MARJORIE CATHERINE WILKINS (MRS. JOHN HENRY DENNIN), coll. adminstr.; b. Barnesville, O., Oct. 5, 1918; d. Charles Walter and Mabel E. (Wilson) Wilkins; A.B., Mt. Union Coll., 1940; M.S., Cath. U. Am., 1964, postgrad., 1967—; m. John Henry Dennin, Jan. 20, 1951. Tchr., Pierpont (O.) Pub. Sch., 1940-42, Dover (O.) High Sch., 1942-44; recreational dir. A.R.C., China, India, 1944-46; librarian, Edison Electric Inst., N.Y.C., 1946-56, Am. Automobile Assn., Washington, 1960-64, Va. Theol. Sem., Alexandria, 1965; dir. learning resources No. Va. Community Coll., Annandale, 1965—. Mem. library adv. com. Va. State Council on Higher Edn., 1966—; mem. library tech. com. Met. Washington Council Govts., 1971—. Mem. Spl. Libraries Assn., Assn. Ednl. Communications and Tech., Am., Southeastern, Va. library assns. Home: 4320 Old Dominion Dr Arlington VA 22207 Office: 8333 Little River Turnpike Annandale VA 22003

DENNING, BERNADINE NEWSOM (MRS. BLAINE DENNING), ednl. adminstr.; b. Detroit, Aug. 17, 1930; d. William Charles and Evelyn Tyler (Pembrook) Newsom; B.S., Eastern Mich. U., 1951; M.Ed., Wayne State U., 1956, Edn. Specialist, 1966, Ed.D., 1970; m. Blaine Denning, Aug. 26, 1956. Tchr., Jefferson Jr. High Sch., Detroit, 1951-59; coordinator Great Cities Sch. Improvement Project, 1959-62; counselor Winship Jr. High Sch., Detroit, 1962-65; intercultural coordinator Detroit pub. schs., 1965-68; asst. dir. Parent-Tchr.-Student Activities, Detroit, 1968-72; dir. Dept. Sch. Vols., Detroit pub. schs., 1971; dir. urban program in edn. U. Mich., Ann Arbor, 1971, dir. spl. studies and projects Sch. Edn., 1972—. Instr. swimming Wayne County chpt. A.R.C., 1947—; asst. dir. Christmas Seal Camp, Chelsea, Mich., 1952-64, Burt R. Shurly Camp, Chelsea, 1964-66; membership chmn. Met. Detroit, YWCA, 1968-69, salute to youth chmn., 1969, chmn. bd. mgmt., 1970-73, mem. met. bd., 1970-73, nat. bd. dirs., chmn. health and environment, 1973; vice chmn. Central dist. Camp Fire Girls, Detroit, 1968-72; chmn. fashion extravaganza March of Dimes, Wayne County, 1972-73. Bd. dirs. Detroit council Camp Fire Girls, 1968—; mem. alumni bd. Wayne State U., 1970—; bd. dirs. Delta Home for Girls, Detroit, 1971-73, Homes for Black Children, Detroit, 1973. Recipient Faculty Women's scholarship, 1949; Joseph Doyle scholarship, 1950; State Bd. Edn. scholarship, 1951; Nat. Found. award, 1972, 73; Charlotte Farnsworth award Campfire Girls, 1972; March of Dimes, 1972. Mem. Am. Assn. U. Women (chpt. dir. 1969-70), Assn. Supervision and Curriculum Devel., Am. Edn. Research Assn., Detroit Women Sch. Adminstrs., Met. Edn. and Cultural Activities Assn., Met. Detroit Soc. Black Ednl. Adminstrs. (dir. 1968-73), Mich. Assn. Supervision and Curriculum Devel. (sec. 1970-71), Nat. Assn. Intergroup Relations Ofcls., Nat. Council Negro Women, N.A.A.C.P. (life), Nat. Soc. for Study Edn., Nat. Community Sch. Edn. Assn., Orgn. Suprs. and Adminstrs., Nat. Sch. Pub. Relations Assn., Nat. Conf. Social Welfare, Delta Kappa Gamma, Beta Sigma Phi, Delta Sigma Theta. Clubs: Health and Physical Education, Women's Economic (Detroit); Faculty Women's (U. Mich.). Home: 3309 Leslie St Detroit MI 48238 Office: 1102 Sch of Edn Univ Mich Ann Arbor MI 48104

DENNIS, BARBARA DUNHAM (MRS. WILLIAM WARREN DENNIS), editor; b. Oak Park, Ill., Aug. 21, 1918; d. Walter Edward and Belle (Shellabarger) Dunham; B.S., U. Ill., 1940, M.S., 1958; m. William Warren Dennis, Nov. 15, 1941; children—William Warren, Jane Ann. Reporter, News-Gazette, Champaign, Ill., 1939-41, Bur. County Republican, Princeton, Ill., 1947-52; editor Inst. Labor and Indsl. Relations U. Ill. at Urbana, 1952-67; mng. editor Jour. Human Resources, Indsl. Relations Research Inst., U. Wis.-Madison, 1967—. Mem. Women in Communications, Inc., Madison Press Club. Author: (with G.G. Somers) Arbitration and Social Change, 1970; Arbitration and the Expanding Role of Neutrals, 1971; Arbitration and the Public Interest, 1972; Labor Arbitration at the Quarter-Century Mark, 1973; Arbitration of Interest Disputes, 1974. Home: 12 Red Center Terrace Madison WI 53717 Office: 4321 Social Sci Bldg U Wis 1180 Observatory Dr Madison WI 53706

DENNIS, BEATRICE FORREST (MRS. EDWARD WIMBERLY DENNIS), physician; b. Vancouver, B.C., Can., Dec. 1, 1915; d. Kenrick Angus and Laurie Millam (Rowan) Forrest; came to U.S., 1925, naturalized, 1945; B.S., La. Poly. Inst., 1940; M.S., Emory U., 1942, M.D., 1948; m. Edward Wimberly Dennis, May 29, 1948; children—Sara Margaret, Edward Forrest, Kathleen Laurie, Kenrick Johnson. Intern Emory U. Hosp., 1948-49; research asst. U. Tex. M.D. Anderson Hosp., 1954-57; resident clin. pathology Baylor Med. Coll., 1966-70, research asso. Inst. for Lipid Research, Houston, 1970—. Mem. Mus. Fine Arts, Houston Symphony Soc., Houston Humane Soc., Houston Alley Theater, A.A.A.S., Nat. Hist. Soc., Smithsonian Instn. Home: 12214 Boheme St Houston TX 77024 Office: 6516 Bertner St Houston TX 77025

DENNIS, DEBBIE KAYE, coll. adminstr.; b. Newberry, S.C., Feb. 7, 1949; d. James Mower and Doris Azalee (Eargle) Dennis; B.A., Lander Coll., 1970; postgrad. U. S.C., 1970-71. Admissions counselor Lander Coll., Greenwood, S.C., 1970-71, dir. admissions, 1971—. Sec.-treas. S.C. High Sch. Coll. Relations Commn., 1973-74. Bd. dirs. Area 6 Tb and Respiratory Disease Assn., 1972—, chmn. cleaner air week poster contest, 1972-73. Mem. Am., Carolinas assns. collegiate registrars and admissions officers, So. Assn. Student Aid Adminstrs., S.C. Assn. Student Financial Aid Adminstrs., Alpha Phi. Home: 11A The Villas Greenwood SC 29646

DENNIS, JOANNE HESS (MRS. CARL E. DENNIS), journalist; b. Syracuse, N.Y., June 7, 1935; d. Bernard John and Mary Louise (Jost) Hess; B.A. in Journalism, Syracuse U., 1957; m. Carl E. Dennis, Aug. 24, 1957; children—Scott, Mary Helen. Communications specialist Crouse-Hinds Co., Syracuse, 1956-68, tour guide, 1956-68, editor house organ, 1961; feature writer Herald Jour., Syracuse, 1968—. Community ambassador from North Syracuse (N.Y.) to Spain, 1954; editor Heart Beats mag. Heart Assn. Upstate N.Y, 1972—. Mem. Women in Communications (v.p. 1970-72), Home: 434 Plymouth Dr Syracuse NY 13206 Office: Herald-Journal Clinton Square Syracuse NY 13201

DENNIS, LILA EGAN (MRS. RALPH E. DENNIS), psychologist; b. Johnstown, O., Apr. 14, 1926; d. Luke Leo and Gladys Lucille (Priest) Egan; B.S. in Edn., Ohio State U., 1966, M.A., 1967, Ph.D. in Psychology, 1971; m. Ralph E. Dennis, July 24, 1948; children—Terri Ann (Mrs. William Rollin), Deborah Ann, Mark James. Psychologist Delaware City Schs., Delaware, O., 1968; clin. psychologist Children's Mental Health Center, Columbus, O., 1968-69; sch. psychologist Columbus pub. schs., 1969—. Cons. to Alexander Graham Bell Sch., 1973—. Mem. Columbus Crisis Intervention Team, 1969. Bd. dirs. Northwest Psychol. Services, Columbus, 1973—. Ohio Youth Commn. grantee, 1968-69; Nat. Def. Edn. Act grantee, 1966-67. Mem. Am. Psychol. Assn., Nat. Assn. Sch. Psychologists, Ohio Sch. Psychologists Assn., Delta Delta Delta, Phi Delta Kappa. Home: 1557 Lafayette Dr Columbus OH 43220 Office: 450 East Fulton St Columbus OH 43210

DENNIS, MARY LEE, hosp. adminstr.; b. Durham, N.C., Mar. 19, 1920; d. William Kenneth and Irene William (Speed) Dennis; grad. Health Adminstrn. Mgmt. Improvement Program, Duke, 1974. With Jefferson Standard Life Ins. Co., 1939-68; admitting officer Watts Hosp., Durham, 1968-71; adminstr. Lenox Baker Cerebral Palsy and Crippled Children's Hosp. of N.C., Durham, 1971—. Charter mem., past treas. Duke Hosp. Vol. Services; mem. exec. services council N.C. Dept. Human Resources, 1972—; mem. Mental Retardation Inter-Agy. Planning Council, Durham, 1972—. Club: Altrusa (pres. 1973—) (Durham). Home: 1310 Leon St Durham NC 27705 Office: 3000 Erwin Rd Durham NC 27705

DENNISON, DOROTHY DELL, artist; b. Beaver, Pa., Feb. 13, 1908; d. Charles Robert and Mary Dell (Bartholomew) Dennison; student (Cresson scholar) Pa. Acad. Fine Arts, 1926-31; m. Joseph Green Butler, June 3, 1946; children—Joseph Green IV, Lorinda Trowbridge. Tchr., Knox Sch., Cooperstown, N.Y., 1939-42, Syracuse U., 1942-45, Russell Sage Coll., Troy, N.Y., 1945-46; exhibited numerous one man shows, including Kennedy Galleries, N.Y.C., 1974. Fellow Pa. Acad. Fine Arts; mem. Jr. League. Home: 1915 Walker Mill Rd Poland OH 44514

DENNY, ALMA, author; b. N.Y.C.; d. Jacob Henry and Pauline (Freed) Denenholz; A.B. cum laude, Hunter Coll., 1927; M.A., Columbia, 1937; m. Theodore Kaplan, July 1, 1928 (dec. Sept. 1964); children—Laura Jane (Mrs. Oliver Popenoe), Elizabeth Pearl (Mrs. Robert M. Secor). Tchr., Far Rockaway (N.Y.) High Sch., 1927-29; sect. mgr. Macy's, 1929-30; editorial asst. Simmons-Boardman Pub. Co., N.Y.C., 1946-49; free lance writer articles, features, humor, 1950-60; syndicated columnist Family Council Gen. Features Corp., 1960-65; asso. editor SIECUS (Sex Information and Edn. Council U.S.) Newsletter, 1965-68. Mem. Soc. Mag. Writers. Editorial bd. Newsletter of N.Y. chpt. Assn. Humanistic Psychology, 1973—. Contbr. articles, features to Retirement Living mag., profl. jours., other mags. Home: 205 W End Av New York City NY 10023

DENNY, CHARLOTTE CURTI (MRS. ERNEST O. DENNY), educator; b. Boston; d. Harry and Olive (Drewett) Curti; diploma Central Islip State Hosp. Sch. Nursing, 1941; B.S. magna cum laude, N.Y. U., 1955; M.A., U. Ky., 1959; postgrad. Coll. City N.Y.; m. Ernest O. Denny, Feb. 16, 1941 (div. 1972); children—Warren, Linda. Pub. health nurse Nassau County (N.Y.), 1949-52; sch. nurse, tchr. Harborfields Sch. Dist., Greenlawn, N.Y., 1954-57; coordinator practical nurses edn. Huntington (N.Y.) High Sch., 1957-58; asst. prof. Coll. Nursing, U. Ky. at Lexington, 1959-66; chmn. dept. nursing Eastern Ky. U., Richmond, 1967—. Mem. steering com. Midwest Continuing Profl. Edn. Nurses project, 1973-75; mem. Ky. Bd. Nursing, 1973-77. Vice pres. Northport-Ocean Av. P.T.A., 1953; chmn. health, nutrition, mental health, exec. council 7th Congl. dist. P.T.A., Ky., 1960-63. Recipient Founder's Day certificate N.Y.U., 1956. Fellow Am. Sch. Health Assn., Am. Pub. Health Assn.; mem. Royal Soc. Health, Am. Nurses Assn., Nat. League Nursing (chmn. health and career com. Ky. 1960-62, 2d v.p. 1968-70), Am. Personnel and Guidance Assn., Ky. Nurses Assn. (pres. dist. 2 1970-72, Ky. dir. 1972-76), Zonta Internat. Home: 3569 Olympia Rd Lexington KY 40502

DENO, EVELYN NEVA DREIR (MRS. JOHN J. DENO), univ. adminstr.; b. Norwalk, Wis., Jan. 8, 1911; d. August William and Jennie (Falke) Dreier; B.S., U. Minn., 1948, M.A., 1950, Ph.D., 1958; m. John J. Deno, Sr., Oct. 3, 1930; children—John Joseph, Stanley Lynn. Tchr. elementary sch. Beaver Dam (Wis.) Pub. Schs., 1930-31; instr. Miss Woods Kindergarten Tng. Sch., Macalester Coll., St. Paul, 1948-50; psychologist U. Minn. Nursery Sch. and Kindergarten, Mpls., 1948-50; instr. Inst. Child Devel., U. Minn., Mpls., 1950-58; dir. spl. edn. and rehab. Mpls. Pub. Schs., 1958-67; dir. Psychol. Edn. Center, U. Minn., 1967-71, prof. ednl. psychology, 1967—; asso. dir. Leadership Tng. Inst. in Spl. Edn., Nat. Center Improvement Edn. Systems, U.S. Office Edn., Mpls., 1971—, cons. Bur. Edn. Handicapped, 1960—. Chmn. statuatory adv. bd. Gifted and Exceptional Children, Minn., 1962-65, 69-71; mem. Instl. Rev. Bd., Faribault State Hosp., Dept. Pub. Welfare, Minn., 1971—. Bd. dirs. Children's Health Center, Mpls., 1968-72, Washburn Child Guidance Center, 1972-74. Recipient Spl. Educator of Year award Minn. Assn. Children with Learning Disabilities, 1971, Outstanding Spl. Educator award Mpls. Civitan Club, 1966. Diplomate Am. Bd. Profl. Psychologists. Mem. N.E.A., Council Exceptional Children (chmn. nat. legislative com. 1962-68), Am., Minn. (pres. 1969-70) psychol. assns., Minn. Psychol. Council (mem. exec. council 1967-70). Home: 4550 Edmund Blvd Minneapolis MN 55406

DENOYER, XENIA BILHORN (MRS. L. PHILIP DENOYER), educator, civic worker; b. Chgo., Sept. 22, 1893; d. John G. and Minnie Samantha (Jacobs) Bilhorn; grad. Chgo. Tchrs. Coll., 1914; student U. Chgo., 1916-27; m. L. Philip Denoyer, Mar. 8, 1930. Tchr. Richard Yates Sch., Chgo., 1914-31; girl scout leader, camp counselor, dir. Girl Scouts Am., Chgo., Wilmette, Kenilworth, Wheeling, Ill., 1919—. Recipient letter commendation, Girl Scouts Am., 1926; Spl. Tributes for 55 years Girl Scout leadership from nat. and local councils Girl Scouts, also from Congressman Samuel H. Young, Ill. Gov. Dan Walker and Pres. Nixon, 1973. Mem. Nat. Wildlife Fedn., Am. Geog. Soc., Am. Nature Assn. Methodist. Club: National Travel (N.Y.C.). Home: PO Box 96 Wheeling IL 60090 also PO Box 116 St Cloud FL 32769

DENSEN-GERBER, JUDIANNE (MRS. MICHAEL M. BADEN), psychiatrist, lawyer; b. N.Y.C., Nov. 13, 1934; d. Gustave A. and Beatrice (Densen) Gerber; A.B. cum laude, Bryn Mawr Coll., 1956; J.D., Columbia Law Sch., 1959; M.D., N.Y. U., 1963; m. Michael M. Baden, June 14, 1958; children—Trissa Austin, Judson Michael, Lindsey Robert, Sarah Densen Baden. Admitted to N.Y. bar, 1961; rotating intern French Hosp., N.Y.C., 1963-64; resident psychiatry Bellevue Hosp., N.Y.C., 1964-65, Met. Hosp., N.Y.C., 1965-67; mem. core staff Addiction Services Agy., N.Y.C., 1966-67; founder, exec. dir. Odyssey House, Inc., psychiat. hosps. for rehab. of narcotics addicts throughout U.S., N.Y.C., 1967—, also clin. dir., 1967-69, exec. dir., 1969—, pres. bd., 1967—; adj. asso. prof. law N.Y. Law Sch.; vis. asso. prof. law U. Utah Law Sch. Vice pres. psychiat. sect. Internat. Forensic Medicine Conf., Budapest, 1967; guest lectr. narcotics addiction N.Y. U. Sch. Medicine and Sch. Law; mem. nat. adv. commn. Criminal Justice Standards and Goals, columnist N.Y. Law Jour., Manchester Union Leader. Founder, pres. bd. dirs., exec. dir. Inst. Women's Wrongs. Recipient Woman of Achievement award N.Y. br. Am. Assn. U. Women, 1970; Myrtle Wreath award Hadassah, 1970; Woman of Greatness award B'nai B'rith, 1971. Fellow Am. Acad. Forensic Scis., Am. Acad. Legal Medicine; mem. A.M.A., N.Y., (com. drug abuse 1968—) New York County med. socs., Soc. Med. Jurisprudence, Am. Acad. Forensic Scis. (chmn. plenary session drug abuse 1969), Am. Bar Assn., Am. Psychiat. Assn., Am., N.Y. County bar assns. Republican. Unitarian. Club: Women's City (N.Y.C.). Author: (with daughter) Drugs, Sex, Parents and You, 1972; We Mainline Dreams: The Odyssey House Story. Contbr. articles to profl. jours. Office: 208-210 East 18th St New York City NY 10003

DENSLOW, MARY ELAINE, newspaper editor; b. Sandusky, O., Jan. 17, 1934; d. Edward Clarence and Margaret Juanita (Carney) Kochendoerfer; grad. high sch.; m. Claude H. Denslow, Sept. 7, 1953. Reporter, Sandusky Register, 1953-55, Clyde (O.) Enterprise, 1956-60; women's editor Fremont (O.) New Messenger, 1960-70; editor Gazette, Bellevue, O., 1970—. Mem. Fremont Meml. Hosp. Women's Aux., 1972—; pres. Fremont Fedn. Women, 1969-70, mem., 1972—. Home: 326 Douglas Dr Bellevue OH 44811 Office: Bellevue Gazette 107 N Sandusky St Bellevue OH 44811

DENSMORE, MARGARET E., physician; b. Los Angeles, Oct. 8, 1922; d. Robert E. and Louise (Black) Densmore; B.A., U. Cal. at Los Angeles, 1943; M.D., Woman's Med. Coll. Pa., 1947; postgrad. U. Pa., 1951-52. Intern Episcopal Hosp., Phila., 1947-48; resident Woman's Hosp. of Phila., 1948-51; practice medicine specializing in obstetrics and gynecology, Phila., 1952—; staff Delaware County Meml. Hosp., Upper Darby, Pa.; chief obstetrics and gynecology Presbyn. Hosp. Diplomate Am. Bd. Obstetrics and Gynecology. Fellow Am. Coll. Obstetrics and Gynecology; mem. A.M.A., Am. Med. Women's Assn., Phila. Obstet. Soc., Am. Com. for Maternal and Child Health, Flying Physicians Assn., Ninety-Nines, Aircraft Owners and Pilots Assn. Presbyn. Club: Medical Women (Phila.). Office: 1001 City Line Av Philadelphia PA 19151

DENSON, CLEMENTINE LENORE LIVELY, leasing co. exec.; b. Elkhart, Tex., Sept. 18, 1917; d. Wesley Carlton and Audrey Daile (Hawthorne) Lively; student Tyler Comml. Coll., 1936; m. Raymond Lawerence Denson, Sept. 3, 1933 (div. Sept. 1945); children—Raymond Larry, Gaile (Mrs. Thomas Craigton Nivens). Sec. bd. OPA, Palestine, Anderson County, Tex., 1945; sec. K Way Equipment Co., Inc., Palestine, Tex., 1945-52, sec.-treas., 1952—, also dir.; dir. K Way Builders Supply Co., Inc. Mem. bus. program adv. com. Anderson County Vocational Center, 1972—. Mem. Anderson County C. of C. Republican. Episcopalian. Mem. Order Eastern Star. Clubs: Harvey Woman's (Palestine); Altrusa (local pres. 1964-65, 70-71). Home: 3 Willow Slough Rd Elkhart TX 75839 Office: PO Box 259 Palestine TX 75801

DENT, FRANCES KELLY, assn. exec.; b. Rome, Ga., Nov. 3, 1925; d. James Frederick and Julia Guy (Thompson) Kelly; student Shorter Coll.; m. Charles Cary Dent, June 19, 1948; children—Charles Frederick, James Kelly. Chief clk. information office Battey Gen. Hosp., Rome, 1944-45; bus. mgr. Medici Corp., med. clinic, Rome, 1962-70; sec. to city mgr., Rome, 1970—; exec. sec. Floyd-Polk Chattooga County Med. Soc., 1954—. Exec. bd. Girl Scouts; chmn. govt. div. Heart Fund, 1974. Presbyn. (past Sunday sch. tchr.). Clubs: Coosa Country, Town and Country Garden (past pres.). Home: 317 E 4th St Rome GA 30161 Office: City of Rome PO Box 1433 Rome GA 30161

DENTON, ALICE DEATHERAGE (MRS. JESSE CAMERON DENTON), librarian; b. Denver, June 12, 1925; d. Cecil Elmer and Anna Estella (Parham) Deatherage; B.A. with honors, Swarthmore Coll., 1947; M.L.S., Tex. Woman's U., 1967; postgrad George Washington U., 1971; m. Jesse Cameron Denton, May 1, 1948; children—Laura Anne, Thomas Cameron. Tchr., Westridge Sch. for Girls, Pasadena, Cal., 1948-49; reference librarian Dallas Pub. Library, 1967-68, U.S. Geol. Survey, Washington, 1968-73; librarian interlibrary loan Paley Library Temple U., Phila., 1973—. Active Girl Scouts Am., 1961-64, Boy Scouts Am., 1962-68; unit chmn. Host Family Program, Dallas, 1964-65. Mem. Am. Library Assn., Spl. Libraries Assn., Am. Assn. U. Women. Home: 111 David Rd Bala Cynwyd PA 19004 Office: Samuel Paley Library Temple University Broad and Montgomery Sts Philadelphia PA 19122

DENTON, ALTA PATRICIA, med. center exec.; b. St. Joseph, Mo., Jan. 4, 1936; d. Don Virgle and Gladys (Dutton) Denton; B.S., Oklahoma City U., 1958; postgrad. U. Chgo., 1958-59. Interviewer, counselor pub. co. Reuben H. Donnelley Corp., Chgo., 1961-62; employment mgr. U. Ill. at Chicago Circle and Med. Center, 1965-68; employment mgr. U. Ill. Med. Center, Chgo., 1962-65, 68-72, asso. dir. personnel services, 1972—. Mem. bus. adv. council Jones Comml. High Sch., 1967—, mem. ednl. council, 1970-71. Mem. Coll. and U. Personnel Assn. (dir. 1971-73, chmn. 1970-71, communications adv. com. 1972-75), Soc. Personnel Adminstrs. (treas. 1972), Internat. Assn. Personnel Women (conf. chmn. 1974), Women in Personnel Chgo. (pres. 1970-71), Chgo. Hosp. Personnel Mgmt. Assn. (sec. 1967-68), Gamma Phi Beta (Lindsey Barbee nat. fellow 1958). Presbyn. Home: 1700 N North Park Av Chicago IL 60614

DENTON, ELEANOR OMER (MRS. CLARK WELLS DENTON), librarian; b. Evanston, Ill., Aug. 23, 1910; d. Lewis and Edith Alice (Nevins) Omer; A.B., Carthage Coll., 1931; M.S., U. Neb., 1933, Ph.D., 1936; B.L.S., U. Ill., 1939; m. Clark Wells Denton, July 21, 1939; 1 dau., Margaret (Mrs. Michael John Siemion). Chem. research librarian Wyandotte (Mich.) Corp., 1939-46, 48—, (name changed to BASF Wyandotte Corp. 1970). Mem. Am. Chem. Soc., Spl. Libraries Assn., Bus. and Profl. Womens Club, Sigma Xi, Iota Sigma Pi, Sigma Delta Epsilon. Republican. Presbyn. Home: 645 Emmons Blvd Wyandotte MI 48192 Office: BASF Wyandotte Corp Wyandotte MI 48192

DENTON, EMMA MANEY, banker; b. Hiawassee, Ga., Nov. 25, 1905; d. Milton M. and Missouri (Eller) Maney; student pvt. schs., Hiawassee, Ga.; m. James Young Denton, May 20, 1920; children—J.C., Evelyn Isabel (Mrs. William T. Groves), Ruth Elois (Mrs. Robert L. Anderson), J. William, Emma Jean (Mrs. Ray W. Anderson). Asso. cashier Bank of Hiawassee, Ga., 1936-70, cashier, 1970—, dir., 1950—. Chmn. county drive Am. Cancer Soc., 1944-60. Mem. D.A.R., Friendship Community Club, Hiawassee Garden Club (charter mem., pres. 1960—). Baptist. Address: Hiawassee GA 30546

DENTON, GISELE ANN PEZZETTA (MRS. LEWIS KARL DENTON), advt. agy. exec.; b. Bari, Italy, Oct. 21, 1937 (parents Am. citizens); d. Erasmus R. and Amelia Claire (Finamore) Pezzetta; B.S. in Bus. Adminstrn., U. Denver, 1961; m. Lewis Karl Denton, May 26, 1961; children—Lewis K. II, Lance Kip. Advt. sales, media liaison Sat. Evening Post, Curtis Pub. Co., Phila., 1955-58; merchandising asst. Valspar Corp., Denver, 1961-66; media research analyst Henderson, Bucknum, Inc., Denver, 1966-68, media dir., 1968-73; v.p., media dir. Lowe, Kojis & Bucknum, Inc., Denver, 1974—. Del. Arapahoe County Republican Conv., 1968-72. Bd. dirs. Ben Franklin Parent-Tchr. Orgn., 1973-74, Il Circolo Italiano. Mem. Denver Advt. Club (mem. edn. com. 1973), Colo. Broadcasters Assn. (mem. edn. com. 1973-74), Sons of Italy, Am. Assn. U. Women, Phi Gamma Nu (alumni pres. 1964-68). Home: 2036 E Mineral Av Littleton CO 80122 Office: PO Box 9569 Denver CO 80209

DENTON, MARY JANE, psychologist; b. Williamsburg, Kan., Dec. 26, 1935; d. Densil R. and Dessie L. (White) Denton; B.A., Friends U., Wichita, Kan., 1957; M.Ed. (fellow), So. Ill. U., 1959; Ed.D. (assistantship), Okla. State U., 1964. Clin. intern Muskogee (Okla.) Guidance Center, 1964-65; psychologist mental health div. Hawaii State Dept. Health, 1967-69; supr. psychol. services San Francisco pub. schs., 1969-70; learning specialist Oakland (Cal.) pub. schs., 1970-72; coordinator opportunity program McClymond's High Sch., Oakland, 1972-73; dir. precision teaching and contingency mgmt. program Oakland pub. schs., 1973—; pvt. practice, San Francisco, 1972—; asso. mem. staff Walnut Creek Hosp., 1974—. Home: 23 Rishell Dr Oakland CA 94619 Office: 3870 Paseo Padre Pkwy C-11 Fremont CA

DENUCCIO, SUSAN HODGES (MRS. PAUL ARMARD DENUCCIO), compensation analyst; b. Indpls., Oct. 26, 1949; d. Earl Franklin and Margarite Elaine (Rambin) Hodges; B.S., Purdue U., 1971, M.S., 1971; M. Pub. Adminstrn., U. Denver, 1973; m. Paul Armard DeNuccio, Feb. 14, 1971. Resident dir. U. Denver, 1971-73; compensation analyst Dayton Hudson Corp., Mpls., 1973—. Mem. Nat. Assn. Student Personnel Adminstrs., Nat. Assn. Women Deans and Counselors, Nat. Orgn. for Women, Am. Compensation Assn., Twin Cities Personnel Assn., Mortar Bd., Alpha Lambda Delta, Phi Mu. Home: 1861 Beaumont St Maplewood MN 55117 Office: 777 Nicollet Mall Minneapolis MN 55117

DEPASQUALE, BARBARA JEAN SORLIEN (MRS. WILLIAM J. DEPASQUALE), musician; b. Fargo, N.D.; d. Leon C. and Norma (Devol) Sorlien; student (scholar) Minn. extension dept. for violin study, 1949-51; Mus.B., Curtis Inst. Music, 1955; student (scholar) Berkshire Music Center, summer 1953, Marlboro (Vt.) Sch. Music, summer 1958; postgrad. (Fulbright scholar) Mozarteum, Salzburg, Austria, 1958-59; m. William J. dePasquale, July 7, 1955. Mem. 1st violin sect. Nat. Symphony Orch., Washington, 1955-58, New Orleans Philharmonic, 1959-63, Phila. Orch., 1963—; mem. Mus. Arts String Quartet (players for Young Audiences concerts), New Orleans, 1959-63; 1st violinist Santa Fe Opera, summer 1961; mem. Bowdoin Coll. Chamber Players, summers 1962-63; duo violin concert tours with husband throughout U.S., Austria, Italy. Recipient Heifetz award Berkshire Music Center, Lenox, Mass., 1953. Mem. Sigma Alpha Iota. Home: 1209 Woodbine Av Penn Valley Narberth PA 19072 Office: 230 S 15th St Philadelphia PA 19102

DEPAULA, GERALDINE FITZGERALD (MRS. CARL J. DEPAULA), physician; b. Utica, N.Y., Aug. 10, 1941; d. John Shanley and Beulah Louise (Gschwind) Fitzgerald; B.A., Vassar, 1963; M.D. with thesis honors, State U. N.Y. at Buffalo, 1968; m. Carl J. DePaula, June 24, 1967; children—Carl Alexander, Geoffrey Reid. Intern Deaconess Hosp., Buffalo, 1968-69; resident psychiatry Eastern Pa. Psychiat. Inst., Phila., 1969-72, chief resident, 1971-72, now dir. continuing med. edn. Home: 8505 Patton Rd Philadelphia PA 19118 Office: Eastern Pennsylvania Psychiat Inst Philadelphia PA 19129

DEPAZZI, EUGENIA ELLEN BOSLEY (MRS. PAZZINO DE'PAZZI), artist; b. Elcador, Ia.; d. Benjamin Harrison and Cecelia Hartlee (Gilman) Bosley; student Ind. U., 1934-38, N.Y. Bus. Sch., 1938-39, L.I. U., 1966-67; studied art under Caterina Baratelli, Rio de Janeiro, 1948-52, Blaue Rider; m. Pazzino de' Pazzi, Aug. 17, 1940; children—Cosimo, Victor Allen. One man show Am. Bible Soc. Nat. Hdqrs., N.Y.C., 1970; exhibited in group shows, including Little Studio, N.Y.C., Pietrantonio, N.Y.C., Jason Gallery, N.Y.C. Parrish Mus., Southampton, L.I., Burliuk Gallery, Hampton Bay, L.I., Westhampton Gallery on L.I., La Guna Gloria Mus., Austin, Tex., Galerie Monmarte, Palm Beach, Fla., Cheekwood Mus., Nashville, Speed Mus., Louisville, Christ Ch. Retrospective, N.Y.C., Mexicano-Norte Americano-Norte Americano Instituto, Monterrey, Mexico, Central Presbyn. Galerie 64 Exhbn., N.Y.C., 1972; represented in permanent collections of Am. Freedom Found. Collection, NASA, Lyndon B. Johnson; participating artist Southampton Coll. Ann. Fine Arts Festivals-Art Exhbns., 1963—; co-chmn., co-founder Westhampton Outdoor Art Show, 1959-73; co-dir. Hampton Art Center and Sch., Quoque, N.Y.; also art tchr. social services for mentally disturbed patients Central Islip Hosp., 1968-69; chmn. Episcopalian Ch. Women fund raising activities; pub. relations work in all media for benefits for South Fork Craftsmen's Guild, Easthampton, L.I., 1960—. Mem. Guild Hall (membership com. 1964-70). Episcopalian. Home: 44 Bayfield Lane The Studio Westhampton Beach NY 11978 also Via Belisario Vinta Florence Italy

DE PÍNERO, EUROPA GONZÁLEZ GARRIGA (MRS. JOSE A. DE PINERO), educator; b. Aguadilla, P.R., Feb. 1, 1918; d. Juan C. Gonzalez Giocoechea and Maria Garriga Chacon; B.A. in Edn., U. P.R., 1938, profl. diploma, 1954; M.A. in Edn., N.Y. U., 1956, Ed.D., 1965; m. Jose A. de Pinero, Dec. 22, 1939; children—Jose Juan, Luis Roberto, Europa Maria (Mrs. Alfredo del Valle), Imgard L. Tchr. elementary, jr. and high schs., prin. P.R. Dept. Pub. Instrn., 1938-58, asst. supt., supt. schs., 1960-65; instr. edn., supr. students U. P.R., 1958-60; prof., chmn. dept. edn. Inter Am. U. P.R., Hato Rey, 1966-70, dean acad. affairs, 1970-73, prof. grad. studies Sch. Edn., 1974—. Mem. cons. com. for devel. vocational and tech. edn. P.R. Dept. Edn.; cons. P.R. Dept. Sch. Prins., 1968—; mem. sch. bd., pres. acad. com. Caribbean Consol. Schs. P.R., 1967-69. Recipient awards for outstanding ednl. work. Mem. Am. Assn. Colls. Tchr. Edn. (Distinguished Achievement award 1969), Assn. for Supervision and Curriculum Devel., Assn. for Childhood Edn. Internat., Am. Assn. for Higher Edn., Nat. Inst. for Advanced Study in Teaching Disadvantaged, Nat. Assn. for Edn. Young Children, Nat. Home Study Council, Am. Acad. Polit. and Social Sci., N.E.A. (life), Tchrs. Assn. P.R., Am. Assn. U. Profs., N.Y. U. Alumni Assn. P.R. (past pres.). Author: Tendencias Ideas Pedagogicas: Su Aplicacion en Puerto Rico, 1971; Accountability and Change in Education, 1972; Schools in Transitition, 1973; El Director de las Escuelas Publicas de Puerto Rico: Sus Problemas, Intereses y Necesidados, 1973; Del Quehacer Educativo Puertorriqueno, 1974. Contbr. articles to ednl. jours. Home: 372 R Lamar St Hato Rey PR 00918

DEPPER, ESTELLE MARLENE, banker; b. Oakland, Cal.; d. Martin S. and Estelle M. Depper; A.B., U. Cal. at Berkeley, 1964, J.D., 1967. Admitted to Cal. bar, 1967; asst. v.p. Wells Fargo Bank, trust dept., San Francisco, 1967—. Mem. Women in Communications, Am., San Francisco, Alameda bar assns., Queen's Bench. Home: 3848 Sacramento St San Francisco CA 94118 Office: PO Box 44002 San Francisco CA 94144

DEPUY, MARY BONNAR (MRS. HENRY C. DEPUY), librarian; b. New Bedford, Mass., Aug. 19, 1917; d. James Miller and Jane (Forsyth) Bonnar; A.B. Colby Coll., 1940; B.S. in Library Sci., Simmons Coll., 1941;; m. Henry C. DePuy, Sept. 29, 1967. Reference librarian N.Y. Pub. Library, N.Y.C., 1941-45; lit. searcher Am. Chem. Soc., N.Y.C., 1945-46; librarian Burroughs Wellcome & Co., Inc., Triangle Park, N.C., 1947—. Cons. H. W. Wilson Co., 1965-70. Mem. adv. council N.C. Central U. Library Sch., 1973—. Mem. Am. Soc. Information Sci., Spl. Libraries Assn. (chmn. pharm. div. 1957-58). Home: 5918 Winthrop Dr Raleigh NC 27612 Office: Burroughs Wellcome & Co Inc 3030 Cornwallis Rd Res Triangle Park NC 27709

DEPWE, MAYDA ANNETTE (MRS. RAYMOND DEPWE), psychologist; b. Frederick, Okla., Dec. 29, 1933; d. Chester and Rachel (Chambers) Cruse; A.A., U. Cal. at Los Angeles, 1954, B.A., 1956; M.Ed., Stephen F. Austin U., 1964; m. Raymond Depwe, Feb. 14, 1958. Ednl. specialist for Marine Corps, Camp Pendleton, Cal., 1956-58; tchr. and counselor Edison Jr. High, Port Arthur, Tex., 1959-62, counselor, 1962-65; asst. dir. pupil personnel services, Port Arthur Ind. Sch. Dist., 1965-71; psychologist West Orange Cove Consol. Ind. Sch. Dist., Orange, Tex., 1971—. Mem. Community Concert Assn., Port Arthur, 1960—; mem. P.T.A., Port Arthur, 1963—. Mem. Am. Psychol. Assn., Am. Personnel and Guidance Assn., Am. Sch. Counselors Assn., Tex. Personnel and Guidance Assn., Tex. State Tchrs. Assn., Council of Exceptional Children, Internat. Transactional Analysis Assn., Phi Beta Kappa. Presbyn. (mem. choir 1969—). Home: 3425 Memorial Blvd Port Arthur TX 77640 Office: Box 1107 Orange TX 77630

DERBECK, JEANNE ENID LUTHMAN, journalist; b. South Bend, Ind., July 14, 1920; d. Theodore Otto and Alva Victoria (Chilberg) Luthman; B.A., Ind. U., 1969; M.A., U. Notre Dame, 1971; 1 dau., Patricia Antonia. Proofreader, South Bend Tribune, 1967-69, gen. assignment reporter, 1970—, youth page editor, 1970-71, action line columnist, 1971—. Grad. fellow U. Notre Dame. Mem. No. Ind. Hist. Soc., Notre Dame English Assn., Phi Beta Kappa, Alpha Mu Gamma. Home: 3112 Rue Renoir St South Bend IN 46615 Office: 225 W Colfax St South Bend IN 46625

DERBY, CHARLOTTE MAY SCHAEDEL (MRS. CLARENCE J. DERBY), civic worker; b. Melrose, Mass., Feb. 7, 1908; d. Charles Seagrave and Mary (Sutherland) Schaedel; B.Secretarial Sci., Boston U., 1929; postgrad. Harvard, summers, 1935, 37; m. Clarence J. Derby, Jan. 14, 1940; children—John Webster, Charles Wilkins. Head comml. dept. Peterborough (N.H.) High Sch., 1929-39; v.p., sec. Derby's Inc., dept. store, Peterborough, 1945-71. Instr., Monadnock Community Coll., 1962-63. Pres., Hosp. Aid Soc., 1942-43; pres. Peterborough Assn. Girl Scouts U.S.A., 1946-50, chmn. state camp com., 1948-50, mem. New Eng. camping com., 1951-57; chmn. blood program Peterborough chpt. A.R.C., 1954-63, mem. exec. com. Vt.-N.H. regional blood program, 1957—, chmn., 1958-61, mem. Eastern Area adv. council, 1962-65, sec., 1964-65; area chmn. Am. Cancer Soc., 1957-59; trustee, treas. Monadnock Community Hosp., 1962—; pres. Peterborough Woman's Club, 1946-47. Recipient Citizen of Year award V.F.W., 1962. Mem. League Women Voters, N.H., Malden, Peterborough (pres. 1959-65) hist. socs., Am. Assn. State and Local History, Am. Assn. U. Women (pres. Monadnock br. 1944-46). Republican. Conglist. (tchr., supt., deaconess). Home: 45 High St Peterborough NH 03458 Office: 30 Grove St Peterborough NH 03458

DERDARIAN, MAE MIKJIAN, pub. relations exec.; b. Detroit, Oct. 31, 1921; d. Paul O. and Sophie (Kalayjian) Mikjian; B.A., Wayne State U., 1943; m. Samuel G. Derdarian, Oct. 11, 1947 (div. June, 1951); 1 dau., Christine Anne. Copywriter, Simons-Michelson Advt. Co., Detroit, 1943-47; continuity dir. radio sta. WJBK, 1947-48, radio sta. WJLB, 1949-55; dir. pub. relations United Community Services Met. Detroit, 1955—. Mem. steering com. Pres.'s Regional Great Lakes Consumer Conf., 1964; mem. Mayor's coms. Better Transp., Detroit Olympics, Good Citizenship, 1961-65; mem. adv. com. Adoption and Foster Care, Mich. Dept. Social Services, 1969—. Named one of fifty outstanding women by Gov. Mich., 1966, Detroit Advt. Women Year, 1965, one of Detroit's top ten working women Central Bus. Dist. Assn. Detroit, 1967, Headliner of Year Theta Sigma Phi, 1972, Women of Wayne State U. Headliner award, 1973. Mem. Pub. Relations Soc. Am., Women in Communications Inc. Clubs: Detroit Press, Women's Economic (dirs. 1971-72, v.p. 1973-74), Women's Advertising (pres. 1961-62) (Detroit). Home: 2676 Heathfield Rd Birmingham MI 48010 Office: 51 W Warren St Detroit MI 48201

DERIAN, PATRICIA MURPHY, Dem. nat. committeewoman; b. N.Y.C.; d. Ronald and Ruby (Haridman) M.; ed. Palos Verdes Coll., Millsaps Coll.; grad. U. Va. Sch. Nursing; m. Paul S. Derian, Mar. 7, 1953; children—Michael Tabore, Thomas Craig, Renee Brooke. Chmn. Women in Miss. for Humphrey-Muskie, 1968; mem. Dem. Nat. Com., 1968—, del. convs., 1968, 72, mem. exec. com. policy council, 1969-73, vice-chmn. rules com., 1972; mem. exec. com., v.p. So. Regional Council, 1973—; Miss. campaign mgr., McGovern/Shriver, 1972; mem. charter commn. Nat. Dem. party. Bd. dirs. Civic Communications Corp., Delta Ministry. Bd. dirs. Miss. Council Human Relations, Center Correctional Justice, Operation Shoestring, Mississippians for Pub. Edn.; nat. bd. dirs. Am. Civil Liberties Union, also bd. dirs. Mem. Gallery Guild, League of Women Voters, Nat. Women's Polit. Caucus. Address: 2349 Twin Lakes Circle Jackson MS 39211

DE RIVERA, DOROTHY PEARL BEHM (MRS. JAMES ENRIQUEZ DE RIVERA), librarian; b. Libertyville, Ill., Mar. 1, 1922; d. Michael L. and Erma Cora (Oryer) Behm; B.A., Mundelein Coll., 1946; M.Ed., Northeastern Ill. U., 1970; postgrad. U. Americas, Mexico City, Mexico, 1955, U. Ariz., 1957, Tex. Western U., 1961, Northeastern N.M. U., 1962; m. James Enriquez de Rivera, Apr. 22, 1946; children—Sue Anne (Mrs. Raymond G. Foss), Charles, Michael, James, John. Owner gift shop, Libertyville, 1944-48; story lady, sta. mgr. KNOG, Nogales, Ariz., 1953-55; producer, master of ceremonies Internat. Variety Show, KOPO-TV, Tucson, 1954-55; radio and TV columnist Nogales Herald, 1954-55; tchr. elementary sch. Nogales, 1956-59, El Paso, Tex., 1959-62, Walker AFB, Roswell, N.M., 1962-63, Deerfield, Ill., 1963-68; elementary sch. librarian, audiovisual coordinator Deerfield (Ill.) Pub. Schs., 1968—, Cadwell Elementary Sch., Deerfield, 1968—. Mem. N.E.A. (life), Ill. Edn. Assn., Nat. Council Tchrs. English, Internat. Reading Assn., A.L.A., Chgo.-Suburban Audiovisual Roundtable, Chgo. Council Fgn. Relations, Ill. Librarians Assn., Ill. Assn. Sch. Librarians, Ill. Audiovisual Assn. for Ednl. Communications, Deerfield Hist. Soc. (dir. 1969-72), Deerfield Tchrs. Assn. (charter mem., pres., 1967-68, dir. 1963-67, social chmn. 1972-73), Mundelein Coll. Alumnae Assn. (mem. governing bd. 1971—, rep. to Internat. Fedn. Cath. Alumnae 1973-74), Alpha Tau Omega Parents Assn. at U. Ia. (pres. 1970-71), Cath. Daus. Am. Roman Catholic. Home: 509 Willow Av Deerfield IL 60015 Office: 445 Pine St Deerfield IL 60015

DERMODY, MARY LOUISE, constrn. co. exec.; b. Zookspur, Ia., June 18, 1917; d. John Andrew and Rose (Pozega) Turkal; grad. Des Moines Bus. Coll., 1935; m. John Daniel Dermondy, Sept. 2, 1938; children—John Paul, Mary (Mrs. John McGrath). With accounting dept. Meredith Publs., Inc., Des Moines, 1936-38, Panama Canal, 1941; sec.-treas. J.D. Dermody Co. Inc., Lancaster, Cal. Project dir. Women in Community Service, Job Corps, 1965—. Chmn. Heart Assn. Antelope Valley, Cal., 1964-74, chmn. phono-cardio-scan program, 1970-74. Democratic precinct chmn., 1958-61; committeewoman Cal. State Dem. Central Com., 1964—; mem. adv. com. Dem. Women's Forum, 1962-75; co-chmn. Robert Kennedy campaign, 1968; observer Dem. Nat. Conv., 1968; Dem. candidate for Cal. Assembly, 1968; coordinator numerous polit. campaigns. Named Vol. of Year in Los Angeles County, 1969, 70; recipient Distinguished Service award Dem. Party, 1969. Mem. Women's Bus. and Profl. Soc., Lancaster C. of C. Rotary-Ann. Home: 44856 15th St W Lancaster CA 93534 Office: 45038 N Yucca Av Lancaster CA 93534

DERNER, CAROL ANN NIEDHAMMER (MRS. GEORGE B. DERNER), librarian; b. Evansville, Ind., May 12, 1934; d. Jacob Christopher and Catherine Loretta (Grant) Niedhammer; B.A. in Am. Lit., Ind. U., 1956, M.A. in Library Sci., 1958;; m. George B. Derner, May 4, 1957. Bookmobile librarian Gary (Ind.) Pub. Library, 1956-57, young adult librarian, head popular library, head extension dept., 1963-67; children's librarian Bloomington (Ind.) Pub. Library, 1958-59, Pub. Libraries Lake County, Ind., 1959-60; librarian Valparaiso (Ind.), 1960-63, then Gary Pub. Library; head librarian Elmwood Park (Ill.) Pub. Library, 1968—. Pres. YWCA, Gary, 1966-67; bd. dirs. League Women Voters, Elmwood Park, 1970—. Mem. Am., Ill. (sec. pub. library sect. 1973-74) library assns., Library Adminstrs. Conf. No. Ill. (sec. 1971-72). Home: 2445 N 77th Av Elmwood Park IL 60635 Office: 7705 Westwood Dr Elmwood Park IL 60635

DEROSE, ANNE KONTAS (MRS. PAUL M. DEROSE), social worker; b. Lansing, Mich., Feb. 3, 1929; d. Charles and Alexandra (Revezika) Kontas; B.A., Mich. State U., 1951, M.S.W., 1965; m. Paul M. DeRose, July 27, 1952; children—Daniel, Marc, Lynne. Staff social worker Dept. Social Services, Lansing, Mich., 1951-53; asst. dir. spl. research project on cholesterol dept. econs. Mich. State U., East Lansing, 1958-60; pvt. instr. music Dunning Group Method, Lansing, 1960-62; staff social worker Family Service Agy., Lansing, 1962-64, Lansing Mental Health Center-Child and Adult Services, 1965-68; lectr., field instr. Sch. Social Work Mich. State U., 1965—, lectr. dept. psychiatry, 1968—. Dir. social work St. Lawrence Community Mental Health Center, Lansing, 1968-69, coordinator community services, 1969—; mem. Capital Area Comprehensive Health Planning Assn. Mem. Tri County Com. on Drug Abuse, 1969-70; mem. exec. bd. Big Sisters of Lansing, 1967-68, adv. bd., 1968-70. Named Social Worker of Year Lansing, 1971-72. Mem. Nat. Assn. Social Workers (exec. bd. 1965-69, v.p. 1968-69), Acad. Certified Social Workers, Mich. State U. Social Work Alumni Assn. (exec. bd. 1965-70), Greater Lansing Social Service Assn. (sec. 1968-69), Community Mental Health Assn. Mich., Am. Assn. Vol. Services Coordinators. Author: Blueprint: A Volunteer Program, 1973. Home: 1232 Hitchingpost Rd East Lansing MI 48823 Office: 1201 W Oakland St Lansing MI 48915

DERREVERE, HARRIET ELIZABETH (MRS. WILLIAM R. DERREVERE), educator, artist; b. Baton Rouge, Mar. 20, 1947; d. Russell Eugene and Geraldine Elizabeth (Moore) Koons; B.F.A., U. Tulsa, 1969; M.A., Western Ill. U., 1971; m. William R. Derrevere, May 16, 1970. Asst. to dir. Philbrook Art Center, Tulsa, 1969-70,

71-73; instr. art Tulsa Jr. Coll., 1973—; exhibited in two person shows at Western Ill. U., Macomb, 1971, Alexandre Hogue Gallery, U. Tulsa, 1971, E. Central State Coll., Ada, Okla., 1972, Accent Framing Ltd., Tulsa, 1972; Philbrook Art Center, 1974; exhibited in group shows at Philbrook Art Center, 1970-73, E. Central State Coll., 1972, U. Tulsa Alexandre Hogue Gallery, 1971, Midwest Women's Art Exhbn., No. Ill. U., DeKalb, 1971, Okla. Mus. Art, Oklahoma City, 1973, Ark. Art Center, Little Rock, 1973; represented in permanent collections at Ark. Art Center, Philbrook Art Center, Tulsa City-County Library. Home: 1347 E 19th St Tulsa OK 74120

DERRICKSON, WINIFRED COX (MRS. HOWARD SICKEL DERRICKSON), librarian; b. Gentry, Ark., Feb. 11, 1916; d. Fred and Alice Josephine (Oakley) Cox; student Central State Tchrs. Coll., 1933-35, Oklahoma City U., 1935-36; B.A., U. Okla., 1937; tchrs. certificate U. Mo., 1968; m. Howard Sickel Derrickson, July 5, 1945; children—Fred Cox (dec.), Ann Lenore. Tchr.-librarian high sch., Pryor, Okla., 1937-38; librarian Pub. Library, Seminole, Okla., 1938-41, Wewoka, Okla., 1941-44; air base librarian U.S. Govt., Richmond, Fla., 1944-45, 7th Naval Dist. librarian, 1945; asst. head dept. Washington U., St. Louis, 1946-47; librarian St. Louis Country Day Sch., St. Louis, 1958—. Mem. Am. Assn. U. Women (state sec. 1944), Bus. and Profl. Women's Club (pres. 1940-41), Greater St. Louis Library Club (treas. 1963-65, pres. 1965-66, mem. council 1967-68), Suburban Librarians (profl. growth chmn. 1973-75). Club: Washington University Woman's (St. Louis). Home: 6312 Pershing Av St Louis MO 63130 Office: 425 N Warson Rd St Louis MO 63124

DERRY, LAURA MILLER (MRS. STEPHEN ARTHUR DERRY), lawyer; b. nr. Canmer, Ky., May 22, 1905; d. Robert Emmett and Cattie Lieu (Rowntree) Miller; student Rutgers U., N.J. State Tchrs. Coll.; A.B., Bowling Green Coll. Commerce, 1933; J.D., U. Louisville, 1936; m. Stephen Arthur Derry, Aug. 12, 1944; 1 dau., Portia Kay. Admitted to Ky. bar, since practiced law Louisville; first woman to try a case before a Ct. Martial of U.S. Army, first woman to win a case involving a capital punishment before a Gen. Ct. Martial; conducted nat. survey of women in pub. service, 1956; survey of women lawyers in pub. service in U.S., 1957. Accredited observer UN, 1946, rep. UN Relief and Rehab. Council meeting, 1946; rep. Pres.'s Hwy. Conf., 1945, 46, Pres.'s Hwy. Safety Conf., Washington, 1956. Mem. patron's com. Internat. Debutante Ball, N.Y., 1969-70. Mem. Internat. Assn. Women Lawyers, Nat. Assn. Women Lawyers (pres. 1946), Am. (del. London meeting 1957), Louisville, Ky. bar assns., Nat. Assn. Parliamentarians (nat. officer, state dir.), Nat. Fedn., Louisville (chmn. legislation com.) bus. and profl. women's clubs, Kappa Beta Pi. Author, compiler: Digest of Women Lawyers and Judges. Contbr. articles to profl. jours. Home: 1815 Yale Dr Louisville KY 40205

DERRY, LOIS BRUHN (MRS. WILLIAM DEAN DERRY), real estate broker; b. Los Angeles, Jan. 26, 1929; d. Albert Theodor and Benina Josephine (Iturburu) Bruhn; m. William Dean Derry, May 24, 1952; children—Ann, William Dean, Carolyn. Various positions title ins., savings and loan cos., 1947-65 real estate broker, San Marino, 1966—. Leader, Girl Scouts U.S.A., 1966-67, 70; pres. Las Hermanitas Guild to Childrens Hosp., Los Angeles, 1972. Mem. San Marino Bd. Realtors (pres. 1973). Roman Catholic. Club: Arcadia Junior Women's (pres. 1964). Home: 595 Old Mill Rd San Marino CA 91108 Office: 2310 Huntington Dr San Marino CA 91108

DERTHICK, HELEN MARIE, banker; b. Mantua, O., Jan. 19, 1918; d. Arthur A. and Emma Louise (Berg) Kuchenbecker; student Steubenville (O.) Bus. Coll., 1950-52; grad. certificate Am. Inst. Banking, 1967; div.; children—James A., David E. Clk. Miners and Mechanics Bank, Steubenville, 1950-52; clk. to sec. to v.p. Broward Nat. Bank, Ft. Lauderdale, Fla., 1952-58; sec. to pres. Coral Ridge Nat. Bank, Ft. Lauderdale, 1958-64, asst. cashier, 1964-69, asst. v.p., 1969—. Named Bus. Woman of Year, Prospect Hall Coll., Ft. Lauderdale, 1971. Mem. Am. Inst. Banking (Merit award Broward County chpt. 1970), Nat. Assn. Bank Women (pres. chpt. 1970-71), Fla. Bankers Assn., Fort Lauderdale C. of C. Mem. Christian Ch. Club: Sunrise Country (Ft. Lauderdale). Home: 6261 NE 19th Av Fort Lauderdale FL 33308 Office: PO Box 11254 Fort Lauderdale FL 33306

DE SAINT PHALLE, THERESE MARIE FREDERICA (BARONESS JEHAN DE DROUAS), author; b. N.Y.C., Mar. 7, 1930; d. Comte Alexandre and Helen (Harper) de Saint Phalle; grad. high sch.; m. Baron Jehan de Drouas, Dec. 30, 1950; 1 son, Henri. Author: (novels) La Mendigote, 1966; La Chandelle, 1967; Le Tournesol, 1968; Le Souverain, 1970, La Clairiere, 1974, also TV films, motion picture scripts, short stories, numerous articles. Mem. Assn. Franz Liszt, Societé Française des Roses, P.E.N., Charles Spaniels Club. Roman Catholic. Editor (with Daniel-Rops) Ecclesia, Lectures Chretiennes, 1949-63; editor Presses de la Cite, 1963-70, Flammarion Pubs., 1971—. Home: 46 Bd Emile Augier Paris 75016 France Office: Flammarion 26 rue Racine Paris 75006 France

DE SALVA, INÉS ENCARNACIÓN (MRS. MARCOS DE SALVÁ), occupational, phys. therapist; b. Rio Piedras, P.R., Sept. 25, 1934; d. Gaspar Encarnación Santana and Adela Canino; certificate occupational therapy and phys. therapy U. P.R., 1957, B.S. magna cum laude, 1967; m. Marcos De Salvá, Dec. 26, 1952; children—Catherine Elizabeth, José Antonio, José Raúl. Staff phys. and occupational therapist Indsl. Hosp., P.R. State Ins. Fund, 1957-61; phys. and occupational therapy supr. nursing home program P.R. Dept. Health, Santurce, 1961-63; student phys. therapy supr. Sch. Phys. and Occupational Therapy, Rio Piedras, 1963; phys. and occupational therapy cons. P.R. Gericulture Commn., Santurce, 1963-65, 65-67; project dir. occupational therapy course P.R. Dept. Edn., Hato Rey, 1965; asst. dir. Project Hope for Aged, Puerto Nuevo, P.R., 1967-68, exec. dir., 1968—. Mem. P.R. Office Econ. Opportunity rep. programs for aged Nat. Council on Aging, Washington, 1968; P.R. del. White House Conf. on Aging, 1971; sec. La Merced High Sch. Parents, Tchrs. and Student Bd., Hato Rey, 1970-74. State Ins. Fund scholar, 1952-57. Mem. Nat. (del. 1961-63), Am. (P.R. chmn. council on practice 1965-66), P.R. (treas. 1962) occupational therapy assns., Am., P.R. (dir. 1965-67) phys. therapy assns., Am. Occupational Therapy Registry, Am., P.R. (dir.) gerontology assns., World Fedn. Occupational Therapists, P.R. Pub. Health Assn. (pres. adminstrv. sect. 1965-67). Editorial bd. Gericulture Bull., 1969. Home: 512 A Juan J Jimenez Hato Rey PR 00918 Office: 6y 13 NE Puerto Nuevo PR 00920

DESANDERS, (ALICE) JANET, journalist; b. Dallas, Dec. 30, 1943; d. William Dwayne and Alice Madeline (Jones) DeSanders; student Whittier Coll., 1961-62; B.S., So. Meth. U., 1965. Asst. to dir. customer relations Neiman-Marcus, Dallas, 1967-68; soc. editor Dallas Times Herald, 1970—; pres. Soc. Publs. Inc., editor, pub. The Soc. Sect. mag., 1972—. Mem. Chi Omega. Address: 3511 N Hall St Apt 201 Dallas TX 75219

DESANTIS, FLORENCE STEVENSON (MRS. ARTHUR A. DESANTIS), editor; b. Bklyn., Aug. 12, 1918; d. George Horton and Florence Marie (Paddock) Stevenson; B.A., Hunter Coll., 1940; M.A., Columbia, 1950; m. Arthur A. DeSantis, Nov. 25, 1950; children—Solange, Arthur L. Tchr., Salem Acad., Linden Hall Acad., 1941-50; advt. promotion asst. Mademoiselle Mag., 1950-53; beauty editor Charm Mag., 1953-56; women's interest editor Bell-McClure Syndicate, 1956-62, United Feature Syndicate, N.Y.C., 1972—. Mem. Phi Beta Kappa. Home: 61-32 228th St Bayside NY 11364 Office: 220 E 42d St New York City NY 10017

DESANTIS, SISTER MARY RAYMOND, educator, librarian; b. Reading, Pa., Sept. 23, 1913; d. Raymond and Anna Marie (Santine) DeSantis; B.S., St. John Coll., Cleve., 1946; M.S. in L.S., Western Res. U., 1957; postgrad. Villanova U., 1970. Tchr. English, Mexico City, 1931-33; tchr. jr. high sch. English and Spanish, Incarnate Word Acad., Cleve., 1964; asst. librarian St. John Coll.; community librarian Sisters of the Incarnate Word. Mem. Cath. Library Assn. (sec.-treas. No. Ohio unit). Editor of Book Rev. Bull. of Cath. Library Assn., 1960-64. Address: 6618 Pearl Rd Cleveland OH 44130

DESAPIO, MARY, investment bank and security co. exec.; b. N.Y.C., Feb. 26, 1929; d. Salvatore and Florence (DeFazio) DeSapio; student N.Y.U. Sch. Commerce, 1952-55, Grad. Sch. Bus., 1957-60. Jr. transp. analyst R.W. Pressprich & Co., Inc., investment bankers, N.Y.C., 1960-64; sr. transp. analyst H. Hentz & Co., stock brokers, 1964-67, Bache & Co., stock brokers, 1967-70; v.p. research Carl Marks & Co., Inc., investment bankers, N.Y.C., 1970—. Vol. worker Spence Chapin Adoption Service, N.Y.C. Mem. N.Y. Soc. Security Analysts, Transp. Research Forum N.Y., Transp. Analysts N.Y., Women's Propeller Club U.S. Republican. Club: Women's Bond (N.Y.C.). Home: 205 3d Av New York City NY 10003 Office: Carl Marks & Co Inc 77 Water St New York City NY 10005

DESCHIN, CELIA SPALTER, educator, social work researcher, author; b. N.Y.C., July 19, 1903; d. Abraham and Yette (Ritoff) Spalter; B.A. cum laude, Smith Coll., 1924; M.S. in Social Work, Columbia, 1942; Ph.D., N.Y. U., 1958; m. Jacob Deschin, Apr. 22, 1929. Tchr. Latin, French, Hartford (Conn.) High Sch., 1924-30; social worker Bklyn. Bur. Social Services and Cons. Center Jewish Family Service, N.Y.C., 1938-43; home service counselor A.R.C., Ohio, 1943-44; welfare counselor War Relocation Authority, Tule Lake, Cal., 1944-45; spl. teaching assignment McGill U. Sch. Social Work, 1945-46; research asso. psychiatry Downstate Med. Center State U. N.Y. at Bklyn., 1948-52; dir. N.Y. Teen-age VD Study Am. Social Health Assn., N.Y.C., 1958-61; prof. research Grad. Sch. Social Work, Adelphi U., 1961-68, prof. emeritus, 1968—; now researcher roots of war and founds. peach; lectr. in field. Mem. bd. Great Neck Com. for Human Rights, 1962—; governing council Am. Jewish Congress, 1968—; participant radio, TV interview, pub. information programs. Fellow Am. Pub. Health Assn., Soc. Sci. Study Sex, Am. Orthopsychiat. Assn. (editorial bd. Jour.); mem. Nat. Assn. Social Workers, Royal Soc. Health Gt. Britain, Am. Sociol. Assn., A.A.A.S., Council Social Work Edn., Am. Assn. U. Profs., Eastern Sociol. Soc., Phi Beta Kappa. Author: The Teenager and VD: A Social Symptom of Our Times, 1969; The Teenager in a Drugged Society: A Symptom of Crisis, 1972. Contbr. articles to profl., popular jours. Home: 6 Wyngate Place Great Neck NY 11021

DESCHNER, ELEANOR ELIZABETH, radiobiologist, cytologist; b. Jersey City, Oct. 18, 1928; d. Fred and Anna Marie (Sichler) Deschner; B.A., Notre Dame Coll. of S.I., 1949; M.S., Fordham U., 1951, Ph.D., 1954; m. Paul Hancock, Oct. 29, 1957; children—Gregory Paul, Laura Anne. Research asso. Columbia Coll. Physicians and Surgeons, 1958-59; research asso. Cornell U. Med. Coll., 1960-68, asst. prof. radiology, 1963—, asst. prof. medicine, 1968—; asso. Sloan-Kettering Inst. for Cancer Research, 1971—; asst. radiobiologist dept. medicine Meml. Hosp. for Cancer and Allied Diseases, N.Y.C., 1972—; asst. prof. biology Sloan-Kettering Grad. Sch. Med. Scis., Cornell U., 1972—. Cons., Controls for Radiation, Inc.; mem. pathology subcom. Nat. Large Bowel Cancer Project. AEC predoctoral fellow Brookhaven Nat. Lab., 1952-54; USPHS postdoctoral fellow, Eng., 1954-57. Mem. Am. Gastroenterol. Assn., Genetics Soc. Am., Royal Soc. Medicine, Radiation Research Soc., Am. Soc. Cell Biology, Am. Inst. Biol. Scis., A.A.A.S., Am. Assn. Cancer Research, N.J. Acad. Sci., Sigma Xi, Kappa Gamma Pi (past chpt. pres.). Roman Catholic. Research in radiobiology and cell kinetics for greater understanding normal, premalignant cell characteristics; test for possible use in early detection colon cancer. Office: 410 E 68th St New York City NY 10021

DESFORGES, JANE (MRS. GERARD DESFORGES), physician; b. Melrose, Mass.; d. Joseph Henry and Alice (Maher) Fay; B.A., Wellesley Coll., 1942; M.D. Tufts Med. Sch., 1945; m. Gerard Desforges, Sept. 11, 1948; children—Gerard, Jane. Intern pathology Mt. Auburn Hosp., Cambridge, Mass., 1945-46, medicine Boston City Hosp., 1946-47, resident, 1948-50; USPHS research fellow hematology Salt Lake Gen. Hosp., 1947-48; research fellow Thorndike Lab., Boston City Hosp., 1950-52; asst. prof. Tufts Med. Sch., Boston, 1952-61, asso. prof., 1961-71, prof., 1971—; asst. dir. Med. Service, Boston City Hosp., 1952-67, asso. dir., 1967-72, acting dir., 1967-68, physician-in-charge Rh Lab., 1952-73, asso. dir. Tufts Hematology Lab., Boston City Hosp., 1954-67, physician-in-charge lab., 1967-73, acting dir. clin. lab., 1967-68; sr. physician New Eng. Med. Center Hosps., 1973—; cons. hematology Malden Hosp., Whidden Meml. Hosp., Charles Choate Meml. Hosp., Melrose-Wakefield Hosp.; lectr. medicine Harvard Med. Sch.; attending physician VA Hosp., Jamaica Plain, Mass., 1960—. Mem. com. automation clin. labs. N1I; adv. com. adverse drug reactions FDA. Mem. adv. com. Oak Ridge Asso. Univs. Trustee Boston Med. Library. Diplomate Am. Bd. Internal Medicine with subsplty. in hematology. Mem. Am. Fedn. Clin. Research, Mass. Med. Soc., Am. Soc. Hematology, Internat. Soc. Hematology, N.Y. Acad. Scis., Am. Soc. Clin. Pathology, A.A.A.S. Asso. editor New Eng. Jour. Medicine, 1960—. Contbr. articles in field to profl. jours. Home: 49 Lake Av Melrose MA 02176 Office: 171 Harrison Av Boston MA 02118

DES GRANGES, PAULINE, city ofcl.; b. Fullerton, Cal., Dec. 2, 1914; d. Paul Ray and Julia (Maino) des Granges; jr. certificate Long Beach Jr. Coll., 1934; B.A., U. Cal. at Berkeley, 1939. Surp. girls and womens activities City of Berkeley Recreation Dept., 1936-41; supr. girls and womens activities City of San Diego Recreation Dept., 1941-43, gen. supr., 1943-46, asst. supt. recreation, 1946-48, supt. recreation, 1948-60, asst. dir. park and recreation, 1960-64, recreation dir., 1964-72, dir. parks and recreation, 1972—. Mem. Cal. Bd. Recreation Personnel, 1953-57, chmn., 1955-57; mem. Cal. Gov.'s Conf. on Aging, White House Conf. on Children and Youth, 1960. Bd. dirs., exec. com. A.R.C., San Diego, 1955-58, 64-67; bd. dirs. San Diego YWCA, 1952-55, 1961-64, San Diego Symphony Assn. Recipient Woman of Valor award Temple Beth Israel Sisterhood, San Diego, 1957; Woman of Achievement award San Diego Women's Service Club Council, 1960, Woman of the Year award, 1966. Fellow Cal. (past pres.), Am. recreation socs.; mem. Nat. Recreation Assn. (adv. com. adminstrn., 1961-63), League Cal. Cities (dir.); hon. mem. Chi Kappa Rho, Delta Kappa Gamma. Club: Altrusa (San Diego). Home: 824 Golden Park Av San Diego CA 92106 Office: Parksand Recreation Dept City Adminstrn Bldg San Diego CA 92101

DESHAIES, LOUISE THOMPSON, librarian; b. Raleigh, N.C., Apr. 13, 1920; d. William Henry and Effie Florence (Avent) Thompson; certificate Peace Coll., Raleigh, N.C., 1938; A.B., Meredith Coll., 1940; M.L.S., U. N.C., 1966; m. Arthur Emilien Deshaies, Dec. 13, 1945 (div. Sept. 1957); children—Louise E. (Mrs. Rudolph Anthony Tempesta, Jr.), Daphne Francine. Tchr. pub. schs. Chatham County, N.C., 1941-44; lab. asst. N.C. State Lab., Raleigh, 1944-46; clk. R.I. Sch. Design Mus., Providence, 1946-48; library asst. Ind. U. Library, 1951-54; tchr. pub. schs., Sampson County, N.C., 1954-56; tchr., Wake County, N.C., 1956-59; library asst. N.C. State U., Raleigh, 1959-63, U. N.C. Library, Chapel Hill, 1963-66; head descriptive adaptive catalog unit U. N.C. Library, Chapel Hill, 1966-72; asst. catalog librarian U. N.C. at Greensboro, 1972—. Mem. Am., N.C. (sec. resources and tech. services div. 1969-71, dir. 1973—), Southeastern, library assns., Friends of the Chapel Hill Public Library, Friends of U. N.C. Library, Guilford Library Club, U.N.C. Alumni Assn. (gen. bd. 1970-71), U.N.C. Sch. Library Sci. Alumni Assn. (pres. 1970-71), Beta Phi Mu. Baptist. Clubs: University of N.C. Faculty, Pilot of Greensboro. Home: 4869 Brompton Dr Greensboro NC 27407

DESICH, HELEN CYNTHIA, govt. ofcl., poet; b. Duluth, Minn., June 5, 1925; d. George and Mildred (Sharich) Desich; diploma Miller Meml. Sch. Nursing, 1952; student U. Minn., 1954-58. Biller Marshall-Wells Co., Duluth, 1943-44; bank remitter First & Am. Nat. Bank, Duluth, 1944-45; biller Kelley-How-Thomson Co., Duluth, 1945-51; geriatric nurse St. Luke's Hosp. Assn., Duluth, 1952-54; pvt. nurse, Mpls., 1954-58; mem. office staff Manpower, Inc., Mpls., 1959-60; clk. Greater Mpls. Girl Scout Council, 1960-63; personnel staffing clk. U.S. Dept. Agr. Mpls., 1964—. Mem. Minn. League of Poets, Mpls. Poetry Soc. (historian 1969—), Midwest Fedn. Chaparral Poets (Sawyers award 1971), Mpls. Soc. Fine Arts, YWCA. Club: Statesman's. Contbr. poems to lit. publs. Home: 1000 West Franklin Minneapolis MN 55405 Office: 123 East Grant St Minneapolis MN 55403

DESJARDINS, HAZEL (MRS. LOUIS HOSEA DESJARDINS), librarian; b. Decatur, Ark., July 7, 1912; d. Walter Raleigh and Mabel Magdelena (Varnado) Fleming; B.S. cum laude, U. Tulsa, 1932; M.A., No. Ariz. U., 1969; m. Louis Hosea Desjardins, Mar. 17, 1939; children—Sara Lynn (Mrs. John E. Dalton), Paula Jean (Mrs. Jay Rutherford). Tutor football team Tulsa U., 1932-33; tchr. nursery sch., Tulsa, 1933-34, tchr. adult edn. astronomy 1939-40; service rep. Southwestern Bell Telephone Co., Tulsa, 1934-39; social reporter Caracas Jour., Venezuela, 1947-49; librarian, asst. to dir. San Jacinto (Tex.) Monument, 1950-51; med. technologist for pediatrician, Houston, 1951-53; spl. tchr. Spanish, Tulsa, part-time 1959-65; operator gift shop, proofreader, publicity writer Gilcrease Mus., Tulsa, 1963-65; tchr. pub. schs., Kingman, Ariz., 1965-66, librarian Manzanita Elementary Sch. Library, 1966—, tchr. adult basic edn. community sch., Kingman, Ariz., 1971-72. Reclassified library Am. Sch., Rio de Janeiro, Brazil, 1955-56; pres. Magic Empire council Girl Scouts Am., 1961-64; mem. Kingman Good Samaritan Com., 1969-72. Recipient Medal of Merit, Brazilian Scouts, 1956, Thanks badge Magic Empire council Girl Scouts U.S.A., 1962. Mem. Kingman (pres. 1966-67), Ariz., Nat. edn. assns., Am., Ariz., Southwest library assns., Am. Assn. Sch. Librarians, Ariz. Fedn. Bus. and Profl. Womens Clubs (dir. dist. 6, 1972—), Republican Educators in Politics, Okla. State Archeal. Soc. (pres. 1941), Internat. Platform Assn., P.E.O., Kappa Delta Pi, Pi Gamma Mu, Lambda Tau (nat. treas. 1959-63), Kappa Kappa Iota (pres. Ariz. chpt. 1972—), Beta Sigma Phi, Phi Kappa Phi, Delta Kappa Gamma. Unitarian. Clubs: International Toastmistress (pres. Mohave club 1970-71), Business and Professional Women's (pres. Kingman 1969-70, 72—) (Kingman, Ariz.). Home: 3945 Butler Av Kingman AZ 86401 Office: 2901 Detroit Av PO Box 8218 Hualapasi Branch Kingman AZ 86401

DES MARAIS, LOUISE (MRS. PHILIP HUBERT DES MARAIS), author; b. Cambridge, Mass., Feb. 28, 1923; d. Louis J.A. and Zoe (Lassagne) Mercier; B.A. in English, Emmanuel Coll., Boston, 1944; m. Philip Hubert Des Marais, Aug. 12, 1950; children—Monica Marie, David (dec.), Louis (dec.). Sec. to dean Mass. Sch. Art, Boston, 1944-45, to headmaster Christopher Columbus Cath. High Sch., Boston, 1945-46; editor, writer Nat. Center of Confraternity of Christian Doctrine, Washington, 1946-50; free lance writer, 1958—. Cons. Nat. Council Cath. Men, Washington, 1969-72; mem. task force on ministry to secular instns. through lay people Nat. Council Chs., 1969-73; mem. parent-educator com. Nat. Center Confraternity Christian Doctrine, 1961-73; nat. chmn. family affairs commn. Nat. Council Cath. Women, 1967-71; sec. bd. dirs. Nat. Council Religion and Pub. Edn., 1974—; mem. Com. Combined Concern, N.Y., 1972—; mem. sponsoring com. Yorkville Counseling Center, N.Y., 1972—; non-govtl. rep. at UN for World Union Cath. Women's Orgns., 1970—, UNICEF steering com., 1973—. Mem. Am. Assn. U. Women (chmn. elementary and secondary edn. com. New Orleans 1957-60), Woman's Nat. Democratic Club (chmn. library com. 1967-68). Author: For Goodness Sake, 1966. Address: 500 A East 87th St New York City NY 10028

DESMOND, ALICE CURTIS (MRS. THOMAS C. DESMOND), writer; b. Southport, Conn. Sept. 19, 1897; d. Lewis Beers and Alice (Beardsley) Curtis; grad. Miss Porter's Sch., Farmington, Conn., 1916; student Parson's Art Sch., N.Y.C., 1920; Litt.D., Russell Sage Coll., 1946; m. Thomas C. Desmond, Aug. 16, 1923. Vice pres., dir. T. C. Desmond & Co., Inc., Colonial Terraces Corp. Recipient Juvenile award Nat. League of Am. Pen Women, 1949. Hon. fellow Rochester Mus. Arts and Scis., 1946. Fellow Soc. Am. Historians; mem. Nat. League Pen Women, Am. Anthrop. Assn., Am. Folk Lore Soc., Am. Assn. U. Women, Soc. Mayflower Descs., Colonial Dames Am., D.A.R., Daus. Founders and Patriots Am., N.Y. State Hist. Assn., Soc. Woman Geographers, Federated Garden Clubs N.Y. State (hon.), N.A.D., Am. Water Color Soc., N.Y. Soc. Artists, Photog. Soc. Am., Royal Photog. Soc. Gt. Britain, Am. Numis. Assn., Am. Philatelic Soc., Nat. Assn. Women Artists, Print Club of Albany, Pen and Brush, Nat. Grange. Episcopalian. Clubs: Women's Nat. Republican, Colony, Jr. League, Collectors (New York City). Author: Far Horizons, 1931; South American Adventures, 1934 (both books endorsed by Carnegie Endowment Internat. Peace); The Lucky Llama, 1939; Soldier of the Sun, 1939; Feathers, 1940; For Cross and King, 1941, Jorge's Journey, 1942 (translated into Portuguese and Swedish, also German; German edit. 1959); Martha Washington, 1942; The Sea Cats, 1944; Glamorous Dolly Madison, 1946; The Talking Tree, 1949 (translated into Swedish, 1956); Alexander Hamilton's Wife, 1952; Barnum Presents: General Tom Thumb, 1954 (translated into French and Dutch languages, 1956); Bewitching Betsy Bonaparte, 1958; Your Flag and Mine, 1960; George Washington's Mother, 1961; Teddy Koala, Mascot of the Marines, 1962; Sword and Pen for George Washington, 1964; Marie Antoinette's Daughter, 1967; Cleopatra's Children, 1971; in numerous anthologies, 1936—, latest being, Told Under Spacious Skies, 1952; A Book of Gladness, 1953; American Backgrounds, 1959; This is Our Land, 1965. Contbr. articles, fiction, verse, to newspapers and mags. Home: Newburgh NY 12550

DESMOND, MURDINA M. MACFARQUHAR, physician; b. Isle of Lewis, Scotland, Nov. 14, 1916; d. Alexander and Margaret Muir (Graham) MacFarquhar; B.A., Smith Coll., 1938; M.D., Temple U., 1942; m. James L. Desmond, July 10, 1948 (dec.); children—Margaret Graham, James Alexander. Intern Lincoln Hosp., N.Y.C., N.Y. Hosp., N.Y.C., 1942-44; resident D.C. Gen. Hosp.,

Washington, 1946-47; fellow pediatrics George Washington U., 1947-48; practice medicine specializing in pediatrics, Houston, 1948—; mem. staff Methodist Hosp., Tex. Children's Hosp., St. Luke's Hosp.; instr. Baylor U., Houston, 1948-53, asst. prof., 1953-57, asso. prof., 1957-65, prof. pediatrics, head neonatology sect., 1965-72, prof. pediatrics and community medicine, 1970—; head Leopold Meyer Center for Developmental Pediatrics, 1972—. Diplomate Am. Bd. Pediatrics. Fellow Am. Assn. Mental Deficiency, Acad. Cerebral Palsy; mem. Am. Soc. Pediatric Research, Am. Pediatric Soc. Research into newborn disease and care. Home: 2210 Bellefontaine St Houston TX 77025 Office: Baylor Coll Medicine 1200 MD Anderson Blvd Houston TX 77025

DESOW-FISHBEIN, LILLIAN (MRS. JACK FISHBEIN), artist; b. Detroit, Feb. 1, 1921; d. Hyman and Esther (Markowitz) Desow; student Cranbrook Acad. Art, 1939-40, Inst. Design, Chgo., 1962-63; m. Jack Fishbein, Jan. 20, 1946; children—Wendy, Shelley. One-man shows Garelick's Gallery, Detroit, 1957, Kovler Gallery, Chgo., 1965; exhibited in numerous group shows including European Traveling Exhbn., 1957, 59, San Francisco Mus. Art, 1957, Boston Arts Festival, 1959, Butler Inst. Am. Art, Youngstown, O., 1957, Library of Congress, 1958, De Cordova and Dana Mus. and Park, Lincoln, Mass., 1959, Detroit Inst. Arts, 1960, Art Inst. Chgo., 1963, St. Paul Art Center, 1966; represented in numerous pvt. and pub. collections. Pvt. tchr. art, lectr. on art, Chgo., 1946—. Recipient numerous awards including Booth Purchase award Detroit Inst. Arts, 1939, Pauline Palmer award Art Inst. Chgo., 1959, Armstrong prize, 1957, hon. mention A.C.A. Gallery, N.Y.C., 1958, 59, Pennell Purchase award Library of Congress, 1958, Merit award St. Paul Art Center, 1963. Mem. Arts Club Chgo., Renaissance Soc. U. Chgo. Address: 3532A N Pine Grove Av Chicago IL 60657

DESY, LOUISE ANNA, med. technologist; b. Montreal, Que., Can., June 17, 1927; d. Lucien and Jeanne (Villeneuve) Desy; student U. Montreal, 1944-45, Ecole de Technologie Medicale, Hotel-Dieu de Montreal, 1945-46; gen. certificate Canadian Soc. Lab. Technologists, 1946; m. Joseph W. Choinski, May 17, 1957 (div. 1967); 1 son, Joseph John. Chief technician St. Joseph's Hosp., Nashua, N.H., 1946-49; sr. hematology technologist St. Luke's Hosp., N.Y.C., 1949-50; research asst. Blood Research Lab., New Eng. Med. Center, Boston, 1950-57; spl. hematology and biochemistry technician Bridgeport (Conn.) Hosp., 1958, with cardiac catheterization sect., 1961; with Park City Hosp., Bridgeport, 1961-62; blood coagulation technologist St. Vincent's Hosp., Bridgeport, 1965-68; supervising technologist spl. hematology N.Y. Med. Coll., N.Y.C., 1967-69; hematology technologist Grade II, Montreal, 1969—. Active Bridgeport chpt. Easter Seal Soc. for Crippled Children and Adults, Conn. chpt. Nat. Hemophilia Found.; sec. women's aux. Rehab. Center, Bridgeport, 1962-63. Mem. Am. Fedn. Clin. Research. Contbr. articles in field to med. jours. Address: CP 274 Succursale Bourassa Montreal PQ H2C 3G2 Canada

DETLOFF, VIRGINIA ALLAN (MRS. WAYNE K. DETLOFF), librarian; b. Port Chester, N.Y., July 27, 1918; d. Alexander and Elsie (Nelson) Allan; A.B., Barnard Coll., 1939; B.L.S. magna cum laude, Syracuse U., 1941; m. Wayne K. Detloff, Mar. 30, 1947; children—Lowell, Bruce. Reference librarian Columbia U. Coll. Physicians and Surgeons, N.Y.C., 1946-47; head librarian Cal. Dept. Pub. Health, San Francisco, 1947-50; U. Ark. Med. Center, Little Rock, 1956-60, C.G. Jung Inst., San Francisco, 1965—. Served to lt. WAVES, 1942-46. Home: 8155 Terrace Dr El Cerrito CA 94530 Office: 2040 Gough St San Francisco CA 94109

DE TORNYAY, RHEBA (MRS. RUDY DE TORNYAY), univ. dean; b. Petaluma, Cal., Apr. 17, 1926; d. Bernard and Ella (Brodsky) Fradkin; A.B., Cal. State U., San Francisco, 1951; M.A., Cal. State U., 1954; Ed.D., Stanford, 1967; m. Rudy de Tornyay, June 4, 1954. Prof., chmn. dept. nursing Cal. State U., San Francisco, 1955-67; prof. nursing U. Cal., San Francisco, 1967-71; prof. nursing, dean Sch. Nursing, U. Cal., Los Angeles, 1971—. Mem. Cal. Bd. Nursing Edn. and Nurse Registration, pres., 1966-67; mem. bd. Cal. Health Manpower Council, 1971-73. Bd. dirs. Assn. for Better Health. Mem. Inst. of Medicine, Nat. Acad. Scis., Am. Acad. Nursing (pres. 1973), Am. (vice chmn. commn. nursing edn. 1968-70), Cal. (pres. 1971-73) nurses assns., Phi Lambda Theta, Sigma Theta Tau. Author: Strategies for Teaching Nursing, 1971. Editorial bd. Jour. Nursing Edn., 1970—; Jour. Nursing Adminstrn., 1971—; Jour. Family Practice, 1972—; Heart and Lung, 1972—. Home: 2148 Mandeville Canyon Rd Los Angeles CA 90049 Office: Sch Nursing Center for Health Sciences U Cal Los Angeles CA 90024

DETTE, ALLIEEN CAIN (MRS. HENRY ERNEST DETTE), banker; b. Dixon, Mo., Feb. 24, 1917; d. William Alexander and Mattie Susan (Bryant) Cain; ed. Dixon pub. schs.; m. Henry Ernest Dette, June 7, 1941; children—Mary Susan (Mrs. Donald R. Butts), William Paul. Bookkeeper State Bank of Dixon, 1936-41, teller, 1951-52, asst. cashier, 1952—. Chmn. Heart Fund, Dixon, 1953-55; sec. P.T.A., Dixon, 1955-56, pres., 1957-59, installing officer, 1960-70; sec. Jessie E. McCully Library, Dixon, 1965—; asst. chmn. planning centennial program, Dixon, 1969. Democrat. Methodist (supt. edn. dept.; mem. adminstrn. bd.). Home: N Ellen St Dixon MO 65459 Office: E 2d St Dixon MO 65459

DETTINGER, JEWEL MITCHELL (MRS. DONALD JAMES DETTINGER), artist; b. Jeffries, La., Mar. 15, 1914; d. Daniel Jefferson and Mary Jane (Campbell) Mitchell; student Montezuma Bapt. Coll., 1934; m. Donald James Dettinger, Feb. 19, 1965; children by previous marriage—Charles Glenn Herbert, Dixie Lou Hall. Auditor Brawley (Cal.) Sch. Dist., 1945-54; mgr. bus. office Bullard Unified Sch. Dist., Fresno, Cal., 1955-58; mgr. Fresno City Coll. Bookstore, 1958-74. Tchr. art pvt. students, Fresno, 1962—. Mem. Fresno Arts Center, Soc. Western Artists. Club: Soroptomist (Fresno). Home: 5883 Midwick Lane Fresno CA 93702

DETTMANN, HELEN MAXINE PATRICK (MRS. EMERON PAUL DETTMANN), editor; b. Mapleton, Ia., Mar. 11, 1925; d. Donald Victor and Jessie Helen (Hasbrouck) Patrick; student Buena Vista Coll., 1943; m. Emeron Paul Dettmann, Sept. 9, 1946; children—Janet (Mrs. Robert Barr), Jean Marie, Julie Faye. Country sch. tchr., Mapleton, Ia., 1943-44; asst. clk. Monona County Selective Service Bd., 1944-46; office sec. J. D. Armstrong Co., Inc., Ames, Ia., 1947-49, Brierly, McCall & Girdner, 1959-61; receptionist Newton (Ia.) Daily News, 1969-70, women's editor, 1970—. Mem. Newton Adult Edn. Adv. Com., 1970—. Mem. Bus. and Profl. Women's Club. Methodist (mem. adminstrv. bd. 1970-72). Mem. Rainbow Girls. Club: Woman's (pres. 1964-65) (Kellogg, Ia.). Home: Route 1 Kellogg IA 50135 Office: 2000 1st Av E Newton IA 50208

DETTMAR, DOROTHY JEAN, psychologist; b. Chgo., Sept. 16, 1924; d. Paul Albert and Rose Mae (McGilvray) Grundman; B.S., Northwestern U., 1945; M.Ed., U. Okla., 1947; postgrad. Purdue U., 1948, U. Chgo., 1948-49; D.Sc., No. U., 1950; m. Robert G. Dettmar, June 13, 1948. Grad. counselor U. Okla., Norman, 1946-47; head resident counselor Purdue U., 1947-48; psychologist Riverside (Ill.) pub. schs., 1948-52, Chgo. pub. schs., 1952-65, Hinsdale (Ill.) pub. schs., 1965-70, Proviso Spl. Edn. Coop., Maywood, Ill., 1970-72, chief psychologist, Posen-Robbins, 1972—. Pvt. practice, 1952—; mem. Ill. Psychologists Exam. Com., 1971—. Diplomate Am. Bd. Profl. Psychology. Mem. Internat. Council Psychologists (editor directory), Nat. Assn. Sch. Psychologists, Am. (chmn. membership com. Ill.), Ill. (asso. sec. clin. sect.) psychol. assns., Kappa Delta Pi. Asso. editor Sch. Psychologist, 1972—. Home: 201 Chanticleer Lane Hinsdale IL 60521

DETWILER, LOUISE BENNETT (MRS. ROYCE DALE DETWILER), pub. health analyst; b. Los Angeles, Sept. 15, 1931; d. Arthur Louis and Hildegarde Mathilde (Hansen) Bennett; B.S., U. Cal. Sch. Pub. Health, 1954; m. Royce Dale Detwiler, May 29, 1955; children—Susan, Nancy. Pub. health analyst San Jose (Cal.) City Health Dept., 1954-61; research analyst Santa Clara County Welfare Dept., San Jose, 1961-65; sr. pub. health analyst Santa Clara County Health Dept., San Jose, 1965—. Cons. records and statistics Cal. State Dept. Health, Berkeley, 1965-71; lectr. pub. health statistics San Jose State U., 1968-69. Mem. Am., Cal. (sec. No. div. 1972) pub. health assns., Am. Statis. Assn., Cal. Conf. Local Pub. Health Statisticians (chmn. 1969-70), U. Cal. Alumni Assn. Office: 2220 Moorpark St San Jose CA 95128

DETWILER, VIRGINIA J. BOARDMAN (MRS. PHILIP DETWILER), civic worker; b. Ann Arbor, Mich., Sept. 7, 1920; d. Harry David and Marguerite (Van Schoick) Boardman; student Coll. William and Mary, 1938-40; B.A. in Polit. Sci., U. Mich., 1942; m. Philip Bell Detwiler, Sept. 14, 1946; children—Anneke Jan (Mrs. Steven MacRostie), Marguerite (Mrs. Jon Barry Telleen), Philip Bell, Virginia Jane. Dir.-commentator woman's program sta. WIBM, Jackson, Mich., 1946; columnist, feature writer, Birmingham (Mich.) Eccentric 1952-55; asso. broker Wallace and Wheeler Realtors, Bellevue, Wash., 1968-73. Co-chmn. publicity Birmingham United Fund drive, 1955; founder, pres. Bellevue Town Hall, 1964-68; mem. steering com. Bellevue Area Self-Improvement Council, 1968; adviser to youth council St. Thomas Episcopal Ch., Medina, 1963; com. chmn. Seattle Art Mus. tour, 1967; bd. mem. Women's Assn. Seattle Symphony; mem. Symphoneve Com., 1971-72; 1959; bd. mem. Birmingham Town Hall, 1959-60. Pres. Beverly-Franklin Republican Women, 1959; del. Mich. Rep. Conv., 1960. Pres., Churchwomen St. Thomas Episcopal Ch., 1969-70, del. to Diocesan Conv., 1968-73, mem. vestry, 1971—. Served as lt. (j.g.) USNR, 1943-46. Mem. League Women Voters, Pi Beta Phi (sec. Mich. Beta assn. 1948, pres. Jackson alumnae 1946, pres. Birmingham alumnae 1954, pres. Bellevue alumnae, del. nat. conv. 1964). Club: Birmingham Athletic (charter). Home: 10202 SE 28th St Bellevue WA 98004

DETZEL, WILMA MARIE CARNELLY (MRS. ARTHUR FRANK DETZEL), cons.; b. Beaver Falls, Pa., Sept. 3, 1911; d. Henry and Mary Magdelene (Mitchell) C.; B.S. in Edn., Geneva Coll., 1933; postgrad. U. Pitts., 1933-34; m. Arthur Frank Detzel, Nov. 27, 1941; 1 son, Donald Arthur. Tchr. women's phys. edn. Beaver (Pa.) High Sch., 1939-41; librarian Geneva Coll., 1945-46, dean women, 1943-45; with YMCA, Erie, Pa., 1960—, women's phys. dir., 1963—, women's rep. Mid-Atlantic region, 1969—, women's fitness cons. Mid-East and Gt. Lakes regions, 1970—. Condr. fitness workshops Pa. State U., 1970. Mem. adv. bd. Springfield (Mass.) Coll., 1969-73, rep. for women's fitness phys. fitness resource center, 1970-73. Recipient Nat. Reader's Digest award Fitness Tng. Inst., 1971; Distinguished Service award Geneva (Pa.) Coll., 1973. Mem. Nat. YMCA Phys. Dirs. Assn. Methodist (trustee). Contbr. articles to nat. mags. Home: 3417 Ellsworth Av Erie PA 16508 Office: 38th and Cherry St Erie PA 16508

DEUPREE, ANNIE JO, educator; b. Denton, Tex., Apr. 15, 1929; d. Frank and Irene (Whiteside) Deupree; B.S., North Tex. State U., 1950, M.S., 1953; Ph.D., Tex. Women's U., 1961. Tchr. phys. edn. Lockhart (Tex.) Ind. Sch. Dist., 1950-51, Lewisville (Tex.) Ind. Sch. Dist., 1951-52, Wichita Falls (Tex.) Ind. Sch. Dist., 1952-54, Georgetown Ind. Sch. Dist., 1954-55, Windham Pub. Schs., Willimantic, Conn., 1955-57; instr. phys. edn. S.W. Tex. State Tchrs. Coll., San Marcos, 1957-59, U. Conn., Storrs, 1960-61; asst. prof. phys. edn. So. Conn. State Coll., New Haven, 1961-64; became asso. prof. phys. edn. N.E. La. State Coll., Monroe, 1964; now prof. health and phys. edn. Midwestern U., Wichita Falls. Mem. Am., So., Tex. (dist. rep. Rep. Council; dist. vice-chmn.), assns. health, phys. edn. and recreation, Nat. Recreation and Park Assn., Nat., So. assns. phys. edn. coll. women, Tex. Assn. Coll. Tchrs., Delta Psi Kappa, Delta Kappa Gamma. Club: Midwestern University Women's. Home: 4209 Cedar Elm Apt 172B Wichita Falls TX 76308

DEUSS, JEAN, librarian; b. Chgo.; d. Edward Louis and Harriet (Goodwin) Deuss; B.A., U. Wis., 1944; M.S., Sch. Library Service Columbia, 1959. Cataloger library N.Y.C. Council Fgn. Relations, 1959-61; head cataloger research library Fed. Res. Bank N.Y., N.Y.C., 1961-68, asst. chief librarian, 1969-70, chief librarian, 1970—. Mem. Spl. Libraries Assn. (nat. treas. 1967-70, pres. N.Y. chpt. 1971-72). Episcopalian. Book reviewer Library Jour. 1961—. Home: 94 Bank St New York City NY 10014 Office: Fed Reserve Bank NY 33 Liberty St New York City NY 10045

DEUTSCH, HELEN TYCE LEWIS, drug co. exec.; b. Charleston, W.Va., Feb. 24, 1918; d. Max and Jennie (Cohen) Lewis; B.S., Ohio State U., 1939; m. Walter Deutsch, Mar. 3, 1940 (div. Sept. 5, 1972); children—Stanley Paul, Barbara Joan (Mrs. Martin Schuster). Pres., dir. Arcade Drug, Inc., Newark, O., 1959—. Registered pharmacist, Ohio. Mem. Am., Ohio, Licking County pharm. assns., Phi Rho Alpha, Alpha Epsilon Phi. Jewish religion (past pres. sisterhood). Home: 51 Riverdale Rd Newark OH 43055 Office: 5 N 3d St Newark OH 43055

DEUTSCH, JUDITH GREENE (MRS. MARSHALL EMANUEL DEUTSCH), educator; b. Jamaica, N.Y., Apr. 18, 1929; d. Charles Shepard and Sadie (Freedman) Greene; B.A., Hunter Coll., 1950; M.A., New Sch. Social Research, 1965; m. Marshall Emanuel Deutsch, June 27, 1947; children—Pamina Margret, Ethan Amadeus, Freeman Sarastro. Tchr. Forest Hills (N.Y.) High Sch., 1950-51, Jr. High Sch. 252, N.Y.C., 1951; dean of women Shawnee Leadership Inst., Rutland, Vt., summer 1959. Mem. N.J. Com. Against Discrimination in Housing, 1955-65; peace edn. chmn. New Eng. Voice of Women, 1967-69; mem. Nashoba Valley Draft Counseling Service, 1968-69; mem. exec. com. Sudbury Human Rights Com., 1967-70; bd. dirs. Boston Indsl. Mission, 1971—; mem. New Eng. Interdist. Religious Edn. Com. (sec. 1969—), Mass. Bay Religious Edn. Dept. Bd. dirs. Satya Community Sch. Mem. Soc. Sci. Study Religion. Unitarian (dir. religious edn., coordinator family advocacy project). Author: Discovering Change; Discovering What People Are Like; Teachers, Prophets, Protestors. Home: 41 Concord Rd Sudbury MA 01776 Office: Harvard Unitarian Ch Harvard MA 01450

DEUTSCH, RUTH FREED (MRS. LAWRENCE DEUTSCH), psychiatrist; b. Bklyn., Nov. 20, 1927; d. Samuel and Celia (Teichberg) Freed; B.A., N.Y.U., 1947; M.D., State U. N.Y., 1951; m. Lawrence Deutsch, June 20, 1948; children—Ezra, Daniel, Joshua. Intern Beth Israel Hosp., N.Y.C., 1951-52; resident psychiatry Kings County Hosp., Bklyn., 1952-55, fellow child psychiatry, 1955-56; fellow child psychiatry S.I. Mental Health Soc., 1968-70; practice medicine specializing in psychiatry; instr. psychiatry Downstate Med. Center State U. N.Y. at Bklyn., 1956-59; staff psychiatrist S.I. Mental Health Soc., 1970-71, Rockland County Mental Health Center, Englewood, N.J., 1970—; also Englewood Hosp. cons. Jewish Welfare Bd., Hackensack, N.J. Diplomate Am. Bd. Psychiatry and Neurology, Am. Bd. Child Psychiatry. Mem. Am. Psychiatry Assn., A.M.A., Am. Acad. Child Psychiatry. Address: 301 Broad Av Englewood NJ 07631

DEVANEY, AMOGENE FOWLER, educator; b. Canyon, Tex., Mar. 2, 1913; d. William Haywood and Odie (Brooks) Fowler; B.A., West Tex. State Tchrs. Coll., 1934, M.A., 1948; Ph.D., N.Y. U., 1965; m. Walter William DeVaney, Dec. 19, 1936; children—Will Earl, David Brooks. Tchr. pub. schs. Vega, Tex., 1934-35, Fritch, Tex., 1935-36; draftsman Dept. Engring. Amarillo (Tex.), 1945-46; tchr. engring. graphics West Tex. State U., Canyon, 1946-47; prof. engring. graphics and math. Amarillo Coll., 1947—, dir. teach aide inst., 1968. Chmn. workshop on testing in engring. graphics Tex. A. and M. U., 1960. Recipient Founders Day award N.Y. U., 1965. Mem. Am. Soc. Engring. Edn. (exec. com. Gulf-S.W. sect. 1950—), Soc. Women Engrs. (chmn. profl. guidance and edn. 1967-69), Tex. Tchrs. Assn. (unit pres. 1964-65), N.E.A., Math. Assn. Am., Tex. Jr. Coll. Tchrs. Assn. (chmn. engring. graphics sect. 1957-59), Am. Assn. U. Women (br. treas. 1955-59), A.A.A.S. Home: 2410 Parker St Amarillo TX 79109

DEVARON, LORNA COOKE, musician, educator; A.B., Wellesley Coll.; A.M., Radcliffe Coll.; studied voice with Olga Averino, Irene Wilson, Conrad Bos, organ with Carl Weinrich, conducting with G. Wallace Woodworth, Robert Shaw, composition with A.T. Davison, Walter Piston, Nadia Boulanger. Condr. choir, asst. prof. music Bryn Mawr (Pa.) Coll., 1943-47; mem. faculty Berskshire Music Center, 1952-66; guest condr. high sch., prep. sch., coll. choral festivals; now condr. chorus and chamber singers New Eng. Conservatory of Music, Boston. Recipient medal for distinguished achievement City of Boston; medal distinguished achievement Grad. Soc. of Radcliffe Coll. Alumnae Assn.; Arts award St. Botolph Club, Boston, 1974. Address: New England Conservatory of Music 290 Huntington Av Boston MA 02115

DEVEREAUX, (DOROTHY) GLORIA DELAPPE (MRS. ALFRED E. DEVEREAUX, JR.), artist; b. Bklyn., May 30, 1922; d. Walter August and Dorothy (Kauffmann) DeLappe; grad. high sch.; m. Alfred E. Devereaux, Jr., June 30, 1940; children—Alfred E. III, Christie. Exhibited numerous group shows including Am. Watercolor Soc., Nat. Arts Club, Catherine Lorillard Wolfe Gallery, Hudson Valley Art Assn., Royal Inst. Painters in Watercolor, Fedn. Brit. Artists, Knickerbocker Artists, Audubon Artists; Manhasset Art Assn., paintings represented in pvt. collections throughout world. Recipient numerous awards including 1st prize water color Locust Valley Art Show, 1967, 2d prize Nassau County Art Soc., 1968, Anna G. Morse award Catherine Lorillard Wolfe show, 1969, Best in Show Bankers Trust Co., Nat. Arts Club Bronze medal watercolor, 1970, Sculpture, 1972, Kathryn Grumbacher medal and certificate, 1972, sculpture award Knickerbocker Artists, 1973, others. Mem. Nat. Arts Club (exhbn. com. 1969-70), Am. Watercolor Soc. Commd. to paint water colors used as top prizes awarded salesmen of year Patriot Life Inst. Co. N.Y.C., 1968. Address: Wardsboro VT 05355

DEVEREAUX, ELIZABETH BELL BAKER, occupational therapist; b. Huntington, W.Va., Oct. 1, 1926; d. Harry Claybourne and Bessie (Franks) Baker; B.S. in Occupational Therapy, Ohio State U., 1949; m. Charles Merritt Devereaux, Aug. 13, 1949 (div. Jan. 1974); children—Gregory Charles, Jan Renee, Steven Mitchell. Exec. dir., chief occupational therapy Wood County Rehab. Center, Parkersburg, W.Va., 1953-61; adj. therapy dir. W.Va. Dept. Mental Health, Charleston, 1965-72; dir. partial hospitalization programs Western Dist. Guidance Clinic, Inc., 1972—, also acting dir. emergency services, 1974—. Mem. task force on rehab. Nat. Council Community Mental Health Centers. Sponsor Sub-Deb Club, 1949-50; active P.T.A., 1957-67; asst. leader Four Rivers council Girl Scouts U.S.A., 1959-66; active Cub Scouts Am., 1958-60, 65-67; chmn. Easter Seal Mothers Parade, 1958. Bd. dirs. Wood County Assn. Retarded Children, Wood County Assn. Crippled Children, Council Alcohol and Drug Abuse, Mid-Ohio Valley Home Health Services; ex officio bd. dirs. Delta Zeta Found., 1970-71. Mem. Am., W.Va. occupational therapy assns., Assn. Community Mental Health-Mental Retardation Program Adminstrs. W.Va. (chmn. com. on state licensing regulations 1972—, mem. peer review com. 1972—, v.p. 1974—), Am. Acad. Polit., Social Sci., Nat. Assn. Activity Therapy and Rehab. Program Dirs. (pres. 1972—), Delta Zeta (named Province IV Woman of Year 1966-67, nat. 1st v.p. 1968-70, nat. pres. 1970-71). Home: 5 Worthington Lane Parkersburg WV 26101 Office: 700 18th St Parkersburg WV 26101

DEVEREUX, DOROTHY LOUISE (MRS. JOHN WILLIAM DEVEREUX), former state legislator; b. Spokane, Wash., Nov. 8, 1911; d. John P. and Olive (Davis) Nelson; R.N., Cal. Luth. Sch. Nursing, Los Angeles, 1931; postgrad. Chgo. Lying-in Hosp., 1932; m. Dr. John William Devereux, Sept. 1, 1934 (dec. Oct. 1968); children—John William, Marvin, Dorothy, Frederick. Part-time asst. to mgr. Lansing and Wilmar hotels, Chgo., 1931-34; clinic nurse Pub. Health Inst., Chgo, 1933; asst. personnel dir., indsl. nurse Wieboldt Dept. Store, Chgo., 1934; asst. to treas. League Rep. Women, 1956-57; mem. Ho. of Reps., Territory of Hawaii, 1958-59; mem. Hawaii Ho. of Reps., 1959-72. Ann. Hiscock lectr. U. of Hawaii, 1969. Pres. Manoa Sch. P.T.A., 1942-43, Punahou Sch. P.T.A., 1956-57, Hawaii Congress P.T.A., 1950-51; bd. mgrs. Nat. Congress P.T.A., 1950-51, mem. platform com., 1951; mem. sch. health com. Hawaii Dept. Pub. Instrn., 1949-51, lay adv. com. ednl. policies, 1950-52; mem. sub-com. exceptional children of Gov.'s Conf. Edn., 1955; Hawaii sch. study adv. com., 1957; pres. Oahu Health Council, 1951-54, exec. com., 1945-55, 56-62, bd. dirs., 1963-67; adviser Oahu Youth Council, 1951-56; chmn. Hawaii adv. com. to Div. Vocational Rehab., 1957-63; mem. Gov.'s Com. Employment Handicapped, 1954—, exec. com., co-chmn. legislative and archtl. barriers com., 1964-72; women's com. Pres.'s Com. on Employment Handicapped, 1962—, mem. subcom. on archtl. barriers, 1965-68; adv. com. Job Survey Project, 1962-65; pres. Oahu Soc. Crippled Children and Adults, 1958-60, dir., exec. com., 1960-63; adv. bd. Hawaii Salvation Army, 1951-70, hon. life mem. adv. bd., 1970—, sec. bd., 1958-59, mem. children's facilities council, 1964—; former bd. dirs. WAIF of Internat. Social Service Hawaii; mem. adv. com. Hawaii Pacific Homes for Aged; rep. from Hawaii women's nat. bd. Med. Coll. Pa.; nat. adv. council vocational rehab. U.S. Dept. Health, Edn. and Welfare, 1960-62; citizens adv. com. Oahu Transp. Study, 1963-67; adv. council Hawaii Comprehensive Health Plan, 1967—; policy bd. Hawaii Rehab. Plan, 1967-69; mem. Fed. Council on Aging, 1974—. Bd. dirs. Health and Community Services Council, Mental Health Assn. Hawaii. Named Hawaii's Mother of Year, 1955; recipient distinguished vol. service award Oahu Health Council, 1959; Distinguished Service award Hawaii Rehab. Assn., 1967; Ann. Kokua (Help) award, Abilities Unltd., 1968. Mem. Cal. Hosp. Nurses Alumnae Assn., Woman's Aux. Honolulu County Med. Soc. (past parliamentarian, chmn. by laws com., mem., exec. bd.), Woman's Aux. Hawaii Med. Assn. (pres. 1957-58, parliamentarian), Hawaii Pub. Health Assn. (hon. life), Nat. Rehab. Assn., Free Kindergarten and Children's Aid Assn. Hawaii, Child and Family Service Assn. Hawaii, Kapiolani Hosp. Woman's Aux. (chmn. by laws com. 1953-57). Republican. Conglist. Home: 2721 Huapala St Honolulu HI 96822

DEVERS, CHARLOTTE MARGUERITE (MRS. WILLIAM PETER DEVERS), library adminstr.; b. N.Y.C., Aug. 10, 1923; d. Edward C. and Charlotte C. (Wilson) Madison; B.A., Cornell U., 1944; M.S., Columbia, 1958; certificate Ballard Sch., 1956; m. William Peter Devers, Dec. 23, 1967. Research librarian Hearst Publs., N.Y.C., 1954-56; librarian TV Bur. Advt., Inc., N.Y.C., 1956-58; head librarian Compton Advt., Inc., N.Y.C., 1956-58; supr. tech. library Gen. Dynamics/Electronics, Rochester, N.Y., 1963-65; mgr. information services Curtiss-Wright Corp., Woodridge, N.J., 1965-68; dir. North Castle Pub. Library, Armonk, N.Y., 1968—. Cons. to CEIR Corp., N.Y.C., 1967-68; guest lectr. U. Buffalo Grad. Sch. Library and Informations Scis., 1968. Co-chmn. Town of North Castle Bicentennial Com. Mem. Friends of North Castle Pub. Library, 1968—. Mem. Pub. Library Dirs. Assn. (pres. 1971), Spl. Libraries Assn. (chmn. editorial bd. 1968-70, pres. N.Y. chpt. 1961-63, sec. Aerospace div. 1967-68, pres. advt. div. 1960-61), A.L.A., Green Acres Garden Club, N.Y. Library Assn., North Castle Hist. Soc., League of Women Voters. Club: Windmill. Co-editor Guide to Special Issues and Indexes of Periodicals, 1963, 2d edit., 1975. Home: Windmill Farm Armonk NY 10504 Office: 19 Whippoorwill Rd East Armonk NY 10504

DEVIEW, LUCILLE LOUISE STARKEY, journalist; b. Detroit, Dec. 9, 1920; d. John Arthur and Viola Louise (Jonske) Starkey; student Wayne State U., 1938-41; m. Harden W. DeView, Nov. 8, 1940 (div. Sept. 1972); children—Harden William, Robin Marie (Mrs. Peeri Pappas). Mng. editor Detroit Area Weekly Newspapers, 1968-71; staff writer Detroit News, 1971—. Vice pres. De View Advt. and Pub. Relations, Traverse City, 1959-66; free lance newspaper writer, 1959-66. Mem. Detroit Mayor's Commn. Aging. Recipient awards including nat. advt. awards, 1963-66, 1st News award Nat. Fedn. Press Women, Inc., 1973; News Merit award Mich. U.P.I., 1973. Mem. Women in Communications, Mich. Women's Press Club (awards 1970-74), Nat. Fedn. Press Women, Inc., Traverse City League Women Voters (co-founder 1964), C. of C., Nat. Orgn. Women, Franklin Village Players (co-founder 1956). Democrat. Christian Scientist. Clubs: Detroit Press, Wayne State Press; Zonta (Traverse City). Home: 2165 Burns St Detroit MI 48214 Office: The Detroit News Detroit MI 48231

DE VITO, ANGELA ANNE, ednl. adminstr.; b. Utica, N.Y., Oct. 26, 1948; d. Silvio Arthur and Jessie (Bianco) DeVito; student Utica Coll., 1966-67, Fairleigh Dickinson U., 1968; B.A., State U. N.Y. at Albany, 1970, M.S., 1971. Guidance Counselor Whitehall (N.Y.) High Sch., 1971-72; adviser office of student life State U. N.Y. at Albany, 1972—, coordinator orientation, 1973—. Mem. Nat. Assn. Women Deans and Counselors (mem. adv. bd., area coordinator), Am., N.Y. personnel and guidance assns., Am. Coll. Personnel Assn. Home: 129 Troy-Schenectady Road Watervliet NY 12189 Office: SUNY A CC137 1400 Washington Av Albany NY 12222

DEVIVO, ANITA, editor; b. New Castle, Pa., June 26, 1930; d. Joseph and Helen (DeMasi) DeVivo; B.A., Youngstown U., 1958; M.A., Brandeis U., 1959. Edit. staff Nat. Parks Mag., Washington, 1959-61; head div. publs. and information Am. Home Econ. Assn., Washington, 1961-68; mgr. publs. Am. Personnel and Guidance Assn., Washington, 1968-71; exec. editor Am. Psychol. Assn., Washington, 1971—. Mem. Common Cause, 1970—, Choral Arts Soc., 1965-72, Amateur Chamber Music Soc., 1952—. Editor: Textile Handbook, 1967; co-editor Personnel and Guidance Jour., 1971; editor Portfolio book photographs, 1971; Publication Manual of the American Psychological Association, 2d edit. Home: 5420 Connecticut Av NW Washington DC 20015 Office: 1200 17th St NW Washington DC 20036

DEVLIN, MARY JANE (MRS. JAMES DONALD DEVLIN), banker; b. Kirksville, Mo., Dec. 8, 1911; d. Warner Everett and Ina Elma (Holloway) Mills; A.B., Wellesley Coll., 1933; m. James Donald Devlin, June 27, 1934; children—Donald Mills, Ina Anne. Tchr. English, Monmouth Coll., 1936-42, 46-47; tchr. math., nav. Monmouth Naval Pre-Flight Sch., 1943-45; with First Nat. Bank, Kirksville, 1960—, pres., 1961—. Mem. Adair County Welfare Adv. Com., Kirksville, 1971—. Bd. dirs. Kirksville Sheltered Workshop, St. Louis area chpt. Nat. Multiple Sclerosis Soc., 1971—. Mem. Kirksville Adair County League Women Voters (dir. 1956-59, 61-68, 71-73, pres. 1959-61, 68-71, 73—), P.E.O., Kappa Alpha Theta. Republican. Presbyn. Club: Monday. Home: 911 E Illinois St Kirksville MO 63501 Office: First National Bank N Elson St Kirksville MO 63501

DEVONSHIRE, LINDA BLANCHE, lawyer; b. Freeport, N.Y., Aug. 27, 1942; d. Charles W. and Florence L. (Benscher) Devonshire; student Cornell U., 1961; B.S. with highest honors, U. Conn., 1964, J.D., 1968. Admitted to Conn. bar, 1968; with Aetna Life & Casualty, Hartford, 1967-74, tax atty., 1968-74, adminstr., 1971-73; asst. counsel law dept. Conn. Mut. Life Ins. Co., Hartford, 1974—. Charter mem. Human Rights Commn. Project, 1968—; active United Fund, 1973. Beatrice Fox Auerbach Found. scholar, 1965. Mem. Conn., Hartford bar assns., Phi Kappa Phi, Beta Gamma Sigma. Home: 45 Eastview Dr Windsor CT 06095 Office: 140 Gardent St Hartford CT 06103

DEVORE, MARGARET BOWEN (MRS. ROBERT N. DEVORE), physician; b. Troy, S.C., Dec. 29, 1930; d. William R. and Ruth (McAlister) Bowen; B.A. magna cum laude, Winthrop Coll., 1951; M.D., Med. Coll. S.C., 1955; m. Robert N. DeVore, Aug. 31, 1952; children—Robert Douglas, Thomas Lee and John Anthony (twins), Margaret Ann and William George (twins). Intern. Med. Coll. S.C., 1955-56; gen. practice Oceana, W.Va., 1957-59, Jackson, S.C., 1959-62; resident anesthesiology, 1962-64; instr. anesthesiology dept. Med. Coll. of Ga., Augusta, 1964-65, asst. prof. anesthesiology, 1966-70, asso. prof., 1970-73, prof., 1973—. Diplomate Am. Bd. Anesthesiology. Mem. A.M.A., Ga., Richmond County med. socs., Am. Soc. Anesthesiologists, Alpha Omega Alpha. Baptist. Home: 405 5th St Jackson SC 29831 Office: Med Coll Ga Augusta GA 30902

DEVRIES, JOAN ANDERSON (MRS. JAN DEVRIES), microbiologist; b. Devizes, Eng., Oct. 27, 1917; d. Boyd and Gladys (Winter) Anderson; B.A., Dalhousie U., 1939; M.D., C.M., McGill U., 1945; m. Jan deVries, Dec. 28, 1940; children—Roberta (Mrs. Hinnerk Gehring), Adriaan. Asst. prof. microbiology McGill U., Montreal, Que., Can., 1946-52, lectr. dept. dental therapeutics, 1952—, asso. prof. faculty dentistry and medicine, 1969—; dir. dept. microbiology Montreal Gen. Hosp., 1952-68; cons. microbiologist to Montreal Childrens Hosp., Montreal Gen. Hosp., Barrie Meml. Hosp., Douglas Hosp., Catherine Booth Hosp. Mem. Canadian Assn. Chemotherapy (dir.), Can. Assn. Med. Microbiologists, Can. Assn. Pub. Health, Can. Med. Assn. Home: 3619 University Apt 2 Montreal PQ H3A 2B3 Canada

DEVRIES, LINDA LEE (MRS. JACK HENRY DEVRIES), educator; b. Monterey Park, Cal., May 4, 1940; d. Clarence Charles and Evelyn May (Partch) Modyman; B.A., U. Redlands, 1961; M.F.A., Boston U., 1962; Ph.D., U. Cal. at Los Angeles, 1973; m. Jack Henry de Vries, June 29, 1962. Instr. Boston U., 1962-63; asst. prof. Northeastern U., Boston, 1963-65; asso. prof. theatre arts La Verne (Cal.) Coll., 1965-74; vis. prof. Pomona Coll., Cal. Inst. Arts, 1974—. Mem. Am. Civil Liberties Union (sec. edn. com. Whittier chpt. 1966-67, mem. bd. 1974—), Am. Theatre Assn., ANTA, Am. Assn. U. Profs., Cal. Democratic Women. Home: 6052 S Bright Whittier CA 90601

DEW, BARBARA FRITSCHI, realtor; b. Honolulu, Sept. 15, 1924; d. Alexander Daniel and Margaret (Pritchard) Fritschi; A.A., U. Cal. at Berkeley, 1944; m. George Wannamaker Dew, July 25, 1945; children—Beverly (Mrs. Peter Eric Van Horne), Jane, Nancy. Real estate salesman Trustco Realty Inc., Honolulu, 1963-70; v.p., sec. Cullen Chee Inc., Honolulu, 1970-71; propr. Barbara Dew Realtor, Honolulu, 1971-73; pres. Real Estators Ltd., Honolulu, 1973—. Mem. Nat., Hawaii (dir. 1974) assns. realtors, Honolulu Bd. Realtors (sec. 1968-69), Assn. Jr. Leagues, Jr. League Honolulu (pres. 1960-61), P.E.O., Pi Beta Phi. Republican. Episcopalian. Office: 333 Queen St Honolulu HI 96813

DEWALD, GRETTA MOLL (MRS. CHARLES F. DEWALD), social worker; b. Kutztown, Pa., Oct. 26, 1929; d. Lloyd A. and M. Olga (Wuchter) Moll; B.A., Agnes Scott Coll., 1950; m. Charles F. Dewald, Dec. 20, 1951; children—Michael Steven, Jonathon Glenn, Henry Lloyd, Janie Patricia, Joseph Charles. Tchr. Eastman (Ga.) High Sch., 1950-51, Bass High Sch., Atlanta, 1951-52; project coordinator Ga. Appalachian Project, Atlanta, 1973—. Lectr. on need for involvement in politics to various civic groups and clubs, 1973—. Mem. Gov's. Commn. on Status of Women, Atlanta, 1972—; mem. Gov's. Commn. on Volunteerism, Atlanta, 1972; chmn. Gov's. Mansion Hostesses, DeKalb County, 1970—. Chmn. Democratic Party of DeKalb County, Ga., 1972—; chmn. Dem. Women of DeKalb, 1970-72; mem. State Dem. Exec. Com., 1970—. Mem. Nat. Assn. for the Edn. of Young Children, Nat. Geog. Soc., Nat. Wildlife Fedn., Save Am.'s Vital Environment (dir. 1973—), Ga. Conservancy, Women's Polit. Caucus, League of Women Voters, Day Care and Child Devel. Council of Am. Presbyn. (elder 1972—). Home: 2231 Kodiak Dr NE Atlanta GA 30345

DEWALL, KAREN MARIE FELLER (MRS. CHARLES E. DEWALL), advt. co. exec.; b. Phoenix, May 31, 1943; d. Merle C. and Agnes Marie (Larson) Feller; A.A., Phoenix Coll., 1968; m. Charles E. DeWall, Sept. 3, 1963; 1 dau., Leslie Karen. Sec., Newspaper Agy. Corp., Salt Lake City, 1963-64, Wade Advt. Agy., Sacramento, 1964-65; media buyer Harwood Advt., Inc., Phoenix, 1967-70; media dir., co-owner DeWall & Assos., Advt., Phoenix, 1971—. Home: 32 W Marlette St Phoenix AZ 85013 Office: 1001 N Central St Phoenix AZ 85004

DEWAR, MILDRED (JO) ELLER (MRS. DONALD NORMAN DEWAR), librarian; b. Wilkesboro, N.C., Nov. 9, 1925; d. Charles Franklin and Golda (Velt) Eller; student Brevard Coll., 1942-44; diploma Jr. Coll, 1944; A.B., Berea Coll., 1946; B.S. in Library Scis., U. N.C., 1948; postgrad. Barry Coll., U. Fla.; m. Donald Norman Dewar, Mar. 6, 1954; 1 dau., Heather. Tchr., librarian Mountain View High Sch., Hays, N.C., 1946-47; chief librarian Tenn. Wesleyan Coll., Athens, 1948-50; dept. head U. Tex. Library, Austin, 1951; librarian U.S. Army Spl. Services, Ft. Jackson, S.C., 1951-52; chief post library system, Ft. Stewart, Ga., 1952-54; librarian Olsen Jr. High Sch., Dania, Fla., 1955-56, Lauderdale Manors Sch., Ft. Lauderdale, Fla., 1956-63; head reader's services Miami-Dade Jr. Coll. Library, Miami, Fla., 1963-70, library dir. South Campus, 1970—. Vis. instr. U. Ga., summer 1967. Co-exec. dir. Nat. Library Week in Fla., 1965-66. Mem. Am. Assn. U. Women (past br. v.p.), Am., Fla. library assns., Nat., Fla. edn. assns., Am., Fla. (past pres.) assns. sch. librarians, Fla. Audio-Visual Assn., Delta Kappa Gamma. Contbr. articles to profl. jours. Home: 3520 Crystal View Ct Coconut Grove FL 33133 Office: 11011 SW 104th St Miami FL 33156

DE WEESE, ELDONNA ROSE, coll. librarian; b. nr. Seneca, Mo., Nov. 7, 1940; d. Osborne Kuhn and Helena Elizabeth (Stelts) De Weese; A.A., S.W. Bapt. Coll., 1960; B.S. in Edn., S.W. Mo. State Coll., 1962; M.S. in L.S. (U.S. Dept. Health, Edn. and Welfare grantee), Kan. State Tchrs. Coll., 1969. Instr. speech and English, librarian Pierce City (Mo.) High Sch., 1962-68; reference librarian S.W. Bapt. Coll., Bolivar, Mo., 1969-72, adminstrv. librarian, 1972—. Mem. adv. council S.W. Mo. Library Network. Mem. A.L.A., Mo. Library Assn. (chmn. nominating com. for jr. mems. round table 1972), Springfield Librarian's Assn. (mem. serials com. 1971—, com. on interlibrary cooperation 1973—). Home: 504 N Benton Bolivar MO 65613

DEWES, BONNIE IRENE, advt. agy. exec.; b. St. Louis; d. Arthur B. and Corinne E. (Schoenle) Dewes; A.B., Maryville Coll. of the Sacred Heart, 1939; postgrad. La. State U., 1940. With D'arcy Advt. Co. (name now D'Arcy MacManus & Masius Advt.), St. Louis, 1942—, account supr., 1961—, v.p., 1957—. Tchr. career courses. Mem. adv. com. Maryville Coll., St. Louis, 1965-71; mem. Pub. Relations Council St. Louis U., 1972—. Named one of ten top advt. women of the nation Am. Advt. Fedn., 1971. Mem. Women's Advt. Club (pres. 1952), Advt. Fedn. Am. (v.p. 1957-58). Club: Press (St. Louis). Home: 14 Clayton Downs St Louis MO 63131 Office: 1 Memorial Dr St Louis MO 63102

DEWEY, PAULINE T., newspaper pub., editor; b. Lyons, Kan., Aug. 2, 1913; d. Ivan L. and Betty Maude (Dalton) Stone; student Kan. State Coll., 1931-32, U So. Cal., 1943; m. J. Sterling Thomas, Feb. 15, 1938 (dec.); children—Betty Claire (dec.), Anthony Thomas (dec.); m. 2d, Franklin Noah Dewey, Jr., Nov. 24, 1952 (dec. June 1968). Editor Airview News, Douglas Aircraft, Santa Monica, Cal., 1942-45; pub. relations mgr. Cal. Intelligence Bur., Los Angeles, 1945-48; owner Thomas & Assos., realtors, Los Angeles, also Palm Springs, Cal., 1948-52; editor, pub. Nevada Times, Las Vegas, 1960—. Former chmn. local Heart Fund drive; mem. Gov.'s com. Mobile Homes and Travel Trailers, 1973—, Citizens' Group Project 701 for City's Master Plan, 1973—. Former trustee Clark County Library, Las Vegas; chmn. bd. R.S.V.P. Recipient Boise Cascade Woman of Year award Los Angeles br. Boise Cascade Co., 1971, Gov.'s citation, 1971, certificates of appreciation from various local orgns. Mem. So. Nev. Park Operators Assn. (hon.), North Las Vegas C. of C. (dir.), Better Bus. Bur., Trailer Coach Assn., Am. Assn. Ret. Persons, League Women Voters. Office: 1537 Las Vegas Blvd N Las Vegas NV 89101 Address: PO Box 4142 North Las Vegas NV 89030

DEWEY, REBECCA ARNELL (MRS. CHARLES SHERMAN DEWEY), cons. psychologist; b. Auburn, Wash., Oct. 11, 1902; d. John Robert and Emma (Hanson) Arnell; B.A., U. Wash., 1926, M.A., 1936; Ph.D. Stanford, 1946; m. Charles Sherman Dewey, Dec. 26, 1942. Tchr. pub. schs., Auburn, Aberdeen, Seattle, Wash., 1921-38; instr. Stanford, 1941-44, U. Nev., summer 1941; asst. prof. U. Ill. at Chgo., 1946-49; cons. psychologist Charles S. Dewey and Assos., 1946—. Fellow A.A.A.S.; mem. A.I.M., Am., Midwestern, Ill. (sec. 1964-69) psychol. assns., Modern Lang. Assn., Indsl. Relations Research Assn., Chgo. Psychol. Club (pres. 1964-65), Women's Share in Pub. Service (v.p. 1967-69), Chgo. Guidance and Personnel Assn., Am. Personnel and Guidance Assn., Interam. Soc. Psychology, Internat. Assn. Applied Psychology, Pi Lambda Theta. Club: Stanford. Contbr. articles to profl. jours. Home: 3130 N Lake Shore Dr Chicago IL 60657 Office: 135 S LaSalle St Chicago IL 60603

DEWITT, CAMILLA JANE, librarian; b. Kingston, N.Y., Dec. 3, 1927; d. Harry Fortnery and Ida (Bettenhausen) DeWitt; B.S., State U. N.Y. at Geneseo, 1950; postgrad. Syracuse U., 1957; M.S., State U. N.Y. at Albany, 1959. Librarian Fallsburg (N.Y.) Central Schs., 1950-51, Scotia-Glenville Central Schs., Scotia, N.Y., 1950-60; librarian Kingston (N.Y.) City Schs., 1960—, J. Watson Bailey Jr. High Sch., 1963—. Mem. N.E.A., Am. Fedn. Tchrs., N.Y. State United Tchrs., Kingston Tchrs. Fedn. Home: 6 Saccoman Av Kingston NY 12401 Office: J Watson Bailey Jr High Sch Kingston NY 12401

DEWITT, CAROLYN KERR, editor; b. Kingston, N.Y., Jan. 24, 1938; d. John Warren and Mildred (Goodnow) DeWitt; B.A., U. Minn., 1959. With McGraw-Hill, Inc., N.Y.C., 1959-65, 73—, copy chief, 1973—; fashion editor Women's Wear Daily, N.Y.C., 1967-69, Home Sewing, N.Y.C., 1969-72. Mem. N.Y. County Democratic Com., 1966—. Contbr. articles to children's and trade mags. Home: 327 W 76th St New York City NY 10023 Office: 1121 Av of Americas New York City NY 10020

DEWITT, ELLEN LOUISE REARDON (MRS. EDWIN ARTHUR DEWITT), town ofcl.; b. Milo, Me., Feb. 20, 1946; d. Joseph Patrick and Eleanor Ida (Mitchell) Reardon; grad. high sch.; m. Edwin Arthur DeWitt, June 24, 1967; 1 son, Steven Edwin. Sec., Employers Liability Ins. Co., Bangor, Me., 1964-67; sec.-clk. B & A R.R., Derby, 1967; legal sec., Milo, Me., 1969-72; selectman, assessor, overseer of the poor Town of Milo, 1973—; justice of peace, 1970—. Civic chmn. Milo Jr. League, 1967. Sec. Piscataquis County (Me.) Democratic Com. 1970-72; mem. budget com. Town of Milo, 1972-74. Mem. Ins. Women Eastern Me., Piscataquis County Extension Assn. Baptist. Mem. Order Eastern Star. Home: Reardon Rd Milo ME 04463

DEWITT, GRETCHEN, librarian; b. Wisconsin Dells, Wis., Nov. 9, 1912; d. Oliver Edmund and Edith (Hanks) DeWitt; B.A., Carroll Coll., 1933; B.S. in L.S., Columbia, 1945; M.A., Wayne U., 1954. Asst. reference dept. Milw. Pub. Library, 1940-48; head of reference and circulation depts. Bryn Mawr (Pa.) Coll., 1948-49; asst. govt. publs., social scis. dept. Detroit Pub. Library, 1949-57; head reference dept. Warder Pub. Library, Springfield, O., 1957-60; head reference services Columbus (O.) Pub. Library, 1961—. Trustee Settlement House, Springfield, 1958-60, sec., 1959-60. Mem. Am. (joint com. on pub. documents 1971—, chmn. 1973—), Ohio (chmn. reference services Round Table 1962, 63, chmn. conf. Registration and Local Information 1963, 67, mem. scholarship and recruitment com. 1968-72), Franklin County library assns., D.A.R. (Ohio State Officers Club), Zonta Internat. (rec. sec. 1966-67, chmn. Springfield Amelia Earhart com. 1958-60, Columbus com. 1972-74, sec. Columbus 1964-66, rec. sec. 1966-67), Beta Phi Mu. Episcopalian (former dir. women's group, St. Monica Guild). Contbr. book revs. and articles to profl. publs. Home: 75 Glenmont Av Columbus OH 43214 Office: 96 South Grant Av Columbus OH 43215

DEWOLF, ROSE DORIS (MRS. BERNARD INGSTER), journalist; b. Reading, Pa., July 18, 1934; d. Lewis Marcus and Pauline (Hirschout) DeWolf; B.S., Temple U., 1956; m. Bernard Ingster, Sept. 30, 1967. Reporter, Doylestown (Pa.) Daily Intelligencer, 1956-60, Camden (N.J.) Courier-Post, 1960-63; reporter-columnist Phila. Inquirer, 1963-69; columnist Phila. Bull., 1969—. TV interviewer WFIL-TV, Phila., 1968-69; TV commentator KYW-TV, Phila., 1971-74. Author: The Bonds of Acrimony, 1970. Home: 2226 Lombard St Philadelphia PA 19146 Office: 30th and Market Sts Philadelphia PA 19101

DEWOLFE, RUTHANNE KATHARINE SOBOTA (MRS. ALAN STEYART DEWOLFE), psychologist; b. Milw., Aug. 13, 1933; d. Erich Max and Mary Elizabeth (Stork) Sobota; student Oberlin Coll., 1951-52; B.A., Heidelberg Coll., 1954; M.S., Northwestern U., 1958, Ph.D., 1960; student John Marshall Law Sch., 1973—; m. Alan Steyart DeWolfe, Aug. 24, 1952; children—Kyle Arend, Hilary Stuart, Elena Maria. Staff psychologist Hines (Ill.) VA Hosp., 1960-62; individual practice psychology, Evanston, Ill., 1962—. Mem. Am., Ill., Midwest psychol. assns., A.A.A.S., Sigma Xi. Mem. Soc. of Friends. Home: 811 Colfax St Evanston IL 60201

DEWSNUP, EVELYN REDMAN (MRS. STANLEY R. DEWSNUP), performer, producer, dir., educator; b. Walla Walla, Wash., Feb. 10, 1924; d. Wynn Henry and Nettie A. (Thompson) Redman; student Sacramento City Coll., 1944; B.A., Stanford, 1946; teaching credentials U. Cal. at Davis, 1970; student Cal. State U. at Sacramento, 1970-71; m. Stanley R. Dewsnup, Feb. 2, 1947; children—Wynn R., Ellen Louise, David Y., Daniel H., Andrew T. With Sta. KNBC, San Francisco, 1945-46; traffic controller KXOA, Sacramento, 1946-47; program dir. KWBR, Oakland, Cal., 1947-50; drama dir., instr. English, Davis Sr. High Sch., 1970—. Cons. Eaglet Theatre, Sacramento; active charitable orgns. Mem. Speech Communication Assn., Internat. Thespian Soc., Sacramento Valley Forensic League, Cal. Speech Assn., Am. Assn. U. Women, Sigma Iota Chi. Mem. Ch. of Jesus Christ of Latter-day Saints. Home: Route 1 Box 2255 Davis CA 95616 Office: 315 W 14th St Davis CA 95616

DEXTER, CAROLYN RACHEL, sociologist, educator; b. Washington; d. Harris Edward and Florence Anna (Isbell) Dexter; B.S., St. Lawrence U., 1948; M.A., Columbia, 1959, Ph.D., 1967. Mgr. safe deposit dept. First Nat. Bank, Poughkeepsie, N.Y., 1948-53; research asst., personnel research IBM, Poughkeepsie, 1953-59; research intern Bur. of Applied Social Research, Columbia, N.Y.C., 1958-60; asst. dir. research Girl Scouts Am., N.Y.C., 1960-65; cons. marketing program evaluation, N.Y.C., 1965-67; sociologist John Hancock Mut. Life Ins. Co., Boston, 1967-69; asst. prof. Pa. State U., Middletown, 1969—. Lectr. methodology Boston U., 1968-69. Treas., Jr. League of Poughkeepsie, N.Y., 1957-58. Recipient grants Columbia U., Pa. State U., 1971-74. Mem. Internat., Am. sociol. assns., Am. Marketing Assn. (pres. central Pa. 1973-74), N.Y. State Safe Deposit Assn. (sec. 1948-53). Home: 660 Boas St Harrisburg PA 17102 Office: Penn State Univ Capitol Campus Middletown PA 17057

DEXTER, HELEN LOUISE, physician; b. Cin., July 28, 1908; d. William Jordan and Katherine (Weston) Taylor; A.B., Bryn Mawr Coll., 1930; M.D., Columbia, 1937; postgrad. U. Cin. Coll. Medicine, 1948-50; m. Morrie W. Dexter, Jan. 27, 1937; children—Katharine, Helen, Elizabeth Taylor (Mrs. Richard T. Potsubay), William Taylor. Began career as intern Jersey City Med. Center, 1938-39; internist Cin. Babies Milk Fund, Maternal Health Clinic, 1938-45; clinician U. Cin. Med. Sch., 1938-48, instr. dept. dermatology, 1948-53; practice medicine specializing in dermatology, Clearwater, Fla., 1954—; dermatology cons. VA, 1955—; investigation of carcinogenic effects of shale oil U.S. Bur. Mines, Rifle, Colo., 1950. Mem. Clearwater P.T.A., Clearwater Power Squadron Aux. Recipient Ina Clay trophy Intercollegiate Ski Champion, 1928-30. Mem. A.M.A., Sec. Investigation Dermatology, Am. Acad. Dermatology, S.E. Dermatol. Assn. (v.p. 1963-64), Fla. Dermatol. Soc. (v.p. 1959), Fla. Soc. Dermatology (pres.), Noah Worcester Dermatol. Soc., Am. Archaeol. Soc., Pan-Am. Dermatol. Soc., Soc. Tropical Dermatology. Presbyn. Club: Clearwater Yacht. Contbr. articles to profl. jours. Home: 409

Bayview Dr Belleair FL 33516 Office: 610 E Druid Dr Clearwater FL 33516

DEYA, LOURDES LENDIAN (MRS. JOSE MIGUEL DEYA), educator; b. Havana, Cuba, Oct. 23, 1925; d. Armando R. Lendian and Alicia L. Colon; student Randolph Macon Woman's Coll., 1943-46, U. Havana, 1959-61; B.A., La. State U., 1962, M.S. in L.S., 1963, postgrad. 1965; m. Jose Miguel Deya, Feb. 3, 1950; children—Michael, George, Alice. Came to U.S., 1961, naturalized. Tchr. Dept. Edn., Havana, 1949-61; asst. cataloger La. State Library, Baton Rouge, 1964-66; prof. cataloging and classification La. State U., Baton Rouge, 1967—; instr. library sci. La. State U. Coll. Edn., 1971—. Faculty adviser La. State U. Library Sch. Grad. Assn., 1969—; cons. on sch. libraries to Govt. Peru, 1972; symposium speaker Inst. Latin-Am. Studies of U. Tex. at Austin—OAS, 1974. U.S. Office Edn. fellow, 1966-67, summer 69. Mem. Baton Rouge Library Club, A.L.A., Am. Assn. U. Profs., La. Tchrs. Assn., Modern Lang. Assn., L'Asamble Francaise, Southwestern, La. library assns., Sacred Heart Alumnae Assn. (pres. 1968-70), Phi Lambda Pi, Phi Sigma Iota, Sigma Delta Pi, Alpha Beta Alpha. K.C. Ladies Aux. Home: 5785 Glenwood Dr Baton Rouge LA 70806

DEZOORT, EDITH JUNE, physician; b. Paterson, N.J., June 26, 1934; d. Wilem and Lavina Mae (Judge) DeZoort; B.S. cum laude, U. Ga., 1956; M.S., Med. Coll. Ga., 1960. Intern Meml. Hosp. Chatham County, Savannah, Ga., 1960-61; resident pediatrics Sinai Hosp. Balt., 1961-62, Talmadge Meml. Hosp., Augusta, Ga., 1962-63; practice medicine specializing in pediatrics, Decatur, Ga., 1963—; chief pediatrics DeKalb Gen. Hosp., Decatur, 1969-71; mem. staff DeKalb Gen., Henrietta Egleston hosps., Decatur. Recipient Bausch Lome award, 1952, Phi Sigma award, 1954. Mem. DeKalb County Med. Soc., Med. Assn. Ga., A.M.A., Phi Beta Kappa, Phi Kappa Phi, Alpha Epsilon Delta, Tau Epsilon Delta, Phi Sigma. Office: 6 Lavista Perimeter Office Park Suite 110 Tucker GA 30084

DHAWAN, SWARAN SETH, civic worker; b. Simla, Himachel Pradesh, India; d. Kesar Chand and Leela (Khanna) Seth; B.S., Miranda House Delhi U., 1953; M.S.W., M.S. U., Baroda, India, 1958; M.S.W., Smith Coll., 1963; 1 dau., Shubanjali Dhawan. Lectr., psychiat. social worker M.S. U., Baroda, 1958-62; asst. dir. profl. services Family and Childrens Soc., Balt., 1963—; dir. social service Taylor Manor Hosp., Ellicot City, Md., 1968—. Bd. dirs. Planned Parenthood Balt. Recipient Spl. award P.E.O., 1962. Mem. Nat. Assn. Social Workers, Internat. Conf. Social Work, Council on Social Work Edn., Family Service Assn. Am., Md. Conf. Social Concern, Am. Soc. for Hosp. Social Work Dirs. Home: 4 Olmsted Green Baltimore MD 21228 Office: 204 W Lanvale St Baltimore MD 21217

DIA, VITA DURAN, ednl. adminstr.; b. Polangui, Albay, P.I., Aug. 23, 1926; d. Leonardo Granada and Luisita Refama (Duran) Dia; B.S. in Edn., Silliman U., P.I., 1950; M.A. in Edn., Philippine Christian Coll., 1956; M.Ed. in Guidance and Counseling (U.S. United Presby. Ch. scholar), U. Ark., 1959; M.S. in Student Personnel Adminstrn., Syracuse U., 1970; came to U.S., 1968. Tchr. high sch. English, United Inst., Legaspi City, P.I., 1950-56, coll. instr. English, 1950-57; instr. English Legaspi Coll., Legaspi City, 1956-57; asst. prof. psychology Silliman U., Dumaqueta City, P.I., 1959-68, counselor to freshmen, 1959-68; resident adviser Syracuse U., N.Y., 1968-70; residence hall dir., counselor, Russell Sage Coll., Troy, N.Y., 1970-73; asst. dean students, residence hall dir. State U. Coll. at Oneonta, N.Y., 1973—. Active Philippine Mental Health Assn., YWCA, Family Planning Assn. Mem. Nat. Assn. Women Deans, Adminstrs. and Counselors, Nat. Assn. Fgn. Student Advisers. Address: Huntington Hall State University College Oneonta NY 13820

DIAL, DONNA KAY, educator; b. Smithers, W.Va., Aug. 7, 1940; d. James Leroy and Helen Rosamond (Curry) Dial; student Milligan Coll., 1958-60, Manatee Jr. Coll., 1961, summer 1960, 62, U. Richmond, 1964-65; B.A., Fla. State U., 1962, M.S., 1964, Ph.D., 1969. Research asst. Fed. Res. Bank, Richmond, Va., 1964; cost analyst, contract reporter Hayes Internat. Corp., Titusville, Fla., 1965-66; instr. econs. U. N.C., Wilmington, 1965, summer, 1967; part-time faculty Fla. State U., Tallahassee, 1966-67, 67-69, research asst. Inst. Human Resources, 1968; asst. prof. econs. Ind. U.-Purdue U., Indpls., 1969—, also supr. Credit Union. Researcher, Model Cities program, Indpls., summer 1970. Recipient teaching award Fla. State U., 1969. Mem. Econ. History Assn., Midwest, So. econ. assns., Appalachian Finance Assn., Am. Acad. Polit. and Social Sci., Omicron Delta Epsilon, Sigma Tau Delta. Mem. Christian Ch. Home: 4257 Fox Harbour E Dr Indianapolis IN 46227 Office: 925 W Michigan St Indianapolis IN 46202

DIAMOND, HINDI ALTMAN (MRS. WALTER DIAMOND), mag. editor; b. N.Y.C., Sept. 11, 1924; d. Saul and Esther (Kijewski) Altman; student C.Z. (Panama) Jr. Coll., 1947-49, U. Miami (Fla.), 1966-69; m. Walter Diamond, Nov. 25, 1943; children—Linda, Stephen, Mark. Reporter, photographer Panama Am., daily English newspaper, 1951-58; Panama corr. for McGraw-Hill Co. and Vision mag., 1951-61; founder, editor Industria Turistica mag. Diamond Pub. Co., South Miami, Fla., 1957—; pub., editor Panama/This Month, 1958-65. Free-lance writer for Miami Herald, Coral Gables Times, also other newspapers, 1966—. Editor newsletter Palmetto High Sch. Parents, Tchrs., Students Assn., 1970—. Bd. dirs. Am. Jewish Com., 1966—, editor Newsletter, 1969—. Mem. Am. Soc. Mag. Photographers (chmn. Fla. chpt. 1960—), Women in Communication. Author: Your Name in the News, 1974. Home: 7250 SW 126th St Miami FL 33156 Office: Industria Turistica Box 52 South Miami FL 33143

DIAMOND, LIEBE DEBORAH SOKOL (MRS. EARL L. DIAMOND), surgeon; b. Balt., Jan. 10, 1931; d. Max and Anne (Hirschhorn) Sokol; A.B. magna cum laude, Smith Coll., 1951; M.D., U. Pa., 1955; m. Earl L. Diamond, Dec. 11, 1960; 1 son, Joshua Moses. Intern Sinai Hosp., Balt., 1955-56, asst. resident gen. surgery, 1956-57; resident orthopedic surgery Hosp. U. Pa., 1957-60; asst. instr. orthopedic surgery U. Pa., 1957-60; instr. orthopedic surgery U. Md., 1960-70, asst. prof., 1970—; dir. resident tng., asst. to chief surgeon Kernan Hosp., Balt., 1961-68, dir. div. clin. research, 1968—. Mem. med. adv. bd. to commr. motor vehicles State of Md., 1960-66. Trustee Balt. Hebrew Coll. Diplomate Am. Bd. Orthopedic Surgery. Fellow A.C.S., Am. Acad. Pediatrics; mem. Am. Acad. Orthopedic Surgery, Am. Acad. Cerebral Palsy, A.A.A.S., Md. Orthopedic Soc. (trustee 1965—, sec.-treas. 1968-71, pres. 1971-72). Address: 833 Park Av Baltimore MD 21201

DIAMOND, MARIAN CLEEVES, educator; b. Glendale, Cal., Nov. 11, 1926; d. Montague and Rosa Marian (Wamphler) Cleeves; B.A., U. Cal. at Berkeley, 1948, M.A., 1949, Ph.D., 1953; postgrad. U. Oslo (Norway), 1948; m. Richard Martin, Dec. 18, 1950; children—Catherine, Richard, Jeffrey, Ann. Research asst. biol. scis. Harvard, 1953-54; instr. zoology Cornell U., Ithaca, N.Y., 1954-58; mem. faculty U. Cal. at San Francisco, 1958-60, mem. faculty U. Cal. at Berkeley, 1964—, asso. prof. physiology and anatomy, 1968—, asso. dean letters and sci., 1970-72. NSF grantee, 1962-63, 66-68, 68-70, 70-72, 71-74; NIH grantee, 1963-64, 63-66. Fellow A.A.A.S.; mem. N.Y. Acad. Scis., Am. Assn. Anatomists, Soc. for Neurosci., Psychoneuroendocrinology Soc., Am. Assn. U. Women (chmn. fellowships 1964—), Sigma Xi, Iota Sigma Pi. Contbr. numerous articles to profl. jours. Home: 574 Santa Clara St Berkeley CA 94707

DIAMONSTEIN, BARBARALEE DWORKIN, writer, radio/TV commentator; b. N.Y.C., Jan. 27; d. Rubin and Sally H. (Simmons) Dworkin; B.A. B.C., N.Y. U., 1952, M.A., 1958, Ph.D., 1963; m. Alan A. Diamonstein, July 22, 1956 (div. 1972). Instr. U. Va., Charlottesville, 1957-58, Coll. William and Mary, Williamsburg, Va., 1959-60; staff asst. The White House, Washington, 1963-66; dir. cultural affairs N.Y.C., 1966-67; dir. forums McCall Corp., N.Y.C., 1967-69; columnist, editor spl. supplements Harper's Bazaar, N.Y.C., 1969-71; contbg. editor Art News, 1972—; free lance writer, radio/TV interviewer, N.Y.C., 1966—; adj. asso. prof. Hunter Coll., 1974—. Commr. N.Y.C. Landmarks Preservation Commn., 1972—; mem. exec. com. N.Y.C. Bicentennial Commn., 1972—. Bd. dirs. Chelsea Theater Center, N.Y.C., 1969—, Bklyn. Acad. Music, 1971—, Film Anthology Archives, 1972—, N.Y. Landmarks Conservancy, 1973—, Municipal Arts Soc., N.Y.C., 1974—. Mem. Author's Guild. Author: Open Secrets: 94 Women in Touch With Our Time, 1972. Editor, pub. Am. Issues Forum, 1974. Home: 4 E 70th St New York City NY 10021

DIAMOS, JO ANN DAVED, lawyer; b. Douglas, Ariz., Dec. 15, 1928; d. Daved George and Elpiniki (Patakas) Diamos; B.A., Stanford, 1950, LL.B., 1953. Individual practice law, Tucson, 1953-61, 70-71; asst. U.S. atty. Dist. of Ariz., 1961-64, 65-69, U.S. atty., 1964-65, asst. fed. pub. defender in charge Tucson office, 1971—. Pres., Pima County Mental Health Assn., 1960-61; founder 1st pres. Com. On Drug Abuse Control, Tucson. Pres., Young Democrats of Tucson, 1956; nat. committeewoman Young Dems. from Ariz., 1956-57; vice chmn. Pima County Dem. Central Com., 1958-60. Home: 55 Calle Clara Vista Tucson AZ 86716 Office: 55 E Broadway Tucson AZ 85701

DIANA, PEARL BUTLER (MRS. LEONARD MATTHEW DIANA), psychologist; b. Frankford, W.Va., May 30, 1920; d. Oza Preston and Lura (Gardner) Butler; B.S., U. N.M., 1937, M.S., 1940; Ph.D., U. Pitts., 1948; m. Leonard Matthew Diana, June 21, 1950; children—Leonard Preston, Susan Claire, Lawrence Gardner. Psychologist, Allegheny County Juvenile Ct., Pitts., 1942-45, Seattle Mental Hygiene Clinic, 1945-46, Staunton Clinic, Pitts., 1947-52; psychol. cons., Richmond, Va., 1961-65; instr., asst. prof. psychology Med. Coll. Va., Richmond, 1963-65; chief psychologist Carnth Meml. Rehab. Center, Dallas, 1967-69; clin. asst. prof. psychology U. Tex., Southwestern Med. Sch., Dallas, 1967-71; cons. psychologist, 1971—. Lectr., U. Pitts., 1948-51. Mem. health adv. com. Dallas City Schs., 1969; mem. Gov.'s Commn. on Status of Women Va., 1965, Gov.'s Com. on Youth, Lake County, Ind., 1955-58. Mem. Am. Assn. U. Women, Am., Southwestern, Tex., Dallas psychol. assns., Dallas Soc. Clin. Psychologists, Nat. Rehab. Assn., Soc. Personality Assessment, League Women Voters, Sigma Xi. Club: Las Colinas Country. Home: 3001 Coronado St Irving TX 75062

DIAS, BETTIE JEAN, educator; b. Pitts., Sept. 27, 1925; d. James Duncan and Catherine M. (Hartman) Dias; B.S., Ohio State U., 1964; M.A. (Dept. Health, Edn. and Welfare scholar 1965-66), U. So. Cal., 1966; postgrad. Med. Coll. Ga. Mem. staff Highland View Hosp., Cleve., 1964-65, asst. chief occupational therapist, 1966-67, chief occupational therapist, 1967; mem. staff occupational therapist Home for Crippled Children, Pitts., 1968; chief occupational therapist Montefiore Hosp., Pitts., 1969-72; asst. prof. occupational therapy and phys. therapy. Med. Coll. Ga., Augusta, 1972—. Served with USN, 1949-59. Mem. Ga. (chmn. clin. practice 1973), Ohio (chmn. membership com. 1964-66), Cleve. Dist. (sec.-treas. 1964-66), Ga. (chmn. com. practice 1973) occupational therapy assns., Am. Soc. Behavioral Kinesiology, Phi Delta Gamma. Editorial bd. Jour. Am. Occupational Therapy Assn., 1968-70. Home: 2535 Crosscreek Rd Hephzibah GA 30815 Office: Med Coll Ga Augusta GA 30904

DIAS, FRANCES JEAN KRACHA, govt. ofcl.; b. Manitowoc, Wis., June 15, 1923; d. Frank Joseph and Beatrice Rosalie (Beale) Kracha; B.A., U. Colo., 1944; postgrad. U. Cal., 1947, Stanford, 1973; m. Julius Edward Dias, Sept. 23, 1947; children—Maryanne, Teresa Frances, Patricia Jean. Asst. history dept. U. Colo., 1943-44; tchr. elementary schs., Baldwin Park, Cal., 1944-45; asst. econ. dept. U. Cal., 1947-48; substitute teaching Oakland, 1947-49; discussion leader U. Cal. Extension Div., 1955-58; city councilman, Palo Alto, 1961-71, mem. planning and procedures com., 1965-66, chmn., 1970-71; founder Sister City Com., mem. bd., 1962-71; chmn. spl. com. for selection city clk., 1966, mayor, 1966-68, vice mayor, 1968-69; field rep. to Congressman Charles S. Gubser, 10th Dist., 1969-71; chmn. fed. exec. bd. Intergovt. Relations Com., 1973—. Santa Clara County rep. exec. com. Assn. Bay Area Govts., 1963-71, city-sch. liaison com., 1965-69, mem. finance com., regional planning com., 1968-71; now regional dir. (1st woman) Office of Def. Civil Preparedness Agy., Santa Rosa, Cal. Mem. League Cal. Cities Com. on Internat. Cooperation, 1962-72, mem. com. on air pollution control Assn. Bay Area Govts., 1965-67; mem. com. on regional govt. Cal. Legislature; hon. life mem. P.T.A.; chmn. 75th Anniversary Com. City Palo Alto; sec. San Francisco Bay Area Olympic Com., 1968-70, chmn. subcom. Gov.'s Earthquake Council, 1972—; mem. Santa Rosa Planning Commn., 1973—. Trustee Palo Alto Community Scholarship Program; bd. dirs. Town Affiliation Assn., 1965-73. U.S., Neighbors Abroad, Martin Luther King Scholarship Fund. Recipient Woman of Achievement award B'nai B'rith, 1965; citation Real Estate Bd., 1967. Mem. Am. Assn. U. Women (parliamentarian 1965-66), Santa Clara County N.G. Commn., Nat. League Cities (com. on internat. municipal cooperation 1963-66, municipal govt. and adminstrn. 1966-71, com. in govtl. relations 1968-71), League Cal. Cities (com. of future 1965-71), Alpha Omicron Pi, Delta Sigma Rho, Pi Gamma Mu, Dialectica. Roman Catholic. Club: Commonwealth (San Francisco). Home: 1010 Winding Ridge Rd Santa Rosa CA 95404 Office: Office Defense Civil Preparedness Agy PO Bos 7287 Santa Rosa CA 95401

DIASIO, CLARA FLORA (MRS. JOSEPH S. DIASIO), ret. physician; b. N.Y.C.; d. Angell and Victoria (Alba-Rosa) Benedict; Ph.G., Columbia, 1923; B.S., N.Y.U., 1925; M.D., N.Y. Med. Coll., 1929; m. Dr. Joseph S. Diasio, Oct. 22, 1933; children—Matthew Roger, Robert Bart. Intern St. Cecilia Hosp., Bklyn., 1929-30; resident pediatrics N.Y. Foundling Hosp., N.Y.C., 1930-31, asst. vis. pediatrician, 1931-36; asst. vis. pediatrician Columbus, N.Y. Postgrad. hosps., 1931-36; asst. allergist St. Lukes Hosp., 1931-36; vis. physician N.Y.C. Dept. Health Baby Clinics, 1931-36; examining physician Western Electric Co., 1943-44; physician Genesee Meml. Hosp., Batavia, N.Y., 1956—; sch. physician Oakfield Ala. Central Sch., Oakfield, N.Y., 1957—; practice medicine, Oakfield. Mem. A.M.A., N.Y., Genesse County (pres. woman's aux. 1951; chmn. disaster med. care com. 1958—; chmn. civil def. com. 1960—) med. socs., Genessee County Cancer Soc. (chmn. ednl. com. 1952-54), Omicron Phi Epsilon. Club: Oakfield Study (pres. 1958). Contbr. articles in field to med. publs. Home: PO Box 213 Culpeper VA 22701

DIBBLE, MARJORIE VEIT (MRS. CHARLES RYDER DIBBLE), educator; b. Bklyn., Jan. 11, 1928; s. William Adam and Marjorie Carmel (Kennedy) Veit; B.S., Hunter Coll., 1949; M.S., U. Tenn., 1950; postgrad. Columbia, 1957-58; m. Charles Ryder Dibble, Aug. 28, 1954; children—Ann Ryder, John Cullen. Faculty Syracuse (N.Y.) U., 1951—, asso. prof., 1967-73, prof., 1973—, chmn. dept. nutrition and food sci., 1973—, acting dean Coll. Human Devel., 1973—. Nutrition cons. Syracuse U. Children's Center, 1969—. Fellow Am. Pub. Health Assn.; mem. Am. Dietetic Assn. (N.Y. pres. 1965-66, del. 1966—), Inst. Food Technologists, N.Y. State Nutrition Council (vice chmn. 1972-74), Omicron Nu. Co-author: Cooper's Nutrition in Health and Disease and Nutrition in Nursing, 1968. Contbr. articles to profl. jours. Home: 848 Livingston Av Syracuse NY 13210

DI BELLA, ANNA (MRS. LOUIS PETER DI BELLA), author; b. Bklyn., Dec. 9, 1933; d. John and Marie (Sciancalepore) Mezzina; B.A., Queens Coll., 1955; M.A., Columbia, 1958; postgrad. Bklyn. Coll., 1960-61; m. Louis Peter Di Bella, Oct. 31, 1959; children—Louis John, Maria, Bettina, John Damian. Psychiat. aide Inst. of Living, Hartford, Conn., 1953-54; adminstrv. asst. Delegation of Lebanon, N.Y.C., 1957-58; claims asst. Marsh & McLennan, Ins., N.Y.C., 1955-57; tchr. English, South High Sch., Valley Stream, N.Y., 1958-60, N.Y.C. Bd. Edn., 1961—; self-employed ins. broker, Bklyn., 1957—; asst. coordinator State Urban Elementary and Secondary Edn. Act, Office of High Schs., N.Y.C. Bd. Edn., 1971-72. Coordinator Nat. League Am. Pen Women art shows Nat. Art Mus. Sport, 1972, Lever House, 1973, Seamen's Bank for Savs.; moderator Poetry Showcase series Donnell Library, N.Y.C., 1972-74. Recipient Leadership award Eastern Centre of Poetry Soc. London and World Poets' Resource Center, 1972. Mem. World, Pa. poetry socs., Nat. League Am. Pen Women (Manhattan br. pres. 1966-70, 74—, treas. 1970-74, N.Y. state pres. 1972-74, North Atlantic regional chmn. radio and TV 1972-74). Club: Women's Press. Author: The Warmth of Presence, 1972. Contbr. poetry to various publs. Address: 877 E 23d St Brooklyn NY 11210

DI BERARDINO, MARIE ANTOINETTE, educator; b. Phila., May 2, 1926; d. Henry and Adelina Martina (Belfi) DiBerardino; B.S., Chestnut Hill Coll., 1948; Ph.D., U. Pa., 1962. Research asst. Inst. for Cancer Research, Phila., 1948-60, research asso., 1960-64, asst, mem., 1964-67; asso. prof. anatomy Med. Coll. Pa., Phila., 1967-71, prof., 1971—. Nat. Cancer Inst. fellow, 1958-60; research grantee NSF, 1967—. Mem. A.A.A.S., Am. Soc. Cell Biology, Am. Soc. Zoologists, Internat. Soc. Developmental Biologists, Soc. for Developmental Biology, Am. Assn. Anatomists. Contbr. articles to profl. jours.

DICARLO, ELLA MERKEL, newspaper editor; b. Plauen, Germany, July 11, 1919; d. Paul Albin and Martha (Paeltz) Merkel; brought to U.S., 1927, naturalized, 1932; student Smith Coll., 1966-67, Holyoke Community Coll., 1967-68, Am. Internat. Coll., 1974; m. Joseph Anthony DiCarlo, Sr., Dec. 28, 1939; children—Sandra, Joseph, Donna, Jeffrey. Free lance writer poetry, religious articles, children's stories, 1937—; with Holyoke (Mass.) Transcript-Telegram, 1968—, asst. wire editor, columnist, 1970-71, news, religion editor, columnist, 1971-73, asst. to editor, columnist, 1973—. Cons. pub. relations Episcopal Diocese, 1970. Charter mem. Holyoke (Mass.) Mus. at Wistariahurst, 1959—; founding mem. Friends Oral History dept. Am. Internat. Coll.; mem. Mayor's Com. Study Local Utilities, 1964-65; coordinator ecumenical Com. Holyoke Centennial. Mem. Republican City Com., 1964—. Bd. dirs. YWCA, Family Service Corp. (both Holyoke), Nat. Conf. Christians and Jews, 1967. Recipient Human Relations award Nat. Conf. Christians and Jews, 1972, 2d prize best news story N.E., A.P., 1971, and several others. Mem. League Women Voters, Holyoke Library Assn. Unitarian-Universalist (lay preacher). Club: Holyoke Women's (pres. 1962-63). Home: 9 Woodbridge St Holyoke MA 01040 Office: 120 Whiting Farms Rd Holyoke MA 01040

DICE, ELIZABETH JANE, educator; b. Urbana, Ill., Apr. 3, 1919; d. Lee Raymond and Dora Sybil (Lemon) Dice; B.Design, U. Mich., 1941, M.Design, 1942; M.A. in Art History, Ind. U., 1967; student Jerry Farnsworth Sch. Painting, 1948, Yale Summer Sch. Painting, 1948, Instito Allende, San Miguel, Mexico, 1956, Ohio State U. Ceramic Workshop, 1962, Penland Sch. Crafts, 1971, 73. Art tchr., Belleville, Mich., 1942, L'Anse, Mich., 1942-45; mem. faculty Miss. State Coll. for Women, Columbus, 1945—, now asso. prof. art. Works exhibited Miss. Art Assn., 1948, 50, 51, 58, 74, Wichita Arts Exhbn., 1948, Soc. Am. Etchers, 1951, Brooks Gallery, Memphis, 1952, 61. Mem. Miss. Edn. Assn. (vice chmn. art sect. 1954, chmn. 1955), Handweavers Guild Am. (Miss. state rep. 1972—). Home: 134 King St Columbus MS 39701

DICE, JANET MARY DILTS (MRS. GEORGE AVERY DICE), occupational therapist; b. Ithaca, Mich., Sept. 20, 1940; d. Leon Francis and Mabel Ruth (Wetzel) Dilts; B.S., Western Mich. U., 1964, M.A. in Occupational Therapy, 1968; m. George Avery Dice, Mar. 3, 1973; 1 dau., Gretchen Marie; children by previous marriage—Susan Jane, David Timothy Somerville. Staff occupational therapist Kalamazoo State Hosp., 1964-65; individual practice occupational therapy, Kalamazoo, 1965-68; dir. occupational therapy Mich. Masonic Home, Alma, 1970-74; occupational therapy cons. C.O.O.R. Intermediate Sch. Dist., Roscommon, Mich., 1974—. Owner beauty shop, Ithaca, Mich., 1973—; sr. extension lectr. Mich. State U., East Lansing, 1972-74. Bd. dirs. Am. Cancer Soc., Gratiot County, Mich. Mem. Am. Assn. U. Women, Ithaca C. of C. Mem. Order Eastern Star. Home: 126 Fulton St Grayling MI 49738

DICHTER, TOBEY ANN GORDON (MRS. MARK SHOLOM DICHTER), editor; b. Phila., Apr. 16, 1944; d. Abraham David and Mezlya (Slobodkin) Gordon; student Pa. State U., 1961-63; B.S. in Journalism, Temple U., 1965, M.Ed., 1968; m. Mark Sholom Dichter, Aug. 17, 1969; 1 dau., Aliza Beth. Coordinator univ. lectures Temple U., Phila., 1965-68; asst. editor Harvard Grad. Sch. Edn., Cambridge, Mass., 1968-69; editor Smith Kline & French News, Phila., 1969-73; editor Dimensions, Smith Kline Corp., Phila., 1973—. Mem. project area com. New Democratic Coalition, 1969-74. Founder respiratory intensive care unit A.D. Gordon Meml. Temple U. Hosp., Phila., 1970. Recipient Printing Silver medal award Neographics, 1971, Bronze medal, 1974; 1st pl. award Internat. Assn. Bus. Communications, 1971,; Gold Quill award, 1974; Graphics award United Fund, 1970, 71, 72, 73. Mem. Women in Communications, Del. Valley Assn. Communicators. Home: 250 S Quince St Philadelphia PA 19107 Office: 1500 Spring Garden Philadelphia PA 19101

DICK, CAROL ANN WEGEHAUPT (MRS. HARRY R. DICK), physician; b. Milw., July 20, 1934; d. H. Wesley and Gladys Florence (Bergholz) Wegehaupt; student U. Wis., 1952-55; M.D., Marquette U., 1960; m. Harry R. Dick, June 10, 1955; children—Brian, Cindy, Carey Lynn, Jeffrey, Jeremy. Intern Milw. Luth. Hosp., 1960-61; staff physician Muirdale Tb Sanatorium, Milw., 1961-62; pub. health physician City Milw. Health Dept., Bur. Maternal and Child Health, 1962-72; staff physician Tb Control Center, Milw., 1972—. Mem. Assn. Physicians and Dentists of Milw. Health Dept. (pres. 1971-72). Home: 5423 W Hemlock Rd Milwaukee WI 53223 Office: 7630 W Mill Rd Milwaukee WI 53218

DICK, ESME JUNE, film critic, cons.; b. Derbyshire, Eng., June 14, 1933; d. Jack and Ellen Amelia (Tickner) Ingledew; m. William Dick, Aug. 21, 1953; children—Paul Adrian, Peter Stephen. Came to U.S., 1956, naturalized, 1963. Coordinator film services Greenwich (Conn.)

Pub. Library, 1964-69; dir. Am. Film Festival, N.Y.C., 1969-72; adminstrv. dir. Ednl. Film Library Assn., N.Y.C., 1969-72; dir. spl. services Eccentric Circle Cinema Workshop, Greenwich, 1972—. Film judge Sinking Creek Film Celebration, Nashville, 1971, 72; film critic USA Festival Dallas, 1973; program coordinator Robert Flaherty Film Seminar, 1974. Sec. bd. dirs. Greenwich Assn. for Retarded Children, 1963-67. Mem. A.L.A. (judge John Cotton Dana award com. 1970—), N.Y. Film Council (treas. 1973—), Film Library Information Council. Founder, mng. editor Film Library Quar., 1967-71; editor Sightline mag., 1969-72; adv. editor com. Films Kids Like (book), 1973. Editor: Film Evaluation Guide Supplement II, 1972; co-editor: Alternatives: A Filmography. Home: 77 Valley Dr Greenwich CT 06830 Office: PO Box 4085 Greenwich CT 06830

DICKENS, DORIS LEE, psychiatrist; b. Roxboro, N.C., Oct. 12; d. Lee Edward and Delma Ernestine (Hester) Dickens; B.S. magna cum laude, Va. Union U., 1960; M.D., Howard U., 1966. Intern, St. Elizabeth's Hosp., Washington, 1966-67, resident, 1967-70; staff psychiatrist, dir. Mental Health Program for Deaf, St. Elizabeths Hosp., Washington, after 1970, now chief program. Bd. dirs. Nat. Health Care Found. for Deaf. Diplomate Nat. Bd. Med. Examiners. Mem. Am. Psychiat. Assn., Washington Psychiat. Soc., Profl. Rehab. Workers for Adult Deaf, Washington Soc. Adolescent Psychiatry, Alpha Kappa Mu, Beta Kappa Chi. Author: How and When Psychiatry Can Help You, 1972; You and Your Doctor. Home: 5250 Oakcrest Dr Oxon Hill MD 20021 Office: 2700 Martin L King Av Washington DC 20032

DICKENS, HELEN OCTAVIA, obstetrician and gynecologist; b. Dayton, O., Feb. 21, 1909; d. Charles and Daisy (Green) Dickens; B.S., U. Ill., 1932, M.D., 1933; M. Med. Scis., U. Pa., 1945; m. Purvis S. Henderson, June 23, 1943; children—Helen Jane, Norman (adopted). Intern Provident Hosp., Chgo., 1934, resident obstetrics and gynecology, 1942-43; resident gynecology Harlem Hosp., N.Y.C., 1943-45, resident obstetrics, 1945-46; practice medicine, Phila., 1945—; asso. prof. obstetrics and gynecology, asso. dean Sch. Medicine, U. Pa.; courtesy staff Woman's Med. Coll. Bd. dirs. Phila. div. Am. Cancer Soc. Named Distinguished Dau. of Pa. by Gov., 1952. Diplomate Am. Bd. Obstetrics and Gynecology. Fellow A.C.S., Internat. Coll. Surgeons, Am. Coll. Obstetrics and Gynecology; mem. Nat. Med. Assn., Pa., Phila. med. socs., Coll. Physicians Phila., Phila. Obstet. Soc., Am. Med. Women's Assn., Pan Am. Med. Women's Alliance (past pres.), Delta Sigma Theta. Episcopalian. Home: 2401 Pennsylvania Av Philadelphia PA 19130 Office: 3400 Spruce St Philadelphia PA 19104

DICKENS, MONICA ENID (MRS. ROY STRATTON), author; b. London, Eng., May 10, 1915; d. Henry Charles and Fanny (Runge) Dickens; student St. Paul's Girls' Sch., London, 1928-33; m. Roy Stratton, Dec. 7, 1951; children—Pamela, Prudence. Came to U.S., 1951. Author numerous books including: The Nightingales are Singing, The Winds of Heaven, The Angel in the Corner, Man Overboard, The Heart of London, Cobbler's Dream, Kate and Emma—The Room Upstairs; The Landlord's Daughter, 1968; The End of the Line, 1970; The House at World's End, 1971; Summer at World's End, 1972; World's End in Winter, 1973; Talking of Horses, 1974. Contbr. articles to mags., newspapers. Address: Box 386 North Falmouth MA 02556

DICKER, JEAN ELIZABETH MORRIS (MRS. HENRY BERNARD DICKER), artist, civic worker; b. East Orange, N.J., May 31, 1906; d. Elmer Presley and Emily (Drotz) M.; grad. Newark Sch. Fine and Applied Art, 1927; student Parsons Sch. Art, N.Y.C., 1928-29, Upsala Coll., 1931-32; m. Joseph William Ellor, Nov. 30, 1929 (dec. Jan. 1968); children—Joy Emily (Mrs. E. James Van Buskirk), Gay Elizabeth Ann (Mrs. William Joseph Paul Smith, Jr.); m. 2d, Henry Bernard Dicker, Apr. 4, 1973. Sketch dept. artist Opalume Sign Co., Newark, 1927; head sketch dept. N.J. Claude Neon Sign Co., Jersey City, 1928-29; financial aid cons. Dean of Student's Office, Upsala Coll., 1959-67; One-man shows East Orange Library, 1945, Time and Life Bldg., N.Y.C., 1948; exhibited in group shows at Newark Mus., 1958, 59, Art Centre of Oranges, 1946-50, Bloomfield Art Club, 1948, Montclair Mus., 1949; tchr. art Montclair Adult Sch., 1947-59, Newark News Craft Classes, 1948-53, Newark Mus., 1958-59. Leader, Brownies, 1943-46, Girl Scouts U.S.A., 1947-48; pres. Franklin Sch. P.T.A., 1945, Clifford Scot High Sch. P.T.A., 1946-47; fund drive chmn. A.R.C., East Orange, 1945; sec. Upsala Women's Aux., 1949; pres. Art Centre of Oranges, 1945-49; vol. tchr. pottery and clay sculptures to blind Diamond Spring Lodge, Denville, N.J., 1960-67. Committee woman Republican Party, 1932. Chmn. bd. dirs. N.J. Found. for Blind, 1960-67. Recipient plaque N.J. Found. for Blind, 1967, citation for outstanding contbn. to Art Centre of Oranges, 1969. Mem. N.J. Rose Soc., Phi Omega Chi, Theta Beta Gamma (adviser 1966-67). Home: Buckhorn Dr RD 1 Belvidere NJ 07823 also 48 Hiram Pond Rd Dennis MA 02638 also 138 Ranchero Village Largo FL 33540

DICKERSON, BONNIE LEE, banker; b. Slaton, Tex., Feb. 14, 1925; d. Charlie Millard and Bessie Lee (Berkley) Biggs; student Tarleton State Coll., 1957-58; m. Ernest Earl Dickerson, Nov. 16, 1945; children—David Duane, Terrell Glenn. With Stephenville Bank & Trust Co. (Tex.), 1956—, asst. cashier, 1962-70, acting cashier, 1970-71, cashier, 1971—. Treas. Salvation Army, Stephenville, 1962-71; treas. Easter Seal Soc., Erath County, Tex., 1962-69; bd. dirs. Stephenville United Fund, 1972-75. Mem. Zonta Internat., Xi Iota Theta, Beta Sigma Phi. Home: 411 Maple Lane Stephenville TX 76401 Office: Stephenville Bank & Trust Co Box 998 Stephenville TX 76401

DICKERSON, IRENE, librarian; b. Mayo, Ky., Oct. 1, 1913; d. Dorestus and Annie Beauford (Parsons) Dickerson; A.B., Centre Coll., 1936; postgrad. U. Ky., 1938-39, 55-56. Tchr. English, librarian Salvisa (Ky.) High Sch., 1936-40; band dir. Fairview High Sch., Bondville, Ky., 1941-55; dir. glee club, Mercer High Sch., Harrodsburg, Ky., 1955-59, librarian, 1955—; pvt. piano and organ tchr., 1945—. Mem. Nat., Ky. edn. assns., Ky. Library Assn., Ky. Assn. Sch. Librarians. Baptist. Home: Rural Route 5 Harrodsburg KY 40330 Office: Mobley Rd Harrodsburg KY 40330

DICKERSON, JANET SMITH (MRS. TERRY L. DICKERSON), coll. adminstr.; b. N.Y.C., Feb. 13, 1944; d. Timothy and Artisse E. (Macomson) Smith; B.A., Western Coll. for Women, 1965; M.Ed., Xavier U., 1968; m. Terry L. Dickerson, Aug. 21, 1965; children—Jill Courtney, Karin Chase. Tchr., counselor Cin. Pub. Schs., 1965-71; instr., counselor ednl. devel. program U. Cin., 1971; dir. supportive services, asso. dean students, asst. prof. Earlham Coll., Richmond, Ind., 1971—. Mem. Richmond Art Assn., 1973—; mem. We Americans, Inc., Richmond, 1973—. Sec. bd. dirs. Trueblood Cooperative Nursery Sch., 1973-74; v.p. bd. dirs. The Children's Sch., Inc., 1974. Mem. Nat. Assn. Women Deans and Counselors. Episcopalian. Office: Earlham College Richmond IN 47374

DICKERSON, MONTIE MAURINE, coll. librarian; b. Bethany, Okla.; d. Lawrence Henry and Ruby Emily (Keeton) Dickerson; A.B., Bethany Nazarene Coll., 1948; M.A., Okla. State U., 1951; M.L.S., U. Okla., 1958. Tchr., Mutual (Okla.) High Sch., 1948-50; teaching fellow Okla. State U., 1950-51; tchr. English, Bethany Nazarene Coll. (Okla.), 1951-58, 59-67; cataloger San Fernando Valley Coll., Northridge, Cal., 1958-59; chief librarian Mid-Am. Nazarene Coll., Olathe, Kan., 1967—. Mem. A.L.A., Phi Delta Lambda, Phi Kappa Phi, Beta Phi Mu. Democrat. Mem. Ch. Nazarene. Home: 1602 Haven Lane Olathe KS 66061

DICKERSON, NANCY HANSCHMAN (MRS. WYATT DICKERSON, JR.), news corr.; b. Wauwatosa, Wis.; d. Frederick R. and Florence (Conners) Hanschman; student Clarke Coll., 1944-46; B.S., U. Wis., 1948; postgrad. Harvard, 1949; Hum. D., Am. Internat. Coll., Springfield, Mass.; m. Wyatt Dickerson, Jr.; children—Elizabeth, Ann, Jane, Michael, and John Frederich. Tchr. Milw. high schs., 1948-50; staff asst. Senate Fgn. Relations Com., Washington, 1951-54; producer news, pub. affairs programs CBS, Washington, 1954-60; corr. CBS News, Washington, 1960-63; news corr. covering Capital for NBC News on TV and radio, 1963-71; TV syndicated news program "Inside Washington", 1971-73; syndicated TV news commentator Newsweek mag., 1973—. lectr.; writer. Recipient awards Albert Einstein Coll. Medicine, Pa. State Coll.; Pioneer award New Eng. Press Assn., 1965; Spirit of Achievement award Albert Einstein Coll., Yeshiva U., 1966; Yale U. asso. fellow, 1972. Mem. Am. Women in Radio and Television (Outstanding Achievement award George Washington chpt. 1966). Club: Washington Nat. Press. Home: Merrywood McLean VA 22101 Office: 1750 Pennsylvania Av NW Washington DC 20006

DICKEY, ANN KUTZ (MRS. CLAYTON L. DICKEY), coll. adminstr.; b. Duluth, Minn., Sept. 30, 1926; d. Karl B. and Leona (Smith) Kutz; A.B. in Polit. Sci., U. Mich., 1947, M.A. (Am. Assn. U. Women fellow), 1967; m. Clayton L. Dickey, Jan. 31, 1948; children—David, Dale. Sales corr. Houghton Mifflin Co., Chgo., 1947; personnel clk. Am. embassy, Paris, France, 1949-50; engaged in pub. relations Milw. Pub. Library, 1950-52; admissions counselor Saginaw Valley Coll., University Center, Mich., 1964-66, registrar, 1967-71, dean student services, 1972—. Mem. Mich. exec. com. Haber Commn. on Polit. Reform Democratic party, 1969. Mem. Am. Assn. U. Women, Mortar Bd., Kappa Alpha Theta, Alpha Lambda Delta. Home: 4606 Roanoke Ct Midland MI 48640 Office: Saginaw Valley College University Center MI 48710

DICKEY, BETTY ALICE (MRS. SAM DICKEY), civic worker; b. Kansas City, Sept. 2, 1924; d. Perl Elmer and Mamie Forrest (Blackwell) Long; A.B., Drury Coll., 1946; postgrad. U. N.C., 1947-48; m. Samuel Stephens Dickey, June 18, 1949; children—Andrew Charles, Stuart Gilbert. Caseworker Greene County Welfare Office, Springfield, Mo., 1946; mem. staff personnel office J. Garfinckel Co., Washington, 1948-49; dir. social services W.E. Handley City Hosp., Springfield, Mo., 1951-56; dir. Greene County Community Planning Council, Springfield, 1966-73; mem. Lakes Country Comprehensive Health Planning Bd., 1971-74, sec., 1971, mem. Task Force on Alcoholism and Related Problems, 1973-74; mem. com. Goals for Springfield, 1972; mem. Child Welfare Adv. Bd., 1970-74; mem. Community Orgn. Against Drug Abuse Bd., 1971-73, Mayor's Commn. on Aging, 1973-74, Alcohol Project Rev. Com. Mo. Dept. Mental Health, 1974-75; sec. U. Mo. Extension Council, 1974. Recipient Ann. Distinguished Service award Greene County Planning Council, 1972. Mem. S.W. Mo. Mus. Assos., Legal Aux Grene County Bar Assn. (pres. 1959), women's Drury Aux. Bd. (treas. 1972), Pi Beta Phi. Presbyn. Club: Twin Oaks Country. Home: 2636 Glenwood Springfield MO 65804

DICKEY, DONNA LEE (MRS. ERNEST MARTIN DICKEY), banker; b. Stanwood, Wash., July 19, 1932; d. Nolan Peter and Erma Dolores (Ross) Leque; ed. Stanwood pub. schs.; m. Ernest Martin Dickey, Nov. 25, 1947; children—Theresa, Martin, James. Teller trainee Nat. Bank Alaska, Anchorage, 1962, savs. poster, 1963, head office teller, 1963-65, asst. head teller, 1965, collection clk., 1965, note teller, 1965, supr. br., Ft. Richardson, 1966-68, head office proof supr., 1968, demand deposit accounting supr., 1969, asst. cashier, 1970, asst. v.p., 1971-73, v.p., 1973—. Vice pres. Creekside Park Grade Sch., Anchorage, 1967-68, pres., 1968-69; treas. Polar Little League, Anchorage, 1967-69. Mem. Nat. Assn. Bank Women, Am. Inst. Banking (consul 1969-72), Anchorage Bus. and Profl. Women's Club. Home: 701 Delaware Pl Anchorage AK 99504 Office: 6831 Arctic Blvd Anchorage AK 99502

DICKEY, HELEN PAULINE, artist; b. Cleve., Jan. 15, 1906; d. John Paul and Caroline Mary (George) McCaslin; student Western Res. U., 1924-26, Toledo U. Museum Sch., 1945-51, also pvt. study; m. Carl O. Dickey, Dec. 25, 1926; (dec. 1926); 1 son, Carl Oyer; m. 2d, Roy Elwood Anderson Sept. 29, 1972. Propr. own art sch., 1959-65; tchr. St. Petersburg (Fla.) Art Club, 1967, 70; dir. St. Petersburg Arts Center Gallery, 1971-73; dir. St. Petersburg Library Gallery, 1965—; mem. Studio Four, 1965-68; one woman exhbns. include Paradigm Gallery, Lakeland, 1966, Art Club St. Petersburg, 1967-70, Fla. Gulf Coast Arts Center, Belleaiv, 1970-75, Muse Gallery, Jr. Coll., Clearwater, 1967, Contemporary Gallery, St. Petersburg (all Fla.); others; represented permanent collections Eckerd Coll., Fla. Power Co., Lowe's Theatres, 1st Fed. Bank, Clearwater. Mem. St. Petersburg Arts Commn. Bd. dirs. St. Petersburg Library Art Gallery Little Theatre, 1965—, Art Gallery Arts Center, 1970-72. Mem. Fla. Artists Group, St. Petersburg Fine Arts Mus., Contemporary Gallery, Stable Artists of Jessada of Clearwater. Address: 1723 Lakewood Dr S St Petersburg FL 33712

DICKEY, JOAN LOUISE, educator; b. East Chicago, Ind., Apr. 30, 1948; d. Joseph Francis and Julie Ann (Marek) Dickey; B.S., Ball State U., 1970, M.A., 1971; postgrad. Western Ky. U., 1971—. Grad. asst. alumni office Ball State U., Muncie, Ind., 1970-71; instr. mass. communications, editor/writer univ. publs. Western Ky. U., Bowling Green, 1971—. Bd. judges Quill and Scroll Journalism Soc., 1971-74, Ia. High Sch. Press Assn., 1972-73, Columbia Scholastic Press Assn., 1972-74; judge So. Ky. 4-H Beauty Pageant, 1972; publicity chmn. March of Dimes Telerama, 1972, 73, 74; youth coordinator March of Dimes Talk-A-Thon, 1973. Recipient award of merit Nat. Found. March of Dimes, 1972, 73. Mem. Ky. Council Edn. in Journalism, Columbia Scholastic Press Advisers Assn., Women in Communications, Kappa Tau Alpha, Alpha Phi Gamma. Home: 2702 Industrial Dr Apt 201-A Bowling Green KY 42101

DICKEY, JULIA EDWARDS (MRS. JOSEPH E. DICKEY), librarian; b. Sioux Falls, S.D., Mar. 6, 1940; d. John Keith and Henrietta Barbara (Zerell) Edwards; student DePauw U., 1958-59; A.B., Ind. U., 1962, M.L.S., 1967, postgrad., 1967—; m. Joseph E. Dickey, June 18, 1959; children—Joseph E., John Edwards. Asst. acquisitions librarian Ind. U. Regional Campus Libraries, 1965-67; head tech. services Bartholomew County Library, Columbus, Ind., 1967-74; reference coordinator Southeastern Ind. Area Library Services Authority, 1974—. Mem. Columbus exec. bd. Mayor's Task Force on Status of Women, 1973—; del. Ind. Sch. Nominating Assembly, 1973-75. Mem. Am., Ind. (dist. chmn. 1972-73) library assns., Library Assts. and Technicians Round Table (chmn. 1968-69), Tech. Services Round Table (chmn. 1971-72, sec. library planning com. 1969-72), Am. Assn. U. Women (pres. 1973—). Home: 1617 McCullough Lane Columbus IN 47201 Office: 536 5th St Columbus IN 47201

DICKINSON, ALICE BRAUNLICH, coll. dean; b. N.Y.C., Apr. 11, 1921; d. Hans and Dorothy (Harding) B.; B.A., U. Mich., 1941, Ph.D., 1952; M.A., Columbia, 1947; m. David J. Dickinson, Dec. 10, 1944; children—Sara, Dan. Asst. project engr. Sperry Gyroscope Co., Garden City, N.Y., 1942-44; mem. staff Mass. Inst. Tech. Radiation Lab., Cambridge, 1944-45; lectr. Pa. State U., 1950-56; vis. prof. U. Baroda, India, 1962, 68, U. Aligarn, India, 1961-62; mem. faculty Smith Coll., 1959—, prof., chmn. math. dept. 1970-73, dean coll., 1973-75; cons. Hampshire Coll., 1965-68. Recipient Hampshire Coll. Founders award, 1970. Mem. Ely Ringing Guild, N.Am. Guild Changeringers, Am. Assn. U. Women. Author: Differential Equations: A Study in Time and Motion, 1972. Home: Graves Rd Ashfield MA 01330 Office: Tyler Annex Smith Coll Northampton MA 01060

DICKINSON, JANE W. (MRS. E.F. SHERWOOD DICKINSON), corp. exec., club woman; b. Kalamazoo, Sept. 27, 1919; d. Charles Herman and Rachel (Whaler) Wagner; student Hollins Coll., 1938-39; B.A., Duke, 1941; M.Ed., Goucher Coll., 1965; m. E.F. Sherwood Dickinson, Oct. 23, 1943; children—Diane Jane Gray, Carolyn Wagner. Exec. sec. Petroleum Industry Com., Balt., 1941-43; exec. sec. Sherwood Feed Mills Inc., Balt., 1943—. Mem. exec. com. Children's Aid Md., 1960-61; mem. bd. women's aux. Balt. Symphony Orch., 1958-60; dist. chmn. Balt. Cancer Drive, 1958; dist. chmn. Balt. Mental Health Drive, 1957; co-chmn. Balt. United Appeal, 1968. Mem. Alpha Delta Phi. Republican. Episcopalian. Clubs: Three Arts (sec. 1958-60, bd. govs. 1960-64, 67—, pres. 1970-72) (Balt.); Women's (bd. govs. 1960-64) (Roland Park); Cliff Dwellers Garden. Home: 1003 Bellemore Rd Baltimore MD 21210

DICKINSON, LENORE MIKALAUSKAS (MRS. JOHN KELLOGG DICKINSON), librarian; b. West Pittston, Pa., Mar. 5, 1919; d. Simon and Katharine (Zuyus) Mikalauskas; student Wayne State U., 1937-41; A.B., Boston U., 1965; M.S. in L.S. (Lilly Found. scholar), Simmons Coll., 1967; m. John Kellogg Dickinson, Apr. 13, 1941; 1 son, Timothy Adam. Bookkeeper, bookseller Personal Book Shop, Boston, 1943-47, Phillips Book Store, Cambridge, Mass., 1954-61; cataloger Andover Harvard Theol. Library, Harvard Div. Sch., Cambridge, Mass., 1961-65, head cataloger, 1965—. Mem. Guild Book Workers, A.L.A., Am. Theol. Library Assn., Am. Recorder Soc. (pres. Boston chpt. 1963-65), Boston Mycological Club. Home: 4 Humboldt St Cambridge MA 02140 Office: 45 Francis Av Cambridge MA 02138

DICKINSON, R. DOROTHEA, govt. ofcl.; b. Bklyn., July 1, 1915; d. Martin and Marion Frances (Haviland) Dickinson; A.B., San Diego State Coll., 1938; B.C.S., Benjamin Franklin U., 1956. Clk., San Diego Gas & Electric Co., 1938-42; legal sec., Los Angeles, 1946, San Francisco, 1946-49, Washington, 1954-56; exec. sec. Congressman John E. Henderson of Ohio, Washington, 1956-59, Congressman Tom Moorehead of Ohio, 1960-61, Congressman Louis C. Wyman of N.H., 1962-63, 66—, Congressman Glenard P. Lipscomb of Cal., 1964, Congressman William L. Dickinson of Ala., 1964-65. Served with WAVES, 1942-46, 50-54; lt. comdr. Res. ret. Mem. Res. Officers Assn., Naval Res. Assn., Am. Assn. Ret. Persons, Ret. Officers Assn. Clubs: Army-Navy (Washington); Capitol Hill (Washington). Office: 410 Cannon House Office Bldg Washington DC 20515

DICKMAN, DORIS MCCULLOUGH (MRS. ROLAND FAVILLE DICKMAN), writer; b. Bridger, Mont.; d. Francis Marion and Bess May (Moore) McCullough; B.A., U. Mont., 1938; postgrad. U.S. Dept. Agr. Grad. Sch., 1952-53, 57-62, 66, U. Md., 1963-64; m. Roland Faville Dickman, June 6, 1938; children—Robert Edward, Laura Ruth (Mrs. John Sidney Alman), Francis William. Clk., sec. U.S. Dept. Agr., Beltsville, Md., Washington, 1941-43, 45-46, 50-53, publs. editor Soil Conservation Service, Beltsville, 1953-61, tech. editor biol. scis. Agrl. Marketing Service, Beltsville, 1961-64, Agrl. Research Service, Hyattsville, and Beltsville, 1964-72, nat. tech. editor plant sci. Agrl. Research Services Beltsville, 1972—. Sigma Delta Chi scholar, 1938. Mem. Soc. Tech. Communication (past chpt. sec., treas.), Internat. Order Jobs Daus. (past guardian sec.), DeMolay Mothers Circle (past pres.), A.A.A.S., Internat. Platform Assn., Shufu Judo Yudanshakai, Women in Communication, Inc. Mem. Order Eastern Star. Clubs: International Toastmistress (pres. Agrivox 1969, editor internat. counc. newsletter); Nat. Press. Home: 11718 Chilcoate Lane Beltsville MD 20705 Office: North Bldg Plant Industry Sta Beltsville MD 20705

DICKSON, BONNIE ELAINE, ednl. adminstr.; b. Murphysboro, Ill., Aug. 6, 1930; d. John A. and Susie (Adams) Dickson; B.S., So. Ill. U., 1952; M.R.E., Southwestern Bapt. Theol. Sem., 1958; Ed.D., So. Bapt. Theol. Sem., 1972. Tchr., Moore High Sch., Farmer City, Ill., 1952-56; state young women's aux. dir. Tex. Women's Missionary Union, Dallas, 1956-58; asst. dir. edn. div. Nat. Women's Missionary Union, Birmingham, Ala., 1958-69; prof. So. Bapt. Theol. Sem., Louisville, 1969-72, dean student affairs, 1972—, Gheens lectr. 1969. Study grantee So. Bapt. Conv., 1969-72. Mem. Orgn. Devel. Network, Nat. Tng. Lab., Assn. Creative Change, Nat. Assn. Women's Deans and Counselors, Am. Personnel and Guidance Assn. Author: The Woman's Missionary Union Program of a Church, 1969. Editor: The 70's: Opportunities for Your Church, 1970. Guest editor Rev. and Expositor, 1974-75. Contbr. articles to profl. jours. Home: 1305 Bluffsprings Ct Louisville KY 40223

DICKSON, LILLIAN DURHAM, author, editor, artist; b. Atlanta; d. Joseph Idelbert and Annie Rosbell (Meeks) Durham; student Sch. Fine Arts, Washington U., St. Louis, 1910-12, Fort Worth Conservatory Music, 1928, Tex. Christian U., 1930-31; m. Henry McHaney Dickson, Sept. 16, 1917 (dec. July, 1956); 1 son, Henry McHaney; m. 2d, B. Houston Cogdell, September 5, 1966 (div.). Propr. real estate firm, Ft. Worth, 1914-59; mgr., supr. Lloyd Surveying and Engring. Co., Houston, 1958-60; mgr. Tarrant County Surveyor's Office, Ft. Worth, 1961-63; dir., mgr. Westbrook Hotel Art Gallery, Ft. Worth, 1963-64, 69, 70, 71, 72; art tchr., propr. Four-Arts Studio, Ft. Worth, 1964—; founder, pub., editor mag. Composers, Authors, Artists Am., 1940—, chief editor, 1940-43, 48-49, contbg. editor, 1943—; contbr. poetry, articles mags., newspapers, 1920—; exhibited paintings in ann. group shows Tex. Fine Arts Soc., Ft. Worth, 1920—, also other regional shows; chmn. Tex. Council Promotion Poetry, Austin, Tex. 1949-59, co-chmn., 1960-66; nat. cultural co-ordinator Avalon Poetry Shrine, San Antonio, 1941-44; Tex. state chmn. Nat. Poetry Day Com., Austin, 1960-65. Recipient award of Merit, Gold medal Tex. Press Woman's Assn., Houston, 1948. Mem. Composers, Authors, Artists Am. (nat. pres. 1940-43, historian, 1948-50, 60-67, hon. life pres., 1944—, organizer Ft. Worth br., pres., 1938, v.p., 1951-52), Nat. League Am. Pen Women (v.p. Ft. Worth br. 1951-52), Ft. Worth Water Color Soc., organizer 1952, bd. dirs., 1952-67, recipient art awards, 1952, 53, 54, 63, 68, 69, 70). Poetry Soc. Tex., Tex. Fine Arts Assn., Ft. Worth Poetry Soc., A.S.C.A.P., Marquis Biog. Library Soc. (adv. mem.). Club: O'Henryettes (Ft. Worth). Author: The Enchanted Mesa, 1937; Amber In The Sun, 1947. Composer: Sentimental Over Texas, 1946. Home: 200 Burnet St Fort Worth TX 76102 Office: Four Arts Studio PO Box 6973 Houston TX

DICKSON, MARY JOAN, lawyer; b. Trenton, N.J., May 15, 1933; d. Vincent J. and Elizabeth (Estok) Dickson; B.S. magna cum laude in Commerce, Rider Coll., 1953; J.D., George Washington U., 1957. Admitted to N.J. bar, 1959; practiced in Trenton, 1962—; asso. Richard J. Hughes, Trenton, 1959-62; with N.J. Legislative Services, Trenton, 1965—, asso. legislative counsel, 1972—. Tchr. real estate and zoning course N.J. Inst. for Continuing Legal Edn., summer 1968. Congl. clk. Congressman Howell of N.J., 1953-54, Congressman Gray of Ill., 1955, Senator Neuberger of Ore., 1956-57. Active Mercer County Heart Fund, 1965, 66, Delaware Valley United Fund, 1967, 68. Rutgers State scholar, 1950-54, Rider Coll. scholar, 1950-53, Seton Hill Coll. scholar, 1950-54, Hungarian-Am. Civic Assn. scholar, 1950. Mem. Trenton Bus. and Profl. Women, Phi Delta Delta, Phi Epsilon Delta. Democrat. Roman Catholic. Home: 805 Chambers St Trenton NJ 08611 Office: 143 E State St Trenton NJ 08608

DICKSON, NAIDA, writer, puzzlesmith; b. Thatcher, Ariz., Apr. 18, 1916; d. Charles Edmund and Daisie (Stout) Richardson; B.S., Utah State U., 1940, M.S., 1944; m. Charles Eugene Dickson, Dec. 25, 1942; children—Charles and Clarence (twins). Social worker in Utah, 1941-43; elementary and jr. high sch. tchr., Utah and Cal., 1939-68; part-time adult edn. tchr., 1968—; children's librarian, Upland, Cal., 1958-59; correctional counselor Cal. Inst. Women, Corona, 1961-62; free-lance writer, 1951—, also puzzlesmith, illustrator. Vol., Right-to-Life-Line, 1972—. Fellow social work Latter-day Saints Ch. Relief Soc., 1940-41. Mem. Soc. Children's Book Writers. Mem. Ch. of Jesus Christ of Latter-day Saints (Sunday sch. tchr. 1936—, pres. word Young Women, 1943-44, stakepublicity dir. 1952-53, pres. Relief Soc. 1955-56, ward newsletter editor 1971-74). Author, illustrator: The Littlest Helper, 1971; In the Meadow, 1971; I'd Like, 1971; The Toad That Couldn't Hop, 1972; Just the Mat for Father Cat, 1972; The Happy Moon, 1972; Big Sister and Tagalong Teddy, 1973; author: The Best Color, 1971; The Story of Harmony Lane, 1971; About Doctors of Long Ago, 1972; The Biography of a Honeybee, 1974; also poems in anthologies, mags. Puzzles published in puzzle mags., 1963—. Address: 23500 The Old Road Space 23 Newhall CA 91321

DICKSON, NELL ROBINS (MRS. ALGERNON RICHARD DICKSON), curator; b. Waterville, Wash., Sept. 21, 1886; d. Samuel C. and Ida Helna (Steiner) Robins; grad. high sch.; m. Algernon Richard Dickson, May 20, 1908; 1 son, Samuel Robin. Clk., U.S. Land Office, Waterville, 1905; librarian Waterville Library, 1919-25; office worker Seattle Grain Co., 1948-56; curator Douglas County Hist. Mus., Waterville, 1959—. Mem. P.E.O. Episcopalian. Mem. Order Eastern Star. Home: Ash St Waterville WA 98558 Office: PO Box 34 Waterville WA 98558

DICKSON, NOVA BRYANT (MRS. EMORY M. MARKS), tchr., counselor, civic worker; b. Whitewright, Tex., Aug. 28, 1917; d. George Fitzgerald and Jewel (Little) Bryant; B.S., Tex. Woman's U., 1939, M.A., 1963; m. Murray S. Dickson, May 30, 1942 (dec. Dec. 1961); children—Frances (Mrs. Robert W. Loveless, Jr.), Margaret Jane (Mrs. Charles Benjamin Masher, Jr.), George Harkey; m. 2d, Emory M. Marks, Apr. 1, 1970. Tchr. English, creative drama, personnel and guidance Am. Inst., Meth. Bd. World Missions, Cochabamba, Bolivia, 1943-60, 65; counselor Collegro Metodista, La Paz, Bolivia, 1962-64; tchr. elementary grades, counselor developing area Austin (Tex.) Pub. Schs., 1940-41, 62, 69, counselor of minority children, 1969-70. Home: 300 E Berger St Santa Fe NM 87501

DICORLETO, HELEN THERESA, ednl. adminstr.; b. Hartford, Conn., Apr. 6, 1918; d. Francesco Antonio and Rosina Julietta (Scavullo) DiCorleto; B.S., Central Conn. State Coll., 1941; M.A., N.Y.U., 1951; postgrad. U. Conn., 1953-55, Boston U., 1957, U. Hartford, 1956-58, Trinity Coll., 1957-58, Bank St. Coll. Edn. (Nat. Def. Edn. Act grantee), 1967-68. Elementary tchr., Hartford Pub. Schs., 1941-54, asst. dir. elementary edn., 1965-67, dir. elementary edn., 1967-70; clin. supr. U. Hartford, 1970—; edn. agt. Tchr. Peace Corps, City of Hartford, 1971-72; dir. Title III Tchr. Interactive Learning Center, 1972—. Mem. Am. Assn. Sch. Adminstrs., Nat., Conn. edn. assns., Zonta Internat., Delta Kappa Gamma. Home: 90 Kane St West Hartford CT 06119 Office: 249 High St Hartford CT 06103

DIDIER, ROSLYN ANN, life ins. co. exec.; b. Ft. Wayne, Ind., Mar. 27, 1924; d. Lester A. and Bertha (Stoll) Didier; grad. Internat. Bus. Coll., 1944. Office mgr. Remington Rand, Inc., Ft. Wayne, 1944-48; sec. to pres. Midwestern United Life Ins. Co., 1948-52, asst. sec. co., 1952-72, sec., 1972—; sec. Transcontinental Motor Inns, Inc. (formerly Midwestern Cos., Inc.), 1959-72, MULIC Cos., Inc., 1972—, MULIC Realty, Inc., 1972—, varied Industry Plan, Inc., 1973—; dir. Jackson Realty Co., Inc., 1962-71, sec.-treas., 1962-72. Home: 621 Tennessee Av Fort Wayne IN 46805 Office: 7551 US Hwy 24 W Fort Wayne IN 46804

DIECKOW, NANCY ELIZABETH, orgn. rep.; b. Cleve., Jan. 16, 1940; d. Howard John and Carolyn Disque (Work) Dieckow; R.N., Swedish Covenant Hosp. Sch. Nursing, 1960; student North Park Coll., 1960-61, Western Res. U., 1963-64. Operating room nurse Swedish Convenant Hosp., Chgo., 1960-61; operating room nurse Univ. Hosps. of Cleve., 1961-64, asst. head nurse orthopedic surgery, 1963-64; operating room nurse U. Tex. Med. Br., Galveston, 1964-65; operating room nurse in charge orthopedic surgery St. Lukes-Tex. Children's Hosp., Houston, 1966-67; office and surg. asst., Houston, 1967-71; South Central regional rep. Pioneer Girls, Houston, 1971—. Nurse, health cons., counseling and adminstr. staff various summer camps. Baptist. Address: 2219 Winrock St Houston TX 77027

DIEFENDERFER, FLORENCE ADELE MORGAN, bank exec.; b. Reading, Pa., Apr. 28, 1916; d. Josiah Foster and Florence (Reiff) Morgan; student Am. Bus. Coll., 1933-35, Am. Inst. Banking, 1957-65, Pa. State U., 1963-64; m. Arthur H. Diefenderfer, Dec. 13, 1935 (div. May 1946); 1 son, Roy M. Exec. sec. Lehigh Valley Transit Co., Allentown, Pa., 1946-56; with Mchts. Nat. Bank, Allentown, 1956—, personnel officer, 1964—, asst. v.p., 1967-72, v.p., 1972—. Charter mem. Muhlenberg Med. Center, 1963—; mem. bus. edn. adv. com. Allentown Sch. Dist., 1966—; mem. banking adv. com. Northampton County Area Community Coll., 1971—. Mem. Lehigh Valley C. of C., Quota Internat. (pres. 1970-71), Am. Inst. Banking (chpt. pres. 1970-71), Nat. Assn. Bank Women, Bank Adminstrn. Inst. Lutheran (mem. ch. council 1967-73; chmn. social ministry 1967-70). Home: Allen House 117 S 4th St Allentown PA 18102 Office: 702 Hamilton St Allentown PA 18101

DIEFENDERFER, OMIE TILTON, educator; b. Fullerton, Pa., June 1, 1910; d. Eugene Edgar and Omie (Tilton) Diefenderfer; B.S. in Edn., Kutztown State Tchrs. Coll., 1931, B.S. in Art Edn., 1952; Ed.M., Temple U., 1955. Tchr., Whitehall Twp. Jr. High Sch., 1931-55; developmental and remedial reading and elementary reading supr. Whitehall Twp. Jr. and Sr. High Sch., 1956-63; reading cons., Whitehall Twp., 1962-63; psychol. examining in Allentown-Bethlehem Guidance Clinic, 1963; reading cons. kindergarten through 12th grade Whitehall-Coplay Joint Sch. System, Hokendauqua, Pa., 1963-73, coordinator spl. program for auditary and visual perceptual handicapped child, 1966-73, reading specialist, 1969-73, now cons. Title I auditory-visual program learning disabilities. Reading cons. Lehigh County Brain Injured Classes, 1968—, LeValle Schs. in Allentown, 1968—; vol. tutor instr. nat. Right to Read program, 1972—. Mem. bd. Council for Children of Allentown State Hosp., 1960—, sec., 1960-61. Recipient certificate of recognition for outstanding service Pa. Assn. Children With Learning Disabilities, 1971; alumni citation in recognition excellence in chosen profession, devotion to pub. service and honor brought upon Alma Mater Kutztown State Coll., 1972. Mem. Whitehall-Coplay Edn. Assn. (parliamentarian 1962—), Internat. Reading Assn. (com. on research and skills, dir., nominating chmn. Lehigh Valley council, mem. bd. of the council), Pa. Assn. Brain Injured Children (v.p. 1965). Nat., Pa. edn. assns., Nat. Congress Parents and Tchrs., Nat. Soc. Study Edn., Woman's Internat. Bowling Congress, Am. Legion Aux., Pa. Assn. for Retarded Children, Kutztown Alumni Assn. Temple U., Fullerton Meml. Assn., Lehigh County Hist. Soc., Gen. Fedn. Women's Clubs, Council Exceptional Children, Internat. Platform Assn., Council for Children with Learning Disabilities (sec. Lehigh Valley chpt., 2d v.p., editor newsletter), Orton Soc. (dir.), Fullerton Fire Co. No. 1 Aux. Republican. Mem. United Ch. of Christ (tchr. Bible Class 1956—, mem. choir). Home: 828 3d Fullerton PA 18052 Office: 2940 MacArthur Rd Whitehall PA 18052

DIEHL, CAROLYN HELEN (MRS. ALBERT L. RUBIN), physician; b. West New York, N.Y., Apr. 8, 1925; d. John Anthony and Estelle Natalie (Vogedes) Diehl; B.A., Cornell U., 1946, M.D., 1950; m. Albert L. Rubin, Sept. 28, 1953; 1 son, Marc. Intern Barnes Hosp. St. Louis, 1950-51, resident, 1951-52; resident Cornell-N.Y. Hosp., 1952-53, 53-54; practice medicine specializing in internal medicine; dir. nurses health service, N.Y. Hosp., N.Y.C., 1954—, asso. dir. employees' health service, 1958—; mem. staff Cornell U. Med. Coll. Mem. Phi Beta Kappa, Alpha Omega Alpha, Phi Kappa Phi, Delta Gamma. Roman Catholic. Home: 220 Allison Court Englewood NJ 07631 Office: NY Hospital 525 E 68th St New York City NY 10021

DIEHL, MARY JANE ELLSWORTH, educator; b. Denville, N.J.; d. Robert George and Angennetta (Keeffe) Ellsworth; B.A., Montclair State Coll., 1940, M.A., 1960; Ed.D., Rutgers, The State U., 1967; m. Edwin D. Diehl, Jan. 14, 1940 (dec. Aug. 1962); children—Digby, Michael. Dir. edn. Middlesex County Health League, New Brunswick, N.J., 1946-49; vice prin., tchr. Montville Twp. Sch., Montville, N.J., 1953-59; team tchr. Mountain Lakes (N.J.) High Sch., 1960-61; profl. asst. adv. services Ednl. Testing Service, Princeton, N.J., 1962-67; asso. prof. Monmouth Coll., West Long Branch, N.J., 1967—, regional coordinator Project Head Start Tng. Program, 1968-69; asst. dir. Project Head Start Tng. Program Rutgers,, summer 1967. Mem. Assn. for Supervision and Curriculum Devel. (nat. bd. mem. 1967—), Am. Assn. U. Women (fellowship chmn. Princeton br. 1968—), N.J. Assn. Supervision and Curriculum Devel. (sec. exec. com. 1962—), N.J. School Women, N.J. Edn. Assn., N.E.A. Home: Poor Farm Rd Harbourton NJ 08534 Office: Monmouth Coll West Long Branch NJ 07764

DIEKEN, GERTRUDE, editor; b. Grundy Center, Ia.; d. J.D. and Louise (Theerman) Dieken; A.B. magna cum laude, Coe Coll., 1932; postgrad. Ia. State Coll., 1937-41. News editor chain weekly newspapers, Grundy County, Ia., 1932-34; home econs. editor Ia. State Coll., 1935-42; home econs. cons. pub. relations dept. E.I. Dupont de Nemours Co., 1942-45; women's editor Farm Jour., Phila., 1945-69, creative dir. Countryside Services, 1969—, also v.p., dir.; editor Town Jour., 1953-55. Mem. sec. agr.'s standing com. home econs. research projects Dept. Agr., 1955-63. Recipient Headliner award Theta Sigma Phi, 1949, Epsilon Sigma Phi award, 1955, Reuben Brigham award Am. Assn. Agrl. Coll. Editors, 1956. Mem. Am. Home Econs. Assn., Women in Communication, Pi Delta Epsilon, Phi Kappa Phi, Alpha Xi Delta. Home: 2031 Locust St Philadelphia PA 19103 Office: Farm Jour Washington Sq Philadelphia PA 19105

DIEL, MARYOLETA BAUMAN, realtor; b. Olney, Ill., Aug. 6, 1924; d. Harry Fredrick and Ices Ernestine (Zerkle) Bauman; student Orlando Jr. Coll., 1964-65, various real estate courses, Fla. Inst. for Continuing Univ. Studies courses, 1965-67; m. Delmar Franklin Diel, Jan. 31, 1944; children—Karen (Mrs. Thomas Albert), Walter D., Timothy F. Real estate saleswoman Grand Bahama Devel. Co., Orlando, Fla., 1965; broker, saleswoman Sam J. Wright Jr. realtor, Winter Park, Fla., 1966-68; v.p., gen. mgr. Carl Brinkman, Inc., realtor, Orlando, 1970—. Presbyn. (pres. Women St. Johns Presbytery 1973-74, deacon, trustee). Home: 3009 Ivel Dr Orlando FL 32806 Office: 2925 E South St Orlando FL 32803

DIEMER, EMMA LOU, musician; b. Kansas City, Mo., Nov. 24, 1927; d. George Willis and Myrtle (Casebolt) Diemer; student Eastman Sch. Music, 1945-46, Ph.D., 1959; student Central Mo. State Coll., 1946-47; B.Mus., Yale, 1949, M.Mus., 1950; postgrad. Berkshire Music Center, 1954-55, Royal Conservatory, Brussels, 1952-53. Tchr. music N.E. Mo. State Coll., summers 1951-52, William Jewell Coll., Liberty, Mo., 1955-57, Kansas City Conservatory Music, 1955-57, Park Coll., Parkville, Mo., 1955-57; Ford Found. composer in residence Arlington (Va.) Secondary Schs., 1959-61; composer-cons. Balt. Pub. Schs., 1964; Arlington Pub. Schs., 1964-65; asst. prof. theory and composition U. Md., College Park, 1965-70; organist Ch. of Reformation, Washington, 1962-71; prof. theory and composition U. Cal. at Santa Barbara, 1971—; lectr. contemporary music, composition; organ, piano recitalist. Recipient Woods Chandler prize Yale, 1950; Delta Omicron composition prize, 1956; prize St. Mark's Ch., Phila.; Edward Benjamin award, 1959; Nat. Presbyn. Ch. award, 1959; Kindler Found. commn., 1963; Nat. City Christian Ch. commn., 1963; award A.S.C.A.P., Nat. Fedn. Music Clubs, 1969. Fulbright scholar, 1952-53. Mem. A.S.C.A.P. (Standard award 1962—), Am. Soc. Univ. Composers, Am. Guild Organists, Mu Phi Epsilon (1st prize for composition 1955, v.p. Washington alumnae chpt. 1963-64). Published compositions include Toccata for Marimba, 1956; O Come, Let Us Sing Unto the Lord, 1961; Fragments from the Mass, 1961; Three Madrigals, 1962; Four Carols for SSA, 1962; Four Piano Teaching Pieces, 1962; Woodwind Quintet 1, 1962; Youth Overture, 1962; Pavane for String Orchestra, 1964; Three Poems of Ogden Nash, 1965; Symphonie Antique, 1966; Ten Hymn Preludes for Organ, 1967; Toccata for Organ, 1967; Fantasie for Organ, 1967; Suite for Band, 1967; Sextet for Piano and Winds, 1968; Sonata for Violin and Piano, 1968; Toccata for Flute Chorus, 1969; Three Mystic Songs for Soprano and Baritone, 1968; Verses from the Rubiayat, 1970; Rondo Concertante for Orchestra, 1970; Fantasy on O Sacred Head for Organ, 1970; Three Aniversary Chorus for Mixed Voice, 1970; Seven Etudes for Piano, 1971; Madrigals Three, 1972; Sonata for Flute and Piano, 1973; The Prophecy for Women's Chorus, 1974, others. Home: 77-A N San Marcos Rd Santa Barbara CA 93111

DIENER, BETTY JANE, marketing cons.; b. Washington, Sept. 15, 1940; d. Edward G. and M. Chambliss (Feild) Diener; A.B., Wellesley Coll., 1962; M.B.A., Harvard, 1964, D.B.A., 1974. Account exec. Young & Rubicam, Inc., N.Y.C., 1964-70; product mgr. consumer products div. Am. Cyanamid Co., Wayne, N.J., 1970-72; marketing cons., 1974—; asst. prof. Case Western Res. U., 1974—. Adviser, Plans for Progress, Washington, 1968-69. Mem. Wellesley Alumnae Class (pres. 1967-72), Harvard Bus. Sch. Doctoral Assn. (pres. 1972-73). Address: 12900 Lake Av #911 Lakewood OH 44107

DIENER, MARY ELEANOR MCMATH, author, advt. agy. exec.; b. Washington, July 20, 1929; d. Mercer Bailey and Margaret Therese (Chase) McMath; student Internat. Coll. Tokyo (Japan), 1947-48; B.A., Manhattanville Coll., 1951; m. William Harrison Diener, Sept. 3, 1951; children—Eric, Paul, Lawrence, Valerie. Mem. econ. staff, reporter co. mag. The World, Gen. Motors of Brazil, Sao Paulo, 1951-52; asst. to Am. dir. Cultural Union of Brazil-U.S., Sao Paulo, 1953-54; dir.-mgr. shopping service, Sao Paulo, 1956-62; feature writer, social critique columnist Brazil Herald, Sao Paulo, 1961-65; pres. Assitencia Social de Vila Alpina, Sao Paulo, 1956-62; editor, display advt. mgr., sales mgr. The Citizen, weekly newspaper, Sarasota, Fla., 1966-67; account rep. Center for Marketing and Research, Sarasota, 1969-71; pres. Diener & Assos., Inc., advt. and ednl. planning and devel. agy., Sarasota and Research Triangle Park, N.C., 1971—. Bd. dirs., parliamentarian Women's Symphony Assn., Sarasota, 1972-74. Mem. Am. Advt. Fedn. (br. officer and dir. 1969-74), Fla. Pub. Relations Assn., Nat. League Am. Pen Women (local pres. 1972-74), Allied Arts Council Sarasota (dir. 1972-74), Sarasota C. of C. Republican. Roman Catholic. Author: When The Sun Goes Down (poetry), 1969. Address: PO Box 12052 50 Park Dr Research Triangle Park NC 27709

DIENHART, CHARLOTTE MARIE, educator; b. Sioux Falls, S.D., Aug. 14, 1923; d. Arthur Peter and Mae (Donahue) Dienhart; B.S., Coll. St. Catherine, 1945; M.S., State U. Ia., 1947; postgrad. U. Minn., 1956-58, Emory U. Sch. Medicine, 1962-64; Ph.D., Mich. State U., 1960. Research asst. U. Minn., 1947-48, grad. teaching asst. physiology, 1957-58; instr. dept. biology Coll. St. Catherine, 1948-57; grad. teaching asst. anatomy Mich. State U., 1958-60; mem. faculty Emory U., Atlanta, 1960—, asst. prof. anatomy, 1966—. Lt. comdr. USNR. Mem. A.A.A.S., N.Y. Acad. Scis., So. Soc. Anatomists, Sigma Xi, Sigma Delta Epsilon, Omicron Nu, Beta Beta Beta. Author: Basic Human Anatomy and Physiology, 1967, 2d edit., 1973. Home: 1943 N Decatur Rd NE Atlanta GA 30307

DIERKING, BARBARA ANNE WENTWORTH (MRS. IRWIN SAMUEL DIERKING), curator; b. Des Moines, Sept. 1, 1945; d. Robert Oral and Helen Anne (Potter) Bower; B.A., U. Ia., 1968; m. Irwin Samuel Dierking, Nov. 29, 1974. Pub. relations officer State Hist. Mus., Des Moines, 1968; adminstrv. sec. intensive care unit U. Ia., Iowa City, 1968-70; curator Hoover Presdl. Library, West Branch, Ia., 1970-71, Ft. Lewis (Wash.) Mil. Mus., 1972—. Mem. Ft. Lewis Bicentennial Celebration Com., 1972—. Mem. Am. Assn. Museums, Am. Assn. State and Local History, Soc. Am. Archivists, Friends Ft. Lewis Mil. Mus. (asso. dir. 1973—). Home: 7516 N 13th St Tacoma WA 98406 Office: Fort Lewis Mil Mus Fort Lewis WA 98433

DIERS, CAROL JEAN (MRS. HERBERT C. TAYLOR), educator; b. Bellingham, Wash., July 16, 1933; d. William Donald and Alice Harriett (West) Diers; B.A., Western Wash. State U., 1956; M.A., U. B.C., 1958; Ph.D., U. Wash., 1961; m. Herbert C. Taylor, Aug. 17, 1973. Tchr. pub. schs., Bellevue, Wash., 1956-57, 58-59; lectr. Olympic Community Coll., Bremerton, Wash., 1961-63; asst. prof. psychology Western Wash. State Coll., 1963-65, asso. prof., 1965-74, prof., 1974—, dir. honor program, 1970-74. Mem. Am. Psychol. Assn., Sigma Xi. Contbr. articles in field to profl. jours. Home: 3004 Cherrywood Av Bellingham WA 98225

DIESSNER, MARGARET CRENSHAW, civic worker; b. Rochester, Minn., May 9, 1922; d. John Lewis and Nell (Bryant) Crenshaw; A.A., Stephens Coll., 1942; student Northwestern U., 1942-43; m. Grant Roy Diessner, Feb. 3, 1948; children—Cathy (Mrs. Kim Clup), Marc Carl, Ann Rowland, Nancy Wostrel. County pres. woman's aux. A.M.A., 1960, state pres., 1966-67, N. Central legislative chmn., 1968-69, dir., 1969-71, chmn. communication com., 1971-73, nat. dir., 1969-73, mem. aux. planning com. for A.M.A. Quality of Life Congress, 1972; charter mem. Meth. Hosp. Aux., Rochester. Served with Armed Forces, 1943-45. Mem. Alice Mayo Soc., Gamma Phi Beta. Episcopalian (dir. Altar Guild 1957, chmn. women's activities 1970). Home: Sunny Slopes Rochester MN 55901

DIETER, NANNIELOU HEPBURN REIER (MRS. GARRET CONKLIN), astronomer; b. Springfield, Ill., June 10, 1926; d. Paul George and Alice (Henderson) Reier; A.B., Goucher Coll., 1948; M.A., Radcliffe Coll., 1957, Ph.D., 1958; m. Garret Conklin, Jan. 12, 1968; children by previous marriage—Amy, Mary Nan. Astronomer, U.S. Coast and Geodetic Survey, Washington, 1948-51, radio astronomy br. U.S. Naval Research Lab., Washington, 1951-55, USAF Cambridge Research Labs., Bedford, Mass., 1958-65, radio astronomy lab. U. Cal. at Berkeley, 1965—. Nat. Acad. Scis. grantee, 1973; NSF fellow, 1958. Recipient Patricia Keyes Glass award for women in sci. in Air Force, 1964. Mem. Internat. Astron. Union, Am. Astron. Soc., Astron. Soc. Pacific. Contbr. articles to profl. jours. Home: 1104 High Ct Berkeley CA 94708 Office: Radio Astronomy Lab U Cal at Berkeley Berkeley CA 94720

DIETRICH, BETTY JEAN BROADY, nursing cons.; b. Sacramento, Oct. 27, 1922; d. Eldon Leroy Broady and Evalena (Engle Broady) Gray; diploma Sacramento Hosp. Sch. Nursing, 1944; B.S., U. Cal. at Berkeley, 1952; M.S., U. Cal. at Los Angeles, 1957; postgrad. U. Cal. at San Francisco, 1967; m. Howard Lynn Dietrich, July 18, 1959. Operating room nurse Sacramento Hosp., 1944-45; office nurse for two internists, Sacramento, 1947-51; head nurse ear-nose-throat surgery unit VA Hosp., San Francisco, 1953-54; asso. clin. prof. U. Cal. Sch. Nursing, San Francisco, 1954-66; asso. coordinator nursing Cal. Regional Med. Programs, Area I, San Francisco, 1967-70; asso. project dir. planning for future of nursing edn. Stanford Sch. Medicine, 1971; project dir. Health Manpower Council Northeastern Cal. Opportunities to Progress Educationally in Nursing, 1974—. Nursing cons. Schs. Nursing and Nursing Services, Santa Rosa Jr. Coll., 1963, Fresno State Coll., 1966, Merritt Hosp., Oakland, Cal., 1966, USPHS Nursing Research Field Center, San Francisco, 1963-64, Health Service and Mental Health Adminstrn, Bethesda, Md., Regional Med. Programs Service, Div. Regional Med. Programs, 1969-70; established nurses continuing edn. programs N.W. Cal. counties. Served with Army Nurse Corps, 1945-46. Mem. San Francisco Health Profession's Council (dir. 1970-72), San Francisco Comprehensive Health Planning Council (dir. 1970-72), Am., San Francisco (pres. 1970-72), Cal. (chair person task force nat. health issues 1972—) nurses assns., Nat. League for Nursing, Common Cause, Nat. Orgn. Women, Sigma Theta Tau. Contbr. articles to profl. pubs. Home: PO Box 141 So Shasta Lake Area Summit City CA 96089

DIETRICH, HELEN RUSSELL, court reporter, conv. service co. exec.; b. Birmingham, Ala., May 4, 1912; d. William Crawford and Lucy Adelaide (Powell) Russell; B.A., Newcomb Coll., 1933; m. Norman Edward Dietrich, July 31, 1935 (div. Oct. 1949); 1 dau., Emilie (Mrs. Henry William Griffin). Sec., ct. reporter 8th Dist. U.S. Navy, 1941-42; founder, pres. Dietrich & Pickett, Inc., court reporting, New Orleans, 1942—; founder, pres. Helen R. Dietrich, Inc., conv. service, New Orleans, 1966—, Habersham Corp., pub., supplier ct. reporting machines, New Orleans, 1966—. Rec. sec. Le Petit Theatre du Vieux Carre, 1964-66. Mem. Nat. Shorthand

Reporters Assn., La. Hist. Soc. (corr. sec. 1962-71), D.A.R., Colonial Dames XVII Century, Dames Magna Charta, Newcomb Alumnae Assn. (2d v.p. 1947-49, treas. 1949-51), Internat. House. Democrat. Episcopalian. Editor, pub.: Of Time and Chase (Edison B. Allen), 1969. Home: 2033 Jefferson Av New Orleans LA 70115 Office: 333 St Charles Av New Orleans LA 70130

DIETSCH, MILDRED KATHRYN POWELL, former clin. psychologist, educator; b. Findlay, O., June 5, 1902; d. Thomas Austin and Fannie (Powell) Dietsch; B.S. in Edn., B.A., Ohio State U., 1920, M.A., 1928; M.A., U. Chgo., 1926; postgrad. U. So. Cal., 1935, Findlay Coll., 1934, 61, Western Res. U., 1941-44; Ph.D., U. Cal. at Berkeley, 1947. Tchr., Glenville High Sch., Cleve., 1920-27; head English dept. city grade schs., Findlay, 1928-35; clin. psychologist Bur. Child Guidance, San Diego, 1935-39, Findlay, 1939-41, Cleve. Bd. Edn., 1941-44, Los Angeles, 1944-46; head psychology dept., prof. Phoenix Coll., 1947-49; tchr., Mission, Tex., 1949-51, Fairfield Sch., Hamilton, O., 1951-55; clin. psychologist Wharton Sch., Findlay, 1955-70; psychologist Mental Hygiene Assn., Findlay, 1954-56, Sch. Migrants Children, 1964-65; individual practice psychol. counseling, 1966-70. Mem. A.A.A.S., Am., Ohio psychol. assns., Am. Assn. U. Women, D.A.R. (registrar 1941, librarian 1961—), Pi Kappa Psi, Gamma Kappa, Pi Lambda Theta. Republican. Methodist. Mem. Order Eastern Star. Home: 1601 S Main St Findlay OH 45840 Retired

DIETZ, ANN F. (MRS. FRANKLIN M. DIETZ, JR.), editor; b. Utica, N.Y., Mar. 3, 1939; d. Carlton Johnson and Violet Lurena (Beecher) Frazier; B.S., Syracuse U., 1960, M.L.S., 1967; m. Franklin M. Dietz, Jr., Oct. 7, 1967; 1 son, Karl Hannes. Cataloger, Cornell U. Library, Ithaca, N.Y., 1965-67; indexer Readers Guide to Periodical Lit., H.W. Wilson Co., Bronx, N.Y., 1967-72, asst. editor, 1972—. Editor, LUNA Monthly Mag., Oradell, N.J., 1969—, Sci. Fiction Times, N.Y.C., 1968-69. Mem. A.L.A., Omicron Nu., Phi Kappa Phi, Beta Phi Mu. Address: 655 Orchard St Oradell NJ 07649

DIETZ, DOROTHY BRILL, artist; b. San Bernardino, Cal.; d. Henry Edward and Anna Mae (Parfitt) Brill; student San Bernardino Jr. Coll., U. So. Cal., Ore. State U., Mills Coll., Coll. of the Desert, Japanese Art Center, San Francisco, 1957, Julian Art Acad., France, 1959. Wash. Sch. Art, 1964; grad. as Licensed Tchr. and Counselor, Unity Sch. Christianity, 1969; student Instituto San Miguel de Allende, Mexico, 1960, Sorbonne and L'Ecole du Cordon Bleu, France, 1959. Exhibited in one man shows at Dietz Galleria, 1959-69, Bank of Am., Palm Desert, Cal., 1962, Ferrall's Playhouse, Palm Springs, 1961; exhibited group shows in Cal., Mexico. Ct. reporter San Bernardino Justice Ct., also San Bernardino Superior Cts., 6 years; practice as interior designer, 1947—. Named Taka Mizu Dietz, Japanese Art Center; recipient Taka Mizu Dietz seal Govt. Japan, 1958; first prize, second prize Nat. Date Festival, Riverside County Fair, Indio, Cal., First, Fifth prizes Nat. contest Nat. League Am. Penwomen, 1962. Mem. Nat. League Am. Pen Women, Inc., Inst. Poetic Sci., Montalvo Assn., Assn. Unity Chs., Alpha Chi Omega. Republican. Club: The Villages Golf and Country. Home: 5336 Cribari Glen San Jose CA 95135

DIETZ, ELISABETH H., educator; b. Chgo., May 12, 1908; d. Bernhard Theodore and Auguste (Erasmi) Hoffmann; B.S., Northwestern U., 1940, M.A., 1942; Ed.D., N.Y. U., 1955; m. Ernest N. Warner, Dec. 18, 1926 (dec.); children—Nadine (Mrs. John Benjamin Rea, Jr.), Theodore Baker Warner; m. 2d, Thomas S. Dietz, Dec. 24, 1953 (div.). Tchr., Deerfield (Ill.) Pub. Schs., 1940-42, Metairie Park Country Day Sch., New Orleans, 1942-44, Edgewood Sch., Scarsdale, N.Y., 1944-50; lt. col. Am. Edn. Mission to Korea, 1952-53; ednl. cons. Am.-Korean Found., 1954; asst. prof. dept. edn. Bklyn. Coll. of City U. N.Y., 1950-52, 54-64, asso. prof., 1964-70, prof., 1971-73, prof. emeritus, 1973—; lectr., cons. in lang. arts and tchr. edn. Mem. exec. bd. Baldwin (N.Y.) Citizens Com., 1961-62; chmn. edn. com. Baldwin Council Human Rights, 1968-69. Trustee, dir. Soc. Preservation Samaritan Culture, 1968-73. Mem. Northwest Maricopa County UN Assn. (chmn. publicity com. 1973—), Am. Assn. U. Women, Internat. Folk Music Council, Soc. Ethnomusicology, Music Educator's Nat. Conf., Am. Soc. for Eastern Arts, Pi Lambda Theta, Delta Kappa Gamma. Editor: (with Thomas Choonbai Park) The Folk Songs of China, Japan, Korea; cons. editor John Day Books in Contemporary Edn.; editor The Urban Edn. Studies, 1965-72; The Rural Edn. Studies; The City is My Home books, American Indians Sing. Author: (with M. B. Olatunji) The Musical Instruments of Africa, 1965; You Can Work in the Health Services, 1968; You Can Work in the Education Services, 1968; You Can Work in the Transportation Industry, 1969; You Can Work in the Communication Industry, 1969; Folk Melodies of the Orient, 1972. Contbr. articles, book revs. to ednl. jours. Home: 9939 Pleasant Valley Rd Sun City AZ 85357

DIETZ, HELEN LOUISE, editor; b. Warren, O.; d. Clarence A. and Grace F. (Weir) Dietz; A.B., U. Pa., 1937. Asst. librarian Biochem. Research Found., Phila., 1937-40; sec. to editor Farm Jour., Phila., 1940-42; copy editor, mgr. editorial dept. W.B. Saunders Co., Phila., 1944-62, sr. editor, 1962-65, asso. nursing editor, also editor Nursing Clinics of N.Am., Am., 1965—. Mem. Phi Beta Kappa. Democrat. Episcopalian. Copy editor (Kinsey, Pomeroy, Martin and Gebhard) Sexual Behavior in the Human Male, 1948, Sexual Behavior in the Human Female, 1953. Office: WB Saunders Co W Washington Sq Philadelphia PA 19105

DIETZ, JANE T., editor; b. Honey Grove, Tex., Apr. 12, 1917; d. Harry Lee and Frances Lucile (Sparkman) Thompson; student Tex. State Coll. for Women, 1934-36; B.A., U. Okla., 1938; 1 son, Thomas Scribner. Soc. editor Clinton (Okla.) Daily News, 1938-40; feature editor Denison (Tex.) Herald, 1940-42; editor publs. Dearborn Stove Co., Dallas, 1953-55; asso. editor The Drilling Contractor mag., pub. Am. Assn. Oilwell Drilling Contractors (name now changed to Internat. Assn. Drilling Contractors), Dallas, 1955-65, mng. editor, 1965—. Mem. Nat. Soc. Magna Charta Dames, Plantagenet Soc., Sovereign Colonial Soc. Ams. Royal Descent, Colonial Order of Crown, Order of Washington, Press Club Dallas, Theta Sigma Phi, Chi Delta Phi. Office: 211 N Ervay Bldg Dallas TX 75201

DIETZ, MARGARET JANE NEUMANN (MRS. RICHARD H. DIETZ), pub. relations exec.; b. Omaha, Apr. 15, 1924; d. Lawrence Louis and Jeanette Amalia (Meile) Neumann; B.A., U. Neb., 1946; M.S., Columbia, 1949; m. Richard H. Dietz, May 30, 1949 (dec. July 1971); children—Henry Louis, Frederick Richard, Susan Margaret, John Lawrence (dec.). Wire editor Kearney (Neb.) Daily Hub, 1946-47; state soc. editor Omaha World-Herald, 1947-48; aide, Akron (O.) Pub. Library, 1963-66, publicity/display dir., editor Owlet, 1966—. Mem. women's bd. Weathervane Community Playhouse, 1962—, trustee, 1972—. Mem. League Women Voters (newsletter editor Akron chpt. 1959-61, 63-65), Ohio Library Assn., Akron Pub. Library Staff Assn. (pres. 1969-70), Mortar Bd., Women in Communications, Inc. (treas. 1972—), Alpha Lambda Delta, Gamma Phi Beta. Club: College (publicity dir. 1954) (Akron). Home: 577 Moreley Av Akron OH 44320 Office: 55 S Main St Akron OH 44326

DIETZ, MARILYN JANE, pub. relations exec.; b. Syracuse, N.Y., Apr. 16, 1926; d. Robert Henry and Irene Jessica (Wakelee) Dietz; student Syracuse U., 1961-65. Community relations asst. United Community Chest & Council, Syracuse, 1956-66; community relations asso. WCNY-TV, Liverpool, N.Y., 1966-69; communications dir. Mchts. Bank, Syracuse, 1969-71; promotion dir. WNYS-TV, Syracuse, 1971; dir. pub. relations St. Camillus Extended Care Facility, Syracuse, 1971—. Columnist Syracuse Post Standard, 1962—, Cath. Sun, Syracuse, 1972—; producer, host Silver and Golden Moments, WCNY-FM, Syracuse, 1972—. Cons., coordinator region 7, White House Conf. on Aging, 1971; cons. pub. relations Gottschalk Research Inst., 1972—, Panam. Assn., 1972—; commr. Met. Commn. on Aging, 1973—; chmn. Community Awareness, 1973—; v.p. Central N.Y. chpt. Arthritis Found., 1973—. Bd. dirs. Civic Morning Musicals, 1973—. Recipient Woman of Achievement award Syracuse Post Standard, 1970; Golden Age award Syracuse Salvation Army, 1972. Mem. Am. Women in Radio and TV (chpt. sec. 1972-74), Pub. Relations Soc. Am., Women in Communications, Bus. and Indsl. Communicators Council, Am. Fedn. Musicians. Episcopalian. Clubs: Syracuse (N.Y.) Press; Stonecrest Supper (Manlius, N.Y.). Contbr. articles in field to profl. jours. Vocalist with Klein Ensemble, 1972—. Home: 123 Annetta St Syracuse NY 13207 Office: 813 Fay Rd Syracuse NY 13219

DI FIGLIA, MARION THERESE, nephrologist; b. N.Y.C., May 15, 1938; d. Samuel Ernest and Clementine (Piazza) Di Figlia; B.S., Queens Coll., 1960; M.D., Med. Coll. Pa., 1964. Intern St. Vincent's Hosp., N.Y.C., 1964-65, resident, 1965-67; fellow nephrology Jefferson Med. Coll. Hosp., Phila., 1967-69; clin. asst. physician medicine St. Vincent's Hosp., N.Y.C.; asst. attending medicine St. Clare's Hosp., N.Y.C., Misericordia Hosp., N.Y.C.; chief nephrology Misericordia and Fordham hosps.; asst. in medicine Jefferson Med. Coll., 1968-69; instr. clin. medicine N.Y. U., 1970—; asst. prof. medicine N.Y. Med. Coll., 1972—. Diplomate Am. Bd. Internal Medicine. Mem. A.C.P., Am. Fedn. Clin. Research, Internat., Am., N.Y. socs. nephrology, A.M.A., Med. Soc. County N.Y., Med. Soc. State N.Y. Office: 600 E 233d St Bronx NY 10466 also 157-16 22d Av Whitestone NY 11357

DIGGS, ANNA JOHNSTON, lawyer; b. Washington, Dec. 9, 1932; d. Virginius Douglass and Hazel (Bramlette) Johnston; grad. Northfield Sch. for Girls, 1950; B.A., Barnard Coll., 1954; LL.B., Yale, 1957; postgrad. Wayne State U., 1969; m. Charles C. Diggs, Jr., Mar. 3, 1960 (div. Nov. 1971); children—Douglass Johnston, Carla Cecile. Admitted to D.C. bar, 1957, Mich. bar, 1960; atty. U.S. Dept. Labor, Washington, 1957-60; asst. prosecutor Wayne County, Detroit, 1962-63; asst. U. S. atty. So. dist. Mich., Detroit, 1966; legislative asst. to husband Congressman Charles Diggs, 1966-70; partner firm Zwerdling, Maurer, Diggs & Papp, 1972—. Instr. labor law Wayne Sch. Indsl. Relations, 1971—. Bd. dirs. Planned Parenthood Detroit, 1968—, YWCA, 1964-66, Delta Home for Girls, Detroit, 1964-66, Moore Sch. for Boys, Detroit, 1968—, Detroit Music Settlement Sch., 1966-68, Neighborhood Service Orgn., Detroit, 1967-72, Big Bros. and Sisters, Detroit, 1969—; bd. visitors Wayne Law Sch., 1971—; budget com. United Community Services, 1972. Mem. 13th dist. Women Democratic party Mich., 1960—, mem. state appeals bd., 1971—. Mem. Wolverine Bar Assn., Mich. Bar Assn., Women Lawyers Detroit, League Women Voters, N.A.A.C.P., Detroit Com. Seven Eastern Women's Colis. Clubs: Women's Econ., Detroit Press. Home: 1361 Joliet Pl Detroit MI 48207 Office: First Nat Bank Bldg Detroit MI 48226

DIGGS, OLIVE MYRL, counselor; b. Mound City, Ill., Apr. 22; d. Charles George and Blanche Weaver (Chambers) Diggs; B.S.C., Northwestern U., 1940; M.A., Roosevelt U., Chgo., 1957. Successively auditor, gen. mgr., editor Chgo. Bee Newspaper, 1929-47; cons. N.Y.A., 1940-43; race relations adviser City Chgo., 1943-49; dir. pub. relations Chgo. Land Clearance Com., 1949-52; asst. dir. Ill. Com. Human Relations, 1952-55; adminstrv. asst. Chgo. Dept. Urban Renewal, 1955—; mem. summer faculty Roosevelt U., 1964. Tech. adviser White House Conf. Children and Youth, 1968-70; mem. open occupancy com. Com. 100. Bd. dirs. Bensenville Home and Soc., 1970-73, Jane Dent Home, Chgo. Met. YWCA. Mem. Am. Assn. U. Women, The Links, Nat. Assn. Coll. Women, Nat. Assn. Housing and Redevel. Ofcls., Alpha Gamma Pi, Delta Sigma Theta. Mem. United Ch. Christ. Contbr. articles to publs. Home: 3001 ML King Dr Chicago IL 60616 Office: 320 N Clark St Chicago IL 60610

DIGIACOMO-GEFFERS, ELIZABETH ANN, nursing adminstr.; b. Mt. Vernon, N.Y., Nov. 8, 1939; d. Vincent and Angelina (Coviello) DiGiacomo; B.A. in Health Edn. and Nursing, Jersey City State Coll., 1961; M.P.H. in Pub. Health Adminstrn., Johns Hopkins, 1967; m. Rodney A. Geffers, Aug. 31, 1973. Tchr. health edn. North Bergen (N.J.) High Sch., 1961-62; supr. Long Beach (Cal.) Meml. Hosp., 1962-63; occupational health nurse Walt Disney Prodns., 1964-65; coordinator sch. health services Huntington (Cal.) Marina High Sch., 1963-65; instr. Sch. Dentistry, U. Md., 1967; asso. dir. pub. health nursing John F. Kennedy Inst., Md., 1967-68; research asst. Johns Hopkins, Balt., 1968; adminstr., supr., head nurse North Hudson (N.J.), Hosp., 1968-70; asst. dir. nursing Cedars-Sinai Med. Center, North Hollywood, Cal., 1970—. Fellow Am. Sch. Health Assn., Am. Pub. Health Assn.; mem. Royal Soc. Health, Am. Assn. U. Women, Am. Nurses Assn. Contbr. numerous articles to profl. jours. Home: 1301 S Atlantic Blvd Monterey Park CA 91754 Office: Cedars Sinai Med Center Fountain Av North Hollywood CA

DIGIOVANNI, JOAN FIMBEL (MRS. PHILIP DIGIOVANNI), educator; b. Jersey City, June 18, 1935; d. Albert Charles and Selma Caroline Kugler; A.A., St. Petersburg Jr. Coll., 1953; B.A., Fla. So. Coll., 1954; M.A., Columbia, 1955; Ph.D., Baylor U., 1961; m. Philip DiGiovanni, June 23, 1956; children—Juliet Paula, Portia Jonquil. Counselor women's residence halls U. Ill. at Urbana, 1955-57; teaching asst., dept. psychology Baylor U., Waco, Tex., 1958-61; asst. prof. psychology Old Dominion Coll., Norfolk, 1961-63, Springfield (Mass.) Coll., 1963-65; dir. counseling services, asso. prof. psychology Western New Eng. Coll., Springfield, Mass., 1965-69, asso. prof., 1969-73, prof., 1973—. Instr. Springfield Hosp. Sch. Nursing, 1964-66. Mem. Am. Assn. U. Profs., Am., New. Eng., Eastern, Mass. psychol. assns., Alpha Kappa Delta, Psi Chi, Alpha Chi. Unitarian Universalist. Home: 910 Plumtree Rd Springfield MA 01119

DILKS, ELEANOR RUTH, educator; b. Richmond, Ind., Jan. 29, 1921; d. William Wright and Bertha Grace (Test) Dilks; B.A., Earlham Coll., 1942; M.S., U. Wis., 1944, Ph.D., 1948. Instr. Earlham Coll., Richmond, Ind., 1942-43, Drury Coll., Springfield, Mo., 1945-47; instr. U. Buffalo, 1947-50, asst. prof., 1950-52; asso. prof. zoology Ill. State U., Normal, 1952-61, prof. zoology, 1961—. NSF faculty fellow, 1957-58. Mem. Marine Biology Assn. (U.K.), Am. Soc. Zoologists, Am. Micros. Soc., Fedn. Ont. Naturalists, Canadian Nature Assn., Ill. Acad. Scis., Australian Natural History Soc., Sigma Xi, Phi Sigma. Club: Altrusa (Bloomington, Ind.). Office: Dept Biol Scis Ill State U Normal IL 61761

DILL, ELSIE JANE (MRS. MURRAY CLAYTON DILL), produce co. exec.; b. Oakland, Cal., May 27, 1930; d. Henry Pierce and Elsie Augusta (Swan) Garin; student San Francisco Coll. Women, 1949, San Jose State, 1951-52; m. Murray Clayton Dill, Sept. 1, 1951; children—George, Gordon, Henry, Katherine, Cynthia. With Garin Co., Salinas, Cal., 1948—, partner, 1950—. Pres. Salinas Fine Arts, 1970-71, Art Unltd., 1972-73; mem. nominating com. Campfire Girls, 1965-68; mem. Salinas Arts Council, 1969-72, Pink Ladies, 1955-58. Mem. Native Daus. Golden West (chmn. art com. 1966-71), Delta Gamma. Republican. Club: Entre Nous (pres. 1967-68). Prin. art work includes mosaic on Palma High Sch. Gym., 1968. Home: 30 Santa Ana Dr Salinas CA 93901 Office: 634 S Sanborn Rd Salinas CA 93901

DILL, JULIA MOORE RUSSELL (MRS. GLENN A. DILL), banker; b. Three Creeks, Ark., May 3, 1909; d. Morgan Alderson and Fannie Lenore (Crawford) Moore; ed. El Dorado (Ark.) pub. schs.; m. Vergil R. Russell, Nov. 17, 1935 (dec. May 1948); 1 dau., Sarah (Mrs. Robert Emry Little, Jr.); m. 2d, Glenn A. Dill, June 21, 1962 (dec. June 1966). Clk. B.W. Reeves &Co., El Dorado, 1929-39; with Nat. Bank Commerce, El Dorado, 1949—, asst. cashier, 1952-70, asst. v.p., 1970—. Mem. Bus. and Profl. Women's Club. Home: 804 N Main St El Dorado AR 71730 Office: Nat Bank Commerce Plaza Washington and Grove Sts El Dorado AR 71730

DILL, JUNE WELLS (MRS. ROBERT GAIL DILL), journalist; b. Columbus, O., June 26, 1914; d. Oakland Caldwell and Elizabeth (Stocklin) Wells; B.F.A., Ohio State U., 1937; m. Robert Gail Dill, June 20, 1942; children—Robert Wells, Jerry Ronald, June Elizabeth, Preston Keith, Kevin Trent. Fashion editor Ohio State Jour., 1937-42; dir. vol. services Western Territorial Hdqrs. Salvation Army, San Francisco, 1944-45; fashion and beauty writer Columbus Dispatch, 1949—. Pub. speaker and fashion show commentator, judge numerous events. Recipient writing awards Ohio Newspaper Women's Assn., 1962, 68, 69, Footwear Inst. Am., 1968-71, Men's Fashion Assn. Am., 1968-69. Mem. Ohio Newspaper Women's Assn., Theta Sigma Phi. Club: Ohio Press. Home: 1988 Waltham Rd Columbus OH 43221 Office: 34 S 3d St Columbus OH 43216

DILL, NANCY NORTON (MRS. GEORGE DILL), educator; b. Winchester, Mass., Aug. 25, 1927; d. Frederick Harwood and Ann Gertrude (Harris) Norton; student Am. Acad. Dramatic Arts, 1945-47; m. George Dill, Dec. 11, 1948; children—Lesley (Mrs. Robert Sagerman), George. Tchr. creative dramatics and pub. speaking, dir., producer Old Greenwich Childrens Theatre, Riverside, Conn., 1959-62; tchr. speech and drama Waynflete Sch., Portland, Me., 1963-68; instr. speech and drama Westbrook Coll., Portland, Me., 1968-72. Mem. Greater Portland Arts Council (pres. 1965-68), Theatre Assn. of Me. (founder 1972). Home: Rural Route 1 Box 233 Yarmouth ME 04096

DILLAHUNT, BETTY JANE, educator; b. Springfield, O., Aug. 18, 1921; d. Earl Farnsworth and Edith (Grube) Doughman; B.S., Wittenberg U., 1946; M.A., Ohio State U., 1953; m. Fred S. Dillahunt, June 10, 1950. Mem. faculty health and phys. edn. Wittenberg U., Springfield, O., 1946—, chmn. women's health and phys. edn. dept., 1967—, asso. prof., 1970—. Founder, co-dir. Valley Farm Field Hockey Camp, Brooklyn, Mich., 1959—; mem. staff A.R.C. Nat. Aquatic Sch., Camp Lutherlyn, Prospect, Pa., intermittently, 1953-65; vice chmn. recreation youth guidance div. Community Welfare Council Springfield, 1964, sec., 1965, treas., 1966-67; chmn. Ohio Commn. on Intercollegiate Sports for Women, 1971—. Bd. mgmt. YMCA Camp Evergreen Mem. Ohio Coll. Assn., A.A.H.P.E.R., Midwest Assn. Health, Phys. Edn. and Recreation, Trans-Miss. Golf Assn. (dir.), U.S. Field Hockey Assn. (chmn. selection com.). Club: Northwood Hills Country (Springfield). Author: Field Hockey for Teachers, 1971. Home: 200 Wenova Dr Springfield OH 45502

DILLARD, GLORIA HANNAH (MRS. LLOYD THOMAS DILLARD II), state ofcl.; b. Zanesville, O., Jan. 6, 1946; d. LeRoy and Alta Laveona (Barnett) Wright; B.A. in Psychology, Muskingum Coll., 1967; m. Lloyd Thomas Dillard II, June 10, 1967; children—Jennifer, Lloyd Thomas III. Counselor Project Peace Skill Center, Cleve., 1967-68; rep. model cities State Ohio. Dept. Economic Community Devel., Columbus, 1973—; neighborhood projects coordinator Community Coordinated Child Care, 1974—. Pres. DARC & Asso. Advt. Co., Columbus, 1973-74. Chmn. fund-raising and Freedom Fund N.A.A.C.P. Bd. dirs. Columbus Community Services Systems, 1972-74, East Central Citizens Orgn., 1972-74. Mem. League Women Voters (bd. dirs. 1969-70), Chi Alpha Nu. Home: 1445 E Broad St Columbus OH 43205 Office: 624 S Ohio St Columbus OH 43205

DILLARD, PEGGY A. ARMSTRONG, social worker; b. Nashville, Aug. 17, 1938; d. Louis Edgar and Margaret (Tucker) Armstrong; A.A., Stephens Coll., 1958; B.A., Stetson U., 1960; M.S.W., U. Tenn., 1963; m. Jerry Wallace Dillard, June 25, 1965 (div.); 1 son, Stephen Louis. Child welfare worker Davidson County Dept. Pub. Welfare, Nashville, 1961-62, sr. child welfare worker, 1963-65, field supr. II, 1965-69; med. social worker Vanderbilt U. Hosp., Nashville, 1971-72; casework supr. Tenn. Prep. Sch., Nashville, 1974—. Mem. Nat. Assn. Social Workers, Acad. Certified Social Workers, Zeta Tau Alpha, Phi Theta Kappa. Democrat. Unitarian. Home: 8300 Sawyer Brown Rd Apt K-306 Nashville TN 37221

DILLARD, RUTH ELAINE ABRAMS (MRS. EDGAR ARCHER DILLARD, JR.), physician; b. Camden, N.J., July 19, 1925; d. Ernest V. and Helen (Schwarz) Abrams; B.A., Mt. Holyoke Coll., 1947; M.D., U. Pa., 1951; m. Edgar Archer Dillard, Jr., June 13, 1951; children—Rebecca Ruth, Barbara Ann, Edgar Archer III. Intern, Jackson Meml. Hosp., Miami, Fla., 1951-52, jr. asst. resident in pediatrics, 1952-53; asst. resident pediatrics Charlotte (N.C.) Meml. Hosp., pvt. practice medicine, Boynton Beach, Fla., 1955-58; instr. U. N.C. at Chapel Hill, 1958-61, 62-63; pediatrician Medico, Jeremie, Haiti, 1961-62; gratuitous service, DaNang, South Vietnam, 1963-65; mem. staff USPHS, Seattle, Wash., 1965-67; instr. U. Wash., Seattle, 1967-70; dir. pediatrics out-patient dept. Harberview Med. Center, 1967-70; asst. prof. U. Tex. at Galveston, 1970—, out patient dept., 1970—. Fellow Am. Acad. Pediatrics; mem. Ambulatory Pediatric Assn., Alpha Omicron Alpha. Home: 8821 Plantation Dr Texas City TX 77590 Office: Dept Pediatrics U Tex Galveston TX 77550

DILLE, JEANETTE HELEN, assn. adminstr.; b. Kenton, O., May 16, 1928; d. Clayton Miller and Helen Claire (Rabberman) Ewing; B.A., Bowling Green State U., 1950; M.S.W., U. Mich., 1960; children—Patrick, Carol (Mrs. Barnet Rhetta), Ronald, Lawrence. Child welfare supr. Wood County Ohio Dept. of Pub. Welfare, Bowling Green, 1954-61, child welfare cons. Northwest area, 1961-62; instr. staff devel. Conn. State Welfare Dept., Hartford, 1962-67, chief div. of staff devel., 1967-69; project dir. Conn. Child Welfare Assn., Inc., 1969—, project dir. Child Advocacy Center, 1971-73. Child welfare cons. to Judiciary Com., Conn. State Legislature, 1972—; adj. prof. child advocacy Union Grad. Sch., Yellow Springs, O., 1973—; lectr. Conn. State and Municipal Police Tng. Acad., Meriden, 1971—; mem. juvenile delinquency prevention sub-com. Planning Com. on Criminal Adminstrn.; mem. adv. com. div. of children and adolescent services, Conn. State Dept. of Mental Health, Dean's Adv. Com. U. Conn. Sch. of Social Work, adv. com. St. Joseph's Coll. Social work program. Mem. Adv. Council, Social Service Asst. Program, Manchester Community Coll. Chmn. Gov.'s Task Force to Study the Adoption Laws in Conn., 1971-72. Mem.

Nat. Assn. Social Workers, Am. Pub. Welfare Assn., Internat. Juvenile Officers Assn., Am. Pub. Health Assn., Acad. of Certified Social Workers. Office: 1040 Prospect Av Hartford CT 06103

DILLEHAY, BETTE HUDGINS (MRS. JOHN ROBERT DILLEHAY), librarian; b. Richmond, Va., Sept. 20, 1935; d. William Joseph and Myrtle Beatrice (Lewis) Hudgins; student Pan Am. Bus. Sch., 1954; B.A., Va. Commonwealth U., 1971; m. John Robert Dillehay, Dec. 21, 1957; 1 dau., Valerie Susan. Adminstrv. asst. Reynolds Metals Co., Richmond, 1954-57, personnel research dir., 1958-59; analyst, marketing research dept. A.H. Robins Co., Richmond, 1960-62, mgr. information services, 1962—. Bd. dirs. Richmond Area Heart Assn. Mem. Am. Soc. Information Scientists, Spl. Libraries Assn. (chmn. 1973-74), Va. Library Assn. (v.p. 1971-72). Club: Quota (Richmond). Home: 1905 Hanover Av Richmond VA 23220 Office: 1407 Cummings Dr Richmond VA 23220

DILLENBERGER, JANE DAGGETT (MRS. JOHN DILLENBERGER), educator; b. Hartford, Wis., Feb. 27, 1916; d. John Minot and Blanche (Morris) Daggett; B.A., U. Chgo., 1940; M.A., Radcliffe Coll., 1944; postgrad. Drew U., 1958-59; m. John Elias Karlin, July 15, 1940 (div. May 1962); children—Bonnie, Christopher (dec.); m. 2d, John Dillenberger, July 19, 1962. Curatorial asst. Chgo. Art Inst., 1940-41; curatorial asst. Newark Mus., 1945-46, dir. exhbn., 1948; head art library and collection Boston Athenaeum, 1944-45; curator catalogue research San Francisco Mus. Art, 1963-65; lectr. Drew Theol. Sem., Madison, N.J., 1950-62, asso. prof. Christianity and the Arts, San Francisco Theol. Sem., 1963-71; asso. prof. theology and arts Grad. Theol. Union, Berkeley, Cal., 1967—. Dir. exhbn. The Hand and the Spirit: Religious Art in Am., 1700-1900, 1972-73. Nat. Endowment Humanities grantee research 19th Century Am. art, 1973-74; Nat. Endowment for Arts grantee research 20th Century Am. art and religion, 1974-75. Fellow Soc. for Art, Religion and Contemporary Culture; mem. Coll. Art Assn., Liturgical Arts Soc., Pacific N.W. Art Historians Assn. Author: Style and Content in Christian Art, 1965; Secular Art with Sacred Themes, 1969; (monograph) The Hand and the Spirit, 1972. Home: 1536 Le Roy Av Berkeley CA 94708 Office: Grad Theol Union 2465 Le Conte Av Berkeley CA 94709

DILLER, BARBARA COX (MRS. THEODORE CRAIG DILLER), civic worker; b. Chgo., July 22, 1909; d. Howard Malcom and Aurelia (Crossette) Cox; B.A., Vassar Coll., 1931; postgrad. U. Chgo. Sch. Bus., 1932-33; m. Theodore Craig Diller, May 16, 1936; children—Anne C. (Mrs. Keir Brooks Sterling), Rebecca C. (Mrs. James R. Howe), and Deborah H. (Mrs. A.M. Triantphyllou). Sec., Chgo. Council Social Agys., 1934-35, for investment counsellor, 1935-36. Chmn. North Shore Vassar Club, 1946-47; leader Girl Scouts U.S.A., Evanston, Ill., 1945-48, Kenilworth, Ill., 1954-57; treas. Lincoln P.T.A., 1947-49, Chgo. Vassar Club, 1954-55; mem. Friends of Sr. Centers, 1960—, dir.; bd. dirs. Fellowship House, 1957-60; treas., dir. League Women Voters, Kenilworth, 1961-64; dir., program chmn. Neighbors of Kenilworth; mem. Fortnightly of Chgo. Home: 416 Cummor Rd Kenilworth IL 60043

DILLER, MARY ANN, coll. dean; b. Kansas City, Mo., Sept. 13, 1924; d. Edward and Willa Vaughn (Gates) Diller; A.B., MacMurray Coll., 1945; A.M., U. Ill., 1948; Ph.D., Mich. State U., 1973. Tchr. history Roxana High Sch., 1945-46; asst. in rhetoric and history U. Ill., 1946-48; tchr. history and English, Belleville (Ill.) Twp. High Sch. and Jr. Coll., 1948-49; tchr. social scis. Danville (Ill.) Jr. Coll., 1949-66, head social sci. dept., 1958-66, dean adult edn., 1966—. Vice pres. Vermilion County Citizens for Community Action, 1964-66; mem. bd. Children's Home of Vermilion County, 1969—; mem. faculty adv. com. Ill. Bd. Higher Edn., 1968-70; mem. exec. com. East Central Ill. Agy. Aging, 1971—. Mem. Nat., Ill., Danville (pres. 1959-60, 63-64) edn. assns., Ill. Adult Edn. Assn. (mem. exec. bd. 1965-70, pres. 1973-74), Pub. Sch. Adult and Continuing Educators of Ill., Assn. Pub. Continuing and Adult Edn. Assn., Adult Edn. Assn. U.S.A., Nat. Council Community Services for Community and Jr. Colls., Am. Assn. for Higher Edn., Am. Assn. U. Women (Danville pres. 1969-70, Ill. bd. mem. 1967-73, Sigma Phi Gamma (pres. 1961-62), Phi Alpha Theta, Delta Kappa Gamma, Kappa Delta Pi, Phi Kappa Phi. Presbyn. Home: 902 W Voorhees St Danville IL 61832

DILLER, MARY BLACK (MRS. MICHAEL ENGEL), artist; b. Lancaster, Pa., Apr. 22; d. William F. and Lida (Scofield) Diller; pvt. study art with Petrovits, Garber, Carles, Thomas Fogarty; m. Michael M. Engel, Sept. 22, 1939. One man shows N.Y. Pub. Library, Reading, Pa., Lancaster, Pa.; group shows Audubon Artists, 1940-65. Pa. Acad. Fine Arts, 1939-41, Art Students League Vet's Exhbn., 1944, Newhouse Gallery, Am.-Brit. Art Center, Pa. state dir. Am. Art. Week, 1938. Recipient Audubon Artist prize 1964. Tiffany Found. fellow. Mem. Nat. Soc. Arts and Letters, also mem. Audubon Artists, Lancaster County (founder; 1st pres. 1937-39, hon. life), Eastern art assns., Am. Artists Profl. League, Kappa Pi (hon. life). Author children's drawing books; also articles in mags. and newspapers. Home: 220 Cabrini Blvd New York City NY 10033

DILLER, PHYLLIS, actress, author; b. Lima, O., July 17, 1917; d. Perry Marcus and Frances Ada (Romshe) Driver; student Sherwood Music Conservatory, Chgo. 1935-37, Bluffton (O.) Coll., 1938-39; m. Sherwood Anderson Diller, Nov. 4, 1939 (div. Sept. 1965); children—Peter III, Sallee, Suzanne, Stephanie, Perry; m. Warde Donovan, Oct. 7, 1965. Theatrical prodns. include Dark at the Top of the Stairs, 1961, Wonderful Town, 1962, Happy Birthday, 1963; played lead in Hello Dolly, Everybody Loves Opal, 1972; numerous appearances TV and radio, concerts, supper clubs and hotels, 1955—; producer, author Phyllis Diller Shows, 1963, 64; rec. artist for Verve Records; pres. Eldorado Enterprises, Inc., 1964—, BAM Prodns., Ltd., 1965, PhilDil Prodns., Ltd., 1966; motion pictures include Boy Did I Get a Wrong Number!, 1966, The Fat Spy, 1966, Eight on the Lam, 1967, Did You Hear the One About the Traveling Saleslady, 1967, The Private Navy of Sgt. O'Farrell, 1967, The Adding Machine, 1969; star The Pruitts of Southampton, TV series, 1966-67. Recipient Star of Yr. award Nat. Assn. Theatre Owners. Hon. life mem. San Francisco Press and Union League Club. Author: Phyllis Diller Tells All About Fang, 1963; Phyllis Diller's Housekeeping Hints, 1966; Phyllis Diller's Marriage Manual; The Complete Mother. Accompanied Bob Hope entertainment group to South Vietnam, Christmas, 1966. Office: PhilDil Prodns Ltd One Dag Hammarskjold Plaza New York City NY 10017

DILLESHAW, FRANCES JOSEPHINE ROTHERMEL (MRS. CHARLES E. DELLESHAW), city ofcl.; b. Cleburne, Tex., May 4, 1917; d. Joseph Antone and Frankie Azlee (Stewart) Rothermel; grad. high sch.; m. Charles E. Dilleshaw, Feb. 12, 1938; 1 son, David Charles. Office sec. County Judges Office, Cleburne, 1937-41, County Agt.'s Office, 1941-42; sec., billing clk. Johnson County Electric Coop., Cleburne, 1950-70; med. sec. Kimbro Med. Clinic, Cleburne, 1971; city clk., city sec., sec. to city mgr. City of Cleburne, 1971—. Pres. Coleman Elementary P.T.A., 1953-54, Jr. High Sch. P.T.A., 1957-58, City County P.T.A., 1959-60. Mem. Assn. City Clks. and Sec. Tex. Baptist. Mem. Order Eastern Star. Home: 503 Bellevue St Cleburne TX 76031 Office: 302 W Henderson St Cleburne TX 76031

DILLING, DIANA JEAN, lawyer; b. Miami, Fla., Aug. 1, 1943; d. Kirkpatrick W. and Betty Ellen (Bronson) Dilling; student Newcomb Coll., 1961-62; B.B.A., Tulane U., 1965; J.D., U. Fla., 1968. Admitted to Ill. bar, 1969, Fla. bar, 1969; mem. firm Dilling and Dilling, Chgo., 1969-71; asst. atty. gen. State of Ill., Chgo., 1971—. Vice pres. Midwest Medic-Aide, Inc., Chgo., 1969-71; dir. Dillman Labs., Ltd., Chgo., 1969-74, Central Ia. Airlines, Ottumwa, 1973-74; treas., dir. P.E.P. Inventions, Inc., Chgo., 1971-74; spl. cons. Aircraft Mfr. and Conversion, Inc., Tuskegee, Ala., 1973-74. Mem. Am., Ill., Fla., Chgo. bar assns., Phi Delta Delta. Republican. Episcopalian. Office: 134 N LaSalle St Chicago IL 60602

DILLMAN, JOAN MARIE, psychologist; b. Chgo., May 15, 1931; d. Laban Lural and Emma Amanda (Vogel) Foster; B.S. in Elementary Edn., 1955; M.S. in Edn., U. Wis.-Milw., 1966, M.S. in Ednl. Psychology (Pupil Personnel fellow), 1968; m. Harold Lee Dillman, Feb. 2, 1951; children—Ken, Bradley, Thomas. Tchr., Hammond, Ind., 1955-56, Cuyahoga Falls, O., 1961-64; grad. asst. U. Wis.-Milw., 1965-68; sch. psychologist Warren (O.) City Schs., 1970-74. Chmn. Pride Com. to evaluate Child Care Vocational Program at Hudson (O.) High Sch., 1974—; mem. curriculum adv. com. Ohio Dept. Mental Health and Mental Retardation; mem. program adv. com. Summit County Bd. Mental Retardation. Bd. dirs. Summit County Council Retarded Children, 1973—. Mem. N.E.A., Ohio, Warren edn. assns., Nat., Ohio, Kent-Akron assns. sch. psychologists, Internat. Reading Assn. (Trumbull Area Reading Council), Trumbell County Community Services, Pi Lambda Theta (pres. chpt. 1966-68). Author: Dillman Tes of Verbal Maturity In Young Children, 1972. Home: 2804 Hudson-Aurora Rd Hudson OH 44236

DILLON, BETTY CRITES, rep. Internat. Civil Aviation Orgn., govt. ofcl.; b. Tucson, July 18, 1923; d. Marvin and Ruby (Kern) C.; student George Washington U.; fellow pub. and internat. affairs Woodrow Wilson Sch., Princeton, 1964-65; 1 dau., Mary Katherine. Sec. San Francisco C. of C., then U.S. C. of C., Washington, 1941-46; spl. asst. to pres. Overseas Nat. Airways, San Francisco, 1948-52, asst. v.p. mgmt., 1958; spl. asst. to dir. FOA, Washington, 1953-58; aviation cons. Lear & Scoutt, 1958-60; air transport examiner, liaison to State Dept., CAB, 1960-65; dep. dir. Peace Corps, Tunisia, Tunis, 1965-67, dir. Ceylon, Colombo, 1967-69, dir. Office Spl. Sers., 1969-71; U.S. minister-rep. Internat. Civil Aviation Orgn., Montreal, Que., Can., 1971—; pres. PAND Corp., Bedford, Ind., 1969—, owner, operator Stonigton farm, Mitchell, Ind. Godfrey Air fellow Am. U., 1954. Recipient certificate sustained meritorious performance CAB, 1964, Fed. Woman's award, 1968. Mem. D.A.R., Bus. and Profl. Women. Nat. Aviation Club, Princeton Alumni Washington, Am. Fgn. Service Assn. Home: 1455 Sherbrooke St W Montreal PQ Canada Office: Internat Civil Aviation Bldg Montreal PQ Canada

DILLON, ELSIE HOPE, ret. educator; b. Lancing, Tenn.; d. Martin and Kathrine (Crawford) Dillon; A.B., Howard Coll., 1926; M.A., U. Ala., 1953. Classroom tchr. Birmingham (Ala.) Pub. Schs., 1927-44; head tchr. Robert E. Lee Elementary Sch., 1944-56, prin., 1956-71. Mem. Jefferson County Adv. Com. for Schs., 1958-61; chmn. schs. div. United Appeal, Birmingham, 1958-61. Bd. dirs. Actors Theatre. Mem. N.E.A. (mem. del. assembly, 1959, 60, 62, mem. election com. 1962), Nat., Ala. (treas. 1961-63) depts. elementary sch. prins., Nat. League Am. Pen Women, Ala. (pres. Dist. V 1962-63), Birmingham (pres. 1958-61, state assembly of dels. 1956-63, editor Bull., 1966—) edn. assns., Ala. Designer Crafts (exhibiting mem. 1973). Kappa Delta Pi, Chi Delta Phi, Delta Kappa Gamma (chpt. 1st v.p. 1951-52, 62-64, state corr. sec. 1961-63, dist. dir. 1964-66, 2d v.p.), Kappa Delta Epsilon. Clubs: Zonta (rec. sec. 1960-61), Birmingham Tchrs. (exec. bd. 1958-64), Birmingham Prins. (v.p. 1952, exec. bd. 1963-64, pres.), Birmingham Arts, Fanelon (treas. 1973-74, program chmn. 1974-75). Author: Brief History of Birmingham Public Schools 1872-1972. Writer column Birmingham Edn. Assn. Bull., 1954—. Home: 3416 Crayrich Dr Birmingham AL 35226

DILLON, EVELYN KATHRYN, educator; b. Cleve.; d. Arthur J. and Edna (Adell) Dillon; B.S., Ohio State U., 1932; M.A., Kent State U., 1942; Ph.D., State U. Ia., 1950. Instr. phys. edn. Parma (O.) High Sch., 1932-40, Old Trail Sch., Akron, O., 1940-44; asst. prof. phys. edn. Wellesley Coll., 1944-53; dir. Camp Gaywood, Oakland, Me., 1950-53; asst. prof., prof., asst. dean Tex. Woman's U., Denton, 1953-61; prof., dir. dept. phys. edn. women Bates Coll., Lewiston, Me., 1961—. Mem. Div. Girls and Women's Sports (chmn. aquatics com. 1948-49, chmn. officiating sect. 1959-60), A.A.H.P.E.R., Me. Assn. Phys. Edn. for Women (pres. 1968-69), Eastern Assn. Phys. Edn. Coll. Women (nominating com. 1967-69), Pi Lambda Theta. Author: Synchronized Swimming Workbook, 1954, 56; (with Landis and Watt) Revised Method of Judging Diving, 1949-51; (with Wells) The Sit and Reach-A Test of Back and Leg Flexibility, 1952. Home: 26 Rita Av Lewiston ME 04240

DILLON, JANE SHANESY, pub. relations exec., govt. ofcl.; b. Eureka, Cal., Aug. 31, 1918; d. Daniel Thomas and Wilhelmina M. (Boyle) Shanesy; student Humboldt State U., 1936-39, Stanford, 1963; m. Leon Mathew Dillon (separated); 1 dau., Barbara Dillon Healy. Free lance pub. relations, San Francisco, 1964-66; dir. pub. relations St. Francis Hotel, San Francisco, 1965-71; pub. information officer Dept. Health, Edn. and Welfare, San Francisco, 1971-73, civil rights div., U.S. Dept. Justice, Washington, 1973-74. Lectr. pub. relations, Fresno, Cal., 1967-68. Pres. Peninsula Symphony Orch., 1960—; mem. Women's Aux., San Francisco Mus. Art, San Francisco Symphony Assn.; vol. pub. relations Peninsula Vols., Inc. Mem. mayor's com. for the Golden Gate Park Centenial, 1969—. Mem. Pub. Relations Soc. Am. (v.p. San Francisco chpt. 1969-70, dir. 1970-75), Bay Area Publicity Club (dir. 1968-69), Nat. Acad. TV Arts and Scis. Club: San Francisco Press. Home: 1360 Montgomery St San Francisco CA 94133 Office: Civil Rights Div US Dept of Justice Washington DC 20530

DILLON, MARCIA NICHOLS (MRS. E. PETER DILLON), ednl. adminstr.; b. Painesville, O., Aug. 9, 1949; d. Milton Harris and Blanche Elizabeth (Ostrander) Nichols; B.A. cum laude, Ohio U., 1971, M.Ed., 1973; m. E. Peter Dillon, Dec. 16, 1972. Resident dir. Ohio U., Athens, 1972-73, Wagner Coll., S.I., N.Y., 1973—. Mem. Nat. Assn. Student Personnel Adminstrs., Nat. Assn. Women Deans, Adminstrs. and Counselors. Address: Harbor View Hall Wagner College Staten Island NY 10301

DILLON, MARY EARHART, educator; b. Kansas City, Mo.; d. Martin L. and Nellie (Edwards) Earhart; Ph.D., Northwestern U., 1940. Instr. Northwestern U., 1941-45, asst. prof. 1946-48; asst. prof. Queens Coll., Flushing, N.Y., 1949-50, asso. prof., 1951-60, prof., 1960—, chmn. dept., 1949-53; pub. relations cons., 1954—; nat. cons. Women's Archives. Radcliffe Coll., 1955—. Research cons. Hist. Research Found., 1960. Mem. Am. Polit. Sci. Assn., Council Edn. Research (dir.), Queens Coll. Assn. (chmn. pub. relations com.), Delta Delta Delta. Author: Frances Willard: From Prayers to Politics, 1944; Biography of Wendell Wilkie, 1952; also articles. Editor paperback series Politics in Government. Home: 45 East End Av New York City NY 10028 Office: Queens Coll Flushing NY 11367

DILLONT, M(AUDE) NATHALIE (MRS. ROBERT M. JOHNSON), physician; b. Maplewood, N.J., Mar. 8, 1910; d. Abel Price and Maude N. (Throckmorton) Dillont; A.B., Vassar Coll., 1931; M.A., Columbia, 1933, M.D., 1939; m. Robert McHardy Johnson, May 16, 1942; children—Sandra Price, Diana Emerson, Cynthia Dillont. Intern Bellevue Hosp., N.Y.C., 1939-42; resident pediatrics Grasslands Hosp., Valhalla, N.Y., 1942-43, chief child psychiatry, 1970-71, practice medicine specializing in pediatrics, Tarrytown, N.Y., 1944-46; sch. physician of Tarrytown (N.Y.), 1947-54; with well-baby clinic Westchester (N.Y.) Health Dept., 1955-62; resident psychiatry N.Y. Med. Coll., 1962-67; dir. walk-in clinic Bronx Lebanon Hosp., Bronx, N.Y., 1967-68, dir. day hosp., 1968-70, supr. psychiatry, 1967-70, chief in-patient service, 1974—; adj. psychiatrist Bronx Lebanon Mental Health Center, 1971-74; instr. psychiatry Einstein Coll. Medicine, 1972—. Pres., Tarrytown Community Concerts, 1948-50, Hudson Valley Symphony Orch., 1952-56. Diplomate Am. Bd. Pediatrics. Mem. A.M.A., N.Y. State, Westchester County med. socs., Am. Psychiat. Assn., Alpha Omega Alpha. Home: 8 Fairview Av Tarrytown NY 10591 Office: Bronx Lebanon Mental Health Center 1285 Fulton Av Bronx NY 10454

DI LORENZO, ADELINE YOLANDA SAELI (MRS. VINCENT DI LORENZO), real estate broker; b. Italy, Oct. 8, 1916; d. Emanuele and Frances (Paturzzo) Saeli; came to U.S., 1923, naturalized, 1928; student U. Md., Monterey Peninsula Coll.; m. Vincent Di Lorenzo, Dec. 13, 1941 (dec. July 1969); children—Vincent, Richard, Yolanda, William, Mark. Real estate broker, Seaside, Cal., 1955—; pres. Adeline D. Lorenzo, real estate and ins., 1957—; pub. Seaside News Sentinel, Pacific Groves Times, Marina Times, Castroville Times, 1964-67; pres. Di Lorenzo Constrn., Seaside, 1971—. Home: 25770 Partridge Pl Carmel CA 93921 Office: 1534 Fremont St Seaside CA 93955

DIMATTIA, JUDY ANNE, coll. adminstr.; b. Buffalo, June 27, 1944; d. Joseph Luke and Colette (Beveridge) Galza; B.A., Russell Sage Coll., 1966; M.Ed., State U. N.Y., Buffalo, 1968; Edn. Specialist, Kent State U., 1970; Ph.D., U. Pitts., 1974; m. A.J. DiMattia, Aug. 23, 1969. Mgr. Georgetown Fabrics, Inc., Buffalo, 1968-69; coordinator Twin Towers, Kent (O.) State U., 1969-71; asso. dir. housing U. Pitts., 1971-72; dir. housing Princeton (N.J.) U., 1972—. Mem. Nat. Assn. Women Deans and Counselors, Nat. Assn. Student Personnel Adminstrs., Am. Personnel and Guidance Assn., Assn. Coll. and Univ. Housing, Ivy League Housing Assn. Home: 56 Ziegler Lane Hamilton Square NJ 08690 Office: Princeton University Upper Madison East Princeton NJ 08540

DIMITROFF, LILLIAN MAURER (MRS. KARL P. DIMITROFF), educator; b. Fresno, O., Jan. 27, 1910; d. Lewis and Elizabeth (Geib) Maurer; A.B., Denison U., 1932; M.A., U. Chgo., 1944; Ph.D., Northwestern U., 1958; m. Karl P. Dimitroff, Oct. 22, 1944. Tchr. elementary and secondary schs., Ohio, N.Y., N.J., Ill., 1932-58; faculty Chgo. State U., 1958—, prof. edn., 1965—, dir. Quality Urban Edn. for Successful Teaching, 1973—. Mem. Nat., (finance chmn. nat. conv.), Ill. councils social studies, Ill. Assn. for Higher Edn., Am. Assn. U. Profs., Am. Assn. U. Women (chmn. edn. com. 1971-73), Chgo. Area Reading Assn., Nat. Soc. for Study Edn., Assn. for Tchr. Educators, Ill. Assn. for Tchr. Educators, Phi Beta Kappa, Phi Alpha Theta, Pi Lambda Theta, Delta Kappa Gamma. Contbr. to numerous publs. Home: 1525 Brummel St Evanston IL 60202 Office: 95th at King Dr Chicago IL 60628

DIMMICK, CAROLYN REABER, judge; b. Seattle, Oct. 24, 1929; d. Maurice C. and Margaret (Taylor) Reaber; B.A., U. Wash., 1951, J.D., 1953; m. Cyrus Dimmick, Sept. 10, 1955; children—Taylor, Dana. Admitted to Wash. bar, 1953; asst. atty. gen., state of Wash., 1953-54; dep. pros. atty. King County, 1955-59, 60-62; practice law, 1959-65; judge Northlake Dist. Ct., 1965-68, N.E. Dist. Ct., 1968—. Mem. Wash., Seattle, Eastside bar assns., Am. Judges Assn. (bd. govs. 1973-77), Allied Arts of Seattle, Phi Delta Delta. Club: Altrusa. Home: 15724 61st St NE Bothell WA 98011 Office: 7425 170 Av NE Redmond WA 98052

DIMOCK, GLADYS OGDEN (MRS. MARSHALL EDWARD DIMOCK), author; b. Pelham Manor, N.Y., Feb. 3, 1908; d. Herbert Gouverneur and Gladys (Frost) Ogden; B.A., Bennington Coll., 1936; m. Marshall Edward Dimock, June 29, 1940; 1 son, Davis Ludlow. Asst. to dir. League of Nations Assn., Geneva, Switzerland, 1927-30; sec. to faculty Bennington Coll., 1932-33, sec., asst. to pres., 1934, pub. relations dir., 1935; research asst. com. on pub. adminstrn. Social Sci. Research Council, Washington, 1935-39; asst. to asst. sec. labor U.S. Dept. Labor, Washington, 1939. Mem. Am. Assn. U. Women (state v.p. 1966-67), Bennington Coll. Alumnae Assn. (dir. 1959-66, pres. bd. 1963-66), N.H.-Vt. Women's Fedn. Unitarian Universalist Assn. (v.p. bd. dirs. 1970—), Unity Circle (pres. Bethel 1964-66, 70—). Author: (with Arthur W. Macmahon and John D. Millett) The Administration of Federal Work Relief, 1941; (with Marshall E. Dimock) American Government in Action, 1947, rev. edit., 1951, Public Adminstration, 1953, rev. edit., 1969, A Home of Our Own, 1963. Home: Scrivelsby Bethel VT 05032

DIMOND, SISTER MARIE THERESE, educator; b. Valdez, Alaska, Nov. 13, 1916; d. Anthony Joseph and Dorothea Frances (Miller) Dimond; A.B., Trinity Coll., 1938; M.S., Cath. U. Am., 1952, Ph.D., 1954. Faculty, Trinity Coll., Washington, 1938-39, 48—, asso. prof., 1957-60, prof., 1960—, chmn. dept., 1958-70, 72—; tchr. Trinity Prep. Sch., Ilchester, Md., 1939-48, Notre Dame High Sch., Moylan, Pa., 1943. Research fellow USPHS, 1956, research grantee, 1956-57, 58-73; sci. faculty fellow NSF, 1959-61. Mem. A.A.A.S., Am. Physiol. Soc., Am. Inst. Biol. Scis.; Am. Soc. Zoologists, Nat. Assn. Biology Tchrs., World Population Soc., Phi Beta Kappa, Sigma Xi. Contbr. articles to profl. jours. Address: Dept Biology Trinity Coll Washington DC 20017

DI MUCCIO, MARY-JO, librarian; b. Hanford, Cal., June 16, 1930; d. Vincent and Theresa (Yovino) Di Muccio; B.A., Immaculate Heart Coll., 1953, M.A., 1960; Ph.D., U.S. Internat. U., 1970. Tchr. parochial schs., Los Angeles, 1949-54, San Francisco, 1954-58; tchr. Govt. of Can., Victoria, B.C., 1958-60; asst. librarian Immaculate Heart Library, Los Angeles, 1960-62, head librarian, 1962-72; prin. librarian City of Sunnyvale, Cal., 1972—. Mem. Catholic, Cal., Am. library assns., Spl. Libraries Assn. Home: 720 C Blair Ct Sunnyvale CA 94087

DINGES, MARGARET JANE (MRS. GEORGE H. DINGES), civic worker; b. Milw., Apr. 18, 1915; d. Edwin and Martha (Sigglekow) Hansen; student Milw. State Tchrs. Coll., 1933-36; m. George H. Dinges, Sept. 3, 1938; children—George E., Thomas R., Carol Pares (Mrs. Phillip Pares). Mem. Milw. Bd. Sch. Dirs., 1962—, pres., 1967-69; bd. control Coop. Edn1. Service Agy. 19, 1965—, chmn., 1965-66, 70—; mem. bd. Wis. Congress P.T.A., 1960—, pres., 1965-67; mem. Am. Edn. Week Com. Met. Milw., 1958—, chmn., 1964-67; mem. Youth Opportunity Bd. Milw.; mem. resolutions com., profl. relations com. Wis. Assn. Sch. Bds., mem. bd. 1968—, v.p. bd., 1972-74, pres., 1974—; regional council Coop. Ednl. Research Lab., Nat. Com. for Support Pub. Schs., Wis. Council United Action in Pub. Edn., Milw. Sch. Tchrs. Annuity and Retirement Fund, Research Council of Great Cities Program for Sch. Improvement. Recipient commendation award Milw. Civil Def. Adminstrn., 1960; named hon. life mem. Wis., 1959, Nat. Congress P.T.A.'s, 1965, Wis. Elementary Sch. Prins. Assn., Nat. Assn. Parliamentarians, 1967. Home: 2794 N Hartung Av Milwaukee WI 53210

DINGHAM, HELEN ALMYRA (MRS. RICHARD GEORGE DINGHAM), librarian; b. Madison, Wis., Dec. 4, 1909; d. Cyril Methodius and Nellie Grace (Moreau) Jansky; B.S., U. Wis., 1930, B.L.S., 1933; m. Richard George Dingham, Dec. 22, 1955; 1 son, Robert Edward. Library asst. Kewanee (Ill.) Pub. Library, 1934-37; cataloger, reader's adviser, asst. to librarian Madison Free Library, 1937-55; reference librarian Alhambra (Cal.) Pub. Library, 1960; reference librarian Ventura (Cal.) Jr. Coll., 1968; head librarian Thacher Sch. for Boys, Ojai, Cal., 1969—. Organizer, pres. Friends Temple City Library. Mem. A.L.A., Cal. Assn. Sch. Librarians, P.E.O. (chpt. rec. sec. 1971), League Women Voters (pres. chpt. 1958), Phi Kappa Phi, Omicron Nu (chpt. pres. 1929-30). Delta Zeta. Methodist. Home: 702 N Ventura St Ojai CA 93023 Office: 5025 Thacher Rd Ojai CA 93033

DINGMAN, ELIZABETH PATERSON, journalist; b. Kingston, Ont., Can., Jan. 27, 1918; d. Thomas Egbert and Mary Richardson (Wright) Paterson; B.A., U. Man., 1940; m. Harold Dingman, Sept. 1945 (dec.); 1 dau., Erica. Reporter, Winnipeg (Man., Can.) Free Press, 1941-42, sub-editor, feature writer, 1951-52; reporter, edn. editor Montreal (Que., Can.) Gazette, 1943-46; asst. editor Beaver, editor Moccasin Telegraph, Hudson's Bay Co., 1952-56; drama script editor Canadian Broadcasting Corp., 1958-59; womens editor, columnist Toronto (Ont.) Telegram, 1959-71; columnist Montreal Star, 1971-72; adminstrv. dir. Ont. Craft Found., 1972—, editor Craft Ont., 1972—. Mem. Women for Polit. Action. Home: 51 Poplar Plains Rd Toronto 7 ON Canada Office: 8 York St Toronto ON Canada

DINGMAN, RITA, nursing cons.; b. Lee County, Ia., Apr. 22, 1919; d. Henry G. and Ellen (Hellman) Dingman; diploma St. John's Hosp., St. Louis, 1945; B.S., St. Louis U., 1948; M.P.H., Yale, 1959. Dental asst., Ft. Madison, Ia., 1936-37; sec. credit dept. W. A. Sheaffer Pen Co., 1937-42; pub. health staff nurse Catholic Charities, Alton, Ill., 1947-49, Alaska Dept. Health, Valdez, 1949-51; rehab. cons. liberty Mut. Ins. Co., Dallas, 1952-58; supr. Vis. Nurse Assn., Houston, 1959-61; asst. chief nurses sect. Colo. Dept. Pub. Health, Denver, 1962—. Mem. adv. council Denver Emergency Preparedness Council; mem. Colo. Emergency Med. Service Council. Mem. exec. com., bd. Mile High A.R.C. Recipient award for service during Hurricane Carla in Houston, A.R.C., 1961; Gov.'s citation for service during floods, 1965, Pfizer award U.S. Civil Def. Council, 1970; Gold Heart award Colo. Heart Assn. Fellow Am. Pub. Health Assn.; mem. Am., Colo. nurses assns., Nat., Colo. leagues nursing, Colo. Pub. Health Assn., Am. (council on cardiovascular nursing), Colo. (exec. com., mem. bd.) heart assns., Colo. Ind. Nursing Assn. (adv. council), Colo. Assn. Pub. Employees, Am., Colo. assns. critical care nurses, Nat., Colo. assns. home health care agys. Roman Catholic. Club: Denver Executives. Home: 409 Adams St Denver CO 80206 Office: 4210 E 11th St Denver CO 80220

DINITZ, ELAINE CHAIFETZ, psychologist; b. N.Y.C., Feb. 19, 1936; d. Nathan and Lillian (Schaefer) Chaifetz; B.A., Hunter Coll., 1956; M.A., Hofstra U., 1969, Ph.D., 1972; div.; children—Richard, Julie. Sch. psychologist pub. schs., Seaford, N.Y., 1970, cons. learning disabilities, 1971-73; sch. psychologist Valley Stream (N.Y.) Union Free Sch. Dist. 13, 1971—; adj. asso. prof. psychology C.W. Post Coll., L.I. U., 1972—; individual practice psychology, Hempstead, N.Y., 1973—; cons. N.Y. State Dept. Social Services, 1974—. Mem. Am., Nassau County psychol. assns., Am. Assn. Advancement Behavior Therapy. Home: 1636 Salem Rd Valley Stream NY 11580 Office: 9 Centre St Hempstead NY 11550

DINKEL, JANET SUE, economist; b. Temperance, Mich., Oct. 26, 1943; d. J. Edward and Betty (Richardson) Dinkel; B.A., Wittenberg U., 1965; M.A., Ohio State U., 1968. Econ. analyst Fed. Res. Bank, Cleve., 1967—. Mem. finance com. Lake Erie Internat. Jetport Project, 1970-71. Lutheran. Home: 2348 Grandview Cleveland Heights OH 44106 Office: PO Box 6387 Cleveland OH 44101

DINKLAGE, LILLIAN BRANDON, counseling psychologist; b. Filbert, S.C., Oct. 31, 1937; d. Isaac Lonnie and Lillian Emily (Robinson) Brandon; A.B., Meredith Coll., 1960; Ed.M., Harvard, 1963, Ed.D., 1968; m. Kenneth Taylor Dinklage, June 17, 1966; 1 son, Joshua Brandon. Statis. asst. Ednl. Testing Service, Princeton, N.J., 1960-62; research, tchr. Harvard Grad. Sch. Edn., 1962-68; guidance counselor Newton (Mass.) pub. schs., 1963-64; psychologist N.H. Children's Aid Soc., 1964-66; mental health coordinator Mystic Valley (Mass.) Mental Health Clinic, 1967-71; psychologist Lesley Coll. Schs. Children, Cambridge, Mass., 1971—. Cons., Peace Corps, 1968-70; pvt. psychol. practice, 1969—; sch. psychologist Lexington (Mass.) Pub. Schs., 1974—. Adv. bd. Green Acres Sch. Fellow Mass. Psychol. Assn.; mem. Am. Psychol. Assn., Pi Lambda Theta, Author: (with others) Career Development: Growth and Crisis, 1970; also monograph. Home: 10 Ivy Rd Belmont MA 02178 Office: 34 Concord Av Cambridge MA 02138

DINO, MARY CATHERINE, curator; b. Binghamton, N.Y., May 24, 1946; d. Andrei and Mary Ann (Merges) Dino; B.A. cum laude, State U. N.Y. Coll. at Geneseo, 1968; postgrad. State U. Coll. N.Y. at Oneonta, 1968-69. Curator of edn. Corning Mus. of Glass, Corning, N.Y., 1969—. Mem. Am. Assn. Museums, N.Y. State Craftsmen (rec. sec. 1973). Home: 16 Indian Pipe Painted Post NY 14870 Office: Corning Museum of Glass Corning NY 14830

DINSMORE, MURIEL HOGAN (MRS. GEORGE A. DINSMORE), newspaper editor; b. Eureka, Cal., May 1, 1929; d. Oscar Walker and Annie Nordina (Johnson) Hogan; A.B., Humboldt State Coll., 1951; m. George Allen Dinsmore, June 11, 1955; children—Samuel, Jeffrey, Tamara, Scot. Sec. to dean adminstrn. Humboldt State Coll., Arcata, Cal., 1951-52; exec. sec., cost accountant Eugene B. Lucas C.P.A., Fortuna, Cal., 1952-56; news corr., feature writer Humboldt Times, 1957-67; women's editor Times-Standard, Eureka, Cal., 1970—. Fund coordinator Fortuna Library Drive, 1957-58; publicity coordinator Dist. Jr. Coll. Organizational Com., 1960-62; founding chmn. Fortuna Art Festival, 1966-69; adviser Christmas Art Festival, 1969—; founding sec. Eureka Heritage Com., 1973. Bd. dirs. Humboldt Arts Council, 1966-70, chmn., 1969-70. Mem. Nat. Trust Historic Preservation, soc. Archtl. Historians. Republican. Home: 2407 G St Eureka CA 95501 Office: 930 6th St Box 3580 Eureka CA 95501

DINWIDDIE, FAYE LOVE (MRS. BENJAMIN F. DINWIDDIE), social worker, author; b. Paris, Tenn.; d. Nelson Watson and Willa (Muzzall) Love; student U. Toledo, 1933-34, U. Denver, 1937-38, U. Mich., 1946; m. John S. Foster, May 23, 1925 (div. 1938); 1 son, John Love Foster (dec.); m. 2d, Benjamin F. Dinwiddie, Oct. 22, 1942 (dec. Mar. 1964). Supr., Dunbar Community Center, Toledo, 1934, dir., 1935-37; newspaper columnist Ohio State Press, Colo. Statesman, Ohio State News, 1937-41; field worker health edn. Toledo and Lucas County Tb Soc., 1944-54; case worker Aid for Aged, Toledo, 1955-56, Lucas County Welfare Dept., 1956-62; family counselor Office Econ. Opportunity for Greater Toledo, acting dir. econ. opportunity center, now editor Community Orbit, 1967—, dir. recruitment Women's Job Corps. Mem. met. planning commn. Toledo C. of C., 1943-46; mem. exec. com. health and welfare sect. Toledo Council Social Agys., 1951-54, chmn. social hygiene com., 1952-54; mem. Toledo Recreation Commn., 1947-52; pres. Coterie Study Group, 1940-41; mem. Study Club; chmn. program devel. Mott br. Toledo-Lucas County Library. Recipient certificate of merit Toledo C. of C., 1953, Ohio Pub. Health Assn., 1954; Key to City of Cleve., 1972. Mem. Am. Pub. Health Assn., N.A.A.C.P., Royal Soc. Health (licentiate), Internat. Platform Assn., Poetry Soc. London, Ohio Soc. N.Y., Common Cause, Smithsonian Assos., Nat. Writers Club, Internat. Black Writers, Centro Studi E Scambi. Baptist. Author: (poems) Song of the Mute, 1970. Contbr. poetry to various publs.; also columns. Home: 1908 Washington St Toledo OH

DINWIDDIE, JANET ISABELLA KITTERMAN, mus. ofcl.; b. Battle Creek, Neb., Aug. 13, 1918; d. Crin Aaron and Jennie Isabella (Edwards) Kitterman; real estate certificate U. R.I., 1954; nursing certificate Tomlinson U., 1969, landscape certificate, 1955, indsl. safety certificate, 1969. Owner dress shop, Sioux City, Ia., 1936-38; with real estate office, Clearwater, Fla., 1939-41; clk. U.S. Civil Service, 1941-44; fire ins. clk. State Farm Ins., Clearwater, 1956-60; hostess Waynesboro (Ga.) Hist. Mus., 1971—; owner Greenhill Farms, Burke County, 1972—. Mem. Ga. Hist. Soc., Burke County Hist. Assn. (sec.-treas. 1971-74). Home: 821 Myrick St Waynesboro GA 30830 Office: 536 Liberty St Waynesboro GA 30830

DION, BARBARA JANE MAGNUSON PHILLIPS (MRS. DEAN JOSEPH DION), realtor; b. Kansas City, Mo., July 28, 1923; d. Charles Edward and Albina Camila (Zetocka) Magnuson; student U. Cal. at Los Angeles, 1960-61; m. Gordon Phillips; children—Gordon, Marsha (Mrs. George McClure), Jeffrey; m. 2d, Dean Joseph Dion, Apr. 10, 1970. Real estate salesman, asst. to broker Grandview Bldg. Co., Gardena, Cal., 1954-58, Palos Verdes, Cal., 1958-63; salesperson Call Realty, Palos Verdes Estates, 1963-68; asso. real estate broker Tarkington Realty, Palos Verdes Estates, 1968—. Bd. dirs. Palos Verdes Bd. Realtors. Mem. Nat. Assn. Real Estate Brokers (co-founder 1969, chpt. pres. 1971-72, dir.). Home: 2501 Via Anacapa Palos Verdes Estates CA 90274 Office: 1 Malaga Cove Plaza PO Box 1026 Palos Verdes Estates CA 90274

DI POTA, HELEN ANNE JOHNSTON (MRS. ANTHONY DI POTA), educator; b. Barre, Vt., Jan. 29, 1911; d. Robert and Margaret B. (Kelley) Johnston; certificate Buffalo State Tchrs. Coll., 1932; Ed.B., U. Buffalo, 1957, M.S., 1960, Ed.D., 1972; m. Anthony Di Pota, June 10, 1935; 1 son, Michael Paul. Clk., Met. Ins. Co., Buffalo, 1932-35; tchr. pub. schs., Buffalo, 1946-48; propr. ceramic supplies Craft Cottage, Kenmore, N.Y., 1948-50; asst. to dir. U. Buffalo, summers 1951-60; prof. social studies, also dir. internat. edn. Erie County Tech. Inst., Williamsville, N.Y., 1960-73, acting asso. dean liberal arts, fgn. student adviser 1961—. Mem. com. for internat. coop. State U. N.Y. Vice pres. Niagara Pub. Affairs Council, 1962-64; treas. Conf. on Community Living, 1964—; chmn. Inter-club Council Western N.Y., 1962-63. Candidate for councilman, Town of Tonawanda, N.Y., 1957, U.S. Ho. of Reps., 1958; sec. Niagara County Democratic Com., 1961-68. Mem. Am. Assn. U. Profs., N.Y. State Polit. Sci. Assn., Western N.Y., Upstate N.Y. sociol. assns., N.Y. State Jr. Coll. Assn. (chmn. commn. for teaching), Bus. and Profl. Women's Club (pres. 1956-57; state scholarship chmn. 1960-62; dist. dir. 1962-64; personal devel. chmn. 1964-66, Woman of Year award 1973), Kenmore Mercy Hosp. Guild (life), Pi Lambda Theta. Episcopalian. Home: 60 Hamlin Sq Williamsville NY 14221 Office: S Youngs Rd Williamsville NY 14221

DIPPO, CATHRYN SUZETTE, statistician; b. Rochester, N.Y., Aug. 1, 1947; d. G. Jack and Alice Louise (Clarke) Dippo; B.S. with spl. honors, George Washington U., 1969; M.A., U. Mich., 1970. Teaching fellow U. Mich. at Ann Arbor, 1969-70; math. statistician Bur. Census, Suitland, Md., 1970—. Mem. Smithsonian Assos., Nat. Archives Assos., Am. Statis. Assn., Alpha Delta Pi. Home: 5807 Marlboro Pike Apt 202 Washington DC 20028 Office: Bur of Census Suitland MD 20233

DIRKS-EDMUNDS, JANE CLAIRE (MRS. MILTON R. EDMUNDS), educator; b. nr. Cotter, Ark., June 9, 1912; d. Peter B. and Lydia (Gates) Dirks; A.B., Linfield Coll., 1937; Ph.D., U. Ill., 1941; m. Milton R. Edmunds, Aug. 11, 1944. Instr. biology, asst. to registrar Linfield Coll., McMinnville, Ore., 1941-44, asst. prof., 1946-48, asso. prof., 1948-60, prof., 1960-74, prof. emeritus, 1974—, acting head biology dept., 1969-70; prof. biology, head dept. Whitworth Coll., 1944-45. Mem. Ore. Acad. Sci. (charter), Pacific N.W. Bird and Mammal Soc. (past v.p. Ore.), Ore. Entomol. Soc., Ecol. Soc. Am., Nature Conservancy, Ore. Marine Biol. Soc, Audubon Soc., Save-the-Redwoods League, Am. Inst. Biol. Scis., Defenders of Wildlife, Sierra Club, Sigma Xi, Phi Sigma, Pi Gamma Mu. Republican. Baptist. Contbr. articles to profl. jours. Home: PO Box 111 McMinnville OR 97128

DIRTADIAN, HELEN, library exec.; b. Utica, N.Y., Jan. 9, 1926; d. Horen and Alise (Nergarian) Dirtadian; A.A., George Washington U., 1948, B.A., 1950; M.A., U. Denver, 1958. Librarian spl. services Dept. Army, Okinawa, 1952-53; asst. dir. State Library Juneau, Alaska, 1958-59, state librarian, 1959-67; dir. Utica Pub. Library, 1968—, Dyna Logics, Inc., 1972—, Central N.Y. Library Resources Council, 1974—. Mem. Am., N.Y., Central N.Y. (treas. 1970) library assns., Am. Assn. U. Women. Episcopalian. Home: 1629 Genesee St Utica NY 13501 Office: 303 Genesee St Utica NY 13501

DI SANTO, GRACE JOHANNE DEMARCO (MRS. FRANK MICHAEL DI SANTO), civic worker; b. Derby, Conn., July 12, 1924; d. Richard and Fannie (DeMarco) De Marco; student N.Y. U. Sch. Journalism, 1941-43; m. Frank Michael Di Santo, Aug. 30, 1946; children—Frank Richard, Bernadette Mary, Roxanne Judith. Newswriter, Australian Asso. Press, N.Y.C., 1942-43; staff reporter Ansonia Sentinel, Derby, Conn., 1943-45; feature writer, drama critic Bridgeport Herald, New Haven, 1945-46; editor monthly bull. Pa. State Coll. Optometry, Phila., 1947-48; free-lance writer, 1949-54. Founder, pres. bd. Investors Ltd., Morganton, N.C., 1966-67. Pres., Catholic Ladies' Guild, Morganton, 1965-66, Morganton Garden Club, 1966-67, Burke County chpt. N.C. Symphony Soc., 1968-70; mem. exec. bd. Community Concerts Assn., 1962-71; mem. Am. Field Service program Burke County, 1969—; active Burke County Heart Fund, Burke County Council Garden Clubs; mem. exec. bd., chmn. room reps. Forest Hill P.T.A., 1968-70. Bd. dirs. Burke county chpt. March of Dimes, 1966—; Burke County chmn. Nat. Humanities Series Woodrow Wilson Nat. Fellowship Found. trustee N.C. Symphony Soc., 1965-68, 69-70. Republican. Roman Catholic (pres. St. Charles Borromeo Ladies Guild 1965-66). Clubs: Schubert Music; Morganton Friday Afternoon Bridge, Lenoir Country (N.C.); Grandfather Golf and Country (Linville, N.C.); Mimosa Hills Golf. Address: 218 Riverside Dr Morganton NC 28655

DI SARIO, DONNA RYNHAM, advt. agy. exec.; b. Phila., Sept. 19, 1945; d. Anthony Rynham and Leona (Lebing) DiSario; B.A., Syracuse U., 1967. Account exec. Allerton, Bermna & Dean, advt. agy., N.Y.C., 1967-69; pres. Rynham Assos., advt. agy., Phila., 1969—. Mem. fashion career bd. Mademoiselle mag., 1969—. Recipient certificate of appreciation Marple-Newtown Jr. C. of C., 1969. Mem. Women in Communications, Phila. Club Advt. Women (dir. 1972—), Syracuse U. Phila. Alumni Club (treas. 1968-70, area fund raising chmn. 1968-70), Phi Mu. Home: 226 W Rittenhouse Sq Philadelphia PA 19103 Office: Suite 2003 Three Penn Center Plaza Philadelphia PA 19102

DISCHER, SISTER MARTHA, health adminstr; b. Louisville, Apr. 17, 1928; d. Louis J. and Evelyn (King) Discher; B.S., Catherine Spalding Coll., 1949; M.S. in Hosp. Adminstrn., St. Louis U., 1964; M.S. in Community Devel., U. Louisville, 1974. Tchr. high schs. Memphis and Bellaire, O., 1958-62; joined Order of Sisters of Charity of Nazareth; 1955; resident in hosp. adminstrn. Mt. Carmel Hosp., Columbus, O. and St. Mary's Hosp., Evansville, Ind., 1963-64; asst. adminstr. St. Joseph Infirmary, Louisville, 1964-65, adminstr., 1965-70; asst. dir. div. med. care Ky. Dept. Health, Frankfort, 1971-72; project dir. community health orientation program for students Kentuckiana Metroversity, Louisville, 1972-74; adminstr. family health center Health Care Louisville, Inc., 1974—; adj. prof. hosp. adminstrn. Xavier U., 1970—. Chmn. hosp. careers com. Hosp. Council Met. Louisville, 1966-68; mem. com. community hosps. Ohio Valley Regional Med. Program, 1968-69; Ky. Hosp. Assn., 1967-69, trustee, 1967-69. Trustee, Ky. Blue-Cross-Blue Shield Assn., 1967-69. Mem. Am. Coll. Hosp. Adminstrs., Am., Ky. pub. health assns., Cath. Hosp. Assn. Home: 3115 Doreen Way Louisville KY 40220 Office: 1809 Standard Av Louisville KY 40210

DISERNIA, PATRICIA SUE RHINEHEARDT, retail exec.; b. Richmond, Va., Oct. 20, 1927; d. John Pascal and Margaret (Ballard) Rhineheardt; student U. N.C., 1941-43; B.A., U. Md., 1945; m. Eugene Anthony Disernia, Apr. 2, 1949; 1 son, David Rudolph. With George Jensen, Inc., N.Y.C., 1945-46, M.C. Flynn, Inc., N.Y.C., 1946-49; asst. fashion editor Girl Scouts U.S.A., 1950-52, fashion and merchandising dir., 1957-67, editor in chief Am. Girl and Leaders mags., 1967-73; dist. mgr. Kaye Corp., 1973-74; dist. fashion merchandiser J.C. Penney Co., 1974—. Cons. in product devel.; nat. polit. speech writer. Mem. Fashion Group, Advt. Women N.Y., League Women Voters (v.p. local chpt.). Home: 656 Westbury Av Westbury NY 11590

DISHMAN, PATRICIA LOUISE, pub. relations exec.; b. Ft. Worth, Oct. 20, 1939; d. Hubert Clinton and Cora Ophelia (Wood) Dishman; B.S., Hardin-Simmons U., 1962; M.A., U. Okla., 1969. Asst. editor The Beam monthly mag. So. Bapt. Radio-TV Commn., Ft. Worth, 1962-63; pub. relations and program dir. Midland (Tex.) YMCA, 1964-68; grad. asst., editorial asst. U. Okla., Norman, 1968; dir. pub. relations and devel. Midland (Tex.) Meml. Hosp., 1969—; partner Custom Concept Copy-writers, pub. relations, Midland, 1971—. Mem. nat. pub. relations council Health and Welfare Services, Inc., 1965—. Mem. Am., Tex. (dist. dir. 1971, dir. 1973, pres.-elect 1974) socs. hosp. pub. relations, Pub. Relations Soc. Am. (asso.), Nat. Assn. for Hosp. Devel., Hardin-Simmons U. Alumni Assn. (chpt. sec. 1968-73), U. Okla. Alumni Assn. Author: 10 Who Overcame, 1966. Home: 3001 W Ohio St # 26 Midland TX 79701 Office: 2200 W Illinois St Midland TX 79701

DISKANT, MARION WHILE (MRS. ANDREW L. DISKANT), educator; b. Cleve., Mar. 13, 1933; d. Stephen W. and Anne (Bridgwater) While; B.A., Baldwin Wallace Coll., 1955; M.S., Case Western Res. U., 1967; m. Andrew L. Diskant; children—Andrew L., Andrea Lee, Wilma Jancuk. Tchr. math. John Adams High Sch., Cleve., 1955-66; chmn. math. dept. Harry E. Davis Jr. High Sch., Cleve., 1966-72; asst. prin. Robert H. Jamison Jr. High Sch., Cleve., 1967-72; asst. prin. Lincoln Jr. High Sch., 1972—. Mem. Ohio Assn. Secondary Sch. Prins., Northeastern Ohio Assn. Sch. Prins., Nat. Assn. Secondary Sch. Prins., Cleve. Edn. Assn. (sec. 1963-64), Ohio Edn. Assn., N.E.A., Northeastern Ohio Tchrs. Assn., Cleve. Math. Club, Inst. Math. Statistics, Delta Kappa Gamma (v.p.). Home: 4948 E 81st St Garfield Heights OH 44125

DISMUKES, HELEN FARRAR, assn. exec.; b. Denver, Aug. 9, 1900; d. Charles Sumner and Anna (Fish) Farrer; student Denver Coll. Speech Arts, 1912-16, Denver U., 1917; jr. certificate cum laude U. Cal. at Berkeley, 1918; student Boston Conservatory Music, 1924, Emerson Sch. Drama and Arts, 1924, Boston U., 1924, U. Philippines, 1930; m. Joseph Walton Dismukes, Dec. 15, 1918; 1 dau., Bonnie Alda (Mrs. Norman Blair). Driver, ambulance div. Motor Corps A.R.C., 1936-42; nat. standards chmn. Sigma Kappa, Indpls., 1962-66, nat. v.p., 1966-71, dist. dir. So. states, 1971-73, dir. Western dist., 1973-74. Mem. San Francisco League Women Voters, 1948-50. Mem. Pro America. Clubs: Alpha (pres. 1973-74); Palo Alto Women's. Home: 1530 Escobite Av Palo Alto CA 94306 Office: 3433 Washington Blvd Indianapolis IN 46205

DISSINGER, JOYCE ANN, journalist; b. Lebanon, Pa., Mar. 2, 1935; d. Russel L. and Bernice A. (Bainbridge) Dissinger; grad. high sch. Sec. to advt. mgr., copywriter WLBR-TV, 1953-54; women's editor, gen. and feature reporter-writer, copy editor Lebanon News Pub. Co., 1954—. Vol. cons. pub. relations Lebanon County chpt., Central Pa. div. A.R.C., 1971—; pub. relations and staff writer Lebanon County Community Chest, Inc., 1970-72. Bd. dirs., sec. bd. Lebanon County Workshop. Mem. Pa. Women's Press Assn., Sigma Delta Chi. Methodist (sec. adminstrv. bd. 1971—). Home: 991 Lilac Lane Lebanon PA 17042 Office: S 8th and Poplar Sts Lebanon PA 17042

DITCHFIELD, ALDA L., educator; b. Shamokin, Pa., July 13, 1911; d. Thomas and Cora (Derk) Ditchfield; B.S., U. Ore., 1943; M.A., Columbia, 1953. Nurse, head nurse, clin. instr., supr. surg. nursing, asst. supr. operating room Allentown (Pa.) Gen. Hosp., 1934-37; dir. nursing service Wheatland (Wyo.) Gen. Hosp., 1937; clin. instr., supr. obstetrics Salt Lake Gen. Hosp. Sch. Nursing, Salt Lake City, 1937-40, supr., asst. hosp. adminstr., 1937-39; dir. nursing service, asst. prof. nursing Med. Coll. Va., Richmond, 1943-46; dir. sch. nursing and nursing service Womans Med. Coll. of Pa., Phila., 1949-52; prof. Med. Coll. Ga. Sch. Nursing, Augusta, 1953-73, now prof. emeritus. Mem. Gov.'s Commn. on Nursing and Nursing Edn. Mem. Am., Ga. (pres. 1967-71) nurses assns., Nat., Ga. (pres. 1960-62) leagues for nursing, Am. Assn. U. Women, Am. Assn. U. Profs., Ga. Heart Assn., Sigma Theta Tau. Contbr. articles to profl. jours. Home 3280 Georgian Woods Circle Decatur GA 30034

DITHRIDGE, BETTY (MRS. ANDREW MORRISON DITHRIDGE), civic worker; b. Los Angeles, Sept. 11, 1920; d. Thomas Edward and Louise (Miles) Mitchell; student U. Cal. at Los Angeles, 1937-39; m. Andrew Morrison Dithridge, May 11, 1940; 1 son, Andrew Morrison. Boy Scout and cub scout leader Los Angeles Orphan's Home Soc., 1952—, sec. extension 1959-64, mem. Los Angeles Jr. Philharmonic Com., 1949—; active Symphonies for Youth Concerts, 1958-59; mem. Friends San Marino Pub. Library, Friends Huntington Library; vol. United Services Orgn., 1969-70; dir. Pasadena chpt. A.R.C., 1961-62, 64-65; bd. dirs. Vol. Bur. Pasadena; chmn. extension com. Los Angeles Orphan's Home Soc., 1964-66; organizer, chmn. San Marino Protection Com., 1971-72; mem. Los Angeles County Grand Jury, 1974—. Recipient awards for work with local youth groups. Mem. Wilshire (chmn. women's bur. 1957-59),

Los Angeles chambers commerce, Assos. Los Angeles City Coll., D.A.R., Alpha Phi. Club: San Marino Garden (corr. sec. 1969-70). Home: 1216 Old Mill Rd San Marino CA 91108

DI TROLIO, RITA MARIE TUNO (MRS. JOEL C. DI TROLIO), state ofcl.; b. Phila., Feb. 19, 1946; d. Angelo A. and Frances (Castrogiovanni) Tuno; A.B., Douglass Coll., 1967; m. Joel C. Di Trolio, Aug. 12, 1967. Jr. planner Bur. Regional Planning-Library, Div. State and Regional Planning, N.J. Dept. Community Affairs, Trenton, 1967-69, sr. planner adminstrv. sect., 1970-72, prin. planner adminstrn. sect., 1972—. Recipient Citation for Outstanding Service, State N.J., 1971. Mem. Council Planning Librarians. Home: 213 Hanson Av Piscataway NJ 08854 Office: 329 W State St Trenton NJ 08625

DITTMAN, MARION MARTHA, editor; b. Chgo., Feb. 24, 1909; d. Ernest C. and Lydia (Karau) Dittman; B.A., M.A., Northwestern U. Formerly editor North Shore News; editorial room staff U. Chgo. Press; editor trade books Rand McNally & Co.; sr. editor Childcraft, Field Enterprises Ednl. Corp., Chgo.; former mng. editor publishing dept., A.L.A., Chgo.; now free lance editor, editorial cons. Mem. Alumna Am. Sch. Classical Studies (Athens, Greece), Council on Fgn. Relations, Phi Beta Kappa, Delta Zeta. Home: 5831 N Kostner Av Chicago IL 60646

DITTMAN, NANCY ANN, educator; b. Buffalo, Mar. 11, 1936; d. Werner Frank and Dorothy Elaine (Herms) Dittman; B.S., Fla. State U., 1958; M.Ed., U. Fla., 1963, Ed.D., U. Colo., 1967. Tchr. high schs., various Fla. cities, 1958-64; instr. State U. N.Y., 1964-66; asst. prof. U. Wyo., Laramie, 1966-68; asst. prof. Ga. State U., 1968-71; asso. prof. bus. and office edn. Va. Commonwealth U., Richmond., 1971—. Cons. office morale, efficiency, cost controls. Mem. N.E.A., Nat., Va. bus. edn. assns., Am., Va. vocational assns., Delta Pi Epsilon, Pi Omega Pi, Kappa Delta Pi. Editor: Armchair Bull., Journal Ga. Bus. Edn. Assn., 1969-71. Contbr. articles to profl. jours. Home: 3809 Delham Dr Richmond VA 23229

DITZHAZY, HELEN ELAINE RINGLE (MRS. JOSEPH ANDREW DITZHAZY, SR.), ednl. adminstr.; b. Evanston, Ill.; d. Albert and Inez (Doty) Ringle; student Western Mich. U., 1944-45; B.S., Mich. State U., 1948, M.A., 1952; postgrad. Wayne State U., 1953-57, Merrill-Palmer Inst., 1960, Bennington Coll. (John Hay fellow), 1961, Inter-Am. U., Mexico, 1966-67; Ph.D., U. Mich., 1972; postgrad. Rockford Coll. (Inst. Devel. Edn. Activities fellow), Finch Coll. (Am. Behavioral Sci. scholar), 1969; m. Joseph Andrew Ditzhazy, Sr., Sept. 11, 1948; children—Joseph Andrew, Carol D'Leine. Dietitian Mich. State U., East Lansing, 1948-50, asst. to mgr., 1950-51, asst. mgr. residence hall, 1951-53, instr. Sch. Edn., 1965; tchr. South Redford Sch. Dist., Detroit, 1954-64, counselor, 1955-64, asst. prin. Lee M. Thurston High Sch., Detroit, 1964-73; prin. Novi (Mich.) High Sch., 1973—. U.S. sec. John D. Ringle Internat. Chmn. scholarship fund raising Dearborn Panhellenic Assn., 1960-64, pres., 1963-64. Mem. Nat., Mich. assns. secondary sch. prins., Aux. Engring. Soc. Detroit, D.A.R. (regent chpt. 1974—), Meadowbrook Homeowners Assn. (v.p. 1973-74), Delta Zeta. Presbyn. Clubs: Soroptimist, Farmington (Mich.) Glen Aquatic. Home: 37990 Tralee Trail Northville MI 48167 Office: 25549 Taft Rd Novi MI 48050

DIVOKY, DIANE (MRS. PETER SCHRAG), writer; b. Cleve., July 10, 1939; d. George Joseph and Rosemary Theresa (Wolf) Divoky; A.B., Trinity Coll., 1961; M.A., Harvard, 1965; m. Peter Schrag, May 24, 1969; 1 son, David Divoky. Tchr. pub. schs., Md. and Mass., 1961-65; reporter Boston Herald, 1965, edn. editor, 1965-67; asso. editor Edn. News, 1967-68; pub. information officer Pub. Edn. Assn., 1969-70; project research dir. N.Y. Civil Liberties Union, 1970-72; sr. editor Learning Mag., Palo Alto, Cal., 1972—. Cons. NBC, ABC, 1973-74. Carnegie-Edn. Writers Assn. travel grantee, 1969. Danforth fellow, 1974. Recipient writing awards Edn. Press, 1969-72, Nat. Council Advancement Edn. Writing, 1972. Mem. Edn. Writers Assn., Trinity Coll. Alumni Assn. (dir. Boston chpt. 1966-67). Author: How Old Will You Be in 1984?, 1969; The Rights of Students, 1974. Contbr. articles to profl. jours. Home: 5963 Manchester Dr Oakland CA 94618 Office: 530 University Av Palo Alto CA 94301

DIVVER, BARBARA ANNE, art gallery exec.; b. Irvington, N.J., Dec. 20, 1941; d. Erwin Nelson and Dorothy (Kreilesheimer) Durchlag; student Wellesley Coll., 1958-60, U. Cal. at Berkeley, 1961-64; m. Albert J. Divver, June 5, 1969. Owner, mgr. Centicore Bookshop, Ann Arbor, Mich., 1964-67; mgr. Brentano's, Boston, 1967-68; dir. promotion Beacon Press, Boston, 1968-69; dir. Impressions Workshop, Boston, 1970-72; mng. dir. Parker St. 470 Gallery, Boston, 1972-73; mng. dir. Harcus Krakow Rosen Sonnabend Gallery, 1973—. Fund raiser McGovern Presdl. Campaign, 1972; co-founder Boston WEB. Home: 51 Marshal St Brookline MA 02146 Office: 7 Newbury St Boston MA 02116

DIX, ANN DAVIS, educator; b. Cadiz, Ky.; d. William Lee and Frances (Broadbent) Davis; B.S., Northwestern U., 1952; m. Maryon Sharpe Dix, June 4, 1924; children—Frances Ann (Mrs. David Warren Wilkinson), Kathryn Sharpe (Mrs. Claude R. Sowle). Founder, dir. North Shore Sch., Chgo., 1938—, North Shore Camp, Chgo., 1939-66; v.p. Midwest Ednl. Guidance and Sch. Placement Center, 1960-65; organizer, dir. French tour for children. Mem. N.E.A., Internat. Reading Assn., Ind. Schs. Assn. of Greater Chgo., Assn. for Childhood Edn., D.A.R. Christian Scientist. Club: Chicago Yacht. Home: 1049 Manor Dr Wilmette IL 60091 Office: 1217 Chase Av Chicago IL 60626

DIX, RUTH KING (MRS. RICHARD D. DIX), physician; b. Bklyn., Dec. 29, 1934; d. Marehant Askren and Grace (Hamilton) King; student U. Cal. Los Angeles, 1952-55; M.D., Women's Med. Coll. Pa., 1959; m. Richard D. Dix, June 5, 1965; children—Stephen Paul, Mary Grace, John Daniel. Intern, Los Angeles County Gen. Hosp., 1959-60, resident, 1960-64; resident City of Hope Med. Center, Duarte, Cal., 1964-65; missionary dr., head obstetrics and gynecology Centre Medical Evangelique, Nyankunde par Bunda, Republic of Zaire, 1966—. Diplomate Am. Bd. Obstetrics and Gynecology. Home: 22020 Placerita Canyon Newhall CA 91321 Office: Nyankunde BR 55 Bunia Republic of Zaire

DIXON, BARBARA JANE, interior designer, cons.; b. South Bend, Ind., Dec. 6, 1933; d. Vincent Alan and Wanda Anita (Rapell) Dixon; student Mich. State U., 1951-55; postgrad. St. Mary's Coll., 1956-57, N.Y. Sch. Design, 1956-58; m. Erwin Delton VanGilder, May 25, 1959; children—Eric Dalton, Marc David. Factory color cons. Smith-Alsop Paint Co., Terre Haute, Ind., 1955-56; archtl. design cons., Mishawaka, Ind., 1956-58; residential-comml. designer, South Bend, Chgo., 1958-63; designer industrialized housing industry, Ga., Fla., Ind., Mich., 1962—; v.p. design Treasure Chest Corp., Sturgis, Mich., 1969, also dir.; design cons. C.O. Smith Ind. Peachtree Housing, Moultrie, Ga., Nobility Homes, Ocala, Fla.; also coordinator trade show displays; writer series on decorating for 2 Mich. newspapers, 1961-63. Officer, Shoreham Village (Mich.) Bd. Zoning, 1960-63. Named Woman of Year, Profl. Model's Club, 1952; recipient 1st pl. furniture design hardwoods Nat. Hardwoods Assn., 1956; 1st pl. Best in Show award, Louisville, Atlanta, 1964-65, 66, 69, 70-74; others. Mem. Design Council Industrialized Housing (award 1974), Nat. Soc. Interior Designers, Mich. State U. Alumni Assn. Permanent guest editor, contbr. Today's Home mag., 1974—. Home: 4212 S Lakeshore Dr St Joseph MI 49085 Office: 178 S Jefferson St Sturgis MI 49091

DIXON, DIANE ELIZABETH, journalist, photographer; b. Phila., Dec. 7, 1934; d. Robert Hugh and Elizabeth Olga (Freeze) Dixon; grad. high sch. Med. asst., Dr. L.G. Fares, Trenton, N.J., 1953-54, Dr. J.B. Lavine, Trenton, 1955-66; freelance writer with articles in TV and movie mags., other popular mags., 1965—; writer monthly horoscope Silver Screen mag., 1971—; staff writer Trentonian, Trenton, 1967—; also home and garden editor, feature writer Saturday mag. Spl. writing projects N.J. State Library for Blind and Handicapped, Library Congress, 1970—; commn. Blind, 1973-74; spl. photog. project children-to-children, Inc., 1973-74. Adviser Rainbow Girls, 1957-63; sec. N.J. Emergency Monitors, Inc., 1968. Recipient Grand Cross of Colors, Rainbow Girls, 1962. Mem. Ewing Hist. Soc., Needlepoint Guild Am., Mercer County Dental Assts. Assn. (charter); past pres.), League Am. Pen Women, Trenton Mus. Soc. Mem. Order Eastern Star. Home: 2321 Route 33 Robbinsville NJ 08691 Office: 600 Perry St Trenton NJ 08602

DIXON, EVA CRAWFORD JOHNSON, librarian; b. Evinston, Fla., Aug. 28, 1909; d. William Alpheus and Willie (Crawford) Johnson; A.B. in Edn. with honors, U. Fla., 1937, M.A., 1948; postgrad. Fla. State U., 1950, Appalachian State Tchrs. Coll., 1955; m. Thomas Gordon Dixon, Dec. 14, 1935 (div. 1944). Tchr., English, librarian Jefferson High Sch., Monticello, Fla., 1945-47; audio-visual dir. Jefferson County Schs., 1948-50; tchr. English, librarian Meigs (Ga.) High Sch., 1954-55; librarian Chipola Jr. Coll., Marianna, Fla., 1955-57, dir. library services, 1958—, chmn. student aid and scholarship com., 1961-65. Recipient Theatre Patron award, Chipola Jr. Coll., 1967. Mem. Jefferson County Edn. Assn. (pres. 1948-50), Fla. Edn. Assn. Honor Socs. (chmn. 1950-51), Bus. and Profl. Women's Club (pres. 1958-59, 62-63, Woman of Achievement award 1971), Fla. Fedn. Bus. Profl. and Women's Clubs (dist. dir. 1962-63), Women of 1st Presbyn. Ch. (pres. 1962-65), Kappa Delta Pi. Contbr. articles to profl. jours. Home: 506 Kelson Av Marianna FL 32446 Office: Chipola Jr Coll Marianna FL 32446

DIXON, GLORIA ANNE (MRS. LEO T. RYAN), physician; b. Athens, Ga., July 19, 1928; d. Ellis Howard and Ann (Norman) Dixon; B.S., U. Ga., 1949; M.D., Med. Coll. Ga., 1953; m. Leo T. Ryan, Dec. 20, 1958; children—Anne Mary, Ellis Truman. Intern, Knoxville (Tenn.) Gen. Hosp., 1953-54; pediatric resident U. Ala., Birmingham, 1954-56; practice medicine, specializing in pediatrics, Birmingham, 1959-69; part-time pediatric clinician Jefferson County (Ala.) Health Dept., 1969—; mem. surg. staff East End Meml. Hosp., Birmingham, 1969—. Pediatric cons. Head Start, Birmingham, 1969-70. Diplomate Am. Bd. Pediatrics. Mem. Am. Acad. Pediatrics, Jefferson County Pediatric Soc., A.M.A., Ala., Jefferson County med. socs., Phi Beta Kappa, Phi Kappa Phi, Sigma Pi Sigma, Alpha Chi Omega. Republican. Methodist. Home: 4237 Harper's Ferry Rd Birmingham AL 35213

DIXON, GRETA KMARIE, coll. dean; b. Somerset, Pa., Jan. 15, 1940; d. Royden Hauger and Ferne (Bowlby) Dixon; B.A., U. South Fla., 1965; M.Ed., U. Portland, 1968; postgrad. Cath. U. Am., 1968-69, U. Ia., 1971—. Med. transcriber, Tampa, Fla., 1959-63; asst. adminstr. Corpus Christi Sch., Temple Terrace, Fla., 1964-66; resident dir. Lewis and Clark Coll., Portland, Ore., 1966-68; dean women Upper Ia. Coll., Fayette, 1969-73. Vol. first-aid div. A.R.C., 1959-66; active Hillsborough County (Fla.) Civil Def. Med. Corps, 1959-66, State of Fla. Civil Def. Med. Corps, 1959-66. Mem. Am. Assn. Higher Edn., Am. Coll. Health Assn., Am. Coll. Personnel Assn., Nat. Assn. Women Adminstrs., Deans and Counselors, Am. Assn. U. Adminstrs., Am. Personnel and Guidance Assn., Am. Assn. U. Adminstrs., Women's Equity Action League (treas. Ia. chpt. 1972—), Nat. Assn. Women Ednl. Adminstrs., Am. Pub. Health Assn. Home: 702 East River Dr Temple Terrace FL 33617

DIXON, HELEN ROBERTA, geologist; b. Belvidere, Ill., Aug. 13, 1927; d. Elmer Lawrence and Helen Amanda (Johnson) Dixon; B.A., Carleton Coll., 1949; M.A., U. Cal. at Berkeley, 1956; Ph.D., Harvard, 1968; children—Dalvin R., Catherine R. Geologist, U.S. Geol. Survey, Denver, 1955—. Vis. lectr. San Diego State Coll., 1969. Fellow Geol. Soc. Am.; mem. Am. Mineral Soc., Am. Geophys. Union. A.A.A.S., Sigma Xi. Home: Route 3 Box 315 Golden CO 80401 Office: US Geol Survey Denver Fed Center Denver CO 80225

DIXON, JEANE P., author, psychic, medium. With real estate brokerage firm, Washington. Author, lectr. and exponent extra-sensory perception, participant various TV discussion programs. Founder Children-to-Children Found., 1964—; chmn. Christmas Seal campaign, Washington, 1968. Recipient Loreto Internat. award Loreto Shrine, Internat. L'Enfant award Holy Family Adoption League; named Woman of Year Internat. Orphans; 1st Anglo hon. Navajo princess. Mem. Nat. League Am. Pen Women, A.S.C.A.P., Internat. Platform Assn. Club: International (Washington). Author: My Life and Prophecies; Reincarnation and Prayers to Live By. Contbr. articles to nat. mags. Address: 1144 18th St NW Washington DC 20036

DIXON, PEGGY ANN HOLMES (MRS. JACK R. DIXON), educator; b. Cleve., June 9, 1928; d. Noel C. and Lillian M. (Armstrong) Holmes; A.B., Western Res. U., 1950; M.S., U. Md., 1954, Ph.D., 1959; m. Jack R. Dixon, Sept. 16, 1950; children—Sally L., Nancy G., Daniel N. Physicist, U.S. Army Chem. Corps, Edgewood, Md., 1950-52; research asso. U. Md., College Park, 1958-61, prof. physics, part-time, 1970—; prof. physics Montgomery Coll., Takoma Park, Md., 1961—. Chmn. Panel on Physics in 2-Yr. Coll., 1968-70. Mem. Am. Assn. Physics Tchrs. (mem. exec. bd. 1973—), A.A.A.S., Am. Assn. U. Profs., Nat. Sci. Tchrs. Assn., Sigma Xi., Sigma Pi Sigma, Iota Sigma Pi, Phi Kappa Phi. Methodist (youth coordinator 1972—). Home: 422 Hillsboro Dr Silver Spring MD 20902

DIXON, REVA EUNICE TAYLOR (MRS. HARRY ELMORE DIXON), civic worker; b. Roanoke, Va., June 24, 1905; d. James Franklin and Virginia Demarris (Perdue) Taylor; piano student Va. Coll., 1922-24; m. Harry Elmore Dixon, Apr. 6, 1926; 1 son, Harry Elmore. Sec., Roanoke Buick Sales Corp., 1926-27; sec., treas. Blue Ridge Motors Corp., Roanoke, 1935-47; profl. parliamentarian for local, state, nat. orgns., 1961—; tchr. parliamentary law to clubs, Va. Western Community Coll., 1971-72, 73-74; parliamentarian for Licensed Practical Nurses, Richmond, Va., Roanoke, 1964-65, 69-71, Credit Union of Va., Roanoke, 1965, 68, 71, Woman's Missionary Union Va. Bristol, Roanoke, 1964-65, Licensed Practical Nurses, 1964-68, 71. Pres., Roanoke Symphony Soc., 1953, Roanoke Symphony Soc. Aux., 1958-60, 73-74, Traveler's Aid Soc., Roanoke, 1962-71, Mary Louise Home of King's Daus., Inc., Roanoke, 1956-65, 73-74; chief, adminstrv. services Roanoke Civil Def., 1950-63; mem. Women's Civil Def., 1960—. Vice chmn. Roanoke Democratic Exec. Com., 1958—; mem. steering com. for Gov. Harrison's election, 1962; pres. Women's Dem. Club Roanoke, 1956-58. Named Mother of Year in Arts and Scis. Retail Mchts., 1957; Woman of Year, Bus. and Profl. Women, 1960. Mem. D.A.R. (regent Col. William Preston chpt. 1971-74, nat. parliamentarian 1968-71, dir. Dist. VII 1974—), Va. State Hort. Soc. (pres. women's aux. 1956-58), Nat. Assn. Parliamentarians (pres. Roanoke unit 1961-62). Baptist (pres. Woman's Missionary Union). Clubs: Woman's (pres. 1947), Bus. and Profl. Woman's (pres. 1948), Thursday Morning Music (pres. 1951-53), Blue Ridge Dist. Va. Fedn. Women's (pres. 1952-54) (Roanoke). Home: 1411 West Dr Lakewood Colony Roanoke VA 24015

DIXON, RUTH HURT FRANKLIN (MRS. D. HARVEY DIXON), broadcasting exec., educator; b. Memphis; d. James Buchanan and Clara Allen (Crutchfield) Hurt; A.B., U. Cal. at Berkeley, 1941; m. O. Thomas Franklin, Nov. 23, 1941 (div. 1950); 1 dau., Pamela Lee; m. 2d, D. Harvey Dixon, Apr. 9, 1955. Women's editor, broadcaster sta. KLX, Oakland, Cal., 1942-44; recreation dir. Service Men's Center, West Palm Beach, Fla., 1944-45; concert singer U.S.O., 1945; by-line columnist East of the Bay, San Francisco Examiner, 1950-56; publicity dir. Lilli Ann, San Francisco, 1953-55; fashion editor San Francisco Today mag., 1958-59; staff writer San Francisco Chronicle, 1961-62; publicist KRON-TV, 1962-64, dir. women's community affairs, 1964; now pub. affairs dir. KWUN Radio, moderator Focal Point; instr. course, use of media Diablo Valley Coll., Contra Costa County. Bd. dirs. Contra Costa County Suicide Prevention Service, Juvenile Hall Aux. Recipient A.P.-Cal. TV Radio ann. award, 1973, award excellence, community affairs div., award merit editorial feature div. Mem. Am. Women in Radio and TV (pres. Golden Gate chpt. 1967-68), Women in Communications, Inc. (past pres. Oakland-Berkeley chpt.), Zeta Tau Alpha. Office: KWUN Radio PO Box 1480 Concord CA 94520

DIXON, SUSAN JANE SCHULTZ (MRS. JON GILBERT DIXON), librarian; b. Bloomington, Ill., June 1, 1939; d. Delbert Lorraine and Virginia (Hartman) Schultz; student Luther Coll., 1957; m. Jon Gilbert Dixon, June 28, 1958; children—Timothy, Thomas, Katrina. With Van Sickles Asso. Pubs., Durand, Ill., 1965-73, editor Durand Gazette, 1969-73, Davis (Ill.) Scope, 1969-72; librarian Rockford (Ill.) Register-Republic, 1973—. Mem. nominating com. Rock River Valley council Girl Scouts U.S.A., 1973—. Bd. dirs. Durand (Ill.) Youth Center, 1971-73, v.p., 1973—. Mem. No. Ill. Editors Assn. (dir. 1973—). Democrat. Methodist. Home: 105 Cynthia Ct Durand IL 61024 Office: News Tower Rockford IL

DIZE, RUTH HARTLEY (MRS. LENWOOD BENNETT DIZE), med. soc. exec.; b. Norfolk, Va., Jan. 19, 1923; d. Herman Newton and Katherine Elizabeth (Eanes) Hartley; student Old Dominion U., 1956-57, U. Va., 1970-72, Tidewater Community Coll., 1972—; m. Lenwood Bennett Dize, Sept. 5, 1942; 1 dau., Jeanne Lynn. Exec. sec. to physician, Norfolk, Va., 1951-60; office mgr. to orthopedic surgery group, Norfolk, 1960-71; exec. sec. Norfolk County Med. Soc., 1971—. Instr. med. office procedures Old Dominion U., Norfolk, 1966; cons. Health careers, Norfolk city schs.; instr. antique porcelain and glass Chesapeake (Va.) city schs., 1972—. Mem. Am. Assn. Med. Soc. Execs., Am. Assn. Med. Assts. (pres. 1969-70), Nat. Assn. Parliamentarians Antique Dealers Assn., Norfolk Toastmistress Club (sec. 1968). Editor Norfolk County Med. Soc. Jour., 1971—. Home: 800 Round Bay Rd Norfolk VA 23502 Office: 1006 Medical Tower Norfolk VA 23507

DOAN, ELEANOR LLOYD, devel. dir.; b. Nampa, Ida., June 4; d. Fred and Gladys (Werth) Doan; B.A., U. Nev., 1936; postgrad. Wheaton Coll., 1937, U. Cal. at Los Angeles. Reporter Nev. State Jour., Reno, 1934, 36; high sch. English tchr., Austin, Nev., 1937-38; merchandising mgr. Christian Publs., Inc., Harrisburg, Pa. and N.Y.C., also William H. Dietz, Chgo., 1938-45; with Gospel Light Pubs., Glendale, Cal., 1945—, now coordinator spl. projects and information services. Formerly co-owner, dir. Tots N Teens, Elko, Nev. Trustee Mustard Seed, missionary bd., Glendale, Cal., Glint, Gospel Lit. Internat.; missionary bd.; sec. Belgu's Sultana Found. Mem. Forest Home Women's Aux. Evang. Press Assn., Nat. Sunday Sch. Assn., Wheaton Alumni Assn., U. Nev. Alumni Assn., Kappa Tau Alpha, Gamma Phi Beta, Chi Delta Phi. Republican. Presbyn. Author, co-author Bible sch. courses, also handcraft and Bible teaching books. Author: Speaker's Sourcebook; Equipment Ency.; Pattern Ency.; Handicraft Ency.; Visual Aid Ency.; Kid Stuff; Food and Fun Craft; More Handcrafts and Fun for Little Ones; Mother's Day Sourcebook; New Speaker's Sourcebook; Finger Fun; Treasury of Inspiration, 1970; Bible Story Picture Book, 1971; 145 Fun to Do Handcrafts, 1972; 157 More Fun to Do Handcrafts, 1972; Riddles and Pun, 1973; Children's Sourcebook, 1974; series on teaching. Home: 1240 Moncado Dr Glendale CA 91207 Office: 110 W Broadway Glendale CA 91204

DOAR, HARRIET FRASER, journalist; b. Charlotte, N.C., Mar. 25, 1912; d. James William and Annie Laurie (MacGillivray) Fraser; student Duke, 1930-31, U. N.C. at Chapel Hill, 1951-53; m. Joseph Graham Doar, Nov. 5, 1932 (div. 1940); children—Jane Maxwell (Mrs. Howard M. Rondthaler), James Fraser. Reporter, women's editor and columnist Charlotte News, 1930-46; interviewer U.S. Employment Service, Charlotte, 1942-44; women's editor Raleigh (N.C.) News and Observer, 1949-51; sec. to curator Mint Mus., Charlotte, 1956-57; with Charlotte Observer, 1959—, book editor, columnist, arts writer, 1962—. Cons. N.C. Arts Council. Bd. dirs. Red Clay Reader Red Clay Books; bd. dirs., founder Dance Guild Greater Charlotte. Mem. N.C. Press Women (co-founder, 1st pres. 1942), Women in Communications, Inc. (pres. Charlotte chpt. 1965-66), Sigma Delta Chi. Democrat. Home: 1250 Kings Dr S Charlotte NC 28207 Office: PO Box 2138 600 S Tryon Charlotte NC 28201

DOBBS, CAROL MAY HARGRAVE (MRS. FRANK QUINN DOBBS), editor; b. Houston, Apr. 5, 1941; d. Tom and Vivian May (Mead) Hargrave; B.S., Sam Houston State U., 1966; m. Frank Quinn Dobbs, June 2, 1962; 1 dau., Holly May. Editor Auto Parts Newsletter, Gulf & Western Industries, Houston, N.Y.C., 1965-68; editor Am. Gen. Ins. Co., Houston, 1968-70, First City Nat. Bank, Houston, 1972-73, State Peace Officers Jour., N.Am. Pub. Co., Houston, 1973—. Mem. Internat. Assn. Bus. Communicators (treas. 1969), Women in Communications (2d v.p. newsletter 1974-75). Mem. Ch. of Christ. Home: 7110 Pine Grove St Houston TX 77018 Office: 1964 W Grey St Houston TX 77019

DOBBS, MATTIWILDA, opera and concert singer, coloratura soprano; b. Atlanta; d. John Wesley and Irene Ophelia (Thompson) Dobbs; B.A. with honors, Spelman Coll., Atlanta, 1946; M.A., Tchrs. Coll. Columbia, 1948; studied voice with Mme. Lotte Leonard, N.Y.C., 1946-50; student Mannes Music Coll., 1948-49, Berkshire Music Festival, 1949; studied French music with Pierre Bernac, Paris, 1950-52; m. Luis Rodriquez Garcia, Apr. 4, 1953 (dec. June 26, 1954); m. 2d, Bengt Janzon, Dec. 23, 1957. Appeared Dutch Opera, Holland Festival, 1952, also recitals, Holland, Paris, Stockholm; appeared LaScala Opera, Milan, Italy, 1953, also concerts Eng., France, Italy, Scandinavia, Austria, Belgium; command performance Covent Garden, London, 1954; concert tours, U.S., 1954—, Australia, 1955, 59, Israel, 1957, 59, USSR, opera and concerts, 1959, Hamburg State Opera, 1961-62; U.S. opera debut, San Francisco Opera, 1955; debut Met. Opera, N.Y.C., 1950, 1956. Recipient 2d prize Marian Anderson awards, 1947; 1st prize Internat. Competition Mus. Performers,

Geneva Conservatory Music, 1951; decorated Order North Star, King Sweden, 1954. John Hay Whitney fellow, Paris, 1950. Conglist. Home: Vastmannagatan 50 Stockholm Sweden Office: care Mrs. Jeanne Rile 424 W Upsal St Philadelphia PA 19119

DOBIE, BEATRICE TORMEY, pub. co. exec.; b. Syracuse, N.Y., Mar. 6, 1922; d. J. George and Beatrice (Tormey) Dobie; B.A., U. Toronto (Ont., Can.), 1944. Asso. editor Forth mag, N.Y.C., 1945-47; with Life mag., N.Y.C., 1947-60, corr., London, Eng., 1954-57, reporter, N.Y.C., 1957-60; chief research Time-Life Books, N.Y.C., 1961—. Club: Overseas Press. Home: 54 Riverside Dr New York City NY 10024 Office: Time & Life Bldg Rockefeller Center New York City NY 10020

DOBLER, LAVINIA GRACE, librarian, author; b. Riverton, Wyo., July 3, 1910; d. George Francis and Grace (Sessions) Dobler; grad. Long Beach (Cal.) Jr. Coll., 1931; B.A., U. Cal., Berkeley, 1933; postgrad. Library Sci., Columbia, 1945-46; postgrad. U. P.R., summer 1936, U. So. Cal., 1940-41, N.Y. U., 1950-52, photography New Sch. Social Research, 1971. Reporter, Long Beach (Cal.) Press-Telegram-Sun, 1928-33; tchr. pub. schs., Riverton, Wyo., 1933-35; tchr. English, Salinas, P.R., 1935-36, Bayamon, P.R., 1936-37; supr. English, Bayamon, Santurce, Rio Piedras dists., P.R., 1937-40; exchange tchr. from P.R., Avenal, Cal., 1940-41; tchr. Long Beach pub. schs., 1941-44; head librarian Scholastic Mags., N.Y.C., 1944—. Mem. Am. Assn. U. Women (v.p. San Juan, P.R., 1937-38), Spl. Libraries Assn. (a founder pub. div. 1949, first nat. chmn. div.), Forum Writers for Young People (1st pres. 1964, pres. 1971-72), Women'a Nat. Book Assn. (sec. N.Y.C. 1955), Nat. Press Women's Assn., Wyo. Hist. Soc. (charter mem.), A.L.A., Westerners, Western Writers Am. Episcopalian. Mem. Order Eastern Star. Author numerous books, including A Business of Their Own, 1958 (Nat. Librarian award, Dodd Mead & Co. 1957), Black Gold at Titusville (Pittsburgh Honor Book award 1960), 1959, Arrow Book of the United Nations (Arrow Book Club selection 1963, 70-74), The Dobler World Directory of Youth Periodicals, 1960, 1965, 70, National Holidays Around the World, 1968; Animals at Work (See Saw Book Club selection 1973) 1973; This Is Your World: Don't Pollute It (Teen Age Book Club selection 1972), 1972; also numerous short stories for young people, articles. Home: 347 E 50th St New York City NY 10022 Office: 50 W 44th St New York City NY 10036

DOBLER, NORMA (MRS. CLIFFORD DOBLER), state legislator, civic worker; b. Haines, Ore., May 2, 1917; d. Lester and Bessie (Bircket) Woodhouse; student U. Cin., 1935-37; B.S. in Bus., U. Ida., 1939; m. Clifford Dobler, June 14, 1941; children—Sharon Louise (Mrs. Rogelio Vega), Carol Marie (Mrs. Gene Harris), Terry Lee. Sec. to registrar U. Ida., 1939-41; sec. to judge, Caldwell, Ida., 1945; sec. Am. Express Co., Seattle, 1943; lab. technician U. Ida. Coll. Forestry, Moscow, 1963-69; mem. Ida. Ho. of Reps., 1973—. Mem. League Women Voters, 1951—, bd. dirs. Moscow, 1953-68, pres. Ida., 1968-71; county adv. bd. trustee Moscow Sch. Dist., 1963-69, vice chmn., 1966-69; bd. dirs. Ida. Sch. Trustees Assn., 1969; leader 4-H Club, 1951-64; pres. Moscow P.T.A., 1958-59, life mem. Methodist (pres. Woman's Soc. Christian Service, 1972, supt. ch. sch. 1953-65, mem. ofcl. bd. 1953-67, 72). Home: 1401 Alpowa St Moscow ID 83843

DOBROGORSKI, OLGA JOHANNA, physician; b. Slonim, Poland, Jan. 28, 1922; d. George and Ida (Amberg) Dobrogorski; student U. Tartu Med. Sch. (Estonia), 1942-44; M.D., U. Erlangen (Germany), 1950; m. Louis A. Platz, Dec. 14, 1962. Came to U.S., 1950, naturalized, 1956. Research pathologist Sarana Labs, Saranac Lake, N.Y., 1954-56, USPHS, Cin., 1956-58; resident pathologist Cin. Gen. Hosp., 1958-61; asso. dir. labs. VA Hosp., Cin., 1961-62; asso. pathologist Good Samaritan Hosp., Cin., 1962—; asst. prof. pathology U. Cin., 1962—. Mem. Am. Soc. Clin. Pathologists, Internat. Acad. Pathology, Coll. Am. Pathologists, Acad. Medicine Cin. Club: Altrusa of Cincinnati. Home: 3508 Cheviot Av Cincinnati OH 45211 Office: Good Samaritan Hospital Cincinnati OH 45220

DOBSON, BRIDGET MCCOLL HURSLEY (MRS. JEROME JOHN DOBSON), television writer; b. Milw., Sept. 1, 1938; d. Frank and Doris (Berger) Hursley; B.A., Stanford, 1960, M.A., 1964; certificate Harvard, 1961; m. Jerome John Dobson, June 16, 1961; children—Mary McColl, Andrew Carmichael. Radio actress Cousin Willie, Los Angeles, 1953, Stan Freeberg Show, Los Angeles, 1954; spl. asst. to v.p. ABC-TV, N.Y.C., 1961; tchr. high sch., Exeter, Cal., Corning, Cal., 1962-64; writer ABC-TV series Gen. Hosp., Chico, Cal., 1966—; asst. prof. Chico State Coll., 1970, 72. Mem. Writers Guild of Am., A.F.R.T.A., Am. Home Soc. Aux. Club: Stanford (sec. 1967-69). Address: 1760 Park Vista Dr Chico CA 95926

DOBSON, CATHERINE ELIZABETH (MRS. JOSEPH ARTHUR DOBSON), realtor; b. Saranac Lake, N.Y., May 30, 1903; d. John Henry and Mayola (Derby) Hatch; student Kansas City Jr. Coll., 1926, Weaver Sch. Real Estate, 1959; m. Joseph A. Dobson, Sept. 4, 1927 (dec. Feb. 1970); children—Robert W., Gloria (Mrs. William Benjamin Potter). Salesman, Howard Cook & Co., Independence, Mo., 1956-59; owner, prin. Dobson Realty, Independence, 1960—; notary pub. Jackson County. Mem. Eastern Jackson County Bd. Realtors (treas., dir. 1966-69), Eastern Jackson County Real Estate Bd. Women's Council (v.p. 1967), Nat. Assn. Real Estate Bds., Bus. and Profl. Women's Club. Mem. Reorganized Ch. Latter Day Saints. Lioness; mem. Order Eastern Star, Social Order Beauceant. Clubs: Sorosis (pres. Independence), Women's. Address: 1450 N River Blvd Independence MO 64050

DOBSON, MARJORIE LUCILLE, librarian; b. Osgood, Ind., May 6, 1922; d. Harry and Mamie C. (Newman) Dobson; B.S., Butler U., 1944; M.S., Carnegie Inst. Tech., 1946. Childrens librarian Indpls. Pub. Library, 1941-56, S. Pasadena (Cal.) Pub. Library, 1957-58; library coordinator Met. Sch. Dist. Washington Twp., Indpls., 1959—. Library storyteller, Channel 6, Indpls., 1951-55; participant A.L.A. Storytelling Festival, Miami Beach, Fla., 1956. Dir. Allisonville Sch. Library-Knapp Sch. Library proj., 1963-66. Mem. N.E.A., Am., Ind. library assns., Ind. State Tchrs. Assn., Ind. Sch. Librarians Assn., Am. Assn. Sch. Librarians, Indpls. Council of Adminstrv. Women in Edn. Contbr. articles to profl. jours. Home: 1052 Ruth Dr Indianapolis IN 46240 Office: 1549 E 85th St Indianapolis IN 46240

DOCHERTY, PATRICIA THOMPSON, retail exec.; b. Columbus, O., May 9, 1917; d. Fred Alexander and Goldie P. (Sandy) Thompson; B.S., Temple U., 1939; m. William Docherty, Jr., June 28, 1941. Supr. phys. edn. pub. schs. Glassboro, N.J., 1939-40, Yeadon, Pa., 1940-41; mgr. Haverford (Pa.) Coll. Bookstore, 1947—. Mem. Nat. Assn. Coll. Stores (mgmt. seminar instr. 1970, 71, 73, chmn. Coll. Store Jour. com. 1973—), Middle Atlantic Coll. Stores Assn., Am. Book Sellers Assn. Home: 3 College Lane Haverford PA 19041 Office: Bookstore Haverford College Haverford PA 19041

DOCKENDORFF, MARGARET ELIZABETH DOUGHTY (MRS. JOHN F. DOCKENDORFF), social work adminstr.; b. Port Jervis, N.Y.; d. Victor A. and Margaret (Wheeler) Doughty; A.B., Asbury Coll., 1949; M.S.W., Rutgers U., 1964; m. John F. Dockendorff, Nov. 29, 1951. Social worker Salvation Army Dor of Hope, Jersey City, 1956-64; asst. dir., social worker Salvation Army Williams Meml. Residence Home for Aged, Flushing, N.Y., 1964-69; dir. social services Salvation Army Williams Meml. Residence Home for Aged, N.Y.C., 1969-70, Salvation Army Wayside Home for Girls, Valley Stream, N.Y., 1970—. Mem. Nat. Assn. Social Workers, Acad. Certified Social Workers, Nat. Conf. Social Welfare, Alumni Assn. Grad. Sch. Social Work of Rutgers U., N.Y. State Conf. Social Welfare. Home: 118 Irving St Leonia NJ 07605 Office: 1461 Dutch Broadway Valley Stream NY 11582

DOCKERAY, MARY JANE PATRICIA, mus. ofcl.; b. Grand Rapids, Mich., Mar. 8, 1927; d. Winfield Clare and Mary Ella (Nye) Dockeray; B.A., Mich. State U., 1949, Ph.D. (Delta Kappa Gamma scholar), 1973. Instr. Nat. Audubon Camps, Me. and Wis., 1957-63; interpretive naturalist Grand Rapids (Mich.) Pub. Mus., 1949—; instr. sci., conservation Mich. State U., Grand Rapids, 1957—; wildlife lectr. Nat. Audubon Soc., U.S. and Can., 1965—. Bd. dirs. Indian Trails Camp for Handicapped Children, 1963—, v.p., 1974. Recipient Delta Kappa Gamma scholarship, 1971. Mem. Am. Assn. Museums (mem. mus. accreditation com. 1971—), Assn. Interpretive Naturalists, Mich. (dir. 1973—), Midwest museums confs., Western Mich. Environmental Action Council (chmn. sites com. 1970-71), Mich. Audubon Soc. (dir. 1967—), Nat. Audubon Soc., Mich. Parks Assn. (dir. 1967—), Mich. State U. Alumni Assn. (chpt. pres. 1973—), Delta Kappa Gamma (v.p. chpt. 1958-60, pres. 1960-62). Author: Let's Go Exploring, 1972. Home: 884 Hollywood NE Grand Rapids MI 49505 Office: 1715 Hillburn Av NW Grand Rapids MI 49505

DOCKETT, LUVENIA DORSEY (MRS. HERBERT DOCKETT), lawyer; b. St. Louis; d. Millard Filmore and Martha (Everett) Dorsey; B.A., Clark Coll., 1938; M.S.W., Atlanta U., 1940; J.D., Detroit Coll. Law, 1950; m. Herbert Dockett, Sept. 12, 1942 (dec. Sept. 1963); 1 dau., Leata. Admitted to Mich. bar, 1951; practiced in Detroit, 1951-56; probation officer Wayne County Juvenile Ct., 1956-62; asst. pros. atty. County of Wayne, 1962—, asst. chief appellate counsel, 1968—; interviewer Mich. Employment Security 1943-48. Legal adviser various civic and community groups. Pres. P.T.A. Boynton Sch., 1961-63. Bd. dirs. Delta Home for Girls. Recipient Woman of Yr. award Prince Hall Grand chpt. State of Mich., Order Eastern Star, 1967; award for outstanding work Wolverine Bar Assn., 1972. Mem. Nat. Dist. Attys. Assn., State Bar Mich. (sec. new criminal law sect. 1972—, sec. constl. law com. 1968—), Am. Judicature Soc., Detroit, Wolverine, Wayne County bar assns., Wayne County Govt. Bar Assn., Nat. Council on Crime and Delinquency, Nat. Assn. Social Workers. Home: Apt 303 650 Chrysler Dr Detroit MI 48207 Office: 1441 St Antoine St Detroit MI 48226

DOCTOR, JUDITH EVA KLEIN (MRS. DANIEL W. DOCTOR), physician; b. Aruba, Netherlands Antilles, Jan. 23, 1936; d. Zoltan and Sarah (Pick) Klein; B.S., U. Mich., 1955; M.D., State U. N.Y. Coll. Medicine, Downstate Med. Center, 1959; m. Daniel W. Doctor, Dec. 21, 1957; children—Laura E., David G., Leslie C., Jonathan Scott. Intern St. Lukes Hosp., N.Y.C., 1959-60; resident N.Y.U. Med. Sch., 1961-62; ophthalmology resident Manhattan Eye, Ear and Throat Hosp., N.Y.C., 1969-72; practice medicine, specializing in ophthalmology, Westport, Conn., 1963—; asst. attending surgeon Manhattan Eye, Ear, Throat Hosp., asso. dir. pediatric diagnostic clinic, asst. attending surgeon Retina Clinic; asst. instr. zoology U. Mich., 1954-55. Diplomate Am. Bd. Ophthalmology. Home: 90 Morningside Dr S Greens Farms CT 06436 Office: 129 Kings Hwy N Westport CT 06880

DODD, FADRA REBECCA DEAN, govt. ofcl.; b. Corinth, Miss., Dec. 23, 1924; d. Sam Richard and Ruby Pearl (Meeks) Dean; student Miss. State U., 1942-43; m. James R. Dodd, Feb. 25, 1945 (div. Dec. 1951); children—James Andre, Myra Kathryn. Dept. circuit clk., Corinth, part-time 1952-57; legal sec. to county atty., Corinth, 1952-57; solicitor, sec. Mut. Ins. Agy., Corinth, 1957-60; circuit ct. clk., county registrar Alcorn County, 1960—. Chmn., Alcorn County Polio Assn., Corinth, 1960. Mem. Circuit Clks. Assn. Miss. (legislative com. 1960-62, 67, 2d v.p. 1963, 1st v.p. 1964, pres. 1965, mem. exec. com. 1966, sec.-treas. 1968-73), C. of C., Tenn.-Miss. Peace Officers Assn., Miss. Assn. Soil Conservation Dist. Commrs. (asso.), Internat. Platform Assn., Bus. and Profl. Women's Clubs (corr. sec. 1968-69, chmn. legislative com. Corinth 1967), Miss. State U. Alumni Assn. (co-chmn. membership com. 1970, pres. 1972). Baptist. Home: 2010 E 6th St Corinth MS 38834 Office: Alcorn County Courthouse Waldron St Corinth MS 38834

DODD, GLORIA LENA (MRS. EVERETT E. DODD), veterinarian; b. Lovelock, Nev., Mar. 3, 1934; d. Jess and Diane Madeline (Quilici) Ralphs; student Northwestern U., 1952-54; U. Cal. at Berkeley, 1954-55; B.S., U. Cal. at Davis, 1956, D.V.M., 1960; m. Everett E. Dodd, Aug. 22, 1958; children—Marlane Diane, Melinda Eileen. Asst. vet. Dr. Williams, Montecito, Cal., 1960-61, Dr. Seymour Roberts, Richmond, Cal., 1961-62, Dr. Mueller, Walnut Creek, Cal., 1962; pvt. practice vet. medicine, Danville, Cal., 1962-73, San Ramon, Cal., 1973—, Asst. med. researcher St. Mary's (Cal.) Coll., 1962—; cons. Vet. Lab., Oakland, Cal., 1973-74. Mem. Native Plants of Cal., Conta Costa County Vet. Med. Assn. Home: Danville CA 94526 Office: 2355 San Ramon Valley Blvd San Ramon CA 94583

DODD, LOIS, artist; b. Montclair, N.J., Apr. 22, 1927; d. Lawrence and Margaret (Vanderhoff) D.; student Cooper Union Art Sch., 1945-48; m. William D. King, Sept. 1948; 1 son, Eli. Exhibited one man shows Tanager Gallery, 1954, 57, 58, 61, 62, Green Mountain Gallery, 1969, 70, 71, Thomas Coll., Waterville, Me., 1973, Green Mountain Gallery, 1974; represented in permanent collections Cooper Union Mus., Whitney Mus. Print Collection, Kalamazoo Art Center, Hilton Hotel Print Collection, Geigy Chem. Corp. Collection, Wadsworth Atheneum, Hartford, Colby Coll. Lectr. Phila. Art Coll., 1963, 65, Bklyn. Coll., 1965-69, 71-73, Queens Coll., 1969, 70; asso. prof. Bklyn. Coll., 1973—. Mem. Cooper Sq. Community Devel. Com., 1960—. Home: 30 E 2d St New York City NY 10003

DODD, NINA PAULINE MOSS (MRS. ARTHUR VAN ZANDT DODD), journalist; b. Wilkinsburg, Pa., June 7, 1928; d. Clair D. and Margaret Bruce (Clark) Moss; B.A., Pa State U., 1950; m. Arthur Van Zandt Dodd, Nov. 22, 1949; children—Mark Reynolds, Randall Clark. Asst. editor Office Chief Mil. History U.S.A., 1950-54; salesman Haley Homes, 1954-55; circulation librarian Wellesley (Mass.) Coll., 1956-57; editor Population Center, U. N.C., 1971; office mgr. Katherine S. Wright, atty., 1971-73; writer, sec. Christian Sci. Com. on Publ. for Chapel Hill, 1973—. Reporter Pa. newspapers, 1948. Mem. Wellesley Town Meeting, 1964-68; vice-chmn. adv. finance com. Town of Wellesley, 1966-68. Bd. dirs. Friends Chapel Hill Pub. Library. Mem. League Women Voters (dir. 1964-66), Women in Communications, Inc., Zeta Tau Alpha (pres. Durham-Chapel Hill alumnae). Republican. Christian Scientist. Contbr. articles to profl. jours. Home: 2101 N Lake Shore Dr Chapel Hill NC 27514 Office: PO Box 208 Chapel Hill NC 27514

DODD, WILMA NEVILLE BEARDSLEE, Democratic nat. committeewoman; b. Ridgely, Tenn., Jan. 2, 1909; m. Claude Dodd. Chmn. Polio Mothers' March, 1945-65; v.p. Nat. Found. Muscular Dystrophy, 1950-60, pres. West Tenn. dist., 1955-58; dir. Lake County (Tenn.) Civil Def., 1950-73, state dir. women's activities civil def., 1958-59, sec.-treas. Tenn. Civil Def. Assn., 1964-67, state rep. U.S. Civil Def. Council, 1968-69, nat. pres. council, 1964-70; mem. Tenn. Gov.'s Employ the Handicapped Com., 1967—, Tenn. Gov.'s Commn. Status of Women, 1967-72. Pres. Lake County Democratic Women's Club, 1958-64; pres. Tenn. Fedn. Dem. Women's Clubs, 1960-61; mem. Tenn. exec. com. Dem. party, vice chmn., 1966—; vice chmn. Tenn. Dem. party, 1970—; del. Dem. nat. conv., 1964, 68, 72; mem. Dem. nat. com. from Tenn., 1972—. Mem. Am. Legion Aux. (unit pres. 1954-55, 60-74). Address: San Souci Farms Ridgely TN 38080

DODDS, JANE BALDWIN (MRS. LEONARD F. DODDS), librarian, artist; b. Greensburg, Pa., Oct. 1, 1916; d. Thomas David and Nethie Nina (Durling) Baldwin; B.S., U. N.M., 1939, postgrad., 1960-70; postgrad. U. Albuquerque, 1967-68, Highlands U., 1967; m. Leonard F. Dodds, June 8, 1941; children—Elizabeth Ann (Mrs. Joe M. Montano), Margaret Jane (Mrs. James W. Burkhead), Thomas David, James Lawrence, John Eric. Tchr. music Harrington Jr. High Sch., Santa Fe, 1939-40; tchr. English, Jefferson Jr. High Sch., Albuquerque, 1957-68; librarian Monroe Jr. High Sch., Albuquerque, 1968-73, Highland High Sch., Albuquerque, 1973—. Mem. United Teaching Profession, N.M. Library Assn. (sec. 1971), Sigma Alpha Iota, Kappa Kappa Gamma. Home: 8911 Northeastern Albuquerque NM 87112 Office: 4700 Cool Av SE Albuquerque NM 87106

DODDS, WINIFRED JEAN, research scientist; b. Shanghai, China, Jan. 4, 1941; d. John Stanley and Winifred Phyllis (Moreton) Willis; D.V.M., U. Toronto, 1964. Asst. prof. physiology Ont. Vet. Coll., U. Toronto, Guelph, Ont., Can., 1964-65; asso. research Scientist div. Labs. and Research N.Y. State Dept. Health, Albany, 1965—. Adj. asso. prof. medicine Albany Med. Coll., 1970—; cons. VA Hosp., Albany, 1968—; mem. adv. com. on animal models div. research resources NIH, 1974—; mem. com. animal models and genetic stocks Inst. Lab. Animals Resources NRC, 1973—. Grantee Nat. Heart and Lung Inst., NIH, 1965—. Mem. Am., Canadian, N.Y. vet. medicine assns., Ont. Veterinarians Assns., Am. Soc. Hematology, Fedn. Am. Socs. Exptl. Biology, Am. Soc. Exptl. Pathology, Am. Heart Assn. (exec. com. thrombosis council 1972-74), Genetics Soc. Am. (com. on maintenance genetic stocks 1973—). Address: Griffin Laboratory Rural Route #1 Slingerlands NY 12159

DODERER, MINNETTE FRERICHS (MRS. FRED H. DODERER), state senator; b. Holland, Ia., May 16, 1923; d. John A. and Sophie (Sherfield) Frerichs; B.A., U. Ia., 1948; m. Fred H. Doderer, Aug. 5, 1944; children—Dennis, Kay Lynn. Mem. Ia. Ho. of Reps., 1964-69, minority whip, 1967-68; mem. Ia. Senate, 1969—. Vice chmn. Ia. Interstate Cooperation Commn., 1965-66. Democratic vice chmn. Johnson County, Ia., 1957-60; Dem. nat. committeewoman, 1968-69; mem. Dem. Nat. Policy Council Elected Ofcls., 1973-74. Bd. dirs. Ia. U. Sch. Religion. Recipient Distinguished Service award Ia. State Edn. Assn., 1969. Mem. UN Assn., League Women Voters. Methodist. Home: 2008 Dunlap St Iowa City IA 52240

DODGE, ALFA DOROTHY MAW (MRS. HAROLD A. DODGE), aircraft tool co. exec.; b. Buffalo; d. Alfred Charles and Lillian (Beyer) Maw; student Chown Bus. Coll., 1916; m. Harold A. Dodge, June 8, 1922; children—Harold A., Dorothy A. (Mrs. Charles L. Plant). Sec. George A. Terry Co., 1941-44, partner, asst. mgr., 1945-62, owner, mgr. 1963—. Mem. Buffalo Philharmonic Women's Com., Albright-Knox Art Gallery Soc., Nat., Buffalo Audubon socs., Am. Forestry Assn., Am. Legion Aux., Am. Mus. Natural History, Buffalo C. of C., Nat. Wildlife Assn., UN Assn. U.S.A., Smithsonian Assos. Mem. Christian Ch. (trustee Chatauqua Assn. Disciples Christ). Club: Zonta (dir.). Home: 4 Mona Dr Buffalo NY 14226 Office: 356 S Elmwood Av Buffalo NY 14201

DODGE, CAROLINE JANE (MRS. JAMES ROGER LATTA), educator; b. Machias, Me., Mar. 4, 1947; d. William Eugene and Elsie (Sirles) Dodge; B.A. with highest honors, U. Me., 1969; M.A., U. Ill., 1970, postgrad., 1970—; m. James Roger Latta, Aug. 4, 1973. Instr. acting, theatre dept. U. Ill., Urbana, 1972, instr. directing, 1972-73; asst. prof. theatre dept. Case Western Res. U., Cleve., 1973—. Mem. Am. Theatre Assn., Phi Beta Kappa, Phi Kappa Phi. Home: 3535 Ingleside Rd Shaker Heights OH 44122 Office: Theatre Dept Eldred Hall Case Western Reserve U Cleveland OH 44106

DODGE, EVA FRANCETTE, physician; b. New Hampton, N.H., July 24, 1896; d. George Francis and Winnie Josephine (Worthem) Dodge; A.B., Ohio Wesleyan U., 1919, H.H.D., 1969; postgrad. Johns Hopkins, 1920-23; M.D., U. Md., 1925; postgrad. U. Vienna, 1930-31. Intern U. Hosp., Balt., 1925-26, resident obstetrics, 1926-27; acting prof. obstetrics Womans Christian Med. Coll., Shanghai, China, 1928-29; obstetric cons. Ala. Dept. Health, Montgomery, 1937-42; practice medicine, Winston-Salem, N.C., 1932-37; asso. med. dir. Planned Parenthood Fedn. Am., N.Y.C., 1943-45; asst. prof. obstetrics and gynecology U. Ark. Sch. Medicine, Little Rock, 1945-46, asso. prof., 1947-60, prof., 1960-64, prof. emerita, 1964—; dir. maternal and infant care project Detroit, 1964-66; dir. East Ark. Family Planning Project, Ark. Health Dept., Little Rock, 1969—. Obstetric cons. Children's Bur., 1940-41. Bd. dirs. New Hampton Sch., 1962—. Named Woman of Yr., Little Rock Democrat, 1951; recipient Alumni award, gold key U. Md. Sch. Medicine, 1967. Fellow A.C.S., Am. Coll. Obstetrics and Gynecology; mem. Am. Med. Womens Assn. (v.p. 1938), Pan Am. Med. Women's Assn. (pres. 1964-66), Pan Am. Assn., A.M.A., Central Assn. Obstetrics and Gynecology, Am. Assn. Sterility, Med. Delta Kappa Gamma. Club: Altrusa (pres. Winston-Salem, N.C. 1933)(Little Rock). Home: Quapaw Tower Little Rock AR 72202

DODGE, SIGNA IRWIN, artist; b. Cleve., Feb., 1936; d. James William and Signa (Glasgow) Irwin; B.A., Conn. Coll. Women, 1958; m. Norton Townshend Dodge, Dec. 27, 1965 (div.). Designer, officer mgr. James Kemble Mills, Inc., San Francisco, 1959-65; sec. Sasaki, Walker & Assos., San Francisco, 1961-62, 63-64; asst. to Western exec. Council on Religion and Internat. Affairs, San Francisco, 1964-65; farm mgr., Mechanicsville, Md., 1966-70; program officer pub. program div. Nat. Endowment for Humanities, Washington, 1970—; instr. adult art history U. Md., 1969; art work represented pvt. collections. Mem. St. Mary's County Art Assn. (dir. 1966-69). Clubs: Women's Nat. Democratic, St. Mary's Garden (dir. 1968-70). Home: 645 A St NE Washington DC 20003 also 16 rue Charlemagne Paris IV France Office: Nat Endowment for Humanities Washington DC 20506

DOEHLER, DOLORES KOTSIAKOS (MRS. ROBERT W. DOEHLER), assn. exec.; b. Chgo., Sept. 6, 1931; d. William C. and Mildred A. (Slouber) Kotsiakos; student MacMurray Coll., 1949-51; B.S., U. Ill., 1954, M.S., 1956; m. Robert W. Doehler, Aug. 22, 1954; children—Lee Anne, David. Office sec., 1949; camp counselor Girl Scouts U.S.A., Wis., 1953; tchr. Champaign (Ill.) Sr. High Sch., 1956-57; phys. edn. tchr. Northwest Suburban YMCA, Des Plaines, Ill., part-time 1961-66; dir. aquatic program, 1966—. Regional aquatic commr. YMCA Nat. Council on Aquatics, 1969—, met. competitive chmn. on swimming, 1972-73. Recipient Phys. Dir. of Yr. award Region YMCA, 1972. Mem. A.A.H.P.E.R., Am. Assn. U. Profs., Phi Beta Phi. Home: 210 Greenfield Dr Glenview IL 60025 Office: 300 E Northwest Hwy Des Plaines IL 60016

DOEHRMAN, MARGERY J., clin. psychologist; b. N.Y.C., Jan. 10, 1945; d. Emanuel George and Greta (Weingartner) Gross; B.A. in Psychology summa cum laude (N.Y. State Regents scholar), U. Rochester, 1966; Ph.D. in Clin. Psychology (USPHS fellow) U. Mich., 1971; m. Steven R. Doehrman, May 5, 1968. Clin. psychologist Psychol. Clinic, U. Mich., Ann Arbor, 1971—, univ. lectr. psychology, 1973—. Pvt. practice psychotherapy, Ann Arbor, 1971—. Mem. Am. Psychol. Assn., Phi Beta Kappa. Home: 1401 Hewett Dr Ann Arbor MI 48103 Office: 1027 E Huron St Ann Arbor MI 48104

DOERING, CATHERINE W. HARTLAUB (MRS. JOHN WARD DOERING), resort hotel exec.; b. Cin., Dec. 30, 1913; d. William M. and Catherine (McGinnis) Hartlaub; grad. Good Samaritan Sch. Nursing (Cin.). 1934; postgrad. Cornell U., 1935; B.B.A., Ohio U., 1971, M.B.A., 1972; m. John Ward Doering, Apr. 22, 1939; children—John Ward, Timothy M., Margaret M., James W., Kathleen A., Lucinda J., Dorothy M. Obstet. supr. Good Samaritan Hosp., Cin., 1935-37; obstet. supr., tchr. Wyckoff Heights Hosp., Bklyn., 1938, Mt. Carmel Hosp., Columbus, O., 1938-39; obstet. supr. Middle Ga. Hosp., Macon, 1943; owner, operator, exec. v.p. Thousand Island Park (N.Y.) Lodge, 1962—; ind. nursing research, 1973-74. Councilwoman, Logan, O., 1954-60. Mem. Logan council Girl Scouts U.S.A., 1955-62, program chmn. 1955, camping chmn., 1959. Mem. Am. Med. Aux., Hocking County (O.) Mental Health Assn., Internat. Platform Assn., St. Joseph Guild for Exceptional Children, Phi Gamma Nu. Roman Catholic. Home: 539 Warner Av Logan OH 43138 Office: Coast Av Thousand Island Park NY 13692

DOETSCH, VIRGINIA LAMB, advt. agy. exec.; b. N.Y.C., Oct. 12, 1920; d. Andrew Thomas and Cameola Weeden (Burns) Lamb; student Northwestern U., 1937-39, Columbia, 1946-47; m. Gunter H. Doetsch, Oct. 12, 1953 (div. Feb. 1972); 1 son, Hugo. Actress, Little Theater and Stock cos., Chgo., Oconomowoc, Wis., Mpls., Bucks County, Pa., Martha's Vineyard, Mass., 1939-44, Red Cross Clubmobile, CBI, Calcutta, India, Kwaiyang, Naning and Shanghai, China, many other towns, 1944-46; copywriter Carson Pirie Scott, Chgo., 1949-50; club dir. Army Spl. Services, Germany, 1951-53; copywriter McCann-Erickson, Frankfurt, Germany, 1954-56; copywriter and pub. relations dir. J. Walter Thompson, Fankfurt, 1954-56; copywriter McCann-Erickson, Chgo., 1958-59; copywriter Tatham-Laird & Kudner, Inc., Chgo., 1959-66, group head, 1966-69, creative supr., v.p., 1969—. Bd. dirs. Jr. Achievement Chgo. Named Chgo. Advt. Woman of Year, AAF Nat. Advt. Woman Year, 1973. Home: 1104 Austin Evanston IL 60202 Office: 625 N Michigan Av Chicago IL 60604

DOGGETT, JANE DAVIS, graphics co. exec.; b. Morristown, Tenn., Nov. 4, 1929; d. Robert Samuel and Anna Katherine (Weesner) Doggett; B.F.A., Tulane U., 1952; M.F.A., Yale, 1956. Founder, Archtl. Graphics Assos., N.Y.C., 1957-60, New Canaan, Conn., 1960, Wilton, Conn., 1963, pres., New Canaan and Wilton, 1962—; adj. prof. U. Bridgeport (Conn.), 1971. Adviser Aesthetics Nat. Joint Com. Uniform Traffic Control Devices, Bur. Pub. Rds. Dept. Trans., 1965—. Mem. Am. Inst. Graphic Arts, Smithsonian Assos., Pi Beta Pi. Presbyn. Originator total graphic design systems airports including Tampa, Fla., Houston, Newark, Pan Am. Terminal, JFK, Madison Sq. Garden, Niagara Falls Conv. Center. Address: 160 Lantern Ridge Rd New Canaan CT 06940 also 2485 E Sunrise Blvd Fort Lauderdale FL 33304

DOHERTY, ANNA MARIE, mag. editor; b. Baldwin, N.Y., Oct. 28, 1929; d. Dennis James and Helen Elizabeth (Koch) Doherty; A.A., Immaculata Coll., 1949; certificate Traphagen Sch. Interior Design, 1950. Asso. food editor This Week mag., N.Y.C., 1952-66, N.Y. Herald Tribune, 1952-66; acting food editor N.Y. World Jour. Tribune, 1966-67; food editor, columnist Suffolk Sun, L.I., N.Y., 1967-69; with Family Circle mag., N.Y.C., 1970—, sr. editor, dir. editorial services, 1971—. Food industry cons., 1965—; free lance food writer, 1966—. Mem. Wine and Food Soc. N.Y. Club: Newswomen's (dir. N.Y.C. 1970-72). Contbr. articles to profl. jours. Home: 154 E 61st St New York City NY 10021 also 4080 Peconic Bay Blvd Laurel NY 11948 Office: 488 Madison Av New York City NY 10022

DOHERTY, ANNE ROSE, clin. psychologist; b. Indpls., May 6, 1928; d. Patrick Joseph and Catherine H. (Bryne) Doherty; B.A. with honors, St. Mary of the Woods Coll., 1962; M.A., Cath. U. Am., 1966, Ph.D., 1969; postdoctoral Inst. Gerontology, U. So. Cal., 1970, 72. Joined Order Sisters St. Mary of the Woods, Roman Cath. Ch., 1953; clin. intern Ind. U. Sch. Medicine, 1967-68; staff psychologist Vigo County Guidance Clinic, Terre Haute, Ind., 1969-71; asst. prof. psychology St. Mary of the Woods Coll., 1969-72; chief clin. psychologist Katherine Hamilton Mental Health Center, Terre Haute, 1971—. Mem. Terre Haute Coordinating Council, Clay County Council on Aging; mem. commn. human devel. Cath. Archdiocese Indpls., 1971-72; adv. com. Ind. Commn. on Aging, 1973—. Bd. overseers St. Meinrad (Ind.) Coll., 1969—; adv. bd. Montessori Sch., Terre Haute, 1970-71. Predoctoral fellow USPHS, 1964-69; postdoctoral fellow Ethel Percy Andrus Inst. Gerontology, 1970-72. Mem. Am., Ind. (sec. 1972-74) psychol. assns., Altrusa Internat., Psi Chi. Author research papers. Home: 2931 Ohio Blvd Terre Haute IN 47803 Office: 620 8th Av Terre Haute IN 47804

DOHERTY, JOAN, educator; b. Doniphan, Mo., July 30, 1931; d. Chester Arthur and Alma (Gerlach) Doherty; student William Woods Coll., 1949-50; B.S., U. Mo., 1953, M.Ed., 1956, Ed.D., U. Mo., 1965, certificate U. Wash., 1968; postgrad. Washington U., 1957, U. Mich., 1959, San Fernando Valley State Coll., 1960, U. Ill., 1961. Elementary supr. Lab. Sch., U. Mo., 1953; elementary tchr. University City, Mo., 1953-54, Jennings, Mo., 1954-57, Clayton, Mo., 1957-63; part time instr. U. Mo., 1960-65, asso. prof. elementary edn., Columbia, 1968—; asst. prof. So. Meth. U., Dallas, 1965-68. Cons. sch. dists. and universities. NSF fellow, 1959, 60, 61, U.S. Office Edn. fellow, 1967-68. Mem. Assn. Supervision and Curriculum Devel., N.E.A., Am. Ednl. Research Assn., Nat. Council Tchrs. Math., Nat. Council Tchrs. English, Nat. Council Social Studies, Mo. Tchrs. Assn., Assn. for Higher Edn., Internat. Reading Assn., Clayton Community Tchrs. Assn. (pres. 1961-62), Pi Lambda Theta (chpt. pres. 1971-72), Delta Kappa Gamma. Republican. Home: 1009 Westport Dr Columbia MO 65201

DOHMS, DORIS A. MOLDENHAUER (MRS. GEORGE W. DOHMS), educator; b. Mt. Morris, Wis.; d. Walter F. and Lillian (Streicher) Moldenhauer; B.E., Wis. State U., 1954; M.S., U. Wis., 1960; m. George W. Dohms, Feb. 14, 1937 (dec. Mar. 1970). Tchr., Sonora Sch., Wautoma, Wis., 1935-37, elementary schs., Waukau, Wis., 1937-41, Fall River, Wis., 1941-42, Windsor, Wis., 1942-43, Token Creek Sch. DeForest, Wis., 1945-47, Cambridge, Wis., 1947-52; tchr. kindergarten Sunnyside Sch., Madison, Wis., 1954-56; tchr. Browning Sch., Milw., 1956-61; tchr. kindergarten Bruce Sch., Milw., 1961-68, supr. Title I, Milw. Pub. Schs., 1968—. Lab. technician Hercules Co., Baraboo, Wis., 1943-45. Sec., Wis. Conservation Curriculum Com., 1957-64, pres., 1964-66; chmn. Milw. Conservation Curriculum Com., 1959-60; 4-H leader conservation 65th St. Club, 1959-61; mem. exec. bd. Wis. Council for Conservation Edn., 1961—, Young Wis. Conservationists, 1964—. Recipient Conservation award Midwest Conservation Conf., 1967. Mem. Milw. Kindergarten Assn. (sec. 1963-66, v.p. 1966-68, pres. 1968-71), Central Assn. Sci. and Math. Tchrs. (sec. 1963, v.p. 1964, pres. 1965), Nat. Sci. Tchrs. Assn., Wis. Soc. for Sci. Tchrs., Assn. for Childhood Edn. Internat., N.E.A., Wis. Edn. Assn., Milw. Tchrs. Edn. Assn., Nat. Audubon Soc., Izaak Walton League, Greater Milw. Alumni, Pi Lambda Theta, Beta Epsilon, Alpha Beta. Home: 17575 Royal Crest Dr Brookfield WI 53005 Office: 5225 W Vliet St Milwaukee WI 53208

DOLAN, BEATRICE DAYTON, educator, social worker; b. Iona, Ida.; d. Wilford Leo and Ellen (Olmstead) Dayton; M.S., U. Ida., 1943; M.S.W., U. So. Cal., 1951; student U. Utah, 1943. Tchr. high schs., Ida., Wash., 1938-43; field rep., dir. home service A.R.C., San Francisco, Honolulu, 1943-47; parole agt. Cal. Youth Authority, Fresno, 1947-48, field rep. in delinquency prevention, Fresno, 1949-51, supervising parole agt., San Francisco, 1952-53, supt. Los Guilucos Sch. for Girls, Santa Rosa, Cal, 1953-62, Ventura Sch. for Girls, Camarillo, Cal., 1962-71; mem. faculty La. Verne Coll.; individual practice social work. Vice-chmn. Cal. Commn. on Status of Women, 1973—; mem. Criminal Justice Center Planning Com., Ventura County. Pres. bd. dirs. Ventura County YWCA, 1974—. Mem. Nat. Conf. Supts. Correctional Instns. Women and Girls (past pres.), Nat. Assn. Tng. Sch. and Juvenile Agys. (past dir.), Nat. Council on Crime and Delinquency, Nat. Conf. Social Welfare, Nat. Assn. Social Workers, Am. Assn. U. Women (div. chmn. 1968-70), Cal. Probation, Parole and Correctional Assn. Club: Zonta. Home: 1910 Terrace Dr Ventura CA 93003

DOLAN, ELEANOR FRANCES, assn. exec.; b. Cambridge, Mass., May 30, 1907; d. Harry Francis and Lillie (McFall) Dolan; B.A., Wellesley Coll., 1929; A.M., Radcliffe Coll., 1928, Ph.D., 1935. With dept. govt. Harvard, 1935-38; asst. prof. govt. Fla. State U., 1938-39; instr. govt. N.Y. U., 1939-41; dean, prof. govt. Mather Coll. of Western Res. U., 1941-50; higher edn. specialist, dir. research Am. Assn. U. Women, 1950-67; edn. specialist, regional coordinator U.S. Office Edn., 1967-73; exec. sec. Nat. Council Adminstrv. Women in Edn., 1973—. Former mem. County Constl. Commn., Ohio. Trustee Citizens League, Cleve., 1943-50. Mem. Nat. Assn. Women Deans, Am. Assn. Higher Edn., Womens Equity Action League, Phi Beta Kappa, Delta Kappa Gamma. Clubs: Capitol Hill, Washington Forum. Contbr. articles on higher edn. women to profl. jours. Home: 1618 Mt Eagle Pl Alexandria VA 22302 Office: 1815 Fort Myer Dr N Arlington VA 22209

DOLAN, ELIZABETH JOAN, lawyer, educator; b. Arlington, Mass., Sept. 10, 1936; d. Bernard J. and Joan (Lombard) Dolan; B.S., Emmanuel Coll., 1958; J.D. cum laude, New Eng. Law Sch., 1963. Mem. faculty Cardinal Cushing Coll., Brookline, Mass., 1959-72, asso. prof., to 1972, admitted to Mass. bar, 1964, Fed. bar, 1966; practice law, Barristers Hall, Boston, 1964-66, Arlington, Mass., 1966—. Mem. alumnae council Emmanuel Coll., 1956-72. Mem. Am., Mass., Middlesex bar assns., Mass. Assn. Women Lawyers, Am. Assn. U. Profs. Address: 67 Ronald Rd Arlington MA 02174

DOLAN, LILLIAN GABEL, librarian; b. Fond du Lac, Wis., Dec. 9, 1911; d. Ferdinand William and Rose (Hollinger) Gabel; B.S. in Elementary Edn., Marian Coll., 1963; M.S. in L.S., U. Wis., 1966; m. Gerald William Dolan, June 9, 1937; children—Mary (Mrs. Donald C. Thelan), Janet (Mrs. Nolan Sauerbreit), Alice (Mrs. Robert Cornett). Tchr. pub. schs., Wis., 1929-37, St. Joseph's Sch., Fond du Lac, 1955-65; librarian Moraine Park Tech. Inst., Fond du Lac, 1966—. Mem. Am., Wis. library assns., Wis. Edn. Assn., Daus. Isabella. Roman Catholic. Home: 355 Doty St Fond du Lac WI 54935 Office: 805 E Johnson St Fond du Lac WI 54935

DOLAND, JOYCE BYRD (MRS. CHARLES WARD DOLAND), occupational therapist; b. Paterson, N.J., Sept. 27, 1942; d. Paul Russel and Joyce Wildalee (Kreager) Byrd; B.S., U. Wash., 1965; m. Charles Ward Doland, Feb. 10, 1968; children—Tara Lenore, Gregory Byrd. Dept. head occupational therapy Bellevue (Wash.) Convalescent Center, 1965; staff therapist occupational therapy dept. Firlands Tb Sanitorium, 1965-70; occupational therapy cons. King County Multiple Sclerosis Assn., Bellevue, Wash., 1971—. Guild ways and means chmn. Children's Orthopedic Hosp., 1972-73. Provisional mem. Jr. League Seattle, 1974—. Bd. dirs. King County Multiple Sclerosis Assn. Mem. Seattle City Panhellenic (pres. 1971), Alpha Xi Delta. Home: 9827 NE 29th St Bellevue WA 98004

DOLAWAY, PHYLLIS WALCOTT, librarian; b. Washington, May 14, 1923; d. Henry Seymour and Imogen (Taylor) Walcott; A.B., De Pauw U., 1944; M.A., Purdue U., 1972; m. Earl Leroy Dolaway, June 12, 1948; children—Peggy (Mrs. Leslie C. Brissette, Jr.), James David. Tchr. pub. schs., La Porte, Ind., 1944-49; supr. media centers La Porte pub. elementary schs., 1967-70, head elementary div. dept. instructional media, 1970—. Vol. host Am. Field Service, 1961-62. Nat. Def. Edn. Act. grantee, 1967. Mem. Am. Assn. Sch. Librarians, Elementary Edn. Assn., Nat., Ind. assns. for ednl. communications and tech., Ind. Sch. Librarians Assn. (membership chmn. 1974—, area vice chmn. 1974), A.L.A., Kappa Kappa Kappa. Episcopalian. Home: 142 Longwood Dr La Porte IN 46350 Office: 910 Harrison St La Porte IN 46350

DOLBEY, MRS. JAMES M. (DOROTHY NICHOLS DOLBEY), city ofcl.; b. Cin., Apr. 28, 1908; d. Herbert Wood and Harriet (Short) Nichols; B.S., U. Cin., 1930; M.S., Columbia, 1934; L.H.D. (hon.), U. Cin., 1969; m. James Morton Dolbey, June 12, 1935; children—James Morton, Elizabeth Nichols (Mrs. Herbert Charles Rule III). Mem. Cin. City Council, 1953-61, acting mayor, 1954, vice-mayor, 1953-55. Dir. Better Housing League, 1950—; dir., chmn. world fellowship com. YWCA, 1950-53; chmn. Mayor's Friendly Relations Com., 1951—, Girl's Week, 1950-53, Girl and Her City Day, 1951—; bd. dirs. Hosp. Care Corp., Goodwill Industries, Garden Center, Central Clinic, Bethesda Home, U. Cin. Recipient Good Neighbor award Wise Temple, 1954, Nat. Citizenship citation from ABC, 1953; named Ohio Mother of 1966. Mem. Ch. Women United (chmn. nat. pub. relations com. 1950-56, nat. pres. 1967-71), Am. Assn. U. Women, Nat. (gen. bd. 1953—), Cin. (exec. com. 1950—) councils chs., Cin. Council Ch. Women (pres. 1948-50), Nat. Conf. Christians and Jews, Cin. Bus. Profl. Women's Clubs, League Women Voters, Nat. Council Chs. of Christ in U.S.A. (v.p. at large 1969—), Phi Beta, Delta Zeta, Delta Kappa Gamma. Methodist. Clubs: Zonta, Cincinnati Woman's, Woman's City, College (Cin.). Home: 5 Twin Hills Ridge Dr Cincinnati OH 45228 Office: Plum at 9th Cincinnati OH 45202

DOLD, HELEN SHUMAKER (MRS. C. NORMAN DOLD), civic worker; b. Prospect, Pa., Oct. 8, 1898; d. Elwood Curtis and Effie (Gailey) Shumaker; A.B., and B.Mus., Denison U., 1921; M.A., U. Wis., 1925; m. Charles Norman Dold, Sept. 24, 1927 (dec. Aug. 1965); children—Charles Norman, John Allen, Robert James, Mary Ann. Instr. English, U. Wis., 1923-25, Rockford (Ill.) Coll., 1925-27. Dir., Rose Exterminatòr Co., Chgo. Bd. mgrs. Woman's Am. Baptist Home Mission Soc., 1942-53, Midwestern v.p., 1951-53; chmn. bd. mgrs. Bapt. Missionary Tng. Sch., 1951-53; corr. sec. Woman's Club of Wilmette (Ill.), 1954-56; regent Skokie Valley chpt. D.A.R., 1958-60; pres. Woman's Bapt. Mission Union of Chgo., 1960-62; mem. North Shore Republican Women's Club. Mem. Mortar Bd. (hon.), Phi Beta Kappa (hon.), Delta Delta Delta, Delta Omicron. Co-author anthology The World Unfolding, 1927. Home: 1350 Greenwood Av Wilmette IL 60091

DOLE, GRACE FULLER, librarian; b. Cambridge, Mass.; d. John Soper and Margaret Fernald Dole; grad. The Masters Sch., Dobbs Ferry, N.Y., 1940; B.A., Bryn Mawr Coll., 1944; M.L.S., Columbia, 1954; m. Paul E. Kohler, Jr., Jan. 22, 1944 (div. May 1946); 1 dau., Margaret (Mrs. Charles E. Nicholson, Jr.). Tchr. French, librarian Low-Heywood Sch., Stamford, Conn., 1948-50; sch. librarian Greenwich (Conn.) Library, 1950-53; with reference dept. N.Y. Pub. Library, N.Y.C., 1954-56; asst. librarian then librarian Benton & Bowles, N.Y.C., 1956-62; reference librarian Ferguson Library, Stamford, Conn., 1962-64; librarian U. Conn.-Stamford Br. and Center, 1964—. Mem. Library Adminstrs. Group Fairfield County. Mem. Spl. Libraries Assn. (head com. new library devel. 1962-63, chmn. publicity 1971—, rec. sec. 1972-73), A.L.A., Am. Artists Profl. League (hon.), Hudson Valley Art Assn. (rec. sec. 1973-74), Margaret F. Dole Contemporary Art Club (v.p. 1973-74), D.A.R., Col. Dames XVII Century, Huguenot Soc. Conn., Panhellenic Assn. (chmn. Fairfield br. 1973-74). Home: 124 Ritch Av Byram CT 10573

DOLGIN, JEANNE RYDELL (MRS. MARTIN DOLGIN), librarian; b. N.Y.C., June 3, 1921; d. Nathan and Celestine (Abeles) Rydell; B.A., Bklyn. Coll., 1944; postgrad. Columbia U., 1944-48, M.S. in Library Sci., 1964; m. Martin Dolgin, Feb. 12, 1950; children—Barbara, Deborah, Stuart. Asst. copy desk Time, Inc., N.Y.C., 1945-52; reference librarian Scarsdale (N.Y.) Pub. Library, 1964-69; asst. prof., reader services librarian Mercy Coll., Dobbs Ferry, N.Y., 1969—. Mem. ad hoc com. Ardsley (N.Y.) Middle Sch., 1967; chmn. Ardsley (N.Y.) Library Com., 1969; vice chmn. Ardsley 75th Anniversary Celebration, 1971. Vice pres. bd. trustees Ardsley Pub. Library, 1971—. Mem. Am., N.Y., Westchester (chmn. coll. librarians sect. 1973—) library assns., Beta Phi Mu. Home: 32 Mt View Av Ardsley NY 10502 Office: Mercy College Dobbs Ferry NY 10522

DOLHINOW, PHYLLIS CAROL JOSCELYN (MRS. JACK L. DOLHINOW), educator; b. Elgin, Ill., Nov. 6, 1933; d. William J. and Fern G. (Fagell) Joscelyn; B.A., Beloit Coll., 1955; A.M., U. Chgo., 1960, Ph.D., 1963; m. Jack L. Dolhinow, June 3, 1968; 1 dau., Rebecca Elizabeth. Lectr. anthropology U. Cal. at Berkeley, 1961-62; fellow Center for Advanced Study in Behavioral Scis., Stanford, Cal., 1962-63; asst. prof. anthropology Columbia, 1963-64; asst. prof. anthropology U. Cal. at Davis, 1964-66, research anthropologist Nat. Center for Primate Biology, 1964-66, asst. prof., Berkeley, 1966-69, asso. prof., 1969-72, prof. anthropology, 1972—. Research grantee in anthropology NSF, 1967-70. Fellow Am. Anthrop. Assn., Am. Assn. Phys. Anthropologists, A.A.A.S.; mem. Am. Assn. Phys. Anthropologists, Wildlife Preservation Soc. India, Am. Ecol. Assn., Internat. Primatological Soc., Am. Assn. U. Profs., Animal Behavior Soc., Am. Inst. Biol. Scis., Phi Beta Kappa, Sigma Xi. Author: Primates: Studies in Adaptation and Variability, 1968; Perspectives on Human Evolution, Vol. I, 1968, Vol. II, 1972; Background for Man, 1971; Primate Patterns, 1972. Asso. editor Am. Jour. Phys. Anthropology, 1963-68. Home: 1819 Thousand Oaks Blvd Berkeley CA 94707

DOLLINGER, ALETHEA MORRISON (MRS. G. GLENN DOLLINGER), physician; b. College View, Neb., July 28, 1909; d. Harvey Arch and Vera (Thompson) Morrison; B.A., Columbia Union Coll., 1937; M.D., Loma Linda U., 1939; m. G. Glenn Dollinger, Nov. 23, 1937; children—Patricia C. (Mrs. Eugene S. Maxson), Armand L. Intern White Meml. Hosp., Los Angeles, 1938-39, resident, 1939-41; practice medicine specializing in anesthesiology, Alhambra, Cal., 1941—; mem. staff Alhambra Community Hosp., chief staff, 1971; instr. dept. anesthesia Loma Linda U., 1941-70. Bd. dirs. San Gabriel Valley Philharmonic Artists Assn. Mem. Pan Am. Med. Womens Assn. (past v.p.). Republican. Mem. Seventh-day Adventist Ch. Club: Quota Internat. (pres. Alhambra club 1949, 56, dist. gov. 1951-53). Home: 115 N Almansor St No 39 Alhambra CA 91801

DOLMAN, VIOLA ELIZABETH SETTER (MRS. BAIRD DOLMAN), realtor; b. Richmond, Kan., Dec. 9, 1922; d. Christopher B. and Bertha (Miller) Setter; B.S., Kan. State U., 1944; M.S., Stanford, 1948; m. Baird Dolman, Apr. 25, 1953; children—David, Laura. Faculty, Stanford Med. Sch., 1948-50, faculty biochemistry dept., 1950-53; real estate broker, Honolulu, 1958—. Pres. Hawaii Assn. for Children with Learning Disabilities, 1970; mem. profl. information com. Am. Cancer Soc., 1967. Bd. dirs. Hawaiian A.R.C., Aloha United Fund. Pub. Health grantee for research, Honolulu, 1953-55. Mem. Farm and Land Brokers Assn., Traders and Exchangers Orgn., Honolulu Bd. Realtors (chmn. multiple listing service com.), Zonta, Sigma Xi. Clubs: Oahu Country, Outrigger Canoe, Waikikii Yacht (Honolulu). Home: 1049 Waiholo St Honolulu HI 96821 Office: 210 Ward Av Honolulu HI 96814

DOLMOVICH, SISTER MIRIAM JOSEPH, coll. adminstr.; b. Pitts., Sept. 5, 1924; d. Joseph J. and Barbara A. (Gregoric) Dolmovich; B.E. in Edn., Duquesne U., 1958; M.B.A. in Bus. Adminstrn., U. Notre Dame, 1962; postgrad U. Neb., 1969, 72. Joined Congregation Sisters Divine Providence, 1949; tchr. bus. edn., Pitts., 1950-68; sec., English corr. Vatican Offices, Rome, Italy, 1968-69; treas. LaRoche Coll., Pitts., 1969—. Mem. Nat., Eastern assns. Coll. and U. Bus. Officers, Coll. and U. Personnel Assn. Address: 9000 Babcock Blvd Pittsburgh PA 15237

DOLOR, MELINDA C. CABARON (MRS. FELICIANO G. DOLOR), physician; b. Cebu City, Philippines, Dec. 1, 1940; d. Francisco C. and Guadalupe C. (Colina) Cabaron; A.A., U. San Carlos, Philippines, 1958; M.D. cum laude, Cebu Inst. Medicine, 1963; m. Feliciano G. Dolor; children—Rowena Joy, Rosemary Ann, Rachel Stella. Instr. microbiology and parasitology Cebu Inst. Medicine, 1963-64; rotating intern Grant Hosp., Columbus, O., 1964-65, resident anatomic pathology and clin. pathology, 1965-69; fellow pediatric pathology Columbus Children's Hosp., 1970-71; asso. pathology, dir. Blood Bank Riverside Meth. Hosp., 1972—. Diplomate Am. Bd. Pathology. Fellow Assn. Clinic Pathologists, Coll. Am. Pathologists; mem. Central Ohio Soc. Pathologists, Am. Women's Med. Assn., Am. Assn. Blood Banks, Intern Acad. Pathologists, Ohio Soc. Pathology, Acad. Medicine Columbus and Franklin County, Ohio Med. Assn., St. Andrew's Women's Club. Home: 5525 Rockport Rd Columbus OH 43220 Office: Riverside Methodist Hospital Columbus OH 43214

DOLOROSA, SISTER MARY GRADY, hosp. adminstr.; b. County Roscommon, Ireland (came to U.S. 1931, naturalized 1942); d. Thomas and Anne (McDonnel) Grady; B.S., Coll. St. Teresa, 1947. Adminstr. Holy Rosary Hosp., Ontario, Ore., 1966-69; med. technologist St. Catherine's Hosp., Kenosha, Wis., 1941-50, supr. clin. labs., 1950-62, asst. adminstr., 1962-66, adminstr., 1969—. Sec. gen. Dominican Sisters of Kenosha, 1951-63; mem. governing bd. Sisters of St. Catherine's Hosp., 1951-63. Pres. Conf. Cath. Hosps., 1968; bd. dirs. A.R.C. of Malheur County, 1966-69; mem. adv. bd. practical nursing program Treasure Valley Coll., Ontario, Ore., 1966-69, sec. adv. bd., 1968-69; mem. corporate bd. Cath. Social Services, Milw., 1969—; mem. resource com. Kenosha County (Wis.) Comprehensive Health Planning for Southeastern Wis., 1969—. Mem. Am. Soc. Med.

Technologists, Am. Coll. Hosp. Adminstrn., Wis. Regional Writers' Assn. Home: 3556 7th Av Kenosha WI 53140 Office: St Catherine's Hosp 3556 7th Av Kenosha WI 53140

DOLORUM, SISTER MARY (ANNE M. LEAVY), med. technologist; b. Westmeath, Ireland; d. John and Catharine (Maguire) Leavy; came to U.S., 1927, naturalized, 1946; student Boston Coll., 1963, 64; B.S., Anna Maria Coll., 1966; M.S., L.I. U., 1972. Trainee, Providence Hosp. Lab., 1931; med. technologist Mercy Hosp. Lab., Springfield, Mass., 1934-39, Farren Meml. Hosp., Montague City, Mass., 1939-42; bacterial-mycol. lab. supr. St. Vincent Hosp. Lab., Worcester, Mass., 1942-46, 50—; lab. supr. Providence Hosp. Lab., Holyoke, Mass., 1946-50. Mem. Am. Soc. Med. Tech., Am. Assn. Blood Banks, Am. Soc. for Microbiology, Mycol. Soc. Am., Internat. Soc. for Human and Animal Mycology, Mass. Assn. Med. Technologists, Am. Assn. Clin. Chemists, Worcester Dist. Med. Technologists Assn. Home: Providence Mother House Holyoke MA 01040 Office: St Vincent Hosp Worcester MA 01604

DOMAN, ELVIRA HAND (MRS. JOHN H. HOLDER), educator; b. N.Y.C.; d. Andrew and Lillian (McClary) Hand; B.A., Hunter Coll., 1955; M.S. in Biology, N.Y. U., 1959; M.A. in Biochemistry (fellow), Columbia, 1960; Ph.D. in Biochemistry (fellow), Rutgers, 1965; m. John H. Holder; children—Paula, Rodney. Jr. technician Univ. Hosp., N.Y.C., 1955-56; sr. technician Sloan Kettering Inst. for Cancer Research, N.Y.C., 1956-57, research asst., 1960-61; research asst. Columbia Coll. Physicians and Surgeons, 1957-58; research asso. Rockefeller U., N.Y.C., 1965-68; lectr. Douglass Coll., New Brunswick, N.J., 1970-73; asst. prof. Seton Hall U., South Orange, N.J., 1973—. Lectr. sickle cell anemia colls., community groups; panelist radio sta. WCTC, New Brunswick, 1973. USPHS pre-doctoral fellow, 1962-64; Sloan-Kettering Inst. fellow, 1965, Rockefeller U., 1965-66. Mem. N.Y., N.J. acads. scis., Am. Chem. Soc., A.A.A.S. Contbr. articles to profl. jours. Home: 172 B Taylor Av East Brunswick NJ 08816 Office: Dept Biology Seton Hall U South Orange NJ 07079

DOMAN, KATHARINE BIGELOW (MRS. NICHOLAS R. DOMAN), civic worker; b. N.Y.C.; d. Mason Huntington and Elizabeth (Macdonald) Bigelow; student Barnard Coll.; m. Carter Chapin Higgins, 1937 (div. 1949); children—Richard Carter, Elizabeth (Mrs. Henry Null IV), Mark Huntington (dec.); m. 2d, Nicholas R. Doman, Aug. 25, 1951; children—Daniel Bigelow, Alexander Macdonald. Co.-dir. Boston Studio and Art Gallery, 1947; art and drama critic St. Augustine (Fla.) News, 1948-49; editorial writer Baker & Funaro, 1949; with Conde Nast, 1949-50. Mem. cts. com. N.Y. Jr. League, 1951-58; active fund-raising coms. Sheltering Arms Children's Service Aux., 1951—; bd. dirs. N.Y. council Nat. Council Crime and Delinquency, 1963-69; mem. Legal Aid Soc. Women's Aux., 1963—; co-chmn. Gov.'s Conf. Women's Role in Crime Prevention, 1968. Bd. dirs. N.Y. Edn. Inst. for Learning and Research, 1964—. Clubs: Woman's City, York, Shelter Island Yacht, Gardiners Bay Country. Home: 1185 Park Av New York City NY 10028

DOMBROWSKI, MADGE COHEA (MRS. CASEY WILLIAM DOMBROWSKI), photography studio exec.; b. Westville, Okla., Sept. 6, 1918; d. William E. and Ina Clyde (Greer) Cohea; B.S., Okla. Coll. for Women, 1939; grad. N.Y. Inst. Photography, 1944, Edwards Sch. of Color, 1941; m. Casey William Dombrowski, July 3, 1943; children—Carol Jo (Mrs. Don Kitchen), Linda Norene (Mrs. Frank Edgell), Peggy Sharon (Mrs. Tom Porter), John Casey, Alan Wayne. Co-partner Cohea Studio, Frederick, Okla., 1938-74; news corr., writer Okla. Pub. Co., Oklahoma City, 1958-74, Lawton (Okla.) Morning Press, 1959-74, Wichita Falls (Tex.) Morning Press, 1958-74; news writer Sta. KTAT, Frederick, Okla., 1960-74. Lectr. on photography to various civic and womens clubs. Publicity chmn. Frederick Community Theater, 1970-72. Bd. dirs. Campfire Girls, 1960-72. Recipient Plaque as Frederick's most useful citizen Lions Club, 1967. Mem. Frederick C. of C., Okla. Coll. for Women Alumni Assn. (dir. 1967-68), Friends of Library. Mem. Christian Ch. Club: Black Kat Bus. Women's (pres. 1943, 60-70) (Frederick). Home: 421 N 12th St Frederick OK 73542 Office: 112 W Grand Av Frederick OK 73542

DOMER, MARILYN ALICE, educator; b. Ft. Wayne, Ind., Apr. 5, 1926; d. Merle Sharon and Irma Belle (Rupley) Domer; A.B., Oberlin Coll., 1949; M.A., Claremont Coll., 1955; Ph.D., Ball State U., 1968. Asst. librarian Fed. Res. Bank, San Francisco, 1950-52; exec. dir. YWCA, Muncie, Ind., 1955-59; camp dir., outdoor recreation dir. YWCA, Pitts., 1959-64; teaching fellow Ball State U., Muncie, 1964-66, instr. sociology, 1966-67, asst. prof. sociology, 1967-68; asso. prof. social sci. George Williams Coll., Downers Grove, Ill., 1968-73, prof. history, 1974—, chmn. faculty senate, 1971-73. Curator Reid Mansion, Chgo., 1968—; mem. Chgo. Art Inst., Field Mus. Natural History. Bd. dirs. Chgo. chpt. Friends of Earth, 1970-72; bd. dirs. YWCA, Chgo., 1971-73, chmn. met. camp com., 1971-73. Mem. Am. Assn. U. Profs. (chpt. pres. 1969-71), Am. Hist. Assn., Orgn. Am. Historians, Phi Gamma Mu, Phi Lambda Theta. Christian Scientist. Author: Exploring Your Values, 1973. Home: 2013 Prairie St Chicago IL 60616 Office: 555 31st St Downers Grove IL 60515

DONAHEY, GERTRUDE WALTON, state ofcl.; b. Goshen, O., Aug. 4, 1908; d. George Sebastian and Mary Ann (Thomas) Walton; grad. bus. coll.; m. John W. Donahey, Apr. 12, 1930 (dec.); 1 son, John William. Pvt. sec., until 1930; now treas. State of Ohio. Sec., mem. exec. com., bd. dirs. Ohio Mental Health Assn. Chmn. operations support Ohio Democratic Com., 1963—, mem.-at-large platform com., 1964, 68; field aide in Central and South Ohio for U.S. Senator Young, 1963-69, then staff asst.; del. Dem. Nat. Conv., 1964, delegate-at-large, mem. platform and resolutions com., 1968. Mem. Municipal Finance Officers Assn., Nat. Assn. Auditors, Comptrollers and Treas. Episcopalian. Home: 2838 Sherwood Rd Columbus OH 43209 Office: State Capital Bldg Columbus OH 43216

DONAHOE, PATRICIA KILROY (MRS. JOHN F. DONAHOE), pediatric surgeon; b. Brookline, Mass., Apr. 12, 1937; d. Lawrence and Sophie T. (Jacoski) K.; B.S. magna cum laude, Boston U., 1958; M.D., Columbia, 1964; m. John F. Donahoe, Aug. 27, 1960; children—Shauna Patrice, J. Tara, John F. Intern, Tufts-New Eng. Center Hosp., 1964-65, resident gen. surgery, 1965-68, chief resident gen. surgery, 1968-69, teaching fellow, 1968-69; research fellow Harvard Med. Sch., 1969-70; sr. resident pediatric surgeon Childrens Hosp., Boston, 1970, Mass. Gen. Hosp., 1970-71; sr. registrar neonatal surgery and pediatric urology Alder Hey Childrens Hosp., Liverpool, Eng., 1971-72; now staff pediatric surgeon Mass. Gen. Hosp., Boston. Recipient Most Outstanding Young Woman of Am. award, 1970. Diplomate Am. Bd. Surgery. Contbr. articles to profl. jours. Address: Mass Gen Hosp Boston MA 02114

DONAHUE, DOROTHY HAZEL, banker; b. Northampton, Mass., Mar. 15, 1916; d. Michael J. and Nora D. (McCarthy) Donahue; student Northampton Comml. Coll., 1935; student Sch. Banking, Williams Coll., 1960. Asst. cashier Northampton Loan & Finance Co., 1936-42; with Northampton Nat. Bank, 1942—, mgr. loan dept. 1958-67, asst. cashier, 1967—, loan and marketing officer, 1972—, asst. v.p., auditor, 1973—. Mem. Bd. Almoners, Northampton, 1960—. Mem. Nat. Assn. Bank Women (vice chmn. Pioneer group 1970-72). Club: Quota International (pres. Northampton). Home: 46 Lilly St Florence MA 01060 Office: 130 Main St Northampton MA 01060

DONAHUE, SHEILA, pathologist; b. Eng., 1916. Resident in pathology Bellevue Hosp., N.Y.C., 1948-50, asst. pathologist, 1950-51, 53-55; asst. in pathology N.Y.U., 1948-51, instr., 1953-55; asst. prof. neuropathology Columbia Coll. Phys. and Surg., 1960-63; asst. prof. pathology Ind. U. Sch. Medicine, Indpls., 1963-66, asso. prof., 1966-70; asso. research scientist N.Y. State Inst. Research on Mental Retardation, 1970—. Served to capt., M.C., Royal Army, 1944-47. Diplomate Am. Bd. Pathology. Address: 1050 Forest Hill Rd Staten Island NY 10314

DONALD, ELIZABETH ANN, educator; b. Edmonton, Alta., Feb. 14, 1926; d. Archibald Scott and Margaret Catherine (Cameron) Donald; B.S., U. Alta., 1949; M.S., Wash. State U., 1955; Ph.D. (fellow 1959-61), Cornell U., 1962. Dietitian U. Alta., Edmonton, 1950-51, mem. faculty, 1969—, prof. econs., 1973—; home economist Expt. Sta., Wash. State U. at Pullman, 1955-59; asst. prof. Cornell U., Ithaca, N.Y., 1962-66, asso. prof., 1966-69. Hatch Fund grantee; NRC Can. grantee. Mem. Am. Inst. Nutrition, Canadian Nutrition Soc., Am. Dietetic Assn., Am. Home Econs. Assn., A.A.A.S., N.Y. Acad. Sci., Sigma Xi, Phi Kappa Phi, Omicron Nu. Club: Faculty (Edmonton). Office: U Alta Edmonton AB Canada

DONALDSON, BRYNA BEVERLY, writer; b. New Rochelle, N.Y., Oct. 22, 1924; d. Alexander and Amy Stevens; B.Mus., U. Wis., 1967; div.; children—Joseph, Janice, Mark. Music tchr., 1942—; photographer, free lance writer articles, stories, songs, poetry. Mem. Madison Area Writers. Author: Paper Piano, 1966; Christmas Songs, 1973. Address: 2544 S Stoughton Rd Madison WI 53716

DONALDSON, DOROTHEA E., lawyer and judge; b. New Rochelle, N.Y.; d. Harnett B. and Amelia J. (Roeck) Donaldson; B.A., Hunter Coll., N.Y.C., 1931; M.A., Tchrs. Coll. Columbia, 1932; J.D., St. John's U., 1935. Tchr. New Rochelle pub. schs., 1932-43; gen. practice law with J. Lester Albertson, New Rochelle, 1943-50; referee and supervising referee N.Y. Workmen's Compensation Bd., 1944-50, presiding judge appeals panel, 1950, 60; chmn. Unemployment Ins. Appeal Bd., 1960-63; judge Ct. of Claims, State of N.Y., 1963—. Trustee St. John's U. Recipient achievement award New Rochelle Bus. and Profl. Women, also Woman of the Year award 1963; Golden Eaglet, Girl Scouts, Benjamin Potoker Meml. Brotherhood award, 1961; Pres.'s medal St. John's U., 1971; named to Hunter Coll. Alumni Hall Fame, 1972. Mem. Inter-Am., Internat., Am., N.Y., Westchester County, New Rochelle bar assns., Bus. and Profl. Women's Club, Beta Sigma Omicron, Iota Tau Tau. Methodist. Club: Westchester County Assn. Home: 65 Brookside Pl New Rochelle NY 10801 Office: 9 S 1st Av Mount Vernon NY 10550

DONALDSON, KAREN MAE (MRS. ARTHUR T. DONALDSON), advt. agy. exec.; b. Thorpe, Wis., July 5, 1941; d. Leon Michael and Mabel Evandale (Taves) Glowacki; grad. high sch.; m. Arthur T. Donaldson, Feb. 13, 1960; children—Arthur T., Susan Ann. With Vivid, Inc., Janesville, Wis., 1957—, v.p., sec., 1963—; mgr. Fairview Mall & Mart, Janesville, 1973—. Group leader Girl Scouts U.S.A., Janesville, 1973-74. Mem. Jr. Republican Women, 1965-70. Mem. Janesville Jaycetts (pres. 1961-66), Elk's Club Aux. Clubs: Janesville Country, Zonta, Star Zenith Boat. Home: 2530 Dartmouth Dr Janesville WI 53545 Office: Hwy 51 South PO Box 307 Janesville WI 53545

DONALDSON, LORRAINE, educator; b. Clearwater, Fla.; d. Lonnie Milton and Lois (Young) Donaldson; B.S. in Bus. Adminstrn., U. Fla., 1960, M.A., 1961; D.B.A., Ind. U., 1965. Research asst. Brookings Inst., Bloomington, Ind., 1963, research asst. Internat. Devel. Research Center, 1962-63; asst. prof. econs. Ga. State U., Atlanta, 1964-66, asso. prof., 1966-70, prof., 1970—. Cons., lectr. econ. edn. for tchrs. Author: Development Planning in Ireland, 1966. Contbr. articles to profl. jours. Home: 1170 Pine Ridge Rd NE Atlanta GA 30324

DONALDSON, MARJORIE CATHERINE, ret. librarian; b. Milw., June 15, 1911; d. Robert Sample and Lenore (Okey) Donaldson; B.A., Rutgers U., 1933. State traveling library, Des Moines, 1933-38; state dir. Iowa WPA Library Project, 1938-39; asst. librarian Ames (Ia.) Pub. Library, 1939-44; with Pasadena (Cal.) Pub. Library, 1944-73, city librarian, 1956-73. Mem. Cal. Library Assn. (pres. pub. libraries sect. 1960), Pub. Library Execs. of So. Cal. (pres. 1957), Pasadena Municipal Employees Assn. (dir. 1952-53), Women's Civic League Pasadena (Woman of Year 1957, sec. 1958), Bus. and Profl. Women's Club (local pres. 1949-50), C. of C. (cultural affairs com. 1955-70). P.E.O. (chpt. pres. 1947). Republican. Presbyn. Clubs: Zonta (pres. 1964-65), Women's City (dir. 1950-56, pres. 1955-56) (Pasadena). Home: 1183 Romney Dr Pasadena CA 91105

DONALDSON, VIRGINIA H., pediatrician; b. Glen Cove, N.Y., 1924; M.D., U. Vt., 1951. Intern Strong Meml. Hosp., Rochester, N.Y., 1951-53, asst. resident pediatrics, 1953-54; asst. resident pediatrics Genesee Hosp., Rochester, 1953, Buffalo Children's Hosp., 1954-55; research fellow pediatrics, 1955-57, Western Res. Hosp., 1955-57, fellow medicine, 1957-62; staff research div. Cleve. Clin.; dir. hematology Shrine Burns Inst., 1967-70, sr. instr. medicine Western Res. U., 1963-67; asso. prof. medicine U. Cinn., until 1971, prof. medicine and pediatrics, 1971—. Diplomate Am. Bd. Pediatrics. Address: Children's Hosp Research Found Elland and Bethesda Avs Cincinnati OH 45229

DONATELLI, ROSEMARY VICTORIA, educator; b. Chgo., Dec. 25, 1929; d. John J. and Anna Helen (Gerwatowski) Donatelli; B.M.E., Mundelein Coll., 1952; M.A., Columbia, 1956; Ph.D., U. Chgo., 1971. Tchr. Chgo. pub. schs., 1952-55, New Rochelle (N.Y.) pub. schs., 1955-57; mem. faculty Loyola U., Chgo., 1957—, prof. history edn., 1957—, Chmn. Founds. Edn., 1972—. Recipient School Bell award N.E.A., 1956. Mem. Philosophy. Edn. Soc., Nat. History Edn. Soc. (sec. 1973-74), Am. Assn. U. Profs. Home: 260 E Chestnut St Chicago IL 60611 Office: Loyola U 820 N Michigan St Chicago IL 60611

DONDERO, GERTRUDE, social agy. exec.; b. Willimantic, Conn.; d. Louis Nelson and Anna (Carey) DonDero; B.S., Boston U., 1932; postgrad. Columbia, 1938, 46, N.Y.U., 1940, New Sch. Drama Workshop, 1945. Dir. summer and winter theatre groups, New Eng., Fla., 1932-42; state dir. for Conn. Fed. Theatre, 1935-37; dir. Greenwich (Conn.) Community Drama Assn., 1937-39; USO Club dir., Ft. Smith, Ark., 1942, program coordinator C.Z., 1943-44, editor weekly page USO on Parade in Panama Am., program cons. stage and radio USO Overseas Dept., Western Hemisphere, 1944-45; speaking, radio engagements Nat. War Fund, Eastern U.S., 1943-45; pub. relations, fund raising counsel Meml. Cancer Center, Profl. Children Sch., Mus. Modern Art, UN Appeal to Children, 1945-52, China Inst. Am., 1952-55, Thomas Alva Edison Found., 1954-55, Stamford (Conn.) Mus. and Nature Center, 1955, Marine Hist. Assn., Mystic, Conn., 1955, Am. Found. Religion and Psychiatry, 1955-57; dir. N.Y. com. Wellesley Coll., 1958-60; dir. devel. Carnegie Hall, 1961-62; nat. exec. dir. Girls Clubs of Am., Inc., 1963—. Dir. N.Y. Jr. League Theatre Workshop, 1947. Recipient meritorious achievement citation Caribbean Def. Command, citation War Dept. Spl. Services Dev., citation N.Y. Com. of Nat. War Fund. Mem. Women's Conf. Group. Clubs: Overseas Press (NYC); Old Kimmul (London). Writer publicity articles, drama criticism, newspapers and mags.; prodn. travel films Hartley Studios, Eng. and France, 1949. Home: Donnybrook Rockrimmon Rd Stamford CT 06903 Office: 133 E 62d St New York City NY 10021

DONDI, DOLORES ALBERTINE, advt. co. exec.; b. Pittsfield, Mass.; d. Didimo A. and Rose (Vanotti) Dondi; student Berkshire Bus. Coll., Davenport Inst. Bus., 1950-51. Sec. Jules L. Klein Advt., Inc., Springfield, Mass., 1952-57, prodn. mgr., 1957-60, media dir., 1960-64, asst. to pres., 1964-68, v.p. client services, 1968—. Mem. Advt. Club Springfield (dir. 1960-64), Springfield Photog. Soc., Springfield C. of C. (v.p. women's div. 1973-74, pres. 1974—). Club: Zonta. Home: 66 Williamsburg Dr Springfield MA 01108 Office: Kimball Towers Penthouse Springfield MA 01103

DONEGAN, SISTER SARA JEAN, educator, dentist; b. Pittsville, Wis., July 20, 1935; d. L. John and Myrtle (Hebert) Donegan; B.S., Mt. Mary Coll., Milw., 1957; D.D.S., Marquette U., 1964, postgrad., 1970. Joined Sisters of Notre Dame, 1957, provincial chpt. del. 1973-75; tchr. math., sci. McDonnell High Sch., Chippewa Falls, Wis., 1958-60, dentist Notre Dame Infirmary, Elm Grove, Wis., 1964—, head dept. dentistry Notre Dame Health Care Center, 1969—. Instr. Marquette U. Sch. Dentistry, Milw., part-time 1964—, asst. clin. prof. fixed prosthodontics, 1972—; instr. math. Mt. Mary Coll., part-time 1968-69. High sch. instr. Confrat. Christian Doctrine, Wauwatosa, 1967-69; del. Milw. Archdiocesan Sisters Council, 1971, mem. health services com., 1971. Recipient Gold Foil Restoration award Acad. Gold Foil Operators, 1964. Mem. Am. Dental Assn., Am. Soc. Geriatric Dentistry, Wis., Waukesha County dental socs., Omicron Kappa Upsilon. Address: 13105 Watertown Plank Rd Elm Grove WI 53122

DONEHOWER, GRACE MILDRED, educator; b. Lidgerwood, N.D., Nov. 19, 1915; d. Ross Floyd and Minnesota (Babcock) Donehower; A.B., Jamestown Coll., 1937; M.A., U. Nev., 1968; postgrad. U. Colo., summer 1940. Tchr., jr. high sch. prin. LaMoure, N.D., 1937-41; jr. exec., auditor Montgomery Ward & Co., St. Paul, 1941-42; prin. Cleveland (N.D.) Pub. Sch., 1942-43, Fargo (N.D.) High Sch., 1943-44; recreation worker A.R.C. Hosp., Naples, Italy, 1944-46; exec. dir. Muncie (Ind.) Girl Scout Council, 1946-49, Sierra Nev. Girl Scout Council, Reno, 1949-58; dir. corr. div. U. Nev., Reno, 1959—, instr. dept. English, part-time 1966-71, acting dean gen. univ. extension, 1969-70, asst. dean gen. univ. extension, 1971—. Mem. Washoe County Community Service Council, 1950-58, pres., 1957-58; Gov.'s com. Status of Women, 1967-70; bd. dirs. Washoe County chpt. Am. Cancer Soc., 1964-66. Recipient Woman of the Year award Nat. Bus. and Profl. Womens Club, 1967. Mem. Nat. U. Extension Assn. (pres.-elect Region VI 1973-74, nat. exec. com. 1974—, nat. bd. dirs. 1973—), Mountain Plains Adult Edn. Assn. (v.p. 1971-72, pres. 1973-74, dir.), Animal Welfare League (bd. dirs. 1968-70), Phi Sigma Alpha. Clubs: Nat. Bus. Profl. Women's (Nev. pres. 1957-58, nat. finance chmn. 1968-69, parliamentarian Western div. 1965-66, 67-68, chmn. nat. personal devel. com. 1970-71), Soroptimist (pres. 1963-64), Soroptimist Fedn. Ams. (dist. sec. 1968-70). Office: U Nev at Reno Gen U Extension Reno NV 89507

DONER, MARY FRANCES, author; b. Port Huron, Mich.; d. James and Mary Jane (O'Rourke) Doner; ed. Columbia. Began writing after leaving coll.; staff writer Dell Pub. Co., N.Y.C., 8 yrs.; music reporter, Boston Traveler, 2 yrs.; contract writer for several publs. N.Y.C. for Alfred H. King, for Penn Pub. Co.; contract writer Doubleday & Co., 1940—, for novels of Gt. Lakes country; speaking, Living Lit., Boston U., 1939, Boston Book Fair, 1938, Meet the Author series Boston Pub. Library, 1946; conducted classes in creative writing Boston Center for Adult Edn., 1943-45, Ludington (Mich.) High Sch., Jr. High and Pub. Library, 1964—. Hon. mem. Internat. Mark Twain Soc., Nat. League of Catholic Women, Women's Lit. Club, Ladies Library Assn., Port Huron, Mich.; mem. Internat. Inst. Arts and Letters, Author's League, Pen and Brush Club (N.Y.C.). Author several novels, later ones: Ravenswood, 1948; Cloud of Arrows, 1950; The Host Rock, 1952; The Salvager, 1958; The Shores of Home, 1961; While the River Flows, 1962; The Wind and the Fog, 1963, Cleavenger Versus Castle—A Case of Breach of Promise and Seduction, 1968; Pere Marquette—Soldier of the Cross, 1969; Return a Stranger, 1970; Thine is The power, 1972; Not by Appointment, 1973; The Darker Star, 1974. Contbr. over 250 short stories and serials to mags. some transcribed into Braille. Home: 210 N Lewis St Ludington MI 49431

DONES DE CARRASCAL, ELOISA MUNOZ (MRS. JOSE DANIEL DE CARRASCAL), physician; b. San Lorenzo, P.R., Oct. 25, 1922; d. Pedro and Maria (Dones) Munoz; B.A. cum laude, U. P.R., 1943, B.S. cum laude, 1943; M.D., Tulane U., 1948; m. Jose Daniel de Carrascal, Dec. 7, 1962; children—Lilia, Maria Eloisa. Intern Arecibo Charity Dist. Hosp., 1948-49, resident, 1949-51; resident in pediatrics San Juan City Hosp., 1949-51; practice medicine specializing in pediatrics, Rio Piedras, P.R., 1951—; chief newborn service San Juan City Hosp., 1951—; instr. clin. pediatrics U. P.R., Med. Center Sch. Medicine, 1951-69, asst. prof., 1969—. Recipient Bronze plaque P.R. Med. Women Assn., 1969, Silver plate, 1973; Bronze plaque distinguished med. services Pediatric Residents Assn. San Juan City Hosp., 1973. NIH grantee, 1962. Diplomate Am. Bd. Pediatrics, Pan Am. Pediatric Sect. Fellow Am. Acad. Pediatrics (chpt. treas. 1964-69), A.M.A.; mem. Am. Med. Womens Assn. (chpt. pres. 1962-66), Royal Soc. Health, Pan Am. Med. Women Alliance, Dominican Pediatric Soc., Tulane Med. Alumni. Democrat. Roman Catholic. Home: C 12 Duke Esquire Tulane Rio Piedras PR 00927 Office: 400 Domenech St Rio Piedras PR 00918

DONLAN, CHARLOTTE PATRICIA (MRS. JAMES HUGHES), physician, radiologist; b. N.Y.C., Nov. 2, 1911; d. William Patrick and Helen A. (Mooney) Donlan; B.A., Hunter Coll., 1933; M.D., Woman's Med. Coll., 1937; m. James Hughes, Feb. 17, 1942; 1 dau., Patricia. Intern N.Y. Infirmary for Women and Children, 1937-38, Strang Clinic, 1938-39; resident N.Y.C. Cancer Inst., 1939-41; radiation therapist Presbyn. Hosp., Vanderbilt Clinic, also instr. radiology Columbia Coll. Phys. and Surg., N.Y.C., 1942-47; radiation therapist Savannah (Ga.) Tumor Clinic, 1947-49; dir. Bur. Cancer Control, D.C. Health Dept., 1949-51; radiation therapist George Washington U. Med. Sch. and Hosp., Washington, 1951-59, asst. prof. Hosp. and Med. Sch., 1955—. Trustee D.C. div. Am. Cancer Soc. 1957—. Recipient Profl. Women of Yr. award Bus. and Profl. Women's Club of D.C., 1956, Fellow Am. Coll. Radiology; mem. Am. Cancer Soc. (profl. edn. com. Va. div.), Am. Assn. U. Profs., Radiol. Soc. N.Am., D.C., Fairfax med. socs., A.M.A., Women's Med. Soc. D.C. (pres. 1960), Georgetown Bus. and Profl. Women's Club, Phi Omega Pi, Alpha Epsilon Iota. Club: Zonta (Washington). Home: 8008 Riverside Bethesda MD 20034 Office: 6305 Castle Pl Falls Church VA 22044

DONLEY, BETTIE LOUX, editor, assn. exec.; b. Drexel Hill, Pa., Nov. 5, 1931; d. Frank Turner and Elizabeth Ida (Kauffman) Loux; B.S., Pa. State U., 1953; m. Marshall O. Donley, Jr., June 12, 1954

(div. Aug. 1971). Prodn. coordinator, editorial research Nat. Geog. Soc., Washington, 1959-69; editor World Traveler mag., dir. publs. Alexander Graham Bell Assn. for Deaf, Washington, 1969—. Mem. forum White House Conf. Children, 1970. Recipient award for picture story Ednl. Press Assn. Am., 1970, award for layout, 1971, award for one-theme issue, 1973, Eleanor Fishburn award for outstanding contbn. to internat. understanding among readers, 1971. Mem. Women in Communications, Ednl. Press Assn. Am., Alpha Gamma Delta, Phi Upsilon Omicron. Democrat. Episcopalian. Club: Silver Spring (Md.) Garden (v.p. 1970-71). Advt. editor Nat. Capital Fedn. Garden Clubs Bull., 1968-73; editor Grace Ch. Messenger, 1971—. Home: 1217 Woodside Pkwy Silver Spring MD 20910 Office: 1537 35th St NW Washington DC 20007

DONLIN, MARY ETTA GRATIOT (MRS. TIMOTHY E. DONLIN), pharmacist; b. Shullsburg, Wis., Aug. 3, 1913; d. Austin Flint and Mercedes (Edge) Gratiot; Ph.G., U. Cal. at San Francisco, 1933; m. Timothy E. Donlin, June 3, 1936 (dec. Jan., 1964). Pharmacist Alameda (Cal.) Drug Co., 1936-40, Owl Drug Co., Oakland, Cal., 1940-46, Gen. Drug Co., Sacramento, 1946-50; pharmacist Sutter Community Hosps., Sacramento, 1950-55, chief pharmacist, 1955—. Mem. Am., Cal. socs. hosp. pharmacists. Mem. Order Eastern Star. Home: 3832 Sherman Way Sacramento CA 95817 Office: 2820 L St Sacramento CA 95816

DONNAN, THOMASIA BATTEN, club woman; b. Palestine, Tex., May 29, 1912; d. John R. and Myrtle Lee (Washburn) Batten; student Tex. State Women's U., 1929-30, Washington U., St. Louis, 1947-48; m. William Varis Donnan, June 24, 1951; 1 dau., Nancy (Mrs. W.O. Beans, Jr.); stepchildren—Marybelle (Mrs. Harry Recker), Carol (Mrs. Thomas Holling), Dwight A. Tchr. rural sch., Cherokee County, Tex., 1931-32; salesman, casher Famous-Barr, St. Louis, 1932-41; with St. Louis Globe-Democrat, 1941-52. Mem. St. Louis Beautification Commn., 1967-69; mem. Glendale Park Bd., 1963-64; landscape design critic, 1966—, master flower show judge, 1969—. Mem. bd. Federated Garden Clubs Mo., 1961-73, asst. dir. East Central Dist., 1961-62; writer, editor The Nat. Gardener, 1969—; pres. Glendale Garden Club, 1960-61, 68-69; pres. St. Louis County Garden Club, 1969-70. Mem. Asso. Garden Clubs Kirkwood (pres. 1957-59), Nat. Council State Garden Clubs, Glendale Women's Club. Methodist. Home: 995 Kirkham Av Glendale MO 63122 Office: 4401 Magnolia Av St Louis MO 63110

DONNELL, BETTY LOUISE SCHMIDT (MRS. ELVIA LEE DONNELL), newspaper exec.; b. Brownfield, Tex., May 6, 1935; d. Frank Frederick and Effie Sina (Burrow) Schmidt; grad. high sch.; m. Elvia Lee Donnell, Dec. 23, 1953; children—Kevin Ray, Marta Kay. Supr. prodn. Canyon (Tex.) News, 1963-68, 71—; editor Swisher County News, Happy, Tex., 1968-70. Sec. Happy Jaycettes, 1969. Home: Route 1 Happy TX 79042 Office: 1500 5th Av Canyon TX 79015

DONNELLY, JUDY ANN, pub. co. exec.; b. Stratford, Conn., Feb. 14, 1942; d. Walter J. and Ann (Cimmarosa) Donnelly; B.A., Barnard Coll., 1963; postgrad. New Sch. Social Research, 1963-64. Editorial asst. children's book dept. Coward-McCann, Inc., N.Y.C., 1964-65; free lance editor, N.Y.C., 1965-66; asst. editor children's books Hastings House Pubs., Inc., N.Y.C., 1966-69, editor-in-chief children's books, 1969—. Mem. Children's Book Council, A.L.A., Woman's Book Assn. Office: 10 E 40th St New York City NY 10016

DONNELLY, LUCIA FAIN BURBAGE, newspaper editor; b. Johnson City, Tenn., Jan. 13, 1915; d. Henry Irving and Kathleen Margaret (Price) Burbage; student East Tenn. State U., 1933-36; m. Harry I. Donnelly, May 19, 1941 (dec. 1964); children—Michael Fain, Lucia Ann (Mrs. Robert Gordon Dudley). Reporter Johnson City (Tenn.) Press Chronicle, 1937-41; reporter Spartanburg (S.C.) Herald Jour., 1941-43, Nashville Banner, 1943-44, Westchester County (N.Y.) Publs., Chappaqua and White Plains, N.Y., 1956-57; asst. editor Town Crier, Westport, Conn., 1957-61; community and information coordinator Westport Bd. Edn., 1961-69; mng. editor Town Crier, 1969-70; editor Westport News, 1970—. Mem. Rep. Town Com., Westport, 1961-69. Recipient gen. excellence award for paper New Eng. Press Assn., 1971, certificate Nat. Editorial Assn., 1973-74. Episcopalian. Home: 2 Scherer Ct Westport CT 06880 Office: 136 Main St Westport CT 06880

DONNELLY, SISTER MARGARET ELIZABETH, coll. dean; b. Detroit, Jan. 11, 1925; d. Joseph Michael and Edna Mae (McCabe) Donnelly; B.S., Coll. Mt. St. Joseph, 1955, B.A., 1957; M.A. in Music, Eastman Sch. Music, 1964; postgrad. Notre Dame U., 1955-58. Joined Sisters of Charity of Cin., 1943; tchr. elementary music parochial schs., Cin., 1945-51, high sch. music, Lansing, Mich., 1951-55, high sch. music, English and theology, Detroit, 1955-57, Pueblo, Colo., 1957-66, high sch. music, humanities and theology, Royal Oak, Mich., 1966-69; dean student affairs Coll. Mt. St. Joseph (O.), 1969—. Mem. Ohio Commn. on Status of Women, 1973—, Catholic Conf. Blue Ribbon Com., 1973—. Mem. Nat. Assn. Women, Nat., Ohio (pres.-elect) assns. women deans, adminstrs. and counselors, Nat. Assn. Student Personnel, Nat. Assn. for Fgn. Student Affairs. Address: College of Mt St Joseph Mount St Joseph OH 45041

DONNELLY, ROSALIE FRANCES DEGIOVANNI (MRS. EDWARD F. DONNELLY), educator; b. Bklyn., Nov. 22, 1926; d. Frank and Rose (Quartuccio) DeGiovanni; B.A., Bklyn. Coll., 1947, M.A., 1953; Ph.D., Columbia, 1961; m. Edward F. Donnelly, Sept. 23, 1962; children—Edward F., Francis. Chief lab. technician allergy lab. Univ. Hosp., N.Y. U., 1947-51; student Columbia Med. Center, Sch. Pub. Health, 1952-54, student, asst. biochemistry dept., 1954-62; research scientist Bionetics Research Labs., Falls Church, Va., 1962-67; asst. research prof. microbiology dept. George Washington U. Med. Sch., Washington, 1968—. Research biologist FDA, 1968—. Recipient Food and Drug Merit award Dept. Health, Edn. and Welfare, 1971. Mem. A.A.A.S., Environmental Mutagen Soc., Am. Soc. Microbiology, N.Y. Acad. Scis., Sigma Xi, Sigma Delta. Home: 1712 Strine Dr McLeon VA 22101 Office: Dept Microbiology George Washington U Washington DC 20006

DONNESON, SEENA SAND, artist; b. N.Y.C., May 2; d. Max and Ann (Silber) Sand; student Pratt Inst., 1941-43, Art Students League, 1943-45, 58; children—Erika, Lisa. One man shows at Chase Gallery, Pietrantonio Gallery, Brooks Meml. Art Gallery, Sheldon Swope Art Gallery, Portland Mus. Art, Tenn. Fine Arts Center, Terrain Gallery, N.Y.C., Western Ill. U., Pensacola (Fla.) Art Center, U. Ariz., others; exhibited in group shows Nat. Assn. Women Artists, Conn. Acad. Fine Arts, Norfolk Mus. Arts and Scis., Bklyn. Mus., San Francisco Mus. Art, DeCordova Mus., Lincoln, Mass., Pratt Graphic Art Center, others; exhibited in fgn. traveling exhibitions T.S.S. Olympia, Am. Gallery of U.S. Embassy, Athens and Salonika, Greece, Brussels (Belgium) Worlds Fair, USIS, 1957-58, Municipal Art Mus., Tokyo, Japan, also on tour throughout Japan, 1960-61, Argentine Artists-NAWA Exchange Exhbn., Museo de Belles Artes, Buenos Aires, Argentina, 1962-63, Scotland, Eng., 1963-64, Contemporary Miniature Prints, 1966—, 15th Nat. Print Exhbn., 1966-68; represented in permanent collections at White Mus. Art, Washington County Mus. Fine Arts, Jacksonville Art Mus., Va. Mus. Fine Arts, Bklyn. Mus., Norfolk Mus., USIA Art in Embassies, Los Angeles County Mus. Fine Arts, Museum Modern Art, N.Y.C., also others; mem. art staff N.Y.U., 1961-62; guest artist Tamarind Lithography Workshop, 1968. Mem. Nassau County Fine Arts Commn. Recipient art awards Suffolk (L.I.) Mus., 1956, Ball State 13th Ann., 1967; Abbott Treadwell meml. prize Nat. Assn. Women Artists, 1966, purchase award Washington State U., 1970; others. Edward MacDowell Found. fellow, 1963, 64. Mem. Artists Equity, Nat. Assn. Women Artists, Profl. Artists Guild, Women in the Arts, Phila. Print Club. Studio: 319 Greenwich St New York City NY 10013

DONNO, ELIZABETH STORY (MRS. DANIEL J. DONNO), educator; b. Kenewick, Wash., June 12, 1921; d. Guy J. and Bertha Elizabeth (Waddell) Story; A.B., Whitman Coll., 1944; A.M., Columbia, 1946, Ph.D., 1959; m. Daniel J. Donno, Dec. 7, 1950. Prof. English lit. Columbia, 1959—. Fulbright fellow, 1949-50; Guggenheim fellow, 1963-64; Henry Huntington fellow, 1970-71. Mem. Renaissance Soc. Am., Modern Lang. Assn., Shakespeare Soc., Modern Humanities Assn., Conf. on Brit. Studies, Phi Beta Kappa. Editor: Metamorphosis of Ajax (Sir John Harington), 1962; Elizabethan Minor Epics, 1963; The Complete Poetry of Andrew Marvell, 1972. Editor Renaissance Quar., 1962—. Home: 29 Claremont Av New York City NY 10027

DONOGHUE, C. EILEEN, ret. educator; b. Holyoke, Mass.; d. Florance J. and Mary (Courtney) Donoghue; A.B., Boston U., 1926; postgrad. summers U. So. Cal., 1929, (Edna White scholar) Am. Acad., Rome, Italy, 1951, (Am. Classical League Scholar) Am. Sch., Athens, Greece, 1957; M.A., Montclair State Coll., 1949. Tchr., New Marlboro (Mass.) High Sch., 1926-27, Charlemont (Mass.) High Sch., 1927-29, Holyoke Jr. High Sch., 1929-31, Bound Brook (N.J.) High Sch., 1931-37, Bloomfield (N.J.) High Sch., 1937-64; instr. Latin, Caldwell (N.J.) Coll. for Women, 1964-70. Mem. Atlantic States (exec. bd. 1951-54), N.J. (pres. 1953-56, mem. exec. bd. 1957—), N.Y., Empire State classical assns., Am. Classical League (mem. elective council 1959-65), Montclair Bus. and Profl. Women (pres. 1963-65), N.J. Bus and Profl. Women's Club (personal devel. chmn. state bd. 1965), Am. Philol. Assn. Contbr. book revs. to profl. jours. Home: 204 Berkeley Av Bloomfield NJ 07003

DONOGHUE, ELIZABETH MARION MACMAHON (MRS. FLORENCE JOSEPH DONOGHUE), mus. curator; b. Castleisland, Kerry, Ireland, Nov. 9, 1896 (parents Am. citizens); d. James and Johanna Mary (Brosnan) MacMahon; B.A., Calvin Coolidge Coll., 1955, M.A., 1956; m. Florence Joseph Donoghue, Apr. 17, 1963 (dec. July 1970). Accountant, Boston Wool Trade, 1914-33; tchr., Everett (Mass.) High Sch., 1934-63; trustee Wenham (Mass.) Hist. Assn. and Mus., Inc., 1956—, curator dolls, 1960—. Driver, Red Cross Motor Corps, Boston, 1939-41, Civilian Def. Motor Corps, Everett, 1941-43. Mem. Antique Toy Collectors Am., Doll Club Gt. Britain, Doll Collectors Am., Emerald Isle, L.I., Ginny doll clubs, League Cath. Women, Mus. Fine Arts Boston, Nat. Ret. Tchrs. Assn., United Fedn. Doll Clubs, Am. Irish Hist. Soc. (life), Christ Child Soc. (life), Soc. Preservation N.E. Antiquities (life), Yesteryears Doll Mus. (life), Eire Soc. Boston (life, editor Bull. 1954-64), Worcester Art Mus., Boston U. Alumni Assn. Contbr. articles to profl. jours. Home: 86 Bradford St Everett MA 02149 Office: 132 Main St Wenham MA 01984

DONOGHUE, MILDRED RANSDORF (MRS. CHARLES DONOGHUE), educator; b. Cleve., Mar. 14, 1929; d. James and Caroline (Sychra) Ransdorf; B.A., U. Mich., 1948; M.A., U. Detroit, 1951; Ed.D., U. Cal. at Los Angeles, 1962; m. Charles Donoghue, July 31, 1948; children—Kathleen, James. Tchr. elementary classroom, Downey, Cal., 1954-59; teaching asst. U. Cal. at Los Angeles, 1960-61, research asst., 1960-61; instr. Immaculate Heart Coll., Los Angeles, 1961-62; asst. prof. edn. Cal. State U., Fullerton, 1962-66, asso. prof., 1966-71, prof., 1971—. Cons. various sch. dists. Mem. Long Beach Regional Arts Council, 1967—. Mem. Nat. Council Tchrs. English, Am. Dialect Soc., Am. Council on Tchrs. of Fgn. Langs., Assn. for Higher Edn., Am. Ednl. Research Assn., Am. Assn. U. Profs., Nat. Soc. for Study Edn., Am. Assn. Tchrs. Spanish and Portuguese, Internat. Reading Assn., Nat. Assn. for Edn. of Young Children, Los Angeles County Med. Assn. Women's Aux., Phi Beta Kappa, Phi Kappa Phi, Pi Lambda Theta. Author: Foreign Languages and the Schools, 1967; Foreign Languages and the Elementary School Child, 1968; The Child and the English Language Arts, 1971. Contbr. articles to profl. jours.

DONOHOE, VICTORIA THERESE, artist and art critic; b. Phila., Mar. 21, 1929; d. Daniel Joseph and Anne (O'Neill) Donohoe; B.A., Rosemont Coll., 1950; M.F.A. (Scholar), U. Pa., 1952; postgrad. scholar Pius XII Inst. Fine Arts Grad. Sch., Florence, Italy. Instr. Rosemont Coll. Art Dept., 1950-52, 54-55; columnist art criticism Standard and Times, Phila., 1959-62; columnist art criticism Phila. Inquirer, 1962—; exhibited group shows, Florence, Italy, Sons of Italy Bldg., and Woodmere Art Gallery, Phila.; represented in permanent collections Villanova (Pa.) U., Merrimack (Mass.) Coll., St. Joseph's Coll., Phila., Holy Child High Curia bldg. Fiesole, Italy, Vatican Library, Rome, also many pvt. collections. Co-chmn. Nat. Juried Liturgical Art Exhibit Phila. Civic Center, 1963. Mem. Phila. Archdiocesan Commn. on Sacred Liturgy, 1972—. Am. Fedn. Arts grantee, 1968. Mem. Pa. Acad. Fine Arts, Phila. Mus. Art, The America-Italy Soc., Mediaeval Acad. Am., Hist. Soc. Pa., Delta Epsilon Sigma (chpt. pres. 1958-66), Soc. Archtl. Historians, Irish Georgian Soc., Geneal. Soc. Pa., Met. Mus. Art, Fairmount Park Art Assn., Mus. Modern Art, U. Pa. Mus. Contbr. to book on outdoor Sculpture in Phila., 1973, also to nat. mags. and publs. Address: 34 Narbrook Park Narberth PA 19072

DONOHUE, AGNES KATHERINE MCNEILL, educator; b. Sheboygan, Wis., Sept. 17, 1917; d. Harry Thomas and Luella (Weinberger) McNeill; B.A., Rosary Coll., 1939; M.A., U. Wis., 1940; Ph.D., Loyola U., Chgo., 1954; m. John Donohue, Aug. 19, 1944 (div. Oct. 1949). Instr. U. Minn., Mpls., 1945-46, U. Ill., Chgo., 1946-54; mem. faculty Barat Coll., 1948-65, prof. English, 1954-63, chmn. dept., 1954-65; prof. English, Loyola U., Chgo., 1965—. Mem. Am. Assn. U. Profs., Modern Lang. Assn., Nat. Council Tchrs. English. Roman Catholic. Author: Casebook on Hawthorne Question, 1962; Casebook on Grapes of Wrath, 1968. Contbr. articles to profl. jours. Home: 1111 Hull Terrace Evanston IL 60202 Office: Loyola U 6525 N Sheridan St Chicago IL 60626

DONOVAN, AILEEN MARTIN WORTHINGTON (MRS. ALFRED D. DONOVAN), lawyer; b. Harrison, Ark., June 26, 1914; d. Joseph Arliss and Aileen (Martin) Worthington; student Coll. St. Elizabeth, 1931-33; LL.B., Fordham U., 1936; m. Alfred Dean Donovan, Aug. 12, 1939; children—Alfred Dean, James Joseph. Admitted to N.J. bar, 1937; asso. Proctor & Nary, Asbury Park, N.J., 1936-39; asso. Ralph H. Jacobson, Maple Wood, N.J., 1957-60, Melville J. Berlow, Newark, 1960-66; mem. firm Oransky, Donovan & Scaraggi, East Orange, N.J., 1966—. Mem. South Orange (N.J.) Bd. Edn., 1964-70. Mem. Essex County, N.J. bar assns. Republican. Roman Catholic. Home: 117 Fairview Av South Orange NJ 07079 Office: 377 S Harrison St East Orange NJ 07018

DONOVAN, EILEEN ROBERTA, ambassador; b. Boston, Apr. 13, 1915; d. William Francis and Mary (Barry) Donovan; grad. Girls Latin Sch., Boston, 1932; B.S. in Edn., Boston Tchrs. Coll., 1936, Ed.M., 1937; student Sch. Mil. Govt., U. Va., also Civil Affairs Tng. Sch. U. Mich., 1944-45; M. Pub. Administrn. (Fgn. Service Inst. fellow 1956), Harvard, 1957; L.H.D., Boston State U., 1973. Tchr. history, pub. schs. of Boston, 1938-43; fgn. service officer Dept. State, 1948—; 2d sec., vice consul Office U.S. Polit. Adviser, Tokyo, Japan, 1948-49; staff Bur. Far Eastern Affairs, Japan-Korea Pub. Affairs, 1949-52; State Dept. mem. Ednl. Exchange Survey Mission to Japan, summer 1949; 2d sec., polit. officer Am. Embassy, Manila, P.I., 1952-54; econ. officer U.S. Consulate Gen., Milan, Italy, 1954-56; chief So. Europe br. Bur. Intelligence and Research, Dept. State, 1957-59, sr. seminar in fgn. policy, 1959; prin. officer, Am. Consul, Barbados, W.I., 1960-62, U.S. consul gen. Barbados and The Windward and Leeward Islands, W.I., 1962-65, dep. dir. Office Caribbean Affairs, 1965-69; ambassador E. and P., Barbados, 1969—; U.S. spl. rep. to Antigua, Dominica, Grenada, St. Christopher-Nevis-Anguilla; St. Lucia, St. Vincent, 1969—. Served to capt. WAC, 1943-46; civilian adv. Japanese women's and secondary edn. to Supreme Comdr. Allied Powers, Tokyo, 1946-48. Recipient Fed. Woman's award, 1969. Mailing address: US Embassy care US NAVFAC FPO New York City NY 09553 Office: US Embassy Bridgetown Barbados West Indies

DONOVAN, EMMA LEE (MRS. ROBERT H. DONOVAN), bank exec.; b. Cisco, Tex., July 5, 1928; d. Gus E. and Emma Lee (Neiman) Wende; student Nixon-Clay Comml. Coll., 1948, Southwestern Grad. Sch. Banking, 1973—; m. Robert H. Donovan, June 12, 1957. With First Nat. Bank, Cisco, 1948—, v.p., 1969—. Sec., March of Dimes, Cisco, 1952-56, Community Chest, Cisco, 1950-54; life mem. Lion's Crippled Children's Camp, Kerrville, Tex., 1964—. Home: Rural Route 3 PO Box 746 Cisco TX 76437 Office: 710 Av D PO Box 1220 Cisco TX 76437

DONOVAN, KATHRYN MARY, librarian; b. Phila., Nov. 24, 1935; d. Francis J. and Mary H. (Dixon) Donovan; B.A., Eastern Coll., 1957; M.S., Drexel U., 1958. Librarian I, Free Library Phila., 1958-59; reference librarian Pennwalt Corp., King of Prussia, Pa., 1959-67, librarian, 1967—. Mem. Am. Chem. Soc., Spl. Libraries Assn. Office: 900 1st Av King of Prussia PA 19406

DONOVAN, MARGARET MARY MACDONELL (MRS. DANIEL JOSEPH DONOVAN), educator; b. Pitts., Dec. 18, 1936; d. Alan Miles and Rachel Beatrice (Van Alystyne) MacDonell; B.S., Marywood Coll., 1958; M.S., So. Conn. State Coll., 1970, postgrad., 1970—; m. Daniel Joseph Donovan, Aug. 22, 1964; 1 adopted son, John M. Tchr. pub. sch., Silver Spring, Md., 1958-59; tchr. mentally retarded Kolburne Sch., Norwalk, Conn., 1959-63, Stamford (Conn.) Pub. Schs., 1963-67; tchr. children with learning disabilities Easton (Conn.) Pub. Schs., 1968—; founder, owner, dir. Glen Mar Home for Boys, Bethlehem, Conn., 1965—. Mem. Am. Assn. Mental Deficiency, N.E.A., Conn., Easton edn. assns., Marywood Alumnae Assn. (pres. Conn. chpt. 1967), Cath. Women's Guild. Roman Catholic. Home: Box 191 Main St Bethlehem CT 06751 Office: 276 Center Rd Easton CT 06612

DONOVAN, RUTH HADLEY (MRS. RICHARD T. DONOVAN), univ. librarian; b. Lincoln, Neb., Dec. 1, 1927; d. Thomas Fredric and Emma Johanna (Reno) Hadley; B.A., U. Wis., 1949, B.L.S., 1950; m. Richard T. Donovan, Dec. 16, 1956; children—Thomas Joseph, Scott Richard. Asst. social studies and documents librarian U. Neb. Libraries, Lincoln, 1950-54; reference librarian U. Nev. Libraries, Reno, 1954-62, asst. dir., 1962-63, 69—, acting serials librarian, 1964, bibliographer, 1967-69. Mem. adv. bd., mem. subcom. on finance Ret. Sr. Vol. Program, Reno, 1973—; mem. Nev. Opera Guild, 1970-72. Mem. Am., Nev. library assns., Am. Assn. U. Women (v.p. 1956-57), Common Cause, Beta Phi Mu, Phi Kappa Phi, Sigma Epsilon Sigma. Home: Box 8352 University Station Reno NV 89507

DONOVAN TOBER, BARBARA STARKEY (MRS. DONALD GIBBS TOBER), editor; b. Summit, N.J., Aug. 19, 1934; d. Rodney Fielding and Maud (Grebbin) Starkey; student Traphagen Sch. Fashion, 1954-56, Fashion Inst. Tech., 1956-58, N.Y. Sch. Interior Design, 1964. Food editor Look mag., 1957; copy editor Vogue Pattern Book, 1958-60; asso. beauty editor Vogue, 1961; dir. womens services Bartell Media Corp., 1961-66; editor-in-chief Bride's Mag., N.Y.C., 1966—; mem. fashion therapy com. Manhattan State Mental Hosp.; mem. adv. bd. Lab. Inst. Merchandising, 1970—. Recipient ALMA award, 1968, Penney-Mo. award, 1972. Mem. Wine and Food Soc., Fashion Group, Cosmetic Career Women, Nat. Home Fashions League, Nat. Council on Family Relations, Am. Soc. Mag. Editors, Pan Pacific and S.E. Asia Womens Assn., Asia Soc., Intercorporate Group, Am. Women in Radio and TV, Nat. Assn. TV Arts and Scis., Nat. Soc. Interior Designers, Am. Inst. Interior Designers, Met. Mus. Art, Mus. Modern Art, Museum Contemporary Crafts. Author: The ABC's of Beauty, 1963. Home: 215 E 68th St New York City NY 10021 Office: 350 Madison Av New York City NY 10017

DOOCY, MADONNA EILEEN, educator; b. Swea City, Ia., Nov. 17, 1934; d. James Howard and Harriet J. (Jensen) Doocy; B.A., Marylhurst Coll., 1959; M.F.A., U. Portland, 1968. Head fine arts dept. St. Mary of Valley High Sch., Beaverton, Ore., 1966-70; head drama dept. La Salle High Sch., Milwaukie, Ore., 1971—, Mt. Hood Community Coll., Bresem, Ore. Roman Catholic. Home: 2943 SE Alder St Portland OR 97214

DOODY, AGNES GRACE (MRS. ARTHUR D. JEFFREY), educator; b. New Haven, Apr. 12, 1930; d. Daniel M. and Carrie (Goodrich) Doody; B.A., Emerson Coll., 1952; M.A., Pa. State U., 1954, Ph.D., 1961; m. Arthur David Jeffrey, Dec. 22, 1962; stepchildren—Drew, Jill. Instr., Genesco (N.Y.) State Coll., 1956-57; mem. faculty U. R.I., Kingston, 1958—, chmn. dept. speech, 1967-74, now prof. speech. Mem. Speech Communication Assn., Eastern Communication Assn. (exec. com. 1967-69, 1st v.p. 1974), New Eng. Speech Assn. (treas. 1966-67, 1st v.p. 1967-68, pres. 1968-69), Am. Forensic Assn., R.I. Speech and Hearing Assn., Nat. Wildlife Fedn., Save-the-Redwood League, Tau Kappa Alpha. Asso. editor Today's Speech, 1968-70. Home: 1 Post Rd Wakefield RI 02879 Office: U RI Kingston RI 02881

DOOLEY, BEATRICE STOUT (MRS. JOHN F. DOOLEY), social worker; b. Seattle, Sept. 4, 1913; d. John W. and Beatrice (Edson) Stout; A.B., U. Cal. at Berkeley, 1935, postgrad., 1943-45; m. John F. Dooley, Mar. 6, 1956; 1 dau., Beatrice (Mrs. Leon Lindberg). Social worker State of Cal., Oakland, 1937-43; chief psychiat. social worker VA, Santa Barbara, Cal., 1945-53, Mental Health Dept., Ventura, Cal., 1953-64; supervising psychiat. social worker Community Services Dept., State Dept. of Health, Ventura, 1964—. Commr. Community Action Comm., 1967-69. Bd. dirs. Ventura County Community Council, Ventura County Mental Health Assn. Mem. Nat. Assn. Social Workers. Democrat. Unitarian. Home: 1496 Brodica Av Ventura CA 93001 Office: 3418 Loma Vista Rd Ventura CA 93003

DOOLEY, DOROTHY COFFEY (MRS. ROBERT P. DOOLEY), ins. co. exec.; b. Sandy Level, Va., Sept. 29, 1913; d. Edgar Littleton and Sadie Lillian (Clements) Coffey; B.A., Va. Comml. Coll., 1929-30; m. Edmun Bruce Lemon, Sept. 17, 1931 (div.); children—Eleanor (Mrs. Gary R.M. Lattimore), Carolyn (Mrs. Noel Phillip Beach), Richard Douglas; m. 2d, Robert Price Dooley, Nov. 17, 1972. Accounting sales dept. Craddock-Terry Shoe Corp., Lynchburg, Va., 1931-39; secretarial, accounting Sam Finley, Inc., Roanoke, Va., 1939-44, J.H. Pence Co., Roanoke, 1955-61; with Estate Life Ins. Co. of Am., Roanoke, 1962—, asst. treas., 1963—. Pres., P.T.A., 1955-56. Baptist. Home: 2761 Diplomat Dr NW Roanoke VA 24019 Office: 1314 S Jefferson St Roanoke VA 24009

DOOLEY, FAY STUART (MRS. ORANDO R. DOOLEY), curator; b. Peshtigo, Wis., July 1, 1914; d. William Thomas and Mattie (Ream) Stuart; m. Harold R. Janzen, Aug. 19, 1933 (dec. Oct. 1955); 1 son, Douglas M.; m. 2d, Orando R. Dooley, Apr. 5, 1958. Curator I, Old Wade House, Greenbush, Wis., 1956-68, curator II Old Wade House and Carriage Museum, Greenbush, Wis., 1968—. Cons. Wis. history U. Wis. at Oshkosh, 1966. Pres., Peshtigo Hist. Cemetery Assn., 1948—. Mem. Wis., Pehtigo, Marinette County (past sec.) hist. socs., Ream Family Assn., Ream Family Hist. Soc., Marinette County Fedn. Women's Clubs (past sec.). Methodist. Club: Women's (Kohler, Wis.). Contbr. articles to profl. jours. Home: 621 Pine Tree Rd Kohler WI 53044 Office: Old Wade House State Park Greenbush WI 53026

DOOLEY, FRANCES JOELLEN (MRS. EMMETT FRANCIS DOOLEY), librarian; b. Wichita Falls, Tex., Sept. 5, 1920; d. Daniel Fletcher and Fanny Elizabeth (Robinson) Luce; B.A., U. Ore., 1949; M.A., U. Denver, 1959; postgrad. U. Cal. at Los Angeles, U. Cal. at Riverside, U. Alaska, Incarnate Word Coll.; m. Emmett Francis Dooley, Sept. 10, 1941; children—Dennis Michael, James Donald, Timothy Daniel, Mark Stephen. Tchr. country sch., Wichita Falls, 1939-41; librarian Riverside Sch. Dist., 1961-65, Tex. Mil. Inst., San Antonio, 1966-68; librarian, head pub. services Riverside City Coll., 1968—. Chmn. profl. growth and sabbatical leave com. Riverside City Coll., 1973-75, mem. Acad. Senate, 1973-75. Mem. Cal., Alaska library assns., Cal. Tchrs. Assn., Faculty Assn. Cal. Community Colls., U. Denver Alumni Assn., Delta Kappa Gamma. So. Baptist. Home: 415 W Highland Av Redlands CA 92373 Office: 4800 Magnolia Riverside CA 92506

DOOLEY, MARIE LOUISE BOYETT, ednl. adminstr.; b. Bryan, Tex.; d. Oran H. and Mary (Mitchell) Boyett; B.S., Tex. Woman's U., 1954, M.S. in Home Econs. Edn., 1956; M.Ed., East Tex. State U., 1961, Ed.D., 1972; m. James C. Dooley, May 5, 1942 (div. Nov. 1966); children—Bobby Curtis, Marilu. Tchr. home econs. Garland Ind. Sch. Dist., 1954-55; tchr. home econs. Richardson Ind. Sch. Dist., 1955-60, counselor, 1958-66; dir. div. drug edn. Tex. Edn. Agy., Austin, 1967—. Mem. Am., Tex. (pub. relations com. 1966) personnel and guidance assns., Am. (membership chmn. 1966, 67), Tex. (pres. 1966-67, exec. bd. 1967) sch. counselors assns., Richardson Edn. Assn. (pres. 1957-58), Tex. Tchrs. Assn., Am. Vocational Assn., North Central Tex. Vocational Guidance Assn. (sec. 1963), Am., Tex. home econs. assns., Phi Sigma Alpha (chpt. charter mem.). Methodist. Club: Altrusa Internat. (chpt. charter mem.). Home: 3 Sugar Shack Austin TX 78746 Office: Tex Edn Agy 201 E 11th St Austin TX 78701

DOOLEY, MURIEL CORNELIA JOHNSON (MRS. ROBERT LEE DOOLEY), occupational therapist; b. Spokane, Wash., Aug. 16, 1944; d. Albert A. and Eliza Mae (Mathews) Johnson; B.S., Ind. U., 1966; certificate prostheticorthotic edn. Northwestern U., 1969; m. Robert Lee Dooley, June 25, 1967; children—Prudence Ann, Daphne Christine. Supr. occupational therapy dept. Holy Cross Hosp., Chgo., 1966-69; occupational therapist Vis. Nurse Assn. Chgo., 1969-71; sr. occupational therapist Cook County Hosp., Chgo., 1971-74; mem. faculty occupational therapy Colo. State U., Ft. Collins, 1974—. Trainee, Tex. Women's U., 1973. Vol. Operation Push, 1972-74; sec. to bd. Community Health Center Englewood, Chgo., 1973. Mem. Ill. Occupational Therapy Assn. (sec. 1971-73). Home: Aggie Village 16-E Fort Collins CO 80521

DOOLIN, SUE ANNE, coll. dean; b. Springfield, Ill., June 27, 1943; d. Timothy Stuart and Elizabeth Sue (Reid) Doolin; B.A., So. Ill. U., 1970, M.A., 1972; postgrad. U. Ia. Elementary tchr. Sacred Heart Sch., Effingham, Ill., 1967; tchr. St. Paul's Jr. High Sch., Highland, Ill., 1968-71; instr. sociology Radford (Va.) Coll., 1971-72; dean women Mt. Mercy Coll., Cedar Rapids, Ia., 1972-74; dean students Waukegan (Ill.) High Sch., 1974—. Mem. Nat., Ia. edn. assns., Midwest Sociological Assn., Nat. Assn. Women Adminstrs., Deans and Counselors, Am. Personnel and Guidance Assn. Democrat. Roman Catholic. Home: 2801 Grandville Ct Apt 109 Waukegan IL 60085 Office: 2325 Brookside St Waukegan IL 60085

DOOLITTLE, DORTHA BAILEY (MRS. ARTHUR K. DOOLITTLE), chemist, educator; b. Oberlin, O., Apr. 16, 1896; d. George Beamon and Elizabeth (Merthe) Bailey; A.B., Oberlin Coll., 1918, Charles M. Hall fellow, 1944-45; postgrad. U. Mich., summer 1918; M.S., U. Ill., 1920; postgrad. (Ellen Richards fellow) Mass. Inst. Tech., 1921-22; m. Arthur King Doolittle, Aug. 8, 1923; children—Robert Frederick II, Elizabeth (Mrs. Donald Charles Peckham). Instr., Oberlin Coll., 1918-19, U. Ill., 1919-21; prof. Oxford Coll. for Women, 1922-23; research asst. Yale, 1923-24; instr. Barnard Coll., Columbia, 1925-26, 27-28, Dearborn Morgan Sch., 1928-31; prof. Kanawha Coll., 1932-39; asso. prof. Morris Harvey Coll., 1939-54; research asst. Union Carbide Chem. Co., 1954-58; asso. prof. W.Va. Inst. Tech., 1958-62; adj. prof. chemistry. Drexel Inst. Tech., 1962-65, asst. prof. Widener Coll. (formerly PMC Colls.), Chester, Pa., 1965-70, emeritus, 1970—. Trustee Arcadia Inst. for Sci. Research, 1959—; pres. Alumni Class, Oberlin Coll., 1963-68, exec. com. class and club presdl. council, also mem. alumni bd., 1967-70, class agt., 1970—. Mem. Am. Assn. U. Women (pres. Charleston 1938-39), Am. Chem. Soc. (nat. council 1950-59), Am. Assn. UN (v.p. 1957-58), Phi Beta Kappa (pres. Charleston 1939-40), Sigma Xi, Iota Sigma Pi, Chi Beta Phi, Delta Kappa Gamma. Author profl. publs. Home: 406 Osborne Lane Wallingford PA 19086 Office: Kirkbride Hall Widener Coll Chester PA

DOORLY, RUTH KIDDER (MRS. PAUL H. DOORLY), educator; b. Somerville, Mass., Oct. 7, 1919; d. Walter G. and Mabel (Seavey) Kidder; A.B., Wheaton Coll. (Norton, Mass.), 1942; Ed.M., Northeastern U., 1962; m. Paul H. Doorly, Aug. 4, 1943. Home tchr. Westwood (Mass.) Sch. Dept., 1950-57, educable class tchr., 1958-64, trainable class tchr., 1964—. Mem. Westwood Art Assn., Friends Westwood Library. Named Mass. Tchr. of Year, Mass. Dept. Edn., 1969. Mem. Westwood, Mass. tchrs. assns., Westwood Hist. Soc. (treas. 1967-69), South Norfolk Assn. Retarded Children, Council Exceptional Children, Old Dedham Wheaton Club, Wheaton Alumnae Assn., Author: Our Jimmy, 1967 (first book on child's level explaining retardation). Home: 46 Churchill Rd Westwood MA 02090 Office: High Sch Nahatan St Westwood MA 02090

DORAN, MADELEINE, educator; b. Salt Lake City, Aug. 12, 1905; d. Frank and Nellie May (Kunkel) Doran; student San Diego State Coll., 1923-25; B.A., Stanford, 1927, Ph.D. (univ. fellow 1928-30), 1930; M.A., U. Ia., 1928; postgrad. Univ. Coll., U. London, 1933; D.Litt. (hon.) Wheaton Coll. (Mass.), 1963. Instr. English, Wellesley Coll., 1930-33, Mary Whiton Calkins vis. prof., 1957; instr. English, U. Wis., 1935-39, asst. prof., 1939-47, asso. prof., 1947-51, prof., 1951-67, Ruth C. Wallerstein prof. English lit., 1967—, mem. Humanities Inst., 1970—; vis. prof. Stanford, spring 1960; grantee Huntington Library, winters 1960, 64; fellow Folger Shakespeare Library, Spring 1964. Guggenheim fellow, 1967-68. Fellow Am. Council Learned Socs., 1933-34, Am. Assn. U. Women, 1946-47. Fellow Am. Acad. Arts and Scis., mem. Modern Lang. Assn. Am. (exec. council 1964-67), Am. Assn. U. Women, Shakespeare Assn. Am., Renaissance Soc. Am. (mem. council 1963-64, 67-70), Malone Soc., Am. Assn. U. Profs., Internat. Assn. U. Profs. English, Nature Conservancy, Friend U. Wis. Arboretum, Friends Elvehjem Art Center U. Wis., Friend Folger Library, Friend Huntington Library, Phi Beta Kappa. Author: Books 2, 3, Henry VI: Their Relation to the Contention and the True Tragedy, 1928; The Text of King Lear, 1931; Endeavors of Art: A Study of Form in Elizabethan Drama, 1954; Something about Swans: Essays, 1973; Time's Foot: Poems, 1974. Editor: If You Know Not Me (by Thomas Heywood), 1934; A Midsummer Night's Dream, Shakespeare, 1959. Contbr. articles, revs. on Shakespeare, Elizabethan drama, Renaissance in learned jours. Office: Dept of English U Wis 600 N Park St Madison WI 53706

DORBECKER, DORIS LORENE, state legislator; b. nr. Kiester, Minn., June 21, 1919; d. Terrence O. and Agnes (McCullough) Phipps; grad. high sch.; m. Orville E. Dorbecker, Jan. 19, 1946; children—Robert E., Jeneil A. Mem. Ind. Ho. of Reps., 1968-74, chmn. elections, 1970—. Mem. Marion County Library Bd., 1966-69; mem. Indpls. Sesquicentennial Commn., 1971. Mem. Indpls. Mayor's Task Force Women. Vice-precinct Committeeman Republican party, 1952-67; del. Rep. state conv., 1962-70. Bd. dirs. Ind. Kidney Found. Served with Waves, USNR, 1943-44. Mem. Am. Legion (charter post) Home: 409 Mellowood Dr Indianapolis IN 46217

DORDET, MATILDA STEUART, art gallery adminstr., artist; b. Montclair, N.J., June 16, 1901; d. James Law and Sarah (Bartow) Steuart; student Sorbonne, U. Paris, Paris art studios, 1923-25; m. Albert Robert Dordet, July 17, 1927 (dec. May 1953). Founder Fantasy Gallery (now F.G. Art Investment Corp.), Washington, 1953, pres., 1953—; v.p. Venable Galleries, Washington, 1970—. Exhibited in group shows at Salon des Femmes Françaises, Paris, Nat. Arts Club, N.Y.C.; represented in pvt. collections. Home: 2122 Massachusetts Av Washington DC 20008 Office: 1742 Connecticut Av Washington DC 20009

DORENKEMPER, CATHERINE ANN FRANK (MRS. CARL J. DORENKEMPER), constrn. co. exec.; b. Mpls., July 4, 1912; d. Guy O. and May A. (McGinnis) Frank; student Coll. St. Teresa, 1931-32, Minot State Tchrs. Coll., 1932-33, U. N.D., 1933-35 U. Minn., 1935-36. Office mgr. Farmers Home Adminstrn., Minot, N.D., 1938-52; corp. sec. Dory Builders, Inc., Mpls., 1965—, Gridor Constrn., Inc., Mpls., 1969—. Home: 6541 Golden Valley Rd Minneapolis MN 55427 Office: 5440 Douglas Dr Minneapolis MN 55429

DOREY, LEONA PIXLEY, psychologist; b. Otter Lake, N.Y., Apr. 19, 1918; d. Stanley Jay and Louise Jackson (Peling) Pixley; R.N., Utica State Hosp. Sch., 1941; B.S., St. Lawrence U., 1962; M.A., Syracuse U., 1964; m. John James Dorey, Feb. 11, 1942 (dec. Jan. 1961); children—John Patrick, Kathleen Ann. Staff nurse Utica (N.Y.) State Hosp., 1941-42; sch. psychologist Bd. of Coop. Ednl. Services, Onondaga County, N.Y., 1964-74; sch. psychologist Ithaca (N.Y.) Sch. Dist., 1974—. mem. staff St. Joseph's Hosp., Out Patient Psychiat. Clinic, 1965-74. Mem. Nat. Assn. Sch. Psychologists, Am. Psychol. Assn., Delta Kappa Gamma, Psi Chi. Home: 354 Horton Rd Newfield NY 14867 Office: Central Elementary Sch Ithaca NY 14850

DORFELD, KATHARINE MAUD PERRY (MRS. HERBERT ALLEN DORFELD), psychiat. social worker; b. Bradford, Pa., July 27, 1909; d. Lytle Flower and Eugenia Celina (Benson) Perry; B.A., Sweet Briar Coll., 1931; M. Social Sci., Western Res. U., 1933; m. Herbert Allen Dorfeld, June 25, 1938; 1 son, William Gurney. Caseworker, Inst. Family Service, Cleve., 1933-34, dist. asst., 1934-37; supr. Dept. Pub. Assistance, Coudersport, Pa., 1937-38; psychiat. social work, supt. Coudersport br. officer Ridgway (Pa.) Area Psychiat. Clinic, 1958-73; dir. dept. community mental health Charles Cole Meml. Hosp., Coudersport, 1973—. Exec. sec. Potter County Tb and Health Soc., 1944-56; pres. Potter County Health Council, 1968—; mem. bd. Coudersport Pub. Library, 1952—, Northwestern Tb and Health Soc., 1968—. Mem. commonwealth com. Women's Med. Coll., Phila. Recipient Benjamin Rush award Potter County Med. Soc., 1949. Mem. Nat. Assn. Social Workers, Acad. Certified Social Workers, Potter County Hist. Soc., Coudersport Bus. and Profl. Women's Club (v.p. 1958-59, 68—, pres. 1959-60), D.A.R. Episcopalian (pres. Church Women 1952-53). Home: 203 Allegany Av Coudersport PA 16915 Office: Charles Cole Meml Hosp Coudersport PA 16915

DORFMAN, MARTA CRYSTAL (MRS. JOSEPH B. DORFMAN), lawyer; b. N.Y.C., May 15, 1916; d. Isidore and Bella G. (Gerber) Crystal; A.A., John Marshall Coll., 1935, LL.B., Coll. Law, 1938; m. Joseph B. Dorfman, July 25, 1937; children—Ilene, Barry. Admitted to N.J. bar, 1940; asso. Abraham Lightdale, Jersey City, 1940-42; individual practice law, North Bergen, N.J., 1942-50; asso. Louis Silver, Jersey City, 1950-56; trial atty. Porter & Clark, Newark, 1956-59; mng. atty. Motor Club Am. Ins. Co., Newark, 1959—, also mem. adv. bd. of co. and subsidiaries. Pres., P.T.A., Yeshiva of Hudson County, 1948-50. Mem. Am., N.J., Essex County bar assns., Am. Judicature Soc., Am. Arbitration Assn. (panel arbitrators). Home: 86 Church St Teaneck NJ 07666 Office: 484 Central Av Newark NJ 07107

DORFMANN, ANIA, pianist, tchr.; b. Odessa, Russia (came to U.S. 1936); degree Paris (France) Conservatory. Tchr., Paris; concert appearances Lieges, Belgium, Paris, London, Eng., throughout Europe; Am. debut, 1936; mem. numerous Am. symphony orchs., also played under Toscanini, 1939, 42, 45, rec. Beethoven C major piano concerto, 1945; tours South Am.; mem. faculty, mus. adviser N.Y. Coll. Music; mem. faculty piano Juilliard Sch. Music, N.Y.C., 1966—; master classes, mus. adviser Stephens Coll., Mo. Office: Juilliard Sch Music 120 Claremont Av New York City NY 10027

DORMAN, BARBARA BRADY (MRS. STUART CALLENDER DORMAN), editor; b. Chgo., Aug. 22, 1923; d. Lawrence Belser and Olive (Klipstein) Brady; student Mt. Vernon Sem., 1939-40, U. Tex., 1940-43; m. Stuart Callender Dorman, Feb. 1, 1944; 1 son, Lawrence Brady. Women's dept. writer Corpus Christi (Tex.) Caller-Times, 1943, spl. feature writer, 1944; N.Y. fashion cor. Dallas Morning News, Corpus Christi Caller-Times, 1948-54; editor Suffolk Times, Greenport, N.Y., 1969—. Corr., On the Sound mag., 1971—. Chmn., Suffolk County chpt. Nat. Multiple Sclerosis Soc., 1961-62; pres. Jr. League North Shore, 1963-65; sec., dir. Suffolk Community Council, 1965-67. Recipient award for best news story N.Y. Press Assn., 1970. Mem. D.A.R., Middle Atlantic Marine Sci. Assn. (dir.), Theta Sigma Phi, Pi Beta Phi. Republican. Roman Catholic. Home: Private Rd Orient NY 11957 Office: 429 Main St Greenport NY 11944

DORN, NATALIE BOROKHOVICH (MRS. ROBERT M. DORN), civic worker; b. N.Y.C.; d. John A. and Marianna (Tresenberg) Borokhovich; student Bklyn. Coll., 1937-40, Pepperdine Coll., 1969-70; m. Ed Reid, July 31, 1938 (div. Apr. 1963); children—Michael John, Douglas Paul; m. 2d, Robert M. Dorn, Nov. 28, 1964. Conover Cover Girl, N.Y.C., 1940-54; TV-radio weekly charm columnist Westchester Recorder, 1954-59; sportswear mgr., buyer Joseph Magnin, Las Vegas, 1959-61; partner Dateline Las Vegas, pub. relations, 1961-62; exec. v.p. Clark County Mental Health Assn., 1961-63; partner, cons. Personnel Placement: Employment Agy. and Convention Coordinator, Las Vegas, 1961-63; account exec. John A. Tetley Co., Los Angeles, 1963-65. Chmn. community health Los Angeles Med. Assn. Aux., 1968-69, chmn. publs. Dist. 5, 1970-71, 2d v.p., program chmn., 1972—; hospitality com. Greek Theatre, 1969—; ednl. chmn. Hollywood Wing, Greek Theatre Assn., 1965—; co-founder Child Abuse Listening Line, 1973. Bd. dirs. Castellmare Mesa Home Owners Assn. Home: 227 Quadro Vecchio Dr Pacific Palisades CA 90272

DORNBUSH, RHEA L., behavioral scientist, educator; b. N.Y.C.; d. Barnett and Betty (Shore) Dornbush; B.A., Queens Coll., 1962, M.A., 1963; Ph.D., City U. N.Y., 1967. Pre-doctoral research fellow Nat. Inst. Mental Health, Queens Coll., Flushing, N.Y., 1964-65; lectr., teaching fellow, research asso., research asst. psychology, 1963-65; asst. prof., lectr. psychology Rutgers U., New Brunswick, N.J., 1965-68; asst. prof. psychiatry N.Y. Med. Coll., 1968-73, asso. prof. psychiatry, 1973—. Mem. Am. Assn. U. Profs., A.A.A.S., Am., Eastern psychol. assns., N.Y. Acad. Sci., Psychonomic Soc., Sigma Xi, Psi Chi. Contbr. articles to profl. jours. Office: 5 E 102d St New York City NY 10029

DORNEY, CATHRYN LAURENTIA KELLY, assn. exec.; b. Sag Harbor, N.Y.; d. Joseph Daniel and Mary Angela (Farmer) Kelly; grad. Maxwell Tng. Sch., Bklyn; student Cortland State U., summers 1928, 29, 31; B.S. in Edn., Fordham U., 1963, postgrad. in guidance and counseling, 1965—; m. James Maurice Dorney, Apr. 7, 1928 (dec. Apr. 1952). Tchr. brs. N.Y.C. Pub. schs.; tchr. health edn., acting chmn. dept. Bushwick High Sch., Bklyn, 1935-42; tchr. health edn. Erasmus Hall High Sch., Bklyn., 1942-71, ret.; exec. dir. Am. Edn. Assn., N.Y.C., 1957—. Actress, Shakespearean repertory, schs., N.Y.C., Tibbets Brook Park, Yonkers, N.Y., Summer Theatre, Saddle River, N.J., 1934-42. Recipient Spl. Edn. citation Queens County Cath. War Vets., 1961, Felicity Buranelli Citizenship medal, 1963, Congress of Freedom award, 1971, 72. Mem. Am. Edn. Assn. (pres. 1954-56), Nat. Soc. Patriotic Women, Third Order St. Francis, Reading Reform Found., Oriel Soc. Flushing, N.Y. and St. Augustine, Fla., Nat. Com. to Free Captive Nations (participant essay contest, celebration N.Y.C. 1960). Editor: Ednl. Signpost 1954-70, columnist. Office: Am Edn Assn 663 Fifth Av New York City NY 10022

DOROTHY, LOU ANN (MRS. MORTON F. DOROTHY, JR.), lawyer; b. Mt. Vernon, Ill., July 19, 1925; d. Obe A. and B. Eva (Milburn) Grant; B.S., U. Ill., 1947; m. Morton F. Dorothy, Jr., Dec. 7, 1946; children—Morton F. III, Syren Jo (Mrs. Claude R. McElvain), John J., Sarah F. Admitted to Ill. bar, 1949; since practiced in Mt. Vernon; mem. firm Dorothy & Dorothy, 1949-67, Lou Ann Dorothy, 1971—; asst. dir. Womble Mountain Legal Aid, Harrisburg, Ill., 1967-68; information rep. to dir. personnel State of Ill., 1968; asst. dir. Peoria (Ill.) Legal Aid, 1968-69; asst. to acting dir. Legal Aid Jackson and Williamson County (Ill.), 1969-71. Bd. dirs. Jefferson County Found. for Vison and Learning Disorders. Mem. Ill., Jefferson County bar assns., Am. Legion Aux. (pres. 1950), Bus. and Profl. Women's Club (sec. luncheon group 1969), Am. Contract Bridae League, Alpha Xi Delta. Republican. Presbyn. Home: 1501 Viola St Mount Vernon IL 62864 Office: 313-314 Rogers Bldg 1002 Main St Mount Vernon IL 62864

DOROUGH, VIRGINIA ANN, banker; b. Birmingham, Ala., Dec. 26, 1930; d. Joseph Southern and Gladyce Mildred (Wilson) Dorough; B.S., U. Ala., 1952, postgrad., 1964-65; postgrad. Ga. State Coll., 1964; certificates Am. Inst. Banking, 1967, 69, 71; grad. Sch. Banking of South, 1973. Tchr. sci. Munford (Ala.) High Sch., 1952, Cahaba Heights Jr. High Sch., Birmingham, 1952-53; loan clk. First Nat. Bank of Birmingham, 1953-55; reservations agt. Eastern Airlines, Birmingham and Atlanta, 1955-64; programmer Exchange Security Bank, Birmingham, 1965-67, systems analyst, 1967—, asst. cashier, 1969—; mem. planning com. U. Ala. Ann. Data Processing Conf., 1968-72. Recipient Bausch & Lomb Hon. Sci. award, 1948. Mem. Am. Inst. Banking, Nat. Assn. Bank Women, Am. Soc. Women Accountants (pres. 1972-73), Mountain Brook Bus. and Profl. Women's Club (pres. 1973-74), Am. Assn. U. Women, Assn. for Computing Machinery. Methodist. Soroptimist; mem. Order Eastern Star (worthy matron 1957-58). Home: 2140 Shadybrook Lane Birmingham AL 35226 Office: Exchange Security Bank PO Box 10247 Birmingham AL 35202

DORRIS, JO FREIDA STRIBLING, univ. adminstr.; b. Walters, Okla., Mar. 4, 1932; d. Jesse B. and Talva (Palmer) Stribling; B.A. in Music cum laude, Okla. Coll. for Women, 1954; M.S. in Psychology, Okla. State U., 1960; Ed.D., Ariz. State U., 1969; m. Nathaniel R. Dorris, June 14, 1958 (div.); children—Richard A., Frances T. Sec., Phillips Petroleum Co., Oklahoma City, 1954-58; instr. evening sch. Hills Bus. Coll., Oklahoma City, 1956-58; residence hall counselor Okla. State U., 1958-60; asst. dean to asso. dean students Ariz. State U., Tempe, 1961-68, dir. residence hall program, 1968-70, dir. orientation, 1970-72; dir. student activities, adj. prof. applied behavioral scis. Okla. State U., Stillwater, 1972—. Regional adviser Intercollegiate Assn. Women Students, 1963-64, Intermountain Assn. Coll. and Univ. Residence Halls, 1968—. Mem. Mohave P.T.A. Mem. Am. Personnel and Guidance Assn., Am. Coll. Personnel Assn., Nat. Assn. Women Deans and Counselors, Hypathia, Delta Kappa Gamma, Kappa Delta Pi, Phi Kappa Phi, Alpha Xi Delta. Baptist. Home: 4230 N Washington St Stillwater OK 74074

DORRIS, PEGGY RAE, educator; b. Holly Bluff, Miss., Feb. 27, 1933; d. Hugh Baskerville and Alta Eugenia (Stampley) Dorris; B.S., Miss. Coll., 1956; M.S., U. Miss., 1963, Ph.D., 1967. High sch. sci. tchr., Benton, Miss., 1956-57, Wilmot, Ark., 1957-61, Pontotoc, Miss., 1961-62; teaching asst. zoology U. Miss., University, 1962-66, research asst. in limnology, summer 1964; asst. prof. biology Henderson State Coll., Arkadelphia, Ark., 1966-68, asso. prof., 1969-72, chmn. dept. biology, 1972—. NSF fellow, 1965, 66. Mem. Am., Paris arachnology socs., Am. Assn. U. Women, Am. Assn. U. Profs., Ark. Audubon Soc., Ark., Henderson edn. assns., Miss. Acad. Scis., Ark. Acad. Sci., Brit. Arachnologists, Kan. Entomol. Soc., Phi Kappa Phi. Contbr. articles to profl. jours. Home: 125 Evonshire St Arkadelphia AR 71923

DORSCH, HELEN E., univ. adminstr.; B.S. in Nursing Edn., Duquesne U., M.S. in Edn. Dean, Sch. Nursing, U. Wis.-Oshkosh; Ph.D., Ohio State U. Adminstr. univ. nursing program U. Wis.-Oshkosh. Office: Sch Nursing Wis State Univ Oshkosh WI 54901

DORSETT, CORA MATHENY, librarian; b. Camden, Ark., July 15, 1921; d. Walter Stanton and Cora (Smith) Matheny; B.S. in Edn. summa cum laude, Centenary Coll. La., 1963; M.S. in L.S., U. Miss.,

1965, Ph.D., 1972; m. George Lehner Dorsett, Apr. 5, 1947; children—Ann, Edward. Tchr. pub. schs., Shreveport, La., 1963-64; dir. Pine Bluff and Jefferson County Pub. Library, Pine Bluff, Ark., 1965—. Alpha Chi fellow, 1962-63; recipient Social Sci. award Chi Omega, 1963. Mem. Am., Ark., Southwestern library assns., Jefferson County Hist. Assn., Kappa Delta Pi. Episcopalian. Home: 1305 W 35th Av Pine Bluff AR 71601 Office: 200 E 8th Av Pine Bluff AR 71601

DORSEY, HELEN, physician; b. Keokuk, Ia., Sept. 25, 1916; d. Frank Blinn and Bertha (Wheeler) Dorsey, Jr.; student U. Tex., 1934-39; M.D., U. Ia., 1943; m. Anthony Christopher Styles, Nov. 20, 1943. Intern Norfolk (Va.) Gen. Hosp., 1943-44, resident, 1944; practice gen. medicine, Hampton, Va., 1944—; head Well-Baby Clinic, Hampton, 1945-62; mem. staff Dixie Hosp., Hampton, also pres. staff, 1959; dir. student health Hampton Inst., 1946-50. Bd. dirs. Peninsula Co-op., Hampton-Newport News, Va. Mem. Hampton (pres.), So. med. socs., Med. Soc. Va., Peninsula Acad. Medicine, A.M.A. Internat. Platform Assn., P.E.O. Clubs: Langley Kennel, Wythe Woman's (Hampton); Soroptimist (Lower Peninsula Va.) Home: 24 Braeman Dr Hampton VA 23369 Office: 148 Clyde St Hampton VA 23369

DORSEY, RHODA MARY, coll. pres.; b. Boston, Sept 9, 1927; d. Thomas Francis and Hedwig (Hoge) Dorsey; B.A. magna cum laude, Smith Coll., 1949; B.A., Cambridge U., 1951, M.A., 1954; Ph.D., U. Minn., 1956; LL.D., Nazereth Coll. of Rochester, 1970. Instr. Goucher Coll., Towson, Md., 1954-57, asst. prof. history, 1957-62, asso. prof., asst. dean, 1962-65, prof., 1965—, dean, 1968-74, also v.p., acting pres., 1973, pres., 1974—; lectr. history Loyola Coll., Balt., 1958-62, Johns Hopkins, 1960-61. Dir. U.S. Fidelity & Guarantee. Mem. Commn. for Hist. and Archtl. Preservation Balt.; mem. commn. higher edn. Middle States Assn.; mem. council Md. Ind. Coll. and Univ. Assn. Mem. adv. panel Archival Project Historic Annapolis, Inc.; mem. Gov.'s Com. for Nat. Register Historic Sites. Trustee Park Sch., Balt.; bd. dirs. House of Good Shepherd, Harford Opera Theater. Mem. Am. Hist. Assn., Orgn. Am. Historians, Md. Hist. Soc. (council). Club: Hamilton Street. Chmn. bd. editors Md. Hist. mag. Home: President's House Goucher Coll Towson MD 21204

DORSHEIMER, GAIL WARD, bank exec.; b. Manchester, Conn., Apr. 10, 1933; d. Anton F. and Mary M. (Egan) Ward; A.B. cum laude, Smith Coll., 1955; postgrad. Bryn Mawr Coll., 1969—; div.; children—Jill, Holly, Sherri. Coll. counseling cons. Psychol. Counseling Center for Students, Immaculata (Pa.) Coll., 1970-71; dir. spl. programs Rosemont (Pa.) Coll., 1972-74; adminstr. Affirmative Action, Girard Bank, Phila., 1974—. Mem. Phila. Coalition of Women Educators and Placement Services, 1974-75. Bd. dirs. Westchester (Pa.) Red Cross, 1970-71. Mem. Nat. Assn. Women Deans and Counselors, Am. Businesswomen Assn., Pa. Assn. Adult Edn., Greater Phila. C. of C. (mem. mgmt. tng. com. 1974-75). Home: 1153 Lake Dr West Chester PA 19380 Office: Rosemont College Rosemont PA 19010

DORTON, SHEILA KAY, advt. agy. exec.; b. Ft. Dodge, Ia., May 4, 1937; d. John Wayne and Vonda E. (Anderson) Dorton; student State U. Ia., 1955-56. Continuity writer WGL-Radio, Ft. Wayne, Ind., 1957-58; continuity dir. KAKE Radio-TV, Wichita, Kan., 1959-60; asst. to radio-TV dir. Wesley Day & Co., advt., Des Moines, 1961-63; copywriter W.B. Doner & Co., advt., Chgo., 1963-65; with Tatham, Laird & Kudner, Inc., advt., Chgo., 1965—, v.p., creative supr., 1970—. Presbyn. Home: 1360 Lake Shore Dr Chicago IL 60610 Office: 625 N Michigan Av Chicago IL 60610

DORTORT, FRANCES K., mental health cons.; b. Basel, Switzerland; d. Edward K. and Ettie Cirel (Schreiber) Dortort; B.S., Temple U., 1950; M.S.W., U. Pa., 1956, postgrad. 1958. Tchr., counselor, social worker elementary schs., Phila., 1952; instr. social case work U. Pa., Phila., 1957-59, asst. prof. psychology, coordinator Psychol. Clinic, 1963—; prof. Nat. Coll. Edn., Evanston, Ill., 1959-60; asso. prof. psychology Lock Haven State Coll., cons., supr. Pa. Welfare Dept., 1961-63; adminstr. mental health retardation program Huntingdon, Juniata and Miflin Counties, Pa. Social work consultant Ford-Wieboldt, Chgo., 1959-62; cons. mental health Fla. Vis. Tchrs. Workshop, Easton Forks Sch. System and Citizens Adv. Com.; lectr. social welfare Temple U., 1968. Mem. Acad. Certified Social Workers, Nat. Assn. Social Workers, Am. Assn. U. Profs., Council Social Work Edn., Soc. Research in Child Devel., Council for Aging, Otto Rank Assn. Contbr. articles to ednl. books, jours. Home: 4878 Roosevelt Blvd Philadelphia PA 19124

DOSCHER, VIRGINIA RUTH (MRS. WILLIAM FREDERICK DOSCHER), govt. ofcl.; b. Pontiac, Mich.; d. Frank Lester and Ruth Henrietta (Johnston) Becker; student Eastern Mich. U., 1932-34; B.A., U. Mich., 1936; postgrad., 1938-40; m. William Frederick Doscher, Feb. 16, 1954. Pub. relations dir. Community Welfare Council, Milw., 1944-54; exec. dir. Nat. Pub. Relations Council for Health and Welfare Services, N.Y.C., 1954-56; cons. to nat., state and local health and welfare orgns., Milw., 1957-65; staff asso. Am. Pub. Welfare Assn., Chgo., 1965-70; corporate sec. Social Devel. and Rev. Corp., Washington, 1970-71; asst. dir. research and evaluation Dept. of Def. Race Relations Inst., Patrick AFB, Fla., 1971—. Mem. Nat. Conf. on Social Welfare. Bd. dirs. Nat. Pub. Relations Council, Child Care Centers of Milw. Mem. Am. Pub. Welfare Assn., Pub. Relations Soc. Am., Federally Employed Women. Editor Public Welfare, 1956-63. Home: 5 Sunflower St Cocoa Beach FL 32931 Office: DRR1/DSR Patrick Air Force Base FL 32925

DOSS, ELLA MAE PERRY (MRS. JAMES MILTON DOSS), educator; b. Grand Prairie, Tex., Nov. 11, 1930; d. John and Edna (Dixon) Perry; B.S., Central State U., Wilberforce, O., 1952; postgrad. Kent State U., 1959-62, Cleve. State U., 1972; m. James Milton Doss, Aug. 26, 1954. Tchr., Cleve. Bd. Edn., 1952-54; tchr. Cuyahoga Bd. Mental Retardation, Cleve., 1956-68; prin. Forest Hill and Brent Schs. for Retarded, 1968—; tchr. Head Start Program, Cleve., summers, 1967, 68, core leader, 1969. Pres. Triangle Civic Club, Cleve., 1956; pres. Entre Nous Social and Civic Club, 1968, treas., 1971-73. Bd. dirs. Parent Vol. Assn. for Retarded, 1971-73. Recipient Distinguished Service award Ohio Assn. Retarded Children, 1969, 70, 73; named Outstanding Profl. of Yr. in Ohio, 1970. Mem. Ohio Assn. Tchrs. of Retarded (pres. 1967-69), Profl. Assn. for Retardation in Ohio (treas. 1971-73), Council for Exceptional Children, Am. Assn. Mental Deficiency, Central State Alumni Assn. (dir. 1965-70, pres. chpt. 1960), Cuyahoga County Assn. Retarded (trustee 1968—), Ohio Assn. Retarded (trustee 1969—), Bus. and Profl. Women, Eta Phi Beta. Democrat. Baptist. Home: 3651 E 140th St Cleveland OH 44120 Office: 3031 Monticello Blvd Cleveland OH 44118

DOSS, MARGOT PATTERSON (MRS. JOHN WHINHAM DOSS), journalist; b. St. Paul, Aug. 22, 1922; d. Eugene Northrop and Irene (Watson) Patterson; B.A., Ill. Wesleyan U., 1943; postgrad. New Sch. Social Research, 1945; m. John Whinham Doss, June 7, 1947; children—Richard Patterson, Alexander McKenzie, John Watson, Grodon Williams. Author newspaper column San Francisco at Your Feet, San Francisco Chronicle, 1961—; mem. staff Milw. Sentinel, 1943-45, Balt. Sun, 1949-53; Midwestern editor Seventeen mag., 1947-48. Tchr. U. Cal. at San Francisco, 1970-74; lectr. San Francisco State U., 1972-73. Bd. dirs. Actor's Workshop, 1960-63; founding dir. Cathedral Sch. for Boys; bd. dirs. Strybing Arboretum Soc.; trustee Four Seasons Found. Recipient Critics Choice of Critics award Venture mag., 1970, Krauskopf award Greater Mission Alliance, 1966. Mem. Friends of Earth, Sierra Club. Clubs: Press, Union League, Garden. Author: San Francisco at Your Feet, 1964; Bay Area at Your Feet, 1970; Golden Gate Park at Your Feet, 1970; Walks for Children in San Francisco, 1970. Contbr. articles to profl. jours. Inventor garbage diverter. Home: 1331 Greenwich St San Francisco CA 94109 also Bolinas CA 94924 Office: 5th and Mission Sts San Francisco CA 94119

DOSS, THERESA, lawyer, state ofcl.; b. Myrtlewood, Ala., Oct. 8, 1939; d. Eddie Edison and Ida (Richards) Doss; A.B., Ohio U., 1961; J.D., Ohio State U., 1964. Admitted to Ohio bar, 1964, Mich. bar, 1966; tchr. social studies jr. high sch., Cleve., 1961; law reference librarian Mich. State Library, 1964-65; program devel. liaison Detroit Archdiocesan Opportunity Program, 1965-66; asst. atty. gen. State of Mich., 1966—. Mem. City of Detroit Pub. Lighting Commn. Mem. Women Lawyers Assn. Mich. (1st v.p. 1972-73, pres. 1973-74), State Bar Mich. (adv. com. jour., mem. character and fitness com. Wayne County chpt., rep. assembly), Am., Detroit (mem. pub. adv. com. 1972), Wolverine (sec. 1967-68, dir. 1969-74), Ohio, Nat. (dir. women's div. 1973, nominating com. 1974—) bar assns. Baptist (trustee ch. 1969—). Home: 2937 W Buena Vista Detroit MI 48238 Office: 1888 State of Mich Bldg Plaza Bldg Detroit MI 48226

DOSSMANN, SISTER ANNE, ednl. adminstr.; b. Houston, Feb. 26, 1933; d. Raoul Niland and Pauline Elizabeth (Britain) Dossmann; B.Mus., Incarnate Word Coll., 1965; M.Ed., Loyola U., 1971. Elementary tchr. St. Patrick's Acad., San Antonio, 1955-56; tchr. St. Catherine of Siena Jr. High Sch., Metairie, La., 1956-60, St. Joan of Arc Jr. High Sch., Weslaco, Tex., 1960-61; St. Mary Magdalen Jr. High Sch., San Antonio, 1961-65; asst. prin.-archbishop Chapelle High Sch., Metairie, La., 1965-68; dean of students Incarnate Word High Sch., San Antonio, 1968-69; dir. admissions Incarnate Word Coll., San Antonio, 1969—. Rep., County Democratic Conv., 1971. Mem. Nat., Great Plains assns. coll. admissions counselors, Cath. Coll. Coordinating Council, Tex. Personnel and Guidance Assn., San Antonio Women Deans and Counselors, Tex. Assn. Collegiate Registrars and Admissions Officers. Address: 4301 Broadway San Antonio TX 78209

DOST, JEANNE EBBERT, educator; b. Walla Walla, Wash., Aug. 12, 1929; d. W.C. and Margie Alice (Patrick) Ebbert; B.A., Wash. State Coll., 1951; A.M., Harvard, 1953, Ph.D., 1959; m. Frank Norman Dost, Sept. 3, 1950; children—Karen Elizabeth, Frederick Ebbert. Instr. dept. econ. Kan. State U., Manhattan, 1956-58, Wash. State U., Pullman, 1960-61; instr. econs., then asso. prof. Ore. State U., Corvallis, 1965—, dir. Women's studies, 1973—. Book rev. editor Annals of Regional Sci. jour. Western Regional Sci. Assn., 1971-73, now mem. editorial bd. Vice pres. Corvallis br. N.A.A.C.P., 1971-73, also mem. exec. bd. Pacific N.W. area conf., 1970-73. Pres. Ore. Women's Polit. Caucus, 1972-73; mem. task force sex discrimination Ore. Bd. Edn., 1973—. NSF fellow, 1970. Mem. Am. Econ. Assn., Royal Econ. Soc., Western Regional Sci. Assn., Phi Kappa Phi. Contbr. articles to profl. jours. Home: 7620 NW Mountain View Dr Corvallis OR 97330

DOSTER, BARBARA HUNNICUTT (MRS. ROBERT OWEN DOSTER II), phys. therapist; b. Greenville, S.C., Nov. 26, 1944; d. James Allen and Virginia Maxgreen (Holland) Hunnicutt; B.S., U. N.C., 1967; m. Robert Owen Doster, June 4, 1966; children—Forest, Brian. Phys. therapist Murdoch Center, Butner, N.C., 1967-68, Wake County Rehab. and Cerebral Palsy Center, Raleigh, N.C., 1969, Meml. Hosp., Charlotte, N.C., 1969-70; phys. therapist, service dir. Mecklenburg Center for Human Devel., Charlotte, 1970-74; phys. therapist Charlotte-Mecklenburg Sch. System, 1974—. Lectr. nursing and psychology depts. U. N.C., Charlotte, 1971-73; cons. United Cerebral Palsy Kindergarten, Charlotte, 1970—, Assn. for Retarded Children, Charlotte, 1970—; mem. mental retardation record com. N.C. Dept. Mental Health, 1971-73. Mem. Am., N.C. phys. therapy assns., Am. Assn. Mental Deficiency. Club: Allen Hills Swim (Charlotte). Home: 1611 Mineral Springs Rd Charlotte NC 28213 Office: 800 S Independence Blvd Charlotte NC 28204

DOSTER, ROSE ELEANOR WILHELM (MRS. JESSE A. DOSTER), artist; b. Balt., May 11, 1938; d. Lewis Milford and Leeanora A. (Naylore) Wilhelm; certificate in illustration and design, Art Instrn. Sch. Mpls., 1956; diploma in design and painting, Md. Inst. Coll. Art, 1960, postgrad., 1960-62; m. Jesse Alfred Doster, Feb. 22, 1958; children—Jeffrey Allen, Roxane Elana. Exhibited in one-man shows at Hampstead Library Gallery, 1969, 70, Aurora Fed. Gallery, Balt., 1969, Goodman Gallery, Ellicott City, Md., 1971, Central Savs. Gallery, Towson, Md., 1971, Parkville (Md.) Library Gallery, 1972, Equitable Trust Bank Reisterstown Gallery, Balt., 1973, others; exhibited in group shows at St. John's Coll., Johns Hopkins, Goodman Gallery, Slayton House, Columbia, Md., Paynter Gallery, Rehoboth, Del, Hilltop House, Harpers Ferry, W.Va., 1974. tchr. drawing, painting and ceramics, 1968—. Active Boy Scouts Am., Girl Scouts U.S. Recipient numerous awards. Mem. Nat. League Am. Pen Women (br. art chmn. 1970-72, 1st v.p. 1972-74), Rehoboth Art League, Md. Craft Council, Md. Inst. Art Alumni Assns., Hanover Art Guild. Home: Box 403-A 119 Shiloh Av Hampstead MD 21074

DOTY, CAROL LEE, editor; b. Colorado Springs, Colo., June 22, 1933; d. George David and Frances Amelia (Bradley) Doty; B.S., Wheaton Coll., 1954; postgrad. Parsons Sch. Design, 1956-57; M.S. (Katherine Sharpe fellow), U. Ill., 1963. Phys. edn. tchr. East Jr. High Sch., Kankakee, Ill., 1954-56; program dir. Herrick House, Bartlett, Ill., 1957-58; tchr. phys. edn. St. Charles (Ill.) Pub. Schs., 1958-59, 60-62, LaGrange (Ill.) Pub. Schs., 1959-60; unit program dir. Honey Rock Camp, Three Lakes, Wis., 1955-58; draftsman for landscape architect, St. Charles, 1958-63; asst. librarian Morton Arboretum, Lisle, Ill., 1963-68, head pub. information, 1969-72, publs. coordinator, 1972—, editor Morton Arboretum Quar., 1966—, instr. adult edn., 1963-69. Mem. hort. council U. Ill. Coop. Extension Service, DuPage County, 1972—, exec. council, 1973—. Trustee Downers Grove Pub. Library, 1971—. Recipient Shapiro award U. Ill., 1963. Mem. I.L.A. Garden Writers Assn. Am., Am. Hort. Soc., Beta Phi Mu. Unitarian. Home: 1921 Curtiss St Downers Grove IL 60515 Office: Morton Aboretum Lisle IL 60532

DOTY, GRESDNA ANN, educator; b. Oelwein, Ia., Feb. 22, 1931; d. James William and Gresdna (Wood) Doty; B.A., U. No. Ia., 1953; M.A., U. Fla., 1957; Ph.D., Ind. U., 1967. Faculty S.W. Tex. State U., San Marcos, 1957-62, 64-65; faculty La. State U., Baton Rouge, 1967—, asso. prof. theatre, 1972—, dir. theatre, 1972—. Mem. Internat. Fedn. for Theatre Research, Am. Theatre Assn., Am. Soc. for Theatre Research, Speech Communication Assn., Soc. for Theatre Research. Author: The Career of Mrs. Anne Brunton Merry in the American Theatre, 1971. Home: 2800 July St #35 Baton Rouge LA 70808

DOUGHERTY, ANNA ELIZABETH, librarian; b. Wilmington, Del., Nov. 8, 1910; d. George Myer and Jennie (Mitchell) Dougherty; A.B., U. Del., 1932; B.S. in L.S., Drexel Inst., 1933; M.S., Columbia, 1948. Student asst. U. Del. Library, 1929-31; govt. publ. librarian Wilmington Inst. Free Library, Wilmington, 1934; library asst. Del. Acad. Medicine, Wilmington, 1934-35; asst. librarian E. I. du Pont de Nemours & Co., Jackson Lab. Patent Library, Deepwater, N.J., 1935-37; reference librarian Bucknell U., 1938-40, head serials dept., 1940-43, head catalog dept., 1943-44; asst. head cataloguer Bryn Mawr Coll. Library, 1944-48; asso. librarian U. Mich. Law Library, 1948-49; classifier Bklyn. Coll. Library, 1949-51; catalog reviser Nat. Library Medicine, Washington, 1951-58, head spl. lang. unit, 1958-59; asst. librarian NIH Library, Bethesda, Md., 1959-63, asst. to chief for program planning, 1963-65. asst. librarian, 1966-67, asst. chief, 1967—. Mem. YWCA, A.L.A., Med. Library Assn. (asso. editor bull. 1952-56, chmn. research group 1970-71), Spl. Libraries Assn. (corr. sec. D.C. chpt. 1957-58), Council Nat. Library Assns. (sec.-treas. 1967-69, joint com. on library edn.), Beta Phi Mu (chpt. pres. 1970-71). Presbyn. Home: 3001 Veazey Terrace NW Washington DC 20008 Office: Nat Inst Health Library Bethesda MD 20014

DOUGHERTY, CAROLYN ANN KRAUS (MRS. GEOGE W. DOUGHERTY), newspaper editor; b. Pana, Ill., June 14, 1921; d. John B. and Gertrude (Wullner) Kraus; grad. high sch.; m. Geoge W. Dougherty, Mar. 14, 1942 (dec. Oct. 31, 1971); 1 son, William X. With Black Mountain (N.C.) News, 1946-53; with Neoga News, Neoga, Ill., 1953—, editor, 1960—. Mem. Ill. Press Assn., So. Ill. Editorial Assn., Ill. Parent Tchr. Assn. (bd. mgrs. 1958-72), Neoga Bus. and Profl. Women's Club. Home: Lake Mattoon Neoga IL 62447 Office: 577 Chestnut St Neoga IL 62447

DOUGHERTY, FLORENCE MARIE HARRY (MRS. PAUL DOUGHERTY), educator; b. Akron, O., Aug. 31, 1914; d. William C. and Mary (Heisser) Harry; B.Ed., Akron U., 1937, M.Ed., 1956; postgrad. Kent State U., 1962-69; m. Paul Dougherty, June 29, 1942. Tchr. Akron pub. schs., 1937-59, resource tchr., cons. math., 1959-62; adminstrv. asst. Greensburg (O.) schs., 1962—; instr. math. Akron U., 1962-64, instr. reading, 1969. Mem. Nat., Ohio, Summit County, Greensburg edn. assns., N.E. Ohio Tchrs. Assn., Ohio Assn. Sch. Adminstrs., Ohio Assn. Supervision and Curriculum Devel., Internat. Reading Assn. (pres.), Am. Assn. Childhood Edn., Am. Assn. U. Women, Comparative Edn. Soc., Kappa Delta Pi, Delta Kappa Gamma. Club: Akron Woman's. Home: 4430 Cottage Grove Rd Uniontown OH 44685 Office: Box 218 Greensburg OH 44232

DOUGHERTY, JEAN HAY, hematologist; b. Mpls.; d. Charles T. and Lydia (Olsen) Hay; B.S., U. Minn., 1940, M.A., 1942; M.D., Yale, 1947; m. Thomas F. Dougherty, Apr. 5, 1941 (dec.); children—Michael Bruce, Ann Marie. Teaching asst. hematology U. Minn., summers 1939-40; teaching asst. anatomy dept. Yale, 1943; instr. medicine 1945-47; head technician Clin. Microscopy Lab., New Haven Hosp., 1944-47; lectr. anatomy U. Utah, Salt Lake City, 1947-48, research instr. pathology and oncology, 1948-51, hematologist Radiobiology Lab., 1952—, research instr. pathology, 1956-63, asst. research prof. pathology, 1963-70, asso. research prof. pathology, 1970—. Mem. Am. Assn. Cancer Research, Radiation Research Soc., N.Y. Acad. Scis., Sigma Xi. Contbr. articles to profl. jours. Office: U Utah Coll Medicine Salt Lake City UT 84132

DOUGHERTY, SISTER JEAN MARY, educator; b. Chgo., July 27, 1926; d. John Edward and Mary Cecile (Dineen) Dougherty; M.A., Siena Heights Coll., 1950; postgrad. Loyola U., Chgo., summers, 1950-56. Tchr. paroachial elementary and high schs., 1946-71; past mem. faculty Siena Heights Coll., Adrian, Mich., Ill. Tchrs. Coll., Chgo., U. Mich., Ann Arbor; instr. English and journalism Barry Coll., Miami, Fla., 1971-74, dir. culture and lecture services, 1972-74, mem. faculty senate, 1971-74, mem. graphics communication com., chmn. workload com., mem. library com. Mem. Nat. Council Publ. Advisers, Women in Communications, Cath. Assn. Tchrs. English (pres. Chgo. chpt. 1967-70). Address: 11300 NE 2d St Miami Shores FL 33161

DOUGHERTY, MARTHA JANE BOCK, lawyer; b. St. Louis, Nov. 10, 1929; d. John Aloysius and Anita Elizabeth (Klaus) Bock; LL.D., St. Louis U., 1954; m. Edward Joseph Dougherty, June 29, 1963; 1 son, John Edward. Admitted to Ill. and Mo. bars, 1954, Fed. Bar, 1956, U.S. Supreme Ct. bar, 1960; practiced law in St. Louis County, Mo., 1954-62, St. Clair County, Ill., 1973—; v.p. Gt. Am. Ins. Agy., Inc., Springfield, Ill., 1963-65; mem. firm Bock & Stenger, Belleville, Ill., 1973—. Mem. Pres.'s Women's Council St. Louis U., 1954. Bd. dirs. East St. Louis Community Concerts, 1959-63, Friends City Art Mus., St. Louis, 1958-62. Recipient Award of Service St. Louis Bar Assn., 1958. Mem. Am., Ill., Mo., St. Louis, St. Clair County bar assns., St. Louis Lawyers Assn. (sec. 1958-63), St. Louis Women's Law Soc. (pres. 1959-60), Mo. Assn. Women Lawyers (v.p. 1959-60), St. Clair County Lawyers Wives, Brotherhood Rwy. and Steamship Clks., McManus Barracks Womens Aux., St. Louis Lawyers Assn., St. Louis U. Alumni Assn., Phi Delta Delta, Delta Theta Tau. Clubs: Junior Women's Schubert (East St. Louis); St. Clair Woman's, The Players. Author: Municipal Delegation to Make Traffic Regulations, 1953. Address: 640 Alhambra Ct East St Louis IL 62205

DOUGHERTY, MARY ALICE, clergyman; b. Campbellville, Ont., Can., Feb. 21, 1907; d. George Fenton and Margaret E. (Zimmerman) Dougherty; B.A., Victoria Coll. U. Toronto (Ont.), 1937, diploma Covenant Coll., 1938, diploma Emmanuel Coll., 1946; postgrad. London (Eng.) U., 1953-54. With Northwestern Fire Ins. Co., Hamilton, Ont., 1929-34; mission rep. to prin. Wen-Teh Girls Middle Sch., Chungking, China, 1938-44; ordained to ministry United Ch. Can., 1947; parish ministry Lucky Lake, Sask., Can., 1946-51, Underwood, Ont., 1951-53, Tehkummah, Ont., 1954-57, Quyon, Que., Can., 1957-60, Merrickville, Ont., 1960-64, Enniskillen, Ont., 1964-69, Vald'Or, Que., 1970, Coe Hill, Ont., 1970-71, Mountjoy United Ch., Timmin, Ont., 1974. Mem. Internat. Assn. Women Ministers (pres. 1970—, hist. custodian). Home: 74 Hyde Park Av Hamilton ON Z8P 4M7 Canada

DOUGLAS, ALICE WIZEMANN, librarian; b. N.Y.C., Nov. 11, 1927; d. Grover William and Emma Elizabeth (Weissner) Wizemann; A.B., Rutgers U., 1949; M.S. in L.S., Case Western Res. U., 1954; m. William Gray Thomson Douglas, Aug. 2, 1952 (div. Jan. 1973); children—James William, Elizabeth Ann. Editorial asst. Aviation Week, McGraw Hill Pub. Co., N.Y.C., 1949-50; librarian, tchr. English, Petersburg, O., 1950-51, Solon Twp., O., 1951-55; librarian Cuyahoga County Regional Reference, Maple Heights, O., 1953; asst. in acquisitions Harvard Law Sch. Library, Cambridge, Mass., 1955-58; librarian E. Jr. High Sch., Watertown, Mass., 1966-68, Sturgis Library, Barnstable, Mass., 1969-73; librarian Sandwich (Mass.) Jr. Sr. High Sch., 1973—. Mem. Mass. Library Assn. (mem. exec. bd. 1973—, nominating com. 1973—), Cape Cod Library Club (v.p. 1971-73, pres. 1973—), League Women Voters. Home: Crestview Dr East Sandwich MA 02537 Office: Box 598 Sandwich MA 02563

DOUGLAS, ALYCE MOEHN (MRS. KENNETH ROOT DOUGLAS), librarian; b. Chgo., July 3, 1906; d. William Albert and Victoria Mary (Lotter) Moehn; teaching certificate Chgo. Normal Sch. Phys. Edn., 1924; B.A., Rosary Coll., 1953, M.A., 1954; m. Kenneth Root Douglas, Aug. 30, 1929; children—Kenneth Root, Charles Henry, Alyce-Martha (Mrs. Frank Sobchak), Dianne Lee (Mrs. Dennis Higgins), Malcolm Root. With Chgo. Pub. Library,

1954—, librarian I Legler Br., 1954-60, head librarian West Town Br., 1960-61, librarian II Austin br., 1961-66, head librarian Toman Br., 1966—. Mem. A.L.A. Contbr. weekly column to Community Reporter, Chgo., 1966—. Home: 1434 Jackson Av River Forest IL 60305 Office: 4005 W 27th St Chicago IL 60623

DOUGLAS, D. JANET, univ. dean; b. Eugene, Ore.; d. Harry and Marguerite (Young) Douglas; B.S., U. Ore., 1946; M.A., Syracuse U., 1948. Asst. dean women U. Colo., Boulder, 1948-53, Ore. State U., Corvallis, 1953-55; dean women Eastern Wash. Coll., Cheney, 1955-59; asso. dean students Cal. State U. at San Jose, 1959-63; dean women, asso. dean students Colo. State U., Ft. Collins, 1963-70; dean women Angelo State U., San Angelo, Tex., 1970—. Adviser Intercoll. Assn. Women Students, 1972. Mem. Gov.'s Com. on Status Women, Colo., 1968-70. Mem. Nat. Assn. Women Deans and Counselors, Am. Assn. U. Women, Mortar Bd., Delta Kappa Gamma. Club: Quota International. Home: Angelo State U San Angelo TX 76901

DOUGLAS, DORIS ELANOR FORD, assn. exec.; b. Douglas, Ga., Dec. 25, 1935; d. Jet and Gladys (Eason) Ford; student Wayne State U., Wayne County Community Coll.; children—André C., Robert K. Community asst. Detroit Bd. Edn., 1967-70; coordinator community services Western YMCA, Detroit, 1970-72, dir. community program, 1972—. Cons. human relations program Detroit Pub. Schs., 1972-73. Pres. Cary Sch. P.T.A., 1967-69, McMillan Jr. High Sch. P.T.A., 1969-70; sch. chmn. Delray United Action Com., 1968-70; area chmn. Muscular Dystrophy, 1969-70; exec. com. Deprived Area Recreation Team, City of Detroit, 1969-70. Recipient Key to City, City of Miami, 1971, Outstanding Service award S.W. Detroit Inter-Agy. Council, 1973. Mem. N.A.A.C.P. (chmn. sch. com. 1969). Home: 8626 Hubbell St Detroit MI 48228 Office: 1601 Clark St Detroit MI 48209

DOUGLAS, DOROTHY RUTH, educator; b. Birmingham, Ala., June 26, 1941; d. Ralph Winfred and Mildred Louise (Bell) Douglas; student Birmingham So. Coll., 1959-62; B.A., Emory U., 1963; postgrad. Tex. Christian U., 1964-65; M.A., U. Ala., 1966, Ed.D. (Ala. Dept. Edn. fellow), 1969. Tchr. retarded children Jefferson County Bd. Edn., Birmingham, Ala., 1963-64; coordinator spl. edn. Walker County Bd. Edn., Lafayette, Ga., 1967-68; instr. U. South Ala., Mobile, from 1968, asst. prof., now asso. prof. spl. edn. Cons. Ga. and Ala. State Depts. Edn. Program for Exceptional Children, Atlanta Pub. Schs., Washington, Clarke and Choctaw Counties. Mem. State Council for Exceptional Children, 1966-67, legislative chmn., 1973-74. Bd. dirs. Group Aid for Retarded Children, United Cerebral Palsy of Mobile County. Ala. Dept. Mental Health grantee, 1971, Bur. Edn. for Handicapped grantee, 1971-72. Mem. Council Exceptional Children, Am. Assn. Mental Deficiency, Assn. Supervision and Curriculum Devel., Internat. Assn. Study Mental Deficiency, Kappa Delta Pi. Home: 281 Bay Front Mobile AL 36605

DOUGLAS, EFFIE MALISSA STINEBAUGH (MRS. LAWRENCE A. DOUGLAS), educator; b. Camden, Ind., Mar. 2, 1908; d. James Gilbert and Mary E. (Reiff) Stinebaugh; A.B., Manchester Coll., 1929; M.S. in Edn., Purdue U., 1961; m. Lawrence A. Douglas, June 5, 1932 (dec.); 1 son, Max W. Douglas. Tchr. Camden High Sch., 1929-32, Deer Creek High Sch., Camden, 1940-44, Carrollton High Sch., Flora, Ind., 1944-48, Flora High Sch., 1948-61; tchr., guidance counselor Carroll High Sch., Flora, 1961-66, dir. guidance, 1966—. Mem. Am., Ind. (sec.), N.W. Central (pres.) personnel and guidance assns., Am., Ind. (area rep. chmn. archives com. 1965-71), sch. counselors assns., Ind. Classroom Tchrs. Assn., Am. Classical League (banker Ind. scholarships 1962—), Ind. Classical Conf., N.E.A., Ind. Tchrs. Assn., Manchester Coll. Alumni Assn. (dir. 1970-73), Ind. Sch. Women's Club, Delta Kappa Gamma (rec. sec. chpt. 1966-68, 1st v.p. 1968-70, pres. 1970-72, inter-council co-ordinating chmn. 1972-74, mem. state publicity and publ. com. 1973-75). Mem. Ch. of Brethren (program planning com. South Central dist. 1970-73). Home: Rural Route 1 Bringhurst IN 46913 Office: Carroll High Sch Rural Route 1 Flora IN 46929

DOUGLAS, HELEN GAHAGAN (MRS. MELVYN DOUGLAS), author, lectr.; b. Boonton, N.J., Nov. 25, 1900; d. Walter and Lillian Rose (Mussen) Gahagan; student Bernard Coll., 1920-22; m. Melvyn Douglas, Apr. 5, 1931; children—Peter Gahagan, Mary Helen. Actress N.Y.C., starred in plays including Young Woodley, 1925, Enchanted April, 1925, Trelawney of the Wells, 1926, Tonight or Never, 1930, Mary Queen of Scotland, 1934, First Lady, 1952; opera singer European tour, 1928-30, 37; star motion picture She, 1935; mem. 79th to 81st congresses from 14th dist. Cal., mem. fgn. affairs com., co-author McMahon-Douglas Bill; U.S. del. Gen. Assembly, UN, 1946. Mem. nat. adv. com. WPA, 1939; del. Jane Addams Peace Assn. to Soviet-Am. Women's Conf., Moscow, USSR, hon. co-chmn. Women's Internat. League for Peace and Freedom, 1964. Del. Democratic Nat. Conv., Dem. Nat. committeewoman from Cal., 1940; vice chmn. Dem. state central com., chmn. women's div., 1941-44. Named Woman of Year, N.Y. Hadassah, 1945, 1 of 12 Outstanding Women of Year, Nat. Council Negro Women, 1945. Mem. Nat. Women's Trade Union League Am. Author: The Eleanor Roosevelt We Remember, 1963. Address: 50 Riverside Dr New York City NY 10024

DOUGLAS, JEANNE MASON (MRS. HARLAN LAMBERT DOUGLAS), ednl. adminstr.; b. Albany, Vt., Oct. 9, 1938; d. Leonard Arnold and Helena Mary (LaRocque) Mason; B.S. in Edn., Johnson State Coll., 1960; postgrad U. Denver, 1966, Colo. State Coll., 1967, U. So. Cal., 1967-68; m. Harlan Lambert Douglas Dec. 2, 1960; 1 son, Mason. Tchr. jr. high sch. and high sch., Morrisville, Vt., 1961-63, White Sands, N.M., 1963-64, Navajo Indian Reservation, Shiprock, N.M., 1965-66, Hindman, Ky., 1966-67; tchr. Alice Lloyd Coll., Pippa Passes, Ky., 1968-69, also adminstr.; tchr. Reading (Pa.) Community Coll., 1972-74, adminstr., 1974—. Cons. instructional devel. colls. Ont., Can., N.Y., Mass., W.Va., Conn., Md., 1971—. Mem. Assn. Ednl. Communications and Tech., Pa. Learning Resources Assn. Contbr. articles to instrn. tech. mags. Home: 279 Parkview Rd St Lawrence Reading PA 19606 Office: Schuylkill and W Greenwich Sts Reading PA 19601

DOUGLAS, OTIS RUFFIN (MRS. CLIFTON O. DOUGLAS), psychologist; b. Youngstown, O., Nov. 5, 1926; d. Clarence and Ida L. (Campbell) Ruffin; B.S., Ohio State U., 1948; postgrad. Youngstown State U., 1957-61; M.S., Akron U., 1970; m. Clifton O. Douglas, Aug. 19, 1957; 1 dau. by previous marriage, Beverly A. Colwell; stepchildren—Clifton, Dennis. With Youngstown Bd. Edn., 1961—, sch. psychologist, 1969—. Bd. dirs. Youngstown Urban League, 1967-74, sec. 1969-71; bd. dirs. Child and Adult Mental Health Center, 1972-74, Campfire Girls, 1970-74; mem. personnel com. YWCA, 1970-74. Mem. Nat. Council Negro Women, N.A.A.C.P., Nat. Assn. Negro Bus. Profl. Women, Nat., Ohio sch. psychologists assns., Nat., Ohio edn. assns., Delta Sigma Theta. Home: 1154 Park Hill Dr Youngstown OH 44502 Office: 1025 W Rayen Av Youngstown OH 44502

DOUGLAS-HAMILTON, MARGARET HAMBRECHT, lawyer; b. Bklyn., July 28, 1941; d. William Matthew and Kathleen (Sheehan) Hambrecht; B.A., Wellesley Coll., 1963; M.A., Syracuse U., 1965; LL.B., Boston U., 1967; m. Diarmald H. Douglas-Hamilton, Oct. 14, 1967. Admitted to Mass. bar, 1967; asso. firm Ely, Bartlett, Brown & Proctor, Boston, 1967-72, asso. firm Bingham, Dana & Gould, Boston, 1972—. Mem. exec. com. Mass. Gov.'s Commn. Status on Women, 1971-72. Republican ward committeeman, 1972. Named one of ten Outstanding Young Leaders Boston Jr. C. of C., 1972. Mem. Am., Mass., Boston bar assns., Mass. Assn. Women Lawyers, Nat. Orgn. Women (Mass. v.p. 1970-71), Mass. Civil Liberties Union (dir. 1972-74), Mass. Women's Polit. Caucus, N.Y. Rug Soc., New Eng. Poetry Soc. (1st prize 1961—; Irene Glascock Meml. prize poetry 1961; Joyce Glueck Meml. prize 1962). Club: Wellesley College (Boston). Home: 39 Pinckney St Boston MA 02114 Office: 100 Federal St Boston MA 02110

DOUGLASS, DONNA JEAN, social worker; b. Walla Walla, Wash., Dec. 17, 1938; d. Donald Stuart Douglass and Jean Douglass Blake; student Mills Coll., 1956-57; B.A., U. Wash., 1960, M.S.W., 1962. Psychiat. social worker mental health div. Tacoma-Pierce County Health Dept., Tacoma, Wash., 1962-64; psychiat. social worker Child Study and Treatment Center, Western State Hosp., Ft. Steilacoom, Wash., 1964-74, chief psychiat. social worker, 1974—. Field instr. U. Wash. Sch. Social Work, 1968-70, 74—. Mem. profl. adv. council Tacoma Mental Health Clinic, 1967-69; profl. rep. Tacoma Comprehensive Mental Health Center, 1966-70; mem. Children's Services Coordinating Com. of Pierce County, 1965-67, 69—; mem. Tacoma Pierce County Mental Health and Mental Retardation Corp., 1966—; fellow N.W. Family Therapy Inst., 1967—. Mem. Nat. Assn. Social Workers (mem. exec. bd. Mt. Rainier chpt. 1965-69, 74—), Acad. Certified Social Workers, Delta Gamma. Episcopalian. Home: Route 4 Box 4779 Gig Harbor WA 98335 Office: Child Study and Treatment Center Ft Steilacoom WA 98494

DOUMIT, ELIZABETH JANE FOSTER (MRS. MITCHELL DOUMIT), civic worker; b. Cathlamet, Wash., Jan. 6, 1909; d. Robert Neil and Ellen (McGill) Foster; student U. Wash., 1926-28, 33, 57; m. Mitchell Doumit, June 6, 1928; children—Michael John (dec. 1953), Mary Elizabeth (Mrs. John Thomas). Bookkeeper, John Doumit & Sons, Cathlamet, 1945-57; tchr. high sch., Cathlamet, 1945-47; income tax service Mitchell Doumit Office, Cathlamet, 1958—. Wash. State del. White House Conf., 1950; mem. Wash. State Council for Children and Youth, 1952-58; mem. adv. bd. Sch. for Mentally Retarded, 1956-58, State Sch. for Blind, State Sch. for Deaf; mem. exec. com. Wash. Gov.'s Mental Health Survey Com., Wash. Gov.'s Phys. Fitness Com., 1957, Gov.'s Com. on Olympic Nat. Forest; leader 4-H Club, 1952-54; pres. Wash. State Fedn. Women's Clubs, 1951-53, endowment trustee, 1958-66, parliamentarian, 1966-68; mem. legislation com. Gen. Fedn. Women's Clubs, 1966-68, parliamentarian Western States conf., 1960-62, 74—, treas., 1962-64, 1st v.p., 1966-68, pres., 1968-70, chmn. Am. Rev. Bicentennial Com., 1972—; pres. Nat. Club Past State Presidents, 1954; active various fund drives; pres. Am. Legion Aux., Cathlamet. Committeewoman, Wash. State Republican Com., 1944-50; mem. exec. com. Wash. State Rep. Central Com., 1948; co-chmn. Western States Women for Nixon, 1960; mem. One Hundred Women for Nixon in U.S., 1968; mem. women's nat. adv. com. for reelection Pres. Nixon, 1972. Pres. Nat. Ahigrenites, 1964-66. Trustee Lower Columbia Coll., 1974—. Recipient citation Gen. Fedn. Women's Clubs, 1956. Address: PO Box 8 Cathlamet WA 98612

DOUTHWAITE, MARY LOUISE (MRS. GEOFFREY KINGSLEY DOUTHWAITE), librarian; b. Portland, Ore., Sept. 7, 1930; d. Charles Francis and Helen Leona (Gibson) Somerville; B.A., Lewis and Clark Coll., 1951; M.Librarianship, U. Wash., 1969; m. Geoffrey Kingsley Douthwaite, Aug. 16, 1952; children—Charles, John, Julia. Librarian, Seattle Pub. Schs., 1969—. Mem. Nat., Wash. edn. assns., Wash. Assn. Sch. Librarians, Seattle Tchrs. Assn., League of Women Voters (dir. 1962-65). Democrat. Mem. Unitarian Ch. Home: 5518 31st St NE Seattle WA 98105 Office: 10750 30th St NE Seattle WA 98125

DOVE, PATRICIA ANN MCGEE (MRS. RALPH NORMAN DOVE), editor; b. Belfield, N.D., Jan. 16, 1932; d. Frederick George and Golden Violet (Honeycutt) McGee; student U. Utah, 1947-52; m. Ralph Norman Dove, Dec. 31, 1954; children—Robert Norman, Susan, Michael George. Stewardess United Air Lines, 1952-54; sec. research div. Raytheon Mfg. Co., Waltham, Mass., 1959; asst. editor Officer's Wives Club Mag., Clark AFB, Philippines, 1962-63, editor, 1963-64; make up artist Max Factor, Philippines and Thailand, 1964-65; editor mag. Indpls. Athletic Club, Indpls., 1969—. Mem. Community Service Council, Indpls., 1972-74. Recipient awards Ind. Bus. Communicators, 1971-73. Mem. Ind. Bus. Communicators, Women in Communications. Home: 5631 E 72d St Indianapolis IN 46250 Office: 350 N Meridian St Indianapolis IN 46204

DOVE, PEARLIE CRAFT, educator; b. Altanta, Dec. 21, 1921; d. Dan Ceicle and Lizzie (Dyer) Craft; A.B., Clark Coll., 1941; M.A., Atlanta U., 1943; Ed.D., U. Colo., 1959; m. Jackson Benjamin Dove, Jan. 20, 1945 (dec. Dec. 1952); 1 dau., Carol Ann. Sec. bus., profl. and indsl. program Phyllis Wheatly YWCA, Atlanta, 1943-45, cons. adult edn. com., 1962—; program dir., sec. Goodwill A.M.E. Ch. Center, Memphis, 1946-47; prof. edn., dir. student teaching Clark Coll., Atlanta, 1949-63, also chmn. dept. edn. and psychology, 1963—, trustee, 1969-72, dir. Feasibility Study USOE Model Elementary Project, 1969-71. Mem. faculty Atlanta U., summers 1960—; cons. tchr. edn. workshop S.C. State Coll., 1960; cons., supervising tchr. advanced study counseling, guidance for elementary, secondary sch. personnel Nat. Def. Edn. Act Inst., Atlanta U., 1967-69; instn. coordinator Atlanta Tchr. Corps Consortium, 1970—; mem. Atlanta Com. Internat. Visitors, 1967—; nat. exec. com. Assn. Tchr. Educators, 1970-73; mem. Inst. Policy Commn. So. Regional Edn. Bd., 1973—. Mem. Atlanta League Women Voters, Ga. Assn. Student Teaching (v.p., editor Newsletter 1965-67, pres. 1967-68), Am. Assn. U. Profs., Ga. Tchr. Edn. Council (exec. com. 1965-67), Atlanta Grad. Pan Hellenic Council (pres. 1960-64), Am. Assn. Colls. for Tchr. Edn. (dir. 1972-75), So. Assn. Colls. and Schs. (Ga. elementary com. 1970—), Delta Sigma Theta (pres. Atlanta chpt. 1962-63, award), Iota Phi Lambda (award), Pi Lambda Theta. Home: 1053 Washington Heights Terrace Atlanta GA 30314

DOW, LOIS WEYMAN, physician; b. Cin., Mar. 11, 1942; d. Albert Dames and Else (Krug) Weyman; B.A. summa cum laude, Cornell U., 1964; M.D. cum laude, Harvard, 1968; m. Alan Wayne Dow, July 23, 1966; 2 children. Intern Bronx Municipal Hosp. Center, Bronx, N.Y., 1968-69; resident Presbyn. Hosp., N.Y.C., 1969-70; practice medicine, teaching and clin. research specializing in internal medicine, hematology and oncology; vis. fellow hematology Coll. Phys. and Surg., Columbia, N.Y.C., 1970-72; instr. NSF Honors High Sch. Program, N.Y.C., 1970-72; instr. dept. medicine, vis. fellow oncology U. Tenn. Coll. Medicine, Memphis, 1972-73, asst. prof. medicine, 1973-74; research asso. St. Jude Children's Research Hosp., Memphis, 1974—. Mem. Am. Fedn. Clin. Research, Am. Soc. Hematology, Memphis-Shelby County Med. Soc., S.E. Cancer Study Group, Mortar Bd., Raven and Serpent, Phi Beta Kappa, Phi Kappa Phi, Alpha Lambda Delta, Alpha Epsilon Delta, Pi Beta Phi. Home: 5408 Sycamore Grove Lane Memphis TN 38117 Office: St Jude Children's Research Hosp 332 N Lauderdale PO Box 318 Memphis TN 38101

DOW, MARGUERITE RUTH, educator; b. Ottawa, Ont., Can., June 13, 1926; d. Gordon Russel and Beatrice (Bott) Dow; B.A., Univ. Coll., U. Toronto, 1949; sr. certificate in drama Banff Sch. Fine Arts, U. Alta., 1956; M.A., U. Toronto, 1970, B.Ed., 1971. Head English dept., librarian Listowel Dist. High Sch., Listowel, Ont., 1950-52, Renfrew (Ont.) Collegiate Inst. and Vocational Sch., 1952-53; tchr. English Brockville (Ont.) Collegiate Inst. and Vocational Sch., 1953-55, Fisher Park High Sch., Ottawa, 1955-59; head English dept. Laurentian High Sch., Ottawa, 1959-65; asso. prof. English U. Western Ont., London, 1965—, prof. English, 1972—. Lectr. Ont. Secondary Sch. Tchrs. Fedn., 1960-62; Critic tchr. Ont. Coll. Edn., U. Toronto, 1963. Bd. dirs. Theatre Found. Ottawa, 1961; mem. Stratford Shakespearean Festival Found. Can., 1965—. Fellow Intercontinental Biog. Assn. (Eng.); mem. Canadian Assn. U. Tchrs., Canadian Coll. Tchrs., Canadian Council Tchrs. English, Nat. Council Tchrs. English, Intercontinental Biog. Assn., Internat. Platform Assn., Canadian Child and Youth Drama Assn. Baptist. Club: University Women's (chmn. 1964-65) (London). Author: The Magic Mask, 1966; Courses of Study in the Theatre Arts, 1969. Editor: Light From Other Windows, 1964. Home: 1231 Richmond St Apt 909 London ON Canada Office: U Western Ont 1137 Western Rd London ON Canada

DOWALIBY, MARGARET SUSANNE, educator, optometrist; b. Dover, N.H., Mar. 5, 1924; d. Abraham E. and Helen (Rizk) Dowaliby; B.S., Los Angeles Coll. Optometry, 1948, O.D., 1950. Mem. faculty So. Cal. Coll. Optometry, Fullerton, 1948—, prof. ophthalmicoptics, 1968—; individual practice optometry, Beverly Hills, Cal., 1959—. Author: Styling of Eyewear, 1954; Modern Eyewear Fashion and Cosmetic Dispensing, 1960; Fundamentals of Cosmetic Dispensing, 1966; Practical Aspects of Ophthalmic Optics, 1973. Contbr. articles to profl. jours. Home: 201 E Chapman Av #72B Placentia CA 92670 Office: So Cal Coll Optometry 2001 Associated Rd Fullerton CA 92631

DOWALIBY, PAULINE AGNES, optometrist; b. Portsmouth, N.H., Nov. 23, 1928; d. Abraham Edward and Helen Josephine (Rizk) Dowaliby; A.A., Los Angeles City Coll., 1948; B. Visual Sci., Los Angeles Coll. Optometry, 1950, D. Optometry, 1951. Individual practice optometry, El Segundo, Cal., 1954-56, Beverly Hills, Cal., 1956—; sch. optometrist Los Angeles City Schs., 1954—. Trustee Los Angeles Coll. Optometry, 1961-63. Named Optometrist of the Year, Los Angeles County Optometric Soc., 1962. Mem. Am. Acad. Optometry, Am., Cal. optometric assns., Los Angeles County Optometric Soc. (sec. 1956), Los Angeles Coll. Optometry Alumni Assn. (pres. 1962), Pi Kappa Rho. Home: 11728 Wilshire Blvd Los Angeles CA 90025 Office: 9465 Wilshire Blvd Beverly Hills CA 90212

DOWD, SISTER RUTH, educator; grad., Manhattanville Coll., 1940; Ph.D. Fordham U., 1955; postgrad. N.Y. U. Joined Soc. Sacred Heart; taught philosophy, Manhattanville Coll.; co-founder, asst. prin. Harlem Prep. Sch.; now prof. edn. Medger Evers Coll., Bklyn. Recipient Woman of Conscience award Nat. Council Women, 1972. Address: Medgar Evers Coll New York City NY 10003*

DOWDELL, DOROTHY FLORENCE KARNS (MRS. JOSEPH DOWDELL), author; b. Reno, May 5, 1910; d. Albert Berdell and Florence (Lusk) Karns; student Sacramento City Coll., 1927-29; A.B., U. Cal. at Berkeley, 1931; postgrad. Sacramento State Coll., 1948-50; m. Joseph Dowdell, June 21, 1931; children—Joan Eva (Mrs. William Robert Moore), John Lawrence. Tchr. elementary schs., Sacramento, 1948-61. Mem. Am. Assn. U. Women (br. dir. 1964-65), Cal. Writers Club (br. pres. 1953-54, 63-64), Authors Guild of Authors League of Am., Cal. Congress P.T.A. (hon. life), P.E.O. (chpt. pres. 1944-46). Episcopalian. Author: Karen Anderson, Illustrator, 1960; Strange Rapture, 1961; Border Nurse, 1963; Roses for Gail, 1964; How to Help Your Child in School, 1964; Tree Farms; Harvest for the Future, 1965; Secrets of the ABC's, 1965; Your Career in Teaching, 1967; Sierra Nevada: The Golden Barrier, 1968; Careers in Horticultural Sciences, 1969; The Japanese Helped Build America, 1970; Your Career in the World of Travel, 1971; The Chinese Helped Build America, 1972; Hawk Over Hollyhedge Manor, 1973. Home: 21549 Old Mine Rd Los Gatos CA 95030

DOWDEY, CAROLYN DECAMPS (MRS. CLIFFORD DOWDEY), librarian; b. Portsmouth, Va., May 24, 1941; d. William Luke and Jessie Woodrow (Willoughby) DeCamps; B.A., Mary Washington Coll., 1963; certificate Fgn. Service Inst., 1964; M.L.S., U. Cal. at Los Angeles, 1967; m. Clifford Dowdey, Sept. 9, 1971. With Nat. Security Agy., Ft. Meade, Md., 1963-66; librarian Va. State Library, Richmond, 1967-68; librarian Chesterfield County Library, Chester, Va., 1968—; adj. faculty Va. Commonwealth U., Richmond, 1969-71. Mem. Am., Va. library assns., Pi Gamma Mu, Beta Phi Mu. Home: 2504 Kensington Av Richmond VA 23220 Office: 4022B W Hundred Rd Chester VA 23831

DOWDY, ELIZABETH GERALDINE, physician; b. Keener, Ala., Aug. 25, 1927; d. Hoyt Wendell and Rubye (Whorton) Dowdy; B.S., U. Ala., 1951, M.D., 1955; Ph.D., U. Miss., 1968. Intern Birmingham Bapt. Hosp., 1955-56, resident anesthesiology, 1956-57, Columbia Presbyn. Hosp., N.Y.C., 1957-59; practice medicine specializing in anesthesiology, 1959—; mem. staff U. Miss. Med. Center, 1960-68; U. Ala. Med. Center, 1959-60, 68—; asst. prof. dept. anesthesiology U. Ala. Sch. Medicine, Birmingham, 1959-60, U. Miss. Sch. Medicine, Jackson, 1960-63; asso. prof., 1963-68, prof. anesthesiology, dir. div. anesthesia research, asso. prof. dept. pharmacology, 1968—, asso. prof. dept. physiology, 1971—. Diplomate Am. Bd. Anesthesiology. Fellow Am. Coll. Anesthesiologists; mem. Am., Ala., Miss. (pres. 1968) socs. anesthesiologists, A.M.A., Ala., Jefferson County med. socs., Internat. Anesthesia Research Soc., Assn. Univ. Anesthetists, Sigma Xi. Contbr. articles in fields of anesthesiology, pharmacology to profl. jours. Office: U Ala Medical Center Birmingham AL 35294

DOWELL, ELIZABETH JEAN AUSTIN (MRS. RICHARD ALLEN DOWELL), banker; b. Loma Linda, Cal., July 11, 1939; d. Lloyd S. and Elinor Jean (Smith) Austin; student Stephens Coll., 1957-58; A.A. in Bus. Adminstrn., Citrus Coll., 1969; B.A. in Bus. Adminstrn., Cal. State Coll. at Fullerton, 1974. m. Richard Allen Dowell, June 14, 1958. Designer, Fashions by Elizabeth Jean, 1957—; real estate lending officer, escrow officer Bank of Am. NT & SA, Monrovia, Cal. 1958-71, asst. mgr., 1971-72, asst. head consumer loans, 1972-73, asst. mgr. br. South Pasadena, Cal., 1974—; owner, operator Elizabeth's Sch. of Design and Sewing, 1966—. Baptist (jr. high sch. youth dir. 1963-69). Club: Zonta (pres. Monrovia 1967-69). Home: PO Box 493 LaVerne CA 91750 Office: Bank Am PO Box 280 South Pasadena CA 91030

DOWLEY, EDITH MARY, educator; b. N.Y.C.; d. Michael F. and Nora (Firth) Dowley; B.A., Marygrove Coll., 1932; M.A., U. Mich., 1935; Ed.D., Stanford, 1951; student Merrill-Palmer Sch., 1933-34. Tchr., Univ. Elementary Sch., U. Mich., Ann Arbor, 1935-43; group supr. Kaiser Co. Child Service Center, Ore. Shipbuilding Corp., Portland, 1943-45; asso., acting head dept. early childhood Merrill Palmer Sch., Detroit, 1945-48; mem. faculty, dept. psychology Stanford, 1949—, asso. prof., 1956—, asso. prof., psychology and edn. 1967-71, prof. psychology and edn., 1971—, dir. Bing Nursery Sch.,

1949—; vis. prof. psychology U. Victoria, summer 1963, U. Hawaii, summer 1967. Nat. cons. Project Heat Start, 1965-67; cons. Project Quest So. N.J., summers, 1971-72; mem. Cal. Task Force on Early Childhood Edn., 1971-72, Gov.'s Conf. on Prevention Developmental Disabilities, 1973. Bd. dirs. Family Service Assn. Mid Peninsula, Palo Alto, Cal., 1968-71, Holy Family Coll., Mission San Jose, Cal., 1971—. Mem. adv. bd. Peninsula Childrens Center, 1960-64, Childrens Health Council, 1973—. Mem. Nat. Assn. Edn. Young Children (dir. 1956-68, v.p. 1960-62), No. Cal. Assn. Nursery Edn. (pres. 1957-59), Soc. Research Child Devel., Am. Assn. U. Profs., Sigma Xi, Kappa Gamma Pi, Pi Lambda Theta. Home: 325 Ambar Way Menlo Park CA 94025 Office: Dept Psychology Stanford U Stanford CA 94305

DOWLING, JACQUES MACCUISTON, sculptor; b. Texarkana, Tex., Oct. 19, 1906; d. Charles Edward and Viola John (Estes) MacCuiston; Tchrs. Certificate, Coll. Marshall, 1923; studied art Loyola U., Frolich's Sch. Fine Art, Los Angeles, N.A.D., Art Students League, N.Y.C. One man shows Fedn. Dallas Artists, 1950, Rush Gallery, 1958, Sartor's Gallery, 1958, Sheraton-Dallas Hotel, 1960; Dallas Meml. Auditorium, 1960; exhibited in group shows at Dallas Mus. Fine Arts, Mus. of N.M., Fedn. Dallas Artists, Sartor's Galleries, Ney Art Mus., Oak Cliff Soc. of Fine Arts, Sartor's Gallery, Shuttles Gallery, Sheraton-Park Internat. Platform Assn., 1966-68, Phillips Mills Art Assn., 1967—, Yardley Ann. Exhbn., 1968—, Tinicum Art Festival, 1968, Woodmere Art Gallery (life mem.), 1973, others; selected sculpture 1st S.W. ann. show Mus. N.M., 1957; represented in permanent collections several corps., many pvt. homes. Mem. Lambertville (N.J.) Bd. Edn. Recipient 1st Sculpture Fedn. Dallas Artists, 1950-54, pinned (all awards jewels), 1961; Hon. Certificate award Dallas Fed. Bus. Assn., 1964; two 1st awards N.J. Fedn. Womens Clubs, 1972, 1st award, 1974, many others. Fellow Internat. Inst. Arts and Letters (life), mem. St. Catherine's Business & Profl. Guild (past pres.), Lambertville Hist. Soc. (sec.), Nat. Hist. Soc., Am. Mus. Natural History, Sr. Citizens Delaware Valley (past pres.), St. Phillip's Chapel Guild, Phillips Mill Assn., Internat. Platform Assn., Internat. Acad. Lit., Arts and Sci. (Tommaso Campanello with gold medal award 1972), C. of C. South Hunterdon (charter). Republican. Episcopalian. Mem. Order Eastern Star (past grand officer; past matron). Clubs: Kalmia (past pres.); Solebury Farmers (pres.); Middle Bucks Chess (charter). Contbr. columns to news chain. Address: 45 York St Lambertville NJ 08530

DOWLING, SYLVIA (MRS. JOHN BENJAMIN DOWLING), broadcasting, advt. exec.; b. Albany, N.Y.; d. Charles and Harriet (Felt) Klarsfeld; student pub. schs.; m. John Benjamin Dowling; children—Susan (Mrs. Rufus Putnam Coes, Jr.), John Benjamin III. Broadcaster, Stas. WOKO, WABY, Albany, WGY, Schenectady; advt. copywriter Young & Rubicam, N.Y.C.; TV supr. Sullivan, Stauffer, Colwell & Bayles, N.Y.C.; v.p. Benton & Bowles, N.Y.C.; asso. creative dir. Am. Home Products Corp., N.Y.C.; newspaper columnist Conn. Sunday Herald, Fairfield County; contbg. editor Fairfield County Mag., Westport; v.p. Radio Stamford (Conn.), Inc.; pub. relations dir. Conn. Assn. Land Surveyors, Fairfield County; now copy dir. Friedman, Rosner, Advt., N.Y.C. Speechwriter, advt. and pub. relations for various Conn. politicians. Named Outstanding Businesswoman of Year, N.Y. Abbe Inst., 1962. Club: Stamford Yacht. Home: Southfield Point Stamford CT 06902 Office: 1414 Av of Americas New York City NY 10019

DOWNEN, MADELINE ELIZABETH MORGAN, hosp. librarian; b. Pontiac, Mich., Aug. 17, 1930; d. Albert Oran and Hazel Marie (Fisk) Morgan; student Ind. U., 1948-50, St. Josephs Calumet Coll., 1968—; certificate hosp. librarianship Am. Hosp. Assn. Inst., 1964; certificate media mgmt. Med. Library Assn., 1972; m. Evan Ray Downen, Dec. 3, 1949 (div. 1968); children—Charles Albert, Linda Carol (Mrs. Dennis Smith), Gregory Lyn. Apprentice med. librarian St. Catherine Hosp., East Chicago, Ind., 1947-50, med. librarian, 1962-65, supr. McGuire Meml. Library, 1965—. Med. library cons. Our Lady of Mercy Hosp., Dyer, Ind., 1969-70; mem. state med. library cons. com. Ind. U. Sch. Medicine, 1973. Pres. East Chicago Mothers Club, 1966-67. Mem. Med. Library Assn., Regional Med. Library Council (by-laws com. representing hosp. library 1971). Mem. Christian Ch. Home: 6730 Alexander Av Hammond IN 46320 Office: 4321 Fir St East Chicago IN 46312

DOWNER, SHERIDA HOOKE (MRS. PAUL ALEXANDER DOWNER), librarian; b. Salt Lake City, Aug. 9, 1948; d. Albert Vernon and Deloris Edith (Alsen) Hooke; B.A. (Ill. State scholar), George Williams Coll., 1970; M.A., Rosary Coll., 1971; m. Paul Alexander Downer, Sept. 14, 1968; 1 dau., Shauna Lori. Librarian, Downers Grove (Ill.) Pub. Library, 1970-71; acquisitions librarian Lewis Coll., Lockport, Ill., 1971, dir. library, 1971—. Mem. A.L.A., Am. Assn. U. Profs., Nat. Council Adminstrv. Women Edn. Home: 46 Oak Lane Lemont IL 60439 Office: Lewis U Library Route 53 Lockport IL 60441

DOWNEY, CHERYL RUTH, motion picture dir.; b. Mpls., Oct. 12, 1944; d. Walter and Ruth C. (Eisele) Downey; B.A. magna cum laude, Gustavus Adolphus Coll., 1966; M.A., U. Cal. at Los Angeles, 1968, Ph.D., 1971. Teaching asst. dept. theater arts U. Cal. at Los Angeles, 1968, 70; dir., tchr. theater arts and English Euclid Sr. High Sch., Cleve., 1968-69; asst. to prodn. supr. Tomorrow Entertainment, Hollywood, Cal., 1971-72; dir., prof. theater arts Los Angeles Harbor Coll., 1972-73; asst. dir. Assn. Motion Picture and TV Producers and Dirs. Guild Am. Program, 1973. Regional screening chmn. Am. Field Service Student Exchange Program, 1972, 73. Bd. dirs., sec. Oakwood Wesley House, Venice, Cal., 1970-73. Chancellor fellow U. Cal. at Los Angeles, 1966-71; student Project Amity among Nations grantee Thailand Nat. Dept. Fine Arts, Bangkok, 1965. Recipient McPherson award U. Minn., 1965. Mem. Dirs. Guild Am., Am. Assn. U. Profs., Am. Theater Assn. Home: 1921 Benedict Canyon Beverly Hills CA 90210

DOWNEY, ELEANOR LONG, med. service adminstr.; b. Birmingham, Ala., Nov. 27, 1942; d. Roger Winston and Pauline (King) Long; A.B., Birmingham So. Coll., 1964; B.S., U. Ala., 1967, postgrad., 1968—; m. Stanford H. Downey, July 4, 1964 (div.); children—Stanford Harmon III, Jonathan Michael. Med. sec. to physician, Birmingham, 1961-63; tchr. Jefferson County Bd. Edn., Ala., 1963-64; research asst. Meml. Inst. of Pathology, Birmingham, 1960-64, research asso., coordinator of research activities, 1964—. Dir. Information and Document Mgmt., Inc., 1974—; cons. Ga. Hosp. Assn., 1972; mem. Internat. Cancer Congress, Kyoto, Japan, 1966. Den leader Birmingham-Vulcan council Boy Scouts Am., 1972-74. Am. Cancer Soc. grantee, 1960. Mem. Ala. Acad. Sci., Internat. Acad. Pathology, Am. Statis. Assn., Am. Assn. Phys. Anthropologists, A.A.A.S., Mem. Nat. Wildlife Fedn., Ala. Zool. Soc. Caucus for Women in Statistics, Kappa Delta Epsilon, Alpha Chi Omega. Mem. Unitarian Ch. (pianist 1970—, tchr. religious edn. program 1972—). Author: (with A.E. Casey) Compilation of Common Physical Measurements on Adult Males of Various Races, 1969. Contbr. articles on clin. pathology, anthropology and measurement theory to sci. publs. Home: 5323 10th Av South Birmingham AL 35222 Office: 1025 South 18th St Birmingham AL 35210

DOWNEY, ISABELLE MATILDA, home economist; b. Opelika, Ala., Jan. 9, 1923; d. Clarence B. and Matilda M. (Grossman) Downey; B.S., Auburn U., 1944; postgrad. (Farm Found. fellow) U. Ark., 1958; M.S. (Sarah Bradley Typson fellow Women's Nat. Farm and Garden Found.), U. Ga., 1960. Asst. home demonstration agt., Pike County, Ala., 1944-46; home demonstration agt., Crenshaw County, Ala., 1946-58; specialist food preservation Coop. Extension Service, Auburn (Ala.) U., 1958—, supr. expanded food and nutrition program Dists. I, III and IV, 1969-71, 72-73. Cons. publ. Putting Food By. County chmn. Cancer Ednl. Services, 1947-50; rural area polio chmn., 1950-53; county information chmn. A.R.C., 1952-56; vol. United Fund, 1970. Mem. Am. Assn. U. Women, Am., Ala. home econs. assns., Wesleyan Service Guild, Epsilon Sigma Pi, Delta Kappa Gamma. Methodist. Author: Food Preservation in Alabama. Contbr. articles to profl. jours. Home: 783 Brenda Av Auburn AL 36830

DOWNING, EDNA C., educator; b. Mpls.; d. Edward Charles Cornelius and Georgia (Brace) Downing; B.S., U. Minn., 1941; M.Ed., Macalester Coll., 1953; postgrad. U. Minn., 1950, 65, 67, 68, 69, State U. Ia., summer 1960, St. Thomas Coll., 1973-74. Tchr. English, Silver Lake (Minn.) High Sch., 1942-44; tchr. English and Latin, dir. speech North St. Paul High Sch., 1944-51; tchr. English, Bryant Jr. High Sch. and Sanford Jr. High Sch., 1951-58; chmn. English dept., tchr. English and Latin Sanford Jr. High Sch., Mpls., 1958—. Supr. student tchrs. U. Minn., 1959—, instr. Coll. Edn., 1967-70, lectr., 1966, 67, 68; lectr. Ia. U., summers 1962-65, Syracuse U., summer 1965; acting cons. in secondary English and humanities Mpls. Pub. Schs., 1970-71; lectr. Minn. Dept. Edn., U. Minn. Workshops, 1965-68; mem. Minn. Lang. Arts Adv. Com.; mem. exec. bd. Women in Edn., 1958-62, 71-72. Recipient Tchr. Excellence award Minn. Edn. Assn., 1964; Tchrs. medal Freedoms Found., 1965, Distinguished Speakers award No. U.S. and Can. Newspaper Circulation Dirs. Assn., 1968; Outstanding Achievement award Mpls. Area Council Tchrs. English, 1969. Mem. Mpls. Area (pres. 1956-57, v.p. 1955-56, sec. 1954-55), Minn. (v.p. 1968, pres. 1969-70, chmn. editorial bd.), Nat. (liaison, profl. relations officer, 1957—, nat. chmn. com. on publs. affiliates 1962-67, cons., dir. 1968—, affiliate relations com. 1973—, com. to write and publish Your Reading 1974—) councils tchrs. English, Minn. Edn. Assn. (pres. English sect. 1964-66), N.E.A., Minn. Classical Conf., U. Minn., Macalester alumni assns., Nat., Minn., Mpls. councils tchrs. English, Delta Kappa Gamma (pres. 1960-62, v.p. 1958-60), Kappa Delta Pi. Methodist. Mem. Order Eastern Star. Author How to Read and Use the Newspaper in English-Units for Grades 7-12. Contbr. articles to profl. jours. Home: 3935 Fremont Av N Minneapolis MN 55412 Office: 36th and 42d Av S Minneapolis MN 55406

DOWNUM, EVELYN ROSE BENSON (MRS. GARLAND DOWNUM), librarian, educator; b. Chgo., Jan. 21, 1916; d. Arthur E. and Rose (Anderson) Benson; student Oshkosh State Coll. (now Wis. State U.), 1933-35; A.B. (hon.), U. Ill., 1937; M.A., U. Tex., 1941; postgrad. Ariz. State Coll. (now No. Ariz. U.), 1955; postgrad. sch. librarianship U. Denver, 1965; m. Garland Downum, June 17, 1939; children—Philip Benson, Carolyn Jean (Mrs. Larry Dale White), Janice Elaine (Mrs. Joe E. Barnett). Instr. history Ariz. State Coll., Flagstaff, 1949, asst. librarian, 1956-59, librarian coll. elementary sch., 1958-66, instr. children's lit., 1965-66, 67—; librarian Thomas Sch., Flagstaff, 1966-67; librarian U. Tng. Sch., No. Ariz. U., Flagstaff, 1967—. Library cons. Flagstaff Headstart Program, 1965; co-dir. European study tour, 1971. Mem. Flagstaff Symphony Guild; sponsor Flagstaff Symphony Orch., 1962—; mem. Ariz. State Coll. Art Gallery, Friends of Osborne and Lillian H. Smith Collections. Bd. dirs. Flagstaff Community Concert Assn., Flagstaff Goodwill Industries. Ariz. Soc. Crippled Children and Adults, Girls' Ranch. Mem. Ariz. Zool. Soc., No. Ariz. Soc. Sci. and Art, Am., Ariz. (dir. sch. libraries div.) library assns., Am. Assn. U. Women (various offices, past state treas., v.p.), Nat. Council Tchrs. English, Internat. Reading Assn., Internat. Youth Library Assn., Children's Lit. Assn., Vereinigung der Freunde der Internationalen Jugend bibliothek, Munich, Beta Sigma Phi (pres. Xi Upsilon), Pi Lambda Theta, Kappa Delta Pi, Gamma Sigma, Delta Kappa Gamma. Republican. Club: Lake Montezuma Country. Book reviewer, Sch. Library Jour., 1964—, Library jour., 1964—. Home: 1609 N Aztec St Flagstaff AZ 86001

DOWTY, MERRILEE ANN, mus. dir.; b. Sacramento, Cal., May 13, 1940; d. William Joseph and Melva Juliet (Offenbach) Gwerder; B.A., U. Cal. at Berkeley, 1963. Sec. advt. dept. Wells Fargo Bank, San Francisco, 1964-65; asst. dir. history room Wells Fargo Bank, San Francisco, 1965-73, dir. history room, 1973—. Nat. Endowment Humanities grantee, 1971. Mem. Spl. Libraries Assn., Western History Assn., Am. Assn. Museums, Am. Assn. State and Local History. Republican. Roman Catholic. Office: 420 Montgomery St San Francisco CA 94104

DOYLE, CHARLOTTE LACKNER (MRS. JAMES J. DOYLE), psychologist, educator; b. Vienna, Austria, June 25, 1937 (came to U.S. 1939, naturalized 1955); d. George and Mary (Meisl) Lackner; B.A. summa cum laude (Woodrow Wilson fellow), Temple U., 1959; M.A., U. Mich., 1961, Ph.D. in psychology, 1964; m. James J. Doyle, Aug. 20, 1959. Teaching fellow U. Mich., 1962-64; instr., asst. prof. psychology Cornell U., 1964-66; mem. faculty Sarah Lawrence Coll., 1966—, prof. psychology, chmn. dept., 1969—. Mem. Am. Psychol. Assn., Phi Beta Kappa. Author: (with W.J. McKeachie) Psychology (textbook). 1966, 2d edit., 1970. Contbr. to profl. publs. Home: 293 Bronxville Rd Bronxville NY 10708

DOYLE, E(MMA) LEE CUNNINGHAM, psychotherapist, educator; b. Noble, Tex., Feb. 9, 1935; d. Dee and Mary (Roland) Cunningham; A.A., Paris Jr. Coll., 1954; B.S. with high honors, E. Tex. State U., 1957, M.Ed., 1958; postgrad. Colo. State Coll., 1965; Ph.D., Fla. State U., 1968; m. Harold Dean Doyle, July 27, 1952 (div. Feb. 1966); children—DeAnna, Delanie. Grad. asst. E. Tex. State U., Commerce, 1957-58, instr., 1958-66; research asso., co-therapist Reproductive Biology Research Found., St. Louis, 1968-69; asso. prof. Cal. State Coll., Long Beach, summer 1969; pvt. practice marriage and family counseling, Dallas, 1969—; prof. family relationships, family devel., and communication in marriage and family Tex. Woman's U., Denton, 1969—. Condr. seminars, lecture series, workshops. Mem. Am. Psychol. Assn., Soc. for Sci. Study of Sex, Am. Assn. Marriage and Family Counselors (bd. dirs. 1971-72), Nat. Council Family Relations (program chmn. 1975), Tex. Council Family Relations (pres. 1965-66), Am. Assn. Sex Educators and Counselors. Home: 6805 Willow Lane Dallas TX 75230 Office: 8616 Northwest Plaza Dallas TX 75225

DOYLE, LEILA ANN, ednl. adminstr.; b. Gary, Ind.; d. Walter William and Agnes Cecilia (Fennell) Doyle; B.S., N.Y. State U., 1936; M.S., Ind. U., 1949; postgrad. U. Chgo., 1945, U. Ill., 1961-62. Sch. media librarian Bailly Jr. High Sch., Gary, Ind., 1962-64, Froebel Sr. High, Gary, 1947-61, Emerson Elementary Sch., Gary, 1937-45; supr. library materials center Gary Pub. Schs., 1964-72; media specialist Ind. Vocational Tech. Coll., Gary, 1972—. Ford Found. fellow, 1954-55. Mem. A.L.A., Ind. Sch. Librarians Assn., Audio-visual Dirs. of Ind., Assn. Ednl. Communications Tech. (mem. standards editorial com. 1973—), Assn. Supervision and Curriculum Devel., Am. Assn. Sch. Librarians (dir. 1968-70), Delta Kappa Gamma. Home: 704 Connecticut St Gary IN 46402 Office: 1440 E 35th Av Gary IN 46409

DOYLE, MARGARET VIRGINIA DAVIS (MRS. WILLIAM V. DOYLE), educator; b. Chelsea, Okla., Sept. 23, 1914; d. John Benjamin and Katharine Alice (Murdoch) Davis; B.S., U. Ark., 1934; Ph.D. (Alumnae fellow 1943-44), U. Chgo., 1945, M.S., 1938; m. William V. Doyle, Dec. 20, 1947; 1 dau., Jean Leslie. Mem. faculty U. Minn., St. Paul, 1938-40, 60—, prof. dept. food sci. and nutrition, 1970—; instr. Conn. Coll., New London, 1940-42; asst. prof. U. Chgo., 1945-53. Cons. food and nutrition. Office Internat. Programs grantee 1970; Hon. Research fellow dept. anthropology, U. London, 1972. Fellow A.A.A.S.; mem. Am. Inst. Nutrition, Am. Bd. Nutrition, Am. Dietetic Assn., Am. Home Econs. Assn., Sigma Xi, Iota Sigma Pi, Sigma Delta Epsilon. Democrat. Episcopalian. Contbr. articles to profl. jours. Home: 1455 W Shryer Av Roseville MN 55113 Office: 225 McNeal Hall U Minn St Paul MN 55101

DOYLE, MARJORIE PATRICIA, nursing educator; b. N.Y.C., Aug. 13, 1922; d. John F. and Ethelyn (Normand) Doyle; diploma Bellevue Sch. Nursing, 1946; B.S., N.Y.U., 1952; M.A. (USPHS scholar 1952), Tchrs. Coll., Columbia, 1953. Staff nurse, pediatric dept. Bellevue Hosp., N.Y.C., 1946-48, head nurse, 1948-50, night supr., 1951-52, asst. supr., clin. instr., 1954-55; dir. playroom, 1953-54; instr. asso. degree nursing program Sch. Gen. Studies, Bklyn. Coll., 1955-63; prof., chmn. div. nursing, health and phys. edn., Suffolk County Community Coll., Selden, N.Y., 1963—. Mem. Bd. Nurse Examiners, N.Y. State Edn. Dept., 1969—; treas. N.Y. State Asso. Degree Nursing Council, 1965-70. Pres. Dist. Women's Democratic Club, Queens County, 1958-62; del. N.Y. State Dem. Conv., 1962; village trustee Village of Lake Grove, 1968—. Recipient edn. service award Suffolk County Community Coll., 1969. Mem. Am., N.Y. State nurses assns., Nurses Assn. Counties of L.I. (chmn. edn. com. 1971-73, mem. speakers bur. 1963—), Nat., So. N.Y. (dir. 1971-73) leagues for nursing, UN Assn. U.S.A., Nassau-Suffolk Tb and Respiratory Diseases Assn. (dir. 1963-69), Mid-Suffolk Bus. and Profl. Women's Club (pres. 1967-69, treas. 1969-70). Club: Zonta (dir. Suffolk County 1966-68, pres. 1968-70). Home: 83 Elliot Av Centereach NY 11720 Office: 533 College Rd Selden NY 11784

DOYLE, SISTER MARY BERNADETTE, hosp. adminstr.; b. Lawrence, Mass., Nov. 3, 1933; d. James Thomas and Viola Mary (Hale) Doyle; diploma Catherine Laboure Sch. Nursing, 1954; B.S., St. Josephs Coll., 1962; M.S., Cath. U., 1967; certificate in exec. devel. hosp. adminstrn., St. Louis U., 1974. Staff nurse St. John's Hosp., Lowell, Mass., 1954-55; head nurse Sisters Hosp., Buffalo, 1956-57; supr. St. Vincent's Hosp., Jacksonville, Fla., 1957-60; supr., instr. St. Agnes Hosp., Balt., 1962-66, 68; adminstrv. asst. div. community services Carney Hosp., Boston, 1968-71; adminstr. St. Margaret's Hosp., Dorchester, Mass., 1971—. Cons. Neponset Health Center, 1969-74. Mem. Uphams Corner Health Com., Dorchester, 1972—. Bd. dirs. Jones Hill Civic Assn., 1971—; trustee St. Mary's Hosp., Troy, N.Y., 1972—, St. Vincents, Bridgeport, Conn., 1973—, Neponset Health Center, Boston, 1969-74, Mass. Cath. Conf., 1972—. Mem. Am. Coll. Hosp. Adminstrs., Am., Mass., Cath. hosp. assns., Mass., New Eng. catholic confs., Am. Pub. Health Assn., Sigma Theta Tau. Democrat. Home and office: 90 Cushing Av Dorchester MA 02125

DOYLE, NANCY MARIE BOLT (MRS. ROBERT J. DOYLE) librarian; b. St. Louis, Oct. 16, 1945; d. Joseph Leroy and Ruth Ann (Laws) Bolt; B.S. in Edn., S.E. Mo. State Coll., 1968; M.L.S., U. Mo. at Columbia, 1970; m. Robert James Doyle, June 4, 1966. Supr. adult basic edn. program Columbia (Mo.) Pub. Sch. Systems, 1971; asst. reference librarian Daniel Boone Regional Library, Columbia, 1971-72; br. librarian Erie County Pub. Library, 1972-73; head reference dept. Meadville (Pa.) Pub. Library, 1973—. Bd. dirs. Freedom to Read Found. Mem. Am. (mem. exec. com. Jr. Mems. Round Table 1971—, pres.-elect 1974; editor Footnotes 1971-73; mem. reference and adult services standards com.), Mo. (exec. sec. 1970-71; exec. com. pub. relations council 1971-72; adult edn. com. 1971-72; state coordinator social responsibilities round table 1971-72; editor Newsletter 1970-71) library assns., Phi Alpha Theta, Beta Phi Mu. Editor: Mo. Directory Trade and Profl. Assns., 1969. Home: 729 Washington St Meadville PA 16335

DOYLE, VERLA DOHERTY (MRS. JACOBS H. DOYLE), club woman; b. Franklin, Pa., Aug. 12, 1912; d. Wilbur Felix and Walza (Magee) Doherty; A.B., St. Francis Xavier Coll. Women, 1936; m. Jacobs H. Doyle, Nov. 10, 1951. Case worker Pa. Dept. Pub. Assistance, Franklin, 1937-41; with U.S.O., Nat. Catholic Community Service, 1941-47, successively asst. club dir., club dir., rep. Tenn. maneuvers, 1943-44, traveling dir. S.E. region U.S., 1944-46; exec. sec. Cath. Youth Orgn., Nashville, 1949-51; bd. dirs. Nashville Diocesan Council Cath. Women, 1951—, sec., 1955-57, pres., 1959-61; nat. youth chmn. Nat. Council Cath. Women, 1958-62; del. Pres.'s White House Conf. Children and Youth, Washington, 1960; bd. dirs. Cath. Youth Orgn., Nashville, 1951-55, Nat. Multiple Sclerosis Soc., Nashville chpt., 1963-64. Alternate del. Democratic Conv. from Tenn., 1952, 56. Mem. Cath. Daus. Am., Cheekwood Cultural Center, St. Xavier Coll. Alumnae, Tenn., Nashville bar auxiliaries. Clubs: Richland Country, Newman (dir. 1963-64), Colonna (treas. 1956, pres. 1958-60) (Nashville). Address: 6117 Robin Hill Rd Nashville TN 37205

DOZIER, BESSIE EUPLE, lawyer; b. Fulton, Miss., Nov. 10, 1908; d. Samuel Lee and Maranda (Googe) Dozier; tchrs. certificate Ala. State Tchrs. Coll., 1933; certificate in bus. adminstrn. Draughon's Bus. Coll., 1939; student Jackson Sch. Law, 1953. Admitted to Miss. bar, 1953; with U.S. Atty.'s Office No. Dist. Miss., Oxford, 1942-62; practiced in Fulton, 1962—; atty. Itawamba County Hosp., Fulton, 1968, Itawamba Jr. Coll., Fulton, 1972, Itawamba County Bd. Suprs., 1965—. Chmn. bd. commrs. U.S. Dist. Ct., 1962. Named Woman of Achievement in Oxford and Lafayette County, Civic Clubs, 1955, Susan B. Anthony award, 1974. Mem. Miss. State Bar, Fed. Bar Assn., Bus. and Profl. Women's Clubs (state pres. 1969-70). Mem. Order Eastern Star. Home: 408 N Cumming St Fulton MS 38843 Office: 111 S Gaither St Fulton MS 38843

DOZIER, MANCE ETRULIA PRESSLEY (MRS. GIBB ALVA DOZIER III), librarian; b. Anderson, S.D., Sept. 23, 1930; d. Mance and Virgie Virginia (Mattison) Pressley; A.B. magna cum laude, Benedict Coll., 1953; M.S., Atlanta U., 1957; m. Gibb Alva Dozier III, May 1, 1955; children—Shirley Mae, Claudette, Gibb Alva IV. Librarian, Whittemore High Sch., Conway, S.C., 1954-70; librarian, Conway Jr. High Sch. (S.C.), 1970—. Interviewer, Am. Research Bur., 1973—. Librarian, Horry County Beautification and Recycling Com., 1972-73; chmn. Mother's March, Nat. Found. March Dimes, Pee Dee area chpt., 1964-65; publicity chmn. Conway Hosp. Aux., 1973. Recipient Carnegie Scholarship, Atlanta U. Sch. Library Service, 1953. Mem. United Teaching Profession, A.L.A. S.C. Library Assn. Club: Chrysanthemum Home and Garden. Home: 1915 Racepath Av Conway SC 29526

DRABBLE, MARGARET, author; b. Sheffield, Eng., May 6, 1939; d. John Frederick and Marie (Bloor) D.; B.A. with 1st class honors, Newnham Coll. Cambridge (Eng.) U., 1960; m. Clive Swift, June, 1960; children—Adam Richard George, Rebecca Margaret, Joseph Samuel. Author novels, also TV play Laura produced in Eng., 1964. Recipient E.M. Forster award, John Llewelyn Rhys Meml. award,

1966, James Tait Black Meml. Book prize, 1968. Author: A Summer Bird-Cage, 1963; The Garrick Year, 1964; The Millstone, 1965; Jerusalem the Golden, 1966; The Waterfall, 1969; The Needle's Eye, 1972; Arnold Bennett, 1974. Contbr. to Brit. lit. jours., nat. mags. Home: 70 Riversdale Rd London N5 England Office: care Weidenfeld & Nicolson 5 Winsley St London W1 England

DRAGON, ROSALINE GLADYS GROSZ (MRS. MICHAEL R. DRAGON), educator; b. Rich Hill, Mo., Aug. 3, 1917; d. Edward and Emma B.C. (Knuth) Grosz; A.B., Valparaiso U., 1938, postgrad., 1938-39; postgrad. U. Minn., 1940, U. Wis., 1944; M.A., U. Mich., 1952, postgrad., 1951-63; m. Michael R. Dragon, Aug. 5, 1950. Tchr. elementary sch., Herington, Kan., 1939-41; tchr. jr. high sch., Appleton, Wis., 1941-42; tchr. social studies jr. high sch., Hamilton, O., 1942-45, Dearborn, Mich., 1945—. Asso. chmn. Photo Guild Ann. Photog. Sch., Marygrove Coll. Recipient numerous awards in photography Greater Detroit Camera Club Council, Ford Motor Camera Club, Photog. Soc. Am., others. Fellow Nat. Council Geog. Edn. (exec. bd. dirs. 1966-67, 70-71), Photog. Soc. Am. (asso., dir. portrait portfolios Pictorial Print div., chmn. internat. chpt. 1973-75); mem. N.E.A., Am. Assn. Geographers, Nat., Mich. councils social studies, Am. Geog. Soc., Mich., Dearborn edn. assns., Photog. Guild Detroit (sec., dir. 1968—, pres. 1968-70), Pi Gamma Mu, Phi Alpha Theta, Pi Lambda Theta. Lutheran. Home: 22434 Cherry Hill Dearborn MI 48124 Office: 4824 Lois St Dearborn MI 48126

DRAGOSITZ, ANNA, ednl. psychologist; b. N.Y.C.; d. Frank and Mary (Barkowitz) Dragositz; B.S., Tchrs. Coll., Columbia, 1940, M.A., 1943. Asso. in guidance lab. Tchrs. Coll., Columbia, 1941-47; head programs and services, coop. test div. Ednl. Testing Service, Princeton, N.J., 1947-49, asst. dir. coop. test div., 1949-52, asso. dir. Evaluation and Adv. Service, 1952-56, dir., 1956-60, asst. to pres., 1960-61, dir. Evaluation and Adv. Service, 1961-69, exec. asso., 1969-70, asso. dir. office information services, 1970—. Sec. Hillcrest Civic Assn., Princeton, 1968-70. Fellow. A.A.A.S.; mem. Am. Assn. for Higher Edn., Am. Coll. Personnel Assn., Am. Ednl. Research Assn., Am., N.J. personnel and guidance assns., Am. Psychol. Assn., Assn. for Measurement and Evaluation in Guidance (del. 1969-71), Eastern Psychol. Assn., Nat. Council on Measurement in Edn. (dir. 1957-60), Nat. Soc. for Study of Edn., Nat. Catholic Ednl. Assn., Pi Lambda Theta, Kappa Delta Pi. Club: Soroptimist. Contbr. articles in field to profl. jours. Home: 36 Woodland Dr Princeton NJ 08540 Office: Ednl Testing Service Princeton NJ 08540

DRAHOLD, LUCILLE EVELYN WALTON, antique shop owner; b. Hugo, Okla., Apr. 13, 1907; d. Winthrop W. and Evelyn (Richardson) Walton; grad. high sch.; m. Otto Drahhold, July 24, 1925; children—Georgene (Mrs. Raymond Hagen), Carol King, Sandra Baker (Mrs. Donald Baker), Byron, Pamela (Mrs. Jeff Bratrud). Owner, tchr. Lucille Drahold's Studio of Dance, Tacoma, Wash., 1925-30; owner, Old Tacoma (Wash.) Antiques Shop, 1960—. Pres., Grant Sch. Presch., 1929; pres. Irving Grade Sch. P.T.A., 1932, Mason Jr. High Sch. P.T.A., 1950; active Tacoma (Wash.) Little Theater; pres. Tacoma (Wash.) Day Nursery, Mecca Club for Crippled Children, 1960. Mem. Nat. Assn. Dealers Antiques, Antique Dealers Pacific N.W., Daus. of Nile. Clubs: Lawn and Tennis, Tacoma Yacht (pres. Shipmates 1955-56). Address: 2223 N 30th St Tacoma WA 98403

DRAKE, BERNEIL LINDBERG MAXEY (MRS. JAMES E. DRAKE, JR.), educator; b. Sioux City, Ia., Nov. 20, 1921; d. Gustav E. and Ruth (Wilson) Lindberg; B.A., Drake U., 1942; M.A., U. Ia., 1947; postgrad., U. Ariz., 1955-70, Ariz. State U., 1962-72, No. Ariz. U., 1964, Cal. Western U., 1964; m. James E. Drake, Jr., Mar. 7, 1959. Statistician, Look Mag., Des Moines, 1940-47; tchr. high sch., Murray and Knoxville, Ia., 1942-44; tchr. Ellsworth Coll., Iowa Falls, Ia., 1945-47; tchr. high sch. system, Phoenix, 1947—, counselor, 1957—. Profl. ch. organist, flautist, Phoenix, 1947—. Adviser SSS, 1967—. Republican precinct committeewoman, Phoenix, 1969—. Mem. Am. Guild Organists (state chmn. 1962-72), Am. Personnel and Guidance Assn., N.E.A., Ariz. Edn. Assn., Daus. of Nile, Delta Zeta, Delta Kappa Gamma, Psi Chi. Lutheran (supt. Sunday sch. 1950-57). Mem. Order Eastern Star. Home: 3426 E Elm St Phoenix AZ 85018 Office: 3415 N 59th Av Phoenix AZ 85031

DRAKE, CAROLINE CURTIS, librarian; b. Hoosick Falls, N.Y., Mar. 22, 1915; d. Henry William and Mary (Bovie) Drake; A.B., Oberlin Coll., 1937; B.S. in L.S., Case Western Res. U., 1938; A.M. in L.S., U. Mich., 1955. Reference asst. Troy (N.Y.) Pub. Library, 1938-44; serials librarian Russell Sage Coll., Troy, 1944-48; asst. librarian Rensselaer Poly. Inst., Troy, 1948-54; engring. librarian U. Notre Dame, South Bend, Ind., 1955-61; circulation librarian Williams Coll., Williamstown, Mass., 1961-62; asst. librarian Sterling-Winthrop Research Inst., Rensselaer, N.Y., 1962-66, librarian, 1966—. Mem. Drug Information Assn., Am. Soc. Information Sci., Med. Library Assn., A.A.A.S., Spl. Libraries Assn. Episcopalian. Home: Bovie Rd Hoosick Falls NY 12090 Office: Columbia Turnpike Rensselaer NY 12144

DRAKE, ELISABETH MERTZ (MRS. ALVIN WILLIAM DRAKE), chem. engr., educator; b. N.Y.C., Dec. 20, 1936; d. John Martin and Ruth (Johnson) Mertz; B.S. in Chem. Engring., Mass. Inst. Tech., 1958, D.Sci., 1966; m. Alvin William Drake, July 31, 1957; 1 son, Alan (dec.). Staff engr. A.D. Little, Inc., Cambridge, Mass., 1958-64, sr. engr. cryogenic processes 1966—. Vis. lectr. U. Cal., Berkeley, 1971; vis. asso. prof. chem. engring. Mass. Inst. Tech., Cambridge, 1973-74. Registered profl. engr. Mass. Mem. Am. Chem. Soc., Am. Inst. Chem. Engrs. (editorial bd. jour. 1970—), Sigma Xi. Patentee in field. Home: 28 Circle Rd Lexington MA 02173 Office: 20 Acorn Park Cambridge MA 02140

DRAKE, JOAN BAKER (MRS. KEVIN GLEN DRAKE), newspaper co. exec.; b. Cleve., Feb. 24, 1944; d. Herbert Charles and Allene Verna (Lambertus) Baker; B.A., Ind. U., 1969; m. Kevin Glen Drake, Jan. 26, 1965. County home demonstration agt. Tex. Agrl. Extension Service, Houston, 1970-71; food editor Los Angeles Herald Examiner, 1971—. Mem. Am. Home Econs. Assn., Home Economists in Bus. (pub. relations chmn. 1973—), Alpha Lambda Delta, Omicron Nu. Home: 8932 Wonderland Av Hollywood CA 90046 Office: PO Box 2416 Terminal Annex Los Angeles CA 90051

DRAKE, MARJORIE ANN (MRS. JOHN WILLIAM DRAKE), real estate broker; b. Jacksonville, Ill., Nov. 22, 1928; d. Arthur Henry and Verna Marie (Middendorf) Kleinschmidt; real estate certification Coll. of the Redwoods, 1971; m. John William Drake, June 20, 1948; children—Marcia (Mrs. Garey Barsanti), Marla, James, Marlene. Various office positions Pacific Lumber Co., Scotia, Cal., 1948-52; bookkeeper Dr. C.R. Schwartz, Fortuna, Cal., 1956; personnel clk. State of Cal., Fortuna, 1961-68; real estate broker Redwood Realty, Fortuna, 1968—. Mem. Nat., Cal. real estate assns., Humboldt County Bd. Realtors (dir. 1972—), Humboldt Bay Quarter Horse Assn. (chmn. fashion show 1973), Fortuna C. of C. (membership chmn. 1971-72, dir. 1974). Republican. Lutheran. Home: 1100 Hilltop Dr Fortuna CA 95540 Office: 1506 Main St Fortuna CA 95540

DRAPER, ELSIE COX (MRS. PORTER R. DRAPER), lawyer; b. Oak Park, Ill.; d. Russell Earl and Edna Agnes (Thome) Cox; B.A. with honors, Ohio Wesleyan U., 1953; J.D., Northwestern U., 1963; m. Charles E. Spears, June 20, 1953 (dec. July 1958); 1 son, Stuart E.; m. 2d, Porter Russell Draper, July 31, 1969; children—Tiffany Joy, Porter Russell; stepchildren—Dianne, Cooper. Admitted to Ill. bar, 1963, Ind. bar, 1971; asso. firm Kirkland & Ellis, Chgo., 1963-70; partner firm Draper & Draper, Gary, Ind., 1971-74; asso. firm Gable, Gotwals, Rubin, Fox, Johnson & Baker, Tulsa, 1974—. Mem. Am. Bar Assn., Phi Beta Kappa, Delta Delta Delta. Editorial staff Northwestern Law Rev., 1961-62, note and comment editor, 1962-63. Office: 2010 Fourth National Bank Bldg Tulsa OK 74119

DRAPER, ETHEL TREW (MRS. HOWARD D. DRAPER), ednl. adminstr.; b. High Point, N.C., Nov. 22, 1918; d. Ernest William and Jennie (Thomas) Trew; B.A. in Elementary Edn. magna cum laude, Atlantic Christian Coll., 1952; M.A., East Carolina U., 1956; postgrad. U. N.C.; m. Howard Dennis Draper, Oct. 10, 1942; 1 son, Howard Dennis. Legal sec. firm W.T. Stauffer, Newport News, Va., 1936-40; sec. Noland Co., Newport News, 1940-43; legal sec. firm Newman & Allaun, Newport News, 1946-49; tchr. pub. schs., Johnston County, N.C., 1952-53, Spring Lake, N.C., 1953-62; gen. elementary supr. Cumberland County Schs., Fayetteville, N.C., 1962-72, dir. fed. programs, 1972—. Mem. Am. Childhood Edn. Internat. (pres. 1970-72), N.C. Assn. Educators (pres. 1974—, past sec., v.p. div. suprs.), N.E.A. (conv. del. 1962), N.C. Edn. Assn. (sec. 1963-64), Am. Bus. Women's Assn. (past sec., pres.), Delta Kappa Gamma. Mem. Order Eastern Star. Home: 3301 Lennox Dr Fayetteville NC 28304 Office: Box 1420 Cumberland County Bd Edn Fayetteville NC 28302

DRAPER, FREDA, opera and concert singer; b. Kansas City, Mo.; d. Frederick and Leila (Burleigh) Faulkner; ed. pub. schs., Kansas City, Mo., Chgo. Mus. Coll.; pupil voice Edna Forsythe, Kansas City, Mo., operatic work with Dino Bigalli, Chgo.; scholarship pupil of Mary Garden; m. Vernon Gerhardt, 1947. Tour soloist Ballet Russe de Monte Carlo, Chgo. Opera Co., 1937-42; sang world premier The Bride of Bagdad, winner of Am. Opera Soc.'s first award, 1940; mem. vocal faculty Northwestern U., 1941-44; with Chgo. Opera Co., 1937-42; has appeared as soloist with leading symphony orchs. of U.S., also as guest nat. radio programs; made seven months tour of P.I. as soloist before armed forces, 1945; appeared in concert and opera on 3 continents, 1952-55; coached oratorio with Charles Baker, N.Y.C.; light opera appearances St. Louis Municipal Opera, Hollywood Prodns., Inc. Recipient Presdl. citation, Medal of Freedom, 1947. Mem. Women's C. of C. Kansas City (hon.), Sigma Alpha Iota, Beta Sigma Phi (internat. hon.). Home: PO Box 636 Dana Point CA 92629

DRAPER, HELEN WISCOMBE (MRS. CECIL MEAD DRAPER), educator; b. Topeka, Dec. 1, 1910; d. Oscar Austin and Verla (Lane) Wiscombe; B.A., U. No. Colo., 1931; M.A., U. Denver, 1942; postgrad. U. Colo., 1961-62; m. Cecil Mead Draper, Mar. 26, 1949; children—Cynthia St. John (Mrs. Dudley Boyd Mattox), Cecily Mead (Mrs. Noll), Virginia Lee (Mrs. Timenes). Tchr., Mesa (Colo.) Pub. Schs., 1931-34; tchr. Denver pub. schs., 1934-66, jr. high schs., 1934-62, South High Sch., 1962-66; chmn. English dept. Gove Jr. High Sch., 1952-55; chmn. guidance dept. Kunsmiller Jr. High Sch., 1957-58. Mem. Greeley (Colo.) Philharmonic Orch., 1928-31, Denver Tchrs. Chorus, 1934-43, Denver Tchrs. Orch., 1934-43; vol., pink lady St. Anthony's Hosp. Recipient Freedoms Found. Teachers' award, 1962. Mem. Salvation Army Aux., Intergroup Edn. Cooperating Schs., P.E.O., Kappa Delta Pi, Alpha Sigma Alpha. Republican. Presbyn. Clubs: Monday of Bow Mar. Composer: The Land Where Nobody Grows Up (children's operetta), 1932. Home: 5350 Ridge Trail Bow-Mar Littleton CO 80123

DRAPER, KAREN FITKIN (MRS. JAMES B. DRAPER), state ofcl.; b. Neptune, N.J., Oct. 31, 1939; student Briarcliff Jr. Coll.; m. James B. Draper; 1 son, 1 dau. Mem. Vt. Bd. Mental Health. Mem. Ward IV Republican Com., Burlington, Vt., Burlington Rep. Com., Chittenden County Rep. Commn., Rep. Women's Com.; now staff asst. Congressman Richard W. Mallary from Vt. Home: 129 Lakewood Pkwy Burlington VT 05401*

DRAPER, MARTHA STARK, ednl. adminstr.; b. Boston, Oct. 16, 1942; d. Charles Stark and Ivy (Willard) Draper; B.A. with honors, U. Pacific, 1964; M.A., Boston U., 1965; student Inst. European Studies, Vienna, Austria. Legal sec. Haley, Bader & Potts, Washington, 1965-67; adminstrv. asst. Communications Satellite Corp., Washington and Geneva, 1967-69; adminstrv. asst. Project MAC, Mass. Inst. Tech., Cambridge, 1969-71, research staff, 1971-72, asso. dir. undergrad. research opportunities program, 1972-74, program coordinator MIT-Detroit Inst. Tech. Assn., 1974—. Home: 35 Homer Av Cambridge MA 02138

DRAPER, VIRGINIA SALLY (MRS. ROBERT F. DRAPER), lawyer, govt. ofcl.; b. Richmond, Va., Sept. 4, 1944; d. Edward and Lucille (Drumgold) Sally; B.S. in Biology, Howard U., 1967, J.D., 1970; m. Robert F. Draper, July 6, 1968. Admitted to D.C. bar, 1970; civil rights atty. U.S. Equal Employment Opportunity Commn., Washington, 1970-71, spl. asst. to chmn., 1971-73; asst. U.S. atty. U.S. Atty.'s Office, Dist. Md., Balt., 1973—. Tchr. pre-law course U. Va., Charlottesville, 1969. Mem. Am. Civil Liberties Union, N.A.A.C.P., Nat. Orgn. Women, Urban League. Recipient Pub. Service award Black Businessman Assn. Niagara Falls, 1973. Mem. Am., Fed., Nat. bar assns. Home: 550 N Broadway Apt 711 Baltimore MD 21205 Office: 111 N Calvert St Baltimore MD 21202

DRASKÓCZY, CAMILLE BALLER (MRS. PAUL R. DRASKÓCZY), physiologist, neurologist; b. Long Branch, N.J., Aug. 7, 1937; d. Melvin David and Marie Lucie (Bronson) Baller; B.A., Wellesley Coll., 1959; Ph.D., Harvard, 1965; M.D., Johns Hopkins, 1972; m. William Henry Olson, June 24, 1961 (div. Oct. 1966); m. 2d, Paul R. Draskóczy, May 3, 1974. Postdoctoral fellow pharmacology Harvard, 1966, instr. pharmacology, 1967, asso. pharmacology, 1968-69; intern New Eng. Deaconess Hosp., 1971-72, resident in medicine, 1972-73; resident neurology Mass. Gen. Hosp., Boston, 1973—. NIH fellow, 1960-65; Woodrow Wilson fellow, 1959-60. Mem. A.C.P., Phi Beta Kappa, Sigma Xi. Home: 35 Yale Av Wakefield MA 01880 Office: Dept Neurology Mass Gen Hosp Fruit St Boston MA 02114

DRATLER, STELLA LYNNE, publisher; b. Vienna, Austria, Nov. 11, 1920; d. Louis and Emily (Lindenbaum) Dratler; came to U.S., 1927; B.B.A., Coll. City N.Y., 1944; m. Adolph Hendler, June 11, 1943; 1 dau., Roberta. Copywriter Charles A. Weeks Advt., N.Y.C., 1937-41; advt. mgr. Jiffy Mfg. Co., Hillside, N.J., 1941-44; pres. Stella L. Dratler Advt., N.Y.C., 1944-71, pub. Fancy Food Merchandiser, Fine Foods & Beverages Internat., 1962-72, Gusto Internat. mag., 1962-72; v.p. Food Forum, N.Y.C., 1972—; cons. in field. Club: Advertising (N.Y.C.). Home: 4580 Broadway New York City NY 10040 Office: 250 W 57th St New York City NY 10019

DRAVES, DOROTHY ENGLE, extension home economist; b. Ochelata, Okla., Nov. 25, 1918; d. James Dow and Genelle (Shelton) Engle; B.S. in Home Econ. Edn., Okla. State U., 1939, postgrad., 1941-42; postgrad. Purdue U., 1949-50; m. Norman Michel Draves, Sept. 29, 1945; 1 dau., Suzanne. Tchr. pub. schs. Chelsea, Okla., 1939-41; asst. home demonstration agt. Payne County, Stillwater, Okla., 1941-42; home demonstration agt. Adair County, Stillwater, 1942-43; asst. home econs. agt. Pinellas County, Largo, Fla., 1962-68, home econs. agt., program leader, 1968—. Mem. Community Services Council, St. Petersburg, Fla., 1968—; mem. health sect. United Fund, Clearwater, Fla., 1960—; mem. gerentology com. United Services Pinellas County, 1970—; mem. Pinellas County chpt. A.R.C., 1940—; mem. Pinellas County Nutrition Com., 1962—; personnel dir. Pink Lady Vols., Morton Plant Hosp., 1958-62. Served with WAVES, USNR, 1943-45. Mem. Am., Fla. home econ. assns., Nat., Fla. (pres. 1968) assns. home econ. agts. Mem. Order Eastern Star. Club: Clearwater Garden. Home: 1660 Magnolia Dr Clearwater FL 33516 Office: PO Box 235 East Bay Dr Fairgrounds Largo FL 33540

DRAY, GERTRUDE (MRS. FRANCIS DRAY), educator; b. Toronto, Ont., Can., Aug. 14, 1909; d. Charles Webster and Jane Elizabeth (Rodd) Ellis; diploma U. Toronto, 1930; B.S., U. Buffalo, 1959; M.S., State U. N.Y., 1967; m. Francis Dray, Oct. 18, 1941; children—Catherine (Mrs. Lee McCue), Alison (Mrs. David Flower). Came to U.S., 1951, naturalized, 1957. Staff therapist Verdun Protestant Hosp., Montreal, Que., Can., 1930-33, Curative Workshop, Toronto, 1933-36; chief occupational therapist Children's Meml. Hosp., Montreal, 1936-40, Dept. Health for Scotland, 1941-42, 45-47, Pinderfield Hosp., Eng., 1947-49, Occupational Therapy Workshop, Montreal, 1949-51, Chronic Disease Research Inst., U. Buffalo, 1951-56, Children's Rehab. Center, Buffalo, 1956-59, Buffalo State Hosp., 1959-62; faculty State U. N.Y. at Buffalo, 1962—, asst. prof. occupational therapy, 1969—. Mem. acad. planning com. Council of Health Sci. Senators, 1973—. Mem. World Fedn. Occupational Therapists, Canadian Assn. Occupational Therapists, Am., N.Y. occupational therapy assns., Am. Assn. U. Profs., Senate Profl. Assn. Club: Faculty (Buffalo). Home: 576 French Rd Depew NY 14043 Office: State U NY 313 Diefendorf Buffalo NY 14214

DRAYSON, DIANE BRANDT (MRS. ROLAND DRAYSON), social worker; b. Lancaster, Pa., Jan. 8, 1938; d. Lewis Clifford and Alma (Webber) Brandt; A.B. magna cum laude, Wittenberg U., 1960; M.A., U. Chgo., 1962; m. S. Roland Drayson, Oct. 12, 1963; children—Kathleen Susan, Christopher David. Clin. social worker VA Hosps., Balt., 1962-63, Ann Arbor, Mich., 1963-64; psychiat. field worker Ypsilanti (Mich.) State Hosp., 1964-66, chief social worker, outpatient clinic, 1966-68; practice psychotherapy, Ann Arbor, 1966—, also practice marriage counselling, 1970—. Field work instr. U. Mich., 1965-67. Bd. dirs., treas. Broadway Drop-In Center. Mem. Nat. Assn. Social Workers, Acad. Certified Social Workers, Internat. Conf. Social Welfare, Council on Social Work Edn., Mich. Assn. Marriage Counselors, League Women Voters, Am. Civil Liberties Union. Club: University of Michigan Faculty Womens. Home: 2577 Bunker Hill Rd Ann Arbor MI 48105 Office: 2301 Huron Pkwy Ann Arbor MI 48104

DREIFUS, CLAUDIA, author; b. N.Y.C., Nov. 24, 1944; d. Henry H. and Marianne J. (Willdorf) Dreifus; B.S., N.Y. U., 1966. Labor organizer Drug and Hosp. Workers Union, N.Y.C., 1967-68; news editor East Village Other, N.Y.C., 1969-71; free lance writer, 1971—. Lectr. on women's liberation at various colls., N.Y., Conn., Pa., 1971—; adj. assoc. prof. journalism N.Y. U., 1974. Vice pres. New Chelsea Democratic Club, N.Y.C., 1967-68. Bd. dirs. Women's Liberation Writing Collective, Inc., 1971—. Mem. Soc. Mag. Writers, Media Women (chairwoman 1971-73), Nat. Orgn. Women, Am. Civil Liberties Union. Author: Radical Life Styles, 1971; Woman's Fate, 1973. Contbr. articles on social and polit. issues to various publs. including McCall's, Nation, Family Circle, N.Y. Times Book Rev. and anthologies. Home: 158 9th Av New York City NY 10011 Office: care Internat Famous Agy 1301 Av of Americas New York City NY

DREIFUS, JOAN FREEHOF (MRS. JORDAN ALBERT DREIFUS), public relations co. exec.; b. Washington, Mar. 11, 1934; d. Hyman Bennett and Sally (Jacobs) Freehof; B.A., U. Md., 1954; M.A., George Washington U., 1960; m. Jordan Albert Dreifus, Feb. 21, 1960; children—Stuart Freehof, Amy Ruth. With Office Pub. Affairs, State Dept., Washington, 1954-57; pub. information officer NIH, Washington, 1957, Dept. Agr., Washington, 1957-60; free lance pub. relations, Los Angeles, 1960—; with Recht & Co., Inc. (name now Admarketing, Inc.), Beverly Hills, Cal., 1967—, dir. pub. relations, 1968—. Pub. relations cons. Los Angeles Library Assn.; pub. relations dir. So. Pacific Coast Region Hadassah. Bd. dirs. Modern Forum, 1966-70, Los Angeles Library Assn., 1972—, Bay Cities Jewish Community Center, Bay Cities Community Relations Council. Mem. Cal. Mus. Sci. and Industry Found., Hadassah (dir., exec. bd. 1960—, pres. 1970-72 Beverly Hills chpt.). Democrat. Jewish religion. Home: 242 Surfview Dr Pacific Palisades CA 90272 Office: 8383 Wilshire Blvd Beverly Hills CA 90211

DREIZEN, FLORENCE MORGENSTERN (MRS. RICHARD BARTH), lawyer; b. Bklyn., Sept. 21, 1918; d. Morris and Rose (Eisenberg) Morgenstern; B.A., Cornell U., 1939; LL.B., Columbia, 1941; m. Nathan Dreizen, Dec. 21, 1945 (dec. 1961); children—Laura (Mrs. Michael Insel), Alison; m. 2d, Richard Barth, Dec. 27, 1970. Admitted to N.Y. bar, 1942; atty. Karelson & Rubin, N.Y.C., 1941-42, Lauterstein, Spiller, Bergerman & Dannett, N.Y.C., 1942-47; atty., exec. asst. to county exec. Eugene H. Nickerson, Nassau County, Mineola, N.Y., 1961-70; counsel N.Y.C. Municipal Service Adminstrn., Mayor's Office of Constrn., N.Y.C., 1970-74; 2d dep. controller City of N.Y., 1974—. Mem. Vocational and Ednl. Commn. Nassau County (N.Y.), 1960-62; sec. Rockville Centre (N.Y.) Sch. Bd., 1960-62; legistlation chmn. Nassau-Suffolk Sch. Bd. Assn., 1961-62. Bd. dirs. S. Shore Child Guidance Assn., Freeport, N.Y., 1957-59, N.Y. State P.T.A., 1959-61, Nassau County P.T.A., 1957-60. Mem. Nassau County Womens Bar Assn. (legislation chmn. 1959-60), N.Y. State Congress P.T.A. (hon.), Phi Beta Kappa. Home: 250 E 65th St New York City NY 10021 Office: Municipal Bldg Room 1818 Chambers St New York City NY 10007

DRELL, ANNIE DEE FLINN (MRS. THEODORE LOUIS DRELL), realtor; b. Fulton, Ky., June 11, 1916; d. Dillingham Dodson and Alma (Bradley) Flinn; student real estate appraising Tulane U., 1966-67; m. Theodore Louis Drell, Aug. 31, 1935; children—Barbara Anne (Mrs. Austin Allen), Robert Louis (dec.), Theodore Louis III, Dee Dodson. Sec.-treas. Ted Drell, advt. art and design, 1939—; real estate agt. Carriere & Harper, New Orleans, 1959-66; broker, 1966-67; v.p. Waguespack, Pratt, Inc., 1967; staff broker Stan Weber & Assos., New Orleans, 1968—. Mem. Methodist Hosp. Woman's Aux., 1968—. Mem. D.A.R. (Charter Bayou St. John chpt. regent chpt. 1958-59, 62-63, treas. 1970-72), Jefferson Bd. Realtors, Nat. Inst. Real Estate Brokers, Nat. Assn. Real Estate Brokers, Jefferson Bd. Realtors, Real Estate Bd. of New Orleans. Baptist. Club: Lake Terrace Women's (rec. sec. 1969-70, pres. 1973-74). (New Orleans). Home: 1336 New York St New Orleans LA 70122 Office: 6244 Argonne Blvd New Orleans LA 70124

DRESKIN, JEANET STECKLER (MRS. E. ARTHUR DRESKIN), artist, educator; b. New Orleans, Sept. 29, 1921; d. William and Beate (Burgas) Steckler; B.F.A., Tulane U., 1942; grad. certificate in med. art Johns Hopkins, 1943; M.F.A., Clemson U.,

1973; m. E. Arthur Dreskin, May 9, 1943; children—Richard Burgas, Stephen Charles, Jeanet Elizabeth, Rena Lynn. Staff artist Am. Mus. Natural History, N.Y.C., 1943-46, dept. anatomy U. Chgo. Med. Sch., 1946-50; instr. drawing and painting Greenville (S.C.) Mus. of Art Sch., 1951-53, 62-74, dir. art sch., 1968-74; teaching asso. Art U. S.C., 1971-74, adj. prof., 1973-74; one-man shows Greenville Mus. Art, 1964, 70, Asheville-Biltmore Coll. U. N.C., 1965, Furman U., 1965, Mus. of Art, Gainesville, Ga., 1966, Columbia (S.C.) Mus. Art, 1966, Erskine Coll., 1966, Ga. Mus. Art, Athens, 1967, Chapel Hill (N.C.) Art Gallery, 1967, Community Art Center, Oak Ridge, 1968, A.L. Lowe Gallery, New Orleans, 1968, U. S.C., Aiken, 1970, Greenwood (S.C.) Mus., 1970, Asheville (N.C.) Mus., 1970, Presbyn. Coll., 1970, Art Center, Spartanburg, S.C., 1971, Sandlapper Gallery, Columbia, S.C., 1971, North Ga. Coll., Dahlonega, 1972, Rudolph Lee Gallery Clemson U., 1973, Sumter Gallery Art, 1973; exhibited in group shows Dulin Gallery Art, Knoxville, 1964, Gibbes Art Gallery, 1952-72, Columbia Mus. Art, 1952-73, Clemson U., 1953, Appalachian Corridors, Charleston, W.Va., 1968, 72, Hunter Gallery Art, Chattanooga, 1967, 74, Central South and Tex., Parthenon, Nashville, 1967, Winston-Salem (N.C.) Gallery Contemporary Art, 1968, 69, 72, 73, Arts Alliance Center, High Mus., Atlanta, 1967-74, Birmingham Mus., 1967, Am. Contemporary Ex. Soc. Four Arts, Palm Beach, Fla., 1968, 70, 1st S.C. State Invitational, 1969, Internat. Platform Assn. Exhbn., Washington, 1969-73, Nat. League Am. Penwomen, Nat. Exhbn., 1966, 70, 72, 74, Dixie Ann. Montgomery Mus. Fine Arts, 1969, 72, Calloway Gardens, Pine Mountain, Ga., 1969, 72, Nat. Arts Club-N.Y.C., 1970-73, S.C. Tricentennial Invitational exhbn., 1970, Nat. Soc. Painters in Casein, 1969, 71, Mint Museum of Art, 1969, 70, 71, 72, South Eastern Graphics Traveling Exhbn., 1973-74, Nat. Assn. Women Artists, N.A.D., N.Y.C., 1969, 70, 71, 72, 73, U.S.A. Traveling Exhbn. Painting and Drawing, 1970-71, 72-74, Chautauqua (N.Y.) Exhbn. Am. Art, 1970, Butler Inst. Am. Art, 1974, Internat. Grand Prix, Cannes, France, 1973, Nat. Watercolor traveling show, 1972-74, I Sette Colle di Roma (Italy), 1974, Tex. Fine Arts Nat. Exhbn., Austin, 1974, others; represented in permanent collections Greenville Mus. Art, Furman U., Ga. Mus. Art, Athens, Columbia Mus. Art, Greenwood Mus., Beaufort Mus., S.C. State Art Collection, S.C. Art Commn., Tex. Fine Art Assn., Austin, Maremont Corp., United Mchts. & Mfrs., Wachovia Bank N.C., Bankers Trust S.C., Nat. Parks Collection, Great Smoky Mountains, Gatlinburg, Tenn., First Fed. Savs. & Loan, Piedmont Industries, C. & S. Nat. Bank of S.C. Greenville City Hall, others. Mem. Recipient awards Sears So. Contemporary Show, 1965, Springs Ann., 1965; 1st pl. and merit awards Greenville Mus. Art, 1950, 57, 58, 64, 69, 71-74, Found. award Carolina Art Assn.-Gibbes Gallery, 1967, 71; Purchase and Merit awards Guild S.C. Artists, 1965, 67, 68, 71, 73; Owen J. Kenan Meml. Merit award Soc. Four Arts, Palm Beach, 1968; W.J. Kaplan Merit award Nat. Soc. Painters in Casein, 1969; Merit award Savannah Art Assn., 1969; M.R. Pool Top Purchase award Greenville Artists Guild, 1969; Bankers Trust Top Purchase award S.C. Tricentennial at Greenwood, 1970, Purchase award Appalachian Corridors exhbn., Charleston, W.Va., 1972, Mus. Purchase award Tex. Fine Arts Assn., 1974, others. Mem. Guild S.C. Artists (mem. adv. bd. 1955-71, 73-74, treas. 1968-69, v.p. 1970-71, pres. 1972-73, chmn. Bicentennial com. 1972-74) Nat. League Am. Pen Women (pres. S.C. 1958-60, 64-66), Artists Equity, Greenville Artists Guild (pres. 1958), Greenville Art Assn. (v.p. 1954-58, 60-62, 64-66), Greenville County Med. Aux. (pres. 1953-54), Nat. Assn. Women Artists (mem. com. 1971-74), Nat. Assn. Med. Artists, Am. Soc. Contemporary Artists Southeastern Graphics Council, Water Color Soc. Ala., Greenville Charity Ball Com. (art chmn.), Greenville County Found. (projects com. 1973-74). Drawings and paintings med. books, jours. including Surgery of Repair (John F. Pick), 1949; Am. Peoples Ency., 1950; Anatomy of Gorilla (Am. Mus. Natural History), 1950; Orthopedic Surgery of Hand (F. Stelling), 1956. Home: 60 Lake Forest Dr Greenville SC 29609

DRESSELHAUS, MILDRED SPIEWAK, educator, engr.; b. Bklyn., Nov. 11, 1930; d. Meyer and Ethel (Teichtheil) Spiewak; A.B., Hunter Coll., 1951; Fulbright fellow Cambridge (Eng.) U., 1951-52; A.M., Radcliffe Coll., 1953; Ph.D. in Physics, U. Chgo., 1958; m. Gene F. Dresselhaus, May 25, 1958; children—Marianne, Carl Eric, Paul David, Eliot Michael. NSF postdoctoral fellow Cornell U., 1958-60; mem. staff Lincoln Lab., Mass. Inst. Tech., 1960-67, Abby Rockefeller Mauze vis. prof., Mass. Inst. Tech., 1967-68, prof. elec. engring., 1968—, asso. head dept. elec. engring., 1972-74, Abby Rockefeller Mauze chair, 1973—; mem. staff Center Materials Sci. and Engring., also vis. Scientist Francis Bitter Nat. Magnet Lab.; vis. prof. Israel Inst. Tech., Technion, summer 1972, also Tokyo, Japan, 1973; cons. NSF. Recipient Hunter Coll. Hall of Fame award, 1972, Radcliffe Coll. Alumni medal, 1973. Fellow Am. Phys. Soc.; mem. N.Y. Acad. Sci., Soc. Women Engrs. (sr.), Fedn. Am. Scientists, I.E.E.E. (sr.), Nat. Acad. Engring., Am. Acad. Arts and Scis. Contbr. articles to profl. jours. Home: 147 Jason St Arlington MA 02174 Office: Mass Inst Tech Cambridge MA 02139

DRESSER, EDNA EARLE, photog. artist; b. Antlers, Okla., Oct. 2, 1918; d. Tony Cornelius and Mary Tennessee (Whitlock) George; pupil of Viva Faye Lefler, Kay Isaacson, Dick Goetz, Leona Turner, Bernice Hinton; advanced photog. artists certificate Okla. Photog. Artists Guild, 1973; m. Billy Ray Dresser, Aug. 6, 1935; children—Jon Michael, James Ronald, Suzanne (Mrs. Clayton Earl Smith). Co-propr. Ray's Studio (formerly George and Son Studio), Chickasha, Okla., 1956—; judge clinics and contests, 1968—; tchr. tole painting Mushroom Gallery and Gift Shop, Chickasha, 1973—; one-man shows Chickasha Pub. Library, 1971-73; group exhbns. in El Reno, Chickasha and Duncan, Okla. Recipient trophy Profl. Photographers Okla., 1960, Southwestern Profl. Photographers Assn., Dallas, 1973. Mem. profl. photographers Okla. (placque 1974), Am., Okla., Am. photog. artists guilds, Chickasha Art Guild (pres. 19—). Home: 1001 S 13th St Chickasha OK 73018 Office: 518 Chickasha Av Chickasha OK 73018

DRESSER, LOUISA (MRS. DONALD W. CAMPBELL), museum curator; b. Worcester, Mass., Oct. 25, 1907; d. Frank Farnum and Josephine Rose (Lincoln) Dresser; A.B., Vassar Coll., 1929; student Harvard, 1932, U. London, 1934, Clark U., 1935-36; H.H.D., Anna Maria Coll., 1973; m. Donald W. Campbell, Sept. 25, 1971. With Worcester Art Mus., 1932—, successively asso. in decorative arts, asso. curator decorative arts, curator decorative arts, acting dir., 1943-46, curator of collection, 1949-72, trustee, 1972—, editor Ann., 1958-70; corporator John Woodman Higgins Armory, Worcester, 1962—, trustee, 1973—; fellow John Simon Guggenheim Meml. Found., 1956-57; Pres. Salisbury Mansion Assos. Corporator Craft-Center, Worcester. Named Woman of Year, Worcester Bus. and Profl. Women's Club, 1960. Mem. Worcester (adv. bd.), Mass. hist. socs., Am. Assn. Museums. Archaeol. Inst. Am. (pres. Worcester soc. 1961-62), Am. Antiquarian Soc., Soc. Arts and Crafts, Boston (trustee). Author: XVII Century Painting in New England, 1935; Early New England Printmakers, 1939; Likeness of America, 1949; co-author: Maine and its Role in American Art, 1963. Editor, joint author The Dial and the Dial Collection, 1959. Contbr. to jours. in field. Home: 17 Beechmont St Worcester MA 01609 Office: 55 Salisbury St Worcester MA 01608

DREUSSI, GINA MARIE, pub. relations exec.; b. Canton, O., Aug. 23, 1949; d. Vitalio Oliver and Adelaide Maria (Casali) Dreussi; B.A. in Journalism, Kent State U., 1971. Journalism internship Barberton (O.) Citizens Hosp., 1970; pub. relations asst. Aultman Hosp., Canton, 1971—. Hosp. vol. A.R.C., 1972—. Mem. Women in Communications, Women's Profl. Journalism Assn., Northeast Ohio Hosp. Pub. Relations Assn., Soc. Profl. Journalists (dir. Buckeye Chpt.). Club: Quota of Canton. Home: 3405 Lincoln St E Canton OH 44707 Office: Aultman Hosp 2600 6th St SW Canton OH 44710

DREVENSTEDT, JEAN, psychologist; b. Louisville, July 13, 1927; d. Eduard A. and Suretta (Redmon) Drevenstedt; B.S. with distinction, Ind. U., 1949; Ph.D., Vanderbilt U., 1965. With prodn. dept. Zimmer-McClaskey-Lewis Advt. Agy., Louisville, 1949-58; USPHS fellow dept. psychiatry and neurology Northwestern U. Med. Sch., Chgo., 1962-63; psychologist Children's Asthma Research Inst. and Hosp., Denver, 1964-65; clin. psychologist, asst. prof. Ohio U., Athens, 1965-71, asso. prof., 1971—. Mem. Am., Midwest, Ohio psychol. assns., A.A.A.S., Mortar Bd., Sigma Xi, Beta Gamma Sigma, Alpha Omicron Pi. Republican. Presbyn. Contbr. articles to profl. jours. Home: 1-102 Monticello Dr Athens OH 45701 Office: Dept Psychology Ohio Univ Athens OH 45701

DREW, ELIZABETH BRENNER, journalist; b. Cin., Nov. 16, 1935; d. William J. and Estelle (Jacobs) Brenner; B.A., Wellesley Coll., 1957; m. J. Patterson Drew, Apr. 11, 1964 (dec. Sept. 1970). Writer, TV commentator Post-Newsweek Stas., Washington, 1973—; Washington editor The Atlantic, 1967-73. Interviewer Thirty Minutes With, Pub. Broadcasting Service, 1971-73. Juror, 1973 Nat. Book Award in Contemporary Affairs. Bd. dirs. Council Fgn. Relations. Recipient award for excellence Soc. Mag. Writers, 1970, Alumnae Achievement award Wellesley Coll., 1973, award for broadcast journalism DuPont-Columbia, 1972-73. Contbr. articles to popular mags. Home: 3112 Woodley Rd NW Washington DC 20008 Office: 1028 Connecticut Av NW Washington DC 20036

DREW, ELIZABETH HARRIET, hist. researcher; b. Houghton, Mich., Jan. 8, 1904; d. Charles Verner and Blanche Sarah (King) Drew; A.B., Vassar Coll., 1924; m. Henry Charles Tomlinson, Mar. 21, 1930 (div. Dec. 1939); 1 son, Charles Verner Drew. Clk. Channel Bookshop, N.Y.C., 1928-29; owner, mgr. Elizabeth Drew Books, 1929-31; dir. Vassar-Smith Players, N.Y.C., 1933-34; dir., stage mgr., dir. Children's Theatre, Beechwood Players Club, Scarborough, N.Y., 1935-40; tchr. drama Scarborough (N.Y.) Sch., 1944-45; dir. Croton Players, Croton-on-Hudson, N.Y., 1949-50, Village Jr. Players, N.Y.C., 1973; researcher on Am. Revolutionary history, 1956—. Mem. Ossining (N.Y.) Community Council, 1949-58, pres., 1955-57; chmn. Ossining Camp Fund, 1949-51, 54-55; dir. Ossining Children's Center, 1947-60, pres., 1956-58; chmn. Ossining Housing Authority, 1951-52; mem. Mayor's Com. N.Y. Shakespeare Festival, 1962-70. Mem. Westchester County Republican Com., 1951-57, N.Y. County Rep. Com., 1961—; asso. leader Rep. Assembly Dist. 64, 1971—. Mem. Am. Assn. for Indian Affairs, Am. Assn. for UN, Am. Mus. Natural History, Mus. Modern Art, Bklyn. Botanic Garden, ANTA, N.Y. Hort. Soc., League Women Voters, Nat. Audubon Soc., Met. Mus., Conn., L.I., Monmouth County, N.J., N.Y.C., R.I. hist. socs. Clubs: Nat. Arts, N.Y.C. Vassar (dir. 1960-65, pres. 1962-65), Women's City (N.Y.C.). Home: 70 E 10th St New York City NY 10003

DREW, FRANCES KATHERINE, librarian; b. Jacksonville, Fla., Dec. 4, 1928; d. Herbert Jackson and Isabella Milling (Williams) Drew; student Mt. St. Joseph Coll., 1947-48; A.B., Wesleyan Coll., 1951; postgrad. (Speech scholar), Wesleyan Conservatory, 1951-52; M.Ed., Emory U., 1954, M. Librarianship, 1959. Tchr. Chatham Jr. High Sch., Savannah, Ga., 1955-57; jr. librarian Savannah Pub. Library, 1957-58; catalog librarian U. Ga. Libraries, Athens, 1959-63; head catalog librarian La. State U., New Orleans, 1963-65; acquisitions librarian Ga. Inst. Tech., Atlanta, 1965-66, catalog librarian, 1966—. Mem. Am. Assn. U. Profs., Poetry Soc. Ga., Ga. Hist. Soc., Fla. Hist. Soc., Ga., Cath., Southeastern, Met. Atlanta, Spl. library assns., D.A.R. Democrat. Roman Catholic (parish librarian 1968—). Home: 710 Peachtree St NE Apt 1224 Atlanta GA 30308

DREW, KATHERINE FISCHER, educator; b. Houston, Sept. 24, 1923; d. Herbert Herman and Martha (Holloway) Fischer; B.A., Rice Inst., 1944, M.A., 1945; Ph.D., Cornell U., 1950; m. Ronald Farinton Drew, July 27, 1951. Instr. history Rice U., 1946-48; asst. history Cornell U., 1948-50; mem. faculty Rice U., 1950—, prof. history, 1964—. Guggenheim fellow, 1959; Fulbright scholar, 1965. Mem. Am. Hist. Assn., Mediaeval Acad. Am., Soc. Legal History, Phi Beta Kappa. Author: The Burgundian Code, 1949; Studies in Lombard Institutions, 1956; Perspectives in Medieval History, 1963; The Barbarian Invasions, 1970; The Lombard Laws, 1973. Contbr. articles to profl. jours. Editor Rice U. Studies, 1967—. Home: 509 Buckingham Houston TX 77024

DREW, KJYSTEN WEPPENER (MRS. CHARLES WILLIAM DREW), educator; b. San Jose, Cal., Feb. 21, 1943; d. Carl Richard and Barbara Swending (Anderson) Weppener; A.A., Hartnell Jr. Coll., 1962; B.A. cum laude (Crown Zellerbach scholar), San Jose State Coll., 1964; m. Charles William Drew, June 15, 1963; children—Ulrike Christine, Melissa Lynn. Tchr. Point Arena (Cal.) elementary sch., 1964-66; tchr. English U.S. Armed Forces Inst., Point Arena, also Kenai, Alaska, 1964-68; ednl. dir. Youth Sci. Center of Monterey County, Salinas, Cal., 1970-73; naturalist Salinas Recreation and Parks Dept., 1974—. Owner Owl Lady; tutor Hartnell Jr. Coll., Salinas, 1971—. Mem. ecology adv. com. Monterey County Office of Edn., 1971-74; campaign mgr. Wyo. State Legislature, 1970. Mem. Audubon Soc., Am. Assn. Univ. Women, Selinas Fine Arts, Phi Beta Phi, Delta Kappa Gamma. Presbyn. Mem. Order Eastern Star. Home: 1310 First Av Salinas CA 93901 Office: River Rd Salinas CA 93901

DREWELOWE, EVE, artist; b. New Hampton, Ia.; d. George Robert and Mary (Martin) Drewelowe; A.B., U. Ia., 1923, A.M., 1924; postgrad. U. Colo., 1954; m. J. Van Ek, June 14, 1923. Exhibited in one-woman shows at Argent Galleries, N.Y.C., 1940, 41, Cedar City, Utah, 1942, Denver Art Mus., 1933, 36, U. Colo., 1930, 33, 36, 37, 40, 44, 49, 62, Henderson Gallery, 1943, 49, Boulder Pub. Library Gallery, 1965, 71, 72, 73, 74; exhibited in group shows including Phila. Art Acad., 1936, Chgo. Art Inst., 1939, World Fair N.Y., 1939, Nat. Assn. Women Artists, UNESCO Traveling Exhbn., Eng., 1949, Kansas City Art Inst., 1940, 42, Nelson Gallery-Atkins Mus., 1960, Joslyn Meml., Omaha, 1956, 60, 62, 70, Denver Art Mus., 1964, 65, 67, 69, Nat. Acad. Galleries, N.Y.C., 1946, Fine Arts Center, Colorado Springs, 1960, Cedar City Ann. Invited Exhbn., 1940-72, U. Ariz., 1967, So. Colo. State Coll., 1967, U. Colo., 1970, Silver Anniversary Exhbn., The Gallery, Central City, Colo., 1972; represented in permanent collections at Harkness House, London, Eng., Coll. So. Utah, U. Ia., U. Colo., Wartburg Coll., Waverly, Ia. Mem. art adv. com. Boulder Pub. Library, 1963-69; juror for Hallmark Art Exhibit; mem. Boulder assembly Colo. Council on Arts and Humanities. Recipient Flower Subject Contest prize Denver Art Mus., 1931, 32, award Colo. State Fair, Tri State, Cheyenne, Wyo., 1956, First prize in oil Boulder Art Assn. Regional Exhbn., 1963. Mem. Artists Equity Assn. (pres. Boulder chpt. 1963-68, acting pres. 1969), Boulder Artists Guild (past pres.), Nat. Artists Equity Assn. (hon. life). Illustrated in Denim and Broadcloth, 1953. Address: 2025 Balsam Dr Boulder CO 80302

DREWES, ARLENE TORGERSON (MRS. WOLFRAM U. DREWES), librarian; b. Denver, Feb. 12, 1928; d. Arnold and Mary Louise (Wallace) Torgerson; B.A. (scholar), U. Colo., 1951; postgrad. U. Syracuse, 1951-55; M.L.S., U. Md., 1968; m. Wolfram U. Drewes, Dec. 9, 1950; children—Kristine, Katrina, Karen. Sec. dept. psychology Syracuse (N.Y.) U., 1951-55, research asst., 1955-57; librarian Nat. Geographic Soc., Washington, 1968—. Active Girl Scouts Am., 1970-72. Student fellow, Internat. Geogra Congress, 1952. Mem. D.C., Spl. Libraries assns. Author: (with Wolfram U. Drewes) Climate and Related Phenomena of the Eastern Slopes of Central Peru, 1957. Home: 5014 River Hill Rd Washington DC 20016 Office: 17th at M Sts NW Washington DC 20036

DREXLER, HAZEL GASSMANN, educator, audiologist, speech pathologist; b. nr. Milford, Pa., Oct. 7, 1921; d. Ralph Cecil and Hazel (Roberts) Gassmann; B.A., Pa. State U., 1942; M.A., 1951; M.S., Purdue U., 1958, Ph.D., 1961; m. Allan B. Drexler, May 9, 1952 (div. Oct. 1963); 1 son, Kim Eric. Engring. asst. Wright Aero. Corp., Patterson, N.J., 1943-44; engring. insp., draftsman U.S. Naval Torpedo Sta., R.I., 1944-45; instr. math. Wilkes Coll., Wilkes-Barre, Pa., 1947-48, Pa. State U., 1948-52, New Haven Tchrs. Coll., 1958-59; audiologist Cin. Speech and Hearing Center, 1961-62; speech pathologist-audiologist in charge audiology dept. Children's Hosp., adj. asst. prof. U. Cin., 1962-66; speech and hearing cons. Children's Neuromuscular Diagnostic Clinic, Cin., 1965-66; clin. co-ordinator audiology and speech pathology dept. Denver Children's Hosp., 1966-69; asso. prof. speech pathology Ore. Coll. Edn., 1969—. Mem. Am. Speech and Hearing Assn., Am. Assn. for Mental Deficiency, Ore. Speech and Hearing Assn., Assn. Jour. Editors (honors), Phi Beta Kappa, Alpha Lambda Delta, Pi Mu Epsilon, Phi Kappa Phi, Sigma Delta Epsilon. Contbr. articles to profl. jours. Home: 401 N Echols St Monmouth OR 97361

DREYFUS, GRACE HAWES (MRS. LOUIS G. DREYFUS, JR.), civic worker; b. Victory, N.Y., Dec. 26, 1892; d. John Bently and Pearl (Van Hoosen) Hawes; student pub. schs. N.Y., Prager Sch., Dresden, Germany; m. Louis G. Dreyfus, Jr., June 14, 1917. Founder, Grace Dreyfus Clinic and Orphanage, Teheran, Iran, 1942; hon. life dir. affiliates U. Cal. at Santa Barbara. Bd. dirs. Welfare Blind, Inc., Washington. Decorated Elmi first class (Iran). Mem. Nat. Inst. Arts and Letters (past pres. Santa Barbara br.), Internat. Platform Assn., The Saint Cecilia Soc. of Santa Barbara, Red Lion and Sun (life mem. Iran), Channel City Women's Forum (charter mem.). Republican. Clubs: Little Town, Valley, Coral Casino (Santa Barbara); Union Interalliee (Paris, France). Home: 370 Hot Springs Rd Santa Barbara CA 93108

DREYFUSS, ANN, educator; b. N.Y.C., Oct. 16, 1938; d. Henry and Doris (Marks) Dreyfuss; B.A., Sarah Lawrence Coll., 1960; M.A., San Diego State Coll., 1965. Vis. tchr. Mt. Vernon Pub. Sch. System/Central Guidance Clinic, 1960-62; exploratory research project live animals in play therapy with emotionally disturbed children San Diego Zoo, 1963-66; research asst. Western Behavioral Scis. Inst., La Jolla, Cal., 1964-66, research asso., 1966-68; mem. staff family therapy Inst./Center for Human Communication, Los Gatos, Cal., 1968-70, dir. Group Center, 1970-71; worked and project sponsored by Israeli Govt. and U. Cal. at Los Angeles, 1970-71; faculty Sonoma State Coll., Rohnert Park, Cal., 1972—; pvt. practice Reichian therapy, San Francisco, 1972—; with Nat. Tng. Labs., Bethel, Me. Mem. Assn. for Humanistic Psychology, Am. Psychol. Assn., Assn. for Transpersonal Psychology. Home: 2648 Bryant St San Francisco CA 94110 Office: Psychology Dept Sonoma State Coll Rohnert Park CA 94928

DREYFUSS, PATRICIA (MRS. M. PETER DREYFUSS), chemist; b. Reading, Pa., Apr. 28, 1932; d. Edmund T. and Anna J. (Oberc) Gajewski; B.S., U. Rochester, 1954; Ph.D. (Sohio fellow, NSF fellow), U. Akron, 1964; m. M. Peter Dreyfuss, Jan. 30, 1954; children—David Daniel, Simeon Karl. Postdoctoral fellow U. Liverpool, Eng., 1963-65; research chemist B.F. Goodrich, Brecksville, O., 1965-71; research asso. Case Western Res. U., Cleve., 1971-73, sr. research asso., 1973-74; research asso. Inst. Polymer Sci., U. Akron, 1974—. Vis. research fellow U. Bristol, Eng., 1972. Mem. W. Suburban Philharmonic Orch., Lakewood, O., 1969—; mem. local bd. 470, SSS, Akron, O., 1972—, sec. Local Bd. 113, 1973—. Am. Assn. U. Women Internat. fellow, 1964-65; NIH Spl. fellow, 1972-73. Mem. Am. Chem. Soc., Am. Assn. U. Women, League Women Voters (treas. 1959-60), Phi Beta Kappa, Delta Phi Alpha. Contbr. articles to profl. jours. Home: 506 W Point Dr Akron OH 44313 Office: Inst Polymer Science U Akron Akron OH 44325

DRIGGS, LOUISE RUST (MRS. EDWIN ODGEN DRIGGS), food cons., writer; b. Sabine Parrish, La., July 19, 1912; d. Milburn James and Lucile Mary (Osborn) Rust; B.J., U. Mo., 1932; B.S., Kan. State U., 1933; M.S., N.Y. U., 1934; m. Edwin Ogden Driggs, June 26, 1937; 1 son, James Ogden. Staff editor Homemakers Bur., Safeway Stores, Oakland, Cal., 1944-47; cons. to various advt. agencies, food cos. and restaurants, 1947—; cons. Spice Islands Co., South San Francisco, Cal., 1955-62; home econs. editor Harvest Years Mag., Berkeley, Cal., 1966-73; writer food nutrition articles in various mags. including Retirement Living, Dynamic Maturity, Two Wheel Trip, Rudder, Sunset. Lectr. home econs. Mills Coll., Oakland, Cal., 1950-51, Cal. State U., San Jose, 1969-70. Mem. nutrition com. Alameda County Heart Assn., Oakland, 1959-69. Mem. Am., Cal. (dist. pres. 1951-52) home econs. assns., Home Economists in Bus. (chpt. pres. 1948-49), U. Mo. Alumni Assn. (dir. No. Cal. 1973), Women in Communications, Inst. Food Technologists, Cal. Writers Club, Cal. Hist. Soc., L'Alliance Francaise, Phi Kappa Phi, Omicron Nu, Chi Omega. Author: Spice Islands Cookbook, 1961; Soups and Stews the World Over, 1971. Home and office: 440 Gravatt Dr Berkeley CA 94705

DRISCOLL, DOROTHY H., scientist, educator; b. Boston, May 30, 1924; d. Frederick J. and Dorothy J. (Connelley) Driscoll; B.S., Radcliffe Coll., 1946; M.A., Smith Coll., 1949. Teaching fellow Smith Coll., Northampton, Mass., 1947, asst. biol. scis., 1948, instr. zoology, 1949-50; research asso. Biophysics Lab., Harvard U., Cambridge, Mass., 1951-55; research asso., health safety officer Nat. Acad. Sci.-Atomic Bomb Casualty Commn., Hiroshima, Japan, 1954-56; tech. specialist Med. Physics div. Brookhaven Nat. Lab., Upton, N.Y., 1956-58, clin. isotopes supr., 1958-60, hosp. lab. asso., 1958-61; research asso. Thomas Jefferson U., Phila., 1961-67, asst. prof., 1967, asso. prof. med. physics, 1967—, coordinator Program for Disadvantaged Youth, 1969—. Cons. Am. Found. Negro Affairs-Access Routes to Med. Careers, 1971—, obstetrics and gynecology St. Barnabas Hosp., 1973—; adj. lectr. radiation health Manhattan Coll., 1965-69. Mem. Am. Assn. Physics Medicine, Soc. Nuclear Medicine, Health Physics Soc., Assn. Advancement Med. Instrumentation, Radiol. Research Soc., Nat. Soc. Magnetic Resonance, Am. Assn. Univ. Profs., N.Y. Acad. Sci., Radiol. Soc. N.Am., Royal Inst. Gt. Britain, Sigma Xi. Home: 561 Judson St Philadelphia PA 19130 Office: Stein Research Center Thomas Jefferson University 920 Chancellor St Philadelphia PA 19107

DRISCOLL, ELEANOR DOLORES, ednl. adminstr.; b. Olean, N.Y., Oct. 18, 1918; d. Eugene and Anna (Moffet) Driscoll; B.A., Alfred U., 1941; M.Ed., Canisius Coll., 1949; postgrad. Columbia, 1954-58. Tchr. English, social studies, Latin, Wayland, N.Y., 1941-44; chief social studies dept., Springville, N.Y., 1944-50; dir. guidance, 1950-56, dir. adult edn., 1950-56; coordinator sch. within sch., Massena, N.Y., 1956-60; dir. instrn. Rush Henrietta Sch., Henrietta, N.Y., 1960-69, dir. ednl. devel., 1969—. Mem. Henrietta Arts Council, Community Playhouse, Civic Music Assn., Rochester, N.Y., 1952-54. Bd. dirs. Bertrand Claffee Hosp., Springville, N.Y., 1954-56. Mem. N.E.A. (life), Internat. Reading Assn., Am. Soc. Curriculum Devel., N.Y. State Tchrs. Assn. (dir. 1953-57), Erie County Tchrs. Assn. (pres. 1950-52), Western N.Y. Assn. Personnel and Guidance (pres. 1950-52). Home: 64 Calkins Rd Rochester NY 14623 Office: 2034 Lehigh Station Rd Henrietta NY 14467

DRISCOLL, FAITH FRANCES, lawyer; b. Everett, Mass., Oct. 11, 1937; d. Francis James and Eleanor Lena (Rushman) Driscoll; B.S. in Elec. Engring. with honors, Northeastern U., 1964; J.D., Suffolk U., 1968. Admitted to Mass. bar, 1969; student engr., Sylvania Electric Products Corp., Needham, Mass., 1961-63; patent atty. Honeywell Informations Systems, Inc., Waltham, Mass., 1964—. Served with USN, 1955-59. Mem. A.B.A., Mass. Women Lawyers Assn., I.E.E.E., Soc. Women Engrs. (rep. to Eng. socs. New Eng.), Mass. Engring. Council. Home: 14 Carlisle Rd Dedham MA 02026 Office: 200 Smith St Waltham MA 02154

DRISCOLL, HARRIET MARY (MRS. EDWIN C. DRISCOLL), banker; b. Sumner, Neb., Oct. 3, 1927; d. Henry S. and Mary Ann (Budin) Clouse; student Nat. Bus. Inst., 1944; m. Edwin C. Driscoll; Oct. 11, 1947; children—Kevin Henry, Kermit James, Klaus Valentine. Sec., Supt. of Schs. and Bd. of Edn., York, Neb., 1945-47; with Francis Wagner Co., El Paso, Tex., 1947-49; v.p. Security State Bank, Sumner, 1949—; agt. E.C. Driscoll Agy., Sumner, 1969—. Roman Catholic. Home: PO Box 43 Sumner NE 68878 Office: PO Box 127 Sumner NE 68878

DRISCOLL, JESSYE SIDES (MRS. CUSTER H. DRISCOLL), librarian; b. Sayre, Okla., Aug. 31, 1912; d. Willie Frank and Anna Lula (York) Sides; B.S., Tex. Wesleyan Coll., 1947; M. Teaching, Southwestern State Coll., Okla., 1960; postgrad. U. Okla., 1962-64; m. Custer H. Driscoll, Nov. 24, 1949; children—T. Roy Carmichael; stepchildren—Bob Driscoll, Don Driscoll. Prin. jr. high sch., Sayre, 1932-43; tchr. Sayre Pub. Schs., 1942-45, 49-56, Amarillo (Tex.) Pub. Schs., 1947-49; librarian Sayre Jr. Coll., 1956—. Mem. N Central Evaluation Com. for Secondary Schs., 1970-73, Okla. Edn. Pilot Program for Libraries, 1966; mem. curriculum com. State Dept. Edn. Okla. Mem. Okla., S.W. Dist. (chmn. 1956-57) library assns., Okla. Edn. Assn., Delta Kappa Gamma (pres. 1966-68). Democrat. Baptist. Mem. Order Eastern Star (past worthy matron). Home: 110 Sides Lane Sayre OK 73662

DRISCOLL, KATHARINE ELIZABETH, lawyer; b. Worcester, Mass., Dec. 29, 1920; d. Patrick Joseph and Delia Agnes (McInerney) Driscoll; A.B., Boston U., 1941, LL.B., 1951, LL.M., 1964. Tchr., Oakfield, (Me.) Pub. Schs., 1946-47; admitted to Mass. bar, 1951; law librarian Liberty Mut. Ins. Co., Boston, 1951-56, atty., 1956-72, asst. counsel, 1973—. Served with USCGR, 1944-46. Mem. Am., Boston bar assns., Phi Beta Kappa. Editor: Boston U. Law Rev., 1949-51. Home: 118 Vernon St Worcester MA 01610 Office: 175 Berkeley St Boston MA 02117

DRISCOLL, SHIRLEY GRIFFITH, physician; b. Pittston, Pa., 1923; M.D., U. Pa., 1949. Intern Mt. Auburn Hosp., Cambridge, Mass., 1949-50; resident in pathology Phila. Gen. Hosp., 1950-51; asst. president Peter Bent Brigham Hosp., Boston, 1954, chief resident pathology, 1954-55; resident pathology Free Hosp. for Women, Brookline, Mass., 1955; resident pathology Boston Lying-in Hosp., 1956, asso. pathologist, 1958-62, pathologist, 1962—; asst. chief lab. service VA Center, Dayton, O., 1956-57, acting chief, 1957; asso. in biochemistry Genetic Clinic, Children's Meml. Hosp., Chgo., 1957-58; asst. instr. pathology U. Pa., 1950-51; teaching fellow Harvard Med. Sch., 1954-56, instr. pathology, 1958-60, asso. pathologist, 1961-66, asst. clin. prof. pathology, 1966-69, asso. prof., 1969—; clin. instr. pathology Ohio State U., 1956-57; instr. pathology Northwestern U., 1957-58. Diplomate Am. Bd. Pathology. Mem. A.A.A.S., Perinatal Research Soc., Mass. Med. Soc., New Eng. Path. Soc., Am. Soc. Clin. Pathologists. Address: 221 Longwood Av Boston MA 02115

DRISKELL, ELOISE WHITEHURST, psychologist; b. Wauchula, Fla., Mar. 19, 1919; d. Wilbur Walton and Lemmie (Carlton) Whitehurst; B.A., Fla. So. Coll., 1939; M.A., Western Carolina U., 1968; children—Jeff Lott, Jess Driskell. Dir. pupil personnel services, sch. psychologist, dir. exceptional children Hardee County Schs., Wauchula, Fla., 1972—. Adviser to registrants Selective Service Bd., 1968—. Delta Kappa Gamma fellow, 1967. Mem. Am., Fla. personnel and guidance assns., Am., Fla. sch. counselors assns., Am. Assn. Mental Deficiency, Nat., Fla. assns. sch. psychologists, Fla. Adminstrs. of Pupil Personnel Services, Fla. Assn. Suprs. of Instrn., Council Adminstrs. of Spl. Edn., Council of Exceptional Children, Bus. and Profl. Womens Club, Delta Kappa Gamma. Democrat. Home: PO Box 517 Wauchula FL 33873

DRIVER, XYLDA IRWIN LOWE, retail store owner; b. Tunica, Miss., Dec. 7, 1898; d. John Thomas and Idella (Irwin) Lowe; student Queens Coll., 1915-16; m. James Skelton Driver, Jr., May 4, 1918 (div. 1939); 1 son, William Richard (dec.). Owner, mgr. Tenn. Terminal Warehouse, Memphis, 1938-41; owner Xylda's Shop, Tunica, 1941—. Presbyn. Clubs: Lison Book, Memphis Country (Memphis). Address: Box 1076 Tunica MS 38676

DROBNYK, WENDY LEIGH, occupational therapist; b. East Orange, N.J., Dec. 14, 1948; d. Wendel Jacob and Kathryn Margarite (Cordes) Drobnyk; B.S., Western Mich. U., 1970; postgrad. U. Minn., 1971. Staff occupational therapist-phys. disabilities U. Minn. Hosp., Mpls., 1970-73; staff occupational therapist-phys. disabilities Fairview Hosp., Mpls., 1973—. Mem. Minn. Occupational Therapists Assn. (sec. 1972-73), Minn. Long Distance Runners Assn., Big Sister Orgn. Club: Sitzmark Ski (Mpls.). Home: 727 13th Av SE Apt 6 Minneapolis MN 55414 Office: 2312 S 6th St Minneapolis MN 55404

DROHLICH, SHIRLEY RUTH, pub. relations counselor; b. St. Louis, June 10, 1921; d. Hyman and Annie (Faierman) Mack; B.A., Harris Tchrs. Coll., 1942; m. Robert A. Drohlich, Apr. 19, 1959; children—Michael L., Lynne M. Mgr. pub. relations Nat. Lumber Mfrs. Assn., Washington, 1946-49; account exec. Fleishman-Hillard, Inc., pub. relations, St. Louis, 1949-53; dir. pub. relations Merc. Trust Co., St. Louis, 1953-56; account exec. Schram-Reiner-Olson, pub. relations, St. Louis, 1956-59; v.p. Robert Drohlich Assos., Inc., pub. relations, St. Louis, 1959—. Bd. dirs. St. Louis Diabetes Assn., 1960-70. Served as lt. USNR, 1943-46. Mem. Pub. Relations Soc. Am., Women's Advt. Club St. Louis (treas. 1953, 2d v.p. 1968, gridiron chmn. 1967). Home: 2 Lynnbrook St Louis MO 63131 Office: 1221 S Brentwood St Louis MO 63117

DROSTE, MILDRED ANNE, coll. dean; b. Ronceverte, W.Va., Feb. 2, 1923; d. Fred William and Pearl Ann (Grassmick) Droste; B.S., Longwood Coll., 1944; Ed.M., U. N.C., 1954. Instr. phys. edn. Va. Intermont Coll., Bristol, 1944-48; asst. prof. phys. edn. Mary Baldwin Coll., Staunton, Va., 1949-53; faculty Mary Washington Coll., Fredericksburg, Va., 1954—, asso. prof. phys. edn., dean of students, 1968—. Instr., Nat. Aquatic Sch., A.R.C., Marlinton, W.Va., 1947-48. Bd. dirs. A.R.C., YMCA. Mem. Nat. Assn. for Women Deans, Adminstrs. and Counselors, So. Assn. Coll. Personnel. Home: 314 Stonewall Dr Fredericksburg VA 22401

DROUGHT, ROSE ALICE, educator; b. Milw.; d. James Thomas and Rose (Hennecke) Drought; student U. Ill., 1924-25, Layton Sch. Art, 1931; B.A., U. Wis., 1924, M.A., 1926, Ph.D. (Carnegie fellow 1929-30), 1931; postgrad. U. Ariz., No. Ariz. U., Ariz. State U. Exec. dir., camp dir. Girl Scouts U.S.A., 1934-48; free lance writer, 1948-54; tchr. spl. edn. Phoenix Elementary Schs., 1954-69; dir. Community Council Project on Aging, 1969—; dir. Area Agy. on Aging, Region I, Ariz., 1974—. Camp planning cons. YMCA, YWCA, ch. camps, pvt. camps, 1935—; dir. internat. camp Adelboden, Switzerland, 1939-1940, Outdoor Edn. Inst., Marquette, U., Milw., summer 1963; guest lectr. Ariz. State U., 1966-69, Glendale Community Coll., 1970, U. Sydney (Australia), 1970; mem. adv. bd. Salvation Army; mem. Phoenix Housing Commn., Phoenix Nutrition Council; chmn. Phoenix Pub. Housing Adv. Bd., 1973—. Recipient Ann. awards Ariz. State Fair, 1953—; Distinguished Service award United Cerebral Palsy Ariz., 1962-63, citation, 1965, certificate of appreciation A.R.C., 1965; Floyd Adams award, 1972; citation Nat. Ret. Tchrs. Assn., 1973; citation of merit Gov. Ariz., 1974. Mem. Ariz. Acad. Pub. Affairs, Am. Camping Assn. (bd. dirs. 1945-48, pres. Coronado sect. 1960-62, v.p. region VIII, 1961-62 campcraft instr. 1960-70), N.E.A., Assn. Outdoor Edn., Council Exceptional Children, Assn. Educators Homebound and Hospitalized Children, Nat. Wildlife Fedn., Nat. Sch. Pub. Relations Assn. (pres. Ariz. chpt. 1968-69), Gerontological Soc., Western Gerontological Soc., Nat. Council on Aging, Delta Kappa Gamma. Democrat. Author: A Camping Manual, 1943; Services and Facilities for Meeting the Needs of Older Americans, 1973; The Community College-A Resource for Older Americans-Older Americans-A Resource for the Community, 1974. Editor: Conservation in Camping, 1952; Phoenix Elementary Classroom Tchrs. Assn. Press, 1965-68; acting editor Camping Mag., 1945-46. Home: 106 W Pierson Phoenix AZ 85013 Office: 1515 E Osborn Rd Phoenix AZ 85014

DROZDA, HELEN DOROTHY, psychiat. social worker; b. Omaha, Mar. 21, 1924; d. Joseph J. and Mary E. (Sabatka) Drozda; B.S., U. Neb., 1955; M.S., So. Ill. U., 1965; postgrad. Tex. Tech. U., 1969, Midwestern U., 1968-69. Supervising group counselor San Diego Probation Dept., 1956-57; health edn. dir. YWCA, Omaha, 1954-56; Y-teen dir. YWCA, Alton, Ill., Bloomington, Ill., Peoria, Ill., 1958-62; guidance dir. Acad. of Our Lady, Peoria, 1962-64, St. Teresa Acad., East St. Louis, Ill., 1964-67, Knox County Pub. Schs., Benjamin, Tex., 1967-69; guidance dir. Wilbarger County Pub. Schs., Vernon, Tex., 1969-70; exec. dir. Burk Guidance and Counseling Services, Burkburnett, Tex., 1970—. Mem. Am. Legion, Air Force Assn., Am. Guidance and Personnel Assn., Nat. Assn. Social Workers, Midwest Soc. Individual Psychology, Tex. Pub. Employees Assn., Tex. Soc. for Social Psychotherapy, Burkburnett C. of C., Nat. Rifle Assn. Home: 820 Sheppard Rd Burkburnett TX 76354 Office: Wichita Falls State Hosp Wichita Fall TX 76300 also Burk Guidance and Counseling Burk Burnett TX 76354

DRUCKENBROD, VERONICA (RONNIE DEANE) (MRS. GERALD DRUCKENBROD), advt. agy. exec.; b. St. Charles, Minn., July 17, 1918; d. John E. and Gertrude M. (Small) Spencer; student Coll. of St. Catherine, 1937-39, U. Wis., 1956-57; m. Gerald Druckenbrod, June 29, 1940; children—Kathleen (Mrs. Frederick Kruger), David, Sara, Robert. Profl. actress summer stock, Minn., 1938-40; copywriter radio sta. KATE Austin, Minn., 1939-41; reporter Duluth (Minn.) Herald, 1942-43; copywriter Stephan & Brady Advt., Madison, Wis., 1965—, v.p., 1967—. Sec., Madison Civic Repertory, 1971—; mem. pub. relations com. Madison Heart Assn., 1973-74, Wis. Kidney Found., 1972-74; mem. Mayor's Cultural Goals Com., 1970-72. Mem. Wis. Regional Writers Assn. Roman Catholic (dir. 1969-72). Club: Madison Advt. Home: 5822 Suffolk Madison WI 53711 Office: 1850 Hoffman St Madison WI 53701

DRUCKER, BERTHA SHAIVITZ SHAY (MRS. JEROME JAMES DRUCKER), business exec., horticulturists; b. Balt., Oct. 12, 1905; d. Morris Theodore and Rosa (Rabinowitch) Shaivitz; M.Dramatic Arts, Phila. Coll. Theatre Arts, 1925; postgrad. U. Pa., 1927-31; m. Harry Shay, Feb. 20, 1927 (dec. July 1963); children—Robert, Jonathan; m. 2d, Jerome James Drucker, Oct. 15, 1972. Actress, 1924-27; directress, concert singer Internat. Radio Program, 1927-31; painter, 1944-55; pres., designer Planters By Bertha Shay. Founder, Am. Jewish Congress, women's div., Phila., 1939, mem. nat. bd., 1945-46, Commn. on Community Cultural Inter-relations, 1945-46. Pres., Montefiore Cemetery Co., 1956—, Am. Cemetery Services, Inc., 1958—, Forest Hills Cemetery, Shalom Meml. Park, 1964, Am. Hort. Services, Inc.; treas. Morlan Internat., Inc. Life mem. Dropsie U. Mem. Am. Acad. Polit. and Social Scis., Pa. Hort. Soc. (life), Am. Jewish Congress Women Aux., Temple U. Sch. Medicine, Am. Friends Hebrew U., Zionist Orgn. Am., Nat. Audubon Soc. Jewish religion. Home: Park Towne N 406 Philadelphia PA 19130 Office: Montefiore Bldg Church Rd at Borbeck St Philadelphia PA 19111

DRUCKER, MARJORIE ANN (KRIS DAHL), mag. editor; b. Grand Forks, N.D., Oct. 25, 1923; d. Sigurd and Stella Justina (Nelson) Vattendahl; B.S., U. Wis. at Superior, 1945; m. Murray Don Drucker; children—Kristina, Karen. Instr. Dorothy Preble Sch. Modeling, Hollywood, Cal., 1946-51; free lance fashion co-ordinating, lecturing, photography, Los Angeles, 1951-56; fashion editor, photographic co-ordinator fgn. assignments Cal. Girl Mag., Beverly Hills, 1956-70; owner, Kris Dahl House, Beverly Hills, 1970—. Recipient awards Cal. State Fair for Cal. Girl Mag., 1964, 65. Club: Mulholland Tennis (Los Angeles). Editor Boxer Rev. (outstanding breed publ. 1966, 68, 70), 1956—. Home: 8760 Appian Way Los Angeles CA 90046 Office: 328 S Beverly Dr Beverly Hills CA 90213

DRUCKER, THERESA, broadcasting co. exec.; b. Phila., Aug. 12, 1933; d. Hyman and Fannie (Rosen) Drucker; B.A., Hunter Coll., 1954. Research analyst Foote, Cone & Belding Advt. Agy., N.Y.C., 1961-63; research dir. Gumbinner-North Advt. Agy., N.Y.C., 1964-67; research mgr. NBC, N.Y.C., 1967—. Mem. Radio and TV Research Council, Hunter Coll. Alumni Assn. (dir. 1972—, asst. treas. 1969-72). Home: 235 E 22nd St New York City NY 10010 Office: 30 Rockefeller Plaza New York City NY 10020

DRUMHELLER, JUNE ELAINE (MRS. JOHN ROBERT DRUMHELLER), retail trade co. exec.; b. Mayfield, Ky., July 7, 1921; d. Clyde and Ethel Sophie (Gustafson) Stephens; A.B. with honors, Olivet Coll., 1943; M.A. in Psychology, U. Mich., 1946; postgrad. U. Tenn., 1959-64; m. John Robert Drumheller, July 22, 1950; children—Fred John, Stephen Thomas. Chief clin. psychologist Kalamazoo State Hosp., 1943-45, 46-47; asst. prof. psychology Kalamazoo Coll., 1947; clin. psychologist VA, Milw., 1948-49; chief clin. psychologist VA Mental Hygiene Clinic, Knoxville, Tenn., 1949-51; psychol. examiner Knoxville city schs., 1956; acting exec. dir. Cecil St. Center, Knoxville, 1964; v.p. Drumheller's Inc., 1967—. Mem. Dulin Gallery Art, Knoxville, Women's Guild Knoxville Symphony Soc. State Coll. scholar U. Mich., 1943-44. Mem. Am. Psychol. Assn., Pi Lambda Theta. Lutheran. Home: 4920 Laurelwood Rd Knoxville TN 37918 Office: 2634 N Broadway Knoxville TN 37917

DRUMMOND, RUTH ALLEN, ret. assn. adminstr.; b. Oregon, Mo., Feb. 20, 1901; d. Francis Collin and Rebecca Jane (Van Buskirk) Allen; B.A., Maryville Coll., 1923; div.; 1 dau., Nancy (Mrs. Alan Kiger). Tchr. high sch., New Point, Mo., 1923-25; with Weiboldt Dept. Stores, Chgo., 1925-29, Montgomery Ward & Co., Chgo., 1935-39; dir. counselling Chgo. Collegiate Bur. Occupations, 1939-43; registrar Registry of Med. Technologists, Am. Soc. Clin. Pathologists, Muncie, Ind., 1943-69. Mem. Altrusa, Am. Soc. Med. Technologists. Presbyn. Home: Apt 8 109 University Av Muncie IN 47303

DRUMMOND, SALLY HAZELET, artist; b. Evanston, Ill., June 4, 1924; d. Craig Potter and Frances (Gillam) Hazelet; student Rollins Coll., 1942-44; B.S., Columbia, 1948; postgrad. Inst. Design, Chgo., 1949-50; M.A., U. Louisville, 1952; m. F. Weichel Drummond, Mar. 25, 1961; 1 son, Craig Potter. Exhibited in one-man shows at Hadley Gallery, Louisville, 1952, Tanager Gallery, N.Y.C., 1955, 57, 60, Green Gallery, N.Y.C., 1962, Fischbach Gallery, N.Y.C., 1968, 72; exhibited in group shows at Am. embassy, Rome, 1953. Fgn. Artists Invitational, Bordighiera, Italy, 1953, Am. Artists Ann., 1960, Whitney Mus., N.Y.C., 1958-59, 64, Green Gallery, 1961. Mus. Modern Art, N.Y.C., 1963; retrospective exhbn. Corcoran Gallery Art, Washington, 1972; rep. permanent collections at Mus. Modern Art, Whitney Mus., Speed Mus., Louisville, Joseph H. Hirshorn, Greenwich, Conn., Hudsons Dept. Store, Detroit, AVCO Corp., Ia. U. Mus., Iowa City, Chase Manhattan Bank, N.Y.C., others. Fullbright grantee to Venice, 1952-53; Guggenheim fellow to France, 1967-68. Home: 371 Wilton Rd E Ridgefield CT 06877

DRURY, HARRIET MARIE (MRS. HAYWARD E. DRURY), publishing co. exec.; b. Kensal, N.D., June 25, 1922; d. Harry N. and Gena (Jorgenson-Barger) Pearson; student Mankato Bus. Coll., 1939-40; m. Hayward E. Drury, Oct. 4, 1944; children—Hayward E., Gay (Mrs. James Murphy), J. Roger, David. With Thompson Yard, Inc., Mankato, Minn., 1940-44; owner, pub. The Shopper, advt. publ., Pipestone, Minn., 1951—. Mem. Pipestone (Minn.) Civic and Commerce, 1951—, dir. 1960-63. Mem. Minn. Shoppers Assn. (pres. 1960). Lutheran. Editor: Minn. Women's Christian Temperance Union paper, 1970—. Address: 305 NE 2d St Pipestone MN 56164

DRURY, REBECCA SUE, coll. dean; b. Henderson, Ky., Sept. 22, 1947; d. George William and Nancy Oressa (Byers) Drury; B.A., Ind. U., 1969, M.S., 1971. Resident counselor De Pauw U., Greencastle, Ind., 1971-72, 72-73; dean women Villanova (Pa.) U., 1973—. Mem. Nat. Assn. for Women Deans, Adminstrs. and Counselors, Ind. U. Alumni Assn., Alpha Lambda Delta, Alpha Kappa Delta. Methodist. Home: 288 Iven Av 2C St David's PA 19087 Office: Dean of Women Tolentine Hall 223 Villanova University Villanova PA 19085

DRYER, DOROTHEA MERRILL (MRS. EDWIN JASON DRYER), lawyer; b. Salt Lake City; d. George Edmund and Lillian (Chapman) Merrill; A.B., Stanford, 1936; LL.B., Yale, 1940; m. Edwin Jason Dryer, Feb. 28, 1942; children—Diana Claire (Mrs. Wright), Faith Ellen. Admitted to Utah bar, 1941; clk. for Chief Justice Wolfe of Utah Supreme Court, 1941; atty. Bur. Immigration, Dept. Justice, Washington, 1941-42; practice law, Salt Lake City, 1943-47, Washington, 1948—; dep. county atty., Salt Lake City, 1947-48; admitted to bar U.S. Supreme Ct., U.S. Ct. Mil. Appeals. Fellow Am. Assn. Criminology; mem. Am., Fed., Utah bar assns., Jr. League of Washington, Nat. Assn. Women Lawyers, Nat. Assn. for Gifted Children, Assn. for the Gifted, Am. Judicature Soc., Internat. Platform Assn., Oral History Assn., Kappa Kappa Gamma. Unitarian. Clubs: Potomac Business and Professional Women's; Nat. Lawyers. Home: 5126 Palisade Lane NW Washington DC 20016 Office: Farm Running Brook Farm Browntown VA 22610

DUB, RUTH DONNA O'KRENT (MRS. ROBERT SHOSTECK), social worker; b. Cin.; d. Julius H. and Mildred (Orlin) O'Krent; B.S., U. Cin., 1936, postgrad. Grad. Sch. Pub. Welfare Adminstrn., 1938; certificate social work Washington Sch. Psychiatry, 1969; m. Leonard M. Dub, Oct. 10, 1937 (dec. Jan. 1962); 1 dau., Petra (Mrs. D. William Subin); m. 2d, Robert Shosteck, Dec. 19, 1970. Interviewer, Ohio State Employment Service, Cin., 1936-37; caseworker Aid to Dependent Children, Cin., 1937-38; A.R.C., Services to Mil. Families, Washington, 1941-43, supr., caseworker, 1961-68; supr. casework Barker Found. Adoption Agy., Washington, 1968-70, exec. dir., 1970—. Mem. Smithsonian Assos., 1965—, Am. Theater Soc., 1955—, Washington Nat. Symphony, 1968—, Acad. Music, Phila., 1967—, Washington Performing Arts Soc., 1967—, nat. women's com. Brandeis U., 1960—, John F. Kennedy Bldg. Fund for Adult Mentally Retarded, 1966—, Friends of Kennedy Center, 1971—, Krishnamurti Found., Ojai, Cal., 1969—, Esalen Inst., Big Sur, Cal., 1968—, Orizon Inst., Washington, 1968—. Mem. Nat. Assn. Social Workers, Nat. Conf. Social Welfare, Internat. Council Social Welfare, Am. Assn. U. Women, Jewish Hist. Soc. Greater Washington. Jewish religion (corr. sec. Temple Sinai Sisterhood 1957-59). Mem. B'nai B'rith Women (exec. chpt. Washington, sec. div. 1971-72, bd. dirs. 1972-74). Home: 5100 Alta Vista Rd Bethesda MD 20014 Office: 4708 Wisconsin Av NW Washington DC 20016

DUBBRIN, LOLA HENNESY (MRS. ALBERT MILES DUBBRIN), real estate co. exec.; b. Bogalusa, La., July 7, 1925; d. Esmond Edward and Ethel Loraine (Simmons) Hennesy; student Huffstetler Bus. Coll., 1943, Santa Rosa Jr. Coll., 1964-67; m. Albert Miles Dubbrin, Mar. 2, 1946; 1 dau., Sonya (Mrs. Dennis De Lugg). With Foreman & Foreman, Mobile, Ala., 1943-46; with L.E. Castner Agys. Boyes Hot Springs, Cal., 1947—, v.p., treas., 1968—. Bd. dirs. Boyes Springs Village Assn., 1970—. Mem. Nat. Assn. Real Estate Bds., Cal., Sonoma County real estate bds., Ins. Womens Assn. (pres. 1968), Sonoma Valley Ins. Agents Assn. (v.p. 1973). Club: Sonoma County Ins. Women (Boyes Hot Springs). Home: PO Box 335 1224 Alberca Rd Boyes Hot Springs CA 95416 Office: 18298 Sonoma Hwy Boyes Hot Springs CA 95416

DUBERSTEIN, HELEN LAURA (MRS. VICTOR LIPTON), poet; b. N.Y.C., June 3, 1926; d. Jacob M. and Beatrice (Lieberman) Duberstein; B.S., Coll. City N.Y., 1947; m. Victor Lipton, Apr. 10, 1949; children—Jacqueline Frances, Irene. Coordinator, First N.Y. Festival Playwrights Cooperative, 1973; rec. artist radio sta. WBAI-FM; coordinator Westbeth Poets, Poetry Workshops; off Broadway plays produced Circle in the Sq., 1967, The Cubiculo, 1971, Theatre for the New City, 1973, 74; playwright in residence Circle Theatre Repertory Co., 1969-72; coordinator poetry readings Theatre for the New City, 1973; poetry readings in Westbeth, Mercer Arts Center, Cubiculo, Theatre for the New City. Recipient various prizes in poetry contests. Nat. Endowment for the Arts grantee, 1972. Mem. Dramatists Guild, Poetry Soc. Am. Author: Succubus/Incubus (poetry), 1972; The Human Dimension (poetry), 1972. Contbr. short stories, poetry, essays to various mags. including Confrontation, Commentary, The Center Forum, Changing Edn., The Outsider. Home: 463 West St Apt 904D New York City NY 10014

DUBICK, PATRICIA MARIE, hotel exec.; b. Bklyn., Apr. 14, 1941; d. Stephen and Katherine (Horbacio) DuB.; B.A., Syracuse U., 1965. Asst. dir. pub. relations/publs. LeMoyne Coll., Syracuse, N.Y., 1967-70; dir. fund-raising/pub. relations Planned Parenthood Assn. Phoenix, 1970-71; advt. copywriter/prodn. mgr. Barnes Assos., Phoenix, 1971-73; advt. copywriter, prodn. mgr. Best Western Motels, Inc., Phoenix, 1973—. Mem. Women in Communications. Home: 4140 N 10th St Phoenix AZ 85014 Office: 2910 Sky Harbor Blvd Phoenix AZ 85034

DUBIEL, DIANE CROWLEY, editor; b. Phila., Aug. 22, 1943; d. Daniel Raymond and Genevieve (Ambrose) Crowley, Jr.; B.A. in Journalism, Pa. State U., 1965; postgrad. Purdue U., 1966—; m. Richard Michael Dubiel, Jan. 22, 1966. Reporter, photographer Herald-Mail, Hagerstown, Md., 1964, Courier-News, Plainfield, N.J., 1965, Jour. and Courier, Lafayette, Ind., 1965-67, Daily Record, Morristown, N.J., 1967-68; editor Purdue Univ. Studies, Lafayette, Ind., 1968—. Mem. Women in Communications. Home: 201 Northwestern Av West Lafayette IN 47906 Office: South Campus Courts-D West Lafayette IN 47907

DU BIN, KARIN ELIZABETH VAN LISSEL (MRS. ALEXANDER DUBIN), educator, author; b. Knoxville Ia.; d. Neilus and Eva (Wilson) Van Lissel; A.B., Parsons Coll., 1926; M.A., Chgo. Theol. Sem., 1937; M.A., U. Mich., 1942; Ph.D., Columbia, 1965; m. Alexander DuBin, Sept. 5, 1947. Actress, Theater of the Air, Berkeley, Cal., 1931-32, Magic of Speech Hour, Chgo., 1935-37; dir. theatre Coll. of Ozarks, 1938-39; speech and theatre dir. Friends U., 1939-40, W.Va. State Coll., 1941-42, Lindenwood Coll., 1942-43; instr. speech City U. N.Y., 1957-59; dir. theatre Hicksville (N.Y.) Sr. High Sch., 1961-63; prof. speech and theatre Bridgewater (Mass.) State Coll., 1965—, dir. verse speaking choir, 1965—. Mem. Am. Assn. U. Women (chmn. writers group N.Y.C. br. 1950-55), Speech Assn. Eastern States, Speech Communication Assn. Am. (nat. chmn. theatre project study group 1965-66), Authors League Am., Dramatists Guild, ANTA, Am. Theatre Assn., Am. Assn. U. Profs., Mass. State Coll. Assn., Pi Kappa Delta, Sigma Tau Delta, Kappa Delta Pi. Author: Connie, Theatre Director, 1946; Verse Choir Lyrics; (play) Grasshoppers; also articles and short stories in nat. mags. Home: 223 Pleasant St Bridgewater MA 02324

DUBROFF, DIANA DOROTHY, lawyer; b. N.Y.C., Mar. 4, 1909; d. Meyer and Gussie (Ginsburg) Leibow; B.A., Hunter Coll., 1928; LL.B., Bklyn. Law Sch., 1931, J.D., 1968; m. Alexander DuBroff, June 25, 1936; children—William, Elinor. Tchr., N.Y.C., 1928-61; admitted to N.Y. bar, 1934; pvt. practice law, N.Y.C.; founder, dir. Nat. Orgn. Insure Support Enforcement, N.Y.C., 1971—, N.O.I.S.E. Children of Divorce Fund, N.Y.C., 1973—, N.O.I.S.E. Abused Children Am., Inc., Washington, 1974—; judge Small Claims Ct., N.Y.C., 1968; hearing officer Parking Violations Bur., N.Y.C., 1968. Founder, Star Civic League, N.Y.C., 1928; organizer, nursery group Forest Hills Jewish Center, N.Y.C., 1942. Fellow Am. Acad. Matrimonial Lawyers (family law com. 1972, chmn. ct. reform 1973—); mem. Am. Arbitration Assn. (arbitrator 1968—), N.Y. State Bar (family law com. 1973—), N.Y. Trial Lawyers Assn. (chmn. family law com. 1973), Am. (mem. family law com. 1968), N.Y., Bronx womens bar assns., N.Y. Women's Bar, Gregarians (founder 1949). Author booklet: Not for Women and Children Only, 1972. Office: 10 Columbus Circle New York City NY 10019

DUCAS, DOROTHY (MRS. JAMES B. HERZOG), pub. relations cons.; b. N.Y.C.; d. Charles and Doris (Pottlitzer) Ducas; B.Lit., Columbia, 1926; m. James B. Herzog, June 7, 1926 (dec. Jan. 1964); children—John, Thomas. Reporter, Bergen Evening Record, N.Y. Herald Tribune, London (Eng.) Sunday Express, N.Y. Evening Post, 1925-29; asso. editor McCall's mag., 1929-30; corr. Internat. News Service, 1930-35; contbr. articles to nat. mags., 1935-49; pub. relations dir. March of Dimes, Nat. Found., 1949-60; founder, chief, mag. bur. OWI, 1942-44; spl. cons. to surgeon gen. USPHS and dir. pub. service Lobsenz Pub. Relations Co., Inc., N.Y.C., 1962-68; spl. cons. Am. Mus. Natural History, Nat. Health Council, 1968-69; pub. relations dir. Nat. Cystic Fibrosis Research Found., 1969-71, pub. relations cons., 1971—; instr. pub. relations N.Y. U., 1961-63; dir. Nat. Pub. Relations Council on Health and Welfare Services, 1952-69. Pulitzer Traveling scholar, 1926. Recipient Headliner's award Theta Sigma Phi, 1944. Mem. Authors League of Am., Pub. Relations Soc. Am., Nat. Assn. Sci. Writers. Clubs: Overseas Press, N.Y. Newswomen's; Washington Press. Author: (with Elizabeth Gorden) More House For Your Money, 1940; Modern Nursing, 1962. Contbr. chpt. on Mrs. Roosevelt, Journalists in Action, 1964, on Dr. Jonas Salk, Heroes for our Time, 1968. Home and office: Box 21A Spring St South Salem NY 10590

DUCKGEISCHEL, MARY CATHERINE, surgeon; b. San Jose, Cal., Dec. 15, 1921; d. John and Mary (Kemper) Duckgeischel; student Coll. Notre Dame, Belmont, Cal., 1940-41, Trinity Coll., Washington, 1945-47, Women's Med. Coll. Pa., 1947-48; M.D., Med. Coll. Va., 1953. Intern, San Francisco City and County Hosp., 1953-54; resident Kaiser Found. Hosp., San Francisco, 1955-59; surgeon Permanente Med. Group, San Francisco, 1959-64, Santa Clara, Cal., 1964—; asst. chief surgery Kaiser Found. Hosp., Santa Clara, 1965—; practice medicine specializing in surgery, San Francisco, 1959-64, Santa Clara, 1964—. Diplomate Am. Bd. Surgery. Fellow A.C.S. Home: 7033 Shirley Dr Oakland CA 94611 Office: 900 Kiely Blvd Santa Clara CA 95051

DUDECK, M. PATRICIA (MRS. CARL F. DUDECK), librarian; b. South Langhorne, Pa., Jan. 12, 1926; d. Arthur and Nellie (Shelley) Peters; B.A., Rutgers U., 1964, M.L.S., 1966; m. Carl F. Dudeck, Apr. 6, 1947 (dec. Jan. 1973); children—Carl Arthur, Barbara Patricia. Lab. technician, organic chemist Johns Manville Research, Manville, N.J., 1944-47; lab. technician microbiology Ethicon, Inc., Somerville, N.J., 1958-65; librarian med. research div. Esso Research & Engring. Co. (now Exxon Research & Engring. Co.), Linden, N.J., 1966—. Mem. adv. bd. Rutgers Grad. Sch. Library Service, 1972-73. Mem. Med. Library Assn., Spl. Libraries Assn. (pres. N.J. chpt. 1972-73), Beta Phi Mu. Home: 810 Route 202-206 N Somerville NJ 08876 Office: Medical Research Division Library PO Box 45 Linden NJ 07036

DUDLEY, DOROTHY NYE, librarian; b. West Salem, Wis., May 15, 1905; d. Lewis Richard and Alice (Nye) Dudley; B.A. (Bible dept. fellow), Ripon Coll., 1927; postgrad. Chgo. Theol. Sem., 1927-28. Librarian West Salem (Wis.) br. LaCrosse County Library, 1940—; clk. Paramount Photo Shop, West Salem, 1944-68. Recipient appreciation award West Salem Lions Club, 1971, Citizens award West Salem, 1973. Mem. West Central Dist. (past sec.), Wis. library assns., West Salem Study Club (past v.p.), Wis. Genealogy Soc., Wis., West Salem (dir.) hist. socs. Presbyn. (elder, wrote local ch. history). Home: 204 W Garland St West Salem WI 54669

DUDLEY, FLORA HELEN (MRS. JOHN CHAPMAN DUDLEY), librarian; b. N.Y.C., Apr. 13, 1919; d. Arno and Flora Helen (Willvonseder) Ehrsam; B.A., Barnard Coll., 1940; M.L.S., Columbia, 1964; m. John Chapman Dudley, June 18, 1941; children—Bruce Chapman, Richard George, David John, Linda Julie (Mrs. Raymond Pyle). Librarian trainee Mamaroneck (N.Y.) Free Library, 1961-64, adult services librarian, 1964-66, asst. dir., 1966—. Pub. relations chmn. Larchmont-Mamaroneck Film Council, 1973. Mem. N.Y. Library Assn. (co-chmn. publicity pub. libraries sect. 1972), Bus. and Profl. Women's Club (program chmn. 1973, membership chmn. 1972-73), League of Women Voters (dir. 1968-70). Club: Mamaroneck (N.Y.) Woman's. Editor, Westchester Library Assn. Bull., 1970—; book reviewer Library Jour., 1974—. Home: 437 Melbourne Av Mamaroneck NY 10543 Office: Prospect Av and Library Lane Mamaroneck NY 10543

DUDLEY, LAURA ELDRIDGE (MRS. KENNETH DUDLEY), librarian; b. Levant, Me., Sept. 21, 1916; d. Elmer L. and Minnie A. (Norton) Eldridge; B.S. in Library Sci., Simmons Coll., 1939; m. Kenneth Dudley, Aug. 6, 1949; children—Deborah Jane, Joan Louise. Cataloger Concord (N.H.) Pub. Library, 1943-45; head reference librarian Portlant (Me.) Pub. Library, 1945-49; order librarian Hofstra Coll., Hempstead, N.Y., 1956-66, head acquisitions librarian, 1967—. Mem. Am. (chmn. nominating com. resources and tech. services div. acquisitions sect. 1973-74, book dealer-librarian relationship com.), N.Y. (chmn. resources and tech. services sect. 1971-73), Nassau County (corresponding sec. coll. and univ. sect. 1968-70, rec. sec. coll. and univ. div. 1970-71) library assns. Home: 1353 Harvey Ct Baldwin NY 11510 Office: Hofstra University Library Hempstead NY 11550

DUDLEY, PATRICIA LOUISE, zoologist, educator; b. Denver, May 22, 1929; d. David Christopher and Carolyn (Latas) Dudley; B.A., U. Colo., 1951, M.A. in Biology, 1953; Ph.D. (NSF fellow), U. Wash., 1957. Research asso. U. Wash., Seattle, 1957-59, instr. marine invertebrate zoology Friday harbor labs., summers 1960, 61; instr. biol. scis. Barnard Coll., Columbia U., N.Y.C., 1959-62, asst. prof., 1962-67, asso. prof., 1967-73, prof., 1973—. Vis. investigator systematics ecology program Marine Biol. Lab., Woods Hole, Mass., 1969, 71. NSF faculty fellow, 1965-66. Mem. A.A.A.S., Am. Soc. Zoologists (sec. invertegrate zoology sect. 1973—), Marine Biol. Assn. U.K., Soc. Systematic Zoology, Am. Assn. Univ. Profs. Author: Development and Systematics of Some Pacific Marine Symbiotic Copepods, 1966. Home: Riverdale NY 10471 Office: Dept Biological Sciences Barnard College Columbia University 606 W 120th St New York NY 10027

DUDLEY, VIRGINIA (EVELYN), artist; b. Spring City, Tenn.; d. Charles Newton and Laura (Thompson) Dudley; student U. Chattanooga, 1937-40, Art Students League. N.Y.C., 1940-45, New Sch. Social Research, 1942-43, 45, Atelier 17, N.Y.C., 1945-46, N.M. Coll., 1947-48, Coll. William and Mary, 1958-59, U. Md., Seoul, Korea, 1959-60; M.F.A., Claremont (Cal.) Grad. Sch., 1950; m. Joseph Spenser Moran, Apr. 20, 1946. Works exhibited Met. Mus. Art, San Francisco Mus. Art, Library of Congress, also London, Eng., San Francisco, Buffalo, Los Angeles, Phila., Vancouver, Washington, others; one-man shows U. Chattanooga, 1943, Hunter Gallery Art, Chattanooga, 1952, Ga. Mus., Athens, 1954, Newport News, Va., 1959, Rome, Ga., 1964, 69, 71, Columbus, Ga., 1970, Macon (Ga.) Mus. Arts and Sci., 1973; represented in permanent collections including Met. Mus. Art, N.Y.C., Library of Congress, Scripps Coll., Ga. Mus. Art, U. Miami, Art Students League N.Y., Everson Mus. Art, Syracuse, Pa. State Mus., Columbus Mus. Arts and Sics., Macon Mus. Arts and Sci.; artist in residence, also asso. prof. art Shorter Coll., Rome, 1964-71; dir. Am. Craftsmen, Studio-Workshop, Virginia Dudley Studios; lectr. on South East Asia and the Orient. Recipient Rosenwald fellowship for painting and lithography, 1943, 1st award So. Highland Handicraft Guild, 1953, Sarasota Found. Craft and Sculpture Show, 1953, Internat. Crafts Show, Canadian Pacific Expn., Vancouver, 1945, Nat. Ceramic Exhbns., Syracuse Mus. Fine Arts, 1956, first prize Chattanooga Area Artists, 1964, others. Art dir. Coronado Playmakers, N.M. State Coll., 1947-48; art editor Rio Grande Writer, lit. mag., 1947-48; staff arts and crafts dir. Hdqrs. 18th U.S. Army, Korea, 1959-61, Eighth Air Force, Westover, Mass., 1961-63. Fellow Internat. Inst. Arts and Letters; mem. So. Highland Handicraft Guild, Soc. Am. Graphic Artists, Am. Crafts Council, Ga. Designer Craftsmen, World Crafts Council, Am. Assn. U. Women, Am. Assn. U. Profs., Chattanooga Art Assn., Royal Asiatic Soc. Address: On Lookout Mountain Route 2 Rising Fawn GA 30738

DUDNEY, DORIS ANN, lawyer; b. Sebring, Fla., June 9, 1934; d. Fred Stanton and Opal (Laine) Dudney; B.A., Vanderbilt U., 1954, LL.B., 1956. Admitted to Fla. bar, 1956, U.S. Supreme Ct. bar, 1971; practiced in Tampa, Fla., 1956—; asso. firm Fowler, White, Gillen, Humkey & Trenam, 1956-61; mem. Fowler, White, Gillen Humkey, Kinney & Boggs, and predecessors, 1961-74. Vice chmn., sec. Law Inc. Hillsborough County (Fla.), 1967-70, pres., chmn. bd. dirs., 1970—. Bd. dirs., vice chmn. YWCA Tampa, 1964-69, 71-74; bd. dirs. Big Sisters, Tampa, 1966-69; bd. dirs., 1st v.p. Hillsborough Assn. Retarded Children; bd. dirs. Mental Health Assn. Hillsborough County, pres., 1973-74; bd. dirs. Giris Club, Tampa, 1966—, pres., 1971—, mem. nat. bd. dirs., 1972—; trustee, sec. Falk Mandel Charity Found.; trustee, exec. com. Tampa-Hillsborough County Drug Abuse Comprehensive Coordinating Office. Named Outstanding Young Woman Am., Vanderbilt U. and Tampa chpt. Am. Assn. U. Women, 1966. Mem. Am., Tampa, Hillsborough County bar assns., The Fla. Bar, Am. Judicature Soc., Am. Assn. U. Women, Greater Tampa C. of C., Nat. Legal Aid and Defenders Assn., League of Women Voters, Am. Dog Owners Assn. (nat. dir.), Order of Coif, Kappa Delta. Republican. Clubs: Zonta Internat. (local pres. 1971-72, lt. gov. dist. 1972-74, gov. dist. 1974—), Tampa Woman's (courtesy), Palma Ceia Golf and Country, Tampa Bay Kennel (dir., show com.), Boston Terriers, The Tower (Tampa). Home: 2407 Ardson Pl Tampa FL 33609 Office: Suite 2001 First Financial Tower Tampa FL 33602

DUEKER, MARILYNN SPANGLET (MRS. GORDON W. DUEKER), statistician, educator; b. Bklyn., Oct. 3, 1925; d. Michael S. and Laura (Brookman) B.A., Hunter Coll., 1945; M.A., U. Cal. at Berkeley, 1947; postgrad N.Y. U., 1968—; m. Gordon W. Dueker, Dec. 28, 1949; children—Lori (Mrs. Mark Hanks), Alice. Asst. prof. statistics Kan. State U., Manhattan, 1947-51; asst. prof. statistics U. Conn. Stamford, 1959—. Mem. Am. Math. Assn., Am. Statis. Assn., Phi Beta Kappa, Sigma Xi., Pi Mu Epsilon. Home: 94 Skyview Dr Stamford CT 06902

DUENSING, JEAN ELIZABETH, editor; b. Sedalia, Mo., Nov. 5, 1919; d. Edwin Arnold and Annabel (Ernst) Duensing; grad. Jefferson City Jr. Coll., 1939; student Sch., Journalsim, U. Mo., 1940-41. Editor house organ Famous Barr Co., St. Louis, Mo., 1941-43; advt. writer and sales rep. Jefferson City (Mo.) News Tribune, 1943-46; advt. mgr. The Purple Shoppe, Jefferson City, Mo., 1946-51; sales dir. sta. KRCG-TV, Jefferson City, 1954-56; continuity dir. KWOS Radio, Jefferson City, 1956-62; home editor Rural Electric Missourian, Jefferson City, 1963-66; asst. mng. editor Missouri Medicine, Jefferson City, 1966-67, mng. editor, 1967—. Publicity chmn. Jefferson City Community Concerts Assn., 1955-73; active Cole County A.R.C.; active Jefferson City Girl Scouts Am. Mem. Mo. Press Women (pres. 1974-75), Zonta Internat. Home: 107 Doehla Dr Jefferson City MO 65101 Office: Missouri Medicine Mo State Med Assn 113 Madison PO Box 1028 Jefferson City MO 65101

DUERK, ALENE BERTHA, naval officer, nurse; b. Defiance, O., Mar. 29, 1920; d. Albert John and Emma Katherine (Dietsch) Duerk; diploma Toledo Hosp. Sch. Nursing, 1941; B.S., Frances Payne Bolton Sch. Nursing, Western Res. U., 1948; Dr. Pub. Service, Bowling Green State U., 1973. Commd. ensign Nurse Corps U.S. Navy, 1943, advanced through grades to rear adminal, 1972; staff nurse Naval Hosp., Portsmouth, Va., 1943-44, charge nurse, 1951, instr. Corps Sch., 1951-56; staff nurse Naval Hosp., Bethesda, Md., 1944-45; staff nurse U.S.S. Benevolence, 1945; staff nurse Naval Hosp., Gt. Lakes, Ill., 1946, chief nurse, 1968-70; inservice coordinator Naval Hosp., Phila., 1956-58; programs officer Naval Recruiting, Chgo., 1958-61; charge nurse Naval Sta., Subic Bay, Philippines, 1961-62; asst. chief nurse Naval Hosp., Yokosuka, Japan, 1965; chief nurse Naval Hosp. Corps Sch., San Diego, 1965-66; spl. asst. for nursing affairs Office of Dept. Asst. Sec. of Def., Washington, 1966-67; dir. Navy Nurse Corps, Washington, 1970—. Mem. Am. Nurses Assn., Nat. League Nursing, Mil. Surgeons U.S., Alumni Toledo Hosp. Sch. Nursing. Home: 506 Highland Pl Alexandria VA 22301 Office: Nursing Div Code 32 Navy Dept Bur Medicine and Surgery Washington DC 20372

DUERST, MARILYN DIANE (MRS. RICHARD WILLIAM DUERST), educator; b. Clinton, Ia., Nov. 30, 1941; d. Harley Merle and Margaret Louise (Eberlein) Moxness; B.A. (NSF scholar 1959, Coll. scholar 1959-60, Minn. Acad. Sci. scholar 1959-60), 1963; M.A., U. Cal. at Berkeley, 1966, postgrad., 1966-67; m. Richard William Duerst, Mar. 1, 1964; children—Karin, Susan, Linda. Translator German-English, Dept. Social Sci., U. Cal. at Berkeley, 1964, teaching asst. Dept. German, 1964-67; instr. German, phys. sci. Dist. One Vocational Tech. Inst., Eau Claire, Wis., 1971—. Mem. Eau Claire Area Ecology Action, 1970-73, mem. exec. bd. 1970-72. Active in Young Republicans and Young Ams. for Freedom, 1959-63. Mem. Am. Council on Teaching of Fgn. Langs., Modern Lang. Assn. Am., Nat. Audubon Soc., Wis. Soc. for Ornithology, Nat. Geog. Soc., Smithsonian Instn., U. Womens Assn. Lutheran (supt. Sunday sch. 1973—). Club: Eau Claire (Wis.) Color Slide (v.p. 1973—). Home: 1511 Hogeboom Av Eau Claire WI 54701 Office: Dist One Vocational Tech Inst Clairemont Av Eau Claire WI 54701

DUEY, BARBARA VOYSEY, orgn. ofcl.; b. Upland, Pa., Feb. 12, 1935; d. Alfred Everett and Revilla Barr (Read) Voysey; B.S. in Med. Tech., Pa. State U., 1957; m. Herbert David Duey, July 13, 1957; children—Jon H., William G., Charles J. Research biochemist Nat. Inst. Dental Research, 1957-58; staff aide, then financial staff aide YWCA of Met. Denver, 1970—. Active P.T.A.; newsletter Girl Scouts; den mother Cub Scouts, 1971-73; mem. Denver Com. Fgn. Relations, 1973—. Mem. League Women Voters (dir. Jefferson County, nat. program chmn. 1968-72, internat. relations chmn. Colo. 1972—), Sigma Sigma Sigma, Alpha Lambda Delta, Phi Sigma, Iota Sigma Pi, Gamma Sigma Delta. Mem. United Ch. of Christ. (ch. sch. supt. 1967-71, deacon 1973—, choir mem.). Club: YW Wives (treas. 1966-67, pres. 1967-68). Home: 12332 W New Mexico Av Lakewood CO 80228 Office: 1545 Tremont Pl Denver CO 80202

DUFF, CHARLOTTE ANN, educator; b. Madison, Wis., June 3, 1926; d. Joseph Henry and Isophene Julia (Schlotthauer) Duff; B.S., U. Wis., 1948; M.A., U. Mich., 1956. Tchr. Oshkosh (Wis.) High Sch., 1948-50; instr. U. Neb., Lincoln, 1950-52; camp and health bd. dir. YWCA, Flint, Mich., 1952-54; teaching fellow U. Mich. at Ann Arbor, 1954-56; prof. phys. edn. Albion (Mich.) Coll., 1956—. Camp counselor, activity specialist, dir. Joy Camps, Hazelhurst, Wis., 1954-56, Camp Kineowatha, Wilton, Me., 1947, Chippewa Trail Camp, Rapid City, Mich., 1948-49, Camp Wabunaki, Hillside, Me., 1950-51, Camp Tyrone, Flint, Mich., 1952-54, 65-68 Quanset Sailing Camps, South Orleans, Mass., 1955-58, Camp Nicolet, Eagle River, Wis., 1959-61, camp cons. Mich. dept. Social Services, 1969—. Mem. Am., Mich. (pres. 1969-70) assns. for health, phys. edn. and recreation, Nat., Midwest (treas. 1973—) assns. for phys. edn. coll. women, Mich. Camping Assn. (leadership chmn. 1963-65), Great Lakes Field Hockey Assn. (chmn. treas. 1961-69), Delta Kappa Gamma. Home: 1133 River's Bend Dr Albion MI 49224 Office: Albion College Albion MI 49224

DUFFE, MARY CLINCH, writer, editor; b. Elmwood, Ill., Aug. 8, 1916; d. Charles Eugene and Irene (Wasson) Clinch; B.J., U. Mo., 1938; M.A., Washington U., St. Louis, 1964; m. Robert William Duffe, Oct. 6, 1942; children—William, Stephen, James, John. Reporter, Peoria (Ill.) Jour. Star, 1939-42; tchr. French and English St. Elizabeth's Acad., St. Louis, 1960-62; instr. French U. Mo., St. Louis, 1963-67; asst. editor St. Louis Commerce Mag., 1967-73; free-lance writer and cons., 1973—. Mem. Women in Communications, Kappa Alpha Theta. Author: Every Elephant, 1972. Home: 3958 Flora Pl St Louis MO 63110

DUFFEL, SARAH COVINGTON, librarian; b. Arkadelphia, Ark., Nov. 2, 1945; d. John Rudolph and Glenna (Stover) Covington; student Hendrix Coll., 1963-65; B.A., U. Ark., 1967; M.S., La. State U., 1968; m. John Anthony Duffel, Aug. 3, 1968; 1 dau., Christy Anne. Librarian I, New Orleans Pub. Library, 1968-69, librarian II, head circulation dept., 1969-73, librarian II information and reference staff, 1974—. Catherine Zeke Caldwell scholar, 1965. Mem. La., Ark. library assns., Beta Phi Mu, Alpha Tau. Methodist. Home: 1405 Aris St Metairie LA 70005 Office: 219 Loyola Av New Orleans LA 70140

DUFFIELD, PAULINE, librarian; b. Sutton, W.Va.; d. John Byrn and Mary (Marlow) Duffield; B.S., George Peabody Coll., 1936, B.S. in Library Sci., 1940. Librarian, Richwood (W.Va.) High Sch., 1930-41, Parker Dist. Library, Greenville, S.C., 1941-43; asst. librarian Vanderbilt U. Sch. Medicine, Nashville, 1944-45, Med. Chirurgical Faculty Md., Balt., 1945-52, Tex. Med. Assn., Austin, 1952—. Mem. Med. Library Assn. (chmn. nominating com. 1968-69), Spl. Library Assn., Tex. Med. Assts., Tex. Council Health Sci. Libraries (sec.-treas. 1968-72). Home: 1219 Castle Hill Austin TX 78703 Office: 1801 N Lamar Blvd Austin TX 78701

DUFFNER, MARGARET CAIN, educator; b. Jacksonville, Ill., Mar. 5, 1919; d. Thomas Raymond and Elizabeth White (Butler) Cain; B.A., MacMurray Coll., 1940; M.A., Northwestern U., 1943; m. John Thomas Duffner, Dec. 26, 1942; children—Thomas, Michael, Mary Elizabeth, Suzanne, Mark, Nancy. Tchr. speech No. Va. Center, U. Va., 1968-70; tchr. speech George Mason U., Fairfax, Va., 1968—, coach forensics, 1971—. Sweepstakes coach numerous tournaments. Recipient award excellence teaching faculty English dept. George Mason U., 1973, Outstanding Service award student govt., 1973, 74, named Tchr. of Year, 1974; named Outstanding Coach in Forensics, Allegheny Regional Tournament, 1971. Mem. Am. Assn. Univ. Profs., Speech Communication Assn. Am., Am. Forensic Assn., So. Speech Communication Assn. Roman Cath. Home: 3802 Ridge Rd Annandale VA 22003 Office: 4400 University Dr Fairfax VA 22030

DUFFY, ESTHER RODGERS (MRS. ROGER FRANCIS DUFFY), librarian; b. Pitts., Aug. 14, 1911; d. Arthur Gregory and Charlotte Catherine (Nagle) Rodgers; B. Music and B.S. in Music Edn., Seton Hill Coll., 1932; postgrad. U. Pitts., 1933, Carnegie Inst.,

1935, Simmons Coll., 1941-42; m. Roger Francis Durry, Nov. 14, 1945; children—Katherine, Mary Anne, Roger. Instr. music Coll. Misericordia, Dallas, Pa., 1932-37; music librarian Cornell U., Ithaca, N.Y., 1937-41; asst. music librarian Columbia U., N.Y.C., 1942-43; research librarian Office Strategic Services, State Dept., 1943-44, Balkans outpost rep. Office War Information, 1944-46, Balkans regional rep. U.S. Information Service, 1946; asst. to pres. Juilliard Sch. Music, N.Y.C., 1947-49; asst. to mng. dir. U.S. Internat. Book Assn., N.Y.C., 1945-47; librarian fine arts Greenwich (Conn.) Library, 1961—. Mem. Music Library Assn., Kappa Gamma Pi. Home: 2 Peters Rd Riverside CT 06878 Office: 101 W Putnam Av Greenwich CT 06830

DUFFY, ISABEL TOOMEY, govt. ofcl.; b. Spearfish, S.D., Dec. 25, 1919; d. Allen and Janet Nadine (Campbell) Toomey; student Black Hills State Coll., 1937-38; B.S., Memphis State U., 1944; B.J., U. Mo., 1945; m. William McFadden Duffy, 1947 (div. 1964); children—Adrienne Elizabeth, William McFadden, Stuart Allan. Reporter, editor A.P., Kansas City, Mo., 1945-47; asst. publicity dir. Internat. House, New Orleans, 1947-52; La. account exec., gen. rep. Merchandising Group, also free lance writer and pub. relations rep., N.Y.C., 1952-68; pub. information officer So. Forest Expt. Sta., U.S. Forest Service, New Orleans, 1968-74, pub. information officer N.E. Forest Expt. Sta., Upper Darby, Pa., 1974—. Mem. adv. bd. Unity Soc. of New Orleans, 1970-72. Recipient Sigma Delta Chi award, 1945; Blue Pencil awards for writing and editing Fed. Editors Assn., 1968-73; Mead Nat. award Mead Paper Co., 1972; Certificate of Merit, U.S. Dept. Agr., 1973. Mem. Nat. Fedn. Press Women, Govt. Information Officers, Conservation Edn. Assn., Internat. Assn. Bus. Communicators, Fed. Editors Assn., Women in Communications (pres. 1969-70, v.p. 1973-74), P.E.O. Home: Drexelview Club Apt 16 W 3200 Township Line Drexel Hill PA 19026 Office: 6816 Market St Upper Darby PA 19082

DUFFY, MARY BROCK (MRS. RICHARD NIXON DUFFY, JR.), physician; b. Meadville, Pa., Feb. 8, 1920; d. George Harrison and Mary (Gibson) Brock; A.B. cum laude, Allegheny Coll., 1941; M.D., U. Pa., 1944; M.P.H., U. N.C., 1962; m. Richard Nixon Duffy, Jr., Feb. 13, 1949; children—Mary Gibson, Richard Nixon III, Randolph Brock, John Chapman. Intern Phila. Gen. Hosp., 1944-45; resident Children's Hosp. Phila., 1945-46, Babies Hosp., Wilmington, N.C., 1946-47; practice medicine specializing in pediatrics, New Bern, N.C., 1947-51; asst. health dir. Knox County Health Dept., Knoxville, Tenn., 1962-67, dir., 1967—; cons. staff U. Tenn. Meml. Hosp. and Research Center, asst. prof. clin. family practice, 1969—. Lectr. U. Tenn. Sch. Health, 1969—. Mem. Health and Welfare Planning Council, Knoxville, 1967-72, Planned Parenthood Bd. Knox County, 1965—, Knoxville-Knox County Community Action Com., 1968—; mem. adv. bd. East Tenn. Arthritis Found., 1969—; med. adviser Knox County Head Start, 1966—, Sr. Citizens Home, Health Aide Service, 1969—, Tenn. State Renal Disease Soc. Bd. drs. East Tenn. Heart Assn. Diplomate Am. Bd. Preventive Medicine. Fellow Am. Coll. Preventive Medicine, Am. Pub. Health Assn. (governing council); mem. A.M.A., Am. Sch. Health Assn., Tenn. Med. Assn., Knoxville Acad. Medicine (exec. com. 1972—), Tenn. Pub. Health Assn. (exec. com. 1969—), Phi Beta Kappa, Alpha Chi Omega. Home: 4055 Valencia Rd Knoxville TN 37919 Office: Knox County Health Dept Knoxville TN 37917

DUFFY, MARY TERESA, lawyer; b. Everett, Mass.; d. John J. and Julia A. (Keough) Duffy; LL.B., Northeastern U., 1932. Asst. mgr., treas. New Ocean House, Swampscott, Mass., 1921-52; mgr. Women's City Club, Boston, 1953-55; admitted to Mass. bar, 1932; practiced in Lynn, Mass., 1955—. Mem. women in council Boston U., 1936-41. Mem. Am. Judicature Soc., Club Mgrs. Assn., Sales Mgrs. Assn., Mass. Assn. Women Lawyers (pres. 1945-46), Swampscott League Women Voters (1st v.p. 1948-50), Bus. and Profl. Women's Club. Clubs: Professional Women's, Women's City, Quota (Boston). Address: 100 Bellevue Rd Lynn MA 01904

DUFNER, MARY ELIZABETH, physician, lawyer; b. Phila., July 1, 1921; d. George Francis and Maude (Moore) Dufner; B.S., Temple U., 1943; M.D., Woman's Med. Coll. Pa., 1949; J.D., Am. U., 1968. Intern, Aultman Hosp., Canton, O., 1949-50; resident Akron (O.) City Hosp., 1950-52, Phila. Gen. Hosp., 1952-54; practice medicine, specializing in pathology, asst. instr. pathology U. Pa. Sch. Medicine, Phila., 1953-54; asso. pathologist Akron City Hosp., 1954-56; asst. pathologist, med. examiner Grasslands Hosp., Valhalla, N.Y., 1957; asso. pathologist Barberton (O.) Citizens' Hosp., 1957-59; instr. Akron City Hosp. Sch. Nursing, 1960-62; dir. dept. pathology Harrisburg (Pa.) State Hosp., 1962-65; lectr. law and medicine Dickinson Sch. Law, Carlisle, Pa., 1964—; writer Matthew Bender & Co., 1967-69; with med. research dept. Hoffmann-La Roche, Inc., 1969—. Chmn. health issues adv. panel Commn. on Med. Malpractice, U.S. Sec. Health, Edn. and Welfare, 1972. Diplomate Am. Bd. Pathology. Fellow Coll. Am. Pathology, Am. Coll. Legal Medicine (mem. com. med. malpractice 1972-74, nominating com. 1973-74), Royal Soc. Health (London); mem. Am. Med. Writers Assn., Pan Am. Med. Assn. Mem. editorial bd. Jour. Legal Medicine, 1972—; feature writer Fed. Register, 2d series. Home: 9617 Leon St Philadelphia PA 19114

DUGAN, APRIL JANET (MRS. KENNETH MICHAEL DUGAN), psychologist; b. Cleve., Jan. 4, 1943; d. Martin Edward and Jeanette Agnes (Guc) Konecek; B.S., St. John Coll. of Cleve., 1965; M.Ed., Kent State U., 1972; m. Kenneth Michael Dugan, Aug. 21, 1965; children—Kenneth Micheal, Kristopher Martin. Sch. psychologist J.A. Garfield Sch. Dist., Garrettsville, O., 1972—. Mem. Nat. Assn. Sch. Psychologists, Ohio Sch. Psychologists Assn., Kappa Delta Pi. Democrat. Roman Catholic. Clubs: Borromean, Isabella Guild (Parma, O.). Home: 6207 Morningside Dr Parma OH 44129 Office: 10207 S R 88 Garrettsville OH 44231

DUGAN, KIMIKO HATTA (MRS. WAYNE ALEXANDER DUGAN), educator; b. Kyoto City, Japan, Oct. 21, 1924; d. Shinzo and Sano (Hatta) Hatta; student U. Md., 1957-58; B.A., Okla. Coll. Women, 1961; M.S., U. Okla., 1965, Ph.D., 1970; m. Wayne Alexander Dugan, Aug. 18, 1947. Grad. fellow dept. anatomy Sch. Medicine, U. Okla., Oklahoma City, 1964-69, instr. dept. anat. sci. Coll. Medicine, 1969-71, asst. prof., 1971—. Mem. A.A.A.S., Am. Assn. U. Women, Am. Chem. Soc., Am. Soc. Zoologists, Electron Microscopy Soc. Am., Sigma Xi. Democrat. Episcopalian. Home: 333 NW 5th St Oklahoma City OK 73102

DUGAN, MARCIA BRUSSEL (MRS. FREDERICK D. DUGAN), pub. relations exec.; b. New Orleans, Aug. 19, 1931; d. Ira J. and Virginia M. (Wiener) Brussel; B.A., Antioch Coll., 1953; m. Frederick D. Dugan, Sept. 7, 1953; children—Michael D., Elizabeth, Margaret. Research chemist Fels Research Inst., Yellow Springs, O., 1951-53, Fed. Nutrition Lab., USPHS, Ithaca, N.Y., 1953-55; instr. math. Keuka Coll., Keuka Park, N.Y., 1958-60, dir. pub. relations, 1972—; tchr. Spanish elementary sch., Penn Yan, N.Y., 1960-62, Penn Yan High Sch., 1970-71. Del. White House Conf. on Aging, 1961; mem. regents adv. council Genesee Valley Higher Edn. Region, N.Y. State, 1972—; chmn. N.Y. Adv. Council Higher Edn. Facilities Planning, 1974—; pres. Central N.Y. Coll. Pub. Relations Council, 1974—. Leader Girl Scouts U.S.A., Penn Yan, 1963-66. Mem. Women's Republican Clubs, 1971—. Mem. Am. Assn. U. Women (chmn. prison rehab. and edn. project N.Y. div. 1972-73). Home: 253 Old County House Rd Penn Yan NY 14527 Office: Keuka College Keuka Park NY 14478

DUHAIME, LIVIA RODRIQUES (MRS. GEORGE H. DUHAIME), nursing educator; b. New Bedford, Mass., Sept. 8, 1919; d. Francisco and Rosa (Fernandes) Rodriques; student Sacred Hearts Acad., 1925-37; R.N., St. Luke's Hosp. Sch. Nursing, 1940; B.S. in Edn., Boston U., 1944, M.Ed., 1950; m. George H. Duhaime, Jan. 29, 1947 (dec. Jan. 1970); 1 dau., Lisa. Staff nurse St. Luke's Hosp., New Bedford, Mass., 1941-42, sci. instr. Sch. Nursing, 1944—, mem. curriculum com., 1947—, admissions and promotions com., 1947—, asst. dir. Sch. Nursing, 1964-66, asso. dir., then dir., 1966—, chmn. curriculum com., 1964—. Judge New Bedford Sci. Fair, 1963-65. Mem. Nat., Southeastern Mass. (pres. 1957-58, v.p. 1963—, mem. careers com., sec. steering com. bd. rev. for accreditation, dept. diploma programs) leagues nursing, Am., Mass. (2d v.p. dist. 3) nurses assns., Am. Greater Boston personnel and guidance assns., St. Luke's Hosp. Sch. Nursing Alumnae (mem. scholarship com. 1960, pres. 1967-69, dir. 1969—), Greater New Bedford Cancer Soc. (chmn. pub. edn. com. 1973), Delta Kappa Gamma, Pi Lambda Theta. Roman Catholic. Home: 148 Hathaway Rd North Dartmouth MA 02747 Office: 101 Page St New Bedford MA 02740

DUHAIME, NINA LEE HUPAYLO (MRS. WILFRED OVID DUHAIME), oil and mining corp. exec.; b. Westbrook, Tex.; d. Walter Frank and Mary (Shockley) Hupaylo; student U. Cal., 1944-45; pvt. study arts and scis., 1934-47; student U. Utah, 1973—; m. Wilfred Ovid DuHaime, Aug. 18, 1944; children—Linda Lee, Donna Irene. Entertainer radio and stage, various cities, 1940-46; operator Bar V Ranch, Taos County, N.M., 1948-53; owner, operator Consol. Interests, Internat., Santa Fe, 1956—; owner, broker Sun Mountain Realty, Santa Fe, 1964—; sec., v.p. Atom, Inc., Santa Fe, Farmington, N.M., 1968—, also dir. Writer N.M. oil activities R.W. Byram & Co., Austin, Tex., 1963—. Active Girl Scouts U.S.A., 1958-66; active Nat. Arthritis Found., N.M. Arthritis Found., other community orgns. Exec. sec. Republican Party, Santa Fe, 1953-54. Recipient awards including Distinguished Service award Dictionary of Internat. Biography, London, Eng., 1969. Fellow Pres.'s Council A.I.M., 1970-71. Mem. A.I.M. (mem. pres.'s council 1969), Internat., S.W. mining assns., Am. Mus. Natural History, Friends of Coll. of Santa Fe, Smithsonian Instn. Assos., Internat. Connoisseurs Green and Red Chile, Internat. Oceanographic Found., Phi Sigma Alpha (chpt. founding pres. 1965). Club: Le Mirador (Vevey, Switzerland). Prodn. partner motion picture, 1967. Weekly columnist Statehouse Reporter, 1965—. Contbr. articles, poetry to pubis. Home: 645 Camino Lejo Santa Fe NM 87501 Office: PO Box 1483 Santa Fe NM 87501

DUHART, EVELINE, librarian; b. Tallahassee, Fla., July 5, 1939; d. Bartow McLin and Madeline (Williams) Duhart; B.S., Fla. A. and M. U., 1960. Head librarian Douglass High Sch., Live Oak (Fla.) Bd. Edn., 1960-68, Suwannee Primary Sch., 1968—. Mem. Nat., Fla. Edn. assns., County Librarians (chmn. 1971-73), Fla. Assn. Media Edn., Suwannee County Edn. Assn., Modernistic Club (v.p. 1970). Baptist. Home: 861 W Delaware St Tallahassee FL 32304 Office: PO Box 92 Live Oak FL 32060

DUKE, ANGELEE MANAGAN (MRS. L.B. DUKE), social worker; b. Lake Charles, La., July 10, 1929; d. Luther Carswell and Leesie Lee (Terral) Managan; student McNeese State Coll., 1946-47; B.A., La. State U., 1950; M.S.W., Worden Sch. Social Service, Our Lady of Lake Coll., 1964; m. Lemuel Bonner Duke, Nov. 23, 1950. Welfare visitor Caddo Parish Welfare Dept., Shreveport, La., 1952-54; asst. probation officer Harris County Juvenile Probation Dept., Houston, 1955-62; caseworker Tex. Inst. for Rehab. and Research, Houston, 1964-65; instr., psychiat. social worker Baylor Coll. Medicine, Dept. Pediatrics and Psychiatry and Tex. Childrens Hosp., Houston, 1965-69; exec. dir. Parent Edn. Project, Houston, 1969-72; dir. parent and family life edn. YWCA, Houston, 1972-73; exec. dir. Mental Health Assn., Houston, 1973—. Vice pres. Western Heights, Inc., Lake Charles, 1969—. Supr. Big Bros. Houston, 1969-71. Mem. Acad. Certified Social Workers, Nat. Assn. Social Workers, D.A.R. Tex. United Community Services, Houston Group Psychotherapy Soc., Internat. Fedn. Parent Edn., Worden Sch. Social Service Alumni Assn. (pres. 1965-69), Psi Chi, Alpha Xi Delta. Club: Tempo Dance (Houston). Home: 2234 Tangley Rd Houston TX 77005 Office: 3208 Austin St Houston TX 77004

DUKE, JUNE TEMPLE, chemist; b. Cambridge, O., June 18, 1922; d. John A. and Edith Evelyn (Tedrick) Temple; student U. Akron, evenings 1942-56, U. Buffalo, 1957-58, Canisius Coll., 1958-59. Chemist, supr. U. Akron (O.) Govt. Labs., 1944-56; research chemist Olin Matheson Chem. Co., Niagara Falls, N.Y., 1956-59; research asso. Standard Oil Ohio, Cleve., 1959—. Fellow A.A.A.S.; mem. Am. Chem. Soc., Sigma Xi. Patentee in field. Home: 28649 Jackson Rd Chagrin Falls OH 44022 Office: 4440 Warrensville Center Rd Cleveland OH 44128

DUKE, MABEL, pub. relations exec.; b. Duke, Ala., Nov. 10, 1916; d. Henry Green and Elizabeth (Pouncey) Duke; student So. Meth. U. Script writer NBC radio newscaster Floyd Gibbons, N.Y.C., 1934-35; mag. writer N.Y.C. and Hollywood film studios, 1935-38; self-employed polit., theatrical pub. relations exec., Dallas, 1938—. Mem. Tex. State Commn. for Women, 1969-71. Mem. Fashion Group Internat., Women in Communications, Freedoms Found., Press Club Dallas, Dallas C. of C. (fine arts com. 1952-60). Home: 10737 D Villager Rd Dallas TX 75230 Office: Davis Bldg 1309 Main St Dallas TX 75202

DUKE, TUTTAN LARSON (MRS. JAMES W. DUKE), ret. librarian; b. Hot Springs, Ark., Mar. 10, 1936; d. Axel Linus and Elsa Linniea (Holgerson) Larson; B.S.E., Henderson State Tchrs. Coll., 1956; M.A. in L.S., George Peabody Coll., 1957; m. James W. Duke, June 23, 1963; 1 dau., Alice Evelyn. Circulation librarian George Peabody Coll., Nashville, 1957-59; sch. librarian Ft. Benning, Ga, 1959-60; reference asst. U. Ark., Fayetteville, 1960-62; reference librarian Neb. State Tchrs. Coll., Chadron, 1962-63; librarian young adult dept. Chgo. Pub. Library, 1963-64, asst. librarian humanities dept., 1964-66. Mem. A.L.A., Am. Assn. Univ. Women (v.p. 1972-74), Beta Phi Mu. Home: 5632 Primrose Av Indianapolis IN 46220

DUKE, VIRGINIA BACON (MRS. H. TRISDOM DUKE III), finance co. exec., civic worker; b. Phila., July 6, 1921; d. Harry Rickards and Dorothy Chappelle (Johnston) Bacon; student Germantown Friends Sch., 1938, Stevens Sch., 1938-40, Pa. Sch. Horticulture for Women, 1940-42; m. H. Trisdom Duke III, Jan. 23, 1942; 1 dau. Susan Chappelle. Office mgr. John Hancock Mut. Life Ins. Co., King of Prussia, Pa., 1961—; v.p. and treas. Profl. Financial Services, Inc., King of Prussia, 1965—. Vice pres. phys. div. Chestnut Hill Community Assn., 1972-74, mem. bd. dirs., 1972—; v.p. Chestnut Hill Teenagers, 1968, treas., 1968-71, v.p., 1971, mem. bd. dirs., 1965—; bd. dirs. Chestnut Hill Hist. Soc., Chestnut Hill Parking Found., 1970—. Named John Hancock Office Mgr. Year, Collins Agy., 1973; recipient Ann. Award for Community Service, Chestnut Hill Community Assn., 1974. Home: 8616 Evergreen Place Philadelphia PA 19118 Office: 150 Allendale Rd King of Prussia PA 19406

DUKERT, BETTY COLE (MRS. JOSEPH MICHAEL DUKERT), broadcasting co. exec.; b. Muskogee, Okla., May 9, 1927; d. Irvan Dill and Ione (Bowman) Cole; student Lindenwood Coll., 1945-46, Drury Coll., 1946-47; B.J., U. Mo., 1949; m. Joseph Michael Dukert, May 18, 1968. With radio sta. KICK, Springfield, Mo., 1949-50; adminstrv. asst. Juvenile Office, Green County, Mo., 1950-52; with WRC-TV/NBC, Washington, 1952-56; asso. producer program Meet the Press, NBC, Washington, 1956—. Recipient Certificate of award Nat. Acad. TV Arts and Scis., 1971; named One of 100 Distinguished Alumna, U. Mo., 1967. Mem. Am. Women in Radio/TV (dir. 1967-68, 72-73), Am. Newspaper Women's Club (program chmn. 1965-66), Radio/TV Corrs. Assn. Club: Washington Press (3d v.p. 1970-71, dir.). Home: 4709 Crescent St Washington DC 20016 Office: H-228 Sheraton Park Hotel Washington DC 20008

DUKES, EVA ALTMAN PAROLLA (MRS. PAUL DUKES), freelance writer, photographer, editor; b. Vienna, Austria, Dec. 18, 1923; d. Heinrich and Theresa (Braun) Altmann; B.A., Hunter Coll. City N.Y., 1945; postgrad. Columbia, 1946; m. Paul Dukes, May 1967. Came to U.S., 1940, naturalized, 1946. Lab. asst. Columbia Coll. Phys. and Surgs., N.Y.C., 1945-46; asst. perfumer Henri Robert, Inc., N.Y.C., 1946-49, de Laire div. Dodge & Olcott, N.Y.C., 1949-51; tech. writer Gen. Aniline & Film Corp., N.Y.C., 1951-59; asso. editor Kirk-Othmer Ency. Chem. Tech., 2d edit., Intersci. Pubs. Inc. (later Intersci. Div. John Wiley & Sons, Inc.), N.Y.C., 1959-69; exec. editor Ency. Food and Food Sci., Wiley-Intersci., N.Y.C., 1969-71; freelance writer and editor, 1971-72; exec. editor sci. Globe Book Co., Inc., N.Y.C., 1972-74; sponsoring editor Marcel Dekker, Inc., 1974—. Mem. Am. Chem. Soc., Inst. Food Technologists, Soc. for Tech. Communication (contbg. editor Chpt. Notes/N.Y. 1967-70), Nat. Assn. Sci. Writers (asso.), Am. Med. Writers Assn. Contbr. articles to profl. jours. Home: 330 E 33d St New York City NY 10016 Office: 270 Madison Av New York City NY 10016

DUKESHIRE, MABEL E., educator; b. Amherst, N.Y., Feb. 1, 1921; d. Henry A. and Ida (Klein) Wolf; B.A. cum laude, Wagner Coll., 1942; Ed.M., U. Buffalo, 1946; Ed.D., Rutgers U., 1966; m. Paul W. Dukeshire, July 13, 1946; children—Joanne Audrey, Paul Wallace. Tchr. secondary schs., 1942-49; mem. faculty Fairleigh Dickinson U., Teaneck, N.J., part-time, 1955-58, prof. math., 1958—. Home: 15 Bancroft Pl Fairlawn NJ 07410 Office: 1000 River Rd Teaneck NJ 07666

DULL, MARY HORAN, ednl. cons.; b. Lakewood, O., Sept. 4, 1920; d. Owen Joseph and Mary Ellen (Gannon) Horan; A.B., U. Mich., 1944, M.A., 1946; m. Robert L. Dull, Dec. 26, 1946; children—Stephen, Michael, Christopher, Amy, Emily, Matthew. Child psychologist Catholic Charities, Cleve., 1945; teaching asst. Inst. Child Welfare, U. Minn., 1945-46; lectr. Western Res. U., Cleve., 1946-47; child psychologist Huron Valley Child Guidance Center, Ypsilanti, Mich., 1947-48; lectr. child devel. and parent edn., Ann Arbor, Mich. and Huntington, N.Y., 1948-55; research asst. Huntington Twp. Mental Health Clinic, 1960-65; cons. N.W. Bergen County Council for Exceptional Children, Wycoff, N.J., 1965-67; dir. Ednl. Devel. Center, Palm Beach, Fla., 1968—. Former mem. bd. dirs. Huntington Twp. Mental Health Clinic, Huntington Vis. Nurses Assn. Mem. Am., Palm Beach County psychol. assns., Assn. for Children with Learning Disabilities, Phi Kappa Phi, Psi Chi. Research on early identification of learning disabilities, curriculum, edn. systems. Home: 210 Colonial Lane Palm Beach FL 33480 Office: 241 Seaview Av Palm Beach FL 33480

DULOHERY, SISTER MARY CORNILE, hosp. adminstr.; b. Longford, Kan., Nov. 10, 1909; d. Cornelius Jerome and Margaret Mary (Berry) Dulohery; R.N., St. Joseph's Hosp. Sch. Nursing, Savannah, Ga.; B.S. in Nursing Edn., M.S., Cath. U. Am. Adminstr., St. Joseph's Infirmary, Atlanta, 1942-52; matron Leprosarium, Trinidad, W.I., 1952-55; dir. St. Joseph's Infirmary Sch. Nursing, Atlanta, 1956-59; adminstr. St. Joseph's Hosp., Savannah, 1960—. Mem. Nat. League for Nursing, Ga. Hosp. Assn. (pres. 1943), Am. Assn. U. Women, Savannah Area C. of C. Home: 11806 McAuley Dr Savannah GA 31406 Office: 11705 Mercy Blvd Savannah GA 31406

DULZER, SISTER MARY KENAN, coll. pres.; b. Cleve., Jan. 20, 1925; d. Edward Fred and Sophia Dulzer; B.S. in Edn., St. John Coll., 1954; M.A. in Theology, U. Notre Dame, 1959; postgrad. Cath. U., 1954, 69; Ph.D. candidate, Kent State U., 1973. Entered Ursuline Order, 1944; tchr. elementary sch., 1946-54; instr. Ursuline Coll., 1956-69, pres. coll., 1969—; asst. novice directress Ursuline Order, 1954-59, novice directress, 1959-69; chmn. Novice Directresses Diocese Cleve., 1966-68. Mem. Orange Community Clergyman's Group; mem. civic adv. bd. Nat. Cystic Fibrosis Found., Cleve., Cleve. Safety Council, mem. Cleve. Commn. Higher Edn.; mem. civic com. Nat. Conf. Christians and Jews. Mem. Asso. Cleve. Colls. (chmn. 1973), Assn. Ind. Colls. and Univs. Ohio, Ohio Found. Ind. Colls., Ohio Coll. Assn. (exec. bd. 1973), Nat. Catholic Ednl. Assn., N.E.A., Am. Council Edn., Asso. Am. Colls., Am. Assn. Higher Edn., Alpha Psi. Address: Ursuline Coll 2600 Lander Rd Cleveland OH 44124

DUMAN, NELLIE MAE FRY (MRS. LOUIS JOSEPH DUMAN), civic worker; b. Denver, July 15, 1927; d. Murray and Jessie (Schott) Fry; B.A., U. Denver, 1948; postgrad. Wayne U., 1948; m. Louis Joseph Duman, Aug. 18, 1946; children—Diana Lynn, Edward Allan, Marilyn Fry. Tchr., Roseville (Mich.) Sch., 1948-49. Pres., Denver chpt. Brandeis U. Nat. Women's Com., 1958-60, nat. bd. mem., 1966-69; sec. Nat. Jewish Hosp. Women's Com., 1965-67, pres. elect, 1967-68; pres. Rose Hosp. Women's Div., Denver, 1968-70; mem. Denver County Ct. Jud. Commn., 1968—; v.p. Denver Lyric Opera Guild, 1968-70, sec. 1968-69, pres., 1970-71; bd. mem. Jr. Symphony Guild, Denver, 1963-64, 66-67; sec. Denver Lyric Opera Bd., 1971-72; sec. Colo. Assn. Hosp. Auxs., 1972—; chmn. CARE luncheon, 1973. Mem. Democratic State Com., 1952—. Mem. Denver League Women Voters, Denver Council Jewish Women (sec. 1960-61). Jewish religion. Club: Faculty Wives (Colo. U. Med. Sch.). Home: 415 Monaco Blvd Denver CO 80220

DU MAURIER, DAPHNE, author; b. London, Eng., May 13, 1907; d. Sir Gerald and Muriel (Beaumont) du Maurier; ed. Camposena, Meudon, Paris; m. Lt. Gen. Sir Frederick Arthur Montague Browning, July 19, 1932; children—Tessa, Flavia, Christian. Created Dame Comdr. Order of British Empire. Author: The Loving Spirit, 1931; I'll Never Be Young Again, 1932; The Progress of Julius, 1933; Gerald—A Portrait, 1935; Jamaica Inn, 1936; The Du Mauriers, 1937; Rebecca, 1938; Happy Christmas, 1940; Come Wind, Come Weather, 1941; Frenchman's Creek, 1941; Hungry Hill, 1943; The King's General, 1945; Castle D'or, 1962; The Glassblowers, 1963. Dramatic works include: The Years Between, 1945; September Tide, 1948; The Parasites, 1949; My Cousin Rachel, 1952; Kiss Me Again, Stranger, 1953; Mary Anne, 1954; The Scapegoat, 1957; The Breaking Point, 1958; The Internal World of Branwell Bronte, 1961; The Glass Blowers, 1963; The Flight of the Falcon, 1965; Vanishing Cornwall, 1967; The House on the Strand, 1969; Don't Look Now, 1971; Not After Midnight, 1971; Rule Britannia, 1973. Fellow Royal Soc. Lit.

Home: Kilmarth Par Cornwall England Office: Address: care Curtis Brown Limited London WC England

DUMONT, VIRGINIA PETERSON (MRS. R. PEASLEE DUMONT), educator; b. Salt Lake City, Jan. 19, 1918; d. Frederick L. and Florence Julia (Carpenter) Peterson; B.A. with honors in English, Mills Coll., 1938; postgrad. (grad. scholar), Bryn Mawr Coll., 1938-39, (spl. fellow), 1939-40; m. R. Peaslee DuMont, Aug. 5, 1940; children—Virginia Patricia (Mrs. Peter Kelly), Peaslee Frederick, Jayne Louise (Mrs. John Mack), Julia Blanche, Peter Bruce, Lorna Elizabeth, Edward Carroll. Home tchr. Piedmont (Cal.) High Sch., 1970-73; pvt. tutor in English and Social Studies, 1970—. Mem. adv. com. on ednl. philosophy Piedmont Unified Sch. Dist., 1967-68. Mem. Mills Coll. Alumnae Assn. (chmn. continuing edn. pilot study 1957-59, nat. gov. 1958-59, dir. Phila. br. 1939, pres. Washington bd. 1946-47, pres. Oakland, Cal. bd. 1969-70), Cal. Writers Club, League Women Voters, Oakland Mus. Assn. Roman Catholic. Contbr. poetry to profl. books. Address: 212 Carmel Av Piedmont CA 94611

DUNAGAN, KATHLYN COSPER (MRS. JOHN CONRAD DUNAGAN), food products co. exec.; b. Shep, Tex., Apr. 7, 1914; d. William Harmon and Lillie Florine (Goode) Cosper; student U. Tex., 1935-37; m. John Conrad Dunagan, Aug. 21, 1933; children—John Charles, Deanna, Carol (Mrs. T. L. Husbands III), Kathleen, William Claiborne. Sec., Midland Hardware Co. (Tex.), 1933, Scruggs Buick Co., Midland, 1934; sec. bookkeeper Monahans Coca-Cola Bottling Co. (Tex.), 1934-35; sec. Anthropology Mus., U. Tex., Austin, 1935-36; sec. to pres. Austin Mut. Life Ins. Co., 1936-37; sec. bookkeeper Monahans First State Bank, 1937-40; corporate dir. and sec. treas. Permiam Coca-Cola Bottling Co., Monahans, 1954—, Sandhills Properties, Inc., Monahans, 1954—, Trans-Pecos Transport Co., Monahans, 1954—. Pres. P.T.A., Monahans, 1946-47; sec. Permiam Basin council Girl Scouts Assn., 1958-62; pres. Friends of Ward County Library, Tex., 1967-69. Mem. bd. Monahans-Wickett Ind. Sch. Dist., sec., 1952-55; v.p. Ward County Parks and Recreation Bd., 1974—. Bd. dirs. Presidential Mus., Odessa, Tex., 1968-70; bd. dirs., co-founder Monahans Youth Center, 1953-60. Named Monahans Woman of Year, 1960, Tex. Outstanding Club Woman, Tex. Fedn. Women's Clubs, 1968; recipient Nat. Civic Beautification Contest award Nat. Council State Garden Clubs, 1966. Mem. Tex. Fedn. Women's Clubs (conservation chmn. 1973—), Monahans C. of C. (dir. women's div. 1970-73). Democrat. Mem. United Methodist Ch. Clubs: Texas Garden (Arbor day chmn. 1970-71), Desert Sands Garden (pres. 1963, project chmn. 1964—), Wednesday Study (pres. 1948-49). Home: 1107 South Dwight Monahans TX 79756 Office: 500 South Main Monahans TX 79756

DUNAWAY, DONNA ELIZABETH KASTLE, computer scientist, co. exec.; b. Ft. Worth, Mar. 16, 1935; d. Joseph A. and Susie (Garrett) Kastle; B.A., Tex. Christian U., 1956; M.S., So. Meth. U., 1969, Ph.D., 1972; children—Diane Elizabeth, Thomas Kastle. Mathematician Gen. Dynamics, Ft. Worth, 1956-57, Humble Oil and Refining Co., Houston, 1957-58; cons. computer sci., Dallas, 1969—; owner, pres. Ditrec Corp. Dallas, 1971—; operations research analyst Atlantic Richfield Co., 1972-73; cons. Tex. Instruments Inc., 1973—; mem. faculty U. Tex. at Dallas, 1974. Mem. Math. Assn. Am., Assn. Computing Machinery, Kappa Kappa Gamma. Republican. Presbyn. Home: 3706 Dartmouth St Dallas TX 75205

DUNAWAY, FAYE, actress; b. Fla., 1941. An original mem. Lincoln Center Repertory Co.; appeared in Hogan's Goat, off-Broadway; played Bonnie in motion picture Bonnie and Clyde, 1967. Recipient Most Promising Newcomer award Brit. Film Acad., 1968. Address: care Warner Bros 4000 Warner Blvd Hollywood CA 90028

DUNBAR, JUNE MINABELLE, coll. adminstr.; b. Los Angeles, June 10, 1926; d. Lancelot Andrew and Minabelle June (Farquhar) Farnum; B.A., U. Redlands, 1948; M.S., U. So. Cal., 1956; m. Waldo Dunbar, Dec. 10, 1955; children—Brian Waldo, Devin Farnum. Psychometrist, U. So. Cal., 1948-51; program dir. Army Spl. Services, Augsberg, Germany, 1951-53; chief psychometrist, vocational counselor U. So. Cal. Vets. Guidance Center, 1954-55; supr. employee counseling Hughes Aircraft Co., 1955-60; marriage counselor Los Angeles Conciliation Ct., 1960-66; instr. psychology and sociology Marymount Coll., Palos Verdes, Cal., 1969-73, dir. women's programs, 1973-74, dir. continuing edn., 1974—. Bd. dirs. Palos Verdes Peninsula Human Relations Council, 1969-70, Family Service Los Angeles, 1958-62. Mem. Am. Psychol. Assn., Nat. Vocational Guidance Assn. (dir. 1959-61), Pi Lambda Theta. Home: 83 Spindrift Dr Portuguese Bend CA 90274 Office: Marymount Coll 6717 Palos Verdes Dr S Palos Verdes CA 90274

DUNBAR, PAMELA JOYCE (MRS. ROBERT DAVID DUNBAR), occupational therapist; b. Kansas City, Mo., Feb. 4, 1946; d. Ross Lowe and Dulcie Dearmin (Baird) Calhoun; B.S. (grant), Kan. U., 1969; m. Robert David Dunbar, June 20, 1966; 1 son, Jeffrey David. Occupational therapist cons. Goodwill Industries, Albuquerque, 1969-70; Albuquerque Pub. Schs., 1970-73; occupational therapist Esperansa Para Nuestros Ninos Sch., Albuquerque, 1973—. Cons. for various pub. schs. and parents of learning disabled children and children with problems. Mem. state bd. of health occupations N.M. Dept. Vocational Edn., Albuquerque, 1970-73. Mem. Nat., N.M. occupational therapy assns., Albuquerque Learning Disability Assn. Home: PO Box 413 Cedar Crest NM 87008 Office: PO Box 12212 Albuquerque NM 87105

DUNBAR, WANDA KERR (MRS. ROBERT A. DUNBAR), advt. exec.; b. Mansfield, O., Oct. 9, 1931; d. Martin Wayne and Blanche B. (Parker) Kerr; student Capital U., 1949-50; B.S. in Journalism, Ohio State U., 1953, postgrad., 1956, 61; student Columbus Sch. Arts and Design, 1957-58; m. Robert A. Dunbar, May 2, 1959; 1 son, Douglas. Pub. relations dir. Columbus Goodwill Industries (O.), 1952, Goodwill Industries and Rehab. Center Dayton (O.), 1953-55; community relations officer, heading promotion of bond issue Slum Clearance Dept. City Columbus, 1955-57; editor internal mag., co. photographer Ross Labs., Columbus, 1957-60; pres., dir. Wanda Kerr Dunbar, Inc., Columbus, 1961—; editor, advt. mgr. Ohio Contractor, Ohio Contractors Assn., 1962—. Sec., Wing 41, Nightingale Cottage Convalescent Home for Children, 1965, pres., 1966. Recipient Mag. award Asso. Contractors Am., 1965; 1st pl. Dayton Community Chest contest in pub. relations, 1953. Mem. Women in Constrn. (charter), Women in Communications, Columbus Area C. of C. (advt. fedn.), Water Mgmt. Assn. Republican. Club: Scioto Boat (Columbus). Home: 2474 Buckley Rd Columbus OH 43220 Office: 1375 W Lane Av Columbus OH 43221

DUNCAN, FRANCES MURPHY, educator; b. Utica, N.Y., June 23, 1920; d. Edward Simon and Elizabeth Myers (Stack) Murphy; B.A., Barnard Coll., Columbia, 1942; M.Ed., Auburn U., 1963, Ed.D., 1969; m. Lee C. Duncan, June 23, 1947 (div. June 1969); children—Lee C., Edward M., Paul H., Elizabeth B., Nancy R., Frances B. Head sci. dept. Arnold Jr. High Sch., Columbus, Ga., 1960-63; tchr. physiology, Spanish, Jordan High Sch., Columbus, 1963-64; tchr. spl. edn. mentally retarded Muscogee County Sch. System, Columbus, 1964-65; instr. spl. edn. Auburn (Ala.) U., 1966-69; asso. dir. Douglas Sch. for Learning Disabilities, Columbus, 1969-70; asst. prof. edn. and spl. edn. Columbus Coll., 1970—. Sec. exec. bd. Muscular Dystrophy Assn., 1968-70; 73-74. Mem. Am. Assn. Mental Deficiency, Am. Assn. U. Profs., Am. Assn. U. Women (pres. 1973—), Council for Exceptional Children (legislative chmn. 1973-74), Ga. Assn. Educators, Kappa Delta Pi, Psi Chi. Roman Catholic. Home: 1811 Alta Vista Dr Columbus GA 31907

DUNCAN, GERTRUDE INEZ (MRS. CLARENCE BARCLAY DUNCAN), ednl. cons.; b. Algona, Ia., Dec. 4, 1896; d. Burke Hamilton and Ariadne (Hartley) Samuels; B.A., Ia. State Tchrs. Coll., 1925; M.A., Columbia, 1926; Ed.D., Temple U., 1942; m. Clarence Barclay Duncan, June 22, 1929; children—Jean Eleanor (Mrs. Robert A. Hollingsead), Robert Barclay. Tchr. rural, village schs., Guthrie and Polk Counties, Ia., 1914-17; dir. municipal playgrounds, phys. dir. Van Wert County YWCA, 1920-21; tchr. health, phys. edn. Des Moines Pub. Schs., 1921-22; instr. health, phys. edn. Des Moines U., summer 1922, State Tchrs. Coll., St. Cloud, Minn., 1922-25; recreation club leader Horace Mann Sch. Columbia, 1926; instr., supr. phys. and health edn. State Tchrs. Coll., Kutztown, Pa., 1926-28, Indiana (Pa.) State Tchrs. Coll., summers 1928-29; asst. prof. health, phys. edn., supr. womens activities Tchrs. Coll. Temple U., 1928-48; tchr. edn. adviser Dept. Pub. Instrn. Commonwealth Pa., Harrisburg, 1960-70; tchr. edn. cons., 1970—; cons. confs. profl. assns. Mem. Parents Com. on Recreation Grammar Sch., Bala-Cynwyd, Pa., 1946-47; tchr. Red Cross first aid to Girl Scouts U.S.A., Bala-Cynwyd, 1946-47; mem. Gov.'s Commn. on Edn., 1960-61; adviser, tchr. edn., certification and related matters; mem. nat. adv. bd. Am. Security Council, 1973-74. Mem. Am. Assn. U. Women (past com. chmn., dir. br.), N.E.A., Pa. Edn. Assn., A.A.H.P.E.R., Am. Social Hygiene Assn., Intercontinental Biograph. Assn. Presbyn. Author: Procedures for Approval of Teacher Education Programs, 1963; Policies, Procedures and Standards for Certification of Professional School Personnel, 1970. Contbr. articles to profl. jours. Home: 4661 Plumosa Dr Yorba Linda CA 92686

DUNCAN, IRMA WAGNER (MRS. DAVID ROBARDSON LINCOLN DUNCAN), chemist; b. Buffalo, Jan. 30, 1912; d. Carl and Emily (Leue) W.; B.A., U. Buffalo, 1933; M.A., U. Chgo., 1935, Ph.D., 1950; m. David Robardson Lincoln Duncan, Mar. 21, 1937; children—David Leue, Paul Robardson. Prof. sci. Colo. Woman's Coll., Denver, 1944-48; asst. prof. chemistry U. Denver, 1951-59; research chemist Arctic Health Research Center, Dept. Health, Edn. and Welfare, Anchorage and Fairbanks, Alaska, 1960—; adj. prof. chemistry Alaska Meth. U., Anchorage, 1960-62. Mem. Alaska Gov.'s Com. Mental Retardation, 1966-72, chmn., 1966, 67; coordinator 1st Spl. Olympics, State Alaska, 1970, coordinator for Fairbanks, 1971. Fellow A.A.A.S. (pres. Cook Inlet br. 1962-63; sec. Alaska div. 1967—); mem. Am. Assn. U. Women, Am. Pub. Health Assn., Arctic Assn. Retarded Children (v.p. 1969), N.Y. Acad. Scis., Sigma Xi. Contbr. articles to profl. jours. Home: Mile 1 McGrath Rd Fairbanks AK 99701 Office: Arctic Health Research Center Fairbanks AK 99701

DUNCAN, JUDY RUTH GIBBS (MRS. WILLIAM CORY DUNCAN), occupational therapist; b. Adrian, Mich., Oct. 24, 1943; d. William Henry and Doris Jeannette (Gregg) Gibbs; student Siena Heights Coll., 1961-62; B.S., Eastern Mich. U., 1965; m. William Cory Duncan, Apr. 16, 1966; children—Andrew Scott, Wendy Lynn. Staff occupational therapist VA Hosp., Balt., 1966-68; staff and supervisory therapist VA Hosp., Ann Arbor, Mich., 1968-69, chief occupational therapy dept., 1969-70. Mem. Am. Occupational Therapy Assn. Methodist. Home: 24789 Apple Crest Novi MI 48050

DUNCAN, KAREN AKINS (MRS. ROBERT CLYDE DUNCAN), educator; b. Grand Rapids, Mich., Nov. 28, 1941; d. Robert William and Marcia Elizabeth (Peterson) Akins; B.S., U. Okla., 1964, M.S., 1968, Ph.D., 1970; m. Robert Clyde Duncan, Dec. 16, 1969; children—David, Donald, John, Paul. Asst. prof., acting dir. sci. applications in computing dept. biometry Med. U. S.C., Charleston, 1969-71, asst. prof., dir. ednl. computing system, coll. dental medicine, 1972—. Trainee in biostatistics NIH, 1966-69. Mem. Am. Statis. Assn., Biometric Soc., Assn. Computing Machinery, Assn. Health Records, Assn. Devel. Computer-Based Instrl. Systems, A.A.A.S. Instl. Research grantee, Med. U. S.C., 1973-74. Home: 72 Norview Dr Charleston SC 29407

DUNCAN, LIGOA (MRS. WILLIAM B. SELIGMANN), art gallery dir., artist-weaver; b. Paris, France; privately tutored; student Akademia Raymond Duncan, fine arts and crafts 1925-41; pvt. study of voice, 1935-44; m. Pierre Merle, 1934; children—Jean-Pierre, Michel; m. 2d, William Benbow Seligmann, May 18, 1956; 1 dau., Doree Duncan. Came to U.S., 1945, naturalized, 1948. Instr. hand weaving and gymnastique Akademia Raymond Duncan, Paris, 1931-44, v.p., 1967—; singing career on radio in France and with U.S. Army Spl. Service in Europe, 1941-45; envoy Dept. Beaux Arts of Edn. of France to U.S., 1945; IBM dept. Blue Cross N.C., 1947; occupational therapy instr. N.Y. State Rockland Hosp., 1947-50; mgr. pottery shop and hand weaver Desert House Crafts, Inc., Tucson, 1950-53; co-chmn. Craft Workshop of Tucson Fine Arts Assn., 1953-54; appeared on folk songs programs on TV Paris and Hollywood, 1952, 55; concerts Carnegie Hall, Town Hall, N.Y.C., 1948, 50, 59—, Internat. Folk Songs, Paris, France, 1970; TV concerts, N.Y.C. and Paris, 1961-64; founder, dir. Ligoa Duncan Arts Center, 1959—; program chmn. Salon Francais Tucson, 1951-54; head of weaving program for handicapped Homecrafters, Inc., 1953-55; dir. Ligoa Duncan Galerie des Arts, 1957—, Ligoa Duncan Gallery; asso. Duncan-Echeverria Galleries, Moorestown, N.J., Rogues Gallery, Allentown, Pa.; dir. fgn. div. exhibits Raymond Duncan Galleries, Paris; singer, lectr. for charities, 1941—; coordinator exchange art shows U.S. and fgn. countries, 1961—. Vice pres. Akademia Raymond Duncan, Paris; chmn. for world tour exhibits for 100th anniversary Festival Raymond Duncan. Mem. N.Y. Conv. and Visitors Bur. Decorated Chevalier de l'Ordre Belgo-Hispanica, Conseiller Culturel (Belgium); recipient certificate merit UNICEF, 1961-71. Mem. Chautauqua Art Assn., Cercle Artistique Francais (mem. com.), Overseas Corrs. French Assn., Pi Delta Phi. Lutheran. Address: 1046 Madison Av New York City NY 10021 also 31 Ruede Seine Paris France Gallery also 825 Madison Av New York City NY 10021

DUNCAN, MARGARET CAROLINE, pediatrician; b. Salt Lake City, 1930; M.D., U. Tex., 1955. Intern King County Hosp., Seattle, 1955-56; resident in pediatrics U. Tex. John Sealy Hosp., 1956-58; resident in neurology Charity Hosp. La., New Orleans, 1958-60, vis. physician neurology and pediatrics, 1961—; fellow pediatric neurology Johns Hopkins Hosp., 1961-63; asso. prof. pediatrics and neurology U. La., 1963—. Diplomate Am. Bd. Psychiatry and Neurology, Am. Bd. Pediatrics. Mem. Am. Assn. on Mental Deficiency. Address: 1542 Tulane Av New Orleans LA 70112

DUNCAN, MARGARET DUNSMORE (MRS. WILLIAM FOWLER DUNCAN), club woman; b. Summit, N.J., Sept. 9, 1920; d. James and Margaret (Montgomery) Dunsmore; student Fresno State Coll., 1941; m. William Fowler Duncan, June 17, 1940; children—William Fowler, Laird Douglas, Fraser Scott. Gray lady A.R.C., Oahu, 1959—, chmn. vols. Langley AFB; active Heart Fund Dr., Neuromuscular Disease Dr.; mem. Los Ninos Guild, Childrens Hosp. Orange County. Mem. Fairfax Hosp. Aux., Clans of Scotland, U.S.A., Scribe, Internat. Platform Assn., Order of Diana, League Women Voters, Beta Sigma Phi (past chpt. pres.). Republican. Presbyn. (chmn. missionary edn. women's assn., mariner, fellowship chmn. 1973, 74, deacon 1974-76). Clubs: Ikebana, Air Force Officers Wives (Washington); Neighborhood Garden; Wheeler AFB Officers Woman's (1st v.p. 1960) (Oahu, Hawaii); Langley Officers Wives, Langley Yacht, Langley Golf; San Clemente Women's. Home: 502 Calle DeSoto San Clemente CA 92672

DUNCAN, MARIE CASTALDI (MRS. CARL PORTER DUNCAN), psychiatrist; b. Providence; d. Gesuelo and Elizabeth (DeAngelis) Castaldi; A.B., Pembroke Coll., 1943; Sc.M. in Psychology, Brown U., 1945; M.D., Northwestern U., 1951; m. Carl Porter Duncan, July 10, 1948. Intern Evanston (Ill.) Hosp., 1950-51; resident Northwestern U., Chgo., 1955-57; practice medicine specializing in psychiatry of adolescents, Evanston, 1957—; attending staff Evanston Hosp.; vis. staff Forest Hosp., Des Plaines, Ill.; asso. in psychiatry Northwestern U. Med. Sch., 1965—; cons. psychiatry Div. Services to Crippled Children, State of Ill., 1960—. Diplomate in psychiatry Am. Bd. Psychiatry and Neurology. Mem. Am., Chgo. (sec.-treas. 1970-72) socs. adolescent psychiatry, Am., Ill. psychiat. assns., A.M.A., Pan Am., Ill. med. assns., Chgo. Med. Soc., Am. Med. Womens Assn., Assn. Community Clinics, Sigma Xi. Home: 615 Central St Evanston IL 60201 Office: 2500 Ridge Av Evanston IL 60201

DUNCAN, PAM, educator; b. Oshkosh, Wis., Aug. 16, 1938; d. James Francis and Gladys (Killam) Duncan; B.A., Wis. State U., 1958; M.A., U. Chgo., 1961; Ph.D., U. Wis., 1968. Psychologist III trainee Div. of Corrections, Madison, Wis., 1962-66; asst. prof. psychology Milton (Wis.) Coll., 1966-67, U. Victoria (B.C., Can.), 1967—. Cons. Family and Children's Service, Victoria, 1967—, Sevenoaks Children's Treatment Centre, Victoria, 1970—. Mem. Canadian, B.C. psychol. assns., A.A.A.S. Editor: Readings in Contemporary Psychology, 1968. Home: 424 Goldstream St Victoria BC Canada

DUNCAN, PATRICIA KAY, securities co. exec.; b. St. Louis, Sept. 15, 1945; d. Harry Sayles and Berenice (Laury) Duncan; B.A. in German, Southwest Mo. State Coll., 1969. Asst. trading dept. Stix Friedman & Co., 1969-72, registered rep., 1970—; with Scherck, Stein & Franc, Inc., St. Louis, 1972-73; registered rep. Sentry Life Ins. Co., Maryland Heights, Mo., 1973—. Mem. Nat. Assn. Security Dealers, Nat. Assn. Life Underwriters, Nat. Fedn. Bus. and Profl. Women, Mo. Bus. and Profl. Women (finance chmn. St. Louis chpt.), YWCA, Alumni Assn. Southwest Mo. State Coll., Gamma Theta Upsilon, Alpha Mu Gamma. Home: 6217 Virginia Av St Louis MO 63111 Office: 12131 Dorsett Rd Maryland Heights MO 63043

DUNCAN, SANDRA JOAN, ednl. adminstr.; b. Nashville, July 25, 1941; d. Ruel Laverne and Lorene Virginia (Ellis) Duncan; B.S., Middle Tenn. State U., 1963; diploma data processing Automation Inst. Middle Tenn., 1968. Records cons. Tab Products Co., Cin., 1967; supr. Minnie Pearl Chicken Systems, Inc., Nashville, 1967-68; systems analyst State Tenn. Dept. Revenue, Nashville, 1968-69; bus. mgr. Shawnee Coll., Ullin, Ill., 1969—. Mem. Am., Ill. assns. sch. bus. ofcls. Mem. Christian Ch. Home: 418 S Court St Marion IL 62959 Office: Shawnee Coll Rd Ullin IL 62992

DUNDAS, MARY JANE, lawyer, govt. ofcl.; b. Waterloo, Ia., Aug. 25, 1943; d. Ross J. and Marie A. (Holland) Dundas; B.A. in Polit. Sci., Cal. State U. at Long Beach, 1966; J.D., Loyola U., Los Angeles, 1970. Admitted to Cal., Ariz. bars, 1971; med. care recovery act officer, personnel claims act officer, Judge Adv. Gen. Corps USN, 1972—, legal assistance officer, 1973—. Asst. staff 14th Naval Dist., Pearl Harbor, Hawaii., Tchr. bus. law Cal. State U., Long Beach, 1971. Mem. Cal., Ariz. bar assns., Cal. Trial Lawyers Assn., Am. Bar Assn., Phi Delta Delta. Roman Catholic. Home: 3139 Ala Ilima Honolulu HI 96818 Office: 14th Naval Dist Law Center Box 110 PFO San Francisco CA 96610

DUNDEE, DOLORES D. SAUNDERS (MRS. HAROLD A. DUNDEE), educator; b. Topeka, Aug. 7, 1927; d. George L. and Mayme (Finnie) Saunders; B.S., Washburn U., 1949; M.A., U. Kan., 1951; Ph.D., U. Mich., 1956; m. Harold A. Dundee, Nov. 3, 1951. Instr. Paterson (N.J.) State Tchrs. Coll., 1957-58; tchr. Clifton (N.J.) High Sch., 1957-58; mem. faculty La. State U., New Orleans, 1958—, prof. biol. scis., 1966—. Flight and ground instr.; cons. aviation safety; mem. Women's Adv. Com. Aviation, 1969-72. Mem. Am. Inst. Biol. Scis., Am. Malacological Union (pres. 1972-73), Assn. Southeastern Biologists, Am. Soc. Zoologists, Malacological Soc. Uruguay, Internat. Pilots Assn., League Women Voters (local v.p. 1969-70, chmn. pub. relations 1968-70). Contbr. articles to sci. jours. Home: 6249 Carlson Dr New Orleans LA 70122

DUNDORE, FANNIE BELLE MORGAN (MRS. MICHAEL JUDSON DUNDORE), pub. health ofcl.; b. Bedford, Va., Aug. 16, 1937; d. Walter Byron and Tressie (Ashwell) Morgan; B.A. in Psychology and Sociology, Madison Coll., 1960; M.S.W., Tulane U., 1965; m. Michael Judson Dundore, Apr. 17, 1968. Social service aide Catawba (Va.) Sanatorium, 1960-63, med. social worker, 1965-69; med. social work cons. bur. crippled children Va. Dept. Health, Roanoke, 1969-71, regional clin. social work supr., after 1971; now with Roanoke County Health Dept., Salem, Va. Active community social service agys.; mem. Mayor's Com. for Employment of Handicapped. Bd. dirs. Madison Coll. Alumni Bd., Va. Council Social Welfare. Named Handicapped Profl. Woman of Year Va. Pilot Clubs, 1970. Mem. Nat. Assn. Social Workers, Va. Council Social Welfare, Acad. Certified Social Workers, Va. Pub. Health Assn., Sigma Sigma Sigma. Episcopalian. Office: Roanoke County Health Dept 510 College Av Salem VA 24153

DUNHAM, BEVERLY DAWN ABRAHAMSEN (MRS. WILLARD EUGENE DUNHAM), newspaper pub.; b. Seattle, Jan. 30, 1932; d. Anders Albert and Marie Amalia (Omdahl) Abrahamsen; student U. Ore., 1951; m. Willard Eugene Dunham, Dec. 24, 1951; children—Willard Eugene III, Delbert Kevin, Meggin Marie. Proofreader, Jesson's Weekly, Fairbanks, Alaska, 1952-53; reporter Seward (Alaska) Seaport Record, 1954; reporter Petticoat Gazette, Seward, 1963-65; editor Sixty Speaks, Seward, 1960-62; owner, pub., editor Seward Phoenix Log, 1966—. Mem. adv. bd. Kenai Peninsula Community Coll., 1968-70; Seward chmn. Alaska Centennial Com., 1965-67. Recipient Nat. Writing award Nat. Fedn. Press Women, 1971, awards Alaska Press Women, 1970, 71, 72. Mem. Nat. Newspaper Assn. (state chmn. 1973-74), Nat., Alaska press women, Alaska Pub. Assn. (pres. 1973-74), Bus. and Profl. Women's Club. Democrat. Episcopalian. Home: Alder St Forest Acres Seward AK 99664 Office: 300 4th Av Seward AK 99664

DUNHAM, RUTH E., physician; b. Chgo., Mar. 29, 1919; d. Charles Joseph and Ruth (Brough) Dunham; B.S., U. Ill., 1940, M.D., 1942; M.P.H., U. Mich., 1947. With Ill. Dept. Pub. Health, 1945-48; commd. asst. surgeon USPHS, 1942-45, 48, advanced through grades to med. dir., 1958; heart disease control program, Newton, Mass., Salisbury, Md., 1948-50; asst. chief outpatient dept. USPHS Hosp., S.I., N.Y., 1951-54, area med. officer Indian Health Program, Portland, Ore., 1954-58, asst. med. adviser Nat. Health Survey,

1958-62, dep. med. officer-in-charge USPHS Hosp., Balt., 1962-63, med. officer in charge, Outpatient Clinic, Washington, 1963-65; regional office program dir. Hill-Burton program Dept. Health, Edn. and Welfare, Denver, 1965-70, Seattle, 1970-72; dep. dir. health care facilities service Hill-Burton program, Rockville, Md., 1972-74. Fellow Am. Pub. Health Assn.; mem. A.M.A. Home: 12000 Old Georgetown Rd Rockville MD 20852

DUNKELBERGER, ELAINE JERVIS (MRS. HAROLD FRANKLIN DUNKELBERGER), librarian; b. Steubenville, O., Sept. 19, 1922; d. Harry and Donna (Merrick) Jervis; B.A., W. Liberty State Coll., 1944; M.A. in L.S., U. Mich., 1961; m. Harold Franklin Dunkelberger, July 3, 1952; 1 stepdau., Theresa Hooper. Tchr., Linden, Mich., Bangor, Mich., Romeo, Mich., 1944-61; librarian elementary sch., Flushing, Mich., 1961—. Nat. Def. Edn. Act. scholar, U. Okla., 1967. Mem. Am. Assn. U. Women. Home: 9103 Fenton Rd Grand Blanc MI 48439 Office: Central Elementary School 525 Coutant St Flushing MI 48433

DUNKIN, ANNE, dancer, choreographer; b. Washington, June 11, 1939; d. Paul Shaner and Gladys (Hammond) Dunkin; B.A. in Humanities, Am. U., 1961; m. Mayo Bradford Willis, June 11, 1962. Dir. Dancer's Studio Md., Kensington, 1968—; founder, creator, co-dir. Qwindo's Window, profl. touring co. for children, 1970—; sec.-treas. Qwindo Found. of Dance Theatre for Children; treas. Broad St. Prodns. Ltd. Sec. Modern Dance Council Washington; v.p. Modern Dance Council. Home: 10200 Capitol View Av Silver Spring MD 20910 Office: 3827 Plyers Mill Rd Kensington MD 20795

DUNKLE, ROBERTA MAE (MRS. HARLEY A. DUNKLE), coll. dean; b. Leatha, Ida., Sept. 26, 1918; d. James Franklin and Maud (Shire) Lanman; B.A., Seattle Pacific Coll., 1965; M.A., Wheaton Coll., 1967; m. Harley A. Dunkle, July 2, 1934; children—Leslie Allen, Gayle (Mrs. Kenneth Ray Clayton), Phillip Alden. Operator fruit ranch, Zillah, Wash., 1945-60; prof. Christian edn., Bible, Cascade Coll., Portland, Ore., 1968-69; residence dir. Houghton (N.Y.) Coll., 1969-71, dean of women, 1971—. Mem. Nat. Assn. Women Deans and Counselors, Am. Assn. U. Women, Christian Assn. Deans of Women. Mem. Ch. of Nazarene. Home: 905 Upland Dr Sunnyside WA 98944 Office: Houghton College Houghton NY 14744

DUNLAP, CONNIE ROBSON (MRS. ROBERT BRUCE DUNLAP), library adminstr.; b. Lansing, Mich., Sept. 9, 1924; d. Frederick Arthur and Laura May (Robinson) Robson; A.B., U. Mich., 1946, A.M., 1952; certificate U. Paris, 1967; m. Robert Bruce Dunlap, Aug. 9, 1947. Jr. circulation librarian U. Mich. Library, Ann Arbor, 1946-52, sr. circulation librarian, 1952-54, asso. circulation librarian, 1954-61, head order dept., 1961-64, head acquisitions dept., 1964-67, head grad. library, 1967—, dep. asso. dir., 1972—, lectr. Sch. of Library Sci., 1965—. Cons. No. Mich. U., 1966, U. S.C., 1969, Duke U., 1973. Mem. nat. adv. com. for cataloging in publ. Library of Congress, 1972—. Foreman, grand jury U.S. Dist. Court, Eastern Dist. of Mich., 1967-69. Democratic precinct worker, Ann Arbor, Mich., 1954-63. Mem. Am. (pres. resources and tech. services 1972-73, div. orgn. com. 1973-74), Mich. library assns., Am. Assn. U. Profs., Am. Soc. for Information Sci. Contbr. various articles and rev. to library jours. Club: University. Home: 1570 Westfield St Ann Arbor MI 48103

DUNLAP, IONE JEANETTE, bank ofcl.; b. Canton, S.D., May 14, 1916; d. Mathias and Olga Amanda (Swanson) Sandbeck; student Nettleton Comml. Coll., Sioux Falls, S.D., 1934-35; m. Walter Templeton Dunlap, Sept. 24, 1943; children—Marla Jan (Mrs. W.F. Adams), Mark, Laurie, Shawn, Lisa. With N.W. Security Nat. Bank, Sioux Falls, 1935-43; with 1st Nat. Bank, Brookings, S.D., 1960—, sec.-bookkeeper. Sec.-treas. United Fund of Brookings, 1970-74. Mem. Trenton Trooper Extension Club (past pres., sec.-treas.). Lutheran (past officer). Home: RFD 1 Aurora SD 57002 Office: First National Bank Brookings SD 57006

DUNLAP, LILLIAN, army officer. Commd. 2d lt. U.S. Army, advanced through grades to brig. gen., 1971; chief Army Nurse Corps, 1971—. Office: Office Surgeon Gen Dept Army Washington DC 20314

DUNLAP, MARTHA VIRGINIA, pub. relations cons.; b. Hankinson, N.D., Mar. 31, 1911; d. Willis and Ida Root (Gordon) Dunlap; B.A., U. Mont., 1932; postgrad. Am. Acad. Art, 1933, Northwestern U., 1934; m. Irving G. Moore, Oct. 19, 1934 (div. 1945); 1 dau., Martha A. Mem. editorial staff Daily Missioulian and Sanders County Independent Ledger, Thompson Falls, Mont., 1928-32; asso. pub. relations Pure Milk Assn., Chgo., 1932-35; editorial dir. Nat. Furniture Warehousemen's Assn., 1935-45; exec. dir. Nat. Truck Leasing System, 1945-69; owner, operator M-D Mgmt., mgmt. and pub. relations cons. firm, Chgo., 1969—; v.p. pub. affairs Ill. Car and Truck Renting and Leasing Assn., Chgo., 1972-74. Mem. Indsl. Editors Assn., Trade Assn. Exec. Forum, Nat. Fedn. Press Women, Am. Assn. U. Women, Women in Communications, Alpha Chi Omega. Clubs: Publicity, Women's Advertising, Press (Chgo.). Editor Furniture Warehouseman, 1935-45; editorial cons. Am. Assn. Nurse Anesthetists, 1944-46. Home: 2317 Geneva Terrace Chicago IL 60614

DUNLAP, MARY RUTH (MRS. LYNN HAWKINS DUNLAP), educator; b. Columbus, Miss., Oct. 25, 1939; d. John Russell and Ruby Elizabeth (Moody) Gallaspy; B.S., Miss. State Coll. for Women, 1961; M.A., U. Miss., 1973; m. Lynn Hawkins Dunlap, June 20, 1968; children—Karen, Hawkins. Tchr. Aberdeen (Miss.) High Sch., 1961-62; asst. editor Tex. and Southwest Hotel-Motel Assn. Mag., San Antonio, 1962-63; tchr., publications adviser N.E. Ind. Sch. Dist., San Antonio, 1963-68; with promotions dept. Houston Post, 1968; tchr., publications adviser Lufkin (Tex.) Ind. Sch. Dist., 1971—. Asst. leader Girl Scouts Am., Lufkin, 1973—, neighborhood publicity chmn., 1973—. Named Outstanding Journalism Tchr., San Antonio Express-News, 1966; recipient Wall St. Jour. scholarship, 1966. Mem. Nat. Sch. Pub. Relations Assn., Women in Communications, Tex. Assn. Journalism Dirs., Tex. State Tchrs. Assn., Classroom Tchrs. Assn., D.A.R. Home: 1503 John Redditt Dr Lufkin TX 75901 Office: 900 E Denman Av Lufkin TX 75901

DUNLAP, NAOMI GIBSON, psychologist; b. Meridian, Tex., Oct. 10, 1911; d. John Wheat and Callie Jane (Taylor) Gibson; B.A., Baylor U., 1949; M.A., U. Tex. at Austin, 1950, Ph.D., 1961; m. Artie Reynolds Dunlap, Nov. 24, 1932 (dec.); 1 dau., Norma Dell (Mrs. Jack Thomas Harris). Clin. psychologist VA Center, Temple, Tex. Home: 3204 W Av T Temple TX 76501 Office: VA Center Temple TX 76501

DUNLAP, PEGGY MAYFIELD (MRS. I. RAY DUNLAP), chemist; b. Austin, Tex., Mar. 24, 1927; d. Ike N. and Ella (Lockwood) Mayfield; B.S. with honors, U. Tex., 1948, Ph.D., 1952; m. I. Ray Dunlap, Dec. 11, 1955 (dec.). Fellow, U. Tex., Austin, 1952-53, spl. instr. chemistry, 1952; sr. research chemist Mobil Oil Corp., Dallas, 1953-67; research asso. Mobil Research & Devel. Corp., Dallas, 1967—. Dir. Stone Gap Indsl. Corp., Duncanville, Tex. Mem. sci. adv. com. Dallas Schs., 1973—; mem. citizens adv. com. on constl. revision Tex. Constl. Revision Commn., Dallas, 1973—. Mem. Tex. Republican Exec. Com., 1971—; del., mem. platform com. Rep. Nat. Conv., 1972; precinct chmn. Rep. party, 1968—. Named Outstanding Rep. Woman of Tex., 1973. Mem. Am. Chem. Soc., Sci. Research Soc. Am., Mobil Mgmt. Assn., C. of C. (postal chmn. 1973—), Sigma Xi, Iota Sigma Pi, Sigma Pi Sigma. Methodist. Mem. Order Eastern Star. Home: 2018 Elmwood St Dallas TX 75224 Office: PO Box 900 Dallas TX 75221

DUNLAP, RAYGENE PAIGE (MRS. THOMAS G. DUNLAP), home economist; b. Monticello, Miss., Jan. 25, 1939; d. R.C. and Sophie (Stephens) Paige; B.S., Mississippi Valley State Coll., 1961; M.S. in Child Devel., U. So. Miss., 1972; m. Thomas G. Dunlap, Dec. 29, 1968; 1 dau., Stephanie Paige. Asso. Negro home demonstrations agt. Newton County, Decatur, Miss., 1961-63; Negro home demonstration agt., Oxford, Miss., 1963-67; asso. extension home economist Jones County, Laurel, Miss., 1968-71, area extension home economist, Laurel, 1971—. Tchr. elementary sch., Monticello, 1967-68. Mem. Nat. (Distinguished Service award 1973), Miss. (Distinguished Service award 1972) assns. extension home economist, Am., Miss., S.E. Dist. (pres. elect 1973), S.E. Miss. (pres. 1974) home econ. assns., Miss. Council Family Relations, Negro Bus. and Profl. Women's Club, Miss. Consumer Assn., U. So. Miss. Alumnae Assn. Methodist. Club: Laurel Federated. Home: 620 S 8th Av Laurel MS 39440 Office: PO Box 448 Laurel MS 39440

DUNN, BARBARA JANE BAXTER, state ofcl.; b. Danbury, Conn., Oct. 24, 1926; d. William Charles and Dorthea (Oestmann) Baxter; B.A., U. Conn., 1948; children—Joanne, Kimberly, James Scott. Tchr. schs., Manchester and East Hartford, Conn., 1952-58; mem. East Hartford Charter Revision Commn., 1961; mem. Town Council, East Hartford, 1963-67; mem. Personnel Bd., East Hartford, 1966-67; mem. Conn. Ho. of Reps., 1967-71; commr. consumer protection State of Conn., 1971—, commr. boxing, 1973—. Mem. com. to study necessity and feasibility of met. gov. in Conn., 1965-67; mem. joint coms. appropriations, edn., rules, constl. amendments State of Conn.; chmn. Nat. Health Services Industries, 1971-73; mem. Conn. Gov.'s Cabinet, 1971—, Conn. Adv. Council Aging, 1971—, Conn. Drug Adv. Council, 1971—, Conn. Comprehensive Health Planning Council, Exec. Com. Human Rights and Opportunities, 1971—, Conn. Joint Council Econ. Edn., Inc., 1971—; adv. bd. Conn. Energy Emergency Agy., 1974—; adv. bd. U.S. Dept. Agr. Meat and Poultry Bd., 1973—; adv. bd. Nat. Consumer Product Safety Commn., 1974—. Sec., East Hartford Family Service Soc., 1960. Mem. East Hartford Republican Party Town Com., 1952-71, sec., 1955, treas., 1958. Trustee Conn. Ednl. TV Bd., 1972—. Mem. East Hartford League Women Voters (dir. 1961), U. Conn. Alumni Council (sec. 1965-72, dir. 1972—), Hartford Panhellenic Assn. (past pres.), Internat. Narcotic Enforcement Officers Assn., Nat. Order Women Legislators, Assn. Food and Drug Ofcls. U.S., U.S. Assn. State, County and City Adminstrv. Ofcls. (bd. 1974—), Delta Zeta. Episcopalian. Home: 1203 Silver Lane East Hartford CT 06118

DUNN, CHARLETA JESSIE (MRS. ROY E. DUNN), ednl. adminstr.; b. Clarendon, Tex., Jan. 18, 1927; d. James Arthur and Ruby Roberta (Burcham) Sisk; student Lamar Coll. Tech., Beaumont, Tex., 1947-48; B.S., West Tex. State U., 1951; M.Edn., 1954; Ed.D., U. Houston, 1966; postgrad. (postdoctoral fellow) U. Tex., 1970-71; m. Roy E. Dunn, Sept. 13, 1947; children—Thomas A., Roy E. III, Sharleta E. Tchr. pub. schs., Amarillo, Tex., 1952-62; asst. prof. U. Houston, 1966-70; pediatric psychologist U. Tex. Med. br., Galveston, 1970-71; dir. appraisal Goose Creek Ind. Sch. Dist., Baytown, Tex., 1971—. Cons. Region III Edn. Service Center, Victoria, Tex., 1968-72. Recipient research fellowship U. Houston, 1964-65, teaching fellowship, 1965-66. Mem. Am., Tex., Southwestern psychol. assns. Author: (poetry) Songs of Sharleta, 1966; World of Work, 1971. Author research publs. Editor: The Junior Listen Hear Program (Jan Slepian and Seidler), 1968. Contbr. articles to profl. jours. Home: 308 Lafayette Lane League City TX 77573 Office: Goose Creek Independent School Dist Baytown TX 77520

DUNN, DOROTHY ANN, lawyer, librarian; b. Mason City, Ia., Mar. 10, 1915; d. Edward Gregory and Laura Helen (Delker) Dunn; B.A., U. Ia., 1936; postgrad. George Washington Law Sch., 1939; J.D., Drake U., 1957. Admitted to Ia. bar, 1957, Cal. bar, 1967; law librarain, instr. Drake Law Sch., Des Moines, 1957-63; reference law librarian U. Cal. at Los Angeles, 1963; title opinion writer Security Title Ins. Co., Los Angeles, 1964-67; asst. reference librarian Los Angeles County Law Library, 1967-70; law librarian, asso. prof. law Pepperdine U. Sch. Law, Anaheim, Cal., 1970—. Acting postmaster Mason City, Ia., 1949-51; dir. Ia. Democratic Women's Assn., 1953. Mem. State Bar Cal., Am. Assn. Law Librarians. Democrat. Roman Catholic. Office: 1520 S Anaheim Blvd Anaheim CA 92803

DUNN, DOROTHY FAY, govt. ofcl.; b. Sidney, Ill.; d. Lafayette and Jeanettie (Thompson) Dunn; B.S., U. Ill., 1939; M.S. in Pub. Health, U. N.C., 1946; Ph.D., Purdue U., 1962; postgrad. U. Minn., U.N.C., summer, 1964. Home mgmt. supr. U.S. Dept. Agr., 1939-43; personnel utilization Fed. Civil Service, 1943-44; home econs. field rep. U. Wis., 1944-45; dir. health edn. Will County Health Dept., Ill., 1946-47; health edn. cons. Ill. Dept. Pub. Health, 1947-51; asso. prof. health sci. U. Ill., 1951-67; prof., head dept. home econs. Western Ky. U., Bowling Green, 1967-68; prof., chmn. home mgmt., econs. and equipment Stout State U., Menomonie, Wis., 1968-71, also mem. environmental council; asst. regional food and drug dir. for consumer affairs FDA, 1971—. Mem. Am. Council on Consumer Interest; mem. Wis. consumer adv. council Dept. Agr. Fellow Am. Pub. Health Assn., A.A.A.S., Am. Coll. Health Assn. (chmn. health edn. sect., program chmn., health edn. chmn.), Am. Sch. Health Assn.; mem. Am., Ill. (past chmn. health com.) assns. home econs., Nat. Assn. Ednl. Broadcasters, Ill. Pub. Health Assn. (sec.-treas., mem. exec. bd., rep. to Am. Pub. Health Assn. governing council), Am. Assn. U. Profs., Am. Assn. U. Women (past chmn. profl. sect.), Ill. Wis. (mem. environmental health com.) pub. health socs., Pub. Health Educators (pres.), Coll. Health Assn., Internat. Platform Assn., Omicron Nu, Sigma Delta Epsilon, Kappa Delta Pi. Contbr. articles to profl. publs. Research in domestic water demand; behavioral characteristics of smokers, Tb. Home: 504 E Chalmers St Champaign IL 61820 Office: FDA-Region V 175 W Jackson St Room A1945 Chicago IL 60604

DUNN, GLADYS MAE, librarian; b. New Brunswick, N.J., Oct. 3, 1917; d. George William and Myrtle May (Meseroll) Dunn; A.B., Douglass Coll., 1939. Organizing asst. Chloe Morse, Inc., library consultants, N.Y.C., 1939-40; sr. library asst. Bridgeport (Conn.) Pub. Library, 1940-43, Paterson (N.J.) Free Pub. Library, 1943-46; mng. editor, asso. editor H.W. Wilson Co., N.Y.C., 1946-50; staff librarian Port Authority of N.Y. and N.J., N.Y.C., 1950—. Mem. Spl. Libraries Assn., Library Pub. Relations Council, N.Y. Library Club (editor 1948-49), N.J. Hist. Soc., English Speaking Union, English-in-Action, Victorian Soc. Home: 146 New St New Brunswick NJ 08901 Office: 1 World Trade Center New York City NY 10048

DUNN, GWYN GUNNISON (MRS. KEITH EDWIN DUNN), occupational therapist; b. Denver, Feb. 26, 1935; d. Hugh and Coralyn (Carey) Gunnison; B.S., Colo. State U., 1956; m. Keith Edwin Dunn, June 30, 1956; children—Kris William, Kelly Allen. Occupational therapist Alaska Native Hosp., Anchorage, 1958-60; staff occupational therapist Fairview State Hosp., Costa Mesa, Cal., 1963-72, supr. occupational therapy student affiliation program, 1970-71; occupational therapist, cons. Garfield Convalescent Hosp., Huntington Beach, Cal., 1972-73, United Ch. Care Center, Garden Grove, Cal., 1972—; tchr. Carl Harvey Sch. for Orthopedically Handicapped, 1974—. Cons. Seaside Hosp. for Exceptional Children, Long Beach, Cal., 1971; instr. U. Cal. at San Diego, 1971—. Sec., Goodwill Industries Alaska, 1958-59. Mem. Am. Occupational Therapy Assn. Address: 2323 Margaret Dr Newport Beach CA 92660

DUNN, KATHLEEN ANN, orgn. exec.; b. Great Falls, Mont., May 17, 1946; d. Charles Eugene and Vernice Elizabeth (Fix) Dunn; B.A., U. Ky., 1968. Tchr., Covington (Ky.) Ind. Schs., 1969; program dir. St. Matthews br. YMCA, Louisville, 1969-73, sr. program dir., 1973—. Mem. Ky., Louisville, So. assns. for children under six, Assn. Profl. Dirs. YMCA (mem. conv. exec. com. 1973—), Am. Camping Assn. (sect. sec. 1971—, council of dels. rep. 1974—). Home: 716 Breckinridge Lane Louisville KY 40207 Office: 4311 Norbourne Blvd Louisville KY 40207

DUNN, MARTHA DAVIS, state govt. ofcl.; b. Malta, O., Feb. 5, 1930; d. George H. and Mabel Freida (Janes) Davis; B.Sc. in Home Econs. Edn., Ohio State U., 1951; M.Sc. in Pub. Health Nutrition, Case Western Res. U., 1966; m. Joseph E. Dunn, Apr. 2, 1971. Processed foods insp. Dept. Agr., 1951-53; home editor Ohio Farmer, Cleve., 1953-59; family life editor Inner City Protestant Parish, Cleve., 1959-62; tchr. home econs., Cleve., 1962-65; adminstr. Cuyahoga County Welfare Dept., Cleve., 1966-71; asst. commnr. Mass. Dept. Pub. Welfare, Boston, 1971—. Recipient Lifeline Am. Trophy award Grocery Mfrs. Am., 1956, Centennial Distinguished Service award Ohio State U., Coll. Agr. and Home Econs., 1970; scholar Martha Holden Jennings Found., 1963. Mem. Am., Ohio (pres. 1958; award excellence and leadership 1968) home econ. assns., Nat. Farm Home Editors Assn. (v.p. 1955-56), Cleve. Home Economists in Bus. (chmn. 1958), Cleve. Home Economists in Health and Welfare (chmn. 1961-63), Cleve. Home Econs. Assn. (pres. 1971), Am. Pub. Welfare Assn. Author textbooks. Home: 151 Tremont St Boston MA 02111 Office: 600 Washington St Boston MA 02111

DUNN, MARTHA SYRING (MRS. ROBERT G. DUNN), coll. adminstr.; b. Tuscaloosa, Ala., Nov. 2, 1930; d. Calvin Patrick and Lillian (Oswalt) Syring; student Judson Coll., 1946-48; B.S., U. Ala., 1960, M.A., 1965, A.A., Ala. A. and M. Coll., 1969; m. Robert G. Dunn, July 8, 1948; children—Steven W., Craig P., Larey E. High sch. tchr., Tuscaloosa County, Ala., 1960-65; elementary and high sch. counselor, dir. guidance, Marshall County, Ala., 1965-71; instr., Snead State Coll., Boaz, Ala., 1969-72, counselor, dir. guidance, internat. student adviser, coordinator activities internat. students, 1972—; pvt. practice as psychologist and psychometrist, Boaz, Ala., 1969—. Psychol. cons. Vocational Rehab., 1967—, Crippled Children's Assn., 1967—, Mental Health Clinics, 1967—; cons. Head Start, 1968-69. Spl. dep. sheriff, Marshall County, Ala., 1968-78; mem. legislative bd. Snead Coll., 1973—, mgr. internat. soccer team, 1973—; active Boy Scouts Am., Girl Scouts Am. Bd. dirs. A.R.C., 1973—. U. Ala., Ala. A. and M. Coll. fellow, 1967-70; Tenn. Valley Edn. Center grantee 1969. Mem. N.E.A., Am. Edn. Assn., Am. Jr. Coll. Assn., Ala. Council Family Relations, Ala. Personnel and Guidance Assn. (pres. 1970), Tuscaloosa Archaelogical Soc., Ala. Hist. Soc. Democrat. Club: Garden (Tuscaloosa). Home: Route 1 Grant AL 35747 Office: Snead Coll Boaz AL 35957

DUNNE, MARY COLLINS (MRS. STEPHEN JOHN DUNNE), author; b. County Down, Ireland, Jan. 15, 1914; d. George William and Brigid Josephine (Byrne) Collins; brought to U.S., 1921, naturalized, 1931; student U. San Francisco City Coll., 1959-62; m. Stephen John Dunne, Jan. 11, 1937; children—Nancy (Mrs. Thomas Roberts), Maryanne (Mrs. Jon Ploof), Bernadette, Christine. Free-lance writer, 1958—. Troop leader Girl Scouts U.S.A., San Francisco, 1956-60. Mem. Cal. Writers Club. Roman Catholic. Author: Alaskan Summer, 1968; Reach Out, Ricardo, 1970; Gregory Gray and the Brave Beast, 1972; Nurse of the Midnight Sun, 1973, Standby Nurse, 1974; also numerous children's stories. Home: 266 Jules Av San Francisco CA 94112

DUNNING, TESSA FRANCES ELEANOR, occupational therapist; b. Whitchurch Shropshire, England, Jan. 11, 1943; d. Gerald Clough and Muriel Ellen (Higham) Dunning; certificate edn. St. Andrews Sch. Occupational Therapy, Northampton, England, 1964; diploma occupational therapy Assn. of Occupational Therapists, U.K., 1964. Came to U.S,, 1967. With, London Borough of Islington, Mental Health Dept., 1964-66; dir. psychiat. day program Mass. Mental Health Center, Boston, 1967-68; occupational therapist, psychiatry unit Tufts New England Med. Center, Boston, 1968-72; head, occupational therapy programs Erich Lindemann Mental Health Center, Boston, 1973—; supr. recreational therapist, psychiatry unit Beth Israel Hosp., Brookline, Mass., 1972—. Instr. clin. psychology Tufts Sch. Occupational Therapy, Boston, 1971. Bd. dir. Met. Cultural Alliance, Boston, 1971—, People's Theatre, Cambridge, Mass., 1968—, pres. 1971-73. Mem. Am., Mass. (program chmn. 1968-69) assns. occupational therapists, Assn. Occupational Therapists (U.K.). Office: Erich Lindemann Mental Health Center Government Center Boston MA 02114

DUNNING, VIRGINIA TEIGELER, author, artist; b. San Francisco, Sept. 4, 1919; d. Herman Fredrick and Julia Pearl (Hardwick) Teigeler; m. Harlan Jackson Dunning, Feb. 20, 1942; 1 son, Gene Harlan. Asso. program dir. KSFO, 1941-45; non-fiction writer Metro-Goldwyn-Mayer, 1938, NBC, 1940. Mem. Another Mother for Peace, Pacific Pioneer Broadcasters. Author: Please Dear God Send Me an Indian, 1972. Contbr. articles to profl. jours. Creator the Little Green Midget, 1971. Home: 4221 Longridge Av Studio City CA 91604

DUNNINGTON, ERMA ELIZABETH, coll. adminstr.; b. Drexel, Mo., Nov. 4, 1931; d. Leslie Crouch and Elizabeth Caroline (Garner) Dunnington; B.S., Central Mo. State U., 1955; M.S. in Edn., U. Kan., 1971. Artist, Hallmark Cards, Inc., Kansas City, Mo., 1955-64; Peace Corp vol., Brazil, 1964-67; Peace Corp tng. instr. U. Wis.-Milw., 1967; research asst., dept. edn. U. Kan. at Lawrence, 1969-71; asst. dean student affairs Elizabethtown (Pa.) Coll., 1971-72; asst. dir. mutual application program Union of Ind. Colls. of Art, Kansas City, Mo., 1972-73, dir., 1973—. Mem. Nat., Mo. assns. for women deans, adminstrs., and counselors, Am. Personnel and Guidance Assn., Am. Coll. Personnel Assn., Am. Assn. for Higher Edn. Home: Box 114 Drexel MO 64742

DUNSCOMB, MARY ANN (MRS. DAVID JEROME DUNSCOMB), newspaper editor; b. Windsor, Ill., Feb. 18, 1935; d. Gerald Paul and Jesse Velma (Brown) Bridges; B.S. with honors, Eastern Ill. U., 1957, postgrad., 1972-74; m. David Jerome Dunscomb, June 2, 1957 (dec.); children—Jon Alan, Mary Alice. Tchr. elementary and high sch. phys. edn., Bement, Ill., 1957-61, elementary, high sch. instrumental music, 1960-61, 66-67; owner, publisher, editor Atwood (Ill.) Herald, 1969—; founder, owner, editor, publisher Tri-County Shopper, Atwood, 1971—. Mem. Atwood (Ill.)

Civic Improvement Corp., 1969—. Bd. dirs. Atwood Area Centennial Corp., 1972—. Mem. Nat. Newspaper Assn., Ill. Community Publishers, Ill. Press Assn., So. Ill. Editorial Assn., Atwood C. of C. (pres. 1973—), Delta Zeta, Phi Kappa Epsilon, Sigma Mu. Mem. United Ch. of Christ (trustee ch. 1972—). Mem. Order Eastern Star. Editor, Atwood's Centennial Hist. Book, 1973. Home: Rural Route 1 Atwood IL 61913 Office: 101 S Main St Atwood IL 61913

DUNTON, FAYE BERNICE (MRS. HARVEY AUSTIN DUNTON), hotel exec.; b. Huntingburg, Ind., Oct. 3, 1922; d. Albert and Lula M. (Kirkoff) Atkins; student Marion Bus. Coll., 1942-44; m. Harvey Austin Dunton, Mar. 24, 1945; children—Larry Austin, Jake Duane. Teletype setter Marion Chronicle, Marion, Ind., 1948-52; sec. Gen. Tire Co., Marion, 1952-55; bookkeeper C & E Distbrs., Inc., Peru, Ind., 1959-64; proofreader Peru Daily Tribune, Peru, 1966-67; mgr. Peru Motor Lodge, 1968—. Treas. P.T.A., Peru, 1958-62; mem. Ladies Aux. of Moose, Peru, 1969—. Mem. Ind. Hotel and Motel Assn. Elkette; mem. Order Eastern Star. Home: 206 East 3rd Peru IN 46970 Office: 23 South Broadway Peru IN 46970

DUNTON, MARY ELIZABETH, mus. ofcl.; b. Seattle, July 6, 1914; d. Ernest Elwood and Elizabeth Marie (Williams) Dunton; B.A., Marylhurst Coll., 1946; M.A., U. Wash., Seattle, 1959. Tchr. elementary and secondary grades pvt. schs., Wash. and Ore., 1934-61; dir. devel. Ft. Wright Coll., Spokane, Wash., 1962-66, dean students, 1967-71, dir. hist. mus., 1964—. Address: W 4000 Randolph Rd Spokane WA 99204

DUNWIDDIE, CHARLOTTE (MRS. D. STANLEY DUNWIDDIE), sculptor; b. Strasbourg, France, June 19, 1907; d. Charles M. and Elsa Alexandra Klein; pvt. study with Prof. Wilhelm Otto, Berlin, Mariano Beulliure, Spain, Alberto Lagos, Buenos Aires; m. D. Stanley Dunwiddie, Feb. 20, 1944 (dec. July 1951). Exhibited in shows N.A.D., Nat. Sculpture Soc., Allied Artists Am., Nat. Arts Club, Am. Artists Profl. League, Hudson Valley Art Assn., Catherine Lorillard Wolfe Art Club, Pen and Brush; represented in permanent collections Marine Corps Mus., Washington, Aqueduct Race Track, N.Y.C., Sem. of Redemptoris Fathers, N.J., Cardinals Palace, Buenos Aires, Ch. of Good Shepherd, Lima, Peru, Ch. of Santa Maria, Bolivia, others; also many pvt. collections. Recipient numerous awards. Fellow Royal Soc. Art, Nat. Sculpture Soc. (sec. 1966-69, 74—); mem. N.A.D. (asso., Ellin P. Speyer prize 1969, Artists Fund prize 1972, 74), Am. Artists Profl. League (dir., pres.'s award 1963), Council of Am. Artist Socs. (v.p. 1963-65), Nat. Arts Club, Allied Artists Am. (Gold medal 1970), Hudson Valley Art Assn., Pen and Brush (pres. 1966-70, gold medals 1958, 62), Soc. Women Geographers, Clubs: Cosmopolitan, Catherine Lorillard Wolfe Art (pres. 1961; gold medal 1960), Salmagundi. Address: 35 E 9th St New York City NY 10003

DUPEPE, EUNICE CLANCY, hotel exec.; b. Kenner, La.; d. Frank James and Vera (Wattigny) Clancy; ed. Soule Coll., New Orleans; m. Vernon Dupepe, Dec. 29, 1933 (div.); children—Frank Clancy, Bryan Vernon, Verna Patrick (Mrs. James Devlin, Jr.). Sec.-treas. Provincial Motels, Inc., New Orleans, 1960—; v.p. Duman Land Investments; sec.-treas. Clancy Investments, Inc. Hostess Le Petit Theatre Du Vieux Carre, 1965, now mem.; hostess Spring Fiesta Tours, 1963, 64, 65—. Mem. La. Landmarks So., Crippled Childrens Hosp. Guild. Beta Beta. Home: 304 Southern Rd Jefferson Parish LA 70123 Office: 1024 Rue Chartres New Orleans LA 70116

DUPLER, DOROTHY, educator; b. Rayensford, Pa., Jan. 1, 1910; d. Alphaeus William and Olive Eleanor (Replogle) Dupler; student Juniata Coll., 1928-29; B.A. Bridgewater Coll., 1931; M.A., Catholic U. Am., 1943; postgrad Columbia, 1947, Denver U., 1951; Ph.D. U. So. Cal., 1961. Clk., Internal Revenue Service, Washington, 1936-41; tchr. Elizabethtown (Pa.) Coll., 1943-44, Lankenau Sch., Phila., 1944-45; mem. faculty La Verne (Cal.) Coll., 1945-74, prof. emerita speech and drama, 1974—, asst. to dean, counselor East China Inst., Taiwan, 1974—. Mem. Am. Assn. U. Women (1st v.p. 1966-68, internat. relations chmn. 1969-74), Speech Communication Assn., Alpha Psi Omega. Office: La Verne College La Verne CA 91750

DUPONT, JACQUELINE LOUISE, nutritionist, educator; b. Plant City, Fla., Mar. 4, 1934; d. Albert Pierre and Bessie Mae (Clemons) Dupont; B.S., Fla. State U., 1955, Ph.D., 1962; M.S., Ia. State U., 1959. Home economist U.S. Dept Agr., Beltsville, Md., 1955-57, research nutrition specialist, 1962-64; asst. prof. biochemistry dept. Howard U., Washington, 1964-66; asst. prof. dept. food sci. and nutrition Colo. State U., Ft. Collins, 1966-69, prof., 1973—. Democratic precinct committeewoman, 1971—. NIH-USPHS grantee, 1971—; recipient Research Career Devel. award, NIH, USPHS, 1972—. Fellow Am. Heart Assn. Council on Arteriosclerosis; mem. Am. Inst. Nutrition, Am. Dietetic Assn., Am. Oil Chemists Soc., N.Y. Acad. Scis., Am. Home Econs. Assn. (nutrition study sect. 1972-76). Editor: Dimensions of Nutritions, 1970. Contbr. articles to profl. jours. Home: 3625 Terry Ridge Rd Fort Collins CO 80521

DUPONT, MARTHA ANNE CAROLINE VERGE (MRS. HENRY ELÉUTHÈRE IRENÉE DUPONT), civic worker; b. Long Beach, Cal.; d. William E. and Martha Anne Caroline (Bready) Verge; student Notre Dame Acad., 1949-53; children—Catherine Foree, William Garey, Christopher H., Martha Anne Caroline, Henri Verge; m. 2d, Henry Eléuthère Irenée duPont, Sept. 25, 1967; children—Sophie Madeleine, Henry Eléuthère Irenée II. A founder The Child Found., Wilmington, Del., 1961, pres., chmn., 1967-72; a founder Del. Pony Club, Wilmington, 1959; pres. Council of Agys. on Children and Youth, 1970-72; mem. Mental Health Assn. Del., 1964-70, Del. Agy. to Reduce Crime, 1970, Nat. Children's Trust, 1973. Trustee Nat. Council on Crime and Delinquency. Mem. Del. Hist. Soc., Am. Civil Liberties Union. Clubs: Wilmington Country; Annapolis (Md.) Yacht; Talbot Country (Easton, Md.). Address: Box 4000 "Montmorency" Greenville DE 19807 also Ellenborough Easton MD 21601 also Gemini Manalapan FL

DUPPSTADT, GLADYS ZUFALL, social worker; b. Somerset, Pa., Jan. 29, 1917; d. Clarence William and Laura (Sufall) Duppstadt; student State Tchrs. Coll., 1935-36; B.A., Pa. State U., 1939; M.S.W., Wayne State U., 1949. Sec. to personnel mgr. Consolidation Coal Co., Somerset, 1940-44; program dir. Y-Teens, YWCA, Bethlehem, Pa., 1944-47; exec. dir. Rouge-Ecorse United Community Centers, River Rouge, Mich., 1949-59, Protestant Community Services, Detroit, 1959-64; exec. sec. social edn. and action and internat. work Nat. Fedn. Settlements and Neighborhood Centers, N.Y.C., 1964-69; cons. Day Care Centers, Mich. Dept. Social Services, 1969—; pres. Detroit Fedn. Settlements and Community Centers, 1959-60. Chmn. River Rouge Human Relations Com., 1952; sec. Mayor's Youth Commn., River Rouge, 1956. Bd. dirs. Co-op Services, Detroit, 1952-56. Mem. Nat. Assn. Social Workers (dir. Met. Detroit 1957-59), Am. Youth Hostels, Detroit Photo Guild, Pi Lambda Theta, Pi Gamma Mu. Mem. Soc. of Friends. Home: 233 Orchard St East Lansing MI 48823 Office: Commerce Bldg Lansing MI 48913

DUPPSTADT, MARY ANN (MRS. ROBERT DUPPSTADT), librarian; b. Somerset, Pa., Sept. 22, 1916; d. Henry Clay and Alma Agatha (Matthews) Miller; B.A., Hood Coll., 1938; B.S., Carnegie Inst. Tech., 1939; m. Robert Duppstadt, Dec. 25, 1941; children—James, Ann (Mrs. Denis Michael), Dorris. Children's librarian Lima (O.) Pub. Library, 1939-42; serials librarian Pa. State Coll., State College, 1942-43; reference librarian Grosvenor Reference Library, Buffalo, 1943-48; sr. librarian Erie County Library, Buffalo, 1949-52; asst. librarian Arlington (Tex.) State Coll., 1952-57; with Ling-Temco Vought, Dallas, 1957—, asst. chief librarian, 1961—. Mem. Spl. Libraries Assn., Beta Phi Mu. Home: 921 E Mitchell St Arlington TX 76010 Office: PO Box 5907 Dallas TX 75222

DUPRÉ, GRACE ANNETTE, portrait painter; b. Spartanburg, S.C.; d. Daniel Allston and Helen Capers (Stevens) DuPre; student Converse Coll. and Converse Coll. Sch. Music, Grand Central Sch. Art, 1931-32; pvt. studies various tchrs., including Wayman Adams and Frank V. DuMond. Solo violinist, tchr. violin; painter, 1932—; several one man shows; works exhibited Fine Arts League of Carolinas, Gibbs Art Gallery, Mint Mus. Charlotte, Blue Ridge, N.C., Allied Artists of Am., Nat. Arts Club, Audubon Artists, Am. Artists Profl. League, Ogunquit (Me.) Nat. Exhbn. of Paintings; ofcl. portrait chief justice S.C. Supreme Ct., justice U.S. Supreme Ct., 1968, pres. Wofford Coll., 1968, gov. of S.C., 1968, also pres. Med. U. S.C., 1973; portraits in permanent collections Columbia U., N.Y.C., Main P.O., N.Y.C., U. Ind. Law Bldg., White House, U.S. Supreme Ct., U.S. 7th Circuit Ct. of Appeals, Chgo., S.C. State House, numerous pub. and ednl. instns., pvt. collections. Recipient various awards including portrait prize Catherine Lorillard Wolfe Art Club ann. show N.Y.C., 1955. Adv. mem. Marquis Biog. Library Soc. Artist mem. Grand Central Art Galleries, Inc., Pen and Brush, Nat. Arts Club, N.Y.C.; mem. Am. Artists Profl. League (nat. exec. bd.), Allied Artists Am., Carolina Art Assn., Gramercy Park Assn., Huguenot Soc. S.C., Portraits, Inc. Clubs: Woman's Music (Spartanburg, S.C.); Catherine Lorillard Wolfe Art (N.Y.C.). Current works include portraits of Paul Hardin III, pres. So. Meth. U., S.C. chief justice Joseph Moss. Studios: 361 Mills Av Spartanburg SC 29302 also 302 S Pine St Spartanburg SC 29302

DUPRIEST, BETTE RUTH HORTON (MRS. DENNIS BLACK DUPRIEST, JR.), club woman; b. Dallas, June 8, 1922; d. Frederick Reece and Frances Mellersh (Martyn) Horton; student Tex. State Coll. for Women, 1941; B.A. in Spanish, B.S. in Journalism, So. Meth. U., 1944; m. Dennis Black DuPriest, Jr., Nov. 28, 1958. Staff, Internat. News Service, Dallas, 1944-45, Dallas Morning News, 1945-49; with Petroleum Engr. Pub. Co., Dallas, 1955-57; translator Spanish and French letters Trinity Portland Cement div. Gen. Portland Cement Co., Dallas, 1950-58. Recipient Sigma Delta Chi scholastic award, 1944. Mem. Maj. James McGregor chpt. Colonial Dames of XVII Century corr. sec., pub. relations chmn. 1967-69, curator 1969-73), Magna Charta Dames (registrar Dallas-Fort Worth 1970-72, historian 1974—), Local History and Geneal. Soc., Colonial Order of Crown, Sovereign Colonial Soc., Ams. Royal Descent, Script and Score, Mortar Bd., Order of Washington, Tenn. Geneal. Soc., Nat. Trust Historic Preservation, Theta Sigma Phi, Sigma Delta Pi, Pi Sigma Alpha, Delta Zeta (chpt. pres. 1942-44, mem. chpt. alumnae adv. bd. 1950-53, 67-68, Dallas chpt. pres. 1955-56). Presbyn. Home: 5621 McCommas Av Dallas TX 75206

DURAN, JUDITH IRMA ARREDONDO (MRS. JULIUS DURAN), occupational therapist; b. McAllen, Tex., Nov. 25, 1939; d. Norberto and Aurora (Montalvo) Arredondo; B.S., Tex. Woman's U., 1963; m. Julius Duran, May 25, 1968; 1 son, Marcos Jaime. Staff therapist Parkland Meml. Hosp., Dallas, 1963-65; chief therapist Sinai Hosp., Balt., 1965-68, Lovelace Clinic, Bataan Rehab. Center, Albuquerque, 1968-73; staff therapist St. Joseph's Hosp., Albuquerque, 1973—. Vis. teaching lectr. Keswich Sch., Balt., 1967-68. Mem. Am., N.M. occupational therapy assns., World Fedn. Occupational Therapists.

DURANT, ARIEL (MRS. WILL DURANT), author; b. Russia, 1898; d. Joseph Michael and Ethel (Appell) Kaufman; came to U.S., 1900, naturalized, 1913; educated privately; hon. degrees including Dr. of Letters, 1968; m. Will Durant, Oct. 31, 1913; 1 dau., Ethel; 1 adopted son, Louis. Engaged in research for and with Will Durant on The Story of Civilization, 1961—. Recipient (with Will Durant) Huntington-Hartford award for lit. for The Age of Louis XIV, 1963; named Woman of Year in Lit., Los Angeles Times, 1965; received Pulitzer prize, 1968. Author: (with Will Durant) The Age of Reason Begins, 1961; The Age of Louis XIV, 1963; The Age of Voltaire, 1965; Rousseau and Revolution, 1967; The Lessons of History, 1968; Interpretations of Life, 1970. Address: 5608 Briarcliff Rd Los Angeles CA 90028

DURANTE, JESSAMINE MARGUERITE, banker; b. Chgo., Mar. 24, 1911; d. Hector Ferdinand and Mary Concetta (Magliano) Durante; Ph.B., U. Chgo., 1932; postgrad. Sch. Financial Pub. Relations, Northwestern U., 1957. With Harris Trust and Savs. Bank, Chgo., 1932—, mgr. Women's banking, 1963-68, asst. v.p., 1968-71, v.p., 1971—. Mem. Art Inst. Chgo.; lectr., personal financial adviser, 1956—. Mem. Assn. Chgo. Bank Women (pres. 1960-61), Nat. Assn. Bank Women, Inc. (mem. career devel. com. 1972-73), Assn. Modern Banking Ill. (pub. information com. 1973—), U. Chgo. Alumni Assn. Republican. Roman Catholic. Contbr. articles to banking jours. Office: 111 W Monroe St Chicago IL 60690 Home: 910 Lake Shore Dr Chicago IL 60611

DURBAHN, JANET SUE (MRS. PAUL A. DURBAHN), newspaper exec.; b. Anoka, Minn., Mar. 23, 1935; d. Cortes Frederick and Erma Rae (Jenks) Reed; student Stephens Coll., 1955; m. Paul A. Durbahn, Aug. 19, 1954; children—Paula, William, Karen, Mark. With Anoka (Minn.) Herald, 1952-54; reporter-circulation Sister Kinney Found., Mpls., 1954-55; reporter, columnist Edina-Morningside Courier, 1962-66; editor Stewartville (Minn.) Star, 1970—. Chmn. Community Awareness, Stewartville, 1971—; mem. United Way Com., Stewartville, 1972—. Mem. adv. bd. Rochester Community Coll., 1972—. Mem. Minn. Press Women, Stewartville C. of C. Methodist. Home: 203 6th Av NW Stewartville MN 55976 Office: Box 365 Stewartville MN 55976

DURDEN, BETTY JEAN (MRS. JESSE N. DURDEN, JR.), univ. adminstr.; b. Jefferson, Ia., Mar. 20, 1923; d. James Harvey and Mina Grace (Downing) Dillavou; B.A., Drake U., 1948, M.S.E. in Guidance and Counseling, 1971; m. Jesse N. Durden, Jr., June 5, 1945; children—Richard, David, Barbara. Dir. adult program YWCA, Des Moines, 1966-69; dir. women's programs continuing edn. Drake U., Des Moines, 1969—, spl. asst. to pres. Equal Opportunity Programs, 1973—. Mem. Gt. Plains States Regional Manpower Adv. Com., 1972—, Ia. Commn. on Status Women, 1972—; chmn. Gov.'s Commn. on Status Women, 1970-72. Served with USNR 1944-45. Mem. Am. Assn. U. Women (pres. Des Moines br. 1964-66), Women's Equity Action League, Adult Edn. Assn. U.S.A. (chmn. sect. on continuing edn. for women), Interstate Assn. Commns. on Status of Women (dir. nat.). Club: Altrusa. Home: 664 56th St Des Moines IA 50312

DURFLINGER, ELIZABETH WARD, educator; b. Ft. Wayne, Ind., July 8, 1912; d. Louis Clinton and Elizabeth Margaret (Fields) Ward; student, Exeter U., Devon, England, 1931-32; B.A., Western Coll., 1933; M.A., U. Cin., 1934, Ph.D., 1939; m. Harry A. Durflinger, July 2, 1949 (div. Feb. 1957). Histology lab. instr. Ecletic Med. Coll., Cin., 1935-36; teaching fellow U. Cin., 1939-40; faculty Butler U., Indpls., 1940—, dean of women, 1940-65; prof. zoology, 1954—. NSF grantee, 1969. Mem. Am. Assn. U. Women, Mortar Bd., Sigma Xi, Phi Kappa Phi, Delta Kappa Gamma, Alpha Lambda Delta. Home: 1010 Oakwood Trail Indianapolis IN 46260 Office: Butler University Indianapolis IN 46208

DURGIN, CAROL EVELYN, occupational therapist; b. Dover, N.H., Sept. 18, 1933; d. Roslyn Caverly and Gertrude Mary (Stacy) Durgin; B.S. in Occupational Therapy, U. N.H., 1956. Occupational therapist VA Hosp., Brockton, Mass., 1957-58, Boston, 1958-60; occupational therapy dir. L.I. Hosp., Boston, 1961-62; occupational therapist Lemuel Shattuck Hosp., Jamaica Plain, Mass., 1962-63, Florence Crittenden Home, Brighton, Mass., 1963, Boston City Hosp., 1963-69; occupational therapy dir. St. Elizabeth's Hosp., Brighton, 1969-71. Mem. Am., Mass. occupational therapy assns., Alpha Xi Delta. Home: 5 Crawford St Apt 8 Cambridge MA 02139

DURHAM, CHRISTINE MEANDERS (MRS. GEORGE HOMER DURHAM II), lawyer, educator; b. Los Angeles, Aug. 3, 1945; d. William Anderson and Louise (Christensen) Meaders; A.B. with high honors, Wellesley Coll., 1967; J.D., Duke, 1971; m. George Homer Durham II, Dec. 29, 1966; children—Jennifer Widtsoe, Meghan Christine. Admitted to N.C. bar, 1971, Utah bar, 1974; practiced in Durham, N.C., 1971-73; asst. dir. legal affairs Physician's Asso. Program, Durham, 1972-73; research asso. dept. community health scis. Duke Med. Center, Durham, 1972-73; legal adviser Older Ams. Resources and Services, Durham, 1971-73; teaching asst. J. Reuben Clark Law Sch., Brigham Young U., Provo, Utah, 1973-74. Mem. Women's Equity Action League, N.C. Women's Polit. Caucus, N.C. Bar, N.C. Bar Assn., Am. Assn. Law Schs. (mem. spl. com. women in legal edn. 1970-71). Democrat. Mem. Ch. of Jesus Christ of Latter-day Saints. Address: 1797 E 9th South Salt Lake City UT 84108

DURHAM, JOAN ELAINE (MRS. LEO DOUGLAS DURHAM), govt. ofcl.; b. Borger, Tex., Dec. 21, 1936; d. J.E. and Ina Ruth (Lackey) Davis; student (scholar), Midwestern U., 1955-56; m. Leo Douglas Durham, Aug. 1, 1970. Sec. to county judge Montague County, Tex., 1956-59; with City of Bowie (Tex.), 1959—, city clk., tax collector, 1965—. Registrar Draft Bd. Local #93, Bowie, 1971—. Mem. C. of C. Baptist. Democrat. Club: Bowie Amity (treas. 1963-64). Home: Rural Route 4 Box 100 Bowie TX 76230 Office; 115 E Tarrant Bowie TX 76230

DURHAM, LUCY ELIZABETH (MRS. DOUGLAS F. DURHAM), banker; b. Atlanta, Nov. 18, 1929; d. George Washington and Elizabeth Ganahl (Black) Sciple; student U. Ga., 1948; grad. Fla. Sch. Banking, U. Fla., 1972; m. Douglas Franklin Durham, Jan. 20, 1951; 1 dau., Sandra Elizabeth. File clk. First Nat. Bank, Atlanta, 1946-48, mgr. installment loan files, 1948-49, loan teller, 1949-51, comml. teller, drive-in teller, savs. teller, relief head teller, 1956-60; comml. teller First Nat. Bank Tampa (Fla.), 1964-66, head teller, 1967-70, asst. mgr. mil. facility, 1968-70, new accounts officer, 1968-72; asst. v.p. 1st Financial Nat. Bank Tampa, 1973-74, v.p., 1974—. Vice pres. elementary sch., Atlanta, 1961; troop leader Girl Scouts Am., 1958-62; charter mem. Piedmont Hosp.'s Women's Aux.; mem. Women's Aux. Tampa Gen. Hosp., bd. dirs., 1963; finance chmn. Gulf Coast Epilepsy Found., 1974—. Mem. Am. Bus. Assn. (treas. 1970-71, pres. 1971-72; Woman of Yr. award 1973), Nat. Assn. Bank Women (1st vice chmn. Gulf Central group, program chmn.), Am. Inst. Banking (dir. 1972—), Credit Mgrs. Assn. (dir. 1974). Episcopalian. Clubs: West Coast Orchid Soc., Palma Cela Golf and Country. Home: 512 Channel Dr Tampa FL 33606 Office: PO Box 17656 Tampa FL 33612

DURICK, ELIZABETH ANNE MCLAUGHLIN, coll. ofcl.; b. N.Y.C., June 6, 1908; d. James Robert and Helen Mary (Dermody) McLaughlin; B.A. in History, Coll. Mt. St. Vincent, 1929; M.A. in History, Fordham U., 1933; postgrad. Katherine Gibbs Soc. Sch., 1935; m. Jeremiah Kinsella Durick, June 10, 1939 (dec. 1960); children—Eileen Mary (Mrs. Lawrence Veladota), Elizabeth Anne (Mrs. Stephen Kinney), Jeremiah K. Editorial asst. Iron Age, weekly mag., 1935-39; instr. communications Jeanne Mance Sch. Nursing, 1955-56; asst. v.p. for pub. relations Champlain Coll., Burlington, Vt., 1957—. Mem. Def. Adv. Com. on Women in Service, 1971—; mem. Burlington Zoning Bd., 1946-49, Burlington Manpower Adv. Com., 1967—. Trustee Vt. Children's Aid Soc., 1966-69. Mem. Am. Coll. Pub. Relations Assn., Vt. Ednl. Pub. Relations Assn. (pres. 1971-72), Am. Assn. Jr. Colls., Vt. Poetry Soc., Athena Club (pres. 1957-58). Home: 25 Greening Av South Burlington VT 05401 Office: 252 S Willard St Burlington VT 05401

DURIEUX, CAROLINE WOGAN, artist, educator; b. New Orleans, Jan. 22, 1896; d. Charles Nicholas and Anna Lovisa (Spelman) Wogan; B.S. in Art, Newcomb Coll. of Tulane U., 1916; M.A. in Art, La. State U., 1949; m. Pierre Durieux, Apr. 14, 1920; 1 son, Charles Wogan. Instr., Newcomb Coll., 1937; asst. prof. Tulane U., 1937-43; instr. La. State U., 1943-45, asst. prof., 1945-52, asso. prof., 1952, prof., 1952-64, prof. emeritus, 1964—; represented in collections Mus. Modern Art, N.Y.C., Phila. Mus. Art, Library of Congress, Washington, N.Y. Pub. Library, Biblioteque National, Paris, Kunst Mus., Basel, Switzerland, others. Grantee for work on electron printing from radioactive drawings La. State U. Council Research, 1952-54, 72—. Illustrator: Gumbo Yaya, 1938. Author: Caroline Durieux Prints and Drawings, 1949. Address: 772 W Chimes St Baton Rouge LA 70802

DURKIN, ANNA JEAN EDMONDSON (MRS. JAMES JOSEPH DURKIN, SR.), coal co. exec.; b. Danville, Pa., Oct. 4, 1914; d. David Edward and Elmira (Foust) Edmondson; B.A., Mt. Holyoke Coll., 1937; m. James Joseph Durkin, Sr., Aug. 17, 1937; children—James Joseph, Edward Edmondson, Carol Durkin (Mrs. Peter Weaver), Barbara (Mrs. Stephen Kirmse). Gen. mgr. Durkin Ins. Office, Dallas, Pa., 1947—; sec. Nat. Diversified Industries, Great Neck, N.Y., 1963-67; budget dir., exec. v.p. Pocono Downs, Inc. Harness Racing Track, Wilkes Barre, Pa., 1965-72; sec., treas. Great Am. Coal Co., Dallas, 1973—. Home: Route 3 Box 399 Shrineview Dallas PA 18612 Office: Route 315 Wilkes Barre PA 18702

DURKIN, CATHERINE MERCEDES, lawyer; b. Cleve., June 4, 1915; d. Edmund J. and Mary (Walsh) Durkin; A.B., Mercyhurst Coll., 1936; J.D., Case Western Res. U., 1948. Admitted to Ohio bar, 1949; with WSB, Dept. Labor, Cleve., 1950-52; practice law, Cleve., 1952-58; mem. firm Schweid & Rini, Cleve., 1958-61, Kane, Ray & Elder, Cleve., 1961-71, Matia Isaac Ray & Elder, 1971-73; staff asst. Rep. James V. Staunton of Ohio, 1970—; spl. counsel to atty. gen. State Ohio, 1971—. Vice-chmn. bd. Mercyhurst Coll., Erie, Pa.; sec. bd. trustees Glen Oak Sch., Gates Mills, O.; bd. dirs. Consumers League Ohio. Recipient Outstanding Alumna award Mercyhurst Coll., 1967. Mem. Am., Ohio, Greater Cleve. bar assns., Phi Alpha Delta. Home: 3141 W 165th St Cleveland OH 44111 Office: 1311 The Superior Bldg Cleveland OH 44114

DURKIN, MARY LUCILE, librarian; b. Battle Creek, Mich.; d. James Henry and Ella M. (McQuillen) Durkin; B.S., Simmons Coll., 1936; B.A., U. Tenn., 1944; M.A., Columbia, 1955; M.L.S., U. Mich.,

1972; postgrad. U. Okla., summer 1973. Librarian, Chattanooga Sch. System, 1938-41; dist. supr. U.S. Govt. Program, Chattanooga, 1941-42; supr. city sch. library and Negro brs., Chattanooga, 1942-44; dir. field clubs A.R.C., Eng., Scotland, Germany, 1944-45; dir. USIS Libraries, Egypt, Morocco, Greece, 1948-58; librarian U.S. Army Aviation Sch., Fort Rucker, Ala., 1959—. Mem. A.L.A., Spl. Libraries Assn., Mil. Librarians Assn., Pi Lambda Theta, Sigma Delta Pi. Home: 207 Westview Dr Enterprise AL 36330 Office: Bldg 5907 Fort Rucker AL 36360

DUROCHER, DORA MAY VAN VLACK (MRS. LINUS F. DUROCHER), author, civic worker; b. nr. Poughkeepsie, N.Y., Dec. 12, 1898; d. William L. and Hattie (Conner) Van Vlack; student nursing Montefiore Hosp.; grad. Eastman Bus. Coll.; m. Linus F. DuRocher, Aug. 7, 1923. Mem. D.A.R., 1956—, N.Y. State chmn. geneal. records, 1959-62, N.Y. State registrar, 1962-65, mem. resolutions N.Y. State com., 1965-66-67, nat. vice chmn. Friends of D.A.R. Mus. Com., 1965—; chpt. regent Dutchess of York chpt. Daus. Am. Colonists, Poughkeepsie, 1957-60, N.Y. State regent, 1965-67, nat. corr. sec. 1967-68, now life nat. v.p. Atlantic Coast sect., nat. chmn. Am. Bicentennial; pres. Margaret Mask chpt. N.Y.C., Colonial Dames of XVII Century, 1958-61, 67—; N.Y. gov. Nat. Soc. Sons and Daus. Pilgrims, 1962-65; N.Y. pres. Nat. Soc. Dames Ct. Honor. 1959-62. Cited by A.R.C. Mem. Order Ams. Armorial Ancestry, Col. Daus. Seventeenth Century (past nat. orgn. sec.), Doll Collectors Am., Nat. Soc. New Eng. Women, Nat. League Am. Pen Women, Huguenot Soc., Vt. Soc. Colonial Dames, Daus. Colonial Wars N.Y. (pres.), Dutch Settlers Albany, Hist. Soc. Vermont, N.Y. Geneal. Biol. Soc., N.Y. Hort. Soc. Baptist. Clubs: Art Study of Poughkeepsie (past pres.), Women's City and County (past pres.), Antique Study (pres. 1972—). Home: 40 Corlies Av Poughkeepsie NY 12601

DURR, BETTY JEAN, librarian; b. McRae, Ga., Dec. 30, 1936; d. Hallie and Leila (Swain) Durr; B.S., Ft. Valley State Coll., 1959; M.S., Atlanta U., 1968. Bookmobile librarian Ocmulgee Regional Library, Eastman, Ga., 1959-69, asst. dir. Ocmulgee Regional Library System, 1969—. Sec., treas. Evereeady Block Club, McRae, Ga., 1971—. Mem. N.A.A.C.P., Am., Ga. library assns. Democrat. Baptist. Club: Ladies of Profession (pres. 1970—) (McRae). Home: 317 N 3rd Av McRae GA 31055 Office: 207 5th Av Eastman GA 31023

DURRETT, BOBBYE RUSSELL (MRS. ROBERT E. DURRETT, JR.), playwright; b. Fort Worth, 1932; d. Robert Mangrun and Elsa (Lange) Russell; student Fairfax Jr. Coll., 1949-50; B.A., Tex. Christian U., 1952, postgrad., 1952-53; m. Robert Ellis Durrett, Jr., June 6, 1956; children—Robert III, Louisa Kathleen. Asst. to dir. Reeder Sch. Theatre and Design, 1952-53; now free lance playwright, especially for children's theater. Pres. Permian Civic Ballet Guild, 1971-72, Burnet P.T.A., 1968-69; mem. bd. mgrs. Jr. Service League, Odessa, Tex., 1959-66, 70-71, community research chmn. 1971-72. Bd. dirs. Odessa Symphony, 1968-69, Symphony Guild, 1965-70, Presdl. Mus., Odessa, 1970—. Mem. Am. Ednl. Theatre Assn., Am. Assn. U. Women. Club: Garden (Odessa). Address: 3112 E 31st St Odessa TX 79762

DURWOOD, MAUREEN WOLKOFF, civic worker; b. Providence, June 14, 1931; d. William and Julianna (Schmelz) Wolkoff; student Pembroke Coll., Brown U., 1949-51; B.A., U. of Mo. at Kansas City, 1968; m. Richard Mark Durwood, June 24, 1950; children—Keith James, Jan Leslie, Dana Ellen. Bd. dirs. women's div. Jewish Fedn. Greater Kansas City, 1961—, chmn. gen. solicitation women's div., v.p., 1974-75; bd. dirs., mem. art com. Brandeis U. Women's Com., 1964—, treas. women's div., pres. chpt., 1972-74, regional v.p., 1974-75, nat. dir., 1974-75; corr. sec. Am. Jewish Com., 1964, v.p., 1971, 72; area co-chmn. Brown U. Bicentennial Devel. Program, 1961-62; bd. dirs., chmn. pub. relations Nat. Council Jewish Women, Greater Kansas City, 1965—; mem. Kansas City Lyric Opera Assn., v.p., 1974—; bd. dirs. Kansas City Legal Aid and Defender Soc., mem. exec. bd., 1972-73; bd. dirs. Planned Parenthood, 1974-75. Mem. Jr. Women's Philharmonic League (dir. 1965), Menorah Hosp. Aux., Kansas City Art Inst. Jewish religion (dir. sisterhood). Home: 6100 Mission Dr Shawnee Mission KS 66208

DURY, MURIEL GOLDMAN (MRS. ABRAHAM DURY), librarian; b. N.Y.C., Dec. 20, 1916; d. Nathan and Jennie (Weinstein) Goldman; B.A., Bklyn. Coll., 1937; postgrad. Columbia, 1939-40; M.L.S., U. Pitts., 1963; m. Abraham Dury, Mar. 16, 1940; children—Ira Michael, David Shepherd. Fellow biology dept. Bklyn. Coll., 1937-40; asso. biochemist Dorn Lab. Med. Research, Bradford, Pa., 1953-59; fellow Falk Med. Library, Pitts., 1962-63; reference librarian Nat. Library Medicine, Bethesda, 1963—. Pres., P.T.A., Bradford, 1956-57. Mem. Beta Phi Mu. Home: 5510 Cornish Rd Bethesda MD 20014 Office: 8600 Rockville Pike Bethesda MD 20014

DUSHANE, HELEN (MRS. JOSEPH DUSHANE), mus. ofcl.; b. Mt. Pleasant, Ia., Jan. 25, 1907; d. Edward and Hazel Dell (Neel) Schwartz; B.S., U. So. Cal., 1931, M.S., 1936; m. Joseph DuShane, Nov. 24, 1945; 1 dau., Renee. Teaching fellow U. So. Cal., Los Angeles, 1928-29, instr. dept. edn., 1928-37; with Los Angeles Bd. Edn., 1938-65; research asso. Los Angeles County Mus., 1965—. Mem. Am. Malacologists Union (treas. 1967), Western Soc. Malacologists (treas. 1968-69), Delta Psi Kappa. Club: Conchological (pres. 1963-64) (Los Angeles). Contbr. articles to profl. jours. Home: 15012 El Soneto Dr Whittier CA 90605 Office: Los Angeles County Museum Exposition Blvd Los Angeles CA 90007

DUSZYNSKI, DIANA OLGA, radiologist; b. Buffalo, Apr. 7, 1917; d. Leonard C. and Marie T. (Rasmus) Duszynski; M.D., State U. N.Y., 1942. Intern Edward Meyer Meml. Hosp., Buffalo, 1942-43, resident, 1943-45; fellowship radiology Lahey Clinic, Boston, 1945-46; asso. attending dept. radiology Buffalo Children's Hosp.; clin. asso. prof. dept. radiology, also dept. nuclear medicine State U. N.Y. at Buffalo. Diplomate Am. Bd. Radiology. Mem. A.M.A., Am. Coll. Radiology, Am. Coll. Nuclear Medicine (charter), Soc. Nuclear Medicine, N.Y. State, Erie County med. socs. Contbr. articles to profl. jours. Office: Department of Radiology Childrens Hospital 219 Bryant St Buffalo NY 14222

DUTOIT, AUDREY LOUISE (MRS. GENE M. BROWN), pub. relations exec.; b. N.Y.C., July 25, 1933; d. Charles L. and Olga (Schmerling) Dutoit; A.B., Duke U., 1954; m. Gene M. Brown, Apr. 17, 1971. Pub. relations asst. Olin Mathieson Chem. Corp., N.Y.C., 1956-62; publicity mgr. Magnavox Co., N.Y.C., 1962-64; with PR Assos., Inc., N.Y.C., 1964—, v.p., 1965—. Mem. Pub. Relations Soc. Am., Fashion Group, Phi Beta Kappa. Presbyn. (trustee 1971-73). Home: 500 E 77th St New York City NY 10021 Office: 575 Madison Av New York City NY 10022

DUTSON, SUSAN BECKWITH (MRS. RAY LORIN DUTSON), editor; b. Delta, Utah, Apr. 18, 1943; d. Frank Sylvanus and Wanda (Peterson) Beckwith; student Utah State Extension, 1962-69; m. Ray Lorin Dutson, Apr. 2, 1960; children—Lewis Ray, Darrin Lee (dec.), Daniel Frank (dec.); stepchildren—Dennis Ray, Cristine Dutson Higgley. Nurses aid West Millard Hosp., 1962-69; linotype operator Chronicle Pub. Co., 1966-70; partner, editor Duwil Pub. Co., pub. Millard County Chronicle, Delta, Utah, 1970—. Pres., Delta High Sch.-Jr. High P.T.A., 1971-73; pres., West Millard Foster Parents, 1973; pres., Tech. Edn. Delta Students, 1972—. Mem. Delta Bus. Assn. (dir. 1972—). Mem. Ch. of Jesus Christ of Latter-day Saints. Home: Box 21 Hinckley UT 84635 Office: Box 248 Delta UT 84624

DUTTON, BERTHA P., anthropologist; b. Algona, Ia., Mar. 29, 1903; d. Orrin Judd and Fannie B. (Stewart) Dutton; student U. Neb., 1929-31; B.A., U. N.M., 1935, M.A., 1937; Ph.D., Columbia, 1952; LL.D., N.M. State U., 1973. Sec. dept. anthropology U. N.M., 1933-36; asst. to dir. Museum N.M., 1936-39, curator ethnology, asso. archaeology, 1939-59, curator of exhibits, 1959-60, curator div. anthropology, 1960-63, curator div. research 1963-65; dir. Mus. Navaho Ceremonial Art, 1966—; N.M. rep. S.W. regional adv. com. Nat. Park Service, 1973—; archaeol. expdns. in Southwestern U.S., Tajumulco, Guatemala, Metapa, Mexico. Regional com. mem. Girl Scouts Am., 1956-57. Bd. dirs. Santa Fe Community Concert Assn., 1959-65. Recipient Alice Fletcher Traveling fellowship, Peru, Bolivia, 1935; Sch. Am. Research grant-in-aid, 1950; Minnie Comnock Blodgett fellowship Am. Assn. U. Women, 1953-54; NSF-Wenner-Gren Found. grantee, 1962-65; Columbus Explns. Fund grantee, 1964-65, 68. Mem. S.W Assn. Indian Affairs (dir. 1946-59, 63—), Soc. Am. Archaeology, Socieded Mexicana de Anthropologia, Southwestern Anthrop. Assn., Ariz. Archaeology and Hist. Soc., No. Ariz. Soc. Sci. and Art, Archeol. Soc. N.M., Old Santa Fe Assn., Soc. Women Geographers, Santa Fe Opera Guild. Author: Happy People, the Huichol Indians, 1962; Sun Father's Way, 1963; Let's Explore-Indian Villages Past and Present, 1970; Friendly People, The Zuni Indians, 1963; New Mexico's Indians of Today, 1968; Indians of the Southwest, 1965; Indians of the American Southwest, 1974. Editor: Pajarito Plateau and its Ancient People, 1953. Contbr. sci. articles to El Palacio, 1935—, and other publs. Office: Mus Navaho Ceremonial Art PO Box 5153 Santa Fe NM 87501

DUTY, ALLENE BEAUMONT (MRS. SPENCER CUMMER DUTY), author; b. Cleve., Jan. 29, 1912; d. John Erwin and Grace Forbes (Allen) Beaumont; B.S., Western Res. U., 1935; diploma Cleve. Sch. Art, 1935; m. Spencer Cummer Duty, Dec. 29, 1936 (dec. June 1973); children—Nancy Allen (Mrs. James Douglas Campbell, Jr.), Spencer Beaumont. Mem. women's adv. council Western Res. Hist. Soc.; mem. jr. council Cleve. Mus. Art; past mem. sr. bd. Amasa Stone House. Author: The Duty Family, 1972; The Forbes Family, 1972; The Taylor Family, 1972; Addenda to Cummer Memoranda, 1972; The Allen Family, 1973. Club: Intown (Cleve.). Home: 2976 Manchester Rd Cleveland OH 44122

DUTY, MRS. ROBERT SUMMERS, JR., club woman; b. Madisonville, Tex., June 8, 1910; d. Edward and Lenda (Geick) Risinger; pvt. tutoring in French, U. Houston, 1948-49; m. Robert Summers Duty, Mar. 27, 1932; 1 dau., Roberta (Mrs. Robert Felton Krouse). Mgr., United Gas Corp., Rosenberg, Tex., 1928-32. Treas., Houston Country Club Womens Assn.; 1st v.p. Houston Geol. Aux.; treas. Briar Rose Garden Club, 1954-55, year book chmn., 1961-62; pres. Ridotto Dance Club, 1961; sec. Women's Circle, 1946-48. Mem. Houston Symphony Soc., 1944-61; neighborhood chmn. Girl Scouts, 1947. Mem. Mus. Fine Arts, English-Speaking Union, Harris County Heritage Soc., Blue Bird Circle. Methodist. Home: 3735 Del Monte Dr Houston TX 77019 also Rhetta D Ranch Route 2 Brenham TX 77833

DUVAL, MARJORIE ANN, librarian; b. Leominster, Mass.; d. Daniel J., Jr. and Margaret L. (Desmond) Duval; tchr.'s diploma New Eng. Conservatory Music, 1943, B.Mus., 1945; M.S., Simmons Coll., 1962. Music tchr., choral condr. Jeanne D'Arc Acad., Milton, Mass., 1946-51; recreation supr. spl. services div. U.S. Dept. Army, Europe, Far East, New Eng., 1951-61; head librarian U. Me., Portland, 1962-72, asso. prof. library service, 1965—, univ. archivist U. Me. at Portland-Gorham, 1972—. Mem. Altrusa Internat. (pres. chpt. 1973-74), Me. (sec. 1971-74), New Eng. (sec. coll. librarians sect. 1970-71) library assns., Library Automation Research and Cons. Assn., Soc. Am. Archivists, New Eng. Archivists, Me. Hist. Soc., Mu Phi Epsilon. Home: 32 Wildwood Blvd Cumberland Foreside Portland ME 04110

DUVALL, CORA LUCILLE (MRS. FORREST DUVALL), newspaper exec.; b. Rising Sun, Ind., Aug. 20, 1915; d. Leonard Carlysle and Jessie Frances (Ballmann) Cofield; grad. high sch.; m. Forrest Duvall, Apr. 21, 1946; children—Carole (Mrs. Richard Powell), Steve, Diane. With various newspapers, Rising Sun and Lawrenceburg, 1938-44; lab. technician, sec. to head of assay dept. Schenley Penicillin Plant, Lawrenceburg, 1944-52; with Ohio County Newspapers, Inc., Rising Sun, 1962—, mng. editor, 1964—. Home: 730 Main St Rising Sun IN 47040 Office: 235 Main St Rising Sun IN 47040

DUVALL, MARY CATHERINE NEILL (MRS. HOWARD G. DUVALL), ednl. adminstr.; b. Tahlequah, Okla., June 9, 1912; d. Percy Phipps and Corinne (Kimmons) Neill; student Belhaven Coll., 1931-32; B.A. with distinction, U. Miss., 1934, M.S., 1936; postgrad. U. Mich., 1937; m. Claude Veazey DeShazo, June 14, 1938 (dec. Jan. 1952); children—Claude Veazey, Mary Corinne (Mrs. John D. Johnson III), Robert Neill; m. 2d, Howard G. Duvall, Apr. 9, 1966 (dec. Nov. 1971). Instr., U. Miss. at University, 1936-37, sec. to chancellor, 1952-58, adminstrv. asst. to chancellor, 1958—; research asst. Ill. Geol. Survey, 1937-38; sec. Miss. Geol. Survey, 1950-52. Adviser, U. Miss. chpt. Mortar Board, 1963-66. Mem. Am. Assn. U. Women (state nominating com. 1966-68, v.p. 1965-66, chmn. fellowship com. 1967-68, 71-72, 73-74), Oxford Heritage Assn. (past dir.), Phi Kappa Phi (past v.p.), Delta Delta Delta, Pi Kappa Pi. Presbyn. (ruling elder). Clubs: Book Lovers (past pres., past treas.), Business and Professional Womens (Oxford). Home: 1415 Jefferson Av Oxford MS 38655

DUXBURY, MARJORY HAZEL, psychologist; b. Winnipeg, Man., Can.; d. Edwin George and Edith May (Connolly) Duxbury; came to U.S., 1967. B.A. in Psychology and English, U. B.C., Can., 1957; M.A. in Rehab. Counseling, U. Ore., 1968, Ph.D. in Counseling Psychology, 1971, certificate Med. Psychology, 1972. Social group worker, Hi-Y dir. YWCA, Vancouver, B.C., 1959-62, New Westminster (B.C.) YM-YWCA, 1962-63; staff psychologist Rehab. Found. of B.C., Vancouver, 1963-67; intern, teaching asst. Counseling Center and Center for Gerontology, VISTA, U. Ore., Eugene, 1970-71, resident med. psychology Med. Sch., Portland, 1971-72; psychologist counseling center U. Washington, Seattle, 1972—. Cons. psychologist William Temple House, Portland, 1971-72. Mem. Am. Psychol. Assn., Pi Lambda Theta. Home: 7038 NE 138th St Kirkland WA 98033 Office: U Wash Counseling Center Seattle WA 98195

DWECK, SUSAN, govt. researcher; b. Washington, July 26, 1943; d. Samuel Ralph and Rena (Cohen) Dweck; B.A., Am. U., 1965; B.A., Am. U., 1965; postgrad. Am. U., 1966-68. Tchr., Montgomery County (Md.) Pub. Schs., 1965-69; research asst., div. research and edn. Univ. Research Corp., Washington, 1969-72; research specialist, evaluation div. Exec. Office of Pres., Office Econ. Opportunity, Washington, 1972-73; research specialist Office Income Security Policy, office of asst. sec. for planning/evaluation Office Sec. U.S. Dept. Health, Edn. and Welfare, Washington, 1973—. Mem. young Jewish leadership com. United Jewish Appeal, 1970—. Active work Democratic polit. campaigns, 1960-73. Home: 3003 Van Ness St NW Washington DC 20008 Office: 330 Independence Av SW Washington DC 20201

DWORKIN, RITA ANNE (MRS. PAUL DWORKIN), librarian; b. Bklyn., Dec. 28, 1928; d. Louis and Helen Beatrice (Rosenfeld) Sokolov; student U. Cal. at Los Angeles, 1946-47; B.A., Bklyn. Coll., 1949; M.S., C.W. Post Coll., 1964; m. Paul Dworkin, Oct. 30, 1949; children—Steven Allen, Betsy Ruth. Trainee, E. Meadow (N.Y.) Pub. Library, 1963-64, asst. reference librarian, 1964-66, head adult services, 1967—. Vice pres. North Merrick (N.Y.) P.T.A., 1961, editor newsletter, 1963. Mem. Nassau County Library Assn. Author: (with Irving Adelman) Modern Drama: A Checklist of Critical Literature, 1967; (with Irving Adelman) The Contemporary Novel: A Checklist of Critical Literature on British and American Novel Since 1945, 1972. Home: 12 McLane Dr Dix Hills NY 11746 Office: East Meadow Public Library Front St East Meadow NY 11554

DWORZAN, HELENE, novelist, poet, playwright; b. Paris, France, Mar. 13, 1925; d. Ansjel and Rebecca (Weiripp) Liberman; came to U.S., 1950, naturalized, 1952; student Lycees Victor Hugo, Paris, 1937-43, New Sch. for Social Research, 1952-53; B.A., Richmond Coll., 1974; m. George R. Dworzan; 1 son, Patrice Olivier. Translator, Robin Internat./Cinerama, N.Y.C., 1954-59; free-lance translator NBC, 1962; editor adviser Chelsea, lit. rev., 1970; tchr. French, Lang. Inst., N.Y.C., 1970-73, Riverdale Country Sch., N.Y.C., 1973; founder Continuum, poetry and fiction readings, 1970, since dir. Recipient novel grant Material Jewish Claims against Germany, 1961, Short Story award Dial Press, 1953. Mem. Authors League Am., Dramatists Guild. Author: (novel) Le Temps de la Chrysalide, 1957; also short stories and poems in various publs. Address: 463 West St New York City NY 10014

DWYER, ETHEL THERSA, psychologist; b. Manchester, N.H., July 30, 1931; d. Joseph George and Florence Theresa (Kittredge) Thibodeau; Mus.B., Boston U., 1953, M.Ed., 1962, certificate of advanced grad. study, 1965, Ed.D., 1968; m. John P. Dwyer, June 22, 1957. Tchr., Miss Jacques Pvt. Sch., 1953-54; asst. dir. Girls Club, 1954-57; tchr. Manchester pub. Schs., 1957-65; instr. Boston U. Sch. Edn., 1962-66; asst. prof. New Eng. Coll., Henniker, N.H., 1965-67; asso. prof. Mt. St. Mary Coll., Hooksett, N.H., 1968-70; staff psychology N.H. Hosp., Concord, 1969-71; pvt. practice as psychologist, Manchester, 1970—. Mem. Am., Eastern, New Eng., N.H. psychol. assns., Am. Ednl. Research Assn., Am. Assn. Elementary, Kindergarten and Nursery Educators, N.E.A. (state rep. 1965-70), N.H. Dental Soc. Women's Aux., Mu Phi Epsilon, Pi Lambda Theta. Home: 2071 N River Rd Manchester NH 03104 Office: 1480 Elm St Manchester NH 03101

DWYER, JEAN AGNES FERGUSON, U.S. magistrate; b. Atlanta, Feb. 14, 1927; d. Frederick Kilby and Rose (Norris) Ferguson; A.B., George Washington U., 1948, LL.B., 1951; 1 dau., Maureen M. Admitted to D.C. bar, 1951, Va. bar, 1965; mem. firm John J. and Jean F. Dwyer, Washington, 1952-72; U.S. magistrate U.S. Dist. Ct., Washington, 1972—. Mem. planning com. Jud. Conf., 1972; mem. criminal rules adv. com. Superior Ct., 1971-72. Mem. Rappahannock League for Environmental Protection. Mem. Women's Bar Assn., D.C., Va. bar assns., Nat. Capitol Great Pyrenees Club, Nat. Council U.S. Magistrates (bd. dirs. 1974—). Home: 7214 Davis Ct McLean VA 22101 Office: US District Courthouse 3d and Constitution Av NW Washington DC 20001

DWYER, MARGARET ANN, coll. dean; b. Syracuse, N.Y.; d. Edward P. and Margaret M. (O'Donnell) Dwyer; A.B., Le Moyne Coll., 1954; M.Ed., Boston Coll., 1956. Tchr. English and Latin, Oswego, N.Y., 1955-56; med. sch. worker St. Joseph's Hosp., Syracuse, 1956-60; registrar Le Moyne Coll., Syracuse, 1960-62, dean of women, 1962-71, asst. acad. dean, 1971-73; exec. asst. to pres. Boston Coll., Chestnut Hill, Mass., 1973—. Chmn. coll. relations bd. Syracuse chpt. A.R.C., 1967-70; mem. consumers' advisers bd. Dey Bros. Dept. Store, 1966-70; sec. St. Mary's Hosp. Adv. Bd., Syracuse, 1965-70. Mem. Nat. Assn. Women Deans and Counselors, Am. Assn. for Higher Edn., Am. Conf. Acad. Deans, Am. Assn. U. Women, Conf. Jesuit Student Personnel Adminstrs. (mem. exec. com.). Home: 44 Linden Sq Wellesley MA 02181 Office: 18 Old Colony Rd Chestnut Hill MA 02167

DWYER, MARIE RITA ROZELLE (MRS. JOHN D. DWYER), educator; b. N.Y.C., Sept. 4, 1915; d. Charles W. and Agnes (Coyle) Rozelle; student L'Assomption, Paris, France, 1932-33; B.A., Notre Dame Coll., 1936; M.A., Fordham U., 1938; student Sorbonne, Paris, summers 1933-37, 52; m. John D. Dwyer, Sept. 8, 1942; children—John Duncan, Joseph Charles, James Gerard, Jerome Valentine. Tchr. French, Fordham U., N.Y.C., 1938-42, Notre Dame Coll., N.Y.C., 1939-40, Coll. of St. Rose, Albany, N.Y., 1949-53, Washington U., St. Louis, 1959-60; faculty French dept. Webster Coll., 1966—; also mem. faculty Met. Coll. St. Louis U.; faculty Meramec Community Coll., St. Louis, 1968-70. Active community fund drives, including Greater St. Louis Fund for Arts and Edn. Bd. dirs. St. Louis Christmas Carols Assn., 1962-66, Parish Council, 1966-67; adult adviser cultural program for young adults Archdiocesan Council Cath. Youth, 1961-67; mem. Archdiocesan Council Laity Charities. Mem. Am. Assn. Tchrs. French (pres. St. Louis chpt. 1955-56), Mo. Acad. Sci. (editorial staff transactions, chmn. linguistics sect., mem. exec. bd., life mem.), Alliance Francaise, Societe Francaise (past sec.), K. C. Aux. (past pres.), A.A.A.S. (rep. Mo. Acad. Sci. Conv. 1973), Notre Dame Coll. Alumnae Assn. (past pres.), Internat. Fedn. Cath. Alumnae (past pres. Albany), Jesuit Mothers Guild (pres. 1963-65), Cath. Women's League (pres. 1964-66, dir. 1966—), Archdiocesan Council Cath. Women (mem. coms. family life teen-age code, corr. sec. 1963-64, pres. 1964-66 South Central dist.), Nat. French Honor Soc., Am. Assn. U. Profs., Modern Lang. Assn., Mo. Modern Lang. Assn. (v.p. 1961-63), Central States Conf. on Teaching Fgn. Langs., Socie'te International de la Linguistique, Linguistic Soc. Am., Fgn. Lang. Assn. Mo. (v.p. 4-Coll. Consortium, v.p. 1972-73), Centro Studie Scambi Internazionali (mem. internat. com.), Smithsonian Instn. Nat. Assos., Pi Delta Phi. Club: St. Louis University Faculty Women's (pres. 1956-58, dir. 1959—). Extensive travel for ednl. and linguistic research. Home: 526 Oakwood St Webster Groves MO 63119

DYAR, JULIA TRAYLOR, advt. exec., assn. adminstr.; b. La Grange, Ga., May 2, 1925; d. James Edward and Gladys (Marchman) Traylor; A.B., La Grange Coll., 1946; m. Hubert Lenhardt Dyar, Jan. 3, 1948 (dec. Oct. 1973). Asso. editor and columnist Royston (Ga.) Record, 1948-58; asst. mgr. Ga. Press Assn., Atlanta, 1958-72, acting mgr., 1972, exec. mgr., 1972—, also corporate sec., 1972—. Corporate sec. Ga. Newspaper Service. Corporate Sec. Ga. Press Ednl. Found., exec. mgr., 1972—. Mem. Women in Communication (sec. 1966, v.p. 1967-68), Atlanta Advt. Club. Democrat. Baptist. Editor: Editor's Forum, 1962—. Home: 1944 Ardmore Rd NW Atlanta GA 30309 Office: 1075 Spring St NW Atlanta GA 30309

DYCK, VELMA HILDEGARDE (MRS. WILLIAM ERWIN DYCK), orthodontist; b. Winnipeg, Man., Can., Dec. 7, 1939; d. Abram Cornelius and Velma Emily (Litz) DeFehr; B.S. with high distinction, U. Minn., 1967, B.A. summa cum laude, 1967, D.D.S.,

1969; M.S. in Orthodontics, Loma Linda U., 1971; m. William Erwin Dyck, June 5, 1959. Came to the U.S., 1962. Bookkeeper, C.A. DeFehr & Sons Ltd., Winnipeg, 1958-62; individual practice orthodontics, Fresno, Cal., 1971—; established dental clinic Hoppa Valley Indian Reservation, Hoppa, Cal., summer 1971. Bd. dirs. Pacific Coll., Fresno. Recipient Alpha Omega award, 1969. Mem. Am., Cal., Fresno Madera dental assns., Am. Assn. Orthodontists, Am. Assn. Women Dentists, Upsilon Alpha, Omicron Kappa Upsilon. Home: 6030 N Briarwood Lane Fresno CA 93705 Office: 2021 N Fresno St Fresno CA 93703

DYE, EDNA MAE (MRS. GEORGE WILLARD DYE), educator; b. Emerson, Neb., Mar. 8, 1911; d. John Frank and Agnes (DeLashmutt) Phillips; normal tng. certificate Ia. State Tchrs. Coll., 1923, B.E., 1926; M.A., Ia. U., 1931; m. George Willard Dye, Mar. 29, 1928 (dec. Apr. 1968); children—Robert F., Philip H., Don Lloyd. Tchr. pub. schs., Oakland, Ia., 1927-28, North Miami, Fla., 1932-33, Ia., 1934-36, Cal., 1940-52; tchr., dir., Pinecrest, Inc., Van Nuys, Cal., 1952—, also 7 pvt. schs. in San Fernando Valley area. Mem. Valley Mental Health Assn., San Fernando Valley Pvt. Schs. Assn. (pres., dir.), Van Nuys C. of C., Cal. Assn. Ind. Schs., Internat. Platform Assn. Methodist. Mem. Order Eastern Star.Home: 5975 Shoup Av Woodland Hills CA 95695

DYER, CHARLOTTE LEAVITT (MRS. GEORGE BELL DYER), educator; b. N.Y.C.; d. Charles Wellford and Clara Gordon (White) Leavitt; student Scarborough Sch., 1918-19, Rosemary Hall, 1920-22, Wykeham Rise, 1923-24, Finch Sch., 1924-25, U. N.M., 1928; B.A. Barnard Coll., 1931; postgrad. Columbia, 1932; A.M., U. Pa., 1948, Ph.D., 1950; m. George Bell Dyer, June 26, 1930. Instr. anthropology Barnard Coll., N.Y.C., field trips to Kutenai Indians, B.C. (Can.), 1928, 31; one of founders Farmers Digest mag., asst. editor, 1937-51; instr. Sch. of Horticulture, Ambler, Pa., 1937-38; instr. Army Gen. Sch., 1950-52, U. Pa., 1947-50, 53-67, Yale, 1957-58; supr. Upper Makefield Twp., Bucks County, Pa., 1971—, chmn., 1974—. Pres. sch. bd. Upper Makefield Twp. Bucks County, Pa., 1957-58; founder (with George Bell Dyer), asso. dir. The Dyer Inst. of Interdisciplinary Studies, New Hope, Pa., 1952. Mem. Pa. Citizens Council Better Schs., 1959; mem. council Rock High Sch. Bd., 1955-67; mem. Gov.'s Council on Rural Devel., 1971. Served with WAAC, 1942; maj. WAC, AUS: U.S. and Europe, 1942-46; at Fort Riley, 1950-52. Decorated European Theater and Army Commendation Ribbon with oak leaf cluster. Fellow Co. Mil. Historians; mem. Alumni Assn. Grad. Sch. Arts and Scis. U. Pa. (co-pres. 1959-62), Acad. Polit. Sci., Am. Acad. Polit. and Social Sci., Colonial Dames Am. (chpt. chmn. new citizens com. 1968—), Bucks County Conservation Fedn. and Open Space (a founder 1969, 1st pres. 1970—), Pi Gamma Mu. Clubs: Cosmopolitan (Phila.); Faculty (U. Pa.). Author: (with George Bell Dyer) The Beginnings of a U.S. Strategic Intelligence System in Latin America, 1950; A Century of Strategic Intelligence Reporting, 1954; A Strategic Intelligence Lesson, 1956; The World Analyst, 1958; Exercises on an Assumption of Violence, 1962; The Cruelest War, 1965; Second Battle of Valcour Island, 1969; co-author numerous monographs in profl. journals. Home: Diabase Farm Box 109 RD 2 New Hope PA 18938

DYER, DOROTHY TUNELL, educator; b. Mpls., Dec. 11, 1895; d. George Henry and Jennie (Ayers) Tunnell; B.S. in Home Econs., Ohio State U., 1918; M.A. in Psychology, U. Minn., 1938; m. John R. Dyer, July 29, 1920 (dec. 1933); children—Jean (Mrs. James Judson), John R., George C. Sec. Mining Town (W.Va.) YWCA, 1918-19, nat. student sec. North Central Field, 1919-20; grad. asst. psychology U. Minn., 1934-35; asst. jr. dean Coll. Arts and Scis., Ohio State U., 1936-37; dean women and asst. prof. psychology Bucknell U., 1937-44; asso. dir. World Student Service Fund, 1942; exec. dir. St. Paul YWCA, 1944-47; asso. prof., chmn. Family Living div., marriage counselor U. Minn., 1947-58; dean Coll. Family Life, Utah State U., 1958-61; marriage counselor No. Utah Mental Health Clinic, 1959-61; dir. Family Life Edn. program Santa Clara County (Cal.), 1963-67; marriage counselor Los Gatos (Cal) Meth. Ch., 1963-67; prof. family relations N.D. State U., Bismarck, after 1967; vis. prof. Mary Coll., Bismarck, 1971; tchr. West Valley Coll. Del. White House Conf. Aging, 1961. Mem. Am. Assn. Marriage Counsellors. Nat. Utah (past v.p.), No. Cal. councils on family relations, Minn. Family Life Council (past sec.), Mpls. Vocational Guidance Assn., Am. Personnel Guidance Assn., Am., Minn. psychol. assns., A.A.A.S., Am., Utah home econs. assns., Rocky Mountain Western psychol. assns., Am. Assn. U. Women, Am. Social Health Assn., Internat. Platform Assn. Methodist. Editor: Sioux Family Life Development, 1970. Contbr. articles in field to profl. jours. Home: 17785 Vista Av Mount Sereno CA 95030

DYER, ELAINE DEDRICKSON, nursing educator; b. Spanish Fork, Utah, Nov. 9, 1923; d. Gilbert and Alberta (Larsen) Dedrickson; B.S., St. Mary of-the-Wasatch Coll., Salt Lake City, 1946; M.S., U. Utah, 1956, Ph.D. (USPHS fellow), 1967; m. Gordon W. Dyer, Sept. 21, 1955. Staff nurse Queen of Angels Hosp., Los Angeles, 1946-47; mem. staff VA Hosp., Salt Lake City, 1947-63, 67—, chief nursing research, 1967—; grad. asst. psychol. lab. U. Utah, 1964-66, asst. research prof. nursing Coll. Nursing, 1967—; asso. prof. nursing Brigham Young U. Coll. Nursing, 1971—; conductor workshops, cons. in field. Mem. task force measuring quality of nursing care VA, 1968-71. Mem. gen. bd. Young Women's Mut. Improvement Assn., 1957-70, past com. chairperson. NIH grantee, 1971-74. Mem. Am., Utah (pres. 1969-71) nurses assns., Am. Psychol. Assn., Nat. League Nursing, Sigma Xi, Kappa Theta Sigma. Mem. Ch. of Jesus Christ of Latter-day Saints. Author: Nurse Performance Description: Criteria, Predictors and Correlates, 1967; co-author: Improved Patient Care Through Problem-Orientated Nursing, 1974. Contbr. articles to profl. jours., sci. papers to profl. meetings. Inventor pressure breathing therapy. Home: 2326 Bryan Av Salt Lake City UT 84108

DYER, GOUDYLOCH ERWIN, state legislator; b. Atlanta, May 28, 1919; d. Edward Jones and Mary Louisa (Browne) Erwin; B.A., Agnes Scott Coll., 1938; postgrad. Columbia, 1939-40; m. Robert Campbell Dyer, Oct. 24, 1940; children—Colin R., Erwin Avery (Mrs. Michael Graham). Book reviewer Chgo. Tribune, 1957-61; polit. panelist radio and TV; mem. Ill. Ho. of Reps., 1968—, chmn. higher edn. com., 1973-74, mem. human resources com., 1973-74, mem. revenue com., 1973—, mem. health care licensure com., 1972—, com. status of women, 1972—, commn. on children, 1973-74. Chmn. Friends of the Forest Preserve, 1966-67. Republican precinct capt., 1962-69; pres. DuPage County (Ill.) Rep. workshops, 1958-59; state bd. mem. Ill. Rep. Workshops, 1958-60; nat. bd. mem. Nat. Council Rep. Workshops, 1960-61; mem. DuPage County Rep. Com., 1961-68; mem. DuPage County Bd., 1961-68. Bd. dirs. Hinsdale Community Nursing Service, Pub. Health Council, DuPage County. Mem. Am. Assn. U. Women, League of Women Voters (pres. Western Springs chpt. 1955-56). Home: 441 E 3d St Hinsdale IL 60521 Office: Capitol Bldg Springfield IL 62706

DYER, LOUISE MARVIN SEEBURGER (MRS. ROBERT WAYNE DYER), assn. exec.; b. Des Moines, Oct. 7, 1919; d. Vernon Raymond and Merze (Marvin) Seeburger; B.S., U. Ia., 1941; m. Robert Wayne Dyer, Sept. 19, 1945; children—Raymond Wayne, George Marvin, Charles Robert, Susan Louise. With actuarial dept. Equitable Life Ins. Co. Ia., Des Moines, 1941-42; sec. Commandants Office. 11th Naval Dist. Hdqrs., San Diego, 1942-45; mem. Bd. Edn. San Diego Unified Sch. Dist., 1965-73, v.p. bd. edn., 1967-68, 72, pres., 1968-69, 73, v.p. Big Fire Assn. Pub. Sch. Dists. Cal., 1973; clumnist Sentinel Newspapers, San Diego, 1970-73. Mem. del. assembly Cal. Sch. Bd. Assn., 1967-73; mem. council Big Cities Bds. Edn., Nat. Sch. Bds. Assn., 1967—, steering com., legislation com., 1970-73. Pres. region 9 Cal. Jr. Coll. Assn. Bd. dirs. San Diego Econ. Opportunity Commn., 1965-67, San Diego region Nat. Conf. Christians and Jews, 1964-67, 70—; adv. bd. U. Cal. at San Diego extension, 1966—; mem. Chancellor's adv. com. Cal. Community Colls., 1971-73; mem. spl. gifts com. San Diego Pub. Library, 1964—. Den mother Cub Scouts, Boy Scouts of Am., 1955-60; leader Girl Scouts of Am., 1963-65. Recipient George Washington honor medal Freedoms Found., 1972. Mem. Am. Assn. U. Women, Family Service League, San Diego Amateur Astronomers, San Diego Hist. Soc., San Diego-Yokohama Friendship Gen. Assembly (v.p. 1964-65), Comprehensive Health Planning Assn. San Diego and Imperial Counties, Kappa Alpha Theta (alumni pres. 1945). Republican. Lutheran. Home: 3412 Browning St San Diego CA 92106

DYER, MERCEDES DOROTEA HABENICHT (MRS. FRED DYER), educator; b. Puiggari, Argentina, July 8, 1917; d. Judson Power and Federica Elisa (Hofer) Habenicht; B.A., Emmanuel Missionary Coll., 1940; postgrad. Mich. State U., 1941, 42, 63; Ind. U., 1969; M.A., U. Mich., 1945, Ph.D., 1961; m. Fred Dyer, June 27, 1954. Tchr., dean of girls Shenandoah Valley Acad., New Market, Va., 1940-41, 43-47, Cedar Lake (Mich.) Acad., 1941-43; dean of women River Plate Coll., Puiggari, 1947-51; dean of women Columbia Union Coll., Takoma Park, Md., 1953-56, dir. guidance, 1956-59, dean students, 1959-61; mem. faculty Andrews U., Berrien Springs, Mich., 1961—, prof. edn., 1964—. Mem. Berrien County adv. com. Manpower Devel. Tng. Act, 1965-69. Pres. Berrien County chpt. Mich. Soc. Mental Health, 1969-71. Mem. N.C., Am., Mich. personnel and guidance assns., Am. Assn. Counselor Edn. and Supervision, Am. Coll. Personnel Assn., Am., Mich. sch. counselor assns., Nat., Mich. assns. women deans and counselors. Club: Altrusa (Benton Harbor-St. Joseph pres. 1965-67). Editor: The Dean's Window, 1956—. Home: 55 4th St Berrien Springs MI 49104

DYER, SALLIE (MRS. ROBERT FRANCIS DYER), genealogist, club woman; b. Washington, Oct. 16, 1891; d. Nathaniel Talmadge and Emma (Hutchins) Worley; student Cazenovia Jr. Coll., 1908-12, George Washington U., 1912-13, Strayer's Bus. Coll., 1914; m. Robert Francis Dyer, Jan. 1, 1926; children—Robert F., Nancie (Mrs. Edward C. Santelmann), Richard Hutchins, David Marcus. Sec., Brit. Embassy, Washington, 1914-15, Adj. Gen.'s. Office, War Dept., 1915-16; owner Dyer's Geneal. Office, Washington, 1914-26. Pres. Washington alumnae club Pi Beta Phi, 1946-47; vice-regent Dorothy Hancock chpt. D.A.R., 1945—, del. to Continental Congress, 1950-73; mem. spl. com. U.S.O., 1941-45, mem. Belasco Theater, 1942-45; nurse's aid A.R.C., 1943-45; mem. woman's bd. George Washington U. Hosp., 1946-56; mem. George Washington U. Alumni Assn. Recipient service award A.R.C., 1945, Golden Arrow award Pi Beta Phi. Mem. So. Dames Am. (charter mem. nat. soc.; state v.p.), Tex. State Geneal. Soc., Md. Hist. Soc. Clubs: Washington, Chevy Chase Woman's, Arts, Army and Navy. Home: 3813 Garrison St NW Washington DC 20016

DYKE, ANNMARIE KIRCHNER (MRS. THEODORE DYKE), lawyer; b. Cleve., Apr. 29, 1936; d. John C. and Elizabeth (Buehner) Kirchner; R.N., St. Vincent Charity Hosp., 1957; B.S. (fellow), St. Louis U., 1964; J.D., Cleve. State U., 1968; m. Theodore Dyke, Aug. 12, 1967; children—Lorianne E., Karla Marie, John Theodore. Staff nurse St. Vincent Charity Hosp., Cleve., 1957-58; office nurse Dr. Pierce H. Mullally, Cleve., 1957-68; charge nurse Firmin Delodge Hosp., St. Louis, 1962-64; admitted to Ohio bar, 1969, since practiced in Cleve.; atty. examiner, hearing officer Ohio Bur. Workmen's Compensation, Cleve., 1971—. Lectr., speaker on nursing and law Sch. Nursing, Cleve., 1969—. Mem. Nat. League Nursing, Ohio Nurses Assn., Am., Cleve., Cuyahoga County bar assns., Women's Lawyers Assn., Nat. Womens Lawyers Assn. Clubs: City, Playhouse (Cleve.). Editor: Cleve. Marshall Law Sch. Law Rev., 1967-68. Home: 1911 Powell Rd Cleveland Heights OH 44118 Office: 1630 Illuminating Bldg Cleveland OH 44115

DYKEMAN, ALICE MARIE JANSEN, pub. relations exec.; b. North Bend, Neb.; d. Cecil V. and Dorothy Lillian (Sillik) Jansen; student Neb. Wesleyan U., 1949-50, So. Meth. U., 1960-69; m. Paul Dykeman, Oct. 15, 1950 (div. Dec. 1960); children—David Clair, Cinda Cecille. Feature writer Biloxi (Miss.) Herald, 1952; women's editor Fremont (Neb.) Guide and Tribune, 1950-54; office mgr. Highland Park Arthur Murray Studio, 1955-57; sales promotion asst. A. Harris & Co., Dallas, 1957-60; account exec. Contact Corp., Dallas, 1960-61; pub. relations dir. Meth. Hosp., Dallas, 1961-72; pub. information officer Region VI, Small Bus. Adminstrn., 1972—; adj. prof. U. Dallas Grad. Sch. Mgmt., 1973—. Mem. exec. com. Nat. Assn. Health and Welfare Ministries, 1969-70; mem. Dallas Health Adv. Bd., 1971-73; chmn. pub. relations com. Dallas Hosp. Council, 1963, 68; mem. publicity com. Dallas County chpt. Am. Cancer Soc., 1965-71, Greater Dallas Council of Chs., 1964-72. Mem. Am., Tex., Dallas (chmn. area pub. relations com. 1965, 66) hosp. assns., Am. Soc. Hosp. Pub. Relations Dirs. (charter mem., area rep. North Tex. 1967-70), Tex. Soc. Pub. Relations Dirs. (charter, pres. 1971), Pub. Relations Soc. Am. (chpt. bd., chpt. pres. 1969, assembly del. 1970-73, S.W. Dist. Sec., 1970, chmn. 1972, nat. eligibility com. 1970, internat. com. 1970-73, edn. com. 1974, asst. gen. chmn. nat. conf. 1971), Dallas Council World Affairs (mem. fgn. visitors com. 1962—), Religious Pub. Relations Council (chpt. charter mem.), Oak Cliff C. of C., Exec. 100. United Methodist. Club: Press (mem. membership com. 1965-69, awards banquet 1969, 71, gridiron show 7 years). Contbr. articles to publs. Home: 3010 Raleigh St Dallas TX 75219 Office: 1720 Regal Row Dallas TX 75235

DYKEMAN, WILMA (MRS. JAMES ROREX STOKELY, JR.), writer; b. Asheville, N.C., May 20, 1920; d. Willard Jerome and Bonnie Cushman (Cole) Dykeman; B.S. in Speech, Northwestern U., 1940; L.H.D., Maryville Coll., 1972; m. James Rorex Stokely, Jr., Oct. 12, 1940; children—Dykeman Cole, James R. III. Lectr. various orgns., 1955—; tchr. numerous writers' confs. Mem. def. adv. com. on Women in the Services, 1967-70. Mem. exec. com. Tenn. Hist. Commn., 1966-71, Tenn. Commn. Humanities. Trustee Berea (Ky.) Coll., 1968—. Recipient Thomas Wolfe Meml. award Western N.C. Hist. Soc., 1955, Hillman award, 1957, Chgo. Friends Am. Writers Waukegan Club award, 1962, Mary Mildred Sullivan medallion, 1971; Guggenheim fellow, 1956. Mem. Am. PEN, Lit. Guild, Author: The French Broad River, 1955; (with husband) Neither Black Nor White, 1957; (with husband) Seeds of Southern Change, 1962; The Tall Woman, 1962; The Far Family, 1966; Prophet of Plenty, 1966; Look to This Day, 1968; (with husband) The Border States, 1968; Return the Innocent Earth, 1973; Too Many People, Too Little Love, 1974. Author numerous short stories and articles. Editorial columnist Look to This Day For News Sentinel, Knoxville, Tenn., 1962—. Address: 405 Clifton Heights Newport TN 37821

DYKES, ELIZABETH PANKRATZ (MRS. J. HARVEY DYKES), coll. librarian; b. Cordell, Okla., Oct. 20, 1910; d. David M. and Elizabeth (Schultz) Pankratz; B.A., Okla. State U., 1956; M.L.S., Tex. Woman's U., 1968; m. J. Harvey Dykes, July 24, 1931; children—Patrick H., Kermit H. Instr. library sci. Okla. State U., 1956-57; reference librarian Okla. Christian Coll., 1962-66; reference librarian Harding Coll., Searcy, Ark., 1967—. Mem. Am. Assn. U. Women (2d v.p. 1973—), Am., Ark., S.W. library assns., Stepping Stones, Beta Phi Mu. Home: 804 W Center St Searcy AR 72143

DYKES, IMELDA JOAN, advt. agy. exec.; b. Baton Rouge, Sept. 10, 1947; d. John Henry and Kathrine Imelda (Degrastino) Dykes; B.A. in Journalism, La. State U., 1969. Editor Land Printing Co., Baton Rouge, 1969-70; prodn. asst. Gulf Pub. Co., Houston, 1970—, prodn. mgr., 1970-72; asst. print buyer McCann-Erickson Advt. Agy., Houston, 1972—. Free-lance producer, designer books and brochures. Mem. ADS. Democrat. Roman Catholic. Home: 614 Kipling St Houston TX 77006 Office: 800 Bell St Houston TX 77002

DYKES, SUSAN FROST, coll. adminstr.; b. Hackensack, N.J., Nov. 23, 1949; d. Norman M. and Constance H. (Harrington) Dykes; B.A., Muskingum Coll., 1971; M.A., Bowling Green U., 1973. Residence hall dir. Muskingum Coll., New Concord, O., 1971-72; residence hall dir., dir. fgn. students and off campus study Otterbein Coll., Westerville, O., 1972-73, admissions counselor, 1973—. Mem. Nat. Assn. for Fgn. Student Affairs, Nat., Ohio assns. for women deans, adminstrs. and counselors, Am. Personnel and Guidance Assn., Cwens, Phi Alpha Theta. Home: 6176 Deewood Loop E Columbus OH 43229 Office: Admissions Office Otterbein College Westerville OH 43801

DYKHOUSE, HERMINA VAN ANKEN (MRS. JACOB DYKHOUSE), educator; b. George, Ia., June 23, 1911; d. Eltje and Tracy (Gruys) VanAnken; B.S., Sioux Falls Coll., 1962; spl. edn. certificate Mankato State Coll., 1962; m. Jacob Dykhouse, May 25, 1937 (dec. Jan. 1956); 1 son, Vance Jacob. Elementary tchr., Ia., Minn., 1950-61; tchr. spl. edn. Luverne (Minn.) High Sch., 1961—. Mem. Nat. (life), Minn., Luverne edn. assns., Council Exceptional Children, Am. Assn. Mental Deficiency, Minn. Assn. Retarded Children, Delta Kappa Gamma. Club: Tourist (pres. 1973-74) (Luverne). Author: (with others) Southwestern Minnesota Special Education Curriculum Guide, 1967. Home: 127 1/2 E Lincoln St Luverne MN 56156 Office: 709 N Kniss St Luverne MN 56156

DYSON, ANNE JANE (MRS. HAROLD FRANCIS DYSON), librarian; b. Amite, La., Mar. 5, 1912; d. Andrew Jackson and Estelle (Vernon) Holton; A.B., La. State U., B.S. in L.S., 1935; m. Harold Francis Dyson, June 18, 1937; 1 dau., Deanna (Mrs. Marshall L. Posey, Jr.). With La. State U. Library, Baton Rouge, 1935—, head humanities div., 1973—. Mem. La. Library Assn., Baton Rouge Library Club. Baptist. Author: (with Helen Palmer) American Drama Criticism, 1970; (with Helen Palmer) European Drama Criticism and Supplement, 1968; (with Helen Palmer) English Novel Explication - Criticism to 1972, 1973. Home: 7575 Jefferson Hwy Baton Rouge LA 70806 Office: Louisana State University Library Baton Rouge University Station LA 70803

DZIEDZIC, BERNADINE VERONICA, savs. and loan exec.; b. Chgo., May 20, 1939; d. Aloysius Sebastian and Victoria (Bolt) Dziedzic; B.A., Mundelein Coll., 1961; grad. Savs. and Loan Grad. Sch., U. Ind., 1969. Controller, Ben. Franklin Savs. & Loan Assn., Chgo., 1961—, asst. sec., 1962—. Mem. Am. Assn. U. Women, Am. Assn. Accountants, Controllers Soc. Am. Savs. and Loan Assn. Home: 3626 S Seeley Av Chicago IL 60609 Office: 1200 Harger Rd Oak Brook IL 60521

EACHO, HILDA BELL (MRS. WILLIAM CARLTON EACHO), club woman; b. Washington, June 30, 1902; d. Thomas and Grace (Bendimire) Bell; student bus. coll.; m. William Carlton Eacho, Dec. 30, 1922; children—William Carlton, Robert Lee. Sec. to v.p. U.S. Housing Corp., Dept. Labor, Washington, 1919-23; pres., mgr. Washington Frosted Foods, Washington Fish Exchange, Cold Storage Co., 1942-46, now dir.; dir. Carlton Fisheries (Morgan City, La.). Episcopalian. Clubs: Washington, Congressional Country (Washington); Surf, La. Gorce (Miami Beach). Home: Shoreham West 2700 Calvert St NW Washington DC 20008 also 5735 La Gorce Dr Miami Beach FL 33140

EADES, LINDA KAY CRANE (MRS. NED EADES), educator; b. Hattiesburg, Miss., Mar. 9, 1945; d. B.F. and Lenora Christine (Blakely) Crane; B.S., William Carey Coll., 1966; M.S., U. So. Miss., 1973; m. Ned Eades, May 26, 1967; 1 son, Ashley. Tchr. Forrest County Agrl. High Sch., Bklyn., Miss., 1966-71; asst. prof. phys. edn. William Carey Coll., Hattiesburg, Miss., 1972—. Mem. A.A.H.P.E.R., Miss. Edn. Assn., Amateur Athletic Union, Delta Kappa Gamma. Home: Rural Route 9 109 Woodheaven Dr Hattiesburg MS 39401

EADS, EDNA CHRISTINA BURCH (MRS. CHARLES P. EADS), state legislator; b. Farmington, Mo., Aug. 8, 1913; d. Alfred and Minnie (Dietzler) Burch; student St. Louis Bus. Coll.; m. Charles P. Eads, Apr. 11, 1934; children—Ronald Wayne, James David, Robert Eugene. Real estate broker, also ins. broker, 1946-66; postmaster, Bonne Terre, Mo., 1954-58; mem. Mo. Ho. of Reps., 1966—, appropriations, local govt., mines and mining coms. Sec. Mo. Republican State Com.; mem. coms. Mo Rep. Assn. Mem. Bus. and Profl. Women's Club, Am. Cancer Soc., C. of C. Conglist. Home: 112 Pine St Bonne Terre MO 63628

EADY, CAROL MURPHY (MRS. KARL E. EADY), nursing adminstr.; b. Cleve., Dec. 3, 1918; d. Alfred John and Beatrice B. (Winternitz) Murphy; diploma St. Luke's Hosp. Sch. Nursing, 1940; B.S. magna cum laude, Baldwin-Wallace Coll., 1943; M.S., Western Res. U., 1955; m. Karl Ernest Eady, July 7, 1945. Ednl. dir. M.B. Johnson Sch. Nursing, Elyria (O.) Meml. Hosp., 1952-57; dir. nursing edn. Mt. Sinai Hosp. Sch. Nursing, Cleve., 1957-62; dir. nursing edn. Michael Reese Hosp. and Med. Center, Chgo., 1962-73; coordinator nursing edn. Area Health Edn. System, U. Ill., 1973—. Mem. nursing adv. com. Nat. Commn. on Nursing and Nursing Edn., 1971-73, nurse tng. act grants rev. com. USPHS, 1968-72. Mem. Nat. League for Nursing (pres. 1973-75). Home: 1115 S Seminary Av Park Ridge IL 60068 Office: 845 S Damen St Chicago IL 60612

EAGER, BEVERLY ANN (MRS LLOYD W. EAGER), pub. relations exec.; b. San Francisco, Nov. 23, 1923; d. Harold Frederick and Ann Elizabeth (Lawler) Taylor; B.A., San Francisco State Coll., 1940-44; m. Lloyd William Eager, Feb. 7, 1942; children—Pamela (Mrs. Paul Sodaski), Sean, Christian, Jason. Women's editor King's Lynn News, Norfolk, Eng., 1964-65; asst. editor The Spectator, Chilton Pub. Co., Phila., 1967-68; pub. relations dir., editor Soroptimist Fedn. of Americas, Phila., 1968—. Mem. Women in Communications (pres. Phila. chpt. 1974-75), Nat. Fedn. Press Women (journalism award 1972), Del. Valley Assn. Communicators. Home: 408 Minden Way Wynnewood PA 19096 Office: 1616 Walnut St Philadelphia PA 19103

EAGER, ELLEN BRASHEARS WATSON (MRS. BAINBRIDGE EAGER), writer, ins. co. exec.; b. Balt., July 8, 1925; d. Mark S. and Susan (Owens) Watson; B.A., Wellesley Coll., 1947; m. Bainbridge Eager, May 29, 1954; children—Mark Watson, Susan Bainbridge.

Reporter Balt. Sun, 1945, 46; instr. Stewart & Co., Balt., 1947-49; asso. editor Johns Hopkins Mag., 1949-54; copy editor Hartford (Conn.) Times, 1954-55; v.p. Bainbridge Eager & Assos., Inc., 1971—. Mem. adv. com. spl. edn. D.C. Schs., 1968—. Episcopalian. Author stories and articles. Home: 3111 Macomb St NW Washington DC 20008

EAGLE, MARJORIE JONES, financial exec.; b. Lebanon, O., Nov. 27, 1920; d. Aldus Clarence and Bertha (Nisewonger) Jones; m. John Milton Eagle, Mar. 25, 1941; 1 son, John Michael. With Nat. Cash Register Co., Dayton, O., 1939-42, Signal Corps Depot, U.S. Army, Dayton, 1943-45; with Pipe Fabricating & Supply Co., Inc., Santa Fe Springs, Cal., 1954—, controller, corporate sec.-treas., 1961—. Mem. Order Easter Star. Home: 1741 Brookdale Av La Habra CA 90631 Office: 9703 S Norwalk Blvd Santa Fe Springs CA 90670

EAGON, CARRIE WILSON, librarian; b. Chattanooga, Aug. 19, 1920; d. Sam D. and Carrie Bell (Robinson) Wilson; B.A., U. Tulsa, 1942; M.L.S., La. State U., 1950; m. Bruce D. Eagon, June 27, 1943; 1 son, Rex W. Mem. staff circulation dept. Tulsa Pub. Library, 1942-43; planning dept. librarian Douglas Aircraft Corp., Tulsa, 1943-44; circulation librarian U. Tulsa, 1945-50; head librarian Jersey Prodn. Research Co., Tulsa, 1955-65; with Esso Prodn. Research, 1965-70, head librarian, Houston, 1965-70; librarian Esso Math & Systems, Florham Park, N.J., 1970-71; librarian Esso Eastern Inc., Houston, 1971—. John Cotton Dana lectr. U. Denver, 1969. Mem. Spl. Libraries Assn., Am. Assn. Law Librarians, Geosci. Information Soc. Home: 3827 Durness Houston TX 77025 Office: PO Box 1415 Houston TX 77001

EAGON, DIANA STANDAHL (MRS. JOHN ALONZO EAGON), lawyer; b. St. Cloud, Minn., July, 18, 1937; d. Roy Francis and Genevieve Alta (Gullander) Standahl; B.A., U. Chgo., 1958, J.D., 1960; m. John Alonzo Eagon, July 3, 1957; children—Leonard, Christopher, Mark. Admitted to Minn. bar, 1968; staff atty. Nat. Legal Aid and Defender Assn., Chgo., 1960-61; practice law in Champaign, Ill., 1962-67, Mpls., 1968—; mem. firms. Mort A. Segall, 1962-67, Crabtree & Eagon, Mpls., 1968-73, Merlin, Starr & Kiefer, Mpls., 1973—. Councilman, New Brighton, Minn., 1972—. Mem. Minn. State (sec. Hennepin County family law com. 1973-75), Hennepin County bar assns., Nat. Assn. Women Lawyers, Minn. Women Lawyers, New Brighton Bus. and Profl. Women (pres. 1971-72). Home: 1503 Mississippi St St Paul MN 55112 Office: 700 Northwestern Federal Bldg Minneapolis MN 55403

EAKES, LAWANA JUNE NANCE (MRS. JOHN W. EAKES), speech pathologist; b. Lonewolf, Okla., June 25, 1931; d. Jack W. and Pearl Ann (Patton) Nance; B.S. in Speech and Speech Therapy, Okla. Coll. Women, 1953; M.S. in Communicative Disorder, U. Okla., 1964, certificate clin. competence, 1967; m. John W. Eakes, Apr. 19, 1952; children—Nancy Ann (Mrs. Bart Kirchoff), Susan Kay, Rodney William, Phillip John, Ricky Don. Speech therapist pub. schs., El Reno, Okla., 1953-55, Chickasha, Okla., 1959-61, 62-63, U. Okla. Med. Center, 1961-62, 64, Vernon (Tex.) schs., 1965-66; supr. speech and hearing dept. Hissom Meml. Center, Tulsa, 1966-68; instr., Chapman Center Communicative Disorders U. Tulsa, 1968-74, asst. prof., 1974—, clin. supr., 1968—; condr. summer camps in speech and reading, 1956-66; lectr., cons. in field. Mem. policy bd. Early Childhood Devel. Center, Tulsa; lang. cons. Tulsa County Early Childhood Devel. program. Adv. bd. Town and Country Sch. Mem. Am., Okla. speech and hearing assns., Am. Assn. Mental Deficiency, Okla. Assn. Children Learning Disabilities, Green Masque, Pi Zeta Kappa, Zeta Phi Eta. Baptist. Author: (with Jeri Brock) Comprehensive Curriculum for Language Development of the Kindergarten Child, 1973; (with Lorene Gibson) Training Auditory Perception, 1973. Home: 1215 E 8th St Sand Springs OK 74063 Office: 600 S College St Tulsa OK 74063

EAKIN, LOIS EUGENIA, librarian; b. Hunt, Tex., Oct. 13, 1935; d. William Eugene and Lena Lois (Sublett) Eakin; A.A., Schreiner Coll., 1955; B.A., U. Tex., 1962; M.L.S., Tex. Woman's U., 1965. Sec. to adminstrv. dean Schreiner Coll., Kerrville, Tex., 1953-60, head librarian, 1962—. Mem. steering com. Fine Arts Council, Kerrville, Tex., 1973. Bd. dirs. Kerrville Concerts Assn., 1968—, pres. 1971—. Named Woman of Year, Am. Bus. Womens Assn., 1971. Mem. Am. Bus. Womens Assn. (chpt. pres. 1971-72), Tex. Library Assn. (dist. chmn. 1973-74), Hill Country Arts Found., C. of C. Home: 1407 Vesper Dr Kerrville TX 78028 Office: Box 4224 Schreiner College Kerrville TX 78028

EALEY, DOROTHY BROWN, psychologist, educator; b. Amarillo, Tex., Sept. 12, 1930; d. Thomas Milton and Juanita (Watts) Brown; B.S. cum laude Okla. Baptist U., 1952; M.A. with honors, Tex. Tech. Coll., 1954; postgrad. Ill. State U., 1956, Northwestern U., 1958-59, also U. Houston. Sch. psychologist Houston Pub. Schs., 1954-59, dir. psychol. services, 1960-70; chief psychologist Edn. Service Center, Houston, 1970-72; individual practice sch. psychologist, Houston, 1973—; asso. prof. psychology North Harris County Coll., Houston, 1973—. Cons. to various sch. dists. Tex. area, 1973—; partner Ednl. Products, Inc., Houston. Bd. dirs. Child Guidance Center, 1970; bd. dirs. childrens com. Harris County Mental Health Assn., 1970—. Recipient Gold Key award Tex. Assn. for Children with Learning Disabilities, 1965. Mem. Am., Tex. (sec. 1972), Southwestern psychol. assns., Nat. Assn. Sch. Psychologists (charter), Tex. Tchrs. Assn., Council for Exceptional Children. Home: 8903 Valley View Lane Houston TX 77036 Office: 2001 Kirby Dr Suite IIII Houston TX 77019

EARL, CLARA EMMA, county ofcl.; b. Lincoln County, Colo., Sept. 30, 1913; d. James Wilson and Hazel Evelyn (Ford) Six; grad. high sch.; m. Raymond Earl, Feb. 5, 1947; children—Claudia (Mrs. Thomas Harvey Thompson), Carlos Raymond. Bookkeeper, Fowler (Colo.) Truck Line, 1944-45; jr. bookkeeper Colo. Milling & Elevator Co., Las Animas, 1946-47; gen. store keeper Howerton's Grocery, Las Animas, 1950-58; nursing asst. Bent County Meml. Hosp., Las Animas, 1963-66; county clk., recorder Bent County, Las Animas, 1967-70, 71—. Mem. State County Clks. Assn. (mem. motor vehicle com. 1967-68, mem. legislation com. 1970-71), Bus. and Profl. Womens Club (pres. 1970-71). Mem. Christian Ch. Mem. Rebecca Lodge. Home: Rural Route 4 Box 1-F Las Animas CO 81054 Office: PO Box 108 Las Animas CO 81054

EARLEY, JEAN LA VERNE (LMRS. CECIL EARLEY), city ofcl.; b. San Benito, Tex., Feb. 18, 1927; d. Denver Cecil and Eula Mae (Trimm) Hance; student N. Tex. State U., 1971, Tex. State Tech. Inst., 1971-72; m. Cecil Earley, June 8, 1946 (dec.); children—Sue Ellen (Mrs. Arthur Barry Elster), Melanie. Office mgr. Palm Fruit Co., San Benito, 1962-64; sec. Dept. of Pub. Works, Harlingen, Tex., 1965-71; city sec. City of Harlingen, 1972—. Owner, citrus and cattle ranch, Harlingen, 1973—. Vice pres. Harlingen Municipal Fed. Credit Union, 1969-71. Mem. Nat., Tex. City, Lower Rio Grande Valley City (sec., treas. 1971) secs. assns. Methodist. Mem. Order Eastern Star. Home: Rural Route 1 Harlingen TX 78550 Office: 118 E Tyler St Harlingen TX 78550

EARLEY, MILDRED CLARK, councilwoman; b. Lead, S.D., July 20, 1925; d. Charles Thomas and Evelyn Jane (Doney) Clark; student Black Hills Tchrs. Coll., 1944-45; m. Willard John Earley, June 8, 1950; 1 dau., Donna (Mrs. John Randolph Roper). Asst. editor Seaton Pub. Co., Lead, 1948-50; adminstr. Caterpillar Tractor Co., Denver, 1951-54; saleswoman Cline & Hardesty Real Estate, Denver, 1954-58; adminstr. Sch. Dist. #12, Thornton, Colo., 1963-66; mem. Denver City Council, 1964—, now pres. Mem. Denver Regional Council Govts., 1972, Colo. Municipal League, 1972. Mem. Westminster (Colo.) C. of C., Beta Sigma Phi (life). Presbyn. Home: 2000 W 92d St #350 Denver CO 80221

EARLY, MADELINE LEVIN, educator; b. Bklyn., Apr. 1, 1912; d. Hyman and Dora (Siegal) Levin; A.B. magna cum laude, Hunter Coll., 1932; M.A., (coll. scholar), Bryn Mawr Coll., 1933, Ph.D. (coll. fellow), 1936; B.S., Bellevue Sch. Nursing, 1945; m. Harold C. Early, Apr. 8, 1949 (div. July 1958); 1 son, Robert Eric. Instr., Hunter Coll., 1935-42; asst. prof. maths. Eastern Mich. U., 1956-59, asso. prof., 1959-67, prof., 1967—. Served with Nursing Corps, USN, 1945-47. Mem. Am. Math. Soc., Am. Assn. U. Profs., Phi Beta Kappa, Pi Mu Epsilon. Home: 2039 Miller Av Ann Arbor MI 48103 Office: Eastern Michigan University Ypsilanti MI 48197

EARLY, MARGUERITE ELIZABETH CHUMLEY (MRS. FREDERICK JUBAL EARLY), civic worker; b. Birmingham, Ala., Jan. 20, 1913; d. Harry Hughes and Marguerite Elizabeth (Nalls) Chumley; Ph.B. U. Chgo., 1934; m. Frederick Jubal Early, May 16, 1958; children—William Dexter Murdock, Harry Justin Murdock. Dir. area information office, Office Civilian Def., Chgo., 1941-43; pres. adv. bd. U. Cal. at Los Angeles YWCA, 1951-53; mem. bd., founding chmn. Los Angeles Citizens' Commn. for Pub. Schs., 1953-54; mem. com. Vol. Bur., Los Angeles, 1951-56; mem. women's bd. San Francisco Mus. Art, 1969—; mem. citizens' adv. com. Los Guilucos Sch. for Girls, Cal. Youth Authority, Sonoma County, 1967-73. Bd. dirs. Nat. Assn. for Mental Health, 1958-63, Fred J. Early, Jr. Found., 1960—; v.p., trustee Nat. Brain Research Found., Chgo., 1962-70; trustee Pacific Med. Center and Presbyn. Hosp., San Francisco, 1961—, v.p., 1970—; regent U. Pacific, Stockton, Cal., 1967—, mem. exec. com., 1969—. Clubs: Francisca (San Francisco); El Real Club Puerta de Hierro (Madrid, Spain). Home: 1100 Sacramento St San Francisco CA 94108

EARLY, MARTHA EVELYN (MRS. PHILIP NOEL MYERS), pathologist; b. Bellefontaine, O., Nov. 5, 1938; d. Paul Miller and Mary Irene (Vore) Early; B.A., Manchester Coll., 1960; M.D., Ohio State U., 1966; m. Philip Noel Myers, Dec. 17, 1960; children—Susan Jill, Ellen June, Amy Beth. Gen. rotating intern Grant Hosp., Columbus, O., 1966-67, resident pathology, 1967-71; asso. pathologist Grant Hosp., Columbus, 1971—. Diplomate Am. Bd. Pathology. Mem. Am. Med. Women's Assn., Acad. Medicine of Franklin County and Columbus, O., Central Ohio Soc. Pathologists, Am. Soc. Clin. Pathologists, Internat. Acad. Pathologists, Coll. Am. Pathologists. Home: 6578 Masefield St Worthington OH 43085 Office: 309 E State St Columbus OH 43215

EARLYWINE, JOSEPHINE LEWIS (MRS. LAYMAN J. WILKINSON), physician; b. Chgo., Feb. 21, 1920; d. Joseph L. and Elsie (Boradman) Earlywine; B.S., Northwestern U., 1940, M.B., 1943, M.D., 1943; m. Layman J. Wilkinson, Dec. 26, 1941; children—Wanda K., Joseph L. Intern Cook County Hosp., Chgo., 1943-44; resident Cook County Children's Hosp., 1944-46; practice medicine, Wilmette, Ill., 1946—; attending staff Evanston Hosp. Assn.; asso. in pediatrics Northwestern U. Med. Sch., 1946-66, asso. prof., 1966—; attending pediatrician The Cradle, Evanston, 1960-65, med. dir., 1965—; attending staff Wilmette Infant Welfare, 1950—, Children's Meml. Hosp., 1964—. Diplomate Am. Bd. Pediatrics. Fellow Am. Acad. Pediatrics; mem. Inst. Medicine Chgo., Chgo. Pediatric Soc., Chgo. Med. Soc., Delta Zeta. Club: Zonta. Home: 1221 Greenwood Wilmette IL 60091 Office: 1149 Wilmette Av Wilmette IL 60091

EASLEY, ELEANOR BEAMER (MRS. HOWARD EASLEY), physician; b. Bellevue, Ida., Mar. 4, 1907; d. James Daniel and Mae (Van Aucken) Beamer; B.A., U. Ida., 1928; A.M., State U. Ia., 1929; M.D., Duke U., 1934; m. Howard Easley, July 25, 1928. Intern, Duke U., Durham, N.C., 1934-35, 36-37, asst. resident, 1935-36, asst. resident obstetrics and gynecology, 1937-40, resident, 1940-41; practice medicine specializing in obstetrics and gynecology, Durham, 1946—; chief obstetrics and gynecology service Watts Hosp., Durham, 1947-53, 64-67, now mem. staff; asso. clin. prof. obstetrics and gynecology Med. Center, Duke U., 1964—; asst. clin. prof. U. N.C. Med. Sch., Chapel Hill, 1953—. Diplomate Am. Bd. Obstetrics and Gynecology. Fellow A.C.S., Am. Coll. Obstetrics and Gynecology; mem. N.C. (past pres.), South Atlantic obstetrics and gynecology socs., N.C. Med. Soc. (past chmn., mem. com. marriage counseling and family life edn. com.). Home: 10 Lebanon Circle Durham NC 27705 Office: 1821 Green St Durham NC 27705

EASLEY, LOYCE (MRS. MACK EASLEY), artist; b. Weatherford, Okla., June 28, 1918; d. Thomas Webster and Anna (Sanders) Rogers; B.F.A., U. Okla., postgrad. work with Leonard Good; postgrad. in elementary edn. U. N.M.; studied with Frederick Taubes; m. Mack Easley, Nov. 17, 1939; children—June, Roger. Art instr. Okmulgee (Okla.) schs., 1946-47, Hobbs (N.M.) schs., 1947-49; exhibited one-woman shows Mus. N.M. at Santa Fe, Maude Sullivan Galleries, El Paso, Tex., Selected Artists' Galleries, N.Y.C., Garden and Art Center, Lubbock, Tex., Botts Meml. Gallery, Albuquerque, Park Gallery, Dallas, S.W. Tex. State Coll., N.M. Jr. Coll., Tex. Technol. Coll.; exhibited two-woman shows Brigham Young U., Provo, Utah, 1970, Tex. Technol. Coll.; exhibited numerous group shows, some of most recent being: 51st Ann. Exhbn. Allied Artists Am. in Nat. Acad. Design, 6th Ann. Exhbn. S.W. Am. Art in Okla. Art Center, All-Okla. Exhbn., 1964, Jr. League Gallery, Oklahoma City, Random House, Dallas, 1963 Alumni Inst. and 50th Anniversary of U. Okla. Art Sch., Sun Carnival Nat. Juried Exhibit at El Paso Mus., 1963 N.M. Artists Biennial Juried Show at Mus. N.M., Nat. Exhibit Universal Arts at Seattle; work selected for various traveling exhibits; represented in permanent collections First Nat. Bank of Santa Fe, State Capitol N.M., El Paso Mus. Art, Roswell (N.M.) Mus. and Art Center, Tex. Technol. Coll. Active civic projects, including founds. for aiding artists, children. Recipient numerous awards for paintings, most recent being: 1st prize 48th Ann. Fiesta Art Exhbn., 1961, 2d prize 50th Fiesta, 1963, (both Mus. N.M.); awards Roswell Circle Exhibit, 1958, S. Plains Art Guild Show, 1959, El Paso Artist's Ann., 1961, Llano Estacado Exhibit, 1968, 72, 73; nominated for Ford Found. competition for mature artists, 1959; commd. col. a.d.c. to gov. N.M. Home: 812 N Dal Paso Hobbs NM 88240

EASON, CAROL NORWOOD (MRS. CALVIN STUART EASON), physician; b. Taylor, Ark., Mar. 17, 1935; d. Yancy Marion and Idelle (Olive) Norwood; B.S., Centenary Coll., La., 1955; postgrad. U. Ark., 1956-57; M.D., U. Tex., 1959; m. Calvin Stuart Eason, Sept. 30, 1955; 1 son, Richard Stuart. Intern, St. Joseph's Hosp., Fort Worth, 1959-60; resident U. Ark., Little Rock, 1961-62; practice medicine, specializing in anesthesiology, Little Rock, 1963—; mem. staff VA Hosp., 1963—, asst. chief anesthesiology, 1970-74, chief anesthesiology, 1974—; asst. prof. anesthesiology U. Ark. Med. Sch. Diplomate Am. Bd. Anesthesiology. Fellow Am. Coll. Anesthesiologists; mem. Am., Ark. (sec. 1971, pres. 1972) socs. anesthesiology, Sigma Xi, Zeta Tau Alpha. Home: 1903 Cedarhurst Dr Benton AR 72015 Office: 300 E Roosevelt Rd Little Rock AR 72206

EASON, HELGA RUTH HALVORSEN (MRS. MORRIS JACKSON EASON), librarian; b. Nebraska City, Neb.; d. Lee Roy and Luella (Strong) Halvorsen; student Evansville (Ind.) Coll., 1924-25; A.B., Ohio Wesleyan U., 1927; B.S., Simmons Coll., 1929; m. Morris Jackson Eason, Nov. 23, 1947. Circulation asst. N.Y. Pub. Library, 1930-39; br. librarian Evansville Pub. Library, 1941-45; head reference dept. Miami (Fla.) Pub. Library, 1947-52, head community relations dept., 1952—. Mem. program com. WTHS-TV Community Television Found. S. Fla., Inc., 1955-70. Sec., bd. dirs. Miami Finance Welfare Employees Fed. Credit Union, 1947-72, sec., 1963-72; bd. dirs. Miami League Women Voters, 1952-53. Recipient certificate of merit Fla. Fedn. Womens Clubs, 1964; John Cotton Dana Publicity awards for library, 1952-54. Mem. Am. (past dir., com. chmn., 2d, v.p. adult services div. 1968-69 rep. reference and adult services dir. to membership com. task force 1971—), Fla. (Nat. Library Week award 66, sect. pres., com. chmn.), Dade County (past pres.) library assns., City Miami Pub. Library Staff Orgn. (past pres.), Nat. League Am. Pen Women (sec., dir., past v.p., editor Owls Feather 1970-72, 1st v.p. Greater Miami br. 1972-74, pres. 1974—), Laramore Rader Poetry Group (pres. 1959-61). Contbr. articles to profl. jours. Home: 152 NE 46th St Miami FL 33137 Office: 1 Biscayne Blvd Miami FL 33132

EAST, CATHERINE SHIPE, govt. ofcl.; b. Barboursville, W.Va., May 15, 1916; d. U. G. and Bertha (Woody) Shipe; A.B., Marshall U., 1943; m. Charles D. East, July 2, 1937 (div. Aug. 1956); children—Mary Ellen, Elizabeth Rose. With Civil Service Commn., 1939-64, successively clk., staff officer, placement officer, program planner as asst. to chief program planning div., coordinating officer Bur. Programs and Standards, chief career service div. Bur. Recruiting and Examining; exec. sec. Inter-departmental Com. Status Women and Citizens' Adv. Council Status Women, Dept. Labor, Washington, 1964—. Unitarian. Home: 5212 N 32d St Arlington VA 22207 Office: Labor Dept 14th and Constitution Avs NW Washington DC 20210

EASTERLING, MARYCATHYREN (MICKEY) GAMBINO (MRS. VERN E. EASTERLING), civic worker; b. New Orleans, Mar. 6, 1931; d. Michel and Ida Marie (CherAmie) Gambino; m. Vern Edward Easterling, Jan. 22, 1956; children—Vern Edward, Nanci Myke. Mem. Le Petit Theatre deVieu Carre Guild, 1964—; patron New Orleans Spring Fiesta Assn., 1964—; mem. Social Welfare Planning Council, 1966-70, mem. spl. ad-hoc com. to study Half-Way House, 1966-67; mem. Delphian Soc. Study Group on Cultural, Polit. and Psychol. Patterns, 1966-69; mem. women's com. Internat. Jazz Festival and 250th Anniversary Celebration Founding New Orleans, 1967-68; mem. women com. WYES-TV Ednl. Sta., 1967-68; chmn., coordinator spl. com. Project Ednl. Theatre, 1970—; mem. La. Council for Social Services, 1964—; mem. New Orleans Fedn. Chs., 1962—; mem. Friends Cabildo, 1968—; mem. La. Bicentennial Commn., 1973—; mem. Vols. Am. Aux., 1968—; mem. Repertory Theater Bd. 1970—, treas., 1972; sec., treas. La. Festivals, 1969—. Bd. govs. Crippled Children's Hosp. Guild, 1962—, corr. sec., 1965-66, 2d v.p., 1966-67, 1st v.p., 1968, pres., 1969-70, immediate past pres., 1970—, trustee, 1969—, sec. bd., 1973—, organizer Jr. Guild, 1962, adviser to Jr. Guild, 1962-65, chmn. Jr. Guild activities, spl. projects chmn., 1963, 70—, gen. chmn. Easter Seal campaign, 1967-68, membership chmn. guild, 1968; nat. trustee Nat. Easter Seal Soc. for Crippled Children and Adults, 1962-65, La.'s vol. rep. to re-orgn. com., 1962-65, mem. Gen. Assembly, 1962-65, nat. del., 1965—; trustee La. Easter Seal Soc., 1962—, sec., 1963, 2d v.p., 1964, 1st v.p., 1965, pres., 1966-67, La. Ho. Dels., 1962—, chmn. Orleans Parish Easter Seal campaign, 1965, vol. exec. dir., 1966-67; trustee Orleans Parish Easter Seal Soc., 1969-70; bd. dirs. Easter Seal Soc. Pontchartrain region, 1970—, chmn. fund raising com., also mem. personel com., 1970—, chmn. membership dr., 1970-71; mem. women's guild New Orleans Opera House Assn., 1964—, 4th v.p., 1973—, chmn. women's div. 1972—, mem. bd. dirs., 1971—; sec. bd. dirs., chmn. fund raising com. Arthritis Found. Greater New Orleans Area, 1970—; sec. bd. dirs., chmn. membership La. Epilepsy Assn. bd. dirs. Broadway theatre League, 1964—, New Orleans Music and Drama Found., 1967-68, Eye Found. Am., 1970—; bd. govs. Nat. Found. March Dimes, 1965-68, sec., 1966-67, 1st v.p. Met. chpt., 1967-68; trustee Crippled Children's Hosp., 1968—; adv. bd., life mem. Delta Festival Regional Ballet Co., 1969—. Recipient Nat. award for outstanding service to crippled children and adults Nat. Easter Seal Soc., 1970, Outstanding Community Service award Goodwill Industries, 1971. Mem. New Orleans area C. of C. (womens aux. 1964—), Internat. Soc. for Rehab. Disabled (chaplain, chmn. membership com.). Methodist (mem. Womens Soc. Christian Service 1964-67; circle leader 1964-65; rec. sec. 1965-66; local, dist. sec. Social Concerns 1966-67). Clubs: Timberlane, Lamplighter (bd. govs. 1970—; chmn. charity fund. com. 1970-71, chmn. membership and fund raising coms.) (New Orleans). Home: 1744 Lakeshore Dr New Orleans LA 70122

EASTLAKE, MARY GAHAGAN, nurse; b. Mt. Jewett, Pa., Nov. 5, 1902; d. John Spencer and Elizabeth (Ledig) Gahagan; R.N., Johns Hopkins Hosp., 1926; B.S., Columbia, 1942, M.A., 1948; m. Fred L. Eastlake, Feb. 12, 1948 (dec.). Head nurse Johns Hopkins Hosp., 1927-32; supr. Panama, C.Z., U.S. Govt., 1932-33; nurse dir. Bur. Indian Affairs, 1933-38, nurse cons., 1938-43, 46-55, USPHS, 1955-66, chief nursing services div. Indian health, ret., 1966. Served lt. to maj. Nurse Corps U.S. Army, 1943-46, ETO. Decorated Bronze Star Medal, Meritorious Service unit plaque; recipient Meritorious Service award USPHS, 1964. Mem. Am. Hosp. Assn., Am. Pub. Health Assn., Am. Nurses Assn., Nat. League Nursing, Johns Hopkins Nurses Alumnae Assn., Tchrs. Coll. Nurses Alumnae Assn., P.E.O. Mem. Order Eastern Star. Author articles in field. Home: Apt 609 5100 Fillmore Av Alexandria VA 22311

EASTLAND, ANNE STACY, owner girl's camp, civic worker; b. Austin, Tex., May 23, 1922; d. William Gillespie and Agnes Lincoln (Doran) Stacy; B.J., U. Tex. at Austin, 1943; m. Seaborn Eastland, Jr., Sept. 7, 1945; children—Stacy Eastland, Nancy (Mrs. Barry Leaton), Richard. Salesman, continuity writer radio sta. KTBC, Austin, 1943-45; part owner Camp Mystic, Hunt, Tex., 1943—. Del. county and state Democratic convs., 1962-68, Dem. Nat. Conv., 1968; sec. Tex. Dem. Exec. Com., 1964, vice chmn., 1966-68; campaign mgr. senatorial elections. Mem. Houston BiCentennial Com.; mem. civic affairs com. Houston C. of C. Mem. Jr. League, Women's Aux. Houston Bar Assn. (past pres.), Bayou City Dem. Women (past pres.), U. Tex. Alumni Assn. (past sec. Houston), P.T.A. (past sec.), Kappa Kappa Gamma. Episcopalian. Clubs: River Oaks Garden, Forest (past pres. women's assn.) (Houston). Address: 255 Pine Hollow Lane Houston TX 77027

EASTLAND, DOROTHY MARGUERITE PAGE (MRS. G. HAMILTON EASTLAND), journalist; b. Waterbury, Conn., May 31, 1921; d. Charles Albert and Gertrude (Dick) Page; student Willimantic Tchrs. Coll., 1953, Conn. Coll., 1964-65, U. Hartford, 1967—; m. G. Hamilton Eastland, Sept. 6, 1941; 1 dau., Jane. Free-lance writer, 1948—; reporter New London (Conn.) Day,

1962-65; asst. news dir. Conn. Coll., 1965-67; editorials writer, book reviewer, feature writer Hartford (Conn.) Courant, 1967—. Recipient bronze plaque Nat. Found. Hwy. Safety, 1972. Home: 35 Virginia Rd RD2 Oakdale CT 06370 Office: 285 Broad St Hartford CT 06115

EASTLAND, ELIZABETH COLEMAN (MRS. JAMES OLIVER EASTLAND), Senator's wife; b. Doddsville, Miss., Nov. 28, 1909; d. Julian Eugene and Ella (Grider) Coleman; A.B., Sophie Newcomb Coll., 1930; m. James Oliver Eastland (U.S. senator from Miss.), July 6, 1932; children—Nell (Mrs. Culberson Amos), Anne (Mrs. Donald Howdeshell), Susan (Mrs. Champ Terney), Woods Eugene. Mem. Phi Mu. Club: Congressional (Washington). Home: 5116 Macomb St NW Washington DC 20016

EASTMAN, JULIANE B. (MRS. THEODORE R. EASTMAN), state legislator; b. Barre, Vt., Feb. 9, 1904; student Goddard Seminary; m. Theodore R. Eastman; 1 son. Mem. Vt. Ho. of Reps., 1971—. Mem. Altrusa Internat. (2d v.p.), Barre League Women Voters, Order Women Legislators. Mem. Universalist Ch. (Assn. Universalist Women). Home: 29 Currier St Barre VT 05641

EASTMAN, MARIE NORTON, psychiat. social worker; b. Boston, Mar. 14, 1919; d. LeRoy M. and Anne (King) Norton; B.A., U. Kan., 1940; M. Social Sci., Smith Coll., 1942; m. Malcolm A. Eastman, Sept. 26, 1942; 1 dau., Ann Marie. Caseworker, Family Soc. Boston, 1942-43, Judge Baker Guidance Center Boston, 1943-48; chief social worker children's unit Inst. Mental Hygiene, Phila., 1948-49; social worker adoption dept. Jackson County Juvenile Ct., Kansas City, 1956-59; faculty cons. dept. social work U. Kan., 1959-60; 62-63; caseworker Jewish Family Service Kansas City, 1960-62, pvt. practice counseling, Kansas City, 1962—; cons. VA Hosp., Wadsworth, Kan., Shamrock House, Kansas City, Jewish Vocational Service Kansas City. Fellow Kan. Soc. Clin. Social Work (sec., rep. to state council); mem. Nat. Assn. Social Workers (past corr. sec. Mo.-Kan. chpt., past chmn. licensing com. Mo.-Kan. chpt., past rep. Mo. State Council, mem. Kan. council of chpts.), Mo. Assn. Social Welfare, Acad. Certified Social Workers, Am. Assn. Family and Marriage (clin. mem.), Phi Beta Kappa, Sigma Kappa. Home: 2505 W 88th St Leawood KS 66206 Office: 425 E 63d St Kansas City MO 64110

EASTON, JOY BROMBERG (MRS. JASON C. EASTON), educator; b. Charleston, W.Va., June 20, 1925; d. Don Alger and Jessie Ora (Young) Bromberg; B.S., W.Va. Wesleyan Coll., 1946; M.S., W.Va. U., 1950; m. Jason Clark Easton, Nov. 24, 1949. High sch. tchr., Md., N.M., 1946-48; instr. W.Va. U., Morgantown, 1955-67, asst. prof. math., 1967—. Mem. History Sci. Soc., Renaissance Soc. Am., Math. Assn. Am., Nat. Council Tchrs. Math. Democrat. Episcopalian. Contbr. articles to Dictionary Scientific Biography, profl. jours. Home: 312 Raymond St Morgantown WV 26505

EASTWOOD, EVALYN GODFREY (MRS. ARTHUR ROBERT EASTWOOD), mfg. co. exec.; b. Ocean City, N.J., Nov. 6, 1923; d. William Van Hook and Arta Lillian (Berry) Shaw; grad. high sch.; m. Arthur Robert Eastwood, Dec. 3, 1943; children—Arthur Robert, Linda (Mrs. William Stanley Schoonmaker), Wendy (Mrs. Robert Michael McDonough). With L.G. Nester Co., Millville, N.J., 1943—, office mgr., 1965—. Mem. Am. Legion Aux. Home: 1627 W Main St Millville NJ 08332 Office: Buck and Sassafras Sts Millville NJ 08332

EATON, ELAINE RUTH DAWSON, librarian; b. Brooklyn Park, Md., Oct. 27, 1919; d. Arthur Paugorman and Mildred Estelle (Merritt) Dawson; B.A., Wilson Coll., 1942; m. Basil Melville Burton, Apr. 5, 1942 (div.); 1 son, Arthur Lloyd. Adminstrv. asst. to dir. dept. information State of Md., Annapolis, 1948-51, asst. state librarian, 1951-66, librarian dept. legislative reference, 1966—, legislative analyst, 1974—. Mem. Am. Assn. Law Librarians, Spl. Librarians Assn., Nat. Microfilm Assn. Home: RD 5 630 Edwards Rd St Margaret's Annapolis MD 21401 Office: Legislative Reference Library PO Box 348 16 Francis St Annapolis MD 21404

EATON, ELSIE DELORES (MRS. JAMES NATHANIEL EATON), univ. librarian; b. Laurinburg, N.C., Nov. 19, 1935; d. Samuel Luke and Sabrina (Campbell) McLeod; B.A., Talladega Coll., 1957; M.S., Syracuse U., 1959; postgrad. summers Columbia, 1960, No. Ill. U., 1968; m. James Nathaniel Eaton, Aug. 6, 1961; children—Sabrina Elizabeth, James Nathaniel, Robert Hilliary, Samuel Kenyatta. Instr. dept. library sci. Fla. A. and M. U., Tallahassee, 1959-63, asst. catalog librarian Coleman Library, 1964-68, head reference dept., 1968, head readers' services div., 1968—, acting dir. libraries, 1969, instr. study skills, basic studies, 1971-72, library rep. faculty senate, 1971-74. Bd. dirs. Camping Opportunities for Children Orgn. Mem. Southeastern, Fla. library assns., Assn. for Women in Higher Edn., Danforth Assos., Delta Sigma Theta, Alpha Beta Alpha. Club: Jack and Jill America. Democrat. Episcopalian. Home: Route 3 Box 1068 Lonnbladh Rd Tallahassee FL 32303

EATON, MARY JAYNE, educator; b. St. Louis, Nov. 14, 1921; d. Guy Walter and Olivia (Brown) Eaton; B.A., Wash. U., St. Louis, 1949; M.A., U. Toledo, 1952; Ph.D., U. Ala., 1968. Dir. psychol. services Madison County Bd. Edn., Huntsville, Ala., 1961-68; faculty Athens (Ala.) Coll., 1968—, asso. prof., chmn. dept. psychology, 1969—, chmn. dept. spl. edn., 1973—. Cons. edn. and psychology; co-owner Jando Cattery, Stillwater, Okla., 1964—. Bd. dir. Friends Family Court, 1972—. Mem. Am., Southwestern psychol. assns., United Burmese Cat Fanciers, Cat Fanciers Assn., Huntsville Felines, Chi Beta Phi, Kappa Delta Phi. Home: Rural Route 2 Box 318 Madison AL 35758 also Rural Route 5 Box 99 Stillwater OK 74074 Office: Athens College Athens AL 35611

EAVES, CAROLYN VIRGINIA, librarian; b. Marlin, Tex., Mar. 24, 1935; d. Lloyd Leroy and Sybial Velma (Odneal) Eaves; student Baylor U., 1953-55; B.A., Tex. Women's U., 1956, M.L.S., 1957. Asst. circulation librarian Stephen F. Austin U., Nacogdoches, Tex., 1957-59; librarian Tex. Christian U., Harris Coll. of Nursing, Ft. Worth, 1959-61; librarian Amon Carter Mus. Western Art, Ft. Worth, 1961-63; acquisition librarian Trinity U., San Antonio, 1963-65; asso. librarian U. Tex., M.D. Anderson Hosp., Houston, 1965-67; head librarian Howard Payne Coll., Brownwood, Tex., 1967—. Mem. Am., Tex., Med. library assns. Home: Rural Route 3 Box 114 Brownwood TX 76801 Office: Howard Payne College Brownwood TX 76801

EBAUGH, ELIZABETH BROWN (MRS. FRANK WRIGHT EBAUGH), civic worker; b. Jacksonville, Tex.; d. John Lemuel and Jewel (Newton) Brown; B.A., U. Colo., 1925; M.A., Tchrs. Coll., Columbia U., 1927; m. Frank Wright Ebaugh, Feb. 22, 1930; 1 dau., Betty Jane (Mrs. Gordon B. McFarland, Jr.). Kindergarten tchr., Port Arthur, Tex., 1927-30. Bd. dirs. Jacksonville Pub. Library, 1944—, pres., 1944-46, curator, organizer Vanishing Texana Mus., 1965—. Mem. Cherokee County Hist. Survey Com., 1964—. Recipient Appreciation plaque Jacksonville Library, 1969. Mem. D.A.R. (charter; registrar 1965—), Chi Omega. Presbyn. (historian 1965-66). Home: 428 S Patton St Jacksonville TX 75766

EBERDT, MARY GERTRUDE, psychologist; b. Ft. Madison, Ia., Dec. 15, 1932; d. Edward J. and Catherine (Storms) Eberdt; B.S., Mt. Angel Coll., 1956; M.Ed., U. Portland, 1958; Ph.D., U. Ore., 1965. Tchr., Evergreen Jr.-Sr. High Sch., Vancouver, Wash., 1958-61, Hudson's Bay High Sch., Vancouver, 1961-62; counseling psychologist Wis. State U., Oshkosh, 1965-71; psychologist Winnebago State Hosp. (Wis.), 1971-72; cons. psychologist Midwestern Psychol. Services, Madison, Wis., 1972-73; cons. community mental health, Green Bay, Wis., 1973-74, Los Angeles, 1974—. Mem. Am. Psychol. Assn., Am. Personnel and Guidance Assn., Soc. for Projective Techniques, Am. Acad. Psychotherapists, Am. Soc. Clin. Hypnosis. Home and office: 202 N LaPeer Dr Beverly Hills CA 90211

EBERHARDT, BARBARA ANNE, TV and theatre producer; b. Orange, N.J., Dec. 20, 1943; d. U. Seth and Barbara Knox (Britten) Eberhardt; B.F.A., Denison U., 1965; M.A., Hunter Coll., 1969; postgrad. Coll. City N.Y., 1971—. Dir., founder theatre program Iona Coll., New Rochelle, N.Y., 1968-71; producer New Playwrights, N.Y.C., 1971-72; asso. producer Women of Year TV spl., 1973, 74; ind. producer-dir. documentary film shorts, 1974—. Mem. Am. Theatre Assn. (co-chmn. region 2, 1971-73), Theatre Festival Assn. (co-chmn. region 4, 1969-71), Nat. Thespian Soc., Inst. for Theatre Design and Tech. Home: 332 W 101st St New York NY 10025

EBERHART, CATHERINE LUCILLE (MRS. CHARLES MORACE EBERHART), retail trade exec., mus. adminstr.; b. Douglas, Wyo., Apr. 21, 1922; d. Eugene Keep and Mary Katherine Lucille (Mangelsen) Farlee; grad. pub. high sch., 1940; m. Charles Morace Eberhart, Dec. 1, 1940; children—Donald Glenn, Ronald Charles. Co-owner, mgr. Western Trading Post, Denver, 1952—; supr., coordinator Chief Iron Shell Mus., Denver, 1969—. Mem. S. Denver Civic Assn., White Buffalo Council Am. Indians, Denver Mus. Natural History, Denver Art Mus. Home: 187 S Zuni Denver CO 80223 Office: Chief Iron Shell Museum 12 W Irvington Denver CO 80223 also Western Trading Post Inc 31 Broadway Denver CO 80203

EBERLE, ROSELYN ANN, pub. relations exec.; b. Chgo., Dec. 6, 1940; d. Christian Chester and Augusta Lyle (Prather) Eberle; student Gulf Park Coll. for Women, 1958-59; B.A., U. Miss., 1963; M.A., Memphis State U., 1973. Copywriter, Cranford Johnson Advt., Inc., Little Rock, 1963; mem. editorial staff Ark. Gazette, Little Rock, 1964-66; Tri State soc. editor Comml. Appeal, Memphis, 1966-69; editorial asst., Memphis State U. Press, 1969-70, editor, 1970-72; asso. editor publs. U. Tenn. Med. Units, 1972-73; account exec. Holiday Inns, Inc., Memphis, 1973—. Mem. Women in Communication, Zeta Tau Alpha. Republican. Methodist. Office: 3754 Lamar Av Memphis TN 38118

EBERT, CHARLOTTE KING, ins. co. exec.; b. Honolulu, Feb. 18, 1914; d. Samuel Wilder and Pauline Nawahineokalai (Evans) King; student Mills Coll., U. Cal. at Berkeley; m. Robert Baldwin Evert II, Dec. 24, 1960; children—Michael and Timothy McAndrews. Adminstrv. sec. to Hawaii delegation U.S. Congress, Washington, 1935-40; gen. agt., mgr. King Ins. Agy., Honolulu, 1955-61; v.p. King, Ltd., real estate, 1964-69; sales rep. Hawaiian Ins. & Guaranty, 1967. Mem. Oahu League Republican Women. Mem. Hawaii Assn. Real Estate Bds., Ins. Women's Club Honolulu, Daus. of Hawaii, Prince Kuhio Hawaiian Civic Club. Home: 700 Richards St Honolulu HI 96813

EBERT, ELOISE Q(UEEN), librarian; b. Scotts Bluff, Neb., Aug. 17, 1911; d. Ernest W. and Daisy (Gamble) Ebert; student Park Coll., 1929-31; B.S., U. Minn., 1936; M.S., U. Ill., 1957. Librarian, Sauk Centre, Minn., 1936-37, Falls City, Neb., 1937-42; post librarian, Ft. Warren, Wyo., 1942-45; AUS librarian, European Command, 1945-49; adminstrv. asst., then asst. state librarian Ore. State Library, Salem, 1949-59, state librarian, 1959—. Sr. trustee Salem Art Assn. Named Woman of Achievement Theta Sigma Phi, 1965. Mem. Am. Assn. State Libraries (pres. 1963-64), A.L.A. (council 1951-57), Pacific N.W. (pres. 1961-62), Ore. (exec. bd.) library assns., Am. Library Trustee Assn. (2d v.p. 1970-71), Am. Assn. U. Women (Ore. internat. relations chmn. 1953-55), League Women Voters (pres. Salem 1953-55). Ore. UN Assn., Ore. Hist. Soc. (dir.), Fedn. Western Outdoor Clubs, Chemeketans, Beta Phi Mu, Alpha Phi, Theta Alpha Phi, Delta Kappa Gamma (state hon. mem.). Home: 1100 Chemeketa St NE Salem OR 97301 Office: Ore State Library Salem OR 97310

EBKEN, RUTH MARJORIE, educator; b. Pitts.; d. William J. and Edith (Poerstel) Ebken; B.F.A., M.F.A., Carnegie-Mellon U.; postgrad. Columbia Tchrs. Coll., summer 1959, U. Pitts., 1956-58, Internat. Sch. Art, 7 summers abroad, Montes Spanish Studio. Tchr. art pub. schs., Dormont, Pa., 1934-35, Pitts., 1935-37; supr. art Pitts. Pub. Schs., 1937-63, dir. art, 1963—. Lectr., cons. Carnegie Mellon U., 1950-53; lectr. U. Pitts., 1960-61, Pa. State U., summer 1962; tour dir. Nat. Art Edn. Assn.-N.E.A., Czechoslovakia, 1966, Greece, 1967, Hawaii, 1967; P.R., 1969. Mem. Nat. Art Edn. Assn. (pres. 1967-69), Eastern Arts Assn. (pres. 1960-62), Nat. Council Adminstrv. Women in Edn. (v.p. 1963-65), Assn. Artists of Pitts., Internat. Soc. for Edn. Through Art, Women's Clan Carnegie-Mellon U. (mem. bd. 1969-71), Adminstrv. Women in Edn. (membership chmn. Pitts. council 1970-71), Delta Kappa Gamma. Club: Altrusa (sec. 1969-71, v.p. 1971-72, pres. 1972-73) (Pitts.). Editor: Prospect and Retrospect, 1960; Art Edn. Bull., 1961-62; mem. editorial adv. bd. Sch. Arts Mag., 1967—. Home: 3210 Niagara St Pittsburgh PA 15213 Office: 341 S Bellefield Av Pittsburgh PA 15213

EBLE, MARY MARTHA COATES (MRS. JOHN F. EBLE), librarian; b. Akron, O., Dec. 6, 1917; d. William Lodge and Josephine (Behra) Coates; B.A., Notre Dame Coll. for Women, 1939; M.S. in L.S., Case Western Res. U., 1967, postgrad., 1967—; m. John F. Eble, May 12, 1941; children—Martha (Mrs. Robert Dickinson), John, Clare (Mrs. Robert Ruffing), Thomas, William, James, Robert. Library clk. Cleveland Heights (O.) High Sch., 1939-40; bookmobile librarian Cuyahoga County Pub. Library, Cleve., 1963; sch. librarian, library-media specialist, coordinator Fairview Park (O.) Bd. Edn., 1963—. Adj. asst. prof. Case Western Res. U. Sch. Library Sci., 1970—. Mem. A.L.A. (E.P. Dutton-John Macrae award 1972), Am., Ohio Assns. sch. librarians, Ednl. Media Council of Ohio, N.E.A., Ohio Edn. Assn., Christ Child Soc., Beta Phi Mu. Home: 22545 Marlys Dr Rocky River OH 44116 Office: 4507 W 213th St Fairview Park OH 44126

EBRIGHT, ELIZABETH JOAN, librarian; b. Baldwin, Kan., Dec. 1, 1911; d. Homer Kingsley and Marie (Moorhead) Ebright; A.B., Baker U., 1933; A.M., U. Kan., 1936; B.S. in L.S., U. Ill., 1938. High sch. and reference librarian Kewanee, Ill., 1938-42; asst. librarian Washburn U., Topeka, 1942-45, librarian, 1945-65, spl. instr. English, Baker U., Baldwin, Kan., 1966—, reader's adviser Univ. Library, 1970-72. Trustee, Baldwin Library Bd., 1965—. Mem. Am., Kan. library assns., Am. Assn. U. Women, Poetry Soc. Kan., Nat. League Am. Pen Women, Nat. Council Tchrs. English, P.E.O., Alpha Chi Omega, Phi Beta Kappa, Beta Phi Mu. Methodist. Clubs: Nat. Quill, Kansas Authors'. Author of poems published in popular mags. Home: Baldwin KS 66006

ECHARD, MARGARET, author; b. Brazil, Ind.; d. Charles C. and Braddie (Porter) Echard; grad. Dillenbeck Sch. Drama. Author numerous plays for McCall-Bridge Stock Co., 1922-29; writer radio serials, Kansas City, Mo. Mem. P.E.N. Author: Stand In For Death, 1940; A Man Without Friends, 1940; Before I Wake, If This Be Treason, 1944; The Dark Fantastic; The Return of Christopher, 1951; The Unbelieving Wife; So Brief A Journey Wife; Born In Wedlock, 1956; Tomorrow At Three; Survival Test; I Met Murder on The Way, 1964; (with Bernard Garbett) Hoofs, Paws and Hands, 1968. Home: 6443 Ivarene Av Hollywood CA 90068

ECHELMAN, SHIRLEY T. (MRS. ELLIOTT J. ECHELMAN), librarian; b. Omaha, Oct. 7, 1934; d. Nathan William and Rose (Ricks) Gimple; student U. Wis., 1952-54; B.Sc., U. Neb., 1956; M.L.S., Rutgers U., 1966; m. Elliott J. Echelman, Oct. 3, 1964. Librarian, BEA Asso., Inc., N.Y.C., 1960-65; research librarian Chem. Bank, N.Y.C., 1966-70, chief librarian, 1971—. Lectr. Rutgers U. Grad. Sch. Library Sci., 1970-71. Mem. editorial adv. bd. Jeffrey Norton Pub. Co., N.Y.C., 1973—; trustee Pub. Affairs Information Service, Inc., N.Y.C., 1972—. Mem. Spl. Libraries Assn. (v.p. N.Y. chpt. 1968-70, chmn. bus. and finance div. 1971-72, div. liaison officer 1972—), Pi Gamma Mu, Beta Phi Mu. Home: 250 W 94th St New York City NY 10025 Office: 20 Pine St New York City NY 10015

ECHOLS, DOROTHY JANE HILLE (MRS. JAMES EWELL ECHOLS, JR.), civic worker; b. Collins, Miss., June 4, 1932; d. Hollie Rich and Bessie Mae (McKenzie) Shoemake; B.S., U. So. Miss., 1954, M.S., 1967; m. James Ewell Echols, Jr., Nov. 12, 1970; children—Kimberly, Scott Alan. Counselor, acad. adviser U. So. Miss., 1965-67, asst. dean women, 1967-68, dean of women, 1968-71. Active P.T.A., Cub Scout Am. Recipient Faculty Outstanding Service award U. So. Miss., 1970-71. Mem. Nat. Assn. Women Deans and Counselors, So. U. Student Govt. Assn. (exec. mem.), Am. Assn. U. Women (1st v.p.), Protestant Women of Chapel, Delta Kappa Gamma, Phi Mu. Mem. Order Eastern Star. Club: Officers Wives (pres. 1972-73 (Ft. McPherson, Ga.) (chmn. Korean welfare com. 1973-74 Seoul). Home: KRE HQ APO San Francisco CA 96301

ECHOLS, IVOR TATUM (MRS. SYLVESTER J. ECHOLS), social worker; b. Oklahoma City, Dec. 28, 1919; d. Israel E. and Katie (Bingley) Tatum; A.B., U. Kan., 1942; postgrad. (A.R.C. scholar) U. Neb., 1945-46; M.S. in Social Work (Nat. Urban League fellow, Porter R. Lee fellow), Columbia, 1952, postgrad. (Nat. Inst. Mental Health fellow), U. So. Cal., 1961-62, D.S.W., 1968; m. Kenneth Johnston, Dec. 28, 1948 (div. June 1951); 1 dau., Kalu Helene; m. 2d, Sylvester J. Echols, June 13, 1954; 1 son, Kim Arnett. Tchr. social studies high sch., Holdenville, Okla., 1942-43, Geary, Okla., 1943-45; caseworker A.R.C., Chgo., 1946-47; resident group worker, Dosoris House for Teen-Age Girls, Community Services Soc., N.Y.C., 1950-51; supr. group work Walnut Grove Center Neighborhood Clubs Clubs, Oklahoma City, 1948-51; program dir. Camp Lookout YWCA, Denver, 1951; dir. program services Presbyn. Neighborhood Services, Detroit, summer 1960, supr. group work Merrill-Palmer Inst., Detroit, 1951-70; asst. dir. Merrill-Palmer Camp, Dryden, Mich., 1951-59; prof. Sch. Social Work, U. Conn., West Hartford, 1970—. Mem. Ad Hoc Com. Citizens Concerned with Equal Ednl. Opportunity, Detroit, 1964—; cons. to N.E.A. Conf. Family Camping Washington, 1959, ednl. film Scott Paper Co., Phila., 1963, 64; summer study skills project Presbyn. Ch. Bd. Nat. Missions, Knoxville, Tenn., 1965—; pres. Protestant Community Services, Detroit, 1969-70. Recipient Sojourner Truth award Detroit chpt. Nat. Assn. Negro Bus. and Profl. Women, 1969. Mem. Nat. Assn. Colored Women's Clubs (participant White House Conf. on Children and Youth 1960), A.M.E. Ministers Wives, Acad. Certified Social Workers, Delta Sigma Theta. Mem. A.M.E. Ch. Home: 51 Chestnut Dr Windsor CT 06095 Office: Sch of Social Work U Conn Westartford CT 06007

ECKARD, JANET MARY BORIS, occupational therapist; b. Phila., Dec. 8, 1946; d. Alfred George and Mary (Takas) Boris; B.A. (scholar) Beaver Coll., 1968; certificate occupational therapy U. Pa. (scholar), 1970; m. Ralph William Eckard, May 1, 1971; children—Christine Mary, Wende Margaret. Staff occupational therapist U.S. Naval Hosp., Phila., 1970-71, Princeton (N.J.) Hosp., 1971. Leader handicapped scouts Freedom Valley Council Girl Scouts U.S., 1973—. Home: 85 Chestnut Cr Richboro PA 18956

ECKARDT, GLADYS EVANGELINE (MRS. KARL PAUL KONRAD ECKARDT), librarian; b. Hartland, N.Y., Sept. 7, 1912; d. Isaac John and Flora Caroline (Hofmeister) Beach; student U. Buffalo, 1930-32; B.A., U. Rochester, 1934; M.A., Rutgers State U., 1958; m. Karl Paul Konrad Eckardt, Oct. 19, 1940; 1 dau., Susan (Mrs. Edward Misiewicz). Dir. Wood-Ridge (N.J.) Pub. Library, 1956-59, Rutherford (N.J.) Pub. Library, 1959—. Trustee Wood-Ridge Pub. Library, 1954-56. Mem. Am., N.J. (sec. 1964-65, chmn. N.J. insts. 1968), Bergen-Passaic (pres. 1964-66) library assns., N.Y. Pub. Relations Council, Bergen County Small Libraries (v.p. 1963), Rutgers Alumni Assn. Home: 535 Moonachie Av Wood Ridge NJ 07075 Office: Park Av Rutherford NJ 07070

ECKBLAD, EDITH GWENDOLYN (MRS. MARSHALL DANIEL ECKBLAD), author; b. Baltic, S.D., Apr. 14, 1923; d. Leander Gerhardt and Louise Marie (Simonson) Berven; student U. Wis., 1940, 61, Wheaton Coll., 1941-42, Union Grove Tchrs. Coll., 1967; m. Marshall Daniel Eckblad, June 9, 1943; children—Mark, Jonathan, James, Nancy, Peter. Sec., J.I. Case Co. also Childrens Service Soc., Racine, Wis., 1943-44; free lance writer, editorial work David C. Cook Pub. Co., Elgin, Ill., 1960-61; substitute tchr. Racine Elementary Schs., 1968-69; tchr. creative writing and workshop Gateway Tech. Inst., Racine, 1972. Guest author Chgo. Reading Round Table, 1967, Pub. Library and Mus. of Sci. and Industry Book Fair, 1969-70. Asso. mem. St. Luke's Hosp. Aux., Racine, 1970—. Mem. Nat. League Am. Pen Women, Council for Wis. Writers (dir.), Wis. Regional Writers. Lutheran. Club: Federated Women's (Racine). Author: Just Marty, 1947; Living With Jesus, 1955; Something for Jesus, 1959; Danny's Straw Hat, 1962; Kindness is a Lot of Things, 1965; A Smile is to Give, 1969; Danny's Orange Christmas Camel, 1970; Soft as the Wind, 1974. Home: 5224 Spring St Racine WI 53406

ECKEL, VIRGINIA ELAINE, librarian; b. Anderson, Ind., Dec. 20, 1924; d. Howard and Edith Irene (Vance) Eckel; B.S., Ball State U., 1946; M.A., George Peabody Coll., 1953. Librarian, Sinclair Coll., Dayton, O., 1946-52; br. librarian Tech. Library, Wright Patterson AFB, O., 1952-61, cataloger, 1961-64, librarian Sch. Systems and Logistics, Air Force Inst. Tech., 1964—. Instr. Wittenberg U., Springfield, O., 1967—. Mem. Spl. Libraries Assn. (chmn. mil. div. 1972-73). Methodist. Home: 2993 Westcott Dr Kettering OH 45420 Office: School of Systems and Logistics Library Air Force Institute of Technology Wright Patterson AFB OH 45433

ECKER, CAROL ADELE (MRS. KENNETH ECKER), veterinarian; b. Mishawaka, Ind., Sept. 26, 1940; d. Marcel and Adele (Sergeant) Van Paemel; D.V.M., Purdue U., 1964; m. Kenneth Ecker, July 1, 1969; 1 son by previous marriage, Larry; 1 dau., Christy. Owner, resident vet. Clayview Animal Clinic and Clayview Farms, South Bend, Ind. 1964—. Active in various 4-H work, 1958—. Mem. St. Joe County Fair Bd., 1972-74; mem. Twp. 4-H Adv. Bd., 1972-74. Recipient Lions Club award for service to 4-H, 1972. Mem. Am., Ind.

quarter horse assns., Hoosier Palomino Assn. (pres. 1962-63), Purdue U. Alumni Assn. (corr. sec. 1964-69). Club: Altrusa (South Bend). Home: 50871 Ironwood Rd Granger IN 46530 Office: 52464 US 31 North South Bend IN 46637

ECKERSLEY, HELEN ELIZABETH PALMER (MRS. ROBERT N. ECKERSLEY), civic worker; b. Akron, O., May 23, 1921; d. Frank Carlton and Gladys (Thompson) Palmer; grad. high sch.; m. Robert N. Eckersley, June 28, 1941; children—Bruce Loc, Richard Laurence, Tari Louise. Troop leader Girl Scouts U.S.A., Waverly, Pa., 1964-68; sec. Scranton (Pa.) Vistas, 1967-70, pres.-elect., 1970-72; chmn. Abington dist. Lackawanna United Fund, 1958-60; hosp. vol. worker Community Med. Center, Scranton, 1964-66; mem. steering com. Abington Meals-on-Wheels; mem. Jr. League Scranton. Mem. Theta Sigma. Clubs: Abington Junior Women's, Waverly Women's (dir.), Country (Scranton). Home: Miller Rd Waverly PA 18471

ECKERT, RUTH MINNIE, coll. dean; b. Kingston, N.Y., July 27, 1922; d. Russell Arthur and Alice Williams (Field) Eckert; student Nyack Coll., 1947-50; B.A., Vennard Coll., 1955; postgrad. State U. Ia., 1956; M.S. in Edn., Drake U., 1959-60. Prof. English, Vennard Coll., University Park, Ia., 1961—. Mem. Christian Assn. Deans of Women (sec. treas. 1972—), Bus. and Profl. Women's Club. Home: University Park IA 52595 Office: Vennard College University Park IA 52595

ECKERT, SHAREN KAY, human factors engr.; b. Painesville, O., Aug. 28, 1945; d. Clayton George and Norma Irene (Champion) Eckert; B.S. in Math., Westminster Coll., 1967; M.S. in Mech. Engring., U. Ariz., 1970. Asso. engr. Lockheed Missiles & Space Co., Sunnyvale, Cal., 1969-72, mgmt. tng. operations personnel devel. program, 1972-73, human factors engr., 1973—. Instr. Opportunities Industrialization Center West, Menlo Park, Cal., 1970-72; cons. Mountain View Planning Commn., 1971. Mem. Mountain View Citizens Liaison Com., 1971-72; mem. adv. bd. El Camino Alcoholism Treatment Center, Sunnyvale, 1974. Mem. Human Factors Soc., Nat. Orgn. Women, Women's Equity Action League, Kappa Mu Epsilon, Phi Mu. Home: PO Box 3 Saratoga CA 95070 Office: D 62-05 B 151 Lockheed Missiles & Space Co Sunnyvale CA 94088

ECKLEY, MARY M., editor; b. Dayton, O.; d. Alexander Munn and Clara (Hoskinson) Eckley; B.S., Simmons Coll., 1943; postgrad. Vassar Coll., 1949; A.M., Columbia, 1952. Asst. editor Everywoman's mag., N.Y.C., 1952-53; asso. editor Good Housekeeping mag., N.Y.C., 1953-58; asso. editor McCall's mag., N.Y.C., 1960-64, sr. editor food sect., 1964—. Active A.R.C., Washington, France, Germany, 1944-49; active N.Y.C. YWCA. Editor The New McCall's Cookbook, 1973. Home: 55 East End Av New York City NY 10028 Office: McCall's Magazine 230 Park Av New York City NY 10017

ECKLOFF, MAURINE CHRISTINE NELSON (MRS. WARREN NATHANIEL ECKLOFF), educator; b. Upland, Neb., Apr. 18, 1928; d. Henry Victor and Christine (Raun) Nelson; student Hastings Coll., 1945-47; B.A., U. Denver, 1948; M.S., Kearney State Coll., 1961; Ph.D., U. Neb., 1974; m. Warren Nathaniel Eckloff, Sept. 3, 1954; children—Nathan, Ann, Ward. Script writer radio sta. KNX-CBS, Los Angeles, 1949; tchr. speech, English pub. schs., Broken Bow, Neb., 1949-50; program mgr., broadcaster radio sta. WGET, Gettysburg, Pa., 1951-52; traffic mgr. KBTV, Denver, 1953-54; telecaster Woman's Voice program KHOL-TV, Kearney, Neb., 1954-51; asst. prof. speech Kearney State Coll., 1962—. Bd. Edn. Minden (Neb.) Pub. Schs., 1972—. Kearney State Coll. research grantee, 1972, 73. Mem. Am. Women in Radio and TV (pres. Neb. chpt. 1958), Am. Assn. Univ. Women (first v.p. Neb. div. 1962-64), Kearney State Coll. Edn. Assn. (pres. 1966-67), Neb. Speech Communication Assn. (first v.p. 1971-73), Speech Communication Assn. Am., Neb. State Edn. Assn., Delta Kappa Gamma, Sigma Tau Delta, Gamma Phi Beta. Methodist (sec. TV, Radio and Film Commn., Neb. conf., 1960-62). Home: Rural Route 1 Minden NE 68959 Office: Kearney State College Kearney NE 68847

ECKMAN, BERTHA ELIZABETH, educator; b. Berlin, Pa.; d. Frank and Augusta (Olson) Eckman; student Cal. Tchrs. Coll., 1929-31; B.S., U. Pitts., 1940, postgrad., 1950-61; in service tng. Ind. Tchrs. Coll., 1959-61. Tchr., Brothers Valley Twp. Sch., Berlin, Pa., 1931-33, Lincoln Twp., Somerset, Pa., 1934, Garrett, Pa., 1934-44, Maple Ridge Sch., 1944—; supervising tchr. California (Pa.) State Tchrs. Coll. Exec. sec. Somerset County Council Christian Edn., 1956—, editor yearbooks, 1958-61; youth counselor Somerset County Youth Camp, 1954—, tchr. young people's class; campaign chmn. A.R.C., Somerset, 1954-57; promotional sec. Somerset Council Sunday Sch. Convs., 1957-68; mem. synodical affairs com. Fgn. Missions West Allegheny Conf. Central Pa.; campaign chmn. Allegheny Luth. Homes Aux., Johnstown, Pa.; pres. Garrett Parish Joint Council Luth. Ch. Am.; exec. sec. Garrett Parish Luth. Ch. Am.; pres. Somerset County aux. Allegheny Luth. Home for the Aged, Johnstown, Pa. Mem. Nat. (del. to centennial conv. 1957, del. to classroom tchrs. conf.), Pa. (pres. Somerset County) edn. assns., United Ch. Women, Nat. Geog. Soc. Educators Beneficial Assn., Delta Kappa Gamma (chpt. pres., dir. work program), Internat. Platform Assn., Marquis Biog. Library Soc. Republican. Lutheran (program coordinator spl. spiritual programs 1936-68). Home: RD 4 Berlin PA 15530 Office: Maple Ridge Sch RD 3 Somerset PA 15501

ECKMAN, BETTY ROSE MICKELSON (MRS. LESTER LLOYD ECKMAN), city ofcl.; b. Killdeer, N.D., Aug. 10, 1919; d. William Godfrey and Myrtle Adelaide (Sexton) Mickelson; grad. high sch., Selah, Wash.; m. Lester Lloyd Eckman, Nov. 24, 1939. Reporter Lewiston (Ida.) Morning Tribune, 1949-58; city treas. City of Clarkston (Wash.), 1958—. Sec., publicity chmn. Asotin County Tb Assn., 1958-65; counselor citizenship awards Boy Scouts Am., 1967—. Mem. Clarkston C. of C. (pres. 1964-65, sec. 1965-67), P.E.O. Methodist (treas. 1955). Mem. Order Eastern Star (past matron), Daus. of Nile. Home: 1505 9th St PO Box 14 Clarkston WA 99403 Office: City Hall 30 5th St Clarkston WA 99403

ECKS, BEATRICE LOUISE, business exec.; b. N.Y.C.; d. Henry Frederick and Clara-Kathryn (Ott) Ecks; A.B., Cornell U.; postgrad. Columbia, N.Y. U., U. Rochester. Dir. Jr. High Sch., Friends Sem., N.Y.C., 1933-44; program adviser, aviation dir. Girl Scouts U.S.A., 1944-49; asst. to pres. Plampin Litho. Co., 1949-51, v.p., 1951-55, dir., 1951-59; owner, operator Bealou Promotions, product introduction and mail order, N.Y.C., 1955-57; v.p. Newtek, Inc., product photography, Long Island City, N.Y., 1956-60, also dir.; dir. I-S Ultd., Inc., 1955—, v.p., 1959—; exec. asst. to pres. Identical Form, Inc., N.Y.C., 1963—; dir., sec. Panhellenic House Assn., 1939-49. Mem. Friendly Visitors of Women's House of Detention. Mem. Advt. Women N.Y., Pi Beta Phi. Episcopalian. Clubs: Underfashions, Pilot (N.Y. pres. 1959-60). Home: 444 E 20th St New York City NY 10009 Office: 17 W 60th St New York City NY 10023

ECKSTEIN, ELEANOR FOLEY, educator; b. Chgo., Mar. 13, 1940; d. Jackson Foley and Edith (Burtch) Eckstein; student Whittier Coll., 1957-59; B.S. (Omicron Nu scholar 1960-61), U. Cal. at Los Angeles, 1961; M.S., U. Wash., 1966; Ph.D. (Mead Johnson award 1968-69), Kan. State U., 1969. Adminstrv. dietitian, head dietary dept. Burien Gen. Hosp., Seattle, 1962-65; instr. instn. mgmt. Carnegie-Mellon U., Pitts., 1966-67; asst. prof. food mgmt. U. Cal. at Berkeley, 1969-73; prof. dietetics Miss State Coll. for Women, Columbus, 1973—. Cons. U.S. Army Natick Labs., 1969-72, dir. dietetics, 1970—. Mem. Am. Dietetic Assn. (mem. scholarship and awards bd. 1970-73), Am. Home Econs. Assn., Am. Assn. U. Women, Am. Assn. U. Profs., Inst. Food Tech., N.Y. Acad. Scis., Computer Applications Council, Sigma Xi, Iota Sigma Pi, Phi Kappa Phi, Omicron Nu. Club: Toastmistress (Seattle). Home: 520 10th St South #22 Columbus MS 39701

EDELEN, SISTER M. LOYOLA, educator; b. Louisville, Mar. 4, 1925; d. Collings J. and Catherine (Feeney) Edelen; B.S., Villanova U., 1955, M.A., 1960. Tchr. elementary sch., Tenn., La., 1948-54; prin., community supr. St. Mark the Evangelist, N.Y.C., 1958-64, Holy Providence, Phila., 1964-65; asst. prof. edn. Blessed Sacrament Coll., Cornwell Heights, Pa., 1964-65; dir. div. edn. Xavier U. La., New Orleans, 1965-67, coordinator ednl. projects, 1968—, supr. Vista, 1968-70, dir. Tchr. Corps, 1968-72, coordinator for career opportunities, 1970—, coordinator community based right to read, 1972—; interagy. career devel. specialist New Orleans Pub. Schs., 1973—. Mem. Archdiocesan Sch. Bd., 1970-71. Pres., Childrens House, Montessori Sch., New Orleans, 1966-71; mem. exec. council Center for Sch. Desegregation, New Orleans, 1968-71; mem. New Orleans Archdiocesan Commn. for Human Rights, 1969—; dir. Neighborhood OEO Recreation Program, 1967—; mem. nat. adv. com. Early Childhood Edn., 1969—; initiator Home Start, 1970. Bd. dirs. Dryodec St YMCA. Mem. Assn. for Supervision and Curriculum Devel., Conf. La. Coll. and Univs. Home: 3912 Pine St New Orleans LA 70125 Office: 3912 Pine St New Orleans LA 70125

EDELMAN, LILY JUDITH PODVIDZ (MRS. NATHAN EDELMAN), educator; b. San Francisco; d. Morris and Rachel (Margolis) Podvidz; B.A., Hunter Coll., 1936; M.A., Columbia, 1938, diploma in adult edn. Tchrs. Coll., 1954; m. Nathan Edelman, May 30, 1936; 1 dau., Jean Louise (dec.). Edn. dir. East and West Assn., N.Y.C., 1941-51; free-lance writer, editor U.S. Dept. State, N.Y.C., 1952-53; exec. sec. Nat. Acad. for Adult Jewish Studies, N.Y.C., 1954-57; dir. Adult Jewish Edn., B'nai B'rith, Washington, 1957—. Mem. Adult Edn. Assn. Nat. Council on Adult Jewish Edn., Jewish Book Council, Phi Beta Kappa. Author: Japan in Story and Pictures, 1953; Israel: New People in an Old Land, 1958, rev., 1969; Hawaii, U.S.A., 1954. Editor, Jewish Heritage mag., 1958—, Jewish Heritage Classic Series; lit. editor Nat. Jewish Monthly. Home: 560 Riverside Dr New York City NY 10027 Office: 1640 Rhode Island Av NW Washington DC 20036

EDELMAN, MARIAN WRIGHT (MRS. PETER B. EDELMAN), lawyer; b. Bennettsville, S.C., June 6, 1939; d. Arthur J. and Maggie (Bowen) Wright; Merrill scholar U. Geneva, U. Paris, 1958-59; B.A., Spelman Coll., 1960; LL.B. (John Hay Whitney fellow 1960-61), Yale, 1963; LL.D. (hon.), Smith Coll., 1969; m. Peter B. Edelman, July 14, 1968; children—Joshua, Jonah. Mem. staff N.A.A.C.P, Legal Defense and Edn. Fund, Inc., N.Y.C., 1963-64, Jackson, Miss., 1964-68, now dir.; partner Washington Research Project, 1968; dir. Children's Def. Fund div., 1973—; dir. Harvard Center Law and Edn., 1971-73. Mem. exec. com. Student Non-Violent Coordinating Com., 1961-63; mem. adv. council Martin Luther King, Jr. Meml. Library; mem. adv. bd. Woodrow Wilson Sch. Princeton U., Hampshire Coll.; mem. Carnegie Council on Children. Bd. dirs. Nat. Office for Rights of the Indigent, Center for Law and Social Policy; trustee Martin Luther King, Jr. Meml. Center, Spelman Coll., Council on Founds.; mem. Yale U. Corp. Recipient Louise Wateman Wise award, 1970; Mademoiselle Mag. award, 1965. Ford Found. grantee, 1966; hon. fellow U. Pa., 1969. Mem. Ams. for Dem. Action (vice chmn.). Home: 19 Carlton Rd Waban MA 02168 Office: 1746 Cambridge St Cambridge MA 02138

EDGE, DELIA L., lawyer; b. Mendenhall, Miss., June 30, 1906; d. Frank Stacey and Claudia (Nicholson) Ledbetter; student Fla. So. Coll., 1925-26; J.D., San Francisco Law Sch., 1952; m. Willis Graham Edge, Nov. 19, 1932; 1 dau., Phyllis Ann (Mrs. Verne Goram Koeppe). Admitted to Cal. bar, 1953; practiced in Oakland, Cal. until 1962; asso. Bledsoe, Smith, Cathcart, Johnson & Rogers, San Francisco, Cal., 1962-71; cons. Hastings-Am. Trial Lawyers Assn. Nat. Coll. Advocacy, San Francisco, 1972—. Pres. Phoenix unit Mt. Diablo therapy Center, 1974. Mem. Am., San Francisco bar assns., State Bar Cal., Queen's Bench (pres. 1965), Iota Tau Tau. Home and office: 6817 Broadway Terrace Oakland CA 94611

EDGE, IDA BACKUS (MRS. ELLIS W. EDGE, JR.), educator; b. Chgo., Sept. 11, 1911; s. Clyde Iling and Olga Martha (Burianek) Backus; B.S. in Edn., Northwestern U., 1932; m. Ellis W. Edge, Jr., Sept. 8, 1939; children—Ellis William, Douglas Robert. Exec. dir. Girl Scouts, U.S.A., Essex County, N.J., 1936-43; tchr. pub. schs., Verona, N.J., 1968—. Trustee Cedar Grove Municipal Library, 1958-76. Mem. N.J. Library Trustee Assn. (dir. 1966-74), N.J., Am. library assns., Am. Library Trustee Assn., N.J. Fedn. Woman's Club (Cecelia Gaines Holland award 1973), Zeta Tau Alpha. Clubs: Cedar Grove Eve. Woman's (dir. 1950-74), Nat. Camping Travelers, Nat. Campers and Hikers, Nat. Holiday Rambler Travel Trailer. Home: 10 Valley View Dr Hickory Hills Bath PA 18014

EDGERTON, MISHEW ELLEN ROGERS (MRS. NORMAN EDWARD EDGERTON), business exec.; b. Raleigh, N.C., Sept. 4, 1904; d. James Rufus and Ellen Mishew (Crudup) Rogers; grad. Nat. Park Sem., 1924; m. Norman Edward Edgerton, Feb. 9, 1929; 1 dau., Mishew Ellen (Mrs. Smith). Pres., Rogers Realty & Ins. Co., 1961—; sec. Raleigh Bonded Warehouse, Inc., 1934—. Mem. D.R., D.A.R., Raleigh Jr. League, Order Crown in Am., Nat. Soc. Colonial Dames Am., N.C. Antiquities Soc. (life), N.C. State Art Soc., Am. Camellia Soc. (charter mem., former judge), Internat. Oceanographic Found. Methodist. Home: Tatton Hall 1625 Oberlin Rd Raleigh NC 27608

EDGERTON, STEPHENIE GROVER, educator; b. Grantsburg, Wis., May 1, 1931; d. Stephen F. and June A. (Strike) Grover; B.A. cum laude, U. Minn., 1952, B.S., 1959, M.A., 1959; Ph.D., U. Ill., 1965; vis. scholar London Sch. Econs. and Polit. Sci., 1967. Asst. prof. U. Wis., Madison, 1965-67; asso. prof. ednl. philosophy N.Y. U., N.Y.C., 1967-72, prof., 1972—, head div. hist. and philosophic founds., 1972-74. Fellow Philosophy Edn. Soc. (mem. exec. bd. 1972-74). Contbr. articles to profl. jours. Home: 100 Bleecker St New York City NY 10012

EDGINGTON, WILBERTA DONART (MRS. GLEN LEROY EDGINGTON), educator, psychologist; b. Glencoe, Okla., July 31, 1913; d. Chauncey and Carolyn (James) Donart; B.S., Okla. State U., 1932, M.S., 1935; postgrad. U. Okla., 1942-43, U. Colo., 1943-44, Purdue U., 1955-56; m. Glen Leroy Edgington, Feb. 14, 1946. Counselor, Stillwater (Okla.) Pub. Schs., 1932-42; instr. WAVE tng. sch. Okla. A. and M. U., Stillwater, 1942-43; chief clk. testing service Signal Corps U.S. Army, Washington, 1943-44; therapist, instr. Wakeman U.S. Army Hosp., Camp Atterbury, Ind., 1945; instr. English, Butler U., Indpls., 1945-46; instr. English, psychology Purdue U., Ft. Wayne, Ind., 1946-50, asst. prof. psychology, 1953-59; asso. prof. English, psychology Huntington (Ind.) Coll., 1946-50; asso. prof. psychology Evansville (Ind.) Coll., 1950-52; faculty St. Francis Coll., Ft. Wayne, 1959—, prof. edn. and psychology, 1959—; coordinator psychol. services East Allen County Schs., New Haven, Ind., 1964—. Mem. Nat. Assn. Sch. Psychologists, Am., Ind. psychol. assns., Phi Kappa Phi, Kappa Delta Pi. Mem. Order Eastern Star. Home: 6103 Beaumont St Fort Wayne IN 46805 Office: 15209 U S 30 East New Haven IN 46774

EDIS, GLORIA TOBY (MRS. MYRON R. SCHOENFELD), pediatrician; b. N.Y.C., Dec. 6, 1939; d. Murray Alvin and Anne (Goldstein) Edis; student Cornell U., 1956-59; M.D., N.Y. U., 1963; m. Myron R. Schoenfeld, June 14, 1959; children—Bradley, Glenn, Dawn, Melody. Intern, Montefiore Hosp., Bronx, N.Y., 1963-64; gen. practice medicine, Yonkers, N.Y., 1964-66; resident pediatrics Babies Hosp., Columbia-Presbyn. Med. Center, N.Y.C., 1966-68; attending pediatrician Lincoln Hosp., Bronx, 1968-70; chief pediatrics Circle Manhattan Med. Group, N.Y.C., 1970—; clin. instr. pediatrics Cornell U. Med. Coll., N.Y.C., 1971—; pediatrician N.Y.C. Health Dept., 1971-73. Fellow Am. Acad. Pediatrics, Westchester Acad. Medicine; mem. A.M.A., Westchester County Med. Assn., Phi Beta Kappa, Alpha Epsilon Delta. Club: Cornell Women's (Westchester, N.Y.). Home: 57 Sprain Rd Scarsdale NY 10583 Office: 123 W 79th St New York City NY 10024

EDMOND, ELIZABETH WATSON, physician; b. Flint, Mich., Feb. 26, 1935; d. Robert and Annie (Watson) Edmond; A.B., Albion Coll., 1956; M.D., U. Mich., 1960. 1 son, Robert Edmond Lins. Intern, Washington Hosp. Center, 1960-61; resident pediatrics Children's Hosp., Washington, 1961-63; fellow pediatric rheumatology Bowman Gray Sch. Medicine, N.C., 1963-64; instr. pediatrics Ohio State U., 1964-65; resident phys. medicine and rehab. Univ. Hosp., Ann Arbor, Mich., 1965-67; instr. phys. medicine and rehab., 1968-72; rep. of phys. medicine and rehab. dept. to pediatric rehab. unit U. Mich. Med. Center, Ann Arbor, 1970-72; practice medicine specializing in pediatrics, Southfield, Mich., 1973—; cons. Bixby Hosp., Adrian, Mich., Mt. Carmel Hosp., Detroit. Mem. Mich. Acad. Phys. Medicine and Rehab., Am. Med. Women's Assn., Internat. Med. Soc. of Paraplegia, Mich., Wayne County med. socs., Am. Assn. Electromyography and Electrodiagnosis, Am. Acad. Phys. Medicine and Rehab., Am. Congress Rehab. Medicine, Am. Acad. Cerebral Palsy. Contbr. articles to profl. pubs. Home: 755 Archwood St Ann Arbor MI 48103 Office: 20905 Greenfield St Southfield MI 48075

EDMONDS, ANNE CAREY, librarian; b. Penang, Malaysia, Dec. 19, 1924; d. William John and Nell (Carey) Edmonds; student U. Reading (Eng.), 1942-44; B.A., Barnard Coll., 1948; M.S. in L.S., Columbia, 1950; M.A., Johns Hopkins, 1959; postgrad. Western Res. U., 1960-61. With War Damage Commn., London, Eng., 1944-46; children's asst. Enoch Pratt Free Library, Balt., 1948-49; reference librarian Sch. Bus. Adminstrn., City Coll. N.Y., 1950-51; reference librarian, then asst. librarian readers' services Goucher Coll., 1951-60; exchange reference librarian European services library BBC, London, 1955; instr. Sch. Library Sci., Syracuse U., summer 1960; librarian Douglass Coll. of Rutgers-The State U., 1961-64, instr. Grad. Sch. Library Service, Rutgers, summer 1962, fall 1963; librarian Mt. Holyoke Coll., 1964—. Mem. A.L.A., Am. Hist. Assn., Am. Assn. U. Profs. Home: 79 Cold Hill Granby MA 01033

EDMONDS, MARY ELIZABETH, pub. relations exec.; b. Stephenville, Tex., Jan. 29, 1949; d. Elrige Cornelius and Martha (Carmichael) Barnette; B.A., Baylor U., 1970; m. Michael Steven Edmonds, Nov. 27, 1971. Mem. pub. relations staff Tex. Christian U., 1970-72; editor regional publ. Sperry & Hutchinson Co., Ft. Worth, 1972—. Vol. Bridge House, home for teenage girls. Bd. dirs. Ft. Worth and Tarrant County YWCA. Mem. Women in Communications, Nat. Secs. Assn., Sigma Delta Chi. Home: 159 Sheffield St Fort Worth TX 76134 Office: 2900 W Seminary St Fort Worth TX 76133

EDMONSON, BARBARA ANN, psychologist, educator; b. Kansas City, Mo., Oct. 15, 1912; d. James Ernest and Hortense Aileen (Taylor) Turner; B.A. in Psychology, U. Mo. at Kansas City, 1951, M.A., 1953; Ed.D. in Spl. Edn., U. Kan., 1970. Dir., Elmhurst Presch. Retarded Children, Kansas City, 1954-61; research asso. Kan. Med. Center, Kansas City, 1964-69, U. Ore., Eugene, 1969-70; dir. psychology tng. Nisonger Center for Developmental Disabilities, Columbus, O., 1970—; asst. prof. psychology Ohio State U., 1970—. U.S. Dept. Health, Edn. and Welfare rehab. research fellow, 1967-68. Mem. Am. Psychol. Assn., Soc. for Research in Child Devel., Am. Assn. Mental Deficiency, Council for Exceptional Children, Nat. Assn. Retarded Citizens (edn. com.), Am. Ednl. Research Assn., Ohio Psychol. Assn. Author: Social Perceptual Training for Community Living, 1969; Test of Social Inference: Demographic, Validity, Data and Scoring Guide, 1974. Home: 3043 Valley Creek Dr Columbus OH 43223 Office: Nisonger Center 1580 Cannon Dr Columbus OH 43210

EDMUNDS, WINIFRED YOUNG (MRS. FREDERICK EDMUNDS), rose nursery exec.; b. Marion, Ind., June 15, 1920; d. Artennis Delno and Rose Elizabeth (Bennett) Young; student Ind. U., 1938-42, U. Ala., 1942-43; m. Frederick Edmunds, June 20, 1959; children (by previous marriage)—Carol (Mrs. John C. Potter), Laura (Mrs. Jerry N. Hager), Philip; 1 stepdau., Cynthia. Reporter, South Bend (Ind.) News Times, 1938, South Bend Tribune, 1943; with Marsh & McLennan, Inc., Portland, Ore., 1955-59, D.K. MacDonald & Co., Inc., Portland, 1959-61; co-owner, mgr. Roses by Fred Edmunds, Wilsonville, Ore., 1961—. Mem. Am., Portland rose socs., All-Am. Rose Selections, Ins. Women's Assn. of Portland, Women in Communication, Wilsonville C. of C., Sigma Kappa. Democrat. Home: 6140 SW Briar Patch Lane Wilsonville OR 97070 Office: 6235 SW Kahle Rd Wilsonville OR 97070

EDMUNDSON, JUDITH MIXON RAMSAY (MRS. JOSEPH A. EDMUNDSON), banker; b. Coal Valley, Ala., Oct. 3, 1938; d. John Robert and Marion Alma (Hinds) Cicero; student Am. Inst. Banking, 1961-62; m. Ted Ashley Ramsay, Jr. Dec. 3, 1954 (div. Oct. 1960); 1 son, Ted Ashley III; m. 2d, Joseph A Edmundson, Aug. 25, 1972. Customer service dept. First Nat. Bank South Miami, 1960-65; asst. v.p. in charge adminstrv. services Inter Nat. Bank Miami, 1965-69; asst. v.p. in charge customer service Coral Gables First Nat. Bank (Fla.), 1969-73; v.p. personnel, office mgr. Biscayne Fed. Savs. and Loan Assn., Miami, 1973—. Mem. Nat. Assn. Bank Women, Bank Adminstrn. Inst., Am. Inst. Banking, Am. Safe Deposit Assn., Savs. and Loan Personnel Assn., Am. Savs. and Loan Inst., Fla. Savs. and Loan League (personnel com.), Coral Gables C. of C., Nat. Assn. Personnel Adminstrn., Personnel Soc. Greater Miami. Club: Soroptimist. Home: 5112 NW 79th Av Apt 308 Miami FL 33166 Office: 1790 Biscayne Blvd Miami FL 33132

EDWARDS, BERNICE JANE LAKIS (MRS. JOHN OLIVER EDWARDS), mfg. co. exec.; b. Chillicothe, Ill., June 12, 1932; d. Alex George and Badia (Ayoub) Lakis; student Internat. Corr. Schs., 1950-55, U. Ill., 1955, 64, Bathel U., 1963-64, Ill. Central Coll., 1968, 73; m. John Oliver Edwards, June 18, 1950; children—Victor L., David Allen, Patricia Ann. Mgr. Spiegel Shopping Center, Pekin, Ill., 1959-62; regional mgr. Mail Order div. J.C. Penney Co., Milw., 1962-65; comptroller Trasco, Inc. div. Goddard & Goddard, Inc., Washington, Ill., 1965-68; pres., gen. mgr., comptroller Fast Printing div. Fleming-Potter, Inc., Peoria, Ill., 1968-69; with Kress Corp., Kress Internat. Corp., Brimfield, Ill., 1969—, corporate sec., treas., 1971—. Mem. Nat. Assn. Accountants, Nat. Assn. Bus. Women,

Christian Bus. Women of Am. Mem. Greek Orthodox Ch. Mem. Order Eastern Star. Home: 445 Edgewood Dr East Peoria IL 61611

EDWARDS, DOROTHY, physician; b. Tallula, Ill., Sept. 3, 1896; d. Samuel Henry and Martha (Mathew) Edwards; B.S., Northwestern U., 1917; M.D., Cornell U., 1922; postgrad. Oxford U. (Eng.), U. Vienna (Austria), U. Zurich (Switzerland), 1926-27; postgrad. (fellow) U. Chgo., 1930-31. Intern, St. Vincent's Hosp., Norfolk, Va., 1922-23, Chgo. Lying-in Hosp., 1923-24; practice medicine specializing in obstetrics and gynecology, Chgo., 1927—; asst. prof. obstetrics and gynecology Rush Med. Sch. Diplomate Bd. Obstetrics and Gynecology. Mem. A.M.A., Ill., Chgo. med. socs. Home: 181 E Lake Shore Dr Chicago IL 60611 Office: 122 S Michigan Av Chicago IL 60603

EDWARDS, DOROTHY BEATRICE (MRS. EDWIN B. EDWARDS, JR.), state legislator; b. Fall River, Mass., Mar. 22, 1924; d. George Albert and Esther (Holland) Jackson; grad. high sch.; m. Edwin B. Edwards, Jr., Nov. 17, 1944; children—E. Branford III, Gary Charles, Debbi Suzanne and Cindy Joanne (twins). Telephone operator New Eng. Telephone Co., Newport, R.I., 1941-42, U.S. Navy Dept., 1942-45; mem. R.I. Ho. of Reps. from dist. 94, 1967—. Mem. Portsmouth (R.I.) Republican Town Com., 1962—, R.I. Rep. State Central Com., 1966—; legislative chmn. R.I. Fedn. Rep. Women, 1968-69. Episcopalian. Address: 25 Cove St Portsmouth RI 02871

EDWARDS, EDNA (MRS. NATHAN HALE EDWARDS), city ofcl.; b. Ellington, Conn., Sept. 17, 1909; d. Frank Joseph and Elna Mariva (Kibbe) Tuttle; grad high sch.; m. Nathan Hale Edwards, Apr. 28, 1928; children—Ralph E., Howard K., Ronald N. Ediphone operator Travelers Ins. Co., Hartford, Conn., 1927-28; assembler Pratt & Whitney Aircraft, East Hartford, Conn., 1943-44; asst. town clk., Ellington, 1952-59, town treas., 1961-73, town clk., 1959—. Sec. Ellington Republican Com., 1960—. Mem. Town Clk's Assn. Conglist. (deaconess, stewardship com.). Mem. Order Eastern Star, Grange (7 deg, treas. 1965—). Club: Federated Women's. Home: 6 Glenwood Rd Ellington CT 06029 Office: City Hall Main St Ellington CT 06029

EDWARDS, ELEANOR RUTH, editor; b. Albany, N.Y., Nov. 4, 1922; d. Frank Cole and Martha Southwell (Leak) Edwards; grad. high sch. Copyholder Williams Press, Inc., Albany, 1940-42, telephone checker, 1942-49, copy editor, 1949-53; proofreader, sr. editorial clk. N.Y. State Dept. State, Albany, 1953-62, prin. editorial clk., 1962-65, editor, 1965—. Home: 111 3d Av Rensselaer NY 12144 Office: 162 Washington Av Albany NY 12225

EDWARDS, ELIZABETH LOVE (MRS. KENNETH R. EDWARDS), business exec., civic worker; b. Ithaca, N.Y.; d. Harry Houser and Anna (Barclay) Love; Mus.B. in Harp, Coll. Fine Arts, Syracuse U., 1935; m. Kenneth R. Edwards, June 1, 1938; 1 dau., Elizabeth Love (Mrs. Jonathan W. Fincke). Profl. harpist, 1935-74, request performance for Chiang Kai Shek, 1932, harpist Grand Rapids (Mich.) Symphony, 1938-47; with Field Enterprises Ednl. Corp., 1954-67, regional mgr., Monroe County, 1959-67; mem. faculty music dept. Capital U., Columbus, O., 1936-38. Pres., St. Cecilia Soc. (music club), Grand Rapids, 1947-49; pres. P.T.A., 1947; pres. Tiotomca area Girl Scouts U.S.A., Ithaca, N.Y., 1952-54; co-chmn. Am. Cancer Soc., Ithaca, 1954-56; head women's council Community Chest, 1956; mem. Babies Welfare, Grand Rapids; active Girl Scouts U.S.; vol. Monroe County Vis. Nurses Assn., Civic Music Assn.; chmn. Perinton chpt. A.R.C., 1968-72, chmn. blood vols. for Rochester-Monroe chpt., also mem. adv. com. vol. council, chmn. Fairport Bloodmobile, 1966-69; vice chmn. Rochester-Monroe County Office Vols., 1971; mem. bd., sec., com. chmn. Zonta Internat. of Rochester. Mem. Rochester Mus. and Sci. Center, Rochester Civic Music Assn. (team capt.), Rochester Meml. Art Gallery, Sigma Kappa (pres. Rochester alumni chpt. 1967-68), Sigma Alpha Iota. Presbyn. (mem. women's bd. Ithaca 1956-57). Died Aug. 9, 1974. Home: 7 Wickford Way Fairport NY 14450

EDWARDS, ESTHER GORDY (MRS. GEORGE H. EDWARDS), entertainment co. exec.; b. Oconee, Ga.; d. Berry and Bertha Ida (Fuller) Gordy; ed. Howard U., 1940-41, Wayne State U., 1941-42; m. George H. Edwards, May 12, 1951; 1 son (by previous marriage), Robert Bullock. With Superior Life Ins. Co., Detroit, 1941-42, U.S. Hdqrs. Army Air Forces, Washington, 1942-43, U.S. War Dept., Detroit, 1944-46; co-owner, gen. mgr. Gordy Printing Co., Detroit, 1947-59; sr. v.p., sec., dir. Motown Record Corp., Detroit, 1959—; sec., dir. Jobete Pub. Co., Inc., Detroit, 1959—; sr. v.p., corporate sec. Motown Industries, Hollywood and Detroit, 1973; exec. com., dir. Detroit Wheels of World Football League; dir. Bank of the Commonwealth. Commr., Detroit's Records Ct. Jury Commn., 1960-62, chmn., 1961-62; mem. Mayor's Study Com. for Cable TV, 1971—; exec. dir. Gordy Found., 1968—; adminstr. Loucye Gordy Wakefield Scholarship Fund, 1968—. Chmn., Wayne County Democratic Women's Com., 1956; Mich. del.-at-large Dem. Nat. Conv., 1960; interim asst. dep. auditor gen. State of Mich., 1960. Bd. dirs. Higher Ednl. Opportunities Com. Wayne State U., Detroit City Theaters Assn., Your Heritage House, Nat. Big Bros. Am., Martin Luther King, Jr. Center for Social Change. Mem. Nat. Acad. Rec. Arts and Scis., Broadcast Music Industries, Am. Women in Radio and TV, Booker T. Washington Bus. Assn., Howard U. Alumni Assn. (v.p. 1945-47), Mich., Greater Detroit (dir. 1973—) chambers commerce, Anthony Wayne Soc. of Wayne State U., Central Bus. Dist. Assn. Detroit (dir.), Alpha Kappa Alpha. Clubs: Gazelles Internat., Economic of Detroit (dir. 1974—).

EDWARDS, FRANCES KATHRYN, pediatrician, diagnostic radiologist, educator; b. Auburn, Ala., Jan. 20, 1923; d. Ralph Lee and Kathryn (McGill) Edwards; student U. Ga., 1942-45, 46; M.D., Med. Coll. Ga., 1950. Intern Crawford W. Long Hosp., Atlanta, 1950-51, pediatric resident, 1951-53; practice medicine specializing in pediatrics Decatur, Ga., 1953-56, specializing in radiology, Atlanta, 1973—; fellow pediatric cardiology Childrens Hosp., Cin., 1956-58; research asso., asst. prof. pediatrics U. Cin., 1958-60; asst. prof. pediatrics Emory U. Sch. Medicine, Atlanta, 1960-63, asso. prof. pediatrics, 1963-72, fellow diagnostic radiology, 1969-72, asst. prof. radiology, 1971-72, asso. prof. radiology and pediatrics Childrens Med. Center, Southwestern Med. Sch., U. Tex., Dallas, 1972-73. Diplomate Am. Bd. Pediatrics; in diagnostic radiology Am. Bd. Radiology. Fellow Am. Coll. Cardiology; mem. So. Soc. Pediatric Research (pres. 1968), Sub-Board Pediatric Cardiology. Home: Apt 20 A 4560 E Ponce De Leon Av Clarkston GA 30021 Office: Suite 255 B Doctors Bldg 490 Peachtree St NE Atlanta GA 30308

EDWARDS, JANE ELIZABETH CAMPBELL (MRS. RICHARD BYRON EDWARDS), author; b. Miles City, Mont., Mar. 31, 1932; d. Christopher Martin and Josephine (Gast) Campbell; m. Richard Byron Edwards, Sept. 26, 1953; children—Linda, Richard, Andrew, Sheila, Patrick. Writing cons. ednl. TV, Santa Clara County Office Edn., 1968-71. Roman Catholic. Author: What Happened to Amy, 1961; (with Gilbert Martinez) The Mexican American: His Life Across Four Centuries, 1973; others; also numerous short stories. Home: 1531 Queenstown Ct Sunnyvale CA 94087

EDWARDS, JULIA SPALDING, journalist; b. Louisville, Oct. 6, 1920; d. James Percival and Margaret (Wathen) Edwards; B.A., Barnard Coll., 1940; M.S., Sch. of Journalism, Columbia, 1942, postgrad. in interant. relations, 1966. Reporter, Balt. Sun, 1942-44; rewriteman Chgo. Daily News, 1944-45; corr. to Frankfurt bur. chief Stars and Stripes, Germany, 1946-48; Washington corr. Pulliam Newspapers, 1949-50; editor USIA, Washington, Tokyo, 1951-52; mng. editor Worldwide Press Service, N.Y.C., 1953-54; dir. pub. information Research Inst. Am., 1955-56; Ind. fgn. corr., writer, editor, N.Y.C., 1957-67; dir. World Affairs Bur., Washington, 1968-73; ind. fgn. corr., 1973—; corr. news agys., mags., Korea, Vietnam, Germany, Japan, others. Mem. Author's Guild. Clubs: Am. Newspaperwomen's, Overseas Press (chmn. Washington com. 1969-73), Nat. Press. Author: The Occupiers, 1967. Home: 250 W 57th St Suite 1527 New York City NY 10019

EDWARDS, JUNE KATHERINE BENNETT (MRS. WILLIAM WAYNE EDWARDS), pub. relations co. exec., aviation cons.; b. N.C., June 4, 1932; d. Roscoe Lee and Lillian Era (Blackburn) Bennett; student U. Tenn., 1962, U. Cal. at Los Angeles, 1967-70, at Bakersfield Coll., 1967-74; m. Lattie Finlayson Reynolds, Jan. 10, 1946 (dec. Dec. 1958); children—Robert Julian, Jacqueline Kay, Katherine Ann; m. 2, William Wayne Edwards, July 17, 1959 Owner, Jack Reynolds Aviation, Candor, N.C., 1946-58, Delray Beach, Fla., 1944-58, Mercury Aviation Candor, Palatka, Fla., 1958-63, June B. Edwards & Assos., Bakersfield, Cal., 1967—. instr. agrl. aviation Bakersfield Coll., 1974—. Agrl. aviation cons., 1963—. Chmn., Bakersfield Coll. Aviation and Aerospace Edn. Com., 1967-70, mem. aviation aerospace adv. com. Cal. Dept. Edn., 1967—; mem. aviation mgmt. adv. com. U. Pepperdine, Los Angeles, 1973—. Bd. dirs. Mission for Children in Mexico. Recipient citation in Aviation Edn., USAF, 1969; Service award FAA, 1969; Aviation Edn. Service award dist. Cal. State Dept. Edn.; commendation for aviation edn. Cal. Legislature, 1969. Mem. Pub. Relations Soc. Am., Am. Women in Radio and TV, Internat. Platform Assn., Kern County Press Club, Cal. Aerospace Edn. Assn. (pres. 1970-71), Nat. Aerospace Edn. Council, Am. Soc. Agrl. Cons., Nat. Pub. Writer's Assn., Bakersfield C. of C., Whirly Girls, Internat. Women Pilots, Ninety-Nines. Mem. editorial adv. staff Aerial Applicator mag., 1973—. Contbr. articles to profl. jours., books. Home: 3100 Durrwood St Bakersfield CA 93304

EDWARDS, KATE F(LOURNOY), portrait painter, artist; b. Marshallville, Ga.; ed. A.I.C., Grande Chaumiere, Paris; also studied with Charles Hawthorne. Works represented in collections: The Capitol, Washington, First Nat. Bank, First Nat. Bank Tower, Budd Terrace, Court House, Westminster Sch., Fed. Res. Bank, Lovett Sch., Aidmore Children's Hosp., Ga. Inst. Tech. (all Atlanta), Mercer U., Wesleyan Coll., Macon, Ga., U. Ga., Wake Forest (N.C.) Coll., Gov.'s Palace, P.R., High Mus. Art, Hdqrs. Bldg., Ft. Benning, Ga., City Library, Dayton, Wash., 4th Nat. Bank, Columbus, Ga., Court House, New Bern, N.C., U. Ill., numerous others. Recipient prizes S.E. Fair Exhbn., 1916, Atlanta Art Assn., 1921. Author: Rhymes for Good Times, 1971. Address: The Darlington 2025 Peachtree Rd NE Atlanta GA 30309

EDWARDS, LELA L'AMOUR HAINES (MRS. ELMER THOMAS EDWARDS, JR.), editor; b. Cuero, Tex., Sept. 5, 1919; d. Paul Graves and Lillian Lidie (Grabow) Haines; B.J., U. Tex., 1940; M.Ed., Tex. A. and M. U., 1967, Ph.D., 1973; m. Elmer Thomas Edwards, Jr., Aug. 21, 1943; children—Thomas Haines, Katherine Anne, Wayne Clay. High sch. English and journalism tchr., publs. adviser sch. dist. information Bryan (Tex.) Pub. Schs., 1958-67; asso. dir. research project, grad. asst. dept. ednl. adminstrn. Tex. A. and M. U., 1967-68; journalism tchr., sch. information officer A & M. Consol. Schs., 1968-71; pubs. editor Tex. Agrl. Extension Service, Tex. A. and M. U., College Station, 1971-74, coordinator information services Office Continuing Edn., 1974—. Active Camp Fire Girls. Nat. Defense Edn. Act English Inst. fellow, 1969; Newspaper Fund, Inc. fellow, 1962. Mem. Am. Assn. Agrl. Coll. Editors Tex. State Tchrs. Assn., (dist. chmn. pub. relations 1970-71), Specialists Assn. Tex. Agrl. Extension Service (dir. 1973-74), So. Assn. Secondary Schs. and Colls. (mem. evaluation team 1966-71), Tex. Assn. Journalism Dirs. (chmn. pub. affairs 1968-70), Women in Communications, Altrusa, Phi Kappa Phi, Kappa Delta Pi, Delta Delta Delta. Democrat. Methodist. Editor: Bryan-College Station C. of C. publs., 1966-70; mem. editorial staff Tex. Agrl. Progress, 1971—.

EDWARDS, LUCILLE WINTERS (MRS. JESSE T. EDWARDS), mfg. co. exec.; b. Valley Center, Kan.; d. Roy Ross and Mary Adeline (Williamson) Winters; student U. Wichita, 1928-30, Wichita Bus. Coll., 1936; m. Jesse Tellis Edwards, July 12, 1947. Tchr. rural schs. Sedgwick County, Kan., 1930-36; clk. A.A.A., Wichita, Kan., 1936-37; with Beech Aircraft Corp., Wichita, 1937—, asst. sec., 1939-72, corp. sec., 1972—; dir. Beech Found. Corp. Bd. dirs. Friends U., Wichita. Mem. Women's Aero. Assn. Kan. Methodist (trustee, finance com.). Club: Altrusa. Home: 1575 Harvard St Wichita KS 67208 Office: 9709 E Central St Wichita KS 67201

EDWARDS, MARIE BABARE, psychologist; b. Tacoma; d. Nick and Mary (Mardesich) Babare; B.A., Stanford, 1948, M.A., 1949; m. Tilden Hampton Edwards (div.); 1 son, Tilden Hampton Edwards III. Counselor guidance center U. So. Cal., Los Angeles, 1950-52; project coordinator So. Cal. Soc. Mental Hygiene, 1952-54; pub. speaker Welfare Fedn. Los Angeles, 1953-57; field rep. Los Angeles County Assn. Mental Health, 1957-58; intern psychologist U. Cal. at Los Angeles, 1958-60; pvt. practice, human relations tng., counselor tng., teaching U. So. Cal., U. Cal. at San Diego, Irvine, Santa Barbara. Mem. Cal., Am., Western, Los Angeles psychol. assns., A.A.A.S., Nat. Acad. Religion and Mental Health, Soc. Advancement Mgmt., So. Cal. Soc. Clin. Hypnosis, Internat. Platform Assn. Author: The Challenge of Being Single, 1974. Office: 6100 Buckingham Pkwy Culver City CA 90230

EDWARDS, MARIGOLD ANNE, educator; b. Auckland, New Zealand, Jan. 14, 1934; d.; Dip. P.E., U. Otago, Dunedin, New Zealand, 1952-54; tchrs. certificate Christchurch (New Zealand) Tchrs. Coll., 1955; B.A., U. Canterbury, Christchurch, 1960; M.Ed., U. Pitts., 1964, Ph.D., 1970. Tchr., Nelson (New Zealand) Coll. for Girls, 1956; officer womens phys. edn. U. Canterbury, 1957-58; instr., warden women's residence U. Sask. (Can.), Saskatoon, 1960-62; lectr. edn. U. Pitts., 1962-67, asst. prof., 1967-70, asso. prof., 1970—. Nat. clinician Lifetime Sports Edn. Project. Served with R.C.A.F., 1961-62. Named Canadian Ladies Singles Squash champion, 1970, 71. Mem. A.A.H.P.E.R., Nat. Found. Health, Phys. Edn. and Recreation, Pa. Assn. Health, Phys. Edn. and Recreation (past v.p. for recreation and health, profl. honor award 1972), Nat. Phys. Edn. Assn. Coll. Women, Eastern Dist., Allegheny County (past sec.), Canadian, New Zealand assns. health, phys. edn. and recreation, Pa. Sports Hall of Fame (chpt. award 1970), U.S. Lawn Tennis Assn., U.S. Womens Squash Racquets Assn., Am. Badminton Assn., Am. Assn. U. Profs., Internat. Council Health, Phys. Edn. and Recreation, Internat. Assn. Phys. Edn. and Sports for Girls and Women, Am. Bus. Womens Assn. (chpt. treas. 1969), U.S. Lawn Tennis Assn. (mem. edn. and research com.), Am. Assn. Advancement Tension Control (chmn. edn. div.), Phi Lambda Theta. Contbr. articles to profl. jours. Capt. U.S. Women's Squash Team, Eng., 1958, Australia and New Zealand, 1972. Home: 4220 Centre Av Pittsburgh PA 15213

EDWARDS, MARY LOUISE, coll. dean; b. Little Rock, Dec. 5, 1944; d. Clincia Dennis and Mable (Moore) Edwards; B.A., Philander Smith Coll., 1967; M.Ed., Colo. State U., 1972. Clk., typist S.A. Jones High Sch., North Little Rock, 1966-68; instr. bus. edn., dean of women Shorter Coll., North Little Rock, Ark., 1968—. Office work Nat. Cash Register Co., Little Rock, 1972-73; typist Select-Aides, Little Rock, summer 1973. Mem. Nat. Council Negro Women, Nat., Ark. bus. edn. assns., Am. Personnel and Guidance Assn., Greater Little Rock Urban League, S.W. Assn. Student Personnel Adminstrs. Baptist (ch. sec. 1966—). Home: 4805 W 22d St Little Rock AR 72204 Office: Shorter Coll 604 Locust St North Little Rock AR 72114

EDWARDS, NETTIE ELIZABETH, ednl. adminstr.; b. Alexandria, La., Oct. 9, 1918; d. John Henry and Sallie Tamson (Donald) Edwards; student Alexandria Bus. Coll., 1936-37, Birmingham-Southern Coll., 1958-59, Nat. Tng. Inst., United Community Funds and Councils Am., 1965-66. Reporter, Alexandria Daily Town Talk, 1942-45; staff writer Brimingham (Ala.) Post, 1945-49; pub. relations dir. Community Chest, Birmingham, 1949-53; dir. information services Pa. United Fund, Phila., 1953-55; asst. exec. dir. Ala. Assn. for Mental Health, Birmingham, 1956-57; pub. relations dir. United Appeal, Birmingham, 1958-68, asst. exec. dir., 1968-71; asst. to pres. for devel. U. Ala., Birmingham, 1971—. Mem. pub. relations com. Ala. Heart Assn., Birmingham. Bd. dirs. Children's Aid Soc., Jefferson-Shelby Lung Assn., Vol. Bur. of Greater Birmingham; adv. com. Jr. League. Recipient First Place awards Nat. Photos for Fedn., 1966-67; citation Pa. United Fund, 1955. Benjamin Franklin fellow Royal Soc. Arts, London; mem. Nat. Pub. Relations Council of Health and Welfare Services (dir. 1967-69), Am. Women in Radio and TV (historian 1968), Colonial Dames Am., D.A.R., First Families of Va., Women in Communications. Presbyn. Club: Lakeview Country (Greensboro, Ala.). Home: 2539 Montevallo Dr Birmingham AL 35223 Office: University Station Birmingham AL 35294

EDWARDS, PHYLLIS AGNES (MRS. THOMAS EDWARDS), clergyman; b. Chgo., Apr. 13, 1917; d. Harry Sherman and Clara Frances (Schmeid) Snyder; B.S., Black Hills Tchrs. Coll., 1951; M.A., Seabury Western Theol. Sem., 1964; m. Thomas Edwards, Dec. 7, 1933;4 children. Ordained to ministry Protestant Episcopalian Ch. as deaconess, 1964, now first woman priest; dir. religious edn. Mission dist., San Francisco, 1964—. Home: 1711 Castro St San Francisco CA 94131 Office: Grace Cathedral 1051 Taylor San Francisco CA 94108*

EDWARDS, PHYLLIS Q., physician; b. Fresno, Cal., Dec. 19, 1916; d. Hiram Wheeler and Vena (Tomlin) Edwards; A.B. with honors, U. Cal. at Los Angeles, 1937; M.D., U. Cal. at San Francisco, 1942; M.P.H. with honors, Harvard Sch. Pub. Health, 1958. Intern, U. Cal. Hosp., San Francisco, 1941-42; resident Barlow Sanitarium, Los Angeles, 1945-49; Tb research USPHS, Washington, 1949-50; with Tb research office WHO, Copenhagen, Denmark, 1950-55; with Tb br. Nat. Communicable Disease Center (Center for Disease Control), USPHS, Washington, 1955-63, Paris, France, 1963-66, Atlanta, 1966—, chief Tb br., Atlanta, 1969—. Diplomate Bd. Preventive Medicine (Pub. Health). Home: 1583 Timberland Rd Atlanta GA 30345 Office: Center for Disease Control Atlanta GA 30333

EDWARDS, RITA LILLIAN, librarian; b. Toronto, Ont., Can., Apr. 5, 1928; d. Gordon Dennis and Kathleen Constance (Bromley) Danby; B.A., U. Toronto, 1951, B.Ed., 1964, M.Ed., 1969, M.L.S., 1971; postgrad. Ont. Coll. Edn., 1952-53; B.Sc.B., U. Ottawa, 1962; m. John Edwards, Dec. 19, 1958. Tchr., Loretto Coll. Sch., Toronto, 1951-52, Ledbury Park Elementary Sch., North York, Ont., 1953-54, Cobden (Ont.) Dist. High Sch., 1954-55, Nickle Dist. Collegiate Sch., Sudbury, Ont., 1955-57; tchr. North Toronto Collegiate Sch., 1960-61; tchr.-librarian Laurentian High Sch., Ottawa, 1961-63; head librarian Bathurst Heights Secondary Sch., Toronto, 1963-68; dir. library services George Brown Coll. Applied Arts and Tech., Toronto, 1968—. Tchr. classification Ryerson Poly. Inst., Toronto, 1968-69. Mem. Ont. Assn. Coll. and Univ. Librarians (chmn. 1973-74), Inst. Profl. Librarians Ont., Ont. Library Assn. Home: 34 Carscadden Dr apt 609 Willowdale ON M2R 2A8 Canada Office PO Box 1015 Station B Toronto ON M5T 2T9 Canada

EDWARDS, RUTH ANN (MRS. EMLYN REESE EDWARDS), librarian; b. Fairmont, W.Va., Jan. 28, 1920; d. Clyde and Gladys (Ferguson) Poling; A.B., Fairmont State Coll., 1941; M.L.S., U. Md., 1970; m. Emlyn Reese Edwards, Dec. 27, 1945; children—M. Jean, L. Thomas. Dir. continuing edn. Sch. of Library and Information Services, U. Md., College Park, 1970; dir. curriculum lab. and library coordinator Bowie (Md.) State Coll., 1971; coll. librarian Wilson Coll., Chambersburg, Pa., 1971—. Instr. Shippensburg (Pa.) State Coll., 1973. Mem. v.p.'s commn. on student affairs U. Md., 1969-70. Trustee Coyle Free Library, Chambersburg, Pa., 1967-68, Congress for Change, Washington, 1969. Mem. Pa. Library Assn., Md. Council of Higher Edn. (mem. ad hoc information net-work study group 1970-71). Home: 1740 Alexander Av Chambersburg PA 17201

EDWARDS, SHIRLEY (MRS. A. GERALD EDWARDS), occupational therapist; b. Phila., Nov. 18, 1932; d. William and Alvina Ore; B.A., City Coll. N.Y., 1955; certificate in occupational therapy Columbia, 1957; M.A., Jersey City State Coll., 1972; postgrad. Rutgers U., 1972—; m. A. Gerald Edwards, Apr. 14, 1956; children—Sandra, Gerald Bruce, Ivan. Occupational therapist Garden Nursing Home, Bklyn., 1959-62, Garfield (N.J.) Pub Schs., 1967-71; pvt. cons. in learning disabilities, Montclair, N.J., 1969—. Adj. instr. dept. reading, mem. staff Right to Read program Jersey City State Coll., 1972-73; instr. Kean Coll. N.J., 1974—. Active P.T.A. Mem. Am. Ednl. Research Assn., Council for Exceptional Children, Am. Occupational Therapy Assn., Assn. for Children with Learning Disabilities, Urban League, N.A.A.C.P. Contbr. articles to profl. jours. Home: 249 N Mountain Av Upper Montclair NJ 07043

EDWARDS, STELLA A., ednl. adminstr.; b. Versailles, Ky.; d. Thomas Wiley and Stella (Dougherty) Edwards; B.A., U. Miami, 1939; M.A., U. Ky., 1955; D.Ed., Columbia, 1964. Cryptographer, USAAF, Homestead, Fla., 1941-43; staff Fgn. Service, Dept. State, Washington, 1944-49; supr., acting dir. div. spl. edn. Ky. Dept. Edn., Frankfort, 1949-56, dir., 1956—. Participant White House Conf. on Children and Youth, Washington, 1960, White House Conf. on Mental Retardation, Warrenton, Va., 1963. Recipient John F. Kennedy Meml. award from Ky. Assn. for Mentally Retarded, 1966. Mem. Am. Assn. Mental Deficiency, Ky. Fedn. Council for Exceptional Children (pres. 1963-65), Nat. Assn. State Dirs. Spl. Edn. (pres. 1968-69), Nat. Council Exceptional Children (gov.-at-large 1965-68, 1st v.p. 1970-71, pres. 1972-73), Kappa Delta Pi, Pi Lambda Theta. Home: 117 Woodford Village Dr Versailles KY 40383 Office: Dept Edn Capital Plaza Tower Frankfort KY 40601

EDWARDS, VIRGINIA CHARLOTTE (MRS. ROBERT LOUIS EDWARDS), psychiatrist; b. Chgo., June 22, 1919; d. Edward and Frances (Geiler) Schooley; student Wright Jr. City Coll., 1939; M.D., U. Ill., 1951; m. Robert Louis Edwards, Oct. 17, 1940; children—Randall Lance, Francis Daryll. Research chemist Continental Can Co., Chgo., 1942; research, control chemist Van Straaten Chem. Co., Chgo., 1944-51; intern, Garfield Park Community Hosp., Chgo., 1951-52; practice gen. medicine, Chgo.,

1952-53, Mansfield and Mt. Vernon, O., 1954-70, specializing in psychiatry, Mansfield, 1972—; resident psychiatry Cleve. Psychiat. Inst., 1970-72; mem. staffs Mt. Vernon (O.) State hosp., 1954-68, Columbus (O.) State Inst., 1968-69, Columbus State Hosp., 1969, Massillon (O.) State Hosp., 1973—. Sec., treas. Assn. Physicians Ohio Dept. Mental Hygiene and Correction, 1957—, hon. pres. 1967; mem. Richland County Mental Health Bd., 1969. Registered profl. engr., Ill. Mem. A.M.A., Ohio, Richland County med. assns., Am. Med. Women's Assn., Chgo. Med. Soc., Alpha Epsilon Iota. Address: 347 Lexington Av Mansfield OH 44907

EDWARDS, WILMA JONES (MRS. SYLVESTER HASSELL EDWARDS), civic worker, b. Harrison, Ark.; d. Albert Grant and Effie Virginia (Harris) Jones; student Kansas City Jr. Coll., 1928-30; m. Sylvester Hassell Edwards, Dec. 2, 1935. Supr. Sinclair Refining Co., Kansas City, Mo., Ft. Worth, 1930-35; owner, mgr. Advt. Letter Service, Ft. Worth, 1946-69. Pres. bd. trustees Minnie L. Maffet Fellowship Fund, 1950, 65. Mem. S.W. Mail Producers Guild (pres. 1946-69), Execs. Secs. (pres. 1958-59), Bus. and Profl. Women's Club (pres. 1957-58), Women in Communication, Mail Advt. Service Assn., Ft. Worth C. of C. Rotarian. Clubs: Altrusa (pres. 1952-53), Woman's, Ft. Worth Boat, Press, Colonial Country (Ft. Worth). Home: Route 9 Box 232 Fort Worth TX 76179 Office: 1410 Throckmorton St Fort Worth TX 76102

EEK, PATRICIA ANN (MRS. NATHANIEL S. EEK), city ofcl.; b. Evanston, Ill., Mar. 2, 1930; d. Paul Cedric and Esther L. (Weyer) Fulton; student Mt. Holyoke Coll., 1947-48; B.S. in Speech, Northwestern U., 1951; m. Nathaniel S. Eek, May 10, 1952; children—Robert Elliott, Konrad Sisson, Erik Peter. Tech. dir. Children's Theatre of Evanston, 1950-51; newswriter Winnetka (Ill.) Talk, publ., 1951-53. Sec. Norman (Okla.) Planning Commn., 1970-72, vice chmn., 1972—, commr., 1969—; treas. Civic Improvement Council of Norman, 1968-69, v.p., 1970-72, pres., 1972-73. Mem. Okla. Planning Congress, Internat. Theatre Pour l'Enfance et la Jeunesse. Republican. Episcopalian. Home: 734 Mccall Norman OK 73069

EEN, ALICE EVELYN MANSFIELD (MRS. LUTHER K. EEN), social worker; b. St. Joseph, Mo.; d. William E. and Anna Bell (Walker) Mansfield; B.S., U. Mo., 1934; M.A., U. Chgo., 1958; m. Luther K. Een, Oct. 7, 1945; children—Carolyn Sue., Thomas Edward, Marolyn Gail. Caseworker, Kansas City Provident Assn., also Mo. Relief and Reconstrn. Commn., 1933-35; child welfare worker, cons. Ia. Dept. Pub. Welfare, 1936-43; psychiat. social worker A.R.C. services to armed forces, 1943-45; asst. field dir. Mental Hygiene Clinic, Amarillo, Tex., 1943-45; casework supr. VA Mental Hygiene Clinic, Denver, 1946-48; case work supr. Family Service Assn., Lincoln, Neb., 1956-58; chief psychiat. med. social work programmer Lincoln Regional Center, 1965—. Social betterment del. to Council of Chs., 1965-69. Mem. Nat. Assn. Social Workers (Neb. pres. 1959, exec. com. 1958-60, chmn. recruitment com. 1961), Neb. Welfare Assn. (chpt. pres. 1958), Neb. Mental Health Assn. Republican. Presbyn. Mem. Order Eastern Star. Home: 1215 S 40th St Lincoln NE 68510 Office: Van Dorn and Folsom Sts Lincoln NE 68501

EGAN, SISTER EILEEN MIRIAM, coll. pres.; b. Boston, Jan. 11, 1925; d. Eugene Owen and Mary Brigid (Condon) Egan; A.B., Spalding Coll., 1956; M.A., Cath. U. Am., 1962, Ph.D. (bd. trustees fellow), 1966. Joined Order Sisters of Charity of Nazareth; chmn. English dept. Spalding Coll., Louisville, 1966-67, v.p. coll., 1968-69, pres., 1969—. Mem. adv. com. Louisville unit Rec. for the Blind; mem. community relations com. Human Relations Commn. Louisville Jefferson County; mem. Louisville Art Assn. Bd. dirs. Louisville Better Bus. Bur., Kentuckiana Metroversity; trustee St. Joseph Infirmary; sec. bd. trustees Ky. Ind. Coll. Found. Inst. Internat. Edn. fellow Oxford (Eng.) U., 1963; Acad. Adminstrn. intern Am. Council on Edn., 1967-68. Mem. Assn. Ind. Coll. Presidents, Nat. Council Accreditation Tchr. Edn., Council Ind. Ky. Colls. and Univs. (v.p.), Nat. Cath. Ednl. Assn. (exec. com. coll. and univ. dept.), Am. Assn. U. Women, English Speaking Union, Assn. Am. Colls. (commn. instl. affairs), Am. Council on Edn. (adv. and nominating coms.). Home: 947 S 4th St Louisville KY 40203

EGAN, ELISABETH TINNERMAN (MRS. ROBERT B. EGAN), resort owner; b. Cleve., Dec. 12, 1919; d. Albert Henry and Ida Veronica (Neubauer) Tinnerman; student Dennison U., 1938-40; B.A., Western Res. U., 1942; m. Robert B. Egan, Dec. 4, 1943 (dec. Sept. 1964); children—Veronica, Robert, John, Elisabeth. Owner, mgr. Rancho Encantado, Santa Fe, N.M., 1967—; dir. Tinnerman Products, Inc., Cleve. Pres. Jones Home for Children, Cleve., 1962-66. Fire chief Tesuque (N.M.) Vol. Fire Dept., 1973-74. Served with WAC, 1942-45. Deocrated Order Brit. Empire. Address: Route 4 Box #57C Santa Fe NM 87501

EGAN, SISTER FRANCIS JOSEPH, librarian; b. Quincy, Mass., Oct. 12, 1911; d. Robert Joseph and Margaret Josephine (Le Vangie) Egan; B.S. in L.S., Villanova U., 1952; M.L.S., Catholic U. Am., 1959. Joined Dominican Sisters Newburgh (N.Y.), 1934; prin. St. Joseph High Sch., Toms River, N.J., 1965-67; dir. library Mt. St. Mary Coll., Newburgh, 1967—. Trustee Southeastern N.Y. Library Resource Council, 1969—. Mem. Am., Catholic, N.Y. Library assns., Catholic Coll. Libraries N.Y., Newburgh Hist. Soc. Home and office: Mount St Mary College Newburgh NY 12550

EGAN, MILDRED IDA SENDKER (MRS. EDWARD JOHN EGAN), educator; b. New Orleans; d. Paul Joseph and Mary (Slasung) Sendker; student Dominican Coll., 1933; Ph.B., Loyola U., New Orleans, 1945, M.Ed., 1953; counselor certificate La. State U., 1958; m. Edward John Egan; children—Jane Mildred, John Edward. Tchr. elementary sch. Holy Savior High Sch., Lockport, La., 1935-40, tchr. high sch., 1942-50, prin. high sch., 1950-52; prin. elementary sch. Our Lady Prompt Succor, White Castle, La., 1940-42; tchr. Sam Barthe Pvt. Sch., New Orleans, 1952-53; tchr. New Orleans pub. schs., 1953-56, counselor, 1956-70, acting supr. guidance, 1965-66; counselor, dept. chmn. John F. Kennedy Sr. High Sch., New Orleans, 1966—, also mem. P.T.A. Piano tchr., Lockport, 1942-52, New Orleans, 1952-56. Mem. Am. Sch. Counselors Assn., Nat. Vocational Guidance Assn., Am., La. personnel and guidance assns., La. Guidance Assn. (pres. 1965-66), Orleans Guidance Counselors Assn. (charter, pres. 1963-65), La. Tchrs. Assn., Am. Assn. U. Women, Loyola U. Alumni Assn., Kaycee Ladies (charter, pres. 1961, 63-64, v.p. 1970-71), Ladies Aux. New Orleans Power Squadron, Kappa Delta Pi. Mem. Pelaya Sultanas Alhambra (charter, pres. 1972-74). Home: 6022 Ponchartrain Blvd New Orleans LA 70124

EGAN, SHIRLEY ANNE, nursing educator; b. Haverhill, Mass., July 11, 1922; d. Rush B. and Beatrice (Bengle) Willard; diploma St. Joseph's Hosp. Sch. Nursing, Nashua, N.H., 1945; B.S. in Nursing Edn., Boston U., 1949, M.S., 1954. Instr. sci. Sturdy Meml. Hosp. Sch. Nursing, Attleboro, Mass., 1949-51; instr. sci. Peter Bent Brigham Hosp. Sch. Nursing, Boston, 1951-53, ednl. dir., 1953-55, asso. dir. Sch. Nursing, 1955-59; nurse edn. adviser AID (formerly ICA), Karachi, Pakistan, 1959-67; prin. Coll. Nursing, Karachi, 1959-67; dir. Vis. Nurse Service, Nashua, N.H., 1967-70; exec. dir. Lowell (Mass.) Vis. Nurse Assn., 1970-71; cons. nursing edn. Pan Am. Health Orgn./WHO to faculty of medicine U. West Indies, Jamaica, 1971-72; med.-surg. coordinator Peter Bent Brigham Hosp. Sch. Nursing, Boston, 1971-73, asso. dir., 1973—. Cons. nursing edn. Pakistan Ministry of Health, Labour and Social Welfare, 1959-67; adviser to editor Pakistan Nursing and Health Rev., 1959-67; exec. bd. Nat. Health Edn. Com., Pakistan. Pres., Nashua Service League, 1973—. Bd. dirs. Nashua Child Care Center, 1968-71; sec. bd. dirs. Matthew Thornton Health Center, Nashua, 1971—. Served as 1st lt. Army Nurse Corps, 1945-47. Mem. Am. Nurses Assn., Trained Nurses Assn. Pakistan, St. Joseph's Sch. Nursing Alumnae Assn., Boston U. Alumnae Assn., Brit. Soc. Health Edn., Sigma Theta Tau. Statis. study grads. Karachi Coll. Nursing. Contbr. articles to profl. publs. Home: 20 Tinker Rd Nashua NH 03060 Office: 721 Huntington Av Boston MA 02115

EGELSTON, MARGUERITE ALICE NORDYKE, librarian; b. Springbook, Ore., Mar. 8, 1914; d. Lewis William and Frances Lucinda (Hoff) Nordyke; B.A., Pacific Coll., 1946; B.S., Ore. Coll. Edn., 1954; M.L.S., U. Portland (Ore.), 1961; m. Elwood Franklin Egelston, July 19, 1936. Tchr., Sandy and St. Helens, Ore., 1947-58; librarian jr. high sch., St. Helens, 1958-62; head librarian State Farm Ins. Co., Bloomington, Ill., 1962—. Mem. Am. Assn. Law Librarians, Spl. Libraries Assn. (chmn. ins. div. 1972-73), Ill. State U. Women's Club. Presbyn. Mem. Order Eastern Star, Daus. Nile. Home: 8 Briarwood Av Bloomington IL 61701 Office: 1 State Farm Plaza Bloomington IL 61701

EGGAR, SAMANTHA, actress; b. London, Eng., 1940. Motion pictures include: The Wild and the Willing, Dr. Crippen, Doctor in Distress, Psyche 59, The Collector, Walk, Don't Run, Return From the Ashes, Doctor Doolittle, Molly Maguires, The Lady in the Car, Walking Stick, The Grove, Light at the Edge of the World. Address: care CMA 8899 Beverly Blvd Los Angeles CA 90048

EGGERTS, LAIMA MUDITE ZVAIGZNE (MRS. ARTHUR H. EGGERTS), med. social worker; b. Latvia; d. Eduards V. and Rosalia (Grinvald) Zvaigzne; D.D.S., State U. Latvia, 1936; M.S. in Social Work, State U. Tenn., 1962; m. Arthur H. Eggerts, Dec. 16, 1930; 1 son, Ragnar Martin. Came to U.S., 1959, naturalized, 1964. Pvt. practice dentistry, Latvia and Germany, 1936-49; organizer, head dental dept. United Christian Hosp., Lahore, Pakistan, 1957-59; psychiat. social worker Overbrook Hosp., Cedar Grove, N.J., 1962-65; med. social worker in geriatrics Lutheran Social Services N.J., Jersey City, 1965—. Cons. social work Luth. Homes of N.J.; lectr. inservice tng. nursing personnel. Served as capt. Pakistan Army Dental Corps, 1950-57. Decorated Republican Commemoration medal (Pakistan). Mem. Nat. Assn. Social Workers, Latvian Med. and Dental Assn. in U.S.A., Acad. Certified Social Workers, U. Tenn. Sch. Social Work Alumni Assn., N.J. Welfare Council, Luth. Conf. on Social Concern, Gerontol. Soc., Gerontol. Soc. N.J. (charter), Daugaviete Sorority. Lutheran. Home: Essex County Hosp Center Cedar Grove NJ 07009 Office: 79 Nelson Av Jersey City NJ 07307

EGGLESTON, RUTH MONROE, librarian; b. Brookneal, Va., Aug. 8, 1923; d. Sam Daniel and Ruth O. (Monroe) Eggleston; B.A. in History, Longwood Coll., 1949; B.S. in L.S., U. N.C., 1952. Children's librarian Richmond (Va.) Pub. Library, 1952-58; librarian Tech. Library, Ft. Lee, Va., 1958-62; librarian Fed. Reserve Bank Richmond (Va.), 1962—. Served with WAVES, 1943-49. Mem. Va. Library Assn. (sec. 1967-69), Spl. Libraries Assn. (pres. Va. chpt. 1966). Home: 1624 Monument Av Richmond VA 23220 Office: Federal Reserve Bank Richmond PO Box 27622 Richmond VA 23261

EGLIN, LELA ADELAIDE HICKOX, optometrist; b. Claude, Tex., Sept. 8, 1916; d. Ira Lester and Elsie (Walters) Hickox; B.S., West Tex. State U., 1937; D.O., So. Cal. Coll. Optometry, 1953; postgrad. East Los Angeles Coll., Los Angeles City Coll.; m. Jack M. Eglin, June 17, 1950 (div. 1961). With accounting dept. Texoma Natural Gas Co., Amarillo, Tex., 1937-40; pvt. practice optometry, Los Angeles, 1953—; sec. Cal. Vision Service, 1963-65. Recipient certificate of honor Wisdom Mag., 1965, award of merit Los Angeles Optometric Soc., 1966; named career woman of year of N.E. Los Angeles, 1969. Mem. Am., Cal., Los Angeles optometric socs., Sesame Lit. Soc., Lincoln Heights C. of C., Pi Kappa Rho, Beta Sigma Phi. Republican. Mem. Ch. of Divine Sci. Contbr. article to profl. jour. Home: 422 Meadowview Dr LaCanada CA 91011 Office: 2731 N Broadway Los Angeles CA 90031

EGLITIS, IRMA, physician; b. Riga, Latvia, Oct. 13, 1907; d. George Juris and Elizabeth (Kronenberg) Liepinsh; M.D. magna cum laude, State U. Latvia, 1931; certificate Creative Problem Solving Inst., State U. N.Y. at Buffalo, 1968; m. John Arnold Eglitis, Apr. 17, 1938. Naturalized Am. citizen, 1956. Asst. instr., jr. instr., instr. gross anatomy, histology and embryology U. Latvia, Riga, 1931-44; instr. gross anatomy Ernst Moritz Arndt U. of Greifswald, Germany, 1944-45; instr. dept. anatomy Coll. Medicine, Ohio State U., 1952-56, asst. prof., 1956-62, asso. prof., 1962-67, prof., 1967—. Diplomate Latvian Bd. of Dermatology and Syphilology. Fellow Ohio Acad. Sci.; mem. Am. Med. Women's Assn. (chmn. com. on med. edn. and practice 1967, 68, nat. sec. 1969, exec. bd. 1969, chmn. resolutions com. 1972), Columbus Women's Med. Assn. (pres. 1961-63, 68, sec. 1958-59, 65-67, v.p. 1959-60), Am. Assn. U. Profs., Council of Inst. for Research in Vision, Am. Assn. Anatomists, Latvian Med. and Dental Assn. in U.S., Assn. Latvian Physicians-Europe; Latvian Biology Assn.-Europe, Sigma Xi. Contbg. author: Anatomy and Histology of the Eye and Orbit in Domestic Animals; The Rabbit in Eye Research Monography. Research in visual apparatus, skin, blood vessels and glandular div. Home: 123 East Lane Av Columbus OH 43201 Office: 1645 Neil Av Columbus OH 43210

EHART, ROSALIE BOSWELL, educator, clubwoman; b. Indpls.; d. John Bruce and Edith K. (Harvey) Boswell; B.A., U. Miami, 1965, postgrad., 1969—; student Barry Coll., 1963-64, M.S. (Nat. Sci. fellow), Colby Coll., 1969; m. William McMein Ehart, Sept. 3, 1944 (div. Aug. 1957); children—Jan Bruce, Penelope Margaret, William McMein. Columnist, Diario las Americas, 1954-55; pres., chmn. bd. Collins Pharmacal Co., 1955-59; tchr. biology Mays Sr. High Sch., Goulds, Fla., 1966-70, Portobello Secondary Sch., Edinburgh, Scotland, 1971-72, Miami Edison Sr. High Sch., 1970-71, 72—. Mem. Women's Congress on Housing, 1956, 57; dir. Am. Homes Com. for Miami Jr. Woman's Club, 1952, dir. social activities, 1953-54, NSF fellow, summers 1966-69; Fulbright fellow, 1971-72. Mem. Dade County Classroom Tchrs. Assn. (mem. human relations commn.), Am. Assn. U. Women, Theosophical Soc., English: Speaking Union. Roman Catholic. Home: 1224 Tangier Coral Gables FL 33134

EHBRECHT, MARTHA ERDMUTHE, psychiatrist; b. Frankfurt, Germany, June 6, 1918; d. August and Selma (Bache) Ehbrecht; M.D., Koenigsberg (Germany) U., 1944. Came to U.S., 1954, naturalized, 1959. Intern, 1956-59; resident Warren State Hosp., Cleve. Inst. Psychiatry, Dayton (O.) Childrens Psychiat. Hosp., 1959-61; practice medicine, specializing in child psychiatry, Dayton, Cherokee, Ia., Buffalo; chief of service Childrens Psychiat. Hosp., West Seneca, N.Y. Diplomate Am. Bd. Psychiatry and Neurology with subsplty. in child psychiatry. Mem. Am. Psychiat. Assn. Address: 1200 East and West Rd West Seneca NY 14224

EHLERS, ELEANOR MAY COLLIER (MRS. FREDERICK BURTON EHLERS), civic worker; b. Klamath Falls, Ore., Apr. 23, 1920; d. Alfred Douglas and Ethel (Foster) Collier; B.A., U. Ore., 1941; secondary tchrs. credentials Stanford, 1942; m. Frederick Burton Ehlers, June 26, 1943; children—Frederick Douglas, Charles Collier. Tchr., Salinas Union High Sch., 1942-43; piano tchr. pvt. lessons, Klamath Falls, 1958—. Mem. Child Guidance Adv. Council, 1956-60; mem. adv. com. Boys and Girls Aid Soc., 1965—; mem. Gov.'s Adv. Com. Arts and Humanities, 1966-67; bd. mem. Friends of Mus. U. Ore., 1966-69, Arts in Ore., 1966-68, Klamath County Colls. for Ore.'s Future, 1968—; chpt. pres. Am. Field Service, 1962-63; mem. Gov.'s Com. Governance of Community Colls., 1967; bd. dirs. Favell Mus. Western Art and Artifacts, 1971—, Community Concert Assn., 1950—, pres., 1966—; established Women's Guild at Presbyn. Intercommunity Hosp., 1965, trustee hosp. sec. bd. trustees, 1962-65, mem. bldg. com. 1962-67, mem. planning com., chmn. edn. and research com. hosp. bd., 1967—. Named Woman of Month, Klamath Herald News, 1965; named grant to Ore. Endowed Fellowship Fund, Am. Assn. U. Women, 1971; recipient greatest Service award Ore. Tech. Inst., 1970-71. Mem. Am. Assn. U. Women (local pres. 1955-56), Klamath Art Assn., P.E.O. (Ore. dir. 1968—), Pi Beta Phi, Mu Phi Epsilon, Pi Lambda Theta. Presbyn. Address: 1338 Pacific Terrace Klamath Falls OR 97601

EHLERS, KATHRYN HAWES (MRS. JAMES D. GABLER), physician; b. Richmond Hill, N.Y., Aug. 22, 1931; d. Albert and Edna (Hawes) Ehlers; A.B., Bryn Mawr Coll., 1953; M.D. Cornell U. (Hannah E. Longshore Meml. Med. scholar 1953-57), (Elsie Strang L'Esperance scholar 1956-57), 1957; m. James D. Gabler, Dec. 5, 1959; children—Jennifer K., Emily E. Intern, N.Y. Hosp., 1957-58, asst. resident pediatrics, 1958-60, fellow in pediatric cardiology Cornell U. Med. Coll., N.Y.C., 1960-64, instr. pediatrics 1964-66, asst. prof., 1966-70, asso. prof. pediatrics, 1970—; practice medicine specializing in pediatric cardiology, N.Y.C., 1958—. Rsearch trainee N.Y. Heart Assn., 1960-62, Am. Heart Assn., 1962-64. Diplomate Am. Bd. Pediatrics, Am. Bd. Pediatric Cardiology. Fellow Am. Coll. Cardiology; mem. N.Y. Heart Assn., Am. Heart Assn., Harvey Soc., Am. Acad. Pediatrics, Alpha Omega Alpha. Contbr. articles in field to profl. jours. Home: 1035 Park Av New York City NY 10028 Office: 525 E 68th St New York City NY 10021

EHLERS, SABINE LILA (MRS. WALTER H. EHLERS), editor; b. Harbin, China, June 26, 1910; d. Joseph and Ann Bardack; B.S., N.Y.U., 1935, grad. work, 1936; m. Walter Henry Ehlers, June 1, 1935; children—Rhea Judith (Mrs. R. John Maxwell), Joyce Reed (Mrs. Esquith), Carol Joan (Mrs. Thomas McMahon). Came to U.S., 1921, naturalized, 1936. Tchr. N.Y. Kindergarten Assn., 1935-37; reporter Mill Valley (Cal.) Record, 1946-50; owner Ideas Promoted, 1951-52; editor, reporter, Honolulu Star-Bulletin, 1950-52; editor U. Hawaii, Honolulu, 1952-53; exec. editor Pearl Harbor Naval Shipyard, 1953-59; writer, editor Polaroid Corp., Cambridge, Mass., 1959-64, publs. cons., 1959-60; free lance editing Florence Heller Sch., Brandeis U., 1961; free-lance editor, writer, and photographer, Topsfield, Mass., 1964—; owner, dir. E & E Assos., Topsfield, 1964—; owner, mgr. Alsa Jewelry, mail order bus.; women's editor weekly newspaper Capital Canon, Tallahassee; corr. Tampa Tribune, 1970—; writer on assignment Fla. Wildlife Mag., 1971—. Recipient award for editorial excellence Hawaii Employers Council, 1953, West Coast indsl. editors' award for best layout, 1955, award for layout pacific Coast Indsl. Editors Awards Program, 1957, Superior Accomplishment award Pearl Harbor Naval Shipyard, 1957; award of excellence for creative advt. Tallahassee Advt. Fedn. Mem. Indsl. Editors of Hawaii (pres.), Fla. State U. Women, Internat. Council of Indsl. Editors. Editor: Kauai Guide Book, 1951, rev. edit. 1957. Author: Hawaiian Legends for Boys and Girls, 1958. Contbr. work in photography. Home: 2006 Lee Av Tallahassee FL 32303 Office: E & E Assos PO Box 6102 Tallahassee FL 32303

EHMANN, JEANNE STETTNER (MRS. WELLINGTON EDWARD EHMANN), educator; b. Ogden, N.Y., Dec. 5, 1920; d. Walter Francis and Bertha Marion (Peck) Stettner; B.A., Keuka Coll., 1942; M.Ed., U. Mass., 1963; postgrad. State U. N.Y., 1966—; m. Wellington Edward Ehmann, Apr. 11, 1942; children—Rik, Christine, Thomas, Constance. Tchr., South Deerfield (Mass.) pub. schs., 1955-58; asso. bur. elementary curriculum devel. N.Y. State Edn. Dept., Albany, 1969; tchr. Averill Park (N.Y.) pub. schs., 1959-73, dir. lang. arts curriculum devel., 1970-71; instr. lang. arts. Russell Sage Coll., Troy, N.Y., 1973—. Editor and cons. Bd. Elementary Curriculum Devel., 1969; owner, mgr. Tamarac Cove Cottages, Schrom Lake, N.Y., 1963—. Mem. Nat. Council Tchrs. English, N.Y. State Assn. Curriculum Devel., N.Y. State Tchrs.' Assn., Internat. Soc. for Study Symbols, Nat. Soc. for Study Edn., N.E.A. Editor: N.Y. State Manual for Operation Snowmobiles, 1970. Home: PO Box 104 Poestenkill NY 12140 Office: Teacher Education Russell Sage College Troy NY 12180

EHRENREICH, EMMA, artist; b. N.Y.C., Sept. 19, 1906; d. William and Rose (Koch) Park; ed. N.A.D., New Sch. Social Research, Coll. City N.Y., L.I. U.; postgrad. Hunter Coll., 1952-55; also studied with Abraham Rattner, Morris Davidson, Robert Motherwell; m. Bernard Ehrenreich, June 24, 1922 (dec.). Exhibited one-woman shows including Contemporary Arts Gallery, N.Y.C., 1953, 55, 59, 62, 64, 66, 68, Silvermine Gallery, Conn., 1958, Artists League Am., 1946, Baryl Mills Gallery, N.Y.C., 1964, 66, 72; exhibited in group shows Bklyn. Soc. Art, 1951, 52, Bklyn. Mus., 1953, 57, 59, 61, Butler Art Inst., 1954, 57, 58, Denver Art Mus., 1955, numerous travelling exhbns. Nat. Assn. Women Artists; represented in permanent collections including Riverside Mus., Met. Mus. Art (both N.Y.C.), Brandeis U., Butler Mus., Denver Mus., Rose Mus., Norfolk Mus., Portland (Ore.) Mus., Time-Life Bldg., Glickenstein Mus., Israel, also pvt. collections. Lectr. art N.Y.C. Bd. Edn., 1962-68; juror nat. exhbns., 1962—. County committeewoman Democratic party, N.Y.C., 1961. Recipient numerous art awards and medals. Mem. Am. Soc. Contemporary Artists (membership chmn. 1970—, dir. 1954—), Nat. Assn. Women Artists (dir. 1968—), N.Y. Soc. Women Artists (chmn. pub. relations 1960-73), Nat. Soc. Painters in Casein and Acrylics (chmn. pub. relations, 1968—), League Present Day Artists (dir. 1966—), Art Edn. Assn. Home: 540 E 20th St New York City NY 10009

EHRGOOD, PAULINE ANNE WORRILOW (MRS. ALLEN HENRY EHRGOOD, JR.), stockbroker; b. Lebanon, Pa., Aug. 20, 1924; d. William Henry and Pauline Emma (Light) Worrilow; grad. Westover Sch., 1942, Pine Manor Jr. Coll., 1944; B.A., Smith Coll., 1946; m. Allen Henry Ehrgood, Jr., June 22, 1946; children—Allen Henry III, William Worrilow, Pauline Anne. Stockbroker, Warren W. York & Co., Inc., investment securities, Allentown, Pa., 1970—. Chmn., St. Fair, Lebanon, 1969. Bd. dirs. Family and Childrens Service, Lebanon; bd. dirs. Home for Widows and Single Women, Lebanon, 1952—, pres. 1961-65, v.p., 1966-68; bd. dirs. Good Samaritan Hosp. Aux., Lebanon; past bd. dirs. Lebanon County council Girl Scouts U.S.A., Jonestown Ch. Home. Mem. Union League Phila. Club: Lebanon Country, Womens (Lebanon). Home: 20 E High St Lebanon PA 17042 Office: 514 Hamilton St Allentown PA 18105

EHRHARDT, ANKE A. (MRS. HEINO F.L. MEYER-BAHLBURG), psychologist; b. Hamburg, Germany, Feb. 20, 1940; d. Herbert and Anne (Horst) Ehrhardt; Vordiplom in Psychology, U. Munchen (Germany), 1962; diplom in Psychology, U. Hamburg, 1964; Ph.D., U. Dusseldorf (Germany), 1969; m. Heino F.L. Meyer-Bahlburg, 1968. Asst. med. psychology, dept. psychiatry and behavioral scis. Johns Hopkins, 1964-66, instr., 1966-69; asst. psychology U. Dusseldorf, 1967-69; asst. research prof. dept. pediatrics State U. N.Y., Buffalo, 1969-73, asso. clin. prof. dept. psychiatry, also asst. research prof. dept. pediatrics, 1973—. Mem. Soc. for Sci. Study Sex, Am. Psychol. Assn., Endocrine Soc., Pediatric Psychology, Deutsche Gesellschaft fur Sexualforschung, Deutsche Gesellschaft fur Psychologie. Author: (with John Money) Man and Woman, Boy and Girl. Contbr. med. articles to profl. jours. Office: Children's Hosp 219 Bryant St Buffalo NY 14222

EHRLE, SALLY IRENE (MRS. RAYMOND EHRLE), govt. ofcl.; b. Cleve., June 11, 1938; d. Lawrence Cottrell and Irene (Siegel) Allen; B.A. in Govt., Miami U., Oxford, O., 1960; postgrad. Western Res. U., 1960-63; M.A., George Washington U., 1966; postgrad. U. So. Cal.-Washington Center, 1974—; m. Raymond Albert Ehrle, Dec. 26, 1964. Personnel clk. Sherwin-Williams Co., Cleve., 1960-61; employment counselor Ohio State Employment Service, Cleve., 1961-63; counseling specialist U.S. Employment Service, Washington, 1963-67; personnel mgmt. adviser Manpower Adminstrn. U.S. Dept. Labor, 1967-68, program dir. part-time employment opportunities for women, 1968, asst. to dir. div. tng. and state personnel mgmt., 1968-70; program analyst Welfare Reform Planning Staff, 1970-71; Am. Polit. Sci. Assn. Congl. fellow, 1971-72; exec. asst. to adminstr. Unemployment Ins. Service, Dept. Labor, 1972—; rep. Pres.'s Commn. on Children and Youth, 1970-71. Vice pres. New Carrollton (Md.) Civic Assn., 1971-72; mem. League Women Voters Prince George's County, Md., 1966—, chmn. New Carrollton unit, 1968-69, mem. county bd. budget com., 1969-70, dir. county bd., 1970-72. Recipient Spl. citation Undersec. Health, Edn. and Welfare, 1972. Mem. Am. Personnel and Guidance Assn. (co-chmn. publicity and pub. relations nat. conv. 1966), Nat. Vocational Guidance Assn., Nat. Capitol Area Personnel and Guidance Assn. (exec. bd. 1964-66, sec. 1965-66), Nat. Employment Counselors Assn. (charter mem., sec. 1964-65), Am. Soc. for Pub. Adminstrn. Home: 8327 Donoghue Dr New Carrollton MD 20784

EHRLICH, ANNETTE, educator; b. Bklyn., Mar. 23, 1931; d. Alexander and Henrietta (Frant) Goldhirsch; B.A., Bklyn. Coll., 1954; M.A., Coll. City N.Y., 1956; Ph.D., McGill U., 1960. Research asso. Northwestern U. Med. Sch., Chgo., 1960-64; vis. scientist Primate Research Center, U. Wash., Seattle, 1964-66; asst. prof. Bowling Green (O.) State U., 1966-69; faculty Cal. State U., Los Angeles, 1969—, asso. prof. psychology, 1971—. Nat. Inst. Mental Health grantee, 1969-73, Grant Found. grantee, 1973. Mem. Internat. Primatological Soc., Am., Eastern Western psychol. assns., A.A.A.S., N.Y. Acad. Sci., Animal Behavior Soc., Assn. Women In Sci., Nat. Orgn. for Women, Sigma Xi, Phi Beta Kappa. Home: 6226 Hollymont Dr Hollywood CA 90068 Office: Psychology Dept Cal State U Los Angeles CA 90032

EHRLICH, DELIA (MRS. JOHN EHRLICH), civic worker; b. San Francisco, Sept. 20, 1930; d. Mortimer and Janet (Choynski) Fleishhacker; student Bryn Mawr Coll., 1948-50; m. John S. Ehrlich, Aug. 27, 1950; children—Joan Delia, John S., Jill Diane, James Sidney. Chmn. Golden gate dist. bd. Children's Home Soc. of Cal., 1966-68, Cal. bd. dirs., 1966-69, dist. bd. dirs., 1970—; chmn. No. Region Cal. Assn. of Adoption Agys., 1966-69, vice chmn., treas., 1970-74; exec. com. and v.p. San Francisco chpt. WAIF, 1965, v.p. chpt., 1968, 72, pres., 1974—, mem. nat. bd., 1973—; adminstrv. vice chmn. JACKIE, 1966-67; bd. dirs. Family Service Agy. San Francisco, 1964-68, Florence Crittenton Home, 1968-69, 70-71, Opera Guild, 1972—, Internat. Traveler's Aid Soc. San Francisco, 1961-67; mem. community com. Plays for Living, 1965—. Mem. Friends of Am. Conservatory Theatre, United Bay Area Crusade, Friends Deps. and Inmates San Francisco County Jail, Friends Delancey St. Found., Com. to Finance New Housing, Roundtable, San Francisco Friends Youth for Understanding, Women's Pub. Interest Com. Clubs: San Francisco Symphony, Metropolitan, Menlo Circus, Villa Taverna.

EHRLICH, EDNA E. GOTTESMAN (MRS. OTTO H. EHRLICH), economist; b. N.Y.C.; d. Herman I. and Pauline (Hellman) Gottesman; B.A. cum laude, Bklyn. Coll., 1943; M.A., Columbia, 1944; Ph.D., New Sch. Social Research, 1960; m. Otto H. Ehrlich, Sept. 28, 1949. Economist, Far Eastern desk fgn. research div. Fed. Res. Bank, N.Y.C., 1944-60, head bus. conditions analysis domestic research div., 1960-62, chief balance of payments div., 1962-67, sr. economist, 1967-72, mgr. internat. research dept., 1972—. Cons. dept. econ. affairs UN, 1951; USIS lectr. Western Germany, 1963-65. Recipient Grad. Faculty Alumni award New Sch., 1960. Mem. Am., Met. (pres. 1970-71) econs. assns., Am. Finance Assn., Downtown Economists Luncheon Group, Internat. Economists Luncheon Group. Author: (with F.M. Tamagna) Japan, (Banking Systems), 1954. Contbr. articles to profl. jours. Home: 250 Prospect St East Orange NJ 07017 Office: 33 Liberty St New York City NY 10045

EHRLICH, GERTRUDE, educator; b. Vienna, Austria, Jan. 7, 1923; d. Josef and Charlotte (Kobak) Ehrlich; B.S., Ga. Coll., 1943; M.A., U. N.C., 1945; Ph.D., U. Tenn., 1953. Came to U.S., 1939, naturalized, 1945. Instr., Oglethorpe U., Atlanta, 1946-50; grad. asst. U. Tenn., Knoxville, 1950-53; instr. U. Md., College Park, 1953-56, asst. prof., 1956-62, asso. prof., 1962-69, prof. math., 1969—. Recipient Distinguished Alumna award Ga. Coll., 1970. Mem. Am. Assn. U. Profs., Am. Math. Soc., Math. Assn. Am., Sigma Xi, Phi Kappa Phi. Author: (with L. W. Cohen) Structure of the Real Number System, 1963; (with J. K. Goldhaber) Algebra, 1970. Asso. editor classroom notes Am. Math. Monthly, 1963-66. Home: 6702 Wells Parkway University Park MD 20782 Office: Math Dept U Md College Park MD 20742

EHRLICH, MARY ANN (MRS. HOWARD G. EHRLICH), plant pathologist; b. Buffalo, July 12, 1926; d. Lewis S. and Loretta (O'Mara) Swaebly; Ph.B., Marquette U., 1947; Ph.D., U. Minn., 1955; m. Howard G. Ehrlich, May 26, 1955; children—Mark Edward, Jennifer Ann. Instr. biology Marquette U., Milw., 1954-57; editorial asst. Jour. Plant Physiology, U. Minn., Mpls., 1957-59; research asso. Duquesne U., Pitts., 1959-72, research plant pathologist, 1972—. Co-investigator NSF research grants, 1960-64, NIH research grants, 1964-70, U.S. Dept. Agr. research grants, 1965-68. Mem. Am. Phytopath. Soc., A.A.A.S., Am. Inst. Biol. Sci., Bot. Soc., Mycological Soc., Sigma Xi, Phi Sigma. Roman Catholic. Home: 313 Twin Hills Dr Pittsburgh PA 15216

EHRLICH, MATHILDE WILHEMINE AUGUSTE (MRS. FRANZ F.S. EHRLICH), librarian; b. Duelmen, Germany, Feb. 16, 1915; d. Lorenz and Maria Anna (Blum) Geis; Abitur summa cum laude, Oberlyzeum, Limburg, Germany, 1934; cum laude Padagogium, Leipsig, Germany, 1936; B.A., St. Peter's Coll., 1966; M.L.S., Pratt Inst., 1969; m. Franz F.S. Ehrlich, Jan. 18, 1939; children—Theodore, Ingrid (Mrs. Jean-Bernard Bayard), Francine. Came to U.S., 1938, naturalized, 1950. Tchr., St. Elizabeth's Sch., London, Eng., 1934-35; dir., tchr. English and French, Egn. Lang. Inst., Koblenz, Germany, 1936-38; tchr. German, German Sch. Verein, N.Y.C., 1944-45; tchr. Latin and French, librarian Holy Rosary Acad., Union City, N.J., 1962-68; head librarian N.Y. Assn. for Blind, N.Y.C., 1969-70, Hudson Cath. High Sch., Jersey City, 1970—. Bd. dirs. Area Library Reference Council, 1970—. Recipient Philosophy medal St. Peter's Coll., 1965; named Outstanding Secondary Educator of Am., 1974. Mem. Am., N.J. library assns., Hudson County Sch. Media Assn., Cath. Library Assn. (dir. No. N.J. unit 1973—), Beta Phi Mu. Roman Catholic. Organizer 1st Braille card catalogue in library of N.Y. Inst. for Blind, 1970. Home: 1606 Palisade Av Union City NJ 07087 Office: 790 Bergen Av Jersey City NJ 07306

EICHELBERGER, ROSA KOHLER (MRS. CLARK MELL EICHELBERGER), civic worker, author; b. Balt., Apr. 28, 1896; d. Jacob George and Mary Elizabeth (Condon) Kohler; student Sorbonne, 1930; m. Clark Mell Eichelberger, Oct. 6, 1924. Playground dir. Children's Playground Assn., Balt., 1916-20; story lady, supt. Radcliffe Chautaugua, nat. tour 1920-28; story lady Hull House, Chgo., 1931-32, Greenwich House, N.Y.C., 1936-38; book rev. editor League of Nations Chronicle and Am. Assn. for the U.N., N.Y.C., 1930-55. Lectr. Am. Assn. for the U.N., 1930-55; mem. speakers research com. UN, 1946—; rep. Women's Nat. Book Assn. to UN Non-govtl. Orgns. and Non-govtl. orgns. U.S. mission to UN. Mem. emergency welfare div. Citizens Welfare Corps, City of N.Y., 1942-45. Mem. county Democratic Com., 1968—. Mem. League Women Voters (leader freedom forums 1941-45), Women's Nat. Book Assn., U.N. Assn. of the U.S.A., Women United for the U.N., East Lyme Hist. Soc. Author: Cal Me Bronko, 1955. Contbr. articles to Scholastic Mag. and numerous young people's publs. Home: 139 E 33rd St New York City NY 10016

EICHHORN, JANICE ELAINE, orgn. exec.; b. St. Louis, Mar. 27, 1938; d. W. Hirschel and Bernice (Saphian) Eichhorn; student U. Ill., Washington U., St. Louis. Mem. office staff U.S. congressmen, 1964-66; asst. U.S. Senator Gaylord Nelson of Wis., 1966-68, dep. adminstrv. asst., 1969-72; exec. asst. to dir. Nat. Council Equal Bus. Opportunity, 1968-69; asst. to Wis. coordinator McGovern for Pres. campaign, 1972; exec. dir. Self-Determination for D.C., 1972—. Mem. D.C. del. Nat. Democratic Conv., 1968. Bd. dirs. Americans for Democratic Action, 1969—, Washington Home Rule Com., 1970—, Southwest Community House, Washington, 1966-70, D.C. Hospitality House, 1975—. Democrat. Home: 512A 6th St SE Washington DC 20003 Office: Self-Determination for DC care Common Cause 2030 M St NW Washington DC 20036

EIDE, IRENE MONSON (MRS. LEIF NORMAN EIDE), educator; b. Hooppole, Ill., Aug. 19, 1914; d. Carl Wilhelm and Betty (Persson) Monson; B.A. (scholar), Concordia Coll., 1936; M.S., Kan. State Coll., 1940; postgrad. (NSF grantee), U. N.D., 1961; m. Leif Norman Eide, Dec. 22, 1942; children—LeRoy Norman, Claire Arthur, Beverly Ellen. Tchr. various high schs., N.D., Mich., Cal., 1936-59; asst. prof. biology, math., registrar U. N.D., Williston, 1959—. Supr. distbn. and sales Shaklee Products, Williston, 1967—. Mem. Am. Assn. U. Women (state topic chmn. 1969-73). Lutheran. Home: 1706 4th Av W Williston ND 58801

EIFLER, ANNE G., home economist; b. Altoona, Pa., Aug. 25, 1908; d. Charles W. and Emily (Cornelius) Eifler; B.S., Pa. State U., 1930; M.S., Cornell U., 1951. Tchr., Altoona Sch. Dist., 1930-46, dir. home econs. and cafeterias, 1946-56; supr. sch. lunch and nutrition Dept. Pub. Instrn., Commonwealth of Pa., Harrisburg, 1956-70; supr. home econs. Pa. Dept. Edn., 1970-73; cons. dietician Hillview Nursing Home, 1973—. Disaster chmn. Blair County br. A.R.C., 1947-57; mem. adv. bd. Altoona Undergrad. Center, Pa. State U., 1940; chmn. adv. bd. Blair County R.S.V.P. Mem. N.E.A., Pa. Edn. Assn. (dist. pres. 1954-56), Am., Pa. home econs. assns., Am. Vocational Assn. (pres. elect home econs. suprs. section), Am. Sch. Food Service Assn., Am. Assn. U. Women (br. corr. sec. 1949-51, br. treas. 1952-53), Delta Kappa Gamma (chpt. pres. 1956). Home: 400 S 22d St Altoona PA 16602

EIKEN, SHIRLEY ANN (MRS. EVERETT H. EIKEN), educator; b. Spring Grove, Minn., Feb. 25, 1939; d. Grant Carlton and Berneice Sylvia (Humble) Wermager; B.A., Luther Coll., 1960; M.S., Winona State Coll., 1963; Ed.D., U. No. Colo., 1965; m. Everett H. Eiken, Mar. 21, 1959; children—Beth Allison, Brett Evan. Tchr. English and bus. edn. Crestwood High Sch., Cresco, Ia., 1960-63, Central High Sch., Greeley, Colo., 1963-64; bus. edn. tchr. Manpower Devel. Tng. Act Adult Edn., 1964-65; prof. bus. adminstrn., Wis. State U. at Whitewater, 1965-66; prof. bus. edn., and office adminstrn. Winona (Minn.) State Coll., 1966—. Recipient Alpha award Delta Pi Epsilon, 1969. Mem. Nat., Minn., North Central bus. edn. assns., Delta Pi Epsilon. Home: Route 1 Minnesota City MN 55959 Office: Winona State College Winona MN 55987

EIKREM, MARGARET ROSEMARIE MCDONOUGH (MRS. LYNWOOD O. EIKREM), realtor; b. Boston; d. William Francis and Margaret F. (McGunigle) McDonough; B.S., Mass. State Coll.; M.Ed., Boston U.; m. Lynwood O. Eikrem, July 13, 1946; children—Margaret Anne, John Paul, Marie Elizabeth, Jeanne Marie. Tchr. pub. schs., Boston, 1939-44; pres. Boston council Girl Scouts U.S.A., 1962-65, exec. dir. Glendale (Cal.) Area, 1966-68; part-time tchr. pub. schs., Glendale, 1968-71; asso. Journey's End Realty Co., LaCanada, Cal., 1969—. Mem. Boston City Fedn. Orgns., 1960—, pres., 1964-65; mem. Mayor's Com. for Better Boston, 1963-65; mem. real estate edn. adv. com. Pasedena City Coll., 1970—; mem. Sierra Madres council Girl Scouts U.S.A., Pasadena, Cal., 1968—; mem. Verdugo Hills (Cal.) Planning Council, 1967-68. Served as ensign USCGR, 1944-46. Mem. Am. Inst. Parliamentarians, Nat. Assn. Parliamentarians, La Canada Bd. Raealtors (pres. salesmen's div. 1971), Boston Parliamentary Law Club (pres. 1962-64), Mass. Fedn. Womens Clubs (dist. dir. 1964-65), Ladies Aux. V.F.W. (state pres. 1961-62). Home: 4902 Alta Canyada Rd La Canada CA 91011 Office: 727 Foothill Blvd La Canada CA 91011

EIL, LOIS HELEN (MRS. HARRY EIL), physician; b. Ashland, Wis., Dec. 25, 1920; d. Abraham and Clara Ida (Frindell) Latts; student Carleton Coll., 1938-39; B.S., U. Minn., 1942, M.S., 1943, M.D., 1946; M.P.H., Columbia, 1967; m. Harry Eil, Mar. 12, 1944; children—Charles, Alison (Mrs. Henry Stolzman), Mitchell. Intern Cumberland Hosp., Bklyn., 1947-48; attending pediatric physician Lincoln Hosp., Bronx, 1953-66; supervising sch. health physician N.Y.C. Health Dept., 1960-66; dir. med. programs Profl. Exam. Service, N.Y.C., 1967-69; dir. medicaid program N.Y. State Health Dept., White Plains region, 1969—. Mem. Am. Pub. Health Assn. Home: 77 Puritan Av Yonkers NY 10710 Office: 901 N Broadway White Plains NY 10603

EINSTEIN, MIMI MATSNER (MRS. ARTHUR W. EINSTEIN, JR.), publishing co. editor; b. N.Y.C., Sept. 21, 1939; d. Eric M. and Brita (Digby-Brown) Matsner; B.A., Hollins Coll., 1961; m. Arthur W. Einstein, Jr., Sept. 10, 1970; children—Nicholas W., Elizabeth J. Publicity asso. Random House, N.Y.C., 1962-64; publicity and advt. mgr. Harcourt Brace Jovanovich, Inc., N.Y.C., 1965-66, editor-in-chief curriculum related books, 1967-70, editor-in-chief children's book dept., 1971—. Mem. Children's Book Council, A.L.A. Home: 2 E 88th St New York City NY 10028 Office: 757 3d Av New York City NY 10017

EINUM, LUCILLE GRACE JOHNSON (MRS. ELMER JOHN EINUM), civic worker; b. New Richmond, Wis., Aug. 13, 1907; d. Willard Joseph and Nora (Unseth) Johnson; grad. Wis. State U., 1926; student U. Minn.; pvt. study voice; m. Elmer John Einum, June 2, 1936; children—Catherine Ann (Mrs. John P. Eimerman), Victoria Lou (dec.). Pres., Wis. Fedn. Music Clubs, 1964-68, bd. dirs., 1949-74, adv. chmn., 1968-72; chmn. TV program Starring Young Wis. Artists, 1968-74; sec.-treas. nat. Council dists. and state presidents Nat. Fedn. Music Clubs, 1966-68, nat. vice-chmn. nat. music week, 1967-69, nat. chmn. nat. music week, 1969-73, nat. bd. dirs., 1971-73, nat. chmn. TV com., 1973; gov.'s appointee to bd. dirs. Wis. Arts Found and Council, 1965-73; 1st state pres. Young Audiences of Wis., 1968—; Midwest regional dir. Nat. Young Audiences, 1970-73; mem. panel Nat. Conf. on Continuing Adult Edn. in Music, U. Wis., 1967—; chmn. 1st Angel Ball Benefit Stout Found., 1968-69; mem. Mayors Adv. Com., 1968— chmn. Wonderful Wis. Week, Rice Lake, 1971. Pres. Barron County Republican Women's Club, 1969-72. Bd. dirs. Wis. Youth Symphony. Adv. chmn. bd. trustees Stout State U. Found. Barron County Campus; bd. govs. Florentine Opera Co., Milw., 1972—. Named Woman of Year, Rice Lake, Fedn. Woman's Clubs, 1966-67; recipient award for support of arts Gov. Wis., 1972; Distinguished Citizens award Am. Assn. U. Women, 1973. Mem. Civic Concert Assn. (bd. dirs. 1951-73, pres. 1969—), Wis. P.T.A. (bd. dirs. 1959-61), Rice Lake Fed. Music Club (life). Delta Omicron. Republican. Presbyn. (choir dir.), Club: Fortnightly Woman's (life, past pres.). Address: 721 N Main St Rice Lake WI 54868

EISEMAN, FANNIE RAPFOGEL (MRS. JACOB B. EISEMAN), library cons.; b. Brklyn.; d. Moses and Lena Rapfogel; Ph.B., Brown U., 1924; B.S. in L.S., Columbia, 1932; m. Jacob B. Eiseman, Aug. 12, 1928 (dec. Aug. 1963). Cataloguer, Columbia Library, N.Y.C., 1920-21, 32; editorial asst. Sch. Library Service, 1936-37; cataloguer Engring, Socs., Library, N.Y.C., 1922-23, 24-26; librarian J. & W. Seligman, N.Y.C., 1926-28; sch. librarian N.Y.C. Bd. Edn., 1939-72, head librarian George W. Wingate High Sch., Bklyn., 1954-72; now library cons. Vis. tchr. dept. library edn. State U. N.Y., Geneseo, summers, 1958-59; speaker, panelist, cons. numerous ednl. and profl. meetings, confs., workshops, 1946-70. Mem. A.L.A., N.Y. Library Assn. (dir. sch. libraries sect. 1967-70), Bklyn. Bot. Garden, Bklyn. Mus., N.Y.C. Sch. Librarians Assn. (v.p. 1948-50, pres. 1950-52), N.Y. Library Club (exec. council 1965-69), Beta Phi Mu. Contbr. numerous articles profl. jours. Home: 10 Plaza St Brooklyn NY 11238

EISEN, EMILY LITTMAN, neuropsychologist; b. N.Y.C., May 14, 1943; d. Benjamin and Ruth (Wertheimer) Littman; B.A., Conn. Coll., 1965; M.A., N.Y. U., 1972, postgrad., 1972—; m. Steven Leslie Eisen, July 23, 1967. Psychology intern Manhattan VA Hosp., N.Y.C., 1968-70; asst. in neuropsychology Montefiore Hosp., Bronx, N.Y., 1969-70; sch. psychologist Shepaug Valley Sch. Dist., Washington, Conn., 1971—. Cons. Waterbury (Conn.) Neurodiagnostics. Bd. dirs. Bethlehem-Morris Vis. Nurses Assn., 1971-73. Ida Brodman scholar. Mem. Am. Psychol. Assn., Internat. Neuropsychol. Soc., Internat. Council Psychologists, Am., Conn. personnel and guidance assns. Home: Box 134 Bethlehem CT 06751 Office: Shepaug Valley Middle High Sch Washington CT 06793

EISENBERG, CAROLA, psychiatrist; b. Buenos Aires, Argentina, Sept. 15, 1917; d. Bernardo and Teodora (Kahan) Blitzman; M.D., U. Buenos Aires, 1944; m. Manfred Guttmacher, Oct. 11, 1946 (dec. Nov. 1966); children—Larry Bernard, Alan Edward; m. 2d, Leon Eisenberg, Aug. 30, 1967. Intern, Instituto Sanchez Picado-Argentina; resident Hospicio de las Mercedes, Argentina; psychiat. fellow Johns Hopkins Hosp., 1945-47; practice medicine, specializing in psychiatry, Balt., 1957-67; asst. prof. psychiatry Johns Hopkins, Balt., 1960-67; physician Student Health Service, Mass. Inst. Tech., 1967-72, dean for student affairs, 1972—; lectr. psychiatry Harvard Med. Sch., 1967—; cons. in psychiatry Mass. Gen. Hosp., 1967—. Fellow Am. Psychiat. Assn.; mem. Am. Med. Women's Assn., Am. Assn. U. Profs., Am. Orthopsychiat. Assn. Home: 9 Clement Circle Cambridge MA 02138 Office: Mass Inst Tech Cambridge MA 02139

EISENBERG, ROSELYN JANE (MRS. WILLIAM VICTOR EISENBERG), microbiologist, educator; b. N.Y.C., Apr. 26, 1940; d. Solomon and Sally (Lichtblau) Goldberg; A.B., Bryn Mawr Coll., 1960; Ph.D., U. Pa., 1965; m. William Victor Eisenberg, Mar. 26, 1961; children—Ruth, Jeffrey. Research asso. U. Pa., Phila., 1968-69, asst. prof. microbiology, 1969—. USPHS postdoctoral fellow, 1966-68; USPHS research grantee, 1969—. Recipient USPHS Career Devel. award, 1972—. Mem. Am. Assn. U. Women, Am. Civil Liberties Union. Research in microbial genetics, physiology. Home: 126 Club House Dr Willingboro NJ 08046 Office: 4010 Locust St Philadelphia PA 19174

EISENBRAUN, JOYCE MARIE (MRS. EDMUND J. EISENBRAUN), radiologist; b. Unity, Wis., Dec. 30, 1926; d. Norman H. and Ella P. (Brehm) Abrahamson; B.S., U. Wis., 1948, M.D., 1951; m. Edmund J. Eisenbraun, Aug. 20, 1949; children—Ellen, Greta, Ann. Intern St. Mary's Hosp., Madison, Wis., 1951-52; resident radiology Wayne State U., Detroit, Mich., 1956-59; acting chief, dept. radiology, Palo Alto (Cal.) Stanford VA Hosp., 1960-61; practice medicine specializing in radiology, Milw., 1961-62, Stillwater, Okla., 1962—, Oklahoma City, 1962—; mem. staff Mercy Hosp., Oklahoma City. Mem. Am., Okla. med. assns., Payne County Med. Soc., Am. Coll. Radiology, Okla. Radiologic Soc., Phi Beta Kappa, Alpha Omega Alpha. Baptist. Home: 1102 Graham Dr Stillwater OK 74074 Office: 501 NW 12th Oklahoma City OK 73103

EISENHART, ELIZABETH WILLIAMS (MRS. EDWIN A. EISENHART), lawyer; b. Roanoke, Va., Feb. 16, 1916; d. John Ashby and Eva Elsie (Wallbridge) Williams; LL.B. cum laude, Southeastern U., 1938, LL.M., 1940; m. Edwin A. Eisenhart, Apr. 22, 1939 (dec. 1971); children—Thomas A., Henry A., Susan (Mrs. Robert Meador). Admitted to U.S. Dist. Ct. for D.C., 1939, U.S. Ct. Appeals for D.C., 1940, U.S. Supreme Ct. bar, 1944, U.S. Dist. Ct. for N.M., 1957, N.M. bar, 1960; asso. firm Ashby Williams, Washington, 1939-42, Butler, Butler & Tausig, Washington, 1942-52, Craig Morton & James O'Toole, Albuquerque, 1960-61; law clk., opinion writer to Chief Justice James M. Compton, Supreme Ct. N.M., Santa Fe, 1961-66; clk. N.M. Ct. Appeals, Santa Fe, 1966-69; ret., 1969. Leader, Girl Scouts U.S.A., Arlington, Va., 1951-53; active Boy Scout and Cub Scout groups. Mem. Bar Assn. D.C., State Bar N.M., Nat., Tex. assns. real estate bds., El Paso Bd. Realtors, Kappa Phi Epsilon. Author: Handbook on Wills, Probate and Administration, 1964. Home: 6411 Los Altos Dr El Paso TX 79912

EISENHOWER, MAMIE GENEVA DOUD, wife former Pres. U.S.; b. Boone, Ia.; Nov. 14, 1896; d. John Sheldon and Elivera M. (Carlson) Doud; ed. Miss Wolcott's Sch.; L.H.D. (hon.), Colo. Woman's Coll., 1946; LL.D. honoris causa, St. Joseph Coll., 1959; m. Dwight David Eisenhower (Pres. U.S. 1953-61), July 1, 1916; 1 son, John Sheldon Doud. Hon. pres. Girl Scouts of Am. Hon. mem.

Woman's Med. Coll. of Pa. Decorated Order of Malta, Italy, 1952, Cavalier Order of So. Cross, Brazil, 1946, Grand Cross Order of Honor and Merit, Cuba, 1953. Mem. Daus. of Colo., Ia. Hist. Soc. (hon.), Distinguished Daus. Pa., D.A.R., Army and Navy Union Aux., Daus. Cin. (hon.). Republican. Presbyn. Home: Gettysburg PA 17325*

EISENSTEIN, ESTHER BENJAMIN (MRS. SAM EISENSTEIN), pediatrician; b. Calcutta, India, Dec. 16, 1935; d. Isaiah M. and Seemah (Jacob) Benjamin; Intermediate Sci. certificate U. Calcutta, 1954, M.B. B.S., 1960; m. Sam Eisenstein, June 24, 1962; children—Sandra Toby, Lana Rachel. Came to U.S., 1964, naturalized, 1972. Rotating intern Jewish Gen. Hosp., Montreal, Que., Can., 1960-61; resident in medicine Montreal Children's Hosp., 1961-62, Queen Mary Vets. Hosp., Montreal, 1962-63; resident in pediatrics Einstein Med. Center, Phila., 1965-66; fellow in pediatrics Jackson Meml. Hosp., Miami Fla., 1967-69, Boston Hosp. for Women, 1969-70; practice medicine specializing in pediatrics, Brookline and Malden, Mass., 1970—; mem. staff Malden Hosp., Children's Hosp. Med. Center, Boston, Carney Hosp., Boston. Instr. pediatrics Harvard Med. Sch., 1970—. Diplomate Am. Bd. Pediatrics. Fellow Am. Acad. Pediatrics; mem. A.M.A. Home: 25 Littell Rd Brookline MA 02146 Office: 2100 Dorchester Av Boston MA 02224

EISERMAN, ARLENE CLAIR, pub. co. exec.; b. Pearl River, N.Y.; d. Frederick Joel and Anna (Behnke) Eiserman; student Bergen Jr. Coll., 1946-48; B.S., Utah State U., 1950; postgrad. Traphagen Sch. Design, 1957, N.Y. U., 1958, Hunter Coll., 1959-60. Research and promotion asst. Archtl. Record, N.Y.C., 1952-56; asst. research dir. Esquire Mag., N.Y.C., 1956-62; research mgr. Am. Machinist, publ. McGraw-Hill, Inc., N.Y.C., 1962-67, marketing service mgr., 1967-69, 1969-71; v.p. marketing services Morgan-Gramplan, Inc., N.Y.C., 1971-72; dist. sales mgr. Postgrad. Medicine McGraw-Hill, Inc., 1972—. Mem. Am. Marketing Assn., Pi Sigma Alpha. Home: 2 Tudor City New York City NY 10017 Office: 1221 Av of Americas New York City NY 10020

EISERT, SANDRA LEE, editor; b. New Albany, Ind., Feb. 23, 1947; d. Erwin Lewis and Norma Lee (Bailey) Eisert; grad. Ind. U., 1973. Asst. picture editor Louisville Times, 1970-71, picture editor, 1971—. Mem. Nat. Press Photographers Assn., Women in Communications. Home: PO Box 3027 Louisville KY 40201 Office: 525 W Broadway Louisville KY 40202

EISING, LUCILE MINELLA, physician; b. Auburndale, Wis., Nov. 5, 1908; d. George Walter and Jessie (Davey) Eising; B.A., Carroll Coll., 1929; M.D., U. Wis., 1933. Intern, Wis. Gen. Hosp., 1933-34; resident Children's Hosp., San Francisco, 1934-35, 36-46, mem. staff, cons. depts. phys. and occupational therapy, 1946-73, cons., 1963—; dir. phys. medicine U. Cal. Hosp., San Francisco, 1948-61, intern phys. therapy, 1935-36; med. supr. curriculum in phys. therapy U. Cal. Sch. Medicine, 1948-58, asst. clin. prof. phys. medicine, 1959—; med. dir. Inst. Neurol. Devel., Belmont, Cal., 1967-71. Cons. phys. therapy dept., mem. med. staff St. Joseph's Hosp., San Francisco, 1969—. Mem. San Francisco exec. com. Muscular Dystrophy Assns. Am., 1970-72. Diplomate Am. Bd. Phys. Medicine and Rehab. Fellow Am. Acad. Cerebral Palsy, Am. Acad. Phys. Medicine and Rehab.; mem. Am. Rheumatism Assn., Am., Cal. med. assns., Nat. Rehab. Assn. (mem. exec. com. San Francisco chpt. 1973—), LeRoy C. Abbott Orthopedic Soc., San Francisco Med. Soc. Home: 1594 11th Av San Francisco CA 94122 Office: U Cal Hosps San Francisco CA 94143

EISING, PATRICIA LAURENE, naturalist; b. Detroit, Jan. 19, 1938; d. Lawrence John and Blanche Hazel (Addicott) Eising; B.S., Mich. State U., 1959, M.A., 1968. Naturalist, Nature Unit, Detroit Dept. Parks and Recreation, 1959-65; naturalist Huron-Clinton Metropolitan Authority, Stony Creek Park, 1965-68, naturalist supr. Kensington Park, Milford, Mich., 1968—. Faculty Wayne State U., 1972—, Univ. Center for Adult Edn., 1972—. Leader 4-H, 1960-66, county conservation leader, 1962-64; vol. leader trainer Girl Scouts Am., 1964—. Recipient Meritorious Service award Assn.-Interpretive Naturalists, 1972. Mem. Assn. Interpretive Naturalists (dir. 1967—), Soc. Am. Foresters, Am. Nature Study Soc. Presbyn. Home: 1935 Alton Circle Walled Lake MI 48088 Office: 2240 W Buno Rd Milford MI 48042

EISLER, RIANE TENNENHAUS, lawyer; b. Vienna, Austria, July 22, 1931; d. David A. and Elisa (Greif) Tennenhaus; came to U.S., 1946; naturalized, 1952; B.A. in Sociology and English magna cum laude, U. Cal. at Los Angeles, 1952, LL.B., 1965; children by previous marriage—Andrea, Loren. Admitted to Cal. bar, 1966; asso. Zagon, Schiff, Hirsch & Levine, Beverly Hills, Cal., 1966-68; pvt. practice law, Los Angeles, 1968—. Dir. legal program Women's Center, 1969-71; lectr. U. Cal. at Los Angeles, 1972, Immaculate Heart Coll., 1972. Bd. dirs. Los Angeles YWCA, 1973—, Women's Clinic, Los Angeles, 1972—. Mem. Los Angeles County Bar Assn., Women Lawyer's Assn., State Bar Assn. Cal., Phi Beta Kappa, Pi Gamma Mu. Contbr. articles to profl. jours. Office: 1028 Selby Av Los Angeles CA 90024

EITZMAN, ARDATH ANN (MRS. WALTER M. EITZMAN, JR.), banker; b. Coshocton, O., June 8, 1938; d. Arthur L. and Jean (Blind) Dickerson; student Ohio State U., 1956-61; m. Walter M. Eitzman, Jr., May 11, 1964; children—Gregory, JoJene. Reporter, Columbus (O.) Dispatch, 1959-60, Kent (O.) Courier, 1961; editor Roadway Express, Akron, O., 1961-63, Sperry Rand Corp., Phoenix, 1963; asst. cashier Ariz. Bank, Phoenix, 1963—. Mem. Internat. Assn. Bus. Communicators (v.p. dist. 1969, Outstanding award 1969), Ariz. Indsl. Editors (pres. 1968), Florence Crittendon Aux., Alpha Delta Pi (pres. 1966). Methodist. Editor: The Ariz. Bank Ledger, 1963-6 Roadway Spotlight, 1961-63. Home: 3636 W Hayward Av Phoenix AZ 85021 Office: 44 W Monroe St Phoenix AZ 85003

EKIRCH, KATHRYN LOUISE, univ. ofcl.; b. N.Y.C., Sept. 21, 1917; d. Arthur and Louise (Borgstede) Ekirch; B.A., Conn. Coll., 1939. Pub. relations practioner R.H. Macy & Co., 1961-66; pub. relations dir., dean women Pace U., Pleasantville, N.Y., 1967-74, asst. v.p. for univ. and community relations, 1974—. Mem. Pub. Relations Soc. Am. (dir. Westchester chpt. 1971—), Pub. Relations Assn. Westchester Colls. and Univs. (pres. 1970-71). Home: 115 Grandview Av White Plains NY 10605 Office: Bedford Rd Pleasantville NY 10570

EKLUND, SUSAN JANE, educator; b. San Antonio, June 2, 1939; d. Theodore Tilden and Jane Mercedes (Kelley) Eklund; student San Antonio Coll., 1957-59; B.A., U. Tex., 1961; M.S., Trinity U., 1961-62; Ph.D., George Peabody Coll., 1970. Psychologist, Houston Ind. Sch. Dist., 1962-65; research asso. Demonstration and Research Center for Early Edn., George Peabody Coll., Nashville, 1967-68; instr. sch. psychology Tchrs. Coll., Columbia, N.Y.C., 1968-69; sch. psychologist White Plains, N.Y., 1968-69; asso. prof. ednl. psychology, dir. sch. psychology tng. program Ind. U., Bloomington, 1969—. Nat. Inst. Mental Health fellow, 1965-68. Mem. Am. Psychol. Assn., A.A.A.S. Home: 3617 Post Rd Bloomington IN 47401

EKSTROM, RUTH BURT, research psychologist; b. Bennington, Vt., July 2, 1931; d. Ralph Amos and Bertha Paisley (Lambert) Burt; A.B., Brown U., 1953; Ed.M., Boston U., 1956; Ed.D., Rutgers U., 1967; m. Lincoln Ekstrom, Nov. 9, 1957. Tchr. pub. schs., Beverly, Mass., 1953-57; research asst. Ednl. Testing Service, 1957-64, profl. asso., 1964-66, dir. documentation services, 1966-68, research psychologist, 1968—. Vis. lectr. Grad. Sch. Edn., Rutgers U., 1958-60. Trustee Brown U., 1972—. Mem. Am. Assn. Higher Edn., Am. Psychol. Assn., Am. Ednl. Research Assn., Nat. Council for Measurement in Edn., Psychometric Soc., Pi Lambda Theta. Co-editor: Kit of Reference Tests for Cognitive Factors, 1963. Contbr. articles to profl. publs. Home: 78 Westerly Rd Princeton NJ 08540 Office: Educational Testing Service Princeton NJ 08540

ELAM, JULIA CORENE, ednl. adminstr.; b. Saxe, Va.; d. William Henry and Mary Jane (Price) Elam; A.B. (scholar), Va. State Coll., 1957, M.A., 1964; D.Arts, Carnegie-Mellon U., 1970. Chmn., English and fgn. lang. dept. Central High Sch., Sussex, Va., 1957-62; instr. English, Va. State Coll., Petersburg, 1960-62; chmn. English and foreign lang. dept. J.E.J. Moore High Sch., Disputanta, Va., 1962-64; faculty Bowie (Md.) State Coll., 1964—, prof. English, dir. ednl. tech. and communication, 1970—. Cons. instructional tech., communication for various ednl. instns., 1970—. Ford Found. study grantee, 1968-70. Mem. Nat., Md. councils tchrs. English, Nat. Assn. Coll. Women, Nat. Assn. Ednl. Broadcasters, Coll. Lang. Assn., Assn. Ednl. Communication Tech., Modern Lang. Assn., Md. Assn. Higher Edn., Delta Sigma Theta. Home: 8670 Brae Brooke Dr Lanham MD 20801 Office: Bowie State College Bowie MD 20715

ELCAN, ANNA BURNETT (MRS. GEORGE HANNAH ELCAN, JR.), home economist; b. Willis, Va., Aug. 19, 1918; d. Eddie Samuel and Iturea Elizabeth (Weeks) Burnett; B.S. magna cum laude, Radford Coll., 1938; postgrad. (Horace A. Mann Found. scholar), Cornell U., 1960, Va. Poly. Inst. and State U., 1961, 67, George Washington U., 1963; m. George Hannah Elcan, Jr., Dec. 4, 1948 (dec. Dec. 1954); children—Anne Burnett (Mrs. David Cyrus Judd), George Hannah III. Tchr. home econs. Willis (Va.) High Sch., 1938-39, Boonsboro High Sch., Lynchburg, Va., 1939-42; extension agt. Va. tech. extension div. Prince Edward Co., Farmville, Va., 1942-48, Campbell County, Rustburg, Va., 1955—. Recipient citation for outstanding service Va. Rural Safety Council, 1957, distinguished service award Nat. Assn. Extension Home Economists, 1962, citation 25 years service to 4-H, 1973. Mem. Nat. (dir. Southern region 1971-73), Va. (pres. 1967-68) assns. extension home economists, Am., Va. (dist. chmn. 1945-46) home econs. assns., Nat., Va. assns. extension 4-H agts., D.A.R., Epsilon Sigma Phi, Kappa Delta Pi, Pi Gamma Mu, Tau Kappa Alpha. Presbyn. (deacon 1968-71, Christian edn. com. 1969-74). Home: 608 Hayes Dr Lynchburg VA 24502 Office: Box 67 Rustburg VA 24588

ELDEFRAWI, AMIRA TOPPOZADA (MRS. MOHYEE ELDIN ELDEFRAWI), neurobiologist; b. Giza, Egypt (came to U.S. 1968).; d. Hussein Khairy and Fadila Ibrahim (Aref) Toppozada; B.S. with distinction, U. Alexandria (Egypt), 1957; Ph.D., U. Cal. at Berkeley, 1960; m. Mohyee Eldin Eldefrawi, July 18, 1957; children—Mohsen, Mona, Mohab. Tchr. asst. U. Cal. at Berkeley, 1960; asst. prof. insect toxicology, U. Alexandria (Egypt), 1961-68; research asso. Cornell U., Ithaca, N.Y., 1968-71, sr. research asso., 1971—. Recipient Grad. Study Fellowship in U.S.A., Egyptian govt., 1959. Mem. Entomol. Soc. Am. Author: Resistance of Insects, Ticks, Mites to Pesticides, 1966. Contbr. articles to profl. jours. Home: 320 N Sunset Dr Ithaca NY 14850 Office: Langmuir Lab Cornell U Ithaca NY 14850

ELDER, HAZEL GASSMAN (MRS. BILLY JUNIOR ELDER), marketing research co. exec.; b. Freeport, Ill., Aug. 17, 1951; d. Oliver August and Leona Gertrude (Pahl) Gassman; grad. high sch.; m. Billy Junior Elder, Nov. 29, 1946. Marketing research interviewer ind. contractor, 1961-64; pres., Marketing Research Field Supervision Service, Hazel Elder Enterprises, Inc., La Mesa, Cal., 1966—; v.p., treas. Billy J. Elder Constrn. Co., Inc., 1973—. Mem. Am. Marketing Assn. (sec. 1968-70), Market Research Assn. (awards com. chmn. 1972-73), San Diego C. of C. (mem. research com. 1971—), San Diego Better Bus. Bur. Mem. Order Eastern Star. Home: 9396 Crest Dr Spring Valley CA 92077 Office: 7700 University Av La Mesa CA 92041

ELDER, SHIRLEY, journalist; b. Oakland, Cal., May 4, 1931; d. James and Marie (Curtis) Elder; B.A., Stanford, 1954; m. Richard Louis Lyons, Mar. 11, 1972. Reporter, Washington Post, 1955; polit. reporter No. Va. Sun, 1957-59, Washington Daily News, 1959-65; congl. reporter Washington Star-News, 1966—, chief congl. corr., 1972—. Home: 1801 Paul Spring Rd Alexandria VA 22307 Office: 225 Virginia Av SE Washington DC 20003

ELDRED, CAROLYN ANNE, psychologist; b. Orange, N.J., Feb. 7, 1945; B.A., Mary Washington Coll., 1966; M.A., George Washington U., 1968, Ph.D., 1971. Research psychologist Nat. Inst. Mental Health, Bethesda, Md., 1966-67, 69-72, Narcotics Treatment Adminstrn., Washington, 1972-74, Westat Research, Inc., Rockville, Md., 1974—. Clin. psychology extern D.C. Gen. Hosp., 1968; intern St. Elizabeths Hosp., Washington, 1969. Credit chair Women's Legal Def. Fund, 1973—; mem. credit, criminal justice coms. D.C. Commn. Status Women, 1973. Nat. Inst. Mental Health trainee, 1968-69. Mem. Am. Psychol. Assn., A.A.A.S., Eastern, D.C. psychol. assns. Research on children's copying errors, marriage, etiology of schizophrenia, drug use in women, effects of drug use on family. Home: 11736 Cherry Grove Dr Gaithersburg MD 20760 Office: 11600 Nebel St Rockville MD 20852

ELDREDGE, MARJORIE LEE BADGE (MRS. INMAN FOWLER ELDREDGE, JR.), city ofcl., real estate broker; b. Bay City, Tex., Sept. 8, 1925; d. George Graham and Ella Marjorie (LeRibeus) Badge; student U. Houston, 1942-44; B.S., La. State U., 1946; postgrad. Lamar U., 1972; m. Inman Fowler Eldredge, Jr., Sept. 1, 1946 (dec. July, 1974); children—George Badge, Frank Inman, Christopher Lee. Free lance newspaper corr., 1959-70; substitute tchr. Silsbee (Tex.) Ind. Sch. Dist., 1970-73; partner Hays-Eldredge Real Estate, Silsbee, 1972—. Mem., sec. City's Charter Change Commn., 1966; mem., sec. City's Safety Com., 1963-66; mem. city council, Silsbee, Tex., 1971—, mayor pro-tem, 1972-73. Bd. dirs., treas., finance chmn. Silsbee (Tex.) Pub. Library. Methodist. Club: Woman's (pres. Silsbee 1965-66). Home: 1230 Maxwell Dr PO Box 1135 Silsbee TX 77656 Office: 915 Hwy 96 S Silsbee TX 77656

ELDRIDGE, JESSIE CANNON, poet, clubwoman; b. Brockton, Mass., Mar. 8, 1914; d. Arthur George and Ella May (Mailman) Cannon; student Mrs. Elliot's Bus. Coll., 1933; m. Warren Sanford Eldridge, Sept. 1, 1934; children—Richard Sanford, William George, James Warren, Charles Prescott. Free-lance poet; newspaper columnist, 1953-57; proprietor answering service, Kingston, Mass. Named Poet Laureate Kingston and Plymouth, Mass., 1950; recipient Danae award. Mem. Nat. Fedn. State Poetry Socs., Mass. Poetry Soc., Writers' Club of Abington, R.I. Writers' Guild, Am. Poetry League, Am. Barders, Jounal Poets, Poesy Club. Author: To A Dream Aspiring, 1948. Home: 35 Maple St Kingston MA 02364

ELDRIDGE, RONNIE MYERS, pub. co. exec.; b. N.Y.C., Jan. 31, 1931; d. Clifford Luckstone and Aimee (Fleck) Myers; A.B., Barnard Coll., 1952; m. Lawrence Eldridge, Mar. 24, 1955 (dec.); children—Daniel, Emily, Lucy. Spl. asst to Mayor N.Y.C., 1969-72; dept. city adminstrn., N.Y.C., 1972; dir. spl. projects Ms. mag., N.Y.C., 1973—; pres. Ms. Marketing, Inc.; exec. dir. Ms. Found.; lectr. New Sch. Social Research. Adviser to Sen. Robert F. Kennedy, 1964-68; dep. campaign mgr. Lindsay for Pres., 1971-72; vice chmn. platform com. Democratic nat. conv., 1972; campaign mgr. Congresswoman Bella Abzug, 1972. Bd. dirs. Woman's Action Alliance; trustee, v.p. Calhoun Sch., N.Y.C. Home: 149 W 93d St New York City NY 10025 Office: 370 Lexington Av New York City NY 10017

ELFAST, SHIRLEY OLIVE, borough clk.; b. West New York, N.J., June 6, 1920; d. Oliver Reuben and Lillian (Burdett) Johnson; student Egan Bus. Sch.; m. Arthur Edward Elfast, Apr. 27, 1974; 1 dau. by previous marriage, Shirley Anne (Mrs. Dennis Paul Polifroni). Sec., Met. Life Ins. Co., 1938-43; sec. Borough Clk.'s Office, Palisades Park, N.J., 1953-66, borough clk., 1967—. Past matron Townley chpt. Order Eastern Star; past mother adviser Townley Assembly, Order Rainbow Girls; past leader Girl Scout Troop. Baptist (tchr. Sunday sch., treas., past pres. missionary guild). Home: 300 E Homestead Av Palisades Park NJ 07650 Office: 275 Broad Av Palisades Park NJ 07650

ELFMAN, ROSE WOLSON MARKS (MRS. HARRY ELFMAN), clin. psychologist; b. Chester, Pa., Apr. 19, 1911; d. Abram William and Gertrude (Herr) Wolson; B.S., U. Pa., 1932, M.A., 1945, Ph.D., 1950; m. Myer Marks, Jan. 28, 1935 (dec. Mar. 1956); children—Avrum William Wolson, Nancy Suzanne (Mrs. Malcolm Silberman); m. 2d, Harry Elfman, June 21, 1958. Spl. class tchr. Chester Pub. Schs., 1932-35; tchr. student nurses Chester Hosp., 1945-50, psychologist in out-patient dept., 1945-56; cons. psychologist Pa. Bur. Rehab., 1950-60, 65—; supr. speech and hearing dept. Delaware County Sch. Dist., Chester, 1956-61; staff psychologist Crozer-Chester Med. Center, 1946—; dir. group therapy program for stroke patients and their families; practice clin. psychology, Chester, 1946—. Past cons. psychologist Neurol. Inst. and Neurol. Clinic for Children, Media; cons. Pa. Nurses aid A.R.C., Chester, 1943-45; cons. Delaware County Intermediate Unit 25 Sch. Dist.; past mem. West Met. Stroke Task Force; cons. Instituto Para La Capacitacion Armonica Del Niño Excepcional, Caracas, Venezuela. Dir. Ohev Sholom Synagogue Center, 1960, Nether Providence Sch. Bd., 1967-71. Bd. govs. Council for Advancement Psychol. Professions and Scis. Fellow Pa. Psychol. Assn. (treas. 1957-59); mem. Am., Eastern psychol. assns., Psychologists in Pvt. Practice (pres. 1970-71, now editor newsletter, editor biog. directory), Am. Psychology and Law Assn., Nat., Pa. rehab. assns., Am., Pa. speech and hearing assns., League Women Voters. Republican. Jewish religion. Mem. Hadassah B'nai B'rith. Author: Delco-Elfman Developmental Achievement Test, 1974. Contbr. articles to profl. jours. Address: Princeton Bldg Wildman Arms Swarthmore PA 19081

ELFSTROM, DOROTHY LILLIAN BETTENCOURT (MRS. WALTER WILLIAM ELFSTROM), author; b. Galveston, Tex.; d. Henry Joseph and Margaret (Rowan) Bettencourt; grad. Draughon's Bus. Coll.; m. Walter William Elfstrom (dec.); children—Dorothy (Mrs. Wade Bailey), Bill, Henry. Recipient 1st pl. awards Nat. Fedn. Press Women, 1963, Tex. Press Women, 1963. Author: Challenge of the Seasons, 1963; Fireside Fancies, 1960; Voyager on the Sea of Life, 1971; Seeker, 1974. Writer various songs including But I Just Can't Say Goodbye; You're Way Behind the Beat, Lovely Galveston; What Are you Trying to Find; At Taps Time I Have a Date With You; Not for Keeps; You Have Shaken Up My World; I Know You've Got to Go; Now You Won't Let Me Be. Contbr. to numerous mags., newspapers; weekly columnist Galveston Island Mirror, Texas City Daily Sun. Home: 3815 Av S Galveston TX 77550

ELGIN, KATHLEEN, author, illustrator; b. Trenton, N.J., Jan. 13, 1923; d. Charles P. and Mary (Poore) Elgin; student Dayton Art Inst., 1939-42, Columbia, 1950-53. Author, illustrator: First Book of Mythology, 1957; First Book of Norse Legends, 1958; Nun, A Gallery of Sisters, 1964; The Human Body; The Eye, The Hand, 1966, The Brain, The Ear, 1967, The Heart, The Male Reproductive System, 1968, The Female Reproductive System, 1968, The Skin, 1969, The Respiratory System, 1969, The Glands, 1970, The Skeleton, 1970, Freedom to Worship: The Quakers, 1968, The Mormons, 1969, The Episcopalians, 1970, The Unitarians, 1971; The Ups and Downs of Drugs, 1971, The Muscles, 1973, The Digestive System, 1973, Twenty Eight Days, 1973; The Fall Down, Skin Your Knee, Break a Bone Book, 1974; illustrator African Treehouse, 1974. Address: Box 425 Ocean Beach NY 11770

ELIASBERG, PHYLLIS WIEDIS, lawyer; b. Bklyn., July 23, 1935; d. Jack and Sadye (Wolf) Wiedis; B.A., Goucher Coll., 1953; postgrad. N.Y. U. Sch. Law, 1953-56; LL.B., San Fernando Valley Coll., 1969; m. Kenneth Charles Eliasberg, Apr. 4, 1956; children—James, David, Jonathan. Admitted to Cal. bar, 1969; staff atty. San Fernando Valley Neighborhood Legal Services, Pacoima, Cal., 1971-72; directing atty., 1972-73; dir. Family Law Center, Canoga Park, Cal., 1972-73; atty. FTC, Los Angeles, 1973; owner, dir. Wave Project, Do-It-Yourself Divorce Center Hdqrs., Van Nuys, Cal., 1973—. Instr. consumer and law U. Cal. at Los Angeles, 1973-74. Mem. Los Angeles Mayor's Spl. Com. on Consumer Protection, 1972-73; mem. planning council United Way, San Fernando Valley, 1972-74. Chairperson, Valley Lawyers for McGovern, 1971-72. Bd. dirs. Consumer Fedn. of Cal., 1973-74. Mem. Am., San Fernando Valley bar assns., Embroiderer's Guild Am. (dir. 1971-74). Home: 17116 Orozco St Granada Hills CA 91344 Office: 7005 Hayvenhurst Av Van Nuys CA 91406

ELIASON, PHYLLIS MARIE, missionary; b. Greenacres, Fla., Dec. 21, 1925; d. John Sylvester and Catherine Marie (Graef) Underhill; B.A. in Psychology, U. Guam, 1971, M.Ed., 1974; m. Albert Augustus Eliason, Oct. 22, 1952 (dec. 1955); children—Phyllis Ann (Mrs. John Worthen), Nancy Louise (Mrs. William Wilkins), James, Albert Augustus. Dir. Child Evangelism Fellowship Palm Beach County Fla., 1957-62; missionary dir. Child Evangelism Fellow, Guam, 1962—; traveling lectr. in U.S., 1966-67, 71-72, 73-74; tchr. trainer Leibenzell Missions Schs., Truk Island, 1968, 70, Bethania Girls Sch., Koror, Palau, 1965, 68. Pres. Guam council Girl Scouts, 1964-65; sec. Guam Shell Club, 1964-65. Named hon. citizens, Huntsville, Ala., 1966. Mem. Council Exceptional Children, Christian Edn. Fellowship of Evang. Tchr. Tng. Assn., Am. Personnel and Guidance Assn., Cal., Hawaiian malacological assns., Am. Assn. U. Women, Underhill Soc. Am., Christian Women's Clubs (prayer adviser 1973), Chi Omicron Gamma. Address: PO Box 905 Agana GU 96910

ELION, GERTRUDE BELLE, research scientist; b. N.Y.C., Jan. 23, 1918; d. Robert and Bertha (Cohen) Elion; A.B., Hunter Coll., 1937; M.S., N.Y. U., 1941; D.Sc., George Washington U., 1969; D.M.S., Brown U., 1969. Lab. asst. biochemistry N.Y. Hosp. Sch. Nursing, 1937; research asst. in organic chemistry Denver Chem. Mfg. Co., N.Y.C., 1938-39; tchr. chemistry and physics N.Y.C. Secondary Schs., 1940-42; food analyst Quaker Maid Co., Bklyn., 1942-43; research asst. in organic synthesis Johnson & Johnson, New

Brunswick, N.J., 1943-44; biochemist Wellcome Research Labs., Tuckahoe, N.Y., 1944-50, sr. research chemist, 1950—, asst. to asso. research dir., 1955-62, asst. to the research dir., 1963-66, head exptl. theory, 1966—, cons. USPHS, 1960-64. Chmn., Gordon Conf. on Coenzymes and Metabolic Pathways. Fellow N.Y. Acad. Scis.; mem. Am. Chem. Soc. (Garvan medal 1968), A.A.A.S., Chem. Soc. (London), Am. Soc. Biol. Chemists, Am. Assn. Cancer Research, Am. Soc. Hematology. Contbr. articles to profl. jours. Patentee in field. Home: 1 Banbury Lane Chapel Hill NC 27514 Office: 3030 Cornwallis Rd Research Triangle Park NC 27709

ELIOTT, KAREN JO, journalist; b. Matador, Tex., Dec. 7, 1947; d. Ted and Bailey Elliott; B.J. with highest honors, U. Tex. at Austin, 1970. Summer intern Houston Chronicle, 1969; edn. editor Dallas Morning News, 1970-71; Washington corr., 1971—; stringer Newsweek mag., 1968-74; corr. consumer affairs Wall St. Jour., 1974—. Mem. Women in Communications, Kappa Alpha Tau. Recipient Sch. Bell award Tex. Tchrs. Assn., 1971. Home: 1523 New Hampshire Av Washington DC 20036 Office: National Press Bldg Washington DC 20004

ELKAN, IDA (MRS. I. RUDOLPH KATZ), educator, composer; b. N.Y.C., Dec. 25, 1894; d. Rudolph and Sarah (Glickman) Elkan; student Hunter Coll., 1912-14, Columbia, 1935; m. I. Rudolph Katz, Jan. 30, 1916; children—Nathaniel, Maxwell B., Leon. Piano tchr. Detroit Inst. Mus. Art, 1926-29, music supr. pub. schs. Detroit, Dearborn (Mich.) Bd. Edn., 1927-29; supr. piano instrn. for sch. tchrs., N.Y.C., 1933-38; dir. piano instrn. Aeolian Piano Co., N.Y.C., 1939-41; established with husband music sch. Ida Elkan Sch. Music, N.Y.C., 1935—, dir., 1935-60; recital pianist, 1925—. Mem. A.S.C.A.P., Am. Fedn. Musicians. Author: Practical Music Theory for Piano, 1939, 58; Piano Sight Reading, 1948; Ear Training—Sight Reading, vol. I, 1926, vol. II, 1933. First Melodious Piano Pieces, 1955; Piano Suite, 1942, 64; Moods, Major and Minor, 1949; Ear Training, Sight Reading and Ensemble for Violin and Piano, 1961 (with I. Rudolph Katz); Birthday Greetings with 8 Variations; Hymn to the United Nations (words by Rev. Ralph Thorn); Sight Reading Studies for Piano, 1972. Address: 408 W 57th St New York City NY 10019

ELKIN, MIRIAM TATE, psychologist; b. Erie, Pa., Aug. 11, 1923; d. Edwin Arthur and Florence May (Petrie) Tate; B.S., U. Pitts., 1944; M.A., State U. Ia., 1947, Ph.D., 1950; m. Albert Elkin, Oct. 10, 1952; children—Dawn, Bradley, Rebecca, Benjamin. Psychologist, Tioga County Community Psychiat. Services, Owego, N.Y., 1969—; psychologist pediatrics dept. U. Kan. Med. Center, Kansas City, 1950-54; psychologist Mental Retardation Project, Muscogee County, Ga., 1958-59. Commr., Human Services Commn. Tioga County, 1973—. Bd. dirs. Creative Play Group, Inc., 1960-72. Mem. Am., N.Y. State psychol. assns., Day Care and Child Devel. Council Am., Girl Scouts Am. Home: Box 29 RD 1 Owego NY 13827 Office: 132 Main St Owego NY 13827

ELKINS, EARLEEN FELDMAN (MRS. RICHARD LONSDALE ELKINS), audiologist; b. South Bend, Ind., Mar. 20, 1933; d. Earl Russell and Vivian Pauline (Paul) Feldman; B.A., U. Md., 1954, M.A., 1956, Ph.D., 1967; m. Richard Lonsdale Elkins, June 19, 1954; children—Robert, Karen, William. Instr., U. Md., College Park, 1954-56, 64-67, asst. research prof. Biocommunications Lab., 1967—; audiologist Walter Reed Army Med. Center, Forest Glen, Md., 1956-57; research asso. Electronic Teaching Labs., Washington, 1960-62; cons. Nat. Inst. Child Health and Human Devel., Bethesda, Md., 1964; audiologist VA Hosp., Washington, 1967—. USPHS grantee, 1970-72. Mem. Am. Speech and Hearing Assn., Acoustical Soc. Am., Sigma Xi, Phi Kappa Phi, Delta Delta Delta. Episcopalian. Contbr. articles to profl. jours. Home: 110 Lillian Lane Silver Spring MD 20904 Office: VA Hosp 50 Irving St NW Washington DC 20422

ELKS, HAZEL HULBERT, librarian; b. Franklin, N.J., June 16, 1916; d. Harry C. and Hazel (Ball) Hulbert; student Library Sch., Trenton State Coll., summer 1938; extension student Rutgers U.; m. David L. Elks, July 6, 1957. With Elizabeth (N.J.) Pub. Library, 1941—, librarian Monroe Av. br., 1946-49, personnel dir,, 1949-62, dir. library, 1962—. Trustee Elizabeth YWCA, 1960-62, Elizabeth League Women Voters, 1959-62, Mem. N.J. Library Assn. (chmn. fed. relations com. 1965—). Home: 1389 Vauxhall Rd Union NJ 07083 Office: 11 S Broad St Elizabeth NJ 07202

ELKUS, LEONORE ROSENBAUM (MRS. JAMES H. ELKUS), TV cons.; b. N.Y.C., Jan. 28, 1914; d. Harold A. and Hulda (Lashanska) Rosenbaum; B.A., Sarah Lawrence Coll., Bronxville, 1935; m. James H. Elkus, June 19, 1935; children—Christopher J., Jonathan H. and Peggy H. (twins). Singer, producer under name Leonore James, radio stas. WCAE and WWSW; singer, producer History of Am. Song, WCAE, Pitts., Let's Explore Music, WWSW, also prod. Fgn. Policy programs; mem. mayor's com. to study need for ednl. TV in Pitts. area, mem. bd. dirs. WQED, Pitts., 1955-74, exec. producer pub. and community affairs, 1962-73; cons. on ednl. TV, 1973—; writer weekly column in various papers W. Pa., 1962—. Bd. dirs. Planned Parenthood Allegheny County, life mem., bd. dirs. Chamber Music Soc. of Pitts.; mem. woman's bd. Allegheny Gen. Hosp.; bd. dirs. Pitts. History and Landmarks Found., Psychol. Services Pitts.; mem. pres.'s council Seton Hill Coll. Recipient medal govt. div. Freedom Found., 1969; named Distinguished Dau. Pa., 1971. Mem. Correctional Services Assn. W. Pa., Internat. Poetry Forum (dir.), Pitts.-Ligonier Women's Club (dir. psychol. services), Am. Assn. U. Women (bd. dirs., div. topic chmn. mass media Pa.). Unitarian. Club: College. Author: (with Jean Whitlock) A Treasury of Art Songs, 1950. Home: Park Plaza Apts 128 N Craig St Pittsburgh PA 15213 Office: WQED 4802 5th Av Pittsburgh PA 15213

ELLEFSEN, BARBARA ANN ROBISON (MRS. ROBERT ELLEFSEN), editor; b. Portland, Ore., July 15, 1933; d. Louis Keith and Marjorie (Work) Robison; student Coll. of Ida., 1951-53, U. Utah, 1969-70; m. Robert Ellefsen, May 16, 1969; 1 dau., Nancy. Sports editor LeGrande (Ore.) Evening-Observer, 1953-54; women's writer Ida. Daily Statesman, Boise, 1955-58; asst. women's editor Tacoma News-Tribune, 1958-59; staff writer Salt Lake Tribune, 1961-67, women's editor, 1967—. Mem. Am., Utah quarter horse assns. Episcopalian. Home: 4210 Caroleen Way Salt Lake City UT 84117 Office: 143 S Main St Salt Lake City UT 84110

ELLENBURG, JANUS YENTSCH (MRS. ROBERT BLANTON ELLENBURG), chemist; b. Linthicum, Md., Jan. 14, 1922; d. Charles William and Bertha Charlotte (Vitt) Yentsch; B.S. cum laude (H.C. Jones fellow), Western Md. Coll., 1942, Sc.D., 1968; m. Robert Blanton Ellenburg, Oct. 16, 1943. Sr. chemist Oak Ridge Nat. Lab., 1956-57; chemist So. Research Inst., Birmingham, Ala., 1957-58; spectroscopist Hayes Internat. Corp., Birmingham, 1958-60, sr. scientist, 1961—; spectroscopist McWayne Cast Iron Pipe Co., Birmingham, 1960-61. Adviser, Bessemer (Ala.) State Tech. Inst., 1971—. Mem. Shades Moutain Civic Assn., Birmingham, 1960-68. Recipient Merit award NASA Inventions and Contbn. Bd., 1970. Mem. Am. Chem. Soc., Am. Inst. Physics, Am. Inst. Aeros. and Astronautics, Royal Soc. for Health (London), Optical Soc. Am. (S.E. regional pres. 1962-64), Beta Beta Beta. Episcopalian. Club: Shades Valley Camera (Birmingham). Contbr. articles to profl. jours. Home: 1133 Lido Dr Birmingham AL 35226

ELLER, NANCY GENEVA TRUXALL (MRS. WALTON G. ELLER), city ofcl.; b. Bergholtz, O., Mar. 17, 1929; d. Lester Harvey and Estella Mildred (Bender) Truxall; grad. high sch., Minerva, O.; m. Walton G. Eller, Mar. 19, 1948; children—Walton G., Sharon L. (Mrs. Jerry Huffman), Terri A. Journeyman, Cronin China Co., Minerva, 1946-49; head cashier Housemart, Streetsboro, O., 1959-61; mgr., instr. U.S. Naval Base, Subic Bay, Philippines, 1963-64; dep. clk. Tarrant County, Crowley, Tex., 1966-67; city sec. City of Crowley, 1967—. Leader, Girl Scouts U.S.A., Subic Bay, 1963. Recipient award Nat. V.F.W., 1973. Mem. City Sec. Assn. Tex., Fleet Res. Assn. (v.p. 1955—). Baptist (sec. 1971-73). Mem. Order Eastern Star. Home: 500 E Mission St Crowley TX 76036 Office: 120 N Hampton St Crowley TX 76036

ELLER, SYLVIA ANTOINETTE PHELPS (MRS. JAMES CRAIG ELLER), educator; b. Somerset, Ky., Aug. 17, 1943; d. Elza Lee and Lois Dean (Jenkins) Phelps; B.A. in English, Berea Coll., 1965; M.A. in English, Appalachian State U., 1967; m. James Craig Eller, Aug. 3, 1962; 1 dau., Jamie Shaun. Prof. English, dir. women's dormitory Truett McConnell Coll., Cleveland, Ga., 1967-70; mem. faculty Louisburg (N.C.) Coll., 1970—, asst. prof. English, 1970-71, dean women, 1971-73, asst. prof. English, 1973—. Vice chmn. Louisburg precinct Republican Party, 1973; del. Rep. State Conv., 1973. Mem. League Women Voters, Am., N.C. assns. womens deans and counselors, South Atlantic Modern Lang. Assn., Am. Assn. U. Women (county v.p. 1971-72), Am. Assn. U. Profs., Nat. Soc. Lit. and the Arts, Phi Kappa Phi, Kappa Delta Pi. Methodist. Clubs: Young Republicans (co-sponsor 1973), Women's (Louisburg Coll.); Green Hill Country, Women's Parchasers, Town and Garden (Louisburg). Home: 306 Sunset Av Louisburg NC 27549

ELLERY, MARILYNNE SHANKS (MRS. WILLIAM ELLERY), educator; b. Toledo, Feb. 16, 1923; d. Erwood S. and Edith (Watson) Shanks; B.S., Ohio Wesleyan U., 1945; M.E., U. Toledo, 1960, student, 1968—; m. William Ellery, Nov. 10, 1945. Tchr. pub. schs., Maumee, O., 1945-50, Toledo, 1950-60; teaching fellow U. Toledo, 1960-61; elementary supr. Bath Local Sch. Dist., Lima, O., 1961-63; prof. elementary edn. Ohio No. U., Ada, 1963—, coordinator elementary student teaching, 1967—; vis. prof. U. Toledo, 1960; dir., coordinator in-service program Ada Elementary Sch., 1973-74. Cons., Hardin County Schs., Ohio, 1966-67. Mem. Am. Assn. U. Women, Assn. Childhood Edn. (state v.p. 1972—), Internat. Reading Assn., Nat. Council Tchrs. English, Nat. Soc. Study Edn., Ohio Consortium Child Devel., Aurora (adviser), Pi Lambda Theta, Kappa Delta Pi, Delta Kappa Gamma (v.p.), Alpha Chi Omega (chpt. pres. 1950-52). Republican. Methodist. Mem. Order Eastern Star. Clubs: Toledo Monnett (pres. 1951-52), Twice Ten Art (pres. 1970-71). Home: 3469 Beverly Dr Toledo OH 43614

ELLETT, MARY SWEENEY (MRS. ROBERT DOUGLAS ELLETT), editor; b. Greensboro, N.C., Dec. 18, 1929; d. William Peet and Emma Belle (Harris) Sweeney; B.A., Randolph-Macon Woman's Coll., 1950; M.A., U. Va., 1974; m. Robert Douglas Ellett, Sept. 8, 1951; children—Martha Lorraine, Jane Harris, James Thompson. Tchr. art and English, Norfolk County, Va., 1950-51; tchr. Lynchburg (Va.) Pub. Schs., 1951-52; caseworker Social Service Bur., Lynchburg, 1953-55; profl. cons. parliamentary procedure Lynchburg (Va.) area, 1958-65; diversional therapist psychiat. unit Va. Bapt. Hosp., Lynchburg, 1967-69; editor Alumnae Bull., Randolph-Macon Woman's Coll., 1971—. Chairwoman women's div. United Fund, 1957; mem. exec. com. Mental Health Assn., 1969. Bd. dirs. YMCA, Family Service, Florence Crittenton, Fine Arts Center. Mem. Randolph-Macon Woman's Coll. Alumnae Assn. (mem. exec. com. 1970—). Methodist. Home: 4209 Hilton Pl Lynchburg VA 24503 Office: Box 307 Lynchburg VA 24503

ELLINGTON, ELIZABETH ROARK, lawyer; b. Colon, Rep. Panama, May 23, 1932; d. Jesse Cox and Elizabeth (Roark) Ellington; B.A., Agnes Scott Coll., 1954; J.D., U. Va., 1959; M.L.S., U. Tex., 1971. Admitted to Tex. bar, 1959; practiced in San Antonio, 1961-69; mem. firm Crites, Ellington, Peterson and Studer; law librarian, lectr. U. Mo., Columbia, 1969-73, law librarian, asso. prof., 1973—. Mem. Am., San Antonio bar assns., State Bar Tex., Kappa Beta Pi (grand registrar 1969-71), Kappa Beta Pi (grand chancellor 1971-73, 2d v.p. 1973—). Presbyn. Home: 2710 W Rollins Rd Columbia MO 65201

ELLINGTON, MARTHA BARA (MRS. THOMAS W. ELLINGTON), psychologist; b. N.Y.C., Sept. 3, 1922; d. Augustus A. and Emily (Quintana) Bara; B.A., Hunter Coll., 1948, M.S., 1959; postgrad. N.Y. U.; m. Thomas W. Ellington, May 11, 1945; children—Stephanie Ellington (Mrs. Duff Albert Brace), Katharine C. (Mrs. Arthur F. Custer), Deborah A., Candice J. Fgn. dept. translator Pub. Nat. Bank & Trust Co., N.Y.C., 1946-48; instr. Gifu U., Japan, summer 1956; instr., guidance counselor U. Md., 1955-57; cons. Mental Health Center, Gifu, summer 1957; asst. to dir. profl. edn., instr. Indsl. Home for Blind, Bklyn., 1958-59; rehab. counselor, student supr. Fountain House Found., N.Y.C., 1959-61, 64-66; supervising probation officer Los Angeles County Probation Dept., Torrance, Cal., 1961-64; research, rehab. counselor Rockland State Hosp., Orangeburg, N.Y., 1966-68; rehab. counselor N.Y. State Dept. Edn., 1968—. Cons. Bklyn. Assn. Mental Health, 1968—. Troop leader Girl Scouts U.S.A., 1955-59. Mem. Am. Personnel and Guidance Assn., Nat. Rehab. Counseling Assn., Am. Assn. U. Women, Alpha Delta Pi, Kappa Delta Pi. Home: 900 W 190th St New York City NY 10040 Office: 225 Park Av S New York City NY 10003

ELLIOT, ELISABETH (MRS. ADDISON HARDIE LEITCH), writer; b. Brussels, Belgium, Dec. 21, 1926 (parents Am. citizens); d. Philip E. and Katharine (Gillingham) Howard; A.B., Wheaton Coll., 1948; m. Philip James Elliot, Oct. 8, 1953 (dec. Jan. 1956); 1 dau., Valerie; m. 2d, Addison Hardie Leitch, Jan. 1, 1969 (dec. Sept. 1973). Missionary to jungle Indians, Ecuador, S.Am., 1952-63. Episcopalian. Author: Through Gates of Splendor, 1957; Shadow of the Almighty, 1958; The Savage My Kinsman, 1960; No Graven Image, 1965; Who Shall Ascend, 1967; The Liberty of Obedience, 1968; Furnace of the Lord, 1969; A Slow and Certain Light, 1973. Contbr. column to Christian Herald mag. Home: 746 Bay Rd Hamilton MA 01936

ELLIOTT, ANNA BURNETT (MRS. DEAN HAMBLIN ELLIOTT), educator, librarian; b. Monte Vista, Colo., Oct. 10, 1917; d. Ernest Clement and Anna (Burnett) Bunker; B.S., Ore. State U., 1940; postgrad. Humboldt State U., part-time 1948-67; M.A. San Jose State U., 1973; m. Dean Hamblin Elliott, June 30, 1947; children—Alison Virginia, Brigid Ann. Stenographer, J. K. Gill, N.W. Mortgage Co., Portland, Ore., 1941; advt., editorial, woman's page editor Coos Bay Times, 1943; continuity writer KVOR, Colorado Springs, 1943-47; KGFN, Grass Valley, Cal., 1948; social worker, Santa Rosa, Cal., 1947-48, Eureka, Cal., 1948-50; music tchr., Eureka, 1950-51; dir. Eureka Parent Nursery Sch., 1956-59; elementary sch. tchr., Eureka, 1959-65; librarian for nine elementary schs., Eureka, 1965—. Bd. dirs. 22d dist. and Eureka council P.T.A. Served with WAC, 1942. Mem. Am. Assn. U. Women (past pres. Humboldt br.), Cal., Eureka tchrs. assns., North Coast Librarians Assn., Cal. Assn. Sch. Librarians, Women in Communications, Delta Zeta. Episcopalian. Home: 1625 Everding Eureka CA 95501 Office: 3200 Walford Av Eureka CA 95501

ELLIOTT, INGER MCCABE (MRS. OSBORN ELLIOTT), textile co. exec.; b. Oslo, Norway, Feb. 23, 1933; d. David and Lova (Katz) Abrahamsen; came to U.S., 1941; naturalized, 1946; A.B. in History with honors Cornell U., 1954; postgrad Harvard, 1955; A.M. (Jean Birdsall fellow), Radcliffe, 1957; m. Osborn Elliott, Oct. 20, 1973; children by previous marriage-Kari McCabe, Alexander McCabe, Molly McCabe. Editor, E. European Student and Youth Service, N.Y.C., 1957-60; photographer Rapho-Guillumette, U.S. and fgn. countries, 1960-73; pres. China Seas, Inc., N.Y.C., 1972—. Tchr., Newton (Mass.) Pub. Schs., 1955-56. Mem. Am. Soc. Mag. Photographers, Phi Beta Kappa. Author: Women Photographers, 1970; A Week in Amy's World, 1970; A Week in Henry's World, 1971; also portfolio in Infinity mag., 1969. Home: 10 Gracie Square New York City NY 10028 Office: China Seas Inc 149 E 72 St New York City NY 10021

ELLIOTT, JANE ELIZABETH (MRS. JACK CALKINS ELLIOTT), coll. dean; b. Kalamazoo, Apr. 20, 1911; d. George Franklin and Florence Elizabeth (Allen) Inch; B.S., U. Mich., 1932, Ph.D., 1959; M.S., Mich. State U., 1949; m. Robert John Smith, Oct. 8, 1932 (dec.); children—George M., Benjamin T., Martha K. (Mrs. Thomas John Kakuk); m. 2d, Jack Calkins Elliott, Apr. 7, 1973. Faculty Mich. State U., E. Lansing, 1943—, asso. prof. geology, 1959-69, asso. prof. Lyman Briggs Coll., 1969-70, prof., asst. dean Lyman Briggs Coll., 1970—. Mem. Geol. Soc. Am., A.A.A.S., Am. Assn. Petroleum Geologists, Nat. Assn. Geology Tchrs., Sigma Xi, Phi Kappa Phi, Alpha Phi. Home: 545 Elizabeth St East Lansing MI 48823

ELLIOTT, JANE HARRISON (MRS. M. LEO ELLIOTT), publishing co. exec.; b. Tampa, Fla., Feb. 6, 1927; d. John Norton and Mary Lou (Bachman) Harrison; student U. Ala., 1945-46; m. M. Leo Elliott, June 15, 1948; children—M. Leo III, Barbara Lynn, Sheila Tracy. With Free Press Pub. Co., Inc., Tampa, 1965—, editor 1971—. Mem. Jr. League of Tampa, Alpha Delta Pi. Democrat. Episcopalian. Home: 902 S Dakota St Tampa FL 33606 Office: 401 E Platt St Tampa FL 33602

ELLIOTT, JOSEPHINE DOROTHEA MIRABELLA (MRS. JOHN BENNETT ELLIOTT), archivist; b. Chgo., Apr. 23, 1912; s. Salvatore Francis and Rosamond (Libonati) Mirabella; Ph.B., U. Chgo., 1932; tchrs. certificate Chgo. Tchrs. Coll., 1933; A.M. (Scholastic scholar), U. Chgo., 1935; postgrad. Ind. State U., 1957-58, Ind. U., 1962; m. John Bennett Elliott, July 30, 1938; 1 dau., Claudia. Tchr. French, Italian, Chgo. Pub. Schs., 1935-38; tchr. lang. arts Evansville (Ind.) Pub. Schs., 1943-46; librarian Workingmen's Inst., New Harmony, Ind., 1958-60; sec. spl. collections U. Chgo. Library, 1960-62; librarian Met. Sch. Dist., Mt. Vernon (Ind.), 1962-72; archivist Ind. State U., Evansville, 1972—. Mem. exec. bd. George Rogers Clark Trail Found.; mem. documents and memorabilia com. New Harmony Meml. Commn.; mem. exec. com. New Harmony (Ind.) Sesquicentennial Celebration, 1964. Mem. Soc. Am. Archivists, Soc. Ind. Archivists, Am. Assn. State and Local History, Conrad Baker Found., Harmonie Assos. (program chmn. 1964—), Golden Raintree Assn. (pres. 1966), Ohio-Wabash Valley Hist. Soc. (dir.), Kappa Kappa Kappa, Delta Kappa Gamma. Democrat. Home: New Harmony IN 47631 also 8600 University Blvd Evansville IN 47712

ELLIOTT, MABEL AGNES, educator, author; b. Liscomb, Ia., May 13, 1898; d. William Lee and Nora Belle (Bash) Elliott; A.B., Northwestern U., 1922, A.M., 1923, Ph.D., 1929. Instr. sociology U. Minn., 1926-27, Stephens Coll., 1927-28; part-time instr. sociology Northwestern U., 1928-29; asst. prof. sociology U. Kan., 1929-37, asso. prof; 1938-47; vis. prof. sociology U. Minn., 1936-37; cons. sociologist Am. Nat. Red Cross, 1946-47; lectr. Am. U., 1947; chmn. dept., prof. sociology Chatham Coll., Pitts., 1947—, Irene Heinz Given prof. sociology (hon.), 1962-65, prof. emeritus, 1965—; Univ. prof. sociology Hunter Coll. City U. N.Y., 1966—; adj. prof. sociology Bklyn. Coll., 1965-66; Phi Beta Kappa lectr., 1959—; Vis. Distinguished prof. of sociology East Tex. State U., Commerce, 1969. Mem. Kan. Temporarary Pub. Welfare Commn., 1931-33; former mem. Pa. Com. Penal Affairs, Mayor's Civic Com., Pitts. Mem. adv. bd. Pitts. Community Councils. Mem. com. Fulbright and Mundt awards in sociology Fgn. Exchange Program; mem. Fulbright screening com., 1956-59. Mem. adv. research com. Mayor's Com. on Human Relations, 1959-65; mem. adv. bd. Community Councils Pitts. Wieboldt research fellow in sociology, 1924, Carola Woerischoffer Meml. fellow in social economy, 1924-26; Fulbright award, U. Bonn, Germany (lectr. criminology), 1955-56; Pitts Woman of Year award, 1957. Fellow Am. Sociol. Assn. (nat. council 1955-58); mem. Eastern Sociol. Soc., Kan. Conf. Social Work (dir. 1930-36; exec. sec. 1933-34; treas. 1936-37), Internat. Sociol. Assn., Soc. Study Social Problems (exec. com. 1953—, pres. 1956-57), Am. Assn. U. Profs., Phi Beta Kappa, Phi Beta Kappa Assos., Alpha Kappa Delta, Alpha Pi Zeta. Democrat. Episcopalian. Clubs: Faculty, University Women. Author several books in sociology, 1926-47; Coercion in Penal Treatment; Past and Present, 1947; Social Disorganization (with F. E. Merrill), 1950, rev. 1961); Crime in Modern Society, 1952 (translated into Serbocroatian 1962), (with others) Marriage and the Family, 1955. Asst. editor Am. Sociol. Rev., 1940-43, Dictionary of Sociology 1944. Contbr. articles and book revs. to profl. jours., also to Ency. Brit. Home: 6164 Tamilynn St San Diego CA 92122

ELLIOTT, MARY HELEN (MRS. TOM JOHNSON ELLIOTT), librarian; b. Nappanee, Ind., May 13, 1937; d. Everett and Charlotte Lillian (Price) Pippen; B.S., Ball State U., 1960; m. Tom Johnson Elliott, June 24, 1961; children—Jennifer Lynn, Tom Johnson, Matthew Everett. Asst. librarian Penn High Sch., Mishawaka, Ind., 1959-60; dist. library supr. Sayville, L.I., N.Y., 1960-61; librarian Grant Los Altos Sch., Albuquerque, 1961-63; dir. Learning Resource Center, Vernon (Tex.) Regional Jr. Coll., 1972—. Library cons. Vernon (Tex.) Center for Drug Dependant Youth, Tex. Dept. Mental Health, 1973—. Leader, Camp Fire Girls, Vernon, 1969—; pres. Wilbarger County Heart Assn., Vernon, 1968—; dir. Wilbarger County Camp Fire Council, Vernon, 1964-72. Mem. Tex. Jr. Coll. Assn., Tex. Library Assn., Mortor Bd., Kappa Delta Pi, Alpha Phi Gamma, Pi Gamma Mu, Alpha Chi Omega. Presbyn. Home: Route 2 Vernon TX 76384

ELLIOTT, MARY RUTH, occupational therapist, educator; b. Muncie, Ind., Dec. 24, 1937; d. William Edward and Alice Margaret (Test) Elliott; B.A. in Biology, Earlham Coll., 1960; certificate U. Buffalo, 1962; M.S. in Edn., Ind. U., 1967. Staff therapist J.W. Riley Hosp., Ind. U., 1962-66; instr. occupational therapy State U. N.Y. at Buffalo, 1968-70, asst. prof., 1970-72; asst. prof. occupational therapy Ind. U., Indpls., 1972-74; grant coordinator for developmental disabilities Mercy Hosp., Urbana, Ill., 1974—. Cons., Buffalo Pub. Sch. System, 1970-72. Mem. World Fedn. Occupational Therapy, Am., Ind. occupational therapy assns., Am. Assn. Mental Retardation. Mem. Soc. Friends. Home: 1805 Lynwood Champaign IL 61820

ELLIOTT, MYRTLE EVELYN KEENER, educator; b. Annawan, Ill., Apr. 11, 1898; d. John William and Mary (Baldwin) Keener; A.B., Cornell Coll., 1921; M.A., Columbia, 1926; postgrad. summers U. Ia., 1928, Ohio State U., 1930, 31, U. Chgo., 1933, San Francisco State Coll., 1949, Fresno State Coll., 1958, 59, 60; m. Leo Louis Elliott, Aug. 10, 1935 (dec. 1948); children—Mary Ellen (Mrs. Jack Agan), Winona (Mrs. Herbert C. Sample), James, Joan. Tchr. pub. high schs., Panora, Ia., 1921-23, Dewitt, Ia., 1923-25; head English dept., dean girls, Kemmerer, Wyo., 1926-29; dean girls and English, Pendelton, Ore., 1929-30; tchr., Ely, Nev., 1930-31; girls' adviser boarding schs. U.S. Indian Service, 1931-35; tchr. Latin and English, Cut Bank, Mont., 1944-46; tchr. older educable retarded children for Kern County Supt. Schs., Bakersfield, Cal., 1949-68; pvt. work with brain damaged and disturbed children. Fellow Am. Assn. Mental Deficiency; mem. Council for Exceptional Children, Cal. Tchrs. Assn., Nat. (hon. life), Cal. (hon. life) congresses parents and tchrs., Catholic Daus. Am., Columbia Tchrs. Coll. Alumni Assn. (past local chmn.), Cornell Coll. Alumni Assn. (sec. Central Valley group 1958—), Am. Assn. U. Women, Internat. Reading Assn., Phi Beta Kappa. Home: 2709 4th St Bakersfield CA 93304

ELLIOTT, NANCY RUTH NOLL (MRS. DONALD EUGENE ELLIOTT), occupational therapist; b. Mason City, Ia., Feb. 23, 1939; d. Earl Raymond and Loretta Elizabeth (Boyd) Noll; B.A., State U. Ia., 1961; postgrad. U. So. Cal., 1962-63, LaSalle Extension U., 1971-73; m. Donald Eugene Elliott, Dec. 27, 1971. Occupational therapist Los Angeles County Gen. Hosp., Los Angeles, 1962-66; commd. 1st lt. USAF, 1966, advanced through grades to capt., 1969; occupational therapist USAF Scott Med Center, Scott AFB, Ill., 1966-68, David Grant USAF Med. Center, Travis AFB, Cal., 1968—. Vol. in cosmetology for disaster planning, 1966—. Vocational Rehab. trainee scholar, 1959-60; decorated USAF Commendation medal. Mem. Am. Occupational Therapy Assn. Home: 420 Sandstone Dr Vacaville CA 95688

ELLIOTT, NEVA MINNIE, judge; b. Damascus, Ore., Apr. 23, 1908; d. John Catou and Minnie (Bohna) Elliott; student Reed Coll., 1931-32, N.W. Coll. Law, 1932; LL.B., Lewis and Clark Coll., 1936; m. Neill Stevens Chinnock, July 15, 1939 (dec. Jan. 1954). Admitted to Ore. bar, 1935, practice in Portland, 1941—; municipal judge, Portland, 1959—; alternate dist. ct. judge, Ore., Portland, 1972—. Mem. Multnomah County (Ore.) Home Rule Com., 1970; vol. counsel YWCA, Portland, 1960-74. Mem. Women's Advt. Club, Portland Advt. Fedn., Am., Ore. bar assns., Quota Internat., Phi Delta Delta. Mem. Daus. of Nile. Home: 3110 W S Fairview Blvd Portland OR 97201 Office: 517 Corbett Bldg Portland OR 97204

ELLIOTT, ROSALIE CONN (MRS. F. SCOTT ELLIOTT), educator, club woman; b. Kosciusko, Miss.; d. Jefferson P. and Ada (Russell) Conn.; B.S., George Peabody Coll. Tchrs., 1924; M.A., U. N.C., 1935; postgrad. U. Chgo., several summers; m. F. Scott Elliott, Dec. 22, 1933; 1 son, F. Scott, Jr. Tchr. Columbia (S.C.) High Sch., 1924-26; tchr. head math. dept. Lee H. Edwards High Sch., Asheville, N.C., 1926-39; math. tchr. Durham (N.C.) High Sch., 1939-46; tchr. English and French, Whitmire (S.C.) High Sch., 1957-65. Past exec. bd., sec. Newberry Civic League; active Crippled Children Soc. Mem. Am. Assn. U. Women (chmn. local lit. div., pres. Newberry br. 1958-60, 70-72, mass. media chmn. state div.), N.E.A., Newberry County Classroom Tchrs. (pres. 1959), Newberry Hist. Soc. N.C. (pres. math. div.), S.C. edn. assns., S.C. Fedn. Women's Clubs (div. chmn. 1951-72, dir. no. dist. 1952-55, chmn. library services 1968-72), Nat. League Am. Pen Women (chmn. Piedmont poetry div.), Am. Legion Aux. (local pres.), Women's Soc. Christian Service (local pres., dist. pres.), U.D.C. (chpt. pres., recorder crosses S.C. div.), D.A.R. (past regent Jasper, state motion picture chmn.), Delta Kappa Gamma (chpt. pres.), Epsilon Sigma Omicron (past chpt. pres.). Methodist (circle leader 1958-73). Club: Woman's (past pres.). Poems included in Nat. Poetry Anthology, 1958-74, S.C. Mag. Home: 718 Glenn St Newberry SC 29108

ELLIS, ANNE LOUISE NOLL (MRS. JOHN THOMAS ELLIS), interior decorator; b. Wahatchee, Tenn., Apr. 1, 1906; d. William Louis and Annie (Thomas) Noll; A.B., Randolph-Macon Woman's Coll., 1927; certificate Master Sch. Interior Decorating, 1932; m. Joseph Ramer Sawyer, Dec. 31, 1927 (dec. Jan. 1939); children—Joanne Noll (Mrs. Frank Tilden Hayes, Jr.), Mary ELizabeth (Mrs. Frank Alexander Knowles, Jr.); m. 2d, John Thomas Ellis, Feb. 9, 1949. English tchr. Cloverdale High Sch., Montgomery, Ala., 1927; sec. to pres. Huntingdon Coll., Montgomery, 1943-50; part-time interior decorator, Montgomery, 1934—. Mem. D.A.R. (chpt. regent, 1950-51; state historian, 1962-67; state chmn. motion pictures, 1967-70, state chaplain 1970—), Daus. Am. Colonists (chpt. regent 1966-69, state chaplain 1967-70, state regent 1970-73, state parliamentarian 1973—), Colonial Dames Seventeenth Century (state 3d v.p. 1973—), Daus. Colonial Wars, Magna Charta Dames (corr. sec. 1973—), Randolph-Macon Women's Alumnae (v.p. chpt. 1967-68, pres. 1968-69), Kappa Delta. Address: 3151 Southview Av Montgomery AL 36106

ELLIS, CAROLYN HARGUS, poet; b. Kingsland, Ark.; d. Calvin and Daisy (Offutt) Hargus; ed. Ark. State Normal Inst.; m. William Robert Ellis (dec. 1935); children—Mary Frances (Mrs. Carl R. Woodring), Janie (Mrs. Hugh Morrison). Tchr. Kingsland Elementary Sch.; receptionist Humble Co., Houston, 1935-59, also columnist bull. Mem. Poetry Soc. Tex. (ann. critic's awards, numerous other prizes), Theta Sigma Phi (1st prize essays Journalism contest Houston chpt. 1961, 62, 64, poetry prize 1961). Contbr. poems to anthologies: Between the Bookends, 1942—, Prairie Schooner Caravan, 1943; Adventures in Poetry, 1946; That Eager Zest, 1961, also mags. including Saturday Rev., Prairie Schooner, Tex. Lit. Quar., Kansas City Poetry mag., St. Regis, Peacock Alley, McCall's, Sat. Eve. Post, Cosmopolitan, The Christian Home, Reader's Digest, Ladies Home Journal, Good Housekeeping, Kaleidograph, Am. mag., and newspapers including Washington Post, Wall St. Jour., N.Y. Times. Home: 2015 Av P Huntsville TX 77340

ELLIS, DOROTHY ANN NAIDEN, librarian; b. Indpls., July 10, 1918; d. James H. and Helen E. (McMinn) Naiden; B.A. cum laude with honors, Brown U., 1940; M.L.S., Case Western Res. U., 1970; m. William Donohue, June 13, 1942; children—William N., Sarah E. Head librarian Rocky River (O.) Sch. Bd., 1946-51, librarian, media coordinator, 1960—. Lectr. Case Western Res. U., 1974. Mem. adv. bd. Sch. Library Sci., Kent State U., 1972-75; mem. adv. bd. ednl. media tech. Cuyahoga Community Coll., 1970; chmn. Met. Cleve. Ednl. Resource Center Operations WVIZ Curriculum Council, 1973-74. Martha Holden Jennings grantee, 1972. Mem. Am. Ednl. Tchr. Assn., Am. Library Assn., Ohio Assn. Sch. Librarians (N.E. dir. 1971-74), Ednl. Media Council Ohio (mem. state standards and certification com. 1971-73), Rocky River Tchrs. Assn., Am. Pilots and Owners Assn. Club: Lakewood (O.) College. Home: 1060 Richmar Dr Westlake OH 44145 Office: 2985 Wooster Rd Rocky River OH 44116

ELLIS, DOROTHY J. CARPENTER (MRS. GENE GREGORY ELLIS), realtor; b. Phila., Aug. 20, 1938; d. Alfred Barrett and Dorothy Aiken (Buzby) Carpenter; student Northwestern U., 1956, U.Miami, 1963; grad. Realtor Inst., 1970; m. Gene Gregory Ellis, Jan. 24, 1959 (dec. May 1962); children—Theresa, Laura, Kathleen. Saleswoman Boehmer & Hedlund, Park Ridge, Ill., 1966-68; saleswoman Baird & Warner, Inc., Des Plaines, Ill., 1968-70; v.p., sales mgr. Rich Port, Realtor, Park Ridge, 1970—. Sec. Einstein Elementary Sch. P.T.A., 1969-71. Mem. Nat. Assn. Realtors (mem. multiple listing com.), Nat. Inst. Real Estate Bds. (mem. Women's Council), Jr. Women's Club Des Plaines, D.A.R., Park Ridge C. of C. Episcopalian. Office: 800 W Higgins Rd Park Ridge IL 60068

ELLIS, EMILY CRAWFORD TAYLOR (MRS. WILLIAM ELLIS), curator; b. Melrose, Mass., Sept. 25, 1898; d. James A. and Annie Charlotte (Stewart) Crawford; B.A., Wellesley Coll., 1921; postgrad. Mass. Inst. Tech., 1925-27; M.S., Harvard, 1928; postgrad. Rutgers U., 1945-49; m. Herbert Lewis Taylor, June 20, 1931 (dec. Jan. 1963); children—Herbert J., John A.C.; m. 2d, William Ellis, Feb. 8, 1965. Editor Houghton Mifflin, Boston, 1926-30, 50; asst. physicist Bell Research Labs., Summit, N.J., 1942-45; research physicist Cornell U., 1946-47; editor 1950-52; tchr. high sch., Bound Brook, N.J., 1945-47; physicist U.S. Army, Fort Monmouth, N.J., 1952-68; dir., curator Drake House Mus., Plainfield, N.J., 1941-63; curator, dir. Herbert Lewis Taylor Archaeol. Mus. and Library, Plainfield, N.J., 1940—. Mem. Am. Meteorol. Soc., Archeol. Soc. N.J. (sec. 1971-74). Mem. Order Eastern Star, Order Amaranth (trustee 1967-75), White Shrine Jerusalem. Author: Along These Shores of Time and Space (poetry), 1958. Contbr. articles to profl. jours. Address: 739 W 8th St Plainfield NJ 07060

ELLIS, FRANCES BYRD SMITH (MRS. H. KIRBY ELLIS), editor; b. Florence, S.C., Sept. 17, 1922; d. Carl Ray and Hallie Carrison (Jordon) Smith; B.A., U. S.C., 1942; grad. Florence Bus. Coll., 1942; postgrad. U. N.C., 1955; m. H. Kirby Ellis, Nov. 9, 1957; 1 son, Elliott H. Knox. Exec. sec. Honolulu Acad. Arts, 1945-49; sec. Fgn. Service, U.S. Dept. State, 1950-53; women's editor Florence Morning News, 1957—. Bd. dirs. County Heart Assn., 1957, Florence County Mental Health Assn. Recipient Scholarship, Civitan, 1965. Mem. Florence Little Theater Guild. Episcopalian. Club: Altrusa (Florence). Home: 1517 Jackson Av Florence SC 29501 Office: 141 S Irby St Florence SC 29501

ELLIS, FRANCES HANKEMEIER, educator; b. Galena, Ill., Jan. 6, 1892; d. Christopher and Elizabeth (Meyer) Hankemeier; A.B., Ind. U., 1914, M.A., 1928; Ph.D., U. Wis., 1939; m. Forrest E. Ellis, June 23, 1917 (dec.). Tchr. Sheridan (Ind.) High Sch., 1914-15, Tech. High Sch., Indpls., 1915-21; instr. German, U. Ind., 1927-39, asst. prof., 1940-50, asso. prof., 1950-57, prof., 1957-62, emeritus, 1962—. Participant Washington Conf. Fgn. Langs. U.S.A., 1953; guest of German Fed. Republic, 1955. Recipient Fulbright research grant, Heidelberg, Germany, 1956-57. Mem. Modern Lang. Assn. (sec. German II sect. 1949-50, chmn. German II sect. 1950-51, chmn. nominating com. 1954-55). Fgn. Langs. in Elementary Schs. (state chmn. for German 1955-60), Lutheran Acad. for Scholarship (nat. sec.; mem. exec. bd. 1947-54), Assn. Tchrs. German State Ind. (pres. 1945-46), Rennaissance Soc. Am., Modern Humanities Research Assn., Am. Assn. U. Women (past mem. exec. com.), Am. Assn. Tchrs. German, Am. Assn. U. Profs. (past local sec.-treas.), Mortar Bd. (hon.), Delta Zeta, Delta Kappa Gamma, Phi Beta Kappa (local pres. 1954-55, nat. v.p. E. Central dist. 1949-52, 56-61, chmn. 1961-63). Republican. Lutheran. Clubs: Univ. (past. v.p.), Language (pres. 1946-47), Women's Faculty (pres. 1949-50). Author: The Early Meisterlieder of Hans Sachs, 1974. Contbr. to publs. including Dict. World Lit., Luth. Scholar, German Quar., Ind. Mag. of History PMLA; also book revs., monographs, articles profl. jours. Home: 522 Ballantine Rd Bloomington IN 47401

ELLIS, JEANNE HOLLAND (MRS. CORNELL FRANKLIN ELLIS), assn. exec.; b. Winston-Salem, N.C., Sept. 17, 1925; d. William and Cora Margaret (Carter) Holland; B.A., N.C. Central U., 1945; M.A., Columbia, 1969; m. Cornell Franklin Ellis, June 10, 1948; children—Cornell Franklin, Larry Tyrone, Michael Bernard. Tchr. J.H. Gunn High Sch., Charlotte, N.C., 1951-55; tchr., counselor John J. Wright High Sch., Fredericksburg, Va., 1957-58; high sch. tchr. Winter Park (Fla.) Bd. Edn., 1958-59; with Child Care Center of Stamford (Conn.) Inc., 1960—, exec. dir. 1966—; exec. dir. Stamford Day Care Program, 1969—; Head Start Program, Stamford, 1971—. Cons. Therapeutic Nursery, 1972—. Chmn. personnel com. Vol. Action Center, Stamford, 1973-75; chmn. nominating com. Child Guidance Clinic, Stamford, 1973; chmn. evaluation com. City Manpower Council, Stamford, 1972—; mem. Mayor's Appointee Title I Adv. Council, Stamford, 1971-73; sec., treas. United Way Exec.'s. Council, Stamford, 1970-71; auditor Norwalk (Conn.) Credit Union, 1970-71; mem. child care adv. council Norwalk Community Coll., 1971—. Mem. Norwalk Negro Dem. Club, 1973-74. Mem. N.A.A.C.P., Assn. for Edn. of Young Children (South Fairfield v.p. 1969-70). Mem. Order Eastern Star. Home: 18 Byrd Rd Norwalk CT 06850 Office: 177 Broad St Stamford CT 06901

ELLIS, JOANNA KAY JONES (MRS. CHARLES WILLIAM ELLIS), psychologist; b. Dallas, Nov. 12, 1942; d. Joseph McCreary and Kathleen (Buchanan) Jones; B.A., So. Methodist U., 1964; Ph.D., U. Tex., 1969; m. Charles William Ellis, June 7, 1969. Clin. psychologist Brown Schs., Austin, Tex., 1965-69; study dir. Child Devel., Evaluation and Research Center U. Tex. at Austin, 1967, instr., 1968-69, intern Counseling Center, 1968; clin. psychologist Harris County Community Mental Health Center, Baytown, Tex., 1969-70; asst. prof. psychology St. Louis Sch. of Medicine, 1970-73; child clin. psychologist Asso. Pediatricians, Tulsa, Okla., 1974—; cons. Dillon Family and Youth Services, 1974—. Office Econ. Opportunity grantee, 1965. Mem. Am., Okla. psychol. assns., Am. Assn. U. Profs., Chi Omega. Home: 5224 S Lewis No 2046 Tulsa OK 74105 Office: 6465 S Yale St Tulsa OK 74135

ELLIS, LOIS JUNE BAUGHMAN (MRS. HOMER GLENN ELLIS), social worker, psychotherapist, civic worker; b. Portland, Ind.; d. Ingall Elwood and Mattie (Brown) Baughman; B.A., Mary Washington Coll., U. Va., 1952; M.S., Tulane U., 1953, postgrad., 1953, 55, 59, 61, 67; m. Homer Glenn Ellis, July 3, 1945; children—Kenneth Glenn, Reyn Katherine. Social worker Orleans Parish Juvenile Ct., New Orleans, 1953-56; social worker adoption Miss. Dept. Pub. Welfare, 1956-59; lectr. field work La. State U., 1960-62; asst. dir. social service East La. State Hosp., Jackson, 1960-62; instr. Tulane U., 1962-63, asst. prof. psychiatry, 1963-67; pvt. practice psychotherapy, dir. Family Service Agy., Fort Smith, Ark., 1966-71; pres. Child and Family Consultants, Inc., 1971—. Cons. mental health Neighborhood Youth Corps, 1966-67; cons. Sparks Manor Nursing Home, 1969-74, Interfaith Center, 1968—, La. Dept. Hosps., 1963-66, Orleans Parish Sch. Bd., 1963-66; Love-to-Share, Inc., 1972—. Mem. hosp. aux. East La. State Hosp., Jackson, 1959-62, St. Edwards Hosp., Fort Smith, 1966-69; chmn. bd. trustees Wilk-Amite County Library, 1960-62; sec. Wilk-Amite chpt. Med. Aux., 1960, pres., 1962; chmn. mental health com. Sebastian Med. Aux., 1967-70; mem. adv. bd. Fort Smith Symphony, 1967-68; bd. dirs. Halfway House, Inc., 1967-68; mem. Govs. Commn. Status Women, 1968-74. Mem. adv. council Benedictine Sisters, Fort Smith, Ark., 1969-72; mem. Whirlpool Scholarship Selection Com., Fort Smith, 1969-72. Fellow Am. Orthopsychiat. Assn.; mem. Am. Assn. U. Women, League Women Voters, Nat. Assn. Mental Health (county v.p. 1966-67), A.M.A. (mem. womans aux. 1954-74), Acad. Certified Social Workers, Alumni Assn. Tulane Sch. Social Work (mem. bd. 1959-60; reporter for postscripts, 1960-62), Internat. Transactional Analysis Assn. (provisional), Am. Group Psychotherapy, Nat. Assn. Social Workers (S.E. La. mental health, psychiat. services chmn. 1962-63), Nat. Assn. Social Workers (leadership tng. program 1968-72). Episcopalian. Home: 4627 Free Ferry Rd Fort Smith AR 72901 Office: 512 S 16th St Fort Smith AR 72901

ELLIS, LUCILLE HAYWOOD (MRS. H. COWEN ELLIS), educator, civic worker; b. Mount Gilead, N.C., Aug. 11, 1922; d. Thomas Franklin and Annie (Brookshire) Haywood; A.A., Mars Hill Coll., 1941; B.A., Meredith Coll., 1943; M.R.E., So. Bapt. Theol. Sem., 1948; Advanced Grad. degree in spl. edn. U. Va., 1970; m. H. Cowen Ellis, May 12, 1944; children—Sandra Cecille, Judith Ellen. Field worker N.C. Bapt. Conv., 1942-43; high sch. tchr. Concord N.C., 1943-44; jour. clk. Tenn. Legislature, Nashville, 1946; state office asst. Woman's Missionary Union, Louisville, 1947; tchr. pub. schs. Jacksonville, Fla., 1949-50; bible tchr. Jacksonville, Etowah, Tenn., Charlottesville, Va., 1948—; youth counselor, 1958—; ednl. therapist with emotionally disturbed children, 1969—. Mem. citizens adv. bd. Juvenile Ct., Charlottesville, 1970—. Mem. ofcl. del. Va. C. of C. Good Will Tour, West Indies, Panama and Jamaica, 1961; leader numerous study tours Orient, Middle East, Australia, Pacific Islands. Mem. Fgn. Mission Bd. Worldwide So. Bapt. Conv., 1966-73; del. Bapt. World Alliance, Tokyo, Japan, 1970, Stockholm, Sweden, 1975. Recipient several awards for dramatic readings. Mem. Philarethian Lit. Soc., Nonpareil Soc., Dodeka, Forensic Council, D.A.R., Ministers Wives Assn. Democrat. Baptist. Clubs: Bible Study, Garden, International Relations. Author denominational articles, spl. bible study books and hist. research with spl. reference to Civil War. Home: 1419 Foxbrook Lane Charlottesville VA 22901

ELLIS, MARGARET RICHARDS, civic worker; b. Ogdensburg, N.Y.; d. Alfred F. and Elizabeth (St. Germaine) Richards; R.N., Bklyn. Hosp., 1924; student Bennington Coll., 1956-60; m. George Adams Ellis, Oct. 22, 1927; 1 dau., Ann (Mrs. A.E. Raynolds). Former v.p. Vt. Copper Co.; former dir. Sulphide Ore Corp. Trustee, incorporator Blackmer Meml. Library, 1955—, Bennington Center Assn., 1954—; mem. women's aux. City Hosp., N.Y.C., 1929-59, Generosity Thrift Shop, N.Y.C., 1930; trustee Bennington Hist. Mus., St. Joseph's Coll. Mem. Vt. Hist. Soc., Vt. Children's Aide Soc. Clubs: Garden (rec. sec. 1930—), Mount Anthony Country (Bennington, Vt.). Home: Parson Dewey House Old Bennington VT 05201

ELLIS, MARJORIE LOU WHEATLEY (MRS. FRANK B. ELLIS), geographer, educator; b. Plainview, Tex., Feb. 4, 1931; d. Elbert Morris and Edith (Pate) Wheatley; B.S., Kan. State Coll., 1951; M.A., So. Meth. U., 1964; postgrad. U. Cal. at Los Angeles, 1964-66; m. Frank B. Ellis, Nov. 18, 1965 (dec. Nov. 1969). Tchr. pub. schs., West Plains, Mo., 1951-53, Joplin, Mo., 1954-56, Merriam, Kan., 1957-60, Rockville, Md., 1961-63; teaching fellow U. Cal. at Los Angeles, 1965; faculty East Tex. State U., Commerce, 1970-71; tchr. geography So. Methodist U., Dallas, 1972-74; instr., coordinator geog. edn. S.W. Tex. State U., San Marcos 1974—. Mem. Assn. Am. Geographers, Am. Geog. Soc., Southwestern Social Sci. Assn., English Speaking Union. Republican. Mem. Disciples of Christ Ch. Clubs: Racquet (Palm Springs, Cal.). Research on history of maps. Office: Dept Geography San Marcos TX 78666

ELLIS, MARTHA SHANNON PERKINS (MRS. RALPH ELKINS ELLIS), lawyer; b. Louisville, Nov. 13, 1918; d. T. Shannon and Margaret (Zapp) Perkins; A.B. cum laude, Duke, 1940; LL.B., U. Louisville, 1943; m. Ralph Elkins Ellis, Sept. 26, 1942; children—Margaret Shannon (Mrs. James A. Donaldson), Martha Elizabeth. Admitted to Ky. bar, 1942; founder, Longview Riding Camp, Stamping Ground, Ky., 1960, owner, dir., 1960—; founder Longview Golf Camp, 1971, Longview Tennis Camp, 1973; asst. atty. gen. State of Ky., 1969—; sec., treas. Longview Golf Course, Inc., 1968—. Organizer, chmn. Scott County chpt. Cerebral Palsy, 1959; mem. bd. Ky. Citizens for Child Welfare, 1960-66, legal adviser, 1960-64, pres., 1965. Mem. Phi Beta Kappa, Pi Beta Phi. Clubs: Longview Swim (sec.-treas. 1969—), Scott County (pres. 1950-51) (Georgetown, Ky.). Home: Longview Farm Stamping Ground KY 40379 Office: Longview Camps Box 471 Georgetown KY 40324

ELLIS, MARY ANN (MRS. JOHN H. ELLIS), librarian; b. St. Louis, Sept. 24, 1926; d. Fred H. and Edna E. (Fleming) Steinmann; A.A., Harris Jr. Coll., 1947; B.S., Washington U., St. Louis, 1949; m. John H. Ellis, Nov. 26, 1966. Librarian, U.S. Air Force, Okinawa, 1949-51, Japan, 1952-54, Germany, 1954-57; librarian Def. Mapping Agy. Aerospace Center, St. Louis, 1958—. Librarian, U.S. Pavilion of the N.Y. World's Fair, 1964. Methodist. Home: 1943 Missouri State Rd Arnold MO 63010 Office: Defense Mapping Agency Aerospace Center/RDSLL 2nd and Arsenal Sts St Louis MO 63118

ELLIS, PAULINE TILLMAN, banker; b. Plant City, Fla., Feb. 7, 1931; d. Jessie James and Grace Pauline (Boutwell) Tillman; ed. Am. Inst. Banking; div.; children—Barbara J. (Mrs. Peter Haag), Steven Lee. With Peoples Bank, N. Ft. Myers, Fla., 1962—, successively bookkeeper, officer in charge comml. and real estate loans, now v.p., comptroller, 1974—. Mem. Nat. Assn. Bank Women, Am. Inst. Banking, Altrusa Internat. (treas. 1973; charter). Lions Aux. (pres. 1956). Home: 77 E North Shore Av North Fort Myers FL 33903 Office: 1288 N Tamiami Trail North Fort Myers FL 33903

ELLISON, ROSE RUTH, physician; b. N.Y.C., 1923; M.D., Columbia, 1948. Intern Maimonides Hosp., Bklyn., 1948-49, asst. resident, 1949-50; research fellow Sloan Kettering Inst., N.Y.C., 1951-54, asst. 1954-60, asso. mem., 1960-62; asso. chief medicine Roswell Park Meml. Inst., Buffalo, 1962-72; chief oncology dept. medicine E.J. Meyer Meml. Hosp., Buffalo, 1972—; research and teaching asst. medicine N.Y. State U. Med. Center, Bklyn., 1950-51; asst. prof. medicine Cornell Med. Sch., 1957-62; asst. research prof. medicine State U. N.Y. Med. Sch., Buffalo, 1964-69, asso. research prof. medicine, 1969-72; asso. prof. medicine State U. N.Y. at Buffalo, 1972—. Diplomate Am. Bd. Internal Medicine with subsplty. in med. oncology. Mem. Am. Fedn. Clin. Research, Am. Assn. for Cancer Research, Am. Soc. Hematology, Am. Soc. Clin. Oncology (sec.-treas. 1970-73, pres., 1974-75) Internat. Soc. Hematology, Am. Soc. for Pharmacology and Exptl. Therapeutics. Address: EJ Meyer Meml Hosp 462 Grider St Buffalo NY 14215

ELLISTON, LURA DUFF (MRS. FRED ADDISON ELLISTON), club woman; b. Leesville, La., May 28, 1907; d. James Edward and Kate (Williamson) Duff; B.A. summa cum laude, Rice Inst., 1928; m. Fred Addison Elliston, May 21, 1932; 1 dau., Lura Duff (Mrs. Eugene Remes). Pres., Jr. Woman's Club, Ft. Worth, 1933-34, Thursday Study Club, Ft. Worth, 1950-51, Friday Lecture Club, Ft. Worth, 1955-56, 61-62; mem. Round Table, Ft. Worth, Tex. Christian U. Fine Arts Found. Guild, Ft. Worth; founder J.E. Duff Fund, Ft. Worth. Bd. dirs. Opera Guild, Ft. Worth, 1950—, Community Theatre, 1963—, Scott Theatre, 1965—, chmn. theater com., 1968—. Recipient Silver and Gold medallions Am. Theater Assn., 1972. Republican. Mem. Disciples of Christ Ch. Home: 2222 Winton Terrace E Fort Worth TX 76109

ELLNER, CAROLYN LIPTON, educator; b. N.Y.C., Jan. 17, 1932; d. Robert Mitchell and Rose (Pearlman) Lipton; A.B. in Philosophy cum laude, Mt. Holyoke Coll., 1953; M.A. in Curriculum and Instrn. (Pres.'s fellow) Columbia, 1956; Ph.D. in Edn. and Behavioral Scis. with distinction, U. Cal. at Los Angeles, 1968; m. Richard Norton Ellner, June 21, 1953; children—David, Alison. Tchr. pub. schs., Malverne, N.Y., 1956, N.Y.C., 1956-59; with Montgomery County pub. schs., Rockville, Md., 1959-62, asst. to dir. staff devel., 1960-61, prin. Potomac Elementary Sch., 1961-62; postgrad. research educationist U. Cal. at Los Angeles, 1964-67, asst. research educationist, 1968; asst. dir. Head Start Evaluation Project, Los Angeles County pub. schs., 1968; asst. prof., dir. tchr. edn. Claremont (Cal.) Grad. Sch., 1968-72, asso. dean, 1972—. Cons. Mental Health Study Los Angeles County Schs., 1969, desegregation project Pasadena City Schs., 1970, ednl. goals study League Women Voters, San Gabriel Valley, 1971—; adminstr. several other projects pub. edn., 1960—. Trustee Oakwood Sch., 1973—, Center Early Edn., Los Angeles, 1974—. Mem. Cal. Council Tchr. Edn. (instl. rep.), Assn. for Master of Arts in Teaching Program (mem. exec. com.), Assn. Childhood Edn. Internat. (mem. Cal. adv. bd.), Am. Ednl. Research Assn., Assn. Supervision and Curriculum Devel., Assn. Tchr. Educators, Nat. Soc. Study Edn. Contbr. articles to profl. jours. Home: 426 S McCadden Pl Los Angeles CA 90020 Office: Harper E 110 Claremont Grad Sch Claremont CA 91711

ELLSTON, JEAN FRANCES PRESSEY (MRS. CLIFFORD ELLSTON, JR.), librarian; b. Providence, Oct. 30, 1935; d. Paul Edwin and Jeanie (Caldwell) Pressey; Ed.B., R.I. Coll., 1956; M.S., U. R.I., 1967; m. Clifford Ellston, Jr., Aug. 20, 1955; children—Clifford III, Paul Robert. Pub. sch. tchr., Smithfield, R.I., 1957-59; operator pvt. kindergarten Emmanuel Ch., Cumberland, R.I., 1964; elementary sch. librarian Cumberland (R.I.) Pub. Schs., 1965-69; high sch. librarian Cumberland High Sch., 1969-70; media specialist North Cumberland Middle Sch., Cumberland, 1971—. Adviser Cumberland High Sch. Library Aides Club, 1969-70. Mem. youth-parent com. The Shen-Le-Mon Civic Center Swim Club, Cumberland, 1966-72. Mem. N.E.A., R.I. Edn. Assn., R.I. Sch. Library Assn., R.I. Library Assn., Cumberland Tchrs. Assn., Friends of the Library. Episcopalian. Club: Cumberland-Lincoln Community Chorus. Home: 44 Lockwood Rd Cumberland RI 02864 Office: Nate Whipple Hwy Cumberland RI 02864

ELLSWEIG, PHYLLIS LEAH, psychotherapist; b. Irvington, N.J., Apr. 19, 1927; d. Sumar and Jeanette (Geffner) Schwartz; B.S., East Stroudsburg (Pa.) State Coll., 1947; Ed.M., Lehigh U., 1966, Ed.D., 1972; m. Martin Richard Ellsweig, Dec. 25, 1947; children—Bruce, Steven. Tchr., Stroud Union High Sch., 1963-66; guidance counselor East Stroudsburg Schs., 1966-68; asst. prof. edn. East Stroudsburg State Coll., 1968; staff psychologist Mental Health Center Carbon, Monroe and Pike Counties, Stroudsburg, 1968—; pvt. practice, 1969—. Pub. speaker, cons. to schs., orgns.; mem. staff Gen. Hosp. Monroe County, East Stroudsburg. Mem. Am. Psychol. Assn., Am. Acad. Psychotherapists, Am. Group Psychotherapy Assn., Assn. for Humanistic Psychology, Nat. Orgn. Women (profl. cons. 1973—), Internat. Assn. Group Psychotherapy. Home: 58 S Green St East Stroudsburg PA 18301 Office: 804 Sarah St Stroudsburg PA 18360 also 125 Stokes Av Stroudsburg PA 18360

ELLSWORTH, LINDA VOLLMAR (MRS. LUCIUS FULLER ELLSWORTH), historian; b. New Prague, Minn., Nov. 22, 1945; d. Roland Emil Frederick and Julia Ann (Pokladnik) Vollmar; B.A. (fellow), Macalester Coll., 1967; postgrad. U. Denver, 1968; M.A. (Hagley Grad. fellow), U. Del., 1969; m. Lucius Fuller Ellsworth, July 3, 1969. Photog. archivist Eleutherian Mills Hist. Library, Wilmington, Del., 1969; historian Historic Pensacola Preservation Bd. Trustees (Fla.), 1969—. Instr. Am. history Pensacola (Fla.) Jr. Coll., 1970-72. Recipient fellowship Nat. Endowment Humanities, 1968-69, fellowship for mus. profls. Nat. Endowment Arts, 1973. Mem. Am. Assn. State and Local History, Fla., Pensacola hist. socs. Editorial asst. Gulf Coast History and Humanities Conf. Proc., 1969—. Home: Route 4 Box 101 Pensacola FL 32504 Office: 200 E Zaragoza St Pensacola FL 32501

ELMALEH, MIRIAN KAISER (MRS. JOSEPH S. ELMALEH), physician; b. Phila., June 12, 1932; d. Alexander A. and Ida F. (Friedman) Kaiser; B.A., U. Pa., 1953, M.D., 1957; m. Joseph S. Elmaleh, Aug. 19, 1956; children—Michael, Francine. Intern, Albert Einstein Med. Center; practice medicine specializing in adolescent medicine, Elkins Park, Pa., 1962—; mem. staff J.F. Kennedy Meml. Hosp., Phila., 1958—, chief auditing officer, 1970—; staff Rolling Hill Hosp., Elkins Park. Mem. A.M.A., Pa., Phila. County med. socs., Am. Soc. Bus. Profl. Women, Am. Med. Women's Assn., Phi Beta Kappa, Pi Gamma Mu. Address: 8251 Old York Rd Elkins Park PA 19117

ELMER, IRENE ELIZABETH, author; b. Portland, Ore., Mar. 1, 1937; d. William Wells and Elizabeth (Goodwin) Elmer; B.A., Mills Coll., 1958; M.A., Smith Coll., 1960. Author juvenile fiction, adult non-fiction, 1961—; free lance editor specializing in coll. texts and scholarly manuscripts, 1969—. Cons. on Brit. and Am. speech patterns for Swiss novelist Hans Ruesch, 1963-65. Mem. Phi Beta Kappa. Author: Benjamin, 1961; Mandragora's Dragon, 1964; The Boy Who Ran Away, 1964; A Lodestone and a Toadstone, 1969; Anthony's Father, 1972. Contbr. articles on aspects of hist. and contemporary popular culture to various mags. Home: 2806 Cherry St Berkeley CA 94705

ELMORE, DOLORES DALY (MRS. COLLIN ELDRED ELMORE), city ofcl.; b. Chesterfield County, Va., Mar. 9, 1930; d. Frank Benjamin and Lillian Essig (Watkins) Daly; grad. high sch.; m. Collin Eldred Elmore, Apr. 13, 1950; children—Collin Eldred, Katherine Gail, Stephen Mark and Michael Lawrence (twins). Gen. office mgr. Frank E. Wiley Ins. Agy., Petersburg, Va., 1947-53; sec. to ednl. adminstr. U.S. Civil Service, Naval Air Sta., Jacksonville, Fla., 1950-52; sec. to personnel mgr. Brown & Williamson Tobacco Corp., Petersburg, Va., 1954-56; ch. sec. Colonial Heights (Va.) Baptist Ch., 1957-59; city clk./clk. council City of Colonial Heights, Va., 1969—. Mem. Internat. Inst. Municipal Clks. Baptist (ch. clk. 1967-69). Home: 624 Fairlie Rd Colonial Heights VA 23834 Office: City Manager's Office Colonial Heights VA 23834

ELMORE, PATRICIA BORGSMILLER, educator; b. Murphysboro, Ill., Nov. 19, 1943; d. Charles Edward and Lillian Resides (Stewart) Borgsmiller; B.A., So. Ill. U., 1965, M.S. in Edn., 1967, Ph.D., 1970; m. Donald Eugene Elmore, Apr. 4, 1970. Instr. dept. guidance and ednl. psychology So. Ill. U., Carbondale, 1967-70, psychometrist, 1968-70, asst. prof., 1970-74, asso. prof., 1974—, coordinator data services, 1970-73, research asso. Student Affairs Research and Evaluation Center, 1973—. Mem. Am. Assn. U. Women, Am. Ednl. Research Assn., Am. Personnel and Guidance Assn., Am. Psychol. Assn., Assn. for Ednl. Data Systems, Nat. Council on Measurement in Edn., Southeastern Psychol. Assn., Kappa Delta Pi, Pi Lambda Theta, Phi Delta Kappa, Pi Mu Epsilon, Alpha Lambda Delta, Alpha Gamma Delta. Contbr. articles to profl. jours. Home: 2141 Elm St PO Box 706 Murphysboro IL 62966 Office: Student Affairs Research and Evaluation Center So Ill U Carbondale IL 62901

ELPERN, BETH SARALYN SCHACHTER (MRS. EDWIN GLADDING BURROWS), broadcaster; b. Chgo., Aug 1, 1942; d. Abraham and Resea (Kutok) Schachter; B.A. in Polit. Sci. (Ill. State scholar 1960-64), U. Chgo., 1964; Certificate of Completion, Ulpan Beit Ziona America, 1966; postgrad. U. Wis., 1967, 72-73; m. Edwin Gladding Burrows, Dec. 7, 1973. Asst. dir. Community Action Commn., Office Equal Opportunity, Madison, Wis., 1966; continuity writer, traffic mgr., coordinal for spl. radio projects Wis. State Broadcasting Service, Madison, 1966-67, writer, producer, editor, 1967-72; writer, researcher Dept. Youth Devel., Madison, Wis., 1972-73; research asst. research and guidance lab. for superior students U. Wis.-Madison, 1973—; media cons. advt., Madison, 1973—; coordinator summer media workshop for minority writers Nat. Center for Audio Experimentation, Madison, 1973—; broadcaster sta. WHA-U. Wis.-Madison, 1966—. Recipient Maj. Edwin H. Armstrong award pub. affairs, 1967, 68, Ohio State award, 1969, 71, 73. Mem. Internat. Platform Assn. Jewish religion. Address: 3512 Green Brier #476 Ann Arbor MI 48105

ELSBERND, SISTER HELEN, educator, chemist; b. Calmar, Ia., Jan. 15, 1938; d. Alois and Loretta (Kuennen) Elsbernd; B.A., Viterbo Coll., 1965; M.S. (Univ. fellow), U. Ill., 1967, Ph.D. (NIH fellow), 1969. Entered Order Franciscan Sisters Perpetual Adoration; jr. high tchr. Sacred Heart Sch., Eau Claire, Wis., 1959-62; sci. and math. tchr. St. Francis High Sch., Provo, Utah, 1963-65; asst. prof. chemistry Viterbo Coll., LaCrosse, Wis., 1969-72, asso. prof., 1972—, chmn. dept., coordinator med. tech., 1970—. Bd. dirs. Dubuque (Ia.) Tri-Hosp. Sch. Med. Tech. Mem. Am. Chem. Soc., A.A.A.S., Midwest Assn. Coll. Chemistry Tchrs. in Liberal Arts Colls., Sigma Xi, Sigma Delta Epsilon. Contbr. articles to profl. jours. Home: 827 Winnebago St LaCrosse WI 54601

ELSON, MIRIAM ALMOND (MRS. ALEX ELSON), psychiat. social worker; b. Chgo.; d. David Moses and Elizabeth (Elson) Almond; B.A., Northwestern U., 1930; M.A., U. Chgo., 1942; m. Alex Elson, July 6, 1933; children—Jacova (Mrs. Allan Silverthorne), Karen (Mrs. Robert O'Neil). Tchr., Lowell Twp. (Ind.) High Sch., 1930-33; research asso. Jewish Children's Bur., 1939-41; supr. adoption div. Ill. Children's Home and Aid Soc., 1945-52; chief psychiat. social worker Student Mental Health Clinic, U. Chgo., 1956—, field work asst. prof. dept. psychiatry, 1966—. Pres., U. Chgo. Lab. Schs. Parents Assn., 1946-48; chmn. parks and recreation com., co-chmn. sculpture com. Hyde Park Kenwood Community Conf., 1953-56, 65-70. Fellow Am. Orthopsychiat. Assn. (membership com. 1965-68); mem. Am. Coll. Health Assn. (program com., del. mental health sect. 1973-75), Nat. Assn. Social Workers. Jewish religion. Contbr. articles to profl. jours. Home: 5642 Dorchester Av Chicago IL 60637 Office: 5743 Drexel Av Chicago IL 60637

ELSON, RUTH MILLER (MRS. ROBERT ELSON), educator; b. Scranton, Pa., Mar. 4, 1917; d. William Charles and Margaret Rucker (Smithson) Miller; B.A. (fellow), Vassar Coll., 1939; M.A., Columbia, 1940, Ph.D., 1952; m. Robert Elson, Jan. 31, 1953; 1 dau., Elizabeth. Instr., Bklyn. Coll., 1942-43; instr. history Vassar, Poughkeepsie, N.Y., 1943-45, 51-53, asst. prof., 1953-58, asso. prof., 1958-60, vis. prof., 1972-73; lectr. Hunter Coll., N.Y.C., 1946-49, 60-62; asst. prof. Rockford (Ill.) Coll., 1949-51; faculty Finch Coll., N.Y.C., 1962—, prof. history, 1970—. Columbia fellow, 1945-46; Vassar faculty fellow, Am. Assn. U. Women fellow, 1957-58; Nat. Endowment for Humanities sr. fellow, 1974-75. Mem. Am. Hist. Soc., Am. Studies Assn. Author: Guardians of Tradition: American Schoolbooks of the 19th Century, 1964. Home: 100 La Salle St New York City NY 10027

ELWELL, MARY ARDELL, educator, author; b. Portland, Me., Apr. 10, 1912; d. Arthur F. and Lida (Harmon) Elwell; B.A., U. N.H., 1949; M.A., Columbia, 1951; Ed.D., Columbia, 1959. Tchr. elementary and secondary schs., Graham, Saco, and Portland, Me., 1935-50; prof., chmn. dept. speech William Paterson Coll., Wayne, N.J., 1951-72, asso-dean tchr. edn., 1972—. Free lance writer, 1951—. Mem. N.J. state Scholarship Commn., 1973—. Mem. Am. Penwomen, Am. Assn. U. Women (pres. 1964-66), Zonta Internat. (pres. 1975), Pi Lambda Theta, Kappa Delta Pi. Author: (with M. Dawson, M. Zollinger and E. Johnson) Language for Daily Use, 1968, 2d edit., 1973. Home: 330 East 33rd St Paterson NJ 07504 Office: 300 Pompton Rd Wayne NJ 07512

ELY, MARICA MCCANN (MRS. NORTHCUTT ELY), interior designer, lectr.; b. Pachuca, Mexico, (parents Am. citizens); d. Warner and Mary (Cook) McCann; B.A., U. Cal. at Berkeley, 1929; grad. interior design Pratt Inst. Art, 1931; m. Northcutt Ely, Dec. 2, 1931; children—Michael N., Craig N., Parry Haines. Prof. Ikebana Sogetsu Sch., Tokyo, Japan, lectr. flower arranging. Past pres. Kenwood Garden Club, Md.; art editor Nat. Capital Garden Club League Flower Arrangement Calendar, Washington, 1957-58; co-founder Delta Gamma Found. for Pre-Sch. Blind Children; bd. dirs. Washington Hearing Soc., 1969-70; bd. dirs. Nat. Library for Blind, Washington. Finalist Jackson-Perkins Nat. Silver Bowl competitions, 1966; recipient Order of Delta Gamma Rose, 1968. Mem. Internat. Platform Assn., Bot. Soc. South Africa, Ikebana Internat., Delta Gamma. Clubs: Berkeley Tennis of Cal. (Berkeley, Cal.); Chevy Chase; Washington Women's. Home and studio: 4200 Massachusetts Av NW Apt 414 Washington DC 20016

ELY, MYRTLE MARGARET MILLER HOVERSON (MRS. ALEXANDER WHITE ELY), sch. adminstr.; b. Brainerd, Minn., May 6, 1911; d. Charles John and Dollie Christina (Miller) Pelkey; B.S., State Tchrs. Coll., Duluth, 1929; M.L.S., U. Minn., 1954; M. Curriculum and Instrn., U. Wis., 1967; m. Arthur Leonard Hoverson, June 5, 1929 (dec. Mar. 1952); children—Charles Leonard, Myrtle Artis, Dolores Elizabeth (Mrs. Edwin Maylin); m. 2d, Alexander White Ely, Dec. 27, 1960 (dec. Aug. 1965). Kindergarten tchr., Nashwauk, Minn., 1928-30; elementary tchr., Mungen, Minn., 1942-45; dir. sch. libraries and audio visual edn. Proctor (Minn.) Ind. Sch. Dist., 1945-60; with Herbert Schenk Middle Sch., Madison, Wis., 1961—, head instructional materials center, 1970—. Organizer presch. and kindergarten class Children's Home, Duluth, Minn., 1929-30. Mem. A.L.A., Nat., Wis., So. Wis. edn. assns. Mem. Order Eastern Star (past worthy matron), White Shrine, Order of Amaranth (past royal matron, now grand marshall State of Wis.). Club: Cloquet (Minn.) Reading (organizer, pres. 1937). Author: Years of the Honey Locust, 1974; also articles. Home: 917 Laurie Dr Madison WI 53711 Office: 520 Schenk St Madison WI 53714

EMBEITA, MARIA Z., educator; Licenciada en Filosofia y Letras, U. Madrid; M.A., U. Chgo.; Ph.D., U. Ill. Charles A. Dana prof. Spanish, Sweet Briar (Va.) Coll. Address: Sweet Briar Coll Sweet Briar VA 24595

EMBERG, RUTH H. BACH (MRS. DONALD JAMES EMBERG), coll. adminstr.; b. Swissvale, Pa., July 29, 1923; d. Anthony and Emily Atwell (Wilson) Bach; student Seton Hill Coll., 1941-42, Pa. State U., 1942-43; B.S., Indiana U. Pa., 1963, M.Ed., 1969; m. Donald James Emberg, Aug. 19, 1944; children—Donald James, Eric V., Lynn Karyl. Draftsman, Westinghouse Electric Co., East Pittsburgh, Pa., 1943; electronics draftsman Femco, Inc., Irwin, Pa., 1952-54; archtl. draftsman J & J Builders, East McKeesport, Pa., 1954-56; engr. Elliott Co., Jeannette, Pa., 1956-58; lab. technician research Carnegie Mellon U., Pitts., 1960; math. tchr. Washington Twp. Sr. High Sch., Apollo, Pa., 1961-66; math. and drafting tchr. Kiski Area Sr. High Sch., Vandergrift, Pa., 1966-71; math. and drafting tchr. Westmoreland County Community Coll., Youngwood, Pa., 1971, adminstr. Kiski Satellite Campus, Vandergrift, 1971—. Mem. Nat. Council Tchrs. Math. Mem. Order Eastern Star.

EMBREE, MARTHA LOUISE, chem. co. exec.; b. Houston, Nov. 30, 1936; d. Elisha Devant and Alma (Bedell) Embree; B.A., U. Houston, 1958. Copy trainee Erwin Wasey, Inc., Houston, 1959, newspaper prodn. mgr., 1959-60; sec. operations, and prodn. asst. KPRC-TV, Houston, 1960-62; copy chief R.S. Townsend Advt. Co., Kansas City, Mo., 1962-63; advt. asst. Chemagro Corp., Kansas City, Mo., 1963-66; free lance copywriter, 1966-68; advt. supr. Glidden-Durkee div. SCM Corp., Jacksonville, Fla., 1968-71, mgr. communications, 1971—. Bd. dirs. Jacksonville Humane Soc., 1973. Mem. N.E. Fla. Bus. Communicators (pres. 1972), Jacksonville Advt. Club (dir. 1972-73), Am. Women in Radio and TV. Home: 14660 Stacey Rd Jacksonville FL 32250 Office: PO Box 389 Jacksonville FL 32250

EMELE, JANE FRANCES, pharmacologist; b. Philipsburg, N.J., Nov. 14, 1925; d. Karl A. and Mary (Shafer) Emele; B.S., Upsala Coll., 1947; M.S., U. Ill., 1949; Ph.D., Yale, 1954. Research asst. Dept. Pharmacology, Schering Corp., Bloomfield, N.J., 1947-48; chief sect. pharmacodynamics Eaton Labs., Norwich Pharmacal Co., Norwich, N.Y., 1954-55; sr. research asso. Warner Lambert Research Inst., Dept. Pharmacology, Morris Plains, N.J., 1955-66, dir. dept. pharmacology Consumer Products Research Div., 1966-70, asso. dir. biol. research, 1970-72, dir. biol. research, 1973—. Mem. fund council Upsala Coll., 1972-74, mem. pres.'s forum, 1973—, fellow coll., 1974—. Bd. dirs. Morris County Health and Welfare Agy., 1965—, Mental Health Bd., Morris County, N.J., 1959—. Named Alumnus of Year, Upsala Coll., 1967. Mem. N.J. (dir. 1960-62), Morris County (dir. 1955—, sec. 1961—, 2d v.p. 1959-61) assns. for mental health, N.Y. Acad. Sci., Am. Soc. for Pharmacology and Exptl. Therapeutics, Am. Therapeutic Soc., Am. Pharm. Assn., Acad. Pharm. Scis., A.A.A.S., W. T. Salter Soc., Upsala Coll., Yale U. Ill. alumni assns., Internat. Soc. Biochem. Pharmacology, Internat. Inflammation Club, Am. Soc. Clin. Pharmacology and Therapeutics, Sigma Delta Epsilon, Chi Delta, Sigma Xi. Club: Zonta. Author numerous articles pub. in profl. jours. Home: 19 Kathleen Place Morris Plains NJ 07950 Office: 170 Tabor Rd Morris Plains NJ 07950

EMERLING, CAROL FRANCES GREENBAUM, lawyer; b. Cleve., Sept. 13, 1930; d. Bernard and Florence (Appelbaum) Greenbaum; student Vassar Coll., 1948-49, Case-Western Res. U., 1949-50; LL.B. summa cum laude, Cleve. Marshall Law Sch., 1955; m. Norton Harvey Noll, Oct. 1, 1950 (dec. 1951); m. 2d, Stanley J. Emerling, May 2, 1953 (div. 1971); children—Keith Stanley, Susan Carol; m. 3d, Jerrold A. Fadem, Aug. 22, 1974. Admitted to Ohio bar, 1955; staff atty. Pub. Defender's Office, Cleve., 1962-69, 1st asst., 1969, atty.-in-charge, 1969-70; regional dir. Cleve. office Fed. Trade Commn., 1970-74, Los Angeles office, 1974—; chmn. Cleve. Fed. Exec. Bd., 1972-73. Mem. Pepper Pike Charter Commn., 1966—, sec., 1966; founder Pepper Pike Civic League, 1956. Mem. bd. overseers Cleve. Marshall Law Coll. of Cleve. State U., 1970—. Trustee, Urban League, Cleve., 1969-72. Mem. Am., Fed., Ohio State, Cuyahoga County, Cleve. bar assns., League Women Voters (chpt. trustee 1955-61), Cleve. State U. Law Alumni Assn. (trustee 1968—, 1st v.p. 1972-73, pres. 1973-74). Club: Vassar (past trustee) (Cleve.). Author: (with Eugene O. Jonckers) The Allergy Cookbook, 1969. Home: 262 18th St Santa Monica CA 90402 Office: 13209 Fed Bldg 11000 Wilshire Blvd Los Angeles CA 90024

EMERLING, MURIEL BERGSON (MRS. KENNETH LLOYD EMERLING), govt. ofcl.; b. N.Y.C., Mar. 7, 1931; d. Samuel and Dora (Deutschman) Bergson; B.S. cum laude, Ohio U., 1953; m. Kenneth Lloyd Emerling, June 21, 1953; children—Sandra Gail, David Martin, Lawrence Charles. With Cleve. Bd. Edn., 1953-56, chmn. faculty, 1956; tchr. South Euclid-Lyndhurst (O.) Bd. Edn., 1967-70; dep. registrar Ohio Bur. Motor Vehicles, Mayfield Heights, 1971—. Chmn. Democratic Registration Com. Cuyahoga County, O., 1970; chmn. Dem. Womens Com. Cuyahoga County, 1970; mem. Cuyahoga County Dem. Exec. Com., 1970-74, vice-chmn., 1972-74; Dem. State Com. Woman, 22nd Congressional Dist., 1970-72; mem. Ohio Dem. Exec. Com., 1970-72. Mem. Council on World Affairs, Citizens League, League Women Voters, Kappa Delta Pi. Home: 933 Glenside Rd South Euclid OH 44121 Office: 6420 Mayfield Rd Mayfield Heights OH 44124

EMERSON, ALICE FREY, univ. dean; b. Durham, N.C., Oct. 26, 1931; d. Alexander Hamilton and Alice (Hubbard) Frey; A.B., Vassar Coll., 1953; Ph.D., Bryn Mawr Coll., 1964; children—Rebecca, Peter. Tchr., Newton (Mass.) High Sch., 1956-58; faculty Bryn Mawr (Pa.) Coll., 1964-66; faculty U. Pa., Phila., 1966—, asst. prof. polit. sci., 1967—, dean women, 1966-69, dean students, 1969—. Mem. bd. overseers vis. com. athletics Harvard, 1973—. Mem. Am. Polit. Sci. Assn., Am. Assn. U. Profs., Nat. Assn. Student Personnel Adminstrs. (mem. at large exec. com. 1973-74, dir. div. profl. relations and legislation 1974—), Am. Council Edn. (acad. affairs commn. 1972-74). Home: 7209 Charlton St Philadelphia PA 19119

EMERSON, ANDI (MRS. EMERSON WEEKS), sales and advt. exec.; b. N.Y.C.; d. Willard Ingham and Ethel (Mole) Emerson; student Barnard Coll., 1947-48; m. George G. Fawcett, Jr., June 18, 1948 (div. May 1958); children—Ann Emerson II, George Gifford III, Christopher Babcock; m. 2d, Kenneth E. Weeks, Feb. 13, 1959 (div. Oct. 1963); 1 dau., Electra Ingham. Account exec. Smith Hagel & Snyder, N.Y.C., 1952-54; pres. Emerson Assos., Inc., N.Y.C., 1954-56; exec. v.p., partner Eugene Stevens, Inc., N.Y.C., 1956-60; pres. Emerson-Weeks, Inc., N.Y.C., 1960—, dir., 1960—; pres., dir. Emerson-Weeks & Towers Corp., 1974—, Emerson House, Inc., N.Y.C., Pub.'s Buying, Inc.; dir. House of Stewart, Inc. Instr. N.Y. U., 1960-65. Block chmn. fund raising A.R.C., Multiple Sclerosis, Nat. Found., Crippled Children, Found. for Blind, 1954-63; vol. worker Childrens Ward, Meml. Hosp., 1964-66, Hosp. for Spl. Surgery, 1967; mem. adv. com. African Students League, 1965-67. Bd. dirs. Violet Oakley Meml. Found., Phila., 1964—. Mem. Direct Mail Advt. Assn., Sales Promotion Execs., Marketing Execs. Club, Mail Order Profls. Group, Soc. Profl. Writers. Clubs: Hundred Million (treas. 1960-61), New York Junior League, Advertising, Barnard. Home: 16 E 96th St New York City NY 10028 Office: 575 Lexington Av New York City NY 10022

EMERSON, DOROTHY, home economist; b. Waltham, Mass.; d. Philip and M. Evelyn (Dewey) Emerson; grad. in home econs. Framingham State Tchrs. Coll.; summer study Dartmouth, Columbia U., Amherst. Tchr. Boston Pub. Schs., Kimball Union Acad. Urban home demonstration agt., Portsmouth, N.H.; county club agt. Sussex County, Del.; prof., asso. state 4-H Club agt. Md. Extension Service, 1923-61, now extension prof. emeritus; now cons. citizenship-leadership div. Nat. 4-H Club Found.; also lectr. on 4-H Club work. Mem. Pen Women, Delta Kappa Gamma (hon.), Epsilon Sigma Phi, Phi Kappa Phi. Author: Scrapbook, 1966; also articles. Home: 3445 S Leisure World Blvd Silver Spring MD 20906 Office: 7100 Connecticut Av Washington DC 20015

EMERSON, EDITH, artist; b. Oxford, O.; d. Alfred and Alice (Edwards) Emerson; student Art Inst., Chgo., 1903-08; Pa. Acad. Fine Arts, 1912-16. Lectr. history of art various colls. and clubs; mem. faculty Agnes Irwin Sch., 1916-27, Phila. Coll. of Art, 1929-36, Coll. Chestnut Hill, dir. Woodmere Art Gallery, 1940—, pres. 1945-46, curator, 1946—, retrospective exhbn. paintings, 1969; illustrator books and mags.; mural and portrait painter; exhibited in group shows at Pa. Acad. Fine Arts, Nat. Acad., Corcoran Gallery, Carnegie Inst., Archtl. League, others; work represented in collections at Phila. Mus. Art, Pa. Acad. Fine Arts, Bryn Mawr Coll., others. Chmn. Regional Council of Community Art Centers, Phila., 1950—; pres. Violet Oakley Meml. Found., 1961—. Recipient Phila. Water Color Club medal, 1964. Mem. Fellowship of Pa. Acad. Fine Arts, Woodmere Art Gallery, Plays and Players (hon.), Nat. Soc. Mural Painters, Phila. Water Color Club, Phila. Mus. of Art, Pa. Acad. Fine Arts, Pa., Germantown, Chestnut Hill hist. socs., Friends of Wissahickon. Christian Scientist. Club: Modern (hon.). Home: 627 St George's Rd Philadelphia PA 19119 Office: 9201 Germantown Av Philadelphia PA 19118

EMERSON, GERALDINE MARIELLEN, biochemist, educator; b. Greensboro, N.C., Dec. 30, 1925; d. William Silas and Buna Launa (Thornton) Blakely; grad. Jacksonville (Fla.) Jr. Coll., 1946; B.A. in Chemistry and Psychology, U. Miami (Fla.), 1949; postgrad. Northwestern U., 1951-52; Ph.D., U. Ala., 1960; m. Jack Drew Emerson, Nov. 26, 1946 (dec. Sept. 1971); 1 son, William Kenneth. Research asst. U. Ala. Med. Center, Birmingham, 1953-59, teaching asst., 1955-60, instr. physiology and biochemistry, 1960-61, instr. biochemistry, 1961-64, asst. prof. biochemistry, 1964—, mem. admissions com. Sch. Dentistry, 1972-74, also mem. Univ. Council, 1973—. Fellow A.A.A.S., Psi Chi; mem. Ala. Acad. Sci. (vice-chmn., v.p. 1966-68), Am. Inst. Chemists (chmn. elect Ala. chpt. 1974), Am. Physiol. Soc., Soc. for Cryobiology, Ala. Soc. Med. History (sec.-treas. 1958-59), N.Y. Acad. Sci., Sigma Xi (treas. Ala. chpt. 1964-66). Contbr. articles on biochemistry and neurophysiology to sci. jours. Home: 2800 Vestavia Forest Place Birmingham AL 35216 Office: Room 217 NBST Univ Station Birmingham AL 35294

EMERSON, MARILYN PARKER (MRS. GARY BURTON EMERSON), editor; b. Howell, Mich., Apr. 6, 1947; d. William Riddle and Josephine Loretta (Russell) Parker; B.A. in Journalism, U. Mich., 1969; m. Gary Burton Emerson, Dec. 18, 1971. Adminstrv. asst. communications dept. Chrysler Corp., Highland Park, Mich. 1969; edn. writer The Daily Eagle, Wayne, Mich., 1969-70; editor Where Mag., Detroit, 1970-71; asst. editor Livingston County Press., Howell, Mich., 1972—. Chmn. pub. relations Howell Area Community Chest, 1973-74. Mem. Women in Communications, Mich. Press Assn. (recipient award Achievement 1973), Mich. Women's Press Club, U. Mich. Alva Gordon Sink Alumnae Group, Zeta Tau Alpha. Home: 11576 Maxfield Blvd Hartland MI 48029 Office: Livingston County Press 111 N Michigan Av Howell MI 48843

EMERSON, ROBERTA SHINN (MRS. ROBERT KENNERLY EMERSON), art mus. ofcl.; b. Indpls., Feb. 14, 1922; d. Lorabee Chanson and Thelma Josephine (Smith) Shinn; student Northwestern U., 1939-41, U. Chgo., 1941-43; A.B., Marshall U., 1965; m. Robert Kennerly Emerson, Sept. 22, 1943; children—Robert Kennerly, Elizabeth Kirkman, Jonathan Pipes. Interim dir. Huntington (W.Va) Galleries, 1967, permanent dir., 1971—, lectr., 1960—. Mem. faculty Marshall U., 1966-67. Mem. Huntington City Charter Bd., 1956-58, W.Va. Commn. on Constl. Revision, 1958-60, Huntington Civil Rights Commn., 1965-67. Recipient Distinguished Citizen award Nat. Municipal League, 1958. Mem. League Women Voters (W.Va. dir., pres. Huntington chpt.), Jr. League (dir. Huntington). Club: Cosmopolitan (N.Y.C.). Home: 706 Ridgewood Rd Huntington WV 25701 Office: Huntington Galleries Park Hills Huntington WV 25701

EMERSON, SUZANNE MICHEL (MRS. DON N. EMERSON), therapist; b. Marion, O., Mar. 13, 1934; d. Paul Devere and Esther (Kent) Michel; student U. Dayton, 1952-53; B.S., Ohio State U., 1953-56; M.A., Loyola U., Los Angeles, 1974; m. Don N. Emerson, Feb. 1, 1972; 1 son, Dane E.M. Little. Staff therapist Ohio State U. Hosp., Columbus, 1956-60; sr. psychiat. therapist VA Hosp., Brentwood, Cal., 1960-61; coordinator adjunctive therapy and adult treatment program Westwood Hosp., Los Angeles, 1961-73; pvt. practice as therapist, also cons., Los Angeles, 1966—. Faculty, Ohio State U., 1956-60, Mt. St. Mary's Coll., Los Angeles, 1962-70, U. So. Cal., Los Angeles, 1971-73, Los Angeles City Coll., 1971-73; cons. Cal. Assn. Mental Health, 1968-69. Recipient grant Dept. Health, Edn. and Welfare, 1958-1962. Mem. So. Cal. Occupational Therapy Assn. (office chmn. 1968-69), Kappa Alpha Theta. Democrat.

EMERY, EMOGENE, educator; b. Howe, Okla., Feb. 25, 1911; d. William Byron and Icie Leolin (Stembridge) Emery; B.A., Okla. Bapt. U., 1931; M.A., U. Okla., 1937; postgrad. summers U. Colo., 1934, U. Wis., 1941, 42, Northwestern U., 1949, 50, Mich. State U., 1958, U. Wash., 1965. Tchr., Shawnee (Okla.) High Sch., 1934-40, Mary Hardin-Baylor Coll., 1940-47, U. Tex., Austin, 1947-54; faculty Hardin-Simmons U., 1954—, now asso. prof. speech. Del., Democratic County Conv., 1972, State Conv., 1974. Mem. Am. Assn. U. Women (bd. dirs. Abilene br. 1973—, parliamentarian state conv. 1973), Altrusa (v.p., dir.), Speech Communication Assn. Am., Tex. Speech Assn., Am. Inst. Parliamentarians. Baptist (Sunday sch. tchr.). Club: Univ. Women's. Contbr. articles to nat. jours. Home: 2473 Clinton St Abilene TX 79603

EMERY, INA NAOMI STANLEY (MRS. FRANK W. EMERY), hist. soc. exec.; b. Kezar Falls, Me., Nov. 7, 1892; d. Preston and Naomi (Stacy) Stanley; student New Eng. Conservatory of Music, 1911-14; m. Frank W. Emery, Nov. 18, 1925. Tchr. schs. in Porter, Me., 1908-09, North Conway, N.H., 1919-21, Kennebunkport and Wells, Me., 1922-24, 35-37, Waterville, Me., 1931-34, Saco, Me., 1938-62. Founder pres. Parsonsfield-Porter Hist. Soc., Kezar Falls, Me., 1946—. Mem. D.A.R. (past regent Saco). Methodist (local historian). Clubs: Historian Literary (Kezar Falls), Ladies' Magazine Reading. Home: Main St Kezar Falls ME 04047 Office: Parsonsfield Porter Hist Soc Box 206 Kezar Falls ME 04047

EMERY, LIN, sculptor; b. N.Y.C.; d. Cornell and Jean (Weill) Emery; sculpture study with Ossip Zadkine, Paris, 1949; welded metal sculpture techniques at Dorothea Denslow Sculpture Center, N.Y.C., 1951; m. Shirley B. Braselman; one son, Brooks Emery. Sculptor; one-man shows include Delgado Mus., 1954, So. Art Mus. Dirs. Assn. at Birmingham Mus., Chattanooga Gallery of Art, Columbia (S.C.) Mus. Art, Norton Gallery of Art, 1955, Sculpture Center, N.Y., 1957, 62, Nashville Fine Arts Center, 1962, Pensacola (Fla.) Art Center, 1958, Lyceum, Havana, Cuba, 1958, Orleans (New Orleans) Gallery, 1960, Marble Arch Gallery, Miami, Fla., 1963, Valley House Gallery, Dallas, 1963, Royal Athena Gallery, N.Y.C., 1964, Delgado Mus., New Orleans, 1964, Gallery Modern Art, Scottsdale, Ariz., 1965, New Orleans Pub. Library, 1965, Mus. N.M., Santa Fe, 1966, Orleans Gallery, 1967, Centennial Mus. Art, 1967; group shows include Women Welders Sculpture Center, N.Y.C., 1952, New Burlington Galleries, London, 1955, Am. Fedn. Arts, 1958, Pa. Acad., 1960, Yoseido Gallery, Tokyo, Japan, 1962, Contemporary Arts Gallery, Manila, Phillippines, 1962, also at USIS Gallery, Hong Kong, 1962, and others; archtl. commns. include 7 statues for St. James Major Ch., New Orleans, 1952, statue for exterior of St. Scholastica Acad., Covington, La., 1954, Pieta for Holy Cross High Sch., New Orleans, 1955, Imperial House, Tampa, Fla., 1960, Morrison Meml., Civic Center, New Orleans, aquamobile Germantown Savs. Bank, Phila., 1965, aquamobile for New Orleans Civic Center, in La., 1966, E. Jefferson Parish Hosp., La., Longue Vue Gardens, Fidelty Plaza, Oklahoma City, 1972, U. S.C., Columbia, 1972; represented in pub. collections including Pensacola Art Center, Fla., Walter P. Chrysler Mus., R.I., Columbia (S.C.) Mus. Delgado Mus., New Orleans, Tex. Instrument Corp., Dallas, Flint Mus., Norton Art Galleries, West Palm Beach, Fla., Huntington Galleries, W.Va.; invitational shows include Flint Invitational, 1966, Birmingham Mus. Religious Art Exhbn. Pres., Orleans Gallery, Inc., New Orleans, 1957; curator New Orleans Internat. House Mission Far East exhbn., 1961; vis. critic Tulane Sch. Architecture, 1967-68. Treas. So. Assn. Sculptors, Inc. Bd. dirs. Nat. Sculpture Center, U. Kan., Lawrence, 1973—. Recipient prizes Nat. Assn. Women Artists, N.Y.C., 1956. Mem. Nat. Assn. Women Artist, N.Y. Sculpture Center, N.Y. Soc. Women Artists. Works reproduced in archtl. publs. Address: 7520 Dominican St New Orleans LA 70118

EMERY, MARGARET ALICE, social worker; b. Hammond, Ind., Apr. 16, 1909; d. David Turner and Carrie B. (Miles) Emery; A.B., Rockford Coll., 1929; M.A. in French, U. Chgo., 1931; postgrad. Sch. Social Service Adminstrn. U. Chgo., part-time 1933-41. Supr. children's services div. Lake County Dept. Pub. Welfare, Gary, Ind., 1937-41, chief case work supr., 1942-44; with Div. Social Services Children's Bur., Washington, 1944-51, asst. dir., 1951-53, asst. to chief for legislation, 1953-58, asst. chief children's bur. Dept. Health, Edn. and Welfare, 1958-63, staff adviser on field relations, civil def., and staff devel. Office U.S. Commr. Welfare, 1964—, spl. asst. to commr. for civil rights, 1966-67, spl. asst. for policy coordination, Office Adminstr. Social and Rehab. Service, 1967-69; asst. prof. social work, dir. rural manpower research and tng. project U. W.Va., Morgantown, 1969-72. Cons. on child welfare children's div. Ind. Dept. Pub. Welfare, Indpls., 1941-42; adviser on family and child welfare Bur. Tech. Assistance UN, Formosa, 1963-64. Recipient Superior Service award Dept. Health, Edn. and Welfare, 1958. Mem. Nat. Assn. Social Workers, Nat. Conf. Social Welfare, Am. Pub. Welfare Assn. Home: 6015 Cairn Terrace Bethesda MD 20034

EMIG, LOIS IRENE MYERS (MRS. JACK W. EMIG), composer; b. Roseville, O., Oct. 12, 1925; d. Earl Francis and Margaret Byrd (Weaver) Myers; B.S. with distinction, Ohio State U., 1946; postgrad. Ohio State U., Queens Coll.; m. Jack Wayne Emig, June 7, 1947; children—Sandra Jill, Keith Jack. Pub. sch. vocal and instrumental music tchr., Ohio and N.Y., 1946-65; pvt. tchr. piano and theory, 1954—; composer and librettist for adult and children's choirs; church organist; works include 9 cantatas, 2 piano books, over 150 varied choral works. Recipient 1st prize, W.Va. Women's Clubs, 1954, 1st prize, Lorenz Children's Anthem contest, 1964. Mem. A.S.C.A.P., Delta Omicron. Contbr. articles to profl. jours. Home and Office: 82 Fletcher Av Valley Stream NY 11580

EMMET, BEULAH HEPBURN (MRS. ROBERT RUTHERFORD MORRIS EMMET), educator; b. Canton, N.Y., Aug. 28, 1890; d. A. Barton and Emily (Eaton) Hepburn; B.A., Wellesley Coll., 1912; m. Robert Rutherford Morris Emmet, Oct. 11, 1912; children—Robert T., Beulah E. (Mrs. Frederick Hiebel), Barton H., John P., Dagny Meister Emmet (Mrs. O'Keefe) (adopted). Tchr., trustee Edgewood Sch., Greenwich, Conn., 1916-42; founder High Mowing Sch. under Waldorf Sch. methods, Wilton, N.H., 1942, now prin., tchr., chmn. bd. Trustee Barton Hepburn Trust. Address: High Mowing Sch Wilton NH 03086

EMMONS, DELLA GOULD (MRS. ALLEN B. EMMONS), writer; b. Glencoe, Minn., Aug. 12, 1890; d. William George and Katherine (Wadel) Gould; B.A., U. Minn., 1912; postgrad. U. Wash., 1937; m. Allen Burdette Emmons, Sept. 20, 1913 (dec. June 1958); children—Kathryn (Mrs. Robert Donald Nettelblad), Allan Gould. Sch. music supr., Sisseton, S.D., 1912-13; writer Wash. State Hist. Com. for Territorial and Lewis and Clark Centennials, 1947-55; script writer Paramount Pictures, Hollywood, 1953. Author: (hist. novels) Sacajawea of the Shoshones (motion picture Far Horizons 1955), 1943, Nothing In Life Is Free, 1955, 12th printing, 1968 (Wash. State Ofl. Centennial novel); Leschi of the Nisquallies, 1965; (pageants) Marcus Whitman, 1922, 23, 24, Ours to the 49th, 1953, On to the Pacific, 1955; (plays) A Territory Is Born, 1953, Out to Win, 1955, Medicine Creek Treaty, 1955; Northwest History in Action (book of 12 plays), 1960; Francis Scott Key-Architect of Freedom award, 1972; symphonic drama Marcus Whitman, 1951, others. Mem. Women's Aux. of Tacoma Indian Hosp., 1957-59; com. mem. Lewis & Clark Recreation Trail Plan. Bd. dirs. Broadway Theatre League, Tacoma. Recipient distinguished service award Wash. Hist. Soc., 1953; internat. achievement award Beta Sigma Phi, 1957; Achievement award Wash. State Press Women, 1966; Golden Acorn award Seattle P.T.A., 1970; Achievement award Fort Lewis, Wash., 1970; also awards various local orgns. Mem. Nat. League Am. Pen Women (nat. chmn. hist. novels contest biennial contest 1964, nat. award for hist. novels 1966), Am. Assn. State and Local History, Internat. Lit. Assn., Wash. Hist. Soc. (curator 1950—), Nat. Ry. Hist. Soc., Am. Assn. U. Women, D.A.R., Internat. Platform Assn., Nat. Press Women (affiliate), Nat. Congress Am. indians (hon.), Beta Sigma Phi. Conglist. Club: Fort Lewis Officers' Wives (hon.). Home: 814 N Lawrence St Tacoma WA 98406

EMMS, JOSEPHA MURRAY, poet; b. Jamaica Plain, Boston, Apr. 21, 1894; d. Joseph Howe and Annie Marie (Welfel) Murray; ed. various writing courses; m. Edward Emms, June 12, 1920 (dec.); 1 dau., Marjorie (Mrs. Frank Robert Pote). Former tchr. drama, expression; judge numerous poetry contests. Author: (plays) Her Son's Sweetheart, 1915; Playing the Game, 1915; Under Suspicion, 1925; A Dream Lesson, 1916; (poetry) April Music, 1962, Epigrams 1946-1960. Recipient certificate of merit N.Y. State Poetry Soc., 2d prize Am. Poetry League Ann. Contest, 1972. Mem. Am. Poetry League, Midwest Chaparral, Poetry Soc. Tex., Poet's Haven, Mass. Poetry Soc. (hon.), Agnes Carr Writer's Club (hon.). Conglist. Home: 205 S Huntington Av Jamaica Plain MA 02130

EMPSON, DORA ROSE (MRS. MANUEL CHARLES ROSENFIELD), physician; b. Scunthorpe, Eng., Jan. 6, 1937; d. Charles William and Dora Alice (Saxby) Empson; M.B., B.S., Royal Free Hosp. Sch. Medicine, U. London (Eng.), 1962; m. Manuel Charles Rosenfield, Dec. 2, 1961; 1 dau., Sarah Elizabeth. Came to U.S., 1962, naturalized, 1965. Intern, Mt. Auburn Hosp., Cambridge, Mass., 1962-63; resident children's service Mass. Gen. Hosp., Boston, 1963-64; resident dept. anesthesia, 1964-67; mem. active med. staff, anesthesiologist Tobey Hosp., Wareham, Mass., 1968-72; staff anesthesiologist Brockton (Mass.) Hosp., 1972—; fellow Radcliffe Inst., Cambridge, 1966—. Recipient gold medal Mass. Hort. Soc., 1971, 72, 73. Diplomate Am. Bd. Anesthesiology. Mem. Brit. Med. Assn., Mass. Med. Soc., Am., Mass. socs. anesthesiologists, Am., New Eng. rose socs. Home: 8 Old Marion Rd Mattapoisett MA 02739 Office: Brockton Hosp Brockton MA 02402

ENELOW, GERTRUDE STRASBERG (MRS. BENJAMIN FRANKLIN ENELOW), educator, lectr.; b. Chgo.; d. Benjamin and Stella (Johnson) Strasberg; student St. Xaviers Coll., 1922-24, U. Chgo., 1918-19; m. Benjamin Franklin Enelow, July 27, 1921 (dec. May 1957). Founder, dir. Gertrude Enelow Sch. of Body Dynamics, Chgo., 1950—; instituted Body Dynamics Programs for Ill. Correctional Instns., Dwight Reformatory, 1967—, Cook County Jail, 1970; mem. faculty Columbia Coll., Chgo., 1969-71; dir. body dynamics, tng. program for RSVP Vols., 1973—; nat. and internat. lectr. for growth centers and univs. Pres. Enelow Found., 1957—; chmn. women's adv. com. Chgo. Bd. Health, 1965-66; guarantor Lyric Opera, 1960—. Bd. dirs. Chgo. Community Music Found., 1963-66, Adult Edn. Council Greater Chgo., Fine Arts Quartet, Urban Gateways of Chgo., Hull House for Sr. Citizens of Met. Chgo., 1965-69, The Villages, Topeka, Friends of Chgo. Pub. Library; mem. adv. bd. Mid Am. Ballet, 1970—, Oasis, 1968—. Recipient award for outstanding service to sr. citizens Adult Edn. Council Greater Chgo., 1970. Mem. Nat. League Am. Pen Women, Chgo. Drama League, Chgo. Assn. Commerce and Industry, United Inventors and Scientists Am., English-Speaking Union, Alliance Francaise, Internat. Platform Assn., Newbery Library Assn., Art Inst. Chgo., Ill. Opera Guild (charter), Chgo. Symphony Soc. (hon. life), Midland Authors. Club: Chicago Press. Author: Body Dynamics, The Zen and Zest of Self-development, 1960; Inner Beauty-Outer Youth, 1970; Joy of Physical Freedom, 1973. Rec. of Body Dynamics and Instant Sleep, 1965. Patentee sleep pillow. Home: 199 E Lake Shore Dr Chicago IL 60611 Office: 900 N Michigan Av Chicago IL 60611

ENG, MARIETTA WAI YING, occupational therapist; b. Honolulu, Jan. 24, 1923; d. Sum Wing and Yau (Lee) Chong; certificate Phila. Sch. Occupational Therapy, 1945; B.S. in Home Econs., U. Hawaii, 1950; M.S. in Occupational Therapy, San Jose (Cal.) State Coll., 1966, tchr.'s certificate Coll. Holy Name, 1971; m. Herc Eng, July 21, 1946; children—Edmund, Linda, Dennis. Occupational therapist Kauikeolani Children's Hosp., Honolulu, 1950; dir. occupational therapy and recreation Hawaii State Hosp., Kaneohe, Oahu, 1953-56; occupational therapist Langley Porter Neuropsychiat. Inst., San Francisco, 1956-65, 66-67; dir. occupational therapy Children's Hosp. Med. Center, Oakland, Cal., 1968-70; ceramics tchr. Havens Sch., Piedmont, Cal., 1971; tchr. emotionally handicapped Webster Elementary Sch., Oakland, 1971-73; occupational therapist, day care coordinator N.E. Community Mental Health, Inc., San Francisco, 1973—. Served as ensign USN, 1945-46. Vocational Rehab. Adminstrn. scholar. Mem. Am. Occupational Therapy Assn. Home: 542 Weldon Av Oakland CA 94610 Office: 615 Grant Av San Francisco CA 94108

ENGEL, GLORIA V., hosp. adminstr., sociologist; b. Los Angeles, Sept. 22, 1921; B.A. in Psychology, U. Cal. at Los Angeles, 1959, M.A., 1962, Ph.D. in Sociology, 1968; m. Benjamin Engel, Apr. 11, 1943; 1 son, Gary. Asst. prof. dept. community medicine and pub. health Sch. Medicine, U. So. Cal., 1969-74; cons. obstetrics and gynecology attending staff Los Angeles County-U. So. Cal. Med. Center, 1970-73, asst. to dir. med. edn., 1971—. Vis. asst. prof. Grad. Sch. Bus. Adminstrn., U. Cal. at Los Angeles, 1970-71; data cons. East Los Angeles Consortium, 1972-73. USPHS trainee. Mem. Am., Pacific sociol. assns., Am. Psychol Assn., Am. Acad. Polit. and Social Scis., Am. Pub. Health Assn., Pi Gamma Mu. Author numerous publs. in field. Home: 3935 Valley Meadow Rd Encino CA 91316 Office: Box 540 1200 N State St Los Angeles CA 90033

ENGEL, MARIE LAMERS (MRS. KARL ENGEL), newspaper editor: b. Kleve am Rhine, Germany, May 24, 1902; d. Gerhard J. and Wilhelmina (Vordermayer) Lamers; student, U. Muenster, 1924; art tchr. degree, Art Acad. and Kunstgewerbeschule, Munich, 1929; m. Karl Engel, Nov. 4, 1930; 1 dau., Therese H. (Mrs. John Weakland). Came to U.S., 1947, naturalized, 1952. Free lance artist, Budapest, Hungary, 1930-47; asst. editor Cin. Freie Presse, 1949-57, owner, publisher, 1957-64; founder, editor, publisher Cin. Kuier, 1964—. Spl. interpreter Immigration & Naturalization Service, FBI, 1958-68. Active Community Chest and Red Cross. Decorated Order of Merit Fed. Republic of Germany, 1972; Good Citizenship award D.A.R., 1952. Home: 925 Purcell Av Cincinnati OH 45205 Office: 432 Walnut St Cincinnati OH 45202

ENGELDER, OPAL LORRAINE (MRS. PAUL OSCAR ENGELDER), real estate co. exec.; b. Harrison, Ark., Jan. 20, 1923; d. John Lester and Ruby Francis (Maloney) Adams; student Barnes Bus. Coll., 1941-44, W. Valley Coll., 1969, 70; m. Paul Oscar Engelder, Mar. 27, 1965; children—Deloris Joan, James Lester. Property mgr. Clair Wilson Realty Co., Campbell, Cal., 1965-69; br. mgr. Star Realty Co., San Jose, Cal., 1969-70; owner Vista Realty Co., Campbell, 1970—. Mem. San Jose Real Estate Bd., Cal. Real Estate Assn., Nat. Assn. Real Estate Bds., Cal. Real Estate Polit. Action, Brit.-Am. Club. Moose. Baptist (sec.-treas. 1968-69). Home: 1245 W Campbell Av Campbell CA 95008 Office: PO Box 237 1245 W Campbell Av Campbell CA 95008

ENGELHARDT, SISTER MARY VERONICE, educator; b. Syracuse, N.Y., Mar. 29, 1912; d. Herman J. and Ellen (Collins) Engelhardt; B.Ed., Cath. U. Am., 1937, M.A., 1938, Ph.D., 1962. Joined 3d Franciscan Order, Minor Conventuals, 1929; instr. St. Francis Normal Sch., Syracuse, 1938-52; diocesan, community supr. schs. Syracuse, 1952-56; lectr. summer sessions Cath. U. Am., 1954-56; dean women Chaminade Coll., Honolulu, 1957-60; clin. instr. reading clinic Child Center Cath. U. Am., 1960, supr. student teaching, 1960-61; asso. prof. edn., psychology, dir. reading, speech clinic Maria Regina Coll., Syracuse, 1962-72, head dept. edn., 1962-68; asst. mother gen. 3d Franciscan Order, 1965-71, personnel dir., 1971—, dir. communications, 1971—; dir. Franciscan Learning Resource Center, 1974—. Mem. Am. Ednl. Research Assn., Internat. Reading Assn., Am. Psychol. Assn. Author: Looking at God's World, 1950; Creatures in God's World, 1951; Learning More About God's World, 1952; co-author Songs About God's World. Address: 1024 Court St Syracuse NY 13208

ENGLAND, BERNICE ELIZABETH HALLREN, chamber of commerce exec.; b. Okla., Nov. 7, 1918; d. Frank Fry and Bernice Amelia (Saeger) Hallren; ed. pub. schs., Chamber of Commerce Inst.; m. Roy Elvin England, June 10, 1939; children—Terrance Patrick, Karen (Mrs. Jean Louis Frant). Sec. dist. office Blue Cross-Blue Sheild, Enid, Okla., 1958-61; part owner, asst. mgr. Pawnee County (Kan.) Credit Bur., 1962-69; sec., mgr. Larned (Kan.) C. of C., 1964—, also part owner, asst. mgr. Larned Credit Bur., 1964-69; part owner England Real Estate and Sales, Larned, Yellow Antique Treasure House, Larned; sec., dir. Larned Centennial, Inc. Pres. Monroe P.T.A., 1957-58. Mem. Kan. Chamber of Execs. (dir.), Bus. and Profl. Women's Club (v.p.). Republican. Mem. Order Eastern Star. Home: 412 W 6th St Larned KS 67550 Office: 502 1/2 Broadway Larned KS 67550

ENGLAND, MARY BELLE, librarian; b. Decaturville, Tenn., Jan. 28, 1923; d. James Stout and Tennessee Belle (Yarbro) England; A.B., Lambuth Coll., 1945; M.A., George Peabody Coll. for Tchrs., 1957, Edn. Specialist, 1965. Tchr. Henderson County Bd. Edn., Lexington, Tenn., 1946-50, College Park (Ga.) High Sch., 1950-56; librarian Fulton County Bd. Edn., Headland High Sch., East Point, Ga., 1956-69; dir. library services Fulton County (Ga.) Bd. Edn., Atlanta, 1969—. Atlanta chpt. English Speaking Union scholar, 1961. Mem. N.E.A., Ga. Edn. Assn. (pres. library dept. 1967-69), A.L.A., South Eastern Library Assn., Delta Kappa Gamma. Methodist. Club: Pilot (East Point, Ga.). Home: 4701 Flat Shoals Rd Villa 40-G Union City GA 30291 Office: 786 Cleveland Av SW Atlanta GA 30315

ENGLANDER, SOPHIA TENDRICH (MRS. MALVIN ENGLANDER), real estate agt.; b. Atlanta, July 24, 1924; d. Joseph and Bessie (Miller) Tendrich; ed. U. Miami; m. Malvin Englander, Mar. 14, 1943; children—Nicki (Mrs. Melvin Grossman, Donna (Mrs. Mark Fleishman), Patti, Tobie, Marla, Joseph. Real estate agt.; organizer First Women's Bank Fla. Vice-chmn. Miami Beach (Fla.)

Housing Authority, 1973—. Democratic State committeewoman, Fla., 1962—; past pres., life mem. Adlai Stevenson Dem. Women's Club. Mem. Fla. Consumers Council, Hebrew Acad. Women (life). Home: 4620 Pinetree Dr Miami Beach FL 33140 Office: care Tendrich Realty Co 11345-A S Dixie Hwy Miami FL 33156

ENGLE, ELOISE KATHERINE HOPPER (MRS. LAURI A. PAANANEN), author; b. Seattle, Apr. 12, 1923; d. Floyd and Lois (Thomas) Hopper; student George Washington U., 1944-47; m. Paul R. Engle, Sept. 7, 1943; children—Paula, David, Margaret; m. 2d, Lauri A. Paananen. Daily columnist Guam News, Agana, 1948-49; free-lance writer women's mags., 1948-58; editor Paradise of Pacific, 1959; contbr. articles to various nat. mags., 1959—; author: Sea Challenge, 1962, Countdown for Cindy, 1962, Dawn Mission, 1962, Princess of Paradise, 1962, Escape, 1963, The Sea of the Bear, 1964, Pararescue, 1964, Sky Rangers, 1964, Earthquake! Alaska's Great Disaster, 1966, Medic, 1966; Winter War: Russo-Finnish Conflict 1939-40, 1973; Last Year In The United States, 1970; Parachutes-How They Work, 1972; National Governments Around the World, 1973. Mem. Air Force Assn., Soc. Mag. Writers. Authors Guild, Soc. Women Geographers. Home: 6348 Crosswoods Dr Falls Church VA 22044

ENGLE, JESSIE LILLIAN, coll. dean; b. Sullivan, Ind., Mar. 18, 1910; d. John Thomas and Sarah Jane (Carrico) Carmichael; grad. Beauty Acad., 1932; student Orlando Jr. Coll., 1968-69, Atlanta Christian Coll., 1966-67, Ky. Christian Coll., 1972-73; m. Carl W. Eagle, Feb. 5, 1933 (dec. 1966); 1 dau., Linda. Owner, operator My Beauty Shop, Sullivan, Ind., 1933-41; operator, mgr. Carl Engle clothing store, Sullivan, 1941-45, asst., 1945-66; dorm dir. Atlanta (Ga.) Christian Coll., 1966-67; with Bullocks Men's Store, LaHabra, Cal., 1970-71; dean of women Ky. Christian Coll., Grayson, 1972—. Pres., Crippled Childrens Orgn., Sullivan, 1941-45, Tb. Soc., Sullivan, 1955-57. Democrat precinct com. woman, 1948-49. Mem. Ch. of Christ. Club: Womans (pres. 1950-52) (Sullivan). Home: 303 Indiana Av Sullivan IN 47882 Office: Kentucky Christian College Grayson KY 41143

ENGLE, MARY ALLEN ENGLISH (MRS. RALPH LANDIS ENGLE, JR.), physician; b. Madill, Okla., Jan. 26, 1922; d. Russell C. and Vera (Apperson) English; A.B., Baylor U., 1942; M.D., Johns Hopkins, 1945; m. Dr. Ralph Landis Engle, Jr., June 7, 1945; children—Ralph Landis III, Marilyn Elizabeth. Intern pediatrics Johns Hopkins Hosp., 1945-46; asst. dir. pediatrics out patient dept., 1946-47; asst. physician cardiac clinic, 1947-48; asst. resident Sydenham Hosp. Contagious Diseases, Balt., 1946; asst. resident N.Y. Hosp., 1948-49, asst. attending pediatrician, 1952-60, asso. attending pediatrician, 1960-62, attending pediatrician, 1962—; instr. pediatrics Johns Hopkins, 1946-48; fellow pediatrics, Cornell, 1949-50; instr. pediatrics, 1950-51, 52-54, asst. prof., 1954-59, asso. prof., 1959-69, prof. pediatrics, 1969—; med. dir. Insts. in Care of Premature Infants, 1952-55, dir. pediatric cardiology, 1963—. Mem. Pres.'s Panel on Heart Disease, 1972; mem. heart adv. com. Joint Commn. Accreditation. Recipient Spence-Chapin award for contbn. pediatrics, 1958; Cummings humanitarian award Am. Coll. Cardiology, 1973. Diplomate in pediatric cardiology Am. Bd. Pediatrics. Mem. Am. Acad. Pediatrics (charter mem. sect. cardiology), Am. (com. on teaching scholars, exec. com. council on cardiovascular disease in the young, internat. com.), N.Y. heart assns., N.Y. Acad. Medicine, Harvey Soc., Soc. Pediatric Research, Am. Coll. Chest Physicians, Assn. European Pediatric Cardiologists (corr.), Am. Coll. Cardiology (master tchr. 1969, 73, long range planning com., trustee), Intersoc. Commn. on Heart Disease Resources (chmn. congenital heart disease), Am. Pediatric Soc., Phi Beta Kappa, Alpha Omega Alpha. Presbyn. Clubs: Pelham Country; International Garden. Editorial bd. Circulation, Am. Jour. Cardiology; sr. editor Chest. Contbr. articles to profl. jours. Home: 1 Country Club Lane Pelham Manor NY 10803 Office: The NY Hosp Cornell Med Coll 525 E 68th St New York City NY 10021

ENGLEBERG, ISA N. (MRS. NIELS CARY ENGLEBERG), educator; b. Jersey City, June 12, 1947; d. Abraham and Florence (Beckman) Natovitz; B.A., George Washington U., 1969; M.A., U. Md., 1971; m. Niels Cary Engleberg, Dec. 21, 1969. Teaching instr., asst. dir. forensic activities U. Md., College Park, 1969-71; lectr. George Washington U., Washington, 1970; asst. prof. speech communications, dir. forensic activities Prince George's Community Coll., Largo, Md., 1971—, community services instr., 1972. Textbook reviewer Houghton Mifflin Co., Boston, 1974-75; play reviewer Montgomery County Sentinel, Rockville, Md., 1973; guest reviewer, actress Washington Shakespeare Festival, 1969. Mem. Nat. Jr. Coll. Speech Assn. (v.p. 1972-76), Am. Forensic Assn., Speech Communication Assn., Eastern Forensic Assn. (mem.-at-large exec. bd.), Forensic Orgn. of Related Colls. in the East (pres. 1971-74), Nat. Orgn. for Women, Common Cause, Mortar Bd., Delta Sigma Rho, Tau Kappa Alpha. Home: 6200 Westchester Park Dr College Park MD 20740 Office: Prince George's Community College 301 Largo Rd Largo MD 20870

ENGLISH, ELIZABETH LOIS, banker, author; b. Macksville, Kan.; d. Alexander G. and Florence (McMorran) English; student pub. schs. Vice pres. Macksville State Bank, 1956-67, pres., 1967—. Mem. Macksville Library Bd. Mem. Internat. Platform Assn., Centro Studi E Scambi Internazionali. Clubs: Research, Kansas Authors. Author: On Wings of Faith, 1956; The Pact and the Psalms, 1957; The Golden Stairway, 1959; The Moving Story, 1962; Progress of the Pilgrim, 1963; The Miracle of Miracles, 1964; Wait-Wait For Yet a Little Longer. Home: Macksville KS 67557 Office: Macksville State Bank Macksville KS 67557

ENGLISH, FANITA BLUMBERG, psychotherapist, lectr.; b. Galatz, Rumania; d. Max and Elena (Gottesman) Blumberg; naturalized 1946; postgrad. Columbia, 1942-43; M.A., Bryn Mawr Coll., 1944, M.Social Service, 1945; m. Maurice English, Apr. 25, 1945; children—Jonathan Brian, Deirdre Elena. Social worker Jewish Bd. Guardians, N.Y.C., 1945; lectr. sociology George Washington U., Washington, 1948-49; dir. Family Service, Alexandria, Va., 1949-50; casework supr. Ridge Farm Residential Treatment Center, Lake Forest, Ill., 1950-56; pvt. practice psychotherapy, Chgo., 1956-70; lectr. U. Chgo., 1968-70, 73, 74; pvt. practice, tchr., lectr. transactional analytic treatment, Phila., N.Y.C., 1970—; founder Phila. Transactional Analysis Seminar, 1970—; dir. Eastern Inst. for Transactional Analysis and Gestalt, Phila., 1971—. Cons. psychotherapy to med. staff trainees Elgin (Ill.) State Hosp., 1963-69; cons., lectr. workshops univs. and social agys. including Chgo. Com. Urban Opportunity, Chgo. Bd. Edn., Ill. Dept. Mental Health, Ill., N.Y. psychiat. assns., U. Chgo., U. Wis., U. Pa., Rutgers U., U. Cal., Marriage Council of Phila., Family Service Assn. Am., Fritz Perls Inst., Germany. Mem. Am. Acad. Certified Social Workers, Am. Group Psychotherapy Assn., Am. Assn. Marriage and Family Counselors, Internat. Coll. Psychosomatic Medicine, Jean Piaget Soc. (dir.); teaching mem. Internat. Transactional Analysis Assn. Home: 1500 Locust St Philadelphia PA 19102 Office: 1530 Locust St 4B Philadelphia PA 19102

ENGLUND, HAZEL BARBARA, occupational therapist; b. St. Paul, Dec. 6, 1941; d. Arnold Ludwig and Marian Julia (Jensen) Englund; B.S., U. Minn., 1965. Occupational therapist Ft. Logan Mental Health Center, 1965-67, U. Colo. Med. Center, 1967—. Mem. Am. Occupational Therapy Assn., Denver Figure Skating Club (dir.). Home: 1225 S Oneida St Denver CO 80222 Office: 4200 E 9th Av Denver CO 80220

ENGSTROM, MARY CLAIRE RANDOLPH (MRS. ALFRED GARVIN ENGSTROM), educator; b. Kansas City, Mo., Oct. 1, 1906; d. Lester Leroy and Florence (Toynbee) Randolph; student St. Teresa Jr. Coll., 1923-25; A.B., B.S., Central Mo. State Tchrs. Coll., Warrensburg, 1928; M.A., U. Mo., Columbia, 1929; Ph.D., U. N.C., 1939; postgrad. Harvard, Yale, 1941-42; m. Alfred Garvin Engstrom, June 10, 1939. Asst. prof., asso. prof. Ark. A. and M. Coll., Monticello, 1929-34; research asso. U. N.C., Chapel Hill, 1942—. Vice pres. Hillsborough Hist. Soc., 1962-63, pres., 1963-64; mem. Historic Hillsborough Commn., 1963—, chmn., 1964-66; mem. Orange County Bicentennial Commn., 1971—. Recipient Cannon Cup award for historic preservation N.C. Soc. for Preservation Antiquities, 1965, Woman of Year award Hillsborough Bus. and Profl. Womens Club, 1966, Book of Golden Deeds award Hillsborough Exchange Club, 1973; medal of Honor, Nat. Soc. D.A.R., 1974. Fellow Am. Assn. U. Women; mem. Soc. Archtl. Historians, Soc. Am. Archivists, Nat. Trust for Hist. Preservation, Am. Assn. for State and Local History, N.C. Soc. for Preservation Antiquities, Chapel Hill Hist. Soc. (dir. 1971—). N.C. Soc. County and Local Historians, N.C. Lit. and Hist. Assn., Phi Beta Kappa. Contbr. articles profl. jours. Home: 403 Lake Shore Lane Chapel Hill NC 27514

ENGSTROM, RUBY MARIA (MRS. CHARLES LOUIS SCHNEIDER), pathologist; b. Duluth, Minn., July 21, 1910; d. Victor Sigfrid and Hannah Maria (Nyquist) Engstrom; B.S., Northwestern U., 1936; M.S., U. Minn., 1946, M.B., 1948, M.D., 1949; m. Charles Louis Schneider, Feb. 26, 1949; children—Charles Louis, Maria, Anna. Dir. nursing Swedish Covenant Hosp., Chgo., 1937-43; teaching asst. in anatomy U. Minn., 1943-46; intern Wayne County Gen. Hosp., 1948-49; resident internal medicine, 1949-50, resident pathology, 1950-54, chief resident pathology, 1954-55, pathologist Cytology and Pathology Lab., 1956—, pathologist, research asso. dept. obstetrics and gynecology, 1959-73; pathologist People's Community, Beyer, Annapolis, Outer Drive hosps., 1959-61. Treas. Coop. Nursery, 1953-54; troop leader Girl Scouts U.S.A. 1961-63; instr. First Aid, 1963-64. Diplomate Am. Bd. Pathology. Fellow Am. Soc. Clin. Pathologists, Coll. Am. Pathologists; mem. Am. Soc. Cytology, Internat. Acad. Pathology, A.M.A., Mich. Soc. Cytology, Mich. Soc. Pathology. Presbyn. (elder 1967-70). Home: 1777 Culver St Dearborn MI 48124 Office: 22148 Michigan St Dearborn MI 48124

ENIX, AGNES LUCILLE, editor; b. Drummond, Okla., Jan. 17, 1933; d. James Robert and Alma Frances (Hodges) Enix; B.S., Okla. State U., 1955; M.S., Northwestern U., 1966. Dietetic intern VA Hosp., Los Angeles, 1955-56; staff dietition, 1956-57; nutritionist Dairy Council Greater Kansas City, Mo., 1957-61; asso. dir. materials devel. Nat. Dairy Council, Chgo., 1961-65; reporter, feature writer Chgo. Tribune, 1966-67; copywriter Rogers & Smith Advt. Agy., Dallas, 1967-68; editor Dallas Mag., Dallas C. of C., 1968—. Mag. cons. Am. Dietetic Assn., 1970-71. Mem. Wednesday Noon Forum YMCA, 1971-72; adv. bd., journalism dept. N. Tex. State U. Recipient award S.W. Journalism Forum, 1970, Journalism award Tex. Med. Assn., 1971, Matrix award Women in Communication, 1971. Mem. Women in Communications, Dallas Press Club, Omicron Nu, Phi Upsilon Omicron, Alpha Delta Pi. Home: 2622 Highland Rd Dallas TX 75228 Office: 1507 Pacific Av Dallas TX 75228

ENNIS, ETHEL LLEWELLYN (MRS. CLYDE E. ARNETT, JR.), singer; b. Balt., Nov. 28, 1932; d. Andrew and Arrabell (Small) Ennis; student Cortez W. Peters Bus. Sch., 1950-52; D.F.A. (hon.), Md. Inst. Art, 1973; m. Jacques Leeds, 1957 (div. May 1965); m. 2d, Clyde E. Arnett, Jr., Aug. 29, 1967. Pianist with male group Balt. area night clubs, 1948; singer local groups East Coast, 1952-55; recorded first LP album with Jubilee, 1955, single with Atco, 1956, albums with Capitol, 1957-58; toured Europe with Benny Goodman band including Brussels World's Fair, 1958; appeared in clubs, N.Y.C., 1958, London, 1959, N.Y.C., Phila., Balt., 1959-63; recorded albums RCA, 1963-66; appeared in night clubs throughout country and London, 1963—, Newport Jazz Festival, 1964, Monterey Jazz Festival, 1965, Aspen Jazz Festival, 1966; regular singer Arthur Godfrey Radio Show, 1966. Benefit performances March of Dimes, Heart Fund, Md. Penitentiary, Cook County Jail, Chgo., 1955-65. Recipient certificate Playboy Jazz Poll, 1960. Mem. Am. Guild Variety Artists, A.F.T.R.A., A.S.C.A.P., Screen Actors Guild. Composer: Little Boy, 1950; Nite Club, 1963. Home: 3113 Leighton Av Baltimore MD 21215

ENNIS, LEE (MRS. DANIEL H. ROSENBLATH), fashion dir.; b. Floral Park, N.Y.; d. Arthur James and Lillian (Kammerer) Ennis; B.S., Muskingum Coll., 1944; student N.Y.U. Sch. of Retailing, 1944-47; m. Daniel H. Rosenblath, Dec. 13, 1948. Asst. buyer, fashion coordinator Bonwit Teller, N.Y.C., 1944-46; promotional stylist Butterick Pattern Co., 1946-48; fashion coordinator Nachman's Dept. Store, Newport News, Va., 1949; v.p. sales Donahue Sales Corp., 1950—. Active scholarship drives Am. Assn. U. Women. Trustee Muskingum Coll. Mem. Am. Women in Radio and TV, Advt. Women N.Y., Fashion Group Inc., Garden City Civic Assn., Muskingum Alumni Assn. (pres. 1958-59), Xi Alpha Nu. Home: 136 Roosevelt St Garden City NY 11530 Office: 41 E 51st St New York City NY 10022

ENOS, SHIRLEY YVONNE (MRS. ROBERT W. ENOS), newspaper co. exec.; b. Sulphur, La., July 19, 1932; d. George Edward and Margie Hellen (Wetherell) Frenzel; B.S., McNeese State U., 1958; m. Robert W. Enos, Feb. 14, 1952; children—Kelly Diane, Tracy Ellen, Michael Scott. Supr. advt. dept. Kinder (La.) News, 1965-67, soc. editor, 1967-70, asst. editor, 1971-72, editor, 1972—. Owner, operator Frenzel Sch. of Dance, Vinton, La., 1962-65. Mem. Nat. Tchr. and Parent Assn., La. Press Assn., La. Press Women of S.W. La. Methodist (asst. ednl. dir. 1971-72). Clubs: Sulphur Garden; La. Press (Sulphur); S.W. La. Advertising (Lake Charles). Home: 307 Cherry Sulphur LA 70663 Office: Drawer AK Kinder LA 70648

ENSLEY, BERNIECE (TONI) MARION ELLISON (MRS. BURT DEWITT ENSLEY), editor; b. Mansville, Alta., Can., June 13, 1912 (parents Am. citizens); d. Emmit Mathew and Ella Marie (Johnson) Ellison; student U. Ore., 1931-33, U. Wash., 1936-55, Cornish Sch. Fine Arts, 1929-31; m. Burt DeWitt Ensley, Oct. 2, 1935; children—Lesli (Mrs. Richard Alan Anderson), Burt DeWitt, Janine (Mrs. Robert E. Lee Fogle III). Stock broker Waddell & Reed, 1965-67; exec. Army and Air Force Exchange Service, Fort Carson, Holloman AFB, 1956-61; editor, pub. Otero County Star, Alamogordo, N.M., 1967-70; sec.-treas., editor Otero County Star, Inc., 1970—. Bd. dirs. March of Dimes. Mem. Nat. Assn. Press Women, Nat. Assn. Pen Women, Nat., N.M. news assns., Alamogordo C. of C., Altrusa. Republican. Roman Catholic. Author: Collected Poems, 1951. Home: 1402 New York Av Alamogordo NM 88310 Office: PO Box 1722 Alamogordo NM 88310

ENSLEY, EVANGELINE WALTON, novelist; b. Indpls., Nov. 24, 1907; d. Marion Edmund and Wilna Eunice (Coyner) Ensley; pvt. edn. Mem. Opera Guild, Nat. Assn. Am. Pen Women. Author: (under pen name Evangeline Walton) The Virgin and The Swine, 1936; Witch House, 1945; The Cross and The Sword, 1956; Son of Darkness, 1957; Island of the Mighty, 1970; Children of Llyr, 1971; Song of Rhiannon, 1972. Address: 2130 E Water St Tucson AZ 85719

EPP, MARGARET A., author; b. Waldheim, Sask., Can., Aug. 1, 1913; d. Henry M. and Agnes (Goossen) Epp; grad. Bethany Bible Inst. (Hepburn, Sask.), 1937; student Prairie Bible Inst. (Three Hills, Alta), 1938-39; U. Sask., 1949. Tchr. history, English, Bethany Bible Inst., Hepburn, Sask., 1945-49; free-lance writer, 1949—. Mennonite. Author: But God Hath Chosen, 1963; Come to My Party, 1964; A Fountain Sealed, 1965; Walk in My Woods, 1967; Prairie Princess 1967; The Princess and the Pelican, 1968; This Moutain is Mine, 1969; The Princess Rides a Panther, 1970; Into All the World, 1973; numerous paperback books and short stories. Home: Waldheim SK Canada

EPPERT, ANN, univ. adminstr.; b. Brazil, Ind., Feb. 12, 1936; d. Franklin Pierce and Eleanor Mary (McAuliffe) Eppert; B.S., Ind. State U., 1957, M.A., 1962; postgrad. Fla. State U., 1971-72. Speech and hearing therapist Fort Wayne (Ind.) Community Schs., 1957-60; asst. dean women Ind. State U., Terre Haute, 1960-68, asst. dean student life, 1968-71, asso. dean, 1972—; counseling psychologist Fla. State U., Tallahasee, 1971-72. Mem. adv. bd. Vols. Am., 1962—, sec. 1963-71, 72-75; mem. United Way Allocations Com., 1970-71. Recipient Arion Found. award, 1953; Hannah Schleuter Meml. award Dr. Joseph Schick, 1957; named Outstanding Woman on Campus, Ind. State U., 1966. Mem. Nat. (sec. Nat. Panhellenic Conf. liaison com. 1969-71), Ind. (v.p. 1968-69, pres. 1970-71, exec. bd. 1973-74) assns. for women deans, adminstrs. and counselors, Am. Assn. Higher Edn., Nat. Assn. Student Personnel Adminstrs., Ind. Tchrs. Assn. (div. sect. vice chmn. 1963-64, chmn. 1964-65), Am. Assn. U. Women (br. 2d v.p. 1965-66), Pamarista, Alpha Omicron Pi (collegiate adv. bd. 1972-75), Lambda Psi Sigma, Alpha Lambda Delta. Club: Ind. State U. Faculty Women's (treas. 1966-67, v.p. 1973-74 Terre Haute). Home: 4676 Poplar St Terre Haute IN 47803

EPPES, MARY ARCHER BEAN (MRS. JAMES VAN DEUSEN EPPES), civic, ch. worker; b. Baguio, Benquet, P.I., Apr. 9, 1908; d. Dr. Robert Bennett and Adelaide Leiper (Martin) Bean; B.A., Sweet Briar Coll., 1929; m. James Van Deusen Eppes, June 27, 1931; children—James Van Deusen, Robert Bennett. Pres. Jr. League Garden Club, Boston, 1948-49; spl. implementation com. Bethlehem (Pa.) Community Council, 1957-58; vice chmn. Fgn. Policy Assn. Lehigh Valley, 1957-59, 70-71, sec., 1963-64; bd. mem. Cambridge (Mass.) chpt. A.R.C., 1947-50, Cambridge Tb and Health Assn., 1946-49, Jr. League of Boston, 1949-50; active canteen corps A.R.C., 1944-50; vol. worker Allentown (Pa.) State Hosp., 1958—. Vice pres., dist. chmn. Episcopal diocese of Mass. and Bethlehem, 1952-54, 58-60, ecumenical relations chmn., 61-62, 63-64; pres. Ch. Women United of Bethlehem, 1956-58, rep. to Community Council, 1966—; state chmn. Christian World Relations commn. United Ch. Women of Pa., 1958-60, mem. nominating com., 1966—; mem. Nat. Council Chs. Commn. Internat. Affairs, 1961-64; mem. bd. Evang. Edn. Soc. Protestant Episcopal Ch., 1965—; pres. Trinity Episcopal Ch. Women, 1969-70; nat. com. Japan Internat. Christian U., 1968—. Mem. Nat. adv. com. on Christian world relations Chmn. Mayor's Com. for UN Week, 1964-65; mem. Mayor's Com. for Beautification Bethlehem, 1965-66; mem. Mayor's Task Force, 1968—, mem. environmental control com., 1970-71. Mem. alumnae council Sweet Briar Coll., 1969-74. Mem. Am. Assn. U. Women (v.p. 1958-59, pres. 1964-65, donor Mary Archer Eppes fellowship 1970), League Women Voters (chmn. com. internat. affairs 1969-70), Nat. Cathedral Assn. (regional chmn. N.E. Pa. 1962 —). Club: Lehigh Faculty Wives (bd. mem. 1958-59, pres. 1959-60). Home: 447 Heckewelder Pl Bethlehem PA 18018

EPPINETTE, SHIRLEY LYNN, educator; b. New Orleans, Apr. 16, 1947; d. Woodie Trevillion and Thelma Elizabeth (Axline) Eppinette; A.A. (Journalism Alumni Assn. scholar), East Los Angeles Coll., 1967; B.A. (Arthur J. Baum journalism scholar), Cal. State U. at Los Angeles, 1969, postgrad., 1969-70. Elementary tchr., Covina-Valley Unified Sch. Dist., 1970-74, San Gabriel (Cal) Sch. Dist., 1974—. Mem. Cal. Tchrs. Assn., San Gabriel Tchrs. Bowling League, Sigma Delta Chi, Theta Sigma Phi. Home: 1717 S 8th St Alhambra CA 91803

EPPINK, HELEN BRENAN (MRS. NORMAN R. EPPINK), artist, educator; b. Springfield, O., Aug. 19, 1910; d. Bayard Richards and Grace (Hewitt) Brenan; student Cleve. Art Inst., 1928-31, John Huntington Poly. Inst., 1931-33, Colo. Fine Arts Center, summer 1945; m. Norman R. Eppink, June 15, 1931; 1 dau., Karen (Mrs. Ricardo B. Ferrari). Head art dept. Coll. of Emporia (Kan.), 1944-48, 49-51, 52-53, 61-73, tchr. Kan. State Tchrs. Coll., Emporia, 1951-52, 60-61, Ottawa (Kan.) U., 1948-51; exhibited in one man shows at Kan. State Tchrs. Coll., 1957, Coll. of Emporia, 1970, 72; exhibited two-men shows Mulvane Mus., Topeka, 1954, Hutchinson (Kan.) Art Assn., 1964, Civic Art Center Gallery, Topeka, 1968, Paine Art Center, Oshkosh, Wis., 1969, Coll. of Emporia, 1972; exhibited in group shows at Cleve. Mus. Art, 1932-38, Kansas City Art Inst., 1939-42, Nelson Art Gallery, 1949, Wichita Art Mus., 1956-61, Joslyn Art Mus., 1956, others; represented in permanent collections at Kan. Fedn. Women's Clubs, Wichita Art Mus, Kan. State U., Manhattan. Vice pres. Emporia Friends of Art, 1968-69. Recipient awards in painting, printmaking Cleve. Mus. Art, Topeka Art Guild exhbns., Kansas City, Mo., Wichita, Kan., Manhattan, others. Home: 2101 Canterbury Rd Emporia KS 66801

EPPS, NONA MANN (MRS. ALTON JACKSON EPPS), city ofcl.; b. Honey Grove, Tex., June 26, 1926; d. William Philip and Edna Mabel (Hulsey) Mann; grad. high sch.; m. Alton Jackson Epps, June 30, 1955; children—Thomas Philip, Mannetta Kay. Sec., bookkeeper Rath Packing Co., Dallas, 1943-48; bookkeeper Superior Wholesale Meat Co., Dallas, 1951-52; cashier Schepps Wholesale Grocer Supply, Dallas, 1952-55, sec., 1960-63, purchasing agt., 1963-66, exec. sec. to v.p., 1966-71; city sec., tax assessor/collector, Ferris, Tex., 1971—. Sec., P.T.A., Ferris, 1957-58, treas., 1958-61; parliamentarian Ellis County P.T.A., 1960-61; active Boy Scouts Am., Girl Scouts U.S.A. Mem. Tex. Assn. Assessing Officers, Assn. City Clks. and Secs. Tex., N. Central Tex. City Secs. Assn. Mem. Ch. of Christ. Home: 205 W 12th St Ferris TX 75125 Office: 201 S Church St Ferris TX 75125

EPPS, ROSELYN ELIZABETH PAYNE (MRS. CHARLES H. EPPS, JR.), physician; b. Little Rock, Dec. 11, 1930; d. William Kenneth and Mattie E. (Beverly) Payne; B.S., Howard U., 1951, M.D., 1955; M.P.H., Johns Hopkins, 1973; m. Charles H. Epps, Jr., June 25, 1955; children—Charles H. III, Kenneth C., Roselyn E., Howard R. Intern, Freedmen's Hosp., Washington, 1955-56, asst. resident pediatrics, 1956-58, chief resident, 1958-59, now mem. attending staff; practice medicine, specializing in pediatrics, Washington, 1960-61; asst. research investigator dept. pediatrics Coll. Medicine, Howard U., 1959-60, instr., 1959-60, asst. prof., 1960-61, clin. asst. prof., 1961-69, clin. asso. prof. pediatrics, 1969—; med.

officer infant and presch. div. Bur. Maternal and Child Health D.C. Dept. Pub. Health, 1961-64, dir. Clinic for Retarded Children, 1964-67, chief infant and presch. div., 1967-71; dir. Children and Youth Project 631, 1970-71; chief Div. Maternal and Child Health, also dir. maternal and child health and crippled children's services, 1971—; mem. attending staff D.C. Gen. Hosp.; cons. Project Headstart, 1968-73. Mem. Pub. Health Adv. Council mental retardation com., 1964-68, Day Care and Child Devel. Council Am.; mem. med. adv. com. Nat. Child Day Care Assn.; mem. devel-disabilities subcom. Health Planning Adv. Com. Vice-pres. bd. trustees Children's Internat. Summer Villages, 1972-74, pres., 1974—; trustee D.C. br. YWCA, 1969—, Washington Performing Arts Soc., 1970-72, 73—, Ford's Theatre, 1974—, Alexander Graham Assn. for Deaf, 1974—, St. John's Child Devel. Center, 1974—. Recipient Alumni award Palmer Meml. Inst., 1968; Fed. Women's award, 1974; citation for voluntary services YWCA, 1974. Fellow Am. Acad. Pediatrics (alternate chmn. for D.C. 1973—, mem. sect. on community pediatrics); mem. Nat. Med. Assn. (womens aux., health chmn. 1967-70), Am. Med. Womens Assn. (chmn. pub. health com. 1973—), Medico-Chirurgical Soc. of D.C. (and womens aux.), Am. Pub, Health Assn., D.C. Pub, Health Assn. (chmn. program com. 1974), D.C. Women's Med. Soc. (pres. 1972-74), Assn. Adminstrv. Women in Edn. (treas. 1972-73), Washington Urban League, Alpha Kappa Alpha. Conglist. Contbr. articles profl. jours. Home: 1775 N Portal Dr NW Washington DC 20012 Office: Suite 807 1875 Connecticut Av NW Washington DC 20009

EPSTEIN, BEATRICE GREENBERG (MRS. LEE EPSTEIN), painter, sculptor; b. N.Y.C., June 2, 1915; d. Morris and Jennie (Korbholz) Greenberg; student N.Y. U., 1934, Art Students League, Craft Students League, 1971-73; m. Lee Epstein, June 28, 1940; children—David G., Phoebe Janet. Dress designer, 1936-55; ind. painter, N.Y.C., 1956—; sculptor, 1971—. Recipient Quinto Maganini prize Silvermine Guild, 1964. Mem. Nat. Assn. Women Artists (Lillian Cotton Meml. award 1972, Charles D. Murphy award for sculpture 1973), Art Students League (life). Home: 112 W 81st St New York City NY 10024 Office: 239 Park Av S New York City NY 10003

EPSTEIN, KATHRYN, radio-television ofcl.; b. Milw., Aug. 11, 1914; d. Benjamin and Rose (Margolis) Epstein; grad. high sch. Various adminstrv. positions U.S. Dept. Agr., 1937-48; sales office mgr. Frankfort Distillers Corp., 1948-51; acting head distilled spirits and wines sect. OPS, 1951-53; partner Jay-Kay Assos., 1953-56; advt. mgr. Leo M. Bernstein Co., 1956-57; asso. editor TV Digest, 1957; sales mgr. radio stas. WDON & WASH-FM, 1957-65; pres., owner Kathryn Epstein Asso., 1965-67; radio-TV information officer USPHS, Health, Edn. and Welfare, 1967—; chmn. women information officers, 1971—. Campaign mgr. March Dimes, 1955-56, coordinator, 1953-55; vice chmn. pub. relations com. Am. Cancer Soc. 1961-63, chmn. tri-div. publicity com., 1963; chmn. spl. events com. Nat. Found. Infantile Paralysis, 1957, chmn. finance com. Brazilian carnival, 1956; mem. publicity com., Pres.'s Com. for Employing Handicapped, 1960-64, John F. Kennedy Center for Performing Arts, 1964. Recipient Service awards U.S. Dept. Agr., 1947, Nat. Found. Infantile Paralysis, 1954; High Quality Performance award Health, Edn. and Welfare-USPHS, 1968, 70. Mem. Nat. Acad. TV Arts and Scis., Am. Women in Radio and TV. Home: 2107 Belvedere Blvd Silver Spring MD 20902 Office: Parklawn Bldg Rockville MD 20852

EPSTEIN, LOIS BARTH, physician; b. Cambridge, Mass., Dec. 29, 1933; d. Benjamin and Mary Frances (Perlmutter) Barth; A.B. cum laude, Radcliffe Coll., 1955; M.D., Harvard, 1959; m. Dr. Charles Joseph Epstein, June 10, 1956; children—David Alexander, Jonathan Akiba, Paul Michael. Resident pathology Peter Bent Brigham Hosp., Boston, 1959-60; intern medicine New Eng. Center Hosp., Boston, 1960-61; research med. officer Lab. Exptl. Pathology of Nat. Inst. Arthritis and Metabolic Diseases, NIH, Bethesda, Md., 1962-63; postdoctoral fellow biol. structure U. Wash., 1963-64; spl. fellow Lab. Exptl. Pathology of Nat. Inst. Arthritis and Metabolic Diseases, and Lab. Immunology of Nat. Inst. Allergy and Infectious Diseases, 1964-66, research med. officer, 1966-67, mem. tng. grants com., allergy and immunology research com., 1972—; asst. research physician Cancer Research Inst. of U. Cal. at San Francisco, 1969-72, asso. research physician, 1972—. Active Cub Scouts, 1969-71. Cancer Coordinating Com. of U. Cal. grantee, 1971-72, Am. Cancer Soc. grantee, 1972-73, Damon Runyon Meml. Fund grantee, 1972-74, N.I.H. grantee, 1974-77; Eleanor Roosevelt Internat. Traveling fellow, vis. scientist tumour immunology unit, dept. zoology Univ. Coll., London, Eng., 1973-74. Mem. Boylston Med. Soc., Am. Fedn. Clin. Research, Am. Assn. Immunologists, Am. Soc. Hematology, Tissue Culture Assn., Western Soc. Clin. Research, Reticuloendothelial Soc. Contbr. articles to profl. jours. Home: 19 Noche Vista Lane Tiburon CA 94920 Office: U Cal Med Sch San Francisco CA 94143

EPSTEIN, SARAH GUNY, library media specialist; b. Providence; d. Maurice and May (Guny) Epstein; student R.I. Coll. Edn., 1943-45, U. Miami, Coral Gables, 1955; B.A., U. R.I., 1957; M.L.S., Pratt Inst., 1958. Asst. catalog dept. Providence Pub. Library, 1946-55; sch. librarian, George J. West Middle Sch., Providence, 1958—. Mem. A.L.A., New Eng. Assn. Sch. Librarians, R.I. Sch. Library Assn. (treas. 1963-65), R.I. Library Assn., Pratt Inst. Grad. Library Sch. Alumni Assn. Jewish religion. Home: 49 Savoy St Providence RI 02906 Office: 145 Beaufort St Providence RI 02908

EPSTEIN, SHERRIE LANDAU (MRS. WALLACE EPSTEIN), psychologist; b. N.Y.C., Jan. 21, 1928; d. Herman and Bertha (Kaplan) Landau; B.A., Hunter Coll., 1949; M.A. City U. N.Y., 1952; postgrad. U. Cal. at San Francisco, U. Cal. at Berkeley; m. Wallace Epstein, June 5, 1949; children—Eve, Gordon, Carolyn. Tchr. N.Y.C. Pub. Schs., 1949-53; parent edn. tchr. Millbrae Coop. Nursery Sch. (Cal.), 1958-60; psychologist Millbrae Elementary Sch. Dist., 1965—. Tchr. learning disabilities Coll. San Mateo Extension; coordinator course Cal. State U. at San Francisco, 1973; lectr. Chapman Coll., 1974. Mem. Family Service Agy., Easter Seal Soc. San Mateo County. Mem. Nat., Cal., San Mateo County (dir.) assns. sch. psychologists, Mental Health Assn. San Mateo County, Cal. Assn. for Neurologically Handicapped Children, Kappa Delta Pi. Author (with others) Child Development Through Literature, 1972. Home: 300 Palm Av Millbrae CA 94030 Office: 1101 Helen Drive Millbrae CA 94030

ERB, DOROTHY LUCIELLE CARSTEN (MRS. EDGAR G. ERB), librarian; b. Hartford, Conn., Dec. 11, 1917; d. Albert Johannessen and Tomine (Ness) Carsten; B.A., Hartwick Coll., 1940; M.S.L.S., Syracuse U., 1962; m. Edgar G. Erb, June 28, 1941; children—Karl Albert, Kari Dorothy (Mrs. Richard Carl Eells), Susan Emilie (Mrs. Donald Lester Haven). Asst. librarian Hyde Park High Sch., Chgo., 1942-43; librarian pub. schs., Syracuse, N.Y., 1958-62; pub. library dir. Solvay, N.Y., 1962-68; supr. (librarian) Reuben H. Donnelley Corp.; elementary librarian Black River, Felts Mills, Great Bend, Natural Bridge, N.Y., 1970-73. Mem. Thousand Island council Girl Scouts U.S.; active Head Start, P.T.A., ednl. groups; mem. bldg. com. Carthage Elementary Sch. Chmn. 16th ward, Am. Cancer Soc., 1967-71; Republican chmn. 16th ward, Syracuse. Childrens story teller Vol. Center Syracuse; book reviewer Womens Clubs, YWCA. Mem. Am., N.Y. library assns., Onondaga-Oswego Sch. Librarians Assn. (orgn. com., charter mem.), Ednl. and Cultural Center, Internat. Reading Assn. (Black River reading council), Onondago and Oswego Counties, Ind. Artist Guild of Central N.Y., Asso. Artists of Syracuse, Sons Norway (financial sec.). Club: College Women's. Home: 2130 US Hwy 101 San Rafael CA 94904

ERB, LILLIAN EDGAR (MRS. DAVID CHARLES ERB), probate judge; b. Stonington, Conn., July 28, 1922; d. Edward and Lillian (Ellis) Matthew; student Eastern Conn. State Coll., 1965-66, U. Conn., 1967-68; m. David Charles Erb, Jan. 28, 1943; children—David Lawrence, Dana Louise, Gregory Barron. Mem. Conn. Ho. of Reps., 1962-71, asst. minority leader, 1971; probate judge, 1971—. Justice of Peace, Groton, Conn, 1954-58, 62-64; mem. Gov.'s Permanent Commn. on Status of Women, 1973—; mem. adv. council Mohegan Community Coll. Mem. Groton Republican Town Com., 1954-73, vice chmn., 1954-58; 1st v.p. Conn. Order Women Legislators, 1969-71; chmn. Rep. State Platform Com., del. Rep. Nat. Conv., 1972. Vice pres., bd. dirs. Conn. Child and Family Service; v.p., bd. dirs. Conn. Student Loan Found., sec., 1966-71; trustee Mystic Oral Sch. Mem. Am. Bar Assn. (asso.), Profl. and Bus. Women's Club, Nat. Coll. Probate Judges, Am. Judicature Soc., Conn. Probate Assembly (exec. bd.), Nat. Assn. Women Legislators, Nat. Council Am. Women, Women's Rep. Club, New London County Women's Rep. Club, Noank Hist. Soc. Roman Catholic. Address: 51 Front St Noank CT 06340

ERDMAN, JEAN MARION, dancer; b. Honolulu; d. John Pinney and Marion Eleanor (Dillingham) Erdman; student Sarah Lawrence Coll., 1934-37, Bennington Summer Sch. Dance, 1937, Martha Graham Dance Co., 1937-42, Sch. Am. Ballet, 1942-43, Jose Fernandez, 1942-43, Mary Pukui, 1944, Hisamatsu Sch. Japanese Dance, 1944; m. Joseph Campbell, May 5, 1938. With J.E. Dance Co., N.Y.C. concerts, U.S.A. tours, 1945-70; solo world tour, 1954-55; author, producer, dir., performer Coach with the Six Insides, N.Y.C., 1962, 67, Spoleto, Paris, Dublin, 1963, Tokyo, 1964, U.S. tours, 1963-67; producer, dir., performer Moon Mysteries, N.Y.C., 1972, 73, U.S. tour, 1974; creator, head dance dept. N.Y. U. Sch. Arts, 1966-71; choreographer Two Gentlemen of Verona, 1971; head dance dept. Tchrs. Coll. Columbia, 1949-51, Bard Coll., 1954-59; artist in residence U. Colo., 1949-56, U. B.C., 1959-61, U. Hawaii, 1962, 69, San Francisco State U., 1966, Pa. State U., 1968, Portland State Coll., 1960, U. Cal. at Los Angeles, 1956, 67, Am. Culture Center, Tokyo, 1955; founding dir. New Dance Group Studio, 1943; co-founder, artistic dir. The Open Eye, 1972; important works include: Tranformations of Medusa, 1942; Daughters of the Lonesome Isle, 1945; Ophelia, 1946; Perilous Chapel, 1949; Solstice, 1950; Changingwoman, 1951; Upon Enchanted Ground, 1951, Fearful Symmetry, 1957. Mem. screening com. dance applicants Fulbright Fellowships, 1958-61, 65-66; screening cons. John Hay Whitney Found., 1959-65, Office Edn., Washington, 1968-70. Recipient Dance Mag. award, 1948-49; Vernon Rice, Obie awards, 1962-63; Choreography award Drama Desk, 1972. Ingram Merrill grantee, 1961. Mem. Assn. Am. Dance Cos. (founding dir. 1966-69), Am. Dance Guild (dir.), Dance Notation Bur., Actor's Equity, Soc. for Stage Dirs. and Choreographers (exec. com. 1973—). Home: 136 Waverly Pl New York City NY 10014 Office: 78 Fifth Av New York City NY 10011

ERDMANN, VIRGINIA MAE, realtor; b. Green Bay, Wis., May 16, 1931; d. Winford Carl and Clara (Shalhoub) Erdmann; B.S., U. Wis., 1953; postgrad. St. Norbert Coll., U. Wis., Marquette U. Direct mail specialist Hardware Mut. Ins. Cos., Stevens Point, Wis., 1953-55; continuity dir. Radio Sta. WJPG, 1956; women's editor Green Bay (Wis.) Press-Gazette, 1956-65; pub. relations counsel to pres. Manpower, Inc., Milw., 1965-68; broker-sales asso. Skogg Real Estate, Inc., Green Bay, Wis., 1973—. Mem. exec. com. Brown County Civic Music Assn., 1962-65; sponsor Brown County Chamber Mus. Soc., 1959-65; mem. Service League, Green Bay, Service League Aux., Neville Pub. Mus. Corp. Bd. dirs. Green Bay Community Theater, 1961-64, Green-Bay-DePere Antiquarian Soc., 1959-65, Brown County unit Am. Cancer Soc., 1970-73. Recipient awards Menswear Retailers Am., Nat. Inst. Men's and Boy's Wear, 1960, 61, 62, 63, Nat. Assn. Home Appliance Mfrs., 1962, Mutation Mink Breeders Assn., 1962-63, Nat. Shoe Inst., 1963, Nat. Fedn. Music Clubs, 1962, 63, 64, Caswell-Massey Ltd., annually 1960-64, Appreciation award Girl Scouts Am., 1963. Mem. Am. Assn. Univ Women (dir. Green Bay br. 1958-64), Wis. Ecol. Soc., Green Bay Bd. Realtors, Fox Valley Advt. Club, Brown County U. Wis. Alumni Assn. (dir. 1956-65), Phi Beta, Gamma Phi Alpha, Coronto Sigma Iota. Republican. Home: 3231 S Webster Av Green Bay WI 54301 Office: 530 S Madison St Green Bay WI 54301

ERHARDT, MARY RUTH CHENOWETH, occupational therapist; b. Mt. Sterling, O., Dec. 10, 1919; d. Walter Scot and Blanche (Rhoades) Chenoweth; B.A. in Elementary Edn., Ohio State U., 1941, B.S. in Occupational Therapy, 1945, M.A. in Spl. Edn., 1969; m. August Wilhelm Erhardt, Apr. 21. 1956 (dec.); children—Laura Louise (dec.), Eberhard, Roland (foster children). Occupational therapist Summit County Receiving Hosp., 1946-49, Chillicothe VA Hosp., 1949-52, Ohio Tb Hosp., Ohio State U. Med. Center, 1952-56, Childrens Convalescent Hosp., Cin. Med. Center, 1956-60, Orient (O.) State Inst. for Mentally Retarded, 1960—. Cons. spl. edn., learning disabilities Pub. Schs. Madison County, O., 1970-72. Mem. Ohio Parks and Recreation Assn. Republican. Lutheran. Home: Rural Route 1 Mt Sterling OH 43143 Office: Orient State Inst Orient OH 43146

ERICKSON, CHARLOTTE JOAN RUDOLPH (MRS. LENNART GOTTFRID ERICKSON), civic worker; b. San Francisco; d. Max and Rebecca (Windreich) Rudolph; student Gallagher Marsh Bus. Coll., San Francisco, 1935; m. Lennart Gottfrid Erickson, Apr. 24, 1937; 1 son, William Scott. Gen. mgr. Universal Molding Co., San Francisco, 1935-39; dir. Charlen Corp., San Mateo, Cal., 1960—. Exec. v.p. founding mem. Spring Opera-San Francisco, 1963—. Pres. Lennart Erickson Found., San Mateo, 1950—. Bd. dirs. San Francisco Sponsors, 1960-65, Merola Meml. Fund, 1960—; founding mem., bd. dirs. San Francisco Chamber Music Soc., San Francisco, 1961—; founder, chmn. Action, San Francisco Opera Co.; bd. dirs. San Francisco Opera Assn. Home: 860 Vista Rd Hillsborough CA 94010

ERICKSON, DEANE FONS HELLER (MRS. JAMES L. ERICKSON), author, biographer; b. Milw., Jan. 14, 1924; d. Edmund J. and Delphine Anne (Ceranski) Fons; student U. Chgo., 1942-44, U. Md., 1948-50; m. David A. Heller, Feb. 12, 1944 (dec. May 1968); children—David Fons, Douglas Bruce; m. 2d, James L. Erickson, May 13, 1972. Reporter Chgo. Sun, 1942-44; editor, writer Jour. Infectious Diseases, U. Chgo. Press, 1946-47; writer for Correlator, Nat. Home Builders' Assn., Washington, 1950; spl. writer Metro Mag., Washington Star 1951-64; spl. writer Potomac Mag., The Washington Post, 1957-67; corr. Miami (Fla.) Herald, 1968-70; contbr. So. Living Mag., Key West, Fla., 1966—. Cons. pub. relations Home Builders Assn., Montgomery County (Md.) Fair, Nat. Assn. Scale Mfrs. Dir. pub. relations Old Island Restoration Found., Key West, 1971. Campaign dir. Montgomery County Democratic Com., 1958. Mem. Soc. Am. Travel Writers, Key West Hist. Soc., Old Island Restoration Found. Author: (with David A. Heller) The Berlin Wall, 1960, Kennedy Cabinet, 1961, Paths of Diplomacy, 1967; Cold War, 1969; Ataturk, Hero of Modern Turkey, 1972. Editor: American Foreign Policy Today, 1970. Home and office: 1502 Vernon Av Key West FL 33040

ERICKSON, ETHEL ELMA (MRS. JESSE W. HOFER), pathologist; b. Chisholm, Minn., July 24, 1914; d. John Erick and Lydia Maria (Ohtonen) Erickson; B.S., U. Minn., 1937, M.D., 1946; m. Jesse W. Hofer, Sept. 14, 1946; children—Elizabeth Ann, Jessica Patrice. Intern, Lenox Hill Hosp., N.Y.C., 1946-47; resident Ill. Research and Ednl. Hosp., Chgo., 1947-50; pathologist, asst. chief lab. service VA Hosp., Houston, 1950-65; pathologist Sharpstown Gen. Hosp., Houston, 1965-69; pathologist, dir. Houston Clin. and Biomedical Lab., 1964—; asst. med. examiner Harris County, Houston, 1969—; clin. asso. prof. pathology Baylor U. Coll. Medicine, 1961—. Mem. A.M.A., Coll. Am. Pathologists, Am. Soc. Clin. Pathologists, Am. Assn. Pathologists and Bacteriologists, Internat. Acad. Pathology, Am. Med. Womens Assn., Tex. Soc. Pathologists, Houston Soc. Clin. Pathologists (pres. 1963-64), Harris County Med. Assn., Nat. Assn. Med. Examiners. Contbr. articles to profl. jours. Home: 3638 Locke Lane Houston TX 77027 Office: 1502 Ben Taub Loop Houston TX 77025

ERICKSON, KAREN LOUISE, educator; b. Covington, Mich., Aug. 4, 1939; d. Godfred Emmanual and Loretta Cecila (Wakeford) Erickson; B.S., Siena Heights Coll., 1960; Ph.D., Purdue U., 1964; postgrad. Cornell U., 1964-65. Asst. prof. chemistry Clark U., Worcester, Mass., 1965-69, asso. prof. chemistry, 1969—; vis. lectr. in chemistry U. Canterbury, Christchurch, New Zealand, 1975. NIH postdoctoral fellow, 1964-65; NIH spl. fellow U. Hawaii, Honolulu, 1972-73. Mem. Am. Chem. Soc., Am. Assn. Univ. Profs. Contbr. articles to profl. jours. Home: 14 Thayer Pond Dr Apt 14 North Oxford MA 01537 Office: Clark U Worcester MA 01610

ERICKSON, ROSEANNE (MRS. LARRY VERLE ERICKSON), hosp. adminstr.; b. Calgary, Alta., Can., Feb. 1, 1935; d. William and Annie (Wasyluck) Mudry; grad. hosp. adminstrn. Calgary Gen. Hosp., 1955; m. Larry Verle Erickson, Sept. 29, 1956. Staff nurse, neurology, urology, emergency Calgary Gen. Hosp., 1955-58, head nurse emergency, 1958-60, head nurse, operating room and recovery room, 1960-66; supr. emergency Foothills Hosp., Calgary, 1966-68, supr. emergency, central supply day care, 1968-70, adminstrv. dir. service depts. and nursing units, 1970—. Mem. Canadian (dir. 1972), Alta. (pres. 1971-73) nursing assns. Home: 3320 Caribou Dr NW Calgary AB Canada Office: Foothills Hospital Calgary AB Canada

ERICKSON, SABRA ROLLINS HOLBROOK (MRS. JOHN B. ERICKSON), author; b. Worcester, Mass.; d. Robert Waddell and Grace (Dickenson) Rollins; B.A., Vassar Coll., 1934; m. John B. Erickson, Oct. 23, 1938; children—Cicely, Romilly. Author childrens books including: Getting to Know the Virgin Islands, 1959; Aluminum from Water, 1960; Berlin, Capital Without a Country, 1961; Getting to Know the Two Germanys, 1966; Getting to Know Canada, 1966; Getting to Know Puerto Rico, 1967; Taming The Columbia River, 1967; Bruno and Karen of Berlin, 1967; Germany, East and West, 1968; The American West Indies, 1969; Sir Tristan of all Time, 1970; A Stranger in My Land, A Life of Francois Villon, 1972; France-The Invisible Revolution, 1973; Joy in Stone, The Cathedral of Rheims, 1973. Editor childrens series Coward McCann, 1950-57; cons. pub. relations various orgns., agys., 1940-60. Democrat. Episcopalian (sec. bishop's com.). Club: Independent Citizens (corr. sec.) (St. John). Address: Box 38 Cruz Bay St John VI 00830

ERICKSON, SAMMYE J. WILLIAMS (MRS. ROY D. ERICKSON), interior designer; b. Wichita Falls, Tex., Dec. 24, 1925; d. Sammy E. and Gladys (Warren) Williams; student Tex. Womans U., 1943, Hardin Coll., 1944, Chouinard Art Inst., 1945-46; m. Roy D. Erickson, Nov. 1, 1946; children—Eric Edwin, Bradford Alan. With Bullock's Interior Design Studio, Los Angeles, 1946-47, interior designer, 1948-52; with Hendrickson's Madison, Wis., 1947-48; sr. interior designer Sammye Jean Erickson Interiors (now Erickson Assos.), Alhambra, Cal., 1952—. Mem. com. profl. women So. Cal. Symphony, Hollywood Bowl Assn.; mem. archtl. guild U. So. Cal. Recipient award for Aspen Villas, Progressive Archtl., 1968. Mem. Am. Inst. Interior Design (pres. Pasadena chpt. 1970-72, nat. dir. 1971—). Lutheran. Home: 328 Bellefontaine St Pasadena CA 91105 Office: 1112 S Garfield St Alhambra CA 91801

ERICSON, CAROLYN REEVES (MRS. JOE ELLIS ERICSON), mus. ofcl.; b. Ft. Stockton, Tex., May 12, 1931; d. Jonathan Floyd and Emma Cornelia (Barrett) Reeves; B.S., Tex. Tech U., 1955; m. Joe Ellis Ericson, June 16, 1955; children—Linda Diane (Mrs. Michael David Devereaux), Joe Reeves, John Ellis. Genealogist, 1955—; editor geneal. query column various Eastern Tex. newspapers, 1969—; curator Stone Fort Mus., Nacogdoches, Tex., 1972—. Mem. Nacogdoches County Hist. Survey Com., 1969-74. Mem. Friends of the Library, Nacogdoches Fedn. Women's Clubs (1st v.p. 1969-71), Tex. Geneal. Soc., Heart of Am. Geneal. Soc., Soverign Colonial Soc. Ams. of Royal Descent, Colonial Order of Crown, Colonial Dames of XVII Century (state curator 1971-73, chpt pres. 1967-69), D.A.R., Daus. of Republic Tex. (registrar gen. 1973—, chpt. historian 1973—), Faculty Wives Ordn. (pres. 1963-64). Methodist. Contbr. articles in field to profl. jours. Home: 1614 Redbud St Nacogdoches TX 75961 Office: Box 6075 Stone Fort Museum Nacogdoches TX 75961

ERICSON, MARY ALICE EATON, educator; b. Portland, Ore., Jan. 14, 1913; d. James Kent and Olive (Clifford) Eaton; B.A. (Durant scholar 1933), Wellesley Coll., 1934; M.A., U. Chgo., 1936; Ph.D., U. N.C., 1940; m. Eston Everett Ericson, June 20, 1940 (dec. 1964); children—Edith Ellen, Emily Eaton. Tchr. pub. schs., Wilmette, Ill., 1935-36; instr. social sci. div. Fla. State Coll. for Women, 1936-38; asst. state statistician Adminstrv. div. N.C. WPA, Raleigh, 1941-42; compiled graphics and statistics for book All These People by Rupert B. Vance, Inst. Research in Social Sci., U. N.C., 1942-44; vis. lectr. in vital statistics Sch. Pub. Health, U. N.C., 1945; instr. geography Mt. Holyoke Coll., 1948; asst. prof. sociology Gustavus Adolphus Coll., St. Peter, Minn., 1948-50, head geography dept., 1950-56, asso. prof. sociology, 1952-59, prof. sociology, 1959-60; resource leader in family relations Am. Friends Service Com. Family Camp, Palmer Lake, Colo., 1956; asst. project adminstr. Columbia U. Sch. Pub. Health and Adminstrv. Medicine, 1958-60; prof. sociology Coe Coll., Cedar Rapids, Ia., 1960—. Rotating staff mem. Central Am. Field Program Asso. Colls. of Midwest, 1966-67; mem. exec. com. Minn. Conservation Edn. Council, 1957-59. Gen. Edn. Bd. fellow, Alpha Kappa Delta; Asso. Colls. of Midwest non-Western studies fellow, 1966-67, 68-69. Mem. Am. Assn. U. Women, Am. Assn. U. Profs., Am. Civil Liberties Union, N.A.A.C.P., Minn., Ia., acads. sci. (cons. geography to editor Procs. 1955-57, chmn. social sci. sect. 1957-58, mem. council 1957-59, editorial com. 1958-59), A.A.A.S., Am., Midwest (chmn. sect. social inequality 1968, chmn. nominating com. 1970, state dir. 1972-74, chmn. sect. voluntary assns. 1974—), Ia. (pres. 1968), Rural sociol. socs., Assn. Am. Geographers, Population Assn. Am., Soc. for Study Social Problems, Phi Beta Kappa. Home: 1615 Keith Dr NE Cedar Rapids IA 52402 Office: Coe Coll Cedar Rapids IA 52402

ERICSSON, EMILY ALICE, semasioloist; b. Maple Hill, Kan., Apr. 6, 1904; d. Herman Carl and Alice (Smith) Ericsson; A.B., U. Kan., 1925, M.A., 1926; postgrad. Sorbonne, 1928-30, U. Mich., 1937. Asso. prof. modern lang. Southwestern Coll., Winfield, Kan., 1934-41, now head dept. research analyst Portuguese area expert, office coordinator information OSS, 1941-45; asst. financial attache Am. Embassy, Lisbon, Portugal, 1945; sec.-treas., fgn. trade analyst writer Ericsson Assos., Inc., 1946-50; internat. economist Dept. Commerce, 1950-51; attache Am. Embassy, Tel Aviv, 1951-53; analyst U.S. Dept. Health, Edn., Welfare, Washington, 1960-61; tchr. Theodore Roosevelt High Sch., Washington; now tchr. McKinley High Sch., Washington. Mem. Capitol Hill-S.E. Citizens Assn., Fedn. Citizens Assns. Recipient Carnegie fellow 1937-40, Rockefeller Geneva Research in-aid, 1941. Mem. Am. Assn. U. Profs. Author: Angola: Resettlement of White Europeans, 1943; Glossary of Consular and Diplomatic Terms English-French French-English, 1945; Little Land, 1950; also other profl. publs. Research and pub. for Spanish speaking people. Home: 3100 Connecticut Av Washington DC 20008 Office: McKinley High Sch Washington DC

ERIKSSON, ANN ELIZABETH MEIKLE (MRS. CARL E.O. ERIKSSON), govt. ofcl.; b. Harrisburg, Pa., Feb. 24, 1927; d. William D. and Irene E. (Jackson) Meikle; B.A., Wilson Coll., 1948; J.D., Dickinson Sch. Law, 1951; m. Carl E.O. Eriksson, Mar. 21, 1959; 1 dau., Ingrid E. Legal researcher Pa. Joint State Govt. Commn., Harrisburg, 1948-52; admitted to Pa. bar, 1952, Ohio bar, 1967; mem. firm Rupp & Meikle, Harrisburg, 1952-59; research atty., asst. dir. Ohio Legislative Service Commn., 1960-71; dir. Ohio Constl. Revision Commn., Columbus, 1971—. Adj. prof. law Ohio State U., 1970—. Mem. Am., Pa., Ohio, Columbus bar assns., Am. Judicature Soc., Am. Assn. U. Women, Am. Soc. for Pub. Adminstrn. (Outstanding Pub. Employee 1967, pres. Central Ohio chpt. 1974-75), Am. Acad. Polit. and Social Scis. Presbyn. Home: 2342 Tremont Rd Columbus OH 43221 Office: 41 S High St Columbus OH 43215

ERLICH, LILLIAN F. (MRS. JOHN J. ERLICH), writer; b. Johnstown, Pa., Mar. 7, 1910; d. Abraham and Bessie (Ginsburg) Feldman; student Cornell U., 1927-28, Columbia, 1929; m. John J. Erlich, May 15, 1930; children—John L., Nina E. (Mrs. Singer). Asso. editor Jr. Lit. Guild, Doubleday Co., 1962-68, 72-73; dir. Child Study Press, Child Study Assn. Am., N.Y.C., 1968-72; freelance writer, 1973—. Mem. Authors Guild Am. Author: (with Eleanor Clymer) Modern American Career Women, 1959; What Jazz Is All About, 1962; (with others) You, Your Child and Drugs, 1971. Home: 9621 SW 77th Av Miami FL 33156

ERNE, NANCY WISWALL (MRS. NED ALLEN ERNE), real estate broker; b. Newton, Mass., July 28, 1921; d. Harold Curtis and Priscilla Molines (Alden) Wiswall; student Westbrook Jr. Coll., 1942; Asso. B.A., Boston Sch. Occupational Therapy, 1944; m. Ned Allen Erne, June 9, 1945; children—Susan (Mrs. Donald Stark), Christine (Mrs. Dwight Lee), Bruce. Occupational therapist Walter Reed Gen. Hosp., Washington, 1944-45; occupational therapist Robert Brigham Hosp., Boston, 1960-65; real estate broker Harold Wiswall, Inc., Wellesley Hills, Mass., 1965—. Mem. town meeting Town of Wellesley, Mass., 1958—, mem. town adv. com., 1965-68. Bd. dirs. Wellesley Jr. Service League, 1952-58, Wellesley, Friendly Aid, 1960-68, Newton-Wellesley Hosp. Aid, 1968, Am. Field Service, 1962-66. Mem. Am. Occupational Therapy Assn., Greater Boston Real Estate Assn. Home: 52 Leighton Rd Wellesley MA 02181 Office: 380 Washington St Wellesley MA 02182

ERNETA, WANDA BALITSCH (MRS. MODESTO ERNETA), mutual fund co. exec.; b. Kirowograd, Russia, Mar. 11, 1935; d. Konstantin Walter and Anna (Adamowsky) Balitsch; came to U.S., 1956, naturalized, 1961; student George Washington U., 1959-60; B.A., Hunter Coll., 1962; M.A., Columbia, 1964; m. Modesto Erneta, Jan. 23, 1970; 1 dau., Nicole. Asst. analyst MacKay Shields Corp., N.Y.C., 1964-66; portfolio mgr., analyst Van Strum & Towne, Inc., N.Y.C., 1966—. Mem. Am. Econ. Assn., N.Y. Soc. Security Analysts, Vols. of Shelter. Home: 8 Princeton Pl Princeton Junction NJ 08550 Office: 280 Park Av New York City NY 10017

ERNST, ALICE HENSON (MRS. RUDOLF H. ERNST), author; b. Washburne, Me.; d. John and Sarah (Pace) Henson; B.A. magna cum laude, U. Wash., 1912, M.A. (Denny fellow), 1913; postgrad. Radcliffe Coll., 1919-20, Yale, 1928; m. Rudolf H. Ernst, 1915 (dec. Oct. 1963). Asso. in English, U. Wash., 1920-23; indsl. corr. N.Y. Evening Post, Seattle, 1920-23; asst. prof. U. Ore., 1924-36, asso. prof. English, 1936-52, research grantee, 1952-54; free-lance writer, 1952—. Mem. Ore. Com. for Performing Arts. Mem. ANTA, Friends of Library, Civic Music Assn., Ore. Hist. Soc., Nat. Press Women, Pacific N.W. Writers Conf., Nat. Wildlife Fedn., Phi Beta Kappa, Mu Phi Epsilon. Republican. Episcopalian. Author: High Country, 1935; Backstage in Xanadu, 1938; The Wolf Ritual of the Northwest Coast, 1948; Trouping in the Oregon Country, 1961. Home: Treetops 194 Sunset Dr Eugene OR 97403

ERNST, KATHRYN FITZGERALD (MRS. JOHN LYMAN ERNST), lit. agt.; b. N.Y.C., Nov. 12, 1942; d. Joseph Michael and Helen Ann (Dougherty) Fitzgerald; B.A. in Econs., Wells Coll., 1963; postgrad. N.Y. U., 1963-64; m. John Lyman Ernst, Dec. 11, 1971. Asst. editor exec. letters Prentice-Hall Pubs., Englewood Cliffs, N.J., 1963-64, asso. editor, 1964-65, asst. editor trade div., 1968, dir. children's books, 1969-74, asst. v.p. trade div., 1972-74; v.p., treas. Manuscript Evaluation Service, Inc., 1974—; confidential asst. to adminstr. pub. affairs Small Bus. Adminstr., Washington, 1965-66; portfolio analyst Donaldson, Lufkin & Jenrette, N.Y.C., 1966-67. Recipient Outstanding Performance award, U.S. govt., 1966, Christopher award Editorial Achievement, Christopher Bros., 1972. Mem. A.L.A., Children's Book Council. Author: Danny and His Thumb, 1973.

ERNST, MELBA BRADSHAW (MRS. ROBERT THOMAS ERNST), food brokerage co. exec.; b. San Antonio, Jan. 10, 1926; d. David Lee and Alta Hope (Howard) Bradshaw; student Julliard Sch. Music, N.Y.C., 1942-43, San Antonio Coll., 1967—; m. Robert Thomas Ernst, Sept. 19, 1943; children—Eileen (Mrs. Dean S. Fox, Mary Elizabeth (Mrs. Richard F. Paxton), Patricia (Mrs. Jim Hutcherson), Robert Christopher. Sec., Bill Lyons Co., San Antonio, Houston, 1967-68, office mgr., 1969—. Named Internat. Sec. of Year, Nat. Secs. Assn., 1973. Mem. Nat. Secs. Assn. Baptist. Home: Route 5 Box 400 San Antonio TX 78211 Office: PO Box 6388 San Antonio TX 78209

ERNST, RHUA HECKART, educator; b. Toledo, May 18, 1939; d. Bernard George and Reba F. (Dask) Liska; B.A., Mary Manse Coll., Toledo, 1960; M.Ed., U. Toledo, 1965, M.A., 1970; student instructional media Stevens Coll., Columbia, Mo., 1969, Miami U., Oxford, O., 1970; m. James W. Ernst, Apr. 4, 1970; children—Ronald Heckart, Erik Heckart. Tchr., Bedford pub. schs., Temperance, Mich., 1960-64; audiovisual dir., librarian Penta County Joint Vocational Sch. and Tech. Coll., Rossford, O., 1965-66; coordinator library tech. assistance program U. Toledo, 1966-67, dir. instructional resources, 1967-71; dir. curriculum devel. program U.S. Office Edn., Washington and U. Toledo, 1971-72; dir. library, audiovisual and television services Tri-Institutional Edn. Facilities, Phila., 1973—; cons. in field. Chmn. Council Library Tech., 1967-68, pres., 1968-69, mem. bd., 1967-71, regional cons., 1972-73; mem. legialtive com. Assn. Ednl. Communications and Tech., 1965—, legislative chmn. Ohio, 1969-71; mem. commn. Media Support Personnel Com., 1969—; mem. com. minority rights Univ. Film Prodn. Assn., 1969-71; mem., pub. relations chmn. Child Abuse Prevention Effort, 1974—. Mem. Child Conservation League; mem. bd. Greenwich (Conn.) Assn. Pub. Schs., 1971-72, Moderate Housing League, 1971-72. Dist. chmn., mem. bd. Democratic Women's Club, 1971-72; publicity chmn. Greenwich Town Com., 1971-72. Fellow U. Toledo, 1964-65. Curriculum devel. grantee U.S. Office Edn., 1970-73. Mem. A.L.A., Health Edn. Media Assn., Med. Library Assn., Spl. Library Assn., Pa. Learning Resources Assn., Pa. Library Assn., League Women Voters, Nat. Assn. Ednl. Broadcasters, Am. Assn. U. Women. Clubs: Greenwich Junior Women's; Junior Saturday (Wayne, Pa.). Author: Cataloging Code for Media Materials, 1970; Library Techinical Assistant: A Suggested Two-Year Curriculum Guide, 1972. Address: 560 Pugh Rd Wayne PA 19087

ERNST, WILMA JANE, sec., club woman; b. Lakeside, O., Aug. 6, 1931; d. William R. and Marrian (Carroll) Brown; ed. Bowling Green State U., Schuster-Martin Sch., Cin., Goodman Theatre Sch., Chgo.; div.; children—Christena Marie, Marrian Sue. Office work Worthy R. Brown & Son, Inc., 1947-51, then sec., clk. Brown's Marina, Lakeside, 1951-66; clk. Fort Firelands, Inc., 1968-69; owner antique bus., 1969-72; sec. Lakeside United Meth. Ch., 1972-73; sec. Catawba Island Club, 1973—; caseworker Ottawa County Welfare Dept., 1974—. Reporter H.B. Magruder Meml. Hosp. Aux., Port Clinton, O., then dir. vols., v.p., and program chmn., pres.; active local P.T.A., Music Boosters group, Girl Scouts U.S.A. Mem. Ohio Fedn. Women's Clubs (dist. officer, state dir., pres. 1972-74). Home: 8132 Lake Blvd Lakeside OH 43440

EROH, AGNES RUTH, educator; b. Weatherly, Pa., Sept. 18, 1914; d. Ralph Arson and Mary Catherine (Hamm) Eroh; B.A., Columbia Union Coll., 1945; M.Ed., Pa. State U., 1958; D.Ed., Boston U., 1964. Mem. faculty Atlantic Union Coll., 1952-69, asso. prof. edn., 1958-66, prof., 1966-69; prof. edn. Loma Linda U. Sch. Edn., Riverside, Cal., 1969—. NSF grantee, 1969-72; Minnemast grantee, 1971. Mem. Nat. Sci. Tchrs. Assn., Nat. Council Tchrs. Math., Pi Lambda Theta. Home: 5083 College St Riverside CA 92505

ERON, MADELINE MARCUS (MRS. LEONARD D. ERON), psychologist; b. New Brunswick, N.J., Sept. 8, 1920; d. Israel and Rae (Becker) Marcus; student U. Mich., 1937-39; B.A., N.Y.U., 1941; M.A., Columbia, 1942; m. Dr. Leonard D. Eron, May 21, 1950; children—Joni Irene, Don Marcus, Barbara Faye. Psychology intern Phila. State Hosp., 1942-43; extern Neurol. Inst. Columbia-Presbyn. Med. Center, N.Y.C., 1943-44; sr. clin. psychologist Inst. for Crippled and Disabled, 1944-51; pvt. practice psychology, New Haven, 1950-55; clin. psychologist Rip Van Winkle Clinic and Found., Hudson, N.Y., 1957-61; clin. psychologist Berkshire Farm for Boys, Canaan, N.Y., 1961-62; pvt. practice retng. brain injured, Iowa City, 1962-63; psychol. cons. Cedar Rapids (Ia.) Community Sch. Dist., 1963-67; engaged in research, Amsterdam, Netherlands, 1967-68; dir. psychol. services U. Ia. Comprehensive Evaluation and Rehab. Center, 1968-69; psychologist Winnetka (Ill.) Pub. Schs., 1969-70; psychol. cons. Glencoe (Ill.) Pub. Schs., 1970-71; psychologist Dist. 68, Skokie, Ill., 1971-72; psychologist Evanston (Ill.) Twp. High Sch., 1972—. Mem. Am., Eastern, Midwestern, N.Y. State, Northeastern N.Y., Ia. (sec. 1965-67), Ill. psychol. assns., Nat. Assn. Sch. Psychologists, Council Exceptional Children, Assn. for Learning Disabilities, Fund for Perceptually Handicapped, Assn. for Precision Teaching, League Women Voters, Psi Chi. Club: University. Home: 1616 Sheridan Rd Wilmette IL 60091

ERRINGTON, NELLIE BALL (MRS. CARL HUGH ERRINGTON), civic worker; b. Soldier, Kan.; d. William Sherman and Eva Mary (Taylor) Ball; diploma Morris Acad. Music, 1954, Wichita Art Center, 1951; student Cal. Sch. Interior Design, 1952, Park Coll., 1953, Stoffell Sch. Reflexology, 1965, Mass Feeding Sch., Denver, 1954; m. Carl Hugh Errington, Nov. 16, 1929; children—Nancy Jane, Mary Jo, Teresa Lynn. Co-owner Bar E Ranch, Goodland, Kan., 1931—. Mem. Kan. Recreation Workshop, Hutchinson, Kan. 1948—, instr. art, 1952-58, bd. dirs., 1950-54, v.p., 1952-54; leader 4-H Club, Ruleton, Kan., 1934-60, bd. dirs. 4-H Found. Kan., Manhattan, 1948-58; instr. mass feeding Civil Def., Goodland, 1954; instr. music Kan. State Youth Music Conf., Manhattan, 1956-57; supr. Ruleton sch. cafeteria, 1948-62; coordinator Meals on Wheels, 1973; pres. Farm Bur. adv. council, Goodland, 1942-46, bd. dirs., 1942-46, chmn. home and community work, 1946-52; bd. dirs. Ruleton March of Dimes, 1953; panelist Kan. State Soil Conservation Conv., Hutchinson, 1954; active Infantile Paralysis, 1941-56, service certificate, 1956. Recipient (with husband) Balanced Farming and Family Living award Kan. State Soil Conservation Assn., 1954; certificate Nat. Safety Council, 1954; Good Neighbor award Radio KXXX, 1954; Leadership award, Kan. State Bd. Agr., 1942, Woman of Year, 1974. Mem. Nat. (life), Kan. (chmn. of Insignia 1958-60, chmn. folklore 1960-62, pres. local club 1956-58, v.p. 1966-67), fedns. music clubs, Nat. Cowbelles Assn., Zonta (pres. Goodland chpt. 1959-60, 66-68, chmn. dist. 1972-74), Kan. Folklore Soc., Puppeteers of Am., Nat. Fedn. Bus. and Profl. Women, Nat. Health Fedn., St. Paul's Women's Guild (pres. 1970-72), Kan. Fedn. Women's Club (pres. local club 1954-55), Internat. Platform Assn., Am. Security Council, UN Assn., Common Cause, Kan. Asso. Garden Clubs (life). Club: Goodland Round Table (pres. 1954-55). Episcopalian. Clubs: Mr. and Mrs. Garden (pres. 1974), Priscilla, Sugar Hills Country. Home: 1102 Arcade St Goodland KS 67735

ERSKINE, HELEN, psychologist, govt. ofcl.; b. Oyen, Alta., Can., Apr. 22, 1916; d. Samuel McMeshan and Hannah (MacKay) Erskine; came to U.S., 1950, naturalized, 1957; R.N., St. Paul's Sch. Nursing, Vancouver, B.C., Can.; B.A., U. B.C., 1948, M.A. in Psychology, 1950; Ph.D., U. Chgo., 1956. With Inst. for Juvenile Research, Chgo., 1957-60, Ill. Inst. Tech., Chgo., 1960-61, Pediatric Diagnostic Center, Johns Hopkins, 1963-64, U. R.I., 1964-67; behavioral research in criminology U.S. Dept. Justice, Washington, 1968—. Served with Canadian Army, 1943-46. Mem. Am. Psychol. Assn. Author: Alcohol and the Criminal Justice System, 1972; also articles. Home: 520 N St SW Washington DC 20024 Office: 633 Indiana Av NW Washington DC 20530

ERSOFF, MARCIE S. FEINGOLD (MRS. STANLEY M. ERSOFF), writer; b. Monticello, N.Y., Aug. 9, 1937; d. Moe and Natalie (Barer) Feingold; student Syracuse U., 1954-55; B.S. summa cum laude, U. Fla., 1958; M.A., U. Miami, 1972; m. Stanley M. Ersoff, Jan. 1, 1960; children—Brett, Seth. Staff writer The Miami Herald, 1958-64; mem. Dade County pub. relations staff Fla. Gubernatorial Campaign, Miami, 1966; journalistic cons. Dept. Pub. Information Dade County Sch. System, Miami, 1967-69; Dade County (Fla.) coordinator Project Pub. Information, Miami, 1967-68; editor newsletter Urban Scene, U. Miami Center for Urban Studies, 1970-72; information specialist Dept. Pub. Information, Dade County Sch. System, Miami, 1972-73; writer feature articles various publs. including Quest, Miami mag., Israel Today, Miami Herald. Bd. dirs. Jewish Family and Childrens Service Bur., Miami, 1964-72; mem. exec. bd. dirs. Project Hope, Miami, 1971-72, Am. Jewish Com., Miami, 1972-73; trustee Dade County Library Adv. Bd., Miami. Acad. grantee U. Miami Center for Urban Studies, 1970-72; recipient pub. service awards Fla. Womens Press Club, 1960, 61. Mem. Women in Communications, Phi Kappa Phi, Kappa Tau Alpha, Alpha Kappa Delta. Home: 149 Shore Dr W Miami FL 33133

ERSTED, RUTH MARION, librarian; b. Brookings, S.D., Oct. 17, 1904; d. Carl T. and Marie (Sigurdson) Ersted; B.S., U. Minn., 1927; M.A., U. Chgo., 1950. Sch. librarian, Hopkins, Minn., 1927-33, Univ. High Sch., Minn., 1933-36; sch. library supr. Minn. Dept. Edn., 1936—; library sci. tchr. summer sessions U. Minn., U. Chgo., Emporia State Coll. Mem. A.L.A. (co-chmn. standards sch. library programs 1960, mem, standards for sch. media programs 1969), Am. Civil Liberties Union, Minn. Assn. Sch. Librarians, Nat., Minn. edn. assns., League Women Voters, Citizens League of Mpls. Unitarian. Author: (with Frances Henne and A. Lohrer) Planning Guide for the High School Library. Address: 5124 Cedar Av S Minneapolis MN 55417

ERTEL, INTA ILZE JANNERS (MRS. PAUL Y. ERTEL), pediatrician; b. Riga, Latvia, Jan. 5, 1932; d. Nikolas B. and Alma M. (Steikmanis) Janners; A.A., Lycoming Coll., 1952; B.S., Mary Washington Coll., 1955; M.D., U. Va., 1959; m. Paul Y. Ertel, Aug. 20, 1955; children—Dace Jacqueline, Lynne Marle. Came to the U.S., 1950, naturalized, 1956. Intern, Cleve. Met. Gen. Hosp., 1959-60; resident pediatrics U. Mich., Ann Arbor, 1960-62, instr. pediatrics, 1962-66, oncology trainee, 1964-66; asst. prof. pediatrics Ohio State U., Columbus, 1966-70, asso. prof. pediatrics, 1970—; pediatric hematologist, oncologist Children's Hosp., Columbus, O., 1966—; practice medicine specializing in pediatrics, Ann Arbor, 1962-66, Columbus, 1966—. Diplomate Am. Bd. Pediatrics. Fellow Am. Acad. Pediatrics; mem. Am. Med. Women's Assn., Central Ohio Pediatric Soc., Midwest Soc. Pediatric Research, Am. Soc. Hematology, Leukemia Soc. Am. (dir. 1971-73). Home: 135 Indian Run Dr Dublin OH 43017 Office: Children's Hospital 561 S 17th St Columbus OH 43205

ERVIN, JANET HALLIDAY (MRS. HOWARD G. ERVIN), author; b. Muncie, Ind., May 29, 1923; d. Everett Clayton and Lois Kathryn (Kidnocker) Halliday; Ph.B., U. Chgo., 1946; m. Howard Guy Ervin, July 3, 1946; children—Howard Guy III, Dennis, David. Reporter, Muncie Evening Press, 1941-44; free lance writer; guest editor-in-chief Mademoiselle mag., 1945; author column Keeping Up with Janet, Toledo Blade; contbr. teen-age fiction, articles to women's mags. author: The White House Cook Book, 1964; (juvenile) Last Trip of the Juno, 1970; (juvenile) More Than Halfway There, 1970. Recipient Vogue Prix de Paris, 1946; Friends Am. Writers' Distinguished Recognition award, 1972. Mem. Council for Wis. Writers, Milw. Fictioneers, U. Chgo. Alumni, Mensa, Theta Sigma Phi. Presbyn. Home: 2450 N 97th St Milwaukee WI 53226

ERVIN, MARGARET BRUCE BELL (MRS. SAM. J. ERVIN), wife senator from N.C.; m. Sam J. Ervin, June 18, 1924; children—Sam J. III, Mrs. Gerald M. Hansler, Mrs. William Edward Smith. Address: 110 Maryland Av NE Washington DC 20002

ERWIN, BRENDA KAY JOHNSTON (MRS. ROY RANDOLPH ERWIN), real estate broker; b. Dallas, Aug. 4, 1949; d. Billy Clyde and Mary Christine (Knowles) Johnston; student El Centro Jr. Coll., 1967-68, North Tex. State U., 1968-70; B. Journalism, U. Tex., 1972; m. Roy Randolph Erwin, Mar. 3, 1972; 1 son, Jarrod Reed. Reporter Gladewater Mirror, Gladewater, Tex., 1971; staff writer Austin (Tex.) Am.-Statesman, 1972; real estate agy. Nat. Resort Communities, Austin, Tex., 1972, Thornton, Murphy & Moore, Austin, 1973—. Recipient Fentress fellowship award Austin Am.-Statesman, 1972. Mem. Austin Bd. Realtors, Tex. Ex-Student Assn., Women in Communications, Sigma Delta Chi. Home: 9444 Spring Hollow St Austin TX 78759 Office: 729 W 23d St Austin TX 78705

ESCALLÓN, MARION SCHMIDT, geologist; b. Chgo., July 25, 1912; d. Harry Logan and Helen (Fraser) Schmidt; B.A., U. Mich., 1933, postgrad., 1933-34; m. Carlos Escallón, June 7, 1941; children—Eduardo Carlos, Roberto Juan. Teaching asst., museum asst. dept. geology U. Mich. at Ann Arbor, 1933-34; asst. to chief geologist, translator Consol. (Sinclair) Oil Corp., N.Y.C., 1935-39; office mgr. in charge geology Tex. Petroleum Co., Bogotá, Colombia, 1939-41; asst. to chief geologist fgn. producing dept. Tex. Co., N.Y.C., 1941; geologist exploration dept. Am. Overseas Petroleum Ltd., N.Y.C., 1955-68; exploration analyst producing dept. eastern hemisphere Texaco, Inc., N.Y.C., 1969—. Mem. Valhalla (N.Y.) High Sch. Curriculum Com. Secondary Edn., 1960. Active Republican primary campaigns, North White Plains, N.Y., 1961, 62. Bd. dirs. A.R.C., North Castle, 1961. Fellow A.A.A.S.; mem. Am. Assn. Petroleum Geologists (sec. Eastern sect. 1957-58; treas. 1969-71), Soc. Petroleum Engrs. Am. Inst. Mining, Metall. and Petroleum Engrs. (dir. N.Y. sect. 1969—), Am. Radio Relay League, Communications Club New Rochelle (dir. 1970, 71). Home: 5 Dunlap Way North White Plains NY 10603 Office: Texaco Inc 135 E 42d St New York City NY 10017

ESCHENBERG, KATHRYN MARCELLA, educator; b. St. Louis, Dec. 12, 1923; B.A., Miami (O.) U., 1946; M.A., U. Colo., 1950; Ph.D. in Zoology, U. Wash. at Seattle, 1957. Asst. in biology and vertebrate physiology U. Colo., 1948-49, instr., 1949-51; asst. in zoology, embryology and cell physiology U. Wash. at Seattle, 1951-56; Nat. Cancer Inst. research fellow Princeton, 1957; asso. prof. zoology, cell biology and embryology Mt. Holyoke Coll., South Hadley, Mass., 1958-64, asso. prof. biol. sci., 1964-70, prof., 1970—, chmn. dept. biol. sci., 1970-72. Mem. A.A.A.S. Research in biochem. embryology, developmental cytology, relation of ploidy to devel. Office: Mount Holyoke Coll South Hadley MA 01075

ESCHMANN, CLARA BELLE HOOKS (MRS. EDGAR ALBERT ESCHMANN, JR.), journalist; b. Americus, Ga., Feb. 12, 1917; d. William Glenn and Clara Belle (Davenport) Hooks; A.B. in Journalism, U. Ga., 1938; m. Edgar Albert Eschmann, Jr., Sept. 30, 1942; children—Mildred (Mrs. John D. Spear), Clare, Edgar Albert III. Society editor Griffin (Ga.) News, 1938-42; dir. publicity Wesleyan Coll., Macon, Ga., 1961-68; food editor Macon Telegraph and News, 1968—. Bd. dirs. Alexander III Sch. P.T.A., 1960-64, A.R.C., Macon, 1964—. Mem. Macon Writers Club (pres. 1972), Theta Sigma Phi. Episcopalian. Home: 1180 S Jackson Springs Rd Macon GA 31201 Office: Macon Telegraph and News PO Box 1467 Macon GA 31208

ESHBAUGH, DOROTHY ELIZABETH EMILY, physician; b. Chgo.; d. C. Harold and Jennie (Hamann) Eshbaugh; B.S., U. Chgo., 1938; M.D., Women's Med. Coll. Pa., 1942. Intern Phila. Gen. Hosp., 1942-43; resident Billings Hosp., St. Lukes Hosp., Chgo., 1943-46; practice medicine, specializing in pathology, Chgo., 1950—; asst. prof. pathology U. Ill., 1955-56, clin. asst. prof., 1957-64, clin. asso. prof. pathology, 1967—; pathologist Michael Reese Hosp., Chgo., 1956—, asst. dir. dept. pathology, 1965—. Diplomate Am. Bd. Pathology. Mem. Am. Med. Women's Assn., A.M.A., Internat. Acad. Pathology, Coll. Am. Pathologists, Chgo. Pathol. Soc., Am. Soc. Clin. Pathologists, Zeta Phi. Home: 8347 Cregier Av Chicago IL 60617 Office: 2929 S Ellis Av Chicago IL 60616

ESHELMAN, ELIZABETH DAVIS (MRS. JOSEPH W. ESHELMAN, JR.), banker, lawyer; b. Montgomery, Ala., Aug. 22, 1924; d. Harwell Goodwin and Lena Chambless (Vail) Davis; B.A., Howard Coll., 1944; LL.B., Cumberland Law Sch., 1964, J.D., 1969; m. Joseph W. Eshelman, Jr., Mar. 18, 1944; children—Joseph W. III, Elizabeth Vail (Mrs. R.D. Crisson). Admitted to Ala. bar, 1964, U.S. Supreme Ct. bar, 1972; practiced in Birmingham, 1964-67; trust officer, bank officer tax div. estate planning Birmingham Trust Nat. Bank, 1967—. Treas. Women's Com. of 100 for Birmingham, 1972-74; mem. Conservative Com. Against Equal Rights Amendment, 1972-73. Bd. dirs. YWCA, 1960-65; bd. dirs. Travelers Aid, mem. finance com., 1969—; mem. alumni bd. Cumberland Law Sch., sec.-treas., 1972—. Mem. Ala. State Bar (mem. consumer protection com. 1971-75), Am., Birmingham (scholarship com. 1972-73) bar assns., Ala. Bankers Assn. (chmn. profl. relations com. trust div. 1972-73), Nat. Bank Women, Southeastern Regional Bank Women, D.A.R., Hypatia Hon. Soc., Alpha Delta Pi, Phi Alpha Delta. Baptist. Co-author: Forms for Wills and Estate Planning, 1967; author: The Corporate Executor's Role in Estate Planning, 1968. Home: 3036 Warrington Rd Birmingham AL 35223 Office: Birmingham Trust National Bank 112-118 N 20th St Birmingham AL 35290

ESKAY, MARION ANITA, ednl. adminstr.; b. N.Y.C., May 2, 1933; d. Leo D. and Ruth (Durst) Miller; B.S., Cornell U., 1954; postgrad. N.J. State Tchrs. Coll., 1955-56, Seton Hall, 1956-57; M.L.S., Queens Coll., 1966; m. Richard S. Eskay, Aug. 16, 1953; children—Marjorie Lauren, Linda Ellen, Julie Ann. Organizer spl. edn. instructional materials center Bd. Coop. Edn. Services II Westchester County, Valhalla, N.Y., 1966-68; creative dir. Pathways Ednl. Programs, Scarsdale, N.Y., 1969-71; curriculum coordinator lang. arts K-12, Pearl River (N.Y.) Pub. Schs., 1971—. Cons. spl. edn. Hunter Coll., 1968-69, tchr., 1968-70; producer radio program Pathways to Children's Lit., sta. WFAS-AM-FM, White Plains, N.Y., 1966-72. Mem. N.E.A., Am. Library Assn. Author: People Profiles Reading Program, 1970; Slavery, Civil War-Reconstruction, 1970; Colonial American Round-Up, 1971, American Indians-Harmony and Discord, 1971. Patentee visual cassette. Home: 26 Sprain Valley Rd Scarsdale NY 10583 Office: Pearl River Sch Franklin Av Pearl River NY 10965

ESPENSCHADE, SYLVIA KATHERINE JOHNSON (MRS. C. WAYNE ESPENSCHADE), pub. relations exec.; b. Detroit, Dec. 19, 1936; d. Alphonse Eskil and Katherine Florence (Reilly) Johnson; student Wayne State U., 1954-56; m. C. Wayne Espenschade, Aug. 20, 1971. Front page editor Detroit Shopping News, 1956-72; promotions mgr. Detroit Symphony Orch., 1972-73, communications mgr., 1973—. Bd. dirs., sec. Detroit Police Athletic League. Recipient Police Citizen citation Detroit Police Dept., 1972; named One of Detroit's Top Ten Working Women, Greater Detroit C. of C., 1971. Mem. Women in Communications, Women's Advt. Club Detroit (sec. 1971-73). Women's Econ. Club Detroit, Founders Soc. Detroit Inst. Arts, Women's Assn. Detroit Symphony Orch., Women Wayne, Pub. Relations Soc. Am. Home: 5254 Falmouth St Troy MI 48084 Office: Ford Auditorium Detroit MI 48226

ESPOSITO, MARGARET LEA, extension home economist; b. Bloomington, Ill., July 5, 1923; d. Charles Andrew and Gladys (Mitchell) Poulton; B.S., Ill. State U., 1961, M.S., 1963, postgrad., 1964—; m. Santine Esposito, Oct. 3, 1942; children—Linda (Mrs. Ronald Lambrecht), Stephen Anthony. With U. Ill. extension service, McLean County, Bloomington, 1962—, asso. extension adviser, 1965-70, extension adviser home econs., 1970—. Editorial bd. newsletter Econ. Opportunities Corp., McLean County, 1970—; Mem. Ill. Council Family Relations, 1962—; sec. Ill. Nutrition Com., 1970-71. Bd. dirs. Salvation Army, Bloomington, 1963—, chmn. bd. dirs., 1972—. Recipient Career Woman of Year award Bus. and Profl. Women's Club, 1971. Mem. Ill., Am. home econs. assns., Home Economists in Homemaking, Ill. (pres. 1972-73), Nat. (chmn. council state presidents, Distinguished Service award 1973) assns. extension home economists, Assn. Commerce (women's div.), MacMurray Alumni Assn. Bloomington-Normal Geneal. Soc. Mem. Ch. of Epiphany. Home: 805 Apple St Normal IL 61761 Office: 202 E Locust St Bloomington IL 61701

ESQUIVEL, ARGELIA VELEZ RODRIGUEZ, educator; b. Havana, Cuba, Nov. 23, 1936; d. Pedro and Maria de las Nieves (Friol) Velez; B.S., and Arts, U. Havana, 1954, Ph.D., 1960; postgrad. (NSF fellow), U. Wis., 1965, Tex. Christian U., 1967-68.; m. Raul Leander Rodriguez, June 6, 1954 (div. Mar. 1969); children—Raul Pedro, Argelia Maria; m. 2d, Ricardo Rafael Esquivel, June 29, 1973. Came to U.S., 1962, naturalized, 1972. Faculty Marianao Inst. and Physics, Havanna, Cuba, 1957-61; asst. prof. math. and physics, chmn. math. dept. Tex. Coll., Tyler, 1962-64; asst. prof. math. Bishop Coll., Dallas, 1964-66, asso. prof., 1966-68, prof., 1968—, dir. of a multi-year-in-service project, 1970—; asso. dir. U. Houston-Bishop Coll. coop. doctoral program in math. edn., 1973—. Mem. evaluation com. on math. for the Thirteen Coll. curriculum program confs., Atlanta, Ga., 1968-71; dir. NSF Coop. Coll.-Sch. sci. projects in math. for Dallas Ind. Sch. Dist., 1972-74. Mem. Nat. Council Tchrs. Math., Tex. Acad. of Sci., Am. Math. Soc., Math. Assn. Am., Am. Assn. U. Profs., A.A.A.S., Am. Assn. U. Women (rep. internat. relations area for Dallas br., 1973-75), Cuban Cath. Assn., Assn. for Grad. Edn. and Research of N. Tex. (mem. math. com., 1969—, mem. computer sci. com., 1969—). Home: 838 Foxboro Lane Dallas TX 75241

ESSELMANN, MARIE TERESA DEMMER (MRS. GEORGE H. ESSELMANN, JR.), microbiologist; b. Union City, Okla., Sept. 30, 1920; d. Leo and Anna (Hentzen) Demmer; B.S., Mt. St. Scholastica Coll., 1943; postgrad. St. Mary's Hosp. Sch. Med. Tech., 1943-44; M.S., U. Louisville, 1961; m. George H. Esselmann, Jr., Nov. 26, 1949. Microbiologist, U.S. Army Borden Gen. Hosp., Chickasha, Okla., 1944-46; U.S. VA Hosp., Oklahoma City, 1946-49; chief dept. immunology VA Hosp., Louisville, 1949—. Named Ky. col. Recipient Okie award, Gov. Oklahoma, 1970. Mem. Am. Bd. Microbiology, Am. Soc. Microbiologists, Am., Ky., Louisville socs. med. technologists, Am. Inst. Biol. Scis., Internat. Fedn. Cath. Alumnae Women Univ. Grads. Club: Mt. St. Scholastica Coll. (pres.). Democrat. Roman Catholic. Home: 1901 Claremoor Dr Anchorage KY 40223 Office: US VA Hosp Dept Immunology Louisville KY 40201

ESSERMAN, RUTH (MRS. NORMAN ESSERMAN), artist; b. Chgo., May 21, 1927; B.A., M.A., U. Ill.; student Art Inst. Chgo.; postgrad. U. Mexico. Exhibited in group shows Denver Art Mus., Mpls. Inst. Art, Chgo. Sun-Times Competition, New Horizons, Roosevelt U., Pan-Am. Exhbn., Hyde Park Competition; resident artist Sybil Shearer Dance Co., 1969-70; instr. art Highland Park (Ill.) High Sch., 1957—, chmn. fine art dept., 1971—. Adviser, U.S. Office Edn., 1967-68; mem. adv. council Ill. Arts Council. Recipient numerous prizes and awards. Mem. Ill. (pres. 1965-66), Nat. (dir.) art edn. assns., Ill. Edn. Assn. Address: 433 Vine St Highland Park IL 60035

ESSEX, CAROLYN HIGHTOWER (MRS. LEO W. ESSEX), clergywoman; b. Aiken, S.C., Nov. 6, 1898; d. Joseph Benjamin and Sarah Frances (Crawford) Hightower; A.B., Research U., 1922; D.D., Coll. Divine Metaphysics, 1923; m. Samuel Timothy Parsons, Jan. 11, 1932 (dec. Oct. 1947); m. 2d, Leo Ward Essex, June 12, 1964 (dec. Apr. 1972). Ordained to ministry Unity Ch., 1938; minister Christ Ch., Unity, Orlando, Fla., 1938—. Tchr's tng. staff, bd. mem. Unity Sch. of Christianity, Lee's Summit, Mo. Mem. Hist. Soc. S.C., Unity Ministers' Assn., D.A.R., Bus. and Profl. Women's Club, Hist. Soc. S.C., Internat. Platform Assn. Clubs: Altrusa (chaplain), Orlando Country, Executive. Home: 84 W Lucerne Circle Orlando FL 32801 Office: 503 S Orange Av Orlando FL 32801

ESTERGREEN, MARION MORGAN, author; b. Albuquerque; d. Francis Marion and Glennie (Holland) Morgan; B.A., U. N.M., 1940; postgrad. U. Wis., 1946-47; m. Paul Henry Estergreen, Mar. 31, 1941; 1 dau., Sheryl Marian. Chmn. adv. bd. Kit Carson Meml. Park, 1950—. Mem. Nat. League Am. Pen Women (charter pres. Taos br. 1950-51), Taos Artists Assn., Taos Opera Guild. Presbyn. Club: Garden (Taos, N.M.). Author: The Real Kit Carson, 1958; Kit Carson: A Portrait in Courage, 1962. Contbr. articles to profl. jours. Home: PO Box 343 Taos NM 78571

ESTERLY, KATHERINE LOUISE, physician; b. Norristown, Pa., Oct. 11, 1925; d. Harold D. and Inez (Morgan) Esterly; B.S., Ursinus Coll., 1947; M.D., Temple U., 1951; postgrad. U. Pa., 1952-53. Intern, Del. Hosp., Wilmington, 1951-52, resident, 1952-54; practice medicine, specializing in pediatrics, Wilmington, 1954—; attending chief Wilmington Med. Center, 1960—; clin. asso. prof. pediatrics Jefferson Med. Coll. Diplomate Am. Bd. Pediatrics. Fellow Am. Acad. Pediatrics; mem. A.M.A. Home: 3200 Centerville Rd Wilmington DE 19807 Office: 1410 Delaware Av Wilmington DE 19806

ESTERLY, NANCY BURTON (MRS. JOHN R. ESTERLY), physician, educator; b. N.Y.C., Apr. 14, 1935; d. Paul Robert and Tanya E. (Pasahow) Burton; B.A., Smith Coll., 1956; M.D., Johns Hopkins, 1960; m. John R. Esterly, June 16, 1957; children—Sarah Burton, Anne Beidler, John Snyder II, Henry Clark II. Pediatric intern Johns Hopkins Hosp., 1960-61, resident, 1961-63, dermatology resident, 1964-67; attending physician Hines VA Hosp., Chgo., cons. dermatology Chgo. State Tb Sanitorium, 1970-73; instr. dept. pediatrics Johns Hopkins Med. Sch., 1967-68; instr. dept. pediatrics U. Chgo., 1968, asst. prof., 1969-70; asst. prof. dept. dermatology U. Ill., Chgo., 1970-72, asso. prof. dept. dermatology and pediatrics, 1972-73; asso. prof. pediatrics U. Chgo., 1973—; dir. div. pediatric dermatology, attending physician Michael Reese Hosp., 1973—. Diplomate Am. Bd. Pediatrics, Am. Bd. Dermatology. Mem. Am. Acad. Dermatology, Soc. for Investigative Dermatology, Soc. Pediatric Research, Phi Beta Kappa, Sigma Xi. Contbr. articles to profl. jours. Home: 6828 S Constance St Chicago IL 60649 Office: Dept Pediatrics Michael Reese Hosp 29th St and Ellis Av Chicago IL 60616

ESTES, CARROLL LYNN, sociologist, educator; b. Fort Worth, May 30, 1938; d. Joe Ewing and Carroll (Cox) Estes; A.B., Stanford, 1959; M.A., So. Meth. U., 1961; Ph.D., U. Cal. at San Diego, 1972; m. Michael C. Thometz, June 27, 1959 (div. Sept. 1965); m. 2d, David H. Gelfand, Apr. 28, 1967; 1 dau., Duskie Lynn. Research asst., asst. study dir. Brandeis U. Social Welfare Research Center, 1962-63; research asso., 1964-65, project dir., 1965-67, vis. lectr. Florence Heller Grad. Sch., 1964-65; research dir. Simmons Coll., 1963-64; asst. prof. social work San Diego State Coll., 1967-72; asst. prof. in residence, dept. psychiatry U. Cal. at San Francisco, 1972—, coordinator human devel. tng. program, 1974—. Mem. Cal. Commn. on Aging, 1974—. Nat. Inst. Mental Health spl. fellow for research, 1970-72. Mem. Am. Civil Liberties Union, Am. Sociol. Assn., Soc. for Psychol. Study Social Issues, Gerontol. Soc., Soc. for Study Social Problems, Alpha Kappa Delta, Pi Beta Phi. Democrat. Author: The Decision-Makers: The Power Structure of Dallas, 1963. Co-author: Protective Services for Older People, 1972. Home: 485 Dewey Blvd San Francisco CA 94116

ESTES, CARROLL VIRGINIA COX (MRS. JOE EWING ESTES), retail store exec.; b. Stephenville, Tex., May 12, 1908; d. Roscoe Edmund and Bertha Delaware (Head) Cox; B.A., So. Meth. U., Dallas, 1928; M.A., Columbia, 1930; m. Joe Ewing Estes, Dec. 1, 1931; children—Carl Lewis II, Carroll Lynn (Mrs. David Harrow Gelfand). Asst. prof. art dept., chmn. dept. Mary Baldwin Coll., Staunton, Va., 1930-31, E. Tex. State U., Commerce, 1931; dir. R.E. Cox Co., Waco, Tex., Berry St. Realty Co., Lancaster St. Realty Co. (both Fort Worth). Active A.R.C., United Fund, Jr. League. Mem. Theta Sigma Phi, Pi Beta Phi. Methodist. Clubs: Woman's, Garden, Dallas, Northwood Country, Chapparral, City (all Dallas). Author: Eavesdropping on Death, 1953; Unhappy New Year, 1954; The Moon Gate, 1955. Address: 5846 Desco Dr Dallas TX 75225

ESTES, EDNA EVA, educator; b. Jasper, Ala., Nov. 23, 1921; d. F. E. and Ethel Etta (Ford) Estes; student Birmingham So. Coll., 1946-47; B.S., U. Ala., 1948, M.S., 1949, Ph.D., 1957. Asst. prof. biology Flora Macdonald Coll., Red Springs, N.C., 1949-53; instr. U. Ala., Mobile, 1953-54, St. Mary's Jr. Coll., St. Mary's City, Md., 1957-59; asst. prof. Del Mar Coll., Corpus Christi, Tex., 1959-60, State Tchrs. Coll., Salisbury, Md., 1960-64; asso. prof. biology Salisbury State Coll., 1964-65, prof. biology, 1965—. Served with WAC, AUS, 1943-45; PTO. Recipient Graham award U. Ala., 1956; So. Fellowship Fund fellow, 1956-57. Mem. A.A.A.S., Am. Assn. U. Women (pres. Salisbury br. 1966—), Bot. Soc. Am., Am. Assn. Plant Physiologists, Southeastern Assn. Biologists, Ala. Acad. Scis., Md. Assn. Higher Edn., Md. Tchrs. Assn., Delta Kappa Gamma, Sigma Xi. Research in phosphorus 32 uptake and localization correlated with photosynthetic factors in higher plants. Home: 514G Georgia Av Salisbury MD 21801

ESTES, MILDRED VALERIE SENDROW, psychologist, educator; b. N.Y.C., Mar. 14, 1919; d. Joseph and Sarah (Ring) Sendrow; B.A., Bklyn. Coll., 1939; postgrad. N.Y. U., 1940-41, Am. U., 1941; M.S. in Edn., University of So. Cal., 1952; m. Gordon W. Estes, Mar. 19, 1945; children—Richard Eileen, Clifford, Joel. Jr. economist OPA, 1941-42, economist, 1945-46; counselor, psychometrist Pacoima Jr. High Sch., 1954-60; tchr., counselor, psychometrist John H. Francis Poly. High Sch., Sun Valley, Cal., 1960-70; sch. psychologist area C, Los Angeles Bd. Edn. Tchr. psychology adult edn. classes, 1960—; lectr. condr. workshops, 1954—; cons. clin. psychology. Lectr. Cal. Dem. Com. Served WAC, 1942-45; MTO. Mem. Los Angeles Reading Council (charter, 1st treas.), California Guidance and Counseling Assn., Pi Lambda Theta, Psi Chi. Home: 1860 N Kingsley Dr Hollywood CA 90027

ESTEY, EMILY ROWLEY (MRS. ELMER ERWIN ESTEY), journalist, author; b. Fabius, N.Y., Nov. 30, 1913; d. Byer Franklin and Myrtle Jane (Brown) Rowley; student Syracuse U., 1942; m. Elmer Erwin Estey, June 26, 1931; children—Lois (Mrs. James A. Brown), Anne (Mrs. Ray McDowell), Patty (Mrs. James Modrak), Myrna (Mrs. James D. Marshall), Elmer Erwin III. Town clk. Town of Pompey, N.Y., 1945-53; columnist Syracuse (N.Y.) Post Standard, 1953-73. Dep. county clk. County of Onondaga Syracuse, 1955-73. Mem. Women in Communications, Nat. League Am. Pen Women, Onondaga County Hist. Assn., Syracuse Press Club. Author: Papa Was Positive, 1965; Lillacs and Mistletoe (poems), 1969; Where Did Yesterday Go., 1970. Home: 16018 Homestead Dr El Paso TX 79927 summer Box 98 Erieville NY

ESTIN, LIBBYADA STRAVER, tech. writer; b. Newark, July 13, 1937; d. Barney and Florence B. (Tenkin) Straver; student Syracuse U., 1955-57; B.S., Columbia, 1960; R.N., Columbia-Presbyn. Med. Center, 1960; certificate N.Y. Sch. Interior Design, 1962. Med. research tech. writer, N.Y.C., 1960-62; pres. Libbyada Estin Interiors, N.Y.C., 1962-65; v.p. advt. and pub. relations Behrman/Estin Inc., N.Y.C., 1965-67; account exec. and dir. pub. relations J.S. Fullerton, Inc., N.Y.C., 1967-68; med. writer L.W. Frohlich & Co., N.Y.C., 1968-69, Intercon Internat. Inc., N.Y.C., 1968-69, Kallir Philips Ross Inc., N.Y.C., 1969-71; copy supr. William Douglas McAdams Inc., N.Y.C., 1971—. Mem. Pub. Relations Soc. Am., Advt. Women N.Y., Am. Advt. Fedns., Am. Med. Writers Assn., Pharm. Advt. Club, Am. Nurses' Assn., Allied Bd. Trade, Columbia-Presbyn. Hosp. Alumnae Assn., Syracuse U. Alumnae Assn., Sigma Theta Tau, Delta Phi Epsilon. Home: 33 E 22nd St New York NY 10010 Office: 110 E 59th St New York NY 10022

ESTLER, SUZANNE ELLEN, coll. adminstr.; b. Paterson, N.J., Sept. 16, 1944; d. Louis Calder and Beatrice Evelyn (Vandervoort) E.; B.A., Douglass Coll., 1966; M.A. in Human Relations, Ohio U., 1969; postgrad. Stanford, 1973—. Resident dir., adminstrv. asst. Ohio U., Athens, 1968-69; asst. dir. residences Dickinson Coll., State U. N.Y. at Binghamton, 1969-70, dir. residences, 1970-71; coordinator student services Dickinson Coll./Coll.-in-the-Woods, State U. N.Y. at Binghamton, 1970-73; research asst. Stanford, part-time 1973—. Recipient State U. N.Y. Binghamton Found. Research award, 1970. Mem. Nat. Assn. Women Deans, Adminstrs., and Counselors, Women's Equity Action League, Douglass Coll. Alumnae Assn. Office: Sch Edn Stanford CA 94305

ESTRADA, DORIS EVELYN PERKINS (MRS. FRANK MARQUIS ESTRADA), librarian; b. Fanshawe, Okla., Dec. 13, 1923; d. William Newton and Nettie Viola (Goss) Perkins; A.A., Graceland Coll., 1944; B.A., Coll. Pacific, 1946; M.L.S., U. Cal. at Berkeley, 1969; m. Frank Marquis Estrada, Oct. 20, 1946; children—Denise (Mrs. Maurice McDonald), William, Alan. Typist clk. Stockton (Cal.) Pub. Library, 1965, library asst., 1965-66, library trainee, 1966-69, librarian I, 1969-72, head children's room, 1970-73, librarian II, 1972—. Active P.T.A. Mem. Young People's Coop. Library Assn. (sec. 1972-73), Beta Phi Mu. Mem. Reorganized Ch. of Jesus Christ of Latter Day Saints (dir. religious edn. 1956-57). Author: Periwinkle Jones, 1965. Home: 5349 E Hobart St Stockton CA 95205

ETEMAD, JACQUELINE GREY, child psychiatrist; b. Palo Alto, Cal., Apr. 16, 1936; d. Roy Leslie and Julia Geraldine (Hansen) Grey; B.A., U. Cal. at Berkeley, 1957, M.D., at San Francisco, 1964; student Antioch Coll., 1952-54; m. Michael A. Etemad, Aug. 11, 1956; children—Gregory Kamran and Jeffrey Keyvan (twins). Intern U. Cal. hosps., San Francisco, 1964-65; resident Langley Porter Inst., San Francisco, 1965-67, fellow child psychiatry, 1967-69, sr. resident child psychiatry, 1969-71, asst. physician, clin. instr., 1971-72, asst. clin. prof., 1973—; practice medicine specializing child psychiatry, San Francisco, 1970-72, Kentfield, Cal., 1972—. Cons. Parent Participation Nursery Schs. San Francisco, 1970-72; dir. Fgn. Exchange Ltd., Inc., San Francisco, 1971. Diplomate Am. Bd. Psychiatry and Neurology. Mem. Am. Psychiat. Assn., Am. Acad. Child Psychiatry, Phi Beta Kappa. Contbr. articles to profl. jours. Office: 1100 Sir Francis Drake Blvd Kentfield CA 94904

ETHERTON, TRUDY SLABY (MRS. WILLIAM M. ETHERTON), state ofcl.; b. South Bend, Ind., June 6, 1942; d. Frank A. and Alice (Michalec) Slaby; B.S., Butler U., 1964, postgrad. 1968; m. William M. Etherton. Tchr., Penn-Harris-Madison Sch. Corp., Mishawaka, Ind., 1964-68; nominee for clk. circuit ct., St. Joseph County, 1966; auditor State of Ind., Indpls., 1968-70, commr. Bur. Motor Vehicles, 1970-72; dir. Washington Liaison Office for State of Ind., 1972-73; acting asso. dir. State and Local Govt. Affairs, 1973; spl. asst. Office of Sec., Dept. Housing and Urban Devel., 1973—. Mem. Marion County Council Republican Women, Nat. Fedn. Rep. Women; pres. Young Republicans, Butler U., 1963-64; mem. exec. com. Nat. Young Reps., 1971-73. Mem. Butler Alumni Assn., Pan Hellenic Orgn., Internat. Platform Assn., South Bend Press Club, Delta Gamma Alumni Assn. Roman Catholic. Republican. Elk. Clubs: Capital Hill (Washington), State Assembly Womens, N.D. Faculty. Home: 5404 Fallwood Dr Indianapolis IN 46220 Office: Office of Secretary Room 10230 HUD 7th and D Sts SW Washington DC 20410

ETIENNE, JEANNE FRANCOISE, printing co. exec.; b. St. Louis, Nov. 24, 1918; d. Leonard Arthur and Kathryn Emily (Sullivan) Etienne; student Wash. U., 1936-38; B.A., U. Cin., 1940 Mgmt. asst. John Shillito Co., Cin., 1940-44; accountant Charles William Deopke Mfg. Co., Cin., 1945-51; with Westerman Print Co., Cin., 1951—, sec., treas., dir., 1960—. Mem. woman's adv. bd. Cin. Summer Opera Assn, 1961—, trustees, 1967—; women's com. Cin. Symphony Orch., 1961—, Cin. Mus. Festival, 1969-71. Trustees Jr. Achievement Greater Cin., Westerman Print Co. Profit Sharing Trust. Mem. Am. Soc. Women Accountants (chpt. pres. 1957-58), Nat. Assn. Accountants (internat. dir.), Cin. Hist. Soc., Cin. Ballet (women's com.), Miami Purchase Assn., Friends of Pub. Library, Stuart Cameron McLeod Soc. Republican. Roman Catholic. Club: Hyde Park Golf and Country. Home: 5841 Robison Rd Cincinnati OH 45213 Office: 2116 Colerain Av Cincinnati OH 45214

ETLING, PATRICIA ANN, educator; b. St. Louis, Mar. 31, 1945; d. Charles Louis and Josephine Julia (Havicon) Etling; B.A., Fontbonne Coll., 1967; postgrad. Forest Park Community Coll., 1967-68, M.E., U. Mo., 1972. With Security Investment Co., St. Louis, 1967; personnel interviewer and job corps recruiter Mo. Employment Security, St. Louis, 1967-68; tchr. speech, pub. speaking and drama, drama coach Kirkwood R-7 Dist. (Mo.), 1968-73; counselor Berkeley (Mo.) Sch. Dist., 1973—. Mem. N.E.A., Mo. Tchrs. Assn., Mo. Guidance Assn., Am., St. Louis personnel and guidance assns., Am., Mo. vocational assns., St. Louis Suburban Tchrs. Assn., Berkeley Community Tchrs. Assn., Suburban Guidance Assn., U. Mo.-St. Louis Alumni Assn. Roman Catholic. Club: Singles, Church Choir, Always on Friday (St. Louis). Home: 7527 Harlan Walk St Louis MO 63123 Office: 8710 Walter St Berkeley MO 63134

ETRA, BLANCHE GOLDMAN (MRS. HARRY ETRA), lawyer; b. N.Y.C., Mar. 8, 1915; d. Jack and Anna (Simon) E.; B.A., Barnard Coll., 1935; J.D., Columbia, 1935; m. Harry Etra, Apr. 19, 1939; children—Aaron, Marshall, Donald, Jonathan. Admitted to N.Y. bar, 1939; mem. firm Hartman, Sheridan, Tekulsky & Pecora, 1939-40; asso. Etra & Etra, N.Y.C., 1940—. Bd. overseers Albert Einstein Coll. Medicine; bd. dirs. United Jewish Appeal Greater N.Y. Recipient Louise Waterman Wise award for pub. service Am. Jewish Congress, 1971. Mem. N.Y. Women's Bar Assn. Home: 35 E 84th St New York City NY 10028 Office: 745 Fifth Av New York City NY 10022

ETTINGER, ALICE, physician; b. Berlin, Germany; M.D., Berlin U., 1926, Freiburg U. (Germany), 1926. Intern, Children's U. Hosp., Berlin, Germany, Moabit City Hosp., Berlin, 1926; asst. in internal medicine 2d U. Clin. Charite, Berlin, 1927-28; asst. X-ray dept. Berlin

Hosp., 1928-30; resident in roentgenology Boston Dispensary, 1932-38; chief radiologist in chief Joseph H. Pratt Diagnostic Hosp., 1938-65; sr. radiologist New Eng. Center Hosp., 1965-70; 1st asst. prof. radiology Tufts Med. Sch., 1943-50, clin. prof. roentgenology, 1950-59, prof. roentgenology, chmn. dept., 1959-65, prof. emeritus, 1965—, coordinator teaching radiology to med. students, 1970—. Diplomate Am. Bd. Radiology. Fellow Am. Coll. Radiology; mem. A.M.A., N.E. Roentgen Ray Soc., Radiol. Soc. N. Am., Am. Roentgen Ray Soc. Address: 171 Harrison Av Boston MA 02111

ETTINGER, ANNA MARIE CONWAY (MRS. RALPH DAVIS ETTINGER), educator; b. Janesville, Wis., Nov. 4, 1925; d. Martin and Anna (Dawson) Conway; B.S., U. Wis., 1946, M.S., 1950; Ph.D., U. Ill., 1967; m. Ralph Davis Ettinger, Apr. 26, 1969. Elementary, high sch. tchr., Barrington, Ill., 1946-49; high sch. tchr., Joliet, Ill., Joliet Jr. Coll., 1950-55; teaching fellow anatomy U. Wis., Madison, 1955-57; instr. anatomy dept. St. Louis Med. Sch., 1957-63; research asst. NSF, U. Ill., Chgo., 1965-66; faculty U. Detroit Dental Center, 1967—, asso. prof. dept. anat. scis., 1969—. Dir. research grant NIH, Detroit, 1969-73. Mem. Am. Assn. U. Profs., Sigma Xi, Omicron Kappa Upsilon. Home: 540 S Holly Rd Fenton MI 48430 Office U Detroit 2985 E Jefferson Av Detroit MI 48207

ETTINGER, CHARLOTTE KAHN (MRS. MORTON ETTINGER), educator; b. Malden, Mass., Jan. 26, 1930; d. Barney Louis and Matilda Louise (Cohen) Kahn; B.A., Emerson Coll., 1950, M.A., 1965; m. Morton Ettinger, Nov. 12, 1950; children—Linda Joyce, Steven, Alan, Jonathan, Mark. Grad. asst. Emerson Coll., 1964; instr. Salem (Mass.) State Coll., 1965-70, asst. prof. speech and theatre, 1970—, chairwoman speech and theatre dept., 1971—. Actress, Marblehead (Mass.) Little Theatre, 1955-65; mem. Marblehead Arts Festival. Mem. Am. Theatre Assn., Speech Communication Assn., New Eng. Theatre Conf. Home: 51 Auburndale Rd Marblehead MA 01945 Office: Salem State Coll Salem MA 01970

ETTLESON, BARBARA LOUISE, univ. adminstr.; b. Chgo., July 14, 1947; d. Leo and Ruth Esther (Wortman) Ettleson; B.S., U. Wis., 1969; M.A., U. Ia., 1972. Tchr., Peabody Elementary Sch., Chgo., 1969-70; head resident U. Ia., Iowa City, 1970-73, extension program asso., inst. pub. affairs, 1974—; area dir. Trenton (N.J.) State Coll., 1973-74. Mem. adv. bd. Women's Resource and Action Center, Iowa City, 1974—. Mem. Am. Personnel and Guidance Assn. Home: 720 N Van Buren St Iowa City IA 52240

ETTLINGER, EDITH, social worker; b. N.Y.C., Dec. 23, 1914; d. Isaac Archibald and Emma (Masur) Elkes; B.A., Hunter Coll., 1934; postgrad. Columbia Sch. Social Work, 1957-58; M.S.W., Fordham U., 1962; m. James R. Wechsler, Aug. 10, 1935 (div. 1950); children—Elizabeth Gail (Mrs. Daniel Berson), Laura (Mrs. Joseph Nodelman); m. 2d, Ernest Ettlinger, July 15, 1952 (div. 1964); 1 stepdau., Joan (Mrs. William K. Herman). Social worker N.Y.C. Dept. Welfare, 1940-44, 49-52, 53-60, Kingsbridge Home and Hosp. for Aged and Infirm, 1952-53; social worker Bur. of Attendance, N.Y.C. Bd. Edn., 1960-66; acting supr. Casework Unit II, E. Harlem office, N.Y.C., 1965-66; Bur. Child Guidance sch. social worker Benjamin Franklin High Sch., N.Y.C., 1966-74; cons. in pvt. practice, 1974—. Cons. social work N.Y.C. Housing Authority, 1964; cons. social worker Congl. Investigation of Aid for Dependent Children, 1964; cons. Head Start, 1966, Non-Public Sch. Program Title I, 1965, 66, Astor Gardens Nursing Home, N.Y.C., 1970. Field instr. Fordham U. Sch. Social Service. Mem. Nat. Assn. Social Workers (mem. steering com. council on schs. 1962-67, chmn. 1967-69; bd. dirs. 1967-69), Acad. Certified Social Workers, Council of Psychiat. Social Workers, N.Y. State Sch. Social Workers Assn. Home: 901 Walton Av New York City NY 10452

ETTRE, KITTY POLONYI (MRS. L.S. ETTRE), elec. equipment mfg. co. exec.; b. Budapest, Hungary, Aug. 19, 1930; d. Eugene and Eva (Hertzka) Polonyi; M.S. Chem. Engring., Tech. U., Budapest, 1952; m. L.S. Ettre, May 16, 1952; 1 dau., Julie Suzanne. Came to U.S., 1958, naturalized, 1965. Chemist Research Inst. Heavy Chem. Industries, Budapest, 1952-54; research chemist Inst. Telecommunication, Budapest, 1954-56; chemist Max Planck Inst. for Biophysics, Frankfurt, Main, Germany, 1957-58; devel. engr. Machlett Labs., Springdale, Conn., 1958-63; pres. Vitta Corp., Wilton, Conn., 1963—. Fellow Inst. Ceramic Engrs.; mem. Am. Soc. Testing and Materials, Am. Chem. Soc., Am. Ceramic Soc., Internat. Soc. Hybrid Microelectronics, Soc. Aerospace Engrs. Contbr. articles to profl. jours. Patentee in field. Home: 157 Grumman Av Norwalk CT 06851 Office: 382 Danbury Rd Wilton CT 06897

EUBANK, MARJORIE HARRELL (MRS. JAMES VINCENT EUBANK, JR.), educator; b. Detroit, Aug. 12, 1914; d. Henry Harrison and Mellie Dott (Fisher) Harrell; student John B. Stetson U., 1933-36; A.B. in Edn., U. Mich., 1937, M.A., 1959, Ph.D., 1968; m. James Vincent Eubank, Jr., Feb. 9, 1941; children—James Harrell, Mellie Elizabeth. Tchr. speech, Miami, Fla., 1937-41; elementary sch. tchr., Warwick, Va., 1951-55, vis. tchr., 1955-56; tchr. speech and drama, Newport News, Va., 1956-60, Utica, Mich., 1960-64; teaching fellow speech dept. U. Mich., 1964-68; prof. speech Va. Commonwealth U., Richmond, 1968-70; speech and theatre edn. coordinator R.I. Coll., Providence, 1970—. Mem. Speech Communication Assn., Speech Assn. Eastern States, Ednl. Theatre Assn. R.I. Home: 95 Olney Av North Providence RI 02911

EUBANK, MIRIAM DOROTHY (MRS. RICHARD WARD JONES), ophthalmologist; b. Kansas City, Mo., July 15, 1909; d. Ambrose Eastin and Dorothy May (Smiley) Eubank; student Kansas City Jr. Coll., 1926-28; A.B., U. Mo., 1930; M.D., U. Kan., 1934; m. Richard Ward Jones, June 25, 1938; children—Richard Mahlon, Judith May (Mrs. Michael Paul Canning), Lawrence Gurdon. Intern, N.Y. Infirmary for Women and Children, N.Y.C., 1934-35; resident Ill. Eye and Ear Infirmary, Chgo., 1935-36; exchange resident Eye Inst., Columbia Med. Center, N.Y.C., 1936, Wilmer Inst., John Hopkins, Balt., 1936, Mayo Clinic, Rochester, Minn., 1937, Cleve. Clinic, 1937; practice medicine specializing in ophthalmology, Evanston, Ill., 1938—; mem. staff Evanston Hosp.; asso. in ophthalmology Northwestern Med. Sch., Chgo., 1944—. Mem. Chgo. Ophthalmol. Soc. (pres. 1969-70), Ill., Chgo. med. socs., Chgo. Inst. Medicine, A.M.A., Am. Acad. Ophthalmology and Otolaryngology, Pan Am. Ophthalmol. Soc., A.C.S., Internat. Coll. Surgery, Am. Assn. Ophthalmology, Delta Gamma (shield award). Conglist. Club: Zonta (merit award) (Evanston). Home: 2618 Orrington Av Evanston IL 60201 Office: 636 Church St Evanston IL 60201

EUBANKS, ELINOR MAE, answering service exec.; b. Park Falls, Wis., Dec. 24, 1911; d. Jay H. and Mabel Edith (Pinkerton) Eubanks; student Northland Coll., Ashland, Wis., 1929-31, U. Minn., 1931-32; B.E., Central State U., Stevens Point, Wis., 1934; postgrad. U. Wis., summer 1935. Tchr. English, Ladysmith (Wis.) High Sch., 1934-37; payroll clk. Dept. Agr., Indio, Cal., 1937; sec. United Date Growers of Cal., Indio, 1937; cashier Cal. Electric Power Co., Indio, 1937-42; social worker Riverside County Welfare Dept., Indio, 1942-46; office mgr. Lone Palm Hotel, Palm Springs, Cal., 1946-47, Wonder Palms Hotel, Palm Springs, 1947; social worker Riverside County Gen. Hosp., Arlington, Cal., 1948; classified advt. mgr. Indio Daily News, 1948-52; sec. Planning Commn., Indio, 1948-54, Indio Merc. Co., 1952-54; owner, mgr. Coachella Valley Answering Service, Indio, 1955—, Answering Palm Desert, 1971—. Mem. Asso. Telephone Answering Exchanges, Inc., Telephone Answering Services of Cal., Order Eastern Star, Sigma Tau Delta, Tau Gamma Beta. Democrat. Presbyn. Address: 45-495 Smurr St Indio CA 92201

EUBANKS, FRANCES OLIVE DOWELL (MRS. ELI T. EUBANKS), oil co. exec.; b. Wellsford, Kan.; d. Frank E and Eva (Thomas) Dowell; student U. Kan., 1945-46; B.S., Kan. State U., 1949, M.S., 1950; m. Eli T. Eubanks, Dec. 23, 1940. Teaching fellow dept. home mgmt. Kan. State Coll., Manhattan, 1949-50; instr. U. Louisville, 1950-51, U. Wash., Seattle, 1951-52; mgr. records dept. Adair Oil Co., Wichita, Kan., 1955—; dir. Augusta Plaza, Inc., Wichita. Sec. Young Democrats Club, U. Kan., 1945-46. Mem. Omicron Nu, Phi Kappa Phi. Home: Route 3 Viola KS 67149 Office: PO Box 7011 Wichita KS 67149

EUDALY, HAZEL MARIE (PEN NAME MARIA SADDLER DE EUDALY), editor; b. Appleton City, Mo., Dec. 22, 1911; d. Russell Godby and Bertha (Piepmeier) Saddler; student William Jewell Coll., 1929-31; B.S. in Edn., Central Mo. State Tchrs. Coll., 1936; M.R.E., Southwestern Bapt. Theol. Sem., 1939, postgrad., 1956-57, 62-63; m. Nathan Hoyt Eudaly, Nov. 22, 1941;children—Richard Milton, Katharine (Mrs. William George Hart), Nathan Hoyt. Tchr. pub. schs., Amsterdam, Mo., 1931-37; with ednl. sects. Bapt. Ch., 1939—, editor, writer Bapt. Spanish Pub. House, Fgn. Mission Bd. El Paso, 1948—. Curriculum cons. Bapt. World Alliance, 1966. Active local chpts. P.T.A., 1960-68, chmn. life edn. com. dist. XV, 1971—; pres. Austin High Sch. chpt. Am. Field Service, 1969—, host 1971-72. Recipient Life Service award Southwest Bapt. Coll. Mem. Sigma Delta Pi. Mem. Order Eastern Star. Author: 19 books in Spanish and English, including: Dickie in Mexico, 1949; Chatting With the Chews, 1950; Object Lessons, 1952; My Helpers, 1957; My Friends, 1958; My Family, 1959; Stories of the New Testament, 1970. Address: PO Box 4255 7000 Alabama El Paso TX 79914

EUPER, SISTER JO ANN, archivist; b. Panama City, Republic of Panama, July 25, 1938; d. Raymond S. and Philomene (Amedeo) Euper; student U. Mich., 1956-58; B.A., Mich. State U., 1960; M.Mus. Edn., U. Kan., 1966, Ph.D. (Nat. Defense Edn. Act grantee), 1973. Music therapist Greystone Park (N.J.) State Hosp., 1960-64, Hosp. Neuro-Psiquiatrico, Tegucigalpa, Honduras, 1966-68; instr. music therapy Lincoln U., Jefferson City, Mo., 1968-69, U. Kan., Lawrence, 1970-71; joined religious order Sch. Sisters of St. Francis, Milw., 1972, research, 1973—; music therapist Alverno Child Devel. Center, Milw., 1972-73. Instr. mental health Hosp. Improvement Program, Larned, Kan., 1965-66; instr. choral and piano Sch. for the Blind, Teguicigalpa, 1966-68; cons. music dept. Alverno Coll., Milw., 1973—. Mem. Nat. Assn. for Music Therapy (mem. exec. com. 1970—). Editor: Jour. Music Therapy, 1970—. Contbr. articles in field to profl. jours.

EURICH, NELL PLOPPER (MRS. ALVIN C. EURICH), ednl. adminstr.; b. Norwood, O., July 28, 1919; d. Clayton W. and Adah (Palmer) Plopper; A.A., Stephens Coll., 1939; A.B., Stanford, 1941, M.A., 1943; Ph.D. in English Lit., Columbia, 1959; m. Alvin C. Eurich, Mar. 15, 1953; children—Juliet Ann, Donald Alan. Dir. Student Union, U. Tex., 1942-43; resident counselor Barnard Coll., 1944-46; asst. to pres. Woman's Found., 1947-49; pub. relations officer State U. N.Y., Albany and N.Y.C., 1949-52; acting pres. Stephens Coll., 1952, dir. devel. N.Y. office, 1953-54; asst. prof. English, Washington Square Coll. N.Y.U., N.Y.C., 1959-64; acad. dean, chmn. ednl. policies com. of bd. New Coll., Sarasota, Fla., 1965—, trustee, 1962—; dir. com. to reorganize curriculum Aspen Pub. High Sch., 1966; dean faculty Vassar Coll., Poughkeepsie, N.Y., 1967-70; provost, dean faculty Manhattanville Coll., Purchase, N.Y., 1970—, prof. English, dir. curriculum devel., 1971—. Cons. Acad. Ednl. Devel., 1970-71; mem. selection com. on fellowships Nat. Endowment for Humanities, 1966-67, cons., 1970-71; mem. spl. com. on liberal studies Am. Assn. Colls., 1966-70; mem. Mid-States selection com. Marshall Fellowships, 1967-68, chmn. Northeastern com. Marshall scholarships, 1969-71; mem. panel judges Fed. Woman's Award, 1969; mem. U.S. Commn. on Ednl. Tech., 1968-69; mem. career minister rev. bd. U.S. Dept. State, 1972; participant Ditchley Conf. V, Eng., 1973. Trustee, Bank Street Coll., N.Y.C., 1953-55, Hudson Guild Neighborhood House, 1947-54, 70-73, Colo. Rocky Mountain Sch., 1965-66, New Coll., Sarasota, Fla., 1962—, Salisbury (Conn.) Sch., 1973—; mem. overseers com. on summer sch. and univ. extension Harvard, 1969—. Mem. Modern Lang. Assn., World Soc. for Ekistics, Nat. Council Women (hon.). Author: Science in Utopia, 1967; Britain's Open University, 1971; contbr. chpt. to Learning for Tomorrow (Alvin Toffler), 1974; also articles to profl. jours. Home: 24 W 55th St New York City NY 10019 also Hubbell Mountain Rd Sherman CT 06784 Office: Manhattanville Coll Purchase NY 10577

EUSTICE, KAREN LEE, cons.; b. Redwood Falls, Minn., Jan. 8, 1937; d. John Donald and Doris Margaret (Gumo) Eustice; student St. Marys Coll., South Bend, Ind., 1955-57; B.A., Coll. St. Catherine, 1959. Exec. dir., camp founder, dir. United Cerebral Palsy, Schenectady, N.Y., 1964-72; cons. occupational therapy United Cerebral Palsy, St. Paul, 1973—. Vice regent Sweet Adelines, Region I, 1972-73, pub. relations Region VI, 1973—; sr. adviser Girl Scouts Am., Schenectady, 1964-65. Mem. Am. Occupational Therapy Assn. Home: 1211 Lakeview Av Minneapolis MN 55416 Office: 1821 University Av St Paul MN 55104

EUTERMOSER, THELMA, mfg. co. exec.; b. Phila., Nov. 20, 1915; d. Frederick Albert and Sophie (Winterstein) Tuckmantel; grad. high sch.; m. Frederick Eutermoser, Apr. 22, 1939 (dec. Sept. 1971); children—Fred, Mark. With Olney Pipe Products Co., Quakertown, Pa., 1959—, treas, 1966—. Baptist (deaconess). Mem. Order Eastern Star. Home: P O Box 305 Trumbauersville PA 18970 Office: 712 Tollgate Rd Quakerstown PA 18951

EUTSLER, LUELLA SHATTUCK (MRS. DANIEL DODGE EUTSLER), librarian; b. Erie, Pa., Oct. 9, 1911; d. Arthur Hill and Pearl Leona (Wiedler) Shattuck; student Edinboro State Tchrs. Coll., 1929-31; B.A., Berea Coll., 1933; M.S., Case Western Reserve U., 1954; m. Daniel Dodge Eutsler, Dec. 26, 1935; children—Patricia (Mrs. Malcolm Gillis), Robert Lee. Librarian, Manassas (Va.) High Sch., 1950-55; reference librarian Wittenberg U. Library, Springfield, O., 1955—, asso. prof., 1974—. Mem. Adminstrv. subcom. Comprehensive Study Springfield City Schs., 1970-71. Recipient Lilly Endowment Study grant Am. Theol. Library Assn., 1959, Nat. Def. Edn. Act grant U. Hawaii, 1968. Mem. Am. Assn. U. Profs., Gen. Soc. Mayflower Descs., Am., Ohio library assns., Clark County Hist. Soc., Phi Kappa Phi, Beta Phi Mu. Republican. Methodist. Home: 370 E Cassilly St Springfield OH 45503

EVANGER, JACQUELINE RUTH GORSUCH (MRS. NORMAN JOHN EVANGER), librarian; b. Cedaredge, Colo., Aug. 11, 1926; d. Scott Davis and Zella Ione (Goddard) Gorsuch; student U. Colo., 1943-45, Western State Coll., 1945-46; m. William Oscar Pyles, Oct. 3, 1946 (div. Oct. 1959); children—William Scott, James Rudd; m. 2d, Norman John Evanger, Apr. 7, 1961. Tech. librarian Climax Molybdenum Co. (Colo.), 1955-56, 59-73; owner Totem Pole, Frisco, Colo., 1956-59; adminstr. records and tech. information Indsl. Mineral Ventures, Inc., Golden, Colo., 1973—. Vice pres. Colo. Labor Council, AFL-CIO, 1971—; pres. Office and Profl. Employees Internat. Union Local, 1967-73. Mem. Colo. Rivers Council, 1971—; trustee Town of Frisco, Summit County, Colo., 1954-59, 71—, chmn. adminstr. com., 1972—; bd. dirs., sec. Summit County Sch. Dist., 1959-61. Chmn. Democratic Central Com., 1972—. Mem. Spl. Libraries Assn. (historian 1971—), Am. Records Mgmt. Assn., Indsl. Relations Research Assn. (mem. on-going program com. 1973-74), Am. Inst. Mining, Metall. and Petroleum Engrs., Summit Hist. Soc. (exec. bd., sec. 1970-73), Summit Citizens Assn. Home: 702 Frisco St Frisco CO 80443 Office: 5920 McIntyre St Golden CO 80401

EVANOFF, DEBORAH A. (MRS. EDMUND A. EVANOFF), retail clothing exec.; b. Chgo., July 14, 1944; s. William David and Crescentia Agnes (Baier) Starnes; Marquette U. Coll. Nursing, 1962-64; m. Edmund A. Evanoff, May 8, 1965; children—Michael, John, Mark. Corporate officer, treas. Evanoff's Inc., Sheboygan Falls, Wis., 1965—, clothing buyer, 1968—. Cath. religious edn. tchr., 1967—. Republican campaign chmn. Sheboygan Falls, 1970, 72. Bd. dirs. Sheboygan Co. Halfway House, 1970-72. Recipient awards of Honor for services Wis. Mental Health Assn., Wis. Assn. Retarded Children, 1970. Mem. Jaycettes (chmn. state mental health and retardation com. 1969-70, state dir. 1970-71, chpt. pres. 1973-74). Roman Catholic (pres. ch. Confrat. Christian Doctrine 1969-74, mem. sch. edn. com. 1971-74). Home: 554 Lynwood Dr Sheboygan Falls WI 53085

EVANS, ALONA ELIZABETH, educator; b. Providence, Feb. 27, 1917; d. Robert R. and Florence (Weatherhead) Evans; A.B., Duke, 1940, Ph.D., 1945. Intern, Personnel Adminstrn. War Dept., 1942; jr. divisional asst. Dept. State, 1942-43; instr. polit. sci. Duke, 1944-45; instr. govt. Westminster Coll., 1945; instr. Wellesley Coll., 1945-48, asst. prof., 1948-52, asso. prof., 1952-58, prof., 1958—, chmn. dept. polit. sci., 1959-70, 72-73, Elizabeth Kimball Kendall prof. polit. sci., 1966—; vis. prof. internat. law Sch. Law, U. Puget Sound, 1973-74; participant 1st Fulbright Inst. in Indian Civilization, Hyderabad, India, summer 1961. Mem. environmental health task force Mass. Office Comprehensive Health Planning, 1969-70. Recipient of Social Science Research Council fellowship, 1948-49; Harbison Fund award Wellesley Coll., 1954-55; fellow in law and polit. sci. Harvard Law Sch., 1961-62, 71-72; Am. Philos. Soc. grantee, 1971-72. Mem. Am. Soc. Internat. Law (exec. council 1956-59, 65-68), Internat. Law Assn. (chmn. Am. br. com. legal problems asylum 1963—, exec. com. 1971—, chmn. com. internat. terrorism London br.), Indian Soc. Internat. Law, Am. Polit. Sci. Assn., Am. Assn. U. Women (bd. dirs. 1963-67, cons. 1968-70; recipient Achievement award 1971), Internat. Fedn. U. Women (council 1963-67), New Eng. Polit. Sci. Assn. (pres. 1966-67), Am. Assn. U. Profs., Phi Beta Kappa. Contbr. legal, polit. sci. jours. Bd. editors Am. Jour. Internat. Law, 1966—. Home: 22 Fiske House Wellesley MA 02181

EVANS, AUDREY ELIZABETH, educator; b. York, Eng., Mar. 6, 1925; d. Llewellyn and Phyllis Mary (Miller) Evans; Licentiate, S.E., Sch. Medicine, Royal Coll. Edinburgh, 1950. Came to U.S., 1957, naturalized, 1962. Physician, tumor therapy Children's Hosp. of Boston, 1957-65; asst. prof., pediatric hematologist U. Chgo., 1965-69; prof. pediatrics U. Pa., 1969—; dir. oncology Children's Hosp. Phila., 1969—. Home: 266 W Rittenhouse Sq Philadelphia PA 19103 Office: Children's Hospital of Phila 34th and Convention Center Blvd Philadelphia PA 19104

EVANS, BARBARA JOAN MARCELO (MRS. FREDERICK J. EVANS), pediatrician; b. Phila., Dec. 28, 1942; d. Arthur and Bertha (Robinson) Marcelo; A.B. (Sons of Italy scholar), Immaculata Coll., 1964; M.D., Women's Med. Coll. Pa., 1968; m. Frederick J. Evans, June 8, 1968; children—Christopher Arthur, David Troy. Intern St. Christophers Hosp. for Children, Phila., 1968-69, resident, 1969-71, fellow in pediatric habilitation, 1971-72; fellowship in pediatric neurology United Cerebral Palsy Research and Ednl. Found., 1972-73; neurodevelopmental cons. Pediatric Group Services, Med. Coll. Pa., 1973—; clin. instr. Temple U. Hosp., 1973—; instr. pediatrics Med. Coll. Pa.; physician St. Christopher's Hosp., Mercy Med. Catholic Center, Med. Coll. Pa. Nat. Inst. Mental Health Fellow Pa. Inst., summers 1965-66. Diplomate Am. Bd. Pediatrics. Fellow Am. Acad. Cerebral Palsy; mem. Am. Acad. Pediatrics, Am. Med. Women's Assn. Home: 3427 Indian Queen Lane Philadelphia PA 19129 Office: 3300 N Henry Av Room 422 H Philadelphia PA 19133

EVANS, BETTY BOLLBACK (MRS. C. HANS EVANS), educator; b. Bklyn., May 28, 1927; d. Anthony J. and Elizabeth (Balzer) Bollback; B.R.E., Nyack Coll., 1949; M.A., N.Y.U., 1951; post-grad. Northwestern U., 1953, Columbia, 1952-57; m. C. Hans Evans, June 10, 1961. Audiologist, Manhattan Eye, Ear, Nose and Throat Hosp., N.Y.C., 1949-54; tchr. Lexington Sch. for Deaf, N.Y.C., 1954-59; supervising tchr. N.Y. Sch. for Deaf, White Plaines, N.Y., 1959-60; ednl. cons. Pa. Sch. for Deaf, Phila., 1960-68; prin. Middle Sch., Pa. Sch. for Deaf, 1968-71; asst. prof. spl. edn. Pa. State U., University Park, 1962-71; specialist in deaf edn. Chester County Child Devel. Center, 1971—. Cons. Nat. Com. on Library Standards for Schs. for Deaf, N.Y., 1965-66; lectr. civic religious and profl. groups. Mem. Chester County Health and Welfare Assn., 1962; social dir. Word of Life Summer Confs., N.Y., 1955-60. Bd. dirs. Heartsease Home for Woman, N.Y.C. Mem. Coatesville Hosp. Aux., Westminster Aux. (pres. 1969), Octarara Hist. Soc., Alexander Graham Bell Assn. for Deaf, Conv. Am. Instrs. for Deaf. Republican. Presbyn. Club: Coatesville Century. Home: 359 E Lincoln Hwy Coatesville PA 19320 Office: 1525 E Lincoln Hwy Coatesville PA 19320

EVANS, CAROL ANN, motel exec.; b. Holden, Mass., Jan. 1, 1941; d. Raymond Betts and Edith Clara (Ekeroth) Evans; ed. U. Ala. With Woodbury & Co., Inc., Worcester, Mass., 1962-65; editor co. newspaper E.F. Laurence Co., Northboro, Mass., 1971; fund raiser, campaign mgr. Owen C. Coogan Co., Worcester, 1972; mgr. Howard Johnson Motor Lodge, West Boylston, Mass., 1973—. Vice pres. Young Republican Club, Worcester, 1968-69; sec. Rutland (Mass.) Rep. Town Com., 1969-70. Served with WAF, 1959-62. Home: 286 Main St Boylston MA 01505 Office: 181 W Boylston St West Boylston MA 01583

EVANS, CAROLYN RUTH, extension communications specialist; b. Lincoln, Neb., Aug. 16, 1927; d. Lloyd Alvin and Mildred May (Griggs) Gerstenberger; B.F.A., U. Ill., 1950; student summers U. Colo., 1948, Knox Coll., 1949; m. James Howard Evans, Sept. 11, 1949; children—James R., Julia A., Paul R., Lisa E. Sales and advt. mgr. Chillicothe Developers, Inc. real estate, (Ill.), 1961-63; profl. practice archtl. renderings, graphic design, Chillicothe, 1961-64; Coop. Extension Service communications specialist Office Agrl. Communications, U. Ill., Urbana, 1967—. Mem. exec. bd. P.T.A., Chillicothe, 1962; den mother Cub Scouts, Chillicothe, 1960-62. Precinct com. woman Republican party, Chillicothe, 1961-64. Recipient Nat. Farm Film Found. award for short films, 1971, Champion Papers award for highest standards in graphic arts, 1971. Mem. Am. Assn. Agrl. Editors, Kappa Kappa Gamma. Mem. Ch. of Christ. Home: 2304 Brookhaven Dr Champaign IL 61820 Office: Mumford Hall Cooperative Extension Service U Ill Urbana IL 61801

EVANS, DORIS LOUISE, crystallographer; b. Weehawken, N.J., July 2, 1923; d. DeWitt F. and Ray A. (Carpenter) Evans; B.A., Hunter Coll., 1943; M.A., N.Y. U., 1945; Ph.D. (NIH fellow), U. London, 1969. Tech. asst. Bell Telephone Labs., 1942-45; microwave engr. Sperry Gyroscope Co., 1945-48; physicist Mt. Sinai Hosp., N.Y.C., 1948-51; asso. research specialist in x-ray diffraction Rutgers U., 1951-59; research asso. Corning Glass Works (N.Y.), 1959—. Tchr. radio and elec. engring., 1947-51. Mem. Am. Crystallographic Assn., Am. Inst. Physics. Research on nucleation and crystallization of metastable glasses, structure of glasses and liquids. Home: RD 1 Watkins Glen NY 14891 Office: Sullivan Park Corning Glass Works Corning NY 14830

EVANS, DAME EDITH (MARY), actress; b. London, Eng., Feb. 8, 1888; d. Edward and Caroline Ellen (Foster) E.; student St. Michael's Sch., Pemlico; D.Litt., London U., 1950, Cambridge, 1951, Oxford, 1954; m. George Booth, 1927 (dec. Jan. 1935). Milliner's apprentice; appeared amateur drama group Streatham Shakespeare Players, as Beatrice in Much Ado About Nothing, 1912; on London stage, 1914-17, on tour Merry Wives of Windsor, Merchant of Venice; created roles of the Serpent, Oracie, She-Ancient in Back to Methuselah, Birmingham Repertory Theatre, 1923; played role of Helena, Midsummer Night's Dream, Drury Lane, 1925; 1st N.Y. stage appearance as Florence Nightingale in Lady with a Lamp, 1931; Broadway performance Katharine Cornell's prodn. Romeo and Juliet, 1934, Daphne Laureola, 1950; motion pictures include Brit. film Queen of Hearts, Dolwyn, Importance of Being Earnest, The Nun's Story, 1959, Look Back in Anger, 1959; Angel recs. Importance of Being Earnest, other Shakespeare roles; London prodns. The Dark is Light Enough, 1954-55; The Chalk Garden, 1956. Entertained troops World War II. Decorated dame comdr. Order Brit. Empire, 1946. Home: Albany Picadilly London W 1 England Office: care Angel Records 38 W 48th St New York City NY 10036*

EVANS, EDITH MAXINE (MRS. DAN EUGENE EVANS), educator; b. Haxtun, Colo., Mar. 10, 1927; d. Gade and Gladys Helena (Gaensmore) Harms; B.S., U. Colo., 1949; M.A. U. No. Colo., 1958; m. Dan Eugene Evans, Aug. 24, 1957; children—Timothy Daniel, Stephanie Jean. Tchr., Alamosa (Colo.) High Sch., 1949-51, Sterling (Colo.) High Sch., 1951-55; instr. bus. Northeastern Jr. Coll., Sterling, 1955—. Mem. Colo. State Vocational Adv. Com. Bus. and Office Edn. for Community Colls. Mem. Sterling City Planning Commn., 1970—, Colo. Adv. Bd. on Tchr. Edn., 1973—. Named Outstanding Young Tchr., Logan County, Colo., 1960. Mem. Nat., Colo., Nat. Bus., Colo. Bus. Mountain Plains bus. edn. assns., League Women Voters (pres. Sterling chpt. 1964-65, chmn. Colo. voters service 1967-71), Delta Pi Epsilon. Democrat. Episcopalian. Home: 1325 Buchanan St Sterling CO 80751

EVANS, ELINOR LUCILE, artist, educator; b. Mont Ida, Kan., Aug. 4, 1914; d. Robert Yantis and Edith (Krone) Evans; B.A., Okla. State U., 1938; M.F.A., Yale, 1954. Instr., asst. prof. Okla. State U., 1946-60, asso. prof. art, 1962-64; lectr. art U. Ill., 1960-62; prof. architecture Rice U., 1964—; exhibited Guggenheim Mus., Mus. Contemporary Crafts, Bklyn. Mus., Chgo. Art Inst., Los Angeles County Mus., Pasadena (Cal.) Art Mus., Nelson Gallery, Kansas City, Dallas Mus. Fine Arts. Recipient Nat. Merit award for tapestry Craftsmen U.S.A., 1966. Home: 7020 Staffordshire St Houston TX 77025

EVANS, ELLA SMITH (MRS. ROBERT KERR EVANS), clubwoman; b. Raleigh, N.C., Sept. 7, 1902; d. Robert Ira and Maggie Nancy (Bagwell) Smith; tchrs. certificate, N.C. State Coll., 1923; certificate Kings Bus. Coll., 1926; m. Robert Kerr Evans, Nov. 9, 1928; children—Nancy Errol (Mrs. Nancy Evans Hainlin), Robert Smith. Tchr., Raleigh pub. schs., 1923-24; adminstrv. sec. to pres. Meredith Coll., Raleigh, 1936; adminstrv. sec. to dean grad. sch. N.C. State Coll., Raleigh, 1927-31; head of hall, gen. hostess state camps N.C. F.F.A.; ofcl. notary public, 1961-64. Mem. Woman's Aux., Lee County Hosp., Opelika, Ala., 1964-65. Mem. U.D.C. (registrar, chmn. membership com., mem. edn. com., del. to state conv. Adm. Semmes chpt. 57, state del. Johnston Pettigrew chpt. 1970—), D.A.R. (chmn. nominating com., hostess chmn. Cashwell-Nash chpt. 1970—, co-chmn. press book, co-chmn. mag. com., registrar, treas. Light Horse Harry Lee chpt. 1968-69; mem. Ala. officers club 1969), Colonial Dames XVII Century (charter mem., v.p., mem. screening com., alternate del. to state conv. Capt. Thomas Yale chpt., spl. nat. award for contbrn. to history of chpt. 1968, chmn. membership com., auditor Sir Walter Raleigh chpt. 1970), Nat., E. Ala. geneal. socs., Jamestowne Soc., Nat. Huguenot Soc., Nat. Soc. So. Dames Am., Nat. Ret. Tchrs. Assn., Nat. Soc. Magna Charta Dames, Soc. Descs. Colonial Clergy, Daus. Am. Colonists (charter mem.; sec.-treas., chaplain chpt. 1968-69), Colonial Order of Crown, Sovereign Colonial Soc., Ams. Royal Descent, Knights Garter, Plantagenet Soc. Democrat. Baptist (v.p. Wesleyan Service Guild 1964-65). Clubs: Woman's of Auburn (over-all hostess chmn. 1965-66), Auburn University Campus, Auburn Minerva (pres. 1956-58), Ala. Minerva Clubs (state pres. 1956-58); Woman's of Raleigh (house furnishings com. 1971-72, Am. Revolution Bicentennial com., reservations com. 1973). Co-compiler: The Captain Thomas Yale Chapter—Colonial Dames XVII Century—1967. Home: Beckanna Apts 508/3939 Glenwood Av Raleigh NC 27612

EVANS, EVALYN MCCOY, lumber co. exec.; b. Chippawa Falls, Wis., Sept. 17, 1907; d. John Edmund and Marjorie Catherine (McKinnon) McCoy; student Wash. State Coll., 1924-27, extension at Spokane, 1948-49, 50, U. Buffalo, 1957, 58-59; m. Robert P. Wallis, May 26, 1927 (div. Aug. 1948); children—Dexter John, R. Jerome, Joseph Winters, Katherine (Mrs. Donald C. Goetzmann); m. 2d, Joseph C.L. Evans, Mar. 17, 1953. Dir. Evans Lumber Co., Buffalo, 1967—, sec., 1969—. Chmn. Buffalo Philharmonic drive, Eggertsville, 1961; chmn. United Fund, Eggertsville, 1962, allocations rev. com., 1963-65, 69-70, 71, spl. handling chmn., 1966-68; vol., mem.'s gallery Albright-Knox Art Gallery, 1964—; mem. women's aux. Salvation Army, 1971—, dir., 1973—; fund chmn. religious edn. program retarded children Buffalo area Council Chs., 1973—. Republican. Club: Buffalo Park Country. Home: 580 LeBrun Rd Eggertsville NY 14226 Office: 1698 Genesee St Buffalo NY 14211

EVANS, GENEVIEVE MARIE (MRS. CARL LEE EVANS), security co. exec.; b. Valparaiso, Ind., May 12, 1931; d. John Selwyn and Henrietta Edna (Kitchell) Horan; grad. high sch.; m. Carl Lee Evans, Sept. 25, 1949; children—Steven Duane, Jennifer Lee, Michael Thomas. With Midwest Appliance and Frozen Foods, Gary, Ind., 1952-56, Barnett Nat. Bank, Deland, Fla., 1957-59, Hamilton Funds, Denver, 1959-67; regional v.p. Westamerica Securities, Denver, 1967—. Chmn., March of Dimes, Deland, 1959. Home: PO Box 1191 Boulder CO 80302 Office: 2777 Canyon St Boulder CO 80302

EVANS, GLORIA BUCHANAN, educator; b. Otsego, Mich., Dec. 25, 1918; d. Edward Lewis and Mattye Martha (Keith) Buchanan; B.S., U. Wis., 1940; M.A. (Rosenwald fellow), Northwestern U., 1948, Ph.D., 1963; m. June 3, 1940 (div.); 1 son, Glenn LeRoy. Personnel placement Chgo. Urban League, 1941; instr. English, LeMoyne Coll., Memphis, 1941-42; faculty Jackson (Miss.) State U., Coll., 1942—, prof. English, speech, and mass communications, 1963—. Mem. Nat. Assn. Ednl. Broadcasters, N.E.A., Speech Communication Assn. Home: 818 S Prentiss St Jackson MS 39209

EVANS, HAZEL (MRS. ROBERT WINFIELD EVANS), civic worker, nat. Democratic committeewoman from Fla.; b. Atlanta, Aug. 16, 1931; d. Alex Pierce and Hazel Deane (Thomas) Robert; grad. Marjorie Webster Jr. Coll., 1951; m. Robert Winfield Evans, Nov. 30, 1968; children by previous marriage—Walter Reed Talley, Jr., Alex Robert Talley. Campaign dir. Manatee County March of Dimes, 1957; state adviser women's activities Nat. Found. Infantile Paralysis, 1957-61; campaign chmn. Manatee County Heart Fund, 1960; pres. Manatee County Heart Council, 1960-63; v.p. Manatee County Mental Health Assn., 1960, chmn. county campaign, 1963; mem. exec. com. Fla. West Coast Symphony, 1962-64, membership chmn., 1962-63; exec. dir. Inauguration Gov. Askew, 1971; mem. Mayor's Adv. Com., St. Petersburg, 1969-71; mem. Gov.'s Pinellas County Adv. Com. commr. Pinellas County Housing Authority, 1971—. Charter mem. Manatee County Dem. Women's Club, 1st v.p., 1956-57, pres., 1957-60; mem. Fla. Dem. Com. from Manatee County, 1962-66, vice chmn. finance com., 1962-66, mem. campaign com., 1962-66, mem. from Pinellas County, 1966—, vice chmn. county liaison com., 1966-70, chmn. women's orgn. Young Dem. Clubs Fla., 1961-62, chmn. ways and means com., 1961-62, state sec., 1962-63, legislative chmn., 1963, state v.p., 1963-64; mem. Manatee County Dem. Exec. Com., 1958-64, treas., 1962, vice chmn., 1962-64, campaign chmn., 1962; mem. Pinellas County Dem. Exec. Com., 1965—, chmn. fund-raising dinner, 1966, mem. exec. adv. com., 1966—, chmn. dinner with govs., 1970; mem. adv. com. Fla. Dem. Exec. Com., 1966-70; mem. Dem. Nat. Com., 1968—, mem. freedom to vote spl. com.; vice chmn. 8th congl. dist. Fla. Dem. Com., 1966—, mem. central com., 1970—, mem. spl. com. rules, 1971; chmn. speakers com. Dem. Women's Clubs Fla., 1962-64; state chmn. women Humphrey-Muskie Pesdl. Campaign, 1968; del. Dem. Nat. Conv., 1964; del. Dem. Nat. Conv., 1968, also mem. credentials com., Fla. housing chmn. Vice pres. Suncoast Heart Assn., 1960-61, 1st v.p., 1962-64, sec., 1961-62, pres., 1965-66, chmn. bd. dirs., 1966-67; mem. state fund raising adv. com. Fla. Heart Assn., 1961-63, bd. dirs., 1962-65; bd. dirs. Manatee County United Appeal, 1961-63, 2d v.p., 1962-63, residential chmn. fund drive, 1962; bd. dirs. Pinellas County United Fund, 1967-70, residential chmn., 1965, 66; bd. dirs. Fla. Assn. Mental Health, 1963-64, mem. legislative com., 1963-65; bd. dirs. Ringling Museums Art Members Guild, 1963-64, v.p., 1962-63, 1st v.p., 1963-64; bd. dirs. Friends of Art of Ringling Museums Art, 1963-64; bd. dirs., mem. exec. com. Ringling Museums Opera Guild, 1963, 64; bd. dirs. Asolo Summer Festival, 1962-64, v.p., 1963-64. Recipient Meritorious Service award Am. Heart Assn., 1960, 64, 66; Pres.'s award Young Dem. Clubs Fla., 1963, 64, Franklin D. Roosevelt award, 1963, Senator George Smathers award, 1962. Mem. Beta Sigma Phi. Home: 1146 41st Av NE St Petersburg FL 33703

EVANS, HELEN HORLACHER (MRS. JOSEPH CARSON EVANS), civic worker; b. Fortville, Ind., June 11, 1920; d. Levi J. and Vaneta (Thomas) Horlacher; B.S., U. Ky., 1941; postgrad. U. Wis., 1941; m. Joseph Carson Evans, Aug. 14, 1948; children—Joseph Carson Jr., Elizabeth Ellen. Tchr. home econs., Versailles, Ky., 1941-42; tng. officer State Regional VA Office, Louisville, 1946-51; later substitute tchr.; friends adminstr. Ky. Ednl. TV, Lexington, 1972—. Pres. elementary, jr. high and high sch. P.T.A.s, Lexington, Ky., 1960-70; head Lexington Heart Fund drive; area capt. United Community Fund, Lexington; pres. Ky. Fedn. Women's Clubs, 1970-72. Served to capt. WAC, 1942-46; ETO. Recipient Service to Mankind award Sertoma, 1972. Mem. Ky. Hist. Soc., Audubon Soc., D.A.R. (chmn. Ky. soc. pub. relations 1968-71, chmn. Ky. soc. resolutions 1971—, chmn. pub. relations Capt. John Waller chpt. 1965—), Mortar Bd., Phi Upsilon Omicron, Phi Beta, Kappa Delta. Address: 281 Taylor Dr Lexington KY 40505

EVANS, ISABEL BICKETT (MRS. FLOYD LEE EVANS), librarian; b. Willow City, N.D., July 17, 1903; d. George Francis and Katherine (Simonieg) Bickett; A.A., St. Joseph Jr. Coll., 1924; postgrad. U. Mo., 1921; m. Floyd Lee Evans, July 28, 1926; children—Mary Ann (Mrs. John Michael Nugent), Alice Carol, Daniel F., Mark V. With St. Joseph Pub. Library 1921—, successively asst. in circulation dept., br. librarian, first asst. circulation, head reference dept., asst. librarian, 1961-63, acting dir., 1963-64, dir., 1964—. Mem. D.A.R., Am., Mo. library assns. Clubs: St. Joseph Women's Press, St. Joseph Art League, Runcie, Phillippine Duchesne Study. Home: 821 N 11th St St Joseph MO 64501 Office: 10th & Felix Sts St Joseph MO 64501

EVANS, JACQUELINE PASCAL, educator; b. Phila., Jan. 12, 1923; d. Edward Wyatt and Jacqueline (Morris) Evans; A.B., Vassar Coll., 1944; M.A., Radcliffe Coll., 1945, Ph.D., 1954. Tchr., Baldwin Sch., Bryn Mawr, Pa., 1945-46; instr. Wilson Coll., Chambersburg, Pa., 1946-49, Wellesley Coll., 1952-53, Smith Coll., 1954-56; asst. prof. Wellesley Coll., 1956-62, asso. prof., 1962-68, prof., 1968—. Mem. Am. Math. Soc., Math. Assn. Am., Am. Assn. U. Profs., Phi Beta Kappa, Sigma Xi. Author: Mathematics: Creation and Study of Form, 1970. Home: 52 S Main St Sherborn MA 01770 Office: Dept Math Wellesley Coll Wellesley MA 02181

EVANS, JANE, religious worker, editor, lectr., writer; b. N.Y.C.; grad. Xavier U., Cin. With Nat. Fedn. Temple Sisterhoods of Union Am. Hebrew Congregations (Reform Judaism), 1933—, now exec. dir.; mem. polit. sci. faculty New Sch. Social Research, N.Y.C. Cons. to U.S. delegation at drafting of UN charter, San Francisco, 1945; past chmn. com. displaced persons Am. Jewish Conf., World War II; head of delegations to UNRRA (now UNRWA) sessions, U.S., Can., Europe; pioneer woman sec., also mem. governing body, exec. com. World Union Progressive Judaism; past pres. Nat. Peace Conf.; past vice-chmn., conf. group, past exec. com. U.S. Nat. Orgns. on UN; mem. nat. panel judges ann. high sch. contest UN; sponsor UN Assn. U.S.A. Named Woman of Achievement, Fedn. Jewish Women's Orgns.; Jane Evans Wood planted by Nat. Fedn. Temple Sisterhoods, Bar Kochba Forest, Israel; recipient numerous citations. Mem. Jewish Braille Inst. Am. (treas., exec. bd.), Commn. Social Action Am. Reform Judaism (chmn. com. world peace), Joint Distbn. Com. (nat. council). Editorial bd. Dimensions mag. Address: 838 Fifth Av New York City NY 10021*

EVANS, JANE ROSSER (MRS. GEORGE F. SHEER), retail store exec.; b. Hannibal, Mo., July 26, 1944; d. Luther Terrell and Katherine (Rosser) Evans; B.A., Vanderbilt U., 1965; student L'Universite D'Aix Marseilles (Aix-en Provence France), 1962, Fashion Inst. Tech., 1965; m. George F. Sheer, 1970. Exec. trainee Genesco, Inc., Nashville, 1965, asst. shoe buyer I. Miller div. Genesco, Inc., N.Y.C., 1965-66, handbag and hosiery buyer, 1966-68, fashion coordinator I. Miller Design Studio, N.Y.C., 1968-70, pres. I. Miller div., 1970-73; mem. adv. bd. Genesco, Inc., v.p. internat. marketing Genesco's Internat. Group, 1973—. Mem. vis. com. Vanderbilt U. Grad. Sch. Mgmt. Mem. Fashion Group, Shoe Women Execs., Young Pres.'s Orgn., U.S. C. of C. (manpower com. 1971-72), Pi Beta Phi. Home: 1000 Park Av New York City NY 10028 Office: 730 Fifth Av New York City NY 10019

EVANS, JEAN MARGARET, savs. and loan exec.; b. Del Norte, Colo., Nov. 2, 1923; d. William Noah and Hattie Bell (Putnam) Evans; B.A. in Music, U. Colo., 1949. Part-owner Evans Produce Co., Del Norte, 1949-58; office mgr. Dr. A.E. Bocock, Del Norte, 1958-63; sec.-treas., mng. officer Del Norte Fed. Savs. and Loan Assn., 1963—; sec., Parker Hill Ty, Del Norte, 1962—. Mem. Colo. Gov.'s Local Affairs Study Commn., 1966-69, sec. finance com. 1966-69. Chmn. bd. trustees Kings Daus. Library, Del Norte. Mem. Gen. Fedn. Women's Clubs (state pres. 1968-70, nat. chmn. resolutions com. 1970—. Home: 582 Columbia Av Del Norte CO 81132 Office: 585 Columbia Av Del Norte CO 81132

EVANS, JOAN BEVERLY (MRS. FRED EVANS), coll. ofcl.; b. Waukegan, Ill., Dec. 31, 1949; d. John Wesley and Ruby Jewel (Macklin) Whitehead; B.S., Ill. State U., 1970, M.S., 1972; m. Fred Evans, Aug. 15, 1970. Resident asst. Ill. State U., Normal, 1969-70, asst. resident dir., 1970-72; asst. dean students Quincy (Ill.) Coll., 1972-73; dir. acad. skills center U. North Fla., Jacksonville, 1973—. Mem. Jacksonville Concert Chorale, 1973—.

EVANS, MRS. JOHN C., civic worker; b. N.Y.C., Jan. 20, 1924; d. Bernard J. and Katherine (Walsh) Markey; B.A., Coll. Mt. St. Vincent, Mt. St. Vincent-on-Hudson, N.Y., 1944; evening student Columbia; m. John Cullen Evans, Jr., Nov. 24, 1951. Rep. N.Y. Telephone Co., 1944; personnel office Sak's 34th, N.Y.C., 1944-45, tng. supr., selling and non-selling depts., 1945-49, spl. assignment for store mgr. 1949-50; non-selling tng. supr. Gimbel Bros., 1950-51. Rep. Gimbels and Sak's 34th at Nat. Conf. of Christian and Jews Retail Group meetings, 1949-50. Instr. textile painting for A.R.C., Chelsea Navy Hosp., 1952-54. Bd. dirs. Marblehead Hosp. Aid Assn., 1954, pres., 1955-58; sec. Mass. Hosp. Assn. Council of Hosp. Auxiliaries, 1957-59, chmn. North Shore region, 1959-61, chmn.-elect, 1961-62, chmn., 1962-64. Exofficio mem. bd. trustees Salem Hosp.; trustee Mary A. Alley Hosp., 1956—, chmn. bd., 1974—. Mem. Alumnae Assn. Coll. Mt. Saint Vincent, Arrangers of Marblehead (chmn. garden therapy 1967—). Clubs: Marblehead Women's Newcomers (pres. 1953). Home: 63 Longview Dr Marblehead MA 01945

EVANS, JONI (MRS. RICHARD EVANS), journalist; b. N.Y.C., Apr. 20, 1942; d. Arthur and Virginia (Sapre) Goldfinger; B.A., U. Pitts., 1963; m. Richard Evans, June 26, 1966. Asst. editor fiction dept. McCalls Mag., N.Y.C., 1963-65; asso. editor fiction dept. Ladies Home Journal, N.Y.C., 1965-67; asso. editor William Morrow & Co., N.Y.C., 1967-70, sr. editor, 1971-74; v.p., dir. subsidiary rights Simon & Schuster, N.Y.C., 1974—. Free-lance reader and reviewer Book of Month Club, 1969—. Contbr. articles N.Y. Mag., N.Y. Times Book Rev., N.Y. Times Mag. Home: 135 E 71st St New York City NY 10021 Office: Simon & Schuster 630 Fifth Av New York City NY 10020

EVANS, JOYCE STEWART (MRS. JOE MACK EVANS), ednl. adminstr.; b. Dallas, Apr. 4, 1933; d. John Benton and Phyllis Joyce (Burnton) Howell; B.S., Tex. Woman's U., Denton, 1964, M.A., 1965; Ph.D. (U.S. Office Edn. fellow), U. Tex., 1971; m. Joe Mack Evans, July 3, 1970; children—Christi, Mark, Phyllis, Patricia, Pamela. Speech therapist Mesquite Ind. (Tex.) Sch. Dist., 1965-66; tchr., speech pathologist Midland (Tex.) Ind. Sch. Dist., 1965-66; research asst. U. Tex., Austin, 1967-68, research asso., 1969, guest lectr. Coll. Edn., 1972-73; spl. project dir., program coordinator early childhood div. S.W. Ednl. Devel. Lab., Austin, 1970—. Cons. Regional Edn. Service Center Workshop, 1969, Title III Program, Birmingham, Ala., 1973. U.S.O. fellow 1964-65, 67-70. Mem. Am. Assn. U. Women, Assn. Edn. Young Children, Am. Edn. Research Assn., Assn. for Retarded Children, Assn. for Children with Learning Disabilities, Council for Exceptional Children (nat. com. on early childhood edn. 1971-73), Jr. League, Nat. Soc. for Study Edn. Episcopalian. Contbr. articles to profl. publs. Home: 5807 Trailridge Circle Austin TX 78731 Office: SW Ednl Devel Lab 211 E 7th Austin TX 78701

EVANS, JUANITA VEVA, lawyer; b. Kearney, Neb., Jan. 24, 1922; d. Lewis Ray and Veva Alwilda (Elliott) Hollingsworth; J.D. summa cum laude, Pepperdine U., 1971; m. Robert David Evans, Jan. 25, 1942; children—Linda (Mrs. Gerald Trautman), Robert David. Various positions, 1939-71; admitted to Cal. bar, 1971; research atty. Cal. 4th Dist. Ct. Appeal, 1971-72; individual practice law, San Bernardino, Cal., 1972-73, 74—; partner Goldie & Evans Law Corp., San Bernardino, 1974. Del., Democratic Primary Conv., 1962; sec. Downtown Dems. Club, 1962. First Am. Title Co., Santa Ana, Cal. scholar, 1971. Mem. Am., Cal., San Bernardino County bar assns., Cal. Trial Lawyers Assn., Am. Assn. U. Women (sec. San Gorgonio br. 1973), Bus. and Profl. Womens. Clubs (v.p. San Bernardino 1973), Zonta, Iota Tau Tau. Home: 3997 Mountain Av San Bernardino CA 92404 Office: 560 N Arrowhead Av San Bernardino CA 92401

EVANS, JUDY LEE, editor; b. Martinez, Cal., Mar. 1, 1944; d. Everett Ward and Beulah Evelyn (Rogers) Evans; B.A., Harding Coll., 1965; standard certificate Am. Inst. Banking, 1970. Relief sec. 1st Nat. Bank, Dallas, 1965, editor, photographer First Family mag., 1965—, communications adminstr., 1969—, editor, photographer 32-1 Hot Line Newsletter, 1972—. Mem. personnel adminstrn. com. Dallas Met. YWCA, 1969-73; chmn. indsl. editors com. Dallas Met. United Fund, 1969-70. Recipient 25 indsl. editing awards including award of excellence Internat. Assn. Bus. Communicators, 1971, Super Banker award, 1972; named Miss First Nat. Bank in Dallas, 1972. Mem. Internat. Assn. Bus. Communicators (3d v.p. Dallas chpt. 1969), Am. Inst. Banking (sec. Dallas chpt. 1967, dir. 1969-72, 2d v.p. 1973, 1st v.p. 1974, chmn. nat. pub. relations com. 1972-73), First Nat. Bank Club (sec. 1967). Mem. Ch. of Christ. Clubs: Chimeras, Slipper (Dallas). Home: 4319 Buena Vista St Dallas TX 75205 Office: PO Box 6031 Dallas TX 75283

EVANS, KATHRYN ANN (MRS. RODNEY LEROY EVANS), govt. ofcl.; b. Denver, May 25, 1939; d. Philip Bernard and Maye A. (Davie) Kail; B.S., Colo. State U., 1962; m. Rodney Leroy Evans, June 11, 1961; children—Bradford Lee, Daniel Joseph, Elizabeth Ann. Tchr. home econs. Telluride (Colo.) Sch., 1965—. Town trustee, Telluride, Colo., 1970-72; mayor pro-tem, Telluride, 1972—; mem. exec. bd., bd. dirs., treas. exec. bd. Region 10 Govt., Telluride, 1973—. Home: Box 82 Telluride CO 81435

EVANS, MARJORIE KRAUS (MRS. CHARLES MICHAEL EVANS), ednl. psychologist; b. Cleve., Apr. 27, 1922; d. Stephen Leopold and Edna Lois (Sill) Kraus; B.A., Flora Stone Mather Coll., 1944; M.S., Case Western Res. U., 1969; m. Charles Michael Evans, June 17, 1942; children—Charles Michael, Roger Kraus, Thomas Samuel, Laurie Tina. Psychologist Title I schs., Cleve., 1969-73, psychologist Cleve. Bd. Edn., 1973—. Certified braille transcriber Library of Congress. Mem. Am., Ohio, Cleve. psychol. assns., Ohio Sch. Psychologists Assn. Home: 17401 Shaker Blvd Cleveland OH 44120 Office: 10600 Quincy St Cleveland OH 44106

EVANS, MARJORIE WOODARD (MRS. GEORGE W. EVANS), lawyer, scientist; b. Denver, Mar. 15, 1921; d. Raymond George and Mary (Garvin) Woodard; B.A., U. Colo., 1942; Ph.D., U. Cal. at Berkeley, 1945; J.D., Stanford, 1972; m. George W. Evans, Jan. 30, 1943 (dec.); children—George Evans, Anne Garvin. Scientist, Cal. Research Corp., Richmond, 1945-46; scientist, cons. N.Y. U.,

Princeton, 1947-51; scientist Armour Research Found., Chgo., 1952-53; scientist, lab. dir. Stanford Research Inst., Menlo Park, Cal., 1953-69, dir. Poulter Lab., 1966-68, exec. dir. phys. sci., 1968-69; partner Evans Assos., Los Altos Hills, Cal., 1969-72; admitted to Cal. bar, 1972; since practiced in Palo Alto. Chmn. program com. 12th Internat. Symposium on Combustion, U. Poitiers (France), 1968. Bd. dirs. Combustion Inst., Zero Population Growth, Inc. Recipient Phoebe Hearst Distinguished Woman award, 1967, George Norlin award U. Colo., 1972. Mem. Am. Bar Assn., Cal. Trial Lawyers Assn., Am. Chem. Soc. Am. Phys. Soc., Am. Inst. Aeros. and Astronautics, Societe de Chimie Physique, Phi Beta Kappa, Sigma Xi, Delta Delta Delta. Club: Commonwealth of Cal. Contbr. numerous articles to sci. and legal jours. Office: 2600 El Camino Real Suite 506 Palo Alto CA 94306

EVANS, MARY JANE (MRS. ROBLEY DWIGHT EVANS), educator; b. Superior, Wis., Apr. 7, 1923; d. Lionel Hanford and Hazel (Newland) Larson; A.A., Ely Jr. Coll., 1942; B.S., Northwestern U., 1944; M.A., Mich. State U., 1955; student Western Res. U., 1944-45, Wis. State Coll., 1952, U. Minn., 1958-60; m. Harrison Wills-Watkins, Jr., July 6, 1946 (div. Mar. 20, 1952); m. 2d, Robley Dwight Evans, Dec. 25, 1961; 1 son, David Rees. Drama tchr. Sunbeam Sch. for Crippled Children, Cleve., 1944-46; mem. childrens theatre staff Cain Park Theatre, Cleveland Heights, O., summers 1944-45; dir. Jr. Civic Theatre, Kalamazoo, 1953-54; grad. asst. Childrens Theatre, Mich. State U., 1954-55, instr., asso. dir. Childrens Theatre, 1955-59; asst. prof. Cal. State U., Northridge, Cal., 1959-64, asso. prof. drama, 1964-69, professor of drama, since 1970—, acting chmn. dept. drama, 1964-66. Cons. Bur. Research, Office Edn., U.S. Dept. Health, Edn. and Welfare, 1965-66, field reader, 1966—; dir. Jr. Red Cross, Whittier, Cal., 1947-51, Whittier Community Theatre, 1949-51; sec. Whittier Community Coordination Council, 1949-51. Mem. Am. Theatre Assn. (sec. Children's Theatre Conf., nat. governing bd. 1958-62, adminstrv. asst. to nat. dir. 1964-65, children's theatre editor Ednl. Theatre Jour. 1968-72, nat. governing bd. 1973—), Cal. (v.p. for elementary schs. 1967-69), ednl. theatre assns., Am. Assn. U. Profs. (chpt. sec. 1960-63, chpt. exec. council 1970-71, chpt. v.p. 1971-72), Western Speech Assn., Delta Zeta, Theta Alpha Phi, Delta Kappa Gamma, Zeta Phi Eta. Republican. Episcopalian. Author: (with Jed H. Davis) Children's Theatre: Play Production for the Child Audience, 1960. Home: 16801 Lassen St Sepulveda CA 91343 Office: Cal State U 18111 Nordhoff St Northridge CA 91324

EVANS, MARY JO (MRS. RICHARD TODD EVANS), biologist; b. Maysville, Mo., Nov. 28, 1935; d. William Lloyd and Lillian Berl (Reeves) Smith; B.A., William Jewell Coll., 1957; M.S. (Research fellow), U. Mo., 1965; Ph.D., U. Tenn., 1968; m. Richard Todd Evans, Apr. 5, 1968; children—David Todd, Douglas Alden. Teaching fellow U. Tenn., Memphis, 1965-66; tng. fellow St. Jude Children's Research Hosp., Memphis, 1966-68; cancer research scientist Roswell Park Meml. Inst., Buffalo, 1968-69, sr. cancer research scientist, 1969—. Mem. Am. Soc. for Microbiology, P.E.O. Home: 23 Chestnut Hill Lane S Williamsville NY 14221 Office: 666 Elm St Buffalo NY 14203

EVANS, MYRNA M., educator; b. Ottawa, Ill., Apr. 3, 1914; d. Charles L. and Jennie M. (Zellers) McAllister; B.S., Ill. State U.. M.S., No. Ill. U., 1959, certificate advanced study, 1961; Ph.D., Lawrence U., 1971; m. Orville A. Evans, July 17, 1937 (dec.). Tchr. elementary schs., Ottawa, 1936-37, 46-48; owner, operator Grove Stables, Ottawa, 1937-42; field supr. Div. Women's and Children's Employment Ill. Dept. Labor, 1942-46; law clk., Ottawa, 1950-53; tchr. speech, coach Marquette High Sch., Ottawa, 1953-58; chmn. speech dept. LaSalle, Peru, Oglesby Jr. Coll., LaSalle, Ill., 1959-66, mem. faculty Ill. Valley Community Coll., Oglesby, 1966—, chmn. speech dept., now chmn. philosophy dept. Mem. Defender's of Wildlife, 1965—, Friends of Animals, Democratic Congl. Dist., 15th Dist, 1948-52. LaSalle County Dem. Com., 1944-48, 1965—. Chmn. Mem. Speech Communication Assn., Central States Speech Assn. Author: Oral Factors in Written Language, 1959; Chrles Stewart Parnell's American Tour, 1961; Psychology of Color, 1973; also videotapes in field. Home: 635 Bennett Av Oglesby IL 61348 Office: Ill Valley Community Coll Office 206 Rural Route 1 Oglesby IL 61348

EVANS, NANCY ANN (MRS. DANIEL JACKSON EVANS), wife of gov. Wash.; b. Spokane, Wash., Mar. 21, 1933; d. William Lawrence and Lilith (Jordan) Bell; B.A., Whitman Coll., Walla Walla, Wash., 1954; postgrad. Eastern Wash. Coll. 1956-58; m. Daniel Jackson Evans, June 6, 1959; children—Daniel Jackson, Mark Lawrence, Bruce McKay. Tchr. pub. schs. Shoreline Sch. Dist., Seattle, 1954-59; wife of gov. Wash., 1964—. Life mem. Retarded Children's Guild, Chilren's Orthopedic Guild; v.p. Seattle Symphony League; nat. chmn. First Ladies for Mental Health Month; mem. adv. bd. Seattle Youth Symphony Orch. Trustee State Capitol Mus., Seattle Symphony Orch., Tacoma Philharmonic Inc., Ballet Northwest, Patrons S. Sound Cultural Activities, Gov.'s Festival of Arts; bd. overseers Whitman Coll. Mem. Am. Assn. U. Women, Fedn. Music Tchrs. (hon. life), Mortar Bd., Delta Gamma, Mu Phi Epsilon, P.E.O. Republican. Conglist. Clubs: Washington Athletic, Corinthian Yacht. Home: Exec Mansion Olympia WA 98501

EVANS, PATRICIA TERRELL (MRS. HARRY LEROY EVANS), state ofcl.; b. New Orleans, June 5, 1931; d. Paul Wallace and Catherine Myrtle (Rappold) Terrell; B.A., Southeastern La. U., 1953; m. Harry Leroy Evans, Aug. 5, 1950; children—Debra, Matthew, Erin. Tchr. elementary sch., Baron Rouge, 1953-55; pub. affairs dir. prodn. and community problems documentaries Sta. WBRZ-TV, Baton Rouge, 1957-74; chief La. Bur. Status Women, 1974—. Cons. reading program for poverty children, 1968. Sponsor Narcotics Anonymous, La. Correctional Inst. for Women, 1971-73; founder Baton Rouge chpt. Cystic Fibrosis Assn., 1967; chmn. youth concerts Baton Rouge Symphony, 1961-62; mem. spl. com. curriculum study Baton Rouge Sch. System, 1970; founder Community Action for Corrections, 1969; mem. Commn. on Status of Women, 1973-74. Bd. dirs. Baton Rouge Ballet Theater, 1959-63. Recipient advt. awards for pub. service Baton Rouge Advt. Club, 1963, 64, 68, 69, awards for pub. service La. Dept. Edn., 1967, award La. Assn. Mental Health, 1971. Mem. Women in Communications (pres. 1966), Women in Politics (dir. 1972-73). Home: 546 Magnolia Wood Baton Rouge LA 70808 Office: State Office Bldg Baton Rouge LA 70801

EVANS, ROSALEEN MALOOLY, music dir.; b. El Paso, Tex.; d. Elias and Mamie (Coury) Malooly; B.A., Colo. Coll., 1945; M.Music, U. So. Cal., 1949; 1 son, John Anthony. Debut as concert pianist Wilshire Ebel Theater, Los Angeles, 1950; profl. operatic appearances Los Angeles Biltmore Theatre, 1949; supper clubs, 1952-60; musical dir. Dallas Summer Musicales, also O'Keefe Center, Toronto, Ont., Can., 1968, Festival Theatre, 1965-71, others; tchr. voice, theater, piano, Los Angeles, 1950, Dallas, 1955, El Paso, 1965—. Adv. bd. Festival Theater, El Paso. Named Woman of the Year for music El Paso Herald Post, 1968. Mem. Nat. Soc. Arts and Letters (v.p. 1970-71), Am. Assn. U. Women, Shakespearean Inst., Am. Ednl. Theatre Assn., Internat. Platform Assn., Mu Phi Epsilon. Club: MacDowell (El Paso). Home: 116 Sutton Pl El Paso TX 79912

EVANS, ROSEMARY KING (MRS. HOWELL DEXTER EVANS), librarian; b. Forsyth, Ga., Nov. 16, 1924; d. Wiley Gwin and Mary (Goggans) King; B.S., Tift Coll., 1957; librarian's certificate Woman's Coll. of Ga., 1963; M. Library Edn., U. Ga., 1972; m. Howell Dexter Evans, June 29, 1945; children—Joseph Williams, Curtis McKenney. Tchr. elementary sch., Forsyth, 1946-48, 54-62; librarian Mary Persons High Sch., Forsyth, 1962-72; catalog librarian Tift Coll., Forsyth, 1972—. Spiritual edn. chmn. P.T.A., 1960-61. Named Star Teacher, 1966. Mem. Nat. Ga., Monroe County (sec. 1959-60, v.p. 1961-62, pres. 1962-63) edn. assns., Ga. (dist. pres. 1965), Southeastern library assns., A.L.A. Methodist (chmn. local edn. bd. 1964-65, chmn. commn. on Christian Vocation 1965—, tchr. adult class). Clubs: Jaycettes, Woman's (1st v.p. 1955-56, chmn. edn. dept. 1959-60, chmn. pub. affairs dept. 1961-62) (Forsyth). Home: Evans Rd Smarr GA 31086 Office: Hardin Library Tift Coll Forsyth GA 31029

EVANS, RUTHANA WILSON (MRS. LIT PARKER EVANS, JR.), educator; b. Roxie, Miss., Mar. 26, 1932; d. James and Luberta (Wade) Wilson; B.S., Tougaloo Coll., 1955; postgrad. (Nat. Def. Edn. Act grantee) U. Ill., 1965, (Nat. Def. Edn. Act grantee) N.C. Coll., 1967; M.S., Delta State Coll., 1971; m. Lit Parker Evans, Jr., Mar. 22, 1957; children—Cedric Glenn, Valerie Denise. Elementary tchr., Shaw, Miss., 1955-57; tchr., curriculum chmn. Nailor Elementary Sch., Cleveland, Miss., 1957-60, tchr., librarian H.M. Nailor Sch., 1960-62, librarian, 1963-64; library supr. Bolivar County Dist. 4 elementary schs., Cleveland, 1965-68; curriculum resources tchr. ednl. tv, Jackson, Miss., 1968-70; librarian Parks and Pearman elementary schs., Cleveland, 1968-70; cons. Greenville (Miss.) Elementary Sch., 1970; edn. dir. Miss. Head Start activities, Cleveland, 1970—. Librarian, Presch. Story Hour, 1964-66, Little Rascals kindergarten, 1966-68; organizer elementary sch. library program Bolivar County, 1969, Dist. 4 Elementary Schs., 1969; job trainer Neighborhood Youth Corps, Cleveland, 1969; trainer man power program Step, Cleveland, 1970—; cons. Indianola (Miss.) presch. activities, 1971; organizer inventory, classification system Head Start, 1970. Sec., Negro's Citizens Com. Cleveland, 1957-61, P.T.A., Shaw, Miss., 1955; active Boy Scouts Am.; librarian Bapt. Tng. Union, Cleveland, 1972—. Mem. Miss. Personnel and Guidance Assn., Miss. Council Human Relations, Miss., Bolivar County tchrs. assns., N.E.A., N.A.A.C.P., Am., Miss. library assns., Miss. Retardation Assn., Negro Voters League. Democrat. Clubs: East Side High Sch. Band Booster (treas. Cleveland 1972-73), Athena Social (treas. 1971, bus. mgr. 1973), Women's (sec. Cleveland 1970). Contbr. articles to profl. jours. Home: 816 Cross St Cleveland MS 38732 Office: 321 S Sharpe St Cleveland MS 38732

EVANS, VIRGINIA JOHN, research biologist; b. Balt., Mar. 19, 1913; d. John Absalom and Stella (Lewis) Evans; A.B., Goucher Coll., 1935; M.S., Johns Hopkins, 1940, Sc.D., 1943. Asst. blood chemistry lab. Johns Hopkins, 1938-39, asst. tissue culture, 1940-41, instr. biochemistry, 1943-44; research biologist Nat. Cancer Inst., 1944-64, head tissue culture sect. Lab. Biology, 1964—. Cons., Tissue Bank, Nat. Naval Med. Center, Bethesda, Md., 1954—. Nat. Cancer Inst. fellow., 1944-46. Mem. Tissue Culture Assn. (chmn. 2d decennial rev. conf. 1966, v.p. 1968, pres. 1972, chmn. local com. 21st ann. meeting 1970), Assn. Cancer Research, Soc. Study Devel. Growth, N.Y. Acad. Scis., Soc. Exptl. Pathology, Internat., Am. socs. cell biology, Cryobiology Soc., Sigma Xi. Contbr. articles on cancer research to profl. jours. Home: 5824 Bradley Blvd Bethesda MD 20014 Office: Nat Cancer Inst Bethesda MD 20014

EVANS, VIRGINIA MORAN, author; b. Dayton, O., Mar. 2, 1909; d. Charles and Grace Evelyn (English) Moran; grad. Miami Jacobs Bus. Coll., 1928; student U. Dayton, 1951-54; m. Albert R. Evans, July 26, 1928 (dec. May 1968); children—David, Ann Virginia (Mrs. John H. Wolf, Jr.), Paul, Alan. Tchr. parochial schs., Dayton, 1957-62; writer poetry, short stories, books of poems: When March Sets Free the River (Am. Weave award), 1946; In Silence and In Thunder, 1951; Flight By Jet (Lyric Mag. Meml. award), 1962; Bee In The Wind, 1965; Eyes of the Tiger, 1970; contbr. nat. mags. Recipient Ohioana Library Sonnet awards, 1957, 59, 62; awards Poetry Soc. Ariz., Federated Poetry Soc. Ind., Ark. Writers Conf., Ark. Poetry Soc., others. Mem. Nat. League of Am. Pen Women (winner 5 nat. awards, corr. sec. Dayton br. 1965—), Poetry Reading Circle of Dayton (pres.), Poetry Soc. Am. (James Joyce award 1973), Dayton Poets' Round Table (past pres.), Poetry Soc. Tex. (several awards), Ohio Poetry Soc. (Gold Key 1955, Lyric Cup 1963), Nat. Fedn. State Poetry Socs. (1st award 1973); Versewriters Guild, Avalon, World Poetry Soc. Poetry editor The Pen Woman, 1970-72. Home: 6161 Noranda Dr Dayton OH 45415

EVE, HENRIETTA JANET, physician; b. Hot Springs, Ark., June 6, 1923; d. John Edward and Henrietta (Jenkins) Eve.; B.A., Fisk U., 1945; M.D., Howard U., 1950; m. Alphonzo Jordan, June 28, 1952 (div. Aug. 1964). Intern Harlem Hosp., N.Y.C., 1950-51; resident Freedman's Hosp., Washington, 1951-54, cardiovascular fellow, 1954-55; adminstrv. physician Internat. Garment Workers N.Y., N.Y.C., 1959-63; med. examiner Bd. Edn., N.Y.C., 1959—; physician Met. Life Ins. Co., N.Y.C., 1959-63; practice medicine, specializing in internal medicine N.Y.C., 1969—; mem. staff Madison Av. Hosp., Trafalgar Hosp.; asst. prof. medicine Howard U., Washington, 1954-56; clin. asso. dept. community medicine Mt. Sinai Sch. Medicine, 1973—. Mem. Nat. Council Negro Women, Coalition of 100 Black Women. Mem. A.M.A., N.Y. State, N.Y. County, Nat., Women's med. assns., Alpha Kappa Alpha. Democrat. Presbyn. Home: 382 Central Park W New York City NY 10025 Office: 158 E 84th St New York City NY 10028

EVEN, CHRISTA-JO CATHERINA ALTIER (MRS. ROBERT LAWRENCE EVEN), librarian; b. Chgo., May 27, 1942; c. Christopher Guy and Charlotte Ruth (Altier) Altier; B.S., Ill. State U., 1964; M.A., No. Ill. U., 1972; m. Robert Lawrence Even, Dec. 30, 1967. Librarian, William Fremd High Sch., Palatine, Ill., 1964-66; librarian Dept. Def., Misawa, Japan, 1966-67; librarian West Aurora High Sch., Aurora, Ill., 1967-68; media dir. Dekalb (Ill.) High Sch., 1969—. Mem. Am., Ill. library assns., Ill., Am. (exec. bd.) assns. sch. librarians, Nat., Ill. edn. assns. Home: 413 Fairmont Dr DeKalb IL 60115 Office: DeKalb High School S 4th St DeKalb IL 60115

EVEN, LUCILLE BARBARA MCWHINNEY (MRS. JOHN THEODORE EVEN), lawyer; b. Peoria, Ill., July 18, 1907; d. Thomas and Mary Magdalena (Rossman) McWhinney; student Bradley U., 1923-25; A.B., U. Ill., 1927; J.D. (Kappa Beta Pi scholar), Chgo. Kent Coll. Law, 1937; postgrad. Governor's State U., 1972-73; m. John Theodore Even, Dec. 30, 1931; children—Mary Jane, John R., Jean Ann. Tchr. English, Peoria Central High Sch., 1931; admitted to Ill. bar, 1937; since practiced in Chgo. and Aurora; chief congl. pub. affairs Office Econ. Opportunity, Region V, Chgo., 1970-73; counsel Fox Valley council Girl Scouts U.S.A., 1945-70, Cath. Social Service, 1950-72. Mem. Ill. Commn. on Children, 1951, 56, 58, 66; mem. adv. council Dept. Children and Family Service, 1962-72; mem. World Refugee Conf., 1958-60; del. White House Conf. on Children and Youth, 1960-61, 70-71; mem. profl. adv. com. Ill. Dept. Corrections, 1970-71, 73—; mem. adv. com. Ill. Bd. Higher Edn., 1968—; mem. Fed. Regional Council Task Force, 1971—, also mem. pub. affairs com.; mem. Council Community Services Pub. Policy Com., 1958-60; mem. adv. com. Phys. Edn. Coll., U. Ill., 1969; mem. Aurora Citizen's Com. on Revenue Sharing and Home Rule, 1972-75; mem. Sch. Dist. Com., 1968—, Integrated Grant Adminstrn., 1972—; mem. pub. policy com. Welfare Council Met. Chgo., 1962—; mem. nat. com. pub. relations Girl Scouts U.S.A., 1965-68; pres. U. Ill. Mothers Assn., 1961-62; active United Fund, United Community Services Met. Chgo. Pres., Republican Women's Club, Aurora, 1959-60; candidate Ill. Legislature, 1958; parlimentarian State Bd. Rep. Women, 1959; mem. State Com. Women for Nixon for Pres., 1968; mem. local com. Ogilvie for Gov., 1968. Mem. Am. Assn. U. Women (nat. bd. 1953-57, state pres. 1949-51), League Women Voters, Diocesan Council Cath. Women, Kappa Beta Pi. Clubs: Altrusa (pres. Aurora 1964-65), Aurora Woman's. Home: 1434 W Downer Pl Aurora IL 60506 Office: 300 S Wacker Dr Chicago IL 60606

EVERETT, KATHRINE ROBINSON (MRS. REUBEN OSCAR EVERETT), lawyer; b. Fayetteville, N.C., Sept 11, 1893; d. Henry McDiarmid and Mary Faison (Hill) Robinson; A.B., U. N.C., 1913, LL.B., 1920; postgrad. Columbia, summers 1917, 19, Cornell U., 1922; LL.D., Duke, 1972; m. Reuben Oscar Everett, June 24, 1926; children—Robinson Oscar. High sch. tchr., Mt. Airy, N.C., 1914-15, Salisbury, N.C., 1915-16; admitted to N.C. bar, 1920, practiced in Fayetteville, 1920-26, Durham, 1944—; mem. firms Robinson & Robinson, Fayetteville, 1920-26; partner Everett, Everett & Everett, attys., Durham, 1957-69, Everett, Everett, & Creech, attys., Durham, 1969—; v.p., treas. Justus Investment Corp., 1945—; dir., sec.-treas. Triangle Telecasters, Inc., Durham, N.C., 1968—; sec.-treas. E & E Devel., Chapel Hill, N.C., 1969—; dir., v.p. Poplar Apts., 1965—; v.p., sec.-treas. Karob, 1965—. Mem. Durham County Welfare Bd., 1934-51, chmn., 1950-51; N.C. region 8 chmn. women's div. War Finance Com., 1942-48, Durham County chmn. Women's div., 1942, permanent chmn. women's div. Durham County, 1945-48; civilian dir. Air Def. Filter Center, Durham County, 1952-58; mem. N.C. War Centennial Commn., 1961-65; past mem. N.C. Caswell Com.; sec. to dir. Research Information Bur., NRC. Washington, 1917-19; pres. P.T.A. City Council, Durham, 1937-39. Vice-chmn. Durham County Democratic Exec. Com., 1936-39, 46-49, 50-54; vice-chmn. Cumberland County Dem. Exec. Com., 1920-26; vice chmn. 6th congl. dist. N.C. Dem. Exec. Com., 1930-38; alderman Durham City Council, 1951-71. Trustee Stonewall Jackson Tng. Sch., Concord, N.C., 1926-44, vice-chmn., 1941-43; trustee Queens Coll., Charlotte, N.C., 1934-41. 44-53. Recipient Alumni Service award U. N.C., Greensboro, 1971. Mem. U.D.C. (pres. Durham 1934-37, 42-44, state pres. 1940-42). Colonial Dames Am. (chmn. Durham Orange Com. 1951-52), D.A.R., Dau. Founders and Patriots Am., U. N.C. Alumni Assn. (pres. Greensboro, N.C. 1926-27). Presbyn. (pres. Woman's Aux. 1931-32). Clubs: Woman's (pres. 1951-53), Tourist Literary, Allied Arts (Durham). Home: 600-2D LaSalle St Holly Hills Apts Durham NC 27705 Office: PO Box 586 Durham NC 27702

EVERETT, MARGARET NEUHAUS, ednl. adminstr.; b. Saginaw, Mich., Mar. 27, 1911; d. Frederick William and Wilhelmina Cresentia (Schwarz) Neuhaus; certified court reporter Gregg Coll., Chgo., 1929; postgrad. U. Mich., 1932-33; m. Franklin Leland Everett, June 14, 1933 (div. Oct. 1969); children—Marilyn Dee Wilson, Stuart Bryan. Mem. faculty Saginaw Bus. Inst., 1930-32; adminstrv. asst. Gt. Lakes Research div. U. Mich., Ann Arbor, 1960-69, adminstrv. asso., 1970—; corp. sec. Gt. Lakes Found., 1966-69, hon. life mem. 1970—. Mem. Internat. Assn. Gt. Lakes Research (sec. pubs. com. 1968-72, Outstanding Service award 1973), PEO (br. pres. 1971-72), U. Mich. Smith Alumnae Group (pres. 1954). Presbyn. Club: Ann Arbor Women's City. Editor, Proceedings ann. conf. on Gt. Lakes Research, 1960-67. Editorial asst. Geochemistry, Internat. Geochem. Soc., 1959-60. Home: 1217 Island Dr Ann Arbor MI 48105

EVERETT, MARIANNE E., ednl. adminstr.; b. Claxton, Ga., Jan. 24, 1926; d. Frank Gibson and Mary Lee (Edwards) Everett; B.A., Salem Coll., Winston-Salem, N.C., 1946; M.A., Tufts U., 1956; profl. diploma Elliot Pearson Sch., 1956; postgrad. Columbia, Harvard, N.Y. U. Tchr., Spence Sch., N.Y.C., 1946-49, Sheffield Terrace Sch., London, Eng., 1949-51; tchr. pub. schs., Great Neck, N.Y. and Ridgewood, N.J., 1951-60; founder, dir. The Everett Sch., N.Y.C., 1960—. Participant traveling seminar to study schs. Italy, Switzerland, Germany, Holland, Denmark, Eng., 1962, course for Am. tchrs. Safron Walden Coll., Essex, Eng., 1971; participant World Conf. on Edn., Asilomar, Cal., 1970; mem. planning com. confs. World Edn. Fellowship, N.Y.C., 1971. Mem. Assn. Supervision and Curriculum Devel., World Council for Curriculum and Instrn. (charter), Nat. Assn. Edn. Young Children, Assn. Child Edn. Internat., Assn. Tchrs. Ind. Schs., Nat. Assn. Child Devel. and Edn., Am. Assn. Elementary-Kindergarten-Nursery Tchrs. Contbr. articles to profl. jours. Home: 47 E 64th St New York City NY 10022

EVERETT, (MINNIE) OLIVIA WILLINGHAM (MRS. RUFUS MARSHALL EVERETT), county ofcl.; b. MaDill County, Okla., Sept. 19, 1914; d. Ephie Leitner and Mary Eudora (Buie) Willingham; ed. Elliott Bus. Coll.; m. Rufus Marshall Everett, May 16, 1931 (dec. 1962); children—Nancy (Mrs. James Pullin), Cleo (Mrs. Lewis Walters), Rufus D., Esther (Mrs. Alvin Frietsch), James D. With Harris County (Tex.) Tax Office, Houston, 1946-56, 63—, now dep. tax assessor-collector. Recipient awards Internat. Poetry Inst., Poetry Soc. Tex. Mem. Internat. Poetry Inst., Poetry Soc. Tex., The Major Poets. Presbyn. Author: (poetry) Come Walk With Me, 1970. Home: 3318 Castledale Houston TX 77016 Office: 301 San Jacinto Houston TX 77002

EVERETT, SHERRY MAE, ednl. adminstr.; b. Pitts., June 25, 1944; d. Edward and Amie Mae (Heath) Everett; B.A., Shaw U., 1966; M.Ed., U. Pitts., 1971, specialist diploma, 1972, postgrad., 1972—. Case worker Pa. State Bd. Assistance, Pitts., 1966; elementary sch. tchr. Pitts. Pub. Sch. System, 1967; vocational counselor Opportunities Industrialization Center, Inc., Pitts., 1968; counselor Allegheny Community Coll., Pitts., 1969; counselor, black studies adviser Carlow Coll., Pitts., 1970; counselor, asst. dir. Center for Career Devel., Morgan State Coll., Balt., 1972—. Cons. Pitts. Model Cities, 1971, Pa. Higher Edn. Office, 1972. Corr. sec. Council of Federated Orgn., Pitts., 1964-67. Recipient Civil Rights award N.A.A.C.P., 1964, Pitts. chpt. Nat. Assn. Black Profl. and Bus. Women Club, Inc., 1965. Mem. Nat. Assn. Women Deans and Counselors, Nat. Assn. Black Profl. and Bus. Womens Club, Inc., Md. Personnel and Guidance Assn. Mem. Order Eastern Star. Home: 6920 Donachie Rd Baltimore MD 21214 Office: Morgan State College Coldspring and Hillen Rds Baltimore MD 21239

EVERHART, KATHRYN MABEL HOSTETTER, jeweler; b. Hanover, Pa., Aug. 11, 1914; d. Amos Irvin and Katie Mabel (Hetrick) Hostetter; grad. Thompson Bus. Coll., 1938; m. William Reed Everhart, Apr. 25, 1938 (div. Nov. 1961); 1 son, William Reed. Owner, Everhart Jewelers, Washington, 1946-52, Cupp Jewelry Store, Fairfax, Va., 1952—, McLean, Va., 1963—. Mem. bd. dirs., adv. council Salvation Army, 1957-60; dir. No. Va. Heart Assn., 1956-60; trustee Fairfax Hosp., 1959-62; mem. No. Va. Community Coll. Bd., 1971—. Mem. Washington Guild of Am. Gem Soc. (pres. 1959-60, Washington Retail Jewelers Assn. (pres. 1962-63), Am. Gem Soc. (dir. 1963-66), Va. State Jewelers Assn. (dir. 1965-69, v.p. 1969-70, pres. 1973—), Retail Jewelers of Am. (vice chmn. adv. council 1968-70), Fairfax County C. of C. (dir. 1956-69, pres. 1969-74, mem.

exec. com. 1972-74), Fairfax City C. of C. (dir. 1964-70). Club: Soroptimist (pres. 1957-58). Home: 10810 Norman Av Fairfax VA 22030 Office: 9966 Main St Fairfax VA 22030

EVERIDGE, MARY JAMES SMITH (MRS. JAMES R. EVERIDGE, SR.), county ofcl.; b. Tampa, Fla., Dec. 16, 1930; d. James Franklin and Mary Ellen (Hancock) Smith; student Fla. State U., 1958; Fla. So. Coll., 1960, U. Fla., 1962; m. James R. Everidge, Sr., Aug. 4, 1946; children—Mary Elizabeth (Mrs. Robert Trout Peters, III), James Ralph. Owner, operator day nursery, Plant City, Fla., 1956-58; dir. Mary Jim Show, WPLA, Plant City, 1963-65; extention worker Plant City Neighborhood Service Center, 1966-68; tax information clk., East office mgr. Hillsborough County (Fla.) Tax Assessor's office, 1968-72; community affairs coordinator Hillsbourough County Div. Children Services, Tampa, 1972—. Mem. Selective Service Bd., 1971—; publicity chmn. East Hillsborough County United Fund Dr., 1960; chmn. Hillsborough County dr. Leukemia Soc. Am., 1971-74, sec. Suncoast chpt., 1972-73, treas., 1974-75; pres. East Hillsborough County P.T.A. Bd., 1958-60, Hillsborough County Council P.T.A.'s, 1961-62. Founder, pres. East Hillsborough County Democratic Women's Club, 1961-62; sec. Hillsborough County Dem. Women's Club, 1972-73; pres. Dem. Women's Clubs of Fla., Inc., 1973-75. Bd. dirs. Hillsborough County chpt. Nat. Found. of March of Dimes, 1964-68, Hillsborough County div. Children Services Vol. League, Inc., 1973, 74. Named Woman of Yr., Plant City Civic Clubs, 1964; recipient Community Service award Plant City Jr. Woman's Club, 1950. Mem. Fla. Fedn. Bus. and Profl. Women's Club (dist. dir. 1973-74), Plant City Bus. and Profl. Women's Club (pres. 1969-70), Nat. Orgn. Women, Fla. Women's Polit. Caucus, Women's Soc. Christian Service (pres. 1965-67). Methodist (supt. youth div. 1950-70). Club: Plant City Junior Woman's (pres. 1954-55). Home: 502 E DeVane St Plant City FL 33566 Office: 3110 Clay Mangum Lane Tampa FL 33618

EVERITT, RUTH CLARK (MRS. HOWARD EVERITT, JR.), theatre dir.; b. Spokane, Wash., Feb. 12, 1934; d. Arthur V. and Ethel Zenora (Mitcham) Clark; student Gonzaga U., 1956-57, U. Cal. at Santa Barbara, 1958-59, Neighborhood Playhouse Sch. Theatre, 1960-61; m. Howard Everitt, Jr., May 13, 1966. Profl. actress, 1962—; dir. Straight Wharf Theatre, Nantucket, Mass., 1968—. Host, Today on Nantucket, Cablevision NCV-3, Nantucket, 1973-74. Bd. dirs. Nantucket Inst., 1972-74. Mem. Actors Equity, Nantucket Arts Council. Home: 59 Fair St Nantucket MA 02554 Office: 58 Main St Nantucket MA 02554 also Delray Beach Playhouse Delray Beach FL 33444

EVERMON, MARGARET DOLORES, psychiatrist; b. Stroudsburg, Pa., May 20, 1935; d. Thomas and Margaret (Poortstra) Evermon; A.B., Barnard Coll., 1955; M.D., Northwestern U., 1959; m. Eli Berman, Apr. 9, 1961 (div. Oct. 1, 1973); children—Peter W., Hilary S. Intern Kings County Hosp., Bklyn., 1959-60, resident 1960-62; resident Allentown (Pa.) State Hosp., 1962-63; practice of medicine specializing in psychiatry, Stroudsburg, 1963—; chief psychiat. service Monroe County Gen. Hosp., East Stroudsburg, Pa., 1966—; med. dir. Mental Health Center of Carbon, Monroe and Pike Counties, Stroudsburg, 1968-72, Guidance Center Northampton and Monroe Counties, Easton, 1963-72. Diplomate Am. Bd. Psychiatry and Neurology. Mem. A.M.A., Pa. Med. Assn., Am. Psychiat. Assn. Address: 125 Stokes Av Stroudsburg PA 18360

EVERS, JEAN GRAF (MRS. CARL G. EVERS), editor, writer; b. Columbus, O., Dec. 27, 1917; d. Ray W. and Marie A. (Dooley) Arms; B.A. summa cum laude, Northwestern U., 1940; m. Don Graf, May 15, 1947 (dec. Nov. 1962); m. 2d, Carl G. Evers, Jan. 22, 1964. Asso. editor House and Garden Mag., N.Y.C., 1942-45, Life Mag., N.Y.C., 1945-47; partner Graf & Graf, pub. relations, N.Y.C., 1947-63; staff pub. relations Am. Carpet Inst., N.Y.C., 1955-57; pub. relations dir. Galbraith-Hoffman, N.Y.C., 1958-60; guest home furniture editor Modern Bride, 1955; guest editor Decorating Supplements and Herald Tribune Sun. mag. Today's Living, N.Y.C., 1960-61; dir. interior furnishings Mohair Council at Kairalla Agy., N.Y.C., 1966-68; contbg. editor Practical Ency. of Good Decorating and Home Improvement, Meredith and Greystone Press, N.Y.C., 1968-70; asst. editor Voices, local tri-city newspaper, Southbury, Conn., 1973-74, editor, 1974—. Press chmn. Tercentennial Celebration, Southbury, Conn., 1972. Recipient Vogue Prix de Paris, 1940. Mem. Nat. Home Fashions League (nat. first v.p. 1973-74, nat. dir. N.Y. chpt. 1972-73), Am. Inst. Designers, Archtl. League of N.Y., Phi Beta Kappa, Delta Gamma. Author: Practical Houses for Contemporary Living, 1954; Doubleday Decorating Books, 1972. Contbr. numerous articles to various women's and home mags. Home: 738 B Heritage Village Southbury CT 06488

EVERS, KATHRYN SCHISSLER HUSSEY, physician; b. Boston, Dec. 14, 1942; d. Joseph Michael and M. Grace (Schissler) Hussey; B.A., Trinity Coll., 1964; M.D., U. Md., 1969; m. Peter Laval Evers, Jan. 19, 1964; 1 son, Peter Aristotle Laval II. Research asst. Psychohormonal Research unit Johns Hopkins Hosp., 1966; Erickson Found. fellow in psychiatry Neuropsychiat. Inst., U. Cal. at Los Angeles, summer 1967; intern St. Agnes Hosp., Balt., 1969-70; resident psychiatry Ft. Logan Mental Health Center, Denver, 1970-73; med. dir., chief psychiatrist Mental Health and Family Services Center, Vancouver, Wash., 1973—. Home: 7708 NE 78th St Vancouver WA 98662

EVERSON, KATHERINE ELIZABETH, extension home economist; b. Thornton, Ida., Apr. 22, 1917; d. Chauncey Richard and Clara (Firth) Hanson; B.S., Ricks Coll., 1956; M.S., Mont. State U., 1958; postgrad. U. Ida., 1956, at Las Vegas, 1960-72; Ednl. Specialist, U. Nev., 1973; m. Calvin Alfred Everson, Jan. 19, 1942; children—Richard, Paul, Barbara (Mrs. Brian Kenneth Spavin). Office mgr. Snake River Mut. Ins. Co., Rexburg, 1948-56; tchr. home econs. Madison County Sch. Dist., Rexburg, 1956-60; home economist Coop. Extension Service U. Nev. at Las Vegas, 1960—. Cons. Bur. Standards, Washington, 1970-72. Mem. Nat. Assn. Extension Home Economists (dir. Western region 1972-74, recipient Distinguished Service award 1970), Nev. Extension Home Econs. Assn. (pres. 1966-68), Nev., (pres. 1972-74), Am. home econs. assns., N.E.A., Am. Vocational Assn., Delta Kappa Gamma, Epsilon Sigma Phi. Contbr. to profl. jours. Address: 300 Las Vegas Blvd S Las Vegas NV 89101

EVERT, YOLANDA, educator; b. Kewanee, Ill., Mar. 22, 1938; d. Charles Anton and Isabel (Srbljanin) Unakis; student U. Ill., 1955-57, Bradley U., 1958; B.A., Millikin U., 1959; M.A., U. Colo., 1964; postgrad. Western Mich. U., 1966; m. E. F. Evert, Mar. 21, 1964; 1 dau., Mara. Tchr., Mendota, Ill., 1959-61, Maywood, Ill., 1961-66; instr. Triton Jr. Coll., River Grove, Ill., 1967-68; instr. English and speech Central YMCA Community Coll., Chgo., 1968—. Mem. Alpha Epsilon Rho, Pi Kappa Delta, Pi Epsilon Delta, Zeta Tau Alpha. Research on relationship between defective speech and spelling disability. Office: 211 W Wacker Dr Chicago IL 60606

EVETT, ALICE ANGELA CALKINS, hosp. adminstr.; b. Waco, Tex., July 13, 1925; d. Harry Radford and Maribelle (Chamberlin) Calkins; student George Washington U., 1942-44; B.A., Baylor U., 1946; M.A., U. Tex., 1951; postgrad. St. Mary's U., 1960, San Antonio Art Inst., 1960-61, Trinity U., 1962-63, San Antonio Coll., 1964; m. Philip John Evett, Sept. 22, 1956 (div. Jan. 1968). Clk., circulation dept. Waco Tribune-Herald, 1946-47; editorial asst. Office Ofcl. Publs., U. Tex., 1950-53; editor, proofreader, bookkeeper U. Tex. Press, 1953-54, bus. mgr., 1954-56; exec. sec. Jack Ammann Photogrammetric Engrs., Inc., San Antonio, 1957-61; editor publs. Am. Security Life Ins. Co., 1961-69, dir. communications, 1969-73; asso. dir. community relations Bexar County Hosp. Dist., San Antonio, 1973—. Recipient Award of Merit, S.W. Conf. Indsl. Editors, 1965; named Editor of Year, Alamo Indsl. Editors Assn., 1970. Mem. Internat. Assn. Bus. Communicators, Alamo Indsl. Editors (pres. 1963, 69-70), San Antonio C. of C. (publs. adv. com. 1974—). Delta Zeta, Sigma Tau Delta. Republican. Home: 111 Grotto St San Antonio TX 78216 Office: 4502 Med Dr San Antonio TX 78284

EWALD, VIRGINIA REYNOLDS (MRS. JOHN B. EWALD, JR.), realtor; b. Atlanta, Nov. 15, 1923; d. Walter and Nellie (Tryon) Reynolds; student Agnes Scott Coll., 1940-42; m. John Benton Ewald, Jr., May 17, 1942; children—John Benton, Virginia Reynolds, Walter W. Saleswoman, River Bend Real Estate, Annapolis, Md., 1966-69, broker, pres., 1970-72; pres. Virginia Ewald Realty, Sherwood Forest, Md., 1972—. dir. Dalfowe, Inc. Mem. Severn Town Club, Annapolis, 1966—. Mem. Anne Arundel County Bd. Realtors. Club: Sherwood Forest. Home: 1003 Clumber Hill Sherwood Forest MD 21405 Office: RFD 1 Box 566 Annapolis MD 21401

EWALT, DELLA MAE, educator; b. Mount Vernon, O., Aug. 30, 1928; d. George Herbert and Katherine Elizabeth (Dague) Cocanower; B.A., Ohio U., 1950; M.A., U. Wis., 1957; postgrad. U. Cin., 1967-68, Miami U., Oxford, O., 1971-72, Beirut Coll. for Women, (Lebanon), 1969; m. Charles E. Ewalt, Aug. 13, 1950 (div. Sept. 1972). Mem. faculty, drama dir., tchr. theater courses, world lit. Lemon-Monroe High Sch., Monroe, O., 1951-53, 55-58, 59—, dean girls, 1955-62. Adv., Tri-Hi-Y., Monroe, 1959-66, Thespian Troupe, 1963—, Nat. Forensic League chpt., 1963—; dir. more than 30 full length plays. Exec. council Council World Affairs, Middletown, O., 1961-69; mem. Middletown Panhellenic Council, 1965; costume parade chmn. Monroe Sesqui-centennial Com., 1967; nat. program dir. Kappa Phi Club for Coll. Women of Meth. Preference, 1950-55. Recipient leaders fellowship YMCA, 1964, Martha Holden Jennings scholarship, 1968-69. Mem. Am. Assn. U. Women (local parliamentarian 1964-65, edn. area rep. and implementation chmn. state div. 1963-66, topic chmn. 1974—), League of Women Voters (bull. editor, exec. bd. 1958-59), Middletown Classroom Tchrs., Nat., Ohio edn. assns., Ohio Speech Assn., Nat. Council Tchrs. English, Am. Ednl. Theatre Assn., Secondary Sch. Theatre Conf., Creative Writing Study Group, Delta Kappa Gamma, Phi Mu Alumnae. Democrat. Methodist. Editor, Continuing Education for Women in Ohio, 1965. Home: 3674-J Village Dr Franklin OH 45005 Office: Lemon-Monroe High Sch Monroe OH 45050

EWAN, MARY VICTORIA TELANDER (MRS. GEORGE EDWIN EWAN), clubwoman; b. Sheridan, Wyo., Apr. 7, 1917; d. John Victor and Mabel (Coffeen) T.; student Wellesley Coll., 1935-36; B.A., U. Colo., 1939; postgrad. in med. tech. Northwestern U., 1939-40; m. George Edwin Ewan, June 10, 1942; children—Robert Allan, Barbara Jeanne, Linda Carol (Mrs. Dana C. Arbaugh), Mary Elizabeth. Med. technician Northwestern U., 1940-42. Pres., P.E.O., 1953-54; state pres. Nat. Soc. Colonial Dames in Wyo., 1957-61; state 1st vice regent D.A.R., Wyo., 1970-72, state regent, 1972-74. Mem. Am. Assn. U. Women, Kappa Alpha Theta. Republican. Conglist. (pres. women's fellowship, 1956-57). Home: 1112 Victoria St Sheridan WY 82801

EWBANK, FRANCES ELIZABETH WHITE (MRS. WILLIAM ALAN EWBANK), educator; b. Detroit, May 20, 1916; d. Andrew Bracken and Mildred Sybilla (Witzel) White; B.A., Wayne State U., 1936, M.A., 1937; Ph.D. (univ. fellow), U. Colo., 1950; m. William Alan Ewbank, July 31, 1964; stepchildren—Wendy (Mrs. Donald Adams), Heather Frances. Instr. English, Detroit pub. high schs., 1937-43, Wheaton (Ill.) Coll., 1943-48; asso. prof. Asbury (Ky.) Coll., 1950-52, prof., 1952-59; prof., chmn. dept. English, Geneva Coll., Beaver Falls, Pa., 1959-64; prof. English, Taylor U., Upland, Ind., 1964—. Chmn. Youngstown (O.) Regional English Conf., 1963. Research grantee British Mus., Asbury Coll., 1956. Mem. Nat. Council Tchrs. English (mem. bibliography of coll. teaching English com. 1961-68), Modern Lang. Assn., Renaissance Soc., Am. Shakespeare Assn., Conf. Christianity and Lit., Midwest Modern Lang. Assn., Ind. Coll. English Assn., Pi Lambda Theta, Phi Alpha Theta. Methodist. Office: Taylor U Upland IN 46989

EWERTS, CAROL ANN, advt. exec.; b. Evergreen Park, Ill., Feb. 22, 1946; d. Charles James and Frieda (Goodyear) Ewerts; A.B., Loyola U. at Chgo., 1968; certificate N.Y. U. Inst. Retail Mgmt., 1974. Asst. to advt. dir. Bramson, Inc., Chgo., 1969-70, advt. dir., 1970-72; div. advt. mgr., men's and children's Carson Pirie Scott & Co., Chgo., 1973—. Newsletter editor 45th ward Young Republicans, 1971-72. Mem. Ad II Chgo. (chmn. finance 1971-72; v.p. 1972-73). Clubs: Carsons Women's, Bavarian. Home: 1200-A Higgins Rd Park Ridge IL 60068 Office: 1 S State St Chicago IL 60603

EWOLDT, VIOLA ESTELLA (MRS. CARL EWOLDT), mus. ofcl.; b. Wood River, Neb., Sept. 20, 1911; d. Joseph Charles and Martha Elisabeth (Guy) Matthews; student pub. schs.; m. Carl Ewoldt, June 9, 1934; 1 son, Joseph Herman. With Cook-Davies Cafeteria, Grand Island, Neb., 1930-34; with Stuhr Dairy Farms, Grand Island, Neb., 1935-61; registrar Stuhr Mus., Grand Island, Neb., 1962—. Mem. Eagles Aux. Presbyn. Club: Hall County Extension (Grand Island). Home: Box 329 Rural Route 2 Grand Island NE 68801 Office: Box 24 Rural Route 2 Grand Island NE 68801

EWY, DONNA HOHMANN (MRS. RODGER FRANK EWY), author: b. Denver, Sept. 1, 1934; d. Lee Kerwith and Irene Lena (Gilberg) Hohmann; B.A., U. Colo., 1956; m. Rodger Frank Ewy, Mar. 1, 1958; children—Marguerite, Suzanne, Rodger, Leon. Tchr., Denver, 1957, San Francisco, 1958, Laurel, Md., 1959, France, 1960. Cons. U. Colo., 1969-72, Colo. Pub. Schs., 1966-74. Pres. Colo. Childbirth Preparation, Denver, 1969-72. Mem. Internat. Childbirth Assn., Am. Soc. Psychophrophy. Author: Preparation for Childbirth, 1970; Preparation for Breastfeeding, 1974. Home: 1315 Norwood Boulder CO 80302

EYERLY, JEANNETTE HYDE, author; b. Topeka, June 7, 1908; d. Robert and Mabel (Young) Hyde; B.A., State U. Ia., 1930; m. Frank Eyerly, Dec. 6, 1932; children—Jane (Mrs. Lawrence Kozuszek), Susan (Mrs. Joseph A. Pichler). Contbr. mags. Am. Home, Am. Girl, Better Homes and Gardens, Ladies' Home Jour., Woman's Home Companion, Coronet, Pageant, Canadian Home Jour., Canadian Star Weekly, McCalls, 1941-57; book reviewer Des Moines Sunday Register; author: Dearest Kate (with Valeria Winkler Griffith), 1961; More Than a Summer Love, 1962; Drop-Out, 1963; The World of Ellen March, 1964; Gretchen's Hill (Susan Glaspell award 1965), 1965; A Girl Like Me, 1966; The Girl Inside, 1968; Escape from Nowhere (Christopher award 1970) 1969; Radigan Cares, 1970; Phaedra Complex, 1971; Bonnie Jo, Go Home, 1972; Good-bye to Budapest, 1974. Tchr. creative writing Des Moines adult edn. classes, 1955-57; lectr. A.P. Mng. Editors Assn., Seattle, 1959, Clarke Coll., 1963, state U. Ia., 1963. Am. Soc. Newspaper Editors Conv., Washington, 1963, State U. Ia., 1966; Speaker New Eng. Library Assn. meeting, 1969, U. Ia., 1969. Bd. dirs. Polk County Mental Health Center; dir. Des Moines Child Guidance Center, 1949-54, St. Joseph Acad. Guild, 1954-57; mem. acquisition com. Des Moines Art Center, 1960-63. Mem. Authors League Am., Nat. Audubon Soc., Ia. Ornithol. Union, Theta Sigma Phi. Roman Catholic. Home: 231 42d St Des Moines IA 50312

EYLER, ANNE AILES (MRS. IRA E. EYLER, JR.), ins. agy. exec.; b. Washington, May 17, 1919; d. Eugene Elliott and Sallie (Cornwell) Ailes; grad. Marjorie Webster Jr. Coll., 1938; m. Ira E. Eyler, Jr., Nov. 26, 1938 (dec. Sept. 1968); children—Ira E. III, George A. Ins. agt. C. Granville Smith & Co., Martinsburg, W.Va., 1956-68, owner 1968—. Mem. Berkeley County Planning Commn., 1964—; mem. Martinsburg Police Civil Service Commn., 1971—. Mem. W.Va., Berkeley County (exec. sec. 1964-68) hist. socs., Gen. Adam Stephen Meml. Assn. (treas. 1961-70), Amateur Trapshooting Assn., Nat. Trust for Hist. Preservation, Assn. State and Local History, W.Va. Conservancy, Martinsburg-Berkeley County C. of C. (dir. 1972-74), Nat. Assn. Ind. Agts. Club: Olde Berkeley Garden (past pres.). Home: Route 6 Martinsburg WV 25401 Office: 102 W King St Martinsburg WV 25401

EYSTER, MARY ELAINE (MRS. ROBERT EUGENE DYE), hematologist; b. York, Pa., Mar. 21, 1935; d. Charles Gable and Marea Viola (Schriver) Eyster; A.B., Duke, 1956, M.D., 1960; m. Robert Eugene Dye, Jan. 2, 1965; children—Robert, Charles. Intern, Cornell U., N.Y. Hosp., 1960-61, resident internal medicine, 1961-63, USPHS trainee, hematology fellow, 1963-66, instr. medicine, 1966-67, univ. asst. prof. medicine, asst. attending hosp. physician, 1967-70; asst. prof. medicine Hershey Med. Center, Pa. State U., 1970-73, asso. prof. medicine, 1973—, chief div. hematology Med. Center, 1973—. Diplomate Am. Bd. Internal Medicine, subsplty. hematology. Fellow A.C.P.; mem. Am. Assn. Blood Banks, Am. Soc. Hematology, Am. Fedn. for Clin. Research, Harvey Soc., Pa. Med. Assn., Pa. Assn. Blood Banks. Home: 51 Woodland Av Hershey PA 17033 Office: Hershey Med Center Pa State U Hershey PA 17033

EZELL, ANNETTE SCHRAM, educator; b. West Frankfort, Ill., June 19, 1940; d. Woodrow C. and Rosa (Franich) Schram; student Evansville Coll., 1957, Protestant Deaconess Hosp. Sch. Nursing, 1957-59, Ind. U., 1959; B.S. in Nursing, U. Nev., 1962, M.S. in Physiology, 1967, postgrad., 1969; m. Ronald L. Ezell, Mar. 28, 1959; children—Michael L., Rona Maria. Staff nurse Washoe Med. Center, Reno, 1962; teaching asst. U. Nev., Reno, 1962-63, instr., 1963-64, 1965-67, asst. prof. nursing, 1967-71; curriculum specialist U. Nev. Med. Sch., 1971-72, project mgr. Fed. Grant Intercampus Nursing Edn. Project, 1969-71, asso. prof. nursing, curriculum specialist rural nurse practitioner program, 1971-73; staff asso. Mountain States Regional Med. Program, 1974—. Cons. nursing edn., TV edn., research methodology; adviser to various research and ednl. bds. Mem. Am. Nev. nurses assns., A.A.A.S., Am. Acad. Arts and Scis., Am. Assn. U. Profs., Am. Nurses Found., Nat. League of Nursing, Nev. Pub. Health Assn., Western Ednl. Soc. for Telecommunications, Phi Kappa Phi. Home: 2205 Blue Heron Ct Verdi NV 89439

FABEN, ESTHER JACKSON (MRS. WALTER WILLIAM FABEN), museum curator; b. Glendale, O., July 17, 1901; d. William and Louisa (Hartmann) Jackson; B.S., Miami U., Oxford, O., 1923; postgrad. U. Minn., 1928; m. Walter William Feben, Aug. 11, 1932. Tchr. vocational home econs. Fremont (O.) Ross High Sch., 1923-32; substitute tchr. Montpelier (O.) pub. schs., 1934-65; curator Williams County Hist. Mus., Montpelier, 1968—. Guardian Campfire Girls, 1932-38; mem. William County Resource Conservation and Devel. Exec. Council, 1971—. Recipient Distinguished Service award Ohio Assn. Garden Clubs, 1963, Woman of Yr. award Bus. and Profl. Women, Montpelier, 1968. Mem. Am. Soc. for State and Local History, Ohio Hist. Soc., Ohio Assn. Garden Clubs (regional dir. 1945-47, state pres. 1950-52), Maumee Valley and Williams County Hist. Soc., Zeta Tau Alpha. Republican. Episcopalian. Club: Montpelier Study; Garden (Pulaski, O.). Contbr. mus. news and weekly garden column to local newspapers. Home: 120 South East Av Montpelier OH 43543

FABIAN, KAREN MARJORIE KARLQUIST (MRS. JOSEPH CHARLES FABIAN), home economist; b. Mpls., Oct. 17, 1935; d. Theodore T. and Margaret (O'Halloran) Karlquist; B.S. in Household Equipment, Ia. State U., 1957; postgrad. U. Colo., 1962-63; m. Joseph Charles Fabian, Oct. 25, 1958; 1 son, Michael Joseph. Student trainee Betty Crocker Gen. Mills, Mpls., 1956; home economist Ind. Mich. Electric Co., Ft. Wayne, Ind., 1957-58, Fairmount Foods, Denver, 1959; home service rep. Pub. Service Co. Colo., Denver, 1960-64; instr. Emily Griffith Opportunity Sch., Denver, 1964, 66, 68-72, mem. homemaking curriculum adv. com., 1964—; home econs. cons., free lance Denver, 1964—. Mem. Denver Art Mus., 1963-69; mem. Denver Symphony Guild, 1965—, jr. bd., 1968—, pres. Denver Jr. Symphony Guild, 1973-74. Mem. Colo., Rocky Mountain (pres. 1963-64) home economists in bus., Colo. Home Econs. Assn. (pres. 1965-66), Denver Area Panhellenic (publicity chmn. 1965-66), Chi Omega (v.p. 1961-62). Conglist. Address: 7177 W 8th Av Denver CO 80215

FABIAN, MYRA LOU WILLIAMSON, counselor; b. Munice, Ind., Sept. 5, 1923; d. Lawrence H. and Laura Ruth (Hiatt) Williamson; B.A., Ball State U., 1944; M.A., Syrauce U., 1950; m. Hans J. Fabian, Aug. 19, 1951; children—Christine Elizabeth, Erik William. Dir. recreational and social activities Edward W. Sparrow Hosp. Sch. Nursing, Lansing, Mich., 1950-51; dir. teen-age program YMCA, Syracuse, N.Y., 1951-54; dean Wilmington (O.) Coll., 1954-56; counselor, tchr. Xenia (O.) pub. schs., 1956-60; counselor, instr. Ohio State U., 1960-64; counselor Center Continuing Edn. for Women, U. Mich. at Ann Arbor, 1965—. Mem. Nat. Assn. Women Deans, Adminstrs. and Counselors, Am. Assn. Personnel and Guidance, Assn. Am. Coll. Personnel, Am. Assn. U. Women. Home: 2320 Walter Dr Ann Arbor MI 48103 Office: 330 Thompson St Ann Arbor MI 48103

FABRAY, NANETTE, actress; b. San Diego, Cal.; d. Raoul and Lillian (McGovern) Fabares; student Los Angeles City Coll.; student Reinhardt Drama Sch., 1938; L.H.D., Gallaudet Coll., 1972; D.F.A., Western Md. Coll., 1972; m. David Tebet, 1947 (div. 1951); m. 2d, Ranald MacDougall, 1957 (dec. 1973). Played leading role in Charlie Chan radio series; mem. cast radio show Showboat; appeared in Max Reinhardt prodns. The Miracle, Six Characters in Search of an Author, Servant with Two Masters; appeared in Broadway prodns. Let's Face It, Meet the People, By Jupiter, Bloomer Girl, High Button Shoes, Arms and the Girl Love Life, Make a Wish, Mr. President, No Hard Feelings; co-star with Sid Caesar on Caesar's Hour, 1954-56; star of TV show The Nanette Fabray Show, 1961-62; appeared in motion pictures Elizabeth and Essex, The Bandwagon, A Child is Born, The Happy Ending, Cockeyed Cowboys. Past campaign chmn. Hope for Hearing Found., U. Cal. at Los Angeles; achmn. Nat. Easter Seal Soc. for Crippled Children, Nat. Mental Assn.; v.p. Nat. Assn. Hearing and Speech Agys., Washington; mem. Pres.'s Com. on Employment of Handicapped. Hon. bd. dirs. Lexington Sch. for Deaf,

N.Y. League for Hard of Hearing, Campaign of Nat. Heart Fund; mem. adv. bd. Deafness Research Center, N.Y. U.; bd. dirs. Nat. Adv. Com. Edn. of Deaf, Muses of Cal. Mus. Found.; trustee Eugene O'Neill Found., Nat. Theatre of Deaf. Recipient two Donaldson awards as best musical actress, best supporting actress in High Button Shoes, 1955; Tony award for best musical actress in Love Life, 1949; Emmy award as best comedienne, 1955-56, best supporting actress, 1955; named Woman of Yr., Radio and TV Editors of Am., 1955; named named Hon. Mayor of Pacific Palisades, 1967-68; named One of 10 Best Dressed Women in Am., 1950; recipient Eleanor Roosevelt Humanitarian award, 1964; Distinguished Achievement award Hollywood High Sch., 1958; Human Relations award Anti-Defamation League, B'nai B'rith, 1969; Achievement award Women's div. Albert Einstein Coll. Medicine, Yeshiva U., 1963; Pres.'s Distinguished Service award Pres.'s Commn. on Employment, 1970; 1st Ann. Cogswell award Gallaudet Coll., 1970; named Woman of Yr., Women's div. Jewish War Vets. Am., 1969, Phi Kappa Zeta, 1969, Phila. Club Advt. Women, 1968. Home: 14360 Sunset Blvd Pacific Palisades CA 90272

FABRIZIO, ANGELINA MARIA, educator, microbiologist; b. Montenero Valcoccharo, Italy; d. Amico Castano and Felicita Francesca (Danese) Fabrizio (parents Am. citizens); B.S., Villa Marie Coll., Erie, Pa., 1944; M.S. (fellow 1944-45), U. Ky., 1947; Ph.D., U. Pa., 1952; certificate Hahnemann Med. Coll. and Hosp., Phila., 1955. Asst. bacteriology U. Ky., 1945-46, instr. Italian, 1946-47; research bacteriologist antibiotics U. Cin. Coll. Medicine, Cin. Gen. Hosp., 1947-48; research asso. exptl. cancer and tissue culture Presbyn. Hosp., Phila., 1951-65; research asso. exptl. cancer and tissue culture Jefferson Med. Coll., Phila., 1965-67, asst. prof. pathology, 1967—; mem. faculty Coll. Grad. Studies, 1971—; instr. U. Pa. Sch. Medicine, 1960; cons. VA Hosp., Coatesville, Pa., 1968—. Fellow Nat. Tb Assn., 1948-51. Fellow A.A.A.S.; mem. Tissue Culture Assn., Am. Soc. Microbiology, N.Y. Acad. Sci., Sigma Xi, Sigma Delta Epsilon (chpt. pres. 1959-60, nat. pres. 1973-74). Home: 2045 Spruce St Philadelphia PA 19103

FACEMYER, ROSEMARY RITA VENEGONI (MRS. A. HARRIS FACEMYER), bldg. and loan assn. exec.; b. Herrin, Ill., May 22, 1928; d. Michael and Mary (Susini) Venegoni; grad. high sch.; m. A. Harris Facemyer, Apr. 15, 1948; children—Marianne (Mrs. Michael Hagstrom), Michael, Richard, Greg. Office mgr. Reynolds & Co., security investors, Bridgeton, N.J., 1961-68; broker, owner Facemyer Real Estate Agy., Bridgeton, 1968—; mng. officer, sec. Cohanzick Bldg. & Loan, Bridgeton, 1968—. Mem. Bridgeton Hosp. Aux., 1950-70. Committeewoman, Republican party, 1955—. Mem. Nat. Assn. Realtor Bds., Cumberland County Bd. Realtors (publicity chmn.). Roman Catholic. Home: 5 Hopewell Rd Bridgeton NJ 08302 Office: 473 N Pearl St Bridgeton NJ 08302

FACEY, VERA LIPTON, educator; b. Halifax, N.S., Can., June 6, 1909; d. Ralph Allen and Eunice Jessie (Young) Facey; B.S. magnum cum laude, Dalhousie U., Halifax, 1936; M.A., Toronto U., 1940, Ph.D., 1946. Came to U.S., 1947, naturalized, 1956. Tchr., N.S. pub. schs., 1928-32, prin., 1936-38; lectr. Dalhousie U., 1940-41, 43-44; mem. faculty N.S. Agrl. Coll., 1945-47; mem. faculty U. N.D., Grand Forks, 1947—, prof. biology, 1961—. Fellow A.A.A.S.; mem. N.D. Acad. Sci. (pres. 1960), Am. Assn. Univ. Profs. (pres. 1967), Bot. Soc. Am., Ecol. Soc. Am., Torrey Bot. Club, Internat., Am. assns. plant taxonomists, Sigma Xi (pres. 1961). Club: Zonta (pres. Grand Forks 1970). Home: 801 Boyd Dr Grand Forks ND 58201

FADELEY, NANCIE PEACOCKE (MRS. EDWARD N. FADELEY), state legislator; b. St. Louis, July 11, 1930; d. Charles Sidney and Nannette (Wood) Peacocke; B.A., Central Methodist Coll., Fayette, Mo., 1952; postgrad. Duke, 1952-53, U. Ore., 1955-74; m. Edward N. Fadeley, June 11, 1953; children—Charles Norman, Shira Nanette. Tchr. pub. schs., St. Joseph, Mo., 1953-54, Eugene, Ore., 1954-57; legislative asst. to Edward N. Fadeley, Ore. Legislature, Eugene, 1961-70; now mem. Ore. Ho. of Reps., Eugene. Free-lance writer. Alternate del. Democratic Nat. Conv., 1968. Bd. dirs. Wesley Found., U. Ore. Mem. P.E.O. (chpt. pres. 1970), Ch. Women United (state legislative chmn.). Methodist. Contbr. numerous articles to popular mags. Home: 260 Sunset Dr Eugene OR 97403

FADEM, JOYCE ABRAMS, assn. exec.; b. Los Angeles, Feb. 25, 1932; d. Arthur Joe and Regina Theresa (Goodman) Abrams; student U. Cal. at Berkeley, 1949-50; A.A., U. Cal. at Los Angeles, 1951, B.A., 1952, M.A., 1961; m. Jerrold A. Fadem (div.); children—Cheryl, Judith. Tchr. Univ. High Sch., Los Angeles, 1953-57; tng. tchr. tchr. tng. program U. Cal. at Los Angeles, 1955-57, 59-60, project writer, 1960-61; mem. faculty social sci. dept. Los Angeles City Coll., 1962-69; instr. Immaculate Heart Coll., Los Angeles, 1967-69; dir. polit. action and legislation Cal. Tchrs. Assn., Los Angeles, 1969-71, polit. edn. exec., 1971—. Cons. Cal. State Dept. Edn., 1964-66. Commr. Los Angeles City Housing Authority, 1974—; mem. Los Angeles Mayor's Labor Mgmt. Adv. Com., 1974—. Mem. Cal. Dem. State Central Com., 1960-64, 1966—; mem. Los Angeles Dem. County Central Com., 1966—; alternate del. Dem. Nat. Convs., 1964, 68; sec. Cal. Dem. Council, 1963-67; coordinator Educators for Alan Cranston, 1968; chmn. Dem. State Central Com. Campaign Conf., 1968. Chmn. tchrs. adv. com. Constnl. Rights Found., Los Angeles, 1962-64. Mem. Nat. Council for Social Studies (com. chmn. 1966, 68-69), So. Cal. Social Sci. Assn. (mem. exec. bd. 1962-73), N.E.A. Home: 427 S McCadden Pl Los Angeles CA 90020 Office: 1125 W 6th St Los Angeles CA 90017

FADER, SHIRLEY SLOAN (MRS. SEYMOUR J. FADER), writer; b. Paterson, N.J., Feb. 24, 1931; d. Samuel Louis and Miriam (Marcus) Sloan; B.S., U. Pa., 1952, M.S., 1953; m. Seymour J. Fader, June 26, 1951; children—Susan Deborah, Steven Micah Kimchi. Writer, journalist, author, Paramus, N.J., 1956—; writer of People and You, Jobmanship columns Family Weekly, 1971—. Mem. Author's Guild, Soc. Mag. Writers. Author: The Princess Who Grew Down, 1968. Address: 377 McKinley Blvd Paramus NJ 07652

FAGALA, MARTHA LU SANDIDGE (MRS. ROSS EVANS FAGALA), city ofcl.; b. Altoga, Tex., Sept. 11, 1907; d. John Harvey and Emilee Fene (Mounger) Sandidge; student Southwestern U., 1959; grad. Collin Meml. Sch. Nursing, 1961; m. Ross Evans, May 27, 1969; children—Dyon Cantrell, Peggie Sue (Mrs. Ronald K. Umphress). Staff nurse Wysong Hosp., McKinney, Tex., 1962-69; councilwoman City Hall, Princeton, Tex., 1971-72, mayor protem, 1972—. Vol., Am. Lung Assn., Dallas, 1973-74; adviser A.R.C., Princeton, 1972-74; chmn. McKinney Collin County Children Retarded Center, 1973-74; vol. nurse Dallas State Fair, Red Cross Children Shelter, 1970-71. Licensed Vocational Nurses Tex. (state bd. dirs. 1968-70, 73, pres. 1968—), C. of C., Women's Missionary Union. Baptist. Mem. Order Eastern Star. Home: 405 N 4th St Princeton TX 75077 Office: City Hall PO Box 68 Princeton TX 75077

FAGAN, SHIRLEY RITA TORRENCE (MRS. CHARLES MERLIN FAGAN), ednl. adminstr.; b. Hammond, La., Oct. 28, 1919; d. Robert Oliver and Viola (O'Brien) Torrence; student Southeastern La. Coll., 1935-37; B.A., La. State U., 1939, M.A., 1940; m. Charles Merlin Fagan, Sept. 13, 1942 (dec.); children—Charles Merlin, James Robert, Thomas Leo. Hosp. vol. coordinator Hammond (La.) State Sch. for Retarded Children, 1964, cottage life supr., 1964-67, cottage life supr. II, 1967-71. edn., tng. adminstr., 1971—. Mem. State Council Mental Retardation Planning, Baton Rouge, 1969—. Mem. La. (bd. dirs. 1965-68), Hammond (pres. 1971-72) assns. for retarded children, Am. Assn. Mental Deficiency, Council Exceptional Children, Royal Soc. Health (asso. London, Eng.). Home: PO Box 277 Hammond LA 70401 Office: Hammond State Sch Route 3 Box 165P Hammond LA 70401

FAGERBURG, JOAN EMELINE, coll. adminstr.; b. Normal, Ill., Nov. 27, 1939; d. Charles F. and Helen (Coupe) Fagerburg; B.A. in Psychology, MacMurray Coll., 1961; M.S. in Edn., Purdue U., 1962, Ph.D. in Coll. Personnel, 1967. Resident dir. Ill. State U. at Normal, 1962-65; grad. asst. Office Admissions, Purdue U., Lafayette, Ind., 1965-66, Office of Dean of Women, 1966-67; asst. dean student affairs and fgn. student adviser No. Ariz. U., Flagstaff, 1967—. Univ. rep. Nat. Assn. Fgn. Student Affairs. Mem. Flagstaff Women's Coordinating Council. Mem. Nat. Assn. Women Deans, Adminstrs. and Counselors (mem. ad hoc com. on continuing edn. women 1968-70), Ariz. Assn. Women Deans, Adminstrs. and Counselors, No. Ariz. Soc. Sci. and Art. Home: 2001 N Navajo Dr Flagstaff AZ 86001 also 2901 E Grandview Dr Bloomington IL 61701

FAGIN, CLAIRE MINTZER (MRS. SAMUEL L. FAGIN), nurse, educator; b. N.Y.C.; d. Harry and Mae (Slatin) Mintzer; B.S., Wagner Coll., 1948; M.A., Columbia, 1951; Ph.D., N.Y. U., 1964; m. Samuel L. Fagin, Feb. 17, 1952; children—Joshua, Charles. Staff nurse Sea View Hosp., S.I., N.Y., 1947, clin. instr., 1947-48; clin. instr. Bellevue Hosp., N.Y.C., 1948-50; psychiat. nurse cons. Nat. League for Nursing, N.Y.C., 1951-52; asst. chief Psychiat. Nursing Service, Clin. Center, NIH, 1953-54; research project coordinator dept. psychiatry Childrens Hosp., Washington, 1956; instr. psychiat.-mental health nursing N.Y. U., 1956-58, asst. prof., 1964-67, dir. grad. programs in psychiat. mental health nursing, 1965-69, asso. prof., 1967-69; prof., also chmn. dept. nursing Herbert H. Lehman Coll., City U. N.Y., Bronx, 1969—. Mem. Task Force II Joint Commn. Mental Health of Children, Washington; cons. Pan Am. Health Orgn., 1972—; mem. expert panel on nursing WHO, 1974—. Recipient Alumni Achievement award 75th Ann. Wagner Coll., 1957, Founders Day award N.Y. U., 1964; named Outstanding Alumna Wagner Coll. Sch. Nursing, 1973. Nat. Inst. for Mental Health fellow, 1950-51, 60-64. Fellow Am. Orthopsychiat. Assn. (dir. 1972—); mem. Am. Nurses Assn., Council Deans Nursing Colls. and Univs. (pres. N.Y. chpt. 1974—), Nat. League for Nursing (com. chmn.), Herman Biggs Soc., Sigma Theta Tau, Pi Lambda Theta. Author: Functions and Qualifications of Psychiatric Nurses, 1953; Effects of Maternal Attendance when Young Children are Hospitalized, 1966; Family Centered Nursing in Community Psychiatry, 1970; Nursing in Child Psychiatry, 1972; Readings in Child and Adolescent Psychiatric Nursing, 1974. Contbr. articles to profl. jours., chpts. in books. Office: Herbert H Lehman Coll City U NY Bronx NY 10468

FAGIN, MARGARET BURCHARD CAIRNCROSS, educator; b. Wauwatosa, Wis.; d. Claude William and Ruth (Ellis) Cairncross; A.B. summa cum laude, Lawrence U.; A.M., U. Chgo., 1941; Ed.D., Syracuse U., 1950. Tchr., dean of girls Bensenville (Ill.) Community High Sch.; dean of women, dir. admissions U. Redlands (Cal.), 1944-48; acting asst. dean of women, asst. dir. grad. course in student personnel for women Syracuse U., 1948-50; dean of women, prof. psychology Carroll Coll., 1950-52; asso. dean students, prof. psychology Chico (Cal.) State Coll., 1952-65; dir. Bus. and Profl. Women's Found., Washington, 1965-66; asso. prof. edn., dir. continuing edn. for women U. Mo. at St. Louis, 1966—. Pres. Adult Edn. Council Greater St. Louis; mem. adv. panel leadership tng. Girl Scout Council Greater St. Louis, 1967—; personnel chmn. Bidwell council Camp Fire Girls, Chico, 1954-64; mem. Gov.'s Commn. on Goals for Mo. Recipient Luther Halsey Gulick award, 1964, Alumnae Achievement award Alpha Chi Omega, 1970. Mem. Nat. (treas. 1953-55), Mo. assns. deans and counselors, Adult Edn. Assn. U.S., Mo. Adult Edn. Assn., Am. Soc. Tng. and Devel., Personnel Women Greater St. Louis, Nat. Univ. Extension Assn., Am. Assn. U. Women (div. pres. 1962-64, mem. ednl. found. 1968—), Phi Beta Kappa, Phi Kappa Phi, Theta Sigma Phi, Delta Kappa Gamma, Pi Lambda Theta, Alpha Chi Omega. Clubs: Altrusa (Waukesha); Zonta (St. Louis). Home: 4647 Redfield Ct St Louis MO 63121

FAGLIE, PEGGY SMITH, hosp. adminstr.; b. San Antonio, Aug. 24, 1916; d. Walter Benthale and Grace (McCollum) Smith; B.S., Southwest Tex. State U., 1938, M.Ed., 1967; m. Jack C. Faglie, May 22, 1938 (div. Jan. 1966); children—Jaclyn (Mrs. William B. Low), Walter Benthale, Jerry Clinton. Vice pres., dir. Guarantee Electric Co., Inc., San Antonio, 1943-57; clinician, lang. clinic Baptist Meml. Hosp., San Antonio, partime, 1965-66; tchr. minimal brain injured San Antonio Sch. Dist., 1964-66, diagnostician Appraisal Center, 1974—; adminstr. Beaumont (Tex.) Remedial Clinic, 1966-74. Mem. Exec. Round Table, 1970—, Southeast Tex. Planning Commn., 1972—, Gov.'s Commn. on Status of Women, 1970-71, Gov.'s Council on Learning Disabilities, 1970—. Mem. Tex. Assn. for Children with Learning Disabilities (dir. 1970—), Tex. Council for Exceptional Children (dir. 1970—), Beaumont Assn. for Mental Health (dir. 1971—), Beaumont Bus. and Profl. Women, Beaumont C. of C. Home: 243 Tophill Rd San Antonio TX 78209 Office: 10333 Broadway San Antonio TX 78217

FAHEY, SHIRLEY ANN NICKOLS, psychologist, educator; b. Omaha, Nov. 7, 1928; d. M. Dwight and Dorothy K. (Bateman) Nickols; B.A. cum laude, Vanderbilt U.; 1957; M.A., U. Fla., 1963, Ph.D., 1964; m. Walter J. Fahey, Nov. 26, 1968; children—Gilbert B. Dickey III, Sharon Ann, Leslie Ann. Grad. asst., grad. fellow, interim instr. dept. psychology U. Fla., 1961-64; asst. prof. psychology Tex. Christian U., 1964-65; asst. prof. psychology Ohio U., Athens 1966-69; asst. prof. psychiatry U. Ariz. Coll. Medicine, Tucson, 1970—. Cons. Ariz. Bd. Tech. Registration, 1969-71. Mem. A.A.A.S., Am. Assn. U. Profs., Am. Assn. U. Women, Assn. for Behavioral Sci. and Med. Edn. (exec. council 1973—), Assn. Women Psychologists, Am., Midwestern, Western psychol. assns., Nat. Orgn. for Women (dir. 1971-73), Phi Beta Kappa, Sigma Xi, Psi Chi. Contbr. articles to profl. jours. Home: 6802 Opatas St Tucson AZ 85715

FAHL, CECI SOULIERE (MRS. EARL CORNELL FAHL, JR.), broadcasting exec.; b. St. Albans, Vt., Aug. 24, 1922; d. Alfred Arthur and Evelyn Helen (L'Ecuyer) Souliere; grad. high sch.; m. Earl Cornell Fahl, Jr., July 28, 1945; 1 son, David Earl. With Radio WWSR AM/FM, St. Albans, 1940—, office supr., 1959—, nat. sales mgr., 1972—. Mem. Target Area Action Program Coordinating Com., St. Albans, 1971—. Recipient Certificate of Appreciation, Kerbs Meml. Hosp., St. Albans, 1966, Distinguished Service award Jr. C. of C., 1972. Mem. Am. Women in Radio and Television (state rep., dir. 1967-68, 71-73), Franklin County Bus. and Profl. Women's Club (pres. 1970-72, chmn. state nominating com. 1973-74). Club: Holy Angels' Mothers (St. Albans). Home: 24 N Elm St St Albans VT 05478 Office: PO Box 270 Swanton Rd St Albans VT 05478

FAHRER, ALISON CLARK (MRS. G. WILLIAM FAHRER, JR.), music publisher, composer, ednl. adminstr.; b. Spokane, Wash., Mar. 29, 1923; d. Levi and Josephine (Forrest) Clark; student U. Wash., Seattle, 1939-40; m. David Demarest, July 22, 1940 (div. Nov. 1965); children—Martha, Charles, Ellen D. (Mrs. Stephen Beers), Jean D. (Mrs. Dean Thresher), David; m. 2d, G. William Fahrer, Jr., Jan. 13, 1967. Pianist, composer, tchr., 1945—; founder Canyon Press, Inc., East Orange, N.J., 1951, pres., 1972—; cons. music edn. Baldwin Piano and Organ Co., Cin., 1966—, dir. edn. div., 1973—. Mem. arts council Cin. Recreation Commn., 1969—. Mem. Music Educators Nat. Conf., Music Pubs. Assn. (dir. 1958-62), Music Industry Council, Isaac Walton League, Islamorada C. of C., Internat. Soc. Music Edn. Author: Elements of Music, 1970. Editor: Canyon Hymnal for Boys and Girls, 1958. Contbr. articles on music to profl. pubjs. Composer various piano and choral works, 1952—. Office: 1801 Gilbert Av Cincinnati OH 45202

FAILING, FRANCES ELIZABETH, educator, artist; b. Canisteo, N.Y.; d. William R. and Lillie (Loomis) F.; grad. Pratt Inst., 1919; B.S., Western Res. U., 1931; M.A., Columbia, 1932. Asst. supr. art pub. schs., Rockford, Ill., 1919-22, City Normal Sch., Rochester, N.Y., 1922-24, Manual Tng. High Sch., Indpls., 1924-27; chmn. art dept. Washington High Sch., Indpls., 1927-55; asst. prof. art Ariz. State U., Tempe, 1956-63; exchange tchr., Farnham, Surrey, Eng., 1934-35, Honolulu, 1949-50; one-man shows at museums, galleries, Houston, Dallas, San Antonio, Cleve., Indpls., Phoenix, univs. Baylor, Ball State, Ind. State, Ariz. State; exhibited in group shows Art Inst. Chgo., Internat. Water Color Exhbn., Bklyn. Mus., Liverpool, Eng., Royal Inst. London, Le Salon, Paris; represented in permanent collections Phoenix Pub. Library, John Herron Art Inst., Indpls., Plymouth Art Club, Eng., Tex. U. at Denton; also pvt. collections. Recipient award Hoosier Salon, 1947; O'Brien Gallery Purchase prize, 1956; Ariz. State Fair prizes, 1956, 58; awards Ind. Art Club, 1951, 52, John Herron Art Mus., 1934, Maricopa (Ariz.) Fair, 1957, 58. Mem. Nat. Assn. Women Artists, N.Y. (Leidy prize 1937), Am. Assn. U. Women, Soc. Mayflower Descs. D.A.R., Delta Kappa Gamma. Home: 516 12th Av NE St Petersburg FL 33701

FAILLA, PATRICIA MCCLEMENT (MRS. GIOACCHINO FAILLA), research scientist; b. N.Y.C., Dec. 22, 1925; d. Morgan Hall and Louise (Yandell) McClement; A.B., Barnard Coll., 1946; Ph.D., Columbia, 1958; m. Gioacchino Failla, Jan. 22, 1949 (dec. Dec. 1961). Asst. physicist physics lab. N.Y.C. Dept. Hosps., 1946-48; research sci. Radiol. Research Lab., Columbia, 1950-60; asso. biophysicist Argonne (Ill.) Nat. Lab., 1960—, asst. dir. radiol. and environmental research div., 1971-73; program coordinator, office of dir., 1973-74, asst. to lab dir., 1974—. Mem. tech. electronic product radiation safety standards com. Dept. Health, Edn. and Welfare, 1973—. Ill. Republican Party precinct committeewoman, 1966-70. AEC fellow, 1948-50. Mem. Radiation Research Soc., Health Physics Soc., A.A.A.S., Biophys. Soc., Am. Assn. Physicists in Medicine, Corp. Marine Biol. Lab., Sci. Research Soc. Am., Phi Beta Kappa, Sigma Xi (mem. com. membership-at-large 1970—), Sigma Pi Sigma. Home: 575 Warren Terrace Hinsdale IL 60521 Office: 9700 S Cass Av Argonne IL 60439

FAIN, JANICE SEARS BLOOM, physicist; b. Hot Springs, Ark., Jan. 8, 1927; d. Landess Aaron and Beatrice Julia (Sears) Bloom; B.A., U. Tex., 1948, M.A., 1950, Ph.D., 1956; m. William Wharton Fain, May 29, 1948; 1 dau., Stephanie Beatrice. Mem. profl. staff SHAPE, Tech. Centre, The Hague, Netherlands, 1961-63; exec. adviser aerospaces sci. dept. Douglas Aircraft Co., Long Beach, Cal., 1963-69; mem. profl. staff Center for Naval Analyses, Arlington, Va., 1966-69; sr. asso. CACI, Inc., Arlington, 1969—. Cons. Hist. Evaluation and Research Orgn., Dun Loring, Va., 1970. Recipient Internat. Postdoctoral fellowship Soroptimist, 1956-57. Mem. Am. Phys. Soc. Home: 5547 29th St NW Washington DC 20015 Office: 1815 Ft Myer Dr Arlington VA 22209

FAIN, ROBIN PAULINE, librarian; b. Jessamine County, Ky., Apr. 14, 1912; d. Larkin D. and Minnie (House) F.; A.B., U. Ky., 1941, M.A., 1952, postgrad., 1956-60, 69; postgrad. U. Denver, 1962. Elementary tchr. Jessamine County Schs., Nicholasville, Ky., 1930-45; high sch. tchr. Wilmore, Ky., 1946-58; librarian Jessamine County High Sch., Nicholasville, Ky., 1958—. Vis. instr. U. Ky., Lexington, 1961, 63-66. Named Outstanding Ky. Sch. Librarian, Ky. Library Trustees Assn., 1967. Mem. Nat., Ky., Central Ky., Jessamine County (pres. 1953-54) edn. assns., Am., Ky. (pres. 1962-63), Central Ky. assns. sch. librarians, Am., Southeastern library assns., Delta Kappa Gamma. Home: Route 2 Nicholasville KY 40356 Office: Jessamine County High School Rural Route 4 Nicholasville KY 40356

FAINSTADT, MARIANNE JIRGAL, educator; b. Evanston, Ill., Dec. 9, 1945; d. George Henry and Lucille Ann (Wood) Jirgal; A.A., Stephens Coll., 1966; B.S., Northwestern U., 1968; M.A., U. Cal. at Los Angeles, 1970; m. Leon Fainstadt, May 15, 1970 (div. 1974). Mem. Judith Scott Dance Co., 1966, Gus Giordano Dancers, 1967-68; head dance div., dept. drama U. Wis.-Stevens Point, 1970-71; chmn. ballet dept., instr. Coll. of St. Teresa, Winona, Minn., 1971-74, asst. prof., 1974—. Coordinator Minn. Collegiate Ballet Co., Winona, 1971—; mem. dance adv. panel S.E. regional Minn. Arts Council, Rochester, 1973—. Mem. Am. Assn. U. Profs., Am. Dance Guild, Am. Soc. for Eastern Arts. Democrat.

FAIR, JUDY ANN HUGHES, librarian; b. Rapid City, S.D., Oct. 6, 1940; d. Robert Raymond and Ruth Margaret (Kleppin) Hughes; B.A. in English Lit., Stanford, 1962; M.L.S., U. Cal. at Berkeley, 1963. Librarian tech. information service Stanford Libraries, 1963-65, internat. documents librarian govt. documents dept., 1965-67, head govt. document dept., 1967-71; head reference dept. George Washington U. Library, Washington, 1972; dir. library Urban Inst., Washington, 1972—. Mem. adv. bd. Clearinghouse and Lab. for Census Data, Arlington, Va., 1972. Sponsor Save the Children Fedn., Norwalk, Conn., 1972—. Mem. A.L.A. (sect. pres. 1971-72; mem. com. 1971—), Spl. Libraries Assn., Am. Soc. Information Scis., Council Planning Librarians, Urban and Microfilm Assn., Stanford Alumni Assn., Oceanic Soc., Sierra Club, Smithsonian Assos., Friends Nat. Zoo, Wilderness Soc. Editorial bd. Microform Review, 1973—. Home: 4390 Lorcom Lane Arlington VA 22207 Office: 2100 M St NW Washington DC 20037

FAIRBANK, JANE DAVENPORT (MRS. WILLIAM MARTIN FAIRBANK), editor, continuing edn. specialist; b. Seattle, Aug. 21, 1918; d. Harold Edwin and Mildred (Foster) Davenport; A.B. magna cum laude, Whitman Coll., 1939; postgrad. U. Wash., 1940-42; m. William Martin Fairbank, Aug. 16, 1941; children—William Martin, Robert Harold, Richard Dana. Teaching asst. U. Wash., Seattle, 1940-42; sci. staff mem. Radiation Lab., Mass. Inst. Tech., Cambridge, 1942-45. Chmn. Second Careers for Women, Stanford, Cal., 1970—; mem. exec. com. Bay Area Consortium Continuing Edn. Women, 1972—; rec. sec. Woodside High Sch. P.T.A., 1961-62, editor Newsletter, 1962-63, 64-65, corr. sec. 1965-66, pres., 1967-68; mem. Canada Coll. Citizens Adv. Com. for Community Edn., 1968—. Mem. Internat. Platform Assn., Whitman Coll. Alumni Assn., Cal. Congress Parents and Tchrs. (hon. life), Mortar Bd., Phi Beta Kappa, Alpha Chi Omega. Mem. United Ch. of Christ. Club: Stanford Faculty Women's (1st v.p. 1969-70, editor Newsletter 1965-67, 71-72). Editor: Radar Maintenance Manual (2 vols.), 1945; Second Careers for Women: A View from the San Francisco Peninsula, 1971. Contbr. articles to sci.

jours. Home: 141 E Floresta Way Menlo Park CA 94025 Office: Second Careers for Women PO Box 9660 Stanford CA 94305

FAIRBANKS, MARY LEE EPLING (MRS. DOUGLAS FAIRBANKS, JR.), civic worker; b. Keystone, W.Va., Dec. 18, 1912; d. Giles Thomas and Nancy (White) Epling; B.S., Lesley Coll., 1933; m. Douglas Fairbanks, Jr., Apr. 22, 1939; children—Daphne (Mrs. David Weston), Victoria (Mrs. Barend Van Gerbig), Melissa (Mrs. Richard Morant). Mem. Am. Soc. Most Venerable Order of Hosp. St. John of Jerusalem; v.p. Sunshine Home for Blind Babies, U.K., 1954—; mem. council Am. Mus. Britain, Bath, U.K. 1960—; v.p. A.R.C., Washington, 1942-45; dame Order Hosp. St. John Jerusalem, U.K., 1952—. Mem. D.A.R. Episcopalian. Home: 50 E 58th St New York City NY 10022 also 255 Emerald Lane Palm Beach FL also 28 The Boltons London SW 10 England

FAIRBANKS, PHYLLIS KELLY (MRS. DOUGLAS A. FAIRBANKS), lawyer; b. Grand Rapids, Mich., Sept. 17, 1930; d. William John and Onahlee Anona (Loyselle) Kelly; A.B., U. Cal. at Los Angeles, 1952, M.A. in Spanish, 1953, LL.B., 1957; m. Douglas A. Fairbanks, May 15, 1965. Admitted to Cal. bar, 1958; practiced in Los Angeles; with Office State Controller, Los Angeles, 1960—. Mem. Am., Los Angeles County bar assns. Clubs: Los Angeles Athletic, Town Hall. Office: 107 S Broadway St Los Angeles CA 91405

FAIRCHILD, CAROL MARGARET, coll. dean; b. Malden, Mass., Mar. 3, 1948; d. Lawrence W. and Margaret M. (Piper) Fairchild; B.S., Ball State U., 1970; M.Ed., Ohio U., 1972. Resident dir. Ohio U., Athens, 1970, asst. area coordinator, 1971, area coordinator, 1972, asst. dir. of residence life, 1972-73; dean of women Berry (Ga.) Coll., 1974—. Mem. Nat., Ohio, Ga. assns. women deans, adminstrs. and counselors, Nat. Assn. Student Personnel Adminstrs. Home and office: Berry College Mount Berry GA 30149

FAIRCHILD, ELVA RUSSELL WHITMAN (MRS. ALEXANDER GRAHAM BELL FAIRCHILD), portrait artist; b. Boston; d. Eldon Russell and Lilian (Gibbs) Whitman; B.S. in Edn., Boston Tchrs. Colls., 1936; study sculpture Gopley Soc. Boston, 1937-38; pvt. study with John Carlson, Miami, 1940; student Philips Art Gallery, Washington, 1945, U. Minn., 1948; m. Alexander Graham Bell Fairchild, June 18, 1938; children—Alice Bell, David II. One-man shows at Mus. Nat. Library Panama, 1953, Mus. of Casa de Esculpturos, Panama, 1970, Gallery Rabbi Witkin U.S.O. C.Z., 1951, Little Gallery, Tivoli Hotel, C.Z., 1958, 62, Casa de la Escultura, Panama; exhibited in group shows at Smithsonian Instn., Washington, Mus. of Panama Art Inst., Gallery Panama N.Am. Assn.; represented in permanent collection at Permanent Gallery of Art of U. Panama, also numerous pvt. collections C.Z., Panama., U.S., S.Am., Europe; executed murals for Children's Home, Bella Vista, also Nat. Mus. Panama; sketches for Hist. Gainesville, Inc., 1973; designer Christmas cards for Nat. Mus. Panama; tchr. pvt. art classes for children, 1945; tchr. painting and portraiture Balboa Coll., 1965-66; tchr. pvt. art classes for adults Morgan's Gardens, 1966, 69; vol. tchr. Helen Keller Sch. of Deaf, 1967, 68. Recipient 1st prize C.Z. Art League, 1942, 1943, 44, 45, 55, 2d prize Panarte Mus., Edificio Malstras, 1964. Mem. C.Z. League Am. Pen Women (pres. 1963-64). Episcopalian. Home and studio: 16 NW 22d Dr Gainesville FL 32601

FAIRCHILD, GYLA MARJORIE SWANSON (MRS. EUGENE FAIRCHILD), occupational therapist; b. Frederic, Wis., Oct. 3, 1918; d. Herman and Maude Louise (Lindvig) Swanson; B.S., Stout Inst., 1940; diploma occupational therapy Phila. Sch. Occupational Therapy, 1946; postgrad. U. Minn., Ia. State U.; m. Eugene Fairchild, Nov. 19, 1947. Tchr. home econs. Wis. High Sch., New Auburn, Arkansaw and Milltown, 1940-45; staff occupational therapist VA Hosp., Palo Alto, Cal., 1946-49, Glenwood Hills Hosp., Mpls., 1949-50, VA Hosp., Mpls., 1951-52; chief, occupational therapy VA Hosp., Iowa City, Ia., 1952—. Pres., Craft Guild of Iowa City, 1963-66. Bd. dir. Fed. Employees Credit Union. Mem. World Fedn. Occupational Therapists, Am. (del. to del. assembly 1970-73), Ia. (pres. 1956-58) occupatonal therapy assns. Methodist. Home: 2517 Friendship St Iowa City IA 52240 Office: Veterans Administration Hospital Iowa City IA 52240

FAIRCHILD, JANE ELECTA KING (MRS. LEROY EDWARD FAIRCHILD), realtor; b. Petaluma, Cal., Aug. 29, 1927; d. James and Mable (Willis) King; B.S., Saline-Johnstone Coll., 1931; m. LeRoy Edward Fairchild, Mar. 2, 1935; children—Carole Janelee (Mrs. Russell Leif), Electa Leigh. Auditor, Gen. Motors, San Francisco, 1939-42; bookkeeper United Motors, San Francisco, 1936-38, Don Gilmore Chevrolet, San Francisco, 1936-38; owner Jane Fairchild Realty, San Rafael, Cal., 1963—. Treas. Marin County Bd. Realtors, 1968-69; mem. Golden Gate Bridge Transp. Adv. Panel Com., San Francisco, 1969-75; chmn. Marin and Sonoma Counties Atty. Gens. Vol. Adv. Council, 1972-75; advisor Order Rainbow for Girls, Petaluma, Cal., 1928. Mem. San Rafael C. of C. (dir. 1973), Women's Council Realtors (pres. Cal. chpt. 1974), U. Cal. Alumni Assn. (life). Mem. Order Eastern Star (worthy matron 1934-35). Home: 3 Woods St San Rafael CA 94901 Office: 412 D St San Rafael CA 94901

FAIRCHILD, RUTH SHERWOOD (MRS. WAYNE LEO FAIRCHILD), civic worker; b. Pierre, S.D., May 19, 1918; d. Mervin C. and Fleta May (Weeks) Sherwood; student Aberdeen Bus. Coll., 1937-38; m. Wayne Leo Fairchild, Sept. 4, 1938; children—Kent, Bruce, Marsha (Mrs. Billy R. Sumpter). Pres. Haakon County Farmers Union, Philip, S.D., 1966-74. Pres. Haakon County Democratic Com., Philip, 1966-70, v.p., 1970-74. Chmn. bd. dirs. Hans P. Peterson Meml. Hosp. Aux., Philip, 1973-74. Presbyn. Club: Get Together (Philip). Home: Star Route Philip SD 57567

FAIRCHILD, SALLY ALEXANDRA (MRS. EDWARD ROSEN), artist; b. N.Y.C., July 19, 1927; d. Henry and Jeannette (Le Bel) Fairchild; student Cooper Union, 1945-48, Coll. City N.Y., 1954-56; B.A. cum laude, Brandeis U., 1958; m. Edward Rosen, June 9, 1959; 1 dau., Carla Jeannette. Exhibited art in shows at Whitney Mus., N.Y.C., Panoras Gallery, N.Y.C., Kretchmer Gallery, N.Y.C., Brandeis U., Waltham, Mass., exhibited in group shows at N.A.D., Lever House, N.Y.C., Memphis State U., Tuskegee (Ala.) Inst., Art Assn. Richmond (Ind.); represented in pvt. collections. Recipient New Mem. prize Nat. Assn. Women Artists, 1970. Mem. Nat. Assn. Women Artists (membership com. 1973-74), Women in Arts. Home: 315 Riverside Dr New York City NY 10025 Office: 310 Riverside Dr New York City NY 10025

FAIRCLOUGH, ELLEN LOUKS COOK (MRS. DAVID HENRY GORDON FAIRCLOUGH), corp. exec.; b. Hamilton, Ont., Can., Jan. 28, 1905; d. Norman Ellsworth and Nellie (Louks) Cook; student pub. schs.; m. David Henry Gordon Fairclough, Jan. 28, 1931; 1 son, Howard Gordon. Accountant, various stock broker offices, Can., 1921-35; accountant E. L. Fairclough, C.P.A., Hamilton, 1935-57; cabinet minister Govt. of Can., Ottawa, 1957-63; corp. sec.-treas. Hamilton Trust & Savs. Corp., 1963—, dir., 1967—. Past Dominion sec. United Empire Loyalists Assn. Trustee, Hamilton United Appeal, 1966—; nat. dir. Canadian Council Christians and Jews, 1957—. Mem. Hamilton City Council, 1946-50; mem. Ho. of Commons, 1950-63. Recipient Queen's Coronation medal, 1953, Cenfedn. medal, 1967. Fellow Inst. Chartered Accountants Ont.; mem. Gen. Accountants Assn., C.P.A. Assn., Hamilton C. of C. (dir. 1972), Girl Guides of Can. Club: Zonta (past pres., dist. gov., now internat. treas.). Home: 25 Stanley Av Hamilton ON 12 Canada Office: 75 James St S Hamilton ON 10 Canada

FAIRLEIGH, MARGARET HILLS (MRS. GEORGE DURELLE FAIRLEIGH), lawyer; b. Atlanta, Apr. 11, 1912; d. Albert Lyman and Georgia (Burns) Hills; LL.B. Woodrow Wilson Coll. Law, 1939; m. George DuRelle Fairleigh, June 29, 1951; stepchildren—Kathryn (Mrs. Roger W. Allen Jr.), Henrietta (Mrs. Charles M. Sparacino). Admitted to Ga. bar, 1940; asso. Poole, Pearce & Hall, Atlanta, 1942-51, partner (name later changed to Poole, Pearce & Cooper), 1951-71; pvt. practice law, Decatur, Ga., 1971—. Dir. Fed. Defender Program, Inc., 1974—. Mem. Atlanta Estate Planning Council, Gov.'s Commn. on Status of Women, 1968-70. Mem. Nat. (state del. 1969-72), Ga. (pres. 1947-48) assns. women lawyers, Atlanta Legal Aid Soc. (pres. 1963-64), Am., Ga., Atlanta, Decatur-DeKalb bar assns., Am. Judicature Soc. Presbyn. Home: 486 Princeton Way NE Atlanta GA 30307 Office: 1 W Court Sq Decatur GA 30030

FAIRLIE, MARGARET CARRICK (MRS. KENNETH ADRIAN RAINE KENNEDY), composer; b. Atlanta, Mar. 27, 1928; d. Andrew Miller and Lucia Cabiness (Peeples) Fairlie; B.S., Julliard Sch. Mus., 1948; Mus.M. (fellow), Converse Sch. Mus., 1955; pvt. study Wallingford Riegger, 1955-57, Ithaca Coll. Instructional Resources Center, 1969-71; m. Kenneth Adrian Raine Kennedy, Aug. 10, 1969. Faculty, Bklyn. Sch. Mus., 1949-51, Converse Sch. Mus., Spartenburg, S.C., 1954-55, Bennington (Vt.) Coll., 1957-58, Jewish Community Center, Atlanta, 1958-59, Hoff-Barthelson Sch. Mus., Scarsdale, N.Y., 1961-63; mus. dir. performing arts Bennett Coll., Millbrook, N.Y., 1963-66; composer in residence for dance Cornell U., Ithaca, N.Y., 1966-68, faculty summer dance program, 1974. Composer score and electronic tape for ednl. TV dance drama, U. Ga., 1967-68; producer films Demons and Dancers of Ceylon, 1971, The Healing Hill, 1973. Mem. Atlanta Community Orch. Com., 1951-54, Atlanta Contemporary Dance Group, 1951-54, Active Voters, 1951-54; chmn. performing arts Atlanta Festival of Arts, 1960-61. MacDowell Colony fellow, 1963, 67; Bennington Composers Conf. Scholar, 1957-58, 61-62. Mem. Am. Mus. Center, Soc. Ethnomusicology, Southeastern Composer's League, Am. Assn. U. Profs., Lamda Chi. Author: Images for the Young Pianist, 1962. Composer: Trio for Piano, Violin and Clarinet, 1957; Concerto for Percussion, 1958, Music for String Quartet and Percussion, 1959; Concerto for Piano and Orchestra, 1960; Set of Four for Piano, 1961; Wind Quintet, 1962; Four Structures for Chamber Group, 1963; Orchestral and electronic score, 1968. Commns. received from Agnes Scott Coll., 1960, Bennington Coll., 1960, Ga. Council Arts, 1968. Home: 63 Hickory Circle Ithaca NY 14850

FAIRMAN, JOAN ALEXANDRA, exec. sec., author; b. Phila., Apr. 11, 1935; d. Alexander Daisley and Florence Mae (Wenner) Fairman; grad. Peirce Jr. Coll., 1953. With Curtis Pub. Co., Phila., 1953-70, exec. sec., writer, 1964-70; exec. sec. Towers, Perrin, Forster & Crosby, Inc., Phila., 1970—. Author of Baba Yaba series Jack and Jill Mag., 1967—; A Penny Saved, 1971. Home: 4147 Elbridge St Philadelphia PA 19135 Office: 3 Penn Center Philadelphia PA 19102

FAIRMAN, PATRICIA ANN, psychologist; b. Tarentum, Pa., July 3, 1937; d. Paul Elwood and June Winifred (Evans) Milliron; B.A. in Psychology, Pa. State U., 1966, M.Ed., 1968. Acting dir. dept. psychology Laurelton (Pa.) State Sch., 1968-69; asso. psychologist Ridgway (Pa.) Psychiat. Center, 1969-72; coordinator Mental Retardation Services, Bradford, Pa., 1972-73, asso. psychol. services, 1973—; cons. in field. Mem. Am. Assn. U. Women, Keystone Soc., Am., Pa. psychol. assns., Am. Personnel and Guidance Assn., Nat. Rehab. Assn., Mortar Bd., Psi Chi, Delta Mu Sigma, Delta Psi Omega. Episcopalian (mem. women's guild). Home: Fairview Rd Kersey PA 15846 Office: Field Social Services Boylston St Bradford PA 16701

FAIRWEATHER, MARION JEANNE, physician; b. Worcester, Mass.; d. John Lee and Marion Gay (Banister) Fairweather; R.N., Hartford Hosp. Sch. of Nursing, 1941; postgrad. Columbia, 1943-44, Boston U., 1944-45; B.S. magna cum laude, Incarnate Word Coll., San Antonio, 1949; M.D., U. Tex., 1954. Nursing supr. obstetrics, Conn., 1945-46; surg. asst. orthopedic surgery, nursing instr. orthopedics and obstetrics, Tex., 1946-49; rotating intern Robert B. Green Meml. Hosp., San Antonio, 1954-55, resident internal medicine, 1955-57; resident internal medicine VA Hosp., Houston, 1957-58; clin. instr. medicine med. sch. Baylor U., 1957-59; fellow internal medicine and cancer research, med. sch. U. Tex., Anderson Hosp. and Tumor Inst., 1958-59; staff dept. internal medicine and endocrinology Brooke Army Med. Center, Ft. Sam Houston, 1959—, chief main hosp. clinics. Mem. Bexar County Civil Def. Moblzn. Fellow Am. Geriatrics Soc.; mem. Tex. Soc. Nuclear Physicians, A.M.A., Internat., Am. med. women's assns., Tex., Bexar County med. socs., Pan-Am. Med. Women's Assn., San Antonio Club of Internists, Internat., Tex. socs. internal medicine Pan-Pacific Surg. Assn. (asso.) Internat. Med. Assembly S.W. Tex., Soc. Nuclear Medicine, Tex. Diabetes Assn., A.C.P. (life), Royal Soc. Health, Am. Rheumatism Assn., S.W. Tex. Archaeol. Soc. (pres. 1972—), Council Internat. Relations, Mil. Order St. Camillus, Assn. Mil. Surgeons U.S., World Med. Assn., Royal Soc. Medicine, Phi Sigma Kappa, Alpha Chi, Alpha Epsilon Iota. Contbr. articles to med. jours. Designer infant rocking bed for resuscitation, 1955. Home: 828 Elizabeth Rd San Antonio TX 78209 Office: Box 146 Brooke Army Med Center Ft Sam Houston TX 78234

FAIVER, ALICE VIOLET ESCKILSEN (MRS. KENNETH L. FAIVER), civic worker; b. Bay City, Mich., May 20; d. Elmer and Nellie (Ward) Esckilsen; student Mt. Pleasand Tchrs. Coll., 1928-29; m. Kenneth L. Faiver, July 1, 1929; children—Joyce Louise (Mrs. John Frank Blackledge), Georgene Alice (Mrs. Bruce Jennings Lundquist) and George (twins). Co-owner Favier's Lobster House, Panacea, Fla., 1960—. Vol., Tallahassee Meml. Hosp. Aux., 1949—, pres., 1957-59, 72—, mem. hosp. municipal bd., 1973-76; trustee Municipal Hosp. Tallahassee; pres. Assn. Fla. Hosp. Auxs., 1962-63, legislation chmn., 1968-69, delegations chmn., 1970-71; treas. Elkettes, 1959, pres., 1964-65. Mem. Internat. Platform Assn. Presbyn. Mem. Order Eastern Star (past worhty patron Davison, Mich.). Club: Altrusa (extension chmn. also treas. 1964-65, pres. Tallahassee 1968-69). Address: PO Box 65 Panacea FL 32346

FALCO, ELVIRA ALLEGRA (MRS. BERL BASS), chemist; b. Bklyn., Dec. 13, 1918; d. Eugene and Laura (Benzaquen) Falco; B.S., Cornell, 1939, M.S., 1940; m. Berl Bass, May 26, 1967; 1 son from previous marriage, William Leuszler. Clin. chemist U. Md. Med. Sch., Md., 1940-41; analyst Davison Chem. Co., Balt., 1941-43; sr. biochemist Burroughs Wellcome Co., Research Triangle, N.C., 1942-56; exec. asst. chem. files Sloan-Kettering Inst., Rye, N.Y., 1959-68, research asso., 1968—. Mem. Am. Chem. Soc. Club: Horseshoe Harbor Yacht (Larchmont, N.Y.). Patentee in field. Home: 115 Pryer Terrace New Rochelle NY 10804 Office: 145 Boston Post Rd Rye NY 10580

FALCO, JUDITH ANDERSON (MRS. FRANK JOSEPH FALCO), broadcasting exec.; b. Mt. Vernon, N.Y., Dec. 31, 1937; d. Howard Service and Ruth Sylvia (Megrath) Anderson; student Reed Coll., 1955—; m. Frank Joseph Falco, June 18, 1960; children—Joseph, Edith, Paul, Ruth. Sec. to v.p. spl. projects R.R. Bowker Co., N.Y.C., 1960-61; copywriter, asst. in programming radio sta. WGLI, Babylon, N.Y., 1973—. Actress numerous local theatre groups; founder, dir., producer Teakettle Players, children's theatre. Mem. Mensa. Home: 115 Haynes Av West Islip NY 11795 Office: WGLI 1290 Peconic Av Babylon NY 11704

FALCONER, HAZEL LUCILLE, lawyer; b. Bismarck, N.D., Aug. 1, 1921; d. William Bentley and Kathryn H. (Lewis) Falconer; grad., Bismarck Jr. Coll., 1939-41; student U. N.D., 1946-47, U. Okla., 1950; m. Nicholas Thomas Devich, June 26, 1947 (div.). Country sch. tchr. Aurora Sch. 1, Goodrich, N.D., 1941-42; sec. Office State Printer, Bismarck, 1942-43, 44-46; property clk., old age assistance div. Pub. Welfare Bd. N.D., Bismarck, 1948-50; sec. geol. div. Cities Service Oil Co., Bismarck, 1951-54; office mgr. Gerlach's Sheet Metal Works, Inc., Bismarck, 1954-70; admitted to N.D. bar, 1969, since practiced in Bismarck. Served with USMC, 1943-44. Mem. N.D. Bar Assn., Burleigh County Pioneer Assn., Burleigh County Pioneer Daus., Bus. and Profl. Women's Assn. Republican. Methodist. Mem. Order Eastern Star. Address: Route 2 Box 123 Bismarck ND 58501

FALCONER, MARY WARING, author; b. Chgo., Mar. 14, 1898; d. Gerard Creagh and Mary Waring (Rode) Falconer; diploma, teaching certificate U. So. Miss. (formerly Miss. Normal Coll.), 1916; diploma Mountainside Hosp. Sch. Nursing, Montclair, N.J., 1921; B.A., San Jose State Coll., 1941, M.A., 1951; postgrad. U. Cal. Extension, San Jose, 1969-70. Tchr. home econs. Wayne County Agrl. High Sch., Clara, Miss., 1916-18; nursing supr. Flushing Hosp. and Dispensary (N.Y.), 1923, tchr. Nursing Sch., 1924-25; tchr. O'Conner Hosp. Sch. Nursing, San Jose, 1927-32, 41-42, 45-63; supr., tchr., asst. dir. nursing Santa Clara Valley Med. Center, San Jose, 1933-39; dir. nurses, head nursing sch. Reid Meml. Hosp., Richmond, Ind., 1943-44; writer, 1951—. Mem. Am. Nurses Assn. (pres. local chpt. 1942), Am. Pharm. Assn. Roman Catholic. Author: The Current Drug Handbook, 1958; (with others) The Drug, The Nurse, The Patient, 1958. Address: 494 Richmond Av San Jose CA 95128

FALCONIERI, VIRGINIA PATRICIA, painter, educator; b. Paterson, N.J., Mar. 18, 1943; d. Nathan J. and Lena M. (Farruggio) Falconieri; student Entwistle Sch. of Art, Ridgewood, N.J., 1959-61, Ridgewood Sch. of Art, 1961-64. One-woman shows at Paterson Mus., 1963-64, Ridgewood Sch. Art, 1964, Art Workshop and Gallery, Hawthorne, N.J., 1965-66, The Studio, Hawthorne, annually 1966—; exhibited in group shows at Mus. Fine Arts, Springfield, Mass., 1963, 64, Arts Club Washington, 1968—, Ahda Artzt Gallery, N.Y.C., 1968—, Pacem in Terris Gallery, N.Y.C., 1969—, Nat. Arts Club N.Y., 1971—, Jersey City Mus., 1970-72, Paterson Mus., 1963-66, Bergen Community Mus., Paramus, N J., 1972—, Salmagundi Club N.Y., 1974; represented in permanent collections Paterson Mus., Bergen Community Mus. Art and Sci., Paramus; instr. oil painting Ridgewood Sch. of Art, 1963-66, Fairlawn (N.J.) Cultural Center, 1964-67, Studio of Virginia Falconieri, Hawthorne. 1966—. Asso. curator Paterson (N.J.) Mus. of Art, 1964—. Recipient Gold medal Gotham Painters, 1968, numerous other awards, 1964—. Mem. Miniature Art Soc. of N.J., Am. Artist Profl. League, Ringwood Manor Assn. of Arts (dir. of children 1964-66), Catharine Lorillard Wolfe Art Club, Gotham Painters N.Y., Burr Artist N.Y., Composers, Authors and Artists Am., Miniature Painters, Sculptors and Gravers Soc., Salmagundi Club, Allied Artists Am. (asso.). Home: 58 Mountain Av Hawthorne NJ 07506 Studio: 228 Lafayette Av Hawthorne NJ 07506

FALES, JERRY LYNN GREER (MRS. DANIEL CARVER FALES), mag. editor; b. New Orleans, May 17, 1943; d. Earnest Frank and Dorothy (Raines) Greer; B.J. (Jesse Jones scholar, Zonta club scholar), U. Tex., 1965; m. Daniel Carver Fales, Dec. 7, 1968. Copy editor Dallas Morning News, 1965-67; asst. editor prodn. Sci. Digest mag., N.Y.C., 1967-70; mng. editor Travel Agt. mag., N.Y.C., 1971; copy editor Metals Week mag., N.Y.C., 1971; prodn. editor House & Garden Guides, mags., N.Y.C., 1972—; free-lance proofreader Finance mag., 1971—. Mem. Women in Communications, U. Tex. Ex-Students Assn. (N.Y.C. sec. 1969-70). Democrat. Methodist. Home: 400 E 55th St Apt 9A New York City NY 10022 Office: 350 Madison Av New York City NY 10017

FALGIATORE, THERSA M., advt. co. exec.; b. Phila., Apr. 18, 1935; d. Amedeo and Mary (Di Gregorio) Falgiatore; B.A., Temple U., 1956; diploma Pierce Coll. Automation, 1966, Charles Morris Price Sch. Advt., 1960; diploma in advt. N.Y. Sch. for Social Research, 1966. Asso. media dir. planning and buying N. W. Ayer, Inc., Phila., 1966; with Ted Bates & Co., Inc., N.Y.C., 1967—, v.p., 1970—, dir. data processing systems dept., 1970—, sr. v.p., 1973—. Mem. N.Y. Data Processing Assn. Club: New York Community Chess (N.Y.C.). Office: Ted Bates and Co Inc 1515 Broadway New York City NY

FALK, ALMA MARTHA (MRS. BYRON A. FALK), educator; b. Chgo., Apr. 18, 1910; d. Henry and Alma (Wolowski) Weihofen; certificate Chgo. Tchrs. Coll., 1932; B.A., George Washington U., 1937, M.A., 1957; m. James E. Curry, Apr. 28, 1934 (dec. Aug. 1972); 1 dau., Aileen Cloonan; m. 2d, Byron A. Falk. Social worker Ill. Relief Commn., 1932-35; tchr. elementary sch. Chgo., 1936-37, 46-47; elementary tchr. Jr. Village Sch., Washington, 1953-57; reading coordinator Washington Pub. Schs., 1957-72; instr. George Washington Reading Clinic, 1957-66; pres. Greater Washington Reading Council, 1966-67. Vol. asst. Civil Def. Milk Sta. Program, San Juan, P.R., 1942-46; instr. Urban Service Corps. of Vols., 1962-66. Recipient citation White House Conf. on Children, 1962. Mem. Am. Assn. U. Women (chmn. bd. 1959-61), Nat. Soc. for Study Edn., Internat. Reading Assn., Am. Fedn. Tchrs., N.E.A., Women's Internat. League for Peace and Freedom, Washington Tchrs. Union (rep. reading specialists 1968-70), Internat. Assn. Gen. Semantics, UN Assn., Phi Delta Gamma. Club: George Washington U. (charter). Home: 1330 New Hampshire Av NW Washington DC 20036

FALK, BARBARA MARIE, psychologist; b. Evergreen Park, Ill., Nov. 16, 1940; d. Walter John and Marie Rose (Pavola) Falk; B.S. in Biology, St. Francis Coll., Loretto, Pa., 1962; M.Ed. in Counseling Psychology, U. Ill., 1969, Ph.D. in Counseling Psychology, 1972. Tchr. biology Community High Sch. Dist. 218, Blue Island Ill., 1966-68, counselor, 1968-70; asst. prof. ednl. psychology U. Ill., Urbana, 1972-73; psychologist, asst. dir. Diagnostic and Treatment Center, St. Louis, 1973—. Mem. faculty, U. Mo. at St. Louis, 1973-74, St. Louis U., 1974—. Mem. Am. Psychol. Assn., Phi Delta Kappa. Home: 14475 Greencastle Dr Apt 3 Chesterfield MO 63017 Office: 607 N Grand Av St Louis MO 63103

FALK, CAROL HELEN, journalist; b. Madison, Wis., Dec. 4, 1941; d. Philip Hadley and Ethel Emma (Mabie) Falk; B.A., U. Wis., 1963; M.S., Columbia, 1964. Newsmarker, Fortune mag., N.Y.C., 1964-65, editorial asst., 1965-66, research asso., 1966-69; staff reporter Wall St. Jour., N.Y.C., 1969-70, Washington, 1970—. Clapp and Poliak fellow. Mem. Mortar Bd., Phi Beta Kappa, Phi Kappa Phi, Conglist. Club: Washington Press. Home: 532 20th St NW Washington DC 20006 Office: Nat Press Bldg Washington DC 20004

FALK, CAROLYN ROSENSTEIN, bacteriologist, ch. worker; b. Elmsford, N.Y., Apr. 28, 1902; d. Louis and Pearl (Asher) Rosenstein; A.B., Smith Coll., 1923; m. K. George Falk, Oct. 16, 1935 (dec. 1953). Lab. asst. N.Y.C. Health Dept., 1923-30, bacteriologist, 1930-57, sr. bacteriologist 1957, ret.; treas. lab. of indsl. hygiene, 1954; specializes in standardization and testing of biologic products, preservations, toxins, antibiotic testing; chmn. N.Y. Met. regional br. Am. Ch. Union, Inc., 1959-61; mem.-at-large United Ch. Women, 1959; sec. bd. govs. Finger Lakes Conf., 2d Province P.E. Ch., 1960-66; treas. Ch. Women United in Manhattan, 1960-64, v.p., 1964-68, pres. 1968-72; diocesan supply chmn. Episcopal Churchwomen, Diocese, N.Y., 1960-66; pres. Assos. Eastern Province Sisters of St. Mary, 1964—, Friends St. Mary's in Field, 1965—; v.p. bd. mgrs. Manhattan div. Council Chs., 1969-71; bd. mgrs. Council of Chs., City N.Y., sec., 1972. Fellow Am. Pub. Health Assn., A.A.A.S.; mem. Soc. Am. Bacteriologists, Am. Assn. Immunologists, Soc. Exptl. Biology and Medicine, N.Y. Acad. Scis., Am. Med. Writers Assn., Royal Soc. for Promotion of Health (London), N.Y. League Women Voters. Episcopalian. Club: Smith College (N.Y.C.). Contbr. articles to sci. jours. Home: 169 E 69th St New York City NY 10021

FALKENRECK, MARY ELIZABETH (MRS. JOHN W. FALKENRECK), ednl. adminstr.; b. Spokane, Wash., Nov. 3; d. James Michael and Mary Elizabeth (Bradley) Duffy; student Marylhurst Coll., 1941-43, Portland State U., 1943, 44, Gonzaga U., 1945, Fort Wright Coll., 1970-73; m. John W. Falkenreck, May 17, 1947; children—Ellen (Mrs. David J. Smith), Robert, Janie. Exec. sec. Wash. Water Power Co., Spokane, 1945-47; asst. to fashion coordinator Bon Marché, Spokane, 1963-65; area rep. Betsy Ross Promotions, 1961-63; registrar Fort Wright Coll., Spokane, 1966—, also mem. admissions com., adminstrv. senate, acad. affairs com., 1967—. Mem. budget panel and task force United Way of Spokane County, 1969—; sec. Spokane P.T.A., 1962-65. Bd. dirs. Spokane Music and Allied Arts Festival, chmn., 1966-67. Recipient Service award United Way of Spokane County, 1972, 73. Mem. Jr. League Spokane (v.p. 1963-64), Am., Pacific assns. collegiate registrars and admission officers. Roman Catholic. Home: 507 W 21st St Spokane WA 99203 Office: W 4000 Randolph Rd Spokane WA 99204

FALKENSTEIN, DOROTHY FRANCES (MRS. ALBERT RANDALL SMITH), physician; b. Ashtabula, O., Mar. 2, 1911; d. Oscar and Nina (Haggerty) Falkenstein; B.A., Ohio State U., 1932, M.D., 1936; postgrad. in pediatrics U. Ia., 1938-40; m. Albert Randall Smith, Sept. 1, 1939; 1 son, Robert Francis. Intern City Hosp., Cleve., 1936-37, resident in chest medicine, 1937-38; resident in pediatrics U. Ia., Iowa City, 1938-39, chief resident in pediatrics, 1939-40; practice medicine specializing in pediatrics and teaching disabled children, Columbus, O., 1940—; asso. clin. prof. pediatrics Ohio State U. Coll. Medicine, Columbus, 1958—; attending staff Univ. Hosp., Children's Hosp., Grant Hosp., Columbus; courtesy staff Mt. Carmel Hosp., Columbus. Mem. Met. Health Council, Columbus, 1954-58; founder, 1st pres., life mem. women's service bd. Grant Hosp. Bd. dirs. Beverly Farm Found, Godfrey, Ill., Ohio State U. Diplomate Am. Bd. Pediatrics. Fellow Am. Acad. Pediatrics (chmn. sch. health com. Ohio chpt.); mem. A.M.A., Am. Med. Women's Assn. (chmn. Nat. Scholarship com.), Pan Am., Ohio med. assns., Central Ohio Pediatric Soc. (pres. 1970-71), Franklin County Assn. Children with Learning Disabilities (dir.), Phi Mu. Clubs: Women's (Starling, O.). Home: 2396 Anson St Columbus OH 43220 Office: 363 E Town St Columbus OH 43215

FALKENSTEIN, JANET LEE, occupational therapist; b. Salem, O., Aug. 20, 1948; d. Alfons Philip and Liesel (Gumpertz) Falkenstein; B.S., Ind. U., 1970, M.S., 1974. Staff occupational therapist Larue D. Carter Meml. Hosp., Indpls., 1970-72, Riley Hosp. for Children, Indpls., 1972—. Mem. Am., Ind. occupational therapy assns., Marion County Mental Health Assn., Marion County Muscular Dystrophy Assn., Pi Theta Epsilon. Democrat. Jewish religion. Home: 5324 Tara Court South Indianapolis IN 46224 Office: 1100 W Michigan St Indianapolis IN 46202

FALL, FRIEDA KAY, artist, art mus. exec.; b. Lebanon, Ind., July 1, 1913; d. Cecil George and Willa Kay (Irvin) Fall; B.A., Tex. State Coll. Women, 1935; M.A., Tex. Woman's U., 1941; m. Joseph Michael Farraday, Mar. 12, 1952 (div. 1952); 1 son, Jonathon Fall Farraday. Tchr. art pub. schs., Center, Tex., 1935-36, Houston, 1936-39, Dallas, 1939-45; owner, operator Frieda Kay Fall Gallery, Dallas, 1945-51; registrar Los Angeles County Mus. History, Sci. and Art, 1951-62; registrar Los Angeles County Mus. of Art, 1963-67, exec. asst. operations, 1967-68, asst. to dep. dir., 1968—. Paintings exhibited in Dallas, Houston, Ft. Worth, San Antonio, N.Y.C., Washington, Phila., traveling exhbns., Tex., La., Tenn., Ala., Ga.; instr. painting and drawing Dallas Mus. Fine Arts, 1938-44; tchr. children's painting classes Los Angeles County Mus., 1961. Recipient awards Tex. State Fair, Dallas Mus. Fine Arts, 1926-32; Edith Penman award ann. exhbn. Nat. Assn. Women Artists, 1938. Fellow internat. Inst. Arts and Letters; mem. Nat. Assn. Women Artists, Dallas Art Assn., Art Historians So. Cal., Am. Assn. Museums (sec., treas. Western regional conf. 1957-59), Internat. Council Museums, Western Assn. Art Museums, Coll. Art Assn., Am. Soc. Archtl. Historians. Republican. Author: Art Objects—Their Care and Preservation, 1967, 71, 73. Contbr. articles to profl. jours. Home: 576 N Kenter Av Brentwood Los Angeles CA 90049 Office: 5905 Wilshire Blvd Los Angeles CA 90036

FALLA, ANITA ELSA, surgeon; b. Jersey City; d. Fernando and Anna (Schumacher) Falla; A.B., Coll. St. Elizabeth, Convent Station, N.J., 1943; M.D., State U. N.Y., 1950. Intern State U. N.Y. Med. Center, Syracuse, 1950-51, resident gen. surgery, 1951-53; resident pediatric surgery Childrens Hosp. Center, Boston, 1953-54; resident gen. surgery Northwestern U. Med. Center, Chgo., 1955-58; chief resident pediatric surgery Buffalo Childrens Hosp., 1959-60; practice medicine specializing in pediatric surgery, Newark, 1960—; asso. dir. surgery, attending pediatric surgeon, dir. pediatric surg. edn., asst. dir. Birth Defects Treatment Center, Children's Hosp. unit United Hosps. Med. Center, Newark; sr. attending pediatric surgeon St. Michaels Med. Center; chief pediatric surgery Children's Hosp. Newark, 1970—; asst. attending surgeon Pediatric Surg. Service Martland Hosp. unit New Jersey Coll. Medicine and Dentistry; cons. pediatric surgeon St. Vincents Med. Center, S.I.; pediatric surgeon Project Hope, 1972; clin. asst. prof. surgery N.J. Coll. Medicine and Dentistry. Trustee CHR-ILL Service, Inc., Montclair, N.J. Diplomate Am. Bd. Surgery. Fellow A.C.S., Am. Acad. Pediatrics; mem. Am. Pediatric Surg. Assn. (charter), Kappa Gamma Pi, Beta Beta Beta. Home: 59 Elm St Millburn NJ 07041 Office: 153 Roseville Av Newark NJ 07107

FALLANDY, YVETTE MARIE, ednl. adminstr.; b. Los Angeles, Dec. 3, 1926; d. Arthur Jules and Elise Blanche (Martin) Fallandy; B.A. in French with honors, U. Cal. at Los Angeles, 1948, Ph.D. in Romance Langs. and Lit., 1957; M.A. in French with honors, U. Ore., 1950. Asst. prof. Mary Washington Coll., Fredericksburg, Va., 1954-59, Skidmore Coll., Saratoga Springs, N.Y., 1959-60, Mills Coll., Oakland, Cal., 1960-64; mem. faculty Cal. State Coll., Rohnert Park, Cal., 1964—, prof. French, 1967—, v.p. acad. affairs, 1974—. Cons. Nat. Endowment of Humanities, 1972—. Mem. Modern Lang. Assn., Am. Assn. Univ. Profs. Home: 2928 Bardy St Santa Rosa CA 95404 Office: 1801 E St Cal State Coll Rohnert Park CA 94928

FALLEY, MARGARET DICKSON (MRS. GEORGE FREDERICK FALLEY), author, genealogist; b. Mpls., Nov. 8, 1898; d. George E. and Edith (Baker) Dickson; B.S., Northwestern U., 1920; m. George Frederick Falley, Mar. 10, 1921 (dec. 1962); children—Katharine (Mrs. Edward H. Bennett, Jr.), Margaret Jane (Mrs. Raymond M. Galt), Carol (Mrs. Warner G. Baird, Jr.), Priscilla (Mrs. Henry W. Apfelbach). Ann. lectr. many years to Am. Inst. Genealogy at Nat. Archives, Washington, Geneal. Inst. Samford U., Birmingham, Ala.; participant Inst. Humanistic Studies, Aspen, Colo., 1967; geneal. lectr. state, tchr. hist. socs., clubs, orgns. Recipient Merit award Nat. Geneal. Soc., 1963. Fellow Am. Soc. Genealogists; Am. rep. council Harleian Soc., London, Eng.; colonial mem. New Eng. Historic Geneal. Soc.; mem. Royal Soc. Antiquaries, Dublin, Ireland, Northwestern U. Alumni Assn. (v.p. 1935-36), Northwestern U. Settlement Sr. Bd. (pres. 1945-46), Colonial Dames Am., D.A.R., Nat. Soc. Descs. Lords of Md. Manors, Daus. of Barons of Runnymeade, Kappa Kappa Gamma (Outstanding Alumnae award 1970). Methodist. Clubs: Union League (Chgo.); Glen View (Golf, Ill.). Author: Richard Falley and Some of His Descendants Including Grover Cleveland, 1952; Palmer Genealogy, Part I (English and Irish Ancestry of George Palmer), 1957; Irish and Scotch-Irish Ancestral Research, 2 vols., 1962. Contbr. articles to geneal. jours. Address: 1500 Sheridan Rd Wilmette IL 60091

FALLON, ANN MARIE, librarian; b. Bronx, N.Y., Mar. 3, 1911; d. Michael James and Elizabeth (Kelly) Fallon; B.S., Villanova U., 1956; M.S. in L.S., Columbia U., 1959; postgrad. Boston U., 1971. Elementary sch. tchr., N.Y., N.J., 1938-59; tchr., librarian Pope Pius XII Diocesan High Sch., Passaic, N.J., 1959-69; acad. librarian Boston U., 1969-73, head reference dept., 1973—, instr. edn. tech. Sch. Edn., 1972-73, vis. lectr., 1973-74. Nat. Def. Edn. Act grantee, 1966. Mem. N.E.A., Nat. Microfilm Assn., A.L.A.; New Eng. Library Assn., Am. Assn. U. Women (sec. 1973—), Boston U., Columbia U. alumni assns., Boston U. Women's Guild, Assn. Ednl. Communications & Tech., Pi Lambda Theta (mem.-at-large). Home: 198 Bay State Rd Boston MA 02215 Office: 771 Commonwealth Av Boston University Boston MA 02215

FALLON, MARGARET AGNES CASSERLY (MRS. FRANCIS X. FALLON), ednl. adminstr.; b. Providence, Feb. 20, 1917; d. James Joseph and Julia (Farrell) Casserly; Ed.B., R.I. Coll., 1938; M.A., Columbia, 1952; m. Francis X. Fallon, Feb. 17, 1945. Tchr. Providence Pub. Schs., 1939-45, N.Y.C. Pub. Schs., 1946-49; asst. prin. Benjamin Cardozo Jr. High Sch., N.Y.C., 1956-60; dist. guidance coordinator Bd. Edn., N.Y.C., 1949-56, borough guidance coordinator Bur. Ednl. and Vocational Guidance, 1960-66, asst. dir. guidance Bur. Ednl. and Vocational Guidance, 1966—. Chmn. adv. council Queens Childrens Hosp., Bellerose, N.Y., mem. bd. visitors, 1974—; mem. N.Y.C. Mayor's Task Force on Child Abuse; chmn. DeMarillac Circle of Ladies of Charity of Diocese of Bklyn., 1955-57. Bd. dirs. Queensboro Council Social Welfare, 1972—. Mem. Am., N.Y. State personnel and guidance assns., Assn. Counselor Edn. and Suprs., Nat. Vocational Guidance Assn., Am. Sch. Counselors Assn. Roman Catholic. Home: 244-11 84th Rd Bellerose NY 11426 Office: 110 Livingston St New York City NY 11201

FALLS, WALDTRAUT MARGRETE GOETZE (MRS. JOHN ALLEN FALLS), librarian; b. N.Y.C., June 28, 1941; d. Otto Paul and Anna Irma (Zander) Goetze; A.B., State U. N.Y. at Albany, 1963, M.A. (scholar), 1964; M.S., Columbia, 1967; m. John Allen Falls, Jr., Dec. 28, 1968; children—John Francis, Michael Gregory. Asst. advt. librarian Curtis Pub. Co., N.Y.C., 1964-65; library asso. N.Y. U. Commerce Library, N.Y.C., 1965-67; librarian, instr. N.Y.C. Community Coll., Bklyn., 1967-69, 70, 73—. Mem. A.L.A., N.Y. Library Club (life). Home: 328 78th St Brooklyn NY 11209 Office: 300 Jay St Brooklyn NY 11201

FALVO, SISTER HELEN, educator; b. Wooster, O.; d. Louis M. and Cornelia (Farcus) Falvo; B.S.E., Siena Heights Coll., 1951; M.A., St. John Coll., 1959; student Mundelein Coll., 1969. Tchr. elementary sch., Dioceses of Cleve. and Youngstown, O., 1944-58; prin. St. Dominic Sch., Youngstown, 1958-64; elementary supr. Dept. of Edn., Diocese of Youngstown, 1965-67, dir. tchr. edn., 1967—; dir. human relations workshop course for tchrs. Walsh Coll., Canton, O., 1969. Prin., supr. Tchr. Edn. Panels, 1955—; panelist Family Life Inst., Youngstown, 1966-69; mem. Christian Action Orgn., 1968—; mem. Youngstown Diocesan Liturgical Commn., 1967—, pastoral planning program com., 1972—; mem. adv. council Area VII, Right to Read, 1971—; adv. council for student teaching Youngstown U., 1972—. Bd. dirs. Community Reading Council, Inc., 1968—. Mem. Nat., Ohio Catholic ednl. assns., Nat., Ohio assns. for supervision and curriculum, N.E. Ohio (exec. com. 1972-73), Ohio sch. suprs. assns., Youngstown Area Urban League, Human Relations Council Canton, Northeastern Ohio Tchrs. Assn., Youngstown Diocesan Elementary Guidance Inst., Youngstown Diocesan Prins. Assn. Home: 147 Jefferson St Youngstown OH 44510 Office: Diocese of Youngstown 144 W Wood St Youngstown OH 44503

FAMARIN, SALLY BASIGA, real estate exec.; b. Mandawe City, Cebu, Philippines, Nov. 11, 1923; d. Severo Ranili and Serapia Seno (Dabon) Basiga; grad. So. Coll., Cebu, 1941; postgrad. Chamberlain Real Estate Sch., 1960, Harlowe Real Estate Sch., 1962, Anthony Sch. Gen. Ins., 1961; m. Carsiolo Tagle Famarin, Feb. 5, 1950; children—Sally Anne (Mrs. Andrew Glenn Davis), Catherine (Mrs. Bruce David Rizotto), Rodolfo Carlito, Rose Marie. Came to U.S., 1950, naturalized, 1952. Accounting, bookkeeper, mgr. ladies' home, Cebu, 1946-50; real estate salesman House of Homes Realty, San Francisco, 1960-61; owner, operator Famarin Realty (name now United Homes Realty 1965—), San Francisco, 1962—; owner, operator Sally's Sunset Villa, ambulatory home for aged, San Francisco, 1972—. Gen. chmn. banquet and ball Golden Jubilee Boy Scouts Philippines-U.S. West Coast region, 1973; chmn. awards Pioneer day picnic Filipino Pioneers Am., Oakland, Cal., 1964. Coordinator com. Filipino-Am. Friends Senator Milton Marks campaign Cal. Senate, 1972; gen. chmn. com. Filipino-Am. Friends Peter Tamaras for San Francisco Bd. Suprs., 1973; active orgn. first Filipino Ind. Polit. Hdqrs., San Francisco; chmn. beauty-talent pageant Filipino Am. Friendship Week, 1974, also gen. co-chmn.; Recipient certificate honor Regular Vets. Assn., 1967; testimonial dinner given in honor Cebu Assn., 1971; certificate honor San Francisco Bd. Suprs.; Outstanding plaque merit Filipino and Am. Soc. Cal., numerous other awards. Mem. Nat. Assn. Real Estate Bds., Cal. Real Estate Assn., San Francisco Real Estate Bd., Nat. Salesman Assn., Am. Soc. Notaries, Cebu Assn. (founder pres. emeritus 1971—, Gold pin), Caballerosde Dimasalang (2d v.p. 1973). Contbr. articles, poems to Filipino and Am. publs. Address: 2207 28th Av San Francisco CA 94116

FAMBROUGH, SALLY EVELYN WALLACE (MRS. TRUMAN E. FAMBROUGH), librarian; b. Woodson, Tex., Aug. 23, 1914; d. James Mullins and Eva (Reeves) Wallace; B.A., Tex. Women's U., 1937; B.L.S., North Tex. State U., 1955; postgrad. Tex. Technol. Coll., 1950-51, Ariz. State U., 1964, U. Wis., 1965, No. Ariz. U., 1967; m. Truman E. Fambrough, Dec. 22, 1940; 1 dau., Jane (Mrs. Ralph Burdick). Tchr. pub. schs. Chico, Tex., 1937-40, Seminole, Tex., 1950-53; librarian pub. schs., Mineral Wells, Tex., 1953-55, Seminole, Tex., 1955-62, Phoenix, 1963-66; dir. Tom Green County Library, San Angelo, Tex., 1962-63; dir. pub. schs. libraries, Flagstaff, Ariz., 1966—. Cons., No. Ariz. Edn. Center, 1967. Mem. Am. Assn. U. Women, N.E.A., Ariz. Edn. Assn., A.L.A., Ariz. Library Assn. (legislative com., pres. sch. div. 1972), Federated Study Club, 20th Century Study Club, Alpha Lambda Sigma, Alpha Delta Kappa. Mem. Christian Ch. Home: 415 W Apache Rd Flagstaff AZ 86001 Office: 2701 N Izabel Flagstaff AZ 86001

FAMEL, YVONNE ROSENGART, bus. exec.; b. Paris, France, Mar. 1, 1891; d. Pierre and Georgette (de Vie) Famel; Brevet Superieur Paris, France, 1906; m. Sylvan Rosangart-Famel, July 3, 1911 (dec. Aug. 1954); 1 dau., Yvonne Marie (Mrs. Rey-Millet Rogers). Came to U.S., 1941, naturalized, 1946. With Famel Labs.; treas. Nat. Investor Fund, Inc., Dover, Del., 1954—; chmn. bd. First Bank Indiantown (Fla.); dir. Chemdrug Corp., N.Y.C., Chmn. bd. dirs. Am. Birth Right Trust Mgmt., Palm Beach, Fla., trustee, founder Am. Birth Right Trust, 1967—. Mem. Soc. Four Arts, Inst. World Affairs, 1946—. Mem. Indiantown C. of C., Roman Catholic. Home: 4 Beach Promenade Copaigue NY 11757 Office: 730 5th Av New York City NY 10019

FAN, JOYCE WANG (MRS. PAUL FAN), educator, chemist; b. Foochow Fukien, China, Oct. 2, 1919; d. Leland and Ada (Pang) Wang; came to U.S., 1938, naturalized, 1964; B.S. magna cum laude in Chemistry and Physics, Wheaton Coll., 1942; M.S. in Chemistry, State U. Ia., 1944, Ph.D., 1946; postgrad. Northwestern U., 1946-47; m. Paul Fan, July 24, 1943; children—Leland, Lawrence. Instr. gen. chemistry U. So. Cal., Los Angeles, 1947-48; asso. prof. chemistry U. Houston, 1949-63, also chmn. div. of Gen. Chemistry, 1954-63; prof. chemistry Houston Bapt. U., 1963—, chmn. div. of sci. and math., 1967-69, chmn. dept., 1963—, chmn. pre-med. adv. com., 1963—. Named Faculty Woman of the Year Houston Baptist U., 1969. Mem. Am. Chem. Soc., Am. Inst. Chemists, Tex. Inst. of Chemists (pres. 1974-76), Am. Chem. Soc. (sec. southeastern Tex. sect. 1972-74). Mem. Chinese Baptist Ch. (Sunday sch. tchr. 1948—, ch. organist 1950—, chmn. bldg. com. 1958—). Contbr. articles on chemistry to sci. jours. Home: 4323 Nenana Houston TX 77035 Office: Houston Baptist University 7502 Fondren Houston TX 77036

FANGER, IRIS MANDEL (MRS. ROBERT DWORET FANGER), educator; b. Chgo., Mar. 15, 1936; d. Leo B. and Beatrice (Hollander) Mandel; B.F.A., Columbia, 1957; M.A., Northwestern U., 1963; Ph.D., Tufts U., 1972; m. Robert Dworet Fanger, Sept. 2, 1956; children—Michael, Laurie. Drama dir. Northwestern U. High Sch. Speech Inst., Evanston, Ill., 1961-63; dir. children's drama Tufts U., Medford, Mass., 1963-67, dir. Magic Circle Theater for Children, 1965-69, 72; lectr. drama Northeastern U., Boston, 1972-73; drama specialist, div. retardation Mass. Dept. Mental Health, Boston, 1973-74; mem. grad. faculty Lesley Coll., Cambridge, Mass., also dean dance center students summer sch. Harvard U., 1974—. Dance reviewer Jewish Advocate, Boston, 1969-73,Christian Sci. Monitor, 1974—; Boston corr., reviewer Dance mag., 1971—; guest lectr. dance York U., Toronto, 1973-74; dir. TV series Can I Borrow A Cookie? WGBH-TV, Boston, 1972-73; cons. children's drama U. N.C., Asheville, 1971-74, Ednl. Devel. Corp., 1973-74. Bd. dirs. Boston Library Creative Drama, 1970-72. Mem. Am. Theatre Assn., Am. Soc. for Theatre Research, Brit. Soc. for Theatre Research, New Eng. Theatre Conf. (chmn. children's theatre div. 1964-66), Société d'Histoire du Theatre, Am. Dance Guild, Alliance Francaise. Contbr. stories on dance and drama to various publs. Translator: Voyage To the Moon (Offenbach), 1972; Grand Duches of Gerolstein (Offenbach), 1968. Home: 190 Dudley St Brookline MA 02146

FANNIN, MARGARET W., social worker; b. Keokuk, Ia.; d. Charles D. and Alma E. (Martin) Fannin; B.A., Culver Stockton Coll., 1933; M.S.W., U. Minn., 1953. Pub. assistance child welfare worker, supr. Lee County Dept. Social Services, Keokuk, Ia., 1939-45, child welfare worker, 1950-51, child welfare cons., Des Moines, 1951-57, dir. Lee County Dept. Social Services, 1957-60; psychiat. social worker, supr., field instr., U. Ia. Grad. Social Work Students, Mt. Pleasant, 1960-66; dir. social services Mental Health Inst., Mt. Pleasant, 1966—, coordinator community services, 1969—; lectr. Ia. Wesleyan Coll., 1973—. Trustee Keokuk Pub. Library, 1949-60. Mem. Ia. Welfare Assn. (dist. pres. 1954), Nat. Assn. Social Workers, Acad. Certified Social Workers, Mt. Pleasant Bus. and Profl. Womens Club (pres. 1967-68), Soc. Hosp. Social Work Dirs., Am. Hosp. Assn. (Ia. area rep.), Social Workers in Health Facilities (pres. Ia. chpt. 1971-72). Episcopalian. Home: 310 S Cherry St Mount Pleasant IA 52641 Office: 1200 E Washington St Mount Pleasant IA 52641

FANNING, KATHERINE WOODRUFF (MRS. LAWRENCE S. FANNING), newspaper pub.; b. Chgo., Oct. 18, 1927; d. Frederick William and Katherine B. (Miller) Woodruff; B.A., Smith Coll., 1949; m. Marshall Field, Jr., May 12, 1950 (div. Aug. 1963); children—Frederick, Katherine, Barbara; m. 2d, Lawrence S. Fanning, Sept. 13, 1966 (dec. Feb. 1971). Reporter, Anchorage Daily News, 1965-66, editor Sunday mag. sect., 1966-67, asst. to pub., 1967-71, pres., pub., 1971—, editor, pub., 1972—. Mem. Anchorage Urban Beautification Commn., 1967-71. Bd. dirs., pres. Anchorage Community Chest, 1973-74. Mem. Anchorage C. of C. (dir.), Alaska Ednl. Broadcasting Commn. Club: Anchorage Press (v.p. 1968-69). Home: 2001 Stanford Dr Anchorage AK 99504 Office: PO Box 1660 Anchorage AK 99510

FANNING, PATRICIA, journalist; b. Odessa, Tex., May 31, 1947; d. James Burton and Delia (Martin) Fanning; B.S. with highest distinction in Journalism, Northwestern U., 1969. Reporter A.P., Chgo., 1969, sta. KDFW-TV, Dallas, 1969-71; free lance writer Washington Post and Nat. Observer, Cin., 1971-72; staff writer Nat. Observer, Silver Spring, Md., 1972—, also asst. to prodn. editor, 1972—. Lectr. Gifted Students Found. Inst., Dallas, 1971. Recipient Tex. State Sch. Bell award Tex. State Tchrs. Assn., 1970. Mem. Washington Press Club, Women in Communications. Home: 316 South Carolina Av SE Washington DC 20003 Office: 11501 Columbia Pike Silver Spring MD 20910

FANT, ELENA NEWSOM BEDFORD (MRS. GEORGE FANT), savs. and loan assn. exec.; b. Bridgeport, Tex., Aug. 15, 1908; d. John Wesley and Beatrice (Acord) Newsom; student Tex. Bus. Coll., 1925-26; m. George Fant, Apr. 26, 1941. With 1st Nat. Bank, Weatherford, Tex., 1926-49, asst. cashier, 1941-45, v.p., dir., 1946-49; with Mut. Bldg. & Loan Assn., Weatherford, 1926—, v.p., 1950-58, pres., 1959—, also chmn. bd. Mem. Weatherford Booster Club; hon. mem. 4-H Club of Parker County; founder George Fant Found., 1963, George Fant-St. Stephens Catholic Ch. Found., 1963; trustee E.D. Farmer Relief Fund. Mem. Soc. Savs. & Loan Controllers, A.I.M. (pres.'s council 1967-69), Weatherford C. of C. (dir. 1974). Clubs: Live Oak Country (Weatherford); Jim Wright Congressional. Home: 508 W Baylor St Weatherford TX 76086 Office: 133 College Av Weatherford TX 76086

FANTARELLA, ANNA MARY FRIONE, concrete co. exec.; b. New Haven, Jan. 21, 1925; d. Domenic Victor and Mary Ella (Velleca) Frione; student summers Albertus Magnus Coll., 1943, U.

Vt., 1944; B.A. in Econs., Trinity Coll., 1945; m. Louis A. Fantarella, June 26, 1945 (div. 1956); 1 son, Richard. With payroll and personnel depts. D.V. Frione & Co., Inc., hwy. constrn. co., New Haven, 1956-60, corporate sec., 1960-71, treas., 1971—, also dir.; sec., dir. Foxon Concrete Corp., New Haven, 1960—; sec., dir. Frione Real Estate Corp., New Haven, 1963-72; sec.-treas., dir. Morgan-Essex Corp., Amdon Corp. Mem. exec. bd. Cub Scouts, Orange council Boy Scouts Am., 1962-64; mem. exec. bd. P.T.A., Orange, 1965-66. Bd. dirs. Benhaven Sch. Autistic Children. Mem. Am. Assn. U. Women (pres. 1970-72), Trinity Coll. Alumnae Assn. (pres. 1961). Roman Catholic. Club: New Haven Women's. Home: 411 Prudden Lane Orange CT 06477 Office: 87 Foxon New Haven CT 06513

FANTASIA, TILIA J., educator; b. Cambridge, Mass., June 19, 1936; d. Francesco and Maria (Vischio) Fantasia; B.S. in Edn., Tufts U., 1958, M.Ed., 1961; Ed.D., Boston U., 1969. Instr., dept. phys. edn. Lasell Jr. Coll., 1958-60, Somerville (Mass.) Pub. Schs., 1960-62; instr. dept. health and phys. edn. Salem (Mass.) State Coll., 1962-66; grad. asst. dept. phys. edn. Boston U., 1966; chmn. dept. phys. edn. Westfield (Mass.) State Coll., 1966-71, asso. prof., 1969-74, prof., 1974—. Mem. Westfield Community Swimming Com., 1968-70. Democratic Ward and City Com., Somerville, 1964-68. Bd. dirs. Westfield chpt. A.R.C. Mem. A.A.H.P.E.R. (v.p. recreation Eastern dist. 1972-74), Mass. Assn. Health, Phys. Edn. and Recreation (v.p. 1968-70), Nat., Eastern (sec. 1975—) assns. phys. edn. for coll. women, Mass. Div. Girls and Womens Sports (ofcl. bd. 1968-70), U.S. Field Hockey Assn., Springfield Bd. of Ofcls. (chmn. 1968-70), Pi Lamda Theta. Home: 87 Thornberry Rd Winchester MA 01890 Office: Westfield State College Western Av Westfield MA 01085

FANUS, PAULINE RIFE (MRS. WILLIAM EDWARD FANUS), librarian; b. New Oxford, Pa., Feb. 14, 1925; d. Maurice Diehl and Bernice Edna (Gable) Rife; B.S., Pa. State U., 1945; M.S. in L.S., Villanova U., 1961; m. William Edward Fanus, June 20, 1944; children—Irene (Mrs. Lewis N. Weaver Jr.), Larry William, Daniel Diehl. Periodical librarian Tex. Coll. Arts & Industries, Kingsville, 1945; tchr. nursery sch. Studio Sch., Wayne, Pa., 1953-55; circulation and reference librarian Franklin Inst., Phila., 1963-66; asst. librarian Ursinus Coll., Collegeville, Pa., 1966; catalog librarian, instr. Eastern Coll., St. Davids, Pa., 1967-71; head librarian Agnes Irwin Sch., Rosemont, Pa., 1971—. Mem. Am. Assn. U. Profs. (chpt. sec. Eastern Coll. 1970-71), Pa. Library Assn. Home: Country Club Rd Phoenixville PA 19460 Office: Agnes Irwin School Rosemont PA 19010

FARCA, MARIE CATHRYN, novelist, photographer; b. Phila., June 6, 1935; d. George and Catherine Ann (Candea) Farca; B.S. in Edn. (state scholar), U Pa., 1957. Tchr., N.J. pub. schs., 1957-74; demonstration tchr. Trenton (N.J.) State Coll., 1963-69; freelance photographer, 1964—. Mem. Authors Guild, Authors League Am., N.E.A., N.J. Edn. Assn., Alpha Omicron Pi. Author: Earth, 1972; Complex Man, 1973. Office: Scott Meredith Literary Agy 580 5th Av New York NY 10036

FARENTHOLD, FRANCES TARLTON (MRS. GEORGE EDWARD FARENTHOLD), lawyer; b. Corpus Christi, Tex., Oct. 2, 1926; d. Benjamin Dudley and Catherine (Bluntzer) Tarlton; A.B., Vassar Coll., 1946; J.D., U. Tex., 1949; LL.D., Hood Coll., 1973, Boston U., 1973; m. George E. Farenthold, Oct. 6, 1950; children—Dudley Tarlton, George Edward, Emilie, James Dougherty, Vincent Bluntzer (dec.). Admitted to Tex. bar, 1949; mem. Tex. Ho. of Reps., 1968-72; dir. legal aide Nueces County, 1965-67; asst. prof. law Tex. So. U., Houston. Mem. Human Relations Com., Corpus Christi, 1963-68, Corpus Christi Citizen's Com. Community Improvement, 1966-68. mem. Tex. adv. com. to U.S. Commn. on Civil Rights, 1968—; chairperson Tex. Com. Nat. Health Security; vice-chairperson Nat. Coalition Human Needs and Budget Priorities; mem. nat. adv. council Am. Civil Liberties Union, Women's Equity Action League; mem. adv. bd. HIU-Minority Tax Research Project. Mem. Orgn. for Preservation Unblemished Shoreline, 1964—. Democratic candidate Gov. Tex., 1972; del. Dem. nat. conv., 1972, 1st woman nominated to be candidate v.p. U.S., 1972. nat. co-chmn. Citizens to Elect McGovern-Shriver, 1972; chairperson Nat. Women's Polit. Caucus. Bd. dirs. Tex. Bill of Rights Found., Mental Health Law Project. Recipient Lyndon B. Johnson Woman of Year award, 1973. Mem. Am. Bar Assn., State Bar Tex. Roman Catholic. Home: 4034 Piping Rock Lane Houston TX 77027 Office: Suite 707 Littlefield Bldg Austin TX 78701

FARHAD, MINA (MRS. VAN VECHTEN BURGER, JR.), radiologist; b. Teheran, Iran, Jan. 1, 1938; d. Ahmed and Jahan Ara (Farhad) Farhad; came to U.S., 1953; B.A. with honors, Barnard Coll., 1957; M.A., Radcliffe Coll., 1958; M.D., Harvard, 1965, Ph.D., 1963; m. Van Vechten Burger, Jr., Nov. 18, 1967; children—Leila, Katrina. Intern, Mt. Auburn Hosp., Cambridge, Mass., 1965-66; resident radiology Sloan Kettering Inst., N.Y. Hosp., 1967-70; staff radiologist N.Y. Hosp., N.Y.C., 1970—, also Lenox Hill Hosp., N.Y.C., 1972—; instr. radiology Cornell Med. Sch., N.Y.C., 1970—. Mem. jr. com. Sloan Kettering Cancer Center. Diplomate Am. Bd. Radiology. Club: Harvard (N.Y.C.). Home: 1088 Park Av New York City NY 10028 Office: 100 E 77th St New York City NY 10021

FARIE, ANN MARIE DIBLASIO (MRS. JOHN CHARLES FARIE), social worker; b. Boston, Nov. 8, 1940; d. James and Mary (Driscoll) DiBlasio; A.B., Emmanuel Coll., 1962; student social work Mass. Eye and Ear Infirmary, 1963-64; M.S.W., Boston Coll., 1964; m. John Charles Farie, June 13, 1964. With DePaul Child Guidance Clinic, Rochester, N.Y., 1964-72, supr., 1969-72; sch. social worker, Fairport, N.Y., 1972-73, Henrietta, N.Y., 1973—. Field instr. U. Buffalo, 1967-68, Carleton U., 1968-71, St. Bernards Sem., 1969-71, Nazareth Coll., 1970-71; mem. staff U. Rochester dept. psychology Primary Mental Health Project, 1973—; cons. parochial, grammar and high schs., 1964—. Mem. task force family and children programs Pittsford (N.Y.) YMCA. Bd. dirs. Mental Health, Monroe County, 1968-71. Mem. Nat. Assn. Social Workers (exec. com. Monroe County chpt. 1970-71), Acad. Certified Social Workers, Rush-Henrietta Edn. Assn. Roman Catholic. Home: 3009 Elmwood Av Rochester NY 14618

FARINA, PENELOPE GLADYS, securities co. exec.; b. Glen Innes, Australia, Mar. 29, 1924; d. Ernest Edward and Constance Marion (Williams) Hall; grad. Presbyn. Ladies Coll., Toowoomba, Australia, 1940; m. Michael M. Farina, Apr. 15, 1944 (div. 1972); 1 son, Richard Anthony. Came to U.S., 1952, naturalized, 1958. Chief clk. U.S. Army, Australia, 1940-45; asst. v.p. Elec. Supply & Service Co., Brisbane, Australia, 1948-52; v.p. Emch. & Co., investment bankers, Milw., 1956-60; asst. treas. Gen. Life Ins. Wis., Milw., 1960-70; treas., dir. GL Securities Corp., Milw., 1960-70; also Gen. Investment Sales Corp.; v.p., asst. sec. Catholic Knights Investment Corp., Milw., 1970-73; v.p., dir. Asso. Equity Investors, Inc., Milw., 1971—; v.p. Met. Entertainment Commn., Inc., Milw., 1971—; v.p., dir. Asso. Equity Investment Sales Ltd., 1973—, Am. Leisure Investment Sales Ltd., 1973—; mem. arbitration panel Am. Stock Exchange, 1970-73. Mem. Wis. Real Estate Brokers, Financial Analysts Fedn., Milw. Investment Analyst Soc. (sec.-treas. 1965-66), Wis. Mortgage Bankers Assn., Am. Arbitration Assn. (nat. panel 1972—). Home: 1914 N Prospect Av Milwaukee WI 53202 Office: 1024 E State St Milwaukee WI 53202

FARINATO, ELEANOR ARCANJO (MRS. UMBERTO ROLAND FARINATO), educator; b. Cambridge, Mass., Oct. 16, 1946; d. Manuel Dos Santos and Ermina (Ponte) Arcanjo; B.A., Boston U., 1968; M.A. in History, Boston Coll., 1971; m. Umberto Roland Farinato, June 21, 1969. Tchr. math. Walnut Hill Sch., Natick, Mass., 1968-70; bilingual tchr. math., sci. Rindge Tech. Sch., Cambridge, Mass., 1970-71; multilingual guidance counselor to fgn. students Cambridge High and Latin Sch., Cambridge, 1971—. Active Cambridge Orgn. Portuguese Ams., 1970-74. Mem. Portuguese Am. Cultural Soc. (corr. sec. 1973-74), Nat. Assn. Women Deans and Counselors, N.E.A., Mass. Sch. Counselors Assn., Mass., Cambridge tchrs. assns., Mass. Personnel and Guidance Assn., Oceanic Soc., Delta Kappa Gamma. Club: Cambridge Faculty. Home: 7 Grenville Rd Watertown MA 02172 Office: Cambridge High and Latin Sch Broadway and Trowbridge Sts Cambridge MA 02138

FARINHOLT, MARY KATHARINE WOLTZ (MRS. WILLIAM WORTHAM FARINHOLT), educator; b. Chapel Hill, N.C., Feb. 5, 1912; d. Albert Edgar and Daisy (Mackie) Woltz; B.A. with honors, Agnes Scott Coll., 1933; M.Ed., Emory U., 1964; m. Holcombe Tucker Green, Oct. 16, 1934; children—Caroline Tucker, Holcombe Tucker; m. 2d, William Wortham Farinholt, July 18, 1959; 1 stepson, Lewis Sharp. Tchr. English, Belmont (N.C.) High Sch., 1933-34; tchr. English Westminster Schs., Atlanta, 1958-59, 64—, dir. Girls' Jr. High Sch., 1964—. Pres. Atlanta Girl Scout Council, 1953, bd. dirs., 1950-53; pres. Child Service Assn. Atlanta, 1956-58; mem. exec. bd. Atlanta Music Club, 1951-59; hon. mem. Child Service and Family Counseling. Trustee Agnes Scott Coll., 1944-45, Appleton Ch. Home, Macon, Ga., 1962-65. Mem. Nat. (jr. high sect. chmn. 1969-70, mem. exec. bd. 1969-70), Ga. (membership chmn. 1969-70) assns. women deans, adminstrs. and counselors, Ga. Assn. Middle Sch. Prins. (state sec.), Mortar Bd. (nat. treas. 1945-47), Phi Beta Kappa, Delta Kappa Gamma. Episcopalian (pres. women's group). Editorial bd. Jour. Nat. Assn. Women Deans, Adminstrs. and Counselors. Home: 567 Peachtree Battle Av Atlanta GA 30305 Office: 1424 W Paces Ferry Rd NW Atlanta GA 30327

FARISS, GERTRUDE HOUK (MRS. CRECENE A. FARISS), assn. exec.; b. Louisville, Feb. 14, 1905; d. Frederick Thayer and Gertrude Nancy (Deane) Houk; B.A., U. Ore., 1925; M.A., Cornell, 1926; postgrad. U. Cal. at Berkeley, 1939; m. Crecene A. Fariss, June 28, 1929. Acad. dean St. Helen's Hall Jr. Coll., Portland, Ore., 1932-46; owner, adminstr. Portland Sch. Tutoring, 1946-52; head St. Helen's Hall, Portland, 1952-69; exec. sec., corporate sec. Clackamas County Bd. Realtors, Lake Oswego, Ore., 1970—. Mem. Pres.'s adv. com. for planning 1960 White House Conf. on Children and Youth, 1958-60; chmn. Gov.'s Com. on Status of Women, 1964-70; mem. Metro Planning Com., 1967-69. Bd. dirs. Ore. Fedn. Rep. Women, 1970; pres. Lake Oswego Rep. Club, 1972. Named Woman of Achievement, Theta Sigma Phi, 1952, Portland Woman of Achievement Ore. Jour., Portland, 1963; recipient Golden Torch award Ore. Fedn. Bus. and Profl. Women, 1966. Mem. Am. Assn. Univ. Women (pres. Portland 1944-46, pres. Ore. 1948-50, mem. nat. bd. 1952-56), Women in Communications, Delta Kappa Gamma. Clubs: Metro Women's (charter mem. Portland, v.p. 1971-72), Altrusa (Portland pres. 1941-42, dist. gov. 1946-48, mem. nat. bd. 1950-52). Home: 16911 SW Bryant Rd Lake Oswego OR 97034 Office: PO Box 218 Lake Oswego OR 97034

FARKAS, BETH GLORIA FISHNER (MRS. DAVID F. FARKAS), occupational therapist; b. Bklyn., Nov. 9, 1949; d. Murray and Eunice (Hendler) Fishner; B.S., Tufts U., 1970; m. David F. Farkas, June 28, 1970. Staff activity therapist Bellevue Psychiat. Hosp., N.Y.C., 1970-71; activity therapy supr. South Beach Psychiat. Center, S.I., N.Y., 1972-74; preceptor Consortium for Occupational Therapy Edn., Orangeburg, N.Y., 1974—. Dept. Health, Edn. and Welfare trainee, 1968-69, 69-70. Recipient Alumni award Tufts U., 1970. Mem. Am. Occupational Therapy Assn., N.Y. Assn. Brain Injured Children, Met. N.Y. Dist. Occupational Therapy Assn. Home: 507 N Midland Av Upper Nyack NY 10960 Office: Consortium for Occupational Therapy Convent Rd Orangeburg NY 10962

FARKAS, FRANCINE MOSS (MRS. ALEXANDER FARKAS), dept. store exec.; student Jackson Coll.; m. Alexander Farkas, 1963; three children. Mgr. photo studio Alexander's, dept. store chain, N.Y.C., fashion coordinator until 1963, fashion dir., 1968-72, v.p. fashion, 1972—; broker Shields and Co., 1964-66, Filor, Bullard and Smyth, N.Y.C., 1966-68. Office: Alexander's Lexington Av at 58th St New York City NY 10022*

FARKAS, JOSANNE GINZBERG (MRS. ROBERT WILLIAM FARKAS), child psychologist; b. Cambridge, Mass., May 1, 1927; d. Alfred Murray and Lillian Rae (Ginsburg) Ginzberg; m. Warren Burroughs, June 14, 1948 (div. 1957); children—Jonathan, Cathy; m. 2d, Robert William Farkas, Mar. 10, 1965; 1 dau., Suzanne. Coordinator research Sch. Indsl. Mgmt., Mass. Inst. Tech., Cambridge, 1958-60; psychologist Newton (Mass.) Pub. Schs., 1962-64; vis. lectr. Pa. State U. at York, 1966-69; psychologist Eastern Mental Health Clinic, Balt. City Health Dept., 1970-72. Cons. child psychologist Inner City Community Mental Health Assn., Balt., 1972—. Committeewoman, Newton Democratic Com., 1958-60. Past mem. bd. dirs. Pa. Mental Health Assn., York Mental Health Assn., Community Progress Council, York Community Arts Council. Am. Psychol. Assn. Home: 304 W Lafayette Ave Baltimore MD 21217 Office: 24 S Calvert St Baltimore MD 21201

FARKAS, RUTH LEWIS (MRS. GEORGE FARKAS), ambassador, personnel and community relations cons.; b. N.Y.C., Dec. 20, 1906; d. Samuel and Jennie (Bach) Lewis; B.A., N.Y. U., 1928, Ed.D. (Founder's Day scholar), 1957; M.A., Columbia, 1932; m. George Farkas, June 17, 1928; children—Alexander Spencer, Robin Lewis, Bruce Russell, Jonathan Dale. Psychol. tutor Fedn. Jewish Charities, N.Y.C., 1941-45; instr. N.Y. U. Sch. Edn., 1949-55; personnel cons., community relations dir. Alexander's, Inc., N.Y.C., 1955-72, also dir., mem. exec. com. Alexander's Dept. Stores, Inc.; pres., Dolma Realty Corp., Ft. Lauderdale, Fla. 1955-71; ambassador to Luxembourg, 1973—. Chmn. pres.'s adv. council N.Y. U. Grad. Sch. Social Work, 1966-74, hon. chmn., 1974—; nat. chmn. Albert Einstein Med. Coll. Women's Div., 1965-68; mem. Women's Council N.Y. State, 1964-71; mem. Pres.'s Com. for Handicapped, 1964-70; founder, mem. Gov.'s Scholastic Program, 1964-71; mem. U.S. Nat. Commn. to UNESCO, 1964-71, mem. exec. com. Behavioral Sci. Commn., 1968-71; part time sociol. cons. U.S. State Dept., 1963, 65, 68; del. Pan Pacific-S.E. Asian Women's Assn. Conf., 1960, 71; v.p. Maferr Found., 1965—; pres. Role Found., 1967—; pres. Bethabraham Hosp., 1963-73; patron Met. Opera Assn. Bd. dirs. Montefiore Hosp., Nat. Council Social Work; trustee N.Y. U., Dr. William Allen White Psychiat. Inst., 1965-73. Recipient honor Pres.'s Com. on Handicapped, 1966; Am. Med. Center Humanitarian award, 1966; Louise Waterman Wise Achievement award, 1968; N.Y. U. Alumnae Achievement award, 1969; Albert Einstein Med. Coll. Women's Div. award, 1973; Founder's Day scholar N.Y. U., 1957. Mem. Met. Mus. Art, N.Y. Philharmonic Assn., Met. Opera Assn. (patron), Fgn. Service Assn. (pub. mem., life), Alumnae Council Tchrs. Coll. Columbia (dir.), Alpha Kappa Delta. Clubs: Harmonie, El Morocco New York University (founder, gov. 1955-58); Capitol Hill (Washington); Palm Beach (Fla.) Country. Patentee roller muff. Home: US Embassy Luxembourg Luxembourg also 389 S Lake Dr Palm Beach FL 33480

FARLEY, CAROL JEAN (MRS. DENNIS SCOTT FARLEY), author; b. Ludington, Mich., Dec. 20, 1936; d. Floyd and Thressa Opal (Moreen) McDole; student Western Mich. U., 1954-56, Mich. State U., 1967-69; m. Dennis Scott Farley, June 21, 1956; children—Denise, Elise, Roderick, Jeannette. Author children's books including Yekapo of Zopo Land, 1958, Mystery of the Fog Man, 1966, Mystery in the Ravine, 1967, Sergeant Finney's Family, 1969, The Bunch on McKellahan Street, 1971; The Most Important Thing in the World, 1974; The Garden Is Doing Fine, 1975; lectr. in field. Active in Scouting programs, 1966-71. Recipient Franklin Watts Mystery medal Franklin Watts, Inc., 1966. Mem. Armed Forces Writers League, Soc. Children's Book Writers, Nat. Orgn. Women. Home: 4411 Medford Dr Annandale VA 22003

FARLEY, DOROTHY GENEVIEVE, social work adminstr.; b. Victoria, B.C., Can.; d. Albert Thomas and Anne (Murphy) Farley; came to U.S., 1949, naturalized, 1956; B.A., U. B.C., 1947, B.S.W. (Laura Holland scholar), 1948; M.S.W., U. Cal. at Berkeley, 1950; adopted children—David, Sheila. Social worker B.C. Provincial Govt., field work instr. U. B.C. Sch. Social Work, 1948-49; psychiat. social worker Family and Children's Service, Berkeley, 1950-51; field rep. Children's Home Soc., Oakland, Cal., 1951; unit supr. children's div. Wash. Dept. Pub. Assistance, Seattle, 1951-52; sr. social worker Florence Crittenton Home, Seattle, 1952-54; supr. Travelers Aid Soc., Seattle, 1954-56; dept. supr. Children's Home Soc. Wash., 1956-58; exec. dir. Ruth Sch. for Girls, Seattle, 1958—. Field work instr. U. Wash. Sch. Social Work, Seattle, 1952-60. Mem. task force and forum mem. White House Conf. for Children. Bd. dirs., Council planning affiliates United Good Neighbors, Seattle, 1969-72. Served to sect. officer RCAF, 1942-45. Mem. Acad. Certified Social Workers (charter), Wash. Assn. Child Care Agys. (exec. com. 1967—), Nat. Assn. Social Workers (chpt. charter mem., chpt. v.p. 1958-59), Sweet Adelines (chpt. pres. 1961-62). Clubs: Women's University (Seattle), Seattle-South Dist. Soroptimist (pres. 1966-67). Home: 319 N 137th Seattle WA 98133 Office: PO Box 10 Burien WA 98166 also 1033 SW 152d St Seattle WA 98166

FARLEY, LEONA PEARLENE BEYER (MRS. JOHN ELLIS FARLEY), editor; b. Mount Carroll, Ill., Mar. 30, 1925; d. Lewis and Lena Hulda (Walthers) Beyer; student Am. Inst. Commerce, Davenport, Ia., 1943; m. John Ellis Farley, May 30, 1947; children—John Ellis, Michael Jay. Reporter, Mirror Democrat. Mount Carroll., 1941-42; asst. soc. editor Democrat and Leader, Davenport, Ia., 1943-47; advt. mgr. Milford (O.) Advertiser, 1963-64, editor, 1965—. Active Old Milford Area, Cin. Nature Center, Unity-By-The Side-Of-The Road. Recipient Citizenship award 6th Congl. Dist., 1972; Am. Press award Milford Area and Ohio Jr. C. of C., 1973. Mem. Tri-City Women's Press Club (pres. 1946-47), Milford Area C. of C. (Pres. award 1970, First Lady of Milford Frontier Days 1973, dir., v.p. 1971-73). Home: 1564 Vera Cruz Pike Milford OH 45150 Office: 4 Main St Milford OH 45150

FARLEY, MARGUERITE MARY, broadcasting ofcl.; b. Phila., May 20, 1930; d. David Francis and Marguerite (Dorsey) Farley; A.B., Chestnut Hill Coll., 1952; postgrad. U. Pa., 1952-53; M.Ed., Temple U., 1966, doctoral candidate, 1971—. Tchr. Phila. pub. schs., 1952-55; radio-TV asst. Phila. Pub. Schs., 1956-70, TV supr., 1970—; coordinator Jr. Town Meeting of Air, WRCV, 1955-58; writer, producer, narrator Magic of Books, WFIL Studio Schoolhouse, 1955-59, writer, originator Americana, 1959-68; writer, producer, narrator Radioland Express, 1955-60; writer, originator, narrator Storyland, 1960-68; tchr.-prod. TV Bookshelf Sta. WHYY-TV, 1958-70, Stories for You, 1965-69, Seed of A Nation, 1969-70. Recipient George Washington Honor, 1960, 62, 63, George Washington Honor Certificate, 1965, George Washington Honor medal, 1966. Mem. Am. Women in Radio and Television (treas. Phila. 1961-62, pres. 1969-70), N.E.A., Nat. Assn. Ednl. Broadcasters, Phila. Assn. Sch. Adminstrs., Assn. Ednl. Communications and Tech., Am. Assn. U. Women, Pa. Learning Resources Assn., Chestnut Hill Coll. Alumnae Assn. (1st v.p. 1963-66). Home: 4614 Disston St Philadelphia PA 19135 Office: Horn Curriculum Center Frankford and Castor Avs Philadelphia PA 19124

FARLEY, ROSE BELLE (MRS. FRANK W. FARLEY), mus. curator; b. Kenedy, Tex., July 8, 1909; d. Charles Hugo and Elisabeth Frances (Schmidt) Kreneck; bus. adminstrn. degree Bee County Bus. Coll., 1934; m. Frank W. Farley, June 3, 1941. Typist, sec., Kathryn O'Connor Found., Goliad, Tex., 1965-67; curator Presidio La Bahia Mus., Goliad, 1968—. Mem. St. Ann Altar Soc. Roman Catholic. Home: Rural Route 2 Box 53-A Goliad TX 77963 Office: La Bahia Museum Box 57 Goliad TX 77963

FARLEY, VIRGINIA MARTEEN AGNEW (MRS. HARRIS FARLEY), home economist; b. Henderson, Ky., June 10, 1911; d. William Stewart and Annie Lou (Secrest) Agnew; student Western Ky. State U., 1928-29; B.S., Murray State Tchrs. Coll., 1939; m. Harris Farley, Dec. 24, 1936. Tchr. Baskett Elementary Sch., Henderson, 1929-36; tchr. Hebbardsville (Ky.) High Sch., 1936-43, prin., 1943-45; nutrition dir. Evansville (Ind.) chpt. A.R.C., 1945-46; chronographer Chrysler Corp., Evansville, 1946-48; lunch dir. Evansville-Vanderburgh Sch. Corp., 1949-73. Cons. Hesmer Foods, Inc., Evansville, Ind., 1973-74. Mem. disaster com. Evansville chpt. A.R.C., 1949-65; mem. Nutrition Council Evansville. Recipient Achievement award Nat. Restaurant Assn., 1954. Mem. Ky. Future Homemakers Am. (hon.), Ind. (life mem.; first pres. 1952-53), Am. (life mem.; pres. 1970-71) schs. food service assns., Kappa Delta Pi. Home: Rural Route 1 Box 335 Henderson KY 42420

FARMER, BARBARA M., social worker, educator; b. Millersburg, Pa., May 18, 1931; d. Richard K. and Mary (Fry) Farmer; B.S., N.J. State Tchrs. Coll. Newark, 1953; M.S., Columbia, 1957. Tchr. pub. sch., Rahway, N.J., 1953-54, St. Christopher's Sch. for Disturbed Children, Dobbs Ferry, N.Y., 1954-55; social worker Dept. Hosp., Bird S. Coler Hosp., N.Y.C., 1957-61; therapeutic community research program Jacobi Hosp., Bronx, N.Y., 1961-64; supr. social service Bronx Municipal Hosp. Center, Albert Einstein Coll. Medicine, Van Etten Hosp., 1964-67, dir. family therapy, asst. dir. Van Etten Home Care Service, 1967-70, social services cons. evaluation unit dept. community health, 1970—. Cons. Berkshire County Rehab. Center, Pittsfield, Mass., 1964-65; instr. dept. medicine and community health Albert Einstein Coll. Medicine, 1967—. Mem. Nat. Assn. Social Workers, Acad. Certified Social Workers, Am. Group Psychotherapy Assn., Physicians Forum, Am. Assn. U. Profs., Am. Pub. Health Assn., Community Council N.Y., Airplane Owners and Pilots Assn., East-African Wildlife Soc. Home: 240 E 82d St New York City NY 10028 Office: Evaluation Unit Bassine Bldg 1300 Morris Park Av Bronx NY 10003

FARMER, ERIN (MRS. CHARLEY WALTON FARMER), club woman; b. Camden, Ala., Oct. 10, 1900; d. Charles Prescott and Jessie (Laird) Atkinson; A.B., Huntington Coll., 1922; m. Charley Walton

Farmer, July 20, 1922; 1 dau., June (Mrs. Harold Everett Causey). Tchr., Samson (Ala.) Schs., 1921, St. Petersburg (Fla.) Schs., 1924-26. Pres. Vineville Garden Club, Macon, Ga., 1939, sec., 1968-70; pres. Shirley Hills Garden Club, 1953, dir., 1951—, now hon. mem.; mem. Morning Garden Club; dir. Garden Club Ga., 1961—; leader Florence Bernd Jr. Garden Club, 1963-64; accredited judge Am. Camellia Soc., 1955-68; trustee Macon YWCA, 1959—, mem. residence com., 1957—, sec., 1959-68. Bd. dirs. Boy's Club, Macon. Mem. D.A.R. Methodist (pres. Bible class 1938). Clubs: Macon Idle Hour Country (Macon and Montgomery, Ala.); College (Montgomery, Ala.); Metropolitan Dinner (Macon). Home: 2691 Stanislaus Circle Macon GA 31204

FARMER, FLORENCE AMELIA, educator; b. Sainte Anne de Bellevue, Que., Can., May 10, 1918; d. John Taylor and Nora Eliza (Pentin) Farmer; B.H.S., McGill U., 1939, M.S., 1944, Ph.D., 1947. Asst. prof. McGill U., Montreal, Que., 1948-59, prof. sch. food sci., 1964—; lectr. U. Madras, (India), 1959-64. Mem. Nutrition Soc. Can., Canadian Inst. Food Sci. and Tech., Canadian Dietetic Assn., Soc. for Nutrition Edn. Mem. Anglican Ch. Home: 30 Maple Av Ste Anne de Bellevue PQ Canada Office: Box 276 Macdonald College PQ H9X3M1 Canada

FARMER, GERALDINE MARY, educator; b. Granum, Alta., Can.; d. Dennis Daniel and Catherine (McKinney) Farmer; B.Ed., U. Alta., 1948; M.A., U. Minn., 1955, Ph.D., 1961. Tchr. Taber (Alta.) High Sch., 1948-57, Salisbury High Sch., Edmonton, Alta., 1957-58; mem. faculty U. Alta., Edmonton, 1960—, prof. bus. edn., 1969—. Mem. bus. edn. curriculum com. Dept. Edn. Alta., 1960—; mem. adv. bd. adult occupational tng. Dept. Manpower and Immigration Can., 1969—. Fellow Canadian Coll. Tchrs.; mem. Adminstrv. Mgmt. Soc. (chpt. pres. 1969-70), Nat. Bus. Edn. Assn., Am. Ednl. Research Assn., Internat. Soc. Bus. Edn., Nat. Soc. Study Edn., Canadian Assn. Bus. Edn. Tchrs. (past pres.), Am. Soc. Curriculum Devel., Bus. and Profl. Womens Club (v.p.), Edmonton Edn. Soc., Delta Pi Epsilon, Pi Lambda Theta, Delta Kappa Gamma. Author: Word Division in the Canadian Business Vocabulary, 1967; (with others) Forkner Shorthand Outlines for the Business Vocabulary, 1971; co-author: Business Transcription, 1973. Home: 1102 11111-87 Av Edmonton AB T6G 0X9 Canada

FARMER, MARGARET KATHLEEN, librarian; b. Montreal, Que., Can., Mar. 20, 1915; B.A., Sir George Williams U., 1953; B.L.S., McGill U., 1954, M.L.S., 1968; certificate Columbia, 1958. Registered nurse Toronto (Ont., Can.) Gen. Hosp., 1936-41, Royal Victoria Hosp., Montreal, 1943-47; clk. IBM dept. Royal Canadian Air Force, Toronto, 1941-42; asst. cataloger Med. Library, McGill U., Montreal, 1947-51, head cataloger, 1952-63, asst. librarian, 1964-68, acting med. librarian, 1968-69, collections librarian, 1969—. Mem. Med. Library Assn., Confedn. Profl. Librarians Que. Office: Med Library McGill U 3655 Drummond St Montreal PQ H3G 1Y6 Canada

FARMER, MARJORIE ELIZABETH, electrochemist; b. Detroit; d. Henry and Jessie (Lodewyck) Farmer; B.A., Mt. Holyoke Coll., 1938. Research electrochemist Pratt & Whitney div. United Aircraft Corp., East Hartford, Conn., 1942-51; electrochemist Chem. Corp., Springfield, Mass., 1953; research electrochemist Convair div. Gen. Dynamics Corp., Pomona, Cal., 1953; electrochemist U.S. Navy Shipyard, Long Beach, Cal., 1954-55; mem. tech. staff Rockwell Internat. Corp., Anaheim, Cal., 1957—, now lead instr. in advanced tng. program in coordination with regional occupation program. Registered profl. engr., Cal. Mem. Am. Electroplaters Soc., New Eng. Anti-Vivisection Soc. Humane Soc. U.S., Pilot Internat. Club, Nat. Assn. Corrosion Engrs., Am. Ordnance Assn. Club: Mt. Holyoke. Contbr. articles to profl. jours. Home: 1123 E Ocean Blvd Long Beach CA 90802 Office: 3370 Miraloma Av Anaheim CA 92803

FARMER, MARTHA LOUISE, educator; b. Cin.; d. William S. and Genevieve (Fye) Farmer; B.A., Wheaton Coll., 1935; postgrad. Wellesley Coll., 1936; M.A., Columbia, 1937, Ed.D., 1956. Asso. prof. Manhattanville Coll. Sacred Heart, 1936-43, 46-48; asso. prof. dept. student life City Coll., City U. N.Y., 1948-69, prof. dept. student personnel services, 1969—. Mem. mgmt. com. Emma Ransom YWCA, N.Y.C., 1958, mem. residence com. 1956-58; mem. jr. high teens com. YWCA, Ridgewood, N.J., 1962—; mem. N.J. com. U.S. Commn. on Civil Rights. Served as lt. USNR (W), 1943-46. Mem. Am. Coll. Personnel Assn. (program com. 1960-62, mem. com. I, 1963-65, chmn. Com. XIII 1965-67, mem. Com. IV 1968—), Am. Personnel and Guidance Assn., Assn. U. Evening Colls., U.S. Assn. Evening Students (chmn. bd. trustees 1970-71), Evening Student Personnel Assn. (pres. 1962-63), Am. Assn. U. Profs., Adult Student Personnel Assn. (chmn. bd. trustees 1968-71). Editor: Student Personnel Services For Adults in Higher Education, 1967; Counseling Services for Adults in Higher Education, 1971. Home: 348 Lake St Upper Saddle River NJ 07458 Office: City Coll NY 138th St and Convent Av New York City NY 10031

FARMER, MURIEL JUNE MACKAY (MRS. HAROLD EDWIN FARMER), educator; b. Boston, June 20, 1930; d. Chauncey Depew and Muriel Augusta (Gilliland) MacKay; B.S., Boston U., 1952, M.Ed., 1953; m. Harold Edwin Farmer, Nov. 25, 1964. Instr., Boston U., 1952-58; tchr. Dennis-Yarmouth Regional Sch., South Yarmouth, Mass., 1958-61, Chatham (Mass.) High Sch., 1961-63; prof., head dept. secretarial sci. Cape Cod Community Coll., West Barnstable, Mass., 1963—, dir. summer session, 1967-70, chmn. adv. com. in secretarial sci., 1970—. Mem. adv. com. Cape Cod Regional Tech. High Sch. Mem. Barnstable County Edn. Assn. (pres. 1964-65, dir. 1962—), N.E.A., Mass. Tchrs. Assn., Eastern Bus. Tchrs. Assn., Mass. Regional Community Coll. Faculty Assn., Mass. Bus. Educators Assn. (newsletter reporter), Pi Omega Pi, Delta Pi Epsilon. Republican. Episcopalian. Home: 50 Cypress Point Way South Yarmouth MA 02664 Office: Route 132 West Barnstable MA 02668

FARMILOE, DOROTHY ALICIA, author, educator; b. Toronto, Ont., Can., Sept. 8, 1920; d. Thomas and Beatrice Daisy (Archer) Roach; B.A., U. Windsor, 1963-67, M.A., 1969; m. Ray Edwin Farmiloe, Sept. 16, 1939 (dec. Oct. 1963); children—Dan, Judith (Mrs. John Long), Linda. Owner, operator Long Point Lodge, Elk Lake, Ont., 1955-63; editor Mainline mag., Windsor, Ont., 1968—; tchr. English, St. Clair Coll., Windsor, 1969—; co-pub. Sesame Press. Active Windsor Poetry Movement, 1966—; organizer poetry readings in libraries and schs., 1966—, poster poem exhibit, Windsor, 1971. Mem. Detroit Women Writers, League Canadian Poets. Author: (poetry) The Lost Island, 1966, 21 x 3, 1967, Poems for Apartment Dwellers, 1970, Winter Orange Mood, 1972, Blue is the Colour of Death, 1973; (play) What Do You Save from a Burning Building, 1973; (anthology) Controverse, 1972; (textbook) Creative Communication, 1974; (novel) And Some in Fire, 1974. Contbr. poems, articles and revs. to profl. publs. Home: 663 1/2 Campbell St Windsor ON Canada

FARNELL, MARGARET ISABEL HAMILTON O'CONNOR (MRS. GERALD GORDON FARNELL), librarian; b. Edmonton, Alta., Can., Sept. 12, 1915; d. George Bligh and Hannah Margaret (Fairlie) O'Connor; B.A., U. Alta., 1936; B.L.S., Simmons Coll., 1937; m. Gerald Gordon Farnell, Feb. 23, 1946; children—George, Douglas, Thomas. Librarian U. Alta., Edmonton, 1937-42, head librarian Rutherford Undergrad. Library, 1963-73, assoc. coordinator Humanities and Social Scis. Library, 1973—. Librarian Brit. Security Coordination, N.Y.C., also Brit. embassies in Port-au-Prince, Haiti, Montevideo, Uruguay, 1942-45. Mem. Jr. League Am., Canadian, Edmonton library assns., Library Assn. Alta., Delta Gamma. Home: 36 St George's Crescent Edmonton AB Canada Office: U Alberta Edmonton AB Canada

FARNES, MARY PATRICIA, physician; b. Portland, Ore., May 16, 1931; d. Cecil Julian and Lucile Augusta (Menges) Farnes; B.A., Willamette U., 1953; M.S., U. Ore., 1956, M.D., 1956. Intern, Presbyn. Hosp., Chgo., 1956-57, resident dept. medicine, 1957-58, USPHS postdoctoral fellow div. hematology, 1959-60; resident medicine R.I. Hosp., Providence, 1960-61, hematologist dept. pathology, cons. oncology, asso. div. hematology, dept. medicine, 1968—; CARE-MEDICO internist Hopital Civil de Benimessous, Algiers, 1963, Kabul, Afghanistan, 1972, asst. prof. medicine Brown U., 1968-74, asso. prof., 1974—. Mem. adv. bd. R.I. Hemophilia Guild, 1968—. Trustee, R.I. Zool. Soc.; bd. govs. R.I. chpt. Am. Cancer Soc. Recipient Alumni citation Willamette U., 1971. USPHS grantee, 1962-70, Am. Cancer Soc. grantee, 1967. Mem. Am. Soc. Cell Biology, Am. Fedn. Clin. Research, Am., Exptl. hematology socs., Med. Com. for Human Rights, Reticuloendothelial Soc., Audubon Soc., Sigma Xi, Alpha Omega Alpha. Editor: Hemic Cells in Vitro, 1969. Contbr. articles on blood and bone marrow differentiation to med. jours. Home: 66 Bowden Av Barrington RI 02806 Office: RI Hosp 593 Eddy St Providence RI 02902

FARNHAM, EMILY, educator, artist; b. Kent, O., May 27, 1912; d. Burt Leonard and Metta (Lake) Farnum; student Cleve. Inst. Art, 1929-30; B.S., Kent State U., 1933; M.A., Ohio State U., 1934, Ph.D., 1959. Instr., Ohio State U., 1934-37, Mich. State U., 1937, Utah State U., 1938-41; head related art dept. Stout State Coll., 1942-45; asst. prof. So. Ill. U., 1947-53, Ohio State U., 1954-55; asso. prof. Mary Baldwin Coll., 1956-62; prof. art history, painting and design East Carolina U., Greenville, N.C., 1962—, chmn. art history dept., 1969-73. One-man shows Ohio State U., Salt Lake City Art Center, So. Ill. U., U. Va., James Sprunt Inst., others. Mem. N.C. Art Commn., 1973-74. Mem. P.E.N., Coll. Art Assn. Am., Am. Assn. U. Women, East Carolina Art Soc., D.A.R. Republican. Conglist. Author: Charles Demuth: Behind a Laughing Mask, 1971. Home: 1108 S Overlook Dr Greenville NC 27834

FARNHAM, FERN HICKS (MRS. WILLARD E. FARNHAM), ret. educator; b. Oakland, Cal., Aug. 23, 1901; d. Lewis Albert and Eva (Pierce) Hicks; B.A., Wellesley Coll., 1922; M.A. in English Lit., Oxford (Eng.) U., 1932; M.A. in French, U. Cal. at Berkeley, 1960; m. Willard E. Farnham, May 9, 1929; children—Anthony Edward, Nicholas Holt. Tchr. English, high sch., Berkeley, 1940-47. Coll. Holy Names, Oakland, Cal., 1960-64; asst. prof. Newton (Mass.) Coll. Sacred Heart, 1964-67, asso. prof. English, 1967-68. Mem. Dante Soc. Am., Mediaeval Acad., Modern Lang. Assn., Société Rencesvals (French), Oxford Soc., Am. Assn. U. Women. Clubs: University Women's (London, Eng.); Wellesley; College Women's. Episcopalian. Contbr. articles to periodicals. Home: 3 Greenwood Common Berkeley CA 94708

FARNHAM, MARY GLADE SIEMER, artist; b. Ross, Cal., Nov. 1, 1924; d. Albert Henry and Mabel (Jones) Siemer; student Marin Jr. Coll., 1942-43, Goucher Coll., 1943-44; B.A., U. Cal. at Berkeley, 1947; m. Neil Farnham, Jan. 28, 1950 (div. Oct. 1972); children—Thomas Ross, Evan Neil, Wendy Marie, William Blair, Hugh Porter. One man shows Dorothy Cabot Best Gallery, Portland Ore., 1962, St. Helen's Hall Gallery, Portland, 1965, Oswego Pub. Library, Lake Oswego, Ore., 1965, 125 S.W. Yamhill St., Portland, 1966, 1st Unitarian Ch., Portland, 1967, U. Ore. Mus. Art, 1972; exhibited in group shows including Library of Congress, U.S. Nat. Mus., Utah, Portland, Seattle, San Francisco, DeYoung, Coos museums, also univ. museums, civic art centers and galleries; represented in permanent collections U. Ore. Mus., Coos Mus., Catlin Gabel Sch., Portland, Portland chpt. A.I.A., Salishan Lodge, Glenden Beach, Ore., Mt. Hood Chem. Co., Portland, Sunriver Properties, Bend, Ore., Ga. Pacific Corp., Portland, also numerous pvt. collections. Pres., Marin County Devel. Co., San Anselmo, Cal., 1969—. Recipient awards including Marin Jr. Coll., Ore. State Fair, Ore. Art Alliance, U.S. Nat. Mus., Wash. State Ann., Seattle Art Mus., Wash. State Art Commn., Richmond (Cal.) Art Center, Long Beach (Cal.) Art Assn., Peninsula Fine Arts Festival, Belmont, Cal., Pacific N.W. Arts and Crafts Fair, Bellevue, Wash., Coos Art Mus. Mem. Portland Museum Art Assn. (sec.), Pi Beta Phi. Episcopalian. Club: Multnomah Athletic (Portland). Address: 2850 NW Westover Rd Portland OR 97210

FARNSWORTH, BEATRICE (MRS. JOHN FARNSWORTH), educator; b. N.Y.C., Feb. 3, 1935; d. Max O. and Letty (Olshansky) Brodsky; B.A., Ind. U., 1955; M.A. (Social Sci. Research Council fellow), Yale, 1956, Ph.D. (Yale fellow), 1959; m. Paul Lauter, June 20, 1953 (div. 1965); children—David, Daniel; m. 2d, John Farnsworth, July 31, 1965; 1 son, Peter Jonathan. Instr. history Hobart Coll., 1962-63; fellow Radcliffe Inst., 1964-65, 66-67; asst. prof. history Wells Coll., Aurora, N.Y., 1965-66, asso. prof., 1968—. Asso. Russian Research Center, Harvard, 1964-65. Recipient George Washington Eggleston award Yale, 1959. Mem. Am. Hist. Assn., Am. Assn. Advancement Slavic Studies. Author: William C. Bullitt and the Soviet Union, 1967. Home: RD 2 Box 515 Seneca Falls NY 13148

FARNSWORTH, PATRICIA NORDSTROM (MRS. EDWARD ALLAN FARNSWORTH), educator; b. Sioux City, Ia., Aug. 18, 1930; d. Clifford and Aris Lucile (Thomas) Nordstrom; B.A., Morningside Coll., 1951; M.S., Columbia, 1952, Ph.D., 1960; m. Edward Allan Farnsworth, May 30, 1952; children—Jeanne Scott, Karen Ladd, Edward Allan, Pamela Ann. Postdoctoral fellow Columbia, 1961-64; asst. prof. Fairleigh Dickinson U., 1964-67; asst. prof. Barnard Coll., 1967-72; asso. prof. Coll. Medicine and Dentistry N.J., Newark, 1972—. Lectr. biophysics Harvard Med. Sch., 1970-72; cons. City N.Y. Health Dept., 1969, Arthur D. Little, Inc., 1971-73; mem. adv. com. Biol. Scis. Curriculum Study, 1973—. Trustee Social Service Fedn., Englewood, N.J., 1965-67. Recipient grants NIH, 1972, Sandoz Found., 1969; Alumni award Morningside Coll., 1971. NIH sr. research fellow, 1971. Mem. Am. Soc. Zoologists, Am. Physiol. Soc., (mem. ednl. com. 1972—), N.Y. Acad. Scis., Sigma Xi. Contbr. articles to profl. jours. Home: 201 Linçoln St Englewood NJ 07631 Office: 100 Bergen St Newark NJ 07103

FARQUHARSON, PATILU, psychologist, educator; b. Luray, Kan., July 25, 1925; d. Hugh Everton and Roberta Carol (Albach) Farquharson; B.A., U. Cal at Berkeley, 1946; M.S., Purdue U., 1948; Ph.D., U. Denver, 1956. Clin. psychologist Mendocino State Hosp., Talmage, Cal., 1948-51, Parsons (Kan.) State Hosp., 1951-52; intern Menorah Med. Center, Kansas City, Mo., 1953-54; instr. U. Denver, 1955-56, asst. prof., 1956-60, also dir. psychol. services for children, 1956-60; sch. psychologist Elk Grove (Cal.) Sch. Dist., 1960—. Lectr., Cal. State U., Sacramento, 1967-74; cons. to pvt. mental hosp., Denver, 1956-58, ednl. psychology rep. Behavioral Scis. Licensing Bd. State of Cal., 1971, 73—, vice chmn., 1973-74. Bd. dirs. Family Services Agy., Sacramento. Am. Bd. Examiners in Profl. Psychology fellow U. Denver, 1969. Mem. Am., Western, Colo. Sch. (pres. 1959-60), Sacramento Valley (sec.-treas. 1962-63, dir. 1963-64). psychol. assns., Internat. Psychologists, Cal. Assn. Sch. Psychologists (sec. 1965-66), Soroptimist Club (v.p. 1968-69, pres. 1969-70). Editorial bd. Jour. Sch. Psychology, 1966— Home: 6917 Briggs Dr Sacramento CA 95828 Office: Elk Grove School District Elk Grove CA 95624

FARR, MILDRED MCCARTY (MRS. FRANKLIN L. FARR), librarian; b. Pleasureville, Ky., Feb. 18, 1920; d. Robert Gill and Tressye Frances (Knight) McCarty; student Transylvania Coll., 1937-38; A.B., U. Ky., 1941, M.S., 1955; m. Franklin L. Farr, Feb. 22, 1966. Librarian, Graham High Sch., Bluefield, Va., 1941-42; office receptionist U. Ky., Lexington, 1943-45; librarian VA Hosp., Lexington, 1945-50, chief library service, 1950—. Ky. chmn. Nat. Library Week, 1960. Mem. Am., Ky. (pres. spl. libraries sect. 1958, sec.-treas. 1965), Lexington (pres. 1961) library assns., Bus. and Profl. Women's Club, Phi Alpha Theta, Kappa Delta Pi, Beta Sigma Phi. Mem. Disciples of Christ Ch. Home: 305 Blueberry Lane Lexington KY 40503 Office: VA Hosp Lexington KY 40507

FARR, TRUDY (MRS. ARTHUR E. FARR), civic worker; b. Watsonville, Cal., Sept. 18, 1925; d. Anthony E. and Mary J. (Rose) Pereira; student pub. schs.; m. Arthur Everal Farr, Sept. 2, 1945; children—Bonnie (Mrs. David Henry), Linda (Mrs. John Poole), Kathy (Mrs. Roger Stewart). Bookkeeper, Valley Pump & Equipment Co., Klamath Falls, Ore., 1953—. Life mem. Nat. and Ore. P.T.A., Roosevelt P.T.A., 1958-59, council pres., 1960-62, Ore. pres., 1969-71, mem. nat. commn., 1971-72, regional v.p. nat. orgn., 1972—; mem. budget com. Ore. United Appeal, 1968—; active Klamath County United Fund, 1964—; mem. State Com. to Study Sex Edn. in Schs., 1968-69, Colls. for Ore.'s Future Com., 1967—, Gov.'s Commn. on Children and Youth, 1966—, Nat. Camp Fire Council, 1966-68; pres. adv. bd. Klamath Mental Health Clinic, 1966-67. Bd. dirs. Camp Fire Girls. Recipient Service award Klamath Council P.T.A., 1970; Seaton award Camp Fire Girls, 1971, Vol. of Year award, 1973; named Woman of Achievement, Quota Club, 1971. Mem. Soroptimists, Beta Sigma Phi. Methodist (tchr. Sunday sch. 1956-59, ofcl. bd. mem.). Home: 2403 Pine Grove Rd Klamath Falls OR 97601 Office: 7364 S 6th St Klamath Falls OR 97601

FARRAGHER, MARY E. KENEFICK (MRS. BERNARD P. FARRAGHER), educator; b. Boston, May 16, 1921; d. William J. and Eva (Bowden) Kenefick; B.S., Boston State Coll., 1942, M.S., 1943; C.A.S., Boston Coll., 1962; m. Bernard P. Farragher, July 1, 1944; children—Joan V. (Mrs. Kevin Sullivan), Katherine M. Tchr. Highland Manor Jr. Coll., Long Branch, N.J., 1943-44; instr. Keyes Coll., Norfolk, Va., 1944-45; dir., founder Coop. Nursery Sch., Newton, Mass., 1953-56; pvt. tutor, Newton, Mass., 1955-58; tutor Manville Sch., Judge Baker Guidance Center, Boston, 1960-61; supr. remedial edn. Newton-Baker Project for Antisocial Boys, Newton, Mass., 1959-63; supr. therapeutic edn. Merrifield Center Project for Emotionally Disturbed Children in Specialized Foster Care, Worcester, Mass., 1963—. Cons., Nazareth Home for Boys, Leicester, Mass., 1965-66; adj. prof. Assumption Coll. Grad. Sch., Worcester, Mass., 1963—; psychoednl. cons., mem. adv. bd. U.S. Office of Edn., In-Service Tng. Inst., Milw. Vocational Tech. and Adult Schs., Milw., 1966—; cons. Youth Guidance Center, Framingham, Mass., 1970-71. Mental Health grantee, 1958, 59. Mem. Am. Orthopsychiat. Assn., Council for Exceptional Children, Assn. for Children with Learning Disabilities. Roman Catholic. Contbr. articles to profl. jours. Home: 44 Navasota Av Worcester MA 01602 Office: 21 Cedar St Worcester MA 01609

FARRAND, AMY GUEST, ret. educator; b. Claymont, Del.; d. Thomas Jefferson and Mary (Ferguson) Lloyd; B.S., U. Del. 1931, postgrad., 1946-51; postgrad. N.Y. U., 1932, Columbia, 1933-35; m. Homer F. Farrand, May 26, 1934. Trainer student tchrs. U. Del., 1934-62; mem. faculty Pierre S. DuPont High Sch., Wilmington, Del., 1935-74, guidance counselor, 1933-74, chmn. social studies dept., 1956-62. Speaker on contemporary historic, econ., polit. and social topics to community and ch. groups, 1935—. Membership chmn. Cedars Civic Assn., 1942-47. Mem. N.E.A., Del., Wilmington (chmn. legislative adv. bd. 1945-47, del. to state assn. 1939-46) edn. assns., Nat., Middle States councils for social studies, Am., Del. personnel and guidance assns., Am. Counselors Assn., Del. Hist. Soc., Women's Soc. Christian Service (sec. 1961-63), D.A.R. Methodist. Mem. Order Eastern Star. Pioneer in field of guidance in pub. schs. of Wilmington. Home: 7 Guest Lane Wilmington DE 19809

FARRAND, JANE MARIE STEPANCHAK (MRS. FRED LENOX), univ. adminstr.; b. Mpls., Nov. 14, 1946; d. John and Alma Jane (Brama) Stepanchak; B.A., U. Minn., 1968; M.S., U. Ore., 1974; m. Fred Lenox, June 10, 1967. Coordinator extended sch. day program Mpls. Bd. Edn., 1968; field dir. inner city Mpls. council Camp Fire Girls, 1968-69; asst. dean students U. Ore., Eugene, 1969—. Exec. dir. YWCA, Eugene, Ore., 1969-72. Mem. exec. bd. Lane County Mental Health Center Adv. Bd., 1972-74; mem. selection com. Aid to Dependent Children Confidence Clinic Adv. Bd., 1972—. Recipient Merit Key award U. Minn. Student Union, 1968. Mem. Nat. Assn. Women Deans, Adminstrs. and Counselors, N.W. Coll. Personnel Assn. Home: 2847 S Louis Lane Eugene OR 97405

FARRAR, CONSTANCE MOSHER (MRS. FRANKLIN ERNEST FARRAR), ins. co. exec.; b. Cambridge, Mass., Aug. 24, 1925; d. Curtis Howard and Jeannette (Shaw) Mosher; C.L.U., Am. Coll. C.L.U.'s, 1961; student Boston U. Met. Coll., 1968; m. Robert Stewart Perkins, Sept. 21, 1946 (div. 1954); 1 son, Bruce Stewart; m. 2d, Franklin Ernest Farrar, Feb. 4, 1961. Chartist, Liberty Mut. Life Ins. Co., N.Y.C., 1945-46; asst. cashier, bookkeeper Columbian Nat. Life Ins. Co., Boston, 1946-51; with New Eng. Mut. Life Ins. Co., Boston, 1951—, dir. brokerage services Downing & Desautels, 1951—. Mem. Boston Estate and Bus. Planning Council, 1959—. C.L.U. Mem. N.A.A.C.P., Internat. Platform Assn., Women Leaders Round Table, Boston Life Underwriters Assn., Nat. Assn. Life Underwriters (Nat. Quality award 1971, 72, 73), Am. Soc. C.L.U.'s (dir. Boston chpt. 1968-69), Golden Key Soc. Episcopalian (lay reader 1973—). Clubs: Zonta Internat. (2d v.p. 1968-69, pres. 1969-71), Toastmistress (pres. Newton 1967-68, pres. Needham 1972-73). Home: 1508 Great Plain Av Needham MA 02192 Office: 10 Post Office Square Boston MA 02109

FARRAR, PATRICIA JEAN HENLEY (MRS. FRANK FARRAR), civic worker; b. Britton, S.D., Aug. 13, 1931; d. Percy D. and Margaret (Schneider) Henley; B.A., U. S.D., 1953; m. Frank L. Farrar, June 5, 1953; children—Jeanne, Sally, Robert, Mary, Anne. Tchr., Summit (S.D.) High Sch., 1953; sec., Britton, 1954-56, part-time 1958-60; dir. Citizens Bank, Enderlin, N.D. Pres., Marshall County chpt. Am. Cancer Soc., 1967, 68, mem., 1972—; mem. St. Mary's Hosp. Aux., 1969—; mem. apparel and textile adv. bd. S.D. State U., 1970—; mem. S.D. Commn. on Status Women, 1969—, S.D. Library Week Com., 1969, S.D. Com. for Pub. Edn. Youth, 1972—, Dean Colton Fine Arts Scholarship Com. U. S.D., 1969—; mem. adv. com. on arts John F. Kennedy Center for Performing Arts, 1972—. Mem. S.D. Edn. Assn., P.E.O., Pi Beta Phi. Republican. Presbyn. Clubs: Britton Study, Britton Garden. Home: 203 9th Av Britton SD 57430

FARRAR, REGINA GERALDINE, social worker; b. Macon, Ga., Feb. 5, 1926; d. Samuel Lee and Ann Regina (Schorr) Farrar; A.B. cum laude, Wesleyan Coll., 1947; M.S.W., Fla. State U., 1954; m. George Nelson Thomas, Jr., Sept. 12, 1947 (div. Sept. 1952). Corr. clk. USAF Directorate of Res. Adminstrn. Officers, Warner Robins AFB, Ga., 1951-52; sr. caseworker A.R.C., Duval County chpt., Jacksonville, Fla., 1954-62; med./psychiat. social worker A.R.C., U.S. Naval Hosp., Jacksonville, Fla., 1962-67; psychiat. social Worker Mental Health Clinic, Jacksonville, Inc. (Fla.), 1967-70; dir. family and social services Jacksonville Parent-Child Center, 1970-71; pvt. practice psychiat. social work, 1971—. Group therapist for spouses of alcoholics Fla. Alcoholics Rehab. Clinic, Jacksonville, 1968-73. Mem. Nat. Assn. Social Workers, Acad. Certified Social Workers, Mental Health Assn. Jacksonville. Home: 2058 Niblick Dr Jacksonville FL 32210 Office: 3599 University Blvd S Suite 203 Jacksonville FL 32216

FARRELL, ANNE ELISABETH ALLABEN (MRS. JAMES KEITHLEY FARRELL), artist, author; b. Roscoe, N.Y., Oct. 3, 1916; d. Charles Moore and Fanny Myra (Jackson) Allaben; B.S., Skidmore Coll., 1939; student Grand Central Sch. Art, 1939-41; m. James Keithley Farrell, Oct. 26, 1946; children—J. Keithley, Anne Althea, Charles A., Susan E., Cynthia E. Free-lance painting and illustrating, N.Y.C., 1942-46; free-lance painting Edward Gross Co. of N.Y.C., Hopewell, Va., 1946-48; free-lance illustrator Bd. Christian Edn., Westminster Press, Phila., 1961-65; writer, illustrator, C.R. Gibson Co. of Norwalk, Conn., Chadds Ford, Pa., 1967—; painter Arthur Kaplan Picture Co. of N.Y.C., 1967—; Bernard Picture Co., N.Y.C., 1967—. Nurses aide A.R.C., 1943-46; collector Heart Fund, 1968-69; mem. Mother's Guild, St. Edmond's Acad., 1959-64, Archmere Acad., 1961-68, Ursuline Acad., Wilmington, Del., 1962-66. Author: Wee Me, 1945; Littlest One, 1956; Nighttime Is a Quiet Time, 1968; Poems For A Little Boy, 1969; Poems For A Little Girl, 1969. Home: Box 370 Fairville Rd Route 1 Chadds Ford PA 19317

FARRELL, EILEEN, singer, soprano; b. Willimantic, Conn., Feb. 13, 1920; d. Michael John and Catherine (Kennedy) Farrell; m. Robert V. Reagan, Apr. 4, 1946; children—Robert V., Kathleen. Made debut as singer Columbia Broadcasting Co., 1941; singer, own program, CBS, 6 yrs.; made opera debut in Il Trovatore with San Francisco Opera; Met. opera debut, 1960; singer with major symphony orchestras in U.S.; toured throughout U.S., South Am., Europe. Address: Herbert Barrett Mgmt Inc 250 W 57th St New York NY 10019

FARRELL, MARGARET ALICE, educator; b. Troy, N.Y., Mar. 9, 1932; d. Edward Arthur and Mary Elizabeth (Madigan) Farrell; A.B., Coll. of St. Rose, 1953; M.Ed., Boston Coll., 1954; Ph.D., Ind. U., 1967. Tchr. math. St. Lawrence Central Sch., Brasher Falls, N.Y., 1954-55, Chatham (N.Y.) Central Sch., 1955-58, Shaker High Sch., Newtonville, N.Y., 1958-60; asst. prof. math. edn. State U. N.Y. at Albany, 1960-65, asso. prof., 1965-73, prof., 1973—. Cons. Capitol area Sch. Dist. Adminstrs. Council, Bur. Continuing Edn., N.Y. State, 1970—. NSF fellow, 1957, 59, 61, 63-65. Mem. Nat. Council Tchrs. Math., Math. Assn. Am., Assn. Math. Tchrs. N.Y. (pres. 1972-73), Sigma Xi, Delta Kappa Gamma, Pi Mu Epsilon, Kappa Gamma Pi. Asso. editor N.Y. State Maths. Tchrs. Jour., 1971—. Contbr. articles to profl. pubs. Home: 32 Oak Rd Delmar NY 12054

FARRELL, SISTER MARY HOWARD, coll. librarian; b. Cleve., Mar. 24, 1927; d. Howard Joseph and Mary Teresa (Finucan) Farrell; B.S. in Edn., St. John Coll., 1959; M.S. in L.S., Case Western Res. U., 1971. Joined Ursuline Community, 1946; tchr. St. Joseph Sch., Cleve., 1947, St. Clare Sch., Lyndhurst, O., 1948-56, St. Jerome Sch., Cleve., 1956-62, Ste. Therese Sch., Garfield Heights, O., 1962-64, Immaculate Conception Sch., Willoughby, O., 1964-66, tchr. St. Mary Magdalene Sch., Willowick, O., 1966-69; asst. prin. St. Ann Sch., Cleveland Heights, O., 1969-71; librarian Villa Angela Acad., Cleve., 1971-72; head librarian Ursuline Coll., Cleve., 1972—. Bibliographer, research guide World Book Ency. Corp., Chgo., 1972. Mem. Am., Cleve., Cath. library assns., Ednl. Media Council Ohio, Asso. Cath. Colls. Cleve. Home: 2600 Lander Rd Cleveland OH 44124

FARRELL, PHYLLIS CHASE (MRS. JOHN JAMES FARRELL, JR.), polit. worker; b. Washington, June 15, 1930; d. Ralph Henry and Ruth (Weihe) Chase; B.S., U. Md., 1952; m. John James Farrell, Jr., May 30, 1953; children—Maureen, John James III, Patrick Kelly, Timothy Douglas. Sec., Mayfair Park, Inc., Savannah, Ga., 1971-73. Mem. adv. council Ga. Crime Information Center, 1974-77. Mem. Ga. Dem. Exec. Com., 1970—; coordinator for Gov. Jimmy Carter, 1970, U.S. Rep. Ronald Ginn, 1972; Savannah campaign mgr. Senator David Gambrell, 1972; del. Dem. Nat. Conv., 1972. Mem. Am. Assn. U. Women (Savannah legislative chmn. 1973-74), League Women Voters (Savannah legislative chmn. 1973-74), D.A.R. (chpt. corr. sec. 1970-74). Club: Mayfair Garden (pres. 1969-70, 71-72, sec. 1972-73 Savannah). Home: 1418 N Camden Circle Savannah GA 31406

FARRELL, SALLIE JOHNSON, librarian; b. Brookhaven, Miss., Dec. 29, 1909; d. William Henry and Ora Lee (Johnson) Farrell; B.A., Miss. State Coll. Women, 1931; B.S. in L.S. cum laude, U. Ill., 1932. Tchr.-librarian Picayune (Miss.) High Sch., 1932-33; asst. Queens Borough Pub. Library, Jamaica, N.Y., 1934-36, Tulane U. Library, 1936; reference librarian La. State Library, Baton Rouge, 1936-38; parish librarian Shreve Meml. Library, Shreveport, 1939, Winn., Rapides and Calcasieu parishes, La., 1940-46; field rep. La. State Library, Baton Rouge, 1946-54, dir. field services, 1954-62, state librarian, 1962—. Mem. U.S.-USSR Libraries Exchange Mission, 1961, La. Bur. on Status Women. Trustee Pub. Affairs Research Council. Mem. Am. (v.p. 1954-55), La. (pres. 1943-44), Southwestern library assns., Nat. Fedn. Bus. and Profl. Women's Clubs, Alpha Delta Kappa, Delta Kappa Gamma. Methodist. Contbr. articles to profl. jours. Home: 1922 Ramsey Dr Baton Rouge LA 70808 Office: La State Library Baton Rouge LA 70821

FARRELL, SUZANNE, ballet dancer; b. Cin.; Ford scholar Sch. Am. Ballet, 1960-61. With N.Y.C. Ballet, 1961-69, soloist, 1963-70, prin. dancer 1965-70; mem. Maurice Bejart Ballet of 20th Century, 1970—; appearances include roles in Don Quixote, Slaughter on 10th Av., 1968, Bach Sonate pasdedeux, Fleur du Mal, Golestan, Nijinsky-Clown of God, Les Triomphes; also appeared in Romeo and Juliet, Bhakti, Bolero, Sacre du Printemps; guest artist Nat. Ballet of Can., 1970; appeared in movie A Midsummer Night's Dream, 1965. Lectr., tchr. U. Cin., 1965. Recipient Spl. Merit award U. Cin., 1965; Mademoiselle Merit award, 1965.

FARRER, IRMANEA VIRGINIA BURCHAM (MRS. GEOFFREY MELBOURNE FARRER), civic leader; b. Tucson, Jan. 25, 1929; d. Gouley Neal and Irma (Emilie) Burcham; B.A., U. Ariz., 1950; m. Geoffrey Melbourne Farrer, Aug. 30, 1950; children—Geoffrey Melbourne, Lynda Cameron, Melissa Ann. Vice pres. Parent Guild, Crippled Childrens Soc. Los Angeles County, 1960; rec. and financial sec. Sr. Silver Spoons div. Womens Aux. Cal. Babies and Childrens Med. Center, 1961; spl. edn. chmn. Inglewood council Nat. Congress Parents and Tchrs., 1961; treas. jr. aux. Assistance League, 1961-63, v.p., 1964, now mem. adv. bd.; sec. Parent Edn. Assn., Francis Blend Sch. for Blind, 1965-67; chmn. Hollywood Bowl Tours, 1966. Trustee Jr. Programs of Cal., 1966-67, corr. sec., 1967; bd. dirs. Docent council Los Angeles County Mus. Art, 1969-70; bd. govs. United Cerebral Palsy Assn., Los Angeles County, 1956-67; founder, adviser Mus. Jrs. of Los Angeles County Mus. of Art, 1965-70; trustee Los Angeles Jr. Art Center, 1971-74. Mem. Nat. Charity League (patroness treas. 1970-72), Delta Delta Delta. Presbyn. Address: 4944 Finley Av Los Angeles CA 90027

FARRIS, ALICE HILD (MRS. GRANT M. FARRIS), library cons.; b. Washington, Dec. 24, 1940; d. Robert Philip and Sara Virginia (Taylor) Hild; A.B., Roanoke Coll., 1962; M.A. (Va. Library fellow), U. Denver, 1963; m. Grant M. Farris, May 16, 1970; 1 dau., Paige Elizabeth. Librarian, Va. Library Extension Div., Richmond, 1963-66; coordinator instructional resources Wyo. Dept. Edn., Cheyenne, 1966-72; library cons., 1967—. Free-lance cons., 1967—. Mem. A.L.A. (council 1969-72), Wyo., Mountain Plains library assns., Wyo. Instructional Media Assn. (exec. sec. 1969-71), League Women Voters (state bd. 1973-74), Am. Assn. U. Women (2d v.p. 1973—). Home and office: 1812 E 21st St Cheyenne WY 82001

FARRIS, GENEVIEVE BAIRD (MRS. FRANK MITCHELL FARRIS, JR.), civic worker; b. New Orleans; d. Thomas Barton and Cecilia K. (Kearny) Baird; grad. Arlington Hall Jr. Coll., 1936; B.A., Agnes Scott Coll., 1938; m. Frank Mitchell Farris, Jr., June 7, 1941; 1 dau., Genevieve Baird (Mrs. William E. Hancock). Press and publs. U.S. Postal Censorship, New Orleans, 1942-44. Area chmn. Heart Fund, Nashville, 1965, United Givers Fund, 1968, 72, 73. Bd. dirs. Nashville Childrens Theatre, 1948—, exec. bd., 1969-72; bd. dirs. Nashville Travelers Aid Soc., 1956—, pres., 1963-64; bd. dirs. Nat. Travelers Aid Soc., 1964-72; dir. Davidson County Hort. Soc., 1968-72, v.p., 1965-67, 71-73, 73-74; sec. bd. Day Care Home Retarded Children, 1970-72, pres., 1973-74. Mem. Davidson County Lawyers Aux. (pres. 1961), Jr. League. Presbyn. Clubs: Bellemeade Country, Centennial. Home: 940 Overton Lea Rd Nashville TN 37220

FARROW, JONELLE MCLEMORE (MRS. BOBBY JAMES FARROW), psychologist, educator; b. Valley Mills, Tex., Feb. 3, 1942; d. Ernest Garth and Evelyn Princella (Carlson) McLemore; B.A., U. Tex., 1964, Ph.D., 1969; m. Bobby James Farrow, Dec. 23, 1965. Lectr. dept. psychology Ind. U., South Bend, 1966-69, asst. prof. psychology, 1969-73, acting chmn. dept. psychology, 1970-72, asso. prof., chmn. dept. psychology, 1973—. Vis. prof. psychology Inst. Psychology Pontifica Universidade Catholica, Rio de Janeiro, Brazil, summer, 1967; research cons. and program devel. Planned Parenthood of Northwest Ind., 1969—; research asso. Latin Am. Population Research Center, summer 1967. Ind. Com. for the Humanities grantee, 1973, Ind. U. South Bend research grantee, 1973. Mem. Am., Rocky Mountain psychol. assns., Psi Chi. Contbr. articles on psychol. characteristics of socio-economic groups and their relationship to family planning to profl. jours. Home: 1508 Hoover Av South Bend IN 46615 Office: Dept of Psychology Indiana University South Bend IN 46615

FARROW, LILA LOUCILE BARBER (MRS. SAM B. FARROW), former editor; b. Oxford, Miss., June 5, 1912; d. William Thomas and Ella Lorena (Bratton) Barber; grad. Freed-Hardeman Coll., 1932; m. Samuel Bray Farrow, May 24, 1938; 1 son, Larry Joe. Tchr., Chester County Schs., 1930-38; adminstrv. asst. to pres. Tenn. Congress Parents and Tchrs., Nashville, 1948-74, editor monthly publ., Tenn. Parent-Tchr., 1954-74. Mem. Nat. (life), Tenn. (life) congresses parents and tchrs. Home: 1925 Rosewood Valley Dr Brentwood TN 37027

FARSACE, DUVERNE KONRICK, poet, sci.-fiction writer; b. Jasper, Tex., Aug. 20, 1923; d. Rudolph Joseph and Vera (Bishop) Konrick; grad. St. Mary's Dominican Coll., New Orleans, 1945; m. Larry Farsace, Aug. 8, 1956. Librarian, New Orleans Pub. Library, 1945-56, Rochester Pub. Library, from 1956; sr. advance reader Lawyer's Co-op. Pub. Co.; poetess, essayist, author sci. fiction short stories: collector, bibliographer. Chmn. La. Poetry Day Com., 1956, co-judge Rochester World Poetry Day, 1958—, co-chmn., 1958—; mem. World Poetry Day Com., co-chmn., co-judge contest, asst. chmn., 1970—; asst. chmn. Western N.Y., World Poetry Day; asst. N.Y. State chmn. Nat. Poetry Day, 1970. Recipient James C. Doty Meml. award for poem, 1948; Allison Nichols prize for best poem of year, Chromotones, 1952, John Francis Sims Meml. award for poem Pine Cathedral, 1955, for Psyche's Sorcery, 1957; Diploma, Greatness and Leadership award United Poets Laureate Internat. and Phillippine Assn. Drs. in Law, 1967; Diploma Di Benemerenza, Centro Studi E Scambi Internationali, Rome, Italy, 1967; Medal for achievement in poetry Pres. of Phillippines, 1968; certificate of recognition for poem Nat. Poetry Day. Mem. Am. Poetry League, Composers, Authors and Artists Am., Avalon World Arts Acad. (hon. life, past dir.-tchr. poetry workshop New Orleans chpt., contbg. editor, asst. nat. councillor 1951-53). Sci. Acad. Rochester, Rochester Astronomy Club, Nat. League Am. Pen Women, Nat., Rochester poetry socs., Acad. Am. Poets (founder), Marquis Biog. Soc., Nolacon. Author: (poems) Flames of Freedom, 1952. Editor: Golden Atom; co-editor Rochester in Poetry, Past and Present, 1958; Golden Atom; Lilac City Lyrics, 1969-71; The Golden Atom Poets of History. Contbr. poetry and short stories to numerous mags., chpts. to books; poems translated and pub. into French, Greek and Spanish. Office: care Golden Atom PO Box 1101 Rochester NY 14603

FASEL, IDA DRAPKIN (MRS. OSCAR FASEL), educator, writer; b. Portland, Me., May 9, 1909; d. I. E. and Lilian (Harwich) Drapkin; B.A. cum laude, Boston U., 1931, M.A., 1945; postgrad. Tex. Woman's U., 1958-59; Ph.D., U. Denver, 1963; m. Oscar A. Fasel, Dec. 24, 1946. Grad. asst. Boston U., 1945-46; instr. English, U. Conn., 1946-50; asst. librarian Okla. Mil. Acad., Claremore, Okla., 1952-54, registrar, 1954-57; reference librarian Midwestern U., 1958-59; instr. in English Colo. Woman's Coll., 1959-62; instr. U. Colo., Denver Center, 1962-64, asst. prof. English, 1964-72, asso. prof., 1972—. Book reviewer Tulsa Sunday World, 1954-57, Wichita Falls Sunday Times, 1957-61. Mem. Modern Lang. Assn. (Rocky Mountain br.), Poetry Soc. Am., Internat. Poetry Soc., Milton Soc. Am., Phi Beta Kappa. Author numerous poems pub. in Christian Sci. Monitor, N.Y. Herald Tribune, Good Housekeeping, The Instructor, Children's Activities, others; included in anthologies. Contbr. critical articles to profl., scholarly mags. Home: 165 Ivy St Denver CO 80220

FASENMYER, SISTER MARY SARAH, univ. dean; b. Kansas City, Kan., Mar. 17, 1923; d. Anthony Charles and Sara (Carey) Fasenmyer; B.S., St. Mary Coll., Leavenworth, Kan., 1952; Ph.D., N.Y.U., 1967. Tchr. St. Patrick's Sch., Butte, Mont., 1946-53; prin. St. Laurence Jr. High Sch., Laramie, Wyo., 1953-60; prin. St. Helena Sch., Helena, Mont., 1960-64; asst. prof. edn. Catholic U. Am., Washington, 1968-70, dir. curriculum Devel. Center, 1968-70, dean Sch. Edn., 1971-73; dean Sch. Edn., St. John's U., Jamaica, N.Y., 1973—. Mem. Am. Assn. Cath. Tchrs. Edn., Am. Assn. Sch. Adminstrn., Assn. Supervision and Curriculum Devel., Nat. Cath. Ednl. Assn. (chmn. tchr. edn. sect.), Kappa Delta Pi. Home: 189-04 64th Av 9D Flushing NY 11365

FASKEN, GENEVA FARLEY (MRS. LEE M. FASKEN), banker; b. Carthage, Mo., Mar. 31, 1921; d. Samuel Charles and Pearl (Pope) Farley; grad. high sch.; student Joiner's Sch. Commerce, 1939-41; m. Lee M. Fasken, May 5, 1942; 1 dau., Melfin Lee (Mrs. William C. Buchanan). Sec., teller, bookkeeper Home Fed. Savs. & Loan Assn., Carthage, 1941-42; sec. First Fed. Savs. & Loan Assn., Colorado Springs, Colo., 1942-44; vacation relief sec., teller, bookkeeper Monterey County Trust and Savs. Bank, King City, Cal., 1944; chief clk. vehicle records sect. Ordnance Office, Camp Crowder, Mo., 1944-46; with Central Nat. Bank Carthage (name now United Mo. Bank Carthage), 1946-51, 54—, asst. trust officer, 1963—, sec., 1968-72, asst. v.p., 1971-72, v.p. trust dept., 1972—; dir. Joplin Tool & Die, Inc., (Mo.). Chmn. bus. and indsl. div. Heart Fund, Carthage, 1971, chmn., 1972. Mem. Nat. Assn. Bank Women (group chmn. Ozark group 1970), Soroptimist Club (corr. sec. 1965, del. 1966, 67, 2d v.p. 1968, 69, 1st v.p. 1970). Methodist (adminstrv. bd. 1965-72; sec. 1966-70). Home: 1710 Missouri Av Carthage MO 64836 Office: PO Box 876 Carthage MO 64836

FASNACHT, BETTY BEEGLE (MRS. RICHARD SHARP FASNACHT), journalist; b. Roaring Spring, Pa., May 19, 1931; d. Earl Ray and Mary Arminta (Myers) Beegle; diploma Phila. Coll. Osteopathy Sch. Nursing, 1952; student piano and organ; m. Richard Sharp Fasnacht, June 14, 1952; children—Richard II, Mary Jean, Mark Steven, Ruth Leslie, Raymon Lore. Mem. operating room staff PCO Hosp., Phila., 1953-54; operating room supr. Portland (Ore.) Osteo. Hosp., 1954-55; nursery staff nurse Phila. Coll. Osteopathy Hosp., 1956; office nurse for husband, Bradford, Pa., part time 1960-69; county editor, writer Bradford Era, 1969-72, city editor, chief photographer, 1972—. Asst. organist 1st U.P. Ch. Bradford, 1962; organist, choirmaster Temple Beth El, Bradford, 1963-66, Grace Luth. Ch., Bradford, 1963-67; cocktail waitress Holiday Inn, Bradford, 1967-68. Apptd. dep. sheriff McKean County, Pa., 1967—; mem. Civil Air Patrol, 1971—. Mem. Nat. Fedn. Bus. and Profl. Women (1st v.p. Bradford chpt. 1970-71), Am. Guild Organists (dean Allegheny chpt. 1967-69, pub. relations chmn. 1969-70). Office: 43 Main St Bradford PA 16701

FASS, SHARON, editor; b. Bklyn., Dec. 21, 1946; d. Paul and Rose (Lassinsky) Abramowitz; B.A. in Journalism, U. Mich., 1967. Editorial trainee McCall Corp., N.Y.C., 1968-69; editorial asst. Saturday Rev. mag., N.Y.C., 1969-72; asst. editor World mag., N.Y.C., 1972-73, Saturday Rev./World mag., N.Y.C., 1973—. Mem. Women in Communications, Alumna Mag. Pubs. Assn., Kappa Tau Alpha.

FASSLER, JOAN GRACE (MRS. LEONARD J. FASSLER), psychologist, author, educator; b. N.Y.C., Sept. 23, 1931; d. Jacob V. and Rose (Sandrowitz) Greenberg; B.B.A., Coll. City N.Y., 1953; M.A., Columbia, 1965; Ph.D. (United Cerebral Palsy Research and Edn. Found. grantee), 1969; m. Leonard J. Fassler, July 26, 1953; children—David Gary, Ellen Beth. Editorial asst. Seventeen at School, N.Y.C., 1954-55, reader Mail editor Seventeen Mag., N.Y.C., 1955-56; research asst. Tchrs. Coll., Columbia U., N.Y.C., 1966-67, project asso., research asso., research cons. Research and Demonstration Center for Edn. Handicapped Children, 1967-72; cons. early childhood programming Videorecord Corp. Am., Westport, Conn., 1970-72; mem. faculty, research asso. Child Study Center, Yale, New Haven, 1972—, chmn. children's lit. adv. com., 1972—. Psychologist, moderator program series Conversations With the Very Young, WNYC radio, N.Y.C., 1970; lectr. summer research workshop coll. tchrs., Columbia U., 1970; vis. faculty psychology dept. U. N.H., Durham, 1971. Demonstration Program grantee Grant Found., 1972-74. Mem. Am. Psychol. Assn., Council for Exceptional Children, Nat. Assn. for Edn. Young Children, Am. Orthopsychiat. Assn. (program com.), Assn. for Childhood Edn. Internat., Psi Chi. Author: The Man of the House, 1969; All Alone with Daddy, 1969; One Little Girl, 1969; Don't Worry Dear, 1971; The Boy With a Problem, 1971; My Grandpa Died Today, 1971; Howie Helps Himself, 1974. Contbr. articles to profl. jours. Home: 80 Hickory Hill Dr Dobbs Ferry NY 10522 Office: 333 Cedar St New Haven CT 06510

FASTEAU, BRENDA SUE FEIGEN, lawyer; b. Chgo., July 7, 1944; d. Arthur Paul and Shirley (Bierman) Feigen; B.A. cum laude in Math., Vassar Coll., 1966; J.D., Harvard, 1969; m. Marc S. Fasteau, Dec. 21, 1968. Admitted to Mass. bar, 1970, N.Y. bar, 1971; chief analyst Boston Redevel. Authority, Boston, 1969; asso. law offices Rosenman, Colin, Kaye, Petschek, Freund & Emil, N.Y.C., 1970; dir. nat. women's rights project Am. Civil Liberties Union, N.Y.C., 1971—. Mem. Nat. Orgn. for Women (nat. legislative v.p. 1970-71), Women's Action Alliance (co-founder, coordinating dir., dir.), Nat. (adv. com.), N.Y. State, New York County women's polit. caucuses. Democrat. Contbr. articles to mags., chpt. to book. Home: 5 Tudor City Pl New York City NY 10017 Office: Am Civil Liberties Union 22 E 40th St New York City NY 10016

FAUBER, JANICE ANNETTE, hist. agy. and mus. ofcl.; b. Duluth, Minn., Oct. 10, 1942; d. Robert James and Muriel Elsie (Carlson) Woodruff; A.B. in Art and History, U. Cal. at Davis, 1964; postgrad. in history Cal. State U., Sacramento, 1965-72; m. Richard Earl Fauber, June 18, 1972. Staff asst. Sacramento City-County Mus. and History Commn., 1964-65, exec. sec., 1965—. Cons. historic preservation City of Columbus (Ga.), 1966; publicity chmn. Sacramento Birthday Celebration, 1966-67, 70-71, 73, vice chmn., 1974, chmn., 1975; exec. com. Sacramento Gold Spike Centennial Celebration, 1969; chmn. Sacramento County History Week Celebration, 1974-75. Campaign worker Democratic Party. Recipient award of merit Am. Assn. State and Local History, 1971. Mem. Conf. Cal. Hist. Socs. (dir.), Am. Assn. Museums (dir. ex officio Western regional conf.), Sacramento County Hist. Soc. (publicity chmn. 1974, newsletter editor 1974, dir. 1975), Friends of Sacramento City and County Mus. (dir. ex officio 1972—), Ecology Information Center Sacramento, Nat. Womens Polit. Caucus, Am. Assn. State and Local History (Cal. awards of merit chmn. 1975), Ams. for Dem. Action. Editor: City of the Plain, Sacramento in the Nineteenth Century, 1969; Western Museums Quar., 1970-74; acting editor Cal. Historian quar., 1974. Monthly contbr. Sacramento Valley Directory and Guide, 1969-72; also articles to hist. publs. Home: 4537 Brandywine Ct Carmichael CA 95608 Office: 1009 7th St Sacramento CA 95814

FAUCHER, ROSE GRACE, librarian; b. Saginaw, Mich., Oct. 29, 1914; d. John Patrick and Helen Augusta (Moses) Faucher; Ph.B., Loyola U., Chgo., 1938; A.B., U. Mich., 1939, A.M., 1944. Library asst. acquisitions dept. U. Mich. Library, 1939-42, library asso. circulation dept., 1944-53, dental librarian Dental Library, 1954-61, asst. head Undergrad. Library, 1961-63, head, 1963—. Mem. Am., Mich., Washtenaw County library assns., Women of Univ. Faculty (pres. 1971-72), Kappa Gamma Pi, Omicron Kappa Upsilon. Home: 601 Sunset Rd Ann Arbor MI 48103

FAULK, LILLIAN MILDRED TIBBELS (MRS. RAYMOND B. FAULK), ednl. adminstr.; b. Smithville, Ark., Aug. 3, 1912; d. Charles D. and Aurelia J. (Shaver) Tibbels; B.S. in Edn., Ark. State Tchrs. Coll., 1940; M.A., George Peabody Coll. for Tchrs., 1947; Ed.D., U. Tenn., 1970; m. Raymond B. Faulk, Mar. 19, 1954 (dec. Aug. 1955). Tchr., Black Rock (Ark.) Elementary Sch., 1936-40; tchr. Hulbert (Ark.)-West Memphis Schs., 1940-49, elementary school prin., now elementary sch. supr. Instr. edn. Ark. State Coll., Jonesboro, summer 1956; chmn. elementary sch. council Ark. Dept. Edn., 1965-68. Named Favorite Tchr. in Ark. and Mo., Memphis Comml. Appeal,

1959; Woman of Year, West Memphis Jr. C. of C., 1966. Mem. N.E.A. (Ark. rep. dept. elementary sch. prins. 1963-69), Ark. Edn. Assn. (mem. com. profl. rights and responsibilities 1965-68), Ark. Assn. Supervision and Curriculum Devel. (pres. 1961-62), Ark. Elementary Sch. Prins. (sec. 1952-53), West Memphis Jr. Aux. (sustaining), Pi Gamma Mu, Kappa Delta Pi, Delta Kappa Gamma (state treas. 1965-67), Alpha Tau (pres. 1960-62). Baptist. Mem. Order Eastern Star. Clubs: West Memphis Quota (pres. 1971-73), Beethoven Music. Home: 508 Gibson St West Memphis AR 72301 Office: Adminstrv Annex 1414 S Avalon West Memphis AR 72301

FAULKNER, ADELE LLOYD, interior designer, color cons.; b. Los Angeles, Dec. 26, 1913; d. Lloyd Lawrence and Coralynn (DeVoe) Lloyd; grad. Woodbury Coll., 1932; m. 2d, William Garl Quinn, Dec. 22, 1963; 1 son (by previous marriage), Lloyd Nelson Faulkner. Pres. Adele Faulkner & Assos., Inc.; syndicated columnist Copley News. Dir. Los Angeles Community Design Center. Fellow Am. Inst. Interior Designers (twice past chpt. pres., v.p. nat. bd. govs., nat. sec. 1972-73, regional v.p. 1973-74, Nat. Design award 1968, 69), Home Fashions League: mem. Nat. Illuminating Engring. Soc. Internat. Platform Assn., Profl. Women for So. Cal. Symphony. Office: Box 112 North Hollywood CA 91603

FAULKNER, ELIZABETH COONLEY, civic worker; b. Chgo., Dec. 3, 1902; d. Avery and Queene (Ferry) Coonley; grad. Madeira Sch., Greenway, Va., 1920; A.B., Vassar Coll., 1924; m. Waldron Faulkner, Nov. 18, 1926; children—Avery Coonley, Winthrop Waldron, Celia Ferry (Mrs. Raymond C. Clevenger III). Tchr., Madeira Sch., 1925-26. Pres. Madeira Sch. Alumnae Assn., 1929-31, bd. dirs., 1943-68; pres. Vassar Coll. Alumnae Assn., 1933-36; pres. Vassar Club D.C., 1942-44; pres. class 1924, Vassar Coll., 1949-60; trustee Vassar Coll., 1958-66; pres. John Eaton Sch. P.T.A., Washington, 1936-38; trustee Potomac Sch., 1948-51; pres. bd. D.C. YWCA, 1951-53, chmn. D.C. com. interpretations and support Nat. Bd., 1952-62, mem. Area Council, 1952-63, mem. Nat. Capital Area, 1964—; chmn. com. curriculums D.C. subcom. White House Conf. Edn., 1956; chmn. women's activities, centennial conv. A.I.A., 1957; pres. women St. Margaret's Episcopal Ch., 1953-55, mem. vestry, 1958-62; pres. Wilmer Conf. Center Corp. Episcopal Diocese D.C., 1960—; mem. bd. Episcopal Center Children, 1962-68. Mem. Am. Assn. U. Women. Clubs: Cosmopolitan (N.Y.C.); Sulgrave (Washington). Address: 3415 36th St NW Washington DC 20016

FAULKNER, MARIANNE OSBORNE (MRS. DOUGLAS CLAUDE FAULKNER), broadcasting exec.; b. Middletown, O., June 14, 1930; d. Arthur Hornung and Caroline Clark (Welch) Osborne;; grad. Middletown Bus. Coll., 1951-52; m. Douglas Claude Faulkner, June 14, 1960; children—Daniel Arthur, Donald Patrick, Gwenda Patrice. Payroll auditor Aeronca Aircraft, Middletown, O., 1956-63; sales service traffic Avco Broadcasting Co., WLW-D, Dayton, O., 1964-67; traffic continuity dir. Springfield Broadcasting, WKEF-TV, Dayton, 1967-70; traffic accounting exec. Metromedia TV Inc. WXIX-TV, Cin., from 1970, then bus. mgr., now v.p. Mem. Community Theatres, Dayton, Middletown Playhouse, Am. Women in Radio and Television (pres. Cin. chpt., chmn. profl. devel. com.; nat. dir. 1974—). Club: Toastmistress. Home: 1769 Forester Dr Cincinnati OH 45240 Office: 10490 Taconic Terrace Cincinnati OH 45215

FAULL, ANNA F(ORWARD), botanist; b. Toronto, Ont., Can., Nov. 13, 1905 (parents Am. citizens); d. Joseph Horace and Annie Bell (Sargent); A.B., Radcliffe Coll., 1927, A.M., 1928, Ph.D., 1934. Research asst. Harvard, 1928-34; tchr. Wheaton Coll., 1934-43, asst. prof. botany, chmn. botany, 1941-43; research in botany, Cambridge, Mass., Houston, 1943—. Mem. Arts and Skills, Boston chpt. A.R.C., 1944-53; mem. Mt. Auburn Hosp. Aux., Cambridge, Mass.; mem. exec. bd. Women's Alliance. Nat., Mass. accredited judge Council of Judges, Garden Club Fedn. of Mass., accredited landscape design critic; flower show cons. East Middlesex Dist. Mem. Bot. Soc. Am., Mass. Hort. Soc., Am. Forestry Assn., Mus. of Sci., Boston, Sargent-Murray-Gilman-Hough-House Assn., Audubon Soc., Cambridge League Women Voters, Cambridge Art Assn., Phi Beta Kappa (treas. Radcliffe chpt. 1963-66), Sigma Xi (sec.-treas. Harvard-Radcliffe chpt. 1970—, nat. exec. bd. 1972-73). Clubs: Appalachian Mountain, Radcliffe of Boston, 1st Parish Garden (pres.). Author and artist drawings, bot. Illustrations. Contbr. papers to sci. jours. and meetings. Address: 72 Fresh Pond Lane Cambridge MA 02138

FAULSTICH, JANET KAY, govt. ofcl.; b. Washington, Dec. 17, 1942; d. Robert Charles and Ruth Virginia (Olson) Faulstich; student, Ia. State U., 1960-61; B.A., Coll. William and Mary, 1964. Asst. Office of Congressman James Roosevelt, Washington, 1965; asst. Office of Congressman Thomas M. Rees, Washington, 1966-68, office mgr., 1969—. Mem. Chi Delta Phi, Gamma Phi Beta. Home: 700 7th St SW Washington DC 20024 Office: 1112 Longworth House Office Bldg Washington DC 20515

FAUNCE, PATRICIA SPENCER (MRS. MICHAEL I. SCHAFER), psychologist, educator; b. Mpls., Mar. 17, 1937; d. Alwin and Rose (Deering) Spencer; B.A. cum laude, U. Minn., 1959, M.A. (Office Vocational Rehab. scholar), 1961, Ph.D. (Soroptomist scholar), 1966; m. Richard W Faunce, June 16, 1962; 1 dau., Stacey Anne; m. 2d, Michael I. Schafer, Feb. 19, 1972. Freshman adviser, coll. counselor Coll. Liberal Arts, U. Minn., 1960-62, sr. adviser and instr., 1964-65, counselor, instr. Student Counseling Bur., 1962-64, 65-66, asst. prof. psychology 1967-71, asso. prof. psychology, 1971—, dir. Univ. Measurement Services Center, 1971—. Mem. com. on edn. Gov.'s Commn. on Status Women, 1965-67; mem. edn. com. Minn. Council on Status Women; adv. bd. U. Minn. YWCA; 1964-66; mem. Walker Art Center, Mpls. Inst. Arts, Center Opera Assn.; mem. U. Minn. Task Force on Equal Opportunity. Bd. dirs. Stagehands League Guthrie Theater Found., 1969-70, edn. chmn. 1969-71, 72-74, sec., program chmn., 1971-72. Soroptomist scholar, 1962-63; Named an Outstanding Young Woman of Am., 1967, Outstanding Young Woman of Minn., 1967. U. Minn. Grad. Sch. research grantee, 1968-69, 69-70; Office Edn. research grantee, 1971-72. Mem. Nat., Minn., Twin City vocation guidance assns., Am. (monograph editorial bd. 1971—), Minn. (treas. 1969-70, pres. 1971-72) coll. personnel assns., Minn., Am. psychol. assns., Mpls. Citizens League, Am., Minn. civil liberties unions, Mpls. League Women Voters, Am. (senator 1971-73), Minn. (sec. 1969-70, membership chmn. 1968-70) personnel and guidance assns., Am. Ednl. Research Assn., N.A.A.C.P., League for Legal Termination Pregnancy, Women's Equity Action League, Council on Univ. Women's Progress, Variety Heart Club, Phi Beta Kappa (sec. Minn. 1969-70, treas. 1970-71, pres. 1971-72), Mortar Bd. (pres. Twin City alumnae assn.). Clubs: University of Minn. Alumnae (treas. 1967-69, dir. 1966-69), Variety. Contbr. articles to psychology jours. Home: 1049 Floral Dr SE East Grand Rapids MI 49506 Office: U Minn Minneapolis MN 55414

FAUNCE, SARAH CUSHING, mus. curator; b. Tulsa, Okla., Aug. 19, 1929; d. George and Helen (Colwell) Faunce; B.A., Wellesley Coll., 1951; M.A. (university fellow), Wash. U., 1958; postgrad. Columbia, 1959-63. History tchr. Hartridge Sch., Plainfield, N.J., 1954-56; teaching asst. in Art History, Barnard Coll., N.Y.C., 1961-63, lectr., 1964; curator of art collection Columbia, N.Y.C., 1965-69, adv. council art history dept., 1970—; curator of paintings and sculpture Bklyn. (N.Y.) Mus., 1969—. Critic Art News Mag., 1961-64; exhbn. cons. Jewish Mus., N.Y.C., 1968-70. Mem. Coll. Art Assn., Municipal Art Soc., The Victorian Soc., Phi Beta Kappa. Democrat. Home: 28 E 92nd St New York City NY 10028 Office: 188 Eastern Parkway Brooklyn NY 11238

FAUST, ALICE LIDA (MRS. GILBERT W. FAUST), educator; b. Richwood, O., Aug. 27, 1923; d. Harry E. and Marcella (Ranney) Peet; B.S., U. Wis., 1944, M.A., 1952, Ph.D., 1961; m. Gilbert W. Faust, June 20, 1971; step-children—Katherine, Marjorie. Served with USNR, 1944-46; tchr. Santiago (Chile) Coll., 1948-50; tchr. West High Sch., Madison, Wis., 1952-55; instr. Temple U., 1955-56, U. Med., 1956-59, U. Wis., summer 1960; asst. prof. Mt. Union Coll., 1959-60; prof. speech and drama U. Wis.-Stevens Point, 1960—, acting head dept., 1965. Dir. Westley Found., Stevens Point, 1964-66. Mem. Nat. Collegiate Players, Speech Assn. Am., Am. Edn. Theater Assn., Am. Nat. Theater and Acad., U.S. Inst. for Theatre Tech., Wis. Speech Assn., Internat. Alliance Theatrical Stage Employes and Moving Picture Machine Operators U.S. and Can., Zeta Phi Eta. Home: 1117 Soo Marie Av Stevens Point WI 54481 Office: U Wis Fine Arts Center Stevens Point WI 54481

FAUST, ANNE SONIA, lawyer; b. Honolulu, Aug. 27, 1936; d. Alfred and Geneva Dora (Barnett) Faust; B.A., U. Hawaii, 1960; certificate of completion Coro Found. Internship in Pub. Affairs, 1961; J.D., Harvard, 1964. Admitted to Hawaii bar, 1964; dep. corp. counsel City and County of Honolulu, 1964-66; asst. researcher Legislative Reference Bur., Honolulu, 1966-69; asso. counsel Legal Aid Soc., Honolulu, 1969-70; dep. atty. gen. State of Hawaii, Honolulu, 1970-72; atty., exec. officer Hawaii Pub. Employment Relations Bd., Honolulu, 1972—. Ex-officio mem. Hawaii Gov's. Commn. on Status of Women, 1971-72. Mem. Am. Bar Assn. (membership chmn. Hawaii 1965), Bar Assn. Hawaii (ethics com. 1973—), Am. Civil Liberties Union (chpt. dir. 1967), Common Cause, Outdoor Circle, Phi Beta Kappa, Phi Kappa Phi. Club: Sierra (Honolulu). Home: 1251 Heulu St Apt A4 Honolulu HI 96822 Office: 550 Halekauwila St Honolulu HI 96813

FAUST, MARGARET SILER (MRS. WILLIAM LANGDON FAUST), educator; b. Tientsin, China. Feb. 22, 1926; d. Charles Arthur and Marion Louise (Pierce) Siler; B.A. with honors, Pomona Coll., 1948; M.A., Stanford, 1951, Ph.D., 1957; m. William Langdon Faust, Aug. 26, 1950; children—Katherine, Ann, Marion. Instr. Scripps Coll., Claremont, Cal., 1958-59, asst. prof., 1960-63, asso. prof., 1963-70, prof. psychology, 1970—, acting dean faculty, 1972-73. Vis. asst. prof. child study Vassar Coll., 1959-60. Mem. head start evaluation team San Bernardino County, 1965-68; coordinator Head Start Evaluation, Ontario, Cal., 1967-69; research coordinator San Bernardino County component, Western Regional Head Start Evaluation and Research Center, U. Cal. at Los Angeles, 1967-69. Grant Found. grantee, 1970-71. Mem. Am. Psychol. Assn., Soc. Research Child Devel., Nat. Assn. Edn. Young Children, Sigma Xi. Contbr. articles to profl. jours. Home: 1100 Harvard St Claremont CA 91711

FAVARO, MARY KAYE ASPERHEIM (MRS. BIAGINO PHILIP FAVARO), pediatrician; b. Edgerton, Wis., Sept. 30, 1934; d. Harold Wilbur and Genevieve Catherine (Hyland) Asperheim; B.S., U. Wis., 1956; M.S., St. Louis Coll. Pharmacy, 1965; M.D., U. Wis., 1969; m. Biagino Philip Favaro, May 31, 1969; children—Justin Peter, Gina Sue. Instr. pharmacology St. Louis U. and St. Mary's Hosp. Sch. Practical Nurses, 1959-64; staff pharmacist U. Hosps., Madison, Wis., 1964-65; intern Albany (N.Y.) Med. Center, 1969-70, resident, 1970-71; resident pediatrics U. S.C., Charleston, 1972-73; asst. prof. pediatrics Med. U. S.C., 1973—. Mem. A.M.A., Am. Med. Women's Assn. Roman Catholic. Author: Pharmacology for Practical Nurses, 1963; The Pharmacologic Basis of Patient Care, 1968. Home: 1866 Capri Dr Charleston SC 29407 Office: Medical University of SC 80 Barre St Charleston SC 29401

FAWCETT, CHARLOTT D. (MRS. CECIL D. FAWCETT), state legislator; b. Delaware County, Ia., Apr. 20, 1911; student Upper Ia. Coll.; m. Cecil C. Fawcett, Jan. 11, 1930; children—Kennedy C., Mrs. Robert Benson. Mem. Pa. Ho. of Reps., 1970—. Past co-chmn. Phila. N.E. Council Vols.; orgn. chmn., past pres. Huntingdon Valley Pub. Library; vol. numerous social agys. Republican Committee Woman, 1960-70, chmn., 1963-70, mem. adv. com.; 3d v.p. Eastern Montgomery Council Rep. Women. Bd. dirs. Montgomery County-Norristown Dist. Center Library, 1964-70. Mem. Montgomery County Citizens Council, Pa. Library Assn., Ambler Bus. and Profl. Women's Club, Nat. Council State Legislators, Order Women Legislators. Home: 2577 High Rd Huntingdon Valley PA 19006

FAWCETT, MARIE ANN FORMANEK (MRS. ROSCOE KENT FAWCETT), civic worker; b. Mpls., Mar. 6, 1914; d. Peter Paul and Mary Ann (Stepanek) Formanek; grad. high sch.; Ph.D. (hon.), Hamilton State U., 1974; m. Roscoe Kent Fawcett, Mar. 16, 1935; children—Roscoe Kent, Peter Formanek, Roger Knowlton II, Stephen Hart. Vol. chmn. Nathaniel Witherell Hosp., Greenwich, 1952-56, chmn. vols., 1956—, now bd. dirs. aux.; chmn. vols. Greenwich Hosp., 1953-54; dist. chmn. A.R.C., Community Chest, Mental Health, 1946-50; vol. mentally retarded children Milbank Sch., Greenwich, 1958-59; vol. numerous charity drives. Bd. dirs. Merry Go Round for Aged, Greenwich, Ct.; bd. dirs., recreation chmn. Merry Go Round Mews for Elderly; bd. dirs. Nathaniel Witherell Hosp. Aux., Cerebral Palsy, Greenwich Philharmonia; bd. dirs. Multiple Sclerosis Soc., 1948—, corr. sec., 1958—. Named Woman of Year, Soroptomist Club, 1967; recipient Fairfield County Community Service award; reference service Am. Bicentennial Research Inst.; award for service to Sr. Citizens; Vol. in Limelight citation for vol. work Greenwich Hosp.; citation for work at Witherell Hosp. from Conn. Dept. Health. Mem. Internat. Platform Assn., Marquis Biog. Library Soc. (adv.). Club: Woman's of Greenwich (various coms.). Address: North St and Hawkwood Lane Greenwich CT 06830

FAWCETT, MARY ISABEL SANDOE (MRS. RICHARD SELDEN FAWCETT), social worker; b. Columbus, O.; d. D. Nevin and Maud (Collins) Sandoe; B.S., Ohio State U., 1930; M.A., Columbia, 1931; postgrad. New Sch. for Social Research, 1959—; m. Richard Selden Fawcett, June 3, 1931; children—Richard N., Joyce, Gay. With Traveler's Aid Soc., N.Y.C., 1931-32; county supr. Emergency Relief Agy., Bergen County, N.J., 1933-34; social worker Children's Aid and Adoption Soc., Orange, N.J., 1935-40, Family and Children's Agy., Montclair, N.J., 1940-44; tchr. adult edn., Livingston, N.J., 1948-49; parent edn. specialist Essex County Coop. Extension Service, U.S. Dept. Agr., Rutgers U., 1950-51; group psychotherapist Essex County Penitentiary, Caldwell, N.J., 1957-61; exec. sec. Family Counseling Service, Belleville, N.J., 1954-64; research specialist Family Service Bur., Newark, 1964-73; individual practice marriage counseling and psychotherapy, 1948—; family psychotherapist Mt. Carmel guild Narcotics Rehab. Center, 1964—. Bd. dirs. Livingston N.J. Coop. Nursery Sch., 1944-46. Mem. Nat. Assn. Social Workers, Acad. Certified Social Workers, Am. Group Psychotherapy Assn. (asso.), Alpha Delta Pi, Sigma Alpha Sigma. Unitarian. Contbr. articles to profl. jours. Home: 321 Lawrence Dr Lanoka Harbor NJ 08734

FAY, JOHANNA, free-lance broadcaster; b. Port Arthur, Tex., Jan. 13, 1919; d. Edmund and Sophie Szafir; student U. Tex., 1950-52, U. Houston, 1952-54; B.S. in Speech, Lamar State Coll. Tech., 1956; m. Hugh Fay, June 5, 1943; children—Coleman Ed, Ralph. Women's dir. radio shows including Theatre of the Air, Book Review Time, This is Your Civil Defense, Fed. Civil Def. Adminstrn., Battle Creek, Mich., 1950-53; producer, writer, master ceremonies Johanna Fay Show, TV, Beaumont, Tex., 1953-55; became pub. service dir. KPAC-TV, Port Arthur, 1955; now free-lance broadcaster radio and TV. Coordinator Women's Activities of Civil Def. and Disaster Relief for Jefferson County; dir. South Jefferson County chpt. A.R.C., 1947—. Mem. Tex. Gov.'s Com. on Human Relations. Recipient numerous nat. and local awards and citations; certificate of merit for distinguished service to community, 1967. Mem. Tex. Assn. Hosp. Auxs. (3d v.p., pub. relations dir. 1953—, mem. state bd., 2d v.p., membership chmn. 1965), Tex. Fedn. Women's Clubs (drama chmn. 4th dist. 1954—), V.F.W. U.S. Aux., Port Arthur Soc. Crippled Children, Am. Women Radio and Television, Thalians (pres.-elect), Jr. Classical League (hon.). Clubs: Symphony, Writers, Port Arthur Choral (pres. 1966). Address: 3030 Lombardy Dr Port Arthur TX 77640

FAYE, MARGARET SCHAEFFER (MRS. ALEXANDER LINDSAY FAYE), govt. ofcl.; b. Tacoma, June 19, 1915; d. Ralph Chester and Hazel Lucille (Estabrook) Schaeffer; student Wellesley Coll., 1932-34; B.A., Stanford, 1936; m. Alexander Lindsay Faye, Dec. 28, 1938; children—Alexander Lindsay, Nancy (Mrs. Xavier Delierre). Dir., Vol. Service Bur., Honolulu, 1954-59, first exec. Hawaii State Commn. on Aging, 1959-63, areawide specialist, 1972-73; 1st exec. Kauai County Com. on Aging, Lihue, Kauai, Hawaii, 1965-72; profl. staff mem. U.S. Senate Spl. Com. on Aging., Washington, 1973—. Columnist, Garden Island Newspaper, Lihue, 1967-72; program interviewer For Your Information, KTOH radio, Lihue, 1968-72. Named Bus. Woman of Year, County Kauai, 1972. Mem. Gerontological Soc., Zonta Club Kauai (pres. 1972), Delta Gamma. Republican. Episcopalian. Home: 700 New Hampshire Av NW Washington DC 20037 Office: New Senate Office Bldg Washington DC 20510

FEAGANS, JAN, govt. ofcl.; b. Rome, N.Y.; B.A., U. Fla., 1958; postgrad. U. N.C., 1962-63, Howard U., 1963-65, 67-68. With Eastern Air Lines, Atlanta, 1958-60; editorial asst. So. Regional Council, Atlanta, 1961-62; mem. faculty Encampment for Citizenship, Riverdale, N.Y., 1962; group leader Operational Crossroads Africa, Tanzania, 1963; research asso. United Planning Orgn., Washington, 1965-67, research cons., 1967; dir. study-in-Africa exchange program, instr. polit. sci. Wis. State U. at Oshkosh, 1968-69; research asst. to dean of faculty Vassar Coll., Poughkeepsie, N.Y., 1969-70; asst. to the pres. State U. N.Y. Coll. at New Paltz, 1970-71; asso. dir. affirmative action program, lectr. dept. polit. sci. U. Pitts., 1971-73; dir. Affirmative Action Program Met. Dade County, Miami, Fla., 1973—. Bd. dirs. Miami Big Bros. and Big Sisters, Inc. Mem. Am. Polit. Sci. Assn., Women's Caucus Polit. Sci., Am. Soc. Pub. Adminstrn., Nat. Orgn. Women, Am. Assn. U. Women, Bus. and Profl. Women, Nat. Women's Polit. Caucus, Am. Soc. for Tng. and Devel., Dade Bus. and Profl. Women. Home: 3609 Avocado Av Miami FL 33133

FEARING, DORIS SINGER (MRS. ROBERT FEARING), educator; b. Adena, O., Sept. 30, 1916; d. Willard Clark and Etta (Masters) Singer; B.A., Waynesburg Coll., 1939; M.A., Ohio State U., 1964; m. Robert Fearing, June 14, 1958. Tchr., Adena High Sch., 1939-41, Bliss Bus. Coll., Columbus, 1942-52, South High Sch., Columbus, 1952-67; tchr. journalism, media, English, Northland High Sch., Columbus, 1967—. Tchr. summer newspaper and yearbook workshop Ohio U., Athens, 1958-73. Mem. Columbus Art Gallery, Columbus Civic Ballet. Recipient Newspaper Fund fellowship Wall Street Jour., 1962. Mem. Nat., Ohio, Columbus edn. assns., Women in Communications (v.p. 1973-74), High Sch. Press Club Central (chmn. 1965), Eta Upsilon Gamma (editor 1967—), Worthington Hist. Soc. (publicity chmn. 1965—), No. Lions Aux. (publicity chmn. 1969), Ohioana Library Assn., Delta Kappa Gamma (publicity chmn. 1970—). Home: 5895 Sinclair Rd Columbus OH 43229 Office: 1919 Northcliff Dr Columbus OH 43229

FEARS, MARY ELIZABETH, ins. pub. relations exec.; b. Walla Walla, Wash., Aug. 5, 1945; d. James Murray and Rubye Elizabeth (McGraw) Fears; B.A. in English, Cal. State U., 1967. Edn. dir. Cal. br. Humane Soc. U.S., Sacramento, 1967-68; pub. relations asst. Unigard Ins., Seattle, 1968-73, pub. relations rep., 1973—. Women's bd. dirs. Evergreen Safety Council, 1971—. Solicitor, United Arts Council Puget Sound, 1970-71. Mem. Wash. Assn. Women Hwy. Safety Leaders (chmn. county fairs 1970-71, dir. dist. V 1971-73, sec. 1970-71, 2nd v.p. 1971-73, pres. 1973-75), Pub. Relations Soc. Am., Nat. Assn. Ins. Women (chmn. Wash. orgn. 1972-73, legislation chmn. Region IX 1974-75), Inst. Women's Assn. Seattle (chmn. pub. relations 1969-71, trustee 1970-71, co-chmn. region IX conf. Seattle 1971, pub. chmn. 1971-72, treas. 1973-74), Wash. Ins. Council (mem. pub. safety com. 1972—, mem. pub. relations tech. com. 1972—), Western Ins. Information Service. Home: 2020 Waverly Place N Seattle WA 98109 Office: 1215 Fourth Av Seattle WA 98161

FEAVEL, YVONNE DOROTHY HENDRICKSON (MRS. JOHN SPENCER FEAVEL), social worker; b. River Falls, Wis., Sept. 15, 1939; d. Solon H. and Lillian (Amundson) Hendrickson; B.S., Wis. State U., 1961; M.S.W., U. Wis., 1964; m. John Spencer Feavel, June 28, 1969; 1 dau., Jennifer Joan. Probation and parole agt. Wis. Dept. Pub. Welfare Div. Corrections, Eau Claire, 1961-62, Madison, 1962-63, social worker Wis. Correctional Instn., Fox Lake, 1963-64; psychiat. social worker Barron-Polk Guidance Clinic, Turtle Lake, Wis., 1964-65, Winnebago County Guidance Center, Neenah, Wis., 1965-66; sch. social worker Oshkosh (Wis.) Area Pub. Schs., 1966—. Mem. Family Life Edn. Study Com., 1968-69; sec. Winnebago County Guidance Center Corp. Bd., 1966-68. Bd. dirs. Winnebago County Mental Health Assn., 1971—, pres., 1973—; bd. dirs. Lost River Sch., 1971—; exec. bd. dirs. Wis. Assn. Mental Health, 1973—. Mem. Nat. Assn. Social Workers, Acad. Certified Social Workers, Nat. Council for Exceptional Children (exec. bd. Winnebagoland chpt. 1968-69), N.E.A., Northeastern, Wis., Oshkosh edn. assns., Wis. (liaison com. chmn. 1968-69), Winnebago County social workers assns. Home: 2423 Palisades Dr Appleton WI 54911 Office: 215 S Eagle St Oshkosh WI 54901

FEBLAND, HARRIET, artist; b. N.Y.C.; B.A., N.Y. U.; student New Sch. Social Research, Art Student's League, Pratt Inst., Eng., France, 1946-57. Exhibited one-man shows Silvermine Guild, Katonah Gallery, Vincent Price Gallery, Rutgers U., N.Y. U., Spectrum Gallery, Seton Hall U., Emory U., Hudson River Mus., Riverside Mus., numerous others; exhibited group shows Carnegie Inst., Riverside Mus., Bklyn. Mus., Mus. Modern Art, N.Y. U.-Loeb Center, Pace Coll., Nat. Acad., Hudson River Mus., Newark State Coll., N.y. State U. at Potsdam-Brainerd Hall Art Gallery, Katonah Gallery, N.Y. Cultural Center, Silvermine Guild Art Gallery, Mus. Modern Art, Paris, France, Drian Gallery, London, Eng., Alwin Gallery, London, many others; represented in permanent collections Emily Lowe Gallery U. Miami, Tweed Gallery U. Minn., Cin. Art

Mus., Hempstead Bank, Sealy Co., Hubert Wilkins Mus., New Sch. Social Research Art Center, others; lectr. modern art appreciation N.Y. U., 1961-62; faculty Westchester Art Workshop, 1967-72; dir., founder Advanced Painters Workshop, New Rochelle, 1962-72. Recipient 1st prize Hudson River Mus., 1969; 1st award Yonkers (N.Y.) Art Assn., 1969; Bea Camhi Meml. award for sculpture, 1972; others. Mem. Artists Equity Assn. (v.p., program dir. N.Y., chmn. Woman's Com. 1973—), League Present Day Artists (dir.), Sculptors League, Coll. Art Assn., Nat. Assn. Women Artists (award for sculpture 1972), Silvermine Guild Artists, Nat. Assn. Women Artists. Home and studio: Premium Point New Rochelle NY 10801

FEDELLE, ESTELLE, artist; b. Chgo.; d. John and Julia (Porebski) Szymanski; student Am. Acad., 1944-47, Northwestern U., 1949-51, Inst. Design, Art Inst. Chgo.; also pvt. study. Exhibited in 47 one-man shows including Wheaton (Ill.) Pub. Library, Liberyville (Ill.) Art League; exhibited in group shows Visual Arts Center, Chgo., Chgo. Pub. Library, Ill. State Fair, Baron Galleries of Chgo. and Las Vegas, Grand Central Gallery, N.Y.C., numerous others; painted portraits; pvt. art tchr., 1950—; dir. Fedelle Sch. Art, Chgo. Recipient 59 awards for painting including Margaret R. Dingle award, 1953; certificate of Merit Distinguished Service in Art, 1967. Mem. Royal Soc. Art London (hon.), Elmhurst Artists Guild, Artists Guild Chgo., Austin-Oak Park-River Forest Art League, Polish Arts Clubs, All-Ill. Soc. Artists, Nat. League Am. Pen Women, Am. Artists Profl. League, Park Ridge, North Shore, Municipal Regent art leagues, Assos. in Art, Internat. Platform Assn., Little Theater Elmwood Park. Author: How To Begin Painting for Fun, 1964; contbg. author: Fun Book on Painting, How to Paint from your Color Slides. Home: 5132 Fletcher St Chicago IL 60641 Office: 5342 W Diversey Av Chicago IL 60639

FEDER, CAROL ZIZMOR (MRS. STUART FEDER), psychologist; b. N.Y.C., July 15, 1937; d. Jesse and Alice (Trubin) Zismor; B.A., U. Rochester, 1959; Ph.D., Adelphi U., 1966; m. Stuart Feder, Apr. 16, 1961; children—Susanna, Adam. Clin. psychology intern Manhattan VA Hosp., N.Y.C., 1962-63; psychologist, N.Y.C., 1969—; sr. psychologist Children's Service Inst. for Medicine, N.Y. U. Med. Center, N.Y.C., 1973—. Cons. Lorge Sch., N.Y.C., 1969—. Postdoctoral fellow, 1971-73. Mem. Am., N.Y. State psychol. assns. Home: 103 E 86th St New York City NY 10028 Office: 400 E 34th St New York City NY

FEDER, IRMA ROSE ROBBINS (MRS. RICHARD YALE FEDER), lawyer; b. Balt., Sept. 28, 1932; d. Bernard S. and Lee (Fraidin) Robbins; B.A. magna cum laude, Hunter Coll., 1953; LL.B., Yale, 1956; m. Richard Yale Feder, Sept. 8, 1957; children—Scott Jay, Brett Marshall, Marsha Robbins. Student research asst. So. dist. N.Y. U.S. Attys. Office, 1955; admitted to N.Y. bar, 1956, Fla. bar, 1960, U.S. Supreme Ct. bar, 1966; staff counsel N.A.A.C.P. Legal Def. and Edn. Fund, N.Y.C., 1956-59; practiced in Miami, Fla., 1959—; asso. firm Hastings, et. al., 1959—. Vis. instr. Miami Dade Jr. Coll., spring 1965. Mem. Am. Civil Liberties Union (cooperating atty. Miami, mem. legal panel 1961—, legal research asst. 1963-64, dir. 1966—, chmn. legal panel 1972). Book critic Miami Rev., 1969-70. Home: 110 N Hibiscus Dr Miami Beach FL 33139 Office: Biscayne Bldg Miami FL 33130

FEDERICO, ROSEMARY BASILE (MRS. VINCENT ARMOND FEDERICO), trophy mfg. co. exec., educator; b. Altoona, Pa., Feb. 22, 1947; d. Leo Carmelo and Catherine (Grillo) Basile; student Pa. State U., 1964-67; B.S., St. Francis Coll., 1970; m. Vincent Armond Federico, July 3, 1971. With Champion Trophy Mfg. Co., Inc., Altoona, Pa., 1970—, v.p., 1970—; tchr. history Maxson Middle Sch., Plainfield, N.J., 1970—. Mem. Nat., N.J., Plainfield (bldg. faculty rep. 1972—) edn. assns., Early Am. Soc., Gamma Sigma Sigma. Home: 748 Carlton Av Plainfield NJ 07060 Office: 1117 9th Av Altoona PA 16602

FEDEROWICZ, SISTER ROSE ANN, educator; b. Orange, Conn., Sept. 5, 1908; d. Ignatius and Susan (Dunaj) Federowicz; B.S., Cath. U. Am., 1940, M.S., 1950, Ph.D., 1962. Tchr., prin. parochial schs., Mass., Pa., N.Y., 1926-54; prof. biology, dept. chmn. Holy Family Coll., Phila., 1954—. Trustee Nazareth Hosp., Phila. Mem. Sigma Xi, Beta Beta Beta. Home: Grant and Frankford Av Philadelphia PA 19114

FEDORKO, MARTHA EVELYN, physician; b. N.Y.C., Sept. 19, 1935; d. Michael and Frances (Mickiewicz) Fedorko; student Coll. Mt. St. Vincent, 1952-55; M.D., State U. N.Y. at Bklyn., 1959. Intern Kings County Hosp., N.Y.C., 1959-60, resident, 1960-62; clin. fellow Pratt Diagnostic Clinic, Boston, 1962-63; fellow Rockefeller U., N.Y.C., 1963-66, asst. prof. 1966-72, asso. prof., 1972—; asso. physician Rockefeller U. Hosp., N.Y.C., 1966-72, physician, 1972—; Leukemia Soc. scholar, 1970—. Mem. Am. Soc. Cell Biology, Am. Soc. Hematology, Sigma Xi. Home: 510 E 6th St New York City NY 10009 Office: Rockefeller University 66th St and York Av New York City NY 10021

FEE, JULIE ANNA CIRILLO (MRS. EDWARD J. FEE, JR.), govt. ofcl.; b. Harrisburg, Pa., Dec. 11, 1942; d. Joseph Anthony and Anna Irene (Calise) Cirillo; B.A., Trinity Coll., 1964; M.S. (Dept. Transp. fellow), Cath. U. Am., 1969; m. Edward J. Fee, Jr., Oct. 3, 1970. Mem. staff, interstate system accident research project Office of Research, Bur. Pub. Roads, Washington, 1964-66; study leader, interstate system accident research Office of Research, Fed. Hwy. Adminstrn., Washington, 1966-68, project mgr., pedestrian safety research project, 1969—, project mgr., rational determination of research and devel. priority targets, 1973—. Chmn. operational effects of geometrics com. Transp. Research Bd., 1973—. Mem. Operations Research Soc. Am. (asso.), Inst. Traffic Engrs. (asso.). Home: 4602 Ordinary Ct Annandale VA 22003 Office: HRS-41 Federal Highway Administration Washington DC 20590

FEELEY, MARCIA CAROL, metal products co. exec., real estate broker; b. Waltham, Mass., Nov. 28, 1946; d. James Joseph and Elvira Margaret (DiVito) Feeley; A.A. with honors, Aquinas Jr. Coll., 1966. Legal sec. Mintz, Levin, Cohn and Glovsky, Boston, 1966, Feeley's Baked Enameling Co., Inc., Quincy, Mass., 1966—. Real estate broker, Quincy, Mass., 1974—. Sec., treas. USCG Aux. Flotilla, Boston, 1967-71; mem. Operation Kindness, Quincy City Hosp., 1961. Mem. Young Democratic Club of Quincy, 1967. Mem. Am. Fedn. Astrologers, New Eng. Astrological Soc. Clubs: Irish Music of Dorchester, Ski, United States Sports of Boston. Home: 1170 Furnace Brook Pkwy Quincy MA 02169 Office: 232-238 Water St Quincy MA 02169

FEEZOR, BETTY DANIELS (MRS. TURNER FEEZOR), home economist, TV commentator; b. Texarkana, Tex., 1925; d. John Buford and Florence (Owen) Daniels; student Tex. State Coll. for Women, 1942-43; B.S., U. Tenn., 1946; m. Turner Feezor; children—Robert Milton, John Daniels, Betty Cole. Home demonstration agt., Tenn. and N.C., 1946-52; home economist sta. WBTV, Charlotte, N.C., 1953—. Recipient First Lady in Food award, 1959; Community Achievement award Charlotte Jr. Women's Club, 1957. Mem. Am. Women in Radio and TV (chpt. pres. 1965-67), Home Econs. Assn., Home Economists in Bus. Author: Betty Feezor's Best; Betty Feezor's Carolina Recipes. Home: 6217 Glenridge Rd Charlotte NC 28211 Office: 1 Julian Price Pl Charlotte NC 28208*

FEHL, PATRICIA KATHERINE, educator; b. Cin., May 29, 1927; d. Norman and Gertrude (Morris) Fehl; A.B. cum laude, DePauw U., 1949; M.S., Ind. U., 1955, Ed.D., 1966. Tchr., Crawfordsville (Ind.) Schs., 1950-52; critic tchr. lab. sch., coll. methods instr. Ind. U., Bloomington, 1952-62; asso. prof. health, phys. edn. and recreation U. Cin., 1962-73, prof., chairperson dept. gen. program Sch. Phys. Edn. W.Va. U., Morgantown, 1973—. Bus. mgr. Girl Scouts U.S.A. camps, summers 1952-55. Mem. profl. and lay edn. com. Heart Assn. of S.W. Ohio, 1967—. Kennedy Found. grantee for workshop in fitness and recreation for mentally retarded, 1966. Fellow Am. Sch. Health Assn.; mem. Am. (v.p. recreation Midwest Dist. 1970, v.p. recreation div. 1973), Ohio (v.p., chmn. div. girls and womens sports 1970-72, meritorious award 1973), assns. for health, phys. edn. and recreation, Ohio Parks and Recreation Assn. (pres. 1972—, Meritorious award 1974), Midwest Assn. for Phys. Edn. for Coll. Women (past chmn. health com., past mem. governing bd.), Am. Pub. Health Assn., Nat. Recreation and Park Assn. (nat. assembly), Am. Camping Assn., Pi Lambda Theta, Delta Kappa Gamma. Co-author: Ohio Secondary Girls Physical Education Curriculum Guide. Contbr. articles to jours. Home: 1336 Cherry Lane Morgantown WV 26505

FEHR, BARBARA JEAN, advt., pub. relations exec.; b. Green Bay, Wis., Feb. 2, 1947; d. Donald B. and Edna May (Butterfield) Rentmeester; B.A., U. Wis., 1969; postgrad. U. Mich., 1972, N.Y. U., 1973. Copywriter/producer WFRV-TV, Green Bay, Wis., 1969-70; pub. relations mgr. Super Valu Stores, Inc., 1970-73; dir. communications Fed. Land Bank, St. Paul, 1973—. Adviser journalism dept. Augsburg Coll., 1972; cons. Nash Finch Co., 1973—; publicity chmn. for upper Midwest, Nat. Agr. Day, Nat. Agri-Marketing Assn., 1974. Recipient 2d Place Internal Communications award Internat. Assn. Bus. Communicators, 1973. Mem. Women in Communications (pres. 1972—), Internat. Assn. Bus. Communicators, Minn. Intermedia Council, Ad Club, Mpls. C. of C. Republican. Author: Yankee Denim Dandies, 1974. Home: 5521 Park Av Minneapolis MN 55417 Office: 357 Jackson St St Paul MN 55101

FEHRENBACH, ALICE O'SULLIVAN, psychologist; b. Denver, Nov. 14, 1910; d. John Alexander and Gertrude (Gaffney) McTammany; A.B., Barnard Coll., 1931; M.A., Denver, 1944, Ph.D., 1955; m. Frank O'Sullivan, July 6, 1940 (dec. Feb. 1941); m. 2d, Carl E. Fehrenbach, June 8, 1953 (dec. 1961). Tchr., Denver Pub. Schs., 1935-47, psychologist, 1948-68; pvt. practice psychology, Denver, 1948—; prof. psychology Regis Coll., 1968—, faculty lectr., 1972, acting dir. counseling service, 1971-73, 74—; vis. lectr. U. Nev.; guest appearances radio, TV series, Denver. Mem. Colo. Bd. Psycholgist Examiners. Bd. dirs. Camp Fire Girls, 1949-55. Diplomate in sch. psychology Am. Bd. Profl. Psychologists. Fellow Am. Psychol. Assn.; mem. Colo. (bd., pres. 1972; distinguished service award 1969), Rocky Mountain (pub. relations officer) psych. assns., English-Speaking Union, Assn. for Specialized Services (pres. 1953-54), Denver Mental Health Assn. (mem. profl. adv. bd.), Columbia U. Women's Club Colo. (founder 1948, pres. 1948-50), Kappa Delta Pi, Delta Kappa Gamma. Author personality test. Contbr. articles to profl. jours. Home: 3232 S Josephine St Denver CO 80210 Office: Regis Coll W 50th at Lowell Sts Denver CO 80221

FEIERABEND, ROSALIND ASTRID LORWIN (MRS. IVO KAREL FEIERABEND), psychologist; b. N.Y.C.; d. Lewis L. and Rose (Strunsky) Lorwin; B.A., Swarthmore Coll., 1947; M.A., U. Cal. at Berkeley, 1952; Ph.D., Yale, 1955; m. Ivo Karel Feierabend, Mar. 31, 1953; children—Susan Beatrice, Thomas Karel, Stephen James. Research asst. dept. psychology Yale, 1952-55, research asso., 1956-58; prin. investigator Coop. Research Project, psychology dept. Washington U., St. Louis, 1959; asst. prof. psychology Cal. Western U., 1960-63; faculty psychology San Diego State U., 1963—, prof., 1970—. Vis. research psychologist Washington U., St. Louis, 1966-67. Fellow Am. Psychol. Assn., A.A.A.S. (co-recipient Socio-Psychol. prize 1966); mem. N.Y. Acad. Scis., Am., San Diego County Western psychol. assns., Am. Acad. Polit. and Social Sci., Soc. Exptl. Social Psychology, Mortar Bd., Phi Beta Kappa, Sigma Xi. Co-editor: Anger, Violence and Politics, 1972. Contbr. articles to profl. jours. Office: Psychology Dept San Diego State U San Diego CA 92115

FEIN, LEAH GOLD (MRS. ALFRED G. FEIN), psychologist; b. Minsk, Russia; d. Jacob Lyon and Sarah Freda (Meltzer) Gold; B.S., Albertus Magnus Coll., 1939; M.A., Yale, 1942; Ph.D. (Marion Talbot fellow), 1944; m. Alfred Gustave Fein, June 10, 1944; 1 son, Ira Hirsh. Health educator New Haven Schs., 1930-43; instr. psychology Carleton Coll., 1944-45; research asso. Conn. Interracial Commn., 1946; prof. U. Bridgeport, 1946-64; individual practice 1948—, specializing in clin., child consultation, 1948—. Clin. cons. Commn. on Alcoholism Clinic, 1952-60; research asso. Soc. for Investigation Human Ecology; therapist Norwalk Psychiat. Clinic, 1952-64; cons. Child Edn. Found., 1953-56; dir. research Sch. Nursing Norwalk Hosp., 1961-64; dir. clin. research cerebral palsy and mental retardation, Waterbury, Conn., 1964-65; asso. prof. Quinnipiac Coll., Hamden, Conn., 1965-66; cons., instr., med. staff N.Y. Hosp.-Cornell Med. Center, White Plains, 1966-67; dir. psychology Psychiat. Treatment Center, N.Y., 1967-68; research asso. Roosevelt Hosp. Child Psychiatry, 1968-69; supr., cons. sch. psychologist Bur. Child Guidance N.Y.C. Board Edn., 1968-70; faculty Greenwich Inst. Psychoanalytic Studies, 1971—; Cons. Inst. Relational Mgmt. Mem. program Com. Internat. Congress Social Psychiatry, 1974. Diplomate clin. psychology Am. Bd. Profl. Psychology. Fellow Soc. Projective Techniques, Am. Acad. Psychotherapists, Internat. Council Psychologists (v.p. 1961-62, pres. 1973-75), Am. Orthopsychiat. Assn., N.Y. Acad. Sci.; mem. Nat. Assn. Gifted (v.p. 1961-62), Internat. Council Women Psychologists (chmn. profl. activities among psychologists), Psychologists in Private Practice (treas. 1972-75), Am. (sec. div. psychotherapy), Conn. psychol. assns., Am. Assn. Group Psychotherapy and Psychodrama (council 1973-75), World Fedn. Mental Health, Nat. Council Jewish Women, Hadassah. Club: Yale (N.Y.C.). Author: The Three Dimensional Personality Test—Reliability, Validity and Clinical Implications, 1960; The Changing School Scene: Challenge to Psychology, 1974. Contbr. to Jour. Clin. Psychology, other profl. jours. Address: 1050 Park Av New York City NY 10028

FEIN, TISHA ANN, pub. relations exec.; b. Los Angeles, Mar. 1, 1946; d. Irving Ashley and Florence (Kohn) Fein; student U. Wis., 1963-65, U. Cal. at Los Angeles, 1966. Casting dir. D'Arcy Advt., N.Y.C., 1966-68; talent agt. Paul Wagner Agy., N.Y.C., 1968-69; talent coordinator Tonight Show, N.Y.C., 1969; publicity dir. Braverman Mirisch, Inc., Los Angeles, 1970—. Asso. producer Marciarose Show, KYW-TV, Phila., 1973. Home: 415 S Willaman Dr Los Angeles CA 90048 Office: 9255 Sunset St Suite 308 Los Angeles CA 90069

FEINBERG, HILDA WARSHAW, educator, librarian; b. Atlanta, Aug. 4, 1915; d. Harry and Emily (Domb) Warshaw; M.Chemistry summa cum laude, U. Ga., 1938; M.L.S. with honors, Columbia, 1963, D.L.S. with honors, 1971; m. Joseph Feinberg, July 1, 1940; children—Stephen, David. Chemist, N.Y. Quinine, 1940; mgr. library services Revlon Research Center, N.Y.C., 1955—. Adj. asst. prof. Queens Coll., Pratt Inst., N.Y.C., 1971—. Mem. Am. Chem. Soc., Spl. Libraries Assn., Am. Soc. Indexers, Med. Library Assn., Am. Soc. Information Sci., Soc. Cosmetic Chemists (head library com. 1968), Cosmetic, Toiletry and Fragrance Assn. (information sci. com.), Phi Beta Kappa, Beta Pi Mu. Author: Book Catalogs, 1971; Cosmetic Perfumery Thesaurus, 1972; Title Derivative Indexing, 1973. Home: 1685 Ocean Av Brooklyn NY 11230 Office: 945 Zerega Av Bronx NY 10473

FEINBERG, LILIAN OKNER (MRS. LEONARD FEINBERG), educator; b. Chgo., Jan. 28, 1917; d. Bernard Samuel and Rose (Tryonsky) Okner; A.B. with honors in English, U. Ill., 1940; M.S., Ia. State U., 1967; m. Leonard Feinberg, Nov. 26, 1938; children—Thomas O. (dec.), Ellen (Mrs. John David Reynolds). Copywriter, Goldblatt Bros., Chgo., 1936-38; resident investigator Market surveys Hearst, J. Walter Thompson, Urbana, Ill., 1939-40; reporter Champaign-Urbana (Ill.) Courier, 1941-43, 44; publicity dir., copywriter R.H. White's, Boston, 1943; asst. in English, U. Ill., Urbana, 1944-46; dir. drama City of Ames (Ia.), 1950-57; instr. English, Ia. State U., Ames, 1952-67, asst. prof., 1967—. Cons. bus. communications, 1965—; ednl. cons. Sta. WOI-TV. Founder community theater, Champaign, Ill., 1941, Actors, Ames, 1956, Children's Theater, Ames, 1949. Bd. dirs. Actors, Ames, 1956-59. Recipient Presdl. citation for drama prodns. for U.S.O., Champaign, 1942, citation for recreation and child welfare contbns. Gov. of Ia., 1956; fellow Wilton Park, Eng., 1972. Mem. Am. Bus. Communication Assn. (dir. 1972—), Women in Communications (treas. 1969-70), League Women Voters, Ia. Council Tchrs. English, Phi Kappa Phi, Phi Sigma Sigma. Unitarian. Author: Unified Exercises, 1961; also articles. Home: 3433 Woodland St Ames IA 50010

FEINBERG, MILDRED, artist, ret. advt. exec.; b. N.Y.C.; d. Joseph and Bessie (Atkin) Feinberg; student Parson's Sch. Design, 1917; grad. Pratt Inst. Fine Arts, 1920; pupil George E. Brown, Joseph Newman, Alex Rodein, Umberto Romano, others; m. Samuel Blumgarten, Dec. 18, 1938 (div. 1941). Partner with twin sister of Twins Advt. Art Service, N.Y.C., 1923-74; illus. children's books, also fashions, 1923—; exhbns. with sister Town House Gallery, Woodstock, N.Y., 1952, Charles Barzansky Galleries, N.Y.C., 1957; group exhbns. Ward Eggleston Galleries, 1953-55, anns. Nat. Assn. Women Artists, 1957—, Tokyo Municipal Art Mus., 1960, Riverside Mus., N.Y.C., 1960, Royal Acad. Galleries, Edinburgh, Scotland, 1963, Royal Soc., Birmingham, Eng., 1964, Nat. Acad. Design ann., 1963, Allied Artists anns., 1961-63; paintings exhibited Lever House, N.Y.C., 1965-68, 72, Palazzo Vecchio, Florence, Italy, 1972, Salvator Rosa Pub. Garden, Naples, Italy, 1972; represented in permanent collections Rose Art Mus., Brandeis U., Norfolk (Va.) Mus. Arts and Scis. Recipient medal honor for painting Nat. Arts Club, 1968. Mem. Nat. Assn. Women Artists (Lillian Cotton Meml. prize 1965), Artists Equity Assn. N.Y., Woodstock Artists Assn. Address: 239 E 79th St New York City NY 10021

FEINGOLD, BARBARA ANN LESSER (MRS. STANLEY FEINGOLD), sch. adminstr.; b. N.Y.C., Nov. 26, 1939; d. Henry and Dorothy (Straus) Lesser; B.A., Queens Coll., 1960; M.A., N.Y. U., 1963, postgrad., 1964—; m. Stanley Feingold, Apr. 15, 1962; children—Cari, Jon. Tchr. retarded children Pub. Sch. 87, Middle Village, N.Y., 1962-65; instr. Mercer Community Coll., Trenton, N.J., 1968-69, Hofstra U., Hempstead, N.Y., 1969; adminstrv. dir., sch. psychologist Little Village Sch., Merrick, N.Y., 1969—. Recipient fed. funds fellowships for tng. leadership personnel N.Y. State, N.Y. U., 1963-65. Mem. Am. Assn. Mental Deficiency, N.Y. Assn. for Emotionally Disturbed Children, Council Exceptional Children, Orton Soc., N.Y. Assn. Brain Injured Children, Nassau County Psychol. Assn. Home: 3497 Howard BLvd Baldwin NY 11510 Office: 2101 William Pl Merrick NY 11566

FEINN, BARBARA ANN, economist; b. Waterbury, Conn., Feb. 16, 1925; d. David Harris and Dora (Brandvein) Feinn; A.B. magna cum laude, Smith Coll., 1946; M.A. (Univ. scholar), Yale, 1947, Ph.D. (Univ. fellow), 1952; certificate Oxford (Eng.) U., 1949. Research economist 1st Nat. City Bank, N.Y.C., 1953-54; asso. economist Office Messrs. Rockefeller, N.Y.C., 1954-61; asst. to dir. N.Y. State Office for Regional Devel., N.Y.C., 1961-62; cons. economist Nelson A. Rockefeller, N.Y.C., 1963-64, Chase Manhattan Bank, 1964-68; sr. council economist N.Y. State Council Econ. Advisers, N.Y.C., 1969-72; chief economist office S.C. Gov., adj. prof. bus. adminstrn. U. S.C., Columbia, 1972—. Dir. Smith Coll. Alumnae Fund Program, N.Y.C., 1965-66, mem. spl. gifts com., 1971. Mem. Am. Econ. Assn., Am. Finance Assn., Am. Statis. Assn., Phi Beta Kappa. Club: Yale (N.Y.C.). Contbr. articles to profl. jours. Home: 200 E 66th St New York City NY 10021 also Box 1199 Quail Run Columbia SC 29206 Office: Gov's Office Columbia SC 29201

FEINSTEIN, DIANNE GOLDMAN (MRS. BERTRAM FEINSTEIN), city ofcl.; b. San Francisco, June 22, 1933; d. Leon and Betty (Rosenburg) Goldman; B.A. in History and Polit. Sci., Stanford, 1955; intern pub. affairs Coro Found., 1955-56; m. Bertram Feinstein, Nov. 11, 1962; 1 dau. from previous marriage, Katherine Anne Berman. Asst., Cal. Indsl. Welfare Commn., 1956-57; mem. Cal. Women's Bd. Terms and Parole, 1962-66, vice chmn., 4 years. Chmn., San Francisco Adv. Com. For Adult Detention, 1968-70; pres. San Francisco City and County Bd. Suprs., 1970-72, 74-76, mem. bd., 1972—. Del. to Cal. Gen. Assembly; mem. Bay Conservation and Devel. Commn., Bay Area Council. Chmn. bd. regents Lone Mountain Coll. Mem. Assn. Bay Area Govts. (exec. com. 1970—). Home: 2030 Lyon St San Francisco CA 94115

FEIR, DOROTHY JEAN, educator; b. St. Louis, Jan. 29, 1929; d. Alex and Lillian (Smith) Feir; B.S., U. Mich., 1950; M.S., U. Wyo., 1956; Ph.D., U. Wis., 1960. Instr. biology U. Buffalo, 1960-61; asst. prof. biology St. Louis U., 1961-64, asso. prof., 1964-67, prof., 1967—. Mem. biology com. Argonne Univs. Assn., 1972—. Contbr. articles to profl. jours. Home: #1 Ballas Cts St Louis MO 63131

FEJES, CLAIRE SPECHT (MRS. JOSEPH FEJES), artist; b. N.Y.C., Dec. 14, 1920; d. Simon and Dvorah (Schneider) Specht; student U. Alaska, 1950—; m. Joseph Fejes, Dec. 21, 1942; children—Mark, Yolande. Tchr. art Fairbanks (Alaska) Pub. Sch., 1949-50; tchr. art, lectr. U. Alaska; mgr., dir. Alaska House, Fairbanks, 1966—; one-woman shows at Frye Art Mus., Seattle, Norfolk (Va.) Mus., Charles Bowers Mus., Santa Ana, Cal., Winblad Gallery, San Francisco, Roko Gallery, N.Y.C., Anchorage Mus. Fine Art, Alaska State Mus., U. Alaska, Alaska House, Larcada Gallery, N.Y.C.; exhibited in group shows at Seattle Art Mus., St. Paul U.S.A. Drawing Show; represented in permanent collections Frye Art Mus., Westpoint Mus., Roko Gallery, U. Alaska, Anchorage Mus. Fine Art, Alaska State Mus., Alaska Gov.'s Mansion, pvt. collections. Lectr. Sheldon Jackson Coll., 1970. State pres. Alaska Crippled Children, 1961. Club: Alaska Press. Author: People of the Noatak, 1966; Enuk, My Son, 1969; illustrator Eskimo Storyteller (Ed Hall). Address: 1003 Cushman St Fairbanks AK 99107

FELD, AUGUSTA GOLDBERG (MRS. BERNARD LESTER FELD), artist; b. Phila., Apr. 18, 1919; d. Nathan and Jennie (Stein) Goldberg; student Fleisher Art Meml. and Music Settlement Sch., 1933-36; B.A., Phila. Coll. Art, 1954; postgrad. Tyler Sch. Fine Arts, 1953-54, Temple U., 1958; M.A., Phila. Acad. Fine Arts, 1962; m. Bernard Lester Feld, Sept. 9, 1940; children—Daniel, Harry, Roy. Tchr. art Phila. Sch. Dist., 1954-66, Art Center, Wallingford, Pa., 1963-64, Haverford (Pa.) High Sch., 1963-65, "Y" Wives, Broomall, Pa., 1965-70; dir. art Hillview-Trout Nursery Sch., Broomall, 1958-68; represented in permanent collections Del. Community Center, Springfield, Pa., Melita Dance Studio, Phila. Recipient Van Sciver award Woodmere Art Gallery, 1962, First prize in Oils Atlantic City C. of C., 1968, First prize print exhbn. Cheltenham Art Center, 1971. Mem. Artist Equity Assn., Pa. Acad. Fine Arts, Phila. Art Alliance, Community Art Center Wallingford, Woodmere Art Gallery, Peale Club Pa., Acad. Fine Arts. Contbr. articles to profl. jours. Home: 2207 Gilham Rd Broomall PA 19008

FELDMAN, DONNA LYNNE, educator; b. Chgo.; d. Nathan and June Marcella (Somers) Feldman; B.S., So. Ill. U., 1966; M.S., Murray State U., 1968. Tchr. English, English Lang. Service, Carbondale, Ill., 1965-66; tchr. communication and oral interpretation Chgo. Com. on Urban Opportunity, 1967, Office of Econ. Opportunity in Ky., Murray, 1968, Com. of Econ. Opportunity in Pa., Wilkes-Barre, 1969; asst. prof. speech Luzerne County Community Coll., Nanticoke, Pa., 1968—, dir. forensics, 1968—. Adviser to delegations Harvard Nat. Model UN, Nat. Model UN, N.Y.C., 1972—. Mem. Eastern Communication Assn., N.E.A., Eastern, Collegiate forensic assns., Pa. Speech Assn., Pa. Ednl. Assn., So. Ill. U., Murray State alumni assns. Mem. Hadassah. Club: Wyo. Valley Ski (Wilkes-Barre). Home: 66 Ashley St Ashley PA 18706

FELDMAN, HELEN STRATTON (MRS. AL FELDMAN), educator; b. Madisonville, Tenn.; d. Walter L. and Ethel (Mason) Stratton; B.S., U. Chattanooga; M.S., U. Tenn., Ed.D., 1958; m. Al Feldman, Jan. 10, 1968. Primary tchr. Monroe County, Tenn.; chemist Oak Ridge Nat. Lab., 1948-53; elementary prin., Knox County, Tenn., 1958-62; ednl. adminstr., Cherry Creek, Colo., 1962—. Vis. prof. Maryville Coll., Tenn. Dept. Edn. and Psychology, U. Tenn. Dept. Ednl. Adminstrn. and Supervision. Mem. Am. Assn. U. Women, N.E.A., Am. Assn. Sch. Adminstrs., Adult Edn. Council Met. Denver, Alpha Delta Kappa, Pi Lambda Theta. Presbyn. Home: 1894 S Oakland St Aurora CO 80010 Office: 4700 S Yosemite Englewood CO 80110

FELDMAN, HILDA (MRS. NEVILLE S. DICKINSON), artist, ret. educator; b. Newark, Nov. 22, 1899; d. Gay L. and Emma B. (Ledig) Feldman; student Newark Sch. Fine and Indsl. Art, 1916-20; m. Neville S. Dickinson, Apr. 30, 1921. Exhibited in numerous one man and group shows in N.Y. and N.J.; work shown throughout U.S., Can., Netherlands, Belgium, Switzerland, Japan; represented in permanent collections at Seton Hall U., South Orange, N.J., Reading Mus. and Art Gallery, Ford Motor Co., Detroit, Marine Hist. Assn., Mystic (Conn.) Seaport; instr. Millburn Adult Sch., 1946-63, Newark Sch. Fine and Indsl. Art, 1923-72. Mem. Am., N.J. watercolor socs., Nat. Assn. Women Artists (Winsor Newton prize 1955, B.W. Hamm prize 1968), Art Gallery South Orange and Maplewood. Home: 507 Richmond Av Maplewood NJ 07040

FELDMAN, MARIANNE LEHMANN (MRS. PHILIP B. FELDMAN), librarian; b. Magdeburg, Germany, Oct. 30, 1927; d. Max and Hilde (Blumenthal) Lehmann; came to U.S., 1937, naturalized, 1948; student Reed Coll., 1945-48; B.A., U. Wash., 1949; postgrad. Lewis and Clark Coll., 1950, Portland State U., 1951, 53, 63, 64; M.L.S., U. Portland, 1967; m. Philip B. Feldman, July 11, 1954; children—Marcia, Nicole, Emily. Sch. dist. librarian, Bellevue, Wash., 1950; tchr., Cottage Grove, Ore., 1951-52, Eugene, Ore., 1952-53, Portland, Ore., 1953-54; librarian Knapp Found. program Roosevelt High Sch., Portland, 1967; research librarian Ore. Hist. Soc., Portland, 1968—. Mem. N.W. Pilot Project Adv. Bd., Portland, 1970-72; active Urban League, Ore. Mus. Sci. and Industry; swimming ofcl. Am. Athletic Union, 1970—. Mem. Spl. Libraries Assn., Am. (chmn. history sect., reference and adult services div. 1973-74), Pacific N.W., Ore. library assns., Nat. Council Jewish Women, Portland Art Assn., Portland Opera Guild. Jewish religion (social action com. 1966-72), Club: Multnomah Athletic (Portland). Home: 6141 SW Seymour St Portland OR 97221 Office: 1230 SW Park St Portland OR 97205

FELDMAN, MARY HELEN KEARNEY, librarian; b. Sapulpa, Okla., July 21, 1920; d. Fabian Earl and Doris Earl (Nave) Kearney; A.A., Monte Cassino Jr. Coll., 1939; postgrad Cin. Conservatory Music, 1939-41; B.S. in Edn., U. Md., 1963; M.S. in L.S., Catholic U. Am., 1965; m. Leon Feldman, Aug 29, 1945 (div. Mar. 1967); children—Jo Kathleen, Michael John, Judith Ellen, Stephen Robert. Tchr., Montgomery County Pub. Schs., Silver Spring, Md., 1963; cataloger U.S. Book Exchange, Washington, 1964; indexer New Catholic Ency., Washington, 1964-66; head tech. services Trinity Coll. Library, Washington, 1965-72; research asst. L.S. dept. Catholic U. Am., Washington, 1966-71; reference librarian Georgetown U. library, Washington, 1970-72; cataloger U.S. Dept. Transp., Washington, 1972—, chief cataloging sect., 1973—. Vice chmn. Democratic precinct, Montgomery County, 1962-64, chmn., 1958-61. Mem. Catholic (chmn. legislative com. 1969-72), Am. (chmn. memberships D.C. chpt. 1968-72), D.C. (sec. 1969-71) library assns., Spl. Libraries Assn. (sec.-treas. transp. div. D.C. chpt. 1973-74, pres. 1974-75), Phi Kappa Phi, Beta Phi Mu (pres. Iota chpt. 1973-74). Editor: (with Joseph R. Judy) Inter-Com, 1971-74, (with Beth Fodor), 1974—; Alumni Forum, Catholic U. Am., 1973—. Home: 7117 Poplar Av Takoma Park MD 20012 Office: 400 7th S W Washington DC 20590

FELDMAN, NANCY KAY GOODMAN, educator; b. Chgo., Oct. 4, 1922; d. Benedict Kay and Irene (Kesner) Goodman; student Vassar Coll., 1940-42, Northwestern U., 1939-40, 42-43; A.B., U. Chgo., 1944, J.D., 1946; m. Raymond G. Feldman, Mar. 2, 1946; children—Richard Goodman, Elizabeth Kay, John Kesner. Mem. faculty U. Tulsa, 1946-50, 58—, asst. prof. sociology, 1959-60, part time lectr., 1960-66, asso. prof. sci., sociology, 1970—; prof. of City, Okla. State U., Tulsa, 1966-70. Bd. dirs. Family and Children's Service, Tulsa Recreation Center for Physically Ltd., Holland Hall Sch. and Parents' Assn., Planned Parenthood, Tulsa Council on Alcoholism, Tulsa Civic Ballet, Council Jewish Women, Philbrook Edn. Com., Okla.; nat. exec. bd. Girl Scouts Am., 1971—. Chmn. adv. Com. to U.S. Civil Rights Commn.; mem. Gov.'s Com. on Children and Youth, Gov.'s Com. Status Women. Recipient U. Chgo. Alumni Assn. Pub. Service citation, 1967; named to Pres. Johnson's Talent Bank of 250 Am. Women, 1966. Mem. Am. Sociol. Assn., Am. Council on Social Work Edn. (del.), S.W. Social Sci. Assn., Okla. Bar Assn., Alpha Kappa Delta, Pi Gamma Mu. Co-author: Tulsa Model Cities Proposal, 1967. Home: 2120 E 46th St Tulsa OK 74105

FELDMAN, ROBIN, editor; b. N.Y.C., June 23, 1948; d. Joseph and Ruth (Gross) Feldman; student Inst. for Youth Leaders from Abroad, Jerusalem, 1966-67; B.A. with honors, Bklyn. Coll., 1971. Advt. prodn. Popular Sci. Pub. Co., N.Y.C., 1967; chief research editor book research div. Fairchild Pubs., Inc., N.Y.C., 1968—. Tutor math. and English, 1961-63. Mem. Zionist Orgn. Am. (ednl. programming v.p. Middle Atlantic States dist. 1967-68). Jewish religion. Home: 504 E 5th St New York City NY 10009 Office: 7 E 12th St New York City NY 10003

FELDMAN, SELMA SCHWARTZ (MRS. ABRAHAM P. FELDMAN), lawyer; b. Cleve., Oct. 6, 1906; d. Jacob and Rose Schwartz; J.D., Cleve. State U., 1928; m. Abraham P. Feldman, Sept. 11, 1932; children—James K., Robert I. Law clk. Treadway & Marlatt, Cleve., 1927-29; admitted to Ohio bar, 1929; lawyer Office of Atty. Gen. Ohio, Cleve., 1929-30; practice law, Akron, O., 1932—; v.p., dir. Stoner Builders, Inc., Akron, Stoner Land Co., Inc., Akron. Mem. Nat. Assn. Women Lawyers, Am. Trial Lawyers Assn., Ohio (mem. family law com. 1973—), Akron (mem. family law com. 1968-74) bar assns. Mem. B'nai B'rith (pres 1935-36). Home: 459 Royal Av Akron OH 44303 Office: 813 2d Nat Bldg Akron OH 44308

FELDMAN, TOBA JEANNE, journalist; b. Chgo., June 13, 1946; d. Jack E. and Margaret H. (Hirsch) Feldman; B.A., U. Cin., 1968. Researcher, writer, reporter Jour. Herald, Dayton, O., 1969-73. Mem. Ohio Gov.'s Task force on Health Care, 1973; chairperson Harrison Twp. Adv. Com. on Transp., 1971-73. Mgr. Curran for City Commn., 1973; pres., Montgomery County Young Democrats, 1972. Mem. Women in Communications, Ohio Newspaper Women's Assn., Ohio, Montgomery County hist. socs., Phi Alpha Theta, Sigma Delta Tau (nat. adviser 1968-69). Home: 5726 Daphne Lane Dayton OH 45415

FELDMEIER, MAXINE ELIZABETH GARRETT (MRS. PAUL FRANCIS FELDMEIER), librarian; b. Grafton, W.Va., July 27, 1911; d. Clarence Melville and Grace May (Snider) Garrett; B.A., Marshall U., 1932; M.S., Fla. State U., 1962; m. Arthur Nelson Davidson, June 25, 1932 (dec. 1963); children—Charles Nelson, Elisabeth Moore (Mrs. Delbert Kimbler, Jr.), Michael A.; m. 2d, Paul Francis Feldmeier, Aug. 1, 1970. Librarian, tchr. Sistersville (W.Va.) High Sch., 1962-64; asst. librarian West Liberty (W.Va.) State Coll., 1964-69; dir. Marshall County Libraries, Moundsville, W.Va., 1969—; regional dir. Miracle Valley Libraries, Moundsville, 1969—. Advisor, cons. pub. libraries, Marshall, Wetzel, Tyler counties, W.Va., 1969—. Mem. planning com. W.Va. Gov.'s Conf. Pub. Libraries, 1973. Recipient State Tng. grant W.Va. Library Commn., 1970. Mem. Am. Assn. U. Profs. (br. treas. 1967-69), Am., W.Va., Tri-State library assns., Am. Assn. U. Women, Tri-City Arts and Humanities Council, Alpha Xi Delta (br. treas. 1964-69). Clubs: Women's (Moundsville, W.Va.); Paden City (W.Va.) Garden. Home: 125 S 4th Av Paden City WV 26159 Office: 700 5th St Moundsville WV 26041

FELDSTEIN, CARLENE BROOKS, psychologist; b. Memphis, Apr. 24, 1932; d. Carl Raymond and Ruby (Hindman) Brooks; B.A., Fairleigh Dickinson U., Teaneck, N.J., 1959; Ph.D. candidate, N.Y. U. Sch. Edn., 1964—; m. Julian M. Feldstein, May 19, 1965; children—Kent Nicholson Lowry, Aaron Carl Feldstein. Psychology intern Inst. Rehab. Medicine, N.Y. U. Med. Center, 1966-67, staff psychologist, 1968-73; lectr., then asst. prof. psychology City U. N.Y., 1972—; pvt. practice psychology, 1973—; instr. Pace U., Westchester, Pleasantville, N.Y., 1973—; mem. faculty new directions Coll. New Rochelle (N.Y.). Nat. Def. Edn. Act fellow, 1964-68. Mem. Am. Psychol. Assn., Internat. Transactional Analysis Assn., Nat. Assn. Family Life, Assn. Humanistic Psychology. Address: 32 Hamilton Rd Scarsdale NY 10583

FELICE, ALICE JAYNE SCHROEDER (MRS. JERRY FELICE), city ofcl.; b. Buffalo, Oct. 13, 1922; d. Walter Theodore and Alice Whilamena (Graf) Mischnick; B.A. cum laude, U. Buffalo, 1944; m. Frederick C. Schroeder, Apr. 15, 1944 (dec. Oct. 1953); children—Pamela Joy (Mrs. Donald A. Schultz), Lee Frederick; m. 2d, Jerry Felice, Dec. 26, 1970. Sec. to chief auditor, income tax div. U.S. Internal Revenue Service, Buffalo, 1943-45; asst. to finance dir. City of Parma Heights, O., 1954-61, finance dir., 1961—, tax adminstr., 1967—. Pres., Parma Park P.T.A., Parma Heights, 1953-54, scholarship chmn. 1953, adult edn. chmn. 1952. Sec., treas. Parma Heights Rep. Club, 1953; Rep. women's ward leader, 1956-58. Mem. Ohio Assn. Tax Adminstrs. (pres. 1973), Municipal Finance Officers Assn. (N.E. Ohio pres. 1971), Chi Omega. Home: 11485 Glendora Lane Parma Heights OH 44130 Office: 6281 Pearl Rd Parma Heights OH 44130

FELL, HILDA WILSON (MRS. HARRY INGRAM FELL), educator; b. Phila., Oct. 19, 1915; d. William Clarke and Susan Annie (Gillespie) Wilson; B.S. in Edn., Temple U., 1940, Ed.M., 1942; Ed.D. (fellow 1954-55), Harvard, 1957; m. Harry Ingram Fell, June 3, 1961; 1 stepson, David. Tchr. Phila. Pub. Schs., 1936-50, elementary sch. prin., 1950-67; asst. prof., chmn. edn. dept., coordinator edn. programs St. Joseph's Coll., Phila., 1967-68, asso. prof., chmn. edn. dept., coordinator edn. programs, 1968—; vis. lectr. edn. U. Pa., summers 1958-63. Adv. council Salvation Army's Ivy House, children's home, 1961—, sec., 1962-74; chmn. appeal bd. Archdiocese Phila. Sch. System, 1968-69; bd. dirs. Our Lady of Angels Coll., Aston, Pa. Recipient scholarship Temple U., 1936. Mem. Am. Assn. Higher Edn., Am. Ednl. Research Assn., Am. Assn. Sch. Adminstrs., Am. Assn. U. Women, World Affairs Council Phila., Pi Lambda Theta (pres. local alumnae chpt. 1958-59). Home: 249 Merion Av Aldan PA 19018 Office: 54th and City Line Philadelphia PA 19131

FELLER, CAROLINE JOSEPHINE, librarian, educator; b. Washington, May 12, 1935; d. Abraham and Alice (Klein) F.; B.A., Sarah Lawrence Coll., 1957; M.S., Columbia, 1958; Ph.D., U. Ore., 1971; m. Peter A. Bauer; 1 child, Hilary A. Children's librarian N.Y. Pub. Library, 1958-60; sch. librarian Eron Prep. Sch., N.Y., 1962-63, Miss Hewitt's classes, 1960-61, Colo. Rocky Mountain Sch., Carbondale, 1963-65; asso. prof. librarianship U. Ore. Sch. Librarianship, Eugene, 1966—. Appeared TV series for children Caroline: Folktales Around the World, KOAC, Portland, 1968; radio series for children Caroline's Corner, KSNO, Aspen, Colo.; producer, instr. Campus of the Air Ore. Ednl. Pub. Broadcasting System KOAC/KOAP-TV, 1973-74. Recipient Ersted award for distinguished teaching, 1968. Mem. Nat. Story League, A.L.A., Puppeteers of Am., Internat. Puppeteers, Ore. Library Assn., Am. Canoe Assn., Nat. Ski Patrol. Club: Sierra. Home: 1607 Lakefront St Lake Oswego OR 97034

FELLERS, HELEN BROADNAX BOWEN (MRS. RUFUS GUSTAVUS FELLERS), librarian; b. Charlotte, N.C., Feb. 9, 1934; d. William Jennings and Helen Broadnax (Nall) Bowen; student Furman U., 1952-53; B.S., Columbia, 1967; postgrad. S.C. Grad. Sch. Edn., 1969, Rutgers U., 1971; m. Rufus Gustavus Fellers, July 15, 1967; children (by previous marriage)—James Ray Lamm, Jr., Helen S. Playsch. instr. Richland County Parks and Recreation Dept., 1955-57; br. librarian Richland County Pub. Library, 1957-71; head librarian Sumter (S.C.) Area Tech. Edn. Center, 1972—. Mem. Columbia Mus. Art, 1963-67, Smithsonian Inst., 1971-73. Mem. S.C., Southeastern library assns., Columbia Jaycettes (v.p. 1962-63), Columbia Drama Soc., Columbia Coll. Alumni Assn. Club: Player's (v.p. Columbia 1967). Home: 1042 Quail Run Columbia SC 29206 Office: 506 Guignard St Sumter SC 29150

FELLIN, OCTAVIA ANTOINETTE, librarian; b. Santa Monica, Cal.; d. Otto P. and Librada (Montoya) Fellin; student U. N.M., 1937-39; B.A., U. Denver, 1941; B.A., in L.S., Rosary Coll., 1942. Asst. librarian, instr. library sci. St. Mary-of-Woods Coll., Terre Haute, Ind., 1942-44; librarian U.S. Army, Burns Gen. Hosp., Santa Fe, 1944-46; post librarian Camp McQuaide, Cal., 1947; librarian Gallup (N.M.) Pub. Library, 1947—; free-lance writer mags., newspapers, 1950—. Dir. Nat. Library Week N.M., 1959. Vice pres., publicity dir. Gallup Community Concerts Assn., 1957-72; organizer Gt. Decision Discussion groups, 1963—; mem. Gallup St. Naming Com., 1958-59, Aging Com., 1964-68; chmn. Gallup Mus. Indian Arts and Crafts, 1964—; mem. publicity com. Gallup Inter-Tribal Indian Ceremonial Assn. 1966-68; mem. N.M. Gov.'s Com. 100 on Aging, 1967-70; chmn. Sr. Citizens Adv. Com., 1970-72; del. N.M. Am. Revolution Bicentennial Commn., 1972; mem. N.M. Library Adv. Council, 1971—; mem. nat. adv. council U.S. Cath. Bishops' Adv. Council, 1970—; organizing chmn. McCounty Hosp. Aux., 1968, editor newsletter, 1972—; chmn. Trick or Treat for UNICEF, 1971—; corr. sec. Latin Am. Mission program, 1973—; pledge chmn. Rancho del Nino San Huberto Home Children, Empalme, Mexico. Recipient Dorothy Canfield Fisher $1,000 Library award, 1961; Outstanding Community Service awards for mus. service Gallup C. of C., also Outstanding Community Service plaque, 1969. Mem. A.L.A., N.M. Library Assn. (v.p., sec., chmn. hist. materials com. 1964-66, salary and tenure com., nat. coordinator N.M. legislative com., com. on pub. library standards 1965—, chmn. com. to extend library services 1969-72), Am. Assn. U. Women (v.p., co-organizer Gallup br., pub. relations dir. 1967—, nominating com. 1968, fellowship and scholarship chmn. 1973—), Plateau Scis. Soc., N.M. Archaeology Assn., N.M. Folklore Soc. (v.p. 1964-65, pres. 1965-66), N.M. Hist. Assn., Gallup Film Soc. (co-organizer, v.p. 1950-58), League Women Voters (v.p. 1953-56), Gallup C. of C. (organizing chmn. women's div. 1972), N.A.A.C.P., Alpha Delta Kappa (hon.). Roman Catholic (Cathedral Guild, Confrat. Christian Doctrine Bd. 1962-64, sec.-treas. diocese Gallup pastoral council 1972—. Cursillo movement). Home: 513 E Mesa Av Gallup NM 87301 Office: 115 W Hill St Gallup NM 87301

FELLMAN, VALERIE MAE DIBBLE (MRS. ALVIN ERIC FELLMAN), occupational therapist; b. Pueblo, Colo., July 3, 1935; d. Edgar Orris and Thelma Mae (Evans) Dibble; A.A., Bakersfield Jr. Coll., 1955; B.A., San Jose State U., 1957; m. Alvin Eric Fellman, May 26, 1961; 1 son, Stephen Eric. Staff occupational therapist Sonoma County Hosp., Santa Rosa, Cal., 1958-59; staff occupational therapist, supr. occupational therapy students Children's Hosp., San Francisco, 1959-62; staff cerebral palsy therapist Alameda County Health Services Agy., Hayward, Cal., 1962-66, staff cerebral palsy therapist, lectr. occupational therapy students, Fremont, Cal., 1969—. Mem. Am. Occupational Therapy Assn. Home: 32933 Lake Bluestone St Fremont CA 94536

FELLOWS, ANN RINGO, TV sta. exec.; b. Bartlesville, Okla., July 15, 1922; d. William Preston and Alberta (Hand) Ringo; B.A. in Advt., U. Okla., 1944; m. Ray Fellows, Dec. 22, 1942 (div. June 1953); children—Cherryl Ann (Mrs. J.D. Douglass) (dec.), Caryl Lynn (Mrs. H.E. Wiles). Promotion mgr. radio sta. KRMG, Tulsa, 1950-52; asst. editor co. pub. Sunray D-X, Tulsa, 1952-54; account exec. Ferguson-Miller & Asso., advt. agy., Tulsa, 1954-55; pub. relations dir. sta. KTEW-TV, Tulsa, 1955—. Lectr. radio, TV U. Tulsa, 1963-64. Pub. relations coordinator Charity Horse Show, Tulsa, 1963-65; mem. ad hoc pub. relations com. Gilerease Mus. Mem. Am. Women Radio and TV (dir. chpt., pub. service chmn., hospitality com., univ. group com.), Women in Communications (dir.). Delta Delta Delta. Presbyn. (mem. ch. choir). Home: 462 S 78th E Av Tulsa OK 74112 Office: KTEW PO Box 3002 Tulsa OK 74101

FELS, MARGARET KATHERINE MCGEARY, educator; b. Erie, Pa., Apr. 29, 1927; d. Charles Porter and Chelsie Adelia (Schenck) McGeary; student Erie Bus. Coll., 1944-45, Grove City Coll., 1945-47; B.A., Chatham Coll., 1949; m. Raymond Lee Fels, Oct. 8, 1949; children—Bryan Lee, Brett Garey. Mem. faculty Behrend Center, Pa. State U., 1949-51; mem. faculty and staff Erie Bus. Center, 1949-53, curriculum coordinator, 1967—, co-dir., 1972—, also v.p. corporate bd. Exec. com. N.W. Pa. Planning Council for Higher Edn. Pres., Erie Council Republican Women, 1961-63, Erie County Federated Council Rep. Women, 1964-65; del. Rep. Nat. Conv., 1964, Nat. Fedn. Rep. Women Conv., 1967; mem. exec. com. Erie County Rep. Com., 1963-66; regional chmn. membership program Pa. Council Rep. Women, 1964-67, bd. dirs., 1965-67; bd. dirs. Fairview Council Rep. Women, 1965-67. Bd. dirs. YWCA, 1957-63, v.p., 1961; sec. Mental Health Bd., 1960; bd. dirs. U.S.O., Erie sponsor Super 60's Bd. Mem. A.A.U.W., Soroptimists (dir.), Carpe Diem Soc. Mercyhurst Coll. (charter), P.E.O. Presbyn. (deacon 1961, elder 1970—, commr. ministerial relations com. Lake Erie Presbytery 71—, pres. ch. women's assn. 1964, 66). Home: 397 Manchester Rd Fairview PA 16415 Office: 246 W 9th St Erie PA 16501

FELSHIN, NINA EVE, writer; b. N.Y.C., Dec. 31, 1944; d. Seon and Dorothy (Cohen) Felshin; B.A., Brandeis U., 1966; M.A., Oberlin Coll., 1967. Asst. to dir. Hanover Gallery, London, Eng., 1967; curatorial asst. Corcoran Gallery, Dupont Center, Washington, 1968-69; asst. curator Corcoran Gallery Art, Washington, 1969-73; free-lance writer, Washington, 1973—. Art cons. AFL-CIO Labor Studies Center, Inc., Washington, 1973—. Kress fellow, 1966; Nat. Endowment for Arts mus. profl. fellow, 1972. Home: 1915 Kalorama Rd NW Washington DC 20009

FENDLER, ELEANOR JOHNSON (MRS. JANOS HUGO FENDLER), educator; b. Danville, Pa., June 27, 1939; d. William Thomas and Ruth Naomi (Miller) Johnson; B.A. (NSF fellow), Bucknell U., 1961; Ph.D. (NSF fellow, Regents fellow), U. Cal. at Santa Barbara, 1966; m. Janos Hugo Fendler, May 29, 1965; 1 son, Michael Thomas Johnson. Research asso. Bucknell U., Lewisburg, Pa., 1961-62; chemistry tchr. Mt. Lebanon Pub. Schs., Pitts., 1962-63; instr. U. Cal. at Santa Barbara, 1963-64, research asso., 1965-66; NASA fellow U. Pitts., 1966-68, research asst. prof., 1968-70; vis. asso. prof. dept. chemistry Tex. A and M U., College Station, 1970—. Recipient NIH Research Career Devel. award, 1971—. Mem. Am. Chem. Soc., Chem. Soc. (Great Britain), Sigma Xi, Phi Beta Kappa, Phi Lambda Upsilon, Alpha Lambda Delta, Kappa Delta Pi, Phi Delta Gamma. Author: Catalysis in Micellar and Macromolecular Systems, 1974. Contbr. numerous articles to profl. jours. Home: 1209 Glade St College Station TX 77840

FENDLER, MIRIAM OLDEN (MRS. HERMAN SEMENOV), lawyer; b. N.Y.C.; d. Max and Ethel (Labowit) Olden; A.B., U. Mich., 1927; LL.B., U. So. Cal., 1929; m. Harold A. Fendler, Mar. 8, 1933; children—Robert H., Douglas M. (dec.); m. 2d, Herman Semenov, Oct. 14, 1973. Admitted to Cal. bar, 1929; practiced in Los Angeles, 1929-51, Beverly Hills, Cal., 1951—. Legislative chmn. P.T.A., Los Angeles. Mem. League Women Voters (pres. Los Angeles, exec. v.p. Cal.), Internat. Fedn. Women Lawyers (hon. life), Delta Sigma Rho, Phi Sigma Sigma (nat. pres.). Home: 865 Comstock Av Los Angeles CA 90024 Office: 9595 Wilshire Blvd Beverly Hills CA 90212

FENERTY, MARJORY RODGERS, editor; b. Manila, Phillippines, Feb. 18, 1912 (parents Am. citizens); d. George William and Anna Hendricks (Rodgers) Wright; B.A., Mt. Holyoke Coll., 1932; A.M., Ohio Wesleyan U., 1933; m. Harold Franklin Fenerty, June 26, 1936. Tchr., Mt. Holyoke Coll., 1933-35, St. Agnes Sch., Albany, N.Y.,

1935-37, Winsor Sch., Boston, 1938-39, Lincoln Sch., Providence, 1940-47; dir. research Pub. Service Research, Inc., Plainfield, N.J., 1966-71; research asso. H.M. Baker Assos., Edison, N.J., 1971—; compiler hist. archives Town of Westwood, Mass., 1960—, acting historian, 1970—; historian First Parish United Ch. Westwood, 1959—. Library trustee, Westwood, 1956-62, Bethel Park, Pa., 1963-65, Edison, 1973—. Mem. Westwood, Dedham (Mass.), N.J. hist. socs., New Eng. Hist. Geneal. Soc., Soc. Preservation New Eng. Antiquities, Am. Assn. State and Local History, Friends Sturbridge Village, Nat. Trust Historic Preservation, Internat. Platform Soc., Am. Water Works Assn. Author: The Meeting House on a Rock, 1959, supplement, 1969; West Dedham and Westwood-300 Years, 1973; also articles. Editor Am. Directory of Water Utilities, 1968. Address: 361 Tampico Dr Palmetto FL 33561

FENILI, MARY LOUISE, coll. dean; b. Vineland, N.J., July 7, 1945; d. Vasco John and Louise (Pennino) Fenili; B.A., Douglass Coll., 1967; M.A., Syracuse U., 1970. Head resident Syracuse (N.Y.) U., 1967-69; head resident U. So. Cal., Los Angeles, 1969-70; asst. dean students, dir. White, Reinhardt and Ege Halls, Mills Coll., Oakland, Cal., 1970-73, asst. dean student services, dir. residential life, 1973—, lectr. English, 1972, dir. Coll. Fed. Credit Union, 1972-74. Mem. Oakland Mus. Assn., 1970—. Recipient Sr. Service award Douglass Coll., 1967. Fellow Am. Acad. Polit. and Social Sci.; mem. Nat. Assn. Women Deans, Adminstrs. and Counselors (placement com. 1973-74), Cal. Assn. Coll. and Univ. Housing officers, Common Cause (dist. liaison 1973), Pi Lambda Theta. Club: Sierra (San Francisco). Home: PO Box 9912 Oakland CA 94613

FENN, JEAN, soprano; b. Ill., 1930; d. George Prentice and Maurine (Hansen) Fenn; A.A., Stephens Coll., 1946. Profl. debut Los Angeles Civic Light Opera, 1950; debut with San Francisco Opera Co., 1952, N.Y.C. Center Opera Co., 1953, Met. Opera Co., 1953—, also New Orleans Grand Opera; Kansas City and St. Louis Light Operas, Denver Opera Assn. Mem. Sigma Alpha Iota. Address: care Met Opera Co Lincoln Center New York City NY 10023

FENNER, MILDRED SANDISON (MRS. H. WOLCOTT FENNER), editor; b. Huntsville, Mo., July 9, 1910; d. John Forte and Minnielee (Holliday) Sandison; B.S., N.W. Mo. State U., 1931; M.A., George Washington U., 1938, Ed.D., 1942; D.Litt., Glassboro (N.J.) State Coll., 1962; m. H. Wolcott Fenner, Feb. 1, 1940. With Today's Edn., N.E.A. Jour., 1931—, as mem. staff, asst. editor, mng. editor, 1931-54, editor, 1954—. Recipient 1st Ann. Distinguished Alumni award N.W. Mo. State U., 1970, George Washington U., 1972. Mem. Am. Newspaper Women's Club, Edn. Writers Assn., Ednl. Press Assn. Am. (nat. sec.-treas. 1951-60, rep. Internat. Ednl. Editors' Workshop, Manila, summer 1956, Amsterdam 1961), Nat. Council Adminstrv. Women in Edn., Am. Assn. U. Women, Horace Mann League (nat. pres. 1972-73), Pi Lambda Theta, Sigma Sigma Sigma. Democrat. Methodist. Author: (with Eleanor Fishburn) Pioneer American Educators, 1944; NEA History, 1945, Discipline in the Classroom, 1969; (with H. Wolcott Fenner) Circus Lure and Legend, 1970; Schools Are People, 1971. Contbr. articles to profl. jours. Home: 530 N St SW Apt S-205 Washington DC 20024 Office: 1201 16th St NW Washington DC 20036

FENNER, PHYLLIS REID, author; b. Almond, N.Y., Oct. 24, 1899; d. William La Verne and Viola (Van Orman) Fenner; A.B., Mt. Holyoke Coll.; B.S. in L.S., Columbia. Librarian, Manhasset, N.Y., 1923-55; instr. story telling St. John's U., Bklyn., 1939—. Mem. Nat. Woman's Book Assn., A.L.A., Pen and Brush, Woman Geographers Soc. Author: There Was a Horse (folktales), 1941; Merry Hearts and Bold, 1942, a Fifth reader; Our Library: The Story of a School Library That Works, 1942; Giants and Witches and a Dragon or Two, 1943; Time to Laugh, 1942; Princesses and Peasant Boys, 1944; Adventure, 1945; Demons and Dervishes, 1946; Fools and Funny Fellows, 1947; With Might and Main, 1948; Horses, Horses, Horses, 1949; Feasts and Frolics, 1949; Cowboys, Cowboys, Cowboys, 1950; Indians, Indians, Indians, 1950; Dogs, Dogs, Dogs, 1951; Yankee Doodle, 1951; Crack of the Bat, 1952; Ghosts, Ghosts, Ghosts, 1952; Circus Parade, 1954; Speed, Speed, Speed, 1954; Fun, Fun, Fun, 1954; The Proof of the Pudding, 1957; Brother Against Brother, 1957; Something Shared, 1959; The Price of Liberty, 1960; Kick-off, 1960; (with Avah Hughes) Entrances and Exits, 1960; Over There, 1961; The Dark and Bloody Ground, 1963; Behind the Wheel, 1964; (with Mary McCrea) Stories for Fun and Adventure, 1961, No Time for Glory, 1962; More Stories for Fun and Adventure, 1964; Danger is the Password, 1965; Quick Pivot, 1965; Open Throttle, 1966; Contraband: Stories of Smuggling, 1967; The Hunter and the Hunted, 1968; Finders Keepers: Stories of Treasure Seekers, 1969, Perilous Ascent: Stories of Mountain Climbing, 1970; Desperate Moments: Stories of Escapes and Hurried Journeys, 1971; Where Speed is King, 1972; Consider the Evidence, 1973. Reviewer: N.Y. Times, library jours. Contbr. stories to ednl. mags., sch. readers. Editorial bd. Cadmus Books, 1945—, Weekly Reader Book Club, 1961—; adv. bd. Children's Digest mag., 1950—. Address: Box 653 Manchester VT 05254

FENNICK, CYNTHIA ALTMAN (MRS. EMANUEL FENNICK), psychologist; b. N.Y.C., Oct. 17, 1934; d. Louis William and Beatrice Irene (Rabinowitz) Altman; B.A., City Coll. N.Y., 1957, M.S., 1961; postgrad. Cornell U., summer 1957, N.Y. U., 1964-68; m. Emanuel Fennick, Nov. 17, 1957; 1 dau., Janine. Tchr. elementary pub. sch. 1957, N.Y.C., 1957-62; group work supr. YM-YWCA, N.Y.C., 1959-63; sch. psychologist Brentwood (N.Y.) Pub. Schs., 1965—. Mem. exec. bd. P.T.A., Commack, N.Y., 1970-71. Mem. exec. bd. Reform Democratic Club, Inwood, Manhattan, 1962. Mem. Nat. Assn. Sch. Psychologists, N.Y. State Sch. Psychologists, N.E.A., N.Y. State, Brentwood tchrs. assns., Suffolk Psychol. Assn. Jewish religion. Home: 21 Adar Lane East Northport NY 11731 Office: Brentwood Pub Schs Psychol Services Brentwood NY 11717

FENOGLIO, CECILIA CHARLOTTE METTLER (MRS. JOHN JAMES FENOGLIO), pathologist; b. N.Y.C., Nov. 28, 1943; d. Fred Albert and Cecilia Charlotte (Asper) Mettler; B.S. with honors, Coll. St. Elizabeth, 1965; M.D., Georgetown U., 1969; m. John James Fenoglio, May 27, 1967; children—Timothy, John. Intern, Columbia-Presbyn. Med. Center, N.Y.C., 1969-70, resident in pathology, 1970-73; postdoctoral fellow tumor immunology Meml. Sloan-Kettering Cancer Center, N.Y.C., 1973; vis. investigator Lab. Cellular Immunobiology, 1974; trainee Nat. Cancer Inst.; instr. pathology Columbia Coll. Phys. and Surg., 1973—. Diplomate Nat. Bd. Med. Examiners. Mem. A.C.P. (asso.), A.A.A.S., Sigma Xi, Beta Beta Beta. Home: Pippin Hill Blairstown NJ 07825 Office: 630 W 168th St New York City NY 10032

FENSHOLT, DOROTHY EUNICE, ret. educator; b. Chgo., Oct. 23, 1911; d. Adolph Herlev and Ethel (Heath) Fensholt; B.S., Northwestern U., 1933, M.S., 1945, Ph.D., 1951; postgrad. Ore. Inst. Marine Biology, 1948, Hopkins Marine Sta., Pacific Grove, Cal., 1949. Market research Fensholt Advt. Agy., Chgo., 1933-37; instr. Northwestern U., 1942-47; asst. prof. Ill. State U., Normal, 1951-55, asso. prof., 1955-61, prof., 1961-74. Mem. Bot. Soc. Am., Phycological Soc. Am., Am. Soc. Microbiology, Phi Beta Kappa, Sigma Xi, Sigma Delta Epsilon. Home: 2404 Loring St San Diego CA 92109

FENSTERMACHER, JEAN MANLEY (MRS. KENNETH L. FENSTERMACHER), coll. adminstr.; b. Volga, W.Va., Feb. 7, 1931; d. Kara Robert and Ida Pearl (Foster) Manley; B.A., Alderson-Broaddus Coll., 1971; M.A. (Title III fellow), W.Va. U., 1972; m. Kenneth L. Fenstermacher, Nov. 30, 1945; children—Kenna Jean (Mrs. Samuel Edward Wright), Nancy Joan, Robin Rebecca (Mrs. Karl Edmund Shaffer). Sec. to dean students Alderson-Broaddus Coll., Philippi, W.Va., 1958-62, adminstr. asst., 1962-68, dir. housing, 1968-71, asst. dean women, 1968-71, dean women, 1971-72, asso. dean students, 1972—. Pres., P.T.A., 1964-65. Mem. So. Counselor Personnel Assn., W.Va. Colls. and Univ. Counselors, W.Va. Student Personnel Adminstrs., Bus. and Profl. Women, Silver Key Hon. Soc. Methodist. Mem. Order Eastern Star, Rebekah. Home: Route 3 Box 38-A Philippi WV 26416

FENTON, ISABELLE BENTLEY (MRS. DONALD MCLEAN FENTON), educator; b. New Rochelle, N.Y., May 13, 1922; d. Bertram Ormand and Louise (McCumber) Bentley; B. Edn., State U. N.Y. Coll., Oneonta, 1943, postgrad, 1953-60; m. Donald McLean Fenton, Jan. 25, 1944; children—Andrea (Mrs. William J. Campbell), John Donald, James Thomas. Tchr., Bayport (N.Y.) Sch., 1943-45, Margaretville (N.Y.) Central Sch., 1949-52, 58—. Mem. coll. council State U. N.Y. Agrl. and Tech. Coll., Delhi, 1972—; mem. presidential search com. State U. Agrl. and Tech. Coll., Delhi, N.Y., 1973-74. Republican committeewoman Town of Middletown (N.Y.), 1951—, sec. Rep. town com., 1956—, vice chmn. Del. County (N.Y.) Rep. Com., 1959-69, 70—, chmn., 1969-70; chmn. Housewives Com. for Gov. Rockefeller, 1970. Bd. dirs. Assn. Council Mems. and Coll. Trustees State U. N.Y. Mem. N.Y. State United Tchrs., Margaretville Tchrs. Assn. (pres. 1963-64), Margaretville P.T.A. (treas. 1959-60), N.E.A., Middletown, Del. County Women's Rep. clubs, Margaretville Meml. Hosp. Aux. Presbyn. Mem. Order Eastern Star. Home: Mountain Av Margaretville NY 12455 Office: Margaretville Central Sch Main St Margaretville NY 12455

FENTON, MARY (MRS. RAY WILLIAM FENTON), pub. relations exec., communications cons.; b. Butte, Mont., Dec. 26, 1920; d. Samuel John and Anna (Sagar) Bukvich; B.A. with honors in Journalism, U. Mont., 1943; m. Ray William Fenton, Apr. 20, 1946; children—Neil, Bruce, Ross, Janis. Reporter, photographer Great Falls (Mont.) Tribune, 1943-46; Mont. corr. Fairchild Publs., Inc., N.Y.C., 1956-64; pub. relations counselor, partner Pub. Relations Assos., Great Falls, 1960—; community coordinator, communications cons. Program for Advanced Children's Edn., Great Falls pub. schs., 1971-74, chmn. Program for Gifted and Talented children. Cons. to Great Falls Symphony Assn., 1970-71, Mont. supr. Am. Research Bur., Great Falls, 1961. Mem. Mont. Commn. on Post-Secondary Edn., 1973. Bd. dirs. Coll. of Great Falls Guild, Great Falls Vol. Action Com.; trustee Mont. Multiple Sclerosis Soc. Mem. Pub. Relations Soc. Am., Am. Women in Radio and TV, Assn. for the Gifted, Council of Exceptional Children, Nat. Assn. Sch. Vols. (coordinator Mont. 1972-74), Great Falls Press Club. Clubs: Fortnightly, Meadow Lark Country. Asso. editor Mont. Rural Electric News, 1966—. Home: 3431 Fifth Av South Great Falls MT 59405 Office: 606 25th St North Great Falls MT 59401

FENWICK, MILLICENT HAMMOND, state ofcl.; b. N.Y.C., Feb. 25, 1910; d. Ogden Haggerty and Mary Picton (Stevens) Hammond; student Foxcroft Sch., Columbia Extension Sch., New Sch. for Social Research; div.; children—Mary (Mrs. Reckford), Hugh. Asso. editor Conde Nast Publs., N.Y., 1938-50; mem. N.J. Gen. Assembly, 1970-73; dir. div. consumer affairs N.J. Dept. Law and Pub. Safety, 1973—. Vice chmn. N.J. adv. com. to U.S. Commn. on Civil Rights. Mem. Bd. Edn., Bernardsville, N.J., 1938-41; mem. Borough Council, 1958-64. Republican. Author: Vogue's Book of Etiquette, 1948. Home: Mendham Rd Bernardsville NJ 07924 Office: 1100 Raymond Blvd Newark NJ 07102

FENWICK, SARA INNIS, educator; b. Lima, O., Dec. 25, 1908; d. Edwin Thomas and Grissie Innis (Greenhow) Fenwick; student Heidelberg Coll., 1926-28; B.A., Western Res. U., 1939; M.A., U. Chgo. Library Sch., 1951. Asst. children's librarian, young people's librarian, head children's work Osterhout Free Library, Wilkes-Barre, Pa., 1931-44; asst. to dir. work with children Enoch Pratt Free Library, Balt., 1944-46; head of work with children Gary (Ind.) Pub. Library, 1946-49; librarian Lab. Sch., U. Chgo., 1949-56, successively asst. prof., asso. prof. Grad. Library Sch., U. Chgo., 1956-71, prof., 1971—. Tchr. summers Ind. U., 1952, 53, Brigham Young U., 1970; cons. Brit. Ednl. Corp., Ency. Brit. Jr. N.E.A. del. to World Confedn. Orgns. of Teaching Profession, Rio de Janeiro, Brazil, 1963; Fulbright sr. lectr. Australian Library Assn., 1964. Recipient Chgo. Area Reading Assn. CARA award, 1971; Chgo. Children's Reading Round Table award, 1974. Mem. Am. Assn. Sch. Librarians (pres. 1962-63), A.L.A. (pres. children's services div. 1971-72), Internat. Reading Assn., Nat. Council Tchrs. English, Assn. for Ednl. Communications and Tech., Pi Lambda Theta, Delta Kappa Gamma. Author: School and Children's Libraries in Australia, 1966. Editor: New Definitions of School Library Service, 1959, A Critical Approach to Children's Literature, 1966. Home: 5550 Dorchester Av Chicago IL 60637

FEREBEE, ANN ELIZABETH, editor; b. Norfolk, Va., Aug. 19, 1931; d. Oscar Benson and Florence Corrine (Swingley) Ferebee; B.A., Barnard Coll., 1953; postgrad. Inst. Fine Arts, 1955-58. Editor Design & Environment jour. RC Publs., Inc., N.Y.C., 1953—. Vis. asso. prof. art and urban environment State U. N.Y., Purchase, 1972—. Author: History of Design from the Victorian Era to the Present, 1971. Picture editor The Camera, Life Library of Photography, 1970. Home: 47 Barrow St New York City NY 10014 Office: 19 W 44th St New York City NY 10036

FERENS, MARCELLA (MRS. JOSEPH J. FERENS), educator; b. Pitts.; d. Ignatius and Marcella (Buzas) Slevinskas; student Greensburg Bus. Coll., 1934-35, Maison Frederic Cosmetology, 1936, Kree Inst. Electrolysis, N.Y., 1952; B.S., U. Pitts., 1957; postgrad. Mid-Western U., 1962; M.Ed., Duquesne U., 1964; m. Joseph J. Ferens, Nov. 27, 1937; children—Joseph Ferens, James. Cosmetologist and electrologist, Manor and Darragh, Pa., 1937—; research in hair regrowth, Darragh, 1954—; tchr. algebra, reading and drama dir. Harold Jr. High Sch., Greensburg, Pa., 1958—; tchr. cosmotology Uniontown (Pa.) Vocational High 1954-55. Insp. Chem. Corps, Dept. of Army, N.Y. 1951. Mem. Nat. Council Tchrs. Math., Nat., Pa. edn. assns. Patentee in field. Home: Box 84 Daragh PA 15625 Office: RFD 6 Greensburg PA 15601

FERGUSON, ANNABELLE EVELYN, ednl. adminstr.; b. Duquesne, Pa., June 17, 1923; d. John and Anna (McWilliams) Ferguson; B.S., U. Pitts., 1944, M.Ed., 1948; Ph.D., U. Md., 1970. Tchr. Titusville (Pa.) Pub. Schs., 1947-50; dir. Y-teen program Titusville YWCA, 1947-50; guidance counselor Howard County, Ellicott City, Md., 1950-58; guidance counselor Anne Arundel County, Severna Park, Md., 1958-59, supr. instrn., 1959-62; supr. guidance Anne Arundel County, Annapolis, Md., 1962-65, Md. Dept. Edn., Balt., 1965-69; dir. pupil services Prince George's County Bd. Edn., Upper Marlboro, Md., 1969-73, central area dir., 1973—. Lectr. grad. schs. Western Md. Coll., Towson State Coll., Bowie State Coll. Served to lt. (j.g.) WAVES, 1944-46. Mem. Am. Assn. Sch. Adminstrs., Nat. Assn. Pupil Personnel Adminstrs., Assn. Supervision and Curriculum Devel., Am. Sch. Counselors Assn. (Adminstr. of Year 1971), Assn. Counselor Edn. and Supervision, Am. (senator 1967-69), Md. (pres. 1967) personnel and guidance assns., Delta Kappa Gamma (chpt. pres. 1956-58). Republican. Methodist. Home: 803 Pin Oak Rd Severna Park MD 21146 Office: Prince George's County Central Area Office Landover MD 20785

FERGUSON, EVA DREIKURS, psychologist, scientist, educator; b. Vienna, Austria, Aug. 28, 1929; d. Rudolf and Sadie (Ellis) Dreikurs; B.A. with honors, U. Ill., 1950; M.A. with honors, Melbourne (Australia) U., 1953; Ph.D., Northwestern U., 1956; m. John A. Ferguson, Jan. 28, 1950 (div. 1969); children—Rodney, Beth, Bruce, Linda. Sociologist, Lady Gowrie Child Center, Melbourne, 1951-52; intern in psychology Ill. Neuropsychiat. Hosp., Chgo., 1954-55; postdoctoral fellow Western Psychiat. Inst., Pitts., 1956-58; psychologist Craig House for Children, Pitts., 1959-62; asst. prof. psychology Melbourne U., 1962-65; asso. prof. psychology So. Ill. U., Edwardsville, 1965-69, prof., 1969—. Recipient award in sociology Chi Omega, 1950. Mem. A.A.A.S. (life), Am. Psychol. Assn., Sigma Xi. Cons. editor Jour. Individual Psychology. Contbr. articles to profl. jours. Office: Dept Psychology So Illinois Univ Edwardsville IL 62025

FERGUSON, FERN ELOIS WILSON (MRS. GEORGE J. FERGUSON), librarian; b. Wheeling, W.Va., Jan. 10, 1913; d. Edwin Dean and Minnie (Hunt) Wilson; A.B., Bethany Coll., W.Va., 1934; B.L.S., U. Ill., 1935; m. George J. Ferguson, Nov. 10, 1937; 1 dau., Joyce Adele (Mrs. Marshall N. Miller). Librarian circulation dept. Northwestern U., Evanston, Ill., 1935-37, Ohio County (W.Va.) Pub. Library, Wheeling, 1937-39; high sch. librarian Wheeling High Sch., 1959-61; head reference dept. Tucson Pub. Library, 1961-65, head, Wilmot Br., 1965-67; librarian Tucson Pub. Schs., 1968-70; librarian Pima County (Ariz.) Schs., 1973—; sec. Uwanta Linen Supply, Inc., Wheeling, 1956—. Mem. Am. Assn. U. Women, D.A.R. (chpt. regent 1959-61, chmn. W.Va. Centennial 1960-61, Ariz. librarian 1970-72, state historian 1972—), A.L.A., Southwestern, Ariz. library assns., Ariz. Hist. Soc. Mem. Christian Ch. (pres. ladies council 1971-72). Mem. Order Eastern Star. Home: 3220 Via Celeste Tucson AZ 85718

FERGUSON, GRACE, lawyer; b. Fredricktown, Mo., May 24, 1905; d. Frank and Charlotte (Cline) Ferguson; student U. La., 1922-24; LL.B., U. Ark., 1926. Admitted to Ark. bar, 1926; legal sec. law firm Mehaffy & Mehaffy, Little Rock, 1926-36; statistician, analyst Bur. Labor Statistics, Little Rock, 1936-66. Mem. Pulaski County Quorum Ct. Bd. dirs. Contact Line, Internat., 1968—, Ark. Youth Homes, 1969—. Mem. Ark. Women Lawyers (pres. 1973-74), Ark. Bar Assn. Democrat. Home: 521 Midland St Little Rock AR 72205

FERGUSON, IRENE LYDIA FUCHS (MRS. CECIL L. FERGUSON), editor; b. Bklyn., June 3, 1934; d. Ernest and Lydia Eleanor (Baumann) Fuchs; B.A., Franklin Coll., 1956; postgrad. Loyola U., 1967-68, Chgo. State U., 1968-69; m. Cecil L. Ferguson, July 16, 1957; 1 son, Mark Lee. With Standard Ednl. Corp., Chgo., 1956—, asst. editor, 1956-60, asso. editor, 1961-65, sr. asso. editor, 1965-69, sr. editor New Standard Ency., 1970—. Mem. Women in Communications. Chgo. Women in Pub., Delta Zeta. Home: 501 E 32d St Chicago IL 60616 Office 130 N Wells St Chicago IL 60606

FERGUSON, JOSEPHINE ANNE LUECKE (MRS. BYRON LEE FERGUSON), ednl. adminstr.; b. Ft. Wayne, Ind., Aug. 30, 1923; d. Christian Herman William and Verma (Hinton) Luecke; A.B., Valparaiso U., 1946; m. Byron Lee Ferguson, Dec. 22, 1945. Placement asst. Ind. U., Bloomington, 1948-50; dir. student services Valparaiso (Ind.) U., 1950-64, dir. financial aid, 1964-65; exec. sec. State Scholarship Commn. of Ind., Indpls., 1965-67; sr. program officer, student financial aid Office Edn., Chgo., 1967—. Cons. Dept. Health, Edn. and Welfare, Office Edn., 1965-67; mem. All-Coll. Scholarship Selection Com. Aid Assns. for Luths., 1965-66; mem. adv. com. Guaranteed Loan Program Pres., Valparaiso U. Guild, 1957-60, vice-chmn. Ind. state unit, 1962-63; speaker to profl. orgns. Mem. Scholarship Assns. Ind. Colls. and Univs. (chmn. 1963-65, sec. 1965-67), Student Financial Aid Commn. of Am. Coll. Personnel Assn. (sec. 1961-64, program coordinator 1966-67), Assn. Coll. Admission Counselors, Assn. Collegiate Registrars and Admission Officers (com. scholarship and aids 1966-67), Kappa Kappa Kappa (corr. sec. 1964-65, scholarship chmn. 1962-66). Club: Zonta. Contbr. numerous articles to profl. jours. Home: 101 Sheffield Dr Valparaiso IN 46383 Office: Office Edn Chicago IL 60601

FERGUSON, LOIS SANDERS (MRS. TOMMY RAY FERGUSON), journalist; b. Pottsboro, Tex., May 4, 1937; d. Freeman and Creola Mae (Odel) Sanders; student N. Tex. State U., 1955-57; m. Tommy Ray Ferguson, Aug. 10, 1956; children—Tomagene, Terry Wayne, Tracy Dale. Society editor Stinnett Star, 1963-66; owner-instr. ABC Kindergarten, 1963-66; editor-pub. Stinnett Leader, 1967-68; editor-mgr. Hutchinson County Herald, 1969-73; corr. Borger (Tex.) News-Herald, Chanel 7 TV, Amarillo, Tex., 1973—; courtroom reporter for criminal cases for news media 84th Jud. Dist. in Hutchinson County, 1972-73. Publicity dir., mem. bldg. com., mem. ways and mean com. Stinnett Community Youth Center Assn., 1973-74; adult leader summer 4-H Club Roadrunners Girls' Track Team, 1973; mem. Stinnett Baseball Assn., 1969-74; neighborhood chmn. Hutchinson County Cancer Crusade, 1973; vol. Heart Fund Drive, 1968-73. Named Girl of Year, Rho Theta chpt. Beta Sigma Phi, 1963. Mem. Hutchinson County Farm Bur., Beta Sigma Phi. Mem. Ch. of Christ (publicity and advt. dir. 1973-74). Club: Morse Telegraph (Stinnett). Home: 421 Morse Box 553 Stinnett TX 79083 Office: 719 Main St Stinnett TX 79083

FERGUSON, MARGARET KATHERINE (MRS. WILLIAM STANLEY FERGUSON), mus. ofcl.; b. Evansville, Ind., Oct. 24, 1906; d. Jacob Fred and Estella (Slinghart) Schumacher; grad. high sch.; m. William Stanley Ferguson, Oct. 17, 1935 (dec.); 1 son, William Stanley. Sec., W.S. Ferguson Co., Cleve., 1925-35; sec. to asst. dir. Univ. Hosps., Cleve., 1955-57; with Cleve. Health Mus. and Edn. Center, 1957—, adminstv. asst., sec. to dir., 1969—. Home: 2685 Euclid Heights Blvd Cleveland OH 44106 Office: 8911 Euclid Av Cleveland OH 44106

FERGUSON, MARY ROSALIE SCHMIDT, telephone co. exec.; b. Indpls., Jan. 1, 1939; d. Francis John and Catherine Marie (Osterman) Schmidt; student Butler U., 1957—; div.; 1 dau., Kimberlie Marie. With Ind. Bell Telephone Co., Indpls., 1957—, office supr., 1965-71, staff asst., 1971-72, staff supr., 1972—. Mem. Indpls. Mus. Art Speaker's Bur., 1973-74, v.p., bd. dirs. bus. unit group, 1973-74. Mem. Am. Bus. Women's Assn. (chpt. pres. 1972-73, 74—, Nat. Bus. Women of Year 1972-73), Jr. Group Ind. State Symphony Soc., Fine Arts Soc. Indpls., Ind. Assn. Retarded Children, League Women Voters. Roman Catholic. Clubs: Ind. Bell Women's (pres. 1972-73), Bell Management (bd. dirs. 1973—) (Indpls.). Home: 6377 Brookline Dr Indianapolis IN 46220 Office: 428 N Meridian St Indianapolis IN 46204

FERGUSON, SARAH (MRS. JAMES GRIFFIN TAYLOR), physician; b. Stephenville, Tex., Aug. 10, 1917; d. Thomas Ewing and Eleanor Eudora (Brachey) Ferguson; student Stephen F. Austin State U., 1933-34; B.A., U. Tex. at Austin, 1936; M.D., U. Tex. at Galveston, 1941; m. James Griffin Taylor, Dec. 23, 1941;

children—Sally (Mrs. William K. Stephenson), Thomas Griffin. Intern Parkland Meml. Hosp., Dallas, 1941-42; practice medicine specializing in pediatrics, Nacogdoches, Tex., 1946—; mem. staff Meml. Hosp., Nacogdoches; contract surgeon U.S. Air Force, Kelly Field, 1943-44; sch. physician North Tex. State U., Denton, 1944-45. Mem. Am., Tex. med. assns., Nacogdoches County Med. Soc. also Women's Aux., Tex. Pediatric Soc., Am. Med. Women's Assn., Phi Beta Kappa, Iota Sigma Pi, Alpha Epsilon Iota. Republican. Episcopalian (mem. guild). Clubs: Alpha Epsilon Iota. Home: 3731 Raguet St Nacogdoches TX 75961 Office: 1301 Raguet St Nacogdoches TX 75961

FERGUSSON, MURIEL MACQUEEN, Canadian senator. Called to N.B. (Can.) bar; since practiced in Grand Falls, N.B.; former mem. Fredericton (N.B.) City Council, also former dep. mayor Fredericton; enforcement counsel Wartime Price and Trade Bd., World War II; mem. Canadian senate, 1953—, speaker, 1972—. Past pres. Provincial Council of Women; regional dir. Dept. Nat. Health and Welfare, Fredericton. Mem. Ind. Order Daus. Empire (edn. sec. N.B. chpt.), Bus. and Profl. Women's Club, Canadian Fedn. Bus. and Profl. Women's Clubs (chmn. internat. relations com.). Home: 102 Waterloo Row Fredericton NB Canada Office: The Senate Ottawa ON Canada

FERKOL, WILMA MAXINE, occupational therapist; b. Ottawa, Kan., Aug. 9, 1938; d. Henry William and Clara Pearl (Alexander) Deitcher; B.A. in Occupational Therapy, U. Kan., 1961; m. Louis Glenn Ferkol, May 25, 1959; children—Gregory, Bradley, Susan, Douglas. Dir. occupational therapy Wheeling (W. Va.) Soc. Crippled Children, 1962-63; lead tchr. Medina (O.) Weekday Sch., 1970-71; occupational therapist New Britain (Conn.) Meml. Hosp., 1973-74; occupational therapist Hartford (Conn.) Rehab. Center, 1974—. Cons. in field. Dir. religious edn. St. Paul's Epis. ch., Medina, 1966-68; mem. St. Peter's Epis. Sch. Bd., Litchfield Park, Ariz., 1972-73. Mem. Alpha Chi Omega. Episcopalian. Home: 9 Lawton Dr Simsbury CT 06070 Office: Hartford Rehab Center Hartford Ct

FERMI, LAURA, author; b. Rome, Italy, June 16, 1907; d. Augusto and Costanza (Romanelli) Capon; student U. Rome, 1926-28; m. Enrico Fermi July 19, 1928 (dec.); children—Nella (Mrs. Nella Weiner), Giulio. Bd. govs. Internat. House Chgo., 1955-65; mem. Women's Bd. U. Chgo. Mem. City Chgo. Air Pollution Control Com., 1960-68. Guggenheim fellow, 1957. Recipient award Friends of Lit., 1968. Mem. League Women Voters. Author: Atoms in the Family, 1954; Atoms For the World, 1957; Mussolini, 1961; The Story of Atomic Energy (juvenile), 1961: (with Ginestra Amaldi) Alchimia Del Tempo Nostro, 1936; (with Gilberto Bernardini) Galileo and the Scientific Revolution 1961; Illustrious Immigrants, 1968. Home: 5532 South Shore Dr Chicago IL 60637

FERN, RUTH KANE (MRS. WALLACE EDWARD FERN), educator; b. Somerville, N.J., May 12, 1919; d. James Aloysius and Marguerite Anne (Carberry) Kane; B.S., Trenton State Coll., 1941; M.A., N.Y.U., 1944; M.A. in Adminstrn., Montclair State Coll., 1953; postgrad. Columbia, 1957-69, New Coll., Oxford, Bedford Coll., U. London; m. Wallace Edward Fern, Sept. 3, 1960. Tchr. sr. English Flemington (N.J.) High Sch., 1941-44; dept. chmn., tchr. sr. English, Passaic Valley High Sch., Little Falls, 1944-51; instr. Newark State Coll., 1951-55, asst. prof., 1955-57, dir. pub. relations, 1952-57; asso. prof. English, edn., William Paterson Coll. of N.J., Wayne, 1958—. Cons., English Lang. Arts, Pequannock (N.J.) Pub. Schs., spring 1966, secondary sch. reading Pompton Lakes Pub. Schs., winter 1972. Vice-pres. Essex County (N.J.) Council State Employees, 1956-57. Flemington (N.J.) Bd. Edn. grantee, 1942-43. Mem. N.E.A. (life mem.), N.J. Edn. Assn. N.J. Assn. Tchrs. English (exec. bd. 1963—), Nat. Council Tchrs. English, Nat. Assn. Tchr. Educators, N.J. Hist. Soc., Delta Kappa Gamma (chpt. pres. 1970-72), Kappa Delta Pi, Pi Lambda Theta (adviser coll. chpt.). Contbr. articles to profl. pubs. Home: 62 Alpine Dr Wayne NJ 07470 Office: 300 Pompton Rd Wayne NJ 07470

FERNANDEZ, ROSE M., ednl. adminstr.; b. Havana, Cuba, Mar. 21, 1940; d. Vicente and Dionisia (Zapatero) Fernandez; came to U.S., 1961, naturalized, 1972; student U. Habana, 1961; B.A. summa cum laude in Sociology (Presdl. scholar) St. Leo Coll., 1970; M.A., U. South Fla., 1971. Tchr. Holy Name Acad., San Antonio, Fla., 1961-64; tchr. and coordinator jr. high sch. curriculum St. Paul's Sch., Jacksonville, Fla., 1964-69; dir. housing St. Leo (Fla.) Coll., 1969-71, dean women, 1971-73; research asst. U. South Fla., Tampa, 1971; coordinator fed. projects Pasco County Sch. Bd., Dade City, Fla., 1973—. Mem. Nat. Assn. Women Deans and Counselors, Am. Assn. Sch. Adminstrs., Fla. Assn. Sch. Suprs., Fla., Nat. women polit. caucuses, Pasco Headstart Adv. Council, Pasco Community Coordinators Council. Home: PO Box 1826 Dade City FL 33252 Office: Fed Projects Office 305 S 14th St Dade City FL 33525

FERNBERG, SHIRLEY CARLOTTA WEISSMAN (MRS. LOUIS PROCTOR FERNBERG), cooking sch. adminstr.; b. Cleve., Feb. 15, 1922; d. Joseph and Kate (Randell) Weissman; B.S., Ohio State U., 1944; occupational therapy diploma Phila. Sch. Occupational Therapy, 1945; M.A., Case Western Res. U., 1968; postgrad. N.Y.U., 1972; certificate Le Cordon Bleu, Paris, France; diploma Culinary Inst. Am., 1968; m. Louis Proctor Fernberg, Jr., Feb. 29, 1948; children—Michael Joseph, Kurt Alan, Laurence Seth. Staff occupational therapist Kingsbridge VA Hosp., Bronx, N.Y., 1945-46; asst. chief, acting chief occupational therapy dept. Crile VA Hosp., Parma, O., 1946-48; supr. occupational therapy Vocational Guidance Rehab. Services, Cleve., 1965; instr. foods Cuyahoga Community Coll., Cleve., 1966-68; owner La Cuisinique Sch. Cookery, Cleve., 1968—; dir. Copco Sch. Creative Cooking, Copco, Inc., N.Y.C., 1968—. Occupational therapy cons. Belmore Manor Extended Care Facility, East Cleveland, O., 1971-72. Publicity chmn. Cub Scouts, Shaker Heights (O.) Boy Scouts Am., 1957-68, P.T.A., 1962-64; mem. benefit planning com. Shaker Lakes Regional Nature Center, 1970—. Mem. World Fedn. Occupational Therapists, Am. Fedn. Radio and TV Artists, Le Confrerie de la Chaine des Rotisseurs, Am., Cleve. Dist. (publicity chmn. 1961) occupational therapy assns., Phi Delta Gamma. Clubs: Garden Clubs Ohio (life mem. Cleve.); Four Seasons Garden (pres. Shaker Heights 1963-65). Author: (with others) The Party in the Park Cookbook. Home: 20696 S Woodland Rd Shaker Heights OH 44122

FERNSTROM, DOROTHY BOND (MRS. KARL DICKSON FERNSTROM), educator; b. Dedham, Mass., Sept. 2, 1919; d. William Holden and Delia Henrietta (Hansen) Bond; B.A., Adelphi U., 1953; M.A., U. Houston, 1964; m. Karl Dickson Fernstrom, Apr. 15, 1945 (dec.); children—John D., Henning II. Exec. dir. Campfire Girls, Cleve., 1955-58; tchr., high sch. counselor Houston Pub. Schs., 1958-66; high sch. counselor Prince George County Pub. Sch., 1966-67; dean women L.I. U., 1967-71; prof. psychology, coordinator vets. affairs Okaloosa-Walton Jr. Coll., Niceville, Fla., 1971—. Served to maj. USMC, 1943-51. Mem. Nat. Assn. Women Deans and Counselors, Am. Assn. U. Women (1st v.p. 1972—), Am. Assn. Jr. Colls., Women Marines Assn., Fla. Assn. Community Colls., Quota, So. Coll. Personnel Assn. Republican. Episcopalian. Club: Eglin Air Force Officers (Eglin AFB, Fla.). Home: 928 Bayshore Dr Niceville FL 32578 Office: Okaloosa-Walton Jr Coll Niceville FL 32578

FERRARA, RUTH RELORDAN (MRS. JOSEPH JAMES FERRARA), assn. exec.; b. Ducktown, Tenn., Nov. 8, 1924; d. Robert Harrison and Lillian (Fralix) Relordan; student pub. schs.; m. Joseph James Ferrara, Oct. 10, 1946; children—James Michael, John Richard. Machinist, Jacksonville (Fla.) Naval Air Sta., 1942-44; with Greyhound Bus Co., Jacksonville, 1944-45; head cashier womens apparel Mangels Ladies Wear, Jacksonville, 1945-46; owner, operator restaurant, Jacksonville, 1946-47, Copperhill, Tenn., 1946-48; bookkeeper Henley & Beckwith, Inc., Jacksonville, 1949-50; mem. purchasing dept. Am. Hardware Corp., New Britain, Conn., 1948-49; sec.-mgr. Greater Jacksonville Fair Assn., 1966-69, dir., 1959-69, exec. sec., 1965-69; pres. Fla. Fedn. Fairs and Livestock Shows, also dir. pub. relations; exec. sec. Fla. Fedn. Fairs, S.C. State Fair, Greenville, 1972—; exec. mgr. Upper S.C. State Fair. Mem. Fla. Agrl. and Livestock Fair Council. Mem. Fla. Council for Aged; mem. aging com. Community Planning Council. Bd. dirs. Jacksonville Fair, 1959-68; sec. Venetia Boys Club, 1958-62; bd. advisers Cathedral Towers. Mem. Gator Bowl Assn., Advt. Club Jacksonville. Democrat. Methodist. Mem. Order Eastern Star. Clubs: Jacksonville Garden (dir. 1960-68), Venetia Manor Garden Circle (pres. 1960-62). Home: 4242 Oristano Rd Jacksonville FL 32210 Office: PO Drawer 7425 Jacksonville FL 32210

FERRARI, MARY SELBY (MRS. FRANK EDWARD FERRARI), poet, educator; b. New Orleans, Aug. 9, 1928; d. Earle Holman and Eloise (Bandi) Selby; B.A., Coll. of New Rochelle, 1950; M.A., N.Y. U., 1969; postgrad. New Sch. for Social Research, 1964-66; m. Frank Edward Ferrari, Feb. 12, 1955; children—Paul, Mary Anne, John, James. Tchr. English, Acad. Mt. St. Ursula, Bronx, N.Y., 1970—. Recipient Dylan Thomas Meml. award for poetry New Sch. for Social Research, 1965. Author: (play) The Heavenly Drugstore, 1969; (poetry) The Flying Glove, 1973. Contbr. poems to anthologies including Another World, Equal Time, Choice, to mags. including Angel Hair, The World, New York Quar. Home: 288 Weaver St Larchmont NY 10538 Office: 330 Bedford Park Blvd Bronx NY 10458

FERRARO, LINDA LEWIS (MRS. DAVID ANTHONY FERRARO), journalist, broadcaster; b. Glendale, W.Va., July 1, 1949; d. Earl William and Laura (Slie) Lewis; B.S. in Journalism, W.Va. U., 1971; m. David Anthony Ferroro, Oct. 2, 1971. Editor, writer The Daily Antheneaum, Morgantown, W.Va., 1969-71; The Westmoreland Star, Murrysville, Pa., 1971-72; dir. news WFRA (AM) WWEN (FM) radio, Franklin, Pa., 1973—. Mem. Women in Communications (sec. 1970-71), Nat. Orgn. Women, League Voters, Sigma Delta Chi (v.p. 1970-71). Home: 939 Elk St Franklin PA 16323 Office: 411 Liberty St Franklin PA 16323

FERREE, MARIE JOSEPHINE, home economist; b. Gays, Ill., Dec. 12, 1922; d. Raymond Kelly and Honore (Casstevens) Ferree; B.S. in Edn., Eastern Ill. State Coll., 1944; M.S., Mich. State U., 1954. Tchr. home econs. secondary schs., Ill., 1944-48; food prodn. mgr. Stouffer Corp., N.Y., Mpls., 1948-51; food service dir. U. N.D., Grand Forks, 1951-53; food marketing information agt., specialist Mich. State U. Agrl. Extension, 1955-64, U. Cal. at Berkeley, 1964—. Mem. food com. Met. San Francisco Def. Bd., U.S. Dept. Agr., 1969—. Mem. Am., Cal. home econs. assns., Inst. Food Technologists (expert panel food safety and nutrition). Home: 1514 Oxford Berkeley CA 94709

FERREE, MARY MERICLE (MRS. H. LANE FERREE), physician; b. Indpls., June 1, 1938; d. Earl William and Ruth Margaret (Fink) Mericle; A.B., Ind. U., 1960, M.D., 1963; m. H. Lane Ferree, Jan. 13, 1968; children—Marjorie, Cathryn. Intern Methodist Hosp., Indpls., 1963-64; resident psychiatry Ind. U. Med. Center, Indpls., 1965-68; staff psychiatrist Hawaii Dept. Health, 1969; staff psychiatrist Kauikeoloani Children's Hosp., Honolulu, 1969-71, acting dir. child guidance clinic, 1970-71; asst. clin. prof. U. Hawaii Sch. Medicine, 1970-71; fellow child psychiatry L.D. Carter Meml. Hosp., Indpls., 1971-73, now staff psychiatrist, coordinator adolescent outpatient services, 1973—; asso. clin. prof. psychiatry Ind. U. Sch. Medicine, 1973—. Mem. Alpha Lambda Delta, Alpha Epsilon Delta, Kappa Alpha Theta. Home: 5450 Washington Blvd Indianapolis IN 46220 Office: Larue Carter Hospital 1315 W 10th St Indianapolis IN 46207

FERRELL, ERNESTINE LAVERA, educator; b. Houston, Miss.; d. Walter and WyNona (Lucus) Ferrell; student Blue Mountain (Miss.) Coll.; B.S., George Peabody Coll. for Tchrs., 1940, M.A., 1950; postgrad. Eastman Sch. Music, Rochester, N.Y., summer 1955. Tchr. math., pub. sch. music, piano, choral Pontotoc High Sch., 1933-40; tchr. piano, choral, pub. sch. music Marks (Miss.) High Sch., 1940-45; music supr. Vicksburg (Miss.) City Schs., 1946-56; choir dir. First Bapt. Ch., Vicksburg, 1945-56; supr. music edn. Miss. Dept. Edn., Jackson, 1956—. Prof. music dept. U. S.C., summer 1958; mem. Tanglewood Symposium Berkshire Music Center, 1967; elementary music clinician Massanetta Music Camp, Harrisburg, Va., U. So. Miss., So. Meth. U.; dir. opera chorus Jackson Opera Guild, 1960-63; clinician workshops for children's choirs in many chs. in South, Children's Chorus So. Bapt. Music Week, Ridgecrest, N.C., Ga. State Bapt. Music Clinic, also elementary music workshop Hardin-Simmons U. Mem. Charles F. Bryan Meml. adv. com. Tenn. Poly. Inst.; adv. panel arts edn. Miss. Arts Council. Bd. dirs. Vicksburg Concert Assn., Community Chorus and Opera Vicksburg. Mem. Miss. Assn. Supervision and Curriculum Devel., Miss. Opera Guild (dir.), Music Educators Nat. Conf. (past pres. So. div.), Nat. Council State Suprs. Music (past sec.), Miss Fedn. Music Clubs (dir., pres. 1973-75), Nat. Fedn. Music Clubs (chmn. dept. music service in community). Am. Guild Organists, Am. Choral Dirs. Assn., Jackson Music Assn., Blue Mountain Coll. Alumni Assn. (past v.p.), Am. Assn. U. Women, Mu Phi Epsilon, Delta Kappa Gamma, Tau Beta Sigma. Editor: Music for Mississippi Schools, 1967, Grades 1-6, 1972. Contbr. to Miss. Notes, Children's Music Leader. Home: 1616 Linden Pl Jackson MS 39202 Office: PO Box 771 Jackson MS 39205

FERRELL, GRAZIA BELL (MRS. HARRISON H. FERRELL), civic worker; b. Buffalo, Aug. 9; d. William Carl and Cora (Sprague) Bell; grad. Chgo. Normal Coll., 1926, W.Va. State Coll., 1941; m. Harrison H. Ferrell, Sept. 15, 1929. Jr. asst. librarian Englewood High Sch. Library, Chgo., 1927-28; tchr. Tennyson Elementary Sch., Chgo., 1928-29, West Dunbar Elementary Sch., 1960-63, 65-68, Inst. Model Sch., 1963-65. Site chmn. Girl Scouts U.S.A., Camp Greenhill, Institute, W.Va., 1947, 48, sec. Camp Clifftop Com., 1949-50; mem. pub. affairs com. YWCA, 1954-60, sec., 1956, dir., 1959-60, co-chmn. pub. affairs com. dir. Kanawha chpt. W.Va. Assn. for Mental Health, 1953-57, 58—, sec., 1954, v.p., 1954, 55, pres. 1956-59, chmn. legislative com., 1954, 55, state bd. dirs., 1955-57, 59-61, 69—, state chmn. pub. information com., 1955-56, chmn. state legislative com., 1955, state 3d v.p., 1969—, bd. dirs. Region 1, 1971—; chpt. del. ann. meeting Nat. Assn. Mental Health, 1956-59, del. dir., 1961-67; mem. women's com. Charleston Symphony Orch., 1969-71; mem. health and med. care div. Kanawha Welfare Council, Kanawha Juvenile Council; chmn. pub. edn. com., mem. steering com. Kanawha Valley Council on Human Relations; mem. W.Va. Gov.'s Interim Com. on Mental Health, 1958; mem. adv. com. Children's Mental Health Services, 1972—. Charter mem. bd. dirs. Charleston Guidance Clinic, 1958-71, sec., 1958-60, pres., 1962-63; mem. exec. com. community relations council Charleston Job Corps, 1969-70, sec., 1971—; Bd. dirs. Mental Health Center of Kanawha Region. Recipient Gold Key award Nat. Assn. for Mental Health, 1967. Mem. W.Va. Edn. Assn., Belles of St. Mary's, Marmet Hosp. Aux., W.Va. Assn. UN, League Women Voters, Am. Assn. U. Women, Alpha Kappa Alpha (life, chpt. pres. 1945, 46, sec. 1956-60, 71—, v.p. 1965-71). Baptist. Dunbar Lioness (1st v.p. 1971-72, pres. 1972-73). Home: 7 Park Av Charleston WV 25302

FERRELL, RUTH MORRIS (MRS. FRANK M. FERRELL), lawyer; b. Portsmouth, Va., Apr. 29, 1928; d. Francis Hubert and Ruth (Whitehead) Morris; B.A., Agnes Scott Coll., 1949; M.A., Emory U., 1952; J.D., U. Pa., 1960; m. Frank M. Ferrell, Apr. 7, 1958. Admitted to Del. bar, 1960, U.S. Supreme Ct. bar; practiced in Wilmington, Del., 1960—; law clk. judges Del. State Cts., 1961-62; dep. atty. gen. Del., 1963-70; head civil div. Del. Atty. Gen's Office, 1967-70; asst. regional atty. Phila. Regional Litigation Center U.S. Equal Employment Opportunity Commn., 1973. Mem. Gov.'s Commn. on Status Women, 1963-68; mem. European adv. council U.S. Dept. State, 1971-72. Pres., Women's Republican Club Wilmington, 1965-67. Trustee Women's Law Fund, Inc.; nat. trustee John Marshall House. Recipient award for outstanding pub. service Rep. Nat. Com. N.E. Regional Women's Conf., 1967. Mem. Am. (chmn. budget and finance com., mem. council local govt. sect.), Del. bar assns., Am. Assn. U. Women, Christina Bus. and Profl. Womens Club (pres.), Mortar Bd., Phi Beta Kappa. Presbyn. Address: 17 Cragmere Rd Wilmington DE 19809

FERRELL, SIBYLE CRIGGER (MRS. ALVIN WARD FERRELL), ednl. adminstr.; b. Speedwell, Va., Aug. 14, 1920; d. Stephen Lonnie and Mary Emma (Spencer) Crigger; B.S., Radford (Va.) Coll., 1942, M.S., 1966; postgrad. U. Va., 1958-70, Va. Poly. Inst. and State U., 1956—; m. Alvin Ward Ferrell, May 12, 1942; children—Janet (Mrs. Harry Beckwith Whitt), Diane (Mrs. Frank Wesley Haden), Linda (Mrs. Kenneth Wayne Edwards). Tchr., supr. Belle Heth Elementary sch., Radford, 1954-59; tchr. Radford High Sch., 1959-64; tchr., supr. McHarg Elementary Sch., Radford, 1964-67; supr. counseling students New River Community Coll., Dublin, Va., 1967—. Mem. com. on testing Va. Community Coll. System, 1967—, Va. Commn. Coll. Admissions and Records, 1969—. Chmn. Cancer, Polio and Heart Drives, 1950-60; pres. P.T.A., 1953; v.p. Blue Ridge council Girl Scouts, 1952-62; sec. Citizens Com. for New Schs., Community Services Com., Radford, 1954—. Mem. Va. Edn. Assn. (com. on local asso. and urban affairs 1968—), Assn. Am. Univ. Women. (chmn. 1957—), Coll. Alumnae, Delta Kappa Gamma, Phi Delta Kappa. Methodist. (altar com. 1973-74). Club: Fairlawn Jr. Woman's (pres. 1952—). Author: Teaching Modern Mathematics-The Discovery Method, 1964. Home: 1201 Downey Radford VA 24141 Office: Box 1127 Dublin VA 24084

FERRER, MARIE IRENE, physician; b. Elberon, N.Y., July 30, 1915; d. Jose Maria and Irene (O'Donohue) F.; B.A., Bryn Mawr Coll., 1937; M.D., Columbia, 1941; 1 adopted dau., Marianne (Mrs. Legato Killian). Intern, Bellevue Hosp., N.Y.C., 1941-43, resident, 1943-44; prof. clin. med. Coll. Phys. and Surgeons Columbia, 1967—; dir. electrocardio-graphic labs. Columbia-Presbyn. Med. Center, 1956—, Doctors Hosp., 1953—. Bd. dirs. N.Y. Heart Assn. Recipient Salute to Women award Republican Women in Industry and Professions, 1966. Mem. Am. Heart Assn. (council on circulation 1967—), N.Y. Acad. Med., Am. Soc. Clin. Investigation, Am. Fed. Clin. Research (emeritus). Club: Cosmopolitan (N.Y.C.). Cardiopulmonary research with Dr. A. Cournand and Dr. D.W. Richards (Nobel prize winners 1956). Home: 200 E 66th St New York City NY 10021

FERRER, SANDRA ANN, stockbrokerage economist; b. N.Y.C., Oct. 3, 1946; d. Roger C. and Doris (Krehnbrink) Van Schoyck; A.A. cum laude, Marymount Coll., 1966; B.A. cum laude, Newton Coll., 1968; postgrad. N.Y. U. Sch. Bus., 1969—; m. Christopher C. Ferrer, May 22, 1971. Analysis individual securities, quality analysis, pricing analysis, growth analysis, economist, analytical statistician firm Fourteen Research Corp., N.Y.C., 1968—. Mem. Nat. Assn. Bus. Economists, N.Y. Soc. Security Analysts (computer applications com.). Home: 33 East End Av New York City NY 10028 Office: 200 E 42d St New York City NY 10017

FERRIER, MARSHA EDDINS (MRS. ROBERT LEON FERRIER, JR.), charitable orgn. exec.; b. Washington, July 29, 1943; d. Henry Adair and Claire Rosamond (Gaskell) Eddins; B.B.A., U. Okla., 1966, J.D., 1970; m. Robert Leon Ferrier, Jr., Oct. 2, 1968. Editorial asst. pub. relations dept. Kerr-McGee Corp., Oklahoma City, 1966-68; free-lance pub. relations in polit. field, 1968-72; spl. asst. to dir. Sch. Indsl. Engring., U. Okla., 1972; exec. dir. United Way of Norman (Okla.), Inc., 1972—. Pres., Interfaith Council of Norman, 1972-74; treas. Assistance League of Norman, Inc., 1971-72, pub. relations chmn., 1973-75; Chmn. pub. relations com. Okla. Republican Com., 1970, editor Okla. Rep. News, 1970-71. Bd. dirs. Norman Homemaker Service. Mem. Women in Communications, Delta Zeta. Mem. Christian Ch. Home: 2557 Cypress St Norman OK 73069 Office: 111 N Peters St Room 201 PO Box 565 Norman OK 73069

FERRIER, SISTER MARY JEANNE, hosp. adminstr.; b. N.Y.C.; d. Henry P. and Loretta M. (Devine) Ferrier; B.S., Fordham U., 1950, M.S., 1956. Tchr. elementary schs., N.Y.C., 1938-45; elementary sch. prin., N.Y.C., 1945-53; pres. Mercy Coll., Dobbs Ferry, N.Y., 1954-59; exec. adminstr. Province of N.Y., 1953-59; chmn. bd. dirs. Mercy Hosp., Watertown, N.Y., Mercy Gen. Hosp., Tupper Lake, N.Y., Sanatorium Gabriels (N.Y.); asst. to chief exec. officer, Bethesda, Md., 1959-65; dir. Sisters of Mercy of Union, Bethesda, Md., 1959-65; dir. personnel, purchasing officer St. Michael's Child Care Home, S.I., N.Y., 1966—; adminstr. St. Francis Hosp., Port Jervis, N.Y., 1966—, pres. bd. trustees, 1966—. Mem. Regional Med. Planning Com., Orange County, N.Y., 1967—; bd. dirs. Orange County Heart Assn., A.R.C. Bd. dirs. Benedictine Hosp., Kingston, N.Y.; trustee United Fund, Port Jervis, N.Y. Mem. Am., Cath. hosp. assns., Hosp. Assn. N.Y. State, Southeastern Hosp. Assn. N.Y. State (pres. 1970—), Am. Acad. Med. Adminstrs. Address: 160 E Main St Port Jervis NY 12771

FERRIS, ELIZABETH ANNE, ednl. adminstr.; b. N.Y.C.; d. Arthur Nelson and Anne (Cooper) Ferris; B.A., Carleton Coll., 1949; M.A., Wayne State U., 1961; grad. student Columbia, 1952. Occupational therapist U.S. Mil. Hosps., 1952-55, Eastern Psychiat. Inst., Phila., 1957-59; founder, dir. ednl. rehab. services Wayne State U., Detroit, 1961—. Pres. regional bd. North Woodward Inter-Faith Center for Racial Justice, Royal Oak, Mich., 1970-71; mem. Royal Oak Human Relations Council, 1966-71; mem. exec. bd. Mich. Wheelchair Athletic Com., 1970—; sec. Arlington Park Property Owner's Assn., Royal Oak, 1966-67; mem. Detroit Archtl. Barriers Com., 1966—, sec., 1967-68; mem. Oakland County Archtl. Barriers Com., 1971—; mem. med. adv. council Mich. Soc. Crippled Children and Adults, 1969—; mem. Southeast Citizens' Dist. Council, 1972-74; chmn. Mich. Com. on Fire and Safety for Handicapped, 1973—; mem. com. on barrier free design Mich. Constrn. Code Commn., 1973—; mem. Mich. archtl. accessibility adv. com. Dept. Edn., 1972—; mem. Mich. Legislative Action Coalition for Handicapped, 1972—, Council Agys.

Serving the Blind, 1972—. Bd. dirs. Farm Home, Inc., Nat. Assn. Physically Handicapped. Mem. Nat., Mich. rehab. assns., Nat. Rehab. Counseling Assn., Nat. Wheelchair Athletic Assn. Home: 1300 Lafayette E Detroit MI 48207

FERRIS, VIRGINIA ROGERS, nematologist, educator; b. Abilene, Kan.; d. Ames P. and Virginia (Lucas) Rogers; student U. Kan., 1945-46; B.A., (Durant scholar), Wellesley Coll., 1949; M.S., Cornell U., 1952, Ph.D. (NSF fellow, Horton-Hallowell fellow), 1954; m. John M. Ferris, June 20, 1953; children—Jeffrey Ames, Susan Virginia. Teaching asst. plant pathology Cornell U., 1949-52, asst. prof. (1st woman prof. in dept.), 1954-55; cons. nematology, West Lafayette, Ind., 1956-65, asst. prof. nematology, entomology Purdue U., 1965-70, asso. prof., 1970-74, prof., 1974—, asst. dean Grad. Sch., 1971—. Recipient H.B. Schleman Gold medallion outstanding woman faculty mem., 1973. Mem. Am. Phytopath. Soc., Helminthological Soc. Washington, Am. Inst. Biol. Scis., Entomol. Soc. Am., Soc. Nematologists (sec. 1965-68, v.p. 1968-69, pres. 1969-70), European Soc. Nematologists, Phi Beta Kappa, Sigma Xi, Mortar Bd. (hon.), Phi Kappa Pi, Kappa Kappa Gamma, Sigma Delta Epsilon, Gamma Sigma Delta (hon.). Asso. editor Nematology News Letter, 1963-66, Jour. Nematology, 1974—. Contbr. articles to sci. jours. Home: 2237 Delaware Dr West Lafayette IN 47906

FERRITER, CLARE (MRS. JOHN T. HACK), artist; b. Dickinson, N.D., June 18, 1913; d. John P. and Katherine (McNertny) Ferriter; student Mass. Coll. Art, 1930; B.F.A., Yale, 1935; M.A., Stanford, 1936; m. John T. Hack, Jan. 23, 1942; children—Katherine Ferriter, John Tilton. Tchr., Coll. De Santa Rosa, Manila, Philippines, 1931-33, MacMurray Coll., Jacksonville, Ill., 1936-38, Westover Sch., Middlebury, Conn., 1940-42; asst. prof. art Cath. U., summer 1966-68, asso. prof. art, summers 1969-74; exhibited one-man shows including Mus. U. P.R., 1962, Corcoran Gallery Art, Washington, 1963, Franz Bader Gallery, Washington, 1964, Bridge Gallery, N.Y.C., 1964, Massillon (O.) Mus., 1966, Cath. U., Washington, 1966, IMF, Washington, 1973; represented in permanent collections including Harvard, Westover Sch., Middlebury, Conn., Cosmos Club, Washington, D.C. Ct. Gen. Sessions, Massillon Mus., George Washington U., U. Del., Newark, Addison Gallery Am. Art, Andover. Recipient awards Balt. Mus. Art, 1966, others. Mem. Washington Watercolor Assn., Soc. Washington Artists (awards 1964, 66, 72), Nat. Assn. Women Artists (awards 1963, 66), Artists Equity Assn. (pres. Washington chpt. 1967-69). Address: 4722 Rodman St NW Washington DC 20016

FERRON, LOIS BERNIECE, govt. ofcl.; b. Julesburg, Colo., Aug. 13, 1924; d. Charles Guy and Inez (Hardee) Sumner; grad. Barnes Sch. Commerce, Denver, 1943; widow; children—Francis R., Diane (Mrs. Dale B. Hays). With Agrl. Stblzn. and Conservation Service, Dept. Agr., 1956—, exec. dir. Custer County (Colo.), 1971—; 4-H leader, 1952—. Sec. Custer County C. of C., 1963—. Clk., Town of Silver Cliff (Colo.), 1953—; vice chmn. Custer County Republican Com., 1954. Mem. Fremont-Custer Hist. Soc., Silver Cliff Community Club. Methodist. Mem. Order Eastern Star (past worthy matron). Clubs: Custer County Women's (pres. 1967); Knife and Fork. Home: 631 Ohio St Silver Cliff CO 81249 Office: 102 S 2d St Westcliffe CO 81252

FERTIG, ILONKA WEST (MRS. EDWARD JOHN FERTIG), mus. dir.; b. Leonia, N.J., Dec. 28, 1903; d. Frederick William and Ilona (Rado) West; student N.Y. Sch. Fine and Applied Art, 1921; m. Edward John Fertig, Oct. 31, 1928. Archtl. tracer Blum & Blum, 1920; office mgr. Muriel Draper, Interior Decorator, 1921-27; sec. Condé Nast, Vanity Fair, Paris, 1927; with Tate & Hall, Decorators, 1928-31; dir. Old Bristol Mus., Pemaquid, Me., 1968—. Chmn. nutrition Civil Def. World War II, Leonia, 1941-42; staff asst. A.R.C., Englewood, N.J., 1941-43. Bd. dirs. Lincoln County Red Cross, 1948-50. Recipient Deborah Morton award Westbrook Jr. Coll., 1970. Mem. Lincoln County Cultural and Hist. Assn. (mem. bd. 1956-70), Pemaquid Hist. Assn. (pres. 1965—). Clubs: Newcastle-Damariscotta (Me.) Woman's (pres. 1948-50), Old Bristol Garden (pres. Damariscotta 1952-53, 58-59). Home: Gentle Cove Pemaquid ME 04558 Office: Harrington Meeting House Pemaquid ME 04558

FERTMAN, JOAN CAROLE (MRS. DONALD A. WOLFF), speech and lang. pathologist; b. N.Y.C., Apr. 3, 1939; d. Carl and Beatrice (Kaufman) Hartman; B.A., U. City N.Y., 1960; M.A., Columbia, 1961; Ph.D., U. So. Cal., 1971; m. Donald A. Wolff, May 22, 1973; 1 son, Kenneth. Adminstr. speech and lang. program pub. schs., Canton, Mass., 1961-65; dir. Community Speech, Lang. and Hearing Services, San Francisco, 1971—; mem. med. staff Mt. Zion Hosp., San Francisco, St. Luke's Hosp., San Francisco; speech and lang. cons. The Child Center, Kentfield, Cal., 1971—, French Hosp., San Francisco, 1971—; mem. faculty Cal. State U. at Hayward, 1973-74. Mem. Am., Cal. hearing and speech assns., Internat. Reading Assn., Am. Psychol. Assn., Council for Exceptional Children, Sigma Alpha Eta. Home: 314 Locust St San Francisco CA 94118 Office: 4141 Geary Blvd San Francisco CA 94118

FESHBACH, NORMA DEITCH (MRS. SEYMOUR FESHBACH), educator; b. N.Y.C., Sept. 5, 1926; d. Samuel and Lena R. (Katz) Deitch; B.S. cum laude, Coll. City N.Y., 1947, certificate clin. psychology, 1949, M.S., 1949; Ph.D. (USPHS fellow), U. Pa., 1956; m. Seymour Feshbach, Aug. 16, 1947; children—Jonathan Stephan, Laura Elizabeth, Andrew David. Asso. research psychologist U. Cal. at Los Angeles, 1964-65, clin. psychologist Neuropsychiat. Inst., 1965, prof. ednl. psychology, 1965—, head. program early childhood devel., 1970—. Editorial cons. Rev. Ednl. Research, Jour. Social Issues, 1970—; ad hoc cons. Merrill Palmer Quar., 1970-72, Nat. Inst. Mental Health Study Panel, 1971-72. Mem. parent adv. council Kenter Canyon Elementary Sch., Los Angeles, 1970-71; faculty adviser Teen Parent and Child Devel., 1970—. Mem. Am. Assn. U. Profs., Am., Cal. edn. research assns., Am., Western, Cal. psychol. assns., Nat. Assn. Edn. Young Children, Soc. Psychol. Study Social Issues, Soc. for Research in Child Devel., Author: (with J. Goodlad and A. Lombard) Early Schooling in England and Israel, 1973. Contbr. articles to profl. pubs. Home: 743 Hanley Av Los Angeles CA 90049

FESLER, ELMA FAYE (MRS. CHAUNCEY FESLER), librarian, educator; b. Eugene, Ore., Oct. 5, 1913; d. John W. and Geneva M. (McCallister) Davis; B.S., Marycrest Coll., 1964; M.S. in L.S., U. Ill., 1969; postgrad. Okla. State U., 1970, Brigham Young U., U. Utah, 1973; m. Chauncey Fesler, May 26, 1936; children—Michael Allen, Gerald Eugene, Judith Marie (Mrs. Thomas Knox). Tchr., rural and consol. schs., Ill., 1933-40, 45-64; mem. faculty in L.S., U. Western Ill., Macomb, 1969—. Cons., Ill. Sch. Evaluation for State Recognition, 1972-73, regional library programs, 1969—. Mem. Am., Ill. Sch. Librarians' assns., A.L.A., Internat. Sch. Librarians Assn.; Ill. Library Assn. (trustee 1955), Nat., Ill. Edn. assns., Am. Assn. U. Profs., Ill. Assn. Tchrs. Eng., Alpha Beta Mu, Delta Kappa Gamma. Home: 133 Holden Dr Macomb IL 61455

FESS, MARILYNN ELAINE (MRS. STEPHEN W. FESS), occupational therapist; b. Casper, Wyo., June 20, 1944; d. Frederick Eugene and Norma Pence (Jarrett) Ewing; B.S., Ind. U., 1967; m. Stephen W. Fess, Nov. 26, 1966. Staff occupational therapist Marion County Gen. Hosp., Indpls., 1966-70; supr. phys. dysfunction unit, 1970-72; supr. adult occupational therapy Ind. U. Med. Center, Indpls., 1972-74, instr. occupational therapy curriculum, 1974—. Cons. to hand surgeons to various hosps. and nursing homes. Mem. exec. bd. Ind. Cerebral Vascular Accident Com., 1973-74. Mem. Ind. Occupational Therapy Assn. (v.p. 1972-73, pres. 1974-76). Home: 2130 Stoneham Dr Indianapolis IN 46260 Office: Occupational Therapy Curriculum 1232 W Michigan St Indianapolis IN 46202

FETHEROLF, MIRIAM MARKHAM (MRS. RICHMOND D. FETHEROLF), newspaper editor; b. Baldwin, Kan., Sept. 28, 1901; d. William Colfax and Carrie (Hoover) Markham; music supr. certificate Baker U., 1922; A.B., Bucknell U., 1923; m. Richmond D. Fetherolf, June 24, 1927 (dec. Oct. 1954); 1 son, Donald Markham. Supr. music Mt. Holly (N.J.) Pub. Schs., 1923-31; food editor Van Nuys (Cal.) News, 1954—, Los Angeles Suburban Newspapers, 1957-65. Vice pres. Van Nuys, Pub. Co., 1956-58, treas., 1958—. Chmn. mothers group Home and Sch., 1945-46, 49-50, chmn. of chairmen, 1947-48. Bd. dirs. A.R.C., Swarthmore, 1950-52. Mem. Cal. Press Women (2d pl. award 1967), Nat. Fedn. Press Women (affiliate), P.E.O., Delta Delta Delta (pres. West Phila. 1947-50). Republican. Presbyn. Club: Old Treasures (pres. 1965-67) (Van Nuys). Home: 17225 Gault St Van Nuys CA 91406 Office: 14539 Sylvan St Van Nuys CA 91401

FETRIDGE, BONNIE JEAN CLARK (MRS. WILLIAM HARRISON FETRIDGE), civic worker; b. Chgo., Feb. 3, 1915; d. Sheldon and Bonnie (Carrington) Clark; student Masters Sch., Dobbs Ferry, N.Y., Finch Coll., N.Y.C.; m. William Harrison Fetridge, June 27, 1941; children—Blakely (Mrs. Harvey H. Bundy III), Clark Worthington. Bd. dirs. region VII, Girl Scouts U.S.A., 1939-43, sec., 1936-38, dir., Chgo., 1936-51, 59-69, v.p. 1946-49, 61-65, chmn. Juliette Low world friendship com., 1959-67, 71-72, mem. nat. program com., 1967-70, mem. Nat. Juliette Low Birthplace Com., 1967-69, mem. nat. adv. bd., 1972—, mem. Internat. Commrs. Adv. Panel, 1973—; mem. women's bd. Chgo. Area council Boy Scouts Am., 1964-69, mem. nat. exploring com., 1973—; mem. Our Cabana Friends com. World Assn. Girl Guides and Girl Scouts, 1969—. Bd. dirs. Jr. League Chgo., 1937-40, Vis. Nurse Assn. Chgo., 1951-58, 61-66, also asst. treas.; women's bd. dirs. Children's Meml. Hosp., 1946-50; bd. dirs., v.p. Latin Sch. Chgo. Alumni Assn., v.p. parents sch. council, 1952-54; mem. women's bd. U.S.O., 1965—, treas., 1969-70, v.p., 1970-74; staff aide A.R.C. Motor Corps, World War II. Mem. Nat. Soc. Colonial Dames Am. (Ill. bd. mgrs. 1962-65, 69—, v.p. 1970-72, state chmn. geneal. information services com. 1972—), Chgo. Dobbs Alumnae Assn. (past pres.), Nat. Soc. D.A.R., English Speaking Union, N.Y. Geneal. and Biog. Soc., New Eng. Historic Geneal. Soc., Conn. Soc. Genealogists, Chgo. Geneal. Soc., Newberry Library Assos., Crerar Library Assos., Antiquarian Soc., Guild Chgo. Hist. Soc., Augustan Soc. Episcopalian. Clubs: Casino, Saddle and Cycle, Woman's Athletic. Home: 2430 Lakeview Av Chicago IL 60614

FEUER, MRS. PAULA, physicist, educator; b. N.Y.C., Feb. 11, 1922; d. Morris and Lottie (Greenwald) Berger; B.A., Hunter Coll., 1941; M.S., Purdue U., 1946, Ph.D., 1951; m. Henry Feuer, Jan. 19, 1946. Instr. physics Purdue U., 1946-55, asst. prof. engrng. scis., 1955-57, asso. prof., 1957-65, prof. aeros., astronautics and engrng., 1965—; vis. prof. physics at Hebrew U., Jerusalem, 1964. Mem. Soc. Engrng. Sci. (founding dir.; treas. 1964-69, Am. Phys. Soc., Am. Assn. U. Profs., Sigma Xi, Pi Mu Epsilon, Sigma Pi Sigma. Club: Canadian Alpine. Author articles sci. jours. Home: 726 Princess Dr West Lafayette IN 47906

FICCO, SISTER MARY DOROTHY, coll. librarian; b. Bklyn., July 10, 1915; d. Alfred Vincent and Carmela A. (DeToro) Ficco; B.S., Fordham U., 1950, M.S., 1955; M.L.S., St. John's U., 1960. Elementary sch. tchr. Archdiocese of N.Y., 1936-60; with Harriman (N.Y.) Coll., 1956—, head librarian, 1960—. Mem. Am., Cath., N.Y. library assns., Nat. Soc. for Study Edn. Address: Harriman Coll Harriman NY 10926

FICELMAN, JUDITH ANNE WEINIG (MRS. MARK L. FICELMAN), bank exec.; b. N.Y.C., Mar. 9, 1946; d. Alexander and Hilda (Friedman) Weinig; B.A., Pa. State U., 1968, postgrad., 1968; m. Mark L. Ficelman, Aug. 11, 1968; 1 son, Robert W. Personnel interviewer Chase Manhattan Bank, N.Y.C., 1968-70, personnel adminstr., 1970—. Vol. worker North Shore Hosp., Manhasset, N.Y., 1960-64. Mem. Alpha Epsilon Phi (v.p.). Home: 5 Road on the Hill Great Neck NY 11023 Office: 1 New York Plaza New York City NY 10015

FICHANDLER, ZELDA DIAMOND (MRS. THOMAS C. FICHANDLER), theatre dir.; b. Boston; d. Harry and Ida (Epstein) Diamond; B.A., Cornell U., 1945; M.A., George Washington U., 1950; L.H.D., Hood Coll., 1962; m. Thomas C. Fichandler, Feb. 17, 1946; children—Hal, Mark. Co-founder Arena Stage, Washington, 1950, producing dir., 1950—, dedicated new Kreeger Theater, 1970, dir. The Devils and Enrico IV, 1963-64, The Skin of Our Teeth, 1965-66, The Three Sisters, 1965-66, The Playboy of the Western World, The Inspector General, Twelfth Night, The Importance of Being Earnest, A Phoenix Too Frequent, Golden Boy, The World of Sholom Aleichem, Witness for the Prosecution, The Browning Version, Romeo and Juliet, The Lady's Not for Burning, Six Characters in Search of an Author, Twelve Angry Men; produced numerous premiers including The Great White Hope, Pueblo, Edith Stein, The Ruling Class, others; v.p., mem. exec. com. Theatre Communications Group. Profl. lectr. dramatic art George Washington U., vis. prof. U. Tex., Austin; Univ. prof., prof. theater arts Boston U. Ford Found. Theatre Dirs. grantee, 1959. Recipient Alumni Achievement award George Washington U., 1970; Ann. award for distinguished service to theater Nat. Theater Conf., 1971; Margo Jones award, 1971. Home: 3120 Newark St NW Washington DC 20008 Office: Arena Stage 6th and M Sts SW Washington DC 20024

FICHTNER, RAE ANN KAUFMAN (MRS. JAY S. FICHTNER), lawyer; b. San Antonio, Mar. 31, 1930; d. Sam and Nona (Kirk) Kaufman; B.A., Tex. Woman's U., 1950; J.D., George Washington U., 1952; LL.M., So. Meth. U., 1972; m. Jay S. Fichtner, Aug. 2, 1954; children—Mark, Kirk. Admitted to D.C. bar, 1952, Tex. bar, 1954, also U.S. Supreme Ct. bar; individual practice, Dallas, 1952-69; mem. firm Blakeley, Blakeley, Hall and Fults, 1952-56, Blakely and Blakeley, 1956-69; asst. city atty. City of Dallas, 1973; legal adviser Dallas Police Dept., 1973—. Instr., Tex. Woman's U., 1964, So. Meth. U. Sch. Law, Dallas, 1971-72, Dallas Police Acad., 1973-74, U. Tex. at Dallas, 1974—. Bd. dirs. Dallas Legal Services, Dallas Council Alcoholism; mem. exec. bd. George Washington U. Sch. Law; dir. bd. expansion Tex. Woman's U. Mem. Internat. Assn. Chiefs of Police, Am. Judicature Soc., Am., Tex. bar assns., Tex. Assn. Police Advisors, Womens Equity Action League, Kappa Beta Pi. Home: 5509 Tanbark St Dallas TX 75229 Office: Legal Liaison Dept Dallas Police Dept City Hall Dallas TX 75201

FIDLER, GAIL SPANGLER (MRS. JAY WAGNER FIDLER), occupational therapist; b. Spencer, Ia., Sept. 28, 1916; d. Warren Whittier and Alma Gail (Bumbaugh) Spangler; B.A., Lebanon Valley Coll., 1938; certificate occupational therapy U. Pa., 1942; m. Jay Wagner Fidler, Apr. 29, 1944; children—Dagny Ann, Eric Jay. Dir. profl. edn., dept. occupational therapy N.Y. State Psychiat. Inst., N.Y.C., 1959-66; asso. in rehab. medicine Coll. Physicians and Surgeons, Columbia, N.Y.C., 1959—; instr. dept. edn. N.Y. U., 1962-68, Boston U., Sargent Coll., 1971—; dir. activities therapy dept. Hillside Hosp., Glen Oaks, N.Y., 1968-71; asso. exec. dir., dir. div. practice, edn. and research Am. Occupational Therapy Assn., Rockville, Md., 1972—. Speaker, cons. to various univs. and hosps. Mem. N.J. Rehab. Com., 1954-62; mem. profl. adv. com. Union County unit N.J. Mental Health Assn., 1954-62; chmn. Parent and Tchr. Edn., Plainfield, N.J., 1957-60. Bd. dirs. Am. Occupational Therapy Found., 1969-72. Fellow Am. Occupational Therapy Assn. (mem. exec. bd. 1958-63, 68-71); mem. World Fedn. Occupational Therapists, Assn. Schs. Allied Health, Am. Pub. Health Assn., Common Cause, Center for Dem. Instns. Author: Occupational Therapy: A Communication Process in Psychiatry, 1964; Introduction to Psychiatric Occupational Therapy, 1954. Editorial bd. Am. Jour. Occupational Therapy, 1966-71. Contbr. articles in field to profl. jours. Home: 732 W 8th St Plainfield NJ 07060 Office: 6000 Executive Blvd Rockville MD 20852

FIEBER, NANCY MARY (MRS. WARREN W. FIEBER), phys. therapist; b. Madison, Wis., Aug. 18, 1929; d. Oscar John and Irene Dorothy (McBain) Hoffland; B.S. in Phys. Medicine U. Wis., 1952; M.A., U. Neb., 1973; m. Warren W. Fieber, Oct. 30, 1954; children—Mary C., Catherine Ann, Susan Elizabeth. Instr., Wis. Easter Seal Cerebral Palsy Center, Madison, 1954-55; staff therapist N.C. Baptist Hosp., Winston-Salem, 1955-56; phys. therapist Lancaster, Wis., also Fond du Lac, Wis., 1957-62; phys. therapist Irving Orthopedic Sch., West Allis, Wis., 1962-64; sr. phys. therapist Meyer Children's Rehab. Inst., Omaha, 1964—. Asst. prof. phys. therapy Coll. Medicine, U. Neb., Omaha, 1974—; cons. Mountain-Plains Regional Deaf Blind Program, 1972—. Mem. Am. Phys. Therapy Assn., Am. Assn. on Mental Deficiency, Council for Exceptional Children, Internat. Bobath Assn., Am. Assn. Univ. Women, League Women Voters, Phi Kappa Phi, Chi Omega. Mem. United Ch. of Christ. Contbr. articles on phys. therapy to profl. publs. Home: 713 S 84th St Omaha NE 68114 Office: 444 S 44th St Omaha NE 68114

FIEDLER, JEAN FELDMAN (MRS. HAROLD FIEDLER), author; b. Pitts.; d. Harry and Diana (Diness) Feldman; B.A., U. Pitts., 1945; postgrad. U. Pitts., Banks St. Coll. Edn., New Sch., N.Y.U.; m. Harold Fiedler, July 5, 1949; children—Judith Laurel, Joan Barbara. Social worker Children's Aid Soc., Pitts., 1945; tchr. high sch. English, Pitts. Schs., 1946-48; copywriter Gimbels Dept. Store, Pitts., 1948; librarian Bklyn. Pub. Library, N.Y., 1949-50; free-lance writer, N.Y., 1950—; substitute tchr. high sch. English, N.Y.C., 1961—; tchr. creative writing Dept. Adult Edn., Bayside High, N.Y., 1963—. Mem. Nat. Women's Book Assn., Authors' Guild of Authors League of Am., Xylon. Author: The Green Thumb Story, 1952; Big Brother Danny, 1953; Teddy and the Ice Cream Man, 1957; The Last Year, 1962; A Yardstick for Jessica, 1964; Jill's Story, 1965; My Special House, 1966; My Special Day, 1967; New Brother, New Sister, 1966; Great American Heroes, 1966; Call Me Juanita, 1968; In Any Spring, 1969; I Know What A Farm Is, 1969; A Break in the Circle, 1971. Author film strip series: Reading Perception, And Then What Happened. Contbr. to mags. Home: 69-23 Bell Blvd Bayside NY 11364

FIELD, CHARLOTTE, assn. exec.; b. Seattle, June 9, 1915; d. Charles Henry and Evelyn Maude (Westcott) Field; B.A., U. Wash., 1936. Fashion coordinator Bon Marche Dept. Store, Seattle, 1940-41, display coordinator, 1941-44, asst. merchandising mgr., 1944-45, asst. rep., N.Y.C., 1945-46; asst. dir. publicity Lord & Taylor Dept. Store, N.Y.C., 1946-47; merchandising coordinator, design cons., asst. to pres. Gump's Dept. Store, San Francisco, 1949-50; account exec. Abbott Kimball Agy., San Francisco, 1951-54; dir. nat. food publicity Wash. State Apple Commn., Seattle, 1957—. Mem. Fashion Group, Advt. and Sales Club, Am. Women in Radio and TV (pres. Evergreen chpt. 1966-67), Nat. Edn. Found. (rep. Am. Women in Radio and TV 1967-68), Nat. Fedn. Press Women. Club: Wash. Athletic. Home: 348 W Olympic Pl Seattle WA 98119 Office: 511 Second West Seattle WA 98119

FIELD, ELIZABETH ASHLOCK (MRS. HENRY LAMAR FIELD), govt. ofcl.; b. Little Rock, Nov. 27, 1915; d. Jesse Vernon and Felecia Irene (Bruner) Ashlock; grad. Little Rock Jr. Coll., 1934; student Washington U., St. Louis, 1934-35, U. Ark., 1962-63; m. Henry Lamar Field, Sept. 8, 1938; children—Elizabeth (Mrs. John Randolph Wassell, Jr.). Dir. historic house mus. Angelo Marre House, 1965-71; dir. Ark. Commemorative Commn., Little Rock, 1972—. Mem. Am. Assn. Museums, Nat. Trust for Historic Preservation, Fine Arts Club Ark., Mus. Sci. and Natural History Little Rock, Am. Clan Gregor Soc., Quapaw Quarter Assn. (pres. 1972-74). Episcopalian. Club: Pleasant Valley Country (Little Rock). Office: 300 W Markham St Little Rock AR 72201

FIELD, F(RANCES) BERNICE, ret. librarian; b. Mankato, Minn., Mar. 7, 1906; d. Merton and Carrie Eva (Tambling) Field; student Am. U., 1925-26; B.A., Carleton Coll., 1927; B.S. in L.S., U. Ill., 1930; M.A. L.S., U. Mich., 1944. Asst. librarian, cataloger Am. U., 1927-30; cataloger Queens Borough Pub. Library, Jamaica, N.Y., 1930-31; asst. cataloger Vassar Coll. Library, 1939-44; serial cataloger Yale Library, New Haven, 1931-39, sr. cataloger, 1944-47, asst. head cataloger in charge serial dept., 1947-52, asst. head catalog dept., 1952-55, head dept., 1955-63, asst. librarian cataloging and classification, 1963-65, asso. librarian tech. services, 1965-74. Recipient Distinguished Alumnus award U. Mich. Sch. Library Sci., 1971; N.Y. Tech. Services Librarians ann. citation, 1974. Mem. A.L.A. (chmn. serials round table 1952-54, pres. resources and tech. services div. 1958-59, chmn. descriptive cataloging com. 1960-66, editorial com. 1963-66; rep. joint com. on union list serials 1957-66; Margaret Mann citation 1966), N.Y. Tech. Services Librarians (pres. 1953-54), Conn. Library Assn., Phi Beta Kappa. Home: 216 Bishop St New Haven CT 06511

FIELD, JOYCE WOLF (MRS. LESLIE A. FIELD), educator; b. Bronx, N.Y., Oct. 1, 1932; d. Abraham and Bella (Kestenbaum) Wolf; B.A., Wayne State U., 1955; postgrad. Ind. U., 1955-58; M.S., Purdue U., 1959; m. Leslie A. Field, Jan. 25, 1953; children—Jeffrey H., Linda K. Social worker, spl. investigator Mich. Dept. Social Welfare, 1953-54; instr. English dept. Purdue U., 1956-64; asst. to editor Jour. Reading, 1964-68; instr. dept. indsl. mgmt. Purdue U., West Lafayette, Ind., 1964—. Pres., Parent Tchr. Orgn., Cumberland Elementary Sch., West Lafayette, 1972-73. Mem. Purdue Women's Caucus (charter, corr. sec., pres.), Women's Equity Action League, Nat. Orgn. for Women, Am. Assn. U. Women Am. Assn. U. Profs. (chmn. subcom. on status women Purdue U.), Phi Beta Kappa (com. om mems. in course Purdue chpt.). Editor: (with Leslie A. Field) Bernard Malamud and the Critics, 1970; Bernard Malamud, 20th Century Views 1974. Home: 625 Avondale St West Lafayette IN 47906

FIELD, JUDITH JUDY (MRS. NATHANIEL LAMSON FIELD), librarian; b. Bucyrus, O., Sept. 30, 1939; d. William Harrison and Eva Gertrude (Miller) Judy; B.B.A., U. Mich., 1961, M.A. in L.S., 1963, M.B.A., 1969; m. Nathaniel Lamson Field, Jan. 25, 1959. Librarian, Bell Telephone Labs., Indpls., 1962-65, U. Mich. Grad.

Sch. Bus. Adminstrn., Ann Arbor, 1965-69; librarian Inst. Internat. Commerce, U. Mich., Ann Arbor, 1969-71, research asso., 1971-72; head gen. reference Flint (Mich.) Pub. Library, 1972—. Mem. Spl. Libraries Assn. (chmn. bus.-finance div. 1972—, sec. Mich. 1971), Am. Soc. Information Sci. (treas. Mich. 1970-72), A.L.A. Author: (with Gunter Dufey) Financial Management in the International Corporation, 1971. Home: 20500 Clement St Northville MI 48167 Office: 1026 E Kearsley St Flint MI 48502

FIELD, MARJORIE MAYER (MRS. LAWRENCE JAMES FIELD), newspaper pub.; b. Mt. Vernon, O., Jan. 14, 1913; d. Joseph R. and Margaret C. (Weber) Mayer; B.A., St. Mary's of Springs Coll., 1933; m. Lawrence James Field, May 7, 1941 (dec. July 1969); 1 son, D. Victor. Profl. concert pianist, accompanist, N.Y.C., 1933-54; pianist Singing Lady TV show Little Lady Story Time, 1952-54; faculty music dept. U. Miami, Coral Gables, Fla., 1956-58; asso. editor Bristol (N.H.) Enterprise, 1962-69, owner, pub., editor, 1969—. Mem. exec. com. N.H. Gov.'s Commn. on Crime and Delinquency, 1973—. Republican. Club: Pasquaney Snowshoe (Bristol). Home: 16 Summer St Bristol NH 03222 Office: 7 Spring St Bristol NH 03222

FIELD, SISTER MARY, librarian; b. Wisconsin Dells, Wis., Jan. 17, 1918; d. Henry Augustus and Georgia Berenice (Coakley) Field; B.A., Rosary Coll., 1939, M.A. in L.S., 1960; M.A., U. Wis., 1940. Joined Dominican Religious Order, 1945; tchr., librarian Medford (Wis.) High Sch., 1942-43, Reedsburg (Wis.) High Sch., 1943-44; librarian Sinsinawa Dominican High Sch. libraries, Ill., Washington, Mont., Okla., 1945-60; reference librarian Rosary Coll., River Forest, Ill., 1960-64, chief librarian, 1964—, mem. com. planning new library bldg., 1966-70. Mem. A.L.A., Cath. Library Assn. (sec. local unit 1962-63), Kappa Delta Pi. Home: 1204 Jackson Av River Forest IL 60305 Office: Rosary College River Forest IL 60305

FIELD, MARY KNAUTH (MRS. RICHARD T. FIELD), civic worker; b. N.Y.C., May 3, 1937; d. Victor Whitman and Marjorie Lord (Strauss) Knauth; student Bryn Mawr Coll., 1954-57; m. Richard T. Field, July 3, 1957; children—Christopher Treadwell, William Hill, Gregory Whitman. Mem. League Women Voters, Vineland, N.J., 1965-68, mem. bd., 1966-68; mem. League Women Voters, Newark, Del., 1968—; mem. League Women Voters Del., mem. bd., 1969-74, chmn. human resources, 1969-71, pres., 1971-72, 1st v.p., 1972-74; co-chmn. Bridgeton Head Start, 1966-68; mem. Del. Edn. Finance Study Com., 1972; pres. W.E. Shue Middle Sch. P.T.A., Newark, 1974—. Bd. dirs. Family Services Cumberland County, Bridgeton, N.J., 1966-68. Episcopalian. Home: 81 Red Mill Rd Newark DE 19711

FIELD, MINNA KAGAN, social worker, author; b. Pruzany, Russian-Poland; d. Simon and Velia (Nitzberg) Kagan; came to U.S., 1920; postgrad. Yale, 1922-23; M.S., Hunter Coll., 1936; postgrad. Columbia Sch. Social Work, 1939; m. Jacob Field, July 27, 1920 (dec. Dec. 1960). Caseworker, supr., research worker Jewish Social Service, N.Y., 1923-40; psychiat. social worker, acting head social service dept. N.Y. State Psychiat. Inst. and Hosp., N.Y., 1940-42; temporary commn. on state hosp. problems as dir. social work and research, 1942-44; dir. social service, asst. to chief, div. social medicine Montefiore Hosp., N.Y.C., 1946-57; in charge casework specialists N.Y. State Dept. Social Welfare, White Plains, 1957-59; supr. rev. unit Westchester County div. Family and Child Welfare, 1963-64; prof. Fla. Internat. U., 1972-73. Mem. adv. com. on home care Jackson Meml. Hosp., 1970—; mem. commn. on aging Greater Miami Jewish Fedn., 1974—; mem. mental health planning com. Comprehensive Health Planning Council S. Fla., 1974—. Bd. dirs. Dade County Mental Health Assn., 1974—. Recipient plaque for Jewish community service, 1955; human resource award Am. Bicentennial Research Inst., 1974. Fellow Am. Orthopsychiat. Assn.; mem. Nat. Assn. Social Workers. Author: Insulin Shock Therapy, 1944; Patients are People, 1953, 3d edit., 1967; Aging with Honor and Dignity, 1968. Editor, compiler: Depth and Extent of the Geriatric Problem, 1969; The Aged, the Family and the Community, 1972. Contbr. articles to profl. jours. Home: 1601 NE 191st St North Miami Beach FL 33162

FIELD, (ROSALIND) PATRICIA ADAMS, physician; b. Bristol, Eng., July 5, 1926; d. Rowland and Doris Annie (Kembery) Adams; student U. Bristol, 1947; M.D., U. Toronto (Ont., Can.), 1950; m. John Field, July 9, 1947 (div. 1963); children—Michael, Colin, Patricia Anne. Came to U.S., 1962, naturalized, 1967. Intern Toronto Western Hosp., 1950-51; resident psychiatry Northwestern U., Chgo., 1962-65, asso. in psychiatry, 1970—, asst. dir. Med. Sch. Psychiatry Clinic, 1965-73; gen. practice medicine, Cooksville (now Mississauga), Ont., 1951-61; practice medicine specializing in psychiatry, Chgo., 1965—; mem. staffs St. Joseph's Hosp., 1965—, Chgo. Wesley Meml. Hosp. (now Northwestern Meml. Hosp.) 1968—; dir. Lakeview Uptown Mental Health Clinic, Chgo. Bd. Health, 1965; staff psychiatrist Suicide Prevention Center, Chgo., 1965-66. Diplomate in psychiatry Am. Bd. Psychiatry and Neurology. Mem. Am., Ill. psychiat. assns., Am. Group Psychotherapy Assn., Alpha Omega Alpha. Home: 1515 N Astor St Chicago IL 60610 Office: 936 N Michigan Av Chicago IL 60611

FIELD, SHIRLEY ADELE, judge; b. Ft. Wayne, Ind., Feb. 27, 1923; d. Abraham Field and Clara (Riddner) Field; student Stephens Coll., 1940-41; A.B., U. Mich., 1943; J.D., Yale, 1946. Admitted to Ore. bar, 1947, since practiced in Portland; mem. Ore. Legislature, 1957-59, 63, 65. Mem. Ore. Gov.'s Com. on Children and Youth Parole and Probation; mem. Interim Com. on Criminal Law, 1959-60, Interim Com. on Pub. Health, 1965-66. White House Conf. on Refugees, 1959, Ore. Adv. Commn. on Civil Rights, 1962—. Ore. Emergency Bd., 1963-64; adv. com. Revision Ore. Ins. Code, 1965. Sec. alternate delegation Republican Nat. Conv., 1952; candidate for state treas., 1960; del., sub-com. chmn., human needs Rep. Platform Com., nat. conv. Chgo., 1960; mem. big city vote com. Rep. Nat. Com., 1961; del., mem. platform com. Rep. Nat. Conv. 1964. Bd. curators Stephens Coll., 1962. Recipient Stephens Coll. Alumnae recognition, 1960. Mem. Ore. Prison Assn. (dir.), Izaak Walton League, Urban League, Am. Assn. U. Women, Ore. Cattlemen's Assn. Home: 7525 SW Kelly St Portland OR 97219 Office: Multnomah County Ct House Portland OR 97419

FIELDEN, GEORGIA FREEMAN (MRS. C. FRANKLIN FIELDEN, JR.), interior designer, residential and comml. cons.; b. Alexandria, La., Aug. 3, 1919; d. John D. and Landis (Barton) Freeman; student fine arts Ward-Belmont, 1932-37, Blue Mountain Coll., 1937-38; B.S., George Peabody Coll., 1941; postgrad. N.Y. Sch. Interior Design, 1953; m. Clarence Franklin Fielden, Jr., July 16, 1942; children—Clarence Franklin III, Landis Michaux. Head dept. arts and crafts Camp Bon Air, Sparta, Tenn., 1939-42; asst. instr. fine arts demonstration sch. Peabody Coll., 1940-41; instr. fine arts Jackson (Miss.) Pub. Schs., 1941-42; lectr., interior designer, Colorado Springs, Colo., 1942-67; design cons., Denver, 1968—. Local pres. P.T.A., 1954-56. Mem. Am. Assn. U. Women, Am. Inst. Interior Designers (Rocky Mountain publicity dir. 1957-58, sec. 1959-60, nat. com. pub. relations 1959-61), Constrn. Specifications Inst., D.A.R., Illuminating Engring. Soc. (asso.), Internat. Platform Assn., Huguenot Soc. of Founders Manakin in Colony Va. Presbyn. Rotary Ann (local v.p. 1959-60), Soroptimist, Contbr. articles to profl. jours. Home: 3554 Cochise Dr NW Atlanta GA 30327 Office: Denver Mdse Mart Denver CO 80216

FIELDERS, MARGARET GRANT, educator; b. Woxall, Pa., Nov. 22, 1914; d. William Grant and Anastasia Deirdre (Cooney) Fielders; B.S. in Edn., Pa. State Coll., 1935; B.S. in L.S., Drexel U., 1947; M.A., Middlebury Coll., 1962, M.Litt., 1973. Children's librarian Wyomissing (Pa.) Pub. Library, 1938-42; librarian La Salle Coll. High Sch., Phila., 1947-54; coll. librarian St. Mary of Springs Coll., Columbus, O., 1954-60, chmn. dept. library sci., dir. honors program Ohio Dominican Coll. (formerly St. Mary of Springs), 1960—, prof. library sci., 1971—. Mem. Ohio Area Honors Exec. Bd., 1972—. Served with WAC, 1942-45. Recipient Drexel U. award for leadership and scholarship, 1947. Mem. Am., Ohio (sec. library edn. Round Table 1971), Columbus (chmn. 1960-62), Cath. (permanent mem. adv. bd.), library assns. Club: Rocky Fork-Headley Hunt (Gahanna, O.). Guest editor Protean, library jour., 1972. Contbr. poems, stories to small mags. Home: 6079 Clark State Rd Columbus OH 43230 Mailing Address: 1216 Sunbury Rd Columbus OH 43219

FIELDING, VERA VICTOREEN (MRS. WENDELL S. FIELDING), pub. relations exec.; b. Pittsfield, Mass., Nov. 9, 1911; d. Walfrid T. and Mary E. (Benson) Victoreen; B.S., Boston U., 1933; m. Wendell S. Fielding, Oct. 25, 1935; children—Vicary J. (Mrs. Frank F. Maxant), Joyce E. (Mrs. Ake L. Bergh). Reporter, photographer, women's page editor Berkshire Eagle, Pittsfield, Mass., 1933-39; photo editor Yankee Mag., Dublin, N.Y., 1939-41; publicity dir. United Community Services, Pittsfield, Mass., 1956-59; pub. relations dir. Pittsfield (Mass.) Gen. Hosp., 1959-67; pub. relations dir. Berkshire Med. Center, Pittsfield, Mass., 1967—. Mem. Pittsfield (Mass.) Sch. Bldg. Commn., 1950-59. Mem. Am. Soc. Hosp. Pub. Relations Dirs. (publs. evaluator 1972-74), Am. Hosp. Assn., Kappa Tau Alpha. Contbr. articles to profl. jours. Home: 121 Fort Hill Av Pittsfield MA 01201 Office: 725 North St Pittsfield MA 01201

FIELDS, CHARLOTTE ABRISCH, pvt. sch. exec.; b. San Diego, May 12, 1935; d. Emil John and Naomi Rachael (Villareal) Abrisch; B.A. cum laude, U. South Fla., 1966, M.A. in Psychology, 1970; m. Harold Lewis Fields, Mar. 1951 (div. Apr. 1960); children—Harold Lewis, Roger Lee, Kathleen Naomi, Kenneth Edgar. Research asst., cons. MacDonald Tng. Center, U. South Fla., 1965-66, ednl. coordinator employment opportunity application project, 1969-71; dir. programming Programmed Instrn., Inc., 1966-70; chmn. bd., pres. Acad. Achievement Center, Inc., Tampa, Fla., 1971—. Mem. Am., Tampa Bay psychol. assns., Gold Key Honor Soc., Psi Chi. Author reading program Further Development, Comparison, and Evaluation of Programmed Instruction for Retarded Children, 1967. Home: 3406 Gables Ct Tampa FL 33609 Office: 7016 N Donald St Tampa FL 33614

FIELDS, JEANETTE SHAMES (MRS. ELLIS K. FIELDS), assn. adminstr.; b. Des Moines; d. Jacob and Freda (Goldblatt) Shames; B.A., U. Chgo., 1942, postgrad., 1944-45; m. Ellis K. Fields, Nov. 18, 1939; children—Jennifer (Mrs. Dov Grunschlag), Diana, Wendy. Feature editor Hyde Park Herald, Chgo., 1950-51; account exec. Herbert Kraus Pub. Relations Co., Chgo., 1960-63; dir. pub. relations Fridstein Fitch & Partners, Chgo., 1965-70; tour dir. Chgo. chpt. Am. Inst. Architects, Chgo., 1969-70; exec. sec. Chgo. Sch. Architecture Found., Chgo., 1970-73, exec. dir., 1973—. Founder, South Shore Commn., Chgo., 1953, South Shore Commn. Art League, 1958, South Shore Open House Com., 1963; mem. Oak Park (Ill.) Tour com., 1972-74, Oak Park Beautiful Com., 1972-73. Bd. dirs. Jewish Family and Community Service, 1970—. Recipient Alumni citation Public Service, U. Chgo., 1966. Mem. Nat. Trust for Historic Preservation, Am. Assn. State and Local History, Soc. Archtl. Historians. Editor, South Shore Plan, 1967. Contbr. articles on popular issues to newspapers, book reviews and articles on architecture to profl. jours. and popular mags. Home: 559 Ashland Av River Forest IL 60305 Office: Glessner House 1800 S Prairie Av Chicago IL 60616

FIELDS, JULIA, writer, educator; b. Uniontown, Ala., Jan. 21, 1938; d. Winston and Maggie (Johnson) Fields; B.S. in English, Knoxville Coll., 1961; M.A. in English, Middlebury Coll., 1972; postgrad. Duke, 1974—; children—Helen Lawrence, Rhoda Lawrence. Tchr. pub. schs.; poet-in-residence East Carolina U., 1971. Woodrow Wilson teaching fellow Miles Coll., 1968; Nat. Endowment for Arts and Humanities grantee, 1969-71. Author: Poems, 1968; East of Moonlight, 1973. Home: PO Box 209 Scotland Neck NC 27874

FIELDS, RUBY DARLENE, phys. therapist, health service adminstr.; b. Fredonia, Kan., Sept. 24, 1926; d. Marion Lee and Maybelle Virginia (Newingham) Fields; B.A., Western State Coll., 1948; M.S. in Edn., Portland State U., 1969. Staff therapist Gonzales (Tex.) Warm Springs Found., 1951, Crippled Children's Service, Truth or Consequences, N.M., 1952; staff and chief therapist Sacred Heart Hosp. and Orthopedic Clinic, Eugene, Ore., 1953-58; staff therapist Crippled Childrens div. U. Ore. Med. Sch., Portland, 1960-68, chief therapist, 1968—, instr. phys. therapy, 1969-74, asst. prof. phys. therapy, 1974—, also tng. dir. univ. affiliated facility, Child Devel. and Rehab. Center, 1969—. Nat. Found. scholar, 1950. Mem. Am., Ore. phys. therapy assns., Am. Assn. on Mental Deficiency. Home: 5200 SW River Rd Hillsboro OR 97123 Office: 3181 SW Sam Jackson Park Rd Portland OR 97201

FIELEKE, CATHARINE NICHOLSON (MRS. LESSLY C.A. FIELEKE), author; b. Ash Grove, Mo., Sept. 27, 1909; d. John Warren and Mattie (Duncan) Nicholson; student Drury Coll., Olivet Coll., U. Chgo.; m. Lessly C.A. Fieleke, Dec. 24, 1929; children—Norman, Sharon (Mrs. Mauj Cohly), Cathy (Mrs. D. Anthony Butterfield), Lessly, Laurel (Mrs. Ezra Shoshani), Curtis, Teresa. Pres., Fieleke Implement Co., 1965-67. Recipient awards Woman's Club, Am. Pen Women, others. Mem. World Soc. Poets Intercontinental, Pen Women (pres. Chgo. br. 1974—), Nat. Writers Club, Internat. Platform Assn., Internat. Biog. Assn., Friends Am. Writers, Children's Reading Round Table, Chgo. Poets and Patrons, Kankakee Area Writers Group. Baptist. Club: Womens. Author: American Poetry Series, 1965; also scripts, ednl. tapes. Home: 312 Ohio St Momence IL 60954

FIELSTRA, HELEN ADAMS (MRS. CLARENCE FIELSTRA), educator; b. Elkhorn, W.Va., Feb. 26, 1921; d. Fred Russell and Clara Sue (Williams) Adams; A.B., U. Cal. at Los Angeles, 1950; M.A., Stanford, 1954, Ed.D., 1967; m. Edmond T. Dooley, Jr., Nov. 15, 1941 (div. 1948); 1 dau., Dereth Conro; m. 2d, Clarence Fielstra, Jan. 1, 1956. Tchr. Santa Monica (Cal.) Unified Sch. Dist., 1947-50; supr. elementary sch. San Diego County Schs., 1950-52; lectr. edn. Stanford, 1953-54, U. Cal. at Los Angeles, 1957-58; gen. elementary supr. Burbank (Cal.) Unified Sch. Dist., 1954-56, Beverly Hills (Cal.) Unified Sch. Dist., 1959-61; faculty edn. Cal. State U. at Northridge, 1961—, prof., 1970—; tng. coordinator Office Econ. Opportunity Tng. and Devel. Center for So. Cal., 1965-66. Cons., speaker curriculum devel. and instructional supervision, 1952—; prin. investigator prospective tchr. grad. fellowship project U.S. Office Edn., 1968-70; dir., prin. investigator NSF Coop. Coll.-Sch. Social Sci. Project, 1972-73, 73-74. Sec.-treas. Hadco, Inc., Los Angeles, Fielstra Publs., Inc., Pacific Palisades. Recipient Cal. State Univs. and Colls. Distinguished Teaching award, 1969, Asso. Student certificate of Service, Cal. State U. at Northridge, 1970. Mem. Am. Ednl. Research Assn., Nat. Soc. for Study Edn., Nat. Council for Social Studies (publs. bd.), N.E.A. (life), Assn. for Supervision and Curriculum Devel., Cal. Assn. for Supervision and Curriculum Devel. (chmn. state com. on supervision in structure pub. edn.), Am. Assn. U. Profs., Assn. Cal. State Coll. Profs., Cal. Higher Edn. Assn. (dir. 1970—, state pres. 1973-74), Cal. Coll. and U. Faculty Assn. (pres. Cal. State U. at Northridge chpt. 1969-70, state v.p. 1970-71, state pres. 1972-73), Delta Kappa Gamma (life, chpt. pres. 1960-62). Democrat. Club: Stanford (Los Angeles); Pacific Palisades Women's. Author: (with L.G. Thomas, A. Coladarci, Lucien Kinney) Perspective on Teaching, 1961; (with Clarence Fielstra) Africa-With Focus on Nigeria, 1963; author numerous curriculum guides, 6 ednl. films. Editorial bd. Cal. Jour. for Instructional Improvement, 1967-70; editor Reading Monograph, 1970, Social Studies in the Elementary School, 1972. Home: 14177 Sunset Blvd Pacific Palisades CA 90272 Office: Cal State U Northridge CA 91324

FIFER, ELLEN ZINSSER (MRS. WILLIAM R. FIFER), physician; b. N.Y.C., Nov. 14, 1924; d. John Sharman and Isabelle (Wadsworth) Zinsser; B.A., Vassar Coll., 1945; M.D., Columbia Coll. Phys. and Surg., 1949; m. William R. Fifer, May 29, 1948; children—Judith, Penman, Alison, William. Intern Hosp. U. Pa., 1949-50; tng. U. Minn. Sch. Pub. Health, 1955-59; pub. health officer City of Bloomington, Minn., 1959-67; health planning dir. Minn. Planning Agy., St. Paul, 1967-73; asst. commr. Minn. Dept. Health, Mpls., 1973—. Mem. Am. Pub. Health Assn. (mem. governing council), Alpha Omega Alpha. Home: 4740 Emerson Av S Minneapolis MN 55409 Office: 717 Delaware St SE Minneapolis MN 55440

FIFER, VIRGINIA BELL, constrn. co. exec.; b. Littlestown, Pa., July 24, 1935; d. Cleason Herbert and Alta Virginia (Ohler) Plunkert; student pub. schs. Gen. contractor Maitland Bros., Co., Inc., Littletown, 1952—, sec., asst. bookkeeper, 1952-56, bookkeeper, asst. office mgr., 1956-61, office mgr., auditor, asst. comptroller, 1961-65, corp. sec., chief security, 1965—. Lutheran. Club: Nat. Travel. Home: 207 E King St Littletown PA 17340 Office: Route 2 Littlestown PA 17340

FIGGE, PHYLLIS ROSS, hosp. exec.; b. St. Paul, Nov. 18, 1929; d. John Henry and Mary A. (Allen) Ross; student U. Minn., 1948-50; m. George R. Figge, Aug. 26, 1950 (dec. 1966); children—Timothy, Theresa, Jill, Julia, John. Weekly columnist Bloomington (Minn.) Suburbanite, 1958-59; daily columnist Chgo. Daily News, 1960-61; dir. community relations St. John's Hosp., St. Paul, 1968—. Tchr. writing Stillwater State Prison, 1967—. Bd. dirs. Face to Face Crisis Center, Inc., Help Enable Alcoholics Receive Treatment. Mem. Pub. Relations Soc. Am., Internat. Assn. Indsl. Editors, Am. Soc. Hosp. Pub. Relations. Club: Minnesota Press. Author: A Widow's Story, 1968; also TV documentary Death and Dying (Edward R. Morrow award), 1973; film Love is to Grow On, 1974. Contbr. articles to newspapers. Home: 1822 Stanford Av St Paul MN 55105 Office: 403 Maria St St Paul MN 55106

FIGUERAS, PATRICIA ANN MCVEIGH, chemist; b. Detroit, Jan. 23, 1933; d. Robert Moore and Charlotte Colley (Jones) McVeigh; B.S., U. Mich., 1953, M.A., 1957, Ph.D., 1958; M.S., U. Minn., 1954; m. John Figueras, May 16, 1970. Research asso., research labs. Eastman Kodak Co., Rochester, N.Y., 1958—. Mem. Am. Chem. Soc. (councilor Rochester sect. 1966-74), Royal Photog. Soc., Sigma Xi, Phi Beta Kappa, Phi Kappa Phi, Alpha Xi Delta. Club: Curling (Rochester). Home: 436 Heritage Dr Rochester NY 14615 Office: Bldg 59 Kodak Park Rochester NY 14650

FIGUEREDO, ANITA VILLEGAS (MRS. WILLIAM J. DOYLE), physician; b. Costa Rica, Aug. 24, 1916; d. Roberto and Sarita (Villegas) Figueredo; A.B., Manhattanville Coll., 1936; M.D., L.I. Coll. Medicine, 1940; m. William J. Doyle, Aug. 8, 1942; children—William, Sarita, John, Thomas, Charles, Anita, Richard, Teresa, Robert. Intern N.Y. Infirmary for Women and Children, 1940-42; asst. resident surgery Meml. Hosp. Cancer Center, N.Y.C., 1942, 43; asst. in surgery Sibley Meml. Hosp., Washington, 1943-44; attending physician Strang Cancer Detection Clinic, N.Y.C., 1945-47; practice medicine and surgery specializing in oncology, La Jolla, Cal., 1948—; surg. staff Scripps Meml. Hosp., La Jolla, 1948—. Pres. La Jolla Civic Orch. Assn., 1964-66; exec. bd. San Diego com. Project Concern, 1967-69; regional chmn. Co-Workers of Mother Teresa in Am., San Diego, 1973—. Trustee La Jolla Town Council, 1956-68, 71-73, v.p., 1966-67, 71-72; chmn. La Jolla Youth and Recreation, 1958-61; bd. dirs. San Diego region Nat. Conf. Christians and Jews, 1967-70; trustee Manhattanville Coll., 1969-71, U. San Diego Coll. for Women, 1968-72; vice-chmn. trustees U. San Diego, 1972—, chmn. acad. affairs com., 1973—. Decorated Pro Ecclesiae et Pontifice, Pope Pius XII, 1954; Equestrian Order Holy Sepulchre Jerusalem, 1970, Pilgrim's Shell, 1972; named Med. Woman of Year, San Diego County, 1954, San Diego Woman of Year, Council Women's Service Clubs, 1958; recipient Americanism award D.A.R., 1961. Mem. A.M.A., Am. Med. Women's Assn. (pres. San Diego chpt. 1953), Cal. Med. Assn., San Diego County Med. Soc., Am. Cancer Soc. (San Diego v.p. 1951, chmn. edn. com. 1951-52), James Ewing Soc., Asso. Alumnae of Sacred Heart (nat. pres. 1959-61), Kappa Gamma Pi (Spiritus Sanctus award 1961). Roman Catholic. Soroptimist (hon.). Home: 417 Coast Blvd La Jolla CA 92037 Office: 418 South Coast Blvd La Jolla CA 92037

FIGURELLI, JENNIFER CONSTANCE, psychologist; b. Jersey City, May 11, 1945; d. Francesco Antonio and Jean (Bigler) Figurelli; B.S., St. Lawrence U., 1966; M.A., U. S.C., 1970; postgrad. U. Calgary, Jersey City State Coll. Research psychologist Alta. (Can.) Mental Hosp., Ponoka, 1967; psychol. research asst. U. Calgary (Alta.), 1968-69; psychologist Columbia (S.C.) Pub. Schs., 1969-70, Jersey City Pub. Schs., 1970—. Adj. prof. psychology St. Peter's Coll., Jersey City, 1970—. Mem. S.C. State Com. on Legalization Abortion, 1970. Mem. Nat., N.J., Jersey City edn. assns., Nat. Assn. Sch. Psychologists (chmn. ad hoc com. 1972-73), Am., N.J., Inter-Am., Southeastern psychol. assns., Internat. Assn. for Applied Psychology, N.J. Assn. for Sch. Psychologists, Soc. for Research in Child Devel., Am. Ednl. Research Assn. Editorial bd. Sch. Psychology Digest. Home: 88 Highland Av Jersey City NJ 07306 Office: 182 Merseles St Jersey City NJ 07302

FILIPPONE, ELLA FINGER (MRS. JOSEPH J. FILIPPONE, III), civic worker; b. Kearny, N.J.; d. Ferdinand and Eliese (Ritzel) Finger; student Katharine Gibbs Sch., 1952-54, Rutgers U., Columbia; postgrad. U. Ill., U. Md.; m. Joseph J. Filippone, Mar 3, 1962; children—Joseph John, Thomas Carl, Andrew Daryl, Frederick Lewis. Sec., Va.-Carolina Chem. Co., 1954-56, Moulin Prodns., N.Y.C., 1956-57; sec. Stricker Research Assos., Inc., 1957-59, v.p., treas., 1959-64, dir., 1960-64, partner, 1961-64, cons., 1964; spl. reporter Bernardsville (N.J.) News, 1970-71. Chmn. bd., pres. Environmental Research Assos., Inc., 1970—. Founder Citizens for Conservation Bernards Twp., 1969, publicity chmn., 1969—; bd. advisers Gill Summer Sch. on Environmental Edn., 1970—; coordinator Passaic River Coalition, 1970, trustee, 1971, chmn., pres., 1972—; bd. advisers N.J. Consortium on Environmental Edn., 1970—; mem. N.J. Gov.'s Green Acres Bond Issue Com.; mem. exec.

com. Environmental Expo 71; chmn. task force on environmental quality N.J. Council of Chs.; chmn. Pre-Stockholm Conf. on Human Environment. Sec., Bernards Twp. Republican Club, 1965-68. Mem. Am. Polit. Sci. Assn., Acad. Polit Sci., Am. Statis. Assn., Am. Econ. Assn., Am. Judicature Soc., Royal Econ. Soc., Nat. Audubon Soc., Nat. Indsl. Conf. Bd., League for Conservation Legislation, Am. Mgmt. Assn., Atomic Indsl. Forum, Nat. Wildlife Fedn., Mus. Natural History, German-Am. C. of C., Smithsonian Assos., UN Assn. U.S.A., No. N.J. Conservation Found. Lutheran. Clubs: Antique Automobile Am. (N.J.); Basking Ridge (N.J.) Garden. Home: 25 Holmesbrook Rd Basking Ridge NJ 07920

FILLER, DOROTHY SANDS (MRS. SAMUEL FILLER), civic worker, bus. exec.; b. Charleston, S.C.; d. Ernest Desi and Hermina (Klein) Sands; B.S. in Edn., Trenton State Coll., 1945; m. Samuel Filler, Feb. 9, 1947; children—Linda Nerine, James Bertram. Tchr., New Hanover Twp. Sch., Wrightstown, N.J., 1945-48; v.p., sec. Filler Farms, Inc., Florence, 1958—, Pine Tree, Inc., Burlington Twp., N.J., 1961—, Samuel Filler Enterprises, Inc., 1964—. Trustee Burlington chpt. Deborah Hosp., 1955-57; chmn. Nat. Library Week, Willingboro, N.J., 1960-61; commr. Burlington County Library, 1972—, N.J. Assn. Library Commrs., 1972—. Sec. bd. trustees Pub. Library Willingboro. Mem. A.L.A., N.J. Library Assn., Am., N.J. library trustee assns., Nat. Council Jewish Women (treas. 1963-64). Jewish religion (trustee religious sch. 1958-60, treas. Sisterhood 1956-57). Rotary Ann. Home: 64 Garland Lane Willingboro NJ 08046 Office: care Pine Tree Inc Sunset Rd Burlington Twp NJ 08016

FILLYAW, MARJORIE LENNEHAN, journalist; b. Yonkers, N.Y., Dec. 14, 1920; d. Emmet Aloysius and Helen (Flaherty) Lennehan; grad. high sch., Miami Beach, Fla.; m. William Fillyaw, Apr. 25, 1942; children—Margaret R. (Mrs. Philip Sosey), Helen T. (Mrs. Gary Bergert). Asso. editor Fla. Catholic, Miami, 1939-42; women's editor North Miami Home News, 1948; sec. St. Rose of Lima Ch. and Sch., Miami Shores, Fla., 1951-59; local news editor The Voice, Miami, 1959—; South Fla. corr. NC News Service, Washington, 1953—. Recipient 3d place award Fla. Press Assn., 1972. Mem. Women in Communications (2d v.p. 1973-74), Miami Council Catholic Women (life), Mercy Hosp. Aux., Sigma Delta Chi. Contbr. articles to profl. jours. Home: 440 NE 110th Terrace Miami FL 33161 Office: 6201 Biscayne Blvd Miami FL 33138

FILMUS, GLADYS NODIFF (MRS. TULLY FILMUS), choreographer; b. N.Y.C.; d. Isaac A. and Sarah (Kirshenbaum) Nodiff; B.A., N.Y. U., 1939; m. Tully Filmus, June 18, 1939; children—Michael Roy, Stephen Isaac. Performing artist modern dance and mime N.Y. City Center, 1936-47; tchr. modern dance Sholem Aleichem Inst., N.Y.C., 1938-47, New Dance Group, N.Y.C., 1939, Henley Sch., N.Y.C., 1954-56, summer classes, Glen Spey, N.Y., 1950-60, Becket, Mass., 1961-68; choreographer New World Dancers, Phila., 1939-43. Mem. exec. bd., chmn. dance dept. North Shore Community Arts Center, 1958-69, v.p., 1971-74, chmn. dance dept., 1973. mem. Dance Council Nassau County, 1964; trustee Great Neck Symphony Soc., 1960-69, 73; mem. Womens Guild exec. bd. Great Neck Symphony, 1967-69. Home: 17 Stuart St Great Neck NY 11023 Summer Studio: Becket MA 01223

FILSINGER, BARBARA MINA, libararian; b. New Brunswick, N.J., May 8, 1936; d. Raymond Carl and Eva Florence (Greiner) Filsinger; B.S. in Edn., Trenton State Coll., 1958; M.L.S., Rutgers U., 1961; postgrad. Trinity Coll., Dublin, Ireland, 1968, U. Copenhagen (Denmark), 1970, U. Wyo., 1971, U. Wis., 1973-74. Librarian, Chathem (N.J.) Jr. High Sch., 1958-60, Syosset (N.Y.) Jr. High Sch., 1961-64, Harcourt, Brace & World Pub. Co., N.Y.C., 1965, Bloomfield (N.J.) Jr. High Sch., 1965-66, Roosevelt Jr. High Sch., Westfield, N.J., 1966—, Scotch Plains (N.J.) Pub. Library, 1968—. Mem. A.L.A., N.E.A., Kappa Delta Pi. Home: 43 Dekker Ct Brick Town NJ 08723 Office: 301 Clark St Westfield NJ 07090

FINAN, LILLIAN, lawyer; b. Middletown, Conn., Feb. 6, 1921; J.D., U. So. Cal., 1957, postgrad. Med. Sch., 1965-66; m. Edward Finan, Feb. 13, 1951; children—Lynn (Mrs. Copp Collins), Monte Morton. Admitted to Cal. bar, 1957, since practiced in Los Angeles and Beverly Hills. Mem. adv. council Cal. Assembly Com. on Med. Malpractice, 1973-74. Bd. govs. Legion Lex-U. So. Cal. Law Sch. Mem. Am. Assn. Trial Lawyers, Am., Los Angeles County, Beverly Hills bar assns., State Bar Cal. (Cal. Med. Assn. com. 1973—), Cal. (head women's rights com. 1972—, gov. 1974—), Los Angeles (gov. 1973—) trial lawyers assns., Women Lawyers Assn. Los Angeles, Nat. Orgn. for Women. Republican. Club: Bel-Air Country (Los Angeles). Office: 1901 Av of Stars Los Angeles CA 90067

FINCH, ALBERTA MAY (MRS. OTTO ROY WEBER), physician; b. Port Jervis, N.Y., Jan. 27, 1926; d. Herbert Leroy and Bertha May (Funnell) Finch; B.S., Pa. State U., 1946; M.D., Temple U., 1950; m. Otto Roy Weber, July 12, 1952; children—Lawrence, Charles, Kathy, Phillip, Jeffrey. Intern Harrisburg (Pa.) Hosp., 1950-51, resident, 1951-52, mem. staff, 1952-62; practice medicine, specializing in pediatrics, Linglestown, Pa., 1952-62; gen. practice medicine, Stroudsburg, Pa., 1962—; physician Pa. Well Baby Clinic Monroe County, 1962—; mem. exec. bd. staff Gen. Hosp. Monroe County, 1971—. Med. adviser Vis. Nurses Assn. Monroe County, 1971—; pres. Planned Parenthood Monroe County, 1970-73; mem. Pa. Bd. for Correlating Activities Social Service Orgns. Monroe County, 1970—; mem. adv. bd. Monroe County Children's Bur., 1972—. Mem. A.M.A., Pa., Monroe County (pres. 1974—) med. socs., Aux. Med. Soc. Monroe County. Methodist. Home: Box 146 RD 5 Stroudsburg PA 18360 Office: 52 Garden St Stroudsburg PA 18360

FINCH, BARBARA LAKE (MRS. JOHN MYLER FINCH), journalist; b. Charleston, W. Va., Jan. 10, 1938; d. Nelson Smith and Mildred (Pearson) Lake; student Agnes Scott Coll., 1955-57; grad in Journalism with honors, U. Ky., 1958; m. John Myler Finch, Oct. 11, 1958; children—Stephen Myler, Sarah Elizabeth. Dir. pub. information Jefferson Coll., Hillsboro, Mo., 1972-73; pub. cons. Arts and Edn. Council Greater St. Louis, 1972-73; pub. relations cons. St. Joseph Hosp., Kirkwood, Mo., 1973—; free lance journalist, 1962—. Mem. Women in Communications (pres. St. Louis profl. chpt. 1970-71). Contbr. articles to popular newspapers and mags. Home: 4777 Towne Centre Dr St Louis MO 63128 Office: 525 Couch Av Kirkwood MO 63122

FINCH, BLANCHE EDITH, realtor; b. Leask, Sask., Can., July 25, 1925; d. Frank and Theresa (Kalman) Nagy; student Welland (Ont.) Bus. Coll., 1943-45, Ga. Real Estate Inst., 1965, 68, U. Ga., Athens, summer 1968; m. Richard A. Schreckengost, Dec. 29, 1945 (div. Sept. 1960); children—Richard E., Daniel; m. 2d, Baxter H. Finch, Oct. 15, 1960 (div. May 1964). Saleswoman Haas & Dod, Atlanta, 1965-66, King-Williams Realty, Smyrna, Ga., 1966-68; pres. Finch Realty Co., Smyrna, 1968-71, Atlanta, 1971—. Mem. campaign com. Gov. Carl Sanders, 1962. Mem. Cobb County C. of C., Cobb County Bd. Realtors, Atlanta Real Estate Bd., Nat. Assn. Real Estate Bds., Cobb 100 Bus. and Devel. Assn. Presbyn. Home: 2479 Peachtree Rd NE Atlanta GA 30305 Office: 3500 Bankhead Hwy Lithia Springs GA 30057

FINCH, OPAL CLAIR LANE (MRS. RALPH FINCH), nurse; b. Mena, Ark., Jan. 31, 1907; d. William Emmet and Lena (Little) Lane; diploma St. Edwards Mercy Hosp., 1928; student Incarnate Word Coll., 1960-61, 61-62; m. Ralph Finch, May 11, 1932; children—Fredrick Lane, Ralph W., Joseph Luther. Nurse, Army and Navy Hosp., Hot Springs, Ark., 1950-55, Brooks Gen. Hosp., Ft. Sam Houston, Tex., 1955-67. Served with Army Nurse Corps, 1928-32. Mem. D.A.R., Women's Overseas Service League, Am. Nurses Assn., Nat. League Nursing. Died Apr. 6, 1974. Home: 114 E Hathaway St San Antonio TX 78209

FINCK, ETHEL JEAN (MRS. FRANK MORTON FINCK), radiologist; b. Los Angeles; d. Samuel Yen and Helen (Ho) Eng; B.A., Pacific Union Coll.; M.D., Cal. Coll. Medicine, 1962; m. Frank Morton Finck, Oct. 29, 1961; children—Brian William, Stuart Alan. Resident radiology Los Angeles County Gen. Hosp., 1964-67; asst. prof. radiology U. Cal. at Irvine, 1964-68, U. So. Cal. Sch. Medicine, 1969—. Mem. Radiol. Soc. N. Am., Am. Coll. Radiology, Am. Coll. Angiology, A.M.A., Cal., Los Angeles med. assns. Contbr. articles to profl. jours. Office: 1200 N State St Los Angeles CA 90033

FINDLAY, MARY EVANS (MRS. DAVID B. FINDLAY, JR.), museum adminstr.; b. Providence, June 15, 1934; d. Robert Alden and Eleanor (Rich) Evans; B.A. in Art History, Smith Coll., 1956; postgrad. Columbia Sch. Architecture, 1970—; m. Peter R. Adams, Sept. 1, 1956 (dec. 1970); children—E. Sinclair, M. Holbrook; m. 2d., David B. Findlay, Jr., June 9, 1973. Catalog research Frick Art Reference Library, 1956-58; research dir. Wilton Hist. Soc., 1970-71; vol. chmn. Wilton Hist. Soc., 1966; chmn. restoration Lockwood-Mathews Mansion Museum of Norwalk, Inc. (Conn.), 1968-74, pres. bd. trustees Lockwood-Mathews Mansion Mus., 1974—; adviser Nat. Trust Historic Preservation, Washington, 1973—, Union R.R. Sta. Trust, New London, Conn., 1973—, mem. adv. bd. Wesleyan Landmarks Middletown, Conn., 1973—. Mem. Norwalk (Conn.) Bicentennial Commn., 1971—. Trustee Wilton Hist. Soc., 1968—, Lockwood-Mathews Mansion, 1968—. Mem. Soc. Archtl. Historians, Assn. Preservation Tech., Victorian Soc. Am. (dir. 1973—). Author: LeGrand Lockwood, 1969; The Lockwood-Mathews Mansion, 1969. Address: 10 Father Peter's Lane New Canaan CT 06840

FINDLEY, HAZEL WINIFRED ROCKWELL (MRS. S. WALKER FINDLEY), occupational therapist; b. Chgo.; d. Alpheus Lynn and Emma (Sperry) Rockwell; student Am. Conservatory Music, 1921-28, U. Chgo., 1929-31, 33, Sch. Art Inst. Chgo., 1945-46; m. S. Walker Findley, Nov. 14, 1931. Occupational therapist in psychiatry Billings Hosp., U. Chgo., 1944-56; dir. occupational therapy Home for Destitute Crippled Children, Chgo., 1956-67; chief occupational therapist Wyler Children's Hosp., Chgo., 1967—. Dir. Community Council for Social Welfare, Palos (Ill.) Area, 1956—, pres., 1958-62; pres. Palos Service League, 1952-54; sec. bd. Libra Sch. for Children with Learning Disabilities, 1970. Founder, pres. Palos Republican Women's Orgn., 1960-62, sec., 1965-66; speakers bur. chmn. Ill. Fedn. Rep. Women, 1962-64, mem. exec. com., 1962—, convs. chmn., 1965-66, 3d v.p., 1973-74; precinct capt. Palos Regular Rep. Orgn., 1962-74; del. Ill. Rep. Conv., 1968, 70; chmn. Ill. dinner Nat. Fedn. Rep. Women, Washington, del. at Large, 1973; alternate del. Rep. Nat. Conv., 1972; mem. Cook County Rep. slate making com., 1973. Mem. Palos Hist. Soc. (sec. 1957-72, dir. 1957—), Palos Park Garden Guild (pres. 1954-56), Palos Play Readers. Presbyn. (elder). Home: 12205 93d Av Palos Park IL 60464 Office: 970 E 59th St Chicago IL 60637

FINE, MARY CAY, psychologist; b. Ft. Worth; d. William Emerson and Margaret Ellen (Cull) Fine; B.S., Tex. Women's U., 1941, B.A., 1941; M.A., Tex. A. and I. U., 1958; postgrad. U. Tex. at Austin, 1959-62. Prin. North Sharyland Sch., Mission, Tex., 1935-40; legal sec. Strickland Ewers and Wilkins, Mission, 1941-43; adminstrv. asst. Dept. Def., Brownsville, Tex., 1943-44, research analyst, adminstrv. asst., Greenwood, Miss., 1943-44, Washington, and Rio de Janeiro, Brazil, 1944-54; adminstrv. asst. Nat. Assn. Broadcasters, Washington, 1954-55; copywriter sta. KRIO, McAllen, Tex., 1955-56; spl. edn. coordinator McAllen schs., LaJoya (Tex.) schs., Weslaco (Tex.) schs., 1956-65; purchasing agt. Reynolds Research and Mfg. Corp., McAllen, 1965-66; dist. psychologist Rio Grande Rehab. Ind. Sch. Dist., Edinburg, Tex., 1967—. Cons. psychologist; Tex. Dept. Pub. Welfare and Hidalgo County Juvenile Dept. Mem. Am., Tex. psychol. assns., Am. Assn. on Mental Deficiency, Council for Exceptional Children, Bus. and Profl. Women, Tex. State Tchr. Assn., N.E.A., Nat., Fed., Tex. (sec. treas. 1968—) press women, Nat., Tex. assns. retarded children, Nat., Tex., Valley personnel and guidance assns., Valley Assn. Sch. Adminstrs., Zonta Club. Home: PO Box 587 Mission TX 78572 Office: PO Box 533 Edinburg TX 78539

FINE, PERLE, artist; b. Boston, May 1, 1908; d. Simon and Sarah (Fine) Fine; studied with Hans Hofmann, Atelier 17; m. Maurice Berezov. One-man shows Marion Willard, DeYoung Mus., Nierendorf, Tanager, Betty Parsons galleries, Graham Gallery, N.Y.C., 1961, 63, 64, 67, Bykert Gallery, 1970, Bykert Gallery in studio, 1970; also has exhibited in nat. group anns. U.S. and abroad; represented in permanent collections Whitney Mus., Smith Coll. Mus., Rutgers U., Los Angeles County Mus., Parrish Mus., Brandeis U., Bklyn. Mus., Mus. Non-Objective Painting Mus. Modern Art; pvt. collections; asso. prof. fine art Hofstra U., vis. prof. art Cornell U., 1961; tchr., lectr. Provincetown Art Assn., pvt. groups. Recipient purchase award for color woodcut Bklyn Mus., 1956; 1st prize for oil painting Silvermine Art Guild, 1961, 1st prize for collage, 1963, award for woodcollage, 1967. Guggenheim scholar; grantee Am. Acad. Arts and Letters, 1974. Mem. Am. Abstract Artists, Fedn. Modern Painters and Sculptors, Guild Hall. Author articles on art. Address: 538 C Old Stone Hwy The Springs NY 11937

FINEGAN, MABEL DAVIDSON (MRS. JAMES H. FINEGAN), realtor; b. Rockyford, Colo.; d. John Adam and Ethel (Basham) Davidson; student Lumbleau Sch. Real Estate, 1946, Pat Compton's Appraisal Sch., 1949, U. Cal. at Los Angeles Extension, 1962-63; m. James H. Finegan, May 21, 1938 (dec.); children—Roy G., Kathy. Bookkeeper, Oxnard Auto Parts (Cal.), 1932-35; real estate broker Coimer Realty, Inglewood, Cal., 1948-49; sec., property mgr., Tozier, Steele & Gill Realtors, Oxnard, 1952-57; realtor with husband, Oxnard, 1957—; pres. Finegan Realtors, 1973, Finegan Investment Co., 1973-74, Asso. Cons., Inc., 1973-74; chmn., pres. Finegan Group of Cos. Mem. Oxnard Community Relations Commn., citizen's adv. com., sec. 1967, v.p. 1968, 69, study com. planning commn., 1967-68, Oxnard Downtown mem. Mail study com., 1967. Mem. Nat. Assn. Real Estate Bds. (organizer Oxnard Chpt. women's council, pres. 1967, gov. So. Cal. women's council 1971-72), Oxnard, Harbor Bd. realtors (Realtor of Year 1965, past pres.), Oxnard, Coast Dist. (pres. 1973-74) bus. and profl clubs, Nat. Assn. Parliamentarians, Cal. Assn. Parliamentarians, Oxnard C. of C. (v.p. 1972-74), Cal. Fedn. Bus. and Profl. Women Clubs (program com. 1974-75, dir. 1974-75). Christian Scientist (past 2d reader, treas. 1972, bd. dirs. 1972-74, pres. 1973). Mem. Order Eastern Star, Jobs Daus. (past guardian). Home: 1505 N F St Oxnard CA 93030 Office: 500 Esplanade Dr Oxnard CA 93030

FINEGOLD, DIANA KLABIN (MRS. RUPERT FINEGOLD), advt. co. exec.; b. N.Y.C., Apr. 22, 1941; d. Lewis L. and Minerva P. (Gold) Klabin; A.B., Columbia U., 1962; postgrad., New Sch. for Social Research, 1964-66, Sch. of Visual Arts, 1965-66; m. Rupert Finegold, June 22, 1969. Copywriter, Simon & Schuster, N.Y.C., 1962-65, Franklin Spier Advt., N.Y.C., 1965-66; advt., promotion mgr. Four Winds Press/Scholastic Inc., N.Y.C., 1966-67; promotion mgr. G.P. Putnam's Sons/Coward-McCann-Geoghegan Publishers, N.Y.C., 1967-69; trade advt. mgr. Macmillan Publishers, N.Y.C., 1969; advt., promotion, publicity mgr. Library Press/Nash Pub., N.Y.C., 1969-71; advt. and sales promotion mgr. Grosset & Dunlap Pubs., N.Y.C., 1971-73; account exec. Denhard & Stewart Advt., Inc., N.Y.C., 1973—. Free lance advt., promotion and pub. relations cons. to various pub. houses. Mem. Women in Pub., N.Y. Copy Club, Pubs. Ad Club. Home: 116 Lafayette Av Brooklyn NY 11217 Office: 20 W 43rd St New York City NY 10036

FINEMAN, CAROL ALSON (MRS. LEWIS TOBIAS FINEMAN), psychologist; b. N.Y.C., Jan. 29, 1943; d. Albert Morris and Evelyn (Gartner) Alson; A.B. cum laude, U. Miami, Coral Gables, Fla., 1963, M.S., 1966, Ph.D., 1970; m. Lewis Tobias Fineman, Sept. 2, 1962. Clin. psychology intern VA Hosp., Miami, Fla., 1968-69; specialist in behavior disorders Dade County Pub. Schs., Coral Gables, 1970-72, spl. edn. psychologist, 1972—. Adj. prof. Miami-Dade Community Coll., 1973—; inservice-evaluation specialist Fla. Learning Resources System, 1973—; adj. prof. U. Miami, 1974—. Mem. edn. and youth services coms., bd. dirs. Dade County Mental Health Assn.; bd. dirs. Dade County Psychiat. Center. Mem. Am. Psychol. Assn., Dade Assn. Sch. Psychologists, Council for Exceptional Children-Council for Children with Behavioral Disorders, Abyssinian Cat Club Am. (regional dir. 1972-73), Magic City Cat Club. Developer psychol. testing procedures. Home: 4242 SW 98th Ave Miami FL 33165 Office: 47 Zamora Av Coral Gables FL 33134

FINEMAN, JOANN BOOZE (MRS. ABRAHAM D. FINEMAN), physician; b. Bloomington, Ind., Jan. 11, 1926; d. Herbert Henry and Nira (Secrest) Booze; A.B., Ind. U., 1945, M.D., 1948; m. Hugh Edward Wilson III, June, 1948 (div. Aug. 1957); children—Hugh Randolph, James Cameron; m. 2d, Abraham D. Fineman, Jan. 25, 1958; 1 dau., Nira Rebecca. Intern New Eng. Hosp., Boston, 1948-49; resident Worcester (Mass.) State Hosp., 1949-50, Mass. Meml. Hosp., Boston, 1951-52; fellow psychiatry Judge Baker Guidance Center and Childrens Med. Center, Boston, 1953-55; teaching fellow Harvard U., 1955; practice medicine specializing in adult and child psychoanalysis and psychotherapy, Boston, 1955—; research asst. Harvard Dept. Social Relations, 1954-56; psychiatrist Childrens Med. Center, Boston, 1955-58; research psychiatrist, child devel. unit Boston U. Sch. medicine, 1956-61, dir. child devel. observation tng. program dept. child psychiatry, 1962-70, asst. clin. prof. child psychiatry 1963-68, asso. clin. prof., 1968—, cons., supr. Infant Devel. Unit, 1970—; asso. attending physician McLean Hosp.; cons. Beaverbrook Child Guidance Clinic, Well-Baby Clinic. Mem. Am. Psychoanalytic Assn., Assn. Child Psychoanalysis, Am. Orthopsychiat. Assn., Am. Acad. Child Psychiatry, Am., No. New Eng. psychiat. assns., New. Eng. Council Child Psychiatry. Contbr. articles to profl. jours. Home: 52 Whitney Tavern Rd Weston MA 02193 Office: Dept Child Psychiatry Boston U Sch Medicine 82 E Concord St Boston MA 02118

FINK, AUGUSTA, writer; b. N.Y.C., Dec. 5, 1916; d. William and Lillian (Graf) Fink; B.A., U. Cal. at Los Angeles, 1937, M.A., 1939. Personnel technician, mgmt. cons. Los Angeles County Civil Service Dept., 1945-60; co-owner Shorebird Bookstore, Palos Verdes Peninsula, Cal., 1960-67; free lance writer, 1967—. Mem. Cal. Hist. Soc., Monterey History and Art Assn. Club: Commonwealth of Cal. Author: Time and the Terraced Land, 1966; To Touch the Sky, 1971; Monterey, the Presence of the Past (Cal. Silver Medal award Commonwealth Club of Cal. 1972), 1972; Adobes in the Sun, 1972. Address: Box 1152 Carmel CA 93921

FINK, KATHRYN FERGUSON (MRS. ROBERT MORGAN FINK), biochemist, educator; b. State Center, Ia., Feb. 13, 1917; d. Frank Hibbard and Katie Carolyn (Meyers) Ferguson; B.A. with high distinction, State U. Ia., 1938; Ph.D., U. Rochester, 1943; m. Robert Morgan Fink, Jan. 6, 1941; children—Patricia (Mrs. Robert Pope), Suzanne Joyce (Mrs. Walter Coppenrath). Asso. clin. prof. biophysics and nuclear medicine U. Cal. at Los Angeles, 1949-63, asso. research biochemist dept. medicine, 1961-66, asso. prof. dept. biophysics and nuclear medicine, 1964-66, biochemist, 1966-67, prof. dept. medicine, 1967—. Research biochemist VA Hosp., Long Beach, Cal., 1950-54, supervising research biochemist, 1954-66. Named U. Cal. at Los Angeles Woman of Sci., 1971; recipient Los Angeles Times Woman of Year award sci., 1971. Mem. Soc. Exptl. Biology and Medicine, Am. Soc. of Biol. Chemists, Sigma Xi, Phi Beta Kappa, Iota Sigma Pi. Research in thyroid, amino acids, purines and pyrimidines to sci. jours. Home: 1804 Rial Lane Los Angeles CA 90024 Office: Dept Medicine UCLA Center for Health Sciences Los Angeles CA 90024

FINKE, LEONDA FROELICH (MRS. ARNOLD I. FINKE), artist; b. Bklyn.; d. Herman and Evelyn (Praeger) Froehlich; student evenings Art Students League, N.Y.C., 1939-42, Ednl. Alliance, 1940-44; m. Arnold I. Finke, Mar. 30, 1947; children—David Nathan, Erica Florence, Rachel Hannah. One-man show Port Washington Library, 1967, Nassau Community Coll., 1969, Harbor Gallery, 1972, Nassau County Mus., 1973; exhibited in group shows at Audubon Artists, 1959-73, Bklyn. Mus., 1960, Hofstra U., 1961, Heckscher Mus., 1961, Adelphi Coll., 1963; Drawings U.S.A., 1963, traveling exhibits 1963-65; Lever House, 1965, 66, 68, Norfolk Mus. Drawing Bienniel, 1965-67, Nat. Assn. Women Artists, 1965—, Pa. Acad. Fine Arts Ann., 1966; Sculpture in permanent collection Norfolk Mus. Arts and Scis.; tchr. sculpture, drawing Nassau Community Coll. Mem. Nat. Sculpture Soc. (award, 1970), Nat. Assn. Women Artists (sculpture awards 1965, 67, 68, 71, 72), Manhasset Art Assn., Audubon Artists (sculpture award 1969, 72, 73), N.Y. Soc. Women Artists. Sculptor bronze and wood figures, drawings. Address: 623 Garden Lane East Meadow NY 11554

FINKEL, JEAN FENTON, architect; b. Welch, W.Va., Nov. 19, 1921; d. James Bristow and Marian Orna Eloise V. (Bornemann) Giltner; student Wheaton Coll., Norton, Mass., 1940, Boston U., 1941-43, Wyndham Coll., Boston, 1944; B.Arch., Western Res. U., 1949; m. Warren Edward Finkel, Jan. 25, 1954 (div. May 1974). Estimator, Roediger Constrn. Co., Cleve., 1947-49; architect Outcalt-Guenther, Architects, Cleve., 1949-50, 54; estimator F.E. Young Constrn. Co., San Diego, 1950-51; designer, job coordinator George A. Fuller, San Diego, 1951-52; architect San Diego Unified Sch. Dist., 1952-53; partner Finkel & Finkel, Architects, Lorain, O., 1954-74. Schweinfurth scholar, 1949. Mem. A.I.A. Important works include Lorain Community Hosp., Murray Ridge Sch., Lorain City Hall. Home and office: 2316 Harborview Blvd Lorain OH 44052

FINKELSTEIN, LUDMILLA SHOKOLY (MRS. BRUNO FINKELSTEIN), physician; b. St. Petersburg (now Leningrad), Russia, Mar. 19, 1913; d. Nicolai Alexander and Vera Timothy (Goliahowski) Shokoly; M.D., U. Belgrade, 1939; m. Bruno M. Finkelstein, Apr. 23, 1946. Came to U.S., 1958, naturalized, 1963.

Various profl. duties, 1940-45; resident phys. medicine and rehab., staff physiatrist Main Army Hosp., Belgrade, Yugoslavia, 1945-51; resident phys. medicine and rehab. Columbia Presbyn. Med. Center, Presbyn. Hosp., N.Y.C., 1959-61, mem. staff, 1962-63; staff phsysiatrist VA Hsop., Hines, Ill., 1964-67, N.Y. State Rehab. Hosp., West Haverstraw, N.Y., 1967-72; Lectr., physiatrist in charge clinic for sch. deformities State Inst. Phys. Edn., Belgrade, 1948-57; asst. rehab. medicine Columbia-Presbyn. Hosp., 1967—; chief phys. medicine and rehab. service VA Hosp., Castle Point, N.Y., 1972—; cons. in field. Diplomate Yugoslavian, Am. bds. phys. medicine and rehab. Mem. Am. Acad. Phys. Medicine and Rehab., Am. Congress Rehab. Medicine, N.Y. Soc. Phys. Medicine and Rehab., Am.-Yugoslav Med. Soc., Am. Physician Fellowship, World Med. Assn. Contbr. articles to fgn. jours. Address: VA Hosp Castle Point NY 12511

FINKELSTEIN, RUTH, physician; b. L.I., N.Y., Mar. 29, 1909; d. Israel and Augusta (Bloom) Finkelstein; grad. Johns Hopkins, 1930, M.D., 1935; m. Harry Greenberg, Oct. 8, 1942 (dec. Oct. 1963); children—Emily Ruth, David. Intern Sinai Hosp., Balt., 1935-36, resident, 1936-38, dir. adolescent gynecology, 1965—; individual practice medicine specializing in gynecology and obstetrics, Balt., 1938—. Cons. gynecology Balt. Health Dept.; cons. Health and Welfare Council Balt., Women's Personal Rights Orgn.; mem. med. adv. bd. Nat. Planned Parenthood World Population, Planned Parenthood Balt.; chmn. med. adv. com. Planned Parenthood Assn. Md., 1974—. Mem. Am. Med. Women's Assn., Am. Assn. Planned Parenthood Physicians, Med. and Chirurg. Soc. Md., Obstet. and Gynecol. Soc. Md., Johns Hopkins Alumni. Jewish religion. Club: Johns Hopkins Faculty. Contbr. articles to sci. jours. Home: 2407 Steele Rd Baltimore MD 21209 Office: 101 W Read St Med Arts Bldg Baltimore MD 21201

FINKLEA, NANCY RUTH GASQUE (MRS. TRACY F. FINKLEA, JR.), govt. ofcl.; b. South Weymouth, Mass., May 4, 1944; d. Samuel Norwood and Mary Elizabeth (Benton) Gasque; A.B. in Journalism, U. S.C., 1965. postgrad., 1966-68; postgrad. U. N.C., 1967; m. Tracy F. Finklea, Jr., Sept. 1, 1966; children—Nancy Elizabeth, Belva Jenkinson. Publs. asst. S.C. Dept. Edn., Columbia, 1965; asst. dir., research asst. Marion County Econ. Opportunity Commn., Marion, S.C., 1965-67; dir. information and planning coordination Dillon-Marion Community Action, Inc., Office Econ. Opportunity, Marion, 1967—. Orientation trainer Head Start, 1966-71, coordinator, 1966-73, mgmt. information system project leader, 1967-73. Sec. Latta Democratic Com., 1966. Bd. dirs. Latta Rescue Squad, 1969-70. Named Young Career Woman of Year, Latta. Bus. and Profl. Woman's Club, 1967. Mem. Women in Communications, Am. Assn. U. Women, U. S.C. Ednl. Found., U. S.C. Alumni Assn., Theta Sigma Phi. Methodist. Mem. Order Eastern Star. Home: 409 W Main St Latta SC 29565 Office: 209 Railroad Av Box 680 Marion SC 29571

FINLAY, WINIFRED LINDSAY, author; b. Newcastle-upon-Tyne, Eng., Apr. 27, 1910; d. James and Susan Lindsay (Crawford) McKissack; B.A., Newcastle U., 1931, D.Th. P.T., 1932, M.A., 1940; m. Evan Finlay, July 25, 1935; 1 dau., Gillian (Mrs. David Hancock). Tchr., Newcastle, Leeds and Stratford-Upon-Avon, 1933-48; lectr., Northampton, Eng., 1950; freelance author, contbr. BBC plays for young people, 1947—. Mem. Soc. Authors. Author 25 books including: Storm over Cheviot, 1955; Folk Tales from the North, 1968; Danger at Black Dyke (best juvenile thriller Mystery Writers Am. 1970), 1968; Beadbonny Ash, 1973. Address: The Old House Walgrave Northampton England

FINLAYSON, ANN LATHROP, author, editor; b. N.Y.C., Mar. 25, 1925; d. Frank Lathrop and Anna (Neacy) Finlayson; B.S. in Journalism, Northwestern U., 1945. Editor pulp mags. Popular Publs., N.Y.C., 1950-51; editor, staff writer True Story, Macfadden Publs., N.Y.C., 1951-60; free lance writer, 1960-63; editor Rutledge Books, Inc., N.Y.C., 1963-64; free lance copy editor, proofreader for book pubs., free lance writer, 1965—; author: Runaway Teen, 1964; A Summer to Remember, 1965; Decathlon Men, 1966; Stars of the Modern Olympics, 1967; Champions at Bat, 1970; Redcoat in Boston, 1971; Rebecca's War, 1972; (with Harold B. Gill) Colonial Virginia, 1973; Greenhorn on the Frontier, 1974; House Cat, 1974; Colonial Maryland, 1974. Home: 33 Western Hwy N Blauvelt NY 10913

FINLEY, SARA CREWS (MRS. WAYNE H. FINLEY), physician; b. Lineville, Ala., Feb. 26, 1930; d. Jessie B. and Jessie E. (Mathews) Crews; B.S., U. Ala., 1951, M.D., 1955; m. Wayne House Finley, July 6, 1952; children—Randall Wayne, Sara Jane. Intern Lloyd Noland Hosp., Fairfield, Ala., 1955-56; NIH fellow pediatrics Univ. Hosp., Birmingham, Ala., 1956-59; NIH trainee med. genetics U. Uppsala (Sweden), 1960-61; asso. prof. pediatrics, asso. dir. lab. med. genetics Sch. Medicine and Dentistry, U. Ala., Birmingham, 1969—; mem. staff U. Hosp., Children's Hosp. Bd. dirs. Aid for Retarded Children. Mem. Am. Soc. Human Genetics, So. Soc. Pediatric Research, Am. Fedn. Clin. Research, Phi Beta Kappa, Sigma Xi, Alpha Epsilon Delta. Home: 2725 Cherokee Rd Birmingham AL 35216 Office: 1720 7th Av S Birmingham AL 35294

FINLEY, THELMA LOUISE SUTLEY, rancher, county judge; b. Center, Colo., July 8, 1902; d. Myron M. and Annie (Chrisman) Sutley; A.B., Colo. State Tchrs. Coll., 1926; M.A., Adams State Coll., 1964; m. Rockard E. Finley, May 25, 1928 (dec.); children—Rockard E., Marianne (Mrs. Ronald G. Whitsitt). Tchr. pub. schs., Center, 1923-25, 63-64, Branson, Colo., 1926-29, Hooper, Colo., 1934-40; partner, bookkeeper Finley Potato Co., Center, 1940-69; municipal judge, Saguache, Colo., to 1973; assisting municipal judge, Center, to 1973. Rep. potato legislative hearings 1960, 61-62. Leader, 4-H, 1920-21, 23-25, 38-44; treas. Woman's Soc. Christian Service, 1953-58; pres. Center Flower Show, 1955-60, 62-66; dir. San Luis Valley Cowbelles, 1955-59, 65—; dir. Center Park Assn., 1959—. Mem. Center Democratic Com., 1932-66, vice chmn., 1934-42, 44-66, chmn., vice chmn., 1942-44; vice chmn. Dem. 3d Congl. Dist., 1955-62, 12th Jud. Dist., 1955-60, 24th Rep. Dist., 1964-66; mem. Colo. Senate, 1959-60, historian Colo. Legislature, 1961-62; mem. Colo. Water Congress, 1959—; mem. Colo. Probation, Parole and Corrections Assn. Treas. Community Council Clubs Center. Recipient Alumni award 4-H, 1966. Mem. Colo., San Luis Valley cattlemen's assns., Center C. of C. (past dir.), Bus. and Profl. Women (pres. 3 times). Methodist. Mem. Order Eastern Star, Rebekah. Home: 111 W 3d St PO Drawer J Center CO 81125

FINLEY, YVONNE ANTOINETTE SMITH (MRS. BENJAMIN F. FINLEY, JR.), social worker; b. St. Louis, Sept. 10, 1936; d. Walter E. and Carenthia (Springfield) Smith; B.S., St. Louis U., 1958, M.S.W., 1962; student spl. courses U. Chgo.; m. Benjamin F. Finley, Jr., Dec. 26, 1962. Casework supr. Ill. Dept. Children and Family Services, 1962-69; social worker Woodlawn Early Childhood Devel. Center, 1971-74. Mem. Joint Citizens for Chestang; sec. Afro-Am. Family and Community Services Inc., 1968-69, now mem. ladies aux.; sec. Whitney M. Young Community Center. Mem. Nat. Assn. Social Workers, Acad. Certified Social Workers, Child Care Assn. Ill., Nat. Assn. Black Social Workers, Black Child Devel. Inst., Black Child Devel. Assn., Alpha Kappa Alpha. Home: 9351 S Cregier St Chicago IL 60617

FINN, FRANCES MARY, educator; b. Pitts., May 6, 1937; d. Stephen Benson and Geraldine Harriet (Weber) Finn; B.S., U. Pitts., 1959, M.S., 1961, Ph.D., 1964; m. Klaus Hofmann, Feb. 26, 1965. Postdoctoral fellow Harvard U., 1964-65; asst. prof. dept. biochemistry U. Pitts., 1969-73, asso. prof., 1973—. Mem. Am. Soc. Biol. Chemists, Am. Chem. Soc. Home: 1467 Mohican Dr Pittsburgh PA 15228

FINN, JOAN LOCKWOOD, communications cons.; b. Plainfield, N.J., June 6, 1929; d. William Albert and Ada Louise (Dayton) Finn; B.A. in Am. History, Radcliffe Coll., 1951; certificate d'attendance U. Paris Sorbonne Coll., 1952. Copywriter, J.C. Penney Co., Inc., 1957-58; jr. account exec. Dudley-Anderson-Yutzey, 1958-61; account exec. Theodore R. Sills & Co., 1961-63, Ted Bates & Co., 1963-67; account supr. Henderson & Roll, 1967-69; dir. press relations Motion Picture Assn. Am., N.Y.C., 1969-70; freelance writer, N.Y.C., 1971-73; communications cons. Coopers & Lybrand, Inc., 1973—; v.p., dir. 285 Riverside Dr. Corp., 1971-73. Mem. steering com. N.Y. Upbeat. Pub. relations, fgn. affairs com. FDR-Woodrow Wilson Democratic Club, 1965. Mem. Pub. Relations Soc. Am., Bus. and Profl. Club (pres.). Democrat. Presbyn. Club: Harvard (N.Y.C.). Author: Heritage of Evil, 1968. Librettist Chicken Little. Editor Diet Ann., 1973, Diet Yearbook, 1973. Contbr. articles to Motor Boating, Ideal Romances, Am. Mercury, Jack O'Dwyer's Newsletters, New Ideas for Figure and Diet, Modern Maturity mags. Home: 285 Riverside Dr New York City NY 10025

FINNAN, ANNE MARY, librarian; b. Scranton, Pa., Jan. 11, 1922; d. Joseph Thomas and Mary Catherine (Healey) Finnan; A.B., Marywood Coll., 1943, B.S. in L.S., 1944; postgrad. George Washington U. Law Sch., 1952-53, Harvard, summer 1968; M.A., Tchrs. Coll., Columbia, 1958. Asst. librarian Mt. St. Agnes Coll., Balt., 1944-45; librarian Glen Burnie (Md.) High Sch., 1945-46, Loyola Coll., Balt., 1946-51; jr. librarian U.S. Supreme Ct., Washington, 1952-54; librarian City Hall div. Fordham U., 1954-69, reference librarian Univ. Library at Lincoln Center, N.Y.C., 1969—. Bd. mgmt. Central br. YWCA, N.Y.C. Mem. A.L.A., Spl. Libraries Assn., Catholic Library Assn., Kappa Delta Pi, Phi Delta Kappa. Roman Catholic. Bibliog. cons. Edn. Yearbook, 1973-74, 74-75. Home: 883 Boulevard East Weehawken NJ 07087 also 714 Hawthorne St Avoca PA 18641 Office: Columbus Av and 60th St New York City NY 10023

FINNERTY, JEAN CLARE, educator; b. N.Y.C.; d. John Joseph and Rose Marie (Bonser) Finnerty; B.A., Manhattan Coll., 1941; M.A., St. John's U., 1946; Ph.D., Fordham U., 1959. Elementary sch. tchr. Cath. schs., Bklyn., 1935-41; secondary sch. tchr. math. Bklyn., 1941-59; grad. adviser secondary schs., over-all supr., curriculum dir. Dept. Edn., Rockville Centre, N.Y., 1959-66, prin. St. Agnes Acad. High Sch., College Point, N.Y., 1966-68; asst. supt. Woodcliff Lake Pub. Schs., N.J., 1968-71; adj. prof. Montclair State Coll. and Seton Hall U., 1968-71; asso. prof. Seton Hall U. Grad. Sch. Adminstrn. and Supervision, South Orange, N.J., 1971—. Cons. several maj. textbook cos. in social studies, 1959-70; instr. coll. math. Manhattan Coll. Extension, 1946-53; instr. English St. Joseph Coll., summers 1942-54; cons. N.Y. State Bd. Regents and Scholarships Exams., 1964, 69; mem. Carnegie team Notre Dame Study and Research Team, 1962-63; dir. in-service math Molloy Coll., L.I., 1959-66. Mem. panel Gov.'s Conf. Nat. Council Christians and Jews, 1959-66; mem. Cath. Interracial Council, Nassau Ecumenical Council, Nassau Community Mental Health Assn., Bklyn. Supt. Schs. Adv. Council, 1959-67; ofcl. observer Internat. Ednl. Conf., Geneva, Switzerland, summer 1964. Mem. Nat. Cath. Edn. Assn. (sec. elementary exec. com. 1960-63, chmn. supr. sect. 1966-68, adv. com. 1968—, chmn. middle states 1970, exec. com. 1959-65, mem. middle states team 1968), N.E.A., Am. Assn. U. Profs., Am. Assn. Supervision Curriculum Devel., Am. Assn. Sch. Adminstrs. Co-author series geography lessons video-taped for Channel 13 TV, 1960-66, 8 spelling books, Spell Correctly, 1965, Evaluative Criteria for the Elementary Catholic Schools, 1965; author: Revolution in Geography, Too?, 1963. Home: 9 St Cloud Pl West Orange NJ 07052 Office: Seton Hall U South Orange NJ 07079

FINNEY, BETTY JANE MACKEY, psychologist, educator; b. N.Y.C., Apr. 11, 1926; d. James Phillip and Agnes (Campbell) Mackey; B.A., Flora Stone Mather Coll., 1946; M.A., Case-Western Res. U., 1958, Ph.D. (grad. fellow), 1968; children—Robbin (Mrs. Kenneth Watkins), Robert William, Wendy L., David C. Instr., Case Western Res. U., Cleve., 1967-68; prof. psychology Millersville (Pa.) State Coll., 1968—; pvt. practice psychology Psychol. Assos. of Lancaster (Pa.), 1971—. Cons. Lancaster Cleft Palate Clinic, 1969-71, Family and Children's Services, 1969—. Mem. Am. Ednl. Research Assn., Nat. Assn. Sch. Psychologists, Am., Pa. psychol. assns. Home: 49 Leaf Park Rd 2 Lancaster PA 17603 Office: Psychology Dept Millersville State Coll Millersville PA 17551

FINNEY, FLORENCE DONADY, state senator; b. L.I. City, N.Y., Mar. 19, 1903; d. William Matthew and Elizabeth (Conroy) Donady; student pub. schs., L.I. City; m. James A. Finney, July 22, 1923; 1 son, James A. Sec. to exec. John W. Thomas, Inc., N.Y.C., 1920-25; sec. to v.p. Guggenheim Bros., N.Y.C., 1928-35; co-partner with husband Suburban Awning Co., 1935—; mem. Conn. Ho. of Reps., 1949-50, 51-52, 53-54; mem. Conn. Senate 1955—, pres. pro tem, 1973-74. Mem. Conn. Legislative Council, 1961-69; mem. Conn. Transp. Authority. 1969-73; asst. sec. Conn. Constl. Conv., 1965. Mem. Greenwich Rep. Town Meeting, 1941—. Mem. Corp. Greenwich Hosp.; bd. dirs. Salvation Army. Mem. Nat. Order Women Legislators. Episcopalian. Home: 10 Riverside Lane Riverside CT 06878 Office: 59 River Rd Cos Cob CT 06807

FINNEY, JACQUELINE JOYCE, mech. contractor exec.; b. McKeesport, Pa., July 22, 1936; d. Elmer Roy and Rita Jane (Hamilton) Campbell; student pub. schs.; m. Ray Finney, Nov. 26, 1954 (div. Dec. 1973); children—Virginia, Diane, Thomas, Colleen, Vicki, Mitchell. With U.S. Piping, Inc., Portage, Ind., 1965—, v.p., 1969—. Mem. Plumbing-Heating-Cooling Contractors Assn., Sheet Metal and Air Conditioning Contractors Nat. Assn. Presbyn. Home: Rural Route #8 Box 360-A Valparaiso IN 46383 Office: PO Box 28 Portage IN 46368

FINNEY, JOAN MARIE MCINROY (MRS. SPENCER W. FINNEY, JR.), city ofcl.; b. Topeka, Kan., Feb. 11, 1925; d. Leonard L. and Mary M. (Sands) McInroy; B.A., Washburn U., 1974; m. Spencer W. Finney, Jr., July 24, 1957; children—Sally, Dick, Mary. Sec. Washington and Topeka offices U.S. Senator Frank Carlson, 1953-69; commr. elections Shawnee County, Kan., 1970-72; adminstrv. asst. to mayor of Topeka, 1973—. Rep. candidate for U.S. Ho. of Reps., 1972; alternate bd. mem. Shawnee County Community Assistance and Action Com., 1973-74; acting dir. Topeka Housing Authority, 1974. Bd. dirs. Big Brother-Big Sister. Mem. Kan. Women's Polit. Caucus, Women Aware, Sigma Alpha Iota. Roman Catholic (mem. bd. dirs., mem. finance com.). Home: 4600 W 19th St Topeka KS 66604 Office: City Hall Topeka KS 66604

FINNEY, KATHERINE, educator; b. Hamilton, O.; d. Harry Glenn and Helen (Weld) Finney; B.A., U. Ark., 1935; M.A., Columbia, 1936, Ph.D., 1944. Mem. faculty Smith Coll., Northampton, Mass., 1937-39, Flora Stone Mather Coll., Western Res. U., Cleve., 1939-43; with Chase Nat. Bank, N.Y.C., 1943-44; mem. faculty Conn. Coll., New London, 1944—, now prof. econs., dir. grad. studies. Dir. Univ. Research Inst. Conn. Mem. Am. Econ. Assn., Am. Finance Assn., Phi Beta Kappa. Author: History of Savings Banks of Northampton, Massachusetts, 1945; Interbank Deposits, 1954. Address: Fanning Hall Conn Coll New London CT 06320

FINNEY, LYNNE DRATLER, lawyer; b. Los Angeles, June 29, 1941; d. Jay and Berenice Tolins (Eunson) Dratler; B.A. cum laude, U. Cal. at Berkeley, 1962; J.D. magna cum laude, Loyola U., Los Angeles, 1967; m. Charles Finney, Jan. 29, 1966. Admitted to Cal. bar, 1968, U.S. Supreme Ct. Bar, 1972; atty. Loeb & Loeb, Los Angeles, 1967-70; instr. Loyola U. Sch. Law, Los Angeles, 1969-70; trial atty. County Counsel Santa Cruz County, Cal., 1970-71; asst. prof. U. Santa Clara (Cal.) Law Sch., 1971-73, dir. Law Clinic, 1971-73; atty., spl. subcom. on investigations House Interstate and Fgn. Commerce Com., Washington, 1973—. Adviser, Council on Legal Edn. Opportunities, Los Angeles, 1969; Chairperson, Com. to Revise San Lorenzo Valley Plan for Residential Devel., 1972-73. Bd. dirs. Legal Aid Soc. Santa Clara County. Recipient Honor award Loyola U., 1967; awards West Pub. Co., 1965, 66, Am. Jurisprudence, 1965-67. Mem. Am. Judicature Soc., Los Angeles County, Santa Clara County bar assns., Barristers Santa Clara County (v.p. 1973), Congl. Staff Club. Home: 1654 29th St NW Washington DC 20007 Office: Rayburn House Office Bldg Washington DC 20515

FINNILA, BIRGIT (MRS. ALLAN FINNILA), contralto; b. Falkenberg, Sweden, Jan. 20, 1931; d. Soren and Helny (Persson) Carlsson; student song and music with concert singer Ingalill Linden, Gothenburg, Sweden, Prof. Roy Henderson, London, Eng.; m. Allan Finnila, Dec. 10, 1950; children—Annika, Ellen, Peter, Orjan, Jeanette. Began singing at an early age; made debut in Gothenburg, 1963; sang with numerous orchs., choral socs. throughout Europe, U.S.A., S.Am., Australia, Asia, including Stockholm Philharmonics, Helsinki City Orch., Danish Radio Orch., Oslo Philharmonic, NDR Orch., Hamburg, Berlin Philharmonic, London Symphony Orch., New Philharmonia, London, Eng., LaScala, Milan, Italy, N.Y. Philharmonic, Balt., Buffalo, Cin., Detroit, Cleve., Houston, Los Angeles, Phila., San Francisco orchs., numerous others; gave recitals in N.Y.C., Chgo., London, cities Europe including Soviet Union; created role Orfeo in Gluck's Orfeo ed Euridice, Lucretia in Britten's Rape of Lucretia at Festival des Flandres, Teodata in Handel's Flavio, Erda in Rheingold and Siegfried, others. Recorded works by Bach, Telemann, Cimarosa, Bruckner, Mahler. Address: c/o Svensk Konsertdirektion AB Junigatan 27 415 15 Goteborg Sweden

FINOCCHIARO, ARLENE CLAIRE, occupational therapist; b. Chgo., Mar. 10, 1943; d. Paul C. and Mary Hazel (Woods) Jung; B.S. in Occupational Therapy, Mt. Mary Coll., Milw., 1965; also spl. courses in field; m. Raymond E. Finocchiaro, Aug. 8, 1970; 1 dau., Deanna Marie. Research occupational therapist Colo. Gen. Hosp., Denver, 1967-70, Fitzsimmons Gen. Hosp., Denver, 1967-70; cons. perceptual motor dysfunction Poe Ednl. Labs., Denver, 1967-70; chief occupational therapy Del Curative Workshop, Wilmington, 1970-73; cons. occupational therapy Formative Play Program, Diamond State Assn. Children with Learning Disabilities, 1974—. Mem. vocational preparation com. Gov. Del. Adv. Council Exceptional Children, 1973. Served with AUS, 1965-67. Mem. Am. (certification com. 1974—), Del. occupational therapy assns., Soc. Behavioral Kinesiology, Beta Beta Beta, Pi Theta Epsilon. Author articles. Home: 208 Sunsey Dr Delaire Wilmington DE 19809

FIORANI, ROSE FLOREY, broadcasting exec.; b. Scranton, Pa., June 9, 1903; d. Frank F. and Marie (Valverde) Florey; student Powell Sch. Bus., 1928; pvt. tutor in drama, 1929; m. Angelo William Fiorani, June 24, 1925 (dec.); children—Eleanor (Mrs. Al Casteili), Rosemary (Mrs. Terrence Gallagher, Jr.). Co-owner, comml. mgr. and broadcaster, radio sta. WPTS, Pittston, Pa., 1953—, pres., 1972—; Mem. exec. bd. Scranton Philharmonic Orch.; pres. Scranton Philharmonic Orch. Assn., 1964—; active A.R.C., City Beautiful Assn., Women's Civic League of Lackawana County, Polio, Cancer and Muscular Dystrophy Assn.; gen. chmn. Scranton Opera Guild, 1942—; founder, v.p. Lucian Guild for Blind Aux., 1954—; co-founder, bd. dirs. Broadway Theatre League Scranton; co-founder St. Mary's Villa Nursing Home for Aged and Sick, 1970, gen. chmn. benefit musicale, 1970, 1st v.p., 1973—; gen. chmn. installation dinner St. Joseph's Orphanage and Hosp. Northeastern Pa., 1970. Vice-chmn. Scranton-Dunmore Sewer Authority, 1972—. Bd. dirs. Lackawana County Mental Health Assn., Pro-Life Pa. Recipient citation VA, 1955; Oscar award Luzerne County United Fund, 1955-59; citation Women's Civic League of Lackawana County, 1959; recipient Amita award N.Y.C., 1961; Lady Equestrian Order of Holy Sepulchre of Jerusalem; citations, Lucian Guild for Blind, also County med. socs., 1963, 64; named Mother of Year, United Mothers Am., 1967. Hon. life mem. Scranton Philharmonic Orch. Soc. (past pres.), Scranton chapter A.R.C.; mem. Hemodyalysis Assn., Scranton C. of C. (dir. 1962), Am. Women in Radio and Television (pres. N.E. Pa. chpt.; gen. chmn. Pa. conf. 1959), Pa. Fedn. Women (radio and TV chmn.), Pittston Hosp. Aux., Mother Cabrini Soc. (trustee), Altar and Rosary Soc., Sacred Heart Enthronement League, St. Lucy's Dramatic Soc. (past pres.), Nat. Council Catholic Women (pub. relations dir. 1949—), Young Musicians Soc. (dir.), Scranton Advt. and Sales Club (plaque for 30 years outstanding service 1962). Club: Columbus of Lackawanna County. Home: 1000 Clay Av Scranton PA 18510 Office: 83 Foote Av Duryea PA 18642

FIORAVANTI, NANCY ELEANOR, bank ofcl.; b. Gloucester, Mass., Apr. 10, 1935; d. Richard Joseph and Evelyn Grace (Souza) Fioravanti; grad. high sch. Various positions and depts. Cape Ann Bank and Trust Co. (successor to Gloucester Safe Deposit & Trust Co.), Gloucester, 1953—, with trust dept., 1959—, asst. trust officer, 1970—. Mem. Nat. Assn. Bank Women. Home: 19 Harvard St Gloucester MA 01930 Office: 154 Main St Gloucester MA 01930

FIORELLA, BARBARA TOHMS, social worker; b. Chgo., July 15, 1927; d. Clifton and Frances (Byrnes) Tohms; B.S., Pa. State U., 1959; M.S.W. (Nat. Inst. Mental Health fellow), Fla. State U., 1962; postgrad. Fla. Atlantic U., 1968; m. Theodore Joseph Fiorella, June 12, 1948 (div. Oct. 1958); children—Stephen Ward, Mark John, Theodore Jeffry, Barbara Lynn. Caseworker Children's Service Bur., Miami, Fla., 1962-64; psychiat. caseworker Jackson Meml. Hosp. Psychiat. Inst., Miami, 1964—; mem. clin. faculty Barry Coll. Grad. Sch. Social Work, Miami, 1972—. Instr. dept. psychiatry U. Miami Med. Sch., 1964—; vis. lectr. social work Fla. Internat. U., 1974. Bd. dirs. Big Sisters of Greater Miami, 1969-71, v.p., 1970-71. Mem. Fla. Juvenile Officer's Assn., Fla. Assn. Clin. Social Workers, Assn. Agy. Field Instrs., Acad. Certified Social Workers. Home: 10235 SW 106th St Miami FL 33156 Office: 1700 NW 10th Av Miami FL 33132

FIORI, GLADYS ELIZABETH BIRDSALL (MRS. JAMES VINCENT FIORI), civic worker; b. Ralston, Pa., Sept. 4, 1924; d. Howard Chester and Agnes Leone (Sampson) Birdsall; student Union-Endicott Sch., 1940-42; m. James Vincent Fiori, Nov. 20, 1948. Instr. traffic dept. N.Y. Telephone Co., Endicott, 1943-49; receptionist Ludlow Motor Carrier Co., Binghamton, N.Y., 1949-52; clk. Guy F. Johnson, Inc., Binghamton, 1952-54; asst. office mgr., head bookkeeping dept. Columbia Gas N.Y., Inc., Endicott, 1954-64; research on family genealogy, Endicott, N.Y., 1964—. Charter mem. Meals on Wheels Western Broome, Inc.; mem. Broome County Bicentennial Commn., 1971—. Reporter for Soule Kindred Newsletter, Duxbury, Mass. Co-founder, Endicott Hist. and Preservation Soc., 1964, 1st sec., treas., 1964—; area chief Broome County United Fund drive, 1967-70. Republican campaign chmn. West Town Union, 1967; Rep. committeewoman Broome County, 1964—; pres. Greater Endicott Women's Rep. Club, 1966-67, dir., 1968-69; mem. West Town Union Rep. Exec. Com., Endicott, 1966—, Nat. Fedn. Rep. Women, Washington, 1964—, N.Y. State Fedn. Rep. Women, N.Y.C., 1964—; mem. Broome County Rep. Women's Club, Johnson City Women's Rep. Club. Mem. N.Y. State Hist. Assn., Tioga County, Lycoming County, Bradford County, Susquehanna County hist. socs., Central N.Y., Tioga County, Orange County geneal. socs., Cobblestone Soc., Central N.Y. Archtl. Soc., Am. Assn. State and Local History, Birdsall Family Reunion Assn. (pres. 1965-66, sec. 1967—), Am. Heritage Soc., D.A.R. (regent Tuscarora chpt. 1972—), Daus. Am. Colonists (1st vice regent Gov. John Cranston chpt. 1974—), Binghamton Civic Club, Am. Legion Aux. Clubs: Endicott Federated Garden (pres. 1970-72), Woman's of Endicott; Monday Afternoon (Binghamton). Home: 928 Neal Rd Endicott NY 13760 Office: PO Box 52 Endicott NY 13760

FIORINA, BETTY VICKNAIR (MRS. A. J. FIORINA), state govt. ofcl.; b. El Paso, 1925; d. Jules A. and Delphine (Souders) Vicknair; student in Bus. Adminstrn., 2 yrs.; m. A. J. Fiorina; children—Tom, Gary. Mem. adminstrv. staff N.M. Legislature, 1949-57; sec. of state State of N.M., 1959-62, 71—; chief clk. N.M. Constl. Conv., 1969. Bd. dirs. A.R.C. Recipient Am. Heritage Found. award Mem. Am. Businesswomen's Assn. Democrat. Office: 713 Don Diego St Santa Fe NM 87501*

FIREBAUGH, FRANCILLE MALOCH (MRS. JOHN DAVID FIREBAUGH), educator; b. El Dorado, Ark., July 15, 1933; d. Delton Verdis and Dorothy (Measeles) Maloch; B.S., U. Ark., 1955; M.S., U. Tenn., 1956; Ph.D. (Phi Upsilon Omicron Nat. Candle fellow) Cornell U., 1962; m. John David Firebaugh, Dec. 28, 1970. Instr. U. Tex., 1956-58; grad. asst. Cornell U., 1958-62; asst. prof. Ohio State U., Columbus, 1962-65, asso. prof. home econs., 1965-68, prof., 1969-73, dir. sch. Home Econs., asso. dean Coll. Agr. and Home Econs., 1973—; prin. family economist Coop. State Research Soc. U.S. Dept. Agr., Washington, 1973. Home mgmt. cons. UAID, U. Udaipur, Rajastan, India, 1970. Mem. summer faculty various univs. Mem. Am., Ohio (chmn. family econs.-home mgmt. sect. 1965-67, pres. 1970-72), Franklin County (scholarship chmn. 1965-66) home econs. assns., Inst. Mgmt. Scis., Omicron Nu, Pi Lambda Theta, Phi Upsilon Omicron, Gamma Sigma Delta, Phi Kappa Phi, Sigma Delta Epsilon. Contbr. articles to profl. jours. Home: 2731 Chester Rd Columbus OH 43221

FIRESTONE, DORIS FLANIGAN (MRS. ROBERT IDEN FIRESTONE), hosp. ofcl.; b. Toledo; d. Edward Yearsly and Carmen (Gamble) Flanigan; B.A., Albion Coll., 1942; postgrad. North Central Coll., 1956-58, U. Ind., 1957-58; m. Robert Iden Firestone, Feb. 13, 1943 (dec. 1958); children—Patricia Lynn (Mrs. Hillard), Susan Ann. With Reeves Advt., Toledo, 1942-43; account exec. Standard Oil Research Labs., Cleve., 1943-45; tchr. art and English, Toledo Bd. Edn., 1960-61; mgr. women's div. Patricia Norman Personnel, Toledo, 1961-62; dir. pub. relations St. Vincent Hosp. and Med. Center, Toledo, 1963—, mem. adminstrv. exec. com., 1966—. Active N.W. Ohio Heart Assn., 1968-70, Am. Cancer Assn., 1965; chmn. publicity council Community Chest, 1969-70, St. Vincent Hosp. and Med. Center Guild, 1963—, Toledo Mus. Art, 1961—, Toledo Symphony Orch., 1968-70, Toledo Opera Club, 1969—; mem. pub. relations com. mental health Internat. Inst. Bd. Dirs., 1969-71; mem. planning com. Nurse Recruitment Hosp. Council of N.W. Ohio, 1969—; active Toledo Safety Council, 1966-70; bd. dirs. N.W. Ohio Practical Nurse Tng. Center, 1968-70; mem. President's Com. on Employment of Handicapped, Washington, 1968-69; bd. dirs. Village Players, 1965—, sec., 1972-73; pres. Village Players Guild, 1967-68. Recipient Ann. Advt. Silver medal award Am. Advt. Fedn., 1967; named Outstanding Advt. Women 5th Dist., 1968. Mem. Women's Advt. Club (pres. 1969), Acad. Hosp. Pub. Relations, Soc. Pub. Relations Dirs., N.W. Ohio Assn. Indsl. Editors, Internat. Assn. Bus. Communicators, Pub. Relations Soc. Am., Am., Catholic hosp. assns., Women in Communications, Delta Gamma, Theta Alpha Phi. Episcopalian. Home: 3901 Elmhurst St Toledo OH 43613 Office: 2213 Cherry St Toledo OH 43608

FIRESTONE, LILLIAN MICHEL (MRS. WILLIAM S. BOAL), pub. relations exec.; b. Harbin, China, Aug. 18, 1932; d. Michael and Celia (Kaplan) Firestone; B.A., Barnard Coll., 1954; m. William S. Boal, Mar. 3, 1971; children—(by previous marriage) Risa C. Levenson, Marc Alfred D'Estaing. Mag. writer, editor, spl. books div. Fawcett Publs., N.Y.C., 1954-60; account exec. Robert S. Taplinger, N.Y.C., 1960-64; pres. Firestone Assos., N.Y.C., 1964—. Lectr. marketing Columbia U. Sch. Pharmacy, 1970, Am. Marketing Assn., 1971. Mem. Fashion Group, Cosmetic Career Women (gov. 1969). Editor Fashion Group Bull., 1972. Address: 43 Fifth Av New York City NY 10003

FIRM, RUTH M., educator; b. Paterson, N.J., July 7, 1912; d. Samuel and Grace (Hemingway) Firm; B.S., M.A., Ph.D., Columbia; m. L. Allen Hangen, 1937 (div.). Hosp. recreation worker Army and Navy hosps. in South Pacific, A.R.C.; mem. faculty Wilson Coll., Chambersburg, Pa., Mt. Holyoke Coll., South Hadley, Mass.; mem. faculty Sweet Briar (Va.) Coll., 1960—, now prof., chmn. art dept. Ford grantee Seminar on S.E. Asia at U. Mich., summer 1964; recipient U. State N.Y. award Seminar on Chinese art history at N.Y. Inst. Fine Arts, summer 1965; Fulbright travel grantee Seminar on Chinese culture, soc., Taiwan, summer 1966; U.S. Dept. Health, Edn. and Welfare grantee to Seminar on Contemporary India, India, summer 1970. Mem. Coll. Art Assn., Archeol. Inst. Am., Assn. for Asian Studies. Home: Sweet Briar Coll Sweet Briar VA 24595

FIRTH, ROXIE ANDREWS (MRS. JACOB G. FIRTH), educator; b. Howell, Mich.; d. John Richard and Lillian (Cline) Andrews; B.S., Wayne State U., 1929; M.A., U. Mich., 1932; grad. Detroit Conservatory Music, 1924; m. Jacob G. Firth, June 25, 1932; children—Gerald M., Barbette Yvonne. Elementary tchr., Royal Oak, Mich. Auditorium, 1918-32; supervising prin. Franklin Sch., Royal Oak, 1917-32; elementary supr. Redford Union Schs., 1934-38; asst. to dir. in charge tchr. placement div. Bur. Appointments, U. Mich., 1938-42; prin. Jerolene Sch., Sturgis, Mich., 1948-52; guidance and reading counselor and dir. reading center Sturgis (Mich.) Pub. Schs., 1959-65; dir. Reading Center for Adult Illiterates, Sturgis, 1969-72. Active Camp Fire Girls. Mem. Am. Assn. U. Women, Nat., Mich. edn. assns., Internat. Reading Assn., Sturgis Bus. and Profl. Woman's Club, Pi Lambda Theta, Delta Kappa Gamma. Methodist (organist, instr. lab. schs.). Club: Sturgis Woman's. Author children's stories. Contbr. articles to various ednl. Jours. Home: 19937 E William Ct Grosse Pointe Woods MI 48236

FISCH, ARLINE MARIE, artist, educator; b. Bklyn., Aug. 21, 1931; d. Nicholas H. and Elizabeth (Fischer) Fisch; B.S. in Art, Skidmore Coll., 1952; M.A. in Art, U. Ill., 1954; postgrad. (Fulbright Found. grantee), Kunsthaadvaerkerskolen, Copenhagen, Denmark, 1956-57. Instr. art Wheaton Coll., Norton, Mass., 1954-56; Skidmore Coll., Saratoga Springs, N.Y., 1958-61; prof. art San Diego State U., 1961—. Summer vis. lectr. Guldsmedshojskolen, Copenhagen, Haystack Mt. Sch. Crafts, Deer Isle, Me., 1965,66, Penland (N.C.) Sch. Crafts, 1968-71, 74; exhibited in one-man shows Pasadena (Cal.) Mus. Art, 1962, Kunstindustrimuseet, Copenhagen, 1967, Mus. Contemporary Crafts, 1968, Goldsmiths' Hall, London, 1971, Lee Nordness Galleries, 1971; exhibited in goup shows Cal. Design 9, 10, 11, 1965, 68, 71, Art of Personal Adornment, 1965, Form and Quality, Munich Internat, 1966-74, Schmuck-Objekte, Zurich, 1971, 1st World Crafts Exhbn., Toronto, 1974; represented in permanent collections Johnson Wax Coll., Worshipful Co. Goldsmiths, Minn. Mus. Art, St. Paul; dealer Lee Nordness Galleries, 1968—. Fulbright research grantee, 1966-67; Danforth Faculty grantee, summers 1959, 60; San Diego State Faculty research grantee, 1970. Named Outstanding Alumna award Skidmore Coll., 1972. Mem. Soc. N.Am. Goldsmiths (founding, sec. treas. 1973—), Haystack Mt. Sch. Crafts (trustee), Am. (trustee), World (U.S. sect.), Crafts councils, Allied Craftsmen San Diego (pres. 1965). Democrat. Roman Catholic. Home: San Diego CA

FISCH, EDITH L., lawyer; b. N.Y.C., Mar. 3, 1923; d. Hyman and Clara (Lond) Fisch; B.A., Bklyn. Coll., 1945; LL.B., Columbia, 1948, LL.M., 1949, J.S.D., 1950; m. Steven L. Werner, Dec. 14, 1963. Admitted to N.Y. State bar, 1948, U.S. Supreme Ct. bar, 1957; asst. to Prof. Richard R. Powell, Columbia, 1948; asso. firm Conrad & Smith, N.Y.C., 1951-57; practiced in N.Y.C., 1957—; pres. Lond Pub. Co., 1958—; Counsel Brodsky, Lenett & Altman, 1973; prof. law N.Y. Law Sch., 1962-65. Legal and tech. adviser to Women Lawyers in U.S., 1957; ednl. dir., trustee Found. for Continuing Legal Edn. Democratic county committeewoman 7th dist., N.Y., 1949-52. Mem. Assn. Bar City N.Y., Nat. Assn. Women Lawyers, N.Y. Women's Bar Assn. (pres. 1970-71), N.Y. State Trial Lawyers Assn., Bklyn. Coll. Lawyers Group, Inc. (rec. sec. 1961-63, bd. govs. 1963-65), Friends of Columbia Libraries, Bklyn. Coll. Alumni Assn., Alumni Assn. Columbia, Acad. Polit. Sci., Nat. Women's Com. Brandeis U. (dir.), Am. Assn. U. Women, Am. Arbitration Assn. (nat. panel). Author: The Cy Pres Doctrine in the U.S., 1950; Lawyers in Industry, 1956; Fisch on N.Y. Law of Evidence, 1959; (with M. Schwartz) State Laws on the Employment of Women, 1953; co-author Charities and Charitable Foundations, 1974. Contbr. numerous articles to profl. publs. Home: 250 W 94th St New York City NY 10025 Office: 1776 Broadway New York City NY 10036

FISCHER, ANNE ROSENBERG (MRS. ERNST FISCHER), social worker; b. Stuttgart, Germany, Aug. 12, 1902; d. Bernhard and Hedwig (Lerchenthal) Rosenberg; came to U.S., 1934, naturalized, 1940; student U. Frankfurt (Germany), 1922-23, U. Heidelberg (Germany), 1923-25; M.S.W., Sch. Social Work, Richmond Profl. Inst., Coll. William and Mary, 1944; m. Ernst Fischer, Mar. 24, 1925; children—George, Eva (Mrs. T. Marx). Supr. Meml. Guidance Clinic, Richmond, Va., 1945-52; welfare specialist Internat. Ednl. Exchange Service, U.S. Dept. State, Germany, 1952, 53, 55; case supr. Children's Aid Soc., Richmond, 1954-55; asst. prof. Sch. Social Work, Richmond Profl. Inst., 1957-60; supr., dir. psychol. social services Meml. Guidance Clinic, Richmond, 1961-64; exec. dir. Jewish Family Services, Richmond, 1965-67; social work cons. Va. Dept. Edn., Richmond, 1968-70; vis. faculty U. Va., Charlottesville, summers 1968-74; cons. project dir. Victor Gollancz Stiftung, Germany, 1956, 60, 64, 67. Bd. dirs. Richmond (Va.) Jewish Community Council, 1965—, Beth Sholom Home of Va., 1968—, Friends' Assn. Children. Recipient Outstanding Alumni of the Year award Sch. Social Work, 1964; Distinguished Service award Beth Sholom Home Va., 1974. Fellow Am. Orthopsychol. Assn.; mem. Nat. Assn. Social Workers, Acad. Certified Social Workers, Va. Council Social Welfare. Home: 3110 Manor Dr Richmond VA 23230

FISCHER, CHARLOTTE FROESE (MRS. PATRICK CARL FISCHER), educator; b. Nikolaivka, USSR, Sept. 21, 1929; d. John David and Helen (Thiessen) Froese; B.A., U. B.C., 1952, M.A., 1954; Ph.D., Cambridge U., 1957; m. Patrick Carl Fischer, Apr. 2, 1967; 1 dau., Carolyn. Instr. math. U. B.C. (Can.), Vancouver, 1957-59, asst. prof. math. and computing centre, 1959-63, asso. prof., 1963-65, prof., 1965-69; vis. prof. U. Waterloo (Ont., Can.), 1968-69, prof. computer sci., 1969-72, prof. applied math., 1972—; prof. computer sci. Pa. State U., 1974—. Research fellow Harvard Coll. Obs., 1963-64; cons. Pacific Oceanographic Group, Nanaimo, B.C., 1957-59. Alfred P. Sloan fellow 1964-68. Mem. Assn. Computing Machinery, Computer Sci. Assn. (dir. 1972-74), Soc. Indsl. and Applied Math., Canadian Information Processing Soc. (sect. pres. 1965-67). Author: Introduction to Programming the IBM 1620, 1964. Editor: Computing Reviews, 1968—, Computer Physics Communications, 1968—. Contbr. papers to profl. publs. Home: 413 Waring Dr State College PA 16801

FISCHER, DOROTHEA JOSEPHINE, artist, educator; b. N.Y.C., Feb. 19, 1915; d. Heinrich Ernst and Paula (Dusselmann) Fischer; B.F.A., Pratt Inst., Bklyn., 1937; M.A., N.Y.U., 1949; postgrad. U. Chgo., 1939, Art Students League, 1940, Am. Sch. Design, 1942, Rutgers U., 1950, U. N.M., Montclair State Coll., 1951, N.Y. U., Columbia, 1952, Bayreuth Festival Master Classes, 1959, 61, Polakov Studio Stage Design, 1961-63. Tchr. art Angola (N.Y.) High Sch., 1937-41, Elizabeth (N.J.) Pub. Schs., 1941-44, Bloomfield (N.J.) High Sch., 1944—, Bloomfield Adult Sch., 1947-49, Bloomfield Art League, 1954-59, East Orange (N.J.) Adult Sch., 1955-67, Essex County Summer Music Sch., Montclair, N.J., 1960; instr. dept. vocational edn. N.Y.U. Sch. Edn., 1957-60; exhibited in one man shows West Essex Art Assn., Verona (N.J.) Pub. Library, 1963, Women's Club, Caldwell, N.J., 1966, Bloomfield High Sch. Art Gallery, 1968, Women's Club, Glen Ridge, N.J., 1969, Bloomfield Pub. Library, 1969, Bloomfield Art League, Bloomfield Civic Center, 1970; exhibited in group shows, N.J., Audubon Artists, N.Y.C., 1971, Nat. Acad., 1971, also juried shows; represented in permanent collections East Orange Hosp., Kessler Inst. for Rehab., West Orange, St. Barnabas Med. Center, Livingston, N.J., Bloomfield High Sch. Art Gallery; free-lance lettering. Judge art shows Essex County; painting demonstrator Essex Water Color Club, Bloomfield Art League, East Orange Library, Womens Aux. Essex County Med. Assn. Bd. dirs. Bayreuth (Germany) Festival Master Classes, N.Y.C. Recipient Essex Water Color Purchase awards, 1965, 67. Mem. Bloomfield Art League (past pres., chmn.), Essex Water Color Club (past pres.), Coll. Art Assn., Nat., N.J. art edn. assns., Eastern Arts Assn., Nat., N.J., Bloomfield edn. assns., Inst. for Study Art in Edn., Internat. Soc. for Edn. Through Art, Am. Artists Profl. League (1st award 1967, Pauline Wick award 1968), Met. Mus. N.Y., Mus. Modern Art N.Y., Montclair Mus. Home: 225 Liberty St Bloomfield NJ 07003 Office: 160 Broad St Bloomfield NJ 07003

FISCHER, EDITH (JEAN) STEINKRAUS (MRS. MARTIN JOHN HENRY FISCHER), musician, composer; b. Portland, Ore.; d. Henry Frank Martin and Alice Elizabeth (Hartley) Steinkraus; B.A., U. Minn., 1942; artist diploma (fellow) Juilliard Grad. Sch. Music, 1947; m. Martin John Henry Fischer, Aug. 19, 1942; children—Susan (Mrs. Jonathan S. Jeans), Joanna (Mrs. Joel K. Simon), Bruce Warren, Andrew Henry. Vocal soloist Mpls. Symphony Orch., Montclair Operetta Club, Chautauqua Opera Co., 1942-68; soloist Temple Emanuel, N.Y.C., mem. Fred Waring Trio, 1945-47; vocal soloist R.I. Philharmonic Orch., Brown U. Orch., 1946-68, Newman Congl. Ch., Rumford, R.I., 1966—; violinist Brown U. Orch., 1953—; adj. prof. voice R.I. Jr. Coll., Providence, 1970—; adj. prof. voice Brown U., 1971—. Appeared as Violetta in La Traviata, Butterfly in Madame Butterfly, Marguerite in Faust, Micaela in Carmen, Mother in Amhl and the Night Visitors, Mimi in La Boheme, others. Organizer children's collections for UNICEF, East Providence, R.I., 1956. Named R.I. Rep. as woman composer, 1969. Mem. Fish. Composer: 5 Canonic Movements, 1970; Book of Sacred Songs-Anthems, 1969, 70; Book of Children's Songs, 1965; also numerous secular songs, chamber music, choral anthems, instrumental solos. Home: 33 Euclid Av Riverside RI 02915

FISCHER, FRANCES HADDEN (MRS. VICTOR BERNARD FISCHER), hotel exec.; b. High Point, N.C., June 9, 1920; d. James Byron and Ola Jane (Smith) Hadden; student Greenville Womens Coll., 1932-36, Cornell U., 1968; m. Victor Bernard Fischer, May 16, 1942; 1 son, James Allen. Vice pres. Credit Union Nat. Assn., Madison, Wis., 1957-67; gen. mgr. Port Royal Plantation Inn, Hilton Head Island, S.C., 1967-73; resident mgr. Island Club Hilton Head, 1973—. Mng. dir. S.C. Credit Union League, 1961-63. Mng. dir. A.R.C., Columbia, S.C., 1961-63; mem. Rock Hill (S.C.) Com. Mental Health, 1965-66. Mem. Women's Bus. and Profl. Group, Jayette's, Jr. League, Beta Sigma Phi. Club: Toastmistress. Home and office: Island Club PO Box 5160 Hilton Head Island SC 29928

FISCHER, GOLDA JOSLYN (MRS. MAYNARD A. JOSLYN), physician; b. Rohatyn, Poland, Mar. 28, 1913; d. Joel and Esther (Strzelisker) Fischer; student U. Vienna, 1933-38, U. South Wales, Cardiff, 1938-40; M.D., Med. Coll. S.C., 1943; m. Maynard Alexander Joslyn, Apr. 19, 1947. Came to U.S., 1940, naturalized, 1947. Intern Jewish Hosp., Cin., 1943; resident Babies Hosp., Phila., 1944, Queens Gen. Hosp., N.Y., 1945; chief resident Children's Hosp., San Francisco, 1946-47; practice medicine specializing in pediatrics, Berkeley, Cal., 1946-58, outpatient pediatric clinics Fairmont, Alameda County Hosp., 1961-70, Crumlin Hosp., Dublin, Ireland, 1971; vis. pediatric cons. Mental Retardation Clinc, Contra-Costa County, Cal., 1972—; staff Alameda County, Herrick Gen., Children's Hosps., San Francisco, Children's Hosp., East Bay, 1947—, Contra-Costa County Hosp., 1972—. Fellow Jerusalem Acad. Medicine; mem. Israel Med. Assn. (charter, exec. com. Am. physicians fellowship com. 1950—, Outstanding Mem. of Year award 1954, corr. mem. 1961—), A.M.A., Cal. Alameda-Contra-Costra med. assns., East Bay Pediatric Soc. Am. Med. Women's Assn., Women's Med. Assn. Israel (hon.), Am. Friends Hebrew U., Am. Council Jewish Women, Zionist Orgn. Am., Pioneer Women, Hadassah (edn. chmn. 1947-53), Women's Am. ORT. Clubs: Women's Physicians (San Francisco); California Writers' (Berkeley). Contbr. articles to profl. jours., mags. Home: 1317 Spruce St Berkeley CA 94709

FISCHER, GRACE MAE, educator; b. Weatherly, Pa., Nov. 25, 1927; d. Alfred Wellington and Clara Elizabeth (Miller) Fischer; B.S., Bucknell U., 1949; M.D., Temple U., 1953; M.S., Drexel U., 1964. Intern, Germantown Dispensary and Hosp., Phila., 1953-54; resident Chestnut Hill Hosp., Phila., 1954-55, mem. staff, 1955-62; gen. practice medicine, Phila., 1955-59; practice medicine specializing in geriatrics, Phila., 1959-62; faculty U. Pa. Sch. Medicine, Bockus Research Inst., Phila., 1964—, asso. prof. physiology, 1972—. Nat. Heart Inst. postdoctoral fellow, 1963-64, spl. fellow, 1965-66; Southeastern Pa. Heart Assn. research grantee, 1970-71. Mem. Am. Physiol. Soc., Am. Assn. U. Profs., Sigma Xi, Phi Beta Kappa, Alpha Omega Alpha. Home: 218 E Meade St Philadelphia PA 19118

FISCHER, IDA ETHEL HARTMEYER (MRS. LOUIS FISCHER), motel exec., b. Pitts., July 23, 1926; d. William John and Ethel Agnes (Curley) Hartmeyer; student U. Md., 1944-45, Strayers Bus. Coll., 1946; m. Rice Miliner, Dec. 10, 1950 (dec. May 1962); children—Rice, Ellen (Mrs. Franklin Dove), Amy; m. Louis Fischer, Feb. 19, 1966 (dec. Nov. 1970). Owner, operator Valencia Motel and Miliner Apts., Laurel, Md., 1950—, Miliner Mgmt. Corp., Laurel, 1971—. Mem. Motel Assn. Am. (dir. Metro chpt. 1969-70, mem. nat. 500 com. 1964, nat. award 1964), Am. Hotel and Motel Assn., Md. Motel Assn., Md. Travel Council, Md. Fedn. Women's Clubs (state chmn. gerontology 1959-60), Laurel C. of C. (dir. 1970-73, certificate of appreciation 1973). Republican. Roman Catholic. Clubs: Woman's, Soroptimist (dir. 1956-73) (Laurel). Address: 10131 Washington Blvd Laurel MD 20810

FISCHER, JEANETTE LUCILLE STOCKETT (MRS. RICHARD ALLEN FISCHER), occupational therapist; b. Albert Lea, Minn., Nov. 13, 1937; d. Stewart Joseph and Bessie Lucille (Junk) Stockett; B.S., Washington U., St. Louis, 1960; m. Richard Allen Fischer, Oct. 22, 1960; children—Richard Arnold, Robert Andrew. Dir. occupational therapy Alexian Bros. Hosp., St. Louis, 1960-62; occupational therapy aide St. Louis State Hosp., 1958-59. Clinic vol. aide A.R.C., 1971-73. Treas., Midland Valley Estates Improvement Assn., 1966-68, 69-70, v.p., 1971-72, pres., 1972-73; treas., Marion Pre-Sch. P.T.A., 1967-68, carnival chmn., 1968-69, v.p., 1969-71, picnic chmn., 1969-73; sch. talent show dir. Boy Scouts Am., 1970-74; mem. St. Louis Civic Ballet, 1973; mem. KETC-TV Ednl. TV, 1971-73. Mem. Am., Mo. (pub. relations chmn. 1965) occupational therapy assns., Alpha Xi Delta. Lutheran. Home: 10025 Pebble Beach Dr Overland MO 63114

FISCHER, LINDA KAY (MRS. HAROLD CHARLES FISCHER), editor; b. Normal, Ill, Jan. 12, 1948; d. Rollin A. and O. Juanita (Hoffman) Henderson; B.A. in History, Ill. Wesleyan U., 1970; M.S. in Journalism, Northwestern U., 1971; m. Harold Charles Fischer, Feb. 26, 1972. Feature writer and copy editor Des Plaines Pub. Co., Des Plaines, Ill., 1971-72; editorial writer John Lehrer & Asso., Mt. Prospect, Ill., 1972-73; promotion supr. Paddock Pubs. Co., Arlington Heights, Ill., 1973—. Mem. Women in Communications, Nat. Fedn. Press Women, Ill. Woman's Press Assn., Beta Sigma Phi, Lambda Delta. Home: 2201 Dorchester Ct Schaumburg IL 60172 Office: 217 W Campbell St Arlington Heights IL 60006

FISCHER, LOUISE, physician; b. New Rochelle, N.Y., Jan. 17, 1911; d. Albert and Alice (Russell) Fischer; B.A., N.Y.U., 1933; M.D., N.Y. Med. Coll., 1937. Intern Jewish Hosp. of Bklyn., 1937-39; resident Bellevue Hosp., N.Y.C., 1939-42; practice medicine specializing in otolaryngology and allergy, N.Y.C., 1955—; mem. staff asst. attending Univ. Hosp., N.Y.C.; asso. prof. otolaryngology N.Y.U. Med. Center, 1960—. Home and office: 445 W 23rd St New York City NY 10011 Office: W 23rd St New York City NY 10011

FISCHER, VIRGINIA TARSEY (MRS. EDGAR E. FISCHER), psychologist; b. Albany, N.Y., Jan. 27, 1917; d. Benjamin Robert and Fannie Rosalind (Warshaw) Tarsey; B.S., Ohio State U., 1939; postgrad. State U. Albany, 1964-67; M.A., St. Rose Coll., 1968; m. Edgar E. Fischer, Sept. 22, 1940; children—Barry Robert, Justine. Psychol. researcher Albany Pub. Sch. System, 1962-66; sch. psychologist Rensselaer (N.Y.) City Sch. Dist., 1966—. Pres. Nat. Women's Com. Brandeis U., Albany, 1953-54, Aus. Daus. of Sarah Jewish Home, Troy, N.Y., 1955-56. Bd. dirs. Daus. of Sarah Home for Aged, Troy, 1956-66. Mem. Nat., N.Y. State assns. sch. psychologists,

Sch. Psychologists Upper New York State, Alpha Epsilon Phi. Jewish religion (v.p. sisterhood 1956-62). Club: Colonie Country (Voorheesville). Home: 37 Clarendon Rd Albany NY 12203 Office: Washington Av Rensselaer NY 12144

FISCHMANN, ALWYCE BETTY (MRS. EUGENE J. FISCHMANN), dermatologist; b. Sydney, Australia, Mar. 5, 1921; d. James Percy and Grace Irene (Spry) Gordon; M.B., B.S., U. Sydney, 1944; m. Eugene Jeno Fischmann, Apr. 16, 1951; children—Ann Michelle, Paul Thomas, Elizabeth Jean. Intern Royal North Shore Hosp., Sydney, 1944-45, resident, 1945-46; fellow dermatology Royal Infirmary, Edinburgh, Scotland, 1946-48; resident med. officer Manchester and Salford Hosp. Skin Diseases, 1948-49; practice medicine specializing in dermatology, Sydney, 1950, Auckland, N.Z., 1951-64; resident dermatology VA Hosp., Washington, 1967; research asso. Med. Women's Coll. Hosp., Toronto, Ont., Can., 1967-68; resident VA Hosp., Washington, 1968-69, chief sect. dermatology, 1970—; asst. hon. dermatologist Royal North Shore Hosp., Sydney, 1949-50, Royal Alexander Hosp. for Children Sydney, 1950-51; asst. prof. medicine Georgetown U., Washington, 1974—. Pres., Auckland Kindergarten Assn., 1962; v.p. Parnell P.T.A., 1963. Mem. A.M.A., Royal Coll. Physicians Edinburgh, Soc. Investigative Dermatology, Am. Acad. Dermatology. Home: 8001 Kerry Lane Chevy Chase MD 20015 Office: VA Hosp 50 Irving St NW Washington DC 20422

FISER, MARY ELIZABETH, lawyer; b. San Francisco, July 16, 1946; d. Gilbert Frank and Wilma Leona (Tomes) Fiser; B.A., Loyola U., New Orleans, 1968; J.D., U. Mo., 1971. Admitted to Mo. bar, 1971; asso. Sheldon D. Grand, atty., St. Louis County, 1970-71; asst. pub. defender, office of pub. defender, 21st Jud. Circuit, St. Louis, 1971—. Mem. Am., St. Louis County, St. Louis Met. bar assns., Cardinal Key Honor Soc., Phi Delta Phi. Roman Catholic. Home: 2229 Summerhouse Dr Apt 13 St Louis MO 63141 Office: Office of Public Defender St Louis County Courthouse Clayton MO 63105

FISH, (CHARLOTTE) RUTH GOODALL, journalist, social worker; b. Alamosa, Colo., Nov. 11, 1892; d. Alfred Alexander and Lavina Jane (Dorris) Goodall; M.S.W., Smith Coll. Sch. Social Work, 1923; postgrad. U. Mich., 1923-24; m. John Clayton Fish, Sept. 24, 1911 (dec. 1921); 1 dau., Dorris F. (Mrs. Leonard J. Coyne). Soc. editor, feature writer Alamosa Courier, 1910-14; news editor Alamosa Jour., A.P. reporter, feature writer Denver Post, Pueblo (Colo.) Star-Jour., 1918-21; disaster relief worker A.R.C., Pueblo, Tulsa, 1921-22; child welfare worker, Pontiac, Mich., 1922-23; med. social worker U. Mich. Hosp., Ann Arbor, 1923-30; dir. med. clinics St. Luke's Hosp., Chgo., 1930-34; dir. emergency relief Taos County, N.M., 1934-36; editor Taos Valley News, 1936; A.P. reporter, Taos County and Santa Fe New Mexican, 1937-46; editor column Wiesbaden (Germany) Post, USAF Hdqrs., 1947-49; dir. visitors' service, sec. Taos County C. of C., 1950-58; A.P. reporter Taos County, 1951-55, U.P.I. reporter, 1955-60; county editor El Crepusculo de Liberdad, Taos, 1958-60; free-lance writer. Substitute tchr. Taos Indian Day Sch., 1938, Taos Municipal Schs., 1942-46; sec. Taos Fiesta Corp., 1935-46, 50-61; chmn. Taos County chpt. N.M. Com. on Aging, 1964—; Social Service cons. County Project on Aging. Mem. Taos Little Theater, Play Readers' Club, 1951—; pres. Holy Cross Hosp. Aux., 1940-44, admissions officer, 1961—. Recipient Civilian Service Cross A.R.C., World War I. Mem. Taos County Hist. Soc. (v.p. 1962—), Am. Assn. Social Workers (charter, Golden Membership award 1966). Democrat. Episcopalian. Clubs: Taos Garden, Playreaders. Home: La Casita Santa Fe Rd Taos NM 87571

FISH, HELEN MARY SCHULTZ (MRS. ARTHUR ELLIOTT), lawyer; b. Newton, Mass., July 18, 1912; d. Christian George and Mary Josephine (Hurley) Schultz; LL.B., Northeastern U., 1935, LL.M., 1938, J.D., 1936; postgrad. Boston U., 1940; m. Arthur Elliott Fish, July 12, 1942. Admitted to Mass. bar, 1936; individual practice law, Boston, 1942—. Bd. dirs. Cath. Charitable Bur., Cambridge, Mass., Tobey Hosp. Guild, Wareham, Mass., Youville Hosp., Cambridge. Dame of St. George. Mem. Mass., Boston, Norfolk bar assns., Mass. Assn. Women Lawyers. Club: Great Neck Golf (Wareham). Home: 817 South St Roslindale MA 02131 Office: 89 State St Boston MA 02109

FISH, JILL HARRIET CARLSON (MRS. WILLIAM D. FISH, JR.), editor; b. Ridgway, Pa., Mar. 10, 1923; d. John Algot and Harriet Marie (Martinson) Carlson; B.S., Grove City Coll., 1945; postgrad. Pa. State U., 1946-48, Mansfield State Coll., 1973—; m. William D. Fish, Jr., Mar. 30, 1946; children—William D. III, John Frederick. Tchr., Coudersport (Pa.) High Sch., 1945-48, No. Potter High Sch., Ulysses, Pa., 1956-57; asso. editor Potter Enterprise, Coudersport, 1957—; corporate sec. Enterprise Pub. Co., Coudersport, 1970—. Co-owner, co-developer Deer Lick Camping Area, Coudersport, 1964-68; tchr. adult classes Coudersport (Pa.) Area Sch., 1969-71. Sec., Council Ch. Women, Coudersport, 1952-54, Potter County Child Welfare Adv. Bd., 1960-62, Potter County chpt. A.R.C., 1972—; program chmn. Coudersport P.T.A., 1960-62; mem. Potter County Christian Ministry to Migrants Com., 1959-64. Mem. Alpha Theta Mu. Presbyn. (finance chmn. 1952-55). Home: 411 N East St Coudersport PA 16915 Office: PO Box 29 Coudersport PA 16915

FISH, MARIE POLAND (MRS. CHARLES JOHN FISH), oceanographer; b. Paterson, N.J., May 22, 1902; d. Addison Brown and Mary (Dennis) Poland; B.A. cum laude, Smith Coll., 1921; D.Sci., U. R.I., 1956; m. Charles John Fish, Feb. 10, 1923; 1 dau. Marilyn (Mrs. J. Barnes Munro, Jr.). Hydrobiologist, U.S. Bur. Fisheries, 1922-27; curator ichthyology Buffalo Mus. Sci., 1928-31; ichthyologist Arcturus Oceanographic Expdn., 1925, Pacific Oceanic Biology project Woods Hole Oceanographic Instn., 1946-50; research asso. Internat. Passamaquoddy Investigations, 1931-33, U.S. Nat. Mus., 1944-46; research asso. Narragansett Marine Lab., U. R.I., Kingston, 1937-39; biol. oceanographer charge Office Naval Research Project Underwater Sound Biol. Origin, 1948-70, instr., 1942-43; ichthyologist State of R.I., 1942-43. Chmn. Kingfish com. USN, 1954—; rep. various confs. USN; cons. USN Atlantic Fleet Tng. Center, Newport, R.I., 1960-70, Submarine Forces Pacific Fleet, Hawaii and Cal., 1960; ofcl. rep. to 11th Pacific Sci. Congress, Tokyo. Instr. first aid A.R.C., Narragansett, 1942-46, chmn. Servicemen's Center, 1943-44; pres. Am. Youth Hostel, Wyoming, R.I., 1942-48, bd. dirs. R.I., 1939-48; pres. Kingston Players, 1936-38. Recipient Women's Centennial Congress award, 1940; achievement award Stamford Mus., 1963; Sophia Smith medal Smith Coll., 1964; Navy Distinguished Pub. Service medal, 1965; Woman of Year award Bus. and Profl. Women's Club, 1967. Mem. Am. Inst. Biol. Scis., A.A.A.S., Am. Soc. Ichthyologists and herpetologists, Soc. Woman Geographers, N.Y. Zool. Soc. (research asso.), Am. Soc. Limnology and Oceanography, Am. Fishery Biologists, Audubon Soc., R.I. Acad. Sci., Wildlife Fedn., Assn. Jr. Leagues Am., League Women Voters, Cocumscussoc, Pettaquamscutt hist. assns., South County Art Assn., Smith Coll. Alumnae Assn., Nat. Fedn. Bus. and Profl. Women's Club, Phi Beta Kappa, Sigma Xi, Phi Sigma. Republican. Presbyn. Clubs: Kingston Music (pres. 1940-42), Triangle (Kingston); South County Art (South Kingston, R.I.); Dunes (Narragansett, R.I.). Author books on bioacoustic research. Contbr. articles to profl. publs. Home: 1291 Kingstowne Rd Kingston RI 02881 Office: Narragansett Marine Lab Grad Sch Oceanography U of RI Kingston RI 02881

FISH, PAMELA RABURN LIVELY, state ofcl.; b. Bossier City, La., June 3, 1945; d. Nelson Hawood and Betty N. (Ray) Raburn; B.A. cum laude in Music Edn., La. Coll., 1968; 1 son, G. Shannon. Dir. music therapy Pinecrest State Sch., Pineville, La., 1967-71; program coordinator for day care services, services dept. of mental retardation La. Dept. Health and Social and Rehab. Services, Baton Rouge, 1971—. Cons. music therapy and program planning for mentally retarded. Mem. Rapides Area Planning Commn., 1971-72. Mem. Nat. Assn. Music Therapists, Am. Assn. Mental Deficiency, Delta Omicron, Alpha Chi. Baptist. Club: Matinee Music. Home: PO Box 747 La Place LA 70068 Office: PO Box 44215 Baton Rouge LA 70802

FISH, RUBY MAE BERTRAM (MRS. FREDERICK GOODRICH FISH), civic worker; b. Sheridan, Wyo., July 24, 1918; d. Ryan Lawrence and Ruby (Beckwith) Bertram; R.N., St. Luke's Hosp., 1936; postgrad. Washington U., St. Louis, 1941; m. Frederick Goodrich Fish, Apr. 12, 1942; children—Bertram Frederick, Lisbeth Ann (Mrs. Charles Jerry Bowling). Staff nurse Huntington Meml. Hosp., Pasadena, Cal., 1941-42; dr.'s office nurse, Denver, 1943-44; travel cons. ACS World Travel Service, Denver, 1964—. Bd. dirs. Jefferson County Easter Seal Soc., 1949—, pres., 1952-53, 56-57, 66-67; pres. Colo. Easter Seal Soc., 1960-61; bd. dirs. Nat. Easter Seal Soc., 1968-69, founds. chmn. nat. ho. of dels., 1973—; bd. dirs. Assistance League Denver, 1968-70, 73-74; mem. Gov.'s Com. Employment Handicapped, 1973—. Mem. Daus. of Nile-El Mejedel. Home: 4646 Bow Mar Dr Littleton CO 80123 Office: 450 S Marions St Denver CO 80209

FISHBEIN, ESTELLE ACKERMAN (MRS. RONALD H. FISHBEIN), lawyer; b. Bronx, N.Y., Sept. 27, 1934; d. Joe and Katie (Ranus) Ackerman; B.A. magna cum laude, Hunter Coll., 1955; LL.B., Yale, 1958; m. Ronald H. Fishbein, June 10, 1956; children—Rand, Jonathan. Admitted to D.C. bar, 1959, Md. bar, 1968; staff atty., office of gen. counsel, old age and survivors ins. div. U.S. Dept. Health, Edn. and Welfare, Washington, 1958-65, sr. staff atty., office of gen. counsel, health ins. div., 1965-68; spl. asst. atty. gen. of Md. for U. Md., Balt., 1968—. Editorial asst. Md. Constnl. Conv., Commn., 1966-67; mem. character com. Ct. of Appeals of Md. for 8th Jud. Circuit, 1972—. Mem. Nat. Assn. Colls. and Univ. Attys. (sec.-treas. 1973-74), Am. Council on Edn. (mem. equal opportunity task force 1973—). Home: Fallscroft Way Lutherville MD 21093 Office: 1 South Calvert St Baltimore MD 21202

FISHBURNE, MAGIE ELIZABETH, utility co. ofcl.; b. Greensboro, N.C., Oct. 16, 1940; d. Edward W. and Lavinia (Wharton) Fishburne; B.A. cum laude, St. Andrews Coll., 1962; M.Ed., U. N.C., Greensboro, 1967, postgrad., 1968. Field rep. St. Andrews Coll., Laurinburg, N.C., 1962-63; tchr. English, Page High Sch., Greensboro, 1963-64; asst. dir. admissions U. N.C. at Charlotte, 1964-66; registrar, dir. admissions Guilford Tech. Inst., Jamestown, N.C., 1967-73; recruitment rep. Carolina Power & Light, Raleigh, N.C., 1973—. Mem. alumni council St. Andrews Coll., Laurinburg, 1974. Mem. Am. Soc. Personnel Adminstrs., N.C. Placement Assn., Wake County Personnel Assn., Alpha Delta Kappa. Clubs: Junior Woman's, Pilot (Raleigh). Office: 336 Fayetteville St Raleigh NC 27602

FISHEL, RACHAEL ROBINSON (MRS. EDWARD KEITH FISHEL), educator; b. Wilmington, N.C., Oct. 13, 1921; d. Jem and Anna (Johnson) Robinson; A.B., U. N.C., 1942; M.Ed., East Carolina U., 1967; m. Edward Keith Fishel, June 20, 1946 (dec. June 1968); children—Edward Keith II, Anna Elizabeth. Tchr., Littleton, N.C., 1942-47; guidance dir. Warren County (N.C.) Schs., Warrenton, 1964-71, dir. instrn., 1971—. Dir. Warren County Headstart Program, summer, 1966. Chmn. Warren County Com. Mental Retardation, 1967—; mem. Franklin-Vance-Warren County Mental Health Council, 1965-67; mem. dist. com. Reynold's Scholarship, U. N.C., Greensboro, 1963; den mother Boy Scouts Am., 1957-59; troop leader Girl Scouts U.S.A., 1959-62. Sec. Littleton Sch. Bd., 1960-62, chmn., 1962-64. Mem. Am., N.C. personnel and guidance assns., Assn. Supervisors and Curriculum Dirs., Am. Sch. Counselors Assn., N.E.A., N.C. (pres. Warren County unit), Warren County (v.p. 1969-71, pres. 1971-72) edn. assns., Dirs. Guidance Services in Eastern N.C. (sec. 1969-70), Kappa Delta Pi, Delta Kappa Gamma (pres. Xi chpt. 1970-72). Democrat. Methodist (v.p. womens soc. Christian services 1969—). Home: 205 College Av Littleton NC 27850 Office: PO Box 110 Warrenton NC 27589

FISHER, ANITA HART, educator; b. Archer City, Tex.; d. Beamont and Annie Lee (Lauderdale) Hart; B.A., Cal. State U., Los Angeles, 1954, M.A., 1956; Ed.D., U. So. Cal., 1963; m. Ira V. Fisher, Jan. 19, 1941; children—Karla (Mrs. John H. Payne), Richard I., Robert A. Instr., Los Angeles City Schs., 1955-56; asst. prof. San Fernando Valley State U., Northridge, Cal., 1956-59; prof. dept. phys. edn. Cal. State U., Los Angeles, 1959—. Founder, ann. dir. Cal. Womens Collegiate Golf Championships, Los Angeles, 1963; mem. Nat. Collegiate Golf Com., 1972—. Mem. Am., Cal. (sponsor Cal. State U. Student unit 1962-71) assns. health, phys. edn. and recreation, Nat. Assn. Phys. Edn. for Coll. Women, Western Soc. Phys. Edn. for Coll. Women, Assn. Intercollegiate Athletics for Women, Pi Lambda Theta (founder, charter, 1st pres. Cal. State U. chpt. 1955). Home: San Clemente CA 92672 Office: 5151 State University Dr Los Angeles CA 90032

FISHER, ANNE ELIZABETH DEDERICK (MRS. HERBERT FISHER), civic worker; b. Keene, N.H.; d. Frederic Van Dyck and Margaret (Gogan) Dederick; A.B., Radcliffe Coll., 1948; postgrad. Harvard, 1948; m. Herbert Fisher, Aug. 8, 1949; children—Emily Ann, Frederic Van Dyck, Mary Martha, John Herbert Newall, Abigail Catherine. Tchr., Concord (Mass.) Pub. Sch., 1949, Chgo. Girls Latin Sch., 1950-51. Dir. Family Service Oakland County, 1959—; commr. Mich. Crippled Childrens Commn., 1960-63; chmn., dir. Oakland County Planning div. Unity Community Services, 1960—; dir. Mich. Soc. for Crippled Children, 1964-68; mem. adv. com. Oakland County Office Econ. Opportunity, 1964—; dir., mem. exec. com. Oakland County Soc. for Crippled Children, 1965—; mem. adv. com. Horizons-Upward Bound-Cranbrook Sch., 1966—; v.p., dir. United Community Services Met. Detroit, 1967—; founder New Horizons Oakland County, 1966, now dir.; dir., sec. Oakland County Vol. Bur., 1967-71; dir. Birmingham Bloomfield Art Assn., Am. Artists Series, 1972—. Democratic precinct del., 1960—. Recipient Community Service award Ford Motor Co., 1966, 67. Home: 150 Brady Lane Bloomfield Hills MI 48013

FISHER, BARBARA EDELSTEIN (MRS. H. KENNETH FISHER), lawyer; b. Duluth, Minn., Apr. 14, 1938; d. Max and Sara Lee (Ginsberg) Edelstein; A.B., Wellesley Coll., 1960; J.D., N.Y. U., 1963, LL.M., 1966; m. H. Kenneth Fisher, July 26, 1964; children—Hugh Edward, Joshua Benjamin, Michael Bernard. Admitted to bar N.Y., 1963, Cal., 1966, Wash., 1970, Ariz., 1973; law clk. So. Dist. N.Y., N.Y.C., 1963; atty. N.Y. Legal Aid Soc., 1964-65, San Francisco Neighborhood Legal Assistance Found., 1966-69; dep. dir. legal services Office Econ. Opportunity, San Francisco, 1969-70, regional dir. legal services, Seattle, 1970-72; individual practice law, Tucson, 1973—; lectr. law U. Ariz. Coll. Law, Tucson, 1973—; dir. Ariz. Pub. Law Advocates, 1973—. Bd. dirs. Seattle Food Banks-Neighbors in Need, 1971-72, Tucson Community Design Center, 1974—. Mem. Am., Pima County bar assns., Nat. Assn. Women Lawyers, Women's Equity Action League, So. Ariz. Hiking Club, Sierra Club. Home: 101 N Sahuara Av Tucson AZ 85711 Office: 201 N Stone Av Tucson AZ 85701

FISHER, DOROTHY LAVERNE WILLIAMS (MRS. OWEN HAROLD FISHER), univ. adminstr.; b. Arcola, Ill., Oct. 1, 1920; d. Paul Beauchamp and Kathryn (Farmer) Williams; A.B., Ball State U., 1942, M.A., 1963; m. Owen Harold Fisher, July 14, 1942; children—Scot Colvin, Alan Harold, Paul William, Margaret Ann. Tchr., Randolph County, Ind., 1945-46; Orangeburg and Stoney Point, N.Y., 1946-47; newswriter Ball State U. News Bur., Muncie, Ind., 1969-72, asst. to dir. pub. information services, 1972—. Mem. Mayor's Drug Commn., 1968. Bd. dirs. Crisis Intervention Center, Aquarius House, Mental Health Assn. Delaware County. Mem. Women in Communications (pres. East Central Ind. chpt. 1972-74), Alpha Phi Gamma, Sigma Tau Delta, Pi Gamma Mu, Pi Omega Pi. Home: 5100 Everett Rd Muncie IN 47302 Office: Pub Information Services Ball State U Muncie IN 47306

FISHER, MRS. DRURY A., club woman; b. Memphis, Nov. 17, 1922; d. Dene Christopher and Mona (Bailey) Patterson; grad. high sch.; m. Drury A. Fisher, May 25, 1941; children—Ginger, Dru. Organizer Les Bonnes Livres, Memphis, 1942, Chickasaw chpt. D.A.R., 1958; pres. Met. Garden Club, 1962; chmn. Heart Fund Tea, Memphis, 1960, 61; decorations chmn. Memphis Cotton Carnival, 1957-60; mem. com. Maid of Cotton Fashion Show, 1961; docent Brooks Art Gallery; chmn. Les Passees, Inc.; clk. Memphis Camellia Soc.; mem. exec. bd. Memphis Symphony League. Episcopalian. Mem. Airplane Operators and Pilots Assn. Clubs: Metropolitan Garden, Shady Grove Garden. Home: 4681 Shady Grove Rd Memphis TN 38117

FISHER, ELIZABETH STILLMAN (MRS. EDWARD JAMISON FISHER, JR.), cons.; b. Kansas City, Kan., Aug. 25, 1909; d. Charles Clark and Rachel (Schermerhorn) Stillman; B.A., U. Mich., 1930; M.A., Ohio State U., 1931, postgrad., 1931-32; m. Edward Jamison Fisher, Jr., Jan. 17, 1935; 1 dau., Mary Elizabeth (Mrs. Mary Fisher Hagen). Missionary Central Brasil Mission, Sao Paulo, Brasil, 1956-60; exec. asst. U.P. Ch., U.S.A., N.Y.C., 1960-64; exec. dir. Coop. Coll. Registry, Inc., Phila., 1964-69; Washington, 1969-72; cons. higher edn. personnel, 1972—. Home: 555 Laurie Lane Apt J-1 Thousand Oaks CA 91360

FISHER, ESTHER OSHIVER (MRS. MITCHELL SALEM FISHER), marriage and divorce counselor; b. Phila., Apr. 5, 1910; d. Harry J. and Rebecca (Saidikoff) Oshiver; B.S., U. Pa., 1929, LL.B., 1932; Ed.D., Columbia Tchrs. Coll., 1962; m. Mitchell Salem Fisher, June 25, 1933; children—Franklin Marvin, Joanne Claire (Mrs. Robert Wang), Wesley Andrew. Chmn. marriage and divorce counseling tng., tchr., supr. Insts. Religion and Health, N.Y.C., 1959—; marriage and divorce counselor, 1959—. Chmn. women's div. Non-Sectarian Anti-Nazi League, 1937-39. Fellow Am. Assn. Marriage and Family Counselors (nat. v.p. 1972-73), Am. Orthopsychiat. Assn.; mem. A.P.A., Soc. for Sci. Study of Sex, Nat. Council on Family Relations, U. Pa. Law Alumni Assn., Hadassah, Delta Phi Epsilon, Kappa Delta Pi, Pi Delta Theta. Author: Help for Today's Troubled Marriages, 1968; Divorce, the New Freedom, 1974; contbg. author Marriage: For and Against, 1972. Contbr. articles to profl. jours. Home: 1050 Park Av New York City NY 10028 Office: 3 W 29th St New York City NY 10001

FISHER, FRANCENIA ELEANORE, plant pathologist; b. Green Cove Springs, Fla., Sept. 23, 1924; d. Roy Dexter and Daisy (Sparkman) Fisher; B.S., Fla. State U., 1945; postgrad. U. Chgo., 1945; M.S., Mich. State U., 1946. Plant pathologist Agrl. Research and Edn. Center, U. Fla., Lake Alfred, 1946—; research and cons. 1946—; cons. U. Cal. at Berkeley, 1972-73. Mem. A.A.A.S., Soc. for Econ. Botany, Am. Phytopath Soc., Mycol. Soc. Am., Fla. Hort. Soc., Seminarium Botanicum (hon.), Ancient Order Ranales (hon.), Internat. Soc. Plant Pathology, Nat. Smithsonian Asso., Internat. Congress Plant Protection, Internat. Orgn. Citrus Virologists, Sigma Xi. Democrat. Episcopalian. Club: Lake Region Yacht and Country (charter Winter Haven). Editor, pub. World Directory of Plant Pathologists. Contbr. articles on citrus diseases caused by fungi, disease resistance, chem. and biol. control, and fungus diseases of insects and mites attacking citrus plants to profl. jours. and trade mags. Home: 1507 W Lake Cannon Dr Winter Haven FL 33880 Office: U of Fla Agrl Research and Edn Center Lake Alfred FL 33850

FISHER, HARRIET HAYES (MRS. WILLIAM S. FISHER), clothing designer; b. Toledo, Feb. 25, 1919; d. Ernest Eugene and Gertrude (Bradley) Hayes; student Ohio State U., 1938; B.A. cum laude, U. Toledo, 1940; postgrad. Parsons Sch. Design, 1940-41; m. Robert H. Raymond, Apr. 6, 1943 (dec. June 1943); m. 2d, William S. Fisher, Sept. 22, 1945 (dec. Jan. 1958); children—William S. II, Nancy Jane, John Hayes. Sportswear designer Petti, Glen Mfg. Co., Milw., 1942-45; sportswear designer Jr. House of Milw., 1945-60, v.p., 1958-60; head designer Jack Winter, Inc., Milw., 1960-72; designer Arthur Jay, 1972-73; cons., freelance designer, 1973—. Mem. Friends of Art, Pi Beta Phi. Republican. Conglist. Address: 1074 E Circle Dr Milwaukee WI 53217

FISHER, JANET ELIZABETH, govt. ofcl., computer systems analyst; b. Green Creek Twp., N.C., Dec. 1, 1928; d. William Mack and Venona Lee (Cole) Fisher; B.A., George Washington U., 1964; postgrad. Cath. U., 1965-70, George Washington U., 1971—. Mem. staff identification div. FBI, Washington, 1945-62; mathematician, crystallographer U.S. Naval Research Lab., Washington, 1963-70; mathematician, computer systems analyst, nonexpendable ordnance div. Naval Ordnance Mgmt. Information Systems, Naval Ordnance Sta., Indian Head, Md., 1970—. Mem. Sci. Research Soc. Am., Am. Math. Soc., Am. Crystallographic Assn., Philos. Soc. Washington, A.A.A.S. Home: 2162 Alice Av No 101 Oxon Hill MD 20021 Office: Nonexpendable Ordnance Div Central NOMIS Office Naval Ordnance Station Indian Head MD 20640

FISHER, JEAN DARLENE ORTH (MRS. EDWARD INMAN FISHER), occupational therapist; b. Whittier, Cal., Sept. 26, 1936; d. Paul Joseph and Elizabeth Georgiene (Garvis) O.; B.A., Mt. St. Mary's Coll., 1958; certificate occupational therapy U. So. Cal., 1960, M.S., 1967; m. Edward Inman Fisher, Aug. 28, 1965; children—Marni Elizabeth, Katherine Suzann. Staff therapist Casa Colina Rehab., Pomona, Cal., 1960-61, Los Angeles County Crippled Children's Service, Whittier, 1962-64, Orange County Crippled Children's Service, Fullerton, 1965-72; founder occupational therapy dept. U. Cal. at Los Angeles Med. Center, 1961-62; feeding cons. mentally retarded children and adults, Orange County, 1973—. Am. Occupational Therapy Assn. ednl. grantee, 1964-65. Mem. Third Order Servants of Mary (sec., treas. So. Cal. chpt. 1960-73). Address: 1201 Valencia Mesa Fullerton CA 92633

FISHER, JOELLEN MAE, educator; b. Racine, Wis., Aug. 23, 1941; d. Ward Kenneth and Helen Jane (Nelson) Fisher; B.S., U. Wis., 1963, M.B.A., 1965. With Donaldson, Lufkin & Jenrette, Inc.,

N.Y.C., 1965-67; instl. research analyst William D. Witter, Inc., bus. instl. brokerage, N.Y.C., 1967-69; corporate sec., investment officer Jennison Assos. Capital Corp., bus. pension fund mgmt., N.Y.C., 1969-73; corporate sec. DCL, Inc., Saddle Brook, N.J., 1973; asst. v.p. First Nat. City Bank, N.Y.C., 1973-74; lectr. finance U. Wis.-Parkside, Kenosha, 1974—. Breeder purebred Arabian horses. Home: Route 1 Box 80 Union Grove WI 53182 Office: U Wis-Parkside Kenosha WI 53140

FISHER, JOSEPHINE ANNIE NICKLESS (MRS. WILLIAM FISHER), physician; b. Paw Paw, Mich., Aug. 30, 1918; d. Percy Herbert and Irene (Smith) Nickless; B.A., Ripon Coll., 1940; M.D., U. Ia., 1944; m. William Fisher, May 27, 1967; stepchildren--Karen (Mrs. Darryl Rogers), Kirk. Intern Norwegian-Am. Hosp., Chgo., 1945; gen. practice medicine, St. Charles, Ill., 1945-62; resident in psychiatry U. Chgo., 1963-65; practice of medicine specializing in psychiatry, St. Charles, 1966—; asso. mem. Mercyville Psychiat. Hosp., Aurora, Ill., 1966—, chmn. med. records com., 1967-69, cons. outpatient dept., 1968-70; active staff Delnor Hosp., St. Charles, sec.-treas. med. staff; cons. staff St. Charles, Community Hosp., Geneva; cons. Community Sch. Dist. 303, St. Charles, 1967-69. Alumni rep., trustee Ripon (Wis.) Coll., 1971—. Mem. Am., Ill. psychiat. assns., Kane County Med. Soc., St. Charles C. of C. (dir. 1950-52). Presbyn. (elder 1966-69). Home: Kingsmill Rd St Charles IL 60174 Office: 24 Mosedale St St Charles IL 60174

FISHER, LILLIAN SHAPIRO (MRS. BERNARD FISHER), lawyer; b. N.Y.C., June 18, 1921; d. Max S. and Betty (Cohen) Shapiro; B.S., Bklyn. Coll., 1942; LL.D. and J.D., U. Ariz., 1963; m. Bernard Fisher, Dec. 22, 1945; children—Marjorie (Mrs. George Cunningham, Jr.), Michael S., Anne S. Admitted to Ariz. bar, 1963; pvt. practice law, Tucson, 1963—. Lectr., U. Ariz., Tucson, 1964-67. Mem. Gov. Adv. Commn. Environmental Quality, 1968—, Tucson Bd. Edn., 1971—); pres. Cerebral Palsy Found, 1971-72. Mem. So. Ariz. Hiking Club, Ariz. Desert Mus., Tucson Art League, Tuscon Cactus and Botan. Garden, Ariz. Bar Assn., Am. Trial Lawyers' Assn., Sierra Club. Office: 5610 E 22nd St Tucson AZ 85711☆

FISHER, LINDA JOYCE BUSS (MRS. JOEL MARSHALL FISHER), govt. ofcl.; b. Mpls., Sept. 1, 1943; d. Maynard M. and Arline I. (Hanson) Buss; A.B., Stanford, 1965; M.A., U. Tex., 1966; m. Joel Marshall Fisher, Aug. 29, 1970; 1 dau., Sara Melinda. Mem. staff lefislative liaison office VA, Washington, 1966-68; manpower specialist U.S. Dept. Labor, Washington and Los Angeles, 1968—. Recipient Outstanding Performance award U.S. Dept. Labor, 1969. Mem. Women in Communications, Stanford Alumni Assn., Cap and Gown, Phi Kappa Phi, Kappa Tau Alpha. Clubs: George Town, Capitol Hill (Washington). Home: 2660 Woodstock Rd Los Angeles CA 90046 Office: 300 N Los Angeles St Los Angeles CA 91001

FISHER, MARGARET BARROW, educator; b. Lockhart, Tex., July 18, 1918; d. Thomas Asbury and Lula Viola (Barrow) Fisher; A.B., U. Tex. at Austin, 1939; M.A., Columbia, 1941, Ph.D., 1953. Mem. staff YWCA, San Francisco, 1941-44, Beaumont, Tex., 1944-45, S.W. regional dir. Nat. Student YWCA, 1947-50, mem. nat. student council, com. on effective citizenship, 1950-53, bd. mem., chmn. pub. affairs com., Buffalo, 1953-55, chmn. young adult com., Oakland, Cal., 1956-58; exec. dir. YWCA, U. Okla., 1945-47; dir. student affairs U. Buffalo, 1953-55; dean students, prof. edn. Mills Coll., 1955-58; coordinator student personnel services Hampton (Va.) Inst., 1958-60; dir. student personnel U. South Fla., Tampa, 1960-63, dean women, 1963-71, asst. v.p. student affairs, 1971—, asso. prof. behavioral scis., 1960-69, prof., 1969—. Mem. adv. commn. on grad. edn. U.S. Office Edn., 1966-70, mem. adv. commn. spl. services to culturally disadvantaged, 1970-72, mem. adv. commn. developing instns., 1973—. Bd. dirs. Fla. Council for Prevention Blindness, Fla. Voluntary Health Assn., Tampa Urban League, Suncoast council Girl Scouts U.S.A.; pres. bd. dirs. Inside the Door. Mem. Acad. Polit. Sci., Am. Acad. Polit. and Social Sci., Am. Assn. U. Women, League Women Voters, Am. Assn. U. Profs., Assn. Higher Edn., A.A.A.S., Nat. Assn. Women Deans and Counselors, Am. Personnel and Guidance Assn. (chmn. 1956-57, woman's sect.), Nat. Vocational Guidance Assn., Am. Recorder Soc., Mortar Bd., Phi Beta Kappa, Delta Gamma, Kappa Delta Pi, Pi Lambda Theta. Democrat. Mem. United Ch. Author: Leadership and Intelligence, 1954; (with Jeanne Noble) College Education as as Personal Development, 1960; (with L. F. Malpass) A Comparison of Programed and Standard Textbooks in College Instruction, 1964. Contbr. articles, line drawings and poetry to profl. jours. Home: 6703 32d St Tampa FL 33610

FISHER, MARJORIE RUTH HORNE (MRS. THOMAS TIMOTHY FISHER), utility co. sec.; b. Uniontown, Pa., Nov. 13, 1927; d. James Edward and Mabel Gertrude (Gerg) Horne; grad. high sch.; m. Thomas Timothy Fisher, Sept. 14, 1946; 1 son, Thomas Michael. Clk., Deffines Dairy, 1943; factory worker Kimberly Clark Co., 1945-46; insp. Globar div. Carborundum Co., 1953-54, plant receptionist, 1954-56, statis. clk., 1956-58; sec., Olin Mathieson Chem. Corp., 1958-60; stenographer Bell Aerosystems, Inc., 1961; sr. stenographer Power Authority State N.Y., Niagara Falls, 1962-71, sec. to supt. power, 1972—. Mem. Civil Service Employees Assn., U.S., Canadian trotting assns., Niagara Power Employees Athletic Assn. Club: McKenzie Social (Niagara Falls). Home: 7701 Recovery Rd Niagara Falls NY 14304 Office: Power Authority State NY PO Box 277 Niagara Falls NY 14302

FISHER, MARTHA ANN, ret. clin. psychologist; b. Susquehanna, Pa., Oct. 28, 1900; d. Charles Ithura and Verna O. (Cook) Fisher; diploma Bloomsburg State Normal, 1925; Mus.B., Susquehanna U., 1933, B.A., 1937; M.A., Bucknell U., 1943; postgrad., Pa. State U., summers 1943-46, 51, 52, 56. Tchr. rural sch., Snyder County, Pa., 1923-24; tchr. elementary schs., Sunbury, Pa., 1925-38, tchr. jr. high sch. music, 1938-40, tchr. mentally retarded classes, 1940-47; dir. guidance Sunbury Area Schs., 1947-59, sch. psychologist, 1947-59; clin. psychologist, dir. treatment, conductor in-service tng. State Correctional Instn., Muncy, Pa., 1947-72. Tchr. advanced psychology Susquehanna U., nights, 1954. Sec. adv. bd. Sunbury Salvation Army, 1930-59. Mem. Am. Assn. U. Women, Am. Assn. Retired Persons, Internat. Council for Exceptional Children (Pa. pres. 1946), Am., Pa. psychol. assns., Pa. Assn. Probation Parole and Correction, Med. Correctional Assn., Ednl. Correctional Assn. Pa., Bus. and Profl. Women's Club (pres. 1948), Northumberland-Snyder County Hist. Soc., Delta Kappa Gamma (chpt. pres. 1950). Methodist. Mem. Order Eastern Star. Clubs: Soroptimist, Iris-Literary, Triangle-Civic. Home: Park Rd Hummel's Wharf PA 17831

FISHER, MARY STUART BLAKELY (MRS. GEORGE ROSS FISHER III), physician; b. Binghamton, N.Y., Aug. 12, 1922; d. Stuart Banyar and Miriam (Brothers) Blakely; A.B., Bryn Mawr Coll., 1944; M.D., Columbia, 1948; m. George Ross Fisher III, Aug. 19, 1950; children—George Ross IV, Miriam, Margaret, Stuart. Intern Mass. Gen. Hosp., Boston, 1948-49; resident Presbyn. Hosp., N.Y.C., 1949-51, Drs. Groover, Christie and Merritt, Washington, 1951-53; radiologist Phila. VA Hosp., 1954-63; dir. diagnostic radiology Phila. Gen. Hosp., 1963—; asst. prof. radiology U. Pa., Phila. Diplomate Am. Bd. Radiology. Fellow Am. Coll. Radiology; mem. A.M.A., Radiol. Soc. N.Am. Home: 203 Chews Landing Rd Haddonfield NJ 08033 Office: X-Ray Dept Phila Gen Hosp Philadelphia PA 19104

FISHER, NELL GIBSON RHODES (MRS. IRVING FISHER), lawyer; b. Stratford, Okla., Sept. 1, 1909; d. David Leslie and Mary Ellen (Sturdivant) Gibson; student Okla. Coll. Women, 1927; LL.B., Oklahoma City Sch. Law, 1941; m. Irving Fisher, Nov. 17, 1951; 1 son (by previous marriage)--Horace Rhodes. Law clk. to Judge A.P. Murrah, U.S. Ct. Appeals, 10th Circuit, Oklahoma City, 1941-52; practiced Oklahoma City, 1952-61; mem. firm Savage, Gibson, Benefield and Shelton; trial examiner Okla. Corp. Commn., Oklahoma City, 1961—. Bd. dirs. Am. Trustee Corp., Lillian Strickler, Inc. Mem. Okla. Women Lawyers Assn., Okla. Bar Assn. Home: 2233 NW 45th St Oklahoma City OK 73112 Office: Jim Thorpe Office Bldg Oklahoma City OK 73105

FISHER, PATRICIA ATKINS (MRS. O.A. KENNETH FISHER), librarian; b. Sault Ste. Marie, Mich., Sept. 22, 1935; d. John Henry and Catherine Donnelda (MacMillan) Atkins; student Mich. Coll. Mining and Tech., 1953-55; B.A., Western Mich. U., 1957; M.A. in L.S., U. Mich., 1961; postgrad U. Colo., 1966-67; m. O.A. Kenneth Fisher, Feb. 9, 1963; 1 dau., Elizabeth. Librarian, Whitehall (Mich.) Pub. Schs., 1957-60, Kalamazoo Pub. Schs., 1961-63, Hild Regional Br., Chgo. Pub. Library, 1963-64, Detroit Pub. Library, 1964-65, Denver Pub. Schs., 1966-67; reference librarian, head reference dept. U. Denver, 1967—. Mem. League Women Voters, Kappa Delta Pi, Pi Gamma Mu. Home: 1337 E Cornell Av Englewood CO 80110 Office: 2150 E Evans St Penrose Library University of Denver Denver CO 80210

FISHER, RHEUA DALE SPICKELMIER (MRS. RICHARD WILLIS FISHER), educator, assn. exec.; b. Willis, Kan., Mar. 28, 1911; d. Thomas Asa and Ella (Compton) Spickelmier; student Baker U., 1928-30; B.S. in Edn., S.W. Mo. State Coll., 1957; M.Ed., U. Mo., 1961; D.Ed. (Delta Kappa Gamma internat. scholar), Okla. State U., 1968; m. Richard Willis Fisher, Mar. 14, 1933; children—Richard Michael, Robert Dale. Tchr., Greene County (Mo.) Schs., 1951-56 tchr., counselor Reorganized Sch. Dist. XII, Springfield, Mo., 1956-66, 67—. Grad. asst. U. Mo., 1962, Okla. State U., 1966-67; instr. S.W. Mo. State Coll., summers, 1968-71. Sec.-treas. Mo.-Ozark Personnel and Guidance Assn., 1965-66, 68-70; 2d v.p. Epsilon chpt. Delta Kappa Gamma, 1965-66, 68-70, 1st v.p., 1970-72, pres., 1972-74. Mem. Springfield Edn. Assn., Mo. State Tchrs. Assn., N.E.A., Mo. Guidance Assn., Am. Personnel and Guidance Assn., Nat. Vocational Guidance Assn., Am. Sch. Counselor Assn., Assn. Measurement and Evaluation in Guidance, Mo. Vocational Assn. Home: 1527 S Holland Av Springfield MO 65804

FISHER, RHODA LEE FEINBERG (MRS. SEYMOUR FISHER), psychologist; b. Chgo., Oct. 10, 1924; d. Isadore Mordecai and Miriam (Margolis) Feinberg; B. Mus. Edn., De Paul U., 1945; M.A., U. Chgo., 1947, Ph.D., 1956; m. Seymour Fisher, Mar. 22, 1947; children—Jerid M., Eve P. Practice psychology, Houston, 1950-61, Syracuse, N.Y., 1969-70, Manlius, N.Y., 1970—; research asst. Baylor Med. Sch., Houston, 1951-53; research asso. Upstate Med. Sch., Syracuse, 1961-63; research psychologist Syracuse Pub. Schs., 1963-69; tchr. courses Women's Study Center, Syracuse U. Mem. Am., Eastern psychol. assns. Contbr. articles to profl. jours. Home: 4855 Armstrong Rd Manlius NY 13104 Office: Kinloch Plaza Manlius NY 13104

FISHER, RUTH KINYON (MRS. ROBERT FISHER), shipping co. exec.; b. Kansas City, Mo., Nov. 8, 1914; d. Henry Hubbard and Mabel (Browne) Kinyon; B.J., U. Mo., 1938; m. Horace Whiteside, 1951 (dec. 1956); m. 2d, Robert Fisher, Sept. 1, 1959 (dec. 1974). Researcher, Time mag., 1938-39; market researcher J. Walter Thompson, 1939-41; research dir. Charles W. Hoyt, 1948-51; free lance taped overseas reporter from Europe for WHCU, CBS, Ithaca, N.Y., 1957-59; mng. dir. Overseas Features Ltd., London, Eng., 1959—; dir. Robert Fisher Packing & Shipping Ltd., Robert Fisher (Holdings) Ltd. Mem. Advt. Fedn. Am. (dir. 1944-46), Am., Internat. Women in Radio and Television, Advt. Women New York, Womens Press Club London, Inst. Dirs. London, Gamma Alpha Chi (nat. pres. 1944-46). Club: Junior Carlton (asso. mem. London). London corr. Travel mag., 1961—. Home: 22 St James Close Prince Albert Rd London NW 8 England also 2171 Gulf Shore Blvd Naples FL 33940 Office: 32 Lexington St London W1 England

FISHER, SUE DUBOIS, photog. co. exec.; b. N.Y.C., May 16, 1934; d. Eugene and Pearl (Brody) Dubois; A.B., U. Miami (Fla.), 1954; m. Ray Fisher, Aug. 9, 1953; children—Andrew, Richard, Julie. Sec.-treas. Ray Fisher Inc., photography, Miami, Fla., 1969—. Free-lance writer and poetess, 1950—; coordinator Wilson Hicks Internat. Conf. Visual Communication. Orginator children's concerts for Dade County sch. children; orginating chmn. vol. work program Fairchild Tropical Garden Miami; pres. Beaux Arts (U. Miami Lowe Museum), 1967-68; founding charter mem., treas. Theatre Arts League, Miami, 1959. Bd. dirs. U. Miami Symphony, Miami Arts Center Helpers, 1972-73; bd/ govs. Young Patronesses of Opera, 1960. Mem. Am. Assn. U. Women, Women in Communications (pres. 1957-59), Viscayans Opera Guild Greater Miami, Friends U. Miami Library, S. Dade Amateur Orchid Soc. Address: 10700 SW 72d Ct Miami FL 33156

FISHER, SUSAN SCHWARZ (MRS. PAUL FISHER), librarian; b. Vienna, Austria, Sept. 24, 1919; d. Ernst and Fritzi (Zuckerbäcker) Schwarz; student Textile Coll., Vienna, 1936-38, U. Minn., summer 1949; m. Paul Fisher, June 5, 1948. Came to U.S., 1948, naturalized, 1950. With Dartmouth Coll. Library, 1948-51, NACA, 1951-54, Dept. Agr., 1954-66; with Library of Congress, Washington, 1966—, asst. sect. head, 1966—. Home: 7024 Bybrook Lane Chevy Chase MD 20015 Office: Library of Congress Washington DC 20540

FISHER, WELTHY HONSINGER (MRS. FREDERICK BOHN FISHER), author, lectr.; b. Rome, N.Y., 1879; d. Abram Walker and Welthy (Sanford) Honsinger; B.A., Syracuse U., 1900, M.A. (hon.), 1921, L.H.D. (hon.), 1965; Litt.D. (hon.), Fla. So. Coll., 1938; L.H.D., Western Coll. for Women, 1963; m. Frederick Bohn Fisher, June 18, 1924 (dec.). Tchr. high sch., Englewood, N.J., 1902-06; prin. and builder Baldwin Sch. for Girls, Nanchang, China, 1906-17; war work in France under YWCA, 1918-19; Chautauqua lectr. on Women of Allies, 1919; editor World Neighbors, N.Y., 1920-24; lectr. on internat. relations; field worker, East and West Asso., 1945, founder Literacy House, Lucknow, U.P., India, 1953. Pres. World Edn., Inc., N.Y.C., 1959-72; hon. pres. World Literacy of Can., Inc., Toronto, Ont., 1959-73, Netherlands Literacy Internat., 1969—; pres. Literacy Internat. Com., New Delhi, India, 1970-73; chaplain World Woman's Party, Washington, 1944; chmn. World Day of Prayer com. United Council Ch. Women. Mem. Women's Nat. Republican Club. Founder Young Farmers Inst., Lucknow, 1966. Recipient George Arents medal for distinguished service in internat. cultural relations, Syracuse U., 1948; Citation for Internat. Edn., Merrill Palmer Inst., Detroit, 1960; Watumull award, 1962; Ramon Magsaysay award, Manila, 1964; Recognitions award Women's Nat. Farm and Garden Assn., 1966; recipient 1968 Nehru Literacy award; Humanitarian award Variety Clubs Internat., 1971. Mem. Am. Assn. U. Women, Syracuse U. Alumnae Assn., Pi Phi, Beta Sigma Phi (hon. internat.), Delta Kappa Gamma (hon. internat.). Clubs: Boston Authors (citation), Women's Professional (Boston); Pen and Brush (N.Y.). Author: Twins Travlogues (Japan, China, India, Korea), 1922; Beyond the Moon Gate, 1924; A String of Chinese Pearls, 1925; The Top of the World, 1926; Freedom, 1930; Frederick Bohn Fisher-World Citizen; Handbook for Ministers' Wives (Women's Press), 1950; To Light a Candle, 1962; prologue and epilogue That Strange Little Brown Man Gandhi (Fred B. Fisher), rev. edition 1970. Home: 523A Heritage Village Southbury CT 06488 Office: 1414 6th Av New York City NY 10019

FISHLER, ESTHER MARIE BAKER (MRS. BENNETT H. FISHLER), ret. librarian; b. Boston, Nov. 25, 1906; d. Alfred Titcomb and Martha (Nichols) Baker; B.A., Wellesley Coll., 1929; B.S., Columbia, 1934; m. Bennett H. Fishler, Mar. 8, 1963. Gen. asst. Albany (N.Y.) Pub. Library, 1931-34; reference librarian George L. Pease Meml. Library, Ridgewood, N.J., 1936-40, dir., 1940-62; dir. Ridgewood Library, 1962—. Trustee Ridgewood Adult Sch., 1948-72, pres., 1953-58. Mem. Am., N.J. (pres. 1950-51) library assns., Bergen and Passaic County Library Club (pres. 1941-42). Clubs: Womans, College. Home: 335 Bedford Rd Ridgewood NJ 07450

FISK, SALLY JEAN, govt. ofcl.; b. Cin., July 11, 1948; d. Harley Bruse and Jean (Brown) Fisk; B.S., Transylvania U., 1970; M.S. in Edn., Ind. U., 1973. Social worker state govt., Covington, Ky., 1970-71; asst. residence hall coordinator Ind. U., Bloomington, 1971-73; personnel mgmt. intern AEC, Argonne, Ill., 1973—. Mem. Nat. Assn. Women Deans, Adminstrs. and Counselors, Am. Coll. Profl. Assn. Home: 404 N LaGrange Rd LaGrange Park IL 60525 Office: 9800 S Cass St Argonne IL 60439

FISKE, VIRGINIA MAYO (MRS. GEORGE FARRINGTON FISKE), biologist, educator; b. Bklyn., Sept. 21, 1910; d. Virginius J. and Lois (Waterbury) Mayo; B.A., Mt. Holyoke Coll., 1932, M.A., 1934; Ph.D., Radcliffe Coll., 1939; m. George Farrington Fiske, Sept. 17, 1938; children—John Mayo, George Farrington, Katharine Reid. Teaching asst. Mt. Holyoke Coll., South Hadley, Mass., 1932-34; head sci. dept. Dana Hall Sch., Wellesley, Mass., 1934-37; tchr. Winsor Sch., Boston, 1937-38, 39-41, 42-43; research asst. Harvard, Cambridge, Mass., 1939-40; researcher in endocrinology Pratt Diagnostic Clinic, Boston, 1942; instr. dept. biol. scis. Wellesley Coll., 1943-50, asst. prof., 1950-56, lectr., 1958-60, asso. prof., 1960-63, prof., 1964—, chmn. dept., 1964-67. Mem. Sherborn (Mass.) Sch. Com., 1955-61. NSF fellow, 1956-57. Mem. Endocrine Soc., Am. Physiol. Soc., A.A.A.S., Phi Beta Kappa, Sigma Xi. Research in endocrinology. Contbr. articles to profl. jours. Home: 27 Hollis St Sherborn MA 01770 Office: Wellesley Coll Wellesley MA 02181

FISSINGER, KAYE SILLERY, performing arts dir.; b. Gary, Ind., May 16, 1944; d. Kenneth Harrison and Frances Cecilia (Flitter) Sillery; student Valparaiso U., 1962-64; B.S. with distinction, Ind. U., 1970; 1 dau., Alisa Kaye. Resident dir., choreographer dept. music Lew Wallace High Sch., Gary, Ind., 1964-67; secondary tchr. theatre and speech arts, dir., choreographer extra-curricular theatre Portage Twp. Sch. Corp., Portage, Ind., 1970-72; adminstrv. asst. Valley Hosp., Van Nuys, Cal., 1972; asst. adminstr. Central Diagnostic Lab., Van Nuys, 1973—. Performing artist Summer of Musicals, Sullivan, Ill., 1962, North Shore Theatre, Beverly, Mass., 1963; choreographer/dir. performing arts Calumet City (Ill.) Theatre Guild, 1964; performing artist Valaparaiso (Ind.) Theatre Guild, 1961-62, choreographer, 1971; dir. performing arts Ind. U. N.W., 1967, 70; performing artist, actress, dancer, singer including Gary (Ind.) Players Guild, 1961, Gary Music Theatre, 1960-61, Gary Children's Theatre, 1960-61, Ind. U. N.W., 1964-69. Recipient scholarships Valparaiso U., 1962-64, Ind. U., 1966-67, 69-70; award Am. Legion, 1962. Mem. Am. Nat. Theatre Acad., Am. Ednl. Theatre Assn., Secondary Sch. Theatre Conf., Nat. Thespian Soc., Ind. State Tchrs. Assn., Portage Assn. Tchrs., Masque and Gavel, Sigma Alpha Iota. Author: (with Michael Harrison) Guito, 1972. Home: 22861 Saticoy St Canoga Park CA 91307 Office: 7660 Gloria Av Van Nuys CA 91406

FITCH, MILDRED BROOKS (MRS. LLOYD DORAN FITCH), lawyer; b. nr. Tolbert, Tex., Nov. 17, 1901; d. Hiram Louis and Mary Emma (Morris) Brooks; student Northeastern State Tchrs. Coll., Tahlequah, Okla., 1921; tchrs. certificate E. Central State Tchrs. Coll., Ada, Okla., 1927; student Bartlesville Bus. Coll., 1928-29; LL.B., Washington Coll. Law, 1939; J.D., Am. U., 1939; m. Lloyd Doran Fitch, Aug. 28, 1921; 1 son, Eugene Brooks. Tchr. pub. schs., Osage County, Okla., 1920-21, Creek County, 1927-28; secretarial positions, Bartlesville, Okla., 1929-35, Washington, 1936-39; admitted to D.C. bar, 1939, Okla. bar, 1940; law clk., sec. to U.S. Dist. Judge, Muskogee, Okla., 1940-41; lawyer Midstates Oil Corp., Tulsa, 1941-52; asso. Martin, Logan, Moyers and Hull, Tulsa, 1952-54; judge Okla. Indsl. Ct., Oklahoma City, 1954-60; pvt. law practice, Tulsa, 1960—. Mem. Pres.'s Com. on Employment of Handicapped, 1958, Gov.'s Com. on Employment of Handicapped, 1956, Mayor's Com. on Employment of Handicapped, 1973—. Precinct co-chmn. Democratic Party, Tulsa, 1940—. Mem. Okla. Assn. Women Lawyers (pres. 1942), Okla., Tulsa County bar assns., Phi Delta Delta, Phi Alpha Delta. Democrat. Mem. Christian Ch. Address: 1637 S Jamestown St Tulsa OK 74112

FITCH, MILDRED LORING, ret. educator; b. Valparaiso, Ind., Aug. 3, 1893; d. Judge Hannibal Hamlin and Emily Ann (Brummitt) Loring; student Lake Forest (Ill.) Coll., 1912-14; B.S., Purdue U., 1937, M.S., 1939; postgrad. Harvard, summers 1938-41; m. Walter Quintin Fitch, Jan 2, 1915 (dec.); 1 dau., Mildred Leah (Mrs. Richard M. Conley). Instr. polit. sci. Purdue U., 1940-45, asst. prof., 1945-51, asso. prof., 1951-61, prof. emeritus, 1961—; lectr., radio commentator nat. and internat. subjects sta. WBAA, Purdue U., until 1970. Mem. Am. Polit. Sci. Assn., Am. Assn. U. Profs., League Women Voters, Am. Assn. U. Women. Presbyn. Contbr. articles to profl. jours. Home: Regency South 3750 Galt Ocean Dr Fort Lauderdale FL 33308

FITCH, VIRGINIA BELLE, realtor; b. Jackson, Mich., Jan. 30, 1920; d. Lyman B. and Norma L. (Squire) Fitch; grad. high sch. sec. archtl. firm Teer, Wickwire, Kressbach & Dabbert, Jackson, 1937-60; saleswoman Nelson Realty, Jackson, 1960-68; broker Ginny Fitch Real Estate, Jackson, 1968—. Sec.-treas. Prin. Activities, Jackson, 1970—; pres., treas. Open Pantry Food Mart, Inc., Jackson, 1971—. City commr., Jackson, 1966-67, commr. Jackson County, 1968-70. Mem. Jackson Bd. Realtors (dir. 1970-73), Jackson Bus. and Profl. Women. Christian Scientist (bd. dirs. 1974—). Home: 534 St Clair St Jackson MI 49202 Office: 706 W Michigan Av Jackson MI 49201

FITE, ALICE EMILY WETTERER (MRS. ROBERT EDWARD FITE), librarian, assn. exec.; b. N.Y.C., Sept. 7, 1926; d. Walter Ader and Alice (Ablanese) Wetterer; B.S., Bob Jones U., 1949; M.S., Columbia, 1951; postgrad. N.Y. U., Ind. U.; m. Robert Edward Fite, Aug. 21, 1948; children—Barbara Lee, Robert Edward. Asst. librarian Queens Borough Pub. Library, Jamaica, N.Y., 1949-51, Sewanhaka High Sch., Floral Park, N.Y., 1951-53; dir. libraries, Plainedge Pub. Schs., Bethpage, N.Y., 1953-56, field rep. personnel, 1954-56; dir. North Bellmore (N.Y.) Pub. Library, 1959-63; librarian Searingtown Elementary Sch., Albertson, N.Y., 1964-66, Aspen Hill Elementary Sch., Rockville, Md., 1967-74; asso. exec. sec. Am. Assn. Sch. Librarians, 1974—; vis. asso. prof. Towson State Coll. Mem. Am. Assn. U. Women, N.E.A., A.L.A., Montgomery County Edn. Assn., Montgomery County Sch. Librarians, Nassau Suffolk Sch. Librarian's

Assn. (past v.p.). Baptist. Contbr. articles to profl. jours. Home: 15205 Wycliffe Ct Rockville MD 20853

FITE, BARBARA ALICE, home economist; b. Weaver, Ala.; d. Howard Wester and Edith (Williamson) Fite; B.S., Ala. Coll., 1955; M.A., U. Ala., 1966, Ed.D., 1973. Home econs. tchr. West Point (Ala.) High Sch., 1955-56; extension home demonstration agt. Ala. Extension Service, Birmingham, 1956-66; specialist in human devel. Ala. Extension Service, Auburn U., 1966—. Sec. Ala. State Adv. Com. Children and Youth, 1967, mem. program planning com., 1968, chmn. pub. relations com., 1973; Ala. planning com. sec. White House Conf. Children and Youth; del. White House Conf. on Children, 1970, White House Conf. on Youth, 1971. Mem. Ala. Home Demonstration Agts. Assn. (treas. 1957-58, nat. conv. chmn. 1959-60), Am. Assn. U. Women, Ala. Coll. Home Econs. Alumni Adv. Council, Nat., Southeastern, Ala. councils family relations, Am., Ala. (liaison to nat. assn. family planning com. 1973) home econs. assns., Ala. Coll., U. Ala. alumni assns., Child Study Assn. Am., Internat. Fedn. Home Econs., Ala. Consumers Assn., Nat. Assn. Edn. Young Child, Assn. Childhood Edn. Internat., Ala. Assn. Young Children, So. Assn. Children Under Six, Kappa Delta Pi, Epsilon Sigma Phi. Roman Catholic (treas. St. Margaret's altar soc. 1960). Home: PO Box 504 Auburn AL 36830

FITTON, CLAIRE JACKSON (MRS. DONALD WEBB FITTON, JR.), theatrical dir; b. West Point, Ga., Aug. 26, 1927; d. William Phillip and Emily Lucille (Cotton) Jackson; B.A., Shorter Coll., 1948; M.A. (fellow) N.Y. U., 1949; M.A. (fellow), Miami U., Oxford, O., 1968; m. Donald Webb Fitton, Jr., June 28, 1952; children—Emily Cotton, Nancy Vaden, Donald Webb, Travis Jackson. Instr. dance Ohio U., Athens, 1949-52; instr. music Hamilton (O.) Pub. Sch. System, 1952-53; instr. dance Miami U., 1967-68, instr. communications and theatre, 1968-72; dir., choreographer plays, musicals, recitals for various orgns., 1949—. Trustee, chmn. bd. Greater Hamilton Civic Theatre; bd. dirs. Planned Parenthood, YWCA. Mem. League Women Voters (mem. bd. 1960-62). Home: 140 Heathwood Lane Hamilton OH 45013

FITTS, SISTER MARY PAULINE, educator, author; b. Ft. Williams, Me.; d. Francis Michael and Pauline (Trutner) Fitts; B.A., D'Youville Coll., Buffalo, 1924; M.A., Catholic U. Am., 1956, Ph.L., 1958, Ph.D., 1960. Tchr. English, French, history, art Grey Nun High Schs., Ogdenburg, N.Y., Buffalo, Phila., Atlanta, 1927-55; prof., chmn. philosophy D'Youville Coll., 1960-73; prof. philosophy Niagara U., 1973—; dir. workshop in writing for Cath. Press, Phila. Regional Writers Conf., 1955-58. Panelist on Communism, WGR-TV, Buffalo, 1966, for Israel Chamber Orch. WBEN-TV, Buffalo, 1968. Mem. Grey Nuns of Sacred Heart, Am. Assn. U. Profs., Am. Assn. U. Women, Am. Soc. for Aesthetics, Am. Catholic chmn. regional conf. 1968-71, v.p., pres.-elect 1974—), Am. philos. assns., Hegel Soc. Am. Author: Hands to the Needy, 1950, 59, 71. Contbr. to New Catholic Ency. Home: 151 East St Buffalo NY 14207

FITZ, CAROLINE MOUL, librarian; b. Hanover, Pa.; d. Earl Samuel and Virginia Washington (Lewis) Fitz; A.B., Wilson Coll., 1941; B.S. in Library Scis., Drexel Inst. Tech., 1942. Asst. cataloger library Drexel Inst. Tech. Phila., 1942-43; asst. librarian Chardon (O.) Pub. Library, 1943-44; head librarian Louisville (O.) Pub. Library, 1944-45; Amityville (N.Y.) Free Library, 1945-49, Norfolk (Va.) Naval Base, 1949-50; library dir. Valley Stream (N.Y.) Pub. Library, 1950-67, Amityville (N.Y.) Pub. Library, 1967—. Trustee Valley Stream Pub. Library, 1974—. Mem. Am., N.Y., Nassau County (sec. 1954-56) library assns., D.A.R., Club: Zonta (pres. L.I. 1965-67, dist. treas. 1974—). Contbr. articles to profl. jours. Home: 12 Ballard Av Valley Stream NY 11580 also 312 Broadway Hanover PA 17331 Office: Public Library Amityville NY 11701

FITZGERALD, A. ANN STRAYER (MRS. L. DALE FITZGERALD), newspaper editor; b. Omaha, June 29, 1930; d. Weir L. and Dorothea Louise (Axtell) Strayer; Bradley U., 1948; m. L. Dale Fitzgerald, Mar 1, 1952; children—Shari, Merrie, Lyndon. Acting editor, Metamora Herald, Inc., Metamora, Ill., 1962; reporter Woodford County Jour., Eureka, Ill., 1963-65; mem. staff Beckman Newspapers, Inc., Metamora, 1965—, gen. mgr., 1965—, editor, 1965—. Chmn. publicity Woodford County Human Services, 1973—, dir., 1973—. Mem. Ill. Press Assn., So. Ill. Editorial Assn. (dir. 1973). Home: Box 8 Metamora IL 61548 Office: Beckman Newspapers Inc 214 E Partridge St Metamora IL 61548

FITZGERALD, ELLA, singer; b. Newport News, Va., Apr. 25, 1918; m. Ray Brown (div. 1953); 1 son, Ray. Singer with Chick Webb Orch., 1934-39; tours throughout U.S., Japan, Europe with Jazz at the Philharmonic troupe, 1948—, with An Evening of Jazz troup in Sweden, Denmark, Norway, France, Belgium, Switzerland, Germany, Italy, 1957; rec. artist for Decca, 1936-55, Verve, 1956—; motion picture in Pete Kelly's Blues, 1955; numerous nightclub appearances, 1956—. Recipient numerous popularity awards from Down Beat mag., Metronome mag., Musicians Poll. Address: 1718 N Sierra Dr Beverly Hills CA 90210*

FITZGERALD, HARRIET, artist, lectr.; b. Danville, Va., Sept. 14, 1904; d. Harrison Robertson and Ida Lee (Flippin) Fitzgerald; A.B., Randolph-Macon Woman's Coll., 1926; student Art Students League, N.Y.C., 1927-29. Tchr. pvt. studio, N.Y.C., 1939-47; dir. Abingdon Sq. Painters, N.Y.C., 1948—; lectr. arts program Assn. Am. Colls., 1955—; vis. lectr. Stratford Coll., Danville, 1957—; one-man shows Va. Mus. Fine Arts, 1942, Charles Barzansky Gallery, N.Y.C., 1944, 46, 47, 50, 58, 64; exhibited in group shows at Milch, and Macbeth Galleries, N.Y.C., Butler Art Inst., Youngstown, O., Daton Mus., Gallery Birmingham Pub. Library, Milch and Macbeth Galleries, ACA Gallery, Norfolk Mus. Art., others; represented in permanent collections Randolph-Macon Woman's Coll., Lynchburg, Va., Lincoln U., Oxford, Pa., Sheldon Swope Gallery, Terre Haute, Ind., S.I. Mus., Bluffton (O.) Coll., Lawrence Coll., Appleton, Wis., Westminster Coll., Fulton, Mo., Randolph-Macon Coll., Ashland, Va., Stratford Coll., Danville, Hines Gallery of Rocky Mount Arts Center. Trustee Randolph-Macon Woman's Coll. Recipient award Am. Artists Congress, 1939; citation for distinguished work in arts Randolph-Macon Woman's Coll., 1960. Mem. Artists Equity Assn., Alumnae Assn. Stratford Coll. (pres. 1961-62, 62-63), Phi Beta Kappa, Pi Gamma Mu, Phi Mu. Club: Woman's Press of N.Y.C. Home: 229 Lady Astor Pl Danville VA 24541 also 62 Bank St New York City NY 10014

FITZGERALD, SISTER JEAN CATHERINE, coll. pres.; b. Green Bay, Wis., Feb. 23, 1927; d. George G. and Agnes (O'Connor) Fitzgerald; B.A., Siena Heights Coll., 1949; M.A., DePaul U., 1955; supervision certificate John Carroll U., 1968; certificate advanced studies in higher edn. U. Chgo., 1969-70. Joined Sisters of St. Dominic of Adrian, Mich.; Tchr. elementary schs., Chgo., Bronxville, N.Y., 1949-59, secondary schs., Cleve. 1959-65; high sch. curriculum cons. Diocesan Sch. Bd., Cleve., 1965-69; acad. v.p. Siena Heights Coll., Adrian, Mich., 1970-74, exec. asst. to Pres., 1974—. Mem. bd. edn., Lansing Diocese, Mich., 1973-75; mem. adv. bd. St. John Sem., Pontiac, Mich., 1973—. Mem. Am. Assn. Higher Edn., Nat. Cath. Edn. Assn., N. Central Assn., Pi Lambda Theta. Address: 1247 E Siena Heights Dr Adrian MI 49221

FITZGERALD, JO DUVALL (MRS. PITT LOOFBOURROW FITZGERALD), humanitarian; b. N.Y.C.; d. J. Sheldon and Martha (Rex) Duvall; m. Pitt Loofbourrow Fitzgerald, Oct. 15, 1955. West coast dir., nat. asso. dir. Am. Bur. Med. Aid for Free China, Los Angeles, 1954—; pres. Am. Creative, Prescott, Ariz., 1960—; cons. Sino-Am. relations, Los Angeles, 1954—; lectr., writer, pub. relations counsellor, 1954—. Bd. dirs. Pasadena chpt. Pro Am., 1962-64. Decorated for vol. humanitarian service Republic of China, 1965. Mem. China Soc., Pasadena Symphony Assn. Republican. Mem. Order Eastern Star. Author: Political Dust Devils, 1964. Home: PO Box 1189 Prescott AZ 86301 Office: 800 Orange Grove Av South Pasadena CA 91030

FITZGERALD, SISTER MARIE CHRISTINE, educator; b. N.Y.C.; d. Francis John and Johannah (O'Neill) Fitzgerald; B.A., D'Youville Coll., Buffalo, 1944; postgrad. U. Havana, Cuba, summer 1945; M.A., Catholic U. Am., 1948; Ph.D. (Spanish Govt. fellow), U. Madrid, Spain, 1954; Ph.D., Western Res. U., 1955. Joined Grey Nuns of the Sacred Heart, 1934; tchr. elementary grades, Buffalo, 1936-37, Atlanta, 1937-40; tchr. high sch. Atlanta, 1940-47; with D'Youville Coll., 1948—, prof., 1958—, head dept. Spanish, 1951-64, dean residents, 1950-52, academic dean, 1954-64, v.p. acad. affairs, 1964-66, now chmn. dept. fgn. lang. Mem. Conf. Community Living, Buffalo, 1956, mem. program com., 1957, vice-chmn. conf., 1958, 66, chmn. conf., 1959, 67, 72; dir. Buffalo Found. Internat. Cooperation, Buffalo Latin Am. AID; chmn. Cath.-Jewish Conf.; chmn. coll. and univ. div. United Fund, 1965—; mem. exec. com. Sisters Assembly, Buffalo, 1971; sec. Buffalo adv. bd. N.Y. State Commn. on Human Rights, 1969—. Recipient Good Neighbor award City Buffalo, 1961, Achievement award Am. Assn. U. Women, 1968, Brotherhood award Nat. Conf. Christians and Jews, 1971. Mem. Internat. Inst. Buenos Vecinos, Modern Lang. Assn., Am. Assn. Tchrs. Spanish and Portuguese (sec.-treas. Buffalo chpt. 1955-57, v.p. 1957-59, pres. 1959), Middle States Assn. Modern Lang. Tchrs. (2d v.p. 1959-61), Nat. Cath. Edn. Assn. (sec. Eastern regional unit coll. and univ. dept. 1961-66, mem. exec. bd., 1963-66), Sigma Delta Pi. Address: D'Youville Coll 320 Porter Av Buffalo NY 14201

FITZGERALD, MARY IRENE, psychologist; b. Hartford, Conn., Dec. 11, 1929; d. Daniel Thomas and Margaret Elinor (Queenin) Fitzgerald; student U. Hartford, 1947-49; A.B., Smith Coll., 1951; M.A., U. Conn., 1960, certificate in sch. psychology, 1962. Underwriting asst. Travelers Ins. Co., Hartford, 1951-52; tchr. elementary and secondary schs., East Hartford, 1952-55, 57-61; guidance counselor Old Saybrook (Conn.) Jr.-Sr. High Sch., 1961-62, Staples High Sch., Westport, Conn., 1962-64; sch. psychologist Windham Bd. Edn., Willimantic, Conn., 1964—. Co-founder, asst. dir. Family Counseling Service, Willimantic, 1973—; active fund raising drives various local charitable orgns. Mem. Nat., Conn. assns. sch. psychologists, Alumnae Assn. Smith Coll., Delta Kappa Gamma. Club: Smith College (Hartford). Home: 12 Garth Rd Manchester CT 06040 Office: 322 Prospect St Willimantic CT 06226

FITZGERALD, PATSY P., social worker; b. Augusta, Ga., Sept. 25, 1938; d. Perry L. and Pearl (Stevens) Fitzgerald; student Tift Coll., 1956-58; B.A., Carson Newman Coll., 1960; M.S.W., Fla. State U., 1965. Tchr. sch. music Fla. Bd. Edn., 1960-61, Ga. Bd. Edn., 1962; pub. welfare worker Richmond County (Ga.) Dept. Family & Children Services, Augusta, 1962, child welfare worker, 1962-63, child welfare supr., 1965-67, casework supr. III, 1968-69, dep. dir., 1969-73, dir. client service Dept. Human Resources, 1973—. Minister music several protestant chs., part-time, 1961-64; instr. Augusta Coll., 1965-68; instr. Paine Coll., 1970; head start cons. Office Econ. Opportunity, 1967-68. Mem. Augusta Community Service Orgn., 1965—; bd. dirs. Augusta Area Tb and Respiratory Disease Assn., 1969-73, mem. adv. com., 1969-70; mem. steering com. Augusta Mental Health Assn., 1969-70, bd. dirs., 1970—; bd. dirs. Alcohol and Drug Abuse Council, 1970—; mem. adv. com. Adult Edn.-Manpower Tng. Center, 1971—; mem. children's emotional health team P.T.A., Augusta, 1971—; mem. adv. bd. Ga. Lung Assn. Mem. Nat. Assn. Social Workers (state council 1969-70), Acad. Certified Social Workers, Ga. Conf. Social Welfare, Ga. Com. Children and Youth, Acad. Polit. and Social Sci., Ga. County Welfare Assn., Child Welfare League Am., Augusta Choral Soc. Democrat. Baptist. Home: 2417 Camelot Dr Augusta GA 30904 Office: PO Box 4507 Martinez GA 30907

FITZGERALD, VIETTA AGNES, former govt. analyst, mgmt. cons.; b. Balt., Aug. 9, 1917; d. John F. and Agnes M. (Little) F.; student Am. U., 1960, George Washington U., 1962-65; A.A., U. Md., 1972. With U.S. govt. service, 1935-73; records adminstr. Social Security Adminstrn., procedures and systems analyst, 1966-73; now mgmt. cons., Balt. Mem. Nat. Microfilm Assn. (former sec., now treas. Md. chpt. 1973), Assn. Records Adminstrs. and Execs., Federally Employed Women, Irish Cultural Assn. Clubs: Ancient Order Hibernians, Emerald Isle. Contbr. articles to profl. jours. Home: 100 Oaklee Village Baltimore MD 21229

FITZHUGH-BELL, KATHLEEN B. SMITH, educator; b. Kansas City, Mo.; d. Ralph A. and Ollie (Bell) Smith; B.A., U. Mo., 1951, M.A., 1954; Ph.D., Purdue U., 1958; m. L.C. Fitzhugh, Oct. 16, 1954 (div. May 1969); m. 2d, B.M. Bell, Feb. 29, 1972. Clin. psychologist, research psychologist New Castle State Hosp., 1958-65, dir. research, 1965-67, cons., 1967—; asst. prof. psychology Ind. U., 1967-69; asso. prof. psychology Tufts U. Med. Sch., Boston, 1969-70; dir. neuropsychology sect., dept. neurology Ind. U. Med. Sch., 1970—, asso. prof., 1971—. Instr. Earlham Coll., 1965-66; cons. Hathorne State Sch., 1969—, Marion County Assn. for Retarded Children. Bd. dirs. YMCA, New Castle, Ind., 1964-66. Mem. Am., Ind. (sec. 1962-66) psychol. assns. Club: Altrusa (pres. 1965-66) (New Castle). Contbr. articles to profl. jours. Address: Riley Hospital 375 Indianapolis IN 46202

FITZROY, NANCY DELOYE (MRS. ROLAND VICTOR FITZROY, JR.), chem. engr.; b. Pittsfield, Mass., Oct. 5, 1927; d. Jules Emile and Mabel Winifred (Burr) DeLoye; B.Chem. Engring., Rensselaer Poly. Inst., 1949; m. Roland Victor Fitzroy, Jr., Mar. 24, 1951. With research and devel. Gen. Electric Co., 1950—; asst. engr. Knolls Atomic Power Lab., Schenectady, 1950-52, devel. engr. Gen. Engring. Lab., 1953-63, thermal engr. Advanced Tech. Labs., 1963-65, heat transfer engr., 1965-71, mgr. heat transfer cons. Corporate Research and Devel., 1971-74, strategy planner, 1974—. Mem. NSF adv. com. engring., 1972-73, adv. com. research, 1973-75. Mem. archtl. com. West Hill Devel., Schenectady, 1972-75; mem. Rensselaer Council Rensselaer Poly. Inst., Troy, N.Y., 1972—, mem. pres.'s hon. degree evaluation com., 1973—. Mem. Am. Soc. M.E. (chmn. sect. 1963-64, regional activities del. 1962-65, mem. goals conf. 1970, working party equal opportunities 1971, policy bd., edn. 1974—), Am. Inst. Chem. Engrs. (hon., life), Soc. Women Engrs. (achievement award 1972), Nat. Soc. Profl. Engrs. (affilate), Nat. Acad. Engring. (bd. on engring. manpower and ednl. policy 1974—), Whirly Girls, Ninety-Nines Internat. Club: Northern Lake George Yacht. Author: My Career as a Heat Transfer Engineer, 1972. Editor: procs. Conf. Career Guidance for Women Entering Engineering, 1973. Home: 2125 Rosendale Rd Schenectady NY 12309 Office: Gen Electric Co CRD Box 8 Schenectady NY 12301

FITZSIMONS, ELEANOR, pub. relations counsel; b. N.Y.C.; d. Ludwig and Helene (Wolf) Brandt; student N.Y. U., 1941-45, New Sch. for Social Research, 1954-55; m. Robert FitzSimons, May 23, 1953 (div. 1972); 1 dau., Leslie Susan. Asso. editor U.S. Trust Co. N.Y., 1943-49; asst. to gen. mgr. Steve Hannagan Assos., 1949-52; asst. to pres. Heublein, Inc., 1957-60; exec. sec., dir. pub. relations Morris Morgenstern Found., N.Y.C., 1960-61; v.p. Louis Weintraub Assos., Inc., 1961-63; exec. v.p. Weintraub & FitzSimons, Inc., N.Y.C., 1963—; v.p. Photo Communications Co., Inc., 1961—; photog. cons. N.Y. Racing Assn., 1961—; contbg. editor L.I. Post, Forest Hills, N.Y., 1962-67; editorial cons. Ridgewood Times, Bklyn., 1968—. Trustee Citizens Budget Commn., N.Y.C. Recipient citation for meritorious service President's Com. on Employment of Handicapped, 1964. Mem. Advt. Women N.Y., Fgn. Press Assn., Pub. Relations Soc. Am., Nat. Council Women. Club: Women's City N.Y. Contbr. articles to newspapers, mags. Home: 254 E 68th St New York City NY 10021 Office: 488 Madison Av New York City NY 10022

FITZSIMONS, RUTH MARIE, educator; b. Pawtucket, R.I.; d. Leo A. and Helena (Hollis) Fitzsimons; B.Ed., R.I. Coll., 1940; M.Ed., Boston U., 1949, D.Ed., 1955; postgrad. Brandeis U., summer 1958, N.Y. U., 1956. Tchr., prin. Warwick (R.I.) Sch. Dept., 1940-49, speech and hearing therapy coordinator, 1949-68; asso. prof. speech pathology U. R.I., Kingston, 1969-73, prof. speech, 1973—. Lectr., Boston U., 1956, 58, 59, U. Me., summer 1966; cons. speech and hearing therapy R.I. Dept. Edn., Providence, 1968-69, cons. Meeting St. Sch. Childrens Rehab. Center, Providence, 1969; cons. editor T.J. Denison & Co., Mpls., 1966—. Mem. R.I. (pres. 1964-65), Am. (legislative councillor 1969-71) speech and hearing assns., Am. Psychol. Assn., Am. Acad. Psychotherapists, Soc. for Research in Child Devel. Author: Stuttering and Personality Dynamics, 1960; Christopher Listens, 1966; Make Believe with Mike, 1968. Contbr. articles to profl. jours. Home: 38 Mystic Dr Warwick RI 02886 Office: Dept Speech U RI Kingston RI 02881

FIXX, ALICE KASMAN, pub. relations co. exec.; b. N.Y.C., Apr. 28, 1943; d. H. Larry and Helen (Sweet) Kasman; A.B. cum laude, Barnard Coll., 1964; M.A., U. Notre Dame, 1965; M. James F. Fixx, 1974. Tchr. English, Riley High Sch., South Bend, Ind., 1965, Star of the Sea Acad., San Francisco, 1965-66; tchr. English and biology Balboa High Sch., San Francisco, 1966-67; tchr. math. Haaren High Sch., N.Y.C., 1967-68; account exec. Partners for Growth, Inc., N.Y.C., 1968-72; account supr. Robert Marston & Assos., Inc., N.Y.C., 1972-73, v.p., 1973—. Home: 37 Crescent Rd Riverside CT 06878 Office: 645 Madison Av New York City NY 10022

FLACK, HANNAH FISK, social worker; b. Chgo., Oct. 13, 1915; d. Henry Bowen and Alice (Abbott) Fisk; B.A., U. Chgo., 1940; M.S.W., U. Pitts., 1962; m. Charles R. Flack, Apr. 26, 1937 (div. May 1968); children—Charlotte (Mrs. Edward Schwyn), Arthur Bowen. Caseworker, Clarion County Bd. Assistance, Clarion, Pa., 1958-60; supr. Indiana County Bd. Assistance, Indiana, Pa., 1961-63, sr. psychiat. social worker Dept. Mental Hygiene, Pomona, Cal., 1963-64; part-time psychiat. social worker Tri-City Mental Health Authority, Pomona, 1963-69, with Lorna Forbes, M.D., Pomona, 1967-69; supervising psychiat. social worker Cal. Dept. Social Welfare, Pomona and El Monte, 1964-69; tng. cons. Cal. Dept. Social Welfare Tng. Bur., Sacramento, 1969-72; program asst. mental retardation Alt. Care Services Unit Cal. Dept. Mental Hygiene, 1972-73; asst. coordinator med. assistance programs Cal. Dept. Health, 1973—. Instr. social work U. So. Cal., 1964-67; participant, La Verne (Cal.) Case Conf., 1964-68, Pomona Case Conf., 1965-68. Mem. bd. Pomona Valley Hearing Soc., 1967-69, pres. Clarion County Library Bd., 1946-48. Mem. Nat. Assn. Social Workers, Am. Orthopsychiat. Assn., Am. Group Psychotherapy Assn., Am. Pub. Welfare Assn., Am. Pub. Health Assn. Episcopalian. Club: Federation of Women's (pres. 1945 Clarion County). Home: Apt 48 2400 Sierra Blvd Sacramento CA 95825 Office: 744 P St Sacramento CA 95814

FLACK, ROBERTA, vocalist; pupil Frederick Wilkerson; grad. Howard U. Jazz vocalist; appeared Mr. Henry's, Washington, now concerts, TV spls.; also numerous recs. Address: care Roberta Flack Enterprises Suite 954 Watergate Six Hundred 600 New Hampshire Av NW Washington DC 20037

FLACK, SHIRLEY JUNE GRAFF (MRS. EDWARD R. FLACK), librarian; b. Mitchell, Neb., Jan. 15, 1934; d. Henry G. and Pauline (Vogel) Graff; student Neb. Western Coll., 1952-53; m. Edward R. Flack, Dec. 19, 1953; children—Janine Kae, Paul Edward. Children's librarian Scottsbluff (Neb.) Pub. Library, 1953-54, asst. librarian 1960-67, then library dir.; dir. N.W. Neb. Regional Library System, 1968—. Sec. Panhandle Library Network Adv. Council, 1970—, Scottsbluff-Gering Community Improvement Council, 1972—; mem. adv. bd. Volunteer Action Center. Mem. Am., Mountain-Plains (chmn. pub. library sect. 1969-70), Neb. (sec. 1973-74; pub. library sect. vice-chmn. 1969-70, chmn. 1970-72), Wyo. library assns., Neb. Ednl. Media Assn., Adult and Continuing Edn. Assn. Neb. Republican. Conglist. Home: 2430 Av C Scottsbluff NE 69361 Office: 1809 3d Av Scottsbluff NE 69361

FLACKE, KLELLA JOAN WAREHAM (MRS. WERNER E. FLACKE), anesthesiologist; b. Evanston, Ill., Dec. 16, 1931; d. Loyal Delbert and Alice Marie (Cummings) Wareham; B.A., Scripps Coll., 1953; M.D., Harvard, 1959; m. Werner E. Flacke, Aug. 7, 1957; children—Christopher, Gary, Timothy. Research asst. dept. surgery Mass. Gen. Hosp., Boston, 1953-55, asst. resident in anesthesia, 1961-64, research fellow in anesthesia, 1964-65, research and clin. fellow, 1965-68, asst. anesthetist, 1968, head anesthesia service Shriners' Burns Inst., 1968-70; intern in pediatrics Boston City Hosp., 1959-60; research fellow in anesthesia Harvard Med. Sch., Boston, 1964-67, research asso. in anesthesia, 1967-69, instr., 1969-70; anesthesiologist VA Hosp., Little Rock, 1971—; asst. prof. anesthesia U. Ark. Med. Center, 1972—. Diplomate Am. Bd. Anesthesiology, Nat. Bd. Med. Examiners. Mem. Am. Coll. Anesthesiology, Am., Ark. socs. anesthesiologists, Mass. Med. Soc. Contbr. articles to med. jours. Home: 10401 W Markham St Little Rock AR 72205 Office: U Ark Medical Center West Markham Little Rock AR 72201

FLAGG, JO ELLEN, librarian; b. Charleston, W. Va., Feb. 8, 1937; d. Henry and Ora (Miller) Flagg; B.S., W. Va. Wesleyan Coll., 1958; M.S. in Library Sci., Case Western Reserve U., 1961; certificate U. Wis., 1968. Library asst. Case Western Reserve U., Cleve., 1961; sci. librarian Oberlin (O.) Coll., 1961-69; librarian Forest Park Community Coll., St. Louis, 1969—. Instr., Washington U., St. Louis, 1973; cons. grad. sch. library sci., Ind. U., Bloomington, 1973-74. Mem. Mo. Assn. Jr. Colls., Am. Library Assn. (chmn. community and jr. coll. library sect., chmn. instrn. and use com. 1972—), League Women Voters (dir. Oberlin, O. chpt. 1961-64), Kappa Phi. Methodist. Home: 4545 Laclede St St Louis MO 63108 Office: Library Forest Park Community College 5600 Oakland Av St Louis MO 63110

FLAGG, MILDRED BUCHANAN (MRS. FRANCIS JOHN FLAGG), writer, lectr.; b. Moravia, N.Y., May 1, 1886; d. B. Frank and Julia (McCormick) Buchanan; A.B., Syracuse U., 1908; M.A., Boston U., 1927, Litt.D., 1963; D.Sc. Oratory, Curry Coll., 1958; L.H.D., Portia Law School, 1965; m. Francis John Flagg, Oct. 7, 1914;

children—David Buchanan (dec.), Julia Buchanan (Mrs. Kenneth A. Williams), Nancy Ferard (Mrs. Robert E. Gibney). Head English dept. high sch., Palmyra, N.Y., 1911-13, Watertown, N.Y., 1913-14; in ednl. work, lectr., writer, 1914—; dir. Am. Students Abroad, 1929-33; dir. Flagstaff Radio Hour, Sta. WCOP Boston, 1935-37; dir. Sta. WXHR. Dir. United Cerebral Palsy Assn. of Mass., 1947-54, Newton Hosp. Aid Assn., 1928—. Boston U. Women's Council, 1931-34, Mass. Com. on Pub. Health, Newton Council for Better World Order, nat. chmn., Books for Norway, 1947-49; chmn. Celebrity Breakfasts, 1945-60; mem. N.E. com. Anatolia Coll., Greece; vice comdr. Women's Field Army for Control of Cancer; trustee Flora Koralsky Scholarship Fund, 1955-60; chmn. bd. cons. Curry Coll.; mem. corp., treas., 1963-66; sponsor Radcliffe Coll. Archives, 1961; dir. Writers Workshop, Newton Tb and Health Assn. Trustee Laubach Literacy Inc., 1970. Mem. Farm and Garden Assn., Mass. Tchrs. Fedn., N.E. Women's Press Assn. (pres. 1931-33), Am. Assn. U. Women (state pres. 1930-32, state chmn. TV-radio 1948-52), Presidents' Club of Mass. (pres. 1937-38), Boston Syracuse Alumnae Assn. (pres. 1920-37), Boston U. Grad. Sch. Alumni Assn. (pres. 1935-37), Newton Center Woman's Club (lit. chmn. 1945-48), Women's City Club Boston, Eliot Woman's Assn. (program chmn. 1961-63), Social Sci. Club, Am. Numismatic Assn., Nat. League Am. Pen Women (pres. Boston br., nat. lectures chmn. 1954-56), N.E.A. (hon. life), Boar's Head, N.Y. Authors League (pres. 1968-70), Zonta Internat., Onaway, Phi Beta Kappa, Theta Sigma Phi, Delta Kappa Gamma. Republican. Conglist. Clubs: Newton Centre Garden, Professional Women's (pres. 1931-33), Boston Authors (pres. 1947-49, 65-67, dir. 1950-52), Boston Travel (program chmn. 1960-62), Newton Community. Author: Community English, 1921; Camera Adventures in Africa, 1935; Plymouth Maid, 1937; Boy of Salem, 1939; Celebrity Chatalogs, 1945; A Lad of Old Nantucket, 1947; Approaching Old Age, 1955; Uncle Sam's Forgotten Children, 1956; Prayer Is My Gyroscope in We Believe in Prayer, 1958; Notable Boston Authors 1900-1966, 1965; Boston Authors—Now and Then, 1967; Profiles of New York Authors, 1972; also articles various publs. Editor: Study Outlines in Pocket Classis, 6 vols., 1921-33; A Certain Rich Man (William Allan White), 1923, 30; The Pen Craft of Authors League. Home: Skyline Apts 753 James St Syracuse NY 13203

FLAGLE, JUDITH RENEE, occupational therapist; b. Greeley, Colo., Sept. 6, 1948; d. Warren Howard and Marian D. (McKeever) Flagle; B.S., Colo. State U., 1970, certificate, 1971. Chief occupational therapist High Plains Easter Seal Rehab. Center, Sterling, Colo., 1971—, inhalation therapy technician, 1972-73. Cons., Rose Arbor Nursing Home, Sterling, 1971—, Sterling Anna C. Petty's Spl. Edn. Sch., 1973—, Perceptual-Motor Screening Clinics, N.E. Colo., 1972, 73, 74. Mem. U.S.A. High Sch. Band and Chorus, 1966; speaker Neb. Tchr.'s Conv., 1973. Mem. Am., Colo. (reporter 1972-73) Occupational Therapy assns., Antique Car Club Am. (sec.-treas. N.E. Colo. chpt, 1972-73), Delta Xi (treas. 1971-72, v.p. 1973-74, pres. 1974—, sec. city council 1973-74, chmn. German dinner 1972). Mem. Rainbow Girls (recipient Grand Cross Color 1966), Order Eastern Star (asso. conductress 1974—). Home: 512 Oak St PO Box 892 Sterling CO 80751 Office: 1406 S 6th Av Sterling CO 80751

FLAHERTY, SISTER ELIZABETH JANE, coll. dean; b. Detroit, Nov. 25, 1931; d. Stephen H. and Helen Marie (Keely) Flaherty; M.A., Siena Heights Coll., 1962; postgrad. Va. Poly. Inst., 1968, U. Detroit, 1969, Mich. State U., 1971. Elementary tchr., Ill., Mich., 1950-60, secondary tchr., counselor Sorrows High Sch., Farmington, Mich., 1961-67, Benedictine High Sch., Detroit, 1967-70; counselor, dean students Siena Heights Coll., Adrian, Mich., 1971—. Vol. counselor Call Someone Concerned, 1971—; publicity chmn., sec. Adrian (Mich.) Area Council Chs., 1972—. Bd. dirs. Detroit Archdiocesan Guidance Council, 1968-70. Recipient Educators Profl. Devel. Act Grant, Va. Poly. Inst., 1968. Roman Catholic. Home: 1480 Village Green Lane Adrian MI 49221

FLAHERTY, MIRIAM IMELDA FLYNN (MRS. LAURENCE S. FLAHERTY), lawyer; b. Waltham, Mass., Jan. 14, 1920; d. John J. and Mary Josephine (Rooney) Flynn; A.B., Emmanuel Coll., 1941; LL.B., Boston U., 1943; m. Laurence S. Flaherty, Feb. 19, 1949. Law clk. Mass. Supreme Ct., Boston, 1945-49; admitted to Mass. bar, 1943, U.S. Supreme Ct., 1957; Flynn & Flynn, Waltham, 1949—. Treas. Waltham Hosp. Assn., 1956-65. Bd. dirs. Waltham Vis. Nurse Assn., 1962-72. Mem. Mass. Bar Assn., Mass. Assn. Women Lawyers (dir. 1962-65). Home: 44 Common St Waltham MA 02154 Office: 411 Main St Waltham MA 02154

FLAIG, PEARL NOWLIN NENO (MRS. EDWARD GUY FLAIG), univ. dean; b. Arkadelphia, Ark., Jan. 25, 1921; d. Edger and Pearl (Adams) Nowlin; B.S., Ouachita Bapt. U., 1943; M.S., Henderson State Coll., 1961; postgrad. Okla. State U., summer 1964, U. Denver, summer 1966; m. Edward Guy Flaig, Mar. 25, 1944; children—Gay, Gail (Mrs. James Davis Russell), Lynda Suzanne. Instr. English, dean of women Ouachita Bapt. U., Arkadelphia, 1959—. Mem. Nat. Assn. Women Deans and Counselors, S.W. Assn. Student Personnel Adminstrs., Am. Assn. Univ. Women, Ark. Personnel and Guidance Assn., Ark. Coll. Personnel Assn., Ark. Assn. Women Deans (pres. elect 1974). Club: Philharmonic Music (Arkadelphia). Home: 10C Pinewood Dr Arkadelphia AR 71923

FLANAGAN, MARY SUE, author, photographer, mus. dir.; b. San Angelo, Tex., July 17, 1926; d. John Thomas and Albert (Powers) Flanagan; student San Angelo Jr. Coll., 1943; B.F.A., U. Denver, 1946; diploma N.Y. Inst. Photography, 1946; postgrad. (Rotary internat. fellow) Trinity Coll., U. Dublin, Ireland, 1952-53, U. Tex., 1959. Reporter, photographer San Angelo Standard-Times, 1947-49, 70th anniversary edit., 1954-55; asso. editor Tex. Sheep and Goat Raisers Mag., San Angelo, 1949-52; coordinator vol. service McKnight State Tb Hosp., Carlsbad, Tex., 1955-59; adminstrv. aide to atty. gen. Tex., Austin, 1959-62; capitol press corr., Austin, 1963-65; mem. adminstrv. staff of Tex. gov., 1966; research asso. Inst. Texan Cultures, 1968-70, asst. to dir., 1970-72; dir. Sam Houston Meml. Mus., Huntsville, Tex., 1972—. Mem. Jr. League of San Antonio. Presbyn. Author: Sam Houston's Texas, 1964 (permanent library at White House, 1966). Home: 1917 20th St Apt 4 Huntsville TX 77340 Office: Sam Houston Meml Museum Huntsville TX 77340

FLANDERS, LEATHA MAY (MRS. FRANKLIN FREDERICK FLANDERS), editor, journalist; b. Hugo, Colo., Sept. 10, 1916; d. Benjamin Harrison and Hazel Verne (Moore) Harris; student Colo. Marinello Beauty Coll., Denver, 1934-35; B.A., U. Colo., 1941; postgrad. Columbia U., Am. Press Inst., 1968; m. Franklin Frederick Flanders, June 29, 1941; children—Francea (Mrs. Howard Phillips), F. Fred. Licensed cosmetologist, Colorado Springs, Colo., 1935-38; with personnel dept. U. Colo., 1938-41; with personnel dept. Lockheed Aircraft Corp., Burbank, Cal., 1943-45; journalist, editor spl. sections Longmont (Colo.) Daily Times Call, 1957—; free lance writer. Pub. relations cons. Girl Scouts Am., 1965-71; state chmn. Status of Women and Internat. Relations, Colo., 1954-55; mem. Longmont Human Relations Commn., 1969-71; chmn. UN Longmont, 1968-72; mem. Longmont City Recreation Commn., 1957-67; organizer, promoter many civic, cultural projects; mem. AP Mng. Editors' Continuing Study Com. on Women's News, 1969, Family News, 1970. Sweepstakes winner Colo. Press Women's Contest, 1970, 73, awards winner Nat. Fedn. Press Women, 1969, 71, 72, 73; named Colo. Woman of Achievement, Colo. Press Women, 1973. Mem. Nat. Fedn. Press Women, Colo. Press Women (program chmn., dist. chmn.; pres. 1974), Sigma Delta Chi, Am. Assn. U. Women (chpt. pres. 1950-51), Beta Sigma Phi (life). Home: 430 Pratt St Longmont CO 80501 Office: 717 4th Av Longmont CO 80501

FLANDERS, RUTH STONE (MRS. PHILLIP RAY FLANDERS), clubwoman; b. Breckenridge, Mich.; d. Arian Warren and Lillie (Clemens) Stone; grad. Mt. Ida Sch., 1924; m. Phillip Ray Flanders, Nov. 14, 1934. First v.p. Sch. Govt. of Detroit, 1971-72, pres., 1972-74. Mem. Mich. Fedn. Music Clubs (life, S.E. dist. pres. 1966-70, corr. sec. 1973—, pub. relations dir. 1973—), Detroit Fine Arts Soc. (treas. 1942-45, dir. 1958—, historian 1961—), West Oakland Hills Lawyers Wives (pres. 1968-69), Fedn. Womens Clubs Met. Detroit (editor Club Womens Bulletin, 1962-66), Womens Assn. Detroit Symphony Orch. (editor Symphony Notes 1957-59, dir. 1966-68, 70-72, hon. life v.p. 1971—, historian 1972—). Clubs: Village Womans (editor Villager 1964-65 Bloomfield Hills, Mich.); Womens City (Detroit dir. 1966-69), Detroit Colony Town. Home: 4688 Brafferton Dr Bloomfield Hills MI 48013

FLANNERY, ROSEMARY MCCARRON (MRS. JOHN F. FLANNERY), lawyer; b. Phila., June 11, 1921; d. Francis A. and Sara D. (Sauer) McCarron; A.B., Chestnut Hill Coll., 1943; LL.B., Villanova U., 1965; m. John F. Flannery, Jan. 21, 1950; children—Mary K., Katherine A., John F. Sports reporter Phila. Inquirer, 1944-49; instr. journalism Rosemont (Pa.) Coll., 1945-53; admitted to Pa. bar, 1965; practiced in Norristown, Pa., 1965—; partner Wisler, Pearlstine, Talone, Craig and Garrity, 1973—. Mem. exec. com. Conf. of County Bar Officers of Pa., 1971-74; bd. dirs. Legal Aid Service Montgomery County, Pa., 1973—. Tchr. Confraternity of Christian doctrine Epiphany of Our Lord Sch., Plymouth Twp, Pa., 1970—. Mem. Exec. Com. of Montgomery County Estate Planning Council, 1973—. Mem. St. Edmund's Home Aux., 1968—. Democratic committeewoman, Whitpain Twp., Pa., 1962—; mem. Selective Service Bd., Norristown, 1972—. Trustee Eastern State Sch. and Hosp., Trevose, Pa. Mem. Am., Pa., Montgomery County (sec. 1971—) bar assns., Montgomery County Trial Lawyers Assn., Ambler Bus. and Profl. Women's Club, St. Francis, St. Vincent's aid assns. Democrat. Roman Catholic. Club: Iris of Philadelphia (dir. 1968—). Home: 666 Midway Lane Blue Bell PA 19422 Office: 515 Swede St Norristown PA 19401

FLASCH, NEVA JOY CHILDERS (MRS. HAROLD ANDREW FLASCH), educator; b. Denison, Tex., Mar. 23, 1932; d. Robert Henry and Ersa Lois (Griffin) Childers; B.A. in Edn., Southeastern State Coll., Durant, Okla., 1951; M.A. in English, Okla. State U., Stillwater, 1954, Ed. D., 1969; m. Harold Andrew Flasch, July 15, 1956; children—Christopher John, Julie Lois, Jeanine Laurie. Tchr. Ardmore (Okla.) High Sch., 1951-53; grad. asst. dept. English, Okla. State U., 1953-54, instr. English, 1954-62; instr. English, Langston (Okla.) U., 1964-66, asst. prof., 1967-68, asso. prof., 1968-69, prof., 1969—, chmn. dept. communication, 1973—. Program dir. YWCA, Guthrie, Okla., 1973-74. Recipient plaque for lit. services Detroit Coordinators Council of Arts, 1973. Mem. Nat., Okla. councils tchrs. English, Kappa Delta Pi. Lutheran (tchr. Sunday sch. 1960-73). Author: Melvin B. Tolson, 1972. Contbr. articles to profl. jours. Home: Route One Coyle OK 73027 Office: Dept Communication Langston Univ Langston OK 73050

FLASHMAN, ALBERTA ROSE COHEN (MRS. BARRY P. FLASHMAN), psychiatrist; b. Newark, Aug. 7, 1934; d. Samuel and Raschen (Solomon) Cohen; B.A., U. Cal. at Los Angeles, 1955; M.D., U. So. Cal., 1960; m. Barry P. Flashman, May 15, 1970; children (by previous marriage)—Rebecca, Judith, Laura. Intern, Los Angeles County Hosp., 1960-61, resident in dermatology, 1962-65; practice medicine specializing in dermatology, Pomona, Cal., 1967-69; Osborne fellow in dermal pathology Armed Forces Inst. Pathology, Washington, 1969-70; Nat. Inst. Mental Health fellow St. Elizabeth Hosp., 1970-71; psychiatry resident U. Md., Balt., 1972-73; practice medicine specializing in psychiatry, Annapolis, 1973—; mem. attending staff Anne Arundel-Gen. Hosp.; clin. instr. U. Md. Med. Sch. Fellow Am. Acad. Dermatology; mem. Am. Psychiat. Assn., Alpha Omega Alpha. Home: Box 416 Severna Park MD 21146 Office: 121 Cathedral St Annapolis MD 21401

FLATO, LINDA JANE RUNYAN (MRS. JOHN RICHARD FLATO), editor; b. Washington, July 3, 1947; d. Howard George and Sarah Jane (Crickenberger) Runyan; B.S., U. Md., 1970; m. John Richard Flato, Jan. 27, 1973. Editorial asst. EDP News Services, Inc., Washington, 1970-71, reporter, 1971-72, asso. editor, 1972—, editor Peripherals Weekly, newsletter, 1972—. Mem. Pub. Relations Soc. Am., Women in Communications, Tau Mu Epsilon, Gamma Phi Beta. Home: 4866 W Braddock Rd Alexandria VA 22311 Office: 7620 Little River Turnpike Annandale VA 22003

FLAX, SERENE (MRS. DONALD FLAX), artist; b. Chgo., May 25, 1925; d. Walter and Florence (Zimmerman) Gottstein; grad. Chgo. Acad. Fine Arts, 1943; student Northwestern U., 1944-45, Art Inst. Chgo., 1946, Inst. Design, Chgo., 1946-47; m. Donald Flax, Feb. 15, 1948;children—Robert, Carole, Patrice. Art dir. advt. agys., Chgo., 1946-48; contbr. to art rental and sales Art Inst. Chgo., 1964—; one-man shows Ontario-East Gallery, Chgo., 1966, Mundelein Coll., Chgo., 1967, Kaummerman Gallery, Racine, Wis., 1962, Barat Coll., Lake Forest, Ill., 1970, Madison (Wis.) Art Center, 1970, Ill. Arts Council, 1973, Ill. State Mus., 1974; exhibited group shows, nat. competitions including Drawings, U.S.A., St. Paul, 1963, Allied Artists Am., N.Y.C., 1963-64, Audubon Soc. Artists, N.Y.C., 1963-64, Am. Water Color Soc., 1964—, Miss. Valley Artists Invitational, Springfield, Ill., 1965, Ill. State Mus. Invitational, Springfield, 1968, 72, Butler Inst. Am. Art, Youngstown, O., 1962—, U. Chgo. Bergman Gallery, 1971, Watercolor U.S.A.; rep. permanent collections Caravan Gallery, Tulsa, Bocour collection, N.Y.C., also many pvt. collections throughout U.S. Chmn. Old Orchard Fesitval, Skokie, Ill., 1965, chmn. exhbns., 1965—; vol. mem. human relations group Lake Forest (Ill.) chpt. Panel Am. Women, 1966—. Recipient travel awards Am. Watercolor Soc., 1963, 64, 65, 66, 67, Cal. Water-color Soc. and Watercolor U.S.A., 1967-68; Bruggers Merit award for transparent watercolor Cal. Watercolor Soc., 1964; 1st prize Evanston (Ill.) Women's Club, 1964; Purchase award Watercolor U.S.A., Springfield (Mo.) Art Mus., 1966, Deerfield High Sch., 1971; Municipal Art League award Chgo. Art Inst., 1969. Mem. Am., Cal. watercolor socs. Contbg. author profl. mags. Address: 268 Moraine Rd Highland Park IL 60035

FLECK, HENRIETTA (MRS. DALE HOUGHTON), educator; b. Papillion, Neb., Sept. 22, 1903; d. John Peter and Wilhelmina (Prinz) Fleck; student Peru (Neb.) Tchrs. Coll., 1921-23; B.S., U. Neb., 1928; M.S., Columbia, 1932; Ph.D., Ohio State U., 1944; D.Sc. (hon.), U. Neb., 1970; m. Dale Houghton, June 6, 1956. Home econs. tchr. Neb. high schs., 1923-27; dietitian in charge metabolic div. Santa Barbara (Cal.) Cottage Hosp., 1928-29; head dept. foods, nutrition U. Del., 1932-42; research asst., bur. ednl. research Ohio State U., 1942-44; chmn. home econs. dept. Ill. State Normal Coll., 1944-46; chmn. home econs. dept. N.Y. U., 1946-71, prof., 1971—; cons. edn. procedures N.Y. Dept. Edn., bus. corps., social orgns., 1946—. Recipient Great Tchr. award N.Y. U., 1973. Mem. N.E.A. (pres. home econs. dept. 1953-55), Am. Home Econ. Assn., A.A.A.S., Am. Dietetic Assn., Am. Ednl. Research Assn., Nat. Council Family Relations, Am. Assn. U. Profs., Nat. Soc. Study Edn., Omicron Nu, Pi Lambda Theta. Author: A Recipe Primer, 1949; How To Evaluate Students, 1953; A First Cook Book for Boys and Girls, 1953; (with Munves) Everybody's Book of Modern Diet and Nutrition, 1955; (with Munves and Fernandez) Exploring Home and Family Living, 1959, 3d edit., 1971, Living with your Family, 1965; Introduction to Nutrition, 2d edit., 1971; The Co-ed Cookbook, 1967; Toward Better Teaching Home Economics, 1968, 2d edit., 1974, Japanese edit., 1972. Editor Macmillan series coll. home econs. text books, 1957-63. Contbg. editor, ednl. advisor Forecast Mag. 1949—. Contbr. articles to profl. jours. Home: 157 E 18th St New York City NY 10003 Office: 537 East Bldg 239 Greene St New York City NY 10003

FLEDDERUS, HELEN THEMO (MRS. J. DYCK FLEDDERUS), librarian; b. Boston, Feb. 16, 1931; d. Pantel and Aphrodite (Shuku) Themo; B.A., Smith Coll., 1951; m. J. Dyck Fledderus, Aug. 27, 1955. Asst. librarian Lamont Library, Harvard U. Library Program, Cambridge, Mass., 1951-52; librarian, George S. Armstrong Co., N.Y.C., 1953-57; reference librarian J. Walter Thompson Co.,N.Y.C., 1958-60; librarian, Reader's Digest Advt. Div., N.Y.C., 1961—. Mem. Spl. Libraries Assn. (sec. N.Y. chpt. 1964-65). N.Y. Library Club. Club: Smith College (N.Y.C.). Home: 10 Mitchell Pl New York City NY 10017 Office: 200 Park Av New York City NY 10017

FLEEGE, VIRGINIA BLANCHE HANSEN (MRS. URBAN H. FLEEGE), educator; b. Jamestown, N.D., July 23, 1925; d. Ross and Mildred (Tofson) Hansen; student Wis. State U., 1943-48; B.A., Marquette U., 1946; postgrad. De Paul U., 1967; m. Urban H. Fleege, Aug. 31, 1948; children—William, Kathleen, Richard, Robert, Maureen, Michael. With pub. relations dept. Wis. Bell Telephone Co., 1943-47; advt. writer Milw. Jour., 1947-48; tchr., demonstrator UNESCO Model Sch. Demonstration Center, Bayambang, Philippines, 1954-56; tchr. Alcuin Montessori Sch., Oak Park, Ill., 1961-65; adminstr., tchr., founder Oak Park Montessori Child Devel. Center, Forest Park, 1965—; mem. faculty dir. Midwest Montessori Tchr. Tng. Center, Chgo., 1966—. Cons. Midwest Montessori Schs., 1966—. Bd. dirs. Elmhurst Montessori Sch., 1965—, Oak Park Montessori Sch., 1966—; mem. Christian Family Movement, 1959-68; mem. adv. bd. St. Mary's Coll., Notre Dame, Ind., 1968—. Mem. Montessori Found. Adv. Com., 1967—. Recipient Montessori Creative award, 1969. Clubs: Original Key, De Paul University Wives (Chgo.). Author: Montessori Index, 1965; Standard Operating Procedures for a Montessori Sch., 1967; Language in the Montessori School, 1971; Montessori Mathematics for Young Children, 1972. Home: 831 Fair Oaks Av Oak Park IL 60302 Office: 16 Lathrop Av Forest Park IL 60130

FLEETWOOD, MARIA FREILE, physician; b. Valparaiso, Chile; d. Alfonso Larrea and Berta (Cordovez) Freile; M.D., U. Chile, 1941, Ph.D., 1946; married; children—Harvey III, Francis Freile. Rockefeller Found. fellow Johns Hopkins Hosp., 1942-44; head research dept. in psychiatry U. Chile, 1944-48, instr. psychiatry, 1944-48, asso. prof. psychophysiology, 1946; head research lab. in psychiatry Cornell U., 1948-54, instr. psychiatry, 1950, clin. asst. prof., 1970—; cons. Clinic for Alcoholism U. Hosp., 1954-55; pvt. practice, N.Y.C., 1951—; teaching staff Huntington Twp. Mental Health Clinic, 1963; sch. psychiatrist N.Y.C. Bd. Edn., 1964—; cons. psychiatrist Family Service, Patterson, N.J., 1955-56, Community Service Soc. Mem. profl. adv. com. Morningside Mental Hygiene Clinic; mem. N.Y. Council on Child Psychiatry. Mem. Am. Spanish med. assns., N.Y. State, N.Y. County med. socs., A.A.A.S., Am. Psychiat. Assn., N.Y. Soc. Clin. Psychiatry, N.Y.C. Med. Soc. on Alcoholism, Soc. for Adolescent Psychiatry, N.Y. Acad. Scis. Author sect. of book, also articles med. jours. Contbg. editor Ann. Survey Psychoanalysis. Address: 11 E 68th St New York City NY 10021

FLEGAL, JEAN ELIZABETH, librarian; b. Zanesville, O.; d. Harry Mitchell and Hazel Ianthe (Purviance) Flegal; B.S., Carnegie Inst. Tech., 1943; M.S. in L.S., Columbia, 1952; M.B.S., N.Y.U., 1967. Sec. to chief chemist Hazel-Atlas Glass Co., Zanesville, 1933-38; sec. to dir. microbiology Merck & Co., Inc., Rahway, N.J., 1943-50; librarian purchasing dept. Union Carbide Corp., N.Y.C., 1951-58, librarian Bus. Library, 1958—. Monitor Recs. for the Blind, N.Y.C., 1972—. Mem. Spl Libraries Assn. (2d v.p. N.Y. chpt. 1955-56, pres. 1958-59, chmn. Inst. Library Planning, 1968, chmn. nominating com. 1960-61, mem. Hdqrs. Operations com. 1964-67). Republican. Methodist. Home: 360 E 55th St New York City NY 10022 Office: 270 Park Av New York City NY 10017

FLEGER, LINDA ALZINA, psychiat. social worker; b. Pitts., d. Philip Arthur and Margaret (Rodgers) Fleger; B.A., Wellesley Coll., 1961; M.S.W., Simmons Coll., 1963. Probation officer Allegheny County Juvenile Ct., Pitts., 1961; med. social worker Mass. Gen. Hosp., Boston, 1962; psychiat. social worker Mass. Mental Health Center, Boston, 1963-69, South Shore Mental Health Center, Quincy, Mass., 1969—. Individual practice psychiat. social work, 1967—. Mem. Nat. Assn. Social Workers, Acad. Certified Social Workers, Mass. Acad. Psychiat. Social Workers. Home: 25 Thatcher St Brookline MA 02146 Office: 1853 Commonwealth Av Brighton MA 02135 also 77 Parking Way Quincy MA 02169

FLEHINGER, BETTY JEANNE ISAACS (MRS. WILLIAM SCHULTZ), mathematician; b. Sandusky, O., Apr. 4, 1922; d. Merritt B. and Edna (Baer) Isaacs; A.B. summa cum laude, Barnard Coll., 1941; M.A. (Grace Potter Rice fellow), Cornell U., 1942; Ph.D. (Pfister fellow), Columbia, 1960; m. William Schultz, Nov. 26, 1970; children (by previous marriage)—Merritt, Lois (Mrs. Arthur Warwick), Joan. Research asst. Columbia, 1952-57; research staff mem. IBM T.J. Watson Research Center, Yorktown Heights, N.Y., 1957—. Vis. prof. biomath. Cornell U. Grad. Sch. Med. Scis., 1965—; cons. dept. pathology Meml. Hosp., 1973—. Fellow A.A.A.S.; mem. Inst. Math. Statistics, Phi Beta Kappa, Sigma Xi. Home: 23 David Dr New Rochelle NY 10804 Office: PO Box 218 Yorktown Heights NY 10598

FLEISCHER, RENEE ALTMAN (MRS. ELLIOT FLEISCHER), physician; b. N.Y.C., June 9, 1934; d. Ben Zion and Helen (Smulin) Altman; A.B., Barnard Coll., 1955; M.D., N.Y. U., 1961; m. Elliot Fleischer, Dec. 19, 1954; children—Corey Bennet, Deborah Ellen, Joshua Mark. Intern, Bronx (N.Y.) Hosp., 1961-62; resident N.Y. VA Hosp., N.Y.C., 1962-65; asst. attending physician medicine L.I. Jewish Med. Center Affiliation, Queens Hosp. Center, 1965—; practice medicine specializing in internal medicine, Jamaica, N.Y., 1966-72, New Hyde Park, N.Y., 1972—; dir. Methadone Maintenance Treatment Program, Queens Hosp. Center, L.I. Jewish Med. Center, Beth Israel Med. Center, 1970—; rec. sec. LaGuardia Med. Group, 1970—, asst. attending physician internal medicine La Guardia Hosp., Forest Hills, N.Y., 1967—; staff internal medicine L.I. Jewish-Hillside Med. Center; asso. prof. medicine State U. N.Y. at Stony Brook. Diplomate Am. Bd. Internal Medicine. Mem. A.M.A., A.A.A.S., Am. Chem. Soc., Am. Med. Women's Assn., Soc. Urban Physicians, N.Y. Acad. Scis., N.Y. State, Queens County med. socs., Am. Soc. Internal Medicine, Barnard Coll. Alumni Assn. Office:

82-68 164th St Jamaica NY 11432 also 271-11 Union Turnpike New Hyde Park NY 11040

FLEISCHMANN, GISELA EBERT (MRS. OTTO FLEISCHMANN), psychiatrist; b. Hamburg, Germany, Mar. 22, 1921 (parents Am. citizens); d. Carl Augustus and Clara (Hasenclever) Ebert; M.D., U. Freiburg, 1944; m. Otto Fleischmann, July 21, 1951; children—Esther M., David. Intern, Poliklinik, U. Zurich (Switzerland), 1945-46; resident in psychiatry S.D. State Hosp., Yankton, 1946-48; resident in psychiatry St. Luke's Hosp., Chgo., 1948-49, VA Hosp., Menninger Sch. Psychiatry, Topeka, 1949-51; practice medicine specializing in psychiatry, Gt. Neck, N.Y., 1963—; mem. staff Menninger Clinic, Topeka, 1951-52, Hillside Hosp., Glen Oaks, N.Y.; med. dir. Jewish Community Service, Rego Park, N.Y. Diplomate Am. Bd. Psychiatry and Neurology. Mem. A.M.A., Nassau Psychiat. Soc., Menninger Sch. Psychiatry Alumni Assn. Democrat. Home and office: 11 Melbourne Rd Great Neck NY 11021

FLEISHHACKER, JANET (MRS. MORTIMER FLEISHHACKER), civic worker; b. San Francisco, Sept. 13, 1908; d. Herbert and Ethel (Berger) Choynski; student pub., pvt. schs.; m. Mortimer Fleishhacker, May 1, 1929; children—Delia (Mrs. John S. Ehrlich), Mortimer, III, David. Treas. women's bd. San Francisco Mus. Art, 1957-59; v.p. Youth Guidance Center, 1950-51; vice chmn. DACOWITS, 1961; v.p. Salesian Boys Club, 1963-64; chmn. bd. Am.-Italy Soc., 1963-64, pres., 1972—; nat. pres. Camp Fire Girls, 1969-72; exec. v.p. Internat. Hospitality Center, San Francisco, 1973—; mem. bd. Bay Area U.S.O., 1974—. Recipient Outstanding Civilian Service medal U.S. Army, 1961; decorated Stella della Solidarita, Republic Italy. Home: 2600 Pacific Av San Francisco CA 94115

FLEISHMAN, DONNA ENGLANDER (MRS. MARK BERNARD FLEISHMAN), pub. relations co. exec.; b. Miami, Fla., Dec. 4, 1947; d. Malvin and Sophia Rachel (Tendrich) Englander; B.J. (Research grantee), U. Tex., 1969; m. Mark Bernard Fleishman, June 11, 1972. Asst. to dir. communications Dept. Housing and Urban Devel., Miami, Fla., 1969; speechwriter gov. Ga., Atlanta, 1970; account exec. Ball & Cohn, pub. relations, Atlanta, 1970-73; asst. pub. information officer Ga. Ho. of Reps., Atlanta, 1971-72; co-owner, v.p. Walburn & Assos., pub. relations, Atlanta, 1973—. Guest lectr. on pub. relations, women in communications. Mem. exec. com. DeKalb County Cancer Soc., 1970-71, Women's Am. Orgn. for Rehab. Through Tng., Atlanta, 1972-73. Youth organizer for John Kennedy and Lyndon Johnson, 1960, 64. Recipient Citation of Merit Muscular Dystrophy Assn. Am., 1972, 73. Mem. Ad Club II, Theta Sigma Phi. Home: 1322 Briarwood Rd NE Atlanta GA 30319 Office: 2 Northside 75 Atlanta GA 30318

FLEIT, MURIEL, psychologist; b. N.Y.C.; B.A., City Coll. N.Y., 1965, M.S., 1967; postgrad. N.Y. U., 1971—. Guidance counselor emotionally disturbed children N.Y.C. Bd. Edn., 1965-67; asst. prof. N.Y.C. Community Coll., 1967—, asst. dir. counseling student services dept., 1973—, adj. prof. social sci. dept., 1967—; pvt. practice psychotherapy, N.Y.C., 1967—. Mem. Am. Assn. U. Profs., Am. Personnel and Guidance Assn., Am. Psychol. Assn., Am. Assn. Jr. Colls., Alpha Psi Omega. Home: 205 W 57th St New York City NY 10019 Office: 300 Jay St Brooklyn NY 11201

FLEMER, HELEN BATEMAN (MRS. ALBERT BISHOP FLEMER), nursery exec.; b. Newark, N.J., May 18, 1918; d. John Frederick and Mabel Grace (Maginness) Bateman; grad. exec. sec. Drake's Bus. Coll., 1936-38; m. Albert Bishop Flemer, Sept. 7, 1940; children—Albert Bishop, John Henry, Suzanne Mabel, Holly Bee. Sec. N.J. Bell Telephone, Newark, 1937-41; v.p. F & F Nurseries, Holmdel, N.J., 1963—. Mem. Bicentenial Com. Monmouth County (N.J.). Charter trustee Mus. Creative Graphics, Shrewsbury, N.J., 1966-67, sec., 1967-70, 72—, pres., 1970-72. Mem. Holmdel Hist. Soc. (dir.). Home: Box 362 Crawford's Corner Rd Holmdel NJ 07733 Office: Box 126 Robert's Rd Holmdel NJ 07733

FLEMING, ALICE CAREW MULCAHEY (MRS. THOMAS J. FLEMING), author; b. New Haven, Dec. 21, 1928; d. Albert Leo and Agnes (Foley) Mulcahey; A.B., Trinity Coll., 1950; M.A., Columbia, 1951; m. Thomas J. Fleming, Jan. 19, 1951; children—Alice, Thomas, David, Richard. Recipient Nat. Media award Family Service Assn. Am., 1973. Mem. P.E.N., Authors Guild. Author: The Key to New York, 1960; Wheels, 1960; A Son of Liberty, 1961; Doctors in Petticoats, 1964; Great Women Teachers, 1965; The Senator from Maine: Margaret Chase Smith, 1969; Alice Freeman Palmer: Pioneer College President, 1970; Reporters At War, 1970; General's Lady, 1971; Highways into History, 1971; Pioneers in Print, 1971; Ida Tarbell, The First of the Muckrakers, 1971; Nine Months, 1972; Psychiatry, What's it All About?, 1972; The Moviemakers, 1973; Trials that Made Headlines, 1974. Editor: Hosannah the Home Run!, 1972. Contbr. articles to mags. Address: 315 E 72d St New York City NY 10021

FLEMING, ANN KARLEN (MRS. WARREN R. FLEMING), lawyer; b. Delta, Colo., Oct. 21, 1938; d. Fredrick Ralph and Ruth Nina (England) Karlen; B.A. in Philosophy, U. Mo., 1967, J.D., 1969; m. Warren R. Fleming, June 14, 1959; children—Julia, Donald Fredrick. Admitted to Mo. bar, 1969. Intern, Pub. Defender's Office, Columbia, Mo., 1967-69; pvt. practice law, Columbia, Mo., 1969—. Vis. lectr. Mid-Mo. Mental Health Center, 1970-73; instr. U. Mo., Columbia, 1970-71. Mem. Columbia (Mo.) Commn. Human Rights, 1973. Republican committeeman, Columbia, 1970-72. Bd. dirs. Columbia YMCA, 1973—, Job Center, 1974—, Planned Parenthood, Columbia, 1969-71. Recipient Am. Civil Liberties award for Service, 1973; Phi Chi Theta service award, 1974. Mem. Nat. Council Juvenile Ct. Judges, Mo., Am. bar assns. Episcopalian. Home: 211 Leslie Lane Columbia MO 65201 Office: 410 Guitar Bldg Columbia MO 65201

FLEMING, DOROTHY JACQUELINE, social worker; b. Mpls., Aug. 21, 1927; d. Robert M. and Eunice (Kendall) Fleming; B.A., St. Olaf Coll., 1949; M.S.W., U. Minn., 1958. Caseworker, Becker County Welfare Dept., Detroit Lakes, Minn., 1949-51; caseworker Hennepin County Welfare Dept., Mpls., 1952-59; supr. child welfare Santa Clara County Welfare Dept., San Jose, Cal., 1959-61; caseworker, supr., asst. dir. psychiat. social work Santa Clara County Mental Health Dept., San Jose, 1961-70; supt. Minn. Correctional Instn. for Women, Shakopee, 1970—. Mem. Nat. Assn. Social Workers (com. chmn.). Home: 8345 Mitchell Rd Eden Prairie MN 55343 Office: Box 7 Shakopee MN 55379

FLEMING, ELAINE BRIGGS (MRS. KENNETH S. FLEMING), club woman; b. Oak Grove, La., July 23, 1912; d. Ollie and Edna (Harper) Briggs; student La. State U., 1934; m. Kenneth Spring Fleming, June 24, 1937; 1 son, Henry Briggs. Mem. D.A.R., 1941—, Ohio registrar, 1962-65, Ohio chaplain, 1965-68, nat. chmn. Americanism and manual for citizenship, 1968-71, 1st v.p. Ohio Officers Club, 1971-73; mem. Nat. Soc. Daus. Colonial Wars, Ohio pres., 1968-71, nat. chaplain, 1971-74; mem. U.D.C., Nat. Soc. Daus. of Founders and Patriots Am., Nat. Soc. Magna Charta Dames, Soc. Descs. Colonial Clergy, Order First Families Miss. (librarian Gen. 1967-68), Nat. Soc. Colonial Daus. 17th Century, Soc. Descs. Colonial Govs., Sovereign Colonial Soc. Ams. Royal Descent, Nat. Soc. Old Plymouth Colony Descs., Jamestown Soc., Order of Crown of Charlemagne U.S.A., Hon. Order Ky. Cols.; Ohio 1st v.p. Dames of Ct. of Honor, 1971-73. Mem. Kappa Delta. Methodist. Mem. Order Eastern Star. Home: 255 Neff Dr Canfield OH 44406

FLEMING, ELYSE SCHWARTZ (MRS. DAVID G. FLEMING), educator; b. N.Y.C., Aug. 3, 1927; d. Benjamin H. and Evanora (Lyon) Schwartz; A.B., Queens Coll., 1948; M.A., U. Cal. at Berkeley, 1952, Ph.D., 1956; m. David G. Fleming, Jan. 30, 1949; 1 son, Neil S. Elementary tchr., Oakland, Cal., 1950-52; psychologist, social worker Douglas County, Kan., 1956-58; asst. prof. dept. edn. Case Western Res. U., Cleve., 1959-63, asso. prof., 1963-72, prof., 1972—, chmn. dept., 1972—. Cons. to various ednl. instns. and agys. Mem. Am. Psychol. Assn., Am. Ednl. Research Assn., Exceptional Children Assn., Cleve. Psychol. Assn., Ohio Assn. for Gifted, Pi Lambda Theta. Contbr. articles to profl. jours. Home: 3714 Atherstone Rd Cleveland Heights OH 44121 Office: Dept Edn Case Western Reserve U Cleveland OH 44106

FLEMING, FRANCES O., librarian; b. Kelso, Wash., Aug. 10, 1924; d. James Taafe and Ona (Ray) Fleming; B.A., Ariz. State U., 1948, M.A., 1950; M.L.S., U. So. Cal., 1955. Librarian, Phoenix Elementary Schs., 1948-57; field librarian U.S. Army Spl. Services, Germany, 1957-58; command librarian, Paris, France, 1958-60; coordinator libraries USAF Dependents Sch., Wiesbaden, Germany, 1960-62; supr. library services Bd. Edn. of Baltimore County, Towson, Md., 1962-68, coordinator library services, 1968—. Workshop cons. Michigan State Library, Lansing, 1955; symposium cons. U. Syracuse, N.Y., 1967. Mem. N.E.A., Am., Md. (v.p. 1965), Ariz. (v.p., editor jour. Ariz. Libraries 1952-54, pres. 1956) library assns., Am. Assn. Sch. Librarians (index editor jour. Sch. Libraries, 1963-65, editor 1966-69, chmn. publs. com. 1965, chmn. standards implementation com. 1969-71), A.L.A. (dir. Young Adult Services div. 1965-66), Assn. Sch. Librarians Md., Beta Phi Mu, Kappa Delta Pi. Home: 1101 Ivywood Lane Towson MD 21204 Office: Dumbarton House Towson MD 21204

FLEMING, JACQUELINE ANTOINETTE, educator, club woman; b. Balt., May 12, 1939; d. Ollie Edward and Sarah Loretta (Watson) Fleming; B.A., U. Md., 1964; M.Spl. Edn., Coppin State Coll., 1970, postgrad., 1973. Tchr. spl. curriculum Balt. pub. schs., chmn. spl. edn. dept., 1971—. Mem. Aux. Provident Hosp.; vol. March of Dimes, 1973. Mem. Nat. Fedn. Rep. Women, Balt., 1969—. Recipient certificate appreciation Aux. Provident Hosp. Mem. Md. League of Women (chmn. recreation 1969-71), Nat. Urban League, YWCA, Negro Coll. Fund, Nat. Assn. Negro Bus. and Profl. Women (life; publicity chmn. 1969-71; exec. com. 1969—), Herbert M. Frisby Hist. Soc. (pres.'s citation 1971, chmn. exptl. studies 1973—), Lambda Kappa Mu (chmn. edn. and scholarship 1973—, award 1971, speaker Brotherhood Week 1972). Baptist (trustee 1970—, mem. Christian edn. com. 1974—). Soroptimist. Home: 3660 Forest Garden Ave Baltimore MD 21207

FLEMING, LOIS VIRGINIA DELAVAN (MRS. PHILIP J. FLEMING), library cons.; b. Toledo, Jan. 25, 1928; d. Millard Terry and Willa Metta Lucille (Symons) DeLavan; B.A., Fla. State U., 1950; M.S., 1965. Advanced M. in L.S., 1968; postgrad. U. Utah, 1968-69; m. Philip Jefferson Fleming, May 18, 1952; children—Mark William, Philip Jefferson, Richard DeLavan. Research librarian Fla. State Advt. Commn., Tallahassee, 1949-52; asst. librarian, instr. Strozier Library, Fla. State U., Tallahassee, 1965-67; community services librarian Palm Beach County Library System, West Palm Beach, Fla., 1970-72; pub. library cons. Fla. State Library, Tallahassee, 1972—. Mem. Manatee County Democratic Com., 1963. Mem. Nat. Assn. Parliamentarians, Aircraft Owners and Pilots Assn., Freedom to Read Found., Adult Edn. Assn. U.S.A., Am. (com. on library service to aging), Southeastern, Fla. (legis. and planning com.) library assns., Fla. Hist. Soc., Fla. Council on Aging, Fla. Adult Edn. Assn., Fla. State U. Alumni Assn. (life), Beta Phi Mu. Home: Route 3 Box 162 Quincy FL 32351 Office: Div Library Services Dept State Supreme Court Bldg Tallahassee FL 32304

FLEMING, LUCILLE ANTOINETTE, realtor; b. Mishawaka, Ind., June 17, 1901; d. William Marks and Margaret (O'Neill) Probasco; grad. high sch.; m. Claude F. Fleming, Dec. 28, 1943. Sec. various comml., profl. firms, 1922-42; prin. realtor, Elkhart, Ind., 1960—; owner Traveler's Inn, Elkhart, 1960—. Mem. Elkhart Med. Aux., 1944—, pres., 1953-54. Mem. Elkhart C. of C., Elkhart Bd. Realtors, Elkhart County Motel Assn. Roman Catholic. Elk; mem. Daus. Isabelle. Clubs: Altrusa International, Four Arts, Elcona Country (charter, Elkhart). Home: 229 W Jackson Blvd Elkhart IN 46514 Office: 220 W Jackson Blvd Elkhart IN 46514

FLEMING, SISTER MARY BLANDINE, hosp. adminstr.; b. Ireland, Aug. 6, 1932; d. Michael John and Nora (Morley) Fleming; postgrad. in hosp. adminstrn. Xavier U. at Cin., 1967. Formerly dir. med. records dept.; asst. hosp. adminstr., then hosp. adminstr. St. Francis Hosp., Tulsa, also trustee, bd. dirs., mem. coms. Mem. Tulsa area health and hosp. planning com., Okla. com. on trauma A.C.S. Recipient award Golden Triangle chpt. Am. Women in Radio, 1968. Mem. Am., Okla., Tulsa hosp. assns., Am. Assn. Med. Records Librarians, Am. Cath. Hosp. Assn. (pres. elect Okla. conf. 1971). Home and office: 6161 S Yale Av Tulsa OK 74136

FLEMING, PEGGY GALE (MRS. GREGORY JENKINS), ice skater; b. San Jose, Cal., July 27, 1948; d. Albert Eugene and Doris Elizabeth (Deal) Fleming; student Colo. Coll., 1966—; m. Gregory Jenkins, June 13, 1970. Profl. ice-skater, 1968—. TV and movie appearances also guest star appearances in Ice Follies. S.W. Pacific and Pacific Coast juvenile ice skating champion, 1960, novice champion, 1961, S.W. Pacific champion in jrs., 2d-place nat. novice, 1962, S.W. Pacific and Pacific Coast sr. champion, 3d nat. jr., 1963, U.S. Ladies champion, 6th pl. in Olympics, 7th pl. in world's championship, 1964, U.S. Ladies champion, 2d N.Am., 3d place in world's championship, 1965, U.S. Ladies champion, Ladies champion of world, 1966, U.S. Ladies champion, N.Am. champion, World Champion, 1967, U.S. Ladies champion, Olympic champion, World champion, 1968. Named Colo. State Woman of the Year, 1967; also Athlete of the Year, ABC-TV; Athlete of Yr. A.P. award, 1968; named to Colo. Hall Fame, 1969. Mem. U.S. Figure Skating Assn. Club: Broadmoor Figure Skating (Colorado Springs, Colo.). Office: Bob Banner Assos 132 S Rodeo Dr Beverly Hills CA 90212

FLEMING, PHYLLIS JANE, physicist, educator; b. Shelbyville, Ind., Oct. 9, 1924; d. Russell P. and Grace (Wheeler) Fleming; B.A., Hanover Coll., 1946; M.S., U. Wis., 1948, Ph.D., 1954. Instr. physics Mt. Holyoke Coll., 1948-50; instr. dept. physics Wellesley (Mass.) Coll., 1953-55, asst. prof., 1955-61, asso. prof., 1961-67, prof. physics, 1967—, dean, 1968-72. Mem. Am. Phys. Soc., Am. Assn. Physics Tchrs., Am. Assn. U. Profs., Sigma Xi. Roman Catholic. Contbr. articles to profl. jours. Home: 668 Washington St Wellesley MA 02181

FLEMING, RUTH, surgeon; b. Poteau, Okla., Nov. 15, 1913; d. William T. and Ora Antoinette (Ellis) Fleming; B.S., U. Ark., 1935; M.D., Washington U., St. Louis. Intern Children's Hosp.-San Francisco, 1939-40, resident, 1940-42; resident St. Joseph's Hosp., San Francisco, 1942-43; preceptor Alison R. Kilgroe, San Francisco, 1943-48; practice medicine specializing in gen. surgery, San Francisco, 1942—; chief surgeon Western Pacific Employees Med. Dept., San Francisco, 1963—; mem. surg. teaching staff Harkness Community Hosp., San Francisco, 1966—. Bd. corporators Med. Coll. Pa., 1973—. Diplomate Am. Bd. Surgery. Fellow A.C.S.; mem. Am. Med. Women's Assn. (nat. pres. 1973), A.M.A., Cal. Med. Assn., San Francisco Med. Soc., Am. Assn. R.R. Surgeons, San Francisco Profl. Women's Club. Club: Women Physician's. Home: 155 Graystone Terrace San Francisco CA 94114 Office: 490 Post St San Francisco CA 94102

FLEMING, SHIRLEY MORAGNE, editor, critic; b. N.Y.C.; d. Berry and Anne (Molloy) Fleming; B.A., Smith Coll., 1952, M.A., 1954. Asst. editor High Fidelity Mag., 1959-65; mng. editor Mus. Am. Mag., N.Y.C., 1965-66, editor, 1966—. Annotator, St. Louis Symphony, 1971-73. Mem. Music Critics Assn., Phi Beta Kappa. Contbr. to Collier's Yearbook, 1969—, Internat. Musician, 1973—, High Fidelity mag., 1959—. Home: 350 1st Av New York City NY 10010 Office: 1 Astor Pl St New York City NY 10036

FLEMING, SUZANNE MARIE, educator; b. Detroit, Feb. 4, 1927; d. Albert Thomas and Rose Evelyn (Smiley) Fleming; B.S., Marygrove Coll., 1957; M.S., U. Mich., 1960, Ph.D., 1963. Instr., Marygrove Coll., Detroit, 1962-64, asst. prof., 1964-67, asso. prof., 1967-72, prof. chemistry, 1972—, chmn. div. natural sci., 1970—. Vis. lectr. U. Mich., 1968-69. Mem. Am. Chem. Soc. (mem. exec. bd. Detroit sect. 1973-74), Am., Mich. (sec.-treas., mem. state council 1973-74, 74-75) insts. chemists, Mich. Coll. Chemistry Tchrs. Assn. (pres. 1975-76), Sigma Xi. Contbr. articles to profl. jours. Home: 121 E Boston Blvd Detroit MI 48202

FLESCH, COLETTE, Luxembourg city ofcl., ed. Wellesley Coll., Fletcher Sch. Law and Diplomacy. With secretariat of council of ministers European Econ. Community, 1964-69; mem. Luxembourg parliament, 1969—, Luxembourg city council, 1970—, mayor, 1970—. Mem. European Parliament, Strasbourg. Mem. Olympic fencing team from Luxembourg, 1960, 64, 68. Address: Office of the Mayor Grand Duchy of Luxembourg

FLESHMAN, CHARLOTTE ELLWOOD (MRS. ALAN FLESHMAN), newspaper editor; b. West Frankfort, Ill., Apr. 12, 1920; d. Carl Grady and Charlotte Ann (Ellwood) Jones; student Beckley Coll., Ind. U., U. Chgo.; m. Alan Fleshman, Mar. 8, 1938; 1 son, Carl Francis. Woman's editor, asst. to mng. editor Gary (Ind.) Post-Tribune, 1941-47; city editor Beckley (W.Va) Post-Herald, 1947-49; co-owner, operator women's retail clothing store, Pontiac, Ill., 1949-57; book reviewer Chgo. Tribune, 1949-51; reporter, photographer, state news supr. Bloomington-Normal (Ill.) Daily Pantagraph, 1951-67; pub. relations Central States Thrasherman's Reunion, Pontiac, 1955-66, Keeley Inst., Dwight, Ill., 1962-65, Winston Churchill Coll., Pontiac, 1965-66, Am. Legion Mountaineer Boys' State, Jackson's Mill, W.Va., 1972; asso. editor Beckley Post-Herald, 1967—; exec. dir. Nine Valley Travel Council, 1973—. Antiques columnist, lectr., appraiser, 1961-67; judge various antique shows, including Ill. State Fair, 1965-67. Mem. W.Va. Ednl. Broadcasting Authority, 1973—; W.Va. lay rep. Pub. Broadcasting Service, 1973—. Treas., W.Va. Fedn. Republican Women, 1969—; mem. W.Va. Rep. State Exec. Com., 1972—. Mem. Nat. Fedn. Press Women, W. Va. Press Women, W.Va. Hist. Soc. Home: 618 Pikeview Dr Beckley WV 25801 Office: PO Box 45 Charleston WV 25301

FLETCHER, ANNE BOSSHARD (MRS. JOHN R. FLETCHER), physician; b. Worcester, Mass., Feb. 3, 1939; d. Henry M. and Anne (Peter) Bosshard; A.B. cum laude, Clark U., 1960; M.D., Washington U., St. Louis, 1964; m. John R. Fletcher, June 16, 1962; children—John, Stephen, David. Intern, U. Rochester (N.Y.), 1964-65; resident R.I. Hosp., Providence, 1965-66; resident Children's Hosp., of D.C., Washington, 1967-68, neonatology fellow, 1968-70, now asso. dir. newborn service; practice medicine specializing in pediatrics and neonatology, Washington, 1970—; cons. in neonatology Holy Cross Hosp., Silver Spring, Md., Washington Hosp. Center; asst. prof. pediatrics George Washington U., Washington, 1970-74, asso. prof., 1974—. Fellow Am. Acad. Pediatrics; mem. Phi Beta Kappa. Home: 11505 Karen Dr Potomac MD 20854 Office: 2125 13th St NW Washington DC 20009

FLETCHER, FRANCES GILMAN, motel exec.; b. Boston, June 29; d. Harry H. and Edythe (Jolles) Gilman; student Boston U., 1940-41; m. Jordan B. Fletcher, Jan. 14, 1943 (dec. May 1967); children—Harold, Susan (Mrs. Arthur Guagliumi), Richard. Adminstrn. asst. customer relations and sales Martin Cerel, realtor, Natick, Mass., 1954-66; adminstrn. asst. Northeast Motel Operation, Inc., doing bus. as Holiday Inn., Newton Lower Falls, Mass., 1967-68, innkeeper, clk., 1968—; gen. mgr. Holiday Inn, Boston-Somerville, 1973—; licensed broker real estate, Mass., 1960—; mem. adv. bd. Community Nat. Bank. Mem. adv. com. Vocational Sch. Retarded Children, 1968-70. Mem. Mass. Hotel Motel Assn. (dir., v.p. 1973—), Nat. Assn. Bus. and Profl. Women, Newton Needham C. of C. (dir.), Altruse Internat. Home: 50 Dinsmore Av Framingham MA 01701 Office: 30 Washington St Somerville MA 02143

FLETCHER, GRACE NIES (MRS. VIVIAN A. FLETCHER), author; b. Townsend, Mass.; d. Leopold A. and Myrtle (Rouse) Nies; A.B., Boston U., 1917; grad. study Ohio Wesleyan U., Columbia; m. Vivian A. Fletcher, Mar. 15, 1924; 1 son, Richard Nies. Asst. dir. publicity Boston U., 1920-24; author mag. articles and stories in nat. mags. including Sat. Eve. Post, Ladies Home Jour., McCall's, Scribner's, Readers Digest and others, 1924—. A founder St. Elizabeth's P.E. Ch., Sudbury. Recipient gold medal N.E. Womens' Press Assn., 1948. Mem. Women in Communications, Phi Beta Kappa. Author: In My Father's House, 1955; Preacher's Kids, 1958; No Marriage In Heaven, 1960; I Was Born Tomorrow, 1961; The Whole World's In His Hand, 1962; The Fabulous Flemings of Kathmandu, 1964; What's Right With Our Young People, 1966; The Bridge of Love, 1967; In Quest of the Least Coin, 1968; Merry Widow, 1970; What's Right with Us Parents, 1972. Address: 3301 Bellaire Dr N Fort Worth TX 76109

FLETCHER, MARY LEE, business exec.; b. Farnborough, England; d. Dugald Angus and Mary Lee (Thurman) Fletcher; B.A., Pembroke Coll., Brown U., 1951. Operations officer C.I.A., Washington, 1951-53; exec. trainee Gimbels, N.Y.C., 1953-54; head researcher Ed Byron TV Prodns., N.Y.C., 1954; copywriter Benton & Bowles, Inc., N.Y.C., 1955-63; creative dir. Alberto-Culver Co., Melrose Park, Ill., 1964-66; advt. and publicity dir. Christian Dior Perfumes, N.Y.C., 1967-71, v.p. advt. and publicity; now v.p. Christian Dior-N.Y. Home: 12 Beekman Pl New York City NY 10022 Office: 498 7th Av New York City NY 10018

FLETCHER, RACHEL GOULINE (MRS. WILLIAM DOUGLAS FLETCHER), stage designer; b. Balt., Nov. 11, 1947; d. David and Gloria Celeste (Shapiro) Gouline; B.A. cum laude, Hofstra U., 1969; M.A., State U. N.Y. at Albany, 1972; postgrad. Rochester Inst. Tech., 1973; m. William Douglas Fletcher, June 10, 1967. Spl. project coordinator Nazareth Coll. Arts Center, Rochester, N.Y., 1971-73, resident designer, lectr., 1970—. Faculty designer U. Rochester Summer Theatre, 1974. Recipient Playwriting award Alpha Psi Omega, 1969. Co-chmn. Ednl. Adv. Council for Secondary Schs., Rochester, 1972-73. Mem. Am. Theatre Assn. (ch-chmn. performance environment program 1973—), Alpha Lambda Delta, Alpha Psi Omega, Sigma Pi, Sigma Kappa Alpha. Home: Apt 4 987 East Av Rochester NY 14607 Office: 4245 East Av Rochester NY 14610

FLETCHER, THELMA RAWLS (MRS. HERBERT HERRICK FLETCHER), bookstore owner, pub.; b. Pleasanton, Tex., Feb. 6, 1905; d. John Fletcher and Agnes (Witten) Rawls; student San Antonio Coll., 1926-27; m. Herbert Herrick Fletcher, Oct. 2, 1927; children—Tyler Herrick, Bernita (Mrs. Kenneth Roland Johnson). Book buyer H. A. Moos, antiquarian book dealer, San Antonio, 1923-27; owner, Fletcher's Books and Anson Jones Press, Houston, 1928-58, Salado, Tex., 1958—. Chmn. antiquarian book acquisitions Friends Temple Pub. Library, 1967-68. Mem. Am. Soc. Appraisers (sr. mem.; internat. bd. examiners 1973-74), Valuers Consortium, D.A.R., U.D.C., Daus. Am. Colonies, Collectors Inst., Tex. State Hist. Assn., Bell County Hist. Soc. (life). Episcopalian. Democrat. Home: Old Chisholm Trail Salado TX 76571 Office: PO Box 65 Salado TX 76571

FLETCHER, WINIFRED FRANCES BELL (MRS. ANDREW RAYMOND FLETCHER), author, playwright; b. Shopiere, Wis.; d. Charles Everett and Frances (Dockstader) Bell; student Wash. State Coll., 1914-16; A.B., Whitman Coll., 1921; m. Andrew Raymond Fletcher, Oct. 12, 1924; children—Edwin James, Andrew Lansing, Frances Elizabeth (Mrs. Charles Harrison Alexander). With Grandview (Wash.) Herald, 1914-15; social worker Hawaiian Bd. Missions, Central Kona Settlement, Kealakekua, Hawaii, 1916-18; music supr. Kohala (Hawaii) Girls Sch., 1921-23; music supr., piano tchr. Mid-Pacific Inst., Honolulu, 1923-24, tchr. music Mira Loma (Cal.) Sch., 1945-48; substitute tchr. Riverside City (Cal.) Schs., 1949-50; dramatic art studio, Beaumont, Cal., 1926-36; dir. Fletcher Players, Beaumont, 1926-36. Den mother Cub Scouts, 1945-46. Recipient Scott-Foresman award, 1965; Writers' Workshop Short Story trophy, 1970. Mem. Nat. League Am. Penwomen (nat. drama chmn. 1954-56, br. pres. 1954-56, 67, 72, named Woman of Year Riverside br. 1970, pres. Riverside br. 1972-74; 1st prize for short, short story "His Own Man" 1972), Cal. State Fedn. Chaparral Poets, Womens Symphony Guild. Conglist. Author: White Tablecloths, 1950; Squiddle the Squid, 1951; Stars Over America, 1954; The Miracle Stone, 1951; Tiki The Monkey Man, 1952; The Golden Heart, 1954; In Joseph's Garden, 1961; Footprints in the Lava, 1967; Hawaii's Bird Paradise, 1967; New Hope for Sandelwood, 1968; My Korean Daughter, 1968; Bird that Almost Wasn't, 1969; His Own Man, 1970; Haka, Son of Thunder, 1971; The Whispering Palm (collected poems), 1972; Hawaii's Immortal Barquentine, 1972; Stained Glass Windows, 1972; Here Comes Mister Deserts, 1973; short stories, articles and poems pub. in numerous mags., anthologies. Home: 4286 6th St Riverside CA 92501

FLETCHER, WINONA LEE (MRS. JOSEPH GRANT FLETCHER), educator; b. Hamlet, N.C., Nov. 25, 1926; d. Henry Franklin and Sarah Belle (Lowdnes) Lee; A.B., Johnson C. Smith U., 1947; M.A., State U. Ia., 1951; Ph.D. (So. Fellowship Fund. fellow), Ind. U., 1968; m. Joseph Grant Fletcher, Mar. 28, 1952; 1 dau., Betty Ann. Sec.-tchr. Delwatt's Radio Inst., Winston-Salem, N.C., 1947-51; mem. faculty Ky. State U., Frankfort, 1951—, prof. speech and theatre, 1968—; mem. faculty Ind. U., Bloomington, 1971-73. Costumer Michiana Summer Theatre, Michigan City, Ind., 1956; costumer, asso. dir. Lincoln U. Summer Theatre, Jefferson City, Mo., 1952-60; dir. cultural affairs Project Upward Bound, exec. sec. Nat. Assn. Drama and Speech, 1958-62; sometimes narrator fashion shows. Mem. Am. Theatre Assn. (dir. 1959-60), Speech Communication Assn., Nat. Council Negro Women, Am. Assn. U. Profs., Southeastern Theatre Conf., So. Speech Communication Assn., Alpha Kappa Alpha. Coll. editor Players mag., 1960-61. contbr. articles to profl. jours. Home: 317 Cold Harbor Dr Frankfort KY 40601

FLICKER, KATHRYN, lawyer; b. Newark, June 15, 1947; d. David Jonas and Judith (Behrin) Flicker; A.B., Ind. U., 1967; J.D., Rutgers U., 1970; m. Michael L. Rosenberg, Dec. 24, 1972. Law clk., chancery div., Superior Ct., N.J., 1970-71; admitted to N.J. bar, 1970; dep. atty. gen. Office Atty. Gen., State N.J., Trenton, 1971—. Bd. dirs. U.S. Com. Sports for Israel. Mem. Am., N.J. State bar assns. Asso. editor Rutgers Camden Law Jour., 1968-69. Home: 50-04 Fox Run Dr Plainsboro NJ 08537 Office: State House Annex Trenton NJ 08625

FLICKINGER, REBECCA JANE MASON (MRS. BERT D. FLICKINGER), journalist, editor; b. Henderson, Tex., Aug. 12, 1943; d. George Truett and Bessie Lou (Price) Mason; A.A., Kilgore Jr. Coll., 1963; B.A., Baylor U., 1965; m. Bert D. Flickinger, Jan. 8, 1966; 1 son, George David. Editor, Kilgore Coll. Newspaper, 1962-63; reporter, asso. editor Baylor U. Newspaper, 1964-65; reporter Orange (Tex.) Leader, 1965—, asst. news editor, 1970-73, news editor, 1973—. Recipient Sch. Bell award Tex. State Tchrs. Assn., 1970, 74, award Orange Sch. Bd., 1968, award Boy Scouts Am., 1971. Mem. Phi Theta Kappa. Republican. Mem. Christian Ch. Home: 1900 Hart Av Orange TX 77630 Office: PO Box 1028 Orange TX 77630

FLIEGLER, DOROTHY SCHERR (MRS. LOUIS A. FLIEGLER), educator; b. N.Y.C., June 19, 1921; d. Morris and Rose E. (Marcus) Scherr; B.A., Hunter Coll., 1942; B.A., Columbia, 1945; m. Louis A. Fleigler, June 29, 1945; children—Gail, Susan. Govt. ordnance insp. N.Y. Ordnance Dept., N.Y.C., 1943-45; occupational therapist Army Hosp., Tilton Gen. Hosp., 1945, N.Y.C. Hosp., Welfare Island, N.Y.C., 1945, VA Hosp., Brentwood Gen. Hosp., Letterman Gen. Hosp., Bronx VA Hosp., 1945-47; tchr. physically handicapped, Syracuse, N.Y., 1956-60; tchr. mentally retarded, Denver, 1960-66; tchr. learning disabled, Akron, O., 1966—. Instr. ceramics U. Wyo., Sheridan, 1953. Bd. dirs. sheltered workshop United Cerebral Palsy Center, Denver, 1954. Mem. B'nai B'rith Women, N.E.A. Home: 1827 Kingsley Av Akron OH 44313 Office: 55 S Portage Path Akron OH

FLIEHR, KATHLEEN VIRGINIA (MRS. RICHARD REID FLIEHR), pub. relations exec.; b. Brainerd, Minn., July 22, 1918; d. Fred E. and Hattie A. (Frisk) Kinsmiller; B.A., U. Minn., 1940; m. Richard Reid Fliehr, June 21, 1941; 1 son, Richard Morgan. Staff advt. dept. Star Jour., Mpls., 1940; editor Golfer-Sportsman Mag., Mpls., 1940-42; twin city corr. Fairchild Pub. Co. of N.Y.C., 1942-45, San Diego corr., 1946-47, Detroit staff, 1947-48; asst. dir. pub. relations Guthrie Theatre, Mpls., 1963-67; partner Morison, Fliehr Assos., art cons., Mpls., 1967-70; cons. to community arts, Mpls., 1970—. Pres., Am. Community Theatre Assn., 1971-73; chmn. Nat. Festival Am. Community Theatres, 1971. Active Abbott Hosp. Aux., A.R.C. Bd. dirs. Theatre in the Round. Mem. Am. Theatre Assn. (U.S. del. to biennial world congress Internat. Amateur Theatre Assn. 1973), Am. Community Theatre Assn. (dir.), League Women Voters, Alpha Omicron Pi. Conglist. Author: (with Bradley G. Morison) In Search of an Audience, 1968. Address: 4501 Belvidere Lane Minneapolis MN 55435

FLIER, MADELEINE ROSS (MRS. THEODORE S. FLIER), city ofcl., lawyer; b. Bronx, N.Y., Jan. 3, 1940; d. Martin and Ella (Schutzman) Ross; J.D., U. San Fernando Valley, 1967; m. Theodore S. Flier, July 5, 1959; children—Nicholas, Anthony, Andrew. Admitted to Cal. bar, 1968; dep. city atty. Office Los Angeles City Atty., Los Angeles, 1968—. Mem. Am., Los Angeles County bar assns., State Bar Cal., Women Lawyers Assn. Los Angeles. Soroptimist, mem. B'Nai B'Rith. Office: 205 S Broadway Los Angeles CA 90051

FLINCHUM, BETTY MAE, educator; b. nr. Dobson, N.C., Dec. 22, 1934; d. Eugene Gaither and Hettie (Denny) Flinchum; B.S., U. N.C., 1957, M.Ed., 1962, postgrad., 1968—; postgrad. Guilford Coll., 1961; Ph.D. La. State U., 1970. Camp counselor, 1954-57; grad. fellow U. N.C., Greensboro, summer 1957, teaching fellow, dormitory counselor, 1962; tchr. Greensboro Pub. Schs., 1957-59, 60-61; day camp dir. Jefferson Country Club, Greensboro, summer 1958-59; Exchange organizer to Eng., Somerset County Council, 1959-60; head dept. phys. edn. Newcomb Coll. Tulane U., 1962-67; group leader to Eng. Expt. in Internat. Living, 1966; cons. for student services A.A.H.P.E.R.-N.E.A., Washington, 1967-72; asso. prof. edn. U. North Fla., Jacksonville, 1972—. Cons. Ford Found. Ednl. Improvement Project, New Orleans; participant Vice President's Conf. on Youth Opportunity, 1968; vis. lectr. George Washington U., 1971-72. Leader, Greensboro council Girl Scouts U.S.A., 1958-59; first aid instr., first aid disaster rep. A.R.C., 1955-67. Bd. dirs. New Orleans YWCA. Mem. N.E.A., A.A.H.P.E.R., D.C. Council Adminstrv. Women, Am. Youth Hostel Assn., Washington Council Expt. in Internat. Living. Democrat. Presbyn. Contbr. articles to profl. jours. Home: 2337 Costa Verde Blvd Apt 301 Jacksonville FL 32250

FLING, JANET LEE, ednl. adminstr.; b. Toledo, Sept. 11, 1945; d. Earl W. and Florence K. (Leupp) Fling; B.S. in Edn., U. Toledo, 1968; B.F.A., U. Pa., 1968, M.F.A., 1971. Teaching asst. U. Pa., Phila., 1969-71; art specialist Marple Newtown Sch. System, Newtown Square, Pa., 1972; dir. admissions and financial aid Moore Coll. Art, Phila., 1972—, chmn. dept. painting, 1973—. Exhibited paintings at Inst. Contemporary Art, U. Pa., Phila., 1970, 71, UN Plaza, N.Y.C., 1971; mem. Coll. Entrance Examination Bd., 1972—, Coll. Scholarship Assembly, 1972—. Recipient grant in aid Art Interest, Inc., Toledo, 1967, Sinclaire Walbridge award Toledo Museum Art, 1968. Mem. Am. Assn. Coll. Registrars and Admissions Officers, Eastern, Pa. assns. financial aid adminstrs., Coll. Art Assn., Nat. Assn. for Women Deans, Adminstrs. and Councellors, Pa. Assn. Coll. Admissions Officers. Home: Apt 75-B Village of Pinerun Lakeview Dr Blackwood NJ 08012

FLINT, DOROTHY JEAN, surgeon; b. Evanston, Ill., Jan. 13, 1926; d. Nelson Chase and Charlotte (Bratter) Flint; B.A. in Chemistry, Mills Coll., 1947, M.A. (chemistry, physics fellow) in Psychology, 1951; postgrad. (Ford Found. fellow), in Psychology U. Ill., 1951-56; postgrad. U. Geneva, Switzerland, 1947-48; M.D., U. Pa., 1960; postgrad. Oak Ridge Inst. Nuclear Studies, 1966. Intern, Cleve. Clinic Hosp., 1960-61; resident neurosurgery U. Pa. Hosp., 1961-65; practice medicine, specializing in pediatric neurosurgery, Media, Pa., 1965—; resident in psychiatry Hahnemann Med. Coll. and Hosp., Phila., 1973—. Diplomate Am. Inst. Hypnosis. Inventor closed ventriculostomy for external cerebrospinal fluid drainage in children, subarachnoid-peritoneal shunt placement without laminectomy. Home: Gardens Plaza 903 Park Pl and Beach Ocean City NJ 08226 Office: Hahnemann Med Coll and Hosp Psychiatry Dept Philadelphia PA 19102

FLINT, ELAINE NELSON (MRS. HOWARD RAYMOND FLINT), librarian; b. Duluth, Minn., July 29, 1917; d. Philip Melvin and Laura Carola (Gronseth) Nelson; student U. Minn., 1935-38; B.A., Coll. St. Scholastica, 1939; B.A. in L.S., U. Mich., 1940; M.A., U. Mont., 1954; postgrad U. Ariz., 1955-57, Ariz. State U., 1959-60; m. Howard Raymond Flint, Nov. 5, 1942; children—Laurel (Mrs. Barry E. Callaway), Karen (Mrs. Dana D. Evans). Asst. documents and serials U. Mont., Missoula, 1940-43, circulation librarian, 1944-47; librarian Instituto Cultural Peruano Norteamericano, Lima, Peru, 1949-51, Centro Ecuatoriano Norteamericano, Quito, Ecuador, 1951-53, Phoenix (Ariz.) elementary sch. dist., 1954-61; librarian West High Sch., Phoenix, 1961-63; librarian Glendale (Ariz) Community Coll., 1963—. Vis. faculty Ariz. State U., Tempe, 1966. Mem. Ariz., S.W. library assns., Western History Assn., Am. Assn. Women in Community Jr. Colls., Am. Assn. U. Profs., Alpha Delta Kappa (sec. 1962-64). Mem. editorial com. Ariz. Blue Book, 1971-72. Home: 6539 N 61st Av Glendale AZ 85301 Office: 6000 W Olive St Glendale AZ 85302

FLINT, GERTRUDE KINSEE, writer; b. Bklyn., Oct. 29, 1909; B.A., Hunter Coll., 1930; M.A., Columbia, 1934; m. Dr. Walter Levy, July 28, 1939; 1 son, James Lewis. Feature writer, soc. editor Greenwich (Conn.) Time, 1937-39; Greenwich corr. N.Y. Herald Tribune, 1937-39; spl. feature writer Bklyn. Eagle Syndicate, 1935-37; free-lance writer, 1960—. Mem. Acad. Polit. Sci., Woman's Press Club of N.Y.C., Pen and Brush. Home: 130 E 75th St New York City NY 10021

FLINT, JANET ALTIC (MRS. ROLAND FLINT), curator; b. Louisville, 1935; B.S. in Painting, Art History, U. Louisville, 1957; M.A., U. Minn., 1969; m. Roland Flint; 2 children. Teaching asst. U. Minn., Mpls., 1957-59; asst. to registrar Walker Art Center, Mpls., 1957-59; asst. also asso. curator Mpls. Inst. Arts, 1959-66; asst. curator Nat. Collection Fine Arts, Smithsonian Instn., Washington, 1969—, curator prints and drawings, 1970—. Mem. Print Council of Am. (trustee), Washington Print Club (adv. bd.). Author: exhibition catalogs. Address: 2104 Huidekoper Pl Washington DC 20007

FLOOD, ELIZABETH GAUCAS, news service exec.; b. Albany, N.Y., Apr. 6, 1933; d. Bernard Relf and Mary Ann (Reid) Gaucas; student Russell Sage Coll., 1952-55; m. div. Legislative corr. N.Y. State Capitol Cuyler News Service, Albany, 1956-67, owner, pres. news service, 1960-74; capitol reporter WRGB-TV, Schenectady, 1966-67; dir. pub. relations N.Y. State Women's Unit, Exec. Chamber, 1967; moderator, speaker various radio and TV shows, panels; owner, operator Elizabeth G. Flood Antiques, Guilderland, N.Y., 1955—. Mem. Legislative Corr. Assn., Overseas Press Club, Sigma Delta Sigma. Club: Women's Press N.Y. State (1st pres. 1966, dir. 1967-70, 74—). Home: 195 Pine Ridge Dr Guilderland NY 12084 Office: State Capitol Albany NY 12224

FLORES, TERESA PENA (MRS. JUAN FLORES), city ofcl.; b. Spofford, Tex., Nov. 12, 1925; d. Adrian and Petra (Dela Rosa) Pena; student North Tex. State U., 1971; m. Juan Flores, Feb. 2, 1945; children—Noelia, Teresa, Johnny, Gloria, Yolanda (Mrs. Victor Ozuna). Cashier, City of Crystal City (Tex.), 1955-65, billing clk., 1965-69, city clk., 1969—. Sec. bd. Crystal City Fire Dept., 1970—. Recipient certificate of appreciation City of Crystal City, 1960. Mem. Assn. City Clks. and Secs. of Tex., Miguel Hidalgo Assn. Home: 204 E Lake St Crystal City TX 78839 Office: PO Drawer 550 Crystal City TX 78839

FLORES-HERNANDEZ, MARIA MONSERRATE (MRS. GILBERTO HERNANDEZ), coll. dean; b. Lajas, P.R., Dec. 14, 1923; d. Juan Monserrate and Maria Josefa (Hernandez) Flores; B.A. in Edn., U. P.R., 1944; M.A., N.Y. U., 1959; Ed.D., Stanford U., 1970; m. Gilberto Hernandez, June 9, 1945; children—Helga Ivette, Helia Ivonne. Tchr. elementary sch., Rio Piedras, P.R., 1942-44; secondary sch., Bayamon, P.R., 1944-47; curriculum technician Central Office, State Dept. Edn., San Juan, P.R., 1948-53, gen. supr. social studies, Hato Rey, P.R., 1953-59; asst. prof. social studies, supr. student teaching U. P.R., Rio Piedras, 1960-62, asso. prof., coordinator student teaching, 1962-64, dir. profl. improvement program of Dominican tchrs., 1963, dir. exptl. program for preparation of secondary sch. tchrs., 1963-66, chmn. dept. curriculum and teaching, 1964-66; asso. prof. edn. Catholic U. P.R., Ponce, 1970-71, dean coll. edn., 1970—, prof., 1971—. Vis. lectr. Fairleigh Dickinson U., Teaneck, N.J., 1959, N.Y. U., N.Y.C., 1969-70. Mem. Nat. Council for the Social Studies, Assn. for Supervision and Curriculum Devel., Am. Assn. Colls. for Tchr. Edn., Am. Acad. Polit. and Social Scis., Am. Assn. for Higher Edn., Am. Mus. Natural History, Stanford Alumni Assn., Pi Lambda Theta. Contbr. articles to profl. jours. Home: 4th St Block E-8 San Jose Development Ponce PR 00731 Office: Catholic University of Puerto Rico Las Americas Av Ponce PR 00731

FLORO, CHARLOTTE OLLERO ASPURIA (MRS. FRANCISCO RODRIGUES FLORO), occupational therapist, educator; b. Maui, Hawaii, Nov. 23, 1926; d. Julian and Patricia (Ollero) Aspuria; student U. Hawaii, 1944-46; B.S. in Occupational Therapy, Milw.-Downer Coll., 1949; M.A. in Psychology, U. Philippines, 1965; m. Francisco Rodrigues Floro, July 24, 1954; children—Mila Lynne, Mark, Sharon, Jeffrey, Phil. Occupational therapist Goldwater Meml. Hosp., N.Y.C., 1949-50, Territorial Hosp., Kaneohe, Hawaii, 1950-52; co-founder, occupational therapist Sch. of Allied Med. Professions, U. Philippines, Manila, 1962, asst. prof. dept. occupational therapy, 1962-73, chmn. dept. occupational therapy, 1962-73, sec. of Sch., 1973—. Mem. Rehab. Internat. Regional Com. for Asia/Pacific, 1973—. Vice pres. Philippine Found. Rehab. Disabled, Inc., 1972—. Served as 1st lt., Women's Specialist Service Corps., AUS, 1952-54. WHO fellow, 1969. Mem. Am. Occupational Therapy Assn., World Fedn. Occupational Therapists, Philippine Mental Health Assn. (dir. 1970-73, v.p. 1973), Psychol. Assn. of the Philippines (dir. 1967-69), Occupational Therapy Assn. of the Philippines (founder, pres. 1965-69). Lion. Home: 929 Epifanio DeLos Santos Av Quezon City Philippines Office: 547 Pedro Gil St Manila Philippines

FLORY, DAISY PARKER (MRS. CLAUDE R. FLORY), educator; b. Charlotte, N.C., Feb. 18, 1915; d. Julius Monroe and Daisy (Kidd) Parker; B.A., Fla. State Coll. for Women, 1937; M.A., U. Va., 1940, Ph.D., 1959; m. Claude R. Flory, Mar. 26, 1973. Instr., Leon High Sch., Tallahassee, 1937-42; instr. Fla. State U., Tallahassee, 1942-47, asst. prof., 1947-57, asso. prof., 1957-65, prof. govt., 1965—, asst. v.p. acad. affairs, 1969-73, dean of faculties, 1973—. Mem. Fla. Gov.'s Study Com. on Personnel, 1954; pres. Le Moyne Art Found., 1967-68. Mem. Fla. Hist. Soc., Tallahassee Hist. Soc. (pres. 1943-45, 61-62), So. Polit. Sci. Assn. (sec. 1960-63), Am. Assn. U. Women (br. pres. 1944-45), Phi Beta Kappa, Phi Kappa Phi, Pi Sigma Alpha, Phi Alpha Theta, Mortar Bd. (editor Jour. 1950-56). Home: 1551 Crestview Av Tallahassee FL 32303

FLORY, (ESTHER) ELAINE, psychologist; b. North English, Ia., Dec. 1, 1942; d. Glen Elmer and Esther (Carter) Flory; A.B., McPherson Coll., 1965; M.S., Kan. State Tchrs. Coll., 1970, Edn. Specialist, 1973. Tchr., Buhler (Kan.) Grade Sch., 1965-69; teaching asst. Kan. State Tchrs. Coll., Emporia, 1969-70, grad. extension instr., 1972—; sch. psychologist Rice County Spl. Edn. Coop., Lyons, Kan., 1970—. Mem. N.E.A., Council for Exceptional Children, Nat., Kan. (chmn. ethical standards com. 1973-75) assns. sch. psychologists. Mem. Ch. of Brethren (chmn. local ch. bd. 1973-74). Home: 531 N Eshelman St McPherson KS 67460 Office: 209 West Av S Lyons KS 67554

FLOWER, ADELAIDE ALBERTI, occupational therapist; b. Chgo., Feb. 16, 1932; d. Charles E. and Josephine (Sesso) Alberti; student Ore. Coll. Edn., 1949-51; B.S. with distinction, San Jose State Coll., 1953; m. John T. Flower, May 4, 1958 (div. 1972); children—Christopher, Clare, Harry, Sarah. Dir. occupational therapy Crippled Children's Hosp., Corpus Christi, Tex., 1954-58; spl. edn. tchr. Austin (Tex.) Ind. Sch. Dist., 1961-62; tchr.-coordinator Northside Ind. Sch. Dist., San Antonio, 1967-70; supr. occupational therapy Santa Rosa-Villa Rosa (psychiat. hosp.), San Antonio, 1970-72; supr. occupational therapist San Antonio State Hosp., 1972—. Adj. faculty dept. allied health scis. U. Tex., Galveston, 1972—. Mem. Am., Tex. occupational therapy assns. Democrat. Roman Catholic. Home: 126 Brees Blvd San Antonio TX 78209 Office: San Antonio State Hosp San Antonio TX 78223

FLOWERS, VIRGINIA ANNE, univ. adminstr.; b. Dothan, Ala.; d. Kyrie Neal and Annie Laurie (Stewart) Flowers; B.A., Fla. State U., 1949; M.Ed., Auburn U., 1958; Ed.D., Duke, 1963. Elementary tchr. Minnie T. Heard Sch., Dothan, Ala., 1949-52; secondary tchr. Dalton (Ga.) High Sch., 1952-55, personnel dir., asst. prin., 1955-61; instr. U.S. history U. Ga. Extension, Dalton, 1960-61; part-time instr. Duke, Durham, N.C., 1961-62, vis. prof., summers 1966, 67, 69, 70, asst. provost, asso. dean Trinity Coll. Arts and Scis. Duke, 1972—, acting vice provost, acting dean, 1973-74, chmn. dept. edn., asst. provost ednl. program devel., Duke, 1974—; asso. prof. edn. Columbia (S.C.) Coll., 1962-66, prof. edn., 1966-68, head dept. edn., 1966-68, asso. dean, 1969-71, dean, 1971-72; prof. elementary edn. Va. Commonwealth U., Richmond, Va., 1968-69, asso. dean Columbia Coll., 1969-71, dean, 1971-72. Mem. N.E.A., Nat. Orgn. Legal Problems in Edn., Am. Ednl. Research Assn., Nat. Soc. for Study Edn., Am. Assn. U. Profs., Soc. Research in Child Devel., Am. Assn. Higher Edn., Nat. Council Adminstrv. Women in Edn., Kappa Delta Epsilon, Kappa Delta Pi, Delta Kappa Gamma, Alpha Kappa Gamma. Research and publs. in field. Home: 2727 Spencer St Durham NC 27705

FLOYD, CLARA BAILEY (MRS. BOOKER T. FLOYD), univ. adminstr.; b. Tallahassee, Sept. 28, 1935; d. Eugene and Luberta (Knight) Bailey; B.S., Fla. A. and M. U., 1957, M.Ed., 1971; m. Booker T. Floyd, May 5, 1956; children—Delbert, Kirkland, Kenton. Sec., tchr., Leon County Sch. System, 1957-60; adminstrv. sec. Fla. A. and M. Hosp., 1960-67; with Fla. A. and M. U., Tallahassee, 1967—, dir. student financial affairs, 1967—. Cons. Fla. Trio Dirs. Confs., 1972-73; cons., resource leader Moten Consortium for Financial Aid and Admissions Dirs., 1973-75; mem. Nat. Task Force Com. Student Aid Common Application, 1974-75. Mem. Nat. Assn. Student Financial Aid (mem. need analysis com. 1973-74), Nat., So., Fla. assns. student financial aid adminstrs. Home: 1104 Joe Louis St Tallahassee FL 32304

FLOYD, MARIA KETTLE, ednl. adminstr.; b. Phila., Feb. 4, 1944; d. Anthony and Margaret (Patrone) Fraietta; student U. Pa., 1962-64; m. Raymond Loran Floyd, Dec. 8, 1973. Dir. Bauder Fashion Coll., Miami, Fla., 1967—. Interior decorator, Miami, 1970—. Mem.

Modeling Assn. Am., Fashion Group Am. Home: 1 Palm Bay Ct Miami FL 33138 Office: 300 Biscayne Blvd Way Miami FL 33131

FLOYD, SUSAN ANN, speech pathologist; b. Marianna, Fla., Feb. 15, 1946; d. Granville Lipscomb and Mary Susan (Massey) Crothers; B.A., Pepperdine U., 1966, M.A., 1967; Ph.D., U. So. Cal., 1974; m. Garland Wayne Floyd, Sept. 11, 1965. Speech and hearing specialist Westminster (Cal.) Sch. Dist., 1967-68, Hawthorne (Cal.) Sch. Dist., 1968-70; instr. Pepperdine U., 1970; teaching asst U. So. Cal., 1970-72, clin. supr. Los Floristas Speech and Hearing Clinic, 1972-73; guest lectr. div. speech pathology and audiology U. Hawaii, 1973; chief speech pathology Pacific Inst. Rehab. Medicine, Honolulu, 1973—. Mem. Am., Hawaii speech and hearing assns., Am. Cancer Soc. Home: 780 Amana St #1804 Honolulu HI 96814 Office: Pacific Inst Rehab Medicine 226 N Kuakini St Honolulu HI 96817

FLOYD, VIOLA CASTON (MRS. HENRY CLYDE FLOYD), civic worker; b. nr. Heath Springs, S.C., Mar. 23, 1901; d. John Durham and Matilda (Ingram) Caston; A.B., Winthrop Coll., 1922; m. Henry Clyde Floyd, Dec. 19, 1924 (dec. Apr. 22, 1967); children—Robert Arthur (dec.), Caroline (dec.). Tchr. elementary sch., Denmark, S.C., 1922-23, Heath Springs, S.C., 1923-25, Sharon, S.C., 1928-29, Lancaster, S.C., 1938-41. Bd. dirs. Lancaster County Hosp., 1964-70; trustee Lancaster County Library, 1956—, Lancaster Ednl. Found., 1962-67; mem. Lancaster County com. S.C. Tricentennial Celebration, 1969-70. Lancaster County Hist. Commn., 1958—; Lancaster County rep. bicentennial com. Catawba Regional Planning Council, 1973—. Pres. Andrew Jackson Bi-Centennial celebration, 1967. Named Lancaster County Woman of Year, 1970, award for Service to community Lancaster Civitan Club. Mem. D.A.R., Daus. 1812, United Daus. Confederacy. Methodist. Club: Lancaster Wednesday Book. Author: Lancaster County, S.C. Tours, 1st edit., 1956, 2d. edit., 1968; Descendants Alexander Ingram, 1957; History Lancaster First Methodist Church, 1962; Floyd-Ervin Family Records, 1963; Descendants William Harper, 1965; Caston and Related Families, 1972. Contbr. articles to mags. and newspapers. Address: PO Box 117 Lancaster SC 29720

FLUCKIGER, ADRIENNE NORTHAM (MRS. JAMES R. FLUCKIGER), librarian; b. Branford, Conn., Aug. 28, 1926; d. Robert Hazen and Alice May (Hill) Northam; B.A., Middlebury Coll., 1947; M.L.S., L.I. U., 1967; m. James R. Fluckiger, Nov. 4, 1949; children—John, James, Anne, Elizabeth. Caseworker, Div. Child Welfare, State of Conn., New Haven, 1947-49; editor Bull. Va. Mus. Fine Arts, Richmond, 1961; trainee Seaford (N.Y.) Pub. Library, 1963-65, children's librarian, 1965-68; children's librarian Syosset (N.Y.) Pub. Library, 1968—, head children's services, 1972—. Mem. N.Y., Nassau County library assns. Democrat. Unitarian. Home: 3964 Marilyn Dr Seaford NY 11783 Office: 225 S Oyster Bay Rd Syosset NY 11791

FLYNN, ANN DE SARNO, state ofcl.; b. Asbury Park, N.J., Oct. 17, 1912; d. John and Carmel De Sarno; grad. Asbury Park High Sch.; m. John Doyle Flynn, Oct. 17, 1947; children—Angela, Ellen. With publ. dept. City Asbury Park, 1941-42; sec. Asbury Park Bur. Health, then registrar vital statistics, 1943-50; owner, operator Flynn's Luncheonette, Asbury Park, 1945-55; owner, operator Flynn's Gift Shop, Asbury Park, 1950-70; adminstrv. sec. div. tax appeals State N.J., 1971—. Active various community drives. Republican committeewoman, Monomouth County, N.J., 1942—, vice chmn. exec. com., 1959; chmn. Monmouth County Bd. Elections, 1963—; pres. Monmouth County Fedn. Rep. Women, 1962-64; alternate del. Rep. nat. conv., 1964, del.-at-large, 1968; mem. N.J. Rep. state com., 1969—, vice-chmn., 1973—; chmn. N.J. Inaugural Ball, Washington, 1972. Recipient award Deborah Jewish Orgn., Asbury Park, 1965; named Rep. Woman of Year N.J. State Fedn., 1971. Mem. Women's Columbian League Monmouth Country (founder, pres. 1958), Bus. and Profl. Women Shore Area (pres. Roman Catholic. Home: 133 Norwood Av Deal NJ 07723

FLYNN, BETTY, journalist; b. Chgo., Aug. 17, 1939; d. Timothy Carver Flynn and Elizabeth Tait Scanlon; B.A. with high honors, U. Wis., 1961. Cityside reporter Mpls. Tribune, 1961-62; cityside reporter Chgo. Daily News, 1962-65, corr. UN, and N.Y.C., 1966—, corr. Washington bur., 1968; Russell Sage fellow U. Wis., Madison, 1965-66. Recipient State award A.P. Mem. UN Corr. Assn. (exec. bd. 1969), Womens Nat. Press Club, White House Corrs. Assn., State Dept. Corr. Assn., Phi Beta Kappa, Sigma Delta Chi. Office: Chicago Daily News 401 N Wabash Av Chicago IL 60611

FLYNN, SISTER MARGARET, religious adminstr.; b. nr. Howell, Mich., Apr. 30, 1918; d. James Cornelius and Margaret Isabel (Walsh) Flynn; B.S., St. Joseph Coll., 1951; M.S.W., U. Mich., 1954; postgrad. U. Ponce (P.R.), 1959. Joined Daus. of Charity of St. Vincent de Paul, 1942; group mother St. Vincent and Sarah Fisher Children's Home, Farmington, Mich., 1950-54; adminstr. LaBoure Center, South Boston, 1954-58, 63-66; supr. Catholic Home Bur., N.Y.C., 1958-63; cons. Nat. Conf. Cath. Charities, Washington, 1967-69; coordinator social welfare East Central Province of Daus. of Charity, Evansville, Inc., 1969—. Mem. Gen. Assembly of Daus. of Charity, Rome, Italy, 1968-69, 74. Cons., Commn. on Aging, 1967-69, Commn. on Families and Children, 1967-69, Commn. on Services to Unmarried Parent, 1967-69, Conf. of Religious of Nat. Conf. Catholic Charities, 1967-69; mem. Nat. Cadre Group, 1971-72. Trustee, Marillac Social Center, Chgo. Mem. Nat. Assn. Social Workers, Nat. Conf. on Social Welfare, Acad. Certified Social Workers, Internat. Council on Social Welfare. Editor: Information Bull. of Nat. Conf. Catholic Charities, 1967-69, Aging, News-Notes, 1967-69. Home and office: Mater Dei Provincial House 9400 New Harmony Rd Evansville IN 47712

FLYNN, SISTER MARIETTA, librarian; b. Pitts., Jan. 4, 1904; d. Patrick Joseph and Catherine Mary (McPaul) Flynn; B.A., Duquesne U., 1933, M.A., 1943; M.S. in L.S., Marywood Coll., 1957. Joined Order Sisters of Charity, 1922; tchr. elementary schs., 1925-30; tchr. Latin and Spanish, Sisters of Charity High Schs., Pitts., 1931-51; librarian Elizabeth Seton High Sch., Pitts., 1952-60, Holy Innocents High Sch., Pitts., 1960-62, Sacred Heart High Sch., Pitts., 1962—. Library supr. Sisters of Charity Elementary Schs., Pitts., 1960—; mem. registration com. Nat. Library Conv., Pitts., 1962; chmn. luncheon and banquet com. Cath. Library Conv., Pitts., 1974. Mem. A.L.A., Catholic (chmn. book week activities West Pa. unit 1960-68, co-chmn. 1969—), Pa., Suburban Pitts. library assns., Nat. Catholic Assn., N.E.A. Democrat. Mem. Cath. supplement com. Sr. High Sch. Catalog for High Sch. Libraries, 1967—. Home: 6225 Walnut St Pittsburgh PA 15206 Office: 6202 Alder St Pittsburgh PA 15206

FOBES, MRS. THEODORE BURGESS (RUTH CARTER FOBES), community service vol.; b. Portland, Me., Aug. 28, 1895; d. George Washburn and Alma (Wiggin) Carter; B.S., Nasson Coll., 1946, L.H.D., 1962; m. Theodore Burgess Fobes, June 7, 1918. Tchr., West Paris and Augusta, 1915-17; substitute tchr. or librarian Portland, 1917-35; v.p. Burgess, Fobes Co., 1935-61, pres., 1961—. Pres. Portland YWCA, 1940-46, hon. mem. bd. 1963—, mem. nat. bd., 1946-52; pres. Portland Council Social Agys., 1946-49; mem. adv. council health and welfare State Me., 1947-62, sec., 1957-62; mem. adv. com. edn. State Me., 1958-62; mem. bd. and reorgn. com. United Fund, 1955-61. Chmn. bd. trustees Nasson Coll., 1955-61, now life mem. bd., asst. sec. bd. and mem. exec. com.; bd. mgrs. Home for Aged, Portland, Me., 1963—. Mem. League of Women Voters (pres. Me. 1951-55, v.p. Portland 1955-57), Me. Welfare Assn., Women's Legislative Council (treas. 1959-61), Women's Lit. Union, Women of Rotary. Conglist. Club: Excelsior. Home: 5 Maiden Cove Lane Cape Cottage Park Cape Elizabeth ME 04107

FOBIL, MARY BARBARA, banker; b. Lafayette, Ind., Dec. 22, 1909; d. Nicholas Daniel and Mary Cecelia (O'Brien) Fobil; grad. Ind. Bus. Coll., Lafayette, 1928; student Am. Inst. Banking, 1955-56. Stenographer law firm Francis J. Murphy, Lafayette, Ind., 1928-29; stenographer, transit clk. City Trust Co., 1929-32; exec. sec. to pres. Fowler Bank City Trust Co., 1932-34; exec. sec. to pres., trust officer Lafayette Nat. Bank, 1934-58; asst. trust officer, 1958-65, asst. v.p., 1966-69, v.p., 1969-74, sr. v.p., 1974—, br. mgr., 1973—. Mem. Nat. Assn. Bank Women, Ind. Bankers Assn. (mem. com. women in banking conf. 1968-69), Am. Inst. Banking. Home: 903 S 10th St Lafayette IN 47905 Office: 337 Columbia St Lafayette IN 47902

FOELLINGER, ELIZABETH RUBY HILLIX (MRS. KENNETH ARTHUR FOELLINGER), educator; b. Menomonie, Wis., Sept. 7, 1914; d. Foster Furman and Ruby Magdelene (Jourdan) Hillix; A.B., Ind. U.; M.S. in Journalism, M.A. in English, Northwestern U.; m. Kenneth Arthur Foellinger, May 11, 1940; children—Patricia Ann, George Edward Smith. Sales promotion dir., publicity KEX, Portland, Ore., 1943-45; womens editor Portland Oregonian, 1945-46; editor house organ Ft. Wayne Mfg. Co., 1950-52; nat. editor Themis, mem. nat. council Zeta Tau Alpha, Evanston, Ill., 1957—; asst. prof. English and journalism Union U., Jackson, Tenn., 1963—. Publicity dir. Ft. Wayne Art League, Am. Cancer Soc., 1949-52, Jackson Symphony League, 1966-68, Youthtown of Tenn., 1968-70. Mem. Nat. Assn. Collegiate Publs. Advisers, Jackson C. of C., Mortar Bd., Alpha Lambda Delta. Mem. Order Eastern Star, Rainbow Girls. Club: Jackson Golf and Country. Office: College Av Union U Jackson TN 38301

FOELLINGER, HELENE R., newspaper publisher; b. Ft. Wayne, Ind., Dec. 12, 1910; d. Oscar G. and Esther Anna (Deuter) Foellinger; A.B., U. Ill., 1932; Litt.D. (hon.), Tri State Coll. Mem. editorial dept. News Pub. Co., publs. of News-Sentinel, Ft. Wayne, Ind., 1932-36, pres. and gen. mgr. 1936—; pres. Ft. Wayne Newspapers, Inc.; dir. Lincoln Nat. Bank & Trust Co., Gen. Telephone Co. Ind. Bd. dirs. Taxpayers Research Assn., Ft. Wayne Philharmonic Orch., Ft. Wayne Better Bus. Bur., Conv. Bur. (also sec.), Ft. Wayne-Allen County Community Chest, Allen County United Fund, Ft. Wayne Horse Show Assn., Ft. Wayne Light Opera Festival (past pres.), Allen County Tb Assn., Allen County Chpt. Nat. Found. for Infantile Paralysis, Allen County unit Ind. Cancer Soc., United War Chest, Ft. Wayne chpt. A.R.C., Jr. Achievement, Ft. Wayne Art Sch., Ft. Wayne Fine Arts Found., Allen County Meml. Coliseum, Ft. Wayne Zool. Soc., Ft. Wayne Found. Mem. Ft. Wayne C. of C. (dir.), Am. Newspaper Assn., Ft. Wayne Exec. Club, Ind.-Purdue Found., U. Ill. Found., Mortar Bd., Phi Beta Kappa, Pi Beta Phi, Pi Mu Epsilon, Psi Iota Xi (past pres.). Lutheran. Clubs: Altrusa (past pres.), Ft. Wayne Country. Home: 4415 Old Mill Rd Fort Wayne IN 46807 Office: 600 W Main St Fort Wayne IN 46802

FOERCH, JO ELLEN (MRS. DAVID C. FOERCH), journalist; b. Indpls., Mar. 25, 1948; d. Henry F. and Mary Ellen (Malloy) Krumm; B.A. cum laude (Trustee scholar), U. So. Cal., 1970; m. David C. Foerch, June 1, 1968. Reporter, Downtowner Newspaper, Los Angeles, 1970; copywriter Ben Franklin Advt., Santa Monica, Cal., 1970-71, Pennington & Richard Assos., Denver, 1972-73; free lance zone writer Denver Post, 1973—. Mem. Women in Communications (pres. Denver chpt. 1973—), Sigma Delta Chi. Home and office: PO Box 86 Dupont CO 80024

FOGARTY, JEAN KAY (MRS. JOSEPH EUGENE FOGARTY), real estate exec.; b. N.Y.C., Sept. 2, 1938; d. William Joseph and Caroline Maude (Hallenbeck) Enright; grad. high sch.; m. Charles Wesley McKay, Oct. 24, 1959 (div. Oct. 1967); children—Charles Wesley, Cynthia Jean, Jill Marie; m. 2, Joseph Eugene Fogarty, Sept. 30, 1971. Salesman, Tom Key Realty, Inc., Anaheim, Cal., 1964-67, sales mgr., 1967-71, div. mgr., 1971; pres. Lincoln Realty, Inc., 1971—. Mem. Visitors Conv. Bur., Anaheim, 1973-74. Mem. Cal. Real Estate Assn. (del. 1974), Anaheim Bd. Realtors (dir. 1974). Club: Los Coyotes Country. Home: 1735 Las Lanas Fullerton CA 92633 Office: 2840 E Lincoln St Anaheim CA 92806

FOGARTY, MARGARET MARY, psychologist; b. New Haven, Feb. 17, 1909; d. James Augustine and Grace Marion (Hyland) Fogarty; diploma New Haven Normal Sch., 1928; B.S., New Britain State Tchrs. Coll., 1939; M.A., Yale, 1944. Tchr. West Haven, Conn., 1928-52; sch. psychologist, dir. psychol. services West Haven Schs., 1952—; pvt. practice, West Haven, 1954—. Mem. adv. com. West Haven Community Devel. Action Plan, adv. bd. West Haven Human Services and Resource Center, Race Relations Com. Mem. Am., New Eng., Conn. psychol. assns., Conn. Assn. Sch. Psychologists (sec. 1961-63, chmn. role and functions com. 1963-65), N.E.A. (life), West Haven Community Service Assn. (sec. 1969-70), West Haven Adminstrs. Group. Roman Catholic. Editor: Study of Role and Function of School Psychological Personnel Working in the Public Schools of Connecticut, 1965. Home: 487 Washington Av West Haven CT 06516 Office: Blake Administration Bldg 25 Ogden St West Haven CT 06516

FOGG, SYLVIA TWIFORD, editor; b. Asheville, N.C.; d. Lloyd D. and Lucy (Vance) Twiford; grad. Cecil's Bus. Coll., 1937; student Western Carolina U., 1963; m. Daniel Anthony Fogg, Nov. 21, 1970; 1 dau. by previous marriage, Nancy (Mrs. Roger C. Sumner). Exec. sec. to area engr. U.S. Corps Engrs., Asheville, 1941-42; exec. sec. to comdt. Bomb Disposal Sch., Aberdeen Proving Ground, Md., 1942-44; exec. sec. Sales Execs. and Mgmt. Club, Asheville, 1954-58; exec. sec. Gerber Products Co., Asheville, 1958-67, editor co. publs., corporate hdqrs., Fremont, Mich., 1967—. Bd. dirs. Asheville Community Theater, 1960-63; chmn. publicity Mayor's Com. Employment of Handicapped, Asheville, 1964-67. Recipient Army-Navy E, 1944; Presdl. citation for employment of handicapped U.S. Pres., 1966, Flying Orchid award Delta Air Lines, 1966. Mem. Mich. Communicators Assn., Internat. Assn. Bus. Communicators, Bus. and Profl. Women (bd. 1961-66). Home: Box 55 Fremont MI 49412 Office: 445 State St Fremont MI 49412

FOGG, VERA VIRGINIA, lawyer; b. nr. Okla., Nov. 4, 1908; d. Charles Robert and Susie Ann (Huddleston) Fogg; student Brantley-Draughon's Bus. Coll., 1926-27; pvt. study law. Admitted to Tex. bar, 1932, Cal. bar, 1957; practiced in Quanah, Tex., 1939-42, Ft. Worth, 1949-52, Tarzana, Cal., 1957-65; asso. firm Mann & Mann, Laredo, Tex., 1935-37, E.G. Aycock, Ft. Worth, 1937-39; county atty. Hardeman County, Quanah, Tex., 1942-48; dep. exec. dir. San Fernando Valley Neighborhood Legal Services, Pacoima, Cal., 1968-69, office dir., 1966-68. Mem. Tex., Cal., Los Angeles County bar assns., Tarzana C. of C. (dir. 1971—), Delphian Soc. (parliamentarian exec. com. Los Angeles assembly chpts.), Soroptimist Club of West Valley (pres. 1967-68). Republican. Baptist. Address: 5317 Mecca Av Tarzana CA 91356

FOHR, JENNY LAURETTE LEVINE (MRS. HENRY DIDEROT FOHR), artist; b. N.Y.C.; d. Samuel and Paula (Pilloff) Levine; B.A., Hunter Coll., 1932; student Alfred U., 1954, U. Colo., 1955-63; m. Henry Diderot Fohr, July 2, 1933; 1 son, Samuel Denis. One-man shows at Bklyn. Mus., Chautauqua, Laurel Gallery, Talents Unltd., Duo and Roko Galleries, Lynn Kottler; exhibited in group shows at N.Y. Whitney Mus., Bklyn. Mus., Riverside Mus., N.J. State Mus., Pa. Acad. Fine Arts, Library of Congress, Nat. Mus., Oakland (Cal.) Art Mus., numerous others; represented in permanent collections at Ciba-Geigy Pharms. of N.Y., Oakland (Cal.) Mus., Library of Congress, Long Beach Island Found. Arts and Scis., N.J., Norfolk (Va.) Mus., John Galt, Inc., Chgo., also pvt. collections. Tchr., Beekman Hill Sch., N.Y.C. Recipient Windsor Newton award, 1966; Paige Electric Corp. award, 1965; Andrew Nelson Whitehead award, 1967; Samuel Mann award 1970; honored in Congl. Record. Mem. Nat. Assn. Women Artists (corr. sec. 1966-68), Am. Color Print Soc., Am. Soc. Contemporary Artists (pres. 1960-61, prize 1971), Painters and Sculptors Soc. N.J. (Gold medal of honor 1964), Pen and Brush, N.Y. Soc. Women Artists, Artist Craftsmen, Provincetown Art Assn. Home: 165 E 32d St New York City NY 10016 Office: 302 E 45th St New York City NY 10017

FOLAND, CAROLYN GENE, health service center adminstr.; b. Columbia, S.C., Mar. 6, 1944; d. Eugene Lee Roy and Louise Julia (Hunter) Foland; B.A., Kan. State U., 1966, M.S., 1969. Dir. pub. information Topeka (Kan.) State Hosp., 1966-71; staff asso. Mental Health Materials Center, N.Y.C., 1971-73; chief mental health communications County of Sacramento, 1973—. Cons. Ft. Logan Mental Health Center, 1968, Kan. State U. Mental Health Mass Communications Program, 1968—, Shawnee Community Mental Health Corp., 1970-71, Nat. Clearinghouse for Drug Abuse Information, 1972-73, Mental Health Assn. Shawnee County, 1973. Mem. adv. bd. Can Help, 1970-71. Mem. Women in Communications, Sacramento Area Mental Health Assn. Editorial bd. Taproots, 1967-70. Home: 200 Selby Ranch Rd Sacramento CA 95825 Office: Dept of Mental Health 2221 Stockton Blvd Sacramento CA 95817

FOLB, BLOSSOM SALTZ DASSIN (MRS. JAY FOLB), artist; b. N.Y.C.; d. Max and Tillie (Walinsky) Saltz; B.A., Hunter Coll.; postgrad. Art Student's League, 1956-58; m. Louis Dassin, 1946 (div. 1953); m. 2d, Jay Folb, Dec. 31, 1954. One-man shows Marble Arch Gallery, 1966, Roerich Mus., 1967, Roerich Mus., 1967; Sala de Exposiciones de la Excma Disputacion Provincial, Malaga, Spain, 1971, Spain, 1972; exhibited in group shows John Myers Gallery, 1954, ACA Gallery, 1954, Ruth Sherman Gallery, 1955, Argent Gallery, 1959, Edinburgh (Scotland) Mus., 1964, Internat. watercolor tour, 1963-65, Royal Birmingham (Eng.) Soc. Artists Galleries, 1963-65, Nat. Assn. Women Artists Traveling Watercolor Show, 1965-67, Vendome Gallery, Pitts., 1965-66, Casino Municipale, Cannes, France, 1966, Henry Clews Found. Chateau de la Napoule, Cannes, 1965, Musee de Cognac, France, 1966, N.Y. World's Fair, 1965, Nat. Acad. Gallery, N.Y.C., 1956—, Nat. Traveling Oil Show Nat. Assn. Women Artists, 1965-67, Lever House, 1966, Mercyhurst Coll., Pa., 1965, Fleming Mus., Vt., 1964-66, Burgos Gallery, N.Y.C., 1966, Marble Arch Gallery, 1963-66, Roehrich Mus., 1967, Gallery 99, Miami, Fla., 1967-68, Casino Municipal, Cannes, France, 1969, La Napoule Art Found., 1969, Group Eight, Artists Equity, 1969, London Pub. Library and Art Mus., 1970, Kenmore Gallery, Phila., 1968-70, Forum Gallery, N.Y.C., 1972; design cons. fine and costume jewelry; head designer Marvella Pearls, 1950-55; tchr. music, art, design high schs. in Manhattan, 1965-66. Trustee Yoga Soc. N.Y. Recipient Heydenryk prize for oil painting, 1960; Lena Newcastle Meml. prize for watercolor, 1962; Margaret N. Cooper prize for oil painting, 1964; Aileen O. Webb prize for watercolor, 1966. Mem. Nat. Assn. Women Artists (exec. bd., fgn. exhbns. chmn. 1968-70), Artists Equity, Internat. Platform Assn. Address: Hotel Alden 225 Central Park West New York City NY 10024

FOLEY, ALICE LORETTA, coll. pres.; b. Clyde, N.Y.; d. David C. and Mary (McGrath) Foley; B.A. magna cum laude, Nazareth Coll., 1930, D.Litt., 1961; M.A., U. Rochester, 1937; postgrad. Columbia, U. Wis., Fordham U. Tchr. pub. schs., Clyde, N.Y., Savannah, N.Y., Rochester, N.Y.; tchr., Brighton, N.Y., 1934-42, asst. prin., 1942-44, prin., 1944-55; asst. supt. instrn. and pupil services, Brighton, N.Y., 1969-71; pres. Nazareth Coll., 1971—. Instr. U. Rochester, Brockport U. Trustee, Rochester Savs. Bank. Mem. N.E.A. (life), N.Y. State Tchrs. Assn. (pres.), Am. Soc. Curriculum Devel., Am. Assn. U. Women, Delta Kappa Gamma, Kappa Gamma Pi. Contbr. articles to profl. jours. Home: 70 Penarrow Rd Rochester NY 14618

FOLEY, ANNA BERNICE WILLIAMS (MRS. WARREN MASSEY FOLEY), library assn. exec.; b. Wigginsville, O., Nov. 20, 1902; s. Karl and Bertye (Young) Williams; student U. Cin., 1920-24, Nanking (China) Lang. Coll., 1926; student Columbia, 1931; grad. certificate Jesus Coll. Oxford (Eng.) U., 1969; m. Warren Massey Foley, Feb. 25, 1924; children—Williams Massey, Karlanne (Mrs. William Scully Hauer). Commentator radio sta. WKRC, Cin., 1934, radio sta. WSAI, Cin., 1938; spl. events coordinator Mabley & Carew Dept. Store, Cin., 1951-66; dir. Martha Kinney Cooper Ohioana Library Assn., Columbus, O., 1966—, also editor Quar. mag., Yearbook, 1966—. Lectr. creative writing; book reviewer Sunday Columbus Dispatch, 1967—. Bd. dirs. Ohio Poetry Day, 1968—. Mem. Am. Women in Radio and Television, Nat. Acad. Radio and Television, English Speaking Union (br. pres. 1966-69), Cin. MacDowell Soc., Ohio Hist. Soc., Ohio Arts Council (mem. lit. panel 1966—), Ohio Press Women, Women in Communication (pres. Columbus, 1973—), Kappa Kappa Gamma. Clubs: Executive of Columbus, Faculty; Cincinnati Women's, Cincinnati Town. Author: (juvenile) Star Stories, 1970. Home: 3440 Olentangy River Rd Columbus OH 43202 Office: 1109 Ohio Depts Bldg Columbus OH 43215

FOLEY, EILEEN, state senator; b. Portsmouth, N.H., Feb. 23, 1918; B.A., Syracuse U.; student U. N.H.; married, 3 children. Dir. Portsmouth (N.H.) Rehab. Center; spl. service work USN; former clk. City Portsmouth; former mayor of Portsmouth; mem. N.H. Senate, now minority leader; mem. N.H. staff U.S. Senator Tom McIntyre. Mem. Def. Adv. Com. Women in Services; mem. Portsmouth Housing Authority, Portsmouth Ednl. Council, Atlantic States Marine Fisheries Commn.; mem. exec. bd. Council Sr. Citizens. adult council Catholic Youth Orgn., mother's guild St. Thomas Aquinas, Immaculate Conception Altar Soc.; mem. state adv. bd. Swiftwater council Girl Scouts U.S.A. Past chmn. Portsmouth Democratic City Commn.; past chmn. Rockingham (N.H.) County Dem. Orgn.; vice-chmn. N.H. State Dem. Com. Bd. dirs. Portsmouth Rehab. Center, Gt. Bay Sch. for Mentally Retarded, U.S.O., N.H. Civil Air Patrol. Served in WACs, 1944-45. Mem. Women's Aux. Am. Legion, Portsmouth C. of C. (dir.). Roman Catholic. K.C. aux. Address: 39 Sunset Rd Portsmouth NH 03301

FOLEY, MARY ALICE DODD (MRS. LAWSON EDGAR FOLEY), piano tchr., civic worker; b. Roanoke, Va., Dec. 24, 1912; d. Cubert Bosworth and Fannie (Hale) Dodd; student St. Louis Inst. Music, 1932, 37, U. Va., 1939-53, Hollins Coll., 1953-55, U. Richmond, 1960-62, U. N.C., summers 1965-67; m. Lawson Edgar Foley, Apr. 12, 1933. Tchr. piano, Roanoke, 1933—. Del., People to

People Travel Program. Mem. Roanoke Music Tchrs. Assn. (parliamentarian 1969-71), Nat. Guild Piano Tchrs., Music Tchrs. Nat. Assn., Va. Music Tchrs. Assn. (state parliamentarian 1969-71, 73-75; 1st v.p. 1968-70, chmn. bd. certification 1971—), Am. Piano Tchrs. Assn., Daus. of Confederacy (pres. 1966-68), Wythe County, New River (charter mem. drama com.) hist. socs., Historic Fincastle, Magna Charta Dames, Soc. Descs. Knights Most Noble Order Garter, Nat., Va. (councilor 1971-74) socs. daus. colonial wars, Huguenot Soc. Va. (rec. sec. 1971-73), Roanoke Hist. Soc., Colonial Dames XVII Century (chpt. pres. 1971-73), D.A.R. (chpt. regent 1968-71, dist. dir. 1971-74, chmn. state friends of museum com. 1974—, dist. parliamentarian 1974—), Alpha Pi Mu (past pres.). Methodist. Home: 6630 Laban Rd Roanoke VA 24019

FOLEY, MARY WELCH, realtor; b. Deer Grove, Ill., Sept. 6, 1904; d. John H. and Minella (Ford) Welch; grad. high sch; m. George F. Foley, Oct. 6, 1936; children—Maureen (Mrs. James A. Norton), Mary Patricia (Mrs. Edward M. Schima). Saleswoman, Standard Edn. Corp., Chgo., 1924-29; office mgr. br., touring counsellor Chgo. Motor Club, Sterling, Ill., 1929-43; owner, Foley Agy., Sterling, Ill., 1945—, also ins. broker, agt. Mem. Art Inst. Chgo. Bd. dirs. Sinissippi Mental Health Center, Dixon, Ill., 1967-69, Sterling Pub. Library, 1967—. Mem. Whiteside County Bd. Realtors (pres. 1960-61), Ill., Nat. assns. real estate bds., Sterling-Rock Falls Ins. Women's Assn., Nat. Assn. Ins. Women., Whiteside County Women's Assn. Democrat. Roman Catholic. Club: Altrusa. Home: 511 W 14th St Sterling IL 61081 Office: 218 1st Av Sterling IL 61081

FOLEY, SUZANNE, curator; b. Detroit, Jan. 10, 1934; A.B., Randolph-Macon Woman's Coll., 1955; M.A., Radcliffe Coll., 1959. Adminstr. sec. Va. Mus. Fine Arts, Richmond, 1955-57, registrar, 1958; research asst. also exhbn. sec. Inst. Contemporary Art, Boston, 1959-61; registrar Walker Art Center, Mpls., 1962, asso. curator, 1962-67; registrar, curator San Francisco Mus. Art, 1967-68, curator, 1968—. Served on local art juries. Recipient fellowship for museum professionals Nat. Endowment for the Arts, 1972. Author: numerous museum exhibition catalogs. Home: Apt 2 2033 Leavenworth St San Francisco CA 94133 Office: San Francisco Mus Art McAllister St at Van Ness Av San Francisco CA 94102

FOLGER, KATHRINE DULIN (MRS. JOHN CLIFFORD FOLGER), civic worker; b. Springfield, Tenn.; d. Hanson Lee and Eugenia (Bell) Dulin; grad. Finch Jr. Coll., 1923; m. John Clifford Folger, Nov. 2, 1929; children—John Dulin, Lee Merritt. Pres. Cumberland Trust Co., Knoxville, Tenn., 1955-63; mng. partner H. L. Dulin Co., Knoxville, 1942-70, partner, 1970—. Pres. Jr. League Knoxville, 1927-29; founder D.C. div. Am. Cancer Soc., 1946; finance chmn. Thrift Shop, 1945-50; mem. women's bd. Children's Hosp., 1943—, Columbia Hosp., 1943—, Washington Hosp. Center, 1939—; past chmn. women's com. Corcoran Art Gallery of Washington; founder Dulin Meml. Gallery of Art, Knoxville, 1961; mem. women's com. Smithsonian Assos., Washington. Trustee, Community Chest, v.p., 1969-71; trustee John F. Kennedy Center, 1970—; pres. Folger Fund. Episcopalian. Clubs: Colony (N.Y.C.); Sulgrave (treas. 1951-53) (Washington); Everglades, Bath and Tennis (Palm Beach, Fla.). Home: 2991 Woodland Dr Washington DC 20008

FOLGER, MARY HELEN DAVIS (MRS. LESLIE ALLEN FOLGER), editor; b. Youngstown, O., Sept. 10, 1929; d. Franklin Porter and Elma Christine (Bruce) Davis; student Kent State U., 1968-71; m. Leslie Allen Folger, May 23, 1947; children—Leslie Allen, Will Raymond, Loretta Jo, Lynette Marie. Asst. editor Valley Views Mag., Solon, O., 1966-71; feature editor Record-Courier, Ravenna, O., 1966-73; exec. editor Garrettsville (O.) Jour., 1973—; founder, mng. editor Western Reserve Mag., Garrettsville, 1973—; free lance writer, 1960—. Mem. Garrettsville Village Council, 1973—, chmn. recreation com., 1973—. Bd. dirs. Portage County United Fund, Portage County Mental Health Exec. Bd. Mem. Ohio Press Women, Ohio Newspaper Women, Women in Communication. Home: 8215 Water St Garrettsville OH 44231 Office: 8098 Main St Garrettsville OH 44231

FOLIN, ELIZABETH FITTON, librarian; b. Hamilton, O., June 6, 1910; d. Samuel D. and Irene (Massee) Fitton; A.B., Oberlin Coll., 1931, M.A., 1939; postgrad. (Inst. Internat. Edn. scholar) Sorbonne, 1935-36. Art librarian Allen Art Museum Library, Oberlin (O.) Coll., 1931-39; head librarian Marquand Art Library, Princeton U., 1939-51, USIS Library, Venice, Italy, 1951-53, Henry Clay Frick Fine Arts Library, U. Pitts., 1966—. Mem. Coll. Art Assn. Am. (chmn. 1st art libraries session 1970), Art Libraries N. Am., Spl. Libraries Assn., Carnegie Inst. of Pitts., Friends of Art Oberlin Coll. Office: Frick Fine Arts Library U Pitts Pittsburgh PA 15260

FOLKER, ROBERTA PUTNAM DUNLAP (MRS. HUGH HOYT FOLKER), educator, orgn. exec.; b. N.S., Can., May 25, 1923; d. James Sedley and Henrietta (Putnam) Dunlap; came to U.S., 1926, naturalized, 1943; A.B., Fla. State Coll. Women, 1943; M.A., Fla. State U., 1959; m. Hugh Hoyt Folker, Feb. 10, 1942; children—Barbara Ann (Mrs. William Frazier Waid), Mary Kathryn. Organizer nursery schs. Orange County Bd. Pub. Instrn., Orlando, Fla., 1943-46; operator pvt. nursery sch. and kindergarten, 1946-50; tchr. Zellwood (Fla.) Elementary Sch., 1950-53; West Central Elementary Sch., Orlando, Fla., 1953-56, Hartsfield Elementary Sch., Tallahassee, 1956-66; elementary resource tchr. Leon Sch. Dist., Tallahassee, 1966-68, area curriculum coordinator, 1968-73, elementary prin. Leon Dist. Schs., Tallahassee, 1973—. Active fund drives March of Dimes, United Fund. Trustee Tallahassee Jr. Mus. Mem. Assn. Childhood Edn. Internat. (state and local coms.; mem. publs. com. 1971—), Fla. (state pres. 1967-69, adviser 1969-71), Leon County (pres. 1964-66) assns. childhood edn., Fla. Edn. Assn. (sect. chmn. 1963-65), Alpha Delta Pi (chpt. pres. 1964-65), Kappa Delta Pi. Presbyn. Home: 2123 Atchena Nene Tallahassee FL 32301 Office: Chaires Elementary School Tallahassee FL 32301

FOLLON, SUE ELLEN, coll. dean; b. Volga, Ia., June 22, 1942; d. Oliver Franklin and Mary Rebecca (Moore) Follon; B.S., Ia. Wesleyan Coll., 1963; postgrad. U. Colo., summer 1966; M.A., U. No. Ia., 1970; postgrad. Ind. U., summer 1973. Secondary tchr. Delwood Community Schs., Delmar, Ia., 1963-67; residence hall dir. U. No. Ia., Cedar Falls, 1967-70; dean women Buena Vista Coll., Storm Lake, 1970—. Mem. Nat., Ia. (pres. 1973) assns. women deans, adminstrs. and counselors, Am. Assn. U. Women, Am. Coll. Personnel Assn., Delta Kappa Gamma, Ia. Women's Polit. Caucus. Home: 100 College Av Storm Lake IA 50588

FOLSOM, GENEVIEVE HUNT (MRS. ROBERT BRUCE FOLSOM), newspaperwoman; b. Leavenworth, Kan., Jan. 11, 1907; d. Devereux and Genevieve Viola (Feidler) Hunt; student U. Utah, 1937-38; m. Robert Bruce Folsom, June 23, 1937; children—Robert Bruce, Richard Kim. Sec., Gillam Advt. Agy., Salt Lake City, 1932-42; with Salt Lake Telegram, 1947-52, garden editor, 1952; garden editor Salt Lake Tribune, Salt Lake City, 1952—. Tchr. gardening Adult Ednl. classes, 1960. Chmn., Salt Lake City clean-up campaign, 1962; coordinator Utah Home and Garden Festival, 1947—, Civic Beautification Awards program, 1948—. Recipient award Nat. Garden Bur., 1959; award Utah Assn. Nurserymen, 1970; Mrs. Utah Beautification, State Utah. Mem. D.A.R., Daus. Am. Colonists (pres. 1938), Women's Archtl. League (pres. 1962). Club: Cottonwood Country. Home: 1595 S 12th E Salt Lake City UT 84105 Office: 143 S Main St Salt Lake City UT 84101

FOLSOM, MARY O'HEARN, educator; b. Dubuque, Ia., Jan. 4, 1916; d. Clarence J. and Marcella M. (Hipman) O'Hearn; A.B., U. Ia., 1939; M.Ed., U. Miami at Coral Gables, 1955; Ph.D., U. Ia., 1958; m. Charles Walton Folsom (div. May 1954); children—Patricia, Charles. Research analyst mil. intelligence, Washington, 1943-45; tchr. elementary schs., Dubuque, 1949-57; prof. edn. U. Miami, Coral Gables, 1958—. Vis. prof. summers U. Ill., 1961, San Jose (Cal.) State Coll., 1964, 65, Stanford U., 1964, 65, Mich. State U., 1969. Recipient Outstanding Tchr. award U. Miami, 1967. Mem. Am. Ednl. Research Assn., Math. Assn. Am., Nat. Council Tchrs. Math., Phi Kappa Phi, Pi Lambda Delta, Alpha Lambda Delta, Delta Kappa Gamma, Delta Kappa Phi. Author: (with others) Elementary Mathematics; Concepts, Properties and Operations Grades K-8, 1966-68. Home: 14150 SW 84th St Miami FL 33143 Office: PO Box 8065 U Miami Coral Gables FL 33124

FOLTA, JEANNETTE RUTH, univ. dean; b. Holyoke, Mass., Aug. 27, 1934; d. Rudolph and Olive Cecile (Roberts) Folta; R.N., Burbank Hosp. Sch. Nursing, 1955; B.S. cum laude, Boston U., 1959; Ph.D., U. Wash., 1963. Clin. instr. psychiat. nursing, Worcester (Mass.) State Hosp., 1955-56; pvt. duty nursing, Boston, 1956-58; pre-doctoral asso. instr. U. Wash., Seattle, 1962-63; co-dir. research tng. U. Cal. Med. Center Sch. Nursing, San Francisco, 1963-66; asso. prof. nursing, sociology Boston U., 1966-69; asso. prof. nursing, sociology and psychiatry U. Vt., Burlington, 1969-72, asst. dean Coll. Arts and Scis., 1972—; cons. Simmons Coll., Boston, Boston U., 1969-70, Nat. Funeral Dir. Assn., 1971—; adv. WHO, Poland, 1971. Vice pres. Champlain Valley Mental Health Council, 1973—. Trustee Counseling Service of Addison County, Vt., 1970—, Planned Parenthood, Burlington, 1970-72. Served to capt. USAF, Nurse Corps Reserves, 1958-66. Mem. Am., Vt. (legislative com. chmn. 1970-72, pres. 1974) nurses assns., Royal Soc. Promotion Health, Community Leaders Am., Contemporary Authors, Am. Sociol. Assn., Nat. League Nursing, Am. Pub. Health Assn., Am. Acad. Polit. and Social Sci., A.A.A.S., Am. Assn. U. Profs., Museum of Nat. History, Alpha Kappa Delta, Sigma Theta Tau. Author: (with Edith Deck) A Sociological Framework for Patient Care, 1966. Contbr. articles to pubs. in field. Home: Snake Mountain Rd Weybridge VT 05753 Office: College Arts and Sciences Univ Vermont Burlington VT 05401

FOLTZ, VIRGINIA CAMPBELL (MRS. DANIEL SHANNON FOLTZ), educator; b. Ashtabula, O., Aug. 3, 1911; d. Hosea William and Grace Evelyn (Griffey) Campbell; B.S., Baldwin Wallace Coll., 1933; M.S., U. Houston, 1966; Ph.D., Tex. Woman's U., 1969; m. Daniel Shannon Foltz, June 12, 1933; children—Richard Campbell, James Lance. Instr., U. Houston, 1963-64; teaching fellow Tex. Woman's U., Denton, 1965; asst. prof. La. Tech. U., Ruston, 1969-70; asst. prof. dept. biology Pan Am. U., Edinburg, Tex., 1970-73, asso. prof., 1973—. Welch Found. fellow, 1968. Mem. A.A.A.S., Genetics Soc. Am., Tex. Assn. Radiation Research, Tex. Acad. Sci., Sigma Xi, Beta Beta Beta. Home: Rural Route 4 Box 225 Mission TX 78572 Office: Dept Biology Pan Am U Edinburg TX 78539

FONDA, JANE, actress; b. N.Y.C.; d. Henry Fonda; student Vassar Coll., 2 years Art Students League, N.Y.C.; pupil acting with Lee Strasberg; m. Roger Vadim, 1966; 1 dau.; m. 2d, Tom Hayden; 1 son. Appeared with father in summer stocks in The Country Girl, Omaha; actress on Broadway, and in movies including: Tall Story, A Walk on the Wild Side, Period of Adjustment, Joy House, Circle of Love, Cat Ballou, The Chapman Report, In the Cool of the Day, Sunday in New York, The Love Cage, La Ronde, Klute, Doll's House; stage plays include There Was a Little Girl, Invitation to a March, The Fun Couple, Strange Interlude. Recipient Acad. award for best actress in Klute, Am. Acad. Motion Picture Arts and Scis. Address: care Famous Artists 9441 Wilshire Dr Beverly Hills CA 90212*

FONDILLER, SHIRLEY HOPE ALPERIN (MRS. HARVEY V. FONDILLER), nurse, educator; b. Holyoke, Mass.; d. Samuel and Rose (Sobiloff) Alperin; grad. Beth Israel Hosp. Sch. Nursing, Boston; B.S., Tchrs. Coll. Columbia, 1962, M.A., 1963, Ed.M., 1971; m. Harvey V. Fondiller, Dec. 27, 1957; 1 son, David Stewart. Staff asst. Am. Nurses' Assn., N.Y.C., 1963-64, dir. ednl. adminstrs., cons. and tchrs. sect., 1964-66, coordinator Am. Nurses Assn.-Nat. League for Nursing careers program, 1967-70; coordinator clin. sessions Am. Nurses Assn., 1971-72. Cons. N.Y. State Asso. Degree Nursing Project, 1964. Mem. Kappa Delta Pi. Writer, columnist Nursing World, 1955-60; film reviewer Am. Jour. Nursing, 1963-64, Film News, 1963-66; writer, dir. The Open Door, radio documentary, 1960; columnist Am. Jour. Nursing, 1971—. Home: 310 W 56th St New York City NY 10019

FONG, ANNABELLE CHING, univ. adminstr.; b. Honolulu, June 9, 1926; d. Foo Lin and Annie (Ling) Ching; B.A., Bowling Green State U., 1947; M.A., Columbia U. Tchrs.'s Coll., 1950; postgrad. U. Hawaii, 1966-69. children—Robert, Brenda, Roanne, Bruce. Extension agt., U. Hawaii, 1947-48; home economist, 1950-53; dir. Ednl. Guidance and Opportunities Community Action Program, 1965-66; project dir. ednl. guidance and opportunities program U.S. Office Edn., Honolulu, 1966-70; became dir. spl. student services U. Hawaii, 1970, now dir. financial aids, instr., 1968-69, mem. task force on equal ednl. opportunity, 1971-72, mem. statewide articulation com., 1972—, statewide high sch. relations com., 1973—. Mem. Western regional exec. com. Coll. Entrance Exam. Bd., 1971-74, chmn., 1973; cons. dept. ednl. psychology Nat. Council Talent Search Dirs., 1969-70; mem. tech. adv. com. Concentrated Employment Program, 1968-70; mem. U.S. Office Edn. Task Force. Bd. govs. U. br. YMCA, 1969-71. Mem. Am., Hawaii (pres. 1971-72) personnel and guidance assns., Asso. Chinese U. Women (pres. 1960) Home: 6370 Hawaii Kai Dr Apt 55 Honolulu HI 96825

FONG, BERNADINE CHUCK, educator, psychologist; b. Palo Alto, Cal., Mar. 8, 1944; d. Frank Y. and Jennie (Tong) Chuck; B.A., Stanford, 1966, M.A., 1968; m. Herbert Harrison Fong, Aug. 12, 1972. Research asst. psychiatry Stanford Med. Sch., 1966-68; psychologist Montessori Presch., Coll. Notre Dame, Belmont, Cal., 1968; instr. City Coll. San Francisco, 1968; tchr. Bing Nursery Sch., Stanford, 1966-68; research asst. Am. Insts. Research, Palo Alto, Cal., 1968-69; instr. Ventura (Cal.) Coll., 1969-70; asst. prof. psychology Foothill Coll., Los Altos Hills, Cal., 1970—. Mem. Am., Western psychol. assns., Cal. Tchrs. Assn., Am. Fedn. Tchrs. Republican. Roman Catholic. Contbr. articles to profl. jours. Home: 917 Stagi Ct Los Altos CA 94022

FONG, ELLYN LO (MRS. HIRAM L. FONG), business exec.; b. Honolulu, Dec. 21, 1911; d. On and Quan (Ching) Lo; B.E., U. Hawaii, 1938; postgrad. Lingnan U., Canton, China; m. Hiram L. Fong (U.S. senator from Hawaii), June 25, 1938; children—Hiram L., Rodney L., Marvin-Allan and Merie-Ellen (twins). Tchr., Dept. Pub. Instrn., Hawaii, 1938; v.p. Market City, Ltd.; partner Kaalaea Farms. Active A.R.C. Mem. Oahu League Republican Women. Mem. Honolulu Symphony Orch. Soc., Am. Legion Aux. Clubs: 86th Congress, University Women's. Home: 1102 Alewa Dr Honolulu HI 96817

FONG, PAULINE LEW (MRS. PATRICK A. FONG), economist; b. White Plains, N.Y., Feb. 23, 1938; d. Frank and Hong Gay (Lee) Lew; A.B. cum laude (William Deiches scholar, Jessie Smith Noyes scholar, Coll. scholar), Barnard Coll., 1959; M.A. (U. Center for Chinese Studies fellow, Nat. Def. Fgn. Lang. fellow), U. Cal., Berkeley, 1964; m. Patrick A. Fong, Aug. 14, 1960; children—Rachel Louise, Joshua Andrew. Research economist U.S. Dept. Labor, summers 1958-59, Marine Fireman's Union, 1965; organizer, bus. agt. Am. Fedn. Govt. Employees, 1964-65; instr. econs. Mills Coll., 1965-66; postgrad. research economist Inst. Indsl. Relations, U. Cal., Berkeley, 1962-65, teaching asso., 1966-67; v.p. planning U. Cal., statewide prin. adminstrv. analyst, 1967-72, asst. dir. program to train neutrals for dispute settlement, 1972-73; dir. mgmt. services, tech. assistance Asian, Inc., San Francisco, 1973—. Certified Laubach Method English instr.; cons. Cal. State Com. on Pub. Edn., San Francisco Chinatown-No. Beach Econ. Devel. Agy., Salvation Army. Mem. Asian Am. Community Alliance Berkeley, 1971—, Oakland Chinese Community Council, 1970— (also dir.), Chinese for Affirmative Action, 1971—, Task Force on Sch. Finance Oakland Pub. Schs. Master Plan Citizens Com., 1971-73, Task Force on Status of Women Berkeley Bd. Edn., 1972-73; Berkeley City Personnel Bd., 1973—; coordinator, founding mem. League Acad. Women, 1971-73; rep. East Bay area Barnard Coll. Admissions Office, 1971—. Mem. Am. Econ. Assn., Western Govtl. Research Assn., U. Art Mus. Council (charter), Cal. Acad. Scis., Am. Civil Liberties Union, Am. Fedn. State, County, Municipal Employees, Bay Area Edn. TV Assn. Home: 939 Arlington Av Berkeley CA 94707 Office: 1610 Bush St San Francisco CA 94109

FONSECA, MARY L., state senator; b. Fall River, Mass., Mar. 30, 1915; B.M.C., Durfee High Sch., 1932. Sec.; mem. Mass. Senate, 1953—. Mem. Democratic City Commn.; mem. Fall River Sch. Com., 1945-53. Mem. Daus. of Isabella, Women on Wheels, Delta Kappa Gamma. Clubs: Quota; Catholic Women's (Fall River); Corky Row aux.; Bus. and Profl. Women's (Boston); Exchangettes. Address: 102 Webster St Fall River MA 02723*

FONTAINE, JOAN (BORN DE HAVILLAND), actress; b. Tokyo, Japan, Oct. 22, 1917; m. Brian Aherne, Aug. 20, 1939 (div. 1944); m. 2d, William Dozier, May 2, 1946; 1 dau., Deborah Lese; adopted dau., Martita Valentina Calderon; m. 3d, Collier Young, Nov. 10, 1952 (div. 1961); m. 4th Alfred Wright, Jr., Feb. 1964 (div. 1969). Has appeared in numerous motion pictures, 1937—; motion pictures include: Rebecca, 1940 (N.Y. Critics award); Suspicion, 1941 (Acad. award); Jane Eyre, 1942; Constant Nymph, 1943; Frenchmen's Creek, 1943; Letter from an Unknown Woman, 1946; Ivy, 1947; September Affair, 1949; Ivanhoe, 1951; Decameron Nights, 1952; Casanova, 1953; Broadway debut in Tea and Sympathy, 1954; Until We Suil, 1957, A Certain Smile; 1958; Tender is the Night; The Devils Own, 1966. Nat. lectr. Recipient Eleanor Roosevelt Humanitarian award, 1966. Club: Deepdale Golf. Address: 160 E 72d St New York City NY 10021

FONTANNE, LYNN, actress; b. London, Eng.; d. Jules Pierre Antoine and Frances Ellen (Thornley) Fontanne; L.H.D., Dartmouth, 1954; m. Alfred Lunt. Made first stage appearance as a child at the Drury Lane Pantomine; first London appearance, 1909; first N.Y.C. appearance as Harriet Bludgeon in Mr. Preedy and the Countess, 1910; played Gertrude in Milestones on tour and later in the revival; small parts in My Lady's Dress, London; then followed, in N.Y. in The Wooing of Eve, Harp of Life, Out There, Happiness, Dulcy, In Love With Love, The Guardsman, Queen Elizabeth, Design for Living, Reunion in Vienna, Point Valaine, Idiot's Delight, Amphitryon, The Sea Gull, Taming of the Shrew, There Shall Be No Night, The Pirate, O Mistress Mine, I Know My Love, Quadrille, 1954, The Great Sebastians, 1956, others. Played in motion picture The Guardsman with Alfred Lunt.

FONTE, JOSEPHINE WHITMAN FRANK (MRS. MICHAEL JOSEPH FONTE), ednl. adminstr.; b. Rochester, N.Y., Dec. 2, 1914; d. Aloysius Balthasar and Josephine (Whitman) Frank; grad. high sch.; m. Michael Joseph Fonte, Sept. 22, 1939; children—Michael Joseph, Susan (Mrs. Kenneth Reynolds), Kathryn (Mrs. Ronald Meier), Timothy, Gerard. News editor Genesee Valley Newspapers, Pittsford, N.Y., 1963-68; community information coordinator, profl. and ednl. journalist cons. Penfield (N.Y.) Central Sch. Dist., 1968—. Columnist, Genesee Valley Newspapers, Pittsford, 1950-68; Pres., P.T.A., Penfield, 1955-57; pres. Penfield Community Chest, 1959-74; pres. Penfield council Girl Scouts Am., 1954-59; town chmn. A.R.C., Penfield, 1954-60. Exec. committeeman Democratic party, 1969-71. Mem. Penfield Heritage Assn., Penfield Rotary Anns (pres. 1969-70), Theta Sigma. Roman Catholic (mem. parish council 1972—). Home: 2124 Penfield Rd Penfield NY 14526 Office: Penfield Central Schs Atlantic Av Penfield NY 14526

FONTENELLE, LYDIA JULIA, educator; b. New Orleans, May 28, 1938; d. Leon Joseph and Lydia Juilette (Dragon) Fontenelle; B.S., La. State U., 1960; Ph.D. (NIH fellow), Tulane U., 1967. Secondary sch. tchr. Bell Chasse, La., 1960-61; lab. technician Tulane U., New Orleans, 1961-63; Nat. Cancer Inst. of Can. fellow McEachern Lab., U. Alta., Edmonton, Can., 1967-69; asst. prof. pharmacology, biochemistry Ida. State U., Pocatello, 1969—. Research grantee Ida. State U. Grad. Faculty, 1970. Mem. Am. Chem. Soc., A.A.A.S., N.Y. Acad. Sci., Gate City Horse Assn., Sigma Xi, Rho Chi. Roman Catholic. Contbr. articles to profl. jours. Office: Coll Pharmacy Ida State Univ Pocatello ID 83209

FONTEYN, DAME MARGOT (MRS. ROBERTO E. ARIAS), ballerina; b. Reigate, Eng., May 18, 1919; Litt.D. honoris causa, Leeds U., 1953; Mus. D. honoris causa, U. London, 1954; Mus. D. (hon.), Oxford U., 1959, U. Manchester, 1966; LL.D. (hon.), Cambridge U., 1962, Edinburgh (Scotland) U., 1963; m. Roberto E. Arias in 1955. Guest artist with Royal Ballet, 1956—. Decorated comdr. Order of British Empire, 1951, Dame Comdr. Order Brit. Empire, 1956; Order of the Lion (Finland); Order Estacio de Sa Brazil; recipient Benjamin Franklin medal Pres. Royal Acad. Dancing, 1954—; mem. Royal Soc. Arts. Address: Royal Opera House Convent Garden London WC2 England

FOOKS, JAQUETTE BETH, travel agt., educator; b. Wichita, Kan., Nov. 27, 1945; d. Leslie Eugene and Dorothy Jean (Hendrix) Fooks; B.A. summa cum laude (acad. scholar), Abilene Christian Coll., 1966; M.A. (univ. fellow), U. Kan., 1968, Ph.D. (univ. fellow), 1970. Asst. prof. and dir. theatre arts Pepperdine U., Los Angeles, 1970-72, Malibu, Cal., 1972-74; travel agt. Atlas Tours and Travel Service, Inc., Toledo, 1974—. Mem. Am. Theatre Assn., Am. Assn. U. Profs. (sec.-treas. local chpt. 1973-74). Home: 2323 Shoreland Toledo OH 43611

FOOTE, BRANGWYN, univ. dean; b. Hanford, Wash., Apr. 28, 1944; d. Ellis and Norma Sophie (Schreiner) Foote; B.A. in Sociology, U. Ariz., 1966; M.A. in Higher Edn., Ohio State U., 1968. Asst. dean women Colo. State Coll., Greeley, 1968-69, acting dean women, 1969-70; asst. prof. teaching psychology and coll. student personnel work U. No. Colo., Greeley, 1968—, dean student affairs, 1970—. Active numerous civic orgns. Mem. Nat. Assn. Women Deans, Adminstrs. and Counselors (regional dir. 1973-74), Colo.-Wyo. Assn.

Women Deans and Counselors, (v.p. 1972, pres. 1975-76), Mortar Bd. Home: 1839 6th Av Greeley CO 80631

FOOTE, FLORENCE MARTINDALE (MRS. CHARLES LEE FOOTE), anatomist, educator; b. Montague City, Mass., June 28, 1911; d. Lawrence Sandin and Mabel (Fields) Martindale; B.A., Mt. Holyoke Coll., 1932, M.A., 1934; Ph.D., U. Ia., 1940; m. Charles Lee Foote, Aug. 25, 1941 (dec. Nov. 27, 1963). Instr. zoology Mt. Holyoke Coll., 1935-38; instr. zoology U. Del., 1940-41; instr. biology Wagner Coll., 1942-44, asst. prof., 1944-47; lectr. zoology, physiology So. Ill. U., Carbondale, 1948-63, asso. prof. physiology, 1963-68, prof. 1968—, research asso., 1957-60, acting chmn. physiology dept., 1971-72. Research asso. College de France, 1960-61. Active A.R.C. Mem. Am. Soc. Zoologists, Am. Assn. Anatomists, Internat. Inst. Embryology, Soc. Developmental Biology, A.A.A.S., Am. Inst. Biol. Sci., Tissue Culture Assn., Am. Assn. U. Women, League Women Voters, P.E.O., Sigma Xi. Iota Sigma Pi. Democrat. Presbyn. Contbr. numerous articles to sci. jours. in U.S., France. Research in field chick embryology, sex devel. in amphibians, tissue culture. Home: 801 Skyline Dr Carbondale IL 62901

FOOTE, JOYCE RUTH STRYKER (MRS. DONALD HENRY FOOTE), librarian; b. Sayville, L.I., N.Y., May 7, 1930; d. Allen Milton and Ruth Myrtie (Esser) Stryker; B.S., State. N.Y. Tchrs. Coll., 1952; postgrad. Hofstra U., 1953-55, State U. N.Y. Coll. at Oneonta, 1960; m. Donald Henry Foote, July 2, 1955; children—Natalie Ruth, Donna Marie. Librarian Bellport (N.Y.) Union Sch., 1952-55; tchr.-librarian Churchville-Chili Central Sch., Churchville, N.Y., 1956-58; campus sch. librarian State U. Coll. at Oneonta, 1960-61, 63-64; cons. librarian Oneonta Consol. Schs., 1966; librarian State U. N.Y. Coll. at Oneonta, Campus Sch., 1967-69; librarian New Berlin (N.Y.) Central Sch., 1971-72; librarian Morris (N.Y.) Central Sch., 1973—. Mem. Morris Centennial Steering Com., 1969-70; sec., Morris Hist. Soc., 1973—; sec., Hillington Cemetery Assn., 1972-74. Sec. bd. assessors Town of Morris, N.Y., 1958-70. Trustee, pres. Village Library, Morris, N.Y. Mem. Central Valley Sch. Librarian's Assn., Suffolk County Librarians Assn. (pres. 1954), Alpha Kappa Phi, Agonian. Republican. Episcopalian. Author: Morris, New York, 1773-1923, 1970. Home: 2 Grove St Morris NY 13808 Office: Morris Central Sch Morris NY 13808

FOOTE, MARCELLE K., librarian; b. Albion, Ind., Nov. 12, 1910; d. George Loomis and Lelia (Kitt) Foote; A.B., Ind. U., 1932; B.S. in L.S., Western Res. U., 1933. Librarian, Albion Pub. Library, 1933-36, Connersville Pub. Library, 1936-56; field cons. Ind. State Library, Indpls., 1956-59; head extension div., 1960-67, dir., 1967—. Chmn. Fayette County chpt. Am. Cancer Soc., 1952-54; mem. Fayette County Adult Edn. Council, 1949-52; sec. Ind. com. on Pub. Records, 1967—, Ind. Library Certification Bd., 1967—, Ind. Am. Rev. Bicentennial Com., 1971—; exec. dir. Ind. Library and Hist. Bldg. Expansion Commn., 1973—; mem. Ind. Com. on Aging and Aged. Named Librarian of Year, Ind. Library Trustee Assn., 1966. Mem. A.L.A. (chmn. jury on citation of trustees 1962), Ind. Library Assn. (pres. 1951-52), Assn. State Libraries (sec. 1963-64), Ind. Sch. Librarians Assn., Am. Legion Aux., Am. Assn. U. Women, Ind. Hist. Soc., Delta Zeta. Presbyn. (deaconess). Mem. Order Eastern Star. Club: Altrusa (dist. treas. 1953-55, dist. Gov. 1957-59, 2d v.p. internat. 1961-63). Home: 5116 LeMans Dr E7 Indianapolis IN 46205 Office: 140 N Senate Av Indianapolis IN 46204

FORBES, ANNE PAPPENHEIMER (MRS. WILLIAM H. FORBES), physician; b. N.Y.C., Nov. 11, 1911; d. Alwin Max and Beatrice (Leo) Pappenheimer; B.A., Radcliffe Coll., 1932; M.D., Columbia, 1936; m. William H. Forbes, Dec. 31, 1935; children—Andrea (Mrs. Scott Schoenfeld), Elise (Mrs. Marc Pachter), Peter, Anthony, Beatrice Anne (Mrs. Robert Manz). Intern, Johns Hopkins U., Balt., 1938; research fellow Mass. Gen. Hosp., Boston, 1939-48, asso. physician, 1965—; mem. faculty Harvard Med. Sch., 1948—, asst. clin. prof. medicine, 1962-70, asso. clin. prof., 1970—; asst. prof. medicine Pahlavi U., Shiraz, Iran, 1967-69. Vis. lectr. Mass. Inst. Tech., Cambridge, 1971—. Mem. Royal Soc. Medicine, Am. Fedn. Clin. Research, Am. Soc. Clin. Investigation, Endocrine Soc., Mass. Med. Soc. Contbr. articles to profl. jours. Home: 304 Adams St Milton MA 02186 Office: Mass Gen Hosp Boston MA 02114

FORBES, CAROLYN HELENE, occupational therapist; b. Jersey City, Nov. 6, 1946; d. William and Lauretta Fitzhenry (Silvers) Forbes; B.S., Loma Linda U., 1969. Staff occupational therapist Rancho Los Amigos Hosp., Downey, Cal., 1970-73; sr. occupational therapist Glendale (Cal.) Adventist Hosp., 1973. Mem. Am., So. Cal. occupational therapy assns., Loma Linda U. Occupational Therapy Alumni Assn. (treas. 1972-73). Mem. Ch. of Seventh Day Adventists. Home: 833 Oakwood Place Pasadena CA 91106 Office: 1509 Wilson Terrace Glendale CA 91206

FORBES, DELORIS FLORINE STANTON (MRS. WILLIAM J. FORBES, JR.) (PEN NAMES STANTON FORBES, TOBIAS WELLS), author; b. Kansas City, Mo., July 10, 1923; d. Lawrence and Florence (Ellis) Stanton; student pub. schs., Wichita, Kan.; m. Argus Marion Daniel, Dec. 20, 1941 (dec. Sept. 1947); m. 2d, William J. Forbes, Jr., Oct. 29, 1948; children—Daniel W., Anne Stanton (Mrs. A. Joseph Lavallee), W. Andrew. Propr., Pierre Lapin and Goetz House, Grand Case, St. Martin, French W.I. Mem. Mystery Writers of Am. Author: If She Should Die, 1961; They're Not Home Yet, 1962; No Questions Asked, 1963; Grieve for the Past, 1963; Terrors of the Earth, 1964; A Matter of Love and Death, 1966; A Business of Bodies, 1966; What Should You Know of Dying, 1967; Dead by the Light of the Moon, 1967; Encounter Darkness, 1967; If Two of Them Are Dead, 1968; Murder Most Fouled Up, 1968; Go to Thy Deathbed, 1968; The Name's Death, Remember Me, 1969; The Young Can Die Protesting, 1969; She Was Only the Sheriff's Daughter, 1970, Dinky Died, 1970; If Laurel Shot Hardy the World Would End, 1970; The Sad Sudden Death of My Fair Lady, 1971; What to Do Till the Undertaker Comes, 1971; One for All and All for Death, 1971; The Foo Dog, 1972; A Deadly Kind of Lonely, 1972; How To Kill a Man, 1972; But I Wouldn't Want To Die There, 1972; A Die in the Country, 1972; Brenda's Murder, 1973; Welcome My Dear to Belfey House, 1973; Some Poisoned by Their Wives, 1974. also others, also short stories. Home: Goetz House Grand Case St Martin French WI 97150

FORBES, DOROTHY TEVORA BELTON, civic worker; b. Indpls., May 29, 1895; d. Charles and Josephine (Bock) Belton; grad. high sch.; m. Ray Forbes, Apr. 8, 1930. Founder, Dorothy Forbes Oxygen Found., Inc., Tucson, 1961, chmn. bd., 1961—; founder Sick Room Loan Chest, Tucson, 1960, chmn., 1961—. Named Woman of Yr., Tucson Advt. Assn., 1961; recipient Kalish award Tucson Jewish Community Center, 1973; Dale Carnegie award, 1965; Cele Petereson award, 1972; Mason-K.C. award 1974. Mem. Nat. Council Jewish Women (hon.), Tucson Symphony Assn. Mem. Order Eastern Star. Club: Tucson Woman's. Address: 4032 E Fort Lowell St Tucson AZ 85712

FORBES, EDITH JAMESON (MRS. WARREN PECK FORBES), librarian; b. Yonkers, N.Y., July 6, 1921; d. William Robert and Edith Jane (Redmond) Jameson; B.A., Coll. New Rochelle, 1942; M.L.S., Pratt Inst., 1963; m. Warren Peck Forbes, Sept. 27, 1947; children—William, Susan, Margaret, Daniel. Sec. to dir. athletics Columbia U., N.Y.C., 1944-47; library clk. Hempstead (N.Y.) Pub. Library, 1955-63; librarian Nassau Community Coll., Garden City, 1963, head of reference, 1965-67, dep. dir. library, 1967—, prof., 1973—, instr. children's lit., 1967—. Mem. N.Y. State, Nassau County library assns., State U. N.Y. Library Assn., Am. Assn. Univ. Profs., Am. Civil Liberties Union. Home: 29 Maryland Av Hempstead NY 11550 Office: Nassau Community College Garden City NY 11530

FORBES, LORNA MIRIAM (MRS. ROBERT CHANEY), psychiatrist; b. Berkeley, Cal., Feb. 28, 1921; d. Louis Charles and Romilda (Smith) Forbes; B.A. in Zoology, U. Cal. at Berkeley, 1942; M.D., Woman's Med. Coll. Pa., 1946; m. Dr. Robert H. Chaney, June 14, 1947; children—Victor Louis, Hollis Roberta, Bradford William. Intern, California Hosp., Los Angeles, 1946-47; resident in surgery New Eng. Hosp., Boston, 1947-50; resident psychiatry Pacific State Hosp., 1951-52, dir. diagnostic and preadmission service, 1952-58; pvt. practice psychiatry, Pomona, Cal., 1958—; psychiat. chief of staff Guidance Center, Exceptional Children's Found., Los Angeles; psychiat. cons. Convent of Good Shepherd, Children's Hosp., Los Angeles, Family Service Agy. of Pomona, also Claremont, Cal., 1961-71; cons. Riverside County Adoptions, 1974—; clin. instr. psychiatry Coll. of Med. Evangelists, 1958-61; asso. clin. prof. of child psychiatry U. So. Cal., 1961—; med. examiner Superior Court, 1958—. Cons., lectr. So. Cal. Sch. Theology, Claremont. Adv. bd. Family Service of Pomona, Dept. of Recreation, Los Angeles, Dept. of Edn. Bur. Vocational Rehab., Pomona, 1971, Community Coop. Nursery Sch., Pomona; cons. Los Angeles County Dept. Adoptions, 1970—, San Bernardino County Welfare, 1972—. Mem. A.M.A., Am., So. Cal. psychiatric socs., Am. Med. Women's Assn., Am. Assn. Mental Deficiency. Author articles profl. jours. Home: 1890 Westwood Pl Pomona CA 91767 Office: 1842 N Garey Av Pomona CA 91767

FORBES, SARAH ELIZABETH, physician; b. Currituck, N.C.; d. Dexter Thomas and Mary (Brock) Forbes; B.A. U. Rochester, 1949; M.D., Med. Coll. Va., 1954. Intern, Norfolk (Va.) Gen. Hosp 1954-55, resident, 1955-58; resident Johnston-Willis Hosp., Richmond, Va., 1956-57; practice medicine specializing in obstetrics and gynecology, Newport News, Va., 1958—; mem. staff, teaching staff Riverside Hosp. Pres., Soc. for Prevention Cruelty to Animals, 1967—; dir., v.p. Cancer Soc., 1971-73, pres., 1973-74; chmn. Research for Cancer Soc., 1961-69; mem. bd. Family Planning Council, 1969—. Fellow Am. Coll. Obstetrics and Gynecology; mem. Tidewater Obstet. and Gynecol. Soc., Va. Peninsula Acad. Medicine (v.p. 1972-73, pres. 1973-74, sec.-treas. 1971-72), Newport News Med. Soc., Va. Med. Soc., A.M.A., Internat. Platform Assn. Home: 5 Merry Point Terrace Newport News VA 23606 Office: 12420 Warwick Blvd Newport News VA 23606

FORCE, MARYANNE TEFFT, mus. ofcl.; b. Peoria, Ill., Apr. 11, 1930; d. Lionel Victor and Marianne Elizabeth (Wilde) Tefft; A.B. in Sociology, Stanford, 1951, A.M. in Sociology, 1952; postgrad. Northwestern U., 1956-57, Walden U., 1974; m. Roland Winfield Force, Sept. 16, 1949. Teaching asst. Stanford, 1951-52, research asso., 1953-54; instr. social sci. San Francisco State Coll., 1953; teaching asst. Stanford, 1951-52, research asso. Tri-Instl. Pacific program, Palau Island, 1954-56; teaching asst. Northwestern U., 1956-57; instr. in anthropology U. Hawaii, Honolulu, 1963-66; coordinator spl. projects Bishop Mus., Honolulu, 1967-70, asso. urban studies, 1972—. Mem. policy bd. Windward Prep. Sch., Kailua, Hawaii, 1974. Mem. Am. Assn. Museums, Hawaii Hist. Soc., Pacific Sociol. Assn., Hawaii Museums Assn., Anthrop. Assn. Hawaii. Author: (with Roland Force) The A. W. Fuller Collection of Pacific Artifacts, 1971; (with Roland Force) Just Our House: A Description and Analysis of Kinship in the Palau Islands, 1972. Contbr. articles to sci. publs. Home: 161 Kalaiopua Pl Honolulu HI 90822 Office: PO Box 6037 Honolulu HI 96818

FORD, SISTER ELINOR RITA, supt. schs.; b. N.Y.C., 1930; d. William and Irene (Hochstrasser) Ford; grad. Fordham U.; Ed.D., Tchrs. Coll. of Columbia; LL.D., Marymount Manhattan Coll., 1973. Joined Order of Sisters of St. Dominic, 1949; tchr. upper elementary grades parochial schs., Bronx, Rockland County, 14 yrs.; chmn. math. and sci. dept. Dominican Coll. of Blauvelt; with office of edn. Roman Catholic Archdiocese N.Y., 1965—, asso. sch. supt. 1970-71, supt., 1972—; first councilor Sisters of St. Dominic, Blauvelt, N.Y., 1971-72. Address: 1011 1st Av New York City NY 10022

FORD, ELIZABETH BLOOMER (MRS. GERALD R. FORD), wife of Pres. of U.S.; b. Chgo., Apr. 8, 1918; d. William Stephenson and Hortence (Neahr) Bloomer; student Bennington Sch. Dance, 1936-38; m. William Warren, 1942 (div. 1947); m. 2d, Gerald R. Ford (38th Pres. U.S.), Oct. 15, 1948; children—Michael Gerald, John Garner, Steven Meigs, Susan Elizabeth. Dancer, Martha Graham Concert Group, N.Y.C., 1939-41; model John Powers Agy., N.Y.C., 1939-41; fashion dir. Herpolscheimer's Dept. Store, Grand Rapids, Mich., 1943-48; dance instr., Grand Rapids, 1932-48. Formerly active Cub Scouts Am.; formerly program chmn. Alexandria (Va.) Cancer Fund Drive; chmn. Heart Sunday, Washington Heart Assn., 1974; pres. Red Cross Senate Wives Club; patron Salvation Army Aux. Ann. Fashion Show Luncheon; active benefits Hosp. for Sick Children, Washington. Dir. League Republican Women; D.C. Episcopalian (Sunday sch. tchr. 1961-64). Home: White House 1600 Pennsylvania Av Washington DC 20500

FORD, EVELYN FRANCES, social work adminstr.; b. Quincy, Mass., Mar. 17, 1908; d. Dennis Joseph and Catherine Cecelia (Ryan) Ford; B.S. in Edn., Boston U., 1946, M.S. in Social Service 1950, postgrad., 1960; postgrad. Boston Coll., 1955. Social worker Quincy (Mass.) Dept. Pub. Welfare, 1932-42; with div. pub. assistance Mass. Dept. Pub. Welfare, 1942—, supr. social service, Greater Boston regional office, Boston, 1963—. Active Girl Scouts U.S.A., Quincy, 1922—, pres. bd. dirs., 1952-53, troop leader, 1931—, bd. dirs. Blue Hill council, 1964-68. Named Citizen of Year Quincy post Jewish War Vets., 1962. Mem. Nat. Assn. Social Workers (charter), Acad. Certified Social Workers (charter), Royal Soc. Health (London, licentiate mem.), Am. Pub. Welfare Assn., Mass. Conf. Social Welfare, Pub. Welfare Conf., Assn. Mass. Dept. Pub. Welfare Employees (vice chmn. 1955-56), Lesley Coll., Boston U. Sch. Edn., Boston U. Sch. Social Work alumni assns., Mass. State Guard Vets. Aux. (Quincy aux. pres. 1944-46, state pres. 1939-40). Clubs: Monday Lunch, Quincy Catholic, Quincy Girl Scout Leaders. Home: 52 Packard's Lane Quincy MA 02169

FORD, HELEN SARRELS, ind. oil operator; b. Anson, Tex., Jan. 23, 1917; d. Reuben Vance and Callie Maye (Carter) Sarrels; student Hardin Simmons U., 1935-36; grad. Draughons Bus. Coll., 1937; m. Philip Holman Ford, Mar. 10, 1941 (div.); children—Diane (Mrs. Diane Duck), John Vance. Civilian tng. adminstr. 2d Air Force, Abilene Air Base, Tex., 1942-45; sec., clk. Grisham-Hunter Corp., Abilene, 1947-50; sec., office mgr. E.F. White Oil Co., Abilene, 1950-55; mgr. John J. Eisner Oil Co., Abilene, Ft. Worth, 1955-70; ind. oil operator and producer, Ft. Worth, 1970—. Home and office: 2016 Grandview Dr Fort Worth TX 76112

FORD, JANE GRIFFITH, chem. co. exec.; b. Anderson, Ind., Mar. 25, 1918; d. Kenneth and Emmaline (Thomas) Griffith; student U. Louisville, 1943-44. Advt. dir. Farm Bur. Ins., Indpls., 1956-73; pub. relations dir. Brulin & Co., Inc., Indpls., 1973—. Named Advt. Woman of Year, Indpls. Ad Club, 1960-61. Mem. Pub. Relations Soc. Am., Women in Communication, Hoosier Press Women Ind., Ind. Bus. Communicators. Club: Civic Theater's Career Wing (Indpls.). Home: 5940 Evanston Av Indianapolis IN 46220 Office: 2920 Martindale St Indianapolis IN 46205

FORD, JEAN (MRS. SAMUEL M. FORD), state legislator, civic worker; b. Miami, Okla., Dec. 28, 1929; d. Clarence N. and Daisy (Flook) Young; B.A. in Sociology, So. Meth. U., 1951; m. Samuel M. Ford, Apr. 9, 1955; children—Janet Lynn, Carla Marie. Recreation specialist A.R.C., 1951-55; tchr.'s aide, Las Vegas Elementary Sch., 1963-64; mem. Nev. Legislature, 1972—. Mem. local bd. League Women Voters, 1964, pres., 1965-67, state bd., 1967-69, state pres., 1969-71; mem. Nev. State Park Commn., 1967-73, Nev. Outdoor Recreation Coordinating Com., 1966-70; policy bd. Rehab. Planning, 1969-71; chmn. ad hoc com. to create pub. library dist. in urban area, 1965-66; chmn. Nev. Air Quality Conf., 1971; mem. citizen's adv. bd. to Toiyabe Nat. Forest, 1970-72; mem. Western regional adv. com. Nat. Park Service, 1974—. Bd. dirs. Nev. Wildlife Fedn., Nat. Conf. Christians and Jews, Clark County Youth Services Commn., Clark County Recycling Center. Mem. Nat. Parks Assn., Wilderness Soc., Common Cause, Nev. Open Spaces Council. Club: Sierra. Republican. Unitarian. Home: 3511 Pueblo Way Las Vegas NV 89109

FORD, LEE ELLEN, scientist, educator, writer, lawyer, editor; b. Auburn, Ind., June 16, 1917; d. Arthur W. and Geneva (Muhn) Ford; B.A., Wittenberg Coll., 1947; M.S., U. Minn., 1949; Ph.D., Ia. State Coll., 1952; J.D., U. Notre Dame, 1972. CPA auditing, 1934-44; asso. prof. biology Gustavus Adolphus Coll., 1950-51, Anderson (Ind.) Coll., 1952-55; vis. prof. biology U. Alta. (Can.), Calgary, 1955-56; asso. prof. biology Pacific Lutheran U., Parkland, Wash., 1956-62; prof. biology and cytogenetics Miss. State Coll. for Women, 1962-64; chief cytogeneticist Pacific N.W. Research Found., Seattle, 1964-65; dir. Canine Genetics Cons. Service, Parkland, Wash., 1963-69; sponsor Companion Collies for the Adult, Jr. Blind, 1955-65; manpower economist Nev. Dept. Labor, also head research unit Nev. Employment Security Dept., Carson City, 1966-68; dir. Genetics Research Lab., Butler, Ind., 1955—, cons. cytogenetics, 1969—; dir. chromosome lab. Inst. Basic Research in Mental Retardation, S.I., N.Y., 1968-69; legislative cons., Butler, 1969—; exec. dir. Legislative Bur., U. Notre Dame Law Sch., also editor New Dimensions in Legislation, 1969-70; practiced in Butler, Ind., 1972—; owner, pub., editor Butler Record Herald, 1972—; exec. asst. for human resources and human rights Gov. of Ind., 1972—; pres. Ford Assos., pubs., Butler, 1972—. Cons. on minority bus., cities and towns Affirmative Action Program. Adult counselor Girl Scouts U.S.A. Mem. or ex-mem. Am. Assn. U. Women, A.A.A.S., Genetics Soc. Am., Am. Human Genetics Soc., Am. Genetic Assn., Am. Inst. Biol. Scis., Am. Soc. Zoologists, La., Miss., Ind., Ia. acads. sci., Bot. Soc. Am., Ecol. Soc. Am., Bus. and Profl. Women's Club. Assn. So. Biologists, Am., Ind., Marion County, Indpls. bar assns., Nat. Assn. Women Lawyers, Nat. Orgn. Women, Am. Women in Sci., Women's Equity Action League, Phi Kappa Phi. Club: Altrusa. Editor: Breeder's Jour., 1958-63, Directory of Women Attys. in U.S.A., 1972; also numerous vols. dog genetics and breeding, and guide dogs for the blind. Contbr. articles on cytogenetics to profl. jours.; active contbr. Am. Kennel Club Gazette, others. Researcher in field. Home: 701 S Federal Av Butler IN 46721

FORD, MAYETTA LEWIS, psychologist; b. Fayetteville, N.C., Oct. 1, 1912; d. John Frank and Margaret Dora (McKoy) Lewis; normal sch. diploma Va. State Coll., 1941, B.S., 1949, M.S., 1959; postgrad. N.C. Central U., summer 1950, Columbia, summer 1961; m. Junious Ford, Apr. 29, 1933 (dec.); 1 dau., Margaret Elizabeth. Tchr. pub. schs., Southampton County, Va., 1941-50, Henderson, N.C., 1950-59, Salisbury, Md., 1959-60; sch. psychologist Norfolk (Va.) Schs., 1960—. Instr. psychology Norfolk State Coll. Evening Sch., 1966—. Chmn., Cavalier Manor Civic League, 1966-73; sec. Portsmouth-Chesapeake Council on Human Relations, 1970—; mem. Portsmouth City Commn. on Museums and Fine Arts; chmn. edn. com. Central Civic Forum, 1968. Mem. Am. Assn. U. Women (edn. com.), Nat. Assn. Coll. Women (pres. Portsmouth br. 1968—), Tidewater (pres. 1969—), Va. assns. sch. psychologists, Tidewater Assn. Retarded Children, Psi Chi, Phi Delta Kappa. Methodist (asst. clk. 1970—, sec. Fgn. Missionary Soc. 1970—). Contbr. articles to profl. publs. Home: 405 Tazewell St Portsmouth VA 23701 Office: 800 E City Hall Av Norfolk VA 23510

FORD, NANCY TORBETT (MRS. CHARLES E. FORD, JR.), banker; b. Tampa, Fla.; d. Ralph S. and Jessie (Newberry) Torbett; B.A., Randolph Macon Woman's Coll., 1948; m. Charles E. Ford, Jr., Apr. 21, 1950; children—Nancy Joan, Charlton Marjorie. Tchr. pub. schs., Tampa, Atlanta, 1950-53; realtor Otto Johnson, Inc., Tampa, 1964-66; pub. relations officer 1st Nat. Bank, Tampa, 1966-69, asst. v.p., 1969-72, v.p., 1972—. Mem. Gov's Commn. on Status of Women, 1966-70, Children's Commn. Hillsborough County, 1965-71; pres. Guidance Center Hillsborough County, 1963-64, Tampa Philharmonic Assn., 1966-70, St. Joseph's Hosp. Devel. Council, 1972-74; bd. dirs. Fla. Gulf Coast Symphony, Inc., 1968-70; v.p., pres. elect United Cerebral Palsy, 1973-74; pres. Jr. League, Tampa, 1964-65. Mem. Nat. Assn. Bank Women, Alpha Delta Pi. Home: 836 Bayside Dr Tampa FL 33609 Office: 1st Financial Tower Tampa FL 33602

FORD, PAULA BAGBY (MRS. JOHN C. FORD), psychologist; b. Murfreesboro, Tenn., Feb. 24, 1945; d. Robert Paul and Faye (Maynard) Bagby; B.S., Ohio State U., 1967, M.A., 1971, postgrad., 1971-72; m. John C. Ford, June 22, 1968; 1 son, Justin Robert. Reading specialist Rosemont Sch. for Girls, Columbus, O., 1967; speech and hearing therapist Upper Arlington City Schs., Columbus, 1967-68, Baltimore County Sch., Md., 1968, Clermont County Schs., Ohio, 1969, Upper Arlington City Schs., Columbus, O., 1969-71; intern sch. psychologist Springfield (O.) Pub. Schs., 1971-72, psychologist, 1974—; sch. psychologist, dir. testing Pickaway County (O.) Schs., 1973-74. Cons., Program Mentally Handicapped, Pickaway County, 1973-74. Treas. Twig 170 of Children's Hosp., Columbus, 1973, v.p., 1974, chmn., 1974. NSF scholar, 1965. Mem. Nat., Ohio edn. assns., Nat., Ohio, Central Ohio assns. sch. psychologists, Ohio Speech and Hearing Assn., Kappa Delta, Sigma Alpha Eta (asso.). Home: 4889 Arthur Place Columbus OH 43220

FORD, RUTH VAN SICKLE (MRS. ALBERT G. FORD), artist, educator; b. Aurora, Ill., Aug. 8, 1897; d. Charles P. and Anna (Miller) Van Sickle; student Chgo. Acad. Fine Arts, 1915-18, Art Students League, summers 1916-17; m. Albert G. Ford, Feb. 7, 1918; 1 dau., Barbara (Mrs. Rodman Turner). One-man shows, Chgo. Art Inst., Grand Central Galleries, N.Y.C., 1947, Mexico City Country Club, Oklahoma City Art Center, 1948, Pomona Coll., Claremont, Cal., Hickory Mus. Art, N.C., 1948, Laguna Beach (Cal.) Art Assn., Centre D'Art, Port-au-Prince, Haiti, 1949, Palmer House Galleries, Chgo., 1949; exhibited in group shows at N.A.D., N.Y.C., Chgo. and Vicinity Artists Show at Chgo. Art Inst., Internat. Water Color Shows, Am. Artists Show at Art Inst., Pa. Acad. Ann. Water Color Show, Nat.

Assn. Women Artists, 1949, Traveling Water Color Show, Oakland (Cal.) Art Gallery, 1949, Argent Gallery, N.Y.C., 1949, Miami Beach (Fla.) Art Center, Chgo. Painter and Sculptors Shows, Am. Water Color Soc., N.Y.C., Water Color, U.S.A., pres., dir. Chgo. Acad. Fine Arts, 1937-60; instr. art Aurora Coll., 1964-72. Recipient numerous art awards. Mem. Conn. Acad., Grand Central Galleries, Chgo. Painters and Sculptors Assn., Salon Women Painters, Nat. Assn. Women Artists N.Y., Artists Guild Chgo. (hon.), Palette and Chisel Acad., Am. Artist Prof. League, Rockport (Mass.) Art Assn., Am. Watercolor Soc., Clinton Art Assn. (asso.), Palette and Chisel (hon.). Home and studio: 69 Central St Aurora IL 60506

FORD, YOLANDE WILLIAMSON (MRS. CLAUDE A. FORD), ednl. adminstr.; b. N.Y.C., May 8, 1929; d. W. Austin and Rose Everett (Williamson) Williamson; B.A., Howard U., 1951, M.A., 1952; m. Claude A. Ford, Aug. 27, 1953; children—Claude A., Diane E. Asst. dir. community programs, pilot communities project Ednl. Devel. Corp., Washington, 1969-71; asst. dir. model sch. div., coordinator coll. and univ. affairs D.C. Pub. Schs., 1971; dir. human relations programs, College Park campus U. Md., 1971—. Cons. Assn. Am. Colls., Urban Research Corp., Volt, Nat. Adv. Council on Vocational Edn. Mem. adv. com. project on status and edn. of women Assn. Am. Colls., 1972-73; mem. Md. Gov.'s Task Force on Desegregation in Higher Edn., 1973-74; pres. Action in Montgomery County, Inc., 1973-74. Mem. governing bd. Urban Inst., Washington Council Chs., 1968-69. Chmn. human relations subcom. Dem. Central Com., Montgomery County, Md., 1973-74; Md. del. Nat. Black Polit. Assembly, 1973. Mem. Nat. Council Negro Women (mem. commn. on black women in higher edn. 1972-74), Md. Assn. Higher Edn., Delta Sigma Theta. Home: 13308 Partridge Dr Silver Spring MD 20904 Office: Room 1112 Main Adminstrn Bldg U Md College Park MD 20742

FORDEN, AMY ADAMS (MRS. WILLIAM THEODORE FORDEN), former museum curator; b. Aurora, N.Y., Feb. 10, 1893; d. William H. and Sara B. (Warner) Adams; grad. high sch.; m. William Theodore Forden, Aug. 29, 1925; children—David W., Mary E. (Mrs. Adelbert W. Whitman). With accounting dept. Spencer Kellogg & Sons, Buffalo, 1919-24; with Buffalo Mus. Sci., 1924-25; tchr. home econs. Buffalo grade schs., 1925-26; curator museums Aurora Hist. Soc., East Aurora, N.Y., 1960-74. Mem. Aurora Hist. Soc. (pres. 1954-57). Home: 50 Hedgerow Dr Hamburg NY 14075

FOREMAN, HELEN PULVER, micropaleontologist; b. West New York, N.J., July 21, 1923; d. Emil Adolph and Fanny Frieda (Walser) Pulver; A.B., Berea Coll., 1946; M.A., Oberlin Coll., 1948; m. Fred Foreman, Jan. 30, 1950. Geologist, U.S. Geol. Survey, 1948-50; research asso. geology dept. Oberlin (O.) Coll., 1960—. Mem. Paleontol. Soc., Paleontol. Research Assn., Sigma Xi. Home: 131 S Professor St Oberlin OH 44074

FOREMAN, LAURA, dancer, choreographer, educator; b. Los Angeles; d. Michael and Gladys (Charnas) Foreman; student Mills Coll., Oakland, Cal. 1955-56; B.S. in Dance, U. Wis., 1959; m. John Everett Watts, Dec. 5, 1963. Mem. Ann Halprin Workshop Group, San Francisco, 1955, Marion Scott Dance Co., N.Y.C., Tamiris-Nagrin Dance Co., N.Y.C., 1962-64, Choreographers Theatre, N.Y.C., 1969—; dir. Laura Foreman Co., N.Y.C., 1966—; founder, dir. Choreographers Theatre and ChoreoConcerts, N.Y.C., 1964—; choreography instr. C.W. Post Coll., L.I., summer 1963; head dance dept. U. Bridgeport, 1960-63; head dance dept. Notre Dame Coll., 1963-70; mem. faculty, dir. dance dept. New Sch. Social Research, N.Y.C., 1967—; commd. dances Channel 31 TV, 1966, Nat. Council Chs., 1967, Cultural Council Found., 1970, 73, Choreographers Theatre, 1970-73, Nat. Endowment for Arts, 1971, 73; dance dir. bd. dirs. Composers & Choreographers Theatre, Inc. Cons., Woodstock Center, N.Y. State Council on Arts. Audition winner Contemporary Dance Prodns., Inc., N.Y.C., 1961. Mem. Nat. Dance Guild, Assn. Am. Dance Cos. (dir.). Choregraphy includes Memorials, Study, A Time, Perimeters, Epicycles, Margins, Signals, glass and shadows, Laura's Dance, songandance, Locrian, Spaces (Collage I-IV), Performanceàdeux. Home: 25 W 19th St New York City NY 10011 Office: New Sch Social Research 66 W 12th St New York City NY 10011

FORER, LUCILLE KREMITH (MRS. BERTRAM R. FORER), clin. psychologist; b. Springfield, Ill.; d. William Frederick and JoAnn Marie (Teubner) Kremith; B.A., U. Tex., 1940; M.A., U. So. Cal., 1942, Ph.D., 1953; m. Bertram R. Forer, Sept. 27, 1941; children—Stephen Keith, William Robert. Personnel officer and adminstrv. officer Office of Adminstr., OPA, Washington, 1942-45; tchr., coordinator testing program psychol. clinic U. Cal. at Los Angeles, 1947-49; asst. prof. psychology Cal. State U., Los Angeles, 1953-58; pvt. practice clin. psychology, 1953—. Psychol. cons., Larri E. Welty Center Ednl. Therapy, Los Angeles, 1969—. Mem. Graphics Council, Los Angeles Mus. Art, 1965—. Bd. dirs. Psychol. Center Los Angeles, 1971-73. Fellow, Soc. Personality Assessment; mem. Am., Western, Cal., Los Angeles County psychol. assns., Hollywood C. of C., League Women Voters, Am. Assn. Univ. Women (chmn. edn. Los Angeles chpt.) Author: Birth Order and Life Roles, 1969. Home and Office: 2170 E Live Oak Dr Los Angeles CA 90068

FORESMAN, MARGARET MILLER, newspaper editor; b. Russell, Ky., Jan. 29, 1920; d. Glenn Earl and Eula Blanche (Haight) Miller; B.A., Pittsburg State Coll., Kan., 1941; children—Elizabeth (Mrs. R.L. Parlett), James L., Robert, Timothy. City editor Key West (Fla.) Citizen, 1952-60, mng. editor, 1960. Mem. Am. Assn. U. Women, Kappa Delta Pi. Presbyn. Home: 1117 Watson St Key West FL 33040 Office: 515 Greene St Key West FL 33040

FORESTER, JEAN MARTHA BROUILLETTE (MRS. JAMES LAWRENCE FORESTER), educator, librarian; b. Port Barre, La., Sept. 7, 1934; d. Joseph Walter and Thelma (Brown) Brouillette; B.S., La. State U., 1955; M.A. (Carnegie fellow 1955-56), George Peabody Coll. Tchrs., 1956; m. James Lawrence Forester, June 2, 1957; children—Jean Martha, James Lawrence. Librarian Howell Elementary Sch., Springhill, La., 1956-58; asst. post librarian Fort Chaffee, Ark., 1958; command librarian Orleans Area Command, U.S. Army, Orleans, France, 1958-59; acquisitions librarian Northwestern State U., Matchitoches, La., 1960; serials librarian La. State U., New Orleans, 1960-66; mem. faculty La. State U., Eunice, 1966—, asst. librarian, asst. prof., 1972—. Active Eunice Assn. Retarded Children. Mem. La. Library Assn. (sect. sec. 1971-72), Delta Kappa Gamma (chpt. parliamentarian 1972—), Alpha Beta Alpha, Phi Gamma Mu, Phi Mu. Democrat. Baptist. Home: 1351 Gregg Av Eunice LA 70535

FORGETT, HEIDI E. KOBER (MRS. VALMORE JOSEPH FORGETT, JR.), corp. exec.; b. Treuberg, Germany, Feb. 27, 1939; d. Otto and Gertrud (Hearich) Kober; student Columbia Union Coll., 1959-60, Fairleigh Dickinson U., 1960-62; m. Valmore Joseph Forgett, Jr., Apr. 28, 1963; children—Diana Lynn, Susan Lee, Valmore Joseph III. Came to U.S., 1954, naturalized, 1959. Corp. sec., treas. Service Armament Co., Ridgefield, N.J., 1959—, Navy Arms Co., Inc., Ridgefield, 1960—, Gt. Am. Arms Corp., Ridgefield, 1960—, Collectors' Arms Inc., Ridgefield, 1964—; dir. Ebbs-Forgett Trading Co. Ltd., Birmingham, Eng. Mem. Ohio Gun Collectors Assn. Republican. Home: Eagle's Roost 60 Pinecrest Dr Woodcliff Lake NJ 07675 also Cannon Hill Farm Box 311B Sussex NJ 07641 Office: 689 Bergen Blvd Ridgefield NJ 07657

FORKER, BARBARA ELLEN, educator; b. Kendallville, Ind., Aug. 28, 1920; d. Frank Rigdon and Bessie (Oviatt) Forker; B.S., Eastern Mich. U., 1942; M.S., Ia. State U., 1950; Ph.D., U. Mich., 1957. Tchr. phys. edn. Wyandotte (Mich.) Pub. Schs., 1942-45; served with A.R.C., European Theater, 1945-47; instr. Ia. State U., Ames, 1948-49, asst. prof., 1949-52, asso. prof., 1952-57, prof. physical edn., 1957—, head dept., 1958—. Chmn. water safety A.R.C., 1951-65; mem. Govs. Council Phys. Fitness, 1958—. Bd. dirs. West Story County chpt. A.R.C., 1960-66, sec., 1961-64. Mem. Ia. (pres. 1958-59), Central Dist. (pres. 1965-66), assns. health, phys. edn. and recreation, Am. Coll. Sports Medicine, A.A.H.P.E.R. (v.p. 1969-70, pres. 1972-73), Nat. (sec. 1966-68), Central (v.p. 1962-64) assns. phys. edn. coll. women, Am. Acad. Phys. Edn. Home: 1108 Wisconsin St Ames IA 50010

FORMAN, BRENDA, govt. ofcl.; b. Hollywood, Cal., Aug. 1, 1936; d. Harrison and Sandra (Carlyle) Forman; B.A., Barnard Coll., 1956; Ph.D. (univ. fellow, Herbert A. Lehman fellow), City U. N.Y., 1969. Free-lance writer juvenile ednl. subjects, 1956-64; systems analyst Mitre Corp., McLean, Va., 1969-73; fgn. affairs analyst Office of Asst. Sec. Def. for Internat. Security Affairs, Washington, 1973—. Speaker various community groups. Fellow European Inst., Columbia U., 1964-65. Mem. Phi Beta Kappa. Author: The Land and People of Nigeria, 1964; The Famous First Name Series, 1964; The Story of Thailand, 1965; America's Place in the World Economy, 1969. Home: 2401 Elba Ct Alexandria VA 22306 Office: OASD/ISA/PP&NSCA Room 4C760 The Pentagon Washington DC 20301

FORNELL, MARTHA STEINMETZ (MRS. EARL WESLEY FORNELL), educator; b. Galveston, Tex., Dec. 19, 1920; d. Joseph Duncan and Martha Lillian (McRee) Steinmetz; B.Mus. cum laude, U. Tex., 1943; postgrad. U. Houston, 1953-56, Lamar U., 1957-60; m. Earl Wesley Fornell, Sept. 20, 1947 (dec. Mar. 1969). Music cons., fgn. program editor Voice of America, USIA, N.Y.C., 1944-46; advt. cons. fed. agys., San Antonio, 1946-47; tchr. music secondary schs., Houston, 1953-56; tchr. art Beaumont (Tex.) Ind. Sch. Dist., 1956—. Vol. sponsor A.R.C., 1958—. Recipient Circuit awards Tex. Fine Arts Assn., 1962-64, Invitational awards, 1964-65. Mem. N.E.A., Mu Phi Epsilon. Contbr. articles to Am.-German Rev. Address: 539 14th St Beaumont TX 77702

FORNEY, DEANNA SUE, univ. adminstr.; b. Somerset, Pa., Mar. 27, 1947; d. Richard Dean and Madge Eileen (Goldsboro) Forney; B.A., Gettysburg Coll., 1969; M.A., Pa. State U., 1971. Social worker Adams County (Pa.) Community Action Agy., 1969; resident hall dir. State U. at Oswego (N.Y.), 1971-72; complex coordinator U. Del., Newark, 1972-74; asso. dir. career services Allegheny Coll., Meadville, Pa., 1974—. Mem. Am. Coll. and Univ. Housing Officers (state rep. to exec. com. 1973-74), Nat. Assn. Student Personnel Adminstrs., Nat. Assn. Women Deans, Adminstrs. and Counselors, Am. Personnel and Guidance Assn., Am., Del. coll. personnel assns., Middle Atlantic Placement Assn., Iota Alpha Delta. Home: 202 B Woodland Heights RD #6 Arthur St Meadville PA 16335 Office: 400 N Main St Allegheny Coll Meadville PA 16335

FORNEY, DOROTHY MARIE ALLARD (MRS. BEECHER W. FORNEY), state ofcl.; b. Haverhill, Mass., Aug. 12, 1918; d. Henry Louis and Yvonne Marie (Chagnon) Allard; student courses trade assn. mgmt. Northwestern U., 1953-54; B. Profl. Studies, Elizabethtown Coll., 1973; m. Beecher William Forney, Nov. 23, 1939; children—Sandra Louise, Lynda Yvonne, Paula Irene. Asst. to exec. dir. Nat. Inst. Locker and Freezer Provisioners, Elizabethtown, Pa., 1951-62; exec. sec. Pa. Assn. Locker and Freezer Provisioners, 1956-67; reporter, feature writer Elizabethtown Chronicle, 1966-67; Eastern corr. Freezer Provisioning Mag., St. Louis, 1963-71; sec. State Senator Richard A. Snyder, Lancaster County, Pa., 1963—, clk. exec. nominations, 1965-66, clk. to mil. affairs and aeros. com., 1967-68; research analyst Pa. Senate minority caucus, 1971-73, exec. research analyst, 1973—. Mem. Parastudy, Inc., Chester Heights, Pa., 1959—, bd. dirs., 1964-66; founder, chmn. Lancaster Psychical Research Group, 1964—; chmn. Elizabethtown area United Campaign, 1966; mem. Elizabethtown Area Music Found.; charter mem. Hist. Restoration Found. Lancaster County, 1967—; mem. Elizabeth Hughes Soc., 1944-52; pub. information officer Nat. Welfare Fraud Assn., 1972—. Republican committeewoman Ward 2, Elizabethtown, 1962—; bd. dirs. Women's Rep. Club, Lancaster, 1963-68; area chmn. Elizabethtown Area Rep. Orgn., Lancaster County, 1970—. Recipient Pub. Service award Nat. Police Officers Assn., Port Charlotte, Fla., 1967. Mem. Pa. Assn. Locker and Freezer Provisioners (editor Cold Facts 1956-67, hon. life), Elizabethtown C. of C. (writer, condr. radio-tv programs, chmn. community information com. 1967-68). Mem. Order Eastern Star. Club: Soroptimist (del. nat. conv. 1963) (Hershey-Elizabethtown). Address: 419 Ridge View Av Elizabethtown PA 17022

FORREST, MURIEL SHOR (MRS. BERNARD J. FORREST), psychologist; b. N.Y.C., Apr. 13, 1924; d. David Arthur and Tovah (Elkes) Shor; B.S. cum laude, Coll. City N.Y., 1960, M.S., 1964; m. Bernard J. Forrest, Apr. 4, 1943; children—April Jill (Mrs. Barry Alan Farber), Wayne Jeffrey. Adminstr. asst., personnel search sect. War Dept., Adj. Gen.'s Office, N.Y.C., 1943-46; clin. asst. ednl. clinic Coll. City N.Y. Sch. Edn., 1964-67; elementary sch. psychologist Edgemont Sch. Dist., Scarsdale, N.Y., 1967—. Program chmn. Ardsley (N.Y.) Elementary P.T.A., 1960-61, 1st v.p., 1961-62. Mem. Am., N.Y. State, Westchester psychol. assns., Nat. Assn. Sch. Psychologists, Coll. City N.Y. City U. Alumni Assn. Home: 4 Markwood Pl Ardsley NY 10502 Office: Edmont Sch Dist Glendale Rd Scarsdale NY 10583

FORREST, VIRGINIA OGDEN RANSON (MRS. WILBUR STUDLEY FORREST), civic leader; b. Balt., June 24, 1896; d. Henry Warfield and Nannie Deaver (Cooper) Ranson; ed. Calvert Sch., Arundell Sch.; m. Frederick Beasley Williamson, Jr., July 5, 1917 (dec. July 1957); children—Virginia (Mrs. Lefferts Hutton), Beverley (Mrs. Winfield Magill), Frederick Beasley III; m. 2d, Wilbur Studley Forrest, Apr. 20, 1960. Dir., Goodall Rubber Co., hon. dir., 1973—. Pres. Jr. League, Elizabeth, N.J., 1924-26, hon. mem., 1944; mem. hostess com. Franklin Inst., Phila., 1941; mem. N.J. Recreation Soc., Elizabeth, 1934-35, rep. N.J. to nat. conv., Chgo., 1935; chmn. New Hope (Pa.) chpt. A.R.C., 1939-43, head flood disaster chpt., 1955, chmn. home service, 1943-45; hon. v.p. New Hope Art Assos., 1940; mem. adv. com. Jonathan Dickinson State Park, Martin County, Fla., 1970—; organizer adviser Bucks County Conservation Alliance. Bd. dirs. Martin County Conservation Alliance, 1966-74, Honey Hollow Watershed Assn., 1969—, Soc. Prevention Cruelty Children Family Welfare Bd., Elizabeth, 1928, YWCA, Elizabeth, 1928, Abington (Pa.) Meml. Hosp. Women's Bd., 1941, Vis. Nurse Assn., New Hope, 1941-49; bd. dirs., 2d v.p. Garden Club, Stuart, Fla., 1951-60; trustee Egnolf Day Nursery, Elizabeth, 1923-36; trustee Holmquist Sch. for Girls, New Hope, Martin County Pub. Library, Stuart, 1958-61; bd. dirs. Free Pub. Library Elizabeth, 1926-39, sec., 1927-36; bd. dirs. Keep Fla. Beautiful Com. Recipient award Fla. Fedn. Garden Clubs, 1961; Gov.'s gold medal conservation award (1st woman recipient), 1961; Gov. Kirk's Conservation award, 1970. Mem. Fla. (recipient award 1960, chmn. Bald Eagle project 1959—, mem. wild life com. 1959—, v.p. 1962-69, hon. v.p. 1970—), Martin County (dir. 1957—, chmn. exec. com. 1973-74), Bucks County (dir., adviser, citation for conservation, 1972) audubon socs., New Hope Hist. Soc. (dir. 1959-60, 67—), Fla. Fedn. Garden Clubs (hon. life), Colonial Dames N.J., Woman Fly Fishers Am. Clubs: Mt. Vernon (Balt.); Hartwood (Monticello, N.Y.); Martin County Anglers (dir. 1966—). Home: The Birches RD 2 New Hope PA 18938

FORSCHNER, JOYCE ELIZABETH HOYNG (MRS. BRIAN EUGENE FORSCHNER), psychologist; b. Celina, O., June 3, 1945; d. Ernest Joseph and Helen Elizabeth (Losche) Hoyng; B.A., U. Dayton, 1967, M.S., 1971; m. Brian Eugene Forschner, July 1, 1972; 1 dau., Joy Christine. Probation counselor Montgomery County Juvenile Ct., Dayton, O., 1967-69; sch. psychologist intern Wilmington (O.) City Schs., 1970-71; sch. psychologist Northridge Local Schs., Dayton, O., 1971-73. Religious edn. tchr., Confrat. Christian Doctrine Program, 1972—; newsletter editor, dir. child care unit Montgomery County Juvenile Ct. Vol. Program, 1973—. Mem. Council Exceptional Children, Nat. Assn. Sch. Psychologists, Ohio, Southwestern Ohio sch. psychologists assns. Democrat. Roman Catholic. Home: 4444 Banning Av Dayton OH 45405

FORSEE, AYLESA, author; b. Kirksville, Mo.; d. Edward Wycliffe and Lena (Moore) Forsee; B.S., S.D. State 1., Mus.B., MacPhail Coll. Music, 1938; M.A., U. Colo., 1939. Tchr., adminstr. Rochester (Minn.) Sr. High Sch., 1939-45; instr. U. Ia., 1945-46; asst. prof. U. Denver, 1946-49; adult educator Denver YWCA, 1949-56; free-lance writer, Boulder, Colo., 1956—; faculty Temple Buell Workshop Children's Lit., Denver, summers 1967, 68. Recipient Helen Dean Fish award, 1956; Colo. Authors' League Top Hand award, 1966, 69. Author: The Whirly Bird, 1955; Miracle for Mingo, 1956; Too Much Dog, 1957; American Women Who Scored Firsts, 1958; Louis Agassiz: Pied Piper of Science, 1958; Frank Lloyd Wright: Rebel in Concrete, 1959; Women Who Reached for Tomorrow, 1960; My Love and I Together, 1961; Beneath Land and Sea, 1962; Albert Einstein: Theoretical Physicist, 1963; William Henry Jackson: Pioneer Photographer of the West, 1964; Pablo Casals: Cellist for Freedom, 1965; Men of Modern Architecture, 1966; Headliners, 1967; Famous Photographers, 1968; Arthur Rubinstein: King of the Keyboard, 1969. Address: 1845 Bluebell Av Boulder CO 80302

FORST, FLORENCE HANDY, educator; b. Pullman, Wash., Aug. 2, 1914; d. Fred Morton and Florence Jane (George) Handy; B.A., Wash. State U., 1936; M.A., Ill. Inst. Tech., 1946; Ph.D., U. Pitts., 1962; m. Edward Forst, Aug. 2, 1941; children—Mary Ann (Mrs. James R. Barbee). Tchr. high sch. Chehalis, Wash., 1936-39; instr. fine arts Pa. State U., 1939-42. Design cons., Chgo., 1943-47; instr. U. Minn. at Mpls., 1949-51; asst. prof. design and edn. Carnegie Inst. Tech., Pitts., 1954-63; asst., then asso. prof., prof. ednl. psychology Cal. State U. at Long Beach, 1963—. Chmn. edn. com. Nat. Orgn. Women, Long Beach, 1971-72. Mem. Am. Ednl. Research Assn., Cal. Ednl. Research Assn., Nat. Assn. Ednl. Communications and Tech., Cal. Audio-visual Assn., Women in Cal. Higher Edn., Cal. Coll. and Univ. Faculty Assn., Soc. Tech. Communications, Internat. Soc. Gen. Semantics (dir.), Phi Beta Kappa, Kappa Alpha Theta. Mng. editor ETC jour. Internat. Soc. Gen. Semantics, 1970—. Home: 5524 Oleta St Long Beach CA 90815

FORSYTH, ARDYS ELIZABETH, curator; b. Waterloo, Ia., Aug. 24, 1913; d. George Lawrence and Lucile B. (Caughlan) Stevens; student Poly. Bus. Sch., Los Angeles, 1932-33; m. David Stewart Forsyth, June 30, 1935; children—David Stewart, Norman Allen (dec.). Vol. community services, 1940—; dir. Centinela Adobe Mus., Los Angeles, 1966-71, curator, 1972—. Field chmn. March of Dimes, 1951-56; sec. Manhattan Beach (Cal.) Community Fair, 1953-54; mem. Am. Field Service Com., 1955-57. Mem. Hist. Soc. Centinela Valley (dir. 1965—), Cal. Congress P.T.A. (hon. life mem.), Euterpe Opera Club (life). Author publs. on Cal. history. Home: 1137 Ronda Dr Manhattan Beach CA 90266

FORSYTH, LOUISE BIRNIE, guidance counselor; b. Quincy, Mass., Sept. 28, 1920; d. George D. and Annie (Birnie) Forsyth; B.S., Mass. State Coll., Bridgewater, 1941; M.A., Coll. William and Mary, 1943; postgrad., Boston U., 1948-60. Tchr., counselor Pembroke (Mass.) High Sch., 1942-43, South Jr. High Sch., Quincy, 1943-57; counselor North Quincy High Sch., 1957-59; head counselor Atlantic Jr. High Sch., Quincy, 1959-65; coordinator city-wide testing program, guidance information services Quincy Pub. Schs., 1965—. Guidance cons. Mass. sch. systems; lectr. to profl. groups. Chmn. Red Cross Youth, Greater Quincy chpt. A.R.C., 1950-64, bd. dirs., 1951—, sec., 1962—, leader A.R.C. internat. study visit to Europe, 1957, mem. adv. com. on internat. activities, 1952—, staff mem. leadership devel. centers, 1950-58, recipient Certificate of Merit, 1964; mem. program adv. com. 1000 So. Artery Sr. Citizen Center, 1965—. Mem. Am. (Sch. Counselor of Yr. award 1973, Guidance Adminstr. of Yr. award 1973, Profl. Writing award 1973), Mass. (pres. 1967-68, exec. sec. 1969-73, Distinguished Leadership award 1973) sch. counselors assns., New Eng. Personnel and Guidance Conf. (chmn. com. printing and mailing, mem. conf. exec. bd. and gov. bd. 1966-69), South Shore Assn. Women in Guidance, Nat. Vocational Guidance Assn., Assn. for Measurement and Evaluation in Guidance, Am., Mass. (1st exec. council 1966-69), Greater Boston personnel and guidance assns., Quincy Edn. Assn., N.E.A., Altrusa, Delta Kappa Gamma. Conglist. (ch. clk. 1960-71, moderator 1972—). Home: 75 Monroe Rd Quincy MA 02169 Office: Quincy Public Schools Quincy MA 02169

FORTENBERRY, DIANE DAWSON, advt. and sales promotion exec.; b. Jackson, Miss., Nov. 24, 1933; d. Hendrix Avera and Kathryn (Howle) Dawson; student Miss. State Coll. for Women, 1951-52, U. Miss., 1953-54; m. Ralph Morgan Fortenberry, Feb. 5, 1955 (div. Feb. 1966); children—Teresa Lynn, Cheryl Diane, Rance Morgan, Steven Ralph. Copywriter, layout artist Kennington's Dept. Store, Jackson, Miss., 1954-55; advt. mgr. Gus Meyer (formerly Giles, Inc.), Jackson, 1955-56; advt. exec. Kennington's Dept. Store, Jackson, 1960-61; women's asst. editor Clarion-Ledger Newspaper, Jackson, 1965-66; advt. and sales promotion mgr. Emporium, Jackson, 1966-71, also dir.; v.p., mgr. Adco Advt. Agy., Jackson, 1971-73; advt. mgr., exec. asst. to pres. George Bell Carpets, Inc., Jackson, 1973—. Exhibited one-man show aux. Wolfe Gallery Jackson Municipal Art Gallery, 1950. Chmn. Officer's Wives Charity Bazaar Pensacola Naval Air Sta., Pensacola, Fla., 1963. Mem. Greater Jackson Advt. Club (chmn. 1st advt. workshop 1967; sec. 1969-71, dir. 1969-71), Phi Mu. Home: 1511 Myrtle St Jackson MS 39202 Office: 932 N State St PO Box 1633 Jackson MS 39206

FORTIER, LILLIAN S., broadcasting exec.; b. New Orleans, Mar. 25; ed. U. Cal., Los Angeles City Coll.; m. Joseph William Fortier (div.); children—Joseph William III, Dwight Drummond, Jacqueline Alma Noble, Alfred Walter. Exec. dir. Fortier Assos., pub. relations, 1959-64; pub. service dir. sta. KPIX-TV, 1964-66; asso. dir. publicity, promotion sta. KQED-TV, 1966-68; dir. dept. pub. information Hunters Point-Bayview Community Health Service, San Francisco, 1968-73; dir. community relations KRON-TV, NBC affiliate, San Francisco, 1973—; women's editor Cal. Voice, 1959—; corr. Region IX Human Needs, publ. Dept. Health, Edn. and Welfare, 1971-73;

conv. Coordinator Golden State Med. Assn., 1971—. Mem. Cal. Gov.'s Com. Status Women, 1964. Recipient Am. Heritage Found. citation, 1964, March of Dimes citation, 1965, Save the Children citation, 1966, Com. Mental Retardation citation, 1966. Mem. Nat. Acad. TV Arts and Scis. (bd. govs.), Am. Women in Radio and TV, N.A.A.C.P., others. Contbr. articles to mags. Home: PO Box 2161 Sta A Berkeley CA Office: KRON-TV Channel 4 San Francisco CA 94119

FORTT, INEZ JULIA LONG (MRS. JAMES GILL FORTT), author; b. Markesan, Wis., Mar. 10, 1902; d. Frederick August and Elizabeth Maria (Schmalz) Long; grad. Milw. State Tchrs. Coll., 1921; B. Liberal Arts, U. Ore., 1952; m. James Gill Fortt, Jan. 31, 1925; children—Elizabeth Margaret (Mrs. Craig Beairsto), Thomas Alden. Research librarian, writer Milw. Jour., 1922-27; librarian Ore. collection U. Ore. Library, Eugene, 1952-64. Mem. Lane County Hist. Preservation Com., 1969-73; chmn. book purchase com. Lane County Mus. Library, 1968—. Honored by designation Inez Long Fortt fellowship Am. Assn. U. Women, 1972, Honorable award Cal. Writer's Contest, 1969. Mem. Nat. League Am. Pen Women (Nat. Columnist award 1974, President's citation 1974, Ore. state pres. 1972-74), Am. Assn. U. Women (historian, dir. Eugene br. 1965-70), Lane County Hist. Soc. (bd. mem. 1968), Nat. Writers Group, Nat. Soc. Lit. and Arts, Am. Assn. Ret. Persons, Western Writers Assn., Ore. Hist. Soc. Republican. Episcopalian. Clubs: Yacht, Lane Rock (sec. Eugene 1970-72). Editor Lane County Historian, 1970—. Author: Hiway Handbook, 1972. Contbr. articles to profl. jours. Home: 3870 Watkins Lane Eugene OR 97405

FOSBENDER, JULE JOANN, librarian; b. Paw Paw, Mich., Aug. 23, 1932; d. Harold L. and Grace (Weaver) Walmer; B.A., Western Mich. U., 1954, M.S. in L.S., 1971; m. Conrad Fosbender, Feb. 12, 1954 (div. Aug. 1960); 1 son, Scott Carl. Librarian, Tecumseh (Mich.) High Sch., 1954-55; dir. library Tecumseh Pub. Library, 1954-67; reference librarian Kalamazoo Library system, 1967-72; dir. Adrian (Mich.) Pub. Library, 1972—. Mem. Am., Mich. (chmn. southwestern Mich. roundtable 1971-72, Lenawee County consortium 1972—) library assns., Adult Edn. Soc. Mich., Mich. Hist. Soc. Home: 1311 Terrace Av Adrian MI 49221 Office: E Church St Adrain MI 49221

FOSHAY, MAXINE VALENTINE SHOTTLAND (MRS. ROBERT LETHBRIDGE FOSHAY), civic worker; b. N.Y.C., Feb. 14, 1921; d. Maximillian Stanford and Violet Gertrude (Turner) Shottland; B.A., Royal Acad. Dramatic Arts, London, Eng., 1943; m. Robert Lethbridge Foshay, Mar. 16, 1956. Field rep. Am. Cancer Soc., N.Y.C. div., 1967-68; dir. fund raising and pub. relations Preventive Medicine Inst., Strang Clinic, 1969-71; dir. fund raising and pub. relations Fedn. Handicapped, N.Y.C., 1971-72; exec. dir. Irvington House, 1972-73; chmn. group affiliates Meml. Sloan Kettering, 1960-66; v.p. Meml. Sloan Kettering Soc., 1966-67; vol. Meml. Sloan Kettering Cancer Soc., 1956—. Mem. Assn. Fund Raising Dirs. (mem. bd. 1972—), Publicity Club N.Y., Daus. Brit. Empire (publicity chmn. N.Y.C. 1973), Advt. Club N.Y. Home: 215 E 68th St New York City NY 10021

FOSSETT, KATHERINE, educator; b. Birmingham, Ala., Feb. 27, 1926; d. Harry Purdy and Flora Gertrude (Waters) Fossett; B.S., Eastern Ky. U., 1945, M.A., 1947; Ed.D., Columbia, 1957; postgrad. George Washington U., 1960, Harvard, 1964. Jr. high sch. tchr., Selma, Ala., 1947-54; asst. dean students Randolph Macon Woman's Coll., Lynchburg, Va., 1955-56; supr. guidance Prince George's County Schs., Upper Marlboro, Md., 1957-61; asst. prof. edn. U. Ala., Tuscaloosa, 1961-62; dir. pupil services Prince George's County Schs., Upper Marlboro, Md., 1962-69; prof., counselor edn., dept. chmn. U. South Ala., Mobile, 1969—. Ford Found. Advancement Edn. fellow, 1954. Recipient Distinguished service award dept. mil. sci. U. South Ala., 1973. Mem. Assn. Higher Edn., Nat. Assn. Women Deans, Adminstrs. and Counselors, Am., Ala. (dist. pres. 1972-74) personnel and guidance assns., Kappa Delta Pi, Pi Lambda Theta, Delta Kappa Gamma, Beta Sigma Phi. Methodist. Home: 4009 Old Shell Rd Apt C23 Mobile AL 36608

FOSSIER, MILDRED, social worker, city ofcl.; b. New Orleans, June 8, 1913; d. Albert Emile and May (Keller) Fossier; B.A., Newcomb Coll., 1935; M.S.W., Tulane U., 1955. Unit supr. dist. U.S. Civil Service Commn., dept. head, personnel analyst recruiting rep., 1942-45; later exec. sec. Real Estate Bd. New Orleans; mem. staff div. child welfare Asso. Catholic Charities, 1955-57; social adminstr. dir. Milne Boys' Home, 1960-63; dir. welfare City of New Orleans, 1963-72, supt. Pkwy. and Park Commn., 1972—. Bd. mem. Area Council on Aging. Mem. Nat. Assn. Social Workers, Acad. Certified Social Workers, Internat. Conf. Social Welfare, La. Conf. Social Workers. Contbr. articles to profl. lit. Home: 8125 Hickory New Orleans LA 70118 Office: City Hall 1300 Perdido New Orleans LA 70112

FOSTER, ADRIENNE BROWN (MRS. JACK P. FOSTER), clubwoman; b. St. Louis, July 20, 1913; d. James Leon and Adah (Wade) Brown; student U. Mo., 1932, Washington U., 1935; B.S. in Edn., Harris Tchrs. Coll., 1936; m. Jackson Perswell Foster, Sept. 10, 1938; 1 dau., Suzenne Wade. Co-owner Foster's Distinctive Furniture, Pampa, Tex., 1951; tchr., St. Louis, 1936-38, Overton, Tex., 1945-48. Judge Tex. Flower Show, 1945—, now chmn. for projects and staging; dist. dir. Am. Cancer Soc., 1957-59, 63-64, exec. bd. Tex. div., 1963-65, bd. dirs., 1966-67, service chmn., 1966-67, pres. Gray County Cancer Assn., 1962-63, dist. service and rehab. chmn., 1973—; mem. internat. relations com. Altrusa Internat., 1960—, pres., Pampa, Tex., 1956-58, vice gov. dist. 9, 1958-60; v.p. Pampa Council Clubs, 1962-63; pres. P.T.A., Overton, 1947-48, pres. council, 1955-56, dist. v.p. 1956-59, dist. parliamentarian, 1958-60; sec. Quivera council Girl Scouts U.S.A., 1960—; sec. Gray County unit A.R.C., 1954-57, chmn. vol. service 1959—; sec. East Tex. Garden Clubs, Inc., 1947-49, Council Social Agys., 1957-59; pres. Overton Garden Club, 1948-49, Adult Edn. Assn., 1953-54, 20th Century Club, 1957-58, 66; rep. Pres.'s Traffic Safety Conf., also White House Conf. on Aging, 1960; patroness Treble Clef Club, 1951—; dir. women's campaign Pampa Youth and Community Center, 1958; polio chmn. Gray County, 1955-56; v.p. Community Concert Assn., 1958-59; rep. Community Concert of Tyler; bd. dirs. Parent Edn. Club, 1955-56, Tex. dist. Federated Women's Clubs, 1957-59, Top of Tex. Found., United Fund Pampa, Pampa Welfare Dental Clinic; bd. dirs., founder Exceptional Children's Assn., 1960—; founder Sr. Center exceptional children's troop Boy Scouts Am.; pres. Panhandle Assn. Red. Cross Chpts., 1964-65; parliamentarian Highland Gen. Hosp. Aux.; mem. bd., treas. Gray County chpt. Nat. Found. Polio and Birth Defects; 1st v.p. Gray County chpt. Retarded Children's Assn., 1966-67; bd. dirs., chmn. spl. events Overton Centennial, 1973; chmn. parks devel. Overton C. of C. Recipient of service awards A.R.C., 1953, 54, 10 Year Service award, award Am. Cancer Soc., 1956, 10 Year Cancer Service award, named Women of Year Beta Sigma Phi, 1954; Girl Scout Nat. Appreciation award, 1959, Girl Scout award, 1965. Mem. U.D.C., League Women Voters (dir.), Beta Sigma Phi (adviser), Delta Kappa Gamma, Delta Sigma Epsilon. Methodist. Clubs: Pampa, Pampa Country, Knife and Fork, Queen Pride Garden (chmn. pub. improvement com.), Wednesday Luncheon and Gad-abouts. Home: Route 1 Box 2 Overton TX 75684 Office: Box 1400 Pampa TX 79065

FOSTER, SISTER ANN AGNES, hosp. adminstr.; b. Bayonne, N.J., Mar. 1, 1926; d. John Joseph and Anna Veronica (Ryan) Foster; B.S., St. Louis U., 1970; M.B.A., Wagner Coll., 1973. Relief nursing supr., dir. inservice St. Francis Hosp., Roslyn, N.Y., 1965-68, adminstr., 1970-73; exec. dir. Divine Providence Shelter, N.Y.C., 1974—. Mem. Health Care Adminstrn. Joint Coll./Community Adv. Com., 1972—; mem. profl. com. Heart Fund Ball, 1973; mem. Rockville Centre Diocesan Review Com. on Ethical and Religious Directives for Cath. Health Facilities, 1972; mem. Expanded Provincial Council Franciscan Missionaries Mary, 1973-74. Bd. dirs. Corp. St. Francis Hosp., Roslyn, N.Y., 1970-73, Nassau-Suffolk Hosp. Council, Inc., 1970-73, St. Raphaels Indsl. Sch. and Home. 40 and 8 scholar, 1968-69. Mem. Am. Nurses Assn., Am. Heart Assn. Address: Divine Providence Shelter 225 E 45th St New York City NY 10017

FOSTER, FLORENCE CHRISTINE, educator; b. Huntsville, Tenn., Jan. 8, 1911; d. Dr. James Irdel and Orlean Florence (Caldwell) Foster; A.B., U. Tenn., 1932; A.M., Columbia, 1934; Ed.D., 1948; student Maryville Coll., 1928-31, Vanderbilt U., summer 1934. Tchr., Huntsville High Sch., 1934; county relief dir. Fed. Emergency Relief Adminstrn., Campbell County, Tenn. (LaFollette), 1935; case supr. Works Progress Adminstrn., Knoxville, 1936; tchr. jr.-sr. high sch., Knoxville City Schs., 1936-39; phys. edn. dir. Guilford (N.C.) Coll., 1939-42, Mary Baldwin Coll., Staunton, Va., 1943-49; prof. phys. edn. Fla. State U., 1949-56; prof., head dept. phys. edn. No. Ill. U., 1956-58; dean of women, prof. phys. edn. Northwestern State Coll., Alva, Okla., 1958-60; dean of women, asso. dean student personnel Central Mo. State Coll., Warrensburg, 1960-64; prof. phys. edn. Delta State Coll., Cleveland, Miss., 1964-66; prof. grad. studies in phys. edn. for men and women N.E. Mo. State U., Kirksville, 1966—; asso. dir. Silver Pines Camp, Roaring Gap, N.C., summers 1948, 49; supr. recreation for women, Oak Ridge, Tenn., summer 1946. Examiner and instr. life savs. A.R.C., 1933-60. Nat. ofcl. W.N.O.R.C. Basketball, 1942-49; v.p. Va. Field Hockey Assn., 1947; sec.-treas. N.C. Bd. Women Ofcls., 1942; chmn. athletic sect. Girls and Women of Va. Health, Phys. Edn. and Recreation Sect., 1946; pres. Fla. sect. Am. Camping Assn., 1952-53. Mem. Nat. (chmn. legislative com.), So. (v.p. 1953-55, pres. 1956-57) assns. for phys. edn. for coll. women, Mo. Assn. Health, Phys. Edn. and Recreation (chmn. sect. health 1972-73), Am. Assn. U. Women (pres. Tallahassee br. 1953, legislative chmn. Kirksville 1971-72 1st v.p. Kirksville br. 1973-74), Bus. and Profl. Women's Club (1st v.p. Cleveland, Miss. 1965-66), Am. Assn. U. Profs. (sec. Kirksville chpt. 1970-71), Alpha Omicron Pi (nat. finance com.). Presbyn. Home: PO Box 743 904 E Deare St Kirksville MO 63501

FOSTER, HARRIET ANDERSEN, ednl. adminstr.; b. Wason Flats, Mont., Apr. 27, 1915; d. Martin Christian and Marion (Villadsen) Andersen; A.A., North Park Coll., 1934; B.A., Wheaton Coll., 1936; M.A., Tchrs. Coll. Columbia U., 1941; m. Elvis R. Foster, Jr., June 14, 1941; children—Harvey Ray, Janet Marian (Mrs. James Dale Weston), Susan Elnora (Mrs. Max Randall Gould, Jr.). Tchr. Sch. Dist. 15, Palatine, Ill., 1938-39, Sch. Dist. 99, Cicero, 1939-41, 44-49; tchr. Consol. Sch. Dist. 15, Palatine, 1954-59, elementary sch. prin., 1959-71, dir. spl. edn., 1971—. Mem. Ill., Nat. edn. assns., Ill. Council for Exceptional Children, Delta Kappa Gamma (exec. bd. 1964—, chpt. pres.). Mem. United Ch. Christ (pres. Women's Guild 1957-58) Home: 220 Old Bridge Rd Palatine IL 60067 Office: 505 S Quentin Rd Palatine IL 60067

FOSTER, HELEN LAURA, geologist; b. Adrian, Mich., Dec. 15, 1919; d. Stanley Allen and Alice Mary (Osborn) Foster; B.S. (scholar) U. Mich., 1941, M.S., 1943, Ph.D. (scholar), 1946. Instr. geology Wellesley (Mass.) Coll., 1946-48; geologist, Mil. Geology br. U.S. Geol. Survey, Tokyo, Japan, 1948-55, 56-57, Ryukyu Islands, 1955-56, Washington, 1958-65, Alaskan geology br., Menlo Park, Cal., 1965—. Teaching fellow in geology U. Mich., 1943-46; instr. geology Summer Field Camp, 1947. Active A.R.C., Potomac Applachian Trail Club. Recipient postdoctoral research grant U. Mich., 1946. Fellow Geol. Soc. Am., A.A.A.S.; mem. Am. Assn. Petroleum Geologists, Arctic Inst., Am. Polar Soc., Am. Geophys. Union (mem. com. on volcanology 1962-64), Japanese Volcanological Soc., Mich. Acad. Sci., Geol. Soc. Washington, Sigma Xi, Phi Beta Kappa, Phi Kappa Phi. Contbr. articles to profl. jours. Home: 270 O'Keefe St Palo Alto CA 94303 Office: 345 Middlefield Rd Menlo Park CA 94025

FOSTER, HELEN MUELLER, lawyer; b. Lawton, Okla., July 14, 1908; d. John and Anna Helen (Stapleton) Mueller; student U. Denver, 1926-30, J.D., 1952; student U. No. Colo., summers, 1931-36; m. Feb. 22, 1936 (div. 1944); 1 son, James F. Tchr. rural pub. schs., Colo., 1926-36; file clk. OPA, Denver, 1942-44, legal sec., 1944-48; legal sec. U.S. Dept. Justice, Denver, 1948-50; adminstrv. sec. U.S. Ct. Appeals, 10th Circuit, Denver, 1950—; admitted to Colo. bar, 1958. Mem. Am., Colo., Denver bar assns. Roman Catholic. Office: PO Box 1984 Denver CO 80901

FOSTER, JOSEPHINE ALEXANDER (MRS. RICHARD HARRISON FOSTER), educator; b. Statesville, N.C., Oct. 5, 1930; d. William Thomas and Vivian (Johnson) Alexander; student Appalachian State U., 1948-50; B.S., U. N.C., 1952, M.Ed., 1955, Ph.D., 1964; m. Richard Harrison Foster, June 9, 1957; children—Richard Harrison, II, Amanda Jeton. Tchr. pub. schs., Mocksville, N.C., 1952-54; head dept. home econs. Columbia (S.C.) Coll., 1955-59; grad. asst. U. N.C., Greensboro, 1954-55, asst. prof., 1959-62, doctoral fellow, 1962-64, dir. manpower devel. and tng. program, 1964-65; chmn. dept. child devel. E. Carolina U. Greenville, 1965-69, dir. staff orientation programs, 1967-68; prof. mgmt. housing and family devel. Coll. Home Econs., Va. Poly Inst. and State U., Blacksburg, 1969-73; chmn. dept. home econs. Appalachian State U., Boone, N.C., 1973—. Cons. day care N.C. Dept. Community Colls., 1967-69, Greene County (N.C.) Program for Children, 1968-69; rep. N.C. Am. Home Econ. Workshop for Low-Income Families, 1964. Mem. Soc. for Research in Child Devel., So. Assn. for Children Under Six, Southeastern Council on Family Relations, Nat. Assn. Home Econs. Adminstrs., Omicron Nu. Home: 401 Stansberry Circle Boone NC 28607

FOSTER, MARGERY SOMERS, economist, educator, univ. dean; b. Boston, Mar. 27, 1914; B.A., Wellesley Coll., 1934; Ph.D. in Social Sci., Radcliffe Coll., 1958. Asst. to actuary New Eng. Mut. Life Ins. Co., 1934-43; dep. comptroller and dir. devel. Wellesley Co., 1946-54; lectr. econs. Harvard, 1956-58; lectr. econs., sec. Coll., Mt. Holyoke Coll., 1958-64; dean coll., prof. econs. Hollins Coll., Roanoke, Va., 1964-67; prof. econs., dean Douglass Coll., Rutgers U., New Brunswick, N.J., 1967—. Dir. Pub. Service Electric & Gas Co. N.J., Prudential Life Ins. Co. Am. Served to lt., Women's Res., USNR, 1943-46. Mem. Am. Econ. Assn., Am. Econ. History Assn., Econ. History Soc., Am. Council Acad. Deans (dir.), Middle States Assn. Colls. and Secondary Schs. (trustee), Phi Beta Kappa. Author: Out of Smalle Beginings, 1962. Research on Am. colonial econ. history, history of edn., pub. finance. Home: 23 Nichol Av New Brunswick NJ 08901 Office: Douglas Coll New Brunswick NJ 08903

FOSTER, MILDRED WILLOUGHBY, city ofcl.; b. Warren, O., May 17, 1923; d. James Andrew Marcus and Georgia Lee (Pickens) Willoughby; grad. Wood Coll., Washington, 1943; postgrad. U. Cal. at Santa Cruz, 1973, 74; m. Alfred James Foster, Nov. 20, 1968; children by previous marriage—Laura Lee Bowen (Mrs. William Arthur Dickenson), Barbara Joan Bowen (Mrs. Mark Splain), Nancy June Bowen, James Allen W. Bowen. Sec. to comml. attache and ambassador Peruvian embassy, Washington, 1941-44; social sec., Washington, 1946-48; sec. Judiciary Com., U.S. Ho. of Reps., other congl. offices, Washington, 1949-59; owner-mgr. Oxnard Office Service Co., Inc. (Cal.), secretarial service, 1959-61; sec. Ventura County Municipal Ct., Oxnard, 1963-65; legal sec. Tiffany, Hunt & Browning, Oxnard, 1965-68; legal sec. City of Oxnard, 1968-72, city clk., 1972—. Co-chmn. South Oxnard drive A.R.C., 1958. Mem. Oxnard Planning Commn., 1951-61, past chmn.; pres. So. Cal. Planning Congress, 1958; mem. Ventura County Grand Jury, 1959. Home: 225 E Guava St Oxnard CA 93030 Office: 305 W 3d St Oxnard CA 93030

FOSTER, PEGGY ANNE BONSACK (MRS. RICHARD HARRY FOSTER), librarian; b. Bonsack, Va., Sept. 4, 1912; d. John Evans and Lela (Saunders) Bonsack; A.B., U. Utah, 1933; M.A., U. Cal. at Berkeley, 1934; m. Richard Harry Foster, Dec. 31, 1938; children—Richard Harry, Mercedes Suarez (Mrs. Roy Wallace McDiarmid, Jr.). Jr. librarian Sacramento Pub. Library, 1935; jr. librarian Oakland (Cal.) Pub. Library, 1935-39, 51-56, sr. librarian, 1956-58, supervising librarian, 1958-60, chief circulation librarian, 1960-67, chief reference librarian, 1967-70, adminstrv. librarian, head adult services, 1970—. Mem. Phi Kappa Phi. Club: Women's Athletic (Oakland). Home: 1693 Grand Av Piedmont CA 94611 Office: 125 14th St Oakland CA 94612

FOSTER, ROBERT ELLEN EWING (MRS. NATHANIEL DAVIS FOSTER), owner apparel mfg. co.; b. Lebanon, Tenn., July 23, 1916; d. Elbert Vance and Mattie Amma (Jennings) Ewing; grad. high sch.; m. Nathaniel Davis Foster, July 20, 1940 (dec. June 1960); children—Helen, Foster Moseley, Ellen Annette (Mrs. Michael Norris), Nancy Sue (Mrs. Thomas Leverette), Robert Nathaniel. Owner, Foster Co., Greenville, Ala., 1960—. Bd. dirs. Ft. Dale Acad., Greenville, 1969—. Mem. Am. Apparel Mfrs. Assn., U.S., Ala., Greenville chambers commerce. Baptist. Clubs: Pilot (v.p. Greenville 1964), Butler County. Home: Fort Dale Rd Greenville AL 36037 Office: Beeland and Thames St Greenville AL 36037

FOSTER, RUTH HELEN AHNERT (MRS. RUSSEL K. FOSTER), food service exec.; b. Milw., Mar. 31, 1914; d. Paul and Emma (Mielke) Ahnert; B.S., Milw.-Downer Coll., 1935; M.S., Cornell U., 1946; m. Russel K. Foster, Apr. 8, 1950. Dietetic intern Western Res. U. Hosps., Cleve., 1935-36; therapeutic dietitian Toledo State Hosp., 1936-38; asst. food service dir. YWCA, Milw., 1938-40; asst. adminstrv. dietitian Doctors Hosp., Washington, 1940-42; asst. food service dir. G. Fox & Co., Hartford, Conn., 1942-44; mgr. dining room, 3 cafeterias Boston Store, Milw., 1946-49; owner, mgr. Ruth Ahnert Food Service, Milw., 1949—; owner Foster House Food Products, Milw., 1958—. Mem. City Safety Commn., 1954-59. Mem. Am. Dietetic Assn., Home Economists in Bus., Omicron Nu Mu, Sigma Delta Epsilon, Phi Delta Gamma. Christian Scientist. Clubs: Woman's, Quota (pres. 1949-50). Home: 2600 Arbor Dr Brookfield WI 53005 Office: 2325 W Wells St Milwaukee WI 53233

FOSTER, RUTH IRENE (MRS. DAVID R. FOSTER), educator; b. Adair County, Ia., Mar. 6, 1916; d. Clyde Manson and Rachel Virginia (Martin) Archer; B.S., Drake U., 1954, M.S., 1962; postgrad. U. Ia., 1969, U. So. Cal., 1970; m. David R. Foster, June 30, 1938. Tchr. rural sch. Adair County (Ia.), 1934-38, Polk County Schs. (Ia.), 1942-54, Des Moines Pub. Schs., 1954—. Mem. Cadre-Tchrs., Central Dist. Ia. State Edn., 1971-72; mem. teaching triad Classroom Tchr. Conf., U. Okla., summer 1969; mem. edn. and certification com. Ia. Dept. Pub. Instrn., 1970—; mem. Ia. Profl. Teaching Practices Commn., 1971—. Republican precinct committeewoman, 1967-69. Recipient Living Meml. scholarship, Delta Kappa Gamma, 1970. Mem. Women's C. of C. (profl.), N.E.A. (del. constl. conv. 1971-72), Des Moines Ed. Assn. (parliamentarian 1972-74), Am. Bus. Women Club, Ia. State Edn. Assn. (dist. pres. 1966-68, rep. World Conf. Orgns. Teaching Profession 1972, mem. instructional profl. devel. com. 1972-74), Nat. (sec. 1967-69), Ia. (pres. 1970-72) assns. classroom tchrs., Kappa Kappa Iota (v.p. state chpt. 1973-74). Republican. Mem. Christian Ch. Mem. Order Eastern Star. Home: 1004 McKinley Des Moines IA 50315

FOSTER, SUSAN JANE, telephone co. exec.; b. Painesville, O., Feb. 22, 1941; d. LaVern Edwin and Catherine Jeanette (Fisher) Foster; B.A., Baldwin-Wallace Coll., 1963; M.B.A., Case Western Res. U., 1970. Asst. accountant Ohio Bell Telephone Co., Cleve., 1963-66, asst. statistician, 1966-68, statistician, 1968-71, dist. mgr., 1971—. Tchr. Reading Improvement Center, Cleve., 1968—; cons. Ohio Bd. Edn. and WVIZ, 1973—; vol. reader Cleve. Soc. for Blind, 1973—. Mem. Am. Marketing Assn. (corr. sec. 1972-73, newsletter editor 1973-74), Phi Mu. Club: Baycrafters (Bay Village, O.). Home: 13234 Franklin Blvd Lakewood OH 44107 Office: 100 Erieview Plaza Room 1031 Cleveland OH 44114

FOSTER, TIAH ANN, psychiatrist; b. Iowa Falls, Ia., Apr. 12, 1942; d. Lee Kenneth and Ruth Helen (Kenney) Foster; student Creighton U., 1960-61, U. Santa Clara, 1961-63; M.D., St. Louis U., 1967. Intern, Fresno (Cal.) Gen. Hosp., 1967-68; resident in anesthesia Santa Clara (Cal.) Valley Med. Center, 1968; resident in psychiatry Agnews State Hosp., San Jose, Cal., San Jose State Coll., Kaiser Hosp., Santa Clara, Mt. Zion Hosp., San Francisco, 1969-72; practice medicine specializing in psychiatry, Santa Clara, 1972—. Cons. Am. Pub. Health Assn. for Continuing Edn. Stewardess World AirWays, 1969. Falk fellow Am. Psychiat. Assn., 1971-72. Mem. Am. Assn. U. Women, Am., No. Cal., Santa Clara County psychiat. assns. Home: 151 Buckingham Dr Santa Clara CA 95050 Office: 160 Saratoga Av Suite 34 Santa Clara CA 95051

FOSTER, VERA ADRIENNE CHANDLER (MRS. L.H. FOSTER), social worker; b. Indianola, Miss.; d. William Henry and Maria (Chandler) Chandler; B.A., Fisk U., 1936; M.A., U. Neb., 1941; M.A., U. Chgo., 1950; m. L.H. Foster, Aug. 27, 1941; children—Adrienne M., L. Hilton. Research asso. Tuskegee Inst., Ala., 1944-48, mental hygienist, 1950; supr. social worker VA Hosp., Tuskegee, 1951—, sr. social worker, 1968—; asso. dir. Tuskegee Inst. Community Edn. Program, 1966-68; field instr. Fla. State U., 1960-68; field instr. U. Ala., 1968—, mem. field edn. com. Sch. Social Work, 1973—, also mem. adv. com.; cons. Macon County Headstart, Follow-Through, 1968—, Sr. Citizens, Preparation for Parenthood, 1970—. Mem. Ala. adv. com. U.S. Civil Rights Commn., 1958—, Ala. Council on Human Relations, Nat. Council Chs., Com. on Responsible Parenthood and Abortion, 1971-72; br. chmn. Women's Internat. League for Peace and Freedom, 1960-66, nat. bd., 1962-66; mem. World Council YWCA, 1961-67, mem. nat. bd., 1964-70; mem. Nat. Com. for Support Pub. Schs., 1969—; mem. adv. com. Model Cities, 1968-70, Leadership Tng. Program for Social Workers; mem. Gov.'s Commn. on Juvenile Correction Instns., 1969-70, Gov.'s Conf. on Children and Youth, 1970, Ala. Youth Services Bd., 1973—; mem. N.A.A.C.P., Links; chmn. Ralph Bunche Meml. awards UN Assn. U.S.A., 1972—. Bd. dirs. Planned Parenthood-World Population, Nat. Conf. Social Welfare, UN Assn. U.S.A.; trustee Fisk U. Recipient Distinguished Service award U. Neb., 1971, U. Chgo., 1972, VA,

1972. Mem. Am. Assn. U. Women, Ch. Women United, Acad. Certified Social Workers, Internat. Council Social Welfare, Nat. Assn. Social Workers (nat. del. assembly 1967; v.p. Ala. chpt. 1972—), Council on Social Work Edn., Nat. (dir.), Ala. (exec. com.) confs. on social welfare, Nat. Orgn. Women, Delta Sigma Theta. Asso. editor: Negro Year Book, 1947. Home: 520 Montgomery Rd Tuskegee Institute AL 36088 Office: VA Hosp Tuskegee AL 36083

FOTO, MARY ELIZABETH SMITH (MRS. STEPHEN ANTHONY FOTO), occupational therapy cons.; b. Iowa Falls, Ia., Sept. 1, 1941; d. Roy D. and Margaret Grace (Binnie) Smith; B.S., U. So. Cal., 1966; m. Stephen Anthony Foto, Aug. 29, 1964; 1 dau., Alison Marie. Clin. affiliate U. So. Cal.-Los Angeles County Med. Center, Rancho Los Amigos, Brentwood VA Hosp., 1966-67; staff therapist Crippled Children's Services Los Angeles County, 1967-68; staff therapist Coll. Vista Convalescent Hosp.; pvt. practice as occupational therapist, Eagle Rock, Cal., 1968-70; head therapist Glen Wheeler Assos., San Gabriel, Cal., 1970-73; cons. Hillhaven Convalescent Hosp., Inc., Tacoma, 1972-74; occupational therapy cons. Blue Cross So. Cal., Los Angeles, 1972—. Tchr. restorative services sect. Western Center Continuing Edn. in Adminstrn. of Health Core Facilities, U. Cal. at Los Angeles, 1971-74; lectr. Loma Linda U. Allied Health Sch., 1973; preclin. instr. U. So. Cal. Sch. Occupational Therapy, 1973, 74; tchr. restorative services Cal. Nursing Home Assn., 1973; lectr. Acad. Speech Pathology, 1974. Cons. Health Programs Evaluation Services, Inc., Los Angeles, 1973—, Westchester Phys. Therapy, Bakersfield, Cal., 1972-74. Mem. Parent involvement Com. All Saints Day Care Center, 1971-74. Mem. Am. (spl. adviser on pvt. practice-nat. legislative com. 1973), So. Cal. (legislative chmn. 1972) occupational therapy assns., Alpha Chi Omega. Republican. Episcopalian. Home: 445 Pilgrim Pl San Marino CA 91108 Office: 3540 Wilshire Blvd Los Angeles CA 90010

FOUGHT, CAROL ANN SHOLLENBERGER (MRS. DONALD EUGENE FOUGHT), ednl. adminstr.; b. Tyrone, Pa., Oct. 1, 1938; d. Carl Alvin and Anna Mary (Miller) Shollenberger; B.S., Pa. State U., 1960; M.S., Long Beach State Coll., 1962; Ph.D., Ohio State U., 1966; m. Donald Eugene Fought, July 11, 1959; children—Bonnie Elizabeth, Bradley Scott, Deborah Lynn. Counselor, Reynoldsburg (O.) Jr. and Sr. High Sch., 1962-64, Bexley (O.) High Sch., 1964-67; asst. dean students Ohio State U., Columbus, 1967-70; dir. continuing edn. Ohio Dominican Coll., Columbus, 1970-71; dir. div. continuing edn. Columbus (O.) Tech. Inst., 1971—. Cons. work incentive program project State of Ohio, 1971-72; cons. women's programs Cuyahoga Community Coll., Eastern Campus, Cleve., 1973. Mem. Ohio Gov.'s Task Force on Continuing Edn. for Aging, 1972—. Leader jr. troop Girl Scouts, Bexley, 1970-72. Mem. Ohio (mem. exec. bd. 1972-74), Central Ohio (pres. 1972-73) adult edn. assns., Nat. (regional rep. 1973—), Ohio (continuing edn. chmn. 1973-74) assns. women deans, adminstrs. and counselors, Ohio Assn. Adult Educators (higher edn. rep. exec. bd. 1974—). Home: 381 S Columbia Av Columbus OH 43209

FOUNTAIN, HELEN VAN ALSTYNE (MRS. KENNETH PIERCE FOUNTAIN), ret. educator, writer; b. Westfield, N.J., Oct. 15, 1906; d. William Becker and Lillian Tyler (DuCharme) Van Alstyne; student Montclair Normal Coll., 1927; B.S., Rutgers U., 1950, M.Ed., 1952; certificate advanced study Wesleyan U., Middletown, Conn., 1962; m. Kenneth Pierce Fountain, June 19, 1928; 1 dau., Marilyn (Mrs. Ellsworth Henry Larkin). Tchr., Parker Sch., Middlesex, N.J., 1927-29, John Runnels Hosp., Scotch Plains, N.J., 1934-41, Deerfield Sch., Mountainside, N.J., 1941-67; lectr. adult edn. 1st-Park Baptist Ch., Plainfield, N.J., 1972-73. Poetry cons. Cooper Hill Writers Conf., East Dover, Vt., 1972-73. Recipient 1st award in poetry Poetry Soc. N.J. and N.H., 1967, 71, 72, Poetry Fellowship of Me., 1973. Mem. Poetry Soc. Am., World Poetry Soc. Intercontinental, Acad. Am. Poets, Poetry Soc. London, N.J., Pa. poetry socs., Poetry Fellowship Me., Plainfield Art Assn. Mem. Order Eastern Star. Club: Monday Afternoon (Plainfield). Author: (poetry) Star Quest, 1967; A Cage of Birds, 1970. Home: 23B Maryland Av Cedar Glen Lakes Whiting NJ 08759

FOUNTAIN, RUTH MCMULLEN (MRS. KEITH WILLIAM FOUNTAIN), city ofcl.; b. Brush, Colo., June 25, 1928; d. George A. and Ruth Ellen (Turner) McMullen; A.B., U. No. Colo., 1964, M.A., 1968; m. Keith William Fountain, Dec. 28, 1952; children—William Keith, Jack A. With Farmers State Bank, Brush, 1947-52; homebound tchr., spl. edn. program Aurora (Colo.) Pub. Schs., 1963-71; mem. city council City of Aurora, (Colo.), 1971—. Pres. Aurora Rep. Women's Club, 1970-71, legislative chmn., 1971-73; chmn. or co-chmn. campaigns U.S. Senate, 1968, state gov., 1970, U.S. Ho. of Reps., 1972. Bd. dirs. Community Services, adv. bd. Community Coll. Bd. Recipient Outstanding Women of Year award Aurora C. of C., 1973. Mem. Am. Assn. Univ. Women (dir. 1970), Aurora Area Bus. and Profl. Women's Club, Colo. Municipal League (dir.), Delta Kappa Gamma (hon.). Home: 12721 E 30th Av Aurora CO 80011 Office: 1470 Emporia St Aurora CO 80010

FOUSE, CLARA MAE JONES (MRS. CLARENCE DUNCAN FOUSE), realtor; b. Tilton, Ga., Apr. 21, 1921; d. Robert L. and Ollie Lucy (Bishop) Jones; student Lindsey Hopkins Vocational Sch., 1957; m. Clarence Duncan Fouse, Nov. 10, 1941; 1 son, Clarence Duncan. Owner, Clara M. Fouse Real Estate, Miami, 1957—; sec.-treas. A A Vacuum Cleaners, Inc., Miami, 1969-74. Chmn. Retarded Children's Com., 1973-74. Alternate del. Republican Nat. Conv., 1960, del., 1964; mem. Rep. Nat. Adv. Com. for Fla., 1966, 67, mem. women's conf. steering com. Mem. Ladies United Comml. Travelers Am. (grand counselor 1972-73), Grand Counselors Assn. Ladies United Comml. Travelers Am., U.S., Can. (pres. 1973-74). Club: Coconut Grove Women's (Miami). Home: 2401 SW 13th St Miami FL 33145 Office: 412 NW 27th Av Miami FL 33125

FOUSHEE, OLA MAIE SUTTENFIELD (MRS. JOHN MCIVER FOUSHEE), painter, columnist; b. Avalon, N.C.; d. Emmett R. and Callie Jane (Keaton) Suttenfield; student U. N.C., intermittently 1953-57, pvt. tchrs.; m. John McIver Foushee, Sept. 5, 1931; children—John McIver, June Keaton. Tchr. arts and crafts Army Convalescent Hosp., 1945, U. N.C.,1946; tchr. art Allied Arts, Durham, N.C., 1955-56; now v.p., adv. mgr. Foushee Realty and Ins. Co., Chapel Hill, N.C., one-man shows in N.C., S.C.; exhibited in group shows, N.C., S.C.; Pa., Va. Lectr. art to women's orgns., P.T.A., art orgns., sch. and profl. groups; mem. art juries. Recipient citation N.C. State Art Soc., 1962. Charter mem. Durham Art Guild; Chapel Hill Jr. Service League; founder Chapel Hill Art Guild, co-founder Asso. Artists of N.C.; mem. Alliance Francaise, Am. Fedn. Arts, State Art Soc. N.C. (life), Phi Mu. Author: Art in North Carolina: Episodes and Developments 1585-1970, 1972. Art columnist Greensboro Daily News, Durham Morning Herald, Rocky Mount Evening Telegram, High Point Enterprise, Charlotte Observer, Wilmington Star and others, 1958-63, Chapel Hill Weekly, 1963—. Home: Chapel Hill NC 27514

FOUST, MARY LOUISE, state ofcl.; b. New Albany, Ind., Oct. 15, 1909; d. David Taylor and Mary Margaret (Rippel) F.; grad. Martin Jr. Coll., Pulaski, Tenn., 1928; A.B. in Econs., Georgetown Coll., 1938; LL.B., U. Louisville, 1944, J.D., 1969; postgrad. in pub. adminstrn. U. Ky., 1958-60. Clk., Bank of Shelbyville (Ky.), 1928-37; accountant, franchise taxes Ky. Dept. Revenue, Frankfort, 1938-42; tax control clk. E.I. duPont de Nemours & Co., Charlestown, Ind., 1942-45; admitted to Ky. bar, 1943; accountant Ky. Div. Pub. Assistance, Frankfort, 1945-49; pub. accountant, San Francisco, 1950, Louisville, 1952-53, Shelbyville, 1953-56, Shelbyville, Lexington, Ky., 1960-69; accounting supr. Gunnison Homes, Inc. subsidiary U.S. Steel Corp., 1951; practiced law in Shelbyville, 1953-56, Shelbyville, Lexington, 1960-69; auditor pub. accounts Commonwealth of Ky., Frankfort, 1956-60, 69—. C.P.A., Ky. Mem. Am. Inst. C.P.A.'s, Am. Women's Soc. C.P.A.'s, Am. Soc. Women Accountants (Ky. pres. 1955-56), Ky. Bar Assn., Women's C. of C. of Ky., Shelbyville Bus. and Profl. Womens Club, D.A.R. (regent Isaac Shelby chpt. 1956-60), Internat. Order King's Daus. and Sons (pres. Ky. br. 1964-68), Beta Alpha Psi (hon.). Democrat. Baptist. Home: Midland Trail West Shelbyville KY 40065 Office: Capitol Annex Frankfort KY 40601

FOWKE, EDITH MARGARET FULTON (MRS. FRANKLIN GEORGE FOWKE), educator; b. Lumsden, Sask., Can., Apr. 30, 1913; d. William Marshall and Margaret (Fyffe) Fulton; student Regina Coll., 1929-31; B.A. with high honours in English and history, U. Sask., 1933, M.A. in English, 1938; LL.D. (hon.), Brock U., 1974; m. Franklin George Fowke, Oct. 1, 1938. Editor, Western Tchr., Saskatoon, Sask., 1937-45; asso. editor Mag. Digest, Toronto, Ont., Can., 1945-50; asso. prof. English dept. York U., Downsview, Ont., 1971—. Mem. Am. Folklore Soc., English Folk Dance and Song Soc., Assn. Canadian U. Tchrs. English, Canadian Assn. U. Tchrs., Canadian Folk Music Soc. (exec. mem.). Author: Folk Songs of Canada, 1954; Folk Songs of Quebec, 1957; Songs of Work and Freedom, 1960; Canada's Story in Song, 1960; Traditional Singers and Songs from Ontario, 1965; More Folk Songs of Canada, 1967; Lumbering Songs from the Northern Woods, 1970; Sally Go Round the Sun, 1969; Penguin Book of Canadian Folk Songs, 1974. Editor Canadian Folk Music Jour., 1973—. Home: 5 Notley Pl Toronto ON M4B 2M7 Canada Office: Ross Bldg 4700 Keele St Downsview ON M3J IP3 Canada

FOWLE, ELEANOR CRANSTON (MRS. JOHN MILLER FOWLE), polit. worker; b. Palo Alto, Cal., Nov. 22, 1909; s. William MacGregor and Carol Edith (Dixon) Cranston; student Stanford, 1928-31; m. John Miller Fowle, June 19, 1929; children—Michael, Linda (Mrs. Linda Burke). Co-chmn. 10th Congl. Dist. Democratic Party, 1964; mem. exec. com. Western States Dem. Conf., 1965; chmn. women's div. No. Cal. Dem. Central Com., 1965-72; women's chmn. Cal. Dem. party, 1966-68, 71-72; state co-chmn. Operation Support, Dem. Nat. Com., 1968; mem. exec. com. Alan Cranston for U.S. Senator, 1968; alternate del. Dem. Nat. Conv., 1968; mem. exec. com. John Tunney for U.S. Senator, 1970. First v.p. Family Service Assn. Palo Alto and Los Altos, 1963-65. Bd. dirs. Community Council No. Santa Clara County, 1963-64. Named Key Dem. Woman of 1971-72, Women's Div., No. Cal. State Central Com., 1973. Mem. League Women Voters (dir. Palo Alto 1960-61), UN Assn. (dir. Palo Alto 1960-61). Home: 27060 Old Trace Rd Los Altos Hills CA 94022

FOWLER, ANNA VIVIETTE LIDELL (MRS. MEL FOWLER), nursing adminstr.; b. Taylor, Tex., Dec. 8, 1920; d. Per Reinhold and Myrtle Marie (Wegstrom) Lidell; grad. Seton Sch. Nursing, 1941; m. Mel Fowler, Sept. 5, 1943; children—James E., Robert M., William W. Nurse new-born nursery St. David's Hosp., Austin, Tex., 1941; pvt. duty nurse, 1943-45; supr. ward for mentally retarded Austin State Sch., 1967-72, supr. pilot project for blind retardates, 1967-68; unit dir. multiple handicapped and retarded persons, Travis State Sch., Austin, 1973—. Mem. Am. Assn. on Mental Deficiency, Tex. Assn. Retarded Children, Tex. Soc. Sculptors (asso.). Home: 8700 Mountainwood Circle Austin TX 78759 Office: Travis State Sch PO Box 430 Austin TX 78767

FOWLER, BEVERLY DAVIS, educator; b. Ord, Neb.; d. Clarence M. and Ida (Bakker) Davis; B.S., U. Neb., 1946; M.S., Purdue U., 1949; Ph.D., U. S.C., 1962; m. Robert Fowler, July 12, 1947 (div. Oct. 1964); children—Robert Davis, William Kevin. Tchr. home econs. Columbia (S.C.) City Schs., 1947-52; tchr., counselor Brookland Cayce (S.C.) City Schs., 1956-59; cons. research homemaking div. State Dept. Edn., 1960-62; counselor U. S.C., Columbia, 1961-62; asst. prof. home econs. U. Neb., Lincoln, 1962-64, asso. prof., 1964-66, asso. dir., 1964-66; prof., chmn. dept. home econs. Murray (Ky.) State U., 1966-69, Western Ill. U., Macomb, 1969—. Headstart cons., 1966-69. Mem. Am. Assn. U. Women, Am., Ill. home econs. assns., Am. Ednl. Research Assn., Nat. Council Adminstrs. Home Econs. (pres. Ill. 1970-71), Am., Ill. vocational assns., Ill. Vocational Home Econs. Tchrs. Assns., Home Economists in Homemaking (counselor Macomb chpt.), Nat., Ill. councils family relations, Kappa Omicron Phi, Alpha Delta Kappa. Home: 801 Meadow Dr Macomb IL 61455

FOWLER, DONA JANE WILSON, educator; b. Muncie, Ind., May 8, 1928; d. Cleo E. and Thelma Irene (Broman) Wilson; B.S., Purdue U., 1955, M.S., 1962, Ph.D., 1965; m. Dale J. Fowler, May 20, 1948 (div. Oct. 1949); children—Ann L. (Mrs. Jack Mastenbrook), J. Sheldon. Research asst. Purdue U., Lafayette, Ind., 1954-55, 61-65; research asso. Eli Lilly Co., Indpls., 1956-60; instr. biology Western Mich. U., Kalamazoo, 1965, asst. prof., 1966-71, asso. prof., 1971—. Guest research scientist CNRS Labs., Gif-sur-Y'vette, France, 1973. Faculty research fellow, 1967; NSF grantee, 1968-70. Mem. A.A.A.S., Am. Inst. Biol. Scis., Am. Soc. Zoologists, Am. Assn. U. Profs., P.E.O., Sigma Xi. Contbr. articles to profl. jours. Home: 722 Grand Pre Kalamazoo MI 49007

FOWLER, ELIZABETH MILLSPAUGH (MRS. PHILIP LIVINGSTON AZOY), reporter, author; b. Newburgh, N.Y., May 24, 1921; d. Anson J. and Hazel (Osterhoudt) Fowler; B.A. in English, Smith Coll., 1942; M.B.A., N.Y.U., 1953; m. Philip Livingston Azoy, Nov. 10, 1950; children—Katrina, Cynthia. Reporter, Buffalo Evening News, 1942-44; copy editor Wall Street Jour., N.Y.C., 1944-46; financial writer Merrill Lynch, Pierce, Fenner & Smith, 1946-56; reporter financial news N.Y. Times, 1956—. Mem. Morristown Jr. League. Episcopalian. Club: York. Lectr. in fields of investments, econs. Author: 90 Days to Fortune, 1965; How To Manage Your Money, 1973; Your Estate, Retirement and Will, 1973; also booklets, articles in field; contbg. author Anatomy of Wall Street, 1968. Home: Mt Kemble Av Morristown NJ 07960 Office: NY Times 229 W 43d St New York City NY 10036

FOWLER, G. FERN (MRS. RUSSELL WINSLOW FOWLER), broadcaster; b. Assumption, Ill.; d. Rawley Egbert and Martha Rachael (Price) Wright; B.S., Purdue U., 1930; m. Russell Winslow Fowler, July 3, 1926. Tchr. home econs. Romney (Ind.) High Sch., 1922-23, Monitor (Ind.) High Sch., 1923-24; supr., tchr. home econs. Danville (Ill.) schs., 1924-26; broadcaster art and craft show WMTV, Madison, Wis., 1953-54; broadcaster landscaping shows WKOW, Madison, 1954-55; broadcaster art and craft show WKOW-TV, Madison, 1954-59; with WKOW Radio, Madison, 1955-56; women's dir., broadcaster Fern Fowler Show, WMTV, Madison, 1959—. Recipient Distinguished Alumnus award Purdue U., 1972. Mem. Women in Communications (pres. 1966-67), Nat. League Am. Pen Women, Am. Women in Radio and TV, Madison Art Guild, Madison Art Assn., Zeta Tau Alpha. Mem. Order Eastern Star. Contbr. monthly column to periodical. Home: 3315 Blackhawk Dr Madison WI 53705 Office: 615 Forward Dr Madison WI 53711

FOWLER, HELEN VIRGINIA, journalist, educator; b. Des Moines, May 2, 1920; d. John Harrison and Hazel Verne (Johnson) Fowler; B.A. in English U. Cal. at Los Angeles, 1947, M.S. in Journalism, 1965. Tchr., English South Bay Union High Sch. Dist., Redondo Beach, Cal., 1949-52; tchr. English, speech and journalism San Pedro High Sch., Los Angeles Unified Sch. Dist., 1952-69; instr. Victor Valley Coll., Victorville, Cal., 1971—; feature writer Mountaineer newspaper, Wrightwood, Cal., 1971—. Rep. faculty Senate Victor Valley Coll., 1973-74. Bd. dirs. High Desert Symphony Assn., Victorville, 1973-76. Newspaper Fund, Inc. fellow, 1961. Mem. Nat. League Am. Penwomen (letters chmn. 1973-74), Delta Kappa Gamma. Editor: Phelan-Pinon Hills Progress, 1971-72. Home: 5618 Lodgepole Dr Wrightwood CA 92397 Office: PO Drawer 00 Victorville CA 92392

FOWLER, KAREN SAUSMAN, naturalist; b. Chgo., Nov. 26, 1945; d. William and Annabel A. (Lofaso) Sausman; B.S., Loyola U., Chgo., 1967; postgrad. U. Redlands, 1968; m. George W. Fowler, Jr., Apr. 24, 1971. Tchr. Palm Springs (Cal.) Unified Sch. Dist., 1968-70; ranger, naturalist Joshua Tree Nat. Monument, Nat. Park Service, 1969-70; dir.-naturalist living desert div. Palm Springs Desert Museum, Palm Desert, Cal., 1970—. Profl. illustrator and photographer; profl. lectr. natural history. Nursery vol. Lincoln Park Zoo, Chgo., 1966-68; vol. mammologist U. Cal. at Riverside, 1971—; mem. Palm Springs Spl. Study Com. on Annexation, 1970-71. Bd. dirs. Desert Protective Council. Mem. Nature Conservancy, Audubon Soc., Nat. Wildlife Fedn., Nat. Parks and Conservation Assn., Am. Assn. Zool. Parks and Aquariums (editor 1971—). Home: 73-305 Salt Cedar St Palm Desert CA 92260 Office: PO Box 390 Palm Desert CA 92260

FOWLER, LUCY BARR (MRS. CHARLES WORTHINGTON FOWLER II), occupational therapist; b. Allentown, Pa., Feb. 19, 1932; d. William Bryce and Lucy Agnes (Chaundy) Barr; B.S. in Phys. Edn., Pa. State U., 1953; certificate occupational therapy U. Pa., 1956; m. Charles Worthington Fowler II, July 21, 1956; children—Charles Worthington III, Ellen Bryce, Timothy Neville. Staff occupational therapist, recreation dir. Palo Verde Psychiat. Hosp., Tucson, 1965-66; staff occupational therapist Neb. Psychiat. Inst.-U. Neb. Med. Center, Omaha, 1970-72; dir. occupational therapy Island of Hope Alcoholic Rehab. and Research Center, Omaha, 1973—. Costume chmn., designer Omaha Ballet Soc.; active (dir.) Omaha Ballet Guild, Omaha Symphony Guild, Omaha Vols. Handicapped Children, Omaha Assistance League. Bd. dirs. Challenge. Mem. Am., Neb. (treas., finance chmn. 1972-74) occupational therapy assns., Nat. Rehab. Assn., Neb. Assn. Alcoholism Counselors, D.A.R., St. Andrews Scottish Soc., Chi Omega (alumnae v.p. 1973-74). Republican Episcopalian. Clubs: Fancy Creek Yacht (Randolph, Kan.); Regency Lake and Tennis (Omaha); Woman's (Allentown, Pa.); Officers Wives' (Offutt AFB, Neb.). Home; 1329 S 93d St Omaha NE 68124 Office: 414 S 13th St Omaha NE 68102

FOWLER, MARILYN LEE LARSON (MRS. GENE FOWLER), civic worker; b. Bertrand, Neb., Dec. 26, 1925; s. Charles Richard and Dorothy Margaret (Stickler) Larson; student Hastings Coll., 1943-44; m. Gene Fowler, Jan. 7, 1945; children—Thomas, Melinda, Richard, Daniel, Felicia. Sec., dir. Fowler Inc., Lexington, Neb., 1971—. Mem. Non-Partisan Nat. Com. for Support Pub. Schs., 1968-72; mem. Neb. Bd. Edn., 1970—, v.p., 1973-74, pres., 1974—; mem. adv. bd. Mid-Am. Arts Alliance, 1973—, Neb. Library Commn., 1974—; mem. Neb. Coordinating Council for Post-secondary Edn., 1974—. Nat. committeewoman Young Democrats of Neb., 1958-64; chmn. (Gosper County Dem. Com. 1964-70; mem. central com. Neb. Dem. Com., 1964-66. Bd. dirs. Lexington Community Hosp. Aux., Community Concert Assn., Lexington, Nebraskans for Pub. Television, 1972—. Recipient Eleanor Roosevelt Meml. award Young Dems. of Neb., 1966. Mem. Fedn. Women's Club, Am. Legion Aux. Home: 1904 Plum Creek Lane Lexington NE 68850

FOWLER, SANDRA LYNN, poet; b. West Columbia, W.Va., Feb. 4, 1937; d. Okey Donly and Ramona Jean (Roach) Fowler; student Franklin Inst., 1956, Palmer Inst. Authorship, 1966. Writer poetry pub. in Cyclo Flame Ann., Internat. Who's Who in Poetry Anthology, Premier Poets, Ocarina, Yearbook Modern Poetry, Bitterroot, Am. Bard, Poet, Madras. Recipient citation of merit Avalon Internat. Poetry Contests, 1963, 64, certificate of merit Accademia Leonardo da Vinci, 1968, 70, medal of honor Centro Studi e Scambi Internazionali, 1967. Mem. Avalon, Centro Studi e Scambi Internazionali (hon. rep. 1969), Internat. Platform Assn., World Poetry Soc. (rep. at large 1969—), United Poets, Democrat. Fundamentalist. Author: (poetry) In the Shape of Sun, 1972. Contbg. editor Ocarina, bi-monthly jour. poetry and aesthetics, 1972—. Address: West Columbia WV 25287

FOWLER, VIOLA PHYLLIS (MRS. WILLIAM WATSON FOWLER), newspaper co. exec.; b. Hayes County, Neb., Feb. 19, 1922; d. George Herman and Minnie May (Ward) Pinn; grad. high sch.; m. William Watson Fowler, Aug. 10, 1941; children—Cheryl (Mrs. John Scott), William Eugene (dec.), Gregory, Vicki (Mrs. Tony Harter). With Hayes Center (Neb.) Times-Republic, Inc., 1963—, mgr., 1969—. Village clk. Village of Hayes Center, 1969—. Mem. Hayes County Hist. Soc., Am. Legion Aux. Conglist. Home: Hayes Center NE 69032 Office: Times-Republican Hayes Center NE 69032

FOWLER, VIRGINIA CHAPLIN (MRS. ARTHUR M. FOWLER, JR.), psychologist; b. Clemson, S.C., Nov. 2, 1946; d. James Ferris and Mary Ellen (Varnadore) Chaplin; B.A., Winthrop Coll., 1968; M.A., U. S.C., 1970; postgrad. U. Tenn., 1971-73; m. Arthur M. Fowler, Jr., Aug. 29, 1970; 1 son, Arthur M. III. Psychol. services worker Knoxville (Tenn.) City Schs., 1970-73, Shelby County Schs., Memphis, 1973-74. Mem. Nat. Assn. Sch. Psychologists, Tenn. Assn. for Psychology in Schs. Home: 5688 Quince Rd Apt 3 Memphis TN 38117 Office: 160 S Hollywood St Memphis TN 38113

FOWLES, JUNE CRAVEN (MRS. LESLIE OMEGA FOWLES), lawyer, govt. ofcl.; b. Olympia, Wash.; d. Sylvester McDonald and Alice (Jessup) Craven; m. Leslie Omega Fowles, Mar. 9, 1935. Admitted to Wash. State bar, 1939; practiced in Olympia; asst. atty. gen. State of Wash., Olympia, 1939; dep. pros. atty. Clark County, State of Wash.; trial atty. U.S. Dept. Justice. Mem. Wash. State Bar. Home: 1709 Water St Olympia WA 98501 Office: 1709 Water Olympia WA 98501

FOWLKES, NANCY LANETTA PINKARD (MRS. VESTER GUY FOWLKES), social worker; b. Athens, Ga.; d. Amos Malone and Nettie (Barnett) Pinkard; B.A., Bennett Coll., 1946; M.A., Syracuse U., 1952; M.S.W., Smith Coll., 1963; m. Vester Guy Fowlkes, June 4, 1955 (dec. May 1965); 1 dau., Wendy Denise. Dir. publicity Bennett Coll., Greensboro, N.C., 1946-47, 49-50; asst. editor Va. Edn. Bull. ofcl. organ Va. State Tchrs. Assn., Richmond, 1950-52; asst. office mgr. Community Service Soc., N.Y.C., 1952-55; social caseworker, asst. supr. Dept. Social Services, Westchester County, White Plains, N.Y., 1959-67, supr. adoption services, 1967—. Mem. adv. bd. White Plains Adult Edn. Sch. First v.p. Eastview Jr. High Sch., 1970-71, area chmn. White Plains Community Chest, 1964; sec. Mount Vernon Concert Group, 1952-54; fund raising co-chmn. Urban League Guild of Westchester, 1967; pres. White Plains Interfaith Council, 1972—. Bd. dirs. Family Service of Westchester, Bethel Meth. Home, Ossining, N.Y. Mem. Nat. Assn. Social Workers, Acad. Certified Social Workers, Jack and Jill of Am. (chpt. pres. 1965-67, regional sec.-treas. 1967-71), Nat. Bus. and Profl. Womens Club (chpt. sec. 1954-56), Internat. Platform Assn., Theta Sigma Phi, Zeta Nu Omega, Alpha Kappa Alpha. Methodist (chmn. adminstrv. bd. 1970-72, ch. trustee 1973—, lay speaker). Club: Regency Bridge (pres. 1963-65, v.p. 1965-67). Home: 107 Valley Rd White Plains NY 10604 Office: County Office Bldg White Plains NY 10601

FOX, BARCY CONDON (MRS. CARL FOX), pub. relations exec.; b. Clarksville, Tenn., Aug. 31, 1945; d. Stephen Patrick and Martha Donnell (Williams) Condon; sutdent Vassar Coll., 1963-64; B.A., St. Louis U., 1967; m. Carl Fox, Oct. 21, 1967. Asst. dir. pub. relations St. Louis Symphony, 1968-69; publs. editor St. Louis Art Mus., 1969-70; dir. communications Maryville Coll., St. Louis, 1970—. Free-lance editor and writer, 1969—; cons. pub. relations, 1969—. Recipient spl. citation, nat. communications competition Am. Coll. Pub. Relations Assn., 1973. Mem. Am. Coll. Pub. Relations Assn., St. Louis Press Club. Editor: 200 Years of Japanese Porcelains, 1969; Museum Monographs II, 1970. Home: 36 Arundel St St Louis MO 63105 Office: 13550 Conway Rd St Louis MO 63141

FOX, CATHERINE LION (MRS. HARRY L. FOX), library rental agy. exec.; b. Balt., Mar. 14, 1908; d. S. John and Ida (Myers) Lion; grad. Md. Inst. Fine Arts and Mechanic Arts, 1930; m. Harry L. Fox, May 29, 1931; children—Richard Lion, Barbara Joan (Mrs. Herbert Fleischer). Office mgr. Fiction Lovers Library Pitts., 1937-45, partner, 1945—; mfrs. rep. 4 top gift lines. Rep., Camp Wingfoot for Girls, Camp Roosevelt for Boys, 1947—. Home: 4314 McCaslin St Pittsburgh PA 15217

FOX, CHRISTY (MRS. LUDLOW SHONNARD, JR.), columnist; m. Ludlow Shonnard, Jr. Columnist, soc. editor Los Angeles Times, 1951—; master of ceremonies KNX radio show; entertainer TV. Office: Los Angeles Times Times Mirror Sq Los Angeles CA 90053

FOX, CLAIRE ELIZABETH GILBRIDE (MRS. STUART AMES FOX), educator, historian; b. Phila.; d. John J. and Claire (Keane) Gilbride; A.B., U. Pa., 1956, M.A., 1960, Ph.D., 1966; M.Ed., Temple U., 1958; m. Stuart Ames Fox, Dec. 3, 1944; children—Richard Stuart, Susan Ames (Mrs. William Patton Graham, III), Jeffrey Keane, Edgar Mark. Tchr., Huntington Jr. High Sch., Abington, Pa., 1956-58, Abington Sr. High Sch., 1958-59; intern teaching program supr. secondary intern tchrs. in math., sci., social studies Temple U., 1959-61, instr., 1964-66; asst. prof. edn. dir. curriculum lab. Beaver Coll., Glenside, Pa., 1966-69; asst. dean, faculty Thomas Jefferson U., Phila., 1969—. Cons. Mercer Mus. Bucks County Hist. Soc., 1969—; cons. in Am. studies. Fellow Coll. Physicians Phila.; mem. Phila. Art Alliance, Am. Assn. History Medicine, Am. Studies Assn., Hist. Soc. Pa., Soc. Hist. Archaeology, Victorian Soc. Am., N.Y. Acad. Scis., Pi Sigma Alpha, Kappa Delta Pi. Club: Manufacturer's Golf and Country (Oreland, Pa.). Contbr. articles to profl. jours. Home: 380 Shady Retreat Rd Doylestown PA 18901

FOX, DOROTHY DAVIS (MRS. WILLIAM FOX, JR.), psychotherapist; b. Ashtabulah, O., Nov. 29, 1925; d. John Robert and Dorotha Beatrice (Stewart) Davis; B.A., Tulane U., 1946; M.S.W., 1949; m. William Fox, Jr., Mar. 3, 1956; children—Dorothy Beatrice, Ann Kathryn. Social worker, supr. Family Service Soc., New Orleans, 1949-56; social worker Akron (O.) Child Guidance Center, 1956, Cleve. Child Guidance Center, 1960-61; psychotherapist, supr. Irene Jossolyn Clinic, Northfield, Ill., 1963—. Cons., Elgin (Ill.) State Hosp., 1971—; treas., dir. Merrill McEnree Fox & Asso., Chgo., 1969—. Mem. New Trier Twp. (Ill.) Child Care Com., 1968-74. Mem. Nat. Assn. Social Workers (liaison rep. clinic to Chgo. chpt. 1973-74), Nat. Acad. Certified Social Workers. Home: 1229 Cleveland St Wilmette IL 60091 Office: 405 Central St Northfield IL 60093

FOX, ELEANOR MAE COHEN (MRS. BYRON E. FOX), lawyer; b. Trenton, N.J., Jan. 18, 1936; d. Herman and Elizabeth (Stein) Cohen; B.A., Vassar Coll., 1956; LL.B., N.Y. U., 1961; m. Byron E. Fox, Mar. 31, 1957; children—Douglas Anthony, Margot Alison, Randall Matthew. Editor high sch. textbooks Cambridge Book Co., N.Y.C., 1956-57; editor labor service publ. Bur. Nat. Affairs, Washington, 1957-58; admitted to N.Y. bar, U.S. Dist. Ct. bars, U.S. Supreme Ct. bar, since practiced in N.Y.C.; asso. firm Simpson Thacher & Bartlett, 1962—, partner firm, 1970—. Mem. Am. (antitrust sect., merger com.), N.Y. State (antitrust sect., Sherman Act com.) bar assns., Assn. Bar City N.Y., Fed. Bar Council (trustee). Author: (with Byron E. Fox) Corporate Acquisitions and Mergers, Vol. 1, 1968, Vol. 2, 1970, Vol. 3, 1973. Contbr. articles to publs.; lectr. on anti-trust law. Home: 69 W 89th St New York City NY 10024 Office: One Battery Park Plaza New York City NY 10004

FOX, FAY LYONEL, writer; b. Williamsburg, Va., Sept. 26, 1913; d. Bertram Lionel and Annie Dorsie (Martin) Parr; student Napa Jr. Coll., 1964-65, Vallejo Jr. Coll., 1967; m. James Erwin Dula, Sr., Apr. 17, 1929; children—James Erwin, Joseph Calloway, Faye Lyonel (Mrs. John J. Hobbs); m. 2d, M. Daniel Dula, Apr. 13, 1960; m. 3d, Harold H. Fox, June 10, 1972. Alphabetizer facts Swens Hist. Index Va., 1929-30; reporter, feature writer, society editor Williamburg bur. Daily Press, Newport News, Va., 1953-60; asst. soc. editor Vallejo (Cal.) Times Herald, 1960; polit. reporter Napa County (Cal., Record, 1961-63, 70-72; dir. publicity 25th Dist. Agrl. Assn., Napa Town and County Fair, 1970-72, program and spl. events dir., 1974; free-lance writer, 1960—. Mem. Am. Bus. Women's Assn. (organizer, cons. Napa chpt. 1973, pres. Napa 1974—; Woman of Year award Vallejo 1972), Women in Communications, N. Bay Press Assn. Democrat. Baptist (various offices). Mem. Order Eastern Star. Author lyrics Alaska, 1959, Pulling Up Stakes, 1959; What Can I Do?, 1962. Compiler, editor: Invitation to Napa County, 1962. Address: 3478 Willis Dr Napa CA 94558

FOX, HAZEL METZ (MRS. ALLAN E. FOX), educator; b. Barton, Md., July 2, 1921; d. Jefferson W. and Blanche (Inskeep) Metz; B.A., Western Md. Coll., 1943, D.Sc., 1969; M.S., Ia. State U., 1947, Ph.D., 1954; m. Allan E. Fox, Jan. 6, 1950; children—Jefferson, Margaret, Allan, Robert, Frank. Tchr. high schs., Allegany County, Md., 1943-45; research asst. Ia. State U., Ames, 1945-47, research asso., 1950-55; research asso. Children's Fund of Mich., Detroit, 1947-50; asso. prof. dept. food and nutrition U. Neb., 1954-62, prof., 1962—, George Holmes prof. food and nutrition, 1968—, chmn. dept., 1963—. Mem. Am. Inst. Nutrition, Am. Dietetic Assn., Am. Home Econs. Assn. (Borden award in human nutrition 1969). Contbr. articles to profl. jours. Home: 1231 N 38th St Lincoln NE 68503

FOX, JEAN CAPLAN (MRS. JOSEPH FOX), lawyer; b. Rockaway Beach, N.Y., Aug. 8, 1920; d. Philip and Selma (Mayer) Caplan; B.A. with distinction in Econs., Temple U., 1941; LL.B., Yale, 1943 (J.D. 1971); m. Joseph Fox, Dec. 19, 1942; children—Philip C., Steven Barry, Berryl C. Admitted to N.Y. State bar, 1945, U.S. Supreme Ct. bar, 1967; asso. firm Koss & Fox, Far Rockaway, N.Y., 1945-48; practiced in Neponsit, N.Y., 1948—. Den leader Cub Scouts U.S., 1955-58; sec. Rockaway Civic Club, 1945-46; mem. N.Y.C. local sch. bd., Queens County, 1956-62, chmn. 1959-60; co-chmn. Yale Alumni Schs. Com. on Admissions, Queens, 1969-71, chmn., 1971—; pres. Parents for Columbia U., 1968-69; pres. Parents Assn. Jr. High Sch. 180, Queens, 1969-72; mem. consultative council Far Rockaway High Sch., 1970—, mem. exec. bd. Parents Assn., 1970, pres. Parents Assn., 1972—; pres. Ad Hoc Parents Assn. Beach Channel High Sch., 1972—. Capt., Rockaway Republican Club, 1960. Named Outstanding Woman, Nat. Council Jewish Women, Rockaway chpt., 1971. Mem. Queens County Women's Bar Assn. (chmn. com. on fed. admissions 1964), Am. Judicature Soc., Queens County Bar Assn., Pi Gamma Mu, Phi Delta Tau. Jewish religion (mem. temple sisterhood). Clubs: Yale Alumni of Queens County (exec. bd. 1968—), Belle Harbor Garden. Address: 144-17 Rockaway Beach Blvd Neponsit NY 11694

FOX, JEAN JOICEY, librarian; b. Toronto, Ont., Can., Apr. 19, 1920; d. William Henry and Gertrude Emily (Eade) Fox; B.A., U. Western Ont., 1945; M.L.S., U. Toronto, 1946. Came to U.S., 1946, naturalized, 1956. Chief gen. reference A.M.A. Library, Chgo., 1962—. Mem. A.L.A., Med. Library Assn., League Women Voters, Common Cause, Am. Civil Liberties Union. Home: 456 Carleton Glen Ellyn IL 60137 Office: 535 N Dearborn St Chicago IL 60610

FOX, LAURA (MRS. VERNON B. FOX), educator; b. Albion, Mich., July 5, 1916; d. Arthur Holmes and Grace (Fellows) Ellerby; A.B., Fla. State U., 1955, M.S., 1958; student Albion Coll., 1938-40; m. Vernon B. Fox, Mar. 22, 1941; children—Karen M., Vernon B., Loraine G. Tchr. biology and chemistry Leon High Sch., Tallahassee, 1955—. Mem. Am. Assn. U. Women, Nat. Assn. Biology Tchrs., Nat. Assn. Sci. Tchrs., Nat. Fla. edn. assn., Kappa Delta Pi. Home: 644 Voncile Av Tallahassee FL 32303

FOX, SISTER MARY ELEANOR, educator; b. Bellevue, Ky., Aug. 14, 1919; d. William Albert and Helen Catherine (Bosch) Fox; A.B., Thomas More Coll., 1942; M.S., Cath. U. Am., 1944; Ph.D., U. Cin., 1962. Faculty, Thomas More Coll., Covington, Ky., 1946—, prof. physics, 1964—. Mem. Diocesan Bd. Edn., 1973—. Trustee St. Claire Med. Center, Morehead, Ky., St. Charles Nursing Home, Covington. Named Outstanding Tchr. of Year, Thomas More Coll., 1971. Mem. Am. Phys. Soc., Am. Assn. Physics Tchrs., Sigma Xi. Home: 1601 Dixie Hwy Covington KY 41011

FOX, MARY ELIZABETH, educator, pianist, lectr., journalist; b. Granger, Tex., June 2, 1918; d. J. S. and Frances (West) Fox; A.B., B.S., Southwestern U., 1931, A.M., 1932; postgrad. U. Tex. Prof. journalism Southwestern U., Georgetown, Tex., 1944—, dir. publicity, 1950—; corr. to UN, 1945—. Del. Williamson County, Tex., Nat. Democratic Convs. Mem. Am. Assn. Profs. Journalism, Nat. Collegiate Players, League Women Voters, Tex. Woman's Press Assn. (pres.), Nat. Fedn. Press Women, Am. Assn. U. Profs., Am. Newspaper Women's Club, Am. Judicature Soc., Acad. Polit. Sci., Tex. Hist. Soc., Am. Assn. U. Women, Brit. Horse Soc., Internat. Platform Assn., Marquis Biog. Library Soc. (adv. bd.), Sigma Phi Alpha, Sigma Tau Delta, Delta Omicron, Pi Epsilon Delta, Pi Delta Epsilon, Delta Delta Delta, Theta Sigma Phi. Methodist. Clubs: Central Tex. Dinner (dir., past pres.), Stagecoach Country (dir.); Music, Writers and Press (London) Ltd. Address: Box 369 Southwestern U Sta Georgetown TX 78626

FOX, MURIEL, pub. relations exec.; b. Newark, Feb. 3, 1928; d. M. Morris and Anne L.(Rubenstein) Fox; student Rollins Coll., 1944-46; B.A. summa cum laude, Barnard Coll., 1948; m. Shepard G. Aronson, July 1, 1955; children—Eric R., Lisa S. Art critic, bridal editor Miami (Fla.) News, 1946; reporter U.P.I., 1946-48; polit. speechwriter, publicist, 1949-50; with Carl Byoir & Assos., N.Y.C., 1950—, TV-radio writer, 1950-52, dir. TV-radio dept., 1952-57, v.p., 1957-74, group v.p., sr. cons., mem. exec. com., 1974—. Mem. nat. comml. panel Am. Arbitration Assn. Co-chmn. Vice Presdl. Task Force on Women, 1968; mem. steering com. Women's Forum, 1974—; mem. Women's Econ. Adv. Com., N.Y.C., 1974—. Bd. dirs. N.Y. Diabetes Assn., 1956-66, Holy Land Conservation Fund. Mem. Am. Women in Radio and TV (dir. 1959-61, chmn. nat. publicity com. 1955-57, chmn. nat. pub. relations com. 1957-59), Nat. Orgn. for Women (founder, v.p. 1967-70, chmn. bd. 1971-73, chmn. nat. adv. com. 1973-74, bd. dirs. Legal Def. and Edn. Fund 1974—). Home: 40 E 83rd St New York City NY 10028 Office: 800 2nd Av New York City NY 10017

FOX, PATRICIA JANE COOMBS (MRS. C. JAMES FOX), author, artist, illustrator; b. Los Angeles, July 23, 1926; d. Donald Gladstone and Katherine (Goodro) Coombs; student DePauw U., 1944-45, Mich. State U., 1945-47; B.A., U. Wash., 1948, M.A., 1950; m. C. James Fox, July 13, 1951; children—Ann Claire, Patricia Taylor. Author: Dorrie's Magic, 1962; The Lost Playground, 1963; Waddy and His Brother, 1963; Dorrie and the Blue Witch, 1964; Dorrie's Play, 1965; Dorrie and the Weatherbox (Jr. Lit. Guild selection), 1966; Dorrie and the Wizard's Spell, 1967; Dorrie and the Witch Doctor, 1967; Dorrie and the Haunted House, 1970; Lisa and the Grompet, 1971; Dorrie and the Birthday Eggs, 1971; Mouse Cafe, 1972; Dorrie and the Goblin, 1972; Dorrie and the Fortune Teller, 1973; Dorrie and the Amazing Magic Elixir, 1974. Illustrator: P.J. My Friend (Gerson), 1968; Lobo (Gretan), 1968; Peri's Bell (Williamson), 1968. Mem. Authors Guild, Pi Beta Phi. Episcopalian. Club: S.I.M.S. Home: 178 Oswegatchie Rd Waterford CT 06385

FOX, RENEE CLAIRE, educator; b. N.Y.C., Feb. 15, 1928; d. Paul Fred and Henrietta (Gold) Fox; A.B. summa cum laude, Smith Coll., 1949; Ph.D., Harvard, 1954; M.A. (hon.), U. Pa., 1971; Sc.D., Med. Coll. Pa., 1974. Teaching fellow Harvard U., 1950-51; research asst. Bur. Applied Social Research, Columbia U., N.Y.C., 1953-55, research asso., 1955-58; lectr., dept. sociology Barnard Coll., Columbia U., N.Y.C., 1955-58, asst. prof., 1958-64, asso. prof., 1964-66; mem. sci. adv. Centre de Recherches Socioloqiques, Kinshasa, Congo, 1963-67; vis. prof. sociology U. Officielle du Congo, Lubumbashi, 1965; lectr. sociology, dept. social relations Harvard U., 1967-69, research fellow Center Internat. Affairs, 1967-68, research asso., 1968-70; vis. prof. Sir George Williams U., Montreal, Que., summer 1968; prof. sociology dept. psychiatry dept. and medicine dept. U. Pa., Phila., 1969—, chmn. dept. sociology, 1972—. John Simon Guggenheim Meml. Found. fellowship, 1962, E. Harris Harbison Gifted Teaching award Danforth Found., 1970, Phi Beta Kappa vis. scholar, 1973-74, 74-75. Fellow African Studies Assn., Am. Sociol. Assn. rep. to Social Sci. Research Council 1970-73 (mem. council 1973—, chmn. med. sociology sect. 1974-75), Am. Acad. Arts and Scis.; mem. A.A.A.S., Am. Assn. U. Profs., Am. Assn. U. Women, Social Sci. Research Council (v.p., dir. 1971-74), Assn. Am. Med. Colls., Eastern Sociol. Soc. (v.p. 1973-74), N.Y. Acad. Scis., Soc. for Scientific Study Religion, Inst. Soc. Ethics and Life Scis. (founder, gov.), Inst. Intercultural Studies (asst. sec., 1969—). Author: Experiment Perilous, 1959; (with Willy DeCraemer) the Emerging Physician, 1968; (with Judith P. Swazey) The Courage to Fail, 1974. Asso. editor: Am. Sociol. Review, 1963-66, Social Sci and Medicine. Contbr. articles in field to profl. jours. Home: 226 W Rittenhouse Sq Philadelphia PA 19103

FOX, RUTH MARY, educator; b. Racine, Wis., May 18, 1891; d. Conrad and Anna (McCormick) Fox; A.B., Rosary Coll., 1912; M.A., U. Wis., 1913; Litt.D., St. Thomas Coll., 1956; L.H.D., Mt. Mary Coll., 1960; postgrad. Stanford, U. Chgo., U. Fribourg (Switzerland); LL.D., Cardinal Stritch Coll., 1974. Head dept. English, Randall Jr. High Sch., Madison, Wis., 1913-17; tchr. Racine High Sch., 1917-21, supr. English, Racine Pub. Schs., 1921-22; instr. English, Milw. State Tchrs. Coll. (merged with U. Wis.—Milw. 1956), 1922-42, head composition workshop, 1942-48, lectr. humanities, 1924-60, prof. humanities, English, 1955-60, prof. emeritus, 1960—; prof. in residence Edgewood Coll., Madison, 1963—; lectr. on Dante, Marquette U., Milw., 1961—, Edgewood Coll., 1963—; vis. prof. Mt. Mary Coll., Cardinal Stritch Coll., Alverno Coll. (all Milw.), Coll. St. Scholastica, Duluth. Founder, Augustinian Hist. Inst., 1944. Recipient Distinguished Work in Human Relations award B'nai B'rith, 1955; Distinguished Teaching in Wis. citation Marquette U., 1956; Magnificat medal Mundelein Coll., 1959; Superior Service award English Assn. Greater Milw., 1960; Gov.'s Awards in the Arts, 1972. Mem. Dante Soc. Am., Wis. Fellowship Poets, Sceptre and Sword, Catholic Poetry Soc., Am. Assn. U. Profs., Medieval and Renaissance Guild, Coll. English Assn., Nat., Wis. councils tchrs. English, State Hist. Soc. Wis., Internat. Platform Assn., Delta Kappa Gamma. Author: Dante Lights the Way, 1958. Contbr. poetry to various publs. including Commonweal, America, N.Y. Times, Spirit, Ava Maria, English Jour., also anthologies including New Poetry out of Wisconsin, 1969; articles to profl. jours. Home: 855 Woodrow St Madison WI 53711

FOX, SARA, copywriter; b. Dallas, June 17, 1907; d. Max and Sarah (Landsberg) Fox; B.Lit., Columbia, 1931; postgrad. U. Ariz., 1972—; m. Leo M. Glassman, 1930 (div. 1947); m. 2d, H.J. Tannenbaum, 1955 (dec. 1970); 1 dau., Leda Glassman (Mrs. F.A. Arensburg). Publicity dir. Helena Rubenstein, Inc., 1931-43; pres. Sara Fox, Inc., Fashion Pub. Relations and Advt., 1943-48; advt. and marketing Helena Rubenstein, Inc., N.Y.C., 1948-61; pres. Fox. Cons., Inc., N.Y.C., 1961-70. Publicity chmn. Am. Assn. Ret. Persons, Green Valley, Ariz., 1972—. Chmn. Democratic N.Y. Boutique, 1968. Named one of top seven N.Y. Advt. Women, 1961. Mem. Fashion Group, Women in Communications. Editor Cosmetics Fair, 1966-67. Patentee cosmetics. Home: 565 Paseo Le Rueda Green Valley AZ 85614

FOX, ZEOLA MISKIMINS, librarian; b. Promise City, Ia., June 7, 1903; d. Henry Elmer and Arminda Alice (Close) Hesseltine; B.S., Mo. State Tchrs. Coll., Kirksville, 1955, M.A. with honors, 1959, postgrad. 1960-62; postgrad. So. Ill. U., 1969; m. Frank Edmonds Miskimins, Oct. 9, 1920 (dec.); children—Harold Hessell, Close Harrison, Rex Edmonds, Wendell Elmer; m. 2d. George Wesley Fox, Oct. 27, 1962 (dec.). Tchr. grade, jr. high schs., Centerville, Ia., 1951-57, high sch. 1957-60; library dir. Indian Hills Community Coll., Centerville, Ia., 1961-73. Leader, 4-H, 1938-42, chmn. County 4-H, 1942-45; sec. twp. Ind. Sch. Bd. 1952-55. Twp. chmn. Republican party, 1940-42. Named County Mother of Year, 1950; recipient Ia. State Fair Blue Ribbon, culinary dept., 1948. Mem. Am., Ia., library assns., Nat., Ia. edn. assns., Faculty Assn. (rec. sec. 1957, 70), Coll. Faculty Assn. (alumni sec. 1966-67), Ia. Higher Edn. Assn., Civic League, Delta Kappa Gamma (sec. 1969-70, pres. 1973—). Methodist. Mem. Order of Eastern Star (worthy matron 1937); mem. White Shrine of Jerusalem (worthy high priestess 1969, 73). Clubs: Community (sec. 1959), Past Matron (pres. 1973-74). Home: Rural Route 1 Plano IA 52581

FOY, ERMA MAE FYFE (MRS. DONALD P. FOY), golf franchising and promotion co. exec.; b. Washington, Nov. 3, 1918; d. John H. and Carrie Irene (Nattress) Fyfe; student Washington Bus. Sch., 1935-36; m. Donald P. Foy, Apr. 17, 1942. Editorial asst. Mfrs. News Bur., Inc., Washington, 1936-40; adminstrv. asst. Nat. Def. Research Com., Washington, 1940-45, Slater System Food Service, Phila., 1953-59; owner, operator Shore Radio, Atlantic City, N.J., 1959-62; exec. asst. to v.p. franchise div. Arnold Palmer Enterprises, Linwood, N.J., 1963-69, dir. promotional services and franchisee relations, 1969-74, chief operational officer, 1974—. Recipient awards for outstanding performance Nat. Def. Research Com. and Naval Bur. Ordnance, 1940-45. Mem. Audubon Soc., Nat. Oceanographic Inst., Am. Heritage Soc., Am. Soc. Notaries, Absecon Island Power Squadron Aux. Club: Yacht (Pleasantville, N.J.). Home: 1217 Bayshore Av Brigantine NJ 08203 Office: 215 Wabash Av Linwood NJ 08221

FOY, LAURETTA BEATY (MRS. ROBERT W. FOY), pilot; b. Oklahoma City; d. Fredrick Ernest and Kathryn Graham (Keffer) Beaty; student Occidental Coll., 1929-32; m. Robert W. Foy, May 16, 1945 (dec. Mar. 1950); children—James C., Ernest, Shawn K. Dancer, Warner Bros., Los Angesles, Cal., 1932-41; pilot Piper Aircraft Corp., Lockheed, Pa., 1940-41; test pilot N.Am. Aviation, Inc., Los Angeles, 1946-48; helicopter pilot, instr. Belmont Aviation Co., Long Beach, Cal., 1962-64, Helicabs, Los Angeles, 1964; chief helicopter pilot Pacific Airmotive Co., Burbank, Cal., 1965-68; chief pilot Southland Helicopter div. Hughes Tool Co. (now Hughes Helicopters), Long Beach, 1968-74, Bell Helicopter Co., Van Nuys Cal., 1974—. Mem. Presdl. Aviation Adv. Commn., Washington, 1970-73, Cal. Gov.'s Aerospace-Aviation Task Force, 1969—; mem. Adv. Com. on Aviation, 1967-70, chmn., 1970. Served with (WASP) USAAF, 1942-44. Decorated Silver Medal award FAA, 1970. Mem. Profl. Helicopter Pilots Assn., 99's, Screen Actors Guild, Musicians Union, Fifinella, Whirly-Girls. Republican. Christian Scientist. Office: Van Nuys Center 7155 Valjean Av Van Nuys CA 91406

FRACCI, CARLA (MRS. BEPPE MENEGATTI), ballet dancer; b. Milan, Italy, Aug. 20, 1938; d. Luigi and Santa Laura (Rocca) Fracci; student Teatro alla Scala Ballet Sch., 1946-55; m. Beppe Menegatti, Oct. 7, 1964. Ballet dancer, 1955—, ballet roles include Cincerella, Giselle, Romeo and Juliet, Don Giovanni, Les Sylphides, Swan Lake, Sleeping Beauty; has appeared in Teatro alla Scala, Teatro dei Parchi, Genoa, Italy, Teatro Verde, Venice, Italy, Empire Theatre, Edinburgh, Scotland, Royal Festival Hall, London, Eng., Coventry Theatre, Eng., NBC-TV, N.Y.C., London Festival Ballet tour, Covent Garden Royal Opera House, London, Teatro Verdi, Trieste, Teatro Communale, Florence, Italy, Civic Opera House, Dallas, Teatro dell 'Opera, Rome, Italy, Bayerischen Staatsoper, Munich, Germany, Wurttembergische Staats-theater, Stuttgart, Germany, Lyric Opera Theatre, Chgo., Teatro Nuovo, Spoleto, Italy, Teatro Regio, Parma, Italy, Teatro Comunale, Bologna, Italy, Royal Theatre, Copenhagen, Denmark, Theatre de l'Opera, Montecarlo, Am. Ballet Theatre tour, State Theatre, N.Y., Jones Hall, Houston, Back Bay Theatre, Boston, Carter Barron Amphiteatro, Washington, Met. Theatre, N.Y.C., others. Home: 5 Via S Spirito 20121 Milan Italy care Dr Dino Meucci 57 Via le Coni Zugma 20144 Milan Italy

FRAGNOLI, NANCY DUGGAN (MRS. BILLY NICHOLAS FRAGNOLI), educator; b. Richmond, Va., Mar. 8, 1926; d. Charles George and Katherine Mae (Humphreys) Duggan; B.S. in Phys. Edn., William and Mary Coll., 1948; postgrad Skidmore Coll., 1966, U. Vt., 1968-70; m. Billy Nicholas Fragnoli, Mar. 8, 1952; children—Katherine Mary, James Joseph. Counselor, Meml. Guidance Clinic, Richmond, 1948-49; phys. corrective therapist McGuire VA Hosp., Richmond, 1949-50; tchr. Glen Lea Sch.,

Henrico County, Va., 1950-52; tchr. phys. edn. Whitehall (N.Y.) Central Sch., 1958—. Adviser, Gay Dolphin Swim Club, Whitehall, 1971—. Mem. N.Y., Tri-County, Whitehall Tchrs. assns., N.Y. Assn. Health and Phys. Edn., A.A.H.P.E.R., Glens Falls Hosp. Guild (pres. 1961-62, 64-65), Delta Kappa Gamma. Home: 258 Broadway St Whitehall NY 12887

FRAIR, CHERYL JO (MRS. LAWRENCE WILLIAM FRAIR), psychologist; b. La Crosse, Wis., Aug. 4, 1944; d. David Albert and Helen Houck (Blomguist) Mayo, Jr.; B.A., Sophia U., Tokyo, Japan, 1964; M.S., Utah State U., 1966, Ph.D. (univ. grantee, univ. research fellow), 1969; m. Lawrence William Frair, Aug. 27, 1968; 1 son, John Lamayo. Psychometrist, Internat. Schs., Bangkok, Thailand, 1967-68, McAuley Neuropsychiatric Inst., San Francisco, 1968-69; staff psychologist Alaska Psychiatric Inst., Anchorage, 1970-73, chief psychologist, 1973—. Pvt. practice psychotherapy, 1970—. Asst. dir. Nat. Inst. Mental Health Staff Devel. grantee, 1972—. Mem. Am., Alaska Psychol. assns. Mem. Christian Ch. Home: 3962 Reka Dr Anchorage AK 99504 Office: 2900 Providence Av Anchorage AK 99504

FRAKES, VERONICA JEAN MCVEAGH, univ. adminstr.; b. N.Y.C., Jan. 5, 1935; d. Joseph and Mary Cecilia (Devlin) McVeagh; student Santa Monica Jr. Coll., 1959-60, 60-64; B.A., Valley State Coll., 1969; postgrad. U. N.M., 1971—. With Woolworth Co., N.Y.C., 1951; office clk. Continental Baking Co. div. U.S. Tabacco Co., N.Y.C., 1951-52; payroll and accounting clk., adminstrv. asst. U. Cal. at Los Angeles, 1954-64; coordinator women's center, div. student affairs U. N.M., Albuquerque, 1972—. Rec. sec. N.M. Women's Polit. Caucus, 1973—. mem. steering com., 1973-74. Mem. Nat. Assn. Women Deans, Adminstrs. and Counselors. Club: Women's Faculty (Albuquerque). Home: Route 4 Box 1095 Los Lunas NM 87031 Office: U NM 1824 La Loma NE Albuquerque NM 87131

FRAME, MRS. HOWARD A. (ANNE PARSONS FRAME), civic worker; b. Berkeley, Cal., Jan. 3, 1904; d. Reginald Hascall and Maude (Bemis) Parsons; A.B., Mills Coll., 1924; postgrad. Columbia, 1924-25; m. Frederic D. Tootell, Apr. 3, 1926 (div. July 1935); children—Geoffrey H., Natalie Oliver; m. 2d, Jasper Ewing Brady (dec. Dec. 1944); 1 son, Hugh Parsons; m. 3d, Howard Andres Frame, Mar. 29, 1948. Dir. Parsons, Hart & Co., Parsons Investment Co., Hillcrest Orchard Corp. Mem. bd. mgmt. Palo Alto br. A.R.C., 1952-60; bd. dirs. Children's Health Council, Palo Alto, 1953-63, 64—, Holbrook-Palmer Recreation Park Found. 1953—; trustee Nat. Recreation and Park Assn., 1966-73, Nat. Recreation Assn., 1948-66; bd. govs. San Francisco Symphony Assn., 1963—; mem. Atherton Park Recreation Commn., 1969-74; bd. dirs. Children's Hosp. at Stanford, 1967—. Mem. League Women Voters, Cal., Chgo., Seattle, San Mateo County hist. socs., Seattle, Mus. Soc., San Francisco Mus. Modern Art. Clubs: Francisca (San Francisco); Woodside-Atherton Garden (dir. 1966-68); Sunset and Seattle Tennis; Casa Abrego (Monterey). Home: 587 Fletcher Dr Atherton CA 94025

FRANCES, EVAN BARBARA (MRS. ALEXANDER FRANCES), author, editor, interior designer; b. N.Y.C., Aug. 19; student Hunter Coll.; A.B. in English Lit. and Journalism, U. Chgo., 1937; M.A., N.Y. U., 1940; postgrad. Am. U.; m. Alexander Frances, Oct. 6, 1946; children—Andrew, James, Scott. Asso. editor Esquire mag., 1942-45, Look mag., 1945-46; feature editor, then mng. editor Pic mag., 1946-50; feature editor House Beautiful, Guide for the Bride, 1950-53; housing and archtl. editor Today's Woman, 1953-54; home furnishings and archtl. editor Family Circle mag., 1954-67; spl. projects editor Ladies' Home Jour., N.Y.C., 1968—. Recipient Scandinavian Design award, 1958; Dorothy Dawe award distinguished journalistic coverage Home Furnishings Industry, 1962, 64, 68; Dallas award, 1963; U. Mo.-J.C. Penney award, 1969. Corporate mem. Am. Inst. Interior Designers; mem. Home Fashions League, Archtl. League. Office: Downe Pub Inc 641 Lexington Av New York City NY 10022

FRANCESA, DORIS TINA, constrn. co. exec.; b. Fayetteville, W.Va., Dec. 22, 1927; d. John Morel and Nona (Stephenson) Francesa; B.A., U. Ga., 1950. Bookkeeper, Acme Constrn. Co., Beckley, W.Va., 1950-52, sec., treas., 1952-65, pres., 1965—; dir., sec., treas. Honey-In-The-Rock Motel, Beckley, 1965—. Home: PO Box 570 Fayetteville WV 25840 Office: PO Box 1660 Beckley WV 25801

FRANCIS, ARLENE (MRS. MARTIN GABLE), actress; b. Boston; d. Aram and Leah (Davis) Kazanjian; student Convent of Mt. St. Vincent, Finch Coll., Theatre Guild Sch.; H.H.D., Am. Internat. Coll., 1965, Keuka Coll., 1966; m. Martin Gabel, May 14, 1946; 1 son, Peter Joseph. Appeared in (plays) The Women, 1937, Orson Welles' Mercury Theatre prodn. of Horse Eats Hat, and Danton's Death, 1938, All That Glitters, 1938, Michael Drops In, 1938, Young Couple Wanted, 1939, Journey to Jerusalem, 1940, The Walking Gentleman, 1942, The Doughgirls, 1942, The Overtons, 1945, The French Touch, 1945, The Cup of Trembling, 1948, (in translation of French play) L'Empereur de Chine, 1949, The Little Blue Light, 1951, Once More With Feeling, Mrs. Dally, 1965, Dinner at Eight, 1966; TV appearances What's My Line, from 1950, Home, 1955-57, also Soldier Parade; mistress of ceremony radio programs What's my Name, Blind Date, Arlene Francis at Sardi's, Family Living; movie appearances include All My Sons, One, Two, Three, 1961, The Thrill of It All, 1963. Dir. Bonwit Teller, N.Y.C. Mem. nat. adv. council U. Utah. Named to U.S. Hall of Fame, 1967. Mem. Am. Fedn. of Radio Artists, Actors Equity Assn., Screen Actors Guild. Author: That Certain Something: The Magic of Charm, 1960. Address: 465 Park Av New York City NY 10022

FRANCIS, CLARA A(VONELLE) HARE (MRS. RICHARD J. FRANCIS), plastics mfg. co. exec.; b. Harrod, O., Mar. 7, 1914; d. William E. and Margret (Thomas) Hare; student Bliss Coll., 1947-49; m. Richard J. Francis, Feb. 4, 1952. Dept. mgr. Walgreen Drug, Columbus, O., 1945-54; sec., treas., dir. Francis Industries, Pataskala, O., 1956—; sec., treas. Richard J. Francis Asso., 1954—; pres. Francis Electronics, 1963—, Francis Industries, 1971—. Lectr. Ohio State U., Columbus, 1948. Active Civil Def., Lima, O., 1942-44; pres., founder Children's Hosp. Twig, Columbus, O., 1950-52. Bd. cons. Basic and Applied Sci. Lab. U. Cin., 1972—. Named Hon. Distinguished Alumni U. Cin., 1972; named Ky. Col., also adm. Neb. Navy. Mem. Pataskala Area C. of C., Bus. and Profl. Womens Club. Baptist. Mem. Order Eastern Star, White Shrine. Clubs: Pataskala Archery (co-founder, v.p. 1957-59), Zonta (sect. dir. 1963-65). Contbr. articles in field. Patentee in field. Office: 11855 Broad St Pataskala OH 43062

FRANCIS, DOROTHY BRENNER (MRS. RICHARD M. FRANCIS), author; b. Lawrence, Kan., Nov. 30, 1926; d. Clayton and Cecile (Goforth) Brenner; Mus.B., U. Kan., 1948; m. Richard M. Francis, Aug. 30, 1950; children—Ann, Patricia. Tchr. music pub. sch., Orange, Cal., 1948-50, Pleasant Hill, Mo., 1950-51, Cache, Okla., 1951-52, Gilman, Ia., 1961-62; tchr. creative writing, Judson Coll., Elgin, Ill., summer 1971, Marshalltown (Ia.) Community Coll., 1971; literary lectr., 1970-72. Vice pres. Marshalltown Community Orchestra Bd., 1970-72. Recipient Bobbs Merrill grant in aid for outstanding juvenile novel-in-progress Ind. U., 1967, award for outstanding juvenile novel-in-progress, 1968. Mem. P.E.O., Mu Phi Epsilon. Methodist. Author: Adventure at Riverton Zoo, 1966; Mystery of the Forgotten Map, 1968; Laugh At The Evil Eye, 1970; Another Kind of Beauty, 1970; Hawaiian Interlude, 1970; Studio Affair, 1972; A Blue Ribbon for Marni, 1973; Nurse on Assignment, 1973; Murder in Hawaii, 1973; Nurse Under Fire, 1973; Nurse in the Caribbean, 1974; Golden Girl, 1974. Home: 1505 Brentwood Terrace Marshalltown IA 50158

FRANCIS, FRANCES ENSEKI, lawyer, economist; b. Los Angeles, May 18, 1940; d. Frank I. and Hannah H. (Tanaka) Enseki; A.B., Dickinson Coll., 1962; LL.B., Yale, 1965; M.Pub. Adminstrn., Harvard, 1969, postgrad., 1970-72; m. Walton J. Francis, June 14, 1969; 1 dau., Margaret M. Asst. to commr. FPC, Washington, 1965-68, atty. Office Gen. Counsel, 1969-70; atty. New Eng. River Basins Commn., Boston, 1971; cons. Energy Policy Project, Washington, 1973—; atty. firm Spiegel & McDiarmid, Washington, 1974—. Mem. Am. Econ. Assn., Am. Bar Assn. Office: 2600 Virginia Av NW Washington DC

FRANCIS, HELEN DANNEFER (MRS. LOWELL ALEXANDER FRANCIS), writer; b. Cuba, Kan., Jan. 2, 1915; d. Edward Rhule and Lily Ann (Nutter) Dannefer; B.A. in English, B.S. in Edn., Ft. Hays Kan. State Coll., 1935; m. Lowell Alexander Francis, June 3, 1935; children—Michael Jackson, John Alexander. Instr. journalism, dir. communications Ft. Hays Kan. State Coll., 1946-53; free-lance writer, 1953—. Mem. adv. panel in creative writing Kan. Arts Commn., 1966; organizational bd. mem. Hays Arts Council, 1965-70; cons. book fairs, Okla., Neb., Kan. Chmn. Hays Council on Human Relations, 1967-68; mem. pub. library bd., Hays, 1947-56. Precinct committeewoman Republican party, Hays, 1950-54; del. state and dist. convs. Bd. dirs. Kan. Adv. Council on Civil Rights, 1952-73, chmn., 1971-72; bd. dirs. Hays Community Day Care, Inc., 1972-74. Recipient Alumni Achievement award Ft. Hays Kan. State Coll., 1972. Mem. League Women Voters (local human resources chmn. 1968-74), N.A.A.C.P., Common Cause (dist. chmn. 1973-74), Phi Kappa Phi. Presbyn. Author: The Phantom Steer, 1953; Double Reverse, 1958; Football Flash, 1961; Basketball Bones, 1962; Martha Norton and Operation Fitness U.S.A., 1963; Big Swat, 1963. Contbr. articles to profl. jours. Home: 401 Walnut St Hays KS 67601

FRANCIS, JANICE ELVINA WATSON (MRS. CARMEN DEAN FRANCIS), newspaper pub.; b. Clyde, Kan., Nov. 20, 1936; d. Maurice French and Vera Mae (Lewis) Watson; grad. high sch.; m. Carmen Dean Francis, Feb. 5, 1955; children—Marvin, Norman, John, Kendal. With Clifton (Kan.) News-Tribune, 1950—, owner, editor, pub., 1966—. Storm spotter Civil Def., Clifton, 1966—. Mem. Kan. Press Assn., C. of C. (chmn. housing com. 1966-71), Am. Legion Aux. (unit publicity chmn. 1967-69), Cath. Daus. Am. (grand regent 1963-65), Sigma Delta Chi. Roman Catholic. Home: 3d and Washington St Clifton KS 66937 Office: PO Box 280 Clifton KS 66937

FRANCIS, MARILYN ANN, editor, poet; b. Columbus, O., Jan. 26, 1920; d. Roy Brooke and Ruth Pauline (Needles) Francis; B.S., Ohio U., 1941. With Western Electric Co., Kearny, N.J., 1941-45, Retail Credit Co., Newark, 1945-51; free lance writer, 1951—; editor Verde Ind., Sedona, Ariz., 1973-74. Lectr., cons. poetry. Cultural dir. Chapel of Holy Cross, Sedona, 1974—. Bd. dirs. Sedona Arts Center, 1961—, v.p., 1973; pres. bd. trustees Sedona Pub. Library, 1967-68; bd. dirs. Winged Arts Gallery Contemporary Art, Sedona. Mem. Poetry Soc. Am., Nat. League Am. Pen Women (Phoenix pres. 1959-61), Centro Studi e Scambi, Alpha Xi Delta. Republican. Club: Soroptimist (pres. Sedona 1967-68). Author: Thunder in the Superstitions, 1959; Tangents at Noon, 1960; Space for Sound, 1961; Mirror Without Glass, 1964; Symbols for Instants, 1965; Radius: Red Rocks, 1972. Home: PO Box 196 Sedona AZ 86336

FRANCISCO, VIRGINIA ROYSTER (MRS. WILLIAM THOMSON FRANCISCO), educator; b. Youngstown, O., Nov. 18, 1942; d. John LeMay and Mary Marjory (Fleming) Royster; B.A. with honors, Mary Baldwin Coll., 1964; M.A., U. Va., 1966; Ph.D., Ind. U., 1974; m. William Thomson Francisco, Jr., Aug. 25, 1972. Instr. dramatic arts Mary Baldwin Coll., Staunton, Va., 1967, asst. prof., 1970—, dir., designer theater, 1970—; dir., designer Oak Grove Theatre, Staunton, Va., 1967—, Theater Wagon Staunton, Va., 1967—. Woodrow Wilson fellow, 1964. Mem. Am. Theatre Assn., Univ. and Coll. Theatre Assn. Home: Route 1 Box 192 Staunton VA 24401

FRANDO, ILDEFONSA ABELLA (MRS. MARIANO A. FRANDO), librarian; b. Tacloban City, Philippines, Jan. 23, 1924; d. Leon and Emilia (Penaflor) Abella; B.S., Divine Word U., 1952; m. Mariano A. Frando, Mar. 11, 1956. Clk., Mcpl. Treas.'s Office, Philippines, 1945-46, Office Justice Peace, 1949-52; tchr. elementary sch., Philippines, 1946-48, tchr. high sch., 1952-55; tchr. Resurrection Elementary Sch., St. Louis, 1956-57; clk.-typist Pius XII Meml. Library, St. Louis U., 1957-63, cataloger, 1963-72, catalog tng. supr., 1972—. Mem. Mo. Library Assn., Spl. Libraries Assn. Home: 2525 Dove Dr Florissant MO 63031 Office: 3655 W Pine St St Louis MO 63108

FRANK, ANNE MORING ROBINS, geophysicist; b. Newton, Mass., Jan. 7, 1919; d. Sidney Swaim and Frances (Lord) Robins; student St. Lawrence U., 1937-38, U. Mich., 1938; A.B., Bryn Mawr Coll., 1940; m. Wilfred R. Frank, Sept. 4, 1943 (dec., Nov. 1966); 1 son, John A. Jr. geologist Ohio Oil Co., Marshall, Ill., 1940-42; geophys. computer Gen. Geophys. Co., Houston, 1942-48; geophys. party chief Tidelands Exploration Co., Houston, 1948-53, rev. geophysicist, 1953-58, chief accountant, corp. sec., 1958-64; sr. accountant Teledyne Exploration Co., Houston, 1964-72, Gulf Coast Geo Data Corp., Houston, 1972—. Mem. Soc. Exploration Geophysicists, Houston Geol. Soc., Houston Gem and Mineral Soc. (treas.), Geophys. Soc. Houston. Home: 5200 Chestnut St Bellaire TX 77401 Office: 816 Americana Bldg Houston TX 77002

FRANK, ELAINE KOENIGSDORF (MRS. RICHARD LAWRENCE WOLF), lawyer; b. Kansas City, Mo., Jan. 24, 1918; d. Henry and Dorothy Belle (Levin) Koenigsdorf; certificate Lindenwood Coll., 1937; student McKay's Bus. Coll., 1948; LL.B., Southwestern U., 1957; m. Richard Lawrence Wolf, July 20, 1961; children—Babette (Mrs. Werner David Meyenberg), Robert Nelson Frank, Jr. Legal sec., Los Angeles, 1948-57; admitted to Cal. bar, 1958; research atty. Los Angeles Superior Ct., 1958-59; atty. Belli, Ashe & Gerry, San Francisco, 1959; research atty. Cal. Supreme Ct.-Cal. Jud. Council, 1959-60; practiced in Los Altos, 1961—; atty.-editor Commerce Clearing House, San Francisco, 1961-62; staff atty. Continuing Edn. of Bar, U. Cal. at Berkeley, 1963—. Mem. curriculum guide com. Cal. Community Colls.; mem. adv. com. legal forms Jud. Council. Mem. Am. Judicature Soc., State Bar Cal. (recorder com. on probate and trust law 1971—), Assn. Acad. Women at Berkeley, Internat. Platform Assn., Iota Tau Tau. Editor, co-author: California Civil Writs, 1970. Home: 102 Montclair Way Los Altos CA 94022 Office: 2150 Shattuck Av Berkeley CA 94704

FRANK, JOAN (BARBARA ANN WEISBECKER), theatre exec.; b. Bklyn., Apr. 19, 1937; d. Frank and Georgiana (Jerico) Weisbecker; grad. high sch. Theatrical performer, 1956-61; owner, producer Saranac Lake (N.Y.) Summer Theatre, 1961-63, Lake Placid (N.Y.) Playhouse, 1964-72; mng. dir. Center for Music, Drama and Art, Lake Placid, 1972—. Bd. dirs. Lake Placid Assn. for Music, Drama and Art, Inc. Mem. Lake Placid C. of C. (dir. 1973—), League Off-Broadway Theatres and Producers. Home: 37 Main St Lake Placid NY 12946 Office: Center for Music Drama and Art Lake Placid NY 12946

FRANK, JUDITH ANNE, social work adminstr.; b. Pitts., Nov. 1, 1937; d. Robert Walter and Dorothy (Mulvey) Frank; B.A., Mount Holyoke Coll., 1959; M.S.W., U. Pa., 1963. Med. research asst. Mass. Gen. Hosp., Boston, 1959-61; caseworker Magee Meml. Hosp., Phila., 1963-70, supr., 1966-70, asst. dir. social service, 1967-70, dir. social service Grad. Hosp., U. Pa., 1970—, lectr. Sch. Social Work, 1970—, mem. curriculum com., 1971—, mem. long-range planning com., 1971—, faculty mem. field agy. work party on communications, 1969-70. Recipient Virginia P. Robinson award U. Pa., 1964. Mem. Nat. Assn. Social Workers (chpt. asst. sec. 1964-67, mem. social legislation and action com. 1969-71, mem. nominating com. 1971—, chmn. com. on inquiry 1972—), Nat., Internat. confs. social welfare, Am. Acad. Social and Polit. Sci., Council Social Work Edn., Am. Assn. U. Women. Home: Brynwood Apts Wynnewood PA 19096 Office: 19th and Lombard Sts Philadelphia PA 19146

FRANK, MARJORIE HOFHEIMER (MRS. CHRIS GABLE), educator; b. N.Y.C., Feb. 25, 1906; d. Arthur and Helen (Milius) Hofheimer; student Columbia Sch. Bus. Adminstrn., 1924; m. Harry Frank, Jr., Oct. 14, 1926 (dec. Mar. 1963); m. 2d, Christopher Gable, Dec. 29, 1969. Dir. service in VA hosps., North Atlantic area A.R.C., 1945-49; asst. exec. dir. Nat. Assn. for Mental Health, N.Y.C., 1949-59; asso. exec. sec. Nat. Family Life Found., 1959-61, asso. exec. dir. Jewish Guild for Blind, N.Y.C., 1961-63; N.Y.C. regional planning rep. N.Y. Dept. Mental Hygiene, 1963-65, asst. to commr. N.Y.C. Community Mental Health Services, 1965-68; instr., adminstrv. asso. dept. psychiatry Columbia; cons. N.Y.C. Comprehensive Health Planning Agy.; coordinator mental health services Gouverneur Hosp., N.Y.C. Health and Hosp. Corp. Dep. comdr. Warren Twp. (N.J.) Civil Def., 1940-45; bd. mem.-at-large Plainfield Council Social Agys., 1944-47; founder, pres. Union County Mental Hygiene Soc., 1944-49; adv. council on citizen participation Community Chests and Councils of Am., 1951-57; mem. bd. Psychoanalytic Research and Devel. Fund; alternate pres. Nathan Hofheimer Found., 1959—. Fellow Am. Pub. Health Assn., Am. Orthopsychiat. Assn. Unitarian. Home: 1155 Park Av New York City NY 10028

FRANK, MARTHA JEAN STEPS (MRS. MANUAL FRANK, JR.), advt. agy. exec.; b. Topeka, Dec. 22, 1939; d. William Emil and Helen Marie (Neimeier) Steps; B.A. cum laude, Kan. State U., 1961; M.A., San Diego State U., 1970; m. Manual Frank, Jr., July 8, 1967; 1 son, Trevor Alan. Editor, Kan. Agrl. Situation, Kan. State U., Manhattan, 1960-62; copywriter Emerson-Franzke Advt. Agy., Topeka, 1962-63; program sec. KOGO Radio, San Diego, 1963-65; v.p. Wilson, Frank & Assos., San Diego, 1965—. Mem. Gamma Phi Beta Alumnae. Home: 6428 Coral Lake Av San Diego CA 92119 Office: 3235 4th Av San Diego CA 92103

FRANK, MARY ANNA, corporate relations exec.; b. Plainfield, N.J.; d. Jacob Alfred and Christine (Manhattan) Frank; student Rutgers U., Upsala Coll., certificate in advt. Tex. Christian U., 1967. With Liberty Mut. Ins. Co., 1941-47; advt. mgr. Am. Handicrafts Co. div. Tandy Corp., East Orange N.J., 1947-53, Tandy Leather Co., Ft. Worth, 1953-64, dir. marketing services Tandy Corp., Ft. Worth, 1964-67, dir. corporate relations, 1967—. Chmn., Ft. Worth unit Postal Customer Council. Bd. dirs. Tarrant County Easter Seal Soc., Ft. Worth Better Bus. Council, Tarrant County Day Care Assn. Named One of Top 10 Women in Advt., Am. Advt. Fedn., 1971; Exec. Woman of Year, Ft. Worth chpt. Zonta Internat., 1973. Mem. Ft. Worth Advt. Club, Ft. Worth Direct Mail Club (pres. 1969), Theta Sigma Phi (treas. 1966-67). Home: 3301 Bellaire Dr Fort Worth TX 76109 Office: 2727 W 7th St Fort Worth TX 76107

FRANK, PAULA FELDMAN (MRS. GORDON D. FRANK), business exec.; b. Tulsa; d. Maurice M. and Sarah (Bergman) Feldman; B.S., Northwestern U., 1954; m. Gordon D. Frank, Dec. 15, 1955; children—Cynthia Jan, Margaret Jill. Directed, wrote and appeared in TV films for Nat. Safety Council, Chgo., 1954-55; appeared in TV commls., 1955-56; treas. Republic S.W. Real Estate Co., Dallas, 1961—, pres. Gaston Av. Inc. Social chmn. Baylor Hosp. Volunteer Corp., Dallas, 1962—; asst. dir. Des Plaines (Ill.) Theater Guild, 1956-57; asst. dir. Pearl Chappell Playhouse, Dallas, 1962-63; asst. dir. Dallas Theater Center, 1964. Mem. Hockaday Alumni Assn. (historian), Idle Wives Book Rev. Club (treas.), Tau Gamma Epsilon, Phi Beta, Sigma Delta Tau. Home: 7123 Currin Dr Dallas TX 75230

FRANK, RUTH ESSER (MRS. ULRICH A. FRANK), educator; b. Cologne, Germany, July 7, 1922; came to U.S., 1939, naturalized, 1946; d. Ernst Samuel and Johanna (Loeb) Esser; B.A., U. N.H., 1955; M.S. in Edn., Temple U., 1958, Ed.D., 1965; m. Ulrich Anton Frank, July 11, 1942; children—Peter Frank, Karin (Mrs. David S. Wasserman), Erica Frank. Classroom tchr. Pennsbury Schs., Fallsington, Pa., 1955-60; supr. intern tchrs., instr. Temple U., Phila., 1960-64; asso. examiner test devel. Ednl. Testing Service, Princeton, 1964-67; prof. edn., coordinator edn. Bucks County Community Coll., Newtown, Pa., 1967—. Ednl. cons. pvt., pub. schs. Pa. Pres., League Women Voters, Levittown, Pa., 1953-55, mem. Hadassah. Sec., Democratic party, Tullytown, Pa., 1954-55. Mem. bd. Childrens House Bucks County, 1965-67. Mem. N.E.A. (life mem., pres. local chpt. 1957-59), Middle Atlantic Assn. Jr. and Community Colls. (dir. exec. bd. 1971-73). Contbr. articles to ednl. jours. Home: 945 Stuart Rd Princeton NJ 08540 Office: Bucks County Community Coll Newtown PA 18940

FRANK, RUTH HERSHFIELD (MRS. ISAIAH FRANK), editor; b. N.Y.C., Dec. 24, 1917; d. Israel and Elsie (Rosenbaum) Hershfield; student U. Mich., 1935-36, B.A., Barnard Coll., 1939; m. Isaiah Frank, Mar. 23, 1941; children—Robert E., Kenneth D. Editor Dell Pub. Co., N.Y.C., 1940-41; with pub. information dept. U. Va., Arlington, 1952-58, Surveys &Research Corp., Washington, 1958-59; editor Washington Center Fgn. Policy Research, 1960-62; asst. exec. dir., editor Nat. Council for Community Services to Internat. Visitors, Washington, 1962—. Mem. League Women Voters, Hadassah. Democrat. Club: Am. Newspaper Women's (Washington). Editor: League Women Voters Bull., Arlington, 1959-61. Home: 3102 Hawthorne St NW Washington DC 20008 Office: 1630 Crescent Pl NW Washington DC 20009

FRANK, RUTH VERD, composer; b. Bristol, Ind.; d. Harvey W. and Laura B. (Mitchell) Kantz; student Moyer Music Sch., Freeburg, Pa.; also pvt. study; m. Murray W. Frank, Aug. 17, 1931. Staff organist (as Ruth Uhl) for sta. WCFL, Chgo., 1934-43; composer, tchr., arranger; piano recitals, Mary Monte Coll., Boca Raton, Country Club, Miami, Kenilwood Hotel. Named to Songwriters Hall of Fame, 1971. Mem. A.S.C.A.P. Club: Chicago Woman's Ideal. Composer: Alone In A Fog, 1938; Set Me Free, 1942; Down Hoosier Way, 1943; Sing A Song (children's book), 1944, Skyway March, 1958. Above the Sun, 1954; Allegheny Way, 1956; Cha-Cha-Stay-Away, 1960; My Indiana, 1964;

Surveyor, 1967; Pondora, 1972; I'm All for You, 1972. Home: 3800 Galt Ocean Dr Fort Lauderdale FL 33308

FRANK, VIRGINIA MARIE, librarian; b. Wadena, Minn., July 18, 1937; d. Herbert Silas and Ruth Amelia (King) Frank; B.A., Westmar Coll., 1959; M.A., U. Minn., 1960; postgrad. Adams State Coll., U. Denver, U. So. Cal. Sch. librarian, tchr. English, McCurdy Sch., Santa Cruz, N.M., 1960-67; librarian Westmar Coll., LeMars, Ia., 1967—, head librarian, 1970—. Mem. Am., Ia. library assns., Librarians of Colls. of Mid-Am. (chmn. 1973—), League Women Voters, United Meth. Women (local pres. 1974—). United Methodist. Home: 900 3rd Av SE LeMars IA 51031

FRANKEL, KIMBERLY CONDE, lawyer; b. Jersey City, Feb. 9, 1945; d. Henry and Maria Philomena (Maiden) Frankel; student U. Ore., 1961-63, B.A., 1965, J.D., 1969; student Portland State U., Pavia, Italy, 1963-64. Admitted to Ore. bar, 1970; law clk. Ore. Ct. Appeals, Salem, 1969-71; dep. dist. atty. Multnomah County, Portland, 1971—. Tchr. Portland Police Bur., 1972-74, Multnomah County Sheriff's Dept., 1972-74; dir. negligent homicide project Dist. Atty.'s Office, 1973. Vol. worker Headstart, also Valley Migrant League, Salem. Mem. Am., Ore. bar, assns., Am. Judicature Soc., Ore. Hist. Soc., Portland Art Assn., Kappa Tau Alpha. Office: Multnomah County Courthouse Portland OR 97204

FRANKENTHALER, HELEN, painter; b. N.Y.C., Dec. 12, 1928; d. Alfred and Martha (Lowenstein) Frankenthaler; B.A., Bennington Coll., 1949; L.H.D. (hon.), Skidmore Coll., 1969; D.F.A., Smith Coll., 1973, Moore Coll. Art, 1974; m. Robert Motherwell, 1958 (div. 1971). One-man shows Tibor de Nagy Gallery, N.Y.C., 1951-58, Jewish Museum, 1960, Emmerich Gallery, 1958-73, Galerie Lawrence, Paris, 1961, 63, Everett Ellin Gallery, Los Angeles, 1961, Galleria dell' Ariete, Milan, Italy, 1962, Bennington (Vt.) Coll., 1962, Kasmin Gallery, London, Eng., 1964, Mirvish Gallery, Toronto, Ont., Can., 1965, 71, Venice Biennale, 1966, Nicolas Wilder Gallery, Cal., Gertrude Kasle Gallery, Mich., 1967, Retrospective Whitney Mus. Art, N.Y.C., 1969, Whitechapel Gallery, London, 1969, Kongresshalle Berlin, Germany, 1969, Kunstverein, Hanover, Germany, 1969, Galerie Godard-LeFort, Montreal, 1971, Heath Gallery, Ga., 1971, John Berggruen Gallery, San Francisco, 1972, Fendrick Gallery, Washington, 1972, Portland (Ore.) Art Mus., 1972, Waddington Galleries II, London, 1973, Janie C. Lee Gallery, Dallas, 1973, Met. Mus. N.Y.C., 1973, Galerie Andre Emmerich, Zurich, 1974; exhibited in group shows Met. Mus. Art, 1969-70, Whitney Mus. annuals 1961, 63, 67, 69, 71; also in U.S., Japan, Germany, Brazil; represented in permanent collections Mus. Modern Art, N.Y.C., Whitney Mus., Carnegie Inst., Pasadena (Cal.) Art Mus., Met. Mus. Art, N.Y.C., numerous others. Tchr. Hunter Coll., N.Y.C., U. Pa., 1965, Yale Grad. Sch., 1966, Calhoun Coll., Yale, 1970, Princeton, 1971, Goucher Coll., 1972; Benjamin West lectr. Swarthmore Coll., 1974. Trustee Bennington Coll., 1967; mem. corp. Yaddo, Saratoga Springs, N.Y., 1974—. Recipient 1st prize Paris Biennale for painting, 1959; Temple Gold medal Pa. Acad. Exhbn., 1968; award Thomas More Coll., Fordham U., 1969; Gold medal Commune Catania, III Bienniale della Grafica D'Arte Florence; Garrett award in 70th Am. exhbn. Art Inst. Chgo., 1972. Fellow Calhoun Coll., Yale; mem. Nat. Inst. Arts and Letters. Home: 173 E 94th St New York City NY 10021 Studio: 117 1/2 E 83d St New York City NY 10028

FRANKFORT, ELLEN, journalist; b. N.Y.C., Oct. 6, 1936; d. Jack and Sylvia (Slote) Frankfort; B.A., Barnard Coll., 1958. Researcher dept. psychiatry Albert Einstein Med. Sch., N.Y.C., 1964-65, Harvard Med. Sch., 1966-68; health columnist Village Voice, N.Y.C., 1970-71; tchr. Calhoun Sch., pub. schs., Beth Jacob Sem. for Women, City and Country Sch., N.Y.C., 1958-64; lectr. in field, 1972—. Coordinator Med. Com. for Human Rights, N.Y.C., 1970; mem. Chelsea-Village Health Council, 1970. Bd. dirs. Women's Med. Group, 1972. Recipient award Media Workshop, 1972. Mem. Soc. Mag. Writers, Media Women, Med. Com. for Human Rights. Author: Classrooms of Miss Ellen Frankfort: Confessions of a Private School Teacher, 1970; Vaginal Politics, 1972. Home: 175 W 12th St New York City NY 10011

FRANKLE, ESTHER DEBORAH ALPERN (MRS. ALLAN HENRY FRANKLE), clin. psychologist; b. Akron, O., Nov. 30, 1918; d. Aaron Harry and Goldie Rae (Alpern) Alpern; student Antioch Coll., 1936-37; B.S., U. Akron, 1940; M.A., U. Chgo., 1948; m. Allan Henry Frankle, June 22, 1947; children—Katherine, Jonathan. Clin psychologist Hilcrest Hosp., Des Moines, Ia., 1947-51; pvt. practice psychology, Des Moines, 1952—. Mem. Am., Ia., Central Ia. psychol. assns., League Women Voters, Psi Chi. Home: 717 54th St Des Moines IA 50312 Office: 550 39th St Des Moines IA 50312

FRANKLIN, ANN YORK (MRS. CARL CECIL FRANKLIN), librarian; b. Friendship, Tenn., Nov. 22, 1923; d. Willard and Mary Lucille (Pennington) York; A.B., U. Louisville, 1944; M.S. in L.S., Nazareth Coll., 1959; M.Ed., Spalding Coll., 1971; m. Carl Cecil Franklin, Oct. 24, 1946; 1 dau., Ann Pennington (Mrs. William M. Redmond, Jr.). Chemist, Brown-Forman Distillers Corp., Louisville, 1944-46; librarian Durrett High Sch., Louisville, 1961-66; vis. librarian Jefferson County Pub. Schs., Louisville, 1966-71, library cons., 1971—. Pres. P.T.A., Louisville, 1959-60. Named Outstanding Ky. Sch. Librarian, Ky. Library Assn., 1964. Mem. Nat., Ky. edn. assns., Am., Ky. (editor bull. 1973—) library assns., Ky. Assn. Sch. Librarians (pres. 1971-72), Ky. Audio-Visual Assn. (treas. 1972-73), Jefferson County Dist. Edn. Assn. Kappa Delta, Delta Kappa Gamma, Kappa Delta Pi. Club: Filson (Louisville). Home: 427 Old Stone Lane Louisville KY 40207

FRANKLIN, CAROLYN KAY STRAFFORD (MRS. JOHN L. FRANKLIN), occupational therapist; b. Indpls., Sept. 6, 1943; d. Glenn L. and Ruth H. (Rafferty) Strafford; B.S. with high distinction, Ind. U., 1966; m. John L. Franklin, Dec. 10, 1966; children—Gregory Lynn, Bradley John. Chief occupational therapist psychiatry Mayo Clinic, Rochester, Minn., 1966-69; chief occupational therapist Sacred Heart Hospice, Austin, Minn., 1969-73; cons. occupational therapy St. Olaf Hosp., also various nursing homes, Austin, 1969—. Mem. Am. Occupational Therapy Assn., Beta Sigma Phi (v.p. Austin 1973-74, pres. 1974-75), Kappa Kappa Kappa (life). Presbyn. Clubs: Home Extension (sec. 1973-74), Winterlude (chmn. 1972) (Austin). Home: 804 7th Av SW Austin MN 55912

FRANKLIN, GEORGIA (MRS. MICHAEL HAROLD FRANKLIN), lawyer; b. Rigby, Ida., Oct. 14, 1934; d. Dean Lloyd and Maxine (Lufkin) Hanni; student Brigham Young U., 1952, Utah State U., 1953; LL.B., Southwestern U., 1961; postgrad. U. Cal. at Los Angeles, 1968-69; m. Michael Harold Franklin, June 14, 1964; children—James, Robert. Exec. adminstr. Am. Fedn. TV and Radio Artists, Los Angeles, 1954-62; admitted to Cal. bar, 1962, since practiced in Los Angeles; asso. Slaff, Mosk & Rudman, Los Angeles, 1967-68. Exec. dir. Composers and Lyricists Guild of Am., Los Angeles, 1962-63; resident counsel Writers Guild Am., Los Angeles, 1963-67; atty. Legal Aid Found. of Los Angeles, 1973—; coordinator Women's Center Legal Program, Los Angeles, 1971, instr. in propria persona divorces, 1972. Bd. dirs. Woman's Place, Elizabeth Fry Center, Casa Montessori. Mem. State Bar Cal., Los Angeles County Bar Assn., Nat. Orgn. for Women (bd. dirs. Los Angeles chpt.), Women Lawyers Assn., Los Angeles Copyright Soc. Home: 826 Glenmont Av Los Angeles CA 90024 Office: 1980 S Vermont Av Los Angeles CA 90007

FRANKLIN, HELENE SALLY, psychotherapist, mgmt. cons.; b. N.Y.C., Mar. 4, 1928; d. Joseph and Elsie (Wolpow) Feldhun; B.A., City U. N.Y., 1965, M.S., 1969; div.; 1 son, Joel. Tchr., N.Y.C. Bd. Edn., Bklyn., 1966-67; psychometrist N.Y. U., 1967-68; psychotherapist Counseling and Psychotherapy Center, Fairlawn, N.J., 1968-70, Center for Counseling, Ridgewood, N.J., 1970-74; exec. dir. Alternative III, Oradell, N.J., 1974—. Lectr., Bergen Community Coll., Paramus, N.J., 1969-70. Mem. Am. Assn. Marriage and Family Counselors (asso.), Am., N.J. psychol. assns., Internat. Transactional Analysis Assn. Home: 1081 Dartmouth St Teaneck NJ 07666 Office: 537 Kinderkamack Rd Oradell NJ 07649

FRANKLIN, MARGARET LAVONA BARNUM (MRS. C. BENJAMIN FRANKLIN), civic worker; b. Caldwell, Kan., June 19, 1905; d. LeGrand Husted and Elva (Biddinger) Barnum; student U. No. Ia., 1923-25, U. Ia., 1937-38; B.A., Washburn U., 1952; m. C. Benjamin Franklin, Jan. 20, 1940; children—Margaret Lee, Benjamin Barnum. Tchr. pub. schs., Union, Ia., 1925-27, Kearney, Neb., 1927-28, Marshalltown, Ia., 1928-40; advance rep. Chautauqua, summers 1926-30. Bd. dirs. state chpt. Nat. Multiple Sclerosis Soc., 1963-66; bd. dirs. Topeka Pub. Library, treas., 1962-65, chmn., 1965-67, sec., 1969-70, bd. rep. to N.E. Kan. Library System, 1968-71; mem. Mayor's Citizens Adv. Com., 1965-67; mem. Topeka Com. for Rescue Italian Art, 1966-67; bd. dirs. Friends of Library, 1969—. Recipient Waldo B. Heywood award for cultural contbn. to Topeka, 1967; named Outstanding Mother of Kan., Alpha Delta Pi, 1971. Mem. Am., Kan. library assns., Shawnee County Hist. Soc. (dir. 1963, 70—, sec., 1964-66), D.A.R. (state chmn. mus. 1968-71), Am. Assn. U. Women, Topeka Art Guild, Topeka Civic Symphony (dir. 1952-57, service honor citation 1960), Doll Collectors Am., Stevengraph Collectors Assn., Marshalltown Community Theatre (pres. 1938-40), Internat. Platform Assn., Nonoso, P.E.O. (president coop. bd. 1964-65, chpt. honoree), Alpha Beta Gamma. Republican. Mem. Christian Ch. Clubs: Western Sorosis (pres. 1960-61), Minerva, Woman's (1st v.p. 1952-54). Home: 4808 W Hills Dr Topeka KS 66606

FRANKLIN-SOMMERLAD, RUTH (MRS. PHILIP LINCOLN SOMMERLAD), mus. dir.; b. Byesville, O., July 2, 1911; d. George Grover and Jennie (Richmond) Shurtz; B.S., M.B., Heidelberg Coll., 1932; m. Philip Lincoln Sommerlad, Nov. 6, 1958 (dec. Jan. 1970); children—Philip Lincoln, Patricia Jean (Mrs. Rollin Buchan Emmons). Dir., mem. adv. bd. Frederick C. Crawford Auto-Aviation Mus. of Western Res. Hist. Soc., Cleve., 1957-73, cons., 1973—; owner, mgr. Specified Maintenance Products, Cleve., 1955—. Mem. adv. bd. Internat. Women's Air and Space Mus. Mem. Am. Assn. Mus.'s, Mid-West Mus. Conf., Soc. of Collectors, Inc., Inter-Mus. Council Cleve., Woman's Advt. Club Cleve., Antique Automobile Club Am. (membership chmn. Ohio), Vet. Motor Car Club Am., Horseless Carriage Club Am., Automobile Old Timers, Inc., H.H. Franklin Club, Classic Car Club Am., Tampa Symphony Guild. Home: Carlton Arms 6911A Concord Dr Tampa FL 33614

FRANKMAN, BETTY SKELTON (MRS. DONALD A. FRANKMAN), realtor, mortgage broker; b. Pensacola, Fla., June 28, 1926; d. David L. and Myrtle (Lowry) Skelton; Ph.D. (hon.), Colo. Christian Coll., 1973; m. Donald A. Frankman, Dec. 31, 1965. Flight instr., profl. aerobatic pilot and test pilot, 1946-53; feminine internat. aerobatic champion, 1948-50; test driver for automotive mfr., 1954-56; advt. exec., v.p., dir. womens advt. and marketing dept. Campbell-Ewald Co., Detroit, 1956-70; pres. 1st Fla. Realty, Inc., Winter Haven, 1971—. Co-producer, writer award winning documentary film which recieved silver award of excellence N.Y. Internat. Film Festival, 1965; driver Art Arfon's jet car Green Monster Cyclops, Bonneville, Utah Salt Flats, 1965 (3 time holder World Land Speed Record for Women 1955, 56, 65). Named One of Detroits Top Ten Career Women, 1964. Mem. Womens Advt. Club Detroit, Parachute Club Am., Exptl. Aircraft Assn., Aircraft Owners and Pilots Assn., Mich. Aeros. and Space Assn., Profl. Race Pilots Assn., Nat. Assn. Realtors, Fla. Assn. Realtors, Nat. Inst. Real Estate Brokers, Nat., Fla. assns. mortgage brokers, Winter Haven Bd. Realtors, Citrus Center Mortgage Brokers. Home: 2200 Havendale Blvd Winter Haven FL 33880 Office: First Fla Realty Inc 1000 1st St S Winter Haven FL 33880

FRANKS, VIRGINIA, health service adminstr.; b. High Springs, Fla., Dec. 31, 1927; d. John Roy and Caroline (Fleet) Franks; A.A., U. N.C., 1955; A.B., U. Chgo., 1957; M.Ed., U. Fla., 1960-61. Tchr. social studies Churchland High Sch., Norfolk County, Va., 1958-60, St. Mary's Sch., Wilmington, N.C., 1964-66; adminstr. Carobell Children's Home, Jacksonville, N.C., 1970—. Mem. Council on Human Resources Onslow County, Jacksonville, 1972—, Onslow County Planning Council on Mental Retardation, 1967-70, 74—. Bd. dirs. Nat. Assn. Pvt. Residential Facilities for Mentally Retarded. Served with USNR, 1950-53. Named Woman of the Year, Jacksonville Jaycees, 1972. Mem. Am. Assn. Mental Deficiency, Nat. Assn. Retarded Citizens. Democrat. Presbyn. Home: 205 Marion Ct Jacksonville NC 28540 Office: 311 Warn PO Box 546 Jacksonville NC 28540

FRANTZ, LOLA HOAG (MRS. RAYMOND HERR FRANTZ), artist; b. Jennings, La., July 14, 1908; d. A. A. and Bertha (Denny) Hoag; student La. Western State U., 1928, Vanderbilt U., 1927-28, George Peabody Coll., 1935; M.A., N.Y. Art Student's League, 1951; m. Alba Heywood, 1928; 1 son, Alba III; m. 2d, Raymond Herr Frantz, Oct. 27, 1946. One man shows Washington County Mus. Fine Arts, Hagerstown, Md., Newton Galleries, N.Y.C., Grand Central Galleries, Vanderbilt, N.Y.; exhibited in group shows at Nat. Acad., N.Y., Corcoran Gallery, Washington, Carnegie Internat., Wade County Ann., Hagerstown, Pa.; represented in permanent collections Peal Mus., Balt., Indiana (Pa.) Mus., Pa. State Tchrs. Coll., Grumbachers Collection, N.Y.C., Mexico Fed. Mus., Acapulco Md. U. Collection, Seton Hall U., Newark. Dir. Wayne Tool Co., Waynesboro. Bd. dirs. St. Frances Hosp., Miami Beach. Recipient 1st award Nat. Acad. N.Y., 1955; 1st award Franklin County (Md.) Art Show, 1960, 61, others. Pub. officer Womens Hosp. Aux., Waynesboro, Pa., 1959—. Pres., Women's Republican Club, Waynesboro, 1958-60, 1st v.p., 1959—. Mem. Internat. Platform Assn. Clubs: Studio (pres. Waynesboro 1961-62); Surf (Miami Beach). Home: 118 Myrtle Av Waynesboro PA 17268

FRANZ, EVELYN JESSIE BIRDSALL (MRS. HENRY P. FRANZ), educator; b. Wallkill, N.Y.; d. Arthur S. and Mary A. (Mack) Birdsall; grad. New Paltz Normal Sch., 1932-35; B.S., Columbia Tchrs. Coll., 1939, M.A., 1944; D.Ed., Rutgers 1958; m. Henry P. Franz, July 21, 1945; 1 son, Conrad Jesse. Tchr. pub. schs., Pleasant Valley, N.Y., 1935-37, Rock Hill, N.Y., 1937-38, Monticello, N.Y., 1938-44; demonstration tchr. Trenton (N.J.) State Coll., 1944-52 asst. prof., 1952-57, asso. prof. edn., 1957-61, prof. coordinator elementary edn., 1961—, chmn. dept. elementary and early childhood edn. Mem. Am. Assn. U. Profs., N.E.A., N.J. Edn. Assn., Nat. Soc. Study Edn., Assn. Student Teaching, Internat. Reading Assn., Nat. Council Tchrs. English, N.J. Reading Tchrs. Assn. (past pres., bd. dirs.), Am. Ednl. Research Assn., Coll. Reading Assn. Theta Phi, Delta Kappa Gamma Alpha Zeta. Clubs: Soroptimist (pres. 1967-68, mem. bd., 1965-66, 1st v.p. 1966-67), Bus. and Profl. Women's Assn. Club: Contemporary of Trenton. Home: 73 Main Blvd Trenton NJ 08618

FRANZ, LYDIA MILLICENT TRUC (MRS. ROBERT FRANZ), real estate exec.; b. Chgo., Jan. 11, 1924; d. Walter and Lydia (Kralovec) Truc; Mus.B., Ill. Wesleyan U., 1944; Mus.M., Northwestern U., 1949; m. Robert Franz, Aug. 27, 1952. Tchr. music pub. schs., Muskegon, Mich., 1947-48; marketing research analyst Grant Advt. Agy., Chgo., 1949; asst. to dir. marketing research Buchen Co., 1949-52; asst. dir. marketing research Sherman Marquette Advt. Co., Chgo., 1952; asst. to pres., dir. media and research Andover Advt. Agy., 1952-55; salesman Boehmer & Hedlund, realty, Barrington, Ill., 1960-63; pres. Country Squire Real Estate, Inc., Barrington, 1963—. Mem. real estate adv. com. William Rainey Harper Coll., Palatine, Ill., 1971—. Served with WAC, 1944-46. Mem. Women in Real Estate (pres. 1966-67), Barrington Bd. Realtors (pres. 1968-69), Ill. Assn. Real Estate Bds. (dir. 1972—, gov. Realtor's Inst. of Ill. 1972—), Nat. Assn. Real Estate Bds., Nat. Inst. Real Estate Brokers, Barrington C. of C. (v.p. 1968-71, pres. 1974, dir. 1972—), Am. Cryptogram Soc., Am. Contract Bridge League, Barrington Bus. and Profl. Women's Club, Sigma Alpha Iota. Republican. Home: 461 Lake Shore Dr Timberlake Barrington IL 60010 Office: 209 Park Av Barrington IL 60010

FRANZ, SISTER MARY PATRICIA, educator; b. Bklyn., Apr. 9, 1920; d. Joseph Michael and Jennie (Bryson) Franz; B.A., Manhattan Coll., 1946; M.A., St. John's U., 1951; M.A., St. Mary's Coll., Notre Dame, Ind., 1961. Tchr. St. Helena Elementary Sch., Bronx, N.Y., 1941-48; chmn. religion dept. Aquinas High Sch., Bronx, 1948-51; instr. St. Agnes Normal Sch., Sparkill, N.Y., 1951-54; postulant mistress, 1951-59; prof. St. Thomas Aquinas Coll., Sparkill, 1954-68, adminstr. theology dept., 1961-65; chmn. social studies dept. Rosary Acad., Sparkill, N.Y., 1971—. Mem. Soc. Cath. Coll. Tchrs. of Sacred Doctrine (mem. exec. com.), Coll. Theology Soc., Am. Acad. Religion, N.Y. State, Nat. councils social studies, Intercontinental Biog. Assn., Am. Assn. Tchrs. Chinese Lang. and Culture, Inst. Judaeo-Christian Studies, Smithsonian Assos. Home: Dominican Convent of Our Lady of the Rosary Sparkill NY 10976 Office: Rt 340 Orangeburg Rd Sparkill NY 10976

FRANZBLAU, ROSE NADLER (MRS. ABRAHAM NORMAN FRANZBLAU), psychologist, journalist; b. Vienna, Austria, Jan. 1, 1905; brought to U.S., 1905; d. Meyer and Rachael (Breitfeld) Nadler; B.A., Hunter Coll., 1926; M.A., Columbia, 1931, Ph.D., 1935; postgrad. U. Heidelberg, summer 1924, Sorbonne, U. Paris, summers, 1926-28; m. Abraham Norman Franzblau, Dec. 21, 1923; children—Michael, Jane (Mrs. Richard A. Isay). Tchr., prin. in religious high schs., N.Y.C., 1927-35; personnel worker, Cin., 1935-37; personnel worker Nat. Youth Adminstrn., Cin., 1937-40, dir. personnel, Cin., Columbus, O., 1940-43, nat. dir. girls tng., Washington, 1943-44; dir. placement, tng. overseas personnel UNRRA, Washington, 1944-46; regional tng. officer OPA, N.Y.C., 1946-47; asso. dir. Internat. Tensions Research Project, 1947-51; daily newspaper columnist N.Y. Post, N.Y.C., 1951—; daily commentator The World of Children, Sta. WCBS, N.Y.C., 1965-70. Lectr., cons. human relations problems; Am. chmn. Girls Town of Italy, 1960—; mem. adv. bd. to psychology dept. U. Jerusalem, 1967—. Recipient awards Albert Einstein Coll. Medicine, Asthma Research Inst., Child Guidance League, Bar Ilan U., Israel. Mem. Hadassah (hon. life), N.A.A.C.P. (hon. life), Sigma Xi. Democrat. Jewish religion. Author: Race Differences in Mental and Physical Traits, Studied in Different Environments, 1935; (with Marie Lane) National Youth Administration: Final Report, 1944; (with Otto Klineberg) Tensions Affecting International Understanding, 1950; (with Abraham N. Franzblau) A Sane and Happy Life: A Family Guide, 1963; The Way It Is Under Twenty, 1964; The Middle Generation, 1971. Contbr. articles to N.Y. Post Mag., Family Circle, Sales Mgmt., Pageant, Cosmopolitan, Seventeen, other popular mags. and profl. jours. Home: 1 Gracie Terrace New York City NY 10028*

FRANZEN, JANICE MARGUERITE GOSNELL (MRS. RALPH OSCAR FRANZEN), mag. editor; b. LaCrosse, Wis., Sept. 24, 1921; d. Wray Towson and Anna Heldena (Renstrom) Gosnell; B.S. cum laude, Wis. State U., LaCrosse, 1943; M.R.E., No. Bapt. Theol. Sem., 1947; m. Ralph Oscar Frenzen, Feb. 15, 1964. Tchr. history, social sci. Galesville (Wis.) High Sch., 1943-45; registrar Christian Writers Inst., Chgo., 1947-49, dir., 1950-63, dir. studies, 1964—, fiction editor Christian Life mag., 1950-63, woman's editor, 1964-72, exec. editor, 1972—. Mem. editorial bd. Creation House, Wheaton, Ill., 1972—; speaker various writers confs. Sec. bd. dirs. Christian Life Missions, 1971—. Mem. Audubon Soc. (DuPage sec. 1972—), Nat. Wildlife Assn. Author: Christian Writers Handbook, 1960, 61. Editor: Christian Author, 1949-54, Christian Writer and Editor, 1955-63. Contbr. articles to various mags. Home: 3N455 Mulberry St West Chicago IL 60185 Office: Gundersen Dr and Schmale Rd Wheaton IL 60187

FRASER, ARVONNE DELRAE SKELTON (MRS. DONALD MACKAY FRASER), civic, polit. worker; b. Lamberton, Minn., Sept. 1, 1925; d. Orland D. and Phyllis (DuFrene) Skelton; B.A., U. Minn., 1948; m. Donald MacKay Fraser, June 30, 1950; children—Thomas Skelton, Mary MacKay, John DuFrene, Lois MacKay, Anne Tallman (dec.), Jean Skelton. Receptionist Humphrey for Senator Com., Mpls., 1948; sec. Democratic-Farmer-Labor Party State Chmn., 1948-51; editor DFL News, 1954-56; vol. staff asst. Office Congressman Fraser, Washington, 1964—. Pres. Marcy (Mpls.) PTA, 1957-59; mem. Washington Integrated Secondary Edn. Com., 1967-69. Vice-chmn. Minn. Dem.-Farmer-Labor Party, 1956-62; asst. mgr. Minn. Citizens for Kennedy-Johnson, 1960; co-chmn. Naftalin for Mayor Com., Mpls., 1961; campaign mgr. Fraser for Congress Com., 1964—; sec. Dem. Congl. Wive's Forum, Washington, 1965-68. Mem. Mpls. Bd. Pub. Welfare, 1961-63; mem. Southwest (Washington) Community House Bd., 1967-69; mem. nat. adv. council Center for Family Planning Program Devel., 1972—; mem. bd. Washington Opportunities for Women, 1971—; nat. v.p. Women's Equity Action League, 1971-72, pres., 1972—, pres. nat. capital chpt., 1971—; convenor Nat. Women's Polit. Caucus, 1971, Minn. Women's Polit. Caucus, 1971; pres. Advise and Consult, Inc.; bd. mem. Women's Equity Fund, Center for Women Policy Studies. Author: Looking Forward to a Career: Government, 1968. Home: 1253 4th St SW Washington DC 20024 Office: House Office Bldg Washington DC 20515

FRASER, ELEANOR RUTH, physician; b. Woodlake, Cal., May 31, 1927; d. Morton William and Dorothy Jean (Harding) Fraser; B.A., Pomona Coll., 1949; M.D., Stanford U., 1954. Intern Los Angeles County Hosp., 1953-54, resident radiology, 1954-57; radiologist Hoag Meml. Hosp., Newport Beach, Cal., 1957-58, St. Joseph Hosp., Orange, Cal., 1957-61; practice medicine, specializing in radiology, Anaheim, Cal., 1961—. Bd. dirs. Lyric Opera Assn. Orange County, Cal., 1970—.Diplomate Am. Bd. Radiology. Mem. A.M.A., A.A.A.S., Pomona Coll. Assos., Phi Beta Kappa. Republican. Presbyn.

Club: Balboa Bay (Newport Beach). Home: 631 Virginia Park Dr Laguna Beach CA 92651 Office: 1661 W Broadway Anaheim CA 92802

FRASER, (META) DOREEN ELIOT, librarian; b. Grenfell, Sask., Can., June 8, 1915; d. Mitchell Campbell and Sara Margaret (Psterson) Fraser; B.A., U. Alta., 1936; B.L.S., U. Toronto, 1937; postgrad. Columbia, 1953. Jr. librarian U. Alta., Edmonton, 1937-40, med. librarian, 1940-42; sr. librarian, adult service B.C. Provincial Library Commn., N. Central Br., Prince George, 1946-47; sr. librarian Vancouver reference div., also 1st asst. fine arts library U. B.C., 1947-49, 1st asst., serials div., 1950-51, med. librarian, travelling regional service, 1951-54, biomed. librarian, 1954-64, hon. lectr. Sch. Librarianship, 1961-64; med.-dental librarian Dalhousie U., Halifax, N.S., 1964-67, health scis. librarian, 1967-72, regional health scis. librarian, asst. prof. Sch. Library Service, 1972—. Cons. B.C. Med. Library Service, 1958-64; asst. librarian Anglican Theol. Coll., Vancouver, 1955-61. Co-Fish head Halifax/Darmouth Fish Service, 1971—. Served to lt. Women's Royal Canadian Naval Service, 1942-46. Mem. Canadian (sec. com. med. sci. libraries 1962-63), Atlantic Provinces, B.C. (pres. 1962-63), N.S., Halifax (chmn. programme com. 1966-67), Med. (pres. N.W. regional group 1957-59, 63-64, internat. editor Bull. 1971—) library assns., Canadian Assn. Coll. and Univ. Libraries, Canadian Assn. Spl. Libraries and Information Services (treas. health sci. sect. 1971-73), Spl. Libraries Assn., Assn. Canadian Med. Colls. (chmn. com. med. sch. libraries 1965-69). Internat. Assn. Documentalists. Club: Ashburn Golf (Halifax). Home: 830 McLean St Apt 32 Halifax NS B3H 2T8 Canada

FRATES, MRS. CLIFFORD LEROY, civic worker; b. Moweaqua, Ill., Jan 15, 1908; d. William James and Gertrude (Gunderson) Rodman; student Pine Manor Jr. Coll., 1924; B.A., U. Okla., 1929; m. Clifford L. Frates, Nov. 15, 1935; children—Rodman A., Kent F. Mem. bd. A.R.C., Oklahoma City; dir Community Fund Bd.; trustee Jane Brooks Sch. Deaf, Okla. Art Center, Okla. Coll. for Women; mem. bd. Okla. State Library; dir. Jr. Leagues of Am.; mem. bd. Okla. Heritage Assn., Allied Arts of Oklahoma City, Oklahoma City Symphony, YWCA; drive chmn. Central Vol. Bur.; chmn. women's div. United Fund; chmn. Art Center drive. Chmn. Oklahoma City Savs. Bond Com.; chmn. Episcopal Women's Conf. Okla.; chmn. Re-act campaign for Oklahoma City Voluntary Action Center, 1971. Named to Okla. Hall of Fame, 1969. Mem. Oklahoma City Art Assn., Phi Beta Kappa (pres. Oklahoma City alumnae 1964-66), Kappa Alpha Theta, Mortar Bds. Republican. Episcopalian (div. chmn. for Christian social relations; mem. Episcopal Bishop and Council. Home: 2607 Warwick Dr Oklahoma City OK 73116

FRAYSER, REGINA, educator; b. Lynchburg, Va., Feb. 18, 1926; d. John Edward and Drusia (Biggs) Frayser; A.B., Randolph-Macon Women's Coll., 1947; A.M., Duke, 1953, Ph.D. (USPHS fellow), 1960. Research asso. medicine Duke, 1957-60, asso. physiology, instr. medicine, 1960-62; asst. prof. medicine Ind. U., Indpls., 1962-63, asst. prof. medicine, physiology, 1963-65, asso. prof. medicine and physiology, 1965-70, prof., 1970-72; prof. research medicine and ophthalmology Med. U. S.C., Charleston, 1972—. Mem. Am. Assn. Anatomists, Microcirculatory Soc., Am. Physiol. Soc., Sigma Xi. Contbr. articles to profl. jours. Office: Dept of Medicine Medical University of SC Charleston SC 29401

FRAZEE, ANNE MARIE (MRS. WILFORD FRAZEE), dept. store exec., artist; b. St. Louis, Mich., Dec. 11, 1923; d. Thomas and Elizabeth Marie (Evica) Olsa; student Cleary Coll., 1943, Famous Artists Schs., 1963-65, 65-68; m. Wilford J. Frazee, Aug. 26, 1944; children—Deborah A. (Mrs. Don T. McCallum), James Steven, Elizabeth Louise. Sec., Nash-Kelvinator Corp., Lansing, Mich., 1943-44; artist Cabana Studios, West Palm Beach, Fla., 1944-45; med. sec. USAAF, Boca Raton, Fla., 1945; sec. Farmers Mut. Liability Co., Indpls., 1946-48, Clyde Smith Agy., Lansing, 1948-49; dept. head accessories Oren's Dept. Stores, Inc., Mt. Pleasant, Mich., 1969—. Artist, part-time, 1964—; exhibited one man shows Cadillac program, 1965; group shows Studio 23, 1965-69, 71, Saginaw Woman's Club, 1965-67, Stone Gallery, Jackson, Mich., 1965-67, Kalamazoo, 1966, Muskegon, 1966, Traverse City, 1966, Charlevoix, 1965-67, Tawas City Show, 1966-68, Midland MidMich. Shows, 1966-68, Temple Israel, 1965, 66, Circle Art Gallery, Mt. Pleasant, 1964-66 68-71, Lioga Duncan Gallery N.Y., 1967. Sec., Child Study Club, 1954-56; v.p. Kinney P.T.A., Mt. Pleasant, 1958-59, pres., 1963, mem. council, 1959-60, council pres., 1960-63; mem. Saginaw Mus. Pres., Isabella County Republican Club, 1956-58. Mem. Mt. Pleasant Art Assn. (publicity dir. program chmn. 1967-71, pres. 1971—), Sacred Heart Altar Soc. (v.p. 1967-69, pres. 1969-71), Cath. Daus. Am., Zonta Internat. Roman Catholic. Home: 1414 E Lincoln Ct Mount Pleasant MI 48858 Office: 127 S Main St Mount Pleasant MI 48858

FRAZEE, JOAN GRANT (MRS. HAROLD DAVID FRAZEE), advt. exec.; b. Bklyn.; d. Charles Joseph and Clearbelle (Futhey) Grant; student Plaza Bus. Sch.; m. John Alden Somerville, Aug. 20, 1940 (div. Feb. 1958); children—Wendy (Mrs. John T. Wall), Grant Alden; m. 2d, Harold David Frazee, Apr. 26, 1958 (dec. Aug. 1964). Account exec. Biow Co., Inc., N.Y.C., 1954-56, Ruthrauff & Ryan, Inc., N.Y.C., 1956-57, Bryan Houston, Inc., N.Y.C., 1957-59, Tatham Laird, Inc., N.Y.C., 1959-62, MacManus, John & Adams, Inc., N.Y.C., 1962-63, William Esty Co., Inc., N.Y.C., 1966—. Sec. Turtle Bay Civic Assn., 1965-66. Sec. Forest Hills Republican Club, 1952-56. Co-founder, mem. bd. dirs. Forest Hills Little League, 1953-56. Roman Catholic. Club: Matterhorn Sports (N.Y.C.). Home: 66 Milton Rd Rye NY 10580 Office: 100 E 42d St New York City NY 10017

FRAZEE, MARIE MARCIA, educator; b. Paterson, N.J., July 4, 1921; d. William Addison and Beatrice (Yost) Frazee, Jr.; A.B., Montclair State Coll., 1943, A.M., 1946; Ed.D., Columbia, 1967. Tchr. Cleveland St. Sch., Orange, N.J., 1943-44; sec., dean of coll. Montclair State Coll., Upper Montclair, N.J., 1946-56, acad. counselor, scheduling officer, asst. prof. edn., 1956-66, acad. counselor, asso. prof., 1966—. Mem. N.E.A., N.J. Edn. Assn., Assn. N.J. State Coll. Faculties, Montclair State Coll. Faculty Assn., Am. Assn. U. Women, N.J. State Employees Assn., Am. Personnel and Guidance Assn., Montclair State Coll. Alumni Assn., Kappa Delta Pi, Pi Lambda Theta. Home: 219 Walnut St Montclair NJ 07042 Office: Montclair State Coll Upper Montclair NJ 07043

FRAZIER, DOLORES LILY THORNHILL (MRS. JOHN HUGH FRAZIER, JR.), civic worker, mining, exploration co. exec.; b. Phila., Jan. 28, 1917; d. Aaron Bates and Minnie (Clark) Thornhill; B.S., U. Pa., 1939, M.S., 1940; m. John Hugh Frazier, Jr., June 14, 1941; children—John Hugh III, Richard Thornhill. Tchr., Upper Darby Sch. Dist., 1941-42; treas. Am. Mining & Exploration Co., Wilmington, Del., Tripoli, Libya, 1965—, dir. Beam & Co., Ithaca, N.Y., P.R.M., Inc., Wilmington Harold E. Hedler Storage, Inc., Newaygo, Mich., 1965-70. Dir. Coopertown Civic Assn., 1954-58; agt. U. Pa. Ann. Giving Campaign, 1954-59, class rep., 1959-64; pres. U. Pa., Alumnae Class, 1964-69. Mem. Republican Women Pa., 1958—. Mem. League Women Voters, Am. Home Econs. Assn., Psi Chpt. House Corp. Delta Delta Delta (pres. 1967-68), Mortar Bd., Pi Lambda Theta. Christian Scientist. Home: 204 Buck Lane Haverford PA 19041 also Outer Dr E 400 E Randolph St Chicago IL 60601 Office: 100 W 10th St Wilmington DE 19899

FRAZIER, OMEGA MOORE, home economist; b. Seaford, Del., Sept. 11, 1911; d. Noah Watson and Eliza Annie (Boyce) Moore; A.B., Morgan State Coll., 1930, B.S., 1958; m. Horatio William Jones, Mar. 12, 1932; 1 son, Horatio William III; 2d, m. John Basil Ray Frazier, June 14, 1969. Pub. sch. tchr., Dover, Del., 1931-44; home economist, 4-H agt. U. Md. Eastern Shore, Wicomico-Somerset Counties, 1944-54; home economist Somerset County, Princess Anne, Md., 1954-69, home economist supervising agt., expanded food and nutrition edn. program, 1969—, home economist and Somerset County chmn., coop. extension service full year headstart operation mainstream Title 1 program, 1971—. Recipient Nat. Distinguished service award for work with migrants, 1966. Farm Found. fellow U. Wis., 1963. Mem. Princess Anne C. of C. (chmn. tri-migrant com. 1955-63, treas. 1963-70), Md. Assn. Home Economists, Am. Home Econs. Assn., Women's Soc. Christian Service (pres. 1964-70), Alpha Kappa Alpha, Epsilon Sigma Phi. Methodist. Clubs: Bridge. Contbr. to publs. in field. Home: 31 Beckford Av Princess Anne MD 21853 Office: Box 277 Princess Anne MD 21853

FREAS, ANNIE BELLE (MRS. MAURICE HENRY FREAS), constrn. co. exec., club woman; b. Delrose, Tenn.; d. James N. and Emma (McLaughlin) Hamilton; diploma Martin Coll., Pulaski, Tenn., 1923; m. Maurice Henry Freas, June 6, 1931. Sec. law firm Bass, Berry & Sims, 1923-24; coml. tchr., bookkeeper Martin Coll., 1924-25; bookkeeping machine operator, head accounting dept., asst. comptroller T. L. Herbert & Sons, W. G. Bush & Co., Sangravl Co., Nashville, 1925-58; bookkeeper, co-owner M. H. Freas, gen. contractor, Nashville, 1958-63; sec., gen. bookkeeper, office mgr. Freas & Houghland Gen. Contractors, Inc., Nashville, 1963-65; sec.-treas. Freas Constrn. Co., Inc., 1965—. Office mgr., pres. Women of Ch., Downtown Presbyn. Ch., 1961—, life membership pin, 1964. Mem. Nashville Republican Com. Recipient medal Underwood Typewriter Co., 1923. Mem. Women in Constrn. (pres. Nashville 1964-66, regional dir. 1966-67, nat. dir. 1966—, named WIC of Yr., 1965), Nat. Assn. Women in Constrn. (nat. chmn. extension and orgn.; chmn. profl. edn. and constrn. Nashville chpt.; chmn. Career Day at Vanderbilt U.), Internat. Platform Assn., Ladies Hermitage Assn., Assn. for Preservation Tenn. Antiquities, Tenn. Bot. Gardens and Fine Art Center. Presbn. (pres. Women of Ch. 1961-62, 64). Clubs: Homemakers (publicity chmn., v.p. 1970-71); Zonta (treas. 1964-69, v.p. 1969-70, chmn. dist. 11-So. states for pub. affairs 1969-71 pres. Nashville 1970-71). Home: 3003 Natchez Trace Nashville TN 37215 Office: 3003 Natchez Trace Nashville TN 37215

FRED, ANN CONWAY, physician; b. Madison, Wis., Mar. 21, 1916; d. Edwin Broun and Rosa Helen (Parrott) Fred; B.A., U. Wis., 1938, M.D., 1951, B.A. in L.S., 1939. Tchr., librarian Foxcroft Sch., Middleburg, Va., 1939-42; tchr. Columbus (O.) Sch. for Girls, 1942-43, Chatham (Va.) Hall, 1943-45; intern Roper Hosp., Charleston, S.C., 1951-52; resident pediatrics Walter Reed Army Hosp., Washington, 1955-57; commnd. 1st. lt. U.S. Army, 1952, advanced through grades to col., 1973; student co. officers course Med. Field Service Sch., Fort Sam Houston, Tex., 1954-55; chief pediatrics Communications Zone, Orleans, France, 1957-59; research in tropical diseases Walter Reed Army Inst. Research, Washington, 1962—, chief dept. disease information Div. Biometrics and Med. Information Processing, 1968—. Decorated Army Commendation medal. Fellow Royal Soc. Health, Assn. Mil. Surgeons U.S.; mem. Gamma Phi Beta. Contbr. articles to profl. jours. Home: 3710 Alton Pl NW Washington DC 20016 Office: Walter Reed Army Inst Research Washington DC 20012

FREDERICH, FAYE THOMAS (MRS. HARRY FREDERICH), real estate broker; b. Rudd, Ia., Feb. 17, 1894; d. Guy and Roxanna (Henson) Thomas; home econs. diploma U. No. Ia., 1914; B.S., U. So. Cal., 1929, M.S., 1934; m. Harry Frederich, Sept. 22, 1923. Tchr. art, home econs. Ia. Secondary Schs., 1915-21; tchr. art Los Angeles Pub. Schs., 1922-57, head art dept., 1942-55, substitute tchr., 1957-63; tchr. home econs., Long Beach, Cal., 1921-22; real estate saleswoman, 1935-55, broker, 1955—; owner Faye Thomas Frederich, Realtor, Los Angeles, 1962—. Mem. Westwood Area Realty Bd. Republican. Mem. Order Eastern Star, White Shriner of Jerusalem. Club: Ebell (Los Angeles). Home: 2103 Glendon Av Los Angeles CA 90025 Office: 10687 Santa Monica Blvd Suite 11 Los Angeles CA 90025

FREDERICK, CLAIRE, psychiatrist; b. New Orleans, 1932; d. Albert Henry and Irene (Hawkins) Cobb; B.A., H. Sophie Newcomb Coll., 1951; M.D., La. State U. Sch. Medicine, 1955; postgrad. Georgetown U., 1964, Wash. Psychoanalytic Inst., 1965-70; m. Arthur Francis Frederick. Instr. psychiatry Med. Coll. Va., 1958-62; supervisory psychiatrist Psychiat. Convalescent and Rehab. Center, Washington, 1962-64; dep. dir. Area C Mental Health Center, Washington, 1964-65; asst. chief psychiatrist D.C. Gen. Hosp., 1965-66; pvt. practice psychoanalysis and psychotherapy, Washington, 1966-72. Med. dir. Washington Luth. Social Services Counseling Inst., 1969-72; psychiat. cons. Luth. Social Services, 1966-72; cons. in child psychiatry Marriage and Family Inst., 1967-69; lectr. group work program Psychiat. Inst. Found., 1967-69, 71-72, mem. faculty, 1972—; area chief Community Mental Health Center, 1972—; cons. operation Headstart, 1972; dir. partial hospitalization Gateways Community Mental Health Center, Los Angeles, 1973—; cons. Los Angeles Unified Sch. Dist., 1972—, Fed. Correctional Inst., Terminal Island, Cal., 1972—, Los Angeles Superior Ct., 1973—. Diplomate Am. Bd. Psychiatry and Neurology. Mem. Med. Com. for Human Rights, 1967—. Mem. Med. Soc. D.C., Am. Psychiat. Soc., Pan Am. Med. Soc., Royal Soc. Health, Am. Geriatrics Soc., Assn. Applied Psychoanalysis, Phi Beta Kappa. Alpha Omega Alpha. Address: 535 Las Casus Av Pacific Palisades CA 90272

FREDERICK, FAITH RAMSAY, artist; b. Battle Creek, Mich.; d. Charles Cornell and Mandana (Edminster) Ramsay; student Radcliffe Coll., Otis Art Inst., Mass. Art Sch.; summer courses George Pearse Ennis Art Sch., The Wayman Adams Sch. of Art, 1934; m. Frank P. Huckins; m. 2d, Brunel Frederick, Apr. 28, 1930. Formerly head art dept., tchr. English, Abbott Acad.; fashion artist William H. Davidow Co., New York; exhibited paintings Lime Rock (Conn.) show, 1933, 6 Greek Theatre shows, Los Angeles, New Hartford, Conn., St. Petersburg, Fla., Dept. State, others. Twice 1st v.p. Las Artistas, Los Angeles. Recipient numerous awards for paintings. Mem. Artists of S.W., Nat. Soc. Arts. and Letters, Nat. League Am. Pen Women (Los Angeles pres. 1964-66, editor Owl news), So. Cal. Woman's Press Club (1st dir., corr. sec.), Las Artistas. Member Republican Party. Clubs: Radcliffe of So. Cal., Wilshire Breakfast, The Freedom. Lectr., writer on art. Address: 5326 1/2 Village Green Los Angeles CA 90016

FREDERICK, HARRIETT ELIZABETH (MRS. ARTHUR JOHN FREDERICK), educator; b. Champaign, Ill., Nov. 26, 1906; d. Jerome Edward and Ida Elizabeth (Harrell) Readhimer; A.B., Northwestern State U. La., 1926; M.A., U. Ill., 1930, Ph.D., 1965; M.A., U. Louisville, 1960; m. Arthur John Frederick, June 18, 1933; children—Arthur Jerome, Richard Harrell, Marian (Mrs. Edward B. Smith), Elizabeth (Mrs. Edward Howe Strachan), Caroline (Mrs. Eugene John Isabelle). Tchr. Latin, history Boyce (La.) High Sch., 1926-27, 28-29, Rankin (Ill.) High Sch., 1929-33; tchr. spl. edn., supr. spl. edn., sch. psychologist Louisville Pub. Schs., 1948-67; lectr. U. Louisville, 1960-67; prof. spl. edn., psychol. cons. Northwestern State U. La., Natchitoches, 1967-72; psychologist Shreveport Mental Health Center, 1972—. Speech and hearing therapist Ky. Soc. Crippled Children, summers 1959-61; supr. student psychologists Mental Health Assn., 1970—; cons. Vocational Rehab. Center, 1970-72; research asst. U. Ill., 1961-62, 63-64; mem. Natchitoches Mental Health Assn.; mem. day care bd. Natchitoches Assn. Retarded Children, 1971-72. Mem. Am. Psychol. Assn., Council for Exceptional Children, Am. Speech and Hearing Assn., Nat. Rehab. Assn., Nat. Assn. Disability Examiners, Phi Kappa Phi, Psi Chi, Eta Sigma Phi, Kappa Delta Pi, Delta Kappa Gamma, Sigma Alpha Eta. Baptist. Mem. Order Eastern Star. Home: PO Box 973 Natchitoches LA 71457

FREDERICK, PAULINE (MRS. CHARLES ROBBINS), ret. radio and TV news corr.; b. Gallitzin, Pa.; d. Matthew Phillip and Susan (Stanley) Frederick; A.B., Am. U., Washington, also A.M.; m. Charles Robbins. State dept. corr. U.S. News; radio editorial asst. H. R. Baukhage, Blue Network and ABC; free-lance Western Newspaper Union, N.A. Newspaper Alliance; also news corr. ABC, 1946-53; news corr. NBC, 1953-72, also UN corr. ABC, NBC; radio anchor man Dem. and Rep. Convs., NBC, 1956. Recipient Headliner award Theta Sigma Phi, 1951, Alfred I. duPont award, 1954, George Foster Peabody award for contbn. to internat. understanding, 1955, Golden Mike award for outstanding woman in radio-TV, McCall's, 1956, 61; voted radio's woman of year for conv. assignment Radio-TV Daily poll, 1957, 61; Honor Medal Journalism U. Mo., 1962; award for contbn. to internat. understanding East-West Center, Honolulu, 1966; first Pa. award for excellence in journalism, 1966; Journalism Achievement award U. So. Cal., 1967, Carr Van Anda Journalism award Ohio U., 1971. Mem. UN Corrs. Assn., Radio-Television Corrs. Assn., Assn. Radio-Television News Analysts. Author: Ten First Ladies of the World.

FREDERICKS, BEULAH MAE, educator; b. Iowa Falls, Ia., Sept. 4, 1929; d. Frank and Golda (Strahorn) Fredericks; student Ellsworth Jr. Coll., 1947-49; B.A., State U. Ia., 1951; M.F.A., Art Inst. Chgo., 1960. Tchr. Dallas Center Ind. Sch. Dist., 1951-57, East Waterloo High Sch., 1960-62; tchr. James Logan High Sch., Union City, Cal., 1962—, chmn. speech-drama dept., 1963-70, dir. dramatics, 1951-71, curriculum asso. fine arts area graded 7-12, 1970-72, asst. prin., 1972—. Mem. No. Cal. Com. for Drama Tchr. Tng., 1970-71. Mem. U. Ia. Alumni Assn., Assn. Cal. Sch. Adminstrs., Phi Beta Kappa. Home: 4473 Alder Av Fremont CA 94536 Office: 1800 H St Union City CA 94536

FREDERICKS, JOAN DELANOY, scientist, govt. ofcl.; b. Dobbs Ferry, N.Y., Feb. 27, 1928; d. Robert B. and Amelia (DeLanoy) Fredericks; A.B., Skidmore Coll., 1949; M.A., Syracuse U., 1954. Research asst. C.F. Kettering Found., Yellow Springs, O., 1949-50, State U. N.Y., Syracuse, 1950-54; research technician Duke U. Med. Center, Durham, N.C., 1954-58; with NIH, Bethesda, Md., 1958—, chemist Nat. Inst. Arthritis and Metabolic Diseases, 1958-63, sci. grants asst. Nat. Heart Inst., head fellowship sect., tng. grants and awards br. Nat. Heart Inst., 1963-70, asst. prog. dir. metabolism Nat. Inst. Arthritis, Metabolic and Digestive Diseases, 1970-72, asst. program dir. for nutrition, 1972-74, acting program dir. for arthritis and orthopedics, 1974—. Mem. Skidmore Coll. Alumnae Assn., Sigma Delta Epsilon. Contbr. articles to profl. jours. Home: 4620 N Park Av Chevy Chase MD 20015 Office: NIH Bethesda MD 20014

FREDRICKSON, MARY FRANCES LONG (MRS. EDWARD FREDRICKSON), journalist; b. Burlington, Ia., Mar. 13, 1915; d. John Edgar and Crystal (Henry) Long; grad. high sch.; student Dale Carnegie, 1967-68; m. Edward E. Fredrickson, Nov. 26, 1935; children—James Edward, Thomas Henry, Lawrence Francis, Dennis Paul. Editor woman's page Lead (S.D.) Daily Call and Deadwood Pioneer-Times, 1958-64, 66-73; exec. sec. Lead C. of C., 1973—. Sec., Lead Bicentennial Com. active U.S.O. Community Concert Assn., Cancer Soc., A.R.C., Heart Fund; v.p. St. Patrick's P.T.A., 1951-53. Recipient Jane McLean award for best piece writing in Lead Woman's Club creative writing contest, 1954. Mem. Nat. League Am. Pen Women (v.p. Black Hills br. 1964-66, pres. 1966-68, pres. S.D. 1968-70), Black Hills Art Assn. (publicity com. 1963-64), S.D. Press Women (1st place critic's rev. 1971, 72). Republican. Roman Catholic. Home: 504 Grand Av Lead SD 57754 Office: 603 W Main St Lead SD 57754

FREEBERN, ELEANOR PEARSE (MRS. RALPH MARTIN FREEBERN), librarian; b. Center Moriches, N.Y., July 17, 1917; d. Erastus R. and Ethel Belle (Robinson) Pearse; B.S., Cornell, 1938; postgrad. Columbia, 1946-47; m. Ralph Martin Freebern, May 8, 1937; children—Douglas Wayne, Gary Brian. Librarian, Halsted Sch., Yonkers, N.Y., 1945-50, Pakistan Mission to UN, N.Y.C., 1950-59; librarian, econs. sect. Rockefeller Family Office, 1959-61; reference librarian J. Walter Thompson Co., advt. agy., N.Y.C., 1961-63; editorial librarian Parade Publs., Inc., N.Y.C., 1963-72; index librarian, editorial asst. Popular Sci. mag., N.Y.C., 1973—. Home: 82 Sherwood Av Ossining NY 10562 Office: 380 Madison Av New York City NY 10017

FREED, CATHERINE CAROL MOORE (MRS. DEBOW FREED), educator; b. Omaha, Dec. 27, 1925; d. Prentice Lauri and Henryetta (Banker) Moore; B.A., B.F.A., U. Tex., 1948; M.A., U. Kan., 1961; m. DeBow Freed, Sept. 10, 1949; 1 son, DeBow II. Mem. Faculty St. Mary's Coll., Xavier, Kan., 1958-59, U. Kan., Lawrence, 1959-61, U. N.M., Albuquerque, 1961-65, Huntingdon Coll., Montgomery, Ala., 1965-67; lectr. in English Ladycliff Coll., Highland Falls, N.Y., 1967-69. Adviser, Albuquerque Sch. System on Gifted Child Edn., 1962-64; speaker and subject of film on purposes and objectives of PTA, 1964; pres. Alliance Community Concert Assn., 1970-74; Alliance area chmn. Blossom women's com. Cleve. Symphony Orch., 1971-74. Mem. Speech Assn. Am., Nat. Council Tchrs. English, Daus. of U.S. Army (pres chpt. Ft. Benning, Ga. 1954-55), Internat. Platform Assn., P.E.O., Mortar Bd., Phi Beta Kappa, Delta Sigma Rho, Pi Kappa Delta, Kappa Phi, Alpha Psi Omega, Alpha Delta Pi. Home: 605 N 6th St Monmouth IL 61462 Office: Office of Pres Monmouth Coll Monmouth IL 61462

FREED, DORIS JONAS (MRS. ARTHUR FREED), lawyer; b. St. Louis, Nov. 12, 1920; d. A. M. and Lillian (Nebenzahl) Fromberg; B.A., N.Y.U., 1951, LL.B., LL.M., J.S.D., 1958; m. James A. Jones (dec. Nov. 1947); 1 dau., Gloria (Mrs. Newell Kane); m. 2d, Arthur Freed, May 17, 1957. Admitted to N.Y. State bar, 1946, Md. bar, U.S. Supreme Ct. bar; practice in N.Y.C.; counsel to firm Delson & Gordon. Am. nat. rappateur 1968 Internat. Bar Conf., Dublin, Ireland. Fellow Am. Acad. Matrimonial Lawyers; mem. Assn. Bar City N.Y. (com. on sex and law, com. on matrimonial law 1965—), Am. Bar Assn. (council and co-chmn. research com. family law sect., bd. editors Family Law Quar., Family Law Newsletter, chmn. com. on divorce laws and procedures, vice chmn. com. on liaison with internat. law com.), Internat. Fedn. Women Lawyers (chmn. com. on domestic relations law), New York County Lawyers Assn. (com. on matrimonial law), Am. Arbitration Assn. (mem. panel arbitrators). Author: (with Ploscowe, Foster and Freed) Cases and Materials on Family Law, 1972; (with Foster) Law and The Family-New York, Vol. I, rev., 1972, Vol. II, 1967; co-author Annual Survey American Family Law, 1966-72, Annual Survey of New York Family Law, 1966-70, 73,

Divorce, American Style, 1969, Charities and Charitable Foundations, 1974; also numerous law rev. articles. Co-author Law and the Family monthly column N.Y. Law Jour. Address: 60 E 42d St Suite 2022 New York City NY 10017

FREED, LAURA E., editor; b. Goodlettsville, Tenn., Sept. 26, 1919; d. J. Walter and Ella Lee (DeBow) Freed; student N.Y. U. Field rep. A.R.C., Europe, 1944-46; with pub. relations dept. Nat. Assn. Ins. Agts., N.Y.C., 1947-49; asso. editor Pub. Relations Jour., N.Y.C., 1949-53; program mgr. Keep Am. Beautiful, Inc., N.Y.C., 1953-71; owner, editor Freed Pub. Co., N.Y.C., 1969—. Environmental cons. Mem. Pub. Relations Soc. Am., Trade Assn. Execs. N.Y., Environmental Writers Assn. Am. Home: 211 E 53d St New York City NY 10022 Office: PO Box 1144 FDR Station New York City NY 10022

FREED, NANCY LEE WURZBURGER (MRS. BERT FREED), pub. relations exec.; b. N.Y.C., Dec. 11, 1923; d. Sigfried Adolph and Dorothy (Kahn) Wurzburger; student Columbia, 1940-43; m. Bert Freed, Feb. 12, 1956; children—Carl, Jennifer; 1 son from previous marriage—Andrew Charles Sutton. Copywriter, Jasper Lynch & Fishel, advt., N.Y.C., 1942-45; asst. advt. dir., pub. relations dir. Jay Thorpe, N.Y.C., 1945-46; account exec. Allen Meltzer, Inc., pub. relations, N.Y.C., 1946-48; asst. producer NBC Network, Vacation Wonderlands, N.Y.C., 1948; owner Nancy Lee Waring, pub. relations, N.Y.C., 1948-50; account supr. Carl Ruff Assos., pub. relations, N.Y.C., 1950-58, Harshe, Rotman & Druck, pub. relations, Los Angeles, 1962-68; pub. relations dir. Art Center Coll. of Design, Los Angeles, 1969-71; pres. Nancy Lee Freed, Pub. Relations, Los Angeles, 1971—. Mem. Pacific Palisades High Sch. Adv. Council, 1971-75. Sec. 60th Assembly Dist. Democratic party, 1969-72; editor Brentwood Dem. Club Newsletter, 1968-71. Chmn. adv. bd. Children's Hosp. Hotline, 1968; bd. dirs. Elizabeth Fry Center, 1973—. Mem. Los Angeles Advt. Women (chmn. ednl. com. 1973-74, dir. 1974). Address: 418 N Bowling Green Way Los Angeles CA 90049

FREEDMAN, ANNE ELLEN GOLDBERG, educator; b. Passaic, N.J., Apr. 6, 1938; d. Sidney and Mollie Clara (Kantor) Goldberg; B.A., Douglas Coll., 1959; M.A. (Woodrow Wilson fellow), U. Cal., Berkeley, 1960; Ph.D., State U. Ia., 1964; m. Philip E. Freedman, Sept. 5, 1960; 1 dau., Sharon Lori. Research asso. Radcliffe Inst. Ind. Study, Cambridge, Mass., 1963-64; instr. Wheaton Coll., Norton, Mass., 1964-65, St. Xavier Coll., Chgo., 1965-66; asst. prof. polit. sci. Roosevelt U., Chgo., 1966-70, asso. prof., chmn. polit. sci. dept., 1970—. Mem. Am. Civil Liberties Union, Am. Polit. Sci. Assn., Am. Acad. Polit. Social Sci., Phi Beta Kappa. Co-author: Voluntary Associations, 1972; author The Planned Society, 1972. Home: 618 A South Blvd Evanston IL 60202 Office: 430 S Michigan Av Chicago IL 60605

FREEDMAN, LAURIE, dancer, educator; b. N.Y.C., July 7, 1945; d. Lionel and Celia Janet (Rubin) Freedman; B.A., Bennington Coll., 1967. Mem. Merry-Go-Rounders Dance Co., N.Y.C., 1967-68; mem. Batsheva Dance Co., Tel Aviv, Israel, 1968—. Tchr. dancing Conn. Coll. Sch. of Dance, New London, 1967-68, Bat-Dor Sch. of Dance, Tel Aviv, 1971—. Tchr. dance programs for various Kibbutzim; choreographer Inter-Kibbutz Dance Co., 1971—. Mem. Batsheva-Bat-Dor Dance Soc. Choreographer: Song of Aeolis, N.Y.C., 1967, Currents, N.Y.C., 1968, Tumble, Tel Aviv, 1972. Office: Batsheva Dance Co 9 SD Haha Skala Tel Aviv Israel

FREEDMAN, SALLY PULLEN (MRS. IRVIN EARL FREEDMAN), store fixture designer and lessor; b. San Antonio, Mar. 4, 1912; d. Saul and Semi (Ruben) Pullen; grad. high sch.; m. Irvin Earl Freedman, Dec. 25, 1936; children—Sidni Rae (Mrs. Melvin P. Greenblat), Patricia, Leslie Dean (Mrs. Stuart Edelman), Daniel Bruce. With Clarks Dollar Stores, San Antonio, 1934, W.T. Grant Co., Houston, 1936; partner I.E. Freedman and Assos., Houston and Silver Spring, Md., 1944—; corporate officer, dir. several leasing corps. Md., Pa., N.J., N.H., N.Y., R.I. Mem. Brandies U. Women's Com. Jewish religion (v.p. Temple Emanuel Sisterhood 1939-40). Club: Internat. (Washington). Address: 1 Eastmoor Dr Silver Spring MD 20901

FREEL, ETHEL LENORE, social worker; b. Soda Springs, Ida., June 7, 1914; d. John Harrison and Mona (Elrod) Turnbull; student Ill. Inst. Tech., 1936-37; M.A. in Social Scis., U. Chgo., 1952; m. Robert M. Freel, Feb. 15, 1946 (dec. Feb. 26, 1966); 1 dau., Bettie Joanne. Job interviewer Ill. Employment Service, Chgo., 1939-42, labor utilization technician, 1943-46; youth counselor Ind. Employment Service, Gary, 1964-65; counselor div. vocational rehab. Ind. Rehab. Service, East Chicago, 1965—. Served to lt. (j.g.) USN, 1944-46. Mem. Nat. Rehab. Assn., Nat. Rehab. Counseling Assn. (pres. Ind. 1971, regional certifying officer 1971), Am. Assn. Mental Deficiency, A.A.A.S., Am. Assn. U. Women. Home: 3343 Kenwood St Hammond IN 46323 Office: 4620 Magoun Av East Chicago IN 46312

FREEMAN, BERNICE, educator; b. LaGrange, Ga., Aug. 8, 1909; d. Thomas Norman and Everette (Jenkins) Freeman; A.B., Tift Coll., 1930; M.A. in English, U. N.C., 1932; Ed.D. in English, Columbia, 1952. Tchr. math. pub. schs., Dublin, Ga., 1930-31; tchr. social studies pub. schs., La Grange, Ga., 1932-42; tchr. social studies, English Peabody Demonstration Sch., Ga. State Coll. Women, 1942-48, prin., tchr. 1948-51; dir. curriculum Troup County Schs., La Grange, 1951-67; asso. prof. edn. West Ga. Coll., Carrollton, 1967-69, prof. edn., 1969—, coordinator secondary edn., 1969-73, chmn. dept. secondary edn., 1973—. Del. Washington Conf. Academically Talented, 1958, White House Conf. Children and Youth, 1960; chmn. English curriculum guide com., Ga. Pub. Schs., 1960-64, mem. steering com., English curriculum guide com., 1965-68; pres. Ga. Dept. Instructional Supervision, 1961-62, co-dir. English Study in Ga., 1951-52. Bd. dirs. Troup-Harris-Cowetta Regional Library. Mem. League Women Voters (pres. Carrollton br. 1970-72), Am. Assn. U. Women (pres. Ga. div. 1957-59), Ga. Council Tchrs. English (pres. 1947-48), Ga. Writers Assn., Ga. Acad. Social Scis., Nat. Council Tchrs. English, Pi Lambda Theta, Kappa Delta Pi, Pi Gamma Mu, Delta Kappa Gamma. Preparation ednl. materials (with Lydia A. Thomas) The Reader's Digest, N.E.A. (exec. com. dept. rural education 1965-69), Reading Skill Builder, Grade 5, Part 3, 1960, (with Bernice Cooper) Grade 1, Part 1, 1963. Home: 305 Park Av LaGrange GA 30240 Office: West Ga Coll Carrollton GA 30117

FREEMAN, BETTY JO, psychologist; b. Butler, Ga., Jan. 7, 1945; d. Frank Patton and Francis Wynell (Andrews) Freeman; A.B summa cum laude, Mercer U., Macon, Ga., 1966; M.A., So. Ill. U., 1968, Ph.D., 1969. Research asso. VA Hosp., Nashville, 1969-71; asst. prof. Fisk U., Nashville, 1971-72; postdoctoral fellow Johns Hopkins Med. Sch., 1972-73; asst. prof. med. psychology Sch. Medicine, U. Cal. at Los Angeles, 1973—; instr. U. Pitts., part-time 1969; instr. U. Balt., 1973. Mem. Am. Psychol. Assn., A.A.A.S., Am. Assn. Mental Deficiency. Contbr. numerous articles to profl. jours. Home: Apt 209 846 4th St Santa Monica CA 90403 Office: Dept Psychiatry Medical Sch Univ Cal Los Angeles CA 90024

FREEMAN, DORIS BRANCH, broadcasting exec.; b. Jackson, Tenn., Mar. 25, 1925; d. Felix Matthew and Martha Belle (Weaks) Branch; student Murray State Tchrs. Coll., 1942-43; m. James H. Freeman, Nov. 21, 1942 (div. 1962); children—Patricia (Mrs. Stephen Little), Cynthia (Mrs. Phillip Haynie), James Vaughn II, Constance Maurine. With radio sta. WDXI, Jackson, 1948—, account exec., broadcaster, 1955—; hostess daily TV show Cousin Tuny, sta. WDXI-TV, Jackson, 1955-67. Promotional dir. Old Hickory Mall, Jackson, 1967—; singer, marimba player. Chmn. pub. relations Reelfoot council Girl Scouts U.S.A., 1968—; West Tenn. chmn. Easter Seals, 1965-66; state chmn. Heart Sunday, Tenn. Heart Assn., 1964-65. Named Jackson-Madison County Woman of Yr., 1962; recipient Distinguished Sales award Jackson Sales and Marketing Exec. Club, 1966, Outstanding Community Service award Lane Coll., 1967, Hon. Dr. Spaceology, USAF Systems Command, 1967, Golden Mike award Am. Women in Radio and TV, 1967. Bd. dirs. Jackson-Madison County A.R.C., Cancer Soc. Named Tenn. Squire. Mem. C. of C. (mem. task force com. 1973—), Am. Women in Radio and TV, Club: Jackson Golf and Country. Composer: Mortgaged Plymouth, 1971. Home: 218 Fairmont St Jackson TN 38301 Office: WDXI Radio Jackson TN 38301

FREEMAN, DORIS CHANIN (MRS. ALAN J. FREEDMAN), art cons., radio show producer; b. N.Y.C., Apr. 25, 1928; d. Irwin S. and Sylvia S. (Schofler) Chanin; B.S., Albright Coll., 1950; M. S.W., Columbia, 1953; m. Alan J. Freedman, June 3, 1951; children—Karen, Nina, Susan. Dir. N.Y.C. dept. Cultural Affairs, 1967-70; producer, moderator weekly radio show Artists in the City, radio sta. WNYC-FM, 1969—. Pres., City Walls, Inc., 1970—. Chmn., Citizens for Artists Housing, 1970-73; v.p. Community Bd. 7, Parks, Recreation and Affairs Com., 1974—, Parks Council, 1972—. Trustee Pratt Inst. Mem. adv. bd. Young Filmaker's Found., 1972—, Vol. Lawyers for the Arts, 1972—. Mem. N.Y. (art cons. 1972—), N.J. (art cons. 1972—) councils on arts, Municipal Art Soc. (chmn. pub. arts council 1971—, v.p. 1973—). Contbr. articles to profl. publs. Address: 25 Central Park W New York City NY 10023

FREEMAN, ELSA S. (MRS. STUART I. FREEMAN), librarian; B.A., Columbia, 1939, B.S., 1940; m. Stuart I. Freeman, 1938. Reference and sch. asst. N.Y. Pub. Library, 1940-41; jr. librarian U.S. Bur. Agrl. Econs., 1941-42; reference asst., sr. reference asst., asst. chief circulation sec. U.S. Dept. Agr. Library, 1941-49; asst. librarian Navy Dept., Bur. Ordnance, 1949-51; head librarian Office of Geography Library, U.S. Dept. Interior, 1951-56; dir. U.S. Dept. Housing and Urban Devel. Library, 1956-71, dir. library and information div., 1971—, mem. fed. women's com., 1970—. Mem. exec. adv. com. Fed. Library Com., 1970-71, also chmn. task force on acquisition library materials and correlation fed. library resources; mem. com. sci. and tech. information and panel information analysis centers Fed. Council for Sci. and Tech., 1970—, librarians' tech. com. Met. Washington Council Govts., 1969—; lectr. in field. Mem. Little Theatre Alexandria. Mem. Spl. Libraries Assn. (chmn. recruitment com. 1955-56; vice chmn. membership com. 1953-55; pres. Washington 1954-55, chmn. conv. program com. 1960-62, chmn. planning bldg. and housing sect. 1965-66), A.L.A. (chmn. bldgs. com. hosp., instn. spl. libraries 1962-64), Internat. Fedn. Library Assns. (chmn. conf. 1974), Assn. Coll. and Research Libraries, Alumni Assn. Columbia, No. Va. Fine Arts Assn., Phi Beta Kappa, Beta Phi Mu. Episcopalian (mem. bd. Christian edn.). Club: Columbian Toastmistress (1st pres.). Editor Progress in Sci. and Tech. Communications, 1970; several brochures Spl. Library Assn.; contbr to mags. Home: 3519 Fort Hill Dr Wilton Woods Alexandria VA 22310 Office: 451 7th St SW Room 8233 Washington DC 20410

FREEMAN, EVELYN SLADE, mgmt. cons.; b. Cleve., July 25, 1940; d. Julius Edward and Jane (Carter) Freeman; B.S., Howard U., 1961; M.A., Tchrs. Coll. Columbia, 1965; M.S. Columbia Sch. Bus., 1972. Vocational counselor N.Y. State Div. Employment, N.Y.C., 1962-64; specialist job devel. and tng. Haryou-Act, Inc., N.Y.C., 1965; exec. v.p. Fields, Freeman Assos., Inc., N.Y.C., 1966—. Cons., Ednl. Testing Service, Princeton, N.J. Mem. exec. com. Harlem br. League of Women Voters, 1970—. Mem. Phi Beta Kappa, Psi Chi, Alpha Kappa Alpha (1st v.p. Tau Omega chpt.). Home: 168 Echo Hill Dr Stamford CT 06903 Office: Suite 1800 51 E 42d St New York City NY 10017

FREEMAN, MRS. FRANKIE M., lawyer; b. Danville, Va.; student Hampton Inst., 1933-36; LL.B., Howard U., 1947; m. Shelby T. Freeman, Jr.; 1 dau. Admitted to Washington bar, Mo. bar, U.S. Supreme Ct. bar; asst. atty. gen. Mo., 1955-56; pvt. practice, 1949-56; clerk U.S. Treasury Dept. Fgn. Funds Control, 1942-44; statistician OPA, 1944-45; commr. U.S. Commn. on Civil Rights, 1964—. Asso. gen. counsel St. Louis Housing and Land Clearance Authorities, 1965—. Active St. Louis br. N.A.A.C.P., YWCA Met. St. Louis. Recipient Outstanding Citizen award Mound City Press Club, 1953; Women of Achievement Nat. Council Negro Women, 1956; Woman of Achievement in pub. affairs, 1965. Bd. dirs. Nat. Council Negro Women. Mem. Am., Nat., Mound City bar assns., Lawyers' Assn. St. Louis, Nat. Assn. Housing and Redevel. Ofcls., Nat. Housing Conf., League Women Voters, Delta Sigma Theta (nat. 1st v.p.). Baptist. Address: 5391 Waterman Av St Louis MO 63112

FREEMAN, LANA RUTH IVESTER (MRS. DUDLEY ROGER FREEMAN), educator; b. Sayre, Okla., July 14, 1941; d. Lando Thurman and Georgia Ruth (Jarvis) Ivester; B.S., Southwestern State Coll., Weatherford, Okla., 1963, M.Ed., 1970; postgrad. No. Ariz. U., 1971; m. Dudley Roger Freeman, June 1, 1959; children—Janet Rene, Joanna Lynn. Tchr. Oney High Sch., Albert, Okla., 1963-66; tchr., drama dir. Liberal (Kan.) High Sch., 1966-69; instr. psychology, counselor Seward County Community Coll., Liberal, Kan., 1969—. Mem. Am. Assn. U. Women (pres. 1971-73), Delta Kappa Gamma, Beta Sigma Phi (pres. 1966). Home: 405 Yale Av Liberal KS 67901

FREEMAN, LINDA WEBSTER, hosp. adminstr.; b. Schenectady, Oct. 13, 1943; d. Robert Grant and Margaret Mary (McDonnell) Webster; R.N., Yale-New Haven Med. Center, 1964; Asso., Russell Sage Coll., 1971; B.S., Union Coll., 1972; m. Robert L. Freeman. Registered nurse specialist N.Y. State Dept. Mental Hygiene, Albany, 1970-72; nursing home adminstr. Highgate Mgmt. Devel. Ltd., Albany, 1972-73; asst. dir.-nursing adminstr. Amsterdam (N.Y.) Meml. Hosp., 1973-74. Recipient Justice Francis Bergan award Russell Sage Coll., 1971. Mem. Am. Nurses Assn., Nat. League Nursing, Am. Assn. Mental Deficiency, Assn. Conf. Dirs. Nursing, Phi Theta Kappa. Address: PO Box 186 Brandywine Sta Schenectady NY 12304

FREEMAN, LOLA LUCILE, librarian; b. Pony, Mont., Feb. 4, 1913; d. James Samuel and Lola May (Carver) Freeman; B.A., Phillips U., 1951; M.A., Butler U., 1959; postgrad. Mont. State U., 1961-62; M.A. in L.S., U. Denver, 1965. Tchr. Weekday Religious Edn. Indpls., 1951-61; tchr., librarian Rudyard (Mont.) Pub. schs., 1962-63; librarian Greybull (Wyo.) High Sch., 1963-66, Drake U., Des Moines, 1966—. Mem. Am., Ia. library assns., Am. Assn. Univ. Profs. (chpt. sec. 1973). Mem. Christian Ch. Home: 2818 Cottage Grove Av Apt 3 Des Moines IA 50311 Office: Cowles Library Drake U Des Moines IA 50311

FREEMAN, SARA LEVIN (MRS. ISADORE FREEMAN), artist; b. Garfield, N.J.; d. Isaac and Blossom (Band) Levin; student Paterson State Coll.; m. Isadore Freeman, July 10, 1938. Exhibited one-man shows including Paterson Mus., Seton Hall U., Fair Lawn Pub. Library, Clinton Theatre Gallery, Library Gallery, County Coll. Morris, Einstein Coll. Medicine, others; exhibited in juried group shows at Montclair Mus., Jersey City Mus., N.J. State Mus., Monmouth Arts Festival, Galerie de la Rose des Vents, Vich, Switzerland, Palazzo Vecchio, Florence, Italy, Ont. (Can.) Library and Arts Center, Oklahoma Art Center, Hunterdon (N.J.) Art Center, L.I. U., others; represented in permanent collections at Paterson Mus., Seton Hall U., Le Chateau de la Napoule, France, Meadox Medicals, Oakland, N.J., also pvt. collections. Mem. Fair Lawn Art Adv. Com., 1968—; program and membership chmn. Friends of Living Arts and Music Enjoyment, 1961-71. Recipient 2d prize in mixed media 4th Internat. Exhbn. Women Artists, Cannes, France, 1969, award Summit Art Center, 1968, 71, Fair Lawn State Show, 1969, 70, Hunterdon County Art Center, 1970, 1st prize Fairleigh Dickinson Ecol. Show, 1971, Community award for contbn. to cultural life in community, 1965. Mem. at. Assn. Women Artists, Artists Equity N.Y., Modern Artists Guild. Address: 13-08 Bellair Av Fair Lawn NJ 07410

FREESE, SHERRY ANNETTE KILPATRICK (MRS. WILLIAM CHARLES FREESE), editor; b. Tabor, Ia., June 10, 1934; d. Charles Francis and Leta Aileen (Ventis) Kilpatrick; B.A. in Journalism, U. Colo., 1957; m. William Charles Freese, Aug. 5, 1961; children—Elizabeth, Mary Kathleen. Tchr. English and journalism Davenport (Ia.) High Sch., 1957-60, Davenport Central High Sch., 1960-61; editor Ia. Motor News, AAA Motor Club Ia., Davenport, 1969—. Active Girl Scouts Am., 1971—. Mem. Women in Communications, Ia. Indsl. Editors Assn. (recipient Editorial Achievement award 1973), Delta Gamma, Republican. Lutheran. Mem. Internat. Assn. Bus. Communicators, P.E.O. Home: 3310 Tremont St Davenport IA 52803 Office: Motor Club Iowa Box 4290 Davenport IA 52808

FREESE, WINIFRED ANDERSON (MRS. ERNEST IRVING FREESE), editor; b. San Diego, Oct. 13, 1913; d. Arthur Leo and Muriel Alice (Cattle) Anderson; student San Diego State Coll., 1933; B.A., Scripps Coll., 1934; M.A., Radliffe Coll., 1935; m. Ernest Irving Freese, Jan. 1, 1937; 1 son, William Arthur. Asst. to curator Huntington Art Gallery, San Marino, Cal., 1936-38; employed with Pacific Mut. Ins. Co., Los Angeles, 1956-61; editorial asst. Huntington Library, San Marino, Cal., 1961-62, asst. editor Huntington Library Quar., 1962—. Historian P.T.A., 1950-52. Mem. Scripps Coll., Radcliffe Coll. alumni assns. Democrat. Episcopalian. Office: 1151 Oxford Rd San Marino CA 91108

FREIFIELD, NORMA ELIZABETH, librarian; b. Edmonton, Alta., Can., June 30, 1917; d. William and Flora Archibald (Clark) Freifield; B.A., U. Alta., 1938; B.L.S., U. Toronto, 1940. Circulation asst. U. Alta. Library, Edmonton, 1941-50, head circulation department library, 1950-70, co-ordinator circulation services, 1970—. Mem. Am., Canadian, Alta. (pres. 1954-55) library assns., Assn. Acad. Staff U. Alta., Canadian Assn. U. Tchrs., Canadian Fedn. U. Women (pres. chpt. 1958-60), Delta Kappa Gamma (pres. chpt. 1964-66). Home: 10409 133d St Edmonton AB T5N 2A2 Canada

FREILICH, ANN, artist; b. Czestochowa, Poland; d. Sam and Sophie (Schwartzberg) Freilich; came to U.S., 1914, naturalized, 1927; student Coll. City N.Y., 1927-30; m. Nathan J. Schutz, Dec. 30, 1942 (div. July 1966); 1 dau., Erica Schutz. One-man show at Roko Gallery, N.Y.C.; exhibited in group shows at Am. Acad. Arts and Letters, Bklyn. Mus., Gallery Modern Art, N.Y.C., Phila. Mus., Jersey City Mus., Toledo Mus. Art; represented in permanent collections Bklyn. Mus., U. Wyo. Art Mus., Laramie, Peabody Mus., Nashville, Syracuse (N.Y.) U. Dir. Bridge Gallery, N.Y.C., 1963-64; tchr. Randall Morgan Art Workshop, Sant' Agata, Italy, 1967. Recipient awards, including Childe Hassam purchase award Am. Acad. Arts and Letters, 1972. Home: 250 W 94th St New York City NY 10025

FREILICHER, JANE, artist; b. Bklyn., Nov. 29, 1924; d. Martin and Bertha (Cummings) Niederhoffer; B.A., Bklyn. Coll.; M.A., Columbia; postgrad. Hans Hofmann Sch.; m. Joseph Hazan, Feb. 17, 1957; 1 dau., Elizabeth. One-man shows at Tibor Denagy Gallery, N.Y.C., 1952—, John Bernard Myers Gallery, N.Y.C., 1971; exhibited in traveling shows Mus. Modern Art, Whitney Ann., 1972; represented in permanent collections at N.Y. U., Loeb Center, Bklyn. Mus., Mus. Modern Art, Brandeis Art Mus., R.I. Mus. Fine Arts, Coll. Art Collection, Stratford, Conn., Whitney Mus., Chase Manhattan Bank. Vis. critic U. Pa. Grad. Sch. Art, spring 1968, 71, Showhegan, Tanglewood, 1968, Carnegie-Mellon U., 1971, Md. Inst. Art, La. State U., 1973. Winner Hallmark Competition, 1960. Am. Assn. U. Women fellow, 1974. Illustrator: Turandot and Other Poems; Paris Review Portfolio, 1965; Poets of the New York School, 1969. Home: 51 Fifth Av New York City NY 10003 also Watermill NY 11976

FREINKEL, RUTH KIMMELSTIEL (MRS. NORBERT FREINKEL), med. educator; b. Hamburg, Germany, Dec. 26, 1926; d. Paul and Lotte (van Biema) Kimmelstiel; came to U.S., 1934, naturalized, 1940; B.A., Randolph-Macon Coll., 1948; M.D., Duke, 1952; m. Norbert Freinkel, June 19, 1955; children—Susan, Andrew, Lisa. Intern, Duke Hosp., Durham, N.C., 1952-53; resident medicine and dermatology Boston City, Mass. Gen. hosps., 1953-54, 56-58; fellow biochemistry Harvard, 1955-56, Cambridge U., 1956-57; instr. dept. dermatology Harvard Med. Sch., 1960-63, asst. prof., 1963-66; asso. prof. dermatology Northwestern U. Med. Sch., Chgo., 1966-72, prof., 1972—. Mem. gen. medicine study sect. NIH, 1972—; mem. sub task force Nat. Program for Dermatology, 1973. Recipient fellowship NRC, 1954-56, grant NIH, 1961—. Diplomate Am. Bd. Dermatology. Mem. Soc. Investigative Dermatology (dir. 1973), Am. Acad. Dermatology, Am. Dermatol. Assn., Central Soc. Clin. Research, Am. Soc. Clin. Investigation. Editorial bd. Jour. Investigative Dermatology, 1972—. Contbr. to publs. in field. Home: 938 Edgemere Ct Evanston IL 60202 Office: 303 E Chicago Av Chicago IL 60611

FREITAG, JULIA LOUISE, physician; b. Allentown, Pa., Nov. 29, 1927; d. Arthur Henry and Ruth Elizabeth (Meaker) Freitag; B.A., Cornell U., 1949, M.D., 1953; M.P.H., Harvard, 1957. Intern, Cleve. City Hosp., 1953-54; resident Upstate Med. Center, Syracuse, N.Y., 1954-55, N.Y. State Dept. Health, Albany, 1955-57; epidemiologist N.Y. State Dept. Health, 1957—, dir. Bur. Epidemiology, 1965-68; dir. Med. Manpower, Albany, 1968—. Lectr., Albany Med. Coll.; mem. adv. council N.Y. Vocational Edn. Diplomate Am. Bd. Preventive Medicine. Mem. Phi Beta Kappa, Phi Beta Phi, Alpha Omega Alpha, Delta Omega. Home: RD 1 Feura Bush NY 12067 Office: 84 Holland Av Albany NY 12208

FREIVOGEL, MARGARET WOLF (MRS. WILLIAM HEIN FREIVOGEL), journalist; b. St. Louis, Mar. 14, 1949; d. William Eugene and Florence Margaret (Dorsey) Wolf; B.A. (Presidential scholar), Stanford, 1971; m. William Hein Freivogel, June 19, 1971. Reporter, St. Louis Post Dispatch, 1971—. Corr. New Times Mag., N.Y.C. Mem. Women in Communications (v.p. St. Louis chpt.

1973-74), Phi Beta Kappa. Home: 3324 LaClede St Louis MO 63103 Office: 900 N 12th St St Louis MO 63101

FRELS, LOIS MARIAN PARNELL (MRS. CALVIN EDWIN FRELS), educator; b. Geneseo, Ill., Nov. 20, 1929; d. Floyd Vinton and Mary Jane (Davis) Parnell; R.N., Moline (Ill.) Pub. Hosp., 1950; student pub. Health U. Minn., Loyola U., Chgo., 1951-54; B.S., Augustana Coll., Rock Island, Ill., 1959; M.A., U. Ia., 1964; diploma for testing, Marianne Frostic Center Ednl. Therapy, Los Angeles, 1969; m. Calvin Edwin Frels, Oct. 28, 1950; children—Mark Edwin, Arlan James. Sch. nurse East Moline Elementary Schs., 1951-54; pub. health work East Moline Vis. Nurses Assn., 1955-57; sch. nurse, project dir., nurse cons. United Twp. High Sch., East Moline, 1957-67; instr. psychology Blackhawk Jr. Coll., Moline, part time 1966-68; tchr., dir. gifted program Silvis (Ill.) Elementary Schs., 1968; counselor Pleasant Valley (Ia.) High Sch., 1969-70; asst. prof. Marycrest Coll., Davenport, Ia., 1970-73; head nursing dept. Ia. Wesleyan Coll., Mt. Pleasant, 1973—. Sec., East Moline Community Resource Council, 1965-67; mem. Riverdale Unit 100 Bd. Edn., Port Byron, Ill., 1964-67, 68—; chmn. Rock Island County Fact Finding Com. White House Conf. Children and Youth, 1970; organizer Little White House Conf. Children and Youth, Rock Island County, 1969; del. White House Conf. on Children and Youth, 1970; 2d v.p. Rock Island County Welfare Council, 1968-70; mem. ednl. task force Rock Island Model Cities Project, 1969-70. Bd. dirs. Opportunity Mentally Handicapped. Ill. Dept. Pub. Instrn. grantee Western Ill. U., 1968. Fellow Am. Sch. Health Assn. (chmn. sch. nurse study com. 1973—); mem. Am., Ill. nurses assns., Am. Personnel and Guidance Assn., Am. Edn. Research Assn., Am. Pub. Health Assn., N.E.A., Ia. Edn. Assn., Soc. for Perception, Royal Soc. Health (London, Eng.), Pi Lambda Theta. Home: Rural Route 1 Box 164 Hillsdale IL 61257 Office: Iowa Wesleyan College Mt Pleasant IA 52641

FRENCH, DOROTHY MAY KAYSER (MRS. LOUIS NUDD FRENCH), writer; b. Milw., Feb. 11, 1926; d. Paul and Gertrude Frances (Ament) Kayser; B.A., U. Wis., 1948; m. Louis Nudd French, July 2, 1948; children—Nancy (Mrs. James T. Kepple), Laura. Soc. editor Shorewood (Wis.) Herald, 1946; women's editor Wis. State Jour., Madison, 1948-50; soc. editor Bartlesville (Okla.) Record, 1951; free-lance writer, 1951—, short stories pub. in Teen, Jack and Jill, Chrysler-Plymouth Spectator, Humpty-Dumpty, Okla. Today, Hi Call. Mem. Women in Communications, Am. Assn. Univ. Women (sec. 1953-55), Mortar Bd., Kappa Delta (pres. 1952-53, 72-74). Author: Mystery of the Old Oil Well, 1963; Swim to Victory, 1969; A Try at Tumbling, 1970; Pioneer Saddle Mystery, 1975. Address: 2136 Starlight Ct Bartlesville OK 74003

FRENCH, EMELYN MAE, mfg. co. exec.; b. Chanute, Kan., June 11, 1909; d. Charles August and Laura Almeda (Moyer) French; grad. Gregg Bus. Coll., 1925. Bond trader (1st woman in U.S.) Thompson Ross & Co., Chgo., 1926-29, Cammack, Clark, Chgo., 1929-33; various positions including legal sec., financial asst. to bank examiners, 1933-38; sec. Am. Steel Foundries, Chgo., 1938-45; hosp. adminstr. Johnson Hosp., Chanute, 1946-50; purchasing agt. Riverside Industries Inc., Tulsa, 1951-72. Mem. Purchasing Mgmt. Assn. Tulsa, Nat. Assn. Purchasing Mgmt. Mem. Royal Neighbors Am. Home: 4911 Old Canton Rd Jackson MS 39211

FRENCH, JANET ANNE BEIGHLE (MRS. ROBERT FRENCH), editor; b. Tacoma, May 19, 1933; d. Dan and Anne (Murray) Beighle; student Western Wash. Coll., 1952-53, Wash. State U., 1953-54; B.S. in Home Econs., Ore. State U., 1955; M.S., U. Wis., 1956; m. Robert French, June 2, 1973. Cook book editor Better Homes and Gardens, Des Moines, 1956-63; home econs. editor Plain Dealer, Cleve., 1963—. Del. White House Conf. Food, Nutrition and Health, Washington, 1969; judge Pillsbury Bake-Off, San Diego, Cal., 1971; adv. com. chmn. Newspaper Food Editors Conf., Chgo., 1969. Recipient award for nutrition writing Carnation Co., 1972, Alma award Am. Home Appliance Mfrs., 1967, 71, Vesta award Am. Meat Inst., 1964. Mem. Am. Home Econs. Assn. (vice chmn. ann. conf. 1969), Home Economists in Bus. (chmn. group 1965), Inst. Food Tech., Newspaper Food Editors and Writers Assn., Nutrition Council Greater Cleve., Common Cause. Sigma Delta Chi. Office: 1801 Superior Av Cleveland OH 44114

FRENCH, SISTER LOUISE, educator; b. Indpls., June 23, 1918; d. Adlai S. and Ann Marie (Burke) French; A.B., Mundelein Coll., 1940; A.M., Marquette U., 1949; Ph.D., St. Louis U., 1961. Joined Sisters of Charity of Blessed Virgin Mary; faculty philosophy dept. Clarke Coll., Dubuque, Ia., 1945-68, prof., 1965-68, dept. chmn., 1957-68; prof. dept. philosophy Mundelein Coll., Chgo., 1968—. Lectr. on contemporary moral theories; ednl. cons. Mem. Am. Catholic, Am. philos. assns., Metaphys. Soc. Contbr. articles to profl. publs. Home: 6363 Sheridan Rd Chicago IL 60660

FRENCH, VARINA CHRISTINE HEINRICH (MRS. HAROLD (DAN) FRENCH), educator; b. Hillsboro, Ore., Nov. 28, 1933; d. Vincent Thomas and Maudie (Hoag) Heinrich; B.S., Pacific U., 1956, M.S., 1965; m. Harold (Dan) French, May 28, 1954; children—Daniel Vincent, Laurie Denise. Tchr. pub. schs., Hillsboro, Ore., 1958-60; asst. prof. health and phys edn. Pacific U., Forest Grove, Ore., 1960—, chmn. dept. health and phys. edn., 1972—. Choreographer, Forest Grove Community Barbershop Ballad Festival, 1956, 61-68; judging commr. No. dist. State of Ore. Gymnastics 1967-68; edn. chmn. Forest Grove Social Action Commn., 1968—; dir. Community Encounter Planning Bd., 1969—, Upward Bound Recreation, 1966; nat. chmn. div. girls and womens sports exams. and ratings com. for gymnastics Olympic Com. for Gymnastics, 1971—; mem. Nat. Collegiate Council for Womens Gymnastics, 1972; v.p. womens com. U.S. Gymnastic Fedn., 1974—. Mem. A.A.H.P.E.R., Ore Assn. Health, Phys. Edn. and Recreation, Western Soc. for Phys. Edn. Coll. Women, Am. Assn. U. Women, U.S. Gymnastic Fedn. (regional chmn. 1968—), No. Ore. Bd. Women Ofcls. (sec. 1963-65), Delta Kappa Gamma. Mem. Disciples of Christ Ch. (deaconess). Home: Route 1 Box 245 Forest Grove OR 97116

FRENTZ, ANNE SUTHERLAND (MRS. LEROY BRAND FRENTZ III), economist; b. Kansas City, Mo., May 25, 1939; d. Richard VanArsdale and Eleanor Given (Thompson) Sutherland; student (Lillian E. Rivers Meml. scholar) U. Cal. at Santa Barbara, 1956-59, Long Beach State Coll., 1959; B.A. (Lillian E. Rivers Meml. scholar), U. Cal. at Berkeley, 1960, postgrad., 1972—; m. LeRoy Brand Frentz III, Dec. 23, 1961; children—Nick Andrew, Sonja Linder, Alexander Steven. Tchr., dept. head, curriculum leader Oakland (Cal.) Pub. Schs., 1961-73; tchr. Am. Mil. Dependents Sch., Chitose, Hokkaido, Japan, 1962-63; cons. Stanford Research Inst., Menlo Park, Cal., 1973—. Dir., Consumers Coop. of Berkeley, Inc., 1969-72; invitee White House Conf. on Food, Nutrition and Health, 1969; mem. Cal. Consumers Counsel Adv. Com., 1969-70. Mem. Alpha Delta Pi. Home: 40 Avis Rd Berkeley CA 94707 Office: Ednl Policy Research Center Stanford Research Inst 333 Ravenswood Av Menlo Park CA 94025

FRESE, ANNE MARIE HORVATH (MRS. HENRY C. FRESE), librarian; b. Chgo., Jan. 5, 1921; d. Frank L. and Juli (Talaber) Horvath; B.A., U. Budapest (Hungary); postgrad. Western Mich. U.; m. Henry C. Frese, Sept. 29, 1945; children—Annemarie (Mrs. Terry Pierce), Henry Jay. With U.S. Steel Corp., Chgo., 1940-45; head librarian Niles (Mich.) Community Library, 1958—. Mem. Berrien County Bicentennial Hist. Commn., Ft. St. Joseph Restoration Commn. Mem. Am., Mich. (sec. pub. library div. 1969-70, pub. relations com. 1970—) library assns., Berrien County Cooperating Libraries, Bus. and Profl. Women's Club, Kappa Delta Pi. Home: 3105 Creek Rd Elvandale Farm Niles MI 49120 Office: Niles Community Library 620 E Main St Niles MI 49120

FREY, DIANE ELIZABETH, educator; b. Quakertown, Pa., Apr. 4, 1945; d. Norman Lawson and Helen Ruth (Snyder) Frey; M.Ed., U. Ill., 1967, Ph.D., 1970. Tchr., Upper Darby (Pa.) Sch. Dist., 1966; dir. psychol. services St. Joseph (Ill.) Ogden High Sch., 1967-69; instr. U. Ill., Champaign, 1969-70; asst. prof. psychology Wright State U., Dayton, O., 1970-73, asso. prof., 1973—, asst. dean Coll. Edn., 1972-74. Psychologist, Dayton Area Psychol. Services, 1972—; cons. Fairborn (O.) Bd. Edn., 1971—, Dayton Childrens Services Bd., 1972—, Montgomery County Mental Retardation Bd., Dayton, 1971—, Clark County Bd. Edn., 1973—, Troy Bd. Edn., 1973—, Peace Studies Inst., 1972-73; psychol. cons. Miami Valley Child Devel., 1972—, Bur. Vocational Rehab., 1974—. Mem. Am. Psychol. Assn., Am. Personnel and Guidance Assn., N.E.A., Kappa Delta Pi. Home: 5011-C Cheswick Ct Dayton OH 45431 Office: Wright State University 325 Millett Hall Dayton OH 45401

FREY, NORMA CLAIRE, psychiat. social worker; b. Buffalo, Apr. 15, 1929; d. Severn Michael and Antoinette (Langlois) Frey; B.A., Ursuline Coll., 1950; M.S.W., McGill U., 1960; postgrad. Tulane U. Sch. Social Work, 1953-54. Tchr., St. Patrick's Elementary Sch., Galveston, Tex., 1950-51; welfare visitor Pub. Assistance Div., La. State Dept. Pub. Welfare, Gretna, La., 1951-53, child welfare worker, child welfare div., Alexandria, La., 1954-56; case aide Social Service Dept., U. Tex. Med. Br., Galveston, 1956-59; psychiat. social worker Tex. Research Inst. Mental Scis., Houston, 1960—. Field instr. U. Houston Sch. Social Work, 1969—; U. Tex. Sch. Social Work, Austin, 1965-66. Mem. St. Joseph's Hosp. Charity League, 1969—, Inst. Internat. Edn., 1964—; active Houston Grand Opera fund dr., 1970—. Mem. Nat. Assn. Social Workers, Acad. Certified Social Workers, Social Group Work Council, Houston Group Psychotherapy Soc., Am. Orthopsychiat. Assn. Contbr. article to profl. jour. Home: 807 S Post Oak Lane No 221 Houston TX 77027 Office: 1300 Moursund St Houston TX 77024

FREYBERG, JOAN TUTTLE, clin. psychologist; b. N.Y.C.; d. Herbert Wesley and Elizabeth Lorraine (Samuel) Tuttle; A.B., Barnard Coll., 1955; M.S. in Sch. Psychology, City U. N.Y., 1967, Ph.D. in Clin. Psychology, 1970; m. Michael Freyberg, Sept. 6, 1955; children—Mark Lawrence, Susan Jane. Lectr. psychology Coll. City N.Y., 1969-70; psychotherapist Lincoln Inst. for Psychotherapy, 1970-72; asso. staff mem., lectr. Postgrad. Center for Mental Health, 1970-74, mem. staff, 1974—; individual practice psychotherapy and testing, 1971—. Psychol. cons. research projects in edn. disadvantaged learners U.S. Office Edn., 1965-69. Mem. Kappa Delta Pi. Co-author: Child's World of Make-Believe, 1973. Editor: Graduate Research in Education and Related Disciplines, 1966-68. Contbr. numerous articles on disadvantaged children, reading disabilities to profl. publs. Home: 4525 Henry Hudson Pkwy New York City NY 10471 Office: 125 E 87th St New York City NY 10028

FREYBERGER, RUTH MATILDA, art educator; b. Reading, Pa., Nov. 15, 1912; d. John Jacob and Hattie Matilda (Holwig) Freyberger; B.S., State Coll., Kutztown, Pa., 1935; M.Ed., Pa. State U., 1939, Ed.D., 1951. Supr. art New Holland (Pa.) Borough Schs., 1935-41; tchr. art Huntingdon (Pa.) Borough Schs., 1941-45,Derry Twp. High Sch., Hershey (Pa.) Jr. Coll., 1945-50; asso. prof. art Ill. State U., Normal, 1951-62, prof., 1962—, also tchr. adult edn., 1961—. Mem. Ill., Nat. art edn. assns., Pa.-German Soc., Pi Lambda Theta, Delta Kappa Gamma. Republican. Lutheran. Contbr. articles to profl. jours. Home: 104 Eisenhower Dr Bloomington IL 61701 Office: Ill State U Normal IL 61761

FRICK, DOROTHY MARY LES MONDE (MRS. RAY J. FRICK), artist, civic worker; b. Green Bay, Wis., Jan. 7, 1912; d. Desire Joseph and Olive Belle (Trask) Les Monde; pvt. study art; m. Ray J. Frick, Aug. 27, 1930 (dec. Aug. 1970); 1 son, William. One-man show at Rahr Civic Center, Manitowoc, Wis., 1963, 66; exhibited in group shows at Green Bay, Madison and Two Rivers, Wis. Active fund drives A.R.C., Am. Cancer Soc.; pres. Little Gallery, Inc., Manitowoc, 1946-47, 66-67, sec., 1967-70, exhibit chmn., 1968-69; mem. City Council of Arts, 1970—. Bd. dirs. Rahr Civic Center, Manitowoc, 1960-68, vice chmn. mus. bd., 1960-68. Mem. Fedn. Women's Clubs, Manitowoc County Hist. Soc. (pres. 1961-63, v.p. 1966-68), Palettiers (sec. 1966-67). Home: 815 Park St Manitowoc WI 54220

FRIEDAN, BETTY, author, feminist leader; b. Peoria, Ill., Feb. 4, 1921; d. Harry and Miriam (Horwitz) Goldstein; B.A. summa cum laude, Smith Coll., 1942; m. Carl Friedan, June 1947 (div. May 1969); children—Daniel, Jonathan, Emily. Research fellow U. Cal. at Berkeley, 1943; lectr. feminism univs., bus. and profl. orgns., polit. groups in U.S. and Europe; founder Nat. Orgn. for Women, 1st pres., 1966-70, chairwoman adv. com., organizer Nat. Women's Polit. Caucas, 1971; organizer, dir. Womans First Bank and Trust Co. Bd. dirs. Legal Def. and Edn. Fund. Recipient Woman of Year award Ladies Home Jour., 1973. Mem. P.E.N., Soc. Mag. Writers, Am. Sociol. Assn., Phi Beta Kappa. Author: The Feminine Mystique, 1963; contbg. editor McCall's mag., 1971; contbr. Harper's, Social Policy, N.Y. Times mag. sect. Address: 1 Lincoln Plaza New York City NY 10023

FRIEDE, ELEANOR KASK, editor, publisher; b. Rochester, N.Y., Nov. 12, 1920; d. John and Claire (Kassick) Kask; B.A. cum laude, Hofstra U., 1942; m. Donald Friede (dec.). Copywriter, McGraw-Hill Book Co., 1942-46; asst. to pres. charge advt., promotion, publicity, editor mag. contingent books Funk & Wagnalls Co., 1946-51; with Pellegrini & Cudahy, 1951-52; in charge advt., publicity, promotion World Pub. Co., 1952-61; co-ordinator Internat. P.E.N. Congress, N.Y.C., 1965-66; marketing dir. Macmillan Pub. Co., Inc., 1966-68, pub. dir. spl. projects dept., sr. editor trade dept., temporary publicity dir., part-time sr. editor, 1968-72, ind. editorial cons., 1972-73; editor, pub. Delacorte Press/Eleanor Friede, 1973—; asso. Creature Enterprises, Inc., Bridgehampton, N.Y., 1973—. Home: 45 W 12th St New York City NY 10011 Office: Delacorte Press 1 Dag Hammarskjold Plaza New York City NY 10017

FRIEDENBERG, MARILYN ROSENFELD (MRS. STANLEY FRIEDENBERG), judge; b. N.Y.C., Oct. 30, 1926; d. Jacob M. and Laura (Miller) Rosenfeld; B.A., Hunter Coll., 1948; LL.B., N.Y. U., 1951; m. Stanley Friedenberg, May 5, 1951; children—Robert, Ellen. Admitted to N.Y. State bar, 1951, practiced in N.Y.C., 1951-53, East Meadow, N.Y., 1953-65; dep. county atty. Nassau County, N.Y., 1965-70; asso. firm Goodman & Dasilva, Carle Place, N.Y., 1971-73; judge Family Ct., Nassau County, N.Y., 1974—. Mem. corrections com. Nassau County Health and Welfare Council, 1967-69; law guardian Nassau County Family Ct. Bd. dirs. Nassau County Law Services Com., 1967-68, Family Ct. Counselling Services. Mem. Nassau County Women's (pres. 1967-68, dir. 1969—), Nassau County (criminal law and procedures com., family law com., juduciary com.), N.Y. State (family law com.) Am. (family law com.) bar assns., Am. Acad. Matrimonial Lawyers, N.Y. Probation and Parole Assn. Home: 80 Wheatley Rd Old Westbury NY 11568 Office: 1200 Old Country Rd Westbury NY 11590

FRIEDER, BERNICE SELDIN (MRS. PHILIP FRIEDER), educator, civic worker; b. Cheyenne, Wyo.; d. Elias David and Sophia (Dvosin) Seldin; B.Mus. with honors., U. Colo.; M.Mus., Northwestern U.; postgrad. N.Y. U.; m. Philip Frieder, June 14, 1944; children—David Seldin, Alice. Tchr. pub. schs., Colo., N.Y. prior to 1950; mem. Nat. Assn. State Bds. Edn., Denver, sec., treas., 1963-64, pres., 1964-65, 65-66, 66-67, chmn. bd., exec. sec., 1968-69, named hon. life mem. 1968; cons. Council Chief State Sch. Officers, 1973—. Mem. child welfare adv. bd. Colo. Dept. Welfare, 1959-65, chmn., 1964; pres. Denver Council Human Relations, 1964; mem. Nat. Adv. Council Title III Higher Edn. Act, 1966-69; mem. Colo. Bd. Edn., 1959-72; vice chmn., chmn. Colo. White House Conf. on children and youth, 1960. Bds. dirs. Denver Jewish Family and Children's Service, 1958-64, Colo. Conf. Social Welfare, 1963-67; trustee Colo. Library, 1959-72; Hon. life mem. Colo. Congress P.T.A.'s. Mem. Nat. Council Jewish Women (nat. dir. 1967—, pres. Western states dist. 1966-67, pres. Denver sect. 1965-66), Colo. Co-ordinating Council Women's Orgns. (pres. 1963-64). Democrat. Home: 201 Jasmine St Denver CO 80220

FRIEDERICH, MARY ANNA (MRS. JOHN STEPHEN SAVAGE), physician; b. Rochester, N.Y., Nov. 15, 1931; d. Lewis Weniger and Mary Jasper (McGinnis) Friederich; student St. Lawrence U., 1949-50; B.A., Cornell U., 1953; M.D., U. Rochester, 1957; m. John Stephen Savage, June 16, 1968; step-children—Steven Timothy, Scott Allen, Sandra Sue. Intern obstetrics, gynecology U. Rochester, 1957-58, resident, 1958-62, chief resident, 1961-62, instr., USPHS trainee, 1962-63, instr. obstetrics, gynecology, psychiatry, asst. obstetrician, gynecologist, psychiatrist, 1963-64, sr. instr., 1964-66, asst. prof., 1966-69, asso. prof., 1969—; asst. obstetrician, gynecologist, psychiatrist Strong Meml. Hosp., Rochester, 1964-66, asso., 1966-69, sr. asso., 1969—. Trustee Rochester Meth. Home. Diplomate Am. Bd. Obstetrics and Gynecology. Fellow Am. Coll. Obstetricians and Gynecologists (com. for splty. div. psychosomatic obstetrics, gynecology); mem. Rochester Acad. Medicine, Am. Psychosomatic Soc., Chi Omega, Alpha Omega Alpha. Methodist. Guest editor: Clinical Obstetrics and Gynecology 13, 1970. Home: 38 Wood Hill Rd Pittsford NY 14534 Office: 260 Crittenden Blvd Rochester NY 14642

FRIEDERSDORF, NANCY WHEELER, educator; b. Erie, Pa.; d. D. and Ella (Herrick) Wheeler; B.S., Purdue U., 1949; M.S., Ind. U., 1957; Ph.D., Purdue U., 1969; m. John L. Friedersdorf, Dec. 27, 1961 (div.) Tchr. phys. edn. Kokomo (Ind.) High Sch., 1949-56, Natrona County High Sch., Casper, Wyo., 1956-58; counselor, tchr. Lake Park High Sch., Medina, Ill., 1958-62, H. E. Wood High Sch., Indpls., 1962-63; counselor Met. Sch. Dist., Perry Twp., Indpls., 1963-67; counselor Office of Dean of Women, Purdue U., Lafayette, Ind., 1967-69, asst. dean of women, 1969—, vis. prof. edn., 1973-74; asst. prof. edn. Butler U., Indpls., 1969-70; Mem. Am., Ind. (pres. 1972-73), Central Ind. (pres. 1965-66) personnel and guidance assns., Am. editor newsletter 1966-69), Ind. sch. counselors assns., Am. Coll. Personnel Assn., Ind. Assn. Womens Deans and Counselors. Home: 124 Tamiami Ct West Lafayette IN 47906

FRIEDLAND, CLAIRE EDITH, research economist; b. N.Y.C., Nov. 20, 1929; d. Joseph M. and Helen (Feinstein) Friedland; B.A., Queens Coll., 1951; postgrad. Brown U., 1951-53; M.A., U. Chgo., 1955. Statistical analyst Fed. Res. Bank Chgo., 1957-59; instr. econs. Roosevelt U., Chgo., summers 1962, 64; research economist Charles R. Walgreen Found. Study Am. Instns., U. Chgo., 1959—. Bd. dirs. Ind. Voters Ill.; bd. dirs. Ill. div. Ams. for Democratic Action, 1966-68, 71-73, mem. polit. action com., 1966-67, chpt. vice chmn., 1971. Mem. Am. Econ. Assn., Phi Beta Kappa. Contbr. articles to profl. jours. Home: 5723 S Dorchester Av Chicago IL 60637 Office: Grad Sch Bus U Chgo Chicago IL 60637

FRIEDMAN, ELISE B., editor; b. Phila., Apr. 18, 1947; d. Martin and Elaine R. (Rosenblatt) Friedman; B.S., Temple U., 1968. Mng. editor Temple U. News, Phila., 1967-68; news editor Moorestown (N.J.) News Chronicle, 1969-73; editor Cherry Hill (N.J.) News, 1973—. Mem. Women In Communications. Home: 107-11 Van Buren Rd Voorhees NJ 08043 Office: 1111 Union Av Cherry Hill NJ 08034

FRIEDMAN, KATHERINE SHAPRIO (MRS. ABRAHAM L. FRIEDMAN), lawyer, govt. ofcl.; b. N.Y.C., Oct. 3, 1918; d. David and Sarah (Jolles) Shapiro; B.A., Hunter Coll., 1937; LL.B. cum laude, N.Y. U.; M.A. in Rehab. Counseling, Seton Hall U., 1973; m. Abraham L. Friedman, Aug. 27, 1950; 1 dau., Nancy Jolles. Admitted to N.Y. bar, 1941, U.S. Supreme Ct. bar, 1949; practiced in N.Y.C.; chmn. rating bd. adjudication div. VA, regional office, Newark, 1957—. Counselor West Orange (N.J.) Family Youth Service, 1971—. Mem. Fed. (sec.), Am. (mem. family law sect. 1960—, adminstrv. law sect. 1962) bar assns., Internat., Nat. assns. women lawyers, Nat. Council Juvenile Ct. Judges, N.Y. County Lawyers Assn., Nat. Rehabilitation Assn., Am. Orthopsychiat. Assn. Address: 16 Amherst Ct Maplewood NJ 07040 also 120 Liberty St New York City NY 10006

FRIEDMAN, LORA RUTH, educator; b. N.Y.C.; d. Milton N. and Esta (Borofsky) Moskowitz; B.S., Coll. City N.Y., 1951, M.A., 1955; postgrad. Rutgers U., 1957, St. Johns U., 1963; diploma in Elementary Adminstrn. and Supervision, Queens Coll., N.Y.C., 1959-61; D.Ed., U. Fla., 1967; div. Elementary sch. tchr., adminstr. N.Y.C. schs., 1952-63; lectr. Queens Coll., N.Y.C., 1961-62; interim instr., grad. asst., grad. fellow U. Fla., 1963-66; asso. prof. edn. Tampa (Fla.) U., 1966-70; asso. prof. curriculum, instrn. U. So. Miss., 1970-72; asso. prof. edn. U. Louisville, 1972-74; asso. prof. edn. Christopher Newport Coll., Newport News, Va., 1974—. Vis. prof. Jacksonville (Fla.) U., summer 1967, U. So. Miss., summer 1968. Mem. U.S. Judo Fedn. (acting sec.), N.E.A., Internat. Reading Assn., Am., Fla. assns. for supervision and curriculum devel., Assn. Childhood Edn. Internat., Am. Ednl. Research Assn., Pi Lambda Theta, Kappa Delta Pi. Home: Newport News VA 23606 Office: Christopher Newport College Newport News VA 23606

FRIEDMAN, MARTHA SCHWABINGER, psychotherapist; b. N.Y.C., Aug. 15, 1915; d. Paul and Mollie (Rothstein) Schwabinger; B.S., Coll. William and Mary, 1937; M.S., Coll. City N.Y., 1958; Ed.D., Columbia, 1970; m. Julius Friedman, Sept. 23, 1939; children—Michael, Joann (Mrs. Michael Urquhart), Peter. Reading clinician Great Neck (N.Y.) Pub. Sch., 1952-60; ednl. counselor, partial hosp. program N.Y. Med. Coll., N.Y.C., 1967—; coordinator Partial Hospitalization Program Met. Community Mental Health Center, 1974—; individual practice as psychotherapist, N.Y.C., 1967—; asst. prof. psychiatry N.Y. Med. Coll., N.Y.C., 1970—; lectr. Hunter Coll., 1967-68, Bank Street Coll., 1967-68. Mem. Am. Psychol. Assn., Am. Group Therapy Assn., Am. Assn. Marriage and Family Counselors, Kappa Delta Pi. Home: 245 E 19th St New York City NY 10003 Office: 5 E 102d St New York City NY 10029

FRIEDMAN, SUSANNAH (MRS. SAMUEL NANNIS), physician; b. Russia, Aug. 25, 1900; d. Moses and Toba (Eisenberg) Friedman; came to U.S., 1910, naturalized, 1920; B.S., Tufts U., 1923; M.D. cum laude, 1926; postgrad. in psychology Boston U., 1933-34; m. Samuel Nannis, Oct. 11, 1942. Intern, L.I. Hosp., 1926-27; intern New Eng. Hosp., Boston, 1927-28, now mem. staff, chief of staff, 1960-61; practice medicine specializing in surgery and urology, Boston, 1934—; mem. staffs Beth Israel, Mass. Gen., Brookline hosps., Boston Dispensary. Fellow Internat. Coll. Surgeons; mem. A.M.A., Internat. Coll. Surgeons, Am. Urol. Soc., Mass., (councilor 1940-73), Norfolk (chmn. mediation and peer rev. 1972-73) med. socs. Mem. Order Eastern Star. Club: Jewish Women's College (pres. 1938-40). Home: 44 Longwood Av Brookline MA 02146 Office: 1101 Beacon St Brookline MA 02146

FRIEDMAN, SYLVIA SCLAR (MRS. ALFRED HENRY FRIEDMAN), psychologist; b. N.Y.C., Apr. 27, 1915; d. Samuel and Virginia (Barzilay) Sclar; diploma in early childhood edn. Mills Tng. Sch., 1937; B.S., N.Y. U., 1937; Ed.M., Temple U., 1958; Ed.D., U. Pa., 1971; m. Alfred Henry Friedman, Dec. 31, 1940; children—Michael Belais, Stephen Belais. Tchr. early childhood edn., N.Y.C., 1937-41; classroom tchr., Bellmawr, N.J., tchr. handicapped children, pub. and pvt. schs., Mt. Holly and Haddon Twp., N.J., 1950-58; psychologist Lindenwold (N.J.) Pub. Schs., 1958-63; psychologist, dept. psychiatry Hahnemann Med. Coll. and Hosp., Phila., 1963-65; counselor, family life edn. discussion leader, dir. workshop for tchrs. and parents, family life and sex edn. Marriage Council Phila., div. family study, dept. psychiatry Sch. Medicine, U. Pa., Phila., 1965-70; coordinator grant for preschool handicapped children div. spl. edn. Sch. Dist. Phila., 1971-72; mem. research team Grad. Sch. Edn. and Med. Sch., U. Pa., Phila., 1972-73, asso. in psychiatry Med. Sch., 1974; pvt. practice as psychologist, marriage and family counselor, Haddon Heights, N.J., 1972—. Vol. worker Columbia Presbyn. Psychiat. Inst., N.Y.C., 1935-36; sector comdr. Civil Def., 1941-43; active worker fund-raising drives various local charitable orgns., 1947-59; capt. local sect. Cancer Drive, 1950; sec. P.T.A., Haddonfield, 1949, chmn. parent edn., 1952, chmn. nominating com., 1953; den mother Cub Scouts, Haddon Heights, 1952-57; lectr. child care and parent edn. at various P.T.A.'s, 1956-65; mem. adv. com. human growth and devel. Sch. Dist. Phila., 1967-70; vol. worker Operation Concern, Oaklyn, N.J., 1971-74. Adv. bd. Parents Without Partners, Pitman, N.J., 1973—. Mem. Am., Eastern, N.J. psychol. assns., N.J. Assn. Sch. Psychologists, Camden County Assn. Psychologists, Internat. Reading Assn., Am. Orthopsychiat. Assn., Psychologists in Pvt. Practice, Am. Assn. Marriage and Family Counselors, N.J. Assn. Marriage and Family Counselors, Women's Am. Orgn. for Rehab. through Tng., League Women Voters, Psi Chi. Address: 1 7th Av Haddon Heights NJ 08035

FRIEHAUF, EDITH MARY HOHN (MRS. HERBERT G. FRIEHAUF), banker; b. Echo, Minn., Mar. 15, 1919; d. Paul and Mary Christina (Lucke) Hohn; student Success Bus. Coll., 1936-37, Morgan County Jr. Coll.,; m. Herbert G. Friehauf, June 9, 1940; children—Gary R., Kathleen Kay (Mrs. Leoncio Reyes). Sec., Central Prsbyn. Ch., Denver, 1937-40, Gem Oil Co., Brush, Colo., 1956; operations supr., credit dept. supr., sec. First Nat. Bank, Brush, 1956-73, asst. cashier, 1973—. Treas., City of Brush, 1972-74. Republican. Methodist (mem. adminstrv. bd. 1944). Club: Music (Treas., sec. Brush 1946-48). Home: PO Box 372 Brush CO 80723 Office: PO Box 525 Brush CO 80723

FRIEL, MARGARET ANNE, psychiatrist; b. Phila., Sept. 5, 1927; d. Edward James and Margaret Mary (Gallen) Friel; B.A., U. Pa., 1949; M.D., Hahnemann Med. Coll., 1953; m. Yale B. Bernstein, June 13, 1960 (div. Mar. 1973); children—Mark Friel, Susan Gallen. Intern, Atlantic City Hosp., 1953-54; resident pediatrics U. Pa. Hosp., Phila., 1954-56; child psychiatry resident Albert Einstein Med. Coll., Phila., 1967-69, resident adult psychiatry, 1969-71; practice medicine specializing in psychiatry, Phila.; asst. prof. pediatrics Med. Coll. Pa., Phila., 1963—; clin. asst. prof. child psychiatry Hahnemann Med. Coll. Diplomate Am. Bd. Pediatrics. Mem. Phila. Pediatric Soc., Am. Acad. Child Psychiatrists, Alpha Omega Alpha. Address: The Philadelphian Apt 11045 Philadelphia PA 19130

FRIEND, CONNIE MAXINE YAGER (MRS. MERRILL B. FRIEND), bus. exec.; b. Mpls., Mar. 5, 1926; d. Jack M. and Florence (Rabinowitz) Yager; B.A., U. Minn., 1946; m. Merrill B. Friend, Sept. 7, 1946; children—Patricia Jane and Stephen Merrill (twins), Judith Ann. Pres., Polit. Research Inst., Encino, Cal., Social Issues Research Council, Encino. Mem. Los Angeles Commn. for Charter Revision, 1968-70, Mayor's Com. on Pollution, 1970—, mem. citizens adv. panel on community affairs Los Angeles Bd. Edn., 1969—. Pres. League Women Voters, Los Angeles, 1965-69. Bd. dirs. Encino Property Owners, 1969—. Mem. Valley U. Women. Home: 4727 Louise Av Encino CA 91316 Office: 18075 Ventura Blvd Encino CA 91316

FRIER, ELIZABETH ALBEE (MRS. HAROLD LESTER FRIER), social worker; b. Grand Rapids, Mich., Nov. 4, 1912; d. Asa LeGrande and Helen (Wanty) Albee; A.B., Vassar Coll., 1934; M.A., Ohio State U., 1939; Ph.D. (hon.), Colo. State Christian Coll., 1973; m. Harold Lester Frier, Dec. 20, 1939; children—Mildred Girven (Mrs. George Hacker), Helen Jane (Mrs. Leroy W. Smith), Anne Lester (Mrs. James Tuttle Cook), Deane Harold, Alan Clark, Mary Elizabeth (Mrs. Larry Swisher). Case worker County Welfare Dept. Mich., Grand Rapids, 1934-36, case supr., Alma, 1936, adminstr., Midland, 1936-38, field rep., Saginaw, 1939-40, dir. Vol. Bur., Grand Rapids, 1941, exec. dir. United Wexford County Chest, Cadillac, Mich., 1959-66; dir. Wexford County Dept. Social Services, Cadillac, 1965-67; adminstr. vol. services Mich. Dept. Social Services, Lansing, 1967—. Regional chmn. White House Conf. on Children and Youth, 1960; regional v.p. Cerebral Palsy Assn. Mich., 1965, mem. nat. finance com., 1971-72, sec. Mich. bd., 1971-72; sec. bd. dirs. United Wexford County Chest, 1945-58. Mem. Nat. Conf. Social Welfare, Am. Pub. Welfare Assn., Nat. Cathedral Assn., Ch. Women United of Mich. (chmn. citizen action), Mich. Assn. Childrens Agys., Assn. Vol. Burs. Am. (dir.), Mich. Assn. Vol. Burs. Republican. Episcopalian. Club: Soroptimist (treas.). Home: 323 N Walnut St Lansing MI 48933 Office: Commerce Center 300 S Capitol St Suite 821 Lansing MI 48926

FRIES, HELEN SERGEANT HAYNES (MRS. STUART G. FRIES), civic leader; b. Atlanta; d. Harwood Syme and Alice (Hobson) Haynes; student Coll. William and Mary, 1935-38; m. Stuart G. Fries, May 5, 1938. Bd mem. Community Ballet Assn., Huntsville, Ala., 1968—; mem. nat. nurses aid com. A.R.C., 1958-59; dir. A.R.C. Aero Club, England, 1943-44; supr. A.R.C. Clubmobile, Europe, 1944-46; mem. womens com. Nat. Symphony Orch., Washington, 1959—. Bd. mem. Madison County Republican Club, 1969-70; mem. nat. council Women's Nat. Rep. Club N.Y., 1963—, chmn. hospitality com., 1963-65; bd. mem. League Rep. Women, 1952-61. Mem. Nat. Soc. Colonial Dames Am., D.A.R., Nat. Trust for Historic Preservation, Va., Valley Forge (Pa.), Eastern Va. hist. socs., Assn. for Preservation Va. Antiquities, Greensboro Soc. Preservation, Tenn. Valley Geneal. Soc., Huntsville Hist. Soc., English Speaking Union. Clubs: Washington, Capitol Hill, Army-Navy Country (Washington); Garden (Redstone Arsenal), Redstone (Ala.) Yacht; Army-Navy (D.C.). Home: care Col Stuart G Fries 577 54 7471 TUSLOG Det 193 Box 1604 APO NY 09289

FRINGS, KETTI, author; b. Columbus, O.; d. Guy H. and Pauline (Sparks) Hartley; student Principia College. Author: (novels) Hold Back the Dawn, 1942; God's Front Porch, 1945; (plays) Mr. Sycamore, 1943, Look Homeward, Angel, 1957; The Long Dream, 1960; (screen plays) Come Back Little Sheba, 1952; About Mr. Leslie, 1954; Fox Fire, The Shrike, 1955. Recipient Pulitzer prize for best play, Look Homeward, Angel, N.Y. Drama Critics Circle award, 1957. Address: New York City NY 10017 also Norwalk CT 06852

FRINGS, MABLE RUTH SMITH (MRS. HUBERT FRINGS), zoologist; b. Shawville, Pa., Apr. 11, 1912; d. Harvey E. and Clara (Straw) Smith; student Lock Haven State Coll., 1930-31; B.S., Pa. State U., 1935; postgrad. U. Okla., 1936-37; m. Hubert Frings, June 9, 1936; 1 son, Carl Frederick. Instr. biology Snead Jr. Coll., Boaz, Ala., 1942-43, Gustavus Adolphus Coll., St. Peter, Minn., 1946-47; research asso. in zoology Pa. State U., University Park, 1949-61, U. Hawaii, Honolulu, 1961-66, U. Okla., Norman, 1966—. Cons. in bio-acoustics Curtis-Wright Corp., Quehanna, Pa., 1958-61, Stanford Research Inst., Palo Alto, Cal., 1959-60, Sunbeam Corp., Chgo., 1961. Recipient Silver medal Pasteur Inst., Paris, France, 1953. Mem. A.A.A.S., Entomol. Soc. Am., Am. Soc. Zoologists, Phi Sigma. Author: Sound Production and Sound Reception by Insects, 1960; Animal Communication, 1964; Concepts of Zoology, 1971. Contbr. articles to profl. jours. Home: 514 College Av Norman OK 73069

FRISCH, SISTER MARY ELIZABETH, educator; b. Covington, Ky., Oct. 18, 1901; d. Anthony and Elizabeth (Buschelman) Frisch; A.B., St. Mary Coll., Monroe, Mich., 1923; M.S., Notre Dame U., 1927; Ph.D., Cath. U. Am., 1939. Tchr. high schs., Covington, 1940; faculty Thomas More Coll., Covington, 1940—, prof. math., 1954—. Mem. Math. Soc. Am., Am. Math. Soc. Address: Thomas More Coll Covington KY 41017

FRISK, DOROTHY JANE, broadcasting exec.; b. Muncie, Ind., Feb. 5, 1921; d. Sumner Burke and Irene (Shirley) Shimp; student Ball State Tchrs. Coll., 1939-40; A.B., Ind. U., 1943; m. Arthur William Frisk, Aug. 24, 1946; children—Gregory Scott, Stephen Gary, Deborah Joan Shidler (Mrs. Peter Wagener), Robert Randall. Women's dir. sta. WJW, Cleve., 1945-46; women's dir. sta. WNDU-TV, South Bend, Ind., 1960-62; now women's dir., producer, hostess show Homemaker's Time sta. WSBT-TV, South Bend. Mem. Kappa Alpha Theta. Republican. Rotary Ann. Home: 1241 Black Oak Dr South Bend IN 46617 Office: 300 W Jefferson Blvd South Bend IN 46601

FRITZ, JO ANN, psychologist; b. Russellville, O., Oct. 24, 1934; d. William Howard and Minnie (Myers) Rickey; adopted d. James Anderson and Mary Kathryn (Ennis) Hanlon; m. Edward Rodney Fritz, Feb. 17, 1951 (div. June 1965); children—Jo Lynne, Barbara Ann (Mrs. Michael Leigh Chinn), James Edward. Tchr., Buford and Lynchbuhg, O., 1961-66, Williamsburg, O., 1966-68; psychologist Hamilton County Schs., Cin., 1968-70, Highland County Schs., Hillsboro, 1970—; pvt. practice as psychologist, Hillsboro and Georgetown, O., 1970—; exec. dir. Brown County Community Mental Health and Mental Retardation Bd., 1973—. NSF scholar, 1967. Mem. Nat. Assn. Sch. Psychologists (charter), Ohio, Southwestern Ohio sch. psychologists assns., Alpha Lambda Delta, Kappa Delta Pi. Home: Route 2 Box 488 Georgetown OH 45121 Office: Box 390 Hillsboro OH 45133

FRITZ, KATHERINE ELIZABETH CAMPBELL (MRS. KENNETH EARL FRITZ), exptl. pathologist; b. Omaha, June 24, 1918; d. Henry Ambler and Katherine Eulah (Shutts) Campbell; B.A., U. Omaha, 1939; M.S., Albany Med. Coll., 1961, Ph.D., 1966; m. Kenneth Earl Fritz, Oct. 15, 1940; children—Gregory Kenneth, Molly (Mrs. Calvin F. Miller). Instr. pathology Albany (N.Y.) Med. Coll., 1966-68, asst. prof., 1968-74, research asso. prof. pathology, 1974—; research biologist VA Hosp., Albany. Mem. Am. Heart Assn. (fellow Council on Arteriosclerosis), Am. Soc. Exptl. Pathology, Am. Soc. Cell Biology, Electron Microscopy Soc. Am., Sigma Xi. Home: 1360 Valencia Rd Schenectady NY 12309 Office: VA Hosp Albany NY 12208

FRIZZELL, MARTHA MCDANOLDS (MRS. THEODORE J. FRIZZELL), state legislator; b. Branchville, N.J., Nov. 18, 1902; d. George A. and Kate E. (Roe) McDanolds; B.S., U. N.H., 1924; postgrad. Columbia; m. Theodore J. Frizzell, June 9, 1927; children—Katharine (Mrs. Edwin E. Blaisdell), Theodora (Mrs. Gordon Duke Duncan), Elizabeth (Mrs. Allyn M. Bascom), Robert T., James A. Mem. N.H. Ho. of Reps., 1951—, chmn. jud. com. Del. N.H. Constl. Conv., 1956, 64, 74; women's chmn. Sullivan County (N.H.) Republican Com., 1956-58; mem. New Eng. Bd. Higher Edn., 1957-64, 69-73, exec. com., 1960-64; moderator Town of Walpole, 1973. Trustee Charlestown (N.H.) Pub. Library. Recipient citation for community service U. N.H. Mem. Farm Bur., Grange, Women's Club (pres.), N.H. Owls (pres. 1963), N.H. Library Trustees Assn. (pres. 1962). Conglist. (trustee N.H. conf.). Author: Second History of Charlestown, N.H., 1955; History of Walpole, N.H. Address: Charlestown NH 03603*

FROEHLICH, EDNA BORG, educator; b. Union City, N.J., July 28, 1918; d. Adolph Frank and Anna Lena (Frese) Borg; B.A. cum laude, Montclair (N.J.) State Coll., 1939; M.A. in Psychology, Columbia Tchrs. Coll., 1956, profl. diploma, 1967, Ed.D., 1970; m. Paul Edward Froehlich, June 27, 1942; children—Pauline (Mrs. Joseph S. Stroman), Kathleen (Mrs. LeRoy W. Osborn), Linda (Mrs. Walter K. Schreyer). Tchr. Emerson High Sch., Union City, N.J., 1939-45, Cresskill (N.J.) Pub. Sch., 1958-60; instr. Fairleigh Dickinson U., Teaneck, N.J., 1959-60; specialist learning disabilities, reading cons., Palisades Park (N.J.) Pub. Sch., 1962-65, coordinator child study, sch. psychologist, 1966-69; clin. psychologist Neurol. Inst., Columbia-Presbyn. Med. Center, summer 1966; instr. Bergen Community Coll., Paramus, N.J., 1970-71; sch. psychologist pub. schs., Glen Rock, N.J., 1970-72, dir. spl. edn., 1972—; pvt. practice psychology, 1973—. Nat. Inst. Mental Health grantee, 1965-66. Mem. Am., N.J., Bergen County psychol. assns., Nat., N.J., Bergen County edn. assns., Council Exceptional Children, Assn. Children With Learning Disabilities, N.J., Bergen County (pres. 1972-73) assns. sch. psychologists, Glen Rock Adminstrs. Assn. Contbr. articles to profl. jours. Home: 208 Engle St Tenafly NJ 07670 Office: Glen Rock Pub Schs Maple Av Glen Rock NJ 07452

FROGGE, BARBARA ERNESTINE, coll. adminstr.; b. Wilburn, Ky., June 24, 1931; d. Frank and Eva (Correll) Frogge; B.M.E., Georgetown Coll., 1952; M.A., Peabody Coll., 1957; postgrad. U. N.C. Stewardess Trans World Airlines, 1953-54; faculty, adminstr. Va. Intermont Coll., Bristol, 1957—, tchr. music, 1957-58, dir. social life, 1958-62, dir. European travel, 1960-66, dir. student life, 1962-67, dir. pub. relations, 1968—. Mem. patent bd. Day Star Corp., 1973. Address: Va Intermont Coll Bristol VA 24201

FROMM, ERIKA (MRS. PAUL FROMM), clin. psychologist, educator; b. Frankfurt, Germany, Dec. 23, 1910; d. Siegfried and Clementine (Stern) Oppenheimer; came to U.S., 1938, naturalized, 1944; Ph.D. magna cum laude, U. Frankfurt, 1933; postgrad. child care program, Chgo. Inst. for Psychoanalysis, 1949-51; m. Paul Fromm, July 20, 1938; 1 dau., Joan (Mrs. Greenstone). Chief psychologist Apeldoorn State Hosp. (Holland), 1935-38; chief psychologist Francis W. Parker Sch., 1944-51; supervising psychologist, Inst. for Juvenile Research, 1951-53; asst. prof. to asso. prof. Northwestern U. Med. Sch., 1954-61; prof. U. Chgo., 1961—. Trustee, Fromm Music Found. Diplomate Am. Bd. Examiners in Profl. Psychology, Am. Bd. Examiners Clin. Hypnosis. Fellow Am. Psychol. Assn. (pres. div. 30, 1972-73), Am. Orthopsychiat. Assn. (dir. 1961-63), A.A.A.S., Soc. Clin. Exptl. Hypnosis (sec. 1965-67, v.p. 1971—); mem. Am. Bd. Psychol. Hypnosis (pres. 1971—), Ill. Psychol. Assn. (council 1951-53, 55-57, bd. examiners 1959-62, v.p. bd. examiners 1960-61), Soc. Projective Techniques, Sigma Xi. Author: (with L. D. Hartman) Intelligence-A Dynamic Approach; (with Thomas M. French) Dream Interpretation, 1964; (with Ronald E. Shor) Hypnosis: Research Development and Perspectives, 1972; also numerous articles in profl. jours. Mem. editorial bd. Jour. Clin. and Exptl. Psychopathology, 1951-59; clin. editor Internat. Jour. Clin. and Exptl. Hypnosis, 1968—. Home: 5715 S Kenwood Av Chicago IL 60637 Office: Dept Behavioral Sciences U Chicago Chicago IL 60637

FROMMER, MARIE, architect; b. Warsaw, Poland; d. b. Salomon Nathan and Anna (Blaufuks) Frommer; Dr. Ing. Dresden Tech. Dipl. Ing. Archit., U. Berlin. With Office Architects, Germany, owner archtl. firm, Berlin, London, N.Y.C., 1945—. Mem. A.I.A. Prin. works include: Swiss Life Ins. Hdqrs., Berlin, Germany, 1938; alteration, interiors for sundry bldgs. for comml. and profl. use, N.Y.C.; also environment devels. Home: 140 W 57th St New York City NY 10019

FRONEBERGER, EILUNED JANE JONES (MRS. HAROLD BURKE FRONEBERGER), occupational therapist; b. Ilion, N.Y., Jan. 17, 1929; d. Lewis Parry and Eliza (Cady) Jones; B.A., U. Rochester, 1950; postgrad. U. Pa., 1950-52, Trinity Coll., 1952-54, Sonoma State Coll., 1973-74; m. Harold Burke Froneberger, Mar. 26, 1972; children (by previous marriage)—Ralph Brancen Green, Margaret Jerene Green; 1 son, Matthew David. Occupational therapist State of Conn., Middletown, 1952-55; occupational therapist State of Cal., Talmage, 1955-58, asst. supr. rehab. services, 1958-71, counselor Dept. of Rehab., 1971—. Cons. Ukiah Valley Rehab. Center, Ft. Bragg Paul Bunyan Assn. for Retarded, Ft. Bragg Employment Office, Regional Occupation Center, spl. edn. dept. Ft. Bragg High Sch.; cons. Area I Mental Retardation/Developmental Disabilities Bd. Mem. Am., No. Cal. occupational therapy assns., Cal. State Employees Assn. (scholarship chmn. 1972-74), Cal. Assn. Rehab. Counselors, Am. Assn. U. Women (gourmet chmn. 1973-75). Mem. Christian Ch. Home: 289 Freitas Av Ukiah CA 95482 Office: 619 S State St Ukiah CA 95482

FROST, AURILLA MAY, newspaper exec.; b. Elgin, Ill., May 2, 1914; d. Paul Arthur and Goldie Irene (Plane) Wagner; grad. high sch.; m. Samuel Russell Frost, Sept. 2, 1946; children—Gloria (Mrs. Jim Brannon), Paula (Mrs. Tom Tomaszewski). Telephone operator Ill. Bell Telephone Co., Lockport, 1935-44; typist Gerlach Barklow Greeting Card Co. Joliet, Ill., 1934-35; PBX operator No. Ill. Cereal, Lockport, Ill., also DuPont Co., Ft. Madison, Ia., 1944-48. With Evening Democrat, Fort Madison, Ia., 1961—, classified mgr., 1966—. Mem. Nat. Assn. Ret. and Vet. Ry. Employees, Assn. Newspaper Classified Advt. Mgrs., Bus. and Profl. Women, Ft. Madison C. of C., Loyal Star Aux., Order Eastern Star, Soroptimists (toastmistress Fort Madison 1966). Home: 409 23rd St Fort Madison IA 52627 Office: 1214 Ave H Fort Madison IA 52627

FROST, DOROTHY ROSE WHITFORD (MRS. WILLIAM M. FROST), educator; b. Stockton, Cal., Mar. 13, 1911; d. Carl Garfield and Clara Jane (Rose) Whitford; B.A., U. Redlands, 1932; M.A., Tex. Western U., 1951; Ed.D., U. Pacific, 1973; m. William M. Frost, June 10, 1934 (dec. 1964); children—Joan (Mrs. Albert Fowler), William M., Robert M., John M. Tchr. English, Shafter (Cal.) High Sch., 1933-34; tchr. English and Latin, East Bakersfield (Cal.) High Sch., 1942-45, Tenafly (N.J.) Jr. High Sch., 1958-64; guidance counselor Tenafly Middle Sch., 1964—. Mem. Nat., N.J. edn. assns., Nat. Assn. Women Deans and Counselors, N.J., Bergen County personnel and guidance assns., Tenafly Tchrs. Assn., Phi Kappa Phi. Home: 16 Terrace St Haworth NJ 07641 Office: Middle School Guidance Dept Tenafly NJ 07670

FROSTIC, GWEN SARA, pub. co. exec.; b. Sandusky, Mich., Apr. 26, 1906; d. Fred W. and Sara (Alexander) Frostic; student Eastern Mich. U., 1924-26, LL.D., 1965; student Western Mich. U., 1928-30, H.H.D., 1971; D.F.A., Mich. State U., 1973. Art tchr. Dearborn (Mich.) pub. schs., 1926-27, Art Metalcraft Studio, Wyandotte, Mich., 1930-41; tool designer Ford Motor Co., Willow Run, Mich., 1941-44; pres. Presscraft Papers, Inc., Benzonia, Mich., 1944—. Mem. Nat. Fedn. Bus. and Profl. Women's Club, P.E.O., Alpha Sigma Tau, Delta Kappa Gamma, Omicron Nu. Mem. Order of Eastern Star. Author: My Michigan, 1956; A Walk With Me, 1958; These Things Are Ours, 1960; A Place On Earth, 1962; To Those Who See, 1964; Wingborne, 1967; Wisps of Mist, 1969; Beyond Time, 1971; Contemplate, 1973. Editor: Mich. Bus. and Profl. Women's Club Publ., 1955-57. Home and office: 5140 River Rd Benzonia MI 49616

FROSTIG, MARIANNE, educator; B.A., New Sch. Social Research, 1948; M.A., Claremont Grad. Sch., 1949; Ph.D., U. So. Cal., 1955. Dir. rehab. program Psychiat. Hosp., Zofiowka, Poland, 1932-37; elementary sch. tchr., Colton and Rialto, Cal., 1945-47; founder, exec. dir. Marianne Frostig Center Ednl. Therapy, Los Angeles, 1947-72, dir. emeritus, 1972—; sch. psychologist Spl. Schs., Los Angeles County, 1949-55; clin. prof. edn. U. So. Cal., Los Angeles, 1966—; prof. edn. Mount St. Mary's Coll., Los Angeles, 1969—. Recipient award Advanced Inst. for Leadership Personnel in Learning Disabilities, 1969; Woman of Year award Los Angeles Times, 1970; Internat. Honor award Internat. Fedn. Learning Disabilities, 1974. Diplomate Am. Bd. Profl. Psychology. Fellow Am. Psychol. Assn., Am. Orthopsychiat. Assn.; mem. Am. Ednl. Research Assn., Am. Assn. Mental Deficiency, Internat. Reading Assn., Soc. for Research in Child Devel., Internat. Assn. for Children with Learning Disabilities (adv. bd. 1968, Golded Key award 1969), Council for Exceptional Children (exec. council 1970—). Author: (with D.W. Lefever, J.R.B. Whittlesey) The Marianne Frostig Developmental Test of Visual Perception, 1964; Move-Grow-Learn, 1969; Movement Education: Theory and Practice, 1970; (with David Horne, Ann-Marie Miller) Pictures and Patterns, 1966, rev. edit., 1972; (with David Horne) The Frostig Program for the Development of Visual Perception, 1964. rev. edit., 1973; (with Phyllis Maslow) Learning Problems in the Classroom, 1973. Home: 1431 Ocean Av Santa Monica CA 90401 Office: 5981 Venice Blvd Los Angeles CA 90034

FROTHINGHAM, ALICE WILSON, author; b. Jersey City, May 10, 1902; d. Charles Self and Sara (Andrews) Wilson; B.A., Mt. Holyoke Coll., 1924; m. Coleridge S. Frothingham, Aug. 11, 1931; 1 dau., Elaine Victoria. Curator of ceramics Hispanic Soc. Am., N.Y.C., 1937-68, now emeritus, hon. sec., 1957—, curator of museum, 1962-66, dir. protem, 1962-65, also mem. adv. bd. Ofcl. rep. 1st Internat. Symposium on Tiles, Lisbon, Portugal, 1971. Decorated Order Civil Merit (Spain); recipient Mitre medal Hispanic Soc. Am.,

1940; Medal of Arts and Lit., 1953, Sorolla medal, 1966, also membership medal, 1968. Mem. Academia de Cordoba, Academia de Bellas Artes de San Fernando, Madrid (corr. mem.), Academia de Bellas Artes y Ciencias Historicas de Toledo (corr. mem.), Com. Internazionale di Patronato of Museo Internazionale deile Ceramiche in Faenza, Italy, 1949—. Author: Catalogue of Hispano-Moresque Pottery, 1936; Sigilate Pottery of the Roman Empire, 1937; Hispanic Glass, 1941; Talavera Pottery, 1944; Lustreware of Spain, 1951; Capodimonte and Buen Retiro Porcelains, Period of Charles III, 1955; Barcelona Glass in Venetian Style, 1956; Spanish Glass, 1964; Tile Panels of Spain (1500-1650), 1969. Contbr. articles to art periodicals. Home: 1650 47th Av N St Petersburg FL 33714 Office: PO Box 2859 St Petersburg FL 33731

FRUECHTENICHT, BARBARA GOETTE, travel agy. exec.; b. Ft. Wayne, Ind., July 26, 1926; d. Fred Henry and Beulah Marie (Baker) Goette; student Valparaiso U., 1944-47; B.A., Ind. U., 1954; postgrad. Purdue U., 1955-56; R.N., Parkview Meml. Hosp., Ft. Wayne, 1961; children—Kip, Carla Marie, Brent. Nurse, Parkview Hosp., Ft. Wayne, 1961-63; women's editor Jour. Gazette, Ft. Wayne, 1963-71, free lance news reporter, 1971—; mgr. Air Holiday Travel Club, Ft. Wayne, 1971—; pres. Bobbie's Fun Times, 1974—. Sec. Kirkwood Park Assn., 1966-72; mem. Philharmonic Women, Women of Philharmonic-Civic Theatre Guild. Bd. dirs. Allen County Mental Health, 1966-70, Am. Cancer Soc., 1968-74. Named Mother of Yr., March of Dimes, 1972; recipient Woman of Yr. award. Mem. Valparaiso U. Alumnae Assn. Republican. Lutheran. Clubs: Summit, Olympia, Pine Valley Country, Press, Fort Wayne Woman's. Home: 2136 Springfield Av Fort Wayne IN 46805 Office: 3402 N Anthony Blvd Fort Wayne IN 46805

FRUEHLING, ROSEMARY THERESE, educator; b. Gilbert, Minn., Jan. 23, 1933; d. John C. and Mary C. (Scalise) Juiffre; A.A., Virginia (Minn.) Jr. Coll., 1952; B.S., U. Minn., 1954, M.A., 1968; m. Donald L. Fruehling, July 23, 1969; 1 dau., Shirley Shanus. Tchr. bus. Red Wing (Minn.) High Sch., 1954-55, Roosevelt High Sch., Mpls., 1955-57, Hopkins (Minn.) High Sch., 1958-65; tchr., coordinator St. Louis Park (Minn.) High Sch., 1965-69; asso. prof. secretarial scis. County Coll. Morris, Dover, N.J., 1969—. Ednl. cons. Warner-Lambert Co., Morristown, N.J., 1971, N.J. Power & Light Co., Sandoz-Wancler, Gen. Mills, Honeywell, Inc. Mem. adv. council Nat. Bus. and Office Career Edn. Curriculum Project; commr. N.J. Pub. Broadcasting Authority. Bd. dirs. Youth Vocational Camps, Minn. Dept. Edn., St. Paul, 1967-68. Recipient Distinguished service award Minn. Dept. Edn., 1967, Service award Minn. Office Edn. Assn., 1968, Distinguished Citation award Nat. Office Edn. Assn., 1969. Mem. Nat. Bus. Edn. Assn., Internat. Platform Assn., N.J., Am. vocational assns., N.J. Office Coordinator's Assn., Office Edn. Assn. (exec. dir. Minn. 1968-69), Delta Pi Epsilon, Kappa Delta. Author: (with Bouchard) Business Correspondence/30, 1971, The Art of Writing Effective Letters, 1971; (with Brasca and LaCombe) A Resource for Cooperative Office Education, 1973; (with Poe) Business Communications: A Problem-Solving Approach, 1973; (with Laird) Psychology and Human Relations, 1974. Home: 6 Raleigh Ct Morristown NJ 07960 Office: Dept Edn County Coll Morris Dover NJ 07801

FRUTO, LIGAYA VICTORIO, writer; b. Philippines; d. Baltazar L. and Fulgencia (Cordero) Victorio; Tchrs. certificate Philippine Normal Coll.; postgrad. in lit. and Spanish, U. Philippines; m. Ramon Reyes (dec. 1944); 1 son, Ramon V. Reyes; m. 2d, Lorenzo C. Fruto, Oct. 1, 1947. Came to U.S., 1946, naturalized, 1960. Tchr., Baguio Normal Coll., Philippines, 2 years; lit. editor Manila Tribune, 2 years; asst. editor Woman's World, 3 years; co-editor Woman's Home Jour., 2 years; editor Light Mag. and Daily News Mag.; later social and women's affairs asst. in press office Pres. Philippine Republic; cultural officer Philippine Consulate Gen., Honolulu, 1946-51; writer Star-Bull., Honolulu, 1952-69; writer short stories. Founder, Ladies Civic Assn., Philippines, World War II; Filipino Women's Civic Club, Honolulu, 1951. Past mem. bd. Hawaii UN Assn., Honolulu YWCA, Girl Scouts U.S.A.; charter mem. Queen's Hosp. Aux., Recipient honors and prizes for short stories. Mem. Women in Communications. Roman Catholic. Author: Yesterday and Other Stories, 1969; also stories included in anthologies. Home: 3598 Alani Dr Honolulu HI 96822

FRY, JOHAN TRILBY (GIFFORD) (MRS. GILBERT WAYNE FRY), occupational therapist, educator; b. Quincy, Mass., Apr. 27, 1937; d. Paul Albert and Mary (Blunt) Gifford; A.A., Westbrook Coll., 1957; B.S. in Edn., Tufts U., 1960; M.A., Western Mich. U., 1971; m. Gilbert Wayne Fry, Dec. 30, 1967; children from previous marriage—Eluned Pihl, Erik Pihl, Kari Pihl. Occupational therapist Lemuel Shattuck Hosp., Boston, 1961-62, St. Mary's Hosp., Mpls., 1962-63, Mpls. Soc. for the Blind, 1964-68, Gaylord Hosp., Wallingford, Conn., 1970-72; asst. prof. dept. occupational therapy Quinnipiac Coll., Hamden, Conn., 1972—. Dept. Health, Edn. and Welfare grantee, 1968. Mem. Am., Conn. occupational therapy assns., Am. Assn. Workers for the Blind. Home: 218 Mansion Rd Cheshire CT 06410 Office: Box 117 Quinnipiac College Hamden CT 06518

FRY, ZELLA JEANNE OLIVER (MRS. ALVIN ABRAM FRY), educator; b. Mayie, B.C., Can., Oct. 30, 1909; d. Walter and Mary (Congdon) Oliver; came to U.S., 1951, naturalized, 1958; B.A., U. Alta., 1931, diploma in secondary edn., 1932, Cert. d'Etudes Francaises, 1936; M.A., Columbia, 1944, postgrad., 1945-51; postgrad. U. B.C., 1940, U. Wash., 1941; m. Alvin Abram Fry, Dec. 29, 1950. Tchr. Alta. pub. schs., 1932-42; asst. prin., sch., High River, S.D.; supervising prin. Lomond Consol. Schs., S.D.; tchr. Edmonton (Alta., Can.) schs., to 1938; univ. demonstration tchr., Alta., 1938-42; lectr. Alta. Normal Schs., 1942-45; asst. prof. lang. arts, theatre U. Alta., Edmonton, 1945-50, asso. prof., 1951; grad. asst. Tchrs. Coll., Columbia, N.Y.C., 1951-52; asso. prof. adolescent psychology Glassboro (N.J.) State Coll., 1953; adj. prof. elementary edn. U. Del., Dover extension center, 1955-57; tchr. Selbyville (Del.) Pub. High Sch., 1955-57; asso. prof. speech, theatre, media studies Kean Coll. N.J. (formerly Newark State Coll.), Union, 1958—. Kappa Delta Pi grantee Kent State U., 1971, 72. Mem. Am. Theatre Assn., Am. Assn. U. Profs., Am. Assn. U. Women (chpt. pres. 1954-55, chmn. state com. on ednl. TV 1954, 55), Am. Coll. and U. Theatre Assn., Nat., N.J. edn. assns., Speech Assn. N.J. (pres. 1970-72, mem. exec. bd. 1972-74), Horatio Alger Soc., Speech Assn. Eastern States, Speech Communication Assn., Kappa Delta Pi, Pi Lambda Theta. Episcopalian. Contbr. to publs. in field. Home: 6 Edgewood Ct North Plainfield NJ 07060 Office: care Kean College NJ V-E 414 Morris Av Union NJ 07083

FRYAR, PEARL STOCK (MRS. FRANK FRYAR), hosp. adminstr.; b. St. Charles, Ida., June 27, 1920; d. George Pointz and Cora Elizabeth (Williamson) Stock; B.S., U. Utah, 1958; postgrad. hosp. adminstrn. Columbia Sch. Continuing Edn., 1964-65; m. Frank Fryar, Aug. 14, 1942; children—Michael Stock, Charles Frank. Lab. technologist Caribou Meml. Hosp., Soda Springs, Ida., 1946-57, Dowell Labs., Mesa, Ariz., 1958-61; adminstr. Caribou Meml. Hosp. and Nursing Home, Soda Springs, Ida., 1961—. Mem. steering com. Battelle Systems Program for Hosps., 1971—. Fellow Am. Coll. Hosp. Adminstrs.; mem. Ida. (pres. 1970-71), Am. hosp. assns., Am. Soc. Clin. Pathologists, Ida. Health Facilities, Am. Coll. Nursing Home Adminstrs., Soda Springs C. of C., Bus. and Profl. Women's Club. Mem. Ch. of Jesus Christ of Latter-day Saints. Home: 260 S Main St Soda Springs ID 83276 Office: 300 South 3d West Soda Springs ID 83276

FRYE, HARRIET BEAVER, retail co. exec.; b. Concord, N.C., Mar. 15, 1940; d. Luther Eugene and Clara (Sherrill) Beaver; student Davidson Coll., summers 1959, 60, U. N.C., 1961; B.A. in History, Duke, 1962; m. Herman Cranford Frye, Apr. 17, 1966 (div. June 1970). Exec. buyer trainee J.B. Ivey & Co., Charlotte, N.C., 1962, buyer, 1962-66; asso. buyer Peck & Peck, N.Y.C., 1966-69; buyer Miller & Rhoads div. Garfinckel's, Brooks Bros. & M&R, Richmond, Va., 1969—. Jr. dress steering com. Frederick Atkins Buying Office, N.Y.C., 1971—. Chmn., Historic Church Hill Candlelight Tour, Richmond, 1971, mem. Church Hill Found., Church Hill Civic Assn., Richmond, 1971—. Mem. Nat., Va. fox hunters assns., Duke Alumni Assn., Kappa Delta. Democrat. Methodist. Clubs: Richmond Ski, Twenty-Three Hundred, Chalet. Home: 200 N 24th St Church Hill Richmond VA 23223 Office: 517 E Broad St Richmond VA 23219

FRYE, HELEN JACKSON, judge; b. Klamath Falls, Ore.; Dec. 10, 1930; d. Earl and Elizabeth Belle (Kirkpatrick) Jackson; B.A. in Eng. Lit. with honors, U. Ore., 1953, M.A., 1961, J.D., 1966; children—Eric, Karen, Heidi. Tchr., Eugene (Ore.) pub. sch., 1957-63; admitted to Ore. bar, 1966; law asso. Riddlesbarger, Pederson, Young & Horn, Eugene, Ore., 1966-68; asso. Husband, Johnson & Frye, Eugene, 1968-71, trial judge ct. gen. jurisdiction, Eugene, 1971—. Vis. lectr. U. Ore., at Eugene, 1970-71. Mem. lay adv. bd. Sacred Heart Hosp., Eugene, 1972; bd. visitors U. Ore. Sch. Law, 1972—. Mem. Am., Ore. bar assns., Ore. Circuit Judges Assn. (treas. 1972-73), Am. Judicature Soc., Bus. and Profl. Women, Phi Beta Kappa, Delta Kappa Gamma. Contbr. articles to profl. jours. Office: Lane County Court House Eugene OR 97401

FRYE, JUDITH ELEEN MINOR (MRS. VERNON LESTER FRYE), printing co. exec.; b. Seattle; d. George Edward and Eleen G. (Hartelius) Minor; student U. Cal. at Los Angeles, evenings 1947-48, U. So. Cal., 1948-53; m. Vernon Lester Frye, Apr. 1, 1954. Accountant, office mgr. Colony Wholesale Liquor, Culver City, Cal., 1947-48; credit mgr. Western Dist. Co., Culver City, 1948-53; partner in restaurants, Palm Springs, Los Angeles, 1948, in date ranch, La Quinta, Cal., 1949-53; partner Imperial Printing, Los Angeles, 1955-67, owner, 1969—; editor New Era Laundry and Cleaning Lines, Los Angeles, 1962—. Mem. Laundry and Cleaning Allied Trades Assn., Internat. Platform Assn., Cal. Coin-Op Assn., Laundry and Dry Cleaning Suppliers Assn., Nat. Automatic Laundry and Cleaning Council, Women in Laundry and Dry Cleaning. Office: 8552-54 Hamilton St Huntington Beach CA 92646

FRYE, SISTER MARY IGNATIA, educator; b. Washington, May 11, 1912; d. George Rex and Mary Lee (Royall) Frye; B.A., Marygrove Coll., 1934; M.S., Catholic U. Am., 1940; Ph.D., 1955; postgrad. N.C. State U., 1963, Va. Poly. Inst., 1964. Instr. chemistry and math. Marygrove Coll., Detroit, 1939-46, asst. prof., 1947-48, asso. prof., 1949-56, prof. math. and physcis., 1957-70, head dept., 1954-70, prof. math. and computer sci., 1970—, chmn. dept. math., 1970-71, 73—, coordinator computer sci. program, 1972—, dir. Computer Center, 1972—. Ford Faculty fellow, 1951-52. Mem. Assn. Computing Machinery, Am. Math. Soc., Math. Assn. Am., Soc. Indsl. and Applied Math., Sigma Xi. Author: Molecular Orbital Calculations of Some Diatomic Molecules, Principally C2, 1955. Address: 8425 W McNichols St Detroit MI 48221

FRYE, PAULINE LEACH, lawyer; b. Chillicothe, O.; d. Omer and Marietta (Moats) Leach; student Am. Inst. Banking; grad. Nat. U. Law (now merged with George Washington U.), 1950; m. Roger Ellis Frye, Dec. 29, 1951; children—Peggy Ann, Judy Maria. Admitted to D.C. bar, 1951, U.S. Supreme Ct. bar, 1959; practiced in Washington, 1951—; asso. firm Murphy & Nelson, 1957—; atty. Econ. Stablzn. Agy., 1951-53. Parliamentarian, N.C. Fedn. Republican Women, 1968—, pres. elect, 1970-71; women's coordinator 8th Congl. Dist. of N.C., Nat. Rep. Congl. Com., 1968; candidate Rep. primary U.S. Congress, 1968; chmn. Pinehurst sect. N.C. Com. for Responsible Legislation, 1971. Mem. N.C., D.C. bar assns., George Washington U. Law Assn., Internat. Platform Assn., Phi Alpha Delta. Ho- me: Polrog Farm Box 322 Pinehurst NC 28374

FRYER, JUDITH EMMA, librarian; b. Pottstown, Pa., Apr. 8, 1940; d. Lewis H. and Dorothy G. (Manwiller) Fryer; B.A., Ursinus Coll., 1965; M.S., Drexel U., 1969. Secretarial positions, 1959-62; tchr. Jefferson Elementary Sch., Pottstown, 1965-66, Owen J. Roberts High Sch., Pottstown, 1967-68; periodicals librarian Ursinus Coll., Collegeville, Pa., 1969—. Vol. librarian Goschenhoppen Folklife Mus. and Library, Green Lane, Pa., 1970—. Mem. Goschenhoppen Historians (sec. 1973—, dir. 1973—). Mem. United Ch. of Christ. Home: 74 E 5th Av Apt K-304 Collegeville PA 19426 Office: Goschenhoppen Folklife Library and Museum Box 476 Green Lane PA 18054

FRYXELL, REGINA CHRISTINA HOLMEN (MRS. FRITIOF M. FRYXELL), musician, educator; b. Morganville, Kan., Nov. 24, 1899; d. John Algot and Amelia (Christensen) Holmen; B.A., Augustana Coll., 1922, Mus.B., 1922, Litt.D., 1961; grad. Juilliard Sch. Music, N.Y.C., 1927; student organ and ch. music in Europe, 1948, 71-72; pvt. study Dr. Leo Sowerby, 1950-68; postgrad. U. Ia., 1967-68; m. Fritiof M. Fryxell, June 22, 1928; children—John, Roald, Redwood. Tchr. piano, theory Augustana Coll., 1922-25, French, 1924-25, organ, 1931-33, 36, piano, 1967-68; teaching asst. Gaston Dethier in organ Juilliard Sch. Music, N.Y.C., 1927-28; instr. organ Knox Coll., 1956-58; tchr. organ Black Hawk Coll., Moline, Ill., 1969—. Tchr. pvt. lessons organ, piano, 1922—; organist chs. Moline, 1922-25, 67—, N.Y.C., 1925-28, Rock Island, Ill., 1928-42, Washington, 1943-46, Davenport, Ia., 1946-67; accompanist piano or organ for singers, instrumentalists, choral groups. Organ recitals various chs. across U.S.; tchr. many ch. music confs.; organist Constituting Conv. Luth. Ch. Am., 1962; mem. Commn. Worship Luth. Ch. Am., 1962-70. Mem. Music Tchrs. Nat. Assn. (mem. panel 1956), Am. Guild Organists (mem. panel regional conv. 1961), Hymn Soc. Am., Luth. Soc. for Worship, Music and Arts, Rock Island Fine Arts Club. Contbr. articles on ch. music to various publs. Composer numerous solos and anthems, liturgical items in Service Book and Hymnal, 4 vols. introits and graduals for choirs. Home: 1331 42d Av Rock Island IL 61201

FUCETOLA, EDITH MARY ASCOLI (MRS. SALVADORE ROPPOLO), radiologic technologist; b. Newark, Aug. 23, 1915; d. Fortunato R. and Rosa (Cerantonio) Ascoli; student Jersey City Med. Center Sch. Radiologic Tech., 1954-56, Essex County Jr. Coll., Orange, N.J., 1956; m. James Fucetola, Nov. 29, 1936; children—Ralph E., James A.; m. 2d, Salvadore Roppolo, Mar. 18, 1972. Student asst. chief radiology Jersey City Med. Center Sch. X-ray Tech., 1956-58; technologist St. Michaels Hosp., Newark, 1957; chief technologist, x-ray dept. head St. Barnabas Med. Center, Livingston, N.J., 1958-65; chief orthopaedic radiologic technologist Montclair Nicola Orthopaedic Group, 1965—. Pres. mothers aux. Boy Scout Troop 1, Kearny, N.J., 1952; vol. womens aux. West Hudson Hosp., Kearny, 1952-56; driver Red Cross Kearny Motor Corps, 1955; N.J. del. U.S. Pub. Health Conf. U. Md., 1966; sec. Service Clubs Montclair, 1967—. Mem. Am. (past conv. chmn.), N.J. (Pres.'s plaque 1967, past pres., com. chmn.) socs. radiologic technologists, Mid-Eastern Conf. Radiologic Technologists (past treas,), Essex County (pres.), Montclair (del., pres. 1970-72) bus. and profl. womens clubs, Am. Registry Radiologic Technologists, League Women Voters, Catholic Daus. Am., St. Raphaels Rosary Soc. Roman Catholic. Club: Arlington Womens (Kearny). Home: 179 S Harrison St Apt 109 East Orange NJ 07018 Office: 200 Highland Av Glenridge NJ 07028

FUCHS, JEANETTE DEBORAH NADLER (MRS. NATHANIEL FUCHS), educator, social worker; b. N.Y.C., June 20, 1908; d. Meyer and Rachel (Breitfeld) Nadler; B.A., Hunter Coll. City of N.Y., 1933; N.S.S., Columbia U., 1942, Ed.D., 1961; m. Nathaniel Fuchs, July 8, 1950 (dec. Jan. 1956). Social investigator N.Y.C. Dept. of Welfare, 1938-39; community group interviewer and sr. intake worker, N.Y.C. Dept. of Welfare 1939-41, acting intake supr., 1941-42; psychiatric case worker Family Consultation Service, Cin., 1943-44; psychiatric social worker Amherst H. Wilder Child Guidance Clinic, 1944-46, sr. psychiatric social worker, 1946-47; psychiat. social worker Westchester Jewish Community Services, 1948; psychiat. cons. East Edn. Nursery Sch., 1950-52; instr. edn. Bklyn. Coll. of City U. of N.Y., 1948-60, asst. prof. edn., 1960-70, asso. prof., 1971—. Recipient fellowship Family Consultation Service of Cin. Fellow Am. Orthopsychiatric Assn., Am. Assn. Workers, World Fedn. for Mental Health, Kappa Delta Pi, Pi Lambda Theta. Contbr. articles to profl. jours. Research on parents of emotionally disturbed children. Home: 55 East End Av New York City NY 10028 Office: Bedford & Av H Brooklyn NY 11210

FUCHS, SOPHIE SCHALET (MRS. BERTRAM FUCHS), pediatrician; b. Lvov, Poland, Oct. 13, 1924; d. Marc and Rosa (Leiter) Schalet; M.D., Charles U., Prague, 1949; m. Bertram Fuchs, Mar. 30, 1952; children—Ronnie M., Marc D. Intern, Knickerbocker Hosp., N.Y.C., 1949-50; asst. resident pediatrics Maimonides Hosp., Bklyn., 1950-51; resident contagious diseases Kingston Av. Hosp., Bklyn., 1951; fellow pediatrics Children's Med. Center, Boston, 1952-53; practice medicine specializing in pediatrics, Hempstead, N.Y., 1958-63, Northport, N.Y., 1963—; mem. staffs Mercy Hosp., Rockville Center, N.Y., L.I. Jewish Hosp., New Hyde Park, N.Y., Nassau County Med. Center, East Meadow, N.Y., 1958-64, Huntington (N.Y.) Hosp., 1963—. Home: 21 Norwood Rd Northport NY 11768 Office: 1026 A Fort Salonga Rd Northport NY 11768

FUDALI, SISTER MARY CONSTANTIA, educator; b. Mpls.; d. Michael Albert and Anna (Pikala) Fudali; B.S., Toledo Tchrs. Coll., 1934; M.S., Notre Dame U., 1942; student Pontifical Inst. Sacred Scis., Regina Mundi, Rome, Italy, 1956-57; Ph.D., Ottawa (Ont., Can.) U., 1964. Joined Order of St. Francis; tchr. math. Central Cath. High Sch., Toledo, 1923-30, 32-51; prin. St. Clare Acad., 1951-66; dir. guidance services St. Clare Acad. and Lourdes Coll., Sylvania, O., 1964—; faculty Notre Dame (Ind.) U., 1966, Toledo, Diocesan Adult Edn. Program, 1967-69. Mem. Sylvania Citizens Recreation Co., 1965-67. Mem. Psychologists Interested in Religious Issues, Nat. Cath. Guidance Conf., Acad. Religion and Mental Health, Nat. Council on Family Relations, Am. Personnel and Guidance Assn., Coll. Theology Soc., Toledo Diocesan Guidance Council (pres. 1967-68), Northwestern Ohio Guidance Council, Ohio Sch. Counselors Assn., Greater Toledo Mental Health Assn., Toledo Area and Sylvania clergy fellowship. Address: 6832 Convent Blvd Sylvania OH 43560

FUERST, SHIRLEY MILLER (MRS. ADOLPH FUERST), artist; b. Bklyn., June 3, 1928; d. Joseph A. and Minna (Lavine) Miller; B.A., Hunter Coll., 1948, M.F.A., 1971; student Bklyn. Mus. Art Sch., 1958-66, Pratt Center for Contemporary Printmaking, 1966-67, Art Students League, 1967-68; m. Adolph Fuerst, July 6, 1951; children—David, Ellen. One-person shows at Gallery 84, Village Art Center; exhibited in group shows at Hudson River Mus., Suffolk Mus., Lovisco Gallery, Roko Gallery, Donnell Art Library, Riverside Mus., Bklyn. Mus., Allentown Art Mus., Mickelson Gallery, Washington, Butler Inst. Am. Art, N.Y. State Fair, Pallazzo Vecchio, Florence, Italy, others; represented in permanent collections James A. Michener Found. Collection 20th Century Am. Art, U. Tex., Allentown Art Mus., others. Recipient 1st prize Pace Coll. Exhbn., 1961, Village Art Center, 1963, merit award with distinction, also merit award with spl. recognition Enjay Art Competition, 1966, graphics award Nat. Assn. Women Artists, 1970. Mem. Nat. Assn. Women Artists, Contemporary Artists, Women in the Arts. Inventor method of painting and/or printing on mylar film using heat diffusion inks, 1970. Address: 266 Marlborough Rd Brooklyn NY 11226

FUGMANN, RUTH ADELE, immunologist; b. Balt., Sept. 7, 1923; d. Charles Louis and Hazel Lufayne (Butts) Fugmann; A.A., Mt. St. Agnes Jr. Coll., 1942; B.S., Johns Hopkins, 1950; M.S., U. Miami, 1964, Ph.D., 1968. Clin. lab. technician Mercy Hosp., Balt., 1942-44; sr. cancer research technician, hematologist Army Chem. Center, Edgewood, Md., 1944-50; research asst., asso. biologist cancer research project Coll. Phys. and Surgs., N.Y.C., 1950-58; research asst., asso. biologist cancer research project Sch. Medicine, U. Miami (Fla.), 1958-61, instr. microbiology, 1968-70; asst. in research Howard Hughes Med. Inst., Miami, 1961-65; research asso. Variety Children's Research Found., Miami, 1965-67; dir. cancer immunology, dept. surgery-research Cath. Med. Center of Bklyn. and Queens, Inc., Jamaica, N.Y., 1969—. Mem. Am. Assn. for Cancer Research, Am. Assn. Immunology, Am. Soc. Microbiology, A.A.A.S., Reticuloendothelial Soc., N.Y. Acad. Sic. Home: 29 Pilgrim Rd Scarsdale NY 10583 Office: 89-15 Woodhaven Blvd Woodhaven NY 11421

FUHRMAN, ESTHER SEGAL (MRS. ROBERT J. FUHRMAN), sculptor, mfg. co. exec.; b. Pitts., Feb. 25, 1939; d. Harry and Lena (Bernstein) Segal; student Pa. State U., 1956-57; B.A., U. Pitts., 1960; pvt. study with Sabastiano Mineo, Hana Geber; m. Robert J. Fuhrman, Oct. 29, 1961; children—Deborah Lynn, Mimi Suzanne, Karen Leigh. Sculptor, specializing in large bronze and acrylic commns. for various bus. firms and pvt. collectors, 1966—; designer, pres. Demika Home Fashion, Inc., mfr. and distbr. acrylic products, N.Y.C., 1972—. Lectr. on sculpture various ednl. groups and instns. Recipient sculpture award Nat. Assn. Women Artists, 1973, 74. Mem. Am. Soc. Contemporary Artists, Artist Craftsmen N.Y., Nat. Assn. Women Artists, N.Y. Soc. Women Artists, Sculptors League, Silvermine Guild Artists. Club: Mill River (N.Y.C.). Home: 4 Essington Lane Dix Hills NY 11746 Office: 10 Sarah Dr Farmingdale NY 11735

FUHS, SISTER PHILIP MARIA, med. service adminstr.; b. South Boston, Mass., Feb. 2, 1914; d. Philip Paul and Margaret Mary (Morrissey) Fuhs; R.N., St. Joseph Infirmary Sch. Nursing, 1938; student Spalding Coll., 1950-53. Joined Sisters of Charity of Nazareth, Ky., 1932; adminstr. Holy Family Hosp., Ensley, Ala., 1956-62, Mercy Hosp., Mount Vernon, O., 1962-73, Sisters of Charity of Nazareth Nursing Facility, Louisville, 1973—. Mem. bd. Ohio Conf. Cath. Hosps., 1966-73. Bd. dirs. Knox County Heart Assn., sec., 1963; bd. dirs. Knox County Joint Vocational Sch., North Central Tech. Sch.; bd. dirs. Knox County Joint Vocational Sch., North Central

Tech. Sch.; bd. dirs. Knox County Health Planning Council, chmn. health facility com. Recipient Distinguished Service plaque Knox County Heart Assn., 1970; Named Woman of the Hour, Mount Vernon C. of C., 1973. Mem. Am. Coll. Hosp. Adminstrs. Address: Russell Hall Nazareth KY 40048

FULCHER, CLAIRE ELEANOR, orgn. cons., educator; b. Los Angeles, Aug. 8, 1925; d. James Herbert and Eleanor (Davis) Fulcher; B.A., Pomona Coll., 1946; M.A., Stanford, 1950; Ed.D., Columbia U., 1955; postgrad. Boston U., 1971-72. Grad. asst. residence hall Stanford, 1947-48, asst. residence hall dir., 1948-49; asst. dean students, instr. biology Palos Verdes Coll., 1950-52; asst. dean student personnel, asso. prof. edn. U. Bridgeport, Conn., 1954-72; dir. Women's Resource Center, YWCA of U.S., N.Y.C., 1972-73. Cons., lectr. edn., women's roles, continuing edn., residence halls. Mem. Campus Ministry Bd., Bridgeport, 1965-72; mem. Every Women's Center, Bridgeport YWCA, 1971—, bd. dirs., 1966-72; state adv. com. on continuing edn. Conn. Bd. Edn. and Commn. on Higher Edn. Mem. Am. Assn. U. Profs., Am. Assn. U. Women (pres. state div. 1966-69, regional v.p. 1969-73, nat. 1st v.p. 1973—), corporate del. convs. (1961-71), Gov.'s Commn. on Status Women Conn., Task Force Edn., Conn. Service Bur. Women's Orgns. (mem. cooperating com. 1966—), Nat. Assn. Women Deans Counselors (life mem., mem. program com. 1967-68), Am. Coll. Personnel Assn. (state membership chmn. 1964—), Am., Conn. (mem. program com. 1965-66) personnel and guidance assns., Conn. Assn. Women Deans and Counselors, P.E.O., Mortar Bd., Delta Kappa Gamma, Pi Lambda Theta, Kappa Delta Pi, Alpha Sigma Lambda. Democrat. Conglist. Author: Techniques of Organizational Effectiveness, 1973. Home: 130 E 18th St New York City NY 10003

FULCOMER, VIRGINIA ANN ROHLF (MRS. CHARLES F. FULCOMER), psychologist; b. Greeley, Minn., Oct. 11, 1916; d. Louis John and Viola Florence (Sybrant) Rohlf; B.A., U. Cal. at Los Angeles, 1956; M.S. in Edn., Westminster Coll., 1959; Ph.D., Case-Western Res. U., 1963; m. Charles F. Fulcomer, Sept. 1, 1938; children—Judith (Mrs. David Willour), Mark, Cheryl (Mrs. David Kriska). Instr., Westminster Coll., New Wilmington, Pa., 1958-62; psychologist, dir. Child Guidance Center, Youngstown, O., 1962-69; pvt. practice cons. and evaluation services, Youngstown, 1969-71; dir. Child and Adult Mental Health Center, Youngstown, 1971—. Mem. Am., Ohio (mem. ethics com. 1969-74) psychol. assns., Psi Chi, Kappa Delta Pi. Presbyn. Home: 1823 5th Av Youngstown OH 44504 Office: 1001 Covington St Youngstown OH 44510

FULD, PAULA ALTMAN (MRS. LAWRENCE FULD), educator, neuropsychologist; b. N.Y.C., Aug. 12, 1938; d. Samuel David and Edna (Birnbach) Altman; student Barnard Coll., 1955-57; B.A., Coll. City N.Y., 1959; M.A., City U. N.Y., 1963; Ph.D., Columbia, 1969; m. Lawrence Fuld, Oct. 12, 1958; 1 son, Eric. Tchr. jr. high sch., N.Y.C., 1959-65; research asst., editorial asst. Columbia Tchrs. Coll., 1965-69; asst. prof. ednl. psychology N.Y. U., 1969-70, Fordham U., Lincoln Center, 1970-72; asst. prof. neurology (psychology) Albert Einstein Coll. Medicine, 1972—; ltd. pvt. practice ednl. therapist, cons., neuropsychologist, N.Y.C., 1961—. Cons. neuropsychology St. Joseph's Sch. for Deaf, Bronx, N.Y. Mem. Internat. Neuropsychology Soc., Am. Psychol. Assn., Internat. Reading Assn. Contbr. articles to profl. jours. Clin. research on learning, performance of children with seizure disorder. Home: 5450 Netherland Av New York City NY 10471 Office: Jacobi Dept Neurology Albert Einstein Coll Medicine Pelham Pkwy and Eastchester Rd Bronx NY 10468

FULDHEIM, DOROTHY, journalist; b. Paterson, N.J., June 26, 1893; d. Herman and Bertha (Wishner) Snell; ed. Milw. Coll., 1914; m. Milton Fuldheim (dec.), W.L. Ulman (dec.); 1 dau., Dorothy Fuldheim Urman. News analyst Scripps-Howard sta. WEWS-TV, Cleve., 1924—; lectr. in field. Recipient Overseas Press Club award, 1959, Ohio Firemen and Police award, 1955, 72, Israeli Freedom award, 1967, Theta Sigma Phi ann. nat. award, 1964, Ohio AFL-CIO award, 1973. Author: I Laughed, I Loved, I Cried, 1965; Where Were the Arabs, 1967; A Thousand Friends, 1974. Home: 13900 Shaker Blvd #216 Cleveland OH 44120 Office: 3001 Euclid Av Cleveland OH 44115

FULFORD, JANICE WALTON (MRS. DAVID ARNOLD FULFORD), librarian; b. Rochester, N.Y., Mar. 19, 1929; d. Herbert William and Marguerite Florine (Earley) Walton; A.B., Houghton Coll., 1950; M.S., Syracuse U., 1951; m. David Arnold Fulford, June 23, 1956. Asst. librarian Houghton (N.Y.) Coll., 1951-53; periodical asst. Syracuse (N.Y.) U., 1953-54; sr. librarian Syracuse Pub. Library, 1954—. Mem. Christian Bus. and Profl. Women's Council, D.A.R. Home: 311 Hutchinson Av Syracuse NY 13207 Office: 1620 W Genesee St Syracuse NY 13204

FULGADO, CARMENCITA QUESADA, ednl. adminstr.; b. Manila, Philippines, Sept. 25, 1940; d. Eliseo Quesada and Pat Castaneda Bunales; came to U.S., 1963, naturalized, 1974; B.A. in Psychology cum laude, U. Philippines, 1961; M.A. in Guidance and Counseling, U. San Francisco, 1966; Ph.D. in Counselor Edn., N.Y. U., 1972; m. Leonardo T. Fulgado, Sept. 7, 1968; 2 children. Vocational counselor Moblzn. for Youth, N.Y.C., 1966-68; counselor St. Vincent's Home for Boys, Bklyn., 1966-67; supr. tng. counselor tng. program div. continuing edn. N.Y.C. Community Coll., 1968-69; asst. prof. counseling, dir. student financial aids, counselor internat. students, dir. summer freshmen orientation program York Coll. of City U. N.Y., Jamaica, 1970—. Instr. psychology Nat. Tchrs. Coll., Manila, 1961-63, U. East, Manila, 1962-63, 65; teaching asst. U. Cal. at Berkeley; instr. spl. course in counseling Cornell U. Extension, 1970. Program cons. Girl Scouts, Los Angeles, 1964; adv. council Office of Mayor, N.Y.C. Urban Corps. Trustee Soc. Christian Unity, N.Y.C. Mgmt. Assn. Philippines grantee, 1965; Univ. Honors scholar, Recipient N.Y. U. Founders Day award, 1972, named Outstanding Filipino Overseas. Mem. Am. Personnel and Guidance Assn., Am. Psychol. Assn., Nat. Assn. Fgn. Student Affairs, N.Y. State Financial Aid Adminstrs. Assn., Asian Soc. Epiphany Parish (v.p.). Author publs. in field. Home: 19 Stuyvesant Oval New York City NY 10009 Office: 150-14 Jamaica Av Jamaica NY 11432

FULKERSON, BETTY FULK (MRS. BAUCUM FULKERSON), editor; b. Little Rock, Aug. 12, 1916; d. Augustus Marion and Elizabeth (Keane) Fulk; diploma Little Rock Jr. Coll., 1935; A.B., Vassar Coll., 1938; m. Baucum Fulkerson, Sept. 21, 1940 (dec. Aug. 1949); children—Catherine Embry, Josephine Bond (dec.). Mgr. Club Travel Agy., Little Rock, 1950-52; woman's editor Ark. Gazette, Little Rock, 1952—. Mem. consumer's affairs com. Ark. Commn. on Status of Women, 1966-70. Past mem. family life bd. Pulaski County Health and Welfare Council; adv. bd. Women's Aux. U. Ark. Med. Center, 1958; bd. dirs. All Saints Episcopal Sch., Vicksburg, Miss., 1961-63. Mem. Phi Theta Kappa, Sigma Delta Chi. Contbg. editor Delta Rev., 1966-70. Home: 1 Beverly Pl Little Rock AR 72207 Office: Ark Gazette 3d and Louisiana St Little Rock AR 72201

FULLER, CHARLOTTE ANN SMITH (MRS. JOSEPH DORCAS FULLER III), educator; b. Meridian, Te., July 27, 1945; d. Melvin Edward and Lillie Mae (Miller) Smith; B.F.A. summa cum laude, Tex. Christian U., 1968, M.F.A., 1969; m. Joseph Dorcas Fuller III, July 14, 1967; 1 son, Joseph Edward. With advt. dept. Tandy Leather Co., Ft. Worth, 1963-64; copywriter So. Bapt. Radio-TV Commn., Ft. Worth, 1966-67; instr. speech Tex. Luth. Coll., Sequin, 1969-71, Tarrant County Jr. Coll., Ft. Worth, 1972—, Tex. Christian U., Ft. Worth, 1972—. Rep. Tex. Christian U. Alumni Council, 1972. Mem. Am. Assn. Univ. Women (1st v.p. 1971), Theta Sigma Phi, Alpha Lambda Delta. Democrat. Baptist. Clubs: TCU Faculty Women's, Newcomers (treas. 1972-73). Home: 6370 Wilton Dr Fort Worth TX 76133

FULLER, ESTHER PIKE (MRS. W. PARMER FULLER, III), mus. ofcl.; b. Washington, Sept. 1, 1918; d. Elias and Alexandra (Smirnova) Yanovsky; B.A. with distinction, George Washington U., 1939; postgrad. George Washington U., 1939-42, Union Theol. Sem., 1942-44; m. James Albert Pike, Jan. 29, 1942; children—Catherine (Mrs. John Charles Patterson, Jr.), Constance, Christopher; m. 2d. W. Parmer Fuller, III, Apr. 21, 1973. Adminstr., Exploratorium, San Francisco, 1969—. Asst. to dir. Dept. Social Relations, Episcopal Diocese N.Y., N.Y.C., 1955-58; mem. editorial bd. Seabury Press, N.Y.C., 1954-58; mem. bd. Urban League, San Francisco, 1959-63; mem. Council for Civic Unity, San Francisco, 1956—; mem. Am. Civil Liberties Union, San Francisco, 1968-70. Mem. Phi Beta Kappa, Phi Delta Delta, Delta Zeta. Episcopalian. Editor, author: Who Is My Neighbor, 1958. Home: 1980 Vallejo St San Francisco CA 94123 Office: The Exploratorium 3601 Lyon St San Francisco CA 94123

FULLER, FLORINE SMITH, librarian; b. Iuka, Miss., Aug. 1, 1920; d. James Carey and Mary Etta (Thomas) Thorne; B.S.E., U. Ark., 1956, M.A., 1959; postgrad. Vanderbilt U., 1960-63; M.A. in L.S., George Peabody Coll. Tchrs., 1961; m. Richard L. Fuller, May 18, 1961; 1 dau., by previous marriage, Juanita Currey Smith (Mrs. Marion Caldwell Harper). Librarian, Nashville Met. Schs., 1956-63; library dir. U. Tenn. at Nashville, 1963—. Mem. A.L.A., Mid-State (exec. council 1971, chmn. 1974-75), Tenn. (chmn. coll. and univ. sect. 1974) library assns., Nashville Area C. of C., Am. Assn. U. Women, Davidson County Profl. Women's Club, Lambda Tau, Phi Alpha Theta. Methodist. Home: 169 Lelawood Circle Nashville TN 37209 Office: 323 McLemore St Nashville TN 37203

FULLER, FRANCES LEONORE (MRS. WORTHINGTON C. MINER), actress; b. Charleston, S.C., Oct. 4, 1907; d. Wallace Watt and Leonore (Byrnes) Fuller; student Manhattanville Coll., 1927-28; L.H.D., Pace U., 1974; m. Worthington C. Miner, Mar. 30, 1929; children—Peter, Margaret (Mrs. Hugh Rawson), Mary Elizabeth. Actress appearing in Broadway plays The Front Page, 1929, Animal Kingdom, 1932, Stage Door, 1937, Home is the Hero, 1952, Lady of the Camellias, 1966; actress appearing in films One Sunday Afteroon, 1933, Girl in the Red Velvet Swing, 1962, They Might be Giants, 1969, Homebodies, 1973; TV actress series Love of Life, 1965-68; tchr. Am. Acad. Dramatic Arts, N.Y.C., 1948-50, 54-74, dir., pres., 1954-64, dir., 1964-74, chmn. bd., 1974—. Mem. Actors Equity Assn., A.F.T.R.A., Screen Actors Guild, Author's League, Broadcast Music Inc. Home: 145 W 58th St New York City NY 10019 Office: 120 Madison Av New York City NY 10016

FULLER, JOAN DIGNAN (MRS. ALFRED W. FULLER), lawyer; b. Boston, Nov. 6, 1928; d. Thomsas Gregory and Hester Clare (Sharkey) Dignan; A.B., Radcliffe Coll., 1950; LL.B., Harvard, 1954; m. Alfred W. Fuller, June 13, 1969; children—Hester L., Bradbury. Admitted to Mass. bar, 1954; asso. Ropes & Gray, Boston, 1962-73, partner, 1973—. Club: Harvard (Boston). Home: 8 Whittier Pl Boston MA 02114 Office: 225 Franklin St Boston MA 02110

FULLER, JUDITH KAY HILDENBRAND (MRS. DONALD EUGENE FULLER), counselor; b. Kankakee, Ill., Mar. 3, 1939; d. Louis Frederick and Katherine Elizabeth (Sheldon) Hildenbrand; student Blackburn Coll., 1957-58; B.A., U. Ill., 1961, M.Ed., 1967; m. Donald Eugene Fuller, Oct. 26, 1963. Tchr. English, J. Sterling Morton High Sch., Cicero, Ill., 1961-64, West Layden High Sch., Northlake, Ill., 1964-66; tchr. English, counselor, transitional year program Coe Coll., Cedar Rapids, Ia., 1967-70; instr., counselor Kirkwood Community Coll., Cedar Rapids, 1970-72; counselor, adminstr. career opportunities program Mt. Mercy Coll., Cedar Rapids, 1972—. Bd. dirs. Hoover Health Council, 1970—. Mem. Nat. Assn. Women Deans, Counselors and Adminstrs., League Women Voters (dir. 1968-72), Women in Communications, Phi Kappa Phi. Home: 223 26th Street Dr NE Cedar Rapids IA 52403 Office: 1330 Elmhurst Dr NE Cedar Rapids IA 52402

FULLER, JULIA MAE, writer-editor; b. Atlanta, Feb. 8, 1941; d. Green Newton and Dora Mae (Hollaway) Fuller; A.B. in Journalism, U. Ga., 1962; postgrad. Ga. State U., 1969—. Asso. editor McFadden Bus. Publs., Atlanta, 1962-64; asst. editor Center for Disease Control, Dept. Health, Edn. and Welfare, Atlanta, 1964-65, editor instructive communications activity, 1965-67, supervisory writer-editor, 1967-73, writer-editor Office of Dir. Tng. Bur., 1973—. Mem. edn. com. CDC Fed. Credit Union, 1974—. Recipient Outstanding Writing Aide award Theta Sigma Phi, 1972. Mem. Am. Med. Writers Assn., Women in Communications, Fed. Editors Assn., Nat. Soc. for Performance and Instrn. (editor Atlanta chpt. 1967), Ga. Pub. Health Assn., CDC Mgmt. Forum (v.p. 1974—). Home: 30 Peachtree Hills Av Atlanta GA 30305 Office: 1600 Clifton Rd Atlanta GA 30333

FULLER, MARY MARGARET STIEHM (MRS. CURTIS GROSS FULLER), editor; b. Lincoln, Neb., Apr. 23, 1914; d. Ewald Ortwin and Marie Daisy (Douglass) Stiehm; B.A., U. Wis., 1938; m. Curtis Gross Fuller, Sept. 24, 1938; children—Nancy Abigail (Mrs. David Abraham), Michael Curtis. Free-lance writer, 1940-52; asst. editor FATE mag., 1952-54, exec. editor, 1954-56, editor, 1956—. Sec., Clark Pub. Co., Highland Park, 1949—; v.p., sec. Woodall Pub. Co., Highland Park, 1965—. Mem. Ill. Soc. Psychic Research (pres. 1966-68), Theta Sigma Phi, Alpha Phi. Home: 815 E Deerpath Rd Lake Forest IL 60045 Office: Highland House 35 Western Av Highland Park IL 60035

FULLER, MURIEL LAURA, educator; b. Holmen, Wis., Sept. 28, 1912; d. Edgar Putnam and Joan (McDonald) Fuller; B.Ed., LaCrosse State Tchrs. Coll., 1935; B.L.S., U. Wis., 1943; M.A., U. Mich., 1956. Tchr. high sch., Birchwood, Wis., 1935-37, Ontario, Wis., 1938-42; asst. librarian LaCrosse (Wis.) Pub. Library, 1943-47, head librarian, 1947-53; pub. library cons. Mich. State Library, 1953-62; lectr. U. Wis. Library Sch., Madison, 1962-63, asst. prof., 1963-66, asso. prof., 1966—, chmn. univ. extension library sci. dept., 1964-72, chmn. communication arts dept., 1972—. Mem. Am. (pres. adult services div. 1962-63, dir. library edn. div. 1967-70), Wis. (pres. 1968-69), library assns., Assn. Am. Library Schs., Adult Edn. Assn. (del. to assembly, 1967-73), Adult Edn. Assn. Wis. (pres. 1972-73), Adult Edn. Assn. Mich. (pres. 1961-62), Ch. and Synagogue Library Assn., Am. Assn. U. Profs. (pres. elect Wis. conf.), Am. Assn. U. Women, Am. Civil Liberties Union, Audubon Soc., Nat. Wildlife Fedn., Wis. Hist. Soc., Altrusa (v.p. 1973—), Capital Community Citizens, Madison Area Library Council. Presbyn. Home: 1347 N Wingra Dr Madison WI 53715 Office: 610 Langdon St Madison WI 53706

FULLER, RUTH L. (MRS. COURTNEY CALLENDER), physician; b. Anderson, S.C., Apr. 26, 1937; d. Samuel L. and Anne (Morgan) Fuller; B.S. magna cum laude, Howard U., 1957; M.D., State U. N.Y., 1961; m. Courtney Callender, June 17, 1961. Intern, Bklyn. Hosp., 1961-62; resident Kings County Hosp. Center, Bklyn., 1962-64, fellow child psychiatry, 1964-66; student, div. psychoanalytic edn. State U. N.Y. Downstate Med. Center, N.Y.C., 1965—; adj. in psychiatry Bronx Lebanon Hosp. Center, 1966; asst. adj. in pediatrics Beth Israel Med. Center, N.Y.C., 1967-68; staff psychiatrist James Weldon Johnson Mental Health Clinic, N.Y.C., 1966-69, psychiat. dir., 1969—. Diplomate Am. Bd. Psychiatry and Neurology. Mem. Am. Psychiat. Assn., N.Y. Council Child Psychiatry, A.M.A., Mental Health Assn. N.Y. and Bronx Counties, N.Y. Acad. Scis., Howard U. Alumni Assn., Esalen Inst., Phi Beta Kappa (nat. candidates council). Home: 311 Convent Av New York City NY 10031

FULLER, SANDRA KAY, assn. exec.; b. Riverdale, Md., May 18, 1945; d. John Nelson and Lana Louise (Renner) Fuller; B.A., U. Md., 1967, postgrad., 1967-69. Resident counselor Shepherd Coll., 1968-69; program dir. YMCA Met. Washington, 1969-71, camp dir., 1971-72, acting exec. dir., program coordinator and camp, 1973; camp dir. YMCA Greater N.Y., 1972. Mem. Community Welfare Council, 1969-73; organizer No. Va. Student Leadership Conf., 1971, No. Va. Day Camp Coalition, 1970-72; instr. A.R.C., 1969-73. Mem. Am. Camping Assn. (dir.), Assn. Profl. Dirs. Methodist.

FULLER, SUE, artist; b. Pitts.; d. Samuel Leslie and Carrie (Cassedy) Fuller; B.A., Carnegie Inst. Tech., 1936; M.A., Columbia, 1939. One man shows at Bertha Schaefer Gallery, McNay Art Inst., San Antonio, Norfolk Mus. Currier Gallery, Corcoran Gallery, Smithsonian Instn., others; exhibited in group shows at Aldrich Mus., Corcoran Gallery, Phila., Mus., Whitney Mus., Bklyn. Mus., others; represented in permanent collections at Addison Gallery Am. Art, Larry Aldrich Mus., Chgo. Art Inst., Des Moines Art Center, Ford Found., Met. Mus., Whitney Mus. Am. Art, Tate Gallery London, Library of Congress, others. Tchr., Pratt Inst., Bklyn., 1964-65. Louis Comfort Tiffany fellow, 1948; John Simon Guggenheim fellow, 1949; Nat. Inst. Arts and Letters grantee, 1950; Eliot Pratt Found. fellow, 1966-68; Mark Rothko Found. grantee, 1973. Producer movie String Composition, 1970. Patentee embedded string compositions. Home: 44 E 63d St New York City NY 10021 Office: Chalette Internat 9 E 88th St New York City NY 10028

FULLERTON, DONNA MAE VOHLKEN (MRS. DONALD T. FULLERTON), owner bookstore; b. Freeport, Ill., Nov. 3, 1931; d. John Henry and Estella Mae (Rawleigh) Vohlken; B.S., U. Wis., 1953; m. Donald T. Fullerton, Aug. 22, 1953; children—Douglas, Stuart, Ann. Staff occupational therapist St. Luke's Hosp., Chgo., 1954-55; staff occupational therapist Neuropsychiat. Inst., U. Ill. Hosps., Chgo., 1955-56, supr. psychiat. occupational therapy dept., 1956-57; psychiat. occupational therapist St. Joseph's Hosp., Marshfield, Wis., 1967-68; owner Brass Lantern Bookshop, Marshfield, 1973—. Pres., Marshfield Art Com., 1966-67; mem. Gov.'s Task Force on No-Fault Ins., 1972-73. Mem. Am. Occupational Therapy Assn., League Women Voters (pres. mems.-at-large unit 1973-74). Democrat. Mem. Soc. of Friends. Home: 917 Martin Dr Marshfield WI 54449 Office: 338 S Central St Marshfield WI 54449

FULLERTON, GAIL JACKSON (MRS. STANLEY JAMES FULLERTON), sociologist; b. Lincoln, Neb., Apr. 29, 1927; d. Earl Warren and Gladys (Marshall) Jackson; B.A., U. Neb., 1949, M.A., 1950; Ph.D., U. Ore., 1954; m. Snell Putney, July 28, 1950 (div. 1966); children—Gregory S., Cindy Gail; m. 2d, Stanley James Fullerton, Mar. 20, 1967. Lectr. sociology Drake U., Des Moines, 1955-57; asst. prof. sociology Fla. State U. at Tallahassee, 1957-60; asso. prof. sociology San Jose (Cal.) State Coll., 1963-72; prof. sociology San Jose (Cal.) State U., 1972, dean grad. studies and research, 1972—. Mem. Am., Pacific sociol. assns., A.A.A.S., Phi Beta Kappa. Author: (with Snell Putney) Normal Neurosis, 1964, The Adjusted American, 1966; Survival in Marriage, 1972. Home: 226 Wave Crest Av Santa Cruz CA 95060 Office: Grad Studies and Research San Jose State University San Jose CA 95192

FULLMER, JUNE ZIMMERMAN (MRS. PAUL PERSHING FULLMER), educator; b. Peoria, Ill., Dec. 16, 1920; d. George Joseph and Ella Otilla (Kahnt) Zimmerman; B.S., Ill. Inst. Tech., 1943, M.S., 1945; Ph.D., Bryn Mawr Coll., 1948; postgrad. Oxford U., 1948-49; m. Paul Pershing Fullmer, June 6, 1953. Asst. prof. chemistry Chatham Coll., 1949-53; asso. prof. chemistry, head dept. Newcomb Coll., Tulane U., 1955-64; asso. prof. Ohio State U., Columbus, 1966-71, prof. history of sci., 1971—; cons. Battelle Meml. Inst., 1971-73. Guggenheim Found. fellow, 1963-64, Am. Council Learned Socs. fellow, 1960-61, Am. Assn. U. Women fellow, 1949-50. Fellow A.A.A.S.; mem. Am. Chem. Soc. (chmn. div. history chemistry 1970-71), History Sci. Soc., Sigma Xi, Phi Beta Kappa (hon.). Author: Sir Humphry Davy's Published Works, 1969, 70. Home: 781 Latham Ct Columbus OH 43214

FULTON, MARY ANN, lawyer, state ofcl.; b. Schenectady, Jan. 3, 1915; d. Gustav and Julia (Petras) Foltanovich; B.A., Wayne U., 1937, J.D., 1959. Admitted to Mich. bar, 1960; practiced in Detroit, 1960-68; asso. George H. Lovequest & William J. Enright, Detroit, 1960-66; atty. Wayne County Neighborhood Legal Services, Detroit, 1968-70; referee Mich. Employment Security Commn., Detroit, 1970—. Instr. Wayne County Community Coll., 1969-71. Mem. Women Lawyers Assn. of Mich. (pres. 1968-69), State Bar of Mich., Am. Numismatic Assn., Friends of Modern Art, Law Study Soc., Pro Musica, Wayne Law Alumni, Phi Alpha Delta. Club: Yachts Women. Home: 2231 Hewitt Av Hamtramck MI 48212 Office: Michigan Employment Security Commission 7310 Woodward Detroit MI 48202

FULTON, VIRGINIA KATHLEEN (MRS. RICHARD FULTON), govt. ofcl., civic worker; b. Webb City, Okla., Feb. 9, 1926; d. Roy Haskell and Ova (Henry) Nunley; B.B.A., North Tex. State U., 1948; m. Richard Lafayette Fulton, July 23, 1949 (dec. Mar. 1970); children—Richard Lafayette, II, Miles Dyer. Sec., spl. edn. div. Tex. Edn. Agy., Austin, 1948-52; sec. Marshall-Wells Co., Billings, Mont., 1952, Bur. Indian Affairs, Billings, 1953-54, St. Alexius Sch. Nursing, Bismarck, N.D., 1954-55, La Habana Corp., Bismarck, 1957-58; sec. tchr. edn. div. North Tex. State U., Denton, 1962; adminstrv. sec. State Planning and Community Affairs Agy., State of Ida., Boise, 1971-73; sr. sec. developmental disabilities sect. Ida. Dept. Environmental and Community Services, 1974—. State pres. League Women Voters N.D., 1969-70, state legis. chmn., lobbyist, 1968-69, pres., Bismarck, 1967-69, del. to nat. conv., 1968, to nat. council, 1969, to regional structures and procedures meeting, 1969; del. to N.D. Gov.'s Conf. on Environment, 1970; mem. N.D. Citizen's Com. for Jud. Improvement, 1966, 68; mem. state com. for Nat. Library Week 1970; treas. Will-Moore Sch. P.T.A., Bismarck, 1965-67; den mother Cub Scouts, 1964-68; pres., Bismarck Petroleum Wives, 1959-60; co-chmn. League Women Voters U.S. 50th anniversary ceremony, 1969. Episcopalian (bd. dirs. women 1968-70). Home: 4024 Mountain View Dr Boise ID 83704

FUNK, ELAINE MYRL BAYER (MRS. SHERMAN MAXWELL FUNK), educator, psychodramatist; b. Boston, Mar. 6, 1921; d. Abraham H. and Miriam (Opp) Bayer; B.S., N.Y. U., 1949; postgrad. Cath. U., 1960-62; M.A., U. Md., 1968; postgrad. Moreno Inst. Psychodrama, 1973-74; m. Sherman Maxwell Funk, Mar. 6, 1953;

children—Katherine Sara, Bernard Eugene. Co-founder Greenwich Mews Theater, N.Y.C., 1946-49; co-founder, dir. Washington Theater Club, Washington, 1958-74; teaching asst. Cath. U., Washington, 1960-62; teaching asst. U. Md., 1965-68, instr., 1967-68; asst. prof. Bowie (Md.) State Coll., 1968—, chmn. speech and theatre dept., 1970—. Theatrical dir. Woodstock Confidential, N.Y.C., 1957, Present Laughter, Tucson, 1958, Madwoman of Chailot, Washington, 1959, Dark of the Moon, 1964, The Crucible, 1968, Gammer Gurton's Needle, 1969, Black Sabbath, 1970, Goin' A Buffalo, 1972; actress The Guardsman, N.Y.C., 1947, Antigone, 1948, Come of Age, 1949, Thunder Rock, Tuscon, 1957, Mattie, the Moron and the Madonna, Washington, 1965. Chmn., Bowie Arts Council, 1963-64; theater cons. City of Bowie, 1965-70; judge State of Md. Drama Festival, 1971-73, Prince Georges County Play Contest, 1968-71; chmn. bd. Bowie Area Com. on Higher Edn., 1962-64. Served with WAC, 1942-45. Named Woman of Achievement, Bus. and Profl. Women's Assn., Bowie, 1970; recipient certificate of achievement Prince George County, 1969. Mem. Am. Theatre Assn., Am. Assn. U. Profs. Democrat. Home: 12416 Stafford Land Bowie MD 20715

FUNK, GRACE EMMALINE TOMLINSON (MRS. JACOB ABRAM FUNK), librarian; b. Saskatoon, Sask., Can., Apr. 20, 1924; d. George James and Edna Martha (Davis) Tomlinson; B.A., U. Sask., 1945; certificate in edn. U. Alta., 1946; B.L.S. (Canadian Library Assn. scholar, B.C. Tchrs. Fedn. scholar), U. B.C., 1967; m. Jacob Abram Funk, July 23, 1945; children—Michael, Jonathan, David. Tchr., Agassiz (B.C.) High Sch., 1947-49, Armstrong (B.C.) High Sch., 1949-50; tchr., librarian Enderby (B.C.) High Sch., 1957-60, Rutland (B.C.) High Sch., 1960-66; elementary sch. librarian South Rutland, B.C., 1967-69, Vernon, B.C., 1969-71, Harwood Demonstration Sch., Vernon, 1971—. Mem. B.C. Sch. Librarians Assn. (sec. 1967-68, editor 1968-69), Okanaga Valley Tchrs. Assn., Delta Kappa Gamma. Home: Rural Route 1 Lumby BC VOE 2GO Canada Office: 2206 45th Av Vernon BC V1T 3M8 Canada

FUNK, HELEN BEATRICE, microbiologist, educator; b. Waverly, Ia., May 23, 1913; d. Joseph Oliver and Maude M. (Stover) Funk; B.A., Ia. State Tchrs. Coll., 1935; M.S. (U. fellow), U. Ia., 1936; Ph.D. (Bacteriol. fellow), U. Wis., 1955. Tchr. secondary sch., Washington, Ill., 1936-42; instr. Milw.-Downer Coll., 1943-46; asst. prof. Barnard Coll., also Columbia U., 1950-56; asso. prof. Goucher Coll., Balt., 1956-61, prof. biol. scis., 1962—. Mem. steering com. Gifted Children's Sci. Seminars, 1959-68. Mem. Am. Soc. for Microbiology (pres. Md. br. 1965-66), Acad. for Microbiology, Soc. Protozoologists, A.A.A.S., Soc. Gen. Microbiology (Brit.). Author: (with Ann M. Lacey) From One Cell To Many, 1966. Contbr. articles to profl. jours. Research on vitamin metabolism of micro-organisms, 1950—. Address: Goucher College Baltimore MD 21204

FUNK, RUTH A. JOHNSON (MRS. FRANK E. FUNK), psychologist; b. Stratford, Conn., Oct. 6, 1927; d. Ambrose A. and Flora (Dufour) Johnson; A.B. magna cum laude, Syracuse U., 1947, M.A., 1951; Ph.D., Purdue U., 1955; m. Frank E. Funk, May 10, 1949; children—Steven Eric, Karen Christine. Ednl. counselor and psychometrist Purdue U., 1952-54; instr., dir. Purdue Reading Clinic, 1954-56; research asso., prin. investigator Syracuse U. Spl. Edn. Dept., 1957-58; pvt. practice, 1959—; cons. clin. psychologist Oneida County Mental Health Bds., 1960—, exec. dir. Mental Health Assn., 1965-67; chief psychologist Robert Soule Clinic, Syracuse, 1968—; cons. Crouse-Irving Detoxication Unit. Past v.p. Wagon Wheel, Limestone Theatre. Recipient Citation Mental Health Assn., 1968, Colgate U. ann. civic award, 1973. Mem. Mental Health Assn. (v.p., program chmn. 1968—), Am., N.Y. (sec. 1969-70), Syracuse (past sec.) psychol. assns., N.Y. State Assn. Mental Health (profl. adv. com.). Clubs: University Women. Author articles in field and musical plays. Author, composer They'd Rather Be Right, 1968; composer Littlest Angel, 1970. Address: 4967 Fayetteville Rd Manlius NY 13104

FURBERSHAW, MARY LOUISE, editor; b. Chgo., July 27, 1917; d. Walter L. and Georgia Frances (Schmitt) Furbershaw; student Northwestern U., 1936, St. Mary's Coll., 1937-38. Expediter Brit. Army staff, Washington, 1941-42; mem. Truman Com. staff, Washington, 1942-43; asst. to dir. BBC field office, Chgo., 1943-46; asst. to v.p. J. Walter Thompson Co., Chgo., 1946-51; midwest editor The Bride's Mag., Conde Nast. Publs., Chgo., 1951-65; free lance writer, editor, Chgo., 1965-68; mng. editor, pub. relations exec. Rand McNally & Co., Skokie, Ill., 1968—. Bd. dirs. Lyric Guild of Evanston, Ill. Mem. Women in Communications (dir. North Shore chpt. 1973—), Fashion Group of Chgo. (treas. 1961-62), English-Speaking Union, Chgo. Women in Publishing. Club: North Shore Public Relations. Home: 650 Michigan Av Evanston IL 60202 Office: 8255 Central Park Av Skokie IL 60076

FURCOLO, LUCY CARRA (MRS. FOSTER FURCOLO), judge; b. Springfield, Mass.; d. Ernest and Tecla (Cipriani) Carra; J.D., New Eng. Sch. Law, 1964; m. Foster Furcolo, Oct. 16, 1967. Secretarial positions with various pvt. firms, 1942-56; exec. asst. Office of Gov. Mass., Boston, 1957-60; pub. utilities commr. State of Mass., 1960-67, mass transp. commr., 1960-64; admitted to Mass. bar, 1964; individual practice law, Springfield, Boston, 1964-68; fed. adminstrv. law judge Dept. Health, Edn. and Welfare, Boston, 1968—. Recipient Amos Taylor Scholarship award Calvin Coolidge Coll., 1964; Distinguished Alumni award Bay Path Jr. Coll., 1973. Mem. Mass. Assn. Women Lawyers, Phi Delta Delta. Home: 18 Lake Shore Dr Wayland MA 01778 Office: JFK Bldg Boston MA 02203

FURMAN, MARGRET LOUISA, univ. ofcl.; b. Bethesda, Md., Apr. 29, 1949; d. Robert Brooke and Eva Jane (Brown) Furman; student Coll. William and Mary, 1967-70, Ed.M., 1974; B.S., Va. Poly. Inst. and State U., 1971. Residence dir. Coll. William and Mary, Williamsburg, Va., 1971-73, dir. summer housing, 1973; asst. to vice chancellor for student affairs U. Mass., Boston, 1974—. Mem. Nat. Assn. Women Deans, Adminstrs. and Counselors, Am. Coll. Personnel Assn., Phi Mu. Roman Catholic (mem. parish bd. 1972-73). Home: 223 Beacon St #8 Boston MA 02116 Office: Harbor Campus U Mass Boston MA 02125

FURNESS, BETTY (MRS. LESLIE MIDGLEY), journalist; b. N.Y.C., Jan. 3, 1916; d. George Choate and Florence (Sturtevant) Furness; student Brearly Sch., N.Y.C., Bennett Sch., Millbrook, N.Y.; m. John Waldo Green, Nov. 26, 1937 (div. Aug. 1943); 1 dau., Barbara Sturtevant; m. 2d, Hugh B. Ernst, Jr., Jan. 3, 1945 (dec. Apr. 1950); m. 3d, Leslie Midgley, Aug. 15, 1967. Motion picture actress, 1932-37, appearing in 35 pictures; appeared in stage plays Golden Boy, My Sister Eileen, Doughgirls; commls. for Westinghouse Corp., 1949-60; own TV shows include Penthouse Party, 1951, Success Story, 1951, Meet Betty Furness, 1953, At Your Beck and Call, 1961, Answering Service—WABC TV, 1962; with CBS radio, Dimensions of A Woman's World, 1962-67, Ask Betty Furness, 1962-67; spl. asst. to pres. for consumer affairs, 1967-69; chmn., exec. dir. N.Y. State Consumer Protection Bd., 1970-71; commr. N.Y.C. Dept. Consumer Affairs, 1973; consumer reporter WNBC-TV News Center, N.Y.C., 1974—. Mem. adv. council to Senate Subcom. on Consumer Affairs, 1970-72; bd. dirs. Consumers Union, 1969—; Common Cause, 1972—; columnist McCall's Mag., 1970, 72. Pres. N.Y. chpt. Acad. TV Arts and Scis., 1961-63. Address: Old Farm Lane Hartsdale NY 10530

FURR, ONETA ROBERTS, educator; b. Anson, Tex., May 24, 1914; d. Jessie J. and Molly (Brown) Roberts; B.S., McMurry Coll., 1937; M.S., N. Tex. State U., 1940, Ed.D. (Annie Webb Blanton scholar, Delta Gamma Gamma scholar), 1968; m. H. Bedford Furr, May 24, 1942. Faculty, Midwestern U., Wichita Falls, Tex., 1950—, asso. prof., 1958-68, prof., 1968—, also dir, early edn., 1968—. Cons. reading programs pub. schs., 1965—. Named Distinguished Alumnus N. Tex. State U., 1969. Mem. Internat. Reading Assn. (state orgn. chmn. 1960-67), Tex. Assn. Improvement Reading (IRA conf. recs. 1965, 66, 68, 71, 73, Book editor TAIR), Wichita Falls Area Reading Council (charter pres. 1959-61), Assn. Childhood Edn. (publicity com. 1965-67), Wichita Falls Kindergarten Assn., Delta Kappa Gamma, Kappa Delta Pi, Pi Lambda Theta. Home: 2615 Bretton St Wichita Falls TX 76308

FUSAN, REGINA ELIZABETH, sch. nursing dean; b. Etna, Pa., Nov. 6, 1920; d. John Ferdinand and Mary Elizabeth (Glasser) Fusan; B.S. in Nursing magna cum laude, Duquesne U., 1943; M.Ed., 1954; postgrad. Tchrs. Coll. Columbia, 1954. Instr. nursing, edn. dir. Montefiore Hosp. Sch. Nursing, Pitts., 1944-49, asso. dir. nursing service, 1949-51; mem. faculty Sch. Nursing Duquesne U., Pitts., 1951—, acting dean, 1962 dean, 1962—. Mem. adv. bd. John J. Kane Hosp., 1968—. Recipient Citizen of Week award radio sta. WJKF, 1951. Mem. Pa. League for Nursing (chmn. 1973—), Am. Nurses Assn., Am. Assn. Higher Edn.; Am. Assn. U. Adminstrs. Home: 67 Prospect St Pittsburgh PA 15223 Office: Sch Nursing Duquesne U Pittsburgh PA 15219

FUSARO, JANIECE ELAINE BARRE (MRS. RAMON M. FUSARO), librarian; b. Detroit, Feb. 7, 1925; d. William and Augusta Rose (Siebenbrunner) Barre; adopted d. Elizabeth Marie (Siebenbrunner) Moses; B.A., U. Minn., 1946, M.A., 1949, B.S. in L.S., 1953, Ph.D., 1968; postgrad. Middlebury Coll., 1949, Stephens Coll., 1968; m. Ramon M. Fusaro, Aug. 4, 1951; children—Lisa Ann, Toni Ann. Teaching asst. German dept. U. Minn., Mpls., 1947-50, acquisitions librarian U. Minn. Library, 1951-53; prof. German, Coll. St. Catherine, St. Paul, 1964-65; librarian Anoka-Ramsey Community Coll., Coon Rapids, Minn., 1965-69, 70-71; program dir. Minn. Higher Edn. Coordinating Commn., St. Paul, 1969-70; community faculty, student adviser Minn. Met. State Coll., St. Paul, 1971—; library cons. Golden Valley Luth. Coll., Minn., 1968, Nat. Coll. Bus., Grand Rapids, S.D., 1972. Dir. statewide library survey Minn. Higher Edn. Coordinating Commn., 1970; mem. Minn. Planning Com. on Library Automation, 1971, Minn. Adv. Com. on Inter-library Cooperation, 1971. Bd. dirs. Riverside Center, Mpls., 1970-74. Named Minn. Librarian of Yr., Minn. Library Assn., 1969. Mem. Minn. Library Assn. (life), A.L.A. (regional chmn. 1968-71), Alpha Lambda Psi. Contbr. articles to profl. jours. Home: 3108 36th Av NE Minneapolis MN 55418 Office: LL90 Metro 7th and Robert St St Paul MN 55101

FUSON, EDNA CATHERINE PHILLIPS (MRS. VERNON RAY FUSON), physician; b. Grayson, Ky., Dec. 28, 1935; d. William Stephen and Edna (Jacobs) Phillips; B.A., Transylvania Coll., 1958; M.D. (NSF grantee), U. Louisville, 1966; m. Vernon Ray Fuson, Aug. 4, 1963. Tchr. sci. pub. schs., Grayson and Bardstown, Ky., 1958-62; intern St. Joseph's Infirmary, Louisville, 1966-67, resident pediatrics, 1967-68; resident pediatrics Duvall Med. Center, Jacksonville, Fla., 1968-69; practice medicine specializing in pediatrics, Winfield, Ala., 1969—. Diplomate Am. Bd. Pediatrics. Fellow Royal Soc. Health; mem. A.M.A., Ala. Med. Soc., Am. Acad. Family Physicians, Order Ky. Cols., Phi Mu. Address: PO Box 112 Jacksonville AL 36265

FUTCH, GRACE BONNER, realtor; b. Manchester, Ga., Sept. 24, 1924; d. Warner Augdon and Johnnye (Brown) Bonner; student Ga. State Coll. for Women, 1941-43, Woodrow Wilson Coll., 1954-55; div.; children—Lynda (Mrs. Andrew Lincoln Creed), Carol Marie. With C.E., U.S. Army, Atlanta, 1943-45, U.S. Civil Service Commn., Atlanta, 1950-52, 3d Army Hdqrs., Atlanta, 1954-55; pres. Realty Center, Inc., Pensacola, Fla., 1960—, Pensacola Beach Realty, Inc. (Fla.), 1972—, N.W. Fla. Investments, Pensacola, 1968—; sec. TOP, Inc., Pensacola, 1965—; sec., dir. Sabine Mortgage & Investment Co., 1972—. Bd. dirs. United Cerebral Palsy N.W. Fla., 1968—, 2d v.p. 1969-70, mem. exec. bd., 1969—, pres. bd. dirs., 1971-72, state pres. 1973-74). Mem. Pensacola Bd. Realtors, Fla. Assn. Realtors, Nat. Assn. Real Estate Bds., Nat. Inst. Real Estate Brokers, Women's Council Realtors (v.p. 1973). Baptist. Club: Zonta (dir. 1964—, pres.-elect 1972—). Home: 204 Sabine Dr Pensacola Beach FL 32561 Office: 2901 N 12th Av Pensacola FL 32503

FUTCH, KATHARINE ANNE FARBER (MRS. GEORGE BLOXHAM FUTCH), civic worker; b. Marshalltown, Ia.; d. Edwin Nott and Cornelia (Coleman) Farber; B.A., Drake U., 1940; m. George Bloxham Futch, Dec. 31, 1960. Sec.-clk. U.S. Army, Des Moines, 1941-42; med. sec., receptionist for dr., Ft. Lauderdale, Fla., 1943-45; A.R.C. aide Broward Gen. Hosp., Ft. Lauderdale, 1942, aide, 1943; asst. pub. relations office Holy Cross Hosp., Ft. Lauderdale, 1968-71; advt. mgr. Broward County Grid Iron Shows, 1968-72, 74. Vol., Holy Cross Hosp., Ft. Lauderdale, 1953-55; den mother Cub Scouts, 1952-54, 56-62; chmn. A.R.C. residential fund raising, Ft. Lauderdale, 1951-52; sr. pres. Children Am. Revolution, Ft. Lauderdale, 1952-54, 67-68, Fla. chmn. pub. relations, 1962-69, sr. treas., 1964-68; mem. D.A.R., 1941—, chpt. treas., 1958-60, chpt. vice regent, 1960-62, regent, 1962-64, Fla. chmn. Constn. Week com., 1964-66, dist. sec., 1964-66, dist.-vice dir., 1966-68, dir., 1968-70, sec. Fla. chpt. Regents Club, 1963-64, treas., 1964-66, 72, pres., 1973-74, Am. Heritage chmn., 1968-71, dist. VIII dir., Fla. state soc. 1970-72; mem. Ft. Lauderdale Mus., 1967-71, Ft. Lauderdale Book-fellows, 1954-72; charter mem. Broward County Women's chpt. Freedoms Found., 1973; mem. West Broward Symphony Guild, 1973—, Ft. Lauderdale Hist. Soc. Recipient various awards for work with D.A.R., other orgns. Mem. Ft. Lauderdale Panhellenic Assn. (2d v.p. 1959-60), Kappa Kappa Gamma (alumna assn. pres. 1947-48), Theta Sigma Phi (sec. 1960-62, v.p. 1962-66), Psi Chi. Republican. Presbyn. Clubs: Ft. Lauderdale Metropolitan Dinner (charter), Coral Ridge Yacht. Home: 4802 NW 27th Terrace Tamarac Lakes Fort Lauderdale FL 33309

FUTTERMAN, ENID SUSAN (MRS. ALAN KUPCHICK), advt. co. exec.; b. Bklyn., Oct. 28, 1943; d. Samuel and Miriam (Gutman) Futterman; A.B., Douglass Coll., 1964; m. Alan Kupchick, May 14, 1971. Copywriter, Grey Advt. Co., N.Y.C., 1964—, v.p., 1970—. Recipient Silver Lion, Cannes Film Festival, 19—, Clio award Am. Tv Commercials Festival, 1973, 74, Andy award Advt. Club N.Y., 1973, 74. Mem. A.S.A.C.P., Copy Club N.Y. Home: 230 E 48th St New York City NY 10017 Office: 777 3rd Av New York City NY 10017

GABEL, EMMA MARGARET, librarian; b. Perkasie, Pa., Aug. 10, 1928; d. William U. and Mary A. (Kramer) Gabel; B.S., Kutztown State Coll., 1950; M.S., Syracuse U., 1957; postgrad. Temple U., 1951-52, Indiana U. of Pa., 1964-65. Librarian, Morrisville (Pa.) Jr. Sr. High Sch., 1950-52; asst. librarian Susquehanna U., Selinsgrove, Pa., 1952-56; asst. librarian Indiana U. of Pa., 1956-66; head cataloger, asst. to dir. Elizabethtown (Pa.) Coll., 1966—. Pres. Woman's Aux. Susquehanna U., 1951-52. Mem. Am., Pa., Lancaster County library assns., Am. Assn. Univ. Profs., Am. Assn. Higher Edn., Elizabeth Hughes Soc., Delta Kappa Gamma, Beta Phi Mu, Sigma Alpha Iota. Home: 531 E Hummelstown St Elizabethtown PA 17022

GABER, JOANNE GARTEN, clin. psychologist; b. N.Y.C.; d. Stanley and Hannah Rosalind (Frank) Garten; B.S. in Edn., Adelphi Coll., 1949; M.A. in Ednl. Psychology, Tchrs. Coll., Columbia, 1950, profl. diploma, 1969; m. Morton Gaber, Aug. 20, 1950 (div.); 1 dau., Evelyn Jean. Ednl. therapist, 1963-67; psychology intern North Jersey Tng. Sch., Totowa, N.J., 1967-68, clin. psychologist, 1969—; psychology intern Middlesex County Mental Health Clinic, 1968-69; adj. clin. psychologist N.J. Coll. Medicine and Dentistry, Jersey City, 1971—. Ednl. therapist Shield of David Inst., Maimonides Inst. for Exceptional Children, 1963-67. Program dir. Play Schs. Assn., 1959, 60. Mem. Am., N.J. psychol. assns., N.J. Assn. for Brain Injured Children, Assn. for Help Retarded Children, Am. Assn. on Mental Deficiency. Home: 28 Highland Cross Rutherford NJ 07070 Office: NJ Tng Sch PO Box 169 Totowa NJ 07511

GABLE, MARTHA ANNE, educator; b. Phila.; d. James F. and Stella (Gingrich) Gable; B.E., Ind. U., 1942; M.Ed., Temple U., 1935. Tchr. Phila. pub. schs., 1926-41, asst. dir. phys. and health edn., Phila., 1942-48, asst. dir. sch. and community relations, 1948-56, dir. radio-TV edn., 1955-66, dir. instrnl. materials, 1966-68; editor Am. Assn. Sch. Adminstrs., 1968-73; cons. ednl. tech., 1973—. Mem. Gov.'s Adv. Commn. Edn., Pa., 1956-58; mem. White House Conf. Edn., 1955; cons. Joint Council Ednl. TV, Washington. Del. Internat. Conf. Ednl. TV, London, 1954; judge Olympic Games, London, 1948, Helsinki, 1952, Melbourne, 1956, Rome, 1960, Tokyo, Japan, 1964. Recipient Temple U. Alumni award, 1964. Mem. Fedn. Women's Clubs (dir. Phila.), Phila. Pub. Relations Assn. (sec.), Am. Women in Radio and TV, N.E.A., Pub. Relations Soc. Am., TV-Radio Advt. Club, Am. Assn. U. Women, Nat. Assn. Edn. Broadcasters, Am. Assn. Sch. Adminstrs., Am. Newspaper Womens Clubs, Adminstrv. Women in Edn. (council), Ednl. Press Assn. Am., Am. Women in Communications. Presbyn. Club: Nat. Press (Washington). Home: 2601 Pkwy Philadelphia PA 19130

GABOR, JEANNE ELIZABETH ZASADIL, charitable fund pub. relations exec.; b. Oak Park, Ill., Dec. 28, 1940; d. Rudolph John and Elizabeth (Voldrich) Zasadil; A.A., Morton Coll., 1960; B.S. cum laude, U. Ill., 1962; m. Richard George Gabor, July 28, 1962 (div. June 1973). Research trainee Wade Advt., Inc., Chgo., 1962-63; asst. editor Food Bus. mag., Chgo., 1964; feature, news editor Vend Mag., Chgo., 1965-67; account exec. Theodore R. Sills, Inc., Chgo., 1967-69; media dir. Community Fund Chgo./Crusade of Mercy, Chgo., 1969—. Recipient Shirley Kreasan Strout award U. Ill., 1961; named Outstanding Woman Grad., Coll. Journalism and Communications, 1962. Mem. Chgo. Assn. Bus. Communicators (pres. 1972, dir.), Pub. Relations Soc. Am., Publicity Club Chgo., Welfare Pub. Relations Forum (dir.), Women in Communications, Instl. Food Editors Conf. (dir. 1969), Restaurant Womens Club Chgo. (pres. elect 1969), Kappa Alpha Theta, Phi Theta Kappa. Home: 175 E Delaware Pl Chicago IL 60611 Office: 72 W Adams St Chicago IL 60603

GABRIEL, ASTERIA MASANGKAY, pediatrician; b. Manila, Philippines, May 20, 1933; d. Juan Reyes and Timotea Vergel Cruz (Masangkay) Gabriel; A.A., U. Santo Tomas, 1951, M.D., 1956. Came to U.S. 1963. Intern, Lowell (Mass.) Gen. Hosp., 1956-57; resident in pediatrics Homer G. Phillips Hosp., St. Louis, 1957-59; resident in psychiatry Harlem Valley State Hosp., Wingdale, N.Y., 1959-61; practice medicine specializing in pediatrics, Paranaque, Rizal, Philippines, 1961-63; vis. pediatrician St. Luke's Hosp., Quezon City, Philippines, 1961-63; staff physician Pineland Hosp. and Tng. Center, Pownal, Me., 1963-65; prin. physician Paul A. Dever State Sch., Taunton, Mass., 1965-68; med. specialist Suffolk Developmental Center, Melville, N.Y., 1968-70; chief of pediatric services, 1970—. Mem. Barrio Council, DonGalo Paranaque, 1962-63. Diplomate Am. Bd. Pediatrics. Fellow Am. Acad. Pediatrics; mem. Am. Assn. Mental Deficiency, Am., N.Y. pub. health assns., Nat. Assn. Residents and Interns. Home: 212 Old South Path Melville NY 11746 Office: Box 788 Melville NY 11746

GABRIEL, ETHEL MARY DE NAGY (MRS. GUSTAVE GABRIEL), record album producer; b. Milmont Park, Pa., Nov. 16, 1921; b. Karoly and Margaret (Horvath) De Nagy; student Temple U., 1939-40, Columbia, 1945, 48; m. Gustave Gabriel, Aug. 10, 1958 (dec. July 1973). Owner dance band EN and Her Royal Men, Pa., 1934-40; trombonist Phila. Women's Symphony Orch., 1939-40; co-owner, tchr. Nagy Ceramic and Liberal Arts Sch., N.Y.C., Pa., 1948-52; artist, repertoire producer RCA record div., 1957—, mem. staff, 1940—. Mem. Nat. Acad. Rec. Arts and Scis., Advt. Women N.Y., Country Music Assn., U.S. Power Squadron Aux. Home: 425 Weaver St Larchmont NY 10538 Office: 1133 Av of Americas New York City NY 10036

GABRIEL, PAT (MRS. GENE F. GABRIEL), club woman; b. Rock Island, Ill., May 2, 1922 d. Max Voyle and Faye (Crist) Wolfe; grad. Canterbury Sch. Fine Arts, 1939; m. Gene Floyd Gabriel, Mar. 8, 1941; 1 dau., Patricia Gene. Soc. columnist Coral Gables Times-Guide, now drama critic. Drama chmn. Morgan Park Jr. Woman's Club, Chgo., 1952-54, 3d Dist. Jrs., 1952-54; children's theatre dir. Beverly Hills Jr. Woman's Club, Chgo., 1954. Dist. coordinator Mothers March of Dimes Chgo., 1952-55, Coral Gables, Fla., 1956-61; publicity chmn. woman's com., pres. woman's com. Variety Children's Hosp.; 2d v.p. women's com. Project Hope; women's campaign mgr. Senator Doyle Carlton, Jr. for Gov., Coral Gables, 1960; pres. Dade County com. Project Hope, 1973-74. Permanent chmn. Coral Gables com. Performing and Allied Arts. Mem. D.A.R. (rec. sec. 1962-64), Fla. Fedn. Women's Clubs (drama co-chmn. 1960-62), Theater Arts League (pres.). Methodist. Club: Coral Gables Senior Women's (1st v.p. 1962-64, pres. 1964-66). Home: 3915 Monserrate St Coral Gables FL 33134

GABRIEL, ROSALINDA VILLARAMA (MRS. RUBEN TAN ONG), psychiatrist; b. Manila, Philippines, Oct. 12, 1939; d. Antonio Paulino and Emerenciana (Villarama) Gabriel; A.A., Far Eastern U., 1955-57, M.D., 1962; m. Ruben Tan Ong, May 15, 1965; children—Rowena Marie, Ryan Anthony. Came to U.S., 1963. Intern, Overlook Hosp., Summit, N.J., 1963-64; resident in pediatrics Newark Beth Israel Hosp., 1964-65, Babies Hosp., Newark, 1965-66; med.-surg. physician Trenton (N.J.) Psychiat. Hosp., 1966-69, resident psychiatry and neurology, 1969-73, asso. dir. tng., 1973—. Home: Station A Trenton NJ 08625 Office: Trenton Psychiat Hosp Trenton NJ 08625

GABRIELSON, ROSAMOND CHRISTINE, nursing adminstr.; b. Los Angeles, Oct. 8, 1925; d. Charles William and Catherine Mary (MacLennan) G.; R.N., Hotel Dieu Sch. Nursing, El Paso, Tex., 1946; B.S. in Psychology, Ariz. State U., 1953, M.A. in Guidance and Counseling, 1958. Staff nurse Copper Queen Hosp., Bisbee, Ariz., 1946-48; nurse pvt. physician, Phoenix, 1948-50; staff nurse VA Hosp., Whipple, Ariz., 1950-51; charge nurse Good Samaritan Hosp., Phoenix, 1951-53, supr., clin. instr., 1953-55, asst. dir. nursing service, 1955-57, asso. dir., 1957-58, dir. nursing service, 1958-65, exec. dir., 1965-71, asso. adminstr. nursing dept., 1972—; participant, speaker numerous workshops; lectr. in field. Mem. health adv. com. Community Council, Phoenix, 1963-64; mem. Pres.'s Health Services Industry Com., 1971-73. Bd. dirs. Vis. Nurse Service, Phoenix, 1963-68, Maricopa County (Ariz.) Council Alcoholism. Mem. Ariz. League Nursing (pres. 1959-60), Ariz. State (treas. dist. 1959-60, pres. 1960-62; state pres. 1965-69), Am. (treas. 1970-72, pres. 1972—) nurses assns., Ariz. Hosp. Assn. (mem. personnel adminstrn. com. 1964-65), Ariz. Bd. Nursing, U. Ariz. Alumnae Assn. (Distinguished Citizen award 1973). Home: 3021 E Whitton St Phoenix AZ 85016 Office: 1033 E McDowell Rd Phoenix AZ 85007

GABRYS, MARY JANE WNUK (MRS. EDWARD WILLIAM GABRYS), newspaperwoman; b. Oil City, Pa., Apr. 16, 1928; d. Vincent Valentine and Mary Cecelia (Malek) Wnuk; student U. Pitts., 1947-49, Western Res. U., 1946-47; m. Edward William Gabrys, July 29, 1950; children—Edward William II, Mary Rebecca. Women's editor News-Herald, Franklin, Pa., 1965—. Press chmn. Franklin Neighborhood council Girl Scouts U.S.A., 1970-72, Verango County Heart Fund, 1971-72. Bd. dirs. Franklin Hosp. Aux., 1963-66. Mem. Pa. Women's Press Assn. (dir.) Franklin Bus. and Profl. Women's Club (v.p. 1970-72), Venango County League Women Voters (charter, chmn. state legislative com.), Catholic Daus. Am. (vice regent Franklin ct. 1958-60). Republican. Roman Catholic. Home: 1336 Otter St Franklin PA 16323 Office: 631 12th St Franklin PA 16323

GADINSKY, MARILYN CLARE LANE (MRS. ED GADINSKY), writer; b. Chgo.; d. Wallace Fredrich and Evelyn Marcele (Winters) Hurter; student U. Miami, 1963; m. S.R. Lane (div. 1968); 1 son, Glenn Edward; m. 2d, Ed Gadinsky, Mar. 9, 1969; stepchildren—Pamela, Brian, Seth. Reporter, photographer Miami News, 1960-66; dir. pub. relations E.J. Scheaffer Advt. Agy., Miami, Fla., 1966-69; free lance writer Miami (Fla.) Herald, 1970—, Nat. Enquirer, 1973—, House and Garden, 1972—. Recipient 6 awards for excellence for work with Miami News. Mem. Women in Communications. Home and office: 5325 Pine Tree Dr Miami Beach FL 33140

GAFFNEY, DOLORES THERESE FITZGERALD, hosp. adminstr.; b. N.Y.C., Sept. 12, 1928; d. John Joseph and Catherine Elizabeth (Cullen) Fitzgerald; student Community Coll.; m. James Francis Gaffney, Oct. 24, 1959; 1 dau., Catherine Regina. Asst. adminstr. Midwood Hosp., Bklyn., 1956-70, adminstr., 1970—. Home: 1535 E 14th St Brooklyn NY 11230 Office: 19 Winthrop St Brooklyn NY 11225

GAFFNEY, ELEANOR AGNES, nurse, educator; b. Lowell, Mass., Apr. 16, 1912; d. James T. and Mary (Deignan) Gaffney; R.N., Tewksbury Hosp., 1934; B.S. in Nursing Edn., Boston U., 1952, M.S. in Nursing Adminstrn., 1957. Nurse Providence Lying-In Hosp., 1934-35; head nurse Tewksbury State Hosp., 1935-42, supr.-instr., 1942-46, asst. prin. sch. nursing, 1946-47, prin., 1947-56, dr. nurses, 1956-59; dir. nursing Lemuel Shattuck Hosp., Boston, 1959-72; adminstr. coordinated home health care Mercy Hosp., Portland, Me., 1973—. asst. prof. clin. nursing Boston U., 1964-72. Chmn. Mass. Bd. Registration in Nursing, 1957-71; mem. Pres. Kennedy's Cons. Com. on Nursing, 1962, Mass. Med., Dental and Nursing Scholarship Bd., 1957-66, Gov.'s Recruitment Com. on Nursing, 1967-68; Gov.'s Standing Com. on Nursing, 1968-72; adv. council Shephard Gill Sch. of Mass. Gen. Hosp., 1970-72; adv. bd. Mental Health After Care program, Portland, 1974—. Bd. dirs. Nat. Council Women U.S.; bd. dirs., health com. United Community Service Greater Boston; bd. dirs. Pine Tree Assn. Community Health Agys. Eleanor A. Gaffney Scholarship Fund established at Laboure Jr. Coll., 1972. Mem. Me. Nurses Assn. (legislative com. 1973—), Nat. League for Nursing, Nat. Assn. for Practical Nurse Edn. and Service (pres. 1958-63), South Portland Pub. Health Nursing Assn. (dir. 1974—). Contbr. articles to profl. jours. Home: Pier Rd Cape Porpoise ME 04014

GAFFNEY, HELEN AGNES, librarian; b. Clayville, N.Y., July 19, 1905; d. Michael George and Sara (Ganey) Gaffney; student Syracuse U., summers 1939-40, Catholic U. Am., summer 1941; B.A., U. Buffalo, 1942; B.S., Columbia, 1943. Reference librarian Hamilton Coll. Library, 1943-53; reference asst. Utica (N.Y.) Pub. Library, 1954-55, 59-60, head children's room, 1961-64, head catalog dept., 1964-68; cataloguer Miami U., Oxford, O., 1969—; dir. library Mohawk Valley Tech. Inst., 1955-59. Mem. Am., Ohio library assns., Ohio Valley Group Tech. Services Librarians, Am. Assn. U. Women, Clinton Hist. Soc., Delta Kappa Gamma. Democrat. Roman Catholic. Club: Altrusa (pres. 1967-69, mem.-at-large), Women's (Oxford). Address: 322 E Withrow Av Oxford OH 45056

GAGE, BETTY MOORE, psychologist; b. Athens, O., Mar. 1, 1936; d. Herbert V. and Goldie (Wemmer) Moore; student Western Coll. for Women, 1954-55, Ohio U., 1956, U. Colo., 1957; B.A., MacMurray Coll., 1958, M.A., 1960; 1 son by previous marriage, Mark S. Grad. asst. MacMurray Coll., Jacksonville, Ill., 1958-60; clin. psychologist Dayton (O.) Children's Psychiat. Hosp., 1960-63, exec., clin. psychologist, dir. group therapy Dayton Child Guidance Center, 1967-74; psychologist Children's Mental Health Center, Xenia, O., 1974—; clin. psychologist Counselling Center, U. Cal. at Berkeley, 1963-64; pvt. practice group therapy, 1972—. Mem. Am., Miami Valley (sec.-treas. 1960-62) psychol. assns., State Affiliated Psychologists and Psychol. Assn., Assn. for Humanistic Psychology. Home: 1805 Brattleboro Ct Kettering OH 45440 Office: Children's Mental Health Center Diamond Acres 206 Home Av Xenia OH 45385

GAGE, DARLEEN NOTEBOOM (MRS. DALE JESSE GAGE), state ofcl.; b. nr. Brookings, S.D., Mar. 9, 1925; d. Mike and Lillian Rose (Husman) Noteboom; m. Dale Jesse Gage, Sept. 10, 1944; children—Gary Gene, Michael Jay, Christopher Dale, Patricia Anne. Sec. U. S.D. Med. Sch., 1948-52; sec. S.D. Ho. of Reps., 1955, 57, 68, 69, 70; mem. S.D. Bd. Edn., 1961-74, pres., 1973-74. Publicity dir. Hughes County (S.D.) Cancer Soc., 1956-67; weekly columnist Sunday Reminder, Pierre, S.D., 1971-73; news editor Pierre Times, 1973-74. Dir. Speaker's Bur. S.D. Republican party, 1968, 70, finance dir., 1970; central Rep. committeewoman, Hughes County, 1970-73. Trustee Council Econ. Edn. S.D., River Park Center, Pierre. Mem. Women's Div. Pierre C. of C., Nat. Secs. Assn. (sec. 1971-72), S.D., Nat. press women. Methodist. Toastmistress. Contbr. articles to Rapid City (S.D.) Jour. Home: 425 5th Av Brandon SD 57005

GAGE, FRANCES MARIE, sculptor; b. Windsor, Ont., Can., Aug. 22, 1924; d. Russell and Jean Mildred (Collver) Gage; grad. Ont. Coll. Art, Toronto, 1951; student Art Students League N.Y., 1954-55, Ecole Des Beaux Arts, Paris, 1955-57. Exhibited one man show Gallery Dresdnere, 1972; exhibited group shows, Toronto, Montreal, Ottawa, Burlington, Kitchener, London; represented in permanent collections at Fanshaw Coll., London, Ont., Med. Sch., London, Med. Scis. Bldg., U. Toronto, Music Bldg. Mt. Allison U., N.B., U. Guelph, Ont., Womens Coll. Hosp., Toronto. Served with Womens Royal Canadian Service, 1944-46. Recipient Rothman Purchase award, 1965, Samuel Bronfman Commemorative medal. Royal Soc. scholar, 1955. Mem. Royal Canadian Acad. Arts Address: 60 Birch Av Toronto ON M4V 1C8 Canada

GAGLIARDI, JANICE KAY CHAREK (MRS. NICK C. GAGLIARDI), occupational therapist; b. Cleve., Mar. 17, 1938; d. Alvin and Helen May (Votypka) Charek; B.S., U. Buffalo, 1960; certificate in interior decorating John Robert Powers Sch., 1970; m. Nick C. Gagliardi, May 27, 1959; children—Donald Philip, David Francis. Occupational therapist Mount View Hosp., Lockport, N.Y., 1960, Buffalo State Hosp., 1961, 67—, Kan. Neurol. Inst., Topeka, 1961-62, Samaritan Lodge Rest Home, Lawrence, Kan., 1962-65. Pack sec., publicity chmn. Cub Scouts, Tonawanda, N.Y., 1972—. Mem. Am., N.Y. State, Niagara Frontier Dist. occupational therapy assns. Home: 747 Brighton Rd Tonawanda NY 14150 Office: 400 Forest Av Buffalo NY 14213

GAGNON, SISTER CLAIRE, hosp. adminstr.; b. St. Prospr, Que., Can., Aug. 12, 1919; d. Benoit and Odile (Perreault) Gagnon; B.S. in Nursing, Seattle U., 1951. Came to U.S., 1940, naturalized, 1950. Nursing supr. St. Vincent Hosp., Portland, Ore., 1951-52, operating room supr., 1957-60; nursing supr. St. Mary Hosp., Walla Walla, Wash., 1952-56, St. Elizabeth Hosp., Yakima, 1960-61; adminstr. St. Peter Hosp., Olympia, 1961—. Mem. Am., Cath. hosp. assns., Am. Coll. Hosp. Adminstrs., Nat. Fire Protection Assn., Assn. Western Hosps., Wash. State Blue Cross Assn. Address: 413 N Lilly Rd Olympia WA 98506

GAIL, MRS. MAXWELL TROWBRIDGE, club woman; b. West Simsbury, Conn.; d. Clarence Campbell and Marguerite (Reynar) Osmun; A.B., Barnard Coll., 1935; ed. The Katherine Gibbs Sch., 1936; m. Parbury Pollen Schmidt, July 14, 1936; children—Parbury, Marguerite Reynar. Mem. bd. dirs., sec. Gen. Office Supply Co. Archives of Am. Art Com. for Nov. Sale, 1960; pres. Barnard Coll. Club Detroit, 1959-64; spl. events chmn. Seven Eastern Women's Colls. Com., 1959; bd. dirs., spl. events chmn., patroness chmn. Camp Oakland, 1960-68; area chmn. Meadow Brook Theater, Oakland U., 1967; mem. Met. Opera Com. of Detroit, 1959; mem. Jr. League of Birmingham, Inc. Bd. dirs. women's com. Cranbrook Art Acad. Mem. Needlework Guild of Am. (sect. pres.). Home: 6190 W Surrey Birmingham MI 48010

GAILEY, MARGUERITE HENRIETTA SAVAGE, nurse; b. San Angelo, Tex., Oct. 2, 1917; d. Oscar Augustus and Virginia Catherine (Warren) Savage; grad. San Angelo Coll., 1937; A.A., Hardin Simmons U., 1951; student U. Me., 1964; m. Luther Lewis Gailey, Nov. 4, 1937 (div. Jan. 1956); children—Catherine Elesynna (Mrs. Jerry MacBetsill), Laura Estalee. Asst. to phys. edn. instr. San Angelo High Sch., 1936-37; with Tom Green County Library, 1937-38; elementary tchr., substitute tchr. Tom Green County Rural Schs., 1938-41; with Civil Service, Goodfellow AFB and San Angelo Army Air Field Bombardier Sch., San Angelo, 1942-46; owner, mgr. restaurant, San Angelo, Tularosa, N.M., 1946-48; floral designer, bookkeeper Leon's Flower Shop, San Angelo, 1948-50; drs. receptionist, bookkeeper, office nurse, med. sec., San Angelo, 1950-53; payroll bookkeeper, cost accountant Warner Constrn. Co., San Angelo, 1954-58; night supr. Bronte (Tex.) Hosp., 1958-62; head nurse Bapt. Meml. Geriatric Hosp., San Angelo, 1962—; pub. relations-program dir. Hotel Cactus, San Angelo, 1966-67. Mem. ad hoc com. Coordinating Bd. Nursing Edn. Nurse cons. Home Fund, San Antonio, 1964-68; personnel-inservice dir. Bapt. Meml. Geriatric Hosp., San Angelo. Mem. Nat. Assn. Practical Nurse Edn. and Service (1st v.p. 1969-73, nat. membership chmn., pres. 1973—), Nat. Council Women, Nat. Ret. Tchrs. Assn., Angelo State U. Ex-Student Assn., Bus. and Profl. Womens Club (named Woman of Yr. 1972), Licensed Vocational Nurses Assn. Tex. (past pres.). Baptist. Odd Fellow (pres. planning bd. all brs. 1973-74, pres. past presidents and past grand masters of Tex. 1973-74), Rebekah (pres. assembly Tex. 1969-70, trustee 1972—). Clubs: Toastmistress (past pres.), Pulliam Home Demonstration. Home: 902 N Main St Apt D13-N San Angelo TX 76901 Office: PO Box 3786 San Angelo TX 76901

GAINER, LINDA LOU (MRS. GARY LUTHER JOHNSON), telephone co. exec.; b. Bellingham, Wash., Feb. 5, 1949; d. William Raymond and Alma May (Snowden); B.A. in Communications, U. Wash., 1971; m. Gary Luther Johnson, Aug. 21, 1971. Communications analyst Gen. Tel., Everett, Wash., 1971-73, pub. affairs mgr., 1973—. Mem. Wash. Press Women, Women in Communications, Nat. Orgn. Women, Nat. Assn. for Edn. Young Children (chmn. publicity Seattle conf. 1973). Home: 7535 Roosevelt Way Seattle WA 98115 Office: 5315 Evergreen Way Everett WA 98201

GAINER, RUBY JACKSON (MRS. HERBERT P. GAINER), educator, civic leader; b. Buena-Vista, Ga.; d. William B. and Lovie (Jones) Jackson; student Miles Meml. Coll., 1932-35; B.S., Ala. State Tchrs, Coll., 1939; M.A. in English and Social Studies, Atlanta U., 1953; postgrad. Fla. A. and M. U., 1962-63, Western Wash. State Coll., 1964, U. Conn., 1965, Okla. State U., 1968. Dr. Humanities (hon.) Selma U., 1968, Daniel Payne Coll., 1971; LL.D. (hon.), Birmingham Bapt, Coll.; Ph.D., Colo. State Christian Coll., 1973; m. Herbert P. Gainer, June 2, 1968; children—Ruby Paulette, James H., Cecil F. Tchr. J. B, Turner High Sch., Milton, Fla., 1947-48, pub. schs., Birmingham, Ala., Washington Jr. High Sch., Pensacola, Fla., 1955-68; guidance counselor Wedgewood Jr.-Sr. High Sch., Pensacola, 1968—; tchr. of English, Woodham High School. Brought 2 successful legal cases against Jefferson County (Ala.) Sch. Bd. for equalization of Negro tchr. salaries, 1946-47, re-instatement Negro tchrs. under Tchr. Tenure Act; organized 1st tchrs. union, Birmingham; also organized local high sch. chpt. Future Tchrs. Am., local tchr. aide and teen service groups, local and county assns. edn.; local capt. Heart Fund, Mothers March of Dimes, Cancer Fund; active local P.T.A., past chmn. Fla. P.T.A. Workshop, 1966; participant Gov. Fla. Conf. Edn., Tallahassee, 1967, Nat. conf. Profl. Rights and Responsibilities, Arlington, Tex., 1968; participant, chmn. numerous profl. ednl. confs. So. U.S.; mem. Escambia County Guidance Council; mem., past officer Fla. Guidance Council. Bd. dirs. Partners for Progress, Pensacola, Escambia County Tb Assn. Named Tchr. of Year, Dist. 1 Fla. State Tchrs. Assn., 1966, also recipient award meritorious service, Distinguished Service award, 1966, DuShane Outstanding Service award, 1967; recipient DuShane Outstanding Dir. award Escambia County Tchrs. Assn., 1967, Distinguished Service award civil, human, profl. rights, 1965; recipient Outstanding Tchr. and Leader award Fla. Edn. Assn., honor award N.E.A., Fla. State Tchrs. Assn., 1966, awards youth, community orgns.; Distinguished Achievement in Edn. award, Outstanding Educator award, Honor award, Recognition Day award, Pub. Service award, Distinguished Community Service award, Parent of Year award, Top Educator award (all 1970), human relations award Student Com. of Woodham High Sch., 1972, others; cited Pitts. Courier, NAACP, 1946-47; Ruby J. Gainer Day proclaimed by mayor Pensacola, 1970, Pensacola's Woman of Year Pensacola Voice Newspaper, 1974. Mem. Jefferson County (past. sec., past pres.), Escambia County (past sec., past pres,), Fla. State (past bd. dirs. dist. 1, past pres. dist. 1, mem. tchr. edn. and profl. standards commn. and evaluation com., bd. advisers dept. classroom tchrs.), Ala. (past. chmn. secondary sch. tchrs.), Am. tchrs. assns., Am. Assn. U. Women, Jefferson County Tchrs. Union (past pres.), N.E.A. (v.p. assn. classroom tchrs. 1969-70), Nat. Council English Tchrs., Nat. Council Social Studies Tchrs., Escambia County League Justice, Future Tchrs. Am. Advisers Council, City-Wide Fedn. Women's Clubs (past officer), Internat. Platform Assn., League Women Voters, Am. Assn. U. Women, Alpha Kappa Alpha (Achievement award S. Atlantic region 1970). Baptist (mem., pres. bd. ushers). Mem. Order Eastern Star. Clubs: Mary M. Bethune, New Idea Art and Study. (Pensacola). Composer: God Planted You Here, Talking to the Moon, It Is Better Not to Know, In the Quiet of the Day. Contbr. articles, poems publs. Address: 1516 W Gadsden St Pensacola FL 32501

GAINES, CHERIE ADELAIDE (MRS. EUGENE M. SWANN), lawyer; b. Queens, N.Y.C., May 17, 1935; d. Charles Oscar and Billie (Robinson) Gaines; B.A., Columbia, 1956; J.D., U. Pa., 1960; m. Eugene M. Swann, Apr. 15, 1960; children—Liana Jane, Eugene Michael. Admitted to Cal. bar, 1963; chief atty. Legal Aid Soc., Oakland, Cal., 1965-70; asst. regional atty. Litigation Center, Equal Employment Opportunity Commn., San Francisco, 1973—; practiced in San Francisco, 1963-65, Oakland, 1973—. Asso. prof. law Golden Gate U., 1970-71, asst. prof. law U. San Francisco, 1971-73; spl. asst. to asst. regional atty. Dept. Housing and Urban Devel., San Francisco, 1971. Founder, Phoenix Elementary Sch., Berkeley, Cal., 1969. Bd. dirs., treas. Consumers Coop., Berkeley. Recipient Commendation plaques Alameda Affirmative Action Com., 1971, Alameda County Human Relations Commn., 1973. Mem. Am. Civil Liberties Union (dir. Berkeley-Albany 1968), Cal., Oakland bar assns., Charles Houston Law Club (v.p. 1972). Episcopalian. Office: 1390 Market St San Francisco CA 94104

GAINES, FRANCES PERLOWSKI (MRS. REUBEN B. GAINES), psychiat. social worker, speech pathologist; b. Chgo.; d. Frank M. and Theodosia (Konczak) Perlowski; B.A., U. Wis., 1926; M.S., Smith Coll., 1927; postgrad. U. Chgo., 1940-41; m. Reuben B. Gaines, Nov. 2, 1932; 1 dau., Kendra Holly. Psychiat. caseworker Mpls. Child Guidance Clinic, 1926-27, Inst. Juvenile Research, Chgo., 1927-29; practice psychiat. social work, speech pathology, Chgo., 1929-56; neuropsychiat. caseworker U.S. Vets. Bur., Chgo., 1928-29; speech pathologist Rush Med. Coll.-Presbyn. Hosp., 1929-40, Children's Meml. Hosp., 1930-42 (both Chgo.), Whiting (Ind.) Sch. System, 1931-33; psychiat. sch. counselor West Chicago (Ill.) Sch. System, 1964-68. Speaker women's clubs, hosp. staffs, sch. and med. orgns. Chmn. northside br. Chgo. Heart Fund, 1958-66. Bd. dirs. Sr. Citizens Com. Chgo., Du Page Mental Health Soc., Wheaton, Ill. Mem. Ill. Psychol. Assn., Nat., Chgo. speech and hearing socs., Woman's Aux. Kane County Med. Soc. (treas. 1973-75), Ill. Garden Club (sec. 1964-65), Pi Lambda Theta. Clubs: Woman's Athletic (Chgo.); St. Charles (Ill.) Country; Dunham Woods Riding (Wayne, Ill.). Contbr. articles to profl. jours., popular mags. Home: Rooster Run Box 185 Wayne IL 60184

GAINES, GAIL ALLYN, physician; b. Topeka, Dec. 11, 1915; d. Otto D. and Agnes E. (Johnson) Gaines; A.B., Washburn Coll., 1941; postgrad. Smith Coll., 1946-47; M.D., Woman's Med. Coll. Pa., 1951; M.A. in English Lit., Western Conn. Coll., 1970; postgrad. Yale, N.Y. Psychiat. Inst. Intern Mary Fletcher Hosp., Burlington, Vt., 1951-52; psychiat. resident Fairfield State Hosp., 1952-54, Grasslands Hosp., 1954-55; supervising psychiatrist Harlem Valley State Hosp., 1955-57; psychiatrist White Plains Clinic, 1957, Mt. Kisco Clinic, 1957-60; dir. Putnam County Community Mental Health Services, Carmel, N.Y. 1958-68; asso. psychiatrist Waterbury Hosp. Clinic, 1959-65, psychiatrist, 1968—; pvt. practice psychiatry, Newtown, Conn., 1958-72; cons. Catholic Family and Community Service, Danbury, Conn., 1968—, Prospect Restoration Health Center, 1973—, Whitewood Manor Convalescent Home, 1973—, New Lakeview Manor Convalescent Home, 1973—; asso. attending Waterbury Hosp., 1973—. Served as capt. AUS, 1942-46. Recipient Hurd Mead fellowship for research, 1954. Diplomate Am. Bd. Psychiatry, Nat. Bd. Med. examiners. Fellow Am. Psychiat. Assn.; mem. New Haven County Med. Soc., A.M.A., Mental Health Assn., Conn. Med. Assn., Zeta Tau Alpha, Zeta Phi. Home: Gainesborough/72 Hale Av Waterbury CT 06708 Office: Waterbury CT 06708

GAINES, LUCILLE SIMCOE (MRS. WILLIAM HARRIS GAINES, JR.), librarian; b. Norfolk, Va., Aug. 30, 1919; d. Walter Taylor and Mary Dare (White) Simcoe; A.B., Randolph-Macon Woman's Coll., 1941; B.S. in L.S., Columbia, 1945; postgrad. Duke, 1945-50; m. William Harris Gaines, Jr., Sept. 22, 1951; children—William Harris, John Ransone. Reference librarian Duke U. Library, Durham, N.C., 1945-50; order librarian Va. State Library, Richmond, 1950-51, head serials sect., 1972—; cataloger Va. Hist. Soc., Richmond, 1956-57, Collegiate Schs., Richmond, 1961-68; head reference dept. Richmond (Va.) Pub. Library, 1970-72. Mem. Va. Library Assn., Phi Beta Kappa, Sigma Kappa. Episcopalian. Home: 1814-A Hanover Av Richmond VA 23220 Office: Virginia State Library Richmond VA 23219

GAINES, MARJORIE L. CHAMBERLAIN (MRS. WOLCOTT S. GAINES), ins. exec.; b. Northboro, Mass., Aug. 26, 1929; d. Charles E. and Margaret M. (Mulchaey) Chamberlain; student pvt. schs.; m. Wolcott S. Gaines, Nov. 24, 1949; children—Karen L., Wolcott S., Brian D. Mgr., State of Me., Keystone State Hosp. Service Agy., Portland, 1963-64; sec., dir. Community Life Ins. Co., Portland, 1964—; sec. Allied Mut. Ins. Co., Portland, 1964-69, First Americal Life Ins. Co., Phoenix, 1966—. Mem. Ins. Women So. Me. Home: 94 Gray Rd Falmouth ME 04105 Office: 2501 Congress St Portland ME 04102

GAINES, NANCY HILL, editor; b. N.Y.C., May 25, 1936; d. Benjamin Harvey and Mabel Elizabeth (Williams) Hill; A.B., U. N.C. at Chapel Hill, 1958; M.A., Ind. U., 1960; m. Donald Frank Gaines, Aug. 11, 1960; children—Elizabeth, Mary Margaret. Women's and gen. news reporter High Point (N.C.) Enterprise, 1958; copy editor Bus. Horizons, 1960-61; editorial asst. Ind. U. Press, 1962-63; editor U. Wis. Press, 1965-66; editor, writer extension editorial services U. Wis., 1966—. Mem. Women in Communications. Author instrn. manuals. Home: 218 S Segoe Rd Madison WI 53705 Office: 432 N Lake St Madison WI 53706

GAINES, NATALIE EVELYN, sculptor; b. Detroit, Dec. 11, 1929; d. Michael and May (Mantin) Gaines; student Detroit Soc. Arts and Crafts, 1945-51, Greason Sch., Detroit, 1949-50. Exhibited one-man shows at Crespi Gallery, N.Y.C., 1958, Glassboro (N.J.) State Coll., 1961; exhibited in group shows at Detroit Inst. Art, 1949, 50, Wayne County Artists Show, Detroit, 1950, Creative Gallery, N.Y.C., 1951, Kirk-in-the Hills Outdoor Art Festival, Detroit, 1952, Crespi Gallery, 1958, 59, 60, Allied Artists Am., N.Y.C., 1958, Archtl. League N.Y., 1969; represented in permanent collections at Glassboro State Coll.; also pvt. collections. Pres., Temple Israel Youth Group, Detroit, 1947-48, Young Adult Council, Detroit, 1950-51; leader jr. div. Allied Jewish Campaign, Detroit, 1947-51; mem. exec. com., co-chmn. program com. Nat. Jewish Youth Council, 1948-50; pub. relations dir. Henry St. Camp Fund drive, Henry St. Friends Com., N.Y.C., 1957. Recipient 3d prize Crespi Gallery Ann. Competition Award Show, 1958; 1st prize Temple Emanu-El Men's Club Ann. Art Exhbn., 1959, 2d prize, 1959, 3d prize, 1962. Mem. Archtl. League N.Y., Artists Equity Assn. N.Y. (summer program chmn. 1957—). Address: 410 E 79th St New York City NY 10021

GAINES, ROSSLYN, psychologist; b. Toronto, Ont., Can.; d. Edward A. and Ruth (Goldin) Stiegel; B.S., Northwestern U., 1948; M.A., U. Chgo., 1961, Ph.D., 1963; m. Joseph A. Gaines, Oct. 15, 1951 (div. 1960); children—Katherine Ellen, John Austin. NIH research fellow, 1960-63; research asst. U. Chgo., 1962, teaching asst., 1962-63, instr., 1963; asst. prof. in residence U. Cal. at Los Angeles, 1963-64, asso. prof. in residence depts. psychiatry and psychology, 1971—; asso. research prof. Gallaudet Coll., Washington, 1964-66; asso. research psychologist Inst. Human Devel., U. Cal. at Berkeley, 1966-71. Research cons. child and ednl. problems, 1962—. Mem. Am., Western psychol. assns., Soc. for Research in Child Devel., Am. Speech and Hearing Assn., Phi Beta Kappa, Sigma Xi. Contbr. articles to profl. jours. Home: 1104 Tigertail Rd Los Angeles CA 90049

GALANE, IRMA ADELE BERESTON, electronic engr.; b. Balt., Aug. 23, 1921; d. Dr. Arthur and Sarah (Hillman) Bereston; B.A., Goucher Coll., 1940; postgrad. Johns Hopkins, 1940-42, Mass. Inst. Tech., 1943, George Washington U., 1945, 65, U. Md., 1958, Army Mgmt. Sch., 1964; 1 dau., Suzanne Felice. Physicist, Naval Ordnance Lab., 1942-43; electronic engr. Navy Bur. Ships, 1943-49, Army Office Chief Signal Officer, 1949-51, Navy Bur. Aeros., 1951-56, Air Research and Devel. Command, USAF, 1956-57, FCC, 1957-60, NASA, 1960-62; supervisory electronic engr. USCG Hdqrs., 1962-64; sci. specialist engring. scis. Library of Congress, 1964-65; project engr. Advanced Aerial Fire Support System, Army Materiel Command, 1965-66; engr. Naval Air Systems Command, 1966-71; electronic engr. Fed. Communications Commn., Spectrum Mgmt. Task Force, 1971—. Registered profl. engr., D.C. Mem. I.E.E.E. (sr.), Am. Inst. Aeros. and Astronautics, Nat. Soc. Profl. Engrs. (chmn. publs. com. 1959-60, co-chmn. civil def. com. 1965, spl. asst. to pres. 1965), Soc. Women Engrs. (sr. mem.; nat. membership chmn. 1952, nat. dir. 1953, mem. nat. scholarship com. 1958), Armed Forces Communications and Electronics Assn., Fedn. Profl. Assn., Am. Ordnance Assn., Johns Hopkins Alumni Assn., A.A.A.S., U.S. Naval Inst., Marine Tech. Soc., Internat. Platform Assn., Smithsonian Inst. (asso.). Editor: The Met. Washington Profl. Engr., 1958-60. Home: 4201 Cathedral Av NW Washington DC 20016

GALANTE, VERA VILLEGAS (MRS. MICHAEL A. GALANTE), ednl. adminstr.; b. N.Y.C., July 31, 1929; d. Jose Antonio and Jennie Rose (Gentile) Villegas; B.A., Hunter Coll., 1950, M.A., 1953; postgrad. St. Johns U., 1967; m. Michael A. Galante, Aug. 23, 1958; children—Gianna, Marie Elena. Adminstrv. asst. Hunter Coll., 1950-53; tchr., Hicksville (N.Y.) Pub. Sch., 1953-56, fgn. lang. supr., 1956—. Supr., TV show, Hablemos Español, WPIX, 1958-59; instr. St. Johns U., 1959, Hofstra U., 1956; cons. N.Y. State Dept. Edn., 1955, 57, 63, 69. Recipient Medal of Guadalupe, 1958, fellowship Columbia U., 1971. Mem. Am. Assn. Tchrs. Spanish, Am. Assn. Tchrs. Italian, Am. Assn. Tchrs. French, Am. Assn. Tchrs. German, Fgn. Lang. Assn. Chmn. Suprs. (pub. relations chmn. 1971), N.Y. State Assn. Fgn. Lang. Tchrs. (dir. 1972), Sigma Delta Pi, Chi Sigma Delta. Office: Hicksville Pub Schs Adminstrn Bldg Division Av Hicksville NY 11801

GALBAN, AGNES SUAREZ, research exec.; b. N.Y.C., July 9, 1929; d. Leandro Suarez and Carmen Victoria (Guerra) Galban; student Coll. New Rochelle, 1945-47; A.B., Barry Coll., 1949; M.L.S., Columbia, 1970. Research librarian Am. Iron and Steel Inst., 1959-68; dir. research Hill & Knowlton, Inc., pub. relations counsel, N.Y.C., 1968-71, v.p. research and library services, 1971—. Mem. Spl. Libraries Assn. (audit com. N.Y. chpt. 1972—, chmn. 1973-74). Home: 520 E 86th St New York City NY 10028 Office: 633 3d Av New York City NY 10017

GALBRAITH, LILYAN KING, educator; b. Smithfield, Pa., Nov. 21, 1902; d. Jasper Thompson and Iona (Ewing) King; B.S., U. W.Va., 1927, M.S., 1946; Ed.D., Pa. State U., 1953; m. Carl Bennett Galbraith, April 28, 1923 (div. 1939). Tchr. home econs., Riversville, W.Va. 1927-29, Clarksburg, W.Va., 1942-44; tchr. trainer W.Va. U., Morgantown, 1944-46; supr. home econs. edn. State Coll., Mansfield, Pa., 1946-53; head home econs. dept. Western Mich. U., Kalamazoo, 1953-55; prof., head home econs. edn. dept. S.D. State U., Brookings, 1955-68; prof. Western Ky. U., Bowling Green, 1968-70; prof. home econs. edn. W.Va. U., 1971-72. Pres., Columbian Lit. Exchange Mansfield, 1950-52; publicity chmn. Tioga County (Pa.) Fedn. Women's Clubs, 1950-51. Recipient citation of merit for meritorious and devoted service to vocational home econ. edn. program in S.D., 1967; named S.D. Home Economist of Yr., 1968. Mem. Home Econs. Assn., N.E.A., Am. Assn. U. Profs., Am. Vocational Assn., Am. Ednl. Research Assn., Am. Assn. U. Women (pres. Brookings br. 1961-63, Uniontown br. 1974-75), Nat. Conf. Home Econs. Tchr. Educators Washington (recorder 1950, evaluation and followup com. 1958), Central Regional Home Econs. Tchr. Educators Conf. (recorder 1953, 55, 57, registration com. 1962, research report 1964), S.D. Homemaking Tchrs. (book com. 1957-61, planning com. 1959-65), Assn. Student Teaching (tri-state nominating com. 1960), Bus. and Profl. Women's Club (pres. Brookings 1967-68, historian 1974-75), S.D. State Coll. Faculty Assn. (adminstrv. council rep. 1961-63), Future Homemakers Am. (hon.), Internat. Platform Assn., Kappa Omicron Phi (chmn. nat. project com. 1954-61), Phi Lambda Theta, Delta Kappa Gamma (pres. chpt. 1964-66, profl. affairs com. chmn. 1972-74), Kappa Delta Pi. Republican. United Methodist (mem. ofcl. bd. pres. Wesleyan Service Guild 1958-60, rec. sec. No. dist. 1958-62, chmn. nominating com. S.D. Wesleyan Service Guild 1961, v.p. Women's group 1971-74). Contbr. articles to profl. publs. Home: 47 Water St Smithfield PA 15478

GALBRAITH, VIRGINIA LEE, educator; b. Boise, Ida.; d. Eugene Robert and Ione (Atkinson) Galbraith; A.B., U. Cal. at Berkeley, 1941, Ph.D., 1954. Instr., Vassar Coll., 1945-47; instr. U. Cal. at Berkeley, 1949-50; prof. econs. Mt. Holyoke Coll., 1950—; vis. prof. U. Minn., summers 1959, 61. Mem. Consumer Council Mass., 1958-63. Mem. Am. Econ. Assn. Democrat. Author: World Trade in Transition, 1965; Trade as an Engine of Growth: Ivory Coast, 1973. Contbr. articles to profl. jours. Home: 7 Greenwood Lane South Hadley MA 01075

GALES, GENEVIEVE SUSAN, city ofcl.; b. Gilbertsville, Ia., Feb. 23, 1912; d. John and Matilda Katherine (Pint) Gales; student U. No. Ia., 1935-36. Operator, Northwestern Bell Telephone Co., 1930-41, 44-46, Chesapeake & Potomac Telephone Co., Washington, 1942-44; med. asst., Waterloo, Ia., 1947-51; sec., bookkeeper Waterloo Thrift Co., 1952-56; accountant Waterloo C. of C., 1956-72; city clk. City of Evansdale (Ia.), 1972—. Mem. consumers' bd. Black's Dept. Store, Waterloo, 1969-70. Mem. Waterloo Womens' Bowling Assn. (treas. 1950-51). Roman Catholic. (mem. ch. council 1969). Club: Altrusa (pres. Waterloo 1969-70). Home: 312 Lafayette St Waterloo IA 50703 Office: 123 Evans Rd Evansdale IA 50707

GALL, ELIZABETH BABCOCK (MRS. JOHN CHRISTIAN GALL, JR.), nurse; b. Markville, Minn., Mar. 27, 1929; d. Paul Rexford and Signe (Swanson) Babcock; student (Tozer Found. scholar) Bethel Coll., 1947-48; diploma Mounds-Midway Sch. Nursing, St. Paul, 1951; B.S. (Tozer Found. scholar) U. Minn., 1955; M.A. in Journalism (Journalism Coop. fellow) U. Mich., 1971; m. John Christian Gall, Jr., June 15, 1955; children—Duane Howard, David Joseph. Gen. and pvt. duty nurse Midway and U. Minn. Hosp., St. Paul and Mpls., 1951-55; pub. health nurse Rochester-Olmsted County, Minn., 1955-56; editorial asst. Latin program U. Mich. at Ann Arbor, 1964-66, grad. asst. research, dept. journalism, 1966-68; nurse, corporate dir. and sec. Human Growth Center, Inc., Ann Arbor, 1973—. Co-founder, accompanist Danville Community Singers, Danville, Pa., 1959-62; co-founder La Leche League Ann Arbor, 1963, leader, 1964-68. Mem. Women in Communications, Sigma Theta Tau, Pi Lambda Theta, Kappa Tau Alpha. Home: 2912 Sheffield Ct Ann Arbor MI 48105 Office: 940 Maiden Lane Ann Arbor MI 48105

GALLAGHER, ALICE KATHERINE, lawyer; b. Tulsa, Feb. 8, 1947; d. James William Gallagher and Katherine Louise (Quinlan) Gallagher Sinclair; student Ecole de Science Politique, Paris, 1967-68; A.B., Hollins Coll., 1969; J.D., U. Tulsa, 1972. Admitted to Okla. bar, 1972; law clk. U.S. Ct. Appeals, 10th Jud. Circuit, Oklahoma City, 1972-73; practice law, Tulsa, 1974—. Mem. Am., Okla. bar assns., Am. Judicature Soc., Jr. League, Phi Delta Phi. Roman Catholic. Home: 2215 E 30th Pl Tulsa OK 74114 Office: Box 1693 Tulsa OK 74101

GALLAGHER, ANNE TIMLIN (MRS. ROBERT H. WISNIEWSKI), mgmt. cons.; b. Wilkes-Barre, Pa., Mar. 21, 1943; d. James Joseph and Ruth Brandon (MacGuffie) Gallagher; A.B., Bucknell U., 1964; m. Robert H. Wisniewski, June 30, 1973. Presentation analyst A.C. Neilsen, N.Y.C., 1964-65; research asso. Gen. Electric Co., N.Y.C., 1965-67, sr. sales rep., computer time-sharing, 1967-69; mgr. financial services Rapidata Co., N.Y.C., 1969-70; mgr. financial markets Computer Scis. Corp., N.Y.C., 1970-73; sr. cons. Arthur Young & Co., N.Y.C., 1973—. Asst. chmn. Am. Statis. Assn. Ann. Forecast Conf. N.Y., 1966, 67. Mem. Am. Statis. Assn., Nat. Assn. Bus. Economists, Met. Econ. Assn., Common Cause. Democrat. Home: 227 E 66th St New York City NY 10021 Office: 277 Park Av New York City NY 10017

GALLAGHER, ARLENE ANN ARDIS (MRS. THOMAS B. GALLAGHER), real estate broker; b. Syracuse, N.Y., May 28, 1932; d. Victor Dempster and Louisa Anna (Grimm) Ardis; student Long Beach Bus. Sch., 1950-51; m. Thomas B. Gallagher, Jan. 5, 1952; chil dren—Thomas, Geri-Ann. Salesman, Pat Robertson Realty, Huntington Beach, Cal., 1965-69; asso. Home Finders Realty, Hunting ton Beach, 1969-72; owner Red Carpet Realtors, Huntington Beach, 1973—. Bd. dirs. Huntington Beach Youth Athletic Assn., 1963-66, pres., 1963. Mem. Nat. Assn. Real Estate Bds. (v.p. Huntington Beach-Fountain Valley women's council 1971-72), Long Beach Bd. Realtors, Huntington Beach-Fountain Valley Bd. Realtors (mem. membership com. 1972, mem. multiple listing com. 1973, chmn. 1974, mem. edn. com. 1974, Million Dollar Club award 1972, 73, 74). Home: 7601 Nancy Dr Huntington Beach CA 92647 Office: 15052 Edwards St Huntington Beach CA 92647

GALLAGHER, HAZEL IRENE, realtor; b. East Providence, R.I., Mar. 3, 1917; d. John E. and Minnie (Healy) Davis; student Providence Coll. Music, 1934-36, Lee Inst., 1960, Boston U., 1967-68; m. Leo H. Gallagher, July 11, 1936 (dec. Sept. 1968); children—Carol (Mrs. John Mark Thomas), Joan (Mrs. Peter P. McNeil), Shirly (Mrs. Joseph F. Stahmer, Jr.). With Gallagher Realty, Foxboro, Mass., 1956—, owner, 1956—, pres., treas., 1969—; dir. Sharon Coop. Bank (Mass.); corporator Foxborough Savs. Bank, 1970—; owner Wanderbub gift shop, East Wareham, Mass., 1973—. Adviser Rainbow Girls, Mansfield, Mass., 1963-67; commr. Foxborough council Girl Scouts U.S., 1943-60, pres., 1948. Mem. Real Estate Bd. Boston, Nat. Assn. Real Estate Bds. Conglist. (deaconess 1954-56). Mem. Order Eastern Star (past matron). Home: 395 Peaceful Lane East Wareham MA 02538 Office: 83 Mechanic St Foxboro MA 02035

GALLAGHER, IDELLA SMITH (MRS. DONALD A. GALLAGHER), found. ofcl., author; b. Union City, N.J., Jan. 1, 1917; d. Fred J. and Louise (Stewart) S.; Ph.B., Marquette U., 1941, M.A., 1943, Ph.D., 1963; postgrad. U. Louvain, Belgium, U. Paris, France; m. Donald A. Gallagher, June 29, 1938; children—Paul B., Maria Noel. Lectr. philosophy Marquette U., 1943-52, 54-56; instr. philosophy Alverno Coll., Milw., 1956-58; asst. prof. philosophy Villanova U., 1958-62; asst. prof. philosophy Boston Coll., 1962-68, asso. prof., 1968-69; asso. prof. philosophy U. Ottawa, 1969-71, prof., 1971-73; projects adminstr. DeRance Found., Milw., 1973—. Mem. Sudbury (Mass.) Com. for Human Rights, 1963-69. Mem. Metaphys. Soc. Am., Am. Cath. Philos. Assn. (exec. council 1967-69), Am. Soc. Aesthetics, Assn. for Realistic Philosophy, Am. Assn. U. Profs., Brit. Soc. Aesthetics, Canadian Philos. Assn., Canadian Assn. U. Tchrs., Phi Alpha Theta, Phi Delta Gamma. Author: (with D. A. Gallagher) The Achievement of Jacques and Raissa Maritain, 1962; The Education of Man, 1962; (with D. A. Gallagher) A Maritain Reader, 1966; (with D.A. Gallagher) St. Augustine—The Catholic and Maniehaean Ways of Life, 1966. Morality in Evolution: The Moral Philosophy of Henri Bergson, 1970. Gen. editor: Christian Culture and Philosophy Series, Bruce Pub. Co., 1965—. Contbr. to New Cath. Ency., also articles to profl. jours. Home: 7714 W Wisconsin Av Wauwatosa WI 53213 Office: DeRance Found 7700 W Bluemound Rd Milwaukee WI 53213

GALLAGHER, SISTER JOYCE EILEEN, educator; b. Ironton, O., Sept. 3, 1937; d. Lawrence James and Frances Irene (Wilson) Gallagher; B.S., Coll. St. Teresa, 1967; M.Ed. (Nat. Def. Edn. Act fellow), Ohio U., 1970; postgrad. Loyola U., Chgo., 1972—. Joined Sisters of St. Francis, 1955; primary tchr. St. Priscilla Sch., Chgo., 1958-59, St. Mary Sch., Portsmouth, O., 1959-63, St. Mary Sch., Owatonna, Minn., 1963-64, Mary E. McCahill Inst., Lake City, 1964-67; tchr. jr. high sci. St. Raphael Sch., Springfield, Minn., 1967-68; instr. psychology and guidance Coll. St. Teresa, Winona, Minn., 1969—. Elementary sch. counselor cons. St. Mary Sch., Winona, 1969-72; grad. asst. Loyola U., Chgo., 1973; intern as asst. to pres. Felician Coll., Chgo., 1974. Mem. Am. Personnel and Guidance Assn., Am. Coll. Personnel Assn., Nat. Assn. Women Deans, Adminstrs. and Counselors, Assn. Am. Higher Edn., Phi Delta Kappa. Home: Coll St Teresa Winona MN 55987 Office: 6364 N Sheridan Rd Chicago IL 60660

GALLAGHER, MARY CATHERINE LLOYD (MRS. WILLIAM RICHARD GALLAGHER), journalist; b. Ashtabula, O., Sept. 6, 1928; d. Charles John and Marie Rose (Parnell) Lloyd; grad. high sch.; m. William Richard Gallagher, Aug. 12, 1950; children—Timothy Patrick, Michael Aloysius, Christopher Corneilus. Operator, Ohio Bell Telephone Co., Ashtabula, 1947-50; mem. staff Record Courier, Kent, O., 1964—. Sec. Mogadore (O.) P.T.A., 1964-65; charter mem. Mogadore Pub. Library. Recipient newspaper awards Ohio Press 1969, 70, 72, 73, Ohio Newspaper Women's Assn., 1969, 70, 71, 73; service award Mogadore Jr. C. of C., 1966; Loyalty Day award V.F.W., 1972-74. Mem. Ohio Press Women, Ohio Newspaper Women's Assn., Mogadore Bus. and Profl. Women's Club (sec. 1965-66), Women in Communications. Home: 4065 Highland Dr Mogadore OH 44260 Office: Record Courier Kent OH 44240

GALLASPY, SARA FULLILOVE (MRS. JOE DEWITT GALLASPY), assn. exec.; b. New Augusta, Miss., Mar. 17, 1923; d. Malcolm David and Sara Edith (Young) Fullilove; B.S., U. So. Miss., 1954; LL.B., Jackson Sch. Law, 1969; m. Joe Dewitt Gallaspy, Dec. 3, 1948; children—Jody, David. Exec. asst. Perry County Schs., New Augusta, 1950-54; asst. cashier Perry County Bank, New Augusta, 1954-57; with Miss. Municipal Assn., Jackson, 1957—, exec. sec., 1960—, editor Miss. Municipalities, 1960—. Admitted to Miss. bar, 1970. Mem. Miss. Soc. Assn. Execs. (sec.-treas. 1962—), Am. Judicature Soc., Miss. Editors and Dirs. Information Assn., Miss. State Bar, Hinds County Bar Assn., U. So. Miss. Alumni Assn., Am. Assn. U. Women. Baptist (adult tchr. Sunday sch.). Mem. Order Eastern Star (past worthy matron). Home: 823 Winn St Jackson MS 39204 Office: 230 Sun-N-Sand Bldg Jackson MS 39202

GALLATIN, JUDITH ESTELE, educator; b. Grand Rapids, Mich., Feb. 15, 1942; d. Victor and Marilyn (Gittlen) Gallatin; B.A., U. Mich., 1962, M.A., 1963, Ph.D., 1967. Lectr. psychology Eastern Mich. U., 1967-68, asst. prof., 1968-72, asso. prof., 1972—; research asso. U. Strathclyde, 1968. Dir. grant to study devel. polit. thinking U.S. Office Edn., 1970-72. Mem. Am., Mich. psychol. assns., Soc. for Research in Child Devel., Am. Asssn. U. Profs. (pres. chpt. 1973-74), Nat. Orgn. Women, Phi Beta Kappa. Author: Adolescence and Individuality, 1975. Contbr. articles to profl. jours. Home: 2738 Golfside St Ann Arbor MI 48197 Office: Dept Psychology Eastern Mich U Ypsilanti MI 48197

GALLENKAMP, PATRICIA BUTLER (MRS. CHARLES B. GALLENKAMP), art gallery adminstr.; b. Roswell, N.M., Oct. 23, 1936; d. Charles E. and Frances (O'Bannon) Butler; B.A. magna cum laude, Smith Coll., 1957; certificate Harvard-Radcliff Program in Bus. Adminstrn., 1958; M.Ed., Harvard, 1959; M.A., U. N.M., 1967; m. Charles B. Gallenkamp, Sept. 2, 1966. Tchr. pub. elementary schs., Concord, Mass., 1959-61; grad. teaching asst. dept. English U. N.M., 1965-67; propr., dir. Janus Galery, Santa Fe, N.M., 1970—. Mem. Phi Kappa Phi. Office: 116-1/2 East Palace Av Santa Fe NM 87501

GALLINGER, JANICE, librarian; b. Melrose, Mass., Sept. 2, 1925; d. Nathan Kraus and Rosamond Louise (Munroe) Gallinger; A.B., Tufts U., 1948; M.L.S., Carnegie Inst. Tech., 1957. Clk., Coll. Nat. Life Ins. Co., Boston, 1948-50; clk. Fgn. Service U.S., Rangoon, Burma, 1950-52, polit. asst., 1952-54, adminstrv. asst., Bonn, Germany, 1954-55; tchr. Lesley-Dearbon Sch., Cambridge, Mass., 1955-56; asst. librarian Erie County Tech. Inst., Buffalo, 1957-65; coll. librarian Plymouth (N.H.) State Coll., 1965—. Exec. dir. Nat. Library Week in N.H., 1969. Recipient Spaulding-Potter Community Service grant, 1973. Mem. Assn. Coll. and Research Libraries (mem. audio-visual com. 1971—, com. on goals 1973—), Am. (council 1971-73), N.H. (mem. exec. bd. 1969-73), New Eng. (mem. scholarship com. 1973—) library assns., Acad. Librarians N.H. (chmn. 1969-71), N.H. Coll. and Univ. Council (chmn. library policy com. 1972-73), Beta Phi Mu. Home: 11 Rogers St Plymouth NH 03264

GALLIVAN, MARION FRANCES VAN ORSDALE (MRS. ROBERT M. GALLIVAN, JR.), librarian; b. Buffalo, Dec. 2, 1940; d. Richard Charles and Marion Elizabeth (Coleman) Van Orsdale; B.A., Syracuse U., 1962, M.S. in L.S., 1963; m. Robert M. Gallivan, Jr., Feb. 3, 1973. Br. librarian, Buffalo and Erie County N.Y. Pub. Library, 1963-65, Order Dept. librarian, 1965-67, assst cons., 1967-70, cons. to community libraries, 1970-74; asst. dir. Mercer County Library System, Trenton, N.J., 1974—. U.S. reference librarian, N.Y. World's Fair, 1965. Mem. Am. (membership com. mem. 1970-73, div. research and devel. com. mem. 1970-74), N.Y. (membership chmn. 1972) library assns., Buffalo and Erie County Pub. Librarians Assn., Wilderness Soc., Beta Phi Mu. Presbyn. Club: Sierra (N.J. chpt.). Home: 190 Washington St Rock Hill NJ 08553 Office: 25 Scotch Rd Trenton NJ 08628

GALLOWAY, EILENE MARIE (MRS. GEORGE BARNES GALLOWAY), govt. ofcl.; b. Kansas City, Mo., May 4, 1906; d. Joseph Locke and Lottie Rose (Harris) Slack; A.B., Swarthmore Coll., 1928; grad. student Am. U., 1937-38, 43; m. George Barnes Galloway, Dec. 23, 1924; children—David Barnes, Jonathan Fuller. Tchr. polit. sci. Swarthmore Coll., 1928-30; editor Student Service, Washington, 1931; staff mem., edn. div. Fed. Emergency Relief Adminstrn., 1934-35; asst. chief information sect., div. spl. information Library of Congress, 1941-43, editor abstracts Legislative Reference Service, 1943-51, nat. def. analyst, 1951-57; specialist in nat. def., 1957-66; sr. specialist internat. relations (nat. security) 1966—; staff mem. Senate Fgn. Relations Com., 1947; professional staff member United States Group of the Interparliamentary Union, 1958-66; cons. Senate Armed Services Com., 1953—, Ford Found., 1958; spl. cons. spl. Senate Com. on Space and Astronautics, 1958; spl. cons. to Senate Com. on Aero and Space Sci., 1958—. Chmn. com. edn. and recreation Washington, 1937-38; forum leader program on adult edn. U.S. Office Edn., 1938; mem. Internat. Astronautical Fedn.'s Internat. Inst. Space Law, 1958—, Am. Rocket Soc.'s Space Law and Sociology Com., 1959—; mem. adv. panel Office Gen. Counsel, NASA, 1971—; adviser outer space delegation U.S. Mission to UN Working Group on Direct Broadcast Satellites, 1973; lectr. U.S. Civil Service Commn., Exec. Seminar Center, Oak Ridge, 1973, 74. Recipient Andrew G. Haley gold medal Internat. Inst. Space Law of Internat. Astronautical Fedn., 1968; Wilton Park fellow, Eng., 1968. U.S. mem. bd. dirs., v.p. Internat. Inst. Space Law, Internat. Astronaut. Fed., 1967—; trustee Theodore Von Karman Meml. Found., 1973—. Mem. League Women Voters (chmn. study groups housing, welfare in D.C., 1937-38, mem. tech. com. on law and sociology), Am. Inst. Aeronautics and Astronautics, World Peace Through Law Center, Am. Soc. Internat. Law, Internat. Acad. Astronautics (corr.) Am. Polit. Sci. Assn., Internat. Studies Assn., Internat. Law Assn., Phi Beta Kappa, Delta Sigma Rho, Kappa Alpha Theta. Episcopalian. Author: Atomic Power: Issues Before Congress, 1946; (with Bernard Brodie) The Atomic Bomb and the Armed Services, 1947; History of United States Military Policy on Reserve Forces, 1775-1957, 1957; Guided Missiles in Foreign Countries, 1957; The Community of Law and Science, 1958; United Nations Ad hoc Committee on Peaceful Uses of Outer Space, 1959; Satellites: AForce for World Peace, World Security and the Peaceful Uses of Outer Space, 1960; International Cooperation and Organization for Outer Space, 1965; Space Treaty Proposals by the United States and U.S.S.R., 1966; Treaty on Principles Governing the Activities of States in the Exploration and Use of Outer Space, Including the Moon and Other Celestial Bodies: Analysis and Background Data, 1967; Remote Sensing of the Earth by Satellites: Legal Problems and Issues, 1973; others. Editor: Space Law Symposium, 1958; The Legal Problems of Space Exploration, 1961; United States International Space Programs, 1965; International Cooperation in Outer Space: A Symposium, 1972; The Role of the United Nations in Earth Resources Satellites, 1972; mem. editorial adv. bd. Jour. Space Law, U. Miss. Law Sch. Home: 4612 29th Pl NW Washington DC 20008 Office: Congressional Research Service Library of Congress Washington DC 20540

GALLOWAY, JUDITH TAYLOR (MRS. WILLIAM DON GALLOWAY), govt. ofcl.; b. Elba, Ala., May 9, 1939; d. Roger Lavelle and Lois (Swain) Taylor; B.A., U. Fla., 1961; J.D., Am. U., 1969; m. William Don Galloway, Sept. 28, 1963; children—Vance William, Leslie Anne. Various positions, 1960-64; congl. aide U.S. Congressman Robert L.F. Sikes, Washington, 1964—. Adviser to Peoples Environmental Research Group, 1972; mem. Legislative Com. Unitarian Universalists Md., 1973, 74. Bd. dirs. Hillandale Citizens Assn., 1973, 74. Mem. Am., Md. bar assns., Women's Bar Assn. Md., Kappa Beta Pi. Club: Hillandale Forest Women's (dir. Silver Spring, Md. 1973-74). Home: 10226 Green Forest Dr Silver Spring MD 20903 Office: House of Representatives 2269 Rayburn Bldg Washington DC 20515

GALLOWAY, LINDA BENNETT (MRS. ERNEST AGNEW GALLOWAY), librarian; b. Dixon, Ky.; d. Charles Wesley and Bonnie (Fugate) Bennett; A.A., Stephens Coll., 1936; A.B., U. Ill., 1938, B.L.S., 1939; postgrad. Cite Universite, Paris, France, 1945; M.A., Vanderbilt U., 1949; postgrad. Western State U., 1961, Murray State

U., 1966, E. Carolina U., 1967, U. N.C., 1968; m. Ernest Agnew Galloway, Sept. 11, 1946; 1 dau., Lisa Linda. Reference librarian Evansville (Ind.) Pub. Library, 1939-41; librarian, Camp Breckinridge, Ky., 1941-44, U.S. Forces, ETO, 1944; historian 15th Army, Bd. Nauheim, Germany, 1945-46; librarian Dixon (Ky.) Pub. Library, 1948-54; coordinator Webster County Schs. Libraries, Dixon, 1961-68; librarian William Street Sch., Goldsboro, N.C., 1967-71; supr. media services Wayne County Schs., Goldsboro, 1971—. Pres. Dixon P.T.A., 1954-55. Bd. dirs. 2d Dist. P.T.A., Dixon, 1965, A.R.C., 1963-65. Recipient nat. fellowship award Delta Delta Delta, 1944; named Tri-State Outstanding Citizen, Evansville Courier, 1952. Mem. Nat., N.C. edn. assns., A.L.A., D.A.R., Am., N.C. library assns., N.C. Assn. Sch. Libraries, N.C. Media Assn., Delta Delta Delta, Delta Kappa Gamma. Democrat. Presbyn. Author: Andrew Jackson, Jr., Son of a President, 1966. Contbr. articles to profl. jours. and children's mags. Home: Walnut Creek Estates Route 9 Goldsboro NC 27530 Office: 301 N Herman St Box GG Goldsboro NC 27530

GALLOWAY, LOUISE JERSAK (MRS. BENJAMIN THOMAS GALLOWAY, JR.), anesthesiologist; b. Kingfisher, Okla., Sept. 14, 1921; d. William Richard and Louise Marie (Pappe) Jersak; student U. Okla., 1938-41; M.D., Tulane U., 1941-44; m. Benjamin Thomas Galloway, Jr., Feb. 23, 1946; children—Thomas Knox, Richard Holt, Mary Ann. Intern St. Joseph's Hosp., San Francisco, 1944-45; residency in anesthesiology Boston City Hosp., 1946-47; resident in anesthesiology Kennedy VA Hosp., Memphis, 1948-49, staff anesthesiologist, 1949-50; practice medicine, specializing in anesthesiology, mem. cons. staff Oteen VA Hosp., Asheville, N.C., 1950-63; practice medicine, specializing in anesthesiology, Brunswick, Ga., 1965—; mem. staff Glynn-Brunswick Meml. Hosp. Bd. dirs. A.R.C. Mem. Am., Ga. med. assns., Glynn County Med. Soc., Am., Ga. socs. anesthesiologists, Am. Med. Women's Assn., Glynn County Med. Aux. Home: 2850 Wildwood Dr Brunswick GA 31520 Office: Glynn-Brunswick Meml Hosp Brunswick GA 31520

GALOP, KATHLEEN PATRICIA, lawyer; b. Newark, Nov. 1, 1946; d. John Francis and Helen Mary (Koch) Galop; student Drew U., 1967; B.A., Caldwell Coll. Women, 1968; J.D., Dickinson Sch. Law, 1971. Admitted to N.J. bar, 1972; asso. Stryker, Tams & Dill, Esqs., Newark, 1971-74; atty. Prudential Ins. Co. Am., Newark, 1974—. Instr. tennis Essex County (N.J.) Park Comm., 1969, 70. Chairperson Newark area N.J. Shakespeare Festival, 1972-74; co-chairperson ticket and subscription sales Newark concert series N.J. Symphony Orch., 1974-75. Mem. Am., N.J., Essex County bar assns., Newark Mus. Assn. Office: Prudential Ins Co Prudential Plaza Newark NJ

GALPER, RUTH ELLEN LEVINE (MRS. WAYNE PROUDFOOT), psychologist, educator; b. N.Y.C., Aug. 9, 1940; d. Benjamin G. and Sylvia (Klein) Levine; A.B. (Nat. Merit scholar), Radcliffe Coll., 1961; Ph.D., N.Y. U., 1969; m. Wayne Proudfoot, Jan. 16, 1972. Nat. Inst. Mental Health tng. fellow, 1965-69; individual practice psychotherapy, 1969-71; asst. prof. psychology Ferkauf Grad. Sch. Humanities and Social Sci., Yeshiva U., N.Y.C., 1969-71; asst. prof. psychology City Coll., City U. N.Y., 1971-74, asso. prof., 1975—. Mem. Am., Eastern psychol. assns., Sigma Xi. Contbr. articles to profl. jours. Home: 514 W 110th St New York City NY 10025

GALT, ALFREDA SILL, pub. relations firm exec.; b. Ithaca, N.Y.; ed. Lincoln Sch. Tchrs. Coll.; m. William E. Galt, July 27, 1944 (dec. Feb. 1955); children—George Egleston, John Payson, Elizabeth Anne. With Jobson Asso., Inc., N.Y.C., 1941—, com. organizer, 1941-52, account exec., 1952-60, v.p., 1960—. Dir. women's div. Brit. War Relief Soc., 1941, Polish War Relief Soc., 1940; bd. dirs., sec., chmn. editorial com. The Lifwynn Found., 1955—. Mem. Pub. Relations Soc. Am., Assn. Humanistic Psychology, Inst. Gen. Semantics. Home: 108 Hillandale Rd Westport CT 06880 Office: 1 Rockefeller Plaza New York City NY 10020

GALVIN, MARGARET ROYCE (MRS. FRANCIS JOSEPH GALVIN, JR.), lawyer; b. Miami, Fla., Mar. 16, 1944; d. Raymond Joseph and Juanita (Jarman) Royce; B.A., MacMurray Coll., 1965; J.D. with honors, John Marshall Law Sch., 1970; m. Francis Joseph Galvin, Jr., Jan. 28, 1972. Sec. to judge U.S. Dist. Ct., Hammond, Ind., 1968-70, law clk., 1970-72; admitted to Ind. bar, 1970; asso. firm Galvin, Galvin & Leeney, Hammond, 1972-74, Galvin and Galvin, Hammond, 1974—. Mem. Am., Ind., Hammond bar assns. Episcopalian. Home: 415 Old Stone Rd Munster IN 46321 Office: 5253 Hohman Av Hammond IN 46320

GALYARDT, CYNTHIA CARSWELL (MRS. MILTON ANDREW GALYARDT), state ofcl.; b. Emporia, Kan., Jan. 1, 1934; d. Jay Horton and Lena (Anderson) Carswell; B.S., Kan. State U., 1955; m. Milton Adnrew Galyardt, Feb. 12, 1955; children—Susan Irene, Thomas Milton, Mark Andrew. Editor, Kan. Bus. Rev., Lawrence, 1966-71; research asst. Kan. Geol. Survey, Lawrence, 1971-72; dir. pub. information Kan. Lung Assn., Topeka, 1972-74; communications coordinator Kan. Commn. on Alcoholism, Topeka, 1974—. Recipient Contest awards Kan. Press Women, 1968, 70, 73. Mem. women in Communications (pres. Lawrence chpt. 1966-68), Pub. Relations Soc. Topeka, Kan. Pub. Health Assn., Lawrence Alumni Assn., D.A.R., Kappa Kappa Gamma. Club: Soroptimist International (Lawrence) Home: 3046 Steven Dr Lawrence KS 66044 Office: 535 Kansas Av Topeka KS

GALYEN, GLADYS JANE, banker; b. Grand Rapids, Mich., July 27, 1904; d. Cyrus Crooks and Mary (Deuel) Shigley; student Western Mich. U.; m. W. Burnette Clancey, Jan. 10, 1922 (div. Aug. 1944);children—Barbara (Mrs. Donald Gruscinski), Joan (Mrs. C. Calvin Rantz), Patricia (Mrs. Jerry Quirin); m. 2d, Thomas A. Galyen, Oct. 11, 1945 (dec. July 1971). With West Mich. Savs Bank, Bangor, 1947—, v.p., cashier, 1969—. Mem. Nat. Assn. Bank Women, D.A.R., Rebekah Odd Fellows. Home: 104 N Walnut St Bangor MI 49013 Office: 220 W Monroe St Bangor MI 49013

GAMACHE, BETTY (SUE) STEVENS (MRS. DENNIS FRANCIS GAMACHE), occupational therapist; b. Indpls., May 4, 1943; d. Lester T. and Elizabeth Ione (Pruitt) Stevens; B.S. in Occupational Therapy, Ind. U., 1967; m. Dennis Francis Gamache, Sept. 6, 1969; 1 dau., Cressa Jayne. Asst. adminstr. Occupational Therapy Dept., Newington (Conn.) Children's Hosp., 1967-74. Cons. at Mansfield (Conn.) Tng. Sch., 1970; lectr. on perceptual-motor disorders New Eng. Council Perceptual-Motor Dysfunction, Conn. State Welfare Conf., 1970. Mem. Hartford (Conn.) YWCA, Greater Hartford Jaycee Wives, 1970-72. U.S. Dept. Health, Edn. and Welfare grantee, 1971-72. Mem. Am., Conn., Student (pres. 1965-66) occupational therapy assns. Home: 595 Main St Cromwell CT 06416 Office: Newington Children's Hospital Newington CT 06111

GAMBAIANI, LINDA KUTSCHBACH (MRS. JOHN VICTOR GAMBAIANI), editor; b. Columbus, O., Dec. 9, 1947; d. William Serage and Helen Joline (Hoyer) Kutschbach; A.A., Stephens Coll., 1967; B.A., DePauw U., 1969; m. John Victor Gambaiani, Aug. 1, 1970. Editorial asst. Charles E. Merrill Pub. Co., Columbus, 1969, prodn. editor, trainee, 1970, prodn. editor, 1970-71, series editor, English, 1971-72, series editor, polit. sci., sociology, history, philosophy, police sci., 1972—. Free-lance indexer, proofreader. Mem. Ohio Commn. on Status of Women, 1972-73. Mem. Women in Communications (rec. sec. 1973-74, 1st v.p. 1974—), Delta Delta Delta. Methodist. Clubs: DePauw University Alumni (sec.-treas. Columbus 1970-71, 2d v.p. 1971-73, pres. 1973-74), Stephens College Alumnae. Home: 84 N Remington Rd Columbus OH 43209 Office: 1300 Alum Creek Dr Columbus OH 43216

GAMBILL, ALICE FRANCES (MRS. ROBERT HART), anesthesiologist; b. Pawhuska, Okla., Jan. 2, 1924; d. Ladd Haskins and Eula Corrine (Wolf) Gambill; A.B., Christian Coll., 1943; B.S., U. Okla., 1945, M.D., 1949; m. Robert Hart, Sept. 1, 1950 (dec. June 1968); children—Martin Gambill, Frances Gayle. Intern, Harris Hosp., Ft. Worth, Tex., 1949-50, resident surgery, 1950-51; resident anesthesiology Okla. Med. Center, Oklahoma City, 1960-62; gen. practice medicine, Ft. Worth, 1951-60, specializing in anesthesiology, Plainview, Tex., 1963-66; cons. Castro County Hosp., Dimitte, Tex., 1964-66; mem. staff Bapt. Meml., Bethany Gen., University, Mercy, Deaconess hosps., Oklahoma City; chief anesthesiology Oklahoma City VA Hosp., 1963; asst. prof. anesthesiology Okla. U. Med. Center, 1963-66, asst. prof. Sch. Inhalation Therapy, 1966-70; med. dir. Variety Health Clinic, Oklahoma City, 1974-74; asst. prof. anesthesiology U. Mo. Med. Center, 1974—. Pres. Traveler's Aid, Ft. Worth, 1956-60; mem. speakers bur. Am. Cancer Soc., Tarrant County, Tex., 1956-60; county med. rep. to Community Action Program of Oklahoma County, 1973. Bd. dirs. Okla. Heart Assn., 1971-73, mem. community service com., 1971-73. Recipient award of Yr., Okla. Heart Assn. Mem. Oklahoma County Med. Soc. (mem. pub. relations com. 1971-73), Women of Variety Club, Altrusa. Home: 1024 Harvard Columbia MO 65201 Office: U Mo Med Center Columbia MO 65201

GAMBLE, JANIE WARD, coll. adminstr.; b. Georgetown, S.C., Nov. 17, 1908; d. Joseph William and Emily (Alston) Ward; licentiate of instrn., S.C. State Coll., 1919; B.S., Allen U., 1954; postgrad. Cheyney State Coll., 1921, Hampton Inst., 1925, Columbia, 1930; m. Lykes David Gamble, Sept. 10, 1942 (dec.). Tchr., Howard High Sch., Georgetown, 1919-42; prin. Oak Grove Elementary Sch., Dillon County, S.C., 1942-50; tchr. Little Miss Muffett Nursery Sch., Washington, 1951; house dir., counselor Allen U., Columbia, S.C., 1952-57, S.C. State Coll., Orangeburg, 1957-73. Mem. Nat. Assn. Women Deans and Counselors, Nat. Assn. Negro Bus. and Profl. Women's Clubs, So. Coll. Personnel Assn., S.C. Employees Assn., Allen U., State Coll. alumni assns., Zeta Phi Beta. Mem. Order Eastern Star, United Order of Tents. Home: 255 Hopkins St SW Atlanta GA 30314 Office: 1806 State College Orangeburg SC 29117

GAMBLE, KATHRYN ELIZABETH, museum dir.; b. Van Wert, O., Aug. 19, 1915; A.B., Oberlin Coll.; M.A., N.Y.U. Grad. Sch. Fine Arts; certificate Newark Mus. Apprentice Course, 1941. Asst. to dir. Montclair (N.J.) Art Mus., 1944-52, dir., 1952—. Mem. Am. Assn. Museums, N.E. Mus. Conf., Museums Council N.J. Office: 3 S Mountain Av at Bloomfield Av Montclair NJ 07042

GAMBLE, RUTH SCALES, financial exec.; b. Amherst, Mass., Oct. 4, 1940; d. Philip Lyle and Elisabeth Davis (Scales) Gamble; B.A., Mt. Holyoke Coll., 1962; M.B.A., Harvard, 1964. Security analyst Bank of Am., San Francisco, 1964-66, L. F. Rothschild & Co., N.Y.C., 1966-68, Faulkner, Dawkins & Sullivan, N.Y.C., 1968-69; financial cons., v.p. Stowell Cons., Inc. N.Y.C., 1969-70; investment analyst Coll. Retirement Equities Fund, N.Y.C., 1970-71, Ford Found., N.Y.C., 1971—. Home: 420 E 55th St New York City NY 10022 Office: 320 E 43d St New York City NY 10017

GAMBRELL, LYDIA JAHN (MRS. FOSTER L. GAMBRELL), educator; b. Cleve., May 18, 1904; d. Carl Friedrich and Marie Sophie (Korlin) Jahn; student Miami U., Oxford, O., 1923-24; B.A., Ohio State U., 1927, M.A., 1928, Ph.D., 1932; D.Sc., Keuka Coll., 1974; m. Foster Lee Gambrell, June 23, 1932; children—Foster Lee, Kenneth Carl. Lab. asst. in zoology Ohio State U., Columbus, 1927-30; instr. physiology and bacteriology Lindenwood Coll., St. Charles, Mo., 1930-32; asst. dept. entomology N.Y. Agrl. Expt. Sta., Geneva, 1935-38; lab. asst. biology Hobart Coll., Geneva, 1945-46; instr. dept. biology Keuka Coll., Keuka Park, N.Y., 1947-54, asso. prof., 1954-58, prof., 1958—, head dept., 1958-69. Mem. Am. Assn. Univ. Profs., Phi Beta Kappa, Chi Beta Phi, Sigma Delta Epsilon. Presbyn. Home: 288 Lafayette Av Geneva NY 14456 Office: Keuka College Keuka Park NY 14478

GAMLEN, DORIS JEAN WAYLAND (MRS. JAMES ELI GAMLEN), advt. agy. exec.; b. Boise, Ida., Dec. 30, 1936; d. Charles Varrell and Grace Alice (Ingersoll) Wayland; student U. Ida., 1955-57; B.A., Coll. Ida., 1959; postgrad. John Robert Powers Modeling-Finishing Sch., 1957, Welcome Wagon Hostess Sch., 1962, San Francisco State U., 1969; m. James Eli Gamlen, Sept. 25, 1965 (dec. Aug. 1973); stepchildren—James Eli, Tom Chester. Asst. mgr. advt., display Bazar Dept. Stores, Boise, 1960-63; mgr. advt.-display Merc. Stores Co., Ida., Ore., Utah, 1963-64; with art dept. Darcy Advt., San Francisco, 1964-65; pub. relations Frederick Gennert & Assos., San Francisco, 1965; pub.-customer relations Bay View Fed. Savs. & Loan, San Francisco, 1965; v.p. pub. relations Western Polymer Corp., Burlingame, Cal., 1968-74; pub. relations dir. Doric Devel. Wenger-Michael Advt., San Francisco, 1974—. Faculty, Peacock Coll., 1961-63; judge Miss Cal. World Pagent, 1965. Active various community drives. Bd. dirs. Mental Health Recovery, Inc., League Handicapped, Symphony, Multiple Sclerosis, Internat. Hospitality. Named San Francisco Mardi Gras Queen, Little Jim Club Children's Hosp., 1968, KABL Citizen of Day. Mem. League Women Voters, Am. Assn. U. Women, D.A.R., Publicity Club, Sons and Daus. Ida. Pioneers. Episcopalian. Club: Commonwealth (San Francisco). Home: 25 Denham Ct Hillsborough CA 94010 Office: Wenger-Michael Advt 760 Market St San Francisco CA

GAMMON, JUANITA LAVERNE, artist, educator; b. McLeansboro, Ill.; d. Lloyd W. and Grace F. (Munsell) Gammon; B.F.A., M.F.A., U. Ill. Exhibited N.Y. Acad. Design, U. Ill., Parkland Coll., others; represented in numerous collections; head art program Parkland Coll., Champaign, Ill., 1967—; free lance illustrator, copywriter, guest lectr., art show judge, condr. workshops. Supr., Champaign County Art Show, 1973—; del. East Central Ill. Cultural Affairs Consortium, 1973—; co-chmn. Urbana Art Fair. Mem. N.E.A., Ill. Art Edn. Assn., Assn. Jr. Colls., Ill. Hist. Soc., U. Ill. Alumni Assn., Art Alumni Assn., Parkland Art Assn. (sponsor), Champaign-Urbana Advt.-Art Club (past treas., dir.). Home: 711 W Healey St Champaign IL 61820

GAMPEL, DOROTHY HUBBARD, psychologist, educator; b. Worcester, Mass., Oct. 1, 1930; d. Clyde W. and Marion (Hodgkinson) Hubbard; B.A. summa cum laude, U. Me., 1952; M.A. in Psychology, Cornell U., 1955; Ph.D., Columbia, 1964; postgrad. Harvard, 1967-69; m. Leonard Gampel, May 15, 1958 (div. Oct. 1962); children—Eric, Alexandra. Instr. Douglas Coll., Rutgers U., New Brunswick, N.J., 1957-58; lectr. psychology Coll. City N.Y., N.Y.C., 1958-64, instr., 1964-65; asst. prof. So. Ill. U. at Carbondale, 1966-67; postdoctoral intern Boston VA Hosp., 1967-69, clin. and research psychologist, 1969-70; sr. research asso. Research Inst. for Ednl. Problems, Cambridge, Mass., 1971-72; asso. prof. psychology U. Mass., Boston, 1972—. Lectr. Northeastern U., Boston, 1967-72. Mem. Am., Mass., Eastern psychol. assns., A.A.A.S., Assn. for the Psychophysiol. Study of Sleep. Guest editor Am. Psychologist, 1972—; cons. editor Jour. Supplement Abstract Service, 1972—. Contbr. articles on perception, verbal learning and research methodology to profl. jours. Home: 273 Conant Rd Weston MA 02193 Office: Psychology Dept College II Univ of Massachusetts Boston Harbor Campus Boston MA 02116

GANDER, LILLIAN KERN (MRS. AKSEL E. GANDER), assn. exec., author; b. Shelbina, Mo., Jan. 13, 1901; d. John William and Susan Tandy (Cochran) Kern; student U. Mo., U. Kan., U. Ia.; m. Aksel E. Gander, Aug. 21, 1921. Asso. editor Gesneriad Saintpaulia News mag., Knoxville, Tenn., 1963—, writer Tips and Techniques column, 1963—, 1st v.p. Santapaulia Internat., 1967-69, 2d v.p., 1969-71, pres., 1971—. Bd. dirs. St. Lukes Hosp. African Violet Cart. Mem. Met. St. Louis African Violet Soc., Am. Gerneriad Soc. Mem. Order Eastern Star. Club: Garden Improvement (Woodson County). Author two books of poetry. Address: 9665 Lilly Jean Dr St Louis MO 63134

GANDHI, INDIRA (NEHRU), Prime Minister of India; b. Allahabad, India, Nov. 19, 1917; d. Jawaharial and Kamala (Koul) Nehru; ed. Ecole Internationale, Geneva, Switzerland, Pupils' Own Sch., Poona, also Bombay, Badminton Sch., Bristol, Eng., Visva Bharati Coll., Shantiniketan, India, Somerville Coll., Oxford (Eng.) U., also hon.D.; D.Litt. (hon.), Andrha U., 1963; hon.D., Agra U., Bangalore U., Vikram U., El Salvador, U. Buenos Aires, Waseda U., Tokyo, Moscow State U., Charles U., Praque; m. Feroze Gandhi, 1942; children—Rajiv, Sanjay. Disciple of Gandhi; formed Vanar Sena, children's orgn. to help Indian Nat. Congress during non-cooperation movement; worked amongst untouchables, popularizing hand-spun cloth and Indian made goods; active student movement India, Eng.; mem. Indian Nat. Congress, 1938—, mem. working com., 1955—, central election com., 1955—, central parliamentary bd., 1958—, pres. Congress, 1959-60; prime minister of India, 1966—; minister atomic energy, 1966—, minister external affairs, 1967-69, minister finance, 1969-70, minister home affairs, 1970—, minister information and broadcasting, 1971—. Ofcl. hostess Prime Minister Nehru, 1947-64. Chmn. Citizens' Central Council, 1962; exec. com. Nat. Def. Fund, 1962; life patron Indian Council Child Welfare; v.p. Internat. Council Child Welfare; mem. Indian delegation UNESCO, 1960-64, also mem. exec. bd. UNESCO; mem. Nat. Integration Council, Indian Nat. Congress, Nat. Inst. Women; chancellor Jawaharlal Nehru U.; founder, pres. Kamala Nehru Vidayalaya; chmn. Bal Bhavan Bd.; founder, chmn. Bal Sahyoq, New Delhi, 1954—; pres. Dakshina Bharat Hindi Prachar Sabha; patron various insts. and socs.; pres. Himalayan Mountaineering Inst., Tibetan Homes Found. Pres. trustees Kamala Nehru Meml. Hosp.; trustee Kasturbi Ghandi Meml. Trust, Gandhi Smarak Nidhi; chmn. Swarj Bhavan Trust. Recipient Mother's award, U.S.A., 1953, citation Columbia U., Yale U. Howland Meml. prize, 1960; Isabella d'Este award (Italy), 1953; diploma of honor Argentine Soc. Protection Animals; named most admired woman French Inst. Pub. Opinion, 1967, 68; most admired person of world Gallup Poll, 1971. Mem. Fed. Film Socs. India (v.p.), Nehru Meml. Mus. and Library Soc. (pres.). Address: 1 Safdarjang Rd New Delhi-11 India

GANDY, EDYTHE EVELYN, lawyer, state ofcl.; b. Hattiesburg, Miss., Sept. 4, 1922; d. Kearney C. and Abbie (Whigham) Gandy; student U. So. Miss., 1939-40; LL.B., U. Miss., 1944. Admitted to Miss. bar, 1944; legislative asst. to Senator Theodore G. Bilbo, Washington, 1944-46; practiced in Hattiesburg, 1947-55; atty. Miss. Dept. Pub. Welfare, Jackson, 1953-58, commr., 1964-67; asst. atty. gen. State of Miss., Jackson, 1959; treas., State of Miss., 1960-64, 68-72; commr. ins., State of Miss., 1972—; mem. Miss. State Bd. Savs. and Loan Assns., Miss. Ins. Commn. Del., Miss. Democratic Convs., 1948-60; mem. Miss. Ho. of Reps., 1948-52. Bd. dirs. Miss. Hosp. and Med. Service. Recipient Jackson Woman of Year award, 1964; named One of Top Ten Women of Sixties in a 3-state area Comml. Appeal Memphis. Mem. Am., Miss. bar assns., Am. Judicature Soc., Miss. Cabinet Women in Pub. Affairs, Miss. Econ. Council, Am. Assn. Women Accountants, Miss. Conf. Social Welfare, Miss. Fedn. Bus. and Profl. Women's Clubs (pres. 1953-54), Congress Parents and Tchrs. Democrat. Baptist. Club: Altrusa (Jackson). Home: 727 Arlington St Jackson MS 39202 Office: Walter Sillers Bldg Jackson MS 39205

GANDY, MARTHA FRANCES, social worker; b. Hattiesburg, Miss., May 4, 1928; d. Kearney C. and Abbie (Whigham) Gandy; B.A., Millsaps Coll., 1949; M.S.W., La. State U., 1962. Visitor, Miss. Dept. Pub. Welfare, Jackson, 1954-58, casework supr., 1958-59, hearing officer, 1959-62, dist. supr., 1962-64, dir. div. adminstrv. services, 1964-67, commnr., 1967-68, dir. Office of Tng., 1968—. Mem. Miss. Women's Cabinet Pub. Affairs. Mem. Miss. Conf. Social Welfare (past chmn. membership com., publs. com.), Nat. Assn. Social Workers, Am. Pub. Welfare Assn., La. State U. Alumni Council, Jackson Bus. and Profl. Women's Club (past chmn. legislation com., civic participation com.). Baptist. Home: 727 Arlington St Jackson MS 39202 Office: PO Box 4321 Fondren Sta Jackson MS 39216

GANICK, NELLENE RICHARDSON (MRS. FRANK P. GANICK), publishing sales exec.; b. Forest Park, Ga., Dec. 11, 1923; d. Otis and Zora Helen (Wootan) Richardson; B.A. in Journalism, U. Ga., 1944; postgrad. U. Tenn., 1949, Peabody Coll., 1963-64; m. Frank P. Ganick, Sept. 14, 1945; children—Gary Paul, Nicholas Richardson. Copywriter, Reliable Stores, Balt., 1946; advt. copywriter Methodist Pub. House, Nashville, 1951-56; copywriter, advt. and sales promotion, book store div. Baptist Sunday Sch. Bd., Nashville, 1956-60, sales promotion specialist, 1960—. Served with WAVES, 1945. Mem. Woman's Nat. Book Assn. (mem. bd. 1971-72), Women in Communications. Baptist. Club: Battlewood Women's (sec.). Home: 723 Cameo Dr Nashville TN 37211 Office: 127 9th Av N Nashville TN 37234

GANNETT, ANN COLE, state legislator; b. Brookline, Mass., Nov. 7, 1916; d. Benjamin Edwards and Ann (Sheafe) Cole; grad. cum laude, Abbott Acad., 1933; student Vassar Coll., 1933-35; m. Thomas B. Gannett, Apr. 18, 1936 (dec.); children—Thomas B., Jr., Ann G. (Mrs. Hurlbut), Benjamin H., Deborah G. (Mrs. Brooks), Peter C. Chmn., Wayland Republican Town Com., 1949-52, mem., 1946—; mem. Mass. Rep. Finance Com., 1952-60; mem. Mass. State Rep. Com., 1952-67; del. Rep. Nat. Conv., 1964, 72; mem. Mass. Ho. of Reps., 1969—. Ednl. aide Mus. Fine Arts, Boston. Trustee Mass. Hosps.; mem. Gov.'s Adv. Com., 1952-54. Roman Catholic. Home: 85 Old Connecticut Path Wayland MA 01778*

GANNON, SISTER ANN IDA, coll. pres.; b. Chgo., 1915; d. George and Hanna (Murphy) Gannon; A.B., Clarke Coll., 1941; A.M., Loyola U., Chgo., 1948; Ph.D., St. Louis U., 1952; hon. degrees Lincoln Coll., 1965, Luther Coll., 1968, Augustana Coll., 1969, Columbia Coll., 1969, Loyola U., 1970, DePaul U., 1972, Ursuline Coll., 1972, Coll. Holy Cross, 1974, Spertus Coll. Judaica, 1974. Mem. Sisters of Charity; tchr. English, St. Mary's High Sch., Chgo., 1941-47; residence, study abroad 1951; chmn. philosophy dept. Mundelein Coll., 1951-57, pres. coll., 1957—. Dir. No. Ill. Gas. Co. Mem. edn. com. Gov.'s Commn. on Status of Women; mem. President's Task Force on Women's Rights and Responsibilities, 1969. Bd. dirs. Girl Scouts U.S.A., 1966—; bd. dirs. N. Central Assn. Colls. and Secondary Schs., 1971—, exec. bd. commn. on instns. higher edn., 1971—, vice chmn., 1972-74. Danforth Found. grantee, 1970-71. Mem. Am. Cath. Philos. Assn. (exec. council 1953-56), Religious Edn. Assn. Am. (pres.), Am. Council Edn. (dir. 1971-74, exec. com. 1973, chmn. 1973-74), Am. Assn. Sch. Adminstrs., Fedn. Ill. Colls.,

Nat. Cath. Edn. Assn., Am. Assn. U. Women, Metaphys. Soc. Am., Assn. Am. Colls. (chmn. 1969). Contbr. articles philos. and edn. jours. Address: 6363 Sheridan Rd Chicago IL 60660

GANO, MARY MYERS (MRS. LOWELL R. GANO), church woman, accountant; b. Indpls., Sept. 29, 1920; d. Claude Faye and Anne (Bates) Myers; student So. Meth. U., 1947-49, U. Cal. at Berkeley, 1949-51; B.A., Sacramento State Coll., 1954; m. Lowell Ralph Gano, Nov. 28, 1940; children—Bates Myers (dec.), Mary Ann (dec.), Douglas Andrew, Elizabeth Ann. Bookkeeper, clerical work, Bethard Wallpaper & Paint Co., Indpls., 1944-46, West Disinfecting Co., Dallas, 1946-47; sr. account clerk U. Cal. at Berkeley Library, 1949-52; accountant, auditor Lyman Straine & Co., C.P.A.'s, Sacramento, 1953-56. Treas. Sacramento Presbytery Camp and Conf. Grounds, 1959-60; vice chmn. Presbyn. Campus Ministry, Sacramento, 1959-60, chmn. bd., 1960-61, chmn. finance com., 1961-62; dir. central area Westminster Found., 1960, 62-63; mem. central area coordinating council United Presbyn. Ch., 1961-64, sec., 1964, sec. adminstrv. com. 1961-64, mem. gen. council Sacramento Presbytery, 1965-66, chmn. budget com., 1974—, trustee Synod of Cal., 1968—, mem. budget task force Synod of Pacific, 1973—; sec. Lake Tahoe Zephyr Point Mgmt. Com., 1968-72, chmn., 1972—; pres. parents assn., asst. treas. Sacramento Country Day Sch., 1965-71. Mem. Jr. Music Sponsors (exec. bd. 1961-64, 67-68, treas. 1962-64), Am. Soc. Women Accountants (chpt. pres. 1956-57, chmn. scholarship 1961-62, pub. relations chmn. 1963-64, dir. 1967-68), U.S. Figure Skating Assn., Am. Soc. Women Accountants (finance chmn. Western regional conf. 1963), Kaiser Found. Hosps. Vol. League (pres. Sacramento chpt. 1971), Alpha Lamba Delta. Presbyn. (elder, trustee 1965-67). Mem. Internat. Order Job's Daus. (guardian sec.), Order Eastern Star. Clubs: Capitol City Figure Skating (bus. mgr. ice show 1966, 67); Tuesday. Home: 3531 El Ricon Way Sacramento CA 95825

GANONG, MARIAN MISH, pub. relations exec.; b. nr. Staunton, Va.; d. Robert Warren Howe and Ligia (Botts) Mish; student Mary Baldwin Coll., 1938; m. James Henry Culpepper, Dec. 1, 1969; children from previous marriage—Jay, Stuart Wentworth. Sec. office mgr. to alumni sec. Va. Mil. Inst., Alumni Assn., Lexington, 1937-39; sec. Van Strum & Towne, Inc., San Francisco, 1940-42; sales rep. Henri Fayette, Inc., Chgo., 1946-53; asso. John J. Greer, A.I.D. & Assos., Georgetown, Washington, 1950-53; sales rep. Walter Lamb, Pebble Beach, Cal., 1953-54; mgr. campagin hdqrs. Teague-For-Congress-Campaign, Monterey, Cal., 1954; rancher, developer Edison A. Holt, Carmel Valley, Cal., 1953-54; social dir. for Walt Disney preparatory to opening Disneyland, Cal., 1955; account co-ordinator Hixson & Jorgensen Advt., 1956-57; dir. contact div. and speakers bur. Knowland for Gov. Campaign, 1958; account exec., West Coast rep. Farson Huff & Northlich Advt. & Pub. Relations, Cin., 1958-59; dir. contact div. Bell-For-Congress Campaign, 1960; pub. relations Frost & Shaffer Advt., Hollywood, Cal., 1959-61; pub. relations dir. Cal. Adoption Found. Holy Family Adoption Service, Los Angeles, 1961-62, Leo J. Shanahan Co., 1962-64; pub. relations Blakiston Ranch, Inc., Chatsworth, 1965-68. Founding dir., horse show chmn. Peacock Hill Nat. Horse Show for Benefit of John Tracy Clinic, Tustin, 1964, 65; coordinator City of Hope Internat. Horse Show, 1968. Founding chmn. Orange County, Freedoms Found. of Valley Forge. Mem. Los Angeles Advt. Women, Inc., Pub. Relations Soc. Am., Newport Harbor C. of C. (dir. women's div.). Republican. Episcopalian. Editor, pub., pres. The Orange Book, 1966-67. Home: #6 Farmington Dr Charlottesville VA 22906

GANSBERG, LUCILLE MATILDA, curriculum cons.; b. Oakland, Cal., Aug. 8, 1908; d. Charles Emil and Henrietta Elizabeth (Ohmen) Gansberg; A.B., U. Cal. at Berkeley, 1929; postgrad. San Francisco State Coll., 1934, 42-44; M.Ed., Mills Coll., 1948; postgrad. Sacramento State Coll., 1964-65. Tchr. high sch., Siskiyou County, Cal., 1930-33, tchr. elementary sch., 1933-47; supr. instrn. Lassen County (Cal.) schs., 1948-51; county supt. of schs. Lassen County, 1951-63; curriculum cons. Sacramento County Schs., 1963-73; cons. to sch. dists., health orgns., 1963—. Council pres. Camp Fire Girls, Inc., Susanville, Cal., 1959-62, Sacramento, 1967-69. Named Woman of Year, Susanville Soroptimist Club, 1961; recipient award of merit Cal. Sch. Health Assn., 1970. Mem. Cal. Fedn. Bus. and Profl. Womens Clubs (local pres. 1953, dist. pres. 1956), UN Assn. U.S.A. (chpt. dir. 1966-73), Phi Beta Kappa, Delta Kappa Gamma. Mem. Order Eastern Star, Ct. of Amaranth.

GANT, LISBETH ANTOINETTE, author, editor; b. Chgo., Apr. 16, 1948; d. Phillip Marshall and Naurice Elizabeth (Jones) Gant, Jr.; B.A. with honors (Ill. State scholor sr. fellow) Kalamazoo Coll., 1968; M.A., Columbia, 1970. Mem. Coll. bd. Conde Nast Pub. Mademoiselle Mag., N.Y.C., 1965, instr. black lit. Borough of Manhattan Community Coll., N.Y., 1970-71, Rutgers U., New Brunswick, N.J., 1971-72, State U. of N.Y. at Stony Brook, 1972-73; West Coast editor Essence Mag., Los Angeles, 1973—. Copy editor Black Theatre Mag., N.Y.C., 1969-72; free lance writer, 1969—. Sec. Sixth Pan African Congress Black World, 1971-72. Chmn. Los Angeles exec. com. United Negro Coll. Fund. Recipient Johnson Meml. Spanish award, 1960, Coretta Scott King award Am. Assn. U. Women, 1970, Richard Wright-Amiri Baraka award, Black World Mag., 1972. Mem. African Heritage Studies Assn. Author: Bibliography of Black American Literature 1746 to 1973, 1974; Resistance to the African Slave Trade, 1974. Contbr. articles on black lit. to popular and lit. mags. Home: 1831 Prosser Av #107 Los Angeles CA 90025 Office: 8560 Sunset Blvd Los Angeles CA 90069

GANZ, IRMA, publishing co. exec.; b. Scranton, Pa., Dec. 25, 1916; d. Jacob and Dora (Weinberger) Ganz; B.A., Pa. State U., 1938; m. Milton Miller, Sept. 3, 1939 (dec.). Dir. Soccer Assos., 1948—; bus. mgr. Jeffrey Lee Syndicate, 1953—; pres. Sportshelf, New Rochelle, N.Y., 1953—; bus. mgr. and dir. Wide World Book Center Ltd., 1966—; mng. editor Soccer News, 1968—. Mem. Soccer Writer's Assn. (pres. 1969-74), Nat. Recreation Assn., A.A.H.P.E.R., Am. Booksellers Assn., Nat. Parks and Recreation Assn., Pa. State U. Alumni Assn., Nat. Sportscasters and Sportswriters Assn., Internat. Platform Assn. Office: 359 North Av New Rochelle NY 10802 also PO Box 634 New Rochelle NY 10802

GANZ, VIVIAN HOFF (MRS. ANDREW GANZ), psychologist; b. N.Y.C., May 27, 1944; d. Fred and Joan (Lamm) Hoff; M.A., Columbia, 1965; m. Andrew R. Ganz, June 5, 1971; 1 dau., Elissa Tamara. Sr. research scientist N.Y. State Psychiat. Inst.-Columbia-Presbyn. Med. Center, N.Y.C., 1965-71; clin. psychologist Springfield (Mass.) Hosp. Med. Center, 1972-73; research psychologist Hillside div. L.I. Jewish-Hillside Med. Center, Glen Oaks, N.Y., 1973—. Mem. Am. Psychol. Assn., Psi Chi. Contbr. research papers to profl. jours. Office: 114 E 72d St New York City NY 10021

GARA, NICOLE, lobbyist, assn. exec.; b. West Palm Beach, Fla., Mar. 25, 1946; d. Nicholas Miklos and Vivian (Suomila) Gara; B.A., Syracuse U., 1968; M.A., N.Y. U., 1970. Dir., registered lobbyist, Congl. liaison A.I.A., Washington, 1971—. Mem. English Speaking Union (treas. unit spl. events 1970-72), Nat. Orgn. Women, League Women Voters. Democrat. Home: 5250 Valley Forge Dr Alexandria VA 22304 Office: 1735 New York Av NW Washington DC 20006

GARBELLANO, NANCY FIDELIA, chem. co. exec.; b. N.Y.C., Nov. 21, 1925; d. Frank and Rose (Masciandaro) Garbellano; grad. high sch. With Lockhead Labs., 1943-45; biller Walter G. Legge Co., Inc., N.Y.C., 1945-53, office mgr., 1953-69, treas., dir., 1969—. Asso. mem. St. Vincents Hosp., 1953—. Mem. Sons of Italy Am. Ladies Aux., N.Y. Heart Assn., Fair Ladies div. Am. Airlines. Home: 1140 81st St Brooklyn NY 11228 Office: 101 Park Av New York City NY 10017

GARCIA, ANN HUGHES (MRS. RAYMOND GARCIA), govt. ofcl.; b. Birmingham, Ala., Nov. 24, 1938; d. Brady Alexander and Juanita Whitfield (Pope) Hughes; B.A., George Washington U., 1962, M.A. (Grad. fellow), 1969; m. Raymond Garcia, Dec. 31, 1970. With U.S. Dept. Commerce, Washington, 1963—, dir. legislative and tariff policy div., 1971—, also del. numerous internat. trade confs. including UN Indsl. Devel. Orgn., UN Conf. on Trade and Devel., GATT. Instr. econs. George Washington U., 1963. Mem. Am. Econs. Assn., Omicron Delta Epsilon. Club: Inn Flying. Home: 4214 Elizabeth Lane Annandale VA 22003 Office: Dept of Commerce Washington DC 20230

GARCIA, CHRISTINA DAVIS (MRS. RICHARD R. GARCIA), assn. exec.; b. San Antonio, Feb. 10, 1947; d. Sheppard G. and Shirley A. (Bradford) Davis; A.A., Del Mar Coll., 1967; B.S., U. Tex., 1969; m. Richard R. Garcia, Mar. 24, 1973. Tchr. journalism Richard King High Sch., Corpus Christi, 1969-71; copy editor Caller-Times Pub. Co., Corpus Christi, 1971-73; pub. information office asst. City of Corpus Christi, 1973; pub. relations mgr. Corpus Christi C. of C., 1973—. Exec. sec. Beautify Corpus Christi Assn., 1973; supr., phone vol. Suicide Prevention Crisis Service, 1971—; vol. worker Head Start, 1972. Mem. Am. Assn. U. Women, Women in Communications, Corpus Christi Advt. Fedn. (asso.), Corpus Christi Press Club (dir. 1973). Democrat. Methodist. Home: 4848 S Alameda Apt 401 Corpus Christi TX 78412 Office: PO Box 640 Corpus Christi TX 78403

GARCIA, JOSEFINA MARGARITA, dancer, nurse, educator; b. Mascota, Jalisco, Mexico, May 2, 1906; d. Manuel Garcia Perez and Margarita (Garcia) Flores; diploma Nat. Coll., Kansas City, Mo., 1933; tchrs. certificate State Tchrs. Coll., Queretaro, Mexico, 1935; R.N., Bethany Hosp. Sch. Nursing, 1939; diploma in psychiat. nursing Inst. of Living, Hartford, Conn., 1941; B.S., Tchrs. Coll., Columbia, 1943, M.A. in Health and Phys. Edn., 1945; Ph.D. in Dance and Related Arts, Tex. Woman's U., 1958. Came to U.S., 1923, naturalized, 1944. Elementary tchr. Methodist Normal Sch., Puebla, Mexico, 1934-36; dir. religious edn., nurse, coordinator phys. edn. George O. Robinson Sch., San Juan, P.R., 1939-40; psychiat. nurse Psychiat. div. N.Y. Hosp., White Plains, 1941-43; tchr. health Poly. Inst., San German, P.R., 1943-44; charge corrective gymnastics Hosp. for Spl. Surgery, N.Y.C., 1944-45; nurse Bellevue Hosp., N.Y.C., 1945-50; tchr., performer La Meri's Ethnologic Center, N.Y.C., 1945-47; lectr., dancer Pearl Buck's East and West Assn., 1947-49; artist, tchr., nurse Jacob's Pillow U. of Dance, Lee, Mass., summers 1949-55; pvt. duty nurse Harkness Pavillion, N.Y.C., 1952-55; supr. psychiat. div. Parkland Meml. Hosp., Dallas, 1956-58; grad. asst. in dance Tex. Woman's U., Denton, 1956-58; chmn. health, phys. edn. and recreation dept. Okla. Coll. for Women, Chickasha, 1958-63 (on leave), instr., 1934-36, 39-40, prof., 1963-64; vis. prof. edn. Miami U., Coral Gables, Fla., 1963-64; dir. dance in dept. health and phys. edn., prof. phys. edn. Madison Coll., Harrisonburg, Va., 1964-67; tchr. of English as secondary lang., bilingual edn. N.Y.C. Bd. Edn. Part-time staff Grady Meml. Hosp., Chickasha, 1962-63; numerous dance recitals and workshops, 1940—; tchr. Mexican and Latin Am. dance Tina Ramirez Dance Studio, N.Y.C.; cons. Sacred Dance Guild; choreographer on Mexican themes Alliance Latin Am. Arts, summer 1973. Fellow A.A.H.P.E.R.; mem. Am., Okla., N.Y. State (dir.) nurses assns., Nat., So., Va. assns. phys. edn. coll. women, ANTA, Okla. Edn. Assn., Va. Assn. Health, Phys. Edn. and Recreation (chmn. 1962-63), Am. Assn. U. Women, Chickasha Bus. and Profl. Women's Club (past chmn. internat. relations com.), Nat. Dance Tchrs. Guild, Nat. Council Arts in Edn., Mus. Natural History, Dance Notation Bur., Internat. Platform Assn., Pan Am. Women's Assn. (dir. 1967—), Dance Film Library Assn. (dir. 1967—), Film Soc (dir.), Profl. Dance Tchrs. Assn., Kappa Delta Pi, Phi Sigma Iota. Contbr. articles on dance to profl. publs., Groliers Ency., Richards Ency. Home: 162 E 80th St New York City NY 10021

GARDINE, JUANITA CONSTANTIA FORBES (MRS. CYPRIAN A. GARDINE), sch. adminstr.; b. St. Croix, V.I., Aug. 6, 1912; d. Alphonso Sebastian and Petrina (Actien) Forbes; B.A., Hunter Coll., 1934; M.A., Columbia, 1940; postgrad. U. Chgo., 1950, N.Y. U., 1960-66; m. Cyprian A. Gardine, Apr. 23, 1942; children—Cyprian A., Vicki Maria Camilla, Letitia Theresa, Richard Whittington. Tchr. elementary schs., 1934-35; tchr. math. high sch., 1935-41, 48-49; acting asst. high sch. prin., 1941; jr. high sch. prin., 1941-47; substitute tchr. math., physics, Montclair, N.J., 1947-48; asst. supt. edn., 1949-55; asso. dean Community Colls., 1955-57; high sch. prin., 1957-58; supr. ednl. statistics, 1958-62; social worker Dept. Welfare, 1962-63; prin. Christiansted (St. Croix) Pub. Grammar Sch., 1963-74; tchr. math. evening session extension classes Cath. U. P.R. Past sec. bd. dirs. St. Croix Fed. chpt. A.R.C., chmn. supervisory com. St. Croix. Fed. Credit Union; past sec. St. Croix Sch. Health Com.; past pres. St. Croix (V.I.) Mental Health Assn. Pres., Tchrs. Assn., 1940, Municipal Employees Assn., 1942. Mem. Am. Statis. Assn., V.I. Fedn. Bus. and Profl. Womens Club (past sec.), Episcopal Ch. Women of V.I. (past chmn. world affairs com., past pres. women of ch.), Christiansted Bus. and Profl. Women's Club (pres.), Daus. King (sec.), Hunter Coll. Alumni Assn. Home: 142 Whim Frederiksted VI 00840 also PO Box 1505 Christiansted St Croix VI 00820 Office: Richmond Christiansted St Croix VI 00820

GARDINER, LILLIAN JOHNSON (MRS. LAURENCE B. GARDINER), author, club woman; b. Humboldt, Tenn., Aug. 15, 1910; d. Tyree LeRoy and Lillian Janette (Campbell) Johnson; student Peabody Coll. and Vanderbilt U., 1928-31, Falls Bus. Coll., Nashville, 1931-32; m. Laurence Bridges Gardiner, Dec. 12, 1944. Author: (with Mrs. L. D. Bejach) Williamson County Marriages 1800-50, 1956; (with Mrs. J. B. Cartwright) North Carolina Land Grants in Tennessee 1778-1791, 1958, Hess-Daviess Family Booklet, 1958; editor, originator Ansearchin' News, organ Memphis Geneal. Soc., 1953-59; editor geneal. column in nat. mag. U.D.C. Named Ky. col., 1967. Mem. Tenn. Civil War Centennial Com.; mem. woman's adv. council, speakers bur. Civil Def.; hon. life mem., dir. woman's bd. Mid-South Fair. Mem. Nat. League Am. Pen Women (br. pres.; state pres.), Tenn. Woman's Press and Authors Club, Sons and Daus. Pilgrims, Memphis Little Theatre (patron), Nat. Geneal. Soc., Colonial Dames Am. (chpt. parliamentarian, v.p.), D.A.R., Daus. Am. Colonists (past Tenn. pres.), Huguenot Soc. (hon. pres. Tenn. 1955—; nat. pres. 1967-69) Descs. Colonial Clergy, Dames Ct. Honor (pres. Tenn. 1961-63, nat. trustee), Decs. Knights Garter, St. George's Chapel Windsor Castle, U.S. Daus. 1812, Assn. Preservation Tenn. Antiquities (chpt. parliamentarian), Order First Families Va., Jamestowne Soc. (dep. gov. Tenn. 1970-72), U.D.C. (chpt. pres. 1958-62), Tenn. Geneal. Soc. (past pres.), Kings Daus. and Sons (leader), Daus. of Barons of Runnemede. Presbyn. Home: 1863 Cowden Av Memphis TN 38104

GARDNER, CAROL RUTH, banker; b. near Hartford, Kan., Mar. 12, 1910; d. Robert Owen and Carrie (Gasche) Gardner; B.S., Kan. State Coll. of Emporia, 1930; student Kan. State U., summer 1934, Gregg Coll., summer 1936, Columbia, summer 1938. Tchr., high sch., Atwood, Kan., 1930-35, Winfield, Kan., 1935-39; sec., office mgr. Pioneer ins. agy., Denver, 1939-44; supr. stenographic pool Trans World Airline, Kansas City, Mo., 1945-46; sec. trust dept. Commerce Bank of Kansas City, N.A., (formerly Commerce Trust Co.), 1946-63, adminstr. probate div. trust dept., 1963-64, asst. trust officer, 1965-66, trust officer, 1967—, asst. v.p., 1972—. Mem. Am. Inst. Banking, Nat. Secs. Assn. (chpt. pres. 1961-62), C. of C. Presbyn. Mem. Order Eastern Star, PEO. Clubs: Womens City, Soroptomist. Home: 4712 Roanoke Pkwy Kansas City MO 64112 Office: Commerce Bank Bldg Kansas City MO 64106

GARDNER, HELEN LOUISE, educator; b. Feb. 13, 1908; B.A. with 1st class honors, Oxford U. (Eng.), 1929, M.A., 1935, D.Litt., 1963. Lectr. Royal Holloway Coll., U. London, 1931-34, U. Birmingham, 1934-41; tutor in English lit. St. Hilda's Coll., 1941-54, reader in Renaissance English lit. U. Oxford, 1954-66, Merton prof. English lit., 1966, also fellow Lady Margaret Hall; vis. prof. U. Cal. at Los Angeles, 1954; Riddell Meml. lectr. U. Durham, 1956; Alexander Meml. lectr. U. Toronto, 1962; Messenger lectr. Cornell U., 1967; Eliot Meml. lectr. U. Kent, 1968. Mem. Robbins Com. on Higher Edn., 1961-63; mem. Council for Nat. Acad. Awards, 1964-67; del. Oxford U. Press, 1959—. Trustee Nat. Portrait Gallery. Decorated dame Order Brit. Empire, 1967; comdr. Order Brit. Empire, 1962. Fellow Royal Soc. Lit., Brit. Acad. Author: The Art of T.S. Eliot, 1949; The Divine Poems of John Donne, 1952; The Metaphysical Poets, 1957; The Business of Criticism, 1959; The Elegies and Songs and Sonnets of John Donne, 1965; A Reading of Paradise Lost, 1965; Religion and Literature, 1971. Editor: (with T. Healey) John Donne: Selected Prose, 1967; Shakespearian and Other Studies (F.P. Wilson), 1969; Faber Book of Religious Verse, 1972; New Oxford Book of English Verse, 1972. Home: Myrtle House Eynsham Oxford England

GARDNER, JO ANN EVANS, psychologist, publisher; b. Latrobe, Pa., Apr. 19, 1925; d. Eugene Everly and Elizabeth Hannah (Atkinson) Evans; B.S., U. Pitts., 1950, M.S., 1960, Ph.D., 1964; m. Gerald Henry Fraser Gardner, Aug. 13, 1950. Asst. prof. psychology Carnegie Mellon U., Pitts., 1965-68, U. Pitts., 1960-70; founder, pres. KNOW, Inc., a women's liberation pub. co., Pitts., 1969—. Mem. Allegheny County Govt. Study Commn., 1972—. Mem. Am. Psychol. Assn. (div. rep. governing council 1974—), Nat. Orgn. for Women (Eastern regional co-dir.), Nat. Women's Polit. Caucus (adv. bd.). Home: 726 St James St Pittsburgh PA 15232 Office: KNOW Inc PO Box 86031 Pittsburgh PA 15221

GARDNER, JOYCE THRESHER (MRS. RUSSELL MENESE GARDNER), club woman, travel cons.; b. Glen Ridge, N.J., Nov. 19, 1922; d. Harold Hayward and Hilda (Gillet) Thresher; student Arlington Hall Jr. Coll., 1939; A.B., Duke, 1944; m. Russell Menese Gardner, Mar. 7, 1946; children—Winthrop Gillet, Page Stansbury, June Thresher. Guest editor Mademoiselle mag., N.Y.C., 1943; asst. promotion mgr. sta. WGBS, Miami, Fla., 1945-46; editor house organ sta. WDNC, Durham, N.C., 1947-48; columnist Personally Speaking, Miami Herald, 1952-54; owner Joyce Gardner Travel Cons., 1968—. Pub. relations dir. Ft. Lauderdale (Fla.) Garden Club, 1951; Children's radio chmn. Jr. League, Miami, 1945-48; pres. Jr. League Sustainers, 1967-68; moderator monthly panel on current issues Miami Herald; radio-TV chmn. Ft. Lauderdale Mus. Arts, 1958-59, lecture chmn., 1960-61, co-chmn. spl. gifts com., 1960-61, bd. dirs., 1959-68, mem. exec. com., 1961-62, rec. sec. 1961-62, founder, corr. sec. Beaux Arts of Ft. Lauderdale, Inc., 1960-61, rec. sec., 1961-62, pres., 1964-66, asso. rep., 1971—; adv. bd. Fort Lauderdale Library, 1963—. Mem. A.L.A., Am. Assn. Museums, Soc. Mayflower Descs. (lt. gov. John Alden Colony), Phi Beta Kappa, Alpha Delta Pi. Democrat. Presbyn. Clubs: Ft. Lauderdale Yacht, Coral Ridge Country (Ft. Lauderdale); Le Club International. Home: 2412 NE 14th St Fort Lauderdale FL 33304 Office: 1109 E Las Olas Blvd Fort Lauderdale FL 33301

GARDNER, LAURA REID (MRS. STEWART FRANKLIN GARDNER), holding co. exec.; b. Elkart, Ind., Aug. 17, 1915; d. Clarence Edward and Clara Sophie (Gardner) Reid; grad. high sch.; m. Stewart Franklin Gardner, Aug. 8, 1936; children—Ann (Mrs. Thomas D. Miller), Stewart Eddy, Susan (Mrs. Richard Bressler). Tchr., Bristol, Ind., Dallas, 1955-67; sec.-treas. Stewart Coach Industries, Bristol, 1946—. Cons. interior decorating. Bd. dirs. March of Dimes, 1950-60, Mental Health, 1963-65, Civic Music, 1955-60, YWCA, 1968. Methodist. Club: Garden (pres. Bristol 1958). Home: Rural Route 2 Box 17 Bristol IN 46507 Office: Stewart Coach Industries Inc Bristol IN 46507

GARDNER, MARILYN, editor; b. Barrington, Ill., 1927; d. Anthony and Elizabeth (Jurs) Gardner; B.A. in Journalism, U. Ill., 1949. Editor Barrington (Ill.) Courier-Rev., 1950-53; reporter women's dept. Milw. Jour., 1953-63, asst. women's editor, 1965-67, women's editor, 1967—. Office: 333 W State St Milwaukee WI 53201

GARDNER, MARY ADELAIDE, educator; b. Kingston, O., July 19, 1920; d. J.P. and Georgia Wyland (Davis) Gardner; A.A., Stephens Coll., 1940; B.A., Ohio State U., 1942, M.A., 1953; postgrad. Evansville Coll., 1942-43, Mexico City Coll., 1952, U. de San Marcos (Peru), 1954-55; Ph.D., U. Minn., 1960. Spl. services Land Upper Austria Area Command, U.S. Army, Austria, 1948-51; program asst. World Affairs Progam, Mpls. Star and Mpls. World Affairs Center, 1957-59; copy editor Mpls. Star, 1960-61; teaching asst. sch. journalism U. Minn., Mpls., 1957-60, lectr. sch. journalism, 1960-61; asst. prof. sch. journalism U. Tex. at Austin, 1961-66; asso. prof. sch. journalism Mich. State U., 1966—, liaison officer USMC, 1966—. Field study Latin Am., Asia, Eastern Europe, Europe, 1972-73, Guatemala and El Salvador, summer 1968; cons. El Norte, Monterrey, Mexico, summers 1970, 72, 74, Corpus Christi Caller Times, summer 1965; hist. researcher Marine Corps Museum, summers 1971, 69, 67; Am. specialist U.S. State Dept. Centro Internacionale de Estudios Superiores Para Am. Latina, Ecuador, summer 1963, Honduras and Columbia, summer 1962. Served with USMC, 1943-46. Recipient Teaching Excellence award, Students Assn. U. Tex., 1966; Stephens Coll. Alumna Recognition award, 1965; commendation Consejo Directivo, U. Antioquia, Columbia, 1962. Buenos Aires fellow to Peru, 1953-54, Mpls. Woman's Club fellow, 1956-57, research fellow, OAS, 1959-60, Tozer Scholarship, 1959-60. Mem. Latin Am. Studies Assn., Assn. for Edn. in Journalism, Midwest Council of Assns. for Latin Am. Studies, Inter Am. Press Assn., Am. Assn. U. Profs., Women in Communications, Delta Sigma, Chi Delta Phi, Kappa Tau Alpha. Author: The Press of Latin America: A Tentative and Selected Bibilography in Spanish and Portuguese, 1973; The Press of Guatemala, 1971. Contbr. articles to profl. jours. Home: 630 Grove St East Lansing MI 48823 Office: Sch Journalism Mich State U East Lansing MI 48824

GARDNER, MILBURN JANICE, advt. co. exec.; b. Fort Smith, Ark., Oct. 24, 1928; d. Alfred Emmett and Dona Catherine (Williams) Gardner; student Memphis State U., 1946-48; m. Joseph James Pinter, Sept. 1949 (div. Dec. 1955). Women's commentator, writer sta. WJPR, Greenville, Miss., 1948; copy dir. sta. WHHM, Memphis, 1949; writer, women's dir., producer sta. WKBW, Buffalo, 1949; radio dir. H.J. Weil, Inc., Buffalo, 1950-56; partner Gardner-Taylor Advt., Inc., Memphis, 1956-72; pres. Jan Gardner & Assos., Inc., 1972—. Mem. Heart Assn., Kidney Found.; active Memphis Arts Council, 1969-71, St. Peter's Orphanage, 1962-64, Easter Seals, 1964-66. Bd. dirs. Goodwill Homes for Children, Memphis-Shelby County March of Dimes, sec., 1966-72; mem. Women's adv. com. Shelby State

Community Coll. Recipient Appreciation award Memphis State U., 1972. Mem. Memphis Advt. Fedn. (pres. 1971-72, named Advt. Woman of the Year 1968), Memphis C. of C., Memphis State U. Alumni Assn., Phi Mu. Club: Soroptimist (pres. 1971-72). Home: 647 West Dr Memphis TN 38112 Office: 3340 Poplar Av Memphis TN 38111

GARDNER, NATALIE NELLIE JAGLOM (MRS. RALPH D. GARDNER), advt. agy. exec.; b. Cernauti, Rumania; d. Abraham and Nadia (Shoenberg) Jaglom; came to U.S., 1939, naturalized, 1946; student Ohio State U., 1943, N.Y. U., 1944, U. Cal. at Berkeley, 1945; m. Ralph David Gardner, Apr. 9, 1952; children—Ralph David, John Jaglom, Peter Jaglom, James Jaglom. Dir. Ralph D. Gardner Advt., N.Y.C., 1955—. Vol., A.R.C., 1944; hosp. vol. Am. Women's Vol. Services, 1944-45. Home: 135 Central Park W New York City NY 10023 Office: 745 5th Av New York City NY 10022

GARDNER, VERA MAY SCOTT (MRS. LEROY N. GARDNER), city ofcl.; b. Detroit, Dec. 29, 1930; d. Clarence A. and Anna I. (Muma) Scott; certificate Jackson Bus. U., 1964; m. LeRoy N. Gardner, Oct. 16, 1971; 1 dau. by previous marriage, Renee (Mrs. Terry Selders). Bookkeeper City of Tecumseh (Mich.), 1949-62, dep. clk., 1962-67, city clk., treas., 1967—. Mem. Lenawee County Election Commn., 1972-74. Trustee Employees' Retirement System, City of Tecumseh. Mem. Municipal Clks. Assn. Mich., Mich. Municipal League (sec. region II, 1970-71), Tecumseh Bus. and Profl. Women's Club. Office: 309 E Chicago Blvd Tecumseh MI 49286

GARDNER, VIRGINIA DICKENS, extension home econs. agt.; b. Marianna, Fla.; d. Andrew and Alma (Dinah) Dickens; B.S., Fla. A. and M., U.; postgrad. Howard U., Prairie View A. and M. Coll., Tuskegee Inst., Cornell U., 1961, U. Fla., 1965, 68, 69, U.N.C. at Greensboro, 1971; M.Ed., N.C. State U., 1972. Coop. extension work agr. and home econs. State of Fla., home demonstration agt., Jackson County, Marianna, Fla., Columbia County, Lake City, Fla., Pinellas County, Clearwater Fla., 1961-63, asst. home demonstration agt., Largo, Fla., 1963-65, asst. county extension home econs. agt., 1965-69, extension home econs. I, Largo, Fla., 1969-70, extension home econs. agt. II, Largo, 1970—. Chmn. Jackson County Health Assn., Marianna, Fla., past sec. Jackson County Tng. Sch. P.T.A., chmn. March of Dimes Drive, Clearwater, 1964; mem. Friends of Ridgecrest Assn., 1962-68. Bd. dirs. Upper Pinellas Council on Human Relations, 1966-68, 71-73, adv. com., 1965-66, 68-71, nominating com., 1971. Named Agent of the Year, Fla. State Assn. Negro Home Demonstration Agents, 1962, also by Nat. Negro Home Demonstration Agts. Assn.; recipient award 4-H Club, Clearwater Heights, Fla. Mem. Fla. Assn. County and Home Demonstration Agts. (past financial sec., past chmn. civic com., past chmn. resolution com., past asst. sec.), Fla. State Assn. Negro Home Demonstration Agts. (pres. 1960-62, v.p. 1974—, mem. conv. com.), Nat. Negro Home Demonstration Agts. Assn. (pres. 1962-64), Am., Fla., West Coast home econs. assns., Nat., Fla. (2d v.p. 1974—, policy com., nominating com., pub. relations com., distinguished service com.) assns. extension home econ. agts., Queen St Community Club (pres.), Rainbow Subdivision Community Club, Epsilon Sigma Phi, Zeta Phi Beta. Baptist (treas. ch. jr. women 1966-69, sec. trustee com.). Office: PO Box 15353 St Petersburg FL 33733

GARIBALDI, MARIE LOUISE, lawyer; b. Jersey City, Nov. 26, 1934; d. Louis Joseph and Marie (Serventi) Garibaldi; B.A., Conn. Coll., 1956; LL.B., Columbia, 1959; LL.M., N.Y. U., 1963. Admitted to N.Y. bar, 1960, N.J. bar, 1965; regional counsel Office Internal Revenue Service, N.Y.C., 1960-66; asso. law firm McCarter & English, Newark, 1966-68; partner firm Riker, Danzig, Sherer & Brown, Newark, 1968—; acting municipal judge, Weehawken, N.J., 1973—. Lectr., N.Y. U. Tax Inst., 1970, Rutgers Continuing Legal Edn., 1971. Chmn., Bd. Adjustment Weehawken, 1970-73, Weehawken Charter Commn., 1969; bd. mgmt. YMCA-YWCA, Newark, 1969—. Mem. N.J. (exec. com. sect. taxation 1973—), Am. (mem. estate and gift com. sect. taxation 1972—), N.J. ins. com. trustee's com. 1973—) bar assns. Contbr. articles to profl. jours. Home: 34 Kingswood Rd Weehawken NJ 07087 Office: 744 Broad St Newark NJ 07102

GARLAND, FRANCES FAY (MRS. GRADY R. GARLAND), realtor; b. Shreveport, La., Sept. 9, 1925; d. Freddie Joe and Virdie Mae (Jaudon) Parker; student pub. schs.; m. Grady R. Garland, Oct. 12, 1944 (div. Aug. 1961); 1 dau., Nancy Gay (Mrs. Ronald Holman). Real estate saleswoman Town & Country Estates, Napa, Cal., 1950-52, realtor, 1952—; pres. Fay Garland, Inc., constrn. co., Napa, 1967—; pres. Napa Fed. Savs. & Loan Assn., 1972—, chmn. com., 1972—; owner Hangin' Tree Retail Store, retail furniture and gift shop, Napa, 1973—; real estate cons. Active City and County Planning Meetings; mem. Queen of Valley Hosp. Found. Nat. Real Estate Assn. Clubs: Silverado Country (Napa); Meadow Brook Country (St. Helena, Cal.). Home: 1142 Broadmoor Dr Napa CA 94558 Office: 3375 California Blvd Napa CA 94558

GARLAND, MARIANNE FRANCES BERRY (MRS. JOHN W. GARLAND), book reviewer; b. Dexter, Kan., Apr. 25, 1909; d. Edward Sanford and Mildred B. (Williamson) Berry; A.A., Stephens Coll., 1928; student Kan. U., 1928-30; m. John W. Garland, Feb. 16, 1929; children—Sally (Mrs. J. R. Foulks), Susanne (Mrs. Don Evans), C. Jepson, John S. Tchr. English and chemistry pub. schs., Perry, O., 1930-32; tchr. elementary sch., Wellington, Kan., 1953-55; wire editor Wellington Daily News, 1940-43; book reviewer for pubs. Wellington, 1960—. Commr. Wellington council Girl Scouts Am., 1940-42. Treas. Sumner County Republican Women, 1965-68. Bd. dirs. Midway Kan. area A.R.C., 1967—; bd. dirs. Wellington (Kan.) Library. Recipient award A.R.C., 1970. Mem. P.E.O., Stephens Coll. Alumnae, Alpha Chi Omega, Theta Alpha Epsilon. Presbyn. Home: 503 Morningside Dr Wellington KS 67152

GARLOCH, LORENA A. (MRS. PAUL H. BYERS), coll. adminstr.; b. North Girard, Pa., Sept. 28, 1908; d. David and Ine E. (Cheeseman) Garloch; student Westminster Coll., 1924-27; A.B. in L.S., U. Mich., 1928; M.A., U. Pitts., 1943, M.Ed., 1967; postgrad. Rutgers U., 1956; m. Paul H. Byers, Aug. 7, 1936. Cataloger Oberlin Coll., 1928-29; order librarian Am. Library, Paris, 1929-31; with U. Pitts., 1931-63, successively reference librarian, dir. pub. services, asst. librarian, acting librarian, 1952-54, univ. librarian and lectr. library sci., 1954-63; asst. prof. Rutgers U. Grad. Sch. Library Service, 1964- 66; asso. prof. Sch. Information and Library Studies, State U. N.Y. at Buffalo, 1966-68; dir. instl. research La. Roche Coll., 1968-71, asst. to pres., 1971-74; dir. coll. placement Cosmopolitan Profl. Employment Agy., 1974—. Mem. Pa. Library Assn. (pres. 1961-62), A.L.A., Soc. Indexers, London, Am. Assn. U. Profs., Sigma Xi, Phi Alpha Theta, Sigma Kappa. Presbyn. Contbr. articles to geog. and profl. jours. Home: 1558 Graham Blvd Pittsburgh PA 15235

GARLUND, ANNA WINIFRED (MRS. GARETH F. GARLUND), lawyer; b. Richmond, Cal., Aug. 8, 1913; d. Guy Arnott and Mary Freda (Dunlop) White; LL.B., San Francisco Law Sch., 1944, J.D., 1968; m. Gareth F. Garlund, Dec. 28, 1940; children—Sara Lee (Mrs. J.A. Estrada), Leslie (Mrs. P. Lupinsky), David (dec.). Admitted to Cal. bar, 1944, U.S. Supreme Ct. bar, 1974; practiced in San Francisco, 1950-59, Porterville, 1969—; adminstrv. sec. to chief justice of Cal. State Supreme Ct., 1940-47; asso. O'Gara & O'Gara, San Francisco, 1950-52, Garlund & Smith, San Francisco, 1952-57; individual practice law, San Francisco, 1957-59, Porterville, Cal., 1960-69, 70—; mem. firm Garlund & Bery, Porterville, 1969-70. Sec. Gateway Broadcasters, Inc., 1960—. Co-founder Co-op Nursery Sch., Porterville, 1961, Co-founder Unitarian fellowship, 1961; mem. com. of mgmt. Porterville YMCA, 1971—. Mem. City Council of Porterville, Cal., 1961-65. Bd. dirs. Tulare County Symphony, chmn. legal affairs com., 1973. Mem. San Francisco (dir. 1959), Tulare County (pres. 1973) bar assns., Queens Bench (pres. 1957). Club: Quota (pres. 1965). Office: 141 East Putnam Av Porterville CA 93257

GARMEL, MARION BESS SIMON (MRS. RAYMOND LOUIS GARMEL), journalist; b. El Paso, Tex., Oct. 15, 1936; d. Marcus and Frieda (Alfman) Simon; student U. Tex., El Paso, 1954-55; B.J., U. Tex., Austin, 1958; m. Raymond Louis Garmel, Nov. 28, 1965. Exec. sec. Nat. Student Assn., Phila., 1958-59, pub. relations dir., 1960-61; dictationist Wall St. Jour., Washington, 1961; librarian, staff writer Nat. Observer, Silver Spring, Md., 1961-70; art columnist Indpls. News, 1971—; also free-lance writer. Recipient 1st Pl. Critics Competition and Feature Story, 2d Pl. Personal Column awards Women's Press Club Ind., 1974. Mem. Nat. Student Assn., Nat. Fedn. Press Women, Nat. Hist. Soc., Hadassah, Women's Zionist Orgn. Am., Women in Communications, Soc. Profl. Journalists, Indpls. Press Club (Journalism award 2d pl. in columnist competition 1973), Delta Phi Epsilon. Democrat. Jewish religion. Home: 226 E 45th St Indianapolis IN 46205 Office: 307 N Pennsylvania St Indianapolis IN 46205

GARMIRE, ELSA, physicist, artist; b. Buffalo; d. Ralph E. and Nelle (Gubser) Meints; A.B. cum laude, Radcliffe Coll., 1961; Ph.D., Mass. Inst. Tech., 1965; m. Gordon Garmire, 1961; children—Lisa Nelle, Marla Victoria. Research fellow Cal. Inst. Tech., Pasadena, 1966-71, lectr., 1972, sr. research fellow applied sci., 1971—. One man show laser art Photosphere Gallery, Hollywood, Cal., 1971; pres. Laser Images, Inc., Los Angeles, 1971-73; cons. Pepsi Cola Pavilion Expo 70. Named Woman of Year, Mademoiselle mag., 1970; recipient Achievement award Soroptimist Los Angeles, 1970. Mem. Am. Phys. Soc., I.E.E.E., Optical Soc. Am., Expts. in Art and Tech. Cal. (v.p., 1969-71), Sigma Xi. Patentee laser devices. Author: Pavilion, 1972. Contbr. articles to profl. jours. Home: 296 S Chester Av Pasadena CA 91106

GARNER, MILDRED MAXINE, educator; b. nr. Liberty, N.C., Mar. 15, 1919; d. Robert Monroe and Maize (Kimrey) Garner; B.A., U. N.C., Greensboro, 1939; M.A., Union Theol. Sem., Columbia, 1946; Ph.D., U. Aberdeen, Scotland, 1952. Tchr. English, Roanoke Rapids (N.C.) High Sch., 1939-40, 41-42; asst. editor Bibl. Recorder, Raleigh, 1940; dir. religious activities U. N.C., Greensboro, 1942-50; asso. prof. religion Meredith Coll., 1952-58; prof. religion Sweet Briar (Va.) Coll., 1958—, dept. chmn., 1961-62, 63-72, 74—, Wallace Eugene Rollins prof., 1969—. Fulbright scholar, 1950-51, 51-52; Program of Advanced Religious Studies fellow Union Theol. Seminary N.Y., 1955-56; Am. Inst. Indian Studies fellow, Poona, India, 1962-63. Mem. Am. Assn. U. Women, Phi Beta Kappa. Republican. Baptist. Home: 123 N Asheboro St Liberty NC 27298 Office: Sweet Briar Coll Sweet Briar VA 24595

GARNSEY, DOROTHY CLARA COWAN (MRS. GEORGE EMMET GARNSEY), artist; b. Deckerville, Mich., Jan. 9, 1919; d. Adam William and Anna Margaret (Binkle) Cowan; student Shimer Coll., 1936-37; B. Design, U. Mich., 1941; B.S., Milw., Downer Coll., 1945; m. George Emmett Garnsey, June 21, 1941; children—Dale Emmett, Susan Elizabeth, William Alan. Clin. tng. Crile Army Hosp., Cleve., 1945-46; chief occupational therapist Crile VA Hosp., Cleve., 1948-51; coordinator for phys. medicine and rehab. Cleve. Clinic, 1952-55. One-woman shows of Oriental brush sumi-e at Stanford Research Inst., 1972, 74, Garden Cafe Gallery, Burlingame, Cal., 1973. Trainer vols. for Welfare Fed. Cleve., 1945-55, also mem. adv. bd., 1948-54; cons. Soc. for Crippled Children of Cleve.; mem. jr. bd. Berea (O.) Community Hosp., 1959-63. Recipient Bunts Found. Research grant Cleve. Clinic, 1952-55. Mem. Berea Fine Arts (program chmn. 1950-51, chmn. 1951-52), Am. Occupational Therapy Assn., San Carlos Fine Arts Assn., Sequoia Arts Assn. Address: 3266 Brittan Av San Carlos CA 94070

GARRARD, JEANNE, editor, educator, writer; b. Birmingham, Ala., Apr. 9, 1923; d. Oscar and Jeanne (Holoman) Garrard; student Stetson U., 1940-42; postgrad. Lindsey Hopkins Hotel Sch., 1959; m. Huber S. Ebersole, Oct. 1, 1957 (div. Nov. 1960). Radio dir., writer, commentator radio sta. WDBO, WLOF, Orlando, Fla., 1942-43; columnist Sentinel-Star, Orlando, 1943; radio commentator, writer for Burdine's, Palm Beach, Fla., 1943, Miami, Fla., 1943-44, radio Sta. WKAT, Miami Beach, Fla., 1944-45; commentator Sta. WIOD, Miami, Fla., 1944, commentator, writer Sta. WGBS, 1945; program dir. Melody, Inc., Miami Beach, 1945-48; writer Grant Advt., Inc., 1946; columnist Miami Beach (Fla.) Sun Star, 1946; writer for sta. WVCG, Coral Gables, Fla., 1949-50; columnist Miami Beach, 1950, Riviera-Times, Coral Gables, Fla., 1950, Miami Daily News, 1950-51; writer for Sta. WIOD, Miami, 1951; feature editor Miami Visitor Publ. Co., Miami Beach, 1952-55, mng. editor, 1955-56, editor, 1956-58; now cons. exec. editor Vis. Pub. Co.; free-lance writer, photographer with work appearing in various publ. including Am. Home mag., Stag mag., numerous newspapers; scout asst. to Better Homes & Gardens, Des Moines, 1959—; asst. mgr., housekeeper Anson Hotel, Surfside, Fla., 1959; asst. to editor, photographer Meredith Pub. Co., Des Moines, 1961; instr. writing adult edn. North Miami (Fla.) High Sch., 1956—; editorial asst. Ortho Garden Guide, Cal. Chem. Co., San Francisco; 1964; exec. editor Beach and Town, Visitor Pub. Co., Miami Beach, 1964—; also writer and pub. relations counselor; sometime lectr. Bd. dirs. Miami Beach Garden Center and Conservatory. Recipient Nat. Lit. Horticulture award Nat. Council Garden Clubs, 1967. Mem. S. Fla. Orchid Soc., Met. Miami Flower Show Assn., Gold Coast Unlimited Orchid Soc. (hon. life mem.), Naples Orchid Soc. (hon. mem.), Theta Sigma Phi (chpt. pres. 1966-67), Pi Beta Phi. Club: Miami Beach Garden (pres. 1966-68). Author: Growing Orchids for Pleasure (Nat. Garden Club Hort. award); Potted; Tropical Flowers of Florida, 1970; Flowers of the Caribbean, 1970; Flowers of the Bahamas, 1970; Flowers of Bermuda, 1970; Fairchild Tropical Garden, 1971; Tropical Flowers, 1973. Contbr. articles to pictorial mags. Home: 5768 Pine Tree Dr Miami Beach FL 33140

GARRARD, MARY MARGARET KERN (MRS. HERBERT L. GARRARD), mag. editor; b. Lafayette, Ind., Nov. 12, 1906; d. Charles B. and Flora (Work) Kern; B.S. magna cum laude, Purdue U., 1927; postgrad. Northwestern U., 1927-28; m. Herbert L. Garrard, Dec. 31, 1932; children—Flora Jane (Mrs. Ronald K. Richard), Bruce Kern, Sara Ann (Mrs. David W. Grepp). Editor Mortar Bd. Quar., 1928-30; asst. editor Union League Club Bull., Chgo., 1930-32; editor Internat. Altrusan, 1932-38, also exec. sec. Altrusa Internat., 1935-38; free-lance writer of articles in nat. and religious press, 1946—; editor Kappa Alpha Theta Mag. 1958-73. Chmn. steering com. City Mgr. Plan, Homewood, Ill., 1952. Recipient Flora Roberts medal Purdue U., 1927. Mem. League Women Voters, Mortar Board, Woman's Press Club Ind., D.A.R., Nat. Fedn. Press Women (nat. award feature story 1965, spl. edit. mag. 1970), Nat. Panhellenic Editors Conf. (chmn. Operation Brass Tacks 1969-71), Women in Communications, Alpha Lambda Delta, Kappa Delta Pi, Kappa Alpha Theta. Presbyn. Women's editor Purdue Alumnus, 1929-30. Author: The Family of Conrad Kern, 1968. Home: 19740 Heather Lane Craig Highlands Noblesville IN 46060

GARRETT, ALICE LUCILE, physician; b. Walla Walla, Wash., Nov. 30, 1922; d. Charles R. and Audrey (Nelson) Garrett; B.S., Wash. State Coll., 1944; M.D., U. So. Cal., 1954. Intern, Los Angeles County Hosp., 1953-54, resident, 1956-58; resident Shriners Hosp., 1955; instr. orthopedic surgery U. So. Cal. Los Angeles, 1959-63, asso. clin. prof., 1963-69, asst. prof., 1963-68; chief cerebral palsy service and children's reconstructive service Rancho Los Amigos Hosp., Downey, Cal., 1959-69; fellow orthopedic surgery Hosp. for Spl. Surgery, N.Y., 1963-64; orthopedic surgeon Los Angeles County Cerebral Palsy Program, 1959-69; asso. clin. prof. orthopedic surgery Columbia, 1969—; dir. surgery service Helen Hayes Hosp., West Haverstraw, N.Y., 1969-72, med. dir., 1972—; mem. staff Columbia Presbyn. Med. Center, N.Y.C. Served to lt. AUS, 1943-46. Diplomate Am. Bd. Orthopaedic Surgery. Mem. Am. Acad. Orthopedic Surgeons, Am. Acad. Cerebral Palsy, Am. Congress Rehab. Medicine, Am. Rheumatism Assn., Am. Orthopedic Foot Soc. Contbr. articles to med. jours. Home: Boxberger Rd Valley Cottage NY 10989 Office: Helen Hayes Hospital West Haverstraw NY 10993

GARRETT, ALINE MAE, psychologist, educator; b. St. Martinville, La., Aug. 28, 1944; d. Anatole Joseph and Aline (Mitchell) Garrett; student Ohio State U., 1962; B.A., U. Southwestern La., 1966; A.M. (fellow), Oberlin Coll., 1968; Ph.D. (Univ. fellow), U. Mass., 1971. Psychometrist Lafayette Parish Sch. Bd., 1967; asst. prof. psychology U. Southwestern La., Lafayette, 1971—. Cons. area head start projects, 1971—, Lafayette Natural History Mus. and Planetarium, 1972—; vol. coordinator tutorial program Am. Assn. U. Women, 1972—. Mem. bishop's adv. com. Diocese of Lafayette; mem. adv. bd. Univ. Year for Action, Univ. Child Care Center. Mem. Am., La., Southeastern psychol. assns., Nat. Assn. Black Psychologists, Soc. for Research in Child Devel., Psi Chi. Democrat. Roman Catholic. Contbr. articles to profl. jours. Home: 615 N Theatre St St Martinville LA 70582 Office: Psychology Dept University of Southwestern La Lafayette LA 70501

GARRETT, ETHEL SHIELDS, civic worker; b. Pitts., May 7, 1896; d. Peter and Cora (Lewis) Shields; grad. Miss Spence Sch., N.Y.C., 1915; m. Harry Darlington, Jr., Jan. 31, 1917 (dec. Jan. 1931); children—Harry III, McCullough, Elaine (Mrs. Anderson Fowler); m. 2d, George Angus Garrett, Apr. 11, 1935. Trustee John F. Kennedy Center Performing Arts; nat. council Met. Opera; mem.-at-large Garden Club Am.; mem. Corcoran Art Gallery, Nat. Trust Historic Preservation. Episcopalian. Home: 2030 24th St NW Washington DC 20008

GARRETT, FLORENCE ROME (MRS. ELMER ELLSWORTH GARRETT), poet; b. Bklyn., Sept. 10, 1912; d. George and Blanche Alice (Smith) Rome; pvt. music edn., 1921-33; m. Elmer Ellsworth Garrett, June 2, 1934; children—Susan, James. Profl. accompanist, N.Y., Conn., 1930-61; tchr. piano, L.I., N.Y., 1930-55; also lectr. poetry and dir. poetry workshops. Chmn. L.I. Poetry Day, 1953; sec. Walt Whitman Soc. Am., 1943-44, exec. chmn., 1945-46. Mem. Democratic Town Com., Roxbury, Conn., 1972, 73. Recipient awards Nat. League Am. Pen Women, 1952, 56, 66, Sharon Creative Arts Found. award, 1965. Fellow Internat. Poetry Soc.; mem. Nat. League Am. Pen Women (br. pres. 1954-56, poetry chmn. Conn. br. 1959-61). Christian Scientist. Author: Edge of Day, 1954; More Than the Quiet Pond, 1969. Authority on haiku poetry form in Japan. Home: Botsford Hill Rd Roxbury CT 06783

GARRETT, JACQUELINE HOPKINS (MRS. KENNETH J. GARRETT), advt. and pub. relations exec.; b. Pontiac, Mich., Feb. 2, 1935; d. Jack Olaf and Fay (Dryden) Morris; student pub. schs.; m. Richard W. Hopkins, Oct. 15, 1953; (dec. Apr. 1965); 1 dau., Casey Hopkins; m. 2d, Kenneth J. Garrett, Nov. 15, 1969. Asso. media dir. J. Walter Thompson Co., Los Angeles, 1956-69; v.p. in charge media Mediators, Inc., Los Angeles, 1969-71, sr. v.p. media, N.Y.C., 1971—. Office: 39 W 55th St New York City NY 10019

GARRETT, LILLIAN ALICE (MRS. SAMUEL KLINGER WORKMAN), artist; b. Beatrice, Neb.; d. Harry M. and Ethel K. (Johnson) Garrett; B.S., U. Neb., 1937; student Archipenko Art Sch., 1938-40; M.S., Ill. Inst. Tech., 1955; m. Samuel Klinger Workman, Mar. 12, 1953. Tchr., New Trier High Sch., Winnetka, Ill., 1941-42; faculty U. Wis., Madison, 1942-44; tchr. Layton Sch. Art, Milw., 1945-48, 53-58, Mpls. Sch. Art, 1950-52, Parsons Sch. Design, N.Y.C., 1965-73. One woman shows at U. Wis., Madison, 1944, Milw. Art Inst., 1944, U. Neb., Lincoln, 1952, Fairweather-Hardin Gallery, Chgo., 1960, Archtl. League, N.Y.C., 1962, West Broadway Gallery, N.Y.C., 1973; exhibited in group shows at Mus. Modern Art, Mus. Contemporary Crafts (both N.Y.C.), Cranbrook Acad., Walker Art Center, Mpls.; numerous pub. and pvt. commns. for paintings, sculptures, screens, fountains, 1960—. Chief designer Louisville Textiles, Inc., 1947-52; curator Everyday Art Gallery, editor Everyday Art Quar., Walker Art Center, Mpls., 1949-50; lectr. various instns. and orgns.; juror art shows. Recipient Louis W. and Maude Hill Found. grant for research in design fundamentals, 1952-53; Internat. Honorary awards for commercial textile desings, 1948, 49; winner bronze fountain sculpture competition U.S. Dept. Housing and Urban Devel. Nat. Community Art Competition, 1973. Author: Visual Design: A Problem-Solving Approach, 1967. Address: RD 1 Riegelsville PA 18077

GARRETT, MARGARET DODGE (MRS. JOHNSON GARRETT), civic worker; b. Beirut, Labanon, Jan. 6, 1917; d. Bayard and Mary (Bliss) Dodge; student Vassar Coll., 1935-36; m. Johnson Garrett, Aug. 5, 1936. Came to U.S., 1934. Dir. exhibitions Balt. Mus. Art, 1939-42; asst. curator, chief inter-Am. sect. Nat. Gallery of Art, Washington, 1942-46. Pres., Jr. Guild Am. Pro-Cathedral, Paris, 1952-54, Am. Women's Group in Paris, 1955-56; sec., Am. Library, Paris, France, 1957-67, v.p., 1967-71, chmn., 1971—. v.p. Am. Aid Soc. Paris, 1954-62, pres., 1962—; v.p. Amis du Musee Franco-Americain de Bierancourt, 1958—. Trustee Evergreen Found., Balt., Margaret Dodge Garrett and Johnson Garrett Found. Mem. Assn. Atlantique, Am. Student Adv. Service, Am. Pro-Cathedral Needlepoint Project. Home: 18 quai d'Orleans Paris 4e France

GARRETT, MARGARET LUCRETIA, psychiatrist; b. Haddonfield, N.J., Sept. 11, 1931; d. Robert Young and Margaret Seagraves (Davis) Garrett; B.S., Bucknell U., 1952; M.D., U. Pa., 1956. Intern, Cooper Hosp., Camden, N.J., 1956-57; resident in psychiatry Yale U., 1959-62, instr. psychiatry, 1962-63, clin. instr. psychiatry, 1963-67; practice medicine, specializing in psychiatry, New Haven, Conn., 1963-67; mem. staff Profl. Assos. of Psychiat. Inst., Washington, 1967—; clin. asst. prof. psychiatry George Washington U., 1967—; candidate Washington Psychoanalytic Inst., 1967—; mem. staff George Washington U. Hosp. Mem. Am. Psychiat. Assn., D.C. Med. Soc., Washington Psychiat. Soc. Home: 2939 Van Ness St NW Washington DC 20008 Office: 2141 K St NW Washington DC 20037

GARRETT, NAOMI MILLS, educator; b. Columbia, S.C., Aug. 24, 1906; d. Casper George and Anna (Threewitts) Garrett; A.B., Benedict Coll., 1927; M.A., Atlanta U., 1937; Ph.D. (fellow), Columbia, 1954. Instr. pub. sch. system, Bessemer City, N.C., 1927-28, Clinton, S.C., 1930-36, Balt., 1941-43; instr. French, Spanish, Kittrell (N.C.) Coll., 1937-40; mem. U.S. Govt. English Teaching Project, Haiti, 1943-44; faculty West Va. State Coll., Institute, 1947-72, fgn. student adviser, 1953-72, chmn., prof. modern fgn. langs., 1958-72; prof. Denison U., Granville, O., 1972—. Translator, Voice o Am., 1946-47. Mem. adv. bd. Opportunities Industrialization Center, 1969—. Rosenwald fellow, 1944-45; Ford fellow, 1951-52, Fulbright fellow, 1958-59. Mem. Am. Assn. U. Women, W.Va. Assn. Mental Health, League Women Voters, Am. Assn. UN, Am. Assn. Tchrs. French, Assn. Dept. Fgn. Langs., Am. Council for Teaching Fgn. Langs., Nat. Assn. Fgn. Student Affairs, Modern Lang. Assn. Author: Renaissance of Haitian Poetry, 1963. Contbr. articles to scholarly revs. Home: PO Box 111 Institute WV 25112 Office: Denison U Granville OH 43023

GARRICK, JEAN, physician; b. Thomasville, Ala., Jan. 14, 1927; d. William Leonard and Ruth Naomi (Doyle) Garrick; B.A., Samford U., 1949; B.S., Johns Hopkins, 1953; M.D., Georgetown U., 1965. Tchr. biology and chemsitry pub. schs., Grove Hill, Ala., 1949-50; intern Balt. City Hosps., 1965-66, resident, 1966-67; fellow Johns Hopkins Sch. Medicine, 1966-67, fellow in pathology, 1967-68; resident Md. Gen. Hosp., Balt., 1967-68; practice medicine specializing in pathology, Montgomery, Ala., 1968-72; now pathologist Mercy Hosp. Jefferson County. former mem. staffs Montgomery, Baptist, St. Margaret's hosps. Former pathology cons. State of Ala. Address: 1515 6th Av S Birmingham AL 35233

GARRIGUE, JEAN, poet; b. Dec. 8, 1914; B.A., U. Chgo., 1937; M.A., U. Ia., 1943. Instr. English lit. U. Ia., 1942-43, Bard Coll., Annandale, N.Y., 1951-52, Queens Coll., Flushing, N.Y., 1952-53, New Sch. for Social Research, N.Y.C., 1955-56, U. Conn. at Storrs, 1960-61, Smith Coll., 1965-66; vis. poet U. Wash., Seattle, 1970. Recipient prize Union League Civic and Arts Found., 1956; Longview award, 1959; Rockefeller grantee in creative writing, 1954; Hudson Rev. fellow in poetry, 1957; Guggenheim fellow, 1960-61; Nat. Inst. Arts and Letters grantee, 1962; Balch prize Va. Quar. Rev., 1966. Author: (poetry) The Ego and the Centaur, 1947; The Monument Rose, 1953; A Water Walk by Villa d'Este, 1959; Country Without Maps, 1965; The Animal Hotel, 1966; New and Selected Poems, 1967; Essays and Prose Poems, in 1970; Studies for An Actress and other Poems, 1973; contbg. author: Thirty-Six Poems and a Few Songs, in Five Young Poets of 1944. Contbr. short stories and novellas to New World Writing, 1954, Cross-Sections, 1947, Botteghe Oscure No. 2; contbr. to Saturday Rev., New Republic, N.Y. Herald Tribune, little mags. Home: 463 West St New York City NY 10014*

GARRISON, ETTA JOSEPHINE GANZ, civic worker; b. Tacoma, Feb. 22, 1905; d. William W. and Josephine (Kuzman) Ganz; student Tacoma Community Coll., 1969-70; m. Lee C. Garrison, Mar. 19, 1929 (dec. Jan. 1969); children—Lee C., William Douglas. Sec., Reid Motor Co., Tacoma, 1923-27; collection mgr. Tacoma Mortgage Co., 1927-29. Vol. tchr. Tacoma Area Literacy Council, 1970—; chmn. Tacoma Beautification Com., 1958-65; Tacoma rep. to Seattle World's Fair, 1958-62; v.p. rural econ. opportunity sect. Pierce County Poverty Program, 1972—; bd. dirs., Pierce County rep. Pierce County Drug Abuse Center, 1967—; mem. Pierce County Law and Justice Com., 1971-72; mem. information com. Pierce County Solid Waste Council, 1969-72. Mem. Ruston Town Council, 1969—, Tocoma Republican Precinct Com., 1958—; treas., past pres. Pierce County Women's Rep. Club. Bd. dirs. Pierce County Drug Alliance, Tacoma, pres., 1974—; bd. dirs. Pierce County Solid Waste Mgmt. Com., Pierce County Equitable Tax Assn., Pierce County Community Action Agy., Pierce County Health Bd. Republican. Roman Catholic. Club: Citywide Garden (Tacoma). Organizer 50 garden clubs for Wash. State Fedn. Garden Clubs, 1954. Address: 5116 N Winnifred St Tacoma WA 98407

GARRISON, EVE JOSEPHSON (MRS. JOSEPH D. GARRISON), artist; b. Boston; d. Wolfe and Sadie (Levinson) Josephson; grad. Art Inst. Chgo., 1930; postgrad. Lawrence Inst. Tech., 1941-43, Wayne U., 1943; m. Joseph David Garrison, 1926; 1 dau., Virginia Dale (Mrs. Eugene Dach). Exhibited in one-man shows Denver Art Mus., 1934, Milw. Art Inst., 1957, Miami Mus. Modern Art, 1961, 65, 73, Duncan Gallery, N.Y.C., 1963, Duncan Gallery, Paris, France, 1963, Drian Gallery, London, Eng., 1964-68, 70, 74, Villanova (Pa.) U., 1966, New Masters Gallery, N.Y.C., 1966, Vincent Price Gallery, 1968, 69, Cliff Dwellers, Chgo., 1971, Galerie Vallombreuse, Biarritz, France, 1972, Rubino Gallery, Chgo., 1973; exhibited in group shows throughout U.S.; represented in permanent collections Miami Mus. Modern Art, Treasury Art Dept., Washington, U. Ill. Urbana, Union League Club, Chgo., Mt. Sinai Hosp., Chgo., Ill. Inst. Tech., others. Mem. Art Inst. Chgo. Alumni Assn., Artists Equity. Works represented in several textbooks. Home: 1410 B Sherwin Chicago IL 60626 Office: 407 S Dearborn St Chicago IL 60605

GARRISON, LAURA ANN, youth counselor; b. Obar, N.M., May 4, 1942; d. George Warren and Cecile (Downing) Garrison; B.S., U. N.M., 1964, M.A., 1968. Teletype operator Dun & Bradstreet, Inc., Albuquerque, 1964-65; youth counselor Employment Security Commn. N.M., Albuquerque, 1965-69; N.M. state coordinator Job Corps, Albuquerque, 1969-72, state supr. counseling and testing, 1972-74; employment specialist Pima Community Coll., Tucson, 1974—. Mem. Am., N.M. personnel and guidance assns., Internat. Assn. Personnel in Employment Security, Nat. Employment Counselors Assn., Nat. Vocational Guidance Assn., Am. Assn. U. Women. Home: 1145 N Catalina Av Tucson AZ 85712 Office: Pima Community Coll Tucson AZ 85709

GARRISON, MARY EDRIS DAVIS (MRS. CLARENCE GRADY GARRISON), employment ofcl.; b. Dalton, Ga., Feb. 8, 1922; d. McAfee Bates and Pryce (Brackett) Davis; student Wesleyan Coll., 1939-42; B.A., U. Tenn., 1943; postgrad. U. Ga., 1958, U. Chattanooga, 1967; m. Clarence Grady Garrison, June 10, 1962; 1 step-son, Kenneth Wayne. Tchr., Whitfield County High Sch., Dalton, 1943-45; employment counselor Ga. Dept. Labor, Dalton, 1945—; selection and referral officer Manpower Devel. and Tng. Act. for Whitfield and Murray Counties. Sec. adv. bd. Salvation Army, 1955—; mem. adv. bd. Dalton Vocational Sch. Practical Nursing, 1966—. Mem. Dalton Bus. and Profl. Womens Club (past pres.), Am. Personnel and Guidance Assn., Nat. Employment Counselors Assn., Internat. Assn. Personnel in Employment Security, League Women Voters, Beta Sigma Phi. Presbyn. Mem. Order Eastern Star. Home: Route 4 Dawnville Rd Dalton GA 30720 Office: 417 W Crawford St Dalton GA 30720

GARRITY, CARLA BEREN (MRS. THOMAS GARRITY), child psychologist; b. Chgo., Aug. 16, 1945; d. Max Erwin and Lois Atlas (Blazer) Beren; B.A. cum laude, State U. N.Y. at Buffalo, 1967; M.A., U. Denver, 1969, Ph.D., 1972; m. Thomas Garrity, Jan. 30, 1964; 1 son, Mark. Psychologist Nat. Jewish Hosp., Denver, 1969-71; cons., Head Start, Denver, 1971-72; psychologist Denver Community Mental Health Center, 1972—. Trustee, Beren Found. Mem. Am., Rocky Mt., Colo. psychol. assns. Democrat. Research in area of acad. success in black ghetto children. Home: 683 S Downing St Denver CO 80209 Office: 529 E 29th St Denver CO 80205

GARRITY, MONIQUE PAUL (MRS. JOHN K. GARRITY), educator; b. Petite-Riviere, Haiti, Mar. 26, 1941; d. Frederic and Germaine (Herard) Paul; B.A. cum laude, Marygrove Coll., 1963; M.A. (fellow), Boston Coll., 1966, Ph.D. (fellow), 1969; m. John K. Garrity, Mar. 15, 1968; 1 son, John K. Came to U.S., 1959. Cons., OECD, Paris, 1967-68; instr. econs. U. Mass., Boston, 1968-69, asst. prof., 1969-70, 71-74, asso. prof., 1974—. asst. prof. Wellesley (Mass.) Coll., 1970-71. Fulbright lectr. U. Dakar, Senegal, 1974—. Bd. dirs. Black Econ. Research Center. Mem. Am. Econ. Assn., African Studies Assn., Am. Assn. U. Profs., Caucus Black Economists. Home: 1222 Cambridge St Cambridge MA 02139 Office: Dept Econs U Mass Boston MA 02125

GARRITY, RUTH ALTHEA ROBERTSON (MRS. EUGENE ROBERT GARRITY), personnel exec.; b. Leominster, Mass., Jan. 11, 1923; d. Ralph Apsley and Gladys Nellie (Thomas) Robertson; grad. high sch.; m. Eugene Robert Garrity, May 31, 1940; children—Judith (Mrs. Stephen Muller), Diane (Mrs. David Barry), Roberta (Mrs. Charles Bennis), Pamela (Mrs. Gary Foster). Receptionist, Asher Co., Fitchburg, Mass., 1964-66, employment supr., 1966-69, dir. personnel and pub. relations, 1969-74, v.p. plant operations, 1974—, also chmn. safety, chmn. security; owner, treas. Miles Kedex Co., Leominster, 1973—; dir. Fitchburg Savs. and Loan Bank, 1973—. Adviser Montachuset Regional Vocational Tech. Sch., 1970—, Jr. Achievement, 1969—; mem. bus. climate com. Third Worcester Senatorial Dist., 3d v.p., 1974—; sponsor Spectrum House for drug addicts, Shirley, Mass., Little League team, Brownie troop; active other community projects. State bd. dirs. Mass. P.T.A., 1955-61; bd. dirs. Leominster Recreation Center; bd. dirs., exec. com. United Fund Fitchburg. Mem. Am. Soc. Personnel Adminstrn., Mass. Congress Parents and Tchrs. (life), C. of C. (mem. personnel com. 1966—), Nat. Wildlife Soc., Fitchburg Art Mus., Montachusett Indsl. Mgmt. Club. (v.p.). Republican. Unitarian (finance chmn., co-chmn. worship and edn.). Home: PO Box 163 Leominster MA 01453 Office: 307 Falulah Rd Fitchburg MA 01420

GARSON, GREER, actress; b. County Down, No. Ireland; d. George and Nina (Greer) Garson; B.A. cum laude, London U.; student Grenoble U.; hon. doctorate Rollins Coll., 1950, Coll. Santa Fe, 1970, Cleve. Inst. Music, 1973; m. 3d, E.E. Fogelson. Debut, London, Eng., 1935; stage plays include Golden Arrow, Vintage Wine, Accent on Youth, Butterfly on the Wheel, Page from a Diary, The Visitor, Mademoiselle, Twelfth Night, School for Scandal, Too True to be Good, The Temptest, Old Music, Auntie Mame; motion pictures include Good-bye Mr. Chips, Pride and Prejudice, Blossoms in the Dust, When Ladies Meet, Mrs. Miniver, Random Harvest, Madame Curie, Mrs. Parkington, Adventure, Desire Me, Valley of Decision, Julia Misbehaves, That Forsythe Woman, The Law and the Lady, Julius Caesar, Scandal at Scourie, Her Twelve Men, Strange Lady in Town, Sunrise at Campobello; appeared in Broadway play Auntie Mame; also Tonight at 8:30, Hollywood, Cal., Captain Brassbound's Conversion, Los Angeles; also various TV performances, Britain and U.S.; adj. prof. So. Meth. U. Mem. Arts Commn., Tex., N.M., Life gov. Women's Hosp., Melbourne, Australia; bd. dirs. Dallas Theatre Center, Dallas Symphony; trustee Dallas Fine Arts Mus.; mem. nat. com. St. John's Coll., Santa Fe; active Greer Garson Theatre Coll. Santa Fe. Recipient Acad. award for performance in Mrs. Miniver, 1943; Golden Globe award for performance in Sunrise at Campobello, 1961; Photoplay Gold medal (2), Brit. Picture-Goer (3), N.M. 4th Ann. award profl. excellence and pub. service. Address: 2010 Republic Bank Bldg Dallas TX 75201

GARTHWAITE, MARION HOOK (MRS. EDWIN LOWELL GARTHWAITE), author; b. Oakland, Cal., Dec. 17, 1893; d. William Perley and Sarah Lloyd (McAllis) Hook; A.B., U. Cal. at Berkeley, 1916; certificate Riverside Library Sch., 1923; m. Edwin Lowell Garthwaite, Oct. 7, 1917; children—Edwin Lowell, Jean (Mrs. John Henry Maddox III). Children's Librarian Madera (Cal.) County Library, 1943-50; children's librarian San Mateo County Library, Redwood City, Cal., 1951-60. Lectr. children's lit., storytelling U. Pacific, 1954-65, U. San Francisco, 1967-73. Recipient Silver medal Commonwealth Club, 1950, Distinguished Woman award Am. Assn. U. Women, 1967. Mem. Am., Cal. library assns. Episcopalian. Author: Tomás and the Red Headed Angel, 1950; Shaken Days, 1952; Coarse Gold Gulch, 1956; Mario, 1960; Locked Crowns, 1963. Home: 3358 Morago Blvd Lafayette CA 94549

GARTNER, AUDREY KATHERINE SCOTT (MRS. DALE WALTER GARTNER), apt. mgr.; b. Grand Island, Neb., Dec. 4, 1947; d. Leonard Edwin and Norma May (Wilcox) Scott; grad. high sch.; m. Dale Walter Gartner, Sept. 25, 1971. Coowner, mgr. apt. complex, Hastings, Neb.; society, food and fashion editor Hastings (Neb.) Tribune, 1970-74. Mem. Hastings Community Theatre; judge Hastings Jr. Miss Pageant, 1970-74; mem., chmn. publicity Mary Lanning Meml. Hosp. Aux., 1974—; co-chmn. publicity Adams County div. Am. Cancer Soc., 1973—. Sec. Adams County Young Republicans, 1971-74. Mem. Women's C. of C. (vice chmn. 1972). Methodist. Club: Hastings Eagle Arie. Home: Route 1 Box 74 Ayr NE 68925 Office: 600 S Colo St Hastings NE 68901

GARVAN, BEATRICE WOOLSEY BRONSON (MRS. ANTHONY N.B. GARVAN), curator; b. N.Y.C., Mar. 9, 1929; d. Francis W. and Helen L. (Silkman) Bronson; B.A., Vassar Coll., 1950; M.A., U. Pa., 1965; m. Barton H. Lippincott, Sept. 16, 1950 (div. Feb. 1969); children—Louise Woolsey, Deborah Wharton, Frances Bronson, Elizabeth Barton; m. Anthony N.B. Garvan, Apr. 26, 1969. Sec. Van Diemen-Lilienfeld Galleries, 1951-53; guide Phila. Mus. Art, 1962-66, curatorial asst., 1966-71, asso. curator, 1971—. Lectr. Germantown Acad., Fort Washington, Pa., 1966-74. Treas. North Penn. Vis. Nurse Assn., 1958; vice-chmn. United Fund Drive North Pa. area, 1959. Mem. Hist. Soc. Pa. (councillor 1965—). Episcopalian. Home: Penllyn Pike Spring House PA 19477 Office: Phila Mus Art Pkwy at 26th St Philadelphia PA 19101

GARVEY, KATHRYN ELLEN (MRS. JAMES JOSEPH GARVEY), journalist; b. Longview, Wash., Oct. 19, 1943; d. John Henry and Mabel Katherine (Green) Keatley; B.A. in Communications, certificate journalism, Wash. State U., 1965; postgrad. Solano Coll., 1971; m. James Joseph Garvey, Dec. 26, 1970. With Vacaville (Cal.) Reporter, 1965—, soc. editor, 1965—, photographer, 1965—; exhibited in one-man photo show Vacaville Art League Gallery, 1967. Publicity chmn. Am. Cancer Soc., Vacaville, Cal., 1968, 69-72. Bd. dirs. Vacaville Fiesta Days, 1968-71, publicity chmn., 1968-71. Union Pacific R.R. grantee, 1961; Solano County 4-H Alumni award, 1967; 1st place photo awards Solano County (Cal.) Fair, 1970-73, 1st pl. award Cal. Newspaper Pubs. Assn., 1973. Mem. Women in Communication, Vacaville Art League. Democrat. Methodist. Clubs: Soroptimist (regional pub. relations chmn. 1970-72, press book chmn. 1970-72, newspaper editor); Soroptimist Fedn. of the Americas (regional press book chmn. 1970-72, mem. regional pub. relations com. 1970-72). Home: 317 Kentucky St Vacaville CA 95688 Office: 318 Main St Vacaville CA 95688

GARVEY, OLIVE WHITE (MRS. RAY HUGH GARVEY), bus. exec.; b. Arkansas City, Kan., July 15, 1893; d. Oliver Holmes and Caroline (Hill) White; A.B., Washburn U., 1914, H.H.D., 1963; Hon. Dr. of Pub. Service, Friends' U., Wichita, 1966; H.H.D., Wilson Coll., 1967; H.L.D., Okla. Christian Coll., 1970; m. Ray Hugh Garvey, July 8, 1916 (dec. June 1959); children—Ruth (Mrs. H. Bernerd Fink), Willard W., James S., Olivia G. (Mrs. George A. Lincoln). Tchr. English, Augusta (Kan.) High Sch., 1914-16; past chmn. bd., dir. Service Oil Co., Colby, Kan., Amortibanc Investment Co., Inc., Wichita, Garvey Grain, Inc., Garvey Elevators, Inc., C-G-F Grain Co., Inc., Lincoln Grain, Inc., World Homes, Inc. and affiliated cos., Petroleum, Inc., Wichita; chmn., dir. Garvey Center, Inc., Wichita, Garvey Inc.; v.p., dir. Topeka Transfer & Storage Co., Garvey, Inc. Mem. regional adv. bd. Internat. Inst. Edn.; mem. Wichita Met. Council 1962—. Chmn., pres., dir. Garvey Found., Wichita; bd. dirs. Garvey Kan. Found., Garvey Tex. Found., Ft. Worth, Lincoln Family Found., Wichita, Kan. 4-H Found., Friends' U., Greater Downtown Wichita; former trustee Washburn Coll.; past bd. dirs. Kan. Dist. YWCA, Wichita YWCA, Wichita YMCA, Congl.-Christian Chs. Bd. Home Missions Sedgwick County United Fund, Wichita Art Mus., Wichita U.S.O.; nat. trustee, bd. govs. Inst. Logopedics. Recipient citation 4-H Club, 1967; service awards; named patron Kan. Press Women, 1967, Salesman of Year, Sales and Mgmt. Execs., 1969; recipient Brotherhood award Nat. Conf. Christians and Jews, 1969, Martin Palmer Humanitarian award Inst. Logopedics, 1970; Distinguished Service award in agr. Kan. State U., 1971. Mem. Nat. League Am. Pen Women (state pres. 1952), Am. Assn. U. Women, Nat. Soc. Colonial Dames Am. (state pres. 1964), Wichita Area C. of C. (dir. 1965-67), P.E.O., Jamestown Soc., Wichita Art Assn., Nonoso, Delta Gamma (Cable award 1965), Phi Kappa Phi. Republican. Conglist. Clubs: Crestview Country, University, Kansas Author's, Twentieth Century (Wichita); Plaza. Author: The Obstacle Race, 1970; also plays, poems, articles. Home: 5051 E Lincoln St Wichita KS 67218 Office: 300 W Douglas St Wichita KS 67202

GARY, GAYLE HARRIET MARGARET (MRS. ARTHUR JOHN GARY), communication exec.; b. N.Y.C., Dec. 23, 1920; d. Michael H. and Lilian E. (Robbins) Summers; student U. Miami, 1939, N.Y.U., 1940-43, Columbia, 1944-46; m. Arthur John Gary, Oct. 28, 1943; 1 dau., Sandra G.M. Pres., owner Gayle Gary Assos., radio and television cons., 1954—; interviewer, producer syndicated radio program Views and People in the News. Pres. Guild of St. Bartholomew P.E. Ch., 1954-56, convocation and diocesan officer, 1954—; mem. prize com. for Debutante Ball; patron, activities com. for Woman's Aux., N.Y. Infirmary, 1950—; mem. Friends of Philharmonic com., 1950—; mem. fund raising com. for women United Hosp. Fund, 1950—; mem. nat. adv. com. for Medico, 1950—; mem. spl. events Eleanor Roosevelt Meml. Found. Com., 1958—; mem. Thrift Shop bd. Goddard Riverside, 1958-64; mem. spl. events Parents League, 1958-64; bd. mem. spl. social service for N.Y.U.-Bellevue Med. Center; mem. exec. com. Hope Cotillion, 1958—; nat. dir. Nat. Radio-TV Com. for Am. observance of Human Rights Week, 1955—; chmn. Daisy Day Week; publicity, finance com. Girl Scouts Am., 1960-62; com. chmn. Girls Friendly Soc. Ball, 1958-60. Co-leader 70 East Assembly Dist. N.Y.C., 1960-70, 73; chmn. pub. relations Nat. Council Women's Nat. Republican Club. Mem. Pub. Relations Soc. Am., Internat. Radio and TV Execs. Soc., Nat. Inst. Social Scis., Religious Pub. Relations Soc. Am., Am. Women in Radio and TV, Hort. Soc. of N.Y., Sea Orgn., Churchwomens Patriotic League, Navy League, Hubbard Assn. Scientologists Internat., English Speaking Union. Republican. Club: Women's Chess of N.Y. (exec. v.p. 1968—). Home: 1212 Fifth Av New York City NY 10029

GARY, JAN, artist; b. Ft. Worth, Feb. 13, 1925; student Art Center Sch., Los Angeles, San Antonio Art Inst. Exhibited in one-man shows Jersey City Mus., 1964, St. Scholastica Acad., Ft. Smith, Ark., 1965, Ark. State Tchrs. Coll., 1965, Centenary Coll. for Women, 1967, Ringwood Manor State Mus., 1968; group shows N.A.D., 1963, 65, Butler Inst. Am. Art, 1963, 66, Montclair Art Mus. State Anns., 1956-62, Newark Museum Festival, 1960, N.J. State Mus., 1956, Witte Meml. Mus., 1949, Silvermine Guild, 1966, Am. Acad. Arts and Letters, 1967, Canton (O.) Art Inst., 1971; traveling exhbns. U.S., Can., Scotland, Eng.; work represented in permanent collections Jersey City Mus., Norfolk Mus. Art and Scis., Butler Inst. Am. Art, Pensacola Art Center, Brandeis U., Wis. State U. at Eau Claire, Carver Mus., Tuskagee Inst. Ala. Asso. dir. Old Bergen Art Guild. Recipient numerous prizes and awards. Mem. Nat. Soc. Painters in Casein, Nat. Assn. Women Artists, Painters and Sculptors Soc., N.J. Watercolor Soc., Audubon Artists, Asso. Artists of N.J. Address: 43 W 33d St Bayonne NJ 07002

GASKILL, MARGARET HELEN JENKINS (MRS. HERBERT LEO GASKILL), lawyer; b. Phila., Sept. 18, 1921; d. Frederick John and Margaret (Swarz) Jenkins; B.S. in Law, U. Wash., 1946, J.D., 1947; m. Herbert Leo Gaskill, Mar. 1, 1944; children—Margaret Vesta, Herbert Leo. Admitted to Wash. bar, 1947, since practiced in Seattle; partner Hardy & Gaskill, 1952-54, Holland &Gaskill, 1954-57; individual practice law, 1958-64; partner Weyer, Sandelin, Sterne & Gaskill, 1964-66, Weyer, Sterne & Gaskill, 1966-69; individual practice, 1969—; judge protem superior ct.; 1961. Mem. Citizens' Adv. Com. Senate Interim Com. Financial Instns., 1973-74. Docent, Seattle Art Mus., 1961-72, now mem. Mem. Am., Wash. State, King County Seattle King County (sec. 1963) bar assns., Am. Trial Lawyers Assn. Phi Delta Delta. Democrat. Home: 4022 E Mercer Way Mercer Island WA 98040 Office: Norton Bldg 2d and Columbia St Seattle WA 98104

GASKILL, MARY HAWTHORNE, constrn. co. exec.; b. Phila., Mar. 25, 1919; d. Robert and Caroline (Spielman) Hawthorne; grad. high sch.; m. Fred Wiegand, Jan. 8, 1938 (dec. Dec. 1958); 1 dau., Mary Anne (Mrs. H.L. Benner); m. 2d, Hewlings J. Gaskill, June 25, 1960; 1 dau., Anne Jean. Pres., Robert Hawthorne, Inc., Phila., 1932—. Mem. Women in Constrn. Home: 422 Tanforan Dr Cherry Hill NJ 08034 Office: 2900 Orthodox St Philadelphia PA 19137

GASPERONI, ELLEN JEAN LIAS (MRS. EMIL GASPERONI), auto wash exec.; b. Rural Valley, Pa.; d. Dale S. and Ruth (Harris) Lias; student Youngstown U., 1952-54, John Carrol U., 1953-54, Westminster Coll., 1951-52; grad. Am. Inst. Banking; m. Emil Gasperoni, May 28, 1955; children—Sam, Emil, Jean Ellen. Bd. dirs. Fill-Up-Up Auto Wash Co., Inc., Ft. Lauderdale, Fla., 1968—, sec., 1968—. Mem. Jr. Business Womens Club (dir. 1962-64). Presbyn. Clubs: Coral Ridge Country, Le Club International (Fort Lauderdale). Home: 4201 NE 25th St Fort Lauderdale FL 33308

GASSERT, MARY ELIZABETH, clin. psychologist; b. Lewistown, Pa., Oct. 3, 1905; d. Samuel P. and Bessie (Muthersbaugh) Gassert; A.B., Juniata Coll., 1928; M.S., Pa. State U., 1936. Tchr. pub. schs., sch. psychologist, Lewistown, 1928-38; dir. guidance, dean girls, sch. psychologist Hershey (Pa.) Pub. Schs., 1939-41; supr. spl. edn. York (Pa.) County Pub. Schs., 1941-71; staff psychologist York Hosp., 1957—; psychol. testing Pa. Dept. Welfare, 1960—; instr. York campus Pa. State U., 1963, 68. Bd. dirs. Children's Service York County, 1956-66, York County Assn. for Retarded Children, 1964-68. Diplomate Am. Bd. Examiners in Profl. Psychology. Mem. Am., Pa.

psychol. assns., Am. Assn. U. Women, Phi Lambda Theta, Psi Chi. Home: 926 McKenzie St York PA 17403

GASSNER, BETTY JANE, mathematician; b. N.Y.C.; d. Abraham and Anna (Goldberg) Gassner; A.B. magna cum laude, Washington Square Coll., 1953; M.S., N.Y.U., 1954, Ph.D., 1956. Grad. asst. N.Y.U., 1954-55; research analyst Remington Rand, N.Y.C., 1957-59; mathematician Autometric, Inc., N.Y.C., 1959-60, Kearfott, Little Falls, N.J., 1960-61, Internat. Electric Corp., Paramus, 1961-62; jr. elec. engr. City of N.Y., 1962-63; mathematician USAAF, Rome, 1963-64; Cecelie Froehlich fellow City U. N.Y., 1965-66; NSF fellow metallurgy Grad. Sch. Engring., N.Y.U., 1966-68; math. specialist Ins. Data Processing Center, 1969-70; jr. examiner N.Y. State Ins. Dept., 1971-72, cons., 1973—. Recipient Women's Badge, Tau Beta Pi, 1964. Mem. Math. Assn. Am., Am. Math Soc., Soc. Actuaries, Mensa, Phi Beta Kappa, Pi Mu Epsilon (past sec.; 1st prize freshman's math. contest 1951), Sigma Pi Sigma (past treas.), Tau Beta Pi. Democrat. Contbr. articles in field. Home: 35 Fort Hill Circle Staten Island NY 10301

GASTEYER, CARLIN EVANS (MRS. HARRY A. GASTEYER), mus. adminstr.; b. Jackson, Mich., Mar. 30, 1917; d. Frank Howard and Marian (Spencer) Evans; student Barnard Coll., 1934-35; m. Harry A. Gasteyer, Jan. 8, 1944; 1 dau., Nancy Catherine. Clk., First Nat. City Bank, 1939-42; statistician Bell Telephone Labs., 1942-45; dir. asst. S.I. Mus., 1956-61; bus. mgr. Mus. of the City of N.Y., 1961-63; mus. adminstr., 1963-66; asst. dir. Monmouth (N.J.) Mus., 1966-67, Mus. of City of N.Y., 1967-70; vice dir. adminstrn. Bklyn. Mus., 1970—. Active Girl Scouts. Co-founder, pres. Jr. Mus. Guild, S.I. Mus., 1956-58. Mem. N.Y.C. Local Sch. Bd. 54, 1960-61. Mem. Am. Assn. Mus., Mus. Council of N.Y.C., N.Y. Cultural Instns. Group. Club: Cosmopolitan. Home: 50 Fort Pl Staten Island NY 10301 Office: 200 Eastern Pkwy Brooklyn NY 11238

GATENBEE, ELIZABETH ROBBINS (MRS. ROBERT JAMES GATENBEE), bearings co. exec.; b. Louisville, Feb. 24, 1916; d. Orlando Douglass and Elizabeth (Holtzhauer) Robbins; spl. student Tarkio Coll., 1955-56; m. Robert James Gatenbee, Sept. 11, 1934; children—Robert James, John Douglass. Sec., Ky. Bearings Service, Inc., Louisville, 1934-48, 57-60, exec. v.p., 1973—, also dir. Home: PO Box 37 Pewee Valley KY 40056 Office: 1524 Algonquin Pkwy Louisville KY 40210

GATES, BARBARA ANN, librarian; b. Worcester, Mass., Apr. 8, 1924; d. William Herbert and Alice Marie (Keating) Gates; B.S., Simmons Coll., 1946; M.L.S., Columbia U., 1953. Cataloger, Ia. State Coll., 1946-49, Vassar Coll. Library, 1949-52; head tech. service Brookline (Mass.) Pub. Library, 1953-60; sr. cataloger Boston U. Library, 1960-62; head serials dept., 1962-67, head reclassification task force, 1967-69; head tech. services librarian Oberlin Coll. (Ohio), 1969-73; librarian/coordinator Interuniv. Council of North Tex. Area, Dallas, 1973—. Instr. pub. library techniques program U. N.H., 1968-70, 72-73. Mem. A.L.A. (chmn. cataloging and classification sect. 1971-72), Tex. Library Assn., Am. Soc. Information Sci., Am. Assn. U. Women. Home: 7951 Cliffbrook Dr Apt 233 Dallas TX 75240 Office: Interuniversity Council of North Tex Area PO Box 30365 Dallas TX 75230

GATES, HELEN ELIZABETH UPTON (MRS. CHARLES WARNER GATES II), civic worker; b. Owasso, Mich., Oct. 8, 1926; d. William Bayly and Beatrice V. (Porteous) Upton; B.A., U. Cal. at Berkeley, 1948; m. Charles Warner Gates II, Dec. 11, 1948; children—Charles Warner III, William Upton, Geoffrey Stephen, Elizabeth Courson. Pres., Laguna Blanca Sch. Mother's Aux., 1967-69; bd. dirs. Music Acad. of West, 1968-69; bd. dirs. women's bd. sec. Santa Barbara (Cal.) Mus. Art, 1965-69; chmn. children's dancing classes Jr. League Santa Barbara, 1966-67; bd. dirs. Jr. League Los Angeles Sustainers, 1973-74. Pres. Montecito Republican Women's Club Fedn., 1969-70. Mem. Gamma Phi Beta. Episcopalian (pres. women 1967-68). Clubs: Garden (corr. sec., dir. 1965-69) (Santa Barbara); Little Town (dir. Santa Barbara 1966-68, membership chmn. 1971-72). Home: 12720 Hanover St Los Angeles CA 90049

GATES, PHILOMENE ASHER (MRS. SAMUEL EUGENE GATES), lawyer; b. Daytona Beach, Fla., Mar. 19, 1918; d. Julius Benjamin and Mary Katherine (Brown) Asher; B.S. Fla. State U., 1938, LL.B., George Washington U., 1942; m. Samuel Eugene Gates, Apr. 26, 1941; children—Gilda (Mrs. Cecil Wray Jr.), Sharon (Mrs. Richard B. Stearns Jr.), Kathe (Mrs. Edwin Williamson). Admitted to D.C. bar, N.Y. State bar; atty. Fed. Register, Dept. of Justice, Washington, 1938-41, OPA, Washington, 1941-42, CAB, Washington, 1943-46, Legal Aid Soc., Washington, 1947-48; individual practice, N.Y.C., 1962—. Mem. com. of legal services Office Econ. Opportunity, Greater N.Y., 1970-74; pres. Girl Scout Council, Greater N.Y., 1973. Trustee Legal Aid Soc., 1966-72, N.Y. Infirmary Hosp., Grosvenor Neighborhood House, N.Y.C., 1951. Mem. Assn. Bar of the City of N.Y. (mem. com. of profl. and jud. ethics 1962), Pi Beta Phi. Episcopalian. Clubs: Cosmopolitan (dir. N.Y.C. 1971-74); Garden Club (Westhampton Beach, N.Y.). Address: 830 Park Av New York City NY 10021

GATEWOOD, MAUD F., artist; b. Yanceyville, N.C., Jan. 8, 1934; d. J. Yancey and Mary Lea (Florance) Gatewood; A.B., U. N.C. Woman's Coll., 1954; M.A., Ohio State U., 1955; postgrad. Harvard, summer 1957, U. Vienna, Acad. of Applied Arts Vienna, 1962-63. Instr. art Huntingdon Coll., 1956-58, Tex. Christian U., 1959-62; asso. prof. U. N.C. at Charlotte, 1964-73; one man shows Heath Gallery, Atlanta, Willard Gallery, N.Y.C., Mint Mus. Art, Winston-Salem Gallery Fine Arts; exhibited in group shows at N.C. Mus. Art, Library of Congress, Dallas Mus. Fine Arts, Denver Mus., many others; represented in permanent collections Mint Mus., Coca-Cola Co., McDonald Corp., N.C. Nat. Bank, pvt. collections. Recipient award for painting Am. Acad. Arts and Letters, 1972; Fulbright grantee, 1962-63. Home: 2309 Pender Pl Charlotte NC 28209

GATLIFF, JANE WANDA, librarian; b. Chillicothe, O.; d. Earl M. and Duanna A. (Thomas) Gatliff; B.S., Wilberforce U., 1939; M.L.S. (Carnegie Library scholar), Atlanta U., 1953. Pvt. sec. Phyllis Wheatley Assn., Cleve., 1941-42; accounting clk. Ohio Bur. Unemployment Compensation, Columbus, 1942-52; librarian Ohio State U., Columbus, 1953—. Mem. A.L.A., Delta Sigma Theta. Episcopalian. Home: 2074 Greenway N Columbus OH 43219 Office: 1858 Neil Av Columbus OH 43210

GATLIN, IRENE MAYE, banker; b. Springfield, Mo., Mar. 27, 1923; d. Clyde A. and Julia A. (Higgins) Tiller; student Rude's Bus. Coll., 1940-42, Sch. Bank Adminstrn., 1962-65, Am. Inst. Banking, 1956-60; 1 dau., Patricia Anne (Mrs. Sonny Thornsberry). Comptroller, Farmers & Mechanics Nat. Bank, Woodbury, N.J., 1962-68; asst. v.p. Peoples Nat. Bank of N.J., Westmont, 1970—. Sec. Gloucester County Citizens Assn. Served with USMCR, 1945-47. Mem. Gloucester County Bus. and Profl. Women (past treas., v.p.). Baptist. Home: 46 Lupton Av Woodbury NJ 08096 Office: PO Box 300 Westmont NJ 08108

GATLIN, LILA LEE (MRS. CARL GATLIN), biologist; b. Hutchinson, Kan., Aug. 23, 1928; d. Henry and Anna (Schoenhoff) Krause; B.S. with honors, U. Tulsa, 1957; M.S., Pa. State U., 1959; Ph.D., U. Tex., 1963; m. Carl Gatlin, Sept. 3, 1947; children—Amy, Jeff, Laura, Jennifer. NIH fellow Genetics Found., U. Tex., Austin, 1964; asst. prof. chemistry Drexel U., Phila., 1965-67; vis. lectr. Bryn Mawr (Pa.) Coll., 1967; asst. research biophysicist Space Scis. Lab., U. Cal. at Berkeley, 1973-74; asso. research geneticist, lectr. U. Cal. at Davis, 1974—. Mem. A.A.A.S., Sigma Xi. Author: Information Theory and the Living System, 1972. Editorial bd. Jour. Molecular Evolution. Contbr. articles in field to profl. jours. Home: 2134 Park Ridge Dr Modesto CA 95355 Office: Genetics Dept U Cal at Davis Davis CA

GATTI, BONNIE MUNRO (MRS. FRANK MICHAEL GATTI), physician; b. N.Y.C., Dec. 22, 1938; d. David Alan and Mary Margaret (Trabulsi) Munro; A.B., Barnard Coll., 1960; M.D., State U. N.Y. at Syracuse, 1966; m. Frank Michael Gatti, Dec. 24, 1961; children—Elizabeth Marie, Jane Karen, Gillian Kathleen, Michael Christopher. Pediatric intern Boston City Hosp., 1966-67; jr. asst. resident pediatrics Children's Hosp. Med. Center, Boston, 1967-68; pediatrician West End-Elmwood Neighborhood Health Center, Providence, 1969-70; fellow emotional aspects pediatric disease Tufts, New Eng. Med. Center, Boston, 1970-71; pediatrician Brookside Park Family Life Center, Jamaica Plain, Mass., 1971—; instr. medicine Peter Bent Brigham Hosp., 1971—. Mem. Congress Racial Equality, Syracuse, N.Y., 1965-66, Boston, 1966-68; sec. admissions com. New Sch. for Children, Dorchester, Mass., 1970-72. Mem. Jamaica Plain Citizens for McCarthy, 1968. Home: 43 Lochstead Av Jamaica Plain MA 02130 Office: 39 Brookside Av Jamaica Plain MA 02130

GATTONE, ALBERTA (MRS. EDMOND GATTONE), lawyer, state ofcl.; b. Mount Vernon, Ind.; d. James A. and Laura (Gifford) Robertson; Ph.B., Marquette U., 1924; J.D., U. So. Cal., 1926; m. Edmond Gattone, Sept. 3, 1934. Admitted to Cal. bar, 1926; dep. atty. gen. Cal., 1933-62. Mem. State Bar Cal., Los Angeles County Bar Assn., Order of Coif, Kappa Beta Pi. Home: 2327 Fargo St Los Angeles CA 90039 also 1625 Hillcrest Dr Laguna Beach CA 92651

GATZ, JOSEPHINE MIRANDA (MRS. ROBERT D. GATZ), educator; b. Falls City, Neb., Jan. 17, 1922; d. Arthur J. and Evelyn Maude (Hart) Weaver; B.Sc., U. Neb., 1944; postgrad., U. Ia., 1944-47; M.Ed. (Coe fellow), U. Wyo., 1959; m. Robert D. Gatz, Sept. 18, 1949; children—John David, Robert Weaver, Joseph Hart. Asst. prof. speech Wesleyan Coll., Macon, Ga., 1947-49; dir. Macon Community Theatre, 1948-49; instr. speech and English, Falls City High Sch., 1955-57, West High Sch., Phoenix, 1961-63; faculty U. Wyo., Laramie, 1957-61, 63-67; faculty, dir. theatre Colby (Kan.) Community Coll., 1967—, dir. Players of Golden Plains, summer stock theatre co., 1968—. Mem. Am. Theatre Assn., Speech Communication Assn., Central States, Kan. (v.p. dist. IV 1972-74), speech assns., Kappa Delta Pi, Delta Kappa Gamma, Pi Beta Phi, P.E.O. Home: 990 W 4th St Colby KS 67701

GAUB, MARGARET LUISE, physician; b. Guatemala City, Guatemala (parents Am. citizens); d. William H. and Margaret (Lattelle) Gaub; B.S. cum laude, U. Wash., 1954, M.D. (Ethel Young Phillips scholar, Group Health Coop. scholar, Nat. Found. Infantile Paralysis fellow, Nat. Inst. Mental Health grantee), 1960. Research asst. zoology dept. U. Wash., 1951, asst. poliomyelitis lab., 1953, research asst. microbiology dept., 1953-54, research asst. for U.S. Army, pharmacology dept., 1959; bacteriologist Seattle-King County Dept. Health, 1954-56; intern surgery Jackson Meml. Hosp., Miami, Fla., 1960-61, resident surgery, 1961-63; research fellow anesthesiology U. Miami Sch. Medicine, 1963-65, resident anesthesiology, 1965-66, instr. anesthesiology, 1966-70, asst. prof. anesthesiology, 1970—; practice medicine specializing in pediatric anesthesiology, 1966—. Mem. Dade County Opera Guild, Greater Miami Philharmonic Soc., 1965—. Recipient Anna C. Dunlap prize Soroptomist Club, 1958-59. Diplomate Am. Bd. Anesthesiology. Fellow Am. Coll. Anesthesiologists; mem. Phi Beta Kappa, Sigma Xi, Phi Sigma, Alpha Epsilon Delta, Iota Sigma Pi, Sigma Epsilon Sigma, Alpha Xi Delta. Contbr. articles to profl. jours. Home: 2451 Brickell Av Miami FL 33129 Office: 6125 SW 31st St Miami FL 33155

GAUEN, MARY JANE ADSIT (MRS. RICHARD E. GAUEN), pub. relations ofcl.; b. Hoopeston, Ill.; d. Joseph Sherman and Eliza Jane (Hickman) Adsit; B.A., U. Ill.; M.A., U. Mich., 1941; m. Richard E. Gauen, July 5, 1940; 1 dau., Susan Carol. Detroit corr. Fairchild Publs., 1942-43; day wire filer, writer weekly drama columns Asso. Press, Detroit, 1943-44; fashion editor, columnist-womens features writer Detroit Free Press, 1944-49; pub. relations dir. of park, recreation and forestry depts. City of Evanston, Ill., 1967—. Mem. Ill. Park and Recreation Soc., D.A.R., Women in Communications (v.p. N. Shore chpt. 1973-74), N. Shore Pub. Relations Club (pres. 1971-72), Zeta Phi Eta, Alpha Gamma Delta. Presbyn. Home: 42 Williamsburg Rd Evanston IL 60203 Office: 1802 Maple Av Evanston IL 60201

GAUFF, SUSAN TYRRELL, advt. and pub. relations exec.; b. Hackensack, N.J., Oct. 19, 1946; d. Donald Eugene and Henrietta Dorothy (Benson) Tyrrell; A.A., Centenary Coll., 1967; m. James Anthony Gauff, Apr. 13, 1973; stepchildren—James Timothy, Janet Lorraine, David Phillip. Exec. sec. Am. Chicle Co. div. Warner-Lambert Co., Morris Plains, N.J., 1967-68; sales analyst market research Warner-Lambert Co., Morris Plains, 1968-69; editorial asst. Western Union Telegraph Co., N.Y.C., 1969-70; pub. relations coordinator Western Union Corp., N.Y.C., 1970-72, account exec. Performance Recognition Assos. div. Western Union Corp., N.Y.C., 1972-73; asso. dir. marketing support Information Dynamics Corp., Reading, Mass., 1973-74; marketing cons., Princeton, N.J., 1974—. Recipient Outstanding Contbns. award Publicity Club N.Y., 1972. Mem. Assn. Indsl. Advertisers, Pub. Relations Soc. Am., Centenary Coll. Alumni Assn. (chmn. chpt./clubs pres.'s bd. 1972-73). Clubs: Bear Hill Golf (Stoneham, Mass.); Publicity of New York (membership com. chmn. 1971-72, sec. 1972-73, dir. 1974-76); Publicity of Boston (chmn. telephone com. 1973-74). Address: 33 Slayback Dr Princeton Junction NJ 08550

GAUGHAN, ELLEN MARGARET, city ofcl.; b. New Bedford, Mass., Dec. 7, 1920; d. Thomas E. and Ellen (Bodkin) Gaughan; grad. Kinyon's Coll., 1939. Asst. city clk. New Bedford, Mass., 1950-70, city clk., 1970—. Author several radio scripts for Ave Maria Radio Hour, Greymoor, N.Y., Cath. Guild, New Bedford. Mem. Internat. Inst. Municipal Clks., Daus. of Isabella, Cath. Theatre Guild.

GAULT, MARY CARMEN EMCH (MRS. THEODORE R. GAULT), librarian; b. Pemberville, O., Mar. 21, 1910; d. John Frederick and Rebecca (Jenkins) Emch; student Bowling Green State U., U. Utah; m. Theodore R. Gault, Oct. 25, 1928; children—Galen, Jeanna Mae (Mrs. John W. Milliron, Jr.), Maurice Allen. Asst. to librarian Weston (O.) Pub. Library, 1959-61, head librarian, 1961—. Adviser 4-H, Weston, 1949-54; first aid instr. A.R.C., Weston, Custar and Hoytville, O., 1953-55. Mem. Ohio Library Assn., Weston C. of C. (trustee 1965-67; sec. 1965-66). Home: 20410 Oak St Weston OH 43569 Office: Corner Main and Locust Sts Weston OH 43569

GAUNCE, MARGARET LONG (MRS. STEWART MACINTYRE GAUNCE), librarian; b. McDaniels, Ky.; d. Patrick Clayborn and Mary Eligabeth (Heilman) Long; A.B., Ky. Wesleyan Coll., 1933; postgrad. U. Ky., 1953-54; M.S., Spalding Coll., 1962; m. Stewart MacIntyre Gaunce, July 31, 1938; children—William MacIntyre, Elizabeth Ann (Mrs. James Fullenwider). English tchr., Henry County Bd. Edn., 1939-43, MercerCounty Bd. Edn., 1949-50; sr. English and Spanish tchr. Henry County Bd. Edn., New Castle, Ky., 1952-56, librarian, 1956—. Coordinator library workshop Spalding Coll., 1962. Mem. N.E.A., Ky., Dist. (pres. 1963) library assns., Ky. Edn. Assn., Ky. A-V Assn., Ky. Assn. Sch. Librarians (treas. 1965), Bus. and Profl. Women's Club, Audubon Soc. Democrat. Methodist (sec. adminstrv. bd. 1970). Club: Women's (Shelbyville, Ky.). Home: Box 378 New Castle KY 40050 Office: Henry County High Sch New Castle KY 40050

GAUSE, EMILYN (LYNNE) MALPASS, writer; b. Atkinson, N.C., July 22, 1927; d. Boney Lee and Myrtle Emma (Everette) Malpass; student Mars Hill Coll., 1944-45, No. Ill. U., 1965, Cape Fear Tech. Inst., 1966, Craven Community Coll., 1973; m. Thomas Sneed Cause, Aug. 19, 1967; children by previous marriage—Linda (Mrs. Mark Sheridan), Larry Leeds. Sec. to editor DeKalb (Ill.) Daily Chronicle, 1965; asst. woman's editor Star News Newspapers, Wilmington, N.C., 1966-67; woman's editor Hanover Sun, Wilmington, 1967; columnist DeKalb County Press, 1968; classified advt. and feature writing Sun Jour., New Bern, N.C., 1973; columnist Pamlico County News, Alliance, N.C., 1974—. Vice pres. New Bern Bus. and Profl. Women's Club, 1971; v.p. New Bern Civic Theatre, 1973, publicity chmn., 1973-74; publicity chmn. Expo '74, craft show, 1974. Recipient award Cal. Poetry Day, 1970, Spearman Assos., 1970; named Today's Outstanding N.C. Citizen sta. WNCT-TV, Greenville, Mar. 1970. Fellow Internat. Poetry Soc. Author: (juvenile) Matu and Matsue, 1973; poems pub. anthologies, newspapers. Home: PO Box 2724 2719 Neuse Blvd New Bern NC 28560 Office: care Pamlico County News PO Box 666 New Bern NC 28560

GAUTHIER, GERALDINE FLORENCE, educator; b. Haverhill, Mass., May 14, 1931; d. Henri M. and Marie Berthe A. (Damphousse) Gauthier; B.S., Mass. Coll. of Pharmacy, 1954, M.S., 1955; A.M., Radcliffe Coll., 1956, Ph.D., 1962. Instr., Brown U., Providence, 1962-63, asst. prof., 1963-64; asst. prof. biology Wellesley (Mass.) Coll., 1964-68, asso. prof., 1968-73, prof., 1973—. Recipient USPHS grants, 1963—, Muscular Dystrophy Assn. of Am. grants, 1970—. Home: 56 Loker St Wayland MA 01778

GAUTIER, AGNES MERCURIO (MRS. EMILIO P. GAUTIER), lawyer; b. N.Y.C., Aug. 27, 1939; d. Paul and Lucrezia (Spano) Mercurio; B.A., Barnard Coll., 1961; J.D., N.Y. U., 1964; m. Emilio P. Gautier, Jan. 19, 1974. Admitted to N.Y. bar, 1964, since practiced in N.Y.C.; v.p. James H. Heineman, Inc., N.Y.C., 1967—; spl. counsel N.Y. Stock Exchange, 1973—. Mem. Am., N.Y. bar assns., N.Y. Women's Bar, Nat. Assn. Women Lawyers. Home: 225 Park Pl Brooklyn NY 11238 Office: 55 Water St New York City NY 10022

GAUVIN, DOROTHY RICE (MRS. ALBERT L. GAUVIN), savs. and loan exec.; b. Navasota, Tex., Mar. 28, 1930; d. Amos Miles and Nancy (Lee) Rice; B.B.A., U. Houston, 1950, M.B.A., 1957; m. Albert L. Gauvin, Dec. 8, 1972; children by previous marriage—David Mark, Barbara Colene. Vice pres., sec. Univ. Savs. Assn., Houston, 1968-72; v.p., personnel mgr. Home Savs. Assn., Houston, 1972—. Instr. Am. Savs. and Loan Inst., also adv. gov., cons. Named Man of Year, Sales Promotion Execs. Assn., 1970. Mem. Am. Savs. and Loan Inst., Am. Soc. Personnel Adminstrs., Lakeside Civic Club, Houston Navy League, Res. Officers Wives Club. Presbyn. Home: 10819 Chevy Chase St Houston TX 77042 Office: PO Box 53509 Houston TX 77052

GAUVREAU, WINIFRED CAROL ROLLINS (MRS. FARREN B. JENSEN), journalist; b. N.Y.C., July 20, 1908; d. Maxwell and Winifred Dorothy (Glaser) Rollins; student Elmira Coll., 1926-29, U. Nev., 1959, 60; m. Emile H. Gauvreau, Dec. 5, 1936 (dec. Oct. 1956); m. Farren B. Jensen, Oct. 14, 1967. Sec. to editor N.Y. Daily Mirrow, N.Y.C., 1930-35; asst. to rotogravure editor Phila. Inquirer, 1936-40; asst. to promotion dir. Radio Sta. WIP, Phila., 1941-42; county editor Suffolk (Va.) News Herald, 1955-57; pub. relations, editor mag. First Nat. Bank Nev., Reno, 1958-64; woman's page editor, columnist Register-Pajaronia, Watsonville, Cal., 1964-70; book review columnist Nev. State Jour., Reno, 1958-71; free lance writer, 1972—. Home: 6 Morehouse Dr Watsonville CA 95076

GAVER, MARY VIRGINIA, librarian, educator; b. Washington, Dec. 10, 1906; d. Clayton Daniel and Ruth L. (Clendening) Gaver; A.B., Randolph-Macon Woman's Coll., 1927; B.S. in L.S., Columbia, 1932, M.S. in L.S., 1938, postgrad. Tchrs. Coll., 1945-50; Litt.D., L.I. U., 1967, Mt. Holyoke Coll., 1968. Librarian, George Washington High Sch., Danville, Va., 1927-37; tech. dir. library project WPA of Va., 1938-39; librarian Scarsdale (N.Y.) High Sch., 1939-42, Trenton (N.J.) State Coll., 1942-54; prof. Grad. Sch. Library Service, Rutgers U., 1954-71; dir. library cons. services Bro-Dart Industries, 1971—, v.p., 1973—; leader-specialist Dept. State, U. Tehran, 1952-53. Carnegie fellow, 1937; recipient Good Teaching award Beta Phi Mu, 1965; Research Council award Rutgers U., 1963; Herbert Putnam Honor Fund award A.L.A., 1963. Mem. Am. (pres. 1966-67), N.J. (pres. 1954-55) library assns., Am. Assn. Sch. Librarians (pres. 1959-60), Woman's Nat. Book Assn. (Constance Lindsay Skinner award 1973), N.E.A., Am. Assn. U. Women, Phi Beta Kappa. Club: Zonta (Trenton). Author: Effectiveness of Centralized Library Service in Elementary Schools, 2d edit., 1962; (with Gonzalo Valezquez) School Libraries of Puerto Rico, 1963; (with Lucyle Hook) The Research Manual, 4th edit. 1969. Editor: Elementary School Library Collection, 8th edit., 1973; Background Readings in Building Library Collections, 1969; Services of Secondary School Media Centers: Evaluation and Development, 1972. Home: 13 Ford Av Somerset NJ 08873 also 300 Virginia Av Danville VA 24540 Office: 124 Church St New Brunswick NJ 08901

GAVILO, HELEN MARIE (MRS. ROBERT DANIEL GAVILO), psychologist; b. Miami, Fla., Sept. 8, 1943; d. Thomas Earl and Elspeth (Kelley) Moore; B.A., Agnes Scott Coll., 1965; M.Ed., W. Ga. Coll., 1968; specialist degree sch. psychology, U. Ga., 1969; m. Robert Daniel Gavilo, June 27, 1970; 1 dau., Laurie Beth. Tchr., Franklin Elementary Sch., Bakersfield, Cal., 1965-66, Jerome Jones Elementary Sch., Atlanta, 1966-67; counselor Miami Dade Community Coll., 1969-70; grad. asst. W. Ga. Coll., Carrollton, 1967-68; sch. psychologist S.W. area office Dade County Bd. Edn., Miami, 1970—. Nat. Def. Edn. Act fellow, 1968-69. Mem. Nat., Fla., Dade County (pres. elect 1972-73) assns. sch. psychologists, Kappa Delta Pi. Home: 16101 SW 87th Ct Miami FL 33157 Office: 9040 SW 79th Av Miami FL 33156

GAVIN, JEANINE HELEN-WAGSTAFF, social psychologist; b. Chgo., Feb. 20, 1931; d. John William and Jean (Thompson) Gavin; B.A., Bradley U., 1954, M.A., 1957; Ph.D., Fla. State U., 1964. Testing cons. Houghton Mifflin Publ., Chgo., 1954-55; tchr. St. Louis Pub. Schs., 1955-56; caseworker Chgo. Dept. Pub. Aid, 1956; psychologist Ill. Dept. Mental Health, Chgo., 1963-66; dir. community and mental health Luth. Gen. and Luth. South hosps.,

1966-71; pvt. practice social psychology, 1963—; dir. psychol. group services Grant Hosp., 1964-71; exec. dir. Retraining and Remotivation Center; now exec. dir. Incentives Inst. Mem. steering com. Inst. Human Ecology, 1966-71. Research fellow Fla. Dept. Pub. Health, 1962. Mem. Am. Psychol. Assn., Am. Sociol. Assn., Am. Population Assn., Am. Pub. Health Assn., Nat. Council on Family Relations, Indsl. Relations Research Assn., Am. Group Psycho-therapy Assn., Psi Chi, Alpha Kappa Delta. Author: Learning in the Guppy, 1960; Attitudes of Public Health Nurses, 1961; Reflections on the Treatment of Schizophrenia, 1964; Group Treatment of Lower Class Schizophrenics, 1965; Behavior Intervention Groups, 1967. Office: 2424 Dempster Des Plaines IL 60016

GAY, CLAUDINE MOSS, physician; b. Alma, Ga., Nov. 30, 1915; d. Fred and Rosa Mae (Mercer) Moss; B.S., Coll. William and Mary, 1935; M.D., U. Va., 1939; m. Lendall C. Gay, June 29, 1940 (dec.); children—Gordon B., Spencer B. Intern Gallenger Hosp., Washington; practice medicine specializing in family practice, Washington, 1940—; mem. staff Sibley Meml. Hosp., Washington. U.S. del. Med. Women's Internat. Congress, 5 times; del. President's Workshop on Non-Govtl. Orgn. Fellow Am. Acad. Family Practice (dir. 1964—; alt. del. to ho. dels. 1964-71); mem. Assn. Med. Women Internat. (del.), D.C. Acad. Gen. Practice (pres.), Am. (councilor orgn. and mgmt. 1972-73, v.p. 1974), D.C. (pres.) med. women's assns., A.M.A., D.C. Med. Soc. (dir., past v.p., mem. nominating com. 1970, relative value study com. 1970—, house and bldg. com. 1971—). Club: Zonta (mem. bd.). Home: 5030 Loughboro Rd NW Washington DC 20016 Office: 403 E Capitol St SE Washington DC 20003

GAY, HELEN, biologist, educator; b. Pittsfield, Mass. Aug. 30, 1918; d. Ulrich and Alice (Gonnet) Gay; B.A., Mt. Holyoke Coll., 1940; M.A., Mills Coll., 1942; Ph.D. (Lalor fellow 1951-54), U. Pa., 1955. Research asst. dept. genetics Carnegie Instn., Cold Spring Harbor L.I., N.Y., 1942, 43, 45-51, asso. in research, 1954-60, asso. cytogeneticist, 1960-62, cytogeneticist, 1962-71, in charge lab., 1963-71; prof. zoology U. Mich., 1962—, asso. chmn. dept., 1973—, lectr. cytology, biology dept. Adelphi Coll., Garden City, N.Y., 1959-62; jr. profl. asst. NIH, Bethesda, Md., 1943-45. Fellow A.A.A.S.; mem. Am. Soc. Zoologists, Internat., Am. socs. cell biology, A.A.A.S., Genetics Soc. Am., Am. Soc. Naturalists, Soc. for Developmental Biology, Sigma Xi. Asso. editor cytology sect. Biol. Abstracts. Contbr. articles to sci. jours. Home: 2650 Heather Way Ann Arbor MI 48104

GAY, KATHLYN RUTH MCGARRAHAN (MRS. ARTHUR LESLIE GAY), author; b. Zion, Ill., Mar. 4, 1930; d. Kenneth Charles and Beatrice Vivian (Anderson) McGarrahan; student No. Ill. U., 1947-49, U. Chgo., 1952; m. Arthur Leslie Gay, Aug. 28, 1948; children—Martin, Douglas, Karen. Pub. relations and publicity Church World Service, 1961-64; advt. copywriter Juhl Advt., Inc., 1966. Writing cons. Lyons & Carnahan, 1969-70, Ginn & Co., 1971, Sci. Research Assos., 1972-73; instr. adult writing for profit, 1972-74. Staff writer polit. campaign Mayor Richard J. Daley, Chgo., 1967; precinct vice committeeman Elkhart County Democratic party, 1970—. Recipient First prize Elkhart County Arts Festival, 1965. Author: Where the People Are, 1969; Careers in Social Service, 1969; The Germans Helped Build America, 1971; A Family Is For Living, 1971; Body Talk, 1974; The River Flows Backward, 1974. Contbr. articles to profl. jours. Address: 1711 E Beardsley St Elkhart IN 46514

GAY, ZHENYA, artist, author; b. Norwood, Mass., Sept. 16; student Columbia, 1919-22, also Solon Borglum, N.Y.C.; pupil of Winold Reiss, N.Y.C., Gaston Dorfinant, Paris, France. Exhibited paintings, drawings and lithographs Davis Galleries, Mexico City, 1927, Montross Gallery, N.Y.C., 1930, Dutton's, N.Y.C., 1931, H.H. de Young Meml. Mus., San Francisco, 1931, Am. Mus. Natural History, N.Y.C., 1935, Rains Galleries, N.Y.C., 1939; costumer, designer Brooks Theatrical Costumes; free-lance motion picture and advt. work. Recipient certificate N.Y. State Assn. Supervision and Curriculum Devel., 1961. Illustrator, author: (juveniles) The Dear Friends, 1959; Look#, 1961; Wonderful Things, 1954; Who Is It?, 1957; Small One, 1958; What's Your Name?, 1955; The Nicest Time of Year, 1960, I'm Tired of Lions, 1961; Who's Afraid?, 1965. Illustrator with lithographs: De Quincey's Confessions of an English Opium-Eater, 1930; Wilde's Ballad of Reading Gaol, 1937; illustrator with line drawings: Poems of Catullus, 1931. Address: 7497 Geo Sickles Rd Saugerties NY 12477

GAYLES, ANNE RICHARDSON, educator; b. Marshallville, Ga., June 4, 1923; d. Franklin J. and Marian (Richardson) Gayles; B.S., Ft. Valley State Coll., 1943; M.A., Columbia, 1949, profl. diploma, 1955; Ed.D., Ind. U., 1961; postgrad. Fisk U., 1944-45; postdoctoral Ore. State U., summer 1962. Tchr. high sch. social studies, Sparta, Ga., 1943-44, Grittin, Ga., 1945-48, Marshallville, Ga., 1947-49; elementary sch. tchr. Mt. Zion Luth. Sch., N.Y.C., 1949-50; instr. sociology Ft. Valley (Ga.) State Coll., 1950-51, 51-52; head dept. sociology Ark. Bapt. Coll., Little Rock, 1950-51; dir. internship tng. Sillman Coll., Tuscaloosa, Ala., 1952-54; asst. prof. social scis., coll. supr. Albany (Ga.) State Coll., 1954-57; faculty Fla. A. and M. U., Tallahassee, 1957—, prof. edn., dir. internship teaching, 1961-62, prof. secondary edn., 1962—, chmn. dept. secondary edn. and founds., 1971-74, coordinator of curriculum and instrn., 1969—. Mem. tchr. edn. program evaluation panel Nat. Council for Accreditation Tchr. Edn., 1966, 68; field reader Bur. Research U.S. Office Edn., 1966-70; spl. cons. Fla. Commn. for Quality Edn., 1967; cons. Ann. Coll. and U. Teaching Workshop, Ore. State U., summer 1962, Choice: Books for Coll. Libraries, 1965-70, Social Studies Council Fla., Evaluation Com. Elementary Schs. Fla.; participant ann. selection outstanding ednl. books NEA Jour., 1966, 74, Internat. Seminar Comparative Edn. Soc., 1967; mem. vis. summer faculty Harvard, 1969. Mem. Assn. Social Sci. Tchrs. (1st v.p. 1966), Fla. Tchrs. Assn. (cons.), Nat. Assn. Coll. Tchrs. Edn., Fla. Assn. Supervision and Curriculum, Fla. Assn. Student Teaching, Nat. Soc. Coll. Tchrs. Edn. (chmn.), Fla. Edn. Assn., Assn. Higher Edn., Assn. Student Teaching, Internat. Platform Assn., Nat. Soc. Profs. Edn. (mem. exec. com.), Pi Gamma Mu, Kappa Delta Pi, Pi Lambda Theta, Delta Sigma Theta, Alpha Kappa Mu. Republican. Methodist. Author: Instructional Planning on the Secondary Level, 1973. Editorial staff Quar. Rev. Higher Education Among Negroes, 1965—. Contbr. numerous articles to profl. jours. Home: 609 Howard Av Tallahassee FL 32304

GAYLOR, BARBARA JEAN, ednl. adminstr.; b. Mishawaka, Ind., May 7, 1929; d. John Frederick and Alberta (Braman) Gaylor; B.S., Western Mich. U., 1951, M.A., 1954; postgrad. Mich. State U., 1957, 63, Western Mich. U., 1958-60. Tchr. home econs. Kalamazoo Pub. Schs., 1951-53; supervising tchr. home econs., adviser Future Homemakers Am., adult edn. tchr. Wayland (Mich.) Community Schs., 1953-56; supervising tchr. Western Mich. U., Kalamazoo, 1956-61; state cons. Home Econs. Edn., Lansing, Mich., 1961-66; head Mich. supr. home econs. Dept. Edn., Lansing, 1966-70, supr. adult vocational edn., 1970-72, supr. bus. and industry work study and co-op. unit, 1972-74, supr. consumer and homemaking edn. unit, 1974—. Mem. nat. adv. bd. Favorite Recipes Press. Mem. N.E.A. (dept. home econs.), Am. Vocational Assn., Am., Mich. (v.p.) home econs. assns., Consumer Alliance of Mich., Nat. Assn. State Suprs. Home Econs., Zonta, Mich. Occupational Edn. Assn., Acad. Am. Educators (hon.), Delta Zeta (charter), Delta Kappa Gamma. Home: 2812 Woodruff Av Lansing MI 48912 Office: PO Box 928 Lansing MI 48904

GAYNER, ESTHER KASMAN (MRS. IRVING C. GAYNER), artist; b. Trenton, N.J., Feb. 3, 1914; d. Leon and Ida Gootl (Morris) Kasman; student Trenton Sch. for Indsl. Arts, 1929-31; B.S., N.J. State Tchrs. Coll., 1935; student Ednl. Alliance Art Sch., 1938-39, New Sch. for Social Research, 1958-73, Museum of Modern Art Sch., 1966, 67; m. Irving C. Gayner, Mar. 17, 1946; children—Stephen Hersch, Jay David. One man show at New Sch. Assos. Gallery, N.Y.C., 1964; exhibited in two-woman show Jewish Community Center Gallery, Wilmington, Del., 1974; in group shows at Audubon Artists Nat. Exhbn., Lever Bros., N.Y.C., Albany (N.Y.) Inst. History and Art, Cayuga Inst. History and Art, Auburn, N.Y., Jesse Besser Mus., Alpena, Mich., Bergen County (N.J.) Mus., Mus. of S.W., Midland, Tex., Oshkosh (Wis.) Pub. Mus., Okla. Art Center, Oklahoma City, Pallazzo Vecchio, Florence, Salvator Rose Pub. Gardens, Naples; represented in permanent collections at Jesse Besser Mus., many pvt. collections in U.S., Eng., and Israel. Recipient Nat. Medal of Honor, Nat. Assn. Women Artists, 1972, Paula Kapp award, 1969. Mem. Nat. Assn. Women Artists (chmn. traveling graphics exhbn. U.S.A. 1971—, pres. 1974—), Artists Equity N.Y. Address: 78-03 Austin St Forest Hills NY 11375

GEARHART, JANE ANNETTE, lawyer; b. Seibert, Colo., Mar. 2, 1918; d. Veron L. and Frances Louise (Taylor) Simpson; B.A., U. Denver, 1940, J.D., 1942, LL.D., 1970; postgrad., Mich. State U., 1948-49; m. Richard Crame Gearhart, July 6, 1946 (div. Oct. 1957); 1 dau., Suzanne (Mrs. David Carroll). Admitted to Colo. bar, 1942, Ore. bar, 1956; student law clk. Legal Aid, Denver, 1941-42; law clk. Schaetzel & Knight, Denver, 1942-43; staff atty. League of Ore. Cities, Eugene, 1957-60; dep. legislative counsel Legislative Counsel Office, Ore. Legislative Assembly, Salem, 1962-73; individual practice law, Salem, 1973—. Served to lt. (j.g.) WAVES, 1943-44. Mem. Ore. State Bar, Marion County Bar Assn. Home and office: 3822 3d Av N Salem OR 97303

GEBBIE, CLEMMA CAROLYN (MRS. DURWARD JAMES GEBBIE), educator; b. Craftsbury Common, Vt., Aug. 12, 1924; d. Ellry Elmore and Mary Matilda (Wheeler) Davis; R.N., Barre City Hosp. Sch. of Nursing, 1945; postgrad. U. Vt., 1945-46, U. Conn., 1946; B.S., Eastern Conn. State Coll., 1963; m. Durward James Gebbie, June 30, 1946; children—Darwin Carl, Donna (Mrs. Paul Schaffer), John Ellry, Bradley James and Brenda Jane (twins), Carol Ann, Linda Ruth. With Mansfield Tng. Sch., Mansfield Depot, Conn., 1948-74, dir. in service tng., 1965-74. Leader, Girl Scouts Am., Storrs, Conn., 1957-59. Mem. Am. Assn. on Mental Deficiency. Republican. Conglist. Home: Box 22 Lyndonville VT 05851

GECHTOFF, SONIA (MRS. JAMES KELLY), artist; b. Phila., Sept. 25, 1926; B.F.A., Phila. Mus. Sch.; m. James Kelly. Exhibited in one-man shows at Dubin Gallery, Phila., 1949, Lucien Labaudt Gallery, 1952, 53, Gallery Six, San Francisco, 1955, de Young Mus., 1957, Ferus Gallery, 1957, 59, Poindexter Gallery, 1959, 60, East Hampton Gallery, 1963; exhibited in group shows at Guggenheim Mus., 1954, Brussels (Belgium) World's Fair, 1958, Carnegie, Mus., 1958, Paris Biennial, 1959, Whitney Mus., 1959, 60, Sao Paulo Biennial, 1961, Abstract Am. Drawings and Watercolors, S.Am Latin Am., 1961-63, Los Angeles County Mus., 1969, East Hampton Gallery, 1966, Westbeth Courtyard galleries, 1971, 72, N.Y. Cultural Center, 1973; represented in collections at U. Cal. at Los Angeles, Oakland Art Mus., San Francisco Mus. Art, San Francisco Art Assn., Singer Co., Inc., Woodward Found., U. Mass., U. Cal. at Davis, Am. Tel. & Tel. Co.; tchr. Cal. Sch. Fine Arts, 1957-58, N.Y.U., 1961-71, Queens Coll., 1970-74; asso. prof. art U. N.M., Albuquerque, 1974—. Recipient award San Francisco Mus. Art, award Santa Barbara Mus. Art; Tamarind fellow, 1963. Address: 463 West St New York City NY 10014

GECKER, EDITH FISHMAN (MRS. LEON GECKER), interior designer; b. N.Y.C.; d. Joseph and Mary (Plitt) Fishman; student Friends Sch.; B.S., Columbia, 1926; m. Leon Gecker, June 6, 1926; 1 dau., Dulcie Jane (Mrs. Stuart Voisin). Interior decorator, 1931—, designer traditional furniture; owner Edith Gecker, interior decorating, N.Y.C. Del. to Inter-Soc. Color Council from Am. Inst. Decorators, 1956-57; mem. adv. council Fashion Com. of State of N.Y., 1963—. Bd. dirs. Grand St. Settlement, N.Y.C., 1932—. Recipient Gold medal devotion WAIF. Fellow Nat. Soc. Interior Designers (life, chmn. delegation Inter Soc. Color Council 1958-68, bd. govs. 1957—, v.p. 1960-61, pres. edn. found. 1963-65, 73-75; Gold medal distinguished service 1973); mem. Am. Inst. Decorators (bd. govs. N.Y. chpt. 1955-57), Am. Arbitration Assn. (mem. nat. panel arbitrators). Address: 600 West End Av New York City NY 10024

GEE, MARGUERITE, writer, editor, pub. relations exec.; b. Houston, June 13, 1944; d. Yum and Mah (Shee) Gee; student U. Tex., 1962-63; B.A., U. Houston, 1968. Pub. relations dir. Hawaii Heart Assn., Honolulu, 1969-72; owner MG Editorial Services, Honolulu, 1972; pub. relations rep. Sheraton Hotels in Hawaii, Honolulu, 1972-73. Bd. dirs. Friends of the Tennent Gallery, 1970-71, sec., 1970-71. Recipient Nelson Prather award for outstanding young communicator Hawaii Communicators Assn., 1972, 1st pl. overall pubs., 1972, 1st pl. mimeograph publs., 1973. Mem. Am. Civil Liberties Union, Hawaii Communicators Assn. (dir. 1970-73), Women in Communications (editor newsletter 1969-71, sec. 1972), Advt. Club II (sec.-treas. 1970-72). Home and office: 1326 Palolo Av Honolulu HI 96816

GEE, RUTH CREW, genealogist; b. Marion, Ia., Mar. 9, 1911; d. Arthur Ellwood and Bertha Alice (Ives) Crew; B.S., U. Ia., 1933; m. Herbert Caran Gee, Mar. 7, 1936; children—Philip Charles, Nancy. Tchr., Marion High Sch., 1934-36. Librarian, Palm Beach County Geneal. Soc., West Palm Beach, Fla., 1969-73. Chmn., West Palm Beach Decent Lit. Com., 1965-67; mem. Bicentennial Steering Com. West Palm Beach, 1973. Mem. D.A.R. (nat. vice chmn. geneal. records com. 1970-72, registrar Fla. soc. 1972-74, chmn. lineage research 1974-76), Daus. Founders and Patriots Am. (state registrar 1967-71, historian 1973—), Dames Ct. of Honor, P.E.O., Chi Omega. Home: 311 Westminster Pl West Palm Beach FL 33405

GEEN, PATRICIA ANN, lawyer; b. Weehawken, N.J., June 13, 1929; d. Arthur Aloysius and Marion Antoinette (Sweeney) Geen; student Albertus Magnus Coll., 1946-49; J.D., Temple U., 1952. Admitted to Conn. bar, 1952; mem. firm James C. Driscoll, Jr., Bethel, Conn., 1952-53; individual practice law Patricia A. Geen, Bethel, 1953-54; atty. First Nat. City Bank N.Y., 1955-60; partner firm Sedensky, Meyer, & Geen, Bethel, 1961—; judge probate dist. Redding, 1974—; instr. Conn. State Tech. Coll., 1970; instr. polit. sci. Albertus Magnus Coll., New Haven, Conn., 1963. Town counsel Town of Redding, Conn., 1970—, Town of Bethel, 1967-69. Mem. nat. council Camp Fire Girls, 1968. Alternate mem. Redding Zoning Bd., 1967-69; Republican State Central committeewoman, 1973-74. Trustee State Colls. for State Conn., 1973—; bd. dirs. United Way of No. Fairfield County (Conn.), 1968, sec., 1970-72, v.p. 1973-74. Mem. Am., Conn. (sec. status of women com. 1972-73, 73-74), Danbury (pres. 1975) bar assns., Am. Judicature Soc., Conn. Assn. Municipal Attys., Bus. Profl. Women's Club of Danbury (pres. 1963), League of Women Voters of Danbury (pres. 1953). Roman Catholic. Home: Huckleberry Rd Redding CT 06896 Office: 1 Diamond Av Bethel CT 06801

GEESLIN, DORINE HAWK (MRS. ROBERT JONES GEESLIN), educator; b. Priceville, Ky., June 22, 1918; d. Benjamin Franklin and Rosa (Avery) Hawk; B.A., Western Ky. U., 1938; M.Ed., U. Louisville, 1959; D.Ed., Fla. State U., 1967; m. Robert Jones Geeslin, May 19, 1938; children—Robert Hawk, Franklin Andrew, Melanie Rose. Tchr. Versailles (Ky.) City Schs., 1950-52, Jefferson County Schs., Louisville, 1952-56; supr. of instrn. Elizabethtown (Ky.) City Schs., 1956-64; research asst. Fla. State U., Tallahassee, 1964-65; dir. reading inst. N. Fla. Jr. Coll., Madison, summer 1965; asst. prof. edn. and human devel. Valdosta State Coll., Ga., 1965-67; reading cons. DeKalb County Schs. Reading Center, Clarkston, Ga., 1967-69; faculty Western Ky. U., 1969—. Mem. Am. Assn. U. Women, Am. Assn. U. Profs., Delta Kappa Gamma (v.p. 1967-68). Presbyn. Democrat. Home: Upton KY 42784 Office: Dept Elementary Edn Western Ky U Bowling Green KY 42101

GEHRIS, MARCIA JEANNE, ednl. adminstr.; b. Reading, Pa., Jan. 10, 1948; d. Leroy Allen and Leona Rebecca (Clouser) Gehris; B.A. cum laude, Lebanon Valley Coll., 1969. Featured vocalist Fred Waring and Pennsylvanians, 1969-70, Arthur Godfrey Radio Show, 1971; asst. marketing div. and customer service Learning Research Assos., N.Y.C., 1971-72; technician instructional media Berks Vocational Tech. Sch., Reading, 1970-71; asst. dean students Lebanon Valley Coll., Annville, Pa., 1972—. Vocalist many civic benefit shows. Mem. Sigma Alpha Iota, Phi Alpha Epsilon. Lutheran. Home: 47A N Prince St Palmyra PA 17078 Office: Lebanon Valley Coll Annville PA 17003

GEIGER, KATHRYN CAROLINE, editor; b. St. Marys, O., Nov. 9, 1905; d. John Frederick and Caroline Elizabeth (Settlage) Geiger; grad. high sch. Reporter, Leader Printing Co., St. Marys, 1923-26, city editor, 1926-44, editor, 1944—. Free lance news reporter Toledo Blade, Dayton (O.) Jour., Dayton Daily News, Lima (O.) Daily News. Pres., St. Marys Sesquicentennial Com., 1932-33, Auglaize County Tb and Health Assn., 1951. City treas. City of St. Marys, 1932-40. Bd. dirs. W. Auglaize chpt. A.R.C., 1934-64, Salvation Army. Mem. Ohio Newspaper Womens Assn., Fraternal Order Police (hon.), St. Marys Future Farmers, St. Marys C. of C. (trustee 1952-55), Jr. C. of C. (hon.). Lutheran (mem. ch. bldg. com. 1964). Club: St. Marys Drama. Author: (with others) The St. Marys Story, 1973. Home: 133 N Wayne St St Marys OH 45885 Office: 102 E Spring St St Marys OH 45885

GEIS, SALLY BROWN (MRS. ROBERT BENN GEIS), educator; b. Salina, Kan., Mar. 20, 1928; d. Porter and Ann (Curphey) Brown; B.A., Stanford, 1949, M.A., 1950; Ph.D. (Nat. Def. Edn. Act fellow), U. Denver, 1967; m. Robert Benn Geis, May 12, 1951; children—J. Raymond, James Porter. Researcher, Council of Social Agys., Kansas City, Mo., 1950-51; teaching asst. U. Denver, 1961-67; faculty Colo. Women's Coll., Denver, 1967—, asso. prof. sociology, 1968—. Cons. program for migrant workers, high sch. equivalency program Office Econ. Opportunity, 1967-69; mem. Gov's. Commn. on the Status of Women for Colo., 1973-74, co-chmn. edn. com., 1973—; mem. nat. bd. of ch. and soc. representing western U.S., United Methodist Ch., 1972—. Del. Democratic state conv., 1964. Mem. Am. Ednl. Studies Assn. (mem. conv. com. 1973-74), Am. Sociol. Assn., Am. Assn. U. Profs., Cap and Gown. Home: 2258 S Milwaukee St Denver CO 80210

GEISER, ELIZABETH ABLE, publishing co. exec.; b. Phillipsburg, N.J., Apr. 28, 1925; d. George W. and Margaret I. (Ross) Geiser; A.B. magna cum laude, Hood Coll., 1947. Promotion mgr. coll. dept. Macmillan Co., N.Y.C., 1947-54; promotion mgr. R.R. Bowker, N.Y.C., 1954-60, sales mgr., 1960-67, dir. marketing, 1967-70, v.p., 1970-73, sr. v.p., pub. book div., 1973—, dir., 1965-68. Lectr. Publishing Procedures Course, Radcliffe Coll., 1966—, Library Sci. Schs. U. Wash., U. So. Cal.; panel mem. TV series The Living Library, 1970. Mem. Publishers' Advt. Club, Publishers Library Promotion Group, Assn. Am. Publishers (sch., library promotion and marketing com. 1972—, adv. council Frankfurt book fair 1971), A.L.A. (pres. exhibits roundtable 1968-70, dir. exhibits roundtable 1968). Presbyn. Contbr. to Manual of Bookselling, a handbook for booksellers, 1969. Home: The Village Green 495 Main St Orange NJ 07050 Office: 1180 Av of the Americas New York City NY 10036

GEISER, FLORAMAE GATES (MRS. DOYLE STANLEY GEISER), editor; b. Davenport, Ia., Apr. 27, 1930; d. Floyd Leon and Mae Jeannette (Hollander) Gates; B.S., Ia. State U., 1952; m. Doyle Stanley Geiser, June 22, 1952; children—David Stanley, Tamara Jane, Andrew Gates. Fashion copywriter Younkers Dept. Store, Des Moines, 1952-54; pub. relations Solar Aircraft, Des Moines, 1954-55; with Ind., Ky. Synod, Lutheran Ch. in Am., Indpls., 1965—, editor, publicity sec., 1965—, asso. editor conv. daily newspaper, 1970. Chmn. dept. communications Ind. Council of Chs., 1971-73; mem. mgmt. com. Office Communications, Luth. Ch. Am., 1972—. Vol. adviser Call for Action, Sta. WFBM, Indpls., 1790-72; mem. com. internat. visitors Indpls. Council on World Affairs, 1966—; v.p. alumnae chpt. Mortar Bd., 1962-63. Mem. Religious Pub. Relations Council, Theta Sigma Phi, Phi Upsilon Omicron, Omicron Nu. Lutheran. Home: 5725 Andover Rd Indianapolis IN 46220 Office: 3733 N Meridian St Indianapolis IN 46208

GEISLER, JOAN MARIE, assn. exec.; b. Dubuque, Ia., May 21, 1930; d. Arthur Peter and Ursula Mary (Graf) Geisler; student Clarke Coll., 1948-50; B.S., Wis. State U., 1963; Elementary tchr. Sheboygan, Wis., 1950-51; sec. Geisler Bros., Dubuque, Ia., 1951-60; exec. dir. Little Cloud Girl Scouts, Dubuque, 1963—. Mem. Ia. State Conservation Commn., Dubuque, 1969-72; mem. Civic Music Assn., 1956-64. Bd. dir. St. Marys Home, 1963-64. Mem. Am. Camping Assn. (v.p. 1969-70), Assn. of Girl Scout Profl. Wokers (finance chmn. 1966). Clubs: Photo (Dubuque); Boat. Home: 998 Kirkwood St Dubuque IA 52001 Office: 666 Loras Blvd Dubuque IA 52001

GEISMAR, HELAINE FELICE, ednl. adminstr.; b. N.Y.C., June 14, 1947; d. Stanley and Muriel Viola (Ernst) Geismar; B.S., Syracuse U., 1968; M.A. (Office of Edn. fellow), Columbia, 1969. Sr. speech and hearing therapist Shield Inst. for Retarded Children, Bronx, N.Y., 1969-73; head speech and hearing therapist Queens Devel. Services for the Mentally Retarded, Long Island, N.Y., 1973; dir. Queens State Sch. Day Center for Severely and Profoundly Retarded Children, Corona, L.I., N.Y., 1973—. Cons. on speech and lang. devel. These Our Treasures Day Care Center, Bronx, 1972; coordinator One-to-One Festivals, N.Y.C., 1972, 73. Vol. adv. council Queens Devel. Services, Corona, 1973—; mem. Steering com. policy and action conf. on the handicapped, N.Y.C., 1972-73; coordinator Mayoral Candidates Conference, policy and action conf. on the Handicapped, N.Y.C., 1973. Mem. Am. Speech and Hearing Assn. (certificate) N.Y. State Speech and Hearing Assn., Am. Assn. Mental Deficiency, Council for Exceptional Children, Parent Edn. Assn. for the Help of Retarded Children (co-chmn. 1973), Zeta Phi Eta, Sigma Alpha Eta. Home: 160 West End Av New York City NY 10023 Office: 37-10 114th St Corona LI NY 11368

GEISNESS, HELEN MOULTON (MRS. JOHN GEISNESS), assn. exec.; b. Seattle, Oct. 9, 1906; d. Myron Dudley and Anna Louise (Conger) Moulton; A.B., U. Wash., 1929, LL.B., 1931; m. John Geisness, July 1, 1933; children—Thomas, Anne (Mrs. John Pangborn). Admitted to Wash. bar, 1931; atty. Seattle-King County Legal Aid, Seattle, 1956-66, dir. lawyer referral, 1960—. Mem. Am., Wash., Seattle-King County (exec. dir. 1966—) bar assns., Order of Coif, Phi Beta Kappa, Phi Delta Delta. Unitarian. Home: 3815 E Pike St Seattle WA 98122 Office: 320 Central Bldg 810 Third Av Seattle WA 98104

GELB, ARLENE (MRS. ARTHUR GELB), advt. agy. exec.; b. N.Y.C., Aug. 13, 1935; d. Murray and Lillian (Golib) Davidson; student, Bklyn. Coll., 1953-54; m. Arthur Gelb, Dec. 25, 1955; children—Jamie, Scott, Stacy. With Gelb Advt., Inc., N.Y.C., 1955-73, pres., 1974—; media dir. Raymond Petrie Advt. Inc., N.Y.C., 1973. Active Birch Sch. P.T.A., Merrick, N.Y. Home: 2080 Holland Way Merrick NY 11566 Office: 280 Madison Av New York City NY 10016

GELB, JUDITH ANNE (MRS. HOWARD S. VOGEL), lawyer; b. N.Y.C., Apr. 5, 1935; d. Joseph and Sarah (Stein) Gelb; B.A. cum laude, Bklyn. Coll., 1955; J.D., COlumbia Law Sch., 1958; m. Howard S. Vogel, June 30, 1962; 1 son, Michael S. Admitted to N.Y. bar, 1959, U.S. Ct. Appeals 2d Circuit, 1960, U.S. Dist. Cts., 1960, U.S. Ct. Mil. Appeals, 1962; confidential asst. to U.S. atty. Eastern Dist. N.Y., Bklyn., 1959-61; asso. Whitman & Ransom, N.Y.C., 1961-70; partner Whitman & Ransom, 1971—. Mem. Fed. Bar Council, N.Y. State, N.Y. Women's (mem. com. on by-laws and com. on taxation 1968-70) bar assns., N.Y. State Dist. Atty.'s Assn., Psi Chi. Democrat. Club: Columbia U. (N.Y.C.). Home: 201 E 36th St New York City NY 10016 Office: 522 Fifth Av New York City NY 10036

GELBER, LOUISE CARP (MRS. MILTON GELBER), lawyer; b. Detroit, Oct. 24, 1921; d. Jacob and Gusta (Schneider) Carp; student Los Angeles City Coll., 1940, U. Mich., 1940-41; B.A., U. Cal. at Berkeley, 1944, J.D., 1944; Ph.D. (hon.), Colo. State Christian Coll., 1973; m. Milton Gelber, July 10, 1943; children—Jack, Bruce, Julie (Mrs. Gary McCoy). Admitted to Cal. bar, 1944; research asst. Judge Roger Traynor, Cal. Supreme Court, San Francisco, 1944-45; partner Gelber & Gelber, El Monte and Arcadia, Cal., 1945—. Judge pro-tem municipal court El Monte Jud. Dist., County of Los Angeles, 1960; lectr. in So. Cal., 1950—. Mem. planning commn. bd. United Way. Asst. treas. Los Angeles County Dem. Com., 1968; mem. exec. com., co-chmn. 24th congressional dist. Dem. State Central Com. 1968; nominee Cal. Senate, 1968. Recipient Award of Honor, El Monte-South El Monte C. of C., 1968. Mem. State Bar Cal., Am., Los Angeles County, Pomona Valley bar assns., Tournament of Roses Assn., League Women Voters, Arcadia C. of C. Mem. Order Eastern Star. Home and office: 1225 Rancho Rd Arcadia CA 91006

GELFOND, JOYCE JEAN LEMMONS (MRS. STEPHEN GELFOND), psychiatrist; b. McAllen, Tex., Jan. 9, 1937; d. George A. and Edith Elizabeth (Adam) Michie; B.S., Okla. U., 1958; M.D., Okla. U., 1966; m. David D. Lemmons, Sept. 16, 1957 (div. Jan. 1959); 1 son, David; m. 2d, Stephen Gelfond, Dec. 30, 1969; children—Jennifer E.T., Jonathan A.L., Benjamin M.F. Med. technologist St. Anthony Hosp., Oklahoma City, 1957-58, McAlester Gen. Hosp., Okla., 1958-60; med. technologist, cytotechnologist Med. Arts Lab. Oklahoma City and Hillcrest Hosp., Tulsa, 1961-62; intern St. Anthony Hosp., Oklahoma City, 1966-67; resident pathology Okla. Med. Sch., 1967-68; resident psychiatry Tulane U., New Orleans, 1968-70, Sheppard-Pratt Hosp., Balt., 1971; resident tchr. Tulane U., 1968-69; cons. psychiatry Morgan State Coll., Balt., 1971; practice medicine specializing psychiatry, Towson, Md., 1971-72, San Antonio, 1972—. Cons., Bexar County Drug Treatment Center. Mem. Am. Soc. Clin. Pathologist, A.M.A., Am. Psychiat. Assn., Alpha Omega Alpha. Jewish religion. Home: 6022 Wildwind Dr San Antonio TX 78239 Office: 6022 Wildwind Dr San Antonio TX 78239

GELLENS, JACQUELINE MARIE WALTRIP (MRS. PAUL J. GELLENS), editor; b. Monett, Mo., Mar. 18, 1928; d. Ralph Claude and Sophia Ola (Jagears) Waltrip; student Monett Jr. Coll., 1946-48, Drury Coll., 1966, Kan. State Coll., 1967, So. Ill. U., 1967, 69, U. Del., 1971; m. Paul J. Gellens, May 23, 1970; 1 son (by previous marriage), Ned Lautaret. Asst. news editor Monett Times, 1944-49, 57-63; news editor Branson (Mo.) Beacon, 1963-66; editor Clay Center (Kan.) Dispatch, 1966-67; asst. city editor Edwardsville (Ill.) Intelligencer, 1967-70; home furnishings editor, feature writer Wilmington (Del.) News-Jour., 1970—. Recipient Hawthorne award Hawthorne Lit. Club, 1948. Mem. Wilmington Bus. and Profl. Women's Club. Republican. Author, editor: (with Jim M. Owen) Jim Owen's Hillbilly Humor, 1970. Home: 605 Brighton Rd Wilmington DE 19809 Office: 813 Orange St Wilmington DE 19899

GELLER, MOLLY S. (MRS. HERMAN GELLER), educator; b. N.Y.C., Jan. 16, 1911; d. Julius and Anna (Cohen) Siegel; B.S., Washington Sq. Coll., 1931; M.S., N.Y. U., 1934, Ph.D., 1962; m. Herman Geller, Apr. 15, 1963; children—Isabelle M. (Mrs. Albert Nalven), Joseph, Rosalind. Teaching fellow N.Y. U. Sch. Edn., 1957-62; asso. prof. biology and sci. edn. William Paterson Coll., Wayne, N.J., 1962—. Cons. on Wetlands vegetation. Trustee Lung Assn., N.J. N.J. Marine Scis. Consortium grantee, 1970. Fellow A.A.A.S.; mem. Nat. Sci. Tchrs. Assn., Am. Littoral Soc. Home: Laurel Lake Lee MA 01238 Office: Box 384 Fort Lee NJ 07024

GELLERT, GEORGIA MARRS (MRS. NATHAN HENRY GELLERT), pub. relations exec.; b. Denver, Oct. 8, 1917; d. William Middelton and Blanche (Boak) Marrs; student U. Denver, 1936-37; m. Winfield Turrell Barber, Jan. 18, 1941 (dec. May 1948); m. 2d, Nathan Henry Gellert, Mar. 12, 1954 (dec. Nov. 1959). Soc. editor Denver Post, 1937-41; tech. writer, editor Consol. Vultee Aircraft, USN Radio and Sound Lab., San Diego, 1944-46; mgr. box office Central City Opera House Assn., Denver, 1948; soc. editor Denver Post, 1949-51; publicity dir. N.A.M., San Francisco, 1951-54; asst. exhibits dir. Seattle Worlds Fair, 1960-62; pub. relations dir. Seattle Center, 1962-64; free lance pub. relations, Seattle, 1964—. Trustee Seattle Symphony Orchestra, 1960—, sec. bd., 1964-65, v.p., mem. exec. com., 1973—; dir. Allied Arts of Seattle, 1960—, treas., 1966-68; dir. Pottery N.W., Seattle, 1966-68; trustee Seattle Childrens Home, 1954-61, pres., 1959-61. Mem. Women in Communications, Found. Preservation Gov.'s Mansion, Pi Beta Phi. Episcopalian. Clubs: Denver Womans Press, Seattle Tennis, Washington Athletic; Rainier. Home: 476 Lake Washington Blvd E Seattle WA 98112 Office: 402 Grosvenor House Seattle WA 98121

GELLHAUS, NANCY LOUISE, pub. relations exec.; b. Waterloo, Ia., Oct. 9, 1946; d. Harvey Wayne and Lois Luella (Gott) Gellhaus; B.S., U. S.D., 1968; postgrad. U. Minn., 1971-74. Asst. to dir. pub. relations Nat. Car Rental Systems, Inc., Mpls., 1969-70; promotions and pub. relations staff Grain Belt Breweries, Mpls., part time 1970; dir. pub. relations Mt. Sinai Hosp. Mpls., 1970-73; customer relations rep. Control Data Corp., Mpls., 1973—. Mem. pub. relations com. Girl Scouts Mpls., 1971-73. Free lance editor, model, demonstrator. Recipient Best Overall Coverage plaque United Fund, 1971, Best Feature plaque, 1972; Pulse nat. awards, 1972; nominated Outstanding Young Woman of Am. Mem. Am. Soc. Hosp. Pub. Relations Dirs., Internat. Assn. Bus. Communicators (dirs.), Twin City Hosp. Assn. (communication council), Women in Communications, Zeta Phi Eta (nat. editor Cameo 1970-71), Alpha Xi Delta. Home: 7430 W 128 St Minneapolis MN 55424 Office: 7801 Computer Av Minneapolis MN 55435

GELLISE, SISTER MARY YVONNE, hosp. exec.; b. Bay City, Mich., Aug. 21, 1934; d. Levi Joseph and Regina (Savage) Gellise; B.S. in Accounting, U. Detroit, 1960; M.Hosp. Adminstrn., St. Louis U., 1965. Jr. accountant Tripp & Laine, C.P.A.'s, Bay City, 1952-55; joined Sister of Mercy, 1955; bus. mgr. Mercy Med. Center, Dubuque, Ia., 1960-63; adminstrv. resident Providence Hosp., Seattle, 1964-65; adminstr. Villa Elizabeth, Grand Rapids, Mich., 1965-67; asso. adminstr. St. Joseph Mercy Hosp., Clinton, Ia., 1967-68; adminstr. St. Joseph Mercy Hosp., Ann Arbor, Mich., 1968—; lectr. hosp. adminstrn. Sch. Pub. Health, U. Mich., 1969. Dir. Ann Arbor Bank. Pres. bd. trustees St. Joseph Mercy Hosp. of Detroit. Named Boss of Year, Arbor Charter chpt. Am. Bus. Women's Assn., 1969. Mem. Hosp. Financial Mgmt. Assn., Am. Coll. Hosp. Adminstrs., Ann Arbor C. of C. (dir.). Address: 326 N Ingalls Ann Arbor MI 48104

GELLMAN, ESTELLE SHEILA (MRS. YALE H. GELLMAN), educator; b. Bklyn., July 27, 1941; d. Jack and Ida (Frankel) Klittnick; B.A., City Coll., 1962; M.A., Tchrs. Coll. Columbia, 1965, Ph.D. (Nat. Def. Edn. Act. fellow), 1968; m. Yale H. Gellman, Aug. 23, 1964; children—Douglas Zane, Russell Marc. Research analyst N.Y. Life Ins. Co., N.Y.C., 1962-63; mem. faculty Hofstra U., Hempstead, N.Y., 1966—, lectr., 1966-67, adj. asst. prof., 1967-68, asst. prof., 1968-72, asso. prof., 1972—. Mem. Am. Ednl. Research Assn., Nat. Council Measurement in Edn., Am. Acad. Polit. and Social Sci., A.A.A.S., Am. Assn. U. Profs., Am., Eastern psychol. assns., Sigma Xi, Psi Chi. Home: 131 Schenck Av Great Neck NY 11021 Office: Dept Ednl Psychology Hofstra U Hempstead NY 11550

GELT, JEANETTE ROSE LEBMAN, state legislator; b. Newburyport, Mass., Aug. 21, 1916; d. Joseph and Agnes (Goldsmith) Lebman; grad. high sch.; m. George Gelt, Nov. 25, 1937; children—Sylvia, Gloria (Mrs. Michael Muskowitz). Del., N.H. Constl. Conv., 1964; mem. N.H. Ho. of Reps., 1965—. Chmn., March of Dimes, 1962-64. Bd. dirs. Salem (N.H.) Mental Health Assn., 1969-71, Salem Vis. Nurses Assn. Mem. Nat. Soc. State legislators (exec. com. Rockingham County 1967—). Republican. Clubs: Salem Garden, Salem Women. Home: 21 Martin Av Salem NH 03079

GENDEL, EVALYN STOLAROFF (MRS. JOSEPH GENDEL), physician; b. New Orleans, Sept. 19, 1922; d. Solomon Aaron and Reva (Dubinski) Stolaroff; B.F.A., Newcomb Coll., 1943; M.D., La. State U., 1949; preceptor Med. Sch., Bristol (Eng.) U., 1947-48; m. Joseph Gendel, Mar. 30, 1947; children—Michael, Peter, Patrice, Steven, Jonathan. Intern, Touro Infirmary, New Orleans, 1949-50, resident orthopedic surgery, 1950-52; gen. practice medicine, Topeka, 1952-56; dir. state polio program Kan. Dept. Health, Topeka, 1957-58, asst. dir. maternal and child health div., 1958-71, chief sch. health sec., 1958-71, dir. maternal and child health, 1971—; lectr. preventive medicine and community health U. Kan. Med. Center, 1959-66, asst. clin. prof. human ecology community health U. Kan. Med. Sch., 1966—. Pres. Kan. Sch. Health Adv. Council, 1960-62, sec.-treas., 1963; med. adviser Topeka City council P.T.A.'s mem. Shawnee County Sch. Health Adv. Council, 1959—; Mem. Surgeon Gen.'s Review Com. on Comprehensive Health Planning Tng. and Studies, USPHS, Dept. Health, Edn. and Welfare, 1968-71; cons. President's Council on Phys. Fitness, 1972—. Pres. bd. dirs. Siecus-Sex Information Edn. Council, 1968-71. Recipient Distinguished Honor award Am. Sch. Health Assn., Houston, 1970; Honor award Kan. Assn. Health Phys. Edn. and Recreation, 1970. Fellow Am. Pub. Health Assn. (chmn. sch. health sect., mem. governing council, mem. population council dir. 1972—), Am. Coll. Sports Medicine, Am. Sch. Health Assn. (governing council, asso. editor Jour. Sch. Health), Am. Coll. Health Assn.; mem. Kan. Pub. Health Assn. (pres. 1964-65), Kan. Med. Aux. (state sch. health chmn.), A.M.A. (chmn. fund raising dr. Edn. Research Found.), Kan. (maternal welfare, sch. health coms., chmn. hearing conservation, venereal disease control coms.), Shawnee County (sch. health com.) med. socs., Am. Assn. Pub. Health Physicians (trustee), Am. Assn. State and Territorial Dirs. Maternal and Child Health and Crippled Children (pres. elect), Alpha Epsilon Iota, Delta Kappa Gamma. Jewish religion. Club: Altrusa (dir. Topeka). Contbr. articles to profl. jours. Home: 3143 Shadow Lane Topeka KS 66604 Office: State Office Bldg Topeka Blvd Topeka KS 66612

GENEAUER, EMILY, art critic, editor, writer; b. N.Y.C.; d. Joseph and Rose (Milch) Geneauer; student Hunter Coll., N.Y.C.; B. Lit., Columbia Sch. Journalism, 1930; m. Frederick Gash, 1935; 1 dau., Constance Lee. Staff writer, art feature writer N.Y. World, 1929-31; art critic, editor N.Y. World-Telegram, 1932-48; art critic N.Y. Herald Tribune, 1948-67; now arts columnist Newsday Syndicate; lectr., broadcaster on art. Mem. Pres.'s Nat. Council on Humanities. Recipient ann. award for writing in specialized field N.Y. Newspaper Women's Club, 1937, for outstanding column in any field, 1949, 56, 58, 60; Grad. Sch. Journalism award Columbia, 1960. Mem. Women in Communications. Author: Best of Art, 1947; Monograph on Toulouse-Lautrec for Met. Mus. of Art, 1953; Biography of Chagall, 1957; Hommage a l'Ecole de Paris, 1961. Address: 243 E 49th St New York City NY 10017

GENETT, ADRIENNE GAYE, mag. editor; b. Glendale, Cal., Apr. 22, 1945; d. James Charles and Gladys Ardella (Miller) Genett; B.A. cum laude, U. Houston, 1967; m. Frederick B. Messmore, Mar. 20, 1971 (div. 1974). Editor, pub. relations rep. Tex. Internat. Airlines, Houston, 1967-69; asst. mgr. pub. relations N. Central Airlines, Mpls., 1969-71; with Webb Co., St. Paul, 1971—, editor, 1972—. Freelance writer and photographer, 1969—. Recipient Mag. Editing award Internat. Indsl. Editors Assn., 1967, 68. Mem. Foremost Women in Communications, Women in Communications, Gamma Alpha Chi. Democrat. Methodist. Author: Contributions of Women: Aviation. Home: 1465 Salem Church Rd # 305 Inver Grove Heights MN 55075 Office: 1999 Shepard Rd St Paul MN 55116

GENIESER, NANCY BRANOM (MRS. WERNER ROBERT GENIESER), physician; b. Aurora, Ill., Dec. 12, 1936; d. Wayne T. and Marie (Speth) Branom; B.A., Wellesley Coll., 1959; M.D., Med. Coll. Pa., 1962; m. Werner Robert Genieser, June 21, 1963; children—Werner Robert, Kevin Scott. Intern, Phila. Gen. Hosp., 1962-63; resident N.Y. U. Med. Center, 1964-67; attending physician Bellevue Hosp., N.Y.C., 1967—; cons. St. Albans Naval Hosp., N.Y.C., St. Vincents Hosp., N.Y.C., Greenpoint Hosp., N.Y.C.; asst. prof. radiology Med. Sch., N.Y. U., N.Y.C., 1967-73, asso. prof. radiology, 1973—. Mem. Pediatric Radiology Soc., A.M.A., N.Y. County Med. Soc. Contbr. profl. jours. Home: Apt 30D 110 Bleecker St New York City NY 10012 Office: 560 1st Av New York City NY 10016

GENIUS, JEANNETTE MORSE (MRS. HUGH FERGUSON MCKEAN), artist; b. Chgo.; d. Richard Millard and Elizabeth (Morse) Genius; student Dana Hall and Pine Manor Jr. Coll.; D.F.A., Rollins Coll., 1962; m. Hugh Ferguson McKean, June 28, 1945. Pres. Winter Park (Fla.) Land Co.; owner, mgr. Center St. Gallery; one man shows at Maitland (Fla.) Research Studio, 1951, Contemporary Arts Gallery, N.Y.C., 1953, 56, 64, Pen and Brush Club, N.Y.C., 1959, Morse Gallery of Art, Winter Park, Fla., 1968, Fla. Fedn. Art, DeBary, 1970, Art Center, Daytona Beach, Fla., 1971; exhibited in group shows at Allied Artists of Am., N.Y., Norton Gallery, Palm Beach, Currier Gallery, Manchester, N.H., Delgado Mus., New Orleans, Contemporary Arts Gallery, N.Y.C., Butler Art Inst., Youngstown, O., Pioneer Gallery, Stockton, Cal., Am. Embassy Gallery, Athens, Greece, Kunst Mus., Berne, Switzerland, Royal Scottish Acad. Galleries, Edinburgh, Royal Birmingham So. Artists, Eng., Museo des Bellas Arts, Argentine, many others; represented in permanent collections at Ga. Mus. Art, Columbus Mus. Arts and Crafts, many pvt. collections. Trustee Rollins Coll.; dir. Morse Gallery Art. Recipient 1st prize Fla. Fedn. Arts, 1948; 2d prize Soc. Four Arts, 1950; Algernon Sydney Sullivan medallion, 1954; 2d prize Pen and Brush Club, N.Y.C., 1953, 1st prize, 1959, 3d, 1962; Cervantes Medal, Hispanic Inst. Fla., 1952; Holiday Mag. Citation of Merit for a beautiful Am., 1968; Fla. Gov.'s award for arts, 1973; others. Mem. Am. Inst. Interior Designers, Nat. Assn. Women Artists (hon. v.p.), Fla. Fedn. Arts, Winter Park C. of C., Fla. Artists Group, N.H. Art Assn., Nat. Arts Club, Artists Equity. Clubs: Junior League (N.Y.C.); Women's Athletic (Chgo.); Women's (Winter Park, Fla.); Rosalind (Orlando, Fla.); Cosmopolitan, Pen and Brush (N.Y.C.); Wonalancet Outdoor (N.H.); Appalachian Mountain. Address: PO Box 40 Winter Park FL 32789

GENN, LILLIAN G. (MRS. EDWARD T. WILKES), journalist; b. N.Y.C., July 17, 1910; d. Abraham and Goldie (Marrow) Genn; student Hunter Coll., 1927-29, New Sch. for Social Research, 1930-31; m. Edward T. Wilkes, June 14, 1940; 1 son, Daniel. Writer radio scripts, off-Broadway plays, 1933; reporter Pub. Ledger Syndicate, Phila., 1937-38, feature writer Sun. mag., 1938-42, fgn. corr., 1942-43; non-fiction editor Argosy Mag., N.Y.C., 1942-49; feature writer Voice of Am. Mag., N.Y.C., 1950; writer syndicated column Newhouse Newspapers, Newark, 1951-52; weekly feature writer N.Am. Newspaper Alliance, 1953-60; N.Y. corr. Modern Maturity Mag., Jour. Am. Assn. of Ret. Persons, N.Y.C., 1968—. Mem. UN Assn. U.S.A., Overseas Press Club Am. Contbr. articles and book revs. to profl. jours.; collaborator med. books for layman. Home: 2 Sutton Place S New York City NY 10022

GENOE, SUE ZUCKER, automotive mfg. co. exec.; b. Chgo., May 30, 1916; d. David and Molly (Tauman) Zucker; coll. grad.; m. Feb. 29, 1956 (widowed). Labor cons. representing mgmt., 1940-69; pres. Gen-O-Ral Processing Corp., Chgo., 1969—. Club: Chicago Press. Home: 3260 N Lake Shore Dr Chicago IL 60657 Office: 166 N Jefferson Chicago IL 60606

GENOVAR, CHRISTINE WOLFE (MRS. WILLIAM GENOVAR), library exec.; b. Wisner, Miss., May 19, 1909; d. Philip Alexander and Ina (Pittman) Wolfe; student Fla. State U., 1927-29; m. Elliott Babcock, Nov. 27, 1935 (dec. 1945); m. 2d, William Genovar, Apr. 1, 1946 (dec. Nov. 1951). With St. Augustine (Fla.) Record, 1929-34, Tallahassee (Fla.) Democrat, 1934; asst. to state safety dir. State of Fla., Tallahassee, 1934-38; chief clk. adminstrn. and personnel Selective Service System, St. Augustine, 1940-47; chief advt. copy writer Bacon, Hartman & Vollbrecht, St. Augustine, also Jacksonville, Fla., 1951-59; pub. relations dir. H & W.B. Drew Printing Co., Jacksonville, 1959-62; asst. mgr. St. Augustine C. of C., 1962-63; pub. relations dir. WQTY Radio, Jacksonville, Fla., 1963-64; pub. relations dir. Jacksonville Pub. Library, 1964—. Mem. League of Am. Pen Women (1st v.p. Jacksonville chpt. 1974), Fla. Pub. Relations Assn. (treas. 1974, sec. 1966), Bus. Communicators of Jacksonville (sec. 1960-61). Democrat. Club: Advertising (sec. Jacksonville 1959-60, dir. 1960-61). Author: Manual of Elementary School Safety, 1936. Home: 1634 Brookwood Rd Jacksonville FL 32207 Office: 122 N Ocean St Jacksonville FL 32202

GENOVESE, ANN LAWRENCE (MRS. HANS-JOACHIM BEYERSDORFF), journalist; b. Washington, July 19, 1941; d. Joseph S. G. and Virginia (Lawrence) Genovese; student George Washington U., 1962; m. Hans-Joachim Beyersdorff, May, 1972. Advt. rep., reporter-photographer Lumberton (N.C.) Robesonian, 3 yrs; worked at state desk, News and Observer, Raleigh, N.C., 1967-69, copy desk, 1969-71; copy editor Atlanta Jour., 1971, editorial asso., 1972—. Office: 72 Marietta St NW PO Box 4689 Atlanta GA 30302*

GENSLEY, JULIANA TOWNSEND (MRS. JOHN FREDERICK GENSLEY, JR.), educator; b. Los Angeles, Feb. 2, 1910; d. James Robert and Mary Beulah (Peauchette) Townsend; B.A., U. Cal. at Los Angeles, 1930, Ed.D., 1962; M.A., Cal. State Coll. at Los Angeles, 1957; m. John Frederick Gensley, Jr., Sept. 23, 1932; children—Robin (Mrs. Donald Leslie Mitchell), James Richard. Tchr. pub. schs., Riverside, Cal., 1931-33, San Marino, Cal., 1937-40, Wiseburn, 1942-51, Redondo Beach, Cal., 1951-62; prof. elementary edn. Cal. State Coll. at Long Beach, 1962—; docent Leonis Adobe, Trippett Ranch State Park; columnist Parent Perspective, Gifted Child Quar. Mem. Child Care Center Commn., Cal. State U. at Long Beach, 1970—; sponsor Long Beach chpt. Student Cal. Tchr. Assn., 1969—; dir. Field Experience Center, Wilmington Park Sch., Los Angeles, 1971—, Tree Registration Program, Calabasas, Cal., 1964—. Named Citizen of Year, Calabasas C. of C., 1971. Mem. Internat. Inst. Nursery Sch. Educators (study coordinator summer 1971), Nat. Assn. Gifted Children (dirs.), N.E.A., Cal. Tchrs. Assn., Cal. Assn. for Gifted, So. Cal., Cal., Nat. assns. edn. young children, Nat. Audubon Soc. Club: Sierra. Home: 24466 Mulholland Hwy Calabasas CA 91302 Office: Cal State U 6101 E 7th St Long Beach CA 90840

GENTEMANN, SISTER MARY ELAINE, educator; b. Fredericksburg, Tex., Oct. 4, 1909; d. John and Mary (Meckel) Gentemann; Mus.B., Our Lady of Lake Coll., 1935, Mus.M., Am. Conservatory Music, 1942; postgrad. Columbia U., 1946-49, Juilliard Sch. Music, 1946-49. Prof. piano and organ Our Lady of Lake Coll., San Antonio, 1929—. Named Composer of Year, Tex. Music Tchrs. Assn., 1963, Composer of Distinction, Nat. Guild Piano Tchrs., 1967; recipient Headliner award Theta Sigma Phi, 1965. Plaque of Distinction, Nat. Cath. Music Educators Assn., 1966, Citation of Honor, 1968. Mem. Am. Musicological Soc., Nat. Guild Piano Tchrs., Nat. Soc. Arts and Letters (mem. adv. council San Antonio chpt. 1963—), Music Tchrs. Nat. Assn., Modern Music Masters, Tex. Study Club, Tex. Manuscript Soc., Tex. Composers Guild, San Antonio Music Tchrs. Assn., San Antonio Choral Soc. (mem. council 1966—), Tex. Music Tchr. Assn., Sigma Alpha Iota. Composer: (piano music) La Danza, 1968; Gay Senorita, 1969; (chorale) Faithful Servant, 1964; (duet) March for Young Americans, 1970; (chorus) Hosanna to the Son of David, Mass for Choir, 1970. Author spl. edn. series We Speak Through Music (5 LP recordings and tchr. manual), 1967; Hymnal, 1960; also piano books making lang. study easy through mus. approach, in German, Spanish, French, Italian. Address: 411 SW 24th St San Antonio TX 78285

GENTILE, CAROLYN DIANE, govt. ofcl.; b. N.Y.C., July 12, 1943; d. Louis and Susan Virginia (Apuzzo) Gentile; B.A., Barnard Coll., 1965; J.D., N.Y. U., 1968. Admitted to N.Y. bar, 1968, U.S. Supreme Ct., 1972, U.S. Dist. Cts. N.Y., 1970; law clk. to judge 9th Circuit C.

Appeals, San Francisco, 1968-69; mem. firm Schulman, Abarbanel & Schlesinger, N.Y.C., 1969-73; dir. div. employee discipline Human Resources Adminstrn., N.Y.C., 1973, asst. adminstr. for labor relations, 1973—. Lectr. labor law N.Y. U. Sch. Law, 1971-73, adj. asso. prof. law, 1973—. Mem. Am., N.Y. bar assns., Assn. Bar City of N.Y. Home: 2960 Grand Concourse New York City NY 10458 Office: 250 Church St New York City NY 10013

GENTILE, SISTER NANNETTE, educator; b. St. Louis, Sept. 10, 1933; d. Peter Michael and Sarah Rose (Pellegrino) Gentile; B.A., Marillac Coll., 1959; M.A. in French, St. Louis U., 1963, Ph.D. in Spanish, 1972. Faculty, Marillac Coll., St. Louis, 1963-73, dean students, 1972-73, asso. prof. modern langs., 1972—; asso. prof. modern langs. St. Mary's Coll., Perryville, Mo., part-time 1971—. Directress novices West Central Province Daus. of Charity of St. Vincent de Paul, St. Louis, 1973—. Translator, interpreter religious community meetings Paris, Rome, 1969-73. Mem. Am. Assn. Tchrs. French (treas. 1972-74), Pi Delta Phi (moderator 1969—). Address: Natural Bridge St St Louis MO 63121

GENTRY, BOBBIE, composer, singer, instrumentalist; b. Miss.; d. Robert H. and Ruby (Shipman) Streeter; ed. North Greenwood Elementary Sch., Greenwood, Miss. and Palm Valley Sch., Palm Springs, Cal.; student Los Angeles Conservatory Music, also U. Cal. at Los Angeles. Began career as sec. and night club entertainer; organized dance and vocal group, Las Vegas, Nev.; co-founder, pres. Gentry Ltd., prodn. and publ. co., Los Angeles; composer for recordings, folk singer, instrumentalist piano and stringed instruments; performed San Remo (Italy) Music Festival, 1967, also for TV including spl. series BBC, London, Eng., shows in Italy, numerous musicals and spls., U.S. Dir. Phoenix Suns profl. basketball team. Recipient awards Best Female Performer, Best New Artist, Best Comtemporary Female Vocal Performance, Nat. Assn. Recording Arts and Scis., 1967, also several nominations, 1967; recipient Achievement award Mlle. Mag., 1967, Most Promising New Vocalist of Year award, 16 Mag.; named to Miss. Hall of Fame, Miss. U.; recipient Grammy awards (3) for Ode to Billie Joe, Nat. Acad. Rec. Arts and Scis., 1968. Composed, recorded: Ode to Billie Joe, Lazy Willie, Chickasaw County Child, Hurry Tuesday Child, Sweet Peony, Ace Insurance Man, Recollection, Casket Vignette, Mornin' Glory, I Saw and Angel Die, Papa Wontcha Let Me Go to Town with You, Jessye 'Lizabeth, Sunday Best, Refractions, Sittin' Pretty, Bugs, Courtyard, Mississippi Delta, Okolona Riverbottom Bank, Reunion. Address: Gentry Ltd 8961 Sunset Blvd Los Angeles CA 90069

GENTRY, EILEEN M. BEYDA (MRS. VERNON L. GENTRY), educator; b. Frontier, Wyo.; d. George and Mary (Besitka) Beyda; B.A., U. Wyo., 1951; M.B.A., Ind. U., 1956, D.B.A., 1967; m. Vernon L. Gentry, June 1967. Tchr., Washakie County High Sch., Worland, Wyo., 1951-55; asst. prof. dept. bus. Colo. State U., 1957-60; teaching asso., dept. bus. edn. and office mgmt. Ind. U. Grad. Sch. Bus., Bloomington, 1960-65; asst. prof. U. Colo. Sch. Bus., Boulder, 1965-72, asso. prof., 1973—; vis. lectr. U. Colo., summer 1959. Mem. Mountain-Plains, Colo., Nat. bus. edn. assns., Colo. Bus. Edn. Forum, Am. Econ. Assn., Beta Gamma Sigma, Delta Pi Epsilon, Phi Gamma Nu. Home: Route 3 Sterling CO 80751 Office: Grad Sch Bus U Colo Boulder CO 80302

GENTRY, GAIL KEITH (MRS. EUGENE HARVEY GENTRY), banker; b. Helena, Ala., July 2, 1936; d. William Brett and Hettie Ruby (Wilson) Keith; student Am. Inst. Banking, 1954-56; m. Eugene Harvey Gentry, Apr. 26, 1957; 1 dau., Cynthia Lee. With Exchange Security Bank, Birmingham, Ala., 1954-72, asst. comptroller, 1965-68, asst. v.p., 1968-72; asst. v.p., cashier Nat. Bank Commerce, 1972—. Active Ann. Spastic Aid of Ala. Telethon, 1955-72; v.p. Chalkville Elementary Sch. P.T.A., 1970-71. Mem. Am. Soc. Women Accountants (past pres. Birmingham chpt., chmn. Eastern regional conf.), Nat. Assn. Bank Women (group chmn.), Ala. Bankers Assn. Methodist (treas. 1965—). Club: The Club (Birmingham). Home: Route 2 Box 557-A Pinson AL 35126 Office: 20 S 20th St Birmingham AL 35203

GENUNG, MARJORIE EVELYNN TOWER (MRS. LOUIS T. GENUNG), librarian; b. Atkinson, Neb., Mar. 12, 1925; d. Albert Ralph and Vera Marie (Rickover) Tower-Tooker; student U. Neb., 1951, Wayne State Coll., 1942-47; B.A., Colo. State Coll., 1966, U. No. Colo., 1970; postgrad. Doane Coll., 1967-68, U. Utah, 1973-74; Ph.D. (hon.), Hamilton U., 1973; m. Louis T. Genung, Feb. 2, 1944; 1 son, Louis Thompson. Elementary tchr. Atkinson pub. schs., 1958-69; librarian Clay County Dist. I-C, Fairfield, Neb., 1972—. Mem. Nat. (life), Neb., Colo. edn. assns., Assn. for Childhood Edn. Internat., Am., Neb. library assns., Nat. Council Tchrs. English, Am. Assn. U. Women, Neb. Media Assn., Neb. Ednl. Media Assn., Am. Nat. Cowbelles, Neb. Cowbelles, D.A.R. (regent 1971, dist. treas. 1968-71), League Women Voters, Women's Soc. Christian Service, Ak-Sar-Ben. Methodist. Mem. Order Eastern Star. Home: 1223 Plesant St Hastings NE 68901 also Atkinson NE 68713 Office: Box 127 Fairfield NE 68938

GEOGHEGAN, SISTER BARBARA, educator; b. N.Y.C.; d. Patrick H. and Mae B. (Schwalbert) Geoghegan; B.A., Coll. Mount St. Joseph, 1928; M.A., Loyola U., Chgo., 1938; Ph.D., Fordham U., 1950. High sch. tchr., Ohio, Mich., 1928-38; prin. St. Sebastian Sch., Chgo., 1938-41, Little Flower High Sch., Royal Oak, Mich., 1941-47; dir. studies Sisters of Charity of Cin., 1950-61; mem. faculty Coll. Mount St. Joseph (O.), 1961—, prof. psychology. Adj. asso. prof. Fordham U., summers, 1955—; cons. to Glenmary Sisters, 1955-59; editorial cons. Harcourt Brace, 1950-55. Mem. Am., Ohio psychol. assns., Cath. Psychol. Assn., Am. Assn. U. Profs., Am. Edn. Research Assn. Author: (with Sister Mary Baptista and W.A. Kelly) Developmental Psychology, 1962; (with Marie B. Pollard) Growing Child in Contemporary Society, 1969. Address: Coll of Mount St Joseph Mount Saint Joseph OH 45051

GEORAS, VENETIA BARBAS (MRS. CONSTANTINE S. GEORAS), physician; b. Athens, Greece; d. Nicholas Theodore and Gerry Constantina (Stamoules) Barbas; M.D., Athens U., 1951; m. Constantine S. Georas, Sept. 18, 1955; children—Daphne A., Helen D., Steve N. Came to U.S., 1954, naturalized, 1960. Intern, Miriam Hosp., Providence, R.I., 1956-57; resident Children's Hosp., Washington, 1954-55, Fordham Hosp., N.Y.C., 1955-56; practice medicine, specializing in pediatrics, Providence, 1956—; research pediatrician Brown U., 1958-62, staff pediatrician Health Services, 1966-70; pediatrician Child Devel. Center, R.I. Hosp., 1968—, coordinator Cystic Fibrosis Clinic, 1970—. Fellow R.I. Heart Assn.; mem. Athens Med. Assn. Home: 450 Lloyd Av Providence RI 02906 Office: Child Devel Center RI Hosp Providence RI 02906

GEORGE, CAROLYN ANN, educator; b. Anna, Ill., July 18, 1941; d. Carroll Griffin and Roberta May (Ervin) Wallace; A.A., Lincoln Coll., 1962; student Ill. Wesleyan U., 1962-63; B.A., So. Ill. U., 1964; m. Michael George, Aug. 8, 1965 (div.); 1 dau., Stephanie Kay. With Lincoln (Ill.) State Sch., 1967—, staff trainer, 1973—. Mem. Central Ill. Health Planning Council, Lincoln, 1972-74. Mem. Am. Assn. Mental Deficiency, Lincoln Coll. Alumni Assn. Presbyn. Mem. Order Eastern Star. Club: Toastmaster (program chmn. Lincoln). Home: 15 Ophir St Lincoln IL 62656 Office: 861 S State St Lincoln IL 62656

GEORGE, LILA-GENE PLOWE KENNEDY (MRS. RICHARD PAINTER GEORGE), composer; b. Sioux City, Ia., Sept. 25, 1918; d. Eugene Preston and Lila Mae (Pickle) Plowe; B.A., U. Okla., 1939, Mus.B., 1940; postgrad. Northwestern U., 1950, Columbia, 1963-65; pvt. study piano with Egon Petri, Silvio Scionti, Herbert Ricker, Edward Steuermann, 1942-63; pvt. study composition with Nadia Boulanger, Fountainebleau, summers 1971-73; m. Richard Painter George, Sept. 11, 1941; children—Eugenia (Mrs. Edward N. Haley), Richard Painter. Solo pianist Okla. Little Symphony, 1935-37, Houston Symphony, 1956; pvt. piano tchr. Latin Am., 1948-52, N.Y., 1961-65, Houston, 1955-60, 71—. Adjudicator contests, Okla., 1940, Tex., 1972—. Recipient Composers award Sigma Alpha Iota, Okla., 1969. Mem. Am. Music Center, Am. Musicological Soc., Tuesday Mus. Club (pres. 1960), Pan Am. Round Table, D.A.R., Sigma Alpha Iota, Chi Delta Phi. Episcopalian. Composer: Horn Trio, 1963; Violin and Piano Sonata, 1964; Madrigals, 1966; Children's Pieces, 1964, 73; Organ Preludes and Postludes, 1965, 73. Home: 2301 Reba Dr Houston TX 77019

GEORGE, LYNDA DAY (MRS. CHRISTOPHER GEORGE), actress; b. San Marcos, Tex., 1946; m. 2d, Christopher George, May 15, 1970; 1 son by previous marriage, Nicky. Formerly model, motion picture actress; actress TV shows Silent Force, Mission Impossible. Mem. Ch. of Jesus Christ of Latter-day Saints. Home: 128 North June St Los Angeles CA 90004 Office: care Bruce Geller Paramount Television 5451 Marathon St Los Angeles CA 90038*

GEORGE, MABEL, ins. underwriter; b. Westfield, Pa., Dec. 22, 1892; d. Lizell and Angie (Dartt) George; B.L., Syracuse U., 1916; M.S., Simmons Coll., 1926. Tchr. English in N.J. high schs., 1916-24; life underwriter Sun Life Assurance Co. Can., Phila., 1928—. Recipient nat. quality award Nat. Life Ins. Assn. C.L.U. Mem. Macaulay Club (hon. life,) Women Leaders Round Table (life), D.A.R., Am. Assn. U. Women (past treas., Emergency Aid of Pa., Mu Phi Epsilon, Phi Mu. Appeared on panel WRCV-TV Invest in America series, 1958. Home: 2120 Chancellor St Philadelphia PA 19103 Office: 1339 Chestnut St Philadelphia PA 19107

GEORGE, MARTHA ALLEN HARDY, automotive corp. exec.; b. Kinston, N.C., Jan. 26, 1938; d. Jesse Edwin and Katherine Marjorie (Allen) Hardy; student N.C. State Coll., 1957; m. Charles George, Apr. 18, 1964 (div.); children—Charles George, Christopher Corey. Editorial asst. pub. relations Nat. Ednl. TV, N.Y.C., 1959-61; asst. to pres. Lionel-Wadsworth, N.Y.C., 1961; personnel Arthur Young & Co., N.Y.C., 1962-63, mgrs. center dept. head, 1964-65; dir., corporate sec. Lee Myles Corp., Maspeth, N.Y., 1966—; account exec. Lee Myles Fleet Repair Service, 1971—. Rec. sec., publicity chmn., vice chmn. A.R.C., Great Neck, N.Y., 1969-72. Home: 88 Croyden Av Great Neck NY 11023 Office: 59-24 Maurice Av Maspeth NY 11378

GEORGE, MARY SHANNON (MRS. FLAVE JOSEPH GEORGE), city and county ofcl.; b. Seattle, May 27, 1916; d. William Day and Agnes (Lovejoy) Shannon; B.A. cum laude, U. Wash., 1937; postgrad. U. Mich., 1937, Columbia, 1938; m. Flave Joseph George; children—Flave Joseph, Karen (Mrs. Perry Van Hook), Christy (Mrs. Peter Cebaus), Shannon (Mrs. Fred Lowrey). Prodn. asst., asst. news editor Pathe News, N.Y.C., 1938-42; mem. fgn. editions staff Readers Digest, Pleasantville, N.Y., 1942-46; columnist Caracas (Venezuela) Daily Jour., 1953-60; councilman City and County of Honolulu, 1969—. Mem. Nat. Air Quality Adv. Bd., 1974. Vice chmn. 1st Hawaii Ethics Commn., 1968; mem. budget com. Aloha United Fund, 1970. Co-founder Citizens Com. on Constl. Conv., 1968. Bd. dirs. Adminstrn. Justice Found., 1967—, Lani-Kailua Outdoor Circle, 1965-66, Hawaii Planned Parenthood, 1970-73, Friends of Foster Garden, Hawaii Med. Services Assn., 1973—. Recipient Jewish Men's Club Brotherhood award, 1974; named Woman of Year, Honolulu Press Club, 1969, Hawaii Fedn. Bus. and Profl. Women, 1970. Mem. League Women Voters (pres. Honolulu 1966-68), Am. Assn. U. Women, John Howard Soc., Mensa, Phi Beta Kappa, Kappa Alpha Theta. Republican. Episcopalian. Author: A Is for Abrazo, 1961. Home: 782-G N Kalaheo Ave Kailua HI 96734 Office: City Hall Honolulu HI 96813

GEORGE, VIRGINIA RUTH STRATFORD (MRS. EDWARD GEORGE), librarian; b. Chgo., Sept. 12, 1927; d. Gifford Winstanley and Bertha Catherine (Nance) Stratford; student Northwestern U., 1945-47; B.S. in Mech. Engring., U. Ky., 1950; M.L.S., U. Wash., 1964; m. Edward George, June 7, 1949; children—Harry G., Catherine D. Research librarian Boeing Sci. Research Labs., Seattle, 1964-70, chief cataloger, 1970-71; supr. Kent tech. library Boeing Co., Seattle, 1971—. Mem. Spl. Libraries Assn., Am. Soc. Information Sci., League Women Voters, Wash. Libraries Assn., Beta Phi Mu. Home: 22608 90th St W Edmonds WA 98020 Office: Boeing Co Kent Library Box 3707 Seattle WA 98124

GEORGI, CHARLOTTE, librarian; b. Pitts.; d. Woldemar Carl and Olga (Mehnert) Georgi; B.A. magna cum laude, U. Buffalo, 1942, M.A., 1943; M.S. in L.S., U. N.C., 1956. Instr., English dept. U. Buffalo, 1942-43; asst. prof. humanities Stephens Coll., Columbia, Mo., 1943-54; head Bus. Adminstrn. Library, U. N.C., 1955-57, chief bus. adminstrn. and social scis. div., 1957-59; chief librarian Grad. Sch. of Mgmt., U. Cal. at Los Angeles, 1959—. Mem. Am., Cal. library assns., Spl. Libraries Assn. (dir. 1966-69, chmn. bus. and finance div. 1963-64, editor Newsletter 1962-63), Am. Assn. U. Profs. (councillor 1966-68, sec. 1968—), Phi Beta Kappa, Pi Lambda Theta, Phi Chi Theta, Beta Phi Mu. Author: The Novel and the Pulitzer Prize, 1918-58, 1958; The Businessman in the Novel, 1959; The Literature of Executive Management; Selected Books and Reference Sources for the International Businessman, 1963; Statistics Sources, 1962, 3d edit., 1971; Encyclopedia of Business Information Sources, 1971; The Arts and the Art of Administration, 1970; Management and the Arts, 1972; The Arts and the World of Business, 1973. Contbr. articles and book revs. to profl. publs. Co-compiler: Sources of Commodity Prices, 1960. Home: 545 Kelton Av Los Angeles CA 90024 Office: Univ California Graduate School of Management Library Los Angeles CA 90024

GERALD, MARTHA WILSON, lawyer; b. Greenville, Miss., Oct. 4, 1919; d. Thomas Eugene and May (Haney) Gerald; student Belhaven Coll., 1937-38; A.B., Millsaps Coll., 1941; LL.B., U. Miss., 1944, J.D., 1968. Admitted to Miss. bar, 1944; practiced in Jackson, 1944—; mem. firm Wells, Thomas & Wells, Jackson, 1944-68, mem. firm Wells, Gerald, Brand, Watters & Cox, 1968—. Mem. Am., Hinds County (pres. 1974-75), Miss. (mem. oil and gas. com. 1974) bar assns., Am. Judicature Soc., Nat. Assn. Women Lawyers, Miss. Oil and Gas Lawyers Assn. (pres. 1965-66), Am. Assn. U. Women, Kappa Delta. Methodist. Home: 1151 Greymont St Jackson MS 39202 Office: PO Box 22 489 Jackson MS 39205

GERALDINE, HILAIRE ANN, lawyer; b. Los Angeles, Nov. 20, 1929; d. Desmond Gavin and Vera Vivian (Smith) Geraldine; B.A., Scripps Coll., 1949; postgrad. U. Cal. at Los Angeles, 1957-59; LL.B., LaSalle Extension U., 1962; 1 son, Blaise Gerald Stoltenberg. Admitted to Cal. bar, 1962; practice law, Long Beach, Cal., 1962-68, Bakersfield, Cal., 1968—. Tchr. pub. speaking for enrichment program St. Francis Sch., Bakersfield, 1972-73. Den mother Cub Scouts Am., Bakersfield, 1970-72. Pres., Bakersfield Rep. Women, 1974. Bd. dirs. YWCA, 1970-72. Mem. Kern County Bar Assn. (dir. 1970-73), Greater Bakersfield C. of C. (pres. women's div. 1971, dir. 1970-72), Hillcrest Bus. and Profl. Womens Club (mem. exec. bd. 1970—), Cal. Women in Chambers of Commerce (parliamentarian 1973—), Womans Club Bakersfield (parliamentarian 1970-71, dir. 1970-72). Home: 409 Hewlett Bakersfield CA 93309 Office: Padre Bldg PO Box 2123 Bakersfield CA 93303

GERAN, RUTH IRIS, biologist; b. Monroe, O.; d. Harry Clayton and Ethel (Kinney) Geran; B.A., Am. U., 1944; M.S., George Washington U., 1954, M. Philosophy in Biology, 1969, Ph.D. in Zoology, 1971. Biologist, Nat. Cancer Inst., Bethesda, Md., 1958—. Mem. Mortar Bd., Am. Soc. Animal Sci., Am. Soc. Zoologists, Beta Beta Beta, Sigma Delta Epsilon. Home: 420 N Oakland St Arlington VA 22203 Office: Nat Cancer Inst Bethesda MD 20014

GERARD, BEVERLY RUTH (MRS. WARREN GAYLE GERARD), educator; b. Drumright, Okla., Oct. 23, 1929; d. Blair Heflin and Alma Rozella (Bates) Crawford; B.Music Edn., Okla. State U., 1954; M.L.S., U. Okla., 1972; m. Warren Gayle Gerard, Dec. 25, 1947; children—Geri Gayle, Sheri Lynn. Tchr. pub. schs., Cleveland, Okla., 1950-51, Medford, Okla., 1951-53, Watonga, Okla., 1953-56, Anadarko, Okla., 1957-61; tchr. mus. ed. Okla. Coll. Liberal Arts, Chickasha, Okla., 1963; librarian, music tchr., edn. specialist Riverside Ind. Sch., Anadarko, Okla., 1963—. Dir. L.S. Inst. U. Okla., Norman, 1969, 70; cons. Inst. Tchrs. Indian Students, 1971-72; panel moderator N.Am. Indian Women's Assn. Conv., 1971. Mem. Nat. Fedn. Fed. Employees (pres. 1968-70), Washita Valley Fine Arts Assn. (treas. 1962-68), Delta Kappa Gamma, Kappa Kappa Iota. Home: Box 160 609 Mission Dr Anadarko OK 73005 Office: Riverside Indian Sch Anadarko Area-Bur Indian Affairs Anadarko OK 73005

GERARD, JOYCE ANN HOWARD (MRS. ROGER GERARD), educator; b. Belleville, Ill., May 1, 1932; d. Lawrence Merle and Blanche Ann (Trout) Howard; B.S., Western Mich. U., 1954, M.A., 1964; postgrad. Boston Coll., 1971—; children—Susan, Scott, Lisa; m. 2d, Roger Lawrence Gerard, Nov. 28, 1970. Staff occupational therapist Kalamazoo State Hosp., 1954-55; staff occupational therapist Battle Creek (Mich.) VA Hosp., 1957-58; tchr., counselor Battle Creek Pub. Schs., 1966-69; instr. Western Mich. U., Kalamazoo, 1969-70; program dir. Boston Coll., 1970-73; asst. prof. spl. edn. San Francisco State U., 1973-74; program dir. learning disabilities U. Santa Clara, Cal., 1974—. Cons. spl. learning disability projects Lexington (Mass.), Salem (Mass.) pub. schs., 1972-73. Mem. Am. Occupational Therapy Assn., Council for Exceptional Children (chpt. pres. 1968-69), Nat. Assn. for Children with Learning Disabilities. Home: 101 Belhaven Dr Los Gatos CA 95030 Office: Dept Edn U Santa Clara Santa Clara CA 95053

GERARD, PAULA (MRS. H.J. RENISON), artist; d.; Paul and Helen (Smith) Gerard; pvt. study art Florence, Venice, Paris, Brussels; student U. Florence, Institut Francais, Florence; student Art Inst. Chgo., 1936-39; m. Herbert J. Renison. One man shows at Bowdoin Coll., Layton Art Gallery, Art Inst. Chgo. Dept. Prints and Drawings, Montgomery Mus. Fine Arts, 1971; exhibited in group shows at Art Inst. Chgo., Print Club Phila., Phila. Art Alliance, Buffalo Print Club, Washington Water Color Club, Corcoran Gallery, Color Print Soc. Phila., N.A.D., Denver Art Mus., San Francisco Art Assn., N.W. Print Makers, Audubon Soc., Sarasota Art Assn., 1960, Washington Water Color Assn., 1963, Chgo. Arts Festival, 1963, Miss Art Assn., 1970, Okla. Art Center, Oklahoma City, 1972; represented in permanent collections in Library of Congress, U. Chgo. Epstein Archives, George F. Harding Mus., Chgo., Earlham Coll., Evansville (Ind.) Mus., Ringling Mus., Sarasota, Fla., Standard Oil, Chgo.; head art dept. N. Central Coll., Naperville, Ill., 1944-45; instr. Layton Sch. Art, Milw., 1945-62; instr. Art Inst. Chgo., 1962-64, asst. prof., 1964-66, asso. prof., 1966-72, prof., 1972—; vis. instr. U. Chgo., 1956, summers 1958-65. Mem. Artists Equity Assn., Renaissance Soc., Art Inst. Alumni Assn., Chgo. Soc. Artists, Am. Assn. U. Profs., Arts Club Chgo. Illustrator: The Great Speckled Bird, 1964. Home: 2043 N Mohwak St Chicago IL 60614

GERBER, ELLA (MRS. SAM KASAKOFF), theatre dir., actress; b. N.Y.C., Aug. 25, 1916; d. Isadore and Esther (Treisman) Gerber; student Columbia, 1943, Shakespeare Inst., U. Birmingham, Stratford-on-Avon, Eng., 1955, N.Y. U., 1963; m. Sam Kasakoff, May 29, 1943. Acting debut with Knickerbocker Players and Playmart Prodns., N.Y.C., 1933-34; appeared in Broadway prodn. Pins and Needles, also touring co., 1938-41; various lead roles on Broadway, Hollywood, Cal., Chgo., 1938-45, Korea, 1946, with U.S. Army Spl. Services, Hawaii, 1946, Japan, 1946-47; appeared in Off-Broadway prodn. The Laundry, 1963, motion picture Barabbas, 1961; dir. numerous prodns. theatres throughout U.S., 1943—, including Miracle Worker, 1964, The Unsinkable Molly Brown, 1964, Milk and Honey, 1964, Guys and Dolls, 1964, Camelot, 1966, Gypsy, 1967, The Miser, Nashville, 1969, Porgy and Bess, Charleston, S.C., 1970, Lisbon, Portugal, 1973, Memphis Opera Theatre, 1972, Casa Manana Theatre, Ft. Worth, 1972, Sch. for Wives, Summertree, 1971, Los Angeles Civic Light Opera Co., 1974, Theatre of Stars, Atlanta, 1974; dir. Hallelujah Train, coll. and univ. tour, 1969; dir. plays Equity Theatre, N.Y.C., 1949—; artistic dir. S.C. Open Road Ensemble, 1973; dir. Madwoman of Chaillot, Duke U., Durham, N.C., 1972; dir., tchr. Arts Six project for arts, Boston, 1969-72; dir. theatrical tours Porgy and Bess, including U.S., 1958, 66-67, Can., 1966-67, Israel, 1966, New Zealand, Australia, 1965; dir. Carousel, Johannesburg, S. Africa, 1968; dir. community theatres, Los Angeles, Miami Beach, Fla., New Orleans; mem. faculty Am. Acad. Dramatic Arts, N.Y.C., 1957-59, 66-67, Am. Mus. and Dramatic Acad., 1967-68. Mem. vis. faculty London Opera Centre (Eng.), 1968. Macdowell Colony fellow, 1966, 67. Mem. Actors Equity Assn., Soc. Stage Dirs. and Choreographers, A.F.T.R.A. Address: 329 E 58th St New York City NY 10022

GERBER, MARCIA LYNN GETZ (MRS. DONALD A. GERBER), physician; b. Bronx, N Y., Feb. 17, 1942; d. George S. and Ruth (Mehlman) Getz; A.B. (Mary Pemberton Nourse fellow), Vassar Coll., 1963; M.D., (N.Y. Arthritis Found. fellow), Columbia U., 1967; m. Donald A. Gerber, June 13, 1964;children—Susan Eve, Andrew James. Intern in internal medicine State U. N.Y., Downstate Med. Center, Bklyn., 1967-68, emergency room physician, 1968, instr. Physician-Student Health Service, 1969—. Trustee, Downstate Nursery Sch., 1971-73, pres., 1972-73. Home: 310 Lenox Rd Brooklyn NY 11226 Office: 450 Clarkson Av Brooklyn NY 11203

GERBRICK, ELIZABETH ANN NUTTALL (MRS. THOMAS MARR GERBRICK), educator; b. West Hickory, Pa., Oct. 29, 1933; d. Theodore and Genevieve (Copeland) Nuttall; B.A., Clarion State Coll., 1955; M.A. (P.T.A. fellowship), U. Denver, 1960; postgrad. U. Md., 1968—; m. Thomas Marr Gerbrick, Apr. 30, 1964. Tchr. Denver Sch. System, 1955-66; spl. edn. tchr. Prince Georges County, Md., 1967—. Spl. edn. cons. Recipient Outstanding Tchr. award Prince George's County Bd. Edn., 1972. Mem. N.E.A., Md., Prince Georges County edn. assns., Am. Assn. Mental Deficiency, Council for Exceptional Children. Mem. Order Eastern Star. Club: Henson Creek Golf (Oxon Hill, Md.). Home: 4324 Hartford Hills Dr Marlow

Heights MD 20023 Office: Barnaby Manor Sch 2627 Owens Rd Oxon Hill MD 20021

GERCKENS, DOSHA PAGE (DOSHA PAGE GERCKENS), prin. pub. schs.; b. Pasadena, Cal.; d. Benjamin F. and Minnie (Ray) Page; A.A., Pasadena City Coll., 1949; B.A., Whittier Coll., 1951; M.A., Claremont Grad. Sch., 1957; m. Richard H. Gerckens, Sept. 30, 1933 (dec. 1956); 1 son, Robert H. With Pasadena Pub. Schs., 1951—, prin. McKinley and Arroyo Schs., 1962-66, Webster Elementary Sch., 1966—. Mem. Women's Civic League, 1966—, chmn. edn. com., 1967—; life mem. P.T.A. Cal., 1964. Mem. Assn. for Childhood Edn. Internat. (pres. So. sect. 1961-63), Cal. Elementary Schs. Adminstrs. Assn., Pasadena Elementary Schs. Adminstrs. Assn., Altrusa Internat. (corr. sec. 1966-68), Pi Lambda Theta, Delta Phi Upsilon (nat. pres. 1954-56), Delta Kappa Gamma. Mem. Order Eastern Star, White Shrine, Daus. Nile. Home: 3640 Fairmeade Rd Pasadena CA 91107

GERDES, SISTER FLORENCE MARIE, educator; b. Blue Island, Ill., Dec. 19, 1919; d. Francis Xavier and Mary Florence (Bennett) Gerdes; Ph.B., DePaul U., Chgo., 1945; M.A., Loyola U. at Chgo., 1954; Ph.D., St. Louis U., 1958. Mem. Congregation Sisters of St. Joseph, 1937—; tchr. classics Nazareth Acad., LaGrange Park, Ill., 1945-65, Rosary Coll., River Forest, Ill., 1965-68, St. Ignatius Coll. Prep., Chgo., 1971—; vis. prof. Loyola U. at Rome (Italy), 1968-69; adminstr. Bethlehem Acad., LaGrange Park, 1969-71. Fulbright grantee, Italy, summer 1961. Recipient Gold Star, Elementary Sch. Library Collection, Bro-Dart Found., Newark, 1970. Semple scholar, Greece, summer 1973. Mem. Chgo. Classical Club, Ill. Classical Conf. Author: The Aeneid: A Retelling for Young Readers, 1969. Home: 1515 W Ogden Av La Grange Park IL 60525 Office: 1079 W Roosevelt Rd Chicago IL 60608

GEREAU, MARY M. CONDON, labor union exec.; b. Winterset, Ia., Oct. 10, 1916; d. David Joseph and Sarah Rose (Stack) Condon; student Mt. Mercy Jr. Coll., 1935-37; B.A. in English, State U. Ia., 1939, M.A. in U.S. History, 1941, postgrad., 1948—; m. Gerald R. Gereau, Jan. 14, 1961. Tchr. English, history high sch., Colo., Ia., 1941-42, Creston, Ia., 1942, 43; program dir. A.R.C., India, 1943-45, field cons. Mont., N.D., S.D., 1945-46; dean students Eastern Mont. Coll. Edn., 1946-48; supt. pub. instrn. Mont., Helena, 1949-57; specialist U.S. Senate Com. Interior Affairs, Washington, 1957, 72—; adviser Pa. Council Edn., Harrisburg, 1957; asst. dir. rural services N.E.A., 1957-61, legislative cons., 1961-73, pres. staff orgn., 1961; dir. legislation Nat. Treasury Employees Union, 1974—. Sec. Mont. Bd. Edn., 1949-57; vice-chmn. Mont. Land Bd., 1949-57; chmn. Mont. Tchrs. Retirement System, 1949-57, council chief state sch. officers, dir., 1953-55, pres., 1956; chmn. nat. com. sch. savs. U.S. Treasury Dept., 1950-56; chmn. Mont. Conf. Children and Youth, 1950; del. White House Conf. Edn., 1955; mem. profl. staff White House Conf. Edn., 1965; nat. chmn. Equal Rights Amendment Ratification Council, 1972—. Del. Democratic Nat. Conv., 1956; mem. platform com. Mont. Dem. Party; exec. dir. Educators for Johnson-Humphrey, 1964, Educators for Humphrey-Muskie 1968; chmn. Women's Joint Congl. Com., 1969-71. Recipient spl. citation V.F.W., 1954; named Conservationist of Year, Mont., 1950; recipient Distinguished Service award Council of Chief State Sch. Officers, 1956; made hon. princess Blackfeet Indian Tribe. Mem. N.E.A. (life), Mont. Edn. Assn. (life), Am. Assn. Sch. Adminstrs., Ednl. Press Assn., Common Cause, Nat. Consumers League, Women's Nat. Democratic Club. Roman Catholic. Home: 1234 Massachusetts Av NW Washington DC 20005 Office: 1730 K St NW Washington DC 20036

GERELICK, MURIEL GOLDBERG (MRS. ROBERT GERELICK), editor; b. N.Y.C., Nov. 13, 1925; d. Sidney and Yetta (Graulich) Goldberg; student Creighton U., 1942-44, U. Neb., 1951-53; m. Robert Gerelick, July 8, 1945; children—Howard, Jerry, Marcia. Account exec. Mort Duff Advt. Agy., Omaha, 1944-49; editor Jewish Press, Omaha, 1964—. Tchr., youth adviser Temple Israel, 1954-64. Mem. Mayors Coms. on Housing and Edn., 1960-64; active various community drives; mem. editorial adv. bd. Am. Friends Hebrew U., 1972—. Recipient Presdl. award Am. Jewish Press Assn., 1967. Mem. Am. Jewish Press Assn. (dir. 1969—), Nat. Council Jewish Women (dir. 1967-69), Anti-Defamation League (dir. 1965—), League Women Voters (treas., dir 1960-64). Jewish religion. Contbr. numerous articles to Jewish publs. Home: 833 N 77th St Omaha NE 68114 Office: 101 N 20th St Omaha NE 68102

GERETY, SALLY MAY, lawyer; b. Elgin, Ill., Oct. 29, 1930; d. Harry Todd and Ethel May (Dolby) Campbell; B.A., U. Denver, 1952; J.D. cum laude, U. Wash., 1955; m. John H. Gerety, Jr., Feb. 1957 (div. Dec. 1958); 1 son, Mason Scott. Admitted to Wash. bar, 1955, N.M. bar, 1971; atty. U.S. AEC, Richland, Wash., 1955-63, asst. chief counsel, 1963, counsel, Los Alamos, N.M., 1963—. Recipient Performance awards AEC, 1960, 68. Mem. State Bar N.M., Wash., Fed. bar assns., Gamma Phi Beta. Democrat. Episcopalian (vestryman 1971—). Clubs: N.M. Kennel (Santa Fe); Los Alamos Dog Obedience; Welsh Terrier of the Jemez. Home: 1063 Pinon Loop Los Alamos NM 87544 Office: US Atomic Energy Commission Los Alamos NM 87544

GERHARDT, LILLIAN NOREEN, mag. editor; b. New Haven, Sept. 28, 1932; d. Victor Herbert and Lillian (Beecher) Gerhardt; B.S., So. Conn. State Coll., 1954; postgrad. U. Chgo., 1961-62. Asst. in reference New Haven Pub. Library, 1954-55; first asst. reference dept. Meriden (Conn.) Pub. Library, 1955-58, head reference dept., 1958-61; asso. editor Kirkus Service, Inc., 1962-66; exec. editor Sch. Library Jour. Book Review, R. R. Bowker Co. Juvenile Projects, N.Y.C., 1966-71; editor-in-chief Sch. Library Jour., 1971—. Lectr. Columbia U. Sch. Library Service, 1969-72. Judge Juvenile Nat. Book award. Mem. A.L.A. (Mildred Batchelder award com. 1970; Newbery Caldecott award com. 1970), Woman's Nat. Book Assn. Sr. editor Best Books for Children, 1967-70; sr. editor, project coordinator SLJ Book Review Cumulative, 1969, Children's Books in Print, 1969; Subject Guide to Children's Books In Print, 1970. Home: 54 W 16th St New York City NY 10011 Office: 1180 Av of Americas New York City NY 10036

GERKE, ROBERTA, free lance writer; b. State Center, Ia., Mar. 2, 1903; d. William H. and Mary (Oehlsen) Gerke; A.B., Mills Coll., 1940. Sec. Cal. Gov. James Rolph, Jr., 1931-33; sec. Louis B. Mayer, Metro-Goldwyn-Mayer Studios. Hollywood, 1933-34; wrote and presented radio program Todays Career Women, 1940-46; pub. relations dir. The Robert Dollar Co., 1946-59; travel dir. Nob Hill Travel Service, 1960—, Jet Travel, Inc., Manila, Philippines, 1963—; Open Doors columnist, State Center (Ia.) Enterprise, 1962-68, Radio Post, Fredericksburg, Tex., 1962-63, Oakland (Cal.) Tribune, 1964-65, Cal. Sr. Citizen News, 1969—. Am. corr. London, covered wedding of Princess Elizabeth, 1947, and coronation, 1953. Recipient Woman of Distinction award City-County Record, San Francisco, 1954; Janice Wilkin Gavel award, Armed Forces Service League, 1963; awards Cal. Press Women, 1970, 72; award Pacific Northwest Writers Conf., 1971. Mem. Cal. Hist. Soc., English-Speaking Union, San Francisco Women's C. of C., Armed Forces Writers League, Washington, Women in Communication. Clubs: Mills (San Francisco); Washington Press. Am. Newspaper Women's (Washington); Cal. Writers; Cal. Press Women; Nat. Fedn. Press Women, Author: Highlights-Dollar Line Case, 1951; Open Doors in Europe, 1953; European Adventure, 1958; also mag. articles. Home: 1233 California St San Francisco CA 94109

GERON, CARY ANN, librarian; b. Dallas, Jan. 30, 1938; d. Cary Wells and Iris Taulene (Blevins) Geron; B.S. in L.S., Tex. Woman's U., 1961. County librarian, Brownfield, Tex., 1961-65; asst. librarian Bapt. Internat. Theol. Sem., Ruschlikon, Switzerland, 1965-67; asst. librarian Golden Gate Theol. Sem., Mill Valley, Cal., 1967-71; librarian Missionary Orientation Library, Foreign Mission Bd. So Bapt. Conv., Pine Mountain, Ga., 1971—. Mem. A.L.A. Address: Missionary Orientation Library Box 535 Pine Mountain GA 31822

GERRARD, LOUISE BURR (MRS. NATHAN LEWIS GERRARD), state ofcl.; b. Chgo., July 13, 1917; d. Maurice and Bebe (Lazar) Burr; A.B., U. Chgo., 1939, A.M., 1940; Ph.D., Columbia, 1969; m. Nathan Lewis Gerrard, May 17, 1936; children—Michael, Steven. With War Dept., 1940-41, O.P.A., 1941-45; lectr. polit. sci., Barnard Coll., also Columbia, 1947-52; dir. research W.Va. Dept. Mental Health, 1964-69; exec. dir. W.Va. Commn. on Aging, Charleston, 1969—. Adj. asso. prof. polit. sci. Coll. Grad. Studies, W.Va. U., 1970—. Active League Women Voters. Mem. Am. Assn. U. Women, Am. Polit. Sci. Assn., Nat. Assn. State Units on Aging (v.p.), Am. Acad. Polit. Sci. Author: The Rural Folk of Appalachia, 1967; (with Nathan Lewis Gerrard) The Holy Ghost People, 1968; also articles in popular and profl. jours. Office: State Capitol Charleston WV 25305 Home: 2100 Kanawha Av SE Charleston WV 25304

GERRITSEN, ELEANOR, social worker; b. Djokjakarta, Java, Indonesia, Oct. 30, 1927; d. Wilhelmus B. and Leonie (de Wilde) Gerritsen; student U. Amsterdam, 1947-49; certificate in katechetics Coll. Ladies of Bethany, Nijmegen, Netherlands, 1959; postgrad. Boston Coll., 1961-62; M.S.W., U. Pitts., 1963. Came to U.S., 1961, naturalized, 1969. Asst. to chief accountant IBM, Amsterdam, Netherlands, 1949-54; youth worker, youth centers, Leiden, The Hague, Netherlands, Ladies of Bethany, 1959-60, ecumenical center, Bilthoven, Netherlands, 1960-61; social worker Vineyard Neighborhood Center, Roman Cath. Diocese Pitts., 1963-70; social worker Craig House-Technoma Workshop, Pitts., 1970-71, supr., 1971-72, dir. Neighborhood Outpatient Center, 1972—. Field instr. Pitts. U. Sch. Social Work, 1971—. North Side Com. on Human Resources, 1965-70, mem. welfare subcom., 1965-66, mem. health and mental health subcom., 1965-70; mem. bd. Residents Council, North View Heights, Pitts., 1962-70; bd. dirs. Craig House-Technoma Workshop, 1969-70; mem. Health and Mental Retardation Citizen's Com., 1969-70, chmn. personnel com., 1969-70; chmn. liaison com. between Citizen's Com. and Adminstrv. Agy., 1969-70. Mem. Nat. Assn. Social Workers. Democrat. Roman Catholic. Home: 443 McKnight Circle Pittsburgh PA 15237

GERSACK, DOROTHY HILL (MRS. JOSEPH ROBERT GERSACK), archivist; b. Livingston, Ill., Oct. 24, 1910; d. Edgar A. and Maude (Linebaugh) Hill; student Western Coll. for Women, Oxford, O., 1929-30, Wittenberg U., 1928-29, 30-31; B.S. in Edn., U. Ill., 1932, B.S. in L.S. cum laude, 1933, M.S., 1937; postgrad. George Washington U. Law Sch., 1939-41; m. Joseph Robert Gersack, Jr., Jan. 27, 1944; 1 dau., Judith Ann (Mrs. Paul M. Vettori). Library asst. Danville (Ill.) Pub. Library, 1926-28, 33-34, Warder Pub. Library, Springfield, O., 1930-31; cataloger U. Ill. Library, Urbana, 1934-36; archivist U.S. Nat. Archives, Washington, 1936—, specialist on legal records, 1950—. Sec., Old Georgetown Rd. Citizens Assn., Bethesda, Md., 1955-58, pres., 1965-68; archivist-historian, mem. procedures com. Bethesda Fire Bd., 1965—, sec., 1969—; vice chmn. Davis Library Adv. Com., Montgomery County, Md., 1966-67, chmn., 1967-68; mem. citizens com. Oakmont, fiscal rev. subcom., 1957-58, ordinance rev. subcom., 1967. Fellow Soc. Am. Archivists (news editor Am. Archivist 1960-68); mem. A.L.A. (del.-at-large history sect. reference and adult services div.), Polit. Study Club Washington, Am. Assn. U. Women, U. Ill. Library Sch. Alumni Assn. (nat. pres. 1941-46), Greater Washington Area Illini Club (sec.-treas. 1942-66, adv. bd. 1966-68), Delta Zeta, Beta Phi Mu. Home: 5600 Oakmont Av Bethesda MD 20034 Office: US Nat Archives Washington DC 20408

GERSBACHER, JANE, lawyer; b. Murphysboro, Ill., June 26, 1941; d. Willard Marion and Eva Nina (Oxford) Gersbacher; student So. Ill. U., 1958-60; B.A., Newcomb Coll., Tulane U., 1961; J.D., U. Ill., 1964. Admitted to Ill. bar, 1964, Cal. bar, 1969; atty. Ill. Legislative Reference Bur., Springfield, Ill., 1964-65; gen. atty. U.S. Dept. Justice, Immigration & Naturalization Service, Chgo., 1965-66, Los Angeles, 1966-73, San Diego, 1973—. Mem. Ill., Cal. bar assns. Home: 1801 Diamond St Apt 3-119 San Diego CA 92109 Office: 2223 El Cajon Blvd San Diego CA 92104

GERSH, ROSEMARIE CECILIA (MRS. EDWARD I. GERSH), camp exec.; b. Ellenville, N.Y., Aug. 6, 1933; d. George Peter and Cecilia Marie (Lechner) Halbig; A.A., Orange County Community Coll., 1954; B.A., Miami U., 1956; postgrad., Hunter Coll., 1961-64; M.A., N.Y. U., 1967; m. Edward I. Gersh, Apr. 14, 1963; children—Roxanne Cecilia, Kevin George. Profl. concert pianist, 1952-56; co-ordinator N.Y. U. Alumni Assn., 1956-58; asst. to exec. v.p. Asso. Products, N.Y.C., 1958-60; tchr. N.Y.C. Jr. High Sch. 117, 1960-64; asst. dir. West Hills Day Camp, Huntington, N.Y., 1964-70, dir., 1970—. Swimming instr. YWCA, N.Y.C., 1957-60. Rep. dist. committeewoman, 1973—. Trustee, founder Wilmington (Del.) Coll., 1967-69; trustee Woodland Acad., Woodbury, N.Y., 1969-74, Crestwood County Day Sch., Melville, N.Y., 1963—. Mem. Am. Camping Assn., Organist Guild Am., League Women Voters, L.I. Pvt. Schs. and Day Camp Assn. (sec. 1966-70, mem. exec. bd. 1966-70). Republican. Home: 324 West Hills Rd Huntington NY 11743 Office: Sweet Hollow Rd Huntington NY 11743

GERSHMAN, SUSAN JANE GILDENBERG, hosp. exec.; b. N.Y.C., Mar. 3, 1938; d. Leon and Jeanne (Goldenberg) Gildenberg; B.A. summa cum laude, Hunter Coll., 1964; M.A. in Psychology, Columbia, 1966, Ph.D. in Psychology (Nat. Def. Act fellow), 1970; m. Lawrence Eugene Gershman, Sept. 29, 1956; children—Gerald Mark, Leslie Rose. Research asst. Center for Research and Edn. in Am. Liberties, Columbia, N.Y.C., 1966, research asso. Research and Devel. Center for Edn. Handicapped Children, 1970-71; instr. Finch Coll., 1969-70; asso. dir. Floating Hosp., N.Y.C., 1971-72, exec. dir., 1972. Mem. Am. Psychol. Assn., Advt. Women N.Y., Direct Mail Marketing Assn., Phi Beta Kappa, Sigma Xi, Psi Chi. Home: 159 Hickory Av Tenafly NJ 07670 Office: 101 Park Av New York City NY 10017

GERSON, LINDA JEAN HANFF (MRS. MERVYN STUART GERSON), occupational therapist; b. N.Y.C., June 13, 1942; d. Joseph Arthur and Ruth (Gilbert) Hanff; B.S. in Occupational Therapy (Dept. Health, Edn. and Welfare grantee), Tufts U., 1964; postgrad. U. Hawaii Sch. Pub. Health, 1973—; m. Mervyn Stuart Gerson, Feb. 14, 1965; children—Laurie Jean, Philip Stuart, Michael Craig. Mem. staff occupational therapy Met. Hosp., N.Y.C., 1964-65, head in-patient div., 1965-66; cons., chief occupational therapist Island Nursing Home, Honolulu, 1971-72, Diamond Head Child Devel. Center, Honolulu, 1972-73, Beverly Manor Convalescent Center, Honolulu, 1973—. Vol. occupational therapist, tutor for exceptional children, 1970—; substitute tchr. Honolulu pub. schs., 1973—. Chmn. by-laws Jr. Guild for Symphony, 1971-72; 2d v.p. Sisterhood Temple Emanuel, Honolulu, 1972; asst. Brownie leader Girl Scouts U.S.A., Kailua, Hawaii, 1972-73, co-cadet troup leader, 1973—; mem. bd. Windward Community Health Council, Kailua, 1972-73; dir. Summer Fun Swimming program, Kailua, 1972-73; water safety instr. A.R.C., 1972—, advanced 1st aides, 1973—, Merit certificate Hawaii chpt., 1973. Mem. Am. Assn. U. Women (br. sec. 1970-73), Am., Hawaii occupational therapy assns., Outdoor Circle, Lawyers Wives. Home: 491 Iana St Kailua HI 96734 Office: 1930 Kam IV Rd Honolulu HI 96819

GERSON, LORRAINE SILVER (MRS. MORTON M. GERSON), lawyer; b. N.Y.C., Feb. 5, 1929; d. Issac and Jean (Shon) Silver; B.A., Bklyn. Coll., 1950; J.D., Seton Hall Law Sch., 1971; m. Morton M. Gerson, Aug. 10, 1952; children—Ann, Loren, Paulette. Retailing mgmt. Bloomingdale's, N.Y.C., 1950-56; admitted to N.J. bar, 1971; dep. atty. gen. State of N.J., Newark, 1971—. Mem. faculty Practicing Law Inst., 1973. Mem. Am., N.J., Essex County bar assns., League Women Voters (chmn. sch. study com. 1967). Home: 9 Glendale Rd Summit NJ 07901 Office: 1100 Raymond Blvd Newark NJ 07102

GERSOVITZ, SARAH VALERIE, painter, printmaker; b. Montreal, Que., Can., Sept. 5, 1920; d. Solomon and Eva (Gampel) Gamer; student MacDonald Coll.; Montreal Mus. Fine Arts, Ecole des Arts appliques, also seminars; m. Benjamin Gersovitz, June 22, 1944; children—Mark, Julia, Jeremy. Tchr. printmaking Bronfman Centre, Montreal, 1972—; seminar course Pointe Claire Cultural Centre, 1973—; one woman exhbns. include Montreal Mus. Fine Arts, 1962, 65, Art Gallery Greater Victoria, 1966, U. Alta., 1966, Burnaby Art Gallery, 1969, Art Gallery Hamilton, 1969, Mt. St. Vincent U., 1971, Coll. St. Louis, 1972, Inst. Cultural Peruano, Lima, 1973, others. Represented in permanent collections Library of Congress, Nat. Gallery South Australia, Inst. Cultural Peruano, Lima, numerous Canadian museums, univs. and embassies; group exhbns. include 3d Internat. Play Group Exhbn., N.Y.C., 1973, Internat. Triennial, Grenchen, Switzerland, 1961, Royal Soc. Painters-Etchers, London, Eng., 1959, 60, 62, 63, La Exposicao Internat. de Gravura, Sao Paulo, Brazil, 1968, Internat. Show, Manchester (N.H.) Inst., 1969, N.A.D., 1975, others U.S. and abroad. Recipient 1st prize Seagram Fine Arts Exposition, 1968; Graphic Art award Winnipeg (Man.) Art Show, 1962, Anaconda award Canadian Soc. Painters-Etchers, 1963, 67; purchase award Nat. Gallery S. Australia, 1967, Dawson Coll., 1974. Mem. Royal Canadian Acad. Arts, Canadian Soc. Graphic Art (jury 1969), Canadian Soc. Painters-Etchers (jury 1965), La Soc. des Artists Professionels (exec. com. 1969). Address: 5173 Mayfair Av Montreal PQ H4V 2E8 Canada

GERST, TOBY MAUREEN (MRS. STEPHEN ARTHUR GERST), judge; b. N.Y.C., July 29, 1943; d. Herman Joseph and Loretta (Burns) Blaivas; student Phoenix City Coll.; B.S., Ariz. State U., 1966; LL.B., U. Ariz.; m. Stephen Arthur Gerst, July 24, 1966; 1 son, Matthew Aaron. Admitted to Ariz. bar; law clk. Ariz. Supreme Court, Phoenix, 1966-70; asst. city atty. prosecutor's office City of Phoenix, 1970-71, judge, city court, 1971—. Lectr. on law to high sch. students. Mem. Women's Aux. Crippled Childrens Hosp. Mem. State Bar Ariz., Kappa Beta Phi. Home: 3614 W Orange St Phoenix AZ 85019 Office: 12 N 4th Av Phoenix AZ 85003

GERSTEN, SANDRA JOAN PESSIN (MRS. AARON L. GERSTEN), lawyer; b. Hartford, Conn.; d. Israel George and Gussie (Marcus) Pessin; B.A., Vassar Coll., 1957; LL.B., U. Conn., 1960; student U. Geneva (Switzerland), 1955-56; m. Aaron L. Gersten, Mar. 29, 1957; children—Peter Samuel, Karen Sue. Admitted to Conn. bar, 1960; individual practice law, West Hartford, 1960—, Past pres. Greater Hartford chpt. Orgn. for Rehab. Through Tng., 1968—. Mem. Conn., Hartford County bar assns., Brandeis Aux., Nat. Assn. Women Lawyers, U. Conn. Law Sch. Alumni Assn. (mem. bd.). Club: Farmington (Conn.). Home: 25 Pioneer Dr West Hartford CT 06117

GERSTENBERGER, DONNA LORINE, educator; b. Wichita Falls, Tex., Dec. 26, 1929; d. Donald Fayette and Mabel (Drinkard) Gerstenberger; A.B., Whitman Coll., 1951; M.A., U. Okla., 1952, Ph.D., 1958. Asst. prof. U. Colo., Boulder, 1958-60; prof. English, U. Wash., Seattle, 1960—, chmn. undergrad. studies, dir. honors program, 1971-74, asso. dean Coll. Arts and Scis., 1974—; author Swallow Press, Chgo., 1960—. Am. Council Learned Socs. grantee, 1962; Am. Philos. Soc. grantee, 1963. Mem. Modern Lang. Assn., Am. Com. for Irish Studies, Am. Assn. U. Profs. Author: J.M. Synge, 1964; Directory of Periodicals, 1974; The American Novel: A Checklist of Twentieth Century Criticism, Vol. I and II, 1970; The Complex Configuration: Modern Verse Drama, 1973; Iris Murdoch, 1974. Editor: Microcosm, 1969. Asso. editor Abstracts of English Studies, 1958-68. Home: 8415 Benotho Pl Mercer Island WA 98040 Office: U Wash Dept English Seattle WA 98105

GERSTER, CAROLYN FRANCES, physician; b. San Francisco; d. Richard Hohn and Evelyn Dagmar (Petersen) Taylor; B.S., U. Ore., 1948, M.D., 1951; m. Josef J. Gerster, Feb. 22, 1958; children—John, Eric, Nils (dec.), Kurt, Mark, Karl. Intern, Queens Hosp., Honolulu, 1951-52; resident Santa Barbara (Cal.) Cottage, 1952-53; Providence Hosp., Portland, Ore., 1953-55; Tb control officer Maricopa County Health Dept., Phoenix, 1959-62; pvt. practice internal medicine, Scottsdale, Ariz., 1962—; mem. staff Scottsdale Meml. Hosp., St. Joseph, St. Luke, Drs. hosps., Phoenix. Vice pres. Maricopa County Heart Assn., 1971-72, pres., 1972-73; mem. Scottsdale Beautification Com., 1970-74; pres. Ariz. Right to Life Com., 1971-72; v.p. Nat. Right to Life Com., 1973—. Served to capt. M.C. AUS, 1955-57. Recipient Award for Outstanding Work in Control of TB award Greater Phoenix TB and Health Assn., 1961, Outstanding Service award Greater Maricopa TB and Respiratory Disease Assn., 1968. Mem. Ariz. Thoracic Soc. (sec.-treas., 1971-72), Ariz. (del. 1970, 74, grievance com., 1970-73), Maricopa County med. assns., Am. Soc. Internal Medicine, A.C.P., Am. Coll. Cardiology. Republican. Episcopalian. Office: 7350 Stetson Dr Scottsdale AZ 85251

GERSTNER, ELIZABETH OSBORNE (MRS. RICHARD MARTIN GERSTNER), physician; b. Flint, Mich., Apr. 15, 1930; d. Donald Sheridan and Ruth Elizabeth (Farnham) Osborne; B.A., Carleton Coll., 1951; M.D., U. Mich., 1955; m. Richard Martin Gerstner, Aug. 15, 1953; children—David, Lynn, Eric, Karl. Intern St. Mary's Hosp., Grand Rapids, Mich., 1955-56; practice medicine, specializing in family planning, Kalamazoo, Mich., 1963—; mem. staff Bronson Hosp., Kalamazoo; physician New Orleans (La.) Health Dept., 1959-61; now med. dir. family planning clinics Kalamazoo County (Mich.). Med. adviser Kalamazoo Bd. Continuing Edn. for Young Women. Mem. Am. Assn. Planned Parenthood Physicians. Home: 2218 Waite Av Kalamazoo MI 49008

GERTSMAN, LILLIAN COPLAN (MRS. S.L. GERTSMAN), clubwoman; b. Ottawa, Ont., Can., Oct. 14, 1918; d. Archibald H. and Lena (Pullan) Coplan; grad. Ottawa Ladies' Coll., 1935; B.A., Queen's U., 1967; m. Sol Lawrence Gertsman, Sept. 1, 1940; children—Audrey (Mrs. Robert S. Amdursky), Cynthia (Mrs. Michael Wyman), Allen, Elizabeth (Mrs. Drew Chatterton), Beverley. Dir. Hull Iron and Steel Foundries Ltd., 1940-46; supply tchr. Ottawa Bd. Edn., 1968-70; home tutor child devel. expt. Carleton U. Chmn. Children of Other Lands for Citizens' Com. on Children, 1961-68; v.p. Internat. House, 1967-71; chmn. Ottawa Council Citizenship and Immigration, 1949-52; coll. convenor of vis. and entertainment Perley Hosp., 1952-62. Bd. dirs. Children's Internat. Summer Villages, 1965-68, Island Lodge, 1964-66, Social Planning Council, 1969-72. pres. 1st Av. Home and Sch. Club, 1951-53; pres. chpt. B'nai B'rith, Ottawa, 1953-54, chmn. Eastern Canada, 1954-55; v.p. Ottawa Home and Sch. Council, 1955-57; pres. Perley Hosp. Aux., 1962-63, Nat. Council Jewish Women, Ottawa, 1971-72; patron Ottawa Civic Symphony; v.p. UNICEF, Ottawa, Carleton, 1972—. Mem. Engineers' Wives (pres. 1957-58), Queen's U. Alumnae (pres. 1968-70), Ottawa Council of Women (pres. 1969-72), Provincial Council Women (v.p. 1972, econs. chmn.), Nat. Council Women (life mem., archivist 1973—), Ottawa Women's Canadian Club (dir. 1963-69), Elizabeth Fry Soc., Hist. Soc. Ottawa, Nat. Art Gallery Assn., Hadassah (chpt. pres. 1953-54). Club: Ottawa Women's University. Home: Champlain Towers 200 Rideau Terrace Apt 1401 Ottawa ON Canada

GERVASI, MILDRED INEZ (MRS. FRANCIS CHARLES GERVASI), librarian; b. DeQueen, Ark.; d. Beverley Johnson and Polly Ann (Sprowles) Quillin; B.S., N. Tex. State U., 1942; M.A. in L.S., George Peabody Coll., 1959; m. Francis Charles Gervasi, Dec. 14, 1945 (dec. Sept. 1955); 1 dau., Beverley Ann (Mrs. John David Van Camp). Acting head music library, North Tex. State U., Denton, 1942, head catalog dept., 1945; head librarian Midwestern U., Wichita Fall, Tex., 1942-45; continuations cataloger U. Rochester, N.Y., 1951-54; head librarian Southwestern U., Georgetown, Tex., 1957—. Cons. Georgetown Friends of Library, 1965—, to library Baptist Temple, 1954. Bd. trustees Georgetown Area Library, 1965-68. Mem. Am. (mem. div. nominating com. 1971, mem. cataloging com. 1968-69), Tex. (chmn. coll. div. 1968-69, chmn. archives history and local hist. dist. chpt. 1966-67, chmn. dist. 1975-76) library assns., Am. Assn. U. Women (pres. Georgetown Br. 1963-65, v.p. 1971-73, chmn. internat. 1972-74), Am. Assn. Higher Edn., Am. Assn. U. Profs., George Peabody Alumni Club, Beta Sigma Phi, Alpha Lambda Sigma. Club: Central Tex. Dinner (dir. 1968-72). Contbr. articles to profl. jours. Home: 1612 Williams Dr Georgetown TX 78626

GERVILLE-REACHE, JOAN (JOY) VIDA, journalist; b. Tettenhall, Staffs, Eng.; d. William and Ethelwyn (Harpham) Millner; grad. high sch.; m. Gaston Gerville-Reache, Sept. 14, 1939 (dec. Jan. 1964). Reporter, womans page editor Wolverhampton (Eng.) Express and Star, 1933-37; subeditor Reuters, London, 1937-46; subeditor, rewrite editor Agence France-Presse, Paris, 1946-66; editorial asst. overseas news div. Christian Sci. Monitor, Boston, 1967-70, editorial writer, 1970—. Mem. Reuters team Paris Peace Conf., 1946. Mem. New Eng. Womens Press Assn., Alliance Francaise. Office: Christian Science Monitor 1 Norway St Boston MA 02115

GESELL, GLORIA PADRON (MRS. HANS GESELL), psychologist; b. St. Croix, U.S. V.I., Mar. 9, 1934; d. Roque and Juana (Cepeda) Padron; B.A., Coll. City N.Y., 1957, M.S., 1960; Ph.D., Ottawa U., 1974; m. Hans Gesell, Nov. 22, 1964. Counselor, Catholic Charities, N.Y.C., 1959-61; extern Child Center, Catholic U., Washington, 1961-62; intern Fairfield State Hosp., Newtown, Conn., 1962-63; trainee Vets. Benefit Office, Washington, 1963-64; from psychologist to chief psychologist Mental Health Clinic, Perth Amboy, N.J., 1965-71; cons. psychologist Bergen (N.J.) Center for Psychol. Services, 1970—, Leonia (N.J.) High Sch., 1971-72, Mt. Carmel Sch., 1973—; pvt. practice psychology, Colonia, N.J., 1970—. Mem. Am., N.J. psychol. assns., Common Cause, Psi Chi. Home: 666 Floyd St Englewood Cliffs NJ 07632 Office: 30 Riveredge Rd Tenafly NJ 07670

GESKE, JANE POPE (MRS. NORMAN A. GESKE), librarian; b. Sutton, Neb., Nov. 27, 1918; d. Dan W. and Carolena (Deines) Pope; B.A., U. Neb. at Omaha, 1941; B.L.S., U. Denver, 1944; m. Norman A. Geske, Sept. 18, 1968. Asst., U. Neb., Omaha, 1944-45; serial records librarian La. State U., 1945-46; serials librarian U. Denver, 1947-52; serials librarian U. Chgo., 1953-60; with Neb. Pub. Library Commn., Lincoln, 1960-71, interim exec. sec., 1969-71, dir., 1973—. Bd. dirs. Neb. Arts Council, 1964-73. Mem. Am., Neb. (past pres.) library assns., Neb. Art Assn. Home: 2628 High St Lincoln NE 68502 Office: State Capitol 1420 P St E Lincoln NE 68509

GESSERT, VIRGINIA GRIFFIN (MRS. CARL F. GESSERT), occupational therapist; b. St. Joseph, Mo., Mar. 11, 1936; d. Frederick Oliver and Virginia Cushing (Saunders) Griffin; B.S., Washington U., St. Louis, 1958; m. Carl F. Gessert, June 7, 1958; children—Steven F., John C. Clin. supr. Rehab. Center Greater St. Louis, 1958-60; sr. staff occupational therapist, supr. rehab. and chronic disease unit Jewish Hosp., St. Louis, 1960-62; cons. occupational therapist St. Vincent's Home, Omaha, Neb., 1968—, dir. therapeutic services, 1971—. Vol. cons. Neb. State Health Dept., Neb. Nursing Home Assn. Activity Dirs.' Tng. Project, 1972-73; mem. health council Midlands Manpower Study Commn., 1973—. Mem. exec. bd. Omaha Vol. Bur.-Vol. Action Center, chmn. forum suprs., 1971—. Mem. supt.'s adv. council Sch. Dist. 66, 1968—, bd. dirs. talented and gifted, 1971-73. Named Outstanding Woman 1973, Omaha Bus. and Profl. Women's Club, 1973. Mem. Am. Assn. U. Women (bd. dirs. Omaha chpt. 1967-70), Am. (chmn. legislation com. 1970-71, recruitment chmn. 1968-72), Neb. occupational therapy assns., Delta Delta Delta. Episcopalian. Home: 1336 S 93d Av Omaha NE 68124 Office: St Vincent's Home 4500 Ames Av Omaha NE 68104

GESSNER, MERLYN (LYNNE) CLARK, author; b. Preston, Cuba, June 10, 1919 (parents Am. citizens); student Portland State Coll., 1962, Phoenix Jr. Coll., 1964; m. Malcolm John Gessner, Apr. 2, 1944; children—Dianne Lynne (Mrs. John B. Doyle) Deborah Dee (Mrs. Dean L. McMann). Bookkeeper, John Ratcliff & Co., Tempe, Ariz., 1972-74. Christian Scientist. Author: Trading Post Girl, 1968, Lightning Slinger, 1968; Ramrod, 1969; Bonnie's Guatemala Adventure, 1970. Home: 6507 E Holly St Scottsdale AZ 85257

GETTS, MRS. CLARK H. (DOROTHY JONES GETTS), radio, TV and concert mgmt. exec.; b. Jersey City; d. Frederic W. and Estelle (Raphun) Jones; grad. pvt. schs.; m. Clark H. Getts, Dec. 30, 1955. Sec., Clark H. Getts, Inc., N.Y.C., 1940—, dir. 1944—; corporate sec. Campagnia Realty Mgmt. Corp., 1965—; program coordinator Longines Chronoscope TV series, 1950-52; exec. dir. Army-Navy-Red Cross radio series The Road Ahead, 1945-46, Jan Struther's Mrs. Miniver radio series, 1945, The Dublin Players theatre tours, 1950-56, Fiesta Mexicana concert tours, 1954-57; represented various individual authors, artists and speakers for their public appearances and other activities. Dir., sec. Am. Inst. for Civic Edn., 1950—. Episcopalian. Office: 663 Fifth Av New York City NY 10022

GETZIN, AMBER DEAN (MRS. NORMAN J. GETZIN), author; b. Depew, N.Y., Dec. 4, 1902; d. Ambertson Myron and Alice Mabel (Robinson) Dean; grad. high sch.; m. Norman J. Getzin, Mar. 1, 1926; 1 dau., Alice (Mrs. Charles Foster Wray). Trustee Avon Free Library. Author: Something for the Birds, 1965; Encounter With Evil, 1967; Deadly Contact, 1969; The Dower Chest, 1971; Be Home By Eleven, 1973; motion picture Last Seen Wearing Bluejeans (Encounter With Evil), 1969. Home: Meadowood West Rush NY 14587

GETZWILLER, POLLY (MRS. MARION H. GETZWILLER), state legislator; b. Luna, N.M., Mar. 8, 1934; d. William T. and Grace Ross (Birdwell) Johnson; m. Marion H. Getzwiller, June 13, 1954; children—Billie Lou, William Albert, Marion Joe. Mem. Ariz. Ho. of Reps.; del. Democratic Nat. Conv., 1968. Mem. Bus. and Profl. Women's Club, Internat. Platform Assn., Colorado River Water Assn., Ariz. Cotton Growers, Farm. Bur. Presbyn. Home: Box 127 Casa Grande AZ 85222

GEWIRTZ, GERRY (MRS. EUGENE FRIEDMAN), editor; b. N.Y.C., Dec. 22, 1920; d. Max and Minnie (Weiss) Gewirtz; B.A., Vassar Coll., 1941; m. Eugene W. Friedman, Nov. 11, 1945; children—John Henry, Robert James. Editor, Package Store Mgmt., 1942-44, Jewelry Mag., 1945-53; freelance editor promotion dept. McCall's Mag., Esquire, 1953-56; free-lance fashion and gifts editor Jewelers Circular Keystone, N.Y.C., 1955-71; editor, pub. The Fashionables, 1971—, The Forecast, 1974—. Bd. dirs. Encampment for Citizenship; trustee Central Synagogue. Mem. N.Y. Fashion Group, Nat. Home Fashions League, Phi Delta Epsilon. Clubs: N.Y. Vassar; Overseas Press. Home: 55 E 86th St New York NY 10028 Office: 420 Madison Av New York City NY 10017

GEYER, GEORGIE ANNE, journalist, author; b. Chgo., Apr. 2, 1935; d. Robert George and Georgie Hazel (Gervens) Geyer; B.S., Northwestern U., 1956; postgrad. (Fulbright scholar) U. Vienna (Austria), 1956-57. Reporter, Southtown Economist, Chgo., 1958; soc. reporter Chgo. Daily News, 1959-60, gen. assignment reporter, 1960-64, Latin Am. corr., 1964-67, roving world corr., 1967—. Active Orgn. for S.W. Community Chgo., 1960—. Recipient 1st prize Am. Newspaper Guild, 1962; 2d prize Ill. Press Editors Assn., 1962; award for best reporting in Latin Am., Overseas Press Club, 1967; Alumni Merit award Northeastern U., 1968; Maria Moors Cabot award Columbia, 1971; Hannah Solomon award Nat. Council Jewish Women, 1973. Mem. Chgo. Council Fgn. Relations (dir.), Mortar Bd., Theta Sigma Chi. Author: The New Latins, 1970; The New 100 Years War, 1972. Contbr. articles to Atlantic Mag., Sat. Rev. Lit., Nat. Observer, New Republic, others. Home: 339 W Barry Av Chicago IL 60657 Office: 401 N Wabash Av Chicago IL 60603

GHATALA, ELIZABETH SCHWENN (MRS. M. HABEEB GHATALA), research psychologist; b. Sparta, Wis., Nov. 27, 1942; d. Fredrick Frank and Margaret (Bagby) Schwenn; B.A. (NSF fellow), Northwestern U., 1964, M.S., 1966; Ph.D. (fellow 1968-70), U. Wis.-Madison, 1970; m. M. Habeeb Ghatala, Apr. 11, 1970. Project asst. Wis. Research and Devel. Center for Cognitive Learning, Madison, 1967-68; adj. asst. prof. U. Cin., 1970; asst. scientist Wis. Research and Devel. Center, Madison, 1971-72; research psychologist Weber State Coll., Ogden, Utah, 1972—; cons. Ogden City Schs., Utah Skills Center. Spencer fellow Nat. Acad. Educators, 1974. Mem. Am. Psychol. Assn., Am. Ednl. Research Assn., Phi Beta Kappa. Author: Conceptual Learning and Development, 1974. Contbr. articles to profl. jours. Home: Apt 208 1785 29th St Ogden UT 84403

GHERING, SISTER MARY VIRGIL, librarian; b. Grand Rapids, Mich., July 18, 1910; d. Henry Christian and Frances Emily (Sharp) Ghering; student Aquinas Coll., 1928-32; A.B., Central Mich. U., 1935; M.S., Marquette U., 1948; postgrad. (NSF faculty fellow) Fordham U., 1957-60; Ph.D., St. Thomas Inst., 1968. Tchr., Cath. Central High Sch., Grand Rapids, 1936-38, Nottawa Twp. Sch. Unit, Rosebud, Mich., 1941-42, Marywood Acad., Grand Rapids, 1942-43, Maple Grove Pub. Schs., New Lothrop, Mich., 1943-49; asst. prof. chemistry Aquinas Coll., Grand Rapids, 1949-57, asso. prof., 1957-61, prof., 1961-68, chmn. dept. phys. scis., 1959-63; librarian St. Thomas Inst., Cin., 1968—. Telephone coordinator Common Cause Ohio, 1973—. Fellow Am. Inst. Chemists. Home: 410 E 5th St Cincinnati OH 45202

GHIGLIERI, SYLVIA MARIE, educator; b. Stockton, Cal., Mar. 13, 1933; d. Sylvio Louis and Aurelia Catherine (Dentone) Ghiglieri; Mus.B. maxima cum laude, Dominican Coll., 1954; diploma Music Acad. of West, 1954; diploma, ConservatoireFontainebleau, France, 1955; Mus. M., U. Pacific, 1960; postgrad. Eastman Sch. Music, 1969, Northwestern U., 1971. Faculty Cal. State Coll., Stanislaus, at Turlock, 1961—, asso. prof. music, 1970—. Concerts in France, Italy, Switzerland, 1955, Cal., 1947—; piano soloist with Modesto and Stockton Symphonies, 1950-69. Com. mem. Turlock Fine Arts Festival, 1966-67. Bd. dirs. Turlock Community Concert, 1962-65, 1970—. Mem. Cal. Music Tchrs. Assn., Music Educators Nat. Conf., Cal. Music Educators Assn., Mu Phi Epsilon (1st prize 1959), Alpha Delta Kappa, Pi Kappa Lambda, Phi Kappa Phi. Democrat. Roman Catholic. Composer: 3 Irish Pieces for Piano, 1959; Psalm 56 for chorus and orch., 1963. Office: Cal State College Stanislaus 800 Monte Vista Av Turlock CA 95380

GHIGLIONE, NANCY GEIGER (MRS. LOREN FRANK GHIGLIONE), newspaper exec.; b. Washington, Jan. 13, 1943; d. Theodore and Frances (Moed) Geiger; B.A., Bryn Mawr Coll., 1965; postgrad. Sorbonne, U. Paris, 1965-66; m. Loren Frank Ghiglione, Feb. 24, 1968; 1 dau., Jessica B. Vice pres. Southbridge (Mass.) Evening News, 1968—. Home: 13 Coolidge Av Southbridge MA 01550 Office: 25 Elm St Southbridge MA 01550

GHOLDSTON, JUNE SCOTT (MRS. WILLIAM EDWARD GHOLDSTON), editor; b. Atlanta, June 14, 1920; d. Walter Wright and Mattie Menla (Eley) Scott; grad. high sch.; m. William Edward Gholdston, May 24, 1942; children—Edward Wright, John Scott. Clk., stenographer Hartford Fire Ins. Co., Atlanta, 1938-41; stenographer FBI, Atlanta, Miami, Fla., 1941-45; stenographer Intelligence and Security, U.S. Army, Camp Kilmer, N.J., 1945-46; editor PTA Bull., Fla. Congress of Parents and Tchrs., Orlando, 1969—. Vol. editor for various newsletters and yearbooks, local PTA's, church and Rotary groups. Sec. to Orange County campaign mgr. Sen. George Smathers, 1950. Mem. Fla. PTA (hon. life), Woman's Soc. Christian Service (hon. life). Democrat. Mem. Ch. of Jesus Christ of Latter-day Saints (sec. Sunday sch. Orlando ward). Home: 821 Rugby St Orlando FL 32804 Office: 1747 Orlando Central Parkway Orlando FL 32809

GIALLOMBARDO, ROSE MARY, educator; b. Willimantic, Conn., Nov. 12, 1925; d. Rosario and Mary (Lidestri) Giallombardo; B.A., U. Conn., 1958; M.A., Northwestern U., 1960, Ph.D., 1965. Lectr. sociology Northwestern U. Dental Sch., Chgo., 1959-61; asst. prof. sociology N.Y.U., 1964-66; research asso., asso. prof. sociology U. Chgo., 1967-73. Mem. Am. Sociol. Assn., Soc. for Study Social Problems, Am. Assn. U. Profs., Nat. Council Crime and Delinquency. Author: Society of Women, 1966; Juvenile Delinquency, 2d edit., 1972; The Social World of Imprisoned Girls, 1974. Home: 1451 E 55th St Chicago IL 60615

GIAMBRONE, ANDREA VETRANO, advt. agy. exec.; b. Bklyn., Sept. 27, 1943; d. Andrew and Theresa (Maida) Vetrano; student N.Y. U., 1960-63, U. Cal. at Los Angeles, 1963-71; m. Frank Joseph Giambrone, Jr., Aug. 10, 1963 (div. Oct. 1970). Sec., Compton Advt., Los Angeles, 1963-64, copywriter, 1964-67; copy supr. Kelly Advt., Los Angeles, 1967-69; sr. copywriter Eisaman, Johns & Laws, Advt., Los Angeles, 1969-71, v.p., copy dir., 1971—. Guest speaker, panelist various advt. seminars. Creator United Crusade Campaign, 1973-74; mem. Los Angeles County Museum Art. Recipient various nat. and regional advt. awards. Mem. Am. Advt. Fedn., Fashion Group, Los Angeles Advt. Women (dir. 1973-74). Office: 6290 Sunset Blvd Los Angeles CA 90028

GIAMMONA, VICTORIA MARIE, newspaper editor; b. Chgo., Mar. 22, 1950; d. Victor C. and Marie Antoinette (Colletti) Giammona; B.S. in Journalism, Northwestern U., 1972. Reporter, Community Publs., Oak Park, Ill., 1972-73, editor, 1973—; pub. Oak Park River Forest World, Elmwood Park-River Grove World, Austin News, Belmont-Cragin News, Montclare-Galewood News Jour., Northwest Jour., Humboldt Park Jour., Hermosa Park Jour., Kelvyn Park Jour. Mem. Northwestern U. Young Alumni Council, Women in Communications, Kappa Delta. Home: 8040 W Addison St Chicago IL 60634 Office: 6905 W North Av Oak Park IL 60302

GIANGRECO, MARIANNE RANSON (MRS. C. JOSEPH GIANGRECO), educator; b. Springfield, Ill., Feb. 1, 1930; d. Gail Brook and Evanda (Potter) Ranson; B.A., Ill. Coll. Jacksonville, 1951; M.S., Gallaudet Coll., 1954; m. C. Joseph Giangreco, June 29, 1949; children—Marianne Evanda, Joseph Brook. Tchr. hearing impaired Ill. Sch. for the Deaf at Jacksonville, 1952-53; instr. hearing impaired Ia. Sch. for the Deaf at Council Bluffs, 1954—; tchr. Council Bluffs Adult Edn., 1968—. Cons. U. No. Colo., 1970. Tree chmn. Historic Gen. Dodge House, 1967. Bd. dirs. S.W. Ia. region Am. Heart Assn., 1968-71, S.W. Ia. Regional Crime Commn. Mem. Alexander Graham Bell Assn., P.E.O. (pres. 1972-73), P.T.A., Am. Assn. U. Women (pres. council Bluffs br. 1964-66), Conv. Am. Schs. for the Deaf. Presbyn. (pres. Council Bluffs Ch. Women United 1967). Author: (with C. Joseph Giangreco) The Education of the Hearing Impaired, 1970; Canoe Country Poems, 1974. Address: Ia Sch for Deaf Council Bluffs IA 51501

GIARRIZZO, GLORIA VIVIAN TORETTA (MRS. CHARLES C. GIARRIZZO), psychologist; b. N.Y.C., Feb. 8, 1924; d. James B. and Alba M. (Tessitore) Toretta; B.A., Hunter Coll., 1944, M.A., 1951; M.S., Cal. State U., 1968; m. Charles C. Giarrizzo, Apr. 7, 1946 (div. 1971); children—Karen Claire, Matthew Charles, David Alexander. Tchr., N.Y.C. schs., 1949-51, San Bernadino (Cal.) city schs., 1961-63; psychologist, educationally handicapped cons. Santa Clara County Office Edn., San Jose, Cal., 1967—. Instr. spl. edn. dept. U. Cal. at San Jose, 1969—; cons. Rubicon Mental Health Center, Fremont, Cal., 1973—. Bd. dirs. Mental Health Assn. Santa Clara County, 1969—, Community Effort for Residential Treatment, San Jose, 1973-74. Mem. N.E.A., Cal. Tchrs. Assn., Council for Exceptional Children (pres. chpt. 1973-74), Am. Psychologist Assn., Nat. Assn. Sch. Psychologists, Cal., Santa Clara County assns. sch. psychologists and psychometrists. Home: 160 Pineview Lane Menlo Park CA 94025 Office: 100 Skyport Dr San Jose CA 95110

GIBAS, GRACE BRADEN (MRS. ANDREW C. GIBAS), editor, pub.; b. Santiago, Chile, S.Am., Aug. 14, 1916; d. Charles Samuel and Grace (McMurray) Braden (parents Am. citizens); B.A., Northwestern U., 1939; m. Andrew C. Gibas, June 11, 1939; children—Murray Albert, Allen Henry, Barbara Jane, Rebecca (Mrs. Greg Gepner). Mem. staff World Christianity, Chgo., 1938-39; co-pub., co-editor Circulating Pines, Circle Pines, Minn., 1959—. Mem. exec. com. Minn. Am. Friends Service Com., 1972—. Recipient 2d pl. best feature story Nat. Editorial Assn. newspaper contest, 1963; 1st pl. excellence in investigative reporting Minn. Newspaper Assn. Better Newspaper Contest, 1968, in sports reporting, govtl. reporting, women's reporting, 1968. Office: 9201 Lexington Av Circle Pines MN 55014

GIBBONS, BARBARA HALLORAN (MRS. WILBUR I. GIBBONS), journalist; b. East Orange, N.J.; d. Frank P. and Marian (Whittlesey) Halloran; student N.J. State Tchrs. Coll., 1953-56, U. Coll. Rutgers, 1958-60; m. Wilbur I. Gibbons, Dec. 16, 1961; 1 dau., Susan. Columnist, Slim Gourmet for United Feature Syndicate, 1971—, Creative Low-Calorie Cooking for Family Circle mag., 1971—, Gourmet Bookshelf, weekly 1972—. Mem. Soc. Mag. Writers. Home: 50 W Shore Trail Lake Mohawk Sparta NJ 07871 Office: care United Features 220 E 42d St New York City NY 10017

GIBBONS, JEAN DICKINSON, educator; b. St. Petersburg, Fla., Mar. 14, 1938; d. John and Alice (Albury) Dickinson; A.B., Duke, 1958, M.A., 1959; Ph.D., Va. Poly. Inst., 1963. Asst. prof. Mercer U., Macon, Ga., 1958-60; asst. prof. U. Cin., 1961-63; asso. prof. U. Pa., Phila., 1963-70; prof., chmn. dept. statistics U. Ala., University, 1970—. Cons. biostatistics U. Cin. Med. Sch., 1962-63. Fulbright scholar, 1973. Mem. Am. Statis. Assn., Inst. Math. Statistics, Phi Beta Kappa, Pi Mu Epsilon, Chi Alpha Phi, Phi Kappa Phi. Asso. editor: Am. Statistician, 1972—. Contbr. articles to profl. jours. Home: 7 Woodridge Tuscaloosa AL 35401 Office: Statistics Dept Box J University Alabama University AL 35486

GIBBONS, MRS. JOHN SHELDON (CELIA VICTORIA TOWNSEND), editor, publisher; b. Fargo, N.D.; d. Harry Alton and Helen (Haag) Townsend; student U. Minn., 1930-33; m. John Sheldon Gibbons, May 1, 1935; children—Mary Vee (Mrs. Kenneth E. Ellenberg), John Townsend. Advt. mgr. Hotel Nicollet, Mpls., 1933-37; contbg. editor children's mags., 1935—; partner Youth Assos. Co., Mpls., 1942-65; pub., art dir. Mines and Escholier mags., 1954-65; founder Bull. Bd. Pictures, Inc., Mpls., 1954, pres., 1954—; founder Periodical Litho Art Co., Mpls., 1962-65, pres., 1962-65. Active St. Paul Internat. House, Friends of Inst., St. Paul Arts and Sci. Center. Republican chairwoman Golden Valley, Minn., 1950; alternate del. Hennepin County Rep. Conv., 1962. Mem. Mpls. Inst. Arts, Ft. Lauderdale Mus. Arts, Art Guild Boca Raton. Delta Zeta. Clubs: Woman's Minikahda; Woman's of Minneapolis; Woman's (Deerfield Beach, Fla.). Home: 1416 Alpine Pass Tyrol Hills Minneapolis MN 55416 Office: 1057 A1A Hillsboro Beach FL 33062

GIBBS, JEANNE OSBORNE, editor, poet; b. Stone Mountain, Ga., June 1, 1920; d. Virgil Waite and Daisy Hampton (Scruggs) Osborne; B.A., Agnes Scott Coll., 1942; divorced; children—Robert Allan, Marilyn Osborne. Mem. editorial staff Atlanta Constitution, 1942; feature writer New London (Conn.) Day, 1943; book reviewer, Atlanta, 1940-48, Atlanta Jour., 1945-48; poetry editor Banner Press, Emory U., 1957-59, book editor Georgia Mag., Decatur, 1957-73. Recipient Robert Martin award N.Y. Poetry Forum, 1973. Mem. World Poetry Soc., Ga. Wrtiers Assn. (lit. achievement award 1971), Poetry Soc. Ga. (John Clare prize 1955), Atlanta Writers Club (pres. 1949-50, named Aurelia Austin Writer of Year in poetry 1971), Phi Beta Kappa. Baptist (pres. Newton class 1973-74). Author: The Other Side of the Water (Author of Year in Poetry award Dixie council of Authors and Journalists 1971), 1970. Contbr. poems to mags. Home: 809 Pinetree Dr Decatur GA 30030

GIBBS, JUNE NESBITT, civic worker; b. Newton, Mass., June 13, 1922; d. Samuel Frederick and Lulu (Glazier) Nesbitt; B.A. in Math., Wellesley Coll., 1943; M.A. in Math., Boston U., 1947; m. Donald T. Gibbs, Dec. 8, 1945; 1 dau., Elizabeth. Republican nat. committeewoman, R.I., 1969—; mem. def. adv. com. Women in Services, 1970—, vice chmn., 1972. Served to lt. (j.g.) USNR, 1942-46. Home: 163 Riverview Av Middletown RI 02840

GIBBS, MARGARET ANDREWS (MRS. FRED C. GIBBS), librarian; b. Onalaska, Tex., Feb. 3, 1914; d. Homer Lee and Pauline (Campbell) Andrews; Asso. Sci., Decatur Bapt. Coll., 1955; B.S. in Edn., N. Tex. State U., 1957; M.L.S. Tex. Woman's U., 1959; m. Fred C. Gibbs, June 4, 1932; children—Helen Marie (Mrs. Orvill Dwayne Boydstun), Sandra Kaye (Mrs. Larry Wayne Milligan). Exec. sec. Decatur (Tex.) Bapt. Coll., 1957-58, head librarian, 1958-65; head librarian Dallas Bapt. Coll., 1965—. Mem. A.L.A. (chmn. spl. projects com.), Southwestern, Tex., Dallas County library assns., Assn. Coll. Research Libraries, Internat. Platform Assn., Tex. Jr. Coll. Tchrs. Assn., Delta Kappa Gamma, Kappa Delta Pi, Alpha Beta Alpha. Contbr. editor: Basic Books for Junior College Libraries: 20,000 Vital Titles, 1963. Home: 3706 Kimballdale Dr Dallas TX 75233 Office: 3000 Florina Dr PO Box 21206 Dallas TX 75211

GIBBY, MABEL ENID KUNCE (MRS. JOHN FRANCIS GIBBY), psychologist; b. St. Louis, Mar. 30, 1926; d. Ralph Waldo and Mabel Enid (Warren) Kunce; student Washington U., St. Louis, 1943-44, postgrad., 1955-56; B.A., Park Coll., 1945; M.A., McCormick Theol. Sem., 1947; postgrad. Columbia, 1948, U. Kansas City, 1949, George Washington U., 1953; M.Ed., U. Mo., 1951, Ed.D., 1952; m. John Francis Gibby, Aug. 27, 1948; children—Janet Marie (Mrs. Kim Williams), Harold Steven, Helen Elizabeth, Diane Louise, John Andrew, Keith Sherridan, Daniel Jay. Dir. religious edn. Westport Presbyn. Ch., Kansas City, Mo., 1947-49; tchr. elementary schs., Kansas City, 1949-50; high sch. counselor Arlington (Va.) Pub. Schs., 1952-54; counselor adult counseling services Washington U., 1955-56; counseling psychologist Coral Gables (Fla.) VA Hosp., 1956—, Miami (Fla.) VA Hosp., 1956—. Recipient Meritorious Service citation Fla. C. of C., 1965, President's Com. on Employment of Handicapped, 1965; commendation for meritorious service Com. on Employment of Physically Handicapped Dade County, 1965, named outstanding rehab. profl., 1966; named Profl. Fed. Employee of Year, Greater Miami Fed. Exec. Council, 1966; Outstanding Fed. Service award Greater Miami Fed. Exec. Council, 1966; Fed. Woman's award U.S. Civil Service Commn., 1968, Community Headliner award Theta Sigma Phi, 1968, Outstanding Alumni award Park Coll., 1968; certificate of appreciation Bur. Customs, U.S. Treasury Dept., 1969, Fla. Dept. Health and Rehab. Services, 1970. Mem. Am., Dade County (past sec.) psychol. assns., Nat., Fla. (past dir. Dade County chpt.) rehab. assns., Nat. Rehab. Counseling Assn. (past sec.). Home: 4501 Granada Blvd Coral Gables FL 33146 Office: 1201 NW 15th St Miami FL 33125

GIBLETT, ELOISE ROSALIE, educator, hematologist; b. Tacoma, Jan. 17, 1921; d. William Richard and Rose (Godfrey) Giblett; B.S., U. Wash., 1942, M.S., 1947, M.D. with honors, 1951. Intern, King County Hosp., Seattle, 1951-52, asst. resident medicine, 1952-53; USPHS postdoctoral research fellow U. Wash. and Postgrad. Sch. Medicine, London, Eng., 1953-55; USPHS postdoctoral trainee genetics Case-Western Res. U., Cleve., 1960; clin. asso. in medicine U. Wash. Sch. Medicine, 1955-57, clin. instr., 1957-58, clin. asst. prof., 1958-61, clin. asso. prof., 1961-66, clin. prof., 1966-67, research prof., 1967—; asso. dir. King County Central Blood Bank, 1955—, head immunogenetics, 1955—. Mem. adv. com. Nat. Blood Resources Program, 1969-72, genetics study sect. NIH, 1972—. Served with WAVES, 1944-46. Mem. Internat., Am. (subcom. on immunohematology 1966-72) socs. hematologists, Am. Soc. Human Genetics (pres. 1973), Am., Brit. socs. immunology, Am. Fedn. Clin. Research, Assn. Am. Physicians, Western Soc. Clin. Research, Western Assn. Physicians, N.Y. Acad. Scis., King County Med. Soc., Sigma Xi, Alpha Omega Alpha. Author: Genetic Markers in Human Blood, 1969. Asso. editor Am. Jour. Human Genetics, 1963-73, Transfusion, 1961—; co-editor brief reports sect. Vox Sanguinis, 1960—. Contbr. articles to profl. jours. Home: 6533 53d NE Seattle WA 98115 Office: King County Central Blood Bank Terry at Madison Seattle WA 98104

GIBNEY, SISTER MARIE HELENE, ednl. adminstr.; b. Newark, June 22, 1936; d. James Ambrose and Helen Loretta (Coggins) Gibney; B.A., Coll. Notre Dame, 1966; M.A., Cath. U. Am., 1969, postgrad., 1970—. Joined Order Sch. Sisters Notre Dame, 1954; tchr. St. Mary's Elementary Sch., Bryantown, Md., 1956-60, Notre Dame High Sch., Bryantown, 1960-67, Archbishop Neale High Sch., La Plata, Md., 1967-68; prin. St. Mary's High Sch., Annapolis, Md., 1968-71; adminstr., dean of admissions Coll. Notre Dame, Balt., 1971—. Choir dir., parish organist St. Mary Ch., Bryantown, 1956-68; parish council officer, Annapolis, 1968-71. Mem. Am. Assn. on Higher Edn., Nat., Balt. assns. secondary sch. prins., Nat. Assn. Coll. Admissions Counselors, Nat. Assn. Collegiate Registrars and Officers of Admission. Club: Glee. Address: 4701 N Charles St Baltimore MD 21210

GIBSON, AUDREY JANE (MRS. QUENTIN H. GIBSON), educator; b. Paris, France, Oct. 5, 1924; d. Gerald Hume and Katharine Kentisbeare (Radford) Pinsent; B.A., Cambridge (Eng.) U., 1946; Ph.D., London U., 1949; m. Quentin H. Gibson, July 21, 1951; children—Katharine J., William G.H., Ursula J., Emma L.M. Commonwealth fund fellow Stanford, Hopkins Marine Sta., Pacific Grove, Cal., 1949-50; research asso. U. Sheffield, Eng., 1951-63; research asso. U. Ill., Urbana, 1961; asst. prof. biology U. Pa., Phila., 1963-65; faculty Cornell U., Ithaca, N.Y., 1966—, asso. prof. biology 1971—. NSF research grantee, 1966—. Mem. Am. Soc. Microbiology, Soc. for Gen. Microbiology, Soc. Biol. Chemists. Home: 98 Dodge Rd Ithaca NY 14850

GIBSON, CAROLYN INGRID LARSON (MRS. C. MARTIN GIBSON), lawyer; b. San Francisco, Mar. 25, 1947; d. Edward Walfred and Doris Louise (Koch) Larson; B.A., Cal. Luth. Coll., 1968; J.D., Hastings Coll. Law, 1971; m. C. Martin Gibson, Oct. 21, 1973. Admitted to Cal. bar, 1972, practiced in San Francisco, 1972; estate tax atty. Internal Revenue Service, San Francisco, 1972—. Mem. alumni assembly Cal. Luth. Coll., Thousand Oaks, 1971—. Mem. Cal. State Bar, San Francisco Bar Assn. (mem. com. 1972—), Phi Alpha Delta. Home: 113 C Oliva Ct Novato CA 94947 Office: 450 Golden Gate Av Room 5216 G San Francisco CA 94102

GIBSON, DOROTHY RAPSON (MRS. JAY EDWARD GIBSON), realtor; b. Los Angeles, Apr. 9, 1924; d. Frederick and Una (Howard) Rapson; B.S., U. Cal. at Los Angeles; m. Jay Edward Gibson, Dec. 2, 1950; children—Stephen Jay, Deborah Louise, Laura Lynn. Dist. dir., camp dir. San Diego council Camp Fire Girls, 1946-49, exec. dir. Mishawaka (Ind.) council, 1949-50, nat. recruiter, 1962-68; real estate sales and broker asso. Bell Realtors, Los Gatos, Cal., 1969—. Bd. dirs. YMCA, Santa Clara County Social Planning Council. Recipient Distinguished Citizens award San Jose City Council, 1972, Gulick award Camp Fire Girls, 1963, Asso. Realtor of Year award Los Gatos/Saratoga Bd. Realtors, 1973, Woman of Achievement award San Jose Mercury and News, 1973. Mem. Am. Assn. Univ. Women (pres. San Jose br. 1963), Gatos/Saratoga Real Estate Bd. (program chmn. 1972). Home: 18236 Seebree Lane Monte Sereno CA 95030 Office: 230 Saratoga Av Los Gatos CA 95030

GIBSON, ELEANOR BEATRICE, library cons.; b. London, Eng., Mar. 8, 1905; d. Harry Hepburn and Anne Elizabeth (White) Gibson; brought to U.S., 1905, derivative citizenship, 1914; A.B., Cornell U., 1928; student St. Joseph's Coll., West Hartford, 1937-38; M.S. in Library Sci., Syracuse U., 1957. With Aetna Life & Casualty Co., Hartford, Conn., 1928-42, librarian research div., 1933-42; librarian Logan Lewis Library, Carrier Corp. Research Center, Syracuse, N.Y., 1947-67, spl. adviser, 1967-70; tech. supr. computerized union catalogue project Conn. State Library, Hartford, 1968-71; now cons. Served from 1st lt. (WAAC) WAC, AUS, 1942-46; capt., 1950-51. Recipient Honors award, Spl. Libraries Assn., 1968, named to Hall of Fame. Mem. Coll. Art Assn. Am., Wadsworth Atheneum, New Britain Mus. Am. Art, Spl. Libraries Assn. (pres. Western N.Y. 1959-60; nat. chmn. metals materials div. 1961-62), Am. Daffodil Soc., Am. Legion, Conn. Hist. Soc., Conn. Hort. Soc., Marquis Biog. Soc., Conn. Acad. Fine Arts, Nat. Audubon Soc., Alumni Assn. Syracuse U. Sch. Library Sci. (pres. 1967-68), Pi Lambda Sigma (pres. 1958-59), Beta Phi Mu (local pres. 1959-60). Republican. Episcopalian. Editor: Guide to Metallurgical Information, 1965. Contbr. articles to profl. jours. Home: 23 Fernridge Rd West Hartford CT 06107

GIBSON, ELIZABETH JUNKIN, librarian; b. Milw.; d. John P. and Katherine F. (Bailey) Junkin; grad. Northrop Collegiate Sch. for Girls, Mpls., U. Minn.; m. Douglas Wood Gibson, Sept. 18, 1942 (div.). With accounting dept. Investors Diversified Services, Mpls., Investors Syndicate Title & Guaranty Co., N.Y.; fashion dept. Town and Country Mag., N.Y.C., 1946-47; librarian Merrill Lynch, Pierce, Fenner & Smith, Inc., N.Y.C., 1948—. Vol. worker Meml. Hosp. for Cancer and Allied Diseases, 1953—. Mem. Nat. Microfilm Assn., N.Y. Jr. League, Records Mgmt. Assn. N.Y., Inc. (dir. 1956—), Spl. Libraries Assn. (vice chmn. financial div. and editor financial div. bull. 1951-52, chmn. financial div. 1952-53, chmn. nominating com. bus. and financial div. 1959-69), Soc. Meml. Cancer Center, Am. Soc. for Information Sci. Home: 414 E 52d St New York City NY 10022 Office: 1 Liberty Plaza 165 Broadway NY 10006

GIBSON, JULIA IMOGENE WYATT (MRS. PAUL GIBSON), educator, librarian; b. Olney, Tex., July 14, 1926; d. Claude Newell and Julia Elizabeth (Wardlow) Wyatt; B.S., U. Chgo., 1947; M.L.S., Tex. Woman's U., 1969; m. Paul Gibson, Sept. 8, 1946; children—Paul Wyatt, Karen Leigh. Bacteriologist, Nalco Chem., Chgo., 1948-51, 54-56; library asst., Austin Coll., Sherman, Tex., 1965-67, cataloger, 1967-69, head tech. services, 1969-70, acting librarian, 1970, coll. librarian, asst. prof., 1971—. Mem. Beta Phi Mu. Home: 1125 Western Hills Sherman TX 75090

GIBSON, MARY ELIZABETH (PSEUDONYM MARALEE G. DAVIS) (MRS. WILLIAM CARTER GIBSON), writer; b. Springfield, Mass., Jan. 9, 1924; d. Francis Clarence and Beatrice Grace (Tait) Gagnier; student, Bay Path Jr. Coll., 1941-42; m. Francis Charles Davis, July 18, 1942 (div. Aug. 1964); children—Beverley Tait (Mrs. William L. Clarke), Susan Olds (Mrs. Ronald Kenneth English), Maralee Ruth Dana (Mrs. Robert Chris); m. 2d, David Joel Thibault, Nov. 9, 1964 (div. Oct. 1967); m. 3d, William Carter Gibson, Jan. 21, 1970. Co-owner dairy farm, Amherst, Mass., 1951-60; with Amherst Jour., 1952-54; with WHMP Radio, Northampton, Mass., intermittently 1955-73; owner Maralee G. Davis, real estate, Amherst, 1956-58; with WHYN Radio-TV, Springfield, Mass., intermittently, 1958-60; with Greenfield (Mass.) Recorder, 1958-62; asst. editor Sportsman's News, Northampton, 1963-64; founder, co-owner, pres., treas. Amherst Employment Service, 1968-69; free lance advt. and writing, 1963—; asso. Heiser Real Estate, Northampton, 1973—. Guest poet WMUL-TV series on poets for ednl. TV, 1971; guest poet and speaker Vt. Writers Seminar, U. Vt., 1970. Treas. Hillcrest Cemetary Marker Service, Springfield, 1972—. Recipient awards for poems Nat. Fedn. Poetry Socs., 1970; citation World Poetry Soc., 1970. Mem. N.H., Ariz., W. Va. poetry socs., World Poetry Soc. Author: (under pseudonym Maralee G. Davis) Soliloquy's Virgin (poetry), 1964; The Valley of Self (poetry), 1969. Contbr. poems to various anthologies. Home: PO Box 697 Amherst MA 01002 Office: Heiser Real Estate 61 Locust St Northampton MA 01060

GIBSON, MARY FRANCES (MRS. WILLIAM C. GIBSON), educator; b. Stuttgart, Ark., Oct. 20, 1913; d. Joseph Carl and Rosamond (James) McCuskey; Asso. Edn., Cottey Coll., 1931; B.S., Ark. State Tchrs. Coll., 1949; m. William C. Gibson, June 12, 1933; 1 dau., Marilyn Jean. Tchr. pub. schs., Humphrey, Ark., 1942-45, Stuttgart, 1945-50, 54—. Mem. Nat., Ark., Arkansas County edn. assns., D.A.R. Mem. Christian Ch. Clubs: Stuttgart Country, Fine Arts (past pres.), Stuttgart Faculty (past pres.). Home: 311 W 7th St Stuttgart AR 72160

GIBSON, VICTORIA GLENNON (MRS. PHIL S. GIBSON), state ofcl.; b. Los Angeles, Mar. 23, 1923; d. Earl Gregory and Regina (Ouellet) Glennon; student Barnard Coll., 1942-43; A.B., Stanford, 1945, LL.B., 1947; m. Phil S. Gibson, Aug. 3, 1954; 1 son, Blaine Alan. Admitted to Cal. bar, 1947, practiced in San Francisco, 1947-54, Carmel, 1970—; research atty. Supreme Ct. Cal., San Francisco, 1947-54; commr. Central Coast Regional Coastal Zone Conservation Commn., Santa Cruz, Cal., 1972—. Teaching asst. Stanford Law Sch., 1962-63. Trustee Monterey Inst. Fgn. Studies, 1971-73. Mem. State Bar Cal., Phi Beta Kappa. Democrat. Home: 4130 Segundo Dr Carmel CA 93921 Office: 701 Ocean St Santa Cruz CA 95060

GIBSON, VIRGINIA NOAH (MRS. WILLIAM EVERETT GIBSON), club woman; b. Cherokee, Kan., Aug. 5, 1907; d. George Ralph and Julia (Kelly) Noah; B.S., Kan. State Coll., 1928; M.S., Kan State U., 1932; m. William Everett Gibson, Jan. 26, 1929. Instr. Am. history Kan. State U., 1940-42. Flower arrangement demonstrator, 1950—; nationally accredited amateur flower show judge, 1960—; lectr. landscape design, 1954-60; chmn. Topeka Flower Show Schs., 1964-66, Kan. state chmn., 1965—; co-chmn. Kan. State Landscape Design Study Courses, 1965—. Grey lady A.R.C., Manhattan, Kan., 1942-58; service chmn. Am. Cancer Soc., Riley County, 1973—. Dir. Kansas Hort. Soc., 1965—. Mem. Kan. Asso. Garden Clubs (pres. 1961-62), Kan. State U. Alumni Assn., Am. Assn. U. Women, Nat. Council State Garden Clubs, Inc. (regional rep. civic devel.), Riley County Hist. Soc., St. Mary's Hosp. Aux., Riley County Fish and Game Assn., Delta Zeta, Phi Delta Gamma, Pi Gamma Mu. Mem. Order Eastern Star. Clubs: Kansas Woman's Day; Town and Country Garden (dir. 1957—), Faculty and Staff Garden (pres. 1959—) (Manhattan). Home: 2216 Claflin Rd Manhattan KS 66502

GIDDENS, ZELMA KIRK (MRS. KENNETH R. GIDDENS), broadcasting co. exec.; b. Lafayette, Ala.; d. James William and Eunice (Rice) Kirk; grad. So. Union Jr. Coll., 1932; student Auburn U., 1934-35; m. Kenneth R. Giddens, May 19, 1934; children—Annsley (Mrs. Thomas H. Buce, Jr.), Therese (Mrs. Sumner Toulmin Greer), Sara Kay. With Sta. WKRG-AM, 1947-55; with Sta. WKRG-AM-FM-TV, Mobile, Ala., 1955—, pres., 1969—. Mem. English Speaking Union (v.p. 1964-69), Smithsonian Assos., Mobile Art Assn., Mobile C. of C. Lion Aux. Clubs: Nat. Press; Am. Newspaper Women's. Home: 2555 N Delwood Dr Mobile AL 36606 Office: 162 St Louis St Mobile AL 36601

GIDDINGS, RUTH ELIZABETH WARNER (MRS. JAMES LOUIS GIDDINGS), mus. curator; b. Yonkers, N.Y., June 17, 1919; d. Earle Horace and Katherine (Johnson) Warner; B.A., U. Ariz., 1941, M.A., 1945; Ph.D., Union Grad. Sch., 1974; m. James Louis Giddings, Dec. 10, 1943 (dec. Dec. 1964); children—James Louis III, Edith Ann, John Russell. Asst. Ariz. State Mus., Tucson, 1941-42, Amerind Found., 1942; archeol. research asst. Expdn. Cape Denbigh, U. Alaska, 1948, Expdn. Kobuk River, Alaska and Kotzebue Sound Area, 1960, 64-67; tchr. lower sch. Moses Brown Sch., Providence, 1964; curator Haffenreffer Mus. Anthropology, Brown U., Bristol, R.I., 1965—, dir. ednl. program, 1969—. Fellow Am. Anthrop. Assn.; mem. A.A.A.S., Soc. for Am. Archaeology, Arctic Inst. N.Am., Alaska Conservation Soc., Archeol. Inst. Am., Audubon Soc. R.I., Sigma Xi. Author: Yaqui Folklore 1942, 67. Editor: (James Louis Giddings) Ancient Men of the Arctic, 1967. Home: Mt Hope Grant Bristol RI 02809

GIDNEY, OLIVE MILBRANDT (MRS. DEAN R. GIDNEY), fashion designer; b. Dallas, May 10, 1916; d. Carl F. and Olive (Villepique) Milbrandt; student Barnard, 1937; m. Dean R. Gidney, July 28, 1941. Buyer B. Atlman & Co., N.Y.C., 1937-61; design dir. Gay Gibson, N.Y.C., 1961-70, Bobbie Brooks, N.Y.C., 1970-72; supr. fashion design Leslie Fay, Inc., N.Y.C., 1972—. Clubs: Shinnecock Hills Golf (Southampton, N.Y.); Mid-Ocean Golf (Bermuda); St. Andrew's Golf (Hastings-on-Hudson, N.Y.); Bridgehampton (N.Y.). Home: 40 Fifth Av New York City NY 10011 Office: 1400 Broadway New York City NY 10018

GIERSBACH, MARION AGNES FISK (MRS. WALTER C. GIERSBACH), educator; b. Oak Park, Ill., July 29, 1900; d. Charles Leon and Marion (Ballou) Fisk; grad. Oberlin Kindergarten Sch. and Coll., 1922; student Bush Conservatory Music and Drama (Chgo.), 1925-26, Cleve. Inst. Art, 1929-30; A.B., Pacific U., 1946; m. Walter C. Giersbach, June 28, 1927; children—Charles W., Walter F., William H. Summer play dir. Chautauquas, 1918-22; tchr. pub. schs., Youngstown, O., 1922-26; dir. City Christian Edn. Program, Gypsum, O., 1927-28; tchr. pub. sch., Cleve., 1928-30; tchr. summer confs., Ill., Ohio, Mont., Ore., 1927-53; drama coach, Modjeska Guild, O., 1929-30; researcher-cartographer Chgo. Theol. Sem., 1930-36; dir. Kindergarten Pacific U., Ore., 1943-45, tchr. dept. history, 1948; lectr. E.C. Brown Trust, Portland, Ore., 1950-52; asst. sec. wills, trusts United Ch. of Christ, N.Y.C., Phila., 1954-63; tchr., counsellor Christian edn. workshops United Ch. of Christ N.J., 1965—. Founder, Tuaiatin Plains Hist. Soc., Forest Grove, Ore., 1948-53, 1st Jr. Hist. Soc. Ore., 1951; pres. Forest Grove Congl. Womens Fellowship, 1949-51; nat. vice moderator Congl. Christian Chs., 1949-51. Bd. dirs. Central Atlantic Conf. United Ch. of Christ. Mem. N.J. Ch. Women United (county dir. 1969-71, chmn. communication 1973—), Ore. Ch. Women United (state pres. 1951-53), Cherry Hill Ch. Women United (pres. 1967-69). Contbr. articles to profl. jours. Home: 100 Saw Mill Rd Cherry Hill NJ 08034

GIES, FRANCES ELIZABETH CARNEY (MRS. JOSEPH GIES), author; b. Ann Arbor, Mich., June 10, 1915; d. Robert John and Frances Sweet (Gibson) Carney; B.A., U. Mich., 1937, M.A., 1939; m. Joseph Gies, Feb. 16, 1940; children—Charles, Jenny, Paul. Tchr. high sch. English, Caro, Mich., 1938-40; reader 20th Century-Fox, 1942-50. Mem. Am. Hist. Soc., Medieval Acad. Am., Phi Beta Kappa, Phi Kappa Phi. Author: Life in a Medieval City, 1969; Leonard of Pisa and the New Mathematics of the Middle Ages, 1970; Merchants and Moneymen, The Commercial Revolution 1000-1500, 1972; Life in a Medieval Castle, 1974. Home: 148 Kimberly Rd Barrington IL 60010

GIESKE, JUDITH PORTER (MRS. JAMES CHAPMAN GIESKE), physician; b. Montclair, N.J., May 27, 1940; d. Thomas R. and Ruth (Koll) Porter; student Wellesley Coll., 1959-61; A.B., Johns Hopkins U., 1962, M.D., 1965; m. James Chapman Gieske, July 19, 1964; children—James Wilkinson Chapman, Thomas Koll Porter, John Hardy Vannort. Intern, Mass. Gen. Hosp., Boston, 1966, resident, 1967, 70-71; pvt. practice medicine, specializing in pediatrics, Milton, Mass., 1971-73, Easton, Md., 1973—; instr. Harvard Med. Sch., 1971-73; staff Easton Meml. Hosp., 1973—. Bd. dirs. Cath. Charitable Bur. Adoption Agy., 1970-73. Radcliffe Inst. fellow. Home: Presquile RFD 1 Box 554 Easton MD 21601 Office: 210 Dover St Easton MD 21601

GIFFEN, SALLIE ANN, ednl. adminstr.; b. Warren, Pa., May 19, 1940; d. Edgar Louis and Glenna Marie (Tiedgen) Giffen; student State U. N.Y., 1958-59; B.S., U. Ala., 1962; postgrad. Loyola Coll., Balt., 1973—. Budget analyst U.S. Office Edn., Dept. Health Edn. Welfare, Washington, 1962-67, financial mgmt. asst., 1967-68; adminstrv. officer Boston U., 1968-71, asst. dean for adminstrn., 1971-72; dir. bus. services U. Md., Balt., 1972, vice chancellor adminstrv. affairs, 1972—. Recipient Superior Service award Dept. Health Edn. and Welfare, 1964. Home: 5668 Stevens Forest Rd Columbia MD 21045 Office: 5401 Wilkens Av Baltimore MD 21228

GIFFORD, MARIAN ELLIS, mus. adminstr.; b. Greencastle, Ind., Apr. 18, 1918; d. Heber Hardin and Erma Ozora (McGuffin) Ellis; A.B., De Pauw U., 1940; postgrad U. Wis., 1942, U. Lousiville, 1956; m. Samuel H. Gifford, 1946 (div. Aug. 1956); 1 dau., Wendy Blythe. Tchr. speech Robinson (Ill.) High Sch., 1941-43; program dir. WKMO radio, Kokomo, Ind., 1943; producer, broadcaster WOWO radio, Ft. Wayne, Ind., 1944-49, WHAS-TV Louisville, 1949-54; fund raiser De Pauw U., Greencastle, Ind., 1959-62, U. Detroit, 1962-64, Lehigh U., Bethlehem, Pa., 1964-67; dir. devel. Indpls. Mus. Art, 1968—. Mem. Dirs. Devel. for Art Mus. (nat. pres. 1973-74), Women in Communications, Nat. Soc. Fund Raisers, Alpha Phi (house bd. Gamma chpt. 1973). Methodist. Home: 3039 W 39th St Indianapolis IN 46208 Office: 1200 W 38th St Indianapolis IN 46208

GIFFORD, MARIE BATTEY (MRS. JOSEPH GIFFORD), radio sta. exec.; b. Cordell, Okla., Jan. 12, 1917; d. John William and Mary (Yoder) Battey; B.F.A., U. Okla., 1937; m. Joseph Gifford, Sept. 2, 1948 (dec. Dec. 1960). Account exec. Sta. KOME, Tulsa, Okla., 1941-44; instr. Baylor U. Sch. Radio, 1944-45; asst. program dir. Sta. KWKH, Shreveport, La., 1945-47; account exec. Sta. KTBS, 1947-55, sales mgr., 1955-57; sales mgr. Sta. KEEL, Inc., 1957-62, gen. mgr., 1962—, v.p., 1964-69; pres. KEEL, also KMBQ, 1969—; v.p. Lin Broadcasting, 1966—. Exec. asst. Shreveport Summer Theatre, 1954-60. Bd. dirs. Community Action Program, 1969-71, Shreveport C. of C., 1967-71. Recipient Humanitarian award Shreveport Negro C. of C., 1969; named Broadcaster of Year, La. Assn. Broadcasters, 1970. Mem. Shreveport Advt. Club pres. 1964-65), Am. Advt. Fedn. (dir. 10th dist. 1964-66), La. Assn. Broadcasters (officer), Chi Omega. Club: Ambassadors (dir. 1969-71). Home: 3818 Akard St Shreveport LA 71105 Office: 710 Spring St Shreveport LA 71120

GIFFORD, PATRICIA JANE (MRS. ROBERT ANDREW BUTSCH), lawyer; b. Indpls., Apr. 13, 1938; d. George Thomas and Jessie Mabel (Martin) Gifford; A.B., Coll. William and Mary, 1960; J.D., Ind. U., 1968; m. Robert Andrew Butsch, Mar. 24, 1973. Tchr. pub. schs., Indpls., 1960-64; admitted to Ind. bar, 1968; asso. firm Runnels & Rademacher, Indpls., 1968-69; Ind. dep. atty. gen., Indpls., 1969-70, asst. atty. gen., 1970-72; partner Moriarty & Gifford, Indpls., 1972—; dep. prosecutor Marion County, Indpls., 1972—. Sec., State House Young Republicans, 1970-71; precinct vice committeewoman, 1972-73. Mem. Am., Ind., Indpls. bar assns., D.A.R., Coll. William and Mary Alumni Soc., Ind. U. Alumni Soc., Kappa Alpha Theta. Mem. Christian Ch. (chmn. dept. Christian edn. 1972-73). Home:

7664 Ivywood Dr Indianapolis IN 46250 Office: 234 E Southern Av Indianapolis IN 46225

GIFFORD, WENDY BLYTHE, bank exec.; b. Louisville, Dec. 12, 1949; d. Samuel Haring and Marian Jane (Ellis) Gifford; B.A., De Pauw U., 1971, postgrad., 1971; postgrad. Ball State U., 1973. Pub. relations asst. Indpls. Mus. Art, 1971-72; dir. pub. information Marian Coll., Indpls., 1972-74, also lectr. journalism, 1972-73; pub. relations rep. Ind. Nat. Bank, Indpls., 1974—. Mem. Women In Communications (sec. Indpls. chpt. 1973-74), Ind. Bus. Communicators, Soc. Profl. Journalists, Sigma Delta Chi, Alpha Phi. Home: 8741 B LeMode Court Indianapolis IN 46268 Office: 1 Indiana Sq Indianapolis IN 46222

GIFFUNI, FLORA BALDINI (MRS. JOSEPH GIFFUNI), artist, ednl. adminstr., interior design co. exec.; b. Naples, Italy, Oct. 26, 1919; d. Carmelo and Anna (Mazza) Baldini; came to U.S., 1921; naturalized, 1940; B.F.A., N.Y. U., 1942, M.F.A., Columbia, 1945; postgrad U. Madrid, Spain, 1959, U. Pisa, Italy, 1960, Institute d'Allende Mex., Mexico, 1966; N.Y. Sch. Interior Design, 1959; Art Students League; m. Joseph Giffuni, June 22, 1941; children—JoAnn (Mrs. Michael Sher), Vincent, Catherine. Exhibited in one man shows Forest Hills Inn, Queens, N.Y., 1966, Pietroantonio Gallery, N.Y.C., 1969, Little Gallery, Barbizon Hotel, N.Y.C., Columbus Club, N.Y.C., 1970, Grist Mill Gallery, Chester, Vt., Art Gallery, Keene, N.H., 1973; exhibited in group shows including Lever House, Am. Artists Profl. League, N.Y.C., 1966, Nat. Acad., N.Y,C., 1970, Nat. Arts Club, N.Y.C., 1971, Nat. Art League, Douglaston, N.Y., 1972, Salmagundi Club, N.Y.C., 1973-74. Dir. Giffuni Studio, Bronx, N.Y., 1942-50 ; instr. art Immaculate Conception Sch., Jamaica Estates, N.Y., 1955-65; pres. F.B.G. Interiors, Jamaica Estates, 1959-74; pres. Flora B. Giffuni Art Sch., Jamaica Estates, 1960-74; dir. Catan Rose Sch. Art, Jamaica Estates, 1962-74, Catharine Lorillarde Wolfe Art Club, N.Y.C., 1973-75. Recipient Amita award Interior Design, Am. Italian Awards for Women Achievement, 1959, ribbon Lever House, Am. Artists Profl. League, 1966; spl. award Nat. Acad., 1970. Mem. Nat. Arts Club (award 1972), Nat. Art League (award 1971, 73), Catharine Lorillarde Wolfe Art Club, Am. Artists Profl. League, Art Students League, Nat. Soc. Interior Designers, Salmagundi Club. Address: 180-16 Dalny Rd Jamaica Estates New York NY 11432

GIGGER, HELEN COLEMAN (MRS. NATHANIEL JAY GIGGER), lawyer; b. Houston, Dec. 24, 1944; d. Samuel and Jessie Lee (Patten) Coleman; B.A., Tex. So. U., 1965, J.D., 1968; m. Nathaniel Jay Gigger, Oct. 25, 1968. Legal proctor Houston Legal Found., 1966-68; planner, program analyst Okla. City and County Community Action Program, 1968-71; admitted to Okla. bar, 1970, since practiced in Oklahoma City; legal counsel, courts planner Okla. Crime Commn., 1971—. Dir., Wayne C. Chandler & Assos., Inc. Registrar edn. task force Urban League, 1972. Mem. N.A.A.C.P. (sec. Okla. state 1971-75, regional chmn. 1973-74), J.J. Bruce Law Soc. (sec. 1973-74), Am., Okla. bar assns., Delta Sigma Theta (nat. parliamentarian 1973—). Mem. Order Eastern Star. Home: 3309 E Forest Park Dr Oklahoma City OK 73121 Office: 5235 N Lincoln St Oklahoma City OK 73105

GIKOW, RUTH, artist; b. Ukraine; d. Boris and Lena (Pohoriles) Gikow; came to U.S., 1922, naturalized, 1928; student Cooper Union Art Sch., 1932-35; m. Jack Levine, Oct. 4, 1946; 1 dau., Susanna. One-man shows Weyhe Gallery, 1946, Grand Central Moderns, 1948, 50, Ganso Gallery, 1952, 53, 54, Rehn Gallery, 1956-58, Nordness Gallery, 1961, Forum Gallery, 1967, 70, 71; group shows at Whitney Gallery, Corcoran Gallery, Washington, others; represented in permanent collections Colby Coll., Springfield Mus., Nat. Acad. Arts and Letters, Brandeis U., Whitney Mus., Met. Mus Art, Mus. Modern Art, Phila. Art Mus.; Illustrated Crime and Punishment, History of Jews in America. Grantee Nat. Inst. Arts and Letters, 1959. Author: Gikow, 1971. Address: 68 Morton St New York City NY 10014

GILB, CORINNE LATHROP, historian, social scientist; b. Lethbridge, Alta., Can., Feb. 19, 1925; d. Glen H. and Vera (Passey) Lathrop; B.A., U. Wash., 1946; M.A., U. Cal., 1951; Ph.D., Radcliffe Coll., 1957; student Alliance Francaise, San Francisco, also Paris, 1967-68, summers 1969-72; m. Tyrell T. Gilb, Aug. 18, 1945; children—Lesley, Tyra Ellen. Teaching asst. dept. history U. Cal., 1950-52, head Regional Cultural History Project, 1953-57, jr. research polit. scientist Inst. Indsl. Relations, 1956-58, asst. research polit. scientist, 1958-59; instr. humanities, dept. history and govt. Mills Coll., 1957-58, lectr. dept. history and govt., 1959-61; acting asso. prof. San Francisco State Coll., summer 1962; research asso. Center for Study of Law and Soc., U. Cal., 1962-66; lectr. San Francisco State Coll., 1964-65, prof., 1965-68; vis. prof. dept. history Wayne State U., 1968-69, prof., 1969—; spl. cons. Cal. Legislature's assembly interim com. revenue and taxation, 1963-64. Sec.-treas. Computrols, Inc. Chmn. human rights Cal. Dem. Issues Conf., 1959; pres. Berkeley Dem. Club, 1959-60; chmn. Kennedy for President campaign in Berkeley and Albany, Cal., 1960; Cal. coordinator Profs. for Johnson for Pres., 1964; bd. dirs., exec. com. Cal. chpt. Ams. for Dem. Action, 1960-63. Guggenheim fellow to France and Yugoslavia, 1967-68. Mem. Am. Polit. Sci. Assn. (world tour seminar 1963), A.A.A.S., Am. Hist. Assn., Am. Studies Assn. (pres. No. Cal. 1960-62), Internat. Assn. for Philosophy of Law and Social Philosophy, Orgn. Am. Historians, Am. Soc. for Polit. and Legal Philosophy, Phi Beta Kappa, Phi Alpha Theta, Alpha Delta Pi Club: Women's Faculty. Author: Hidden Hierarchies: The Professions and Government, 1966; also articles in field. Home: 111 El Camino Real Berkeley CA 94705

GILBERT, ALICE LEE, judge; b. Chgo., May 16, 1932; d. Alfred O. and Rebecca (Shamis) Gilbert; student Wellesley Coll., 1950-53; J.D., Northwestern U., 1956; postgrad. Nat. Coll. State Judiciary, 1969-73; children—Owen, Greg, Dean. Admitted to Mich. bar, 1957; practiced in Livonia, 1957-68; justice of the peace Bloomfield Twp., State of Mich., 1961-65; justice for city of Bloomfield Hills, Mich., 1963-65; dist. judge 48th jud. dist., State of Mich., Bloomfield Hills, 1968—. Mem. Law Enforcement and Criminal Justice Planning Council; lectr. Inst. of Continuing Legal Edn. Wayne State U., Oakland County Police Acad., Mich., 1970—; cons. on civil and polit. rights to Gov.'s Commn. on Status of Women; mem. Study of Traffic Cts. and Prosecution in Oakland County; mem. Study Com. on Jud. Definition. Mem. Bloomfield Hills Youth Guidance Com.; active No. Oakland County council Girl Scouts Am. Mem. Mich. (pres. 1969-70), Oakland County (chmn. 1970) dist. judges assns. Home: 4714 Pickering Rd Birmingham MI 48010 Office: 2709 Telegraph Rd Bloomfield Hills MI 48013

GILBERT, ALMA CARMEL MAGGIORE (MRS. RICHARD B. GILBERT), broadcasting exec.; b. Canton, O.; d. Vincent D. and Florence A. (Manack) Maggiore; grad. Mt. Marie Acad., Canton; m. Richard B. Gilbert, July 17, 1953; 1 son, Gary Richard. Dir., treas., program dir. KPOK, Scottsdale (Ariz.) Broadcasting Co., 1955-58, Ariz. Aircasters, Inc., 1955-58; dir., v.p., sec., program dir. KYND, KYND Radio Corp., Aircasters, Inc., Tempe, Ariz., 1960-66; dir., v.p., sec. KXTC, also Aircasters, Inc., Ariz. Communications Corp., (all Phoenix), 1968—. Home: Box 182 Scottsdale AZ 85252 Office: Hotel Westward Ho Phoenix AZ 85004

GILBERT, ANNE WIELAND (MRS. GEORGE GALE GILBERT III), journalist; b. Chgo., May 1, 1927; d. David and Joy (Arnold) Wieland; B.S., Northwestern U., 1949; m. George Gale Gilbert III, Apr. 7, 1953; children—Douglas, Christopher. Columnist, Chgo. Daily News, 1971—, also syndicated in N.Y. News, 1973—, San Francisco Chronicle, 1973—. Reporter NBC-TV Sunday in Chgo., 1973; guest expert NBC-TV, N.Y.C. Today, 1974—; producer WSNS-TV spl. Collectors World, 1971; free lance writer; pub. relations cons. Chgo. Community Music Found. 1968-73. Mem. Chgo. Press Club, Alpha Gamma Delta. Presbyterian. Author: Antique Hunters Guide: For Freaks and Fanciers, 1974. Address: 932-15th St Wilmette IL 60091

GILBERT, CAROL JEANNE, theatre mgr.; b. Camden, N.J., Feb. 13, 1943; d. Ross Oswald and Jeanne Marie Gilbert (Porr) Fuller; B.S., Millersville (Pa.) State Coll., 1965; postgrad. Temple U. Tchr. English and drama Woodrow Wilson High Sch., Levittown, Pa., 1965-68; dir. pub. relations Theatre-in-the-Park, Trenton, N.J., summers 1967-69; tchr. English and drama Penn Manor High Sch., Millersville, 1968-69; mem. staff Bucks County Theatre Co., Bucks County Playhouse, New Hope, Pa., 1969—, asst. mng. dir., dir. ednl. projects, sec.-treas., 1972—. Mem. New Hope C. of C. Home: PO Box 302 Street Rd Lahaska PA 18931 Office: PO Box 223 S Main St New Hope PA 18938

GILBERT, EDITH PORTER (MRS. JACK HITE GILBERT), contract writer; b. Glen Carlyn, Va.; d. Herbert W. and Augusta (Brindley) Porter; B.A., U. Wis.; m. Jack Hite Gilbert, Feb. 12, 1955. Newspaper reporter Milw. Jour., Burlington (Wis.) Standard, 1930-31; govt. information specialist FHA and Housing and Home Finance Agy., Washington, 1938-59, 62-65, acting dep. adminstr. Housing and Home Finance Agy., 1960-61; spl. asst. to sec. Housing and Urban Devel., Washington, 1965-73. Sec., Georgetown Citizens Assn., 1955-61, v.p., 1962-63, treas., 1964-66. Mem. Womens Nat. Press Club (treas. 1954-55), Am. Newspaper Womens Club (dir. 1964-65, 69-71, gov. 1974—), Sigma Kappa. Episcopalian. Contbr. articles to profl. jours. Home: 3336 O St NW Washington DC 20007 Office: 451 7th St SW Washington DC 20410

GILBERT, HARRIET SMITH (MRS. PAUL LAWRENCE GILBERT), physician; b. Phila., June 22, 1930; d. Joseph Lewis and Jeanne Sylvia (Orkin) Smith; A.B., Bryn Mawr Coll., 1951; M.D., Columbia U., 1955; m. Paul Lawrence Gilbert, Jan. 3, 1957; children—Laura Ellen, David Scott, Daniel Mark. Intern, Mt. Sinai Hosp., N.Y.C., 1955-56, asst. resident internal medicine, 1956-58, research asst., 1961-63, research asso., 1963-64, asst. prof. medicine Mt. Sinai Sch. Medicine, 1966-69, asso. prof. medicine, 1969—; mem. staff Mt. Sinai Hosp., N.Y.C.; consulting hematologist Elmhurst (N.Y.) Hosp., 1964—; attending hematologist VA Hosp., Bronx, N.Y., 1971-73, cons. hematologist, 1973—. Bd. dirs. Research Found. City Univ. N.Y., 1971—. Am. Cancer Soc. grantee, 1965—. Diplomate Nat. Bd. Med. Examiners, Am. Bd. Internal Medicine. Fellow A.C.P.; mem. Am. Soc. Hematology, Harvey Soc., Am. Fedn. Clinical Research, Biophys. Soc. Home: 685 West End Av New York City NY 10025 Office: 19 E 98th St New York City NY 10029

GILBERT, JUDITH ARLENE, lawyer; b. Los Angeles, Jan. 9, 1946; d. Beril B. and Dorothy Marilyn (Stern) Gilbert; student U. Cal. at Berkeley, 1963-64; B.A., U. Cal. at Los Angeles, 1967; J.D., Harvard, 1970. Admitted to Cal. bar, 1971; practiced in Los Angeles; asso., firm Rosenfeld, Myer & Susman, 1970-72, Quittner, Stutman, Treister & Glatt, Los Angeles, 1973—. Mem. Los Angeles County Com. Human Resources. Active Girl Scouts Am., Cystic Fibrosis, City of Hope. Mem. Beverly Hills Law Wives, Women Lawyers Assn., Lawyers Club Los Angeles, Cal., Los Angeles bar assns., Am. Arbitration Assn. Thespians, Collegian Singers, Brick Muller Soc., Internat. Law Club (social co-chmn. 19—), Phi Beta Kappa, Gamma Delta Epsilon, Pi Gamma Mu, Omega Delta Epsilon, Tower and Flame, Phi Chi, Delta Phi Epsilon. Clubs: Sutherland (sec.-treas. 19—). Home: 320 S Clark Dr #308 Los Angeles CA 90048 Office: Ahmanson Center E Penthouse 3701 Wilshire Blvd Los Angeles CA 90010

GILBERT, LELA SIEBERT (MRS. ARNOLD R. GILBERT), lawyer, real estate broker; b. Goessel, Kan., Apr. 3, 1916; d. Wesley and Matilda Anna (Woerz) Siebert; A.B., U. Kan., 1938, J.D., 1942, M.A. in Polit. Sci., 1946; postgrad polit. sci. U. Colo., 1964-68; m. Arnold R. Gilbert, Mar., 1942; 1 dau., Nancy Ann (Mrs. Stuart A. Ring). Admitted to Kan. bar, 1942, Mo. bar, 1943, Colo. bar, 1944; atty. solicitor's office Dept. Agr., Kansas City, Mo., 1942-43; real estate broker, Denver, 1944-47; landman Cal. Co., Denver, 1947-48; atty., office mgr. Scott & Scott, oil brokers, Denver, 1948-51; partner Gilbert & Gilbert, Denver, 1951—. Mem. Colo. Ho. of Reps., 1957-63; instr. polit. sci. U. Colo., Boulder, 1965-66; instr. bus. law Met. State Coll., Denver, 1968-69. Mem. Colo. Apt. Owners Assn., 1972—, WE CARE, 1972—, pres. Am. Legion Aux., 1968-69. Bd. dirs. Rocky Mountain Kidney Found. Mem. Colo., Denver bar assns., Am. Bus. Womens Assn. (chpt. pres. 1968-69), Zonta Internat., Lakewood Bus. and Profl. Womens Club, Bus. and Profl. Womens Club Denver (pres. 1967-68), Lakewood C. of C., Phi Beta Kappa, Pi Sigma Alpha, Pi Lambda Theta. Club: Lincoln of Colorado (pres. 1972-73). Home: 12693 W Alabama Way Lakewood CO 80228 Office: 10600 W Alameda Av Lakewood CO 80226

GILBERT, MARGARET SHEA (MRS. W. PAUL GILBERT), biologist, educator; b. Canton, O., Feb. 25, 1908; d. Mortimer J. and Louisa (Schneider) Shea; B.A., Oberlin Coll.; M.A., Wellesley Coll.; Ph.D., Cornell U.; m. W. Paul Gilbert, June 22, 1932; children—Joan (Mrs. Jerry Domer), Judith (Mrs. Joseph Blazek), Margaret. Prof. biology Lawrence U., Appleton, Wis., 1946-66, Hawaii Loa Coll., Honolulu, 1966; now prof. ocular anatomy Coll. Optometry, Pacific U., Forest Grove, Ore. Recipient Edward Uhrig award for excellence in teaching. Mem. Am. Assn. Anatomists, Teratology Soc., Am. Inst. Biol. Scis., League Women Voters (past treas., pres., dir. Appleton), Phi Beta Kappa, Sigma Xi, Phi Kappa Phi. Author: Biography of the Unborn, 1939, rev. edit., 1963; Synopsis of Scientific Terminology for Optometrists, 1970. Home: 2605 15th Av Forest Grove OR 97116 Office: Coll Optometry Pacific U Forest Grove OR 97116

GILBERT, MARY ELLIN (MRS. NEVIN ERNST GILBERT), hotel exec., educator; b. Windber, Pa., July 24, 1930; d. Thomas Leo and Elizabeth Jean (Walsh) Guiney; B.S. in Art Edn., Pa. State U., 1972; m. Nevin Ernst Gilbert, Apr. 24, 1950; children—Glen, Gretchen, Amy. Co-owner Bedford Beverage Co. (Pa.), 1961-65; co-owner Hillcrest Inn, Bedford, 1965—; art instr. Hollidaysburg (Pa.) Jr. High Sch., 1973—; art instr. night classes Bedford Heritage Commn., 1973—. Mem. Young Republican Exec. Bd., Cambria County, Pa., 1957-58; committeewoman Richland Twp., Cambria County, 1957-59. Mem. Allied Artists of Johnstown, U.S. Trotting Assn. Address: RD 2 Bedford PA 15522

GILBERT, MARY PORTER JORDAN, coll. adminstr.; b. New Haven; d. William Amos and Marion (Porter) Jordan; A.B., Vassar Coll., 1945; A.M., Wesleyan U., Middletown, Conn., 1947; m. N. Charlton Gilbert, June 7, 1947 (div. Jan. 1957); 1 son, Charlton H. Tchr., Porter Sch., Tucson, 1946-47; tchr. Prospect Hill Sch., New Haven, 1948-50; staff Elmo Roper & Assos., N.Y.C., 1958-59; adminstrv. dir. Office Pub. Relations, Vassar Coll., Poughkeepsie, N.Y., 1959—. Rep., Town Meeting, Hamden, Conn., 1953-55. Bd. dirs. Jr. League New Haven, 1953-57. Mem. Am. Coll. Pub. Relations Assn., Jr. League Poughkeepsie. Club: Vassar. Home: Vassar Garden Apts Poughkeepsie NY 12603

GILBERT, MILDRED MAXINE, home economist; b. nr. Wadley, Ala., Jan. 5, 1921; d. Marvin Wilson and Grace Leona (Kewley) Gilbert; B.S., Auburn U., 1944, M.S., 1964. Asst. home demonstration agt. Butler County (Ala.), 1944-46, Washington County (Ala.), 1946-47, Jackson County (Ala.), 1947-49; home demonstration agt. Blount County (Ala.), 1949-64, asso. county extension chmn., 1964—. Vice pres. United Way, 1974—; pres. Blount County Needy Sch. Children's Assn., 1973—. Recipient Distinguished Service award Nat. Assn. Extension Home Economists, 1963. Mem. Phi Kappa Phi, Omicron Nu. Club: Oneonta Bus. and Profl. Women's (pres. 1969-72). Home: 616 2d Av W Oneonta AL 35121 Office: PO 2d Av Oneonta AL 35121

GILBERT, MIRIAM (MRS. ABE PRESBERG), literary agt.; b. N.Y.C., Dec. 1, 1919; d. Charles and Kate (Kinstler) Goldstein; B.A., Hunter Coll., 1940; m. Abe Presberg, June 18, 1944; children—Karen Laurie, Andrea Claire. Sec. sales dept. Robert M. McBride Co., 1941-43; mng. editor Didier Pub. Co., 1943-45; publicity dir. Arco Pub. Co., 1945-46; mng. dir. Island Press, 1946-48; dir. Authors and Pubs. Service, 1949—; copy editor Coronet mag., 1973. Recipient Brotherhood award Nat. Conf. Christians and Jews, 1962. Author: I Wish I Were A Giraffe, 1945; Eli Whitney: Master Craftsman, 1956; Jane Addams, World Neighbor, 1960; Henry Ford, 1962; The Prophet Isaiah, 1963; Money and Mud, 1964; Shy Girl: The Story of Eleanor Roosevelt, 1965; First Party, 1966; Glory Be, 1967; Rosie, The Oldest Horse in St. Augustine, 1967; This is My Country, 1968; Care and Development of Your Baby, 1969; A Doctor Discusses Breast Feeding, 1970; Roundup of Horses, 1973; also articles and short stories in various U.S. and fgn. mags. Address: 146-47 29th Av Flushing NY 11354

GILBERTSEN, DOROTHY AGNES BUELL (MRS. CECIL REINHART GILBERTSEN), coll. dean; b. Lake Geneva, Wis.; d. Ralph Arthur and Tena (Knudsen) Buell; B.A., Beloit Coll., 1934; m. Cecil Reinhart Gilbertsen, Aug. 6, 1938; children—James, Alice (Mrs. Robert Pearson Stone), Richard. Tchr. English and Latin, Randolph (Wis.) High Sch., 1934-36; tchr. English Columbus (Wis.) High Sch., 1937; tchr. English and Latin, Janesville (Wis.) High Sch., 1938; dean women Beloit (Wis.) Coll. 1965—. Mem. Bd. Edn., Janesville, 1949-68, pres., 1952, 67. Named Mem. of the Year Wis. Sch. Bd., 1966. Mem. Nat. Assn. Women Deans and Counselors, Am. Assn. U. Women (2d v.p. Wis. div. 1963-65), Phi Beta Kappa, Mortar Bd. Home: 1016 E Milwaukee St Janesville WI 53545 Office: Beloit Coll Beloit WI 53511

GILBERTSON, EVA LABELLE, physician; b. Maddock, N.D., Dec. 23, 1916; d. Henry and Anna (Brandrud) Gilbertson; B.A., U. N.D., 1939; M.D., Temple U., 1941; M.S., U. Minn., 1945. Intern Emanuel Hosp., Portland, Ore., 1941-42; resident, fellow in radiology Mayo Clinic, Rochester, Minn., 1942-46; radiologist Portland (Ore.) Clinic, 1946-49; practice medicine, specializing in radiology, Seattle, 1949—; mem. staff Children's Orthopedic Hosp.; clin. asst. prof. radiology U. Wash., 1951—. Mem. A.M.A., Radiol. Soc. N. Am., Am. Roentgen Ray Soc., Wash. State Radiol. Soc. (pres. 1960-61). Home: 3243 Cascadia Av S Seattle WA 98144 Office: 706 Summit Av Seattle WA 98104

GILBERTSON, VELMA ANNETTA KINGMAN (MRS. HOWARD BURTON GILBERTSON), bus. exec.; b. Rialto, Cal., Oct. 9, 1907; d. Harry Clark and Minnie Annetta (Gaultney) Kingman; student San Bernardino Bus. Coll., 1925-26; m. Thomas C. Bowles, Oct. 25, 1936 (div. Oct. 1952); m. Howard Burton Gilbertson, June 5, 1954;children—Pamela Elaine Bowles, Caron Sue. Pres. Monticello Hotels, Beverly Hills, Cal., 1960—; v.p. Manhattan Homes, Inc., Beverly Hills, Cal., 1952—. Pres. Hope Guild, Inc., 1954. Clubs: Balboa Bay Newport Beach, Cal. Home: 13622 Rushmore Lane Santa Ana CA 92705 Office: 130 S Robertson Blvd Beverly Hills CA 90211 also PO Box 825 Tustin CA 92680

GILBERTSON, VIRGINIA MABRY (MRS. WALLACE CORNELL GILBERTSON), piano tchr.; b. Memphis, Dec. 2, 1914; d. Edgar Duval and Ina (Woods) Mabry; student Memphis State U., 1932-34; B.M., De Shazo Coll. Music, 1936; studied with Edwin Hughes, N.Y.C., 1944-64; m. Wallace Cornell Gilbertson, Apr. 21, 1935;children—Jon Wallace, Virginia Mabry, Cynthia Anne. Asso. tchr. De Shazo Coll. Music, Memphis, 1936-41; pvt. piano tchr., Wilmington, N.C., 1941-42, Charlotte, N.C., 1942-49, Fremont, O., 1949-57, New Canaan, Conn., 1957-60, Kinnelon, N.J., 1960-72; dir. music Charlotte Country Day Sch., 1944-46; accompanist Silvermine Guild Artists, New Canaan, Conn., 1957-60, New Canaan Town Players, 1957-60, Westport (Conn.) Community Theatre, 1958-63, Westport Madrigal Singers, 1958-59. Bd. dirs. Smoke Rise Players, 1970, Friends of the Library, Edgecombe County, 1973-74. Recipient 1st prize Tenn. contest Nat. Fedn. Music Clubs, 1930. Mem. A.S.C.A.P., Am. Guild Authors and Composers, Edgecombe County Hist. Soc. (sec.) Internat. Platform Assn., D.A.R., Pi Mu. Club: Women of Smoke Rise (Kinnelon). Club: Magazine. Composer, co-author Next to Heaven, 1960; One Bronze Fealther (for N.J. tricentennial), 1964; several songs, 1955-65. Home and office: Tarboro NC 27886 also 587 Kent Brook Terr Smoke Rise Kinnelon NJ 07405

GILCHRIST, AGNES ADDISON, archtl. historian; b. Phila., Dec. 25, 1907; d. William Henry F. and Eleanor (Adams) Addison; A.B., Wellesley Coll., 1930; M.A., U. Pa., 1933, Ph.D., 1938; Carnegie scholar, Brevet d'art de la Sorbonne, Paris, 1934; certificate Courtauld Inst., London, 1936; m. John Mason Gilchrist, Sept. 26, 1942;children—John Addison, James Huntington. Instr. Tex. State Coll. for Women, Denton, 1931-32; instr. history U. Pa., 1934-36, fine arts, 1934-41; adj. prof. Randolph-Macon Coll., 1941-42; lectr. N.Y.U., 1948-49; archtl. historian div. design and constrn., Nat. Park Service, Phila., 1957-58; archtl. research Sleepy Hollow Restorations, Tarrytown, N.Y., 1959-60, N.Y.C. Landmarks Preservation Commn., 1962-64; mem. Archtl. Rev. Bd., Mt. Vernon, N.Y., 1961—; researcher Nat. Portrait Gallery, 1966-67. Recipient Carnegie scholarship Fogg Mus., Harvard, summers 1935, 40, Brunner fellowship N.Y. chpt. A.I.A., 1955, grant Am. Council Learned Socs., 1967. Mem. Soc. Archtl. Historians (pres. 1954), Landmark and Hist. Soc. Mt. Vernon (pres. 1964-66), Municipal Art Soc. (dir. 1951-58), Art Alliance of Phila., Mus. Modern Art, Coll. Art Assn., Am. Assn. U. Women. Author: Romanticism and the Gothic Revival, 1938; Portraits in the University of Pennsylvania, 1940; William Strickland, 1950. Home: 286 E Sidney Av Mount Vernon NY 10553

GILCHRIST, ELIZABETH BRENDA, editor; b. Coulsdon, Surrey, Eng. (parents Am. citizens); d. Huntington and Elizabeth (Brace) Gilchrist; B.A., Smith Coll. Asst. Durlacher Bros. Art Gallery, N.Y.C., 1954-57; art adminstrn. asst. Brussels World's Fair, Belgium, 1957-58; fund raiser Mus. Modern Art, N.Y.C., 1959-62; reporter Show Mag., N.Y.C., 1962-64; staff writer Am. Heritage Pub. Co., N.Y.C., 1964; sr. editor Praeger Pubs., N.Y.C., 1965—. Bd. dirs. Drawing Soc., mem. exec. com., 1960—. Mem. Soc. Archtl. Historians, Coll. Art Assn., Am. Assn. Museums, Victorian Soc. in

Am. Club: Deer Isle Yacht. Translator: Marc Chagall: The Ceiling of the Paris Opera (Jacques Lassaigne), 1966. Home: 175 W 93rd St New York City NY 10025 Office: 111 Fourth Av New York City NY 10003

GILCHRIST, MARTHA JEAN SCOTT (MRS. GEORGE EDWARD GILCHRIST), librarian; b. Indpls., Jan. 12, 1912; d. Robert Harvey and Bessie (Masten) Scott; student Butler U., 1931-35, Columbia, summer 1944; m. George Edward Gilchrist, May 30, 1937; 1 son, George Scott. Clerical asst. catalog dept. Indpls. Pub. Library, 1927-37; clerical asst. Joint Reference Library, Pub. Adminstrn. Service, Chgo., 1938-43, cataloger, reference asst., 1945-63, librarian, 1963-67, asso. librarian, 1967-74, acting librarian, 1974—; asst. order dept. Post Library, Ft. Monmouth, N.J., 1944. Mem. Spl. Libraries Assn., Alpha Chi Omega. Editor: (with Marianne Yates) Administrative Reorganization of State Governments, 1948. Home: 5842 Harper Av Chicago IL 60637 Office: 1313 E 60th St Chicago IL 60637

GILDEA, SISTER MARIANNA, educator; b. Luzerne, Pa., May 22, 1907; d. David Bernard and Anna B. (Gilboy) Gildea; A.B., Coll. Misericordia, 1928; M.A., Catholic U. Am., 1940, Ph.D., 1943; post-doctoral Western Res. French House, summer 1949, Regina Mundi Inst. Sacred Studies, Rome, Italy, 1956. Tchr., Luzerne High Sch., 1928-30, Sacred Heart High Sch., Plains, Pa., 1933-34; instr. Latin, Coll. Misericordia, Dallas, Pa., 1934-39, prof., 1943—, dean, 1957-67, dir. grad. studies, 1967—; regional coordinator Sisters of Mercy, 1969-71; asst. provincial adminstr. Sisters of Mercy, 1971-73; dir. placement Coll. of Misericordia, 1973—. Instr. Cath. U. Am., Cath. Sisters Coll., Washington, 1942-43; dir. Cath. Action Radio Program, 1952-53. Mem. Pa. Adv. Com. Undergrad. Tchr. Edn.; gen. adv. bd. Religious Sisters of Mercy of Union. Recipient Amita award, 1966. Mem. Modern Lang. Assn., Am. Assn. French Tchrs., Am. Assn. German Tchrs., Am. Assn. Italian Tchrs., Internat. Platform Assn. Author: Expressions of Religious Thought and Feeling in Chansons de Geste, 1943; Living the Little Office, 1955. Home and office: College Misericordia Dallas PA 18612

GILES, MARTHA ANN MARTIN (MRS. TED ANDREW GILES), librarian; b. Birmingham, Ala., Nov. 27, 1927; d. Philip Dodd and Julia Massey (Nelson) Martin; A.B., Ala. Coll., 1948; M.A., Emory U., 1949; m. Ted Andrew Giles, Dec. 22, 1949; children—Deborah Joan, Andrea Dorian. Reference librarian Atlanta Pub. Library, 1950-52, 63-67; asst. librarian Kennesaw Jr. Coll., Marietta, Ga., 1967-73, acting head librarian, 1969-70, 71-72, asso. librarian, 1973—. Mem. Southeastern, Ga. (mem. membership com.) library assns. Presbyn. (deacon). Home: 250 Alpine Dr Roswell GA 30075 Office: Kennesaw Jr Coll Marietta GA 30061

GILES, ROSALIND, social worker, state ofcl.; b. Chrisney, Ind., Aug. 2, 1910; d. Henry C. and Mayme (Miller) Giles; A.B., So. Meth. U., 1933; postgrad. Tulane Sch. Social Work, 1934-35, Sch. Social Service Adminstrn., U. Chgo., 1944-45. Caseworker, Tex. Relief Commn., 1933-36; with child welfare div. Tex. Dept. Pub. Welfare, 1936-68, successively caseworker, unit supr., regional supr., asst. dir., 1936-48, dir., 1948-68, regional adminstr. Dallas met. area, 1968—. Mem. Citizens Planning Commn., Austin, Tex.; mem. welfare com. task force Goals for Dallas; chmn. supportive services sub-com. Manpower Planning Com. N. Central Tex. Council Govt. Mem. Child Welfare League Am. (chmn. S.W. regional conf. 1952), Nat. Assn. Social Workers, Tex. Social Welfare Assn., Am. Pub. Welfare Assn. (chmn. state dirs. programs for children and youth 1966-67), Family Service Assn., Phi Mu. Club: Altrusa (pres. 1957). Home: 6856 Gaston Av Dallas TX 75214 Office: Old County Courthouse Dallas TX 75202

GILFORD, DOROTHY MORROW, govt. ofcl.; b. Ottumwa, Ia., Feb. 19, 1919; d. Frank Bliss and Mabel Irene (Coate) Morrow; B.S. in Math. magna cum laude, U. Wash., 1940, M.S. in Math., 1942; grad. student Bryn Mawr Coll., also Columbia; m. Leon Gilford, Mar. 31, 1950. Teaching fellow U. Wash., 1940-42; instr. math. Seattle Coll., 1942; lectr. statistics Bryn Mawr Coll., 1944-45; asst. prof. math. George Washington U., 1945-48, lectr., 1948-50; biometrician CAA, 1948-51; sampling expert FTC, 1951-55; head math. statistics br. Office Naval Research, 1955-58, head logistics and math. statistics br., 1959-61, dir. math. sci. div., 1962-71; asst. commr. Nat. Center Edn. Statistics, 1971—. Mem. adv. panel math. scis. NSF, 1958-59; mem. Presdl. Study Group Careers for Women, 1966—. Recipient Fed. Woman's award, 1965. Fellow A.A.A.S., Am. Math. Soc., Inst. Math. Statistics (rep. conf. bd. math. socs. 1963—, program sec. 1960-65), Am. Statis. Assn. (dir. 1961-63), Royal Statis. Soc.; mem. Inst. Mgmt. Scis., Internat. Statis. Inst. Editor: Naval Research Logistics Quar., 1959—; (with Scarf and Shelley) Multistage Inventory Models and Techniques, 1963; Monograph Series on Mathematical Methods in Logistics, 1963—; (with others) Research Program Effectiveness, 1966. Home: 6602 Rivercrest Ct NW Washington DC 20016

GILHULY, KATHLEEN BLACKBURN (MRS. EUGENE F. X. GILHULY), designer, ret. educator; b. N.Y.C.; d. Richard and Catherine (Davis) Blackburn; student N.Y. U., 1931-32; m. Eugene F.X. Gilhuly, Apr. 1, 1933. Buyer, Macy's 1930-37, Lord & Taylor, 1937-39; designer-owner Wedding Shop, 1939-42; buyer Arnold Constable, 1942-43, Milgrim's, 1943, Macy's, 1943-51; instr. Barmore Sch., 1951-53; designer-owner Lori Veils, Ltd., N.Y.C., 1951-57; editor Bridal Wear Mag. and News Digest, N.Y.C., 1959-60; design instr. Bennett Coll., Millbrook, N.Y., 1962-66, asst. prof., 1967-69, asso. prof., 1970-72, prof. emeritus, 1972—. Mem. nat. adv. bd. Bride's Mag. and Modern Bride Mag., 1944-48; cons. Bachrach, photographer, 1945-46; cons. Ziff-Davis Pub. Co., 1947-48; free lance writer Hearst, radio, NBC, CBS; organizer, condr. lecture series Sch. For Brides, N.Y. Town Hall, 1942, Bennett Coll. European Summer Fashion Seminar, 1967, 70. Organist, choir master, dir. Cath. Youth Orgn., Bangall, 1954-67; pres. Am. Legion Aux., 1955; v.p. Home Bur., 1956; master Stanford Grange 808, 1961. Vice pres. Dutchess County Womens Democratic Club, 1959-60. Recipient Youth Service award N.Y. Diocesan Cath. Youth Orgn., 1960, Community Service award Stanford Lions Club, 1961. Mem. Am. Assn. U. Profs., Fashion Group N.Y. Home: Creamery Rd Stanfordville NY 12581

GILKEY, JANE, occupational therapist; b. Kansas City, Mo., Jan. 17, 1932; d. Harry Melvin and Jane (Swofford) Gilkey; B.S. in Occupational Therapy, Washington U., St. Louis, 1955. Dir. occupational therapy Crippled Children's Nursery Sch., Kansas City, Mo., 1956-61, Children's Cardiac Center, Kansas City, 1961-63; dir. occupational therapy pediatric sect. Menorah Med. Center, Kansas City, 1961-63, dir. pediatric occupational therapy, 1966-67; mem. staff Wednesday mag., Kansas City, Mo., 1962-63; soc. editor The Beirut (Lebanon), 1963-64, Daily News, Beirut, 1964-66; dir. occupational therapy Warrensburg (Mo.) Nursing and Med. Center, 1967-68, cons., 1970—; organizer, dir. homebound program for handicapped, Easter Seal homecraft shop Easter Seal Soc., Kansas City, 1967-68; dir. family ednl. program Cath. Social Center for Island of St. Croix, U.S. V.I. Antipoverty Program, 1968-69; organizer occupational therapy program Masonic Home of Mo., St. Louis, 1970; dir. phys. disabilities St. Marys Hosp., Kansas City, 1970—, dir. occupational therapy, 1974—. Founder, Jr. Women's Philharmonic Assn., Kansas City, 1960. Mem. Am., Kan. occupational therapy assns., Nat. League Am. Pen Women, Kappa Epsilon Alpha. Home: 5000 Oak St Apt 1104N Kansas City MO 64112 Office: St Mary's Hosp 101 Memorial Dr Kansas City MO 64108

GILKEY, MARGARET JANE, educator; b. Indiana, Pa.; d. Thomas Enright and Margaret (Brinkman) Gilkey; B.A., diploma in art, Fla. So. Coll.; M.Ed., Pa. State U., 1949; postgrad. Duke, 1938, Applachian State Tchrs. Coll., 1944, U. Miami, 1950-53. Elementary tchr., head social studies dept. Lakeland (Fla.) pub. schs., 1935-39; head guidance program Miami Beach (Fla.) High Sch., 1940-53; art tchr. Shenandoah Jr. High Sch., Miami, 1939-40; dir. guidance services Dade County (Fla.) pub. schs., 1953-69, dir. pupil personnel services, 1969-71; instr. adult div. U. Miami, 1954—. Bd. dirs. Welfare Planning Council, Dade County, 1958-61, Family and Children's Services of Dade County, 1970—, Jr. Achievement; ednl. com. Mental Health Soc. Miami, 1953—; exec. com. Family and Child Care Div. of Welfare Planning Council Dade County, 1953-60; bd. dirs. Nurses' Tng. Program of Jackson Meml. Hosp., 1959—, Children's Center, 1964-68; exec. bd. Dade County Com. Children and Youth, 1962-65, Crippled Children's Soc., 1971—; mem. Nat. Merit Scholarship Adv. Council, 1961-65; panel on guidance Coll. Entrance Exam. Bd., 1963-66; mem. Coll. Entrance Exam. Bd. Scholarship Assembly, 1969-71, com. on exams., 1969-73, trustee bd., 1970-74; mem. panel on counseling and selection Manpower Devel. and Tng. Adv. Com., 1964-67; mem. Def. Adv. Com. on Women in the Services, 1961-63, chmn., 1963; mem. 3d Army Adv. Council, 1959-68; mem. S.E. regional manpower adv. Council Dept. Labor, 1965-67. Recipient Outstanding Woman Educator of Dade County award Miami Daily News, 1958, Headliner award Theta Sigma Phi, 1959; award of merit to edn. Alpha Chi Omega, 1962; Outstanding service award Fla. Assn. Deans and Counselors, 1963, Distinguished Service award Am. Osteo. Assn. Aux., 1963; Alumni Distinguished Service award Fla. So. Coll., 1969. Mem. Nat. Vocational Guidance Assn. (trustee 1957-58), Am. Personnel and Guidance Assn. (state membership chmn. 1956-62), Nat., Fla. (pres. 1958-59) assns. deans and counselors, N.E.A., Fla. Edn. Assn., Am. Sch. Counselors Assn., Assn. Counselors, Educators and Suprs., Nat. Council on Measurements in Edn., Assn. Supervision and Curriculum Devel. Assn. Measurement and Evaluation in Guidance, Am. Vocational Assn., Fla. Ednl. Research Assn., P.E.O., Delta Kappa Gamma (founder Fla. chpt., recipient Achievement award 1971), Alpha Chi Omega. Methodist (mem. adminstrv. bd. 1962—). Editorial bd. Am. Personnel and Guidance Assn. Jour., 1967-70. Home: 919 Tendilla Av Coral Gables FL 33134

GILL, BETTY BAINBRIDGE (MRS. JOSEPH MAX GILL), county ofcl.; b. Farmington, W.Va., Jan. 10, 1921; d. William Wayne and Nelle Grant (Jones) Bainbridge; student W.Va. Bus. Coll., 1938; m. Joseph Max Gill, Sept. 27, 1950. Chief office sec. Ray's Jewelry Co., Fairmont, W.Va., 1939-53; mgr. Central Small Loan Exchange, Fairmont, 1953-73; county commr., Fairmont, 1973—. Sec., 1st v.p. YWCA, Fairmont, 1954-57; active Co-op Shop for Mental Retarded, Fairmont, 1973—, Marion County Sr. Citizens Center, Fairmont, 1973—, Marion County Bd. Health, Fairmont, 1973—; mem. W.Va. Drug Abuse Adv. Council, 1973—; mem. Marion County Planning Commn. Pres. W.Va. Fedn. Dem. Women, 1968-71; treas. Nat. Fedn. Dem. Women, 1972—. Mem. V.F.W. Aux., League Women Voters. Moose. Club: Quota of Fairmont. Home: 1150 Avalon Rd Fairmont WV 26554 Office: Marion County Ct House Adams St Fairmont WV 26554

GILL, ELEANOR MARGARET KEATING, ednl. adminstr.; b. Waltham, Mass., Oct. 6, 1914; d. John Paul and Margaret Josephine (Power) Keating; B.A., Brown U., 1935; M.N., Yale, 1938; M.S., Boston U., 1960; div.; children—Marcia Mason, Timothy, Deborah (Mrs. Martin Sequeros). Instr., Sch. Nursing, Yale, 1938-42; instr., then asst. prof. Boston U., 1952-64; adminstrv. supr. Boston U. Med. Center, 1964-67; dean Sch. Nursing, U. Conn. at Storrs, 1967—; cons. dept. nursing Coll. V.I. Pres., League of Women Voters, Westwood, Mass., 1954-56. Mem. Am. Nurses Assn., Conn. Nurses Assn. (mem. edn. com. 1968-71, chmn. 1971—), Nat. League for Nursing, Am. Assn. Deans Colls. Nursing. Home: Nutmeg Village Talcottville Rd Vernon CT 06066

GILL, EVELYN EILEEN MURPHY, city ofcl.; b. Cherryvale, Kan., Feb. 4, 1921; d. George M. and Olive T. (Spencer) Murphy; grad. high sch.; m. Richard L. Gill, Mar. 10, 1942 (dec. 1971); children—James H., Mary (Mrs. W.O. King, Jr.), Troy B. Asst. bookkeeper Consol. Motors, Inc., Phoenix, 1942-43; bookkeeper Artesia Pharmacy (N.M.), 1955-57; teller Artesia Savs. and Loan Assn., 1957-59; loan clk. Currier Abstract Co., Artesia, 1959-62; sec., treas. Merm's Constrn., Inc., Artesia, 1965-68; mgr., dir. pub. housing FHA, Artesia, 1968—. Pres., Hermosa P.T.A., 1957-58; sec. Bulldog Parents and Boosters, 1960-61. Mem. Artesia Desk and Derrick Club (pres. 1967), Women's Soc. Christian Service. Methodist. Women of Moose (recorder Artesia 1970-71). Home: 816 Mann Av Artesia NM 88210 Office: PO Box 1326 Artesia NM 88210

GILL, GLENDA FRANCES MCNIELL (MRS. FRANK BENINGTON GILL), pediatric hematologist; b. Memphis, Apr. 2, 1939; d. James Franklin and Theresa Bernice (Sewell) McNiell; B.S. with honors, U. Chgo., 1961, M.D. with honors, 1965; M.P.H., U. Mich., 1967; m. Frank Bennington Gill, June 19, 1965. Pediatric intern U. Mich., 1965-66, pediatric resident, 1968-69; fellow in pediatric hematology Cardeza Found., Jefferson U., Phila., 1970-72, research fellow in pediatrics, 1970-72; instr. pediatrics U. Pa., Phila., 1972-73, asst. prof., 1973—; asst. physician Children's Hosp. Phila., 1972—. Diplomate Am. Bd. Pediatrics. Mem. Sigma Xi, Alpha Omega Alpha, Delta Omega. Home: 108 Lee Circle Bryn Mawr PA 19010 Office: 1740 Bainbridge Philadelphia PA 19047

GILL, JOCELYN RUTH, astronomer; b. Flagstaff, Ariz., Oct. 29, 1916; d. Thomas B. and Sarah (Bailey) Gill; A.B. in Math., Wellesley Coll., 1938; S.M. in Astronomy and Astrophysics, U. Chgo., 1941; Ph.D. in Astronomy, Yale, 1959. Lab. asst., instr. astronomy Mt. Holyoke Coll., 1940-42; staff mem. radiation lab. Mass. Inst. Tech, 1942-45; from instr. to asst. prof. astronomy Smith Coll., 1945-52; grad. work, teaching asst. U. Cal. at Berkeley, 1946-48; asst. prof., then acting chmn. dept. astronomy Mt. Holyoke Coll., 1952-57; asso. prof. astronomy and math. Ariz. State Coll., 1959-60; vis. lectr. Wellesley Coll., 1960-61; staff scientist Office Astronomy and Solar Physics, Office Space Sci., NASA, Washington, 1961-63, with manned space sci. div., 1963-66, chief in-flight scis., 1963-66, staff scientist, manned flight expts. office Office Space Sci. and Applications, 1966-68, program scientist for manned flight expts., physics and astronomy programs, 1968—; made solar eclipse flight, 1963. Named woman of yr. Nat. Multiple Sclerosis Soc., 1966; recipient Woman's Federal award class 1966, 1966; Achievement award Proviso High Sch., 1969, Wellesley Coll., 1970. Fellow A.A.A.S.; mem. Am. Astron. Soc., Nantucket Maria Mitchell Assn., Washington Philos. Soc., Am. Assn. Variable Star Observers, N.Y. Acad. Scis., Sigma Xi. Presbyn. Club: Zonta (mem. med. scholarship com.). Home: 2140 Pogue Av Cincinnati OH 45208

GILL, MARGARET ANN GASKINS (MRS. STEPHEN PASCHALL GILL), lawyer; b. St. Louis, Mar. 2, 1940; d. Richard Williams and Margaret (Cambage) Gaskins; B.A., Wellesley Coll., 1962; postgrad. Boston U., 1962-64; J.D., U. Cal. at Berkeley, 1965; m. Stephen Paschall Gill, Dec. 21, 1961. Admitted to Cal. bar, 1966; asso., Pillsbury, Madison & Sutro, San Francisco, 1966-73, partner, 1973—. Home: 32 Flood Circle Atherton CA 94025 Office: 225 Bush St San Francisco CA 94104

GILL, SABRA HALL (MRS. WILLIAM L. GILL), public information ofcl.; b. Houston, Mar. 1, 1941; d. James A. and Susie Margaret (Jageman) Hall; B.S., U. Houston, 1963; m. William L. Gill, Jan. 26, 1973. Pub. information asst. Houston Natural Gas Corp., 1963-65, pub. information supr., 1965-72, mgr. information services, 1972—. Publicity chmn. Job Fair, 1973. Active Houston Livestock Show and Rodeo Assn., Houston Mus. Fine Arts, Houston Ballet Found. Recipient pub. relations achievement award Am. Gas Assn., 1967, achievement for mgmt. award Internat. Council Indsl. Editors, 1968. Mem. Houston Advt. Club (dir. 1968-70, editor 1968—), Pub. Relations Soc. Am. (dir. Houston chpt. 1973—, sec. 1974), Nat. Alliance Businessmen (pub. relations chmn. Houston), Internat. Assn. Bus. Communicators, Am. Advt. Fedn., Houston C. of C. (communications/information com.), U. Houston Alumni Fedn., Gamma Alpha Chi (charter mem., 1st pres. Houston), Theta Sigma Phi, Kappa Tau Alpha, Alpha Chi Omega. Home: 5140 Chevy Chase Apt 8 Houston TX 77027 Office: PO Box 1188 Houston TX 77002

GILLELAND, MARTHA JANE, educator; b. Monroe, La., Sept. 9, 1940; d. Ray Orion and Myrtle (Bacle) Gilleland; B.A., La. Poly. U., 1962; Ph.D., La. State U., 1968. Research asso. Edsel B. Ford Inst. for Med. Research, Detroit, 1968-70; research fellow Northwestern U., Evanston Ill., 1970-72; asso. prof. chemistry Cal. State Coll., Bakersfield, 1972—. Mem. Am. Chem. Soc., A.A.A.S., Am. Fedn. Scientists, Cal. Assn. Coll. Tchrs., N.Y. Acad. Scis., Sigma Xi, Iota Sigma Pi. Contbr. articles to profl. jours. Home: 6430 Stockdale Bakersfield CA 93309

GILLEN, MARY DOHERTY, lawyer; b. Whiting, Ind., Mar. 21, 1917; d. John and Rose Teresa (Sharkey) Doherty; student Newark State Tchrs. Coll., 1934-36; B.S. in Edn., Fordham U., 1947, J.D., 1964; m. Hugh H. Gillen, Nov. 14, 1936 (dec. Oct. 1937); children—John J., Denis H. (twins). Sec., Procter & Gamble Mfg. Co., S.I., N.Y., 1938-61; admitted to N.J. bar, 1965; asso. Joseph G. Barbieri, Elizabeth, 1965-73, firm Pollis, Williams, Pappas & Dillon, Elizabeth, 1973—. Mem. Elizabeth City Council, 1956-59, councilwoman at large, 1961-66, council pres. 1962; mem. bd. Pub. Works, City of Elizabeth, 1959-61, Planning Bd., City of Elizabeth, 1960-63. Trustee Union Coll., 1974. Mem. Assn. Trial Lawyers, Am. (mem. N.J. exec. com. 1973-74, treas. N.J. br. 1974), Am., N.J., Union County (chmn. workmen's compensation com. 1971) bar assns., Compensation Assn. N.J. (Union County ethics com. 1974—), Cath. Daus. Am. Democrat. Roman Catholic. Club: Soroptimist (Elizabeth, N.J.). Home: 335 Rosehill Pl Elizabeth NJ 07202 Office: 125 Broad St 11th Floor Elizabeth NJ 07201

GILLES, HELEN ELAINE MARTIN (MRS. PAUL W. GILLES), physician; b. Paola, Kan., Sept. 23, 1922; d. Montie A. and Hazel (Upham) Martin; B.A., U. Kan., 1943, M.D., 1945; m. Paul W. Gilles, Dec. 22, 1944; children—Timothy, Rebecca, Kathleen. Intern, San Francisco Children's Hosp., 1945-46; resident Children's Hosp. of East Bay, Oakland, Cal., 1946-48; mem. staff Lawrence (Kan.) Meml. Hosp.; pvt. practice medicine, specializing in pediatrics, Lawrence, 1948—. Lectr. clin. pharmacology, occupational therapy U. Kan. at Lawrence. Mem. Lawrence Human Relations Commn., 1960-64, Lawrence Unified Sch. Dist. Bd. Edn., 1969—. Diplomate Am. Bd. Pediatrics. Home: 1301 Iowa St Lawrence KS 66044 Office: care Med Art Center Lawrence KS 66044

GILLES, MATHILDA ANN, sch. adminstr.; b. Spring Hill, Minn., Jan. 12, 1907; d. Peter John and Gertrude (Buermann) Gilles; grad. Mt. Angel Coll., 1936, Ed.D., 1965; B.A., San Francisco State Coll., 1945; M.Ed., U. Ore., 1952; postgrad. U. Utah, summer 1951, U. Mont., 1953, Northwestern U., summers 1954, 55, Stanford, summer 1956, U. Mich, summer 1959, U. Hawaii, summer 1960, U. N.M., summer 1962, U. P.R., summer, 1963. Teacher rural and city schs., Ore., 1924-26, 28-40; tchr. city schs., Salem, Ore., 1940—, prin. Richmond Elementary Sch., 1946-69, Four Corners Elementary Sch., Salem, 1969-71; mem. staff, elementary sch. prins.' workshop U. Denver, 1958. Mem. White House Conf. on Fitness for Am. Youth, Annapolis, 1956, White House Conf. on Edn., 1955. Active Community Chest, A.R.C., March of Dimes campaigns; mem. Salem Sister City Commn., 1965. Recipient Victory Loan award of merit, 1945; Valley Forge sch. library award Freedom Found., 1953, 54, 56, 57, Freedom's Found. Prin. Sch. award, 1958, George Washington honor medal, 1955, 59, 60, distinguished service award, 61, 62, 63, 64, 65, Am. Educators award, 1966. Mem. Nat., Ore. congresses parents and tchrs., Nat., Ore. (pres. 1950-52) elementary sch. prins. assns., Nat. (pres. dept. elementary sch. prins. 1956-57, vice chmn. Def. Commn. for Democracy Thru Edn., 1959-60, chmn., 1960-61; chmn. commn. profl. rights and responsibilities 1961-62; del. to World Confedn. Orgns. Teaching Professions, India 1961, Rio de Janeiro, 1963, Addis Ababa 1965), Ore. (pres. 1961-62) edn. assns., Am. Assn. Sch. Adminstrs., Am., Ore. assns. for supervision and curriculum devel., Nat. Sch. Pub. Relations Assn., Nat. Council Adminstrv. Women in Edn. (mem. exec. bd. 1966-67, v.p. 1967-69, pres. 1969-71, membership chmn. 1971—), Oregon UN Assn., Am. Assn. U. Women, Bus. and Profl. Women's Club, Delta Kappa Gamma (pres. Ore. 1957-59), Pi Lambda Theta. Club: Zonta. Editorial adv. bd. Leads for the Elementary School Principal, 1953-54. Contbr. articles to ednl. jours. Home: 695 Court St NE Salem OR 97301

GILLESPIE, DOROTHY MURIEL (MRS. BERNARD ISRAEL), artist; b. Roanoke, Va., June 29, 1920; d. Earl Vivian and Lillian (Foster) Gillespie; student Md. Inst. Art, 1938-41, Clay Club, N.Y.C., 1943-44, Stanley William Hayter's Atelier 17, 1945, Art Students League, 1944; m. Bernard Israel, May 29, 1946; children—Dorien Gillespie, Gary Gillespie, Richard Gillespie. One man shows include Barzansky Galleries, N.Y.C., Miami (Fla.) Mus. Modern Art, Lowe Art Gallery, U. Miami; Inst. Contemporary Art, Lima, Peru; Gallerie Das Fenster, Frankfurt, Germany, Coll. St. Marys of Springs, Columbus, O., Va. Poly. Inst., L.I. U., Gertrude Stein Gallery, N.Y., Columbia U., Spl. Events Series Ritual '71 at N.Y. U.; exhibited N.Y. Cultural Center, 1973, N.Y. U., 1973, Women's Interart Center, N.Y.C., 1973; represented in numerous permanent collections; own radio show Dorothy Gillespie Show, WHBI, N.Y.C., 1967-73. Recipient numerous painting awards, 1931—. Patentee ednl. game, 1967. Address: 135 Mac Dougal St New York City NY 10012

GILLESPIE, MARCIA ANN, mag. editor; b. Rockville Centre, N.Y., July 10, 1944; d. Charles Marshall and Ethel (Young) Gillespie; B.A. with honors in Am. Studies, Lake Forest Coll., 1966. Researcher, Time-Life Books, N.Y.C., 1966-70; mng. editor Essence mag., N.Y.C., 1970-71, editor-in-chief, 1971—. Adv. bd. Community News Service, N.Y.C. Recipient Alumni Distinguished Service citation Lake Forest Coll., 1973. Mem. Am. Soc. Mag. Editors, Nat. Council

Negro Women. Home: 15 W 72d St New York City NY 10023 Office: 300 E 42d St New York City NY 10017

GILLESPIE, NANCY CAROLYN, mus. dir.; b. Balt., Oct. 6, 1936; d. Raymond and Mary Ada (Ainsworth) Cockey; student DePauw U., 1954-56, Md. Inst. Coll. Art, 1957; B.A. in Art, Towson State Coll., 1968; certificate U. N.C., 1973; children—Dale Raymond, Lauren Sebret. Instr. art N.C. Central U., Durham, 1969-70, 70-71, acting chmn. dept. art, 1971-73, acting dir. univ. mus., 1971-73, dir., 1973—, also chmn. bd.; cons. in field. Founder, sponsor ann. Festival Children's Art, Durham. Mem. Coll. Art Assn., Kappa Pi. Address: NC Central U Mus Art Durham NC 27701

GILLESPIE, RITA, broadcasting exec.; b. London, Eng.; d. John Drysdale and Marjorie (Fullbrook) Gillespie; ed. Lady Eleanor Holles Sch., London, 1939-45, Pittman's Bus. Coll., 1945-46. Sec., then prodn. asst. BBC, London, 1946-55; prodn. asst. ATV, London, 1955-56; free-lance TV stage mgr., London, 1956-58; free-lance TV dir., London, 1958-63, Hollywood, Cal., 1963—; shows include Shindig (Beatles First Spl.), Andy Williams spl., Tom Jones Show, others. Mem. Dirs. Guild Am. Author TV show formats. Home: 5922 Tuxedo Terrace Los Angeles CA 90028 also 8 Heather Pl Rural Route 4 Brampton ON Canada and 20 Summerland Grange London N 10 England

GILLESPIE, ROXANI MANOU (MRS. J. CHRISTOPHER GILLESPIE), ins. co. exec.; b. Athens, Greece, Apr. 19, 1941; d. Pericles C. and Helen C. (Zavitzianou) Manou; student Athens U., 1964; LL.B., Boston Coll., 1967; m. J. Christopher Gillespie, Dec. 2, 1963; children—Margaret, Constantine. Came to U.S., 1964, naturalized, 1969. Admitted to bars Cal., Mass.; claims rep. Indsl. Indemnity Co., San Francisco, 1970-71, atty., 1971-73, sr. atty., 1973—, asst. sec., 1973—. Mem. Am. Field Service, Am., Cal. Bar assns. Clubs: Stock Exchange, Lawyers' of San Francisco. Office: 255 California St San Francisco CA 94120

GILLETT, MARGARET, educator; b. Wingham, Australia, Feb. 1, 1930; d. Leslie Frank and Janet (Vickers) Gillett; B.A., U. Sydney, 1950; M.A., Russell Sage Coll., 1958; Ed.D., Columbia, 1961. Tchr. English, Australia, Eng., 1950-54; edn. officer Colombo Plan Sect., Commonwealth Office Edn., Australia, 1954-57; asst. prof. edn. Dalhousie U., Halifax, N.S., Can., 1961-62; registrar Haile Selassie I U., Addis Ababa, Ethiopia, 1962-64; asso. prof. edn. McGill U., Montreal, Que., Can., 1964-67, prof., 1967—. Cons. Social Sci. and Humanities Div., Can. Council, 1965—; bd. internat. cons. Religion in Edn. Found. Recipient Scholarship Altrusa Internat., 1957, grad. award Columbia, 1960. Mem. Comparative and Internat. Edn. Soc. Can. (v.p. 1968-71), Am. Ednl. Studies Assn. (mem. exec. 1972—). Author: A History of Education - Thought and Practice, 1966; (with Monika Kehoe) The Laurel and the Poppy, 1967; Educational Technology, 1973. Editor: Readings in the History of Education, 1969; (with John Laska) Foundation Studies in Education: Justifications and New Directions, 1973. Founding editor McGill Jour. Edn., 1966—. Cons. editor: Educational Studies, 1970—. Contbr. articles to profl. jours. Home: 1400 Pine Av W Apt 1305 Montreal PQ H3G 1B1 Canada Office: Faculty Edn McGill U Montreal PQ Canada

GILLETTE, JEANETTE LOUISE, freelance writer, photographer, editor; b. McCamey, Tex., July 1, 1940; d. Robert M. and Olive Louise (Gill) Gillette; B.A., U. N.M., 1963. Reference librarian Tom Green County Library, San Angelo, Tex., 1963; reporter San Angelo Standard-Times, 1963-65, sci. writer, 1965-69; freelance mag. Writer, 1969—; editor Shoppers Exchange Weekly, 1972; cons. pub. relations. Recipient A.A.A.S.-Westinghouse Sci. Writing award, 1967, Area Soil and Water Conservation Dist.'s award for service to water conservation, 1967-68. Mem. A.A.A.S., Tex. Acad. Sci. (editor newsletter 1969-70), San Angelo Geol. Soc. (past pres.). Author: Brush—The Water Thief, 1967. Address: 302 W 37th St San Angelo TX 76901

GILLHAM, OTHA WADE (MRS. PHIL M. GILLHAM), librarian; b. Adamsville, Tenn., Sept. 20, 1919; d. M. B. and Bertha (Johnson) Wade; student Freed-Hardeman Coll., 1937-39; B.S., Union U., Jackson, Tenn., 1949; M.S., U. Tenn., 1954; m. Phil M. Gillham, Nov. 29, 1945. Elementary tchr. Hardin County (Tenn.) Sch., 1940-44, 50-57, tchr. English and social studies, 1944-45; librarian Central High Sch., Savannah, Tenn., 1957-69; library supr. Hardin County, Tenn., 1969—. Chmn. bd. trustees Hardin County Pub. Library. Mem. N.E.A. (life), A.L.A., Am. Assn. U. Women, Tenn. Library Assn., Tenn., West Tenn., Hardin County tchrs. assns., Bus. and Profl. Women's Club, Delta Kappa Gamma, Friends Hardin County Library (v.p. 1969-72). Home: Crump TN 38327 Office: Hardin County Educational Center 616 Harlem St Savannah TN 38372

GILLIAM, JOSEPHINE CALDWELL, oil co. exec.; b. Bowie, Tex., June 8, 1912; d. John Walter and Josephine (Ribble) Caldwell; student Trinity U., 1929-30; m. Raymond Arnold Gilliam, June 3, 1932. Typist, Elliott & Waldron Abstract Cos. Inc., Athens, Tex., 1932-35, titleman, 1935-40; mgr. Elliott & Waldron, Pittsburg, Tex., 1940-42; staff fiduciary trust suit Shell Oil Co., Houston, 1942-43, sr. title clk. land dept., 1943-50; mgr. land dept., corporate asst. sec. J. Ray McDermott & Co., Houston, 1951-68; mgr. land dept., corporate asst. sec. TransOcean Oil Inc., Houston, 1968—, corporate asst. sec. brs. J. Ray McDermott Can., Ltd., 1967-71; asst. sec. TransOcean Oil Can. Ltd., 1971—, TransOcean Oil (U.K.) Ltd., 1971—, TransOcean Oil (U.K.) Inc., 1971—. Mem. Am. Bus. Women's Assn. (pres. 1967-68, Woman of Year 1965-66, editor Shamrock chpt. monthly mag. Blarney Stone 1970-71). Home: 10626 Chevy Chase Houston TX 77042 Office: First City East Bldg Houston TX 77002

GILLIAM, MARY ANN ENGEL (MRS. JAMES MELVIN GILLIAM), pediatrician; b. Oklahoma City, Nov. 10, 1943; d. Joseph Michael and Mary Amelia (Reinhart) Engel; student Our Lady of the Lake Coll., 1960-63; M.D., U. Okla., 1968; m. James Melvin Gilliam, June 25, 1966; children—Laura Ann, Sandra Marie. Straight pediatric intern Hosp. St. Raphael, New Haven, Conn., 1968-69, asst. resident, 1969-70, chief resident pediatrics, 1970-71; affiliate asst. resident Yale New Haven Hosp., 1970; practice medicine, specializing in pediatrics, New Haven, 1971—; mem. med. staff, house staff com. Hosp. of St. Raphael, Yale New Haven Hosp. Sch. physician, well child conf. physician New Haven and Hamden (Conn.) Health Dept., 1971-74. Pres. Little Medics Nursery, Inc., 1969-70. Mem. Conn. State, New Haven County med. socs., U. Women's Orgn., Hosp. St. Raphael House Staff Assn. (pres. 1969). Roman Catholic. Clubs: Yale Newcomers (New Haven); High Lane. Address: 1732 Whitney Av Hamden CT 06517

GILLIES, PATRICIA ANN MYERS (MRS. ROBERT WILLIAM GILLIES), govt. worker; b. Berkeley, Cal., Sept. 23, 1929; d. William W. and Barbara (Weddle) Myers; student San Jose State Coll., 1947-48, 51-52; A.B., Fresno State Coll., 1954, M.A., 1961; m. Robert William Gillies, Sept. 17, 1948 (div. Dec. 1967); children—Catherine I., Coila L. Tchr. biology Parlier (Cal.) Unified Sch. Dist., 1955-56; insps. aide U.S. Dept. Agr. Processed Products Inspection, Fresno, Cal., 1956-58; tech. asst. Fresno State Coll., 1958-59; pub. health biologist Cal. Dept. Pub. Health, Fresno, 1959—. Trustee, Consol. Mosquito Abatement Dist., 1974—. Mem. Entomol. Soc. Am., Am., Cal. mosquito control assns., San Joaquin Entomology Assn. Cal. Soc. Vector Ecologist. Contbr. articles to profl. jours. Home: 9360 E Clinton St Fresno CA 93727 Office: 5545 E Shields Av Fresno CA 93727

GILLILAN, LOIS A., physician; b. Springville, Utah, June 15, 1911; d. Lewis W. and Ellen (Benson) Gillilan; B.A., Mt. Holyoke Coll., 1935; A.M., Vassar Coll., 1937; Ph.D., U. Mich., 1940; M.D., U. Pitts., 1947. Asst. in physiology Vassar Coll., Poughkeepsie, N.Y., 1935-38; instr. anatomy U. Pitts., 1942-45; intern Med. Center Hosps., Pitts., 1947-48; asst. prof. hygiene, med. adv. for women U. Ill., Champaign-Urbana, 1948-49; asst. prof. anatomy Grad. Sch. Medicine, U. Pa., Phila., 1949-51, asso. prof., 1951-60; research asso. neuroanatomy, dept. neurology Phila. Gen. Hosp., 1958-60; asso. prof. anatomy U. Ky., Lexington, 1960-63, prof., 1963—; cons. neurology VA Hosp., Lexington, 1963-65. Bd. dirs. Presbyn. Child Welfare Agy., Buckhorn, Ky., 1967-72. Fellow Royal Soc. Health (hon.), Council on Cardiovascular Disease; mem. Am. Assn. Anatomists, Phila. Neurol. Soc. (2d v.p. 1959), Am. Acad. Neurology, Am. Neurol. Assn., Am. Assn. Neuropathologists, Phi Sigma, Sigma Xi, Alpha Omega Alpha. Research in blood supply to central nervous system. Home: 954 Wolf Run Rd Lexington KY 40504 Office: Dept Anatomy Coll Medicine U Ky Lexington KY 40506

GILLIM, MARION HAMILTON, educator, economist; b. Owensboro, Ky., Apr. 12, 1909; d. Parvin Douglas and Marion (Reid) Gillim; A.B., Mt. Holyoke Coll., 1930; M.A., Columbia, 1938, Ph.D., 1944. Instr. high sch., Owensboro, Ky., 1932-39, econs. and sociology N.J. Coll. Women, 1941-42; mem. faculty Mt. Holyoke Coll., 1942-49; mem. research staff Nat. Bur. Econ. Research, 1943; internat. cons. labor statistics Central and S. Am., Bur. Labor Statistics, 1949-52, 55-56; mem. faculty Barnard Coll., N.Y.C., 1952—, prof. econs., 1962—, chmn. dept., 1955-63, 67-68, 71—, Brookings research prof., 1957-58. Mem. Am. Acad. Polit. Sci., Am. Assn. U. Profs., Am. Assn. U. Women, Am., Met. econ. assns., Am. Statis. Assn., Internat. Fiscal Assn., Internat. Inst. Pub. Finance, Latin Am. Studies Assn., Nat. Tax Assn., Tax Inst. Am., Phi Beta Kappa. Club: Cosmopolitan (N.Y.C.). Author: The Incidence of Excess Profits Taxation, 1945. Contbr. articles to profl. jours. Home: 1505 Griffith Av Owensboro KY 42301 Office: Barnard Coll New York City NY 10027

GILLIN, CAROLINE JULIA, govt. ofcl.; b. Alpena, Mich., Sept. 16, 1932; d. Thomas F. and Frances (Kendziorski) Gillin; B.A. magna cum laude, Mercy Coll. Detroit, 1960; M.Ed., Wayne State U., 1964, Ed.D., 1969. Tchr. parochial schs., Detroit, Lansing and Ia., 1952-62; faculty, adminstr. tchr. edn. Mercy Coll. Detroit, 1962-70; sr. program specialist U.S. Office Edn., Tchr. Corps, Washington, 1970—. Research asst. Mt. Clements (Mich.) Community Sch. Dist., 1967; Project REMIDY Wayne County Intermediate Sch. Dist., 1968-69. Bur. Research grantee; U.S. Office Edn. fellow. Mem. Am. Assn. for Higher Edn., Assn. Tchr. Educators, Am. Edn. Research Assn., Lambda Iota Tau, Delta Epsilon Sigma, Kappa Delta Pi, Phi Delta Kappa. Democrat. Roman Catholic. Home: 1100 6th St SW Washington DC 20024 Office: US Office Edn Tchr Corps Washington DC 20202

GILLING, LUCILLE GLICK (MRS. WILLIAM GILLING), artist; b. Hamilton, Mo.; d. Manassah M. and Eva (Morgan) Glick; student Kansas City Art Inst., 1925-27, N.Y. Sch. Fine and Applied Arts, 1927-28, Queens U., summers 1953, 54; m. William Gilling, May 2, 1942; 1 son, Joseph. One man shows at Pascal Gallery, Toronto, Ont., Can., Dorothy Butchart Gallery Leith, Ontario, 1966, Sobot Gallery, Toronto, Ont., 1968, Marjorie Kauffman Graphics, Houston, 1972; exhibited in 2-man shows at Sonneck Gallery Kitchener, Ont., Alice Peck Gallery, Burlington, Ont., Tom Thompson Meml. Art Gallery, Owen Sound, Ont., 1964, Gallery House Sol, Georgetown, Ont.; exhibited in group shows Royal Ont. Mus., Art Gallery Toronto, Montreal Mus., Fine Art, Winnipeg Art Gallery, others; represented in permanent collections Victoria and Albert Mus., London, Eng., Nat. Library of Can. (Ottawa), Montreal Mus. Fine Art, Toronto Central Library, McGill U., numerous others. Recipient Sterling Trust award, 1959; Anaconda award Merit, 1968. Mem. Soc. Canadian Painter-Etchers and Engravers. Club: Toronto Heliconian. Pub. portfolios of etchings The Canterbury Tales, 1966, Don Quixote, 1968. Home: 178 Alfred Av Willowdale ON Canada

GILLIO, CAROLYN IRENE MOLL (MRS. FRANK GILLIO), psychotherapist; b. Wells, Minn., Jan. 1, 1931; d. William John and Antonia (Augst) Moll; B.A., Gustavus Adolphus Coll., 1952; postgrad. U. Chgo., 1952-53; M.A., U. Cal. at Berkeley, 1955; m. Cesar Padilla, 1953 (div. 1966); children—Paula Mark, Julie; m. 2d, Frank Gillio, May 24, 1969. With Luth. Home Finding Soc., Chgo., 1952-53; with Family Service Assn. of Santa Clara County (Cal.), 1958-68, supr. Sunnyvale (Cal.) dist. office, 1964-68; pvt. practice psychotherapy, Sunnyvale, 1968—. Chmn. Sunnyvale Coordinating Council, 1967-68; mem. central care com. Comprehensive Mental Health Planning Com., Sunnyvale, 1965-67; bd. mem. North County Social Planning Council, 1968—; troop committeewoman Boy Scouts Am., Sunnyvale, 1965—; chmn. Santa Clara County Health and Welfare Commn., 1972—; mem. affirmative action adv. com. Sunnyvale Sch. Dist. Sch. Bd. Recipient Distinguished Service award Family Service Assn. Santa Clara County, 1968. Mem. Nat. Assn. Social Workers (sec. 1968), Soc. Clin. Social Workers (mem. ethics and ins. coms. 1970). Democrat. Home: 869 Cumberland Av Sunnyvale CA 94087 Office: Mid Peninsula Psychiat Med Clinic 990 W Fremont St Sunnyvale CA 94087

GILLIOM, BONNIE LEE CHERP (MRS. M. EUGENE GILLIOM), educator; b. Mansfield, O., Mar. 1, 1933; d. Gregor Leonard and Rella Hildegard (Jacobs) Cherp; student U. Wis., 1953; A.B., Heidelberg Coll., 1955; M.A., Ohio State U., 1961, Ph.D. in Ednl. Communications, 1971; m. M. Eugene Gilliom, Dec. 29, 1956; children—Gregor William, Julia Lee. Tchr., Thomas Jefferson Jr. High Sch., Cleve., 1955-58; dept. head Berea (O.) High Sch., 1958-59; tchr. TV, Columbus (O.) Pub. Schs., 1959-62; writer, producer talent sta. WOSU-TV, Columbus, 1959-62, sta. WPIX-TV, San Francisco, 1962-64, Nat. Instructional Television, Cleve., 1966-68; lectr. San Francisco State Coll., 1962-65; prof. children's creative movement Ohio State U., Columbus, 1971—. Cons., instructional TV tchr., demonstrator Gen. Electric Co., Syracuse, N.Y., 1962-64; TV tchr., writer, producer Gt. Plains Nat. Instructional TV Library, 1962-69; vol. trainer Peace Corps, 1964; guest lectr., demonstrator Kan. Legislature, Kan. Sch. Bd., profl. assns., colls. and univs., 1958—. Recipient 1st place award Inst. for Ednl. Radio and Television, 1962. Mem. A.A.H.P.E.R., Nat. Assn. Study Edn., Nat. Acad. TV Arts and Scis. (edn. com. 1971), Nat. Assn. Ednl. Broadcasters, N.W. Council on Human Relations, Kappa Delta Pi, Pi Delta Epsilon, Pi Lambda Theta. Democrat. Methodist. Author: Basic Movement Education for Children: Rationale and Teaching Units, 1970; (with Anne Zimmer) ITV: Promise into Practice, 1972; also contbr. chpts. to books. Home: 2495 Haverford Rd Columbus OH 43220

GILLIS, JOANE GAYLORD (MRS. FRANK JOSEPH GILLIS), actress, writer-dir.; b. Bloomfield, N.J., Sept. 27, 1909; d. Melcom Vartan and Grace Margaret (Rooney) Gaylord; student Whittier Coll., 1931-33, San Jose State Coll., 1945-48, U. Cal. at Los Angeles, 1952-54; m. Frank Joseph Gillis, June 30, 1934; 1 son, Ronald Blair. Appeared in Broadway prodns. including George M. Cohan's-Merry Malones, 1927-38, Lawrence Webers-Twinkle Twinkle, 1926-27; under contract Fox Films, 1929-30, Pathe Studio, 1930-31, Metro Goldwyn Mayer, 1931-33; writer, dir., producer To G.I. Joe With Love, 1944, Fashion Ala Mode, 1948; creator-dir. children's simulated TV sta. K.I.D.S., 1949; asst. The California Story, 1950; TV actress Jack Benny, Red Skelton shows, Hazel, Dr. Kildaire, Gladys, others; dir., tchr. Joane Gaylord Center of Performing Arts, Los Angeles, 1969—; creator-producer Neptune's Network, 1974. Recipient awards for work on war bond drives U.S. Treasury Dept., 1942-45. Mem. Am. Fedn. Radio and TV Artists, Am. Women in Radio and TV, Acad. TV Arts and Scis., Screen Actors Guild, League of Women Voters (radio and tv chmn. 1949-52), Hollywood Studio Club Alumni Assn. (pres. 1961-63). Home: 10524 Selkirk Lane Los Angeles CA 90024

GILLIS, NANCY CROCKETT (MRS. RALPH L. GILLIS), social worker; b. Kansas City, Mo., June 3, 1912; d. Clarence M. and Jane (Young) Crockett; B.S., U. Mo., Columbia, 1933; M.S.W., Washington U., St. Louis, 1949; m. Ralph L. Gillis, Nov. 29, 1934; 1 son, Charles C. Casework supr. Jackson County Office, State Dept. Welfare, Kansas City, Mo., 1933-44; field work supr. Washington U. Sch. Social Work, 1940-47; med. social worker Alfred Benjamin Dispensary, Kansas City, 1944-47; chief social worker Rehab. Inst., Kansas City, 1964-66; dir. social service dept. Menorah Med. Center, Kansas City, 1966—; cons. social service Smithville (Mo.) Community Hosp., 1968-69; cons. social service dept. Jackson County Pub. Hosp., 1969-71, Bros. of Mercy ECF, Bapt. Meml. Hosp., 1971-72, Shawnee Mission Med. Center, 1972, Hillhaven Convalescent Center, Inc., 1971—; field supr. U. Mo., Columbia Grad. Sch. Social Work, 1968—. Pres., sec., bd. dirs. Childrens Cardiac Center; v.p., sec., bd. dirs. Womans City Club; sec., v.p., bd. dirs. Greater Kansas City Travelers Aid Soc.; bd. dirs., acting exec. dir. Gillis Home for Children. Mem. Acad. Certified Social Workers, Nat. Assn. Social Workers, Nat., Mo. (dir. Kansas City area div.) confs. social welfare, Am. Hosp. Assn., Am. Soc. for Hosp. Social Work Dirs. (chpt. chmn., area rep.), Phi Mu. Presbyn. Home: 1239 W 67th Terrace Kansas City MO 64113 Office: 4949 Rockhill Rd Kansas City MO 64110

GILLIS, RUTH JEANETTE KATHAN (MRS. FRANK JAMES GILLIS), librarian; b. Tulsa, July 26, 1921; d. William Wallace and Edith Viola (Parrish) Kathan; student Wayne State U., 1948-52, Barnard Coll., 1953; B.A., U. Minn., 1960, M.A., 1964; m. Frank James Gillis, Sept. 13, 1943; 1 son, Christopher Jay. Librarian, Univ. Elementary Sch., U. Minn., Mpls., 1962-64; librarian Univ. Elementary Sch., Ind. U., Bloomington, 1964—, univ. vis. lectr., 1969—. Served with WAC, 1943-45. Mem. A.L.A., Nat. Council Tchrs. English, N.E.A., Ind. Tchrs. Assn., Ind. Sch. Librarians Assn., Beta Phi Mu, Pi Lambda Theta. Democrat. Contbr. articles to profl. jours. Home: 3508 Morningside Dr Bloomington IN 47401 Office: University Elementary School Highway 46 Bypass Bloomington IN 47401

GILMARTIN, AMY JEAN, educator; b. Red Bluff, Cal., Oct. 15, 1932; d. Ruy H. and Margaret Helena (Harvey) Finch; B.A., Pomona Coll., 1954; M.Sc., U. Hawaii, 1956, Ph.D. (Am. Assn. U. Women fellow), 1968; m. Malvern Gilmartin, June 8, 1954 (div. 1974); children—Malvern Gilmartin III, Dale Moana, Sheila Ann, Ian Harvey. With Hawaii Agr. Expt. Sta., Honolulu, 1954-56; curator Herbarium, U. B.C., Vancouver, Can., 1956-58; vis. prof. Sch. Natural Scis., Ecuador, 1962-64; mus. vis. researcher San Diego Natural Hist. Mus., 1964; Smithsonian Instn. fellow botany, 1967, 70; prof. biology Monterey (Cal.) Peninsula Coll., 1971—. Cons. environmental impact studies. Adviser, Seaside (Cal.) Planning Dept., 1973—; adviser in plantings Monterey (Cal.) Parks and Recreation Dept., 1971-72. Research grantee NSF, 1971-73, 74-76, Soc. Sigma Xi, 1961-62, Am. Philos. Soc., 1968-69, Nat. Geog. Soc., 1969. Mem. Internat. Bromeliad Soc. (dir. 1971—), Sociedad de Ciencas Naturales (Ecuador), Sigma Xi. Author: Bromeliaceae of Ecuador, 1972. Contbr. articles to profl. jours. Home: 981 David Av Monterey CA 93940

GILMORE, ARABY ALLEN, advt., promotion exec.; b. Summit, N.J.; d. Robert C. and Arabella (Allen) Keith Gilmore; B.A., Smith Coll. Copywriter CBS, N.Y.C., 1947-52; copywriter Radio Advt. Bur., N.Y.C., 1952-55; copywriter Look Mag., N.Y.C., 1955-64, copy chief, 1964-70, mgr. sales promotion, 1970-71; asst. marketing dir. Good Housekeeping Mag. N.Y.C., 1972—. Free lance writer, 1970—. Recreation staff asst. A.R.C., S.W. Pacific, 1944-46. Mem. Advt. Women of N.Y. (dir. 1969-71), Nat. Council of Women (chmn. trades and professions 1968-70). Home: 145 East 92nd St New York City NY 10028 Office: 959 8th Av New York City NY 10019

GILMORE, JOAN ELIZABETH, newspaper editor; b. Waukegan, Ill., May 14, 1927; d. Joseph and Helen Ruth (Parks) Gilmore; B.A. in English, Drury Coll., 1951. Asst. soc. editor Springfield (Mo.) Newspapers, Inc., 1951-52; women's editor Muskogee (Okla.) Phoenix and Times Democrat, 1952; women's editor, fashion editor Daily Oklahoman and Oklahoma City Times, 1952—; lectr. U. Okla., Okla. State U., 1971-73. Past pres. Oklahoma City Regional Fashion Group, 1962; mem. women's com. Mummers Theatre. Bd. dirs. Oklahoma City Symphony Soc. Recipient award for communications Nat. Fedn. Colored Women's Clubs, 1970. Mem. Okla. Art Center Assn., D.A.R., Women in Communications (pres. Oklahoma City profl. chpt. 1960, Outstanding Achievement award Oklahoma City chpt. 1974), Sigma Delta Chi (dir.). Home: 3321 NW 52d St Oklahoma City OK 73112 Office: PO Box 25125 Oklahoma City OK 73125

GILMORE, MARJORIE HAVENS (MRS. HUGH REDLAND GILMORE), lawyer, club woman; b. N.Y.C., Aug. 16, 1918; d. William Westerfield and Elsie (Medl) Havens; A.B., Hunter Coll., 1938; J.D., Columbia, 1941; m. Hugh Redland Gilmore, May 8, 1942; children—Douglas Hugh, Anne Charlotte, Joan Louise. Admitted to N.Y. State bar, 1941, Va. bar, 1968; research asst. N.Y. Law Revision Commn., 1941-42; asso. firm Spence, Windels, Walser, Hotchkiss & Angell, N.Y.C., 1942, Chadbourne, Wallace, Parke & Whiteside, N.Y.C., 1942-43; atty. U.S. Army, Washington, 1948-53. Sec., Thomas Jefferson Jr. High Sch. P.T.A., 1956-58; parliamentarian Wakefield High Sch. P.T.A., 1959-60, chmn. citizenship com., 1960-61; publicity chmn. Patrick Henry Sch. P.T.A., sec., 1964-65; parliamentarian Nottingham P.T.A., 1966-69; mem. extra-curricular activities com. Arlington County Sch. Bd.; area chmn. fund drive Cancer Soc., 1955-56; active Girl Scouts U.S.A., 1963-70; mem. '41 com. Columbia Law Sch. Fund. Recipient Constl. Law award Hunter Coll., 1938. Mem. Columbia Law Sch. Alumni Assn., Alpha Sigma Rho. Presbyn. Club: Williamsburg Woman's of Arlington (corr. sec. 1970-72, 1st v.p. 1972-74, pres. 1974—). Home: 3020 N Nottingham St Arlington VA 22207

GILMOUR, KAY ELLEN, physician; b. Syracuse, N.Y., July 29, 1942; d. Robert Fulton and Mildred Florence (Seckner) Gilmour; B.S., U. Fla., 1963, M.D., 1967. Fellow in internal medicine Johns Hopkins Hosp., 1967-69; fellow in cardiology U. Ala. Hosp., 1969-71; practice medicine specializing in adult cardiology, Jacksonville, Fla., 1971—; mem. staff Meml., Bapt., Univ., Jacksonville Gen., St. Vincent's hosps., Jacksonville; asst. prof. U. Fla. Sch. Medicine, 1972—. Asst. fire div. surgeon dept. pub. safety, Jacksonville, Fla., 1972—. Mem. A.C.P. Home: 1347 Morier St Jacksonville FL 32207 Office: 2549 Park St Jacksonville FL 32202

GILOT, FRANCOISE, painter; b. Neuilly-sur-Seine, France, Nov. 26, 1921; d. Emile Armand and Madeleine (Renoult) G.; B.A., Sorbonne, Paris, 1938; student law and lit., 1939-41; degree English lit. Cambridge (Eng.) U.; student painting Endre Rozsda's Studio, Paris, 1941-42, drawing Souverbie Studio, Acad. Julian and Acad. Sect. d'Or., 1943-45; influenced by Picasso, 1943, 46-53, Matisse, 1946; m. Jonas E. Salk, 1970. Painter under contract Galerie Louise Leiris, Paris, 1951-56, Galerie Coard, Paris, 1958-68, Galerie F. Mayor, London, Eng., 1958-68, Dalzell Hatfield Gallery, Los Angeles, 1969—, Montcalm Galleries, 1970—, Mary Moore Gallery, La Jolla, Cal., 1971—; one man exhbns. include 43 rue Boissy d'Anglas, Paris, 1943, Galerie La Hune, Paris, 1951, Galerie Louise Leiris, 1952, Galerie Folklore, Lyons, France, 1953, Galerie Coard, 1959, 61, 63, 66, 68, 70, Mayor Gallery, London, 1960, 62, Mrs. Herbert C. Morris gallery, Phila., 1962, David Findley Gallery, 1965, Von der Hue Gallery, 1965, Galleria d'arte 32 Milano, 1965, Galleria Santo Stephano Venise, 1966, Chapman Kelly Atelier, Dallas, 1966-70, Galleria Dantesca, Turin, Italy, 1969, Dalzell Hatfield Gallery, 1969, Southampton (N.Y.) Mus. Art, 1970, Hackley Art Gallery, Muskegon, Mich., 1971, Grand Rapids (Mich.) Art Mus., 1973, U. San Diego, 1974, numerous others; group exhbns. include Salon des Surindepdennts, Paris, 1945, Leicester Gallery, London, 1953, 68, Gallery Alex Vomel, Dusseldorf, Germany, 1954, Univ Paris/Bruxelles, 1957, Centro Culturel and Artisque de France-Amerique, 1957, Salon de Mei, Paris, 1951-56, Ecole de Paris, Gallerie Charpentier, 1956-60, Salon des Tuilaries, Paris, 1959-62, Dalzell Hatfield Gallery, Los Angeles, 1969, 71; lithographer Asso. Am. Artists, N.Y.C., 1961—; designer scenery Janine Charrat, 1953, ballet Heracles, 1953. Theatre des Champs Elysees; rep. permanent collections Musieed'Art Moderne, Paris, Mus. Modern Art, N.Y.C., Jacksonville Art Mus., Wichita Art Mus., others, also pvt. collections. Author: Life with Picasso, 1964. Illustrator: Pages d'Amour (Andre Verdet), 1951; Pouvoir tout dire (Paul Eluard), 1952; Infus Amour (Andre Miguel), 1953; Vignettes pour les Vignerons (J. Prevert), 1953. Address: 40 Rue Lauriston Paris XVI France also 2444 Ellentown Rd La Jolla CA 92037

GILROY, SUE ANNE STARNES (MRS. RICHARD D. GILROY), city ofcl.; b. Crawfordsville, Ind., June 28, 1948; d. Carl Richard and Kathryn Helen (Myers) Starnes; B.A., DePauw U., 1970; postgrad. Ind. U., 1973—; m. Richard D. Gilroy, Aug. 4, 1973. Projects asso. Office of Mayor, City of Indpls., 1970-71, neighborhood coordinator, 1971-73, staff dir., 1973—. Mem. adv. council Equal Housing Opportunity, 1971-73; mem. vol. bur. Indpls. Community Service Council, 1971-73. Chmn. Youth for Mayor Lugar, 1971; Marion County co-chmn. Young Voters for Pres., 1972. Bd. dirs., sec. Indpls. Legal Services Orgn., 1972—. Mem. Women in Communications, DePauw U. Alumni Assn. (dir. 1971-74), Kappa Alpha Theta (chmn. adv. bd. 1972-73). Mem. Christian Ch. Home: 5696 N Delaware St Indianapolis IN 46220 Office: 2501 City County Bldg Indianapolis IN 46204

GILSON, SALLY SEKIKO KONDO (MRS. CARROLL DUANE GILSON), real estate broker; b. Tokyo, Japan, Feb. 28, 1939; d. Truichi and Mitue (Takahashi) Kondo; came to U.S., 1959, naturalized, 1965; student Pierce Coll., 1965-68; m. Carroll Duane Gilson, Aug. 25, 1959; children—Glenn Alan, Michael. Press information sec. Embassy of Pakistan, Tokyo, 1957; social sec. to ambassador of Pakistan, 1958; pres. Hearth Realty, Inc., Northridge, Cal., 1968—. Lectr. various groups and orgns. Mem. Nat., Cal. real estate assns. Home: 719 De Garmo St San Fernando CA 91324 Office: 18449 Devonshire St Northridge CA 91324

GIMBUTAS, MARIJA BIRUTĖ ALSEIKA, educator; b. Vilnius, Lithuania, Jan. 23, 1921; d. Daniel and Veronika (Janulaitis) Alseika; diploma in archaeology Vilnius U., 1942; Ph.D., Tubingen U., 1946; m. Jurgis Gimbutas, July 12, 1941 (div. Apr. 1964); children—Danute, Zivile, Rasa-Julie. Came to U.S., 1949, naturalized, 1955. Prof. European archaeology and Indo-European studies U. Cal. at Los Angeles, 1963—, curator old world archaeology Museum Cultural History, 1966—. Fellow Center for Advanced Study, Stanford, 1961-62, Netherlands Inst. for Advanced Study, Wassenaar, 1973-74. NSF fellow, 1968-69; 73-74, Smithsonian Instn. fellow, 1967-71, Wenner-Gren fellow, 1956, 71, Kress fellow, 1967-74; named Woman of Yr., Los Angeles Times, 1968. Author: The Prehistory of Eastern Europe, 1956; The Bronze Age of Central and Eastern Europe, 1965; The Slavs, 1971; The Gods and Goddesses of Old Europe, 1974. Editor archaeology sect. Jour. Indo-European Studies, 1973. Contbr. articles to profl. jours. Home: 21434 Entrada Rd Topanga CA 90290 Office: 5288 Buchhe Hall U Cal at Los Angeles Los Angeles CA 90024

GING, ROSALIE J. JHUNG (MRS. NELSON GING), physician; b. Detroit; d. Yangpil and Dorothy (Lee) Jhung; M.D., U. Mich., 1945; m. Nelson Ging, Sept. 25, 1945; children—Constance, George. Intern New Eng. Hosp. for Women and Children, Boston, 1945-46; resident U. Kan. Med. Sch., 1953-54; staff psychiatrist Kansas City (Mo.) VA Hosp., 1954-56, Ann Arbor (Mich.) VA Hosp., 1956-58; asst. chief psychiatrist Ann Arbor VA Hosp., 1958-60, chief psychiatry service, 1960—; asst. prof. psychiatry U. Mich. Med. Sch., 1960—. Diplomate Am. Bd. Psychiatry and Neurology. Fellow Am. Psychiat. Assn.; mem. A.M.A., Mich. Med. Soc., Central Electroencphalograph Soc. Contbr. articles to profl. jours. Home: 4670 Midway Dr Route 1 Ann Arbor MI 43108 Office: VA Hosp Ann Arbor MI 48104

GINGERY, ZERLYNE SMITH (MRS. CLARENCE LOUIS GINGERY), retired educator; b. Autaugaville, Ala., Aug. 18; d. Morgan McClain and Minnie (Dantzler) Smith; student Fla. State Coll. Women, 1922-24; B.A., U. Miami, Coral Gables, Fla., 1938; m. Otis Sale King, June 19, 1930 (dec. Feb. 1960); 1 dau., Mary Elizabeth (Mrs. Donald L. Bain); m. 2d, Clarence Louis Gingery, Oct. 5, 1963. Tchr., Allapattah Elementary Sch., Miami, Fla., 1924-47. Mem. U.D.C. (pres. 1962-63), Hist. Soc., Opera Guild, Miami Shores C. of C. Methodist (pres. Womens Soc. Christian Service 1959-61, circle leader; ofcl. bd.). Mem. Order Eastern Star, Daus. of Nile, White Shrine. Clubs: Miami Woman's (mem. conservation com., mem. chorus), Flamingo Dinner, Miami Garden (treas.); Retired Teachers (mem. adminstrv. bd.). Home: 151 NE 93d St Miami Shores FL 33138

GINGRICH, DOROTHEA LOHOFF, journalist; b. Lane County, Kan., May 7, 1911; d. Paul and Emma (Thon) Lohoff; student Washington U., 1927-29; B.J., U. Mo. (outstanding woman journalism student), 1931, M.A., 1941; m. R. G. Schlegel, Aug. 29, 1933 (div.); 1 dau., Sandra Kay (Mrs. Tucker Hollamon); m. 2d, Jack Edward Gingrich, July 27, 1941; 1 son, Paul Schuyler. Editor West Plains (Mo.) Jour., 1931-33; dir. journalism and publicity Mary Hardin-Baylor Coll., Belton, Tex., 1936-41, dir. Centennial pub. relations, 1944-45; mem. journalism faculty Tex. Christian U., 1947-49; asso. editor Seguin (Tex.) Enterprise, 1951-53, woman's page, 1953-55, featured columnist, 1954—; corr. San Antonio Light, 1951—; head journalism dept. Tex. Luth. Coll. Girl Scout commr., Robstown, Tex., mem. council Ft. Worth, Seguin, Tex.; pres. Seguin Friends of Library, 1961, hon. life mem.; trustee County Library, 1961—, chmn. bd. 1965—. Region V mem. Women's Civil Def. Council. Recipient Headliner award Theta Sigma Phi, San Antonio, 1956; 1st place award for column South Tex. Press Assn., 1957; distinction in journalism Tex. Centennial Rangerette Commn., 1936; 1st place award in state for newspaper column Tex. Women's Press Assn., 1960, 61, 63, 65, 66, 67, 69; 1st place Tex. Press Assn., 1960; 3d place Nat. Fedn. Press Women's contest, 1960; Outstanding Community Service award Seguin and Guadalupe County C. of C., 1970; Devoted Service plaque Library Bd., 1970; named Library Trustee of Year, Tex. Library Assn., 1965, chmn. Trustee, Round Table, 1970. Mem. Women's Soc. Christian Service (pres. 1957), Tex. Press Women, Inc. (pres. 1968-69), Nat. Fedn. Press Women (2d v.p. 1969-70, historian 1973—), Am. Assn. U. Women (state bd. mem., past pres.), Am. Coll. Pub. Assn. (pres. Tex.-Okla. dist. 1941), Tex. Fedn. Women's Clubs (dist. chmn. edn. dept. 1961-64, pres. Alamo dist. 1968-70, state div. chmn.), Conservation Soc., Tex. Assn. Coll. Jour. Tchrs. (pres. 1959), Nat. Soc. Arts and Letters (parliamentarian San Antonio 1972-74), Zonta Internat. (dir. 1973, historian 1973), Women's Soc. Christian Service, Theta Sigma Phi (past nat., sec., v.p., regional dir.; distinguished service award 1962), Delta Delta Delta (nat. pub. relations chmn.), Beta Sigma Phi (hon.; order Rose degree 1970), Kappa Tau Alpha, Delta Kappa Gamma. Methodist (steward). Clubs: San Antonio Woman's (chmn. heritage dept. 1973); Seguin Shakespeare (pres 1965—), Delphian (pres.). Home: 1120 N King St Apt 210 Seguin TX 78155 Office: Seguin Enterprise N Austin St Seguin Tx 78155

GINN, ROSEMARY LUCAS (MRS. M. STANLEY GINN), mem. Republican Nat. Com., club woman; b. Columbia, Mo., Aug. 28, 1912; d. Reuben E. and Mary (Bewick) Lucas; B.A., U. Mo., 1933, grad. student, 1933-34, 58-59; m. Milton Stanley Ginn, June 21, 1934; children—Nancy Bewick, Sally Reuben. Dir. Mo. Stores Co., Columbia, 1939—. Mem. budget coms. United Funds, Columbia, 1955, 56, 57, dir. 1957; mem. Columbia Bd. Health, 1956-59; bd. dirs. Boone County Hosp. Aux.; adviser Columbia Council Clubs, 1956-59. Pres. Lawrence County (Mo.) Women's Republican Club, 1937-38, Boone County (Mo.), 1948-49; pres. Fedn. Rep. Women's Clubs Mo., 1959-61; bd. dirs. Nat. Fedn. Rep. Women, 1959-61; Rep. nat. com. woman for Mo., 1960—, chmn. del. and orgn. com. Rep. Nat. Com., 1969-72, mem. rule 29 com.; dist. v.p. State Young Rep. Club, 1948; del. county, dist. and state Rep. convs. 1948-52, 56, alternate del. at large Mo. to nat. Rep. Conv. 1956, del.-at-large, 1968; permanent sec. Rep. State Conv. of Mo., 1956; mem. Nat. Mortar Bd. Found., 1956—. Recipient Faculty-Alumni award U. Mo., 1971. Mem. Assn. Coll. Honor Socs. (rep. Mortar Bd. 1949-58, exec. council 1953, pres. 1955-57, rep. nat. conf. of frats. and socs. 1956), Mortar Bd. (sect. dir. 1935-45; nat. dir. expansion, 1945-48, nat. pres. 1948-55, U. Mo. alumni citation of merit, 1963), Nat. Assn. Women Deans and Counselors, Am. Assn. U. Women, Am. Legion Aux. (counsellor Mo. Girls State 1956-64), League Women Voters, Kings Daus., Phi Beta Kappa, Alpha Kappa Delta, Delta Sigma Rho, Alpha Pi Zeta, Delta Delta Delta. Baptist. Clubs: Hawkeye Beagle, Tuesday, Columbia Country (Mo.). Address: 303 West Blvd S Columbia MO 65201

GINN, SOPHIE (MRS. PAUL PASTER), soprano, educator, opera dir.; b. N.Y.C., Oct. 29, 1933; d. Stanley and Lillian (Piwowarczyk) Ginn; B.S., Juilliard Sch. Music, 1956, M.S., 1958; m. Paul Paster, Feb. 18, 1954; 1 son, Paul Alex. Appeared in The Mighty Casey—CBS-TV, N.Y.C., 1955, The Veil—N.Y. Opera Theatre, 1955; recital at Kaufmann Hall, N.Y.C., 1956; appeared in Faust—Hotel Pierre, 1957; soloist with Camarata Singers, 1958; N.Y. Town Hall debut, 1958; soloist with Goldman Band—Central Park, 1960-61; with N.Y.C. Opera Co., 1961; appeared in No For An Answer, Blitzstein-Circle-in-the-Square Theatre, 1962; soloist under Robert Shaw Beethoven's Ninth Symphony—Meadow Brook, Rochester, Mich., 1967, La Traviata, La Boheme, Il Trovatore, Carmen, O., Verdi Requiem, Midland (Mich.) Symphony, 1968, Akron Symphony, 1969; Capriccio with Cleve. Orch.; performed world premiere Shadow Wood (by Warren Benson); soloist Bach Festival, Berea, O., 1970; soloist Forever Young (by Elwell) Cleve. Arts Festival, 1971; soloist with Severance String Quartet, 1972; guest performer Nat. Mu Phi Epsilon Conv., 1972; soloist Ohio Chamber Orch., 1973; soloist, asst. dir. opera performances, Graz, Austria, 1973; pvt. voice tchr., dir. Glee Club Rhodes Prep. Sch., N.Y.C., 1957-59; instr. music North Tex. State U., Denton, 1959; asst. prof. music Bowling Green (O.) State U., 1961-66; dir. opera Baldwin-Wallace Conservatory, Berea, O., 1968—. Organizer Festival-Shakespeare in Vocal Music, 1964, Synartesis Series at Baldwin-Wallace Coll., 1970. Den mother Pack 323 Cub Scout council Boy Scouts Am., 1964-65. Caruso Meml. scholar 1958-59; recipient N.Y. Singing Tchrs. Assn. Recital award, 1958, William Matheus Sullivan Mus. Found. award, 1958, Y Young Artist award, 1956, Marcella Sembrich-Kochanska Nat. Voice Contest prize, 1954. Baldwin-Wallace faculty grantee, Graz, Austria, 1973. Mem. Nat. Assn. Tchrs. Singing, Central Opera Service, Mu Phi Epsilon. Club: Fortnightly. Home: 519 Karen Dr Berea OH 44017

GINOCCHIO, RUTH ARLENE, banker; b. Woodhaven, N.Y., Aug. 27, 1929; d. Charles Louis and Sybilla Katherine (Hugel) Ginocchio; student Queens Coll., 1952-53, Am. Inst. Banking, 1967-68, Adelphi U., 1970. With Richmond Hill Savs. Bank (N.Y.) 1947—, asst. br. mgr., 1970—. Mem. Savs. Bank Women N.Y., Officers Forum Group VI. Presbyn. (deacon 1965-71, ch. blood bank chmn. 1968-71, fair co-chmn. 1967-72). Club: XYZ (project chmn. N.Y.C. 1971-72). Home: 91-37 89 St Woodhaven NY 11421 also Whitfield Rd Accord NY 12404 Office: 115-20 Jamaica Av Richmond Hill NY 11418

GINSBERG, SADIE-VERA DASHEW, machinery co. exec.; b. Balt., Mar. 21, 1901; d. Jacob and Eve (Chircus) Dashew; B.A., Goucher Coll., 1922; postgrad. Johns Hopkins; m. Leon M. Ginsberg, June 15, 1922; 1 dau., Judith (Mrs. Melvin Bender). Exec. dir. Child Study Assn. Balt., 1925-46; part-time instr., cons. early childhood edn. McCoy Coll., dept. edn. Johns Hopkins, 1945-65, vis. lectr. day care Sch. Hygiene and Pub. Health, 1946-66; co-ordinator Head Start Tng. Project for Balt., U. Md., 1965—; project officer U.S. Office Econ. Opportunity for Parent and Child Centers, 1967-69; sec.-treas. J. Dashew, Inc., Balt., 1948-66, exec. dir., 1962-63, pres., 1966—; exec. dir. Children's Guild, Balt., 1962-63, hon. chmn., 1953—; instr. cons., dept. early childhood edn. U. Md., 1963-67; vis. lectr. Towson (Md.) State Coll., 1971-72; cons. Nat. Day Care Licensing Study-Task Force on Fire and Bldg. Codes, 1971-72; planning cons. in early childhood edn. for Columbia, Md., Rouse Co., 1965-68; cons. med. staff John F. Kennedy Inst., Johns Hopkins Hosp., 1973—; cons. in-service early childhood tng. Univ. Hosp., Balt., 1973—. Charter mem., vice chmn. U.S. Nat. Com. for Early Childhood Edn., 1952-56, chmn. nominations, 1952, 56, 70-72; chmn. state adv. com. on day care Md. State Dept. Social Services, 1969-72; mem. adv. com. on early childhood edn. Md. State Dept. Edn., 1970—, mem. adv. com. on licensing for child day care Md. Dept. Health and Mental Hygiene, 1972—; treas. Md. 4C Com., 1970-74; hon. chmn. Md. Com. for Day Care of Children, 1946—; mem. bd. sci. advisers Med. Research Inst., Worcester, Mass., 1962—; mem. adv. com. Demonstration Day Care Center, Towson State Coll., 1971—; chmn. com. on day care services, Kennedy Inst., Johns Hosp., Balt., 1971—, mem. women's bd. Kennedy Inst. Council, 1972—; bd. advisers infant and presch. developmental programs Inst. Rehab. Medicine, N.Y. U., Hosp. Med. Center. Active Balt. Mus. Art, Balt. League Women Voters, Balt. Symphony Orch. Assn., women's aux. Brandeis U., Friends of Library Johns Hopkins U., Friends of Library Goucher Coll. Md. Recipient Hannah G. Solomon award Nat. Council Jewish Women Balt. chpt. 1969; named Woman of Year, Balt. Fedn. Jewish Women's Orgns., 1951; Outstanding Woman of Year, Nat. Camp Fire Girls, 1971; Louise Waterman Wise Community Service award Women's div. Am. Jewish Congress, 1972; Exceptional Service award Child Study Assn. Md., 1973. Mem. Assn. for Childhood Edn. Internat. (life, chmn. gifts and bequests com. 1967-73, mem. finance com. 1972—), Nat. Assn. for Edn. Young Children (life), Interagy. Council (chmn. 1971—), Day Care and Child Devel. Council Am. (vice chmn. bd. dirs. 1959-66, chmn. 1966-67), Md. Ornithol. Soc., Md. Acad. Scis., UN Assn. Md., Am. Assn. U. Women, Chamber Music Soc. Balt., English Speaking Union, Goucher Coll. Alumnae, Johns Hopkins U. Alumni Assn., Hadassah Med. Orgn. (life), Md. Assn. for Childhood Edn., Pi Lambda Theta. Contbr., editor articles to tech. jours. Home: 58 Olmsted Green Baltimore MD 21210 Office: 417 W Baltimore St Baltimore MD 21201

GINSBURG, HELEN LACHS (MRS. NATHAN GINSBURG), social scientist, educator; b. N.Y.C.; d. William and Anna (Riegelhaupt) Lachs; B.A., Queens Coll.; M.A., New Sch. for Social Research, Ph.D., 1967; m. Nathan Ginsburg. Research asst. Twentieth Century Fund, N.Y.C., 1956-61; research asso. New Sch. for Social Research, N.Y.C., 1962-63; lectr. Queensborough Coll., N.Y.C., 1965-66; instr. L.I. U., Bklyn., 1966-67, asst. prof. econs., 1967-73; research asso. prof. N.Y. U., 1973—. Mem. Am. Econ. Assn., Indsl. Relations Research Assn., Assn. for Evolutionary Econs. Author: Poverty, Economics, and Society, 1972. Contbr. to University and Community: A New Partnership, 1971. Home: 41-90 Frame Pl Flushing NY 11355 Office: NYU Center for Studies in Income Maintenance Policy 35 Fifth Av New York City NY 10003

GINSBURG, IONA BARBARA HOROWITZ (MRS. SELIG M. GINSBURG), physician; b. Bklyn., Dec. 2, 1931; d. A. Eugene and Gertrude (Seidman) Horowitz; A.B., Vassar Coll., 1953; M.D., Coll. Physicians and Surgeons, 1957; m. Selig M. Ginsburg, Aug. 15, 1954; children—Elizabeth, Jessica. Intern, Mt. Sinai Hosp., N.Y.C., 1957-58; resident N.Y. State Psychiat. Inst., N.Y.C., 1958-61; practice medicine specializing in psychiatry, N.Y.C., 1961—; mem. staff N.Y. Psychiat. Inst.; instr. psychiatry Columbia U., 1962—. Diplomate Am. Bd. Psychiatry and Neurology. Mem. A.M.A., Am. Psychiat. Assn., N.Y. Soc. for Clin. Psychiatry, N.Y. Acad. Scis., Soc. for Adolescent Psychiatry, Met. Coll. Mental Health Assn. (exec. com., treas.), Phi Beta Kappa, Alpha Omega Alpha. Office: 55 E 86th St New York City NY 10028

GINSBURG, MIRRA, editor, translator; b. Russia, June 10, 1919; d. Joseph and Bronia (Geier) Ginsburg. Came to U.S., 1933, naturalized, 1941. Self-employed as editor and translator from Russian and Yiddish into English. Grantee Nat. Translation Center, Austin, Tex., 1967. Mem. P.E.N. Editor, translator: (Soviet satire) Fatal Eggs, 1965; (sci. fiction) Last Door to Aiya, 1968, Ultimate Threshold, 1970; (by Yevgeny Zamyatin) (stories) Dragon, 1966, (essays) Soviet Heretic, 1970; (novel) We, 1972; (by M. Bulgakov) Master and Margarita, 1967, Heart of a Dog, 1968, Life of Monsieur de Moliere, 1970, (play) Flight, 1969; (by Chingiz Aitmatov) White Ship, 1972; (by Dostoevsky) Notes From Underground, 1974; (juvenile) Diary of Nina Kosterina, 1968; (folklore retold) Master of the Winds, 1970, Three Rolls and One Doughnut, 1970, Kaha Bird, 1971, One Trick Too Many, 1972, The Lazies, 1973, How Wilka Went to Sea, 1974. Address: 150 W 96th St New York City NY 10025

GINSBURG, (RUTH) ANN FORMAN (MRS. VICTOR GINSBURG), biochemist; b. Porterville, Cal., Jan. 17, 1932; d. Maurice W. and Ruth (Harris) Forman; B.A. with honors in biochemistry, U. Cal. at Berkeley, 1954, M.A., 1956; Ph.D., George Washington U., 1964; m. Victor Ginsburg, May 27, 1955; children—Mark, Lisa. Biochemist, Nat. Inst. Arthritis and Metabolic Diseases, NIH, Bethesda, Md., 1956-58, 63-64, Nat. Inst. Dental Research, 1964—, Nat. Heart and Lung Inst., 1966—. Mem. Am. Soc. Biol. Chemists, Phi Beta Kappa, Sigma Xi, Iota Sigma Pi. Home: 6905 Loch Lomond Dr Bethesda MD 20034 Office: Nat Heart and Lung Inst NIH Bethesda MD 20014

GINSBURG, RUTH BADER, educator; b. Bklyn., Mar. 15, 1933; d. Nathan and Celia (Amster) Bader; B.A., Cornell U., 1954; postgrad. Harvard Law Sch., 1956-58; J.D. (Kent scholar), Columbia, 1959; LL.D., Lund (Sweden) U., 1969; m. Martin David Ginsburg, June 23, 1954; children—Jane Carol, James Steven. Admitted to N.Y. bar, 1959, U.S. Supreme Ct. bar; law clk. to dist. judge So. Dist. N.Y., 1959-61; research asso. Columbia Law Sch. Project on Internat. Procedure, 1961-62, asso. dir., 1962-63; asst. prof. law Rutgers U., Newark, 1963-65, asso. prof., 1966-69, prof., 1969-72; prof. law Columbia, N.Y.C., 1972—. Chmn. com. on women in legal edn. Assn. Am. Law Schs., 1971-73; mem. exec. com. Assn. Am. Law Schs., 1971-73; bd. dirs. Woman's Law Fund, 1972—; coordinator women's rights project Am. Civil Liberties Union, 1971-73, gen. counsel, 1973—. Mem. Am. Bar Assn. (chmn. com. on comparative procedure and practice 1970-73, bd. editors jour. 1972—), Bar Assn. N.Y.C. (exec. com. 1974—, com. on post-admission legal edn.), Am. Law Inst., Am. Fgn. Law Assn. (dir. 1970—, v.p. 1973—), Council on Fgn. Relations, Phi Beta Kappa (vis. scholar 1973-74), Phi Kappa Phi. Author: (with Anders Bruzelius) Civil Procedure in Sweden, 1965, The Swedish Code of Judicial Procedure, 1968; A Selective Survey of English Language Studies on Scandinavian Law, 1970; (with others) Constitutional Aspects of Sex-Based Discrimination, 1974; Sex-Based Discrimination, Text, Cases and Materials, 1974. Bd. editors Am. Jour. Comparative Law, 1966-72. Contbr. articles to legal jours. Home: 150 E 69th St New York City NY 10021

GINSPARG, SYLVIA LEVINE, psychologist; b. Chgo., July 22, 1931; d. Sidney and Helen (Wineberg) Levine; A.B., Roosevelt U., 1951, A.M., 1953; Ph.D., Washington U., St. Louis, 1956; children—Joel Harvey, Daniel Norman. Clin. intern Chgo. Med. Sch. Clinics, Mt. Sinai Hosp., 1952-53; research psychologist Washington U. Sch. Medicine-Malcolm Bliss Psychopathic Hosp., St. Louis, 1953-54; psychol. intern community child guidance clinic Washington U., St. Louis, 1954-55, psychol. asst., 1955-56; chief psychologist children's service Larue Carter Meml. Hosp., Indpls., 1956-57; psychol. cons. Family and Children's Service Greater St. Louis, also pvt. practice psychology, St. Louis, 1957-60; research psychologist longitudinal studies of child devel. Menninger Found., Topeka, Kan., 1960-65, staff psychologist, div. law and psychiatry, 1966-72, psychoterapist child clin. services, 1970—, faculty mem. div. indsl. mental health, 1971—, asst. dir. div. sch. mental health, 1972—; staff psychologist child study unit Kan. Neurol. Inst., Topeka, 1965-66; mem. faculty Menninger Sch. Psychiatry, Topeka, 1973—.

Mem. Am., Kan. (chmn. social action com. 1970-71), Mo., Topeka psychol. assns., Am. Orthopsychiat. Assn. (mem. editorial bd. 1973), Am. Psychology-Law Soc., Am. Assn. Suicidology, Am. Assn. Correctional Psychologists, Psychologists Interested in Study of Psychoanalysis (program chmn. 1970—), Sigma Xi. Contbr. to publs. in field. Home: 2706 Indian Trail Topeka KS 66614 Office: Box 829 Menninger Found Topeka KS 66614

GINTHER, RUTH MARGARET, mus. exec.; b. Niagara Falls, N.Y., July 31, 1903; d. Charles Joseph and Jennie (Engel) McCarthy; student Niagara U., 1944-45, U. Buffalo, 1952-56, 58; m. Joseph G. Ginther, Dec. 13, 1922 (annulled); 1 dau., Jeane M. (Mrs. W.E. Hauth). Dir. specifications div. Carbon Products div. Union Carbide Corp., Niagara Falls, 1924-69; curator costumes Niagara County (N.Y.) Hist. Mus., 1969—; social service worker Health Assn. Niagara County; resource person women's div. N.Y. State Dept. Commerce. Lectr. antique costumes. Mem. Niagara Falls City Commn., 1959—, chmn., 1963; pres. Niagara Council Women's Assns., 1961; sec. Operation Petticoat Progress, 1966; mem. Niagara Falls Meml. Hosp Aux. Sec. bd. dirs. Niagara Falls A.R.C., Niagara Falls Philharmonic Orch.; bd. control Niagara Falls festivals; treas. bd. Odd Fellow and Rebekah Home Assn., Lockport, N.Y. Mem. Republican Women's Forum. Recipient VIM citation N.Y. State Bus. and Profl. Women's Club, 1964; Key to Lockport Falls (N.Y.); Seal of Niagara Falls; named Outstanding Woman Community, 1970. Mem. Niagara Falls Philharmonic Guild (pres.), Niagara Falls (dir.), Niagara County (chmn. women's div. 1966) hist. socs., Nat. Conf. Christians and Jews (dir.), Bus. and Profl. Women's Club (pres. chpt. 1946; sec. N.Y. State fedn. 1948-50), Niagara Area C. of C., Am. Bus. Women's Assn., Beta Sigma Psi. Presbyn. (pub. relations worker). Mem. Rebekah (dist. dep. pres. Western NY.). Clubs: Quota (pres. 1956, dist. lt. gov. 1964, gov. N.Y. State), Niagara Falls Garden (pres. 1943), Niagara Frontier Country. Home: 1135 Garrett Av Niagara Falls NY 14305 Office: 3625 Highland Av Niagara Falls NY 14305

GINZLER, HELEN BELL, librarian; b. Detroit, May 4, 1920; d. Joseph and Dora (Mishkin) Bell; B.A., Wayne State U., 1964, M.S. in Library Sci., 1967; m. Emanuel Mortimer Ginzler, Jan. 19, 1944; children—James Arthur, Frances Jean (Mrs. Harvey Rubin), Dorene Beth. Adminstr. North Farmington High Sch. Library, Farmington, Mich., 1965-67; coordinator multi-media center Brother Rice High Sch. Library, Brimingham, Mich., 1967—. Program dir. Women's Am. ORT, Oak Park, Mich., 1970—; bd. dirs. Alpa Nu Parents Club, Detroit, 1970—, sec., 1973-74. Named Outstanding Sr. Woman Wayne State U., 1964. Mem. Am., Mich., Catholic library assns., Mich. Sch. Librarians Assn., Mich. Audiovisual Assn. Home: 21971 Avon Oak Park MI 48237 Office: 7101 Laser Rd Birmingham MI 48010

GIORGI, CELIA ANN COLORADO (MRS. ANGELO JOSEPH GIORGI), coll. adminstr.; b. Antioch, Cal., June 27, 1927; d. Santos and Angelina (Martinez) Colorado; m. Angelo Joseph Giorgi, Sept. 21, 1952; 1 dau., Loretta Margaret. Social worker Fresno (Cal.) County Welfare Dept., 1969-70; dir. personnel services St. Mary's Coll., Moraga, Cal., 1972—; dir., asst., cons. Sisters of the Holy Trinity, Fresno. Mem. League of Women Voters of Diablo Valley, Personnel Mgmt. Assn. of Aztlan, Assn. of Ind. Cal. Colls. and Univs., Childrens Home Soc. Roman Catholic. Home: 327 Constance Pl Moraga CA 94556 Office: St Marys Coll of Cal Moraga CA 94575

GIRA, CATHERINE RUSSELL (MRS. JOSEPH ANDREW GIRA), educator; b. Fayette City, Pa.; d. John Anthony and Mary (Stephen) Russell; B.A., California (Pa.) State Coll., 1953; M.Ed., Johns Hopkins, 1957, M.L.A., 1972; M. Joseph Andrew Gira, July 17, 1954; children—Cheryl Ann, Thomas Russell. Tchr. pub. schs., Baltimore County, 1953-60, chmn. English dept., 1959-60; writing cons. Md. Dept. Edn., Balt., 1961—; instr. writing courses Johns Hopkins, 1964-68; asso. prof. English and coordinator writing courses U. Balt., 1965—. Mem. N.E.A., Md. Council Tchrs. English, Tchrs. Assn. Baltimore County, Coll. English Assn., Coll. Conf. on Composition and Communication, Am. Assn. U. Profs., Phi Delta Gamma (nat. pres.), Pi Lambda Theta, Kappa Delta Pi. Home: 10450 Green Mountain Circle Columbia MD 21044

GIRARD, MARY ELOISE SABEL (MRS. RICHARD A. GIRARD), personnel cons.; b. Huntington, W.Va., Oct. 8, 1912; d. Isaac Herbert and Minnie (McLaughlin) Sabel; B.A., Randolph-Macon Women's Coll., 1934; M.S., N.Y.U., 1935; m. Richard A. Girard, June 16, 1965. Personnel mgr. Ohrbach's, Inc., Newark, 1935-44, N.Y.C., 1944-63, v.p., 1969-72; personnel cons., 1972—; instr. City Coll. N.Y., 1952-53, sch. retailing N.Y.U., 1954; guest panelist ednl. forums and radio. Mem. adv. commn. State U. N.Y., 1946—; trustee Distributive Edn. Found. of N.Y.C., Inc. Mem. Assn. Personnel Women (pres. No. N.J., 1940-41), Personnel Club N.Y. (v.p. 1952-54), Eastern Coll. Personnel Officers, Internat. Assn. Personnel Women, Internat. Transactional Analysis Soc., Zeta Tau Alpha Alumni Assn., Tau Kappa Alpha, Eta Mu Pi. Presbyn. Contbr. articles retail trade and personnel publs. Home: 390 First Av New York City NY 10010 Office: 390 1st Av New York City NY 10010

GIRARD, WANDA GLORIA MISKOWIEC (MRS. DEAN L. GIRARD), physician; b. La Jara, Colo., Aug. 31, 1930; d. Adalbert and Josephine (Gonzales) Miskowiec; B.A., U. Colo., 1952, M.D., 1955; m. Dean L. Girard, June 20, 1955; children—Michele Therese, Dean Clayton, Stephanie Ann, Denise Marie, Phillip Damian, David Miskowiec. Intern, St. Josephs Hosp., Denver, 1955-56; practice medicine, specializing in anesthesiology; staff Santa Fe, Mennonite hosps., La Junta, Colo., VA. Hosp., Fort Lyon, Colo., 1956-65; pub. health physician Otero County Health Dept., 1956-65, med. cons., programs coordinator, 1971-73; med. health officer Otero County, 1974—. Mem. licensed practical nursing adv. com. Otero Jr. Coll., 1972—. Asst. leader Girl Scouts U.S.A., 1966-68; swimming instr. A.R.C., 1963-65; dir. student health program St. Patrick Parocial Sch., 1960-65; mem. adv. bd. Mennonite Hosp. Sch. Practical Nursing, 1960-65; mem. Loma Vista Bldg. Corp., 1960-71, Region 6 Comprehensive Health Planning Assn., La Junta Parochial Sch. Bd. Mem. A.M.A., Colo., Otero County, Denver med. socs., Colo. Pub. Health Assn., U. Colo. Alumni Assn., P.E.O., Alpha Omicron Pi. Roman Catholic. Clubs: Faculty Wives Medical School. Home: 77 Circle Dr La Junta CO 81050

GIRGUS, JOAN STERN, psychologist, coll. dean; b. Albany, N.Y., Mar. 21, 1942; d. William Bernet and Louise (Mayer) Stern; B.A., Sarah Lawrence Coll., 1963; M.A., The Grad. Faculty New Sch. for Social Research, 1965, Ph.D. (NSF fellow, NIH fellow), 1969; m. Joel Joseph Girgus, June 18, 1966. Asst. prof. dept psychology Coll. City N.Y., N.Y.C., 1969-72, asso. prof., 1972—, asso. dean div. social sci., 1972—. Faculty Research grantee City U. N.Y., 1971-74, Nat. Inst. Child Health and Human Devel. Research grantee, 1972-75. Mem. Am., Eastern Psychol. assns., Psychonomic Soc., Sigma Xi. Contbr. articles and chpts. to profl. jours. and books. Home: 163 W 17th St New York City NY 10011 Office: Div Social Science Shepard 118 City College of City U New York Convent Av and 138th St New York City NY 10031

GITCHELL, MAZIE, lawyer; b. Evart, Mich., Apr. 16, 1894; d. Benjamin Franklin and Mary Elizabeth (Smith) Gitchell; student Mich. State U., 1910-11, 26, Mich. Central U., 1912-13; LL.B., Wayne U., 1936. Tchr. Jr. High Sch., Dimondale, Mich., 1913-15; asst. to pres. Grange Life Ins. Co., Lansing, Mich., 1915-30; actuarial, statis. work Maccabees Life Ins. Co., Detroit, 1930-32; admitted to Mich. bar, 1936, since practiced in Detroit and Hartland; now small farm operator; adjudicator, mortgage loan examiner for VA, purchasing agent, and claims officer Dept. of Army, Detroit and Centerline, Mich., 1944-60. Mem. Mich. Bar Assn., Alpha Sigma Tau, Kappa Alpha Theta. Home: 13055 Dunham Rd Hartland MI 48029

GITOMER, IRENE STOLLER (MRS. IRVING GITOMER), librarian; b. Edinburgh, Scotland, June 14, 1924; d. Ellis and Alice (Davis) Stoller; came to U.S., 1927, naturalized 1935; B.A., Rutgers U., 1961; M.S. in L.S., Drexel U., 1962; m. Irving Gitomer, Dec. 23, 1944; children—David, Jonathan, Philip, Ellen, Daniel. Adminstrv. asst. to dean Drexel Grad. Sch. L.S., Phila., 1960, dir. pub. relations, 1961, instr., 1965; dir. Cherry Hill (N.J.) Free Pub. Library, 1962-70; library cons., 1970-71; dir. Madison Twp. (N.J.) Free Public Library, 1971—. Instr., Phila. Comm. Coll., 1968-69, Glassboro State Coll., 1969. Mem. Burlington County Human Relations Commn. Bd. dirs. Drexel U. Alumni, 1974—. Mem. A.L.A., Am., N.J. library trustees assns., Spl. Libraries Assn., Am., Pa. library assns., Library Pub. Relations Council, Catholic, Jewish, N.J. (chmn. recruitment com. 1965-67, 2d v.p. 1966-67, chmn. scholarhip com. 1968-70, chmn. exhibits com. 1970-73, mem. at large exec. bd. 1972-75), Camden county (pres. 1966) library assns., Library Pub. Relations Assn. (pres. 1968-69), Am. Civil Liberties Union (exec. bd. So. Jersey), League Women Voters, Women's Polit. Caucus, Beta Phi Mu, Phi Kappa Phi. Club: Zonta (chmn. service project 1965). Home: 18 Oriole Way Moorestown NJ 08057

GIVEN, BARBARA KNIGHT (MRS. BRUCE WILLARD GIVEN), educator; b. Quenemo, Kan., July 17, 1935; d. Henry Taylor and Lucile M. (Jolley) Knight; A.A., Colo. Woman's Coll., 1955; B.A., Kan. State U., 1958; M.Ed., U. Ore., 1967; Ph.D., Cath. U. Am., 1974; m. Bruce Willard Given, June 7, 1959; children—Bryce Walton, Bethany Kay. Elementary tchr., Wichita, Kan., 1958-59, Eugene, Ore., 1959-61; cons., scriptwriter, mentally retarded deaf project Cath. U. Am., Washington, 1966-69, instr. mentally retarded, 1967; cons. project Lang. Improvement to Facilitate Edn., N.E.A., 1969; dir. spl. edn., instr. pediatrics John F. Kennedy Inst., Johns Hopkins, Balt., 1969-70; teaching asst. Cath. U. Am., Washington, 1971-72; tchr. learning disabilities Fairfax County (Va.) Pub. Schs., 1972-73; asst. prof. spl. edn. George Mason U., Fairfax, 1973—. Mem. Council for Exceptional Children, Am. Assn. Mental Deficiency, Va., Fairfax County tchrs. assns., N.E.A., Internat. Soc. for Edn. Through Art. Home: 3113 Shadeland Dr Falls Church VA 22044 Office: 4400 University Dr Fairfax VA 22030

GIVEN, PHYLLIS E., state legislator; b. Pomeroy, O.; d. Ray and Ethel (Jones) Evans; ed. pub. schs.; student Columbus Bus. Coll., W.Va. U., Morris Harvey Coll.; m. Harold C. Given, Dec. 25, 1946 (dec.); children—Barbara Lynn, Harold Edward. Mem. exec. council Kanawha County P.T.A.; mem. nat. consumers adv. council Kroger Co.; mem. Ednl. Task Force; mem. non-traditional study task force for higher edn. W.Va. Bd. Regents; mem. adv. panel on missions and goals W.Va. State Coll. Mem. W.Va. Ho. of Dels. from Kanawha County, 1970—. Mem. Kanawha County Democratic Women; v.p. W.Va. Fedn. Dem. Women. Mem. Nat. Soc. State Legislators (exec. com.), Nat. Legislative Conf. (intergovtl. relations com.), Order Ky. Cols., League of Women Voters. Home: 915 Somerset Dr Charleston WV 25302*

GLADDEN, FRANCENE, social worker; b. Pine Bluff, Ark., July 14, 1945; d. Fred and Ruth Virginia (Ridgway) Gladden; student Tex. Woman's U., 1963-65; B.A., So. State Coll., 1966; postgrad. State Coll. Ark., 1970-71. Caseworker, Ark. Dept. Pub. Welfare, McGehee, 1966-67; castworker Ark. Children's Colony, Conway, 1967-68, social worker, acting dir. social service McRae Unit, Alexander, 1968-69; social worker rehab. service Boys Tng. Sch., Pine Bluff, 1969—. Mem. Am. Assn. Mental Deficiency, Nat. Rehab. Assn., Nat. Rehab. Counseling Assn., Ark. Conf. on Social Welfare, Tau Beta Sigma. Methodist. Home: 1714 W 11th St Pine Bluff AR 71601 Office: Route 8 Box 982 Pine Bluff AR 71601

GLADDING, ELINOR DOROTHY HARTNELL (MRS. EDWARD K. GLADDING), chemist; b. Cheltenham, Md., June 5, 1912; d. George and Lillian (Freeman) Hartnell; A.B., Lynchburg Coll., 1932; B.S. in L.S., George Peabody Coll., 1933; M.A., Johns Hopkins, 1945, Ph.D., 1948; m. Edward K. Gladding, Mar. 6, 1954. Asst. librarian, tech. library Chem. Warfare Service, Edgewood Arsenal, 1938-42; sr. chemist survey anti-malarial drugs Johns Hopkins, 1943-46, patent chemist organic chems. dept. E. I. duPont de Nemours & Co., Wilmington, Del., 1948-58, elastomer chems. dept., 1958-74. Mem. Am. Chem. Soc., Nat. Audubon Soc., Nat. Wildlife Fedn., Wilderness Soc. Club: Appalachian Mountain. Home: 2401 Pennsylvania Av Wilmington DE 19806 Office: E I duPont de Nemours & Co Wilmington DE 19898

GLADFELTER, VALERIE GARBER (MRS. DAVID DREWS GLADFELTER), social worker; b. Phila., May 18, 1938; d. Samuel and Beatrice (Gillman) Garber; B.A., Brandeis U., 1959; M.S.W., Rutgers U., 1964; m. David Drews Gladfelter, July 13, 1968; 1 son, Stephen Garber. Social worker Norristown (Pa.) State Hosp., 1959-60, Camden (N.J.) Psychiat. Hosp., 1960-62; chief social worker Temple Med. Sch. unit, dir. Phila. Day Treatment Center, Eastern State Sch. and Hosp., Trevose, Pa., 1964-68; regional supr. N.J. Div. Mental Retardation, 1968-70; individual practice marriage and family counseling, Willingboro, N.J., 1970—. Mem. co-adj. faculty Rutgers Grad. Sch. Social Work, 1972—, also field instr.; field instr. U. Pa. Grad. Sch. Social Work, 1965-68; instr. Temple U. Med. Sch., 1967-68; cons. Willingboro (N.J.) Police Dept., 1973—; mem. N.J. Bd. Marriage Counselor Examiners, 1973—. Vice-chmn. Willingboro Twp. (N.J.) Human Relations Commn., 1970-72, chmn., 1972-74. Bd. dirs. Mercer St. Friends Center, Trenton, N.J., 1965-68, Counselling Center, Willingboro, N.J., 1973. Brandeis Nat. scholar, 1955-56, Nat. Inst. Mental Health fellow Rutgers Grad. Sch. Social Work, 1963-64. Mem. Am. Assn. Marriage and Family Counselors, Nat. Assn. Social Workers (mem. council on social work edn. 1965). Mem. Soc. of Friends. Home: 109 Tyler Dr Willingboro NJ 08046

GLADISH, MARY LOUISE, educator, librarian; b. Prospect, Tenn., May 15, 1920; d. William L. and Cleo (Potts) Gladish; B.S. in Home Econs., U. Tenn., 1941, M.S. in Pub. Health, U. N.C., 1944; M.A., U. Chgo., 1948; student Harvard Sch. Pub. Health, 1948-49; course med. librarianship Emory U., 1964; M.L.S., George Peabody Coll., 1966. Home econs. tchr. Hornbeak (Tenn.) High Sch., 1941-43; health educator Camp Forrest Dist. Health Dept., Manchester, Tenn., 1944-45, Lee County Health Dept., Tupelo, Miss., 1945-47; asso. prof. health edn. East Tenn. State U., Johnson City, 1958-63; now med. research librarian Vanderbilt U. Med. Library, Nashville. Active Girl Scouts. Bd.; mem. Washington County chpt. A.R.C., Johnson City, 1961-63; mem. Goodwill Industries Aux., Nashville Mental Health Assn., Lookout Nashville; vol. worker A.R.C., Cheekwood Gift Shop, Vanderbilt Hosp. Gift Shop. Fellow Soc. Pub. Health Educators (charter), Am. Pub. Health Assn. (mem. governing council health edn. sect. So. br. 1962-64), Am. Nat. Council Health Edn. of Pub., Internat. Union Health Edn.; mem. Southeastern, Tenn. (chmn. spl. libraries sect. 1969-72), Midstate library assns., Med. Library Assn. (chmn. curriculum com. 1972-73), So. Med. Library Assn., Vanderbilt Soc. Hist. Medicine, Am. Assn. U. Women, Women's Nat. Book Assn., Tenn. Bot. Gardens and Fine Arts Center, English Speaking Union, Tenn. Folklore Soc., Ladies Hermitage Soc., Beta Phi Mu, Delta Kappa Gamma, Kappa Delta Pi, Pi Lambda Theta. Clubs: Pilot (extension chmn. dist. VII 1960-62), University, Nashville Library. Co-author: Classification For Medical Literature, 5th edit. Home: 6501 Harding Rd Nashville TN 37205 Office: Vanderbilt U Med Library Nashville TN 37232

GLADSTONE, SUZANNE PINK (MRS. MARK B. GLADSTONE), clin. psychologist; b. N.Y.C., Sept. 20, 1935; d. Lester Winthrop and Beatrice Joan (Meister) Pink; B.S., Pa. State U., 1957; Degree Superieur U. Paris, Sorbonne, 1958; M.S., Utah State U., 1962; Ph.D., U. Md., 1971; m. Mark B. Gladstone, Feb. 3, 1957; 1 dau., Leslie Anne. Teaching asst. U. Md., 1965-66; psychology trainee VA Hosp., Washington, Balt., 1966-70; clin. psychologist, chief psychologist out-patient services Area C, Community Mental Health Center, Washington, 1971—. Pvt. practice psychology, 1972—. Mem. Am., D.C., Md. psychol. assns., Am. Civil Liberties Union, Am. Humanist Assn., Psi Chi. Mem. Ethical Soc. (Sunday sch. council). Home: 7704 Westfield Dr Bethesda MD 20034 Office: Area C-Community Mental Health Center 1905 E St SE Washington DC 20003

GLANTZ, ANNE FURNEAUX WATSON, editor; b. Balt., Feb. 1, 1914; d. Richard Furneaux and Mary Kate (Darby) Watson; student George Washington U., 1932-34, Johns Hopkins, 1949-50, Richmond Profl. Inst., 1958-59, U. Cal. at Los Angeles, 1966, 68; m. Albert L. Glantz, Jan. 27, 1934 (div. June 1948); 1 dau., Martha-Anne. Copy chief advt. Thalhimers Co., Richmond, Va., 1956-58, Advt. Counsellors of Ariz., Phoenix, 1958-60; advt. copywriter Robinson's of Cal., Los Angeles, 1960-62, I. Magnin & Co., Los Angeles, 1962-64; exec. editor SCW, Inc., Chatsworth, Cal., 1964—. Sustaining mem. Republican Party, 1972—. Bd. dirs. Lung Assn. Los Angeles County. Mem. Women in Communications, Cal. Fedn. Music Clubs. Sigma Kappa.

GLANZ, LENORE MARIE, librarian; b. Chgo., Sept. 16, 1933; d. Leon Thomas and Maria Magdalena (Shiverski) Glanz; B.A., U. Ill., 1954, M.A. (Laurence Larson fellow), 1957, M.S. in L.S., 1960; Ph.D., Loyola U., Chgo., 1972. Residence halls counsellor U. Ill., Urbana, 1955-59; reference librarian Chgo. Pub. Library, 1960-61; bibliographic researcher U. Ill. Library, Urbana, 1959-60; research librarian Field Enterprises Edn. Corp., Chgo., 1961—. Mem. Am. Hist. Assn., Am. Soc. for Legal History, Spl. Libraries Assn. (asst. editor chpt. newsletter 1967-68, editor 1974—), Am. Civil Liberties Union, Chgo. Council on Fgn. Relations, Loyola U. Alumni Assn. (adv. bd. 1973), Mask and Bauble, Phi Alpah Theta. Home: 6151 W Roscoe St Chicago IL 60660 Office: Merchandise Mart Plaza Chicago IL 60654

GLASER, HELEN L. HOFSOMMER (MRS. ROBERT JOY GLASER), physician; b. St. Louis, May 25, 1924; d. Armin C. and Aphrodite (Jannopoulo) Hofsommer; B.S., Washington U. (St. Louis), 1947, M.D., 1947; m. Robert Joy Glaser, Apr. 1, 1949; children—Sally Louise, Joseph II, Robert Joy. Intern, St. Louis City Hosp., 1947-48; resident St. Louis Childrens Hosp., 1948-50; practice medicine specializing in pediatrics, Webster Groves, Mo., 1950-57; mem. staff St. Louis Children's, Colo. Gen. hosps.; instr. pediatrics U. Colo., Denver, 1957-61, asst. prof., 1961-63; clin. asso. pediatrics Harvard Med. Sch., Boston, 1963-65; asso. in medicine, asso. in medicine in child health Boston Childrens Hosp. Med. Center, 1963-64, sr. asso., 1964-65, asst. dir. child health div., patient care coordinator, 1964-65; chief pediatrician Mass. Mental Health Center, Boston, 1964-65; asst. med. dir. Childrens Hosp. at Stanford, Palo Alto, Cal., 1965-70; clin. asst. prof. pediatrics Stanford U. Sch. Medicine, 1965-70; resident in psychiatry Stanford Med. Center, 1970-71, 72-74, N.Y. State Psychiat. Hosp., 1971-72; faculty asso. East House, Radcliffe Coll., 1964-65. Bd. dirs. Community Assn. for the Retarded, Palo Alto, 1966-70, Family Service Assn. Mid-Peninsula, 1967-69; profl. adv. com. Peninsula Childrens Center, Palo Alto, 1966-70. Mem. Ambulatory Pediatric Assn., Western Soc. for Pediatric Research, Am. Orthopsychiat. Assn., Am. Assn. for Child Care in Hosp. (v.p. 1969-70, pres. 1971), Am. Psychiat. Assn. Author: (with others) Changing Hospital Environments for Children, 1972. Contbr. articles in field to profl. jours. Home: 1 Elm Pl Atherton CA 94025 Office: Dept Psychiatry Stanford Med Center Stanford CA 94305

GLASER, KAREN MCKEE, univ. dean; b. Wichita, Kan., Apr. 28, 1938; d. Roy and Dorothy (Simmons) Glaser; Mus.B., Lindenwood Coll. for Women, 1960; M.S., Ind. U., 1962. Resident Asst. Ind. U. residence halls, Bloomington, 1960-61, asst. head counselor, dean of students staff, 1960-62; personnel coordinator charge women's residence halls U. N.M., Albuquerque, 1962-66, asst. dean of women, 1966-68, asso. dean women, 1968-70, asso. dean students, 1970-71, dean students, 1971—. Mem. community concerts membership dr., Albuquerque, 1963. Mem. Am. Personnel and Guidance Assn., Nat. (membership, affiliation com. 1963-64), N.M. (pres. 1967-71), assns. women deans and counselors, Nat. Council Adminstrv. Women in Edn., Am. Assn. for Higher Edn., Nat. Assn. Women Deans, Adminstrs. and Counselors, N.M. Women's Polit. Caucus, Phi Kappa Phi. Mu Phi Epsilon (sec. Albuquerque alumnae), Pi Kappa Lambda. Home: 13 Casa Hermosa NE Albuquerque NM 87112

GLASER, RENEE, journalist; b. East Prussia, Germany, Sept. 9, 1929; d. Kurt and Magda Glaser; came to U.S., 1938; B.A., Wilson Coll., 1950; M.S. in Journalism, Columbia, 1954. State editor Williamsport (Pa.) Gazette and Bull., 1951-53; reporter Bridgeport (Conn.) Herald, 1954-55, N.Y.C. Post., 1956-59; producer WOR-TV and radio, N.Y.C., 1960; writer ABC-TV, N.Y.C., 1961; producer, also reporter Channel 13-TV, N.Y.C., 1962-64; information officer Human Resources Adminstr., N.Y.C., 1965-68; news dir. WRVR-FM, N.Y.C., 1969, host Urban Affairs Report, 1969; editor Facts On File, N.Y.C., 1970-72; writer, N.Y.C., 1972—. Recipient N.Y. Women's Press Club award, 1954; Freedoms Found. George Washington Honor medal, 1960, George Polk award, 1963. Address: 332 W 83d St New York City NY 10024

GLASGOW, BONNIE JEAN LOYD (MRS. CHARLES WAYNE GLASGOW), assn. exec., librarian; b. Chgo., June 28, 1942; d. Hugh S. and Lillian M. (Sharitt) Loyd; B.A. cum laude, N. Tex. State U., 1964, postgrad., 1974—; M.S., La. State U., 1967; m. Charles Wayne Glasgow, Jan. 25, 1964. Asst. tech. services librarian N.C. State Library, Raleigh, 1967-68; interlibrary loan and documents librarian Tex. Women's U., Denton, 1968-70; co-dir. Inst. for Study of Ch. and Soc., Denton, 1970—. Mem. A.L.A., Phi Kappa Phi, Alpha Chi, Beta Phi Mu, Pi Sigma Alpha, Phi Alpha Theta, Kappa Delta Pi. Home: 2716 Nottingham Dr Denton TX 76201 Office: 2716 Nottingham Dr Denton TX 76201

GLASGOW, JANIS MARILYN, educator; b. Wooster, O., Aug. 24, 1934; d. Paul Ellsworth and Edna (Smith) Glasgow; B.A., Western Res. U., 1956; postgrad. Universite de Bordeaux, France, 1956-57, Sorbonne (Fulbright scholar), 1957; M.A., U. Wis., 1958; Ph.D., U. Cal. at Los Angeles, 1966. Teaching asst. French, U. Wis., Madison, 1957-58, U. Cal. at Los Angeles, 1958-62; asst. prof. French, Cal. State U. at San Diego, 1962-68, asso. prof. French, 1968—, chmn. dept. French and Italian, 1972-73. Vis. prof. U. Paris, 1973-74. Mem. Union Francaise de San Diego, 1964—, treas., 1967-69, pres., 1971; mem. Alliance Francaise, San Diego, 1962-68. Robert V. Merrill grad. scholar French, 1959-60, Univ. fellow, 1961-62. Mem. Am. Assn. Tchrs. French, Assn. Internationale des Etudes Francaises, Phi Beta Kappa (sec.-treas. Epsilon assn. 1968-70, pres. 1972-73), Phi Sigma Iota, Pi Delta Phi, Alpha Mu Gamma. Home: 713 N Grant St Wooster OH 44691 Office: Dept of French and Italian Cal State U San Diego CA 92115

GLASS, DOROTHEA DANIELS (MRS. ROBERT E. GLASS), physiatrist; b. N.Y.C., July 4, 1920; d. Maurice B. and Anna (Kleegman) Daniels; B.A., Cornell U., 1940; M.D., Woman's Med. Coll. Pa., 1954; postgrad. U. Pa., 1960-61; m. Robert E. Glass, June 23, 1940; children—Anne (Mrs. Steven Roth), Deborah, Catherine, Eugene. Intern, Albert Einstein Med. Center, No. div., Phila., N.Y., 1954-55; resident phys. medicine and rehab. VA Hosp., Phila., 1959-62; gen. practice medicine, Phila., 1956-59; maternal and child health clinician Dept. of Pub. Health, City of Phila., 1956-59; with Phila. Pulmonary Neoplasm Research Project, 1956-57; chief phys. medicine and rehab. VA Hosp., Coatesville, Pa., 1962-63; asst. clin. dir. phys. medicine and rehab. Jefferson Med. Coll. Hosp., Phila., 1963-66; physiatrist Camden County stroke program Cooper Hosp., Camden, N.J., 1963-66; chief phys. medicine and rehab. VA Hosp., Phila., 1966-68; med. dir. Moss Rehab. Hosp., Phila., 1968—; chmn. div. phys. medicine Albert Einstein Med. Center, Phila., 1971—; cons. VA Hosp., Phila., 1968—; asso. prof. Temple U. Med. Sch., Phila., 1968-73, prof., 1973—; Lois Mattox Miller fellow Women's Med. Coll. Pa., 1954. Diplomate Am. Bd. Phys. Medicine and Rehab. Fellow Council Cerebro-Vascular Disease, Royal Coll. Health; mem. Am. Congress Rehab. Medicine, Am. Acad. Phys. Medicine and Rehab., Am. Heart Assn., A.M.A., Internat. Assn. Rehab. Facilities, Assn. Med. Rehab. Dirs. and Coordinators, Assn. Advancement Med. Electronics, Internat. Rehab. Med. Assn., Pa. Thoracic Soc., Am. Coll. Angiology, Laennec Soc., Coll. Physicians, Alpha Omega Alpha. Clubs: Georgetown (Md.) Yacht; Peale (Phila.). Office: 12th and Tabor Rd Philadelphia PA 19141

GLASS, LAUREL ELLEN, scientist, educator; b. Selma, Cal., Oct. 1, 1923; d. Sydney Leon and Marie (Damron) Glass; B.A., U. Cal. at Berkeley, 1950; Ph.D., Duke, 1958; M.D., U. Cal. at San Francisco, 1974. Asst. prof. anatomy U. Cal. Med. Sch., San Francisco, 1958-66, asso. prof., 1966-72, prof., 1972—. Mem. San Francisco Bd. Edn., 1967-71, pres., 1969, chmn. budget com., 1970; mem. steering com. council Big Cities Bds. Edn., Nat. Sch. Bds. Assn., 1969-71; past mem. adv. coms. Bay Area Social Planning Council, Project Concern, Cameron House, Cal. Med. Clinic for Psychotherapy. Bd. dirs. Constl. Rights Found.; trustee Glide Found., 1965—, San Francisco City Coll., 1969-70; regent Lone Mountain Coll., 1973—. Recipient Distinguished Citizen award Council for Civic Unity, 1969; Distinguished Woman award San Francisco Examiner, 1970, Chancellor's award for pub. service, 1971. Mem. Developmental Biology Soc., Am. Assn. Anatomists, Am. Soc. Cell Biology, Soc. Study Reprodn., Am. Soc. Zoologists, Phi Beta Kappa, Sigma Xi. Methodist (trustee). Contbr. numerous articles to profl. publs. Home: 2233 9th Av San Francisco CA 94116

GLASSBERG, GWENDOLYN REVILDA KROMAN DARLING, portrait artist, poet; b. Phila., Mar. 19, 1927; d. Hugo Edward Kroman and Mary Marian (Piltz) Darling; grad. high sch.; m. Rubin Glassberg, Apr. 3, 1945; children—Sandra, Evelyn (Mrs. Barry O. Hodson), Fay (Mrs. Leslie M. Brooks, Jr.). Receptionist, Bishop Studio Photography, West Chester, Pa., 1966-71; portrait artist, West Chester, 1973—. Fellow Internat. Poetry Soc.; mem. Pa. Poetry Soc., Am. Poets Fellowship, Accademia Leonardo da Vinci (hon. rep. diploma), Am. Poetry League, Internat. Platform Assn., Chester County Art Assn. Poems rep. in anthologies. Address: 302 E Marshall St Apt 438 West Chester PA 19380

GLASSER, CLAIRE SKALETZKY (MRS. JASHA L. GLASSER), occupational therapist; b. N.Y.C., Aug. 3, 1927; d. Julius and Fanny (Fischer) Skaletzky; B.S., Columbia, 1949; M.A., N.Y. U., 1958, postgrad. 1959, 74; m. Jasha L. Glasser, Jan. 16, 1949; children—Marc Joseph, Theodore Gary. Dir. occupational therapy New Haven Curative Workshop, 1949-50; occupational therapist Bellevue Hosp., N.Y.C., 1950-51; dir. occupational therapy N.Y. Hosp., N.Y.C., 1951-56, instr. occupational therapy, 1956-60; occupational therapist Tri-Hosp. Home Care Program of Passaic (N.J.), 1969—. Lectr. to various univs. and orgns.; cons. Am. Pub. Health Assn., N.Y.C., 1962-67, Home Health Services Passaic County, 1967-71. Chmn. women's res. Boy Scouts Am., Cedar Grove, N.J., 1972—, mem. pack com. Cub Scouts, 1972-73. Bd. dirs. women's com. N.J. Symphony Orch., Montclair, 1970-71, mem. women's com., 1967—; bd. dirs. P.T.A., Cedar Grove, 1966-72, v.p., 1971-72. Mem. Am. (unit chmn. 1956-58), N.Y. (pres. 1954-56, chmn. com. 1953-62), N.J. (chmn. spl. interest group 1974—) occupational therapy assns. Author: (with others) Physician's Occupational Therapy Reference Guide, 1958. Home: 17 Brookshire Dr Cedar Grove NJ 07009 Office: Tri-Hospital Home Care Program of Passaic Beth Israel Hospital Passaic NJ 07055

GLASSER, JOYCE FERN, ednl. adminstr.; b. Chgo., Apr. 8, 1938; d. Daniel D. and Sylvia Thelma (Goldstein) Glasser; B.A., Lake Forest Coll., 1959; M.Ed., Nat. Coll. Edn., 1964. Learning center dir. Ridge Sch., Elk Grove Village, Ill., 1966-68; prin. Grant Elementary Sch., Elgin, Ill., 1968-74; dir. Title III Project, Mundelein, Ill., 1974—. Condr. workshops, lectr., 1972—. Mem. Nat., Ill. assns. women's deans, adminstrs. and counselors, Ill. Prins. Assn. Author: The Elementary School Learning Center for Independent Study, 1971. Home: 2205 Fulle St Rolling Meadows IL 60008 Office: 200 W Maple Av Mundelein IL 60060

GLASSER, SELMA SUZANNE GOLDSTEIN, writer, b. N.Y.C., Jan. 2; d. Morris and Clara (Dlugash) Goldstein; grad. high sch.; m. Allen Glasser, Nov. 18, 1948 (dec.); children—Gary, Gloria. Humor writer for Joan Rivers; fillers appear in newspapers and mags. including Playboy, Harper's, Good Housekeeping, Wall Street Jour., Saturday Evening Post, Med. World News, Am. Journal of Nursing, Family Weekly, Nat. Tattler, N.Y. News, Los Angeles Times, Todays Family, others; regular columnist General Contests, Duluth, Minn., 1971-74. Recipient cash prize, Vantage Press Poetry award, 1973. Clubs: Bklyn. Contest (pres.) Bklyn. Writers (pres.). Author: Glasser Guide to Filler Writing, 1973; Fell's Official Guide to Prize Contests and How to Win Them, 1974. Address: 241 Dahill Rd Brooklyn NY 11218

GLASSON, MURIEL ADA, educator; b. Almena, Kan., Dec. 16, 1900; d. Fred John and May (Williams) G.; B.S., U. Neb., 1934; postgrad. Kan. State Coll., Columbia, Colo. State Coll., (Internat. Sch. Art Study award 1945) Quadalajara (Mexico) U., U. Cal. at Berkeley, (A.R.C. Study award 1951) Whitworth Coll., Cornell U. Tchr. home econs., Spivey, Kan., 1934-36, Cedar Point, Kan., 1936-38, Sylvan Grove, Kan., 1938-42, Highland, Kan., 1942-43, Waterville, Wash., 1943-45, Lindsay, Cal., 1946, Port Angeles, Wash., 1946-52, 53-56, 57—. Del. Internat. Congress Home Econs., Edinburgh, Scotland, 1953; Balt., 1958; chmn. com. internat. students U. Wash., Seattle, 1959. Fulbright scholar, Netherlands, 1952-53, Burma, 1956-57; Asia Found. grantee, 1957, Sears, Roebuck & Co. Found. award, 1960. Mem. Tchrs. Credit Union (v.p. 1950-53, 58-60), Am. Home Econs. Assn. (internat. chmn. Wash. 1953-54), Wash. Olympic Peninsula Home Economists (area chmn.), Olympic Home Economists (pres. 1953-56), Am. Assn. U. Women (legislative chmn. So. Kan. 1934-36), Bus. and Profl. Women's Club (v.p. Lindsay 1946), Wash. Orthopedic Aux., (pres.), D.A.R. (chpt. treas., regent 1964-65, dir. Ranier chpt.), Internat. Platform Assn., Soc. Colonial Dames. Conglist. (past bd. mem.). Rebekah (past noble grand); mem. Order Eastern Star. Contbr. articles to profl. publs. Home: 308 E Republican St Seattle WA 98102

GLATER, RUTH A. B. (MRS. JULIUS GLATER), plant scientist; b. N.Y.C., Aug. 11, 1919; d. Jacob and Jennie (Friedland) Bobrov; B.A., Hunter Coll., 1939; M.A., Columbia, 1941; Ph.D., U. Cal. at Los Angeles, 1951; m. Julius Glater, Dec. 31, 1953; children—Selina I., Sara E. Research, teaching asst. U. Cal. at Los Angeles, 1947-51; research botanist Los Angeles County Air Pollution Control Dist., 1951-58; research botanist U. Cal. at Los Angeles, 1961—; teaching, cons. in biology D.Environment program U. Cal. at Los Angeles. Served from ensign to lt. (j.g.) WAVES, 1943-45. Mem. A.A.A.S., Am. Phytopathol. Soc., Am. Bot. Soc., Air Pollution Control Assn., Sigma Xi. Contbr. articles to profl. jours. Home: 3230 Kelton Av Los Angeles CA 90034 Office: U Cal Los Angeles CA 90024

GLAUSER, ELINOR MIKELBERG, med. educator; b. Phila., Aug. 24, 1931; d. Henry Brinton and Rose Rena (Minkin) Mikelberg; B.A., U. Pa., 1952; M.D., Med. Coll. Pa., 1957; m. Stanley C. Glauser, Feb. 16, 1952; children—Terry Ann, Tracy Andrew, Todd Adam. Intern, Hosp. Med. Coll. Pa., 1957-58; post-doctoral fellow U. Pa. Sch. Medicine, 1958-59; fellow exptl. medicine Cambridge (Eng.) U., 1959-60; fellow medicine Harvard, 1960-61; asso. medicine Med. Coll. Pa., 1961-63; asso. prof. medicine Temple U. Sch. Medicine, 1963—. Kate Hurd Mead fellow, 1959-61; Nat. Found. fellow, 1955-57; NIH fellow, 1961-63; Am. Thoracic Soc. fellow, 1958-59, 63-65. Mem. Am. Physiol. Soc., Am. Soc. Pharmacology and Exptl. Therapeutics, Am. Thoracic Soc., A.A.A.S., Am. Chem. Soc., Phila. Physiol. Soc., A.M.A., Pa. Thoracic Soc., Laennec Soc., Phila. Club Med. Women, Phi Beta Kappa (bd. dirs. Gamma assn.). Contbr. articles to profl. jours. Home: 630 Richards Rd RD 1 Wayne PA 19087 Office: 3400 N Broad St Philadelphia PA 19140

GLAZE, NADA STUART (MRS. FRANK D. GLAZE), banker; b. Camden, Ala.; d. James Edgar and Alba (Steen) Stuart; m. Frank D. Glaze. Sec., asst. to mgr. Fairfield br. First Nat. Bank of Birmingham (Ala.), 1941-52, asst. cashier, 1956-64; teller Seattle First Nat. Bank, Spokane, Wash., 1952-53; sec. Straus-Frank Co., San Antonio, 1953-54; mgr. ladies div. First Nat. Bank, Louisville, 1967—. Mem. Am. Bus. Women's Assn. (chmn. contact com. Louisville chpt. 1971), Nat. Assn. Bank Women (vice chmn. Louisville group 1971, chmn. 1972, membership chmn. Ky. group 1970-71, vice chmn. 1972, chmn. 1973, nat. exec. com. 1971—, chmn. quadregional conf. 1974). Baptist. Office: First Nat Bank Box 1019 Louisville KY 40201

GLAZER, ESTHER (MRS. IRWIN HOFFMAN), violinist; b. Chgo.; d. Louis and Sarah (Zeidman) Glazer; grad. (fellow 1944-48), Juilliard Sch. Music, 1948; m. Irwin Hoffman, Feb. 20, 1946; children—Joel, Gary, Toby, Deborah. Debut as concert violinist at age 9, Chgo.; concerts in U.S., Can., Europe, Israel, S.Am.; appeared with various orchs., including Chgo. Symphony, Royal Philharmonic, Brit. Broadcasting Co. Symphony; mem. music faculty U. B.C., 1961-64; now artist in residence U. Tampa (Fla.). Recipient Naumburg award, 1950. Performed world premieres of new compositions, including first Chgo. performance Violin Concerto (Schoenberg). Home: 1901 Brightwaters Blvd St Petersburg FL 33704

GLEASON, ELIZABETH GERTRUDE HOOPER (MRS. CHARLES SHERMAN GLEASON), physician; b. Boston, July 4, 1921; d. William Elsworth and Grace Wright (Robinson) Hooper; B.S., Tufts Coll., 1943, M.D., 1946; m. Charles Sherman Gleason, Dec. 6, 1947; children—William H., Pamela A., Susan E., Robert C., Amy L. Intern, Newton-Wellesley Hosp., Newton, Mass., 1946-47; resident anesthesia Syracuse Med. Center, 1948; gen. practice medicine, Wareham, Mass., 1950—; mem. active staff Tobey Hosp., Wareham, Mass., pres. staff, 1969-70; courtesy staff Barnstable County Hosp., Pocasset, Mass., 1974—; qualified physician Taunton (Mass.) State Hosp., 1974—. Pres., founding mem. Wareham (Mass.) Drug Com., 1971—. Trustee Friends Acad., North Dartmouth, Mass., 1965-70; bd. dirs. Wareham Area Counseling Service Inc., 1973—. Mem. Am. Med. Women's Assn., Mass., Barnstable County med. socs. Address: 121 High St Wareham MA 02571

GLEASON, JACQUELINE, statistician; b. Lowell, Mass., Dec. 13, 1925; d. Fred J. and Helen T. (O'Donnell) Gleason; A.B., Trinity Coll., 1947; M.A., Cath. U., 1951. With Human Resources Research Office, George Washington U., Washington, 1952-62; with Fed. Govt. Washington, statistician Exec. Office of Pres., 1970-73, Gen. Services Adminstrn. Office Preparedness, 1973—. Mem. Am. Statis. Assn. Home: 4601 22d Av Washington DC 20018 Office: 1800 F St NW Washington DC 20405

GLEASON, JEAN BERKO (MRS. ANDREW MATTEI GLEASON), psycholinguist; b. Cleve., Dec. 19, 1931; d. Arthur E. and Alice (Gelbberger) Berko; A.B., Radcliffe College, 1953, A.M., 1955, Ph.D., 1958; m. Andrew Mattei Gleason, Jan. 26, 1959; children—Katherine, Pamela, Cynthia. USPHS fellow Mass. Inst. Tech., 1958-59; with Inst. for Def. Analyses, Princeton, N.J., 1960-61; research asso. U.S. VA Hosp., Boston, 1961—; prin. research asso. dept. psychiatry Harvard Med. Sch., 1970-72; vis. asst. prof. dept. psychology Boston U., 1972-73, vis. asso. prof., 1973—; research asso. Harvard Grad. Sch. Edn., 1968-70. Mem. Cambridge Civic Assn., 1961—, Am. Civil Liberties Union, Boston, 1965—. Mem. Am., New Eng. psychol. assns., Linguistic Soc. Am., Radcliffe Grad. Soc. (v.p. 1965, pres. 1971-73), Radcliffe Coll. Alumnae Assn. (dir. 1969-72), Acad. Aphasia, Soc. for Research in Child Devel., Phi Beta Kappa (pres. Radcliffe chpt. 1965-68). Editorial bd. Child Devel., 1971—; asso. editor Jour. Speech and Hearing Research, 1972-73. Contbr. articles to profl. jours. Home: 110 Larchwood Dr Cambridge MA 02138 Office: Dept Psychology Boston University 64 Cummington St Boston MA 02215

GLEASON, NORMA LOUVAIN HINZ (MRS. DENIS J. GLEASON), writer; b. St. Paul, Aug. 23, 1914; d. Max C. and Blanche (Whiteaker) Hinz; grad. high sch.; m. Jack E. Salter, June 15, 1944 (div. Nov. 1949); children—Joan (Mrs. Theodore F. Homer), Susan (Mrs. William Jones); m. 2d, Denis J. Gleason, June 12, 1956. Columnists Point of View reprinted in press sect. Reader's Digest, 1965; writer several syndicated columns; writer children's puzzles for Cartoon Features Syndicates, 1963; editor Davison (Mich.) Index, 1966; reporter Lapeer (Mich.) County Press, 1967—; mgr. Gleason Features newspaper syndicate. Contbr. to newspapers, mags. including Christian Sci. Monitor, Farm Jour., Calling All Girls, Sat. Rev. Home: 848 Lincoln St Lapeer MI 48446 Office: Lapeer County Press 69 W Nepessing St Lapeer MI 48446

GLEAVE, G(ERTRUDE) MARGARET, occupational therapist; b. Potlatch, Ida., Jan. 23, 1911; d. Frederich and Gertrude (Gleave) Gleave; student Washington U., St. Louis, 1931-35. Staff occupational therapist R.J. Delano Sch., Kansas City, Mo., 1935-37; staff occupational therapist Ind. U. Med. Center, Indpls., 1937-45; exec. dir. Del. Curative Workshop, Wilmington, 1945-50; exec. dir. Curative Workshop of Racine, Wis., 1950-73, adminstrv. cons., 1973—. Ann. lectr. U. Ill., Chgo. Mem. Am. (award of merit 1967, past treas., chmn.), Wis. occupational therapy assns., Nat. Rehab. Assn., Assn. Rehab. Center (past dir.), Nat. Assn. Sheltered Workshops (past dir.). Contbr. to textbooks: Principles of Occupational Therapy, 1947-54; Occupational Therapy, 1963-71. Contbr. articles to profl. jours. Home: 1356 Howard St Racine WI 53404 Office: 2335 Northwestern Av Racine WI 53404

GLEBERMAN, MIRIAM RIVKIN (MRS. J. HARVEY GLEBERMAN), furniture co. exec.; b. S.I., N.Y., Apr. 8, 1923; d. Joseph and Sarah (Mink) Rivkin; B.S., N.Y. U., 1943; student N.Y. Sch. Interior Design, 1954; m. J. Harvey Gleberman, Nov. 18, 1948; children—Joan, Ellen, Joseph. Tng. dir. Abraham & Straus, Bklyn., 1943-53, cons. customer services, 1953-55; exec. v.p. J.H. Harvey, Inc., retail furniture chain, 1955—. Mem. bus. adminstrn. faculty Coll. City N.Y., 1943-55; guest speaker various women's clubs and consumer panels. Mem. Nat. Home Fashions League, Interior Design Soc., Nat. Home Furnishings Assn. Jewish religion. Club: Elmwood County (White Plains, N.Y.). Home: 164 Brewster Rd Scarsdale NY 10583 Office: 53 Tarrytown Rd White Plains NY 10607

GLENDY, MARGARET ELIZABETH MORIARTY (MRS. ROBERT EARLE GLENDY), physician; b. Boston, Feb. 26, 1898; d. Patrick William and Julia (Lombard) Moriarty; B.S., Simmons Coll., 1919; M.D., U. Va., 1931; m. Robert Earle Glendy, Aug. 16, 1933; children—Robert Earle, David Gardner, Elizabeth (Mrs. A. Arthur J. Hull). Research chemist pediatric dept. Mass. Gen. Hosp., Boston, 1919-27, intern, 1931-32, resident pediatric dept., 1932-33; instr. pediatrics Harvard Med. Sch., 1933-45; practice medicine specializing in pediatrics, Boston, 1933-45, Roanoke, Va., 1946—; rheumatic fever clinician Va. Health Dept., Roanoke, 1946-57; well baby clinician, Roanoke, 1946—. Mem. Roanoke Area Drug Abuse Control Council, 1970-72; health chmn. Roanoke Central Council P.T.A., Va. Congress P.T.A., 1948-60; acting health commr., Roanoke, 1948, 68, health commr., 1957-63. Bd. dirs. YWCA, Nat. Found., Am. Heart Assn., Tb Assn., Am. Cancer Soc., Burrell Meml. Hosp. Recipient Brotherhood award Nat. Council Christians and Jews, 1970; named Woman of Year, Bus. and Profl. Women's Club, 1955, Roanoke Mchts. Assn., 1960. Mem. Phi Beta Kappa, Sigma Xi, Alpha Omega Alpha. Address: 3806 Heatherton Rd SW Roanoke VA 24014

GLENN, LINDA LOUISE, mental retardation programs adminstr.; b. Munich Germany, Oct. 12, 1947; d. Robert Clinton and Ann (Field) Glenn; came to U.S., 1949, naturalized, 1968; B.S. in Phys. Edn., U. Miss., 1968, M.Ed. in Spl. Edn., 1969; Ph.D. in Ednl. Adminstrn. and Bus. Adminstrn., U. Kan., 1974. Research asst. Neb. Psychiat. Inst., Omaha, 1969; dir. research and planning Omaha Assn. for Retarded Children, 1969-70; dir. research Eastern Neb. Community Office of Retardation, Omaha, 1970-72, exec. dir., 1974—; dir. Bur. Child Research, U. Kan., Lawrence, 1973-74. Cons. in devel. disabilities and mental retardation; owner Cenergy, Kansas City, Mo., 1973—. Mem. conf. execs. Assn. for Retarded Children, 1969-70, pres.'s adv. council Omaha Assn. for Retarded Children, 1970-72, Omaha Community Coordinated Child Care Adv. Council, 1971-72, Douglas County Mental Health Adv. Com., 1971-72, Comprehensive Area Manpower Planning Council, 1970-71, Comprehensive Health Planning Council of Midlands, 1971-72, Eastern Neb., Western Ia. Regional Corrections Adv. Bds., 1970-71, tech. review task force Neb. Office Mental Retardation, 1969-70. Bd. dirs. Madonna Sch. for Exceptional Children, 1971-72. Mem. Am. Assn. on Mental Deficiency, Council for Exceptional Children, Nat. Rehab. Assn., Nat., Greater Omaha (mem. planning com. 1970-72, dir. 1972), Neb. (chmn. human and legal rights com. 1972), Douglas County, Kan., assns. for Retarded Children. Author: (with W. Wolfensberger) Program Analysis of Service Systems (PASS), 1973; System Advisory Structure-Position Paper on ENCOR Advisory Committees, 1971. Contbr. articles to profl. jours. Office: Eastern Neb Community Office of Retardation 116 S 42d St Omaha NE 68131

GLENN, RHONDA FAYE, TV broadcaster; b. Jacksonville, Fla., May 6, 1946; d. Ranford Eugene and Rhanolda (Ritch) Glenn; student Palm Beach Jr. Coll., 1964-66. Reporter, Palm Beach Post-Times, West Palm Beach, 1966-67; columnist Miami (Fla.) Herald, 1968-69; reporter news and weather Sta. WAVY-TV, Portsmouth, Va., 1969—. Chmn. Lloyd Liebler Meml. Golf Tournament, Portsmouth, 1971. Winner Middle-Atlantic Women's Golf Championship, 1969. Republican. Home: 4390 Point West Dr Portsmouth VA 23704 Office: 801 Middle St Portsmouth VA 23704

GLENNIE, ATHENA JEAN, pub. relations exec., editor; b. Internat. Falls, Minn., July 12, 1935; d. John Demitrious and Mabel Elizabeth (Powers) Phaklides; student Hibbing Jr. Coll., 1953-54, U. Wis., 1954-66; m. William Angelo Fena, Sept. 18, 1953 (div. Mar. 1968); m. 2d, George Arthur Glennie, Feb. 15, 1974. Reporter, society editor Hibbing (Minn.) Daily Tribune, 1953-54; editorial asst. South Milw. Voice Jour., 1966-68, mng. editor, 1968-72, asst. to pub., 1972—. Bd. mgrs. South Shore br. YMCA, 1971-73. Mem. Women in Communications, League of Women Voters Asso. editor U.S. History Time Concepts, 1967; Story of the Afro-American, 1969; N.Am. Curling News, 1970—. Home: 7638 W Waterford Milwaukee WI 53220 Office: 723 Milwaukee Av South Milwaukee WI 53172

GLENNON, MARGARET KELLY (MRS. LAWRENCE E. GLENNON, JR.), city ofcl.; b. Dobbs Ferry, N.Y., Dec. 22, 1909; d. Thomas C. and Ann E. (Michaely) Kelly; student McDowell Sch. Fashion Art, 1941-44, accounting Columbia Sch. Bus., 1937-40; m. Lawrence E. Glennon, Jr., May 22, 1948. Dep. clk., Village of Dobbs Ferry, 1928-37, treas., 1931-72, clk., receiver of taxes, budget officer, 1937-72, now ret. Pres., Young Women's Republican Club, Dobbs Ferry, 1940-46; bd. dirs. Dobbs Ferry Rep. Club, 1945-49, sec., 1955-57; sec. Greenbrugh Women's Rep. Club, 1952-54. Bd. dirs. A.R.C., Dobbs Ferry, 1957-60. Mem. Music Box Canteen, N.Y.C., 1941-45; mem. canteen hosp. com. Kingsbridge Vets. Hosp., N.Y.C., 1945-49. Home: 316 Oak St Melbourne Beach FL 32951

GLESER, GOLDINE TECKLA COHNBERG (MRS. SOL M. GLESER), educator; b. St. Louis; d. Julius and Lena (Goldberg) Cohnberg; A.B., Washington U., St. Louis, 1935, M.S., 1936, Ph.D., 1950; m. Sol M. Gleser, June 4, 1936; children—Leon J., Malcolm A., Judith A. Instr. math. Washington U., 1947-49, research asst., 1948-50, research asst. in anatomy, 1950-51, research asst. to research asso. in neuropsychiatry, 1950-54, research asso. in anatomy, 1956-57; from research asst. to asso. prof. dept. edn. U. Ill., 1957-63; from asst. prof. to prof. psychology U. Cin. Med. Sch., 1956—, dir. psychology div., dept. psychiatry, 1967—. Fellow Am., Ohio psychol.

assns., A.A.A.S., Am. Coll. Neuropsychopharmacology, Am. Statis. Assn.; mem. Psychometric Soc., Cin. (pres. 1957-58, 65-66), Midwest psychol. assns., Soc. Multivariate Exptl. Psychology, N.Y. Acad. Scis., Phi Beta Kappa, Sigma Xi. Author books. Contbr. articles to profl. jours. Home: 3604 Lansdowne Av Cincinnati OH 45236

GLICK, GINA PHILLIPS MORAN (MRS. L. MICHAEL GLICK), physician, educator; b. Chgo., Dec. 6, 1931; d. Edward Langan and Virginia (Phillips) Moran; student Mundelein Coll., 1953; M.D., Loyola U., Chgo., 1956; m. L. Michael Glick, Feb. 9, 1957; children—Mark Michael, Celeste Michele, Felicia Michele, Matthew Michael. Intern, Mercy Hosp., Chgo., 1956-57; resident Chgo. Wesley Meml. Hosp., 1957-59; practice medicine specializing in anesthesiology, Cumberland, Md., 1959—; chmn. dept. anesthesia Sacred Heart Hosp., Cumberland; U. Md. clin. instr. anesthesia Balt. City Hosps., 1964-70. Legislative chmn. Md. Emergency Care Adv. Council, 1971—. Diplomate Am. Bd. Anesthesiology. Mem. Am. Coll. Anesthesiologists, Md.-D.C. Soc. Anesthesiologists (pres. sect. I 1971, sects. I and II 1972), Soc. Critical Care Medicine. Home: 126 N Smallwood St Cumberland MD 21502

GLICK, HARRIET BRIER (MRS. MILTON GLICK), theatre sch. dir.; b. Phila., Aug. 29, 1922; d. Ben and Gertrude (Lerner) Brier; grad. Phila. Sch. Drama Art, 1941; student U. Pa., 1940-42, St. Joseph Coll., 1965, Barnes Found., 1969-73; m. Bernard Fine, May 23, 1942 (div. Mar. 1971); children—Diane (Mrs. Edward Davids), Kenneth; m. Milton Glick, Mar. 19, 1971. Practice tchr. Phila. Sch. System, 1962; dir. children's theater, New Hope, Bucks County, 1963; dir. high sch. theater Cornelia Otis Skinner Playhouse, Lower Meion Sch. System, 1967; instr. improvisational theater Harcum Jr. Coll., 1967, Main Line Sch., 1971; tchr. Lower Merion Sch. Dist., 1971-74; dir. children Bala Cynwdy Library, Narberth, Pa., 1964-74; instr. creative dramatics Merion Elementary Sch., 1971; dir. Belmont Hills Sch., Narberth, Pa., 1972—. Mem. Am. Ednl. Theater Assn. Author: What Makes An Actor and Artist and Not Just A Performer, 1969. Home: 605 Conshohocken State Rd Penn Valley Narberth PA 19072 Office: 6 E Lancaster Av Ardmore PA 19003

GLICKLICH, LUCILLE B. (MRS. MARVIN GLICKLICH), physician; b. Fond du Lac, Wis., Jan. 10, 1926; d. Peter and Freda (Pevnick) Barash; B.A., U. Wis., 1947, M.D., 1950; m. Marvin Glicklich, Sept. 12, 1948; children—Daniel Gale, Anne M., Peter Allen, Lynn B., Barry J. Intern Youngstown (O.) Hosp. Assn., 1950-51; resident Milw. Children's Hosp., 1951-53, resident in psychiatry, 1967-69, resident in child psychiatry, 1969-71; instr. pediatrics U. Ill., 1956-57; asst. prof. pediatrics Med. Coll. Wis., 1957—, asst. prof. psychiatry, 1971—; practice medicine, specializing in pediatrics, Milw., 1957-67, in psychiatry, 1971—; mem. staff Milw. Children's Hosp., Wilwaukee County Gen. Hosp.; med. dir. Cerebral Palsy Clinic, 1959-60; med. coordinator Handicapped Children's Center, 1961-64; chief med. cons. Milw. Pub. Schs. Dept. Exceptional Edn., 1965-67; med. cons. Easter Seals Child Devel. Program, 1965-67. Mem. task force Mental Health and Retardation Planning Com., 1965—; mem. Milw. Bd. Jewish Edn., 1969—. Diplomate Am. Bd. Pediatrics. Mem. Am. Acad. Cerebral Palsy, Am. Acad. Pediatrics, Am. Psychiat. Assn., Am. Acad. Child Psychiatry, A.M.A., Milw. Pediatrics Soc., Milw. County Med. Soc., Alpha Epsilon Iota. Home: 5220 N Lake Dr Whitefish WI 53217

GLICKMAN, BETTE WALTERS, lawyer; b. Norristown, Pa., Sept. 5, 1946; d. Albert Bradford and Elizabeth Moore (Daymon) Walters; B.A., U. Pitts., 1967; J.D., Temple U., 1970, LL.M. in Taxation, 1974; m. Jay Charles Glickman, Jan. 8, 1972. Admitted to Pa. bar, 1970; law clk., asso. counsel William R. Cooper, Lansdale, 1969-72; student staff asst. legal aid br. Temple U., 1967-70; practice law, N. Wales, Pa., 1972—; house counsel Alco Standard Corp., Valley Forge, Pa., 1973—; spl. asst. to pub. defender Montgomery County, 1973—; staff atty. Montgomery County Legal Aid Service, 1970, bd. dirs., 1973—. Sponsor N. Penn High Sch. Sr. Career Study Program, 1972-73, 73-74; referral work with Women in Transition, 1973—; dir. Community Orgn. for Personal Enrichment, 1971—. Recipient Legal Aid award Temple U. Law Sch., 1970. Mem. Am., Pa., Montgomery County bar assns., Nat. Assn. Women Lawyers, Montgomery County Estate Planning Council, Indoor Light Gardening Soc. Republican. Address: English Village 6 C-2 North Wales PA 19454

GLICKMAN, LAURA LEE, lawyer; b. Bklyn., Apr. 26, 1946; d. Daniel Bernard and Miriam K. (Friedman) Glickman; A.B. with honors, U. Cal. at Los Angeles, 1967, J.D., 1970. Admitted to Cal. bar; practiced Pacoima, Cal., 1971-72, Los Angeles, 1972—; staff atty. San Fernando Valley Neighborhood Legal Services, Inc., Pacoima, Cal., 1971-72, directing atty., 1972; clin. supervising atty. Legal Aid Found. Los Angeles, 1972-74; asso. firm Sarnoff and Lieberman, Los Angeles, 1974—. Adj. clin. prof. Loyola U. Sch. Law, Los Angeles, 1972—. Mem. Am. Civil Liberties Union Lawyers Com., 1972—. Recipient Bancroft-Whitney award, 1968, Appellate Advocacy award U. Cal. at Los Angeles Law Sch., 1970. Mem. State Bar Cal., Bar U.S. Dist. Ct., Los Angeles County Bar Assn., U. Cal. at Los Angeles Law Alumni Assn. Office: 6404 Wilshire Blvd Suite 1020 Los Angeles CA 90048

GLICKMAN, SARA REBECCA GOLDSHLAG (MRS. ARTHUR GLICKMAN), editor; b. N.Y.C., July 10, 1923; d. Nathan and Mary (Rosenzweig) Goldshlag; A.B., Ohio State U., 1944, B.A. cum laude, 1944; m. Arthur Glickman, Jan. 27, 1946; children—Alan Robert, Mindy Ellen. A founder Nat. Council Adoptive Parents Orgns., 1964, asst. editor Nat. Adoptalk, 1965-68, editor, 1968—; founder Adoptive Parents Com. of N.J., 1960, legislative chmn., 1961-68. Bd. dirs. Spaulding for Children, adoption agy. Mem. Nat. Council Jewish Women, O.R.T., Am. Jewish Congress, Bergen County Artists Assn. Home: 538 Rutland Av Teaneck NJ 07666 Office: Nat Council Adoptive Parents Orgns Box 543 Teaneck NJ 07666

GLIDDON, STELLA (MRS. REVERDY THOMAS GLIDDON), journalist; b. Fredericksburg, Tex., Apr. 13, 1897; d. Charles and Mary (Kuenemann) Klaerner; student St. Anthony's Bus. Coll., 1917-18; m. Reverdy Thomas Gliddon, June 20, 1920 (dec. Jan. 1940); stepchildren—Inez (Mrs. N. M. Johnson), Sofie Marie (Mrs. J. R. Odiorne); children—Merrill (Mrs. Philip Holquin), Reverdy Thomas, Roselyn (Mrs. John Bustin), Charles, James Franklin (dec.), Martha (Mrs. Howard D. Schulze). Soc. editor Fredericksburg Standard, 1917—; asst. editor Record-Courier, Johnson City, Tex., 1940, owner, editor, pub., 1940-68, editor, 1969—; postmaster, Johnson City, 1944-67. Pres., Johnson City P.T.A., 1945; pres. Johnson City Women's Civic Club, 1947; mother adviser Johnson City Assembly, Order Rainbow For Girls, 1948; pres. March Dimes, 1948; treas. Nat. Found., 1965; mem. Blanco County Hist. Survey. Recipient Bronze plaque for outstanding service to soil conservation Ft. Worth Press, 1953. Mem. Blanco County Hist. Assn. (charter), Theta Sigma Phi. Christian Scientist. Mem. Order Eastern Star. Club: Community Garden (pres. 1968). Presented Hist. Medallion to Lyndon B. Johnson's Boyhood Home, 1965. Home: Johnson City TX 78636 Office: Box 205 Johnson City TX 78636

GLIDEWELL, LINDA SUE, journalist; b. Denver, Aug. 10, 1943; d. Albert Edward and Marjorie Effie (McDowell) Glidewell; student Colo. State Coll., 1961-63, U. Cal. at Berkeley, 1963-65; m. Willie P. Mears, Apr. 15, 1972; 1 dau., Erin Kelly Mears. Asst. pub. relations dir. Carson/Roberts Advt., 1965-66; asst. to beauty editor Vogue Mag., 1967-68; publicity mgr. Clinique Labs., div. Estee Lauder Inc., 1968-69; account coordinator Saul Bass & Assos., 1969-70; fashion and beauty editor Los Angeles Herald-Examiner, 1970-72; free lance writer, 1972—. Beauty lectr. Pacific & Orient Lines cruises, 1971-72. Mem. Theta Sigma Phi. Democrat. Home: 444 S Maple Dr Beverly Hills CA 90212

GLISSMAN, CATHERINE JEAN BOX (MRS. HANS HENRY CHRISTIAN GLISSMAN), physician; b. Belle Plaine, Ia., Dec. 18, 1921; d. Richard and Ina Mathilda (Viall) Box; B.A., U. Ia., 1943, M.D., 1949; M.S., U. Rochester, 1945; m. Hans Henry Christian Glissman, Dec. 29, 1953; 1 step-son, Richard Glissman. Intern, U. Kan. Med. Center, Kansas City, 1949-50; resident St. Lukes-Presbyn. Hosp., Chgo., 1950-51, Neb. Psychiat. Inst., Omaha, 1951-53; psychiatrist VA Mental Hygiene Clinic, Des Moines, 1954-56, Child Guidance Center, 1957-59, Broadlawns Gen. Hosp., 1959-66; W. Central Mental Health Clinic, 1967-71, med. dir., 1967-71; pvt. practice medicine specializing psychiatry, Des Moines, 1954—. State cons. Ia. Div. Vocational Rehab., 1954—. Mem. Womens Profl. League Des Moines (pres. 1961), Am., Ia. (pres. 1958) med. womens assns., A.M.A., Ia., Polk County med. socs., Am. Psychiat. Assn., N.Y. Acad. Scis., Nat. Rehab. Assn. Home: 2031 70th St Des Moines IA 50322 Office: 1414 Woodland Des Moines IA 50302

GLIST, ALICE, food co. exec.; b. Chgo.; d. Hyman and Minnie (Ulis) Glist; student spl. courses U. Cal. at Los Angeles, 1959, 60; m. Brooks Teyburn Pierce, Jan. 20, 1944 (div. Dec. 1950). With Community Laundry, 1935-40, Hollywood Ranch Market, 1940-44, Technicolor Studios, 1944-46; film technician Pathe Studios, 1945-47; founder, pres. PerAls Cheesecake, Inc., Los Angeles, 1947—; partner Baklava Co., Los Angeles, 1961—; co-owner Bakers Dozen, Los Angeles, 1963-67. Worker mental health. Mem. United Restaurants Owners Assn. (dir. 1965—), Food Execs. of Los Angeles, Chefs de Cuisine, Garfield Alumni Assn., Far West Ski Assn. Democrat. Clubs: Standard, German Shepard (Am.). Died July 27, 1972. Address: 3115 S San Pedro Los Angeles CA 90011

GLOGAU, LILLIAN FLATOW FLEISCHER (MRS. JEROME N. GLOGAU), ednl. adminstr.; b. N.Y.C., Feb. 15, 1925; d. Henry and Diana (Heller) Flatow; B.A. cum laude, Bklyn. Coll., 1946; M.A., Columbia, 1949; Ed.D., N.Y.U., 1969; m. Jerome N. Glogau, Nov. 20, 1963; children—Jordan, Laurence, Alexander. Tchr., N.Y.C. Schs., 1946-49; tchr. Plainview (N.Y.) Schs., 1959-61, adminstr., 1961-66; prin. Spring Valley (N.Y.) Schs., 1966—; pres. Pragmatix, ednl. corp., South Orange, N.J. Lectr., cons. to sch. dists. Recipient Found. Day award N.Y.U., 1970. Mem. P.T.A. (life), Am. Assn. Sch. Adminstrs., Am. Soc. Curriculum Devel., N.Y. State Sch. Adminstrs. Assn., Kappa Delta Pi, Pi Lambda Theta. Author: Nongraded Primary, 1967; You and N.Y. City, 1970; Let's See, 1971; The Elementary School Media Center, 1972. Contbr. articles to profl. jours. Home: 515 Rehill Ct River Vale NJ 07675 Office: East Ramapo Central School District 4 Spring Valley NY 10977

GLOS, MARGARET TAFT BEACH (MRS. STANLEY GLOS), assn. exec.; b. N.Y.C.; d. Stewart Taft and Josephine (Cushman) Beach; B.A. summa cum laude, Smith Coll., 1958; postgrad. Columbia, 1959-61; m. Stanley Glos, June 1, 1961; children—Alexander Beach, Maya Cushman. Editor, Nucleonics Mag., McGraw Hill Co., 1959-66; asst. mng. editor Sci. Research Mag., 1966-67; exec. dir. mng. editor Soc. Nuclear Medicine, N.Y.C., 1967—. Editorial cons. Grolier Corp., 1961-63. Bd. dirs. British Am. Ednl. Found. Mem. Am. Astronomical Soc., Soc. Nuclear Medicine, Phi Beta Kappa, Sigma Xi. Contbr. articles to profl. jours. Home: 129 E 94th St New York City NY 10028 Office: 475 Park Av S New York City NY 10016

GLOVER, BETTY S., musician; b. Hudson, Ill., Jan. 24, 1923; Mus. B., Mus. M., Cin. Conservatory of Music, student of Ernest N. Glover. Prin. trombonist Kansas City Philharmonic, 1944-48, Columbus (O.) Philharmonic, 1948-49; bass trombonist Cin. Symphony Orch., 1952—. Adj.-asso. prof. also dir. Brass Choir, Conservatory of Music, U. Cin. Mem. Pi Kappa Lambda, Sigma Alpha Iota. Home: 8791 Cottonwood Dr Cincinnati OH 45231

GLOVER, ROSALIE HARWOOD, club woman; b. Richmond, Va., Nov. 22, 1892; d. Charles Whitlock and Marie (Haggarty) Harwood; student pvt. schs., Richmond; m. Henry Lee Finlayson, Feb. 11, 1920 (dec. Oct. 1937); 1 son, Henry Lee; m. 2d, Robert O. Glover, Apr. 18, 1938. Formerly with Liberty Loan at Planters Nat. Bank, Richmond. Vol. worker, A.R.C., World War I and II, Navy Relief Soc., World War II. Mem. Colonial Dames of Am., Jamestown Soc. Clubs: Virginia Country, Colony, Catholic Woman's (Richmond, Va.). Home: 4308 Cambridge Rd Richmond VA 23221

GLOVER, SANDRA JEAN, entomologist; b. Mansfield, La., Jan. 19, 1939; d. Charles Pickett and Johnnie Ruth (Williams) Glover; B.S., Northwestern State U., Natchitoches, La., 1961; M.Ed., U. Ga., 1965, Ph.D., 1968. Tchr., Fair Park High Sch., Shreveport, 1961-64; grad. research asst. U. Ga., 1965-68; asso. prof. Miss. State Coll. Women, 1968; aquatic biologist Fed. Water Pollution Control Adminstrn., Dept. Interior, Kansas City, Mo., 1968; asst. prof. biology Appalachian State U., Boone, N.C., 1969—. NSF summer inst. grantee, 1964; NSF-Acad. Year Inst. grantee U. Ga., 1964-65; Dept. Agr. grantee, 1965-68; postdoctoral fellow U. Ga., 1968-69. Mem. Am. Assn. U. Women (Boone br. area rep. 1971-72), Assn. Southeastern Biologists, Entomol. Soc. Am., Ga. Entomol. Soc., Sigma Xi, Delta Zeta (corr. sec. 1957-61, exec. com. 1960-61). Author: Biology: The Laboratory, 1970. Office: Dept Biology Appalachian State U Boone NC 28607

GLUBOK, SHIRLEY ASTOR (MRS. ALFRED H. TAMARIN), author, lectr.; b. St. Louis, June 15, 1933; d. Yale I. and Ann (Astor) Glubok; B.A., Washington U., St. Louis; M.A., Columbia Tchrs. Coll., 1958; m. Alfred H. Tamarin, Feb. 25, 1968. Lectr. history of art Met. Mus. of Art, N.Y.C., 1958—. Mem. Am. Assn. Mus., Archael. Inst. Am., Washington U. Archaeol. Assn., Authors League Am. Author: The Art of Ancient Egypt, 1962; The Art of Lands in the Bible, 1963; The Art of Ancient Greece, 1963; The Art of the North American Indian, 1964; The Art of the Eskimo, 1964; The Art of Ancient Rome, 1965; The Art of Africa, 1965; Fall of the Aztecs, 1965; Art and Archaeology, 1966; The Art of Ancient Peru, 1966; The Art of the Etruscans, 1967; Fall of the Incas, 1967; Discovering Tutankhamun's Tomb, 1968; The Art of Ancient Mexico, 1968; Knights in Armor, 1969; Home and Child Life in Colonial Days, 1969; The Art of India, 1969; Discovering the Royal Tombs at Ur, 1969; The Art of Japan, 1970; The Art of Colonial America, 1970; Digging in Assyria, 1970; The Art of the Southwest Indians, 1971; The Art of the Old West, 1971; The Art of the New American Nation, 1972; The Art of the Spanish in the United States and Puerto Rico, 1972; The Art of China, 1973; The Art of America from Jackson to Lincoln, 1973; The Art of America in the Gilded Age, 1974. Home: 50 E 72d St New York City NY 10021

GLUECK, HELEN IGLAUER (MRS. NELSON GLUECK), med. educator; b. Cin., Feb. 4, 1907; d. Samuel and Helen (Ransohoff) Iglauer; B.A., U. Wis., 1929; M.D., U. Cin., 1934; m. Nelson Glueck, Mar. 26, 1931; 1 son, Charles. Intern, Cin. Gen. Hosp., 1934-35, resident in medicine, 1935-36; Research fellow May Inst., Jewish Hosp., 1939-43; dir. coagulation lab. dept. medicine U. Cin. Coll. Medicine, 1956—, prof. medicine, 1965—. Mem. Internat. Soc. Hematology, Central Soc. Clin. Research, Alpha Omega Alpha. Clubs: University, Losantiville Country (Cin.). Home: 162 Glenmary Av Cincinnati OH 45220

GOBBIE, EVELYN MAUDE, judge; b. London, Eng., June 24, 1921; d. Francis Julian and Evelyn Mary (Marshall) Gobbie; student St. Joseph Coll., West Hartford, Conn., 1938-39; J.D. summa cum laude, U. Miami (Fla.), 1957; m. John Kennedy Birley, July 21, 1945 (div. May 1949). Admitted to Fla. bar, 1957, U.S. Ct. Appeals, 1957, U.S. Dist. Ct., 1957; asso. firm Perry Nichols, Miami, 1957-58, William Grimes, Bradenton, Fla., 1958-63; pvt. practice in Sarasota Fla., 1963-72; city prosecutor City of Palmetto (Fla.), 1958-63, City of Sarasota, 1966-67; chief municipal judge, Sarasota, 1967-72; municipal judge, Longboat Key, Fla., 1969-72; circuit judge 12th Jud. Circuit, 1973—. Lectr. law U. Miami Law Sch., 1957-58. Served with Women's Aux., RAF, 1941-46. Mem. Am. Trial Lawyers Assn., Acad. Fla. Trial Lawyers, Am. Judicature Soc., Fla. Conf. Circuit Judges, 12th Jud. Circuit (sec.-treas. 1963—), Fla. Bar, Sarasota County Bar Assn. (sec. 1966-68), Am. Bus. Women (Woman of Yr., Sarasota chpt. 1967), Sarasota C. of C. (better bus. com. 1964—), Kappa Beta Pi, Phi Kappa Phi. Home: Forest Lakes Village 2424 Clubhouse Circle Apt 102 Sarasota FL 33580 Office: Sarasota County Courthouse Sarasota FL 33577

GOBELI, LAURETTA LAING WIMMER (MRS. MURRAY JEROME GOBELI), banker; b. Draper, N.C., Feb. 7, 1921; d. William Lehman and Lila (Hill) Laing; student Va. So. Coll., U. Va. Extension, Am. Savs. and Loan Inst.; m. Charles W. Wimmer, Apr. 3, 1945 (dec. Aug. 1960); 1 son, Lee; m. 2d, Murray Jerome Gobeli, Sept. 17, 1966; stepchildren-Gary, Joseph, Murray John. Asst. sec., S.W. Va. Savs. & Loan Assn., Roanoke, 1949-66; personnel officer 1st Agrl. Nat. Bank, Pittsfield, Mass., 1966—. Mem. regional adv. council Pittsfield Dept. Edn., 1972—. Mem. Am. Savs. and Loan Inst. (chpt. pres. 1963-64), Nat. Assn. Bank Women, Pittsfield C. of C. (manpower com. 1969-71), Wesleyan Service Guild (treas. Roanoke 1964-66). Methodist. Home: 24 Notch Rd North Adams MA 01247 Office: 100 North St Pittsfield MA 01201

GOBLE, ELISE JOAN HOLLENBERG (MRS. JOHN LEWIS GOBLE), physician; b. Winnipeg, Man., Can., Jan. 23, 1932; d. Michael Samuel and Sarah (Corbin) Hollenberg; M.D., U. Man., 1956; m. John Lewis Goble, Oct. 4, 1956; children—John Robert, Michael William. Came to U.S., 1956, naturalized, 1960. Intern Vancouver (B.C., Can.) Gen. Hosp., 1955-56; resident Columbia-Presbyn. Med. Center, N.Y.C., 1956-59, chief resident, 1959; practice medicine specializing in gen. ophthalmology, San Mateo, Cal., 1959-61, specializing in pediatric ophthalmology, 1961—; mem. staffs Mills Meml. Hosp., San Mateo, Peninsula Hosp., Burlingame, Sequoia Hosp., Redwood City, Cal. Fellow Am. Acad. Ophthalmology and Otolaryngology, A.C.S.; mem. A.M.A., Cal. Med. Assn., San Mateo County Med. Soc. Home: 2007 New Brunswick Dr San Mateo CA 94402 Office: 101 S San Mateo Dr San Mateo CA 94401

GOCEK, MATILDA ARKENBOUT (MRS. JOHN A. GOCEK), librarian; b. Hoboken, N.J., Feb. 18, 1923; d. Jacob Richard and Mathilda (Meyer) Arkenbout; A.A., Orange County Community Coll., 1961; B.A., N.Y. State U. Coll. at New Paltz, 1964; M.L.S., N.Y. State U. Coll. at Albany, 1967; m. Harry Francis Decker, May 15, 1939 (div. Nov. 1955); children—Ruth Ann (Mrs. Donald Case), Dianne Karen (Mrs. Ralph McKinstrie); m. 2d, John A. Gocek, Nov. 18, 1956; 1 son, John Jacob. Librarian, Monroe (N.Y.) Free Library, 1958-61, Tuxedo Park (N.Y.) Library, 1963—. Library cons. Tuxedo Union Free Sch., 1967-69. Ofcl. historian Town of Tuxedo, 1973—; chmn. Tuxedo Bicentennial Commn., 1974—. Trustee Tuxedo Park Sch. Mem. Orange-Sullivan Pub. (pres. 1967-70), N.Y., Am. library assns., Dirs. Assn. (sec. exec. bd. 1974—), Southeastern N.Y. Library Reference Resource Council. Author: The Tuxedo Park Library: Social Aspects of Growth, 1901-1940, 1969; Benedict Arnold: Reader's Guide and Bibliography, 1972; Orange County, N.Y.: Reader's Guide and Bibliography, 1973. Editor: Library Research Assos., 1968; Dialogue monthly newsletter. Home: Dunderberg Rd Monroe NY 10950 Office: Tuxedo Park NY 10987

GODDARD, ESTHER CHRISTINE (MRS. ROBERT HUTCHINGS GODDARD), editor; b. Worcester, Mass.; d. August William and Augusta (Johnson) Kisk; student Bates Coll., 1920-22; B.S., Johns Hopkins U., 1945; M.A., Clark U., 1951, L.H.D., 1972; Sc.D., Nasson Coll., 1961, Worcester Poly. Inst., 1969, Anna Maria Coll., 1970; m. Robert Hutchings Goddard, June 21, 1924 (dec. Aug. 1945). Editor books with Dr. G. Edward Pendray: Rocket Development, 1947, The Papers of Robert H. Goddard, 3 vols., 1970; contbr. articles on space exploration to various publns., 1946—; bd. dirs. Age Center of Worcester (Mass.) Area, Inc., 1963-70; dir. First Fed. Savs. and Loan Assn., 1965-73. Mem. exec. bd. Mass. chpt. Arthritis Found., 1964—; trustee Med. Research Inst. Worcester, 1965-70, Clark U., Worcester, 1964-72; mem. adv. bd. Anna Maria Coll., Paxton, 1965-72; mem. adv. historic landmark com. City of Worcester, 1966-70; hon. mem. dir.'s council Worcester Sci. Center, 1970—. Named Woman of the Year, Worcester Bus. and Profl. Women's Club, 1958, Nat. League Am. Pen Women, 1972. Fellow Am. Astronautical Soc.; mem. Am. Inst. Aero. and Astronautics (hon.), Air Force Assn. (hon.), Am. Assn. U. Women (outstanding mem.), Soroptimists (hon. mem. Worcester). Club: Nat. Space (bd. govs. Washington), Boston Authors. Home: 1 Tallawanda Dr Worcester MA 01603

GODDEN, RUMER, author; b. Sussex, Eng., Dec. 10, 1907; d. Arthur Leigh and Katherine Norah Godden; ed. Moira House, Eastbourne; m. Laurance S. Foster, Mar. 9, 1934; children—Jennifer Jane, Paula Mary; m. 2d, J. L. Haynes-Dixon, Nov. 26, 1949. Author books including: Black Narcissus, 1939; The River, 1946; A Candle for St. Jude, 1948; A Breath of Air, 1950; In Noah's Ark (poetry), 1950; Kingfishers Catch Fire, 1953; An Episode of Sparrows, 1955; The Greengage Summer, 1958; China Court, 1961; The Battle of the Villa Fiorita, 1964; Prayers From The Ark, 1964; The Feather Duster, 1964; The Creatures' Choir, 1967; The Kitchen Madonna, 1967; Two Under the Indian Sun, 1967; Swans and Turtles (short stories) 1968; In This House of Brede, 1969; Shiva's Pigeons, 1972; (children's book) The Diddakoi, 1972. Contbr. to many children's books. Home: 4 Mermaid St Rye East Sussex England

GODENNE, GHISLAINE DUDLEY, physician; b. Brussels, Belgium; d. Pierre and Olive Dudley (Short) Godenne; grad. Ecole Catholique de Service Social, Brussels, 1946; B.S., Universite Catholique de Louvain Louvain Belgium, 1948, M.D., 1952. Came to U.S., 1951. Intern Providence Hosp., Washington, 1951-52, resident pediatrics, 1952-54; fellow pediatrics Mayo Clinic, Rochester, Minn., 1954-57; fellow pediatric research Johns Hopkins U., 1957-58, asso. prof. mental hygiene, psychiatry, pediatrics, 1966—, prof. psychology, 1973—; resident psychiatry Johns Hopkins Hosp., Balt., 1958-62, chief adolescent psychiat. service, 1964-73; dir. counseling and psychiat. services John Hopkins U., 1973—; mem. staffs various hosps., Balt. grad. Balt.-Washington Psychoanalytic Inst., 1972. Cons. psychiatrist Clyburn Children's Home, Balt., 1960, Catonsville (Md.) Community Coll., 1968—, Good Shepherd Center, 1970—. Bd. dirs. Balt. Girl Scouts Assn., 1958-60, Met. Balt. Assn. for Mental Health, Inc., 1965-69, Florence Crittendon Home, 1966-68. Fulbright grantee 1951-52, Parke & David-Research Investigation grantee, 1957, Gen. Practitioner grantee Nat. Inst. Mental Health, 1961-63; Md. Richmond fellow, 1971—; recipient Career Teaching award, 1963-65; decorated chevalier Order of Leopold (Belgium). Fellow A.C.P., Am. Psychiat. Assn., Am. Pub. Health Assn., Inc., Am. Orthopsychiat. assn.; mem. Md. Soc. Adolescent Psychiatry (pres 1968-69), Md. Psychiat. Soc. (chmn. program com. 1969-70), Md. State Conf. Social Welfare (mem. child welfare com. 1961-64), Am. Soc. Adolescent Psychiatry (v.p. 1974—), Am. Soc. Adolescent Medicine, Am. Psychosomatic Soc., Am. Assn. U. Profs. Home: 15 Edgevale Rd Baltimore MD 21210

GODERSKY, LOIS GARNET SHOFF (MRS. GEORGE EDWIN GODERSKY), pathologist; b. Flora, Ind., Aug. 10, 1917; d. John Frank and Jennie Garnet (Moudy) Shoff; A.B., Ind. U., 1939, M.D., 1942; m. George Edwin Godersky, Sept. 14, 1940; children—Christine (Mrs. Philip Gubbins), Janet (Mrs. Anthony Ingraffea), John Carl, Andrea, Peter. Intern, Ind. U. Med. Center, 1943-44, St. Joseph Hosp., South Bend, Ind., 1962-63; resident pathology South Bend Med. Found., 1963-67, staff pathologist, 1967—; vis. asst. prof. microbiology dept. U. Notre Dame, South Bend, 1971-72. Active St. Joseph County Cancer Soc. Mem. A.M.A., Am. Soc. Clin. Pathologists, Coll. Am. Pathologists. Address: 3018 Robinhood Lane South Bend IN 46614

GODFREY, REBECCA TAUB (MRS. PETER SIMON GODFREY), cellist, assn. exec.; b. N.Y.C.; d. Morris and Pauline (Mahler) Taub; B.A., Bklyn. Coll., 1939; M.A., Columbia, 1942; m. Peter Simon Godfrey, Feb. 19, 1938; children—Eric Philip, Robin Lincoln, Naomi Welcome. Nursery sch. tchr., 1937, 38-39; psychiat. social worker Jewish Family Soc., N.Y.C., 1942-43; cellist Charleston Symphony Orch., 1943-69; exec. dir. Charleston Chamber Music Soc., 1956—; originator, designer TV series The Musical Ombudsman, also co-producer, host. Cellist, first chair Charleston (W.Va.) Chamber Music Soc., 1944-55; tchr. cello, 1938—; cons. family relations, concert mgmt.; lectr. mus. subjects with psychiat. implications. Mem. women's com. Charleston Symphony Orch.; pres. women's com. Charleston Chamber Music Soc., 1943-56; founder Charleston Cinema Soc., 1947, exec. dir., 1947-56; pres. Interstate Impact Com., 1969; bd. dirs. Charleston Area Youth Symphony; treas. Charleston Draft Information Center, 1968-70; co-founder Suburban Watershed Assn., Charleston, 1961; v.p. so. region Catholic Charities, Diocese of Wheeling, W.Va. Mem. Assn. Coll. and Univ. Concert Mgrs., Internat. Violocello Soc., League Women Voters, Nat. Wildlife Fedn., Nat. Audubon Soc., Citizens for Protection Environment W.Va., Environmental Def. Fund, Ams. Democratic Action, Am. Civil Liberties Union. Writer mus. subjects. Home: 1409 Meadowcrest Lane Charleston WV 25314

GODIN, NICOLE, physician; b. Niort, France, June 8, 1933; d. Maurice and Madeleine (Betin) Godin; B.A.-B.S.C., Lycee Fenelon, Paris, France, 1951; diploma scis. Sorbonne U., Paris, France, 1952; M.D., U. Paris, 1958; m. Robert R. Castro, Oct. 10, 1959; children—Isabelle, Michael. Came to U.S., 1961. Rotating intern, Covington, Ky., 1958-59; resident internal medicine Hosp. Jean Talon, Montreal, Que., Can., 1959-61, U. Hosp., Madison, Wis., 1961-64; practice medicine, specializing in internal medicine, Ottawa, Ill., 1968—; mem. staff Ottawa Community Hosp. Mem. A.M.A., Ill., LaSalle County med. socs., Am. Coll. Chest Physicians. Home: 210 Forest Park Pl Ottawa IL 61350 Office: 113 W Glover St Ottawa IL 61350

GODOWSKY, FRANCES GERSHWIN (MRS. LEOPOLD GODOWSKY), artist; b. N.Y.C.; d. Morris and Rose (Bruskin) Gershwin; student Columbia, 1930, N.Y.U., 1940, extension U. Rochester, 1933; m. Leopold Godowsky, Nov. 2, 1930; children—Sandra (Mrs. Edward Hume), Leopold III, Georgia (Mrs. David Keidan), Nadia. One man shows at Kipins Gallery, Westport, Conn., Silvermine Guild, New Caanan, Conn., Westerly Gallery, N.Y.C., Phoenix Gallery, N.Y.C.; exhibited in numerous group shows; represented in pvt. and permanent collections including Wadsworth Atheneum, Hartford, Conn., N.Y.U., Newark Mus., Cornell Art Mus., Ithaca, N.Y., Eisenhower Coll. Recipient Grand Prix medal Internat. Women's Exhbn., France, 1969. Address: 45 Sutton Pl S New York City NY 10022

GODWIN, FRANCES LOUISE ELLIOTT (MRS. CHARLES MARION GODWIN), librarian; b. Colorado City, Tex., May 13, 1920; d. Lewis Beall and Elizabeth Anna (Wilson) Elliott; B.A. in L.S., Tex. Woman's U., 1941; M.Ed., Hardin-Simmons U., 1969; m. Charles Marion Godwin, June 14, 1942; children—Marilyn Louise (Mrs. Robert Dean Brookshear), Joyce Elaine (Mrs. Lewis E. Buchanan). Librarian, Pecos High Sch., 1941-42, Colorado High Sch., 1942-43, 45-48, 62—. Ore. State Library, 1943-44; audio-visual coordinator Colorado City Ind. Sch. Dist. Sponsor dist. III Teen-Age Library Assn., Hutchinson P.T.A., 1954-60; vol. A.R.C., Community Chest fund drives. Mem. A.L.A., Tex. Library Assn., Tex. State Tchrs. Assn. (life), Am., Tex. assns. sch. librarians, N.E.A., Poetry Soc. Tex., Am. Assn. U. Women, Tex. Assn. Ednl. Tech., Order Rainbow Girls (past mother adviser), Daus. of Nile, Delta Kappa Gamma. Methodist (past pres., life mem. Womens Soc. Christian Service, treas. women's group, coordinator adult ministries). Mem. Order Eastern Star. Home: 735 E 16th St Colorado City TX 79512 Office: 12th and Chestnut Sts Colorado City TX 79512

GODWIN, GAIL, author; b. Bessemer, Ala., June 18, 1937; d. Mose Winston and Kathleen (Krahenbuhl) Godwin; student Peace Jr. Coll., 1955-57; B.A. in Journalism, U. N.C., 1959; M.A. in English, U. Ia., 1968; Ph.D., 1971; postgrad. (Center for Advanced Study fellow), U. Ill., 1971-72. Reporter, Miami (Fla.) Herald, 1959-60; writer, cons. U.S. Govt. Tourist Office, London, Eng., 1961-65; editorial staff writer Sat. Eve. Post, N.Y.C., 1966-67; instr. English, U. Ia., Iowa City, 1968-71; lectr. Ia. Writers Workshop, Iowa City, 1972-73; free lance writer, 1973—. Mem. Modern Lang. Assn. Author: The Perfectionists, 1970; Glass People, 1972; The Odd Woman, 1974. Contbr. fiction, lit. articles to popular mags., profl. jours. Office: c/o Paul R Reynolds Inc 599 5th Av New York City NY 10017

GOEBEL, SISTER MARISTELLA, educator; b. Racine, Wis., Sept. 10, 1915; d. James Nicholas and Henrietta Marie (Rademacher) Goebel; B.S., Edgewood Coll., 1944; M.A., Cath. U. Am., 1947, Ph.D. (scholar), 1966; postgrad. U. Chgo., 1953. Tchr. English, Cathedral High Sch., Sioux Falls, S.D., 1946-47, Heart of Mary High Sch., Mobile, Ala., 1947-49; mem. faculty Rosary Coll., River Forest, Ill., 1949—, asso. prof. psychology, 1966—. Clin. psychologist Hines VA Hosp., Hines, Ill., 1970—; cons. Dominican Sisters, Sinsinawa, Wis., 1966—. Recipient Research grants Nat. Inst. Mental Health, 1962, 63, 66, Third Place award Nat. Psi Chi, 1963. Mem. A.A.A.S., Am., Wis., Ill. (sect. sec., treas. 1973—) psychol. assns., Psychologists Interested in Religious Issues, Soc. for Clin. and Exptl. Hypnosis, Psi Chi. Roman Catholic. Home: 7900 W Division St River Forest IL 60305 Office: Hines VA Hosp Hines IL 60141

GOEDICKE, PATRICIA MCKENNA (MRS. LEONARD WALLACE ROBINSON), poet; b. Boston, Mass., June 21, 1931; d. John Bernard and Helen Victoria (Mulvey) McKenna; B.A., Middlebury Coll., 1953; M.A., Ohio U., 1963; m. Leonard Wallace Robinson, Dec. 7, 1969. Editorial asst. Harcourt Brace and Jovanovich, Inc., Publishers, N.Y.C., 1953-54; research asst. Columbia Phys. and Surgs., N.Y.C., 1954-55; editorial asst. T.Y. Crowell, publishers, N.Y.C., 1955-56. Lectr. English, Ohio U., 1963-67, Hunter Coll., 1968-71; lectr. poetry Instituto Allende, Mexico, 1972—. Recipient award Nat. Endowment for the Arts, 1969-70, award Borestone Mountain, 1969. Mem. Modern Lang. Assn., Poetry Assn. Am., Phi Beta Kappa. Author: Between Oceans, 1968. Author numerous poems published in numerous mags. including Saturday Review, Poetry The Nation, New York Times, Kenyon Review, Iowa Review, New York Quarterly, New American Review. Home: Aptdo 462 San Miguel de Allende Guanajuato Mexico

GOEN, MURIEL, psychologist; b. Parkersburg, W.Va., Apr. 1, 1903; d. George William and Edna May (Killingsworth) Goen. Tchr. Milo Elementary Sch., 1925-40; head ednl. program Franklin County Ct. of Domestic Relations, 1940-49; head spl. edn. Columbus Pub. Schs., 1949-50; with Dept. of Child Study, Columbus, 1950—; tchr. adult edn. courses, 1945—. Diplomate Am. Bd. Profl. Psychology. Mem. A.A.A.S., N.E.A. (life), Am. Psychol. Assn., Internat. Platform Assn., Delta Kappa Gamma. Office: Columbus Bd Edn 61 S 6th St Columbus OH

GOETTE, MARY HOWE, educator; b. St. Paul, Aug. 11, 1924; d. Herbert Jacob and Irene Mary (Howe) Goette; B.A. cum laude, U. Minn., 1945, M.A., 1951, Ph.D., 1970. Psychometrist, Duluth (Minn.) State Tchrs. Coll., 1945-46; instr. polit. sci. and psychology Rochester (Minn.) Community Coll., 1946—. Mem. Am., Minn. (mem. exec. com. 1973-74) polit. sci. assns., Am. Psychol. Assn., Minn. Community Coll. Faculty Assn. (dir. 1973-74), Rochester Bus. and Profl. Women's Club (past pres.), Delta Kappa Gamma. Episcopalian. Home: 807 6th St SW Rochester MN 55901

GOETTEL, ELINOR PRAEGER (MRS. GERARD LOUIS GOETTEL), author; b. Bangkok, Thailand, Aug. 14, 1930 (parents Am. citizens); d. Otto and Carrie-Will (Coffman) Praeger; A.B., Duke, 1951; m. Gerard Louis Goettel, June 4, 1951; children—Sheryl, Glenn, James. Free lance writer Crowell-Collier Edn. Corp., N.Y.C., 1965, Ednl. Audio-Visual, Pleasantville, N.Y., 1967-68, Columbia U. Press, N.Y.C., 1966-67, 72—. Mem. Phi Beta Kappa. Author: Eagle of the Philippines: President Manuel Quezon, 1970; America's Wars - Why?, 1972. Home: 6 Chamberlain St Rye NY 10580

GOETTLING, GISELA ERIKA KRAUSE, educator; b. Berlin, Germany, Aug. 15, 1926; d. Gustav Reinhold and Gertrud (Weiberg) Krause; voice teaching diploma (full scholar) Staatliches Prüfungsamt, Staatlichhochschule für Musik, Hamburg, Germany, 1951, opera singing diploma Deutsche Bühnengenossenschaft, 1953; m. Woldemar Peter Goettling, Feb. 4, 1956 (dec. Jan. 1970); 1 dau., Kira Xenia; m. 2d, Baldwin Ford, July 10, 1971 (dec. Oct. 1971). Came to U.S., 1957, naturalized, 1965. Gen. music tchr. Staatliche Jugendmusikschule, Hamburg, 1951-56, Staatliche Gewerbe and Hauswirtschaftschule, Hamburg, 1956-57; owner pvt. voice studio, Hamburg, 1950-57, Chgo., 1963-66; tchr. voice, mem. vocal bd. Cosmopolitan Sch. Music, Chgo., 1960-63; gen. music tchr. Harris Sch., Chgo., 1961-64; tchr. gen. music, voice tng., vocal ensembles U. Chgo. Lab. Schs., 1964—; tchr. voice Am. Conservatory, Chgo., 1966—, Harper Coll., Palatine, Ill., 1971—. Recitals in Germany, Denmark, 1950-57; concert tour, Germany, Denmark, Sweden, France, 1968. Mem. Nat. Assn. Tchrs. Singing (chpt. bd. dirs. 1968-70, chpt. chmn. student evaluation auditions 1970-72), Music Tchrs. Nat. Assn. (judge divisional contest 1974). Home: 126 Ashley Ct Hoffman Estates IL 60172 Office: Am Conservatory 410 S Michigan Av Chicago IL 60172 also U Chgo Lab Sch 1362 E 59th St Chicago IL 60637

GOFF, ANN SPINKS (MRS. JOHN PATRICK GOFF), psychologist; b. El Paso, Tex., Aug. 1, 1940; d. William Barney and Virginia Lillian (Bunicke) Spinks; B.A., U. Tex., El Paso, 1967, M.A., 1969; m. John Patrick Goff, May 27, 1971; children—Kelly, Leslie. Teaching asst. U. Tex., 1967-68; staff psychologist Child Guidance Center, El Paso, 1968-73, asst. dir. psychol. services, 1973—. Cons. Prude Ranch, Ft. Davis, Tex., 1973—; group co-therapist, El Paso, 1971, pvt. psychol. testing, El Paso, 1970—. Mem. Am., Tex psychol. assns., Tex. Assn. for Children with Learning Disabilities, Mental Health Assn. Home: 815 Driver Circle El Paso TX 79903 Office: 1501 N Mesa St El Paso TX 79902

GOFF, ANNE MARIE, physician; b. Dublin, Ireland, June 16, 1931; d. Patrick Lawrence and Mary Elizabeth (Farrell) Digan; M.D., Nat. U., Dublin, 1960, B.Sci., 1962; m. Richard Goff, Apr. 24, 1950; 1 dau., Valerie. Came to U.S., 1964, naturalized, 1971. Intern, St. Vincent's Hosp., Dublin, 1960-61; resident St. Vincent's Hosp., Dublin, also Bellevue Hosp., N.Y. U. and Boston; research fellow Boston U. Med. Centre, 1964; chief resident Bellevue Hosp. Pulmonary Service, N.Y.C., 1966; instr. Boston U. Sch. Medicine, 1967, asst. prof., 1968-73, asso. clin. prof. medicine, 1973—; dir. chest service Brockton Hosp., 1973—; pulmonary cons. Hosp. for Crippled Children, Canton, Mass., Cape Cod Hosp., Hyannis, Mass., University Hosp., Boston VA Hosp., Boston City Hosp. Fellow Am. Coll. Chest Physicians; mem. Royal Coll. Physicians Ireland, Royal Coll. Physicians Glasgow, Am. Thoracic Soc., Brit. Med. Assn., Irish Med. Assn., Mass. Med. Soc. Clin. research lung disease. Home: Chateau Cardinale Reservoir St Brockton MA 02401 Office: Brockton Hospital Brockton MA 02402

GOFF, HARRIET ALICE (MRS. CHARLES HAROLD GOFF), banker; b. Wataga, Ill., June 10, 1912; d. Joseph E. and Ida May (Moore) Van Huffel; grad. high sch.; m. Charles Harold Goff, Oct. 25, 1930; children—Harold Eugene, Gary Alan, Charles Joseph. With Farmers Nat. Bank, Knoxville, Ill., 1958—, asst. cashier, 1967—. Persifer Twp. assessor, 1956-66. Pres., Knoxville High Sch. PTA, 1953-55. Republican. Mem. Christian Ch. (treas. 1966—, Christian Women's Fellowship pres. 1956-57, treas. 1961—, deaconess 1957—). Mem. Order Eastern Star. Home: Rural Route Knoxville IL 61448 Office: E Main St Knoxville IL 61448

GOFF, REGINA MARY (MRS. JOSIAH F. HENRY JR.), educator; b. St. Louis; d. Ward Wellington and Annabelle (Young) Goff; B.A. in Edn., Northwestern U., 1934; M.A., Columbia, 1940, Ph.D., 1948; m. Josiah F. Henry, Jr., Sept. 23, 1960. Dir. nursery sch., St. Louis, 1935; tchr. kindergarten, Kansas City, Kan., 1936-39; instr. Lincoln U., Jefferson City, Mo., 1940-46; dir. student teaching Stowe Tchrs. Coll., St. Louis, 1947-48; prof. child devel. Fla. A. and M. Coll., Tallahassee, also supr. Fla. Dept. Edn., 1949-50; mem. faculty Morgan State Coll., Balt., 1950-65, chmn. dept. edn., 1963-65; asst. commr., office of programs for disadvantaged U.S. Office Edn., Washington, 1965-71; prof. U. Md., 1971—. Cons. Ministry Edn. Iran, 1955-56. Mem. child welfare com. Md. Conf. and Welfare, 1960-62; pres. Urban League Md., 1961-63, bd. dirs., 1959-64; bd. dirs. UN of Md., Children's Guild Md. Recipient Pub. Service in Edn. awards Urban League Balt., 1963, St. Louis Assn. Negro Women's Clubs, 1965. Nat. and Profl. Bus. Women's Clubs, 1966, Alpha Kappa Alpha, 1966; Rockefeller Found. fellow, 1945-46. Mem. Am. Psychol. Assn., Md. Assn. Tchr. Edn. (pres.), N.E.A., Pi Lambda Theta, Kappa Delta Pi, Psi Chi, Alpha Kappa Alpha. Democrat. Roman Catholic. Contbr. articles on ednl. studies, cultural influence on personality devel. to ednl. jours. Home: 2306 Montebello Terrace Baltimore MD 21214

GOFFSTEIN, MARILYN BROOKE (M.B. GOFFSTEIN), author; b. St. Paul, Dec. 20, 1940; d. Albert Arthur and Esther Edith (Rose) Goffstein; B.A., Bennington Coll., 1962; m. Peter Schaaf, Aug. 15, 1965. One-woman showings in pen and ink and water color include Wakefield Gallery, N.Y.C., 1961, 62, 65, St. Paul Art Inst., 1961, Suzanne Kohn Gallery, 1966; lectr. New Sch., 1971, 74, Bank St. Coll. Edn., N.Y.C., 1971, Young Authors Conf., East Lansing Pub. Schs., 1973. Author, illustrator: The Gats! (honor book Children's Spring Book Festival), 1966; Sleepy People (Am. Inst. Graphic Arts Children's Book shows 1965-66), 1966; Brookie and Her Lamb, 1967; Across the Sea (Am. Inst. Graphic Arts Children's Book shows 1967-68, N.Y. Times best children's books 1967-68), 1968; Goldie the Dollmaker (N.Y. Times best children's books 1969-70), 1969; Two Piano Tuners, 1970; (novel) The Underside of the Leaf, 1972; (picture book with record) A Little Schubert, 1972; Me and My Captain, 1974. Address: 697 West End Av New York City NY 10025

GOHR, LEORA HELEN BREITAG (MRS. KENNETH GOHR), psychologist; b. Beaver Dam, Wis., Aug. 16, 1913; d. William and Pauline (Goetsch) Breitag; B.S., U. Wis., 1955, M.S., 1960, postgrad., 1965; m. Kenneth Gohr, June 16, 1962. Tchr., Dodge County Schs., Juneau, Wis., 1932-47, Columbus (Wis.) Pub. Schs., 1955-60; prin. Burnett State Graded Sch., Burnett, Wis., 1947-55; supr. Fond du Lac (Wis.) County Schs., 1960-65; psychologist Columbus Schs., 1965—. Mem. Nat. Assn. Sch. Psychologists, Wis. Psychol. Assn., Internat. Wis. reading assns., Madison Reading Council (sec. 1969-70), N.E.A., Wis. Edn. Assn., Pi Lambda Theta. Home: Route 1 Fall River WI 53932 Office: 200 W School St Columbus WI 53925

GOIN, MARCIA STEWART KRAFT (MRS. JOHN MOREHEAD GOIN), physician; b. Portsmouth, N.H., June 27, 1932; d. Wendell Everett and Dorothy (Spurr) Kraft; B.A., Middlebury Coll., 1954; M.D., Yale, 1958; m. John Morehead Goin, Mar. 5, 1960; children—Suzanne Jennifer, Jessica Michele. Med. intern U. Cal. Hosp., San Francisco, 1958-59; psychiat. resident Los Angeles County Gen. Hosp., Los Angeles, 1959-62, asst. dir. psychiat. outpatient clinic, 1962-68, staff psychiatrist psychiat. outpatient clinic, 1968—; practice psychiatry, Los Angeles, part-time 1962—; asso. clin. prof. U. So. Cal. Med. Sch., 1965—. Recipient certificate of humanitarian service for vol. work in South Vietnam, A.M.A., 1966. Mem. Am., So. Cal. (membership com. 1962—) psychiat. assns., So. Cal. Psychoanalytic Inst. Contbr. articles to profl. jours. Home: 2500 Park Oak Dr Los Angeles CA 90068 Office: 1127 Wilshire Blvd Los Angeles CA 90017

GOINS, LOUISE COPENING (MRS. WALTER L. GOINS), educator; b. Lenoir, N.C., Nov. 18, 1913; d. Vance and Bessie (Jones) Copening; A.B., Bennett Coll., 1935; M.Ed., Boston U., 1952; m. Walter L. Goins, Aug. 23, 1941; 1 dau., Bessie Louise. Tchr., Lenoir City Schs., 1935-47, Morganton, (N.C.) City Schs., 1948—. Asst. prin. Mt. View Elementary Sch., Morganton, 1966-67. Mem. Welfare Adv. Council of Lenoir, 1947-52, Lenoir Recreation Adv. Council, 1968-69. Trustee by-laws com. Woman's Civic Club, pres., 1964-65. Mem. N.C. Council Negro Women, Northwestern Profl. Women's Club (treas. 1970-74), Delta Sigma Theta. Home: 632 Stage St Lenoir NC 28645

GOKBORA, MARY JANE MCKEE, social worker; b. Mankato, Minn.; d. John Cecil and Claire (Nieberle) McKee; B.A., U. Ia., 1946, M.S.W., 1958; m. Ahmet Gokbora, Jan. 11, 1946 (div. June 1956); children—Gail M. (Mrs. William Hurst), Erol K. Pub. assistance worker Ia. Dept. Social Welfare, Linn County, 1951-56; child welfare worker, Marshall and Tama Counties, 1958-59; psychiat. social worker, mental health team Div. Mental Health, Ia. Bd. Control State Instns., 1959-60; dir. social services Ia. State Tng. Sch. for Boys, Eldora, 1960-62; supt. Mo. State Tng. Sch. for Girls, Chillicothe, 1962-71; social work cons. to Mo. Law Enforcement Assistance Council, Jefferson City, Women in Community Service, Lincoln, Neb., St. Francis Homes, Albany, N.Y., 1971—. Mem. Am. Assn. U. Women, Nat. Fedn. Bus. and Profl. Womens Clubs, Mo. Assn. Social Welfare, Mo. Correctional Assn., U. Ia. Alumni Assn., Nat. Assn. Social Workers (chpt. v.p. 1965-66), Nat. Council Crime and Delinquency, Joint Commn. Correctional Manpower and Tng., Mo. Council Children and Youth, Nat. Assn. Tng. Schs. and Juvenile Agys. (v.p. 1963--), Nat. Conf. Supts. of Correctional Instns. for Girls and Women (pres. 1965-66), Acad. Certified Social Workers. Episcopalian. Home: 22 Tulip Terrace Elnora NY 12065 Office: 62 S Swan St Albany NY 12210

GOLAN, MARGO ELIZABETH, business exec.; b. Lafayette, Ind., Aug. 23, 1916; d. Charles Fenton and Sarah Elizabeth (Fisher) May; grad. high sch.; m. Samuel L. Golan, Dec. 2, 1944 (dec. Dec. 1969); 1 dau., Kim (Mrs. Marvin Chancellor Norton, Jr.); stepchildren--Leonard Walter, Frederick Joseph. With Kauffman & Wulf Dept. Store, Hammond, Ind., 1935-36; dept. head Goldblatt Bros., Inc., Hammond, 1936-42; with Holiday Inn, Key West Fla., 1960—, innkeeper, 1962—; dir. Key West & Lower Keys Devel. Corp. Chmn. Monroe County Advt. Commn., 1969-74; mem. Monroe County Master-Plan Adv. Council. Mem. Key West C. of C. (dir., recipient Community Service award 1971), Internat. Assn. Holiday Inns (advt. com. 1971, reservation com. 1972). Club: Key West Women's (dir., recipient Outstanding Mem. award 1972). Home: 2 Go-Lane Key West FL 33040 Office: 1111 N Roosevelt Blvd Key West FL 33040

GOLD, CLAIRE SANDRA (MRS. JULIUS GOLD), ednl. adminstr.; b. Hoboken, N.J., Dec. 15, 1932; d. Max and Rose (Welger) Pineles; B.A., U. Pa., 1953; postgrad. Yale, 1953-54; M.A., Fairfield U., 1964, postgrad., 1968; m. Julius Gold, Sept. 3, 1952; children—Lauren, Jehv. Sch. psychologist, Ridgefield, Conn., 1964-65; sch. psychologist Westport (Conn.) Bd. Edn., 1965-68, dir. spl. edn., 1968-73, asst. supt., 1973—. Cons. Conn. and N.Y. adv. bds. Office Econ. Opportunity, mem. Drug Adv. Bd. Conn., 1973—, Mental Health Consortium Bd., Norwalk, Conn., 1972. Ednl. Profl. Devel. Act grantee, 1968; Title III Fed. grantee, 1972; State Conn. grantee, 1972; Title VI Fed. grantee, 1974. Mem. League Women Voters (v.p. 1959-61), Nat., Conn., Westport edn. assns., Nat., Conn. assns. sch. psychologists, Am. Assn. Mental Deficiency, Am. Personnel and Guidance Assn., Assn. Measurement and Evaluation Guidance, Council Exceptional Children, Conn. Sch. Counsellor Assn., Soc. to Aid Retarded, Conn. Assn. Pupil Personnel Adminstrs., Conn. Assn. Child Learning Disabilities. Club: Jewish Community Center (bd. govs. 1965-69). Office: 15 N Morningside Dr Westport CT 06880

GOLD, DELAYNE DEDRICK (MRS. LAURENCE J. GOLD), pub. relations co. exec.; b. N.Y., July 15, 1938; d. Gilman Teal and Helen A. (Smullen) Dedrick; B.A., Manhattanville Coll., 1960; postgrad. N.Y. U., 1961--; m. Laurence James Gold, Mar. 20, 1968.

Research librarian pub. relations dept. Olin Matheison Chem. Corp., N.Y.C., 1960-62; publicity coordinator Magnavox Co., N.Y.C., 1962-65; pub. relations supr. Rowland Co., N.Y.C., 1965-68; exec. v.p. Irving L. Straus Assos., N.Y.C., 1968—, pres. Straus Advt. div. Democrat. Roman Catholic. Home: 355 E 72d St New York City NY 10021 Office: 475 Park Av S New York City NY 10016

GOLD, JEANETTE BRENNER GOLDMAN (MRS. IRVING M. GOLD), realtor; b. Evansville, Ind., Nov. 2, 1922; d. Louis and Alice (Goldberg) Goldman; grad. high sch.; m. Irving M. Gold, Nov. 10, 1963; children—Jeffrey Brenner, Jeri Ellen Brenner. Property dir. Key Properties Mgmt., 1960-71; broker, owner Prime Property Mgmt., San Carlos, Cal., 1971—. Mem. Inst. Real Estate Mgmt. Elk. Home: 5 Portfino Ct San Carlos CA 94070 Office: 1150 Morse Blvd San Carlos CA 94070

GOLD, LEAH, painter, printmaker; d.; Morris B. and Hannah (Sklar) G.; art student Ruth Reeves Workshop, New Sch. Social Research, Hans Hofmann Sch. Fine Arts, Contemporaries Workshop, Bklyn. Mus. Art Sch. Exhibited in group shows including Bklyn. Mus., Provincetown Art Assn., Cape Cod Art Assn., Nat. Acad. Galleries, Stedelijk Mus. Amsterdam, Am. Jewish Tercentenary Exhbn., Nat. Philatelic Mus., N.Y.C. Center Gallery, Riverside Mus., Soc. Am. Graphic Artists, print Clubs Albany, Phila., Am. Color Print Soc., Painters and Sculptors Soc. N.J., Silvermine Guild Artists, Nat. Soc. Casein Painters, Asso. Am. Artists, Internat. Art Galleries, other galleries, museums in U.S., Holland, Belgium, Switzerland; purchase by Collectors Am. Art; traveling exhbns.; exhibited two-man award show Art Center Gallery, N.Y.C., two-man shows Cunningham and Walsh, N.Y.C., Hudson Guild Gallery, East Coast Gallery Provincetown, United Fedn. Tchrs. Gallery. Recipient hon. mention Artists Equity Assn., 1953, purchase prize for fabric design Birmingham Mus., 1956; prizes Painters and Sculptors Soc. N.J., Nat. Assn. Women Artists; 1st prize for sculpture Bklyn. Soc. Artists; prize watercolor, Painters and Sculptors Soc., N.J.; hon. mention for stained glass relief Design Derby, Miami, 1960; prizes for graphics and casein paintings Village Art Center, N.Y.C. Mem. Artists Equity Assn., Nat. Assn. Women Artists, Am. Soc. Contemporary Artists, Met. Painters and Sculptors, Provincetown (Mass.) Art Assn., Painters and Sculptors Soc. N.J., League Present Day Artists, East Coast Gallery Provincetown. Home and studio: 330 W 28th St New York City NY 10001

GOLD, SADIE ZUSSMAN (MRS. MILTON GOLD), editor; b. London, Eng., Apr. 2, 1921; d. Solomon and Rachel (Needleman) Zussman; grad. high sch.; m. Milton Gold, Oct. 16, 1959. Came to U.S., 1958, naturalized, 1963. Reporter, Daily Express, London, 1946-53, Sunday Pictorial, London, 1953-58; press officer British Information Services, N.Y.C., 1958-60; asst. to pres. pub. relations Am. Assembly Columbia, N.Y.C., 1961-62; asst. to pres. Simulmatics Corp., N.Y.C., 1962-65; editor British-Am. Trade News, British-Am. C. of C., N.Y.C., 1965-74; now free lance writer. Served with AUS, 1942-45. Recipient Medal of Freedom, U.S. Govt., 1946. Mem. Audubon Soc. Home: 4101 Cathedral Av NW Washington DC 20016

GOLD, SALLY, editor; b. N.Y.C., Sept. 12, 1908; d. Morris and Hannah (Greenstein) Tannenbaum; student Bklyn. Coll., 1941-43; m. Victor Gold, Jan. 12, 1941; children—Jon H., Errol S. Appeared in Broadway show Applause, 1937; model Rosanna Dresses, 1937-38; advt. exec. Indsl. Plants Corp., N.Y.C., 1938-53, dir., tchr. Magic Cottage Nursery Sch. and Camp Victor Day Camp, Long Beach, N.Y., 1954-64; columnist One Woman's Opinion, L.I. Ind. newspaper, Long Beach, 1964—, mng. editor, since 1971—. Lectr., Weight Watchers, 1964-72; owner Desperate Club, 1972-74. Vice pres. Orgn. Rehab. Tng., Long Beach; 1st pres. Nat. Council Emotionally Disturbed Children. Vice pres., function chmn. Long Beach Womens Democratic Club, 1953-63. Recipient certificates of appreciation Long Beach Police Dept., 1972, Am. Cancer Soc., 1972, plaque Army Dept., 1973. Mem. Nassau Press Assn., Sisterhood Cong. Mt. Sinai Bklyn., Am. Jewish Congress (v.p.), Forester (1st pres). Home: 116 Riverside Blvd Long Beach NY 11561 Office: 120 W Park Av Long Beach NY 11561

GOLD, SONIA STEINMAN (MRS. BELA GOLD), educator; b. N.Y.C., Dec. 17, 1917; d. Isaac and Mary (Singerman) Steinman; B.A., Hunter Coll., 1938; postgrad. Am. U., 1939-40, Columbia, 1940-41; Ph.D., U. Pitts., 1956; m. Bela Gold, July 5, 1938; 1 son, Robert. Economist, Treasury Dept., Washington, 1943-47; instr. Chatham Coll., Pitts., 1951-54; asst. prof. Carnegie-Mellon U., Pitts., 1959-66; asso. prof. John Carroll U., Cleve., 1967-72, prof. econs., 1972—. Radcliffe Inst. scholar, Cambridge, Mass., 1966-68. Mem. Am. Econ. Assn., A.A.A.S., Am. Assn. U. Profs. Contbr. articles to profl. jours. Home: 2901 Litchfield Rd Shaker Heights OH 44120 Office: Econs Dept John Carroll U Cleveland OH 44120

GOLDBERG, ANN BARBARA COGAN (MRS. STEPHEN P. GOLDBERG), occupational therapist; b. N.Y.C., May 3, 1939; d. Allan D. and Phyllis S. (Schultz) Cogan; B.S. in Occupational Therapy, U. Fla., 1961; m. Stephen P. Goldberg, May 24, 1970. Staff therapist Del. Curative Workshop, Wilmington, 1962-64; sr. therapist Inst. Rehab. Medicine, N.Y.C., 1964-67; chief occupational therapist Lubin Rehab. Center, Hosp. Albert Einstein Coll. Medicine, Bronx, N.Y., 1967—. Instr. N.Y. U., 1967-69, Columbia Sch. Occupational Therapy, 1970—. Recipient grant Office Vocational Rehab., 1963. Mem. Am. Occupational Therapy Assn. (mem. com. 1967-69). Home: 67 N Court Roslyn Heights NY 11577 Office: 1600 Tenbroeck Av Bronx NY 10461

GOLDBERG, DOROTHY K. (MRS. ARTHUR J. GOLDBERG), artist, author; b. St. Louis; B.A., U. Chgo.; student Art Inst. Chgo., various pvt. tchrs.; m. Arthur J. Goldberg; children—Robert, Barbara (Mrs. David A. Cramer). Exhibited in numerous one-man shows; program dir. Asso. Artists Gallery. vol. recruiter for programs to combat juvenile delinquency, Washington; active Urban Service Corps, Counsellors Aides Program, Widening Horizons Program, art enrichment programs; active Friends of Juvenile Ct., 1964; responsible for numerous meetings U.S. Mission to UN Am. women's group clubs, including Congl. wives' tours. Bd. dirs. UN Assn., Nat. Sch. Vol. Program. Author: The Creative Woman, 1963. Contbr. articles to mags. Home: 2801 New Mexico Av Washington DC 20007

GOLDBERG, ETHEL KARAN, psychologist, educator; b. Camden, N.J., June 10, 1943; d. Harry J. and Rose (Spivak) Goldberg; B.S. with honors, Temple U., 1965, M.Ed. with honors (N.J. state scholar, univ. scholar 1961-65), 1968, Ed.D. with honors (grad. fellow), 1971. Research asst. Temple U., Phila., 1967-68; research asso. Research for Better Schs., Inc., Phila., 1967-68; staff psychologist Pa. State U. at Chester, summer, 1969; tchr. psychol. testing and counseling theories to med. interns and residents, supr. paraprofls. Phila. Gen. Hosp., 1970-72; staff clin. psychologist Dept. Psychiatry Phila. Gen. Hosp., 1970-72, City Phila. Health Dept., 1972-73; ednl. researcher and evaluator Bd. Edn., Phila., 1973—. Mem. Am., Eastern, Pa. psychol. assns., Am., Pa., Phila. personnel and guidance assns., Phila. Soc. Clin. Psychology, Am. Ednl. Research Assn., Phi Delta Gamma, Alpha Lambda Delta. Home: 265 South 22nd St Philadelphia PA 19103 Office: Office of Research and Evaluation 4th floor Board of Education Philadelphia PA 19101

GOLDBERG, FAYE JOAN GIRSH (MRS. LEON I. GOLDBERG), educator; b. Phila., May 5, 1933; d. Jack Gould and Rose (Rosenberg) Girsh; A.B., Temple U., 1954; M.A., Boston U., 1955; Ed.D., Harvard, 1962; m. Leon I. Goldberg, Feb. 20, 1958; children—Mark, Claudia. Clin. psychologist Mass. Mental Health Center, Boston, 1958-59; social sci. analyst Nat. Inst. Mental Health, Bethesda, Md., 1959-61; instr. psychiatry Emory U., Atlanta, 1960-61; mem. faculty Morehouse Coll., Atlanta, 1965—, asso. prof. psychology, acting chmn. dept., 1969-73, prof., dir. drug tng. program, 1973—. Mem. DeKalb County Bond Study Commn., 1969-70, Criminal Justice Commn., 1969-70. Mem. exec. com. DeKalb County Democratic Party, 1966-71; mem. Ga. Democrat Exec. Com., 1966-70. Mem. Am., Ga., Southeastern psychol. assns., Soc. for Research in Child Devel., Soc. for Psychol. Study Social Issues, Am. Assn. U. Profs. (chpt. sec. 1968—), Am. Civil Liberties Union (dir. Ga. bd. 1966—). Contbr. articles to profl. jours. Address: care Dr Leon I Goldberg Pharmacology Dept U Chgo Med Sch Chicago IL 60637

GOLDBERG, HARLEAN FADER (MRS. LEONARD GOLDBERG), weight reduction orgn. exec.; b. Bklyn., June 1, 1932; d. Moe and Marjorie (Cullens) Fader; student Bklyn. Coll., 1949-51; m. Leonard Goldberg, Mar. 30, 1969; children—Terry, Janet, Randi, Warren. Pres., Weight Watchers of S.I. Inc., 1965-69; v.p. Weight Watchers of Syracuse Inc. (N.Y.), 1968—; sec. Select-A-Size Ltd., Syracuse, 1972—; pres. Shape Shoppes Inc., Syracuse, 1974—. Dir. W.W. Franchisee Assn. Inc., N.Y.C., 1972-73, mem. purchasing com., 1971-73, chmn. emergency fund com., 1972—. Bd. dirs. Jewish Family Service Bur., Syracuse, 1973—. Club: Syracuse University Hardwood (bd. dirs. 1973—, corr. sec. 1972—). Home: 5263 Jamesville Rd Dewitt NY 13214 Office: 5858 E Molloy Rd Syracuse NY 13211

GOLDBERG, JEANINE JACOBS (MRS. GERALD S. GOLDBERG), lawyer; b. Phila., Sept. 27, 1939; d. Louis and Mollie (Capter) Jacobs; B.S., U. Pa., 1960; LL.B., Harvard, 1963; m. Gerald S. Goldberg, Nov. 23, 1967. Admitted to Pa. bar, 1963, D.C. bar, 1964, U.S. Supreme Ct. bar, 1967, Conn. bar, 1970; trial atty. tax div. U.S. Dept. Justice, Washington, 1963-69; asso., Copelon & Schiff, New Haven, 1969-71, Cohen & Wolf, Bridgeport, Conn., 1972—. Mem. White House Conf. on Children and Youth, 1960, Gov's Conf. on Children and Youth Pa., 1960—, Pa. 100,000 Ambassadors, 1965—, Council for Internat. Visitors, 1957—. Govt. trustee, v.p. United Jewish Appeal, 1964-69. Mem. Nat. Assn. Women Lawyers (life), Am., Conn., New Haven County, Bridgeport bar assns., Nat. Panhellenic Conf., Harvard Law Sch. Assn. Conn., Kappa Beta Pi, Phi Sigma Sigma (nat. pres. 1969—), Kappa Delta Epsilon, Pi Lambda Theta, Pi Gamma Mu, Pi Delta Phi. Jewish religion (bd. mem. 1970—). Home: 952 Rainbow Trail Orange CT 06477 Office: 10 Middle St Bridgeport CT 06604

GOLDBERG, LEE WINICKI (MRS. FRANK M. GOLDBERG), furniture co. exec.; b. Laredo, Tex., Nov. 20, 1932; d. Frank and Goldie (Ostrowiak) Winicki; student San Diego State U., 1951-52; m. Frank M. Goldberg, Aug. 17, 1952; children—Susan Arlene, Edward Lewis, Anne Carri. With United Furniture Co., Inc., San Diego, 1953—, corporate sec., dir., 1963—, dir. environmental interiors, 1970—. Den mother Boy Scouts Am., San Diego, 1965; vol. Am. Cancer Soc., San Diego, 1964-69; chmn. jr. matrons United Jewish Fedn., San Diego, 1958; del. So. Pacific Coast region Hadassah Conv., 1960, pres. Galilee group San Diego chpt., 1960-61. Recipient Hadassah Service award San Diego chpt., 1958-59. Mem. Nat. Home Furnishings Inst. Democrat. Jewish religion.

GOLDBERG, LORRAINE HAZEL, clin. psychologist; b. Chgo., Oct. 9, 1928; d. Morris J. and Rose Helen (Edelstein) Goldberg; B.S., U. Ill., 1950, M.S., 1951; Ph.D., Ill. Inst. Tech., 1973. Supr. adult counseling service Jewish Vocational Service, Chgo., 1957-67; psychologist student counseling service U. Ill. at Chgo. Circle, 1967—, also coordinator group psychotherapy program; individual practice psychology, Chgo., 1957-62, 72—; cons. Psychiat. Inst. Circuit Ct. Cook County. Supr. adult vols. B'nai B'rith Youth Orgn. Mem. Am., Ill. (charter mem., sec. social issues sect.) psychol. assns., Ill. Group Psychotherapy Soc. (mem. constrn. revision com., elections com.). Research on psychotherapy, attitudes of clin. psychologists toward their patients. Home: Apt 23-E 4170 N Marine Dr Chicago IL 60613 Office: 601 S Morgan St Chicago IL 60680

GOLDBERG, LUCIANNE CUMMINGS STEINBERGER (MRS. SIDNEY GOLDBERG), editor; b. Boston, Apr. 29, 1935; d. Raymond Leonard and Lucy Jane (Moseley) Steinberger; student Va. Intermont Coll., 1951-53; m. Sidney Goldberg, Apr. 10, 1966; children—Joshua John Zolman, Jonah Jacob. Merchandising mgr. Washington Post, 1956-60; press aide Citizens for Lyndon Baines Johnson for Pres., 1960-61; congl. liaison Carl Byoir & Assos., 1961-62; pres., owner Cummings & Assos., Washington, 1961-66; news editor Women's News Service, N.Y.C., 1967—. Mem. Aux. Mounted Police, N.Y.C. Police Dept., 1973—. Mem. Pussycat League (nat. chmn. 1969—), Newswomen's Club N.Y. (mem. bd. govs. 1973-74). Author: Purr, Baby, Purr - The Case Against Women's Lib, 1971. Home: 255 W 84th St New York City NY 10024 Office: 220 E 42d St New York City NY 10016

GOLDBERG, MARGERY HELEN (MRS. LEONARD JACOBS), physician; b. Lecompfe, La., Nov. 29, 1915; d. Abraham and Bessie (Myers) Goldberg; B.S., La. State U., 1937; M.D., Tulane U., 1941; m. Leonard Jacobs, June 28, 1942; children—Joseph L. (dec.), Carl D. Intern, Women's Hosp., Phila., 1941-42; practice medicine, specializing in child psychiatry, Phila., 1943-59; physician, Community Health Service, Phila., 1943-48, Phila. Schs., 1948-59, Los Angeles City Schs., 1960—; Nat. Inst. Mental Health fellow in child psychiatry U. So. Cal.-Los Angeles County Hosp., 1967-68. Mem. Physicians Assn. Los Angeles Schs. (treas. 1968-71, pres. 1972—), Alpha Lambda Delta, Alpha Epsilon Iota, Gamma Nu. Home: 236 N Bundy Dr Los Angeles CA 90049 Office: Los Angeles City Schs 450 N Grand St Los Angeles CA 90012

GOLDBERG, NORMA LEE BOONE (MRS. ALLEN F. GOLDBERG), physician; b. Roseburg, Ore., July 22, 1931; d. William James and Helen (Wilson) Boone; B.A., Stanford, 1954, M.D., 1957; m. Allen Fred Goldberg, Feb. 15, 1960; children—Nancy Renee, David Samuel. Intern, resident U. Ill., 1957-59, clin. instr. anesthesiology, Med. Sch., 1963-68; resident U. Cal. at San Francisco, 1959-60; staff anesthesiologist St. Luke's Hosp., San Francisco, 1962; asst. anesthesiologist Western Res. U., Cleve., 1962-63; staff anesthesiologist Hines (Ill.) VA Hosp., 1963-64, attending anesthesiologist, 1965-69, in charge inhalation therapy, asst. sect. chief pulmonary disease, 1969—; clin. asst. prof. medicine U. Ill. Abraham Lincoln Sch. Medicine, Chgo., 1968—, asst. prof. medicine 1969—. Diplomate Am. Bd. Anesthesiology. Fellow Am. Coll. Anesthesiologists, Am. Coll. Chest Physicians; mem. Internat. Anesthesia Research Soc., Am. Soc. Anesthesiology, A.M.A., Ill., Chgo. med. socs., Chgo. Soc. Anesthesiologists. Contbr. articles to profl. jours. Address: 8500 W Carol St Niles IL 60648

GOLDBERG, VIRGINIA LUCIE EAGAN (MRS. RAYMOND ROBERT GOLDBERG), fashion illustrator; b. Lebanon, Pa., Feb. 27, 1914; d. Charles Daniel and Clara Evelyn (Euston) Eagan; grad. nursing U. Buffalo, 1937; pvt. study art with Raymond Goldberg, 1940-42, John Pike, 1969-70; m. Raymond Robert Goldberg, Oct. 16, 1942. Social worker Meadowbrook Hosp., E. Meadow, L.I., N.Y., 1940-42, dir. social service dept., 1943-47; art dir. Martin Trencher, Inc., Garden City, N.Y., 1953—; fashion illustrator, copy writer Raymond Goldberg Advt., Rockville Centre, L.I., N.Y., 1948—. Instr. watercolor and oil painting N.Y. Program of Continuing Edn., Rockville Centre, N.Y., 1970—, also pvt. students. Recipient awards Knickerbocker Artists, 1973, Malverne Artists, 1971-72, Long Beach Art Assn., 1970-71, others. Fellow Am. Artists Profl. League; mem. Long Beach Art Assn. (bd. govs. 1969-74), Art League of Nassau County, N.Y. (bd. govs. 1968-74, editor newsletter 1967-71), Nat. Art League, Malverne Artists of L.I., Miniature Art Soc. N.J. Address: 126 Princeton Rd Rockville Centre NY 11570

GOLDEN, CONSTANCE ADELLA WALRUFF (MRS. WILLIAM ALBERT GOLDEN), radio sta. mgr.; b. San Diego, Feb. 20, 1930; d. Charles Albert and Esther Beryl (Huebner) Walruff; student U. Kan., 1946-48; m. William Albert Golden, Oct. 17, 1949; children—Susan (Mrs. Timothy J. Scovill), Wendy Lee. Owner, editor Shopping Guide Publ., Oslo, Norway, 1965-68; radio time salesman Radio Sta. WJMD, 1968, Radio Sta. WEZR, 1969; gen. mgr. Radio Sta. WEZS, Richmond, Va., 1970—. Bd. dirs. No. Va. council Girl Scouts U.S.A., 1963-64, troop leader, 1964-65. Mem. Republican Steering Com. Fairfax County (Va.), 1955-57, exec. sec. dist. com., 1963-65. Mem. Richmond (dir. 1971-72), Washington advt. clubs, Sales and Marketing Execs. Club, Greater Richmond Broadcasters (pres. 1973). Club: Pilot Internat. (Fairfax, Va.). Home: Hughes Creek Farm Route 1 Box 127A Powhatan VA 23139 Office: 5900 Midlothian Pike Richmond VA 23225

GOLDEN, HILDA HERTZ (MRS. MORRIS GOLDEN), educator; b. Berlin, Germany; d. Paul and Hanna (Gernsheimer) Hertz; came to U.S., 1939, naturalized, 1945; A.B., Skidmore Coll., 1942; M.A., Duke, 1944, Ph.D., 1950; m. Morris Golden, Apr. 11, 1954; children—Olivia, Daniel. Instr. sociology Ga. State Coll. Women, 1945-46, Randolph-Macom Woman's Coll., 1946-49; research asso. Bur. Applied Social Research Columbia, 1949-55; asst. prof. U. Mass., Amherst, 1962-70, asso. prof. sociology, 1970—. Mem. Am. Sociol. Assn., Population Assn. Am., Internat. Union for Sci. Study Population, Phi Beta Kappa. Contbr. articles to profl. jours. and encys. Home: 49 Ridgecrest Rd Amherst MA 01002

GOLDEN, JEAN DACE (MRS. GILBERT E. DUNNING), physician; b. Monroe, Mich., Mar. 26, 1923; d. Oliver John and Mary Ann (McNally) Golden; B.A., Mary Grove Coll., 1944; M.S., U. Mich., 1948, M.D., 1956; m. Gilbert E. Dunning, Jan. 28, 1967. Intern, Presbyn. Hosp., Phila., 1956-57, resident surgery, 1957-58, resident in gynecology, 1962-63; resident surgery Detroit Gen. Hosp. U. Wayne, 1958-62; practice medicine, specializing in gen. surgery, Monroe, Mich., 1963-67, Stroudsburg, Pa., 1967—; mem. active staff Monroe County Gen. Hosp.; lab. instr. anatomy U. Pa., 1957-58. Div. sci. rep. Pa. div. Am. Cancer Soc., 1973—. Bd. dirs. Mich. Cancer Soc., Monroe, 1964-67, Am. Cancer Soc., Stroudsburg, Pa., 1967—, Mental Health Soc., 1967-71, Pregnancy Counseling Service, Scranton Diocese, 1973—; mem. panel over-the-counter preparation FDA, 1973—; Monroe County regional rep. Delaware Valley Regional Med. Program, 1972—. Diplomate Am. Bd. Surgery. Fellow A.C.S.; mem. A.M.A., Pa., Monroe County med. assns., Pan Pacific Surg. Assn., Am. Colon and Rectal Surg. Assn., Midwest Surg. Soc. Home: Crestview Rd Stroudsburg PA 18360 Office: 175 E Brown St East Stroudsburg PA 18301

GOLDEN, JESSIE GRAY (MRS. JOE BOB GOLDEN), librarian; b. Seagoville, Tex., Oct. 23, 1903; d. William Tapley and Eula Lavina (Herring) Gray; B.A., W. Tex. U., 1929; postgrad. N. Tex. U., 1948; m. Joe Bob Golden, July 29, 1928; children—Jeanelle Zellane (Mrs. Lawrence Henry Warburton, Jr.), Joe Bob. Librarian, prin. Kaufman County, Tex., 1924-27; tchr. Wichita County, Tex., 1927-44; tchr., dir. Camp Fire Girls, Bonham, Tex., 1946-49; docent Tex. State Library, Austin, 1953-65, genealogy librarian, 1965—. Chmn., Daus. Republic Mus. Com., 1969—; dist. officer P.T.A., 1942-49; mem. Woman's Forum Bd., Wichita Falls, Tex., 1940-44. Democratic election judge, 1968-71. Mem. Austin Geneal. Soc. (dir. 1969-72), Am. Assn. U. Women, Daus. Republic Tex. (chmn. mus. com. 1969—), Tex. Woman's Forum (pres. Vernon Tex. 1952-53), Santa Rosa Hort. Soc. (treas. 1951-53), Alpha Story League (pres. 1941-43). Baptist (Sunday sch. tchr.). Clubs: Bonham Garden (pres. 1947-49); Austin Woman's. Home: 2100 Hartford Rd Austin TX 78703 Office: 1201 Brazos Austin TX 78701

GOLDEN, MARY ANN HESSION (MRS. JAMES W. GOLDEN), psychologist; b. Peoria, Ill., May 18, 1947; d. Robert Louis and Anna Mary (Chiotte) Hession; A.B., U. So. Cal., 1969, M.S., 1970, sch. psychology credential, 1973; m. James W. Golden, Aug. 8, 1970; 1 son, John Anthony. Intern sch. psychology Children's Hosp., Los Angeles, 1970; sch. psychologist ednl. service unit 3, dept. psychology, Omaha, 1970-73; sch. psychologist, pupil personnel services Glendale (Cal.) Unified Sch. Dist., 1973—. Pres., Jr. Vols. of St. Luke Hosp., Pasadena, 1964-65. Recipient grant NSF, 1964. Mem. Nat., Cal. assns. sch. psychologists. Home: 3050 Oneida St Pasadena CA 91107 Office: 223 N Jackson St Glendale CA 91206

GOLDEN, ROSIE PEARL HACKETT (MRS. RUSSELL D. GOLDEN), mus. ofcl.; b. Ceres, Cal., Aug. 6, 1929; d. Frank Thornton and Lillian Josephine (Visher) Hackett; student Central Cal. Comml. Coll., 1945-46; m. Russell D. Golden, Mar. 5, 1950; children—Daniel E., Sheila A., David R. Stenographer, Bank of Am., Fresno, Cal., 1945-46; office mgr. Bay Valley Land Co., Fresno, 1946-51; sec. Claremore (Okla.) C. of C., 1963-65; exec. sec. J.M. Davis Gun Mus., Claremore, 1965-74; dir. Claremore Coll. Found., 1974—. Pres. Claremore Credit Women Internat., 1968-69; dir. Okla. State Credit Women Internat., 1968-69; mem. Okla. State Chamber Tourist Com., 1970-71; den mother Cub Scouts Am., Germany, 1958-62; neighborhood chmn. Claremore Girl Scouts, 1962-65. Mem. Okla. Mus. Assn. (sec., treas. 1971-73), Claremore C. of C. (dir. 1967-70), Credit Women Internat. Bus. and Profl. Women. Methodist. Home: 102 E 11th St Claremore OK 74017 Office: College Hill Claremore OK 74017

GOLDENBERG, PEARL PHYLLIS LEVINSON (MRS. HAROLD GOLDENBERG), educator; b. Chgo., Aug. 13, 1929; d. Israel and Tillie (Gash) Levinson; B.S., U. Ill., 1950; M.A., Mich. State U., 1962; m. Harold Goldenberg, Aug. 6, 1950; children—Debra, Joel, Risa, Donna. First grade tchr. Berrien Springs Pub. Schs., 1961-63; type A tchr. Benton Harbor (Mich.) Pub. Schs., 1963-68, Grand Ledge (Mich.) Pub. Schs., 1968—. Pres., Berrien County Assn. Retarded Children, 1967; v.p. Eaton County Assn. Retarded Children, 1969-72, pres., 1973—; leader S.W. Mich. council Girl Scouts Am., 1963-71. Jewish religion. Mem. B'nai B'rith. Home: 7131 St Joseph St Grand Ledge MI 48837 Office: 615 Jones St Holbrook Sch Grand Ledge MI 48837

GOLDHABER, GERTRUDE SCHARFF (MRS. MAURICE GOLDHABER), physicist; b. Mannheim, Germany, July 14, 1911; d. Otto and Nelly (Steinharter) Scharff; student univs. of Freiburg, Zurich, Berlin; Ph.D., U. Munich, 1935; m. Maurice Goldhaber, May

24, 1939; children—Alfred Scharff, Michael Henry. Came to U.S., 1939, naturalized, 1944. Research asso. Imperial Coll., London, 1935-39; research physicist U. Ill., Champaign, 1939-48; asst. prof., 1948-50; asso. physicist Brookhaven Nat. Lab., Upton, N.Y., 1950-58, physicist, 1958-62, sr. physicist, 1962—. Cons. to nuclear data group NRC, 1966; AEC Labs., 1946—. Mem. research adv. com. NSF, 1973—; mem. Com. on Problems of Women in Physics, 1971; mem. physics vis. com. Harvard, 1973—; chmn. ad hoc panel on nuclear data compilations, NRC-Nat. Acad. Sci. Com. on Nuclear Sci., 1969-71. Trustee Nat. Accelerator Lab. Univ. Research Assn., Batavia, Ill. Fellow Am. Phys. Soc. (program com. nuclear physics div. 1973—); mem. Nat. Acad. Scis. (report rev. com. 1973—), Sigma Xi. Editorial com. Ann. Revs. Nuclear Sci., 1972—. Home: 91 S Gillette Av Bayport Long Island NY 11705 Office: Brookhaven Nat Lab Upton Long Island NY 11973

GOLDIN, AUGUSTA REIDER (MRS. OSCAR GOLDIN), educator; b. N.Y.C., Oct. 28, 1906; d. Jacob and Fanny (Harris) Reider; B.A., Hunter Coll., 1927; M.S., City U. N.Y., 1929; Ed.D., Columbia, 1947; m. Oscar Goldin, Oct. 25, 1933; children—Kenneth, Valerie. Tchr. elementary and jr. high sch., N.Y.C., 1928-44; prin., N.Y.C., 1944-71; asst. prof. edn. St. John's U., N.Y.C., 1971—. Syndicated feature writer Universal Sci. News, Inc., Newspaper Enterprise Assn.; columnist S.I. Advance. Recipient scholarships, Nat. Audubon Soc. Mem. Nat. Council Adminstrv. Women, Council Supervisory Assns., Nat. Audubon Soc., Doctorate Assn. N.Y. Educators. Author: 7 books in Let's Read and Find Out Sci. Series, 1963-69; How to Release the Learning Power in Children, 1970; To Build a Skyscraper, 1974. Contbr. to Instructor Mag., Grade Tchr., Scholastic Tchr. Home: 590 Bard Av Staten Island NY 10310 Office: St John's U Staten Island New York City NY 10301

GOLDIN, KATE SMITH (MRS. WILLIAM R. GOLDIN), editor; b. Monroe, Ga., May 8, 1910; d. William Oscar and Jessie Lou (Rogers) McConnell; student So. Bus. Coll., 1926, U. Ga., 1927; m. Floyd Clifford Smith, Aug. 17, 1927 (dec. Oct. 1966); m. William B. Goldin, Apr. 28, 1967. With new bus. dept. First Nat. Bank Atlanta, 1931-40; with Bowdon (Ga.) Bull., 1940—, editor, 1944—. Recipient Certificate of Merit, Am. Cancer Soc., 1971, Certificate of Merit, Heart Fund, 1972, Certificate, U.S. Navy Recruiting Program, 1956. Mem. Pub's. Aux. (recipient recognition Editor of Week 1963), Ga. Press Assn., Bowdon Merchants Assn. (pub. chmn. 1970—), Women's Soc. Christian Service. Methodist. Contbr. stories and articles to Atlanta-Journal Mag., 1930—. Home: City Hall Av Bowden GA 30108 Office: The Bowdon Bulletin Bowdon GA 30108

GOLDMAN, ELLEN MYNETTE EASON (MRS. JAMES OSWALD GOLDMAN), lawyer; b. Kosciusko, Miss., Apr. 11, 1921; d. Van Vernon and Nellie Clayton (Vaughan) Eason; B.A., Miss. State Coll. for Women, 1941; M.A., U. Miss., 1960, J.D., 1970; m. James Oswald Goldman, July 31, 1947; 1 son, James Oswald. Admitted to Miss. bar, 1970; with E & J Enterprises, Marks, Miss., 1965—, v.p., 1965—; practiced in Marks, 1970—. Sec. City Beautification, Marks, 1971-73; docent Brooks Meml. Art Gallery, Memphis, 1973. Mem. Am. Trial Lawyers Assn., Am. Judicature Soc., Am. (mem. practice handbook com.), Miss., Quitman County (sec. 1970—) bar assns., Mensa, Herb Soc. Am. Embroiderer's Guild Am., Marks C. of C. (pres. 1970-73), Kappa Beta Pi, Delta Kappa Gamma. Home: 551 Lamar St Marks MS 38646 Office: 231 Chestnut St Marks MS 38646

GOLDMAN, GAIL H., social worker; b. Boston, Jan. 26, 1937; d. Louis A. and Molly (London) Goldman; A.A., Boston U., 1956, M.S., 1960; B.A., U. Buffalo, 1958. Jr. caseworker Univ. Hosp., Mass. Meml. Hosps., Boston, 1960-63; instr. field work Boston U. Sch. Social Work, 1961-63; sr. caseworker Yale New Haven Hosp., 1963—; instr. social work-medicine Yale U., 1964—. Cons. social worker New Haven Ostomy Assn. Mem. Nat. Assn. Social Workers, Nat. Conf. Social Welfare, Acad. Certified Social Workers, Ostomy Assn. New Haven, Sigma Delta Tau. Home: 37A Willard St New Haven CT 06515 Office: Yale New Haven Hosp 789 Howard Av New Haven CT 06501

GOLDMAN, LOUISE PAUL (MRS. DAN E. GOLDMAN), instl. exec.; b. Chgo., July 17, 1917; d. George and Sophia (Marshak) Paul; B.B.A., U. Chgo., 1947; postgrad. Purdue N. Central, 1955, 57, 58, 60; m. Dan E. Goldman, June 5, 1937; children—Barbara (Mrs. Gerald Hundt), Dan E., Lawrence, David. With Fred Newman, Inc., Chgo., 1935-38; with YMCA, Michigan City, Ind., 1955—, program supr., 1959—. Den mother Cub Scouts Am., Chgo., 1947-49, Michigan City, 1952-55; pres. Council on Aging, Michigan City, 1971—. Bd. dirs. Mental Health Assn., 1954-55, Community Service Council, 1966-70; mem. bd. dirs. PACT, 1973-74, mem. steering com., 1972-73, treas., 1973-74. Recipient Mother of Year award in recreation Chgo. Met. Welfare Council, 1949, Woman of Achievement award LaPort Herald Argus, N.A.A.C.P., 1971. Democrat. Jewish religion. Mem. Hadassah. Home: 539 Cole Court Michigan City IN 46360 Office: 120 W 7th St Michigan City IN 46360

GOLDMAN, MARIANNE, cons.; b. San Francisco, Dec. 25, 1923; d. Richard Samuel and Alice Gertrude (Wertheim) Goldman; B.A., Stanford, 1944. Copy girl/reporter San Francisco Chronicle, 1945-46; vol. co-ordinator Red Cross, San Francisco, 1946-48; promotion asst. KCBS Radio, San Francisco, 1950-54; dir. pub. relations KQED-TV, San Francisco, 1954-63; cons. Stanford, 1965; dir. symposium on Asian Art Brundage Collection, deYoung Mus., San Francisco, 1967-68; cons. communications Asso. Councils Arts, N.Y.C., 1969-70, San Francisco Mus. Art, 1970-72; cons. for Wilson Riles, Cal. State Supt. Edn., San Francisco, 1973—. Vice pres. United Jewish Community Centers, San Francisco, 1968-72; sec. Women's Pub. Interest com. San Francisco Symphony Assn.; sec. Lombard Hill Improvement Assn. Mem. Telegraph Hill Neighborhood Assn. (pres. 1967-70). Home: 1025 Lombard St San Francisco CA 94109

GOLDMAN, NANCY GAY CANEDY (MRS. LEONARD C. GOLDMAN), educator; b. North Adams, Mass., May 29, 1932; d. Donald Otis and Florence (Hicks) Canedy; B.S., Skidmore Coll., 1954; M.S., State U. N.Y., 1961; postgrad. Rensselaer Poly. Inst., 1971—; m. V. Misurelli, Aug. 27, 1955 (annulment Dec. 1961); m. 2d, Leonard C. Goldman, July 19, 1963; 1 son, David Bennett. Tchr., Johnstown (N.Y.) High Sch., 1954-55, Saratoga Springs (N.Y.) High Sch., 1955-57; instr. in bus. Skidmore Coll., Saratoga Springs, 1957-61; asst. prof. adminstrv. services State U. N.Y., Albany, 1961-70; adj. prof. bus. Howard Community Coll., Columbia, Md., 1972; lectr. in field. Mem. Bus. Tchrs. Assn., Eastern Bus. Tchrs. Assn., Am. Bus. Writing Assn., Skidmore Coll. Alumnae Assn., Nat. Council Tchrs. English, Delta Pi Epsilon. Contbr. articles to profl. jours. Home: 8967 Queen Maria Ct Columbia MD 21045

GOLDMAN, RUTH GOLDBLATT (MRS. HAROLD L. GOLDMAN), lawyer; b. Chgo., July 6, 1921; d. Harry and Henrietta (Cadkin) Goldblatt; B.S., U. Chgo., 1942, J.D., 1947; m. Harold L. Goldman, Apr. 14, 1946; children—Amy, Debbie, Frances, Richard. Psychology intern Michael Reese Hosp., 1942; admitted to Ill. bar, 1948; since practiced in Chgo.; instr. USAF, 1943-45; atty. Jewish Family and Community Service, 1947-50, Devoe, Shadur & Krupp, Chgo., 1968—. Faculty mem. Greenerfields, Inc., Northfield, Ill., 1971—; cooperating atty. Am. Civil Liberties Union, 1971-73. Pres. Ravinia Sch. P.T.A., 1961-62. Mem. Highland Park (Ill.) Bd. Edn., 1963-69, pres., 1967-69. Mem. League Women Voters (dir. 1961-65), Am. Civil Liberties Union (mem. women's rights com. 1971—), Chgo. Bar Assn. (mem. probate com.), Chgo. Council Lawyers (mem. women's rights com.). Home: 953 Wildwood Lane Highland Park IL 60035 Office: 208 S LaSalle St Chicago IL 60604

GOLDMAN, SHERLI EVENS (MRS. ERWIN GOLDMAN), advt. and pub. relations exec.; b. Orlando, Fla.; d. Harold William and Marjorie (Foster) Evens; A.B., U. Cal. at Los Angeles, 1964, M.A., 1968; m. Erwin Goldman, Jan. 4, 1955; children—Adam, Audrey. Pub. relations rep. Xerox Data Systems, 1969-70; advt. mgr. Basic/Four Corp., Los Angeles, 1971—. Mem. Modern Lang. Assn., Writers Guild Am. West (co-chairperson women's group 1971-72). Democrat. Roman Catholic. Author: Mary McCarthy: A Bibliography, 1968. Writer (with Erwin Goldman) prodns. for TV programs. Home: 3985 Mandeville Canyon Rd Los Angeles CA 90049 Office: 18552 MacArthur Blvd Irvine CA 92707

GOLDSBERRY, GWENYTH DAWN (MRS. EDWARD E. GOLDSBERRY), newspaper exec.; b. Whangarei, New Zealand, Dec. 15, 1923; d. Percy and Rhoda (Spear) Wiles; student pub. schs.; m. Edward E. Goldsberry, July 4, 1944; children—David Eugene, Daniel Paul. Came to U.S., 1945, naturalized, 1957. With Univ. Park News, Denver, 1957-69; pub. Colo. Prospector, Denver, 1969—. Mem. S.E. Denver Civic Assn., 1960-65. Mem. English Speaking Union, Nat. History Soc., Western History Assn., State Hist. Soc. Colo., hist. socs. Summit County, Arvada, Julesburg. Republican. Home and office: 4760 E Idaho Place Denver CO 80222

GOLDSCHLAGER, NORA BARBARA FOX (MRS. ARNOLD WILLIAM GOLDSCHLAGER), cardiologist; b. N.Y.C., Dec. 10, 1939; d. Theodore T. and Nina U. (Urkovetsky) Fox; A.B., Barnard Coll., 1961; M.D., N.Y.U., 1965; m. Arnold William Goldschlager, June 3, 1962; children—Nina Lee, Hilary Anne. Intern, Montefiore Hosp., N.Y.C., 1965-66, med. resident, 1966-68; fellow in cardiology Wayne State U., Detroit, 1968-69; fellow in cardiology Presbyn. Hosp. Pacific Med. Center, San Francisco, 1969-70, research cardiologist, 1970—; practice medicine specializing in cardiology, San Francisco, 1970—; asst. prof. medicine U. Cal. Sch. Medicine, San Francisco, 1971—. Diplomate Am. Bd. Medicine. Fellow Am. Heart Assn. Council Clin. Cardiology, Am. Coll. Cardiology, A.C.P.; mem. Phi Beta Kappa. Home: 2744 Summit Dr Burlingame CA 94010 Office: Presbyn Hospital San Francisco CA 94115

GOLDSCHMIDT, FAITH MARCY KNABE, microbiologist; b. Springfield, Mass., Sept. 25, 1940; d. Henry Walter and Ruth (Dupree) Knabe; B.A., Clark U., 1962; M.A., Smith Coll., 1963; postgrad. Rutgers U., 1964-67; m. Paul Robert Goldschmidt, June 16, 1963 (div. Nov. 1973); 1 son, Jeffrey Scott. Research asst. Inst. Microbiology, Rutgers, The State U., New Brunswick, N.J., 1964-65; research microbiologist Johnson & Johnson, North Brunswick, N.J., 1967—. Mem. A.A.A.S., Am. Inst. Biol. Scis., Am. Soc. Microbiology, N.Y. Acad. Scis., Theobald Smith Soc., Sigma Xi. Home: 61 Herbert Dr East Brunswick NJ 08816 Office: Route 1 North Brunswick NJ 08903

GOLDSMITH, BARBARA, writer, editor; b. N.Y.C., May 18, 1931; d. Joseph I. and Evelyn (Cronson) Lubin; B.A., Wellesley Coll., 1953; M.A., Columbia, 1955; children—Andrew, Alice, John. Entertainment editor Womans Home Companion, N.Y.C., 1954-57; contbr. N.Y. Herald Tribune, Esquire mag., New Yorker, 1957-64; contbg. editor N.Y. Mag., 1966-71; sr. editor Harpers Bazaar mag., N.Y.C., 1970—. TV spl. writer documentaries and entertainments; lectr. N.Y. U., 1969. Mem. jr. council Mus. Modern Art, N.Y.C., 1951-73; dir. Parks Council of N.Y.C., 1965—; mem. acquisitions com. Friends of Whitney Mus. Art, 1964-69; mem. pres's council Mus. of City N.Y., 1970—. Author: The Straw Man, 1974. Home: 655 Park Av New York City NY 10021

GOLDSMITH, DONNA LEE LASSILA (MRS. JAMES HARRY GOLDSMITH), assn. exec.; b. Pitts., June 11, 1938; d. Elmer John and Esther Irene (Schweitzer) Lassila; student Syracuse U., 1970, Mich. State U., 1971, 72, 73, U. Notre Dame, 1974; m. James Harry Goldsmith, Feb. 6, 1964; children—James, David, Scott. Exec. sec. U.S. Steel Co., Pitts., 1955-57, Rockwell Mfg. Co., Pitts., 1962-64; exec. dir. Penn Hills C. of C., Pitts., 1969—. Mem. Columbia Hosp. Women's Aux., Pa. C. of C. Execs. Clubs: Wilkinsburg Junior Womens (dir. 1965-70), Alcoma Country (Pitts.). Home: 550 Springdale Dr Pittsburgh PA 15235 Office: Penn Hills C of C 85 Universal Rd Pittsburgh PA 15235

GOLDSMITH, ELAINE BAUER (MRS. RICHARD W. GOLDSMITH), lawyer; b. N.Y.C., Nov. 24, 1931; d. Morris K. and Estelle (Rapoport) Bauer; B.A., U. Mich., 1954; J.D., Seton Hall U., 1971; m. Richard W. Goldsmith, June 24, 1951; children—Steven, Thomas, Patricia. Admitted to N.J. bar, 1971; law clk. to county ct. judge Somerset County, N.J., 1971-72; mem. firm Borrus, Goldin & Foley, New Brunswick, N.J., 1971-72; pvt. practice law, Somerville, N.J., 1973—. Adj. prof. Seton Hall U., South Orange, N.J., 1973. Mem. Nat. Council Jewish Women (nat. com. 1972-73), Am. Assn. U. Women, N.J. Bar, Am., Somerset County bar assns., Women's Aux. Somerset County Med. Assn., Zonta, Nat. Orgn. for Women, Kappa Beta Pi. Home: 115 Vanderveer Av Somerville NJ 08876 Office: 39 Mechanic St Somerville NJ 08876

GOLDSMITH, ILSE SONDRA (MRS. ALFRED GOLDSMITH), author; b. Munich, Germany, Sept. 9, 1933; d. Joseph and Bettina (Bendit) Weinberg; came to U.S., 1939, naturalized, 1945; B.A. in Bio-chemistry, Hunter Coll., 1955; M.A., Albany State U., 1960; m. Alfred Goldsmith, Feb. 19, 1956; children—Jeffrey Mitchell, Stephen Blaine. Med. researcher Mt. Sinai Hosp., N.Y.C., 1954-56; chemist Gen. Electric Co., Schenectady, 1956-59. Lectr. schs. and colls. in Orange County, N.Y., 1959—; sec. bd. dirs. United Vision Services, Inc., Middletown, N.Y., 1972. Pres. M.H.A. Nursery, Middletown, 1969-70. Mem. Am. Chem. Soc., League Women Voters, Horton Hosp. Aux. (pres. 1973-75, dir. 1969-71, v.p. 1971-73), Inter Faith Council. Jewish religion. Mem. Hadassah, Sisterhood. Club: Women's University (pres. 1968) (Middletown). Author: Anatomy for Children, 1960; Why You Get Sick and How You Get Well, 1970. Home and office: Park Court Middletown NY 10940

GOLDSMITH, JOANNE TEMAH SCHWITZGOLD (MRS. DAVID H. GOLDSMITH), civic worker; b. Wilmington, Del., June 28, 1933; d. Max and Rose (Ruggiero) Schwitzgold; B.A., U. Md., 1955; m. David H. Goldsmith, June 13, 1954; children—Michael Jay, Melinda Robin, Melanie Ann. Adminstrv. asst. Jewish War Vets., Washington, 1955-56; adminstrv. sec. Dept. Navy, Washington, 1956-57. Mem. Health and Welfare Council Nat. Capitol Area, 1971—; mem. Health and Welfare Council Prince Georges County, Md., 1972—; Mem. bd. Nat. Conf. Christians and Jews Nat. Capitol area, 1972—; exec. bd. Day Care Assn. Prince Georges County, 1970—; exec. bd. Prince Georges County council P.T.A., 1968—; v.p. Bd. Edn. Prince George's County, 1972-73. Chief Democratic election judge, 1967-70. Mem. Gamma Phi Beta (province officer 1962-69). Jewish religion (exec. bd. sisterhood 1970—). Home: 2212 Marbury Dr District Heights MD 20028

GOLDSMITH, MAVIS NORTHROUP (MRS. GEORGE M. GOLDSMITH), realtor; b. Alhambra, Cal., Feb. 23, 1922; d. Benjamin Porter and Myrtle Stevanna (Lines) Northrup; student Phoenix Jr. Coll., 1940-41; m. George M. Goldsmith, June 24, 1963; children—Kimberly (Mrs. Michael Gilson), Joseph Porter Bucknam. Salesman Mann Realty, Oxnard, Cal., 1960-62; realtor, owner Channel Island Realty, Oxnard, Cal., 1962—. Mem. Nat. Assn. Real Estate Brokers (chpt. pres. women's council 1966, mem. governing council 1963—), Oxnard Harbor Bd. Realtors (pres. 1974, dir.,), Cal. Real Estate Assn. (state dir. 1973-74), Oxnard C. of C. Home: 3307 Harbor Blvd Oxnard CA 93030 Office: 3921 Ocean Dr Oxnard CA 93030

GOLDSMITH, ROSEMARY GUMPERT (MRS. GEORGE GOLDSMITH), violist; b. Duesseldorf, Germany, Jan. 6, 1917; d. Julian and Else (Hayn) Gumpert; student Conservatory Duesseldorf, 1933-36, Samuel Lifshey, Henri Marteau and Anna Hegener; m. George G. Goldsmith, Dec. 13, 1938; children—Peter, Martin. Came to U.S., 1941, naturalized, 1947. Violist, Pitts. Symphony, 1944-46; asst. prin. violist St. Louis Symphony, 1947-67; soloist numerous recitals and chamber-music, 1947-67; violist Cleve. Orch., 1967—; mem. Severance String Quartet, 1969—. Home: 3698 Tolland Rd Shaker Heights OH 44122 Office: care Severance Hall Cleveland OH 44106

GOLDSTEIN, DORA BENEDICT (MRS. AVRAM GOLDSTEIN), univ. pharmacologist; b. Milton, Mass., Apr. 25, 1922; d. George Wheeler and Marjory (Pierce) Benedict; Bryn Mawr Coll., 1940-43, Stanford, 1945; M.D., Harvard, 1949; m. Avram Goldstein, Aug. 29, 1947; children—Margaret (Mrs. William Bradley Wallace), Daniel, Joshua, Michael. Fellow dept. bacteriology and immunology Harvard Med. Sch., Boston, 1953-55; research asso. dept. pharmacology Stanford Sch. Medicine, 1955-70, sr. scientist, 1970—. Mem. N.A.A.C.P. (local exec. bd. 1964-68), Am. Soc. Pharmacology and Exptl. Therapeutics, Am. Soc. Biol. Chemists, Alpha Omega Alpha. Home: 735 Dolores St Stanford CA 94305

GOLDSTEIN, ELAYNE, broadcasting exec.; b. Chgo.; d. Philip and Sara (Chankin) Goldstein; student U. Ill., Northwestern U., U. Chgo. Asso. creative dir. Leo Burnett Co., Inc., Chgo., 1960-71; asso. creative dir., v.p. Grey-North Advt., Chgo., 1971-73; asso. producer, writer Channel 11, Chgo., 1973—. Mem. Alpha Lamda Delta. Office: Channel 11 5400 N St Louis St Chicago IL 60025

GOLDSTEIN, ESTELLE LORAINE GOLDSTAUB (MRS. MAC GOLDSTEIN), librarian; b. N.Y.C., Jan. 30, 1921; d. Frank L. and Paula (Czaban) Goldstaub; B.A., N.Y. U., 1934; M.L.S., Pratt Inst., 1959; postgrad. Columbia, 1939, Rutgers Grad. Sch. Library Sci., 1958; m. Mac Goldstein, Mar. 18, 1936; 1 son, Paul J. With advt. dept. N.Y. Times, 1934-36; br. librarian Queens Borough Pub. Library, N.Y.C., 1957-61, regional librarian, 1962-63, spl. dept. asst., 1963-64; coordinator childrens services Smithtown (N.Y.) Library, 1964-68; asst. dir. adult services Elmont Pub. Library, 1968-70; adult services specialist Nassau Library System, Garden City, L.I., N.Y., 1970—. Mem. Am., N.Y., Nassau County library assns., Beta Phi Mu. Home: 83-15 Lefferts Blvd Kew Gardens Long Island NY 11415 Office: Roosevelt Field Lower Concourse Garden City Long Island NY 11530

GOLDSTEIN, IRIS BALSHAN (MRS. BERNARD S. GOLDSTEIN), psychologist, educator; b. Newark, N.J., Mar. 31, 1936; d. Leo I. and Dorothy (Reiser) Balshan; B.A., U. Cal. at Los Angeles, 1957, M.A., 1960, Ph.D., 1961, Nat. Inst. Mental Health Postdoctoral fellow, 1966-69; m. Bernard S. Goldstein, June 10, 1962; children—Mark, Gary. Research psychologist Psychosomatic and Psychiat. Inst., Michael Reese Hosp., Chgo., 1961-64; lectr. U. Cal. at Los Angeles, 1964-66, Loyola U., Los Angeles, 1971—. Mem. Am. Psychol. Assn., Soc. for Psychophysiol. Research, Psychosomatic Soc., Phi Beta Kappa, Sigma Xi. Contbr. chpt. to Handbook of Psychophysiology, 1972; articles to profl. jours. Home: 3700 Crownridge Dr Sherman Oaks CA 91403

GOLDSTEIN, MARION ZUCKER, psychiatrist; b. Berlin, Germany, Apr. 30, 1932; d. Julian and Gertrude (Feige); B.S., Queens Coll., 1953; M.S., U. Ill., 1954; M.D., Albert Einstein Coll. Medicine, 1959; m. Elliott J. Goldstein, May 28, 1961; children—Lillian Rachel, Naomi Sussannah. Research asst. biology dept. Brookhaven Nat. Lab., 1958; intern Bklyn. Jewish Hosp., 1959-60; psychiat. resident Hillside Hosp., Glen Oaks, L.I., N.Y., 1960-61, Western Psychiat. Inst. and Clinic, Pitts., 1961-63; staff psychiatrist Haverford (Pa.) State Hosp., 1964, Devereaux Found., Devon Pa., 1965; staff psychiatrist St. Francis Hosp. Community Mental Health Center, Pitts., 1965—, dir. Day Center Services, 1970—; clin. asst. prof. Western Psychiat. Inst. and Clinic, Pitts., 1974—; pvt. practice psychiatry, Pitts., 1965—; psychiatrist Student Health Services, U. Pitts., 1969—. Bd. dirs. chpt. Center for Creative Work with Children, Univs. Cities Ministries, 1969-71. Diplomate Am. Bd. Psychiatry and Neurology. Mem. Am., World, Pa. psychiat. socs., Pitts. Neuropsychiat. Soc., A.M.A., Pa., Allegheny County med. socs. Office: 121 University Pl Pittsburgh PA 15213

GOLDSTEIN, MARJORIE TUNICK (MRS. HERBERT GOLDSTEIN), educator; b. Port Chester, N.Y., Oct. 20, 1940; d. Abraham and Gertrude (Gluckman) Tunick; B.S., Syracuse U., 1961; M.A., George Washington U., 1968; postgrad. Yeshiva U., 1972—; m. Herbert Goldstein, May 27, 1973. Tchr. spl. edn. Lancaster (Pa.) City Schs., 1962-63, Hempfield (Pa.) Pub. Schs., 1963-64, Montgomery County (Md.) Pub. Schs., 1964-65; ednl. specialist Bur. Edn. for Handicapped, U.S. Office Edn., Dept. Health, Edn. and Welfare, Washington, 1965-69; coordinator field operations, curriculum research and devel. center in mental retardation Yeshiva U., N.Y.C., 1969—. Mem. Council for Exceptional Children, Am. Assn. Mental Deficiency, Council Adminstrs. Spl. Edn. Democrat. Jewish religion. Home: 85 4th Av 3FF New York City NY 10003

GOLDSTEIN, MYRNA EDITH, journalist; b. Rochester, N.Y., Aug. 5, 1948; d. Earl and Evelyn (Cohen) Goldstein; B.S. in Journalism, Northwestern U., 1970; postgrad. N.Y. U., 1971, New Sch. for Social Research, 1972-73. Editorial asst., also writer Consol. Book Pubs., Evanston, Ill., 1966; market editor apparel div. Daily News Record, Fairchild Publs. Inc., N.Y.C., 1971-73; contbg. editor AC & R Pub. Relations Inc., N.Y.C., 1973—. Writer, Bklyn., 1973-74, Rochester, 1974—. Pub. relations dir. New Village Theatre, N.Y.C., 1971-72. Mem. Mag. Pubs. Assn. (summer intern 1969), N.Y. Women in Communications, Women in Communications. Contbr. to No. Am. Newspaper Alliance, Fawcett Publs., Inc., N.Y.C. Home and office: 222 Council Rock Av Rochester NY 14610

GOLDSTEIN, PEGGY JANET ROSENFELD (MRS. E. ERNEST GOLDSTEIN), sculptor; b. N.Y.C., Jan. 16, 1921; d. Francis Mortimer and Ruth (Schram) Rosenfeld; A.B., Smith Coll., 1941; student Art Inst. Chgo., 1941-42, Academie de la Grande Chaumiere, 1952-53, 53-54; m. E. Ernest Goldstein, June 22, 1941; children—Susan Martha (Mrs. I. I. Lipsitch), Daniel Frank. Exhibited one-man shows, Creative Gallery, N.Y.C., 1951, 53, Springfield (Mass.) Mus. Fine Arts, others, Washington, Tex., Galerie Lambert, Paris; exhibited in group shows Salon de la Jeune Sculpture, Galerie

Simone Badinier, Salon de Mai, Galerie Bernheim Jeune (all Paris, France), Corcoran Gallery Art, Smithsonian Instn., Washington, Riverside Mus., N.Y.C., El Museo de Bellas Artes, Buenos Aires, Argentina, USIS tour, others; represented many pvt. collections. Tchr. clay modeling Anacosta Neighborhood Mus., Washington, 1967-68. Co-recipient 1st prize sculpture Soc. Washington Artists, 1954; recipient 2d prize profl. sculpture Washington Outdoor Show, 1954, Tex. Fine Arts Assn., 1955; award Ball State Tchrs. Coll., Muncie, Ind., 1961. Mem. Nat. Assn. Women Artists. Contbr. articles to profl. jours. Address: 6 Sq Emmanuel Chabrier Paris 17 France

GOLDSTEIN, SHIRLEY ILGOVSKY, psychiat. social worker; b. N.Y.C., July 8, 1931; d. Henry and Mamie (Solomon) Ilgovsky; B.S., U. Mich., 1951; M.S., Smith Coll., 1953; m. Irving Goldstein, June 27, 1955 (div. Dec. 1972); children—Leslie Deborah, Mark Jonathan. Social worker Boston State Hosp., 1953-55; sr. social worker Douglas Thom Guild Guidance Clinic, Boston, 1955-57; researcher Florence Heller Sch., Brandeis U., Waltham, Mass., 1963-64; head social worker McLean Hosp. Out-Patient Clinic, Belmont, Mass., 1964-69, supr. casework, 1969-71, coordinator social work tng., 1971—. Instr. Boston U. Sch. Social Work, 1964-73, adj. prof., 1973—; faculty Simmons Coll. Sch. Social Work, 1973, asso. clin. prof. Smith Coll. Sch. Social Work, 1973-74. Mem. Nat. Assn. Social Workers, Am. Orthopsychiat. Assn., Acad. Certified Social Workers, Mass. Acad. Psychiat. Social Workers, Group Psychotherapy Assn., Acad. Clin. Social Work, Boston Geriatric Soc., Nat. Assn. Smith Coll. Sch. for Social Work Alumni (pres. 1969-73). Home: 31 Peacock Farm Rd Lexington MA 02173 Office: 115 Mill St Belmont MA 02178

GOLDSTEIN, SONJA (MRS. JOSEPH GOLDSTEIN), lawyer; b. Leipzig, Germany, Dec. 20, 1926; d. Osias Oscar and Charlotte (Rosenfeld) Lambek; B.S. in Econs., London Sch. Econs., 1947; LL.B., Yale, 1952; m. Joseph Goldstein, Aug. 3, 1947; children—Joshua, Anne, Jeremiah, Daniel. Came to U.S., 1948, naturalized, 1951. Admitted to D.C. bar, 1952, Conn. bar, 1962; atty. NLRB, Washington, 1952-53; mem. firm Sachs, Sachs & Sachs, New Haven, 1964—. Mem. Woodbridge (Conn.) Town Planning and Zoning Commn., 1972—. Bd. dirs. Family Service, 1968-70. Home: 40 Overhill Rd Woodbridge CT 06525 Office: 99 Cherry St Milford CT 06460

GOLDSTEIN, THELMA WEINMAN (MRS. MILTON S. GOLDSTEIN), shoe co. exec.; b. N.Y.C., Nov. 8, 1922; d. Bernard and Rae (Kaplowitz) Weinman; B.A. in Sociology and Psychology, Queen's Coll., 1943; grad. N.Y. Sch. Interior Design, 1958; M.Ed. in Guidance and Counseling, Millersville (Pa.) State Coll., 1970; m. Milton S. Goldstein, July 17, 1943; children—David Joel, Shari Esta. Mem. summer office staff Five Star Shoe Mfg. Co., N.Y.C., 1940-42; field and social worker N.Y.C. Park Dept., summer 1944; asst.-treas. Empire Shoe Mfg. Co. Inc., Elizabethtown, Pa., 1947—; interviewer radio sta. WGAL, 1956-73. Pres. Lancaster chpt. Hadassah, 1965-67, chmn. subcom. pub. information, human relations com.; coordinator vols. aftercare services Lancaster Guidance Clinic; bd. dirs. local League Women Voters. Mem. Am. Assn. U. Women, Pi Lambda Theta. Democrat. Jewish religion. Home: 1409 Center Rd Lancaster PA 17603 Office: Empire Shoe Mfg Co Inc Washington and Poplar St Elizabethtown PA 17022

GOLDSTON, EMMA ANNE SMITH (MRS. EDGAR C. GOLDSTON), physician; b. Norfolk, Va., Jan 2, 1923; d. Albert Cromwell and Georgie (Foreman) Smith; B.S., Coll. William and Mary, 1944; M.D., Med. Coll. Va., 1956; postgrad. U. Richmond, 1951-52, U. Minn. Mayo Grad. Sch. Medicine, 1960-64, 73-74; m. Edgar C. Goldston, July 18, 1953; children—Edgar C., Jr., Maryanne Foreman, Georgieanne Maxwell. With Dept. Pub. Health, Norfolk, 1944-51, Communicable Disease Center, Atlanta, 1948; gen. rotating intern Norfolk Gen. Hosp., 1956-57, resident pediatrician, 1959; pvt. practice obstetrics, Virginia Beach, 1958; fellow pediatrics, hematology Mayo Grad. Sch. Medicine, 1960-64; practice medicine specializing in pediatrics, Rochester, Minn., 1964—, Austin, Minn., 1965—; mem. staff St. Olaf Hosp., Austin; pediatrician Olmsted Health Dept.; pediatric cons. State of Minn., 1966. Leader, River Trails council Girl Scouts U.S.A. Smith Found. Meml. med. grantee, 1954-56. Mem. So. Minn., Minn. State med. assns., A.M.A. (mem. Zumbro Valley women's aux. bd. 1965-66), Zumbro Valley Med. Soc., Am. Med. Womens Assn., A.A.A.S., Northwestern Pediatric Soc., Am., Minn. pub. health assns., Gt. Plains Assn. for Perinatal Care, Alumni Assn. Mayo Grad. Sch. Medicine, D.A.R., Kappa Delta, Alpha Epsilon Iota. Episcopalian. Clubs: Zonta International (Rochester); Norfolk Yacht and Country. Home: 1138 7th St SW Rochester MN 55901 Office: 101 NW 14th St Austin MN 55912

GOLDTHORPE, MARY JANE, librarian; b. Duluth, Minn., June 29, 1945; d. Clarence J. and Matilda J. (Debalock) Goldthorpe; student U. Pitts., 1963; B.S., East Stroudsburg State Coll., 1967; M.L.S., Rutgers U., 1968; certificate of advanced study U. Chgo., 1971. Tchr. math. Bristol Twp. Sch. Dist., Edgeley, Pa., 1967; coordinator data services Technol. Inst. Library, Northwestern U., Evanston, Ill., 1968-70; cons. Far West Lab. for Ednl. Research and Devel., San Francisco, 1972; librarian San Francisco Pub. Library, 1973—. Mem. Am. Soc. for Information Scis., Sigma Zeta. Office: San Francisco Public Library Civic Center San Francisco CA 94102

GOLDTHWAITE, ANIELA PRISCILLA GORCZYCA (MRS. FRANK H. GOLDTHWAITE), wholesale trade exec.; b. nr. Fort Worth, May 24, 1912; d. Fred S. and Samie (Leahy) Gorczyca; student pvt. sch.; m. Frank Henry Goldthwaite, June 20, 1934; children—Aniela Priscilla (Mrs. Hugh Pitts), Frances (Mrs. William D. Read), Frank Henry. Pres., Goldthwaite's of Fort Worth, Dallas, Houston, San Antonio, 1960—. Sec., treas. Fort Worth Recreation Bd., 1955-57; pres. Women's U.S. Golf Assn., 1950-52, Tex. Women's Golf Assn., 1949-50. Recipient Merit award Profl. Golfers Assn. Am., 1962. Episcopalian. Clubs: Barnaby, Rivercrest Country, Colonial Country, Ridglea Country, Fort Worth (all Fort Worth). Home: 2328 Medford Ct W Fort Worth TX 76109 Office: 1401 Foch St Fort Worth TX 76107

GOLDWATER, MARGARET JOHNSON (MRS. BARRY MORRIS GOLDWATER), wife U.S. senator from Ariz.; d. Ray Prescott and Anna (Davies) Johnson; grad. Mt. Vernon Jr. Coll., Washington, 1931; m. Barry Morris Goldwater, Sept. 22, 1934; children—Joanne (Mrs. Eugene Butler), Barry Morris, Michael, Margaret (Mrs. Richard A. Holt). Active Blood Bank, Phoenix; founder Planned Parenthood Ariz. Bd. dirs. Meml. Hosp. Home: PO Box 1601 Scottsdale AZ 85252

GOLIN, BARBARA ANNE KEEFE (MRS. SANFORD GOLIN), psychologist, educator; b. Tulsa, May 17, 1932; d. James Loyal and Frances (Harrison) Keefe; B.A., Newcomb Coll., 1954; postgrad. Tulane U., 1954-56; Ph.D., U. Ia., 1960; m. Sanford Golin, Dec. 31, 1957; children—Carol Elaine, Eric James, Sarah Lisa. Grad. teaching asst. Tulane U., 1954-56; grad. teaching asst. U. Ia., 1956-57, counselor trainee, counseling center, 1957-58; clin. psychology trainee VA Hosp., Knoxville, Ia., 1959-60; instr. psychology U. Wis., Milw., part-time, 1960-65, assessment officer Peace Corps Tng. Center, 1964-65; mem. faculty dept. spl. edn. and rehab. U. Pitts. (Pa.), 1966—, asso. prof., 1968-71, prof., 1971—, asso. coordinator rehab. counselor tng. program, 1969—. Mem. Am. Psychol. Assn., Am. Personnel and Guidance Assn., Nat. Rehab. Assn. Home: 209 Seneca Dr Pittsburgh PA 15228

GOLLIN, PEARL REIFFEL, pediatrician; b. Chgo., May 25, 1924; d. Michael I. and Ethel (Zwick) Reiffel; B.S. in Medicine magna cum laude, U. Ill., 1945, M.D. cum laude, 1947; m. Harvey A. Gollin, Oct. 9, 1948; children—Susanne, Joan, Roberta. Intern, Cook County Hosp., Chgo., 1947-49, resident, 1949-51; practice medicine specializing in pediatrics, Chgo., 1951—; mem. asso. attending staff Cook County Hosp., 1951-56, also mem. faculty Chgo. Med. Sch.; mem. staff Columbus, Edgewater, Skokie Valley Community hosps. Active local Easter Seal Soc. Bd. dirs. Jerome D. Solomon Med. Research Found. Women's Am. ORT, Hadassah. Mem. Inst. Medicine Chgo., Council Fgn. Relations, Phi Beta Kappa, Alpha Omega Alpha. Home: 6510 N Keating St Lincolnwood IL 60646 Office: 6120 N Lincoln Av Chicago IL 60645

GOLLOTTE, GWEN HAND (MRS. WILFRED E. GOLLOTTE), pub. relations exec.; b. Meridian, Miss., Apr. 11, 1928; d. Preston James and Beulah (Cross) Hand; student Biloxi Hosp. Sch. Nursing, 1945-47, N.Y. sch. Interior Design, 1960-62, Jefferson Davis Jr. Coll., 1963-64; m. Wilfred E. Gollotte, Aug. 1, 1948; children—Diane (Mrs. Daniel Migues), Vicki Jeanne, Geoffrey. Asst. to program dir. Radio Sta. WJXN, Jackson, Miss., 1947-48; women's program dir. Radio Sta. WLOX, Biloxi, Miss., 1948-51; interior decorator Merchiston-Hall Galleries, Biloxi, 1960-63; pub. relations dir. Gulf Pines council Girl Scouts U.S.A., Hattiesburg, Miss., 1963-69; exec. dir. Biloxi Council on Aging, 1969-71, Harrison, Hancock and Jackson County Areawide Program for Elderly, 1961-73; founder, pres., dir. Gwen Gollotte Pub. Relations, Inc., Biloxi, 1973—. Cons.-tchr. personality devel. course Sacred Heart Girls High Sch., 1961. Bd. dirs. Gulf Coast Mental Health Assn., 1970-72, Harrison County Tb and Respiratory Disease Assn., 1969-71, Cath. Charities Housing, Inc., Diocese Natchez-Jackson, 1971—; v.p. bd. dirs. Gulf Coast Symphony, 1964—, Gulf Pines council Girl Scouts U.S.A., 1963-65, 72-73. Named Outstanding Beta Sigma Phi of Year, 1951, 54. Mem. Pub. Relations Soc. Am. (accredited mem.; Miss. pres. 1973, sec. Mid-South dist. 1974), Miss. Women's Cabinet Pub. Affairs, Miss. Press Women, Biloxi C. of C. Home: 1345 Lafayette St Biloxi MS 39530 Office: PO Box 385 Biloxi MS 39531

GOLOMB, SYLVIA LILLIAN GALLANT(MRS. IRVING L. GOLOMB), marriage counselor; b. N.Y.C., Dec. 3, 1917; d. Louis and Fay (Leavitt) Gallant; B.A., Hunter Coll. 1938; postgrad. Cornell U., 1940; M.S., Western Res. U., 1946; m. Irving L. Golomb, Jan. 26, 1947; children—Jolie Beth, Abby Loren. Economist, editor confidential transp. report WPB, Washington, 1942-45; caseworker Jewish Child Care Assn., N.Y.C., 1946-47; family and children's counselor East Manhattan Consultation Center, Jewish Family Service, 1947-49; youth counselor N.Y.C. Youth Bd., 1949-51; dir. community chest nursery and casework services Day Nursery of Oranges, Orange, N.J., 1951-54; casework supr. Children's Village, Dobbs Ferry, N.Y., 1954-55; research asst., research dept. N.Y.C. Youth Bd., 1955-56; dir. Family Counselling Unit, N.Y. State Supreme Ct., N.Y.C., 1956-67; supervising marital counsellor, conciliation bur. N.Y. State Supreme Ct., N.Y.C., 1967-73; supr. casework Cardinal McCloskey Sch. and Home, White Plains, N.Y., 1974—. Supr. student field work tng. N.Y. Sch. Social Work, 1953-54. Treas. Cultural Arts Com., Mamaroneck, N.Y., 1962-63; mem. hospitality com. Westchester Orchestral Workshop, 1963-64; mem. bd. Community Concerts Assn. Larchmont-Mamaroneck, 1969. Mem. Nat. Assn. Social Workers, Acad. Certified Social Workers. Home: 139 Highview St Mamaroneck NY 10543 Office: Cardinal McCloskey Sch and Home Mamaroneck Av White Plains NY

GOLSETH, ANNE ELIZABETH, ednl. adminstr.; b. Mpls., Feb. 10, 1937; d. Ralph Gustav and Marian (Nelson) Golseth; B.A., U. Colo., 1959; M.A., Cornell U., 1962; Ednl. Specialist, Mich. State U., 1968, Ph.D., 1974. Asst. dean students Mills Coll., Oakland, Cal., 1962-64; asst. dean women Kent (O.) State U., 1965-67; asst. prof., dean women U. N.D., Grand Forks, 1968-71; mem. faculty, asst. dir. edn. and research, dean students office Mich. State U., East Lansing, 1973-74; dir. advt. services U. Cal. at Davis, 1974—. Mem. def. adv. com. Women in Services, 1970-73. Mem. Am. Assn. Univ. Women, Am. Assn. Higher Edn., Nat. Assn. Student Personnel Adminstrs., Nat. Assn. Woman Deans, Adminstrs. and Counselors, Phi Beta Kappa, Gamma Phi Beta. Home: 800 Adams St #4 Davis CA 95616

GOLSON, FLORENCE (MRS. WINTON WADKINS BATEMAN), musician; b. Fort Deposit, Ala., Dec. 4, 1891; d. Howell Rose and Alabama (Goldsmith) Golson; student Tenn. Sch. for Blind, Nashville, 1913-15, Huntington Coll., Montgomery, Ala., 1916-17; diploma Cin. Conservatory Music, 1920, postgrad., 1920-21; pvt. study N.Y.C., 1921-22; postgrad. summers Cin. Conservatory Music, 1928, 44, Am. Conservatory Music, Chgo., 1946, U. South, Sewanee, Tenn., work under Roy Harris, 1950; m. Winton Wadkins Bateman, Mar. 22, 1923 (dec. June 1942). Concerts in Eastern and Midwestern states, 1920-23; lectr., song recitals Ga., Ala., La., 1923-42; dir. Montgomery (Ala.) Music Study Club Chorus, 1936-46; pvt. voice instr. College Park, Ga., 1924-36, Montgomery, Wetumpka, Ala., 1943-67; composer 7 songs and choral works, pub. 1918-23. Premier performance cantata A Spring Symphony, Rubenstein Club, N.Y.C., 1921. Mem. Ala. Fedn. Music Clubs (bd. dedicated Florence Golson Bateman studio at Transylvania Music Camp, Brevard, N.C.), Nat. Fedn. Music Clubs (life), College Park Music Club (hon. life), Montgomery Music Study Club (chmn. internat. music relations 1962—), League Am. Pen Women (past pres. Montgomery br.), Fine Arts Club Wetumpka (pres.), So. Composers League, Delta Kappa Gamma (hon.), Mu Phi Epsilon. Baptist. Home: 311 Government St Wetumpka AL 36092

GOLUMBIC, NORMA RICHMAN (MRS. CALVIN GOLUMBIC), govt. ofcl.; b. Bklyn.; d. Isador and Sophie (Kattan) Richman; B.A., Bklyn. Coll., 1936; M.S. in Organic Chemistry, U. Ia., 1938; m. Calvin Golumbic, May 10, 1946; 1 dau., Isabel (Mrs. John F. Davison). Chemist U.S. Bur. Mines, Pitts., 1942-50; publ. writer U.S. Dept. Agr., Washington, 1955; sci. writer and asst. chief research information br. Nat. Cancer Inst., Bethesda Md., 1955-69; pub. information officer div. nursing Bur. Health Manpower Edn., Bethesda, 1969-74; sci. writer Nat. Cancer Inst., 1974—. Fellow Am. Inst. Chemists; mem. Am. Chem. Soc., A.A.A.S., Nat. Assn. Sci. Writers. Author: (with H.H. Storch and R.B. Anderson) The Fischer-Tropsch and Related Syntheses, 1951; contbg. author Pres. Commn. Heart Disease, Cancer and Stroke, 1965. Home: 6000 Highboro Dr Bethesda MD 20034 Office: Nat Insts Health Rockville Pike Bethesda MD 20014

GOMES, BERTHA RUTH, real estate broker; b. Bridgeport, Ala., Dec. 23, 1924; d. Marion Baxter and Bertha Texas (Howard) Evans; grad. high sch.; 1 dau., Judy Carolyn (Mrs. Ennis Rowe). Owner-broker Pride Properties, 1969—; dir. Hacienda Fed. Savs. Mem. Cal. Real Estate Assn., Oxnard Harbor Bd. Realtors, Womens Council of Real Estate (v.p. 1974—). Home: 735 Ivywood Dr Oxnard CA 93030 Office: 152 E Pleasant Valley Rd Oxnard CA 93030

GOMEZ, ANA LYDIA MAS (MRS EDMUNDO GOMEZ), ret. govt. ofcl.; b. San Juan, P.R., Sept. 30, 1913; d. Jose and Concepcion (Marti) Mas Nadal; B.A., U. P.R., 1937; M.A., Columbia, 1948; m. Edmundo Gomez, Dec. 24, 1934. Jr. econ. analyst U.S. Dept. State, 1945-48, agrl. econ. asst., econ. officer, 1948-52, asst. agrl. attache, 1952-54, econ. officer, attache, 1965-73; asst. agrl. attache U.S. Dept. Agr., 1954-65. Recipient Superior Service award U.S. Dept. Agr., 1956. Mem. Am. Econ. Assn., Am. Statis. Assn. Home: Explanada 1210 Lomas de Chapultepec Mexico 10 DF Mexico

GOMEZ, CELIA MARIA MALDONADO (MRS. JOHN GOMEZ), educator; b. Fresno, Cal., Nov. 1, 1945; d. Luis I. and Mercedes (Rodriguez) Maldonado; B.S., Cal. State U., 1967, postgrad., 1971—; m. John Gomez, Aug. 5, 1972; 1 son, Joaquin Juan. Personnel analyst Fresno (Cal.) Co., 1967-69; employment security officer State of Cal. Dept. of Human Resources Devel., Fresno, Cal., 1969-71; counselor Fresno (Cal.) City Coll., 1971—. Sec. People to People Council, 1968-69; chmn. East Fresno Service Center Citizens Adv. Council, 1973—. Mem. Am. Soc. for Pub. Adminstrn. (exec. council 1971, sec.), Assn. Mexican Am. Educators, Mexican Manpower Devel. Assn., Phi Chi Theta. Home: 4409 N Thorne St Fresno CA 93705

GONCE, NANCY CUMMINGS (MRS. ROBERT L. GONCE), librarian; b. Birmingham, Ala., May 21, 1939; d. Truman and Mozelle (Brown) Cummings; B.S., U. Ala., 1961; M.A., George Peabody Coll., 1961; m. Robert L. Gonce, Aug. 26, 1961; children—Nancy Suzanne, Elizabeth Mozelle. Reader's adviser Friedman Library, Tuscaloosa, Ala., 1960; area librarian Ala. Pub. Library Service, State of Ala., 1961-66, field rep., 1966-67; librarian, profl. library Muscle Shoals Mental Health Center, Florence, Ala., 1972—. Chmn. library com. Citizens Study of Florence City Schs., 1969-70; mem. Ala. Adv. Council on Libraries, 1972—. Bd. dirs. St. Bartholomews Kindergarten, 1970-72. Mem. Am. Assn. Univ. Women (br. pres. 1969-71, div. legislative chmn. 1972-74), Ala. Library Assn. (pres. friends and trustees div. 1968-69), Alpha Beta Alpha, Alpha Theta, Epsilon Sigma Alpha. Home: 213 Colonial Dr Florence AL 35630 Office: 635 W College St Florence AL 35630

GONG, MERY LEE, data processor; b. Cleve., June 14, 1931; d. Wing and Swee (Woo) Gong; B.S., Ohio State U., 1954. With Ohio State U. Instruction and Research Computer Center, Columbus, 1954—, computer operator, 1954-56, programmer, cons., 1956-61, operations supr., 1961-65, adminstrv. asst., 1965-72, asst. dir., 1972—. Computer cons. Cole-Layer-Trumble Co.; instr. Ohio State U. continuing edn. Children's Hosp., Columbus, 1969. Mem. Am. Mgmt. Assn., Assn. Computing Machinery, Data Processing Mgmt. Assn., Air Force Assn., Assn. for Systems Mgmt., Ohio State U. Alumni Assn., Northwest Area Council for Human Relations, League of Women Voters, Ohio Commn. on Status of Women, Upper Arlington Civic Assn., Columbus Area Civil Rights Council. Club: Quota (Columbus). Home: 1776 Ridgecliff Rd Columbus OH 43221 Office: 1971 Neil Av Columbus OH 43210

GONYEA, MEREDITH ANN, state ofcl., ednl. adminstr.; b. Springfield, Mass., May 23, 1938; d. Edward Alex and Loretta Elizabeth (Seymour) Gonyea; B.S., U. Mass., 1960; Ph.D., U. Mich., 1971. Asst. dir. adminstrv. research Ohio State U., Columbus, 1970-72, asst. prof. pub. adminstrn., 1970-73; dir. faculty study Dept. Higher Edn., Trenton, N.J., 1973—. Cons. U. Mich., U. Mass. Grad. Sch., 1967-70. Mem. Am. Assn. U. Profs., A.A.A.S., Assn. Computer Machinery, Inst. Mgmt. Sci., Assn. Instl. Research, Am. Soc. Pub. Adminstrn., Am. Assn. for Higher Edn., Sigma Xi. Home: 1201 Linden Av Yardley PA 19067 Office: 225 W State St Trenton NJ 08625

GONYOW, MARY EVELYN, educator; b. Burlington, Vt., May 11, 1913; d. Charles William and Ann (Mckenna) Gonyow; student Conn. State Hosp. Tng. Sch. Nurses, Middletown, 1932-35; B.S., U. Vt., 1948; M.A., N.Y. U., 1953. Head nurse Conn. State Hosp., 1936-43, 46, acting edn. dir., 1948-49; gen. duty nurse U.S. Army Hosp. Ships: Acadia and Chateau Thierry- European, African, Middle Eastern and Asiatic Pacific Theaters, 1943-45; instr. N.Y. Hosp. Westchester div., White Plains, 1949-56; asst. prof. Syracuse (N.Y.) U., 1956-64; asso. prof. Northeastern U., Boston, 1964—, archivist, 1973—. Reference source Library Human Resources Am. Bicentennial Research Inst., 1973—. Sponsor, Am. Indian child Save the Children Fedn., 1967—. Mem. Am. Assn. U. Profs., Am. Nurses Assn., Nat. League Nursing, Nat. Wildlife Fedn. (asso. mem.), Pi Lambda Theta. Home: 32 Rockland St West Roxbury MA 02132 Office: 360 Huntington Av Boston MA 02115

GONZALEZ, NANCIE LOUDON SOLIEN, anthropologist, educator; b. Chgo., Dec. 9, 1929; d. Archibald N. and Dorothy (Ayers) Loudon; B.S., U. N.D., 1951; M.A., U. Mich., 1955, Ph.D., 1959; m. children—Ian, Kevin, Tania. Instr. nutrition Jamestown Coll., 1952-53; prof. anthropology U. San Carlos (Guatemala), summers 1957, 61, 62, 63; vis. lectr. anthropology U. Cal. at Berkeley, 1959-60; research anthropologist Inst. Nutrition of Central Am. and Panama, 1961-63; vis. asst. prof. sociology and anthropology U. N.M., 1965, asso. prof., 1965-69; prof., asst. chmn. anthropology U. Ia., 1969-70, prof., chmn. anthropology, 1970-72; prof., chmn. anthropology Boston U., 1972—. Fellow Am. Anthrop. Assn., Soc. for Applied Anthropology, mem. Am. Ethnological Soc., Current Anthropology, Latin Am. Studies Assn., Phi Beta Kappa, Sigma Xi, Phi Kappa Phi, Phi Upsilon Omicron. Author: A Heritage of Pride: The Spanish-Americans of New Mexico, 1969; Black Carib Household Structure; A Study of Migration and Modernization, 1969. Home: 296 Nashoba Rd Concord MA 01742

GONZALEZ, SISTER PAULA, educator; b. Albuquerque, Oct. 25, 1932; d. Hilario C. and Emilia Anna (Sanchez) Gonzalez; A.B., Coll. Mt. St. Joseph, 1952; M.S. (USPHS fellow), Cath. U. Am., 1962, Ph.D., 1966. Sci. instr. Regina Sch. Nursing, Albuquerque, 1952-54; sci. tchr. Seton High Sch., Cin., 1955-60; asst. prof. biology Coll. Mount St. Joseph (O.), 1965-73, asso. prof., 1973—, chmn. dept., 1969-72. Cons., developer Minicourse Devel. Project, Purdue U., Lafayette, Ind., 1973-74. Mem. Right to Life, Inc., Cin. Mem. Nat. Assn. Biol. Tchrs., Nat. Sci. Tchrs. Assn., Am. Inst. Biol. Sci., Ohio Acad. Sci., Audio-Tutorial Congress, Inst. Soc., Ethics and Life Scis., Sigma Xi. Home: 5776 Delhi St Cincinnati OH 45233 Office: Dept Biology Coll Mount St Joseph Mount St Joseph OH 45051

GONZÁLEZ, SARITA GALLARDO, Republican nat. committeewoman; b. Caguas, P.R., May 12, 1932; d. Hostos Miguel and Sara J. (Jiménez) Gallardo; student Mt. St. Mary's Acad., Plainfield, N.J., 1944-47; B.A., Coll. Mt. St. Vincent, 1952; postgrad. Institut des Hautes Etudes, Fribourg, Switzerland, 1950-51, New Sch. Social Research, 1952-53; m. Wallace Gonzáles-Oliver, Dec. 21, 1952; children—Wallace M., George A. Dir. Bank San Juan, Santurce; mem. Republican nat. com. from P.R. Pres. Ponce (P.R.) Mus. Fund Raising campaign, 1973-74. Mem. Am. Translators Assn. Home: PO Box 192 San Juan PR 00902

GOOD, ANNE LEEPER (MRS. JOHN CARTER GOOD), civic worker; b. Jackson, Tenn., Nov. 10, 1923; d. Robert Allen and Ola (Crittenden) Leeper; A.B., B.S. cum laude, Lambuth Coll., 1944; m.

John Carter Good, Oct. 28, 1945; children—John Robert, Carter Crittenden, William Allen. Co-chmn. Introduction to Washington com. The Hospitality and Information Service, 1968-71, treas., 1971—; membership chmn. Spanish Portuguese Study Group, 1968-69, v.p., 1969-70, pres., 1970-71; mem. ladies' bd. House of Mercy, 1970—, treas., 1972-74. Bd. dirs. D.C. br. Nat. Capitol Area YWCA, 1973—, rec. sec., 1974—; bd. dirs. Hannah Harrison Career Sch., 1971—; bd. dirs. Rosemount Infant Day Care Center, 1972—, v.p., 1974—; bd. dirs. Washington chpt. Achievement Rewards for Coll. Scientists, 1971-72, Alliance Francaise, Club d'Amitie Franco-Internationale. Clubs: St. Albans School Mothers (pres. Washington 1964-65), Air Force Officers Wives (mem. bd. Washington 1959-61). Home: 3712 Fordham Rd NW Washington DC 20016

GOOD, JOSEPHINE LOUISE, polit. party ofcl.; b. Denver, Mar. 10, 1918; d. George Washington and Lena Pearl (Wooley) Good; student Parks Sch. Bus., 1935. Typist, payroll div. Colo. office WPA, Denver, 1936-39; sec. to pres. Fageol Motor Sales Co., Seattle, 1939-40; sec. SEC, Washington, 1940-42; supr. stenographic pool Exec. Office for Price, OPA, Washington, 1942-43; sec. to mem. congress, Washington, 1945-53; cofidential and adminstr. aide to postmaster gen., Washington, 1953-56; conv. dir., asst. to chmn. Rep. Nat. Com., Washington, 1956—. Mem. Def. Adv. com. Women in Service, 1974. Served with U.S. Coast Guard Women's Res., 1943-45. Roman Catholic. Home: 3900 Tunlaw Rd NW Washington DC 20007 Office: 310 1st St SE Washington DC 20003

GOODE, JULIA PRATT, coll. dean; b. Martin, Ga., Feb. 26, 1929; d. James McMullin and Mary Agatha (Hall) Goode; B.A. in Chemistry, Agnes Scott Coll., 1950; M.S. in Chemistry, Emory U., 1952. Lab. technician Pub. Health Dept. State of Ga., Atlanta, 1948-50, chemist, 1950-53; asst. dir. to agrl. research Tenn. Corp., Atlanta, 1953-56; chmn. sci. depts. Fulton County Bd. Edn., Atlanta, Ga., 1956-66; asso. prof. Baptist Coll., Charleston, S.C., 1966-69; asst. prof. med. tech. Med. U. S.C., Charleston, 1969-71, adminstrv. co-ordinator med. tech. program, 1971-73, asst. dean Coll. of Allied Health Scis., Charleston, since 1973—. NSF grantee, 1964. Mem. Am. Chem. Soc., Ga. Acad. Sci., Am. Soc. Allied Health Professions, Chi Beta Phi. Club: Altrusa Internat. (pres. 1971-72). Home: 418 Trapier Dr Charleston SC 29412

GOODE, MATTIE FAY, constrn. co. exec.; b. Concho County, Tex., Jan. 13, 1922; d. Rora Arthur and Berenice Ethel (Miller) Stephens; student San Angelo Jr. Coll., 1940-42; m. James David Goode, Feb. 14, 1942; children—J. Carolyn (Mrs. Willard W. Mullins), Elizabeth A. (Mrs. Marcus Kirkpatrick Martin), Vivian Lea. Formerly bookkeeper, sec. James D. Goode Co., San Angelo, Tex.; formerly sec.-treas. James D. Goode Constrn. Inc., San Angelo, now v.p. Mem. Order Eastern Star, Social Order of Beauceant (past chair officer, pres. 1972, oracle 1973). Home: 3137 Chatterton Dr San Angelo TX 76901 Office: 912 S Oakes St San Angelo TX 76901

GOODEN, OPAL, editor, writer; b. Ft. Worth, Oct. 13, 1911; d. Juewell and Winnifred (Eastus) Gooden; A.B., Tex. Christian U., 1931; student U. Chgo., 1931-33, Chgo. Theol. Sem., 1931-33. Writer, Paterson (N.J.) Call, 1937-38, Youth Employment Project, WPA, Duluth, Minn., 1938; mem. program staff YWCA, Summit, N.J., 1939-42; writer, internat. specialist U.S. Dept. Labor, Washington, 1942-47; free lance writer, 1947-49; information officer U.S. War Claims Comm., Washington, 1949-51; writer, editor Internat. Press Service, USIS, Washington, 1951-53; careers cons., editor Am. Assn. Med. Social Workers, Nat. Assn. Social Workers, Washington, 1954-56; personnel asst., editor Miners Meml. Hosp. Assn., Washington, 1957-64; editor, adminstrv. asst. United Mine Works of Am. Welfare and Retirement Fund, Washington, 1964-74; editorial cons. Health and Med. Care, 1974—. Mem. Citizens Assn. Georgetown; v.p. Friends Non-Profit Housing, Inc., 1965-71. Bd. dirs. Ionia R. Whipper Home, 1969-72. Fellow Am. Pub. Health Assn.; mem. D.C. Pub. Health Assn., Am. Med. Writers Assn. (chpt. sec. 1967-68), Am. Newspaper Womens Club (2d v.p. 1963-64), Nat. Trust for Historic Preservation, Sierra Club, Washington Nat. Press Club. Democrat. Mem. Soc. of Friends. Home: 3320 Dent Pl NW Washington DC 20007 Office: 3320 Dent Pl NW Washington DC 20007

GOODEN, RUTH GARDNER (MRS. FRANCIS W. GOODEN), civic worker; b. Glenn, Okla., Jan. 14, 1908; d. William S. and Edda (Williams) Gardner; student Okla. State U., 1926-27; m. Francis W. Gooden, July 28, 1927; children—George Marvin, William Josiah. Pres., P.T.A., Kingfisher, Okla., 1941-42; den mother Cub Scouts Am., 1945-49; bd. dirs. United Fund, 1964-66; v.p. Okla. Outdoor Council, 1955-57; gen. chmn. Kingfisher County Diamond Jubilee Celebration, 1964; pres. Council of Garden Clubs, 1949-50; sec.-treas. Okla. Garden Clubs, 1951-55, pres., 1955-57, S. Central regional dir., 1957-59, nat. bird chmn., 1963-65, state parliamentarian, landscape design study chmn., 1963-65, chmn. regional roadside devel., 1967-69, dist. garden therapy chmn., 1971—, state bird chmn., 1973—; dir. Nat. Council Garden Clubs, 1955-65; dir., sec. Okla. Christian Found., 1966—; pres. Kingfisher Ch. Women United, 1967-68; v.p. Okla. Church Women United, 1970-73, state chmn. fall forum, 1970; pres. Kingfisher study Club, 1969-70; dir. Memory Lane, 1970—, pres., 1972-73; v.p. bd. mgrs. United Christian Missionary Soc., 1967-68; state bd. Okla. Assn. Christian Chs., 1962-65, pres., 1964-65; supt. horticulture and arrangements Kingfisher County Fair, 1959—; northwest dist. chmn. Okla. div. Am. Cancer Soc., 1972—. Named Ark. Traveler, 1958, Okla. Merit Mother, 1963; Okla. Mother of Yr., 1974. Mem. D.A.R. (regent 1963-64, v.p. dist. 1971-73), Okla. Onithol. Soc. (sec.-treas. 1958-65), Central Okla. Hemerocallis Soc. (pres. 1962-64), Nat. Council Garden Clubs (life), Okla. Garden Clubs (life). Mem. Christian Ch. (tchr., supt. Sunday Sch., financial sec., deaconess, state treas. Christian Women's Fellowship 1958-60, v.p. 1961-62, pres. 1962-64). Mem. Order Eastern Star (worthy matron 1939, dist. dep. 1942, mem. grand com. 1942-45, 56-66). Home: 304 S 6th St Kingfisher OK 73750

GOODENOUGH, IRENE WISEMAN (MRS. JOHN BANNISTER GOODENOUGH), educator; b. Ottawa, Ont., Can., June 28, 1924; d. Peter and May Catherine (Johnston) Wiseman; A.B., Asbury Coll., 1944; M.A., U. Mich., 1945; postgrad. U. Chgo., 1946-48; m. John Bannister Goodenough, June 16, 1951. Tchr., Barnard Sch. Boys, N.Y.C., 1949-51, Shady Hill Sch., Cambridge, Mass., 1954-55; faculty resident Mass. Inst. Tech., 1954-60, faculty adviser Fgn. Students Summer Program, 1956, faculty adviser married students wives, 1958-64; prof. history, philosophy Mass. Bay Community Coll., Watertown, Mass., 1964—; prof. history U. Without Walls, Roxbury, Mass., 1971. Dir. women's program Internat. Conf. Magnetism, Boston, 1967; asso. Movement Internat. Des Responsables Chretiens, Paris, France, mem. internat. confs., 1958, 62, 64. Mem. housing com. Mass. Inst. Tech., 1961-64, mem. art com., 1966-71. Mem. Am. Assn. U. Profs. Home: 100 Memorial Dr Cambridge MA 02142 Office: 57 Stanley Av Watertown MA 02172

GOODENOUGH, URSULA WILTSHIRE (MRS. ROBERT PAUL LEVINE), educator; b. Queens Village, N.Y., Mar. 16, 1943; d. Erwin Ramsdell and Evelyn Ivy (Wiltshire) Goodenough; student Radcliffe Coll., 1961; B.A., Barnard Coll., 1963; M.A., Columbia, 1965; Ph.D., Harvard, 1969; m. Robert Paul Levine, Aug. 15, 1969; children—Jason Ramsdell, Mathea Wiltshire. Asst. prof. biology Harvard, Cambridge, Mass., 1971—. NIH fellow, 1964-71; NIH research grantee, 1972-73. Mem. Am. Soc. for Cell Biology, Genetics Soc. Am., Phi Beta Kappa, Sigma Xi. Home: 89 Irving St Cambridge MA 02138

GOODHEART, BARBARA JEAN PETERSON (MRS. CLYDE R. GOODHEART), writer; b. Chgo., July 13, 1934; d. Victor Theodore and Jean Veronica (Smyth) Peterson; B.A., Northwestern U., 1955; m. Clyde R. Goodheart, Dec. 26, 1953; children—Kenneth James, Karen Jean, Diane Louise. Free-lance writer Deerfield (Ill.) Rev., 1965-66, Soc. for Visual Edn., 1968, Scott, Foresman & Co., 1972; v.p., sec., dir. BioLabs, Inc., Northbrook, Ill., 1969—. Mem. Soc. Mag. Writers, Am. Med. Writers Assn., Kappa Delta. Author: A Year On the Desert, 1969. Contbr. articles to mags., also chpts. to various books. Address: 15 Sheffield Ct Deerfield IL 60015

GOODLAND, ELIZABETH SERING, newspaper editor; b. Redlands, Cal., Mar. 28, 1905; d. John R. and Alice G. (Corrie) Sering; student U. Redlands, 1924-27, U. Cal. at Berkeley, 1927; m. Max E. Goodland, June 24, 1946; 1 son by former marriage, Richard Edward Lownes. Soc. editor San Marino (Cal.) Tribune, 1941-43, 47-53; personnel sec. Los Angeles Daily News, 1943-47; with Los Angeles Times, 1953-62, soc. editor, 1956-60; club editor, 1960-62; with women's dept. Pasadena (Cal.) Ind. Star News, 1965—, now women's editor. Mem. Theta Sigma Phi (nat. pres. 1967-68). Home: 1808 Hanscom Dr South Pasadena CA 91030 winter: 2091 Calle Felicia Palm Springs CA 92262

GOODLATTE, JEANNE ROE PRICE (MRS. ARTHUR RICHARDSON GOODLATTE), civic worker, journalist; b. Chgo., Aug. 29, 1911; d. Clarence Virgil and Jeanne Marie (Roe) Price; Principia Jr. Coll., 1931; student U. Chgo., 1931-32; m. Arthur Richardson Goodlatte, Apr. 15, 1937; children—Arthur Richardson, William S., James T., Peter R. East Longmeadow (Mass.) news corr. Springfield Union, 1952-70, Longmeadow News, Enfield, Conn., 1969—. Chmn. East Longmeadow Hist. Commn., 1970—; mem. East Longmeadow Bicentennial Commn., 1974—; mem. East Longmeadow Master Plan Study Com., 1974—. Trustee East Longmeadow Hist Commn. Trust Fund. Mem. Jr. League of Springfield. Conglist. Club: Women's Community (dir. East Longmeadow 1972—). Home: 33 Greenacre Lane East Longmeadow MA 01028 Office: East Longmeadow Hist Commn Town Hall East Longmeadow MA 01028

GOODMAN, CORINNE LOUISE RICHARDSON, lawyer; b. St. Louis, Sept. 17, 1937; d. Orville Willcott and Martha Louise (Corn) Richardson; A.B., Washington U., 1958, J.D., 1960, postgrad. 1964-65; m. Harold S. Goodman, May 12, 1966 (div.); 1 son, James Richardson. Admitted to Mo. bar, 1960; practiced in St. Louis, 1960-66; legal adviser St. Louis County Juvenile Ct., Clayton, Mo., 1966—. Gen. aid for solicitation of funds United Fund, Am. Cancer Soc., 1965-67; mem. Mo. Commn. on Status of Women, 1972—. Mem. Am., Mo., St. Louis County bar assns., Am. Judicature Soc., Lawyers Assn. St. Louis, Am. Soc. Internat. Law, Pi Beta Phi (treas. 1957). Contbr. articles to profl. jours. Home: 7474 York Dr Clayton MO 63105 Office: 501 S Brentwood St Clayton MO 63105

GOODMAN, DENISE WINTER, journalist; b. Akron, O., July 12, 1939; d. Adolph Edward and Denise May (Winter) Goodman; B.A., Ohio State U., 1961; postgrad., N.Y. U., 1964-65. Asst. news editor, dept. of information Nat. Council of Chs., N.Y.C., 1964-65; urban affairs writer Dayton (O.) Jour. Herald, 1961-64, 65-73; asst. editor Belfast (Me.) Rep. Jour., 1973—. Free lance writer, 1973—. Mem. Mortar Bd., Theta Sigma Phi. Home: Box 46 Searsport ME 04974 Office: Belfast Republican Journal Belfast ME 04915

GOODMAN, DORIS, physician; b. Cleve., June 18, 1925; d. Mathias and Helen (Marks) Goodman; B.S., Ohio State U., 1947; M.D., Woman's Med. Coll. Pa., 1960. Intern, U. Chgo. Clinics, 1960-61; resident Phila. VA Hosp., 1961-64; practice medicine specializing in cardiology, Phila., 1965—; mem. staff Grad. Hosp. U. Pa., Phila., Phila. Gen. Hosp.; asso. medicine U. Pa., 1970-73, asst. prof. medicine, 1973—. Fellow Am. Coll. Cardiology, A.C.P.; mem. Alpha Omega Alpha. Home: 7901 Henry Av Philadelphia PA 19128 Office: Graduate Hosp Pa Philadelphia PA 19146

GOODMAN, ELLEN HOLTZ, journalist; b. Newton, Mass., Apr. 11, 1941; d. Jackson Jacob and Edith (Weinstein) Holtz; B.A. cum laude, Radcliffe, 1963; Nieman fellow Harvard, 1973-74; 1 dau., Katherine Anne. Researcher, reporter Newsweek, mag., 1963-65; feature writer Detroit Free Press, 1965-67; feature writer, columnist Boston Globe, 1967—. Named New Eng. Newspaper Woman of Year, New Eng. Press Assn., 1968; recipient Catherine O'Brien award Stanley Home Products 1971, Media award Mass. Commn. Status Women, 1974. Nieman fellow Harvard, 1974. Home: 66 Stanton Rd Brookline MA 02146 Office: Boston Globe Boston MA 02102

GOODMAN, EVELYN KITTENPLAN, banker; b. Richmond, Va., Dec. 30, 1924; d. Philip and Hannah (Harfeld) Kittenplan; certificate Am. Inst. Banking, 1959, 63; certificate commerce U. Richmond, 1965; grad. Rutgers U. Stonier Grad. Sch. Banking, 1973; m. Bernard Stuart Goodman, June 14, 1947; children—Debra Sue, John William. With Central Nat. Bank Richmond, 1941—, operations officer, 1968—. Active Richmond Jewish Community Center; co-chmn. group div. United Jewish Welfare Fund drive Richmond Jewish Community Council, 1956-57. Mem. Nat. Assn. Bank Women (chmn. Commonwealth group 1970-71, So. Atlantic regional scholarship award 1972; named Jean Arnot Reid Bank Woman of Year 1948, Regional scholar 1970), Am. Inst. Banking (pres. Richmond 1968-69, Banker of Year Richmond chpt. 1973), Altrusa Internat., pres. Richmond 1973-74), Cross Keys. Jewish religion. Home: 4308 Augusta Av Richmond VA 23230 Office: 219 E Broad St Richmond VA 23261

GOODMAN, HARRIET WILINSKY (MRS. SYLVAN A. GOODMAN), marketing cons.; b. Boston; d. Charles F. and Jeanette (Isenberg) Wilinsky; student Wellesley Coll., 1923-24; B.A., Barnard Coll., 1927; m. Sylvan A. Goodman, Aug. 25, 1933. Psychologist Judge Baker Guidance Center, Boston, 1927-29; copywriter R. H. White Co., Boston, 1930-31; advt. mgr. E. T. Slattery Co., Boston, 1931-43; fashion dir. William Filene's Sons Co., Boston, 1943-45, sales promotion mgr., 1945-68, mem. mgmt. bd., 1945—, v.p. sales promotion div., 1968-73; dir. Wilinsky-Goodman Marketing Services, 1973—. Asso. in retailing Simmons Coll., Boston, 1964—. Named Bus. Woman of the Year, Boston Bus. and Profl. Women's Club, 1952, Advt. Woman of the Year, Greater Boston Advt. Club, 1961. Mem. Nat. Retail Mchts. Assn. (dir. 1968-71), Boston Better Bus. Bur. (dir. 1957—), Fashion Group Boston (regional dir. 1943-45), Fashion Group N.Y., Boston C. of C. (dir. 1951-54), Boston Retail Trade Bd., Asso. Merchandising Corp. Publicity Dirs. Group (chmn. 1954-55), Com. Young Audiences (dir. Boston 1964—), Advt. Club Greater Boston (dir. 1961-63), Bus. and Profl. Women's Club, Phi Beta Kappa. Club: Nat. Altrusa Boston. Author: Careers and Opportunities in Retailing, 1970. Home: 51 Beacon St Boston MA 02108 Office: 151 Tremont St Boston MA 02101

GOODMAN, JANET SILVERMAN (MRS. DAVID J. GOODMAN), psychologist; b. N.Y.C., July 9, 1939; d. Arthur and Pearl (Hut) Silverman; B.A., Smith Coll., 1962; B.A. with honors, Univ. Coll., London, Eng., 1964, Ph.D., 1968; m. David J. Goodman, Sept. 9, 1962; children—Leila D., Alissa T. Research scientist N.Y. State Psychiat. Inst., N.Y.C., 1970-71; project mgr. Human Resources Lab., Am. Tel.&Tel., N.Y.C., 1972-74; sr. vis. research fellow dept. elec. engring. sci. U. Essex, Eng., 1974—. Vice pres. Pelamay Products, Inc., Carteret, N.J. Mem. Brit. Psychol. Soc., Am. Psychol. Assn., Met. Assn. for Applied Psychology. Contbr. articles to profl. jours. Home: 15 Collingham Rd London SW5 England Office: Dept Elec Engring Sci U Essex Wivenhoe Park Colchester Essex England

GOODMAN, JULIA ANN, psychol. cons., hosp. adminstr.; b. Denver, Aug. 6, 1911; d. George Cody and Anna (Bond) Goodman; grad. Long Beach Jr. Coll., 1931; B.A., U. Cal. at Los Angeles, 1948; M.S., Purdue U., 1949, postgrad, 1949-50. Chief psychologist Child Guidance Clinic, Lansing, Mich., 1950-51; staff psychologist Mich. Children's Inst., Ann Arbor, 1951-54; asst. supervising psychologist U. Mich. Med. Center, Children's Psychiat. Hosp., Ann Arbor, 1954-56; pvt. practice psychol. cons., 1956—; staff psychologist, clin. coordinator Cath. Social Services, Port Huron, Mich., 1956-64; chief psychologist, clin. coordinator U.S. Dept. Health, Edn. and Welfare, Highland Park (Mich.) Bd. Edn., 1964-68; co-founder, asso dir. William Beaumont Hosp., Neuro-Edn. Center, Royal Oak, Mich., 1968—. Mem. Am., Mich. psychol. assns., Acad. Religion and Mental Health, Internat. Council Psychologists, Cons. Psychologists in Pvt. Practice. Home: 2222 Parkwood St Ann Arbor MI 48104 Office: 525 Southfield St Birmingham MI 48009

GOODMAN, URSULA SALTSMAN, pub. relations exec.; b. Haileyville, Okla., Apr. 24, 1910; d. Thomas Francis and Allie (Carley) Saltsman; B.A., U. Okla., 1936, M.A., 1970; 1 dau., Sula Grace. Spl. rep. U. Okla., Norman, 1936-43; asst. mgr. promotion dept. Capper Publs., Inc., Topeka, Kan., 1943-55; promotion asst., Southwest market U.S. Savs. Bonds, Treasury Dept., 1955-58; area pub. information specialist Indian Health Service, U.S. Dept. Health, Edn. and Welfare, Oklahoma City, 1958—. Guest lectr. on profl. pub. information in pub. health at various schs. journalism and medicine. Mem. Nat. Press Women, Women in Communications, Am. Women in Radio and TV, Internat. Assn. Bus. Communicators, Puppeteers Am., Phi Beta Kappa. Club: Pilot (Oklahoma City). Home: 1614 NW Britton Rd Oklahoma City OK 73120 Office: 388 Old Post Office Bldg Oklahoma City OK 73102

GOODNIGHT, MARIE LOUISE (MRS. CLARENCE JAMES GOODNIGHT), educator; b. Blue Island, Ill., Aug. 27, 1916; d. Rudolph Worley and Louise Sophia (Blatt) Ostendorf; A.A., Thornton Jr. Coll., 1936; student Colo. Coll., 1936-37; B.S., Kan. State U., 1938; M.S., U. Ill., 1939; postgrad. Purdue U., 1955-57; m. Clarence James Goodnight, Aug. 25, 1940; children—Ann Marie, Charles James. Instr. zoology U. Ill., Urbana, 1938-39, 42-44, research asst., 1943-44; instr. Purdue U., Lafayette, Ind., 1946-53, 59-65; instr. Western Mich. U., Kalamazoo, 1972, research asso. in biology, 1972—. Spl. writer Kalamazoo Nature Center, 1970—. Bd. dirs. Mich. Children's Aid Soc., 1967-70, Kalamazoo Community Concerts, 1972—. Recipient fellowship Am. Philos. Soc., 1950, grant Am. Assn. Univ. Women, 1973. Mem. Am. Assn. Univ. Women (publicity chmn. 1972-73), Sigma Xi, Phi Kappa Phi, Sigma Delta Epsilon. Democrat. Mem. Unitarian Ch. Author: (with C.J. Goodnight) Zoology, 1954; (with C.J. Goodnight, R.R. Armacost) Biology: An Introduction to the Science of Life, 1962; (with C.J. Goodnight, P. Gray) General Zoology, 1964. Contbr. articles to profl. jours. Home: 1633 Chevy Chase Blvd Kalamazoo MI 49008

GOODRICH, MARGARET, librarian; b. Cheyenne, Wyo., Dec. 5, 1909; d. Ralph Dickinson and Margaret (Knight) Goodrich; B.A., U. Wyo., 1931; B.L.S., Columbia, 1932. Librarian, Carbon County Pub. Library, Rawlins, Wyo., 1937-41; spl. services librarian U.S. Army, Ft. F.E. Warren, Wyo., 1941-45, Germany, 1945-47, Ft. Dix, N.Y., 1951-54; librarian John D. Rockefeller, Jr. Offices, N.Y.C., 1947-51; dir. W. Tex. Am. heritage project A.L.A., Lubbock, Tex., 1954-55; reference librarian Lubbock Pub. Library, 1955-57; staff mem. Denver Pub. Library, 1957-62; post librarian Fitzsimons Gen. Hosp., Denver, 1962-66, Ft. Sam Houston, Tex., 1966-68, Hdqrs. USARV Spl. Services Library Br., 1968-71, Fort Polk, La., 1971-73, Fort Bliss, Tex., 1973, Fort Hood, Tex., 1973-74; librarian Fitzsimmons Army Med. Center, Denver, 1974—. Recipient civilian merit award U.S. Army, 1946, certificate of achievement, 1973. Mem. A.L.A., Library Pub. Relations Council (treas. 1949-51), Colo., Tex. library assns., Adult Edn. Assn., D.A.R., Armed Forces Mgmt. Assn., P.E.O., Pi Beta Phi. Republican. Episcopalian. Home: 1255 Ash St Denver CO 80220 Office: Fitzsimmons Army Med Center Denver CO 80240

GOODRICH, MARGRIT HUBMANN (MRS. MURRAY H. GOODRICH), educator; b. Lengnau, Blel, Switzerland; d. Erwin J. and Rosa (Michel) Hubmann; came to U.S., 1942, naturalized, 1948; Asso. Applied Scis., Queens Coll., 1959; B.S., N.Y. U., 1961, M.A., 1963; Ph.D. in Psychology, U.S. Internat. U., San Diego, 1973; m. Murray H. Goodrich, May 25, 1963. Sec.-registrar nat. bd. YWCA, N.Y.C., 1955-57; intern oncological nursing Meml. Hosp. for Cancer and Allied Diseases, N.Y.C., 1959-61; pub. health nurse Dept. Pub. Health, City N.Y., 1961-62; coordinator inservice edn. Scripps Meml. Hosp., La Jolla, Cal., 1963-66; asst. prof. nursing San Diego State Coll., 1966-70; postgrad. fellow clin. psychology Mercy Hosp. and Med. Center, San Diego, 1973-74, staff psychologist mental health out-patient services, 1974—; marriage, family and child counselor, 1971—. Mem. Am. (dir.), Cal. (past chmn. membership com.) nurses assn., Nat., Cal. leagues for nursing, Am. Cancer Soc. (profl. edn. com., chmn. nursing edn. subcom. Cal. div. 1969—), Am. Pub. Health Assn., San Diego Heart Assn. (nursing edn. com.), San Diego County Psychol. Assn., Cal. Assn. Marriage and Family Counselors, Ninety-Nines, Internat. Orgn. Women Pilots, Assn. for Humanistic Psychology, Sigma Theta Tau, Pi Lambda Theta. Home: 5132 Pacifica Dr San Diego CA 92109

GOODRICH, NANCY ANN NEEDHAM (MRS. GEORGE HERBERT GOODRICH), educator; b. Cleve., Nov. 10, 1927; d. Delos N. and Florence (Duval) Needham; B.A. in Polit. Sci., Mt. Holyoke Coll., 1948; m. George Herbert Goodrich, Sept. 3, 1949; children—George Herbert, Craig Needham, Thomas Abrams. Mem. jr. exec. tng. course Time Inc., N.Y.C., 1948-49; broadcaster, dir. women's program radio sta. WCHV, Charlottesville, Va., 1949-52; moderator, producer program The 25th Hour sta. WTOP-TV, Washington, 1957-62; v.p., exec. producer Washington Tapes Inc., Washington, 1965-74; dir. studies Nat. Cathedral Sch. for Girls, Washington, 1974—. Founding pres. Jr. Goodwill Guild, Washington, 1952-54; sec. Jr. League, Washington, 1957, pres., 1962-64. Vice chmn. D.C. com. arts Nixon-Agnew campaign, Washington, 1968; mem. Inaugural Ball Com., 1968-69. Writer, moderator program WETA-TV.

GOODRIDGE, MARJORIE STEWART, educator; b. New Castle, Ind., Jan. 23, 1926; B.A., Miami U., Oxford, O., 1948; M.S. in Edn., Ind. U., 1952; Ph.D., Ohio State U., 1969. Tchr. Lemon-Monroe High Sch., Monroe, O., 1948-50; head residence hall dir. U. Fla., 1952-57; asst. dean women U. Cin., 1957-66, acting dean women, 1966-67, dean women, 1967-72, asst. prof. edn., 1967-73, asso. dean student devel., 1972-73. Former mem. Ohio Commn. Status Women. Mem. Am. Assn. U. Women, Mortar Bd., Kappa Delta Pi, Pi Lambda Delta. Home: 4234 Gulf of Mexico Dr Sarasota FL 33577

GOODROW, SISTER ESTHER MARIE, educator; b. Creede, Colo.; d. Joseph Douglas and Josephine (Lorber) Goodrow; ed. Loretto Ednl. Center, Nerinx, Ky., 1933-35; B.A., Loretto Heights Coll., 1940; M.A., St. Louis U., 1950, Ph.D., 1955. Tchr. pub. schs., Antonito, Colo., 1927-28, Del Norte, Colo., 1928-32, Loretto, Ky., 1935-40; tchr. history Inst. Bishop Toolen High Sch., Mobile, Ala., 1940-50; instr. Webster Coll., St. Louis, 1950-56; prof. Loretto Heights Coll., Loretto, Colo., 1956—, chmn. history dept., 1956-68, chmn. emeritus history dept., 1968—, moderator Internat. Relations Club, 1956-65; vis. prof. Chapman Coll. Afloat, 1968. Dir. Am. Studies workshop Coe Found., 1957-61, Nat. Def. Edn. Act History Inst., 1965, 66, 67, 68; mem. adv. com. Rocky Mountain div. UN Speaker Services, Denver, 1960—. Mem. Gov.'s Council on Juvenile Delinquency, 1967—. Fulbright participant summer Inst. in Chinese Civilization, Tunghaig U., Taichung, Taiwan, 1963. Mem. Am. Hist. Assn., Am. Studies Assn. (pres. Rocky Mountain div. 1960-61), Western History Assn., Rocky Mountain Social Sci. Assn. (exec. council), Colo. Council for Social Studies, Internat. Studies Assn. Author: Mobile During the Civil War, 1950; contbr. article to New Catholic Ency., 1966. Address: 3001 S Federal Blvd Denver CO 80236

GOODSTEIN, ANITA SHAFER (MRS. MARVIN ELIAS GOODSTEIN), educator; b. Bklyn., Sept. 12, 1929; d. William and Sadye (Schulman) Shafer; B.A., Mount Holyoke Coll., 1951; M.A., Cornell U., 1953, Ph.D., 1959; m. Marvin Elias Goodstein, June 14, 1953; children—Sarah Gina, Eban Saul. Instr., U. of South, Sewanee, Tenn., 1963-67, asst. prof., 1967-71, asso. prof. dept. history, 1971—. Social Sci. Research Council grantee, 1968-69. Mem. Am., So. hist. assns., Orgn. Am. Historians, Phi Beta Kappa. Author: Biography of a Businessman, 1963. Home: Sewanee TN 37375

GOODSTEIN, MADELINE PRAGER (MRS. JULIAN GOODSTEIN), educator; b. N.Y.C., Oct. 23, 1920; d. Julius and Henrietta (Goldfarb) Prager; B.A. cum laude, Bklyn. Coll., 1941; M.S., Poly. Inst. Bklyn., 1948; Ed.D., Columbia, 1968; m. Julian Goodstein, Jan 12, 1947; children—Elaine (Mrs. Jacques Robinson), Barbara, Ronald. Chemist, Trubeck Labs., East Rutherford, N.J., 1941-48; faculty Bklyn. Coll., 1959-62, U. Hartford (Conn.), 1963-64; faculty Central Conn. State Coll., New Britain, 1967—, asso. prof. chemistry, 1972—. Recipient Outstanding Educator award Outstanding Educators Am., 1973. Fellow Am. Inst. Chemists; mem. Nat. Assn. for Research in Sci. Teaching, Am. Chem. Soc. (Curriculum com. div. of chem. edn. 1969-73), Nat. Sci. Tchrs. Assn. (N.E. com. coll. sci. teaching 1973-74). Home: 6 Woodland Dr Woodbridge CT 06525 Office: Dept Chemistry Central Conn State College New Britain CT 06050

GOODWIN, BARBARA HALL (MRS. CHARLES A. GOODWIN), ednl. adminstr.; b. Brookline, Mass., May 25, 1908; d. Morris Andrew and Frances (Jouett) Hall; A.B., Smith Coll., 1930; M.Ed., Emory U., 1957; specialist in edn. degree, U. Ga., 1971; m. Charles A. Goodwin, July 24, 1932; children—Priscilla (Mrs. John Allen Bennett), Constance (Mrs. Roscoe Earl Luke), Jonathan Hall. Tchr. pub. schs., Atlanta, 1953-66; lead tchr. Nat. Tchr. Corps, pub. schs. Atlanta, 1966-67, resource tchr., 1967-71; curriculum developer for early childhood edn. pub. schs., Atlanta, 1971—. Instr. first aid Red Cross, 1940-43; chmn. Community Fund, 1945-50. Mem. Nat., Ga., Atlanta edn. assns., Ga. (pres.), Atlanta (pres. 1963-65) assns. for childhood edn., Ga. Dept. Instructional Supervision, Assn. for Childhood Edn. Internat. (chmn. conf. planning com. 1970, v.p. 1970—), Assn. for Supervision and Curriculum Devel., Internat. Reading Assn., Ga. Assn. on Young Children, Am. Assn. U. Women, Atlanta League Women Voters, Atlanta Smith Coll. Club, Delta Kappa Gamma. Home: 1732 N Rock Springs Rd NE Atlanta GA 30324 Office: 2930 Forrest Hills Dr SW Atlanta GA 30315

GOODWIN, DOROTHY CHENEY, educator; b. Hartford, Conn., Sept. 2, 1914; d. Charles Archibald and Ruth (Cheney) Goodwin; A.B., Smith Coll., 1937; Ph.D., U. Conn., 1957. With various agencies Fed. Govt., 1937-45; librarian Food and Agr. Orgn., UN, Washington, 1945-46; agrl. economist Allied Powers in Japan, 1946-52; faculty U. Conn., Storrs, 1957-71, now asso. prof. econs. Asst. provost, dir. instl. research Conn. Natural Gas Corp., 1972—. Chmn. Joshua's Tract Conservation and Historic Trust, Windham Planning Retion, Conn., 1968—; mem. Mansfield (Conn.) Bd. Tax Rev., 1961-74. Mem. Mansfield Town Council, 1971—; mem. Dem. Town Com., Storrs, 1965. Vice chmn. bd. trustees Hartford Coll. for Women, 1960; mem. bd. regents U. Hartford, 1971—; bd. dirs. U. Conn. Found., 1966—; trustee Conn. chpt. Nature Conservancy, 1970—; exec. bd. Indian Trails council Eastern Conn. Boy Scouts Am., 1973; corporator Windham Community Meml. Hosp., 1971, Hartford Hosp., 1972. Mem. League Women Voters, Assn. for Instl. Research. Democrat. Episcopalian. Home: 447 Browns Rd Storrs CT 06268

GOODWIN, KATHLEEN WATSON (MRS. JOHN R. GOODWIN), state legislator; b. Bath, Me., Nov. 13, 1940; d. Nathan Wilbur and Kathleen Violet (Leonard) Watson; student U. Me., 1960-62; grad. Bliss Coll., 1963; m. John R. Goodwin, July 12, 1969; 1 son, Jonathan Eaton. Mem. Me. Ho. of Reps., Augusta, 1969—. Chmn., Me. Com. on Aging, 1971—; mem. Natural Resources Council Me. Sec., Me. Democratic Com., 1968—; vice chmn. Me. Dem. Platform Com., 1970; sec. Bath City Dem. Com., 1963-66; treas. Sagadahoc County Dem. Com., 1964-65. Mem. Nat. Soc. State Legislators (gov.). Roman Catholic. Home: 409 High St Bath ME 04530 Office: State House Augusta ME 04330

GOODWIN, NANCY LEE, educator; b. Peoria, Ill., Aug. 11, 1939; d. Raymond Darrell and Mildred Louise (Brown) Goodwin; B.A. (Nat. Meth. scholar, Nat. Merit scholar), MacMurray Coll., 1961; M.A., U. Colo., 1963; Ph.D., U. Ill., 1971. Tchr., Roosevelt Jr. High Sch., Peoria, 1961-62; counselor U. Ill., Urbana, Ill., 1963-66; staff asso., asst. prof. edn. measurement U. Ill., Chgo., 1967-71; asso. prof. statistics Fla. Internat. U., Miami, 1971—, also dir. Cons. Mid-Am. Computer Corp., First Chance Network U.S. Office Edn., 1972—. Mem. Com. on Ill. Govt., Higher Edn. Task Force. Mem. Vol. Action Center, Miami, 1972—; active Girl Scouts U.S.A., 1971—. Recipient Merit award Chgo. Tchrs. Assn., 1969; citation Girl Scouts U.S.A., 1973. Mem. N.E.A., Am. Assn. Higher Edn., Am. Ednl. Research Assn., Assn. for Instl. Research. Home: 8500 SW 109th Av Miami FL 33143

GOODWIN, NORMA JEAN, physician; b. Norfolk, Va., May 14, 1937; d. Stephen C. and Helen (Jefferson) Goodwin; B.S., Va. State Coll., 1956; M.D., Med. Coll. Va., 1961. Intern, resident, chief resident in internal medicine Kings County Hosp. Center, Bklyn., 1961-65, clin. asst. in medicine, 1965-67, asst. vis. physician in medicine, 1967—; clin. asst. instr. medicine State U. N.Y., Downstate Med. Center, Bklyn., 1964-65, asst. instr. medicine, 1965-67, instr. medicine, 1967-70, asst. prof. medicine, 1970—, clin. dir. hemodialysis unit, 1967-69, dir. unit, 1969-71; v.p. for community health and ambulatory care services N.Y.C. Health and Hosps. Corp., 1971—. Past pres., treas. Provident Clin. Soc. Bklyn. Inc., 1967-69, pres., 1969-72; mem. health task force N.Y. Urban Coalition; cons. U.S. Dept. Health, Edn. and Welfare; mem. health services research study group Nat. Center Health Services Research and Devel., Health Services and Mental Health Adminstrn. Dept. Health, Edn., Welfare; mem. regional adv. group N.Y. Met. Regional Med. Program; past 1st vice chmn. Bedford Stuyvesant Comprehensive Health Planning Council; mem. health sci. career adv. com. La Guardia City U. N.Y. Bd. dirs. McDonough St. Community Center, N.Y. Assn. Ambulatory Care, N.Y.C. Comprehensive Health Planning Agy.; trustee Atlanta U. Center Fellow nephrology NIH, 1965-67. Mem. Am. Soc. Nephrology, N.A.A.C.P., Nat. Urban League, Am. Soc. Artificial Internal Organs, Royal Soc. Health, N.Y., Internat. socs. nephrology, Nat. Med. Assn., Bklyn. Soc. Internal Medicine, Soc. Urban Physicians, Kings County Med. Soc., N.Y. Heart Assn. (dir.), Am. Pub. Health Assn., Pub. Health Assn. N.Y.C. (com. policy and legislation), Ambulatory Pediatric Assn., Internat. Platform Assn., Sigma Xi, Alpha Kappa Mu, Beta Kappa Chi. Lectr. on renal disease; contbr. articles to med. jours., chpt. to book. Home: 747 E 37th St Brooklyn NY 11210 Office: 125 Worth St New York City NY 10013

GOOLD, NANCY JEAN, therapist; b. Hinsdale, Ill., Feb. 26, 1946; d. Robert Charles and Florence Harrington (Wilson) Goold; student Ill. Wesleyan U., 1964-65; B.S., U. Ia., 1969. Asst. dir. occupational therapy Upstate Med. Center, Syracuse, N.Y., 1969-71; staff therapist Michael Reese Hosp., Chgo., 1971; sr. staff therapist Rehab. Inst. Chgo., 1971-74, supr., 1974—. Mem. research team Central N.Y. Regional Med. Program, 1970-71; recruitment chmn. Ill. Occupational Therapy Assn., 1973—, co-worker task force, 1973—. Dir. Vols. for Dawn Clark Netsch, Ill. State Senator, 1973. Rehab. Services Adminstrn. scholar, 1970. Mem. Am., Ill. occupational therapy assns., Sheffield Neighbors Assn., Alpha Gamma Delta. Democrat. Episcopalian. Clubs: Sandburg, Lakeshore Ski (Chgo.). Home: 2140 Lincoln Park W Chicago IL 60614 Office: 345 E Superior St Chicago IL 60611

GOOR, JEANETTE MINDEL, govt. ofcl.; b. N.Y.C., July 31, 1914; d. Isaac and Esther (Eventoff) Mindel; B.A., Hunter Coll., 1934; m. Charles G. Goor, July 7, 1935; children—Ronald Stephen, Robert Mindell. Analyst Ceir, Inc., Bethesda, Md., 1955-66; mgmt. information specialist U.S. Office Edn., Washington, 1966—. First pres. Buckingham Coop. Nursery and Kindergarten, Arlington, Va., 1944-45. Home: 3133 Patterson St NW Washington DC 20015 Office: US Office Edn 400 Maryland Av SW Washington DC 20202

GOPLERUD, ELIZABETH JANE, physician; b. Osage, Ia., Sept. 26, 1919; d. Clifford Peder and Ethel Lucia (Cromer) Goplerud; B.A., Grinnell Coll., 1941; M.D., U. Ia., 1944. Intern, Cin. Gen. Hosp.; resident obstetrics and gynecology Johns Hopkins Hosp., Balt., 1944-48; chief obstetrics and gynecology Palmerton (Pa.) Hosp., 1948—; v.p. Palmerton Visiting Nurse Assn., 1950—; mem. Panther Valley Cancer Soc. Recipient Golden Deeds award Exchange Club, 1967. Diplomate Am. Bd. Obstetrics and Gynecology. Fellow Am. Coll. Obstetricians and Gynecologists; mem. A.M.A., Pa., Carbon County med. socs. Home: 821 1st St Palmerton PA 18071 Office: Palmerton Hospital Palmerton PA 18071

GORDON, ANNE ISABEL, coll. adminstr.; b. Spotsylvania County, Va., Dec. 25, 1921; d. James Addison and Essie William (Payne) Gordon; grad. Mary Washington Coll., 1942. Office sec., recruiter U.S. Dept. Agr., Raleigh, N.C., 1942-44; interviewer USES, 1944-47; pvt. sec. to contractor, Fredericksburg, Va., 1947-50; accountant, office mgr. Chrysler Corp., Fredericksburg, 1950-54; real estate, ins. broker Gen. Realty Corp., Fredericksburg, 1954-55; dir. placement Mary Washington Coll., Fredericksburg, 1955—. Pres., College Heights Civic Assn., 1969-70. Mem. So. (pres. 1971-72), Va. (pres. 1967-68, editor newsletter 1968—) coll. placement assns., Bus. and Profl. Women's Club (pres. 1951-53), D.A.R. (chpt. regent 1968-71), Nat. Trust for Historic Preservation, Mary Washington Coll. Alumnae Assn. (mem. nat. bd. 1968-71), Beta Sigma Phi (pres. 1961-62), Club: Potomac Regents (pres. 1971-72). Home: 1208 Thornton St Fredericksburg VA 22401

GORDON, BETTY REBECCA (MRS. ARNOLD GORDON), ins. co. exec.; b. N.Y.C., Sept. 24, 1934; d. Max and Mary (Ligorio) Van Dyke; B.S., Bklyn. Coll., 1956; postgrad. Cooper Union Sch. Engring., 1956-59, Bklyn. Coll. Grad. Sch., Coll. Ins., N.Y. U., 1960-68; m. Arnold Gordon, Dec. 14, 1968; 1 son, Michael. Mathematician materials lab., gyro-navigational div. N.Y. Naval Shipyard, 1958-60; with Standard Security Life Ins. Co., N.Y.C., 1960—, 2d v.p. systems, 1968—. Pvt. instrn. math., programming. Mem. Assn. Computing Machinery, Data Processing Mgmt. Assn. (sec., 1971-72), Assn. Computer Programmers and Analysts (sr.), Soc. for Information Sci. Home: 67-67 Burns St Forest Hills NY 11375 Office: 111 5th Av New York City NY 10003

GORDON, CLARA SOS (MRS. OTTO GORDON), cancer researcher; b. Budapest, Hungary, Aug. 27, 1929; d. Ernest and Irma (Kohn) Sos; Masters Degree, Chem.E., Tech. U., Budapest, 1953; m. Otto Gordon, Mar. 11, 1953. Came to U.S., 1957, naturalized, 1964. Cancer researcher Sloan Kettering Inst., N.Y.C., 1957-61, Columbia U., Francis Delafield Hosp., N.Y.C., 1961-64, Research Inst. for Skeletomuscular Diseases, Hosp. for Joint Diseases, N.Y.C., 1964-73; research asst. Sloan Kettering Inst., N.Y.C., 1973—. Home: 104-20 Queens Blvd Forest Hills NY 11375 Office: 425 E 68th St New York City NY 10035

GORDON, CONNI GERALDINE, artist, entertainer; b. New Britain, Conn., June 28, 1923; d. Jack Wadsworth and Rhea Ruth (Robinson) Gordon; grad. Naval Tng. Sch., Coll. William and Mary, 1945; student Columbia Sch. Fine Art, 1945-48, Columbia Tchrs. Coll., 1945-48; certificate Ecole des Beaux Arts, Fontainebleau, France, 1948; certificate fine arts and art history New Sch. Social Research, 1952; student N.Y. State U., 1952. Originated use of art participation as form of entertainment, 1940; originator, dir. hairdressers' art course M. Louis Hair Design Inst., N.Y.C., 1946-47; condr. audience participation paint parties for various art, conv., women's groups, France, 1948—; artist, exhibitor Palace of Fontainebleau (France), 1949; founder, dir. Conni Gordon Art Schs., 1950—; founder, star Paint Party TV shows, personal appearance shows, 1950—; dir. art activities Concord Hotel, Kiamesha Lake, N.Y., 1951-54; chmn. bd. dirs. Conni Gordon, Inc. of Fla., Miami Beach, 1959—; pres. Palette Prodns., Inc. of Fla., Miami, 1972—. Vol. art tchr. community service TV, Miami, 1954—, Miami City Jail, 1964-65; art tchr. Police Athletic League, 1960-63; lectr. U. China, Hong Kong, 1971-72; tchr. mentally retarded groups, Dade County, Fla., 1960—; active telethons and fund-raising various charitable orgns., 1940—; dir. spl. art activity VA Hosp, Miami, 1968-72. Served with U.S. Women Marine Corps, 1943-45. Recipient awards for recognition of vol. services. Mem. A.F.T.R.A., Screen Actors Guild, Nat. Art Materials Trade Assn., Hobby Industry Am., Miami Better Bus. Bur., Miami C. of C., Women Marine League, Sunflower Soc., Lowe Mus. U. Miami. Author: Conni Gordon Art Course, corr. course, 1960, self-teaching art course, 1969; You Can Paint In Minutes, 1959; art course series, 1963—. Patentee in field. Originator 4 step paint-in-minutes method. Home: 528 Lincoln Rd Miami Beach FL 33139 Office: 530 Lincoln Rd Miami Beach FL 33139

GORDON, DARLINE KATHRYN, radio sta. exec.; b. Clinton, Ia., June 19, 1911; d. Amos Walton and Kathryne (Cosgrove) Gordon; student Wartburg Coll., Clinton, Ia., 1930-32. Reporter The Courier, Grants Pass, Ore., 1928; state editor Clinton Herald, Clinton, 1929-36; home lighting advisor Interstate Power Co., 1936-38; continuity dir. radio sta. WMRO, Aurora, Ill., 1938-41; sales mgr. radio sta. KROS, Clinton, 1941—. Mem. Clinton City Council, 1964-65, 66-67, 68-69, 70-71; mem. Clinton Police and Fire Retirement Bd., 1972—. Chmn. Clinton County chpt. Nat. Found., 1939-59; pres. Clinton Jr. Achievement Bd., 1969-71. Named Woman of the Year, Clinton, Ia., 1955; recipient Order of the Rose, Beta Sigma Phi, 1956. Mem. Clinton Bus. and Profl. Women's Club (past pres.), C. of C., Daus. of Isabella, Am. Legion Aux., AMVETS Aux. (pres. Ia. 1949-50, nat. pres., 1952-53, nat. parliamentarian, 1959—), Beta Sigma Phi. Roman Catholic. Home: 547 6th Av S Clinton IA 52732 Office: Jacobsen Bldg Clinton IA 52732

GORDON, EDITH MIRIAM, soprano, tchr.; b. Canton, O., July 11, 1924; d. Harry and Sarah (Axelrod) Gordon; diploma (Margaret McGill scholar), Juilliard Sch. Music, 1948; m. Louis M. Ainsberg, May 30, 1964; children—Mark Sherman, Sharon Ainsberg. Soloist, Tanglewood and Paris Opera Ballet's prodn. of Milhaud's Salade, 1948; leading role in Menotti's The Telephone and The Medium on Broadway also nat. tour, 1949-50, CBS-TV Omnibus, 1952; soloist Little Orch. Soc. in world premiere of Babar, The Elephant, 1954-61; leading soprano Goldovsky Opera Theatre in Barber of Seville, 1956; lead soprano Chautauqua Opera, 1961; soloist Cleve. Symphony, 1959-61, Boston Symphony, 1961, City Symphony of N.Y., 1964, Bronx Arts Ensemble Orch., 1974-75; tchr. voice Riverdale Sch. of Music, 1964—; concert tour in Israel, 1964; appeared at Hudson River Mus., Yonkers; Carnegie Hall recital, 1974. Mem. selection panel Bronx Council on Arts, 1974-75. Recipient Alice M. Ditson award Juilliard Sch. Music. Recorded Mozart's, Impresario for Mercury Records; rec. artist Tikva Records. Mem. N.Y. Singing Tchrs. Assn. Home: 4525 Henry Hudson Pkwy Riverdale NY 10471

GORDON, ELIZABETH WHITNEY BUFFUM (MRS. EDWARD GORDON), club woman; b. Pitts.; d. Frederick Delano and Helen (Kerruish) Buffum; A.B., Vassar Coll.; m. John Erwin Beaumont II, June 20, 1940 (div. 1954); children—John Erwin III, Peter Whitney; m. 2d, Theodore Valtses, Dec. 3, 1955 (div. 1967). Mem. adv. bd. Am. Real Property Fedn., 1955-57, Surety Trust Co., Wakefield, Mass., 1963-64. Bd. dirs. Lucy Jackson chpt. D.A.R., 1959-65, mem. Old State House chpt.; bd. dirs. Melrose chpt. A.R.C., 1960-64, YMCA, 1961-65. Vice pres. Mass. Women's Republican Club, 1961-64. Mem. Buffum Family Assn. (asst. historian 1959-63), Miami Jr. League, New Eng. Hist. and Geneal. Soc., Bostonian Soc., Nat. Security Council. Clubs: Vassar (Miami), Surf. Address: PO Box 6156 Surfside FL 33154 also Miami Beach FL

GORDON, ETHEL MAE (MRS. MAXIE SYLVESTER GORDON), educator; b. Antreville, S.C., Nov. 16, 1911; d. Robert Oliver and Olivia Beatrice (Smith) McAdams; A.B., Benedict Coll., 1939; M.Ed., Temple U., 1955; postgrad. Mich. State U., 1966, Harvard, 1969; m. Maxie Sylvester Gordon, June 6, 1940; children—Maxie Sylvester, Thomas Asbury. Pub. sch. tchr., Anderson and Anderson County, S.C., 1934-39, 40-42; asst. librarian Benedict Coll., Columbia, S.C., 1943-44, bookstore mgr., 1947-53, asso. prof. edn., elementary tchr.-trainer, 1955—. Tchr. of missions Summer Religious Insts., 1962-73; historian women's aux. Nat. Bapt. Conv., 1966-73; assns. tchr. Nat. Sunday Sch., 1967-73, Bapt. Tng. Union Congress, 1966-73. Recipient plaques Woman's Aux. Nat. Bapt. Conv. U.S.A., 1971, S.C. Assn. Ministers Wives, 1973. Mem. Internat. Reading Assn., N.A.A.C.P., N.E.A., Nat. Assn. Coll. Women, Assn. Tchr. Educators, League Women Voters, Council on Human Relations, Sigma Gamma Rho. Mem. Order Eastern Star. Home: 2221 Marguerette St Columbia SC 29204

GORDON, EVELYN WALKER (MRS. REUBEN J. GORDON), statistician; b. Washington, May 1, 1918; d. Lawrence Eugene and Bertha (Beckman) Walker; B.A., U. Md., 1962, M.A., 1963; Ph.D., Am. U., 1969; m. Reuben J. Gordon, July 1, 1939; children—Judith (Mrs. Robert L. Denningham), Peter A. Instr. sociology U. Md., College Park, 1963-67, research asst. USPHS grantee Dental Health Project, 1964-66; research asso. Met. Washington Council of Govts., 1967-68; pub. health adviser Health Services Adminstrn., Washington, 1968-70, asst. chief, consumer survey div., 1970-71; supervisory survey statistician Hosp. Discharge Survey, Dept. Health, Edn. and Welfare, Rockville, Md., 1971-73, survey statistician Consumer Statistics Survey Staff, FDA, 1973—. Recipient award Dept. Housing and Urban Devel., 1969. Mem. Am., D.C. sociol. assns., D.C. Pub. Health Assn., Assn. for Consumer Research, Phi Beta Kappa, Phi Kappa Phi, Alpha Kappa Delta, Psi Chi. Home: 6109 Lombard St Cheverly MD 20785 Office: 5600 Fishers Lane Rockville MD 20852

GORDON, FLORENCE LARUE, entertainer; b. Plainfield, N.J., Feb. 4, 1942; d. James and Sara (Minnick) LaRue; A.A. in Elementary Edn., Los Angeles City Coll., 1965; B.A. in Elementary Edn., Cal. State Coll. at Los Angeles, 1967; m. Marcus M. Gordon, Jr., Apr. 23, 1969. Original mem. of 5th Dimension singing group, 1966—; rec. artist Bell Rec. Corp. Named Miss Grand Talent in Miss Bronze Cal. Pageant, 1964, Miss Val Verde, 1965. Home: 13577 D'Este Dr Pacific Palisades CA 90272 Office: 1022 N Palm St Los Angeles CA 90049

GORDON, GUANETTA STEWART (MRS. LYNELL F. GORDON), writer, poet; b. Kansas City, Mo.; d. Samuel Lewis and Minnie Anna (Brown) Stewart; ed. Baker U., 1922-24, U. Kan., 1945-46; m. Lynell F. Gordon; children—Stewart Lynell, Krista Sharon (Mrs. Morris). Radio dramatist sta. KMBC, Kansas City, Mo., 1927-28; radio script writer, dramatist, Brownsville, Tex., sta., 1929-30; lectr., book reviewer, Kansas City, Mo. area, 1934-40; free lance writer, 1936—; author: Songs of the Wind, 1953; Under the Rainbow Arch, 1965; Petals From the Moon, 1971; Shadow Within the Flame, 1973; also poetry various mags. Recipient feature writing awards Nat. League Am. Pen Women, 1st place, 1954, 2d place, 1954, 3d place, 1956, spl. award for quantity of good articles submitted to 1956 contest; named Kan. Poet of Year, Midwest Fedn. Chaparrals, 1966, 2d award Poetry Soc. Va., 1966, 2d award Kan. Authors Club, 1970, many other awards in prose and poetry. Mem. Nat. League Am. Pen Women (pres. Alexander br. 1956-58, nat. 1st v.p. 1970-72), Am. Poetry League, D.A.R., Poetry Soc. Va., World Poetry Soc. (distinguished service citation 1970), Ariz., Phoenix (pres. 1973) poetry socs., Poetry Soc. Am., Midwest Fedn. Chaparral Poets, Delta Delta Delta. Address: 12238 Riviera Dr Sun City AZ 85351

GORDON, HELEN LEE, ednl. cons.; b. Chgo., Dec. 8, 1912; d. Louis and Rose (Ganetzkin) Appelman; B.A. in Edn., U. Chgo., 1935; M.A. in Psychology, U. Minn., 1949; M.A. in Spl. Edn. and Mental Retardation, U. Denver; m. William Gordon, Jan. 5, 1935; children—Irene Linda, Lawrence Edward, Lee David. Head tchr., dir.

pre-schs. Jewish Community Center, Denver, 1949-53; day camp dir. Jewish Community Center, Portland, Ore., 1953-56; head tchr., dir. Jewish Community Center Pre-Sch., Portland, 1963-67; Headstart and day care coordinator Portland Met. Steering Com., 1967-70; cons. to program devel. coordinator, also to exec. dir. Met. Area Community Coordinated Child Care Council, Portland, 1970—. Mem. bd. Nat. Assn. Retarded Children, 1962-68, chmn. com. child care services, 1967-71; mem. bd. Day Care and Child Devel. Council Am., 1970—; 1st chmn. Ore. Assn. Edn. Young Children, 1963. Recipient Rosemary Dybwad Internat. award in mental retardation, 1968; Kelly Low Labor award, 1970; Woman of Achievement award Ore. Jour., 1971; Portland State U. Day Care Center changed name to Helen L. Gordon Child Devel. Program, 1972. Mem. Am. Assn. Mental Deficiency, Council Exceptional Children, N.E.A., Nat. Assn. Edn. Young Children, Child Welfare League, Nat. Assn. Community Devel., Am. Civil Liberties Union, Common Cause, Nat. Council Jewish Women, P.T.A., Women's Internat. League Peace and Freedom, Another Mother for Peace. Democrat. Home: 5022 SE 45th St Portland OR 97206

GORDON, JANET HILL, lawyer; b. N.Y.C., Jan. 11, 1915; d. James P. and Florine P. (Hall) Hill; B.F.A., Syracuse U., 1935; LL.B. magna cum laude, Bklyn. Law Sch., 1940; m. William J. Gordon, May 1, 1942; 1 dau., Gail Hill. County atty. Chenango County, 1944-46; formerly mem. firm Gordon & Hill. Mem. N.Y. State Assembly, 1946-58, N.Y. State Senate, 1958-62; commr. counciliation 6th Jud. Dist. N.Y. 1967-73. Trustee Chenango Supreme Ct. Library, Norwich, N.Y., 1964-74. Vice chmn. county Rep. Party, 1940-42, state committeewoman, 1942-46; vice chmn. com. on marriage and family counseling Family Law Sect., Am. Bar Assn.; del. N.Y. State Constl. Conv., 1967; N.Y. State del. to White House Conf. on Children, 1970. Mem. N.Y. State, Am., Chenango County bar assns., Bus. and Profl. Women, Am. Legion Aux., V.F.W. Aux., D.A.R., Nat. Order Women Legislators, Plymouth, Chenango County granges, Phi Delta Delta, Gamma Phi Beta, Delta Kappa Gamma. Episcopalian. Mem. Order Eastern Star. Home: Woodchuck Hill Farm Norwich NY 13815 Office: 23 N Broad St Norwich NY 13815

GORDON, JOAN LOIS HONKALA (MRS. JAMES R. GORDON), broadcasting exec.; b. Painesville, O., Jan. 29, 1935; d. M.R. and Betty (Sutch) Honkala; B.A., Bowling Green State U., 1957; B.S. in Edn., Ohio State U., 1959; m. James R. Gordon, Aug. 17, 1957; children—Kevin, Melissa. Asst. cataloger Elyria (O.) Pub. Library, 1957-58; newspaper columnist The Star, newspaper, Columbus, 1958-59; pub. relations asst. Swan Dry Cleaners, Columbus, 1958; tchr. English and journalism Bowling Green High Sch., 1959-61; editorial asst., publs. office Bowling Green State U., 1961-62, proofreader, publs. office, 1962-67; radio-TV editor Sentinel-Tribune, Bowling Green, 1966-72, county editor, 1969-72; dir. pub. information and devel. WBGU-TV, Bowling Green, 1972—. Instr. journalism Bowling Green State U., 1969. Publicity chmn. Wood County Christmas Seal Campaign, 1968-69; chmn. publicity and advt. Miss Bowling Green Pageant, 1969-72; chmn. publicity Wheeled Meals, 1971-73; leader Brownie Scouts, 1971-73; service unit dir. Bowling Green Girl Scouts, 1973-74; pres. Wood County Easter Seal Soc., 1973-74. Bd. dirs., chmn. pub. relations com. Maumee Valley council Girl Scouts, 1964-69. Recipient chpt. degree Future Farmers Am., 1972. Mem. Am. Assn. U. Women (br. pres. 1969-71), Women in Communications, Ohio Newspaperwomen's Assn., Alpha Phi. Methodist (sec. edn. commn. 1969-72). Club: Toledo Press. Home: 1446 Conneaut Av Bowling Green OH 43402 Office: Bowling Green State U Bowling Green OH 43403

GORDON, JULIA WEBER, educator; b. Athenia, N.J., Dec. 29, 1911; d. John and Pearl Weber; B.A., N.J. Coll. for Women, 1933; M.A., Tchrs. Coll. Columbia, 1940; Ed.D., U. Md., 1952; L.H.D. (hon.), Rutgers U., 1966; m. Philip Gordon, Nov. 24, 1954. Tchr. pub. schs. Warren County, N.J., 1933-40, rural supr., 1940-48; asst. prof. edn. U. Md., 1949-51; cons. child study groups in Tex., La., Md., N.J., 1949-51; cons. child and youth study N.J. Dept. Edn., 1951-57, dir. Office Child and Youth Study, 1957-68; prof., founder, dir. Center for Human Devel., Fairleigh Dickinson U., Rutherford, N.J., 1968-71; ednl. writer and cons., 1971—. Recipient award N.J. Assn. Sch. Psychologists, 1970; Distinguished Achievement award Fairleigh Dickinson U., 1971; inducted into Douglass Soc. for Women of Achievement, 1973. Fellow Inst. Child Study of U. Md.; mem. N.J. Assn. Supervision and Curriculum Devel. (past pres.), Nat. (life), N.J. edn. assns., Nat. Assn. Supervision and Curriculum Devel., Humanistic Psychology Assn., Assn. for Childhood Edn. Internat., Psychosynthesis Research Found., Tri State Council Family Life, Am. Ednl. Research Assn., Phi Beta Kappa. Author: My Country School Diary, 1946, 70; also mag. articles. Home: 117 Crestview Dr Princeton NJ 08540

GORDON, LEAH SHANKS (MRS. JOHN GORDON), journalist; b. Sharon, Pa., May 16, 1934; d. A. Martin and Mildred Jacoby (Freedman) Shanks; B.A., Bryn Mawr Coll., 1956; m. John Gordon, July 30, 1961. With Doubleday & Co., N.Y.C., 1956-58, Engring.-News Records mag., N.Y.C., 1958-60; gen. assignment researcher-reporter Time mag., N.Y.C., 1960-64, art researcher-reporter, 1964-68, asst. chief researchers and reporters, 1968-73, researcher reporters sr. staff, 1973—. Partner Leah & John Gordon Gallery, N.Y.C., 1965—. Freelance writer N.Y. Times, 1970—, Natural History mag., 1972—, N.Y. Mag., Art News, 1973—, Smithsonian, 1974—. Home: 313 W 57th St New York City NY 10019 Office: Time Mag c/o Time Inc Rockefeller Center New York City NY 10020

GORDON, LINDA CAROL, advt. agy. exec.; b. Coral Gables, Fla., Apr. 24, 1949; d. Arnold and Estelle (Berke) Gordon; student Miami Dade Community Coll., 1967-72, U. Miami, 1972-. With Creative Dirs., Inc., Coral Gables, Fla., 1969—, media dir., 1970—. Advt. cons. Third Eye Prodns., Coral Gables, 1972—. Mem. Young Democratic Club Dade County. Mem. Advt. Fedn. Greater Miami. Clubs: Ad II Miami (Fla.). Home: 498 NW 165th St Rd North Miami FL 33169 Office: 262 Almeria Av Coral Gables FL 33134

GORDON, LOIS GOLDFEIN (MRS. ALAN LEE GORDON), educator; b. Englewood, N.J., Nov. 13, 1938; d. Irving David and Betty (Davis) Goldfein; B.A. (Nat. Merit supplementary scholar, Barbour scholar), U. Mich., 1960; postgrad, Columbia, 1960-61; M.A., U. Wis., 1962, Ph.D. (Dissertation Completion fellow), 1966; m. Alan Lee Gordon, Nov. 13, 1961; 1 son, Robert Michael. Teaching asst. U. Wis., 1962-64; lectr. Coll. City N.Y., 1964-66; asst. prof. U. Mo., Kansas City, 1966-68; asso. prof. English, Fairleigh Dickinson U., Teaneck, N.J., 1968—. Cons. U. Mo. Press, 1968-69. Research grantee, U. Mo., 1968. Mem. Internat. Bach Soc., Modern Lang. Assn. Jewish religion. Author: Stratagems to Uncover Nakedness: The Dramas of Harold Pinter, 1969. Asst. editor Lit. and Psychology, 1968-71. Contbr. articles to profl. jours. Home: 300 Central Park W New York City NY 10024 Office: Dept English Fairleigh Dickinson U Teaneck NJ 07666

GORDON, MATHILDE WEINSTEIN (MRS. MAX GORDON), psychotherapist, educator; b. Lemburg, Poland, July 1, 1907; d. Joseph and Anna (Chidekel) Weinstein; brought to U.S., 1907; naturalized, 1916; B.A., Washington Square Coll., N.Y. U., 1947; M.A., Columbia U., 1965; m. Max Gordon, Sept. 15, 1930; children—David Michael, Nicholas Karl, Patricia Vivian. Mem. staff Psychiat. Inst., Columbia Sch. Social Work, N.Y.C., 1943-72; asst. prof. Pace U., N.Y.C., 1966-72, adj. asso. prof. psychology, 1972—. Lectr. Taft High Sch., Bronx, N.Y., 1963-66, Tchr's. Coll., Columbia U., N.Y.C., 1965; mem. staff Community Guidance Service, N.Y.C., 1969—; pvt. practice psychotherapy, 1966—. Mem. N.Y. Assn. Marriage and Family Counselors (rec. sec. 1968—), Am. Psychol. Assn., Am. Assn. U. Profs. Home: 270 Ft Washington Av New York City NY 10032 Office: 265 Central Park W New York City NY 10024

GORDON, MILDRED, author; b. Eureka, Kan., July 24, 1912; d. Hanson W. and Rosamond (Kaiser) Nixon; B.A., U. Ariz., 1935; m. Gordon Gordon, Nov. 10, 1932. Corr., UP, Tucson, 1935-36; editor Arizona mag., Tucson, 1936-37; freelance mag. writer, 1938-42; author with husband, Encino, Cal., 1950—; books 19 novels including Undercover Cat, The Tumult and the Joy, Talking Bug, Power Play, The Informant; also filmscripts Experiment in Terror, That Darn Cat. Recipient Edgar Allen Poe award for Talking Bug, Mystery Writers Am. Mem. Writers Guild. Home: 4431 Petit Av Encino CA 91316

GORDON, MILDRED HARRIET GROSS (MRS. IVAN H. GORDON), hosp. exec.; b. Phila., Mar. 13, 1934; d. Nathan and Kate (Segal) Gross; student U. Pa., 1952-56; B.S., Kutztown (Pa.) State Coll., 1960; M.S. (Falk Found. fellow), Med. Coll. Pa., 1970, Ph.D. in Psychiatry (fellow), 1972; m. Ivan H. Gordon, June 13, 1954; 1 dau., Radene Lara. Tchr. sci. pub. schs., 1961-66; with Family Guidance Center, 1966-70; dir. dept. psychiatry Mental Health Treatment Center, Reading Hosp., West Reading, 1972—. Clin. instr. dept. psychiatry Med. Coll. Pa., Phila., 1972—; mem. Pa. Gov.'s Council on Drug and Alcohol Abuse, 1972—. Bd. dirs. Confront, 1971-73, Council on Chem. Abuse, 1971-73. Mem. Am. Psychol. Assn. Home: 1850 Oak Lane Reading PA 19604 Office: Reading Hospital K Bldg West Reading PA 19602

GORDON, MYRA, organic chemist; b. Mt. Vernon, N.Y., Dec. 12, 1939; d. David M. and Grace S. (Aronson) Gordon; A.B., Mt. Holyoke Coll., 1960; Ph.D., U. Pitts., 1965; asst. prof. chemistry dept. Tulane U., New Orleans, 1966-69; sr. sci. officer chemistry dept. U. Western Ont., London, Ont., Can., 1972-74; chemist Isotopes div. Merck, Sharp & Dohme Can., London, 1974—. Mem. Sigma Xi. Office: 1209 Richmond St Box 606 London ON N6A 3L7 Canada

GORDON, PATRICIA BETTY ASTRID (MRS. ALBAN GORDON), playwright; b. London, Eng., Mar. 20, 1909; d. Louis and Rebecca Nina (Shapira) Meyer; student Cheltenham Ladies' Coll., 1924-27; m. Alban Gordon, Jan. 23, 1937. Justice of the Peace, Dorking, Surrey, Eng., 1961—. Mem. Dorking Artists Assn., Sussex Artists Assn., N-Weald Group. Playwright: Snow Cakes, 1959, Magic Carpet, 1966, Brief Suspicion, 1960, Thought for the Morrow, 1957, Beggar my Neighbor, 1957, Three's Company, 1958, Mid Autumn Madness, 1959, Sauce for the Gander, 1959, The Wonderful Day, 1961, Tangled Web, 1966. Home: The Studio Mynthurst Leigh near Reigate Surrey England

GORDON, ROSE MARY JOHNSON, psychologist; b. Savannah, Ga., Apr. 11, 1934; d. Ezra and Rosemary Lucy (Williams) Johnson; B.A., Fisk U., 1956, M.A. (Danforth fellow), 1957; postgrad. Roosevelt U., 1965-66, Northeastern U., Chgo., 1966-67. Psychol. intern pediatrics dept. Meharry Med. Coll., 1955-56; instr. psychology Fisk U., 1957-60; cons. Easter Seal Soc., Nashville, 1959-60; instr. Meharry Sch. Nursing, 1958-60; psychologist Chgo. Bd. Edn., 1961—. Mem. Jr. Governing Bd. Chgo. Symphony Orch., 1970—. Mem. Am. Psychol. Assn., Phi Beta Kappa (pres. Delta chpt. 1959-60), Beta Kappa Chi, Alpha Kappa Alpha. Conglist. (mem. choir 1962—). Office: 228 N La Salle St Room 724 Chicago IL 60601

GORDON, ROSE (MRS. ALEXANDER GORDON), city ofcl.; m. Alexander Gordon; 3 children. Former mem. Dade Status of Women Commn.; former chmn. Miami Planning and Zoning Bd.; mem. Miami City Commn., 1971—. Home: 1890 S Bayshore Dr Miami FL 33133

GORDON, SHIRLEY MARION FILBERT (MRS. GEORGE E. GORDON), occupational therapist; b. St. Louis, July 7, 1924; d. Louis Felix and Erna Louise (Thalinger) Filbert; B.S. in Occupational Therapy, Washington U., St. Louis, 1947; m. George E. Gordon, June 15, 1946; children—Pamela (Mrs. Roger Steenbergen), Donna. Graphic artist Audio-Visual Library, Stephens Coll., Columbia, Mo., 1947-49; tchr. Hansel and Gretel Nursery Sch., Glendale, Mo., 1953-56; occupational therapist Old Folks Home, Kirkwood, Mo., 1962—, Blind Girls Home, Kirkwood, Mo., 1971—. Cons. occupational therapy Edgewater Nursing Home, St. Louis, 1966-67. Mem. Am., Mo. (v.p. 1966-67) occupational therapy assns., Alpha Chi Omega. Presbyn. Mem. Order Eastern Star. Co-author, editor: Manual on Occupational Therapy in Nursing Homes, 1969. Home: 952 Cleveland Av Kirkwood MO 63122 Office: 711 S Kirkwood Rd Kirkwood MO 63122

GORDON, SOPHIE REITER, drug co. exec.; b. Pitts., May 11, 1899; d. Cadmus Zaccheus and Katherine (Acheson) Gordon; A.B. cum laude, Smith Coll., 1922; M.A., Brown U., 1924. Grad. asst. in biology Woman's Coll., Brown U., 1922-23; asst. serology lab. Columbia Coll. Phys. and Surg., 1925; dir. clin. lab., N.Y.C., 1925-48; established Gordon Wheat Germ Co., N.Y.C., 1939, Gordon Pharms. div., 1946. Mem. N.Y. Acad. Sci., Bus. and Profl. Women's Group (pres. 1946-48), Sigma Delta Epsilon (treas. 1968-71). Episcopalian. Club: Altrusa (N.Y.C. rec. sec. 1954-56), bd. dirs. 1964-66, 68-70, editor newsletter 1959-69). Author article, monographs for med. profession. Research related to treatment of vascular disease, particularly in smokers. Patentee in field. Home and office: 61 Scarborough Pl Holiday City at Berkeley Toms River NJ 08753

GORDON, SUSAN JOAN, gastroenterologist; b. Atlantic City, Aug. 14, 1942; d. Maurice Bear and Muriel (Hoffman) Gordon; student Goucher Coll., 1959-62; M.D., Jefferson Med. Coll., 1966. Intern in internal medicine Hahnemann Med. Coll. Hosp., Phila., 1966-67; resident in internal medicine Thomas Jefferson U. Hosp., Phila., 1967-69, fellow in gastroenterology, 1969-71; practice medicine specializing in gastroenterology, Phila., 1971—; instr. medicine Thomas Jefferson U., Phila., 1971-73, asst. prof. medicine, 1973—; coordinator jr. student teaching program in medicine, 1971—. Recipient William J. Potter prize Jefferson Med. Coll., 1966. Diplomate Am. Bd. Internal Medicine, also diplomate in gastroenterology. Mem. Alpha Omega Alpha. Home: 2201 Pennsylvania Av Philadelphia PA 19130 Office: 1025 Walnut St Philadelphia PA 19107

GORDON, TANIA ELAINE (MRS. CHARLES GORDON, JR.), occupational therapist; b. Lincoln, Ill., Dec. 5, 1937; d. Charles Loren and Frances Evelyn (Renner) Stringer; Assoc. Arts and Sci., Lincoln Jr. Coll., 1958; B.S., U. Ill., 1961; m. Charles Gordon, Jr., Nov. 24, 1960; children—Charles Michael, Laura Lynn, Jon Brian. Occupational therapist Lincoln State Sch., home for retarded, 1961-62, Bird S. Coler Chronic Disease Hosp. and Home, Welfare Island, N.Y., 1964-65; cons. occupational therapist Am. Health and Rehab. Inst., Convalescent Home, Plantation, Fla., 1972—, Alden House, nursing facility, Ft. Lauderdale, Fla., 1973-74. Mem. Am. Assn. Occupational Therapists, Realtors Assn. Fla., Ft. Lauderdale Bd. Realtors. Home: 7061 SW 18th St Plantation FL 33317 Office: 3260 N State Rd 7 Ft Lauderdale FL 33313

GORDON, VINETA EMELDA HINDS (MRS. VINCENT HOOVER ADAMA GORDON), educator; b. Jamaica, West Indies, Nov. 29, 1929; d. Edgar Balentine and Muriel Belmadore (Reid) Hinds; B.A., Morris Brown Coll., 1959; M.A., N.Y. U., 1961; m. Vincent Hoover Adama Gordon, Nov. 25, 1962; children—Jacqueline Mae, Anna Marie, Vincent Hoover Adams. Came to U.S., 1962, naturalized, 1966. Chmn. dept. English Paul Quinn Coll., Waco, Tex., 1961-62; tchr. English, Christiansted High Sch., St. Croix, V.I., 1962-66, 69-70; coordinator of reading all jr. high schs., St. Croix, 1967-68; instr. English, Coll. of V.I., St. Croix, 1971—; tchr. English St. Croix Central High Sch., 1971—. 1st v.p. Council of Chs., St. Croix, 1970-72; sec. Gov.'s Com. of Social Affairs, St. Croix, 1970-71. Chmn. bd. edn. Caribbean Community Sch., 1969-71. Recipient Outstanding Tchrs. award Paul Quinn Coll., 1961-62, V.I. Dept. Edn., 1969-70. Mem. Internat. Reading Assn., Nat. Soc. for the Study of Edn., Nat. Council Tchrs. English, Women's Missionary Soc., Ch. Women United St. Croix (pres.), Bus. and Profl. Womens Club, C. of C. (mem. civic searchlight com.). Methodist. Author of Jamaica's theme song words and music God Bless Our Native Land, 1962. Home: Grove Place St Croix VI Office: Box 156 Christiansted St Croix VI 00820

GORE, DOROTHY JEAN, educator; b. Oklahoma City, May 1, 1926; d. Robert Wallace and Leta Pauline (Killian) Gore; B.S., Principia Coll., 1948; M.S., U. Ill., 1952; Ph.D., U. Wis., 1963. Asst. geologist Ill. State Geol. Survey, Urbana, 1948-52; asst. prof. geology Principia Coll., Elsah, Ill., 1952-65; asso. prof. earth scis. So. Ill. U., Edwardsville, 1965—. Pres., Elsah Hills Corp., 1963—. Leader, Girl Scouts Am., Elsah, 1958—. Mem. Nat. Assn. Geology Tchrs., Mineralogical Soc. Am., Ill. Acad. Scis., Geol. Soc. Am., Wilderness Soc., Sierra Club (mem. exec. com. Piasa Palisades, Ill. 1972—). Sigma Xi, Delta Kappa Gamma. Home: 5 Elsah Hills Dr Rural Route 1 Elsah IL 62028 Office: Box 45 Earth Sciences Dept Southern Illinois University Edwardsville IL 62025

GORE, LOUISE CANTRELL (MRS. JOHN LENOX GORE), poet, exec.; b. Banks County, Ga., May 21, 1917; d. Charlie Bond and Hattie Ethel (Hood) Cantrell; m. John Lenox Gore, Oct. 27, 1944; children—Donald, Barbara (Mrs. Bible), Ethelyn (Mrs. Stephan Holland), Stephen, Gregory. Speaker on poetry in various schs; judge poetry contests. Mem. Alaska Centennial Poetry Commn., Anchorage, 1967. Mem. Internat. Platform Assn., World Poetry Soc. Intercontinental, Avalon Poetry Soc., Creative Writing Group. Author: Soul of the Bearded Seal (poems), 1967. Poetry represented in spl. centennial anthology Alaskan poets One Hundred Years of Alaska Poetry, 1967; poetry included in anthology poems on L.P. record Alaska (Alaska Centennial Com.), 1967. Home: 102 W Maryland Phoenix AZ 85013

GOREAU, LAURRAINE ROBERTA, editor, composer, playwright; b. New Orleans, Sept. 27, 1918; d. Nelson G. and Anna (Wilson) Goreau; student La. State U., 1938-39, U. N.C., 1940. Censor supr., instr., editor Office of Censorship, 1941-43; writer newspaper and radio publicity, recruitment rep. Navy Dept., 1943-44; telegraph editor Daily Advertiser, Lafayette, La., 1944-45, mng. editor, chief editorial writer, 1945-52; writer CBS, Hollywood, Cal., 1952-53; mng. editor, chief editorial writer Superior (Wis.) Evening Telegram, 1953-56; TV producer, moderator Press Conf., Good News; dir. Sage of Park Point, Arrowhead TV Network, Duluth, Minn., 1953-54; writer, dir., moderator Top News, KDAL-TV, Duluth, 1954-55; women's editor New Orleans Item, 1956-58, New Orleans States-Item, 1958—; writer semi-weekly column c'est la vie, 1957—; free-lance writer newspapers, mags., U.S., Eng., Australia. Mem. women's guild New Orleans Opera House Assn., 1957-58. Bd. dirs. Jr. Philharmonic Assn., 1952-58. Mem. Nat., La. fedns. press women, Le Petit Theatre de Vieux Carre. Presbyn. Clubs: Nat. Press, New Orleans Press. Composer: Shrimp Boy, 1948; When You Close Your Eyes, 1949; Whambrain, Mary Ann, Could I, 1951; I Cry Inside, 1952; Borrowed Bliss, 1952; Voodoo, 1953; Ain't It So, 1953; New Orleans Street Cries, 1953; Show Me a City Like New Orleans, 1962; I've Got to Walk, Lord—Hold My Hand, 1963; Whenever You're Lonely, 1965; Never You Mind, 1965; Walk With Him, Children, 1965. Author: Next Time Blue, 1943, Dark Bayou, 1940, Museum Piece, 1952 (plays); Donahue for Governor (dramatic monologues), 1956. Home: 538 St Peter St New Orleans LA Office: 601 North St New Orleans LA

GORECKI, SISTER MARY TIBURTIA, librarian; b. Balt., Nov. 25, 1921; s. Peter and Wanda (Chotkowski) G.; B.S., Mt. St. Joseph, 1953; M.S. in L.S., Marywood Coll., 1964; postgrad. Appalachian State U., 1970. Tchr., Corpus Christi Sch., Buffalo, 1941-46, St. Vincent Sch., 1946-56, St. Sebastian Sch., Dearborn, 1956-60, St. Mary Sch., Hamburg, N.Y., 1960-66; librarian Hilbert Coll., Hamburg, N.Y., 1966—. Recipient President's medal Hilbert Coll., 1974. Mem. Am., Cath. (pres. Western N.Y. 1966-70), N.Y. library assns., Western N.Y. Cath. Librarians Conf., Western N.Y. Ednl. Communications Council (bd. mem. 1971—), N.Y. State Assn. Jr. Colls. Home: 5286 S Park Av Hamburg NY 14075

GORELICK, MOLLY CHERNOW (MRS. LEON GORELICK), educator, psychologist; b. N.Y.C., Sept. 17, 1920; d. Morris and Jean (Zabraun) Chernow; A.B., U. Cal. at Los Angeles, 1948, M.A., 1955, Ed.D., 1962; m. Leon Gorelick, Apr. 12, 1941; children—Walter, Peter. Tchr., counselor Los Angeles City Bd. Edn., 1948-61; tchr. tng., counselor U. Cal. at Los Angeles, 1957-63, instr., 1961-63, supr. psychology clinic sch., 1963; chief guidance services Exceptional Children's Found., Los Angeles, 1963-70; prof. Cal. State U., Northridge, Cal., 1970—; project dir. U.S. Dept. Health, Edn. and Welfare grant, 1971—. Vis. asst. prof. edn. U. So. Cal., 1964-66; research project dir. U.S. Dept. Health, Edn. and Welfare, Vocational Rehab. Adminstrn., Los Angeles, 1964-66. Owner, dir. Hi-Ho Day Camp, 1950-57; cons. Riverside County Schs., 1962-70. Mem. adv. bd. U. Cal. at Los Angeles Sch. Social Welfare, Cal. State Regional Diagnostic Center at Children's Hosp., Los Angeles, Mirman Sch. for Gifted Children, Cal. Ednl. Center, Friendship Day Camp. Mem. Am., Western psychol. assns., Am. Assn. on Mental Deficiency (dir.), N.E.A., Council for Exceptional Children, Nat. Rehab. Assn., Phi Beta Kappa, Pi Lambda Theta, Pi Gamma Mu. Co-author: Rescue series, 5 vols., 1967-68. Contbr. articles to profl. jours. Home: 600 N June St Los Angeles CA 90004 Office: California State University Northridge CA 01324

GORENCE, PATRICIA JOSETTA, journalist, educator; b. Sheboygan, Wis., Mar. 16, 1943; d. Joseph and Antonia (Marinsheck) Gorence; B.A., Marquette U., 1965; M.A., U. Wis., 1968; m. John Michael Bach, July 11, 1969; children—Amy Jane, Mara Jo. Gen. assignment, legislative reporter So. Courier, Montgomery, Ala., 1967; gen. assignment reporter Waukesha (Wis.) Freeman, 1968-69; research coordinator Alverno Coll. Research Center Women, Milw., part-time, 1970-71; researcher, writer Council on Urban Life, Milw., 1970-73; instr. polit. sci. Carroll Coll., Waukesha, Wis., 1973—. Instr. continuing edn. dept. Marquette U., Milw., 1973; asso. bd. mem. Southeastern Wis. Housing Corp., Burlington, 1972—. Mem.

women's rights com. Am. Civil Liberties Union, Milw., 1971—; sec., treas. Housing Action Coalition, Milw., 1971-74; mem. Wis. state adv. com. Civil Rights Comm., Chgo., 1972—. Recipient Wis. legislative scholarship U. Wis., 1961-62. Mem. Women in Communications, Marquette U. Coll. Journalism Alumni Bd. (chmn. communications com. 1973), Midwest Polit. Sci. Assn. Home: 2754 N Hackett Av Milwaukee WI 53211

GORENSTEIN, SHIRLEY SLOTKIN (MRS. SAMUEL GORENSTEIN), educator; b. N.Y.C., Mar. 4, 1928; d. Harry and Mary (Pfeffer) Slotkin; B.A., Queens Coll., 1949; M.A., Columbia, 1953, Ph.D. (Am. Assn. U. Women fellow), 1963; m. Samuel Gorenstein, July 3, 1948; children—Ethan, Gabriel. Lectr., Queens Coll., Flushing, N.Y., 1962; faculty Columbia, N.Y.C., 1963—, asst. prof. dept. anthropology, 1971-74, asso. prof., 1974—. NSF grantee, 1965. Fellow Am. Anthrop. Assn. (chmn. com. on status of women 1971-72), A.A.A.S., Latin Am. Studies Assn. Author: Introduction to Archaeology, 1965; Tepexi El Viejo, 1973; Not Forever on Earth, 1974. Home: 29 Longview Dr Scarsdale NY 10583 Office: Dept Anthropology Columbia New York City NY 10027

GORHAM, THELMA REA THURSTON educator, writer; b. Kansas City, Mo., Feb. 21, 1913; d. Frank and Bertha (Smith) Thurston; A.B., U. Minn., 1935, M.A., 1951, postgrad. 1959, 68—; m. Richard R. Gorham, Jr., Aug. 30, 1941 (div. Apr. 1960); 1 son, Darryl Theodore. Bur. news editor, reporter, feature writer Call, Kansas City, Mo., 1935; reporter St. Louis Call, 1941-42; asst. dir. pub. relations Hampton (Va.) Inst., 1941-42; editor Apache Sentinel, U.S. Army, Ft. Huachuca, Ariz., 1942-44; news editor, feature writer Los Angeles Sentinel, 1945; accredited UN corr., San Francisco, 1945; mng. editor pro-tem Crisis, N.Y.C., 1946; news editor East Bay office San Francisco Sun-Reporter, 1947-51; exec. editor Step-Up, 1953-54; asst. prof. journalism Lincoln U., Jefferson City, Mo., 1954-55; mng. editor Okla. Eagle, Tulsa, 1954-55; asst. prof. English, journalism So. U., Baton Rouge, 1955-56; exec. editor Black Dispatch, Oklahoma City, 1960-62; tchr. Central High Sch., Kansas City, Mo., 1961-63; dir. pub. relations, asso. prof. journalism Fla. A. and M. U., Tallahassee, 1963-66, asso. prof., 1966-68, asso. prof. journalism and mass communication, faculty adviser student publs., 1971—, also head div. journalism and mass communication; cons. research, curriculum devel. Twin Cities Opportunities and Industrialization Center, Mpls., 1968-71, exec. dir., 1968-71; instr. communication U. Minn., 1968-71. Dir. Gorham Enterprises, Oakland, Cal., 1946-52. Publicist, writer Alameda County Health and TB Assn., Oakland, San Francisco, N.A.A.C.P., Am. Friends Service Com., San Francisco, Fannie Walls Children's Home and Day Nursery, Oakland, all 1945-47; group work program dir. St. Louis County br. YWCA Clayton, Mo., 1952; editor Bldg. A Better State, Mo. Assn. Social Welfare, 1951-52; asst. to chmn. St. Louis com. on gt. books St. Louis Pub. Library, 1953-54; pres. Creston Hills Sch. P.T.A., Oklahoma City, 1956-58; research editor U.S. Negro World, 1962—; v.p., program chmn. Tallahassee Human Relations Council, 1966-67, exec. com., 1965—; mem. speakers bur. San Francisco Council for Civic Unity, 1946-47; mem. exec. bd. Friends Homer G. Phillips Hosp., St. Louis, 1951-53; bd. adminstrn. Kansas City Yates br. YWCA, 1936-41; mem. exec. com. Tulsa Urban League, 1954-55; chmn. exec. bd. Friends Fla. A. and M. U. Hosp., Tallahassee, 1965—; mem. Gov.'s Task Force on Equal Ednl. Opportunity, 1970—; mem. citizen's adv. com. to adminstrn. Mpls. Pub. Schs.; bd. dirs. Urban Coalition Mpls.; bd. dirs. Tallahasse chpt. Am. Civil Liberties Union, Tallahassee Urban League Guild. Ford Found. fellow, 1959-60. Recipient Media citation for integration editorial series Okla. Eagle, Nat. Conf. Christians and Jews, 1954; N. Tulsa Community Service citation plaque, 1954; Golden Key Appreciation award Twin Cities Opportunities Indslzn. Centers, Mpls., 1970; Outstanding Service award Mpls. Urban League, 1971. Mem. Am. Bus. Women's Assn., Minn. Press Women, Am. Assn. U. Women (chmn. publicity Tallahassee br.), Women in Communications, Sigma Epsilon Sigma, Alpha Kappa Alpha, Pi Gamma Mu. Mem. Baha'i Faith (mem. U.S. nat. interracial service com., pub. information service com. 1960-62, nat. pub. information com. 1971-73, coordinator proclamation com., teaching com. N. Fla. dist.). Author: Meeting The Challenge of Change, 1963. Home: 3509 Sunnyside Dr Tallahassee FL 32304

GORMAN, DOROTHY LA RUE GREGG (MRS. JACK W. GORMAN), artist; b. Burnside, Pa., Apr. 4, 1917; d. Kay Anson and Grace Sarah (Wetzel) Gregg; student U. Pa., 1967-73; m. Jack Williams Gorman, Feb. 10, 1938; children—Jack Williams, Kay LeRoy. One-man shows at Indiana (Pa.) Art Assn., Flood Mus., Wash.; exhibited in group shows at Indiana (Pa.) U., Lever House, N.Y.C.; represented in permanent collections at Johnstown (Pa.) City Hall, Cambria County Hosp., Ebensburg Pub. Library, Colver Hosp., Johnstown Flood Museum, Miners Hosp., Spangler, Pa., also pvt. collections; tchr. pvt. classes art, 1968—; owner, tchr. classes in drawing, pastel, oil, printmaking and ceramics North Light Studio, Ebensburg, Pa., 1972—. Fellow Am. Artists Profl. League (founder, rec. sec.); mem. Allied Artists Johnstown (dir. 1966-68), Pitts. Print Group, Indiana Art Assn., Allied Artists Johnstown, Cambria County Hist. Soc. D.A.R. Home and studio: RD 1 Box 29 Ebensburg PA 15931

GORMAN, ETHEL MILLER, health services adminstr.; b. Birmingham, Ala., Oct. 20, 1911; d. Beauregard and Ethel Therese (Jungell) Miller; student Howard Coll., 1928-29; A.B. cum laude, Rollins Coll., 1932; postgrad. Washington U., St. Louis, 1937, Tulane U., 1959; m. Thomas C. Gorman, Apr. 11, 1939; children—Beauregard, Terry Carrol (Mrs. Raymond J. Salassi, Jr.). Caseworker Social Security Commn., St. Joseph, Mo., 1937; social work interviewer WPA, Birmingham (Ala.) Welfare Dept., 1938; child welfare worker Children's Aid Soc., Birmingham, 1953-54; probation officer Jefferson County Juvenile and Domestic Relations Ct., Birmingham, 1954-59; information specialist Jefferson County Assn. for Mental Health, Brimingham, 1959-70, exec. dir., 1970—, editor Newsletter, 1959-70. Sec. adv. bd. Lee McBride White Sch., 1963-64; acting exec. Jefferson, Blount, St. Clair Mental Health Authority, 1969-70, sec., 1969-73. Bd. dirs. Planned Parenthood Ala., 1969-71, Crisis Center Jefferson County, 1970. Recipient First prize Playwriting Fla. Allied Arts Contest, 1932, Novel prize Ala. Writers Conclave, 1953. Mem. Ala. Hist. Assn., Jefferson County Child Devel. Council (v.p. 1973), Sierra Club (mem. exec. com. 1973), Mental Health Assn. (dir. staff council 1964-70, editor nat. newsletter 1964-70), Zonta, Phi Mu. Unitarian-Universalist (pres. ch. 1964-66). Author: Red Acres, 1953. Contbr. articles and stories to popular mags. Home: 409 St Charles St Birmingham AL 35209 Office: 3600 S 8th Av Birmingham AL 35222

GORMAN, SISTER M(ARY) ADELE FRANCIS, educator; b. Balt.; d. John Divin and Marguerite (Meyer) Gorman; student Johns Hopkins, summers 1940-42; B.A. cum laude, Coll. Notre Dame of Md., 1941; M.A., Villanova U., 1955; Ph.D., U. Notre Dame, 1962; postgrad. Goucher Coll., summer 1956, Loyola U. (Balt.), 1957-58, Mt. St. Mary (Emmitsburg, Md.), 1944-45, U. Denver, 1971. Labor statistics clk. Am. Oil Co., Shell Oil Co., Standard Oil Co., Balt., 1932-34, Fisher Body Corp., Gen. Motors Co., Balt., 1934-38; tchr. Towson Catholic High Sch., Balt., 1941-58, 62-64, Mt. St. Mary Coll., Emmitsburg extension, 1957-58; Villanova U. Extension, Aston, Pa., 1961-62; asst. prof. Our Lady of Angels Coll., Glen Riddle, 1964-65, asso. prof. history and polit. sci., 1965-72, prof., 1972—, dean of women, 1965-66, chmn. div. history and social scis., 1966—. Hostess, U.S.O., Balt., 1941-43; mem. Cardinal's Human Relations Com., Phila.; sec. Pa. Council for Social Studies; mem. steering com. Sisters Com., Cardinal's Human Relations Com. and Sisters Involved in CEF, also exec. com., trustee; mem. govt. com. CICU; archivist Sisters St. Francis, Phila.; mem. lecture bur. Franciscan Sisters' Fedn. Named as Outstanding Tchr., Kanzanjian Assn.; George Washington Honor medal Freedoms Found., 1973, 74. Mem. Am. (women's com., pres.), Pa. Catholic hist. assns., Am. Soc. Ch. History, Polit. Sci. Acad., Am. Polit. Sci. Assn., Middle States (exec. bd.), Nat., Pa. (sec., v.p.) councils for social studies, Am. Acad. Polit. and Social Scis., Nat. Cath., Balt. Cath. (sec. 1956-57, publicity dir. 1955-58) forensic leagues, Ch. Women United, Pa. Hist. Soc., Kappa Gamma Pi (ecumenical program planning com.). Republican. Contbr. articles to profl. jours. Address: Our Lady of Angels Coll Aston PA 19014

GORME, EYDIE, singer; b. N.Y.C., 1932; m. Steven Lawrence, 1958. Export mgr. theatrical equipment co. to 1952; 1st profl. engagement as vocalist Tommy Tucker's band; various night club engagements; mem. Steve Allen's TV troupe Tonight Show, 1954, co-star summer replacement show, 1958; appeared Copacobana, N.Y.C., 1957; recs. include Too Close For Comfort, Mama TeachMe to Dance.*

GORMICAN, ANNETTE THERESE, educator; b. Fond du Lac, Wis., Apr. 26, 1924; d. James Thomas (dec.) and Marion (Meyer) (dec.) Gormican; B.S., Coll. St. Catherine, 1946; M.S., U. Ia., 1947, Ph.D. (Mary Swartz Rose fellow), 1965. Asst. prof. U. Minn., St. Paul, 1952-60; ednl. dir. dietetics U. Wis. Med. Center, Madison, 1961-62; asst. prof. U. Neb. Coll. Medicine, Omaha, 1965-66; faculty, dir. dietetic internship U. Wis., Madison, 1967—, asso. prof. dept. nutritional sci., 1971—. Recipient Dietary Products Found. award Am. Hosp. Supply Corp., 1969. Fellow Am. Inst. Chemists; mem. Am. Dietetic Assn., N.Y. Acad. Sci., A.A.A.S., Am. Pub. Health Assn., Am. Acad. Polit. and Social Sci., Phi Beta Kappa, Sigma Xi. Roman Catholic. Author: Controlling Diabetes with Diet, 1971. Home: 3124 Harvey St Madison WI 53705

GORN, JANICE LEONORA JACOBY (MRS. LION ALBERT GORN), educator; b. N.Y.C., Mar. 23, 1915; d. Morris and Emilie (Joseph) Jacoby; B.F.A., N.Y.U., 1938; M.A. 1954, Ph.D., 1963; m. Lion Albert Gorn, Jan. 18, 1940 (dec. Nov. 1943). Med. technician Dr. Nathaniel Uhr and Dr. Alfred G. Selinger, internists, N.Y.C., 1939-42; asst. registrar Grad. Sch. Social Work, Columbia U., N.Y.C., 1942-55; asst. to dir., chief editor Council on Social Work Edn., N.Y.C., 1955-58; teaching fellow N.Y.U., 1958-59; asst. prof. history and philosophy of edn. Paterson State Coll. (N.J.), 1959-61; asst. prof., asso. prof. edn. N.Y.U. Sch. Edn., N.Y.C., 1961-69, prof. interdisciplinary studies, 1969—. Cons. Caldwell (N.J.) Coll., Morristown (N.J.) Boys Benedictine Secondary Sch., R.I. Coll., others. Trustee, William Hodson Community Center, N.Y.C., 1959-60. Mem. Am. Hist. Assn., Council on Social Work Edn., Philosophy of Edn. Soc., Smithsonian Assos., History of Sci. Soc. Nat. Soc. for Study of Edn., History Edn. Soc., Am. Assn. U. Profs. Author: Style Guide for the Writing of Scholarly Papers, Masters' Theses and Doctoral Dissertations, 1973. Contbr. articles to profl. jours. and books. Home: 60 E 12th St New York City NY 10003

GORNEY, SONDRA FRIEDA KATTLOVE (MRS. JAY GORNEY), communications exec.; b. LeCompte, La., Jan. 19, 1918; d. David and Tania (Reichenbach) Kattlove; student Drake U., 1935-36; B.A., U. Cal. at Los Angeles, 1945; postgrad. Chgo. U., 1946-47, N.Y. U., 1948-49, Columbia, 1960-61; m. Jay Gorney, Jan. 27, 1943; children--Karen Lynn (Mrs. Kenneth Golden), Daniel Frederick. Asso. editor PIC Mag., N.Y.C., 1941, Los Angeles, 1942; co-chmn. mus. play dept. Dramatic Workshop, New Sch., N.Y.C., 1948-53, Am. Theatre Wing, N.Y.C., 1953-57; dir. mag. services Girl Scouts U.S.A., N.Y.C., 1957-60; dir. pub. relations Girls Clubs Am., Inc., N.Y.C., 1960-62, Inst. Internat. Edn., N.Y.C., 1962-68; publicity coordinator Nat. Multiple Sclerosis Soc., N.Y.C., 1968; exec. dir. Information Center on the Mature Woman, N.Y.C., 1968—. Mem. Pub. Relations Soc. Am. (pres. N.Y.C. chpt. 1974—, chmn. nat. edn. com., 1972-73), Women Execs. in Pub. Relations, N.Y. Women in Communications (matrix award 1973), Am. Women in Radio and TV (chmn. ednl. found. com. N.Y.C. chpt. 1968). Co-author: After Forty: How Women Can Achieve Fulfillment, 1973. Home: 270 W End Av New York City NY 10023 Office: 515 Madison Av New York City NY 10022

GORSKI, MARILYN NEUHAUS (MRS. LEO GORSKI), educator; b. Chgo., Apr. 7, 1933; d. Harold Walter and Pearl Lillian (Mudge) Neuhaus; B.S., DePaul U., 1955; M.A., Roosevelt U., 1964; m. Leo Gorski, June 22, 1957. Dir. women's recreation Jewish Peoples Ins., Chgo., 1952-55; faculty Mundelein Coll., Chgo., 1955—, asst. prof. phys. edn., 1967—. Co-pres., owner Midwest Burglar Alarm Co., Chgo., 1971—. Mem. Rosemont Community Voters League, 1973-74; active A.R.C. Recipient award A.R.C., 1973. Mem. Am. Assn. U. Profs., Laramie Av. Bus. Assn. Aux. (pres. 1972-73). Home: 9614 W Higgins Rd Rosemont IL 60018 Office: 2916 N Oak Park St Chicago IL 60634

GORSLINE, DORIS EILEEN SULLENBERGER, editor; b. Piqua, O., July 11, 1928; d. Louis O. and Bessie Elizabeth (Williams) Sullenberger; student Sinclair Community Coll., 1963-69, U. Dayton, 1965, 74, Coll. Dayton Art Inst., 1973; m. Don Lee Gorsline, Apr. 10, 1953; 1 son, David Lee. Women's editor Piqua Daily Call, 1957-60; staff writer Dayton (O.) Daily News, 1960-65; publicity asst. Sinclair Community Coll., Dayton, 1965-69; publs. editor Miami Valley Hosp., Dayton, 1969—. Mem. Women's Polit. Caucus, 1972—. Recipient awards for writing Ohio Newspaper Women's Assn., 1961-64; editing award Ohio Assn. Bus. Communicators, 1972. Mem. Women in Communications (chpt. pres. 1968), Internat. Assn. Bus. Communicators, Pub. Relations for Health S.W. Ohio, Miami Valley Hosp. Soc. Home: 219 Aberdeen Av Dayton OH 45419 Office: 1 Wyoming St Dayton OH 45409

GOSNELL, ELIZABETH TUCKER (MRS. WILLIAM B. GOSNELL), poet, editor, broadcaster; b. Little Rock, Apr. 21, 1921; d. Henry Hennegin and Katharine (Duke) Tucker; B.A., Duke, 1942; m. William Burton Gosnell, Sept. 24, 1943; 1 dau., Katherine Amanda Wells. Author: The Poet Who Was A Painter Of Souls, 1969; Silk And Silence, 1971; editor poetry column Advance Monticellonian, McGehee Times, 1966—; hostess After Glow program sta. KHBM, 1971—. Instr. creative writing Art Camp, S.E. Ark. Arts and Sci. Center, 1970; leader South and West Poetry Workshop, Pine Bluff, 1969. Troop leader Ark. Post council Girl Scouts U.S.A., 1953-62, pres. council, 1960-62, bd. dirs., 1958-60; founder Holiday Sch., Drew County. Recipient Thanks badge Girl Scouts U.S.A., 1962. Fellow Internat. Poetry Soc. (founding); mem. Internat. Biog. Assn., Drew County Hist. Soc. (dir.), Poetry Soc. Am., World Poetry Soc. Intercontinental (dir.), United Poets Laureate Internat., Poets Roundtable Ark., Ky., Ill. poetry socs., South and West Lit. Assn. (sec. 1967—), Sorosis, Delta Delta Delta. Episcopalian (vestry 1970—, treas. 1969, mem. Diocesan Liturgical Commn. 1971-72). Home: 803 N Slemons St Monticello AR 71655

GOSS, AMY DANIELS (MRS. GALEN LEWIS GOSS), ednl. adminstr.; b. Scranton, Pa., Oct. 10, 1942; d. Lloyd George and Ruth Miriam (Schumaker) Daniels; B.S., Bloomsburg State Coll., 1964; M.Ed., Ohio U., 1967; postgrad. Syracuse U., 1971-72; m. Galen Lewis Goss, Nov. 18, 1972. Tchr. Abington Heights Schs., Clarks Summit, Pa., 1964-66, 69-70; head resident adviser Mich. State U., East Lansing, 1967-69; asst. dean women Shippensburg (Pa.) State Coll., 1970-73; coordinator student activities No. Va. Community Coll., Alexandria, 1973—. Mem. Nat. Assn. Student Personnel Adminstrs., Nat. Assn. Women Deans, Adminstrs. and Counselors, Am. Personnel and Guidance Assn., Am. Coll. Personnel Assn., Am. Assn. Higher Edn. Home: 5750 Drake Court Alexandria VA 22311 Office: 3001 North Beauregard Alexandria VA 22311

GOSS, DOROTHY KNAPP (MRS. JONATHAN CARVER GOSS), librarian; b. Canton, O., Dec. 2, 1919; d. Ernest Walter and Maude Agnes (Copella) Knapp; student Alfred U., 1938-39, McMaster U., 1939-40, U. Toronto, 1940-41, Masters Sch., Boston, 1941-42; m. Jonathan Carver Goss, Sept. 18, 1943; 1 son, Jonathan Carver. Supr. tech. information services Ramo-Wooldridge div., TRW Systems, Inc., 1954-61; sr. lit. analyst Aerospace Corp., 1961-64; adminstrv. librarian NASA, 1964-67; librarian Rand Corp., 1968-70; head librarian Hughes Helicopters div. Summa Corp., Culver City, Cal., 1970—. Lectr., U. Cal. at Los Angeles, 1967. Mem. Spl. Libraries Assn., Am. Soc. Information Sci. Home: 12421 Rochedale Lane Los Angeles CA 90040 Office: Centinela and Teale Sts Culver City CA 90230

GOSS, MARY ELSTON (MRS. HENRY GOSS), educator, social worker; b. Tuscaloosa, Ala., June 11, 1910; d. William and Electa (Jones) Elston; A.B., U. Chgo., 1943, M.A., 1952; student Columbia, summers 1926, 27, 29, Ala. State Tchrs. Coll., 1924, 25, 33; m. Harry A Doss, July 17, 1934 (dec. 1936); 1 son, Harry A.; m. 2d, Henry Goss, Nov. 27, 1948. Tchr. Birmingham pub. schs., 1926-34, 36-41; med. social worker Jefferson County Bd. of Health, Birmingham, Ala., 1941-44, A.R.C., Chgo., 1944-46, VA Regional Office, Chgo., Hines Hosp., Cook County Hosp., 1946-54; asst. prof. med. social work Coll. of Medicine, U. Ill., 1954—, also field instr. Jane Addams Grad. Sch. Social Work. Mem. Acad. Certified Social Workers, Nat. Assn. Social Workers, Council on Social Work Edn., Am. Assn. U. Women. Democrat. African Methodist Episcopal. Club: Chicago Dentists Wives. Contbr. profl. jours. Home: 8238 E Eberhart Av Chicago IL 60619

GOSSELIN, RACHEL YVONNE NEPVEU (MRS. GEORGE GOSSELIN), educator; b. Allenstown, N.H., Feb. 12, 1912; d. Agenor and Laura Louise (Verville) Nepveu; R.N., St. Mary's Hosp. Sch. Nursing, Lewiston, Me., 1937; Registered Med. Librarian, St. Vincent de Paul Hosp., Sherbrooke, Can., 1944; B.S. in Nursing Edn., U. Ottawa, 1956; m. George Gosselin, Apr. 18, 1960; children—Louise, Richard, Robert. Supr., St. Mary's Hosp., Lewiston, 1937-38; instr., dir. St. Anthony Hosp. Sch. Nursing, Le Pas, Man., Can., 1938-54; dir. St. Louis Hosp. Sch. Nursing, Berlin, N.H., 1954-60; instr., sec. faculty Moore Gen. Hosp., Goffstown, N.H., 1960-64; dir. health services, prof. anatomy and physiology N.H. Coll., Manchester, 1964-74. Mem. Am., N.H. nurses assns., Am., New Eng. coll. health assns., Mil. Order Purple Heart Aux. Author: Anatomy and Physiology, 1965, rev. edit., 1973; Medical Terminology, 1966. Home: 907 Hayward St Manchester NH 03103

GOSSELIN, RUTH SMITH, physician; b. Yonkers, N.Y., Aug. 15, 1913; d. Walter Everett and Grace May (Andrae) Smith; A.B., Smith Coll., 1935; M.D., U. Rochester, 1949; m. Robert Edmond Gosselin, June 26, 1948; children—Peter Gordon, Andrea Lee. Rotating intern Rochester (N.Y.) Gen. Hosp., 1949-50, resident in pathology, 1950-51; univ. physician U. Rochester, 1954-56; gen. practitioner with Lyme (N.H.) Med. Assos., 1959—; attending physician Dartmouth Health Service, 1966—; mem. clin. staff Mary Hitchcock Meml. Hosp., Hanover, N.H., 1966—. Mem. med. adv. com. Planned Parenthood, Lebanon, N.H.; trustee, mem. profl. adv. com. Community Health Services, Norwich, Vt., 1970—. Mem. Am. Acad. Family Physicians, N.H., Grafton County med. socs. Home: Elm St Norwich VT 05055 Office: Lyme Medical Associates Lyme NH 03768 also Dartmouth College Health Service Hanover NH 03755

GOSSETT, OUIDA GRIFFITH (MRS. JAMES W. GOSSETT), club woman; b. Nocona, Tex., Aug. 15; d. Marvin Grey and Louise (Stewart) Griffith; student Tex. Woman's U., 1935-37, Baylor U., 1938-41, U. Tex., 1951-53; m. James William Gossett, Apr. 3, 1944; children—James Richard, William Griffith. Head nurse Baylor U. Hosp., 1941-42. Dir. ret. citizens program Nueces Activity Center, 1965-67, Lakeside Act. Center, 1967-71; asst. supr. Parks and Recreation Dept., 1971-72; program cons. Gov.'s Com. on Aging, 1972—. Served USNR, 1942-44. Mem. Women's Aux. Tex. Dental Assn. (silver lining chmn. 1953-54, dental health council 1954-57, 3d v.p. 1957-58, state pres. 1959-60, adminstrv. com. 1962-65), Austin Heritage Soc., Adult Services Council, Tex. Recreation and Park Soc., Friends of Austin Pub. Library, Women of Univ. Presbyn. Ch., Austin Dist. Dental Aux. (pres. 1950-51), North Austin Rotary-Anns. Presbyn. Club: Westwood Country. Home: 3401 River Rd Austin TX 78703

GOSWITZ, HELEN ANN VODOPICK (MRS. FRANCIS GOSWITZ), physician; b. Milw., Apr. 29, 1931; d. John and Anna (Ribar) Vodopick; B.S., Marquette U., 1953, M.D., 1956; m. Francis Goswitz, June 2, 1956; children—Mary, Francis, Gregory. Intern U. Ia., Iowa City, 1956-57, internal medicine resident, 1957-60; post resident asst. nuclear medicine Oak Ridge (Tenn.) Inst. Nuclear Studies, 1960-61; fellow hematology, instr. medicine U. Ia., Iowa City, 1961-63; fellow hematology U. Utah, Salt Lake City, 1963-65; sr. research clinician Oak Ridge Asso. Univs., 1965—. Recipient Schering award Schering Corp., Bloomfield, N.J., 1956. Mem. A.M.A., Soc. Nuclear Medicine, Am. Soc. Hematology, Am. Cancer Soc. Contbr. articles to sci. jours. Home: 107 Berwick Dr Oak Ridge TN 37830 Office: Oak Ridge Asso Univs PO Box 117 Oak Ridge TN 37830

GOTHARD, DONITA E., educator, psychologist, educator; b. Minden, La., June 9, 1932; d. Donald Elmer and Nita (Brunt) Gothard; B.A., Northwestern State U. La., 1954, M.Ed., 1961; Ph.D., U. Ala., 1970. Tchr., Bossier (La.) Parish Schs., 1954-61, counselor, 1961-67; dir. human relations Caddo (La.) Parish Schs., 1970-71, sch. psychologist, 1971-73; asst. prof. psychology La. State U., Shreveport, 1973—. Bd. dirs. Sentry Schs., Shreveport. Mem. Am., Southwestern, La. psychol. assns., La. Tchrs. Assn., Assn. for Children with Learning Disabilities. Home: 4748 Dixie Garden Dr Shreveport LA 71105

GOTHIA, SISTER BLANCHE, media coordinator; b. Port Arthur, Tex., Oct. 27, 1930; d. Elton Joseph and Blanche (Landry) Gothia; B.A., Dominican Coll., 1960; M.L.S., Tex. Women's U., 1973. Joined Dominican Sisters, 1948; tchr. elementary, secondary schs., 1950-69; tchr. St. Anthony's Cathedral Sch., Beaumont, Tex., 1964-67, prin., 1965-67; audio-visual dir. St. Agnes Acad., Houston, 1967-69, media coordinator, 1969—. Mem. Am., Tex., Cath. (vice chmn., chmn. elect Bishop Byrne Gulf Coast unit) library assns., Assn. Ednl. Communications and Tech. (co-chmn. Tex. legislative com. 1970—),

Tex. Assn. Ednl. Tech., Am. Film Inst., Houston Film Tchrs. Assn. (dir.). Home and office: 9000 Bellaire Blvd Houston TX 77036

GOTLIB, LORRAINE, lawyer; b. Toronto, Ont., Can., May 13, 1931; B.A., U. Toronto, 1952; grad. Osgoode Hall. Admitted to Ont. bar, 1959; partner firm McMillian, Binch, Toronto. Named Queen's Counsel, 1973. Mem. Canadian Bar Assn. Mem. County of York Law Assn., Women's Law Assn. Ont., Kappa Beta Pi. Clubs: Royal Canadian Yacht, Toronto Ski, Eglinton Equestrian. Address: 20 King St W Toronto ON Canada

GOTSIS, STAVRULA PERUTSEAS (MRS. FABIAN PETER GOTSIS), physician; b. Tseria, Greece, May 20, 1924; d. Christos Eustratiou and Filanthi Gregoriou (Tavularea) Perutseas; M.D., Nat. U. Athens, 1949; m. Fabian Peter Gotsis, July 25, 1959; children—Philene, Lia. Came to U.S., 1950, naturalized, 1952. Intern, South Shore, Cook County hosps., Chgo., 1950-51; resident gen. surgery Loyola U.-Mercy Hosp., Chgo., 1951-54, plastic and reconstructive surgery U. Wis. Clinics, Madison, 1954-56; practice medicine specializing in plastic and reconstructive surgery, Chgo, 1957—; mem. staff St. Francis Hosp., Blue Island, Ill., Meml. Hosp., Harvey, Ill., St. James Hosp., Chicago Heights, Ill., Palos Community Hosp., Palos Heights, Ill. Cons. South Suburban Hosp., Hazel Crest, Ill. Mem. A.M.A., Ill. Med. Soc. Home: 9114 W 126th St Palos Park IL 60464 Office: 1255 W 127th St Chicago IL 60643

GOTT, GAIL KATHRYN SCHEERE (MRS. RUDOLPH GOTT), journalist; b. San Francisco, May 6, 1919; d. Fred Holmes and Marion (Kelley) Scheere; student Stockton Jr. Coll., 1937-40; m. Rudolph Gott, Apr. 11, 1953; 1 stepson, Rudy. Women's program dir. for radio sta. KWG, Stockton, Cal., 1945-50; reporter and feature writer Stockton Daily Evening Record, 1950-71. Hon. policewoman; mem. founding bd. Stockton Civic Theatre. Recipient citizens award Sheriff Michael N. Canlis. Mem. Salvation Army Aux. Home: 3024 Wallace Av Stockton CA 95204 Office: PO Box 900 Stockton CA 95201

GOTT, HELEN THERESA, newspaper editor; b. Jersey City, July 2, 1942; d. William E. and Cynthia (Williams) Gott; B.A., Syracuse U., 1963; M.Internat. Affairs (Whitney Found. grantee), Columbia, 1965. Summer intern Washington Post, 1964; gen. assignment reporter Kansas City (Mo.) Star, 1965-71, religion editor, 1971—. Bd. advisers Sch. Discovery. Mem. United Prayer Movement, Religion Newswriters Assn., Women in Communications. Editor The New Birth. Home: 2455 N 57th St Kansas City KS 66104 Office: Kansas City Star 1729 Grand Av Kansas City MO 64108

GOTTESMAN, ELEANOR GLUCKMAN BELL (MRS. CALLMAN GOTTESMAN), psychologist; b. Cleve., May 24, 1914; d. George and Jeannette E. (Klein) Gluckman; student Northwestern U., 1934-36; B.A. in Psychology, George Washington U., 1947, M.A. in Clin. Psychology, 1963; m. Callman Gottesman, Aug. 2, 1964; children from previous marriage—Erika Bell (Mrs. John Arthur Greenberger), Barbara Bell. Psychologist, psychotherapist D.C. Gen. Hosp., Washington, 1961-64; with Bethesda (Md.) Community Psychiat. Clinic, 1961-64; psychologist Nassau County Schs., Rockville Center, East Rockaway, Hempstead, N.Y., 1965-70; exec. psychologist Richardson, Bellows, Henry, mgmt. consultants, N.Y.C., Washington, 1970-71; psychologist Pleasantville (N.Y.) Cottage Sch., Jewish Child Care Assn., 1973—. Mem. Am. Psychol. Assn., Psi Chi. Originator body image identification test. Home: 1 W 72d St New York City NY 10023 Office: Pleasantville Cottage School Pleasantville NY 10570

GOTTFRIED, DEANNE FOSTER (MRS. SIDNEY GOTTFRIED), physician; b. Boston, Jan. 9, 1932; d. Jacob and Edythe (Robinson) Foster; B.A., Wellesley Coll., 1953; M.D., Tufts U., 1957; M.P.H., U. Cal. at Berkeley, 1964; m. Sidney Gottfried, Dec. 30, 1962; children—Jay Adam, Johannah. Intern, San Francisco Gen. Hosp., 1957-58; resident Children's Hosp., Oakland, Cal., 1958-60; USPHS fellow in infectious disease Yale Sch. Med., U. Cal. Sch. Medicine, 1960-62; postgrad. research physician U. Cal. at San Francisco, 1962-63, asst. clin. prof., 1966—; dist. health officer San Francisco Dept. Pub. Health, 1964—. Diplomate Am. Bd. Preventive Medicine. Fellow Am. Acad. Preventive Medicine; mem. A.M.A., Am., Cal. pub. health assns., Cal. Med. Assn., Cal. Acad. Preventive Medicine, San Francisco Med. Soc. Jewish religion. Office: 1301 Pierce St San Francisco CA 94115

GOTTRON, MARTHA VIRGINIA, journalist; b. Cleve., Nov. 2, 1943; d. Donald Lawrence and Helen Graham (Gaither) Gottron; B.A. in Polit. Sci., Ohio Wesleyan U., 1965. Research asst. Republican Nat. Com., 1965-67; polit. writer Congl. Quar., Washington, 1967-69, legislative writer, 1972—; information analyst Nat. Jour., 1970. Mem. Pi Sigma Alpha. Home: 1728 20th St Washington DC 20009 Office: 1414 22d St NW Washington DC 20036

GOUDGE, ELIZABETH DE BEAUCHAMP, Brit. author; b. Somerset, Eng., Apr. 24, 1900; d. Henry Leighton and Ida de Beauchamp (Collenette) Goudge; student Art. Sch. Reading (Eng.) U., 1920-22. Began as handicraft tchr., 1922; profl. writer, 1932—. Fellow Royal Soc. of Lit.; mem. P.E.N. Club. Mem. Ch. of Eng. Author: Island Magic, 1932; Middle Window, 1933; City of Bells, 1934; Pedlar's Pack, 1935; Towers in the Mist, 1936; Three Plays, 1937; Sister of the Angels, 1938; The Bird in the Tree, 1940; Smoky-House, 1940; The Golden Skylark, 1941; The Castle-on-the-Hill, 1941; The Blue Hills, 1942; Green Dolphin Street, 1944 (chosen by Lit. Guild, U.S.A.; won Metro-Goldwyn-Mayer prize); The Little White Horse (juvenile); winner Carnegie medal (Eng.); Pilgrims Inn (Lit. Guild selection); God So Loved the World; Gentian Hill; The Valley of Song (juvenile); The Heart of the Family; The Rosemary Tree, 1956; The White Witch, 1957; My God and My All, 1959; The Dean's Watch, 1960; The Scent of Water, 1963; A Book of Comfort, 1964; A Diary of Prayer, 1966; The Child From the Sea, 1970; The Lost Angel, 1971. Address: Rose Cottage Peppard Common Henley-on-Thames England

GOUGE, RUTH LOUISE, physician; b. Bristol, Tenn, Jan. 23, 1919; d. Horace E. and Lucy Adelaide (Leach) Gouge; R.N., Miami Valley Hosp. Sch. Nursing, Dayton, O., 1940; B.A., U. Denver, 1948, J.D., 1965; M.D., U. Colo., 1951. Registered nurse Miami Valley Hosp., 1940-41; intern St. Luke's Hosp., Denver, 1951-52; gen. practice medicine, Littleton, Colo., 1951-68; physician student health service, teaching faculty U. Colo., Boulder, 1968—. Served with Nurse Corps, USNR, 1943-46. Fellow Am. Coll. Legal Medicine; mem., Am., Colo. bar assns., Am. Acad. Family Physicians, Am. Med. Women's Assn., Am. Assn. Women Lawyers. Contbr. articles to profl. publs. Home: 900 Mountainview St Apt 108 Longmont CO 80501 Office: University of Colo Boulder CO 80203

GOUGE, SUSAN CORNELIA JONES (MRS. JOHN OSCAR GOUGE), microbiologist; b. Chgo., Apr. 18, 1924; d. Harry LeRoy and Gladys (Moon) Jones; student Am. U., Washington, 1942-43, La. Coll., 1944-45; B.S., George Washington U., 1948; postgrad. Georgetown U., 1966-70; m. John Oscar Gouge, Aug. 7, 1943; children—John Ronald, Richard Michael, Claudia Renee. Med. technician Children's Hosp. Research Lab., Washington, 1948-49; bacteriologist George Washington U. Research Lab., D.C. Gen. Hosp., 1950-53; med. microbiologist Walter Reed Army Inst. Research, Washington, 1953-61; research asst. Dental Research, Walter Reed Med. Center, 1961-62; microbiologist antibiotics div. FDA, 1962-63; supr. quality control John D. Copanos Co., Pharms., Balt., 1963-64; research tng. asst., infectious diseases and tropical medicine Howard U. Med. Sch., 1964-65; research asso. Georgetown U. Lab. Infectious Diseases, D.C. Gen. Hosp., 1966-69; mycologist Georgetown U. Hosp. Lab., 1969-70; microbiologist The Research Found. of The Washington Hosp. Center, 1971-73; dir. quality control Bio-Medium Corp., 1973—. Sec. to exec. bd. Bethesda Project Awareness, 1970-71; cons. lead poisoning detection testing project D.C. Office Vols. for Internat. Tech. Assistance, 1970-71, recipient medal for community service. Mem. Nat. Capital Harp Ensemble, 1941-65. Mem. Women's Suburban Democratic Club. Mem. A.A.A.S., Am. Soc. for Microbiology, Am. Assn. Clin. Chemists, Am. Astronautical Soc., Albertus Magnus Guild, Capital Bus. and Profl. Women's Club (rec. sec. 1973-74, 1st v.p. 1974—), Pi Kappa Delta. Roman Catholic. Home: 4101 Maryland Av Washington DC 20016 Office: Bio-Medium Corp 8841 Brookville Rd Silver Spring MD 20910

GOUGH, ELLEN DORIS SCHREIEGG (MRS. JOHN THOMAS GOUGH), physician; b. Thannhausen, Germany, Sept. 10, 1925; d. Hans and Margarete Agnes Maria (Schurmeyer) Schreiegg; M.D. cum laude, Ludwig-Maximillan U., Munich, Germany, 1952; m. John Thomas Gough, Apr. 7, 1958; children—Frances-Marie, Catherine Elizabeth. Came to U.S., 1956, naturalized, 1961. Intern U. Hosp., Munich, Germany, 1951-52; resident, City Hosp., Weissenhorn, City Hosp. Castrop-Rauxel, Germany, 1952-56; intern, Drs. Hosp., Seattle, 1957-58; resident Swedish Hosp., Seattle, 1958-59; practice medicine, specializing in obstetrics and gynecology; sr. research asso., dept. pharmacology U. Wash., Seattle, 1970—. Home: 6850 36th St NE Seattle WA 98115

GOUGH, JESSIE POST (MRS. HERBERT FREDERICK GOUGH), educator; b. Nakon Sri Tamaraj, Thailand, Jan. 26, 1907 (parents Am. citizens); d. Richard Walter and Mame (Stebbins) Post; B.A., Maryville Coll., 1927; M.A. in English, U. Chgo., 1928; Ed.D., U. Ga., 1965; m. Herbert Frederick Gough, June 30, 1934; children—Joan Acland (Mrs. Alexander Reed), Herbert Frederick. Tchr. English, Linden Hall, Lititz, Pa., 1930-32; tchr. Fairyland Sch., Lookout Mountain, Tenn., 1955-64; research asst. English curriculum studies center U. Ga., 1964-65; assoc. prof. elementary edn. LaGrange (Ga.) Coll., 1965-73, prof., 1973—. Prof., N.W. Ga. area tchr. edn. services, 1969-71. Mem. Walker County (Ga.) Curriculum Council, 1959-61, Walker County Ednl. Planning Bd., 1958-60. Mem. Am. Ednl. Research Assn., Nat. Soc. Study Edn., Nat. Council Social Studies, E. Tenn. Hist. Soc., Nat., Ga. edn. assns., Delta Kappa Gamma, Kappa Delta Pi. Home: 401 Ridley Av LaGrange GA 30240

GOUGH, PATRICIA MARIE, educator; b. Eagle River, Wis., Jan. 13, 1937; d. Frank C. and Eleanor Martina (Johnson) Gough; B.S., U. Wis., 1958; M.S., U. Minn., 1961, Ph.D., 1966. Research chemist Nat. Center for Disease Control, USPHS, Dept. Health, Edn. and Welfare, Atlanta, 1967-68; asst. prof. Vet. Med. Research Inst., Ia. State U., Ames, 1968-72, asso. prof., 1972—. Mem. Am. Chem. Soc., Am. Soc. for Microbiology, A.A.A.S., Wildlife Disease Assn., Sigma Xi, Omicron Nu, Phi Kappa Phi. Home: Rural Route 2 Ames IA 50010

GOULD, ALTHEA O'HANLON (MRS. LESLIE GOULD), club woman; b. N.Y.C.; d. George Theodore and Minnie (Grau) Mundorff; grad. Centenary Jr. Coll.; student Conn. Coll., Columbia; m. Leslie Gould, June 14, 1957; children by previous marriage—Elizabeth (Mrs. Thor Andersen), Mary Jane (Mrs. Charles Carson). Asst. dir. Vol. Services, Office Civilian Def., 1942-44; asst. v.p. Capital Airlines, 1959-61, dir. passenger service, 1946-59; pres. Horizon House Corp.; dir. Palmer Nat. Bank & Trust Co., Naples, Fla. Mem. nat. bd. Family Welfare Assn. of Am., 1945-47; bd. dirs. Travelers Aid Assn., Washington, 1959-62, Family Service Assn., Washington, 1952-54; pres. Presbyn. Sr. Services of N.Y., 1964-69, pres. Ft. Schuyler House Corp., 1968-72, Horizon House Naples, 1973. Mem. Nat. Inst. Social Scis., English Speaking Union. Clubs: Comedy (asso.), Cosmopolitan (N.Y.C.); Nat. Women's Democratic, Women's Advertising of Washington (hon. mem., past pres.), Am. Newspaper Women's; Royal Poinciana (Naples, Fla.). Home: 3951 Gulf Shore Blvd Naples FL 33940

GOULD, BETTY LOUISE KOONTZ, educator; b. Atwood, Ind., Mar. 3, 1935; d. Donald H. and Opal Lee (Stidham) Koontz; B.A., Simpson Coll., 1957; postgrad. U. Ia., Ia. State U., Drake U., U. No. Ia., Okla. State U.; m. James J. Gould, Dec. 22, 1957 (div. Oct. 1970); 1 son, John Prescott. Tchr., Moravia (Ia.) Community Schs., 1963-64, 66-67; tchr. English and speech, coach forensics Lake City (Ia.) Community Schs., Westview High Sch., 1967—. Vol. worker Pied Piper Day Care, Indianola, Ia., 1969—; dir. live nativity scene, Lake City, 1970-72. Mem. Speech Communication Assn., Central States Speech Assn., Ia., Lake City ednl. assns., Blackfriars, Alpha Kappa Delta, Phi Beta Phi. Home: 204 W Jefferson St Lake City IA 51449 Office: Westview High Sch Lake City IA 51449

GOULD, JANE AUERBACH SCHWARTZ (MRS. JAY GOULD), coll. adminstr.; b. Pleasantville, N.Y., Mar. 25, 1918; d. Irvin H. and Helen (Hays) Auerbach; student New Coll., Columbia U., 1935-37; B.A., Barnard Coll., 1940; M.A., Tchrs. Coll., Columbia U., 1970; m. Bernard M. Schwartz, Aug. 4, 1942 (dec. Jan. 1967); children—Nancy, David; m. 2d, Jay M. Gould, Oct. 17, 1969. Asst. dir. Alumnae Adv. Center, N.Y.C., 1953-65; dir. placement and career planning Barnard Coll., N.Y.C., 1965-72, dir. Womens Center, 1972—, in charge Community Service Workshops, 1966-68. Mem. exec. com. Barnard Coll. Women's Center, 1971-72. Bd. dirs. Seven Coll. Vocational workshops, 1962-66. Mem. Eastern Coll. Personnel Officers, Women's Equity Action League, Am. Personnel and Guidance Assn., Nat. Assn. Women Deans and Counselors. Contbr. articles to ednl. jours. Home: 302 W 86th St New York City NY 10024

GOULD, KATHLEEN SIMPSON (MRS. VINCENT W. GOULD, JR.), ins. and real estate exec.; b. Ellenville, N.Y., Feb. 12, 1914; d. Richard Gardiner and Nellie (Merritt) Simpson; student Stetson U., 1932; m. Vincent W. Gould, Jr., Dec. 26, 1931 (dec. Apr. 1947) children—Vincent W. III, Robert Simpson, William Howard. Sec.-treas. V.W. Gould Agy., Inc., DeLand, Fla., 1947—; pres. Athens Realty Co., DeLand, Fla., 1947—. Pres. DeLand and West Volusia Bd. Realtors, Inc., 1971. Bd. dirs. Community Mental Health Center; v.p. Volusia County Guidance Center. Recipient Woman Realtor of the Year award, Fla. Assn. Realtors, 1969. Mem. Fla. Assn. Realtors (corp. sec. 1969—, dist. v.p. 1964), Nat. Assn. Real Estate Bds. (gov. womens council 1969-70, regional v.p. women's council 1971, exec. com. 1974). Home: 108 Oakland Dr DeLand FL 32720 Office: PO Box 165 DeLand FL 32720

GOULD, MARY DALRYMPLE (MRS. CHARLES P. GOULD), hosp. adminstr.; b. Pasadena, Cal., Aug. 28, 1911; d. Glenford and Marguerite (Vedder) Dalrymple; B.E., U. Cal. at Los Angeles, 1933; m. Charles Perry Gould, Sept. 1, 1934; children—Thomas Charles, Mary (Mrs. Robert K. Lancefield), Ann Frank (Mrs. Lynn Thomason). Psychiat. social worker Los Angeles County, Cal., 1933-41; owner, adminstr. Charter Oak Psychiat. Hosp., Covina, Cal., 1941-63, adminstr., 1963—. Mem. Gov.'s Adv. Com. on Children and Youth, 1960-73, chmn., 1967-73; treas. Nat. Council of State Coms. on Children and Youth, 1971-74. Mem. Nat. Assn. Pvt. Psychiat. Hosps. (Western regional chmn. 1961-71), Am., Cal. (psychiat. hosp. com. 1956—, sec. 1956-62) hosp. assns., Assn. Western Hosps., Phi Omega Pi (local pres. 1932-33). Home: 1200 Old Mill Rd San Marino CA 91108 Office: 19757 E Covina Blvd Covina CA 91722

GOULD, MILLICENT (MRS. LEON N. GOULD), interior designer; b. Mt. Vernon, N.Y.; d. Harry and Anna Matilda (Kagan) Uslan; pvt. study art and interior design; m. Leon N. Gould, Nov. 24, 1938; children—Richard, Alan. Pres., Millicent Gould Interiors, Inc., Scarsdale, N.Y., 1950—. Mem. Am. Inst. Interior Designers, Soroptimists. Home: 27 Leatherstocking Lane Scarsdale NY 10583

GOULDEN, ANNE MCDOWELL (MRS. JAMES JEPSON GOULDEN), govt. ofcl.; b. Waynesville, N.C., Jan. 1, 1910; d. Charles Harper and Isabella Wadley (Josselyn) McDowell; B.A., U. N.C., 1931; m. James Jepson Goulden, June 20, 1931; 1 dau., Linda Wightman. With U.S. AEC, Oak Ridge, 1961—, publs. editor Tech. Information Center, 1961—. Mayor, City of Norris, Tenn., 1970-72; mem. city council Norris, 1970—. Leader, Girl Scouts U.S.A., Knoxville, Norris, 1933-50. Mem. Am. Woman's Club of Iran (pres. 1954-55). Home: 13 E Circle Rd Norris TN 37828

GOULDER, CAROLJEAN HEMPSTEAD (MRS. LLOYD LYNTON GOULDER, JR.), sch. psychologist; b. Houston, Minn., Apr. 9, 1933; d. Orson George and Jean (Lischer) Hempstead; B.S., Hamline U., 1956; M.A., R.I. Coll., 1972; m. Lloyd Lynton Goulder, Jr., May 26, 1956; children—Jean, David, Ann. Dept. head, instr. Highsmith Hosp. Sch. Nursing, Fayetteville, N.C., 1956-57; instr. Deaconess Hosp. Sch. Nursing, Boston, 1957-58; dir. sch. psychol. services Burrillville Pub. Schs., Harrisville, R.I., 1972—. Cons., Mary C. Wheeler Sch., Providence, 1970-73. Mem. Am. (asso.), Mass. (asso.) psychol. assns., Council Exceptional Children, Children with Learning Disabilities. Conglist. Home: 85 Old Farm Lane Attleboro MA 02703 Office: Burrillville Schools Harrisville RI 02830

GOULDER, GRACE (MRS. ROBERT J. IZANT), author; b. Cleve., Mar. 27, 1893; d. Charles and Marian (Clements) Goulder; B.A., Vassar Coll., 1914; postgrad. Western Reserve U., 1936; m. Robert J. Izant, Oct. 18, 1919; children—Robert J., Jonathan G. (dec.), Mary (Mrs. Eugene D. White). Mem. editorial staff Cleve. Plain Dealer, 1914-17; mem. nat. bd. YMCA, N.Y.C., 1917-18; publicity writer Internat. YWCA, France, also Germany, Eng., 1918-19; writer, photographer Plain Dealer Sunday Mag., Cleve., 1942-69. Mem. Ohio Am. Revolution Bicentennial Adv. Commn., Columbus, 1970. Trustee Hudson Heritage Assn. Western Res. Early Settlers, Ohioana Library, Columbus, Western Reserve Hist. Soc. Recipient Ohio Gov.'s award, 1949, Prize for Lit. Kulas Found. Women's City Club, Cleve., 1965. Mem. Soc. of Friends. Author: This is Ohio, 1953, rev. edit., 1965; Ohio Scenes and Citizens, 1964; John D. Rockefeller, the Cleveland Years, 1973. Address: 250 College St Hudson OH 44236

GOWDEY, MARILYN PATRICIA, educator; b. Burlington, Vt., Oct. 6, 1944; d. Philip Edwin and Barbara (West) Gowdey; student Middlebury Coll., 1962-64; A.B., Cornell U., 1966; M.A. in English and Edn., U. Chgo., 1969. Tchr. English and performing arts Central YMCA High Sch., Chgo., 1967—, co-chmn. English dept., 1968-72, chmn., 1974—, co-developer humanities program in fine and performing arts, 1971. Mem. Phi Beta Kappa, Phi Kappa Phi. Home: 415 W Rosalyn Pl Chicago IL 60614 Office: Central YMCA High Sch 19 S LaSalle St Chicago IL 60603

GOYAK, ELIZABETH FAIRBAIRN (MRS. EDWARD A. GOYAK), pub. relations exec.; b. Chgo., 1922; d. Lewis and Berenice (Bowers) Fairbairn; B.Ed., So. Ill. U., 1943; postgrad. Northwestern U., 1943-44; m. Edward A. Goyak. Formerly reporter Chgo. Tribune, INS, Chgo. Jour. Commerce; account exec., account supr. A. Cushman & Assos., Gardner, Jones & Co., until 1960; with Daniel J. Edelman, Inc., Chgo., 1960—, v.p., 1968—. Pres. Matteson (Ill.) Pub. Library Bd., 1971-74. Mem. Pub. Relations Soc. Am. (accredited), Nat. Home Fashions League (v.p. Chgo. chpt. 1967, 70-74). Club: Publicity (dir., sec. 1958-61, 71-74) (Chgo.). Home: 21310 Butterfield Pkwy Matteson IL 60443 Office: 221 N LaSalle St Chicago IL 60601

GRABER, DORIS A. (MRS. T.M. GRABER), polit. scientist, editor, author; b. St. Louis, Nov. 11, 1923; d. E. Appel and Martha (Insel); A.B., Washington U., St. Louis, 1940; M.A., 1941; Ph.D., Columbia, 1947; m. T. M. Graber, June 15, 1941; children—Lee Winston, Thomas Woodrow, Jack Douglas, Jim Murray, Susan Doris. Feature writer St. Louis County Observer, University City Tribune, St. Louis, 1937-41; civilian dir. U.S. Army Ednl. Reconditioning Program, Camp Maxey, Tex., 1942-43; editor U.S. Supreme Ct. Digest, Legal Periodical Digest, Commerce Clearing House, Chgo., 1945-46; lectr. polit. sci. Northwestern U., U. Chgo., N. Park Coll., 1947-52; research asso. Center for Study of Am. Fgn. and Mil. Policy, U. Chgo., 1950-71; text book editor Harper & Row, Evanston, Ill., 1956-63; asso. prof. polit. sci. U. Ill., 1963-70, prof. polit. sci., 1970—. Mem. Am. Assn. Pub. Opinion Research, Midwest Polit. Sci. Assn. (pres. 1972-73), London Inst. World Affairs, Am., Internat. polit. scis. assns., Am. Soc. Internat. Law, Am. Acad. Polit. and Social Sci., League Women Voters, Pi Sigma Alpha, Phi Beta Kappa. Author: The Development of the Law of Belligerent Occupation, 1949; Crisis Diplomacy; A History of U.S. Intervention Policies and Practices, 1959; Public Opinion, The President, and Foreign Policy, 1968; Verbal Behavior and Politics, 1974. Contbr. articles to profl. jours. Home: 2895 Sheridan Pl Evanston IL 60201

GRABER, JEAN WEBER (MRS. RICHARD REX GRABER), ornithologist; b. Cedar Point, Kan., Sept. 12, 1924; d. Charles W. and Bertha Christina (Graves) Weber; B.S., Washburn Municipal U., 1945; M.A., U. Mich., 1949; Ph.D. (NSF fellow), U. Okla., 1958; m. Richard Rex Graber, Nov. 25, 1945; Med. technologist Lattimore Labs., Topeka, 1945-48, Stormont-Vail Hosp., 1952; research asso. animal sci. dept. U. Ill., Urbana, 1960-68, research asst. prof., 1968-72; wildlife specialist Ill. Natural History Survey, Urbana, 1972—. Mem. Am. Ornithol. Union, Southwestern Assn. Naturalists, Sigma Xi, Phi Sigma. Contbr. articles to profl. jours. Home: 109 W Franklin St Urbana IL 61801 Office: Natural Resources Bldg Urbana IL 61801

GRABOWSKI, CLAIRE JUSTINE HESS, artist, poet; b. San Antonio, May 26, 1932; d. Leonard Mark and Mary Antoinette (Rodesney) Hess; B.A., Fontbonne Coll., St. Louis, 1954; student San Antonio Art Inst., 1961-62, Art League Houston, 1966-70, 13-10 Studio, Houston, 1968-71; m. Paul Richard Grabowski, Sept. 1, 1956; children—Jean Elizabeth, Paul Richard II, Jon Daniel. One woman shows Brooks AFB, 1964, Ring Library, Houston, 1969, Framemakers Shop, 1972, Cinima Gallery, Louisville, 1975; numerous gallery exhibits in San Antonio, Houston and Louisville; lectr., poetry reader. Mem. internat. com. Centro Studi e Scambi Internat., Rome, 1971. Girl Scout art badge tchr. Recipient awards River Art Group competition, 1967, Nat. League Am. Pen Women, 1970-72; also awards poetry. Poetry Soc. Tex. Fellow Internat. Poetry Soc.; mem. Acad. Internat. Leonardo da Vinci, Nat. League Am. Pen

Women, Poetry Soc. Tex., Ky. Poetry Soc., Women Artists of Am. West, Southwest Watercolor Soc. Author: Thursday's Child, works included in anthologies. Address: 7117 Greengate Ct Louisville KY 40222

GRABOWSKI, SISTER MARY BONAVENTURE, ednl. adminstr.; b. Balt., Nov. 19, 1918; d. Ignatius and Veronica (Ryciak) Grabowski; B.A., Villanova U., 1953; M.A., Fordham U., 1959. Joined Congregation Sisters of St. Felix of Cantalice, 1935; elementary tchr. parochial schs., N.J., Pa., Del., 1935-38; tchr. math. and sci. St. Anthony High Sch., Jersey City, St. Joseph High Sch., Camden, N.J., 1948-67; asso. prof. math. Felician Coll., Lodi, N.J., 1967—, registrar, 1968—. Mem. constns. commn. Congregations, 1967—, sec., 1970-74. Active in various civic, community projects. Mem. Nat. Council Tchrs. Math., Assn. Collegiate Registrars and Adminstrn. Officers. Democrat. Address: Felician Sisters Convent 260 S Main St Lodi NJ 07644

GRACE, PRINCESS OF MONACO (GRACE PATRICIA KELLY), b. Phila., Nov. 12, 1929; d. John Brendan and Margaret (Majer) Kelly; student Acad. of Assumption, Stevens Sch. (both Phila.), Am. Acad. Dramatic Arts, N.Y.C.; m. Rainier III, Prince of Monaco, Apr. 19, 1956; children—Caroline Louise Marguerite, Albert Alexander Louis Pierre, Stephanie Mary Elizabeth. Actress in plays, TV, motion pictures, 1949-56; Broadway debut play The Father, 1949; motion pictures include: High Noon, Mogambo, Dial M for Murder, Rear Window, The Country Girl, Bridges at Toko-Ri, To Catch a Thief, The Swan, High Society. Recipient Acad. Award for role in Country Girl, 1954. Pres. Monegasque Red Cross, Garden Club of Monaco, Princess Grace Found.; chmn. organizing com. Centennial of Monte Carlo; hon. pres. Monaco-U.S.A., Girl Guides of Monaco, A.M.A.D.E., Irish-Am. Cultural Inst. Decorated lady Equestrian Order of Holy Sepulchre of Jerusalem, Order St.-Charles. Address: Principality of Monaco The Palace Principality of Monaco

GRACH, THELMA BLOOM (MRS. PAUL GRACH), educator, mfg. corp. exec.; b. Chgo., Dec. 13, 1916; d. Philip and Sarah Goldie (Stein) Bloom; student Moser Bus. Coll., 1933-34; m. Paul Grach, May 26, 1940; children—Bonita Joyce (Mrs. Peter Allen Wallach), Brian Stewart, Mark Steven. Typist Sears Roebuck Co., Chgo., 1934-35; with Fred Willner, Inc., Chgo., 1935-42; v.p. Western Broom Works, Inc., Oak Park, Ill., 1954—, realtor Av. Realty and Mortgage Co., Oak Park, 1972-74; salesperson Gagliardo Realty, River Forest, Ill., 1974—. Vice pres. Mark-Western Corp., Oak Park, 1972—; violinist Orch. Hall, Chgo., 1933, Chgo. World's Fair, 1934, Pres. West Suburban Hadassah, Oak Park, 1953-55, exec. v.p., 1955-62; chmn. Parent Tchrs. Council B'Nai Israel Congregation, Chgo., 1958; chmn. Blue Ribbon Ball, Oak Park, 1958—. Named Hadassah Woman of Year, 1957-58. Home: 224 S Oak Park Av Oak Park IL 60302 Office: 7375 W North Av River Forest IL 60305

GRAD, MARJORIE ANN, physician; b. Cin., Nov. 16, 1921; d. Edward A. and Anna Mary (Brandt) Grad; B.Sc., U. Cin., 1943, M.D., 1947. Rotating intern Cin. Deaconess Hosp., 1947-48, instr. Sch. Nursing, 1948-50, pres. med. and dental staff, 1965; postgrad. anesthesiology Cin. Gen. Hosp., 1950; instr. phys. diagnosis U. Cin. Med. Center, 1948-49; family practice medicine, Cin., 1948—; mem. attending staff Deaconess, Good Samaritan, Providence hosps.; mem. courtesy staff Bethesda, Children's hosps. Diplomate Am. Bd. Family Practice. Mem. A.M.A., Ohio Med. Assn., Am. Women's Med. Assn., Cin. Acad. Medicine, Cin. Anesthesiology Soc., Am. Acad. Family Practice, Ohio Acad. Family Practice, S.W. Ohio Soc. Family Physicians (pres. 1972-74), Ohio (pres.), No. nut growers assns., Cin. Woman's Rotary (past pres.), Cin. Med. Women's Assn. (past pres., past sec.). Presbyn. Contbr. med. jours. Home: 3237 Jessup Rd Cincinnati OH 45239 Office: 7225 Colerain Av Cincinnati OH 45223

GRADEL, DOROTHY VIRGINIA MENG (MRS. GEORGE A. GRADEL), educator; b. Rochester, N.Y., Apr. 30, 1918; d. Arthur E. and Isobel (Lockington) Meng; R.N., Rochester Gen. Hosp. Sch. Nursing, 1946; A.B., Sacramento State Coll., 1952, M.A., 1954; Ed.D., Wash. State U., 1965; m. George A. Gradel, Feb. 11, 1952. Staff nurse Sutter Hosp., Sacramento, Cal., 1947-51; instr. Sacramento Jr. Coll., 1951-52, Ft. Worth Vocational Nursing Sch., 1959-61, Incarnate Word Coll., 1964-67; dir. nursing edn. S.W. Fla Tb Hosp., 1952-53; asst. prof. edn., Sacramento State Coll., 1967-71; exec. dir. Project Homestart, Binghamton, N.Y., 1971-72; asso. prof. health scis.-nursing Broome Community Coll., Binghamton, 1973—. Mem. Am. Nurses Assn., Assn. Supr. and Curriculum Devel., N.Y. Tchrs. Assn., Nat. League Nursing, Am. Assn. for Higher Edn., Nat. Council on Family Relations, Am. Assn. Sex Educators and Counselors, Am. Assn. U. Profs. Home: 27 Newberry Dr Endicott NY 13760 Office: Broome Community Coll Binghamton NY 13901

GRADISAR, HELEN MARGARET, coll. adminstr.; b. Bridgeville, Pa., July 1, 1922; d. Frank Luke and Elizabeth Helen (Pogacnik) Gradisar; B.S. in Bus. Adminstrn., Duquesne U., 1944. Jr. accountant Carnegie-Ill. Steel Corp., Pitts., 1943-50; asst. dir. alumni relations Duquesne U., Pitts., 1950-67; registrar Rosemont (Pa.) Coll., 1967-68; registrar Carlow Coll., Pitts., 1968—, asst. dean coll., 1974—. Mem. Duquesne U. Alumnae Assn. (pres. 1948-49), Cath. Daus. Am., Epsilon Eta Phi. Democrat. Roman Catholic. Home: 657 Chestnut St Bridgeville PA 15017 Office: 3333 5th Av Pittsburgh PA 15213

GRADWOHL, JANICE LINDQUIST, judge; b. Norfolk, Neb., May 4, 1929; d. Emil Sigfried and Edythe Marie (Cotton) Lindquist; student Colo. Woman's Coll., 1947-48; A.B., U. Neb., 1951, J.D., 1954; postgrad. in law Harvard, 1956-57; m. John Mayer Gradwohl, May 29, 1954; children—Ann, Jill, John. Admitted to Neb. bar, 1954, U.S. Supreme Ct. bar, 1967; legal asst. Hdqrs. Air Materiel Command, USAF, Wright-Patterson AFB, O., 1954-56; asst. to dir. World Tax Series, Harvard Law Sch., 1956-57; practice law firm Max Kier, then firm Kier, Cobb & Luedtke, Lincoln, Neb., 1957-65; dep. county atty. Lancaster County, Lincoln, 1965-74; judge Municipal Ct., Lincoln, 1974—. Former mem. study com. on child abuse Neb. Com. for Children and Youth, also former mem. study com. on juvenile legislation; instr. seminars Police Officers Assn. Neb., Nat. Assn. Dist. Attys., Neb. County Judges Assn. Trustee U. Neb. Found. Mem. Neb. (chmn. com. family law), Lincoln-Lancaster County bar assns., Am. Judicature Soc., Am. Judges Assn., Nat. Safety Council. Home: 2925 Jackson Dr Lincoln NE 68502 Office: County-City Bldg 555 S 10th St Lincoln NE 68508

GRADY, ROSLYN MARIE TOOMEY (MRS. MICHAEL J. GRADY, JR.), ednl. adminstr.; b. Providence, June 27, 1931; d. Martin John and Rose Ann (McKenna) Toomey; B.Ed. R. I. Coll., 1952; M.A., U. Ala., 1964, Ph.D., 1968; m. Michael J. Grady, Jr., Mar. 14, 1953; children—Kevin, Brian, Michael J. III, Martin, Sean. Teaching fellow U. Ala., 1963-64; sch. psychologist Colorado Springs (Colo.) Pub. Sch. Dist. 11, 1965-66, dir. research, 1967—. Pres., Grady Research Assos., Inc., 1971—; grad. instr. U. Colo., Colorado Springs, 1967-70, 73—. Recipient Outstanding Research award Colo. chpt. Internat. Reading Assn., 1969, 70, 71. Mem. Colo. Assn. Sch. Execs. (dir. 1972-74, pres. Colorado Springs chpt. 1970, Outstanding Ednl. Specialist award 1973), Am. Ednl. Research Assn., Am., El Paso County (pres. 1969) psychol. assns. Club: Soroptomist. Author: Grady Adjustment Battery, 1966. Home: 4604 El Camino Dr Colorado Springs CO 80918 Office: 1115 N El Paso St Colorado Springs CO 80903

GRAEBNER, JUDITH ANNE, physician; b. St. Paul, Oct. 29, 1939; d. Robert Carl and Dorothy Lucille (Roehnisch) Graebner; B.S. U. Minn., 1959; M.D., Howard U., 1968; postgrad. George Washington U., Washington, 1963-64; m. Michael B. Hogan, Nov. 1, 1969. Am. Heart Assn. cardiology fellow Howard U., Washington, 1964-68; intern D.C. Gen. Hosp., Washington, 1968-69; pvt. practice family medicine, Silver Spring, Md., 1970—. Active sex and drug edn., local schs. Diplomate Am. Bd. Med. Examiners. Mem. A.M.A., Md. Med. Chirug. Faculty, Montgomery County Med. Soc., Am. Acad. Family Practice, Nat. Orgn. Women. Republican. Home and office: 1404 Hampshire West Ct Silver Spring MD 20903

GRAEME, MARY LEE, pharmacologist; b. Valentines, Va., Aug. 20, 1922; d. Atwell Joseph and Maben Huff (Clary) Clary; B.A., U. Richmond, 1944; postgrad. U. N.C., 1944-45; m. Jock Laurie Graeme, Dec. 29, 1953 (div. Apr. 1961). S.B., Penick grantee, endocrinological project U. Mich., 1946-47; with Ciba, Summit, N.J., 1947-51, Johnson & Johnson Research Found., New Brunswick, 1951-56, Ethicon, Inc., Somerville, 1956-60, Ortho Research Found., Raritan, N.J., 1960-61; with Geigy Pharms., Ardsley, N.Y., 1961—, sect. head gen. pharmacology Geigy Research, 1961-71, sect. head metabolic diseases, 1971—. Mem. Am. Soc. Exptl. Biology, Inflammation Research Assn. (sec. 1971—), Research Assn. Am. Republican. Episcopalian. Contbr. articles to profl. jours. Office: Saw Mill River Rd Ardsley NY 10502

GRAF, SISTER MARY OLGA, ednl. adminstr.; b. La Crosse, Wis., Apr. 19, 1914; d. William Peter and Olga (Brudlos) Graf; M.A., U. Minn., 1960; postgrad. U. Fribourg (Switzerland), 1950, Loyola U., Chgo., 1962, Ind. U., 1963-64. Asst. prin. Lourdes High Sch., Rochester, Minn., 1955-61, Pacelli High Sch., Austin, Minn., 1961-68; dean students Coll. St. Teresa, Winona, Minn., 1969—. Nat. Def. Edn. Act grantee in guidance and counseling Loyola U., 1962; Monetary award Coll. St. Teresa, 1949. Mem. Minn. Cath. Edn. Assn. (sec. 1958-62), Nat. Assn. Women's Deans and Counselors, Minn. Cath. Edn. Assn. (sec. 1958-62). Address: Coll St Teresa Winona MN 55987

GRAFLY, DOROTHY, writer; b. Paris, France, July 29, 1896 (parents Am. citizens); d. Charles and Frances (Sekeles) Grafly; B.A., Wellesley, 1918; grad. work under Prof. George P. Baker of Harvard, 1918-19; m. Charles Hawkins Drummond, Aug. 9, 1946. Art critic Phila. North Am., 1920-25, art editor, editorial and feature writer, 1925; art editor Public Ledger, Phila., 1925-34; art critic Evening Pub. Ledger, 1934; art editor Phila. Record, 1934-42; Phila. corr. Am. Mag. of Art, to 1928; curator collections Drexel Inst., 1934-45; dir. mag. publicity Phila. Art Alliance, 1944-48; dir. research and art Philip Ragan Assos., 1942-48, contbg. critic Art Digest (under name of Dorothy Drummond), to 1953; art editor Tempos mag., Phila., 1955-59, also Evening and Sunday Bull., 1956-70; lectr. art Temple U., 1938-39, Drexel Inst., 1940-42. Recipient prize for one-act play Plays and Players Club, Phila., 1921; named Distinguished Dau. Pa., 1960; recipient 1st citation Da Vinci Art Alliance, 1961; medal of achievement Phila. Art Alliance, 1968; City of Phila. citation, 1972. Fellow in perpetuity Pa. Acad. Fine Arts, 1957. Mem. Art Alliance, Alumnae Assn. Wellesley Coll., New Century Guild (Phila.), Pa. Acad. Fine Arts (hon.), Phila. Water Color Club (hon.), Nat. Travel, Nat. Geog., Am. Assn. Museums, Phila. Mus. Art, Am. Fedn. Arts. Club: Altrusa (charter mem.; pres. 1930-32) (Phila.). Wrote and produced Masque of Night, Masque of Life, The Phoenix, Metamorphosis, Images—all produced Gloucester, Mass., 1914-20. Author: History of Philadelphia Print Club, 1929; series Am. art biographies under title Parade of American Art, 1936-37; series of articles dealing with living European sculptors, nat. What Sells series, Am. Artist, 1948-49. Contbr. Dictionary of Am. Biography; Ency. Brit., Ency. Americana, Notable Am. Women, to mags. Editor-pub. of Art in Focus. Lectr. on art. One of six American critics invited by Chgo. Art Inst. to broadcast over nat. hook-up at opening of 1934 Century of Progress Expn. Art Exhbn. Address: 131 N 20th St Philadelphia PA 19103 (summer) Lanesville MA 01930

GRAFMAN, LAURA RUTH SAMUELS (MRS. DAYTON FOWLER GRAFMAN), coll. adminstr.; b. Chgo., May 8, 1932; d. Paul H. and Revella (Budwig) Samuels; student Grinnell Coll., 1948-49, Art Inst. Chgo., 1957-58; m. Dayton Fowler Grafman, June 4, 1950; 1 dau., Lynn Alyce. Admissions counselor, Chgo. area rep. Ill. Wesleyan U., Bloomington, 1952-54, Bradley U., Peoria, Ill., 1954-56, Nat. Coll. Edn., Evanston, Ill., 1963-64, counselor for financial assistance, 1965-69, dir. financial aid, 1969—, chmn. council on financial assistance, 1969-70, 72—. Mem. Fed. Regional Financial Aid Rev. Panel, 1971; mem. financial need adv. com. Ill. State Scholarship Commn., 1974—. Mem. Ill. (chmn. resolutions com. 1973-74), Midwest (resolutions com. 1973-74), assn. student financial aid adminstrs. Home: 1516 Hinman Av Evanston IL 60201 Office: 2840 Sheridan Rd Evanston IL 60201

GRAFSTEIN, BERNICE (MRS. HOWARD SHANET), neurophysiologist; b. Toronto, Ont., Can., Sept. 17, 1929; d. Max and Dora (Firestein) Grafstein; B.A., U. Toronto, 1951; Ph.D., McGill U., 1954; m. Howard Shanet, Oct. 10, 1963; 1 son, Laurence Paul. Lectr. dept. physiology McGill U., Montreal, Que., 1954-55, asst. prof. physiology, 1957-62; hon. research asst. dept. anatomy Univ. Coll., London, Eng., 1955-57; asst. prof. Rockefeller U., N.Y.C., 1962-69, adj. asso. prof., 1969—; asso. prof. physiology Cornell U. Med. Coll., N.Y.C., 1969-73, prof., 1973—. Trustee Grass Found. Mem. A.A.A.S., Am., Canadian physiol. socs., Internat. Brain Research Orgn., Soc. for Neurosci. (councillor). Home: 1235 Park Av New York City NY 10028 Office: Cornell U Med Coll New York City NY 10021

GRAFTON, ERNESTINE, educator; b. Hubbard, Tex., Jan. 17, 1913; d. Louis Dormer and Connie Imogene (Newton) Grafton; A.B., Trinity U., San Antonio, 1933; B.L.S., U. Okla., 1934; M.A., U. Chgo., 1940; M.S. in Adult Edn., Coll. City N.Y., 1972. Student asst. Library Trinity U., 1930-33; reference asst. circulation dept. Cin. Pub. Library, 1936-41; tri-county librarian Person, Caswell, Orange County Libraries (N.C.), 1941-45; head extension div. Va. State Library, Richmond, 1945-56; dir. Ia. State Traveling Library, Des Moines, 1956-71; basic edn. tchr. RCA-MCDA Region VIII, Bklyn., 1971—. Bldg. cons. for pub. libraries. Treas. Ia. Council For Community Improvement, 1961-62, v.p., 1962-65, pres., 1965—. Named Va. Woman of Yr., 1951; recipient Achievement award Mo. Valley Adult Edn. Assn., 1963, Ia. Adult Edn. Assn., 1970. Mem. Am. (council mem. at large), Ia. (exec. com.) library assns., Ia. (exec. com., past pres., chmn. nominations and elections com.), Mo. Valley adult edn. assns., Assn. State Library, UN Assn. U.S.A., United World Federalists, League Women Voters, Pi Gamma Mu, Kappa Delta Pi. Editor: N.C. Libraries, 1942-44, Va. Library Bull., 1945-56, Ia. Library Quar., 1956-71. Home: 330 3d Av New York City NY 10010

GRAHAM, ADA COGAN (MRS. FRANK GRAHAM JR.), author; b. Dayton, O., Aug. 22, 1931; d. James D. and Jeannette S. (Steller) Cogan; A.B., Hunter Coll., 1957; m. Frank Graham, Jr., Oct. 31, 1953. Tchr. pub., pvt. schs., N.Y., 1957-59, Me., 1965-69; author, Milbridge, Me., 1969—. A founder, dir. Narraguagus Childhood Devel. Assn., 1971, Children's Summer Nature Program, 1968—. Me. Humanities Council, 1973—; mem. Me. Family Planning Assn. (dir.) 1973—. Recipient Outstanding Sci. Books for Children award Nat. Sci. Tchrs. Assn. and Children's Book Council, 1972. Author: (with Frank Graham Jr.) The Great American Shopping Cart, 1969; Wildlife Rescue, 1970; Puffin Island, 1971; The Mystery of the Everglades, 1972, Dooryard Garden, 1974; The Careless Animal, 1975. Co-author, co-editor: Audubon Primer series: Let's Discover the Floor of the Forest, Let's Discover Changes Everywhere, Let's Discover Birds in Our World, Let's Discover the Winter Woods, 1974. Address: Milbridge ME 04658

GRAHAM, FRANCES KEESLER (MRS. DAVID GRAHAM), psychologist; b. Canastota, N.Y., Aug. 1, 1918; d. Clyde C. and Norma (Van Surdam) Keesler; B.A., Pa. State U., 1938; Ph.D., Yale, 1942; m. David T. Graham, June 14, 1941; children—Norma, Andrew, Polly. Psychologist, St. Louis Psychiat. Clinic, 1942-44; instr., research asso. Washington U. Sch. Medicine, 1942-48, 53-57; instr. Barnard Coll., 1948-51; research asso. U. Wis. Sch. Medicine, 1957-64, asso. prof., 1964-68, prof. dept. pediatrics, 1968—, prof. dept. psychology, 1969—. Research scientist awardee Nat. Inst. Mental Health, 1964-74, exptl. psychology study sect., 1970-74. Fellow Am. Psychol. Assn. (sec.-treas. div. physiol. and comparative psychology 1963-69, sec.-treas. div. developmental psychology 1962-65); mem. Soc. Research Child Devel. (mem. governing council 1965-71, pres.-elect 1973), Soc. Psychophysiol. Research (dir. 1968-71, 73—, pres. 1973-74), Nat. Research Council, Midwestern Psychol. Assn., League Women Voters, Phi Beta Kappa, Sigma Xi, Kappa Kappa Gamma. Bd. editors Child Devel., 1966-68, Jour. Exptl. Child Psychology, 1964-67, Jour. Exptl. Psychology, 1968-73; bd. editors Psychophysiology, 1968-69, asso. editor, 1969-70. Home: 2927 Harvard Dr Madison WI 53705

GRAHAM, JANE (MRS. JOSEPH WESLEY GRAHAM), advt. exec.; b. Rice Tex., Mar. 4, 1922; d. William Edward and Kathryn Ruth (McKay) Tidwell; student Tex. State Coll. Women, 1938-39, Abilene Christian Coll., 1939-40, N. Tex. State Coll., 1941; m. Joseph Wesley Graham, Jan. 5, 1946; 1 dau., Kathryn Ann. Profl. singer, radio, 1941-49; producer, writer radio-TV drama, N.Y.C., 1948-56; v.p. United Nat. Films, Dallas, 1957-59; with Tracy-Locke, Glenn Advt., Dallas, 1964-66, Bloom Advt., Dallas, 1966-67; owner Jane Graham Advt. and Editorial Services, Dallas, 1967—. Active United Fund. Recipient numerous awards Dallas Advt. League. Mem. Fashion Group, Dallas Advt. League, Press Club, Theta Sigma Phi. Editor S.W. Advt. and Marketing, 1966-71. Contbr. articles to profl. jours. Home: 5843 E University Blvd Dallas TX 75206 Office: 2818 Apparel Mart Dallas TX 75207

GRAHAM, JEANA BLACK (MRS. ROBERT V. GRAHAM), librettist, choral dir.; b. Rochester, N.Y., Sept. 20, 1914; d. Donald Mitchell and Edith (Parshall) Black; Mus.B., Eastman Sch. Music, 1937; postgrad. in archeology Divinity Sch. Pacific, 1950; m. Robert V. Graham, Dec. 20, 1936; children—Robin Donald, Ross Lee, Tad Laury, Paul David, Jared Mark. Tchr. English, Rikkyo Jo Gakuin, Tokyo, Japan, 1951-53; kitchen dir. Pima County Hosp., Tucson, 1955-70; dir. Leeward Choral Soc., Waianae, Hawaii, 1970—. Free lance writer, 1960—; tchr. piano, organ, voice; dir. music Schofield Chapel, Hawaii. Mem. cultural com. Model Cities Program. Recipient awards for community service as dir. choral soc. Mem. Am. Music Tchrs. Assn., Nat. Guild Piano Tchrs., Honolulu Morning Music Club, Prairie Quill Club, Choristers Guild, Friends of Madge Tennett Art Galleries (charter). Writer cantata librettos including Lo! A Star; The Sower and the Seed; Golgotha; Dawn of Redeeming Grace; Barefoot School; Jonah's Tale of a Whale (musical), others; writer libretto Paul in Chains (opera); textwriter numerous single choral works; also articles, poems. Home: Box 586 Waianae HI 96792

GRAHAM, JORY, author, columnist; b. Chgo., Feb. 7, 1925; d. Ralph A. and Rose-Frances (Kramer) Reis; student U. Chgo., 1940-43. Columnist Jory Graham's City, Chgo. Sun-Times. Adv. bd. St. Leonard's House, 1962-64; mem. bd. Children's Reading Round Table, 1966-67. Mem. Soc. Midland Authors, Soc. Am. Travel Writers, Sigma Delta Chi. Club: Arts of Chicago. Author: I'm Driving My Analyst Crazy, 1959; Children On a Farm, 1962; Katie's Zoo, 1964; Chicago: An Extraordinary Guide, 1968, rev. edit., 1973; Instant Chicago: How to Cope, 1973; also booklets. Editor: The Wagon and the Star: A Study of American Community Initiative, 1966. Address: 2801 Sheridan Rd Chicago IL 60657

GRAHAM, JUDITH, physician; b. Des Moines, July 23, 1932; d. W. Walter and Elizabeth (Haw) Graham; B.A. cum laude, U. Colo., 1953; M.D., State U. Ia., 1957. Intern, resident State U. Ia., 1957-61, NIH diabetes trainee, 1961-62; practice medicine, specializing in internal medicine, Alhambra, Cal., 1962-67, Gt. Falls, Mont., 1967—; instr. internal medicine State U. Ia., 1961-62; clin. instr. internal medicine Loma Linda U., 1962-67, U. So. Cal., 1964-67; staff Gt. Falls (Mont.) Clinic; cons. VA Hosp., Ft. Harrison, Mont. Mem. adv. com. Mont. State U. Coll. Nursing Postgrad. Continuing Edn. Project, 1972-73; mem. planning com. Mont. Gov.'s Conf. on Nursing and Nursing Edn., 1971-72. Diplomate Am. Bd. Internal Medicine. Mem. A.M.A., Mont. Med. Assn., Am. Soc. Internal Medicine, Am., Mont. (dir., v.p. 1971—) diabetes assns., Am., Mont. (pres. 1973-74, dir. 1969—) heart assns., Trail Riders of Canadian Rockies (council 1970—, v.p. 1974—), Phi Beta Kappa, Alpha Omega Alpha, Pi Beta Phi. Presbyn. Home: 71 Devonshire St Great Falls MT 59405 Office: 1220 Central Great Falls MT 59401

GRAHAM, KATHARINE, newspaper co. exec.; b. N.Y.C., June 16, 1917; d. Eugene and Agnes (Ernst) Meyer; student Vassar Coll., 1935-36; A.B., U. Chgo., 1938; m. Philip L. Graham, June 5, 1940 (dec. 1963); children—Elizabeth Morris (Mrs. Elizabeth Weymouth), Donald Edward, William Welsh, Stephen Meyer. Reporter San Francisco News, 1938-39; pres. Washington Post Co., 1963-73, chmn. bd., chief exec. officer, 1973—; dir. Bowaters Mersey Paper Co. Ltd., Allied Chem. Corp. Trustee George Washington U., Com. for Econ. Devel., U. Chgo., Nat. Center Resource Recovery, Urban Inst., Fed. City Council; adv. com. John F. Kennedy Sch. Govt. for Inst. Politics, Harvard; mem. Conf. Bd., Newspaper Advt. Bur. Mem. Sigma Delta Chi, Theta Sigma Phi. Clubs: Washington Press, 1925 F Street, Nat. Press (Washington); Cosmopolitan (N.Y.C.). Home: 2920 R St NW Washington DC 20007 Office: 1150 15th St NW Washington DC 20005

GRAHAM, LAURA MARGARET (LAURA GRAHAM FORBES), artist; b. Washington, Ind.; d. Ray Austin and Eugenia Bruce (Winston) Graham; student Sacred Heart Convents (Grosse Point, Mich., Noroton, Conn., N.Y.C.) Westover and Nightingale Schs.; studied art Art Students League, with Bridgman and Frank du Mond; Grand Central Art Sch.; Traphagen Art Sch.; pvt. study with Mead Schaeffer, Henry Rittenberg and Edward Dufner, N.A.; grad. Sch. Adult Edn., N.Y. U., 1965; m. Clifford Lee Forbes, May 4, 1940 (div. 1949); 1 son, Clifford Lee. Exhibited paintings John Herron Art Mus., Indpls., N.Y. Water Color Club, Am. Water Color Soc., N.A.D. (youngest artist exhibiting Nov. 1932), Pa. Acad., Boston Art Club, Montclair Art Mus., World's Fair 1940, Contemporary Art Bldg., Conn. Acad. Fine Arts Exhibit, Allied Arts of Am., Ogunquit (Me.)

Art Center, 50th Anniversary Celebration Westover Sch., Newport Art Assn. A sponsor N.Y.U. Chamber Music Concert, 1954—, concerts in Washington Sq. Park, 1954-55. Recipient Alexander Wall prize, 1943, Allied Artists Am. exhbn., N.Y. Nat. Arts Club, 1st prize for painting, 1939; 2d prize, 1940, 41, hon. mention, 1947, 48, 72; hon. mention Allied Artists, 1948, Art Assn. Ogunquit, Maine, 1947, 49; hon. mention and war bond, Terry Art Exhbn., Miami, Fla., 1952. Mem. Nat. Assn. Women Artists, N.Y. Hist. Soc., Museum City N.Y., N.Y. U. Alumni Assn., Allied Artists of Am., Conn. Acad. Fine Arts (artist mem.), Nat. Trust for Historic Preservation, Friends of the Philharmonic, Am. Artists Profl. League, Art Students League (life). Clubs: Nat. Arts, Women's Nat. Republican, Pen and Brush, (N.Y.C.). Address: 10 Washington Sq N New York City NY 10003

GRAHAM, LOIS, educator; b. Troy, N.Y., Apr. 4, 1925; d. Paul Seabrook and Marion Isabelle (Cooley) Graham; student Rensselaer Poly. Inst., 1942-45; B.Mech. Engring., M.S., Ill. Inst. Tech., 1949, Ph.D., 1959; m. Sanford A. Weil, Apr. 28, 1967. Test engr. Carrier Corp., Syracuse, N.Y., 1945-46; grad. asst. Ill. Inst. Tech., Chgo., 1946-48, jr. research engr., 1948-49, instr., 1949-53, asst. prof., 1953-59, asso. prof., 1959—, asst. chmn. dept. mech. engring., 1950-70, asso. dir. edn. and experience Engring. Program Center, 1974—. Bd. dirs. Ada S. McKinley Community Services, 1959-64, sec., 1962-63. Mem. Am. Assn. U. Profs., Am. Soc. Engring. Edn., Am. Soc. M.E. (chmn. K-18 cryogenic heat transfer com. 1971—), Am. Soc. Heating, Refrigerating and Air-Conditioning Engrs., Soc. Women Engrs. (pres. 1955-56), Sigma Xi, Pi Tau Sigma. Home: 5901 N Sheridan Rd Chicago IL 60660

GRAHAM, LOLA AMADA (BEALL) (MRS. JOHN JACKSON GRAHAM), photographer, author; b. nr. Bremen, Ga., Nov. 12, 1896; d. John Gainer and Nancy Caroline Idella (Reid) Beall; student Florence Normal Sch., 1914; m. John Jackson Graham, Aug. 3, 1916; children—Billy Duane, John Thomas, Helen (Mrs. D. Hall), Donald, Beverly (Mrs. Bob Forson). Tchr. elementary pub. sch., Centerdale, Ala., 1914, Eva, Ala., 1915; free lance photographer and writer, 1950—; editor poetry column Mobile (Ala.) Home News, 1968-69. Recipient numerous nat. prizes, 1950—. Mem. Ina Coolbrith Poetry Soc., Chapparal Poets. Contbr. photographs to Ency. Britannica, numerous mags. and books. Address: 225-93 Mt Hermon Rd Scotts Valley CA 95066

GRAHAM, LORRAINE HUNT, state legislator; b. Burlington, Vt., July 20, 1925; d. Elzor L. and Leona Mae (Gelinas) Hunt; grad. high sch.; m. Foster J. Graham, Sept. 2, 1946; children—Lealand, Foster J. II, Deborah, Dana Darryl, Bryan, Stacey Jo. Typist engring. dept. Bell Aircraft, 1944-45; with traffic dept. New Eng. Tel. & Tel., 1945-52; investigator Centralized Traffic Investigation, Burlington, Vt., 1962-65; mem. Vt. Ho. of Reps., 1966—; sch. commr., 1970—. Chmn. Burlington Property and Bldg. Com.; mem. Democratic City and Ward Com., 1960—. Bd. dirs. Vt. A Child with Learning Disabilities. Recipient President's award Children with Learning Disabilities, 1968. Mem. Nat. (pres. 1973-74), Vt. orders women legislators, Fanny Allen Aux., Sch. and Home Assn. Rice Meml. High Sch. Roman Catholic. Clubs: National Guard Officers Wives, Rice High Booster (Burlington). Home: 280 N Winooski Av Burlington VT 05401 Office: State House Montpelier VT 05602

GRAHAM, SISTER M. JOANNE, hosp. adminstr.; b. Hot Springs, S.D., Mar. 8, 1935; d. Edmund Albert and Eunice Florentine (Kinghorn) Graham; R.N., St. Elizabeth Hosp. Sch. Nursing, Lincoln, Neb., 1955; B.S., St. Louis U., 1958, M.H.A., 1966. Joined Benedictine Sisters of Annunciation, 1958; nurse St. Alexius Hosp., Bismarck, N.D., 1958-64, adminstr., 1966—; nurse St. Elizabeth Hosp., Lincoln, Neb., 1955-56. Mem. faculty home study program Sch. Hosp. Adminstrn., U. Minn., 1969—. Trustee Mary Coll., 1968—, sec., 1968—; bd. dirs., sec., mem. exec. com. N.D. South Central Health Planning Council, 1969—; trustee, mem. exec. com. Blue Cross of N.D., 1970—, 2d vice chmn., 1971—. Mem. Am. Coll. Hosp. Adminstrs., N.D. Hosp. Assn. (pres. 1974—). Address: St Alexius Hosp PO Box 1658 Bismarck ND 58501

GRAHAM, MARGARET EDNA (MRS. WILLIAM B. GRAHAM), club woman; b. Weedsport, N.Y.; d. James Leo and Grace (Van Duzer) Kanaley; grad. St. Xavier Coll., 1932; m. William Burden Graham, June 15, 1940; children—William J., Elizabeth Ann (Mrs. Dennis Muckermann), Margaret Edna (now Mrs. Benson Caswell), and Robert Byron. Past president of the American Assn. Maternal and Infant Health; mem. women's bd. De Paul U.; past sec. Chgo. Chamber Music Soc.; governing mem. Orchestral Assn.; mem. woman's bd. Mercy Hosp., Ill. Children's Home and Aid Soc., Children's Meml. Hosp., Chgo. Rehab. Inst., Loyola U., De Paul U., English Speaking Union, U. Chgo., U. Chgo. Cancer Research Found., Chgo. Symphony; mem. U.S.O.; vice chmn. women's bd., trustee Ravinia Festival; bd. govs. Ill. Club Cath. Women; mem. bd. Kenilworth Home and Garden Club. Clubs: Women's Athletic, Casino (Chgo.); Westmoreland, Mid Am., Kenilworth, Indian Hill, Eldorado Country; Tres Vidas (Mexico). Home: 40 Devonshire Lane Kenilworth IL 60043

GRAHAM, MARJORIE FRANCES, pub. relations and advt. exec.; b. El Paso, Tex., July 13, 1933; d. Ewing Wendell and Fontaine (Williamson) Graham; student U. Tex., 1951-52; B.J., U. Mo., 1954; M.S., Boston U., 1966. Edn. editor El Paso Times, 1955-67; pres. Radford Sch. for Girls, El Paso, 1968-73; pres. Pan-Am. Pub. Relations and Advt., El Paso, 1973—. Mem. woman's com. El Paso Symphony Orch. Assn. Bd. dirs. U. Civic Ballet, El Paso Hist. Soc. Recipient Walter Williams award in creative writing Mo. Writers Guild, 1954. Ford Found. fellow Urban Journalism Center, Northwestern U. Medill Sch. Journalism, 1967. Mem. Nat. Fedn. Press Women (1st pl. writing contest 1964, 67), Tex. Press Women (dist. pres. 1964-65), Nat. Soc. Arts and Letters, Pan Am. Round Table, Assn. U. Women, Pub. Relations Soc. Am. (accredited), D.A.R., Theta Sigma Phi, Tau Mu Epsilon, Zeta Tau Alpha. Republican. Presbyn. Home: 2915 Federal Av El Paso TX 79930 Office: 108 Texas Av El Paso TX 79901

GRAHAM, MARJORIE RUTH KILLEBREW (MRS. CARL FRANCIS GRAHAM), ednl. adminstr.; b. Kansas City, Mo., Sept. 25, 1915; s. Robert Herman and Edith Cruce (Tyler) Killebrew; B.A., U. Okla., 1936; M.A., U. Mich., 1969; m. Carl Francis Graham, Apr. 27, 1941; children—David Carl, Nancy (Mrs. James R. Flink), Carol Ann. Reference librarian Kansas City (Kan.) Pub. Library, 1936-40; librarian LaQuinta High Sch., Garden Grove, Cal., 1963-67, Central High Sch., 1967-71, Ottawa High Sch., Grand Rapids, Mich., 1971-73; supr. instructional media, Grand Rapids, 1973—. Lectr. library sci. U. Mich., 1970—. Pres., Garden Grove P.T.A. council, 1963-65. Mem. A.L.A., Am. Assn. Sch. Librarians, Mich. Assn. for Media in Edn., Mich. Assn. Sch. Curriculum Devel., Assn. for Ednl. Communications and Tech., Phi Beta Kappa, Beta Phi Mu, Delta Kappa Gamma, Gamma Phi Beta. Republican. Methodist (trustee 1965-66). Club: University Mich. Alumnae (group pres. Grand Rapids 1973-74). Home: 2648 Berwyck Rd SE East Grand Rapids MI 49506 Office: 143 Bostwick NE Grand Rapids MI 49502

GRAHAM, MARTHA, dancer, choreographer, teacher; b. Pitts.; studied with Ruth St. Denis; LL.D., Bard Coll., Harvard, 1966, also numerous others. Co-founder Dance Repertory Theatre, N.Y.C., 1930; founder Martha Graham Dance Company; has created more than 150 dance theatre works; solo performances several leading orchestral groups; Guggenheim fellow, 1932-39; dir. Martha Graham Sch. Contemporary Dance, Inc., N.Y.C.; faculty Neighborhood Sch. of Theatre, Juilliard Sch. Music; fgn. tours, 1950, 54, 55, 56, 58, 62, 67, 68. Fellow Am. Acad. Arts and Scis. Recipient Capezio award, 1959, Aspen award in the humanities, 1965, Creative Arts Awards medal Brandeis U., 1968, award for distinguished service to the arts Nat. Inst. Arts and Letters, 1970. Author: Notebooks of Martha Graham, 1973. Address: 316 E 63d St New York City NY 10021

GRAHAM, SISTER MARY JUDE, educator; b. Omaha, Neb., July 3, 1919; d. John Henry and Arda (Olden) Graham; B.S. in Edn., Coll. St. Mary (Omaha), 1952; M.A. in Philosophy, Marquette U., 1967; postgrad. Catholic U., 1967, DePaul U., Chgo., 1968, U. Neb., 1970-71. Joined Religious Sisters of Mercy, 1937; tchr. elementary schs., Lincoln, Neb., 1940-43, Denver, 1943-47, Greeley, Colo., 1948-52, Balta, N.D., 1947-48; tchr., adminstr. parochial schs. Omaha, 1952-54, Greeley, 1954-60; mem. faculty Coll. St. Mary, Omaha, 1960—, asst. prof. philosophy, 1966-71, asso. prof. 1971—, also chmn. dept., 1961—. Mem. Am. Catholic Philos. Assn., Mountain Plains Philos. Conf., Am. Philos. Assn., Omaha Club Bus. and Profl. Women. Roman Catholic. Home: 7506 Hascall St Omaha NE 68124 Office: 1901 S 72d St Omaha NE 68124

GRAHAM, MARYLEN, ednl. adminstr.; b. Lindale, Tex., May 4, 1942; d. Alvis Lee and Eara Pauline (Praytor) Graham; A.A., Tyler Jr. Coll., 1962; B.S., N. Tex. State U., 1965, M.Ed., 1971; M.R.E., Southwestern Bapt. Theol. Sem., 1971. Tchr., Alvarado (Tex.) Pub. Schs., 1965-67, Crowley (Tex.) Pub. Schs., 1967-69; counselor in residence Eastern Ky. U., Richmond, 1971-72; dean women S.W. Bapt. Coll., Bolivar, Mo., 1972-73; counselor Irving (Tex.) Pub. Schs., 1973—. Mem. Nat. Assn. Women Deans and Counselors, Nat. Assn. Christian Deans, Am., Tex. personnel and guidance assns. Home: 1831 W Pioneer Apt 202 Irving TX 75061 Office: 600 E 6th St Irving TX 75060

GRAHAM, PATRICIA ALBJERG (MRS. LOREN R. GRAHAM), educator; b. Lafayette, Ind., Feb. 9, 1935; d. Victor L. and Marguerite (Hall) Albjerg; B.S., Purdue U., 1955, M.S., 1957; Ph.D., Columbia, 1964; m. Loren R. Graham, Sept. 6, 1955; 1 dau., Marguerite Elizabeth. Tchr. high sch., Norfolk, Va., 1955-56, 57-58, N.Y.C., 1958-60; lectr., asst. prof. Ind. U., 1964-66; asst. prof. Barnard Coll. and Columbia Tchrs. Coll., N.Y.C., 1965-68, asso. prof., 1968-72, prof., 1972-74; dean Radcliffe Inst., Cambridge, Mass., 1974—; prof. Harvard, Cambridge, 1974—. Am. Council on Edn. fellow Princeton, 1969-70. Bd. dirs. Dalton Sch., 1973—. Guggenheim fellow, 1972-73; Radcliffe Inst. fellow, 1972-73. Mem. History Edn. Soc. (pres. 1972-73), Phi Beta Kappa. Episcopalian. Author: Progressive Education: From Arcady to Academe, 1967; Community and Class in American Education: 1865-1918, 1974; (with W. Todd Furniss) Women in Higher Education, 1974. Home: 39 Garden St Cambridge MA 02138

GRAHAM, RETA LILLIAN, educator; b. Milford, Me., June 28, 1925; d. William Patrick and Ida (Cote) Graham; student Midland Coll., Fremont, Neb., 1944-46; B.A., U. Me., 1949; M.A., U. Neb., 1954; Ed.D., U. Md., 1964. Head English and speech dept. Hartington (Neb.) City Schs., 1949-53; grad. teaching asst., instr. speech U. Neb., 1953-54; instr. speech, acting dean of women Aroostook State Coll., Presque Isle, Me., summers 1954, 56; asst. prof. speech, 1964-65, asso. prof., 1965-66, prof., 1966—; instr. speech, dir. speech correction program U. Me., 1954-55; instr. speech, supr. speech student tchr. tng. Fresno (Cal.) State Coll., 1955-56; 1st lt., instr. speech WAC Sch., Ft. McClellan, Ala., 1957-59; grad. teaching asst. U. Md., 1960-61; pvt. bus., instr. speech, speech cons., Arlington, Va., 1962-64. Cons., lectr. speech. Mem. Speech Communication Assn., Speech Assn. Eastern States, Me. Speech Assn., Me. Speech and Hearing Assn., Internat., Eastern communication assns., Internat. Platform Assn., Nat. Geog. Soc., Phi Omega, Cardinal Key, Pi Delta Epsilon. Home: Davenport St Milford ME 04461 Office: U Me Presque Isle 181 Main St Presque Isle ME 04769

GRAHAM, VIRGINIA, TV-radio commentator; b. Chgo., July 4, 1912; d. David Stanley and Bessie (Feiges) Komiss; attended Francis W. Parker Sch., Chgo., Nat. Park Sem., Washington; B.A., U. Chgo.; M.A., Northwestern U.; m. Harry W. Guttenburg, May 2, 1935; 1 dau., Lynn (Mrs. Seymour M. Boffrer). Radio writer, 1936-38; emcee Internat. Beauty Show, 1947-51; TV performer on shows including Dave Garroway Show, Where Was I, NBC, 1950, Food for Thought, Channel 5, N.Y.C., 1951-57, This is Your Life, NBC, 1956; co-hostess radio show Week Day, NBC, 1956; goodwill ambassador Clairol Co., 1961; emcee Girl Talk, ABC, after 1962. Active Am. Cancer Soc., March of Dimes, Kidney Found., A.R.C., mental health, cerebral palsy orgns., others; appeared numerous fund-raising telethons. Named Woman of Yr., K.P., 1957, Am. Cancer Soc., 1961; Internat. Woman of Yr., Women's Clubs of Am., 1959; many citations for civic activities. Author: (with Jean Black) There Goes What's Her Name, 1965. Home: 1025 Fifth Av New York City NY 10028 Office: 12 W 45th St New York City NY 10036

GRAHAME, MRS. ORVILLE FRANCIS (PAULA PATTON GRAHAME), artist, club woman; b. Clearfield, Ia.; d. Harry T. and Bertha J. (Jacobs) Patton; B.A., U. Ia., 1926; m. Orville F. Grahame, Nov. 3, 1923; 1 dau., Sarah (Mrs. Cairns). Artist and sculptor exhibited at Independent Artists, N.Y.C., Worcester Art Mus., Rockport Art Assn. Dir. Protective Assn. of Can., 1962-70. Corporator Worcester Girls Club, Home for Blind; corporator, dir. Edward Street Day Nursery, 1954-60, Children's Friend Soc., 1963-67; pres. Unitarian Women's Alliance, 1966-68, dir. Youth Guidance Center, 1963-67; founder art scholarship fund U. Ia., Distinguished Service award U. Ia., 1969. Mem. Worcester Hist. Soc., Natural History Soc., Art Museum, Music Festival Assn., Worcester Orchestral Soc., Rockport Art Assn., Am. Assn. U. Women (pres. Worcester br. 1959-61), League Women Voters. Unitarian. Clubs: Worcester County Women's Republican, Women's, Westboro Country. Author: Palimpsest Stories, 1929-30. Editor Memorial Hospital News, 1951-54. Home: 6 Bancroft Tower Rd Worcester MA 01609

GRAINGER, NESSA (MRS. MURRAY GRAINGER), artist; b. Atlantic City, Sept. 15, 1929; d. Barnet and Pauline (Gittelman) Posner; student U. Miami, 1947, Pa. State U., 1948, Phila. Mus. Sch. Art, 1949-51, Tyler Sch. Fine Art, 1952-54; m. Murray Grainger, Dec. 19, 1964; children—Richard, Margie. Exhibited in one-man shows at Little Falls (N.J.) Library, 1973, South Orange (N.J.) Library, 1973-74, Newark Library, 1974, Annex Gallery, Montclair, N.J., Berkeley Savs. & Loan, Millburn, N.J., 1972, Liberty Savs. & Loan, South Orange, 1972-73; exhibited in group shows at Phila. Mus. Art, Civic Center Mus., Phila., Phila. Art Alliance, Nat. Acad., N.Y.C., Morris Mus., N.J., Jersey City Mus., Newark Library; represented in many pvt. collections. Vice pres. Art Gallery, South Orange, Maplewood, 1971-73. Recipient Silver medal Ocean City Cultural Art Center, 1972; 1st watercolor award Art Center of the Oranges, 1972; 1st abstract watercolor award Painters and Sculptors, 1972; 1st in abstract painting Miniature Art Soc., 1973; 1st in mixed colors Little Falls Library, 1973; 1st in contemporary watercolors Festival of Arts, 1973, Florham Park, 1973. Mem. Nat. Assn. Women Artists (Aileen O'Webb award for watercolors 1973, corr. sec. 1974-76), N.J. Water Color Soc. (Art for Arthritis award 1972, corr.). Address: 48 Duffield Dr South Orange NJ 07079

GRALEY, FRANCES MARY, coll. adminstr.; b. Buffalo, Apr. 28, 1930; d. James Theodore and Frances Florence (Wargula) Graley; ed. U. Buffalo, U. Toronto. With Mfrs. & Traders Trust Co., Buffalo, 1948-53, Ford Motor Co., Oakville, Ont., Can., 1953-59; fund campaign mgr. Buffalo Philharmonic Orch., 1959-66; treas., office mgr. Q-R-S Music Rolls, Inc., Buffalo, 1966-71; adminstr. grants State Univ. Coll. at Buffalo, 1971—. Mem. Buffalo Philharmonic Women's Com., Nat. Secretaries Assn. Democrat. Roman Cath. Home: 34 Warren Av Kenmore NY 14217 Office: 1300 Elmwood Av Buffalo NY 14222

GRAM, MARGARET A., educator; b. Shevlin, Minn., Feb. 2, 1907; d. Rev. J. C. and Caroline (Alveson) Gram; B.A., Hunter Coll., 1929; M.A., Columbia, 1936; postgrad. N.Y.U., 1938-43. Faculty, Hunter Coll., 1929-38; faculty Queens Coll., Flushing, N.Y., 1938-46; asst. prof., 1946-50, asso. prof., 1950-59, prof., 1959-74, prof. emeritus, 1974—, chmn. dept., 1940-73, dir. coll. food service, 1938-62, Army food service, Unit 3222 Army Specialized Tng. Program, 1943-44. Cons. bldg. com. for Queens Coll. dining hall, 1957-60; mem. adv. com. to bd. control Concordia Coll., Bronxville, N.Y., 1955-58, 60-62, 63-66. Named Distinguished Tchr. of Year, Queens Coll., 1971; recipient Servant of Christ award Concordia Coll., 1974; Spl. award N.Y. State Home Econs. Assn., 1974. Mem. Am. Home Econs. Assn., Am. Assn. U. Women, Luth. Edn. Soc., Bowne House Hist. Soc., Kappa Delta Pi, Phi Upsilon Omicron. Lutheran. Home: 49-27 166th St Flushing NY 11365 Office: Queens Coll Flushing NY 11367

GRAMBS, JEAN DRESDEN (MRS. HAROLD GRAMBS), educator; b. Pigeon Point, Cal.; d. Abraham and Esther (Dresden) Schwartz; A.B., Reed Coll., 1940; M.A., Stanford, 1941, Ed.D., 1948; m. Harold Grambs, June 18, 1945; children—Marya, Sarah, Peter. Tchr. pub. schs., Cal., 1941-43; instr. Stanford, 1948-49, asst. prof., 1949-53; supr. adult edn. Prince George County, Md., 1955-58; lectr. edn. U. Md., College Park, 1955-61, asso. prof. edn., 1961-67, prof., 1967—. Cons. Ednl. Devel. Corp., 1965-68, Office of Edn. Tchr. Corps, 1966-70, Abt Assos., 1972. Robert Kennedy Meml. Commn. of Inquiry into High Sch. Journalism, 1972-73. Ford Found. faculty fellow, 1952-53; research grantee U. Md. Mem. Nat. Council Social Studies (dir.), Am. Ednl. Studies Assn. (exec. bd. 1971-74), Soc. for Psychol. Study Social Issues, Am. Ednl. Research Assn., Council on Anthropology and Edn., A.A.A.S., Am. Assn. U. Profs., Am. Civil Liberties Union, Phi Beta Kappa. Author: Schools, Scholars and Society, 1965; Inter-group Education — Methods and Materials, 1968; (with others) Modern Methods in Secondary Education, 1952, rev. edit., 1958, 70; Black Image: Education Copes with Color, 1971; Black Self-Concept, 1972; Sex: Does it Make A Difference?, 1975. Contbr. articles to profl. publs. Home: 8502 49th Av College Park MD 20740

GRAMSE, ERNA LILLIAN, librarian; b. Holyoke, Mass., May 31, 1911; d. Edward R. and Karolina (Kraushar) Gramse; A.B., Mount Holyoke Coll., 1932; M.A., Cornell U., 1933, postgrad., 1934-35. Asst. chemistry Wheaton Coll., Norton, Mass., 1933-34; asst. tech. librarian Texaco, Inc., N.Y.C., 1935-46; head central information service FMC Corp., N.Y.C., 1946—. Mem. Am. Inst. Chemists (hon., nat. sec. 1968-72, dir. 1972—, chmn. N.Y. chpt. 1974—), mem. Am. Chem. Soc., Am. Soc. for Information Sci., Spl. Libraries Assn. (dir. N.Y. chpt. 1950-52), Sigma Delta Epsilon. Republican. Lutheran. Home: 45 Tudor City Place New York City NY 10017 Office: 633 3d Av New York City NY 10017

GRAND, ANN HUTTON (MRS. WILLIAM HERBERT GRAND), city-county ofcl.; b. Vancouver, B.C., Can., Dec. 27, 1918; d. John Edward Hutton and Jean (Shaw) Jeremy; B.A., U. B.C., 1940; postgrad. U. Ore.; m. William Herbert Grand, Nov. 3, 1942; 1 son, Jeremy Herbert. Came to U.S., 1945, naturalized, 1958. In charge Portland office League Ore. Cities, Portland, 1958-63; adminstrv. asst. Met. Study Commn., Portland, 1963-65; exec. sec. Ore. Port Authorities Commn., Portland, 1966-69; asst. City Club of Portland, 1970-71; asst. dir. City-County Charter Commn., Portland, 1971-74; pub. information officer Ore. Land Conservation and Devel. Commn., Portland, 1974—. Bd. dirs., mem. exec. com. Met. Area Perspective, 1964—. Mem. Women in Communications (dir. 1967), Ore. Press Women, League Women Voters (dir. Portland 1959). Home: 2675 SW Braemar Ct Portland OR 97201 Office: 1600 SW 4th St Portland OR 97201

GRAND, HELEN TOMSON (MRS. HENRY G. GRAND), psychologist, educator; b. N.Y.C.; d. Israel and Sarah (Sidlin) Tomson; Ph.D., N.Y.U., 1959; m. Henry G. Grand, May 9, 1936; children—Robert, Walter, Laura (Mrs. Robert Bartels). Tchr. elementary schs., 1930-50; guidance counselor N.Y.C. Bd. Edn., 1950-55; sch. psychologist Briarcliff Manor, N.Y., 1955-60; practice psychoanalysis and psychotherapy, N.Y.C., 1961—; lectr. psychotherapy Postgrad. Center Mental Health, N.Y.C., 1965—, supr. individual and group psychotherapy, 1968—; clin. instr. psychiatry Albert Einstein Coll. Medicine, Bronx, N.Y.C., 1967-68; asst. clin. prof. psychiatry N.Y. Med. Coll., N.Y.C., 1968—. Mem. Am., N.Y. psychol. assns., Am. Group Psychotherapy Assn. Address: 320 E 18th St New York City NY 10003

GRANESE, MARY ALICE, librarian; b. Wakefield, Mass., Apr. 28, 1914; d. Andrew and Madeline (DeFazio) Granese; A.B., Radcliffe Coll., 1936. Asst. librarian U.S. Rubber Co., Passaic, N.J., 1937-38; lit. searcher Gen. Chem. Co., Long Island City, N.Y., 1939-42; librarian Burroughs Wellcome Co., Tuckahoe, N.Y., 1942-43; chemist Melrose Labs. (Mass.), 1943-51; documents librarian Mass. Inst. Tech. Lincoln Lab., Lexington, 1951—. Mem. Am. Soc. for Information Sci., Spl. Libraries Assn. Home: 26 Franklin St Wakefield MA 01880 Office: 244 Wood St Lexington MA 02173

GRANGE, KATHLEEN MARY, educator; b. Preston, Eng., July 11, 1926; d. Joseph and Bertha (Bleazard) Grange; B.A. with honors in English and Philosophy, U. Birmingham (Eng.), 1947; diploma in edn., U. London (Eng.), 1948; Ph.D. in English (Clarke fellow), U. Cal. at Los Angeles, 1960, postdoctoral certificate in history medicine, 1964. Came to U.S., 1955, naturalized, 1964. Tchr. English, King Edward's VI Sch., 1948-50, then 2 Swiss finishing schs., 1950-51; historian Internat. Refugee Orgn., also tchr. Am. forces in Europe, 1951-52; tchr. English, U. Cal. at Los Angeles, 1956-60; prof. English, philosophy and world religion Compton (Cal.) Coll., 1964—. Nat. Inst. Mental Health grantee, 1960-64. Mem. Am. Assn. History Medicine, Cal. Tchrs. Assn. Author pamphlet The Slang of Watts, 1968, also articles on history psychiatry and psychology. Address: 1111 E Artesia Blvd Compton CA 90221

GRANGER, GRACE TOLIVAR, artist; b. N.Y.C.; d. (foster parents) Angel M. and Anna (Gabriel) Tolivar; student pub. schs., New Orleans; studied art at Francis T. Nicholls Sch., Harry Nolan Studio

Painting, Albert Rieker Studio Sculpture, New Orleans Art Sch., Grand Central Sch. Art N.Y.C.; m. Amedee P. Granger, Jr., Feb. 26, 1931 (div.). Conducted dept. store classes in batik and fabric painting, 1929; artist in batik design, murals, ceramics, sculpture, original doll creations, costumes, display designs, figures in papier mache and Mardi Gras balls and parades; head art dept. Jr. Univ. of New Orleans. One man show La. State Library, 1959, Royal Gallery, New Orleans, 1959, U. S.E. La., Lafayette. Artifacts and watercolors rep. 2000 yrs. of Paris fashion, for celebration 2000th birthday of Paris; exhibited La. Folklor Soc.; represented in pvt. doll collections, Conn. Dept. Edn., Bd. Edn., River Forest, Ill., Mus. State Hist. Soc. Wis. Executed life size figures of Gen. Andrew Jackson, Jean Lafitte, and others for exhibit of Battle of New Orleans Conf. in Secret Chamber Mus. of Old Absinthe House, 1950. Recipient 1st prize sculpture New Orleans Art Sch., 1927; popular prize for painting Delgado Mus., 1934; 1st prize ceramics Pirates Alley Outdoor Art Show, 1943, 2d prize ceramics and 2d prize graphic arts, 1947; 1st prize ceramics, Little Gallery, 1946; 1st prize water color painting, La. div. Nat. League Am. Pen Women, 1961; 1st prize watercolor, 2d prize oil Whitney Nat. Bank Competition, New Orleans, 1969; 1st prize oil painting, 1st prize watercolor Fedn. Women's Clubs in New Orleans, 1971. Mem. Art Assn. New Orleans, Women's Guild of New Orleans Opera House Assn., New Orleans Spring Fiesta Assn., France Amerique, La. Hist. Soc., Nat. League Am. Pen Woman (art chmn. La. br.), La. Folklore Soc., La. Poetry Soc. (pres. 1962—). Roman Catholic. Democrat. Contbrs. to Arts, New Orleans Display; Lectr. art and hist. character dolls, design, sculptural displays before schs., clubs, assns. Home: 626 Bourbon St New Orleans LA 70130

GRANGER, NANCY WHITTEMORE (MRS. WILLIAM N. GRANGER), ednl. adminstr.; b. Holyoke, Mass., June 8, 1938; d. Willis Homans and Dorothy Wendell (Gile) Whittemore; B.Ed., Plymouth State Coll., 1959; M.Ed., Boston U., 1962; M.P.E., Springfield Coll., 1965, certificate advanced study, 1970; m. William N. Granger, Feb. 15, 1973. Dir. girls phys. edn. Tenney High Sch., Methuen, Mass., 1959-62; head resident Springfield (Mass.) Coll., 1962-65, asst. dean students, 1966-70; asst. dean of women U. Me., Orono, 1965-66; with North Adams (Mass.) State Coll., 1971—, dir. intramural programs, 1973—. Bd. dirs. No. Berkshire United Community Services; mem. exec. bd. Greylock A.B.C. Inc., 1972—. Mem. Nat. Intramural Assn., Nat. Assn. Student Personnel Adminstrs. (mem. human rights com. 1973-74). Home: PO Box 24 Williamstown MA 01267 Office: Church St North Adams State College North Adams MA 01247

GRANGER, PATRICIA ROSE, educator; b. Hammond, Ind., Apr. 17, 1948; d. Lee and Patricia Rose (Lynch) Granger; certificate U. Innsbruck (Austria), 1964; B.A., U. Wis., 1970; M.A., Columbia, 1973. Caseworker, Lake County Dept. Pub. Welfare, Gary, Ind., 1970-71; coordinator student activities Brookdale Community Coll., Lincroft, N.J., 1971-73, counselor, 1973—. Mem. Nat. Assn. Woman Deans Adminstrs. and Counselors (mem. community coll. steering com. 1973-75), Am. Personnel and Guidance Assn., Assn. Coll. Unions Internat., Kappa Kappa Gamma Alumni Assn. Home: 2131 Aldrin Rd Apt 5A Ocean Township NJ 07712 Office: 765 Newman Springs Rd Lincroft NJ 07738

GRANICHER, BETH ROBINSON (MRS. BRUCE JUSTICE GRANICHER), librarian; b. San Luis Obispo, Cal., Aug. 24, 1931; d. Herbert Catherwood and Neva Lee (Robinson) Grundell; B.A., U. Cal. at Berkeley, 1953, M.L.S., 1968; m. Bruce Justice Granicher, Aug. 15, 1953; children—Jill, William, James. Periodicals librarian Holy Names Coll. Library, Oakland, Cal., 1969-70, chief librarian, 1970—. Mem. Am., Cal. library assns., Catholic Library Assn., U. Cal. Library Sch. Alumni Assn., Beta Phi Mu. Republican. Lutheran. Home: 1009 Knightwood Ct Walnut Creek CA 94596 Office: 3500 Mountain Blvd Oakland CA 94619

GRANNIS, AINSLIE DINWIDDIE, former city ofcl.; b. New Orleans, July 18, 1938; d. George Summey and Augusta Rosser (Benners) Dinwiddie; student Smith Coll., 1956-57, Tulane U., 1958, La. State U., 1958-62; m. Alexander Banks Grannis, June 6, 1971; 1 son, George Wilcox Snellings. Asst. editor Newsweek Mag., N.Y.C., 1965-69; contributing editor Bus. Week Mag., N.Y.C., 1969-71; dir. pvt. involvement programs Parks, Recreation and Cultural Affairs Adminstrn., N.Y.C., 1973-74. Mem. The Parks Council, Sierra Club, Civil Liberties Union. Club: City of N.Y. Home: 501 E 87th St New York City NY 10028

GRANNIS, FLORENCE SPRAGUE, librarian; b. Wash., Oct. 9, 1919; d. F.I. and Bertha Lee (Silva) Sprague; B.A. in Sociology cum laude, U. Wash., 1950, B.A. in L.S., 1951; M.S. in L.S., U. So. Cal., 1961; div.; children—David, Linda (Mrs. Leonard Good), Christopher. Charge Seattle Library for Blind, 1952-60; librarian Ia. Library for Blind, 1960—; asst. dir. Ia. Commn. Blind, 1960—; co-editor Ia. Transcriber, 1964—. Mem. Am. (chmn. round table library service to blind 1967), Ia. library assns., Spl. Libraries Assn., Nat. Braille Assn., Assn. Edn. Visually Handicapped, Ia. Assn. Preservation Historic Landmarks, African Violet Soc. Am., Des Moines Eve. African Violet Club, Am. Iris Soc. Contbr. articles in field. Address: 524 4th St Des Moines IA 50309

GRANO, BARBARA SUE KOPRIVER (MRS. JAMES NICHOLAS GRANO), pub. relations cons.; b. Kansas City, Mo., Mar. 13, 1949; d. Edward Otto and Terry (Minor) Kopriver; B.A., Ohio State U., 1971; m. James Nicholas Grano, Mar. 13, 1971. Pub. relations dir. Ohio Arts Council, 1970-71; pub. information specialist Columbus (O.) Dept. Devel., 1972-74; dir. pub. relations Designers and Communicators, 1974—. Free-lance pub. relations cons., 1972—. Mem. Central Ohio Bicentennial Observance Com. Trustee Better Environment for Everyone, Inc., 1973—. Recipient Bee award for pub. service Better Environment for Everyone, Inc., 1973, Young Republican award Capital City Young Rep. Club, 1973. Mem. Women in Communications (chmn. publicity clinic 1973), Phi Mu (Outstanding sr. award 1971). Republican. Roman Catholic. Home: 1959 Wickford Rd Columbus OH 43221 Office: Designers and Communicators 423 Granville Sq Worthington OH 43085

GRANT, ELIZABETH BRUBAKER (MRS. BEN J. GRANT), artist; b. St. Paul, Apr. 3, 1917; d. Delmer Dawson and Maude (Spear) Brubaker; student Sarah Lawrence Coll., 1934-37; m. Ben J. Grant, Aug. 9, 1938; children—William Dowman, Richard Martin, Martha Watts (Mrs. Mark A. Bedner). One-man shows Down East Gallery, Washington, Port Royal Inn, Hilton Head, S.C., 1970, Red Piano Gallery, Hilton Head Island, S.C., 1973; exhibited in group shows at Nat. Press Club Ann. Art Shows, Washington Soc. Artists Show, 1962. Recipient First Popular prize Washington Religious Art Exhibit, 1962, 65, Congl. Club Art Show, 1964, St. Andrews Religious Art Exhibit, 1964, 65, Best of Show Nat. Capitol Garden Club Show, 1956, 62. Mem. Nat. Capital Area Fedn. Garden Clubs, Artists Equity Assn. Conglist. Clubs: Kenwood Golf and Country (Bethesda, Md.); Plantation (Hilton Head). Home: 7000 Orkney Pkwy Bethesda MD 20034 also North Sea Pines Dr Hilton Head Island SC 29928

GRANT, EVVA H., writer, editor; b. Rock Island, Ill., Feb. 22; d. Morris and Ida (Learner) Handelman; A.B., Augustana Coll., 1934; A.M., State U. Ia., 1937; m. Herman Grant, June 5, 1934; 1 son, David. Tchr. pre-sch. and parent edn., St. Louis, 1936-37; editor P.T.A. mag., 1940—, editor-in-chief Nat. Congress Parents-Tchr., 1940-72; asso. Boutwell, Crane & Moseley Assos., 1972—; interpreter (voice P.T.A.) on Baxters radio program sponsored by P.T.A. and NBC. Vis. lectr. Northwestern U., summers 1945, 46; mem. edn. faculty Lincoln Acad. Ill. Cons. pub. adv. bd. FOA, 1954; lectr. child devel. and parent edn. Sec. U.S. nat. Com. Internat. Union Family Orgns., 1963-65. Mem. bd. visitors Singer Learning Centers for Early Childhood Edn. Mem. Ednl. Press Assn. Am. (pres. 1941-43, exec. com. 1943-45), Edn. Writers Assn., Am. Child Guidance Found. (adv. bd.), N.E.A., Sigma Xi (asso.), Delta Kappa Gamma. Cons. editor: Community Life in a Democracy (Nat. Congress Parents and Teachers), 1942; editor: Guiding Children as They Grow, 1959, P.T.A. Guide to What's Happening in Education, 1965. Author: Parents and Teachers as Partners, 1952, rev. edit., 1971. Contbr. to ednl. jours. Home: 2600 N Lakeview Chicago IL 60614 Office: 52 Vanderbilt Av New York City NY 10017

GRANT, JUANITA G., librarian; b. Princeton, W. Va., July 25, 1930; d. William Randle and Cora (Fitch) Grant; B.S., Concord Coll., 1953; B.S. in L.S., U. N.C., 1955; M.Liberal Arts, Johns Hopkins U., 1970. Librarian, Spl. Services, U.S. Army, Germany, France, 1956-58; asst. librarian Carson Newman Coll., Jefferson City, Tenn., 1959-63; librarian Judson Coll., Marion, Ala., 1964-67; dir. Blount Library, Averett Coll., Danville, Va., 1967—. Mem. A.L.A., Southeastern, Va. library assns., Am. Hist. Soc., Danville Hist. Soc. Baptist. Club: Wednesday (Danville). Home: 126 Primrose Ct Danville VA 24541

GRANT, TONI GALE (MRS. NEIL HOLLANDER), clin. psychologist; b. N.Y.C., Apr. 3, 1942; d. Joseph and Blanche (Walker) Grant; B.A., Vassar Coll., 1964; M.S., Syracuse U., 1968, Ph.D., 1970; m. Neil Hollander, May 14, 1965; 1 dau., Kimberly Grant. Intern, VA Hosp., Southeastern Mental Health Center, Sioux Falls, S.D., 1968-69; individual practice pvt. and group psychotherapy, Hollywood, Cal., 1972—; moderator, psychol. cons. sta. KGBS, Storer Broadcasting, Los Angeles. Bd. govs. Am. Acad. of Achievement, 1974. Mem. Am. Psychol. Assn., Internat. Transactional Analysis Assn., Los Angeles Group Psychotherapy Assn., Group Psychotherapy Assn. So. Cal. Contbr. articles to profl. jours. Office: West Hollywood CA 90069

GRANVILLE, NORMA BELLE, hematologist; b. Lynn, Mass., Dec. 12, 1923; d. Zanford D. and Alta May (McIntire) Granville; R.N., Syracuse U., 1944, A.B., 1948, M.D., 1952. Intern, Albany Hosp., 1952-53, resident, 1953-54, fellow, 1954-55; chief med. resident St. Francis Hosp., 1955-56; blood research fellow Blood Research Lab., New Eng. Center Hosp., 1956-58; dir. hematology service St. Francis Hosp., Hartford, Conn., 1958—; cons. hematologist Newington Hosp. Crippled Children, 1963—, Newington Hosp., VA, 1964—, Rocky Hill Soldier's Home, 1969—, Windham Meml. Hosp., 1969—; asst. prof. medicine U. Conn. Med. and Dental Sch., 1969—. Served with USNR, 1944-46. Damon Runyon Cancer Research grantee, 1956-58. Fellow A.C.P.; mem. Am. Soc. Hematology, Hartford County Med. Assn., A.M.A., Conn. Med. Soc. Home: 126 Clover St Windsor CT 06095 Office: 114 Woodland St Hartford CT 06105

GRASS, ELLEN ROBINSON, med. instrument co. exec.; b. Taunton, Mass., Mar. 29, 1914; d. Francis J. and Laura (Waldron) Robinson; A.B. in Biology, Radcliffe Coll., 1935, M.A., 1936; LL.D., Regis Coll., 1970; m. Albert M. Grass, June 28, 1936; children—Robert W., Henry J. Clk., sales mgr., treas. Grass Instrument Co., Quincy, Mass., 1935—. Pres., sec. Grass Found., 1967—; pres. Am. Epilepsy Fedn., 1959-60, Internat. Bur. Epilepsy, 1966—; sr. v.p. Epilepsy Found. Am., 1967—; mem. Mass. Developmental Disabilities Council, 1971; mem. adv. council Nat. Inst. Neurol. Disease and Stroke, 1969-73; mem. corp. Marine Biol. Lab., Woods Hole, Mass., 1969—; vis. com. Bd. Overseers to Grad. Sch. Arts and Scis., Harvard, 1970—; developmental disabilities adv. com. Social Rehab. Services, Dept. Health, Edn. and Welfare, Region I, 1971; mem. Nat. Commn. on Multiple Sclerosis, 1973-74. Trustee, Regis Coll., Weston, Mass., 1974—. Porter fellow Am. Physiol. Soc., 1936. Mem. Eastern, So., Central, Western electroencephalographic socs., Phi Beta Kappa. Home: 77 Reservoir Rd Quincy MA 02170 Office: 101 Old Colony Av Quincy MA 02169

GRASSELLI, JEANETTE GECSY (MRS. ROBERT K. GRASSELLI), chemist; b. Cleve., Aug. 4, 1928; d. Nicholas W. and Veronica (Varga) G.; B.S., Ohio U., 1950; M.S., Western Res. U., 1958; m. Robert K. Grasselli, July 20, 1957. Jr. chemist Standard Oil Co., Cleve., 1950-56, tech. specialist, 1957-64, supr. molecular spectroscopy sect., 1965—. Lectr., Case Western Res. U., Cleve., 1967-73, Canisius Coll., Buffalo, 1967-69; spl. cons. infrared spectroscopy Cleve. Council World Affairs, 1964—. Recipient Chem. Profession award Cleve. Chem. Soc.-Cleve. Chem. Engrs. Soc., 1963; certificate of merit Ohio U., 1965. Mem. Fedn. Analytical Chemistry and Spectroscopy Socs. (chmn. governing bd. 1971-73); mem. Soc. for Applied Spectroscopy (nat. pres. 1970), Coblentz Soc. (bd. mgrs. 1968-71), Phi Beta Kappa, Iota Sigma Pi. Editor: Atlas of Spectral Data and Physical Constants for Organic Compounds, 1973; (with Ed Brame) Practical Spectroscopy (M. Dekker), 1974. Mem. adv. bd. Analytical Chemistry, 1972-74. Contbr. articles to profl. publs. Home: 130 Greentree Rd Chagrin Falls OH 44022 Office: 4440 Warrensville Rd Cleveland OH 44128

GRASSI, MADELLE LYONS HEGELER, art broker; b. Danville, Ill.; s. Edward C. and Madelle (Lyons) Hegeler; student Northwestern U., 1948; B.A., Vassar Coll., 1952; M.A., Sorbonne, Paris, France, 1954; postgrad. Ecole du Louvre, Paris, 1955; m. Luigi A. Grassi, Nov. 29, 1962 (div. Oct., 1969); children—Cornelia Maria, Giovanna Camilla. Dir. pub. relations, saleswoman French & Co., N.Y.C., 1956-58, fgn. rep., 1959-60; self-employed art broker, Paris, N.Y.C., 1960—. Mem. Delta Delta Delta. Republican. Episcopalian. Home: Brigadune PO Box 214 Southampton NY 11968 also 41 Quai d'Orsay Paris 7 France Office: 35 E 76th St New York City NY 10021

GRASSO, DORIS TENEYCK (MRS. DOMINIC LAWRENCE GRASSO), artist; b. Sullivan County, N.Y., May 3, 1914; d. Eugene Oscar and Elsie (TenEyck) Teschner; student Ednl. Alliance, N.Y.C., 1957-57; student art centers and pvt. art tng.; m. Dominic Lawrence Grasso, Nov. 29, 1933; children—Robert Eugene, Virginia Ann. Art dir., instr. Doris Grasso Sch. Fine Arts, Bayonne, N.J., 1952-61; exhibited in numerous group shows, including Thomson Gallery, N.Y.C., Pen and Brush Club, N.Y.C., Terry Art Inst., Miami, Fla., Newark Art Mus., Montclair (N.J.) Art Mus., Lever House, N.Y.C., Nat. Arts Club, N.Y.C.; one man shows Burr Gallery, N.Y.C., Bennett Coll., Bayonne Pub. Library, others; represented in Paul Whitener Meml. Collection, Hickory (N.C.) Mus. Art, George B. Burr Permanent Collection, N.Y.C., Bambergers Collection Famous People N.J., Jersey City Art Mus. Trustee, Jersey City Mus. Art, 1955-57. Recipient Pauline Wick award, 1961, Windsor Newton awards, 1958, 61, Jersey City Mus. award, 1958; gold medallion Jersey Jour. award, gold medal Woman's Club, 1963; award for nat. achievement in art Amita, Inc., 1966; 1st award for sculpture Fedn. Women's Clubs, Ridgewood, N.J., 1971; 1st sculpture award Womens Club, Atlantic City, N.J., 1971; others. Fellow Am. Artists Profl. League, Internat. Arts and Letters (Switzerland); mem. Burr Artists, Hudson Artists (pres. 1960-62), Jersey City Mus. Assn., N.J. Painters and Sculptors Soc. (dir., rec. sec.), Trailside Art Mus. (permanent mem.), Essex Watercolor Soc. Bayonne Mus. Arts, Whistler Art Soc., Burr Galleries, Village Art Center Galleries, Sarasota Mus. Art Assn., Hunterdon Art Center Assn., Newark Art Center, Hudson Artists (dir.), Gotham Painters Rutherford, Plainfield art assns., Rockport Artists Assn. (asso.), Elks Aux. (pres. 1950-52), Ch. Guild (pres. 1950-52). Club: Bayonne Women's (art chmn.). Address: 88 W 32d St Bayonne NJ 07002 also Doris TenEyck Grasso Gallery 15 Langsford St Lanesville Cape Ann Gloucester MA 01930

GRASSO, ELLA T. (MRS. THOMAS A. GRASSO), gov. Conn.; b. Windsor Locks, Conn., May 10, 1919; d. James and Maria (Oliva) Tambussi; student pvt. schs.; B.A. magna cum laude, Mt. Holyoke Coll., 1940, M.A., 1942; m. Thomas A. Grasso, Aug. 31, 1942; children—Susane, James. Asst. dept. econs. and sociology Mt. Holyoke Coll., 1942; asst. state dir. research War Manpower Commn., 1943-46. Mem. Conn. Legislature, 1953, 55, asst. house leader, 1955; state sec. State of Conn., 1958-70; mem. 92d Congress from 6th Dist. Conn.; gov. Conn., 1975—. Democratic nat. committeewoman from Conn., 1956-58, chmn. platform com., 1956—, co-chmn. resolution com. Nat. Dem. Conv., 1964; del. Conn. Constl. Conv., Dem. floor leader; chmn. planning com. Gov's Commn. Status Women, also mem. commn.; adv. bd. Hartford chpt. Am. Com. Italian Migration. Hon. mem. bd. Urban League; mem. Com. 100 U Hartford; adviser Mental Health Planning Com., 1964; hon. chmn. Red Cross Campaign, Conn. 1964; state chmn. of Cystic Fibrosis Assn., 1966; mem. Windsor Locks Pub. Library Bd.; trustee Conn. Opera Assn. Recipient Amita award as outstanding woman of Italian parentage, 1959; Am. Heritage award, 1961; Americanism award B'nai B'rith, 1963; Italian-Am. Gold Medal, 1963; leadership award Assn. Retarded Children, 1963; Silver Apple award Conn. Edn. Assn., 1964; Woman of Year, Bus. and Profl. Woman's Club, Hartford, 1964; Distinguished Service citation Am. Legion Aux., 1965; citation for devotion ideals edn. Kappa Delta Pi; others. Mem. Am. Assn. U. Women, Nat. Assn. Secs. of State, League Women Voters, Order Sons Italy in Am., Regina Elena Soc., Council of Cath. Women. Clubs: Mt. Holyoke (Hartford); Pilot. Address: 13 Olive St Windsor Locks CT 06096

GRAU, SHIRLEY ANN (MRS. JAMES KERN FEIBLEMAN), author; b. New Orleans, July 8, 1929; d. Adolph and Katherine (Onions) Grau; B.A., Tulane U., 1950; m. James Kern Feiblemen, Aug. 4, 1955; children—Ian J., Nora M., William L., Katherine S. Writer for Holiday, The New Yorker, New World Writing, Mademoiselle, Sat. Eve. Post, The Atlantic, The Reporter, 1954—. Recipient Pulitzer prize for fiction, 1965. Author: The Black Prince and Other Stories, 1955; The Hard Blue Sky, 1958; The House on Coliseum Street, 1961; The Keepers of the House, 1964. Mem. Phi Beta Kappa. Address: care Brandt & Brandt 101 Park Av New York City NY 10017

GRAVATT, JOAN HARRIET STACY (MRS. ROBERT H. GRAVATT, JR.), govt. ofcl.; b. Plainfield, N.J.; d. Henry E.R. and Grace (Lipsius) Stacy; A.B. cum laude, Smith Coll., 1937; M.A., Am. U., 1948; m. Robert H. Gravatt, Jr., Oct. 9, 1954; 1 son, Robert H. Economist, WPB, Washington, 1942-44; chief air priorities sect., 1944-45; chief air cargo priorities sect. U.S. Dept. State, Washington, 1945-46, divisional asst. comml. policy div., 1946-47, fgn. affairs officer Office of Aviation, 1948—. Mem. U.S. delegation confs. Internat. Civil Aviation Orgn., 1948-74. Mem. Internat. Aviation Club (membership chmn. 1965-66). Clubs: Smith College of Hartford (publicity chmn. 1940); Smith College of Washington (treas. 1958-60). Internat. editor Jour. Air Law and Commerce, 1948-52. Home: 6319 Kenhowe Dr Bethesda MD 20034 Office: Dept of State Washington DC 20520

GRAVES, (ALTA FRANCES) JUDY (MRS. HAROLD NATHAN GRAVES, JR.), writer; b. Collinsville, Okla.; d. Joseph Richard and Pearl (Furnish) Judy; B.A., W.Va. U., 1934; M.S., Columbia, 1936; m. Harold Nathan Graves, Jr., July 9, 1937; children—Stephen T., Thomas Perry, Michael A. Reporter Charleston (W.Va.) Daily Mail, 1934-35; edn. editor Lit. Digest, 1936-37; asso. editor Pathfinder Mag., 1938-39; mng. editor N.J. Ednl. Rev., 1939-40; story editor Audience Research Inst., Princeton, N.J., 1941; chief edn. sect., war savs. staff U.S. Treasury Dept., 1941-42, editorial asst. to asst. to. Sec. of Treasury, 1943, editor Minuteman war finance div., 1943-44; editor Cancer Control Letter, Nat. Cancer Inst., 1948-49; editor Gist, Nat. Com. Careers in Med. Tech., 1957-62, ann. Directory of Pathology Tng. Programs, 1968—; coordinating editor The Future of Medical Education, Duke Press, 1973; author health pamphlets, film discussion guides, film script Pub. Affairs Com., 1962-64; information counsel Intersoc. Com. Pathology Information, Bethesda, Md., 1964—; pres. Information Services, Inc., Bethesda, 1969—. Chmn. women's hospitality com. ann. meeting World Bank, 1965, 69. Vice chmn. Democratic Precinct, Montgomery County, Md., chmn. publicity Kensington Dem. Club, 1952-56, Werner for Congress Com., 1952, Woman's Suburban Dem. Club, Montgomery County, 1957-61; dir. publicity Montgomery County campaign com. John F. Kennedy, 1960; mem. Inaugural Ball Com., 1960, 64. Mem. Nat. Assn. Sci. Writers, Am. Med. Writers Assn., Kappa Tau Alpha, Delta Gamma. Mem. Christian Ch. Home: 4816 Grantham Av Chevy Chase MD 20015 Office: Information Services Inc 9650 Rockville Pike Bethesda MD 20014

GRAVES, AVIS JEANETTE RUTHVEN (MRS. WILLIAM H. GRAVES III), educator, ednl. psychologist; b. Cades, S.C., Nov. 15, 1943; d. William Geta and Vera (Jeffords) Ruthven; B.A., Winthrop Coll., 1965; postgrad. Merrill-Palmer Inst., 1964-65; M.Ed., U. Fla., 1967, Ed.D., 1971; m. William H. Graves, III, Aug. 21, 1965. Instr. community coll. edn. Miss. State U., 1968-69, instr. ednl. psychology, 1969-72, asst. prof. ednl. psychology, 1972-74, asso. prof., 1975—. Mem. Am., Southeastern, Miss. psychol. assns., Am. Assn. U. Profs., Am. Ednl. Research Assn., Nat. Council Measurement in Edn., Miss. State U. Edn. Assn. (sec.-treas. 1969-71), Phi Kappa Phi. Presbyn. Contbr. articles to profl. jours. Home: 206 Windsor Rd Starkville MS 39759 Office: Drawer EP Mississippi State MS 39762

GRAVES, CONSTANCE JEAN LAFFOON, physician; b. DuQuoin, Ill., May 30, 1924; d. Fred James and Florence (Eaton) Laffoon; student So. Ill. U., 1941-43; A.B., U. Chgo., 1945; M.D. with distinction, Northwestern U., 1950; m. James H. Graves, Dec. 22, 1944 (div. June 1949). Intern Chgo. Wesley Meml. Hosp., 1950-51, resident in anesthesiology, 1952-54, attending staff anesthesiology, 1954-65; mem. faculty Northwestern U. Med. Sch., 1954-65; instr. U. Utah Coll. Medicine, 1966-68, asst. prof. anesthesiology, 1968-74; attending physician U. Utah Med. Center, Salt Lake City, 1966-74. Cons. Salt Lake VA Hosp., 1966-74; vis. staff Intermountain Shriner's Hosp. for Crippled Children, 1966-71; active staff San Jose (Cal.) Hosp. and Health Center, Santa Teresa Hosp., San Jose, 1974—. Diplomate Am. Bd. Anesthesiology. Fellow Am. Coll. Anesthesiologists; mem. A.M.A., A.A.A.S., Internat. Anesthesia Research Soc., Am., Cal. socs. anesthesiologists, Cal., Santa Clara County med. assns., Alpha Omega Alpha. Home: 20051 Northwood Dr Cupertino CA 95014 Office: 25 N 14th St Suite 560 San Jose CA 95112

GRAVES, DOROTHY LOU IRISH (MRS. BRUCE B. GRAVES), banker; b. Hurley, N.M., Feb. 10, 1925; d. R. Levon and Lucretia Alice (Dunbar) Irish; student Meadows-Draughn Bus. Sch., 1945-46; m. Paul Orban Barron, Apr. 5, 1942 (dec. Oct. 1961); children—Charlotte L. Linda K., Paul Levon; m. 2d, Bruce B. Graves, Aug. 29, 1962. Sec. Samuel G. Wiener Co., Shreveport, La., 1946-47; bookkeeper Haslam Lumber Co. (Tex.), 1950-52; bookkeeper Tex. State Bank, Joaquin, 1952-55, asst. cashier, 1955-67, cashier, 1967—. Bd. dirs. Joaquin Cemetery Perpetual Fund Com. Presbyn. Mem. Order Eastern Star. Home: Box 95 Joaquin TX 75954 Office: Box 98 Texas State Bank Joaquin TX 75954

GRAVES, ELEANOR MACKENZIE (MRS. RALPH GRAVES), publ. co. exec.; b. N.Y.C., Sept. 28, 1926; d. Luther Burns and Rena (Glogau) MacKenzie; B.A. magna cum laude, Barnard Coll., 1948; children by previous marriage—William White Parish Jr., Alexander Parish; m. Ralph Graves, Oct. 27, 1958; children—Sara Evans, Andrew Donaldson. With Time, Inc., 1948—, reporter Life Mag., 1948-52, editor, 1952-60, sr. editor, 1960-64, dir. programming Time-Life Films, 1971-73, exec. producer, 1973—, v.p., 1973—. Author: Great Dinners From Life, 1969; Best of Everything Cookbook, 1971. Contbr. articles to popular mags. Home: 1158 5th Av New York City NY 10029 Office: Time-Life Films Time Life Bldg Rockefeller Center NY 10020

GRAVES, ELIZABETH ANN, librarian; b. Stamford, Conn., July 1, 1929; d. Thomas Ashley and Esther (Brittain) Graves; B.A. in Music, Wells Coll., 1951; M.Music in Musicology, Boston U., 1958; M.L.S., Simmons Coll., 1963. Sec. TV dept. Am. Bible Soc., N.Y.C., 1953-54; sec. to editor-in-chief Allyn & Bacon, Inc., Boston, 1954-56; head sch. fine and applied arts library Boston U. Libraries, 1959-64, head circulation, 1967-68, head audio dept., 1968—. Mem. Music Library Assn., Am. Musicol. Soc. Club: Republican (Boston). Home: 9 Claflin Rd Brookline MA 02146 Office: 771 Commonwealth Av Boston MA 02215

GRAVES, (GRACE) PAULINE BERG (MRS. LYLE LEVERNE GRAVES), journalist; b. Salt Lake City; d. Carl Ingebret and Blanch (Hurlbut) Berg; A.A., Glendale Jr. Coll., 1934; B.S. cum laude, U. So. Cal., 1937; m. Lyle Leverne Graves, Oct. 16, 1937; children—Dennis Leverne, Terry Lou (Mrs. Jim R. Davis). Copywriter, Barker Bros. Furnishings Store, Los Angeles, 1937-42; freelance writer specializing in home ideas, Los Angeles, 1938—. Mem. Trojan League (v.p. 1969), Theta Sigma Phi (chpt. pres. 1960), Pi Beta Phi. Republican. Author: Distinctive Ideas, 1947. Contbr. articles to Los Angeles Times Home Mags, Better Homes and Gardens, others; syndicated newspaper columnist Try This, 1952—. Address: 6307 Riggs Pl Los Angeles CA 90045

GRAVES, JEANNE REINERT (MRS. CHARLES EDGAR GRAVES), audio-visual producer; b. Memphis, Jan. 22, 1941; d. John Carl and Helen (Barnett) Reinert; B.J., U. Tex., 1962; m. Charles Edgar Graves, Aug. 15, 1964; children—Barbara Michelle, John Justin. Amusements editor Beaumont (Tex.) Jour., 1962-63; sci. writer and editor Sci. Digest, N.Y.C., 1964-73; pres. Voices Am., Short Hills, N.J., 1972—. Mem. Women in Communications, Nat. Assn. Sci. Writers, League Women Voters (dir. Berkeley Heights, Millburn, N.J. 1968-72, pres. Essex County, N.J. 1973—). Home: 80 Hemlock Rd Short Hills NJ 07078 Office: 80 Hemlock Rd Short Hills NJ 07078

GRAVLEE, PAULINE ELIZABETH, univ. dean; b. Birmingham, Ala., June 5, 1924; d. Walter Sylvester and Pearl (Tanner) Gravlee; student U. Ala., 1943-45; A.B., Samford U., 1948; M.A., George Peabody Coll., 1951; postgrad. Inst. for Ednl. Mgmt., Harvard, 1972. Clerk-typist Tenn. Coal, Iron and R.R. Co., Fairfield, Ala., 1942-45; sec. counseling service Samford U., Birmingham, Ala., 1948-49; psychology instr. Mary Hardin-Baylor Coll., Belton, Tx., 1949-50; dean women Va. Intermont Coll., Bristol, 1951-54; dean women U. North Ala. at Florence, 1954-73, dean student life, 1973—. Chmn. Citizens Adv. Council, 1972—. Bd. dirs. Met. N.W. Ala., 1974—; bd. govs. Am. Educators Life Ins. Co. Chmn. Nat. Found., Lauderdale County chpt., 1963—. Mem. Am. Assn. U. Women (pres. Ala. div. 1968-70), Ala. Assn. Women Deans and Counselors (pres. 1960-62), Ala. Guidance Assn. (v.p. 1959), Phi Kappa Phi. Baptist. Home: 2304 Bower Dr Florence AL 35630

GRAVLEY, ERNESTINE HUDLOW (MRS. LOUPE H. GRAVLEY), author; b. Russellville, Ark., Feb. 4, 1918; d. Joseph Ernest and Mary (Mullins) Hudlow; student Ark. State Tchrs. Coll., 1940, Ouachita Coll., 1947, U. Okla., 1956, Harding Coll., 1959, Newspaper Inst., N.Y.C., 1960; m. Loupe Hames Gravley, Jan. 12, 1940; children—Almalou (Mrs. Jerry L. Cowan), Carol Ann (Mrs. Larry Floyd Fugit). Newspaper reporter, columnist Shawnee News-Star, 1970—; staff writer Daily Oklahoman, Oklahoma City, 1970—; free-lance mag. writer, 1946—; staff cons. Ark. Writers Conf., Little Rock, 1946—. Mem. staff asso. dist. judge 23d jud. dist., Okla., 1967—. Mem. Nat. League Am. Pen Women (2d v.p. Ark. Pioneer br. 1948-50, 68-70), Ark., Okla. hist. assns., Okla. Writers Fedn. (pres. Shawnee chpt., exec. bd. 1968—, state pres. 1972—), Beta Sigma Phi. Author: Hang on to the Willows, 1958, rev. 1968; A History of Pottawatomie County, other books. Contbr. articles, short stories to mags. Home: 1225 Sherry Lane Shawnee OK 74801 Office: Office of Dist Judge Courthouse Shawnee OK 74801

GRAY, ALMA MARCUS (MRS. DONALD MILTON GRAY), physicist; b. Rotterdam, Netherlands, Oct. 1, 1925; d. Eugen and Jette (Blazer) Marcus; B.S., McGill U., 1948, M.S., 1950; Ph.D., Rensselaer Poly. Inst., 1964; m. Donald Milton Gray, May 21, 1967. Came to U.S., 1953, naturalized, 1958. Mathematician, NRC Can., Ottawa, 1948, 49-50, research asst., 1953-54; fellow U. Ill., 1950-52; research asst. McGill U., Montreal, 1952-53; research engr. Sprague Electric Co., North Adams, Mass., 1954-59; research physicist Watervliet (N.Y.) Arsenal, 1964—. Chmn., Town of Brunswick (N.Y.) Conservation Adv. Council, 1973—; mem. Environmental Planning Lobby, 1971—. Mem. Am. Phys. Soc. Club: Adirondack Mountain (Albany, N.Y.). Contbr. articles to profl. publs. Home: 36 Oxford Circle Troy NY 12180 Office: Watervliet Arsenal Watervliet NY 12180

GRAY, AMELIA COBB, educator; b. Washington, May 1, 1939; d. William Montague and Hilda (Smith) Cobb; B.A., Carleton Coll., 1960; M.F.A., Yale, 1963; m. Leander Gray, July 2, 1963 (div. Mar. 1970); 1 son, Leander C. Tchr. French, Jonathan Law High Sch., Milford, Conn., 1963-67; part-time instr. Fed. City Coll., Washington, 1970; asst. prof. speech and drama D.C. Tchrs. Coll., Washington, 1970—. Drama cons. One America, Inc., 1971-72. Mem. Am. Theatre Assn., Am. Fedn. Tchrs. (local v.p. 1973-74). Unitarian. Home: 2218 Washington Av Silver Spring MD 20910 Office: DC Tchrs College 2565 Georgia Av NW Washington DC 20001

GRAY, ANN EVALYNN, pub. relations exec.; b. Canton, O., Nov. 23, 1922; d. Donald Shafer and Dorothy Mary (Cramblet) Gray; B.A., Kent State U., 1948. Reporter, photographer Courier Tribune, Kent, O., 1947-48; dir. pub. relations Aultman Hosp., Canton, 1948-52, Mercy and Timken Mercy Hosps., Canton, 1954-61, Akron City Hosp., Akron, 1963—; cons. hosp. pub. relations, 1961-62; dir. personnel Mt. Sinai Hosp., Cleve., 1962-63. Trustee Am. Cancer Soc., Akron, Summit County Kidney Found., Akron. Served with USNR, 1943-45, 52-54; now Res. Named Distinguished Alumnus, Sch. Journalism, Kent State U., 1968. Mem. Am. Assn. U. Women, Bus. and Profl. Women, Naval Res. Assn., Women in Communications, U.S. Naval Inst., Kent State U. Alumnae Assn. (sec. bd. trustees 1956-58), Akron Hosp. Council (chmn. pub. relations com. 1970—), Am. Legion. Club: Akron Press. Contbr. articles to profl. jours. Home: 458 Spaulding Dr Kent OH 44240 Office: 525 E Market St Akron OH 44309

GRAY, BARBARA JEAN ALDRIDGE (MRS. WILLIAM S. GRAY), oil co. exec.; b. Indpls., Sept. 24, 1924; d. Frank M. and Odessa (King) Aldridge; student Ward-Belmont Coll., 1943-45; m. William S. Gray, June 15, 1946; children—David Bradford, Sharron Aldridge. Treas., Middle States Oil Co., Lakewood, O., 1960-68, treas., sec., 1969—, v.p., gen. mgr., 1970—. Active A.R.C.; mem. blood program adv. com. Vol. Bur., Welfare Fedn., 1965—; mem. children's bd. Lakewood Hosp., 1951-52; dir. vols. Sunny Acres Hosp., 1969—. Mem. Women's Golf Assn. (pres. 1959). Methodist (Council on Ministries 1972—). Clubs: Westwood Country (Rocky River, O.); Union (Cleve.); Rolling Rock (Ligonier, Pa.). Home: 1269 E Melrose Dr Westlake OH 44145 Office: 14812 Detroit Av Lakewood OH 44107

GRAY, DORIS MARY KAVANAGH (MRS. JOHN GRAY), physician, cardiologist; b. Carleton, Que., Can., Sept. 15, 1930; d. Alfred John and Evelyn Philomen (Bujold) Kavanagh; M.D., Ottawa U., 1954; m. John Gray, July 22, 1953; children—Cynthia, John, Andrea. Intern, Ottawa Gen. Hosp., 1953-54; resident Henry Ford Hosp., Detroit, 1954-59; practice medicine, specializing in cardiology, Vancouver, B.C., 1959—; chief div. cardiology St. Paul's Hosp., Vancouver, 1959—; asst. prof. medicine U. B.C., 1968—; cons. cardiologist Children's Hosp. B.C., 1960—. Mem. med. adv. bd. B.C. Heart Found., 1967-72. Diplomate Am. Bd. Internal Medicine. Fellow Royal Coll. Physicians, A.C.P., Am. Coll. Cardiology; mem. Canadian Cardiovascular Soc. (counciler on bd. dirs. 1969-72), Vancouver Heart Assn. (pres. 1965). Home: 1638 W 49th St Vancouver BC Canada Office: 1081 Burrard St Vancouver BC Canada

GRAY, ETHEL MCCULLOUGH, ch. ofcl.; b. Hastings, Fla., July 29, 1912; d. Charles Henry and Cuba (Doak) McCullough; grad. high sch.; m. Bruce Gray, Jan. 30, 1929 (dec. Aug. 1962); children—Donna (Mrs. Donald L. Myhre), Jennie (Mrs. James J. Boyer), David Bruce, Dale Marie, Alan Neil. Owner-operator Gray Farms, Putnam County, Fla., 1962—. Coop. weather observer U.S. Weather Bur., 1962—. Mem. World Methodist Council, 1966—; del. Gen. Conf. Meth. Ch., 1968, del. Jurisdictional Conf., 1968, pres. Womans Soc. Fla. Conf., 1966-70, del. Spl. Session of Gen. Conf. United Meth. Church, 1968; del. World Meth. Council, 1971, del. gen. conf., 1972; pres. Fla. Council of Chs., 1972—. Mem. womens adv. bd. Bethune Cookman Coll., Daytona Beach, Fla. Trustee Paine Coll., Augusta, Ga. Mem. Putnam-St. Johns County Farm Bur., (past dir.), Fla. Planter, Fla. Fruit and Vegetable Assn. Home: PO Box 36 Hastings FL 32045 Office: Route 1 Box 330 East Palatka FL 32031

GRAY, GEORGIA NEESE, banker; b. Richland, Kan.; d. Albert and Ellen (O'Sullivan) Neese; A.B., Washburn Coll., 1921, D.B.A. (hon.), 1966; student Sargent's, 1921-22; L.H.D., Russell Sage Coll., 1950; m. George M. Clark, Jan. 21, 1929; m. 2d, Andrew J. Gray, 1953. Began as actress, 1923; asst. cashier, Richland (Kan.) State Bank, 1935-37, pres., 1937—; pres. Capital City State Bank & Trust Co., Topeka; treas. of U.S., 1949-53. Mem. Commn. on Jud. Qualifications for Supreme Ct. Kan. Democratic nat. committeewoman, 1936-64; hon. chmn. Villages project C. of C. Bd. dirs. Kan. Am. Automobile Assn., 1950—; bd. dirs., former chmn. Kan. div. Am. Cancer Soc.; mem. bd. exec. campaign and maj. gifts com. Georgetown U.; bd. dirs. Seven Steps Found., Harry S. Truman Library Inst.; bd. regents Washburn U.; chmn. Alpha Phi Found., 1962-63; mem. nat. bd. Womens Med. Coll. Pa. Recipient Distinguished Alumni award Washburn U., 1950. Mem. Am. Bus. Women's Assn., Nat. Assn. Bank Women, Topeka C. of C., Met. Bus. and Profl. Womens Club, Alpha Phi (nat. trustee), Alpha Phi Upsilon, Theta Sigma Phi. Clubs: Soroptimist (hon. life), Met. Zonta, Topeka Country. Address: Box 1433 Topeka KS 66601

GRAY, GRACE WARNER, educator; b. Chgo., Nov. 20, 1924; d. William Scott and Beatrice Warner (Jardine) Gray; B.A., Mt. Holyoke Coll., 1945; Ph.D., U. Mich., 1951; postgrad. Marquette U. Med. Sch., 1958-61. Jr. research pharmacologist William S. Merrell Co., Cin., 1945-47; sr. research pharmacologist Bristol Labs., Syracuse, N.Y., 1951-54; instr. pharmacology Marquette U. Med. Sch., Milw., 1954-57, asst. prof., 1957-63; USPHS trainee U. Tenn. Med. Sch., Memphis, 1963-64; asst. prof. pharmacology Woman's Med. Coll., Phila., 1964-66; research asso. U. Pa. Med. Sch., Phila., 1966-67; asst. prof. vet. pharmacology U. Minn., St. Paul, 1967-71, asso. prof., 1971—. Mem. Am. Soc. Pharmacology and Exptl. Therapeutics, League Women Voters, Phi Beta Kappa. Unitarian. Home: 12 Sunset Lane North Oaks St Paul MN 55110

GRAY, HANNA HOLBORN (MRS. CHARLES MONTGOMERY GRAY), univ. adminstr.; b. Heidelberg, Germany, Oct. 25, 1930; d. Hajo and Annemarie (Bettman) Holborn; came to U.S., 1934; naturalized, 1940; A.B., Bryn Mawr Coll., 1950; Ph.D., Harvard, 1957; M.A. (hon.), Yale, 1971; m. Charles Montgomery Gray, June 19, 1954; Instr., Bryn Mawr (Pa.) Coll., 1953-54; instr. Harvard, 1957-59, asst. prof., 1959-60; asst. prof. U. Chgo., 1961-64, asso. prof., 1964-72; prof. Northwestern U., Evanston, Ill., dean Coll. Arts and Scis., 1972-74; provost Yale, New Haven, 1974—, successor trustee, 1971-74. Phi Beta Kappa vis. scholar, 1971-72. Mem. NRC, Nat. Council on Humanities. Bd. dirs. Am. Council on Edn., Am. Council Learned Socs.; trustee Carnegie Found. for Advancement of Teaching, Inst. for Advanced Study. Newberry Library fellow, 1960-61; Center for Advanced Study in the Behavioral Scis. fellow, 1966-67. Fellow Am. Acad. Arts and Scis.; mem. Assembly Behavioral and Social Scis., Am. Hist. Assn., Renaissance Soc. Am. Editor: (with Charles Gray) Journal of Modern History, 1965-70. Contbr. articles to profl. jours. Home: 35 Hillhouse Av New Haven CT 06511

GRAY, HARRIETT KIMBALL TAYLOR (MRS. JS GRAY), civic worker; b. Adrian, Mich., June 2, 1892; d. Howard Thorne and Maude (Howell) Taylor; student Colonial Sch., Washington, Adrian Coll., 1911-12, N.Y. Secretarial Sch., 1917-18; m. JS Gray, Sept. 10, 1912; children—Thorne (Mrs. David Charles Hawley), Grattan, Whitmore. Sec., War Camp Community Service Hdqrs., N.Y.C., 1918; lectr. on world travels, 1952—. Chmn., Monroe (Mich.) Community Concert Assn., 1940-45, pres., 1945-50; co-chmn. women's aux. Monroe Nat. Def., 1943-44; charter mem. Monroe Thrift Shop Assn., 1952—, v.p., 1958-59; mem. Mayor's Fine Arts Commn., 1967. Mem. Women's Republican Club. Recipeint award for creative writing in poetry Mich. Fedn. Women's Club, 1940. Mem. D.A.R. Republican. Christian Scientist. Clubs: Women's City (Detroit); Monroe (Mich.) Country. Home: 448 N Macomb St Monroe MI 48161

GRAY, HELEN SMITH (MRS. STANLEY NOYES GRAY), assn. exec.; b. Kansas City, Mo., Apr. 1, 1919; d. Delbert O. and Cordie E. (Goodwin) Smith; student Bethany Coll., 1937-38, 41; Mus.B. Edn., Tulsa U., 1941; m. Stanley Noyes Gray, June 10, 1945; 1 dau., Janet (Mrs. Edwin Bailey Robinson). Tchr. Woodbine (Kan.) High Sch., 1941-42; tchr. instrumental music, city grade schs., Webster Groves, Mo., 1953-56; mem. radio-TV staff U. Tex., Austin, 1957-62; field exec. Girl Scouts U.S.A., 1962—, Mem. Am. Camping Assn. (standards chmn. 1968—), Assn. Girl Scout Profls., Sigma Alpha Iota, Alpha Epsilon Rho, Kappa Delta. Republican. Home: 4730 S Columbia Pl Tulsa OK 74105 Office: 2432 E 51st St Tulsa OK 74105

GRAY, JESSIE KERR, librarian; b. Scotland; d. William and Nancy (Wilson) Gray; student So. Ill. U., 1950-53, U. Wis., 1954-55. Asst. librarian Marion (Ill.) Carnegie Library, 1947-59, librarian, 1959—. Sec., Williamson County Quas Que Centennial, 1964. Mem. Marion Bus. & Profl. Woman's Club (past pres.), Friends of Library, Am., Ill., Williamson County library assns., Ill. Hist. Soc., Marion Meml. Hosp. Aux., Ill. Adult Edn. Assn. Mem. Christian Ch. Club: Marion Woman's (past pres.). Home: 402 S Madison Marion IL 62959 Office: S Market Marion IL 62959

GRAY, JO ANNE HASTINGS, Republican nat. committeewoman; b. Birmingham, Ala., Dec. 1, 1921; d. Littleberry Byrd Haley and Virginia Irene (Jenkins) Haley Hastings; B.A., U. Colo., 1943; postgrad. U. Denver, 1943; m. Daniel Gray, Apr. 29, 1946; children—Daniel Allan, Robert Byrd. Stewardess Continental Airlines, 1943-46, asst. chief stewardess, dir. stewardess tng., 1946; tchr. stewardess tng. Denver U., 1947. State co-chmn. Goldwater campaign, 1964; Republican precinct committeewoman, 1960—; mem. Rep. Roundtable, 1963—; clk. Colo. senate, 1963-65; chmn. pub. relations Rep. Women's Club, 1965—; county Rep. tng. chmn., Denver, 1965—; mem. Rep. Nat. Com. from Colo. Coordinator Bus. and Indsl. Polit. Action Com.; mem. Planned Parenthood Colo.; chmn. P.T.A.; discussion leader Great Books, Jr. Great Books. Bd. dirs. U. Colo. Devel. Found. Mem. U. Colo. Alumni Assn. (pres. 1959, dir. 1958-60), Delta Gamma. Presbyn. Address: 2850 E Flora Pl Denver CO 80210

GRAY, KATHARINE MEEKER (MRS. HORACE GRAY), civic worker; b. Chgo., Feb. 1, 1894; d. Arthur and Grace (Murray) Meeker; student pvt. schs., N.Y.C.; m. Horace Gray, Oct. 16, 1915; children—Horace, Arthur M., Joan. Bd. dirs. Infant's Hosp., Boston, 1920-23; pres. Jr. League Santa Barbara, 1925-27; bd. dirs. San Francisco Mus. Art, 1930-50; commr. Housing Authority, City and County of San Francisco, 1943-46; bd. dirs. Nat. Housing Conf., Washington, 1945-63, San Francisco Planning and Housing Assn., 1944-50; dep. dir. vol. services Western region A.R.C., 1945-50; bd. dirs. Music Acad. West, Santa Barbara, 1949-61, Am. Assn. UN, 1951-56; bd. dirs. League Women Voters, San Francisco, 1947-50, pres., Santa Barbara, 1950-55, So. v.p. Cal., 1956-58; pres. Welfare Planning Council Santa Barbara, 1955-60, Pacific Coast Festival Assn., 1953-56, Santa Barbara Symphony Orch. Assn., 1959-60; pres. Women's com. Community Arts Music Assn., 1951-54, bd. dirs., 1951-53; bd. dirs. Community Chest, 1954-60; regional v.p. Cal. Assn. Health and Welfare, 1959-62; bd. dirs. Residence for Teen Age Girls, 1960-62, Affiliates U. Cal., Santa Barbara, 1961-66, Freedom Community Clinic of Santa Barbara; So. v.p. Citizens Planning Assn. Santa Barbara County, 1960-70, hon. v.p. 1972; bd. dirs. Family Service Agy., 1961-63, hon. v.p., 1963—; pres. Planned Parenthood Santa Barbara County, 1964-69, hon. v.p., 1969—; mem. Nat. Com. on U.S.-China Relations, N.Y.C., 1966—; bd. dirs. Channel City Women's Forum, 1966—, Summer Sch. World Affairs, 1963-65; chmn. Santa Barbara Council of Family Life Edn., 1972; hon. life mem. Am. Soc. Planning Ofcls., 1972. Named Woman of the Year by Advt. and Merchandising Club of Santa Barbara, 1957; Gold Feather award Women's Com. of Community Chest, 1961. Home: 122 Olive Mill Lane Santa Barbara CA 93103

GRAY, LAURIE WILLIAMS (MRS. JAMES EVERETT GRAY), univ. librarian; b. Tunica County, Miss.; d. Thomas Sylvester and Ira Emma (Sharp) Williams; A.B., Miss. State Coll. for Women, 1933; M.A., Murray State U., 1955, postgrad., summers 1956-58; M.A., George Peabody Coll. for Tchrs., 1963; m. Roy Hall Ikerd, July 3, 1933 (dec. 1958); 1 dau., Carroll (Mrs. Raymond George Ammar); m. 2d, James Everett Gray, Dec. 18, 1967. Librarian, Heath High Sch., West Paducah, Ky., 1955-58; faculty Murray (Ky.) State U., 1958—, coordinator tech. services, 1974—. Treas., St. Marys High Sch. P.T.A., Paducah, 1954. Mem. Nat., Ky. edn. assns., Ky., Southeastern library 1st Dist. (pres. 1958-59) assns., Nat. Council for the Social Studies, Nat. Geog. Soc., 1st Dist. Edn. Assn., Kappa Delta Pi (sec. 1969-70). Home: 1510 Martin Chapel Rd Murray KY 42071

GRAY, MARJORIE COX (MRS. E.L. GRAY), nurse; b. Rock Hill, S.C., Oct. 8, 1926; d. Jennings M. and Miriam (King) Cox; student Duke, Sacred Heart Coll., Queens Evening Coll., Ga. State Coll., U. N.C.; grad. Mercy Sch. Nursing, 1946; m. Edward L. Gray, Mar. 4, 1950; 1 son, Hugh Edward. Office nurse Dr. D.B. Mizell, Charlotte, N.C., 1946-48; asst. dir. nurses Mercy Hosp., Charlotte, 1948-51; nursing services dir. Mecklenburg County (N.C.) chpt. A.R.C., 1951-54; dir., owner Home Care Vis. Nurse Service, Charlotte, 1954-57; supervisory nurse Southeastern region Exxon Co., Charlotte, 1957-61, job analyst, 1961-63, adminstr. employment and pub. relations, 1963—; real estate broker, 1973—. Instr. trainer Mecklenburg County chpt. A.R.C., 1951—; ednl. com. Heart Services, Charlotte, 1959—. Bd. dirs. Mecklenburg County chpt. Am. Cancer Soc., 1958—, Mecklenburg County Diabetes Assn. Recipient Community Service awards Jr. Woman's Club, 1957, Mecklenburg County chpt. Am. Cancer Soc., 1961. Mem. N.C. (sec. 1960-63, dir. 1948), Dist. 5 N.C. State (dir. 1961, pres. 1959-60) nurses assns., Mercy Hosp. Alumni Assn. (2d v.p. 1964), Carolina Clowns (charter mem.), N.C. Assn. Indsl. Nurses (sec. 1962—), Internat. Platform Assn. Clubs: Toastmistress (sec. 1964, rep. 1965, speech contest award 1964, 65); Jr. Woman's (dir., state communications chmn.). Contbr. articles to profl. jours. Home: 1210 Dilworth Rd Charlotte NC 28203 Office: Exxon Co PO Box 420 Charlotte NC 28201

GRAY, MARY JANE (MRS. THOMAS DAY SEYMOUR BASSETT), physician, educator; b. Columbus, O., June 13, 1924; d. Claude M. and Gladys H. (McClung) Gray; B.A., Swarthmore Coll., 1941-45; M.D., Washington U., 1949; D. Med. Sci., Columbia U., 1953; m. Thomas Day Seymour Bassett, June 15, 1963; stepchildren—John, Elizabeth, Miriam (Mrs. Douglas French), Margot. Intern, internal medicine Barnes Hosp., Washington U., St. Louis, 1949-50; resident obstetrics and gynecology Sloane Hosp. for Women, Columbia Presbyn. Med. Center, N.Y.C., 1950-53, Barnes Foster fellow, research, 1953-54; chief resident obstetrics Sloane Hosp. for Women, Columbia Presbyn. Med. Center, N.Y.C., 1954, chief resident gynecology, 1956; trainee Marriage Council of Phila., dept psychiatry U. Pa., 1970-71; Barnes Foster fellow The Radiumhemmet, Stockholm, Sweden, 1955; asst. zoology dept. Wesleyan U., Middletown, Conn., 1945; instr. obstetrics and gynecology Columbia U. Coll. Phys. and Surg., 1956-60; asst. prof. obstetrics and gynecology U. Vt. Coll. Medicine, 1960-61, asso. prof., 1961-71, prof., 1971—; mem. staff Med. Center Hosp. Vt., Burlington; vis. asso. prof. St. Michael's Coll. Grad. Sch., 1968, U. Pa., 1970-71; chmn. med. adv. bd. Planned Parenthood Vt., 1965-69; med. dir., 1969-70; chmn. Com. to Revise Vt. Abortion Law, 1968-70; examiner Am. Bd. Obstetricians and Gynecologists, 1969-71. Diplomate Am. Bd. Obstetrics and Gynecology. Mem. Nat. Assn. for Repeal

Abortion Laws (bd. dirs. 1971—), Soc. Gynecologic Investigation, Am. Coll. Obstetricians and Gynecologists, A.A.A.S., Grove Conf., Soc. Scientific Study Sex, Nat. Council Family Relations, Am. Assn. Sex Educators and Counselors, Assn. Profs. Gynecology and Obstetrics (exec. com.), Am. Civil Liberties Union (dir. Vt. chpt.), Sigma Xi. Cons. editor Medical Aspect of Human Sexuality. Home: 179 N Prospect St Burlington VT 05401 Office: Department Obstetrics and Gynecology Given Bldg University of Vermont Burlington VT 05401

GRAY, MAY HARRIS (MRS. THOMAS VIRGIL GRAY), writer; b. Canton, Ky.; d. James Robert and Mary Priscilla (Bridges) Harris; student Northeastern La. Bus. Coll., Fort Smith, Ark., 1917-18; m. Thomas Virgil Gray, June 19, 1920;children—Jean (Mrs. Louis H. Peer), Dorothy (Mrs. Joseph Beech Edwards), Thomas Virgil. Co-owner COIN-Stores, Fort Smith, Ark. and Oklahoma, Tex., 1946—. Mem. womans bd. Sparks Meml. Hosp., Fort Smith, 1936—. Recipient John Gould Fletcher Poetry award, 1964, 68; Jesse Stuart award, 1967; Dylan Thomas award, 1968; Poet Laureate's citation, 1966; 1st Place award Nat. League Am. Pen Women, 1970. Mem. Ft. Smith Poets Roundtable Group (co-founder), Acad. Am. Poets, Nat. Fedn. State Poetry Socs., Nat. League Am. Pen Women (treas. 1968-69), Poetry Soc. Am. (life), Poets Roundtable Ark., University City Poetry Club, P.E.O. (chpt. pres. 1960-61), D.A.R. Baptist. Club: Explorers. Author: In the Garden, 1935; The Voice of the Sea, 1963; Moment Before Summer, 1970. poems pub. in various mags., anthologies, newspapers. Home: 1315-55 Terrace Fort Smith AR 72901 Office: 2300 Rogers Av Fort Smith AR 72901

GRAY, MERLE, ret. educator; b. Portersville, Ind. June 21, 1897; d. John D. and Emma (Rudolph) Gray; Ph.B., U. Chgo., 1934; M.A., Columbia, 1939; Litt.D., Oakland City Coll., 1967. Tchr. rural schs., Pike County, Ind., 1918-19; tchr., Petersburg, Ind., 1919-21; tchr., Hammond, Ind., 1921-28, dir. elementary edn., 1928-58; author, editor Silver Burdett Co., Morristown, N.J., 1958-61. Chmn. mayor's com. for care of children in war time, 1941-43, Ind. Council for Children and Youth, 1953-55. Mem. Assn. for Childhood Edn. Internat. (pres. 1955-57, mem. U.S. com. on childhood edn. 1955—), N.E.A., Am. Assn. U. Women, Nat. League Am. Pen Women, League Women Voters, Delta Kappa Gamma, P.E.O. Presbyn. Author: (with others) Making Sure of Arithmetic, 1947; Modern Mathematics Through Discovery, 1-6, 1966, 70. Home: 1308 Southdowns Dr Bloomington IN 47401

GRAY, MIRIAM MARY, educator; b. Nevada, Mo., Nov. 29, 1905; d. Chester H. and Pearl (Welch) Gray; A.A., Cottey Coll., 1925; B.S., U. Mo., 1927; M.A., Columbia, 1932, Ed.D., 1943. Tchr. phys. edn. high sch. and jr. coll., Moberly, Mo., 1927-30, jr. and sr. high sch., Chickasha, Okla., 1930-31, elementary and jr. high sch., Tulsa, 1934-41; phys. edn. dir. The Knox Sch. for Girls, Cooperstown, N.Y., 1932-33; instr. phys. and health edn. U. Tex., 1943-46; asso. prof. health and phys. edn. Ill. State U., 1946-57, prof., 1957-72, emerita, 1972—, dance coordinator, 1946-69; dir. advanced study insts. U.S. Office Edn., summers 1968, 69. Hon. fellow A.A.H.P.E.R. (chmn. midwest dance sect. 1954-55, chmn. nat. sect. on dance 1958-60, editor dance div. 1966-70, program chmn. conf. on dance as a discipline 1965; v.p., chmn. dance div. 1970-73, dir. 1971-72, nat. dance assn. parliamentarian 1974—); mem. Nat., Ill. edn. assns., Ill. Assn. Health Phys. Edn. and Recreation, Nat. (nat. editorial com. 1955-60, editor biennial publ. 1957-59), Midwest assns. for phys. edn. of coll. women, Internat. Assn. Phys. Edn. and Sports for Girls and Women, Nat. Found. for Health, Phys. Edn. and Recreation, Internat. Council Health, Phys. Edn. and Recreation, Am. Dance Guild, Sacred Dance Guild, Com. on Research in Dance (dir. 1969-73, parliamentarian 1973-74), Nat. Conf. Grad. Edn. (editorial com. 1967), Dance Notation Bur., Am. Dance Therapy Assn., Ill. Square Dance Callers Assn. (roving dir. 1955-57, central dir. 1960-62), Ill. Fedn. Square Dance Clubs (devel. chmn., editor newsletter 1955-57), Vernon County Hist. Soc. (dir. 1973—, corr. sec. 1974—), Am. Assn. U. Profs. (chpt. pres. 1953-54, Ill. conf. pres. 1955), Nat., Mo., Vernon County (sec.-treas. 1973-74, pres. 1974—) ret. tchrs. assns., Am. Assn. Ret. Persons, Bus. and Profl. Women's Club, Delta Kappa Gamma (2d v.p. 1964-66), Phi Lambda Theta, Kappa Delta Pi, Phi Theta Kappa. Clubs: Idlers (pres. 1963-64), Nevada Camera. Author: The Physical Education Demonstration, 1946; A Century of Growth, 1951. Editor: Purposeful Action, Workshop Report of NAPECW, 1956. Co-editor; Designs for Dance, 1968. Contbr. to profl., ednl. and lay publs. Dance dir. centennial pageants: The Past Is Prologue, 1955; With Faith in the Future, 1957. Editor: Focus on Dance V, Composition, 1969. Address: The Wayside Route 1 Nevada MO 64772

GRAY, SANDRA RAE (MRS. DONALD N. GRAY, JR.), educator; b. East Palestine, O., Nov. 8, 1932; d. Kenneth Ray and Nina Olivia (Jamsen) Morris; B.A., Cal. State U. at Fullerton, 1967, M.A., 1974; m. Donald N. Gray, Jr., Nov. 9, 1951; children—Pamela, Donald N. III, Douglas. Tchr., dir. forensics Ramona High Sch., Riverside, Cal., 1968-71; tchr., dir. forensics Tustin (Cal.) High Sch., 1971—. Mem. Cal. Speech Assn. (mem. exec. bd. 1973—), Western Speech Communication Assn., Speech Communication Assn. Am., Orange County Speech League (pres. 1973—), Cal. High Sch. Speech Assn., State Speech Council (area IV chmn. 1973—), Nat. Forensic League (mem. dist. com. 1973—). Home: 13671 Falmouth Dr Tustin CA 92680 Office: Tustin High School 1171 Laguna Rd Tustin CA 92680

GRAY, SHEILA HAFTER, psychiatrist, psychoanalyst; b. N.Y.C., Oct. 19, 1930; M.D., Harvard, 1958; certificate Washington Psychoanalytic Inst., 1969; m. Oscar Shalom Gray, Apr. 8, 1967. Intern, St. Elizabeth's Hosp., Washington, 1958-59; resident, McLean Hosp., Belmont, Mass., 1959-61; Clin. Research fellow Mass. Gen. Hosp., Boston, 1961-62; staff psychiatrist Chestnut Lodge, Inc., Rockville, Md., 1962-64; practice medicine, specializing in psychiatry and psychoanalysis, Chevy Chase, Md., 1964—; clin. asst. prof. psychiatry U. Md. Sch. Medicine, Balt., 1968—; instr. Washington Psychoanalytic Inst., 1971—; mem. staff Suburban Hosp., Bethesda, U. Md. Hosp., Balt. Physician mem. Commn. on Mental Health, Superior Ct. of D.C., 1972—. Mem. Am. Psychiat. Assn., Am. Psychoanalytic Assn., Washington Psychoanalytic Soc. Office: 4740 Chevy Chase Dr Chevy Chase MD 20015

GRAY, SUZANNE KALDECK (MRS. IRA C. GRAY), librarian; b. Vienna, Austria, Dec. 30, 1924; d. Rudolph and Martha (Porges) Kaldeck; B.S., Simmons Coll., 1945, M.S., 1967; m. Ira C. Gray, July 17, 1949; children—Alan R., Janet M. Research chemist Bird & Son, E. Walpole, Mass., 1945-49; spl. projects F.A. Countway Library of Medicine, Boston, 1964-66; with Boston Pub. Library, 1968—, coordinator sci., 1971—. Asst. prof. Bridgewater (Mass.) State Coll., 1973. Mem. Mass. State Sci. Fair Com., Boston, 1972—. Mem. Am. Library Assn., Spl. Libraries Assn. Home: 50 Moose Hill St Sharon MA 02067 Office: PO Box 286 Boston MA 02117

GRAY, VIRGINIA MAXINE POMROY (MRS. EDGAR L. GRAY), educator; b. Nitro, W.Va., Oct. 3, 1928; d. Henry Evan and Ruth (Roberts) Pomroy; B.A., W.Va. U., 1952, M.A., 1955; student Glenville State Coll., summer 1947; postgrad. Barry Coll., 1957; Ph.D., Bowling Green State U., 1973; m. Edgar L. Gray, June 1, 1963. Tchr. Blackhill Sch., Wirt County, W.Va., 1947-48, Wirt County High Sch., Elizabeth, W.Va., 1952-53, Ocala (Fla.) High Sch., 1954-55, N. Miami Sr. High Sch., Miami, Fla., 1955-59; asst. prof. speech and drama Morris Harvey Coll., 1959-62, head dept. speech and drama, 1962-71, asso. prof., 1969-71; asso. prof. speech and drama W.Va. State Coll., Institute, 1971—, chmn. dept. speech and drama, 1971—. Mem. State Democratic Women's Assn., Am. Assn. U. Profs., D.A.R., Speech Assn. Am., Speech Assn. Eastern States, N.E.A., W.Va. Ednl. Assn., W.Va. Speech Assn. (pres. 1971-72), Alpha Delta Kappa (pres. 1963), Delta Zeta (dir. coll. chpt. 1961). Baptist. Mem. Order Eastern Star. Home: 303 McKinley Av Charleston WV 25314

GRAYBURN, KATHRYN BARNWELL, journalist; b. Atlanta, Apr. 12, 1923; d. William Habersham and Martha (Ryder) Barnwell; student U. Ga., 1940, Am. U., 1945; m. Jack Grayburn, May 4, 1946 (div.); children—Gayle (Mrs. Raymond E. Smith), John Edward III. Staff writer Atlanta Constn., 1941-44, soc. editor, columnist, 1960-68; with Southwestern area A.R.C., Atlanta, 1943-44; soc. and fashion editor Neighbor Newspapers, Marietta, Ga., 1970—. Writer, N.Y. U., N.Y.C., 1968. Bd. dirs. Leukemia Soc. Am., Inc., Atlanta, 1972—, residential chmn., 1972-73; bd. dirs. Alliance Theatre Aux., Atlanta, 1973—, Dixie Council Authors and Editors, Atlanta, 1973—. Recipient State Soc. Coverage award Ga. Press Assn., 1970, 71; award Nat. Newspaper Assn., 1972; Centennial Citation Cherokee chpt. D.A.R., Atlanta, 1973. Clubs: Music, Piedmont Driving, Chattahoochee Plantation (Atlanta). Contbr. short stories to mags. Office: 120 Copeland Rd Atlanta GA 30342

GRAYE, MARY M. PECKHAM (MRS. DIRK V. GRAYE), banker; b. Okmulgee, Okla.; d. Miles N. and Pearl (Menefee) Peckham; B.S., Kan. State Coll., 1951; postgrad. U. Wis. 1958, Grad. Sch. Banking, 1968; m. Dirk V. Graye, Apr. 26, 1951. Mem. dist. mgmt. staff Sears & Roebuck Co., Blackwell, Okla., 1941-49; joined First Wis. Nat. Bank of Madison, 1958—, dir. personnel, 1958-66, asst. v.p., dir. personnel, 1966-68, v.p., dir. personnel, 1968—, also dir. Bd. dirs. YWCA, 1965—, chmn. personnel com., 1969—, mem. exec. com., 1969-73; mem. Equal Opportunities Commn., Dane County Affirmative Action Commn., 1973—; mem. citizens senate United Way; bd. dirs. Jr. Achievement, 1973—, Madison Met. Distributive Edn. Assn., 1972—. Recipient Boss of Year award Madison Jaycees, 1971. Mem. Am. (exec. com. 1973—, affirmative action com. 1973—), Wis. (bank mgmt. com. 1972—) bankers assns., Am. Soc. for Personnel Adminstrn., Indsl. Relations Assn. Wis., North Central Region and Wis. Bank Women, League Women Voters, Nat. Assn. Bank Women, Adminstrn. Mgmt. Soc., Madison Theater Guild, Madison Art Assn. Home: 3311 Topping Rd Madison WI 53705 Office: 905 University Av Madison WI 53715

GRAYE, MYTROLENE L., educator; b. Jackson, Tenn.; d. James A. Zachery and Frances (Hamby) Graye; student Lane Coll., 1926-28; B.S., Agrl. and Tech. State U. N.C., 1937; M.A., Columbia, 1945, Profl. diploma, 1955; postgrad. U. Me., 1958, Mich. State U., 1959, U. Hawaii, 1960, U. Wis., 1961, U. P.R., 1963, Yeshiva U., 1966. Classroom tchr. Fairview Elementary Sch., High Point, N.C., 1928-32, teaching prin., 1932-45, supervising prin., 1954-68; now tchr. N.Y.C. Sch. System, faculty John Finley Campus Sch., N.Y.C.; workshop participant several N.E.A. nat. summer confs. Mem. vis. com. So. Assn. Accreditation Greensboro City Schs., 1960-61, Guilford County Schs., 1964. Chmn. div. local chpt. N.C. Symphony Soc.; mem. girl scout planning bd., com. mem. Girl Scouts, 1954-64; chmn. personnel com. YWCA, 1945-53; mem. project United Fund, 1963-64. Recipient Woman of Yr. award Zeta Phi Beta, 1950; So. Edn. Found. grantee, 1956. Mem. N.E.A. (recorded nat. confs., mem. spl. com. ann. meetings 1955), Am. (v.p. 1958-61, state com. 1957-58), N.C. (past chmn. principals dept., past chmn. div. elementary edn., sec. bd. dirs. credit union 1961-64) tchrs. assns., Assn. Supervision and Curriculum Devel., Assn. Childhood Edn. Internat., Nat. Council Adminstrv. Women Edn., N.Y. State United Tchrs. Inc., Nat. Soc. Study Edn., Nat. Council Negro Women's Clubs, N.C., High Point federated women's clubs, Guilford Pan-Hellenic Council (sec. 1945-64), Bronx-Manhattan Friends Symphony of New World, M.M.S. (adv.), Zeta Phi Beta. Methodist (bd. stewards), mem. adminstrv. bd., sec. chancel choir). Contbr. articles to profl. jours. Editor: The Rooster Crows, 1961—. Home: Lenox Terrace Apts 25 W 132d St New York City NY 10037 Office: 425 W 130th St New York City NY 10027

GRAYER, MERYL ROMAINE, ins. co. exec.; b. N.Y.C., Mar. 7, 1931; d. Harry and Betty (Hurwick) Grayer; B.S., N.Y. U., 1948, M.A., 1949; C.L. U., Am. Coll. Life Underwriters; postgrad. N.Y. Sch. Bus., 1958, Sobelsohn Sch., 1958-59, Am. Inst. Property and Liability Underwriters, 1973—; m. Steven S. Held, June 14, 1962; children—Melody Anderson, Morgan Meredyth. Exec. asst. Federated Brokerage Group, N.Y.C., 1958; asst. v.p. Standard Security Life Ins. Co. N.Y., N.Y.C., 1959-69; corporate asst. sec. Madison Life Ins. Co., N.Y.C., 1969-71, also corporate sec. Asso. Madison Cos., Inc., N.Y.C., 1969-71; mgr. performance improvement and product marketing cons. Met. Life Ins. Co., N.Y.C., 1972—; adj. asst. prof. Coll. Ins., N.Y.C., 1973—; lectr. in field. Mem. fund-raising com. Alumni Fedn. N.Y. U. Mem. Am. Soc. C.L.U.'s (dir. N.Y. chpt. 1972-74), N.Y. League Bus. and Profl. Women (dir. 1973-76), Golden Key Soc., Nat. Assn. Life Underwriters, Am. Mgmt. Assn., Assos. Lincoln Center, Friends City Center. Editor Life Underwriters Bull., 1973—. Contbr. articles to profl. jours. Home: 130 E 18th St New York City NY 10003 Office: 1 Madison Av New York City NY 10010

GRAYSON, BARBARA CAROL FERGUSON, ins. underwriter; b. Port Angeles, Wash., Jan. 13, 1940; d. T. Lawson and Margaret Rose (Edmisten) Ferguson; B.A., U. Wash., 1971; m. Gary Alyn Grayson, Mar. 4, 1960 (div. Aug. 1965). With Union Ins. Soc. of Canton (China), 1958-66, asst. claims mgr., 1963-66; free-lance advt. researcher, 1971-72; adminstrv. asst. Crown Life Co., Seattle, 1972-73; comml. property underwriter Chubb/Pacific Indemnity Group, Seattle, 1973-74, Tampa, Fla., 1974—. Mem. Women in Communications, Ins. Women's Assn. Seattle (chmn. publicity 1973-74), Seattle Advt. Fedn. Republican. Home: 10455 Carrollbrook Circle Tampa FL 33618 Office: 5200 Kannedy Blvd Tampa FL

GRAYZEL, ESTHERANN FINK (MRS. ARTHUR I. GRAYZEL), physician; b. Chgo., Apr. 5, 1934; d. J. Lester and Rose (Fradkin) Fink; B.A., Radcliffe Coll., 1955; M.D., Northwestern U., 1960; m. Arthur I. Grayzel, June 16, 1957; children—Jonathan, Susan, David. Intern, Bellevue Hosp., N.Y.C., 1960-61, resident, 1961-62, 64-65; resident Manchester (Eng.) Royal Infirmary, 1962-63, Montefiore Hosp., N.Y.C., 1963-64; practice medicine specializing in internal medicine-endocrinology, N.Y.C., 1965-67, Bronx, N.Y., 1967—; asst. dir. med. edn., attending endocrinologist Hosp. for Joint Diseases, N.Y.C., 1965-67; instr. Albert Einstein Coll. Medicine, Bronx, N.Y., 1967-69, asst. prof. medicine, 1970—; attending physician Bronx Municipal Hosp. Center, 1967—. Diplomate Am. Bd. Internal Medicine. Mem. Endocrine Soc. Club: Radcliffe (Westchester, N.Y.). Home: Larchmont NY 10538 Office: 1600 Tenbroeck Av Bronx NY 10461

GRAZIANO, FLORENCE VERONICA MERCOLINO (MRS. NATALE GRAZIANO), artist; b. Plainfield, N.J., Aug. 23, 1924; d. Michael and Florence (Sheriff) Mercolino; grad. Muhlenberg Hosp. Sch. Nursing, 1948; student R.I. Sch. Design, Columbus Coll. Art and Design, 1963—, Art Students League, 1968-70; m. Natale Graziano, Dec. 11, 1954. Exhibited in one-man shows Chase Gallery, N.Y.C., Bullock's-Wilshire Gallery, Los Angeles, Washington County Mus. Fine Arts, Hagerstown, Md. in group shows throughout N.J., Crespi Gallary, N.Y.C., Mansfield Art Gallery, Columbus, O., Marion, O.; represented in permanent collections at Columbus Coll. Art and Design, Rutgers U., Eureka Coll., U. Me., Wittenberg U., Coll. City N.Y., Payne Whitney Clinic, Washington County Mus. Fine Arts, Hagerstown, Sheldon Swope Art Gallery, Terre Haute, Ind., others. Dir., instr. Graziano Sch. Fine Arts, N.J. Mem. Plainfield, Westfield art assns., Art Students League N.Y., Am. Artists Profl. League, Allied Artists of N.Y.C. (asso.), Pen and Brush N.Y., Painters and Sculptors Soc. N.J. Clubs: Salmagundi, Nat. Arts (N.Y.C.). Address: 1413 Highland Av Plainfield NJ 07060

GRAZIER, MARGARET HAYES (MRS. ROBERT THEODORE GRAZIER), educator; b. Denver, Dec. 19, 1916; d. Warren Chauncey and Rosetta Ernestine (Bankwitz) Hayes; B.A., U. No. Colo., 1938, M.A., 1941; diploma library sci. U. Denver, 1937-38; postgrad. U. Chgo., 1952-53; m. Robert Theodore Grazier, July 27, 1957. Supr. sch. libraries Greeley, Colo., 1939-42; librarian Lake Forest (Ill.) High Sch., 1942-45; library cons. W.K. Kellogg Found., Battle Creek, Mich., 1945-46; dir. pub. service div. U. Denver Libraries, 1946-48; asst. prof. Coll. Librarianship, U. Denver, 1948-52; asst. prof. Grad. Library Sch., U. Chgo., 1953-56; librarian Birmingham (Mich.) secondary schs., 1956-65; prof. div. library sci. Wayne State U., Detroit, 1965—; vis. instr. U. Mich., summers 1957-65. Cons. U.S. Office Edn., 1965-71, H.W. Wilson Co., 1962-71. Mem. A.L.A. (mem. council 1960-64, 72-74), Am. Assn. Sch. Librarians (2d v.p. 1970-71), Mich. Assn. for Media in Edn., Assn. for Ednl. Communications and Tech., Assn. for Supervision and Curriculum Devel., Am. Civil Liberties Union, Right to Read Found., Am. Assn. U. Profs. Contbr. articles to profl. jours. Home: 17565 Pennington St Detroit MI 48221 Office: Room 315 Kresge Edn Library Wayne State U Detroit MI 48202

GRAZIOLI, MARGARET, librarian; b. Weehawken, N.J., Aug. 28, 1917; d. Russell A. and Mary (Wilson) Keenan; B.A., Rutgers U., 1938; m. Roger Grazioli, Aug. 28, 1937; children—Kathleen (Mrs. Paul Freitag), Roger. Children's librarian Weehawken Pub. Library, 1956-61, dir., 1966—, also trustee; dir. Secaucus (N.J.) Pub. Library, 1961—. A founder Sr. Citizens Secaucus, 1962, now gold card holder; v.p. publicity Secaucus Child Guidance; chmn. Secaucus Girl Scout drive, 1968-69, Weehawken A.R.C., 1956-57; 8th dist. chmn. Garden's Conservation, Women's Clubs, 1969-72; v.p. Secaucus Child Guidance, 1969-71; chmn. UN Observance for Secaucus, 1967—; sec. Secaucus Citizens Against Narcotics, 1969-71; Secaucus rep. on drugs Mayor's Council Hudson County, 1971-72. Named Woman of Achievement for outstanding library work Jersey Jour., 1967. Mem. Am., N.J., Hudson County (pres. 1968-72) library assns., Woodrow Wilson P.T.A. Weehawken (pres. 1957-61), Weehawken Hist. Soc. (charter), Secaucus Bus. and Profl. Women, Deborah. Elk. Clubs: Weehawken Garden (chmn. flower show 1966, 70, pres. 1967-69); Secaucus Women's (garden chmn. 1969-70). Home: 4 Mill Rodge Rd Secaucus NJ 07094 Office: Secaucus Plaza Secaucus NJ 07094 also 49 Hauxhurst Av Weehawken NJ 07097

GREACEN, NAN, artist; b. Giverny, France; d. Edmund and Ethol (Booth) Greacen; student Friends Sem. N.Y.C., 1914-21, Bearley Sch., 1921-26, Grand Central Sch. Art, 1926-30; m. Rene Bard Faure, Dec. 9, 1935; children—Nancy F. Waesche, Renee F. Bane. Instr. painting Grand Central Art Sch., 1931-45; one-man exhibits Montross Gallery, N.Y.C., Guild Hall, East Hampton, Grand Central Art Galleries; exhibited Corocoran Gallery, World's Fair, N.A.D. Recipient Hallgarten prize Nat. Acad., 1936; National Arts Club medal, 1937; Montclair Art Museum medal, 1938; Flower Painting award, 1939; mems. annual award National Arts Club, 1940; Grand Central award, 1941; Cooper prize Nat. Assn. Women Artists, 1942; 1st prize Hudson Valley Art Assn., 1947; Julian Detmer award, 1950; 1st prize Yonkers Art Exhibit, Jane Peterson prize for flower painting Allied Artists Ann., 1st prize Scarsdale Art Assn., 1951; silver medal Katherine Lorillard Wolfe Woman's Exhibit, 1953; portrait prize Scarsdale Art Exhibit, 1955; Chester Eldredge award Hudson Valley Art Assn., 1956; 1st prize $500, Manhattan Savs. Bank Exhibit, 1963; 1st prize Westchester Art Tchrs. Exhbn., 1963; Nat. Academician, 1962; 1st prize Arts Club Ann., 1964; Best in Show, Katherine Lorillard Wolfe Women's Exhibit, 1965; Kathleen Grumbacker medal Nat. Arts Club, 1969; 1st in oil and best in show St. Augustine Honor Show, 1972; water color award Fla. Water Color Soc., 1973. Mem. N.A.D., Allied Artists Am. Nat. Arts Club, Painters and Sculptors Gallery Assn., Nat. Assn. Women Artists, Audubon Artists, Hudson Valley Art Assn. (gold medal 1966, Newington award 1970), St. Augustine Art Assn. Clubs: Ponte Vedra, Sawgrass (Ponte Vedra Beach, Fla.). Author: Still Life Is Exciting, 1969; The Magic of Flower Painting, 1970. Home: 184 San Juan Dr Ponte Vedra Beach FL 32082

GREASER, CONSTANCE UDEAN, publishing co. exec.; b. San Diego, Jan. 18, 1938; d. Lloyd Edward and Udean (Rohr) Greaser; B.A., San Diego State Coll., 1959; postgrad. U. Copenhagen Grad. Sch. Fgn. Students, 1963, Georgetown U. Sch. Fgn. Service, 1967; M.A., U. So. Cal., 1968. Advt., publicity mgr. Crofton Co., San Diego, 1959-62; supr. engring. support services div. Arcata Data Mgmt., Hawthorne, Cal., 1962-67; mgr. computerized typesetting dept. Continental Graphics, Los Angeles, 1967-70; v.p. Sage Publs., Inc., Beverly Hills, Cal., 1970—. Publicity dir. National City March of Dimes Parade, 1961-62. Mem. Nat. Mgmt. Assn. (local sec. 1967), So. Cal. Bookbuilders Assn., Women in Communication. Editor: Urban Research News, 1970—; mng. editor Comparative Polit. Studies, 1971—. Contbr. articles to various publs. Home: 4735C La Villa Marina Marina Del Rey CA 90291 Office: 275 S Beverly Dr Beverly Hills CA 90212

GREAVES, ALISON ASH, physician; b. Evanston, Ill., Dec. 15, 1928; d. William Henry and Edythe (Tower) Ash; A.A., Blackburn Coll., 1950; Ph.B., Northwestern U., 1953; M.D., U. Ill., 1962, M.P.H., 1974; m. Robert Greaves, June 9, 1962; children—Edmund, Cordelia. Intern Cook County Hosp., Chgo., 1962-63; resident in pediatrics Children's Meml. Hosp., Chgo., 1963-65; physician Chgo. Bd. Health, 1965-66; med. dir. Infant Welfare Soc. Chgo., 1966-73, cons., 1973—; asso. mem. faculty Northwestern U., Chgo. Med. technician Arabian Am. Oil Co., Saudi Arabia, 1956-58. Diplomate Am. Bd. Pediatrics. Fellow Am. Acad. Pediatrics; mem. Alpha Omega Alpha. Home: 117 Custer Av Evanston IL 60202

GREAVES, BETTINA BIEN (MRS. PERCY L. GREAVES, JR.), economist; b. Washington, July 21, 1917; d. Van Tuyl Hart and Bertha (Conn) Bien; B.A., Wheaton Coll., 1938; postgrad. Strayer Sch. Bus., 1939, N.Y. U., 1951-52; M.L.S., Columbia, 1967; m. Percy L. Greaves, June 26, 1971. Various secretarial positions, 1939-42; adminstrv. asst. Fgn. Econ. Adminstrn., La Paz, Bolivia, Vienna, Austria, 1943-46, sec. export dept. Smith, Kline & French, Phila., 1946-47; asst. to exec. dir. Found. for Freedom, Washington, 1947-48; office mgr. Thomas L. Phillips, realtor, Washington, 1948-51; sr. staff mem., dir. debate materials program Found. for Econ. Edn., Inc., Irvington-on-Hudson, N.Y., 1951—. Mem. A.L.A., Am. Econ. Assn., Am. Hist. Assn. Compiler: The Works of Ludwig von Mises, 1970; translator 3 monographs by Ludwig von Mises; contbr. Toward

Liberty, Mises Festsohrift, 1971, also to profl. jours. Home: 19 Pine Lane Irvington-on-Hudson NY 10533 Office: 30 S Broadway Irvington-on-Hudson NY 10533

GREBE, ZEL(PHA) ESTHER (MRS. TED GREBE), pub. relations exec.; b. Aberdeen, S.D., June 15, 1922; d. William and Lola (Bonebrake) Grosvenor; A.A., Colo. Women's Coll., 1942; B.A., U. Denver, 1944; m. Charles Lind, June 14, 1944 (div. Oct. 1958); m. 2d, Ted Grebe, June 16, 1960. Tchr., Denver pub. schs., 1944-47; dir. fgn. and personal shopping service Denver Dry Goods Co., 1952-57; asst. sec. Columbia Savs. and Loan Assn., Denver, 1960-72, savs. mgr., 1961-64, asst. dir. pub. relations, 1964-68, dir. pub. relations, 1968-72; asst. dir. pub. relations MCA Financial, Denver, 1972—. Mem. pub. relations council Denver Art Mus., 1968—; mem. pub. relations com. Mile Hi council Girl Scouts Am., 1969-72. Named Woman of Year, Am. Bus. Women's Assn., 1968; recipient outstanding alumnae citation Colo. Women's Coll., 1970. Mem. Am. (Colo. dep. gov. 1968-70), Denver (chmn. bd. 1966-68) savs. and loan insts., Am. Women in Radio and TV (chmn. regional conf. 1969-70, pres. 1971-72), Pub. Relations Soc. Am. (Colo. v.p. 1974), Phi Beta Kappa. Club: Soroptimist (Denver). Home: 1990 Quebec St Denver CO 80220 Office: MCA Financial Colo State Bank Bldg Suite 1100 1600 Broadway Denver CO 80202

GREELEY, JEANNE WINIFRED GRANT (MRS. HORACE GREELEY), dermatologist; b. Bklyn., May 6, 1926; d. Edward T. and Florence Elizabeth (Hernandez) Grant; B.S., N.Y. U., 1958; M.D., Women's Med. Coll. Pa., 1962; m. Horace Greeley, Jan. 1, 1953; children—Grant Horace, Norman Horace. Intern, Bklyn. Hosp., 1962-63; resident internal medicine VA Hosp., Bklyn., 1963-64; resident dermatology King County Hosp., Bklyn., 1964-66; fellow dermatology N.Y. U. Postgrad. Med. Sch., 1966-67; asst. attending dermatology Bklyn. Cumberland Hosp., Luth. Med. Center, Bklyn.; dermatology and allergy staff Internat. Longshoremen's Med. Center, Bklyn., 1968—, Internat. Sales and Prodn. Union Med. Center, Bklyn., 1967—; dir. Dr. Horace Greeley's Lab., Bklyn., 1967—. Mem. A.M.A., N.Y. State, King County med. socs., Alumni Women's Med. Coll. Pa. Home: 7609 Ridge Blvd Brooklyn NY 11209 Office: 140 Clinton St Brooklyn NY 11201

GREELIS, THELMA E. TRIMBLE (MRS. DAVID E. GREELIS), banker; b. Watervliet, N.Y.; d. Richard Elliott and Eliza (Gummer) Trimble; student pub. schs.; m. David E. Greelis, June 14, 1941 (dec. Jan. 1960). With Nat. City Bank, Troy, N.Y., 1926-59, successively clerk, teller, gen. bookkeeper, sec., 1926-38, mgr. personal loan dept., 1938-48, asst. cashier, 1948-59; asst. cashier State Bank of Albany, Troy, 1959—. Treas., Rensselaer County Tb and Pub. Health Assn., Inc., 1967—; treas., mem. exec. com. United Urban Ministry of Troy, Inc., 1970—. First v.p. bd. women mgrs. Bethesda Home, 1966—, bd. dirs., mem. investment com., 1973—; bd. dirs., treas. Capital Dist. unit Am. Lung Assn., 1973—; bd. dirs., mem. investment com. Troy Ann. Conf., United Methodist Ch., 1973—, also mem. exec. com. Council on Ministries, Bennington-Troy Dist. Mem. Nat. Assn. Bank Women, Credit Women Internat. (unit dir. 1961—), N.Y. State Bankers Assn., Am. Inst. Banking, Greater Troy C. of C. Methodist. Club: Troy. Home: 1331 3d Av Watervilet NY 12189 Office: 59 3d St Troy NY 12181

GREEN, ADELINE ULANOVE MANDEL (MRS. MAURICE L. GREEN), social worker; b. St. Paul; d. Meyer and Eva (Ulanove) Ulanove; B.S., U. Minn., 1933, M.S.W., 1955; m. Nathan G. Mandel, July 13, 1938 (div. July 1962); children—Meta Susan (Mrs. Richard Katzoff), Myra (Mrs. Jeffery Halpern); m. 2d, Maurice L. Green, Aug. 31, 1969. Investigator, Ramsey County Mothers Aid and Aid to Dependent Children, Ramsey County Welfare Bd., St. Paul, 1933-37; psychiat. social worker Wilder Child Guidance Clinic, St. Paul, 1938; psychiat. social worker, supr. out patient psychiatry clinic U. Minn. Hosps., Mpls., 1955-68, supr., clin. instr. psychiatry social service, out patient psychiatry clinic, 1968-69; pvt. practice family and marriage counseling. Pres. St. Paul sect. Council Jewish Women, 1950-54; chmn. Diagnostic Clinic for Rheumatic Fever-Wilder Clinic, St. Paul, 1952-54. Mem. Nat. Assn. Social Workers, Acad. Certified, Social Workers, Minn. Welfare Conf., Am. Assn. Marriage Counselors, Brandeis U. Women. Democrat. Jewish religion. Home: 1696 Miller Av Los Altos CA 94022

GREEN, AGNES ANN, chemist, educator; b. Alvin, Ill., Aug. 15, 1912; d. Charles F. and Mabel Ann (Tilletson) Green; B.A. (Mary Young Moore scholar), Immaculate Heart Coll., 1934; M.S., U. So. Cal., 1942; Ph.D., Stanford, 1946. Asst. prof. chemistry Immaculate Heart Coll., Los Angeles, 1942-46, asso. prof., 1946-52, prof., 1952—, chmn. chemistry dept., 1948-72. Vis. prof. chemistry Brown U., Providence, 1965-66. NIH fellow, 1965-66. Mem. Cal. Assn. Chemistry Tchrs. (pres. 1959-60, 66-67), Am. Chem. Soc. (chmn. So. Cal. sect. 1972-73), A.A.A.S., Assn. Women in Sci. Contbr. articles to profl. jours. Home: 1832 N Garfield Pl Los Angeles CA 90028

GREEN, ALICE, librarian; b. nr. Burlington, Kan., Sept. 20, 1916; d. Roy J. and Eliza (Carleton) Green; student Amarillo Coll., 1933-35, W. Tex. State Coll., 1935-37; B.S. in Library Sci., U. Okla., 1938. Librarian Tex. Mil. Coll., Terrell, 1938-39; gen. asst. Tex. State Library, Austin, 1939-41; asst. librarian Amarillo Pub. Library, 1941-47, librarian, 1947—. Mem. Am., Southwestern Tex. library assns., Am. Assn. U. Women, Delta Kappa Gamma. Club: Altrusa. Home: 3704 Clearwell St Amarillo TX 79109 Office: Amarillo Pub Library Amarillo TX 79105

GREEN, ALICE LOLA COHN (MRS. ROBERT H. GREEN), educator; b. N.Y.C., Mar. 24, 1924; d. Jack and Sid Rita (Brandwein) Cohn; B.A. (N.Y. State scholar), Bklyn. Coll., 1944; M.A. (Univ. Out-of-State scholar), U. Wis., 1946; tchr. certification Northwestern U., 1959; m. Robert H. Green, Oct. 18, 1947; children—Franklin Jay, Merrill Adam. Free-lance writer Los Angeles Times, 1947-49; mem. editorial staff Parents' mag., N.Y.C., 1946-47, 49-51; tchr. English, Niles Twp. High Sch., Skokie, Ill., 1959-67, New Trier Twp. High Sch., Winnetka, 1967—. Mem. N.E.A., Nat. Council Tchrs. English, New Trier Twp. Edn. Assn. (mem. grievance com. 1969-72), Women in Communications. Jewish religion (mem. scholarship com. synagogue 1969-70). Home: 9214 Harding Av Evanston IL 60203 Office: New Trier Twp High Sch 385 Winnetka Av Winnetka IL 60093

GREEN, ALICE OLDS, govt. ofcl.; b. Grand Junction, Colo.; d. James Arthur and Lucy (Olds) Green; student Northwestern U. Various positions Dept. of Labor, Ill. State Employment Service, Chgo., 1942—, tng. supr., 1961-74, methods and procedures adviser, 1974—. Care fund officer Dayton Cemetery Assn., 1964-66, 68-70, v.p., 1967-68, pres., 1970-71. Mem. Am. Soc. for Tng. and Devel., Ill. Tng. Dirs. Assn., Chgo. Council on Fgn. Relations, LaSalle County Hist. Soc., Phi Chi Theta. Home: 5040 Marine Dr Chicago IL 60640 Office: 165 N Canal St Chicago IL 60606

GREEN, ARLINE REA, aquatic coach, instr.; b. Indpls., June 30, 1926; d. Arlie Leslie and Bessie Glenn (Custer) Rea; A.B., Ind. U., 1947; B.S., U. Ariz., 1963, M.Ed., 1964; m. Robert Harper Green, Dec. 27, 1947 (div. 1967); children—Robert Harper, John Custer. Radio program hostess, dance instr., Tucson, 1942-43; lifeguard, instr., Tucson, 1945-46; aquatic and dance counselor, Me., 1947; head swimming instr. Riviera Club, Indpls., 1948-49; radio program hostess, Indpls., 1948-49; head instr., coach, Washington Court House, O., 1950-59; coach, instr. Highland Vista Aquatic Club, Tucson, 1960-66; TV commls. KVOA, Tucson, 1962; asst. instr. U. Ariz., 1963-64; owner, instr. Rincon Swim Sch., Tucson, 1963—; synchronized swim chmn. for Ariz.; mem. U.S. Amateur Athletic Union Synchronized Swim Com., 1967-70; instr. water safety A.R.C., 1946—. Recipient award for humanity A.R.C., 1965, Jantzens Internat. Age Group Swim Coach award, 1966. Mem. Am. Swim Coaches Assn., So. Ariz. Aquatic Assn., Amateur Athletic Union U.S. and Ariz. (sec. 1974), A.A.H.P.E.R., D.A.R. (past pres. Jr. D.A.R.), Nat. Thespian Soc., Nat. Honor Soc., Swimming Hall of Fame (life), Zeta Tau Alpha, Pi Lambda Theta, Delta Psi Kappa. Address: 9424 E Sierra Av Tucson AZ 85710

GREEN, BARBARA ANN, journalist; b. Richmond, Va., June 18, 1944; d. Arnold Thomas and Ida Lucille (Bransford) Green; B.A., Mary Washington Coll., 1966; postgrad. Va. Commonwealth U., 1968, 73. Intern Richmond Newspapers, 1966-67, reporter, 1967-70, critic, 1968—, picture editor, 1970-72, bus. writer, 1972-74, cultural and gen. assignment reporter, 1974—. Mem. Va. Mus. Fine Arts. Office: 333 E Grace St Richmond VA 23219

GREEN, BEATRICE THERESA GOULD (MRS. GEORGE GREEN), psychologist; b. Windsor, Vt.; d. Herman and Gertrude (Black) Gould; B.S., Boston U., 1938; B.S., Simmons Sch. Social Work, 1939; M.A., Clark U., 1963, Ed.D., 1974; m. George Green, Oct. 13, 1940; children—Robert Hart, Richard Bradley. Caseworker, Childrens Aid Soc., Boston, 1939; tchr. English, Malden (Mass.) Sch. System, 1940; counselor Clark U., Worcester, Mass., 1962-63; 1st exec. dir. Internat. Center of Worcester, 1964; ednl. psychologist Worcester (Mass.) Sch. System, 1965-66; founder, adminstrv. supr. Berkshire Theatre Festival, Stockbridge, Mass., 1966-68; ednl. co-ordinator, dir. research Berkshire Regional Ednl. Theatre, Pittsfield, Mass., 1968-71; co-producer Berkshire Community Theatre, Lenox, Mass., 1971-74; counselor So. Berkshire Free Psychol. Clinic, 1973—. Mem. Worcester Citizens Plan "E" Assn., 1954-74; vol. Worcester Youth Guidance Center, 1947-50. Bd. dirs. Jewish Family Service Worcester, 1960-61, Berkshire Lyric Theatre. Mem. Am. Assn. U. Women (treas. 1960), League Women Voters, Nat. Council Jewish Women (v.p. 1958-59), Am. Personnel and Guidance Assn., Nat. Assn. Fgn. Student Affairs, Am., Mass. psychol. assns., Am. Nat. Theatre and Acad., Internat. Platform Assn., New Eng. Theatre Conf. for Humanistic Psychology, N.E.A., Mass. Assn. Children with Learning Disabilities, Am. Ednl. Research Assn., Am. Ednl. Theatre Assn., Internat. Communication Assn. Home: 47 East St Stockbridge MA 01262

GREEN, BEVERLY DORIS (MRS. WILLIAM HOWARD GREEN), advt. agy. exec.; b. Klamath Falls, Ore., Apr. 8, 1925; d. Jacob Ernest and Kathryn Bell (Bryan) Brunton; student (scholar) Northwestern U., summer 1942; B.A. (Phi Beta Patroness' scholar), U. Ore., 1953; m. William Howard Green, June 19, 1954; children—William Harrison, Blakely Alan. Host, writer, producer Story Lady, Coffee Break shows KUGN, Eugene, Ore., 1948-54, Two Early, KVAL-TV, Eugene, 1954-64; with Green Assos., Eugene, 1963—, pres., gen. mgr., 1970—. Pres., Lane County (Ore.) Assn. for Retarded Children, 1969-70; mem. adv. bd. Eugene chpt. Jr. League, 1968—, United Way, 1968-72. Named Ad Man of Year, Eugene-Springfield Advt. Club, 1969. Mem. Women in Communications, Phi Beta Kappa, Phi Beta. Author: Out Of The Shadows, 1965. Editor: Bev's Coffee Break Cookbook, 1965. Home: 3505 Dulles Av Eugene OR 97401 Office: 1174 W 7th Av PO Box 2565 Eugene OR 97401

GREEN, CORENA CRASE (MRS. HAROLD FRANCIS GREEN), newspaper editor; b. Grass Valley, Cal., Apr. 7, 1917; d. James Carter and Drucilla Grace (Hicks) Crase; student U. Cal. at Berkeley, 1934-35, postgrad. 1938-39; A.B., Stanford, 1938; m. Harold Francis Green, Dec. 16, 1950; children—Elizabeth (Mrs. Douglas Marr Duncan), James Carter, Richard Holman. Tchr., Oakland (Cal.) pub. schs., 1939-43; sec. to personnel mgr. Am. Trust Co., San Francisco, 1945-48; reporter San Rafael (Cal.) Ind. Jour., 1956-64; reporter, editor Palos Verdes Peninsula (Cal.) News, 1964—. Pres. Marin County (Cal.) council Girl Scouts U.S.A., 1960-62. Bd. dirs. Marin County Red Cross, 1960-64. Served with WAVES, 1943-45. Mem. Am. Assn. Univ. Women (financial sec. Marin County br. 1956, recipient Status of Women award 1971), Nat. Fedn. Press Women (recipient writing awards 1969, 70, 71, 72), Los Angeles Press Club, S.W. Press Assn. (treas. 1970-73), Cal. Press Women, Cap and Gown, Sierra Club, Audubon Soc., Am. Cetacean Soc., Palos Verdes Peninsula Oceanographic Soc., P.T.A. (hon. life), Theta Sigma Phi. Home: 5710 Scotwood Dr Palos Verdes Peninsula CA 90274 Office: PO Box 2400 Palos Verdes Peninsula CA 90274

GREEN, DOROTHY BURKETT (MRS. LONSDALE B. GREEN), bus. exec., club woman; b. Raleigh, N.C., Oct. 28, 1902; d. Charles William and Laura (Weisman) Burkett; B.A., Vassar Coll., 1924; m. Lonsdale Bruce Green, Jan. 8, 1938. Riding tchr. Barnard Camp for Girls, Vt., 1920-24; interior decorator, N.Y.C. and Miami Beach, Fla., 1928—; real estate broker, 1943—; partner Hotel Devon, Miami Beach, 1950-59; partner House Closing & Maintenance Co., 1938-50. Pres., Vassar Club Dade County, 1950-60, John Foster Dulles chpt. Womans Cancer Assn. U. Miami, 1960-62; registrar Biscayne chpt. D.A.R., 1958-60, vice regent, 1960-62, regent, 1962-64, treasurer, 1966-68, state insignia chmn., 1958-60, state chmn. D.A.R. mag. advt., 1960-62, recipient nat. award for Insignia, 1960, nat. award mag. advt., 1962-64, rec. sec. Fla. soc., 1964-66, state chmn. Am. heritage com., 1963-64, nat. vice chmn. D.A.R. mag. advt. com. 1965-68, state chmn. membership com. 1967-68, U.S.A. bicentennial com., 1968-72, pres. Fla. Officers Club, 1969-70, registrar Biscayne chpt., 1970-72, treas. chpt., 1972-74, regent chpt., 1974—; state chmn. colonial courier, Daus. Am. Colonists, 1961-64, chpt. regent, 1964-67, rec. sec. Fla. soc., 1967-68, registrar Gov. John West chpt., 1970-73; Fla. chmn. U.S.A. bicentennial com. U.S. Daus. of 1812, 1973—; trustee Third Century, U.S.A., Miami, 1972—. Club: La Gorce Country (chmn. womans golf assn. 1952-53; chmn. bridge com. 1971-73). Author: Horseback Riding, 1922; Canary Birds, 1931. Home: 5121 North Bay Rd Miami Beach FL 33140

GREEN, EDITH, congresswoman; b. Trent, S.D.; d. James Vaughn and Julia (Hunt) Starrett; student Williamette U., 1927-29; B.S., U. Ore., 1939; 32 hon. degrees; children—James S., Richard A. Tchr. sch., Salem, Ore., 1930-41; comml. radio work KALE, Portland, Ore., 1944-45, free lance, 1943-47; dir. pub. relations Ore. Edn. Assn.; Dem. candidate for sec. state, 1952; mem. 84-93d congresses, 3d Ore. Dist., mem. appropriations com. Del. Inter-Parliamentary Conf., Switzerland, 1957; congl. del. NATO Conf., London, 1959. Del.-at-large Dem. Nat. Conv., 1956, 60, 64, 68. Recipient B'nai B'rith Brotherhood Award, 1956; Woman of the Year award Amvets Aux., 1958; distinguished service award Am. Coll. Pub. Relations Assn.; honored by Nat. Council Jewish Women, YWCA; Top Hat award Bus. and Profl. Women; Outstanding Service to Handicapped award Goodwill Industries Am., 1964; E. B. McNaughton award Am. Civil Liberties Union, 1966; distinguished service award U. Ore., 1967; Pres.'s award Nat. Rehab. Assn., 1967; Distinguished Service award Council Chief State Sch. Officers, 1967; Edn. Citizen of Year, Ore. Edn. Assn., 1967; Distinguished Pub. Service award County Los Angeles, 1968; Distinguished Service award N.E.A., 1968; Conde Nast award Georgetown U. Student Body, 1969; Distinction award Nat. Council Adm. Women in Edn., 1971; Distinguished Service award Nat. Assn. Trade and Tech. Schs., 1971; Citation World Conv. Chs. of Christ, 1971, Abram L. Sachar award, 1972, Distinguished Service award Ore. U., 1972, Outstanding Service award Nat. Assn. Student Personnel Adminstrn., 1972, Citation of Appreciation Am. Legion, 1972; ann. award Ore. Pub. Health Assn., 1973; Simon LeMoyne medal LeMoyne Coll., 1973; Distinguished Service award Pres.'s Com. on Employment Handicapped, 1974; Ann. Achievement award Am. Assn. U. Women, 1974. Mem. Christian Ch. Office: US Court House Portland OR 97205 also 1501 Longworth Bldg Washington DC 20515

GREEN, ELEANOR BROOME SAMUELS (MRS. LEON GREEN, JR.), museum ofcl.; b. Covina, Cal.; d. Charles and Eleanor (Broome) Samuels; A.B., Vassar Coll., 1949; M.A., George Washington U., 1971, Ph.D., 1973; m. Leon Green, Jr., Apr. 14, 1951; children—John Anderson, Emily Broome, Charles Leon. Curator, Washington Gallery Modern Art, Washington, 1964-67; curator contemporary art Corcoran Gallery Art, Washington, 1967-71; dir. art gallery U. Md., College Park, 1971—. Mem. Am. Assn. Museums, Jr. League of Washington. Author exhbn. catalogues. Contbr. articles to profl. jours. Home: 5140 Westpath Way Washington DC 20016 also Villa Green Porto Cervo Sardegna Italy Office: Art Gallery U Md College Park MD 20742

GREEN, ELEANOR KUHLMAN, govt. ofcl.; b. Wellsburg, W.Va., Feb. 5, 1908; d. Alfred George B. and Minerva (Kramer) G.; B.A. in Edn., U. Fla., 1940, M.A. in Edn., 1943, Ed.D., 1956; m. Arthur Sylvester Green, Dec. 20, 1935 (dec.); 1 son, Arthur Willard. Tchr. Brooksville, Fla., 1926-29, Newport Richey, Fla., 1930-35, Gainesville, Fla., 1938-40; mem. faculty U. Fla., 1940-62, asso. prof. edn. U. Fla., 1948-62; tchr. edn. adviser AID, Ankara, Turkey, 1962-66; tchr. edn. adviser, Saigon, 1966-69, edn. adviser, 1969, edn. dir. tchr. edn., 1970—. Recipient Meritorious Honor award AID, 1969; medal of honor (Vietnam), 1970. Mem. N.E.A., Am. Acad. Polit. Sci., Phi Kappa Phi, Phi Delta Kappa, Delta Kappa Gamma. Home: 1200 N Nash St Arlington VA 22209 Office: AID Dept State Washington DC 20523

GREEN, ELECTA DINGUS (MRS. LOUIS DOUGLAS GREEN), dentist; b. Guthrie, Okla.; d. James Andrew and Electa Maude (Longdon) Dingus; B.S., Tuskegee Inst., 1937; postgrad. Tenn. State U., 1942-44; D.D.S., Meharry Med. Coll., 1948; m. Louis Douglas Green, Aug. 19, 1939; children—Elna (Mrs. Lee Maur Benefee), Janice (Mrs. Aubry Carter Douglas). Tchr. pub. schs., Wagoner, Okla., 1937-38; research asst. Tuskegee Inst. Sch. Edn., Ala., 1938-39; tchr. pub. sch. Tuskegee Inst. High Sch., 1939-42; exec. sec. dept. edn. Tenn. Bd. Edn., 1943-44; practice dentistry, Birmingham, Ala., 1948-57, Cleve., 1957—. Organizer, founder Ellsberry Community Club, Birmingham, 1950-57, pres., 1956-57; mem. Birmingham council Girl Scouts U.S.A., 1954-57, mem. area council camping com., Cleve., 1958-60. Mem. Am., Ohio dental assns., Cleve. Dental Soc., Forrest City Dental Study Club, Cleve. Acad. Dental Studies, Delta Sigma Theta. Methodist. Soroptomist. Home: 25203 Duffield Rd Beachwood OH 44122 Office: 2475 E 22d St Cleveland OH 44115

GREEN, ELIZABETH ADINE HERKIMER, music educator; b. Mobile, Ala., Aug. 21, 1906; d. Albert Wingate and Mary Elizabeth (Timmerman) Green; B.S., Wheaton (Ill.) Coll., 1928; Mus.M., Northwestern U., 1938; pupil orchestral conducting with Nicolai Malko, violin with Ivan Galamian. Tchr. violin, orch. condr. Waterloo (Ia.) pub. schs., 1928-41, Ann Arbor (Mich.) pub. schs., 1942-55; mem. faculty U. Mich., 1945—, prof. music, 1963—; guest prof. Ohio State U., summer 1951, Calvin Coll., Grand Rapids, Mich., summer 1971; clinician in U.S. and Can. Mem. judging panel 3d Nicolai Malko Meml. Internat. Conducting competition for young condrs., Copenhagen, 1971. Mem. Music Educators Nat. Conf., Am. String Tchrs. Assn., Nat. Sch. Orch. Assn., Am. Assn. U. Profs., Delta Omicron, Pi Kappa Lambda. Author: Orchestral Bowings and Routines, 2d edit., 1957; The Modern Conductor, 2d edit., 1969; Teaching Stringed Instruments in Classes, 1967; The Conductor and His Score, 1975; also numerous articles. Composer: Twelve Modern Etudes for Violin, 1964, other works. Home: 1225 Ferdon Rd Ann Arbor MI 48104

GREEN, EMMA ALICE, librarian; b. Coffey County, Kan., Sept. 20, 1916; d. Roy J. and Eliza Keithline (Carleton) Green; student Amarillo Coll., 1934-36, W. Tex. State U., 1936-37; B.A., Okla. U., 1938. Librarian, Tex. Mil. Coll., Terrell, 1938-39; gen. asst. extension div. Tex. State Library, Austin, 1939-41; asst. librarian Amarillo (Tex.) Pub. Library, 1941-47, city librarian, 1947—. Mem. Am., Tex. (chmn. pub. library div. 1973—) library assns., Amarillo C. of C. Club: Altrusa (Amarillo). Home: 3704 Clearwell St Amarillo TX 79109 Office: 1000 Polk St Amarillo TX 79105

GREEN, EVELYN LUCILE, ch. exec.; b. Cuero, Tex., July 31, 1913; d. John Leighton and Lucy (Oates) Green; A.B., Tex. Christian U., 1934; B.R.E., Presbyn. Sch. Christian Edn., Richmond, Va., 1936; H.H.D., Ark. Coll., 1964. Dir. Christian edn. Synod. Okla., 1936-42, Broadway Presbyn. Ch., Ft. Worth, 1942-45, Brazos Presbytery, Houston, 1945-50; sec. program div. Bd. Women's Work, Presbyn. Ch. U.S., 1950-60, exec. sec., Atlanta, 1960—. Mem. gen. bd. Nat. Council Chs., 1965—; rep. Presbyn. Ch. U.S. to gen. assembly World Council Chs., New Delhi, India, 1961; del. women's dept. World Presbyn. Alliance, Frankfurt, Germany, 1964; mem. U.S. Conf., World Council Chs., 1961—; guest speaker Congress Women's Socs. Presbyn. Ch. Brazil, Rio de Janeiro, 1966, guest tchr. gen. conf. Women's Socs. Presbyn. Ch. Congo, 1967; del. gen. council World Alliance Ref. Chs., Nairobi, Kenya, 1970. Mem. program planning com. YWCA, Atlanta, 1960—; mem. women's planning com. Japan Internat. Christian U., 1961—. Mem. Am. Assn. U. Women. Presbyn. (deacon). Club: Altrusa (Atlanta). Home: 236 Clarion Av Decatur GA 30030 Office: 31 Ponce de Leon Av NE Atlanta GA 30308

GREEN, GERALDINE DOROTHY, petroleum co. exec.; b. N.Y.C., July 14, 1938; d. Edward and Lula Madeline (Albro) Chisholm; student accounting Coll. City N.Y., 1962-64; J.D., St. John's U., 1968. Tax accountant Lybrand, Ross Bros. & Montgomery, C.P.A.'s, N.Y.C., 1966-68; admitted to N.Y. Bar, 1968; atty. IBM Corp., Armonk, N.Y., Washington and Los Angeles, 1968-72; corporate finance atty., asst. sec. Atlantic Richfield Co., Los Angeles, 1972—. Spl. counsel to Western regional dir. N.A.A.C.P., 1972—, v.p. Hollywood (Cal.) br., 1973—, recipient Freedom award, 1973; counsel to exec. dir. Los Angeles Urban League, 1972—, recipient Community Service award, 1973. Mem. Am., Nat., Beverly Hills bar assns., Cal. State Bar (com. on corps.), Nat. Legal Aid and Defender Assn., Los Angeles Women Lawyers Assn., Langston Law Club, Lawyers Club Los Angeles, Office: 515 S Flower St Los Angeles CA 90071

GREEN, GLORIA FRANCES REED (MRS. ARTHUR DALE GREEN), nurse educator; b. Ottumwa, Ia.; d. John D. and Minnie May (James) Reed; grad. Jennie Edmundson Meml. Hosp. Sch.

Nursing, Council Bluffs, Ia., 1942; B.S. in Nursing Edn., Creighton U., 1949; m. Arthur Dale Green, Apr. 8, 1949 (dec. 1971); children—Karen May, Robert Dale. Supr., Meml. Hosp., Cheyenne, Wyo., 1944-46; clin. instr. div. of nursing Loretto Heights Coll., St. Anthony Hosp., Denver, 1949-50; clin. instr. Mercy Hosp. Sch. Nursing, Denver, 1953; dir. Neb. Western Coll. Sch. Practical Nursing, Scottsbluff, 1972—; clin. instr. St. Anthony Hosp. Sch. Practical Nursing, Denver, 1957-60, acting dir., 1960-61, dir., 1961-70. Chmn., Colo. Conf. Schs. of Practical Nursing, 1958, 66. Sponsor med. explorer troop Wyo.-Neb. Area council Boy Scouts Am. Bd. dirs., chmn. disaster nursing subcom. Scottsbluff County chpt. A.R.C. Mem. Nat. Assn. for Practical Nurse Edn. and Service (dir. 1966-70, chmn. accrediting rev. bd. 1969-71, cons. for workshops, 1970—), Am. Nurses Assn., Neb. Edn. Assn. Baptist (trustee 1969). Home: 623 E 26th St Scottsbluff NE 69361

GREEN, HANNAH OPPENHEIMER (MRS. ROBERT W. GREEN), biochemist; b. Dusseldorf, Germany, Oct. 14, 1935; d. Walter and Luise (Morgenstern) Oppenheimer; B.S., Carnegie Mellon U., 1957; M.S., Cornell U., 1960, Ph.D., 1964; m. Robert W. Green, May 21, 1966; children—Catherine Martha, Linda Elizabeth. Came to U.S., 1940, naturalized, 1946. Chemist, Jones & Laughlin Steel Corp., Pitts., 1957-58; research asso. dept. biochemistry and biophysics U. Hawaii, Honolulu, 1964-67; research asso. depts. biochemistry, physiology, pharmacology Duke Med. Center, Durham, N.C., 1969, 70-71, 73; information specialist N.C. Sci. and Tech. Research Center, Research Triangle Park, 1973—. Mem. Am. Chem. Soc., Sigma Xi, Phi Kappa Phi. Home: 1610 Sycamore St Durham NC 27707

GREEN, HELEN BAGENSTOSE (MRS. SAMUEL M. GREEN), educator; b. Bklyn., Aug. 10, 1909; d. Harvey Lee and Mary (Stuart) Bagenstose; B.A., Wellesley Coll., 1931, M.A., 1933; Ph.D., U. Conn., 1963; m. Samuel Magee Green, June 23, 1934; children—Jonathan Standish, Samuel Adams, Gwynthlyn Hoage. Lectr. psychology Trinity Coll., Hartford, Conn., 1964-67; asso. prof. psychology Wesleyan U., Middletown, Conn., 1968-71; prof. dept. psychology, supr. mental health worker program Middlesex Community Coll., Middletown, 1972—. Co-dir. Service Corps Research Project, Conn. Dept. Mental Health, 1964-66. Mem. Am. Psychol. Assn., Inter-Am. Soc. Psychology, Internat. Soc. for Study of Time. Contbr. articles to profl. jours. Home: 256 Oak Hill-Meriden Rd Middletown CT 06457

GREEN, JEAN CATHERINE (MRS. FRANK H. GREEN), editor; b. Pekin, Ind.; d. William L. and Jessie (Scott) Green; A.B., M.S., Ind. U.; m. Frank H. Green, July 1, 1938; children—David Lot, John Charles, William Louis. Feature writer woman's page Washington Times, 1934-36, Washington Post, 1936-38; editor Hoosier Dr.'s Wife, 1949—; contbg. editor M.D.'s Wife, Rushville, Inc., 1965—; columnist Rushville Republican, 1963—. Mem. editorial adv. bd. to women's aux. A.M.A., 1970—, Internat. Platform Assn., 1969—. State v.p. Aux. to Ind. State Hosp. Assn., 1954-56, Rushville Sch. Bd., 1945-49; mem. regional bd. Sch. Bd., 1957-59. Mem. Woman's Press Club Ind. (1st Pl. editorial 1964-65, 70), Press Club Washington, Am. Fedn. Press Woman. Author: The First Twenty Five Years Indiana Academy of General Practice and Family Physicians, 1973; One Hundred and Fifty Years of Medicine in Family Practice, 1972. Home: 516 N Morgan St Rushville IN 46173

GREEN, JEANNINE ANN SHIVERS, mgmt. research exec.; b. Baton Rouge, La., July 11, 1939; d. James McLaurin and Jeannetee (Perkins) Shivers; B.A., U. Conn., 1961; M.A., U. Wis., 1963. Information specialist Conf. Bd., Inc., N.Y.C., 1966, mgr. information center, 1966-68, dir. information services div., 1968—. Speaker and/or cons. mgmt. devel., tng. equal employment opportunity; speaker on crime prevention to various civic groups. Mem. Brownstone Revival Com., N.Y.C., 1969-72; chmn. crime com. Boerum Hill Assn., 1971; mem. Mayor's Urban Task Force, N.Y.C., 1973—. Mem. Am. Soc. Indexers, Am. Documentation Inst., Am. Mgmt. Assn., Am. Soc. Tng. Dirs., Information Industry Assn., Pi Beta Phi, Spl. Libraries Assn., Econ. Think Tank for Women. Home: 201 E 22d St New York City NY 10010 Office: 845 3d Av New York City NY 10022

GREEN, JOAN LUCILLE, educator; b. Salt Lake City, Apr. 21, 1930; d. Harold J. and Louise (Nave) Green; diploma in nursing Holy Cross Hosp., 1953; B.S., St. Mary-of-the-Wasatch, 1953; M.S., Cath. U. Am., 1960; Ph.D. in Higher Edn., U. Cal. at Berkeley, 1974. Staff nurse St. Mary's Hosp., San Francisco, 1954-55; instr. Franklin Hosp. Sch. Nursing, San Franciso, 1955-56; med.-surg. nursing clin. coordinator St. Mary's Hosp. Coll. Nursing, San Francisco, 1956-58; faculty Sch. Nursing, U. San Francisco, 1960—, prof., 1973—, research project dir., curriculum evaluation, 1966-73, asst. dean, 1974—. Chmn. nursing edn. com. San Francisco Heart Assn., 1962-66, bd. govs., 1961-66, mem. profl. edn. com., 1964-66. Mem. Am., Cal. nurses assns., Nat. League Nursing, Am. Assn. U. Profs., Am. Ednl. Research Assn., Am. Assn. Higher Edn., Council Nurse Researchers. Home: 51 Calvert Av South San Francisco CA 94080

GREEN, JOYCE HENS (MRS. SAMUEL GREEN), judge; b. N.Y.C., Nov. 13, 1928; d. James Stanley and Hedy (Bucher) Hens; B.A., U. Md., 1949; LL.B., George Washington U., 1951; m. Samuel Green, Sept. 25, 1965; children—James Harry, Michael Timothy, June Heather. Admitted to the D.C. bar, 1951, Va. bar, 1956; pvt. practice law, Washington, 1951-68, Arlington, Va., 1956-68; partner (with husband) Green & Green, Washington, until 1968; asso. judge, D.C. Ct. Gen. Sessions, 1968-71, Superior Ct. D.C., 1971—. Trustee D.C. div. Am. Cancer Soc., 1963—. Recipient certificate merit for outstanding profl. achievement D.C. Profl. Panhellenic Assn., 1968. Fellow Am. Acad. Matrimonial Lawyers; mem. Am., Va., Arlington County, D.C. Women's (pres. 1960-62) bar. assns., Bar Assn. D.C., Unified Bar D.C., Nat. Lawyers Club, Kappa Beta Pi. Home: 1714 N Glebe Rd Arlington VA 22207 Office: DC Superior Ct 4th and E Sts NW Washington DC 20001

GREEN, JOYCE WRIGHT (MRS. ALFRED LOUIS GREEN), nurse, educator; b. Key West, Fla., Aug. 23, 1940; d. Wayne Glenworth and Mary Rose (Yurgenc) Wright; student Mary Washington Coll., 1958-60; B.S. in Nursing, U. Va., 1962; M.N. in Nursing, U. Fla., 1968; postgrad. Central Conn. State Coll., 1973—; m. Alfred Louis Green, Aug. 10, 1968; 1 son, Glenworth Edward. Instr. pub. health U. Fla. Sch. Nursing, Gainesville, 1968-69, research asst., 1968-69; instr. dept. pediatrics Mailman Center for Child Devel., U. Miami (Fla.), 1969-70; asst. prof. nursing Quinnipiac Coll., Hamden, Conn., 1970—. Instr., Parents Assn. for Childbirth Edn., Hartford, Conn., 1972—, dir. child birth edn., 1973—. Served to lt. USNR, 1962-67. Mem. Am., Conn., Fla. (chmn. rules com. 1969-70) nurses assns., Am. Assn. for Maternal and Child Health, Am. Assn. U. Women, Civic Music Assn. Home: 62 Richmond Lane West Hartford CT 06107 Office: 1680 Albany Av Hartford CT 06105

GREEN, JUNE LAZENBY (MRS. JOHN CAWLEY GREEN), fed. judge; b. Arnold, Md., Jan. 23, 1914; d. Eugene H. and Jessie T. (Briggs) Lazenby; J.D., Am. U., 1941; m. John Cawley Green, Sept. 5, 1936. Admitted to Md. bar, 1943, D.C. bar, 1945; individual practice law, Washington, 1947-68, Annapolis, Md., 1950-68; claims adjuster Lumbermans Mut. Casualty Co., Washington, 1942-43, claims atty., 1943-47; apptd. judge U.S. Dist. Ct., D.C., 1968—. Bar examiner, Washington, 1963-68. Named Woman Lawyer of Yr., 1965. Fellow Am. Acad. Matrimonial Lawyers; mem. Inter-Am., Am., Md. bar assns., Bar Assn. D.C. (dir. 1966-68), Women's Bar Assn. D.C. (pres. 1955-57), Kappa Beta Pi. Clubs: Nat. Lawyers, Zonta. Home: 261 Joyce Lane Arnold MD 21012 Office: US Ct House 3d and Constitution Av NW Washington DC 20001

GREEN, KAREN MARGUERITE (MRS. DENNIS R. GREEN), health services adminstr.; b. Oelwin, Ia., Feb. 2, 1941; d. Clifford Raymond and Marguerite Pearl (Krueger) Johnson; student U. Neb., 1959-61; R.N., Neb. Meth. Hosp. Sch. Nursing, 1963; m. Dennis R. Green, Nov. 7, 1964; children—Erin Ruth, Eric Russell. Staff nurse diagnostic and evaluation team Glenwood (Ia.) State Hosp. Sch., 1965-67, dir. foster grandparent program, 1967-68, leader treatment team, 1969-72; dir. devel. maximation programs Eastern Neb. Community Office Retardation, Omaha, 1972—. Cons. profl. and program services com. United Cerebral Palsey Omaha, 1973—. Sec. S.W. Ia. Drug Abuse Council, 1969. Served with USAF, 1964-65. Mem. Am. Assn. Mental Deficiency, Omaha Assn. for Retarded Citizens. Home: Route 1 Pacific Junction IA 51561 Office: 4102 Woolworth St Omaha NE 68105

GREEN, LEONA MILDRED THACHER (MRS. HOWARD WHIPPLE GREEN), club woman; b. Herington, Kan.; d. Frank Eugene and Cecilia Imogene (Dittrich) Thacher; A.B., Colo. Coll.; m. Howard Whipple Green, Nov. 30, 1919; children—Patricia Anne (Mrs. David Charles Miller), Howard Thacher. Tchr., Canal Zone, 1917-19, Colorado Springs, 1912-17; area dir. Civilian War Services, Cleveland Heights, O., 1942-44; bd. dirs. Cleve. Mental Health Assn., 1947-53, Cleve. Guidance Center, 1944-49. Nat. corr. sec. Daus. Am. Colonists, 1949-52, nat. v.p., 1952-55, hon. nat. v.p., 1955—; pres. Ohio ct. Women Descendants Ancient and Honorable Arty. Co., 1959-62, nat. chaplain, 1962-65, nat. pres., 1965-68; pres. Ohio chpt. Daus. Founders and Patriots Am., 1961-62; mem. Order of Crown of Charlemagne, Colonial Dames Am., Americans of Armorial Descent, D.A.R., Dames Court of Honor, Sons and Daus. of Pilgrims, Nat. Huguenot Soc., Daus. Barons of Runnymede, Colonial Daus. 17th Century, Daus. Colonial Wars, Nat. Soc. New Eng. Women, Order of Crown in Am., P.E.O. Presbyn. Club: College (Cleve.). Died Feb. 2, 1974. Home: 2231 Delamere Dr Cleveland Heights OH 44106

GREEN, LUCILE ALBERTA WOLFE (MRS. ARTHUR R. ISITT), educator; b. Fenchow, Shansi, China, on April 24, 1917 ; d. Jesse Benjamin and Clara (Husted) Wolfe; student Yenching U., Peking, China, 1933-35; B.A. magna cum laude, Pomona Coll., 1937; M.A., Claremont Coll., 1939; Ph.D., Ohio State U., 1957; m. John H. Green, 1939 (div.); children—Sidney Wolfe, Nelson Wesley; m. 2d, Arthur R. Isitt, 1970. Instr., Lincoln Coll., 1946-50, Ohio State U., 1951-56; asst. prof. Otterbein Coll., Westerville, O., 1953-56; prof. humanities and philosophy Merritt Coll., Oakland, Cal., 1957—, chmn. dept. humanities, 1960-62, 66—; lectr. on world govt., problems of peace, 1965—. Active World Com. for a World Constl. Conv., 1963—; del. World Constl. Conv., Switzerland, 1968; chmn. World Ecology Com. Trustee, pres. bd. Acad. World Studies, San Francisco. Mem. World Future Soc., World Federalists, Am. Humanist Assn., Cal. Humanities Assn. (co-chmn. ann. conf. 1974), World Constn. and Parliament Assn. (v.p.), Phi Beta Kappa. Unitarian (trustee). Author: The Human Spirit in the Atomic Age, 1961; Human Value in the Atomic Age, 1963; also numerous articles on gen. edn., relation sci. and humanities, and problems of peace. Co-editor The Worried Woman's Guide to Peace Through World Law, 1965. Home: 774 Colusa Av El Cerrito CA 94530 Office: Merritt Coll 12500 Campus Dr Oakland CA 94619

GREEN, MAE RABACH (MRS. SAM GREEN), artist; b. N.Y.C., Sept. 14, 1930; d. Philip and Clara (Donnenfeld) Rabach; grad. Pratt Inst., 1951; student U. N.M., 1953-54; m. Sam Green, Feb. 1, 1953; children—Michelle, Tracy, Dori Sue, Marshall. Textile designer Black Studios, N.Y.C., 1950; one-man shows at Jonson Gallery, Albuquerque, Malvina Miller Gallery, San Francisco; exhibited in group shows at Perspective Gallery, N.Y.C., Fiesta Show Mus., N.M., Los Griegos Library, N.A.D., N.Y.C., Malvina Miller Gallery, Cassidy Gallery, Albuquerque, Mus. N.M., El Paso Mus., Jonson Gallery, Albuquerque; represented in permanent collections Jonson collection U. N.M., Pub. Service Co. N.M. Flower Show judge State N.M., 1962; active United Community Fund. Recipient Bronze medal Pratt Inst., 1951, Nat. award for wallpaper and drapery Nat. Inst. Design, 1950. Home: 1521 Sagebrush Trail SE Albuquerque NM 87123

GREEN, MARGARET, educator; b. Shamrock, La., Mar. 27, 1917; d. Samuel Lafayette and Bessie Amee (Brown) Green; B.S., La. State U., 1937; M.S., Emory U., 1939; Ph.D., U. Wis., 1952. Bacteriologist, Charity Hosp., Shreveport, La., 1939-42; instr. bacteriology La. State U., Baton Rouge, 1942-47, asst. prof., 1952-55, asso. prof., 1956-65, prof., 1966-68; prof., head dept. microbiology U. Ala. at Tuscaloosa, 1968—. NSF Sr. Sci. fellow, 1966-67. Mem. A.A.A.S., Am. Chem. Soc., Am. Soc. Microbiology (nat. councillor 1957-59), Sigma Xi. Home: 7 Rhonda Dr Tuscaloosa AL 35401

GREEN, MARGARET MURPHY (MRS. FRANCIS J. GREEN), educator, author; b. Lawrence, Mass., Sept. 1, 1926; d. William A. and Margaret M. (Donovan) Murphy; A.B., Am. U., 1965; m. Francis J. Green, Dec. 31, 1949; children—Ellen (Mrs. Russell Byrne), Frank, William, Mary. Tchr., English, Fairfax, Va., 1965—. Named Fairfax County Tchr. Year, Sch. Adminstrs. and Tchrs. Fairfax County, 1972-73. Mem. Nat. Council Tchrs. English, Nat., Va. edn. assns. Roman Catholic. Author: Defender of the Constitution, 1962; Man Behind the Legend, 1964; President of the Confederacy, 1963, Radical of the Revolution, 1971. Home: 6920 Fern Lane Annandale VA 22003 Office: WT Woodson High Sch 9525 Main St Fairfax VA 22030

GREEN, MARJORIE ELEANORE BERG (MRS. LOY F. GREEN), music tchr.; b. Wellsville, O.; d. Carl A. and Flora (Kampman) Berg; B.A., Case-Western Reserve U., 1932; Mus.B., Baldwin Wallace Coll., 1957; postgrad. Case-Western Res. U., 1958-61; m. Loy F. Green, Oct. 3, 1931; children—Wayne Francis, Linda Lee. Tchr. piano and organ, Berea, O., 1957—; co-ordinator Bach Festivals, Baldwin-Wallace Coll., 1955-70. Past pres. womens com. Baldwin-Wallace Conservatory; dir. Town and Gown Concert Series, 1958-72. Exec. v.p. S.W. Women's Republican Club. Mem. Nat., Ohio music tchrs. assns., Internat. Platform Assn., Mu Phi Epsilon, Delta Zeta (past alumni pres.), Phi Delta Gamma. Clubs: Berea Fine Arts (pres. 1969-70), Zonta (treas. 1969-70, pres. 1972-74), Three Arts, Chopin. Home: 1851 King James Pkwy Westlake OH 44145

GREEN, MARTHA DORIS BARKER, obstetrician, gynecologist; b. Piedmont, Ala., Feb. 26, 1922; d. Norwood E. and Carrie Lou (Stewart) Barker; B.A., Vanderbilt U., 1943; M.D., U. Tenn., 1946; children—Robert Lee III, Norwood E. Intern, Jefferson-Hillman Hosp., Birmingham, Ala., 1946-47, resident, 1947-50; practice medicine, specializing in obstetrics and gynecology, Birmingham, Ala., 1952—; mem. staff Bapt. Med. Centers, South Highlands Hosp., Brookwood Hosp. (all Birmingham); asst. clin. prof. obstetrics and gynecology U. Ala. Med. Center, 1961—. Diplomate Am. Bd. Obstetrics and Gynecology. Fellow Am. Coll. Obstetricians and Gynecologists. Home: 86 Country Club Blvd Birmingham AL 35213 Office: 1601 11th Av S Birmingham AL 35205

GREEN, MARY ELOISE, educator; b. East Liberty, O., June 10, 1903; d. Milton M. and Sylvia (Creviston) Green; student Ohio Wesleyan U., 1920-21; B.S., Ohio State U., 1928, M.S., 1933; Ph.D., Ia. State U., 1949. Tchr. elementary schs., East Liberty, 1923-26; tchr. home econs. Monroe Twp. High Sch., West Liberty, 1928-37; instr. home econs. edn. Ohio Wesleyan U., Delaware, 1937-39; instr. foods and nutrition Ohio State U., Columbus, 1939-45, asst. prof., 1946-54, asso. prof., 1955-67, prof., 1968-72, prof. emeritus, 1972—; research fellow Ia. State U., 1947-49; vis. prof. foods and nutrition Ball State Tchrs. Coll., Muncie, Ind., summer 1950, Okla. State U., summer 1965, Indiana U. of Pa., summers 1968, 70. Fellow A.A.A.S.; mem. Am. Home Econs. Assn., Am. Dietetic Assn., Inst. Food Technologists, Am. Assn. Cereal Chemists, Ohio Pub. Health Assn., Am. Assn. U. Women, Pi Lambda Theta, Kappa Delta Pi, Iota Sigma Pi, Sigma Delta Epsilon, Omicron Nu. Home: 116 W Como Av Columbus OH 43202

GREEN, MARY GRACE, psychologist; b. N.Y.C., Oct. 11, 1916; d. James John and Kathryn Josephine (Ryan) Green; B.S., Rosary Coll., 1936; M.A., U. Minn., 1942; M.A., Fordham U., 1961; Ph.D., St. John's U., 1971. Instr. chemistry and math. Coll. Edn., Great Falls, Mont., 1937-41; tchr. chemistry Central High Sch., Valley Stream, N.Y., 1942-44, tchr. health, 1946-64, sch. psychologist, 1964-71; guidance counselor Oceanside (N.Y.) High Sch., 1944-45; statistician Am. Cancer Soc., N.Y.C., 1945-46; pvt. practice psychol. cons., 1971—. Bd. dirs. Drug Prevention Program, Valley Stream, 1971—. Mem. Am., Eastern psychol. assns., Nat. Assn. Sch. Psychologists. Contbr. articles on drug use to profl. jours. Home: 41 Fletcher Av Valley Stream NY 11580

GREEN, MARY HOSTLER, physician; b. Pitts., Feb. 13, 1913; d. Henry Albert and Mary Jane (Smith) Hostler; A.B. magna cum laude, Chatham Coll., 1934; M.S., U. Cin., 1940; M.D., U. Pitts., 1947; m. Melvin William Green, Aug. 27, 1938 (div. Apr. 1944). Research asst. Mellon Inst., Pitts., 1934-38; control chemist food products Am. Products Co., Cin., 1938-39; instr. biochemistry U. Cin. Med. Sch., 1939-40; research biochemistry, quantitative bacteriology Christ Hosp. Inst. Research, Cin., 1940-41; Renziehausen research fellow Children's Hosp., Pitts., 1941-44, resident pathology, 1949-52; intern, Mercy Hosp., Pitts., 1947-48; asst. pathologist, asst. prof. research in pathology Children's Hosp. and U. Pitts. Sch. Medicine, 1952-55; resident medicine St. Marg Meml. Hosp., Pitts., 1955-56; practice medicine specializing in internal medicine, Pitts., 1956—; mem. staffs Suburban Gen., St. John Gen. hosps., Pitts., Mem. Am., Pa., Allegheny med. assns., Am. Diabetes Assn., Am. Bus. Women's Assn., Sigma Xi, Alpha Omega Alpha. Republican. Episcopalian. Contbr. articles to profl. publs. Address: 826 California Av Pittsburgh PA 15202

GREEN, MARY JANE (MRS. JAMES RIGNEY GREEN), librarian; b. Sedan, Kan., Mar. 9, 1941; d. Charles Wheeler and Helen Beatrice (Casement) Martin; B.S. in Edn., Kan. State Tchrs. Coll., Emporia, 1963, M.S. in L.S., 1967; m. James Rigney Green, Apr. 18, 1970. English instr. Sherman County Community High Sch., Goodland, Kan., 1963-65; cataloger, librarian Midwest Research Inst., Kansas City, Mo., 1967-68, head librarian, 1968-70; cataloger U. Kan., Lawrence, 1970-72, head cataloger, 1972-74, acting personnel dir., 1974—. Mem. Spl. Libraries Assn. (chpt. publicity chmn. 1967-68, sec. 1968-69, dir. 1969-70, recruitment chmn. 1970-71), Am. Assn. U. Profs., Am. Soc. Information Sci., A.L.A., Kan. Library Assn., Delta Zeta (chpt. pres. 1962), Pi Lambda Theta. Home: 523 Kasold Dr Lawrence KS 66044

GREEN, MARY JOANN HILDYARD (MRS. FORBES JOHN GREEN), occupational therapist; b. Hutchinson, Kan., Apr. 18, 1940; d. Arthur Thomas and Vida Grace (Welker) Hildyard; B.S., Western Mich. U., 1963; m. Forbes John Green, June 23, 1973. Staff therapist St. Joseph's Hosp., St. Paul, 1963-65; supr. occupational therapy Minn. Residential Treatment Center, Lino Lakes, 1965-68; psychiat. instr., supr. clin. practice Kyushu Coll. Rehab., Kitakyushu, Japan, 1968-70; supr. occupational therapy Louise Whitbeck Fraser Sch., Richfield, Minn., 1970-74; hon. mem. faculty Coll. St. Catherine, St. Paul, 1973—. Bd. dirs. Richfield Sweet Adelines, Inc., 1972-73. Mem. Am., Minn. occupational therapy assns., Mental Retardation Spl. Interest Group (chmn. 1972-73), Minn. Ceramic Assn., Single Persons for Tax Equality Assn. (bd. dirs. 1971-73, nat. sec., 1971-73). Home: 14419 Locke Lane Houston TX 77077

GREEN, MAXINE WISE (MRS. ALVIN E. GREEN), polit. worker; b. Vincennes, Ind., Feb. 7, 1917; d. Raymond Franklin and Iva (Copple) Wise; grad. high sch.; m. Alvin E. Green, Apr. 16, 1938; children—William Charles, Alvin E. Sec., Cal. assemblyman 1963-66; sec. regional office for Gov. Reagan, San Diego, 1967; field rep. Senator Jack Schrade, San Diego, 1967-68; field rep. Senator Burgener, San Diego, 1968-73; dist. rep. Congressman Burgener, 43d dist., San Diego, 1973—. Pres., Longfellow Sch. P.T.A., San Diego, 1953-54, Marston Sch. P.T.A., 1957-58; life mem. P.T.A., women's chmn. United Fund, San Diego, 1959, pres. Clairemont Woman's Club, 1955-57. Pres., Republican Women's Club, 1966-67; mem. Rep. State Central Com., 1963—; ex-officio mem. San Diego County Rep. Central Com., 1966—; mem. Rep. Assos., 1974—, San Diego Fedn. Rep. Women. Recipient Clairemont Woman of Year award Clairemont Women's Club, 1957; Woman of Valor award for community services City of San Diego, 1959. Mem. Globe Guilders, Country Friends. Home: 2847 Arnott San Diego CA 92110 Office: 7860 Mission Center Ct San Diego CA 92108

GREEN, MYRTLE H., retail store exec.; b. Des Moines, Apr. 9, 1908; d. Joseph Lloyd and Estelle Burke (Craven) Green; student Drake U., 1928-30; postgrad. Des Moines Coll. Law, 1933-36. Circulation and promotion staff Register & Tribune, Des Moines, 1926-37; fashion promoter, radio personality under name June Marlowe Wieboldt Stores, Inc., Chgo., 1937-56, advt. mgr., 1956-63, sales promotion mgr., 1963, v.p., 1963—, also dir. Chmn. State St. Council Promotion Com., Chgo., 1974-76. Named Chgo. Advt. Woman of Year, 1966. Mem. Chgo. Fashion Group (mem. council 1968-70), Women's Advt. Club Chgo. Home: 1212 Asbury St Evanston IL 60202 Office: 1 N State St Chicago IL 60602

GREEN, NETTIE LUTHER CLECKLER (MRS. CLATIS GREEN), univ. adminstr.; b. Arab, Ala.; d. Gordon and Evie (Story) Cleckler; B.S., U. Ala., 1957, M.A., 1961; m. Clatis Green, May 31, 1924 (dec. June 1954). Residence dir. U. Ala., 1956-59; dean girls Menaul Sch., Albuquerque, 1959-60; resident counselor, instr. Shepherd Coll., Shepherdstown, W.Va., 1961-63; resident counselor Stephens Coll., Columbia, Mo., 1963-64, Wis. State U., Eau Claire, 1964-66, Troy (Ala.) State U., 1966-69; dir. social activities U. Wis.-Eau Claire, 1969—. Mem. Nat. Assn. Women Deans and Counselors, Assn. Wis. State U. Faculties, Ala. Alumni Assn., N.E.A., Am. Assn. U. Women, Women's Soc. Christian Service (pres. 1940-43). Methodist. Address: Davies Center U Wis Eau Claire WI 54701

GREEN, PAULA, advt. exec.; b. Hollywood, Cal., Sept. 18, 1927; d. Myron and Elizabeth (Grobstein) Green; B.A., U. Cal., 1944; m. John Glucksman, July 1, 1948; 1 son, Joel. Vice pres., creative supt. Doyle, Dane Bernbach, N.Y.C., 1956-69; pres. Green, Dolmatch, Inc., 1969—. Dir. Palisades Life Ins. Co. Bd. dirs. Am. Cancer Soc. Named Copywriter of Year Am. TV Festival, 1961; recipient Gold Key, AWARE Internat. Andy award, 1970, Minerva award, 1971, Saturday Rev. award, 1971. Office: Green Dolmatch Inc 500 Fifth Av New York City NY 10036

GREEN, REBA JUNE LONG (MRS. B.J. GREEN), broadcaster; b. Yale, Okla., June 29, 1920; d. Asa M. and Ida May (Allison) Long; student Va. Intermont Coll., 1938-40; A.B. magna cum laude, U. Redlands, 1942; m. Ralph H. Brumet, Nov. 7, 1943 (div. Mar. 1964); children—Ralph H., Barbara Lee, Linda May; m. 2d, B.J. Green, Apr. 21, 1965. With publicity dept. David O. Selznick, Culver City, Cal., 1942-43; with WORI Radio, Bristol, Tenn.-Va., 1951-53; broadcaster, moderator show WFHG Radio, Bristol, Va., 1953—; free-lancer sta. WKAZ, Charleston, W.Va., 1960-64, WKOY, Bluefield, W.Va., 1960-69. Speaker at various civic meetings. Pres. Border Child, Bristol, Va., 1956-57. Bd. advisers Va. Intermont Coll., 1973—; mem. bd. dirs. Dogwood Players, 1965-66. Mem. Am. Women in Radio and TV, Women in Communications, Bristol Ladies Golf Assn., Phi Theta Kappa, Phi Rho Pi. Clubs: Three Arts (Bristol, Va.); Child Study (Bristol, Va.). Home: 101 Haverhill Bristol VA 24201 Office: WFHG Valley Dr Bristol VA 24201

GREEN, ROSE BASILE (MRS. RAYMOND S. GREEN), educator, author; b. New Rochelle, N.Y., Dec. 19, 1914; d. Salvatore and Caroline (Galgano) Basile; B.A., Coll. New Rochelle, 1935; M.A., Columbia, 1941; Ph.D., U. Pa., 1962; m. Raymond S. Green, June 20, 1942; children—Carol-Rae (Mrs. Alfred Robert Hoffmann), Raymond Ferguson St. John. Tchr., Torrington (Conn.) High Sch., 1936-42; writer, researcher Fed. Writers Project, 1935-36; free-lance script writer Cavalcade of Am., NBC, 1940-42; asso. prof. English, univ. registrar Tampa (Fla.) U., 1942-43; spl. instr. English, Temple U., Phila., 1953-57; prof. dept. English, Cabrini Coll., Radnor, Pa., 1957-70, chmn. dept., 1957-70. Mem. lit. com. Phila. Art Alliance. Bd. dirs. Phila. Grand Opera Co. Mem. Am. Acad. Polit. and Social Sci., Am. Studies Assn., Am. Assn. U. Women, Nat. Council Tchrs. English, Am.-Italy Soc. (dir. 1952—), Eastern Pa. Coll. New Rochelle Alumnae (pres. 1951-54), Kappa Gamma Pi. Club: Cosmopolitan (Phila.). Author: Cabrinian Philosophy of Education, 1967; (poetry) To Reason Why, 1971, Primo Vino, 1974; (criticism) The Italian-American Novel, 1974. Editor faculty jour. A-Zimuth, 1963-70. Home: Route 2824 Manor Rd Philadelphia PA 19128

GREEN, RUTH RELKIN (MRS. DARWIN GREEN), psychologist, educator; b. N.Y.C., Apr. 9, 1929; d. William and Ethel (Trachtenberg) Relkin; B.S., Coll. City N.Y., 1950; M.A., Columbia, 1952; m. Darwin Green, Sept. 2, 1950;children—Robert Leslie, Sandor Allen. Intake interviewer Div. Vocational Rehab., N.Y.C., 1950-51; part-time instr. dept. edn. psychology N.Y. U., 1967-71; dir. counseling services N.Y. League for Hard of Hearing, N.Y.C., 1951—, asst. adminstrv. dir., 1969—. Cons. psychology Center for Deafness Research, N.Y. U., 1966—; guest lectr. several univ., colls., and assns., 1952-53. Corr. sec. Camp Av. Sch., P.T.A., 1961-62, treas., 1963-64, mem. bd., 1959-65; treas., mem. bd. Nassau Center for Emotionally Disturbed Children, Merrick Aux., 1960-65; mem. Govs. Com. to Employ the Handicapped, 1962-65. Recipient Citation of Honor N.Y. League for Hard of Hearing, 1966. Mem. Am. Psychol. Assn., Nat. Rehab. Assn., Nat. Rehab. Counseling Assn., Am. Personnel and Guidance Assn., Nat. Vocational Guidance Assn., Psychol. Assn. for Study of Hearing (an original founders 1967, mem. exec. com. 1967—). Home: 1669 Hendrickson Av Merrick NY 11566 Office: 71 W 23d St New York City NY 10010

GREEN, SHARON HULTNER (MRS. MORT GREEN), lawyer; b. Wallace, Ida., Apr. 4, 1938; d. Henry Harold and Violet Myrtle (Werner) Hultner; B.A. magna cum laude, Cal. State Coll., 1965; J.D., U. Cal. at Los Angeles Law Sch., 1968; m. Mort Green, Feb. 24, 1961; children—Devon Marie, Stacy Allison. Admitted to Cal. bar, 1969; asso. Kadison, Pfaelzer, Woodard & Quinn, Los Angeles, 1967-68; house counsel, corporate sec. Synanon Found., Inc., Santa Monica and Oakland, Cal., 1969—; asso. firm Sullivan, Jones & Archer, San Francisco, 1973—; counsel Sickle Cell Anemia Research and Edn. Found., San Francisco, 1973—, Peter Maurin House Neighborhood Found., Oakland, 1973—. Mem. Alameda Lawyers Club, Barristers Los Angeles, Am., Cal. bar assns. Home: 2240 24th St San Francisco CA 94107 Office: 2100 Crocker Plaza San Francisco CA 94104

GREENBERG, ABBY JOAN, pediatrician; b. N.Y.C., July 8, 1935; d. Irving and Ruth (Gellert) Schlein; A.B., U. Rochester, 1955; M.D., State U. N.Y. Downstate Med. Center, 1959; m. Gerald Martin Greenberg, June 23, 1955; children—Leonard Marc, Scott Kenneth, Carolyn Beth. Intern pediatrics Kings County Hosp., Bklyn., 1959-60; resident pediatrics N.Y. Hosp., 1960-62; fellow pediatric nephrology Cornell U.-N.Y. Hosp., 1962-66; med. editor Physicians Publns., N.Y.C., 1966-72; clinician Nassau County Dept. Health, 1968—; pvt. cons. pediatrics nephrology, 1968—; asst. attending dept. pediatrics Nassau County Med. Center, East Meadow, N.Y., 1973—; instr. pediatrics State U. N.Y. at Stony Brook Sch. Medicine, 1973—, Adelphi U. Sch. Nursing, Garden City, N.Y., 1973—. Mem. bd. East Williston Sch. Dist. P.T.A., 1968—, treas. coordinating council, 1971-73. Bd. dirs. Westwood Civic Assn., 1969—. Recipient 1st ann. Samuel Z. Levine prize N.Y. Hosp., 1962. Diplomate Am. Bd. Pediatrics. Mem. Alpha Omega Alpha. Contbr. articles to med. jours. Address: 12 Candy Lane Roslyn Heights NY 11577

GREENBERG, BETTY ZELDA, physician; b. Pitts., Apr. 25, 1932; d. Merle and Doris Gertrude (Bendes) Spandau; B.A., Adelphi Coll., 1952; M.D., U. Geneva (Switzerland), 1957; m. Julian Greenberg, Mar. 3, 1957; children—Roberta, Bruce, Michael. Intern Beth-El Hosp., Bklyn., 1958; resident internal medicine and chest diseases Dallas VA Hosp., 1959-60; pvt. practice internal medicine, Elmont, N.Y., 1963—; mem. staff Franklin Gen., South Nassau Communities hosps. Home: 515 Hungary Harbor Rd North Woodmere NY 11581 Office: 1554 Dutch Broadway Elmont NY 11003

GREENBERG, DEBORAH, banker, lawyer; b. London, Eng.; d. Joseph and Sarah (Bedofsky) Greenberg; student Am. Inst. Banking Boston U., Mass. U.; J.D., Northeastern U., 1941, LL.M., 1943; m. Nathan Feldman, June 9, 1970. Naturalized, 1934. Admitted to Mass. bar, 1945; with Boston Safe Deposit and Trust Co., 1932—, asst. trust officer, 1958-62, legal officer 1962—. Guest lectr. Mass. U., Harvard. Pres., bus. profl. group Boston chpt. Hadassah, 1965—, first v.p., 1963-64, chmn. youth Aliyah com., 1963-64, past chmn. com. on bequests and wills New Eng. region, v.p. New Eng., 1968—; active Combined Jewish Philanthropies Town meeting mem., Brookline, 1968—. Mem. Am. (tax sect., com. on estate and gift taxes), Boston (com. on fed. taxation, corporate counsel com.), Mass. (com. grievances) bar assns., Mass. (chmn. speakers bur., pres. 1955-56), Nat. (Mass state del.) assns. women lawyers, Boston Estate and Bus. Planning Council, Northeastern U. Law Sch. Alumni Assn., Nat. Assn. Bank Women (program com. No. New Eng. group, 1962), Am. Inst. of Banking, Kappa Beta Pi (past dean alumnae chpt). Club: Jewish Women's College (pres. Boston 1963-65). Asso. editor Women Lawyers Jour., 1964-65. Home: 141 Sea St Quincy MA 02169

GREENBERG, ELINOR RAE (MRS. MANUEL GREENBERG), coll. adminstr.; b. Bklyn., Nov. 13, 1932; d. Ray and Susan (Weiss) Miller; B.A., Mt. Holyoke Coll., 1953; M.A., U. Wis., 1954; m. Manuel Greenberg, Dec. 26, 1955; children—Andrea, Julie, Michael. Teaching asst. U. Wis., Madison, 1953-54; speech pathologist United Cerebral Palsy Center, Denver, 1954-56, Nat. Jewish Hosp., Denver, 1956-60; dir. and speech pathologist Arapahoe Soc. for Crippled Children and Adults, Denver, 1967-69; instr. speech U. Colo., Denver, 1967-69; dir. U. Without Walls and other spl. programs Loretto Heights Coll., Denver, 1971—, instr. sociology, 1968, 70. Chmn., panel Eastern Liberal Arts Colls., Denver, 1964—; chmn., mem. Littleton (Colo.) Council for Human Relations, 1964-69; mem. adv. council Colo. Commn. on Higher Edn., 1972—. Bd. dirs. Colo. Conf. of Social Welfare, 1972—, Colo. Consortium on Higher Edn., 1970-73, United Negro Coll. Fund, 1964-69 Named to Denver Post Hall of Fame, 1968; named Citizen of Year Omega Psi-Phi, 1966, Woman of Decade, Littleton Newspapers, 1970; recipient Distinguished Service award Littleton Edn. Assn., 1968. Mem. Am., Colo. speech and hearing assns., Colo. Mt. Holyoke Alumnae Assn. (bd. dirs. 1963-64), Cherry Knolls Civic Assn., Anti Defamation League (bd. dirs. 1964-71). Democrat. Jewish religion. Contbr. articles to profl. jours. Home: 6725 S Adams Way Littleton CO 80122 Office: 3001 S Federal Blvd Denver CO 80236

GREENBERG, ESTHER FRANCES SIEGEL (MRS. ARTHUR GREENBERG), librarian; b. N.Y.C., May 25, 1923; d. Louis and Rose (Weisman) Siegel; B.S., N.Y. U., 1944; M.S., Western Res. U., 1963; m. Arthur Greenberg, Sept. 7, 1946; children—Eric, Paul. Supr. test sample purchasing Consumers Union U.S., Inc., 1947-53; adult services asst. Cleveland Heights-University Heights Pub. Library, 1961-63; cataloger Case Inst. Tech., 1963-64, chief cataloger, 1964-67; chief cataloger Case Western Res. U., Cleve., 1968-74, asst. head tech. services, 1971-74; coordinator systems, research and staff devel., 1974—. Cons., Ohio Coll. Library Center, 1973—; mem. adv. bd. Cuyahoga Community Coll. Library Tech. Program, 1968—; study team mem., mgmt. rev. and analysis program Assn. Research Libraries, 1974—; com. mem. Ad Hoc Discussion Group on Serials Data Bases, 1974—. Fellow Council Library Resources; mem. A.L.A., Am. Assn. U. Profs., Acad. Library Assn. Ohio (dir. 1974—). Tri-State Assn. Coll. and Research Libraries (dir. 1973—), No. Ohio Tech. Services Librarians (dir. 1971-73), Beta Phi Mu. Home: 3562 Bendemeer Rd Cleveland OH 44118 Office: 11161 East Blvd Cleveland OH 44106

GREENBERG, FLORA HARRIET BUDNICK (MRS. DAVID GREENBERG), psychologist; b. N.Y.C., Feb. 14, 1912; d. Abraham and Stella Frances (Poliakoff) Budnick; B.S., N.Y.U., 1932; M.A., Columbia, 1934; student Julliard Sch. Music, 1928-29; m. David Greenberg, Sept. 6, 1935; children—Henry M., Victor. Social worker, N.Y.C., 1935-40; pvt. practice as psychologist and remedial tchr., Wingdale, N.Y., 1956-63; librarian, psychologist Green Chimneys Sch., Brewster, N.Y., 1963-66, sch. psychologist, 1966—. Pres. P.T.A., Wingdale, N.Y., 1945-47; chmn. A.R.C., Wingdale unit, 1960-61. Bd. dirs. Hudson Valley Philharmonic Soc. Mem. Am., Mid-Hudson psychol. assns., N.Y. State Assn. Educators Emotionally Disturbed, P.T.A. (life). Home: Sherman CT 06784 Office: Green Chimneys School Brewster NY 10509

GREENBERG, FLORINE ALEXANDRIA, educator, psychologist; b. Roanoke Rapids, N.C., July 1, 1937; d. Mooney and Rose Sarah (Reisner) Greenberg; B.A., Barnard Coll., 1959; M.A., Columbia, 1960; M.Ed., U. Md., 1966; Ed. E. (Nat. Def Edn. Act fellow), George Washington U., 1972. Tchr., N.Y.C. Pub. Schs., 1960-61, Balt. Pub. Schs., 1961-66, counselor, 1966-70; prof. psychology No. Va. Community Coll., Annandale, Va., 1972—. Lectr., George Washington U., Washington, 1972; cons. Prince George County (Md.) Pub. Schs., Washinton Opportunities for Women, 1972—, Alexandria (Va.) Mental Health Assn., 1973—; counselor, cons. Hebrew U. Jerusalem, Israel. Mem. Am., Washington, Va. psychol. assns., Am. Personnel and Guidance Assn., Internat. Assn. Ednl. and Vocational Guidance, Phi Delta Gamma, Pi Lambda Theta. Democrat. Jewish religion. Mem. Hadassah, B'nai B'rith Women. Author: Teenage Pregnancy, 1972; Counseling the Disadvantage, 1969, Symbolism in Projective Designs, 1974. Home: 4201 S 31st St Arlington VA 22206 Office: Va Community Coll 8333 Little River Turnpike Annandale VA 22003

GREENBERG, LAURY REINER (MRS. JERRY GREENBERG), camp dir.; b. N.Y.C., July 11, 1927; d. Louis Leon and Minnie (Berkowitz) Reiner: B.A., Queens Coll., 1948; postgrad. Hunter Coll., 1949-50; m. Jerry Greenberg, Sept. 12, 1948; children—Mara Sue, Mark Daniel, Lida Beth. Statistician, Boy Scouts Am., N.Y.C., 1948-49, Paramount Movies, N.Y.C., 1949-50; camp dir., owner Camp Birchwood, West Goshen, Conn., 1947—. Mem. Am., Conn. camping assns., Assn. Pvt. Camps, Conn. Camp Dirs. Assn. Home: 140 Ash Dr Roslyn NY 11576

GREENBERG, NAOMI FRANCES SCHUBIN (MRS. DAVID GREENBERG), occupational therapist; b. Hoboken, N.J., Nov. 21, 1937; d. William and Edith (Pencak) Schubin; student U. Mich., 1955-57; B.S., Columbia, 1960, M.P.H., 1971; postgrad. N.Y. U., State U. N.Y. at Bklyn.; m. David Greenberg, June 25, 1961; children—Seth Nolan, Ariel Myles. Supr. occupational therapy Coler Hosp., N.Y.C., 1960-65; rehab. coordinator N.Y. Med. Coll., 1965-68; cons. community rehab. N.Y.C. Med. and Health Research Assn., 1969-70; cons. activity program Proprietory Nursing Homes, N.Y.C., 1968—; asso. prof., dir. occupational therapy LaGuardia Community Coll., City U. N.Y., N.Y.C., 1973—. Tchr., cons. N.Y. State Health Facilities Assn., 1973; tchr. Jewish Home and Hosp. for Aged-Zeman Center, 1971. Mem. Health Task Force staff Community Council, 1973; mem. health careers com. United Hosp. Fund, 1966; mem. West Side Interagy. Council for Aging, 1970-73. Bd. dirs. River Park Nursery Sch., 1971. Recipient various traineeships. Mem. World Fedn. Occupational Therapists, Am. Pub. Health Assn., Am. Occupational Therapy Assn. (mem. council edn. 1973—), Am. Acad. Health Adminstrn., Young Israel Women (membership chmn. 1970). Club: Women's City. Home: 365 Maple St West Hempstead NY 11552 Office: LaGuardia Community Coll 31-10 Thomson Av Long Island City NY 11101

GREENBLATT, GERTRUDE ROGERS (MRS. MILTON GREENBLATT), psychiatrist; b. Boston; d. Thomas Eugene and Margaret (Kerrigan) Rogers; A.B., Radcliffe Coll., 1936; M.D., Tufts U., 1940; m. Milton Greenblatt, June 10, 1941; children—David John, Daniel Lawrence. Charlton teaching fellow Tufts Med. Sch. 1940-41; intern in pediatrics Johns Hopkins Hosp., Balt., 1941-42; resident in psychiatry Mass. Mental Health Center, Boston, 1942-45, sr. psychiatrist, 1945-49, asst. dir. children's unit, 1950-59; fellow in child psychiatry Judge Baker Guidance Center, Boston, 1949-50; instr. psychiatry Harvard Med. Sch., Boston, 1950-73; dir. psychiatry children's unit Met. State Hosp., Waltham, Mass., 1959-73. Spl. lectr. psychiatry Simmons Sch. Social Work, Boston, 1950-64. Mem. New Eng. Council Child Psychiatry (v.p. 1963-65, dir. 1965-73), Mass. Med. Soc. Home: 3326 Longridge Terrace Los Angeles CA 91403

GREENBLATT, IDA M. SCHECHTMAN (MRS. HAROLD GREENBLATT), lawyer; b. Dec. 25, 1903; d. Mac and Goldie Esther (Klugman) Schechtman; grad. St. Lawrence U.; LL.B., Bklyn. Law Sch., 1923; m. Harold Greenblatt, June 27, 1925; children—Walter, Carol D. (Mrs. Alvin J. Corbin). Admitted to N.Y. bar, 1923, U.S. Mil. Ct. of Appeals, 1956, U.S. Supreme Ct. bar, 1969; pvt. practice, 1935—. Chmn. legal adv. services to Armed Forces, 1943-46; chmn. spl. com. Legal Rights of Mentally Ill. Pres. Am. Med. Center, Dallas, 1954.; now staff aid Suicide Prevention Bureau, Dallas. Bd. dirs. Dallas Mental Health Assn., Angels, Inc. (mentally retarded). Recipient UN fellowship award, award Dallas Bar Assn., 1973. Mem. Internat. Fedn. Women Lawyers (treas., chmn. scholarship com., del. to UN 1969, past pres.), Nat. Assn. Women Lawyers (assembly del., recipient Merit Service award, 1968, chmn. family law), Nat. (UN fellow 1969), Tex. (speakers bur. dist. world affairs chmn.) fedns. bus. and profl. womens clubs, Town North Bus. and Profl. Women's Club (pres.; Famous Woman of Year award 1972), Council Jewish Women, Hadassah (internat. scholarship chmn., Am. affairs chmn.), Council World Affairs, UN Orgn. Dallas, Iota Tau Tau (internat. supreme chancellor, editor jour.). Mem. B'nai B'rith (mem. bd. 1955, 56). Author: New Aspects of our Immigration Laws, 1969. Contbr. articles to profl. jours.

GREENBLATT, JUDITH, govt. ofcl.; b. Brotmansville, N.J.; d. Morris and Ida (Lipman) Greenblatt; B.S. in Edn., U. Pa., 1935. Interviewer Fla. State Employment Service, 1941-47, sr. interviewer, 1947-55; corr. Am. Tel. & Tel. Co., N.Y.C., 1955-56; counselor N.Y. Assn. New Ams., 1957; interviewer, N.Y. State Employment Service, 1957-62, sr. interviewer, 1962-67, sr. counselor, 1967—. Authorized U. Pa. Alumni rep. admissions office, 1957—, class rep. U. Pa. ann. giving campaign, 1973, 74. Mem. Am. Personnel and Guidance Assn., Internat. Assn. Personnel in Employment Security. Home: 20 W 72d St New York City NY 10023 Office: 349 E 149th St Bronx NY 10451

GREENE, ADELE SHUMINER, pub. relations exec.; b. Newark, Sept. 16, 1925; d. Adolph and Sara (Schubert) Shuminer; student N.Y. U., 1942-44, Julliard Sch. Music, 1942-44, New Sch. for Social Research, 1944-47; 1 son, Joshua Michael. Asst. to pres. Cobleigh & Gordon, N.Y.C., 1962-63; account coordinator Gaynor & Ducas, N.Y.C., 1963-64; account exec. Ruder & Finn, Inc., N.Y.C., 1964-66, sr. asso., 1966-68, v.p., 1968-72, sr. v.p., 1972—. Instr. pub. relations and community affairs N.Y. U., 1974. Bd. dirs. Queens Symphony Orch. Mem. Pub. Relations Soc. Am. Author: (with Charles Mangel) Teen-Age Leadership, 1971. Home: 30 W 60th St New York City NY 10023 Office: 110 E 59th St New York City NY 10022

GREENE, BARBARA ESTELLA, educator; b. Joliet, Ill., May 9, 1935; d. Howard Lyle and Helen Jean (Koenig) Greene; student Fla. So. Coll., 1953-55, Ohio State U., 1955-56; B.S., Fla. So. Coll., 1957; M.S., Fla. State U., 1962, Ph.D., 1966. Instr. dept. food sci. and nutrition, researcher Agrl. Expt. Sta., Colo. State U., 1966-68; asst. prof. food sci. and nutrition, dept. food tech., researcher Agrl. Expt. Sta., Ia. State U., 1969; asst. prof. food and nutrition, researcher Agrl. Expt. Sta., U. Ga., Athens, 1969—. Mem. Ga. Conservancy, 1970—, sec., 1973. Mem. Inst. Food Technologists (sec. Dixie sect. 1973—), Alpha Delta Pi. Contbr. articles to profl. jours. Home: 100 W Whitehead Terrace Athens GA 30601

GREENE, EDEE NIELSEN (MRS. JOSEPH RUKENBROD), editor; b. Newark; d. Henry Meyer and Emily (Sudworth) Nielsen; m. Thomas G. Greene, May 30, 1934 (div. July 1951); children—Thomas James, Helen (Mrs. Leslie Johnson); m. Joseph Rukenbrod, Jan. 15, 1955. Mag. editor, women's editor Orlando (Fla.) Sentinel, 1951-57; women's editor Ft. Lauderdale (Fla.) News, 1957-69; exec. women's editor Gore Pub. Co., Ft. Lauderdale, Fla., 1969—. Vice pres. Broward County Community Service Council, 1973-74. Bd. dirs. Broward County United Way. Mem. Fla. Press Club (bd. mem. 1960—, pres. 1963-65), Theta Sigma Phi, Sigma Delta Chi. Home: 860 Allamanda Ct Plantation FL 33317 Office: PO Box 131 Fort Lauderdale FL 33302

GREENE, ELIZABETH A. (MRS. LEROY GREENE), state legislator; b. North Hampton, N.H.; ed. U. N.H.; m. Leroy Greene; 3 children. Mem. N.H. Ho. of Reps., 1961—, now asst. majority leader. Mem. N.H. Air Pollution Commn., 1970-73; chmn. N.H. Solid Waste Com., 1973—. Trustee Rye Library. Mem. Order Women Legislators. Republican. Address: 399 South Rd Rye NH 03870

GREENE, GWENDOLYN MOESKOPS (MRS. ROBERT EDWIN GREENE), librarian; b. Los Angeles, Aug. 5, 1926; d. Leroy Bristol and Antoinette Maria (Moeskops) Chick; B.A. in History, San Diego State Coll., 1951; M.S. in Library Sci., U. So. Cal., 1957; m. Robert Edwin Greene, Aug. 10, 1957; 1 dau., Catherine. Librarian, San Diego State Coll., 1956-57; asst. librarian Mary Baldwin Coll., Staunton, Va., 1964-65, Mira Costa Coll., Oceanside, Cal., 1968—. Mem. Nat. Trust for Historic Preservation, Cal. Library Assn., San Diego Hist. Soc., Assn. for Preservation Va. Antiquities. Home: 819 Neptune Av Encinitas CA 92024 Office: One Barnard Dr Oceanside CA 92054

GREENE, HATTIE BRYANT WITT, sch. adminstr., editor; b. Birmingham, Ala.; d. Henry and Ernestine (Webb) Bryant; A.B., Miles Coll., 1956; M.L.S., George Peabody Coll., 1966; LL.D., Daniel Payne Coll., 1968; m. Edward P. Greene, Dec. 19, 1960 (dec.); children—Edward L., Meldodie (Mrs. Lewis Wright), Charles, Barbara (Mrs. William Kindred), Taylor W. Librarian, Washington Sch., 1938-50; sec. United Appeal, Birmingham, 1940-60; librarian Brunetta C. Hill Sch., 1950-71; prin. John J. Eagan Sch., Birmingham, 1971—; editor A.M.E. Women's Missionary Mag., Proud Americans, 1971—. Dir. Christian edn. A.M.E. Ch., Ala., 1940-71. Leader B.C. Hill Sch. council Girl Scouts Am., 1970—, leader Brownie troop, 1973—. Bd. dirs. U. Hosp. Vol. Aux. Named Instr. Mag. Tchr. of Month, 1966; recipient citation outstanding ednl. leadership Miles Coll., 1973. Mem. N.E.A. (life), Ala. Assn. Clubs (named Woman of Year 1970), Birmingham Fedn. Clubs (past pres.), Birmingham Assn. Classroom Tchrs. (past pres.), N.A.A.C.P., Zeta Phi Beta (named Woman of Year 1950, basileus Alpha Sigma Zeta chpt. 1971—). Club: Imperial (treas.). Home: 1023 N 5th St Birmingham AL 35204 Office: 1716 31st Av N Birmingham AL 35207

GREENE, HELEN WIPPICH (MRS. JEROME DAVIS GREENE II), marketing exec.; b. Glen Cove, N.Y., Mar. 21, 1932; d. Hans G. and Antonia E. (Fluthmann) Wippich; B.S., U. Vt., 1953; m. Jerome Davis Greene II, Sept. 18, 1971. Asst. mgr. market research Young & Rubicam Advt., N.Y.C., 1953-60; sr. project dir. Benton & Bowles Advt., N.Y.C., 1960-61; v.p., dir. research C.E. Hooper, N.Y.C., 1961-70; dir. research services Eastern Air Lines, N.Y.C., 1970-73; acct. exec. Burlington Industries, N.Y.C., 1974—. Bd. dirs. Dessoff Chorus. Mem. Am. Marketing Assn., Am. Assn. Pub. Opinion Research, U. Vt. N.Y. Alumni Assn. (pres. 1969-71). Home: 30 W 60th St New York City NY 10023 Office: 1345 Av of Americas New York City NY 10019

GREENE, JANET EILEEN (MRS. LAURENCE E. GREENE), editor, state ofcl.; b. Clevel., July 14, 1943; d. Paul Wilbert and Edna Mae (Farrar) Duncan; B.A. in Journalism, Ohio State U., 1965; m. Laurence E. Greene, May 13, 1967. Communications writer Ohio

Dept. Transp. Columbus, 1965-66; chief copywriter Fixzit System, Inc., Columbus, 1966-67; chief publs. writer and editor Ohio State Hwy. Patrol, Columbus, 1967—. Exec. v.p. Laurence Greene & Asso., Columbus, 1966-67. Active Boy Scouts Am., 1966—; vol. adviser Franklin County (O.) Law Enforcement Explorer Post. Mem. Women in Communications, U.S. Judo Assn. (chmn. com. for recreation therapy Central Ohio chpt., 1967—), Ohio State U. Alumnae Assn., Westerville Judo Club (pres. 1972—), Judo Fedn. Ohio (v.p. 1966-68). Home: 5418 Lisbon Place Westerville OH 43081 Office: 660 E Main St Columbus OH 43205

GREENE, JANICE BRIECE (MRS. GERALD MICHAEL GREENE), psychologist; b. Oklahoma City, Dec. 14, 1940; d. Harold Jack and Loretta Margaret (Nicklas) Briece; B.A., Kan. State Coll., 1964; postgrad., 1967-69; M.S., U. Okla., 1966, Ph.D., 1971; m. Gerald Michael Greene, Jan. 28, 1967; children—Erin Kylie, Kegan Ellery. Clin. psychologist Osawatomie (Kan.) State Hosp., 1969; supr. Vocational Rehab. Service, Oklahoma City, 1970-71; clin. psychologist Yacorzynski, Greene, Blechman & Asso., Kenilworth, Ill., 1972—. Psychol. cons. Headstart, Chgo., 1972-73; lectr. psychology Kan. U., Lawrence, 1966-67. Mem. Panamanian Psychol. Assn., Psi Chi (sec. Kan. chpt. 1966-67, sec.-treas. U. Okla. chpt. 1964-66), Am., Ill. psychol. assns., Kappa Delta Phi. Home: 2327 Castalian Circle Northbrook IL 60062 Office: 450 N Green Bay Rd Kenilworth IL 60043

GREENE, KATHARINE BRADFORD (MRS. EDWARD BARROWS GREENE), psychologist; b. Laramie, Wyo., Mar. 18, 1897; d. Frank Pierrepont and Helen Hope (Wadsworth) Graves; student Ohio State U., 1913-14; B.S., U. Pa., 1916; A.B., Vassar Coll., 1917; Ph.D., Columbia, 1923; postgrad. U. Mich., 1952-56; m. Edward Barrows Greene, Aug. 14, 1926; children—Hope (Mrs. Robert MacIntyre), Helen (Mrs. William M. Jagger), Frank Pierrepont, Beth, (Mrs. William C. Self), Edward. Faculty, U. Del., Newark, 1918, Russell Sage Coll., Troy, N.Y., 1923-25; faculty edn. U. Mich., Ann Arbor, 1927-35, lectr. genetic psychology, 1936-37, lectr., 1937-52; marriage counselor Washtenaw County Circuit Ct., Ann Arbor, 1952-53, Wayne County Circuit Ct., Detroit, 1953-62; pvt. practice marriage counseling Detroit, 1962-68; pvt. practice clin. psychologist, Fairhope, Ala., 1968—; clin. psychologist Center for Counseling, Fairhope, 1973—. Lectr. behavioral problems Ohio State U., Columbus, summers 1935-36; dir. Sherwood Sch., Bloomfield Hills, Mich., 1940-47. Diplomate Am. Bd. Examiners in Profl. Psychology. Fellow Am. Psychol. Assn., Soc. for Child Psychology; mem. Nat. Assn. Social Workers (charter), Ala. Psychol. Assn. (emeritus), Am. Assn. Marriage and Family Counsellors, Pi Lambda Theta. Home: 360 Satsuma St Fairhope AL 36532 Office: Center for Counseling N Sect St Fairhope AL 36532

GREENE, MAXINE MEYER (MRS. ORVILLE N. GREENE), educator; b. N.Y.C., Dec. 23, 1917; d. Max C. and Lily (Greenfield) Meyer; B.A., Barnard Coll., 1938; M.A., N.Y. U., 1949; Ph.D., 1955; m. 2d, Orville N. Greene, Aug. 2, 1947; children—Linda, Timothy F. Instr. philosophy and history edn. N.Y. U., 1949, instr. English edn., 1957-59, asst. prof., 1959-60, asso. prof. edn., 1960-62; asst. prof. English, Montclair (N.J.) State Coll., 1956-57; asso. prof. edn. Bklyn. Coll., 1962-65; vis. lectr. Tchrs. Coll., Columbia, N.Y.C., 1963, asso. prof. English, 1965-67, prof., 1967—, prof. philosophy and edn., 1973—, editor Tchrs. Coll. Record, 1965-70. Vis. asst. prof. U. Hawaii, summer 1960, vis. asso. prof., summer 1962; dir. Harlem Edn. Program, 1963-66; cons., writer philosophy edn. project U. Ill., summer 1965. Mem. Nat. Council Tchrs. English, Modern Lang. Assn., Am. Assn. U. Profs., Philosophy Edn. Soc. (program chmn. 1964-65, pres. 1966-67), Middle Atlantic States Philosophy Edn. Soc. (pres. 1965-67), John Dewey Soc. for Study Edn. and Culture (exec. bd. 1963-65, lectr. chmn.), Phi Beta Kappa, Kappa Delta Pi. Author: The Public School and The Private Vision, 1965; Existential Encounters for Teachers, 1967; Teacher as Stranger, 1973. Editor Rev. of Research in Edn., 1974—. Contbr. articles to profl. publs., mags. Home: 1080 Fifth Av New York City NY 10028

GREENE, SUE SHIDAKER (MRS. WILLIAM A. GREENE), civic worker; b. Wilmington, O., Feb. 20, 1938; d. Wayne Harvey and Genieve Eleanor (Turner) Shidaker; A.B., Ohio Wesleyan U., 1960; postgrad. Duke, 1961, Ohio State U., 1964-66, U. Alaska, 1970-71; m. William A. Greene, Dec. 27, 1966; children—Jeffrey David, Karen Elizabeth. Youth program dir. Ohio dist. YWCA, Columbus, 1960; tchr. English and lang. arts Durham (N.C.) High Sch., 1960-62, Hayes High Sch., Delaware, O., 1962-65, Worthington (O.) High Sch., 1965-66, Lathrop High Sch., Fairbanks, Alaska, 1967-68, West High Sch., Anchorage, 1968-69. Pres. League Women Voters of Alaska, 1971-72; co-chmn. Anchorage Citizens Adv. Com. on Year-Round Schs., 1971-72; mem. Anchorage Sch. Bd., 1972—, pres., 1972-73, v.p., 1973-74. Bd. dirs. Anchorage Mental Health Assn., 1970-71. Recipient Outstanding Young Educator of Alaska award, 1968. Mem. Assn. Alaska Sch. Bds. (pres. 1973-74), Kappa Alpha Theta. Home: 1385 Bennington Dr Anchorage AK 99504

GREENE, WILDA WITT (MRS. WALLACE S. GREENE, JR.), author; b. Falkville, Ala.; d. Frank Thomas and Ida Dixie (Lovelady) Witt; student pub. schs.; m. Wallace S. Greene, Jr., Mar. 2, 1936; 1 dau., Donna (Mrs. William T. Miller). Author: Visitation Evangelism, 1955; The Disturbing Christ: A Devotional Study of Hebrews, 1968; contbg. author Broadman Devotional Annual, 1973; numerous articles in field for religious publs. Mem. Nat. League of Am. Pen Women (pres. Nashville br.), Authors Guild, Internat. Platform Assn. Clubs: Tenn. Woman's Press and Authors; Nashville Womans' Press and Authors. Address: 5020 Dovecote Dr Nashville TN 37220

GREENE, ZULA BENNINGTON (MRS. MILTON WILLARD GREENE), journalist; b. nr. Quincy, Mo., Mar. 2, 1895; d. Jacob Anders and Margaret Ann (Holley) Bennington; student U. Colo., 1914-16; m. Milton Willard Greene, June 26, 1918; children—Margaret, Edward, Willard, Dorothy (Mrs. Richard Hanger). Tchr. Center (Colo.) pub. schs., 1916-18; columnist various weekly newspapers, 1925—; columnist Topeka Daily Capital, 1933—. Pres. Topeka Civic Theatre, 1957-58. Bd. dirs. Friends of Topeka Pub. Library, 1968—, Performing Arts for Children, 1970—, Hillhaven Convalescent Home, 1965—. Named Outstanding Newspaper Woman of Yr., Theta Sigma Phi (Women in Communications), 1959, 1969. Mem. Kan. Hist. Soc. (life), Women in Communications, Shawnee County Hist. Assn. (dir. 1964-68), Tau Delta Pi (hon.). Republican. Conglist. Clubs: Minerva Literary and Music, Nautilus (hon.). Home: 1205 Mulvane St Topeka KS 66604 Office: 616 Jefferson St Topeka KS 66605

GREENFIELD, MEG, journalist; b. Seattle, Dec. 27, 1930; d. Lewis James and Lorraine (Nathan) Greenfield; B.A. summa cum laude, Smith Coll., 1952; postgrad. (Fulbright scholar) Newham Coll., Cambridge U., 1952-53. Researcher, Reporter Mag., 1957-61, staff writer, 1961-62, Washington corr., 1962-65, Washington editor, 1965-68; editorial writer Washington Post, 1968-70, dep. editor editorial page, 1970—. Mem. Am. Soc. Newspaper Editors, Phi Beta Kappa. Home: 3318 R St NW Washington DC 20007 Office: 1150 15th St NW Washington DC 20005

GREENFIELD, NANCY LEE (MRS. MELVIN C. GREENFIELD), physician; b. Newark, Oct. 10, 1936; d. Hubert J. and Ethel (Haskin) Reis; B.A., Barnard Coll., 1958; M.D., State U. N.Y., 1962; m. Melvin C. Greenfield, Mar. 8, 1958; children—Gloria Haskin, Jacqueline Louise, Johnathan C. Intern, U. Miami (Fla.) Sch. Medicine, Jackson Meml. Hosp., 1962, resident pediatrics, 1963-65, resident psychiatry, 1965-68; dir. psychiatry Variety Children's Hosp., Coral Gables, Fla., 1968—; clin. instr. dept. pediatrics, dept. psychiatry U. Miami, 1968—; dir. adolescent unit Montanari Clin. Sch. and Residential Treatment Center, Hialeah, Fla., 1968—. Psychiat. cons. Cystic Fibrosis Assn. Mem. Am., Fla. Women's med. assns., Dade County Med. Soc., Am., S. Fla. psychiat. socs., Greater Miami Pediatric Soc., Alpha Omega Alpha. Home: 9497 SW 92d St Miami FL 33156 Office: 8740 N Kendall Dr Miami FL 33156

GREENFIELD, THELMA CAROLINE NELSON (MRS. STANLEY BRIAN GREENFIELD), educator; b. Portland, Ore., Sept. 11, 1922; d. Ivar Emanuel and Lulu Ruth (Maxwell) Nelson; B.A., U. Ore., 1944, M.A., 1947; Ph.D., U. Wis., 1952; m. Stanley Brian Greenfield, Jan. 22, 1951; children—Tamma, Sayre. Instr., U. Wis. Extension, 1952-54, Queens Coll. Sch. Gen. Studies, 1955-59; asst. prof. English, U. Ore., Eugene, 1963-67, asso. prof., 1967-73, prof., 1973—. Guest lectr. John Hay Summer Insts., 1963-65; resource leader Shakespeare Camp, 1968—. Recipient Arthur Pratt award U. Ore., 1944, award Inst. Internat. Edn., 1950. Mem. Modern Lang. Assn., Shakespeare Assn. Am., Renaissance Soc. Am., Am. Assn. U. Profs., Phi Beta Kappa, Pi Lambda Theta. Author: The Induction in Elizabethan Drama, 1969. Editor: (with Waldo McNeir) Pacific Coast Studies in Shakespeare, 1966. Home: 2056 Orchard St Eugene OR 97403

GREENGLASS, BARBARA SHAFRAN (MRS. MILTON GREENGLASS), mental health center exec.; b. Boston, Dec. 7, 1929; d. Samuel Paul and Anna Lillian (Slotnick) Shafran; B.S., Wheelock Coll., 1950, M.S., 1968; m. Milton Greenglass, Dec. 25, 1949; children—Donald, Robert, Susan. Nursery sch. tchr. South Shore Mental Health Center, Quincy, Mass., 1960-65; head supervising tchr., 1966-67, asso. dir., 1968—; instr., supr. Wheelock Coll., Boston, 1967-68. Cons. Washtenaw County Mental Health Center, Ann Arbor, Mich., 1971-72. Mem. Council for Children, Quincy, Mass., 1972—; mem. adv. com. Amego, Inc., Quincy, 1971—. Mem. Council for Exceptional Children, Boston Assn. for Edn. of Young Children. Home: 132 Central St Hingham MA 02043 Office: 77 Parking Way Quincy MA 02069

GREENHILL, BARBARA CHRISTEN, librarian; b. Lakewood, O., Nov. 17, 1917; d. Thomas Peter and Mary Emmeline (England) Christen; B.A., Western Res. U., 1939, B.S. in L.S., 1944; children—Laurie Ann, Ian William. Tchr., Willoughby, O., 1939-42; reference librarian, history dept. Cleve. Pub. Library, 1942-56; sch. librarian Chagrin Falls (O.) Schs., 1960—. Mem. Internat. Assn. Sch. Librarianship, Women's Nat. Book Assn., N.E.A., Ohio, Chagrin Falls (mem. exec. bd. 1971-73) edn. assns., Ohio Assn. Sch. Librarians. Home: Chagrin Falls OH 44022 Office: 400 W Washington St Chagrin Falls OH 44022

GREENHOUSE, LINDA JOYCE, journalist; b. N.Y.C., Jan. 9, 1947; d. Herman Robert and Dorothy Eleanor (Greenlick) Greenhouse; B.A., Radcliffe Coll., 1968. Asst., N.Y. Times, 1968-69, local staff reporter, 1969-73, state polit. reporter, 1974—. Club: Radcliffe (N.Y.C.). Contbr. articles to profl. jours. Office: 229 W 43d St New York City NY 10036

GREENHUT, IRENE ELINOR TATMAN (MRS. L.W. POLLARD), physician; b. nr. Union Mills, Ind., Apr. 8, 1920; d. Chester Arthur and Olivia (Fogg) Tatman; B.A. magna cum laude, Taylor U., 1942; M.S., Purdue U., 1944; Ph.D., U. Wis., 1948; M.D., Ind. U., 1952; m. J. William Greenhut, Jan. 20, 1945 (div. Jan. 1964); 1 dau., Mary Beth; m. 2d, L.W. Pollard, July 1, 1972. Instr., asst. chemistry, biochemistry Taylor U., Upland, Ind., 1939-42, Purdue U., 1942-44, Ind. U., 1947-51; intern Los Angeles County Harbor Gen. Hosp., Torrance, Cal., 1952-53; resident Pacific State Hosp., Spadra, Cal., 1953-54; practice medicine specializing in pediatrics, Redondo Beach, Cal., 1954-62; sch. physician Torrance Unified Sch. Dist., 1962-70; with U. Cal. Med. Sch., Irvine, 1970-72, Monterey County Health Dept., Monterey, Cal., 1972—. Cons. in learning problems of children. Chmn. sch. edn. Heart Assn., Los Angeles County. Mem. A.M.A., Cal., Los Angeles County med. assns., Am. Acad. Pediatrics, Los Angeles County Pediatric Soc., Am. Med. Writers' Assn. (v.p. Los Angeles County br. 1966-67, treas. 1967-68), Audubon Soc. Republican. Presbyn. Home: 8580 Carmel Valley Rd Carmel CA 93921 Office: Monterey County Health Dept 1200 Aguajito Rd Monterey CA 93940

GREENIG, PATRICIA FAYE (MRS. ROBERT MELVIN GREENIG), psychologist; b. Chgo., Mar. 12, 1929; d. Elliott Fisher and Anna (Sachs) Brown; B.A. summa cum laude, Hunter Coll., 1965; M.S. (Helen Gates Putnam fellow), Vassar Coll., 1967; postgrad. New Sch. for Social Research, Syracuse U.; m. Robert Melvin Greenig, Feb. 4, 1949; 1 son, Douglas Scott. Exec. sec. Burlington Industries, N.Y.C., 1957-61; instr. psychology Finch Coll., N.Y.C., 1967-68; sch. psychologist Bd. Co-op. Ednl. Services, Verona, N.Y., 1970—. Mem. Nat., N.Y. assns. sch. psychologists, Am., N.Y. psychol. assns., Sch. Psychologists Upstate N.Y., Council for Exceptional Children, Assn. Children with Learning Disabilities, Phi Beta Kappa, Psi Chi. Home: 5167 Winterton Dr Fayetteville NY 13066 Office: Morrisville-Eaton Central Sch Morrisville NY 13408

GREENLEAF, BARBARA KAYE (MRS. JONATHAN WHITMAN GREENLEAF), author; b. N.Y.C., July 1, 1942; d. Louis Cutler and Alice Lois (Ginsberg) Kaye; B.A., Vassar Coll., 1963; m. Jonathan Whitman Greenleaf, July 29, 1965; children—Caroline Kaye, Catherine Kaye. Asst. editor art and architecture The New Book Knowledge, Grolier, Inc., N.Y.C., 1963-64; writer book and edn. div. N.Y. Times, 1964-66; freelance filmstrip writer Eyegate House, N.Y.C., 1966; tech. writer, editorial adviser Rockland Psychiat. Research Center, 1974—. Mem. League Women Voters (bd. mem., 1971-73). Author: America Fever, 1970; Forward March to Freedom, 1971. Contbr. articles to newspapers and women's jours. Home: 5 Birch Grove Dr Armonk NY 10504

GREENLEAF, ELIZABETH A., educator; b. Winthrop, Mass., Nov. 4, 1919; d. Herrick E. H. and L. Blanche (Bryant) Greenleaf; A.B., DePauw U., 1941; M.A., U. Wis., 1947; Ed.D., Ind. U., 1952. Tchr., counselor pub. schs., Ind., 1941-50; dir. activities center, asst. prof. guidance So. Ill. U., Carbondale, 1952-57; asso. dean students, dean of women San Jose (Cal.), State U., 1957-59; asst. dean students, dir. residence hall counseling Ind. U., Bloomington, 1959-69, asst. prof. edn., 1959-63, asso. prof., 1963-67, prof., 1967—, chmn. dept. student personnel adminstrn. Mem. Am. Assn. U. Women (br. pres. 1966-68), Am. Coll. Personnel Assn. (nat. pres. 1967-68), Am. Personnel and Guidance Assn. (dir. 1967-68, mem. senate 1964-67, 69-72), Nat. Assn. Women Deans (sect. pres. 1965-67, nat. pres. 1971-72), Delta Kappa Gamma (Ind. pres. 1969-71). Contbr. articles to profl. jours. Home: 914 Meadowbrook St Bloomington IN 47401

GREENLEAF, JEAN HOPE RADDE, psychiat. case worker; b. Cleve., Apr. 8, 1915; d. Otto Carl and Lois (McCabe) Radde; B.A., U. Buffalo, 1937, M.S., 1939; M.S. Edn., Canisius Coll., 1972; m. John A. Greenleaf, June 7, 1941 (div.); children—William John, David Otto. Case worker Erie County Dept. Social Welfare, Buffalo, 1938-39, Children's Center, New Haven, 1939-44; supr. Church Mission of Help, Dunkirk, N.Y., 1952-64, Westfield (N.Y.) Counseling Service, 1964-65; case worker Mental Health Clinic, Mayville, N.Y., 1963-65; counselor State U. Coll., Fredonia, N.Y., 1965-72; with Child Guidance Clinic, Clearwater, Fla., 1972—. Field work instr. for students in social welfare, 1943-53. Bd. dirs., sec. Dunkirk-Fredonia Counseling Service, Dunkirk, N.Y., 1966-72. Mem. Planned Parenthood Assn., Am. Assn. U. Women, Am. Assn. U. Profs., Am., Western N.Y., N.Y. personnel and guidance assns., Nat. Assn. Social Workers, Am. Assn. Humanistic Psychology, Acad. Certified Social Workers. Episcopalian (pres., sec. 1955-60). Home: 2042 Australia Way W Apt 36 Clearwater FL 33515 Office: Child Guidance Clinic Clearwater FL 33516

GREENSPAN, CAROL M., educator; b. N.Y.C., July 13, 1933; d. A. Albert and Florence (Bass) Greenspan; B.A., U. Ill., 1953; Ed.M., Harvard, 1960, A.M., 1961; Ph.D., Columbia, 1968. Chem. patent searcher Shell Devel. Co., 1954; technician Oakknoll Naval Hosp., 1955; tchr. math. Claremont Jr. High Sch., 1956-57; tchr. chemistry Castlemont High Sch., Oakland, Cal., 1957-59; sci. dir. Microbiol. genetics and physiology NSF High Sch. Student Insts., 1965; instr. biochemistry for med. students Columbia, 1965; postdoctoral fellow Nat. Jewish Hosp. Research Center, Denver, 1968-70; research asso., med. genetics fellow U. Ore. Med. Sch., Portland, 1970-73; asst. prof. chemistry Old Dominion U., Norfolk, Va., 1973—. Tchr. human genetics Eastern Va. Med. Sch., 1973—. Mem. Ore. Gov.'s. Human Rights Commn., 1972; gov. Ad Hoc Affirmative Action Com., Portland, Ore., 1973; NIH tng. grantee, 1960-66; Radcliffe fellow, 1970-71; NIH postdoctoral fellow, 1968-70, NIH med. genetics fellow, 1971-73; U. Colo. Univ. fellow, 1966-68. Mem. N.A.A.C.P., A.A.A.S., Am. Chem. Soc., N.Y., Va. acads. scis., Am. Civil Liberties Union, Women for Polit. Action, Common Cause (Dist. Congl. Dist. II rep. Tidewater Equal Rights Amendment coalition), Sigma Xi, Phi Beta Kappa, Phi Kappa Phi. Home: 7728 Enfield Av Norfolk VA 23505

GREENWALD, BARBARA TOBY ORLIN (MRS. ANDREW GREENWALD), occupational therapist; b. Manhattan, N.Y., May 12, 1946; d. Harold James and Miriam Sarah (Babes) Orlin; A.B., Barnard Coll., 1967; certificate occupational therapy Columbia, 1968; m. Andrew Greenwald, Mar. 14, 1968. Occupational therapist Beth Abraham Hosp., Bronx, N.Y., 1969-71, sr. occupational therapist, 1971-74, supr. occupational therapy, 1974—. Mem. Am., Met. N.Y. occupational therapy assns. Mem. B'nai B'rith. Home: 250 E 73d St New York City NY 10021 Office: 612 Allerton Av Bronx NY 10467

GREENWALD, PATRICIA BRAUNSTEIN (MRS. JAMES L. GREENWALD), advt. co. exec.; b. N.Y.C., Sept. 9, 1930; d. Charles and Rose (Nathanson) Braunstein; B.S., Western Res. U., 1951; M.A., Columbia, 1953; m. James L. Greenwald, Dec. 18, 1960; 1 son, Thomas. Lectr. dept. speech City Coll., Baruch Sch., 1951-53; speech pathologist Ittleson Center Child Research, 1953-58; asso. research dir. Marplan, McCann-Erickson, 1958-68; v.p., dir. research deGarmo, Inc., N.Y.C., 1971—. Contbr. articles to profl. jours. Home: 785 Park Av New York City NY 10021 Office: 605 3d Av New York City NY 10016

GREENWALD, SHEILA ELLEN (MRS. GEORGE E. GREEN), author; b. N.Y.C., May 26, 1934; d. Julius and Florence (Friedman) Greenwald; B.A., Sarah Laurence Coll., 1956; m. George E. Green, Feb. 18, 1960; children—Sam, Ben. Mem. Authors Guild, Authors League Am. Author: A Metropolitan Love Story, 1961; Willie Bryant and The Flying Otis, 1971; The Hot Day, 1971; Mat Pit and the Tunnel Tenants, 1972; Amanda Snap, 1972; The Secret Museum, 1974. Contbr. articles to profl. jours. Home: 175 Riverside Dr New York City NY 10024

GREENWOOD, ERMA GRIFFITH, lawyer; b. Honaker, Va., Feb. 10, 1917; d. Arthur Tazewell and Maude (Catron) Griffith; A.B., Duke, 1937, LL.B., 1939; m. Porter Greenwood, Dec. 21, 1939 (div. June 1951). Admitted to Va. bar, 1938, Tenn. bar, 1943; partner Griffith & Greenwood, Lebanon, Va., 1939-43; asso. Poore, Kramer & Overton, Knoxville, Tenn., 1943-48; partner Kramer, Dye, McNabb & Greenwood, Knoxville, 1948-63; sr. partner Kramer, Dye, Greenwood, Johnson & Rayson, 1963—. Sec. central com. East Tenn. Community Improvement Program, 1959, pres., 1963; mem. budget com. Community Services Council, Knoxville, 1961-63, admissions com., planning council, 1964; sec. Vol. Rescue Squad, 1965—. Bd. dirs. Tenn. River and Tributaries Assn., Cooper Inst. Bus., Travelers Aid Soc. Knoxville, Knox County chpt. A.R.C.; bd. visitors Duke Law Sch., 1973—. Mem. Am., Tenn. (past pres. woman's conf., chmn. ins. sect. 1963-64), Knox County bar assns., Bus. and Profl. Women's Club, Tau Kappa Alpha. Methodist. Clubs: Quota (gov. 23d dist. 1969-70), Deane Hill Country. Home: 3305 Montlake Dr Knoxville TN 37920 Office: Valley Fidelity Bank Bldg Knoxville TN 37901

GREENWOOD, THERESA MAE WINFREY (MRS. CHARLES H. GREENWOOD), writer; b. Cairo, Ill., Dec. 28, 1936; d. Hubert Augustus and Lillian Theresa (Williams) Winfrey; B.Music Edn. (Tri Delta scholar), Millikin U., 1959; M.A., Ball State U., 1963, Ed.D. (fellow), 1975; m. Charles H. Greenwood, June 26, 1960; children—Lisa Renee, Marc Charles. Tchr. music East Chicago (Ind.) pub. schs., 1959-61; tchr. elementary schs., Muncie, Ind., 1962-68; acad. counselor Ball State U., Muncie, 1971-72; columnist Muncie Evening Press, 1969-73. Singer Civic Theater, Muncie, 1968. Bd. dirs. A.R.C., 1971-73, United Fund, 1971-73, EIC-TV, 1971-73; adv. bd. Huffer Day Care Center. Ford Found. fellow Ball State U., Muncie, 1974. Mem. Pi Lambda Theta, Kappa Delta Pi, Sigma Alpha Iota. Methodist (mem. bd. social concern 1964-65, mem. bd. ministries, 1972-74). Author: Psalms of a Black Mother, 1970. Contbr. poems, short stories and articles to publs., including Friends, Vital Christianity, others. Home: 2100 Lincolnshire Dr Muncie IN 47304

GREER, ARLINE EBERT, journalist; b. Bklyn., Nov. 10, 1928; d. Philip and Mollie (Grosswirth) Ebert; B.A. cum laude, Bklyn. Coll., 1950; M.A., Bryn Mawr Coll., 1951; m. Melvin Greer, Dec. 16, 1951; children—Jonathan Michael, Richard Alden, Alison Elizabeth, David Matthew. Cons. pub. relations Merck & Co., N.Y.C., 1951-52; editor Where mag., N.Y.C., 1952-56; med., sci. writer U. Fla. Teaching Hosp., Gainesville, 1964-65; drama critic, feature writer, columnist Gainesville Sun, 1968—. Mem. Women in Communications (historian, publicity chmn. 1973—), Phi Beta Kappa. Editor: U. Fla. Med. Guild Newsletter, 1963-69. Home: 2058 NW 14th Av Gainesville FL 32605 Office: 101 SE 2d Pl Gainesville FL 32601

GREER, DOROTHY LUCILLE LEECH (MRS. THOMAS KEISTER GREER), bus. exec.; b. Fort Morgan, Colo., Nov. 5, 1921; d. Laurance Blakely and Lucille Otis (Gill) Leech; student Mills Coll., 1939-40; B.A., San Diego State Coll., 1943; m. Thomas Keister Greer, Jan. 9, 1943; children—Nancy Tallaferro (Mrs. William Nelson Alexander II), Giles Carter, Celeste Claiborne. Tchr., Franklin County Schs., Rocky Mount, Va., 1944-45, 48-49, Roanoke (Va.) City

Schs., 1949-51; dir., sec.-treas. Franklin County Times, Inc., Rocky Mount, 1968—. Mem. central com. Assistance League So. Cal., Los Angeles, 1952-54; mem. patrons com. Internat. Debutante Ball, 1969-71. Mem. D.A.R., Internat. Platform Assn. Christian Scientist. Clubs: Willow Creek Country (sec.-dir. Rocky Mount 1962-64); Roanoke Country; San Diego Yacht. Home: The Grove Rocky Mount VA 24151

GREER, GERMAINE, author, feminist; b. nr. Melbourne, Australia, Jan. 29, 1939; d. Eric Reginald and Margaret May Mary (Lafrank) Greer; B.A. with honors in English and French Lit., U. Melbourne, 1959; M.A. with honors in English, U. Sydney (Australia), 1961; Ph.D. (Commonwealth scholar), Newnham Coll. of Cambridge U. (Eng.), 1964; m. May 1968 (div.). Lectr. English, U. Warwick (Eng.), 1967—. Author: The Female Eunuch, 1970. Address: care Curtis Brown Ltd 1 Craven Hill London W2 3EN England

GREER, LEORA BETTIE QUARLES (MRS. JOHN DOZIER GREER), nurse; b. Edgefield, S.C., Nov. 3, 1914; d. Martin Luther and Bettie (Bledsoe) Quarles; student U. N.C., 1955-56, N.Y.U., 1965; m. John Dozier Greer, May 1, 1937; children—John Dozier, Betty Clara. Staff nurse Vanderbilt U. Hosp., 1937-38; staff nurse, head nurse Crawford W. Long Hosp., Atlanta, 1938; staff nurse Emory U. Hosp., 1939; doctors asst. Dr. Marvin A. Mitchell, Atlanta, 1939-42; clinic nurse Clayton County Health Dept., Jonesboro, Ga., 1952-53; staff nurse, 1953-59; pub. health nursing supr. Crippled Children's Service, Ga. Dept. Pub. Health, Atlanta, 1959-69; asst. dir. nursing Ga. Retardation Center, 1969—. Vol. blood bank worker A.R.C., 1949. Mem. Am., Ga. (sec. nursing sect. 1956-57) pub. health assns., Am., Ga. nurses assns., Ga. Mental Health Assn., Am. Assn. Mental Deficiency, Nat. League Nurses, Ga. League Nurses, Ga., Clayton County Tb assns. Methodist. Home: 4455 Cain Circle Tucker GA 30084 Office: Ga Retardation Center 4770 N Peachtree Rd Atlanta GA 30341

GREER, REBECCA ELLEN, author, editor; b. Washington, Oct. 15, 1935; d. Frank Upton and May (Mann) Greer; B.S., U. Fla., 1957. Asst. editor Parents' Mag., N.Y.C., 1958-60, Ladies' Home Jour., N.Y.C. 1960-61; editor-in-chief Teen Age Mag., N.Y.C. 1962-63; features editor Brides Mag. N.Y.C., 1965-68; articles editor Woman's Day mag., 1968—. Instr., New Sch. for Social Research, N.Y.C., 1973—, U. Miss. Writers Conf., 1972, Rollins Coll. Writers Conf., 1973. Recipient Key to N.Y.C. for work with Dag Hammerskold Meml. Fund, 1965. Mem. Delta Gamma, Theta Sigma Phi (v.p., program chmn. N.Y. chpt. 1961-63, recipient the Sound of Success award 1970). Author: The Book for Brides, 1965; The Bride's Book of Etiquette, 1966; Why Isn't a Nice Girl Like You Married?, 1969; also articles for popular mags. Home: 50 King St New York City NY 10014 Office: 1515 Broadway New York City NY 10036

GREER, SANDRA CHARLENE THOMASON (MRS. WILLIAM LOUIS GREER), phys. chemist; b. Greenville, S.C., Jan. 7, 1945; d. Charles Williams and Sara Louise (Childress) Thomason; B.S. (Nat. Merit scholar), Furman U., 1966; M.S. (Woodrow Wilson fellow), U. Chgo., 1968, Ph.D., 1969; m. William Louis Greer, Mar. 17, 1968; children—Andrew Sean, Michael Geoffrey. Research chemist Nat. Bur. Standards, Gaithersburg, Md., 1969—. Mem. Am. Phys. Soc., Am. Chem. Soc., Assn. Women in Sci., Nat. Orgn. for Women, Am. Civil Liberties Union. Democrat. Home: 721 Owens St Rockville MD 20850 Office: Nat Bur Standards Gaithersburg MD 20234

GREESON, GEORGIANA WHITE, librarian; b. Capps, Ark., Mar. 26, 1921; d. James L. and Agnes (Calvert) White; student Hendrix Coll., 1939-40; B.A., Ark. State Tchrs. Coll., 1943; B.S. in L.S., La. State U., 1951; m. William H. Greeson, Jan. 16, 1946 (div. 1953); 1 dau., Patricia Evlin. Tchr., English jr. high sch., Harrison, Ark., 1943-44; library asst., librarian N. Ark. Regional Library, Harrison, 1944-53; children's librarian Los Angeles Pub. Library, 1954; librarian Phillips County Library, Helena, Ark., 1955-57, St. Charles Parish Library, Hahnville, La., 1958—. Mem. Am., La., (past sec. pub. library sect.) library assns. Home: Route 2 Box 34C Luling LA 70070 Office: St Charles Parish Library Hahnville LA 70057

GREESON, JUDITH GALE, librarian; b. Indpls., Oct. 3, 1946; d. George Albert and Floris Irene (Cobb) Greeson; B.A., Ind. Central Coll., 1969; M.L.S., Ind. U., 1970. Asst. librarian, instr. library sci. Huntington (Ind.) Coll., 1970-71, coordinator library services, instr. library sci., 1971—. Media certification adv. com. for tchr. edn. and certification com. Ind. Dept. Pub. Instrn., 1971—. Mem. Beta Phi Mu. Presbyn. Club: Civic Newcomer's (sec. 1973) (Huntington). Home: 926 Opal St Huntington IN 46750 Office: 2303 College Av Huntington IN 46750

GREGG, DOROTHY ELIZABETH (MRS. PAUL HUGHLING SCOTT), educator, bus. exec.; b. Tempe, Ariz.; d. Alfred Tennyson and Mamie (Walker) Gregg; B.A., U. Tex., 1944, M.A. (grad. fellow), 1945; Ph.D. (all-univ. grad. fellow), Columbia, 1951; L.H.D. (hon.), 1967; m. Paul Hughling Scott, 1952; children—Kimberly, Gregg. Student tchr. U. Tex., 1941-44; lectr. Columbia, 1946-52; asst. prof. econs., 1952-54; tchr. econ. history Barnard Coll., 1953; tchr. evening courses New Sch. for Social Research, N.Y.C., 1956-57; research cons. to mgmt. cons. firms, N.Y.C., Chgo., 1954-58; researcher, pub. relations research sect. U.S. Steel Corp., N.Y.C., 1958-60, asst. staff dir. ednl. services, 1960-68, asst. dir. pub. relations, 1968-74; dir. corporate pub. relations Celanese Corp., 1974—; asso. prof. Grad. Sch. Bus., Pace Coll., 1962-64. Spl. research asst., N.Y. coordinator to Sen. Jacob K. Javits, N.Y.C., 1957; spl. cons. to ECA, Washington, 1952; spl. research asst. to head, financial div. Nat. Bur. Econ. Research, 1951-52; speaker before ednl., profl., polit. groups. Co-chmn. consumer com. woman's council N.Y. State Dept. Commerce, 1963—. Bd. dirs. Greater N.Y. Safety Council, N.Y.C. Recipient Top Hat award Nat. Fedn. Bus. and Profl. Women's Clubs, 1968; Sound of Success award Theta Sigma Phi, 1969; named Nat. Advt. Woman of Year, Am. Advt. Fedn., 1968, Advt. Woman of Year in N.Y.C., 1968, Outstanding Woman of Year, Toastmistress Club, 1969. Advt. Women of N.Y. (dir.), Pub. Relations Soc. Am., Com. on Women in Pub. Relations (chmn. bd. dirs.), Bus. and Profl. Women N.Y.C., Am. Woman's Assn. (dir.), Grad. Faculties Alumni Assn. Columbia, Am. Econ. Assn., Joint Council on Econ. Edn., Am. Acad. Polit. and Social Sci., Am. Sociol. Assn., Phi Beta Kappa, Pi Sigma Alpha. Clubs: Zonta (dir. N.Y.C.), Lotos (asso.), Columbia U. Biographer businessmen for Harvard. Contbr. articles to profl. mags. P. F. Collier & Son Ency. Home: 299 Riverside Dr New York City NY 10025 Office: 71 Broadway New York City NY 10006

GREGG, GRACE LOUISE STOLLAR, physician; b. Pitts., Nov. 25, 1919; d. Bert Lee and Grace May (Stewart) Stollar; B.S., U. Pitts., 1941, M.D., 1943; m. Frank John Gregg, Sept. 18, 1945; children—John S., David L., Thomas A., Mary G. Intern Mercy Hosp., Pitts., 1943; asst., then chief resident pediatrics Children's Hosp., Pitts., 1943-45, asst. cardiologist, 1945-51, dir. devel. clinic, 1968—; cons. pediatrics, 1951-64; asst. dean student affairs U. Pitts. Sch. Medicine, 1971—, asso. prof. pediatrics, 1971—. Mem. Am. Acad. Pediatrics, Midwest Soc. Pediatric Research, Am. Assn. Mental Deficiency, Soc. Research Child Devel., A.M.A., Pitts. Pediatric Soc., Alpha Omega Alpha. Home: 110 Millview Dr Pittsburgh PA 15238 Office: Children's Hosp Pittsburgh PA 15213

GREGG, MARGARET MARY, social worker; b. Girard, Kan., May 28, 1916; d. George Harry and Lucile (Burgett) Gregg; B.A., Mary Hardin-Baylor Coll., 1937; M.A., U. Chgo., 1954. Social worker Baylor U. Hosp., Dallas 1937-42; pub. welfare worker Tex. Dept. Pub. Welfare, 1942-45, pub. welfare supr., 1945-49, cons. instns.-child welfare, 1954-55, dir. field staff pub. assistance, 1956-67, asst. dir. program adminstrn., 1967—; case work cons. Tex. Youth Devel. Council, 1949-53. Pres. Extend-A-Care, Inc., Austin, 1969—; pres. Austin chpt. Tex. United Community Services, 1960; mem. Bd. Nat. Ministries, Presbyn. Ch. in U.S., 1972—, mem. Commn. on New Synod Boundaries, 1971—; pres. Austin Urban Council, 1973. Bd. dirs. Presbyn. Children's Home and Service Agy. Mem. Nat. Assn. Social Workers (chpt. pres. 1956-58), Am. Pub. Welfare Assn. (mem. bd. 1967-69), Presbyn. (elder, mem. adv. com. ch. in community 1963-67). Club: Altrusa (Austin, Tex.). Home: 6404 Wilbur Dr Austin TX 78757 Office: John H. Reagan Bldg Austin TX 78701

GREGGS, ELIZABETH MAY BUSHELL (MRS. RAYMOND JOHN GREGGS), librarian; b. Delta, Colo., Nov. 7, 1925; d. Joseph Perkins and Ruby May (Stanford) Bushell; student Colo. Coll., 1943-44; B.A., U. Denver, 1948; m. Raymond John Greggs, Aug. 16, 1952; children—David M., Geoffrey B., Timothy C., Daniel R. Children's librarian Grand Junction (Colo.) Pub. Library, 1944-46, Chelan County Library, 1948, Wenatchee Pub. Library, 1948-52, Seattle Pub. Library, 1952-53; dir. children's library Renton Pub. Library, 1957-61, br. supr. and children's services, 1963-67; area children's supr. King County Library, Seattle, 1968—. Cons., organizer Tutor Center Library, Seattle South Community Coll., 1969—. Mem. Bond Issue Citizens Group to build a new Renton Library, 1958, 59. Recipient Hon. Service to Youth award Cedar River dist. Boy Scouts Am., 1971. Mem., Am. (Boy Scout com. children's services div. 1973—), Wash. (exec. bd. children's and young adult services div. 1970—) library assns., King County Right to Read Council (co-chmn. 1973—), Pierce-King County Reading Council, Wash. State Literacy Council (exec. bd. 1971—), Puget Sound Orton Soc. Methodist. Editor: Cayas Newsletter, 1971—. Home: 800 Lynnwood Av NE Renton WA 98055 Office: 300 8th Av N Seattle WA 98109

GREGORIUS, BEVERLY JUNE, gynecologist, obstetrician; b. Ottawa, Ill., June 21, 1915; d. Henry Godfrey and Arline (Barry) Pruette; B.S., Madison Coll., 1935; M.D., Loma Linda U., 1946, M.S., 1952; m. Hans Harvey Gregorius, Apr. 6, 1939; 1 dau., Joan Marie (Mrs. Jeffrey Mason Jones). Intern Los Angeles County Gen. Hosp., 1946-47; resident White Meml. Hosp., Los Angeles, 1949-52, pvt. practice, Burbank, Cal., 1952—; asst. clin. prof. obstetrics and gynecology Loma Linda U., 1953—, also U. So. Cal. Diplomate Am. Bd. Obstetrics and Gynecology. Fellow A.C.S., Am. Coll. Obstetrics and Gynecology, Internat. Coll. Surgeons. Home: 4355 Forman Av North Hollywood CA 91602 Office: 2121 W Magnolia St Burbank CA 91506

GREGORY, ANGELA, sculptor; b. New Orleans, Oct. 18, 1903; d. William Benjamin and Selina Elizabeth (Bres) Gregory; B.Design, Art Sch. Newcomb Coll., 1925; certificate Parsons Sch. Design, Paris, 1926; student Pvt. Studio Bourdelle, Paris, 1926-28, Academie de la Grande Chaumiere Paris, 1926; M.A. in Architecture, Tulane U., 1940. Important works include: Criminal Cts., New Orleans, 1928-29, La. State Capitol, 1930, St. Landry Parish Courthouse, Opelousas, La., 1940, various bldgs. Tulane U., St. Gabriel Cath. Ch., 1952, St. Louis Archdiocesan Adminstrn. Bldg., 1961, McDonogh Monument, New Orleans, 1938, Bienville Monument, New Orleans, 1955, Gen. H.W. Allen Monument, Port Allen, La., 1961; various portrait bas relief memls.; sculptural decorations for John XXIII Library, 1967, Albertus Magnus Hall, 1972 (both St. Mary's Dominican Coll.); numerous medals and coin medals including Sesquicentennial Battle New Orleans medal. Artist-in-residence Newcomb Coll., 1940-41; state supr. art program WPA, 1941-42; sculptor-in-residence St. Mary's Dominican Coll., New Orleans, 1962—. Cons. La. Gettysburg Meml. Com., 1967-71. Shell Cos. Found. grantee, 1971. Fellow Nat. Sculpture Soc.; mem. Le Petit Salon (hon.), Delta Kappa Gamma (hon. life). Democrat. Unitarian. Home: 630 Pine St New Orleans LA 70118

GREGORY, CLARA HALE (MRS. GEORGE GROOT GREGORY), physician; b. Palmyra, N.Y., Nov. 17, 1890; d. Frank Herbert and Amanda Carpenter (Reynolds) Hale; M.D., Syracuse Med. Coll., 1912; m. George Groot Gregory, Sept. 15, 1915;children—Anne (Mrs. Paul L. Bunce), Jean (Mrs. Ralph Louis Meenger), George Groot, David Hale. Intern, Women's and Children's Hosp., Syracuse; practice medicine specializing in gen. practice, Syracuse; asst. police surgeon City of Syracuse, N.Y., 1913-18; sr. Tb physician Onondaga Sanatorium, Syracuse, 1944-59; ret. Home: 7058 Fayetteville Rd Fayetteville NY 13066

GREGORY, CYNTHIA KATHLEEN (MRS. TERRENCE S. ORR), ballerina; b. Los Angeles, July 8, 1946; d. Konstantin and Marcelle (Tremblay) Gregory; grad. high sch.; m. Terrence S. Orr, May 14, 1966. Ford Found. scholar San Francisco Ballet, 1961, soloist, 1962-65; with Am. Ballet Theatre, N.Y.C., 1965—, soloist, 1966, prin. dancer, 1967—; appeared on TV with San Francisco Opera, 1963-64, in film Girl Most Likely, 1955. Home: 310 W 94th St New York City NY 10025 Office: 1619 Broadway New York City NY 10019

GREGORY, ENA, realtor; b. Sydney, Australia, Apr. 16, 1915; d. Arthur James and Jessie (Prior) Gregory; grad. high sch.; m. Albert S. Rogell, Dec. 23, 1930; m. 2d, Frank G. Nolan, Nov. 5, 1937; m. 3d, James T. Talbot, May 2, 1951 (dec. 1955). Came to U.S., 1923, naturalized, 1935. Motion picture star Universal Film Corp., Hollywood, Cal., 1927-37; realtor Gregory Realty Co., South Laguna, Cal., 1944—. Head com. South Laguna Planning, 1961-65. Mem. Laguna Beach Bd. Realtors (chmn. com. 1967-70). Office: 31645 Coast Hwy South Laguna CA 92677

GREGORY, GWENDOLYN H., lawyer, govt. ofcl.; b. Denver, Sept. 28, 1937; d. Stanford W. and Gertrude (Hurt) Gregory; B.A., U. Denver, 1959, J.D., 1963. Admitted to Colo. bar, 1963, practiced in Denver, 1963-69; atty. Office of Gen. Counsel, Food, Drugs and Environmental Health div. Dept. Health, Edn. and Welfare, Washington, 1969-71, confidential asst. to dir. Office for Civil Rights, 1971-73, dir. Office Policy Communication, Office for Civil Rights, 1973—. Substitute tchr., pub. schs., Denver, 1960-63. Mem. bd. dirs. Colo. Cystic Fibrosis Soc., 1968-69. Mem. Am., Colo., Arapahoe, Denver, Fed. bar assns., Kappa Delta, Kappa Beta Pi, Zeta Phi Eta (pres. 1958-59). Republican. Episcopalian. Home: 2615 P Street NW Washington DC 20007 Office: 330 Independence Av SW Washington DC 20024

GREGORY, MARJORIE BUTLER (MRS. HARBERT C. GREGORY), home economist; b. Quincy, Fla., Nov. 19, 1917; d. David Arthur and Sophia Regena (Garland) Butler; B.S. in Home Econs., Fla. State U., 1938; m. Harbert C. Gregory, June 28, 1939; children—Harbert Scott, Joe Garland. Tchr. home econs. Chattahoochee (Fla.) High Sch., 1938-39; substitute tchr. home econs. Quincy (Fla.) High Sch., 1939-42; supr. Gadsden County Canning Center, Quincy, 1942-43; supr. county lunch room, Gadsden County, 1943-46; extension home econs. program leader, head agt., Gadsden County, 1952—. Program dir. for county extension home econs. programs. Adviser, Glenn Julia Park, Mt. Pleasant, Fla., 1950—. Recipient service to county award Charles F. DuPont Found., 1969; Meritorious Service award in field safety Fla. Hwy. Patrol 1968. Mem. Nat., Fla. home econs. assns., Nat., Fla. extension home econs. agts. assns., Quincy Womans Club, Epsilon Sigma Phi. Presbyn. (mem. Womens Circle 1939—, pres. 1966-67, adviser to young people, mem. witness com. 1971-72). Club: Gadsden Country. Home: 336 N 9th St Quincy FL 32351 Office: 410 E Jefferson St Quincy Fl 32351

GREGORY, RUTH WILHELMENE, librarian; b. West Point, Neb., Feb. 20, 1910; d. Edward George and Wilhelmene (Plieth) Gregory; A.B., U. Neb., 1933; Library Sci., U. Wis., 1938. Gen. library asst. Lincoln (Neb.) City Library, 1934-36; librarian editorial dept. Rotarian mag., Chgo., 1937; acting librarian Stevens Point (Wis.) Pub. Library, 1938-39; asso. librarian Waukegan (Ill.) Pub. 1938-39, head librarian, 1939—; instr. Drexel Grad. Sch. L.S., summer 1962. Bd. dirs. Family Service Agy., 1954-69, North Lake County Mental Health Soc., 1954-62. Sec. Waukegan City Planning Commn., 1950-57. Sec. bd. dirs. Lake County Mus. History, 1961-64. Mem. A.L.A. (exec. sec. div. pub. libraries 1966-68; v.p. presidents and editors Round Table, 1948-49; mem. council, 1951-54; chmn. jury on citation of trustees 1952-53; pres. pub. libraries div. 1954-55; mem. exec. bd. 1956-60, chmn. coordinating com. on materials 1959-62, chmn. standards com. 1960-61), Ill. Library Assn. (pres. 1947-48, mem. planning bd., 1951-54), Am. Assn. U. Women (pres. local br. 1949-51), League Women Voters, Lake County Women's Indsl. Mgmt. Club (hon.), Kappa Delta, P.E.O. Clubs: Chicago Library; Woman's (Waukegan), Altrusa (hon.). Author: (with L.L. Stoffel) Public Libraries in Cooperative Systems, 1971. Editor: Public Libraries, 1947-48; Waukegan Ill., Its Past Its Present. Home: 2035 Walnut St Waukegan IL 60085 Office: Waukegan Pub Library Waukegan IL 60085

GREGORY, SARA MCDOWELL, librarian; b. Conyers, Ga., Apr. 30, 1917; d. Luther Milton and Lillian Blanche (Parker) McDowell; B.S. in Chemistry, Ga. Coll., Milledgeville, 1939; M.A. in Librarianship, George Peabody Coll., 1964; m. John Willis Gregory, Jan. 27, 1946; children—John Willis, Charles Luther. Tchr. math. and chemistry Douglas (Ga.) High Sch., 1939-40, LaGrange High Sch., 1940-42; Ga. Mil. Coll., 1942, O'Keefe High Sch., Atlanta, 1945-47, Oxford Coll. of Emory U., 1947-49; chemist Davidson Chem. Corp., Balt., 1942-45; asst. librarian Oxford Coll., 1958-64, librarian, 1964—; tchr. Peabody Library Sch., summers 1966, 67. Mem. vis. team to evaluate libraries for accreditation So. Assn. Schs. and Colls. Recipient Memory Dedication, 1967, Spokesman award, 1970. Mem. Am., Southeastern, Ga. library assns., Delta Kappa Gamma, Beta Phi Mu, Phi Kappa Phi. Methodist (steward). Home: 884 Cornish Mountain Rd Covington GA 30209 Office: Oxford Coll Oxford GA 30267

GREGORY, STEPHANIE ANN (MRS. SHELDON CHERTOW), physician; b. Vineland, N.J., June 23, 1940; d. Stephen N. and Andonetta (Mainiero) Gregory; B.S., Boston Coll., 1961; M.D., Med. Coll. Pa., 1965; m. Sheldon Chertow, Feb. 2, 1970; children—Elizabeth Anne, Jennifer Marie, Daniel Stephen. Intern, Presbyn.-St. Luke's Hosp., Chgo., 1965-66, resident, 1966-69; practice medicine specializing in internal medicine, hematology, Chgo.; mem. attending staff Rush-Presbyn. St. Lukes Med. Center, Chgo., 1970—, asst. prof. medicine, 1972—. Schweppe Research fellow, 1969-72. Diplomate Am. Bd. Internal Medicine. Mem. A.C.P., Am. Fedn. Clin. Research, Chgo. Soc. Internal Medicine, Internat. Soc. Exptl. Hematology, Am. Soc. Hematology, Sigma Xi, Alpha Omega Alpha. Home: 147 Dempster Evanston IL 60201 Office: 1753 W Congress Pkwy Chicago IL 60612

GREGORY, VIRGINIA LOIS SULLENGER (MRS. JAMES LEE GREGORY), univ. librarian; b. Crittenden County, Ky., Mar. 29, 1912; d. William David and Mary Lee (Paris) Sullenger; A.B., U. Ky., 1933; M.A., Murray State Coll., 1960; M.L.S., George Peabody Coll., 1968; m. James Lee Gregoy, June 4, 1932; children—Lucy Lee (Mrs. John Daniel Quertermous), James William, Richard Davis, John Scott, Rose Marie. Sec. to county judge Crittenden County, Marion, Ky., 1935-39; high sch. librarian Crittenden County Bd. Edn., 1955-68; reference librarian Murray (Ky.) State U., 1968—. Mem. Ky. Adv. Com. on Tchr. Edn. and Certification, 1967-68. Mem. Am., Southeastern, Ky. library assns., Ky. Assn. Sch. Librarians (pres. 1967-68), N.E.A., Ky. Edn. Assn., Ky. Hist. Soc., Beta Phi Mu, Kappa Delta Pi. Republican. Mem. Disciples of Christ Ch. Author: Afro-Americans, 1972; Natural Resources and Environment, 1973. Home: 108 Broach Av S Murray KY 42071

GREGORY, VIRGINIA WHITNEY (MRS. LINWOOD E. GREGORY), clubwoman; b. Pittsfield, Mass., July 10, 1912; d. Laurence Haines and Frances (Taylor) Whitney; A.B., Smith Coll., 1934; Ph.D. (hon.), Colo. State Christian Coll., 1973; m. Stephen W. Irwin, Aug. 1, 1939; m. 2d, Linwood E. Gregory, Sept. 23, 1950. Sec., Wise, Hobbs & Seaver, Boston, 1935-37, Clarke & Co., Boston, 1937-39, Mass. Women's Def. Corps, Boston, 1941-44, New Products Research Corp., 1945-50, also dir. Bd. dirs., 2d v.p. charge vis. nurses Women's Civic Club, 1957-59; regent Jane McCrea chpt. D.A.R., 1959-61, pres. Capital Dist. Council, 1970-72, N.Y. State chmn. mag. advt. com., 1971—; pres. Glens Falls Colony Nat. Soc. New Eng. Women, 1966-68, corr. sec. Glens Falls Colony New Eng. Women, 1970-72; pres. Welcome Wagon, Newcomers Club, 1953-54, Hosp. Guild, 1951-75; sponsor N.Y. State Assn. Crippled Children, Glens Falls Operetta Club, Glens Falls Concert Assn.; 1st v.p. Glens Falls Club Coll. Women, 1955-56; sec. bd. dirs. Health Assn., Warren County, 1958-64; 1st v.p. Am. Assn. U. Women, 1952-54; pres. Camera Club, 1961-62; bd. dirs. League Women Voters, 1957-60; pres. Alumni Couples Club, Presbyn. Ch., 1954-55; mem. N.Y. Huguenot Soc. (chmn. membership com. to 1975), Glens Falls Hist. Assn. (sponsor), Nat. Soc. Daus. of Founders Patriots of Am., Smithsonian Instn. (charter), Boston Smith Coll. Club, Glens Falls Country Club. Recipient award for work with Mass. Def. Corps from gov. Mass., 1943, certificate Palomino Horse Breeders Assn. Am., Inc., Commendation N.Y. Civil Def. Commn., certificate Nat. Police Officers Assn. Am. Home: 12 North Rd Glens Falls NY 12801

GREGSON, MARGARET, aircraft design specialist; b. Steelton, Pa.; d. John and Edith (Goodell) Gregson; B.A. summa cum laude in Math., Bryn Mawr Coll., 1928; M.A. in Math., U. Cal. at Los Angeles, 1939. Statistician, Peoples Gas Light & Coke Co., Chgo., 1929-38; math. tchr. Compton (Cal.) Jr. Coll., 1941-43; aircraft engr. Northrop Aircraft Co., 1947-49; aircraft engr. Lockheed Aircraft Corp., Burbank, Cal., 1943-47, 50-71, design specialist structures, 1966-71, cons., 1971—. Bryn Mawr European fellow, 1928. Mem. Am. Inst. Aeros. and Astronautics, Am. Helicopter Soc. Republican. Episcopalian. Clubs: Chicago Women's Junior City (pres. 1930), Bryn Mawr So. Cal. (pres. 1959-63). Home: PO Box 208 Hesperia CA 92345

GREIBACH, SHEILA ADELE (MRS. JACK WEBSTER CARLYLE), educator; b. N.Y.C., Oct. 6, 1939; d. Emil Henry and Miriam (Ungar) Greibach; A.B., Radcliffe Coll., 1960, M.A., 1962; Ph.D., Harvard, 1963; m. Jack Webster Carlyle, Mar. 22, 1970. Lectr.

Harvard U., Cambridge, Mass., 1963-65, asst. prof., 1965-69; asso. prof. dept. system sci. U. Cal. at Los Angeles, 1969-72, prof., 1972—. Cons. System Devel. Corp., Santa Monica, 1964-70. Recipient fellowship NSF, 1960-63, research grant, 1970—. Mem. Am. Math. Soc., Phi Beta Kappa, Sigma Xi. Mng. editor Math. Systems Theory. Contbr. articles to profl. jours. Office: 4531 Boelter Hall U Cal Los Angeles CA 90024

GREICHUS, YVONNE ARLIE THOMPSON (MRS. ALGIRDAS GREICHUS), educator, chemist; b. Whitefish, Mont., Aug. 4, 1926; d. Merle Sutherland and Clara Elisabeth (Bergman) Thompson; B.A., Reed Coll., 1949; M.S., U. Wyo., 1960, Ph.D., 1964; m. Algirdas Greichus, Feb. 7, 1951; children—Marcia Jan., Margo Jill, Mark George, Michael Bruce. Asso. prof. biochemistry S.D. State U., Brookings, 1963—. Named An Outstanding Educator Am. Stanford Research Inst. fellow, 1960-63; grantee Water Resources Inst., 1967-70, NSF, 1971-74. Mem. Am. Chem. Soc., A.A.A.S., S.D. Acad. Sci., Sigma Xi, Gamma Sigma Delta. Contbr. articles to profl. jours. Home: 348 Eastern Av Brookings SD 57006

GREINER, PHYLLIS KEITH GOODWIN (MRS. KEITH G. GREINER), sch. adminstr.; b. nr. Eggleston, Va.; d. John Earl and Glenna (Williams) Goodwin; student Radford Coll., 1928-30; U. Va. Extension, 1935-45; B.S., Roanoke Coll., 1953; M.Ed., Va. Poly. Inst., 1959; m. Charles B. Greiner, Mar. 24, 1932 (dec. Jan. 1954); 1 dau., Carolyn Ruth Odell. Tchr., Houston Pub. Schs., 1930-45, 50-53; tchr. kindergarten North Cross Pvt. Sch., Salem, 1945-50; tchr. Roanoke City Pub. Schs., 1953-61; prin. Washington Heights and Westside Schs., Roanoke, 1961-64, Acad. St. Sch., Salem, 1964-68, Burlington Sch., Roanoke, Va., 1968—. Box office mgr. Roanoke Valley Drama Assn., Salem, summers 1957, 58; mem. edn. com. Govs. Commn. on Status of Women, 1965. Mem. Am. Assn. U. Women, N.E.A., Va. State, Va. Dist. Roanoke County edn. assns., Nat., Va., Roanoke County prins. assns., Nat. (exec. bd. 1966-68), Va. (pres. 1966-68), Roanoke Valley (pres. 1964-66) councils adminstrv. women in edn., Internat. Platform Assn., Early Am. Soc., Citizens Com. on Status Women in Va., Va. Mental Health Assn., Smithsonian Instn., Internat. Reading Assn., Colonial Dames XVII Century, Alpha Delta Kappa. Methodist. Home: 124 Lewis Av Salem VA 24153 Office: 6533 Peters Creek Rd NW Roanoke VA 24019

GREITZER, CAROL, city ofcl.; grad. Hunter Coll. M.A. in English Lit., N.Y. U.; 1 dau., Elizabeth. Former copywriter; mem. N.Y. City Council, 1969—. First pres. Nat. Assn. Repeal Abortion Laws (name now Nat. Abortion Rights Action League); founder N.Y.C. Parks Council; mem. Com. for Artists Housing; chmn. Transit Riders Action Com.; founder Women's Advocacy Com. Leader Democratic Dist., 1961-69. Address: 59 W 12th St New York City NY 10011

GREIWE, HERMINA HOPPE (MRS. RAYMOND E. GREIWE), librarian; b. Cin.; d. Henry and Francesca (Wuebben) Hoppe; A.B., U. Cin., 1921; M.A., U. Ky., 1957; m. Raymond E. Greiwe, Jan. 15, 1926; children—Thomas H., Don Paul, Frances (Mrs. John Frederick Glaser). Counselor, Wright Aero. Co., 1942-45; librarian Cin. and Hamilton County Pub. Library, Cin., 1945-68. Mem. Cin. Council on Alcoholism, 1955-70; archivist Cin. Group for Study Parapsychology, 1962-71. Mem. Nat. Security Council, 1972—. Mem. A.L.A., Ohio Library Assn., Cin. Hist. Soc., Friends of Library Assn., Nat. Trust Historic Preservation, Nat. Council Catholic Laity, Cin. Art Mus., Morality in Media, Inc., Nat. Arthritis Found., Citizens for Decency through Law, Theta Phi Alpha. Home: Box 43652 Cincinnati OH 45243

GREMILLION, EFFIE GILLIS, clin. social worker; b. Excelsior, La., Nov. 9, 1906; d. Joseph Benjiman and Ada Helen (Phillips) Gillis; student La. Coll., 1949-50; B.A., Tex. U., 1950-53; M.S.W., Wordens Sch. Social Service, 1958; m. Wiley J. Gremillion, Feb. 4, 1928 (div. Mar. 1947); children—Barbara Margaret (Mrs. Linton Bowman, III), Dona Madrice (Mrs. William Weaver Harris), Effie Jeanne (Mrs. Michael Dennis O'Callaghan). Social worker Austin State Hosp., 1954-57; clin. social worker VA Hosp., Shreveport, La., 1958—, mem. intensive psychiatry service, 1965—, dir. psychodrama, 1967—. Treas., Austin-Travis County Assn. Mental Health, 1956-57. Bd. dirs. Cadd-Bossier chpt. La. Assn. Mental Health. Mem. Nat. Assn. Social Workers, Acad. Certified Social Workers. Methodist. Home: 2829 Doles Pl Shreveport LA 71104 Office: VA Hosp 510 E Stoner St Shreveport LA 71130

GRENE, ETHEL MAY (MRS. DAVID GRENE), physician; b. Chgo.; d. Edward William and Libby (Greengard) Weiss; B.S., U. Chgo., 1956, M.D., 1959; m. David Grene, Dec. 23, 1961; children—Andrew, Gregory. Intern, Cook County Hosp., Chgo., 1959-60; gen. practice medicine, Chgo., 1960—; mem. staff Woodlawn, Ill. Central hosps., Chgo. Home: 1380 E Hyde Park Blvd Chicago IL 60615 Office: 1126 E 59th St Chicago IL 60637

GRENIER, MILDRED LUCILLE (MRS. JOSEPH GRENIER), author; b. Maysville, Mo.; d. Clarence Wood and Mary Ann (Bottorff) Bromley; student Maryville State U., 1937-42, Mo. Western Coll., 1973-74; m. Joseph Grenier, Dec. 24, 1942; 1 dau., Candace. Pub. sch. tchr., Osborn, Mo., and Columbia, S.C., 1936-46. Mem. Nat. League Am. Pen Women, Mo. Writers League. Author: Christmas Every Day, 1961; How Big is the Sky, 1968; How Kids Earn Cash, 1970; Cash In, 1970; The Wagon and the Star, 1971; God Made the World, 1972; Money in Minutes, 1974. Contbr. articles to profl. jours. Home: 1811 Lovers Lane Heights St Joseph MO 64505

GRENNAN, LAURIE MURRAY (MRS. PAUL JOHN GRENNAN), educator; b. Newport News, Va., Apr. 9, 1920; d. Guy Powers and Mary Alice (Harrell) Murray; B.A., Randolph-Macon Woman's Coll., 1941; M.A., Wellesley Coll., 1942; Ph.D. (NSF faculty fellow), Ia. State U., 1966; m. Paul John Grennan, July 19, 1945 (div. Mar. 1959); children—Eileen (Mrs. Michael May), James, Philip, Laurie (Mrs. Saide Marashi), Jean. Chemist, E.I. duPont de Nemours & Co., Inc., Waynesboro, Va., 1942-44; instr. chemistry Randolph-Macon Woman's Coll., Lynchburg, Va., 1944-45; chemist Refined Syrups and Sugars, Yonkers, N.Y., 1951-52, Mt. Sinai Hosp., Milw., 1955-58; instr. chemistry Milw. Downer Coll., 1958-62; asst. prof. chemistry U. Tenn., Martin, 1965-69, asso. prof., 1969—. Mem. Am. Chem. Soc., Am. Assn. U. Women, Sigma Xi, Iota Sigma Pi, Phi Kappa Phi. Episcopalian. Home: Route 4 Minosa Dr Martin TN 38237

GREY, LUCILLE JONES (MRS. HUGH MORTON GREY, JR.), orgn. exec.; b. Cuyahoga Falls, O., Apr. 15, 1922; d. Mark Barber and Nellie (James) Jones; student U. Miami, 1939-41, Rollins Coll., 1941, U. Fla., summer 1942, Cornell U., 1942-43; m. Hugh Morton Grey, Jr., Sept. 27, 1943; children—Leslie (now Mrs. Eugene Juston Harper), Hugh Morton Grey III, Roderic, and Helen Valerie. Organizing pres. Beaux Arts of Lowe Gallery, Coral Gables, Fla., 1952, Town and Country Garden Club, Concord, N.C., 1956; chmn. vol. guides Mus. Sci. and Natural History, Miami, 1952-54; guide Childrens Mus., Charlotte, N.C., 1955-56; leader Girl Scouts, Concord, 1954-55, Cub Scouts, Concord, 1956-57; pres. Coll. Club of Venice (Fla.) Area, 1960-61, Band Parents Club, Venice, 1960-61; jr. chmn. Garden Club of Venice, 1960-62; bd. dirs. P.T.A., Merrick Demonstration Sch., 1951-52, Miami Music Club, 1951-53; mem. womens planning com. Venice Yacht Club, 1961-62; sustaining chmn. Sarasota Jr. Welfare League, 1967-68; mem. bd. Family Service Assn. Sarasota, 1968-70; mem. bd., rec. sec. Women's Library Assn. of New Coll., Sarasota, 1967-69. Mem. Jr. League of Miami, D.A.R. (regent 1973-74), Fine Arts Soc. Sarasota (charter), Upson Family Assn. Am., Kappa Kappa Gamma (organizing pres. Sarasota County chpt. 1962). Methodist. Home: 604 Narvaezi St Venice FL 33595

GREY, MARILYN LOUISE, psychologist; b. Portland, Ore., Dec. 23, 1938; d. Leslie Cecil and Louise (Misun) Grey; B.Ed., Central Wash. State Coll., 1960, B.A., 1962, M.Ed., 1966. Grad. asst. Central Wash. State Coll., 1961-62; sch. psychologist Arlington (Wash.) Sch. Dist., 1962-66; sch. psychologist Snohomish and Monroe Sch. Dists., 1966-67, Edmonds (Wash.) Sch. Dist., 1967—. Mem. Nat. Assn. Sch. Psychologists (regional dir. 1973-74, dir.), N.E.A., Wash., Edmonds edn. assns., Psi Chi. Mailing Address: 12203 Maplewood Av Edmonds WA 98020 Office: 3800 196th St Lynnwood WA 98036

GRIBBIN, PATRICIA HAMMONS (MRS. HUGH GORDON GRIBBIN), bus. exec.; b. Ventura, Cal.; d. Hal Valentine and Rena Sessions (Willoughby) Hammons; student Ventura Jr. Coll., 1937-39; m. Hugh Gordon Gribbin, Jan. 22, 1943; children—Bruce Gordon, Katharine Carson (Mrs. Charles Wayne Yates). Stenographer-bookkeeper Hughes Pontiac Co., Ventura, 1935-37; asst. mgr., bookkeeper Pacific Finance Co., Ventura, 1937-39; stenographer, cashier Ventura Theatre, 1937-40; stenographer engring. dept. contractors Pacific Naval Air Bases, Pearl Harbor, 1940-41, sec. to civilian personnel dir., Port Hueneme, Cal., 1942; sec. to personnel dir. Hawaiian Constructors, Honolulu, 1941-42; stenographer, officer personnel, sec. U.S. Navy, Pearl Harbor, 1942-43; sec. Rolling Hills Archtl. Com. and Rolling Hills Community Assn. (Cal.), dep. city clk., 1959-60; asst. mgr., sec. to mgr. Palos Verdes Homes Assn., Palos Verdes Estates, Cal., 1960-62, mgr., corporate sec., bldg. commr., dir. finance, 1962—; exec. sec.-treas. Palos Verdes Art Jury, Palos Verdes Estates, 1960—. Area chmn. A.R.C., Palos Verdes Estates, 1959; pres. Needlework Guild, Portuguese Bend chpt., 1958, Peninsula chpt. Nat. Charity League, 1959-62. Mem. 40 Leaguers Ventura County (charter, founder). Republican. Club: Soroptomist (Redondo Beach, Cal.). Home: 204 Via Las Vegas Palos Verdes Estates CA 90274 Office: 340 Palos Verdes Dr W Palos Verdes Estates CA 90274

GRIBBONS, JACKIE M., educator; b. Cleve., Aug. 29, 1932; d. John Louis and Minnie (Krall) Gribbons; B.S., Bowling Green State U., 1954; M.A., Western Res. U., 1960. Teaching cons. Grand Rapids (Mich.) Bd. Edn., 1954-55; tchr. Willoughby-East Lake (O.) Schs., 1955-59; resident adviser Bowling Green, (O.) State U., 1959-60, asst. dean women, 1960-66; dean women U. Vt., 1966—. Bd. dirs. Miss Vt. Scholarship Found., 1970. Mem. New Eng. Regional Manpower Adv. Commn., 1971-74. Named Outstanding Young Women Am., 1965-66. Mem. Nat. Assn. Women Deans, Adminstrs. and Counselors (chmn. profl. devel. and standards com. 1972—, Commn. on Profl. Employment Practices 1973), Nat. Assn. Student Personnel Adminstrs. (regional adv. com. 1971-73), Vt. Student Personnel and Guidance Assn. (sec.-treas. 1972-73), Mortar Bd., Chi Omega. Home: RD 1 Box 119 East Charlotte Hinesburg VT 05461 Office: Dean of Women U VT Burlington VT 05401

GRIDLEY, BERYL SMITH (MRS. HENRY NORMAN GRIDLEY), educator; b. Vermillion, O.; d. George W. and Alzona (Minkler) Smith; A.B. cum laude, U. Wash., 1923, M.A., 1931; postgrad. Sch. Social Work, U. Wash., 1935-37, San Francisco State Coll., 1955; m. Henry Norman Gridley, June 24, 1928 (dec. Sept. 1954). Girls adviser Cleveland High Sch., Seattle, 1924-28; prin. Woodside Sch. for Handicapped Children, Highline Sch. Dist., 1951-65; exec. dir. Assn. Retarded Children King County chpt., Seattle, 1965-70; case worker Family Counseling, Seattle, 1937-39, King County Juvenile Ct., Seattle, 1939-40, 1943-46; case worker, dir. Fed. Transient Bur., Seattle and Portland, 1932-35; consumer rep. OPA, west coast, 1941-43; asst. state dir. mental health State of Washington, 1946-49. Recipient Matrix award, 1970. Mem. Adminstrn. Women in Edn., Am. Assn. U. Women (past pres.), Nat. Assn. Social Work, Am. Assn. Mental Deficiency, Royal Soc. Health London, Mortar Bd., Pi Lambda Theta, Delta Kappa Gamma, Alpha Chi Omega. Home: Judson Park 23600 Marine View Dr Seattle WA 98188

GRIDLEY, MARION ELEANOR, author; b. White Plains, N.Y., Nov. 16, 1906; d. William Thomson and Ada Antoinette (Robertson) Gridley; student Northwestern U., 1954-55; m. Robinson Johnson, May 15, 1932 (div. 1948). Pub. relations dir. Children's Meml. Hosp., Chgo., 1943-46, Chgo. YWCA, 1946-48, Chgo. Med. Sch., 1948-57, Francis W. Parker Sch., Chgo., 1961-62, Convenient Food Mart, Chgo., 1970-74. Pub. relations dir. Ill. Heart Assn., Chgo., 1946-48; pub., editor Amerindian, 1972—. Recipient numerous awards. Mem. Nat. Fedn. Press Women, Ill. Woman's Press Assn. (Women of Year award), Midland Authors, D.A.R. Republican. Episcopalian. Author: Indians of Today, 1936, 4th edit., 1970; Indians of Yesterday, 1940; Pocahontas, 1948; Hiawatha, 1950; Indian Legends of American Scenes, 1959, rev. edit., 1972; Jamie's Dog, 1961; American's Indian Statues, 1966; Contemporary American Indian Leaders, 1972; Maria Tallchief, 1973; American Indian Women, 1973; and others. Home and office: 1263 W Pratt Blvd Chicago IL 60626

GRIDLEY, NANCY CLARKE, editor; b. Yonkers, N.Y., Apr. 26, 1943; d. Allen Hubert, Jr. and Mabel Blanche (Clarke) Gridley; B.S., Houghton Coll., 1965; M.A., Syracuse U., 1967. Asst. editor News for You, Syracuse, N.Y., 1967-70, editor, 1970—. Mem. Women in Communications, Ednl. Press Assn. Am., Syracuse Press Club. Baptist. Home: 2425 E Genesee St Syracuse NY 13210 Office: Box 131 Syracuse NY 13210

GRIEGER, PAULINE JOY MORRIS (MRS. RONALD ALTON GRIEGER), home economist; b. Cando, N.D., Feb. 4, 1938; d. Paul Ellis and Hildreth (Keen) Morris; B.S., N.D. State U., 1960, postgrad., 1960-66; m. Ronald Alton Grieger, July 28, 1962. Home econs. tchr. N.D. High Schs., 1960-63, 65-67; extension clothing specialist N.D. Coop. Extension Service. N.D. State U., Fargo, 1963-65; asst. consumer edn. dir. Johnson Wax, Racine, Wis., 1967-73, consumer edn. dir., 1973—. Mem. Adv. com. for proposed program in consumer edn. Racine Unified Schs., 1970-72. Trustee, Johnson Wax Fund, Inc., 1973—. Recipient Shield award Home Economists in Bus., 1969. Mem. Am., (2d v.p. N.D. 1964-66). Wis. (program chmn. S.E. dist. 1969) home econs. assns., Home Economists in Bus. (Wis. group newsletter editor 1968-70, chmn.-elect 1970-71, chmn. 1971-72, nominating chmn. 1972-73), Am. Women in Radio and TV (Wis. chpt. sec. 1970-71, treas. 1971-72, pres. elect 1972-73, pres. 1973—), Nat. Home Fashions League. Home: 177 Westminster Sq Racine WI 53402 Office: 1525 Howe St Racine WI 53403

GRIER, ELEANOR MEACHAM (MRS. PAUL LIVINGSTON GRIER), librarian; b. Acton, Ind., Mar. 22, 1920; d. Oscar Frederick and Edna Irene (Neal) Meacham; A.B., Ind. U., 1944; B.A. in L.S., U. Mich., 1947; m. Paul Livingston Grier, Aug. 16, 1947. With catalog dept. Ind. U., Bloomington, 1943-44; stenographer Army Dept., Indpls., 1944-45; with catalog and circulation depts. U. Mich. Library, Ann Arbor, 1945-47; sec. to pres. Hampden-Sydney (Va.) Coll., 1947-53, asst. catalog librarian, 1961-65, acquisitions librarian, 1965—. Mem. Assn. for Preservation Va. Antiquities, Phi Beta Kappa, Phi Kappa Phi. Presbyn. Club: College Hill (Hampden-Sydney). Home: PO Box 7 Hampden-Sydney VA 23943

GRIER, EUNICE SHERIDAN (MRS. GEORGE W. GRIER), social scientist; b. Stamford, Conn., July 19, 1927; d. Charles J. and Velma (Viles) Sheridan; B.S. with honors in Journalism, U. Pa., 1948, postgrad. in sociology, 1950-51; m. George W. Grier, Apr. 9, 1949; children—Sheryl Lynn, Suzanne Lauren, Leigh Robert. Writer, Am. Friends Service Com., Phila., 1950-52; cons., 1958-59; rep. for research N.Y. State Commn. against Discrimination, N.Y.C., 1957-60; staff asso. Washington Center for Met. Studies, 1961-65, sr. asso., 1972—; dir. research U.S. Commn. Civil Rights, 1965-71. Cons., Fund for Republic, Inc., 1954-55, Commn. on Race and Housing, 1955-57, Pa. Dept. Labor and Industry, 1958, Anti-Defamation League of B'nai B'rith, 1959, U. Pa. Inst. for Urban Studies, 1956-57, 63. Mem. nat. adv. com. community relations sect. Am. Friends Service Com., 1963-70. Mem. Nat. Assn. Intergroup Relations Ofcls. (chmn. research commn. 1963). Author: (with husband) Privately Developed Interacial Housing, 1960; Equality and Beyond, 1966. Contbr. numerous articles and monographs to profl. pubis. Home: 6532 E Halbert Rd Bethesda MD 20034 Office: 1717 Massachusetts Av NW Washington DC 20036

GRIER, FRANCES BELLE POWNER (MRS. JOSEPH GRIER), writer; b. Harristown, Ill.; d. Charles Tracey and Olive Rebecca (Davis) Powner; student U. Ariz., 1916, 27-45; m. Joseph Grier, Apr. 15, 1930 (dec. Nov. 1959); 1 son, Joseph Lemon. Tchr. elementary schs., Greensburg, Ind., 1901-03; clk. Marshall Field & Co., Chgo., 1903-05, Caxton Co., Chgo., 1906-11; editor, mem. firm Charles T. Powner Co., Chgo., 1912-27; asst. to librarian U. Ariz., 1927-30; Lectr. on Mark Twain. Tchr., Community Ch. Leadership Tng. Schs., Tucson, 1939-41. Mem. P.E.O., Nat. League Am. Pen Women (br. pres. Tucson 1939-40, Ariz. state pres. 1950-52), Alumni Assn. U. Ariz. (life), Hist. Soc. Decatur County, Ariz. State Hist. Soc. Republican. Presbyn. (elder). Translator from Spanish: Life of Joaquin Murrieta, 1925. Author: California Cook Book, 1925. Collector 1st edits. works Mark Twain, donated collection to U. Ariz., 1962. Home: 845 E Bonita L30 Pomona CA 91767

GRIESBAUM, JANET LEE, zoo adminstr.; b. St. Louis, Mar. 16, 1943; d. Edgar Joseph and Ella June (Mohrmann) Griesbaum; B.A. with honors, DePauw U., 1965. Newsroom girl Friday, KTVI-TV, St. Louis, 1965-66; community relations asst. Jr. Coll. Dist., St. Louis, 1966-68; adminstrv. asst. to chmn. Stix, Baer & Fuller Co., St. Louis, 1968-73; asst. to dir. community relations St. Louis Zoo, St. Louis, 1973—. Mem. exec. com. Young Republican, 1966—. Mem. Women in Communications (corr. sec. 1969), St. Louis Geneal. Soc., Mound City Archeol. Soc., St. Louis Ski Club. Home: 1966 Hunting Lake Ct Apt 301 Kirkwood MO 63122 Office: Forest Park St. Louis MO 63110

GRIEST, ELINOR PRESTON, editor; b. Lancaster, Pa., Dec. 1, 1921; d. Ellwood and Carolyn (Hutton) Griest; B.A., Swarthmore Coll, 1943; student Sorbonne (Paris), 1948-49. Dir. mail advt., coll. textbook dept. Henry Holt & Co., Publishers, N.Y.C., 1943-46; writer Ofcl. History, O.S.S., Washington, 1946-47; information officer Econ. Cooperation Adminstrn., Paris, France, 1949-51; reporter Washington bur. Reader's Digest, 1951-60, asso. editor, N.Y.C., 1960—. Mem. Swarthmore Coll. Alumni Council, 1968-71. Mem. Washington Press Club, Am. Newspaper Womens Club (past bd. govs.), Overseas Press Club. Home: 25 E 10th St New York City NY 10003 Office: 200 Park Av New York City NY 10017

GRIFFEL, PAMELA KATHERINE, music educator; b. Iowa Falls, Ia., Jan. 8, 1945; d. Ralph Heinrich and Katherine Teresa (Ashley) Griffel; student U. No. Ia., 1963-65; Mus.B., Ind. U., 1968, Mus.M., 1969. Grad. asst. in piano Ind. U., 1968-69; instr. piano and music lit. St. Mary's Coll., Notre Dame, Ind., 1969-72; instr. piano and class piano Sch. Fine Arts, U. Kan., Lawrence, 1972—. Soloist, Waterloo Symphony Orch., 1962, U. No. Ia. Orch., 1964; solo recitals in Mich., Ind., Chgo., Kan., Mo., Ia., 1961—; accompanist, Ind., 1965—. Mem. Am. Assn. U. Women, Music Tchrs. Assn.-Kan. Music Tchrs. Assn., Sigma Alpha Iota. Home: 1517 W 9th St Apt 21 Lawrence KS 66044

GRIFFIN, BARBARA JEAN KLABIUS (MRS. DONALD NEILSON GRIFFIN), real estate broker; b. Detroit, Nov. 7, 1937; d. Edward Prince and Dora Elizabeth (Brainard) Goocher; grad. Anthony Real Estate Sch., 1967; broker De Anza Jr. Coll., 1968-70; m. John Adam Klabius, Apr. 27, 1957 (div. May 1970); children—Kimberly Eve, John Adam, Samantha Lynn; m. 2d, Donald Neilson Griffin, Dec. 29, 1973. Sales agent Action Realty, San Jose, Cal., 1967; asst. mgr. Lad Realty, San Jose, 1969; broker, realtor Fireside Realty, San Jose, 1970-72; owner, real estate broker Barbara Griffin Realty, San Jose, 1973—. Chmn. for atty. gen. Cal., Los Gatos, 1969—; citizens adviser to the atty. gen., 1971—. Mem. Nat. Assn. Realtors, Cal. Real Estate Assn., San Jose Real Estate Bd., Asso. Investment and Exchange Counselors, Los Gatos Art League. Home: 849 Lilac Way Los Gatos CA 95030 Office: 1142 S Winchester San Jose CA 95128

GRIFFIN, BETTY SPRAGENS, judge; b. Lebanon, Ky., Aug. 10, 1928; d. William Henry and Eleanor Lillian (Brewer) Spragens; J.D., U. Ky., 1951; m. Gerald Robin Griffin, Mar. 23, 1951 (div. Jan. 1974); children—Susan O'Hara, Leigh Spragens. Admitted to Ky. bar, 1951; individual practice law, Lexington, Ky., 1969-71; friend of the ct. Fayette Circuit Ct., 1971—; judge pro tem Municipal Ct., Lexington, 1970-73. Asst. chmn. publicity Jr. League Horse Show, 1964; head of parents com. Lexington Sch., 1966-68; mem. state exec. com. White House Council on Children and Youth, 1969; pres. Spragens Fund, 1965—. Co-chmn. Dem. Com. Fayette County, 1960. Bd. dirs. Jr. League, 1964-65; bd. dirs. Florence Crittenden Home, 1964-65, pres., 1968-69. Mem. Ky., Fayette County bar assns., Blue Grass Tennis Assn. (dir. 1966-69, treas. 1967-68). Presbyn. Home: 1323 Prather Rd Lexington KY 40502 Office: 2d Floor Fayette County Court House Lexington KY 40507

GRIFFIN, CAROL LEE, psychologist; b. Quincy, Mass., Dec. 31, 1936; d. Carroll Thomas and Jeanette (Lee) Griffin; A.B. magna cum laude, Boston U., 1958, M.A., 1959, Ph.D., 1967. Intern psychology Brockton (Mass.) VA Hosp., 1959-60, VA Outpatient Clinic, Boston, 1961-62, South Shore Mental Health Center, Quincy, 1960-61; staff psychologist South Shore Mental Health Center, Quincy, 1961-68; mental health cons. Quincy Pub. Schs., 1965-68, dir. pupil personnel services, 1968—. Cons., Boston YWCA, 1965-66; research asso. Simmons Coll. Sch. Social Work, 1966-69; practice of psychology, Quincy, 1964-70; cons. South Shore Mental Health Center, 1968-70; lectr. Emerson Coll., 1968-70. Chmn. young adult com. Boston YWCA, 1967-69, mem. bd. dirs., 1967-70; mem. Youth Commn., 1973—. Clk., bd. dirs. Survival, Inc., 1970—; bd. dirs. Protestant Social Service Bur., 1971—. Mem. Am., Mass. psychol. assns., Am. Orthopsychiat. Assn., Nat. Assn. Pupil Personnel Adminstrs., Mass. Sch. Counselors Assn., Delta Kappa Gamma (1st v.p. 1972—). Conglist. Club: Altrusa (dir. 1965-66). Home: 81 Macy St Quincy MA 02169 Office: Quincy Pub Schs Quincy MA 02169

GRIFFIN, EILEEN PATRICIA, judge; b. Springfield, Mass., Mar. 10, 1921; d. Jeremiah J. and Hannah M. (O'Rouke) Griffin; student Northeastern U., 1940-45; LL.B., Boston U., 1949; J.D., New Eng. Sch. Law, 1971. Admitted to Mass. bar, 1949; mem. Barry, Landers & Griffin, Springfield, Mass., 1951-64; judge Dist. Ct., Palmer, Mass., 1964-73, Superior Ct., Boston, 1973—. Mem. Springfield City Council 1961-64. Mem. Bus. and Profl. Women's Club. Club: Quota (Springfield). Home: 160 Maple St Springfield MA 01105 Office: Superior Ct Boston MA 02108

GRIFFIN, EMILIE RUSSELL DIETRICH (MRS. HENRY WILLIAM GRIFFIN), advt. copywriter; b. New Orleans, July 22, 1936; d. Norman Edward and Helen (Russell) Dietrich; B.A., Newcomb Coll., Tulane U., 1957; m. Henry William Griffin, Aug. 31, 1963; children—Lucy Adelaide, Henry Francis, Sarah Jeannette. Guest editor Mademoiselle, N.Y.C., summer 1956; reporter New Orleans Item, 1957-58; advt. copywriter-producer Swigart & Evans, Inc., New Orleans, 1958-59; copywriter Fuller & Smith & Ross, Inc., N.Y.C., 1959-62; copy group head Norman, Craig & Kummel, Inc., N.Y.C., 1962-64; copy group head, sr. creative group supr. Compton Advt., Inc., N.Y.C., 1964-70, v.p., 1968-70; copywriter, cons. Gen. Foods Corp., Procter & Gamble Co., others, 1970—; dir. children's advt. rev., nat. advt. div. Council Better Bus. Burs., Inc., N.Y.C., 1974—. Recipient Playscript award La. Council for Music and Performing Arts, 1971. Mem. D.A.R., Southampton Colonial Soc., La. Hist. Soc., Phi Beta Kappa. Home: 110 Audley St Kew Gardens NY 11415 Office: 845 3d Av New York City NY 10022

GRIFFIN, HARRIET ELIZABETH, educator; b. Parker County, Tex.; d. Minter Crozier and Lillian (Sumner) Griffin; B.A., Tex. Christian U., 1932, M.A., 1935; postgrad. U. Tex., Colo. State U, U. Cal. at Los Angeles, U. So. Cal. English tchr. Milsap pub. schs., 1933-35; tchr. Ft. Worth pub. sch., 1935-47, dean Tech. High Sch, also supr. Adult Evening Sch., 1947-63, coordinator guidance testing and vis. tchrs., 1963-67, dir. profl. relations, 1967—. Del. World Confederation Orgn. of Teaching Professions, Korea, 1966, Ireland, 1968, London, 1972; producer radio program Edn. Today. Bd. dirs. Big Brothers of Tarrant County, Conf. Christians and Jews, Family Service, Nat. Youth Corps, Travelers Aid, Ft. Worth Traffic Safety Commn.; bd. mgrs., legislative chmn. Tex. Congress Parents and Tchrs.; vice chmn. Ft. Worth Mayor's Com. Status of Women, Ft. Worth Mayor's Com. on Youth Opportunity; treas. Community Action Agy. Mem. N.E.A., Am. Assn. U. Women, Fort Worth Sch. Adminstrs., Bus. and Profl. Women's Club, Tex. Tchrs. Assn. (pres. 1966), Council Adminstrv. Women (past pres.), C. of C. (edn. com. women's div.), Kappa Kappa Iota (hon.), Delta Kappa Gamma, Kappa Delta Pi. Clubs: Altrusa (past pres.), Woman's, Shakespeare. Author ednl. column. One Small Voice, Ft. Worth Press (Sch. Bell award 4 yrs.). Contbr. articles to profl. publs. Home: 2555 Greene Av Ft Worth TX 76109 Office: 3210 W Lancaster Fort Worth TX 76107

GRIFFIN, JACQUELINE PERRY (MRS. CHARLES W. GRIFFIN, JR.), educator; b. Manila, Philippine Islands, Dec. 21, 1927; d. Emil Bates and Amalia Marie (Erbach) Perry; B.A., George Washington U., 1948; M.A., Montclair State Coll., 1968; m. Charles W. Griffin, Jr., Nov. 26, 1949; 1 dau., Janis. Research asst. hist. div. Dept. Army, 1948-50; sec. Am. Friends Service Com., 1950-52; prof. English Essex County Coll., Newark, 1968—. Mem. bd. edn., Cherry Hill Twp., N.J., 1959-60. Recipient Fed. Teaching Fellowship Grant, 1966-68. Mem. Nat. Council Tchrs. English, N.J. Edn. Assn. Author: Sentence Strategies, 1971. Home: 62 Indian Spring Trail Denville NJ 07834 Office: 31 Clinton St Newark NJ 07102

GRIFFIN, MARJORIE (MRS. ROBERT P. GRIFFIN), wife of U.S. Senator; b. Ludington, Mich.; d. William E. and Eva (Krogen) Anderson; A.B. Central Mich. U.; postgrad. U. Mich., U. Mexico; m. Robert P. Griffin, May 10, 1947; children—Paul Robert, Richard Allen, James Anderson, Martha Jill. Tchr. Greenville (Mich.) High Sch., 1944-46; asst. reference librarian Central Mich. U. Library, 1946-47; tchr., librarian Slauson Jr. High Sch., Ann Arbor, Mich., 1947-50; substitute tchr. Traverse City (Mich.) High Sch., 1950-54. Mem. exec. bd. Senate Wives A.R.C. Mem. Nat. Womens Adv. Com. Nixon-Agnew; v.p. Republican Congressional Wives Club. Recipient 75th Anniversary award Central Mich. U., 1968. Conglist. Clubs: Congressional (Washington), Mich. Bus. and Profl. Women's. Home: 1320 Peninsula Ct Traverse City MI 59684 also 2500 Q St NW Washington DC 20016

GRIFFIN, MARY ELIZABETH WILSON (MRS. DONALD F. GRIFFIN), metals mfg. co. exec., educator; b. Yuba City, Cal., May 24, 1932; d. Zacharias Walters and Mary (Nickerson) Wilson; A.A., Yuba Coll., 1952; A.B. cum laude (Cal. Congress P.T.A. scholar), Chico State Coll., 1954; postgrad. Sacramento State Coll., 1956, San Francisco State Coll., 1957-58; m. Donald F. Griffin, Sept. 6, 1958; children—John Malcolm, Mimi Elizabeth, Zachary Paul. Tchr. pub. elementary schs., Santa Rosa, Cal., 1954-57; asso. prof. edn. San Francisco State Coll., 1957-59, temporary tchr. Campus Elementary Sch., 1960-67; v.p. Griffin Metal Products, San Francisco, 1960-63, sec.-treas., 1963—; tchr. South San Francisco Unified Sch. Dist., 1973—. Treas. library trust fund French-Am. Bi-Lingual Sch., San Francisco, 1965-67; active P.T.A., 1967—, dir. county parent edn. program, 1972—; mem. Millbrae Beautification Com., 1971—. Recipient appreciation certificate Cub Scouts Am., 1969, 70, 71, Hon. Service award Cal. Congress P.T.A., 1973. Democrat. Presbyn. Club: Millbrae (Cal.) Woman's. Home: 67 Aura Vista Millbrae CA 94030 Office: 1320 Underwood Av San Francisco CA 94124

GRIFFIN, MARY RUFFIN ROBERTSON (MRS. ORMOND BISHOP GRIFFIN), educator; b. Stoneville, N.C., Aug. 24, 1915; d. Samuel Ruffin and Daisy (Joyce) Robertson; R.N., Roanoke Rapids (N.C.) Hosp. Sch. Nursing, 1938; B.S. in Pub. Health Nursing, Peabody Coll. for Tchrs., 1947; M.P.H. U. N.C., 1965; postgrad. E. Carolina U., 1962-63; m. Ormond Bishop Griffin, Dec. 28, 1947. Sch. nurse Roanoke Rapids (N.C.) high sch., 1938-41; field health supr. U.S. Govt. Nat. Youth Adminstrn., Kinston, N.C., 1941; mem. infirmary nursing staff E. Carolina U., Greenville, 1941-42; pub. health nurse Chatham County Health Dept., Pittsboro, N.C., 1942-46, Greensboro Health Dept., 1947, Halifax County Health Dept. (N.C.), 1953-62; nurse Dr. K. Mathiesen, Pittsboro, 1948; pvt. duty Mathiesen Clinic, Pittsboro, 1949-52; instr. pub. health nursing East Carolina U., 1962-65; prof. East Tenn. State U., Johnson City, 1965—. Tchr. home nursing A.R.C., 1942-44. Precinct chmn. Democratic party, Haw River Twp., Moncure, N.C. Fellow Am. Pub. Health Assn.; mem. N.C., Blountville (Tenn.) bus. and profl. women's club, Tenn. Pub. Health Assn., Am., N.C. (dist. pres. 1964) nurses assns. Nat., Am. leagues for nursing, Tenn., East Tenn. edn. assns. Baptist. Home: Rural Delivery Blountville TN 37617 Office: East Tenn State U Johnson City TN 37601

GRIFFIN, MARY VELMA SHOTWELL (MRS. JAMES LEONARD GRIFFIN), author; b. nr. Carrollton, O., Aug. 11, 1904; d. Winfield Scott and Eva Anaz (Smith) Shotwell; certificate elementary edn., Kent State U., 1925; m. James Leonard Griffin, Oct. 2, 1929. Accordionist, Radio Sta. WTAM, Cleve., 1926, Chatuauqua and Lyceum circuits, 1927-28, Accordion Gypsies, 1931-48, Ringling Bros.-Barnum and Bailey Circus, 1935-36; tchr. pub. schs., Ohio, 1922-65; ret., 1965; now free lance writer. Gray lady, A.R.C., 1967—. Bd. dirs. Bell-Herron Scholarship Found., 1965—; pres. Carroll County Hist. Soc., 1965-67, dir., 1963—, curator, 1967—. Mem. N.E.A., Carroll County Ret. Tchrs. Assn., Ohio, Carroll County (pres. 1964-65) edn. assns., Ohio Hist. Soc., Ohioana Library Assn. (county chmn. 1958—). Republican. Methodist. Rebekah; mem. Order Eastern Star. Author: Fair Prize, 1956; Circus Daze, 1957; Mystery Mansion, 1958; numerous short stories pub. in popular mags. Home: 6 Arch St Dellroy OH 44620

GRIFFIN, RUTH COWLES MCCRUM, educator; b. Hartford, Conn., Oct. 4, 1923; d. Robert Carlisle and Amy Frances (Sawyer) McCrum; student Hartford Coll. for Women, 1942-44, Tufts U., 1944-46; B.S., U. Hartford, 1966, M.Ed., 1967; Ph.D., U. Conn., 1973; m. Carl E. Griffin, 1958 (div.); 1 son, Robert Douglas. Dir. occupational therapy Newington (Conn.) Childrens Hosp., 1946-54, St. Francis Hosp., Hartford, Conn., 1955-57; asst. dir. edn. and research-occupational therapy Norwich (Conn.) State Hosp., 1957-58; asst. dir. dept. ednl. therapy Inst. of Living, Hartford, Conn., 1959-68; prof., dir. occupational therapy Quinnipiac Coll., Hamden, Conn., 1969—, co-chmn. dept. therapeutic and rehabilitative scis., 1972—. Project dir. educator devel. workshops U. Conn., Storrs, 1970—, Ohio State U., Columbus, 1971; mem. nat. adv. council on vocational rehab. Rehab. Services Adminstrn., Dept. Health, Edn. and Welfare, Washington, 1972-73; mem. adv. bd. occupational therapy program Manchester (Conn.) Community Coll., 1969—, Towson State Coll., Balt., 1973—. Social and Rehab. Service grantee Dept. Health, Edn. and Welfare, 1968-69. Mem. World Fedn. Occupational Therapists, Am., Conn. (pres. 1951-53) occupational therapy assns., Am. Assn. U. Profs., Conn. Rehab. Assn., West Hartford C. of C. (edn. com. 1974—). Club: Quota (New Haven). Home: 23 Westfield Rd West Hartford CT 06119 Office: Quinnipiac Coll Hamden CT 06518

GRIFFIN, RUTH LEWIN (MRS. JOHN KENNETH GRIFFIN), former state legislator, nurse; b. Fall River, Mass., July 9, 1925; d. Perez Otis and May Dorothy (Bailey) Lewin; grad. Wentworth Hosp. Sch. Nursing, Dover, N.H., 1946; m. John Kenneth Griffin, Oct. 4, 1947; children—Joan Kathleen (Mrs. David Welles Maloney), John Kenneth, Michael Joseph, Joyce Elaine, Timothy Gerard. Mem. N.H. Ho. of Reps., 1971-73; 1st Dist. del. Republican Nat. Com., 1972, mem. com. on resolutions, Miami Beach, 1972; del. N.H. Rep. Conv., 1971-73, mem. platform com., 1973; mem. Portsmouth (N.H.) Bd. Edn., 1974—. Mem. pub. health and welfare com. N.H. Gen. Ct., 1971-73, clk. fish and game com., 1973. Mem. D.A.R., Order Women Legislators. Methodist (trustee). Home: 479 Richards Av Portsmouth NH 03801

GRIFFIN, TREVA ANN (MRS. ROBERT MILTON LEE GRIFFIN), banker; b. Holloway, O., Dec. 6, 1931; d. Muriel Wesley and Linnie Harried (Van Curen) Evans; certificate Am. Inst. of Banking Sch., 1971; grad. Grad. Sch. Banking, U. Wis., 1974; m. Robert Milton Lee Griffin, Dec. 9, 1951; children—Judith Ann, Robert Lee. Bookkeeper, Phil-Mor, Inc., Steubenville, O., 1949-51; cashier U.S. Army, Camp Breckinridge, Ky., 1952-53; exec. officer in charge personnel and adminstrn. Comml. Nat. Bank, Flushing, O., 1969—. Mem. Nat. Assn. Bank Women, Am. Inst. of Banking, Belmont County Hist. Soc. Home: Circle Dr Flushing OH 43977 Office: PO Box 7 Flushing OH 43977

GRIFFIN, VIRGINIA JUNE KIESSLING (MRS. GEORGE D. J. GRIFFIN), govt. ofcl; b. Cin., June 27, 1923; d. Frederick John and Beatrice (Niebaum) Kiessling; B.A. cum laude, U. Cin., 1948, M.A., 1947, postgrad., 1972-74; m. George D. J. Griffin, Feb. 15, 1947; children—George D.J. III, Deborah, Brian Frederic, Nancy Jayne. Mem. Bd. Edn., Cin., 1967—. Chmn. Over the Rhine Task Force Cin. Model Cities Program, 1970-72. Chmn. bd. trustees Cin. Tech. Coll. 1972-73. Mem. Nat., Ohio sch. bds. assns., Am. Ednl. Research Assn., Policy Studies Orgn., Am. Audubon Soc., Am. Assn. Sch. Adminstrs., Womans Aux. Acad. Medicine Gen. Bd., Sierra Club. Home: 2780 Dunaway Av Cincinnati OH 45211

GRIFFITH, ELEANOR B., state ofcl.; b. Carrollton, Mo., 1926; student Central Methodist Coll. Asst. sec., trust officer Excelsior Trust Co. Bank. Mem. Excelsior Springs (Mo.) Bd. Edn., former pres., former treas.; mem. Mo. Bd. Edn., 1970—, now v.p. Mem. Bus. and Profl. Women's Club, Mo. Fedn. Women's Clubs, Nat. Assn. State Bds. Edn. Democrat. Methodist. Home: 906 Magnolia W Excelsior Springs MO 64024

GRIFFITH, ELIZABETH DICKERSON, ret. educator, orgn. exec.; b. Washington, June 26, 1907; d. Harold Clarke and Grace Emma (Adams) Griffith; A.B., George Washington U., 1937, M.A., 1943; postgrad. Cath. U., 1940-41, D.C. Tchrs. Coll., 1958-59. Tchr. Janney Sch., Washington, 1927-28, Park View Sch., 1928-32; tchr. sci. and phys. edn. Buchanan Sch., 1932-33, remedial instrn. tchr., 1933-47; remedial instrn. tchr. research dept., D.C. Pub. Schs., 1947-55, research asst., pupil appraisal, study and attendance dept., 1955-63, sch. psychologist, pupil appraisal and study dept., Pupil Personnel Services, 1963-64; asst. exec. sec. D.C. Edn. Assn., 1964-65, serving as exec. sec., 1965-68, ret. water front dir. Camp Matoaka, St. Leonard, Md., 1928-58. Mem. N.E.A. (hon. v.p. 1954-56, state dir. 1951-54), D.C. Classroom Tchrs. Council (chmn. 1956-57), D.C. Edn. Assn. (pres. 1957-59), Am. Assn. U. Women, Nat. Council of Adminstrv. Women in Edn. (chmn. awards com. 1973-74), Elementary Classroom Tchrs. Assn., (legislative chmn. 1950-68, pres. 1948-50), D.C. Ret. Tchrs. Assn. (pres. 1974-76), D.C. Congress of Parents and Tchrs., Pi Lambda Theta (chpt. pres. 1938-39), Phi Delta Gamma (chpt. pres. 1952-53) Delta Kappa Gamma (pres. D.C. br. 1959—). Methodist. Home: 3601 Connecticut Av NW Washington DC 20008

GRIFFITH, LUCILLE, educator; b. Bessville, Mo., Oct. 25, 1905; d. Laurence C. and Carolina (Mabuce) Griffith; A.B., Belhaven Coll., 1929; M.A., Tulane U., 1942; Ph.D., Brown U., 1957. Tchr. pub. high schs., Miss., 1929-42; head history dept., East Miss. Jr. Coll., 1942-46; instr. history Ala. Coll., 1946-57, prof., 1957—, acting chmn. department social scis., 1966-68, chmn., 1968-73. Past dir. Community Chest. Chmn. bd. Montevallo Town Library. Mem. Am., So. hist. assns., Ala., Va. hist. socs., Am. Studies Assn., Am. Assn. Univ. Profs., Am. Assn. Univ. Women (2d v.p. 1959-61, nat. com. on higher edn. 1959-63, past pres. Montevallo br., pres. Ala. div. 1962-64, nat. com. fellowships to Am. women 1969-73). Author: Yours Till Death, 1951; History of Alabama, 1962; The Virginia House of Burgesses, 1750-1774, 1963; History of Alabama College, 1969; Alabama: A Documentary History to 1900, 1972; also numerous articles pub. in profl. jours. Editor: Anne Royall's Letters From Alabama 1817-1822, 1969; I Always Wore My Topi: The Burma Letters of Ethel Mabure, 1916-1921, 1974. Home: 163 Plowman St Montevallo AL 35115

GRIFFITH, MARY BETH (MRS. CHARLES H. GRIFFITH), librarian; b. Prescott, Ark., Oct. 15, 1905; d. George Jefferson and Laura Bailey (Johnson) Terry; student Galloway Coll., Ark. Coll.; B.A. in Speech, U. Ark., 1954; postgrad. Tex. Woman's U.; m. Charles Howard Griffith, June 14, 1930; 1 son Charles Howard (died in Korea). Former high sch. tchr., Ark., Ala.; regional librarian, supr. 6 county area White River Regional Library, Batesville, 1945—. Mem. Ark. Library Assn. (chmn. pub. library sect. 1947, treas. 1959, pres. 1966, mem. nominating com. 1972, chmn. Nat. Library Week 1961), Pi Beta Phi. Democrat. Methodist. Home: 658 Boswell St Batesville AR 72501 Office: 110 Broad St Batesville AR 72501

GRIFFITH, MARY IRENE, physician; b. Ruffin, N.C., July 1, 1909; d. Harry and Nannie (Dameron) Griffith; student Woman's Coll., U. N.C., 1926-29, U. N.C., 1932-33; M.D., U. Tenn., 1942. Intern N.C. Bapt. Hosp., Winston-Salem, N.C., 1942, obstetrics, gynecology staff, 1942, now men. staff; intern Johns Hopkins Hosp., 1942-43, asst. resident 1943-44, resident obstetrics, 1944-45; asst. resident pathology Boston Lying-In Hosp., 1945, Free Hosp. for Women, 1945-46; practice medicine, specializing in obstetrics, gynecology, Winston-Salem, N.C., 1946—; asso. prof. obstetrics and gynecology Bowman Gray Sch. Medicine, 1968—; med. cons. Nigeria, Ire Welfare Center, W. Africa, 1954, 62, Bapt. Hosp., Paraguay, 1956. Bd. dirs. Friendship House. Diplomate Am. Bd. Obstetrics and Gynecology. Fellow Am. Coll. Obstetricians and Gynecologists; mem. A.M.A., Am. Med. Women's Assn., Alpha Epsilon Iota, Alpha Omega Alpha. Baptist. Club: Altrusa. Contbr. articles to profl. jours. Home: 419 S Hawthorne Rd Winston-Salem NC 27103 Office: 207 S Hawthorne Rd Winston-Salem NC 27103

GRIFFITH, MARY LOUISE KILPATRICK (MRS. EMLYN I. GRIFFITH), civic worker; b. Gadsden, Ala., Mar. 22, 1926; d. Lewis A. and Willie (Reid) Kilpatrick; A.B., Huntingdon Coll., 1947; m. Emlyn I. Griffith, Aug. 13, 1946; children—William L., James R. Pres. Evergreen Twig, hosp. charity group, Rome, 1966-67; bd. dirs. Rome Art and Community Center, 1967-72; mem. Bd. Edn. Rome City Sch. Dist., 1967—; bd. dirs. Rome chpt. Am. Field Service, 1969—; trustees planning com. Kirkland Coll., 1969—; trustee Utica Coll. Found., 1974—. Pres. Rome Home, 1973—; permanent adviser Rome Newcomers Club. Recipient Rose for Living award Rotary Club, 1973. Presbyn. Mem. P.E.O. (pres. 1965-66), N.Y. State, Oneida County sch. bds. assns., Am. Assn. U. Women. Club: Wednesday Morning (pres. Rome 1968-70). Home: Golf Course Rd Rome NY 13440

GRIFFITH, ROBERTA JEAN (MRS. RAYMOND S. SCHILLMOELLER), artist; b. Hillsdale, Mich., May 14, 1937; d. Robert Charles and Jane (Randolph) Griffith; student U. Mich., 1952-53, 55-57, Instituto Allende (San Miguel de Allende, Mex.), 1957-58, Mich. State U., 1959, N.Y.U., summer 1966; B.F.A., Chouinard Art Inst., 1960; M.F.A., So. Ill. U., 1962; Fulbright grantee, Massana Sch., Barcelona, Spain, 1962-64; m. Raymond S. Schillmoeller, Mar. 26, 1966; children—David Robert, Raymond Mark. Jr. counselor Camp Ak-o-Mak, Can., summer 1954; with Latin Am. Inst., So. Ill. U., Carbondale, summer 1961, teaching asst. Spanish, fgn. lang. dept. So. Ill. U., 1961-62; tchr. art Am. Sch., Barcelona, Spain, spring 1964; asst. ceramic designer Design Technics, N.Y.C., 1965-66; prof. art Hartwick Coll., Oneonta, N.Y., 1966—, chmn. dept. art, 1974—; one-man shows Aspen (Colo.) Gallery, So. Ill. U. Mus., Old Mill Gallery, Tinton Falls, N.J., DeMena Gallery, N.Y.C., Hartwick Mus., others; exhibited in group shows Brooks Meml. Gallery, Memphis, Chouinard Art Inst., Los Angeles, E. Stroudsburg State Coll. Gallery, DeMena Gallery, N.Y.C. Bklyn. Mus., Joe and Emily Lowe Art Gallery, Coral Gables, Fla.; others; represented in permanent collections at U. Mich., So. Ill. U., E. Stroudsburg State Coll., Ateneo of Madrid, Fulbright Commn. of Madrid, others. Fulbright grantee, 1962-64. Mem. Am. Crafts Council, Artist-Craftsmen of N.Y., Coll. Art Assn. Am., Am. Assn. U. Women, Am. Assn. U. Profs., League Women Voters, Cooperstown Art Assn., Upper Catskill Council on Arts (sec.). Home: 32 Main St Otego NY 13825 Office: Hartwick Coll Oneonta NY 13820

GRIFFITHS, ANITA NETHKEN (MRS. JAMES T. GRIFFITHS), ednl. counselor; b. Des Moines, Nov. 17; d. Harley Joseph and Gwendolyn Maude (Taylor) Nethken; B.S., La. Inst. Tech., 1937; M.S., Ia. State U., 1939; Ed.D., U. Fla., 1966; m. James Thompson Griffiths, Sept. 7, 1939; children—Kenneth Alan, Roger Dale. Prof. psychology Polk Jr. Coll., Winter Haven, Fla., 1966-67; asso. prof. edn. U. South Fla., Tampa, 1967-68; ednl. psychologist Byron Harless & Assos., Tampa, 1968-69; pvt. practice ednl. counseling, Lakeland, Fla., 1969—. Bd. dirs. Polk County Asso. Children with Learning Disabilities. Mem. Am., Fla., So. psychol. assns., Fla. Assn. Sch. Psychologists, Nat. Assn. for Children with Learning Disabilities, Am. Personnel and Guidance Assn. Contbr. articles to profl. jours. Home: Route 1 Box 655 West Lake Eloise Terrace Winter Haven FL 33880 Office: PO Box 230 Lakeland FL 33802

GRIFFITHS, MARTHA W., lawyer, congresswoman; b. Pierce City, Mo.; d. Charles Elbridge and Nelle (Sullinger) Wright; A.B., U. Mo., 1934; LL.B., U. Mich., 1940; hon. degrees Eastern Mich. U., 1963, Mercy Coll., 1966, Mich. State U., 1966, Wilson Coll., 1971, Hood Coll., 1972, Queens Coll., 1972, Keuka Coll., 1972, No. Mich. U., 1973, Schoolcraft Coll., 1973, Cedar Crest Coll., 1973; m. Hicks G. Griffiths. Admitted to Mich. bar, 1941; contract negotiator Detroit Ordnance Dist., 1942-46; mem. Griffiths & Griffiths, Detroit, 1946—; judge, recorder Recorder's Ct., City of Detroit, 1953; mem. 84th to 93d congresses, 17th Dist. Mich., mem. joint econ. com., house coms. ways and means. Mem. Detroit City Election Commn., 1953; mem. Mich. Ho. of Reps., 1949-52. Am. del. Interparliamentary Union Council Meeting, Rome, Italy, 1962. Named Outstanding Congresswoman of Yr., Central Bus. Dist. Detroit, 1962; Woman of Yr., Soroptimist Club, Detroit, 1962, Woman of Year in Pub. Affairs, Ladies Home Jour., 1974. Office: Longworth Office Bldg Washington DC 20515 also 26547 Grand River Detroit MI 48240

GRIGG, MARY MONICA IRIMESCU (MRS. EMANUEL R.N. GRIGG), psychiatrist; b. Bucharest, Rumania; d. Stefan and Elena (Gutulescu) Irimescu; M.D., U. Bucharest, 1947; m. Emanuel R.N. Grigg, Dec. 15, 1946; children—Steven A., Madeleine M., Richard A., Sandra L., Susan K., Louise J., Charles L., John J., Peter A. Came to U.S., 1949, naturalized, 1954. Intern Women and Children's Hosp., Chgo., 1952-53; staff physician Kankakee (Ill.) State Hosp., 1953-58; staff physician Chgo.-Read Mental Health Center, 1968-70; resident Dept. psychiatry Loyola U. Med. Center, Maywood, Ill., 1970-73, now mem. staff; psychiatrist Mercyville Hosp., Aurora, Ill., 1973—. Diplomate Am. Bd. Psychiatry. Club: Oak Park. Home: Box 2038 Oak Park IL 60303 Office: Suite 220 Oakbrook Professional Bldg Oak Brook IL 60521

GRIGG, VIRGINIA CAFFEE (MRS. CHARLES MEADE GRIGG), librarian; b. Balt., Mar. 5, 1924; d. John Staub and Ruth Mary (Kellogg) Caffee; A.B., Randolph-Macon Womans Coll., 1945; B.L.S., U. N.C., 1949; m. Charles Meade Grigg, Aug. 23, 1947; children—Charles Meade, John, Joseph, Ruth. Instr., U. N.C., Chapel Hill, 1949-50, librarian Sociol. City and Regional Planning Library, 1949-50; librarian Tochwotten br. Providence Pub. Library, 1953-55; asst. librarian Leon County Pub. Library, Tallahassee, 1955-59; instr. Fla. State U. Library Sch., 1960-63; pub. library cons., bur. chief Fla. State Library, Tallahassee, 1963-70, acting state library dir., 1972, chief Bur. Library Devel., 1972—. Cons., Asso. Consultants in Edn., Inc., 1971. Mem. A.L.A., Southeastern, Fla. library assns., P.T.A., Eastern Shore Hist. Soc., LeMoyne Art Found., Pi Beta Phi. Democrat. Presbyn. Club: Tallahassee Woman's. Home: 2500

Harriman Circle Tallahassee FL 32303 Office: Florida State Library Supreme Court Bldg Tallahassee FL 32304

GRIGGS, MARY LEA FISKEN (MRS. EVERETT G. GRIGGS II), conservationist; b. Seattle, May 27, 1901; d. Archibald James and Mary (Gazzam) Fisken; student U. Wash., 1919-20; m. Everett G. Griggs II, July 8, 1922; children—Mary Lea (Mrs. Edward H. Morgan), Nancy Elizabeth Daugherty, Everett G. III. Pres., Tomolla Tree Farm, Inc. Conservation cons. to schs., 1945-60. Past pres. Tacoma Philharmonic Orchestra. Bd. dirs. Natural Resources Forum, Wash.; hon. trustee Keep Wash. Green. Mem. Soc. Am. Foresters (hon.), Colonial Dames of Am., Jr. League Tacoma (past pres.), U. Wash. Coll. Forestry Alumni Assn. (hon.). Clubs: Tacoma Country and Golf; Sunset, Seattle Garden (hon.); Tacoma Garden; Garden of America. Home: 22340 Jansky Rd E Graham WA 98338

GRIGGS, RUTH MARIE PRICE (MRS. PAUL PHILIP GRIGGS), educator; b. Linton, Ind., Aug. 11, 1911; d. Roy Evans and Mary Blanche (Hays) Price; B.S., Butler U., 1933; postgrad. U. So. Cal., 1938, Northwestern U., 1939; M.A., U. Wyo., 1944; postgrad. (Newspaper Fund fellow) U. Minn., 1967; m. Paul Philip Griggs, Aug. 4, 1940. Tchr., Warren Central High Sch., Indpls., 1934-37, Howe High Sch., Indpls., 1938-46; faculty Butler U., Indpls., 1947; tchr. journalism, dir. publs. Broad Ripple High Sch., Indpls., 1948—. Instr. journalism, evening div. Butler U., Indpls., 1972—. Recipient award Freedoms Found., 1955, 73, gold key Columbia U., 1964, nat. award Journalism Edn. Assn., 1965, Ind. Journalism Tchr. of Yr. award Ind. High Sch. Press Assn., 1965, Ind. Scholastic Journalism award Ball State U., 1967, Nat. Journalism Tchr. of Yr. award Wall St. Jour., 1968, Pioneer award Nat. Scholastic Press Assn., 1970; named Outstanding Woman Journalism in Ind., Women in Communications, 1969. Mem. Women in Communications (nat. exec. sec. 1938-40, Indpls. pres. 1970), N.E.A., Ind. Tchrs. Assn., Journalism Edn. Assn. (2d v.p. 1963-65), nat. pres. 1967-69), Ind. High Sch. Press Assn. (state pres. 1972), Columbia Scholastic Advisers Assn., Delta Zeta, Kappa Delta Pi, Kappa Tau Alpha, Tau Kappa Alpha, Phi Kappa Phi. Author: (with J. Gable, K. Keilman) Handbook for High School Journalism, 1957; (with others) A Teacher's Guide to High School Journalism, 1965. Home: 6055 Crestview Dr Indianapolis IN 46220 Office: 1115 Broad Ripple Av Indianapolis IN 46220

GRIGORIADIS, MARY (MRS. MICHAEL D. GRIGORIADIS), artist; b. Jersey City, June 23, 1942; d. George and Anna (Peliotis) Livitsanos; B.A., Barnard Coll., 1963; M.A., Columbia, 1965; m. Michael D. Grigoriadis, July 25, 1965; 1 dau., Vanessa Maia. One woman shows A.I.R. Gallery, N.Y.C., 1972; exhibited in group shows Internat. House Columbia, 1965, IBM, White Plains N.Y., 1966, Goddard-Riverside Community Center, N.Y.C., 1971, A.M. Sachs Gallery, N.Y.C., 1971, Lerner-Misrachi Gallery, N.Y.C., 1972, Whitney Mus., 1973, Am. Acad. Arts and Letters, 1974, Mus. of Phila. Civic Center, 1974; represented in permanent collection Chase Manhattan Bank, N.Y.C. Founding mem. A.I.R. woman's gallery, N.Y.C., 1972—; sec., asst. to curator Guggenheim Mus., N.Y.C., 1965-66; lectr. Madison (Wis.) Art Center, 1967; lectr. art, N.Y.C., 1970-73. Home: 382 Central Park West 20P New York City NY 10025

GRIGSBY, MARGARET ELIZABETH, physician; b. Prairie View, Tex., Jan. 16, 1923; d. John Richard and Lee (Hankins) Grigsby; B.S., Prairie View State Coll., 1943; M.D., U. Mich., 1948. Intern Homer G. Phillips Hosp., St. Louis, 1948-49, asst. resident medicine, 1949-50; asst. resident Freedmen's Hosp., Washington, 1950-51, asst. physician, 1952-56, attending physician, 1956; pvt. practice, 1953-54, cons. practice, 1952—; instr. medicine Howard U., 1952-57, asst. prof., 1957-60, asso. prof., 1960-66, prof., 1966—, also chief of infectious diseases, sect. of internal med., 1952-71, lectr. Sch. Social Work 1955-59, administrv. asst. dept. medicine, 1961-63; epidemiologist USPHS, Ibadan, Nigeria, 1966-68; hon. vis. prof. preventive and social medicine U. Ibadan; cons. AID, U.S. Dept. State, 1970-71; mem. adv. com. Anti-Infective Agts., FDA, 1970-72. Rockefeller Found. fellow Harvard Med. Sch., research Thorndike Meml. Lab. infectious diseases Boston City Hosp., 1951-52; China Med. Bd. fellow tropical medicine U. P.R., 1956; Commonwealth Fund fellow U. London 1962-63; diploma in tropical medicine and hygiene, London. Diplomate Nat. Bd. Med. Examiners, Am. Bd. Internal Medicine. Asian flu adv. com. D.C., 1957, 58, 59. Fellow A.C.P.; mem. A.M.A., Nat. Med. Assn., Med. Soc. D.C., Am. Assn. U. Profs., Royal, Am. socs. tropical med. and hygiene, Am. Pub. Health Assn., Medico-Chirur. Soc. D.C., Assn. Former Interns and Residents of Freedman's Hosp., Bus. and Profl. Women's Club, Pasteur Med. Reading Club, Prairie View Alumni, Sigma Xi, Alpha Epsilon Iota, Alpha Kappa Mu, Alpha Kappa Alpha. Contbr. articles to med. jours. Home: 3256 Chestnut St NW Washington DC 20015 Office: Howard U Washington DC 20001

GRILLO, JOANN, mezzo soprano; b. Bklyn., May 14, 1939; d. John D. and Lucile (DePierre) Grillo; student Hunter Coll., 1957-59, N.Y. Coll. Music, Am. Acad. Dramatic Arts; studied voice with Marinka Gurewich, Kathryn Long courses Met. Opera; m. Anthony Correra, Aug. 8, 1965; m. 2d, Richard Kness, July 1967; 1 son, John. Appeared in Aida, Madame Butterfly, N.Y. City Opera, 1962; made European debut in Werther at Gran Teatro Liceo, Barcelona, 1963; appeared in Carmen with Paris Opera Teatro San Carlo, Naples, as Ammeris in Aida at Zurich Stadttheatre, Bellas Artes of Mexico City, 1963, Israel Nat. Opera, Opera of Marseille, 1964, as Charlotte in Werther at Paris Opera Comique, 1971, as Carmen with Teatro Liceo, Barcelona, Spain, 1973; made debut with Met. Opera, N.Y.C., 1963, resident artist, 1963—; toured U.S. for Civic Concert Orgn., 1959, 61; presented concerts in Europe, Latin Am. Roman Catholic; guest artist operas of Hamburg, Dusseldorf, Geneva, Frankfurt, 1967—. Home: 1550 75th St Brooklyn NY 10028 Office: Met Opera Assn New York City NY 10018

GRIMES, DOREEN, educator; b. Weatherford, Tex., Feb. 1, 1932; d. Clarence Milton and Berta Stevens (Keaton) Grimes; Mus.B., So. Methodist U., 1951, Mus.M., 1952; Ph.D., North Tex. State U., 1961. Dir. Grimes Sch. Music, Weatherford, Tex., 1952-62; chmn. theory dept. Eastern N.M. U., 1962-71; prof., coordinator music Angelo State U., San Angelo, Tex., 1971—. Theory cons. N.M. Music Tchrs. Assn., 1967—. Precinct sec. Democratic party, 1970-71. Recipient 1st place N.M. Fedn. Women's Clubs Lit. Contest, 1971. Mem. Music Tchrs. Nat. Assn., Music Educators Nat. Conf., Tex. Music Educators Assn., Tex. Music Tchrs. Assn., Tex. Fedn. Music Clubs (pres. Dist. 11), Phi Kappa Phi, Sigma Alpha Iota. Composer: numerous compositions including A Day in the Country (piano), 1956; The Canyon (choir), 1962; Piece for 2 Pianos, 1972; (opera) Drugstore Panorama, 1971. Research in electronic music, using computers with music. Home: 3202 Lindenwood Dr San Angelo TX 76901

GRIMES, EVA MARIE SCHIFFER (MRS. HUBERT N. GRIMES), radiologist; b. Budapest, Hungary; d. Ernest and Elizabeth (Tornai) Schiffer; student U. Budapest, 1952-56; M.D., Northwestern U., 1959; m. Hubert N. Grimes, Dec. 27, 1966; children—John Floyd, Matthew Ernest. Came to U.S., 1956, naturalized, 1962. Intern, Passavant Meml. Hosp., Chgo., 1959-60; radiology resident Mayo Clinic, Rochester, Minn., 1960-63; practice medicine specializing in radiology, Oakland, Cal., 1963-64, Indpls., 1964—; mem. staff Methodist, Winona Meml. hosps. (both Indpls.). Mem. A.M.A., Ind. Med. Assn., Marion County Med. Soc., Northwestern U. Med. Alumni Assn., Mayo Alumni Assn. Home: 6001 Buckskin Circle Indianapolis IN 46250

GRIMES, KAREN LESLIE, educator; b. York, Pa., July 24, 1951; d. Samuel and Delores Jeanette (Myers) Grimes; B.A., Lincoln U., 1973; postgrad. Tufts U., 1973—. Arts and crafts dir., tchr. arts and crafts, supr. York (Pa.) Recreation Commn., summers 1971—. Mem. Nat. Council of Negro Women, Am. Ednl. Theatre Assn., Alpha Chi, Alpha Kappa Alpha. Home: 2504 Joppa Rd York PA 17403

GRIMES, MARY CATHERINE, former nursing orgn. exec.; b. N.Y.C.; d. Patrick A. and Mary (Foley) Grimes; R.N., Manhattan State Hosp. Sch. Nursing, 1937; B.S., N.Y. U., 1947, M.A., 1948. Charge nurse Coney Island Hosp., Bklyn., 1938-40; teaching supr. Fordham Hosp. Sch. Nursing, Bronx, N.Y., 1941-42; commd. ensign USN, 1942, advanced through grades to comdr., 1965; charge nurse U.S. Naval Hosp., Charleston, S.C., 1942-43; instr. Hosp. Corps Sch., Bainbridge, Md., 1943-44; flight nurse Air Evacuation VRE-Squadron, Pacific, 1945, VR-1 Squadron Naval Air Sta., Patuxent River, Md., 1948-52; liaison officer Sch. Aviation Medicine, Randolph Field, Tex., Gunter AFB, Montgomery, Ala., surg. supr. St. Albans Naval Hosp., 1953; instr. Sch. Aviation Medicine, Pensacola, Fla., 1954; ednl. coordinator U.S. Naval Hosp., Bethesda, Md., asst. chief nursing service, 1955-58; chief nursing service U.S. Naval Hosp., Annapolis, Md., 1958-59; head Nurse Corps Res. liaison br. Nursing Div., Bur. Medicine and Surgery, Navy Dept., Washington, 1959-65; ret., 1965; dir. dept. practical nursing programs Nat. League Nursing, N.Y.C., 1965-68, dir. hosp. and related instnl. nursing services, 1968-70. Decorated various theatre medals; recipient certificate of merit for distinguished and outstanding service to Med. Dept. Navy, 1965. Mem. D.C. (past 1st v.p.) Nurses Assn., Assn. Mil. Surgeons (1st chmn. Nurse Corps sect.), Aerospace Med. Assn. (v.p. 1969), A.A.A.S., N.Y.U. Sch. Edn. Alumni, Kappa Delta Pi, Pi Lambda Theta. Address: 180 Cabrini Blvd New York City NY 10033

GRIMM, DOROTHY JEAN, librarian; b. Milw., July 12, 1917; d. Edward Wesley and Mary (Hume) Burgess; student Milw. Downer Coll., 1934-36, Milw. State Tchrs. Coll., 1936-37; Ph.B., Marquette U., 1939; B.S. in L.S., Western Res. U., 1944; m. Egon Grimm, Jan. 11, 1941 (dec. 1953); children—Catherine, Virginia (Mrs. John Robert Potter). Clk. librarian South Division High Sch., Milw., 1939-42; library asst. Milw. Pub. Library, 1942-44, reference librarian, 1944-45; mem. staff San Diego Pub. Library (Cal.), 1954—, librarian, 1959, sr. librarian, 1959—. Mem. Am. Civil Liberites Union, Cal., Am. library assns., Mission Bay Bus and Profl. Woman's Club (sec. 1973-74), Common Cause. Home: 1675 Law St San Diego CA 92109 Office: 820 E St San Diego CA 92101

GRIMSLEY, EDITH ELLINGTON (MRS. CHRISSIE G. GRIMSLEY, JR.), educator; b. nr. Danville, Ga., Aug. 24, 1929; d D. Elmer and Ethel (Gray) Ellington; B.S., Ga. State Coll. for Women, 1952; M.A., Columbia, 1959, Ed.D., 1968; m. Chrissie G. Grimsley, Jr., June 25, 1949. Tchr., Putnam County Schs., Eatonton, Ga., 1948-49; tchr. Twiggs County Schs., Danville, Ga., 1949-54; tchr. Bibb County Schs., Macon, Ga., 1954-63, curriculum dir., 1963-66, coordinator elementary curriculum, 1967-68; asst. prof. Coll. Edn., U. Ga., Athens, 1968-73, asso. prof., 1973—. Vis. prof. Mercer U., Macon, summers 1965-66. Recipient McKibben Lane award for excellence in teaching, 1963. World Book Ency. Gen. fellow in Tchrs. Coll., 1966. Mem. Assn. for Supervision and Curriculum Devel. (nat. dir.), Ga. Assn. Curriculum and Instructional Supervision (pres.), Nat. Council Tchrs. Math., Kappa Delta Pi, Delta Kappa Gamma. Home: 6 S Stratford Dr Athens GA 30601

GRINDLE, EVELYN STAPLES, clergywoman; b. Penobscot, Me., Mar. 13, 1912; d. George Medbury and Lizzie (Berry) Staples; student Normal Sch., Machias, Me., summer 1929, Meth. Conf. Theol. Corr. Courses, 1944-51; m. Shirley Harold Grindle, Aug. 22, 1931 (dec. Dec. 1958); children—Ivan Terrance, Judith Sandra. Tchr. pub. schs., Warren, Me., 1929-30, Verona, Me., 1930-31; ordained to ministry Meth. Ch. as deacon, 1949, as elder, 1951; pastor South Penobscot (Me.) Meth. Ch., 1944-49, West Penobscot, 1944-54, North Brooksville, 1949-50, Penobscot, 1946-48, North Penobscot, 1952-58, Trenton (Me.) Union Ch., 1955-56, Surry and Ellsworth Ch., 1954-61, Winterport and Ellingwood Corner chs., 1961-65, Wayne Community Ch., N. Wayne United Meth. Ch., 1965-70, Wilton United Meth. Ch., 1970—. Pres. Women Ministers Me. Meth. Conf., 1956. Mem. Internat., Am. (corr. sec. 1966-67), N.E. (pres. 1956-58) assns. Women ministers, Grange. Home: 88 Depot St Wilton ME 04294

GRINELL, SHEILA, mus. dir.; b. N.Y.C., July 15, 1945; d. Richard and Martha (Mimiless) Grinell; B.A., Harvard, 1966; M.A., U. Cal. at Berkeley, 1968. Co-dir. exhibits and programs The Exploratorium, San Francisco, 1970—. Cons. Illusions exhbn. Inst. Contemporary Arts, London, Eng., 1973—; Fulbright teaching asst., 1966-67. Hon. Woodrow Wilson fellow, 1967-68. Home: 2539 Polk St San Francisco CA 94109 Office: 3601 Lyon St San Francisco CA 94123

GRIPALDI, PAULINE P. BENNETT (MRS. BENEDICT VICTOR GRIPALDI), educator; b. Danbury, Conn.; d. Chauncey and Clara (Beacon) Bennett; student, Rutgers U., 1956-58; m. Benedict Victor Gripaldi, Jan. 27, 1952; 1 son, Peter. Training supr. Brass Rail Restaurant, Inc., N.Y.C., 1947-52; beauty operator, Newark, 1952-54; instr. Park Beauty Sch., Newark, 1954-56, supr., 1956-70; tng. coordinator Wilfred Beauty Schs., N.Y., N.J., Conn., 1970-72; staff asst. Nat. Assn. Cosmetology Schs., 1972—. Cons., Milady Pub. Co. Pres., Nat. Tchrs. Ednl. Council, 1966-68. Editor: Cosmetology Instr., 1966—. Home: 9 Carteret Rd Livingston NJ 07039 Office: 599 S Livingston Av Livingston NJ 07039

GRISHAM, EDITH PEARL MOLES, librarian; b. Pinch, W.Va., Mar. 27, 1926; d. Lawrence Edward and Effie (Christy) Moles; A.A., San Antonio Coll., 1958; B.B.A. cum laude, St. Marys U., 1961; postgrad. Our Lady of Lake U., 1964; M.L.S., Tex. Womans U., 1973. Billing and sales service asst. Uvalde Rock Asphalt Co., San Antonio, 1953-62; office mgr. Data Processing Center, Inc., San Antonio, 1962-64; serials librarian Houston Pub. Library, 1964-65; head lit. and biography dept., 1966-68, head bus. and tech. dept., 1968-73; head tech. library engring. div. Brown & Root, Inc., Houston, 1973—. Served with USAAF, 1944-53. Mem. Am., Tex., Southwestern, Spl. library assns., Kappa Pi Sigma, Alpha Beta Alpha. Club: Houston Library. Home: 3219 Rice Blvd Houston TX 77005 Office: PO Box 3 Houston TX 77001

GRISHMAN, EDITH P., physician; b. Berlin, Germany, May 5, 1914; d. S. and Alice (Maass) Peltesohn; student U. Berlin, 1932-36, U. Leipzig, 1936-37; M.D., U. Leipzig, 1937; m. Arthur Grishman, Jan. 12, 1939; children—Peter, Ralph. Came to U.S., 1939, naturalized, 1944. Intern, Berlin, 1938; practice medicine, specializing in pathology, Mt. Sinai Hosp., N.Y.C., 1940-45; asso. pathologist City Hosp., Elmhurst, N.Y.; asst. prof. pathology Mt. Sinai Med. Sch., N.Y.C., 1966—. Fellwo Am. Coll. Pathologists; mem. Am. Assn. Pathology and Bacteriology, N.Y. County, N.Y. State med. socs. Home: 322 Central Park W New York City NY 10025

GRISSOM, KATHY RENE, psychiat. social worker; b. Russellville, Ala., Feb. 16, 1948; d. Edison Ford and Carrie Viola (Duncan) Grissom; B.A., Samford U., 1970; M.A., U. Ala., 1971. Counselor Samford U., Birmingham, Ala., 1968-70; counselor U. Ala., Tuscaloosa, 1970-72; psychiat. social worker Bryce State Mental Hosp., Tuscaloosa, 1972—. Mem. Nat. Assn. Women Deans, Adminstrs. and Counselors, Ala. Assn. Women Deans, Adminstrs. and Counselors, Phi Gamma Mu. Home: 1514 10th St Apt 6-A Tuscaloosa AL 35401 Office: Bryce Hosp Tuscaloosa AL 35401

GRISWOLD, JULIA HUEY (MRS. EMMETT O'NEAL GRISWOLD), lawyer, state ofcl.; b. New Brockton, Ala., July 8, 1917; d. Walton Sellers and Katie Mae (Rowe) Huey; tchrs. certificate Troy State U., 1958; A.B., U. Ala., 1939, LL.B., 1941, J.D., 1972; m. Emmett O'Neal Griswold, Nov. 28, 1935 (dec. Mar. 1957); children—Kathryn Hope (Mrs. William L. Lambert), Emmett O'Neal, Nita Huey. Admitted to Ala. bar, 1941; partner Griswold & Griswold Attys., Enterprise, Ala., 1941-42; ins. dept. clk. Tenn.-Eastman Corp., Kingsport, Tenn., 1942-44; tchr. social studies Daleville (Ala.) Jr. High Sch., 1958-59; asst. atty. gen. Ala. Dept. Pensions and Security, Montgomery, 1961-63, Hwy. Dept., 1963—. Mem. Ala. Bar., Ala. Fedn. Women's Clubs (dir. 1948-50, mem. exec. bd. 1948-50), Colonial Dames XVII Centry. Methodist. Clubs: Twentieth Century Chautaugua, Pierian (Enterprise). Home: 714 W Lee St Enterprise AL 36330 Office: 11 S Union St Montgomery AL 36104

GRISWOLD, MARY BROOKS (MRS. A. WHITNEY GRISWOLD), state legislator; b. Scranton, Pa., June 11, 1906; d. John H. and Augusta (Archbald) Brooks; B.A., Smith Coll., 1928; m. A. Whitney Griswold, June 10, 1930 (dec.); children—Sarah (Mrs. R.G. Leahy), Mary (Mrs. J.O. Flender), Susanna W., A. Whitney. Mem. Conn. Ho. of Reps., 1967—. Dir., Conn. Savs. Bank. Del. Conn. Constl. Conv., 1965. Trustee, Quinnipiac Coll. Democrat. Address: 280 Livingston St New Haven CT 06511

GRIVICICH, DONNA JAMISON BOUDREAU, psychologist, educator; b. Antigo, Wis., June 8, 1921; d. Emil Joeseph and Alice Mae (Atkins) Boudreau; B.A., Drew U., 1954; M.A., Tchrs. Coll., Columbia, 1957; teaching certificate Newark State Tchrs. Coll., 1958; postgrad. Rutgers U., 1958-60; m. Robert John Grivicich, Feb. 14, 1965; children from previous marriage—Judith Jamison (Mrs. Robert B. Haig), Elaine Jamison (Mrs. Paul Timler), Carl Timler, Erin Ullery. Tchr. elementary schs., New Vernon, N.J., 1954-60; asst. prof. Newark State Coll., 1960-64; tng. officer, counselor Ojibway Job Corps, Marenisco, Mich., 1965-68; asst. prof. psychology Gogebic Community Coll., Ironwood, Mich., 1969—. Bd. dirs. N.J. Urban League, 1958-60, Nat. council YMCA, 1954-56. Mem. Am. Psychol. Assn., Am. Assn. U. Profs., N.A.A.C.P. (past dir. N.J.), Kappa Delta Pi, Pi Lambda Theta. Home: Box 80 Marenisco MI 49947 Office: Gogebic Community College Ironwood MI 49938

GRIZZLE, MARY R. (MRS. BEN F. GRIZZLE), state legislator; b. Lawrence County, O., Aug. 19, 1921; ed. Portsmouth Interstate Bus. Coll.; m. Ben F. Grizzle; children—Henry, Polley, Lorena, Mary Alice, Betty, Jeanne. Mem. Fla. Ho. of Reps., 1963—, mem. coms. on bus. regulation, environmental protection, appropriations. Chmn. Fla. Commn. on Status of Women; govt. rep. Nat. Conf. Women Community Leaders for Hwy. Safety; active P.T.A.; mem. Pinellas County (Fla.) Civil Service Com., Pinellas County Planning Com. Former town commr.; Republican precinct committeewoman; past pres. Women's Rep. Com. Named One of Ten Outstanding Women, St. Petersburg Times, 1966. Mem. League Women Voters, Largo Bus. and Profl. Womens Club, Altrusa, Woman's Club, Nat. Soc. Arts and Letters. Episcopalian. Author: (with others) Thimbleful of History. Home: 120 Gulf Blvd Belleair Shore Indian Rocks Beach FL 33535 Office: Room 505 Coachman Bldg 503 Cleveland St Clearwater FL 33515

GROCH, JUDITH GOLDSTEIN (MRS. WILBERT MINOWITZ), author, editor; b. N.Y.C., May 14, 1929; d. Eli and Caroline (Kleppner) Goldstein; student Vassar Coll., 1946-48; B.S. cum laude, Columbia, 1952; m. Sigmund Noel Groch, May 31, 1953 (dec. Nov. 1961); m. 2d, Wilbert Minowitz, Oct. 6, 1962; children—Deborah, Emily; 1 stepson, Peter. Asso. editor Med. World News, 1973—. Recipient Nat. Mass Media award Thomas Alva Edison Found., 1963. Mem. Phi Beta Kappa. Author: You and Your Brain, 1963; The Right to Create, 1969. Home: 168 W 86th St New York City NY 10024

GRODECOEUR, FRANCES LOUISE, ednl. adminstr.; b. Monongahela, Pa., Dec. 7, 1916; d. Louis Aristide and Marjorie Douglas (Geekie) Grodecoeur; B.A., Coll. of William and Mary, 1939. Head sales, stock, book dept. Joseph Horne Co., Pitts., 1939-44; asst. librarian U.S. Steel Corp., Pitts., 1944-47; interviewer, asst. employment mgr. Joseph Horne Co., 1947-49, employee services mgr., asst. personnel dir., 1949-63; asso. dir. coll. admissions Carnegie Mellon U., Pitts., 1963-74, asst. dir. estate planning, 1974—. Mem. Western Pa. Women Deans, Counselors and Personnel Workers, Nat. Assn. for Women Deans, Adminstrs. and Counselors, Pa. Assn. Women Deans and Counselors, Am. Coll. Pub. Relations Assn., Alpha Chi Omega. Presbyn. Home: 810 Howard St Monongahela PA 15063 Office: Carnegie Mellon U 5000 Forbes Av Pittsburgh PA 15213

GRODINS, SYLVIA VIOLA JOHNSON (MRS. FRED S. GRODINS), interior designer; b. DeKalb, Ill., May 7, 1916; d. Andrew and Henrika (Anderson) Johnson; student No. U., 1934-35; grad. Augustana Sch. Nursing, 1939; grad. N.Y. Sch. Interior Design, 1954; m. Fred S. Grodins, Mar. 28, 1942. Pvt. duty nursing, Chgo. hosps., 1939-41; interior designer Pond's Interiors, Evanston, 1948-56, Interior Design, Inc., Chgo., 1956-58; owner Creative Studio, Chgo., 1958—. Mem. Alumnae Assn. Augustana Hosp. Sch. Nursing, Am. Inst. Interior Designers, Soc. Archtl. Historians. Home: 26 Chuckwagon Rd Rolling Hills CA 90274 Office: 200 E Walton Av Chicago IL 60611 also 2325 Palos Verdes Dr W Palos Verdes Estates CA 90274

GRODMAN, PYRRHA GLADYS, physician; b. State Line, Miss., Sept. 27, 1918; d. Bennett Desiderius and Rosalind Jeanne (Jackson) Grodman; student Bklyn. Coll., 1932; B.A., L.I. U., 1936; postgrad. Columbia, 1943-47; B.S., N.Y. U., 1944, M.A., 1946; M.D., Woman's Med. Coll. Pa., 1948. Research biochemist Richard Morton Koster Research Labs., N.Y.C., 1940-43; editorial asso. Bklyn. Med. Press, N.Y. Sci. Press, Exptl. Medicine and Surgery, 1941-48; intern Cumberland Hosp., Bklyn., 1948-49, surg. resident, 1949-50; surg. resident Norfolk (Va.) Gen. Hosp., 1951-52; path. resident Providence Hosp., Portland, Ore., 1955-57, St. Joseph's Infirmary, Atlanta, 1958-59; physician, surgeon Bur. Indian Affairs, U.S. Interior Dept., 1950-51; mining surgeon, physician Phelps Dodge Corp., Clifton and Morenci, Ariz., 1952-55; instr. U. Ore. Med. and Dental Sch., Portland, 1955-57, Emory U. Med., Dental schs., Atlanta, 1958-65; dir. Med. Diagnostic and Research Labs., Atlanta, pathologist various hosps. in Ga. and Tenn., 1958-65, in La., Ark., Miss., 1965—; dir. Monroe (La.) Med. Diagnostic Labs., 1965—. Bd. dirs. Monroe chpt. Am. Cancer Soc. Fellow Am. Cancer Soc., 1959-60. Fellow Coll. Am. Pathologists, Am. Soc. Clin. Pathologists,

A.C.P., Royal Soc. Physicians (London), Royal Soc. Health (London); mem. Monroe C. of C., Dallas Art Mus., Masur Mus. Art, Atheneum, N.Y. Acad. Scis., Am. Mus. Natural History, Air-Medics Assn., Am. Cytological Soc., Pan Am. Med. Assn., Am., Internat. med. women's assns., A.M.A., So. Med. Assn., La. Soc. Pathologists, Am. Geriatrics Soc. (founding fellow So. div.), Smithsonian Inst., Internat. Oceanographic Inst., Internat. Platform Assn., Audubon Soc., Am. Forestry Assn. Home: PO Box 853 Monroe LA 71201 Office: PO Box 1913 Monroe LA 71201

GRODSKY, LILLIAN SCHWARTZ (MRS. JOSEPH GRODSKY), psychiat. social worker; b. N.Y.C.; d. Samuel and Pauline (Danziger) Schwartz; B.S. Rutgers U., 1960, M.S.W., 1964; m. Joseph Grodsky, Sept. 5, 1943; children—Robert Joel, Gilbert Alan. Social worker N.J. Bur. Childrens Services, New Brunswick, N.J., 1961-65; chief psychiat. social worker Raritan Bay Mental Health Center, Perth Amboy, N.J., 1965—; pvt. practice psychotherapy, Somerville, N.J., 1967—. Mem. Nat. Assn. Social Workers, (chmn. N.J. chpt. inst. 1970-73), Am. Group Psychotherapy Assn., Nat. Psychol. Assn. for Psychoanalysis, Am. Assn. Marriage and Family Counselors. Home: 92 Green St Somerville NJ 08876 Office: 1 E High St Somerville NJ 08876

GROEGER, ELFRIEDE MARIA, psychiatrist; b. Vienna, Austria, Sept. 11, 1934; d. Hofrat Johann and Erika Karoline (Huss) Korber; student U. Vienna (Austria), 1953-59; physician diploma U. Basle (Switzerland), 1963, M.D., 1965; m. Theodor O. Groeger, Apr. 22, 1957; children—Theodor C., Alexander M. Came to U.S., 1965, naturalized, 1972. Intern St. Barnabas Med. Center, Livingston, N.J., 1966; resident N.J. State Hosp., Greystonepark, 1967-70, psychiatrist, 1970-72; psychiatrist Essex County Guidance Center, East Orange, N.J., 1970—; asst. psychiatrist St. Michael's Med. Center, East Orange, N.J. Mem. A.M.A., N.J., Essex County med. assns. Address: 2 Collamore Circle West Orange NJ 07052 also St Michael's Medical Center East Orange NJ

GROESBECK, DOROTHY GRIFFIN (MRS. ARTHUR J. GROESBECK, JR.), civic worker; b. Marysville, Kan., July 29, 1916; d. Walter T. and Nelle (Williams) Griffin; student Washburn U., 1934-35; m. Arthur J. Groesbeck, Jr., Feb. 13, 1937; children—Arthur J. III, Douglas G., Alan W., Deborah. Vol., Meml. Hosp., 1957-66; pres. Manhattan Area (Kan.) P.T.A. Council, 1960, Manhattan elementary, jr. and sr. high sch. P.T.A.'s, 1956-59; women's chmn. United Fund, 1960; pres. Manhattan Library Bd., 1956-61; pres. Manhattan Bd. Edn., 1961-69; mem. Kan. Bd. Edn., 1969—; hon. life mem. P.T.A. Precinct Republican committeewoman 1954-70; vice chmn. Riley County Rep. Com., 1958-70; vice chmn. 2d Dist. Rep. Com. 1966-72. Mem. P.E.O. Methodist. Home: 3100 Arbor Dr Manhattan KS 66502

GROEZINGER, CATHARINE HOMANS CONNER (MRS. THEODORE GROEZINGER), physician; b. San Francisco, Apr. 27, 1917; d. Robert Leonard and Margaretta Gladys (Dambmann) Conner; student San Mateo Jr. Coll., 1933-35; A.A., San Jose State Coll., 1940; A.B., U. Cal. at Berkeley, 1942, M.D., 1944, M.P.H., 1966; m. Theodore Groezinger, Feb. 19, 1965. Intern, San Francisco County Hosp., 1944-46; physician student health service women's service, U. Cal., 1947-62; resident in pub. health Berkeley City Health Dept., 1964-65, San Francisco City and County Health Dept., 1967-68; practice medicine specializing in pub. health and preventive medicine, San Francisco; dist. med. officer San Francisco City and County Health Dept., 1968-74, physician specialist, 1974—. Mem. Nat. Safety Council, Cal. Med. Assn., Am., Cal. med. polit. action coms., A.M.A., Am., No. Cal. pub. health assns., Cal., Almeda-Contra Costa med. assns., Cal. State Employees Assn., San Francisco Heart Assn., Pub. Health League Cal., U. Cal., U. Cal. Med. Sch., U. Cal. Sch. Pub. Health alumni assns., Phi Beta Kappa, Alpha Omega Alpha. Home: 2262 27th Av San Francisco CA 94116 Office: 1351 24th Av San Francisco CA 94122

GROMMONS, JOYCE ANN STRATFORD, systems analyst; b. Louisville, Oct. 4, 1930; d. Gifford Winstanley and Bertha Catherine (Nance) Stratford; B.S., U. Wash., 1954; m. Harry Frances Grommons, Dec. 31, 1954 (div. Feb. 1963); children—Catherine Marie, Teresa Anne. Research engr. Boeing Co., Seattle, 1955-67; systems programmer U. Wash., Seattle, 1967—. Home: 3046 NE 98th St Seattle WA 98115

GRONDIN, FRANCES GRACE (MRS. J.W. GEORGES GRONDIN), broadcaster; b. Worcester, Mass., July 25, 1932; d. Joseph Anthony and Rose Ester (Belculfine) Franchi; R.N., Meml. Hosp. Sch. Nursing, 1953; student Jackson Coll. Women, 1953-54; m. J.W. Georges Grondin, Jan. 29, 1955; children—Georges, Jean-Paul, Joseph, Rosanne. Supr., Rochester (N.Y.) Gen. Hosp., 1956-58, Hotel Dieu Hosp., Moncton, N.B., Can., 1958-59; free-lance broadcaster CBC radio, Moncton, 1974—. Pres., Meals on Wheels, 1972-73, mem. adv. bd., 1973-74. Mem. adv. bd. YMCA, 1971-72, East End Boys Club, 1972-74; bd. dirs. Moncton Flying Sch., 1966-68. Mem. Can. Assn. for Children with Learning Disabilities (treas. 1971-3), Muncton Council Women (chmn. recreation 1973-74, mem. exec. bd. 1973-74), Moncton Drug Aid Assn. (exec. sec. 1971-72), Atlantic Symphony Assn. (chmn. variety show 1972), Moncton Flying Club, Mountain Ridge Golf Club, Moncton Gun Club, Can. Okners and Pilots Assn., Maritime Provinces Colt Stakes Assn., U.S. Trotting Assn. Roman Catholic. Home: 294 Westmount Blvd Moncton NB Canada

GRONER, BEVERLY ANNE (MRS. SAMUEL BRIAN GRONER), lawyer; b. Des Moines, Jan. 31, 1922; d. Benjamin L. and Annabelle B. (Miller) Zavat; student Drake U., 1939-40, Cath. U., 1954-56; J.D., Am. U., 1959; m. Samuel Brian Groner, Dec. 17, 1962; children by previous marriage—Morrilou (Mrs. Raymond Morell), Lewis Anthony Davis, Andrew G. Davis. Admitted to Md. bar, 1959, U.S. Supreme Court, 1963, D.C. bar, 1965; mem. firm Groner & Groner, Bethesda, Md., 1962—. Lectr. wills and estates Montgomery Coll., Rockville, Md., 1972-73; mem. faculty domestic relations div. Montgomery-Prince George's Continuing Legal Edn. Inst., 1974—; mem. Md. Gov.'s Commn. to Study Implementation of Equal Rights Amendment, 1974—. Fellow Am. Acad. Matrimonial Lawyers; mem. D.C. Bar (steering com. family law div. 1974—), Am., Md. (vice chmn. family law sect. 1974—), Montgomery County (chmn. com. bar liaison with domestic relations master 1974—) bar assns., Phi Alpha Delta. Home: 6710 Western Av Chevy Chase MD 20015 Office: Suite 304 Perpetual Bldg Bethesda MD 20014

GRONICK, PATRICIA ANN JACOBSEN (MRS. JOSEPH GRONICK), educator; b. Madison, S.D., May 1, 1931; d. Jay C. and Lauretta (Lynch) Jacobsen; B.S., Pa. State U., 1952; M.Ed., Kent State U., 1970; postgrad. John Carroll U., 1972—; m. Joseph Gronick, Aug. 12, 1950; 1 son, Joseph Patrick Michael. Home economist to regional home econs. dir. West Penn. Power Co., Pitts., 1952-61; nat. home econs. dir. Cleve. Range Co., 1961-70; distributive edn. coordinator for Mayfield, Richmond Heights, Orange, Bratenahli and Beachwood Sch. Systems, 1970—; cons. photog. food layouts, 1960-61. Mem. Cleve. Social Health and Welfare Assn., Am. Home Econs. Assn., Am. Assn. U. Women, Elec. Woman's Round Table, Internat. Fedn. U. Women, Cath. Daus. Am., Home Economists in Bus. Club: Woman's (rec. sec. Cleve. 1962, parliamentarian 1965-66). Home: 1126 Winston Rd Cleveland OH 44121 Office: Beachwood High Sch 25100 Fairmont Blvd Cleveland OH 44122

GROOVER, ELOISE TARPLEY (MRS. HENRY FINN GROOVER, JR.), state ofcl.; b. Leesburg, Ga., Feb. 14, 1918; d. William Edward and Annie Lou (Roberts) Tarpley; A.B., Ga. State Coll. for Women, 1939; M.A., Fla. State U., 1955; m. Henry Finn Groover, Jr., Mar. 22, 1969; 1 son (by previous marriage), John Edward Jones. Tchr., Miller County High Sch., Colquitt, Ga., 1939-52, librarian, 1952-61; instr. Fla. State U., 1961-64; library cons. Fla. Dept. Edn., Tallahassee, 1964-65, adminstr. ednl. media, 1965—. Faculty U. Ga., Albany Center, 1956-60. Mem. A.L.A., Assn. State Sch. Library Suprs. (chmn. 1964-65), Ga. Edn. Assn. (pres. library dept. 1957-59), Ga. (pres. 1958-61), Fla. (chmn. children's and young people's sect. 1966), Southeastern library assns., Fla. Assn. Sch. Librarians (exec. sec. 1964-73), Assn. for Ednl. Communications Tech., Fla. Assn. for Media in Edn., Delta Kappa Gamma, Beta Phi Mu. Home: 1711 Country Club Dr Tallahassee FL 32301 Office: Fla Dept Edn Tallahassee FL 32304

GROPPE, CHRISTINE CARLSON, nutrition specialist; b. Lincoln, Neb., Aug. 15, 1911; d. William E. and Hilda Ollie (Warner) Carlson; B.Sc. in Home Econs., U. Neb., 1932; M.Sc. in Nutrition, Mich. State U., 1940; m. Albert Groppe, Oct. 3, 1942; children—Connie (Mrs. Floyd Brumley), Lynn (Mrs. Gary Hardaway). Home demonstration agt., Neb., 1935-38; nutrition specialist Agr. Extension, Ohio State U., 1940-42; home adviser Agr. Extension Alameda County, U. Cal. at Hayward, 1952-65; nutrition specialist U. Cal. at Berkeley, 1965-71; nutrition tchr. Peace Corps, Hemet, Cal., 1969; nutrition cons. AID, El Salvador, 1971-72, Yonsei U., Seoul, Korea, 1972—. Mem. Am. Home Econs. Assn., Inst. Food Tech., Phi Upsilon Omicron, Sigma Kappa. Writer numerous bulls. on nutrition. Home: care Mrs EL Anderson 2840 Kucera Dr Lincoln NE 68502

GROSECLOSE, MARGARET ANN, home economist; b. Marion, Va., Nov. 16, 1930; d. Roy Eugene and Thelma Alice (Robinson) Groseclose; B.S., Madison Coll., 1952; M.S., U. Tenn., 1958. Home demonstration agt. Va. Poly. Inst. Extension, Tazewell County, 1952-57, Roanoke County, 1959, clothing specialist Extension div., 1960-70; asst. dir. family resources Va. Poly. Inst. and State U. Extension div., Blacksburg, 1970-74, dir. family resources, 1974—. Mem. Am., Va. home econs. assns., Va. Extension Service Assn. (pres. 1970), Am., Va. adult edn. assns., Epsilon Sigma Phi, Phi Delta Kappa. Methodist. Home: 605 Montgomery St Blacksburg VA 24060

GROSS, CAROLINE LORD (MRS. MARTIN L. GROSS), govt. ofcl.; b. Laconia, N.H., May 5, 1940; d. William Shepard and Marion (Manns) Lord; A.B., Radcliffe Coll., 1963; M.A.T., Harvard, 1964; m. Martin L. Gross, Nov. 5, 1960. Research asst. Supr. Schs., Concord, N.H., 1965-66, N.H. Legislative com. ann. sessions, Concord, 1966, N.H. Fiscal com. 1967-68; adminstrv. asst. N.H. gov., Concord, 1969-70; coordinator N.H. fed. funds, Concord, 1971-72; supr. checklist, Concord, 1969—. Mem. N.H. Commn. Status Women, 1972-75; del. N.H. Republican Conv., 1968, 70, 74; legislative policy asst. N.H. Ho. of Reps., 1974—. Trustee Concord Library, 1974—. League Women Voters, N.H. Council Better Schs. Home: 15 Rumford St Concord NH 03301 Office: Office of the Speaker State House Concord NH 03301

GROSS, LYDIA ELIZABETH, educator; b. Lock Haven, Pa.; d. Charles Edward and Susan (Ranck) Gross; student Lock Haven State Coll., 1923-25; B.S., Tchrs. Coll., Columbia, 1932, M.A., 1937; postgrad. Duke, summer 1945, Pa. State U., 1962-64. Tchr. Willimantic (Conn.) State Coll., 1935-46; faculty Lock Haven State Coll., 1946-53, prin. Campus Sch., dir. elementary edn., 1953-63, dir. elementary edn., 1963-72; prof. emerita Alaska Methodist U., Anchorage, 1972-73. Recipient Gold Key Columbia Scholastic Press Assn., 1960. Mem. Pa. Ednl. Assn., N.E.A., Am. Assn. U. Women, Nat. Soc. for Study Edn., Am. Acad. Polit. and Social Sci., Am. Assn. U. Profs., Am. Guild Organists, Assn. Childhood Edn. Internat., Delta Kappa Gamma, Phi Lambda Theta. Lutheran. Author: How a Town Grew in New England, 1964. Home: 411 Guardlock Dr Lock Haven PA 17745

GROSS, MARTHA FLORENCE, mfrs. and pubs. rep.; b. Lithuania, Jan. 31, 1902; d. Label and Chaya (Krenez) Grosbard; ed. Europe, also U.S. pub. schs. Came to U.S., 1914, naturalized, 1949. Mfrs. rep. Berkshire Traveller Press, Stockbridge, Mass., Borden Pub. Co., Alhambra, Cal., Books 'n' Things, North Hollywood, Cal., Pabst Breweries. Vol. worker Phila. Gen. Hosp., 1935-40. Mem. Women's Nat. Book Assn., Friends of Lit. Hadassah. Home: 2909 Sheridan Rd Chicago IL 60657

GROSS, MIRIAM ZELLER (MRS. RUSSELL CHARLES GROSS), writer, coll. editor; b. Hennepin, Ill., Oct. 28, 1896; d. Julius Christian and Emma Alice (Bryant) Zeller; student Coll. Puget Sound, 1912-13, U. Miss., 1913-15; A.B., Huntington Coll., 1916; M.A., U. Chgo., 1921; postgrad. Sch. Journalism Temple U., 1927-29, Robert Morris Sch. of Advt., 1930-32; m. Frank Ogden, Dec. 26, 1917 (dec. 1918); m. 2d, Russell Charles Gross Nov. 26, 1927; 1 dau., Ruth Adora (Mrs. Thomas Charles Bove). Instr. music and dramatics, Sulligent, Ala., 1917; tchr. and instr., Ala., Miss., P.I., Ohio, 1918-26; dir. pub. relations Phila. County Med. Soc. and Woman's Med. Coll. of Pa., 1928-34; dir. ethical div. White Labs, Newark, 1934-39; asst. dir. advt. and sales promotion Ethicon Suture Lab. div. Johnson & Johnson, New Brunswick, N.J., 1942-46; free lance writer, lectr., interpreting advances in med. scis., 1946-47; devel. cons. Wagner Coll., S.I., 1957—. Mem. N.Y. Acad. Sci., D.A.R., Advt. Women N.Y., Am. Coll. Pub. Relations, Soc. Mayflower Descs., Women Descs. Ancient and Honorable Order Arty. (nat. historian), Women Descs. Founders and Patriots (past pres. N.J.), Dames Court of Honor, Order Crown Charlemagne in U.S.A., Huguenot Soc. U.S., Daus. 1812 (nat. com. chmn., past pres. N.J. chpt., state rec. sec.), Descs. Colonial Clergy, Descs. Colonial Govs., Order Three Crusades 1096-1192, Order Americans Armorial Ancestry, Daus. Colonial Wars, Descs. King William I, Brit.-Am. Soc., Internat. Platform Soc. Community Club of the Oranges, Kappa Delta. Author: The Ethicon Book of Sutures, 1946; (with Hinton D. Jouez, M.D.) My Fight to conquer Multiple Sclerosis, 1952. Compiler and editor: Poems, Verses, Meditations by Julius Christian Zeller, 1945. Contbr.: Science Yearbook, 1945, 46, 47; med. articles to nat. mags. including Sat. Eve. Post, McCall's, Readers Digest. Address: 180 Walnut St Montclair NJ 07042

GROSS, PATRICIA ROBINSON (MRS. MARVIN A. GROSS), real estate, bus. financial and investment cons.; b. Balt., Aug. 25, 1933; d. Manford and Frances (Clements) Robinson; A.B., U. Miami, 1953; m. Marvin A. Gross, Dec. 26, 1960; children—Terri Lee, Michael. Trainee, Julius Garfinkle, Washington, 1947-50; exec. tng. dept. Lord & Taylors, N.Y.C., 1953-55; ready to wear buyer Farnsworth-Reed, Ltd., Washington, 1959, Allied Stores, Jordan Marsh, Fla., 1958-63; pres., treas. boutiques Lerob, Inc., also Ltd. Edits., N. Miami Beach and So. Miami, Fla., 1964-72; v.p. The Wall St. Co., Miami, 1971-74, Keyes Co., North Miami Beach, 1974—. Guest instr. local colls.; guest author local fashion and news publns. Active various community drives; v.p. Greater Miami Jewish Fedn. Pub.-Community Relations; chmn. Greater Miami's Date With Press; mem. U.S. President's Com. for Women of Achievement; mem. com. of 100, chmn. underwriting com. Miami Ballet Soc.; patron, mem. membership com. Dade County Mus. Sci. Coordinating Gov., Mayor and Senatorial campaign, 1964-66. Recipient Service award, U. Miami, 1953, Golden Keys award, Theta Sigma Phi, Phi Sigma Sigma, 1953. Mem. Greater Miami, North Miami Beach chambers commerce, Women in Communication, Theta Sigma Phi (v.p. 1952-53), Phi Sigma Sigma (pres. 1952-53, nat. officer 1954-56), Gamma Alpha Chi, Alpha Sigma Upsilon. Home: 19527 NE 22d Av North Miami Beach FL 33180 Office: 510 NE 167th St North Miami Beach FL 33162

GROSS, PHYLLIS PENNEBAKER, educator; b. Exeter, Cal., July 18, 1915; d. William Glen and Palma L. (Buckman) Pennebaker; A.A., San Mateo Jr. Coll., 1935; B.S., San Jose State Coll., 1937; M.A., Stanford U., 1939; m. Joseph Gross, Oct. 20, 1940 (div. 1954); chidlren—William Joseph, Patricia Dianne (Mrs. Cass T. Grimm). High sch. biology tchr., Madera, Cal., 1939-41, Grants Pass, Ore., 1945-46, Sequoia High Sch., Redwood City, Cal., 1949-51, Modesto (Cal.) High Sch., 1954-65; faculty Cal. State U., Hayward, 1965—, prof. biology, 1970—. Chmn. Cal. Inter-Sci. Council, 1971-73. Shell fellow, 1968. Mem. Nat. Sci. Tchrs. Assn. (chmn. Western regional conf. 1970), A.A.A.S., Nat. Assn. for Research in Sci. Teaching (asso.), Am. Inst. Biol. Scis., Assn. Edn. Tchrs. in Sci., Cal. Tchrs. Assn. (mem. exec. bd. 1971-73), Nat. Assn. Biology Tchrs. Author: (with Esther Railton) Teaching Science in an Outdoor Environment, 1972. Home: 16680 Armstrong Woods Rd Guerneville CA 95446 Office: Dept Biological Sciences California State University Hayward CA 94542

GROSS, RUTH TAUBENHAUS, physician, educator; b. Bryan, Tex., June 24, 1920; d. Jacob J. and Esther (Hirshenson) Taubenhaus; B.A., Barnard Coll., 1941; M.D., Columbia, 1944; m. Reuben H. Gross, Jr., Aug. 22, 1942, (div. June 1952); 1 son, Gary E. Instr. Radcliffe Infirmary, Oxford, Eng., 1949-50; instr. pediatrics Stanford (Cal.) Med. Sch., 1950-53, asst. prof., 1953-56, asso. prof., 1956-60, acting exec. dept. pediatrics, 1957-59, prof., 1973—, asso. dean for student affairs, 1973—; asso. prof. pediatrics and co-dir. div. human genet. Albert Einstein Coll. Medicine, N.Y.C., 1960-64, prof. pediatrics, 1964-66; clin. prof. pediatrics U. Cal. Med. Center, San Francisco, 1966-73; dir. dept. pediatrics Mt. Zion Hosp. and Med. Center, San Francisco, 1966-73, dir. comprehensive child care project, 1967-69. Commonwealth Fund postdoctoral fellow to study human genetics Istituto de Genetica, Pavia, Italy, 1959-60. Mem. A.A.A.S., Am. Fedn. for Clin. Research, Am. Pediatric Soc., Am. Physiol. Soc., Am. Soc. Hematology, Am. Pub. Health Assn., Am. Soc. Human Genetics, Harvey Soc., N.Y. Acad. Scis., Soc. for Exptl. Biology and Medicine, Soc. for Pediatric Research, Am. Acad. Pediatrics, Ambulatory Pediatric Assn., Phi Beta Kappa, Alpha Omega Alpha, Sigma Xi. Contbr. articles to profl. jours. Home: 405 Davis Ct San Francisco CA 94111 Office: Stanford Medical School Stanford CA 94305

GROSS, SUSAN RENEE, home economist; b. Lewistown, Pa., Mar. 3, 1946; d. George Thomas and Julia (Celia) Moeller; dietetics degree Immaculata Coll., Phila., 1968; postgrad. Drexel U.; m. Michael Edward Gross, July 27, 1968. Dietitian Norfolk Gen. Hosp. (Va.), 1968-69, Hempstead Gen. Hosp. (N.Y.), 1970; extension home economist Atlantic County Extension Service, Rutgers-The State U. N.J., Mays Landing, 1970—. Sec. Atlantic County Nutrition Council, 1970—; mem. adv. com. Atlantic County div. Medicare, 1971—; chmn. equal employment opportunity adv. com. N.J. State Extension Service, 1971—, Zonta Internat., 1971-73. Mem. hostess com. Miss Am. Pageant. Mem. Am., N.J., So. Counties (chmn. newsletter) home econs. assns., N.J. Assn. Extension Home Economists (exec. bd.). Home: 2050 Cedar Bridge Rd Northfield NJ 08225 Office: 1200 W Harding Hwy Mays Landing NJ 08330

GROSSBERG, JOSETTE BRUGEROLLE (MRS. SIDNEY EDWARD GROSSBERG), anesthesiologist; b. LaRochelle, France, May 24, 1929; d. Rene Pierre and Marguerite Raymonde (Bouyer) Brugerolle; student Coll. Rochelle, U. Poitiers, France, 1940-46; B.S., U. Paris, 1947, M.D., 1954, diploma anesthesiology, 1954; m. Sidney Edward Grossberg, May 20, 1959; children—Daniel Eliot, Leslie David. Came to U.S., 1959, naturalized, 1968. Anesthesiologist, Faculty of Medicine, U. Strasbourg, France, 1954-55, St. Joseph Hosp., Valence, France, 1955-57; resident anesthesiology Duke U. Hosp., Durham, N.C., 1958, Lutheran Deaconess Hosp., Mpls., 1959; intern The French Hosp., N.Y.C., 1965-66; resident anesthesiology Milwaukee County Gen. Hosp., 1967-69; attending physician anesthesiology Mount Sinai Hosp., Milw., 1970—; instr. dept. anesthesiology Milw. County Gen. Hosp., 1969-70; clin. asst. prof. dept. anesthesiology Med. Coll. Wis., Milw., 1970—. Brit. Council scholar, 1958-59. Diplomate Am. Bd. Anesthesiology. Mem. A.M.A., Am. Soc. Anesthesiology, Wis. Soc. Anesthesiology, Internat. Research Soc. Anesthesiology. Home: 3005 E Kenwood Blvd Milwaukee WI 53211 Office: Mount Sinai Hosp 948 N 12th St Milwaukee WI 53233

GROSSHOLTZ, JEAN, educator; b. McKean, Pa., Apr. 17, 1929; d. Theodore George and Hazel Vincent (Kearns) Grossholtz; B.A., Pa. State U., 1956; M.A., U. Denver, 1957; Ph.D. (Fulbright fellow), Mass. Inst. Tech., 1961. Faculty, Mount Holyoke Coll., South Hadley, Mass., 1961—, prof. polit. sci., 1972—. Sr. specialist E.W. Center, U. Hawaii, Honolulu, 1968-69; vis. lectr. Flinders U., South Australia, 1972. Served with WAC, 1949-53. Recipient NSF fellowship, 1965-66. Mem. Nat. Womens Polit. Caucus, Am. Polit. Sci. Assn., Am. Assn. Univ. Profs., Am. Civil Liberties Union, Assn. Asian Studies. Home: 10 Jewett Lane South Hadley MA 01075

GROSSI, MARGARET THORNE (MRS. CARLO GROSSI), physician, med. services adminstr.; b. Babylon, N.Y., May 10, 1928; d. George R. and Margaret H. (Devlin) Thorne; B.A., Notre Dame Coll. S.I., 1949; M.D., Georgetown U., 1953; M.P.H., Columbia, 1967; m. Carlo E. Grossi, Dec. 11, 1954; children—Eugene, Mary, Elizabeth, Sarah. Intern, Cornell Med. div. Bellevue Hosp., N.Y.C., 1953-54, resident in pediatrics, 1954-55, Pediatric fellow N.Y. Hosp., 1956-57; asso. attending pediatrician N.Y. Hosp., 1970—; dir. Bur. Child Health N.Y.C. Dept. Health, 1970—; asso. clin. prof. pediatrics Cornell U. Med. Coll., 1970—. Fellow Am. Acad. Pediatrics; mem. Am. Pub. Health Assn. Home: 520 E 82d St New York City NY 10028 Office: 125 Worth St New York City NY 10013

GROSSMAN, ANNE RAFSKY, interior decorator; b. N.Y.C., Dec. 20, 1922; d. Henry A. and Bertha (Fischel) Rafsky; student Adelphi Coll., 1940-42; B.S., Columbia, 1944; m. Harry Grossman Aug. 6, 1950;children—Sandra Kay, Ilene Hope. Partner interior decorating firm Jo-Ann Designs, N.Y.C., 1957-67; owner Anne R. Grossman Interiors, N.Y.C., 1967—. Trustee, treas. Henry A. Rafsky Research Fund, Inc.; bd. dirs. N.Y. chpt. WAIF. Mem. Nat. Soc. Interior Designers, Inc., Nat. Council Jewish Women. Mem. B'nai B'rith. Club: Alpine Country. Address: 25 Sutton Pl New York City NY 10022

GROSSMAN, ELISE (MRS. SEARLES AARON GROSSMAN), city ofcl.; b. Beaumont, Tex., May 24, 1925; d. Maurice and Rose Lillian (Greenberg) Moskowitz; B.A. in Psychology, U. Tex., 1945; m.

Searles Aaron Grossman, Jan. 27, 1946 (dec. Dec. 1972); children—Allida, Sherry Lynn, Scott Alan. Mem. juvenile delinquency task force Del. Gov.'s Com. Law Enforcement and Adminstrn. of Justice, 1960-65; pres. Wilmington (Del.) Council P.T.A.'s, 1967-69; mem. Del. Vocational Adv. Council, 1969-70; v.p. Del. Bd. Edn., 1970—; community analyst dept. planning and devel. City of Wilmington, 1973-74; coordinator community relations Del. Tech. and Community Coll., Wilmington, 1974—; field reader region III equal ednl. opportunities program U.S. Office Edn., 1973—. Mem. Wilmington Mayor's Adv. Com. Urban Renewal, 1965-72; mem. community relation com. Del. Jewish Fedn., 1967-72. Bd. dirs. Wilmington Child Guidance Center. Recipient Hannah G. Solomon award Wilminton sect. Nat. Council Jewish Women, 1972. Mem. League of Women Voters Del. (dir. 1960-65; v.p. 1964-65). Democrat. Jewish religion. Address: 4004 Coleridge Rd Wilmington DE 19802

GROSSMAN, PATRICIA DUNLAP, entomologist; b. Columbus, O., Mar. 2, 1939; d. Erle Peter and Alyce Florence (Dunlap) Grossman; B.S. in Agr., Tex. Technol. Coll., 1963. Agrl. research technician div. entomology U.S. Dept. Agr., Kerrville, Tex., 1963-67; entomologist U.S. Dept. Def., USAF Epidemiological Lab., Lackland, AFB, Tex., 1967-68; insect identification pineapple juices Quality Control Lab., Del Monte Corp., Honolulu, 1970-71; lab. technician insect identification Bishop Mus., Honolulu, 1971—; water microbiologist I, City and County of Honolulu Bd. Water Supply, 1973; biol. technician Hawaiian hornfly project U.S. Dept. Agr., Halawa, Hawaii, 1974—. Vice pres. Hawaii Epilepsy Soc., 1971-72, treas., 1972, sec., chmn. membership com., 1973, Merit certificate, 1973; planning com. chmn. for med. seminar on epilepsy, Epilepsy Found. Am., Honolulu, 1971; mem. Am. Bicentennial Research Inst. Library Human Resources. Mem. Entomol. Soc. Am., Agettes (sec. 1962-63). Club: Women's Propeller (project chmn. 1969-70) (Honolulu). Contbr. articles to tech. jours. Home: 3093 Pualei Circle Honolulu HI 96815

GROSSMANN, MARY ANN (MRS. TOM THOMSEN, JR.), journalist; b. St. Paul, Sept. 6, 1938; d. Vern P. and Marion (Lehmann) Grossmann; B.A., Macalester Coll., 1960; m. Tom Thomsen, Jr., Oct. 28, 1961. Reporter, U.P.I., Mpls. Bur., 1960-61; gen. assignment reporter St. Paul Pioneer Press, 1961-63; fashion writer St. Paul Dispatch & Pioneer Press, 1963-66, soc. and women's editor, 1966—. Bd. dirs. Theatre in the Round, Mpls., Fashion Group; mem. alumni bd. Macalester Coll. Home: 214 W Curtis St West St Paul MN 55118 Office: 55 E 4TH St St Paul MN 55101

GROSVENOR, DONNA KERKAM (MRS. GILBERT M. GROSVENOR), journalist; b. Washington, July 16, 1938; d. John Freeman and Eleanor (Beck) Kerkam; B.A., Sweet Briar Coll., 1960; m. Gilbert Melville Grosvenor, June 16, 1961; children—Gilbert Hovey, Alexandra Rowland. Various assignments Nat. Geog. mag. and Nat. Geog. Sch. Bull., Nat. Geog. spl. publs. book Pandas, 1973, Egypt, East Africa, Ceylon, Monaco, Indonesia, Washington, 1961—. Sec., Jr. League, Washington, 1966-67; mem. Smithsonian Assos. Ladies Com., 1967-69; mem. bd. Friends Nat. Zoo, 1968—, Child Health Center of Childrens Hosp., 1965—; mem. exec. com. Project Hope, 1967-68; mem. governing bd. Nat. Cathedral Sch., 1972—. Mem. Soc. Woman Geographers, Nat. Cathedral Sch. Alumni Assn. (exec. bd., sec. 1965-68). Clubs: Sulgrave, Washington. Home: 1259 Crest Lane McLean VA 22101

GROSVENOR, VERTA MAE SMART, writer; b. Fairfax, S.C., Apr. 4; d. Frank and Clara (Ritter) Smart; student pub. schs., Phila.; div.; children—Kali, Chandra. Writer-in-residence Conn. State Coll., 1972, Penn Community Center, Frogmore, S.C., 1973. Author: Vibration Cooking, 1970; Thursdays and Every Other Sunday Off, 1972; Speaking of Everything, 1974. Contbr. articles to popular mags. including Redbook, McCalls. Home: 311 W 97th St New York City NY 10025

GROTH, BETTY, conservationist, author; b. Oak Park, Ill.; d. Herman A. and Bertha L. (Luepke) Groth; grad. Vassar Coll., 1932. Sec., Oak Park YMCA, 1935-42; sec. Ill. Commn. for Handicapped Children, 1943-46; pvt. sec. Chgo. Assn. of Commerce and Industry, 1947-53, Chgo. Heart Assn., 1953—. Mem. Save-The-Dunes Council, N. Central Audubon Council; sec., dir. Natural Resources Council of Ill., 1967-71, v.p., 1969-71; v.p., dir. Du Page County Clean Streams, 1967-69; founder, chmn. No. Conservation Cabinet, 1971—. Mem. Nat. Audubon Soc., Ill. Audubon Soc. (v.p. conservation, dir. 1962-73, sec. bd. dirs. 1973-74), Du Page Audubon Soc., Nat. Wildlife Fedn., Morton Arboretum, Am. Bald Eagle Club. Baptist. Club: Chgo. Vassar. Author: Open Spaces in Illinois, 1962; Surprise in the North Woods, 1966; Wildlife by John Burroughs Cabin, 1967; King's Ransom to Save a Prairie, 1968; Ivory Bills Found Alive in Texas Big Thicket, 1969; Great Swamp Wildlife Refuge Versus Jetport, 1970; The Fate of Thorn Creek Woods, 1971; Man's Dominion of the Green Earth, 1972; Country Estate, 1973; King of Sky, Land and Water, 1974. Contbr. articles to profl. jours. Home: Ten-O-Seven Front St Lisle IL 60532

GROTZINGER, LAUREL ANN, educator; b. Truman, Minn., Apr. 15, 1935; d. Edward F. and Marian Gertrude (Greeley) Grotzinger; A.B., Carleton Coll., 1957; M.S., U. Ill., 1958, Ph.D., 1964. Instr., asst. librarian Ill. State U., 1958-62; asst. prof. Western Mich. U., Kalamazoo, 1964-66, asso. prof., 1966-68, prof., 1968—, asst. dir. Sch. Librarianship, 1965-72. Mem. A.L.A. (sec.-treas. Library History Roundtable 1973-74), Assn. Am. Library Schs., Am. Soc. Information Sci., Mich. Library Assn., Am. Assn. U. Profs. (sec. W.M. chpt. 1968-70), Phi Beta Kappa, Beta Phi Mu (v.p., pres. Kappa chpt.), Pi Delta Epsilon, Alpha Beta Alpha. Author: The Power and the Dignity, Scarecrow, 1966; mem. editorial bd. Jour. Edn. for Librarianship, 1973—. articles. Home: 313 Solon Av Kalamazoo MI 49007

GROUT, GERALDINE ISABEL HALE (MRS. JOHN MARSHALL), nursing home adminstr.; b. Leominster, Mass.; d. Ashley Garfield and Lula (Robbins) Hale; B.S. in Comml. Ednl., Boston U., 1947, M.Ed. in Bus. Edn., 1950; D.Ed., Ind. U., 1961; m. John Marshall, Apr. 21, 1957. Billing clk., sec. E.E. Miles Co., South Lancaster, Mass., 1941-44; bus. tchr. Troy (N.H.) High Sch., 1947-49; tchr. South Lancaster Acad., 1950-53; asso. prof. bus. edn. Columbia Union Coll., Takoma Park, Md., 1953-57, 60-64, Atlantic Union Coll., South Lancaster, 1964-69; adminstr. Hale Convalescent and Nursing Home, West Groton, Mass., 1964—. Mem. Am. Assn. U. Profs., Nat. Bus. Edn. Assn., Am. Coll. Nursing Home Adminstrs., Delta Pi Epsilon, Pi Omega Pi. Office: Main St South Lancaster MA 01561

GROUT, RUTH ELLEN, cons.; b. Princeton, Mass., Oct. 4, 1901; d. Edgar Homer and Laura Maria (Miller) Grout; A.B., Mt. Holyoke Coll., 1923; M.P.H., Yale, 1930, Ph.D. (Mary Pemberton Nourse Meml. fellow), 1939. Tchr. biology, Bristol, Conn., also New Haven, 1923-31; dir. health edn. study Cattaraugus County, N.Y., 1931-38; cons. TVA, Chattanooga, 1939-42; cons. on sch. health Office Edn., FSA, Washington, 1942-43; asso. prof. pub. health edn. U. Minn., Mpls., 1943-52, prof., dir. program in health edn., 1953-67, prof. emeritus, 1967—. Cons. health edn. WHO, European region, 1952-53, 56-57, Thailand, 1959, African region, 1962, Mediterranean region, 1966, Malaysia, 1968, Geneva, 1970-71; cons. AID, Jamaica, 1969-71; cons. Chapel Hill Council on Aging, Chapel Hill, N.C., 1972—. Trustee Chapel Hill (N.C.) Resident Retirement Center; bd. dirs. Chapel Hill Day Care Center. Recipient Prentiss award Cleve. Health Mus., 1958. Fellow Am. Pub. Health Assn. (chmn. pub. health edn. sect. 1952-53, mem. governing council 1959-60), Soc. for Pub. Health Edn. (hon.); mem. Am. Assn. Ret. Persons, Am. Assn. Univ. Women, Delta Omega. Mem. United Ch. (sec. bd. trustees 1973—). Author: Health Teaching in Schools, 1948, 5th edit., 1968. Contbr. articles in field to profl. jours. Home: 6 Brandon Rd Chapel Hill NC 27514

GROVE, JEAN DONNER (MRS. EDWARD R. GROVE), sculptor; b. Washington, May 15, 1912; d. Frederick Gregory and Georgia V. (Gartrell) Donner; student Cornell U., 1932, Hill Sch. of Sculpture, 1934-35, Corcoran Sch. of Art, 1935-37, 42-44, Cath. U. Am., 1936-37, Phila. Mus. Art Sch., 1967; B.S., Wilson Tchrs. Coll., 1939; m. Edward R. Grove, June 24, 1936; children—David Donner, Eric Donner. Exhibited in one-man shows at Wilson Tchrs. Coll., Washington, 1939, Cayuga Mus. History and Art, Auburn, N.Y., 1964, Episcopal Acad. Gallery, Phila., 1966; exhibited in group shows at Pa. Acad. Fine Arts, Phila., 1947, 48, 51, 53, N.A.D., N.Y.C., 1949, Nat. Sculpture Soc. at Archtl. League, N.Y.C., Topeka, 1957 and Lever House, N.Y.C., 1974, Art U.S.A., Madison Sq. Garden, N.Y.C., 1958, Corcoran Gallery Art, Washington, 1943-47, Internat. Gallery, Washington, 1946, Phila. Mus. Art, 1955, 59, 62, Phila. Art Alliance, 1957, 60, 66, Phila. Civic Center, 1968, Flagler Art Center, West Palm Beach, Fla., 1972, Norton Gallery Art, West Palm Beach, 1974; represented in permanent collections at Rosenwald Collection, Phila., Ch. of Holy Comforter, Drexel Hill, Pa., Fine Arts Commn., City Hall, Phila. Sculptor numerous portrait commns., garden figures and fountains, 1940—. Recipient 1st prize sculpture met. reg. Nat. Mus. Washington, 1946; 1st prize Sculpture Arts Club, 1946, Portrait prize, 1947; Morris Goodman award John Herron Art Mus., Indpls., 1957; Competition prize for design and sculpture Artists Equity Phila. 1960; others. Mem. Nat. Sculpture Soc., Artists Equity Assn. (dir. Phila. chpt. 1964-66), Am. Fedn. Arts, Soc. of Four Arts, Norton Gallery Art, Soc. Washington Artists, English Speaking Union, Animal Rescue League of Palm Beaches (com. chmn. 1972—), St. Mary's Guild of Episcopal Ch. Women (v.p. 1974—), Kappa Delta Pi. Address: Sea-Lake Studio 3215 S Flagler Dr West Palm Beach FL 33405

GROVE, KATHRYN MOWREY (MRS. D. DWIGHT GROVE), church worker; b. Harrisburg, Pa., Jan. 11, 1914; d. D. Floyd and Eva (Shearer) Mowrey; A.B. cum laude, Lebanon Valley Coll., 1934; m. D. Dwight Grove, July 11, 1939; children—David, Carol. Tchr. high sch., New Cumberland, Pa., 1934-39. Missionary, Evang. U.B. Ch., Sierra Leone, West Africa, 1939-41; mem. bd. Christian edn. East Pa. Conf., 1957-62, children's work council, 1957-62; mem. council adminstrn. Pa. Council Chs., 1964-68; mem. fgn. student com., dept. united ch. women Greater Phila. Council Chs., 1960-64; pres. Women's Soc. World Service, Phila. 3d Ch., 1964-67; pres. East Pa. Conf. br. Women's Soc. World Service, 1957-62, mem. gen. program com., 1957-62, mem. com. leadership edn., 1963-67, dept. health and welfare, 1963-67, mem. nat. council, 1963-68; pres. Gen. Women's Soc. World Service; sec. jud. council United Methodist Ch., 1968—. Founder Jr. Story League, New Cumberland, 1936; pres. Phila. Story League, 1955-57; chmn. 20th biennial conv. Nat. Story League, Phila., 1964; pres. Birney Sch. P.T.A., Phila., 1960-61; speaker various ch. meetings, conv. confs. Mem. women's planning com. Japan Internat. Christian U. Found., Inc. Trustee, Lebanon Valley Coll., 1968—, Logan United Meth. Ch., 1971—. Mem. Am. Assn. U. Women, Pa. Folklore Soc., Elfreth's Assn. Republican. Mem. Order Eastern Star. Contbr. articles to religious publs. Home: 5025 N Marvine St Philadelphia PA 19141

GROVER, ARLENE HARRIS (MRS. ROSCOE A. GROVER), librarian; b. Ithaca, N.Y., May 25, 1909; d. Franklin Stewart and Estella (Spilsbury) Harris; B.A., Brigham Young U., 1929, M.A., 1934; postgrad. Columbia, 1931-32, U. Utah, 1960-62; m. Roscoe A. Grover, Sept. 14, 1934; children—Franklin, Alice (Mrs. Rodney Bagley), John, Martha (Mrs. James D. Gardner), Paul, Nancy (Mrs. Robert A. Frampton), Margaret, Stephen. Tchr. Coll. So. Utah, Cedar City, 1946-50; librarian VA Hosp., Salt Lake City, 1960-62; librarian, dir. tech. services Utah State Library, Salt Lake City, 1962—. Vice pres., sec. Utah Congress Parents and Tchrs., 1956-62. Bd. dirs. Utah sect. League Women Voters, 1958-60. Mem. Utah (pres. 1971-72), Mountain Plains, Am. library assns. Mem. Ch. Jesus Christ of Latter-day Saints. Home: 62 Virginia St Salt Lake City UT 84103 Office: 2150 S 300 W Suite 16 Salt Lake City UT 84115

GROVER, PATRICIA PINCHERRI HINTON, newspaper columnist; b. Altoona, Pa., Aug. 3, 1920; d. Samuel and Anna Marie (Buontempo) Pincherri; grad. Zeth Bus. Coll., 1944; m. M.R. Hinton, Mar. 6, 1940 (div. June 1946); 1 son, Dennis; m. 2d, Carl A. Grover, Nov. 6, 1965. With Altoona Mirror, 1944—, editorial and feature writer, columnist, 1944—, sec. to pres. and pub., 1953—; sec. to bd. dirs. Altoona Printing & Supply Co., 1959—; dir., sec.-treas. Himes Printing Co., State College, Pa. Recipient George Washington gold medal Freedoms Found.; named Woman of Yr. in Achievement, 1964-65. Sec. of Year, Altoona Area Chamber of Commerce. Mem. Blair County Music Assn., Nat. Fedn. Women's Press Assn., Bus. and Profl. Woman's Club, Pa. Women's Press Assn. (pres. 1962, nat. dir. state N.Y., Pa.), Nat. Secs. Assn., Sigma Delta Chi. Author TV script, plays, articles for mags. Home: 700 Ruskin Dr Altoona PA 16602 Office: 1000 Green Av Altoona PA 16601

GROVES, DOLORES HALE, ednl. adminstr.; b. Denver, Jan. 12, 1921; d: Moses Solomon and Grace Helen (Bradford) Hale; B.F.A., U. Colo., 1943; M.A., Denver U., 1963; postgrad. (art scholar), U. Colo., U. No. Colo.; m. Harry E. Groves, May 2, 1944 (div. Aug. 1948); 1 son, Sheridon Hale. Art tchr., R.T. Coles Jr. and Vocational High Sch., Kansas City, Mo., 1943-45; art instr. So. U., Baton Rouge, 1945-46; health educator Denver Tb Soc., 1948-51; govt. employee Air Force Finance Center, 1951-56; art tchr., counselor Manual High Sch., Denver, 1956-66; dean Cole Jr. High Sch., 1966-72; asst. prin. Kunsmiller Jr. High Sch., Denver, 1972—. Chmn., Task Force for Minority Concerns, 1973-74; active Urban League, United Negro Coll. Fund, Salvation Army. Health fellow, U. Colo., 1949. Mem. N.A.A.C.P., Nat. Assn. Women Deans, Adminstrs. and Counselors (exec. bd. as elementary and jr. sch. sect. chmn. 1974—, chmn. task force on minority concerns 1973-74), Denver Adminstrs. and Suprs. Assn., Am. Personnel and Guidance Assn., Colo.-Wyo. Women Deans, Adminstrs. and Counselors (historian 1967, jr. high sch. rep., exec. bd. 1972-73), Denver Deans (sec. 1967-68), Denver Educators Art Assn. (pres. 1959), Alpha Kappa Alpha (life, pres. 1951-53). Club: West Point Mothers (Denver). Home: 1223 Race St Denver CO 80206 Office: 2250 S Quitman St Denver CO 80219

GROWNEY, MARGARET BERG, lawyer, nursing home exec.; b. Wilkinsburg, Pa., Dec. 9, 1918; d. Albert Leonard and Teresa Marie (Nolan) Berg; A.B., Stetson U., 1949; J.D., 1951; m. Honore S. McKeown, 1951 (dec. 1953); m. 2d, Lawrence M. Growney, 1956 (div. 1973); children—Helen Mary McKeown, Honora Stephana McKeown, Laurence Michael, Gerard Anthony. Admitted to Fla. bar, 1951; mem. firm McKeown & McKeown, West Palm Beach, Fla., 1951-53, individual practice, 1953—; adminstr., pres. Alhambra Nursing Home, Inc., St. Petersburg, Fla., 1969—. Served with WAVES, 1944-45. Mem. Nat. Assn. Women Lawyers, Am. Nursing Home Assn., Fla. Bar, St. Petersburg Bar Assn., Fla. Assn. Women Lawyers, Fla. Nursing Home Assn., D.A.V., Phi Alpha Delta. Address: 2000 80th St N St Petersburg FL 33710

GRUBB, BETTY ANNE, real estate broker; b. Lincoln, Neb., July 17, 1923; d. Lyle Afton and Thelma Mae (Emerson) Bowers; B.A., Bob Jones U., 1946; postgrad. Yale Lang. Sch., 1960; m. Royal Harwood Grubb, Sr., Dec. 24, 1946; children—Royal Harwood, Karen L., Marilyn R. Salesman, Morgan Realty Co., Dayton, O., 1965-67, Bay & Beach Realty, Corona del Mar, Cal., 1968-71, Wesley Taylor Co., Inc., Newport Beach, Cal., 1970-71; owner, real estate broker Betty A. Grubb Realty, Newport Beach, Cal., 1971—. Pres., Embassy Wives Club, Tokyo, 1963. Mem. Newport Beach C. of C., Newport Harbor-Costa Mesa Bd. Realtors (chmn. hospitality com. 1972, chmn. multiple listing com. 1973-74), Sigma Kappa Rho. Home: 2433 Blackthorn St Newport Beach CA 92660 Office: 567 San Nicolas Dr Newport Center Newport Beach CA 92660

GRUBBS, ETHEL LAURANCE, home economist; b. LaCrosse, Kan., July 28, 1917; d. Pleasant Hubert and Ruth Irene (Bitter) Grubbs; B.S. in Home Econs. and Sci., Maryville Coll., 1940; postgrad. N.C. State U., 1941, 45, U. Ark., 1951, U. Ga., 1963; M.S., Va. Poly. Inst. and State U., 1966. Home econs. tchr. Nancy Reynolds Meml. High Sch., Westfield, N.C., 1940-43; lab. technician Hercules Powder Co., Radford, Va., 1943-45; home econs. tchr. Germanton (N.C.) High Sch., 1945-48; home demonstration agt. Patrick County, Va., 1948-55; home demonstration agt.-at-large Va. Poly. Inst., Blacksburg, 1955-66; extension specialist home econs. Va. Poly. Inst. and State U., Blacksburg, 1966—, extension specialist family resources, 1972—. Mem. Com. Gov.'s Conf. on Aging, 1971. Recipient recognition for distinguished service Nat. Assn. Extension Home Economists, 1965. Mem. Va. Extension Service Assn., Va. Assn. Extension Home Economists, Am., Va. home econs. assns., Adult Edn. Assn. U.S.A., Gerontological Soc. Am., Epsilon Sigma Phi. Home: PO Box 275 Blacksburg VA 24060

GRUBE, JUANITA SMITH (MRS. OLIVER CHRISTEN GRUBE), county ofcl.; b. Hale Center, Tex., Sept. 6, 1922; d. Ernest Clyde and Addie Neoma (Scudder) Smith; student N.M. Highlands U., 1942-43; m. Oliver Christen Grube, June 9, 1946; 1 son, Bobby Lyn. Dept. to tax assessor, Eddy County, Carlsbad, N.M., 1943-47, dep. tax assessor, 1950-58, clk. for civil def., 1959-60, tax assessor, 1961-64, 69-72, chief dep. assessor, 1965-68, 73—; clk. Lance, 1947-48; bookkeeper Corner Drug, 1948. Tax assessor N.M. Tax Commn., 1955-57. Mem. Statehood Commemoration Commn., 1972. Treas., Carlsbad Democratic Women's Club, 1968-69. Mem. Am. Bus. Women's Assn. (pres. 1968, Am. Bus. Woman of Year 1971), Carlsbad Bus. and Profl. Women's Club, N.M. Assessing Officers Assn. (v.p. 1971-72, pres. 1972-73), N.M. Hist. Soc. of S.W. Home: 303 N Ash St PO Box 314 Carlsbad NM 88220 Office: PO Box 729 Carlsbad NM 88220

GRUBEL, HELEN KATHERINE TEAL (MRS. RALPH OSWALD GRUBEL), city ofcl.; b. Cin., Feb. 14, 1922; d. Frederick Irving and Katherine Olive (Tompkins) Teal; student Dyke Bus. Coll., 1940; m. Ralph Oswald Grubel, Oct. 24, 1970. Sec. to dir. finance, city mgr. City of East Cleveland, O., 1940-67; dir. finance Village of Chagrin Falls, O., 1967-70; dir. finance City of Mentor, O., 1970—. Mem. exec. bd. Central Income Tax Agy., Clevel., 1972-74. Mem. Municipal Finance Officers Assn. U.S. and Can., Municipal Finance Officers Assn. Ohio, Municipal Finance Officers Assn. N.E. Ohio (pres. 1974—), Ohio Municipal League (trustee 1972-74). Baptist (mem. bd. social concern 1972-74). Home: 2250 Par Lane 719 Willoughby Hills OH 44094 Office: 8383 Mentor Av Mentor OH 44060

GRUBER, BONNIE JEAN (MRS. JOHN EDWARD GRUBER), journalist; b. Superior, Wis., Mar. 26, 1938; d. Barney B. and Helga M. (Becklund) Barstow; student Wis. State Coll., 1956-57; B.S., U. Wis., 1960; m. John Edward Gruber, May 12, 1962; children—Richard John, Timothy John. Journalism intern Clintonville (Wis.) Tribune-Gazette, 1958; editor Daily Cardinal, Madison, Wis., 1959; reporter Appleton (Wis.) Post-Crescent, 1960-61; newsman U.P.I., Madison, Wis., 1961-62; free lance journalist, 1969—. Mem. Women in Communications (chpt. historian 1969-72, v.p. 1974—), Luth. Ch. Library Assn. (chpt. sec. 1973). Lutheran (publicity chmn. 1967—). Editor: The Unfaced Suit Made Easy (Helen Price and Lois Farnsworth), 1971; Knits Made Easy (Helen Price), 1972. Editor, Communicator, 1973—. Home: 1430 Drake St Madison WI 53711

GRUBER, KATHERINE BARBARA KRAUTH (MRS. HAROLD EDWARD GRUBER), assn. exec.; b. Astoria, N.Y., Oct. 16, 1931; d. Edward Charles and Barbara (Knab) Krauth; student Hofstra U., 1949-50; m. Harold Edward Gruber, July 5, 1953; children—Edward, Kathrine I. and Babette L. (twins). Head sec. physics lab. Sylvania Electric Co., N.Y.C. and Bayside, N.Y., 1953-58; adminstrv. sec. to engring. dir. Huyck Systems Co., Huntington Station, 1960-63; sr. sec. Airborne Instruments Lab., Deer Park, N.Y., 1965-69; office mgr. Smithtown (N.Y.) YMCA, 1969-70, program dir., 1970-74, sr. dir., 1974—. Vice pres. Branch Civic Assn., 1968. Mem. Assn. Profl. Dirs. YMCA's. Republican. Home: 14 Cresthill Pl Smithtown NY 11787 Office: PO Box 607 Edgewood Av Smithtown NY 11787

GRUCCIO, LILLIAN JOAN (MRS. WILLIAM TAYLOR HARRINGTON THORMAN), lawyer; b. Camden, N.J.; d. Joseph and Millie (Fornataro) Gruccio; grad. Steelman Bus. Sch., Camden, 1945; A.A., Rutgers U., 1947, LL.B., 1951, LL.D., 1968. Admitted to N.J. bar, 1952, to U.S. Supreme Ct. bar, 1960; asso. firm Frank C. Propert, Camden, 1952-55, Lewis and Hutchinson, and successor firms, Camden, 1955-61; with legal dept. Campbell Soup Co., Camden, 1955; practiced in Pennsauken, N.J., 1961-73, Medford, N.J., 1973—. Mem. Camden City Juvenile Conf. Com., 1957-62; mem. Camden County Health and Welfare Council, 1957-61. Bd. dirs. Camden and Vicinity YWCA, 1959-67, chmn. adult program com., 1957-67, fashion show com., 1967; budget com. United Fund of Camden County, 1968. Mem. Am., N.J., Camden County, Burlington County bar assns., Rutgers U. Law Sch. Alumni Assn. (chancellor South Jersey div. 1962, bd. mgrs. 1952-64), South Jersey Pub. Relations Assn., Pennsauken (charter, 1st v.p., mem. legislative com. 1967-72, corr. sec. 1972-73, chmn. personality devel. com. 1972-73) Burlington County (scholarship com. 1974, legislative com. 1974) bus. and profl. women's clubs, LeisureTowne Civic League (rec. sec. 1974—). Clubs: Laurel Oak Country, Zonta of Greater Camden (charter 1st v.p. 1962, chmn. pub. affairs and status of women com. 1958-63, chmn. fashion show com. 1968, rec. sec. 1959-61, bd. dirs. 1959-62, 68-69, chmn. safety com. 1972-73), Aux. United Republican (chmn. legislative com. 1971-72). Home: 63 Sheffield Pl Vincentown NJ 08088 Office: Cedarbrook Bldg Taunton Blvd Medford NJ 08055

GRUEN, NINA JAFFE (MRS. CLAUDE GRUEN), sociologist; b. Cin., Dec. 14, 1933; d. Leslie Auer and Rosa (Shor) Jaffe; B.A. with honors, U. Cin., 1962, M.A., 1963; m. Claude Gruen, Sept. 11, 1960; children—Lester Walter, Dale Jaffe, Adam Samuel, Joshua Claude, Aaron Nathaniel. Lectr., U. Cin., 1963-64, U. Ky., Covington,

1963-64; cons. Arthur D. Little, Inc., San Francisco, 1966-70; v.p., prin. sociologist Gruen, Gruen & Asso., San Francisco, 1970—. Recipient NSF grant, 1964. Mem. Am. Sociol. Assn., Western and Internat. Regional Sci. Assn., Am. Soc. Planning Ofcls., Am. Assn. Pub. Opinion Research, Phi Beta Kappa, Psi Chi. Co-author: Low and Moderate Income Housing in the Suburbs: An Analysis for the Dayton, Ohio Region, 1972. Contbr. articles in field to profl. jours. Home: 8649 Don Carol Dr El Cerrito CA 94530 Office: Suite 3009 Ferry Bldg San Francisco CA 94111

GRUENBERG, GLADYS WALLEMAN, educator; b. Milw., June 22, 1920; d. John M. and Olive A. (Glassner) Walleman; A.B., Marquette U., 1940; A.M., St. Louis U., 1949, Ph.D., 1952; m. Harold Gruenberg, Dec. 28, 1946; children—Sandra, Dorothy, Daniel. Sec. Marquette Labor Sch., 1941-42; exec. sec. Asso. Unions Am., 1942-44; field examiner NLRB, St. Louis, 1944-46; research, edn. dir. Retail, Wholesale and Dept. Stor Union CIO, St. Louis, 1946-47; asst. prof. econs. St. Louis U., 1949-55, asso. prof., 1969—, cons. grievance handling workshop Labor Sch., 1957; cons. arbitration workshop Pub. Personnel Assn., 1969, retirement workshop Inst. Applied Gerontology, 1974. Mem. arbitration panel Fed. Med. and Conciliation Service, 1971—. Mem. Am. Arbitration Assn. (mem. nat. labor arbitration panel 1969—), Indsl. Relations Research Assn. (sec. Gateway chpt. 1973—), Am. Soc. Personnel Adminstrn., Am. Assn. U. Profs. (v.p. St. Louis U. chpt. 1974—), Am., Midwest, So., Mo. econs. assns., Soc. Profls. in Dispute Resolution (charter), Southwest Social Scis. Assn., Delta Sigma Rho, Beta Gamma Sigma, Pi Gamma Mu. Editorial asst. New Cath. Ency., 1960-62. Home: 801 Jackson Av St Louis MO 63130 Office: 3674 Lindell Blvd St Louis MO 63108

GRUHIN, LOIS ANN, lawyer; b. East Orange, N.J., Apr. 17, 1947; d. Robert Charles and Pauline Clara (Rosenblum) Gruhin; B.A., Rutgers U., 1968; J.D. magna cum laude (Carl Mann scholar 1969-70; Ben F. Washer Scholar 1970; Louis D. Brandeis scholar 1971), U. Louisville, 1971. Admitted to Ky. Ct. Appeals, 1971, Supreme Ct. N.J., 1971, U.S. Dist. Ct. N.J., 1971, Supreme Ct. N.Y., 1973; asso. Marshall, Bratter, Greene, Allison & Tucker, N.Y.C., 1971-72; in house counsel Ohio Bell Telephone Co., Cleve., 1972—. Ohio bar assns., Am., Essex County (N.J.) bar assns., Bar Assn. Greater Cleve., Kappa Beta Pi, Phi Kappa Phi. Home: 6809 Mayfield Rd Mayfield Heights OH 44124 Office: Ohio Bell Telephone Co Room 1422 100 Erieview Plaza Cleveland OH 44114

GRUM, VINCENTA MARY, librarian; b. Carbondale, Pa., June 15, 1945; d. Frank Joseph and Louise Jeannette (Markunas) Grum; B.S., Kutztown State Coll., 1967; M.S., Marywood Coll., 1971. Br. librarian Forest City br. Susquehanna County (Pa.) Pub. Library, Forest City, Pa., 1967-69; reference librarian Bethlehem (Pa.) Pub. Library, 1970-71; librarian Lackawanna Jr. Coll., Scranton, Pa., 1971—. Mem. Am., Pa. library assns., Bus. and Profl. Women's Club, Phi Alpha Theta. Home: 311 Vine St Forest City PA 18421 Office: 635 Linden St Scranton PA 18503

GRUMBINE, CECILY GARDNER (MRS. ANTHONY J. LEMBACH), clin. psychologist; b. Chgo., Aug. 9, 1926; d. Walter and Anna (Allen) Gardner; M.A. (scholar), U. Chgo., 1953, Ph.D. (scholar), 1957; m. Robert Grumbine (dec.); children—Robert Eugene, Margaret-Mary; m. 2d, Anthony J. Lembach, Sept. 30, 1961; stepchildren—Michael, David, Madelon. Tchr., Lab. Sch., U. Chgo., 1952-56; clin. psychologist II, Inst. Juvenile Research, Chgo., 1956-57; dean women, asst. prof. psychology Colo. State Coll. (now U. No. Colo.), Greeley, 1957-59; dir. Counseling Service of No. Colo., Greeley, Ft. Collins, 1959-65, 68—, part-time psychologist, 1965-68; team psychol. Ft. Logan Mental Health Center, Denver, 1965-66, div. psychologist, 1966-68; v.p. Ace Travel Service, Greeley, 1966-67. Invited del. 4th Ann. Conf. Am. Women Leaders, 1966, 5th Ann. Conf., 1967. Fellow Internat. Council Psychologists (dir. 1960-62, 67-69, editor Newsletter 1960-63, chmn. publs. com. 1963-65, internat. pres. 1965-67), Am. Orthopsychiat. Assn.; mem. Am., Rocky Mountain, Colo. psychol. assns., Colo. Soc. for Psychologists in Pvt. Practice, (pres. 1967-69), Nat., Colo. assns. women deans and counselors, Am. Assn. U. Women (1st v.p. Greeley br. 1960-63), Colo. Women Psychologists (sec. 1972—), Soc. Clin. and Exptl. Hypnosis, Assn. Psychologists In Marital and Family Therapy), Nat. Assn. Parliamentarians (pres. Greeley unit 1969-72, 1st v.p. 1970-71, 1st v.p. Colo. assn. 1972-74, pres. registered unit Colo. 1974—), Bus. and Profl. Women's Club Loveland (2d v.p. 1970-71, sec. 1972-73, pres. 1973-74), D.A.V. Aux. (comdr. Greeley aux. 8, 1970-71, 74—, state exec. com. 1971-72, state adj. 1972-74, Nat., Colo. press women, Phi Chi Theta (pres. Denver area alumnae 1960-62, South Central dist. dir. 1962-64; named one of 3 outstanding women in Chgo. area 1957, sec. 1964-65, pres. 1966-68), Greeley Bus. and Profl. Women's Club (trustee project K 1973—), Gold Key, Mortar Bd., Pi Lambda Theta, Gamma Alpha Chi (nat. sec.-treas. 1946), Iota Sigma Epsilon, Beta Sigma Phi (pres. Theta chpt. 1966-67, treas. Gamma Omega chpt. 1971-72). Roman Catholic. Clubs: Toastmistress (pres. Greeley club 1962); Altrusa (chmn. internat. relations com.), Greeley Woman's (program chmn. 1971-72, chmn. home and edn. dept. 1972-73, 2d v.p. 1974—). Office: First Nat Bank Bldg 1025 9th Av Greeley CO 80631

GRUNDFEST, SANDRA LEAH URY (MRS. JERRY GRUNDFEST), univ. ofcl.; b. N.Y.C., Sept. 27, 1933; d. Milton and Frieda (Tanz) Ury; B.A. cum laude, Barnard Coll., 1954; M.Ed., Rutgers U., 1966, D.Ed. (Nat. Def. Edn. Act fellow), 1970; m. Jerry Grundfest, Dec. 25, 1954; children—Leslie, Robert. Lectr. Grad. Sch. Edn., Rutgers U., New Brunswick, N.J., 1968-71; asst. dir. career services Princeton (N.J.), 1971—. Mem. Franklin Twp. Bd. End., 1974—. Mem. Am. Personnel and Guidance Assn., Am. Psychol. Assn., Eastern Coll. Personnel Officers, Middle Atlantic Placement Assn. Office: Career Services Clio Hall Princeton University Princeton NJ 08540

GRUNDMAN, ROSE ANN, educator; b. Chgo., Oct. 30, 1926; d. Paul Albert and Rose (McGilvray) Grundman; B.S., Northwestern U., 1947, M.S., 1948. Instr. math. U. Ariz., 1948-49, U. Ill. Med. Center, Chgo., 1949-57, asst. prof. math., statistics and computer sci., 1957-72, asso. prof., 1972—. Mem. Am. Math. Soc., Math. Assn. Am., A.A.A.S., Am. Statis. Assn., Am. Assn. U. Profs. (sec.-treas. chpt. 1960-72), Am. Pharm. Assn., Phi Beta Kappa, Sigma Xi, Chi Omega. Methodist. Contbr. numerous articles to profl. jours. Home: 2626 Lakeview St Chicago IL 60614

GRUNDY, BETTY LOU BOTTOMS (MRS. DAVID MATHER GRUNDY), physician; b. Dothan, Ala., Jan. 3, 1940; d. Wilmer Rudolph and Marie (Brandon) Bottoms; student Huntingdon Coll., 1956-59; M.D., U. Fla., 1963; m. David Mather Grundy, June 3, 1963; 1 dau., Jennifer Marie. Intern, Rose Meml. Hosp., Denver, 1963-64; resident Peter Bent Brigham Hosp., Boston, 1965-67; practice medicine, Lead, S.D., 1964-65, specializing in anesthesiology, Saginaw, Mich., 1967—; chmn. dept. anesthesiology St. Luke's Hosp.; asst. clin. prof. surgery Mich. State U. med. adviser Mich. Soc. Inhalation Therapy. Bd. dirs. Saginaw Tb and Respiratory Disease Assn., 1968-69, Mich. Tb and Respiratory Disease Assn., 1968-69. Diplomate Am. Bd. Anesthesiology. Fellow Am. Coll. Anesthesiologists; mem. Associated Anesthesiologists Saginaw (v.p. 1968-70, asst. treas. 1969—, sec. 1970—), A.M.A., Am. Soc. Anesthesiologists. Club: Quota. Home: 8771 White Beech Dr Saginaw MI 48603 Office: 1232 N Michigan Av Saginaw MI 48602

GRUNER, VIRGINIA SHAW (MRS. GEORGE JOHN GRUNER), club woman; b. Chgo., Feb. 19, 1912; d. Neil John and Rose (Tenwick) Shaw; grad. Chgo. Tchrs. Coll., 1931; B.S., Northwestern U., 1932; m. George John Gruner, Nov. 6, 1935; children—Valerie Dale, Diane Rae. Tchr., Parker Practice Sch. of Chgo., Chgo. Tchrs. Coll., 1935-40. Active Girl Scouts Am., 1949-53; v.p. Factotums, Scarsdale (N.Y.) Woman's Club, 1953; mem. member's guild High Mus. Art, Atlanta. Recipient Civic Achievement award City of Chgo. Mem. Internat. Platform Assn., Pi Lambda Theta, Cui Bono, Alpha Omicron Pi. Republican. Presbyn. Clubs: Scarsdale Golf (chmn. women's golf assn. 1954-56); American Yacht (Rye, N.Y.); Coral Ridge Country (Ft. Lauderdale, Fla.). Home: 140 Maison Pl Cross Creek NW Atlanta GA 30327

GRUNNET, MARGARET LOUISE (MRS. IRVING NOEL EINHORN), physician; b. Mpls., Feb. 20, 1936; d. Leslie Nels and Grace Harriet (Thomson) Grunnet; B.A., U. Minn., 1958, B.S., M.D., 1962; M.S. in Pathology, Ohio State U., 1969; m. Irving Noel Einhorn, Mar. 10, 1972; stepchildren—Jeffrey Einhorn, Franne Ruth Einhorn, Eric Carl Einhorn, Stanley Glenn Einhorn. Straight med. intern, U. Minn. Hosp., Mpls., 1962-63, resident psychiatry U. Pa. Hosp., 1963-64; resident anatomical pathology Presbyn.-U. Pa. Hosp., 1965-67; fellow neuropathology Phila. Gen. Hosp., 1967-68, Ohio State U. Hosp., Columbus, 1968-69; instr. pathology Ohio State U., 1969; asst. prof. neurology and pathology U. Utah, Salt Lake City, 1970—. Mem. A.M.A., Am. Assn. Neuropathologists, Phi Beta Kappa, Alpha Omega Alpha. Home: 4353 Zarahemla Dr Salt Lake City UT 84117 Office: University of Utah Hospital Salt Lake City UT 84112

GRUPE, AUDREY JEAN, educator; b. Elgin, Ill., Mar. 18, 1929; d. Victor Louis and Emma Elizabeth (Kasten) Grupe; B.S. in Edn., Ill. State U., 1951; M.S., U. Ill., 1955, Ph.D., 1961. Tchr. pub. sch., Bloominton, Ill., 1951-53; sch. psychologist North Shore Schs., Glen Head, N.Y., 1958-63, chief sch. psychologist, 1963-68; asso. prof. psychology Ill. State U., Normal, 1968—, also coordinator grad. program in sch. psychology. Mem. Am., Ill. psychol. assns., Council Exceptional Children, Delta Kappa Gamma. Democrat. Lutheran. Home: RFD 4 Bloomington IL 61701 Office: Dept Psychology Ill State U Normal IL 61761

GRYDE, CAROL JOAN, hosp. adminstr.; b. nr. Edinburg, N.D., July 9, 1940; d. Edwin and Myrtle Christine (Sunderland) G.; student (Am. Legion Aux. scholar), U. Ore., 1958-59; B.S., San Jose State Coll., 1963; postgrad. Columbia, 1971—. Staff occupational therapist Burke Rehab. Center, White Plains, N.Y., 1964-66; with Army Dept., 1966-67; supr. occupational therapy Conn. Mental Health Center, New Haven, 1968-69; chief occupational therapy Fordham Hosp., Bronx, N.Y., 1969-73; chief occupational therapy Jacobi Hosp.-Albert Einstein Med. Coll., Bronx, 1973—. Cons., Misericordia Home Care Program, Bronx, 1969-70, Bronx Devel. Services, 1973—; clin. lectr. Columbia U. Occupational Therapy Sch., N.Y.C., 1971—. Recipient tng. grant Office Vocational Rehab., 1963. Mem. World Fedn. Occupational Therapists, UN Assn., Am., N.Y. State (bd. mem. dist. 1969-73) occupational therapy assns. Democrat. Home: 1296 Midland Av Yonkers NY 10704 Office: Room 2N27 Jacobi-Eastchester Rd at Pelham Pkwy Bronx NY 10461

GUASCO, JEAN ACKERS (MRS. DANTE V. GUASCO), librarian; b. Lancaster O.; d. Raymond McKinley and Elsie (Moran) Ackers; student Capitol U., 1939-40; B.S., Ohio State U., 1943, M.A., 1945; M.S., Columbia, 1953; m. Dante V. Guasco, Feb. 14, 1946. Tchr. Mifflin High Sch., Columbus, O., 1942-46; librarian Rogers Jr. High Sch., Stamford, Conn., 1946-48; library asst. U.S. Navy Underwater Sound Library, New London, Conn., 1948-49; circulation librarian U. Conn., Storrs, 1949-51; asst. librarian Ft. Jay Post, 1st Army Reference Library, Governors Island, N.Y.C., 1951-53; reference librarian McGraw-Hill, Inc., N.Y.C., 1953-54, asso. librarian, 1954-60, chief librarian, 1960—. Mem. Am. Library Assn., Am. Soc. Information Sci., Nat. Microfilm Assn., Spl. Libraries Assn. (chmn. pub. div. 1968-69), N.Y. Library Club, Beta Phi Mu. Home: 5425 Fieldston Rd Bronx NY 10471 Office: 1221 Av of Americas New York City NY 10020

GUBBINS, JOAN MARGARET (MRS. DALE GEORGE GUBBINS), state senator; b. N.Y.C., July 2, 1929; d. Arthur L. and Margaret (Hedge) Barton; student U. Ill., 1947-49; m. Dale George Gubbins, May 6, 1949; children—Gregory Dale, Carol Jane. Mem. Ind. Senate, 1969—. Research chmn. Ind. Goldwater for Pres. Com., 1964; del. Ind. Republican State Conv., 1966, 68, 70; Rep. precinct committeewoman, Indpls., 1966-70. Bd. dirs. Com. for Constl. Govt. Mem. Nat. Fedn. Rep. Women, Ind. State Legislators Club, Citizens Forum, Poet's Corner (hon.), Nat. Assn. Pro Am., Am. Contract Bridge League, Central Ind. Bridge Assn. Presbyn. Home: 1000 E 81st St Indianapolis IN 46240

GUDGEN, MARJORIE GLORIA, art edn. dir.; b. Independence, Kan.; d. Herbert Truman and Emma (Billington) Gudgen; B.S., Kan. State Tchrs. Coll., 1936; M.S., U. Kan., 1952; postgrad. West Tex. State U., 1958. Art instr., prin. art supr. Coffeyville (Kan.) pub. schs., 1929-52; art cons. Galveston (Tex.) Ind. Sch. Dist., 1952-57; dir. art edn. Amarillo (Tex.) Ind. Sch. Dist., 1957-74. Chmn. adv. com. local Scholastic Art Awards contest, Amarillo, 1964-74, mem., 1974-75. Bd. dirs. Amarillo Art Center. Mem. Amarillo C. of C. (mem. fine arts council 1963—), N.E.A., Tex. State Tchrs. Assn., Nat. Art Edn. Assn., Tex. Art Edn. Assn. (pres. 1962-64), Amarillo Fine Arts Soc., Delta Kappa Gamma, Pi Lambda Theta, Kappa Delta Pi. Methodist. Selected to participate in Programa De Educacion Interamericana, 1968. Home: 1205 Jackson Amarillo TX 79101

GUDIKSEN, KAREN JEAN STOUT (MRS. PAUL HALBORG GUDIKSEN), psychiatrist; b. Seattle, Nov. 29, 1939; d. John Edward and Ellen Marie (Jensen) Stout; B.S., U. Wash., 1962, M.D., 1965; m. Paul Halborg Gudiksen, Aug. 17, 1963. Rotating intern Va. Mason Hosp., Seattle, 1965-66; psychiatry resident U. Wash., 1966-67, Langley Porter Neuropsychiat. Inst., San Francisco, 1967-69; staff psychiatrist Alameda County Health Care Services Agy., 1969-74; practice medicine, specializing in psychiatry and forensic psychiatry, Oakland, Cal., 1972—; mem. staff Fairmont Hosp., San Leandro, Cal. Diplomate Am. Bd. Psychiatry and Neurology. Mem. Am. Psychiat. Assn., A.M.A., Cal., Alameda-Contra Costa med. assns., No. Cal. Psychiat. Soc., Sierra Club, Mortar Bd., Alpha Epsilon Delta. Home: 4721 Mira Vista Dr Castro Valley CA 94546 Office: 15400 Foothill Blvd San Leandro CA 94578

GUDSCHINSKY, SARAH CAROLINE, linguist, educator; b. Bay City, Mich., May 8, 1919; d. Eduard E. and Ursula E. (MacFalane) Gudschinsky; B.Sc., Central State Tchrs. Coll., 1940; M.A. U. Pa., 1956, Ph.D. (Joseph Bennett fellow), 1958. Tchr. rural pub. schs., Mich., 1937-47; mem. Summer Inst. Linguistics and Wycliffe Bible Translators, Santa Ana, Cal., 1948—; field worker Huautá de Jiminez, Mexico, 1948-55; linguistic supr. Summer Inst. Linguistics, Brazil, 1958-66, internat. literacy supr. and co-ordinator, 1966—, also dir.; prof. linguistics U. Tex., Arlington, 1970—. Lectr. in various univs. in Latin Am., Africa, Asia, Australia and New Guinea, 1958—. Bd. dirs. Wycliffe Bible Translators Inc., 1973—. Mem. Linguistic Soc. Am., Internat. Reading Assn., Asso. Current Anthropology. Author: Handbook of Literacy, 1951; Proto-Popotecan: A Comparative Study of Popolocan and Mixtecan, 1959; How to Learn an Unwritten Language, 1967; A Manual of Literacy for Illiterate Peoples, 1973. Address: 7500 W Camp Wisdom Rd Dallas TX 75211

GUEDEN, HILDE, concert singer; b. Vienna, Austria, Sept. 15, 1922; d. Italo F. and Frieda (Brammer) Geiringer; student Acad. Music, Vienna, also dramatics with Max Reinhardt Sch.; m. Lacy L. Hermann, Feb. 28, 1952; 1 son, Robert Joseph. Operatic debut Zurich State Opera, 1939; lyric, coloratura soprano; debut Staatsoper, Munich, Germany, 1941, Royal Opera, Rome, 1942; appeared Salzburg Festivals, 1946—; debut LaScala, 1946, Met. Opera, 1951; mem. Vienna State Opera, 1947—; also participated concert tours European cities, orch. concerts with Phila., Chgo. orchs.; TV programs Eng., U.S. Recipient title Kammersangerin, Pres. of Austria, 1950; Austrian Grand Cross of Honour for Sci. and Art. Mem. Royal Naval Assn., Sigma Alpha Iota. Home: 1 Sutton Pl S New York City NY 10022 Office: Met Opera New York City NY 10023

GUENTHER, ANNETTE DOROTHY REHM (MRS. WILLIAM FREDERICK GUENTHER), educator; b. Bklyn., July 26, 1915; d. Frederick George William and Rose Irene (Delfoe) Rehm; B.S., Austin Peay State U., 1952; M.Ed., Temple U., 1955; postgrad. Rutgers U., Syracuse U., Trenton State Coll., U. Conn.; m. William Frederick Guenther, June 25, 1941. Tchr. kindergarten, West Palm Beach, Fla., 1933-41, Moury County Schs. (Tenn.), 1946-49, Mercerville (N.J.) Elementary Sch., 1952-53, Trenton State Coll. Demonstration Schs., 1953-54, Princeton (N.J.) Elementary Schs., 1954-56; tchr. elementary grades, Trenton, 1956-62; dir. reading clinic Jr. High Sch. 3, Trenton, 1962-64; learning disabilities specialist Lawrence Twp. (N.J.) Elementary Schs., 1964-67; county curriculum specialist, lang. arts, communication skills, arts and humanities and early childhood edn. Bucks County Office of Supt. of Schs., Doylestown, Pa., 1968—; instr. Trenton State Coll. Extension Div., 1958-62, Pa. State U. Continuing Edn. Div., 1972—. Mem. Gov.'s Com. for Child Devel. Programs, 1971—, also mem. exec. com., 1973—. Mem. Am. Assn. Elementary, Kindergarten and Nursery Educators (nat. pres. 1971-72), Am. Assn. U. Women, Assn. Childhood Edn. Internat., Assn. for Supervision and Curriculum Devel., Internat. Reading Assn., N.E.A. (life), Nat. Assn. for Edn. of Young Children, N.J. Edn. Assn., Pa. Edn. Assn., U.S. Nat. Com. and World Orgn. for Early Childhood Edn., World Confedn. Orgn. Teaching Professions (U.S. del., com. for pre-sch. edn.), Kappa Delta Pi, Delta Kappa Gamma. Contbr. articles to profl. jours. Editor in chief N.J. Reading Instrn. Jour., 1969-70. Home: Yorkshire Rd RD 4 Doylestown PA 18901 Office: Ansley Bldg Old Easton Rd Doylestown PA 18901

GUERCIA, ROSEMARIE ADELINE CANTOR (MRS. ANTHONY T. GUERCIA), physician; b. Bklyn., Mar. 8, 1926; d. Hyman and Josephine Mary (Baldwin) Cantor; B.S., Queens Coll., 1946; M.D., N.Y. Med. Coll., 1950; m. Anthony T. Guercia, June 26, 1949; children—Nancy, Darcy. Rotating intern Flushing Hosp., 1950-51; asst. resident pediatrics Greenpoint Hosp., 1951-52; chief resident pediatrics City Hosp., Welfare Island, N.Y., 1952-53; practice medicine specializing in pediatrics, Rego Park, N.Y., 1953-56, Jericho, N.Y., 1956—; clinician N.Y. City Health Dept., 1953—, Nassau County Health Dept., 1963—; clin. asst. pediatrics City Hosp., 1953-54, asst. pediatrician, 1954-58. Address: 30 Birchwood Park Dr Jericho NY 11753

GUERIN, POLLY (PAULINE), pub. relations, advt. and fashion cons.; b. N.Y.C.; d. George Germaine and Blanche (Ruest) Guerin; student Coll. City N.Y., 1950-53, (Fashion Group scholar) Fashion Inst. Tech., 1953-55; m. Hal L. Cohen, 1971. Fashion editor Women's Wear Daily, N.Y.C., 1951-58; asso. fashion dir. Amos Parrish & Co., N.Y.C., 1958-61; promotion and advt. dir. Abaco Fabrics Corp., N.Y.C., 1961-64; fashion coordinator Baar & Beards, Inc., N.Y.C., 1964-65; pub. relations and edn. dir. Lovable Co., N.Y.C., 1965-68; apparel publicity mgr. Monsanto Co., N.Y.C., 1968-69; owner Polly Guerin Advt./Pub. Relations, pub. relations and fashions cons., N.Y.C., 1969—. Instr. pub. relations and publicity Fashion Inst. Tech., 1965-67; instr. fashion coordination Pratt Inst., 1968-69; opera and consert singer Nostalgia Musicale, 1972. Recipient Mayor's certificate appreciation N.Y.C., 1965. Mem. Fashion Group, Advt. Women N.Y., Publicity Club N.Y. (Distinguished Service award 1966, dir., luncheon chmn. 1973—), Advt. Club N.Y. (women's interest cons. 1968-69, advt. and marketing course com. 1973—, bd. dirs. 1974—), Am. Women in Radio and Television, Nat. Acad. Television Arts and Scis. Author: Fashion Writing, 1972. Writer syndicated column Pollytalk, 1968—. Address: 15 Park Av New York City NY 10016

GUERNSEY, JANET BROWN (MRS. WILLIAM GUERNSEY), educator; b. Germantown, Pa., May 2, 1913; d. Clarence M. and Luella (Conwell) Brown; A.B., Wellesley Coll., 1935; A.M., Harvard, 1948; Ph.D., Mass. Inst. Tech., 1955; m. William G. Guernsey, June 20, 1936; children—Richard M., David W., Michael W., Robert G., Madeleine. Instr. dept. physics Wellesley Coll., 1942-48, asst. prof., 1948-55, asso. prof., 1955-61, prof., 1961-70, Louise S. McDowell prof. physics, 1970—, also chmn. dept. Mem. A.A.A.S., Am. Phys. Soc., Am. Assn. Physics Tchrs. (v.p. 1973-74), Am. Assn. U. Profs., Phi Beta Kappa, Sigma Xi. Home: Sabrina Farm Wellesley MA 02181

GUERRANT, DORIS JEANNE (MRS. SAMUEL SAUNDERS GUERRANT III), vocational psychologist; b. Jersey City, Sept. 23, 1931; d. Walter Vincent and Emma Catherine (Eichhorn) Talbot; B.A. cum laude, Roanoke Coll., 1968; M.S., Radford Coll., 1972; m. Samuel Saunders Guerrant, III, June 5, 1963; children—Priscilla Jeanne, Diana Nadine, Douglas Gordon, Margaret Anne. Tchr. educable mentally retarded Jefferson High Sch., Roanoke, Va., 1968-70; dir. vocational evaluation Goodwill Industries, Roanoke, 1970-74; psychologist Roanoke Area Drug Abuse Control Council, 1974—. Cons. Opportunities Industrialization Center, 1972-73. Mem. Council for Exceptional Children (treas. 1970-72). Editorial adv. bd. Vocational Evaluation and Work Adjustment Bull., 1973—. Home: 2415 S Jefferson St Roanoke VA 24014 Office: 1322 2d St SW Roanoke VA 24016

GUERRERO, JOSEPHINE CAMARILLO, city ofcl.; b. Chgo., Nov. 18, 1919; d. Joseph and Erlinda (Cervantez) Camarillo; student San Jose Met. Adult Edn., 1947-72. With Milpitas (Cal.) Post Office, 1947—, asst. postmaster, 1966—; owner, operator Milpitas Cleaners, 1938-48; bookkeeper, salesgirl Samuel Pyes Jeweler, San Jose, Cal., 1944-47. Planning commr., Milpitas, 1955-58; library commr., Santa Clara County, Cal., 1963—, City of Milpitas, 1965—; adv. bd. mem. to bd. trustees San Jose City Coll., 1968; Green Thumb civic beautification chmn., 1962. Named Woman of Year, Milpitas Green Thumb Club, 1962. Mem. Women Appointive Polit. Opportunities, Milpitas Bus. and Profl. Women's Club (pres. 1960, 63, 72), Milpitas C. of C. (v.p. 1973), Star of Sea Credit Union (pres. 1956-66). Roman Catholic (mem. ch. council). Home: 135 Spence Av Milpitas CA 95035 Office: 40 E Carlo St Milpitas CA 95035

GUESON, EMERITA TORRES, obstetrician, gynecologist; b. Angeles City, Philippines, Jan. 4, 1942; d. Pedro Guanzon and Lina Suarez (Torres) Gueson; A.A., U. St. Tomas, 1958, M.D., 1963. Came to U.S., 1964. Rotating intern Germantown Hosp., Phila., 1964-65; gen. practice resident Community Gen. Hosp., Reading, Pa., 1965-66; obstetrics-gynecology resident Phila. Gen. Hosp., 1966-70; gynecology research cons. U. Pa. Dental Sch., Phila., 1970; practice medicine specializing in obstetrics and gynecology, Bristol, Pa., 1971-72; mem. staff Nazareth Hosp., Phila. Human resource Am. Bicentennial Research Inst. Jr. fellow Am. Coll. Obstetricians and Gynecologists; mem. Am. Fertility and Sterility Soc., Blockley Obstet. Soc., A.M.A. (achievement award for continuing med. edn. 1970-73), Pa., Philadelphia County med. socs., Pa. Assn. for Retarded Children. Home: 6305 Forge Turn Neshaminy Valley Cornwells Heights PA 19020 Office: 900 Old Orchard Lane Bristol PA 19007 also 3101 Cottman Av Philadelphia PA 19149

GUGGENHEIM, MALVINA HALBERSTAM (MRS. WOLF GUGGENHEIM), educator; b. Poland, May 2, 1937; d. Marcus and Pearl (Halberstam) Halberstam; came to U.S., 1947, naturalized, 1952; B.A., Bklyn. Coll., 1957; M.Internat. Affairs, Columbia, 1964, J.D., 1961; m. Wolf Guggenheim, Aug. 13, 1963; children—Arye, Achiezer. Admitted to N.Y. bar, 1962, Cal. bar, 1968; law clk. to So. dist. judge, N.Y.C., 1961-62; research asso. project on internat. procedure Columbia Law Sch., N.Y.C., 1962-63; asst. dist. atty. N.Y. County, N.Y.C., 1963-67; mem. firm Rifkind & Sterling, Los Angeles, 1968-69; sr. atty. Nat. Legal Program on Health Problems of the Poor, U. Cal. at Los Angeles, 1969-70; asso. prof. law Loyola U., Los Angeles, 1970-71, prof., 1971—. Vis. prof. law U. So. Cal., Los Angeles, 1972-73; mem. nat. adv. council Video-Tape Project on Women and Law, 1973—; faculty adviser Loyola Soc. Internat. Law, Los Angeles, 1971—. Kent scholar, 1959, 61; Stone scholar, 1960. Recipient Jane Marks Murphy award Columbia Law Sch., 1959. Mem. Am., Los Angeles County (com. on arbitration 1973—) bar assns., State Bar Cal., Am. Soc. Internat. Law (panel on constn. and conduct Am. fgn. policy 1973—), Am. Judicature Soc., Assn. Am. Law Schs. (com. on fgn. exchange of law tchrs. and students 1972), World Peace through Law Center (exec. com. sect. on internat. legal edn., 1973—), Center for Study Democratic Instns., Columbia Law Sch. Alumni Assn., Phi Beta Kappa. Contbr. articles to profl. jours. Home: 1204 S Camden Dr Los Angeles CA 90035

GUGGENHEIMER, ELINOR COLEMAN (MRS. RANDOLPH GUGGENHEIMER), city planner; b. N.Y.C.; d. Nathan and Lillian (Fox) C.; student Vassar Coll., 1929-31; B.A., Barnard Coll., 1934; postgrad. Tchrs. Coll., Columbia, 1951-52, Pratt Inst. Tech., 1962; m. Randolph Guggenheimer, June 2, 1932; children—Charles S., Randolph. Mem. N.Y.C. Planning Commn., 1961-68; moderator program Straight Talk, WOR-TV, 1971-74; commr. N.Y.C. Dept. Consumer Affairs, 1974—; faculty New Sch. Social Research. Founder, hon. pres. Day Care Council City N.Y.; Day Care and Child Devel. Council Am.; chmn. program planning com. Community Council Greater N.Y., 1970—, bd. dirs., 1958—; bd. dirs. Nat. Recreation and Park Assn., 1965—, Community Service Soc., 1954—, Citizen's com. for Children, 1952—, United Neighborhood Houses, 1948—, N.Y. Fund for Children, 1956—, Jewish Assn. for Services to the Aged, 1969—, State Adv. Com. on Pub. Community Coll. Study, 1967-69. Chmn. adv. council N.Y.C. Democratic Com.; mem. policy com. Nat. Women's Polit. Caucus, 1970-72. Hon. trustee Edn. Alliance. Recipient Pearl Merrill award League Parent Edn., 1962, Louise Waterman Wise award Am. Jewish Congress, 1964. Mem. Fedn. Jewish Philanthropies (trustee 1953—). Clubs: Cosmopolitan, Women's City (N.Y.C.). Author: Recreation Planning in Urban Areas, 1969. Contbr. articles to profl. jours. Home: 1095 Park Av New York City NY 10028

GUHA, LOUISE DORA HARSHBARGER, bus. exec.; b. Plymouth, Ind.; d. Paul Revere and Dora L. (Croxton) Harshbarger; student pub. schs.; grad. Gracie Inst. Hypnosis, N.Y.C., 1966; m. P. Kumar Guha, Aug. 21, 1953 (div. May 1967). Sec., Capehart Farnsworth Television and Radio, Ft. Wayne, also bookkeeper Tokheim Oil Tank & Pump Co., Ft. Wayne, 1938-42; bookkeeper, stenographer N.Y. Testing Labs., N.Y.C., 1942-43; sec. to treas. J. G. White & Co., Inc., N.Y.C., 1943-52; corp. sec., asst. treas. Soya Corp., N.Y.C., 1952, White Securities Corp., N.Y.C., 1952-66; found. sec. White Found., 1952—, also treas., dir., mem. Found.; corp. sec. Ill. Cities Water Co., N.Y. and Robinson, Ill., 1952-63, corp. sec., asst. treas. successor co. Eastern Ill. Water Co., N.Y. and Robinson, 1963-73; sec.-asst. treas. Water Securities Co., 1963-73, Indsl. Water Supply Co., 1953-73 (both N.Y. and Robinson); staff Finance mag., N.Y.C., 1973—. Mem. Tagore Soc. N.Y., N.Y. Jazz Soc., Business and Profl. Women's Club, Duke Ellington Soc., Sikh Cultural Soc., Pan Pacific and S.E. Asia Women's Assn. U.S.A. Roman Catholic. Home: 322 E 4th St New York City NY 10009 Office: 5 E 75th St New York City NY 10021

GUIDO, ANGELINA (MRS. HAROLD M. SILVER), ophthalmologist; b. Morgantown, W.Va., Nov. 11, 1924; d. Salvatore and Julia Angelina (Gallo) Guido; B.A., W.Va. U., 1945, B.S., 1947; M.D., U. Md., 1949; postgrad. Harvard, 1950-51; m. Harold M. Silver, Aug. 10, 1958; children—Dorothy Nan, Richard Frank, Michael Guido. Intern, Pitts. Med. Center, 1949-50; resident Univ. Hosp., Balt., 1951-53; fellow in ophthalmology Johns Hopkins Hosp., Balt., 1953-54; practice medicine specializing in ophthalmology, Balt., 1954-59. Active Boy Scouts Am. Mem. A.M.A., Am. Acad. Ophthalmology, D.C. Med. Soc. Address: 8029 Herb Farm Dr Bethesda MD 20034

GUILD, ALICE WALTA (MRS. ROBERT WYLIE GUILD), advt. and pub. relations exec.; b. San Francisco, July 6, 1934; d. Walter Emmet and Muriel Beatrice (MacFarlane) Flanders; A.A., Colo. Woman's Coll., Denver, 1954; m. Robert Wylie Guild, Oct. 23, 1954; children—Maric Drue, Walter Flanders, Diane Scott, Alice MacFarlane. Comml. artist Star-Bull. Printing Co., Honolulu, 1954; asst. advt. and pub. relations mgr. M. McInerny, Ltd., Honolulu, 1954-55; free lance comml. artist, Honolulu, 1955-67; dir. advt. and pub. relations Security Diamond Co., Honolulu, 1967-74; advt. and promotion mgr. Ala. Moana Center, Honolulu, 1974—. Vol. worker Mental Health Assn., Hawaii Heart Assn., Friends of the East-West Center, Am. Cancer Soc. Sec. Gov.'s Commn. on the Year 2000, 1971—; mem. Citizen's Adv. Com. on the Civic Center Master Plan, Honolulu, 1965-70; precinct worker Republican Com., Hawaii, 1959-74. Mem. adv. com., Goodwill Industries of Hawaii, 1973—. Bd. dirs. Friends of Iloani Palace, corr. sec., 1965-69; bd. dirs. Aloha United Fund, Honolulu, Jr. League of Honolulu, 1956-75, pres., 1969-70; bd. dirs. Child and Family Service, Honolulu, 1957-63. Recipient Riley H. Allen award Hawaii Newspaper Agy., 1970, 73. Mem. Am. Advt. Fedn., Punahou Alumni Assn., Daus. of Hawaii. Home: 2106 Keeaumoku St Honolulu HI 96822 Office: 3200 Ala Moana Center Honolulu HI 96814

GUILD, CAROL ELIZABETH (MRS. WILLIAM H. GUILD), telecaster, producer; b. Minnet, Wash.; d. David Pringle and Grace (McFadden) Williams; student U. Nev., 1937-40, Pasadena Community Playhouse, 1940-41, Keystone Jr. Coll., Pa., 1966, Pa. State U., 1972; m. William H. Guild; children—Diane, Nita, William H., Ruth. Broadcaster, telecaster, producer KOH, Reno, KOLOTV, Reno, 1951-59, KPIX, San Francisco, 1958-59, WAFM, Miami, Fla., 1959-60, Monitor, NBC, N.Y.C., 1958-61, WDAU-WNEP-TV, Scranton, Pa., 1960-63, daily shows Carol and Friends, Time With Carol, Magic Window, A Visit with Carol, Party Line, PBS-WVIA-TV, Scranton, 1966—. Mem. Nev. Gov.'s Welfare Com., 1958-59. Vice chmn. Lyon County (Nev.) Republicans, 1956-58. Bd. dirs. Crippled Children's Soc. Scranton. Mem. Delta Delta Delta, Beta Sigma Phi. Mem. Order Eastern Star. Home: Route 1 Box 69 New Milford PA 18834 Office: WVIA-TV Old Boston Rd Pittston PA 18640

GUILD, HARRIET GRIGGS, physician; b. Windham, Conn., Aug. 11, 1899; d. Frank Eugene and Harriet Exton (Clarke) Guild; A.B., Vassar Coll., 1920; M.D., John Hopkins U., 1925. Intern Johns Hopkins Hosp., 1925-26, intern pediatrics, 1926-27, asst. resident pediatrics, 1927-28, dir. pediatrics dispensary, 1928-30, instr. pediatrics, 1928-34, asso., 1934-45, asso. prof., 1945-65, asso. prof. emeritus, 1965—; practice medicine specializing in pediatrics, Balt., 1965—; asso. cons. Sinai Hosp., Balt., 1958—, Union Meml. Hosp., Balt., 1965—, pediatric cons. Windham Community Meml. Hosp., Willimantic, Conn., 1940—. Mem. med. adv. bd. Partridge Sch. Rehab. Center, 1956-64. Trustee, mem. med. adv. bd. Md. Kidney Found. Recipient Elizabeth Blackwell award N.Y. Infirmary, 1958, research grant Md. Kidney Found., 1960-70. Mem. Soc. Pediatric Research, Am. Pediatric Soc., Am. Acad. Pediatrics, Am. Diabetes Assn., Am. Soc. Human Genetics, Nat. Kidney Found., N.Y. Acad. Scis., Am., Pan-Am. med. assns., Md. Soc. Med. Research, Am. Museum Nat. History, Johns Hopkins Med. Assn., Johns Hopkins Surgical Assn., Pediatric Sect. Balt. Med. Soc., Nat. Hist. Soc., Phi Beta Kappa, Sigma Xi, Alpha Omega Alpha. Conglist. Contbr. articles to profl. jours., med. textbooks. Home: 4422 Marble Hall Rd Baltimore MD 21218 Office: 550 N Broadway Baltimore MD 21205

GUILFORD, JOAN SHERIDAN, psychologist; b. Lincoln, Neb., Sept. 28, 1928; d. Joy Paul and Ruth S. (Burke) Guilford; A.A., Bradford Jr. Coll., 1947; B.A., U. Neb., 1949; M.A., U. So. Cal., 1951, Ph.D., 1962; m. Irving J. Budnoff, Mar. 17, 1963 (div. June 1966); m. F.B. McClung, Sept. 1, 1951 (div. Feb. 1958); children—Jacqueline M., Scott S., Michael P.; m. 3d, Frederick L. McGuire, Nov. 16, 1972. Psychologist, Sheridan Supply Co., Beverly Hills, Cal., 1951-62; sr. research scientist Am. Inst. Research Los Angeles, 1962-66, dir. Los Angeles office, 1963-66; prin. engring. scientist Douglas Aircraft Co., 1966-67; dir. grant project Holy Cross Hosp., 1967-69; dir. research Sheridan Psychol. Services, 1969; sr. behavioral scientist Gen. Behavioral Systems, Inc., 1969-71; exec. dir. Sheridan Psychol. Services, Inc., 1971—. Mem. Am., Western psychol. assns., Human Factors Soc., Sigma Xi, Phi Kappa Phi, Alpha Phi. Democrat. Episcopalian. Home: 220 City Blvd W Apt 112 Orange CA 92668

GUILFORD, MARY THERESA BACON (MRS. MORTON GUILFORD), realtor; b. Pleasantville, N.Y., Sept. 4, 1934; d. Arnold O. and Bridget (Goonan) Bacon; grad. high sch.; m. Morton Guilford, Feb. 8, 1956; children—Carolyn, Louis, David, Evelyn. Dir. M. Goldfarb My Florist, Inc., N.Y.C., 1962-74; v.p. Arcadia-Gardens, Pitts., 1967—, Ossining, N.Y., 1964—; real estate saleswoman, 1972—; notary pub., 1972—. Home: 1339 N Doheny Dr Los Angeles CA 90026

GUIN, GRACE HUGHES, pathologist; b. Birmingham, Ala., July 23, 1912; d. Ernest Smith and Grace (Hawkins) Hughes; B.S., Birmingham So. Coll., 1938; M.D., Vanderbilt, 1943; postgrad. Harvard, 1948; m. Joel B. Guin, Oct. 21, 1942 (div.); 1 dau., Grace Hawkins. Intern Albany (N.Y.) Hosp., 1945-46; asst. surgeon USPHS, Washington, 1946-50; post doctoral fellow Nat. Cancer Inst., 1950; resident pathology Garfield Meml. Hosp., 1950-52; resident pathology Children's Hospital, Washington, 1952-53; asso. clin. prof. pediatrics Georgetown U., 1960-70, chmn. dept. pathology, 1960-65; fellow pathology Meml. Center, N.Y.C., 1953-54; asst. clin. prof. pathology George Washington U. Sch. Medicine, 1960-71, asso. prof., 1971—; asso. pathologist Arlington Hosp., 1964-67; asst. to dir. pathology and allied services VA, Washington, 1967—. Diplomate in pathologic anatomy and clin. pathology Am. Bd. Pathology. Fellow Am. Soc. Clin. Pathologists, Coll. Am. Pathologists (mem. com. for systematized nomenclature pathology 1968—, com. lab. mgmt. and planning 1969—); mem. N.Y. Acad. Scis., D.C. Med. Soc. (v.p. 1963), Washington Soc. Pathologists, D.A.R., Phi Beta Kappa. Republican. Contbr. articles to med. jours. Home: 3600 N Abingdon St Arlington VA 22207 Office: VA Pathology Service Central Office 810 Vermont Av NW Washington 20420

GUINEY, MARCELLA BEFFA, nutritionist, dietitian; b. Summit, N.J., July 26, 1922; d. Louis George and Ida (Steinmetz) Beffa; B.S. in Home Econs. magna cum laude, St. Joseph Coll., 1943; M.S. in Instl. Mgmt., Columbia, 1945; m. William Francis Guiney, Jr., Apr. 21, 1956; children—William Francis III, Liam, John, Marcia Ann. Intern N.J. Coop. Course, Newark, 1944; asst. dietitian Roosevelt Hosp., N.Y.C., 1944-45; nutritionist Nat. Dairy Council, 1945-47, cons. greater N.Y. program, 1963-66, program dir., 1966-68; chief dietary dept. Am. U. Beirut (Lebanon) Hosp., 1947-50; nutritionist, pub. relations Borden Co., N.Y.C., 1951-52; exec. dir. Dairy Council Westchester County (N.Y.), White Plains, 1952-58; exec. dir. Dairy Council Met. N.Y., 1969—. Chmn. Food and Nutrition Council Greater N.Y., 1971-72. Mem. Am., Greater N.Y. (pres. 1955-56) dietetic assns., N.Y. State Nutrition Council, Am. Home Econs. Assn., Internat. Fedn. Home Econs., Am., N.Y. pub. health assns., Soc. Nutrition Edn., Nat. Council Catholic Women. Home: 51 Burning Tree Rd Greenwich CT 06830 Office: 60 E 42d St New York City NY 10017

GUINN, JACQUELINE DORIS (MRS. JAMES OLIVER GRANT), dentist; b. Birmingham, Ala., May 18, 1933; d. Henry Davis and Ethel Lois (Sewell) Guinn; B.S., Talladega Coll., 1954; D.D.S., Meharry Med. Coll., 1958; m. James Oliver Grant, Nov. 24, 1960; children—Jacques, Jo Lynn, Jason. Intern, Guggenheim Dental Clinic, N.Y.C., 1958; pvt. practice dentistry, Cleve., 1958—. Mem. Mount Pleasant Community Council. Recipient certificate of thanks Jobs Corps for Women. Mem. Am., Ohio dental assns., Assn. Am. Women Dentists, Forest City Dental Study Club, Cleve. Dental Soc., Alpha Kappa Alpha. Home: 17300 Liomond Blvd Cleveland OH 44120 Office: 14809 Kinsman Rd Cleveland OH 44120

GUINN, NORA (MRS. CHARLES W. GUINN), dist. judge; b. Akiak, Alaska, Nov. 11, 1920; d. Joseph N. and Annie (Wassilli) Venes; grad. high sch.; m. Charles W. Guinn, Jan. 27, 1941; children—Susan (Mrs. Kevin Murphy), Charles J., John, Robert, Judith, Margaret, James, Shelley, Cindy. Tchrs. aide Bur. Indian Affairs, Tunuvok, Nelson Island, 1942-45; magistrate State of Alaska, Bethel, 1959-68; dist. judge 4th dist. State of Alaska, Bethel, 1968—. Pres., Kuskokwim Valley Native Assn., 1969-70; mem. Gov.'s Adv. White House Bd. on Youth; adv. bd. East Sea Title III; mem. Alaska Gov.'s Bd. Criminal Justice. Bd. dirs. Alaska Legal Service. Home: Box 143 Bethel AK 99559 Office: Box 93 Bethel AK 99559

GUINZBURG, RUTH LEWY (MRS. FREDERIC V. GUINZBURG), artist; b. N.Y.C., May 25; d. Sigmund and Bertha (Epstein) Lewy; A.B., Barnard Coll., 1919; postgrad. U. Rome, 1923, U. Florence, 1925, Sorbonne, 1927; M.A., Columbia, 1930; m. Frederic V. Guinzburg, Feb. 22, 1920; children—Kate (Mrs. William E. Fox, Jr.), Betty (Mrs. Thomas Caufield, Jr.). Exhibited in group shows in Mexico City, Mexico, 1935, Paris, France, 1927, Delphic Studio, N.Y.C., 1936, County Center, White Plains, N.Y., 1962, Contemporary Arts, N.Y.C., 1963; represented in pvt. collections. Tchr., Chiselhurst Studio, N.Y.C., 1930—. Chmn. arts and skills Grasslands Hosp., 1940-42; chmn. arts and skills corps Westchester County, 1942-45; chmn. art exhibits Hawaii chpt. World Brotherhood, 1958-62. Recipient prize for lithograph Hudson Valley Art Assn., 1945, watercolor prize Westchester County Center, 1960. Mem. Nat. Sculpture Assn. (allied asso.), Nat. Assn. Women Artists. Home and studio: Chappaqua NY 10514

GUITE, SUZANNE (MRS. ALBERTO TOMMI), sculptor; b. Perce-Gaspe, Que., Can., Oct. 12, 1927; d. E.J. and Aline (Cyr) Guite; B.A., Inst. Design, Chgo., 1947, M.A., Scuola di Belle Arte, Florence, Italy, 1950; m. Alberto Tommi, May 29, 1950; children—Thomas M. Josee, Michelle, Frederic. One woman shows Cercle Universitaire, Montreal, 1952, Galerie Agnes Lefort, Montreal, 1953, Roberson Gallery, Ottawa, 1954, Cercle Universitaire, Que., 1955, Risher's Gallery, Mexico, 1956, Galeria 60, Florence, 1960, Gallerilibre, Montreal, 1963, Princeton U., 1967, Maisons des Art Chicoutimi, 1967, Galerie Whitney, Montreal, 1970, Musee Rodin, Paris, 1970, Boston U., 1971, Columbia (S.C.) Art Mus., 1971, Los Angeles Mus., 1971, Gallery Ingenu, Toronto, 1971, Nat. Art Center, Thor Gallery, Louisville, 1972, Galerie du Parc Trois Rivieres, 1972, Ottawa, 1972, Nat. Art Center, Ottawa, 1973, Douglass Coll., New Brunswick, N.J., 1974; exhibited in group shows Musee D'Art Moderne, Sao Paolo, Brazil, 1959, Expo 67, Montreal, Toronto City Hall, 1967, U. Waterloo, 1969, Musee D'Art Contemporain, Montreal, 1970, Galerie Espace, Montreal, 1972, others; executed murals Cathedral San Miguel de Allende, Mexico, New Carlisle Courthouse, Que., Can., sculptures Montreal Expo, 1967; represented in permanent collection Que. Provincial Mus. Founder, dir. classes Perce Art Center, 1955-72; Recipient prize Que. Provincial Exhbn., 1954. Mem. Sculptors Soc. Can., Soc. Sculptors of Quebec. Address: CP 144 Perce PQ Canada

GULLAHORN, JEANNE DORIS ERARD (MRS. JOHN TAYLOR GULLAHORN), educator; b. Springfield, Mass., Mar. 11, 1932; d. Hector Langevin and Malvina (Lanctot) Erard; A.B. summa cum laude, Radcliffe Coll., 1954; M.A., U. Kan., 1958; Ph.D., Mich. State U., 1964; student U. Paris (France), 1954-55; m. John Taylor Gullahorn, May 7, 1955; children—Gregory Maurice, Lorraine Lynn, Leslie Joan. Asst. prof., dept. psychology Mich. State U., East Lansing, 1965-69, asso. prof., 1969-74, prof., 1974—. Cons., System Devel. Corp., 1961-65; vis. scientist, Santa Monica, Cal., 1965-66; vis. prof. Univ. Coll., Cardiff, Wales, 1972-73. NSF coop. grad. fellow, 1959-61, NSF research grantee, 1965-69, Nat. Inst. Mental Health research grantee, 1968-70. Mem. Midwest Soc. Multivariate Exptl. Psychology (sec.-treas. 1969-71), Am. Psychol. Assn., Am. Sociol. Assn., Am. Humanist Assn., Phi Beta Kappa, Sigma Xi, Phi Kappa Phi. Contbr. articles to profl. jours. Office: Dept Psychology Mich State Univ East Lansing MI 48823

GULLATT, MARY JANE, editor; b. Phenix City, Ala., Oct. 6, 1932; d. Claude Bertram and Julia (Hornsby) Gullatt; A.B., U. Ala., 1954. Reporter, Tuscaloosa (Ala.) News, 1954-58; edn. reporter Pensacola (Fla.) News, 1958-60; govt. reporter Columbus (Ga.) Enquirer, 1960-66, 71-72; editor, pub. Phenix Citizen-Herald, 1966-70, 73—. Mem. Aux. Cobb Hosp., Phenix City, 1969—; mem. Phenix City-Russell County Library Bd., 1968—, treas. 1968-70. Bd. dirs. Russell County unit Am. Cancer Soc. Mem. Nat. Newspaper Assn., Ala. Press Assn., Phenix City-Russell County C. of C. Methodist (sec. adminstrv. bd. 1973—). Office: 1507 5th Av Phenix City AL 36867

GULLETTE, ETHEL MAE BISHOP, pianist; b. St. Paul, Mar. 29, 1908; d. Clarence Eugene and Alma (Beckman) Bishop; Mus.B., Mac Phail Sch. Music, Mpls., 1928; B.A., U. Minn., 1931; diploma Juilliard Sch. Music, 1936; pvt. study piano with Donald N. Ferguson, James Friskin; m. William Brandon Gullette, Sept. 5, 1936; children—Ethel Mae, Charlene Ann. Concertized as pianist, accompanist, Middle West, also radio appearances, 1925-33; voice accompanist Juilliard Sch. Music, 1934-48; pvt. tchr. piano, N.Y.C., 1934-48; concert pianist Eastern U.S., 1933—; duo-pianist, accompanist, Fairfield County, Conn., 1951—; mem. New Canaan Piano Quartet, 1960-68; duo-piano concerts, N.J., Conn., N.Y.C., 1967—; concerts Fairfield Hills Hosp., Newton, Conn., 1957-71; concerts, Savannah, Ga., 1972, Hilton Head Island, S.C., 1972, Beaufort, S.C., 1972, Scarsdale, N.Y., 1972-74; accompanist Darien Troupers, 1968, 69, accompanist New Canaan High Sch. Summer theater, 1972-73, duo piano concerts Springtime Open House, 1973, 74; accompanist Art Song Guild Schumann Lieder Concerts, 1974. Mem. New Canaan Town Players, 1952—, accompanist, 1958-63, 73; mem., accompanist Nutmeg Music Theatre, 1957-61, Demi-Opera Co., Brookfield (Conn.) Summer Theatre, 1961, others. Bd. govs., rehearsal pianist Norwalk (Conn.) Symphony Orch., 1955-62; bd. dirs. New Canaan Community Concerts Assn., 1961-69, membership chmn., 1967-69; active fund drives charitable orgns. Co-pres. New Canaan High Sch. Parent's Council, 1964-65. Recipient citations for work in cancer and Red Cross drives. Mem. N.Y. Singing Tchrs. Assn., New Canaan Hist. Soc. (photographer Gown Exhibits 1968—), Darien Community Assn. (chmn. duo piano group; bd. dirs. 1962-64, duo piano publicity chmn. 1966-68, 70-71, 74-75), New Canaan Library, New Canaan Audubon Soc., Norwalk Symphony Womens Assn., Am. Shakespeare Guild (fund raising chmn. New Canaan com. 1955), Am. Assn. U. Women (charter), Friends of N.Y. Philharmonic Orch., Fairfield County Panhellenic (New Canaan chmn. recommendation com. 1965-67), Juilliard Alumni Assn., U. Minn. Alumni Assn. (past dir. N.Y.), Mu Phi Epsilon, Delta Zeta (charter; pres. local alumnae chpt. 1961-63). Conglist. (sec. ch. music com. 1964-67). Clubs: Schubert (St. Paul); Atlantic Beach (L.I., N.Y.); Schubert (Stamford). Home: 85 West Hills Rd New Canaan CT 06840

GULLEY, ROSEMARIE CHARMAINE, news announcer; b. Louisville, Nov. 8, 1942; d. Ernest Lee and Marie (Powell) Gulley; B.A., Roosevelt U., 1964. With auditing dept., part-time, Michael Reese Hosp., Chgo., 1961-63; sec. Bertrand Goldberg & Assos., Chgo., 1963; successively sec., exec. sec., asst. exec. dir., exec. dir. Ind. Voters of Ill., Chgo., 1965-72; staff news announcer Sta. WLS, Chgo., 1972-73; hostess talk show Sta. WLS-TV, 1972—, TV news reporter, 1973—. Cons. on all ind. campaigns, Chgo. Publicity dir. Mid-South Health Planning Orgn., Chgo., 1970—. Bd. dirs. South Shore YMCA; chmn. pub. affairs com. Adult Edn. Council Greater Chgo. Recipient radio sta.'s Great Guy award, 1970. Mem. Nat. Acad. Television Arts and Scis. (dir.), Nat. Acad. Radio and Television Artists, Women in Broadcasting, League Women Voters. Home: 5115 S Ingleside Av Chicago IL 60615 Office: 190 N State St Chicago IL 60601

GUMM, JEANNE ELIZABETH RITZ, pub. relations exec.; b. Pitts., Feb. 11, 1925; d. Robert Steel and Ruby Ellen (Wyld) Ritz; student Chatham Coll., 1943-44, Gettysburg Coll., 1945; 1 son, Robert McKay. Buyer, Rosenbaums Dept. Store, Pitts., 1946-48; dir. Redpath-Horner Chataqua, Kansas City, Mo., 1949-52; writer Continental Casualty Co., 1955-58; copywriter Quaid Advt., Chgo., 1959; prodn. dir. Wilk Advt., 1960-63; writer, Combined Ins. Co.,

1964-68; account supr. Daniel J. Edelman, Chgo., 1968—, v.p., 1972—. Mem. Com. on Ill. Govt., 1970—; mem. Pub. Welfare Coalition, 1969-71; chmn. Community Action Commn., 1972—; mem. exec. com. Citizens Health Orgn., 1972—. Pub. relations dir. Ind. Precinct Orgn., 1968-69, ward coordinator, 1969-72, exec. dir., 1973-74. Mem. Am. Civil Liberties Union. Presbyn. (ruling elder 1967—). Home: 1951 N Howe St Chicago IL 60614 Office: 221 N La Salle St Chicago IL 60601

GUNDACKER, ELAINE MARIE TIMM (MRS. HARRY P. GUNDACKER), assn. exec.; b. New Hampton, Ia., June 11, 1933; d. Alvin J. and Myra Mae (Meta) Timm; student Upper Ia. Coll., 1958-59; m. Harry P. Gundacker, Aug. 8, 1969; 1 dau. by previous marriage—Constance Heitman (Mrs. Clark Heitman); stepchildren—Kurt, Kristin, Erik, Jenifer (Mrs. Ben Britton). Asst. city clk., City of New Hampton, Ia., 1957-63; city clk., finance dir. City of Geneseo, Ill., 1966-71; city clk. City of Oelwein, Ia., 1971-73; field rep. Municipal League Field Service, 1973—. Mem. N.W. Ill. Municipal Assn. (sec. 1970-71). Lutheran. Home: PO Box 144 New Hampton IA 50659 Office: League Iowa Municipalities 444 Ins Exchange Bldg Des Moines IA 50309

GUNDERSEN, KATHRYN IONE COHEN, occupational therapist; b. Chgo., Mar. 4, 1945; d. Maurice and Bettie (Landsman) Cohen; B.S., U. Ia., 1967; certificate Ia. Coll. Medicine, 1968; m. June 15, 1974. Intern, Michael Reese Hosp. and Med. Center, Chgo., 1967-68, Cerebral Palsy Center, U. Ind. Med. Campus, 1968, VA Hosp., Wood, Wis., 1968; staff therapist West Side VA Hosp., Chgo., 1968-74. Teaching staff U. Ill. Sch. Asso. Med. Scis., 1971-74. Active Irving Park YMCA Mixed Chorus. Mem. Am., Ill. (continuing ed. com. 1970-74) occupational therapy assns., King Arthur, Kings and Queens bowling leagues, Beta Sigma Phi (chpt. sec. 1970-71, v.p. 1971-72, pres. 1972-74, corr. sec. Chgo. met. area council 1973-74). Jewish religion. Home: 1723 Alamitas St Monrovia CA 91016

GUNDERSON, DOROTHY RUSSELL PIERCE (MRS. JAMES HAROLD GUNDERSON), broadcaster; b. Augusta, Ga.; d. Benjamin Eugene and Essie (Hankinson) Pierce; student Brenau Coll., 1930-32, Columbia, 1932-33; certificate audiometry U. Cal. at Los Angeles, 1943; m. Everly Mahin Davis, Jr., Aug. 21, 1932 (dec. Oct. 1936); 1 son, John Everly Pierce; m. 2d, James Harold Gunderson, Feb. 14, 1961. Vice pres., asst. mgr., acct. exec. Western States Radio, Santa Barbara, Cal., 1953-67, daily program Kist Coffee Call radio sta. KIST, 1953-67; dir. pub. affairs Sta. KMUZ, Santa Barbara, Cal., 1967-71, daily program Dorothy Davis Show, 1967-71; ret., 1971. Co-chmn. CARE, Santa Barbara, Cal., 1965-68; mem. adv. bd. Am. Cancer Soc., Santa Barbara, 1956—, Salvation Army, 1955-73; asso. mem. Childrens Home Soc. Mem. Santa Barbara Advt. Club (sec.-treas. 1959-61), Alpha Delta Pi Alumni. Presbyn. Club: Soroptimist (Santa Barbara) (charter pres.). Mailing Address: 3405 Madrona Dr Santa Barbara CA 93105

GUNDRUM, L. JUNE, corp. exec.; b. East St. Louis, Ill.; d. Norman H. and Fern (Seibel) Gundrum; student Rockford Coll., 1943-44; B.S., U. Chgo., 1947. Chemist, U.S. Dept. Agr., Peoria, Ill., 1948-50, tech. editor, 1950-51; tech. writer E. I. duPont de Nemours, Wilmington, Del., 1951-58; tech. writer Amoco Chem. Corp., Chgo., 1958-65, advt. mgr., 1965—. Vice chmn. pub. relations com. Soc. Plastics Industry. Mem. Assn. Indsl. Advertisers (chpt. dir. 1969-71, treas. 1971-72), Am. Chem. Soc., Soc. Tech. Communicators, Woman's Advt. Club of Chgo., Assn. Nat. Advertisers. Office: 200 E Randolph Dr Chicago IL 60601

GUNDRY, GENEVIEVE LYDIAN (MRS. L. MELVIN GUNDRY), lawyer; d. W. Forrest and Julia (Russell) Dutton; B.A., J.D.; m. L. Melvin Gundry; children—Leslie D., James A. Admitted to Ill. bar, 1933; mem. firm Gundry & Gundry, Galena, Ill., 1933—. Lectr. various univs. and orgns. Chmn. Mayor's Hist. Adv. Council, 1945-74; mem. Ill. Youth Commn., 1956-72, Gov.'s Adv. Council, 1968-72, Ill. Hist. Sites Commn., 1964-72. Bd. dirs. Ill. Big Bros. and Sisters, 1958-74. Home: 200 Bench St Galena IL 61036

GUNN, BARBARA AILEEN WELLS, home economist, univ. ofcl.; b. Dallas, Ore., Sept. 21, 1926; d. Clifford F. and Olive Marietta (Stevens) Wells; B.S., U. Ore., 1948; M.A., U. Cal. at Los Angeles, 1954; Ph.D., Stanford, 1960; m. Rex B. Gunn, June 13, 1945; children—Rex Brenner (dec.), Mary Katharine, Sally Ann. Tchr. jr. high and high sch., Palo Alto, Cal., 1948-58, Lake Arrowhead, Cal., 1948-58; sch. counselor, Lake Arrowhead, 1958-68; dir. San Bernardino Area Mental Health Assn., 1968-69; human relations specialist agrl. extension U. Cal. at Davis, 1969-73; program leader home econs. coop. extension U. Nev., Reno, 1973—. Am. Home Econs. Assn. Found. Intercity fellow, 1970. Mem. Nat. Council Family Relations, Am. Home Econs. Assn., Am. Sociol. Assn., Soc. for Study Social Problems, Cal. Personnel and Guidance Assn., Cal. Marriage Counselor Assn., Day Care and Child Devel. Council Am. Home: 1151 Skyline Blvd Reno NV 89502

GUNN, SISTER MARY LAURA, hosp. adminstr.; b. Memphis, Jan. 20, 1927; d. John F. and Selmena J. (Denegri) Gunn; diploma in nursing Mercy Hosp. Sch. Nursing, Hamilton, O., 1951; B.S. in Nursing, Our Lady of Cincinnati Coll., 1951; M. Hosp. Adminstrn., St. Louis U., 1960. Staff nurse Our Lady of Mercy Hosp., Cin., 1951; with St. Mary's Meml. Hosp., Knoxville, 1951-66, asst. adminstr., personnel dir., 1960-63, adminstr., 1963-66; adminstr. Our Lady of Mercy Hosp., Owensboro, Ky., 1966—. Vice pres. bd. trustees Sisters of Mercy of Nashville, Tenn., Inc., 1963-66; pres. corporate bd. trustees Sisters of Mercy of Ky., 1966—. Vice pres. bd. Owensboro-Daviess County Mental Health Center, 1967-73, 74—; bd. dirs. Owensboro-Daviess County Mental Health Assn., 1967—, Tri-State Health Planning Council, 1972—; mem. exec. com. Green River Area Health Planning Council; sec. bd. dirs. Green River Area Med. Program, 1969—; mem. Green River Mental Health Adv. Council, Ky. Comprehensive Health Planning Council; sec. adv. com. Home Health Care Agy., Daviess County Health Dept.; bd. dirs. Ret. Sr. Vols. Program. Mem. Am. Coll. Hosp. Adminstrs., Am., Cath., Ky. (trustee) hosp. assns., Council Community Services Execs. (mem. exec. com. 1972—), Twin Lakes Hosp. Conf. (pres. 1973), Owensboro C. of C. Address: 1006 Ford Av Owensboro KY 42301

GUNN, MICHELA FAITH (MRS. MARTIN B. GELBER), psychiatrist; b. Chgo., Feb. 27, 1940; d. Samuel Albert and Elsie Lottie (Chestler) Gunn; B.S. cum laude, U. Miami, 1961, M.D., 1965; m. Martin B. Gelber, Jan. 22, 1970. Intern, Los Angeles County-U. So. Cal. Med. Center, Los Angeles, 1965-66, psychiat. resident, 1966-70, attending physician, 1970—, ward chief adolescent crisis ward, 1970—; practice medicine specializing in psychiatry, Beverly Hills, Cal., 1970—; courtesy staff Westwood Hosp., 1970—, Meml. Hosp.; clin. asst. prof. child psychiatry U. So. Cal. Sch. Medicine, 1970—. Mem. Am. Psychiat. Assn., So. Cal. Psychiat. Soc. (adolescent sect.), Am. Psychoanalytic Assn. (affiliate), So. Cal. Soc. Child Psychiatry, Los Angeles Psychoanalytical Inst. Home: 10576 Troon Av Los Angeles CA 90064 Office: 360 N Bedford Dr Beverly Hills CA 90210

GUNSON, NELLIE HUTCHINSON (MRS. WILLIAM E. GUNSON), educator; b. Fayetteville, Tenn., Apr. 12, 1907; d. Thomas L. and Mettie Lou (Beard) Hutchinson; student Bryson Coll., 1923-24; diploma Murray State Tchrs. Normal, 1925; B.S., Murfreesboro State Tchrs. Coll., 1931; M.A., Peabody Coll. Tchrs., 1940; postgrad. U. Md., 1952-53, summers 1960-61, 63, 65, fall 1963-64, Syracuse U., 1955-56; m. William E. Gunson, May 29, 1934. Tchr., Elora (Tenn.) Sch., 1925-26, Watertown (Tenn.) Sch., 1926-30, Andrew Jackson Sch., Kingsport, Tenn., 1931-34, Oakwood Sch., Woodlawn, Tenn., 1934-35, Jordan Springs Sch., Woodlawn, 1935-42, Brooklyn Pg., Balt., 1945-52, Belle Grove, Balt., 1952-53, Glendale, Glen Burnie, Md., 1953-55; accountant timekeeping and accounting dept. Glenn L. Martin Aircraft Co., Middle River, Md., 1942-45; teaching prin. spl. edn. Sunnyside Sch., Glen Burnie, 1955-56; supervising prin. spl. edn. Sunnyside, Sunnydale, Sunny Meadow Schs., Glen Burnie, 1956-58, Sunnyside, Sunny Glen, Sunny Meadow, 1958-59, Sunnyside, Sunny Glen, 1959-66; asst. in spl. edn. Bd. Edn., Anne Arundel County, Md., 1966-73; specialist in spl. edn. Bd. Edn. Area III, Anne Arundel County, 1973—. Demonstration tchr. spl. edn. summer workshop U. Md., 1957. Worker to establish programs for retarded children Ann. Swim Week, Glen Burnie, 1959-61. Summer Recreation Program, Glen Burnie, Cub Scouts, Boy Scouts, Brownies, Anne Arundel County, 1959-61. Bd. dirs. Bella Mache Residential Home, Sheltered Workshop Anne Arundel County. Mem. Assn. Childhood Edn. (pres. Montgomery County 1937-38, del. conv. Cin. 1923, 38), Council Exceptional Children (pres. 1958-59, del. state conv. 1960), Am. Assn. on Mental Deficiency, Assn. Ednl. Leaders Anne Arundel County, Nat., Md., Anne Arundel County assns. retarded children, Delta Kappa Gamma (chpt. rec. sec., chpt. corr. sec., chpt. treas.). Methodist (tchr. class retarded children; mem. ch. adminstrv. bd.). Mem. Order Eastern Star. Home: 213 2d Av SW Glen Burnie MD 21061 Office: Bd Edn Anne Arundel County Area III Box 1691 Millersville MD 21108

GUPTA, RUTH CHURCH (MRS. KAMIMI K. GUPTA), lawyer; b. Orland, Cal., June 4, 1917; d. James Bryon and May (Thorn) Church; A.B., Mills Coll., 1938; J.D., Hastings Coll. Law, San Francisco, 1948; m. Kamini K. Gupta, Nov. 23, 1939. Clk. to transp. atty. W. P. Fuller & Co., 1938-54; admitted to Cal. bar, 1949, since in practice with husband as Gupta & Gupta. Bd. dirs. Planned Parenthood of San Francisco, 1957-58; dir. San Francisco Lung Assn.; mem. Gov.'s Conf. on Aging. Mem. citizens legislative adv. com. to Cal. Legislature, 1957-61; commr. Regional Water Pollution Control Bd., 1959-65, Cal. Water Quality Control Bd., 1964-67, Cal. Constnl. Revision Commn., 1964-73; treas. Californians Against Smog; mem. San Francisco Mayor's Com. on Status of Women, 1971—; mem. adv. council Bay Area Air Pollution Control Bd., vice chmn., 1974. Mem. Democratic state and county central coms. Mem. Queen's Bench (pres. 1953), State Bar Cal., San Francisco Bar Assn., Nat. Assn. Women Lawyers, San Francisco Council Dist. Mchts. Assns. (pres. 1962), UN Assn. U.S.A., League Women Voters, Cal. Fedn. Bus. and Profl. Women's Clubs (legislative advocate 1955—, pres. 1963-64), Sierra Club, Am. Assn. U. Women, Marina Mchts. Assn. (dir.), Sierra Club, Delta Kappa Gamma (hon.), Kappa Beta Pi (past chpt. dean). Club: Lawyers' (bd. govs. 1970—, treas. 1972, 2d v.p. 1974) (San Francisco). Address: 2237 Chestnut St San Francisco CA 94123

GURALNICK, LILLIAN, statistician; b. N.Y.C., Jan. 16, 1915; d. Jacob and Minnie (Eisenbud) Guralnick; B.A. cum laude, Bklyn. Coll., 1934; M.Sc. (Rockefeller fellow), Johns Hopkins, 1950. Statistician, N.Y.C. Health Dept., 1938-45, Nat. Center for Health Statistics, Washington, 1946-66, Social Security Adminstrn., Washington, 1966—. Adj. prof. sch. pub. health U. N.C. at Chapel Hill, 1971—. Fellow Am. Pub. Health Assn.; mem. Am. Statis. Assn., Internat. Union Sci. Study Population. Contbr. articles to profl. jours. Home: 510 N St S W Washington DC 20024 Office: 1875 Conn Av N W Washington DC 20009

GURD, RUTH SIGHTS (MRS. FRANK ROSS NEWMAN GURD), neurochemist; b. Chgo., Sept. 17, 1927; d. Warren Preston and Frances Helen (Coleman) Sights; B.S. U. Mich., 1949; M.D., Washington U., 1957; m. Frank Ross Newman Gurd, June 12, 1956; children—Martha Helen, Charles Baillie. Research asso. Presbyn. Hosp., Chgo., 1949-51, Washington U. Sch. Medicine, 1951-52; fellow physiology Cornell U. Med. Coll., N.Y.C., 1957-58; med. cons. Aerospace Research Application Center Ind. U., Bloomington, 1962-65, sr. research asso., 1966—, asst. prof. biochemistry in med. scis., 1972—. Predoctoral fellow NSF, 1954; fellow Washington U. Med. Sch., 1955; Life Ins. Med. Research Fund fellow, 1957-58. Mem. Soc. Neurosci., Mortar Bd., Kappa Kappa Gamma. Home: 2600 Fairoaks Lane Bloomington IN 47401

GURLEY, LAVERNE TOLLEY (MRS. KENNETH W. GURLEY, SR.), educator; b. Calhoun City, Miss.; d. F. Wesley and Sarah J. (Hearington) Tolley; student U. Tenn., 1951-52; B.A., Northeastern Ill. U., 1973; m. Kenneth W. Gurley, May 22, 1939; children—Charlotte Ann (Mrs. James D. Crouch), Kenneth W. Instr. radiology U. Tenn., 1961-70, asst. prof., 1970-73, asso. prof. radiologic tech., 1973—. Fellow Am. Soc. Radiologic Technologists (counselor 1966-67); mem. Tenn. Soc. Radiologic Technologists (v.p. 1965), Assn. Univ. Radiologic Technologists (chmn. 1973—). Contbr. to profl. jours. Home: 2894 Danville Cove Memphis TN 38118 Office: 800 Madison Av Memphis TN 38163

GURNEE, RITA MAE (MRS. ROBERT TOWNSEND GURNEE), librarian; b. Allentown, Pa., Sept. 6, 1922; d. John A. and Uanna (Maier) Frati; student Sch. Bus. Practice and Speech, 1940-41; B.A., U. So. Cal., 1951, M.L.S., 1952; m. Robert Townsend Gurnee, Jan. 28, 1945. Asst. sec. to publisher Bus. Week, N.Y.C., 1940-41; make-up man Bus. Week advt., 1946-48; reference librarian Pasadena (Cal.) Pub. Library, 1952-57; asst. librarian Electro-Data Corp., Pasadena, 1957-59; reference librarian Mt. San Antonio Coll., Walnut, Cal., 1959—, occupation information specialist, 1969—. Served with WAVES, 1942-45. Mem. Spl. Libraries Assn. (dir. pub. relations so. Cal. chpt. 1955-56, chmn. recruitment 1960-61, chmn. profl. devel. 1956-57), Cal. Library Assn. (chmn. documents com. 1955-56, pres. reference librarian round table 1956-57), U. So. Cal. Library Sch. Alumni Assn. (pres. 1962-63), Libraria Sodalitas (sec. 1965-66, dir. 1967-74), Am. Assn. U. Women (pres. Covina chpt. 1968-70), Beta Phi Mu (pres. Beta chpt. 1961-62). Home: 927 S Shasta St West Covina CA 91791 Office: 1100 N Grand Av Walnut CA 91789

GURSKIS, EUGENIA ELENORA (MRS. VLADAS PAUZA), obstetrician-gynecologist; b. Cicero, Ill., Mar. 8, 1916; d. Anthony P. and Josephine (Zauras) Gurskis; M.D., U. Ill., 1941; m. Vladas Pauza, June 27, 1953; children—Anthony Gurskis, Walter Gurskis. Intern, Norwegian-Am. Hosp., Chgo., 1941, Woman's Hosp., Detroit, 1942; resident Woman's Hosp., 1942-45; practice medicine specializing in obstetrics and gynecology, Detroit, 1946—; major attending physician in obstetrics-gynecology Hutzel Hosp., Detroit. Mem. Lithuanian Displaced Persons Com., 1948-53; pres. Lithuanian chpt. Internat. Inst., 1953. Fellow A.C.S., Am. Coll. Obstetrics-Gynecology, mem. A.M.A., Am. Med. Women's Assn., Mich. Soc. Obstetrics-Gynecology, Mich. State, Wayne County med. socs. Home: 14154 Archdale St Detroit MI 48227 Office: Fisher Bldg Detroit MI 48202

GURWITSCH, ALICE RAJA STERN (MRS. ARON GURWITSCH), artist; b. Fulda, Germany, May 19, 1900; d. Jonas and Hilda (Schamberg) Stern; student Sch. for Applied Art, Nurnberg, Germany, 1922-25, New Sch. for Social Research N.Y. Art Students League, 1958-59, painting with Carl Nelson, Boston, 1953-60, printmaking New Sch. for Social Research, 1965-70; m. Aron Gurwitsch, Apr. 23, 1929. Came to U.S., 1940, naturalized, 1945. Exhibited individual shows at Gallery Cambridge Art Assn., Bush-Reissinger Mus., Twentieth Century Club, Boston, Lynn Kottler Gallery, N.Y.C., 1970; exhibited group shows including Audubon Artists, N.Y.C., Nat. Art Club, N.Y., Print Club Albany, N.Y., Lever House Show, N.Y.C., Nat. Assn. Women Artists Anns., traveling graphics exhbns. through numerous states, Italy, 1969, 71; represented in pvt. collections. Mem. Nat. Assn. Women Artists. Address: 820 W End Av New York City NY 10025

GUSRAE, RACHEL SCHULMAN, social worker; b. Slutzk, Russia; d. Falk and Betty (Baron) Schulman; came to U.S., 1921, naturalized, 1926; B.A., Hunter Coll., 1930; certificate in social work Tng. Sch. for Jewish Social Work, 1931; M.Social Service, Grad. Sch. for Jewish Social Work, 1934; postgrad. Columbia Sch. of Social Work, 1930-45; m. Gustave B. Gusrae, Aug. 1, 1931; 1 son, Bert Lee. Caseworker, Jewish Family Service, 1931-34; sr. caseworker, field work supr., 1934-40; casework supr. Nat. Refugee Service, N.Y.C., 1940-42, Jewish Hosp. Bklyn., 1942-45; dir. social service dept., adminstrv. dir., chief psychiat. social worker, dept. neuropsychiatry Jamaica (N.Y.) Hosp., 1945-63; coordinator profl. services Rehab. Center, Queens Neuro-psychiat. Inst., Jackson Heights, L.I., N.Y., 1963-65; owner Rachel Gusrae Assos., Counseling Service, Jamaica, 1963—. A founder, adminstrv. dir. South Queens Mental Health Clinic, 1953-57; psychiat. social work cons. Queens chpt. League for Mentally Ill Children, 1956-60, Lifeline Center for Child Devel., Jamaica, 1960-63; cons. Samaritan Halfway House, 1966—. Vice pres., chmn. edn. com. Queens County Mental Health Soc., 1960-62, also mem. bd.; mem. profl. adv. com. Queensboro Council for Social Welfare, 1945-47, mem. program com., 1947-55, chmn. mental health div., 1950-56, chmn. mental health dir. com., 1958-59, mem. com. on youthful offenders, 1955; Queensboro rep. to mental health div. Community Council Greater N.Y., 1952-62. Recipient certificate appreciation City N.Y.; Protection Services, U.S. Citizens Def. Corps., 1945; SSS, N.Y.C. Hdqrs., 1945; certificate of merit South Jamaica Community Council, 1957; cited for distinguished service Queens County Mental Health Soc., 1960, 62. Fellow Am. Orthopsychiat. Assn.; mem. N.Y. State Assn. for Mental Health (dir. 1960-62), Nat. Assn. Social Workers, Acad. Certified Social Workers, World Fedn. for Mental Health, Assn. for Improvement Mental Health, Alumni Assn. Columbia U. Sch. Social Work, Internat. Platform Assn. Author booklet: You, Your Patient, and the Social Service Department, 1947. Contbr. articles to profl. jours. Address: 138-34 Coolidge Av Jamaica NY 11435

GUSS, CAROLYN, educator; b. Indpls., June 11, 1910; d. Edward M. and Mary Edna (Kealing) Guss; A.B., Butler U., 1929; postgrad. Chgo. U., 1930; M.S., Ind. U., 1942, Ed.D., 1952. Tchr. high sch. Latin and English, Kingman, Ind., 1929-35; tchr. high sch. Latin, English, librarian, Amo, Inc., 1935-42; prof. edn. Ind. U., Bloomington, 1942—. Trustee Delta Kappa Gamma Ednl. Found. Mem. Am. Assn. U. Profs., Am. Assn. U. Women (br. pres. 1954-56), Council on Non-Theatrical Internat. Events (life), Assn. Edn. Communications and Tech. (dir. 1960-62), Assn. Supervision and Curriculum Devel., Audio-Visual Instrn. Dirs. Ind. (award for distinguished service to edn. 1965, pres. 1958-59), Ednl. Film Library Assn. (nat. pres. 1970-71), Nat. Soc. Study Edn., Delta Kappa Gamma (Internat. Achievement award 1963, internat. pres. 1964-66), Phi Kappa Phi, Pi Lambda Theta. Club: School Women's (Indpls.). Author: (with Margaret Rufsvold) Guides to Educational Media, 1971. Contbr. articles to profl. jours. Home: Rural Route 2 Box 292 Bloomington IN 47401

GUSSEN, RUTH MARCUS (MRS. JOHN GUSSEN), physician; b. N.Y.C., May 6, 1925; d. Joseph and Charlotte (Herman) Marcus; B.A., Cornell U., 1946, M.D., 1950; m. John Gussen, Dec. 25, 1949; 1 son, James Leo. Intern, Bellevue Hosp., N.Y.C., 1950-51, resident, 1951-54; asst. in pathology N.Y. U. Med. Coll., 1950-54; asst. chief pathologist Vets. Adminstrn., Oklahoma City, 1955-58; instr. pathology U. Okla. Sch. Med. 1955-58; asso. dir. Otology Research Lab., Cedars-Sinai Med. Center, Los Angeles, 1964-66; asso. physician diplomate Dept. of Surgery, U. Cal. at Los Angeles, Sch. of Medicine, 1966—, dir. Temporal Bone Lab., 1967—, asst. prof. pathology, 1967-73, asso. prof., 1973—. NIH Research grantee, 1966—. Diplomate Am. Bd. Pathology. Asso. fellow Am. Acad. Ophthalmology and Otolaryngology (research com. 1971—). Contbr. articles to med. jours. Office: 31-34 Rehab Center Univ Cal Los Angeles CA 90024 also 620 Clinton Pl Beverly Hills CA 90210

GUSTAFERRI, ANNA JEANNETTE, psychologist, b. Jamaica, N.Y.; d. Alfred A. and Rose (Ciranna) Gustaferri; diploma St. Mary's Hosp. Sch. Nursing, 1948; B.S in Nursing, St. John's U., 1964, M.A., 1969. Supr., Jamaica Hosp., 1948-56; adminstrv. supr. Terrace Heights Hosp., Hollis, N.Y., 1956; psychol. clin. specialist LaGuardia Hosp., Forest Hills, N.Y., 1968-70, supr., 1968—; pvt. practice psychol. testing, and cons., 1970—. Mem. Am., N.Y. State psychol. assns., Am. Nurses Assn., N.Y. State Nursing Assn., Am. Heart Assn., Am. Assn. Critical Care Nurses, St. John's Alumnae Assn., Italian Charites Am. Home: 141 38 84 Rd Jamaica NY 11435

GUSTAFSON, FRANCES SANDRA BURDISON (MRS. DAVID ALAN GUSTAFSON), lawyer; b. Greenwood, Miss., Oct. 26, 1946; d. Hugh Francis and Neva Betha (Sanders) Burdison; A.A., Northwest Jr. Coll., Senatobia, Miss., 1966; B.A., U. Miss., 1968, J.D., 1971; m. David Alan Gustafson, Aug. 26, 1972. Admitted to Miss. bar, 1971; counselor family services dept. Juvenile Ct. Memphis and Shelby County (Tenn.), 1971-73; asso. Garner, Whitten & Garner, Hernando, Miss., 1974—. Mem. Am., Miss., Desoto County bar assns., Nat. Women's Political Caucus. Lutheran. Home: 1603 Desoto Cove Southaven MS 38671 Office: 19 Union St Hernando MS 38632

GUSTAFSON, MARJORIE LILLIAN, educator; b. Galesburg, Ill., Apr. 17, 1920; d. Carl J. and Anna (Johnson) Gustafson; A.B., Knox Coll., 1942; M.A., U. Ill., 1953; postgrad. U. Wis., summers 1943, 47-48, Middlebury Coll., 1945, N.Y. Berlitz Sch., 1955, Harvard, 1958, Centre U. de Pau, France, 1969. French tchr. Wayland Acad., Beaver Dam, Wis., 1942-45, 47-50, 52-53, Holland Hall, Tulsa, 1945-47; English tchr. Cours Complémentaire, Paris, Lycée, Guingamp, Brittany, 1950-51; dean women Estherville (Ia.) Jr. Coll., 1953-54; head lang dept. Milw. Downer Sem., 1954-57; asst. prin. Tudor Hall Sch., Indpls., 1957-62; dean, St. Katharine's Sch., Davenport, Ia., 1962-63; dean women MacMurray Coll., Jacksonville, Ill., 1963-66, asst. prof. fgn. langs., 1963-70, asso. prof., 1970—. Mem. Am. Assn. U. Women (pres. 1967-69), Am. Assn. Tchrs. French, Assn. Lang. Lab. Dirs., Morgan County Hist. Soc., Phi Beta Kappa, Pi Delta Phi, Alpha Lambda Delta. Author: Le Cornemuseur et son chien, 1969. Home: 1419 Lakelawn Dr S Jacksonville IL 62650

GUSTAFSON, SARAH REGAL (MRS. ELTON T. GUSTAFSON), author, editor; b. Kishinev, Rumania, Apr. 20, 1902; d. Benjamin and Hilda (Gdansky) Regal; came to U.S., 1914, naturalized, 1920; B.A., Hunter Coll., 1926; M.S., N.Y. U., 1928; Ph.D., Columbia, 1935; m. Elton T. Gustafson, Dec. 8, 1953 (dec. Apr. 1969); children—Olin Riedman, Eric Riedman. Instr. physiology Hunter Coll., N.Y.C., 1926-30; asst. prof. physiology and biology Bklyn. Coll., 1930-52; dir. med. lit. Hoffmann-La Roche, Nutley, N.J., 1958-67, cons., 1967—. Mem. vis. sci. program Fla. Acad. Sci., 1969—. Recipient Med. Communications award Am. Med. Writers Assn., 1967. A.M.A. grantee, 1933. Fellow Am. Med. Writers Assn. (mem. bd. 1970-71), Sci. Research Soc. Am., Sigma Xi. Author: Physiology of Work and Play, 1950; Psychochemotherapy, 1963, 66; (with Charles H. Carter) Drugs in Neurospastic Disorders, 1965; The Pediatric Patient, 1963-69. Address: 7 Palmetto Way Jensen Beach FL 33457

GUSTAITIS, RASA JULIA (MRS. MELVIN MOSS), journalist; b. Kaunas, Lithuania, May 19, 1934; d. Antanas and Brone (Alexsandraviclute) Gustaitis; brought to U.S., 1947, naturalized, 1953; B.A., Oberlin Coll., 1956; M.S. in Journalism, Columbia, 1960; m. Melvin Moss, Nov. 25, 1969; 1 dau., Usha Antonia. Reporter, Washington Post, 1960-65, N.Y. Herald Tribune, N.Y.C., 1965-66; free-lance writer, San Francisco, 1966—. Mem. Living Creatures Assos. (asso.). Author: Melissa Hayden: Ballerina, 1967; Mixed-Up Max, 1968; Turning On, 1968; Wholly Round, 1972. Contbr. articles to numerous popular mags. Home: 359 Jersey St San Francisco CA 94114

GUSTISON, ELIZABETH SUTTON, assn. exec.; b. Seattle, 1903; d. William Comegys and Mary (Skinner) Sutton; A.B., U. Wash., 1926, postgrad. Law Sch., 1932-35; m. Virgil Gustison, Aug. 22, 1935 (div. Oct. 1953). Dir. Mus. History and Industry, Seattle, 1953-65. Pres., Pro American, 1945; chmn. friendly exchange sale Children's Orthopedic Hosp., 1939-41. Named Woman of Yr. Quota Club, 1961. Mem. Fashion Group Am., D.A.R., Delta Zeta. Republican. Episcopalian. Clubs: Sunset; Seattle Yacht. Home: Apt 503 1220 Boren Av Seattle WA 98101 Office: 2161 E Hamlin St Seattle WA 98102

GUTFRUCHT, RUTH EMMA, educator, artist; b. Rochester, N.Y.; d. Rudolph A. and Marian (Skinner) Gutfrucht; diploma (fellow) Rochester Inst. Tech., 1939, B.F.A., 1959, M.F.A., 1966; student Cleve. Inst. Art, 1954, Syracuse U., 1959; pvt. study Umberto Romano, Gloucester, Mass., 1955. Free lance artist, 1939—; wallpaper designer Roehlen Engraving Works, 1939-42; indsl. designer Fred Grover Assos., 1942-43; communications designer Burroughs Co., 1943-47; faculty Rochester Inst. Tech., 1947—, prof. communication design, 1973—, mem. faculty council, 1969-73; art tchr. Nazareth Coll., part-time 1951-52; art adviser, designer publs. Rochester, Inst. Tech. 1947—. Exhibited group shows Albany Inst. Art, 1960, Meml. Art Gallery, Rochester, 1950, 59, 60, 71, Rundel Gallery, Rochester, 1950, 54, 58-64, Bevier Gallery, Rochester, 1948-51, 58, 61, 63-64, 67, 70, 71, 72, 73, 74, Smithsonian Inst., Washington, 1959, 64, Goodland (Kan.) Art Gallery, 1959. Mem. Am. Assn. U. Profs. (chpt. treas. 1959-64), Alumni Assn. (mem. exec. council 1954-56), Meml. Art Gallery, Soc. Scribes and Illuminators, Soc. Italic Handwriting. Clubs: Rochester Art, Adirondack Center for the Arts, Burroughs Audubon Nature, Print (sec. 1960-62, pres. 1962-65) (Rochester). Home: 58 Rand Pl Pittsford NY 14534 Office: 1 Lomb Memorial Dr Rochester NY 14623

GUTH, CARYL JOY (MRS. JOHN FALSTAD), anesthesiologist; b. Peoria, Ill., Sept. 17, 1935; d. Walter Christian and Helen Josephine (Whitaker) Guth; A.A., Mars Hill Jr. Coll., 1955; B.S. cum laude, Wake Forest U., 1957; postgrad. N.C. Baptist Hosp. Sch. Cytology, 1957-58; M.D., Bowman Gray Sch. of Medicine, 1962; m. John Falstad, Aug. 24, 1968. Intern, U. Kan. Med. Center, Kansas City, 1962-63; resident in anesthesiology U. Pa. Hosp., Phila., 1963-65; instr. anesthesia Bowman Gray Sch. of Medicine, Winston-Salem, N.C., 1965; anesthesiology fellow Queen Victoria Hosp., E. Grinsted, Sussex, England, 1966; vis. instr. anesthesia U. Nijmegan, Netherlands, 1966; chief anesthesia Kaiser Med. Center, Santa Clara, Cal., 1967; anesthesiologist Mills Meml. Hosp., San Mateo, Cal., 1967—, asst. chief anesthesiologist, 1969-71; pvt. practice medicine, specializing in anesthesiology, San Mateo, 1967—. Mem. bldg. com. Mills Meml. Hosp., 1971—, mem. acute care, surgery rev. coms., 1972—, governing exec. com., 1974—. Diplomate Am. Bd. Anesthesiology. Mem. Am. Soc. Anesthesiology, No. Cal. Soc. Anesthesiology, A.M.A., Cal., San Mateo county med. assns., Am. Med. Tennis Assn., Beta Beta Beta, Alpha Epsilon Delta, Kappa Mu Epsilon. Patentee gen. anesthesia mask and chin holder. Home: 821 N Humboldt St San Mateo CA 94401 Office: 100 S Ellsworth St San Mateo CA 94401

GUTH, PATRICIA SNYDER (MRS. B. ARNOLD GUTH), ednl. adminstr.; b. Palmerton, Pa., Feb. 23, 1933; d. Mark Samford and Sara May (Kern) Snyder; B.S., Kutztown State Coll., 1954; M.S., U. Pa., 1963, postgrad., 1968—; postgrad. Lehigh U., 1966; m. B. Arnold Guth, Aug. 27, 1960. Tchr., Central Bucks Sch. Dist., Doylestown, Pa., 1954-58; tchr. Pennridge Sch. Dist., Perkasie, Pa., 1958-60, curriculum asst., 1960-61, dir. elementary edn., 1961-66, adminstrv. asst., 1966—. Instr. continuing edn. Pa. State U., 1963-68; cons. reading and lang. arts. Dir., coordinator Fed. Edn. Projects; chmn. Nat. Elementary Prins. Conv., 1972; alternate mem. child devel. and day care com. Pa. Gov.'s Council for Human Resources. Bd. dirs. Bucks County A.R.C., 1970-73, chmn. nominating com., 1971—. Mem. Am. Assn. Sch. Adminstrs., Nat., Mideastern, Bucks County (pres. 1964-65, 74—, v.p. 1973-74) assns. supervision and curriculum devel., Internat. Reading Assn., (council pres. 1964-65, dir., workshop chmn. state conv. 1974), N.E.A., Kappa Delta Pi. Mem. United Ch. of Christ. Home: 127 S 4th St Perkasie PA 18944 Office: 601 N 7th St Perkasie PA 18944

GUTHMAN, GERTRUDE JUDITH, educator; b. Chgo.; d. Samuel David and Lena (Morrison) Guthman; B.S. in Edn., Northwestern U., 1932; L.S., U. Ill., 1944. Tchr., librarian pub. high schs., Chgo., 1934-61; cultural resources co-ordinator Chgo. Bd. Edn., 1961—; dir. cultural enrichment project Chgo. elementary and high schs. Title III Elementary and Secondary Edn. Act, 1967-70; tchr. library sci. grad. schs. Northeastern Ill. U. (formerly Chgo. Tchrs. Coll.), U. Wis., DePaul U., Chgo., evenings, summers, 1956-65. Mem. letters and drama assembly Adult Edn. Council, Chgo.; mem. Citizens' Com. Survey Chgo. Pub. Library; liaison with pvt. and community theater orgns. and repertory cos. for play performances schs. Chgo. Bd. dirs. Chgo. founders group Nat. Repertory Theatre. Recipient recognition award Chgo. Drama Tchrs. Assn., 1968. Mem. Am. Nat. Theatre and Acad., Art Inst. Chgo., Chgo. Drama Tchrs. Assn. Contbr. articles to profl. jours. Office: Bd of Edn 228 N LaSalle St Chicago IL 60601

GUTHRIE, ELEANOR Y., lawyer; b. Annawan, Ill., Aug. 12, 1915; d. James M. and Nell (Stevenson) Young; B.A., U. Ill., 1937; LL.B., Chgo.-Kent Coll. Law, 1940; m. George B. Guthrie, Dec. 26, 1941; 1 son, Richard Y. Editor, Commerce Clearing House, Inc., 1940-42; lawyer Defrees & Fiske, Chgo., 1942-52, partner, 1952—. Pres. Joint Com. on Woman's Ct. and Detention Home, Chgo., 1957-58; vol. worker teen-age program Erie Neighborhood House, 1954-62; mem. com. on social security Ill. C. of C.; bd. dirs., mem. loop center com. YWCA; bd. dirs. U.S.O., 1969-73; asst. sec. U.S.O. of Chgo., 1971-72; v.p., bd. dirs. YWCA, Chgo. Delegate Women's Share in Pub. Service, also Ill. Women's Conf. on Legislation. Mem. Women's Bar Assn. Ill. (pres. 1950-51), Nat. Assn. Women Lawyers (state del. 1952, labor law com.), Am. (mem. labor sect., vice chmn. occupational health and safety labor sect. 1972-73, mem. fed. labor standards legislative com.), Chgo. (mem. labor law, house grievance coms., chmn. house com. 1970-72) bar assns., Alliance Bus. and Profl. Women Chgo. (pres. 1964-65), Nat. (asst. parliamentarian 1958, parliamentarian 1973-74), Ill. (parliamentarian 1958—) fedns. bus. and profl. women's clubs, Am. Assn. U. Women, Internat. Platform Assn., Zeta Phi Eta. Conglist. Clubs: Pilot (pres. 1955-56), Executive (Chgo.). Home: 547 Belleforte Av Oak Park IL 60302 Office: 105 S La Salle St Chicago IL 60603

GUTHRIE, JANICE ELAINE, business exec.; b. Muscatine, Ia., Apr. 21, 1925; d. Guy Marion and Mary U. (Yakle) Guthrie; high sch. grad. Pub. relations rep. western div. Am. Airlines, Los Angeles, 1942-49; editorial promotion writer Los Angeles Times, 1949-50; dir. publicity, City of Palm Springs, Cal., 1950-54; dir. pub. relations Interstate Brands Corp., Kansas City, Mo., 1954-70; asst. dir. pub. relations Castle & Cooke, Inc., Honolulu, 1970-73; dir. pub. relations Bank of Hawaii, Honolulu, 1973—. Mem. Am. Women in Radio and TV (pres. So. Cal. chpt. 1960-61), Am. Inst. Banking, Pub. Relations Soc. Am., Hawaii C. of C., Theta Sigma Phi, (pres. Hawaii chpt. 1973-74). Clubs: Honolulu Press; Outdoor Circle. Home: 1521 Punahou St Honolulu HI 96822 Office: Financial Plaza of Pacific Honolulu HI 96813

GUTHRIE, JOANNAE UTLEY, ednl. adminstr., restaurant exec.; b. Springfield, O., Nov. 12, 1922; d. Robert and Opal Puckett (Guthrie) Utley; student Santiago (Chile) Sch. Art, 1944-45, Sch. Fine Arts, Caracas, Venezuela, 1949; m. Diego Ibarra Palacios de la Torre, 1944 (div.); 1 son, Roberto Antonio Ibarra Guthrie; m. 2d, Maurice B. Morgan, 1953 (div.); 1 son, John William Morgan Guthrie; m. 3d, Henry A. Smith, 1964 (div.). Cartographer Goodyear Tire and Rubber Co., Akron, O., 1940-44; with Mainbocher, N.Y.C., 1951; interior decorator, N.Y.C., 1951-53; mgmt. trainee Polsky's Dept. Store, Akron, 1954-56; writer, dir., performer WEWSTV, Cleve., 1958; interior designer Akron, 1962, Marvin Interior Decorators, Akron, 1963, Town and Country Decorators, Akron, 1963, Cottington Interior Decorators, Glen Ellyn, Ill., 1964; farm owner, mgr., 1967—; pres. Phoenix Acad. Cultural Exploration and Design, Wheaton, Ill., also Madison, Wis., 1967—, pres., 1971—; owner Ovens of Brittany, Inc., Madison, 1971—; partner Guthrie-McKean Bldg. Partnership, Madison, 1971—. Lectr. ancient philosophy and religions, 1960—. Mem. Theosophical Soc. Am. Author: Prospectus for Living Design, 1970. Home: 1711-15 Kendall Av Madison WI 53705 Office: 310 State St Trine Madison WI 53703

GUTHRIE, LOUISE CALBERT (MRS. MARSHALL BECK GUTHRIE), ednl. adminstr.; b. Shelbyville, Ind., May 28, 1917; d. Charles Watson and Nola Alice (Fryer) Calbert; B.A., U. Ky., 1940; postgrad. U. Pa., 1943-44; m. Marshall Beck Guthrie, Sept. 14, 1941; children—Michael Beck III, Marion Lee (Mrs. Eric Charles Zwarg), Mark Bruce. Reporter, feature writer Louisville Courier-Jour., 1938-41; asst. dir. personnel U. Pa., Phila., 1941-46; dir. pub. relations Upper Merion Area Sch. Dist., King Prussia, Pa., 1966—. Cons. in pub. relations; head Lexington Herald-Leader news bur., Georgetown, Ky., 1940-41. Active Emergency Aid Pa., Phila.; mem. doctors' wives com. U. Pa., Phila.; mem. Montgomery County (Pa.) Med. Aux., 1958—, Phila. Coll. Physicians Med. Aux., 1965—, U. Pa. Study Council Group E in Pub. Relations, 1967-74. Bd. dirs. Nearly New Shop, Hosp. U. Pa., Phila., 1955-68. Mem. Nat., Pa. sch. pub. relations assns., Pub. Relations Soc. Am., Ednl. Press, Women in Communications (chpt. v.p. 1939-40), Upper Merion Bus. and Profl. Women's Club, League Women Voters. Republican. Episcopalian. Home: Guthrie Rd Wayne PA 19087 Office: 435 Crossfield Rd King of Prussia PA 19406

GUTHRIE, VERA MARIA GRINSTEAD (MRS. CHARLES SNOW GUTHRIE), educator; b. Glasgow, Ky., Oct. 5, 1930; d. James David and Gracie T. (Vance) Grinstead; A.B., Western Ky. State Coll., 1953; M.S., in L.S., U. Ky., 1957, Ed.D., 1973; m. Charles Snow Guthrie, Dec. 25, 1973. Classroom tchr. elementary sch., Barren County, Ky., 1949-51; tchr., librarian Glasgow (Ky.) High Sch., 1953-54; librarian Reddick (Fla.) Sch., 1954-56, Vine Grove (Ky.) Sch., 1957-58; prof. library sci. Western Ky. U., Bowling Green, 1958—, head dept. library sci., 1973—. Named one of Outstanding Young Women of Am., 1965. Mem. Am. Assn. U. Women (pres. 1961-63), A.L.A., Ky. (pres. 1969), Southeastern library assns. Democrat. Baptist (adult Sunday sch. tchr. 1971-72). Home: 518 Regents Av Bowling Green KY 42101

GUTIERREZ, ELSA MARISSA (MRS. JAIME A. AQUERON), civil engr.; b. Mayaguez, P.R., Oct. 5, 1951; d. Andres and Lydia (Desa) Gutierrez; B.S., U. P.R., 1972; m. Jaime A. Aqueron, Feb. 9, 1974. Civil engr. E. Olivieri & Asso., engrs. and mgmt. cons., Hato Rey, P.R., 1973; civil engr. P.R. Hwy. Authority, Aguadilla (P.R.) regional officer, 1973—. P.R. Hwys. Authority scholar, 1970-71; recipient honor certificate of merit Lions Club, 1965. Mem. Am. Soc. C.E. (chpt. sec. 1971), Am. Concrete Inst. Home: PO Box 2245 Mayaguez PR 00708 Office: care Regional Office PR Hwy Authority Aguadilla PR

GUTMAN, JUDITH MARA, author, historian; b. N.Y.C., May 22, 1928; d. Victor and Anna (Zimmerman) Markowitz; B.A., Queens Coll., 1949; M.S., Bank Street Edn., 1959; m. Herbert Gutman, June 18, 1950; children—Marta Ruth, Nell Lisa. Dir., Montefiore Nursery Sch., N.Y.C., 1954-57. lectr. Hunter Coll., N.Y.C., 1958-59; tchr. Stoughton (Wis.) elementary schs., 1952. Lectr., U. Wis., 1953, cons., 1954. Mem. Author's Guild. Author: The Colonial Venture, 1966; Lewis W. Hine and the American Social Conscience, 1967; Is America Used Up?, 1973; Lewis W. Hine: Two Perspectives, 1974. Co-author: The Making of American Society, 1972. Address: 97 6th Av Nyack NY 10960

GUY, BESSIE MAE, coll. dean; b. Seattle, Feb. 20, 1912; d. Oliver Leslie and Bessie E. (Horsfall) Guy; student U. Wash., 1933-35; B.A., Northwest Coll., 1959. Missionary to Am. Indians, Port Gamble, Wash., 1939-41; asst. minister Evangel Temple, Bremerton, Wash., 1941-55, Oakland (Cal.) Temple, 1955-56; dean women Northwest Coll., Kirkland, Wash., 1958—. Mem. Christian Assn. Women and Counselors (regional chmn. 1961-67). Mem. Assembly of God. Home: 10624 NE 47th Pl Kirkland WA 98033

GUY, CORRIS HOPE, food industry cons.; b. Seattle; d. Kirby Odgers and Mabel (Stradley) Guy; B.S., U. Wash., 1934. Home economist Puget Sound Power & Light, 1934-37, Hawaiian Electric Co., 1937-42, So. Cal. Gas Co., 1942-46; dir. consumer service Helms Bakeries, 1946-67, v.p., dir. pub. relations, 1967-69; food industry cons., Beverly Hills, Cal., 1969—. Producer, star Milady, KTLA-TV, 1947-48, Tricks 'n Treats, 1948-65, Cooking with Corris, 1966—; food editor Western Family mag., 1957-59. Dir. nutrition, canteen A.R.C., Southeast dist., 1942-46; chmn. consumer adv. com. Nat. Turkey Fedn. Bd. dirs. Profl. Women for Los Angeles Symphony-Hollywood Bowl. Recipient Los Angeles Advt. Women's award best TV show produced by a woman, 1948. Mem. Home Economists in Bus. (pres. 1954-56, chmn. adv. com. 1961-63, chmn. nominating com. 1963—, chmn. internat. relations com., 1964—), Execs. Secs. (pres. 1954-55, organizing officer Boston chpt. 1964, conv. chmn. 1968), Am., Cal. (chmn. bienniel conv. 1963, chmn. profl. standards com. 1964—) home econs. assns., Mortar Bd., Zeta Tau Alpha. Club: Totem. Home: 1030 Hilts Av Los Angeles CA 90024 Office: PO Box 1961 Beverly Hills CA 90213

GUY, HERMANNA MARGUERITE GROENIGER (MRS. JOHN ALBERT GUY), mech. contracting co. exec.; b. Columbus, O., Aug. 25, 1918; d. William Charles and Hermanna Marguerite (Greiner) Groeniger; student Ohio State U., 1936-39; m. John Albert Guy, June 1, 1939; children—John Albert, William H., Barbara A. Treas., dir. J.A. Guy, Inc., Dublin, O., 1953—. Mem. Columbus Gallery Fine Arts, Ohio State U. Assn. (life). Mem. Community Ch. Mem. Order Eastern Star. Club: Brookside Country. Home: 7192 Dublin Rd Dublin OH 43017 Office: 24 N High St Dublin OH 43017

GUY, JULIANNA ROYAL (MRS. ROBERT I. GUY), accountant; b. East Aurora, N.Y., Sept. 15, 1926; d. Osmon and Carolyn (Merritt) Royal II; B.A., Pomona Coll., 1948; accounting U. Cal., Los Angeles, 1957-59; m. Charles A. Shiner, 1950 (div. 1955). Supr. gen. ledger sect. Occidental Life Ins. Co., Los Angeles, 1948-50; sec., bookkeeper Lightfoot Studio, Pasadena, Cal., 1950-53; staff auditor Arthur Young & Co., C.P.A.'s, Los Angeles, 1953-58; bus. mgr. KCOP Television, Inc., Los Angeles, 1959-69; dir. bus. affairs, TV broadcast div. Chris Craft Industries, 1969-70; controller No. TV Inc., Anchorage, 1970-72; financial cons. radio and TV, 1972; personnel dir. Laventhol, Krekstein, Horwath and Horwath, C.P.A.'s, Seattle, 1973—. C.P.A., Cal., Alaska, Wash. Mem. Am. Inst. C.P.A.'s, Am. Women's Soc. C.P.A.'s (nat. dir. 1963-64, 72-73, 74—, treas. 1973-74), Wash. Soc. C.P.A.'s, Am. Soc. Women Accountants (pres. Los Angeles chpt. 1961-62, Most Valuable mem. 1961-62), Am. Women in Radio and TV (pres. So. Cal. chpt. 1969-70, Merit award 1968), Inst. Broadcasting Financial Mgmt. (dir. 1961-62). Contbr. articles to profl. jours. Home: 7554 44th Av SW Seattle WA 98136

GUY, L(EONA) RUTH, educator; b. Kemp, Tex.; d. Henry Luther and Minnie Elizabeth (Murphy) Guy; A.B., Baylor U., 1934, M.S., 1948; Ph.D., Stanford, 1953. Med. technologist Dallas Med. and Surg. Clinic, 1934-36, Ryan Clinic, Midland, Tex., 1936-39; chief med. technologist Hendrick Meml. Hosp., Abilene, 1939-46; research asst. Baylor U. Hosp., Dallas, 1946-50, instr. Dental Coll., Dallas, 1948-50; research asst. Irwin Meml. Blood Bank, San Francisco, 1950-51; teaching asst. Stanford U., 1951, research fellow, 1952-53; mem. faculty U. Tex. Southwestern Med. Sch., Dallas, 1953—, asso. prof. dept. pathology, 1965—, prof. med. tech., 1972—, chmn. dept. med. tech., 1970—. Asso. dir. blood bank Parkland Meml. Hosp., Dallas, 1953—; cons. immunology and blood banking VA hosps., Dallas, 1961—, Temple, Tex., 1964—; cons. in blood banking China Med. Bd. N.Y., 1969-70; cons. Inst. Forensic Sci., Dallas, 1972—. Mem. adv. bd. Dallas County Big Sisters, 1966-68; med. adv. bd. Dallas chpt. Nat. Hemophilia Found., 1964—. Trudeau Research fellow., Nat. Tb Assn., 1952, 53; recipient award for excellence in field of medicine Dallas Bus. and Profl. Women's Club, 1963. Mem. Am. (coordinator South Central dist. clearing house 1958—, John Elliott award 1973), South Central (pres. 1964-65) assns. blood banks, Acad. Clin. Lab. Physicians and Scientists, N.Y. Acad. Scis., Am. Soc. Clin. Pathologists (asso. mem., mem. council immunohematology 1972—), Am. Soc. Microbiology, Bus. and Profl. Women's Club Dallas (pres. 1970-71), Sigma Xi. Baptist. Club: Zonta (Dallas) (pres. 1962). Contbr. articles to profl. jours. Home: 3016 Leahy St Dallas TX 75229 Office: 5323 Harry Hines Blvd Dallas TX 75235

GUZIK, JOHANNA LOUISE (MRS. WALTER JOSEPH GUZIK, JR.), editor; b. Cleve., Dec. 27, 1933; d. Joseph Martin and Anna (Krivonak) Leposky; student, Western Res. U., 1952-54; Ohio U., 1954-56; m. Walter Joseph Guzik, Jr., Aug. 21, 1954; children—Erik John, Erin Jann, Evie Anna. Editor, Halle Bros. Dept. Store, Cleve., 1956-57; sec. to pub. relations dir. Lazarus Dept. Store, Columbus, O., 1957-58; sec. to state architect State of Ohio, Columbus, 1958-63; with Paul Worth Assos., pub. relations, Columbus, 1963-64; editor Motor Travel Mag., Columbus, 1964—. Lectr. Marysville (O.) Women's Reformatory, 1965-73. Mem. Midwest Travel Writers Assn. (treas. 1971—). Club: Ad (Columbus). Home: 1640 Ridgeway Place Columbus OH 43212 Office: Suite 1201 8 E Long St Columbus OH 43215

GUZMAN, LILIA SANCHEZ, physician; b. Lopez, Quezon, Philippines, May 24, 1933; d. Nicanor Villaneuva and Rosario (Villaneuva) Sanchez Guzman; A.A., U. St. Tomas, Manila, P.I., 1950, M.D., 1955. Intern, Univ. St. Tomas Hosp., Philippines, 1955, St. John's Riverside Hosp., Yonkers, N.Y., 1957; resident internal medicine Fordham Hosp., Bronx, N.Y., 1958-62; teaching fellow internal medicine Ellis Hosp., Schenectady, 1967-69, asso. staff internal medicine, 1970-72, asst. attending in medicine, 1973—; practice internal medicine, Schenectady, 1971—. Cons. internal medicine Vets. Meml. Hosp., Philippines, 1962-67. Recipient Physician's Recognition award A.M.A., 1969, 72. Fellow Am. Coll. Chest Physicians; mem. Am. Coll. Cardiology (affiliate), Philippine Med. Assn., A.M.A. Home: 28 Woodcrest Dr Scotia NY 12302 Office: 1101 Nott St Schenectady NY 12308

GWIN, DOROTHY JEAN BIRD (MRS. CLINTON D. GWIN), educator; b. Tex., June 26, 1934; d. Joseph William and Elva Gracie (Elledge) Bird; B.B.A., East Tex. State U., 1954, M.S., 1955; Ed.D., U. Kan., 1958; m. Clinton Dale Gwin, Nov. 24, 1964; 1 son, Clinton Bird. Tchr. Thomas Jefferson High Sch., Port Arthur, Tex., 1954-55; head resident counsglor U. Kan., Manhattan, 1955-57; psychologist Caddo Parish Sch. Bd., Shreveport, La., 1958-67; prof. edn. and psychology Centenary Coll., Shreveport, 1967—. Bd. dirs. Child Guidance Center, 1960-64, Parent League, 1966-69, 73—, Vols. of Am., 1966-69. Mem. Am. Psychol. Assn., Am. Personnel and Guidance Assn., Am. Assn. U. Profs. Home: 3402 Madison Park Shreveport LA 71104

GWON, NANCY VIRGINIA (MRS. LANG YICK CHIN), physician; b. N.Y.C., Nov. 9, 1939; d. William Yim and Mamie (Lee) Gwon; B.A. summa cum laude, Hunter Coll., 1960; M.D. summa cum laude, State U. N.Y., 1964; M.P.H., Johns Hopkins, 1966; m. Lang Yick Chin, Sept. 1, 1968; children—Kevin, Michael. Instr. dept. environmental medicine State U. N.Y., 1967-68; asso. staff New Eng. Med. Center Hosps., 1970-72; internist E. Boston Health Clinic, 1970-71; clin. cons. Boston City Hosp., 1971-72; now internist East Boston Health Clinic. Lectr., Hunter Coll., 1965. Recipient Salk award, 1960, Janet Glasgow award Am. Med. Woman's Assn., 1964, Mitchell award State U. N.Y., 1964. Mem. Phi Beta Kappa, Alpha Omega Alpha. Editor: Headache Rounds, Faulkner Hosp., Boston, 1969-71. Contbr. articles to profl. jours. Address: 4 Robinwood Av Boston MA 02130

GYEMANT, INA LEVIN (MRS. ROBERT ERNEST GYEMANT), lawyer; b. San Francisco, Aug. 2, 1943; d. Manuel and Mildred Lita (Woloski) Levin; A.B., U. Cal. at Berkeley, 1965; J.D., Hastings Coll. of Law, 1968; m. Robert Ernest Gyemant, June 7, 1970; children—Robert Ernest, Anne Elizabeth. Admitted to Cal. bar, 1969; clk. chief justice Cal. Supreme Ct., 1969; dep. pub. defender City and County of San Francisco, 1970; individual practice law, San

Francisco, 1971; dep. atty. gen. State of Cal., San Francisco, 1972—. Mem. Am., San Francisco bar assns., State Bar Cal., Queen's Bench, Foster Parents Assn., Alpha Epsilon Phi. Republican. Clubs: Commonwealth Club of Cal. (sec. law enforcement sect. 1973—); Barrister's; San Francisco Lawyers; Criminal Trial Lawyers; Met.; Los Altos (Cal.) Golf and Country; Variety Club of N. Cal. (San Francisco); San Francisco Lawyer's Wives. Office: 6000 State Bldg San Francisco CA 94102

GYLDENVAND, LILY MYRTLE, mag. editor; b. LaMoure, N.D., May 26, 1917; d. Ole Christian and Karen Gunillea (Myhr) Gyldenvand; B.A., Concordia Coll., 1939. Sec., dept. Christian edn. Evang. Luth. Ch., Mpls., 1939-41, CCC, U.S. Dept. Agr., Mpls., 1941-52; adminstrv. and editorial asst., office pub. relations Evang. Luth. Ch., Mpls., 1952-60; editor Scope mag. Augsburg Pub. House, Mpls., 1960—. Recipient award of merit Asso. Ch. Press, 1967. Mem. Lutheran Editors and Mgrs. Assn., Asso. Ch. Press, Luth. Daus. of Reformation (nat. pres. 1948-54). Author: Beyond All Doubt, 1949; What Am I Saying?, 1952; Of All Things, 1956; So You're Only Human?, 1957; What Am I Praying?, 1964; Call Her Blessed, 1967; Invitation to Joy, 1969; (with Alida Storaasli) If God So Loved Me, 1965, Established in the Faith, 1966, Called to Be Agents of Reconciliation, 1966. Home: 2088 Fry St St Paul MN 55113 Office: 426 S 5th St Minneapolis MN 55415

HAACK, LOUISE BENDER, educator; b. Washington, Jan. 26, 1925; d. Emil George John and Sophie Frances (Knapp) Bender; B.A., George Washington U., 1948, M.A., 1959; M.A. in Teaching Math. (NSF fellow), U. Wash., 1963; m. Clifford W. Haack, June 16, 1946 (div. 1959); children—Carolyn, Linda. Lectr. math. George Washington U., 1947-49, tech. editor Logistics Research Project, 1950-52; tchr. math. Fairfax County Pub. Schs., Annandale, Va., 1955-60, Seattle Pub. Schs., 1960-61; instr. math. U. Wash., Seattle, 1961-62; tchr. math. Arlington County (Va.) Pub. Schs., 1962-67; supr. math. Fairfax County Pub. Schs., 1967—. Chmn. Md.-D.C.-Va. Regional Math. Conf., 1969-72; charter mem. speakers bur. Common Cause. Mem. N.E.A. (life), Va., Fairfax edn. assns., Nat., Fairfax math. suprs. groups, Nat. Council Tchrs. Math. (life), A.A.A.S., Math. Assn. Am., Pi Mu Epsilon, Delta, Zeta. Mem. Ch. of Christ (mem. choir 1967—). Home: 6604 Kerns Rd Falls Church VA 22042

HAACK, MARY LOUISE, educator; b. Elgin, Ill., Oct. 12, 1930; d. Clarence Maxium and Opal Alma (Woocott) Haack; student Estherville Jr. Coll., 1948-49; A.B., Augustana Coll., 1952; M.Mus., U. Mich., 1960; postgrad. Eastman Sch. Music, U. S.C., U. Ga. Instr. Martin Luther Coll., New Ulm, Minn., 1953-59; asst. prof. music Berry Coll., Mt. Berry, Ga., 1960—. Mem. Nat. Fedn. of Music Clubs (Ga. jr. counselor 1970—), Am. Assn. U. Women, Am. Assn. U. Profs., Music Tchrs. Nat. Assn., Rome Music Tchrs. Assn., Sigma Alpha Iota (sponsor chpt.). Lutheran. Club: Berry Woman's (Mt. Berry). Home: One Knollwood Dr Rome GA 30149 Office: Berry College Box 553 Mount Berry GA 30149

HAAG, JESSIE HELEN, educator; b. Reading, Pa., Apr. 7, 1917; d. Charles Milton and Helen (Sell) Haag; B.S., Temple U., 1939, M.Ed., 1943, Ed.D., 1950. Health educator Lansdale (Pa.) Pub. Schs., 1939-46; dir. health edn. Lebanon Valley (Pa.) Coll., 1946-47; health educator State Tchrs. Coll., West Chester, Pa., 1947-50; asst. prof. U. Tex., Austin, 1950-56, asso. prof., 1956-67, prof., 1967—. Cons. joint com. on health problems in edn. N.E.A., A.M.A.; cons. FDA, Washington. Recipient award Internat. Tech. Exhbn. Health Edn., Union Internationale Pour L'Education Sanitaire De La Population, 1956. Fellow Am. Pub. Health Assn., Am. Sch. Health Assn. (Distinguished Service award, research council), A.A.A.S., Royal Soc. Health, London, A.A.H.P.E.R. (exec. council sch. health div., research council, Honor award So. dist.); mem. A.M.A. (cons. 8th nat. conf. physicians and schs.), Internat. Union Health Edn., Am. Assn. U. Profs., Tex. Assn. Health, Phys. Edn. and Recreation (recipient State Honor award), Am. Col. Health Assn., Pi Lambda Theta, Delta Psi Kappa. Author: Checklist Appraising Elementary and Secondary School Health Program, 1951; School Health Program, 1958, rev., 1965, fgn. edit., 1968, 3d. edit., 1972; Physiology, 1959; School Health Practices in the United States, 1961; Health Education for Young Adults, 1965; Teacher's Edition for Health Education for Young Adults, 1965; FDA's Life Protection Series, 1968; Focusing on Health, 1973, also tchr.'s edit., 1973; Toward Sexual Maturity-Tchr.'s Reference, 1973; abstract writer, sch. health, Excerpta Medica, Amsterdam. Mem. editorial bd. Research Quar., Am. Jour. Pub. Health; asso. editor TAHPER Jour., Completed Research in Health, Phys. Edn. and Recreation. Contbr. to World Congress on Teaching Professions; also profl. jours. Home: 4519 Apache Pass Austin TX 78745

HAAGE, CATHERINE MARIE (MRS. LOUIS KACMARYNSKI), coll. dean; b. Reading, Pa.; d. John Augustus and Katherine (O'Reilly) Haage; B.A., Trinity Coll., Washington, 1923; M.A., U. Pa., 1927, Ph.D., 1932; m. Louis Kacmarynski, June 25, 1938; 1 dau., Katharine Louise. Tchr. Latin, social studies secondary schs., Reading, 1923-33; chmn. edn. dept. St. Mary of Woods Coll., Terre Haute, Ind., 1933-38; lectr. edn. dept. Hunter Coll., N.Y.C., 1940-59; dir. tchr. tng. Coll. New Rochelle (N.Y.), 1958-72, dir. reading program, 1970—, dean grad. sch., 1973—. Cons. Cath. Family Inst., 1948-55. Mem. N.E.A., Nat. Cath. Edn. Assn., Assn. Tchr. Educators, Nat. Soc. Coll. Tchrs. Edn., Am. Assn. U. Profs., Nat. Council Tchrs. English, N.Y. State Tchrs. Assn. Home: 49 Askins Pl New Rochelle NY 10801

HAAKER, ANN MARIE, educator; b. Chgo., Nov. 22, 1919; d. Edward Bernard and Marie Louise (Miller) Haaker; B.A., U. Tex., 1941; M.A., Claremont Grad. Sch., 1952; Ph.D., Shakespeare Inst., U. Birmingham (Eng.), 1960. Clk., fgn. service Am. embassy, Mexico City, Mex., 1944-45; asst. prof. U. Md. Overseas, Brize Norton, Oxford, Eng., 1954-55, Pasadena (Cal.) City Coll., 1960-65; prof. English, Cal. State U., Fullerton, 1965—, grad. coordinator English, 1969-72. Mem. Modern Lang. Assn., Am. Assn. U. Profs., Renaissance Soc. Am., Shakespeare Assn. Am., Philol. Assn. Pacific Coast, Western Shakespeare Conf. Editor: The Antipodes (Richard Brome), 1966; The Jovial Crew (Richard Brome), 1968. Contbg. author: Renaissance Drama, 1968, 72; Research Opportunities in Renaissance Drama, 1972, also other publs. Home: 31551 Crystal Sands Dr Laguna Niguel CA 92677 Office: Dept English Cal State U at Fullerton CA 92634

HAAS, ELEANOR ALTER (MRS. PETER RALPH HAAS), pub. relations cons.; b. Jersey City, Mar. 12, 1932; d. Nicholas Mark and Eleanor (Cochran) Alter de Csanytalek; B.A., Smith Coll., 1953; certificate N.Y. Sch. Interior Design, 1960; m. Peter Ralph Haas, Oct. 22, 1966. Exec. sec. MCA Artists, Ltd., N.Y.C., 1954-56; exec. sec. Young & Rubicam, Inc., N.Y.C., 1956-58; exec. sec. J. Walter Thompson Co., N.Y.C., 1958-59; exec. sec. Stanford Research Inst., N.Y.C., 1959, Deafness Research Found., N.Y.C., 1960, Earl Newsom & Co., N.Y.C., 1961-65; account exec. Ruder & Finn, Inc., N.Y.C., 1965-68; founder, sr. partner The Haas Group, N.Y.C., 1968—. Bd. dirs. Co-Workers Devel. Corp., N.Y.C. Mem. Am. Mgmt. Assn., Pub. Relations Soc. Am., Women Execs. in Pub. Relations, Environmental Writers Assn., Nat. Women's Polit. Caucus, Nat. Soc. Fund Raisers. Home: 171 West 79th St New York City NY 10024 Office: 59 East 54th St New York City NY 10022

HAAS, RUTH ALICE, coll. pres.; b. Syracuse, N.Y., Mar. 30, 1903; d. Frederick W. and Mary E. (Marra) Haas; A.B., Syracuse U., 1924, B.S., 1925, M.A., 1928, LL.D., 1946; postgrad. Yale, 1933-35; Ed.D., R.I. Coll. Edn.; LL.D., Albertus Magnus U., 1973, U. Hartford, 1974. Tchr. history and civics Watertown (N.Y.) High Sch., 1924-27; instr. polit. sci. Maxwell Sch. Citizenship, Syracuse U., 1927-31; asst. personnel dept., 1928-31; dean Western Conn. State Coll., Danbury, 1931-46, pres., 1946—. Mem. Conn. Commn. on Cooperation with Fed. Authorities in Matters of Higher Edn., New Eng. Bd. Higher Edn. Trustee Danbury Library; trustee Danbury Hosp. Mem. Eastern States Assn. Profl. Schs. for Tchrs. (pres. 1947), New Eng. Assn. Tchrs. Colls. (pres. 1949), Conn. Council Higher Edn. (pres. 1959—), Am. Assn. U. Women, N.E.A., Conn. Edn. Assn., Kappa Delta Pi, Alpha Kappa Delta, Delta Kappa Gamma. Address: Western Conn State College Danbury CT 06810

HAAS, SONIA BOGIN (MRS. FRANCIS HAAS), psychologist; b. Poland, May 7, 1923; d. Solomon and Esther P. (Yagudin) Bogin; came to U.S., 1938, naturalized, 1944; Asso. of Edn., Drake U., 1946; B.A., Roosevelt U., 1947; M.A., U. N.M., 1954; m. Francis Haas, Aug. 9, 1942; children—Marcia (Mrs. Edward Mazria), Linda (Mrs. David Tarr), Sandra, Ellen. Tchr. Dade (Fla.) County Pub. Schs., 1956-57, sch. psychologist 1957—. Mem. Fla. (dir. 1965-66), Dade (sec. 1967-68) assns. sch. psychologists, Am., Fla., Dade County psychol. assns., Fla. Edn. Assn., Alpha Delta Kappa. Democrat. Home: 3430 Royal Palm Av Miami Beach FL 33140 Office: 14027 NE 16th Court N Miami FL 33161

HAAS, THELMA ROBERTS SUMNER (MRS. CHARLES ELMER HAAS), educator; b. Dade City, Fla., Feb. 28, 1910; d. Jefferson Davis and Mittie (Roberts) Sumner; B.A., Fla. State U., 1931; postgrad. Duke, summers 1935-36; M.Ed. in Personnel Services, U. Fla., 1963; m. Charles Elmer Haas, June 11, 1938; children—Donald Victor, Edith H. Hill. Tchr. English and history B. Franklin Jr. High Sch., Tampa, Fla., 1931-34, Andrew Jackson Sr. High Sch., Jacksonville, Fla., 1939-45; tchr English, H. B. Plant Sr. High Sch., Tampa, 1934-38; tchr. sci. and health North Shore Elementary-Jr. High Sch., Jacksonville, 1954-57; tchr. history Andrew Jackson Sr. High Sch., Jacksonville, 1957-61, guidance counselor, 1961-69, dean girls, 1970—; dean girls Oceanway Jr. High Sch., Jacksonville, 1969-70. Sec. Marigold Circle Garden Club, 1953-54, v.p., 1954-55; mem. Civic Music Assn., Friends of Pub. Library, Jacksonville Fedn. Garden Clubs, 1952-56. Mem. N.E.A., Fla. Edn. Assn., Am., Fla. personnel and guidance assns., Fla. Deans and Counselors Assn., Nat., Fla. assns. Secondary Sch. prins., Am. Assn. U. Women (pres. Tampa br. 1936-38, Jacksonville br. 1939-40, Fla. treas. 1936-37, chmn. fellowships 1965-66), Mortar Bd., Delta Kappa Gamma (chpt. pres. 1964-66, parliamentarian 1966-68, pres. coordinating council 1966-68, chaplain 1969-70), Alpha Chi Alpha, Pi Lambda Theta, Kappa Delta Pi (corr. sec. 1968-70), Phi Mu. Democrat. Baptist. Home: 332 W 69th St Jacksonville FL 32208 Office: Andrew Jackson Sr High Sch 3816 Main St Jacksonville FL 32206

HAASE, ANN MARIE BERNAZZA (MRS. RICHARD FRANK HAASE), educator; b. Poughkeepsie, N.Y., Jan. 3, 1942; d. Leonard David and Ann Jane (Peluse) Bernazza; B.S., State U. N.Y. at New Paltz, 1963; M.A., U. Conn. at Storrs, 1967, Ph.D., 1969; m. Richard Frank Haase, Mar. 27, 1971. Asso. prof. edn. U. Hartford West Hartford, Conn., 1968-72; asso. prof. nursing research U. Mass. at Amherst, 1972—, vis. lectr., 1971-72; cons. New Eng. Program Tchr. Edn., Durham, N.H., 1970-72, Conn. Research Commn., 1970-71. Mem. New Eng. Ednl. Research Orgn. (program chmn. 1971-72, v.p. 1970-71, pres. 1972-73), Am. Psychol. Assn., Am. Ednl. Research Assn., Nat. Reading Conf., Assn. Supervision and Curriculum Devel., Phi Kappa Phi. Author: (with R.H. Bloomer) Reading and Typing: A Linguistic Phonetic Approach, 7 books in primary reading, 1969. Contbr. articles to profl. publs. Home: RFD 3 327 Long Plain Rd Amherst MA 01002

HABAN, SISTER M. TERESINE, educator; b. Columbus, O., Jan. 15, 1914; d. Stephan and Anna (Kollar) Haban; A.B., Coll. St. Francis, 1935, Mus.B., 1940; Mus.M., Chgo. Musical Coll., 1942; Ph.D., Eastman Sch. Music, 1957. Faculty Coll. St. Francis, Joliet, Ill., 1941-74, prof. music, 1958-74, chmn. music dept., 1959-70; asso. prof. music theory West. Chester (Pa.) State Coll., 1974—. Mem. Coll. Music Soc., Ch. Music Assn. Am., Delta Epsilon Sigma. Author: The Hymnody of the Roman Catholic Church, 1956; The Bells of St. Francis (musical score), 1965. Composer of various musical compositions.

HABAN, MARY FRANCES, librarian, educator; b. Columbus, O., Jan. 6, 1935; d. Stephen P. and Frances (Zollner) Haban; B.A magna cum laude, Coll. Mt. St. Joseph, 1956; M.L.S., Carnegie Inst. Tech., 1959; postgrad. Nat. Def. Edn. Act Inst. for Sch. Librarians, U. Denver, 1965; Ph.D., U. Pitts., 1971. Tchr. English and Math. high sch., Cin., 1956-58; librarian Carnegie Library of Pitts., 1960-62, 70; librarian Central Dist. Catholic High Sch., Pitts., 1962-66; asst. prof., dir. library sci. edn. Duquesne U., Pitts., 1966-68; asso. prof., head library sci. dept. Madison Coll., Harrisonburg, Va., 1970—. Recipient Distinguished Research award Pi Lamba Theta, 1972. Mem. A.L.A., N.E.A., Va. Edn. Assn., Va. Library Assn., Va. Assn. for Ednl. Communications and Tech., Am. Assn. U. Profs., Beta Phi Mu, Alpha Beta Alpha. Contbr. articles to profl. jours. Address: Dept of Library Science Madison College Harrisonburg VA 22801

HABEEB, VIRGINIA THABET, editor; b. Charleston, W. Va.; d. Mitchell Joseph and Rose M. (Couri) Thabet; A.B. in Vocational Home Econs., Marshall U., 1946; secretarial degree Bluefield Coll., 1943; m. Mitchell H. Habeeb. Home service adviser Appalachian Electric Power Co., Abingdon, Va., 1946-49; with Crosley div. Avco Mfg. Corp., Cin., 1949-54; staff mem. field home econs. program, regional home economist, dir. nat. home econs. tng. program; woman's editor, daily show WCHS-TV, Charleston, 1954-55; asso. home equipment editor Am. Home mag., N.Y.C., 1955-58, home equipment editor, 1958-62, food and equipment editor, 1962-69, mng. editor mag., 1969-70, dir. editorial services, 1970—; contbg. editor Ladies Home Jour., 1972—, Modern Bride mag., 1973—, Girl Talk mag., 1972—. Former mem. home com. Greater N.Y. Safety Council; mem. home conf. com. Nat. Safety Council; mem. consumer com. Nat. Assn. Home Builders. Mem. Am. Home Econs. Assn., Elec. Women's Round Table (chmn. N.Y. chpt. 1962-63, nat. dir. elec. women, nat. v.p. 1964-66), Advt. Women of N.Y. (dir. 1971-72), Home Economists in Bus. (nat. chmn. housing and household equipment com. 1959-60), Am. Women Internat. Understanding, Nat. Major Appliance Consumer Action Panel. Episcopalian (pres. women of ch.). Author: The Little Chef's Book, 1953; Learn to Cook Book, 1966; Ladies Home Journal Art of Homemaking, 1973. Editor: Handbook of Household Equipment Terminology, 1956-60, American Home All-Purpose Cook Book. Office: 200 E 62d St New York City NY 10021

HABER, RUTH BOSS, clin. psychologist, educator; b. Danbury, Conn., Aug. 23, 1932; d. Mendell and Bertha (Kurtz) Boss; B.A., U. Mich., 1954; M.A., Harvard, 1955, Ph.D., 1959; m. Ralph Haber, July 12, 1961 (div. July 1974); children—Sabrina, Rebecca. Postdoctoral fellow with Judge Baker Child Guidance Ct., Boston, 1958-60; staff psychologist Douglas Thom Child Guidance Clinic, Boston, 1960-61; clin. asst. Strong Meml. Hosp., U. Rochester (N.Y.), 1964—, prof. psychology, 1964—. Cons., Allenscreek Psychiat. Group, Rochester, 1973—, United Cerebral Palsy Assn., Rochester, 1968—. USPHS fellow, 1958-60. Mem. Am. Psychol. Assn. Democrat. Home: 55 Avon Rd Rochester NY 14625

HABERMAN, FERN STURM (MRS. BEN HABERMAN), corp. exec.; b. Bklyn.; d. Mark and Sophie (Heller) Sturm; m. Ben Haberman (dec. 1967); children—Mitchell L., Mark Aaron. Owner, Direct Image Alum. Plate and Supply, 1953-59, Direct Image Corp., Monterey Park, Cal., 1959—, Chgo., 1965—, Long Island, N.Y., 1967—, pres., treas., 1967—. Tchr. piano and cello, 1950—. Mem. Printing Industries Am., Nat. Assn. Photo Lithographers, Graphic Arts Tech. Found. Research and devel. supplies for graphic arts. Home: 9920 Toluca Lake Av North Hollywood CA 91602 Office: 1350 S Monterey Pass Rd Monterey Park CA 91754

HABERMANN, HELEN M., educator; b. N.Y.C., Sept. 13, 1927; d. Hans Otto and Katherine (Hansen) Habermann; A.B., State U. N.Y. at Albany, 1949; M.S., U. Conn., 1951; Ph.D., U. Minn., 1956. Research asso. Research Inst., U. Chgo., 1956-57; postdoctoral fellow Hopkins Marine Sta., Stanford U., Pacific Grove, Cal., 1957-58; asst. prof. biol. scis. Goucher Coll., Towson, Md., 1958-64, asso. prof., 1964-70, prof., 1970—, chmn. dept. biol. scis., 1963-66. Vis. investigator dept. plant biology Carnegie Instn. Washington, Stanford, Cal., summer 1959, Pflanzenphysiologisches Institut, U. Gottingen (Germany), summers 1960, 62. NIH spl. research fellow, 1966-67. Author: (with G.B. Moment) Biology: A Full Spectrum, 1973. Home: 801 Beaverbank Circle Towson MD 21204

HABRYL, JOY, psychologist; b. Chgo., July 30, 1937; d. Fred F. and Claire (Gard) Habryl; B.S., Northwestern U., 1958, Ph.D., 1971; M.A., Radcliffe Coll., 1960. Tchr., Evanston Twp. (Ill.) High Sch., 1959-67; clin. psychologist Wis. State U., LaCrosse, 1969-70, VA, Chgo., 1970—. Reading cons. Sci. Research Assos., Chgo., 1963-64. Mem. Human Relations Council LaCrosse, 1969—, Catholic Interracial Council, 1969—. Bd. dirs. jr. governing bd. Chgo. Symphony Orch., 1968—. Mem. Am., Ill. psychol. assns., Am. Personnel and Guidance Assn., Ill. Vocational Guidance Assn., Ill. Acad. Criminology. Home: 4943 N Francisco Av Chicago IL 60625 Office: VA Hosp Downey IL 60004

HACK, JEAN VICKERS, social work adminstr.; b. Sask., Can., Feb. 14, 1918; d. Joseph W. and Madge (Douglas) Vickers; B.A., Howard Payne Coll., 1949, M.Ed., 1955; M.S.W., U. N.C., 1958; div.; children—Gerald R., Herman E. High sch. tchr., Dallas, Tex., 1949-54; dean women Howard Payne Coll., Brownwood, Tex., 1954-56; social work supr. dept. child care Bapt. Gen. Conv., Oklahoma City, 1956—. Mem. steering com. Okla. Conf. Children and Youth, 1970. Mem. Nat. Assn. Social Workers (chpt. pres. 1969-71), Acad. Certified Social Workers, Register of Social Workers (Okla.), Okla. Health and Welfare Assn. (central area chmn. 1967-68; conf. chmn. 1973), Alpha Chi. Baptist (tchr. bible study 1943—). Address: 1141 N Robinson St Oklahoma City OK 73103

HACK, KATHRYN ELIZABETH, banker; b. Paris, Tex., July 31, 1922; d. Charlie and Ora (Dodson) Hack; student Trinity U., 1960-61, San Antonio Coll., 1955-60; B.S., Am. U., 1962; M.B.A., Trinity U., 1966. Sec. investment dept. Nat. Bank Commerce, San Antonio, 1947-61, adminstrv. asst. trust dept., 1961—, asst. trust officer, 1969—. Instr. accounting San Antonio Coll., 1967—. Mem. Am. Assn. U. Women, Nat. Assn. Bank Women. Baptist. Home: 511 La Jara Blvd San Antonio TX 78209 Office: PO Box 121 San Antonio TX 78291

HACKEL, STELLA BLOOMBERG, lawyer; b. Burlington, Vt., Dec. 27, 1926; d. Hyman and Esther (Pocher) Bloomberg; student U. Vt., 1943-45; J.D. cum laude, Boston U., 1948; m. Donald Herman Hackel, Aug. 14, 1949; children—Susan Jane, Cynthia Anne. Admitted to Vt., Mass. bars, 1948; practiced in Burlington, 1948-49, Rutland, Vt., 1949-59, 73—; city prosecutor, Rutland, 1957-63; commr. Vt. Dept. Employment Security, 1963-73. Mem. Vt. Adv. Com. on Mental Retardation, Interdeptl. Council on Aging, Commn. on Status Women, Human Resource Inter-Agy. Com., Emergency Resource Priorities Bd., Information Planning Council, Legislative Council Equal Opportunity Com.; ex-officio mem. Nat. Manpower Adv. Com., 1971-72, Fed. Adv. Council on Unemployment Ins., 1971-72. Pres. Rutland Girl Scouts Leaders Assn., 1949-50, Rutland League Voters, 1951-53, Rutland Council Jewish Women, 1955-56; chmn. women's div. Rutland Community Chest drive, 1952, Rutland County-Vt. Assn. for Blind, 1953-56. Pres. Rutland County Democratic Women's Assn., 1956-63; treas. Rutland City Dem. Com., 1957-63; former rep. office of women's activities of Dem. Nat. Com. on Regional Council I of Women's Civil Def. Councils. Mem. Vt. bd. Girl Scouts U.S.A. Mem. Vt., Rutland County (pres. 1973—) bar assns., Bus. and Profl. Women's Club, Am. Assn. U. Women (treas. Rutland 1951-55, pres. Rutland County br. 1961-62), Vt. Council Social Agys., League Women Voters, Am. Soc. Pub. Adminstrn., Interstate Conf. Employment Security Agys. (v.p. region I, 1966-68, legislative com. 1969, sr. v.p. 1970-71, pres. 1971-72), Delta Phi Epsilon. Clubs: Emblem (dir. 1960-63), Rutland Country. Home: 43 North St Extension Rutland VT 05701 Office: Mead Bldg Montpelier VT 05701

HACKER, ANNE MELCHER, pub. relations ofcl.; b. Omaha, May 9, 1939; d. John Frederic and Mary Jane (Mercer) Melcher; B.A., U. Minn., 1961; M.S., Rensselaer Poly. Inst., 1969; m. James Walter Hacker, Aug. 30, 1969; 1 dau., Jane Elizabeth. Information analyst U.S. Govt., Frankfurt, West Germany, 1961-64; radio-TV producer U. Minn., 1964-65; press officer to gov. Minn., 1965-66; tech. writer-editor Control Data Corp., Mpls., 1966, Boeing Co., Seattle, 1967-69; pub. relations dir. Bellevue (Wash.) Hosp., 1970-72. Free lance writer, editor. Chmn., Seattle Symphony Family Concert. Fund raiser, campaigner, dir. various polit. campaigns. Mem. Soc. Tech. Writers and Pubs., Women in Communications, Mensa, Theta Sigma Phi. Home: 4327 158th Pl SE Bellevue WA 98006

HACKER, ELAINE MARY (MRS. EDWARD MAZZOTTA), physician; b. Clontarf, Minn., Feb. 24, 1925; d. George Henry and Emma (Jansen) Hacker; B.A. magna cum laude, U. Minn., 1946, B.S., 1947, M.B., 1949, M.D., 1950; m. Edward Mazzotta, June 21, 1955; children—Catherine Marion, George Edward. Intern, Detroit Receiving Hosp., 1949-50, asst. and chief resident in obstetrics and gynecology, 1951-54; resident obstetrics Maternity Hosp., Mpls., 1950-51; staff obstetrician and gynecologist Blain Clinic, Detroit, 1954-56; practice medicine specializing in obstetrics and gynecology, Detroit, 1956—, Grosse Pointe Woods, Mich., 1960—; staff Hutzel, Deaconess, Holy Cross hosps., Detroit, Cottage Hosp., Grosse Pointe; clin. instr. dept. obstetrics and gynecology Wayne State U., 1954—. Bd. dirs. Grosse Pointe Assn. for Retarded Children. Diplomate Am. Bd. Obstetrics and Gynecology. Mem. A.M.A., Mich., Wayne

County med. socs., Am. Coll. Obstetrics and Gynecology, Mich. Soc. Obstetrics and Gynecology, Alpha Epsilon Iota. Home: 26 Christine Dr Grosse Pointe Farms MI 48236 Office: 19557 Mack Av Grosse Pointe Woods MI 48236

HACKETT, BARBARA K. (MRS. PATRICK E. HACKETT), lawyer; b. Detroit, Mar. 17, 1928; d. Martin J. and Bessie (Kobe) Kloka; Ph.B., U. Detroit, 1948; J.D., 1950; m. Patrick E. Hackett, Apr. 19, 1952; children—Marie Susan, Carol Mary, Lynn M., Margaret M., Mary Patricia, Elizabeth, Sarah. Admitted Mich. bar, 1950; atty. for Mich. Wis. Pipe Line Co., Detroit, 1950-51; law clk. U.S. Dist. Ct., Detroit, 1951-52; mem. firm McGraw, Sullivan, Ferguson, Detroit, 1952-53; practiced in Dearborn, Mich., 1953-67, Dearborn Heights, Mich., 1972; mem. firm Hackett & Hackett, 1953-67; chief law clk. Mich. Ct. Appeals, 1965-67; asst. pros. atty., Wayne County, Mich., 1967-72; magistrate U.S. Dist. Ct., Eastern Dist. Mich., 1973—. Mem. State Bar Mich., Am., Fed., Detroit bar assns., Woman Lawyers' Assn. of Mich., Nat. Women Lawyers' Assn., U. Detroit Law Alumni Assn., Nat. Assn. R.R. Trial Counsel, Nat. Dist. Attys. Assn., Kappa Beta Pi, Pi Kappa Delta, Gamma Pi Epsilon. Office: 1027 Federal Bldg Detroit MI 48226

HACKETT, FLORENCE (MRS. RICHARD WILBUR HACKETT), motel exec.; b. Akron, O., Sept. 7, 1915; d. John and Lillian (Stiner) Ban; grad. high sch.; m. Richard Wilbur Hackett, May 15, 1937; children—Richard N., Robert J., Elaine (Mrs. John Wesley Ruttle). With Dinner Bell Inn and Motel, Inc., Rehoboth Beach, Del., 1959—, motel mgr., 1963—. Charter mem. Rehoboth Beach League Women Voters. Home: 19 Silver Lake Dr Rehoboth Beach DE 19971 Office: 2 Christian St Rehoboth Beach DE 19971

HACKETT, HELEN RAYNER (MRS. ROBERT E. HACKETT), realtor; b. Manila, P.I., Dec. 30, 1910; d. Earnest Adolphus and Klara Augusta (Bruske) Rayner; B.S. in Edn., U. So. Cal., 1935; m. Robert E. Hackett, Jan. 3, 1969. With Robert E. Lynch, Realtor, Clayton, Mo., 1950-54; sales mgr. Al Elam, Inc., Realtors, Lake Ozark, Mo., 1954-62; owner Helen R. Huber, Realtor, Osage Beach, Mo., 1963—; co-partner G-H Investment Co., Osage Beach, 1968—; co-owner Osage Beach Properties, Inc., Osage Beach, 1961—, sec.-treas., 1961—. Mem. Osage Beach Bus. and Profl. Women, Lake Ozarks Bd. Realtors (sec. 1966-68), Bagnell Dam Area Bd. Realtors (organizer, charter pres.), Phi Mu. Episcopalian. Home: Lake Rd 54-22 Osage Beach MO 65065 Office: Hwy 54 at Lake Rd 54-22 Osage Beach MO 65065

HACKETT, LAURA LYMAN (MRS. FREDERICK K. HACKETT), coll. dean; b. Oberlin, O., Apr. 19, 1916; d. Eugene W. and Mary (Ely) Lyman; A.B., Smith Coll., 1936; M.A., Occidental Coll., 1955; m. Frederick K. Hackett, June 22, 1959; children—Eugene L., Julie M. (Mrs. Charles S. Hernandez), Sybil L. Faculty, Santa Barbara (Cal.) City Coll., 1949-59; tchr. Farmingdale (N.Y.) High Sch., 1959; faculty Suffolk County Community Coll., Selden, N.Y., 1960—, prof., chmn. humanities div., 1964-74, dean of instruction, Western Campus, Brentwood, N.Y., 1974—. Mem. League of Women Voters, Am. Civil Liberties Union. Club: Adirondack Mountain (N.Y.). Author: (with Richard Williamson) Anatomy of Reading, 1965, Design for a Composition, 1966. Home: 19 Hawkins Rd Stony Brook NY 11790 Office: Suffolk County Community College Western Campus Crooked Hill Rd Brentwood NY 11717

HACKETT, SARAH LEGARE SMITH (MRS. JAMES DOMINICK HACKETT), ch. worker; b. Balt., Mar. 12, 1918; d. Horace Taylor and Sarah Mabel (Wolf) Smith; student Johns Hopkins, 1943-44; m. James Dominick Hackett, Oct. 4, 1958; 1 son, Rory Taylor. Asst. to buyer Hutzler Bros. Co., Balt., 1935-41, ward clk. Johns Hopkins Hosp., 1942-45; showroom mgr., designer Flower Modes, Ltd., N.Y.C., 1946-48; fashion editor, reporter Women's Wear Daily, N.Y.C., 1948-54, display advt. solicitor, 1954-58. Pres. United Ch. Women, Great Neck, N.Y., 1961-62, chmn. World Day of Prayer, 1964-66; chmn. World Community Day, 1965; pres. Episcopal Ch. Women of All Saints' Ch., 1961-63, 66-73, chmn. women exec. bd., 1963-66; vice chmn. youth program Gt. Neck chpt. A.R.C., 1967-68, mem. bd., 1967-74. Mem. Internat. Platform Assn., Advt. Club N.Y., Inc., Nat. Trust for Historic Preservation, Nat. Hist. Soc., L.I. Fedn. Women's Clubs Inc. (drama chmn. 1973-75). Club: Woman's (publicity chmn. 1965-66; program chmn. 1966-68, 1st v.p. 1968-70, 73-74, pres. 1970-72, 74—) (Gt. Neck). Home: 8 Lowell Rd Port Washington NY 11050

HACKING, ELEANOR MILLS, educator; b. New Bedford, Mass., Dec. 29, 1934; d. Sidney and Stella Elizabeth (Talbot) Hacking; B.A., Houghton Coll., 1956; Ed.M., Boston U., 1964; C.A.G.S., Boston U., 1972; postgrad. R.I. Coll., 1968-70, Gesell Inst. Child Devel., 1968; certificate U. Hartford, 1972. Tchr. grades 1 and 2 Fairhaven (Mass.) Pub. Schs., 1956-68, elementary reading and lang. arts specialist, 1968—. Asst. prof. Southeastern Mass. U., North Dartmouth, 1972. Mem. town meeting, Fairhaven, 1973-76. Recipient Sara E. Chase Scholarship awards Delta Kappa Gamma Honor Soc. Internat., 1963, 64. Mem. N.E.A. (life), Internat. Reading Assn., Nat. Soc. Study Edn., Mass. Assn. Children with Learning Disabilities, Mass., Fairhaven tchrs. assns., Delta Kappa Gamma. Home: 34 Hamlet St Fairhaven MA 02719 Office: 128 Washington St Fairhaven MA 02719

HACKL, MURIEL FORSTER (MRS. ALPHONS J. HACKL), graphics co. exec.; b. N.Y.C., Feb. 11, 1924; d. Englebert Michael and Johanna (Barisch) Forster; student Hunter Coll., 1942-45, George Washington U., 1946-50; m. Alphons J. Hackl, Feb. 2, 1946; 1 son John R. With soft drink industry trade assn., 1946-48; advt. mgr., v.p., sec. Colortone Press Creative Graphics Inc., Washington, 1948—; v.p., sec., asso. publisher Acropolis Books, Ltd., Washington, 1965—. Recipient Pub. Service award Am. Advt. Fedn., 1964, certificate White House Beautification Com., 1966; named Nat. Advt. Woman of Year, 1972, D.C. Advt. Woman of Year, 1972. Mem. Women's Advt. Club Washington (past pres.), Am. Assn. U. Women. Home: 3077 Cleveland Av NW Washington DC 20008 Office: Colortone Bldg 2400 17th St NW Washington DC 20009

HACKLEMAN, WAUNETA ADELENE (PSEUDONYM VAL MASON), writer; b. Anderson, Ind., Jan. 7, 1915; d. John Dudley and Jennie Mae (Foreman) Mason; grad. Durham Bus. Coll., Phoenix, 1961, Fairmount Sch. Nursing, 1954; student Phoenix Coll., Glendale Community Coll., U. Ariz.; m. John Emory Hackleman, Sept. 20, 1933; 1 son, John Stephen. Nurse, lab. technician, 1949-57; sec. Salt River Project, 1957—, now sr. office sec. Treas. Ariz. Mother's Com.; state chmn. U.S. Savs. Bonds, 1971. Mem. Nat. League Am. Pen Women (pres. Phoenix, pres. Ariz., nat. elections bd., nat. music bd., editor state mag., 1st pl. award for monthly publ. 1973), Nat. Fedn. State Poetry Socs. (past nat. membership chmn., nat. treas. 1972-74, 3d nat. v.p., Nat. Tribute award 1974), Bus. and Profl. Women's Clubs (pres. Phoenix 1972-73, Woman of Year 1973, poet laureate 1973). Republican. Mem. Ch. of Nazarene (pres. Missionary Soc., Ch. Mother of Year 1967). Author: Soliloquies in Verse. Contbr. column to Phoenix Gazette; poems to various publs. Home: 5532 W Monterosa St Phoenix AZ 85031 Office: Box 607 Glendale AZ 85311

HACKMAN, HELEN ANNA HENRIETTE, home economist; b. New Melle, Mo., Oct. 8, 1908; d. John Henry and Lydia Eliza (Meier) Hackman; A.B., Central Wesleyan Coll., Warrenton, Mo., 1929; B.S., U. Mo., 1942; postgrad. U. Wis., 1934, U. Mo., 1942, U. Colo., 1953, U. Ariz., 1974. Prin., Wright City High Sch., 1929; home econs. tchr., Cape Girardeau, Mo., 1930-42; sr. extension adviser home econs. U. Ill., Pittsfield, 1942—. Dietitian, buyer Oshkosh Wis. Camp Fire Girls Camp, summers 1935, 36, 37; sec.-treas. Western Ill. 4-H Camp Assn., 1952-54; mem. Western Ill. Fair Bd. Com., Griggsville, 1946—; v.p. Tri-county Assn. for Handicapped, 1960—; tech. cons. White House Conf., 1960, 70; pres. Pike County Heart Assn., 1969, organizer Family Planning Centers, Diabetic and Blood Pressure Clinics, Pike County Health Dept., 1971. Bd. dirs. Pike County Mental Health. Recipient Distinguished Service award Nat. Home Demonstration Agts. Assn., 1952; Meritorious Service award Heart Assn., 1960, 61. Mem. Ill. Home Adviser's Assn. (sec. 1948), Nat. Assn. Extension Home Economists (3d v.p. 1951-53, pub. relations chmn. 1951-53), Am. Home Econs. Assn. (sec. Ill. nutrition com. 1967-69), Epsilon Sigma Phi (chief 1962), Gamma Sigma Delta. Home: 230 S Illinois St Pittsfield IL 62363 Office: PO Box 227 Hwy 36 East Pittsfield IL 62363

HACKMAN, JEANNE FRANCES LEIGHTON (MRS. JOHN EDWARD HACKMAN), assn. exec.; b. Austin, Minn., July 1, 1940; d. Charles William and Margaret (Fisch) Leighton; student U. Minn., 1961-62; B.S., Coll. St. Teresa, 1962; postgrad. Niagara U., 1964-65; m. John Edward Hackman, Aug. 28, 1964; children—Jennifer, Jonathan Leighton. Research, Proctor & Gamble Co., 1962-64; asst. dir. Dairy Council of Niagara Frontier, 1964-66; program dir. Lexington (Ky.) Dairy Council, 1966-69; exec. dir. Dairy Council Ky. and So. Ind., Inc., Louisville, 1969-73, Dairy Council of Mid South, 1973-74; dir. spl. programs and industry relations S.E. United Dairy Industry Assn., Atlanta, 1974—. Chmn. Gov.'s Commn. on Nutrition, 1972—; mem. Gov.'s Agrl. Council Consumer Edn., 1973—. Mem. Agys. Exec. Club in Blue Grass (sec.-treas. 1967-68, pres. 1969), Farm, Press, Radio Assn. Ky. (sec.-treas. 1966-70, 1st v.p. 1970—), Am., Ky. home econs. assns., Am. Pub. Health Assn., Blue Grass Dietetics Assn., Dairy Tech. Soc., Woman Aux. A.M.A. (pres. 1972—), Teresan Alumni, Pub. Relations Soc. Am. (sec. Ky. chpt. 1972—), Nutrition Club Louisville, Cin. Home Economists in Bus. Club: Zonta (pres. Lexington 1968-70). Home: 2452 Heather Way Lexington KY 40503 Office: 1501 Phoenix Blvd Atlanta GA 30349

HACKMAN, M. EILEEN, educator; b. Coopersburg, Pa., July 4, 1922; d. Marcuse Henry and Florence Ellen (Hartman) Hackman; B.A., Wheaton Coll., 1944; M.S., U. Pa., 1952; postgrad. U. Ariz., 1958-59, U. Denver, 1959-61. Asso. prof. Wheaton (Ill.) Coll., 1945-58; camp dir. Honey Rock, Three Lakes, Wis., 1954-58; tchr. Denver pub. schs., 1959-64; mem. faculty Elmhurst (Ill.) Coll., 1964—, asst. prof. phys. edn., 1964—, chmn. phys. edn. dept., 1973—. Dir. Deer Run Girls' Camp, Alton, N.H., 1964-73. Mem. Am. Camping Assn., Christian Camping Internat., A.A.H.P.E.R. Home: 401 N Scott St Wheaton IL 60187 Office: 190 Prospect Av Elmhurst IL 60126

HACKMAN, MARY COOK MACATEE (MRS. EMORY EDWIN HACKMAN), lawyer; b. Huntington, W.Va., Dec. 2, 1911; d. Charles Augustus and Martha Charlotte (Murphy) Macatee; J.D., Am. U., 1960; m. Emory Edwin Hackman, Nov. 29, 1934; 1 son, Emory Edwin. Admitted to Va. bar, 1962, D.C. bar, 1971, U.S. Supreme Ct., 1972; practiced in Arlington, Va., 1962—; mem. adv. bd. Fidelity Nat. Bank, Arlington, 1965-66. Polit. columnist No. Va. Sun Newspaper, 1956-57. Pres., Arlington Civic Fedn., 1960-62; vice chmn. No. Va. Regional Park Authority, 1959-70. Editor campaign com. Freehill for Congress, 1958. Recipient Trophy for Civic Endeavor, Washington Evening Star, 1957. Mem. Am., Arlington bar assns., Va. State Bar, D.C. Women's Bar, Arlingtonians for a Better County (treas. 1956), Kappa Beta Pi. Democrat. Pub., Arlington (Va.) Citizen Weekly newspaper, 1956-57. Home: 3104 N Inglewood St Arlington VA 22207 Office: 2009 N 14th St Arlington VA 22201

HACKMAN, PEARL E(STELLA), physician; b. nr. Sunneytown, Pa.; d. Joseph B. and Jennie V. (Heany) Hackman; student Temple U., 1916-18; B.S., Pa. State U., 1920; M.D., Woman's Med. Coll., 1924. Intern, Reading (Pa.) Gen. Hosp., 1924-25; gen. practice ophthalmology, asst. gen. practitioner, part-time sch. health and san. inspection, Reading, 1926-43; indsl. medicine E. I. duPont deNemours & Co., Penn's Grove, N.J., 1944-45; gen. practice eye, ear, nose and throat, Canton, O., 1945-46; dir. maternal and child welfare, sch. health physician Lansing and Ingham County Health Dept., Lansing, Mich., 1946-49; gen. practice, hosp. adminstrn. U.S. Indian Service, Navajo Indian Reservation in Ariz., N.M., Utah, Colo., 1950-52; physician Milw. Health Dept. Maternal and Child Welfare Dept., 1952; gen. psychiatry State Hosp., Cleve., 1952-53; psychiatrist, acting chief internal medicine, surgery, geriatrics, chief outpatient services and admissions officer VA Neuropsychiat. Hosp., Gulfport, 1953-65, ret., 1965. Diplomate Nat. Bd. Med. Examiners. Fellow Royal Soc. Health; mem. A.M.A., Miss., Coast Counties med. socs., A.A.A.S., Internat. Platform Assn., Am. Assn. Ret. Persons, Airline Passenger Assn., Nat. Hist. Soc., Smithsonian Assos., Defenders of Wildlife, Am. Security Council (adv. bd.), Marquis Biog. Library Soc. (adv. mem.), Nat. Hist. Soc. (founding mem.), Nat. Assn. R.R. Passengers. Address: PO Box 6115 Gulfport MS 39501

HACKNEY, ELLEN ELIZABETH, editor; b. Indpls., Sept. 24, 1938; d. Glendon Earle and Helen Augusta (Schoelch) Hackney; A.B., Ind. U., 1960. Editorial asst. Hardware Retailing, Indpls., 1960-67, asso. editor, 1967-69, copy editor, 1969-73, sr. editor, 1973—. Mem. Women in Communications, Inc. (treas. Indpls. chpt. 1972—). Methodist. Home: 319 N Graham Av Indianapolis IN 46219 Office: 964 N Pennsylvania St Indianapolis IN 46204

HACKNEY, MYRTLE VIVIAN, editor; b. nr. Greenbrier, Tenn., Nov. 1, 1914; d. Jordan and Minnie Melissa (Castelow) Hackney; student pub. schs., Nashville. Asst. editor Sunday Sch. Bd. of So. Bapt. Conv., Nashville, 1951—; asst. lit. editor The Music Leader, 1966—, Young Musicians, 1966—, Music Makers, 1966—; writer Sunday Sch. curriculum materials. Mem. Nat. League Am. Pen Women (treas.), Tenn. Fedn. Bapt. Bus. Women (chmn. commn. study), Tenn. Womens Press and Authors Club. Author: Invitation to Prayer, 1965; co-author Hyms to Know and Sing, 1973. Home: 1304 Stainback Av Nashville TN 37207 Office: 127 Ninth Av N Nashville TN 37234

HADDAD, MARY ANN CRESSLER (MRS. RICHARD M. HADDAD), educator; b. Shippensburg, Pa., Apr. 5, 1932; d. Donald Ira and Viola (Sprecher) Cressler; B.S., Shippensburg State Coll., 1953, postgrad., 1967-68; M.Ed., Pa. State U., 1958; m. Richard M. Haddad, Aug. 19, 1967; 1 dau., Suzanne E. Elementary tchr. Shippensburg (Pa.) Area Schs., 1953-56; research asst. dept. child devel.-family relations Pa. State U., Coll. Home Econs., 1958; guidance counselor York (Pa.) City Schs., William Penn Sr. High Sch., 1958-61; guidance counselor jr.-sr. high sch. USAF Dependents Schs., Pacific Area, Misawa, Japan, 1961-62, European area, Tripoli, Libya, N. Africa, 1963-67; guidance counselor high sch., Wiesbaden, Germany, 1962-63, ednl. testing specialist/counselor, Aviano, Italy, 1969-70. Mem. Am., Keystone personnel and guidance assns., Am. Sch. Counselors' Assn., N.E.A., Overseas Edn. Assn., Iota Alpha Delta. Club: Desert Explorers' (Tripoli, Libya-Sahara Desert).

HADDEN, FRANCES ROOTS, pianist, composer, music educator; b. Kuling, Kiangsi, China, Aug. 24, 1910; d. Logan Herbert and Eliza (McCook) Roots; A.B., Mt. Holyoke Coll., 1932; pvt. study piano with E. Robert Schmitz, 1930-35; M. Mus., U. Mich., 1967; m. Richard Moulton Hadden, Aug. 23, 1947. Debut as pianist, Hankow, China, 1932; appearances as concert pianist in U.S., Europe, Far East, 1932-40; duo-pianist with husband, 1941—; participant dramatico-mus cultural missions to critical world areas, 1946-64; prof. music Mackinac Coll., 1967-70; concertizing Piano Duologues with the Haddens, 1970—; tours Mich. Council for Arts, 1971—, tours Far East including People's Republic China, 1972; performance White House, 1973. Mem. Cultural Action Com. Mich. Upper Penninsula Com. for Area Progress. Composer (for two pianos) Arch Rock-A Rock Excursion, 1971, Lu Shan Suite, 1973, (stageplays) The Forgotten Factor, 1941, A Statesman's Dream, 1945, The Good Road, 1947, Take It To The World, 1951, Jotham Valley, 1951, The Crowning Experience, 1958, Asian Musical Turning of the Tide, 1958, Pickle Hill, 1959, The Hurricane, 1960, The Tiger, 1960; (motion pictures) The Forgotten Factor, 1953, Jotham Valley, 1953, The Crowning Experience, 1960, Voice of the Hurricane, 1964; (songs) Sweet Potato Pie, Chinese Christmas Cradle Song, Arch Rock, We're All the Same Underneath, I'm The Luckiest Girl Alive, Spin Those Propellers, Look to the Mountains, Turning of the Tide, and others. Co-dir. Peter Howard's stageplay The Boss, Japanese prodn., Tokyo, 1955; world tour accompanist mezzo-soprano Muriel Smith, 1960; world tour with mus. Space Is So Startling, 1962-64. Mem. A.S.C.A.P. (spl. awards 1966-73), Am. Fedn. Musicians, Soc. for Ethnomusicology, Internat. Soc. Music Edn., Internat. Platform Assn. Phi Beta Kappa. Club: Mount Holyoke (N.Y.C.). First Am. concert artist to appear Red China since 1949. Home: Cedar Point Mackinac Island MI 49757

HADDOCK, ALICE FLORINE SHARP (MRS. CECIL LEONARD HADDOCK), extension agt.; b. Roswell, N.M., Oct. 21, 1922; d. Roscoe Ray and Flora Kitty (Hebison) Sharp; B.A., Eastern N.M. U., 1944; M.A., U. N.M., 1963; m. Cecil Leonard Haddock, Mar. 17, 1946; children—Leslie Cecilia (Mrs. Kenneth M. Brazelton), Linda Jean (Mrs. John Lomasney). County extension agt. Agrl. Extension Service, Lea County, Lovington, N.M., 1944-46; substitute tchr. Albuquerque Pub. Schs., 1956-57; 4-H agt. Coop. Extension Service, Bernalillo County, Albuquerque, 1957-67, county home agt., 1967-71; dist. supr. N.M. Co-op. Extension Service, 1971—. Mem. Albuquerque Community Council, 1965-68, Farm Found. scholar Colo. State U., 1958, 71. Recipient Distinguished Service award Nat. Assn. Extension Home Economists, 1970. Mem. Am., N.M. home econs. assns., N.M. Home Agts. Assn. (pres. 1969-70), Albuquerque Home Econs. Club, Epsilon Sigma Phi. Office: 1020 Tijeras NE Albuquerque NM 87106

HADEK, SUZANNE EUGENIA, security analyst; b. N.Y.C., July 27, 1946; d. Charles Gregory VII and Eugenia (Wenger) Hadek; student Syracuse U., 1964-65; B.A. (N.Y. State Regents Coll. scholar 1964), Adelphi U., 1968; M.B.A., N.Y.U., 1969. Security analyst Irving Trust Co., N.Y.C., 1969—, now asst. v.p. Recipient Nat. Merit Scholar Letter of Commendation, scholarship Oyster Bay-East Norwich Kiwanis Club. Mem. N.Y. Soc. Security Analysts, Financial Women's Assn. N.Y., N.Y.U. Bus. Forum, Adelphi U. Alumni Fedn. Club: New York University Alumni, New York University Finance. Home: 55 Lawrence Hill Rd Huntington NY 11743 Office: Irving Trust Co 1 Wall St New York NY 10015

HADFIELD, SHIRLEY CATHERINE THORNSKAR (MRS. ROBERT WILBUR HADFIELD), govt. ofcl.; b. Alliance, Neb., Oct. 23, 1918; d. Theo and Dessie Maude (Schulte) Thornskar; grad. high sch.; m. Robert Wilbur Hadfield, July 28, 1943; children—Carol Susan, Robin Wendy. Sec., Hall County Welfare Dept., Grand Island, Neb., 1936-38; sec., chief statistician div. placement and unemployed ins. State of Neb., Lincoln, 1938-40, hearings stenographer and reporter appeals tribunal, 1940-43; legal sec. Security Title and Trust Co., also firm Birkman, Beckman, Stanard & Vance, San Antonio, 1943-44; sec. to research leader U.S. Dept. Agr., Lincoln, 1960—. Active in P.T.A., 1954—, treas. state P.T.A., 1973—; sec. Roberts Park Improvement Assn., Lincoln, 1953-54. Bd. dirs. Camp Fire Girls, 1970-71, leader, 1958-68. Recipient Certificate of Merit, U.S. Dept. Agr., 1968. Mem. Neb. P.T.A. (life). Democrat. Presbyn. Clubs: Towne Club Mothers Club (pres. 1970-72), U.S. Dept. Agr. (pres. 1973—) (Lincoln). Editor Neb. Parent Tchr. bull., 1968-72, The Foghorn, 1968-70. Home: 5020 Everett Lincoln NE 68506 Office: Room 5 Agrl Engring U Neb Lincoln NE 68503

HADGOPOULOS, SARALYN POOLE (MRS. GEORGE JOHN HADGOPOULOS), educator; b. Atlanta, Aug. 31, 1931; d. George Grady Poole and Sarah (Wimberly) Shaw; student Vassar Coll., 1949-51, Sorbonne, Paris, 1951, U. Ga., 1952; B.S., Columbia, 1955; M.A., N.Y.U., 1961; Ph.D., Emory U., 1965; m. George John Hadgopoulos, Nov. 23, 1963; 1 son, John George de Haven. Tchr. Miami (Fla.) Edison Sr. High Sch., 1958-60; asso. prof. English, Slippery Rock (Pa.) State Coll., 1967-69; prof. Tidewater Center, George Washington U., Little Creek, Va., 1972—, also prof. Program for Afloat Coll. Edn. in conjunction with USN, 1973—. Mem. Inst. Linguists London (Eng.), Modern Lang. Assn. Am., Nat. Council Tchrs. English, Archaeol. Inst. Am. Author: Poems of North Africa, 1973. Address: PO Box 5582 Bayside Sta Virginia Beach VA 23455

HADLEY, ESTELLE ARNOLD (MRS. RICHARD H. HADLEY), lawyer; b. Custer, S.D., Sept. 9, 1907; d. John E. and Lydia (Cowalske) Arnold; J.D., Westminster Law Sch., 1931; m. Frank S. Morrison, June 22, 1929 (div. Aug. 1952); 1 dau., Lea (Mrs. Russell John Schroeder); m. 2d, Richard Hanna Hadley, May 16, 1958. Admitted to Colo. bar, 1933; practiced in Denver, 1933-35, Commerce City, Colo., 1958—; dep. dist. atty., Adams County, Colo., 1961-62; asst. city magistrate Commerce City, 1966-67. Editorial asst. Am. Statis. Inst., Washington, 1943-46. Mem. Players of Denver, 1968—, League Women Voters Adams County, 1967. Publicity chmn. Adams County Jane Jefferson Democratic Club, 1967-68, pres., 1969, historian, 1970; mem. exec. bd. Adams County Dem. Central Com., 1967-68. Mem. Commerce City Bus. and Profl. Women's Club (organizer, pres. 1963), Adams County C. of C. Club: Toastmistress Mile High (Denver). Home: 7101 E 62d Av Commerce City CO 80022 Office: 6496 E 73d Av Commerce City CO 80022

HADLEY, SUSAN JANE (MRS. DAVID S. BIBERMAN), physician; b. Madison, Wis., Sept. 30, 1919; d. Frederick Brown and Jenny Elizabeth (Potts) Hadley; B.A., U. Wis., 1941; M.D., Cornell U., 1944; m. David S. Biberman, May 23, 1951; children—David Hadley, Elizabeth Anne. Intern, Bellevue Hosp., 1944-45, resident, 1945-46; resident N.Y. Hosp., 1946-48, asst. dir. central labs., 1951-64, dir. lab. microbiology, 1964-70, chief pulmonary clinic, 1964—; fellow, instr. N.Y. U., 1948-51; asst. prof. medicine Cornell U. Med. Coll., 1952-68, asso. prof., 1968-72, prof., 1972—, asst. to chmn. dept. medicine, 1965—. Mem. clin. labs. adv. com. City N.Y. Dept. Health, 1968-73. Mem. Harvey Soc., Am. Thoracic Soc., Royal Soc. Medicine, N.Y. Acad. Medicine, N.Y. Trudeau Soc., Phi Beta Kappa, Alpha Omega Alpha. Club: Cosmopolitan (N.Y.C.). Home:

1035 5th Av New York City NY 10028 Office: 1300 York Av New York City NY 10021

HADRA, RUTH, educator; b. Magdeburg, Germany, June 8, 1914; d. Arthur and Lina (Ahlfeld) Hadra; came to U.S., 1940, naturalized, 1946; B.S. in Occupational Therapy, U. Pa. Staff therapist N.J. State Hosp., Trenton, 1946-47; asst. dir. occupational therapy Children's Rehab. Inst., Reisterstown, Md., 1947-55; research Nat. Insts. Neurol. Diseases and Blindness, NIH, Bethesda, Md., 1955-57; chief therapist United Cerebral Palsy, Cin., 1957-63; instr. occupational therapy U. Ill. Coll. of Medicine, Chgo., 1964-74, asst. prof., 1974—. Named Outstanding Occupational Therapist, Ohio Occupational Therapy Assn., 1962—. Mem. Am., Ill. occupational therapy assns., World Fedn. of Occupational Therapy. Contbr. to profl. publs. Office: University of Illinois 840 S Wood St Chicago IL 60612

HAEFELI, MARLAN GRAUL (MRS. CHARLES AUGUST HAEFELI), banker; b. Bklyn., Jan. 9, 1916; d. Frank Joseph and Katherine Veronica (Ludwig) Graul; student N.Y.U., 1949-51; grad. Sch. Financial Pub. Relations, Northwestern U., 1958, Grad. Sch. Savs. Banking, Brown U., 1962; m. Charles August Haefeli, Oct. 4, 1941. Asst. to advt. dir. Am. Express Co., N.Y.C., 1933-46; sec. treas. corp. Sweetser, Byrne & Harrington, Inc., N.Y.C., 1946; exec. asst. to pres. charge personnel, labor relations Schranz & Bieber Co., Inc., N.Y.C., 1947-48; exec. asst. charge personnel C. V. Starr & Co., N.Y.C., 1953-54; exec. asst. to pres. Prudential Savs. Bank, Bklyn., 1954-57, pub. relations officer, 1957-61, asst. v.p., pub. relations officer, 1961-67, sec. to adv. com., 1961-71, asst. v.p., officer in charge Nassau County Office, 1967-68; pub. relations cons., 1968-70; adminstrv. asst. corporate planning and marketing Valley Nat. Bank, Phoenix, 1970-72, asst. v.p., dir. spl. promotions, 1972—. Mem. Savs. Bank Women N.Y. (hon., past pres.), Nat. Assn. Bank Women, Advt. Women N.Y. (life), Am. Advt. Fedn., Bank Marketing Assn., Pub. Relations Soc. Am. Home: 207 W Clarendon St Phoenix AZ 85013 Office: Valley Nat Bank Main Office Phoenix AZ 85004

HAERTEL, LOIS STEBEN (MRS. JOHN DAVID HAERTEL), educator, aquatic ecologist; b. Hinsdale, Ill., Dec. 16, 1939; d. Roy Edwin and Velma Rose (Graue) Steben; B.S., U. Ill., 1961, M.S., 1963; Ph.D., Ore. State U., 1969; m. John David Haertel, June 15, 1962; children—Michael, Patrick. Asst. oceanography dept. Ore. State U., 1963-65; asst. prof. S.D. State U., Brookings, 1969—. USPHS-Dept. Interior predoctoral fellow, 1966-68; grantee Office Water Resources, 1970-72, 74—, S.D. Agrl. Expt. Sta., 1971-73, 74—. Mem. Ecol. Soc. Am., Am. Soc. Limnology and Oceanography, Phi Beta Kappa, Gamma Sigma Delta, Phi Kappa Phi. Democrat. Lutheran. Contbr. articles to profl. jours. Home: 1924 Derdall St Brookings SD 57006 Office: Botany-Biology Dept SD State U Brookings SD 57006

HAFF, ELINOR MAUDE HUNTOON (MRS. FORREST PALMER HAFF), ret. librarian; b. Sayville, N.Y.; d. Charles Henry and Bertha (Clock) Huntoon; A.B., Adelphi Coll., 1924; postgrad. Columbia U., 1930, 37; m. Forrest Palmer Haff, Aug. 30, 1929. Kindergarten-primary tchr. Bay Shore pub. schs., 1924-35; librarian, dir. Sayville Library, 1937-70. Founder, pres. Wet Paints Studio Group, 1949. Mem. D.A.R. (regent), Suffold County Library Assn. (founder, past pres.), Sayville Hist. Soc. (dir.), Internat. Platform Assn., Sigma Kappa. Conglist. (pres. women's fellowship 1973). Club: Sayville Garden (pres. 1973); South Shore College Women's (pres. 1967-69). Home: 29 Edwards St Sayville NY 11782

HAFFER, GLORIA SCHOTTENSTEIN (MRS. MYLES HAFFER), dept. store exec.; b. Cin., Jan. 28, 1941; d. Benjamin and Dorothy (Signer) Schottenstein; student H. Sophie Newcomb Coll., 1958-60; B.A., U. Cin., 1962; m. Myles Haffer, Jan. 28, 1962; children—Beth, Stephen. Caseworker, Hamilton County (O.) Welfare Dept., 1962-64; buyer, Ben's Dept. Store, Cin., 1964—; sec. Haffer Advt., Inc., 1968—; asst. sec. White Oak Shopping Center, Inc., Cin., 1960—. Bd. dirs. Bonds for Israel, 1968-72, Jewish Fedn. of Cin., 1968-71, Jewish Family Serivce, 1972, Council of Jewish Women, 1965-71, United Appeal, 1968-71. Mem. Alpha Epsilon Phi. Clubs: Cincinnati, Crest Hills Country (Cin.). Home: 8300 Arborcrest Dr Cincinnati OH 45236 Office: 721 Central Av Cincinnati OH 45202

HAFFNER, MARLENE ELISABETH (MRS. WILLIAM HENRY JOSEPH HAFFNER), physician; b. Cumberland, Md., Mar. 22, 1941; d. Ludwig and Gusty Elisabeth (Waldstein) Brings; student Western Res. U., 1958-61; M.D., George Washington U., 1965; m. William Henry Joseph Haffner, Aug. 17, 1963; children—Stephanie Elisabeth, Andrea Jean. Intern, George Washington U. Hosp., 1965-66; fellow dermatology Columbia-Presbyn. Med. Center, N.Y.C., 1966-67; resident internal medicine St. Lukes Med. Center, N.Y.C., 1967-69; fellow hematology Albert Einstein Sch. Medicine, N.Y.C., 1969-71, clin. instr. medicine, 1969-71, chief dept. internal medicine Gallup (N.M.) Indian Med. Center, 1971-74; chief med. service Navajo Area Indian Health Service, Window Rock, Ariz., 1974—; cons. internal medicine Navajo Indian Reservation. Diplomate Am. Bd. Internal Medicine. Mem. A.C.P., Am. Coll. Clin. Pharmacology, Mortar Board, Alpha Epsilon Phi, Iota Sigma Pi. Home: 317 S Wyatt St Gallup NM 87301 Office: PO Box 1337 Gallup NM 87301

HAFT, GAIL SELDEN KLEIN (MRS. JACOB ISRAEL HAFT), physician; b. N.Y.C., Mar. 5, 1938; d. Herbert and Pearl (Mittleman) Klein; A.B., Vassar Coll., 1959; M.D., U. Rochester, 1963; m. Jacob Israel Haft, Mar. 27, 1964; children—Bethanne Donna, Ian David Aaron. Intern, Albert Einstein Coll. Medicine, N.Y.C., 1963-64, pediatric resident, 1964-65; pediatrician, N.Y.C. Dept. Health, 1965-67; pediatric resident Mt. Sinai Hosp., N.Y.C., 1967-68; sch. physician, Englewood Cliffs, N.Y., 1970-71; utilization rev. physician Fordham Hosp., N.Y.C., 1973—; pediatrician Westchester County Health Dept., 1972—; instr. pediatrics Mt. Sinai Sch. Medicine, 1967-68. Diplomate Nat. Bd. Med. Examiners, Am. Bd. Pediatrics.

HAGE, ELIZABETH BERNICE, librarian; b. Madelia, Minn., May 12, 1911; d. George S. and Hanna M. (Borresen) Hage; student LaCrosse State Tchrs. Coll., 1929-30; A.B., Carleton Coll., 1933; B.L.S., U. Wis., 1937. Librarian, Wahpeton (N.D.) Pub. Library, 1937-39; 1st asst. circulation dept. Davenport (Ia.) Public Library, 1939-40; supr. WPA, Des Moines 1940-42; county librarian Pub. Library, Virginia, Minn., 1942-45; librarian Lyon County Library, Marshall, Minn., 1945-48; reference librarian Appleton (Wis.) Public Library, 1948-49; librarian Scott County Library, Eldridge, Ia., 1950-57; dir. Prince George's County Meml. Library, Hyattsville, Md., 1957—. Mem. Prince George County Adv. Youth Action Com., 1968—, Health Planning Adv. Com., 1969-72. Mem. A.L.A. (chmn. PLA legislative com. 1968), Md. Library Assn. (pres. 1963), D.C. Library Assn. (exec. bd. 1963), Md. Pub. Library Adminstrs. Assn. (pres. 1964). Home: 200 Dorset Rd Laurel MD 20810 Office: 6532 Adelphi Rd Hyattsville MD 20782

HAGEDORN, JUDITH WRIGHT (MRS. FRANK HAGEDORN), psychologist; b. Independence, Kan.; d. John L. and Thelma V. (Rooks) Wright; B.A., U. Tulsa, 1961, M.A., 1965, Ed.D., 1969; m. Frank Hagedorn, Aug. 19, 1960. Individual practice psychology, 1969—. Co-moderator Move Closer to Your World, teenage talk show, KTUL-TV, Tulsa, 1970—; lectr. in field. Mem. Am., Tulsa (pres. 1968-69) psychol. assns. Author: (with Janet Kizziar) Gemini: The Psychology and Phenomena of Twins, 1974. Home: 11441 S 87th E Av Bixby OK 74008 Office: 2651 E 21st St Tulsa OK 74114

HAGEMAN, SHARON POST (MRS. PAUL THOMAS JOHN HAGEMAN), occupational therapist; b. Wellsville, N.Y., Sept. 21, 1945; d. Philip Bramwell and Irene Louise (Claire) Post; B.A., Alfred U., 1967; Occupational Therapist certificate Va. Commonwealth U., 1970, postgrad., 1970—; m. Paul Thomas John Hageman, Mar. 21, 1970. Occupational therapy instr. Craig State Sch., Sonyea, N.Y., 1968, occupational therapy trainee II, 1969; staff therapist West Seneca (N.Y.) State Sch., 1970; sr. occupational therapist J.N. Adam State Sch., Perrysburg, N.Y., 1970-72, head occupational therapist, 1972-73, program coordinator, head occupational therapist, 1973—. Lectr., Erie Community Coll., 1970-73. Pres., J.N. Adam Employees Fed. Credit Union, 1972—. Mem. Am. Occupational Therapy Assn., Nat. Rehab. Assn. Republican. Home: 102 Buffalo St Gowanda NY 14070 Office: JN Adam State Sch Perrysburg NY 14129

HAGEN, LOIS BLANCHE, editor, author; b. Westby, Wis.; d. Reuben and Blanche (Nichols) Hagen; B.A., U. Wis., 1941. children—Ellen, Aboya. Reporter, U.P.I., Chgo., 1941-42; editorial researcher Time Mag., N.Y.C., 1942-43; radio news editor U.P.I., 1944-47; home furnishings editor Milw. Jour., 1947—. Recipient awards Dorothy-Dawe-Am. Furniture Mart, 1950, 51, 58, 63, 68, 70, 73; U. Mo.-Penney award, 1965; Apollo award Summer and Casual Furniture Mfrs. Assn., 1955; certificate of Achievement, Am. Inst. Interior Designers, 1962; award Burlington House, 1971, 72; Writers Hall of Fame, So. Furniture Market, 1972; Press award Nat. Soc. Interior Designers, 1973. Mem. Phi Kappa Phi, Sigma Delta Chi. Clubs: Chicago Press, Milwaukee Press. Home: 9217 N 70th St Milwaukee WI 53223 Office: 333 W State St Milwaukee WI 43201

HAGENER, ANTOINETTE RADER (MRS. LOUIS W. HAGENER), mus. ofcl.; b. Buffalo, Nov. 22, 1926; d. Joseph and Angele (Von Wulpen) Rader; A.B., U. Denver, 1946; m. Louis W. Hagener, June 8, 1947; children—Louis I., Anne (Mrs. Eric Oksendahl), Jeffry, Jim. Lab. technician Good Samaritan Hosp., Phoenix, 1946; sci. tchr. Westminister (Colo.) High Sch., 1946-47, S. High Sch., Denver, 1947-49; lab. technician Vita Rich Dairy, Havre, Mont., 1953-68; curator H. Earl Clack Meml. Mus., Havre, 1963—. Health chmn. Mont. P.T.A., 1966-68, 70-72; chmn. Havre (Mont.) Mental Health Assn., 1971-73; mem. City of Havre Park and Recreation Bd., 1971—. Trustee Mont. Hist. Soc., 1970—, sec. exec. bd. 1972—. Recipient Mus. award Am. Assn. for State Local History, 1972. Mem. Am. Assn. U. Women (pres. No. Mont. br. 1962-64, dir. Mont. div., v.p. 1972—), Mus. Assn. Mont. (dir., pres. 1972—), League Women Voters, P.E.O., Mont. Inst. of Arts. Methodist. Author: (with Louis W. Hagener) Edible Wild Plants of North Central Montana, 1973. Contbr. articles to profl. jours. Home: 612 17th St Havre MT 59501 Office: H Earl Clack Meml Mus Havre MT 59501

HAGENSTEIN, RUTH H. (MRS. W. D. HAGENSTEIN), civic worker; b. Everett, Wash.; d. Andrew and Mabel (Walker) Johnson; B.A. magna cum laude, U. Wash., 1937, M.S., 1939; m. William D. Hagenstein, Sept. 2, 1940. Psychologist, Western State Custodial Sch., Buckley, Wash., 1939-40; personnel technician Wash. State Merit System, Seattle, 1944, U.S. Civil Service Commn., Washington, 1945. Mem. Ore. Water Resources Bd., 1960-69, chmn., 1965-66; mem., on exec. com. Portland (Ore.) Met. Study Commn., 1963-71; bd. dirs. Parry Center for Children, 1964-71, chmn. program services com., 1964-66, pres., 1967-69; mem. priorities com. Community Council, 1961-66, children's residential treatment com., 1963-67; mem. Bonneville Regional Adv. Council, 1970—; chmn. program com., bd. dirs. Christie Sch., 1971—; mem. Portland-Multnomah County Consol. Charter Commn., 1971-73; Pres.'s Nat. Adv. Council on Edn. Disadvantaged Children, 1971—; mem. Portland Concentrated Crime Reduction Task Force, 1972—; v.p. Ore. United Appeal, 1973—; bd. dirs. Tri. County Met. Transp. Dist. of Ore., 1974—. Vice chmn. in charge precinct orgn. Multnomah County Republican Central Com., 1960-63; edn. chmn. Ore. Rep. Central Com., 1959-60. Named Portland Woman of Accomplishment, 1973. Mem. Am. Assn. U. Women (state legislative chmn. 1963-64), League Women Voters (Portland pres. 1951-53, Ore. 1st v.p. 1953-54), Phi Beta Kappa. Home: 3062 S W Fairmount Blvd Portland OR 97201

HAGERTY, HARRIET MAY, editor, artist; b. Potsdam, N.Y., July 14, 1909; d. John Alexander and Johanna (Stolte) May; student Rochester Inst. Tech., 1929; pupil Berta Frey, Karl Laurell; m. Cornelius Hagerty, Feb. 16, 1943; 1 son, John May. With various textile firms, Chatham, N.Y., 1966-69; exhibited one-man show Pen and Brush Club, 1963, Trias Gallery, summer 1966; exhibited group shows at Northeast Craftsman, Worcester (Mass.) Mus. Contemporary Crafts; represented in permanent collection Cooper Hewitt Mus. Republican county committeewoman, 1961-74. Recipient Best in Show award Pen & Brush Club, 1962; Best Use of Color award New Eng. States Weaving Sem., Amherst, Mass., 1965; certificate merit Artist Craftsmen, 1966; Cooper Union Mus. award wool yardage, 1967. Mem. Pen and Brush Club (pres. 1972), N.Y. Guild of Handweavers. Clubs: Chatiemac (North Creek, N.Y.); North Creek (N.Y.) Hunting and Fishing. Contbr. articles on weaving to various pubs. Home: 15 W 67th St New York City NY 10023 Office: 220 Fifth Av New York City NY 10001

HAGERTY, MARGARET SOMERS FREY (MRS. FRANCIS W. HAGERTY), broadcasting exec.; b. Moline, Ill.; d. Harry and Helen (Somers) Frey; student Christian Coll., 1937-38, Parsons Coll., 1938-39; B.A., Grinnell Coll., 1941; m. Francis W. Hagerty, Apr. 30, 1960. Acting city editor Fairfield (Ia.) Daily Ledger, 1943-44; office mgr., prodn. mgr., media dir., sec.-bookkeeper R. L. Sines & Assos. Advt., San Francisco, 1946-47; tchr. pub. schs., Newburg, Ia., 1948; promotion asst. radio sta. KOMO, 1948-50, promotion mgr., 1950-53; advt. and promotion mgr. KOMO-TV, Seattle, 1953-72, mgr. press relations, 1972—. Mem. Nat. Acad. Television Arts and Scis., P.E.O., Broadcast Promotion Assn. Methodist. Home: 6543 46th St NE Seattle WA 98115 Office: 100 4th Av N Seattle WA 98109

HAGERTY, NANCY DAINES, ednl. researcher; b. Murray, Utah, Sept. 25, 1935; d. Leland Albert and Bernice (Burbidge) Daines; B.S. in Sociology, Brigham Young U., 1961; M.A. in Psychology, Columbia, 1964; Ph.D. in Ednl. Research, Fla. State U., 1970; m. Everett Hagerty, July 18, 1958 (div. Sept. 1973); children—Lonn James, Colleen Kay, Shawn Marie. Tchr., Greer Elementary Sch., Hope Farm, N.Y., 1966-67; lectr. U. B.C., Vancouver, 1970; cons. Center for Continuing Edn., 1971—. Cons. to local schs. on individualizing ednl. process, 1971—. U.S. Office Edn. fellow in Computer-Assisted Instruction, 1967-69. Mem. Am. Psychol. Assn., Am. Ednl. Research Assn. Author: (with Walter Dick) Reliability and Validity, 1971; A General Systems Approach Model for Developing Instructional Materials, 1971; Individualizing Instruction, 1972.

HAGGIE, HELEN JEAN MORROW (MRS. ANTHONY JAMISON HAGGIE), editor; b. Scottsbluff, Neb., Aug. 3, 1913; d. William and Philomena (Congdon) Morrow; B.A., U. Neb., 1933; m. Anthony Jamison Haggie, Apr. 15, 1938 (dec.); 1 dau., Kate (Mrs. A.L. Ellison). Tchr., Scottsbluff High Sch., 1933-38; city editor Telescope, Bellville, Kan., 1948-50; with Lincoln (Neb.) Jour., 1950—, peoples editor, art, cultural, fashion writer, 1974—. Tutor athletic dept. U. Neb., 1962-72. Neb. com. Bundles for Britain, 1940-41; vol. A.R.C., 1941-45; vol. head dispensary Moston Club, London, Eng., 1941-45; mem. Cath. Bishops Com. Civil Rights, 1961-64; mem. Govs. Commn. Status Women, 1965-72, chmn., 1971-72; mem. Neb. Com. to Select Poet Laureate, 1974—. Bd. dirs. Cath. Social Bur., 1960-65; bd. dirs. Vol. Bur., also pres., 1967-71. Named Neb. Woman of Year, Theta Sigma Chi. Mem. Am. Assn. Univ. Women, Sigma Delta Chi. Clubs: Omaha Press; Lincoln University. Home: 2317 S 27th St Lincoln NE 68502 Office: 9th and P Sts Lincoln NE 68501

HAGIN, ROSA A., psychologist; b. Elizabeth, N.J., June 14, 1921; d. William N. and Jennie B. (Smith) Hagin; B.S., N.J. State Coll., 1941; M.A., N.Y. U., 1944, Ph.D., 1955. Dir. spl. services Roselle (N.J.) Bd. Edn., 1951-58, Irvington (N.J.) Bd. Edn., 1958-61; fellow clin. psychology N.Y. U. Sch. Medicine, 1949-51, instr., 1961-64, asst. prof., 1964-69, research asso. prof. psychology, 1969—; pvt. practice psychology, N.Y.C., 1955—. Co-dir. Learning Disorders Unit. Diplomate Am. Bd. Profl. Psychology. Fellow Am. Psychol. Assn., Am. Orthopsychiat. Assn.; mem. Am. Assn. Mental Deficiency, Orton Soc., N.E.A. (life), N.J. Psychol. Assn., N.Y. Assn. Clin. Psychologists. Contbr. articles to profl. jours. Home: 15 Canterbury Pl Cranford NJ 07016 Office: 200 E 33d St New York City NY 10016

HAGLICH, SISTER BIANCA, artist, educator; b. Lussin, Italy, Feb. 4, 1927; d. Anthony and Frances (Picinich) Haglich; came to U.S., 1934; certificate Central Park Sch. Art, 1945; B.A., Marymount Coll., 1953; M.A., Notre Dame U., 1962; postgrad. Acad. Fine Art, Perugia and Florence, Italy, 1959, Finland, 1968-69, Eng., 1971. Designer, Kress Display Dept., N.Y.C., 1947-48; tchr. elementary sch., Marymount Jr. Sch., Tarrytown, N.Y., 1948-52; tchr. high sch., Tarrytown, 1950-61; tchr. art Marymount Coll., Tarrytown, 1962—, asst. prof., 1964-71, chmn. dept. art, 1970-74, asso. prof., 1971—; one-man shows at Finnish Festival, Marymount Coll.; exhibited in group shows at U. Notre Dame Gallery, Rochester Festival Religious Art, Yorktown Jewish Center Art Show; represented in pvt. collections. Recipient 1st prize New Rochelle Women's Art Exhbn., 1966, 2d prize Art in Park, Tarrytown, 1966. Mem. Am. Assn. U. Profs., Coll. Art Assn., Catholic Fine Art Soc. (publicity chmn. 1963-64). Met. Mus. Art. Address: Marymount Coll Tarrytown NY 10591

HAGLOCK, LOUISE MCCLELLAN (MRS. FREDRICK WILLIAM HAGLOCK), city ofcl.; b. Nashville, Sept. 28, 1914; d. William David and Betty Evelyn (Hooper) Nichols; student Beckwith Bus. Inst., 1943-44; m. Fredrick William Haglock, July 11, 1948; children—Anita (Mrs. Daniel Ray Paisley), David. Bookkeeper Ridgeway Feed Store, New Philadelphia, O., 1944-45, Midway Lumber Co., Dover, O., 1946-49; with Kuhn Motors, Inc., Sugar Creek, O., 1950-72, Dover, 1972; auditor City of Dover, 1972—. Mem. Bus. and Profl. Women's Club. Republican. Mem. Moravian Ch. Home: 205 N Fairview Av Dover OH 44622 Office: City Bldg City of Dover OH 44622

HAGLUND, KRISTINE ANN, mus. ofcl.; b. Denver, Sept. 1, 1947; d. Erik E. and Bernice L. (Kimel) Haglund; B.A., U. Colo., 1969. Curator, Buffalo Bill Meml. Mus., Golden, Colo., 1967—. Lectr. to various clubs and schs. Mem. Colo.-Wyo. Assn. Museums (dir. 1971—), Mountain Plains Museums Conf., Phi Beta Kappa. Home: 6911 W 24th Av Lakewood CO 80215 Office: Rural Route 5 Box 950 Golden CO 80401

HAGMAN, JEAN CASSELS, mus. ofcl.; b. Des Moines, Sept. 17, 1947; d. Harlan Lawrence and Mary Anna (Cassels) Hagman; student No. Mich. U., 1965-66; B.A., Mich. State U., 1969; M.A., Wayne State U., 1971. Dir. edn. Grand Rapids (Mich.) Art Mus., 1970—. Mem. Am. Assn. U. Women. Episcopalian. Club: Zonta (corr. sec. Grand Rapids 1973—). Home: 4117-12 Crooked Tree SW Wyoming MI 49509 Office: 230 E Fulton Grand Rapids MI 49502

HAGOOD, ANNABEL DUNHAM, educator; b. Hattiesburg, Miss., Feb. 7, 1924; d. John H. and Bella (Smith) Dunham; A.B., Southwestern La. Inst., 1944; M.A., U. Wis., 1946; grad. study 1947-49; m. William Knox Hagood, June 6, 1950 (div. Sept. 1969). Asst. dir. debate and drama Southwestern La. Inst., 1944-45; asst. counselor U. Wis., 1945-46; Instr. U. Ala., 1946-49. asst. prof., 1949-57, asso. prof. speech, 1957-63, prof., 1963—, dir. forensics, 1946—, mem. univ. council, 1961-62, 70-71, coach College Bowl team, 1962, chmn. student acad. affairs Coll. Arts and Scis., 1969-71, chmn. arts and scis. faculty senate, 1972-73. Adv. com. contests and awards Alexander Hamilton Bicentennial Commn., 1956-57. Trustee Nat. Debate Tournament Com., chmn., 1968-69, treas., 1972-73. Mem. Am. Forensic Assn. (successively So. gov., sec.-treas., v.p., nat. pres. 1956-57, chmn. finance com. 1964-65, chmn. profl. relations com. 1968-70), Speech Assn. Am. (chmn. com. on internat. discussion and debate 1953-54-55), So., (chmn. com. time and place 1951, tournament dir. 1956), Ala. speech assns., Phi Kappa Phi, Pi Kappa Delta, Tau Kappa Alpha (nat. pres. 1960-63, chmn. speaker of year Bd. of Award Delta Sigma Rho-Tau Kappa Alpha). Author chpts. in books and articles in profl. jours. Editor: The Register, 1956, 57. Home: One Wood Manor Apts Tuscaloosa AL 35401

HAHN, ARLENE CLARA, librarian; b. Frackville, Pa., Nov. 26, 1928; d. Philip and Mildred Nellie (Richards) Hahn; B.S., Kutztown State Coll. Pa., 1950; M.L.S., George Peabody U., 1954. Librarian, U.S. Army Post Library, Fort Monmouth, N.J., 1955—; in charge U.S. Air Force Libraries, Korea, 1967-68. Recipient John Cotton Dana award A.L.A., 1967, 68, 71, 72, 73. Mem. Am. Assn. U. Women, Fed. Librarians. Clubs: Fort Monmouth Officers; Peninsula House Beach (Seabright, N.J.). Home: 38 Country Club Rd Eatontown NJ 07724 Office: Post Library Fort Monmouth NJ 07703

HAHN, BEVRA YVONNE HANNAHS (MRS. THEODORE JOHN MILFORD HAHN), rheumatologist; b. Wheeling, W.Va., Dec. 9, 1939; d. Chester Hobart and Isa May (Quillen) Hannahs; B.S., Ohio State U., 1960; M.D., Johns Hopkins, 1964; m. Theodore John Milford Hahn, May 3, 1964; children—Alysanne Yvonne, April Dianne. Intern, Washington U., St. Louis, 1964-65, resident in medicine, 1965-66; fellow rheumatology Johns Hopkins, 1966-69; practice medicine, specializing in rheumatology, St. Louis, 1969—; instr. medicine Washington U., St. Louis, 1969-71; clin. investigator VA, 1970-73; research and edn. asso. St. Louis VA Hosp., 1969-70, clin. investigator, 1970-73, chief rheumatology, 1972—, asst. chief medicine, 1973—; asst. prof. medicine and preventive medicine Washington U., St. Louis, 1971—. Bd. dirs. Mo. Com. Legalized Abortion. Mem. Am. Rheumatism Assn., Eastern Mo. Arthritis Found., St. Louis Rheumatism Soc., St. Louis Soc. Internal Medicine, Phi Beta Kappa. Methodist. Contbr. articles to profl. jours. Home: 62 Willow Brook Dr St Louis MO 63141 Office: 4566 Scott Av St Louis MO 63110

HAHN, EMILY, author; b. St. Louis, Jan. 14, 1905; d. Isaac Newton and Hannah (Schoen) Hahn; B.S. U. Wis., 1926 student Columbia, 1928-29, Oxford (Eng.), 1934-35; m. Charles R. Boxer, Nov. 28, 1945;

children—Carola, Amanda. Mining engr. Deko Oil Co., St. Louis, 1926; courier, Santa Fe, 1927-28; instr. geology, Hunter Coll., N.Y.C., 1929-30; with Red Cross in Belgian Congo, 1930-31; writer stories, scenarios, N.Y.C., Hollywood, also travels and newspaper work in Eng., the Continent and North Africa, 1931-32; instr. English, Customs Coll., Shanghai, also writer, 1935-38, Chungking, 1940; instr. Customs U., Hong Kong, 1941. Author: including China to Me, 1944; Hong Kong Holiday, 1946; China A to Z, 1946; Picture Story of China, 1946; Raffles of Singapore, 1946; Miss Jill, 1947; England to Me, 1949; Purple Passage, 1950; Love Conquers Nothing, 1952; Chiang Kai-Shek, 1955; Diamond, 1956; The Tiger House Party, 1959; Fractured Emerald, 1971; On the Side of the Apes, 1971. Interned by Japanese govt., 1941; returned to U.S. on Gripsholm, 1943. Address: care Brandt & Brandt 101 Park Av New York City NY 10017

HAHN, HANNELORE, writer; b. Dresden, Germany; d. Arthur and Helene (Brach) Hahn; came to U.S., 1938, naturalized, 1943; B.A. in Comparative Lit., U. So. Cal., 1952; 1 dau., Tatiana. Cons., mem. staff Parks, Recreation and Cultural Affairs Adminstrn., N.Y.C., 1966—; exhibit coordinator U.S. Pavillion, Expo '67, Montreal, 1965-66; founder, dir. Phoenix House Poetry Workshops, N.Y.C., 1970-73. Chairperson lit. Internat. Women's Arts Festival, 1974—; producer, dir. Women/Voices/1975, Internat. Women's Year, N.Y.C., 1975. Author: Take a Giant Step, 1960. Translator Scientific Correspondence of Albert Einstein, 1963-64. Address: 1628 York Av New York City NY 10028

HAHN, HARRIET LOUISE PAINE (MRS. CHARLESS HAHN), editor; b. Gatun, Panama, June 3, 1919; d. Alan Grant and Clara deNormandie (Abercrombie) Paine; student Reed Coll., 1936-38; B.A., U. Chgo., 1940; m. Charless Hahn, Dec. 27, 1940; 1 dau., Padraig (Mrs. Theodore A. Brennen). Free lance mural painter, Winnetka, Ill., 1941-45; head lower and middle sch. art dept. N. Shore Country Day Sch., Winnetka, 1956-63; editor trade papers All Am. Publishers Service, Inc., Chgo., 1963—. Bd. dirs. North Shore Art League, 1941-48, pres., 1946-48; Family Service of Winnetka-Northfield, 1965-71, sec. bd., 1970-71; bd. dirs. YWCA, 1973—; treas., 1974. Club: Chgo. Press. Home: 370 Walnut St Winnetka IL 60093 Office: 9 S Clinton St Chicago IL 60606

HAHN, SISTER MARY, health service exec.; b. Kinsley, Kan., Aug. 30, 1939; d. Lawrence Constantine and Margaret Louise (Roepka) Hahn; B.S. in Edn., Sacred Heart Coll., 1963; postgrad. Kan. State U., 1965; M.S. in Spl. Edn., Fort Hays (Kan.) State Coll., 1970. Tchr. parochial schs., Kan., 1959-69; dir., founder Hope, Inc., Gt. Bend, Kan., 1969-72; dir. Barton County Community Mental Retardation Center, Inc., Great Bend, Kan., 1972—. Chmn. Extended Services Commn., Gt. Bend, 1971-74; dir. Hope Work Activity Center, Gt. Bend, 1971. Vice pres. Kan. Recreation Workshop, 1973-74. Joseph Kennedy grantee, 1969-70. Mem. Kan. Assn. Rehab. Facilities, Council for Exceptional Children (chmn. membership 1973—), Barton County Assn. Retarded Citizens. Club: Soroptomist (v.p. 1972-74, pres. 1974—) (Gt. Bend). Home: 3600 Broadway Great Bend KS 67530 Office: 1500 Polk St Great Bend KS 67530

HAHN, ODESSA ELIZABETH MILFORD (MRS. THEODORE JOHN HAHN), civic worker, educator; b. Columbus, Ga.; d. Jefferson Davis and Odessa (Norris) Milford; A.B., Randolph-Macon Woman's Coll.; M.A., George Washington U., 1960; postgrad. Johns Hopkins, 1934, 35, 58, 65, U. Md., 1959, Loyola Coll., 1965; m. Theodore John Hahn, Aug. 15, 1935; children—Theodore John, Davis Milford. Social worker Family Welfare Assn., Balt., 1933; tchr. So. High Sch., 1933-35, Eastern High Sch., 1958-66 (all Balt.); asso. prof. psychology Community Coll. Balt., 1967—, chmn. community lectr. series, 1967-68. Adviser series tv programs WMAR-TV. Publicity dir., head women's div., a founder Nat. Found. for Mentally Retarded and Handicapped Children, 1950-56; founder Gladys M. Dorsey Scholarship Fund, 1964—; mem. Md. Congress Parents and Tchrs.; founder, hon. life pres. women Civitan Club, 1952-56; exec. reservist Dept. Labor; bd. visitors, bd. dirs. Morgan State Coll. Mem. Am. Psychol. Assn., Eastern, Southeastern, Md. psychol. assns., So. Psychol. and Philos. Assn., Md. Tchrs. Assn., D.A.R. (dir. 1937-40), Am. Assn. U. Profs. (chpt. v.p. 1971-72), N.E.A., Randolph-Macon Woman's Coll. Alumnae Assn. (pres. 1937-39, pub. relations dir. Md., alumnae adviser for nat. publicity endowment campaign 1956), Phi Beta Kappa, Pi Gamma Mu, Psi Chi, Phi Delta Gamma. Democrat. Presbyn. Clubs: Three Arts of Homeland (dir. 1942-45), Womens of Roland Park. Home: 5720 Cross Country Blvd Baltimore MD 21209 Office: 2901 Liberty Heights Av Baltimore MD 21215

HAHNE, HELEN JO, banker, b. Chgo., Dec. 31, 1929; d. Oliver A. and Opal J. (Andrews) Hahne; B.S., U. Ill., 1950; M.S., U. Chgo., 1952; J.D., Northwestern U., 1957. Admitted to Ill. bar, 1957; practiced in Chgo., 1957—; law clk. Woodson, Pattishell & Garner, 1957-59; asst. v.p. First Nat. Bank Chgo., 1959—. Mem. Am. Bankers Assn., Women's, Ill. Chgo. bar assns., Phi Beta Kappa, Delta Gamma. Office: 1 First Nat Plaza Floor Chicago IL 60670

HAHNEL, GERMAINE RITA, physician; b. Cleve., Sept. 3, 1931; d. John and Charlotte Frances (Schmotzer) Hahnel; A.B., Ohio U., 1953; M.D., U. Cin., 1957. Intern, St. Louis City Hosp., 1957-58, resident, 1958-59; gen. practice medicine, North Olmsted, O., 1959—. Diplomate Am. Bd. Family Practice. Mem. A.M.A., Am. Med. Women's Assn. Home: 27407 Blossom Blvd North Olmsted OH 44070 Office: 25300 Lorain Rd North Olmsted OH 44070

HAIGHT, MILDRED LUCILE SHERMAN (MRS. LYNDON A. HAIGHT), educator, artist; b. Collingswood, N.J.; d. George and Edna (Wygant) Sherman; B.S. in Edn. magma cum laude, Syracuse U., 1933, M.S., 1938, postgrad. in arts, 1960-64; m. Lyndon A. Haight, Sept. 8, 1932; children—Jean (Mrs. George Remington), Christine (Mrs. William A. Clegg), Gary L.S. Tchr., supr. Syracuse (N.Y.) U. Nursery Sch., 1926-33; tchr. Syracuse U., 1933, 42, Nurses Tng. Sch. Syracuse Meml. Hosp., 1938-43; supr. Nursery Sch.-Parent Edn. City Syracuse, 1934-36, State N.Y., 1936-38; tchr. of tchrs. for Migrant Schs. at King Ferry, N.Y., 1946-50; supr. nursery and kindergarten div. Logan Sch., Auburn, N.Y., 1944-50; tchr. art Geneva, Waterloo, Auburn Adult Program, 1963-70; prof. art Auburn (N.Y.) Community Coll., 1964—. Exhibited in shows including Cayuga Mus., Auburn, Moravia, N.Y., Albany State Capitol, Lakeside Galleries, Skaneateles, N.Y., Rochester, N.Y., Insel Galleries, N.Y.C., Binghampton, N.Y., Mystic, Conn., P.R., Washington; represented permanent collection Syracuse U., pvt. collections. Active A.R.C., United Fund, P.T.A.; den mother Cub Scouts, Auburn, 1954-56; drive chmn. Civic Music Assn.; active ch. worker, Sunday Sch. supt. 20 years, mem. ch. and state bd., officer ch. dist. bd., mem. dist. evaluation com. 1971—. Mem. bd. Cayugo County council Girl Scouts U.S.A., 1952-55; trustee Cuyuga Mus. History Art, 1955—, chmn. art div., 1956—; 1st pres. Friends Seymour Library, 1968-71. Recipient numerous art awards. Mem. Am. Assn. U. Profs., Internat. Platform Assn., Auburn Coll. Club (pres. 1948-50), Syracuse U. Alumna Club (sec. 1946-49, v.p., scholarship chmn. 1957-60), Finger Lakes Art Retreat Group, Pi Lambda Theta. Home: 149 North St Auburn NY 13021

HAIL, BARBARA ANDREWS (MRS. EDWARD G. HAIL), mus. ofcl.; b. Phila., Nov. 2, 1930; d. James Wickersham and Elizabeth Alice (Woolridge) Kirk; student (Elisha Benjamin Andrews scholar), Brown U., 1948-50; A.B., Cornell U., 1952, A.M., 1953; postgrad. (Danforth Grad. fellow), Columbia, 1965-67; m. Peter B. Andrews, Dec. 23, 1950 (dec. 1964); children—Clinton J., Elizabeth D., Cynthia K.; m. 2d, Edward G. Hail, May 29, 1969; stepchildren—Ted, Andrew, Peter, Elinor. Tchr. history high sch., Ithaca, N.Y., 1953-54; edn. coordinator Haffenreffer Mus. Anthropology, Brown U., Bristol, R.I., 1968-72, asst. curator, 1972—. Mem. R.I. Women's Intergroup Com. 1971-72. Mem. R.I. New Democratic Coalition, 1971-72. Mem. Am. Assn. Museums, Phi Beta Kappa. Club: Lake Placid (N.Y.). Home: 220 Rumstick Point Rd Barrington RI 02806 Office: Haffenreffer Museum Mount Hope Grant Bristol RI 02809

HAINES, MILDRED ALICE MORRIS (MRS. CURTIS WILLIAM HAINES), educator; b. Oberlin, O., Jan. 5, 1899; d. George William and Hattie Maud (Watkins) Morris; A.B., Oberlin Coll., 1920; M.A., U. Chgo., 1921; postgrad. (scholar 1921-22, fellow 1923-24), U. Chgo., 1923-24, 29, Case-Western Res. U., 1933, 35; m. Curtis William Haines, July 9, 1931. Tchr., Wellington, O., 1921-23, Bryn Mawr Coll., 1924-26; dean girls, Shaker Heights, O., 1926-56; dir. guidance Oberlin High Sch., 1956-58; tchr. Stuart Hall, Staunton, Va., 1958-61, 63-64; substitute tchr. Lake Ridge Acad., North Ridgeville, O., 1972—. Trustee St. Lucie County Hist. Soc., Ft. Pierce, Fla., 1966-69; bd. dirs. Lorain County Hist. Soc., 1970-72. Mem. Ohio Women Deans, Ohio State Hist. Soc., Phi Beta Kappa, Delta Kappa Gamma. Home: 807 West Av Elyria OH 44035

HAINES, NANCY ANN STUTLER, librarian; b. Akron, O., Aug. 25, 1934; d. Ernest Lynn and Sophrona Rebecca (Pepper) Stutler; student U. Akron, 1952-54; B.A., Kent State U., 1956; m. Clifford Frank Haines, Aug. 20, 1960 (div.). Jr. asst. librarian E. Br. Library, Akron, 1956-59; hosp. librarian VA Hosp., Northampton, Mass., 1959-61; med. librarian VA Hosp., Brecksville, O., 1961-65, chief librarian, 1965—. Mem. Med. Library Assn., N.E. Ohio Med. Library Assn., Zeta Tau Alpha. Home: 7035 Carriage Hill Brecksville OH 44141 Office: 10000 Brecksville Rd Brecksville OH 44141

HAINES, THELMA MINNIE LOUISE, educator; b. Brant, N.Y., Feb. 24, 1914; d. Harry Lee and Bertha Alvina (Nordblum) Haines; B.S., State U. N.Y. Coll. at Buffalo, 1935, M.S., 1951, postgrad., 1953-59. Tchr. elementary schs., Canisteo, N.Y., 1935-36, Tonawanda, N.Y., 1937-55; primary tchr. State U. N.Y. Coll. at Buffalo, Coll. Learning Lab. (formerly Campus Sch.), 1955-70, primary group chmn., 1969-70, asso. prof. intermediate dept. math. and social studies, 1970—, chmn. dept., 1971-72, demonstration tchr., supr. coll. jr. and sr. participants, student tchrs., 1955—. Mem. women's aux. DeGraff Meml. Hosp. NSF fellow, 1959. Mem. N.E.A., United Univ. Professions, Bus. and Profl. Women of Tonawandas, Pi Lambda Theta. Presbyn. (trustee, elder). Home: 81 Harriet St Tonawanda NY 14150 Office: State U New York 1300 Elmwood Av Buffalo NY 14222

HAINJE, NANNIE MARGUERITE, obstetrician and gynecologist; b. Brewton, Ala., Apr. 15, 1919; d. John Abe and Willie Thomas (Etheridge) Hainje; B.A. with honors, Mt. Holyoke Coll., 1940; M.D., Duke, 1944; m. Foo Chu, Mar. 27, 1948; children—Janice, David, Carol. Resident pathology Boston Lying-in-Hosp., also Free Hosp. Women, Brookline, 1944-45; research fellow medicine Bellevue Hosp., N.Y.C., 1945-46; house officer obstetrics and gynecology Johns Hopkins Hosp., 1946-47; asst. resident gynecology Royal Victoria Hosp., Montreal, Can., 1947; resident gynecology and obstetrics Woman's Med. Coll. Hosp., Phila., 1948-49; asst. attending Strang Cancer Prevention Clinic, Meml. Hosp., N.Y.C., 1949-58; asso. attending Lincoln Hosp., Bronx, N.Y., 1949-59; individual practice obstetrics and gynecology, Tarrytown, N.Y., 1950—; mem. staff Phelps Meml. Hosp., North Tarrytown, now dep. chief obstetrics and gynecology. Pres., Hainje's Inc. Mem. med. adv. bd. Planned Parenthood, Westchester County. Trustee, treas. Scarborough Sch. Mem. A.M.A., Westchester County Med. Soc., Westchester Obstet. Soc., Am. Coll. Obstetricians and Gynecologists, Am. Soc. Abdominal Surgeons, Am. Soc. Psychoprophylaxis in Childbirth. Clubs: Hill and Dale Garden (Tarrytown); Soroptimist (Hudson Valley, N.Y.). Home: 116 Altamont Av Tarrytown NY 10591 Office: 67 Neperan Rd Tarrytown NY 10591

HAINSKI, MARTHA ELVIRA BARRIONUEVO (MRS. STEVEN HAINSKI), chemist; b. Buenos Aires, Argentina, Feb. 18, 1932; d. Ricardo Barrionvero and Balbina Bargados; Dr. Chemistry, U. Buenos Aires, 1957; m. Steven Hainski, Sept. 22, 1964; 1 dau., Alexandra Martha. Came to U.S., 1957, naturalized, 1962. Postdoctoral research asso. Wayne State U., Detroit, 1957-58, Phila. Gen. Hosp., 1958-63; fellow in clin. pathology NIH, Phila., 1963-66; dir. protein chemistry research Hyland Labs., Los Angeles, 1966-70; mgr. devel. Abbott Sci. Labs., Los Angeles, 1970—. NIH fellow, 1963. Fellow Am. Inst. Chemists; mem. Am. Chem. Soc., Nat. Orgn. Women (pres. Los Angeles chpt. 1967—). Republican. Roman Catholic. Office: 5555 Valley Blvd Los Angeles CA 90032

HALASI-KUN, ELISABETH CHRISTINA SZORAD (MRS. GEORGE J. HALASI-KUN), educator; b. Versec, Austria-Hungary, Oct. 18, 1919; d. Nicholaus and Mary Juliana (Honig) Szorad; came to U.S., 1958, naturalized, 1963; B.S., Columbia, 1966, M.A., 1968; M.Ed., U. Munich, 1967; Ph.D., N.Y. U., 1972; m. George J. Halasi-Kun, Mar. 10, 1945; children—Beatrice P. (Mrs. Ulrich A. Maniak), Georgie E. Asst. to librarian Barnard Coll., N.Y.C., 1961-66; instr. German, head German div. Marymount Manhattan Coll., N.Y.C., 1965-69; asso., Columbia, N.Y.C., 1971—. Recipient Founders award N.Y. U., 1973. Mem. Am. Assn. U. Profs., Modern Lang. Assn., Internat. Lenau Soc., Delta Phi Alpha. Author: Oral Epic Poetry of the South-Slavs, 1968; Historical, Cultural and Social Influences in the Epics of Nicholaus Lenau, 1973. Home: 31 Knowles Av Pennington NJ 08534 Office: 70 Morningside Dr New York City NY 10027

HALBERG, LYNNEA JANE, coll. dean; b. Springfield, Ill., Sept. 3, 1943; d. LeRoy Albin and Betty Jane (Ewing) Halberg; B.A., Eastern Ill. U., 1965; M.Ed., U. Ill., 1972. Coordinator counseling services, prof. ednl. psychology Blackburn Coll., Carlinville, Ill., 1969-72; dean students So. Seminary Jr. Coll., Buena Vista, Va., 1973—. Mem. Am., Ill. personnel and guidance assns., Am., Ill. coll. personnel assns., Am. Assn. U. Women, Pi Beta Phi. Home: 2664 Walnut Av Buena Vista VA 24416

HALBROOKS, ELIZABETH STAPLES (MRS. WILLIAM R. HALBROOKS), publishing co. exec.; b. Southboro, Mass., Jan. 13, 1918; d. Frederick Clifton and Elizabeth Yerkes (Flanders) Staples; B.A., Wellesley Coll., 1940; M.Ed., Tufts U., 1960; m. Arthur T. Dyer, Jr., Sept. 6, 1941 (dec. 1960); children—Deborah (Mrs. Paul H. Fenton), Elizabeth Sprague, David Stevens; m. 2d, William R. Halbrooks, Sept. 9, 1967. Sec. Boston Office, Parents' Mag., 1941, sociology dept. Wellesley Coll., 1941-42, 56-59; tchr. kindergarten pub. schs., Medway, Mass., 1961; bus. mgr. The Horn Book, Inc., Boston, 1963—, v.p., 1969—, dir., 1971—. Mem. Pubs. Library Promotion Group. Clubs: Wellesley College. Home: 22 Chatham Circle Wellesley Hills MA 02181 Office: 585 Boylston St Boston MA 02116

HALE, ARLENE, author; b. New London, Ia., June 16, 1924; d. Ira Tate and Florence (Hand) H.; student New London Coll. Commerce, Burlington, Ia., 1941. Free-lance writer, New London, 1950—. Mem. Mystery Writers of Am., Author's Guild, Inc. Author: The Reluctant Heart, 1958; Tender Harvest, 1959; Blossoms in the Wind, 1959; The Reluctant Stranger, 1960; School Nurse 1960; Be My Love, 1961; Dr. Myra Comes Home, 1962; Listen to Your Heart, 1962; Ghost Town's Secret, 1962; The Hungry Heart, 1962; Wait for Love, 1963; Leave it to Nurse Kathy, 1963; Dude Ranch Nurse, 1963; The Girl from Sherman Oaks, 1964; Symptoms of Love, 1964; Nurse Marcie's Island, 1964; Nurse Conner Comes Home, 1964; Nurse Shelley Decides, 1964; Nurse On The Run, 1965; Disaster Area Nurse, 1965; Private Duty for Nurse Scott, 1965; Nurse on Leave, 1965; Chicago Nurse, 1965; Camp Nurse, 1965; Emergency for Nurse Selena, 1966; Mountain Nurse, 1966; Lake Resort Nurse, 1966; Nothing But A Stranger, 1966; Community Nurse, 1967; Nurse on the Beach, 1967; Stay with Me, Love, 1967; Doctor's Daughter, 1967; The Lady Is a Nurse, 1967; University Nurse, 1967; Emergency Call, 1968; Private Nurse, 1968; Nurse in Residence, 1968; The Bend in the River, 1968; Dr. Barry's Nurse, 1968; Whistle Stop Nurse, 1968; Stranger on the Beach, 1969; A Nurse for Sand Castle, 1969; A Happy Ending, 1969; Crossroads for Nurse Cathy, 1969; Nurse Roger's Discovery, 1969; Private Hospital, 1970; Orphanage Nurse, 1970; Holiday to Fear, 1970; Share Your Heart, 1970; When Love Returns, 1970; The New Nurses, 1970; Special Duty, 1970; Nurse Jean's Strange Case, 1970; The Season of Love, 1971; Executive Nurse, 1971; Walk Softly, Doctor, 1971; The Runaway Heart, 1971; The Secret Longing, 1971; Dark Flames, 1971; The Nurse from Mulberry Square, 1971; The Shining Mountain, 1972; A Time for Us, 1972; The Reunion, 1972; Promise of Tomorrow, 1972; Goodbye to Yesterday, 1972; (pseudonym Gail Everett) Love is the Winner, 1960; Love of Laura, 1961; Search for Love, 1962; Teach Me to Love, 1962; Designs on Love, 1963; Journey for a Nurse, 1966; When Summer Ends, 1968; My Favorite Nurse, 1968; The Way to the Heart, 1970; (under pseudonym Louise Christopher) Robin West: Nurse's Aide, 1963; Robin West: Freshman Nurse, 1964; (pseudonym Lynn Williams) Once Upon a Nightmare, 1971; Lake of the Wind, 1971; Where Is Jane?, 1972; Shadows Over Seascape, 1972; Picture Her Missing, 1973; Rendezvous with Danger, 1973; Secret of Hedges Hall, 1973; Threads of Intrique, 1973; (under pseudonym Will Kirkland) Trouble on the Rim Rock, 1972. Methodist. Address: 416 E Main St New London IA 52645

HALE, FRANCES, librarian; b. Brockton, Mass., June 8, 1912; d. Chester Stanley and Frances (Thomson) Hale; B.S., Simmons Coll., 1934; M.A., Hofstra Coll., 1958. Head cataloger Brockton (Mass.) Pub. Library, 1935-41; chief catalog div. Schenectady Pub. Library, 1941-45; library dir. Floral Park (N.Y.) Pub. Library, 1945-59, Garden City (N.Y.) Pub. Library, 1959—; profl. lectr. Pratt Inst. Library Sch., Bklyn., 1952-55. Mem. pub. librarians exam. com. N.Y. State Bd. Regents, 1957-59. Mem. Am., N.Y., Nassau County (pres. 1950-52) library assns., Library Pub. Relations Council, Am. Assn. U. Women, N.E. Historic Geneal. Soc., D.A.R. (vice regent Lord Stirling chpt., 1959-62), Bus. and Profl. Women's Club (pres. Nassau County 1952-54), Soc. Mayflower Descs., Mass. Library Assn. Republican. Clubs: Soroptimist (pres. Central Nassau club 1956-58), Woman's. Home: 70 Tulip Av Floral Park NY 11001 Office: 60 7th St Garden City NY 11530

HALE, HELENE ELEANOR, advt. agy. exec., realtor; b. Mpls., Mar. 23, 1918; d. Gale P. and Ellen Reta (Harris) Hilyer; B.S., U. Minn., 1938, M.A., 1940; m. William Jasper Hale, Jr. (div. 1969); children—Indira (Mrs. Marcus O. Tucker), William. Bd. suprs. County Hawaii, 1955-63, chmn., chief exec. officer, 1963-65; pres. Hale Cons., Inc., Hilo, Hawaii, 1965—; pres. Hawaii Isle Realty, Ltd., Hilo, 1972—. Instr. San Diego State Coll., 1945-47, U. Hawaii, 1966-67. Bd. dirs. YWCA, 1971, pres., 1971; treas., bd. dirs. Pan Pacific Found.; pres. Big Island Local Devel. Corp. Mem. Hawaii Island Bd. Realtors (v.p. 1972, pres. 1973), Hawaii Hotel Assn., League Women Voters, Hawaii Island C. of C. (legislative chmn. 1972), Japanese C. of C. and Industry (dir., chmn. econ. devel. 1974). Home: 262 Anela St Hilo HI 96720 Office: 38 Kalakaua St Hilo HI 96720

HALEY, SISTER MARY ALICE, educator; b. Ogdensburg, N.Y., May 25, 1925; d. Stephen Philip and Katherine Mary (Garvey) Haley; A.B., Creighton U., 1954; M.A., St. Louis U., 1964, Ph.D. in Philosophy, 1971. Joined Servite Sisters, 1942; tchr. elementary sch. Holy Ghost Sch., Omaha, 1945-49; tchr. math., religion, Latin, Servite High Sch., Detroit, 1949-62; instr. philosophy St. Louis U., 1968-70; asst. prof. philosophy Creighton U., Omaha, 1970—. Chmn. com. for revision of Constns. of Servite Sisters, 1970—; mem. Internat. Commn. on Constns. of Servite Sisters; mem. Sisters' Council of Omaha, Omaha Archdiocese Bd. Arbitration, 1971-73. NSF grantee, summers 1958, 59, 60, 61. Mem. Am. Catholic Philos. Assn., Phi Sigma Tau. Democrat. Home: 2904 North 45th St Omaha NE 68104 Office: R 203 Wareham Hall Creighton University Omaha NE

HALEY, THEODOSIA DORIS SHIMER, Christian sci. practioner; b. Hartley, W.Va.; d. Elbridge Ellsworth and Celestine (Elliott) Shimer; student Marshall Coll., 1924-27; m. Charles Haley, July 15, 1927; 1 dau., Gloria Doris (Mrs. Arthur Shaw). Mem. Mother ch., First Ch. of Christ Scientist, Boston, 1934—, 7th Ch. of Christ Scientist, N.Y.C., 1955—, 2d reader Seventh Ch. of Christ Scientist, N.Y.C., 1957-60; C.S. practitioner, Huntington, W.Va., 1939-52, Rego Park, L.I., N.Y., 1953-54, N.Y.C., 1954—; circulation rep. Christian Sci. Pub. Soc., Boston, for Christian Sci. Jour., Christian Sci. Quar., Christian Sci. Sentinel, Christian Sci. Monitor, Charleston, S.C. and Huntington, W.Va., 1938-44. Trustee Seventh Ch. of Christ Scientist, N.Y.C., 1956, 61-64, 69-71. Address: 375 Riverside Dr Mew York City NY 10025

HALFMAN, HAZEL LINTON (MRS. WILLIAM A. HALFMAN), librarian; b. Ft. Atkinson, Wis.; d. Frank A. and Florence P. (Shafer) Linton; B.A., Carroll Coll., Waukesha, Wis., 1934; M.A., U. Wis., Madison, 1957; postgrad. U. Okla., summer 1967; m. William A. Halfman, July 4, 1936; children—William R., Catherine L. (Mrs. Donald Bayer). Pub. librarian, Jefferson, Wis., 1953-55; high sch. librarian, Menomonee Falls, Wis., 1955-66, coordinator sch. library services, 1966—. Mem. Wis., Menomonee Falls edn. assns., A.L.A., Waukesha County (past pres.), Met. Sch. library assns., Wis. Assn. Sch. Librarians (mem. audiovisual cataloging manual com.), Beta Phi Mu. Home: W169 N8730 Sheridan Dr Menomonee Falls WI 53051 Office: W132 N8779 Hwy 145 Menomonee Falls WI 53051

HALFON, ANN HALFON (MRS. RAYMOND HALFON), ednl. adminstr.; b. N.Y.C., Sept. 16, 1916; d. Abraham Saul and Rachel (Hougnou) Halfon; M.L.S., Columbia, 1940, postgrad., 1956; postgrad. Bklyn. Coll., 1955; m. Raymond Halfon, May 26, 1940; children—Jerald William, Robin (Mrs. Jules Licht). Tchr. library N.Y.C. Bd. Edn., 1954-62, supr., asst. adminstrv. dir., 1962-71, asst. dir., specialist in library adminstrn., budgeting, fed. funds, elementary library media center services, 1972—. Active Sephardic Home for

Aged, 1965—, Rhodes League of Bros. Aid Soc., 1950—. Mem. Am., N.Y. library assns., N.Y.C. Sch. Librarians Assn., Book League of N.Y. Home: 1534 E 7th St Brooklyn NY 11230 Office: 110 Livingston St Brooklyn NY 11201

HALFORD, HANNAH MORE KELLET (MRS. JOHN H. HALFORD), civic worker; b. Fernwood, Pa., June 23, 1888; d. John and Jane (Tetley) Kellett; student Drexel Inst. Sch. Tech., 1906-08, U. Pa., 1909-11, Sch. Hort. for Women, Ambler, Pa., 1923-33; m. John H. Halford, Nov. 25, 1914; children—John H., Jane Tetley (Mrs. Charles E. Parker, Jr.). Vice pres. Norristown (Pa.) Garden Club, 1921-23; pres. womens bd. Christian Assn., U. Pa., Phila., 1945-48; pres. Chinese cultural group Internat. House, Phila., 1947-50; pres. Conversational Club, Norristown, 1947; mem. Preservation of Hist. Landmarks, Phila.; mem. Coll. Club Bowdoin Women, Brunswick, Me.; mem. Emergency Aid, Phila. Bd. dirs. Valley Forge (Pa.) Hist. Soc. and Mus., Pa. Presbyn. (dir. Westminster Guild, 1940-61, of 1st Presbyn. Ch., Norristown, directing its mission work). Donor (with husband) early Americana and English and Am. paintings to Bowdoin Coll. Mus. Art, Valley Forge Mus., Caleb Pusey House. Home: Foulkeways E-9 Gwynedd PA 19436

HALINA, MME. (HALINA JOZEFA LUTOMSKI, MRS. FLOYD MARTIN LUTOMSKI), dance educator, choreographer; b. Lwow, Poland, Feb. 4, 1929; d. Adam and Katarzyna (Jezierska) Dziekan; student Warsaw Opera Ballet Sch., 1936-38, Wielke Theatre, Lwow, 1939-41; grad. Politechnik, Lwow, 1944; m. Floyd Martin Lutomski, Oct. 31, 1946; children—Norbert Michael, Ilona Maria, Kevin. Came to U.S., 1947, naturalized, 1950. Dancer, Warsaw Opera Ballet, 1938-39, World's Olympiade, Kiev, Russia, 1939, U.S.O., Germany, 1945-46; producer Dance Capades, 1948—; tchr. Nat. Dance Tchrs. Orgns., U.S., P.R., 1950; choreographer children's and classical ballets Kimbo Dance Records, 1954—; founder, artistic dir., choreographer Elmira-Corning Ballet, Inc., 1955—; coordinator, also dir. ednl. programs; lectr.; producer choreographer Four Seasons, 1950, Fairy Doll, 1951, Sleeping Beauty, 1953, 59, 65-67, Nutcracker, 1954, Hansel and Gretel, 1955, Cinderella, 1957, Les Ballet de Elements, 1958, Schlagobers. 1959, Gaite Parisienne, 1960-61, La Boutique Fantasque, 1961, adaptation of Les Sylphides, 1962, Swan Lake, 1952-64, Masquerade, 1962-63, Snow Maiden, 1964, Copelia, 1965, 70, Karnival Kontrasts, 1966, La Bayadere, 1966, Nutcracker, 1969, Cinderella, 1968, Aurora's Wedding, 1971; dir. choreographer ballet Nutcracker for Elmira-Corning Ballet, 1965-66, also Red-White and Blue, Comedia del Arte, Masque; directed Les Petits Riens, 1967; dir., choreographer Wooden Prince, 1971, Americana, 1972, La Fille Mal Gardee, 1972, Vignette's Classique-Comedia, 1973, Sylvia, 1974; lectr. Steuben, Chenung, No. Pa. counties; supr. ballet records Roper label; rep. ballet dept. for Dance Educators Am. to Nat. Council Dance Tchrs' Orgns.; dir. Sch. Dance Arts, Elmira, N.Y., Corning, N.Y.; lectr. Elmira-Corning Sch. Dists., 1969-72, Schulyer County Schs., 1968-71. Recipient Steuben Crystal and Gold award Corning community. Mem. Dance Educators Am. (chmn. ballet exam., com. 1966-67, exec. bd. 1967-69, exec. dir. 1969-71). Roman Catholic. Recs. 8 ballet albums Roper Label. Home: 933 Fassett Rd Elmira NY 14905 Office: 410-14 W Gray St Elmira NY 14905 also 171 Cedar St Corning NY 14830

HALL, ALICE JOYCE, writer; b. Spirit Lake, Ia., May 16, 1936; d. Glen R. and Ruth A. (Gable) Hall; B.A., Mills Coll., 1958; M.A., George Washington U., 1970. Editorial asst. Nat. Geog. mag., Washington, 1964-66, editorial staff, 1967—. Clubs: Washington Press, Mills Coll. Office: National Geographic Washington DC 20036

HALL, CYNTHIA HOLCOMB, judge; b. Los Angeles, Feb. 19, 1929; d. Harold Romeyn and Mildred Gould (Kick) Holcomb; A.B., Stanford, 1951, J.D., 1954; LL.M., N.Y. U., 1960; 1 dau., Desma Letitia Holcomb; m. 2d, John Harris Hall, June 6, 1970; 1 son, Harris Holcomb. Admitted to Ariz. bar, 1954, Cal. bar, 1956; law clk. to Judge Richard H. Chambers U.S. Ct. Appeals 9th circuit, 1954-55; trial atty. tax div. Dept. Justice, 1960-64; atty.-adviser Office Tax Legislative Counsel Treasury Dept., 1964-66; mem. firm Braverman & Holcomb, Beverly Hills, Cal., 1966-72; judge U.S. Tax Ct., 1972—. Served to lt. (j.g.) USNR, 1951-53. Home: 2820 E California Blvd Pasadena CA 91107 Office: US Tax Ct Box 70 Washington DC 20044

HALL, DORIS MADELINE JANITSCHEK (MRS. DOUGLAS E. HALL), public relations exec.; b. Jersey City, July 31, 1931; d. Rudolph M. and Viola (Geils) Janitschek; student Stevens Acad., 1946-49; B.S., Skidmore Coll., 1953; m. Raymond H. Farrant, July 18, 1959; m. 2d, Douglas E. Hall, May 10, 1969. Asst. to v.p., sales promotion dir. Bates Fabrics, Inc., 1955-57; fashion and publicity dir. Cavendish Trading Corp., 1957-59; publicity mgr. fashions and home furnishing Celanese Fibers Marketing Co., N.Y.C., 1959-65; pub. relations mgr. fashions Uniroyal, Inc., N.Y.C., 1966-72; account exec. Grey & Davis, Inc., N.Y.C., 1972-74; mgr. strategic planning communications and competitive analysis Gen. Electric Co., Fairfield, Conn., 1974—. Named Ky. col. Mem. Am. Home Econs. Assn., Home Economists in Bus., Fashion Group, Am. Inst. Interior Designers, Nat. Home Fashions League. Lutheran. Home: 30 Ten O'Clock Lane Weston CT 06880 Office: Gen Electric Co Fairfield CT 06430

HALL, DOROTHY KATHERINE SHEETS (MRS. JOHN JOSEPH HALL), therapist, motel owner; b. Chillicothe, O., Aug. 20, 1924; d. John Anton and Charlotte Celine (Kiedrowski) Sheets; B.S. (Alumni scholar), Ohio State U., 1949; m. John Joseph Hall, Apr. 1, 1949; children—John Terrance, Ronald Wendall. Research therapist Muscular Dystrophy Clinic, U. Hosps. of Cleve., 1957-63; therapist psychiatry dept. VA Hosp., Cleve., 1963-66; owner High Country Lodge, Alto, N.M., 1966—. Mem. Beta Sigma Phi. Methodist. Mem. Order Eastern Star. Home and office: High Country Lodge Box 137 Alto NM 88312

HALL, ELVAJEAN, librarian; b. Hamilton, Ill.; d. Henry Nelson and Nellie (Hyer) Hall; A.B., Oberlin Coll., 1930; certificate U. Wis. Library Sch., 1932; M.L.S., Columbia, 1941. Asst. librarian Milw.-Downer Coll., 1932-33; librarian high sch., Elgin, Ill., 1934-37, Milw. U. Sch., 1937-42, Stephens Coll., Columbia, Mo., 1944-46; supr. sch. libraries, Jackson, Mich., 1942-44, Newton, Mass., 1946—. Instr. Mass. Dept. Edn., 1948; cons. Sch. Library Jour., 1958-63, Grolier Soc., 1959; cons., sch. library expert Library Services br. U.S. Office Edn., Washington, spring 1960; cons. library program Chung Chi Coll., Hong Kong, 1962-63; lectr. Univ. Coll., Dublin, summers 1967-69. Mem. A.L.A., Nat. League Am. Pen Women (pres. Boston 1970-72), Am. Assn. Sch. Librarians (nat. recruitment chmn. 1956), N.E.A., Mass. (chmn. 1948-49), New Eng. sch. library assns., Assn. for Supervision and Curriculum Devel., Women's Nat. Book Assn. (pres. Boston chpt. 1957-59; nat. dir. 1957-62, nat. sec. 1960-62), Authors Guild Am., Am. Assn. U. Women, Kappa Delta, Delta Kappa Gamma. Republican. Author: Books To Build On, 1955; Land and People of Argentina, 1960-72; Pilgrim Stories, 1962; Argentina Pueblo y Costumbres, 1962; Land and People of Norway, 1963, 72; Pilgrim Neighbors, 1964; The Volga: Lifeline of Russia, 1965; Land and People of Czechoslovakia, 1966; Hong Kong, 1967; The Psalms, 1968; Picture Map Geography of Eastern Europe, 1968; The Proverbs, 1970; Battle for Sales, 1973; Careers in Marketing and Distribution, 1974. Contbr. articles to ednl. and library jours. Home: 233 Commonwealth Av Boston MA 02116 Office: 88 Chestnut St West Newton MA 02165

HALL, ESTHER JANE WOOD (MRS. JULIAN KENNIS HALL), educator; b. Gadsden, Ala., Sept. 18, 1911; d. Henry William and Emma Virginia (Crowe) Wood; B.S., Samford U., Birmingham, Ala., 1939; M.S., U. Tex., 1953, Ph.D., 1957; postdoctoral studies in jurisprudence U. Tenn., 1969, 71; m. Julian Kennis Hall, Jan. 13, 1949; 1 dau., Virginia Ann. Pharmacist, Fairview Pharmacy, Birmingham, 1929-39; prodn. control mgr. statistician Warren-Teed Products Co., Columbus, O., 1939-44; label cons., dir., asst. prodn. control mgr. S. E. Massengill Co., Bristol, Tenn., 1944-46; asst. prof. Howard Coll., Birmingham, 1946-47; asst. prof. Coll. Pharmacy, U. Tex. at Austin, 1947-61, asso. prof., 1961—, also dir. area pharmacy and health care adminstrn.; cons. Am. Pub. Health Assn., Washington, 1961; spl. research Walgreen Co., Chgo., 1960; dir. Tex. Prescription Survey, Gosselin, Dedham, Mass. Chmn. manpower com. The Pharm. Found., U. Tex. Coll. Pharmacy, 1956—; friends hist. pharmacy Med. Coll. Va., 1965-70. Mem. com. Pharmacy Edn. State Tex. Coordinating Bd. Schs. Faculty fellow Am. Found. for Pharm. Edn., 1953-57; recipient Lederle Lab. faculty award, 1965, 67; participant Pharmacy Industry Forum, Princeton, 1959, Pharmacy Adminstrv. Seminar, Walgreen Co., Chgo., 1953, 60, 67, Dept. Justice Bur. Narcotics and Dangerous Drugs Nat. Tng. Inst., 1972, U. Okla. Health Care Adminstrn. Tng. Inst., 1972, others. Fellow A.A.A.S.; faculty fellow Am. Coll. Apothecaries (chmn. com. on edn., mem. hosp. com.; sec. Tex.); mem. Am. Assn. Colls. of Pharmacy (chmn. sec. tchrs. pharmacy adminstrn., mem. com. curriculum, future enrollment), Am. (sec. hist. sect. state historian, visual edn. com. Tex., chmn. survey com.), Capital Area pharm. assns., Am. Inst. History of Pharmacy, (council), W. Tex. Hist. Soc. (Project Hope com. 1965), Am. Inst. Indsl. Engrs., Am. Soc. Hosp. Pharmacists, Am. Assn. Indsl. Engrs. (asso.), Royal Soc. Health Eng., Rho Chi, Kappa Epsilon (grand council editor), Sigma Iota Epsilon, Phi Mu (adviser). Episcopalian. Club: University (Austin). Author: (with A. H. Chute) The Pharmacist in Retail Distribution, 1953, 55, 60, 63; Teachers Guide, 1960; Study Guide for Pharmaceutical Jurisprudence, 1951, 56, 67; (with Henry M. Burlage) Pharmaceutical Abstracts, 1963-69; (with C. A. Walker) Manuals for Pharmacy Administration, 1969; various other manuals. Contbr. to Am. Profl. Pharmacist, Am. Jour. Pharmacy Edn., Prac. Edition, Am. Pharm. Assn. Jour., Co. Pharm. Jour., Tex. Jour. Pharmacy, Tex. Pharmacy, Am. Druggist, Drug Standards, Dissertation Abstracts, Jour. Am. Hosp. Assn., Pa. Med. Jour., Hosp. Pharmacy, NARD Jour., Walgreen World, Tex. State Hist. Jour., 1959—. Home: The Westgate 1122 Colorado St Austin TX 78701

HALL, EVELYN LOUISE LONG (MRS. RICHARD MALCOLM HALL), county ofcl.; b. Hillsboro, Ind., Nov. 8, 1921; d. David Paul and Lelah (Hershberger) Long; student pub. schs.; m. Richard Malcolm Hall, Sept. 11, 1942; 1 son, Robert Malcolm. Clerical worker Indiana Farmers Mut. Ins. Co., Indpls., 1939-42, Fountain County Assessor's Office, Covington, Ind., 1951-56; county assessor Fountain County, 1956—. Bd. dirs. Fountain County Tb Assn., 1955—, 1st v.p., 1969-72; bd. dirs. West Central Ind. Lung Assn., 1973—. Past pres. Attica Women's Republican Club, v.p., 1972; sec. Fountain County Women's Republican Club, 1969-74, 2d v.p., 1974—. Mem. Ind. County Assessors Assn. Home: Route 4 Veedersburg IN 47987 Office: Court House Covington IN 47918

HALL, GEORGETTE BROCKMAN (MRS. NORMAN BERNARD HALL, JR.), librarian; b. New Orleans; d. Thomas Harry and Gertrude Christine (Ott) Brockman; B.A., Tulane U., 1937; M.L.S., George Peabody Coll. for Tchrs., 1966; m. Norman Bernard Hall, Jr., Dec. 28, 1938; 1 dau., Lynne Gertrude (Mrs. Ralph Wood Pringle). Tchr. English, journalism, Spanish, librarian Bay St. Louis (Miss.) High Sch., 1946-62; librarian Chalmette (La.) High Sch., 1962—, St. Bernard Parish Community Coll., 1967—. Mem. St. Bernard Parish, La. tchrs. assns., Am. Assn. U. Women, Beta Phi Alpha, Delta Kappa Gamma. Clubs: Diamondhead (Miss.) Country, Diamondhead Yacht. Author: House on Rampart Street, 1954; The Sicilian, 1975. Home: Aila St Diamondhead Bay St Louis MS 39520 Office: 1101 E Judge Perez Dr Chalmette LA 70043

HALL, GERALDINE ADELINE BOHANNON (MRS. LESLIE STANDISH HALL), lawyer; b. San Francisco, Sept. 7, 1896; d. David Eugene and Elizabeth Jane (Bosch) Bohannon; B.A., U. Cal. at Berkeley, 1921, J.D., 1923; m. Leslie Standish Hall, Oct. 30, 1923 (dec. 1947); children—Ruth (Mrs. John Paul Juhl), John Standish, Emily (Mrs. Emil J. Simoncini). Admitted to Cal. bar, 1923; asso. Breed & Burpee, Oakland, Cal., 1923-24, Charles W. Fisher, Oakland, 1923-25; pvt. practice law, Oakland, Cal., 1925—. Legislative chmn., leader, organizer various P.T.A.s, ch. groups, clubs; mem. World Affairs Council, San Francisco, 1956-61; chmn. health and safety, parliamentarian Rockridge Improvement Club, 1925-35; v.p., parliamentarian Women in Legal Profession San Francisco Bay Area, 1923—; Alameda County chpt. UN. Mem. League Women Voters, Alpha Delta Pi Mothers Club, Kappa Beta Pi. Republican. Episcopalian. Clubs: Rockridge Woman's, Federated Women's (Oakland). Address: 6016 Broadway Oakland CA 94618

HALL, GUINIVERE BRYAN, utility co. exec.; b. Sand Coulee, Mont.; d. Charles Stanley and Blanche Verniere (Meehan) Hall; B.S., N. Y. U., 1973. Asst. buyer Meier & Frank Co., Portland, Ore., 1939-43; storekeeper U.S. Coast Guard, N.Y.C., 1943-45; reporter N.Y. Herald Tribune, N.Y.C., 1946-59; dep. commr. in charge career programs for women N.Y. State Commerce, Albany, 1959-71; urban affairs supr. N.Y. Telephone, N.Y.C., 1971—. Bd. advisors Nat. Coalition on Research in Women's Edn., 1972—; bd. dirs. Elder Craftsmen, Inc., 1960—; mem. com. aging Community Service Soc., 1973—; bd. mgrs. YWCA N.Y., 1973—. Named Woman of Year, Westchester Fedn. Women's Clubs, 1971. Mem. Bus. and Profl. Womens Club, N.Y. Personnel Mgmt. Assn., Women Execs. Pub. Relations (v.p. 1973—), Newspaper Women N.Y. Club: Zonta (N.Y.C.). Home: 55 Park Av New York City NY 10016 Office: 1411 Broadway New York City NY 10018

HALL, HELEN, broadcasting co. exec.; b. Kansas City, Mo.; d. Earnest F. and Helen C. (Drees) Hall; student Wellesley Coll., 1938; m. Elmer L. Knoedler, Dec. 21, 1941 (div. Nov. 1953). Star, Barbara Welles Show, WOR-TV, N.Y.C., 1948-54; roving reporter NBC Monitor, N.Y.C., 1955-63; Home Show, N.Y.C., 1956-58; broadcaster-commentator Today Show, N.Y.C., 1956-58; broadcaster, producer One Woman N.Y., WCBS Radio, N.Y.C., 1963-70; star Helen Hall Show, N.Y.C., 1970—. Mem. Am. Women in Radio and TV (N.Y.C. chpt. pres. 1957, dir. 1969-70). Club: Wellesley (N.Y.C.). Home: 333 E 79th St New York City NY 10021 Office: 240 West 60th St New York City NY 10023

HALL, JO EVANS (MRS. DAVID HALL), wife Gov. Okla.; b. Ark., Feb. 3, 1934; d. Ruth (Ashcraft) Evans; student Ark. State Tchrs. Coll., 1951-53; grad. Am. Airlines Stewardess Sch., 1954; m. David Hall, 1956; children—Nancy, Douglas, Julie. Stewardess Am. Airlines, N.Y.C., 1955; sec. Dresser Engring., 1956-57. Precinct co-chmn. Democrat Party. Presbyn. Home: 820 NE 23d St Oklahoma City OK 73105

HALL, JUDITH ESTES, psychologist; b. Oklahoma City, Sept. 10, 1940; d. Lester Clayton and Ora Katie (Young) Estes; student Lindenwood Coll., 1958-59, David Lipscomb Coll., 1959; B.A. cum laude, Auburn U., 1961; M.A., U. N.C., 1965; Ph.D., U. Ala. at Tuscaloosa, 1969; m. Robert Clyde Hall, May 31, 1964; 1 son, Chadlee Derek. Clin. psychologist Spartanburg (S.C.) Mental Health Center, 1964-65; asst. prof. psychology Limestone Coll., Gaffney, S.C., 1965-67; co-dir. hosp. improvement project Partlow State Sch. and Hosp., Tuscaloosa, 1969-70; asst. prof. exptl. psychology dept. psychiatry U. Ala. Sch. Medicine, Birmingham, also staff psychologist Center for Developmental and Learning Disorders, 1970—. Cons. scientist U. Ala. Hosps. and Clinics, Birmingham; tchr. mental retardation and behavior modification Jefferson State Jr. Coll.; state and fed. research and devel. sex edn. for mentally retarded. Mem. Ala. Bd. Examiners in Psychology, 1972—, chmn., 1974—. Mem. Am. Psychol. Assn., Am. Assn. Mental Deficiency, Am. Acad. Mental Retardation, Soc. Research in Child Devel., Southeastern, Ala. psychol. assns., Southeastern Assn. Advancement Behavior Therapy. Contbr. articles to profl. jours. and chpts. to books. Home: 128 Ski Lodge Dr Birmingham AL 35209 Office: 1720 7th Av S Birmingham AL 35294

HALL, LEE, artist, educator; b. Lexington, N.C., Dec. 15, 1934; d. Robert and Florence (Fitzgerald) Hall; B.F.A., U. N.C., 1955; A.M., N.Y.U., 1959, Ph.D., 1965; postgrad. (Am. Philos. Soc. research grantee), Warburg Inst. U. London, 1965. Asst. prof. art N.Y. State U., Potsdam, 1958-60; asso. prof. art, chmn. dept. Keuka Coll., Keuka Park, N.Y., 1960-62; asso. prof. art, Winthrop Coll., Rock Hill, S.C., 1962-65; chmn. art dept. Drew U., Madison, N.J., 1965-74; dean visual arts State U. N.Y., Purchase, 1974—. Artist, one-man shows Winston-Salem (N.C.) Gallery Fine Arts, 1958-65, U. Ore., Eugene, 1961, Keuka Coll., 1962, Furman U., Greenville, S.C., 1966, Jersey City State Coll., 1966, also Ruth White Gallery, N.Y.C., 1969; exhibited in group shows at Arts Gallery, N.Y.C., 1957, Forum, N.Y.C., 1957, Stendig N.Y.C., 1958, 59, Mercury Gallery, London, 1965-66; represented in permanent collections Finch Coll. Mus., Hudson River Mus. APS grantee, 1965, 68. Recipient prizes and awards Forsyth County Art Exhbn., 1955, Winston-Salem Gallery Fine Arts, 1958-61, 64, Witherspoon Internat. Paper in Art Exhbn., 1965. Dir. Research Project on Pres. Kennedy's Influence on Art, Drew U. and Kennedy Library; panelist Nat. Endowment for Humanities, 1972—. Mem. Am. Assn. U. Profs., Am. Assn. U. Women, Coll. Art Assn., Soc. for Aesthetics, Pi Lambda Theta, Alpha Psi Omega. Staff writer N.J. Music and Arts Mag.; contbr. to Collier's Ency., other publs. Office: Visual Arts State U NY Purchase NY 10577

HALL, LILLIAN LEVERN, hotel exec.; b. Cleveland, Tenn., June 23, 1936; d. Bruce William and Mable Hooper (Morgan) Hooper; student U. Chattanooga, 1958-60; m. William Lynn Hall, June 6, 1955; children—Keyoda Flichia, Kimitia Subrena. Supr. deaf mutes with on the job tng., 1955-60; with physiology dept. State of Tenn., 1962-65; mgr. Howard Johnson Motor Lodges, Chattanooga, 1966—. Substitute tchr. Bradley County Sch. System, 1955. Mem. Am., Tenn., Chattanooga hotel and motel assns. Republican. Office: 6616 Ringgold Rd Chattanooga TN 37412

HALL, LOIS BAXTER (MRS. RICHARD WESLEY HALL), ret. librarian; b. nr. Sudlersville, Md., Aug. 3, 1912; d. Rollison and Florence (Hall) Baxter; student Washington Coll., Md., 1929-31; A.B., U. Ala., 1933; postgrad. U. Md., 1934, 36, 57, 58, 60; M.L.S., Western Md. U., 1959; m. Richard Wesley Hall, June 18, 1938; children—Lois Elaine (Mrs. Richard Allen Staufenberger), Richard Wesley. Secondary sch. English tchr. Millington (Md.) High Sch., 1934-42; tchr.-librarian Preston (Md.) High Sch., 1956-59, Denton (Md.) Jr. High Sch., 1959-62; librarian-media specialist N. Caroline High Sch., Denton, 1963-73; ret., 1973. Sec., nominating chmn. Ednl. Media Md., 1967-69; co-chmn. book awards Wye Inst., 1965-68; mem. curriculum com., library chmn. Talbot and Caroline counties, 1966. Mem. Caroline County Tchrs. Assn. (sec. 1962-64), Caroline County Credit Assn. (publicity and supervisory coms. 1968—), Kappa Delta Pi, Psi Chi. Methodist. Mem. Order Eastern Star. Club: Woman's (pres. Preston, Md. 1955-57). Home: Route 3 Box 92 Princess Anne MD 21858

HALL, MARJORY (MRS. TAYLOR B. YEAKLEY, PSEUDONYMS CAROL MORSE, LUCILE BLAIR), author; b. Pittsfield, Mass., May 16, 1908; d. Walter Atwood and Lucile (Reynolds) Hall; A.B., Wellesley Coll., 1930; postgrad. Columbia, Harvard; m. Taylor Blair Yeakley, Oct. 30, 1937. Advt., editorial and promotion depts. Curtis Pub. Co., 1931-42; account exec., v.p. H. B. Humphrey Alley & Richards, Inc., 1942-56; free-lance writer, 1956—; travel and resort editor Yankee Mag., 1946-72. Mem. Authors Guild, Tau Zeta Epsilon. Club: North Shore Wellesley. Author (fiction for girls): Success in Reserve, 1941; Bread and Butter, 1942; After a Fashion, 1944; Model Child, 1945; Copy Kate, 1947; Your Young Life, 1949; Linda Clayton, 1951; Saralee's Silver Spoon, 1952; A Year from Now, 1952; Greetings from Glenna, 1953; Star Island, 1953; Orchids for Anita, 1954; Paper Moon, 1954; A Picnic for Judy, 1955; Star Island Again, 1955; Morning Glory, 1956; Mirror, Mirror, 1956; Cathy and Her Castle, 1957; Straw Hat Summer, 1957; The Glass House, 1958; Carnival Cruise, 1958; Three Stars for Star Island, 1958; White Collar Girl, 1959; Romance at Courtesy Bend, 1959; The Magic Word, 1959; Roundabout Robin, 1959; A Hatbox for Mimi, 1960; Tomorrow Is Another Day, 1960; Bright Red Ribbon, 1961; Whirl of Fashion, 1961; A Green Light for Sandy, 1961; Rita Rings a Bell, 1962; To Paris and Love, 1962; Fanfare for Two, 1963; Judy North: Drum Majorette, 1963; See the Red Sky, 1963; One Perfect Rose, 1964; A Hatful of Gold, 1964; Double Trouble, 1964; A Valentine for Vinnie, 1965; Drumbeat on the Shore, 1965; Clotheshorse, 1966; Treasure Tree, 1966; Three Cheers for Polly, 1967; Look at Me!, 1967; Another Kind of Courage, 1967; Mystery at Lions Gate, 1967; The Gold Lined Box, 1968; The Whistle Stop Mystery, 1969; The Seventh Star, 1969; Quite Contrary, 1970; Beneath Another Sun, 1970; The Carved Wooden Ring, 1972; Rosamunda, 1974; The Other Girl, 1974. Address: 572 Commonwealth Lane Sarasota FL 33581

HALL, MARY NETTLETON, physician; b. New Haven, Jan. 12, 1920; d. Joseph and Mary Ethel (Nettleton) Hall; B.A., Conn. Coll., 1941; M.S., Yale, 1943; M.D., Albany Med. Coll., 1948. Intern in internal medicine Albany Hosp., 1948-49; resident in psychiatry Middletown Hosp., 1949-50; resident in pediatrics Yale-New Haven Hosp., 1950-51; practice medicine, gen. practice, Clinton, Conn., 1951-62; dir. student health service Conn. Coll., New London, 1962—. Bd. dirs. Planned Parenthood League Conn. Mem. Am., New Eng. (pres. 1972-73) coll. health assns., A.M.A., Conn., New London County med. socs., Phi Beta Kappa. Home: 88 Smith St Niantic CT 06357 Office: Conn Coll New London CT 06320

HALL, NAN, advt. co. exec.; b. Cleve., Sept. 28, 1925; d. Edward Francis and Jane (Quinn) Haflinger; student, Ashland Coll., 1943-44. With Lang, Fisher & Stashower Advt., Inc., Cleve., 1950—, broadcast coordinator, radio-TV dept., 1952—. Mem. Cleve. Center on Alcoholism and Drug Abuse, 1972-73. Mem. Am. Women in Radio and TV, Foremost Women in Communications. Home: 27105

Normandy Rd Bay Village OH 44140 Office: 1010 Euclid Bldg Cleveland OH 44115

HALL, NAN GILLASPY (MRS. HAROLD CALEB HALL), coll. adminstr.; b. St. Louis, Dec. 29, 1927; d. Joseph Leslie and Hattie Mai (Adams) Gillaspy; B.S., La. State U., 1947; M.A.S., U. Ala., 1974; m. Harold Caleb Hall, Aug. 15, 1947; children—Wendy, Robin, April. Exec. sec. Kaiser Aluminum & Chem. Corp., Baton Rouge, 1953-58, owner Your Sec., Huntsville, Ala., 1958-64; registrar U. Ala., Huntsville, 1964-72, registrar, dir. admissions and records, 1972—. Mem. Am., Ala. assns., coll. registrars and admissions officers, Phi Mu. Club: Soroptimist (Huntsville, Ala.). Home: 4115 Coffee Circle Huntsville AL 35805

HALL, NANCY CATHERINE, microbiologist; b. Winnipeg, Man., Can.; d. Joseph Richard and Myrtle (MacPherson) Hall; R.N., Winnipeg Gen. Hosp., 1938; B.Sc., McGill U., 1948, M.Sc., 1950; Ph.D., Leland Stanford U., 1962. Jr. sci. lab. asst. clin. bacteriology McGill U., 1948-50; supr. new antibiotic research Ayerst, McKenna, & Harrison, Ltd., Montreal, Que., Can., 1950-53; research asst. U. Cal. Med. Center, San Francisco, 1954-55, Palo Alto Med. Research Found., 1955-57, Leland Stanford U., 1957-59; mgr. microbiology dept. Barnes-Hind Pharms., Inc., Sunnyvale, Cal., 1959—; also research asso. Sch. Dentistry, U. Cal. at San Francisco Med. Center. Decorated Asso. Royal Red Cross, Bronze Oak Leaf. Served as lt. (Nursing Sister) M.C., Royal Canadian Army, 1939-45. Fellow Royal Soc. Health; mem. Am. Soc. Microbiology, Soc. Gen. Microbiology, Canadian Soc. Microbiologists, Soc. Indsl. Microbiology, Am. Inst. Biol. Scis., Parenteral Drug Assn., N.Y. Acad. Scis., A.A.A.S., Man. Assn. Registered Nurses, Med. Mycol. Soc. of Ams., Sigma Xi. Contbr. articles to profl. publs. Home: 4242 Pomona St Palo Alto CA 94306 Office: Barnes-Hind Pharms Inc 895 Kifer Rd Sunnyvale CA 94086

HALL, NANCY J. (MRS. C. G. HALL), state ofcl.; b. Prescott, Ark.; d. George Sim and Minnie (Bryan) Johnson; student pub. schs.; m. C. G. Hall, Oct. 5, 1929; 1 dau., Nancy Anne (Mrs. R. Robert Bailey). Head stenographer Ark. Hwy. Commn., 1925-30; asst. Sec. of State, State of Ark., 1937-61, sec. of State, 1961-63, state treas., 1963—. Mem. Women's C. of C., Bus. and Profl. Women's Club, Daus. 1812, U.D.C. Democrat. Presbyn. Club: Zonta. Home: 4206 Woodlawn Little Rock AR 72205 Office: State Capital Bldg Little Rock AR 72201

HALL, NATALIE GRACE, editor; b. Bklyn., July 25, 1941; d. Nathan Isaac and Margaret Ingeborg (Sabelstrom) Hall; student U. Pacific, 1959-61; B.A., Am. U., 1963; postgrad. U. Cal. at Los Angeles, 1963-64. Asst. editor Bldg. News, Inc., Los Angeles, 1964-65; woman's editor Daily Sun-Post, San Clemente, Cal., 1966-67; reporter-photographer Press-Herald, Torrance, Cal., 1967-70; woman's editor Daily Rev., Burbank, Cal., 1970—. Recipient Copley Ring of Truth awards, 1970, 71, 72; certificate of excellence Valley Press Club, 1971, award, 1972. Mem. Theta Sigma Phi. Clubs: Sierra (Los Angeles); Valley Press (dir. 1974—). Home: 4232 Mary Ellen 3 Studio City CA 91604 Office: 228 E Orange Grove St Burbank CA 91502

HALL, PENELOPE COKER, TV show hostess; b. Charlotte, N.C., Mar. 19, 1933; d. James Lide and Elizabeth (Boatwright) Coker; student Sarah Lawrence Coll., 1950-53; m. William P. Wilson, July 18, 1963 (div. 1972); 1 dau., Eliza; m. Mortimer W. Hall, Dec. 8, 1972. Writer, asso. producer NBC-TV, 1960-63; reporter Ten O'Clock News, WNEW-TV, N.Y.C., 1969-70, hostess The New Yorkers program, 1967-68; hostess Wrap Up, N.Y.C., 1960, 10 Around Town, Phila., 1964. Sr. editor Celebrity Register, Cleveland Amory, 1959—. Mem. Author's Guild, Actors Equity Assn., Screen Actors Guild, A.F.T.R.A. Clubs: Piping Rock (Locust Valley, N.Y.); Goldens Bridge Hunt (North Salem, N.Y.). Author: Fancy and the Cement Patch, 1964; The Wish Bottle, 1965. Home: 355 E 72d St New York City NY 10021

HALL, REBECCA EDNA LAWRENCE (MRS. JOHN H. HALL, JR.), extension agt.; b. Durham, N.C., Jan. 20, 1922; d. Charlie Mangumn and Mary (Pratt) Lawrence; B.S., Bennett Coll., 1942; postgrad. N.C. Central U., 1946, N.C. State U., 1957, 60, 63, 67, Southeastern Community Coll., 1968; m. John H. Hall, Jr., Sept. 24, 1949; 1 son, Charles B. Home econs. extension agt., Wilmington, N.C., 1944—; home econs. tchr., Forest City, N.C., 1943-44. Program dir. Turnkey III Home Ownership Program, 1971—. Sec., YWCA, 1948; merit badge leader Cape Fear council Girl Scouts U.S.A., 1946. Bd. dirs. Mental Health, Sencland Crafts, New Hanover County Drug Abuse. Named Woman of the Year, Wilmington Jour., 1954, Omega Psi Phi, 1969. Mem. Am. Home Econs. Assn., Links, Jack and Jill Am., Nat., N.C. assns. extension home economists, Alpha Kappa Alpha, Epsilon Psi Phi. Episcopalian. Home: 389 S Kerr Av Wilmington NC 28401 Office: 222 Division Dr Wilmington NC 28401

HALL, SOPHIA HARRIET, lawyer, county ofcl.; b. Chgo., July 10, 1943; d. John B. and Beverly N. (Doyle) Hall; B.S., U. Wis., 1964; J.D., Northwestern U., 1967. Admitted to Ill. bar, 1967; asso. lawyer McCoy, Ming & Black, Chgo., 1967—. Adminstrv. asst. to Cook County Clk., Chgo., 1973; dep. clk. Cook County Bd. Commrs., Chgo., 1973—. Bd. dirs. Chgo. Legal Assistance Found., 1972. Mem. Nat., Ill., Cook County (Civil Rights award 1973, 3d v.p. 1971-72, 1st v.p. 1973), Chgo. bar assns., Women's Bar Assn. Ill., N.A.A.C.P. (chmn. legal redress com. Ill. conf. 1973—). Home: 1301 E Madison Park Chicago IL 60615 Office: County Bldg Chicago IL 60602

HALL, SUE MARION, educator; b. Omaha; d. Frederick M. and Rosamond (Peterson) Hall; B.S., U. Neb., 1930; M.S., U. So. Cal., 1937; Ph.D., Ohio State U., 1948. Tchr. phys. edn. Minne Lusa Sch., Omaha, 1930-32, North Jr. and Central High Sch., Sioux City, Ia., 1932-37; instr. phys. edn. U. Minn., Mpls., 1937-38; tchr. phys. edn. for girls, Falls City, Neb., 1939-40; prof., dept. health, phys. edn. and recreation, U. Louisville, 1940—. Del. White House Conf. on Children, 1950; chmn. Louisville-Jefferson County Sch. Health Council, 1951-53; del. internat. Congress Phys. Edn. and Sports for Girls and Women, 1949, 61. Named hon. Ky. col., 1963. Mem. A.A.H.P.E.R. (So. dist. pres. 1961-62, So. dist. honor award 1959, mgr. So. dist. conv. 1957-58, v.p. div. girls and womens sports So. dist. 1957-58, chpt. or nat. membership dir. for Ky. 1958-60, nat. publicity dir. for Ky. 1957-59), Ky. Assn. Health, Phys. Edn. and Recreation (pres. 1950, honor award 1955, Mustaine award 1962, Sue Hall Day award 1955, 50th Anniversary certificate of achievement 1960, chmn. past pres. com. 1971—), Am. Assn. U. Women (br. pres. 1953-55), Nat., So. assns. phys. edn. for coll. women, Alpha Psi Delta (hon.), Delta Kappa Gamma, Gamma Phi Beta, Mortar Bd., Falls City Womens Golf Assn. Clubs: Louisville Arts, Plantation Swim, Beckham Bird. Home: 1518 Herr Lane Louisville KY 40222

HALL, TEODORA DE LEON (MRS. JAMES N. HALL), pediatrician; b. Baliuag, Bulacan, Philippines, May 21, 1935; d. Delfin Trinidad and Soledad (Geronimo) De Leon; A.A., U. Santo Tomas, 1952, M.D., 1957; m. James N. Hall, Mar. 27, 1967. Came to U.S., 1958, naturalized, 1971. Intern St. Thomas U. Hosp., Manila, P.I., 1956-57; rotating intern Truesdale Hosp., Fall River, Mass., 1958-59; resident in obstetrics and gynecology Quincy (Mass.) City Hosp., 1959-60; resident in gen. practice Wyandotte (Mich.) Gen. Hosp., 1960-62; resident in pediatrics Children's Meml. Hosp., Omaha, 1962-64; instr. pediatrics Sch. Medicine, Creighton U., Omaha, 1967-70, asst. prof., 1970-73, clinic dir. pediatrics, 1972-73; mem. staff St. Joseph Meml. Hosp., Douglas County Hosp. Diplomate Am. Acad. Pediatrics. Fellow Am. Acad. Pediatrics; mem. Douglas County Med. Soc., Neb. Pediatric Soc. Home: 4716 S 79th Av Ralston NE 68127

HALL, VIOLA MABEL, educator; b. Sheridan, N.Y.; d. Richard and Mabelle (Wood) Hall; student Syracuse City Normal Sch., 1937; B.S., Syracuse U., 1942, M.S., 1948, certificate advanced standing, 1958; postgrad. Oslo U., summer 1966. Tchr., Salt City Sch., Liverpool, N.Y., 1938-44, Cleveland Sch., Syracuse, N.Y., 1944-47, Sumner Sch., Syracuse, 1947-49; prin. Cleveland Sch., 1949-51, Frazer Sch., 1951-56, Seymour Sch., 1956-65, Frank C. McCarthy Sch., 1965 (all Syracuse). Condr. travelogues for civic groups, 1950—; treas. N.Y. Fedn. Exceptional Children, 1959-62; pres. Evang. Family Service, 1960, 61, Salt City P.T.A., 1939-41, Frank C. McCarthy P.T.A., 1967; organizer Mothers' Club, Cleveland Sch., 1950, P.T.A., Frazer Sch., 1955, Mothers' Club, Seymour Sch., 1956. Bd. dirs. Huntington Family Center, Central Dist P.T.A., also chmn. exceptional children com.; bd. dirs. local Planned Parenthood. Recipient citation for Outstanding Work, Nat. Council Negro Women, Lambda Kappa Mu, 1964, Citation for Outstanding Work to Mentally Retarded Friends of Retarded, 1970. Mem. N.E.A., Nat., N.Y. State, Syracuse (past pres.) councils exceptional children, Syracuse Assn. Adminstrs. and Suprs., N.Y. State Tchrs. Assn., Nat., N.Y. State elementary prins. assns., N.Y. State Assn. Tchrs. for Mentally Retarded (charter mem. state, county chpt.), Nat., N.Y. State Onondaga (dir.) assns. retarded children, N.Y. State Congress Parents and Tchrs. (life mem.), Syracuse Rehab. Association, Women's Christian Bus. and Profl. Group (pres. 1963-67), Am. Bus. Women's Assn. (Woman of Year, pres. Syracuse chpt. 1967), Syracuse U. Alumnae Club (life), Nat. Missions U.P. Ch. U.S. (hon.), Am. Assn. U. Women, Pi Lambda Theta (life), Delta Kappa Gamma. Presbyn. (Sunday sch. work 1933—, supt. and tchr. jr. dept., chmn. Christian edn. com.). Author: Marching Forward Thru the Years, 1942, rev., 1961. Home: 4230 Polaris Course Liverpool NY 13088 Office: 116 W Glen Av Syracuse NY 13205

HALLAM, BEVERLY LINNEY, artist; b. Lynn, Mass., Nov. 22, 1923; d. Edwin Francis Hallam and Alice (Linney) Hallam Murphy; B.S. Edn., Mass. Coll. Art, 1945; postgrad. Cranbrook Acad. Art, Mich., 1948; M.F.A., Syracuse U., 1953. One-man shows Joe and Emily Lowe Art Center, Syracuse U., 1953, DeCordova Mus., Lincoln, Mass., 1954, Shore Galleries, Boston, 1959, 62, 68, 73, 74, Nasson Coll., Springvale, Me., 1967, Witte Meml. Mus., San Antonio, 1968, U. Me., 1969, Lamont Gallery, Exeter, N.H., 1969, Addison Gallery Am. Art Retrospective, Andover, Mass., 1971, Fitchburg Art Mus., 1972, Fairweather Hardin Gallery, Chgo., 1972, Hobe Sound (Fla.) Galleries, 1973; two-man show Inst. Contemporary Art, Boston, 1956; exhibited in group shows Barn Gallery, 1954—, Busch-Reisinger Mus., Harvard, 1956, 59, 60, Portland (Me.) Mus., 1959, Mus. Fine Arts, Boston, 1960—, Inst. Contemporary Art, 1960, 63, 68, Pace Gallery, Boston, 1962, Stanhope Gallery, Boston, 1962, DeCordova Mus., 1963, 64, 68, 69, 70, 71, Fitchburg (Mass.) Art Mus., 1963, Ward-Nasse Gallery, Boston, 1964, Ogunquit (Me.), Mus. Art, 1964, R.I. Arts Festival, 1966, Smithsonian Instn., Washington, 1966, Farnsworth Mus., Rockland, Me., 1967, Am. Watercolor Soc. traveling exhbn., 1967, City Hall, Boston, 1970, Watercolor U.S.A., Springfield, Mo., 1968. Represented in permanent collections including Brandeis U., Worcester (Mass.) Art Mus., U. Mass., Corcoran Gallery Am. Art, Washington, Witte Meml. Mus., San Antonio, Tex., Kresge Art Center Gallery, Decordova Mus., Lincoln, Mass., Addison Gallery Am. Art, Andover, Mass., Lamont Gallery, Exeter, N.H., Fitchburg Art Mus., Mus. Art Ogunquit, Me., Portland Mus. Me., U. Me., Currier Gallery Art, Manchester, N.H., also pvt. collections U.S. and Can. Chmn. art dept. Lasell Jr. Coll., Auburndale, Mass., 1945-49; asso. prof. Mass. Coll. Art, 1949-62; lectr., 1962—. Recipient Pearl Safir award Silvermine Guild Artists, New Canaan, Conn., 1955; painting prize Boston Arts Festival, 1957; Blanche E. Colman Found. award 1960; Hatfield awards Boston Soc. Watercolor Painters, 1960, 64, 1st prize, Edwin T. Webster award, 1962; A.H. Benoit award in graphics Art-Ogunquit, Barn Gallery, Ogunquit, Me., 1967. Mem. Ogunquit Art Assn. (pres. 1964), Am. Fedn. Arts. Author: Beverly Hallam: Paintings, Drawings and Monotypes, 1956-71, 1971. Pioneer in use of polyvinyl acetate as a painting medium. Home: Surf Point York ME 03909

HALLENBECK, PHYLLIS NEWTON, psychologist; b. N.Y.C., Nov. 15, 1921; d. Philip and Thora (Few) Newton; B.S., Kent State U., 1944; M.A., Western Res. U., 1955, Ph.D., 1964; m. Charles Hallenbeck, Jr., Aug. 18, 1955 (div. June 1963); children—Arthur David, Ann. Research asst. Highland View Hosp., Cleve., 1960-62; research asso. Vocational Guidance and Rehab. Service, Cleve., 1964-66; clin. psychologist Lake County Mental Health Clinic, Mentor, O., 1966-69; instr. psychology Lakeland Community Coll., Painesville, O., 1967-69; dir. psychology Sagamore Hills Children's Psychiat. Hosp., Northfield, O., 1969—. Founder, dir. Flowerledge Sch. for Retarded Children, Geneva, O., 1946—; dir. Hallenbeck Psycho-Ed. Center, Willoughby, O., 1972—. Mem. Am., Ohio, Cleve. psychol. assns., Am. Assn. Mental Deficiency, Cleve. Acad. Cons. Psychologists, Council for Exceptional Children, Orton Soc. Contbr. articles to profl. jours. Home: 4805 Wood St Willoughby OH 44094 Office: PO Box 345 Northfield OH 44067

HALLER, CAROL ANN KLEPINGER (MRS. GERALD J. HALLER), educator, pathologist; b. Lafayette, Ind., Nov. 26, 1933; d. Harry Edwin and Katherine Dorothy (Frasch) Klepinger; student MacMurray Coll., 1951-52; A.B., Ind. U., 1955, M.D., 1958; m. Gerald J. Haller, Feb. 20, 1965. Intern, St. Lukes Hosp., Denver, 1958-59; resident, obstetrics, gynecology Meth. Hosp., Indpls., 1959-60, pathology, 1961-65; asso. pathologist VA Hosp., Wood, Wis., 1966-67; asso. pathologist Milw. Children's Hosp., 1967-69, cons. in neuropathology, 1973—; asst. prof. pathology Marquette Med. Sch., 1967-69, Loyola U. Med. Center, Maywood, Ill., 1970—; cons. in neuropathology Hines (Ill.) VA Hosp., U. Ill. Med. Sch., Rockford, 1974—. Neuropathology fellow, 1970-72. Diplomate Am. Bd. Pathology. Mem. A.M.A., Coll. Am. Pathologists, Am. Soc. Clin. Pathology, Assn. Clin. Scientists, Ind. Assn. Pathology, Chgo. Pathology Soc., Ill., Chgo. med. socs. Home: 2241 N Clifton St Chicago IL 60614 Office: 2160 S 1st Av Maywood IL 60153

HALLER, OLGA, pediatrician; b. Schwennigen, Germany, Oct. 13, 1912; d. Christian and Christine (Schlenker) Haller; came to U.S., 1925, naturalized, 1930; B.A., Columbia, 1934; M.D., U. Heidelberg, Germany, 1939. Intern, Norwegian Hosp., Bklyn., 1939-40, St. James Hosp., Newark, 1940-41; resident, Mass. Meml. Hosp., Boston, 1941-42, Boston Floating Hosp., 1942-43; practice medicine specializing in pediatrics, Newark, 1943—; chief staff Babies' Hosp., Newark, 1966-69; asso. clin. prof. pediatrics N.J. Coll. Medicine and Dentistry, 1966—. Mem. WHO. Trustee, v.p. bd. Essex County Blood Bank. Diplomate Am. Bd. Pediatrics. Fellow Am. Acad. Pediatrics; mem. A.M.A., Am. Med. Women's Assn., Home: 275 Prospect St East Orange NJ 07017 Office: 182 Roseville Av Newark NJ 07107

HALLEY, MARGARET CAROLINE KOHLHEPP (MRS. MAX J. HALLEY), physician; b. Dannenberg, Germany, July 21, 1895; d. August and Josephine (Wolff) Kohlhepp; student meds. schs. in Gottingen, Munich, Berlin, Germany, 1914-19, state bd. examination, Berlin, 1919; m. Max J. Halley, July 9, 1926; children—Max M., Marianne (Mrs. Jules Chametzky, Renate (Mrs. Paul Duchesneau). Intern, Rudolph Virchow Hosp., Berlin, 1919-20; resident, 1920-22; resident Kaiserin Frederick's Children's Hosp., Berlin, 1923; gen. practice medicine, Wesermunde, Germany, 1924-36; mem. staff Bellevue Hosp., N.Y.C., 1936; practice medicine specializing in gen. medicine, Olean, N.Y., 1937—; mem. staff St. Francis Hosp., Olean; dir. bloodbank Olean Gen. Hosp., 1940-45, now mem. staff. Mem. Med. Soc. N.Y., Cattaraugus County Med. Soc., A.M.A., Women's Med. Soc. N.Y. Address: 144 S Union St Olean NY 14760

HALLGREN, CONSTANCE THERESE, therapist; b. Norway, Mich., Apr. 1, 1936; d. Harold Anton and Amelia Rose (Zanon) Hallgren; B.S., Eastern Mich. U., 1958; postgrad. McGill U., Northwestern U. Occupational therapist psychiatry Hines (Ill.) VA Hosp., 1959-63, supr. gen. medicine and surgery, 1963-68; with R&E Hosp., U. Ill., Chgo., 1968-69; with Madden Zone Center, Hines, 1969—, activity therapy coordinator, 1970—. Mem. Am., Ill. (standards com. 1973) occupational therapy assns. Home: 2037 S 15th Av Broadview IL 60153 Office: 1200 S 1st Av Hines IL 60141

HALLIDAY, BESSIE EARLE HENDERSON (MRS. HOWARD LAY HALLIDAY), educator; b. Pasadena, Tex., Oct. 15, 1919; d. James Lee and Alma Bell (Ridens) Henderson; B.S. in Home Econs., U. Tex., 1940; postgrad. So. Methodist U., summer 1956, Tex. A. and M. U.; M.A., Sam Houston State Coll., 1962; m. Howard Lay Halliday, Jan. 25, 1945; children—Connie Beryl (Mrs. Morris Kagan), Sondra Alma (Mrs. J. Mathis Weaver). Tchr. pub. schs., Galena Park, Tex., 1941-42, 56-65, Houston, 1944-45; tchr., dir. Halliday Pvt. Sch., Galena Park, 1945-55; asst. chemist Gulf Portland Cement, Houston, 1942-43; typist Brown & Root, Houston, 1943-44; instr. home econs. Sam Houston State Coll., summers 1962-63; chmn. home econs. dept. San Jacinto Coll., Pasadena, 1966—, chmn. home econs. div., 1973—. Pres., Galena Park Elementary P.T.A., 1951-52, Galena Park Jr. High P.T.A., 1953-54; mem. speakers bur. Am. Heart Assn. Mem. Vocational Homemaking Tchrs. Assn. Tex. (area chmn. 1956-57, 62-63), Tex. Tchrs. Assn. (coll. rep.), Am., Tex. home econs. assns., Tex. Jr. Coll. Tchrs. Assn. (past chmn. home econs. sect.), Baptist Bus. Women's Union, Tex. P.T.A. (life), Tex. Elec. Women's Round Table (charter, fellowship chmn.), Nat. (life), Tex. (life) sch. food service assns., Tex. Execs. in Home Econs., Adult Edn. Assn., Nat. Assn. Pub. Continuing and Adult Edn. Beta Sigma Phi (program chmn. 1946-51), Eta Epsilon Kappa. Baptist (teaching staff). Clubs: Galena Park Garden (program chmn. 1945-50); Fairfield Bay Community; Faculty Women's San Jacinto. Home: 1506 7th St Galena Park TX 77547

HALLIDAY, LAURA ALICE MCCARTY (MRS. JAMES G. HALLIDAY), ednl. adminstr.; b. Lehighton, Pa., Aug. 11, 1928; d. Eugene James and Edna Elizabeth (Goldsworthy) McCarty; B.S., Mansfield State Coll., 1950; M.Ed., Lehigh U., 1962; D.Ed., Pa. State U., 1971; m. James G. Halliday, July 8, 1960 (dec.); 1 dau., Bonnie Lynn. Tchr. home econs. Emmaus (Pa.) High Sch., 1950-59; vocational cons. Pa. Dept. Edn., Harrisburg, 1959—; instr. home econs. edn. grad. sch. Pa. State U., 1971-72; cons. vocational career edn. grad. program, Lehigh U., 1972—. Elementary Secondary Edn. Act grantee Pa. Dept. Edn., 1968. Mem. N.E.A. (life), Am. Vocational Assn. (life), Am. (life), Pa. home econs. assns., Vocational Adminstrs. Pa., Pa. Home Econs. Tchr. Educators Assn., Omicron Nu. Mem. Order Eastern Star. Home: RD 1 Box 211G Stroudsburg PA 18360 Office: 4577 Tilghman St Allentown PA 18104

HALLINAN, PATRICIA AUGUSTA (MRS. CHARLES STANTON HARROD), physician; b. San Francisco, Aug. 29, 1916; d. Patrick and Elizabeth (Sheehan) Hallinan; A.B., Stanford, 1939; M.D., Stanford, 1943; m. Charles Stanton Harrod, Dec. 8, 1942; children—Charles Patrick, Stephen Anthony, David Gregory, Michael Dennis, Patrick Vincent. Intern, San Francisco Gen. Hosp., 1942-43; resident, 1943-44; physician San Francisco Pub. Health Dept., 1943-50; dir. Employees Health Service, A.R.C., San Francisco, 1955-61; asst. health officer Marin County, 1961-68; practice medicine San Francisco Gen. Hosp., 1944—; mem. staff St. Joseph's Hosp., French Hosp., Children's Hosp. (all San Francisco), Ross Hosp., Marin County. Lobbied for passage of battered child legislation, Cal., 1971; mem. Gov. Reagan's Citizen's Com. to Rev. Welfare Reforms, 1971; mem. med. adv. bd. Respite Home for Retarded, 1968, Genetic Counseling Clinic, Marin Speech and Hearing Center, 1968. Bd. dirs. Marin Home Care Services, 1968. Recipient award for services to genetic counseling clinic March of Dimes, 1968. Mem. A.M.A. Club: Commonwealth (San Francisco). Home: 25 Allen Av Ross CA 94957 Office: 1030 Sir Francis Drake Blvd Kentfield CA 94904

HALLORAN, GERTRUDE RYAN (MRS. LEO J.J. HALLORAN), judge; b. Gloucester, Mass., July 3, 1892; d. Stephen Joseph and Mary Joseph (Glynn) Ryan; LL.B., Portia Law Sch., 1925; LL.M., Boston U., 1948; A.B., Boston U., 1953, postgrad., 1953-56; J.D., New Eng. Sch. Law, 1969; m. Leo J. Halloran, Oct, 12, 1927; (dec. July 1953). Admitted to Mass. bar, 1926; practiced in Boston, 1926-38; mem. firm Halloran, Halloran and Madden, 1926-38; spl. justice Dist. Ct. East Norfolk, Quincy, Mass., 1938-73. Mem. Internat. Fedn. Women Lawyers, Am., Fed., Quincy, Norfolk County bar assns., Mass. Assn. Women Lawyers, Nat. Hist. Soc., Phi Beta Kappa. Clubs: Boston, Professional Women's, Boston University Women Graduates. Home: 102 Wilson Av Wollaston MA 02170

HALLUM, GYDA ALMIRA, psychologist; b. Foxhome, Minn.; d. John O. and Emma (Smerud) Hallum; B.A., Trinity U., 1951, M.A., 1955; M.S., Tex. Arts and Industries Coll., 1958; Ph.D. (U.S. Dept. Health, Edn., and Welfare fellow) U. Tex., 1962. Caseworker, psychometrist Children's Service Bur., San Antonio, 1948-51; spl. investigator Harris County Probation Dept., Houston, 1951-52; supr. med. and psychiat. social service, acting clin. psychologist U.S. Naval Hosp., Corpus Christi, Tex., 1954-57; spl. services tchr. Harlingen (Tex.) Ind. Sch. Dist., 1958-59; chief clin. psychologist El Paso (Tex.) Child Guidance Center, 1962-63; asst. prof. Tex. Western Coll., U. Tex., El Paso, 1964, asso. prof., 1965, lectr., Extension Div., 1964; research psychologist Abilene (Tex.) State Sch., 1965-66; program coordinator Austin (Tex.) State Sch., 1966-67; chief psychologist Gulf Bend Center Diagnostic Clinic, Victoria, Tex., 1968-70; practice psychology, Corpus Christi, El Paso, Abilene, Austin, 1955-70, Victoria, Tex., 1970—. Cons., Pre-Sch. for Deaf and Hearing Handicapped, El Paso, 1963-65, Canutillo (Tex.) Ind. Sch. Dist., 1964-65, West Tex. Rehab. Center, Abilene, 1965-66, Region III Edn. Service Center, Victoria, 1971-73; lectr. Victoria Center U. Houston, 1973—. Recipient Best Poem of Year award Avalon Mag., 1947, 1st prize Nat. Penwomen's Contest, 1946, 2d prize Corpus Christi Art Show, 1955. Mem. Am., Southwestern, Tex. psychol. assns., Internat. Assn. Cross Cultural Psychology, Am. Soc. Clin. Hypnosis, Alpha Chi. Writer poetry, 1945-50, pageant Saga of Spring Grove, 1947. Contbr. articles to profl. jours; inventor. Home: 104 N Liberty St Victoria TX 77901 Office: 2701 N Azalea Victoria TX 77901

HALLUM, ROSEMARY NORA, educator; b. Oakland, Cal.; d. Fred Fain and Edna Henrietta (Becker) Hallum; A.B. with highest honors, U. Cal. at Berkeley, 1954; gen. elementary teaching credential U. of Pacific, 1955; M.A. with honors, Cal. State U., 1960. Accompanist, asst. tchr. in dance studios; pvt. piano tchr.; teaching asst. U. Cal. at Berkeley, 1954-55; high sch. English tchr., elementary sch. tchr., social dance tchr., workshop clinician ednl. writer, West coast cons. Ednl. Activities, Inc., Oakland, Cal., 1955-74. Mem. A.S.C.A.P., Musicians Union, Oakland Edn. Assn., Cal. Tchrs. Assn., Phi Beta Kappa, Pi Lambda Theta, Delta Kappa Gamma. Roman Catholic. Club: Cal. Writers (Oakland). Early childhood cons., contbg. author New Dimensions in music textbook series, 1970. Author: Boxing, 1973; Safe Motorcycle Riding, 1973; Kookie The Motorcycle Racing Dog, 1973; MotoCross Racing, 1973; Dr. Marcus A. Foster, 1974. Producer various filmstrips and records. Address: 1021 Otis Dr Alameda CA 94501

HALOW, MARY, lawyer, govt. ofcl.; b. Juarez, Mexico, June 5, 1932 (parents Am. citizens); d. Beshure Joseph and Afifie (Khoury) Halow; B.A., George Washington U., 1956, LL.B., 1960; postgrad. (Nat. Inst. Pub. Affairs Career Edn. Award grantee), Cornell U., 1966-67. Admitted to Washington bar, 1961; editorial asst. AEC, Washington, 1957-60, agreements specialist, 1960-72, spl. asst. to commr., 1972-73, asst. to chmn. bd. contract appeals, 1973—. Mem. Washington, Fed. bar assns. Home: 6812 Brookville Rd Chevy Chase MD 20015 Office: US Atomic Energy Commission Washington DC 20545

HALPER, ROSE LEE SCHAINMAN (MRS. CHARLES H. HALPER), artist; b. Bklyn., Apr. 2, 1937; d. Edward I. and Mae (Chalkin) Schainman; student Vassar Coll., 1955-57; B.S. in Art Edn., Skidmore Coll., 1959; m. Charles H. Halper, June 14, 1959; children—David Grad, Jan Rachel. Art tchr. Horace Greeley High Sch., Chappaqua, N.Y., 1959-60; one-man shows Stamford (Conn.) Mus., 1963, York Gallery, N.Y.C., 1968, Fairfield U., 1969, Avanti Gallery, N.Y.C., 1971, Mus. Art, Sci. and Industry, Bridgeport, Conn., 1972, Skidmore Coll., 1973, Union Am. Hebrew Congregations, N.Y.C., 1973, Lincoln Center Mus. Performing Arts, N.Y.C., 1974; 2 man show Vassar Coll., 1969.; represented in permanent collection Mrs. Martin Luther King, 1964, Theodore Bikel. Art tchr. adults; instr. art sch. vol. program, Bridgeport, 1969-74. Mem. Caucus of Concerned Democrats. Bd. dirs. Sch. Vol. Assn. Bridgeport, 1972-74. Mem. World Affairs Center (dir.), Conn. Childbirth Assn. Lamaze Method (founder, pres. emeritus 1965-67, information dir.), Vassar and Skidmore alumnae clubs Fairfield County. Jewish religion (trustee, mem. temple sisterhood, co-chmn. social action com. 1970-73, chmn. art com. 1973-74). Mem. Hadassah. Author: To Life, 1972. Address: 21 Little Fox Lane Westport CT 06880

HALPERN, PHYLLIS CAMILLE SCHACHTER (MRS. SIDNEY B. HALPERN), lawyer; b. Phila., June 2, 1928; d. Nathan and Anna (Freilich) Schachter; B.A., U. Pa., 1949, LL.B., 1951; m. Sidney B. Halpern, Dec. 23, 1951; children—Baruch, Nikki. Admitted to Pa. bar, 1952; asso. Gerber & Gelfand, Phila., 1952-66; counsel Plymouth Mut. Life Ins. Co., Phila., 1964-67, Food Fair Stores, Inc., Phila., 1968—. Guest lectr. U. Pa., 1953-54. Mem. Pres.'s Com. for Aged, 1962. Mem. Am., Pa., Phila. (mem. services and communications 1967—, services com. 1970—) bar assns. Home: 1025 Friendship St Philadelphia PA 19111 Office: 101 N 33d St Philadelphia PA 19101

HALPERT, SYLVIA SIDRANSKY, social worker; b. N.Y.C., Feb. 26, 1914; d. Morris and Elizabeth (Katz) Sidransky; M.S., Cath. U. Am., 1945, D.Social Welfare, 1965; certificate in psychiatry Washington Sch. Psychiatry, 1949; m. Harold P. Halpert, Apr. 27, 1937. Psychiat. social worker Washington Inst. Mental Hygiene, 1945-62; social research educator Howard U., 1965-68; social worker Marriage and Family Inst. Washington, 1966-70; pvt. practice psychiat. social work, Washington, 1950—. Cons. Head Start Program, 1968-71; mem. profl. adv. bd. D.C. Inst. Mental Hygiene, 1968—. Fellow Am. Orthopsychiat. Assn.; mem. Council on Social Work Edn., Acad. Certified Social Workers, Nat. Assn. Social Workers, Am. Sociol. Assn. Address: 4606 Bayard Blvd Washington DC 20016

HALPIN, SISTER MARLENE, acad. dean; b. N.Y.C., Oct 14, 1927; d. William J. and Elsie (Etzold) Halpin; B.A., St. John's U., 1956; M.A., Catholic U. Am., 1957, Ph.D., 1963; postdoctoral studies Columbia, 1964, N.Y.U., 1965, Adelphi U., 1971. Elementary tchr. St. Thomas the Apostle, Woodhaven, N.Y., 1947-52; tchr. religion, Latin and English, St. Agnes, Rockville Centre, N.Y., 1952-56; instr. philosophy Molloy Coll., 1956-59, asso. prof., chmn. dept. philosophy 1963-67, prof., acad. dean, 1967-74; dir. continuing edn., prof. philosophy Aquinas Inst. Theology, Dubuque, Ia., 1974—; prof. philosophy, chmn. dept. religion St. Agnes, 1959-61, chmn. div. philosophy and theology, 1964-65. Instr. English St. Joseph's Dunwoodie affiliation, N.Y., summer 1956; vis. prof. Sacred Heart Coll., Belmont Abbey, N.C., 1964-65; pres. sisters adv. council Rockville Centre Diocese of N.Y.; cons. N.Y. State Edn. Dept.; dir. insts. Trustee, mem. exec. com. Nassau Higher Edn. Consortium, 1972-74. Mem. Am. Cath. Philos. Assn., Am. Soc. Christian Ethics (dir.), Dominican Ednl. Assn. (founding pres. Amityville chpt. 1966, dir.), Eastern Assn. Coll. Deans, Metaphys. Soc. Am., Nat. Cath. Edn. Assn., N.E.A., Charles Pierce Soc., Delta Epsilon Sigma, Lambda Iota Tau. Contbr. articles periodicals. Office: 2570 Asbury Rd Dubuque IA 52001

HALPRIN, ANN SCHUMAN (MRS. LAWRENCE HALPRIN), dancer; b. Wilmette, Ill., July 13, 1920; d. Isadore and Ida (Schiff) Schuman; student Bennington Summer Sch. Dancer, 1938-39; B.S. in Dance, U. Wis., 1943; m. Lawrence Halprin, Sept. 19, 1940; children—Daria, Rana. Founder, choreographer, dir., performer Dancers' Workshop of San Francisco, 1954—; appeared in films Four in the Afternoon, The Bed, Parades and Changes, The Bust, Ann, a Portrait, others; performed Am. Festival of Dance, 1972, N.Y.C. Center, 1972; master tchr. Esalen Inst., U. Cal. at Berkeley, U. Cal. at Los Angeles, U. Ill., Reed Coll., Harvard Sch. Design, Environmental Sch. Design, U. Cal., San Francisco State Coll., U. Mich., Mass. Inst. Tech., Case Western Res. U., Lake Erie Coll.; founded dance dept. Studio Watts Sch. Arts; dance cons. Chinese Cultural Center, San Francisco; performed maj. works: Venice Opera House, Sweden, Finland, Poland, Canada; gave month-long presentation Expo '70, Osaka, Japan; choreographed The Prophetess, The Lonely Ones, Visions, Birds of America or Gardens without Walls, Esponsizione, Visage, The Five Legged Stool, Parades and Changes, Apt. 6, The Bath, Ceremony of Us, Evocation to the Cement Spirit, New Time Shuffle; produced Animal Legend, Transformations and Initiations. Mem. Regional Bay Area Arts Council, San Francisco Arts Resources Devel. Com.; founder, dir. Marin Dance Coop.; participant Alternate Pursuits Conf., San Diego, 1972, Action for Human Settlements Conf., Greece, 1972; Workshop Leader Internat. Congress Arts, Religion and Architecture, Jerusalem, 1973, Young Pres.'s Am., Hawaii, 1973. Mem. dance com. Pasadena Mus. Art. Recipient choreographer's grant Nat. Endowment Arts, 1969; Guggenheim fellow for expts. in Kinetic theatre, 1970. Mem. Assn. Am. Dance, Conscientious Artists Am. Author: When A School Comes Home; Exit to Enter and Collected Writings. Founder Impulse mag. Home: 15 Ravine Way Kentfield CA 94904 Office: 321 Divisadero St San Francisco CA 94123

HALSELL, GRACE ELEANOR, author; b. Lubbock, Tex., May 7, 1923; d. Harry H. and Ruth (Shanks) Halsell; student Tex. Technol. Coll., 1939-42, Columbia, 1943-44, Tex. Christian Coll., 1945-51, Sorbonne, 1956-57. With Avalanche-Jour., Lubbock, 1942-44, Ft. Worth Star-Telegram, 1945-51; Free lance writer various newspapers, 1952-57; columnist Japan Times, 1958, Hong Kong Tiger-Standard, 1959, La Prensa. Lima, Peru, 1960-62; staff writer Pres. Johnson, 1965-68. Clubs: Womans Nat. Press, Am. Newspaper Womens (program chmn. 1967-68). Author: Getting To Know Peru, 1964; Getting To Know Guatemala, Honduras, 1964; Getting To Know Colombia, 1964; Peru, 1961; Soul Sister, 1969; (with Charles Evers) Evers, 1971; Black-White Sex, 1972; Bessie Yellowhair, 1973. Address: 2401 Calvert St NW Washington DC 20008

HALSEY, JULIA MCELHINNEY WALKER (MRS. JAMES HERRON HALSEY), civic worker; b. Great Falls, Mont., Nov. 8, 1905; d. John Perry and Julia (McElhinney) Walker; A.B., U. Ill., 1927; postgrad. Ind. U., 1934-35; m. James Herron Halsey, June 18, 1930; children—James Herron, John Easton, George Rogers. Elementary tchr., Harvey, Ill., 1927-30; social studies tchr. MacJannet Schs., Paris, France, 1930-33. Founder, exec. dir. Camp Counselor Internat. Exchange Program in cooperation with Centre d'Entrainement aux Methodes d'Education Active de France and Federation Nationale des Cooperatives de Consommation d'Entrainemant de France, 1959—; founder, exec. dir. U.S. Com. for Consejo Argentino de Intercambio Estudiantil, 1968—; chmn. Am. Mothers Com. Conn., 1962-65, dir., 1965—; county v.p. Women's Internat. League for Peace and Freedom, 1966-68; v.p. Greater Bridgeport Council Chs., 1966, chmn. family life dept., 1966—, chmn. Family Life Edn. Confs., 1967—; chmn. Community Com. on Day Care for Children of Working Mothers, 1968—; founder Conn. Widows and Widowers Assn., 1972; Conn. rep. Franco-Am. Com. for Ednl. Travel and Study; bd. dirs. Greater Bridgeport Symphony Soc., 1967—, Student Exchange-Work Program, 1969—; Bridgeport Internat. Inst., 1969—; Arts Commn., 1969—; founder, dir. Speech and Hearing Clinic Greater Bridgeport, 1958-66, v.p., 1962-66; founder-dir. L'Alliance Francaise, Fairfield County, 1959—. Named Conn. Mother of Yr., Am. Mothers Com.; 1961. Mem. Am. Assn. U. Women, Conn. UN Assn. (sec. 1963-67, hon. chmn. 1968—), League Women Voters, Alpha Gamma Delta. Conglist. Clubs: Brooklawn Country (Bridgeport). Home: 491 University Av Bridgeport CT 06604

HALSEY, LINDA ANN, editor; b. Bay City, Mich., Jan. 16, 1939; d. Edgar Clay and Mildred Agnes (Proud) Britton; B.A., U. Mich., 1961, postgrad., 1961-63; M.A., Hunter Coll., 1967; m. John Robert Halsey, Sept. 5, 1967; children—Norman Edgar. Editorial asst. Doubleday & Co., Inc., N.Y.C., 1963-66; editor Mus. Anthropology, U. Mich., 1966-67, U. N.C. Press, 1967-69; publs. editor U. Wis. Extension, 1969—. Mem. Women in Communications (sec. Madison profl. chpt. 1974—). Home: 4922 Knox Lane Madison WI 53711 Office: 432 N Lake St Madison WI 53706

HALTER, KAREN ANN JACOBSON (MRS. BRADLEY AHERN), occupational therapist; b. Milw., Aug. 22, 1942; d. Elmer Bernard and Erma Mary (Fraenzl) Jacobson; student San Diego State U., 1960-62; B.S., San Jose State U., 1964; postgrad. U. Cal. at Santa Barbara, 1972; m. Bradley Ahern, Dec. 18, 1971; 1 son, Steven John. Occupational therapist Camarillo (Cal.) State Hosp., 1965-68; sr. occupational therapist Ventura County Mental Health Dept., Oxnard (Cal.) Day Treatment Center, 1968-74. Occupational therapy cons. Oxnard Manor Convalescent Hosp., 1970-71; ceramics tchr. Pleasant Valley Recreation Dist., Camarillo, 1969. Bd. dirs. Resocialization Center, Oxnard, 1971-72. Mem. Rehab. Services Assn., Am., So. Cal. occupational therapy assns., Tri-San Occupational Therapy Dist. (v.p. 1971-72), Alpha Gamma Delta. Home: 3582 E Barca St Camarillo CA 93010

HALVORSON, VIRGINIA MARKLE (MRS. NEWMAN T. HALVORSON), civic worker; b. Detroit, Oct. 19, 1910; d. Stanton Jay and Henrietta (Westbrook) Markle; student Briarcliff Coll., 1927-29; m. Newman T. Halvorson, Dec. 1, 1934; children—Newman T., Sigrid (Mrs. L. Richard Freese, Jr.), Karin (Mrs. William A. Hillhouse II). Pres. Women's Com. Cleve. Orch., 1967-69; v.p. Women's Assn. Symphony Orchs., 1969-71; chmn. jr. council Cleve. Mus. Art, 1971-73. Trustee, Lake Erie Opera Theater, 1965-71, Cleve. Inst. Music, 1966—, YWCA, 1966-71, Briarcliff Coll., 1970-73, Garden Center Greater Cleve., 1971—. Home: Woodstock Rd Gates Mills OH 44040

HAMANN, MARJORIE ANN RAUWERDINK (MRS. VINCENT LAWRENCE HAMANN), home economist; b. Sheboygan, Wis., July 2, 1939; d. Harvard Melvin and Dorothy Margaret (Duenk) Rauwerdink; B.S., Stout State U., 1961; M.Ed., U. Minn., 1973; m. Vincent Lawrence Hamann, Feb. 23, 1963; children—John Christopher, Sandra Nicole. Extension home economist U. Minn., Washington County, Stillwater, 1961—. Mem. Minn. Home Econs. Assn. (v.p. membership 1971-72), Minn. Assn. Extension Home Economists (pres. 1972-73), St. Croix Valley Home Economists, Epsilon Sigma Phi, Phi Upsilon Omicron. Mem. Order Eastern Star. Home: 1304 W Pine St Stillwater MN 55082 Office: 6081 Oxboro Av N Stillwater MN 55082

HAMANT, CELESTINE, ednl. adminstr.; b. Indpls., June 20, 1940; d. Celestine John and Julia Agnes (Long) Hamant; B.A., St. Mary of the Woods Coll., 1962; certificate Wash. U., St. Louis, 1964; M.S., Butler U., 1971. Staff occupational therapist Cerebral Palsy Clinic, Ind. U. Med. Center, Indpls., 1964-68, dir. occupational therapy service, 1974—; asst. prof., supr. dept. occupational therapy, supr. clin. edn. Riley Hosp. for Children, Indpls., 1969—. Cons. in care and mgmt. of severely retarded in instns. in various states. Mem. Am., Ind. occupational therapy assns. Home: 5915 Carvel Av Indianapolis IN 46220 Office: 1100 W Michigan St Indianapolis IN 46202

HAMBLETT, RUTH MITCHELL, cons.; b. Iroquois Falls, Ont., Can., Sept. 16, 1928; d. Frank Leslie and Edith Louise (Barnes) Mitchell; Occupational Therapist, U. Toronto, 1949; m. David Coombs Hamblett, Sept. 9, 1950; children—Susan (Mrs. Richard Wyrwicz), Robert, Jonathan, Frank. Came to U.S., 1950, naturalized, 1958. Staff occupational therapist Allen Meml. Hosp., Montreal, Que., Can., 1949-50, Mass. Gen. Hosp., Boston, 1950-51; occupational therapist Manchester (N.H.) Rehab. Easter Seal, 1951-52; occupational therapist cons. Hillsborough County Nursing Home, Goffstown, N.H., 1958-73, Hillsborough County House Corrections, 1973. Occupational therapist Community Music Concerts, Nashua, N.H., 1950-73. Mem. Am., Canadian occupational therapy assns. Home: 21 Columbia Av Nashua NH 03060 Office: Hillsborough County House Correction Goffstown NH 03060

HAMBLIN, FRANCES HARDER MURPHY (MRS. FRANCIS DOW HAMBLIN), educator; b. Amsterdam, N.Y., Feb. 12, 1915; d. J. Harvey and Sara Frances (Harder) Murphy; A.B. magna cum laude, Wells Coll., 1935; M.A. (Spl. fellow), Brown U., 1937, Ph.D., 1940; m. Francis Dow Hamblin, Dec. 18, 1944; children—Nathan Chipman II, Peter Dow. Instr., Wells Coll., Aurora, N.Y., 1938-39, 43-46, asst. prof. philosophy and psychology, 1946-48; instr. philosophy and psychology Lawrence Coll., Appleton, Wis., 1942-43; asst. prof. philosophy U. Rochester (N.Y.), 1948-49, sr. lectr., 1955-64; lectr. philosophy Rochester (N.Y.) Inst. Tech., 1962-63, asso. prof., 1963-66, prof., 1966—. Mem. Am. Philos. Assn., Creighton Club, A.A.A.S., Am. Assn. U. Profs., Phi Beta Kappa. Home: 345 Westminster Rd Rochester NY 14607

HAMBRICK, ERNESTINE, physician; b. Griffin, Ga., Mar. 31, 1941; d. Jack Daniel and Nannie Rubens (Harper) Hambrick; B.S., U. Md., 1963; M.D. (scholar), U. Ill., 1967. Surg. intern Cook County Hosp., Chgo., 1967-68, gen. surgery resident, 1968-72, fellow in colon and rectal surgery, 1972-73. Asst. prof. surgery U. Ill. Abraham Lincoln Sch. Medicine. Diplomate Am. Bd. Surgery, Am. Bd. Colon and Rectal Surgery. Fellow A.C.S.; asso. fellow Am. Soc. Colon and Rectal Surgeons; mem. Chgo. Med. Soc. Mem. Moody Ch. Home: 2625BS Indiana Av Chicago IL 60616 Office: 1825 W Harrison St Chicago IL 60612 also 30 N Michigan Av Chicago IL 60602

HAMBURG, MARIAN VIRGINIA (MRS. MORRIS HAMBURG), educator; b. St. Louis, Oct. 20, 1918; d. Oliver John and Hazel (Klein) Miller; student U. Wis., 1936-37; B.Sc., U. Mo., 1940; M.A., N.Y. U., 1945; Ed.D., Columbia, 1955; m. Morris Hamburg, Dec. 27, 1955; children—Jean, Jacalyn. Dir. health edn. YWCA, Chgo., 1946-48; health edn. coordinator Stephen F. Austin State U., Nacogdoches, Tex., 1948-49; sch. health cons. Nassau County Tb. and Pub. Health Assn., Garden City, N.Y., 1949-51; asst. dir. pub. edn. The Nat. Found., N.Y.C., 1951-54; sch. health cons. Am. Heart Assn., N.Y.C., 1954-64; mem. faculty N.Y. U., N.Y.C., 1964—, asso. prof. edn., 1966-69, prof., 1969—, also dir. health edn., 1967—. Mem. White House Conf. Food Nutrition and Health, 1969; mem. com. sch. health and health careers Am. Heart Assn., 1964-66; mem. com. community programs Nat. Council YMCA, 1968; mem. task force sch. health edn. study Nat. Health Council, 1965-68; del. of Nat. Interagency Council Smoking and Health to World Smoking Conf., 1967; mem. adv. com. health edn. N.Y. State Dept. Edn., 1967—, com. flouridation N.Y. State Dental Soc., 1969—; chmn. task force on pub. edn. N.Y. State Alcoholism Com., 1972-73; mem. exec. com. N.Y. State Gov.'s Task Force on Alcohol Problems, 1973—, N.Y. State Council on Critical Health Problems, 1972—. USPHS grantee, 1966-67, U.S. Office Edn. grantee, 1967-70, N.Y. State Dept. Edn. grantee, 1968—; recipient Women's Centennial Honor award U. Mo., 1968. Fellow Am. Pub. Health Assn. (chmn. sch. health sect. 1962-64), A.A.H.P.E.R. (mem. rep. assembly 1966-68), Am. Sch. Health Assn. (recipient Distinguished Service award 1969; mem. research council 1963-69); mem. N.Y. State Assn. Health, Phys. Edn. and Recreation (recipient Distinguished Service award 1970; v.p. for health edn. 1966-67), Soc. State Dirs. Health, Phys. Edn. and Recreation, Am. Coll. Health Assn. (mem. research com. 1965-67), Soc. Pub. Health Educators, Sex Information and Edn. Council of U.S., Mortar Bd., Eta Sigma Gamma, Pi Lambda Theta. Author: (with Morris Hamburg) Health & Social Problems in Schools, 1968. Contbr. articles to profl. jours. Home: 933 Lincoln Av Baldwin NY 11510 Office: Sch Edn New York Univ Washington Square New York City NY 10003

HAMDAN, BARBARA E. BRUNET (MRS. HUSSEIN M. HAMDAN), physician; b. North Adams, Mass., June 23, 1932; d. A. Paul and Ellen (Andrews) Brunet; B.A., Coll. Our Lady of Elms, 1954; M.D., U. Vt., 1958; m. Hussein M. Hamdan, Oct. 1, 1957; children—Ziad, Nabil, Karim, Sharif, Amira, Khalil, Tarik, Rashid. Intern, Seton Hall Med. Center, Jersey City, 1958, St. Francis Hosp., Trenton, N.J., 1959-60; resident N.J. Neuropsychiat. Inst., Princeton, N.J., 1960-65; staff psychiatrist Catholic Charities Guidance Clinic, Trenton, N.J., 1965-67; practice medicine specializing in child psychiatry, Princeton, 1967—; cons. Willis Sch. for Psychoednl. Therapy, 1966, Princeton Child Devel. Center, 1972. Mem. A.M.A., Am., N.J. neuropsychiat. assns., N.J. Pub Health Assn., Orton Soc., Am. Med. Women's Assn., Am. Acad. Child Psychiatry, Am. Acad. Orthomolecular Psychiatry, N.Y. Acad. Scis., Am. Schizophrenia Found. Roman Catholic. Address: Cherry Hill Rd RD 5 Box 165 Princeton NJ 08540

HAMEISTER, LAVON LOUETTA, social worker; b. Blairstown, Ia., Nov. 27, 1922; d. George Frederick and Bertha (Anderson) Hameister; B.A., U. Ia., 1944; postgrad. N.Y. Sch. Social Work, Columbia, 1945-46, U. Minn. Sch. Social Work, summer 1952; M.A., U. Chgo., 1959. Child welfare practitioner Fayette County Dept. Social Welfare, West Union, Ia., 1946-56; dist. cons. services in child welfare and pub. assistance Ia. Dept. Social Services, Des Moines, 1956-58, dist. field rep., 1959-64, regional supr., 1964-65, supr., specialist supervision, adminstrn, Bur. Staff Devel., 1965-66, chief Bur. Staff Devel., 1966-68, chief div. staff devel. and tng., 1968-73, asst. dir. Office Staff Devel. and Tng., 1973—. Active in drive to remodel, enlarge Oelwein (Ia.) Mercy Hosp., 1952. Mem. Bus. and Profl. Women's Club (chpt. sec. 1950-52), Am. Assn. U. Women, Nat. Assn. Social Workers (chpt. sec.-elect 1958-59), Am. Pub. Welfare Assn., Ia. Welfare Assn. Home: 3440 Grand Av Des Moines IA 50312 Office: Robert Lucas State Office Bldg Des Moines IA 50309

HAMER, LOIS VIOLA, community services cons.; b. Waterloo, Ia., Mar. 10, 1916; d. Orville Lavan and Lydia (Shafford) Hamer; B.A., U. No. Ia., 1937; M.A., Northwestern U., 1941. Tchr., prin. Baldwin (Ia.) High Sch., 1937-39; prin. Carson (Ia.) Pub. Sch., 1940-43; employee orientation, personnel dept. Umatilla (Ore.) Ordnance Depot, 1943-44; program dir. Radio Sta. KODL, also dean of girls Dalles High Sch., The Dalles Ore., 1944-45; dir. Christian edn. and youth work 1st Congl. Ch., Salem, Ore., 1945-49, parish dir., Klamath Falls, Ore., 1949-50; ch. sch. worker, dept. Christian edn. Congl. Conf. So. Cal. and S.W., Los Angeles, 1950-54; minister of Christian edn. 1st Congl. Ch., Albuquerque, 1954-55; dir. Christian edn. Mont. Congl. Conf. and Congl. Christian Conf. of N.D., hdqrs. Miles City, Mont., 1955-59; exec. sec. Los Angeles Office of Fellowship of Reconciliation, 1959-62; vol. U.S. Peace Corps, Thailand, 1962-64; lectr. Stewardship Council of United Ch. of Christ, throughout U.S., 1964-65, mem. peace task force, 1971—; curriculum coordinator Community Skill Center, West Coast Trade Schs., Los Angeles, 1966; spl. counselor Seven Seas Div., Chapman Coll., Orange, Cal., 1966-67; cons. Protestant Community Services of Los Angeles Council Chs., 1966-69; dir. Program Ret. Citizens, Los Angeles, 1969-73; coordinator employee relations and community relations Embree Buses, 1973-74; dir. sr. adult program Valley Community Coll., Van Nuys, 1974—. Cons., So. Cal. Ch. Consultants, Los Angeles. Bd. dirs. Los Angeles br. Womens Internat. League for Peace and Freedom, 1965—, br. pres., 1969-71, nat. dir., 1966-68, 70, sr. cons. to internat. exec. com., 1971—, mem. internat. team to South Vietnam, 1971. Mem. Fellowship of Reconciliation (dir. 1959-62), Am. Assn. U. Women, UN Assn. Conglist. (deaconess). Home: 3755 Glenfeliz Blvd Los Angeles CA 90039 Office: 4603 Prospect Av Los Angeles CA 90027 also 5800 Fulton Av Van Nuys CA 91401

HAMER, MARILYN SCHNEIDER, textile co. exec.; b. St. Louis; d. Paul J. and Alvina (Fleer) Schneider; A.A., Pine Manor Jr. Coll., 1950; m. Warren G. Hamer, Mar. 10, 1973. Pub. relations exec. DuPont Co., N.Y.C., 1962-70; account exec. Glick & Lorwin, N.Y.C.,

1971-73; dir. advt. and pub. relations Bloomcraft, N.Y.C., 1973—. Mem. Pub. Relations Soc. Am., The Fashion Group, Home Fashions League. Office: 295 Fifth Av New York City NY 10016

HAMILL, BERTHA ELIZABETH AMMANN, educator; b. Corbin, Kan., Sept. 24, 1906; d. Carl Albert and Julia Evelyn (Fierce) Ammann; B.S., Kan. State Coll., 1938; M.A., Colo. State U., 1942; postgrad. N.Y., Tchrs. Coll., Columbia, Okla. State U., Okla. U., Temple U.; m. Harold C. Hamill, May 28, 1930 (div. Nov. 1932); 1 dau., Phyllis Lovell (Mrs. T. Ray Graham). Librarian Harper City (Kan.) Pub. Library, 1924-26; tchr. art Oxford (Kan.) pub. schs., 1928-30, Ft. Scott (Kan.) pub. schs., 1938-41; head art dept. Ft. Scott (Kan.) Jr. Coll., 1941-45; asst. prof. art Central State U., Edmond, Okla., 1945-73, asso. prof. art, chmn. art dept., 1973—. Exhibited art in Kan., Okla., Tex., Colo., N.M., Mo., Ark., N.Y. Mem. Nat., Okla. edn. assns., Am. Assn. U. Women, Am. Assn. U. Profs., Okla. Art Edn. Assn., Oklahoma City Art Center Assn., Delta Zeta, Delta Kappa Gamma, Kappa Kappa Iota, Kappa Pi. Club: Cambridge. Home: 133 Ann Arbor Edmond OK 73034

HAMILTON, CLARA EDDY (MRS. HENRY W. SCHOENBORN), physiologist; b. New Haven, Mar. 14, 1923; d. William Ferguson and Helen Folsom (Dula) Hamilton; B.A., U. Ga., 1942; M.A., U. Ill., 1944, Ph.D., 1946; m. Henry W. Schoenborn, Dec. 19, 1955 (dec. 1967). Asst. prof. U. Ga., Athens, 1946-55, asso. prof., 1955-56; exec. sec. physiology study sect. NIH Div. Research Grants, Bethesda, Md., 1956—. Mem. A.A.A.S., Am. Soc. Zoologists, Am. Physiol. Soc., Sigma Xi, Phi Beta Kappa. Home: 15424 Tierra Dr Silver Spring MD 20906 Office: Div Research Grants NIH Bethesda MD 20014

HAMILTON, DOROTHY ISABELLE (MRS. HARRY DALE HAMILTON), author; b. Muncie, Ind., Sept. 25, 1906; d. Garry C. and Mary (Bartle) Drumm; student Ball State U., 1924-25, Ind. U., 1961; m. Harry Dale Hamilton, Sept. 30, 1926; children—Dale, Kathryn, Carolyn, Lois, Stephen, Frances, David. Tutor, Liberty-Perry Sch. Corp., Selma, Ind., 1964-73. Mem. Order Eastern Star. Author: Anitas Choice, 1971; Charco, 1971; Christmas for Holly, 1971; The Killdeer, 1972; Tony Savala, 1972; Jim Musco, 1972; Settled Furrows, 1972; Kerry, 1973; Mindy, 1973; The Quail, 1973; The Blue Caboose, 1973; Jason, 1974; The Gift of a Home, 1974; The Eagle, 1974; Bus Boys at Big Bend, 1974. Home and office: Rural Route 1 Box 351 Selma IN 47383

HAMILTON, ELYNOR ELIZABETH BUTLER (MRS. BENJAMIN M. HAMILTON), educator; b. Memphis, Sept. 26, 1938; d. George Washington and Sue (Etheredge) Butler; student Winthrop Coll., 1956-58; B.A. in Dance, Fla. State U., 1960; M.A. in Dance, Tex. Women's U., 1964; M.A. in Theatre, U. Miss., 1970; m. Benjamin Mason Hamilton, Aug. 8, 1964; 1 dau., Margaret Sue. Instr. dance U. Miss., 1960-63, also dir. U. dancers; dir. concert dance group U. Ga., Athens; choreographer speech and theater dept. U. Miss., 1965, grad. asst., 1969-70; instr. dance St. Mary Coll., Xavier, Kan., also dir. St. Mary Concert Dancers, 1965-66; instr. extension course, Coll. William and Mary, 1970-71. Dance cons. Meridian (Miss.) High Schs., 1961; choreographer program WKNO-TV, Memphis, 1962; producer shows, WGAU-TV Athens Ga., 1963-64; writer, choreographer, producer 2 shows KFEQ-TV, St. Joseph, Mo., 1966; mem. Mary Michael dancers, 1970-72; instr. D.C. Tchrs. Coll., spring 1971; tchr. modern dance Ascension Acad., Alexandria, Va., 1971-73, Pope Dance Studio, 1971-73; dance instr. Schofield Barracks Youth Activities, Hawaii, 1973—. Bd. dirs. Modern Dance Council of Washington, 1970-73. Mem. Am., Ga., Miss. (dance chmn. 1961-63) assns. health, phys. edn. and recreation, Nat., So. assns. phys. edn. coll. women, D.A.R., North Miss. Chi Omega Alumnae. Conducted workshops, dance programs for profl. assns., phys. edn. tchrs., coll. events, Miss., Ga., Washington, 1961—. Home: Box 216 Jonestown MS 38639

HAMILTON, GINGER IRENE, animal psychologist; b. Portsmouth, O., Feb. 21, 1935; d. Edward Sherman and Arlie Daisy (Waring) Hamilton; B.S. with honors, Ohio U., 1959; M.A., Ohio State U., 1967, Ph.D. (USPHS fellow), 1969. Tchr. math. and sci. pub. schs., Ohio, Fla., Hawaii, Cal., 1956-61; research psychologist Fla. Atlantic Ocean Sci., Boca Raton, 1969-70; supr. research Montgomery County Pub. Schs., Rockville, Md., 1970—; cons. in animal psychology, Wheaton, Md., 1972—. Mem. Am., Midwestern, Md. psychol. assns., A.A.A.S., Psi Chi, Phi Kappa Phi. Contbg. author: Your Animal's Health from A to Z (McKeown and Strimple), 1973. Office: Consultants in Animal Psychology 11151 Georgia Av Wheaton MD 20902

HAMILTON, GRACE TOWNS (MRS. HENRY COOKE HAMILTON), state legislator; b. Atlanta, Feb. 10, 1907; d. George Alexander and Nellie (McNair) Towns; A.B., Atlanta U., 1927; M.A., Ohio State U., 1929; m. Henry Cooke Hamilton, June 12, 1930; 1 dau., Eleanor Towns (Mrs. Charles Benjamin Payne, Jr.). Girls work sec. YWCA, Columbus, O., 1927-28, nat. program staff coll. and community divs., N.Y.C., 1936-43, cons. community relations, 1960-62; instr. Atlanta Sch. Social Work, 1928-29; instr. psychology Clark Coll., Atlanta, 1929-30, LeMoyne Coll., Memphis, 1930-34; dir. Survey White Collar and Skilled Negro Workers, Memphis, 1935-36; asso. dir. So. Regional Council, Atlanta, 1954-55; exec. dir. Atlanta Urban League, 1943-60; community relations cons. Hamilton Assos., Atlanta, 1961-67; dir. Atlanta Youth Council, 1966; mem. Ga. Ho. of Reps., 1965—. Vice chmn. Atlanta Charter Commn., 1971-73. Past mem. exec. com. Citizens Adv. Com. for Urban Renewal, Atlanta; mem. Ga. Gov.'s Commn. on Status Women; mem. Nat. Citizens Adv. Commn. Recreation and Natural Beauty, 1966; mem. exec. com. So. Regional Council; mem. Ga. Gov.'s Spl. Council on Family Planning, Fulton-DeKalb Hosp. Authority, 1971; mem. exec. bd. Ga. div. Nat. Conf. Christians and Jews. Mem. Fulton County Democratic Exec. Com., 1970—, Ga. Dem. Exec. Com., 1971—. Bd. dirs. Gate City Day Nursery Assn.; trustee Meharry Med. Coll., Atlanta U. Rosenwald fellow, 1947-48. Recipient numerous awards, 1965—, including Distinguished Achievement award Atlanta U. Alumnae Assn., 1965, certificate of appreciation Atlanta Urban League, 1970, citation for pub. service Sta. WSB-TV, 1972, Nonpartisan Community Service award Fulton County Republican Women, 1971, Good Neighbor award Nat. Conf. Christians and Jews, 1973, Law Day-Liberty Bell award Atlanta Bar Assn., 1974; named Alumnus of Year, Atlanta U., 1969. Mem. Nat. Order Women Legislators, Internat. Conf. Social Work, Nat. Conf. Social Welfare. Conglist. Address: 582 University Pl NW Atlanta GA 30314

HAMILTON, JEAN FRANCES, educator; b. Akron, O., Mar. 19, 1921; d. James and Katharine (Martin) Hamilton; B.S. in Edn., U. Akron, 1942; postgrad. U. Wis., summers 1943-44; M.A., U. Ia., 1947, Ph.D., 1950. Elementary tchr. Manchester (O.) Pub. Schs., 1942-43, Akron Pub. Schs., 1943-44; instr., supr. 5th grade Moorhead (Minn.) State Coll., 1944-46; instr. Exptl. Sch., U. Ia., 1946-50; asst. prof. elementary edn. Butler U., Indpls., 1950-51; asst. prof. Wayne State U., Detroit, 1951-59, asso. prof. elementary edn., 1959-65, prof., 1965—, dir. Nat. Def. Edn. Act Reading Inst., summer 1965. Prof., vis. lectr. U. R.I., summer 1966; cons. lang. arts suprs., Edinburgh, Scotland, 1970. Mem. task force on reading Mich. Dept. Pub. Instrn., 1966-67, chmn. subcom. reading, 1967-69, mem. communications skills com., 1972; mem. adv. com. Mich. Edn. Dept. Right to Read, 1973-74. Recipient certificate of recognition, certificate of merit Council Chs., 1963. Nat. Def. Edn. Act Title VI grantee U.S. Office Edn., 1965. Mem. Internat. (chmn. citation awards com. 1968-70, citation of appreciation 1972), Mich. (pres. 1961-62, editorial bd. Jour. 1972—) reading assns., Am. Assn. U. Profs., Am. Ednl. Research Assn., Nat. Council Tchrs. English, Pi Lambda Theta, Delta Kappa Gamma, Alpha Delta Pi. Contbr. articles to profl. jours. Home: 21110 Dartmouth Dr Southfield MI 48076 Office: Coll Edn Wayne State U Detroit MI 48202

HAMILTON, JEAN TYREE, civic worker, writer; b. Lexington, Mo., June 6, 1909; d. Clement and Maude (Duncan) Tyree; A.A., Christian Coll., 1929; B.S. in Edn., U. Mo., 1932, postgrad., 1932; m. Henry W. Hamilton, Feb. 24, 1940; children—James Tyree, Anne. Engaged in restoration Anderson House, Lexington, Mo., 1937; leader Girl Scouts U.S.A., 1943-51, mem. exec. council, 1954-60; leader Cub Scouts, 1951-53; chmn. Saline County Library Campaign, 1952; chmn. women's div. City Red Cross Drive, 1956, City Cancer Drive, 1957; chmn. Lewis and Clark Saline County Commn., 1966—; mem. Gov.'s Conf. on Natural Beauty, 1967; v.p., chmn. restoration com. Friends of Arrow Rock, 1960—; mem. Nat. Park Service Historic Sites Conf., 1968-69; mem. Com. for Restoration Saline County (Mo.) Courthouse, 1972—. Dep. assessor Lafayette County (Mo.), 1932-37, county treas., 1937-40; mem. gas rationing panel, 1942-46. Bd. dirs. Mar-Saline Retirement Home, 1973—. Mem. Am. Heritage Soc., Mo. Museums Assn., Mo., Ia., Okla., Ark. anthrop. socs., Mont., S.D., Neb., Mo. hist. socs., D.A.R. (regent 1950-52), Colonial Dames Am. (treas. 1970—), P.E.O. (pres. 1963-65). Democrat. Mem. Disciples of Christ. Author: Arrow Rock, Where Wheels Started West, 1963, rev. edit., 1973; Sections of Saline County History, 1967; Abel J. Vanmeter, His Park and His Diary, 1971; Sections Shelby County, Missouri History, 1973; (with Henry W. Hamilton) Remington Schuyler, Artist and Writer, 1969; The Sioux of the Rosebud, A History in Pictures, 1971; Clay Pipes From Pamplin, 1972; Embossed Copper Plates for Spiro, 1973. Home: 537 E Eastwood St Marshall MO 65340

HAMILTON, LILLIE BELLE DRAKE (MRS. VICTOR NORRIS HAMILTON), educator; b. College Park, Ga., July 15, 1919; d. Charley Grady and Lillie Vesta (Gullatt) Drake; B.A., Agnes Scott Coll., 1940; M.A., Middlebury Coll., 1948; postgrad. San Marcos U., Lima, Peru, 1950; m. Victor Norris Hamilton, May 20, 1953; children—Cynthia Belle, Hilary Phyllis. Tchr. Latin and Spanish, Fulton County Bd. Edn., Atlanta, 1940—, Women's Tchr. Tng. Coll., Tripoli, Libya, 1951-53, Agnes Scott Coll., Decatur, Ga., 1948-51; mem. gov.'s staff State of Ga., 1968-69. Mem. Spanish lang. seminar Nat. U. Mex., Mexico City, 1947. Chmn. Pan Am. Student Forum for Ga., 1946-48; mem. Ga. Adv. Council on Fgn. Langs., 1969—; sr. counsellor Nat. Spanish Honor Soc., 1972-73. Named Ga. Latin Tchr. of Yr., 1968-69. Mem. Jr. Classical League (Ga. Spanish Tchr. Yr. award 1972, chmn. Ga. chpt.; mem. nat. governing bd. 1974—), Am. Assn. Tchrs. Spanish and Portuguese (Master Tchr. 1967), Fgn. Lang. Assn. Ga. (pres. 1973—), Am. Assn. Tchrs. Spanish (pres. Ga. chpt. 1970-72), Women's Caucus on Modern Langs., Am. Classical League (ofcl. del. 6th Internat. Congress Classical Studies, Madrid 1974), S. Atlantic Modern Lang. Assn., Classical Assn. of Mid West and South, Ga. Assn. Educators, N.E.A. So. Lang. Conf. (mem. adv. council), Delta Kappa Gamma (pres. Beta Nu chpt. 1974—). Home: 6201 Roosevelt Rd Union City GA 30291 Office: College Park High School College Park GA 30337

HAMILTON, MARGARET LETITIA, pub. co. exec.; b. Galt, Ont., Can.; d. Norman and Myrtle Venetia (Townley) Hamilton. Business mgr. Evening Reporter, Galt, Ont., Can., 1949-52, asso. pub., gen. mgr., 1953-54; exec. asst. to gen. mgr. Thomson Newspapers Ltd., Toronto, Ont., 1955-56, exec. asst. to mng. dir., 1957-69, v.p., asst. mng. dir., 1969—; v.p. Thomson Newspapers, Inc., Des Plaines, Ill., 1969—; dir. Thomson-Brush-Moore Newspapers, Inc., Oxnard Pub. Co., San Gabriel Valley Tribune, Inc., Humboldt Newspapers, Inc., Replacement Sales Ltd., County Newspapers Ltd., Film Type Ltd., Moorefield Investments Ltd. Vice chmn. Canadian Advt. Adv. Bd. Bd. dirs. Advt. Bur. Canadian Daily Newspapers. Mem. Canadian Daily Newspapers Pubs. Assn. (dir. 1958—), Inst. Newspapers Controllers and Finance Officers, Ont. Provincial Dailies Assn., Canadian Press, Commonwealth Press Union, Internat. Press Inst. Clubs: Zonta (v.p., dir. 1961-69), Granite (Toronto); Country (Galt). Home: 9 Deer Park Crescent Toronto ON Canada also 64 Blair Rd Galt ON Canada Office: 65 Queen St W Thomson Bldg Toronto ON Canada

HAMILTON, MARION HOPE, ednl. adminstr.; b. N.Y.C., Nov. 16, 1913; d. John Sym and Christine Martin (McGinnis) Hamilton; B.A., Hollins Coll., 1935; M.A., U. Va., 1940, Ph.D., 1952. Sec. Cooper Union, N.Y.C., 1936-38; editorial asst. McGraw-Hill, 1940-41; advt. mgr. Bur. Publs. Columbia, 1941-42; club dir. A.R.C., Eng., 1942-46; dean students U. Richmond (Va.), 1946-50; asst. prof. English, Wellesley Coll., 1952-55; headmistress Ellis Sch., Pitts., 1955-63, Williams Sch., New London, Conn., 1963—. Bd. dirs. YMCA, Thames Sci. Center, New London Sch. Nursing. Mem. Nat. Assn. Prins. Schs. for Girls (pres. 1973-75). Democrat. Presbyn. Home: 6 Best View Rd Quaker Hill CT 06375 Office: Williams Sch Mohegan Av New London CT 06320

HAMILTON, MARY K., lawyer; b. Denver, Aug. 3, 1926; d. Henry H. and Helen (Clancy) Kerr; B.S., Simmons Coll., 1948; LL.B., U. Toledo, 1958; m. William A. Hamilton, June 15, 1957; children—Lucia Mary, Henry Kerr, John Allen, Peter Dempsey. Exec. sec. Toledo Bar Assn., 1955-58; admitted to Ohio bar, 1958; staff atty. Toledo Legal Aid Soc., 1959-61; mem. firm Cobourn, Yager, Smith & Falvey, Toledo, 1960-69; asst. trust officer Toledo Trust Co., 1969-70, trust officer, 1970-73, sr. trust officer, 1973—, mgr. probate div., 1971—. Mem. policy com. Toledo Legal Aid Soc., 1963-66. Discussion leader Republican. Workshops, Lucas County, O., 1963-66. Mem. Ohio, Toledo (sec. 1964-74) bar assns., Am. Inst. Banking, Nat. Assn. Women Bankers, U. Toledo Coll. Law Alumni Assn. (exec. com. 1971—), Jr. League Toledo. Home: 2647 Pemberton Dr Toledo OH 43606 Office: Toledo Trust Bldg Toledo OH 43603

HAMILTON, MARY TOWNSEND, educator; b. N.Y.C., Mar. 26, 1926; d. Landon McDuffie and Anna Treadwell (Blanton) Townsend; B.A., Wellesley Coll., 1946; Ph.D., U. Pa., 1969; m. Daniel C. Hamilton, May 29, 1954 (div. Apr. 1969). Instr. econs. Wharton Sch. U. Pa., Phila., 1958-59; research asst. Am. Bankers Assn., N.Y.C., 1947; econ. analyst Standard Oil Co. N.J., N.Y.C., 1947-52; research asso. U. Chgo., 1964-71; prof. finance Sch. Bus. Adminstrn. and Grad. Sch. Bus. Loyola U. at Chgo., 1972—, chmn. dept. finance, 1972—; price commr. Econ. Stabilization Program, 1972-73, vice-chmn. food adv. com., 1973; cons. Ford Motor Co., 1963-64, Chadwell, Keck, Kayser & McLaren law firm, Chgo., 1965, White House Task Force, 1967, Carnegie Commn. Higher Edn., Chgo. group, 1968, law firm Seyfarth, Shaw, Fairweather & Geraldson, 1967-71, Chgo. Council Human Relations, 1968-69, Commn. Founds. and Pvt. Philantrhopy, 1969-70, DUSOF constrn. combine, Weston, Ill., 1969-70, ad hoc adv. panel Equal Employment Opportunity Commn., 1971; lectr. U. Chgo. Tng. Program, Ill. State Employment Service, 1972. Bd. dirs. Chgo. Lying-in-Hosp., 1960—, v.p., 1962-65. Ford Found. fellow, 1959-60; Sr. Durant scholar, 1946. Jr. Durant Scholar, 1945. Mem. Am. Econ. Assn., Am. Finance Assn., Indsl. Relations Research Assn., Pi Gamma Mu. Home: 5807 Dorchester St Chicago IL 60637

HAMILTON, NANCY MILLER (MRS. RALPH E. HAMILTON), journalist; b. El Paso, Aug. 22, 1929; d. Harold Fred and Corinne (Miller) Miller; B.A., U. Tex., El Paso, 1949, M.A., 1954; m. Ralph E. Hamilton, June 15, 1968; stepchildren—James, Jeanne. Reporter, El Paso Times, 1950-59; pub. relations specialist El Paso Pub. Schs., 1959-68; reporter El Paso Herald-Post, 1972—. Mem. Delta Kappa Gamma. Democrat. Methodist. Home: 10329 Rushing Rd El Paso TX 79924 Office: PO Drawer 20 El Paso TX 79999

HAMILTON, PEARL BASS (MRS. WILLIAM BENJAMIN HAMILTON), oil operator; b. Claude, Tex., Sept. 3, 1892; d. Agesilaus Wilson and Rosa Ella (Reeder) Walker; student Poly. Coll. Ft. Worth, 1908-11, Belcourt Sem., Washington, 1911-13; m. William Benjamin Hamilton, Sept. 22, 1913; children—William Walker, John Martin. Pres., owner Elwyn, Inc., Wichita Falls, Tex., 1931-68; co-owner W.B. Hamilton Estate, Wichita Falls, 1968—. Sustaining mem. N.W. Tex. council Boy Scouts Am., 1971-72. Pres. Wichita Falls Women's Forum, 1941-43, Wichita Falls Symphony, 1952-55; pres. Bethania Hosp. Aux., Wichita Falls Gen. Hosp. Aux. Bd. dirs. Hopecrest Lodge, Alcoholics Anonymous. Named Mrs. Symphony, Wichita Falls Symphony, 1952-55, Woman of Year, Altrusa Club, 1958. Mem. Nat. Western Stock Show Assn. Denver, Am. Symphony Orch. League, Izaak Walton League, Nat. Trust for Historic Preservation, Wichita Falls C. of C. Methodist (pres. Women's Soc. Christian Service), Rotary Ann. Clubs: Altrusa, Wichita Falls Garden, Wichita Musicians, So. Meth. U. Mothers, Knife and Fork, Wichita, Wichita Falls Country, Farm and Ranch (hon.). Home: 1106 Brook St Wichita Falls TX 76301 Office: Hamilton Bldg Wichita Falls TX 76301

HAMILTON, PHEBE E. THORNE (MRS. WILLIAM GARNETT HAMILTON), civic worker; b. New Haven, Conn., Feb. 21, 1941; d. Lewis and Helen Presten (Ellis) Thorne; A.A., Bradford Jr. Coll., 1961; B.S., Columbia, 1964; m. William Garnett Hamilton, June 1, 1964; 1 step-son, William G., 1 adopted son, Lewis Thorne. Part-time registered nurse Roosevelt Hosp., N.Y.C., 1965-68; nurse Columbia Med. Center, N.Y.C., 1968-69, med. supr., part-time 1971—; owner, mgr. Uplands Farm, Keene Valley, N.Y. Asst. dir. Children's theater Henry St. Settlement, 1964—, bd. dirs., 1970—, also chmn. benefit com.; bd. dirs. Bradford Jr. Coll., 1970—; bd. govs. Westover Sch. Club: Keene Valley Country (dir.). Home: 55 Central Park W New York City NY 10023

HAMILTON, RHODA LILLIAN ROSEN, educator; b. Chgo., May 8, 1915; d. Reinhold August and Olga (Peterson) Rosen; student Moser Coll., Chgo., 1932-33; B.S. in Edn., U. Wis., 1953; postgrad., Ohio State U., 1959-60, Mich. State U., 1971, Yale, 1972, Loma Linda U., 1972; M.A.T., Rollins Coll., 1967; m. Douglas Edward Hamilton, Jan. 23, 1936 (div. Feb. 1952); children—Perry Douglas, John Richard, Exec. sec. to pres. Ansul Chem. Co., Marinette Wis., 1934-36; personnel counselor Burneice Larsons's Med. Bur., Chgo., 1954-56; adminstrv. asst. to Ernst C. Schmidt, Lake Geneva, Wis., 1956-58; dir. student employment Ohio State U., 1958-60; tchr. English to speakers of other langs., Istanbul, Turkey, 1960-65; counselor Groveland (Fla.) High Sch., 1965-68; counselor Overseas Dependents Sch., Okinawa, 1968—. Co-owner plumbing, heating bus., Marinette, Wis., 1943-49; journalist Rockford (Ill.) Morning Star, 1956-58, Istanbul (Turkey) A.P., 1960; vol. instr. U.S. citizenship classes, Okinawa, 1971-72. Mem. Am. Personnel and Guidance Assn., Nat. Vocational Guidance Assn., Assn. Measurement and Evaluation in Guidance, Am. Fedn. Govt. Employees (v.p. Okinawa dist.), Federally Employed Women (program chmn. Okinawa chpt.), Nat. Council Measurement in Edn., Am. Sch. Counselor Assn., Phi Delta Gamma. Mem. Order Eastern Star. Club: Ikebana Internat. Author poetry on Middle East, 1959-64. Home: 255 E Waldo St Groveland FL 32736 Office: DOD ODS Mercy Elementary School PO Box M-143 APO San Francisco CA 96248

HAMILTON, SEENA MADELINE (MRS. S. K. FINEBERG), broadcaster, writer, children's travel exec.; b. N.Y.C., Feb. 8, 1928; d. Leonard K. and Helen H. (Brahms) Hamilton; student Coll. William and Mary, 1943-47; m. S.K. Fineberg, Aug. 18, 1950; 1 son, Bryan Scott. With press dept. WTOP, Washington, 1948-49; dir. advt. and pub. relations E.B. Marks, pubs., N.Y.C., 1949-51; sr. editor Apt. Life Mag., Inc., N.Y.C., 1951-52; asso. editor Today's Family, N.Y.C., 1952-54; editor, pub. Hotel Gazette, N.Y.C., 1954-61; pres. Gulliver's Trails, children's and conv. travel service, N.Y.C., since 1961—. Cons. and lectr. on youth market; producer, co-host radio program You and Your Health, WMCA, N.Y.C. Founder, chmn. Easter Bowl Jr. Indoor Tennis Championships, 1968. Mem. U.S. Lawn Tennis Assn., N.Y.C. Conv. and Visitors Bur. Clubs: Armonk (N.Y.) Tennis; Jockey (Miami, Fla.). Author: N.Y. on the Family Plan, 1965. Contbr. articles to various publs. Home: 450 E 63d St New York City NY 10021 Office: 1161 York Av New York City NY 10021

HAMILTON, SYLVIA WALINOW (MRS. RAY A. HAMILTON), pub. relations exec.; b. Kansas City, Kan., Nov. 24, 1919; d. Joseph and Eva (Lasik) Walinow; student Kansas City (Kan.) Jr. Coll., 1936-38; m. Ray A. Hamilton, Nov. 20, 1948. Dir. pub. service Radio Sta. KCKN, Kansas City, Kan., 1945-48; dir. pub. relations 5-County Heart Am. United Campaign, Kansas City, Mo., 1948-58, asso. dir. in charge pub. relations, 1958-73; nat. pub. relations dir. V.F.W. Aux., Kansas City, 1973—. Pub. relations cons. to study of Bay Area United Crusade, San Francisco, 1965. Recipient Silver Anvil award for best program in philanthropic field Am. Pub. Relations Assn., 1958. Mem. Kansas City Pub. Relations Soc. (pres. 1960, dir. 1965—), Kansas City Indsl. Editors Assn. (pres. 1960-61), Women's C. of C., Advt. and Sales Club, United Community Funds and Councils Am. (nat. pub. relations com. 1956—, chmn. midwest regional conf. 1962), Theta Sigma Phi. Home: 2138 Normandy Lane Kansas City KS 64116 Office: 406 W 34th ST Kansas City MO 64111

HAMILTON, VALDENE DELAVAN (MRS. JESSE E. HAMILTON), financial planner; b. Brownfield, Tex., Apr. 4, 1925; d. John Futher and Edna Bessie (Aytes) Dumas; student Tex. Tech U., 1965-67; m. James Henry DeLavan, Nov. 23, 1944 (dec.); children—James Neil, Lonnie Clark; m. 2d, Jesse E. Hamilton, Aug. 8, 1964. Partner, DeLavan Bros., Lubbock, Tex., 1954-73; exec. v.p., sec., treas., dir. Financial Planners of Am., Inc., Lubbock, 1970-73; v.p., sec., treas., dir. Mgmt. Co. of Am., Inc., Lubbock, Financial Plans Data Corp., Lubbock, W.L. Jenkins & Co., Inc., Lubbock. Den mother Cub Scouts Am., Lubbock, 1960-61, Lubbock Pub. Schs. P.T.A., 1954-67. Mem. Internat. Assn. Financial Planners, Assn. Cons. Actuaries, Hammond Organ Soc. (v.p. 1960-63), Mem. Ch. of Christ (mem. estate and trust council 1967-69). Home: 3511 39th St Lubbock TX 79413 Office: Suite 33 Briercroft Office Park Lubbock TX 79412

HAMILTON, VELMA FERN BELL, educator; b. Pontotoc, Miss., Feb. 28, 1910; d. Walter and Melvina Grace (Allen) Bell; A.B., Beloit Coll., 1930; M.A., U. Wis., 1933; m. Henry Lemuel Hamilton, June 18, 1934; children—Harry Lemuel, Patricia Grace (Mrs. Maung Byi),

Muriel Elizabeth. With Bennett Coll., Greensboro, N.C., 1930-36; with Tougaloo (Miss.) Coll., 1939-42; with Madison (Wis.) Area Tech. Coll., 1950—, chmn. gen. studies, 1970—. Cons.-examiner N. Central Assn. Colls. and Secondary Schs., 1969—. Mem. Nat. Bd. for Home and Ministries, United Chs. of Christ, 1971—. Adv. bd. YWCA, Madison, 1970—; mem. state bd. Wis. Arts Council, 1973—; corporate mem. bd. Meth. Hosp., Madison, 1968—. Named Citizen of Year, Madison Newspaper Guild, 1962. Mem. Wis. Adult Edn. Assn. (bd.), Delta Kappa Gamma. Club: Zonta (Madison). Home: 918 Pontiac Trail Madison WI 53711 Office: 211 N Carroll St Madison WI 53703

HAMLETT, IONA CUYLER, psychologist; b. Austin, Tex., Dec. 12, 1901; d. Robert Henry and Sarah Iona (McBryde) Cuyler; A.B., U. Tex., 1922, A.M., 1923; Ph.D., U. Ind., 1934; m. G. W. Deluz Hamlett, Aug. 29, 1923 (div. 1934); children—Iona Helen (Mrs. James Richard Mensch), Sarah Suzanne (Mrs. Gordon M. Haggard). Ednl., clin. psychologist Ft. Wayne (Ind.) State Hosp. and Tng. Center, 1934-72, dir. dept. psychol. services, 1966-72; pvt. practice psychology, Ft. Wayne, 1972—. Fellow Am. Assn. on Mental Deficiency (chmn. Gt. Lakes region 1963), Am. Psychol. Assn., Internat. Council Psychologists; mem. Ind. Psychol. Assn. (diplomate clin. psychology), Allen County Assn. Mental Health. Presbyn. Home: Box 5131 Hazelwood Sta Fort Wayne IN 46805 Office: 3010 E State Blvd Fort Wayne IN 46805

HAMLIN, LEONORA HOUSTON (MRS. CLYDE HAMLIN), educator; b. Mobile, Ala.; d. Paul Leonard and Isabella (Jackson) Houston; B.S. in Sociology, Howard U., 1944; M.S. in Social Work, Boston U., 1946; postgrad. Wayne State U.; Ph.D. in Edn., U. Mich., 1971; m. Clyde Alfonza Hamlin, Jan. 1, 1950; children—Teri Denise, Karla, Kurt. Med. social worker Boston City Hosp., 1946-49; social worker Downriver (Mich.) Family Service, 1950-54; sch. social worker River Rouge (Mich.) schs., 1954-57; tchr. Westwood Community Schs., Inkster, Mich., 1957-61, sch. social worker, 1961-72; sch. social work cons. Mich. Dept. Edn., 1972—; part-time instr. Wayne State U., 1967—; vis. lectr. U. Mich., 1968—, cons. Bur. Sch. Service, 1970—. Bd. dirs. Mich. Council Family Relation, 1954-62, treas., 1957-60; bd. spl. project Neighborhood Service Orgn., 1964-67, social work supr., 1966-67; bd. dirs. Western Wayne County YWCA, 1964-68, co-chmn. county program com., 1963-67, v.p., 1965-66; bd. dirs. Northwestern Child Guidance Clin., 1963—, Family and Neighborhood Services, 1972—. Mem. Mich. (chmn. River Rouge legislative com., mem. state service com. 1965-67, tchrs. conf. regional planning com. 1965-66, dist. del. rep, assembly 1964), Dearborn Dist. 8 (pres. 1960-62, membership chmn. 1963-65) edn. assns., Mich. Sch. Social Workers Assn. (region A treas. 1955-56, sec. 1963-64, state corr. sec. 1965-67), Midwest Sch. Social Work Assn. (dir. 1972—, pres. 1973-74), Assn. Supervision and Curriculum Devel., Nat. Assn. Social Workers, Acad. Certified Social Workers, Alpha Kappa Alpha (chpt. pres. 1960-61, treas. 1964-72). Democrat. Home: 27206 Kitch Av Inkster MI 48141

HAMLIN, ROXIE MONA (MRS. RONALD A. HAMLIN), therapist; b. Presque Isle, Me., Oct. 21, 1946; d. Rodney F. and Faylene Alice (Nickerson) Black; B.S. cum laude, Boston U., 1968; m. Ronald A. Hamlin, Dec. 22, 1967. Cons. spl. edn. Am. schs., Nurnberg, West Germany, 1970; staff therapist John T. Berry Rehab. Center, North Reading, Mass., 1970-72, head therapist, 1972-74; occupational therapist Project Me. Stream, Child Devel. and Family Resource Center, Cumberland Center, Me., 1974—. Pvt. practice evaluations and treatment, Salem, N.H., 1971. Mem. Am., Mass., No. New Eng. occupational therapy assns. Home: C-14 Juniper East Yarmouth ME 04096 Office: Project Me Stream Main St Cumberland Center ME 04021

HAMM, MARIE ROBERSON (MRS. STANLEY RYAN KETCHAM), author; b. Mpls., May 16, 1917; d. Gustav J. and Marie (Anderson) Norstrom; student Barnard Coll., 1935-36; m. Stanley Ryan Ketcham, Nov. 24, 1970. Accessory buyer Best & Co., N.Y.C., 1937-43; asso. editor Harper's Bazaar, N.Y.C., 1943-45; founder, owner, mgr. Gourmet Accessory Shops, N.Y.C. and Greenwich, Conn., 1946-52; pub. relations account exec. Robinson Hannagan, N.Y.C., 1953-54; with Batten, Barton, Durstine & Osborne, N.Y.C., 1954-70, account supr., 1970. Mem. Nat. Home Fashions League, Am. Women in Radio and TV. Author: The Chafing Dish Cook Book, 1949; The Casserole Cook Book, 1951; The Complete Barbecue Book, 1952; The Complete Small Appliance Cook Book, 1952; The Meat Cookbook, 1953; The Poultry Cookbook, 1954; The Buffet Cookbook, 1954; The Famous American Recipes Cook Book, 1955; The Second Chafing Dish Cookbook, 1963; Money in the Bank Cookbook, 1968; Fondue Cookbook, 1970; Blender Cookbook, 1971; Italian Cookbook, 1972; The Natural Foods Cookbook, 1973; Gifts from Your Kitchen Cookbook, 1973. Editor expanded Woman's Day Ency. of Cookery, 22 vols., 1973-74. Contbr. articles to mags. Address: 360 E 72d St New York City NY 10021

HAMM, RUTH THELMA (MRS. JAMES JUSTIN HAMM), clubwoman; b. Torrington, Wyo., July 3, 1915; d. Frank Leslie and Harriet Belle (Merwin) Bitting; m. James Justin Hamm, July 22, 1936. With stock and bond dept. First Nat. Bank, Miami, Fla., 1934; bookkeeper Prairie Farms, Bloomington, Ill., 1939-40; mgr. Lettershop, Bloomington, 1940-45; reporter The Daily Pantagraph, Bloomington, 1940-44; with Dept. Labor, Div. Placement and Unemployment Compensation, Bloomington, 1945-50; with Office Rent stblzn., Bloomington, 1950-52, acting area rent dir., 1952. Chmn. fund raising drives A.R.C., 1940-41, Community Chest, 1955-56, Hudson Twp. chpt. Am. Cancer Soc., 1958-59, United Fund, 1960-62; leader 4-H Club, 1954-64; vice-chmn. exec. com. Christian Rural Overseas Program, McLean County, Ill., 1973-75. Trustee, Tamassee D.A.R. Sch. (S.C.), 1968-74. Named outstanding 4-H Club leader, McLean County, Ill., 1964; recipient endowment Pin Children Am. Revolution, 1965, good citizenship medal S.A.R., 1966; mem. D.A.R. (chpt. regent, 1956-58, state chmn) The Flag of the U.S.A. com., 1959-61, state dir., 1961-63, state registrar, 1963-65, state regent, 1967-69, nat. vice chmn. sch. com., 1969-71, pres. state officers club, 1969-70, state chmn. Bells on Independence Day, 1967-69, v.p. Gen. Nat. Soc., 1969-72, sec. v.p. gen. club, 1970-71, mem. nat. resolutions com., 1972-74, chmn. Ill. State Room in Meml. Continental Hall, Washington, 1969-73, Children of the Am. Revolution (sr. state pres.; 1965-67, nat. vice. chmn., 1965-68), Homemakers Extension Assn. (pres. McLean County, Ill. 1959-62), Nat. Soc. Daus. Founders and Patriots Am. (councilor Ill. chpt. 1969-72, chmn. membership com. 1970-73, chmn. preservation and restoration records com. 1973—), Colonial Daus. of the Seventeenth Century (rec. sec. 1973—), Nat. Trust for Historic Preservation, Internat. Platform Assn., Ill. State Hist. Soc., Friends of the Mus. (life mem.), Ill. State Geneal. Soc. (charter mem.), Bloomington Normal Geneal. Soc., Smithsonian Assos. Republican. Presbyn. Editor: Prairie State News, 1965-67, Historic Illinois, 1968. Wrote and produced sesquicentennial pageant From Wilderness to Statehood, McLean County Fair, 1968. Contbr. articles to D.A.R. mag., 1969. Home: 101 S Broadway Hudson IL 61748

HAMMARGREN, BETTY LOU CECELIA, librarian; b. Kilkenny, Minn., Dec. 17, 1926; d. Edward Richard and Elizabeth Christine (Mach) Hammargren; B.S., Coll. St. Catherine, 1948; postgrad. U Notre Dame, 1951-52. Cataloger, U. Santa Clara (Cal.), 1948-50, U. Notre Dame (Ind.), 1950-53, Ramsey County Library, St. Paul, 1953; exec. sec. Golden Rule Dept. Store, St. Paul, 1954; reference dept. asst. Mpls. Pub. Library, 1954-55, asst. brs., 1955-58, cataloger, 1958—. Research librarian Normandin Publs., St. Paul, 1968—. Mem. Cath. (chmn. parish and lending libraries sect. 1967-68), Ch. and Synagogue (pres. 1972-73), Am., Minn. library assns., St. Joseph Hosp. Aux., Mpls. Pub. Library Staff Assn. (pres. 1973-74), Am. Legion Aux., Retreats Internat. Roman Catholic. Club: National Travel. Editor: Parish and Lending Libraries News, 1967-68, Parish and Community Library News, 1973—. Home: 1440 Randolph Av St Paul MN 55105 Office: 300 Nicollet Mall Minneapolis MN 55401

HAMMEKE, PATRICIA LOUISE (MRS. MICHAEL DENNIS HAMMEKE), occupational therapist; b. Indpls., Mar. 7, 1948; d. Charles William and Mary Alice (Kenny) Barth; B.S., Ind. U., 1970; m. Michael Dennis Hammeke, July 4, 1970; 1 son, Joseph William. Occupational therapist in psychiatry Creighton Meml. St. Joseph Hosp., Omaha, 1970-71, supr. occupational therapy, 1971—. Juvenile ct. probation officer, Omaha, 1970-71; mem. Douglas County Mental Health Adv. Bd., Omaha, 1973—. Mem. World Fedn. Occupational Therapists, Am. (steering com. in psychiatry 1971—, chmn. spl. interest group in psychiatry, region VII 1971—, mem. continuing certification task force in psychiatry 1974—), Neb. (pres. 1972-73, state chmn. council on practice 1973—) occupational therapy assns., Ind. U. Alumni Assn., Phi Theta Epsilon. Home: 5107 Dodge St Omaha NE 68132 Office: 2305 10th St Omaha NE 68108

HAMMER, JANE AMELIA ROSS (MRS. PHILIP GIBBON HAMMER), violinist; b. Charlotte, N.C., Apr. 9, 1916; d. Otho Bescent and Lucy (Harris) Ross; B.A., U. N.C., 1936, M.A. (Kenan fellow), 1937; postgrad. Radcliffe Coll., 1938-39, New Eng. Conservatory, 1938-39; m. Philip Gibbon Hammer, Aug. 27, 1937; children—Philip, Thomas Ross, Michael Levering. Tchr. philosophy Spelman Coll., Atlanta, 1946-58; violinist Atlanta Symphony, 1947-52; charter mem. N.C. Symphony and Symphony Quartet, Chapel Hill, 1934-37; program dir. Overseas Edn. Fund U.S. League Women Voters, Washington, 1962-63, mem. staff Edn. Fund, 1964-65, trustee, 1965-68, chmn. Nat. Inner-City Citizenship Edn. Project, Washington, 1966-73; pres., violinist Friday Morning Music Club, Washington, 1973—. Pres. Margaret Mitchell Sch. P.T.A., Atlanta, 1960-61; gen. chmn. Atlanta Orgns. Assisting Schs., for peaceful integration, 1960-61. Mem. Women's Nat. Democratic Club, Washington, 1962—. Bd. dirs. Trinity Sch., Atlanta, 1960-61; trustee Dag Hammarskjold Coll., Columbia, Md., 1969-73. Recipient Presidential pen D.C. League Women Voters, 1965; Good Housekeeping mag. Civics award, 1962. Mem. Ga. Philosophy Assn. (sec. 1949-52), So. Soc. Philosophy of Religion, Hegel Soc. So. Soc. Philosophy and Psychology, Phi Beta Kappa, Chi Omega. Club: Country (Bethesda, Md.). Home: 5152 Manning Pl Washington DC 20016

HAMMER, LILLIAN, poet; b. Lodz, Poland; d. Mendel and Rachel (Spigelman) Ries; ed. coll.; m. Liola Ris; children—Ruth Mannal Aronson, Helen Hammer. Author: Waves of Fire, 1972; also numerous individual published poems; works represented in anthologies. Recipient numerous awards in internat. and nat. poetry competitions. Mem. Found. Fellows, World Poetry Soc. Inter-continental, World Poets and Resource Center, Ill. Poetry Soc., Soc. Lit. Designates of title of Danae (life), Internat. Clober Poetry Assn. Home: 2820 Bronx Park E Bronx NY 10467

HAMMERL, JEAN NEWELL, editor; b. Detroit, Feb. 16, 1944; d. Norman and Aileen Elizabeth (Spangler) Hammerl; student U. Mich., 1962-63; B.A. in Journalism, Wayne State U., 1968. Publs. editor Detroit Macomb Hosp. Assn., 1966-68; advt. copywriter S.S. Kresge Co., Detroit, 1968; plant editor Chrysler Corp., Highland Park, Mich., 1968-70; publs. editor Wayne State U. Sch. Medicine, Detroit, 1970—. Cons. sci. editing. Mem. Women in Communications, Inc., Am. Alumni Council, Detroit Press Club. Home: 1960 Golfview Dr Troy MI 48084 Office: 540 E Canfield Av Detroit MI 48201

HAMMOND, CARVEL BIGHAM LEE (MRS. A.R. HAMMOND), author, artist; b. Mpls., Apr. 2, 1910; d. Abraham Lincoln and Rebecca (Lung) Bigham; student Mpls. Sch. Art. U. Minn.; m. Kermit Anton Lee, May 18, 1934 (dec.); children—Kermit Anton, Lorita Gail; m. 2d, A.R. Hammond, Jan. 15, 1970. Art dir., advt. mgr. illus. lecture artist, conv. booth planner, 1932; designer ofcl. seals for religious and charitable orgns., clubs; designer murals; display coordinator; designer workbooks, conv. booth, fair exhibits for temperance groups, materials for N.E.A., ednl. materials for numerous publishers, aids to train handicapped children U. Minn., others. Mem. W.C.T.U., Federated Garden Clubs Am., Internat. Platform Assn. Lutheran. Author, artist: Art Activities, 1956; The Art Guide, 1959, Tender Tyrant, 1961; The Library Bulletin Board Guide, 1965. Artist, illustrator: The Kindergarten, 1-6th Grade logs; Count Fingers, Count Toes; Creative Art Ideas—Grades Kindergarten thru 6th; Fingerplay Approach to Dramatization; Bessie, the Messy Penguin; Johnny Hop's Adventure; Porkadot; Finger Playtime; Springboards to Science; Creative Handwork Ideas; Wading Into Science; Learning How to Use The Five Senses; Discovering Science Through Experiments; Teaching Resources for the Kindergarten-Primary Teacher. Author (with Lorita Lee), artist: The Bulletin Board Guide series, also Instructor's Manual; The Sunday Sch. Bulletin Board Guide; The Decoration Guide; the Crafts Guide Series; The Art Project Guide Series, The Health Bulletin Board Guide, The Music Guide '68. Contbr. to mags., newspapers, ednl. publs. Home: 7329 Colfax Av S Minneapolis MN 55423

HAMMOND, JANE LAURA, librarian; b. nr. Nashua, Ia.; d. Frank D. and Pauline (Flint) Hammond; B.A., U. Dubuque, 1950; M.S., Columbia, 1952; J.D., Villanova U., 1965. Catalogue, Harvard Law Library, 1952-54; asst. librarian Villanova (Pa.) U. Sch. Law, 1954-62, librarian, 1962—, prof. law, 1965—; admitted to Pa. bar, 1965. Adj. prof. Drexel U., 1971—. Mem. Am. Assn. Law Libraries (sec. 1965-70, v.p., pres.-elect 1974—), Council Nat. Library Assns. (sec.-treas. 1971-72), Spl. Libraries Assn., Am. Library Assn., Pa. Bar Assn., P.E.O. Episcopalian. Office: Villanova U Villanova PA 19085

HAMMOND, MRS. JOHNSON F. (LOUISE E. SELLERGREN), singer; b. Colorado Srings, Colo.; d. Casper and Hannah (Henning) Sellergren; grad. (scholar in voice) Chgo. Mus. Coll., 1927; m. Johnson F. Hammond, Feb. 25, 1935 (dec.). Pub. appearances lyric soprano, active in church, radio, concert, light opera, 1922-35; as protege of Estelle Leibling, appeared in number of Shubert prodns., N.Y.C., 1930; with Chgo. Operetta Co., 1934. Mem. Nat. Soc. Arts and Letters (Chgo. pres. 1956; nat. trustee 1962—), McDowell Soc. Allied Arts (program chmn. 1958-60), Ill. Opera Guild, Lakeview Music Soc., Musicians Club of Women (dir.), Evanston Lyric Opera Guild (dir.), Phi Mu Gamma (pres. Chgo. 1956). Clubs: Arts (Washington, Chgo.); Edgewater Golf, Arts, University. Address: 5555 Sheridan Rd Chicago IL 60640

HAMMOND, LUCY SADIE MARIE TAYLOR (MRS. ROBERT E. HAMMOND), extension agt.; b. Junction City, Ky., June 16, 1927; d. George and Mary Hannah (Dunaway) Taylor; B.S., Ky. State Coll., 1950; M.S., Fla. A. and M. U., 1963; M.S. in Community Devel., U. Louisville, 1974; m. Robert E. Hammond, June 7, 1958; 1 son, Robert Edwin II. Staff dietician VA Hosp., Canandaigua, N.Y., 1952-53, head dietician, 1953-57; head dietician, acting asst. chief Vets. Hosp., Cin., 1957-58; chief dietician Fla. A. and M. Hosp., Tallahassee, 1958-66; vol. cons. Fla. Hosp. Assn., Fla. A. and M. Hosp., 1966-67; asst. county extension home econs. agt., Leon County, Fla., 1966; area extension agt. Blue Grass area U. Ky. Extension Service, 1967-70; extension program coordinator for foods and nutrition U. Ky., Lexington, 1970—. Bd. dirs. Neighborly Orgn. Women, Inc., 1968-70. Recipient 1st Place award Epsilon Sigma Phi, 1969. Mem. Am., Ky. (sec. 1970-72) dietetic assns., Nutrition Edn. Soc., Lexington Montessori Soc., Ky. Nutrition Council. Baptist. Home: 1141 Brairwood St Lexington KY 40507 Office: 1312 S Lime St Lexington KY 40506

HAMMOND, MAUDIE THOMAS, realtor, dancer, critic; b. Rexburg, Ida.; d. Ward J. and Loretta (Eckersell) Thomas; student Mills Coll., 1957, various courses U. Cal., Berkeley, 1963—; m. M.H. Hammond, June 21, 1946 (div. Sept. 1964); children—Dianne Simone, Matthew Henry. Profl. dancer, N.Y.C., 1942-46; tchr., owner Maudie Hammond Sch. Dance, Orinda, Cal., 1959-64; owner The Hammond Real Estate Co., Orinda, Cal., 1964—. Performer on local TV variety and talk shows, 1945-72. Active Girl, Boy scouts Am., Brownies, P.T.A., 1954-60. Mem. Contra Costa Bd. Realtors, Nat. Orgn. Women, League Women Voters, Cal. Acad. Scis., KQED Ednl. Tv. Office: 2 Vashell Way Orinda CA 94563

HAMMOND, MILDRED ALLERTON, librarian; b. N.Y.C., Sept. 2, 1909; d. Joseph Irish and Mary (Stoeth) Hammond; A.B., Hunter Coll., 1930; B.S., Columbia, 1933. Library clk. Standard & Poors, Inc., N.Y.C., 1933-34; librarian Goldman, Sachs & Co., 1934-39; tchr. pub. schs., N.Y.C., 1930-32, 1939-40; reference librarian Queens Boro Pub. Library, 1940-41; post librarian U.S. Army, Ft. Hamilton, N.Y., 1941-46, chief librarian, service club dir., Alaska, 1946-49, post librarian, Ft. Jay, N.Y., 1949-55; staff librarian 1st U.S. Army, Governor's Island, N.Y., 1955-65; chief library br. FAA, Eastern region, 1965—. Mem. A.L.A., N.Y. Library Assn., Am. Soc. Information Scis., Spl. Libraries Assn., Booksellers League of N.Y. Home: 86-43 123d St Richmond Hill NY 11418 Office: FAA Eastern Region Library J F Kennedy Internat Airport Jamaica NY 11430

HAMMONTREE, MARIE GERTRUDE, author; b. Jefferson County, Ind., June 19, 1913; d. Harry Clay and Hattie Agnes (Means) Hammontree; B.A., Butler U., Indpls., 1949. With Bobbs-Merrill Co., Indpls., 1934-42, Ind. U. Med. Center, Indpls., 1942-48, Travel Enterprises, Inc., N.Y.C., 1949-50, U.S. Dept. Justice, Indpls., 1950—; author: Will and Charlie Mayo, Doctor's Boys, 1954; A.P. Giannini, Boy of San Francisco, 1956; Albert Einstein, Young Thinker, 1961; Mohandas Gandhi, Boy of Principle, 1966; Walt Disney, Young Movie Maker, 1969. Mem. Nat. League Am. Pen Women, Women in Communications, Sigma Tau Delta, Phi Kappa Phi. Home: 930 N Bosart Av Indianapolis IN 46201

HAMPERS, LAVONNE JOYCE OHL (MRS. CONSTANTINE L. HAMPERS), lawyer; b. Mt. Vernon, Ind., Sept. 30, 1938; d. Arthur Joseph and Ruby Fern (Lopp) Ohl; student Ind. U., 1956-59, Northwestern U., 1959-61; LL.M., Boston U. Sch. Law, 1969; LL.B., Boston Coll., 1967, J.D., 1969; m. Constantine L. Hampers, May 16, 1964; children—Louis, Mark, Douglas. Gen. mgr. Staff Research Asso. and Indsl. Systems, Inc., Chgo., 1959-64; admitted to Mass. bar, 1967; atty. Wilson, Curran, Malkasian & Winward, Boston, 1968—. Mem. League Women Voters (mem. com. 1973), Am., Mass., Boston bar assns., Women's Aux. Greek Orthodox. Club: Country (Wellesley Hills, Mass.). Office: 19 Congress St Boston MA 02109

HAMPSON, ZENA (MRS. THOMAS M. HAMPSON, PSEUDONYM ZENA COLLIER), writer; b. London, Eng., Jan. 21, 1926; d. Ben and Rebecca (Capinsky) Feldman; m. Lou Shumsky, May 3, 1945 (div. 1967); children—Jeffrey A., Paul E.; m. 2d, Thomas M. Hampson, Dec. 30, 1969. Free-lance writer, 1953—; short stories pub. in mags., including McCalls, Woman's Day, Canadian Home Jour., Alfred Hitchcock Mystery Mag. lit. mags., including Prairie Schooner, Univ. Rev., Lit. Rev., articles for various mags.; tchr. writers workshop, adult edn., Rochester, 1968—. Mem. Friends Univ. of Rochester Libraries. Bd. dirs. Friends Rochester Pub. Library, 1967-70. Mem. Women in Communications, Mystery Writers Am., Am. Civil Liberties Union (state dir. 1966-67, Genesee Valley chpt. dir. 1966-67, 74—). Author: (books for children; under pseudonymn Jane Collier) The Year of the Dream, 1962, A Tangled Web, 1967; (with Lou Shumsky) First Flight, 1962, Shutterbug, 1963. Address: 83 Berkeley St Rochester NY 14607

HAMPTON, CAROLYN HUTCHINS (MRS. CAROL DEAN HAMPTON), educator; b. Glen Alpine, N.C., Dec. 11, 1936; d. Hugh Caldwell and Mary Eleanor (Patton) Hutchins; B.S. cum laude, Appalachina State U., 1959; M.S. in Zoology, U. Tenn., 1961, Ph.D. in Zoology (AEC fellow 1961-63), U. Tenn., 1963; m. Carol Dean Hampton, Dec. 22, 1963; 1 son, Frederick Bennett. Asst. prof. U. N.C., Charlotte, 1963-65; asst. prof. biology Longwood Coll., Farmville, Va., 1965-66; asso. prof. sci. edn. East Carolina U., Greenville, N.C., 1966—. Cons. to book cos. and various sch. systems, 1966—. Dir. NSF Inst. for High Sch. Biology Tchrs., 1969-70. Mem. Am. Inst. Biol. Scis., Assn. Southeastern Biologists, N.C. Acad. Scis., Am. Assn. U. Profs., Sigma Xi. Lutheran (pres. Luth. Ch. Women 1974). Contbr. articles to profl. jours. Home: Route 7 Box 206 Greenville NC 27834

HAMPTON, LUCILE PAQUIN SMITH (MRS. LAWRENCE CHARLES HAMPTON), pub. relations exec., artist; b. Dubuque, Ia., Jan. 7, 1904; d. Albert Hugo and Lola (Lichtenberger) Smith; student Dubuque Acad. Music (Ia.), 1911-21; diploma Chgo. Acad. Fine Arts, 1923; postgrad. Pasadena City Coll., 1947-48, 64, 67-68; U. Cal. at Los Angeles, 1965-66; B.A. in Art, Cal. State U. at Los Angeles, 1973; m. Lawrence Charles Hampton, Dec. 16, 1930 (dec. Apr. 4, 1960); children—Lawrence Charles, Nancy (Mrs. Merle Willis Asper, Jr.), Elizabeth Mary (Mrs. John Erskine). Artist advt. dept. Union Lithographing Co., Little Rock, 1923-24; art dir. advt. dept. M. Rich & Bros. Co., Atlanta, 1924-25; head fashion layout artist advt. dept. May Co., Los Angeles, 1925-29; sr. artist advt. dept. David Jones Ltd., Sydney, Australia, 1929-30; tchr. art essentials and history of art Anoakia Sch. Girls, Arcadia, Cal., 1963-66; substitute tchr. San Marino (Cal.) Unified Sch. Dist., 1973—; free lance artist Lucile Hampton Greeting Cards, San Marino, Cal., 1960—. Mem. Girl Scout Leader's Club, San Marino, Cal., 1948-56, pres., 1950-51, leader troop, 1948-56; active bd. P.T.A., Stoneman Sch., San Marino, 1942, South Pasadena (Cal.) High Sch., 1950-55. Mem. P.E.O. (chpt. pres. 1955-56), D.A.R. (chpt. regent 1960-61), Children of the Am. Revolution (sr. pres. chpt. 1958-64, social dir. cotillion ball 1958-59), Am. Assn. U. Women, Kappa Pi, Gamma Tau. Republican. Presbyn. Clubs: Euterpe Opera Reading (bd. dirs. 1956-59), Women's Athletic (Los Angeles); Pacific Coast; San Marino Women's. Home: 2775 Mesa Verde Dr East #G-106 Costa Mesa CA 92626

HAMPTON, LUCILLE CHARLOTTE, sculptor, painter; b. Bklyn., July 22, 1922; d. Harold Highfield and Lucy Jane Montgomery (Kelly) Hampton; student Columbia Bible Coll., 1948-49; Asso. Studies, Bklyn. Coll., 1954; student N.Y. U., 1956-57, 67. Sculptor-painter Am. West; designed Foxburg (Pa.) War Meml., 1938; nat. exhibits: Catharine Lorillard Wolfe Art Club, 1969, 72, 73, Hudson Valley Art Assn., 1970, 73, Allied Artists Am., N.A.D., 1971, Am. Artists Profl. League, Lever House, 1973, 74; bronze sculptures, oil paintings in pvt. internat. collections; permanent sculpture exhibit Kennedy Gallery, N.Y.C., Maintrail Galleries, Ariz., Hampton Galleries, Ariz., Galeria del Sol, N.M.; pvt. tchr. sculpting; lectr. Am. West art and bronze casting. Recipient Mrs. John Newington award Hudson Valley Art Assn., 1970; award Council Am. Artists Socs., 1972, 74. Mem. Am. Artists Profl. League (Anna Hyatt Huntington award 1973), Catharine Lorillard Wolfe Art Club. Home: 734 Ocean Av Brooklyn NY 11226 Office: 2 Broadway Room 1161 New York City NY 10004

HAMRICK, MARJORIE EVELYN VANDILL (MRS. FORREST G. HAMRICK), civic worker; b. Pine Bluff, Ark., Mar. 12, 1921; d. William Alphonse and Permelia (Medlen) Vandill; student Vanderbilt U., 1940-42; B.A., Barnard Coll., 1946; m. Forrest G. Hamrick, Apr. 14, 1955. Sec. to chief personnel dept. Pine Bluff (Ark.) Arsenal, 1942-44; with Dept. Polit. and Security Council Affairs, UN, N.Y.C., 1946-56, asst. polit. officer, 1950-56, assigned UN Spl. Commn. on Balkans, Salonika and Athens, Greece, 1947-49. Bd. dirs. Va. Day Nursery, Inc., N.Y.C., 1957—, pres., 1961-63, treas., 1966-70; com. mem. Yorkville Community Assn., Inc., N.Y.C., 1957—, bd. dirs., 1961—, chmn. dance com., 1969-70; corr. sec. Garden Club, East Hampton, N.Y., 1970-73, pres., 1973—. Club: Colony (N.Y.C.). Home: 840 Park Av New York City NY 10021 also Apaquogue Rd East Hampton NY 11937

HAMRICK, RUTH MASHBURN (MRS. DOW C. HAMRICK), librarian; b. Jasper, Ga., June 18, 1911; d. William Alfred and Ella (Poole) Mashburn; B.S. in Edn., U. Ga., then postgrad.; postgrad. Western Carolina U.; m. Dow C. Hamrick, Apr. 16, 1933. Tchr. Gilmer County (Ga.) High Sch., 1940-48; dir. Cherry Log Child Devel., Ellijay, Ga., 1966-68; librarian Ellijay Elementary Sch., 1968-74; also librarian Gilmer County Pub. Library, 1970-74. Chmn. Gilmer County Planning and Devel. Council; sec. Gilmer County Disaster Relief Assn. Trustee Tallulah Falls Sch., 1962-64. Recipient Gilmer County Vol. award Am. Cancer Soc., 1965, State Fund award, 1965. Clubs: Woman's (pres.) (Ellijay); Georgia Federated Woman's (pres. dist. 1962-64). Methodist (pres. local Woman's Soc. Christian Service 1950-54, dist. v.p. 1950, del. World Conf. 1961). Home: 62 River St Ellijay GA 30540 Office: 1 Library St Ellijay GA 30540

HAMRIN, JOY, truancy officer; b. Lexington, Minn.; d. Christopher Nelson and Sarah Lenore (Hays) Hamrin; B.A., Hamline U., 1919; M.A., U. Minn., 1941; postgrad. Sioux Falls Coll., U. S.D., Glassboro Coll., U. Hawaii. Teaching asst., fellow in physics U. Minn., Mpls., 1919-21; tchr. Sioux Falls (S.D.) Sr. High Sch., 1925-68; truancy officer pub. schs., Sioux Falls, 1969—. Chmn. interviewing com. exchange tchrs. U.S. Office Edn., 1955—; hon. life mem. P.T.A. Recipient Award of Merit, Sch. of Mines, 1952; A.R.C., 1958; Meritorious award State U. S.D., 1960; S.D. Educators award, 1962. Mem. Nat., S.D. (dir. 1952-68, pres. 1952) edn. assns., Internat. Platform Assn., Nat. Ret. Tchrs. Assn., P.E.O. (pres. 1947-48), Sioux Falls C. of C. (mem. exec. bd. women's div.), Women's Soc. Christian Service, Marquis Biog. Library Soc. (adv. mem.), Delta Kappa Gamma (state founder, pres. local chpt. 1951-52), Pi Mu Epsilon. Methodist. Mem. Order Eastern Star, Rebekah Lodge. Home: 805 W 18th St Apt 2 Sioux Falls SD 57105

HANAS, ANNA LORA SAVIGE (MRS. SYLVESTER HANAS), coll. adminstr.; b. Brooklyn, Pa., Aug. 1, 1917; d. Charles Jay and Jennie Lee (Miller) Savige; grad. Dean Coll. Bus., Kingston, Pa., 1936; student Phoenix Art Inst., N.Y.C., 1938-39, Art Students' League, N.Y.C., part time 1940-41; m. Sylvester Hanas, Mar. 25, 1941; children—Andrea Lee (Mrs. Michael Graham), Carole May (Mrs. Richard Arnott), Jay Savige. Sec., dir. profl. dept. Bristol-Myers Co., N.Y.C., 1939-41; sec., v.p. plant protection Curtiss-Wright Corp., Cheektowaga, N.Y., 1942-43; part-time work with pvt. sch. and ins. co., 1940's; recorder Corning (N.Y.) Community Coll., 1959-63, registrar, 1963—. Mem. Bus. and Profl. Women's Club Corning, Middle States Assn. Registrars and Officers of Admission, Am. Assn. Collegiate Registrars and Admissions Officers. Republican. Methodist (mem. choir). Home: 220 W 1st St Corning NY 14830

HANAVAN, MARYROSE, coll. adminstr.; b. N.Y.C., Nov. 16, 1920; d. William Lawrence and Mary Virginia (Taylor) Hanavan; A.B. in Math., Manhattanville Coll., Purchase, N.Y., 1942; M.S. in Indsl. Engring., Columbia, 1948; student numerous specialized courses. Traffic engr. N.Y.C. Dept. Traffic, 1949-52; tech. writer, editor du Pont Co., 1952-58, Vitro Labs., West Orange, N.J., 1958-62, engr. specialist data and information systems div. Internat. Tel. & Tel., 1962-64, Polaris div. Sperry Gyroscope Corp., 1964-65; tchr. math. high schs. in N.J., 1967-69; dir. student financial aid Englewood Cliffs (N.J.) Coll., 1969-74; research analyst, information systems and planning Cath. U. Am., Washington, 1974—. Served to lt. (j.g.) USNR, 1944-46. Mem. Am. Soc. M.E., Am. Inst. Aeros. and Astronautics, Soc. Tech. Communications (sec.-treas. chpt. 1957), N.J. Assn. Financial Aid Adminstrs., Manhattanville Coll. Alumni Assn. (chpt. treas. 1957-58, chpt. corr. sec. 1962-64), Catholic TV Guild Wilmington (dir. 1957), Engring. Women's Club N.Y.C. (chmn. evening group 1951). Home: 10401 Grosvenor Pl Rockville MD 20852 Office: Information Systems and Planning Office Catholic U Washington DC 20064

HANAWALT, PRISCILLA WEBBER (MRS. CLARE H. HANAWALT), coll. adminstr.; b. Salem, Mass., Mar. 25, 1918; d. Harry E. and Alice B. (Edwards) Webber; B.A., U. Wash., 1939; m. Clare H. Hanawalt, June 29, 1941; children—Alan E., Janet E. Asst. to deans Reed Coll., Portland, Ore., 1960-70, acting dean students, 1970-71, dean students, 1971—. Mem. Nat., Ore. assns. women deans and counselors. Home: 1751 Hillcrest Dr West Linn OR 97068 Office: Reed College Portland OR 97202

HANBACK, JACQUELINE TANKERSLEY (MRS. WILLIAM F. HANBACK), rehab. counselor; b. Jacksonville, Ill., Nov. 18, 1926; d. James H. and Mary E. (Hamilton) Tankersley; grad. MacMurray Coll., Jacksonville, 1948; M.A., U. Ill., 1965, postgrad., 1966; m. William F. Hanback, Apr. 9, 1950; 1 dau., Mary Murla. Tchr., Jacksonville, 1948-60; program dir. Elm City Rehab. Center, Jacksonville, 1960-63, profl. adv. com., 1967—; rehab. counselor for psychiatrically disabled Div. Vocational Rehab., Jacksonville, 1963—. Mem. profl. adv. com. accreditation council for psychiat. facilities Joint Commn. on Accreditation Hosps., 1971. Mem. Scott County Sch. Unit 1 Bd. Edn., 1966—, Interagy. of Morgan County, 1967—; mem. bd. Four Rivers Spl. Edn. Dist., 1972—, chmn. operating bd. and council, 1973—; vice chmn. Two Rivers div. Ill. Assn. Sch. Bds., 1974. Mem. Am. Personnel and Guidance Assn., Am. Rehab. Counselors Assn., Nat. (pres.'s counsel 1969-71, del. 1967-70, treas. 1973, pres.-elect Gt. Lakes region 1974), Ill. (research award com. 1972) rehab. counseling assns., Nat. (sec.-treas. 1972-73), Ill. (sec. 1966, dir. 1967-69, pres. 1969, nat. membership chmn. 1970-72) rehab. assns., Ill. Welfare Assn. (vice chmn. dist. 1971-73, chmn. 1969—). Club: Soroptimist (vice chmn. 1973). Home: Rural Route 1 Winchester IL 62694 Office: 1440 W Walnut St Jacksonville IL 62650

HANCH, VIRGINIA PAULINE CARTY (MRS. WILLIAM CHARLES HANCH, SR.), gift store owner; b. Montezuma, Ind., Jan. 13, 1922; d. Harvey Arthur and Ethel May (Heslar) Carty; student Ind. U., 1957-58; m. William Carles Hanch, Sr., Jan. 14, 1942; children—William Charles, Carolyn Sue, Marilyn Marie. With Jessup Jewelry Store, San Diego, 1942-44; photographer CAA, El Toro, Cal., 1944-45; asst. to driver's licenses supr. Ind. State House, 1949-50, supt. microfilm, 1950-51; purchasing agt., bookkeeper Ind. State Tax Bd., Indpls., 1951-52; purchasing agt. Ind. Conservation Dept., 1952-53; comptroller Weir Cook Municipal Airport, Indpls., 1956-62; dining room mgr. Indpls. Motor Speedway, 1962-66; owner Home of the 500 Gift Shop, Weir Cook Airport, Indpls., 1968—; owner Jet Set Boutique, Indpls., 1969—, The Seagull, 1974—. Tchr. 4-H, 1939. Hostess for nat. Chairwoman Democratic Com., 1950, for gov.'s wife, 1950. Com. mem. Indpls. Sesquicentennial Cook Book, 1971. Mem. Indpls. Conv. and Visitors Bur., Indpls. C. of C., 500 Festival Assn. Episcopalian. Club: Fox Cliff Country. Owner of Copyright and designer of Indpls. Home of the 500 Book, 1971, designer men and womens racing jackets, race towles, Indpls. charms, dragster racer charm. Home: Rural Route 2 Box 295 Plainfield IN 46168 Office: Box 41524 Weir Cook Municipal Airport Indianapolis IN 46241

HANCHETT, BONNY JEAN HOWLAND (MRS. ROSS A. HANCHETT), newspaper editor; b. Muskegon, Mich., July 26, 1920; d. Val Mott and Dorothy Louise (Mitchell) Howland; B.A., Wash. State U., 1942; m. Ross Allen Hanchett, Jan. 4, 1943; children—Val Howland, Mary Elizabeth, Roberta Lee, Jon Allen, Kathryn Ann. Soc. editor Everett Daily Herald, 1943-44; reporter Burbank Daily Herald, 1944; propr. dress shop, Everett, Wash., 1950-53; editor Lewis River News, Woodland, Wash. 1953-55, Clear Lake Observer-Am., 1955—; Lake County corr. Press Democrat, Santa Rosa, also Sacramento Bee. Former trustee Lower Lake Elementary Sch. Dist. Mem. Bus. and Profl. Women's Club, Clear Lake C. of C. (pres. 1974), Bus. and Profl. Women's Club, Theta Sigma Phi. Clubs: Soroptimist, Emblem. Home: PO Box 218 Lower Lake CA 95457

HANCOCK, CAROL HELEN BROOKS (MRS. TAYLOR HANCOCK), law firm exec.; b. Los Angeles, July 10, 1941; d. John Howard and Carol G. (Henley) Brooks; student Los Angeles City Coll., 1959, U. Fla., 1959-61; m. Roger Lester Edwards, Aug. 22, 1959 (div. Dec. 1964); 1 dau., Laura Anne; m. 2d, Taylor Hancock, Mar. 29, 1969; 1 dau., April. Sec., Latta & Co., pub. relations, Glendale, Cal., 1956-59; head sec. field services, dept. ednl. adminstrn. U. Fla., Gainesville, 1959-60, exec. sec.-supr. pathology dept. Health Center, 1963; asst. office mgr.-bookkeeper Jim Hope Elec., Inc., Gainesville, 1960-63; office mgr. Lincoln Estates, Inc., Gainesville, 1963-65; dir. Gallerie La Colline, Paris, France, 1965; v.p. Bolo Corp., Los Angeles, 1966-69, v.p. Bolo Internat. Ltd., Nassau, Bahamas, 1968-69; exec. dir. Orangefair Mall, Fullerton, Cal., 1969-71; gen. partner Feminist Book Club, Los Angeles, 1972-73, Affirmative Action Mgmt. Cons., Los Angeles, 1973—; bus. mgr. firm Greenberg, Bernhard, Weiss & Karma, Inc., Los Angeles, 1973—; dir. Bo-Lomb South, Inc., Bo-Lomb West, Inc., Los Angeles. Republican. Episcopalian. Address: 811 W 7th St Los Angeles CA 90017

HANCOCK, FRANCES LOUISE (MRS. FRANCIS CECIL GORE HANCOCK), lawyer; b. Toledo, Apr. 18, 1924; d. Jacob and Clara (Sklar) Kazansky; student San Diego State Coll., U. Cal. at Los Angeles; A.B., Hastings Coll. Law, U. Cal.; m. Francis Cecil Gore Hancock, Feb. 18, 1950; children—Phillip Austin, Madeline Gilda. Social worker San Diego Juvenile Ct., 1945-46; social worker Florence Crittenton Home, San Francisco, 1949; admitted to Cal. bar, 1956; practiced in San Francisco, 1957—; asst. dir. Bur. Family Relations, Office of Dist. Atty. San Francisco, 1951-54; adult probation officer, San Francisco, 1954-56. Exec. bd. Community Effort for Disturbed Children, San Francisco; bd. dirs. San Francisco Women's Rehab. Found., San Francisco Montessori Sch., Tamalpais Montessori Center for Disturbed Children. Mem. Am., San Francisco bar assns., Am., Cal. trial lawyers assns., State Bar Cal., Queens Bench (sec.-treas. 1959), San Francisco Lawyers Club. Home: 1 Edgehill Way San Francisco CA 94127 Office: 35 Vicente St San Francisco CA 94127

HANCOCK, GERALDINE RUTH COOPER (MRS. TYRONZA M. HANCOCK), city ofcl.; b. Springfield, Mo., June 23, 1925; d. Essie and Edith (Young) Cooper; B.S., Lincoln U., 1946; postgrad. Chgo. Tchrs. Coll., 1946-48, U. Chgo., 1947; m. Tyronza M. Hancock, Sept. 6, 1948; 1 son, Anthony C. Sec. dept. zoology U. Chgo., 1946-47; sec. dept. publicity United Packing House Workers Internat., 1947-48; tchr. high sch., Chgo., 1948-53; bookkeeper Ill. Fed. Savs. and Loan Assn., 1953-54; asst. housing mgr. Chgo. Housing Authority, 1954—. Mem. Nat. Assn. Housing and Redevel. Ofcls. Club: First Nighters. Home: 9304 S Lowe St Chicago IL 60620 Office: 454 E Pershing Rd Chicago IL 60653

HANCOCK, JOHANNA BERTHA, speech pathologist, audiologist; b. Louisville, June 1, 1935; d. James Duffy and Marie (Seelbach) Hancock; student Coll. of Notre Dame, Md., 1953-54, Loyola U. of Los Angeles, summer 1956; B.S. in Speech, Marquette U., 1957; M.A. in Speech Therapy, Catholic U. Am., 1959; postgrad. Western Res. U., 1957, U. Md., 1958, George Washington U., 1958; M.A. in Psychology, U. Louisville, 1967. Pvt. practice as speech pathologist and audiologist, Louisville, 1959—; part-time therapist Rehab. Center, Inc., Louisville, 1957, United Cerebral Palsy of Greater Louisville, 1959-60, Louisville Deaf-Oral Sch., 1959; instr. dept speech and communications Bellarmine Coll., Louisville, 1959-61, chmn. dept. 1961-62. Cons. therapist Cleft Palate Clinic, Ky. Commn. for Handicapped Children (vol.); audiologist in residence Changhua Christian Hosp., Changhua Hsien, Taiwan, 1969. Mem. bd. Jefferson County Med. Soc. Woman's Aux.; mem. Younger Woman's Club of Louisville, Spinsters Cotillion. Recipient certificate appreciation Nat. A.R.C.; Distinguished Alumni Achievement award Marquette U. Sch. Speech, 1966. Mem. Am., Ky. (exec. council) Louisville, Cal. speech and hearing assns., Internat. Council for Exceptional Children, Speech Assn. Am., Am. Acad. Pvt. Practice in Speech Pathology and Audiology, Am. Cleft Palate Assn., Alexander Graham Bell Assn. for Parents and Tchrs. of Deaf, Am. Assn. U. Profs., Am. Hearing Assn., Jr. Circle of Queen's Daus., Psi Chi, Tau Kappa Alpha (hon.), Sigma Alpha Eta (hon.). Contbr. articles to profl. jours. Home: 80 Valley Rd Louisville KY 40204 Office: Suite 3412 Med Arts Bldg 1169 Eastern Pkwy Louisville KY 40217

HANCOCK, MARY LOUISE, state ofcl.; b. Franklin, N.H., July 5, 1920; d. Herbert and Amanda Louise (Lambert) Hancock; A.B., U. N.H., 1942. Stenographer, N.H. Bd. Edn., 1942-43; with N.H. Travel Div., 1943-44; research librarian, planning asso., asst. planning dir., planning dir. N.H. Dept. Resources and Econ. Devel. (formerly N.H. Planning and Devel. Commn.), 1944-70; planning dir. N.H. planning project Office of Gov. John W. King, 1963-65; dir. Office State Planning, Office of N.H. Gov., Concord, 1970—. Sec.-treas. N.H. Planning & Zoning Assn., 1951—; mem. N.H. Water Supply and Pollution Control Commn., 1960—, N.H. Commn. on Status Women, 1964-68; N.H. rep. Conn. River Basin Coordinating Coms., 1964—; chmn. N.H. Council of Resources and Devel., 1965—; gov.'s rep. Bur. of Outdoor Recreation, 1965-68; mem. Concord Sch. Bd., 1955-64, Concord Planning Bd., 1967-72, Concord Bd. Adjustment, 1972—, Central N.H. Regional Planning Commn., 1968-72; co-chmn. Grace E. Weston Scholarship Com., 1950—; project dir. N.H. Trails Study Adv. Com., 1972—; mem. N.H. Spl. Bd. on Dredge and Fill, 1969—, N.H. Open Space Land Study Commn., 1971—, N.H. Rural Devel. Exec. Com., State Capital-City Planning Bd., 1967—, N.H. Adv. Council for Higher Edn. Act of 1965; mem. evaluation com. N.H. Bulk Power Supply Facility Site, 1971—; mem. adv. com. N.H. Water Resources Research Center, 1972—; mem. exec. bd. N.H.-Vt. Devel. Council, Inc., 1967—; N.H. liaison rep. to U.S. Water Resources Council. Bd. dirs. New Homes for N.H., Inc. Mem. Am. Inst. Planners (Distinguished Service award New Eng. chpt. 1969), Am. Soc. Planning Ofcls., Council State Planning Agys., N.H. Art Assn., N.H. Audubon Soc., U. N.H. Alumni Assn. (dir. 1953-56, 66-69, meritorious service award and medal 1955), Harlem Inst. Fashion (New Eng. dir. 1968—), Am. Heritage Found., N.H. Hist. Soc. Club: Woman's College (pres. 1960-62) (Concord). Home: 33 Washington St Concord NH 03301 Office: State House Annex Concord NH 03301

HAND, MARY GERTRUDE, psychologist; b. New Milford, Pa., Apr. 15, 1916; d. Martin Francis and Ellen Veronica (Tierney) Hand; certificate Mansfield State Tchrs. Coll., 1937; B.S., Pa. State U., 1946, M.Ed., 1947, D.Ed., 1964. Tchr., New Milford (Pa.) Pub. Schs., 1937-45; sch. psychologist West Orange (N.J.) Bd. Edn., 1947-63, Westfield (N.J.) Bd. Edn., 1963—. Served with WAC, 1943-45. Mem. Nat., N.J. edn. assns., Am., N.J. psychol. assns., N.J. Assn. Sch. Psychologists. Home: 53B Duncan Hill Apts Westfield NJ 07090 Office: 302 Elm St Westfield NJ 07090

HANDLER, FRANCES CLARK (MRS. FRANK STEVENSON HANDLER), educator, writer, assn. exec.; b. Maplewood, N.H., Feb. 28; d. Frank and Marie (Jamia) Clark; B.S. in Bus. Machine Teaching, Boston U., B.B.S. in Accounting, A.B. in Banking and Finance; m. Frank Stevenson Handler, Sept. 21, 1946. Instr. accounting Burroughs Sch., Boston, later collaborating writer poetry books, hist. novels, autobiographies, children's books. Lectr. on women's vocations Barry Coll., Miami, Fla., 1965—; founder, nat. dir. Fla. State Poetry Day, Inc. and Nat. Poetry Day Com., 1965—; mem. Congressman Pepper's Com. on Youth Affairs; internat. bd. dirs. World Poetry Day Com.; spl. adviser World Congress Poets, Taiwan, 1973. Named hon. poet laureate UN Day, Philippines, 1967, Md. Com. 100, 1971, 72, 73; Litt. D., Internat. Research Socs., U. Asia, Pakistan, 1968; recipient medal of Achievement, Nat. Poetry Day Com.; King Journalism award, 1971-72. C.P.A., Mass. Mem. United Poets Laureate Internat. (award, 1967, membership chmn. 1968—), World (internat. dir.), Fla. State (founder, sec., treas. 1965—, editor, pub. Flamingo 1969-70), Nev. (hon. life) poetry socs., Fla. Arts Council, Ia. Poetry Day Assn. (hon. life.). Nat. League Am. Pen. Women (treas. Coral Gables, Fla. br. 1963—), Hotel Accountants Assn. (pres. 1947-51). Author: Reina Mercedes, 1956, Canberra, 1957; Nobel Goes to Heaven, 1970; Nurses Notes, 1971; Beyond the Silent River, 1971; collaborator: Encyclopedia of Jazz, Devastators, 1971; 1955, Selected Poems, Memorial Award Books, 1966-72; The World is a Contrast. Editor: Selected Poems-Memorial Award Book and Internat. Hall of Fame books, 1969-72; Governor's Book, 1971-72; 9 Muses I and II, 1971-72. Home: 1110 N Venetian Dr Miami Beach FL 33139

HANDLER, JANICE, govt. lawyer; b. Newark, July 9, 1945; d. Lester Robert and Rose Mildred (Reider) Handler; B.A., Douglass Coll., 1967; J.D., Rutgers U., 1970. Admitted to N.Y. bar, 1971; law clk. to U.S. dist. judge So. Dist. N.Y., 1970-71; atty. Fried Frank Harris Shriver & Jacobson, N.Y.C., 1971-72; trial atty. SEC, N.Y.C., 1972—. Vol. research asst. to N.Y. state legislator, 1971-72. Mem. Am., N.Y. State bar assns., Assn. Bar City N.Y. (young lawyers com. 1973—), Phi Beta Kappa, Phi Sigma Alpha. Jewish religion. Office: 26 Federal Plaza New York City NY 10007

HANDLER, JUNE MOSS (MRS. MORTON D. HANDLER), educator; b. N.Y.C., Apr. 6, 1923; d. Maximilian and Grace D. (Leff) Moss; A.B. in English, Pembroke Coll., 1943; M.S. in Early Childhood Edn., Bank Street Coll., 1955; Ed.D. (Childcraft fellow) Tchrs. Coll. Columbia, 1966; m. Morton D. Handler, Mar. 3, 1946; children—Peter Moss, Roberta Lynn (Mrs. Richard Polton). Copywriter various advt. agys., 1943-46; dir.-tchr. Temple Coop. Nursery Sch., Westwood, N.J., 1955-62; adj. instr. Newark State Coll., 1963-64; reading specialist Englewood (N.J.) pub. schs., 1964-65; asso. prof. Newark State Coll., 1965-68, prof. early childhood edn., 1968—, chmn. early childhood edn., 1970-73; cons. Head Start, Infant Day Care programs. Vol. childrens ward Hackensack (N.J.) Hosp., 1954-55; asst. packmaster Bergen council Boy Scouts Am., 1956; leader Bergen County council Girl Scouts U.S.A., 1956-58; v.p. Teaneck League Better Schs., 1952-55; edn. chmn. and youth chmn. Nat. Council Jewish Women, Teaneck, 1952; mem. N.J. Task Force on Performance Criteria, 1973—, on Childcare Licensing, 1973—. Recipient Merit recognition Newark State Coll., 1971, 72; Research grantee B'nai B'rith on prejudice, 1964. Mem. Concerned Educators Devel. Early Childhood (co-chmn. N.J. 1971—), Assn. Childhood Edn. Internat., Nat. Assn. Edn. Young Children, N.J. Edn. Assn., Am. Civil Liberties Union, Pi Lambda Theta, Kappa Delta Pi. Jewish religion (mem. temple). Home: 440 Kensington Rd Teaneck NJ 07666

HANDLER, RUTH MOSKO (MRS. ELLIOT HANDLER), toy and leisure products co. exec.; b. Denver, Nov. 4, 1916; d. Jacob Joseph and Ida M.; student U. Denver, 1935-36; m. Elliot Handler, June 26, 1938; children—Kenneth Robert, Barbara Joyce. Formed Mattel, Inc., Hawthorne, Cal., 1945, exec. v.p., 1945-67, pres., 1967-73, co-chmn. bd., 1973—. Mem. exec. com., chmn. sub-council on product safety President's Nat. Bus. Council for Consumers Affairs, 1971—; mem. adv. com. on econ. role women Council Econ. Advisers, 1972—. Founder mem. Los Angeles Music Center, 1965, bd. dirs. Center Theater Group, 1971; mem. bus. adv. council White House Conf. Children and Youth, 1970. Asso. U. So. Cal., 1967—. Bd. dirs. Vista Del Mar Child Care Service. Named Outstanding Bus. Woman, Nat. Assn. Accountants, 1961, Couple of Year City Hope, 1963, Woman of Year in Bus., Los Angeles Times, 1968. One of Outstanding Women in Am. Ladies Home Jour., 1971; Advt. Woman of Year, Western States Advt. Agys. Assn., 1972, Brotherhood award So. Cal. Region, Nat. Conf. Christians and Jews, 1972. Office: 5150 Rosecrans Av Hawthorne CA 90250

HANDLER, SHIRLEY WOLZ, educator; b. Marshall, Tex., Jan. 2, 1925; d. George Anthony and Shirley (Wolz) Handler; A.A., East Tex. Bapt. Coll., 1943; M.A. (Teaching fellow 1945-46), U. Tex., 1947, B.A., 1945; Ph.D., U. Okla., 1958. Mem. faculty East Tex. Bapt. Coll., Marshall, 1947—, prof., chmn. dept. biology, 1953—. Pres. Am. Cancer Soc., Harrison County, 1967-68, mem. bd. dirs., 1955—; corr. sec. Marshall (Tex.) Community Concert Assn., 1958—; 2d v.p. Marshall Symphony Soc., Marshall, Tex., 1972—. Bd. dirs. Tex. Fine Arts Soc., 1968—. Mem. A.A.A.S., Nat. Assn. Biology Tchrs., Am. Inst. Biol. Scis., Am. Soc. Human Genetics, Am. Genetics Assn., Am. Assn. Med. Colls., Am. Chem. Soc., Delta Kappa Gamma, Southwestern Assn. Naturalists, Beta Sigma Phi (pres. 1967-68, Girl of Year 1968). Methodist. Home: 203 E Crockett St Marshall TX 76570 Office: E Tex Bapt Coll Marshall TX 75670

HANDLOFF, NORMA BRAM (MRS. SAMUEL HANDLOFF), state ofcl.; b. Phila., Feb. 24, 1913; d. Israel and Sadie (Weisgold) Bram; B.S. in Edn. with honors, Temple U., 1935; certificate police-community relations Mich. State U., 1958; m. Samuel Handloff, June 19, 1938; children—Susanna Hope (Mrs. Dennis C. Ehn), Deborah Joyce (Mrs. Barry N. Cornwall). Tchr., Chester (Pa.) High Sch., 1936-41; commr. Newark (Del.) Housing Authority, 1961-66, mayor, 1966-73; exec. dir. Del. Agy. to Reduce Crime, Wilmington, 1973—. Mem. Gov.'s Com. on Ednl. TV, 1963-64, Del. Commn. on Children and Youth, 1965-70, Gov.'s Commn. on Status of Women, 1966-70; edn. chmn. Del. div. Am. Cancer Soc., 1956-64; mem. distbn. com. Del. Found., 1963—; v.p. Overseas Edn. Fund, 1963-66. Democratic nominee for U.S. Congress, 1972. Bd. dirs. WHYY-TV. Mem. Del. League Local Govts. (v.p. 1966-73), Am. Assn. U. Women (pres. Newark br. 1950-52), League Women Voters (pres. Newark br. 1955, Del. br. 1958-61), Del. Ednl. TV Assn. (pres. 1963-64), Bus. and Profl. Women, Nat. Conf. State Criminal Justice Planning Adminstrs., Soroptimists, Delta Kappa Gamma. Home: 4 Kent Way Newark DE 19711 Office: 1101 Washington St Wilmington DE 19801

HANDRUP, BERNARDA, coll. dean; b. Chgo.; d. Bernhard and Mathilde (Babel) Handrup; B.A. in Biology, Alverno Coll., Milw., 1950; M.A. in Physics, U. Wis., 1950, Ph.D., 1960. Faculty physics Alverno Coll., 1953-70, acad. dean, 1970—. Mem. Am. Assn. Physics Tchrs., Am. Assn. Higher Edn., Sigma Xi. Home: 3401 S 39th St Milwaukee WI 53215

HANDSAKER, MARJORIE LINFIELD (MRS. MORRISON HANDSAKER), economist; b. Cambridge, Mass., Apr. 2, 1905; d. Bertram French and Eltha Nona (Brown) Linfield; A.B., Radcliffe Coll., 1925, A.M., 1930; fellow U. Chgo., 1930-32; m. Morrison Handsaker, Aug. 25, 1934; 1 dau., Alice (Mrs. David E. Kidder). Editor Labor Bull., Ill. Dept. Labor, Chgo., 1932-33; chief statis. sect., compliance div. NRA, Washington, 1934-36; instr. Occidental Coll., Los Angeles, 1942-43; lectr. Moravian Coll., Bethlehem, Pa., 1959, part-time, 1962-63; research asso. of husband in fields of econs. indsl. relations, Easton, Pa., 1946—,. Lectr. for USIS, Eng., 1957-58, Japan, 1964-65. Mem. Am. Econ. Assn., Indsl. Relations Research Assn., Soc. Profls. in Dispute Resolution (editorial bd. 1974), League Women Voters, Phi Beta Kappa. Author: (with Morrison Handsaker) The Submission Agreement in Contract Arbitration, 1962; also various studies pub. in profl. jours. Home: 717 W Lafayette St Easton PA 18042 Office: Lafayette Coll Easton PA 18042

HANDY, IMENA A. ALLISON (MRS. DONALD A. HANDY), ret. social worker; b. Troy, Ala.; d. William Henry and Annie Laurie (Harmon) Allison; grad. Troy State Tchrs. Coll., 1927; B.S., Ohio State U., 1940; M.S., Smith Coll., 1941; D.Social Work, Case Western Res. U., 1968; m. Donald A. Handy, Oct. 24, 1941. Disaster rep. Nat. A.R.C., Washington, 1936-41; asst. mgr. Cin. and Hamilton County chpt. A.R.C., 1942-53; dir. Family Service Disaster Service, Nat. A.R.C., Washington, 1953-59; chief clin. social work research VA, Brecksville, O., 1962—. Chmn., Workshop Ohio Welfare Conf. on Supervision, 1963, workshop on Problems of Aging, 1964; mem. VA Central Office Commn. on Social Work Research, 1964-74. Mem. Nat. Assn. Social Workers. Club: Altrusa (Akron, O.). Contbr. articles to profl. jours. Home: 2309 Park Av Richmond VA 23220

HANES, LEE DUNCAN, hosp. adminstr.; b. Kansas City, Mo., June 2, 1927; d. Elmer Lee and Edna Beryl (Ingram) Duncan; B.S. in Pharmacy, U. Mo., Kansas City, 1949; M.D., U. Kan., 1954; m. Robert Landon Hanes (dec.); 1 son, William Duncan. Resident psychiatry Greater Kansas City Mental Health Found., 1956-59, asst. clin. dir., dir. group therapy, 1959-69; asst. commr. mental health N.Y. State Dept. Mental Hygiene, 1969-70; dir. St. Lawrence State Hosp., Ogdensburg, N.Y., 1970—; clin. instr. psychiatry U. Mo., 1959-62, asst. clin. prof., 1962-69. Diplomate Am. Bd. Psychiatry and Neurology. Fellow Am. Psychiat. Assn., Am. Orthopsychiatry Assn.; mem. A.M.A., Am. Group Psychotherapy Assn., Assn. Med. Supts. Mental Hosps. Club: Zonta. Author: Day Care of Psychiatric Patients, 1964. Address: St Lawrence State Hosp Ogdensburg NY 13669

HANEVOLD, LOIS, broadcasting co. exec.; b. Birmingham, Ga., June 16, 1918; d. Julius Marshall and Carrie Edna (Redd) Lennard; A.B., U. Ga., 1940; postgrad. Emory U., 1948; m. Robert Benjamin Hanevold, Apr. 8, 1943; children—Barbara, Robert, Coral. Asst. to editor Kappa Alpha mag., Atlanta, 1940; copy chief WCSC-TV, Charleston, S.C., 1946-58; sales prodn. and continuity dir. WSB Radio, Atlanta, 1958—. Free lance radio writer for various agys. Gen. chmn. Atlanta Dogwood Festival, 1974; treas. Pres.'s Council Atlanta, 1970. Recipient Golden Mike award Coll. Women in Broadcasting, 1973. Mem. Am. Women in Radio and TV (nat. sec., treas. 1970-72), C. of C. (dir.). Home: 2682 Harrington Dr Decatur GA 30033 Office: WSB Radio 1601 W Peachtree St Atlanta GA 30309

HANEY, CAROL, ret. educator; b. Mpls., Aug. 29, 1905; d. William Leslie and Clara Elizabeth (Haslip) Haney; student Eveleth (Minn.) Jr. Coll., 1922-24; B.A. cum laude, Macalester Coll., 1929; postgrad. U. Minn., summer 1961. Tchr. jr. and sr. high schs., Eveleth, 1929-69. Mem. modern fgn. langs. adv. com. Minn. Dept. Edn., 1962-65, mem. state adv. com. tchr. edn., 1964-68; faculty rep. High Sch. P.T.A. Exec. Bd., 1965-66; sec. Eveleth City Charter Commn., 1958-68; mem. Eveleth Citizens Com., 1957; mem. Eveleth City Library Bd., 1955-68, now chmn.; m. Eveleth Bd. Edn., 1971—. Chmn. Eveleth Pub. Library Bd., 1973-74. Recipient Valley Forge Tchrs. medal Freedoms Found., 1965. Mem. N.E.A. (life), Minn. (English adv. com., ex officio dir., dep. commr. ethics comm., sec.-treas. English sect. 1968-70), N.E. Minn. (sec. 1959-69, chmn. English sect. 1957-59, 61-65), Eveleth (chmn. salary com. 1950-61, 65—) edn. assns., Am., Minn. library assns., Nat., Minn. (adv. bd. 1959-65, com. articulation secondary and coll. English) councils tchrs. English, Am. Assn. U. Women, Northeast Ret. Tchrs. Assn. Minn. (chmn. legislative com.), Pi Phi Epsilon, Delta Kappa Gamma (pres. chpt. 1972-74). Presbyn. (deacon, mem. session, trustee 1970-73, pres. session 1973—). Contbr. articles to profl. jours. Mem. adv. bd. Ency. Brit. Home: 726 Hayes St Eveleth MN 55734 Office: Sr High Sch Eveleth MN 55734

HANEY, LUCIE RENEE, psychiatrist; b. Dallas, July 4, 1942; d. Charles Oscar and Corinna Lutherine (Wilson) Haney; B.A., U. Tex., 1964; M.D. (Maffat scholar), Southwestern Med. Sch., Dallas, 1968. Intern Baylor U. Med. Center, 1968-69; resident psychiatry Sheppard and Enoch Pratt Hosp., Towson, Md., 1969—, fellow child psychiatry, 1972-73; chief resident, fellow child psychiatry U. South Fla., 1973-74, instr. dept. psychiatry, 1973-74, staff psychiatrist St. Joseph's Hosp., Tampa, Fla. Mem. Am. Psychiat. Assn., Am. Soc. Adolescent Psychiatry, Hillsborough County Med. Assn. Home: Route 1 Box 221 Hutchenson Rd Tampa FL 33618 Office: St Joseph's Hosp Mental Health Center 3001 W Buffalo St Tampa FL 33607

HANFORD, DIANA LUCILLE, ednl. adminstr.; b. Middletown, Conn., Feb. 28, 1940; d. Jay and Ida Elizabeth (Sandin) Hanford; B.A. with high honors, U. Conn., 1962; M.A. (Conn. Commn. Higher Edn. scholar), Wesleyan U., Middletown, 1967. Systems analyst trainee Aetna Life and affiliated cos., Hartford, Conn., 1962-63; tchr. social science and history The Beard Sch., Orange, N.J., 1963-66; asst. dir. admissions, tchr. history Westover Sch., Middlebury, Conn., 1967-68, dir. admissions, tchr. history, 1968-72; dir. financial aid Westbrook Coll., Portland, Me., 1972-73; asso. dir. admissions Wilson Coll., Chambersburg, Pa., 1973—. Friend Westover Sch., Wesleyan U., Westbrook Coll. Mem. Japan Soc., U. Conn. Alumni Assn., Nat. Assn. Coll. Admissions Counselors, Am. Assn. Collegiate Registrars and Admissions Officers, Coll. Entrance Exam. Bd., Am. Coll. Testing, Phi Beta Kappa, Phi Alpha Theta, Phi Kappa Phi, Pi Sigma Alpha. Republican. Home: 1328 Edgar Av Chambersburg PA 17201

HANFT, ETHEL WITFORD NATTRASS (MRS. REX LEROY HANFT), livestock exec.; b. Durham County, Eng., Apr. 16, 1911; d. William Henderson and Beatrice Elmira (Dobson) Nattrass; grad. Wright's Bus. Coll., 1932, Midland Radio Sch., 1942, Famous Writers Sch., 1973; m. Rex Leroy Hanft, Sept. 15, 1944; 1 son, Vern Richard. Operator Bell Telephone Co., Pitts., 1929-31; waitress, hostess, N.Y.C., 1931-42; instr. Morse Code, WAC, U.S. Army, Sioux Falls, S.D., 1943-44, radio operator Hdqrs. 8th Air Force, Eng., 1944-45; with Wapello Livestock Auction, Inc. (Ia.), 1947—, v.p., 1947—, sec., 1947—; free-lance writer. Committeewoman Wapello, vice chmn. Louisa County (Ia.) Dem. Party, 1960-66, 67-71. Aid Meml. Hosp., Burlington, Ia., 1963-64; mem. Vol. Action Center. Served with WAC, 1943-45. Mem. Am. Legion Aux. (pres. Wapello 1961), Musser Fine Art Mus., Heritage Assn., YWCA, Gen. Hosp. Aux., Nat. Press Women. Club: Ethics Federated Women's. Presbyn. (trustee 1963-66, deacon 1968). Address: Apt 6 1222 Vista Ct Muscatine IA 52761

HANFT, RUTH S. SAMUELS (MRS. HERBERT HANFT), economist; b. N.Y.C., July 12, 1929; d. Max Joseph and Ethel (Schechter) Samuels; B.S., Cornell U., 1949; M.A., Hunter Coll., 1963; m. Herbert Hanft, June 17, 1951; children—Marjorie Jane, Jonathan Mark. Cons., Urban Med. Econs. Project, Hunter Coll., N.Y.C. and D.C. Dept. Health, 1962-63; health economist Office of Research and Statistics, Social Security Adminstrn., Washington, 1964-66; chief grants mgmt., health div. Office Econ. Opportunity, Washington, 1966-68; sr. health analyst Office of Asst. Sec. Planning and Evaluation, Dept. Health, Edn. and Welfare, Washington, 1968-71, spl. asst., asst. sec. health, 1971-72; sr. research asso. Inst. Medicine-Nat. Acad. Scis., Washington, 1972—. Fellow Am. Pub. Health Assn., Royal Soc. Health. Jewish religion. Contbr. articles to profl. jours. Home: 411 N Lee St Alexandria VA 22304 Office: 2101 Constitution Av NW Washington DC 20201

HANKS, HELEN CHAPPELL (MRS. STEDMAN SHUMWAY HANKS), ceramic sculptor, author; b. Chgo., Mar. 31, 1889; d. Henry Whitehill and Mary Robinson (Rand) Chappell; student Chateau De Dieudonne, Paris, France, 1903-04; m. Stedman Shumway Hanks, May 20, 1952. Ceramic sculptress, 1930-37, exhibited in group shows, New Canaan, Conn. Club: Colony. Co-author: Frontiers Are Not Borders, 1955. Office: 19 E 72d St New York City NY 10021

HANKS, NANCY, govt. ofcl.; b. Miami Beach, Fla., Dec. 31, 1927; d. Bryan Cayce and Virginia (Wooding) Hanks; student U. Colo., 1946, Oxford (Eng.) U., 1948; A.B. magna cum laude, Duke, 1949; D.F.A. (hon.), Pratt Inst., 1970, U. Mich., 1971, U. Pa., 1972, Washington U., St. Louis, 1972, Conservatory Music of P.R., 1972; D.H.L., Princeton, 1971, Hofstra U., 1971, Ill. Wesleyan U., 1972, Kenyon Coll., 1972, Williams Coll., 1972, U. So. Cal., 1973, George Washington U., 1973, Mich. State U., 1973. Mem. staff ODM, 1951-52; mem. Pres.'s Adv. Com. Govt. Orgn., 1953; asst. to undersec. Dept. Health, Edn. and Welfare, 1953-54; spl. asst. Spl. Projects Office, White House, 1955; asst. to Nelson A. Rockefeller, N.Y.C., 1956-59; asso. Laurance S. Rockefeller, 1959-69, exec. sec. spl. studies project Rockefeller Bros. Fund, 1956-69; chmn. Nat. Endowment for Arts and Nat. Council on Arts, 1969—. Adviser Outdoor Recreation Resources Rev. Commn., 1961-62. Mem. Phi Beta Kappa, Phi Kappa Delta, Kappa Alpha Theta, Sigma Alpha Iota. Clubs: Capitol Hill (Washington); Cosmopolitan (N.Y.C.). Office: McPherson Bldg 1425 K St NW Washington DC 20506

HANLEY, EVELYN ALICE, educator, author; b. Atlanta; d. James Bourke and Alice (Wanamaker) Hanley; A.B., Bklyn. Coll.; A.M., N.Y.U.; Ph.D. Formerly fellow in English, Hunter Coll., N.Y.C., now asst, prof., 1966—; former instr. Bklyn. Coll., Adelphi Coll., Garden City, N.Y. Recipient Parker Lloyd-Smith prize in poetry, Charles Dickens Commemorative medal, 1970; Certificate of Merit in poetry and criticism, London, 1973. Mem. Modern Lang, Assn. Am., Nat. Council Tchrs. English, Am. Assn. U. Profs., English Grad. Assn. of N.Y.U. (charter). Author: Stoicism in Major English Poets of the Nineteenth Century, 1964; Poetic Profiles, 1962; Antiphony (poetry), 1963; Nature in Theme and Symbol: Wordsworth to Eliot, 1972. Contbr. articles and book revs. to profl. publs., poetry to mags., anthologies, newspapers; series of articles on Dante, Michelangelo, Leopardi, Raphael, and Petrarch in Italian Times mag. Home: 82-64 170th St Jamaica NY 11432 Office: Hunter Coll 695 Park Av New York City NY 10021

HANLEY, MARY CAROLYN DUKE (MRS. JOHN THOMAS HANLEY), librarian; b. Henny, Ill., Jan. 8, 1922; d. Clarence O. and Margaret (Jones) Duke; A.B., Kalamazoo Coll., 1944; M.S., U. Ill., 1962; m. John Thomas Hanley, Oct. 22, 1945; children—Judith Ellen, Joan Marie, John Thomas, Barbara Brooks, Michael Davies. With children's dept. Kalamazoo Pub. Library, 1944-45; clk. circulation dept. U. Ill. Library, 1958-59, serials asst., 1959-63; librarian U. Minn. Library, Mpls., 1963-65, librarian, instr. catalog dept., 1965—, head cataloguer sci. sect., 1966-69, head biomed. library catalog dept., 1969—, asst. prof., librarian, 1972—. Mem. Am., Minn., Med., Spl. (pres. Minn. chpt. 1970-71) library assns., Am. Soc. Information Sci. Home: 5705 Lawndale Lane Hamel MN 55340

HANLON, GRISELDA FRANCES GUTCHECK (MRS. WALLACE E. HANLON), educator; b. Anaconda, Mont., Jan. 25, 1922; d. Charles Alexander and Louise (Nechimer) Gutcheck; B.S. in Entomology, Mont. State U., 1943; D.V.M., U. Minn., 1952, M.S., 1955; m. Wallace E. Hanlon, July 1, 1960. Research asst. U. Cal., San Francisco, 1943-44; research fellow U. Minn., St. Paul, 1952-55, faculty, 1955—, prof. radiology, 1973—. Served with USNR, 1943-44. Diplomate Am. Coll. Vet. Radiology. Mem. Educators Vet. Radiol. Sci. (sec. 1968-69), Am. (pres. 1971-72), Brit. vet. radiol. socs., Am. Vet. Med. Assn., Internat. Assn. Vet. Radiology, Radiology Soc. N.Am. Contbr. articles to profl. jours. Home: 333 Capitol View Av W St Paul MN 55113 Office: Vet Hosps U Minn St Paul MN 55101

HANLON, PAULINE LUCY, assn. exec.; b. Boston, Sept. 2, 1942; d. William Augusta and Maria (Beristine) Hanlon; Asso. B.S., Mt. Ida. Jr. Coll., 1963; B.S., Northeastern U., 1971. Case worker for teens New Eng. Home, Boston, 1966-67; asst., teen-age dept. Boston YWCA, 1967-69, dir. outdoor edn. center, 1969—; dir. resident camp Blazing Trail Camp, Denmark, Me., 1969-74; cons. infield. Mem. Am. Camping Assn., Me. Camp Dirs. Assn. Club: Appalachian Mountain. Home: Denmark ME 04022 Office: 140 Clarendon St Boston MA 02116

HANNA, DOLORES DIANE KALAJIAN (MRS. HERBERT L. HANNA), lawyer; b. Chgo., Dec. 5, 1927; d. George Vosgerchian and Victoria (Ignatius) Kalajian; B.A., Ohio U., 1949; J.D., Chgo.-Kent Coll. Law, 1952; m. Herbert L. Hanna, Jan. 30, 1954. Admitted to Ill. bar, 1952; editor state tax dept. Commerce Clearing House, Chgo., 1949-57; mem. firm Fitch, Even & Tabin & Luedeka, Chgo., 1957-65, partner, 1965-73; atty. law dept. Kraftco Corp., Chgo., 1973—. Bd. dirs. Mary Bartelme Home for Girls, Chgo., 1966—. Mem. Am., Ill., Chgo. (bd. mgrs. 1971-73, vice chmn. patent and trademark com., mem. com. on inquiry 1965-71) bar assns., Women's Bar Assn. Ill. (pres. 1962-63), Alliance Bus. Profl. Women (1st v.p. 1967-68), Kappa Beta Pi (chpt. dean 1951). Home: 431 W Oakdale Av Chicago IL 60657 Office: Kraftco Ct Glenview IL 60025

HANNA, LAVONE AGNES, educator; b. Clay Center, Kan.; d. George William and Mary Alice (Gillespie) Hanna; A.A., Lindenwood Coll., 1916, Litt.D., 1953; B.A., U. Wis., 1919; M.A., U. Chgo., 1927; Ed.D., Stanford, 1943. Tchr., Clay County High Sch., Clay Center, 1920-23, Bartlesville (Okla.) High Sch. and Jr. Coll., 1923-31; tchr., dir. gen. edn. secondary schs., Tulsa, 1931-39; research asso. Stanford, 1939-43, asst. prof., 1943-44; dir. curriculum Long Beach (Cal.) Pub. Schs., 1943-47; prof. edn. San Francisco State U., 1947-61, emeritus prof., 1961—. Vis. prof. Am. U. Beirut, Lebanon, 1957-58. Mem. exec. bd. Nat. Conf. Christians and Jews, San Francisco, 1948—. Mem. Nat. Council for Social Studies, Nat. (exec. com. 1958-62), Cal. (pres. 1945-46) assns. for supervision and cirriculum devel., Phi Beta Kappa, Pi Lambda Theta, Delta Kappa Gamma. Republican. Presbyn. Author: (with G. Potter, N. Hagamon) Unit Teaching in the Elementary Schools, 1955, rev., 1963; (with I.J. Quillen) Education for Social Competence, 1948, rev., 1961; Facing Life's Problems, 1955; Challenges for a Free People, 1964; (with G. Potter, R. Reynolds) Dynamic Approach to Elementary Social Studies: Unit Teaching, 1973. Contbr. articles to profl. jours. Home: 15 Berenda Way Menlo Park CA 94025

HANNA, MARY ANN JONES (MRS. ALBERT KENNETH HANNA), librarian; b. Greencastle, Ind., Aug. 8, 1920; d. Benjamin Frank and Bernice (Allen) Jones; A.B., DePauw U., 1942; B.S. in L.S., U. Ill., 1944; M.L.S., Western Mich. U., 1969; m. Albert Kenneth Hanna, May 27, 1944; children—Susanne, Donovan Allen. Tchr., English, Deshler (O.) High Sch., 1942-43; pub. sch. librarian, Cleve., 1944-46, Clarkston, Ga., 1951-54, Birmingham, Ala., 1954-58; librarian U. Ala. Extension Center, Birmingham, 1958-60; sch. library cons. Mich. State Library, Lansing, 1960-67; head sch. library cons., adminstr. Title II, E.S.E.A., Bur. Library Services, Mich. Dept. Edn., 1967-72; coordinator library specialist program, state library services Mich. Dept. Edn., Lansing, 1972—. Mem. Am., Mich. library assns., Am., Mich. assns. sch. librarians, P.E.O., Kappa Alpha Theta. Home: 1446 Roxburgh St East Lansing MI 48823 Office: 735 E Michigan Av Lansing MI 48913

HANNA, MARY MARGARET MELSON (MRS. JOHN ALDEN HANNA), librarian; b. nr. Rolfe, Ia., Oct. 17, 1913; d. Randall and Fern Sigourney (Beers) Melson; B.A., Morningside Coll., 1934; postgrad. U. Ia., 1936, Ia. State U., 1937, U. No. Ia., 1956; M.A., U. Wis., 1966; m. John Alden Hanna, Aug. 17, 1938 (dec. 1963); children—Carolyn (Mrs. Gary Clinton Snell), Frank Richard, Cynthia (dec. 1947). Tchr. English, Milford (Ia.) High Sch., 1934-37; prin. Ankeny (Ia.) High Sch., 1937-38; tchr. English, Blairsburg (Ia.) High Sch., 1957-59; tchr. Am. lit. Webster City (Ia.) High Sch., 1959-64; dir. Kendall Young Library, Webster City, 1966—. Asst. sec. Kendall Young Library and Trust Estate, 1966—. Mem. Ia. Library Assn., Bus. and Profl. Women, P.E.O. Republican. Methodist. Club: Women's (Webster City). Home: 1404 Grove St Webster City IA 50595 Office: 1201 Willson Av Webster City IA 50595

HANNAN, GRETCHEN ELIZABETH RELYEA (MRS. ROBERT JOSEPH HANNAN), merchandising exec.; b. Hudson, N.Y., Feb. 5, 1922; d. Charles Miller and Edna (Pulver) Relyea; B.A., Barnard Coll., 1943; m. Robert Joseph Hannan, Apr. 16, 1955 (dec. Mar. 1963); children—Robert Charles, Alan Richard, William Sprague. Adminstrv. asst. Calvert Distilling Co., Balt., 1943-46; asst. buyer Jordan Marsh Co., Boston, 1946-47, buyer, 1947-51, dept. mgr., Framingham, Mass., 1951-55; asst. buyer Carson Pirie Scott & Co., Chgo., 1956-57, buyer, 1957-66, divisional mdse. mgr., 1966-70, inventory control officer, 1970-71, dir. loss prevention, 1971-72, mdse. reports controller, 1972-73, dir. tng., 1973—. Publicity worker Cub Scouts, 1965-71; active fund drives Boy Scouts Am., 1964, Crusade of Mercy, 1965; group chmn. fund drive Am. Cancer Soc., 1967; fund raising chmn. class 1943 Barnard Coll., 1968-73; mem. operating effectiveness com. Community Fund Chgo., 1972—. Mem. D.A.R., Huguenot Hist. Soc., Alumnae Assn. Barnard Coll. Republican. Clubs: Barnard College (Chgo.); Olympia Fields (Ill.) Country. Home: 908 Argyle Av Flossmoor IL 60422 Office: 1 S State St Chicago IL 60603

HANNEMAN, AUDRE LOUISE, pub. co. editor; b. Council Bluffs, Ia., July 27, 1926; d. Homer William and Nettie (Smith) Hanneman; grad. high sch. Indexer Sweet's Catalog System, McGraw-Hill, Inc., N.Y.C., 1963-69, index editor, McGraw-Hill Book Co., 1969—. Mem. Am. Soc. Indexers, Bibliog. Soc. Am.; life mem. N.A.A.C.P. Author: Ernest Hemingway: A Comprehensive Bibliography, 1967. Home: 2 Horatio St New York City NY 10014 Office: 1221 Av of Americas New York City NY 10020

HANNIGAN, MARGARET MARY HOPKINS (MRS. CHARLES A. HANNIGAN), physician; b. Boston, Feb. 22, 1924; d. Thomas William and Margaret Mary (Downing) Hopkins; student Emmanuel Coll., 1941-44; M.D., Tufts Coll., 1948; m. Charles A. Hannigan, Sept. 2, 1950; children—Charles, Margaret, John, Matthew, Patricia, Katherine. Intern, Boston City Hosp., 1948-50; asst. resident Columbia-Presbyn. Hosp., 1950-52, U. Ala. Jefferson-Hillman, 1953; practice medicine specializing in dermatology, Auburn, Me., 1955—; mem. cons. staff Central Me. Gen. Hosp., Lewiston, Togus VA Hosp.; mem. courtesy staff St. Mary's Gen. Hosp., Lewiston, Me., Stephens Meml. Hosp., Norway, Me. Mem. health services bd. Community Coordinated Child Care, Lewiston, 1971—; leader Kennebec council Girl Scouts U.S.A., 1970-72. Mem. adv. bd. dirs. Area Health Edn. Com.; bd. dirs., pres. Child and Family Mental Health Services; bd. dirs. Home Health Services, Tri-County, Me., pres., 1972. Mem. Am. Acad. Dermatology, New Eng. Dermatology Assn., Me. Med. Assn., Androscoggin County Med. Soc. Roman Catholic (parish council 1970—). Home: RFD 2 West Auburn ME 04210 Office: 10 High St Lewiston ME 04240

HANNON, PATRICIA BERRY, univ. exec.; b. Columbus, O., Feb. 12, 1923; d. Maurice Denver and Mary (Funk) Berry; B.S., Ohio State U., 1944, postgrad., 1945, 60; postgrad. Otterbein Coll., 1960-61; m. Escalus E. Elliott, Jr., Apr. 1944 (div. May 1962); 1 son, Escalus E. III; m. 2d, Edward J. Hannon, Jan. 7, 1966. Instr. dept. fine arts Ohio State U., 1945-46; art supr., tchr. Gahanna (O.) Pub. Schs., 1960-61; mem. art guide com. Franklin County Bd. Edn., 1960-61; mem. pub. relations community coms. and Childrens Hosp., 1962; exec. sec. Columbus Town Meeting Assn., producer-dir. Columbus Town Meeting Forum, 1963-72; tech. asso. community relations Center for Vocational Edn., Ohio State U., 1972—. Pres. bd. trustees West Side and Ohio Av. Day Care Centers Assn., 1958-60; gen. chmn. Twig Bazaar, 1950, mem. exec. com., 1950-60; gen. chmn. Twigs of Childrens Hosp., 1955-57. Recipient certificate of merit Franklin County Bd. Edn., 1961. Mem. Am. Acad. Television Arts and Scis. (past chpt. sec.), Pi Lambda Theta, Delta Phi Delta, Kappa Kappa Gamma. Office: 1900 Kenny Rd Columbus OH 43210

HANOUSEK, JANE ANN JOHNSON (MRS. FRANK L. HANOUSEK), editor; b. Wakefield, Mich., Jan. 14, 1939; d. Arthur Theodore and Agnes Evelyn (Gustafson) Johnson; B.S., U. Wis., 1961; m. Frank L. Hanousek, July 10, 1965; 1 son, Frank Louis. Reporter, Ironwood (Mich.) Daily Globe, 1960; mem. women's staff Dubuque (Ia.) Telegraph Herald, 1961-64; receptionist, copywriter radio sta. KMAQ, Maquoketa, Ia., 1964-65; gen. news reporter Wausau (Wis.) Daily Record-Herald, 1966-68, family living editor, 1968—. Mem. Wausau Area Fine Arts Council Com., 1970-72, Wausau Mayor's Commn. on Status of Women, 1971—, Wausau Child Care Center Com., 1971—; pub. relations chmn. Birch Trails council Girl Scouts U.S., 1973—; mem. adv. bd. Wausau YWCA, 1973—; active Easton Sch. P.T.A. Mem. Central Wis. Press Club, U. Wis. at Stevens Point Alumni Assn. Episcopalian. Home: Route 1 Box 122 Ringle WI 54471 Office: 800 Scott St Wausau WI 54401

HANSCHU, BONNIE JEAN, occupational therapist; b. Mason City, Ia., Mar. 4, 1946; d. Kermit Lee and Aili Hilja (Wehkala) Hanschu; student Gustavus Adolphus Coll., 1963-65; B.S., U. N.D., 1968. With Anoka (Minn.) State Hosp., 1969—, dir. rehab. therapy program, 1971—; dir. occupational therapy asst. program Duluth Area Vocational Tech. Inst., 1971—. Mem. Young Republican League, 1971-73. Mem. Am., Minn., Arrowhead Dist. occupational therapy assns., Am., Minn. vocational assns. Club: Altrusa (dir. Duluth, Minn., v.p. 1974). Home: 4217 Luverne St Duluth MN 55804 Office: 2101 Trinity Rd Duluth MN 55811

HANSEN, CAROL LYNN, home economist; b. Milw., Dec. 31, 1938; d. Victor P. and Liane (Johannsen) Hansen; B.S., U. Wis., 1960. Home service rep. Wis. Electric Power Co., Milw., 1960-62; asst. dir. Dairy Council Milw., 1962-63; asst. consumer edn. dir. Johnson Wax, Racine, Wis., 1963-66, consumer edn. dir., 1967-72, exec. dir. Consumer Services Center, 1972—. Mem. citizen's steering com. on vocational edn. Racine Unified Sch. Dist. Mem. Home Economists in Bus. (North Central regional adviser 1969-70, co-chmn. nat. adv. com. 1971-72, chmn. nat. housing furniture and equipment com. 1972-74), Am. Home Econs. Assn. (nat. meeting program com. 1967-68, sec. nat. housing, furnishings and equipment com. 1970-72, mem. internat. program com. 1973-74), Am. Women in Radio and Television (East Central regional conf. chmn. 1969-70, pres. Badger chpt. 1969-70), Elec. Women's Round Table (nat. scholarship selection com. 1967-69), Soc. Consumer Affairs Profls. in Bus. (membership com. 1973—), Nat. Home Fashions League. Tech. cons. Jour. Home Econs., 1972-73. Home: 2914 N Main St Racine WI 53402 Office: 1525 Howe St Racine WI 53403

HANSEN, CHARLOTTE LORRAINE HELGESON (MRS. GORDON H. HANSEN), editor; b. Jamestown, N.D., June 1, 1922; d. Louis Sebern and Ida Ethelyne (Clough) Helgeson; student Jamestown Coll., 1940-41; B.S., U. Minn., 1944; m. Gordon H. Hansen, Oct, 31, 1945; 1 dau., Jo-Ida Charlotte. Hematologist, Hanford Engrng. Co., Richland, Wash., 1944-45; serologist Tex. Dept. Health, Wichita Falls, 1945-46; instr. microbiology Jamestown Coll., 1951-61; food editor Jamestown Sun, 1949—; sec.-treas. Hansen Bros., Inc.; dir. Jamestown First Nat. Bank. Mother adviser Rainbow Girls, 1964-73. Pres., United Fund, Jamestown council Girl Scouts Am.; bd. dirs. Camp Rokiwan, James River Sr. Citizens. Recipient Grand Cross of Color, Rainbow Girls, 1940, Thanks badge Girl Scouts Am., 1964; named Merit Mother of N.D., 1969; named Outstanding Woman of N.D. in Civics and Community Services, 1974. Mem. Am. Assn. U. Women, Nat. Fedn. Press Women, N.D. Press Women, Am. Legion Aux., P.E.O., Zonta, Theta Tau Sigma, Delta Kappa Gamma, Sigma Delta Chi. Methodist. Mem. Order Eastern Star. Clubs: Wednesday, Civic Music. Author: Kitchen Magic, 1964; Favorites of My Family, 1972. Home: 309 11th Av NE Jamestown ND 58401 Office: 121 2d St NW Jamestown ND 58401

HANSEN, EILEEN ARDYCE, lawyer; b. Hampton, Neb.; d. George W. and Hannah (Nilson) Hansen; A.A., Am. U., 1956, B.S., 1958, J.D., 1962. Sec., Bur. Ships. Navy Dept., Washington, 1942-46; adminstrv. officer Nat. Bur. Standards, Dept. Commerce, Washington, 1946-62; admitted to Neb. bar, 1962, D.C. bar, 1964, U.S. Supreme Ct. 1970; exec. asst. to dir. for strategic tech. (formerly Ballistic Missile Def. Office, Project Defender), Advanced Research Projects Agy., Office Sec. Def., Washington, 1962-72, cons., 1973-74; partner firm Smith and Hansen, 1973—. Recipient Meritorious Service award and medal Sec. Def., 1973. Mem. Women's Bar Assn. D.C. (rec. sec. 1965-67, corr. sec. 1967-68, dir. 1969-71, v.p. 1971-72), Neb., Omaha, D.C. bar assns., Am. Soc. Internat. Law, Philos. Soc. Washington, Nat. Lawyers Club, Kappa Beta Pi (nat. grand registrar 1965-69, grand chancellor 1969-71, 2d asso. grand dean for N.Am. 1971-73, chmn. bd. dirs., 1st v.p. 1973—). Home: 929 S 70th Plaza Omaha NE 68106 also Hampton NE 68843 Office: 1022 1st Nat Bank Bldg Omaha NE 68102

HANSEN, FLORENCE MARIE CONGIOLOSI (MRS. JAMES S. HANSEN), social worker; b. Middletown, N.Y., Jan. 7, 1934; d. Joseph James and Florence (Harrigan) Congiolosi; B.A., Coll. New Rochelle, 1955; M.S.W., Fla. State U., 1960; m. James S. Hansen, June 16, 1959; 1 dau., Florence M. Caseworker, Orange County Dept. Pub. Welfare, N.Y., 1955-57, Catholic Welfare Bur., Miami, Fla., 1957-58; supr. Catholic Family Service, Spokane, Wash., 1960, Cuban Children's Program, Spokane, 1962-66; founder, dir. social service dept., adminstr. supr. Spokane and Inland Empire artificial kidney center Sacred Heart Med. Center, Spokane, 1967—. Asst. in program devel. St. Margaret's Hall, Spokane, 1961-62; mem. budget and planning div. United Way, 1964—, chmn. projects com., 1972—; active work with Cuban refugees; mem. Kidney disease adv. com. Wash.-Alaska Regional Med. Program, 1972—. Mem. Nat. Assn. Social Workers (pres. Inland Empire chpt. 1972-74), Acad. Certified Social Workers (charter), Am. Soc. Hosp. Social Work Dirs. Roman Catholic. Home: 5609 Northwest Blvd Spokane WA 99205 Office: Sacred Heart Med Center W 101 8th St Spokane WA 99204

HANSEN, JULIA BUTLER, congresswoman, author; b. Portland, Ore., June 14, 1907; d. Don C. and Maude (Kimball) Butler; student Ore. State Coll., 1924-26; A.B., U. Wash., 1930; LL.D. (hon.), St. Mary's Coll., Ind.; m. Henry A. Hansen, July 15, 1939; 1 son, David Kimball. Mem. Wash. Ho. of Reps., 1939-60, mincrity leader, 1953-55, past speaker pro tem, chmn. hwys. com.; mem. 86th-93d congresses from 3d Dist. Wash., mem. appropriations com.; chmn. Joint Fact Finding mem. Nat. Rivers and Harbors Congress; chmn. Interior Sub-com. on Appropriations; mem. Transp. Subcom. on Appropriations. Democratic state committeewoman, 1936-60. Mem. Am. Assn. U. Women, D.A.R., Clark County Hist. Soc., Longview Bus. and Profl. Women's Club, Delta Kappa Gamma (hon.) Author: Singing Paddies, 1935; also poetry, feature articles. Home: Cathlamet WA 98612 Office: Cannon Bldg Washington DC 20515 also 3305 O St NW Washington DC 20007

HANSEN, KATHRYN GERTRUDE, ret. state ofcl., assn. editor; b. Gardner, Ill., May 24, 1912; d. Harry J. and Marguerite (Gaston) Hansen; B.S. with honors, U. Ill., 1934, M.S., 1936. Personnel asst. U. Ill., Urbana, 1945-46, supr. tng. and activities, 1946-47, personnel officer, instr. psychology, 1947-52, exec. sec. U. Civil Service System Ill., also sec. for merit bd., 1952-61, adminstrv. officer, sec. merit bd., 1961-68, dir. system, 1968-72; para-legal asst. firm Webber, Balbach, Theis and Follmer, Urbana, Ill., 1972—; also lectr., cons. personnel practice. Mem. bd. U. YWCA, 1952-55, chmn., 1954-55. Mem. Coll. and Univ. Personnel Assn. (hon., life mem., editor Jour. 1955-73, Newsletter, Internat. pres. 1967-68), Annuitants Assn. State Univs. Retirement System Ill. (state sec.-treas. 1974—), Altrusa Internat., U. Ill. Alumni Assn. (life), Campus Round Table U. Ill., Nat. League Am. Pen Women, Am. Assn. U. Women (state 1st v.p. 1958-60), Bus. and Profl. Women's Club, Levis Faculty Center, Champaign-Urbana Symphony Guild, Delta Kappa Gamma (state pres. 1961-63), Phi Mu (life), Kappa Delta Pi, Kappa Tau Alpha. Author: (with others) A Plan of Position Classification for Colleges and Universities; A Classification Plan for Staff Positions at Colleges and Universities, 1968. Editor: The Illini Worker, 1946-52; Campus Pathways, 1952-61; This is Your Civil Service Handbook, 1960-67. Author, editor publs. on personnel practices. Home: 1004 E Harding Dr Urbana IL 61801 Office: 202 Lincoln Sq Urbana IL 61801

HANSEN, LINDA WORKMAN, journalist; b. Binghamton, N.Y., Apr. 15, 1942; d. Robert Walter and Charlotte Elizabeth (Benz) Workman; B.A. in Social Sci., Elmira Coll., 1963; postgrad. in journalism Syracuse U., 1967-68; postgrad. in social sci. State U. N.Y. at Oswego, 1963, U. Rochester, 1970-71; m. Eric H. Hansen III, July 3, 1965; 1 son, Bruce Geddes. Tchr., Skaneateles, then Sidney, N.Y., 1963-66; with Gannett Pub. Co., 1966—, feature writer, asst. family editor Binghamton Evening Press, 1966-67, feature writer Times-Union, Rochester, N.Y., 1968—, drama critic, 1972—. Recipient 2d pl. award feature category N.Y. State Asso. Press Assn., 1973. Mem. Women in Communications, Newspaper Guild (exec. bd., finance com.), Sigma Delta Chi. Episcopalian. Home: 64 Pershing Dr Rochester NY 14609 Office: 55 Exchange St Rochester NY 14614

HANSEN, PHOEBE JANE HALLENBERG (MRS. ROBERT EUGENE HANSEN), city ofcl.; b. Fargo, N.D.; d. Herbert and Marjory (Marsh) Hallenberg; B.A., U. Minn., 1935, M.A., 1974; m. Robert Eugene Hansen, May 7, 1936 (dec.); children—Barret Eugene, Phoebe (Mrs. John Paul Nelson). Advt. copy writer Dayton's Dept. Store, Mpls., 1936-40, house organ editor, 1954-55, spl. events dir., 1955-56; spl. events dir. Donaldson's Dept. Store, Mpls., 1956-67; dir. pub. relations Weight Watchers, Mpls., 1968-70; coordinator cultural arts Mpls. Park and Recreation Bd., 1970—. Bd. dirs. Sr. Citizens Centers, Mpls., 1965-70; bd. dirs. Internat. Center for Students and Visitors, U. Minn., Mpls., 1965-70, chmn. pub. relations, 1965-70; bd. dirs. Walker Arts Center, Mpls., 1959-64, v.p., 1963-64; bd. dirs. Minn. Opera Co. Assn. Mem. Mpls. C. of C. (dir. women's div. 1964-67), Arts Forum (pres. 1973-74), Minn. Recreation and Park Assn., Children's Theatre Assn., Chi Omega. Club: Minnesota Collectors (sec. 1963-65). Home: 1963 S Sheridan Av Minneapolis MN 55405 Office: Mpls Park and Recreation Bd 250 S 4th St Minneapolis MN 55415

HANSEN, SHARON LEE, microbiologist; b. Corry, Pa. July 4, 1938; d. Andrew and Audrey (Mason) Hansen; B.S., Beaver Coll., 1960; M.S., U. Md., 1970. Research asst. U. Pa. Hosp., Phila., 1960-61; head dept. bacteriology Franklin Sq. Hosp., Balt., 1961-62; head clin. study center labs. U. Md. Hosp., 1962-63; asst. to head Bioquest Quality Control, Cockeysville, Md., 1963-69; dir. microbiology Micro Tech Labs., Balt., 1969-71; chief microbiologist VA Hosp., Balt., 1971—. Mem. Am. Soc. for Microbiology, Am. Soc. Clin. Pathologists, Am. Inst. Biol. Scis., Am. Soc. Med. Technologists, Am. Pub. Health Assn., Internat. Food Technologists, Am. Pub. Health Assn., Md. Acad. Scis. Democrat. Presbyn. Home: 1543 Kennewick Rd Baltimore MD 21218 Office: Lab Service VA Hosp 3900 Loch Raven Blvd Baltimore MD 21218

HANSON, ANNE COFFIN (MRS. BERNARD ALAN HANSON), educator; b. Kinston, N.C., Dec. 12, 1921; d. Francis Joseph Howells and Annie Roulhac (Coffin) Coffin; B.F.A., U. So. Cal., 1943; M.A. in Creative Arts, U. N.C., 1951; Ph.D., Bryn Mawr Coll., 1962; m. Bernard Alan Hanson, June 27, 1961; children by previous marriage—James Warfield Garson, Robert Coffin Garson, Ann Blaine Garson. Instr., Albright Art Sch., U. Buffalo (N.Y.), 1955-58; vis. asso. prof. art Cornell U., 1963; asst. prof. Swarthmore Coll., 1963-64, Bryn Mawr Coll., 1964-68; dir. Internat. Study Center, Mus. Modern Art, N.Y.C., 1968-69; prof. history of art Yale U., 1970—. Nat. Endowment for the Humanities fellow, 1967-68, Am. Council Learned Socs. grantee, summer 1963. Mem. Coll. Art Assn. Am. (pres. 1972-74). Author: Jacopo della Quercia's Fonte Gaia, 1965, Edouard Manet, 1966. Contbr. articles to profl. pubs. Mem. editorial bd. The Art Bulletin, 1971—; editor monograph series Coll. Art Assn., 1968-70. Home: 28 Lincoln St New Haven CT 06511 Office: Dept History Art 56 High St Yale University New Haven CT 06520

HANSON, BETTE LEE (MRS. ROGER W. HANSON), broadcast exec.; b. Superior, Wis., Aug. 10; d. Reuben B. and Dena K. (Knudsen) Johnson; Mus.B., U. Ia.; m. Roger W. Hanson, Dec. 27, 1948; children—Heidi, Eric. Women's program dir. WAPI Radio and TV, Birmingham, Ala., 1957—, feature reporter WAPI News, 1970—; lectr. Pres. women's com. Spain Rehab. Center, 1971—. Recipient numerous awards for excellence in journalism A.P. and U.P., 1957, 58, 59, 65, 66, 68, 70, 71. Mem. Am. Assn. U. Women, Am. Women in Radio and TV, Sigma Delta Chi. Home: 1734 Woodbine Dr Birmingham AL 35216 Office: PO Box 1310 Birmingham AL 35201

HANSON, BONNIE JOAN, editor; b. Clear Lake, Ia., June 20, 1929; d. Lester Leland and Elizabeth (Dull) Hanson; student Mpls. Sch. Fine Art, 1950, Bethany Fellowship Missionary Tng. Center, 1953-55. Editor Floodtide mag.; artist Christian Lit. Crusade, Fort Washington, Pa., 1955—. Lutheran. Author: Teenage Rebel, 1966; Born Wild, 1968; A Strange, Lonely Feeling, 1972. Address: 701 Pennsylvania Av Fort Washington PA 19034

HANSON, KATIE LOU CRAFT, educator; b. Edmund, S.C., Dec. 18, 1914; d. Dallas Ristmus and Annie (Shumpert) Craft; A.B., U. S.C., 1936, M.A., 1939; Ed.D., Columbia, 1950; postgrad. Union Theol. Sem., 1946, (S.C. Scholar) George Peabody Coll., 1940, George Washington U., 1944-45; m. Eugene Nelson Hanson, June 29, 1950; children—Louise (Mrs. Ronald Gossard), Jennifer. Tchr., prin. pub. elementary schs., S.C., 1936-42; campus sch. tchr. Sue Bennet Coll., London, Ky., 1947-48; mem. faculty Ohio Northern U., Ada, asso. prof., 1955-57, prof., 1957—. Served to lt. WAVE, USNR, 1942-45. Mem. Internat. Reading Assn. (pres. Ohio council 1955-56; chmn. Ohio chpt. 1966—), Katie Lou Hanson Reading Council (pres. 1972), Am. Assn. U. Women, Assn. for Curriculum Devel., Internat. Platform Assn., Kappa Delta Pi, Delta Kappa Gamma. Democrat. Lutheran. Club: Twice-Ten Women's (Ada, O.). Contbr. articles to profl. jours. Home: Route 2 Ada OH 45810

HANSON, NOEL ADRIENNE (MRS. JOSEPH PERRY HANSON), reporter; b. Liberty, N.C., Oct. 12, 1909; d. Alfred Barton and Theodora Anne (Parrott) Highfill; A.A., King's Bus. Coll., 1928; postgrad. Boston U., 1955-56, U. Mass., 1957-58; m. Joseph Perry Hanson, Sept. 22, 1930 (dec. Mar. 1968); children—Mary (Mrs. Martin Joseph Salmon), Natli A., Joseph Edward, Douglas MacArthur. Mgr., Art's Gas Sta., Orange, Mass., 1928-30; supr. first aid sewing project, Orange, 1933-35; asst. mgr. sch. lunch program, Bolton, Mass., 1945-59; supr. quality control H.H. Scott, Inc., Maynard, Mass., 1959-72; reporter Worcester Telegram, Bolton, 1952—. Sec., Bolton Pub. Health Com., 1944—, Bolton Citizen's Assn., 1954—; Bolton rep. to area council Office for Children, 1973—; sec., treas. Bolton 4-H Club Com., 1965-73, Mass. Council for Pub. Schs., 1955-56. Mem. Ft. Devens, Bolton (dir. 1969—, corporate clk. 1969—, sec. 1964—) hist. socs., Bay State, Lancaster League hist. socs., Bolton Sr. Citizen's Club. Club: Thursday Evening Guild. Home: 124 Main St Bolton MA 01740

HANSON, PAULINE DAVIS (MRS. WILLIAM FRANK HANSON), lawyer; b. Selma, Cal., July 13, 1922; d. Rees Peter and Georgia Way (Johnston) Davis; A.A., Reedley Community Coll., 1941; B.A., U. Pacific, 1943; J.D., Stanford, 1946; m. William Frank Hanson, June 19, 1947; children—Nels, Victor and Alfred (twins). Admitted to Cal. bar, 1946; asst. to assemblyman from 33d Dist. of Cal., 1959-61; sr. atty. Ct. Appeals, 5th Dist., Fresno, Cal., 1961—. Bd. dirs. San Joaquin Valley Town Hall, Inc., Fresno. Mem. Am., Fresno County bar assns., State Bar Cal., Cal. State Attys., Am. Assn. U. Women. Mem. Order Eastern Star. Club: Soroptimist (Fresno).

HANSON, PHYLLIS MARIE GEIS (MRS. HOWARD H. HANSON), realtor; b. Sioux Falls, S.D.; d. William H. and Jane Irene (Manley) Geis; student Nettleton Bus. Coll., 1943; m. H.S. Eidy, Mar. 8, 1942 (div. 1947); m. 2d, Howard H. Hanson, Apr. 23, 1954; 1 son, Phillip G. Co-owner, mgr. hotel, 1942-43; asst. mgr. State Theatre, asst. to dir. for Eastern S.D., Minn. Amusement Co., 1943-45; owner, operator Brunch House Cafe, 1947; founder home econs. dept. L.C. Lippert Co., Sioux Falls, 1948, dir., 1949-54; salesman Dorothy Poulos, Real Estate, Pierre, S.D., 1959; partner Poulos & Hanson, Real Estate, Pierre, 1961—. Mem. Central S.D. Bd. Realtors, 1959—, sec., 1961, treas., 1962, pres., 1963, v.p., 1973, chmn. state real estate conv., 1963, named Realtor of Year, 1963, 73; mem. S.D. Bd. Realtors, 1959—, Women's Council Realtors. Mem. S.D. Assn. for Blind, 1954—. Mem. Nat. Assn. Real Estate Bds., Nat. Brokers Inst., S.D. Assn. Realtors (dir. 1971-73, 73-75), Pierre C. of C. (dir. 1966-69, treas. 1967-69, exec. bd. 1967-69), U.S. (mem. tourist and conv. com. 1964-65), Pierre (dir. 1973-74) chambers commerce, Beta Sigma Phi (host pres. state conv. 1966). Roman Catholic (pres. band 1963). Home: 417 W 2d St Pierre SD 57501 Office: 302 Coteau St Pierre SD 57501

HANSON, SERENE GERENE RUST (MRS. HUBERT O. HANSON), savs. and loan exec.; b. Grantsburg, Wis.; d. Anton O. and Clare (Sather) Rust; student Tulsa Bus. Coll., Woodbury Coll., 1934-35; grad. diploma Am. Savs. and Loan Inst., 1960; m. Hubert O. Hanson, June 15, 1941 (dec. Mar. 1968). Supr., Midwest Fed. Savs. & Loan Assn., Mpls., 1955-64, asst. sec., 1964-71, asst. v.p., 1971-72, v.p., 1972—. Minn. speech dir. Am. Savings & Loan Inst., 1963-69, dep. gov. Minn., 1968-69. Program chmn. Minn. Safety Council, 1965-67, vice chmn. women's div., 1972-74, chmn., 1974—; treas. Crippled Child Relief, 1954-57, pres., 1971-73; mem. promotion com. Downtown Council of Mpls., 1963-66, 69-74. Recipient Good Neighbor award Sta. WCCO, N.W. Ford Dealers, N.W. Orient Airlines, 1971. Mem. UN Assn. Minn. (dir. 1969-70, 3d v.p. 1970-74, 2d v.p. 1974—), Mpls. C. of C., Internat. Platform Assn., Minn. Sunshine (exec. com. 1950-55). Club: Zonta (treas. 1968-69, v.p. 1971-73, pres. 1973—) (Mpls.). Contbr. to Comml. West mag. Home: 8235 Oakmere Rd Minneapolis MN 55438 Office: 801 Nicollet Mall Minneapolis MN 55402

HANSON, SHIRLEY JEAN (MRS. DUWAYNE EDWARD HANSON), editor; b. Independence, Kan., Mar. 18, 1934; d. Carl Leon and Clarissa Mabel (Reynolds) Musgrove; student Independence Jr. Coll., 1953; m. DuWayne Edward Hanson, June 13, 1953; children—Gregory, Perry. Operator, Southwestern Bell Tel. Co., Independence and Neodesha, Kan., 1951-61; office clk. Wilson County Hosp., Neodesha, 1961-63; sec. Bacon Ins. & Real Estate Co., Neodesha, 1963-64; editor Neodesha Register, 1964—, feature writer, columnist, bookkeeper, 1964—. Cons. high sch. journalism, 1970. Bd. dirs. Community Fund, 1966-67. Mem. Nat., Kan. (contest winner 1970, 71, 72, 73) press assns., Nat., Kan. (contest winner 1973) presswomen, Wilson County Hosp. Aux., Republican. Lutheran. Club: Independence Country, Women's Golf Assn. Home: 723 N 9th St Neodesha KS 66757 Office: PO Box 210 810 Main St Neodesha KS 66757

HANSON, VIRGINIA GORDON (MRS. HAROLD E. HANSON), editor; b. Oquawka, Ill., Oct. 27, 1898; d. James Walker and Mary Angela (Hickok) Gordon; student Am. U., 1947-48; George Washington U., 1953-54; m. Harold E. Hanson, June 5, 1926 (dec. 1972); 1 son, James E. Publs. editor U.S. Dept. Justice, Bur. Prisons, Washington, 1942-62; editor Am. Theosophist, Wheaton, Ill., 1962—; sr. editor Thesophical Pub. House, Wheaton, 1973—. Mem. Nat. League Am. Penwomen. Author: A Man Should Rejoice, 1944. Contbr. articles to theosophical publs. Home: PO Box 270 Wheaton IL 60187 Office: 1926 N Main St Wheaton IL 60187

HANUS, ANN, ins. co. exec.; b. N.Y.C.; Jan. 9, 1915; d. Adolf and Louisa (Nemec) Hanus; B.B.A. magna cum laude, Coll. City N.Y., 1957. Mgr. premium collection and accounting Guardian Life Ins. Co. Am., N.Y.C., 1959-63, assisted in design and installation consol. life computer system, 1964-68, dir. computer systems, 1969-71, dir. programming, 1972-73, asst. v.p. data processing, 1973—. Mem. Beta Gamma Sigma, Beta Alpha Psi. Home: 444 E 20th St New York City NY 10009 Office: 201 Park Av S New York City NY 10003

HANWIT, MURIEL BADIN (MRS. WILLIAM HANWIT), occupational therapist; b. Bronx, N.Y., Feb. 28, 1944; d. Joseph and Lillian S. (Weinstein) Badin; B.A., N.Y. U., 1965, certificate occupational therapy, 1967, M.A., 1974; m. William Hanwit, Sept. 10, 1967; 1 dau., Alison. Evaluation counselor Occupational Tng. Center for Handicapped, Morristown, N.J., 1967-69; sr. occupational therapist N.Y. State Sch. for Mentally Retarded, Letchworth Village, Thiells, N.Y., 1969—. Vocational Rehab. Adminstrn. grantee, 1965-67. Mem. Am. Occupational Therapy Assn., N.J. Assn. for Retarded Children. 41 Marcia Rd Ringwood NJ 07456 Office: Letchworth Village Thiells NY 10984

HANZALEK, ASTRID (LUISE) TEICHER, state legislator; b. N.Y.C., Jan. 6, 1928; d. Arthur Albin and Luise Gertrud (Funke) Teicher; grad. Concordia Coll., 1947; B.S., U. Pa., 1949; m. Frederick J. Hanzalek, Nov. 11, 1955. Mem. Conn. Ho. of Reps., 1970—, now also asst. majority leader. Dir., Suffield Center Corp.; trustee Suffield Savs. Bank. Past v.p. Conn. Travelers Aid Soc.; mem. Edn. Commn. of States, Conn. Edn. Council; sec. Suffield Citizens Adv. Com., 1966—. Vice pres. 6th Congl. Dist.-East Women's Republican Club, 1968—. Bd. dirs. Greater Hartford Community Council, Suffield Women's Republican Club, Emergency Aid Assn., Suffield, Conn. Mem. Conn. Womens Golf Assn. (dir. 1970—), Nat., Conn. orders women legislators, Nat. Legislative Conf. (energy com.), Alpha Chi Omega. Lutheran. Home: 155 S Main St Suffield CT 06078

HANZEL, MARSHA WEINSTEIN (MRS. JEFFREY SHELDON HANZEL), journalist; b. Columbus, O., Oct. 3, 1947; d. Marcus Leroy and Eleanor Frances (Reich) Weinstein; B.J., U. Mo., 1969; postgrad. U. Va., 1970-71. Staff writer Norfolk (Va.) Virginian-Pilot, 1969-70; editor Norfolk Naval Sta. newspaper, 1972-73; staff writer Hartford (Conn.) Courant, 1973—. Free lance photographer, 1972—. Mem. Women in Communications, Nat. Fedn., Va. press women. Home: 10 King Arthur Way Apt 5 Newington CT 06111 Office: Hartford Courant 285 Broad St Hartford CT 06115

HAPGOOD, POLLY PRENTICE, civic worker; b. Hartford, Conn.; d. Frank and Mary (Merrill) Prentice; student Bennett Coll., 1920-22; m. Thomas Emerson Hapgood, Sept. 30, 1922 (div. Mar. 1948); children—Frank Prentice, Polly (Mrs. Andrew Fuller Mitchell). Dir., sec. Woodland Nursery Sch.; chmn. Jr. League Child Health Clinics; mem. Red Cross Nurses Aide Corps, Santa Fe, 1936-56. Bd. dirs. Humane Ednl. League, North St. Settlement, Conn. Soc. Mental Health, Hartford County Mental Health Soc. Mem. League Women Voters (pres. 1934-35), D.A.R., Soc. Mayflower Descs. (charter N.M.). Episcopalian. Contbr. articles to profl. jours. Home: 5100 Constitution St NE Albuquerque NM 87110

HARADINE, JANE CAROL (MRS. WILLARD HARADINE), newspaperwoman; b. Hibbing, Minn., Jan. 14, 1934; d. Simon Alexander and Lillian Helen (Arkkola) Simonson; student U. Minn., 1951-52; R.N., St. Luke's Hosp. Sch. Nursing, 1954; m. Eugene VanderVeer, Oct. 1, 1954 (div. Nov. 1969); children—Kimberly Ann, Debra Lynn, Pamela Sue; m. 2d, Willard Haradine, Dec. 31, 1970. Registered nurse, Grand Rapids, Mich., 1955-60; with Fideler Co., Grand Rapids, 1960-66, editorial supr., 1961-63; reporter Belding (Mich.) Banner-News, 1966-68; med. reporter Grand Rapids (Mich.) Press, 1968—. Mem. Mich. Women's Press Club (sec. 1970-73). Home: 944 Northlawn St NE Grand Rapids MI 49505 Office: The Grand Rapids Press Vandenberg Center Grand Rapids MI 49502

HARADON, VIRGINIA ELIZABETH INGLES (MRS. CLAYTON BARTLETT HARADON), ednl. therapist; b. Redfield, S.D., July 27, 1913; d. Thomas Jefferson and Della May (Hooker) Ingles; B.A., U. Omaha, 1946, M.A., 1948; postgrad. research U. Neb. Med. Sch., 1946; M.Ed., Trinity U., 1959; M.S.W. in psychiatric social work (USPHS grantee) Worden Sch. Social Service, Our Lady of Lake Coll., 1961; m. Alvin James Maes, June 1, 1936 (dec. 1944); m. 2d, Clayton Bartlett Haradon, May 10, 1946; children—John Bartlett, Susan. Newspaper reporter suburban Los Angeles, 1933, 36; research asst. on relocation Japanese-Ams. sociology dept. U. Cal. at Los Angeles, 1944; psychol. testing, retarded and disturbed children, psych. clinic U. Omaha, also psychodiagnostic testing, family therapy A. E. Bennett Neuropsychiat. Found., Omaha, 1945-47; instr. Marriage and Family, U. Omaha, 1947-48; certified psychologist schs. Locust Valley and Bethpage (both N.Y.), sch. cons. Nassau County (N.Y.) Probation Dept., 1956-58, also marriage and family counselor Family Welfare Assn. Nassau County, summer 1957; psychol. interne Valley Stream (N.Y.) Summer Reading Sch. (study of dyslexia), summer 1958, pvt. practice counseling, ednl. therapy, San Antonio, 1962—; instr. marriage and family Our Lady of Lake Coll., San Antonio, 1970; cons. San Antonio Lit. Council, YWCA, Juvenile Intervention Program. Mem. Community Com. for Mental Health Clinic, Glen Cove, N.Y., 1958. Bd. dirs. Beautify San Antonio Assn., Arts Council San Antonio. Mem. Am. Assn. Marriage and Family Counselors, Am. Personnel and Guidance Assn., Assn. Children with Learning Disabilities, Nat. Assn. Social Workers, N.E.A., A.A.A.S., Family Therapy Assn. Tex., Acad. Certified Social Workers, Acad. Religion and Mental Health (sec., treas. San Antonio chpt. 1966), San Antonio Group Psychotherapy and Group Process Soc. (exec. council 1973-74), Internat. Transactional Analysis Assn., A.S.C.A.P., Nat. Acad. Popular Music, Delphian Soc., Alpha Kappa Delta. Composed, pub. When Are You Comin' Home, Joe (also RCA recorded), 1955; Welcome to Texas, 1968; In Tribute to Trinity; others. Contbr. articles to profl. publs. Home: 614 Fresno Dr San Antonio TX 78212 Office: Suite 4 Kelly Bldg 2003 San Pedro Av San Antonio TX 78212

HARBAUGH, JANE WORTH, univ. dean; b. Balt., Apr. 24, 1930; d. Vernon Leslie and Charlotte (Kirby) Harbaugh; A.B., Tufts Coll., 1952; M.A., Fletcher Sch. Law and Diplomacy, 1953, Ph.D., 1957. Instr. history, polit. sci. U. Chattanooga, 1957-59, asst. prof., 1959-62, asso. prof. 1962-65, prof., chmn. dept. history, 1965-69; dean Coll. Arts and Scis., U. Tenn., Chattanooga, 1969—. Rockefeller Found. research grantee, 1956; recipient Evans Found. award, 1963; fellow Center East Asian Studies, Harvard, 1960-61. Mem. ad hoc com. adv. editorial bd. U. State N.Y., 1965; v.p. Adult Edn. Council Chattanooga Area, 1962-64, dir., 1958-60. Mem. Am. Assn. U. Profs., Assn. for Asian Studies (chmn. com. on undergrad. edn. 1966-68). Democrat. Home: 720 Maryland Circle Chattanooga TN 37412

HARBIN, SHIRLEY MEVERNA (MRS. DEAN T. HARBIN), city ofcl.; b. Santa Cruz, Cal., Feb. 26, 1932; d. Fordyce Owen and Lillian Meverna (Erickson) Pengilly; student Muskegon Community Coll., 1950-52; B.A., U. Mich., 1954, M.A., 1960; postgrad. Wayne U., 1963; m. Dean T. Harbin, Dec. 27, 1956; children—Joseph Brian, Paul Dean. Tchr., Pontiac (Mich.) High Sch., 1954-57; social dir. U. Mich. English Lang. Inst., Ann Arbor, summers 1954-55; with Dunston's Florists, Pontiac, Mich., part-time, 1954-57; tchr. Ypsilanti (Mich.) Jr. High Sch., 1957-60; costumer Assn. Performing Arts, U. Mich., Ann Arbor, tchr. creative drama Ann Arbor Bd. Edn., dir. summer performing arts Camp Homestead Acres, Chelsea, Mich., 1961-63; drama dir. Detroit Parks and Recreation, 1963-69; performing arts dir. City of Detroit Dept. Parks and Recreation, 1970—. Instr., Wayne County Community Coll., 1970—; program asst. WWJ TV children's show Oopsie, 1971—; cons. Oakland U., Mott Found. Continuing Edn. Creative Drama, 1965. Pres., Detroit Theatre Council, 1970—. Bd. dirs. Detroit Met. Black Arts, Inc., sec.-treas., 1970—; bd. dirs. Detroit City Theatre Assn. of Detroit Inst. Arts, festival chmn., 1972; nat. publicity chmn. Children's Theatre Assn., co-chmn. Mich. Children's Theatre Conf., Kalamazoo, 1970; conv. speaker Mich. Parks and Recreation Assn., Lansing, Mich., 1972, chmn. cultural arts, 1973—; co-chmn. Internat. Theatre Olympiad and Symposium hosted by Detroit Met. Theatre Council, 1975. Mem. Internat. Assn. Theatre for Children and Youth (coordinator Show and Tell the World for Internat. Festival, Albany, N.Y., 1972), Am. Community Theatre Assn. (chmn. royalty research com.), Community Theatre Assn. Mich. (bd. dirs. 1965—). Editor: Theatre-the Michigan Scene, newsletter Community Theatre Assn. Mich., 1965-69, editor directory, 1969—; (poems) Many Voices, One Dream. Founder, editor: Detroit Theatre Council Newsletter, 1970—. Home: 15081 Rockdale St Detroit MI 48223 Office: 2735 W Warren St Detroit MI 48208

HARBOUR, JEANNE DULAS (MRS. HOWARD HARBOUR), child psychiatrist; b. Labatut, France, Feb. 9, 1921; d. Pierre and Dorothy (Stafas) Dulas; M.D., Sch. Medicine, Paris, France, 1947; M.D., Wis. U., 1968; m. Howard Harbour, June 15, 1962. Came to U.S., 1958, naturalized, 1967. Sch. pub. health med. insp., France, 1948-58; intern Presbyn.-St. Luke's Hosp., Chgo., 1958-59, resident, 1959-61; clin. asst. psychiatry Ill. U., 1959-61; fellow psychiatry McGill U., 1962, Toronto U., 1963; fellow child psychiatry Chapel Hill Meml. Hosp., N.C. U., 1964-65; cons. child psychiatry North Shore Hosp., Winnetka, Ill., 1966-67, Mendota State Hosp., Madison, Wis., 1968-71; clin. instr. Wis. U., Madison, 1968-71; attending child psychiatrist Children's Meml. Hosp., Chgo.; clin. asso. prof. dept. psychiatry Loyola U., Chgo., 1973—. Diplomate in child psychiatry Am. Bd. Psychiatry and Neurology. Fellow Am. Orthopsychiat. Assn.; mem. A.M.A., Am. Psychiat. Assn., Ill. Med. Soc., Am. Med. Womens Assn., Internat. Platform Assn. Research on color blindness of sch. children. Home: Naperville IL 60540 Office: Loyola U Medical Center Maywood IL 60153

HARD, MARGARET AILEEN MCGREGOR (MRS. ARTHUR R. HARD), educator; b. Mortlach, Sask., Can., June 26, 1919; s. Thomas William and Minnie Isadore (Dobson) McGregor; B.S., U. Sask., 1940; M.S., U. Wis., 1942; m. Arthur R. Hard, Dec. 29, 1948; children—Margaret Jean, Robert. Research chemist Wash. State U., Pullman, 1942-43, instr., 1944-45, asst. prof., 1946-51, asso. prof., 1952-57, prof. food and nutrition Coll. Home Econs., 1957—, chmn. home econs. research center, 1951—, acting dean Coll. Home Econs., 1973—. Named Woman of Year Bus. and Profl. Women, 1953. Mem. Am. Chem. Soc., Am. Home Econs. Assn., Inst. Food Technologists, Omicron Nu, Phi Kappa Phi, Sigma Xi, Delta Gamma (Rose award 1974). Episcopalian. Contbr. articles to various publs. Home: SE 1000 Spring St Pullman WA 99163 Office: 308 White Hall Wash State U Pullman WA 99163

HARDAWAY, PAMELA LYNN, advt. exec.; b. N.Y.C., May 16, 1942; d. Joseph Anthony and Frances (Nestor) Kundle; A.A.S., State U. N.Y. at Farmingdale, 1962; m. Herman B. Hardaway, Dec. 26, 1971; stepchildren—Janie, Hugh, Carla. Copywriter, Norman, Craig & Kumel, N.Y.C., 1962-67, Joe Sacco & Friends, N.Y.C., 1967-68; v.p., creative dir. Erwin Wasey Advt., Los Angeles, 1968—; instr.'s asst. effective pub. speaking and human relations course Dale Carnegie Sch., 1969—. Recipient Internat. Broadcasting award, 1969, CLIO award Am. TV and Radio Commls. Festival, 1970. Office: 5455 Wilshire Blvd Los Angeles CA 90036

HARDEN, CLAUDIA JEAN (MRS. JAMES EDWARD HARDEN), broadcasting exec.; b. Elgin, Ill., Oct. 22, 1943; d. Howard Walter and Dorothy (Hanauer) Griesbach; student State U. Iowa, 1961-62; B.A., Northwestern U., 1964; m. James Edward Harden, Aug. 13, 1966; 1 dau., Jana Elizabeth. Continuity writer ABC, Chgo., 1964-65; asst. dir. continuity WFLD-TV, Chgo., 1965-66; sec.-treas. Harden Broadcasting Co., Long Beach, Cal., 1969—; exec. producer KNAC Radio (owned by Harden Broadcasting), Long Beach, 1969—. Asst. election cons. KNBC-TV, Los Angeles, 1968—. Office: Suite 1000 320 Pine Av Long Beach CA 90812

HARDEN, MARGARET ANNE (MRS. JAMES ALEXANDER HARDEN, JR.), retail trade exec., real estate developer; b. Elizabeth City, Va., July 23, 1936; d. Dayton Roosevelt and Edna Mae (Allen) Sulfridge; student Colo. State U., 1954-56, 66-68; student N.Y. Sch. Interior Design, 1973—; m. James Alexander Harden, Jr., Aug. 6, 1960; 1 dau., Pamela Ruth. Co-propr. Valley Vet. Supply Co., Ft. Collins, Colo., 1960—; co-propr. Nedrah A A Devel. Co., Ft. Collins, 1966—; propr. Anne's Antiques and Decorator Furnishings, Ft. Collins, 1968—. Lectr. antique appraising; interior designer, 1968—. County chmn. Multiple Sclerosis Drive, 1969; charter mem. Ft. Collins Symphony Guild. Mem. Nat. Assn. Dealers in Antiques, LaPorte Community Involvement Com., Nedrah Acres Archtl. Assn., Larimer County, Albany County Wyo. stockgrowers assns., Colo. Cattleman's Assn., Kappa Delta. Presbyn. (elder 1973). Democrat. Club: Country ofen Ft. Collins. Home: 1801 Country Club Rd Fort Collins CO 80521 also PO Box 710 Fort Collins CO 80522 Office: 131 Lincoln Av Fort Collins CO

HARDEN, OLETA ELIZABETH (MRS. DENNIS CLARENCE HARDEN), educator, ednl. adminstr.; b. Jamestown, Ky., Nov. 22, 1935; d. Stanley Virgil and Myrtie Alice (Stearns) McWhorter; B.A., Western Ky. U., 1956; M.A. in English, U. Ark., 1958, Ph.D. in English, 1965; m. Dennis Clarence Harden, July 23, 1966. Teaching asst. U. Ark., Fayetteville, 1956-57, 58-59, 61-63; instr. S.W. Mo. State Coll., Springfield, 1957-58, Murray (Ky.) U., 1959-61; asst. prof. English, Northeastern State Coll., Tahlequah, Okla., 1963-65; asst. prof. Wichita (Kan.) State U., 1965-66; asst. prof. English Wright State U., Dayton, O., 1966-68, asso. prof., 1968-72, prof., 1972—, asst. chmn. English dept., 1967-70, asst. dean coll. liberal arts, 1971-73, asso. dean, 1973-74, exec. dir. Gen. Univ. Services, 1974—. Wright State U. Research and Devel. grantee, 1969, Found. grantee, 1971. Mem. Modern Lang. Assn., Coll. English Assn., Am. Assn. U. Profs. Author: Maria Edgeworth's Art of Prose Fiction, 1971. Home: 2618 Big Woods Trail Fairborn OH 45324 Office: Gen Univ Services Wright State University 7751 Colonel Glenn Hwy Dayton OH 45431

HARDER, LOIS MAYBELLE, educator; b. Berwyn, Ill., Aug. 30, 1932; d. Clarence Louis and Rose (Johnson) Harder; B.S., Mary Washington Coll., 1953; M.S., MacMurray Coll., 1954; postgrad. N.Y.U., 1960-61. Instr. asst. prof. phys. edn. MacMurray Coll., 1953-60; asst. prof. Goucher Coll., Towson, Md., 1963-69. Riding dir. Camp. Illahee, N.C., 1953; instr. Mary Washington Coll., summer 1961; mem. div. girls and womens sports Nat. Riding Com., 1970—. Instr. life sav. and swimming A.R.C., 1953-67. Mem. Am. Assn. U. Profs., Am. Assn. U. Women, A.A.H.P.E.R., Am. Horse Shows Assn., Va. Horse Show Assn. Republican. Presbyn. Home: 715 Deacon Rd Fredericksburg VA 22401

HARDER, MARTHA BROWN, univ. adminstr.; b. Linden, Tenn., Dec. 31, 1933; d. Edmund Green and Bonnie (Kirk) Harder; B.S., George Peabody Coll., Tchrs., 1955; M.A. Austin Peay State Coll., Clarksville, Tenn., 1958; Ed.D., Auburn (Ala.) U., 1973. Tchr., Clarksville city schs., 1955-58, Cumberland Coll., Lebanon, Tenn., 1953-63; dean students Lander Coll., Greenwood, S.C., 1963-66; dean women Va. Poly. Inst., Blacksburg, 1966-68, dean for student program, 1968-71, asst. dir. spl. acad. programs, 1973—. Mem. Nat., Regional assns. women deans and counselors, So. Coll. Personnel Assn. (sec. 1966-68), Nat. Collegiate Honor Council, Kappa Delta Pi. Delta Kappa Gamma. Home: Carlton Scott Apts Blacksburg VA 24060

HARDESTY, HELEN POPE (MRS. JOSEPH DONNER HARDESTY), civic worker; b. Memphis, Aug. 28, 1914; d. Ashby G. and Adah (Lyons) Pope; grad. high sch.; m. Joseph Donner Hardesty, Sept. 18, 1935; children—Joseph Donner, Eugene Arthur. Hon. mem. Memphis City Beautiful Commn., 1949-59; mem. Mayor's Youth Opportunity Com. Health, Edn. and Welfare, 1967; pres. Memphis and Selby County Ch. Women United, 1966-67; Tenn. pres. Ch. Women United, 1968—, mem. nat. bd., 1971—; v.p. Tenn. Council Chs., 1968—; state rep. U.S. Com. for UNICEF, 1967—; mem. exec. bd. Methodist Hosp. Aux., Bethlehem Center Community House. Named Most Outstanding Woman Memphis Inter-Denominational Fellowship, 1967. Mem. Womans Soc. Christian Service (life, past pres., dist. exec. bd., chmn. Christian social relations Memphis Conf. 1971-73). Methodist. Club: Jackson Terrace Garden (past pres. Memphis). Home: 3161 Caradine St Memphis TN 38112

HARDGRAVE, DOROTHY OPAL (MRS. NORRIS HARWELL HARDGRAVE), coll. bookstore mgr.; b. nr. Covington, Tex., Oct. 5, 1918; d. William David and Mildred (King) Burnett; grad. high sch.; m. Norris Harwell Hardgrave, Oct. 1, 1940; 1 dau., Patricia Ann (Mrs. Johnny Leon Coker). Asst. dir. Bapt. Student Union, Corsicana, Tex., 1962-63; mgr. bookstore Navarro Jr. Coll., Corsicana, 1963—. Coordinator girls div. Navarro County Youth Exposition, 1961—. Mem. P.T.A. (life), Nat. Bookstores. Democrat. Baptist (tng. union dir. 1963—). Clubs: Altrusa, Navarro Faculty. Home: PO Box 92 Corsicana TX 75110 Office: PO Box 1170 Corsicana TX 75110

HARDIE, RUTH DION (MRS. THOMAS G. HARDIE), writer; b. Providence, Oct. 14, 1926; d. Albert Louis and Anna (Nelson) Dion; A.B., Skidmore Coll., 1948; m. Thomas G. Hardie, Dec. 23, 1950; children—Todd, Louise, Thomas Gary 3d, Elizabeth. Editor, Vogue, N.Y.C., London, Paris, 1948-50; fashion editor Paris (France) Rev., 1951, Pathfinder mag., 1951-52; free-lance writer, 1952-60; columnist Balt. News-Am., 1961-64, Balt. Sun, 1966-73; free-lance writer features in newspapers and mags. Recipient Outstanding Alumni award Skidmore Coll., 1972. Episcopalian. Author: View from the Hill, 1971. Contbg. Editor House and Garden mag. Address: Thornhill Farm Glyndon MD 21071

HARDIE, VIRGINIA SMITH, psychologist; b. Sycamore, Ga., June 12, 1907; d. Wilbur Riddick and Pearl (Fields) Smith; student Agnes Scott Coll., 1925-27; A.B., LaGrange Coll., 1929; M.A., U. Ga., 1933; postgrad., Columbia, N.Y. U., 1948-49, U. N.C., 1951; Ed.D. (Colo. Bus. and Profl. Women fellow), U. Colo., 1955; m. Newton Gary Hardie, Apr. 14, 1936 (dec. Nov. 1958); children—Sue (Mrs. Glenwood Jefferson Mitchell), Newton Gary. Tchr., Columbus (Ga.) High Sch., 1935-40, Atlanta and Fulton County high schs., 1940-43; supr., coordinator counseling and rehab. U.S. Army Hosp. Service, 1943-48; owner, dir. pvt. counseling offices, N.Y.C., Augusta, Ga., 1948-54; dir. counseling and placement Atlanta and Fulton County schs., 1948-50; dir. guidance Richmond County schs., Augusta, 1950-54; counselor, trainer Cole. Dept. Vocational Edn., Denver, 1954-55; acting asst. prof. edn. U. Colo., 1954-55; prof. gerontology Adult Continuing Edn. Center, Clemson (S.C.) Coll., 1957, 58, psychologist, dir. counseling clinic, 1962—; asso. prof. ednl. psychology U. Tenn., 1959-62. Vis. prof. various colls. and univs.; dir. S.C. Nat. Bank, Clemson; psychol. cons. U.S. Dept. Health, Edn. and Welfare. Bd. dirs. Presbyn. Coll., Clinton, S.C. Mem. Am., S.C. (tri-county pres. 1963-64) personnel and guidance assns., Am., Southeastern, S.C. psychol. assns., S.C. Mental Health Assn. (pres. 1969, pres. 1974, sec. bd.), Am. Assn. U. Profs., Am. Assn. U. Women (1st v.p. Clemson chpt. 1955-56), Bus. and Profl. Women, League Women Voters, Pi Lambda Theta, Kappa Delta Pi, Kappa Alpha Theta. Presbyn. (elder 1973). Club: Altrusa (Atlanta). Author: Women at Work, 1955. Contbr. articles to profl. lit. Home: PO Box 86 Pendleton SC 29670

HARDIN, CAROLYN MYRICK, educator, physiologist; b. New Albany, Ind., Dec. 31, 1929; d. James Madison and Olive Cleon (Venner) Myrick; student U. Md., 1946-48; B.A., George Washington U., 1958, M.A., 1959, Ph.D., 1969; postgrad. Cath. U. Am., 1959-61. Lab. instr. physiology dept. George Washington U. Med. Center, 1965-69; instr. psychiatry Meharry Med. Coll., Nashville, 1969-70, asst. prof. psychiatry, 1970-71, asst. prof. pharmacology and psychiatry, 1971—. NIH-Nat. Heart Inst. fellow, 1964-69. Mem. A.A.A.S., Sigma Xi. Democrat. Methodist. Club: University (Nashville). Research, publs. in brain research. Home: 1906 South St Nashville TN 37212

HARDIN, ELIZABETH COOPER (MRS. JOHN R. HARDIN), civic worker; b. Dayton, O., Aug. 29, 1901; d. Hugh L. and Frances (Graves) Cooper; grad. Finch Jr. Coll., 1921; student sculpture under Salem Borglum, 1922; m. John R. Hardin, Nov. 24, 1924; children—John R., Frances H. (Mrs. Cornelius J. Reid, Jr.). Exhibited Nat. Sculpture Soc., N.Y.C., 1923; Cleve. Mus., 1922. Chmn. nurses aid A.R.C., Newark, 1944-46. Trustee St. Barnabas Hosp., Newark, 1926-50; bd. mgrs. Vis. Nurses Assn., Newark, 1930-49; trustee Newark Mus., 1935—, v.p., 1943—; trustee Morristown (N.J.) Meml. Hosp., 1952. Club: Cosmopolitan (N.Y.C.). Home: Old Gladston Rd Chester NJ 07930

HARDIN, LUCILLE (MRS. SIDNEY LANIER HARDIN), book reviewer; b. Fate, Tex., Sept. 26, 1899; d. Thomas Preston and Ina Pearl (Davidson) McGraw; student So. Meth. U., 1919-20, 36, 50, U. Dallas, 1959-60; m. J. B. Hill, Sept. 26, 1920 (dec. 1949) children—Peggy Lucille (Mrs. John C. Taylor), J.B., Joy Hill (Mrs. Charles Flach), Martha (Mrs. Tommy Prince), Thomas, David; m. 2d, Sidney Lanier Hardin, Aug. 31, 1957. Profl. reviewer books for book clubs, civic clubs and publs., 1949—. Mem. Delphians, Dallas Story League, Bus. and Profl. Women's Club. Baptist. Rebekah, Maccabees; mem. Order Eastern Star. Club: Zonta. Home: 121 Austin Blvd Edinburg TX 78539 Office: 6362 Malcolm St Dallas TX 75214

HARDIN, NANCY ABOLIN, editor; b. Balt., Sept. 27, 1938; d. Louis C.M. and Elizabeth (King) Abolin; B.A., Wellesley Coll., 1959; M.A., Columbia Grad. Sch., 1961; postgrad. U. Cal. at Berkeley, 1961—, Harvard, 1957, U. London, 1958. With Grolier, Inc., N.Y.C., 1961-64; reporter Television Age Weekly, N.Y.C., 1965; researcher Time, Inc., N.Y.C., 1965-66; asst. editor New American Review, N.Y.C., 1967-70; asso. editor New Am. Library, N.Y.C., 1969-70, editor, 1970-71; sr. editor Pocket Books div. Simon & Schuster, pub. co., N.Y.C., 1971, sr. editor Bantam Books, 1972-74; v.p. Ziegler-Ross Agy., Los Angeles, 1974—. Home: 1330 N Harper St Los Angeles CA 90046 Office: 9255 Sunset Blvd Los Angeles CA 90069

HARDIN, VERALEE BLACKBURN (MRS. COMFORT BURGESS HARDIN, JR.), educator; b. Stoutland, Mo., May 18, 1925; d. Aubrey Res and Della Mae (Calkin) Blackburn; B.S. in Edn., S.W. Mo. State Coll., 1953; M.Ed., U. Mo., 1958, Ed.D., 1964; m. Comfort Burgess Hardin, Jr., Sept. 11, 1944. Tchr. elementary schs., Stoutland and Springfield, Mo., 1944-46, 52-56; tchr. jr. high sch., Stoutland, 1946-68, prin. elementary sch., 1948-52; instr. U. Mo. at Columbia, 1957-64, asst. prof. edn., 1964-67, asso. prof. edn., 1967-71, prof. edn., 1971—, dir. Clinic Disabled Learners, 1957—. Cons. Title III, Prevention of Reading Difficulties, Port Angeles, Wash., 1969, 70, 71, 72; ednl. cons. series of films Study Skills, Coronet Films, 1970-71, 71-72; cons. In-service Edn. for Tchrs. of Disabled Learners and Culturally Disadvantaged, Springfield, 1970-71; participant ann. meeting Am. Acad. Pediatrics, St. Louis, 1971. Mem. adv. bd. Miriam Sch., St. Louis. Recipient E.M. Carter award U. Mo. at Columbia, 1958, Faculty-Alumni award, 1972. Mem. Internat. Reading Assn. (pres. Mo. council 1968-69), Mo. Assn. Children with Learning Disabilities (adv. bd. 1969-73, Distinguished Service award 1972), Pi Lambda Theta (pres. 1967-68), Delta Kappa Gamma (pres. 1970-72). Contbr. articles to profl. jours. Home: 1016 Bourn Av Columbia MO 65201

HARDING, ANITA MAE HUTCHINSON (MRS. JOHN FRANCIS HARDING), comml. designer; b. Pittsfield, Mass., Oct. 10, 1911; d. Harry Clifford and Gertrude (Latimer) Hutchinson; student Katherine Gibbs Sch., Boston, 1929-30; m. John Francis Harding, Sept. 2, 1934; 1 dau., Deborah Ann. Model, John Robert Powers Agy., 1935-40; model or emcee various charitable orgns., 1941-55; creator clothes pin doll Pegmalion, Inc., N.Y.C., 1950, pot pourri and packaging Ashbro Imports, Paris, France, N.Y.C., 1960; designer hand-painted lunch boxes Earl Kelley Sch., N.Y.C., 1967; Mem. benefit com. Lenox Hill Neighborhood Assn., King Coit Sch., 1951; mem. advt. com., prizes com., gifts and membership com. N.Y. Infirmary Com., 1957-67, chmn. benefit luncheon and fashion show, Danbury Conn., 1963; mem. adv. com. Candlewood Theatre, New Fairfield, Conn., 1963; mem. advt. com., chmn. theatre benefit for Danbury Hosp., 1965; mem. com. Arthritis Found., N.Y.C. Home: PO Box 218 New Fairfield CT 06810 also 136 E 56th St New York City NY 10022 also Blackberry Hill Farm East Lake Rd Danbury CT 06810

HARDING, FRANCES KELLER, physician; b. College Place, Wash., June 3, 1906; d. Peter Martin and Florence (Armstrong) Keller; B.S., Walla Walla Coll., 1925; M.D., Loma Linda U., 1929; m. Warren G. Harding 2d, Dec. 23, 1926; children—Florence (Mrs. Roy Burnett Hiscock II), Carolyn (Mrs. Werner Motzel), Peter M. Martin. Intern. Hollywood Presbyn. Hosp., Los Angeles, 1929-30; studied in Edinburgh, Scotland; resident Sydney (Australia) Sanitarium and Hosp., 1933-38; practice medicine, specializing in obstetrics and gynecology, Sydney, 8 years; specializing in med. gynecology, Columbus, O., 1941—; asst. prof. student health dept. Ohio State U.,

1946, also lectr. dept. medicine and adj. lectr. health edn.; adj. lectr. health edn. Dennison U., Ohio Wesleyan U., Oberlin Coll., Capital U., Otterbein U. Pres., Met. Health Council, Columbus 1950-52; mem. Community Chest Finance Com. and bd., 1953-58; bd. dirs., pres., mem. med. adv. bd. Planned Parenthood, of Columbus; bd. dirs. Planned Parenthood World Population; mem. bd. Florence Crittenden Home, 1963; mem. Columbus Council Social Agys.; chmn. Ohio Health Edn. Com.; bd. dirs. Columbus Pub. Health Nurses Assn. Recipient Women of Year award Am. Med. Women's Assn., 1959. Mem. A.M.A., Brit., Ohio, Columbus and Franklin County med. assns., Am. Pub. Health Assn., Royal Coll. Physicians and Surgeons (Edinburgh, Scotland), Royal Soc. for Promotion Health (Eng.), Am. Sch. Health Assn., Planned Parenthood Physicians U.S.A., Am. Med. Women's Assn. (dir., lectr., v.p., pres. 1972, com. chmn.), Zonta (pres. Columbus br.), Mortar Bd. (hon.). Contbr. articles to med. jours. Home: 3660 Westerville Rd Columbus OH 43224 Office: 463 E Town St Columbus OH 43215

HARDING, LOIS ELAINE DUPREY (MRS. CHARLES ELMER HARDING), ednl. adminstr.; b. Neche, N.D., Dec. 29, 1912; d. Maxime and Della Lenore (Shelly) DuPrey; student U. N.D., 1934-35; B.S., Lincoln U., 1966, postgrad., 1967-68; postgrad. U. Mo., 1968; m. Charles Elmer Harding, Dec. 29, 1939; children—Charles Maxime, Blake E., Terry Vance. Vocational adjustment coordinator Ft. Leonardwood-Waynesville (Mo.) Sch. System, 1966-68; ednl. supr. Rolla (Mo.) Regional Diagnostic Clinic, 1968-70; founder Skills Builder Sch., Rolla, Mo., 1970, dir., instr., 1970—; ednl. cons. Waynesville-Ft. Leonard Wood Sch. System. Regional v.p. Mo. Assn. Retarded Children, 1969-71. Bd. dirs. Cerebral Palsy Assn. Mem. Am. Assn. U. Women (pres. Rolla br. 1969-71), Am. Assn. Mental Deficiency, Nat. Assn. Autistic Children, Council Exceptional Children, Nat. Rehab. Assn., Assn. Classroom Tchrs. (dist. pres. 1968-69; pres.'s com. 1969-70), Mo. Assn. Children with Learning Disabilities, Mo. Assn. Mental Health, Rolla C. of C., Delta Kappa Gamma, Kappa Kappa Iota. Clubs: Federated Women's, Federated Garden (Rolla). Home: 1520 McCutchen Dr Rolla MO 65401 Office: 305 W 9th St Rolla MO 65401

HARDING, MARY KATHERINE, math. statistician; b. Washington; d. Raymond Dent and Armida (Chicca) Harding; A.B., Trinity Coll., Washington, 1946. Mathematician, Applied Physics Lab., Johns Hopkins, 1946-49, Dept. Def., Washington, 1949-58; math. statistician Bur. Mines, Dept. Interior, Washington, 1958—. Mem. Am. Statis. Assn. Author govt. bulls. Home: 8800 Lynnhurst Dr Fairfax VA 22030 Office: 4015 Wilson Blvd Arlington VA 22203

HARDING, VIRGINIA LEE DODGE (MRS. FRED J. HARDING, JR.), photographer; b. St. Paul, Apr. 25, 1920; d. Ethiel John and Lucille Mary (Rieger) Dodge; student U. Minn., 1937-39, 1947; m. Jerrold Stoll, Feb. 8, 1947 (div. 1959); children—Nelson, Gina, Christopher, Carrie; m. 2d, Fred J. Harding, Jr., Aug. 25, 1968. Staff writer Manson-Gold Advt. Agy., Mpls., 1938-40, Radio Sta. WDGY, Mpls., 1940-42, Pacific Coast Advt. Agy., San Francisco, 1947-49; civilian writer Army Dept., Camp Crowder, Mo., 1942-43; staff writer, producer Blue Network, San Francisco, Chgo., 1943-45; part-time dir. San Francisco Photography Center, 1961-65; asst. Instructional Materials Center, Palo Alto (Cal.) Unified Sch. Dist., 1966-67, information specialist, 1967-69. Cons., contbr. San Francisco Mus. Art exhibit, 1962; cons. Cal. Dept. Edn., 1965-66; contbg. photographer Urban Life Picture Series, 1965-67; exhibited photographs in shows at San Francisco Mus. Art, M.H. DeYoung Mus., San Francisco, Stanford U., Focus Gallery, San Francisco, Cal. State U., San Francisco, Crown-Zellerbach Plaza, San Francisco, George Eastman House, Rochester, N.Y., Parents Mag. Gallery, N.Y.C., Kaiser Center, Oakland, Cal., Palo Alto Children's Theatre, Jr. Mus., Palo Alto, others; represented in permanent art collections Oakland Mus., San Francisco. Mem. steering com. San Francisco Art Festival, 1955; chmn. pub. information com. Youth Arts, Palo Alto, 1968-69; photography rep. Citizens Adv. Planning Com., Palo Alto Cultural Center, 1969-70. Recipient First place purchase award San Francisco Ann. Art Festival for group documentary exhibit San Francisco Weekend, 1955, certificate award Dept. State, U.S. Am. for Art in the Embassies program, 1968. Mem. Bay Area Photographers (chmn. 1955-57), Am. Soc. Mag. Photographers San Francisco (treas. 1965-66), Am. Soc. Photographers in Communication, Council for Arts, Mid-Peninsula Writers Workshop. Club: Mothers (Ore. State U., Corvallis). Contbr. photographs to numerous mags. Address: PO Box 2308 Stanford CA 94305

HARDY, BARBARA L., real estate broker; b. Oklahoma City, Okla., Oct. 15, 1939; d. Leonard and Lorine (Fulbright) Richmond; A.A., Diablo Valley Coll., 1959; real estate certificate Merritt Coll., 1965; m. Melvin S. Hardy, Aug. 6, 1960; children—Debra, Edward. Clk.-stenographer U.S. Naval Legal Dept., Treasure Island, Cal., 1959-64; real estate broker, Best Buy Realty, Oakland, Cal., 1965—. Sec., Woodland Community Action Council. Active East Bay Democratic Club. Mem. Nat. Assn. Realtors, Cal. Real Estate Assn., Asso. Real Property Brokers, Order Eastern Star. Club: Winchester Rifle. Home: 7750 Surrey Lane Oakland CA 94605 Office: 10067 MacArthur Blvd Oakland CA 94605

HARDY, ELIZA HUNTON CALDWELL (MRS. EDWARD ADAMS HARDY), physician; b. Danville, Ky., Oct. 22, 1910; d. Charles Wickliffe and Virginia Everett (Taylor) Caldwell; A.B., Centre Coll., Danville, 1932; M.D., Vanderbilt U., 1936; m. Edward Adams Hardy, May 18, 1940; children—Virginia (Mrs. John Pierce Chase, Jr.), Helen Tyler, William Logan, Elizabeth Clemens. Intern, Duke Hosp., Durham, N.C., 1936-38; asso. resident pediatrics Bellevue Hosp., N.Y.C., 1938-39, resident pediatrics, 1940; pvt. practice medicine specializing in pediatrics, Pelham, N.Y., 1941—; attending pediatrician Mount Vernon, (N.Y.) Hosp., 1960—. Mem. Narcotics Guidance Council, Pelham, 1970—. Fellow Am. Acad. Pediatrics; mem. Westchester Acad. Medicine (pres. 1973—), A.M.A., Jr. League. Republican. Presbyn. Clubs: Pelham Manor, International Garden (Pelham). Address: 145 Corlies Av Pelham NY 10803

HARDY, EVELYN, writer, broadcaster; b. Phila.; d. Thornton and Beulah (Greenough) Hardy; B.A., Smith Coll., U. London. Author and broadcaster of scripts Third Programme, BBC, London; lectr. English lit., Anglo-Romanesque Art, other subjects Bristol U., Nat. Portrait Gallery, London, Allington Castle, Thomas Hardy festival, others. Leverhulme Research grantee for investigation of Thomas Hardy manuscripts, 1955-57, Soc. of Authors grantee. Club: University Women's, London. Author: Donne: A Spirit in Conflict, 1942; Swift: The Conjured Spirit, 1949; Swift: Selected Prose with Introduction, 1950; Summer in Another World, 1950; Thomas Hardy: A Critical Biography, 1954, Survivors of the Armada, 1966; Midnight Festival (poems), 1968. Editor: Thomas Hardy's Notebooks, 1955; Some Recollections by Emma Hardy (with Robert Gittings), 1961. One Rare Fair Woman: Letters of Thomas Hardy to Florence Henniker (with F.B. Pinion), 1972. Office: care Peter Janson-Smith Ltd 31 Newington Green London N16 England

HARDY, HARRIET LOUISE, physician; b. Arlington, Mass., Sept. 23, 1906; d. Horace Dexter and Harriet (Decker) Hardy; A.B., Wellesley Coll., 1928; M.D., Cornell U., 1932. Intern, resident Phila. Gen. Hosp., 1932-34; physician Northfield Sem., East Northfield, Mass., also pvt. practice, 1934-39; coll. physician, head dept. health edn. Radcliffe Coll., Cambridge, Mass., 1939-45; grad. asst. medicine Mass. Gen. Hosp., 1940-43, asst. in medicine, 1943-50, asst. physician, 1950-51, asso. physician, 1951—, chief occupational med. clinic, 1949-61; mem. bd. consultation, 1971—; health div. group leader Los Alamos Sci. Lab., AEC, 1948-49, cons., 1949-64; asso. physician charge occupational med. service Mass. Inst. Tech., 1949-50, asst. med. dir. charge occupational med. service, 1950-71, lectr. dept. civil and san. engring., 1951-54, 61-62; instr. indsl. hygiene Harvard Sch. Pub. Health, 1947-52, asst. prof. preventive medicine Harvard Med. Sch., 1955-58, asso. prof., 1958-59, lectr. medicine, 1959-71, clin. prof., 1971—; lectr. medicine Tufts Med. Sch., 1955-65; cons. Atomic Research Center, Ames, Ia., 1949-61, com. on social and occupational health WHO, 1951-70, ILO, Geneva, Switzerland, 1950-65; sr. cons. occupational medicine Lemuel Shattuck Hosp., Boston, 1955—; cons. internal medicine VA Hosp., Boston, 1961—. cons. div. biology and medicine AEC, 1949-64; attached worker dept. occupational health London Sch. Hygiene, 1963—; mem. com. on fish protein concentrate Nat. Acad. Sci., 1963-68; mem. research com. Med. Found., Boston, 1966-67; mem. med. adv. com. United Mine Workers, 1969—; mem. adv. com. to university health services Princeton, 1970—; mem. supersonic transport panel on environmental research Dept. Commerce, 1971—; vis. prof. medicine Dartmouth Coll., 1971—, adj. prof. environmental studies, 1971. Named Med. Women of Year, Am. Med. Woman's Assn., 1955, Bus. and Profl. Woman of Year, 1963; recipient Hardy Family award, 1965, Alice Hamilton award N.Y. Acad. Scis., 1971; Distinguished award Cornell Med. Coll., 1972. Diplomate Nat. Bd. Med. Examiners, Am. Bd. Preventive Medicine. Fellow A.C.P., Indsl. Med. Assn. (Merit in Authorship award 1964, Knudson award 1965); mem. Mass. Med. Soc. (com. on occupational health 1949-64), Am. Acad. Occupational Medicine (award of merit 1971), Am. Indsl. Hygiene Assn., Am. Conf. Govtl. Indsl. Hygienists, New Eng. Indsl. Med. Assn. (v.p. 1967-68), Mass. Thoracic Soc. (council 1967-68), Assn. Am. Physicians, Internat. Assn. Occupational Health (permanent commn.), Royal Soc. Medicine (affiliate), Phi Beta Kappa, Sigma Xi (hon.), Alpha Omega Alpha (hon.), Delta Omega. Author: (with Alice Hamilton) Industrial Toxicology, 1949; Dangerous Occupations sec. Ency. Brit., 1961; also chpts. in books, numerous med. articles and papers. Editorial bd. Clin. Pharmacology and Therapeutics. Contbr. numerous articles to med. jours. Address: Sandy Pond Rd Lincoln MA 01773

HARDY, HAZEL NETTLESHIP, broadcasting co. exec.; b. Warsaw, N.Y., Apr. 13, 1944; d. Charles Robert and Marion Virginia (Templin) Nettleship; B.A., William Smith Coll., 1965; M.A., U. Mo., 1967; m. Joseph Hardy, Feb. 4, 1967. Reporter, Broadcasting mag., N.Y.C., 1967-70; publicist NBC, 1970; A.P. editor Westinghouse Broadcasting Co., N.Y.C., 1970-72; dir. corporate information ABC, N.Y.C., 1973—. Mem. Nat. Acad. TV Arts and Scis., Women in Communications, William Smith Coll. Alumnae Assn. (v.p.). Home: 320 Central Park W New York City NY 10025 Office: 1330 Av of Americas New York City NY 10019

HARDY, MADELINE ISOBEL, educator; b. London, Ont., Can., Dec. 22, 1931; d. Homer Joseph and Bella (Corsaut) Hardy; B.S., Columbia U., 1960; M.Ed., U. Toronto, 1966, Ed.D., 1968. Tchr., cons. to tchrs. London (Can.) Bd. Edn., 1953-67; prof. elementary edn. U. Western Ontario, London, 1967-73; coordinator edn. exceptional students York U., Toronto, 1973—. Adminstr. profl. devel. courses Ont. Dept. Edn., 1969-70. Recipient travel and study grant British Council, 1969. Mem. The Council for Exceptional Children in Can. (chmn. 1972-73). Author: Standards for Educators of Exceptional Children in Canada, 1971. Contbr. articles to profl. pubs. Home: 15 Park Hill Ct Apt 603 Brampton ON Canada Office: Faculty Edn York Univ 4700 Keele St Downsview ON Canada

HARDY, ZELMA BOYD (MRS. GEORGE CHAPPELL HARDY), city ofcl.; b. Gamburg, Mo., May 23, 1907; d. James S. and Ellen Elizabeth (Sewell) Boyd; B.A., So. Meth. U., 1931; M.A. (H.E. Butt fellow), U. Tex., 1950; m. George Chappell Hardy, Mar. 1, 1930; children—Anna Beth (Mrs. Richard B. Felner), George Chappell. Tchr. English, Westover, Tex., 1932-33, Nolan, Tex., 1942-43, Snow Hills, N.C., 1944-46, Tivy High Sch., Kerrville, Tex., 1946-58, Alamo Heights High Sch., San Antonio, 1958-62; asso. prof. English, Schreiner Coll., Kerrville, 1962-69; mayor of Kerrville, 1973—. Dir. Capital Eye TV News Program, Austin, 1970—. Pres. Tivy High Sch. P.T.A., Kerrville, 1952-53; chmn. Kerrville Community Service Council, 1970-72, United Fund Drive Kerr County, 1971. Bd. dirs. local United Fund. Mem. city council City of Kerrville, 1970—. Recipient Hogg Found. fellowship, 1954, Am. Studies Coe fellowship, 1958. Mem. Am. Assn. Univ. Women (local pres. 1972-74). Methodist (mem. S.W. Tex. conf. on ministries 1972—). Club: Kerrville Literary (pres. 1962-64). Author: (with Joseph Slate) Of This Time, 1970. Home: 303 Spence St Kerrville TX 78028 Office: 600 Main St Kerrville TX 78028

HARE, DAPHNE KEAN (MRS. PETER HEWITT HARE), med. educator; b. Palmerton, Pa., Jan. 19, 1937; d. Clare Hibberd and Lucile (Lawrence) Kean; B.A. with honors in Physics, Barnard Coll., 1958; M.D., Cornell U., 1962; m. Peter Hewitt Hare, May 30, 1959; children—Clare Kean, Gwendolyn Meigs. Intern, Buffalo Gen. Hosp., 1963-64, resident, 1964-65; NIH fellow State U. N.Y., Buffalo, 1965-68, asst. research prof., 1968-70, asst. prof. medicine and biophysics, 1970—. Cons. Johann Gutenberg U., Mainz, Germany, Free U. of West Berlin; mem. tng. grant com. NIH, 1971-73. United Health Found. Western N.Y. grantee, 1969-70; NIH grantee, 1970-73; VA Clin. Investigator grantee, 1972. Mem. Biophys. Soc. (chmn. com. profl. opportunities for women 1973-74, mem. biophysics council 1974—), Am. Nephrology Soc., Am. Assn. U. Profs., A.A.A.S., N.Y. Acad. Sci., Am. Civil Liberties Union (chpt. dir. 1968—, chpt. dir., chpt. v.p. 1972—), Nat. Orgn. Women (chpt. pres. 1970-71). Home: 219 Depew Av Buffalo NY 14214

HARELICK, MARJORIE ALMA, psychiatrist; b. Bayonne, N.J., Feb. 3, 1943; d. Samuel and Beatrice (Wolosin) Harelick; B.A., Antioch Coll., 1965; M.D., Ohio State U., 1969. Intern, Highland Gen. Hosp., Oakland, Cal., 1969-70; residence in psychiatry St. Elizabeths Hosp., Washington, 1970-72; fellow in child psychiatry Woodburn Center Community Mental Health, 1972-74; staff child psychiatrist, out-patient unit Mt. Vernon Center for Community Mental Health, Alexandria, Va., 1974—; pvt. practice psychiatry; cons. Inst. Marriage and Family Relations, Springfield, Va.; staff psychiatrist St. Elizabeth's Hosp., Washington. Smith Kline and French Fgn. fellow, 1968. Mem. Am. Psychiat. Assn., D.C. Psychiat. Soc. Home: 5219 N 12th St Arlington VA 22205 Office: Mt Vernon Center for Community Mental Health 8119 Holland Rd Alexandria VA 22306

HARGIS, BETTY JEAN, immunologist; b. Madison, Ind., Aug. 14, 1925; d. Carleton Edwin and Margaret Emma (Geile) Hargis; B.S., Purdue U., 1947; M.A., Boston U., 1958, Ph.D., 1967. Chief research asst. Peter Bent Brigham Hosp., Boston, 1955-62; research asst. Children's Cancer Research Found., Boston, 1963—; research asso. pathology Children's Hosp. Med. Center, Boston, 1971—. Mem. Am. Assn. Immunologists, A.A.A.S., Sigma Xi. Mem. Order Eastern Star. Club: Guild of Opera Company (Boston). Contbr. articles to sci. jours. Home: 115 Park St Brookline MA 02146 Office: 35 Binney St Boston MA 02115

HARGRAVE, ROWENA ADELINE (MRS. HAROLD HARGRAVE), author; b. Boonville, Ind., Dec. 12, 1906; d. Berry Little and Anna Laura (Stephens) Hullett; student, Oakland City Coll., 1924-25; B.S., Ind. State U., 1949; M.A., U. Chgo., 1962; m. Harold Hargrave, June 4, 1935; 1 dau., Ruth Davis. Tchr. elementary schs. Warrick County, Boonville, 1925-29, La Porte (Ind.) Community Schs., 1929-39, 1942-71; summer instr. reading clinic U. Chgo., 1963, 65. Reading cons. for tchrs. workshops and convs., 1953-65. Mem. La Porte Community Hosp. Aux., 1967-74. Mem. Nat. Ret. Tchrs. Assn., Internat. Reading Assn., Am. Assn. U. Women (pres. 1955-56), Delta Kappa Gamma (pres. 1972-74), Pi Lambda Theta. Mem. Order Eastern Star. Clubs: Little Theatre, Women's Literary (La Porte). Author: Speedboat, 1951, rev., 1971; Streamliner, 1951, rev., 1971; Jet Plane, 1951, rev., 1971; Rocket, 1951, rev., 1971; Atomic Submarine, 1951, rev., 1971; Space Ship, 1951, rev., 1971; co-author: Extending Reading Skills, levels 7, 8, 9, 1974-75. Home: 1808 Monroe St La Porte IN 46350

HARGRAVE, VICTORIA E(LIZABETH), librarian; b. Ripon, Wis., Aug. 22, 1913; d. Alexander Walter and Estelle Winifred (Swanson) Hargrave; A.B., Ripon Coll., 1934; library diploma U. Wis., 1938; M.A., U. Chgo., 1947; postgrad. U. Cal. at Los Angeles, 1970. Tchr. Brandon (Wis.) High Sch., 1934-37; extension librarian Ia. State Coll. Library, 1938-44; librarian Ripon Coll., 1944-46, MacMurray Coll., Jacksonville, Ill., 1947—. Mem. adv. council librarians U. Ill. Grad. Sch. Library Service, 1962-64. Mem. A.L.A., Am. Assn. U. Women, League Women Voters. Home: 1017 W College Av Jacksonville IL 62650

HARGREAVES, GLADYS, materials engr.; b. Tifton, Ga., Jan. 21; d. Leon Abraham and Harriet Elizabeth (Blitch) Hargreaves; student Tift Coll., 1927-30; B.S., U. Ga., 1935, M.S., 1941. Tchr. high sch., Ashburn and Georgetown, Ga., 1930-34; jr. physicist Signal Corps Research Labs., Fort Monmouth, N.J., 1942-43; instr. physics U. Ga., Athens, 1943-44; physicist Tenn. Eastman Corp., Kingsport, 1944-50, Tufts U. Sch. Dental Medicine, Boston, 1952-56; research asso. Naval Air Engring. Center, Phila., 1956-67; with Naval Air Devel. Center, Warminster, Pa., 1967—, materials engr., 1970—. Fellow A.A.A.S., Am. Inst. Chemists; mem. Am. Chem. Soc. (div. dir. 1963-66, 1971-74; councilor 1971-73, 73—), Grad. Women in Sci. (treas. 1964-65, pres. 1968), Am. Phys. Soc., N.J. Acad. Sci., N.Y. Micros. Soc. Contbr. articles to various sci. publs. Home: 316 O'Sharon Way Jamesburg NJ 08831 Office: Naval Air Devel Center AVTD Code 30224 Warminster PA 18974

HARIMAN, EMMA LOU COWGER (MRS. GEORGE E. HARIMAN), hosp. adminstr.; b. Morganfield, Kentucky; d. Robert Donald and Zorah Almeda (Cowgur) Cowger; grad. Aurora Bus. Coll., 1921; student various nursing, extension, night schs.; m. George E. Hariman, Jan. 14, 1923; 1 son, Donald George. Adminstr. Hariman Sanatorium, Chiropractic Clinic and Hosp., Grand Forks, N.D., 1924—. Sec. N.D. Presbyn. Women's Synodical, 1927-35, pres., 1936-40; pres. Pembina Presbyterial, 1953-56; mem. Nat. Com. for Prevention and Control Delinquency, 1946—; mem. group to discuss nation's problems in which women and women's orgns. can play spl. role, Washington, 1963; pres. N.D. Council United Ch. Women; mem. N.D. Gov.'s Com. on Migrant Workers, Gov.'s Com. Status of Women, 1964, Gov.'s Council on Human Resources, 1970; area coordinator Women in Community Service, 1967—; chmn. com. for solicitation funds and selecting location Internat. Friendship House; mem. Grand Forks Mayor's Citizens Adv. Com.; chmn. Task Force on Overall Planning, Housing and Zoning; mem. Gov.'s Com. N.D. Women for Hwy. Safety. Bd. dirs. Salvation Army. Fellow Internat. Chiropractic Coll.; mem. Nat. Chiropractic Aux. (past sec., v.p.), Am. Legion Aux., N.D. Conf. Social Welfare, Grand Forks Bus. and Profl. Women's Club, Grand Forks Hist. Soc. (dir.), Fedn. Women's Clubs, League Women Voters, Internat. Assn. Rebekah Assemblies. Mem. Order Eastern Star, Rebekah (internat. pres. 1946-48). Club: Zonta (Grand Forks). Author articles various publs. Home: 2912 University Av Grand Forks ND 58201 Office: 2002 University Av Grand Forks ND 58201

HARING, ARDYCE ELAINE, quantitative analyst; b. Franklin, Neb., Sept. 5, 1937; d. Alfon Charles and Ethel Lucinda (Pocock) Haring; B.S., U. Neb., 1959; M.S., U. Wis., 1960, Ph.D., 1965. Grad. research asst. U. Wis., 1959-60, instr. journalism, 1961-65, asst. prof. dept. agrl. journalism, 1965-68; sr. research exec. Grey Advt. Agy., N.Y.C., 1968-70; sr. quantitative analyst Human Resources Adminstrn. of N.Y.C., 1971-74; dir. program evaluation Orange County Community Mental Health Center, Goshen, N.Y., 1974—. Adj. asst. prof. communication arts and scis. dept. Queens Coll., Flushing, N.Y., 1971-73. Mem. Sigma Xi. Research and publs. in evaluation of social programs, cross cultural communications patterns. Home: 262 W 91st St New York City NY 10024 Office: Orange County Community Mental Health Center Goshen NY 10924

HARING, OLGA MUNK, physician; b. Oradea, Austria, Aug. 25, 1917; d. Moris and Ilona (Lindenbaum) Munk; B.A., U. Vienna, Austria, 1938; M.D., U. Leon, Nicaragua, 1939; 1 dau., Claire (Mrs. Mark Golan). Rotating intern Mt. Sinai Hosp., Chgo., 1952; resident in medicine Chgo. Wesley Meml. Hosp., 1960-61, Cook County Hosp., Chgo., 1961-62; practice medicine specializing in cardiology, Chgo., 1965—; mem. staff Passavant Meml. Hosp., Chgo.; asso. prof. medicine Northwestern U. Med. Sch., Chgo., 1970—. Fellow A.C.P., Am. Coll. Cardiology; mem. Am. Assn. U. Profs. (treas. 1973-75), Sigma Xi. Home: 1201 Judson Av Evanston IL 60202 Office: Searle Bldg 303 E Chicago Av Chicago IL 60611

HARKER, BERNICE, psychiatrist, osteopath, physician, surgeon; b. Chgo., Aug. 26, 1898; d. Ray Clarkson and Lulu (Abernathy) Harker; student Pomona Coll., 1916-18; B.A., U. So. Cal., 1920; D.O., Coll. Osteo. Phys. and Surg., 1925. Intern Mont Sano Osteo. Hosp., Los Angeles, 1926; mem. clinic staff P.T.A., 1927-29; clin. student Merrill Psychiat. Sanitarium, Venice, Cal., 1937-38; mem. attending staff in psychiatry Los Angeles County Osteo. Hosp., 1939-54; mem. psychiat. staff Meyers Clinic, 1947-49; tchr. Christian Clinic Class for psychiat. study, 1941-54; med. dir. Compton (Cal.) Counseling Service, 1959-61; psychiat. cons. S.W. Counseling Service, Los Angeles, 1965-72. Mem. nat. adv. council Camps Farthest Out of N. Am., 1965-68. Diplomate Am. Osteo. Bd. Neurol. and Psychiatry. Mem. Am. Coll. Neuropsychiatrists, Osteo. Physicians and Surgeons Cal. (dir. 1966-71), Hollywood Physicians and Surgeons Club, Bus. and Profl. Women's Club. Methodist. Home: Apt 8 1541 N Detroit St Hollywood CA 90046

HARKINS, SISTER MARY ELIZABETH CATHERINE, ednl. adminstr.; b. Carthage, Miss., Aug. 21, 1914; d. Peter T. and Sudie (Thornton) Harkins; diploma Mercy Hosp. Sch. Nursing, New Orleans, 1946; B.S., St. Mary Coll., 1950; M.S., Cath. U., 1962; Ph.D. candidate, Fla. State U., 1974—. Floor supr. Mercy Hosp., Vicksburg, Miss., 1946-48; children's supr., 1948-50; instr. Sch. Nursing, 1951-57, asst. edn. dir. Mercy Hosp. Sch. Nursing, 1957-60, dir., 1962-66; dean U. So. Miss. Sch. Nursing, Hattiesburg, 1966—. Mem. task force levels of care categorization Miss. Health Planning Adv.

Council; mem. joint practice com. Miss. Nurses Assn.-Miss. State Med. Assn.; mem. div. comprehensive health planning Office of Gov. Miss. Charter fellow Acad. Nursing; mem. Miss. Nurses' Bd. Examination and Registration (pres. 1968-69), Miss. Bd. Nursing (pres. 1973), Miss. Nurses' Assn. (pres. 1963-67, 72—), Am. Nurses Assn. (mem. by-laws com. 1968, resolutions com. 1974), Nat. League Nursing, Am. Assn. U. Women (pres. local chpt. 1969-70), Am. Assn. Higher Edn., Sigma Theta Tau, Delta Kappa Gamma, Phi Kappa Phi, Kappa Delta Phi. Home: 610 Southern Av Hattiesburg MS 39401 Office: Box 95 Southern Station Hattiesburg MS 39401

HARKNESS, DOLORES PRISCILLA SCHWARTZ (MRS. RAWLAND HARKNESS), savs. and loan exec.; b. Ryder, N.D., Dec. 5, 1926; d. Alexander C. and Anna C. (Carlsen) Schwartz; grad. diploma Am. Savs. and Loan Inst., Chgo., 1963; student Grad. Sch. Savs. and Loan Assn., U. Ind., 1964-65; m. Rawland Harkness, Sept. 13, 1968; children—Nancy, Marcella, Michael; stepchildren—Todd, Pamela. Teller, First Nat. Bank, Minot, N.D., 1945-49; with Minot Fed. Savs. and Loan Assn., 1953—, corp. sec., 1965-67, v.p., 1967—. Mem. Street Lighting Com., City of Minot, 1970; panel mem. Minot High Sch. chpt. Distributive Edn. Club, 1966-69. Mem. Minot C. of C. (subchmn. health safety com. 1971—), Business and Professional Women's Club (pres. 1961, northwest dir. 1970—), Am. Legion Aux. Roman Catholic. Club: Minot Country. Home: 609 24th St NW Minot ND 58701 Office: 123 1st St SW Minot ND 58701

HARKNESS, REBEKAH WEST (MRS. WILLIAM HALE HARKNESS), composer, cultural and sci. founds. adminstr.; b. St. Louis, Apr. 17, 1915; d. Allen T. and Rebekah (Semple) West; student Rossman & John Burroughs Schs., St. Louis, Fermata Sch., Aiken, S.C., Boulanger Sch. of Composition, Fountainbleau, France, Dalcroze Sch., N.Y.C.; m. Dickson Pierce, 1938; children—Allen West, Anne Terry; m. 2d, William Hale Harkness, 1947; 1 dau., Edith Hale. Composer: Safari, 1955; Mediterranean Moods, 1957; Musical Chairs, 1958; Journey to Love, 1957; Barcelona Suite, 1960; Gift of the Magi, 1959; Letters to Japan, 1960; others. Founder, pres. Rebekah Harkness Found., 1959—, Harkness Ballet, 1964, Harkness House for Ballet Arts, 1965—. Bd. dirs. William Hale Harkness Found. also pres.; bd. dirs. Soc. for a More Beautiful Nat. Capitol; mem. Pres.'s Council on Youth Opportunity, Washington. Decorated Officer of Merite Cultural and Artistique, France, 1966; recipient N.Y.C. Handel award, 1967, Marquis de Cuevas prize U. de la Dance, Paris, 1965, Congressional Record citations, 1965, 66, Shield award Am. Indian and Eskimo Cultural Found., 1967. Address: 4 E 75th St New York City NY 10021

HARKNESS, SARAH PILLSBURY, architect; b. Swampscott, Mass., July 8, 1914; d. Samuel H. and Helen (Watters) Pillsbury; certificate M.Arch., Smith Coll., grad. Sch. Architecture and Landscape Architecture, 1940; D.Fine Arts, Bates Coll., 1974; m. John C. Harkness, June 14, 1941; children—Sara, Joan, Nell, Timothy, Alice, Frederick, John Pillsbury. Designer office Eleanor Raymond, architect, Boston, 1938-39; draughtsman Peter & Stubbins, architects, Boston, 1939-40; agt. for Artek-Pascoe, under name Pillsbury & Vaughan, Boston, 1940-41; designer Dan Cooper, Inc., N.Y.C., 1941-43; designer circulating exhbns. Mus. Modern Art, 1943-44; partner Architects Collaborative, Cambridge, Mass., 1945—. Vis. critic Harvard Grad. Sch. Design, 1973, 74. Mem. A.I.A. (chmn. commn. on bldg. design 1972, dir. New Eng. region 1974). Home: 34 Moon Hill Rd Lexington MA 02173 Office: 46 Brattle St Cambridge MA 02138

HARKRIDER, ANNE PRATKA (MRS. WILLIAM WALTON HARKRIDER, JR.), mil. officer, therapist; b. Houston, May 1, 1948; d. Robert Frank and Violet Augustine (Janicek) Pratka; student U. Tex. at Austin, 1966-68; B.S., U. Tex. Sch. Allied Health Scis., 1970; m. William Walton Harkrider, Jr., Aug. 29, 1970. Commd. 2d lt. USPHS, 1971, advanced through grades to 1st lt. 1972; staff occupational therapist USPHS Hosp., New Orleans, 1970—, dep. chief occupational therapy dept., 1973—. Fed. Health Programs Service Research grantee, 1972—. Mem. Am., La. (treas. 1973—) occupational therapy assns. Roman Catholic. Editor: La. Occupational Therapy Newsletter, 1971—. Home: 554 Rosa Av Metairie LA 70005 Office: 210 State St New Orleans LA 70118

HARLAN, DONNA BELAT (MRS. HAROLD HARLAN), librarian; b. Columbus, O., Dec. 19, 1926; d. John Ralph and Beryl (Ayers) Belat; A.A., Stephens Coll., 1946; B.A., Morris Harvey Coll., 1948; M.L.S., Columbia, 1950; m. Harold O. Harlan, Apr. 27, 1951; children—Harold O., John B. Cons., W. Va. Library Commn., Charleston, 1950-51, 62-65; br. librarian Racine (Wis.) Pub. Library, cataloger, 1952; cataloger Fed. Res. Bank, Chgo., 1953-54; staff and tng. officer U. Pitts., 1965-66; head librarian Ind. U. at South Bend, 1966—, prof. library sci., 1969—. Mem. Am. Assn. U. Women (legislative dir. 1971-73), A.L.A., Am. Assn. U. Profs., Modern Lang. Assn., Zonta Internat. Home: 1411 Northside Blvd South Bend IN 46615 Office: 1825 Northside Blvd South Bend IN 46615

HARLAN, ROMA CHRISTINE, portrait painter; b. Warsaw, Ind.; d. Charles William and Fern (McCormick) Harlan; student Purdue U.; Art Inst. Chgo. One-man shows Lake Shore Club Chgo., Little Gallery of Esquire Theater, Chgo., Purdue U., Hoosier Salon, Indpls., All.-Ill. Soc. Fine Arts, Kaufmann's Gallery, Chgo., Lafayette (Ind.) Art Assn., Arts Club Chgo.; exhibited numerous group shows; represented in permanent collections at U.S. Supreme Ct., D.C. Fed. Ct. House, Nat. Guard Bldg., Washington, Nat. Fedn. Bus. and Profl. Women's Clubs, Washington. Art chmn. D.C. Fedn. Women's Clubs. Daus. of Ind. scholar. Mem. Ind. State Art Assn. Presbyn. Club: Arts (Washington). Address: 1600 South Joyce St Arlington VA 22202

HARLEN, ADA JANE PAULSON (MRS. HARRY CHARLES HARLEN), lawyer; b. Havre, Mont., Nov. 2, 1924; d. Oliver C. and Lillian A. (Rindy) Paulson; diploma in law LaSalle Extension U., Chgo., 1966; m. Harry Charles Harlen, Apr. 7, 1946; children—Craig D., Steven S., Thomas K. Legal sec. Burns & Thomas, Chinook, Mont., 1942-44, county atty., Chinook, 1944-46, Mahan & Marchi, Helena, Mont., 1952-54, Loble & Picotte, Helena, 1954-69; asst. city treas. Helena, 1946-49; admitted to Mont. bar, 1969; asso. atty. Loble, Picotte & Loble, Helena, 1969-73; partner Loble, Picotte, Loble, Pauly & Sternhagen, Helena, 1973—. Den mother Cub Scouts Am., Helena, 1957-61, 68-69. Mem. Am., Mont. (com. on uniform probate code 1973—), 1st Jud. Dist. (pres. 1974-75) bar assns., Nat. Assn. Women Lawyers, Nat., Mont. (bar liason officer 1972—), Helena (pres. 1959, Legal Sec. of Year 1959, Boss of Year 1972) legal secs. assns., Helena Bus. and Profl. Women (1st v.p. 1972), Sons of Norway, Am. Bus. Women's Assn. (Boss of Year 1971), Bus. and Profl. Women's Club. Lutheran (mem., sec. council 1973—). Home: 822 Breckenridge St Helena MT 59601 Office: 833 N Main St PO Box 176 Helena MT 59601

HARMAN, ESTELLE KARCHMER (MRS. SAMUEL HARMAN), owner acting workshop; b. Beaumont, Tex., Sept. 11; d. Alexander and Ethel Ida (Ray) Karchmer; A.A., Los Angeles City Coll., 1942; B.A., U. Cal., 1945; M.A., U. So. Cal., 1947, postgrad., 1948-52; m. Samuel Harman, Aug. 31, 1947; children—Deborah Ann, Alexis Melinda, Eden Kay. Instr. U. Cal., Theatre Arts, 1946-50; head talent, test dir. Universal Studios, Universal City, Cal., 1950-53; owner, dir. Estelle Harman Actors' Workshop, Los Angeles, 1953—. Coached polit. candidates for platform communication for live performances and TV. Mem. Am. Ednl. Theatre Assn., Am. Nat. Theatre Assn., Internat. Platform Assn., Mortar Bd., Zeta Phi Eta. Office: 522 N LaBrea St Los Angeles CA 90036

HARMAN, JEANNE PERKINS (MRS. HARRY ELLIOTT HARMAN III), author; b. Baxter Springs, Kan.; d. Enoch and Maude (Himes) P.; B.A. magna cum laude, Smith Coll., 1939; m. Harry Elliott Harman III, Mar. 28, 1949; 1 dau., Jeanne Anne. Staff writer Life mag., N.Y.C., 1942-49; corr. Time, Life, Sports Illus. mags., Charlotte Amalie, St. Thomas, V.I., 1949—; tchr. journalism U. Miami (Fla.), 1953-54; corr. N.Y. Times, 1956—; editor, pub. Here's How mag., St. Thomas, 1958—; author spl. articles for various mags. Mem. Am. Soc. Travel Writers, Internat. Platform Assn., Phi Beta Kappa, Kappa Kappa Gamma. Club: Overseas Press. Author: The Love Junk, 1951; Such Is Life, 1956; The Virgins: Magic Islands, 1961; Fielding's Guide to the Caribbean and the Bahamas, 1969-75; Harman's Official Guide to Cruise Ships, 1971; Best Buys in the Caribbean, 1974-75. Address: 2014 Wood Valley Dr Valdosta GA 31601

HARMER, RUTH MULVEY, educator, free lance writer; b. N.Y.C., June 18, 1919; d. Charles Watt and Mary (Gierloff) Mulvey; student Boston U., 1938-40; A.B., Barnard Coll., 1941, M.A. Columbia, 1942; Ph.D., U. So. Cal., 1972; m. Lowell Harmer, Oct. 31, 1950; 1 dau., Felicia. Reporter Hartford (Conn.) Courant, 1942-44, Washington Times-Harald, 1944-46; editor Mexico City Herald and News, Modern Mexico mag., 1947-51; prof. Cal. State Poly. U., Pomona, 1962--; free lance writer, 1951—. Mem. P.E.N. Club: Washington Nat. Press. Author: Good Food from Mexico, 1950; The High Cost of Dying, 1963; Unfit for Human Consumption, 1971. Home: 437 Crane Blvd Los Angeles CA 90065 Office: Cal State Poly Univ Pomona CA 91766

HARMEYER, VIRGINIA MURPHY (MRS. EDWARD JOHN HARMEYER), educator; b. Blakely, Ga., Oct. 23, 1915; d. James K. and Frances S. (Peurifoy) Murphy; B.S., Northwestern State U., 1959; M.Nursing, Emory U., 1961; postgrad. Murray State U., 1971, U. Tex., 1972; m. Edward John Harmeyer, May 8, 1943; children—Barbara Elizabeth, Frances Evelyn (Mrs. Tom Ridenour). Asst. prof. nursing Northwestern State U., Natchitoches, La., 1960-64; maternal and child health cons. Utah State Dept. of Pub. Health, Salt Lake City, 1964-67; asso. prof. dept. nursing Murray State U., Murray, Ky., 1967-72; prof., dir. div. nursing Valdosta (Ga.) State Coll., 1972—. Served with Nurse Corps, USNR, 1942-43. Mem. Nat. League for Nursing (state recruitment com. chmn. 1964-67), Am. Nurses Assn., Am., Ky. pub. health assns., Alpha Delta Kappa. Club: Quota (Valdosta, Ga.). Home: 2504 Deborah Dr Valdosta GA 31601

HARMON, ADELAIDE THERESA, educator; b. N.Y.C., May 10, 1929; d. Edward William and Margaret Frances (Lambert) Harmon; B.S. magna cum laude, Fordham U., 1955, M.S. in Physics, 1964; Ph.D. (Cardinal Spellman fellow), N.Y. U., 1969. Divisional chmn. dept. natural sci. St. Thomas Aquinas Coll., Sparkill, N.Y., 1967-69, cons. financial aid fed. programs, 1967-71; asst. prof. math. edn. York Coll. City U. N.Y., Jamaica, 1969-74; coll. rep. Gordon project-Pub. Sch. 134, 1970—. Math. coordinator Title I, Sch. Adv. Bd. St. Agnes Sch., Sparkill, 1967—. Recipient Founders' Day award N.Y. U., 1969. NSF fellow Kan. State U., Lawrence, 1969. Mem. N.Y. State Tchrs. Math. Assn. (presdl. council), Am. Math. Assn., Nat. Council Tchrs. Math. Home: 560 Shasta Av Morro Bay CA 93442 Office: Cal Poly State U San Luis Obispo CA 93407

HARMON, CAROLINE HOFF (MRS. PAUL C. HARMON), paper co. exec.; b. Elizabeth, N.J., Apr. 4, 1927; d. Carl Herman and Marie (Bergmann) Hoff; student Am. Conservatory Music, 1945-47, Latin Am. Inst., 1955-56; B.S. magna cum laude, N.Y.U. Sch. Commerce, 1961, postgrad. Sch. Law, 1961, M.A. in Adminstrn. in Higher Edn., 1964, postgrad. Sch. Arts and Scis., 1964-68; m. Paul C. Harmon, Sept. 12, 1959. Various secretarial positions Chgo., N.Y.C., 1945-56; corp. sec. and office mgr. Nat. Coll. Club Program, Inc., N.Y.C., 1957-59; asst. to v.p. sales Fawcett-Dearing Printing Co., N.Y.C., 1959-60; asst. to corp. sec. U.S. Industries, Inc., N.Y.C., 1960-66; adminstr. Nigerian project N.Y.U., N.Y.C., 1966-68; asst. to v.p. and sec. Celanese Corp., N.Y.C., 1968-72; coordinator corporate equal opportunity Internat. Paper Co., N.Y.C., 1973—. Writer, lectr. U.S. and Can. on problems of evening edn. and devel. programs geared to adult, employed students especially women in bus. adminstrn.; research contbn. Pres. Kennedy's Comm. on Status of Women. Recipient N.Y.U. Pres. Certificate Achievement, 1961. Mem. Internat. Assn. Evening Student Councils (founder 1960, treas.), Evening Students Personnel Assn. (past dir.), N.Y.U. Sch. Commerce Alumni Assn. (past dir., sec.), Am. Acad. Polit. and Social Sci., N.Y.U. Club, Am. Mgmt. Assn., Women's Equity Action League (adv. bd. N.J. Chpt. 1972—); Assn. Legal Adminstrs., Bus. and Profl. Women's Club, Am. Assembly Collegiate Schs. Bus. (mem. equal opportunity com. 1973—), Profl. Panhellenic Assn. (mem. finance com. 1972—, rules com. 1972—), Internat. Platform Assn., Phi Chi Theta (v.p. 1966-70; nat. pres. 1970—), Beta Gamma Sigma Alumni. Home: 2 Brantwood Terrace Short Hills NJ 07078 Office: 220 E 42d St New York City NY 10017

HARMON, LUCY, educator; b. Richards, Mo.; d. Franklin and Eva (Knox) Harmon; A.A., Cottey Coll., 1914; B.S., Kan. State Coll., Pittsburg, 1922; M.A., U. Chgo., 1926; Ph.D., N.Y.U., 1934. Tchr. pub. schs., Richards, Mo., 1914-18, Nevada, Mo., 1918-20, McAlester, Okla., 1920-21; instr. Kan. State Coll., 1921-22, asso. prof., 1922-31; prof. English, N.Y. State U. at Geneseo, 1934—, dean, 1934-50. Hon. asso. Danforth Found. Recipient award for distinguished service in edn. to nation and state N.Y. State, 1964. Mem. Modern Lang. Assn., Am. Assn. U. Profs., Am. Assn. U. Women (Woman of Yr. award), N.Y. State Fedn. Women's Clubs (v.p. 1966—), Soc. Protection Children, Formers Club (permanent mem.), Livingston County Hist. Soc. (life), Sigma Tau Delta, Delta Kappa Gamma. Home: 19 South St Geneseo NY 14454

HARMON, REBECCA LAMAR (MRS. NOLAN BAILEY HARMON), author, coll. trustee; b. Rockville, Md., July 23, 1896; d. George Holt and Edith (Stonestreet) Lamar; A.B., Randolph-Macon Woman's Coll., 1916; m. Nolan Bailey Harmon, June 20, 1923; children—Nolan Bailey III, George Lamar. Tchr. Disputana (Va.) High Sch., 1917; translator U.S. Com. Pub. Information Food Adminstrn., Washington, 1917-19; translator A.R.C. hdqrs., Washington, 1919-20, head translation bur., 1920-21; tng. dir. Ohrbach's Inc., Newark, 1943-56; now author. Trustee Randolph-Macon Coll., Randolph-Macon Woman's Coll., 1930—; mem. exec. com. Randolph-Macon Woman's Coll. Bd., 1940-70. Mem. Nat. Alumnae Assn. Randolph Macon Woman's Coll. (pres. 1942-44), Am. Sam Hon. Soc., Phi Beta Kappa, Alpha Omicron Pi. Methodist. Author: Susanna, Mother of the Wesleys, 1968. Contbr. articles, stories to various mags., jours. Home: 998 Springdale Rd NE Atlanta GA 30306

HARMON, VERNA LEOLA CLAY (MRS. FLOYD HARMON), med. assistance cons.; b. Roselm, O.; d. William Oliver and Minnie (Jackson) Clay; R.N., W.A. Foote Hosp. Tng. Sch., 1925; student Cin. Coll. Embalming, 1950; m. Floyd Harmon, May 8, 1926 (dec. Nov. 1971); 1 dau., Geraldine (Mrs. Jack Schauweker) (dec. 1966). Pvt. duty nurse, Albion, Mich., Jackson, Mich., Ann Arbor, Mich., Niles, Mich., Ft. Wayne, Ind., Dayton, O., Findlay, O., McComb, O., 1925-48; office nurse, Dayton, 1927-28; adminstrv. asst. Miller-McComb Hosp., 1948-50; exec. sec., nurse cons. Am. Cancer Soc. of Hancock County, O., 1951-59; co-owner, asst. Harmon Funeral Home, McComb, 1930-66; med. assistance cons. Toledo dist. Ohio Dept. Pub. Welfare, 1966-69, adminstrv. specialist utilization rev. commn. Bur. Med. Assistance, 1969-70, adminstrv. specialist utilization Rev. Bur., Columbus, 1970-71; field rep. Ohio Soc. for Crippled Children and Adults, Columbus, 1962-65. Instr. classes home nursing A.R.C., 1942-43, mem. adv. com. Home Health Nursing Service Hancock County, 1967—; sec. to adv. council Home Health Agy. Findlay-Hancock County, 1969-70, 74-75, pres. Hancock County Cancer Soc., 1974-75. Dist. chmn. religion Gen. Fedn. Women's Club, 1960-62; mem. Nat. Council on Aging; former coordinator aging Hancock County for Ohio Commn. on Aging; charter pres. McComb Community Garden Club. Trustee Blanchard Valley Hosp., Findlay, 1968-72; life bd. dirs. Hancock County unit Am. Cancer Soc., v.p., 1972. Recipient citation Am. Cancer Soc., 1958, meritorious service citation Ohio Pub. Health Dept., 1961. Mem. Ohio Funeral Dirs. Assn., Bus. and Profl. Women's Club, Am. Assn. Ret. Persons, Smithsonian Assos., Progress Study Club McComb (pres. 1955-56), Nat. Rep. Women's Assn., Ohio Pub. Health Assn., Nat. Rehab. Counseling Assn., Am., Ohio nurses assns., Ohio Rehab. Assn., Blanchard Valley Hosp. Assn. Methodist. Mem. Order Eastern Star. Clubs: National Travel; Zonta (charter Findlay). Home: 201 E Pearl St Findlay OH 45840

HARMOND, THELMA E. MOORE (MRS. EDWARD HUGH HARMOND), educator; b. Hubert, Ga., Sept. 3, 1920; d. John Leon and Estelle (Chauncey) Moore; grad. Ga. State Tchrs. Coll., 1937; B.S., Ft. Valley State Coll., 1944; M.Ed., Atlanta U., 1945; Ph.D., Ohio State U., 1965; m. Edward Hugh Harmond, Mar. 17, 1951; children—Gale Cuthbert, Fern Estelle, Cherry Suzanne. Demonstrn. tchr. State Tchrs. Coll. Lab. Sch., Forsyth, Ga., 1937; tchr. Starr High Sch., Thomaston, Ga., 1938-39; tchr., prin. Lab. Schs., Montgomery, Ga., 1939-43; supr. Jeanes, Cordele, Ga., 1945-48; mem. faculty Savannah State Coll. (Ga.), 1948—, prof. tchr. edn., 1966—, chmn. dept., 1966—, chmn. grad. edn. dept., 1968—. Chmn. Ga. Adv. Group on Tchr. Edn. Policy, 1973-74. Am. Assn. Colls. for Tchr. Edn. fellow to study Brit. Primary Schs., 1972. Mem. Ga. Tchrs. and Ednl. Assn. for Student Teaching, Assn. for Childhood Edn., Ga. Council Econ. Edn. (trustee), Internat. Assn. for Supervision and Curriculum Devel., Acad. Council on Tchr. Edn. (chmn.-elect leadership for undergrad. and grad. edn. univ. system), Nat. Council for Accreditation Tchr. Edn., Am. Assn. Colls. for Tchr. Edn., Kappa Delta Pi, Pi Lambda Theta. Presbyn. (trustee). Contbr. articles to profl. jours. Home: Grove Point Rd Route 4 Box 375 Savannah GA 31405 Office: Savannah State Coll Savannah GA 31404

HARMS, LOUISE IVIE (MRS. WILLARD DANIEL HARMS), librarian; b. Birmingham, Ala., June 25, 1924; d. Henry J. and Lola Belle (Hicks) Ivie; B.S., U. Ala., 1944; B.S., George Peabody Coll., 1946; m. Willard Daniel Harms, Oct. 17, 1955; children—Dennis Leon, Daniel Lee, Willard Daniel. Asst. librarian Coll. Edn. Library, U. Ala., University, 1944-45, head cataloger, 1948-51; reference asst. George Peabody Coll. for Tchrs., Nashville, 1945-46; cataloger Allegheny Coll. Library, Meadville, Pa., 1946-47; 1st asst. cataloger U. Ark. Library, Fayetteville, 1947; depot librarian spl. services libraries U.S. Army, Europe, 1951-55, library adminstr. spl. activities div., 1958-63; English tchr. Sweetwater (Tenn.) High Sch., 1963-64; asst. librarian Merner Pfeiffer Library, Tenn. Wesleyan Coll., Athens, 1964-65, head librarian, 1965—. Pres., Sweetwater P.T.A., 1973—. Mem. Am., Tenn., Southeastern, E. Tenn. (sec. 1972-73) library assns., Am. Assn. U. Profs. (sec., treas. 1970-72, pres. 1973—), Alpha Beta Alpha, Kappa Delta Pi, V.F.W. Aux. Democrat. Presbyn. Home: 20 Hickory Lane Sweetwater TN 37874 Office: Tennessee Wesleyan College Athens TN 37303

HARMS, NANCY LU, antique store owner; b. LaSalle, Ill., June 6, 1944; d. George William and Vivian Wilma (Anderson) Norquist; student Carl Sandburg Coll., 1968-73; m. Ronald F. Harms, Apr. 13, 1964; children—Brad Elliot, Brent Joseph. Owner, Americana Antiques, Galesburg, Ill., 1965—; bookkeeper Midwest Builders, Inc., Galesburg, 1966-73; bookkeeper Johnson Bldg. Systems, Galesburg, 1973—. Lectr., exhibitor antiques. Mem. Nat. Assn. Dealers in Antiques, Early Am. Soc. Contbr. articles to trade publs. and magazines. Restored hist. landmark, Galesburg, 1973. Home and Office: 435 N Kellogg St Galesburg IL 61401

HARMSTONE, TERESA RAKOWSKA, educator; b. Poznan, Poland, Aug. 12, 1927; d. Tadeusz Jan and Jadwiga Wanda (Kopczynska) Rakowski; B.A., McGill U., 1950; A.M., Radcliffe Coll., 1952; Ph.D., Harvard, 1966; m. Richard C. Harmstone, Apr. 1955 (div. Mar. 1965); 1 son, Andrew Tadeusz. Came to U.S., 1950, naturalized, 1955. Research analyst fgn. areas studies div. Am. U., Washington, 1957-61; instr. polit. sci. Douglass Coll. Rutgers U., New Brunswick, N.J., 1961-65; asst. prof. Carleton U., Ottawa, Ont., 1966-68, asso. prof., 1968-74, prof., 1974—, supr. grad. studies, 1968-70, dir. Inst. Soviet and East European Studies, 1973—; exec. dir. League Women Voters U.S., Washington, 1970-72. Am. Assn. U. Women fellow, 1963-64. Mem. Am., Canadian polit. sci. assns., Am. Assn. Advancement Slavic Studies, Am., Canadian assns. univ. profs., Canadian Assn. Slavists. Author: Russia and Nationalism in Soviet Central Asia, 1970. Editor (with A. Bromke) Communist States in Disarray, 1972. Home: 21 Farnham Crescent Ottawa ON Canada

HARNETT, LILA BEVERLY (MRS. JOEL WILLIAM HARNETT), writer; b. Bklyn., Oct. 4, 1926; d. Milton Samuel and Claire S. (Merahn) Mogan; B.A., Bklyn. Coll., 1946; postgrad. New Sch. for Social Research, 1947-50; m. Joel William Harnett, Feb. 4, 1951. Personnel exec. Walter Lowen Agy., N.Y.C., 1947-52; pub. Bus. Atomics Report, N.Y.C., 1953-63; weekly columnist N.Y. State Newspapers, 1964—. Chmn. Friends Council Whitney Mus. Am. Art, 1965—. Mem. Met. Opera Guild, Friends of City Center, Overseas Press Club. Club: Town Tennis (gov.). Home and office: 2 Sutton Place S New York City NY 10022

HARNEY, SISTER MARY KIERAN, hosp. adminstr.; b. Brinsmade, N.D., Feb. 6, 1926; d. James Kyran and Ellen Catherine (Holland) Harney; B.S. in Nursing summa cum laude, Catholic U. Am., 1955, M.H.A., St. Louis U., 1959. Supr., clin. instr. pediatric nursing Mercy Hosp., Des Moines, 1949-55, instr., 1955-57; asst. adminstr. Mercy Hosp., Denver, 1959-62, adminstr., 1962-73, pres. governing bd., 1973—. Sec.-treas. Met. Denver Hosp. Council, 1961, pres., 1969. Dir. finance Sisters of Mercy, Omaha Province, 1972—. Bd. dirs. Mercy Hosp., Denver, also Red Bluff, Cal., Des Moines; regional adv. bd. Am. Hosp. Assn., 1972—. Fellow Am. Coll. Hosp. Adminstrs.; mem. Colo. Conf. Cath. Hosps. (pres. 1962-63), Catholic (sec. 1971-74, chmn. elect 1974—), Colo. (pres. 1970) hosp. assns., St. Louis U. Alumni Assn. Hosp. Adminstrs. (treas. 1962-63, pres. 1969-70). Address: Mercy Hosp E 16th and Milwaukee St Denver CO 80206

HARNOIS, BARBARA MAY, town ofcl.; b. N. Grafton, Mass., Aug. 21, 1922; d. Edmund E. and Lucy C. (Snow) Harnois; student David Hale Fanning Sch. for Girls, 1940-42; Cosmotologist, Quinsigamond Jr. Coll., 1971. Hairdresser, Deluxe Beauty Salon, Westborough, Mass., 1942-48, Modern Beauty Shop, Westborough, 1948-49, 53-63, drill press operator Marcus Mason Co., Westborough, 1949-53; with Bay State Abrasives, Westborough, 1963-68; bookkeeper Town of Westborough, 1968-70, town accountant, 1970—. Mem. Mass. Municipal Auditors and Accountants Assn. Home: 14A Cedar St Westborough MA 01581 Office: Town Hall West Main St Westborough MA 01581

HARNSBERGER, CAROLINE THOMAS (MRS. AUDLEY E. HARNSBERGER), author; b. Columbus, O., Apr. 12, 1902; d. James Oscar and Edith (Hiss) Thomas; student Juilliard Sch. Music, 1922-25, Paris Conservatoire de Musique, 1925-26, Ohio State U., 1929, Northwestern U., 1954-56; m. Audley E. Harnsberger, May 18, 1926; children—Donald A., Robert T., Ann (Mrs. Peter J. Atkinson). Violinist, Women's Symphony, Chgo., 1926-33, Evanston (Ill.) Symphony Orch., 1946—; founder, owner Hallock Music House, Northfield, Ill., 1964-73; propr. Music in Northfield, 1973—. Mem. Nat. League Am. Pen Women, Midland Authors, Women in Communications. Conglist. Clubs: North Shore Musicians; 99's; Winnetka Music; Music (Evanston). Author: Mark Twain at Your Fingertips, 1948; The Lincoln Treasury, 1950; A Man of Courage, 1952; Mark Twain, Family Man, 1960; Mark Twain's Views of Religion, 1961; Pilot's Ready Reference, 1962, 72; A Treasury of Presidential Quotations, 1964; Bernard Shaw: Selections of His Wit and Wisdom, 1965; Everyone's Mark Twain, 1972. Home: 775 Sumac Lane Winnetka IL 60093 Office: 446 Central Av Northfield IL 60093

HARNSBERGER, THERESE COSCARELLI (MRS. FREDERICK OWEN HARNSBERGER), librarian; b. Muskegon, Mich.; d. Charles and Julia (Borrell) Coscarelli; B.A. cum laude, Marymount Coll., 1952; M.L.S., U. So. Cal., 1953; postgrad. Rosary Coll., River Forest, Ill., 1955-56, U. Cal Los Angeles Extension, 1960-61; m. Frederick Owen Harnsberger, Dec. 24, 1962; 1 son, Lindsey Carleton. Free-lance writer, 1950—; librarian San Marino (Cal.) High Sch., 1953-56; cataloger, cons. San Marino Hall, South Pasadena, Cal., 1956-61; librarian Los Angeles State Coll., 1956-59; librarian dist. library Covina-Valley Unified Sch. Dist., Covina, Cal., 1959—; librarian Los Angeles Trade Tech. Coll., part-time 1972—, Pasadena City Coll. Library, 1973—. Chmn. spiritual values com. Covina Cordinating Council, 1964-66; telephone chmn. Fremont Sch. P.T.A., Alhambra. Mem. Cal. Assn. Sch. Librarians (chmn. legislative com.), Covina Tchrs. Assn., Am. Assn. U. Women (historian 1972-73), U. So. Cal. Grad. Sch. Library Sci. (life), League Women Voters, Am. Nutrition Soc. (chpt. Newsletter chmn.), Pi Lambda Theta. Office: 2809 W Hellman Av Alhambra CA 91803

HARP, SYBIL CHANCE (MRS. JAN L. HARP), mag. editor; b. Passaic, N.J., June 22, 1931; d. Percival H. and Sybil Dorothy (James) Chance; A.B., Wilson Coll., 1953; postgrad. (Fulbright grant), U. Utrecht, Netherlands, 1953-54; m. Jan L. Harp, Jan. 15, 1955; children—Sybil Angelique, John Henry, Peter Marcel, Sandra Elizabeth. Editor, Creative Crafts Mag., Newton, N.J., 1967—. Mem. Municipal Pool Commn., Ramsey, N.J., 1972-73. Mem. Am. Craftsmen's Council, Hobby Industry Assn. Am. (chmn. pubs. sect. 1972—), Phi Beta Kappa. Home: PO Box 99 Stillwater NJ 07875 Office: PO Box 700 Newton NJ 07860

HARPER, CAROL ELY (MRS. MAURICE WILSON HARPER), editor; b. Monroe City, Mo.; d. Aurelius Wesley and Annie Belle (Adkisson) Ely; certificate (scholar), Whitman Coll., 1928; B.A., U. Wash., 1952; M.A., 1959; postgrad. U. Birmingham (Eng.), 1954; m. Maurice Wilson Harper, Mar. 11, 1925; children—Maurice Ely, Carol-Maura (Mrs. Charles Anthony Kiselyak). Tchr. pub. sch. Walla Walla County (Wash.), 1923-24; Eastern Ore. corr. Oregonian, Portland, 1934-36; co-founder Experiment Mag., Walla Walla, 1944, bus. mgr., 1947-48, editor, 1949—; editor Experimenter, 1944-46, Campus Directory, U. Wash., 1973; free lance editor, 1970—. Founder, Eastern Ore. Music Project, 1937, Walla Walla (Wash.) Little Theater, 1944, Experiment Theatre, 1958. Mem. Nat. Fedn. Press Women, Internat. Platform Assn., Internat. Aril Soc., Wash. Press Women, Pioneer Assn. State of Wash., D.A.R., Arena, Actors Equity. Author: To a Faulty Lover (poetry), 1946; Distichs for a Dancer (poetry) 1950. Editor: (drama anthology) Experiment Theatre One, 1960. Contbr. poetry and prose to various mags. and anthologies. Home: 6565 NE Windermere Rd Seattle WA 98105

HARPER, ELSA RUTH CROOKS (MRS. JOHN JAY HARPER), educator, author, composer; b. Beallsville, O., Feb. 17, 1906; d. George W. and Ada Sarah (Wright) Crooks; Edn. degree Kent. State U., 1935; student Elliott Comml. Coll., 1927-28, West Liberty Coll., 1923, U. Utah, 1961-62; diploma U.S. Sch. Music, 1950, Lincoln Sch. Practical Nursing, 1957; m. John Jay Harper, Apr. 3, 1963 (dec.); 1 son, Keith. Tchr. Powhatan, O., 1930-50, Beallsville, O., 1950-58, Bucyrus, O., 1959-63, Barnesville (O.)-Somerton Consol. Schs., 1963-66. Organizer, Beallsville Kindergarten, 1961. Pres., Federated Woman's Club, Beallsville, 1973. Mem. Arts and Crafts Bd. Monroe County, 1973-74. Bd. trustees Rebekah Lodge, Powhatan, 1945-48; house parent Omaha Boys Sch., 1969—. Mem. U.S. Trotting Assn., O. and Pa. Commn. Racing, Nat., O. ret. tchrs. assns., Sr. Citizens (pres. 1968-70), Hist. Soc. Republican. Mem. Eastern Star. Clubs: Homemakers (Jerusalem, O.); Friendship (Powhatan). Composer: Songs for Kindergarten, 1962; Read a Poem Its Good for the Soul, 1970. Address: Box 35 Jerusalem OH 43747

HARPER, FLORENCE RUTH (MRS. EDWIN M. HARPER), produce co. exec.; b. Buhl, Ida., Feb. 3, 1928; d. Arley and Isabella Frances (Clark) Smith; grad. high sch.; m. John W. Hardin, Feb. 19, 1946 (div. Sept. 1965); children—John Wesley, Jeffrey Steven; m. 2d, Edwin M. Harper, Nov. 24, 1966; 1 dau., Megnild Jane. With Ashworth Motor Co., Twin Falls, Ida., 1954-58; office mgr. E.S. Harper Co., Inc., Twin Falls, Ida., 1958—, corporate sec., 1964—, dir. 1969—; sec., treas., dir. G & H Land and Cattle Co., Twin Falls, Ida., 1962—. Mem. Magic Valley Hosp. Aux. (2d v.p., mem. exec. bd. 1973-74). Republican. Methodist (adult edn. commn. 1972-73). Clubs: Blue Lake Country. Home: 290 Lincoln St Twin Falls ID 83301 Office: 198 Gem St Twin Falls ID 83301

HARPER, JENNIE AMABEL MCINTOSH (MRS. JOSEPH HARPER), educator; b. Bath, N.B., Can., Apr. 21, 1913; d. John K. and Mabel C. (Dalling) McIntosh; B.S., U. N.B., 1936; M.S., U. Me., 1938; Ph.D., Cornell U., 1941; m. Joseph Harper, Oct. 12, 1950 (dec. 1962); children—Nathan, Joseph. Came to U.S., 1936, naturalized, 1950. Faculty, Ain Shams U., Cairo, Egypt, 1965-67; faculty So. Ill. U., Carbondale, 1957—, prof., 1969—; vis. prof., chmn. home econs. U. Sierra Leone, 1974—. Fulbright grantee, 1965-67, 72. Mem. Am. Home Econs. Assn. (chmn. fellowships com. 1973-75), Asian Soc., Inst. Food Technologists. Home: 501 S Oakland St Carbondale IL 62901 Office: So Ill Univ Carbondale IL 62901

HARPER, MARGARET EARL MCCONNELL (MRS. GARY L. HARPER), educator; b. Princeton, Ind.; d. Earl F. and Gertrude W. (Williams) McConnell; A.B., Ind. U., 1946, M.C.S., 1947, Ph.D., 1963; postgrad. U. Mo., 1950-51, U. Cal. at Los Angeles, 1952, U. Wis., 1955; m. Gary L. Harper, Dec. 29, 1964. Asst. prof. English, Oakland City Coll., (Ind.), 1947-61, U. Md., overseas campus, Ramstein AFB, West Germany, 1964-66, U. Evansville (Ind.), 1966-67; prof. English, Oakland City Coll. (Ind.), 1962-64, 69—, dir. dramatics 1947-64, 69—, chmn. div. langs. and lit., 1969-72. Mem. D.A.R., Am. Assn. U. Profs., Nat. Council Tchrs. English, Ind. Council Tchrs. English, Am. Theatre Assn., Nat. Trust for Hist. Preservation, Ind., Gibson County hist. socs., Am. Philatelic Soc., Am. Soc. Theatre Research, Alpha Phi Gamma (nat. v.p. 1955; nat. exec. sec. 1957-64), Theta Sigma Phi, Delta Kappa Gamma, Kappa Kappa Kappa, Alpha Psi Omega. Republican. Methodist. Mem. Order Eastern Star. Club: Oakland City College. Home: 231 N Madison St Oakland City IN 47660

HARPER, MARTHA ANN KELLY, banker; b. Elk City, Okla., Aug. 17, 1929; d. Olin Lake and Cora Agnes (Gowdy) Kelly; student Okla. Bapt. U., 1947-48; grad. Okla. Intermediate Sch. Banking, 1972; m. Donald Earl Harper, Aug. 21, 1948 (div. 1969); 1 son, David Kent. Asst. cashier Farmers Nat. Bank, Elk City, Okla., 1955-60, asst. v.p., 1960-65, cashier, 1965-66, v.p., cashier, 1966—, also dir. Sec.-treas. Elk City (Okla.) United Fund. Bd. dirs. Elk City United Fund. Mem. Nat. Assn. Bank Women, Okla. Bank Women (mem. com.), Okla. Bankers Assn. (mem. bank mgmt. com. state Okla. 1971-72, mem. edn. and service sect. 1973-74, operations com. 1973-74). Baptist. Home: 915 N Washington St Elk City OK 73644 Office: 101 N Main St Elk City OK 73644

HARPER, PAMELA DAE, assn. exec.; b. Marion, O., Nov. 25, 1945; d. Wayne Harold and Dorothy Elnor (Sechrist) Harper; B.A., Ohio Wesleyan U., 1967. Field dir. Camp Fire Girls, Columbus, O., 1967-69, dist. dir., 1969-70, cons., 1970-72, exec. dir., 1972—. Active Young Women Committed to Action, Hunger Task Force, Am. Field Service, YMCA; mem. Gov.'s Home and Safety Com.; mem. profl. adv. com. United Way. Mem. League Women Voters. Home: 2581 Scioto View Columbus OH 43221 Office: 718 S High St Columbus OH 43206

HARPER, WILHELMINA, editor; b. Farmington, Me.; d. William and Bertha (Tauber) Harper; spl. courses Columbia, N.Y.U., N.Y. State Library Sch. Childrens librarian, br. librarian Poppenhusen br. Queensboro (N.Y.) Pub. Library, 1908-18; first asst. Camp Library, Pelham Bay Naval Tng. Sta., N.Y., 1918-19; library organizer for YMCA, Brest, France, 1919; asst. to Edward C. Carter dir. YMCA Overseas Service, 1920; organizer, supr. childrens work Kern County Free Library, Bakersfield, Cal., 1921-28; organizer Redwood City (Cal.) Pub. Library, 1929, librarian, 1930-54; editor, compiler childrens books, 1918—; instr. childrens lit. Sch. Librarianship U. Cal., 1929, Riverside Library Sch., summers 1929, 32, San Jose (Cal.) State Tchrs. Coll., summer 1929. Mem. A.L.A. Author: Ghosts and Goblins, 1936, 65; Merry Christmas To You, 1936, 65; The Harvest Feast, 1938, 65; Easter Chimes, 1941, 65; The Gunniwolf, 1967. Died Dec. 23, 1973. Home: 2385 Waverley St Palo Alto CA 94301

HARRAGAN, BETTY LEHAN, cons.; b. Milw., June 2, 1921; d. Charles Joseph and Marie Ann (Caswell) Lehan; student Milw. State Tchrs. Coll., 1939-41; A.B., Marquette U., 1944; A.M., Columbia, 1947; m. David Joseph Harragan, Jan. 2, 1962 (dec.); 1 dau., Kathleen Ann. Research asst. CBS, N.Y.C., 1945-46; publicist Newell-Emmett Advt. Agy., N.Y.C., 1947-49; womens editor co. publs. N.Y. Telephone Co., N.Y.C., 1950-56; with Ruth Lundgren Co., N.Y.C., 1957-63, v.p., 1960-63; sr. writer pub. relations dept. J. Walter Thompson Co., N.Y.C., 1963-72; pres. Betty Harragan & Affiliates, N.Y.C., 1972—. Lectr., New Sch. for Social Research, 1971-73, N.Y. U., 1974. Bd. dirs. Life Workshops, Mem. Nat. Orgn. for Women (chpt. pub. relations coordinator 1972, dir., corr. sec. 1973—), Publicity Club of N.Y., Assn. Feminist Consultants (founding mem., pub. relations dir. 1972-73), Women's Polit. Caucus. Address: 541 E 20th St New York City NY 10010

HARRALL, FRANCES BOONE (MRS. E. RUSSELL HARRALL), realtor; b. Greensboro, N.C., Mar. 2, 1907; d. Robert Philemon and Effie (Geringer) Boone; student pub. schs. and bus. coll.; m. E. H. Young, Mar. 1, 1924 (div. 1941); children—Miriam (Mrs. Robert Gordon Kvarnes), Richard Franklin; m. 2d, Edwin Russell Harrall, Apr. 25, 1943. With Cone Mills, N.Y.C., 1927-42, Children's Home of Balt., 1943-46; dist. mgr. Beauty Counselors, Inc., 1956, nat. sect. mgr., 1957-61, div. mgr., 1961-63; realtor Russell T. Baker & Co., Inc., Lutherville, Md., 1963—. Mem. Md. Hist. Soc., English-Speaking Union, Women's Civic League, P.E.O., So. Dames Am. (nat. v.p.), Realtors Million Dollar Club (life), Internat. Platform Assn. Episcopalian. Clubs: Little Garden, Dulaney Springs Golf. Home: Nepenthe 1505 E Phoenix Rd Route 1 Phoenix MD 21131 Office: 1629 York Rd Lutherville MD 21093

HARRELL, IRENE BURK (MRS. ALLEN WAYLAN HARRELL), author; b. Howard City, Mich., Mar. 10, 1927; d. Howard Lofton and Marguerite Luella (Weatherby) Burk; B.A., summa cum laude, Ohio State U., 1948; B.S. in L.S., U. N.C., 1949; m. Allen Waylan Harrell, June 22, 1952; children—Thomas Burk, Alice Elizabeth, James Britton, Susan Irene, Marguerite Owens, Maria Weatherby (adopted). Librarian, Westerville (O.) Pub. Library, 1949-52; dept. librarian Sociology, Anthropology and City Planning Library, U. N.C., Chapel Hill, 1952-53; dir. Halifax County (N.C.) Library, 1953-54; with C.L. Hardy Library, Atlantic Christian Coll., 1958-64, head librarian, 1962-64; self employed writer. Mem. Phi Beta Kappa. Author: Prayerables; Meditations of a Homemaker, 1967, Good Marriages Grow; A Book for Wives, 1968, God Ventures; True Accounts of God in the Lives of Men, 1970, Lo, I Am with You; Prayersteps to Faith (also titled Miracles Through Prayer), 1970, Ordinary Days with an Extraordinary God; Prayerables II, 1971, The Opposite Sex, 1972; Black Tracks: Nineteen Years on the Mainline, by Floyd Miles as told to Irene Burk Harrell, 1972; (with J.H. Walker, Jr. and Lucille Walker) God's Living Room, 1972; Security Blankets-Family Size, 1973; Muddy Sneakers and Other Family Hassles, 1974; (with Harold Hill) How to Live Like a King's Kid, 1974; The Windows of Heaven: Prayerables III, 1974. Editor: Logos, Internat., 1969—. Home: 408 Pearson St Wilson NC 27893

HARRELL, JEAN GABBERT, educator; b. Berkeley, Cal., Sept. 28, 1921; d. Harry and Florence (Doyle) Gabbert; A.B., U. Cal., Berkeley, 1943; Ph.B., Columbia U., 1950; m. Elwood C. Harrell, June 1, 1948 (dec. Nov. 1963); children—Scott F., Gail L. (Mrs. Philip Lindberg), Brian G. Instr., Mount Holyoke Coll., 1945-47; asst. prof. philosophy Cal. State Univ., Hayward, 1964-68, asso. prof., 1968-72, prof., 1972—. Author introduction, compiler: Aesthetics in 20th Century Poland, 1972. Editor: Volume 1, History of Aesthetics (in English translation of book by W. Tatarkiewicz). Home: 615 Euclid Av Berkeley CA 94708 Office: Department of Philosophy California State Univ Hayward CA 94542

HARRELL, KILDA MALCOLM, author; b. Oswego, N.Y.,; d. William S. and Anna (Mannering) Malcolm; m. Rudolph T. Harrell, June 16, 1919; children—Thomas Malcolm, Robert Malcolm, Betty Jeanne (Mrs. Turner C. Trippe). Dir. Harrell Bros. & Campbell Ins. Co., 1953—. Trustee Maret Sch., Washington, 1938—. Mem. Nat. League Am. Pen Women, Nat. Soc. Arts and Letters, Pan-Am. Liaison Com. Women's Orgns., D.A.R., Cum Laude Soc. Episcopalian. Clubs: Washington, Columbia Country. Author: Look Before You Leap, Then Go to South America, 1950. Contbr. articles to mags.; illustrated travel lectures. Home: 5101 Ridgefield Rd Bethesda MD 20016

HARRIETT, (H. WILCOXEN), artist, writer, puppeteer; b. Lewistown, Ill., May 12, 1905; d. George Ray and Sylvia (Black) Wilcoxen; student Western Ill. Tchrs. Coll., 1924-27; part time or evening student Knox Coll., Galesburg, Ill., Acad. Fine Arts., San Diego, Pepin Fashion Acad., Mpls., Walker Art Center, Mpls. Sch. Art, Dunwoody Indsl, Inst., Art Students League, The von Hesse Studios of Effective Speech and Human Relations, N.Y.U., Betty Cashman Drama Studios; m. Harold Ginnings, June 22, 1928 (div.); 1 dau. Brett. Exhibited in group shows at Portraits, Inc., Hotel Pierre, N.Y.C., Old Bklyn. Heights, Batten, Barton, Durstine and Osborn, Inc., Ted Bates Company, J. Walter Thompson, Hammacher Schlemmer, pvt. showings; represented permanent collection Meml. Library Western Ill. U., Lila Acheson Wallace Meml. Library, Lewistown, Ill.; appearance as actress on NBC-TV, 1957, also asst. producer puppet show; produced original show for children The Magic Slate, 1956 on NYU-TV, appearance as guest artist WABD-TV, 1953; actress CBS-TV, 1961—; appearance in The Mirage, 1965; also guest panelist on Girl Talk, ABC-TV, 1966; mem. little theatre troupe Fable Valley Puppets, 1961-62; tchr. commerce Meredosia (Ill.) High Sch., 1927-28; tutored in commerce, Galesburg, Ill., 1928-30; tchr. English Berlitz Sch. Langs., Mpls., 1943—; substitute art tchr. Mpls. Schs., 1943—; insp., artist war plants, Mpls., 1943—; apprenticeship Colwell Press, 1944—; free-lance writing, designing, illustrating, 1944—; asst. to art dir. Grosset & Dunlap, Inc., 1959-62; asst. editor The Book of Knowledge, Grolier, Inc., 1962-63; med. editor-writer Macfadden-Bartel Corp., 1963-73; writing instr. Famous Schs., Westport, Conn., 1966-67; arts and features editor Employees' Newsletter, St. Clare's Hosp. and Health Center, 1969-72; asso. editor The Gold Leaf Question and Answer Library, Interior Design, 1964; book designer, illustrator Harvey House, Inc., 1964-67; commns. include parties for children, portraits of children and pets, and puppets. Mem. Modern Mus. Modern Art, Met. Mus. Art. Ghostwriting for presdl. campaign. Mem. Soc. Illustrators, Nat. Acad. Television Arts and Scis., Art Students League, Am. Fedn. of Television and Radio Artists, Screen Actors Guild, Puppetry Guild Greater N.Y. (liaison officer 1964-65), Puppeteers of Am. Republican. Author, illustrator: Animal ABC, 1949; It Is Easy to Draw, 1951-52; The Travel Play and Coloring Book, 1960; Saint Francis and His Friends (children's story), 1954; Froggie Went A-Courtin', 1967; First Lady of India: The Story of Indira Gandhi, 1969; book designer and illustrator: The Professor and the Mysterious Box, 1964; The Professor and the Vanishing Flags, 1965. Contbg. editor Leisure Mag., 1959. Illustrator: My First Adventure in Pianoland, 1953; The Bear Family, 1966; illustrator, designer Baby's Own Horoscope, 1971. Address: 135 E 54th St New York City NY 10022

HARRIGAN, JOAN (MRS. JOHN JOSEPH HARRIGAN), ednl. cons.; b. Syracuse, Kan., Oct. 12, 1927; d. Edward Dewey and Elizabeth Leora (Berg) Burnside; A.B., Colo. State Coll. Edn., 1949; M.A., U. Denver, 1961, postgrad., 1969—; m. John Joseph Harrigan, Sept. 5, 1949; 1 son, John Patrick. Tchr., sch. librarian, Colo., 1950-64; state sch. library cons. Colo. Dept. Edn., 1965-69, dir. library planning, research and evaluation, 1969-72, specialist on sch. improvement process team, 1972—. Cons., U.S. Office Edn., 1970, S.D. Dept. Pub. Instrn., 1973; workshop dir. Western Interstate Com. Higher Edn., 1970. Mem. Colo. Edn. Assn. (pres. Western Colo. tchrs. div. 1956-57), Capitol Hill (pres. 1968-69), Nat. (Colo. ofcl. del. 1968-71) edn. assns., Colo. Assn. Sch. Execs. (dept. vice chmn. 1968-70), Am., Colo. library assns., Kappa Delta Pi (local v.p. 1971-73). Author bibliographies and monographs. Editor: Colo. State Library Newsletter, 1969-71. Home: 2640 S Lowell Blvd Denver CO 80219 Office: Colo Dept Edn State Office Bldg Denver CO 80203

HARRINGTON, ARLENE NORCOTT (MRS. MILTON E. HARRINGTON), real estate broker; b. Crossett, Ark., Mar. 23, 1908; d. Joseph Copeland and Fanny (Howell) Norcott; certificate real estate U. Cal. at Los Angeles, 1973; m. Milton E. Harrington, Feb. 2, 1936; children—Joanna (Mrs. Jay Lintner), Susan Arlene (Mrs. Richard Wilenken), John Milton. Co-owner Harrington Realty, Palos Verdes Estates, Cal., 1964—, real estate broker, 1969—. United Methodist (sec. state bd. of ch. women 1960-64). Club: Palos Verdes Estates (Cal.) Women's. Home: 5670 Whitecliff Rancho Palos Verdes CA 90274 Office: #24 Malaga Cove Plaza PO Box 122 Palos Verdes Estates CA 90274

HARRINGTON, EUNICE KNISS (MRS. WAYNE W. HARRINGTON), ch. assn. exec.; b. Sutton, Neb.; d. Peter and Katherine (Ulmer) Kniss; student U. Neb., 1927, York Coll., 1932; L.H.D., Neb. Wesleyan U., 1961; m. Wayne W. Harrington, July 11, 1928; 1 son, Thomas Wayne. Tchr. pub. schs., Neb., 1926-32; v.p., sec. W.W. Harrington, Inc., Fairmont, Neb., 1937-48. Pres., Neb. Conf. Woman's Soc. Christian Service, 1951-53; nat. pres. women's div. Bd. Missions, United Methodist Ch., 1968—; v.p. gen. bd. of missions United Meth. Ch., Omaha, 1968—; mem. adv. coms. various Meth.-related social agys. and mission schs. Named Layman of Year, Neb. Conf. Meth. Ch., 1963. Mem. League of Women Voters, P.E.O. Sisterhood. Mem. Order Eastern Star. Address: 4903 California St Omaha NE 68132

HARRINGTON, HARRIETT BEALE (MRS. PATRICK W. HARRINGTON), assn. exec.; b. Oneonta, N.Y., June 22, 1920; d. Frederick Grant and Olive Beryl (Christy) Beale; student Nazareth Coll.; m. Patrick W. Harrington, Aug. 14, 1943; children—Patricia, Kevin, Timothy, Laura. With Landmark Soc. of Western N.Y., Rochester, 1962—, dir., 1967—. Cons. N.Y. State Council on the Arts, 1967—; mem. N.Y. State Bd. for Historic Preservation, 1973—; chmn. N.Y. State Com. for Nat. Register, 1973—; bd. advisers Nat. Trust for Hist. Preservation, 1973—. Fellow Rochester Mus. and Sci. Center; mem. Victorian Soc. Am. (dir. 1973—). Club: Penfield (N.Y.) Country. Home: 225 Mulberry St Rochester NY 14620 Office: 130 Spring St Rochester NY 14608

HARRINGTON, MARY PAULSON, religious journalist; b. Chgo.; d. Henry T. and Evelina (Belden) Paulson; B.A., Oberlin Coll., 1946; M.A., Chgo. Theol. Sem., 1956; postgrad. Northwestern U., 1946-49; m. Gordon K. Harrington, Sept. 7, 1957; children—Jonathan Henry, Charles Scranton. Newspaper reporter, editor House Organ, Chgo., 1946-49; mem. editorial staff Music Educators Jour., Chgo., 1949-50; publicist Nat. Council Chs., N.Y.C., 1950-51; mem. press staff Second Assembly World Council Chs., Evanston, Ill., 1954; mgr. midwest office Office of Communication, Congl. Christian Chs., Evang. and Reformed Ch., United Ch. of Christ, Chgo., 1955-59; staff writer United Ch. Herald, 1959-61; free-lance writer, 1961—; corr. Religious News Service, 1962—. Chmn. dept. communication Ind. Council Chs., 1960-63, chmn. radio-TV com.; chmn. state publicity, promotion Ind. Chain Missions, 1960-62. Past pres. Internat. House, Chgo.; dir. Internat. House Assn., 1958-60; co-founder, treas. Coop. Community Nursery Sch., Ogden, 1969-71. Recipient Ecumenical Service Citation, Ind. Council Chs., 1962; certificate of merit in writing Iota Sigma Epsilon, 1959, 66, 67, 68, 69, 72; 1st award, mag. article, Wis. Regional Writers Assn., 1969. Mem. Nat. Religious Publicity Council (treas. Chgo. chpt. 1958-59), Am. Assn. U. Women,

Wis. Regional Writers Assn. (program chmn. spring conf. 1968), League Women Voters (dir. Kenosha 1968-69, sec. Ogden 1970-73), Nat. League Am. Pen Women (gen. chmn. Utah ann. conv. 1973), Weber State Coll. Women's Assn. (chmn. book group 1970-72, spl. interests groups 1972-73, mem. program com. 1971-72, traditions and policy-making com. 1972—, sec. 1974—), Women in Communications (frat. adviser U.S.C. organizing student chpt. 1962-63, Beta Chi student chpt. U.S.C. 1964-65), Iota Sigma Epsilon. Mem. United Ch. Christ (program chmn. women's fellowship 1968-69, v.p. Utah women's fellowship 1972—, vice moderator 1973—). Clubs: Quill (Columbia); Oberlin Women's (past sec.) (Chgo.); Welcome Wagon (Kenosha); Carthage College Women's. Contbr. articles to ednl. and religious periodicals. Home: 722 Boughton St Ogden UT 84403 also care H T Paulson 936 N Harvey Av Oak Park IL 60302

HARRIS, ANNA SHAPIRO (MRS. SIDNEY H. HARRIS), educator; b. N.Y.C.; d. Samuel and Rachel (Gochberg) Shapiro; B.A. (Regent scholar), Hunter Coll., 1928; M.S. in Edn., Coll. City N.Y., 1933; Ph.D., N.Y. U., 1962; m. Sidney H. Harris, June 29, 1930; children—Stephen M., Victor A. Tchr., N.Y.C., 1930-40; sch. psychologist Mt. Vernon (N.Y.) Bd. Edn., 1957-62, supr. reading, 1965-70; dir. reading clinic Moblzn. for Youth, N.Y.C., 1963-65; asso. prof. edn. Manhattan Coll., Bronx, N.Y., 1970—. Cons., Nat. Assessment for Ednl. Progress, 1970—. Mem. Am. Psychol. Assn., Am. Assn. U. Profs., Internat. Reading Assn., Nat. Tchrs. English, Westchester Reading Assn. (program chmn. 1970-71), Kappa Delta Pi, Pi Lambda Theta. Jewish religion. Author: (with Nila B. Smith) Graded Selections for Informal Reading Diagnosis, 1963. Contbr. articles and book reviews to profl. jours. Home: 324 Claremont Av Mount Vernon NY 10552 Office: Manhattan College Bronx NY 10471

HARRIS, AUDREY ELLEN FEGLEY (MRS. JACK MCALLISTER HARRIS), author; b. Phila., Nov. 6, 1916; d. Raymond J. and Audrey Mills (Vogt) Fegley; A.A., Coll. San Mateo, 1937; m. Jack McAllister Harris, Nov. 12, 1938; children—Claudia Jean (Mrs. David W. McCarley), Diane Roberta (Mrs. John Maddux), David Jack. Sec. ins. and law, San Francisco, 1937-42; sec., editorial asst. to Dr. Hilda Taba, edn. author, Millbrae, Cal., 1951-57; sec., pub. relations writer Coll. San Mateo (Cal.), 1957-59; exec. sec. Cal. Tchrs. Assn., working editor Cal. Higher Edn. News Briefs, 1959-65. Active P.T.A., Girl Scouts Am. Mem. Nat. Fedn. Press Women, Cal. Press Women, Cal. Writers Club (pres. Peninsula br. 1971-72), Millbrae Hist. Soc. (historian 1971-73). Author: History of Millbrae, 1972. Contbr. articles to profl. jours., mags., newspapers. Home: Route 1 Box 85 San Luis Obispo CA 93401

HARRIS, BARBARA HULL (MRS. F. CHANDLER HARRIS), social agy. adminstr.; b. Los Angeles, Nov. 1, 1921; d. Hamilton and Marion (Eimers) Baird; student U. Cal. at Los Angeles, 1939-41, 45-47; m. F. Chandler Harris, Aug. 10, 1946; children—Victoria, Randolph Boyd. Pres., Victoria Originals, 1955-62; partner J.B. Assos., cons., 1971-73; statewide dir. vols. Children's Home Soc. Cal., 1971—. Pres., Silver Spoons vol. group Cal. Pediatric Center, 1958; Los Angeles County Heart Sunday chmn. Los Angeles County Heart Assn., 1965, bd. dirs., 1966-69; mem. exec. com. Hollywood Bowl Vols., 1966—, chmn. vols., 1971; chmn. Coll. Alumni of Assistance League, 1962; mem. exec. com. Assistance League So. Cal., 1964-71, 72—, house com. chmn., 1964-71, chmn. personnel practices com., 1967-71, corr. sec., 1968-70, 3d v.p., 1972-74; bd. dirs., 1964—; bd. dirs. Nat. Charity League, Los Angeles, 1965-69, sec., 1967, 3d v.p., 1968; ways and means chmn., dir. Los Angeles Am. Horse Show, 1969; dir. Coronet Debutante Ball, 1968, ball bd. chmn., 1969-70, mem. ball bd., 1969—; pres. So. Cal. alumni council Alpha Phi, 1961, financial adviser to chpts. U. So. Cal., 1961-72, U. Cal. at Los Angeles, 1965-72; benefit chmn. Gold Shield, 1969, 1st v.p., 1970-72. Recipient Outstanding Service award Los Angeles County Heart Assn., 1965; Ivy award as outstanding Alpha Phi alumna So. Cal., 1969. Home: 7774 Skyhill Dr Hollywood CA 90068

HARRIS, BETTYE SUE (MRS. SAMUEL CALVIN HARRIS), city ofcl.; b. Memphis, Dec. 13, 1933; d. Thomas Edward and Mary (Coggin) Edmonds; B.S. in Bus. Adminstrn. and Govt., Tex. Women's U., Denton, 1954; m. Samuel Calvin Harris, Aug. 20, 1954; children—Steve, Ann. With Dallas County (Tex.) Health Dept., 1962-65; with City of Lewisville (Tex.), 1965—, dir. personnel, 1970—, city sec., 1971—. Mem. Bus. and Profl. Women's Clubs, Toastmistresses. Home: 163 Yale St Lewisville TX 75067 Office: 151 W Church St Lewisville TX 75067

HARRIS, CONSTANCE MARIA (MRS. JOHN JOSEPH HARRIS), pub. co. exec.; b. N.Y.C., Apr. 25, 1920; d. Salvatore Thomas and Rose (Zerilli) Costanza; B.A., Coll. New Rochelle, 1941; m. John Joseph Harris, June 1, 1946; children—Constance (Mrs. James Patrick McGonagle), Tonine (Mrs. Richard J. Fogliano), Thomas, Eugenia. With Fletcher Smith Studios, N.Y.C., 1942-43; asst. advt. mgr., fashion artist Michael's Dept. Store, Newark, 1943-44; layout makeup artist Fashion Advt. Agy., N.Y.C., 1944-48; staff artist WTVI-TV, Fort Pierce, Fla., 1958-59; job printing artist, mgr. Fort Pierce Press, 1959-65; account exec., advt. mgr. News Tribune, Ft. Pierce, 1965-72; account exec. Vero Beach (Fla.) Press Jour., 1972-73; account exec. News Tribune, Ft. Pierce, Fla., 1973—. Recipient 2d place awards Southeastern U.S. Newspaper Advt. competition sponsored Internat. Harvestor Corp., 1968, 69. Mem. Am. Assn. U. Women. Roman Catholic. Home: 4056 Greenwood Dr Fort Pierce FL 33450

HARRIS, DORIS JEWELL SEELYE (MRS. GEORGE SILAS HARRIS), ednl. adminstr.; b. Potosi, Tex., Aug. 26, 1916; d. Clyde Vernal and Grace Luta (Welch) Seelye; B.A., Abilene Christian Coll., 1938; M.Ed., McMurry Coll., 1952; postgrad U. Tex., 1960-66; m. George Silas Harris, Sept. 25, 1943. Tchr. English, Holliday, Tex., 1940-44; tchr. English and speech Jefferson Jr. High Sch., Abilene, Tex., 1948-71; dir. information services Abilene Ind. Sch. Dist., 1971-74; regional cons. Tex. State Tchrs. Assn., Austin, 1974—. Active Abilene chpt. A.R.C. Bd. dirs. Abilene Mental Health. Recipient Alumni citation Abilene Christian Coll., 1971. Mem. N.E.A. (dir. Tex. 1971-74), Am. Bus. Women's Assn., Tex. Classroom Tchrs. Assn. (pres. 1965-66), Tex. State Tchrs. Assn. (pres. 1970-71), Delta Kappa Gamma. Democrat. Mem. Ch. of Christ. Home: 784 Westwood St Abilene TX 79603 Office: Box 981 Abilene TX 79604

HARRIS, DOROTHY BEIDLEMAN (MRS. STEPHEN RICHARDSON HARRIS), educator; b. Bristol, Tenn., June 1, 1928; d. Samuel and Florence Elizabeth (Tiggs) Beidleman; B.S., Livingstone Coll., 1950; postgrad. Tenn. A. and I. State U., 1959; postgrad. U. Va., 1959; M.A., East Tenn. State U., 1965, Va. Poly. Inst., 1973; m. Stephen Richardson Harris, Dec. 23, 1958; 1 dau., Stephanie (Mrs. Arthur Sterling Morris). High sch. math. tchr. Aiken, S.C., 1950-51; elementary tchr., basketball coach, homebound tchr. Slater Sch., Bristol, Tenn., 1952-59; tchr. high sch. math., counselor William C. Jason High Sch., Georgetown, Del., 1960-65; freshman counselor Del. State Coll., 1966-67, asst. testing program, 1966-68, dean women, dean students, 1967-68; counselor Del. Tech. and Community Coll., Georgetown, 1968-70; counselor Va. Highlands Community Coll., Abington, Va., 1970-71, dir. placement, 1971-72, coordinator student services sci. and engring. div., 1971—. Ednl. chmn. Drug Council, Bristol, Tenn.-Va., 1972-73. Mem. Am., Va. personnel guidance assns., Placement Assn., Womens Counselors and Deans Assn., Delta Sigma Theta. Methodist (vice-chmn. united Meth. women 1973—, sec. vocations). Mem. Order Eastern Star. Clubs: Monday Evening, Community Service (Bristol, Tenn.). Home: 917 E State St Bristol TN 32760 Office: College Placement Office Virginia Highlands Community College Abingdon VA 24210

HARRIS, DOROTHY JEAN, ednl. adminstr.; b. Docena, Ala., June 29, 1942; d. Starling T. and Bernice Edwards (Harris) Edwards; B.S., N.C. Agrl. and Tech. State U., 1964, M.S. (NSF grantee), 1969. Tchr., Williston High Sch., Wilmington, N.C., 1964-67, John T. Hoggard High Sch., 1968-69; counselor Bennett Coll., Greensboro, N.C., 1969-70, dir. curriculum program, 1970—, chmn. freshman studies, 1973—. Mem. Am. Chem. Soc., Am. Assn. U. Profs., Beta Kappa Chi, Alpha Kappa Mu, Alpha Kappa Alpha. Mem. United Ch. of Christ. Home: 606 W Meadowview Rd Greensboro NC 27406

HARRIS, DOROTHY VIRGINIA, educator; b. Fishersville, Va., July 19, 1931; d. Edgar Lee and Harriet (Gibson) Harris; B.S., Madison Coll., 1953; M.S., U. N.C., 1958; Ph.D. (Oscar Mayer fellow), U. Ia., 1965; postgrad. Pa. State U., 1967-69. Instr. Va. Pub. Schs., Augusta County, 1953-54, Hollins Coll., 1954-56, U. N.C. at Greensboro, 1956-63, U. Ia., 1963-65, Madison Coll., Harrisonburg, Va., 1965-66; asst. prof., research asso. Human Performance Research Lab., Pa. State U., University Park, 1966-70, asso. prof. phys. edn., 1970-73, prof. phys. edn., 1973—. Active various community drives. USPHS postdoctoral research tng. fellow, 1967-70. Mem. A.A.A.S., N.Am. Soc. for Psychology of Sport and Phys. Activity (pres. 1974-75), Internat. Soc. for Sport Psychology, Internat. Sport Sociology Com., Am. Coll. Sports Medicine, Am., Pa. assns. health, phys. edn. and recreation, Nat., Eastern (v.p. 1972-73) assns. phys. edn. for coll. women, Am. Camping Assn., Alpha Sigma Alpha. Contbr. articles to profl. jours. Author: Involvement in Sport: A Somatopsychic Rationale for Physical Activity. Editor, DGWS Research Reports: Women in Sports; Women and Sport. Home: 235 Circle Dr State College PA 16801 Office: White Bldg Pennsylvania State Univ University Park PA 16802

HARRIS, ETHEL SEIDMAN (MRS. ARNOLD S. HARRIS), found. exec.; b. Camden, N.J., Jan. 13, 1920; d. Louis and Sarah (Cutler) Seidman; student Strayers Bus. Coll., 1938; m. Arnold S. Harris, Dec. 22, 1946 (dec. 1957); children—Barbara, Noreen, Alan. Founder, pres. Harris Employment Service, 1959—; pres. Harris Bus. Sch., Camden, 1965—; dir. personnel Peoples Nat. Bank of N.J., 1969-70. Mem. Council Human Relations, Haddonfield Arts and Crafts League (chmn. ways and means com. 1963). Sec., bd. dirs. Kidney Diease Found.; bd. dirs., playing mem. Haddonfield Symphony Orch.; founder, chmn. Haddon Twp. Ann. Teenage Art Exhibit; commr. Haddon Twp. Housing Authority; vice chmn. Camden County Manpower Adv. Com.; chmn. Bus. and Profl. Women, Allied Jewish Appeal; adv. bd. South Jersey Council for Performing Arts; exec. bd. Big Bros. Camden County; budget com. United Fund Camden County; mem. Jewish Community Relations Council. Named Haddon Twp. Mother of Year, Suburban Newspaper Group, 1963. Mem. Nat., N.J. (v.p. 1962, ethics com. 1972) pvt. employment agys. assns., Nat. Secs. Assn. (chmn. ways and means com.), South Jersey Pub. Relations Assn., Camden C. of C. (chmn. civic affairs com.), Camden Better Bus. Bur. Club: Zonta (chmn. service com. Camden 1963). Home: 701 Crystal Lake Av Haddonfield NJ 08033 Office: 8 Haddon Av Camden NJ 08103 also 1847 E Route 70 Cherry Hill NJ 08003 and 23 W High St Glassboro NJ 08028

HARRIS, FRANCES ALVORD (MRS. HUGH W. HARRIS), cons., ret. radio-TV broadcaster; b. Detroit, Apr. 19, 1909; d. William Roy and Edith (Vosburgh) Alvord; A.B., Grinnell Coll., 1929; m. Hugh William Harris, Sept. 24, 1932; children—Patricia Anne (Mrs. Floyd A. Metz), Hugh William, Robert Alvord. With advt. dept. Himelhoch Bros. & Co., Detroit, 1929-31; broadcaster as Julia Hayes, Robert P. Gust Co., 1931-34; tng. and personnel dept. Ernst Kern Co., 1935-36; broadcaster as Nancy Dixon, Young & Rubicam, Inc., 1939-42; women's editor sta. WWJ, Detroit, 1943-64, spl. features coordinator, 1964-74; prin. Fran Harris & Assos., cons. to social agys., instns., orgns., Detroit, 1974—. Mem. exec. bd. Wayne County chpt. Mich. Soc. for Mental Health, 1953-63; chmn. Mental Health Week, 1958-59; publicity com. YWCA, 1945, 2d v.p., 1963; mem. publicity com. Tri-County League for Nursing, 1956-61; publicity chmn. Met. Detroit YWCA Bd. Dirs., 1961-66, exec. com., 1962-67; campaign dist. chmn. United Found., 1959, unit chmn., 1960-61, chmn. speakers bur., 1974; exec. bd. United Found. Women's Orgn., 1962-64; governing bd. United Community Services Women's Com., 1961-66; bd. dirs. United Community Services, 1964-67; bd. dirs. Homemaker Service Met. Detroit, pres., 1969-70; bd. dirs. Vis. Nurse Assn., pres., 1974—; bd. dirs. Camp Fire Girls of Detroit, mem. nat. council, 1967-72, mem. nat. bd., exec. com., 1970—; bd. dirs. Well Being Service Aging, 1969-74, Sr. Center, 1971—, Friends Detroit Pub. library, 1972—, Friends Children's Museum, 1972-74; trustee Detroit Com. Alcoholism, 1961-64; mem. Mayor's Com. for Freedom Festival, 1959, chmn. women's activities, 1965; mem. Mayor's Com. for UN Week 1959. Mem. Gov.'s Commn. Status of Women, 1962-69, Mich. State Women's Commn., 1969—; mem. nat. council Homemaker Service, 1970-73; mem. adv. com. to trustees Grinnell Coll.; mem. bd. control Ferris State Coll., 1968—; mem. def. adv. com. Women in the Services, 1970-73, chmn., 1973; program chmn. Met. Detroit YMCA, 1973—. Recipient Grinnell Coll. Alumni award, 1959, Mental Health Soc. Mich. award, 1958, Theta Sigma Phi Headliner award for Mich., 1951, nat., 1952; Women's Advt. Club of Detroit Civic award, 1957; named Advt. Women of Year, Detroit, 1958, Soroptimist Woman of Year, 1965; Fran Harris Day in her honor, Detroit, 1960. Mem. Am. Women in Radio and TV (pres. Detroit chpts. 1957-58, gen. chmn. nat. conv. 1966, Outstanding Community Service award 1972), Women's Advt. Club of Detroit (pres. 1959-60, mem. bd. 1974—), UN Assn. U.S.A. (dir. Detroit chpt. 1962-65, Mich. div. bd. 1963-65), Advt. Fedn. (nat. v.p. women's activities 1964-67), Nat. Fedn. Press Women (hon.), Women in Communications (pres. Detroit 1950-51; del. to Asian-Am. Women in Broadcasting Conf. 1966, nat. 1st v.p. 1968-71, nat. pres. 1971-73, chmn. Communications Conf. Ams., 1968, del. III World Congress Women Journalists 1973), Pi Epsilon Delta. Episcopalian (communications com. local congregation and Diocese of Mich. 1965-66). Club: Press (Detroit). Home and office: 8120 E Jefferson Detroit MI 48214

HARRIS, FRANCES KAY (MRS. LEWIS HARRIS), radio broadcaster, editor; b. Galveston, Tex., Aug. 26, 1917; d. Samuel Simon and Lillian (Jacobson) Kay; student U. Tex., 1934-36, Am. Acad. Dramatic Arts, 1937-38; m. Lewis Harris, Aug. 22, 1939; children—John Kay, Tracy Kay. Broadcaster daily radio program KGBC, Galveston, Tex., 1948—; travel editor Galveston News, 1966—. Pres. Citizens Charter Com., Galveston, 1961-62; sec. Citizens Charter Commn., Galveston, 1960-61. Mem. Galveston League Women Voters (pres. 1957-60). Jewish religion. Home: 3001 Beluche Dr Galveston TX 77550 Office: KGBC Pelican Island Galveston TX 77550 also Galveston Daily News Galveston TX 77550

HARRIS, GRACE SALZMAN, city ofcl.; b. Pitts., July 12, 1929; d. Jacob Leon and Esther Libby (Siff) Salzman; B.A. in Edn., U. Pitts., 1951, J.D., 1968; m. Robert S. Harris, Oct. 3, 1953; children—Andrea Sue, Rachel Leigh, Jonathan Wayne. Tchr. pub. schs., Pitts., 1951-67; admitted to Pa. bar, 1968; law clk. Baskin, Boreman, Wilner, Sachs, Gondelman & Craig, Pitts., 1967; law clk. to judge U.S. Dist. Ct. Western Dist. Pa., 1968-69; practice law, Pitts., 1970—; asst. city solicitor, Pitts., 1970—. Adj. prof. bus. law Allegheny Community Coll., 1969-71. Cluster chmn. Allderdice Cluster Bd. Edn., 1972—. Bd. dirs. Squirrel Hill Urban Coalition, 1972—, co-chmn. edn. task force. Mem. Am., Pa. (pub. records com. chmn.), Allegheny County (citizenship com., dir. municipal and sch. solicitors com.) bar assns., Am. Judicature Soc., Am. Civil Liberties Union, Pitts. History and Landmarks Found., Carnegie Inst., Alpha Epsilon Phi Alumnae, Pi Lambda Theta, Phi Eta Sigma, Phi Gamma Delta. Clubs: Women's Internat. (U. Pitts.), Parkway. Home: 6567 Bartlett St Pittsburgh PA 15217 Office: City-County Bldg Pittsburgh PA 15219

HARRIS, HARRIET (MRS. STUART RODNEY YURMAN), dermatologist; b. Cambridge, N.Y., June 18, 1936; d. Benjamin Raphael and Helen Monica (Decker) Harris; A.B., Skidmore Coll., 1957; M.D., State U. N.Y. at Bklyn., 1961; m. Stuart Rodney Yurman, Aug. 16, 1959; 1 dau., Blair Ann. Intern medicine Kings County Hosp., N.Y.C., 1961-62; resident dermatology N.Y. U. Med. Center, N.Y.C., 1962-65, chief resident, 1965, instr. dermatology, 1965-66, asst. prof. clin. dermatology, 1971—; practice dermatology, S.I., N.Y., 1966—; asso. attending dermatology St. Vincent Med. Center, Seaview Hosp., S.I., Bellevue Hosp., N.Y.C. Diplomate Am. Bd. Dermatology. Fellow Am. Acad. Dermatology. Address: 1545 Victory Blvd Staten Island NY 10314

HARRIS, JANET DOROTHEA, ret. educator; b. Boston, Feb. 13, 1915; d. Ralph and Linna (Ehrenfried) Harris; B.S. in Edn., Boston U., 1936, M.Ed., 1946. Tchr. pub. schs., Winchendon, Mass., 1937-40; tchr. remedial reading pub. schs., Farmington, Conn., 1940-43; tchr. pub. schs., West Hartford, Conn., 1943-50, Newton, Mass., 1950-72. Mem. Assn. Supervision and Curriculum Devel., Internat. Reading Assn., Palm Beach Roundtable, Art Mus. Palm Beach, Newton Tchrs. Assn., Photog. Soc. Am., Internat. Platform Assn. Club: Lake Worth Camera. Author articles in field. Home: Lake Clarke Gardens 2615 S Garden Dr Apt 201 Lake Worth FL 33460

HARRIS, JANET UROVSKY, author; b. Newark, Apr. 17, 1928; d. Nathan and Ida (Lachow) Urovsky; student U. Mo., 1948; B.S. in Edn., Ohio U., 1950; children—Michael, Clint. Critic, N.Y. Times Book Review, N.Y.C., 1969—; lectr. Eng., C.W. Post Coll., Greenvale, N.Y., 1970, State U. N.Y., Glen Cove, 1971. Trustee, Nathan Urovsky-George Washington Trust, 1963—. Recipient Outstanding Books of Year award N.Y. Times, 1970. Mem. Women's Press Club N.Y.C. (recipient award for contbn. to lit. of social protest 1971), Author's League, Author's Guild, Congress of Racial Equality (Nassau sec., 1965-69), Nat. Orgn. for Women, Interracial Book Council (mem. exec. bd.). Author: Crisis in Corrections, 1973; A Single Standard, 1971; The Long Freedom Road, 1967; Black Pride, 1969; Students in Revolt, 1970. Home and office: 120 Lena Av Freeport NY 11520

HARRIS, JEAN COLLINS, educator; b. Cairo, U.A.R., Dec. 4, 1927; d. Erdman and Harriette (Pope) Harris; A.B., Smith Coll., 1949; M.A., Radcliffe Coll., 1954, Ph.D., 1961. Tchr., Winchester-Thurston Sch., Pitts., 1949-53; instr. dept. art Mt. Holyoke Coll., South Hadley, Mass., 1957-61, asst. prof., 1961-67, asso. prof., from 1967—, now prof. Chmn. Mt. Holyoke Friends of Art, 1963-69; mem. South Hadley Sch. Bldg. Com., 1967-69. Mem. Coll. Art Assn. Am., Am. Assn. U. Profs. Home: 6 Greenwood Lane South Hadley MA 01075

HARRIS, JEAN LOUISE, physician; b. Richmond, Va., Nov. 24, 1931; d. Vernon Joseph and Jean Louise (Pace) Harris; B.S., Va. Union U., 1951; M.D., Med. Coll. Va., 1955; m. Leslie John Ellis, Jr., Sept. 25, 1955; children—Karen Denise, Pamela Diane, Cynthia Suzanne. Intern, Med. Coll. Va., Richmond, 1955-56, resident internal medicine, 1956-57, fellow, 1957-58; fellow Strong Meml. Hosp.-U. Rochester (N.Y.) Sch. Medicine, 1958-60; research asso. Walter Reed Army Inst. Research, Washington, 1960-63; practice medicine, specializing in internal medicine, allergy, Washington, 1964-71; instr. medicine Howard U. Coll. Medicine, Washington, 1960-68, asst. prof. dept. community health practice, 1969—; lectr. dept. med. care and hosps. Johns Hopkins, Balt., 1971—; asst. clin. prof. dept. community medicine Charles R. Drew Postgrad. Med. Sch., Los Angeles, 1970—; adj. asst. prof. dept. preventive and social medicine U. Cal. at Los Angeles, 1970—; chief bur. resources devel. D.C. Dept. Health, 1967-69; exec. dir. Nat. Med. Assn. Found., Washington, 1970-73; prof. dept. family practice Va. Commonwealth U., 1973—, also dir. Center Community Health. Cons. div. health manpower intelligence Dept. Health, Edn. and Welfare, 1969—. Bd. dirs. Health Facilities Planning Council, Travelers Aid Soc. Recipient East End Civic Assn. award, 1955. Fellow Royal Soc. Health (Eng.); mem. Am. Acad. Med. Adminstrs., Am. Pub. Health Assn., Am. Assn. Hosp. Planning, Nat. Assn. for Community Devel., Dist. Med. Soc., Nat. Med. Assn., Med. Chirurgical Soc. D.C., Beta Kappa Chi, Alpha Kappa Mu, Sigma Xi. Home: 3318 Chatham Rd Richmond VA 23227 Office: 11th and Marshall Sts Richmond VA 23219

HARRIS, JESSIE G. (MRS. HUBERT LAMAR HARRIS), ednl. adminstr.; b. Athens, Ga., May 12, 1909; d. Wiley Jackson and Dora (Hilley) Ginn; B.B.A., U. Ga., 1956; A.B., Ga. State U., 1960; m. Hubert Lamar Harris, Nov. 25, 1930; children—Mary Ann (Mrs. William Holley), Hubert Lamar, Dorothy (Mrs. Ronald Zazworksy), Martha Susan (Mrs. R. R. McCue, Jr.). Various secretarial positions, ins. and law offices, 1923-30; sec. div. gen. extension U. Ga., 1930-35, asst. dir. div. gen. extension, 1935-47; assisted with compilation survey Univ. System Ga., Atlanta, 1949-50, adminstrv. asst. to regents, 1951-63, asst. exec. sec., 1963-67, asso. exec. sec., 1967-72, asst. vice chancellor personnel, 1972—. Asst. exec. dir. Ga. Scholarship Commn., 1965-66; asso. exec. sec. Ga. med. Edn. Bd., 1952-72. Mem. Am. Assn. U. Women (chmn. study group 1964-66, treas. 1972-73), Crimson Key Honor Soc., Mortar Bd., Phi Chi Theta, Delta Mu Delta, Psi Chi. Club: Atlanta Writers. Home: 765 Douglas Rd NE Atlanta GA 30342 Office: 244 Washington St NW Atlanta GA 30334

HARRIS, JOY FRANCES ROEBUCK, realtor; b. Little Rock, Apr. 18, 1925; d. William Robert and Maude (Childress) Roebuck; student Rice U., 1941-43; m. John N. Garner, June 10, 1943 (dec. Feb. 1954); 1 dau., Joy Dianne; m. 2d, Paul Harris, Sept. 3, 1955 (div. Aug. 1968). Mgr., Arthur Murray Sch. of Dance, Little Rock, 1947-51; confidential sec., asst. to v.p. Kansas City Title Ins. Co., Ark., 1951-63; sec.-treas. Paul Harris & Assos., 1961-66; exec. sec. Ark. Land Title Assn., 1961-67, Ark. Alstractors Bd. Examiners, 1961-67; real estate salesman Paul Harris & Assos., 1961-66, Jernigan & Co., 1966-70, Block Realty Co., 1970— (all Little Rock). Mem. Little Rock and North Little Rock Bd. Realtors, Ark. Realtors Assn., Nat. Assn. Realtors (womens council realtors 1964—, v.p. Little Rock chpt. 1973, pres. Little Rock chpt. 1974), Ark. Home Builders Assn. (asso.), Am. Ark. (editor monthly 1961-67) land title assn. Methodist. Club: Kappa Kappa Gamma Mothers (editor yearbook 1966). Editor The

Titleman, 1961-67. Home: 7004 Princess Dr Little Rock AR 72205 Office: Markham and State Sts Little Rock AR 72203

HARRIS, JUDITH ANN, pediatrician; b. Clay, Ky., Mar. 19, 1939; d. Mansel Clifton and Anna Mae (Whitledge) Harris; B.A., U. Tex., 1961; M.D., Tulane U., 1965. Intern, Charity Hosp., New Orleans, 1965-66, resident in pediatrics Tulane service, 1966-68; instr. pediatrics Tulane U., New Orleans, 1968-70, asst. prof., 1970-71, clin. asst. prof., 1971-73, asst. chief sect. pulmonary diseases, dept. pediatrics, 1968-73; asst. prof. pediatrics La. State U. Med. Sch., 1973—; practice pediatrics, New Orleans, 1971-73; mem. staffs Charity Hosp. La., Touro Infirmary (both New Orleans). Dir. Tulane Pediatric Chest Clinic, 1970—; asst. dir. New Orleans Cystic Fibrosis Clinic, 1968—; dir. Developmental Disability Center for Children, 1973—. Diplomate Am. Bd. Pediatrics. Fellow Am. Acad. Pediatrics, Am. Coll. Chest Physicians; mem. Am. Thoracic Soc. (sec. sci. assembly on pediatrics 1970-71), La. Tb and Respiratory Disease Assn. (mem. S.E. area council bd. 1970-71, state bd. 1972—), Phi Beta Kappa, Alpha Lambda Delta, Alpha Epsilon Delta. Home: 3209 State St Dr New Orleans LA 70125 Office: Bldg 144 1100 Florida Av New Orleans LA 70119

HARRIS, JULIE, actress; b. Grosse Pointe Park, Mich., Dec. 2, 1925; d. William Pickett and Elsie (Smith) Harris; student Perry Mansfield Theatre Work Shop, 1941-43, Yale Drama Sch., 1945; m. Jay I. Julien, Aug. 12, 1946; m. 2d, Manning Gurian, Oct. 21, 1954; 1 son, Peter. Appeared in plays: Sundown Beach, 1948; The Young and Fair, 1948-49; Magnolia Alley, 1949; Montserrat, 1949; The Member of the Wedding, 1950-51; I Am a Camera, 1951-52, (film), 1956; The Lark, 1956; Little Moon of Alban 1960; Poacher's Daughter, 1960 (film); tour, Broadway, The Warm Peninsula. Recipient Antoinette Perry award, 1956, East of Eden (one of 10 outstanding films, 1955). Address: care Actors' Equity 226 W 47th St New York City NY 10019

HARRIS, KAREN ILENE PITZELE (MRS. ARTHUR HARRIS), occupational therapist cons.; b. Chgo., May 27, 1944; d. Oser Sherman and Helen (Schutzbank) Pitzele; B.S., Ind. U., 1966; m. Arthur Harris, Nov. 23, 1968; children—Jerald David, Judith Fran. Staff occupational therapist St. Joseph's Hosp., Chgo., 1966-68, dir. occupational therapy, 1968-70; occupational therapist cons. Wrightwood Extended Care, Chgo., 1968-70, Edgewater Phys. Therapy Assn., Chgo., 1971-72, Riveria Manor Nursing Home, Chicago Heights, Ill., 1972—. Mem. Am., Ill. occupational therapy assns., Nat. Council Jewish Women (personnel chmn. 1973-74). Author: Daily Living with Arthritis, 1967. Home: 20347 Fairfield St Olympia Fields IL 60461

HARRIS, KATHERINE SAFFORD (MRS. GEORGE HARRIS), educator; b. Lowell, Mass., Sept. 3, 1925; d. Truman Henry and Katherine Morgan (Wardwell) Safford; B.A., Radcliffe Coll., 1947; Ph.D., Harvard, 1954; m. George Harris, Oct. 2, 1952; children—Maud, Louise. Research asso. Haskins Labs., N.Y.C., 1952—; faculty City U. N.Y., 1969—, prof. speech and hearing scis., 1970—. Fellow Am. Speech and Hearing Assn., Acoustical Soc. Am.; mem. Am. Assn. Phonetic Scis. (sec. 1973—). Home: 864 Carroll St Brooklyn NY 11215 Office: 33 W 42nd St New York City NY 10036

HARRIS, LA DONNA CRAWFORD (MRS. FRED R. HARRIS), civic worker; b. nr. Temple, Okla., Feb. 15, 1931; d. William and Lily (Tabbytite) Crawford; student pub. schs.; m. Fred R. Harris (U.S. Senator), Apr. 8, 1949; children—Kathryn, Byron, Laura. Mem. Lawton (Okla.) Community Human Relations Council, 1964—; mem. exec. bd. S.W. Human Relations Center, U. Okla.; bd. advisers Lawton Indian Edn. Project; founder, pres. Oklahomans for Indian Opportunity, Norman, 1965, now hon. pres.; founder, pres. Americans for Indian Opportunity; mem. edn. com. Mus. of Gt. Plains, Lawton; chmn. pub. affairs dept. Lawton Women's Forum, 1960-62; chmn. Women's Nat. Adv. Council on Poverty, 1967; mem. Nat. Com. Against Discrimination in Housing, Nat. Rural Housing Conf.; chmn. Nat. Health Forum, 1970; mem. nat. steering com., chmn. health task force Urban Coalition; mem. Joint Commn. on Mental Health; mem. Nat. Indian Opportunity Council, chmn. com. on urban and off-reservation Indians, 1968; nat. bd. dirs. Girl Scouts. Trustee Antioch Coll.; bd. visitors U. Okla.; bd. dirs. Nat. Assn. Mental Health, Nat. Health Council, Nat. Urban League, Goodwill Industries, Lawton, Okla. Mental Health Assn., Okla. Health and Welfare Assn. Home: 1120 Cherry St Lawton OK 73501 also 1104 Waverly Way McLean VA 22101

HARRIS, LAURILYN JAY, educator; b. Cin., Dec. 23, 1944; d. Thomas Lloyd and Ruth Marie (Weil) Harris; B.A., Ind. U., 1966; M.A., U. Ia., 1970, Ph.D., 1972. Vis. asst. prof. dept. drama U. Okla., Norman, summer 1972; research-lectr. dept. theatre U. Mass., Amherst, 1973-74; asst. prof. dept. speech Wash. State U., Pullman, 1974—. Mem. Speech Communication Assn., Am. Theatre Assn., Mediaeval Acad. Am., Am. Assn. U. Profs., Am. Civil Liberties Union, Early English Text Soc., Phi Beta Kappa, Alpha Lambda Delta, Eta Sigma Phi. Office: Dept Speech Wash State U Pullman WA 99163

HARRIS, LOUISE, author; b. Warwick, R.I., Sept. 28, 1903; d. Samuel P. and Faustine M. (Borden) Harris; A.B., Brown U., 1926; pvt. study organ with T. Tertius Noble, N.Y., 1938-42. Sec., Samuel P. Harris, Inc., 1928-42; tchr. piano and organ, ch. organist, recitalist, Providence, 1928-46. Fellow Intercontinental Biog. Assn.; mem. Internat. Platform Assn., Am. Guild Organists, Hymn Soc. Am., Audubon Soc., Brown Alumnae Assn., Nat. Trust Historic Preservation, Nat., R.I., Western R.I., East Providence hist. socs. Am. Heritage Soc., Am. Mus. Natural History, Smithsonian Assos. Author: A Comprehensive Bibliography of C.A. Stephebs, 1965; None But the Best, 1966; A Chuckle and A Laugh, 1967; The Star of the Youth's Companion, 1969; The Flag Over the Schoolhouse, 1971. Compiler: Under the Sea in the Salvador (C.A. Stephens), 1969; C.A. Stephens Looks at Norway, 1970; Charles Adams Tales (C.A. Stephens), 1973. Home: 15 Jay St Rumford RI 02916 Office: Box 1926 Brown U Providence RI 02912

HARRIS, LYNETTE ELAINE, social worker; b. Ft. Riley, Kan.; d. Cleo K. and Wilma (Baumgartner) Harris; B.S., Fla. State U.; M.S.W., Washington, U., St. Louis, 1963. Asso. dir. Grace Hill Settlement House, St. Louis, 1961—; asso. dir. Consol. Neighborhood Services, Inc., St. Louis, 1971—. Field instr. Washington U. Sch. Social Work, 1964—, St. Louis U. Sch. Social Work, U. Mo. Sch. Social Work, Columbia. Mem. Nat. Assn. Social Workers, Acad. Certified Social Workers, Nat. Fedn. Settlements, Alumni Assn. George Warren Brown Sch. Social Work Washington U. (dir. 1968—, pres. 1972—), Alpha Omicron Pi. Lutheran. Home: 1745 Herault Pl St Louis MO 63125 Office: 2600 Hadley St St Louis MO 63106

HARRIS, MARCELLA H. EASON (MRS. HARLEY EUGENE HARRIS), social worker; b. Augusta, Ark., Apr. 19, 1925; d. William Harvey and Hazel Faye (Haraway) Eason; B.A., Wilberforce U., 1947; M.S.W., Loyola U. (Chgo.), 1961; m. Harley Eugene Harris, June 15, 1952. Child welfare worker Ill. Dept. Pub. Welfare, 1952-54, caseworker Family Consultation Service, 1954-64; clin. social worker Winnebago County Mental Health Clinic, Rockford, Ill., 1964—. Mem. Rockford Bd. Edn., 1965—, sec., 1965-69. Recipient Francis Blair award Ill. Edn. Assn., 1970, Service above Self award Rockford Rotary Club, 1971. Mem. Nat. Assn. Social Workers (chpt. vice chmn. 1960-61), Ill. Welfare Assn., Acad. Certified Social Workers, Nat. Council Negro Women, Rockford Jr. League (hon.), Am. Assn. U. Women, Delta Kappa Gamma (hon.), Alpha Kappa Alpha. Club: Taus Sevice. Home: 2014 Chestnut St Rockford IL 61102 Office: 304 N Main St Rockford Ill 61102

HARRIS, MARGARET ANN (MRS. HENRY WILLIAM HARRIS), pathologist; b. Morrison, Ill., May 1, 1922; d. William Edward and Lucretia Grace (Maynard) Roberts; B.A., U. Wis., 1944, M.D., 1946; m. Henry William Harris, Nov. 29, 1950; children—Henry William, John Roberts, James Philip. Intern, Luth. Hosp., La Crosse, Wis., 1946-47, resident surgery, 1947-49; mem. staff Gundersen Clinic, La Crosse, 1949-53; resident pediatric pathology St. Christopher Hosp. for Children, Phila., 1961-64; resident pathology Lankenau Hosp., Phila., 1965-66; resident pathology Nassau Hosp., Mineola, N.Y., 1968-71, fellow pathology, 1971-72, asst. pathologist, 1973—; mem. staff pathology dept. South Nassau Communities Hosp., 1972-73. Home: 14 Seabury Rd Garden City NY 11530 Office: Nassau Hosp Mineola NY 11501

HARRIS, MARGARET ELEANORE PHILLIPS (MRS. QUINTON P. HARRIS), librarian; b. Linden, Va., June 23, 1915; d. John Lloyd and Marie (Ernst) Phillips; B.A., William and Mary Coll., 1938; B.L.S., U. Wis., 1939; postgrad. U. Alaska, 1956, 65, 70-72.; m. Quinton Harris, Oct. 5, 1943; children—Patricia Marie (Mrs. Melvin Grant Lortie), John Lloyd, Nancy Lynn. Librarian, Warren County (Ill.) Pub. Library, 1939-41; asst. librarian Main Library, Kern County Pub. Library, Bakersfield, Cal., 1941-42; interviewer Alaska Employment Service, Fairbanks, 1956-58; head readers services U. Alaska Library, Fairbanks, 1958-60, head cataloging dept., 1960-63, documents librarian, 1963-71, spl. assignment, 1972—, also asst. prof. library sci. Cons. librarian Fairbanks Sch. Dist., 1961-63, Fairbanks Evang. Lutheran Ch., 1946—. Mem. Hamilton Acres Pub. Utilities Bd., 1955-57; treas. Nordale Sch. P.T.A., 1954-55, Lathrop High Sch. rep. Central Council, 1959-60, state chmn. for reading and library service and audio-visual services, 1961-63; treas. Pony and Colt Baseball League Fairbanks, 1961-62; sponsor Bluebird group Campfire Girls, 1961; mem. Alaska Sch. Survey Com., 1962, Fairbanks Urban Beautification Commn., 1970-71; mem. Pioneer Park Bd. Fairbanks, 1969-73. Com. mem. Know Your Constl. Conv. Candidates Com., 1955; co-chmn. Hamilton Acres Precinct Republican Com., 1956-57; chmn. Mamie Eisenhower book project Fairbanks Rep. Women's Club, 1966-71. Served with WAVES, 1942-44. Mem. Am. (state chmn. for recruitment 1965-70), Pacific N.W. (state chmn. for recruitment 1963-70), Alaska (chmn. Fairbanks 1963-65, state pres. 1966-67, conv. chmn. 1964-65, mem. coms.) library assns., Aux. Pioneers of Alaska (marshall 1968, chaplain 1969), Alaska, Tanana Yukon (pres. 1970-71) hist. socs., Am. Assn. for State and Local History, Arctic Inst. N.Am., Students Internat. Mediation Soc. Club: Hamilton Acres Women's (pres. 1954-55). Author: Decennial Year History of Alaska Library Association, 1970; A Contribution to Regional Bibliography: Alaska, A Pilot Study in Indexing, 1972. Compiler, Directory of Alaska Libraries and Library Personnel, 1963, 65-68, 71. Contbr. to Ency. Library and Information Sci., 1968, Alaska, 1972. Home: PO Box 3102 Fairbanks AK 99701 Office: U Alaska Library Fairbanks AK 99701

HARRIS, MARGARET MAY (MRS. JOHN H. HARRIS, JR.), coll. adminstr.; b. St. Thomas, Ont., Can., Mar. 14, 1929; d. Howard H. and Rena L. (Hebberd) Hyndman; student Spring Arbor Coll., 1946-51; m. John H. Harris, Jr., June 16, 1951; children—Diane (Mrs. Dan Kurtz), Robert, Ronald, Douglas. Came to U.S., 1946, naturalized, 1953. Order typist purchasing dept. Western Electric Co., Indpls., 1951-52; sec. to dean of students, placement sec. Spring Arbor (Mich.) Coll., 1966-71, dir. of placement and career counseling, 1971—. Mem. Alpha Kappa Sigma. Methodist. Home: 3765 Chapel Rd Spring Arbor MI 49283

HARRIS, MARGARET PARSONS (MRS. JOHN MALCOLM HARRIS), civic worker; b. Tampa, Fla.; d. William H., Jr. and Bonnie (Crews) Parsons; student Fla. State U.; B.A., U. N.C., 1945; m. John Malcolm Harris, Aug. 16, 1946; children—John Malcolm, William D., Donna M. Mem. women's com. Houston Symphony Soc. Bd. dirs. Houston Grand Opera Assn., Gulf Coast Arthritis Found. Mem. Harris County Heritage Soc., Women's Inst. Houston, Mus. Fine Arts, Friends of Bayou Bend, Delta Delta Delta. Republican. Episcopalian. Clubs: Racquet, Briar, University, Champions Golf (Houston). Home: 2928 Del Monte Dr Houston TX 77019

HARRIS, MARION AGNES DELANEY (MRS. JAMIE LEE HARRIS), assn. exec.; b. Knoxville, Tenn., Jan. 28, 1944; d. William J. and Lena M. (Guilford) Delaney; B.A., U. Tenn., 1965, M.A., 1968; m. Jamie Lee Harris, Nov. 23, 1973; 1 dau., Kimberly F. Delaney. Instr. speech Knoxville (Tenn.) Coll., 1966-68; tng. specialist in adult edn. and devel. Girl Scouts of U.S.A., region III, Atlanta, 1968-73; council cons., 1973—. Cons., trainer Coll. Ednl. Achievement Program, Knoxville, 1967—. Mem. Ga. Council Human Relations. Girl Scouts U.S.A. grantee, 1970. Mem. Ga. Women's Polit. Caucus, Atlanta Urban League, So. Christian Leadership Conf., Ga. Adult Edn. Council, Speech Communication Assn., League Women Voters. Democrat. Home: 2909 Campbellton Rd SW #4-C Atlanta GA 30311 Office: 2531 Briarcliff Rd NE Suite 217 Atlanta GA 30329

HARRIS, M(ARTHA) ISABEL, coll. dean; b. Farwell, Mich., Aug. 9, 1914; d. John Bradley and Lillian Jane (Wallace) Harris; B.S., U. Mich., 1934; diploma nursing Johns Hopkins Hosp., 1937; Ed.M. (Nat. Inst. Mental Health grantee), U. Minn., 1951, Ph.D., 1962. Psychiat. nursing Johns Hopkins Hosp., Balt., 1938-40, Wayne County Gen. Hosp., Eloise, Mich., 1940-42, 46-47, U. Minn., Hosps., Mpls., 1947-51; dean, faculty U. Minn. Sch. Nursing, Mpls., 1969—. Mem. rev. com., profl. nurse traineeship program U.S. Dept. Health, Edn. and Welfare, 1962-65, mem. rev. com. constrn. of nurse tng. facilities, 1965-68; cons. div. hosp. and med. facilities Bur. Health Services, 1967-70. Mem. adv. council Am. Nurses Found., 1961-66. Served with Army Nurse Corps, 1942-46. Commonwealth Fund grantee, 1956-59. Mem. Nat. League for Nursing, Am. Nurses Assn., Am. Assn. Deans of Nursing, Sigma Theta Tau, Pi Lambda Theta, Psi Chi. Home: 2415 W 22d St Minneapolis MN 55405

HARRIS, MARY JO, educator; b. Birmingham, Ala., Aug. 20, 1929; d. Albert Cleveland and Mary Elizabeth (McPherson) Harris; B.A., U. Montevallo, 1950; M.A., U. Ala., 1954, Ph.D., 1963. Tchr. elementary grades Anniston Bd. Edn., 1950-51, Birmingham (Ala.) Bd. Edn., 1951-55, USAF Dependents' Schs., Libya, Germany, and Norway, 1955-58; asst. prof. elementary edn. Northwestern State Coll., Natchitoches, La., 1963-65; mem. faculty U.S. Ala., Mobile, 1965—, prof. early childhood and elementary edn., 1972—. Cons. to various sch. bds. in La. and Ala.; mem. supervisory panel Ala., Fla., Ga. Inst. Early Childhood Edn., 1970-74. Bd. dirs. Child Day Care Centers, Mobile, 1969—. Mem. Nat., Ala. edn. assns., Assn. Supervision and Curriculum Devel., Alpha Delta Kappa. Reviewer of books for Choice mag., 1968—. Home: 4363 Antares Lane Mobile AL 36609

HARRIS, MAY DIANE (MRS. AUGUST WATKINS HARRIS, JR.), mus. ofcl.; b. El Paso, Tex., Jan. 12, 1928; d. Sampson Oliver and May Belle (Brownlee) Miller; student, Penn Hall Jr. Coll., 1944-46; B.A., U. Tex., 1948; postgrad. Columbia U., 1948, U. Americas, 1963, U. Tex., 1965, 73; m. August Watkins Harris, Jr., Mar. 2, 1963; children—August Watkins III, Diane Banford. With Rheinhold Pub. Co., N.Y.C., 1952; tchr. Houston Ind. Sch. Dist., 1954-56; sec., editor W.S. Benson Pub. Co., Austin, 1956-62; with Elisabet Ney Mus., Austin, Tex., 1969—, dir. mus. programs, 1970—. Mem. Am. Assn. Museums, Fine Arts Soc. Tex. (dir. 1970-72), Tex. Museums Assn. (dir. 1971-72, editor 1971-72), Mountain Plains Mus. Conf., Jr. League of Austin, Heritage Soc., State Hist. Assn., Kappa Alpha Theta.

HARRIS, NADINE CLAIRE (MRS. DONALD HARRIS), educator; b. Tours, France, Oct. 9, 1935; d. Yves Jules and Paulette Sarah (Weill) Oppert; came to U.S., 1946; B.A., U. Minn., 1957; certificat d'etudes superieures, Sorbonne, U. Paris, 1961; m. Donald Harris, June 23, 1959; children—Daniel Yves, Jeremy W. Lang. tchr. Lanco, Paris, 1962-64; tchr. Faculte de Droit et de Scis. Economiques, Paris, 1965-68; French audio-visual tchr. New Eng. Conservatory Music, Boston, 1969—. Home: 465 Clinton Rd Chestnut Hill MA 02167 Office: 290 Huntington Av Boston MA 02115

HARRIS, NANCY TOLL (MRS. DAN EDWARD HARRIS), civic worker; b. Los Angeles, Feb. 14, 1929; d. Gerald S. and Maisie (Maxfield) Toll; B.A., Stanford, 1950; m. Dan Edward Harris, Mar. 22, 1952; children—Anne Joy, Sally Marie, Peter Toll. Residential chmn. United Crusade, San Fernando Valley area, 1966, group moblzn. chmn., Los Angeles County, 1967-69; benefit chmn. Resthaven Aux., 1968; treas. Los Angeles region Vol. Bur., 1968-69; mem. gen. bd. United Way, 1969-71, San Fernando Valley area bd., 1966-72; chmn. spl. gifts div. United Crusade, San Fernando Valley area, 1969-70; pres. Vol. Bur., Los Angeles, 1969-71; dir. vol. coordination Mental Health Assn. Orange County, 1971-72, asso. dir. programs, 1972—; mem. Stanford Assos., 1971-74. Chmn. Orange County Dirs. Vols. Agys., 1973-74; regional chmn. Orange County, Stanford Quad. Campaign, 1973-74. Home: 109 Via Ravenna Newport Beach CA 92660

HARRIS, NARVIE MOZELLE JORDAN (MRS. JOSEPH L. HARRIS), educator; b. Wrightsville, Ga.; d. James E. and Anna (Hobbs) Jordan; A.B., Clark Coll., Atlanta, 1939; M.Ed., Atlanta U., 1944; postgrad. Tuskegee Inst., Tenn. State A. and I. U., Grambling Coll., Wayne State U., U. Ga., Athens, Ga. State U.; m. Joseph L. Harris, Nov. 19, 1945; 1 dau., Daryll (Mrs. Michael Griffin). Tchr., Fowlstown (Ga.) Elementary Sch., 1939-41, Shoal Creek Jr. High Sch., Locust Grove, Ga., 1941-42, Edison (Ga.) High Sch., 1942-43; supr. instrn. DeKalb County Schs., Decatur, Ga., 1944—, also ednl. dir. Head Start Program, 1966, 69; lectr. in field. Pres. Atlanta dist. P.T.A., 1953-59; sec. Ga. Congress Colored Parents and Tchrs., 1963-65, v.p., 1965-66, pres., 1967-71, co-author history of orgn., 1970; chmn. sch. edn. Ga. Congress P.T.A., 1970-73, now bd. mgrs.; mem. adv. bd., steering and program com. Ga. Gov.'s Conf. on Edn., Gov.'s Task Force on Edn., 1967-71; cons. on edn., 1944—; mem. exec. com. Ga. Commn. on Children and Youth, 1967-70; pres. Royal Oaks Manor Community Club, 1962-64, sec., 1970-73; mem. com. Georgians United for Edn., 1973-74, Gov.'s United for Edn. Com. Mem. adv. bd. DeKalb County YWCA; bd. dirs. Met. Atlanta chpt. A.R.C., 1972—, mem. service to mil. families com., 1970-72, mem. adv. bd., 1969—, bd. dirs. DeKalb chpt. Recipient awards for services in and to edn., including Meritorious Service award Clark Coll., 1966. Mem. Nat. Congress Colored Parents and Tchrs. (life, pres. 1967-71), Urban League, Ga. Tchrs. and Educators Assn. (past dir. Region 3, dir.), Ga. Assn. Curriculum and Supervision, Internat. Reading Assn., Ga. Assn. Curriculum Dirs., Assn. Childhood Edn., Ga. Assn. Instructional Suprs., Ga. Assn. Supervision and Instrn. (4th dist. dir. 1974—), Assn. Curriculum Devel. and Supervision, Ga. Tchrs. Assn., Ga. Edn. Assn., Ga. (chmn. pub. relations com. 1973-74) DeKalb (ethics com. 1973-74) assns. educators, N.E.A., Iota Phi Lambda (Bronze Woman of Year 1965), Delta Sigma Theta (past pres., citations 1959, 65, 67). Baptist (chmn. woman's day 1960—). Home: 815 Woodmere Dr NW Atlanta GA 30318 Office: Ct House Bldg Decatur GA 30030

HARRIS, NELL, pub. relations real estate exec.; b. Palestine, Tex.; d. Thomas Jefferson and Nellie (Hester) Harris; A.B., Rice U.; student Baylor U. Coll. Medicine, 1943-45; postgrad. Mayo Clinic, U. Minn., 1945; certificate phys. therapy, U. Tex., 1947; student hosp. adminstrn., U. Chgo. 1948, 50; m. Charles Y. Swartz (div. Mar. 1947); children—Charles Harris, Mary Nell (Mrs. Charles E. Richards Jr.), Thomas Byrne; m. 2d, Bruce Stone, Jan. 12, 1952 (div. May 1963). Formerly engaged in rehab. handicapped children; established Hedgecroft Clinic for complete treatment polio victims, Houston, 1942, owner, 1942-48, incorporated as non-profit corp., 1948, chmn. bd., dir., 1948-51, exec. dir., trustee 1951-58, dir., trustee, 1958-62 (center gen. rehab.); cons. orgn. and operation health and hosp. facilities, 1962-64; free-lance counselor pub. relations and advt., 1964—; pres. Hosp. Adv. Services, Inc., 1962—; pres. Nell Harris Assos., Inc., theatre and concert mgmt. Trustee Hedgecroft Hosp.; sponsor Houston Horse Show. Past pres. Houston Hosp. Council. Elected nominee Am. Coll. Hosp. Adminstrs. Mem. Advt. Fedn. Am., Am. Women in Radio and TV, Achievement Rewards for Coll. Scientists Found. Episcopalian. Clubs: Advertising, Altrusa (Houston); Farm and Ranch; College Women's; Scribbler's; Junior League Luncheon. Contbr. articles profl. publs. Address: 448 N Post Oak Lane Houston TX 77024

HARRIS, PATRICIA ROBERTS, lawyer, educator; b. Mattoon, Ill., May 31, 1924; d. Bert Fitzgerald and Hildren Brodie (Johnson) Roberts; A.B., Howard U., 1945; J.D., George Washington U., 1960; postgrad. U. Chgo., 1945-47, Am. U., 1949-50; LL.D., Lindenwood Coll., Morgan State Coll., 1967, Russell Sage Coll., Dartmouth, Tufts U., 1970, Johns Hopkins, MacMurray Coll., U. Md., Williams Coll., 1971, Ripon Coll., Brown U., 1972, Wilberforce U., 1973, Aquinas Coll., 1973, Colby Coll., 1973, Brandeis U., 1973; D.C.L., Beaver Coll., 1968; D.H.L., Miami U., 1967, Newton Coll. of Sacred Heart, 1972; D.P.Sc., Rollins Coll., 1974; m. William Beasley Harris, Sept. 1, 1955. Program dir. YWCA, Chgo., 1946-49; asst. dir. Am. Council Human Rights, 1949-53; exec. dir. Delta Sigma Theta, 1953-59; admitted to D.C. bar, 1960, U.S. Supreme Ct. bar, 1963, trial atty. Dept. Justice, 1960-61; asso. dean students, lectr. law Howard U., 1961-63, asso. prof. law, 1963-67, prof. law, 1967-69, dean Sch. Law, 1969; partner firm Fried, Frank, Harris, Shriver & Kampelman, Washington, 1970—; mem. U.S.-P.R. Commn. Status P.R., 1964-66; U.S. ambassador to Luxembourg, 1965-67. Dir. Chase Manhattan Bank, IBM, Scott Paper Co., 20th Century Fund. Alternate U.S. del. to 21st-22d Gen. Assemblies of UN, 1966-67. Mem. Carnegie Commn. on Future Higher Edn., 1970-73; mem. adv. bd. Marshall Scholarship Program. Co-chmn. Nat. Womens Com. Civil Rights, 1963-64; vice chmn. Nat. Capitol Area Civil Liberties Union, 1962-65; exec. bd. D.C. chpt. N.A.A.C.P., 1963-65; bd. dirs. Legal Def. Fund, 1967—, UN Assn., 1967-71; bd. dirs. Georgetown U., Nat. Merit Scholarship Corp.; chmn. welfare com. Urban League D.C., 1961-65; mem. Com. on Grievances, U.S. Dist. Ct., D.C., 1970—; mem. council Rockefeller U., 1973—. Del., Democratic Nat. Conv., 1964, chmn. credentials com., 1972; presdl. elector D.C., 1964;

mem.-at-large Dem. Nat. Com., 1973—. Decorated Order of Oaken Crown (Luxembourg). Mem. Am., Fed., D.C. bar assns., Order of Coif, Phi Beta Kappa, Delta Sigma Theta, Kappa Beta Pi. Clubs: Cosmopolitan (N.Y.C.); Internat. (Washington). Home: 1742 Holly St NW Washington DC 20012 Office: 600 New Hampshire Av NW Washington DC 20037

HARRIS, POLLY ADAIR ELSTEIN (MRS. PAUL HARRIS), pub. relations exec.; b. Kansas City, Mo., Dec. 18, 1924; d. Mordy A. and Lyllian (Harris) Elstein; A.A., Kansas City Jr. Coll., 1943; B.S. in Psychology, U. Mo. at Kansas City, 1945; m. Paul Harris, Mar. 31, 1949. Mem. bus. staff U. Mo., Kansas City, 1945-49; radio broadcaster, writer El Paso, Tex., 1950-55; writer, accountant exec., pub. relations dir. Mithoff Advt., 1956-68; pub. relations dir. Empire Club, Empire Aircraft; head Harris & Harris Pub. Relations, 1968—. Fashion-hair-style TV commentator, 1958—; publicity dir. El Paso-Southwestern Sun Carnival, 1959—; speaker on Civic Theater, Press Club Gridiron Show; dir. El Paso Theater Downtown; dir. hist. pageants State Nat. Bank. Mem. City Bd. Devel., 1972—. Recipient feature writing award Tex. Press Women, awards Voice of Am.; named Woman of Yr., Herald-Post, 1971-72. Mem. El Paso Advt. Club (dir., Achievement award 1959, 60, 61, Outstanding Mem. award 1964, v.p. 1971, pres. 1972), Internat. Platform Assn. Clubs: Press (dir.), Empire (dir.), Bullfight (El Paso). Home: 6212 Papago Dr El Paso TX 79905 Office: 2810 Montana St El Paso TX 79903

HARRIS, SARAH LUCILLE, librarian; b. Evanston, Wyo.; d Matthew T. and Mary Ellen (Baker) Harris; A.A., Westminster Coll., Salt Lake City, 1936; B.A., U. Utah, 1938; B.L.S., U. Denver, 1947. Librarian, Judge Meml. High Sch., Salt Lake City, 1939-43; asst. circulation dept. Salt Lake City Pub. Library, 1943-49, head circulation dept., 1949-52, asst. librarian, 1952—. Mem. A.L.A., Mountain-Plains (past treas.), Utah (past pres.) library assns., Delta Kappa Gamma. Clubs: Zonta (corr. sec., past pres.), YWCA Trl (past pres.). Home: 136 Lincoln St Salt Lake City UT 84102 Office: 209 E 5th S Salt Lake City UT 84111

HARRIS, TAMSEN HOLBROOK (MRS. JOHN K. HARRIS, JR.), judge; b. Hartford, Conn., June 16, 1939; d. George Treat and Marjorie S. (Pike) Holbrook; B.A., Wilson Coll., 1961; J.D., U. Conn., 1964; m. John K. Harris, Jr., Aug. 14, 1965; children—Miranda, George, Douglas. Admitted to Conn. bar, 1964; asst. law librarian U. Conn. Sch. Law, 1964-68; practice law, Brooklyn, Conn., 1968—; judge of probate, Brooklyn, 1970—. Bd. dirs. Brooklyn Hist. Soc. Mem. Windham County Bar Assn. Home: RFD 3 Day St Danielson CT 06239 Office: Town Hall Brooklyn CT 06234

HARRIS, TERESA ANN, social work adminstr.; b. Ft. Niagara, N.Y., July 1, 1935; d. Carl Hill and Margaret Mary (Markey) Harris; B.A., Coll. Our Lady of Elms, 1956; M.Ed., Springfield (Mass.) Coll., 1961; M.S.W., U. Conn., 1963. Dir. social service Mercy Hosp., Springfield, 1956-61; psychat. social worker Area Mental Health Clinic, Holyoke, Mass., 1963-66; social worker Children's Study Home, Springfield, 1966-71, asst. to dir., 1971—. Tchr., Am. Internat. Coll., 1967—; social work cons. to various children's programs. Mem. ednl. task force Springfield Model Cities, 1968-70, health and social service task force, 1970—. Bd. dirs. Casa Credit Union, 1965—, v.p., 1967—; bd. dirs. Casa Hispanoamericana, 1965-71. Mem. Nat. Assn. Social Workers, Acad. Certified Social Workers, Mass. Conf. Social Welfare, Am. Group Therapy Assn., Am. Orthopsychiat. Assn., Soroptimist Internat. Home: 101 Mulberry St Springfield MA 01105 Office: 44 Sherman St Springfield MA 01109

HARRISON, ADA M(ARGERY), educator; b. Sask., Can.; d. Lewis Douglas and Florence Gladys (Ryan) Harrison; came to U.S., 1921, naturalized, 1941; B.A. in Econs., State Coll. Wash., 1941; Ph.D. in Econs., Radcliffe Coll., 1952. With price div. OPA, Denver and Washington, 1943-46; mem. faculty Carleton Coll., Northfield, Minn., 1948—, prof. econs., chmn. dept., 1958—. Research fellow Brookings Instn., 1957-58. Mem. Am., Midwest econs. assns., Phi Beta Kappa. Home: 417 Union St Norfolk MN 55057

HARRISON, ANNA JANE, chemist, educator; b. Benton City, Mo., Dec. 23, 1912; d. Albert S. J. and Mary (Jones) Harrison; student Lindenwood Coll., 1929-31; A.B., U. Mo., 1933, B.S., 1935, M.A., 1937, Ph.D., 1940. Instr. chemistry Newcomb Coll., 1940-45; asst. prof. chemistry Mt. Holyoke Coll., 1945-47, asso. prof., 1947-50, prof., 1950—, chmn. dept. chemistry, 1960-66. Mem. Nat. Sci. Bd., 1972—. Recipient Frank Forrest award Am. Ceramic Soc., 1948; award Mfg. Chemists Assn., 1969. Am. Assn. U. Women Sarah Berliner fellow Cambridge U., Eng., 1952-53; Petroleum Research Fund Am. Chem. Soc. Internat. fellow NRC of Can., 1959-60. Mem. Am. Chem. Soc. (chmn. div. chem. edn. 1971), Sigma Xi. Contbr. articles to profl. jours. Home: South Hadley MA 01075

HARRISON, BEATRICE ALTA (MRS. MYRON V. HARRISON), civic worker; b. Norma, N.J., Sept. 13, 1905; d. Aaron and Hannie (Levin) Coltun; student N.Y. U., 1948; m. Myron Victor Harrison, Dec. 22, 1927; 1 son, David C. Chpt. pres. B'nai B'rith, Phila., 1941-42; chmn. Anti-Defamation League Activities B'nai B'rith Council, Phila., 1942-43; chmn. Anti-Defamation League Activities B'nai B'rith Dist., 1943-45; dir. 1st Phila. B'nai B'rith Women's Anti-Defamation League, 1945-47, dir. women's dept. nat. office, N.Y.C., 1947-52; asso. dir. Anti-Defamation League, Phila., 1952-64; sec. B'nai B'rith House Greater Phila., 1972; mem. Pa. Gov.'s Commn. on Pub. Edn., 1955-58. Sec., v.p. Alumni and Friends Settlement Music Sch., 1958—; v.p. Singing City, 1966-69, bd. dirs., 1969—. Named Woman of Yr. Temple Isreal, 1963; citation Mitrana Sch., Phila., 1961; numerous other citations. Mem. Pa. Ballet Guild. Jewish religion. Home: Latches Lane Apts Merion PA 19066

HARRISON, CARMELITA RUTH DEIMEL (MRS. MARION EDWYN HARRISON), civic worker; b. Washington, Nov. 2, 1930; d. Henry Lito and Ruth (Grady) Deimel; A.B., Duke, 1952; degree for Cours de Civilization, Sorbonne, U. Paris, 1951; m. Marion Edwyn Harrison, Sept. 6, 1952; children—Angelique Marie, Marion Edwyn III, Henry Deimel. Research analyst Nat. Security Agy., 1952-55. Mem. bd. Arlington Com. of 100, 1963-64; pres. Service League of No. Va., 1968-69; mem. Arlington com. Latch Key Care for Children, 1969-70; corr. sec. Women's Com. for Washington Nat. Symphony, 1969-70, commr. Va. Commn. for Children and Youth, 1971—; del. White House Conf. for Children, 1970; childhood chmn. No. Va. Mental Health Assn., 1970-73; chmn. regional com. for disturbed children Mental Health and Mental Retardation Services Bds. of Arlington, Alexandria, Fairfax and Prince William, 1971—; youth chmn. women's com. Nat. Symphony Orch., 1971-73. Publicity chmn. Arlington Republican Club, 1967-68; Arlington chmn. Ladies for Lin Holton for Gov., 1969. Trustee, Arlington Hosp., 1971—; bd. dirs. Wolf Trap Assos., 1973—. Mem. Alpha Phi (pres. alumnae chpt. 1959-61). Club: Washington. Home: 4526 N 41st St Arlington VA 22207

HARRISON, CELESTE BERYL STEPHENS (MRS. DILLARD HARRISON), advt. co. exec.; b. nr. Carnesville, Ga., Oct. 21, 1922; d. Tatum Grover and Sadie Senoia (Davis) Stephens; grad. N. Ga. Coll., 1941; B.S., U. Ga., 1943; m. Dillard Harrison, Aug. 4, 1968; 1 dau., Martha September. Tchr., McDuffie County High Sch., Thomson, Ga., 1943-44; with Grizzard Advt., Inc., Atlanta, 1944—, v.p., prodn. mgr., 1957—. Tchr. juvenile delinquents, Atlanta, part-time 1957-58. Mem. adv. com. Christian City, Red Oak, Ga., 1958-59. Mem. Women's Chamber. Mem. Christian Ch. Club: Downtown Pilot (Atlanta). Home: Route 4 Kings Dr Douglasville GA 30134 Office: 1144 Mailing Av SE Atlanta GA 30315

HARRISON, EVELYN BYRD, educator, archaeologist; b. Charlottesville, Va., June 5, 1920; d. William Byrd and Eva (Detamore) Harrison; A.B., Barnard Coll., 1941; A.M., Columbia, 1943, Ph.D., 1952; postgrad. Bryn Mawr Coll., 1942-43. Instr. classics U. Cin., 1951-53; asst. prof. fine arts, archaeology Columbia U., 1955-59, asso. prof., 1959-67, prof., 1967-70; prof. art and archaeology Princeton, 1970—. Mem. Archaeol. Inst. Am., Soc. Promotion Hellenic Studies, German Archaeol. Inst. (corr. mem.). Author: The Athenian Agora, I, Portrait Sculpture, 1953; Agora XI, Archaic and Archaistic Sculpture, 1965. Contbr. articles Hesperia, Am. Jour. Archaeology. Home: 84 Western Way Princeton NJ 08540

HARRISON, JEAN ANN SAIGE (MRS. JOHN RUBEN HARRISON, JR.), banker; b. Highland Springs, Va., Feb. 12, 1929; d. Walter Clair and Theresa (Coughlan) Saige; grad. high sch.; m. John Ruben Harrison, Jr., Aug. 3, 1947; children—Pamela Gayle, Michael Saige. Accounting clk. Western Electric Co., Winston-Salem, N.C., 1947-49; accounting clk. Wachovia Bank & Trust Co., Winston-Salem, 1950-55, payroll clk., 1955-66, asst. sec., mgr. payroll, 1966-67, asst. v.p., 1967-69, v.p., 1969—. Active various community drives; mem. Mayor's Com. Equal Status Women, 1973—. Mem. Nat. Assn. Bank Women (vice chmn. N.C. group 1969, chmn. 1970-71, mem. nat. editorial com. 1971-72, chmn. edn. com. Southeastern region 1972-73), Am. Inst. Banking, N.C. Bankers Assn. (v.p. women's div. 1974—), Bank Adminstrs. Inst., Catholic Daus. Am. (N.C. state monitor 1960-66). Clubs: Toastmasters, Altrusa (treas. 1974—). Home: 1454 Capri Rd Winston-Salem NC 27103 Office: Wachovia Bldg Winston-Salem NC 27102

HARRISON, JOAN, producer; b. Guildford, Eng., June 20, 1909; d. Walter and Amelia (Muir) Harrison; ed. Sorbonne, Paris, France, also St. Hugh's Coll., Oxford U.; m. Eric Ambler, Oct. 11, 1958. Author screenplays in Eng., The Girl Was Young, 1937, Jamaica Inn, 1938; author screenplays in U.S., Rebecca, 1940, Fgn. Correspondent, 1941, Suspicion, 1943; producer motion pictures Phantom Lady, 1945, Uncle Harry, 1946, They Won't Believe Me, 1947, Ride the Pink Horse, 1948; producer TV program Alfred Hitchcock Presents, 1953-65; exec. producer TV series Journey to The Unknown, after 1968. Home: 10640 Taranto Way Los Angeles CA 90024

HARRISON, LINDA SPARKS, physician; b. Schenectady, Jan. 9, 1943; d. Lawrence Fenelon and Ethel Mae (Butler) Jeffrey; B.A., Russell Sage Coll., 1964; M.D., U. Ky., 1968. Intern, U. Ky. Med. Center, Lexington, 1968-69; resident internal medicine Tampa (Fla.) Gen. Hosp., 1969-71, fellow endocrinology and nephrology, 1971-72; practice medicine specializing in nephrology and endocrinology, 1972—; med. dir. Meml. Hosp. Tampa; dir. dialysis BMA of Tampa. Diplomate Am. Bd. Internal Medicine. Mem. Nat., Fla. kidney founds., A.C.P. (asso.), Am. Soc. Nephrology, Alpha Omega Alpha. Home: 628 Jamaica Av Tampa FL 33606 Office: 2901 Swann Av Tampa FL 33609

HARRISON, LORNA ANN WELSH (MRS. JAMES DAVIS HARRISON, JR.), civic worker; b. Greenwich, Conn., Jan. 4, 1933; d. James Whitelaw and Lorraine (Rutherford) Kennedy; student Bennett Jr. Coll., 1951-52; m. James Davis Harrison, Jr., Sept. 2, 1961. Sec. to advt. dir. Reynolds Metals Co., Richmond, Va., 1959-60, sec. to gen. mgr., internat. div., 1958-59; pub. relations dir. Richmond Area Community Chest, 1957; asst. buyer Thalhimers Dept. Store, Richmond, Va., 1954-56. Mem. Happy Hills Hosp. Womens Bd., 1966—, v.p., 1968-74; mem. Childrens Hosp. Womens Bd., Balt., 1966—, corr. sec., 1968-70, exec. com., 1973-74; mem. patrons com. United Cerebral Palsey Benefit, 1968; mem. Md. Com. for Day Care for Children, 1968—; mem. Balt. Area Council on Alcoholism, 1966—, bd. dirs., mem. exec. com., 1970—; mem. exec. bd. Md.-D.C. Assn. Child Care in Hosps., 1970—; del. Md. Assn. Hosp. Auxs., 1970—; bd. dirs., 1971—. Mem. Johns Hopkins Hosp. Womens Aux., Sheppard-Pratt Hosp. Aux., Federated Garden Clubs of Md. (conservation chmn. 1969-71). Republican. Epsicopalian. Clubs: Mt. Vernon, Junior Luncheon, Ivy Garden (sec. 1968-70, corr. sec. 1973—). Home: 6132 Allwood Ct Baltimore MD 21210

HARRISON, LULLELIA MARIE WALKER (MRS. ALEXANDER HARRISON, SR.), educator; b. Houston, Jan. 24, 1913; d. Franklin Pierce and Etta (Day) Walker; B.A., Wiley Coll., 1932; postgrad. U. Chgo., 1938-39; M.Ed., Tex. So. U., 1957; m. Alexander Harrison, Sr., July 9, 1933; children—Charles W., Alexander. Tchr. English, Jack Yates High Sch., Houston, 1939-56, counselor, 1956-58; counselor Ryan Jr. High Sch., Houston, 1958—. Mem. com. on adminstrn. Blue Triangle YWCA, 1959—; sec. bd. dirs. Neighborhood Centers, Day Care Assn., Houston, 1968—; pres. policy bd. Child Care Council Greater Houston, 1972—; vol. adviser Nat. Found.-March Dimes, 1972—. Bd. dirs. DePelchin Faith Home for Dependent Children, Houston, Community Welfare Planning Assn. Mem. Tex., Houston tchrs. assns., Houston Sch. Counselors Assn., Houston Council Greek Letter Orgns., Houston League Bus. and Profl. Women (founder, pres. 1963-67), Nat. Assn. Negro Bus. and Profl. Womens Clubs (gov. South Central dist.), Zeta Phi Beta (regional dir. 1936-43, nat. pres. 1943-48, nat. exec. sec. 1948-61, nat. project coordinator 1972—, life mem. nat. bd. 1948—). Methodist. Home: 3210 S MacGregor Way Houston TX 77021 Office: 2610 Elgin St Houston TX 77004

HARRISON, MARGARET ANN, pediatrician; b. Chgo., Aug. 24, 1937; d. Augustus N. and Maurice (Whittington) Harrison; A.A., Little Rock Jr. Coll., 1956; student Ouachita Bapt. U., 1956-57; B.S., U. Ark., 1959, M.D., 1963. Intern, U. Okla. Med. Center, 1963-64; resident pediatrics U. Ark. Med. Center, 1964-66; fellow hematology Children's Hosp. Mich., Detroit, 1966-67; practice medicine specializing in pediatrics, Eldorado, Ark., 1967-73; asst. prof. pediatrics U. Ark. Sch. Medicine, 1974—; mem. staff Warner Brown, Union Meml. hosps., El Dorado, 1967-73; clin. instr. U. Ark. Med. Center, 1967-73; lectr. Sch. Nursing, So. State Coll., Magnolia, Ark., 1971-73. Mem. sch. bd., v.p. Children's House Learning, El Dorado, 1971-72. Bd. dirs. Community Coordinated Child Care Center. Diplomate Am. Bd. Pediatrics. Mem. Ark. Soc. Hematologists, Am., Ark. acads. pediatrics, Ark., Union County med. socs., Alpha Omega Alpha. Baptist. Home: 1812 Reservoir Rd Little Rock AR 72207 Office: 4301 W Markham Little Rock AR 72202

HARRISON, MARGARET NORMA (MRS. JULIAN RAVENEL HARRISON III), museum ofcl.; b. N.Y.C., Feb. 25, 1938; d. Charles and Margaret (Gamble) Marquardt; B.S., Bucknell U., 1959; M.A., Duke U., 1963; m. Julian Ravenel Harrison III, June 11, 1960; children—Charles, Susan. Instr. biology Western Carolina Coll., Cullowhee, N.C., 1960-61; research asst. biochemistry Med. Coll. S.C., Charleston, 1964-67; summer instr. biology Coll. of Charleston, 1967, 68; curator edn. Charleston Museum, 1969—. Home: 805 Robert E Lee Charleston SC 29412 Office: 121 Rutledge Av Charleston SC 29401

HARRISON, MARGIT GARTHE (MRS. CHARLES HARRISON), pharmacist, frat. exec.; b. Longmont, Colo., Apr. 28, 1916; d. Magnus E. and Hanna (Hagen) Garthe; B.S., Washington State Coll., 1940; m. Charles William Harrison, Oct. 7, 1942. Pharmacist Harry Race Druggist, Ketchikan, Alaska, 1940-43, Higgin's Drugstore, Pullman, Wash., 1943-45, Currin's for Drugs, Portland, Ore., 1945-48; chief pharmacist hosp. of Nucleonics div. Gen. Electric Co., Richland, Wash., 1948-56; chief pharmacist Kadlec Methodist Hosp., 1950-64; pharmacist Visger Drug, Kennewick, Wash., 1964-66; dir. pharmacy service Kennewick Gen. Hosp., 1966—; pres. Marcha Lab., Inc., hand cream mfrs., Pasco, Wash., 1966—. Mem. Lambda Kappa Sigma (nat. pres. 1950-52, expansion chmn. 1950-54, western dist. supr. 1954-56, nat. v.p. 1956-58, hon. adviser, 1958—, chmn. scholarship com. 1958—. Home: Pasco Heights Route 1 Box 50 Pasco WA 99301 Office: Kennewick Gen Hosp Kennewick WA 99336

HARRISON, MARJORIE HALL (MRS. JAMES A. HARRISON), educator; b. Nottingham, Eng.; d. Henry and Edith Elizabeth (Banks) Hall; B.Sc. with honors in Math., U. Alta. (Can.), 1936; Ph.D. in Astronomy and Astrophysics, U. Chgo., 1947; m. James A. Harrison, Dec. 16, 1942; children—James C., Allen Ray. Faculty, Tex. Christian U., Ft. Worth., 1962-64; faculty Sam Houston State U., Huntsville, Tex., 1964—, prof. physics, 1971—. Fellow Royal Astron. Soc., Tex. Acad. Sci.; mem. Am. Astron. Soc., Sigma Xi, Sigma Pi Sigma. Contbr. articles to astrophys. jours. Home: 2405 Av S Huntsville TX 77340

HARRISON, NINA BERNELLE YATES (MRS. JAMES WILLIAM HARRISON, JR.), religious orgn. exec.; b. Sadler, Tex., Sept. 12, 1914; d. Thomas Edward and Barbara Frances (Grounds) Yates; student Draughon's Bus. Coll., 1935-36, Rutherford Met. Sch. Bus., 1937-38; m. James William Harrison, Jr., Feb. 14, 1942. With accounting dept. Standard-Brand, Dallas, 1938-39; with annuity bd. So. Bapt. Conv., Dallas, 1939—, dir. actuarial services, 1963-69, dir. research and actuarial services, 1970—. Methodist (North Tex. Conf. Bd. Pensions). Home: 6126 Averill Way Dallas TX 75225 Office: Annuity Bd So Bapt Conv 511 N Akard Bldg Dallas TX 75201

HARRISON, ROSALIE THORNTON (MRS. PORTER H. HARRISON), educator; b. Birmingham, Ala., Jan. 24, 1917; d. John William and Zora (Whetstone) Thornton; A.B., Samford U., 1937; M.A., U. Ala., 1945; postgrad. Tchrs. Coll., Columbia, Catholic U. Am., George Washington U., Am. U., U. Md., D.C. Tchrs. Coll.; m. Porter Harmon Harrison, Apr. 12, 1941; 1 son, Porter Harmon. Tchr., Pinson (Ala.) Sch., 1937-41; tchr., asst. prin. Avondale Estates (Ga.) Elementary Sch., 1941-45; asst. tchr. Horace Mann-Lincoln Sch. of Tchrs. Coll., Columbia, 1946; instr. English, Samford U., 1948; tchr. Lakeview Sch., Birmingham, 1948-49, Hazelwood and McFerran Sch., Louisville, 1950-53; with D.C. Pub. Schs., 1956—; tchr. Congress Heights Elementary Sch., Washington, 1956-63; guidance counselor Barnard Elementary Sch., Washington, 1963—; tchr. Children's Sch., U. Ala., summers 1939-41; adminstr. D.C. Project Head Start, summers 1966-69, coordinator parent program, summers 1968-69; prin. Congress Heights-Savoy Elementary Summer Sch., 1971, Blow-Bowen Elementary Summer Sch., 1972. Del. Congress of Baptist World Alliance, Rio de Janeiro, Brazil, 1960, Miami, Fla., 1965; dir. D.C. Bapt. Conv. Summer Mission Camp Girls, 1955; dir. Bapt. Tng. Union, Riverside Bapt. Ch., Washington, 1954-65, also mem. choir, council, mem. numerous coms., officer, 1953—. Mem. N.E.A. (life), Am., Nat. Capital personnel and guidance assns., Council for Exeptional Children, D.C. Counselors Assn., Am. Assn. Sex Educators and Counselors, Columbian Women of George Washington U., Alpha Delta Kappa (pres. chpt.). Clubs: Research, Ministers Wives (Washington). Home: 3828 17th Pl NE Washington DC 20018 Office: 5th and Decatur Sts Washington DC 20011

HARRISON, RUTH JANET DINKINS (MRS. WILLIAM MELVIN HARRISON), banker; b. Columbus, Ind., June 27, 1926; d. Chester Newton and Mary Sophia (Schulz) Dinkins; grad. high sch.; m. William Melvin Harrison, July 21, 1946; 1 son, David Carter. Loan interviewer installment loan dept. Irwin Union Bank & Trust Co., Inc., Columbus, 1956-57, mgr. charge account banking dept., 1957-60, mgr. new accounts dept., 1960-62, dir. pub. relations and advt., 1962-63, asst. cashier, dir. pub. relations and advt., 1963-66, asst. v.p., dir. pub. relations and advt., 1966-73, v.p. marketing, 1973—. Co-chmn. indsl. div. United Fund, 1974. Mem. exec. com. Ind. Sch. Bd. Nominating Assembly, 1970-73, mem. nominating com., 1974. Bd. dirs. Bartholomew County Library Assn., 1968-71, Ind. Consumer Adv. Council. Mem. Nat. Assn. Bank Women (nat. pres. 1971-72, trustee found.), Am. Bankers Assn. (mem. exec. com. marketing/savs. div. 1968-70, governing council 1973, fund econ. edn. com. 1973-74), Bank Marketing Assn. (mem. nominating com. 1971, communications council 1973-75), Ind. Bankers Assn. (ex-officio mem. women in banking com. 1970-72), C. of C. (mem. community promotion com. 1969-71, dir. 1972-74), Psi Iota Xi. Club: Zonta (pres. 1964) (Columbus). Methodist (mem. ofcl. bd. 1968-70). Home: 3417 Woodland Pl Columbus IN 47201 Office: 500 Washington St Columbus IN 47201

HARRISON, VIRGINIA FERN BROWNE (MRS. LLOYD J. HARRISON), assn. exec.; b. Seattle, Dec. 26, 1907; d. William Nye and Zona Fern (DeLong) Browne; student Arrillaga Music Coll., 1925-28, Stanford, summers 1925-28, Portland U., summer 1938, U. Santa Clara, 1966; m. Lloyd James Harrison, Feb. 20, 1933; children—Lewis A., Wesley E. Piano tchr., San Francisco, 1928-30, Portland, Ore., 1930-33, Clatskanie, Ore., 1936—; mgr. candy dept. Fred Meyer, Inc., 1932-36; night operator, rate operator West Coast Telephone Co., Clatskanie, Ore., 1943-65; exec. sec., mgr. Clatskanie (Ore.) C. of C., 1966—; freelance writer, newspaper corr. Daily Astorian, Astoria, Ore., also Longview (Wash.) Daily News, 1957-73; corr. St. Helen's (Ore.) Chronicle, 1973—. Sec., P.T.A., Columbia County, 1952-53, pres. county council, 1953-55; mem. Gov.'s Com. for Pres.'s Conf. on Edn., 1955-56; dir. patient care Columbia County March of Dimes, 1954-57; founder, dir. waterbabies program Clatskanie Pool, 1968, dir., 1966-71. D.C., Clatsop and Tillamook Counties, Am. Field Service Exchange Student Program, 1956—. Recipient Distinguished Service award Clatskanie-Westport Jaycee's, 1968; $25,000 for best receipe Nat. Pineapple Growers Assn. Cooking Classic, 1972. Presbyn. (Sunday Sch. Supt. 1947-57). Home: Route 1 Box 423 Clatskanie OR 97016 Office: PO Box 635 Clatskanie OR 97016

HARRISON-ROSS, PHYLLIS, pediatrician, psychiatrist; b. Detroit, Aug. 14, 1936; d. Harold J. and Edna (Smith) Harrison; B.A., Albion Coll., 1956; M.D., Wayne State U., 1959; m. Edgar L. Ross, 1970. Intern, Cornell Med. Coll., 1959-60, resident pediatrics, 1960-62, instr., 1961-62; resident adult and child psychiatry Albert Einstein Med. Coll., 1962-66, asst. prof. psychiatry and pediatrics, 1966—; sch. psychiatrist N.Y.C. Bd. Edn., 1966—; practice medicine specializing in adult and child psychiatry, N.Y.C., 1966—; dir. Met. Hosp. Community Mental Health Center, 1973—; prof. clin. psychiatry N.Y. Med. Coll., 1973—. Chmn., N.Y. council United Negro Coll. Fund, 1967-71; mem. N.Y. Gov.'s Commn. on Quality Cost Edn., 1969—; commr. UN, N.Y.C. Parks Com., 1968—; mem. council Empire State Coll. of State U. N.Y., 1971—; moderator TV series All About Parents, 1971—; mem. Pres.'s Nat. Adv. Council on

Drug Abuse Prevention, 1972. Bd. dirs. N.Y. Urban League; trustee Mills Coll., N.Y., Bank Street Coll., Children's Television Workshop. Recipient World of Soul award United Negro Coll. Fund, 1969. Mem. Am. Psychiat. Assn. Address: 41 Central Park W New York City NY 10023

HARRISS, MARY RUTH (MRS. WILLIAM EDWARD HARRISS), writer; b. Mound City, Ill., Nov. 3, 1938; d. Rohan Aloysius and Mary Amanda (Ewers) Lutz; B.S. in Communications, So. Ill. U., 1960; m. William Edward Harriss, Aug. 20, 1960; children—Katherine Jeannine, Jennifer Lynne. Asst. social dir. Student Union, U. Ill., Chgo. Circle, 1960-61; research asst. Earle Ludgin Advt. Agy., Chgo., 1961; copywriter Montgomery Ward, Chgo., 1961-64; free lance advt. copywriter Macy's, San Francisco, 1967, Western Girl, Inc., San Francisco, 1968. Active writer's profl. sect. Vol. Bur., Chgo., 1961; mem. bd., publicity chmn. Letterman Gen. Hosp. Officer's Wives Club, San Francisco, 1967-68; mem. bd., field office chmn., hosp. disaster chmn. A.R.C., Ft. Hood, Tex., 1969-70; publicity chmn. Riverside County (Cal.) Med. Assn. Aux., 1971, internat. health chmn., 1973—, mem. Camelia Ball com., 1971; writer, editor Clean Air Now newsletter, 1971-73; cultural arts chmn. Alcott P.T.A., Riverside, 1972-73; flyer chmn. Youth Concert Series Bd., 1972-73; elementary sch. docent Jr. League-Lung Assn. Polluted Air Project, 1972-73; mem. community research com. Jr. League, 1973—; mem. make up com. Children's Theatre, 1972-73. Mem. So. Cal. alumni bd. So. Ill. U., 1971—. Recipient St. Louis Advt. Club award, 1960; Service award Ft. Hood Officers Wives Club, 1970; Ft. Hood A.R.C. Service award, 1970; Jr. League Recognition award for docent program, 1973. Mem. Women in Communications, (mem. fashion show com. San Antonio chpt.). Presbyn. (choir sec. 1971—, mem. ch. support commn. 1973—). Clubs: Canyon Crest Country, Riverside Swim and Tennis. Home: 5423 Provence Pl Riverside CA 92506

HARROD, EMMA KRALL (MRS. DAVID BIDWELL HARROD), physician; b. Eaton, O., Feb. 25, 1930; d. Bert L. and Mildred I. (Wolverton) Krall; B.A. cum laude, Miami U., 1952; M.D., Harvard, 1957; m. David Bidwell Harrod, June 15, 1954; children—David A., Eric B., Mary Ellen, Richard. Intern, U. Minn. Hosps., 1957-58; fellow genetics Roswell Park Meml. Inst., Buffalo, N.Y., 1963-66; resident pediatrics Buffalo Children's Hosp., 1966-67; dir. Birth Defects Center, 1968-70; dir. maternal and child health services Erie County Health Dept., 1970—, dep. commr., 1972—; asst. clin. prof. pediatrics State U. N.Y., dir. Rand Capital Corp., Buffalo, 1971—. Bd. dirs. YWCA, Day Care Council Erie County. Mem. Am. Acad. Pediatrics, Am. Soc. Human Genetics, Teratology Assn., Am. Pub. Health Assn., A.A.A.S. Club: Zonta. Home: 174 Morris Av Buffalo NY 14214 Office: Erie County Health Dept 95 Franklin St Buffalo NY 14202

HARROLD, JOANNE (MRS. RICHARD HARRY GAINES), lawyer; b. Maywood, Cal., July 28, 1943; d. Ludwell Dyson and Kathryn Francis (Ramage) Lansdale; student Santa Ana Jr. Coll., 1964-66; LL.B. magna cum laude, Western State U., 1970; m. Richard Harry Gaines, Jan. 22, 1972; children by previous marriage—David James O., Daniel Dyson O. Admitted to Cal. bar, 1971; atty. Pub. Defenders Office of Orange County, Santa Ana, Cal., 1970—. Supr. Juvenile Ct. Western State U., Anaheim, Cal., 1970-71; prof. Citrus Belt Law Sch., Riverside, Cal., 1971-72. Recipient Corpus Juris Segundum award West Pub. Co., 1966, 67; Am. Jurisprudence award Bancroft-Whitney Co., 1966, 67, 68, 69, 70. Mem. Orange County Bar Assn., Pub. Defenders Assn. Cal., Iota Tau Tau. Republican. Baptist. Club: Anaheim (Cal.) Figure Skating. Office: Office Pub Defender 700 Civic Center Dr Santa Ana CA 92701

HARROWER, LEONTINE LYLE (TINA), mem. Republican Nat. Com.; b. N.Y.C., Feb. 12, 1926; d. William Gordon and Leontine (de Sabla) Lyle; grad. Miss Hewitt's Sch., 1944; m. Norman Harrower, Jr., Sept. 1, 1945; children—Harriet Greeley, Norman III, Mary Stuart. Co-chmn., Conn. Vols. for Nixon-Lodge, 1960; mem. campaign staff mayoralty, congl. and senatorial candidates, Conn., 1961-62; co-chmn. Conn. for Scranton for Pres. Com., 1964; alternate del. Rep. Nat. Conv., 1964, del., 1968, mem. arrangements, platform coms., 1968; mem. Rep. Nat. Com. for Conn., 1964-72; exec. bd. Young Rep. Nat. Fedn. Mem. adv. com. Center Am. Women in Politics-Eagleton Inst. Politics Rutgers U. Home: 144 Edgehill Rd New Haven CT 06511

HARSHBARGER, HELEN MARY SHIFFMAN (MRS. HOWARD FRANCIS HARSHBARGER), tax exec.; b. Ft. Wayne, Ind., Mar. 18, 1916; d. Jacob and Frances Helen (Wright) Shiffman; A.B., U. Chgo., 1937; m. Howard Francis Harshbarger, Dec. 6, 1941; children—Howard David, Warren Francis, Robert Leon, Lisa Helen. Tchr., Plainfield (Ill.) High Sch., 1937-40, 59-60, Rock Island (Ill.) Central Sch., 1940-41; exec. sec. tax dept. Chgo. gen. offices Kraft Foods, 1941-43; tchr. Aurora (Ill.) West High Sch., 1943-45; owner, operator Helen S. Harshbarger Tax Service, Plainfield, 1946—. Will County chmn. Com. for 1970 Ill. Constn., 1970, Ill. dir., 1968-70; mem. Ill. Gen. Assembly Commn. on Status of Women, 1971—; dist. legislation chmn. P.T.A., 1961-62; mem. Bd. Edn. Plainfield Dist. 202, 1960-66; mem. Will County Bd., 1972—; mem. Ill. Com. Legislative Reform, 1973—. Bd. dirs. Ill. Com. for Cts. and Justice, sr. services center Will County. Named Will County Republican Woman of Year, 1974—. Mem. Am. Assn. U. Women (Joliet pres. 1946-48, Ill. v.p. 1950-52), League Women Voters (Joliet pres. 1968-70, Ill. task force on county govt. 1971—), Joliet Bus. and Profl. Women, Ill. Assn. Sch. Bds. (pres. Three Rivers div. 1963-66), Will County Farm Bur. (chmn. women's com. 1964-70), Ill. Congress Parents and Tchrs. (life), Phi Beta Kappa, Delta Kappa Gamma. Christian Scientist (1st reader 1969-72). Address: RFD 4 Box 114A Plainfield IL 60544

HART, AGNES (MRS. JOSEF PRESSER), artist; b. Meriden, Conn.; d. Edward J. and Adelina (Dauphinais) Hart; student, Ringling Coll., 1936-38, Ia. State U., 1945; m. Josef Presser, Dec., 1941 (dec. Apr. 1967). Exhibited solo shows including Roko Gallery, N.Y.C., 1948, Contemporary Arts, N.Y.C., 1954, Coward Gallery, 1956, Rice Gallery, N.Y.C., 1961, 62, Mercer U., Macon, Ga., 1962, Gladstone Gallery, Woodstock, N.Y., 1963, Phoenix Gallery, N.Y.C., 1970, 72, 74, Rudolph Galleries, Coral Gables, Fla., 1973; exhibited in group shows including Met. Mus. of Art, N.A.D., Bklyn. Mus., Pa. Acad., Phila. Art Alliance, Va. Acad. Fine Arts, Toledo Mus., Springfield Mus. Fine Art, Chgo. Inst., Riverside Mus., Art U.S.A., Butler Art Inst., N.Y. Cultural Center, Berkshire Art Assn., Eight at Phoenix, Galerie Interieur, Zurich, Switzerland; represented in permanent collections at Norfolk Mus. Arts and Sci., Met. Mus. of Art, Terry Art Inst., Wichita State U., Whatcom Mus. History and Art, also pvt. collections; tchr. Art Students League, N.Y.C., 1965—, Dalton Sch., N.Y.C., 1961-64, Birch Wathen Sch., N.Y.C., 1946-47, Williamsburg Housing and Anna Maria (Fla.) Sch., 1952, Childrens Workshop at Parnassus Square, Woodstock, N.Y., summer 1952-58, Guild of Craftsmen, Woodstock, 1960-62; mem. Phoenix Gallery, N.Y.C., Polari Gallery, Woodstock, Rudolph Galleries, Coral Gables. Yaddo fellow, 1948-49. Mem. Am. Soc. Contemporary Artists, Woodstock Artists Assn. (exhibiting mem., mem. exec. bd. 1955-56), Kaaterskill Group (founding mem., chmn. 1958-59). Home: Maverick Rd Woodstock NY 12498 Studio: 30 E 14th St New York City NY 10003

HART, ALLIE CARROLL, state ofcl., archivist; b. Madison, Ga., June 28, 1913; d. Joseph Martin and Maud (Atkinson) Hart; A.B., Brenau Coll., 1935; M.A., U. Ga., 1939. Serials cataloger U. Ga. Libraries, Athens, 1948-57; asst. state archivist Ga. Dept. Archives and History, Atlanta, 1957-64, dir. dept., 1964—; founder, dir. Archives Inst. Ga. Dept. Archives and History-Emory U., 1967—; co-founder Tri-State Archives and Records Conf.; mem. tech. adv. com. Westville Historic Handcrafts, Inc., 1973—. Mem. Ga. Heritage Trust Adv. Commn.; ex-officio mem. Ga. Commn. Nat. Bicentennial Celebration, 1970; mem. adv. bd. Inman Park Restoration, Inc., 1971—; mem. com. Commn. Archives and History United Methodist Ch., 1972—, mem. commn. North Ga. Conf., 1972—. Trustee R.J. Taylor, Jr., Found., 1971—; mem. operations com. Richard B. Russell Found., 1971; adv. bd. Foxfire Fund, Inc., Rabun Gap, Ga., 1973—. Richard J. Reynolds grantee Coastal Island research. Fellow Soc. Am. Archivists; mem. Ga. Geneal. Soc. (founder), Soc. Ga. Archivists (founder), Ga. Hist. Soc. (curator), Soc. Am. Archivists (council), Nat. Microfilm Assn., Southeastern Archaeol. Conf., Oral History Assn., D.A.R., Phi Beta Kappa, Phi Alpha Theta, Alpha Delta. Democrat. Methodist. Home: 18 Peachtree Circle NE Atlanta GA 30309 Office: 330 Capitol Av SE Atlanta GA 30334

HART, BELLE ASHBURN OLIVER (MRS. HAROLD CLIFFORD HART), club woman; b. Suffolk, Va., July 30, 1902; d. Samuel Columbus and Eureka (Ashburn) Oliver; student Mary Washington Coll., Fredericksburg, Va., 1920-22; A.B., George Washington U., 1944; m. James Wesley Simmons, Apr. 27, 1926 (div. Apr. 1929); children—Belle Oliver (Mrs. Wm. E. Traver II), John Oliver; m. 2d, Harold Clifford Hart, Oct. 15, 1934 (dec.). Tchr. Martha Washington Coll., Abingdon, Va., 1922-23, Harpers Ferry (W.Va.) High Sch., 1923-24, Hopewell (Va.) High Sch., 1924-26, 28-29; asst. prin., Tenacre, Mass., 1938-39; asst. state service officer Dept. Pub. Welfare, Richmond, Va., 1929-31; adminstrv. asst. U.S. Dept. Justice, Washington, 1931-33; sec. NRA, Fed. Emergency Relief Adminstrn., U.S. Govt., 1933-34; nat. def. WPB, Washington, 1940-44; exec. sec. woman's aux. Episcopal Diocese Mass., Boston, 1945-48; asso. John M. Hancock, Lehman Bros., N.Y.C., 1948-54. Pres. Boston chpt. U.D.C., 1945-47, 58-59, rec. sec. gen., 1955-57. Pres., Wellesley Council Ch. Women, 1958-60. Mem. bd. Northfield League, 1955—. Dir. Mass. N.E. Grenfell Assn., Belleair Beach Property Owners Assn., 1965—. Mem. D.A.R. (regent Amos Mills chpt. Wellesley 1961-63), Mary Washington Coll. Alumnae Assn. (pres. 1941-44), Am. Assn. U. Women, Belleair Beach Garden Club (pres. 1967-69), Federated Hills Garden Club (charter mem., rec. sec. 1956, pres. 1961-62, sustaining mem.). Episcopalian (directress ch. altar guild, exec. sec. women's work Diocese Mass. 1945-48). Club: Bath (St. Petersburg Beach, Fla.). Address: 117 5th St Belleair Beach FL 33535

HART, EVA AULTMAN (MRS. FRANK EDWARD HART, JR.), educator; b. Memphis, Nov. 23, 1946; d. Howard H. and Ida LaVerne (Wicker) Aultman; B. Music Edn., Miss. Coll., 1968; Mus.M., U. Miss., 1970, postgrad., 1972; m. Frank Edward Hart, Jr., Oct. 7, 1973. Teaching fellow U. Miss., Oxford, 1968-70, admissions counselor, 1970-73; prof. music in voice Miss. Coll., Clinton, 1973—. Performer, Spring Street U.S.A., TV series, Nashville, 1971-74; active Jackson Music Assn. Mem. Nat. Opera Assn., Actor's Equity Assn., Music Educators Nat. Conf., Nat. Assn. Women Deans and Counselors, Delta Omicron. Home: 302 Beauregard Village Clinton MS 39056

HART, JACQUELINE SPOERER, physician; b. Balt., July 11, 1934; d. Paul M. and Lillian (Spoerer) Hart; B.A., Rice Inst., 1956; M.D., U. Tex. at Galveston, 1961. Intern, John Sealy Hosp., Galveston, 1961-62, resident internal medicine, 1962-65, internal medicine fellow endocrinology and metabolism, 1965-66; internal medicine fellow oncology and hematology M.D. Anderson Hosp. and Tumor Inst., Houston, 1966-67, asst. prof. medicine, 1969—; practice medicine specializing in internal medicine, Houston, 1967—. Exec. sec. Lymphoma Task Force, Nat. Cancer Inst., Washington. Fellow Royal Soc. Health; mem. A.M.A., So., Tex. med. assns., World, Harris County med. socs., Postgrad. Med. Assembly South Tex., S.W. Cancer Chemotherapy Group for Cancer Research, Leukemia Soc. Am., Am. Soc. Clin. Oncology, Am. Soc. Hematology, Am. Med. Women's Assn. N.Y. Acad. Scis., Am. Soc. Internal Medicine, Doctors Club, Mu Delta, Alpha Epsilon Iota. Club: Mayfair University (Houston). Home: 5301 Brae Burn Dr Bellaire TX 77401 Office: MD Anderson Hospital and Tumor Institute 6723 Bertner Av Houston TX 77025

HART, JANET, govt. ofcl.; b. Cin., July 8, 1917; d. Hornell Norris and Ella (Brockhausen) Hart; B.A., Swarthmore Coll., 1937; LL.B., Duke, 1954; m. Harry A. Sylvester, Sept. 2, 1954; children—Barbara Diebold (Mrs. Thomas Ashton Wick), Beatrice Diebold (Mrs. Michael John Berry), John Diebold. Admitted to D.C. bar, 1955; asso. Paul, Weiss, Rifkind, Wharton, & Garrison, Washington, 1954-58; asst. counsel legal div. bd. gov. Fed. Res. System, Washington, 1958-61, sr. atty., 1962-68, asst. dir. div. supervision and regulation, 1968-74; dep. dir. Office Saver and Consumer Affairs, 1974—. Mem. D.C. Bar (steering com., dir. corporate finance and securities law), Am. Judicature Soc., Am. Assn. U. Women, Order of Coif. Mem. Soc. of Friends. Home: 3330 Upland Terrace NW Washington DC 20015 Office: Fed Res System Constitution Av and 20th St NW Washington DC 20551

HART, JUSTINA CARSKADON (MRS. CHARLES HYDE HART), artist; b. Clarksburg, W.Va.; d. Justin Milton and Bessie Welling (Compton) Carskadon; student Randolph Macon Women's Coll., 1927-28; grad. Parson Sch. Design, N.Y.C., and Paris br., 1931; m. Charles Hyde Hart, Jan. 21, 1933 (dec. Dec. 1957); children—Charles Milton, John Carskadon. One-man shows at Newcomb-Macklin Gallery, N.Y., 1949, Urban Gallery, N.Y., 1955, Bodley Gallery, N.Y., 1963, Fairmont (W.Va.) State Coll., 1972, W.Va. U., 1972; exhibited in group shows at N.Y. World's Fair, 1964, Norton Art Mus., West Palm Beach Fla., 1973-74, W.Va. U., Morgantown, Creative Arts Center, W.Va. U., Compass Gallery, Nantucket, Mass., 1973; represented in permanent collections at Peabody Mus., Nashville, Witte Meml. Mus., San Antonio, Evansville (Ind.) Mus. Fine Arts and Sci., Washington County Mus., Hagestown, Md., asso. Bodley Gallery, N.Y.C., 1963-64. Founder, dir. Clarksburg Art Center, 1942-48. Recipient 1st prize Norton's Art Gallery, 1949. Mem. Internat. Platform Assn., W.Va. State Fedn. Garden Clubs (v.p. 1941-43), Assn. for Research and Enlightenment. Republican. Episcopalian. Clubs: Goff Plaza Garden (hon.), Clarksburg Country. Address: 716 Brightridge Dr Bridgeport WV 26330

HART, MARTHA JOY, journalist; b. Tuscon, Aug. 4, 1948; d. John Rene and Margaret (Jackson) Hart; student McMurry Coll., 1965-67; B.A. with honors, U. N.M., 1969; M.S., Kan. State U., 1971; m. Gerald Hunter, 1974. Summer intern Good Housekeeping Mag. and Media/Scope Mag., N.Y.C., 1968; reporter Odessa (Tex.) American, 1969; summer intern Boston State Hosp., 1970; with St. Petersburg (Fla.) Times, 1971-74, consumer writer, 1972-74; reporter Tulsa Tribune, 1974—. Vis. instr. dept. communications U. Tulsa, 1973-74; cons. Beyond the Mirror of Soc. conf., Kan. State U., 1973. Mem. founding com. Women's Center, St. Petersburg, Fla., 1973, mem. coordinating com., 1973. Fellow Nat. Inst. Mental Health, 1969-71; named Outstanding Grad. journalism dept. Kan. State U., 1971. Mem. Women in Communication, Phi Kappa Phi, Sigma Delta Chi. Democrat. Contbr. articles to profl. jours. Address: 1309 E 21st St Apt 212 Tulsa OK 74114

HART, PHYLLIS G. PETERS (MRS. COVELL J. HART), clin. psychologist; b. Battle Creek, Mich., Sept. 2, 1935; d. Robert V. and Winnie G. (White) Peters; A.B., Mich. State U., 1960, M.A., 1961; Ph.D., Northwestern U., 1965; m. Covell J. Hart, Aug. 17, 1968; children—Ken, David, James. Psychologist, VA Hosp., Chgo., 1962-65; clin. psychologist Ill. Dept. Mental Health, Chgo., 1965—, chief of service, 1973—, asst. subregion dir., 1968—. Instr. Moody Evening Coll., Chgo., 1968, Wheaton (Ill.) Coll., 1971—. Co-founder, treas. Hart to Heart, Inc., 1974—. Bd. dirs. Maine Twp. Mental Health Center, Park Ridge, Ill., 1969-72. Recipient Alumni award Kellogg Community Coll., 1968. Mem. Am., Ill. psychol. assns., Christian Assn. for Psychol. Studies, Am. Group Psychotherapy Assn. Presbyn. (co-pastor). Home: 7 Darby Lane Deerfield IL 60015 Office: 4200 N Oak Park Av Chicago IL 60634

HART, SYLVIA ELIZABETH, coll. dean; b. Milw., July 26, 1928; d. Peter Michael and Sylvia Christina (Streff) Hart; R.N., Sacred Heart Sch. Nursing, 1949; B.S. in Nursing Alverno Coll., 1952; M.S. in Nursing, Catholic U. Am., 1962; Ph.D., N.Y. U., 1967. Staff nurse Waupun (Wis.) Meml. Hosp., 1952-54; med. pediatric supr. St. Joseph Hosp., Beaver Dam, Wis., 1954-60; chmn. nursing dept. Alverno Coll., Milw., 1962-64; asst. prof. nursing N.Y. U., N.Y.C., 1966-69; asso. prof. sch. nursing State U. N.Y., Buffalo, 1969-72, asso. dean, 1969-72; prof. and dean sch. nursing U. Tenn., Knoxville, 1972—. Cons. curriculum Molloy Coll., Kan. State U., 1970—. Mem. N.Y. (pres. 1970-72), Nat. leagues nursing, Am. Assn. Univ. Profs., N.Y. Acad. Scis., Am. Nurses Assn. Home: Route 18 Knoxville TN 37921 Office: 804 Volunteer Blvd Knoxville TN 37916

HART, UNA EILEEN LYNCH, chem. co. exec.; b. White Plains, N.Y., Feb. 23, 1926; d. Thomas Henry and Eileen (Quinn) Lynch; A.B., N.Y. U., 1945, M.S., 1947; Ph.D., Purdue U., 1952; m. Bernard Peter Hart, Sept. 27, 1952; children—Patricia Eileen, Maureen Jane, Una Anne. Research chemist Am. Cyanamid Corp., Bound Brook, N.J., 1952-53; head lead-acid battery research Gould, Inc., St. Paul, 1961-63; head chem. research Univac div. Sperry Rand Co., St. Paul 1964-69; v.p. research and devel. Oh Dear Labs. Inc., odor control, St. Paul, 1969-74; dir. Philmon & Hart Labs., Inc., Mpls., 1974—. Instr. biochemistry N.Y. Med. Coll., Elmford, N.Y., 1955-58; instr. physiology U. Minn., 1959-61. Mem. Archdiocesan Bd. Edn., 1972—. Mem. Am. Chem. Soc., A.A.A.S., Harvey Soc., Am. Assn. U. Women, Sigma Xi. Roman Catholic. Patentee in field. Home: 1750 Summit Av St Paul MN 55105 Office: 661 Western Av N St Paul MN 55103

HART, VIRGINIA BYRNES SHEAHAN (MRS. EDWARD HART), govt. ofcl.; b. Worcester, Mass.; d. Edward P. and Katherine (Byrnes) Sheahan; A.B., Clark U., 1945; M.A., Am. U., 1959; m. Edward Hart, Dec. 30, 1948; children—Susan J., Edward Wales, Cherie. Corr., Worcester Telegram, 1943-45; asst. editor fgn. policy bull. Dept. State, Washington, 1946-47; asst. producer nat. radio program Is Congress Doing Its Job, 1947; pub. relations dir. Korean Affairs Inst., Washington, 1948; features corr. Far East Service, Voice of Am., 1949-53; free-lance writer, 1954-59; staff cons. Fgn. Leaders Exchange Program, Am. Council on Edn., 1960; pub. information officer Office Vocational and Manpower Tng., U.S. Office Edn., 1961-64; asst. for communications to commr. Indian affairs Indian Affairs Bur., Washington, 1964-70; pub. affairs officer to sec. of interior Dept. Interior, Washington, 1970-74, asso. dir. pub. affairs, 1974—. Dir. Career Devel. Program in Communication, Am. U., Washington, 1968-72. Recipient awards for outstanding publs. Fed. Editors Assn., 1966, 67; Dept. Interior nominee Fed. Woman of Year, 1972. Mem. League Women Voters (chmn. water resources com. D.C. div. 1958-59), Women's Nat. Press Club (treas., mem. bd. 1969-70), Govt. Pub. Information Officers Assn. (dir. 1967-72, v.p. 1971). Clubs: Nat. Press, Washington Press, Am. Newspaper Women's. Contbr. articles to profl. jours. Office: Dept of Interior Washington DC 20240

HARTEL, ROSARY VERA NIX (MRS. STEPHEN CAMILLE HARTEL), civic worker; b. New Orleans, Oct. 22, 1914; d. James Thomas and Vera (Malter) Nix; B.A., Newcomb Coll., 1935; M.A., Columbia, 1936; m. Stephen Camille Hartel, July 2, 1942; children—Mary Nix (Mrs. Robert James Brent, Jr.), Rosary Vera (Mrs. John Terence O'Brien), Stephen Camille, Joseph Francis. Nat. bd. dirs. Girl Scouts U.S.A., 1960-72, mem. nat. communications com., 1970-72, pres. bd. dirs. S.E. La. council, 1958-59; mem. Western hemisphere com. World Assn. Girl Guides and Girl Scouts, 1969-73; bd. mem. New Orleans chpt. Nat. Conf. Christians and Jews, 1962-65; mem. budget com. United Fund Greater New Orleans, 1959-72; mem. archdiocesan com. Catholic Girl Scouting, 1954-69; founder Hosp. Library Assn. of Sacred Heart, 1955, chmn., 1963-67; mem. adv. bd. Convent of Good Shepherd, New Orleans, 1966-70, sec., 1967-70; bd. dirs. YWCA, New Orleans, 1971—, pres., 1973—. Recipient Pro Ecclesia et Pontifice, Pope Pius XII, 1958. Mem. Am. Assn. U. Women, La. Hist. Soc., English Speaking Union, D.A.R., Causeries du Lundi, Chi Omega. Clubs: New Orleans Country, Orleans. Home: 54 Fontainebleau Dr New Orleans LA 70125

HARTIGAN, GRACE, artist; b. Newark, Mar. 28, 1922; d. Matthew A. and Grace (Orvis) Hartigan; student pvt. art classes; D.Fine Arts, Moore Coll., Phila., 1969; m. Robert L. Jachens, May, 1941 (div. 1948); 1 son, Jeffrey A.; m. 2d, Robert Keene, Dec. 14, 1959 (div. 1960); m. 3d, Winston H. Price, Dec. 24, 1960. One-man shows Tibor de Nagy Gallery, N.Y.C., 1951-55, 57-59, Vassar Coll. Art Gallery, 1954, Robert Keene Gallery, Southampton, N.Y., 1957-59, Gres Gallery, Washington, 1960, Chatham Coll., Pitts., 1960, Martha Jackson Gallery, 1962, 64, 67, 70, U. Minn., 1963, U. Chgo., 1967, Gertrude Kasle Gallery, Detroit, 1970; exhibited in group shows Mus. Modern Art, 1955-56, 69, Jewish Mus., N.Y.C., 1957, 3d Internat. Contemporary Art Exhbn., India, 1957, 4th Internat. Art Exhbn., Japan, 1957, IV Bienal, Sao Paulo, 1957, New Am. Painting Show, Europe, 1958-59, World's Fair, Brussels, 1958, Columbus (O.) Gallery Fine Arts, 1960, Walker Art Center, Mpls., 1960, U. Mich. Art Mus., 1961, Guggenheim Mus., 1961, 69, USIA Exhbn., Europe, 1961, Mus. of Ghent, 1964, Norfolk Mus. Arts and Scis., 1964, Am. Fedn. Arts, 1964, Whitney Mus. Am. Art, 1965, Finch Coll. Mus. Art, 1965, Drexel Inst. Tech., 1966, Kent State U., 1966, Flint Inst., 1966, U. Ill., 1967, 69, Md. Inst. Coll. Art, 1967, Nat. Gallery, 1968, Pa. Acad. Fine Arts, 1968, Ft. Worth Art Center, 1968, Detroit Inst. Arts, 1968, La Jolla Mus., 1969, Phila. Art Alliance, 1969, Toledo Mus., 1969; represented in collections Mus. Modern Art, N.Y.C., Walker Art Center, Mpls., Whitney Mus., N.Y.C., Chgo. Art Inst., Met. Mus., Raleigh (N.C.) Mus., Providence Mus., Bklyn. Mus., Mpls. Mus., Albright-Knox Art Gallery, Buffalo, Carnegie Inst., Pitts., William Rockhill Nelson Gallery Art, Kansas City, Kan., Washington U. Art Gallery, St. Louis, Vassar Coll. Art Gallery, New Paltz (N.Y.) Mus., Rose Art Gallery, Brandeis U., Balt. Mus., Israel Mus., Jerusalem, Wadsworth Atheneum, New Sch. for Social Research, Princeton U., U. Chgo., Nat. Collection Fine Arts, Grand Rapids Mus., Phila. Mus., Okla. Art Center, St. Louis Mus., also numerous pvt. collections. Address: 1701 1/2 Eastern Av Baltimore MD 21231

HARTKE, MARTHA TIERNAN (MRS. VANCE HARTKE), wife U.S. Senator, civic worker; b. Richmond, Ind., Mar. 14, 1920; d. Edward A. and Margaret Tiernan; B.S., Ind. U., 1942; m. Vance Hartke (U.S. senator from Ind.), June 12, 1943; children—Sandra, Jan Alan, Wayne, Keith, Paul, Anita, Nadine. Former tchr. Mentally Retarded Sch. Active Lutheran Guild. Trustee Internat. Freedom from Hunger Found.; past sec. Harvard Law Sch. Mem. Alpha Omicron Pi. Club: U.S. Senate Wives. Home: 6500 Kerns Ct Falls Church VA 22044

HARTLEY, ELLEN RAPHAEL (MRS. WILLIAM BROWN HARTLEY), journalist; b. Dortmund, Germany, Jan. 1, 1915; d. Gustave and Elizabeth (Steinweg) Raphael; grad. Schiller Lyceum, 1932; m. William Brown Hartley, Oct. 7, 1957. Arrived in U.S., 1951, naturalized, 1962. Asst. advt. prodn. mgr. Sales Mgmt., N.Y.C., 1952-53, head records and research dept. 1954-55; prodn. control mgr. Grant Advt. Agy., Inc., Miami, Fla., 1956; billing supr. So. Advt. Inc., Miami, 1956-57; journalist, Miami, 1957—, author, 1957—. Founder and adminstrv. asst. South eastern Writers Conf., 1970, 71. Served with WAAF, 1943-46. Mem. Soc. Mag. Writers. Author: The Ellen Knauff Story, 1952, reprinted 1974; (with William B. Hartley), Your Important Years, 1962; Young Living, 1963; A Woman Set Apart, 1963; Eine Tapfere Frau, 1964; Osceola-The Unconquered Indian, 1973. Contbr. articles to popular mags. Address: 5747 SW 82d St South Miami FL 33142

HARTLEY, HELENA CATHERINE PETRICH, antique dealer; b. Lawrence, Mass., Dec. 2, 1917; d. Peter and Victoria (Dudek) Petrich; grad. high sch.; m. Winston J. Hartley, Sept. 23, 1939; 1 son, Denton H. Antique dealer, appraiser Hartley's Barn, Pelham, N.H., 1940—. Mem. Appraisers Assn. Am., Antique Dealers Assn. N.H., N.H. Hist. Soc. Address: Mammoth Rd Pelham NH 03076

HARTLEY, VIRGINIA HAWGOOD GJEMSO (MRS. FRED HARTLEY), realtor; b. Everett, Wash., Aug. 14, 1916; d. Einar S. and Josie Elma (West) Gjemso; B.S., U. Wash., 1940; m. Arthur Phillip Hawgood, Feb. 22, 1944; children—Katherine (Mrs. John Wilson Baker III), Christine (Mrs. Russell Reighley), Arthur Phillip; m. 2d, Fred Hartley, May 16, 1973. Salesman, Wynn Norton Co., La Canada, Cal., 1955-59; mgr. Jonnie L. Ross Co., La Canada, 1959-62; owner La Canada Valley Realty, 1962—, Hawgood Assos., La Canada, Palm Dessert, Cal., 1972—. Pres., Children's Home Soc., Indio, Cal., 1974. Mem. La Canada Multiple Listing Assn. (pres. 1969), La Canada (pres. 1973-74, dir.), Palm Dessert bds. realtors, Cal. Real Estate Assn., Nat. Assn. Realtors (pres. La Canada chpt. women's council 1969-73). Club: Indian Wells Country (Cal.). Home: Casa Dorado A15 Indian Wells CA 92260 Office: UC Bank Bldg 650 Foothill La Canada CA 91011

HARTMAN, BETTY GRANT, educator; b. Geneva, O., Feb. 1, 1922; d. Albert Findley and Nellie (Hesser) Hartman; A.B., MacMurray Coll., 1943, M.S., 1947; Ph.D., Ohio State U., 1958. Girls phys. edn. tchr. Barstow Sch. for Girls, Kansas City, Mo., 1943-45, Kansas City (Mo.) Pub. Schs., 1945-46; grad. asst. MacMurray Coll., Jacksonville, Ill., 1946-47; instr. Carnegie Inst. Tech., Pitts., 1947-49; asst. prof. Madison Coll., Harrisonburg, Va., 1949-55; grad. asst. Ohio State U., Columbus, 1955-56, instr., 1956-58; asso. prof., dept. head women's phys. edn. MacMurray Coll., Jacksonville, 1958-61; asso. prof., dept. chmn. women's phys. edn. U. Conn., Storrs, 1961-66; prof. women's phys. edn. Kent (O.) State U., 1966—, chmn. dept., 1966-71. Mem. Ohio adv. council, girls secondary phys. edn. Ohio Dept. Edn., 1967-72; chmn. curriculum com. for devel. of curriculum guide for girls secondary phys. edn. Ohio Dept. Edn., 1968-71. Mem. Am. (chmn. div. girls and women's sports 1971-74, v.p. 1971-74), Eastern (editor newsletter 1965-66), Midwest (mem. constn. com. 1959-61), Conn. (pres. 1965-66, Honor award 1966), Ohio (Profl. Merit award 1973; chmn. editorial com.) assns. health, phys. edn. and recreation, Conn. (sec. 1962-63), Ill. (chmn., sec. 1960-61) bds. women ofcls., Ill. Assn. for Profl. Preparation (chmn. constn. com. 1959-61). Author: (with M.A. Sanborn) Issues in Physical Education, 1970. Editor: Curriculum Guide for Girls' Secondary Physical Education for the State of Ohio, 1970; Evaluative Criteria for Secondary Physical Education for State of Ohio. Contbr. articles to profl. jours. Home: 200 Valleyview St Kent OH 44240

HARTMAN, CATHERINE RUDISILL (MRS. HAROLD R. HARTMAN), educator; b. Biscoe, N.C., Mar. 24, 1916; d. Jacob Andrew and Annie (Dietz) Rudisill; B.S., Appalachian State Tchrs. Coll., 1944; M.A., Columbia, 1950, profl. diploma Tchrs. Coll., 1959; student U. London, Heidelberg U., summer 1953, N.Y.U., summer 1954, U. Cal. at Los Angeles, summer 1956; m. Harold R. Hartman, Dec. 26, 1962. Primary tchr. Park Grace Sch., Kings Mountain, N.C., 1936-39; elementary, music tchr. Oakhurst Sch., Charlotte, N.C., 1939-44, Gary Sch., Tampa, Fla., 1945-47; elementary supr. schs. Gaston County Schs., Gastonia, N.C., 1947-55, dir. instrn., 1955-61, asst. supt. in charge instrn., 1961-63; asso. prof. edn. William Paterson Coll. of N.J., Wayne, 1964—, chmn. gen. elementary program com. for curriculum revision, 1967-68, chmn. dept. secondary edn., 1972—. Mem. Assn. Supervision and Curriculum Devel. of N.E.A. (nat. dir. 1958-61), Nat. Conf. Christians and Jews (Carolinas regional dir. 1952-63), Am. Assn. U. Women (dir. Charlotte 1953-55), Assn. Childhood Edn. (life, treas. N.C. 1955-57, adviser Gaston County br. 1955-63), N.J. Edn. Assn., Assn. N.J. State Coll. and Univ. Profs., Am. Assn. Sch. Adminstrs. (life), Delta Kappa Gamma, Kappa Delta Pi, Pi Lambda Theta. Presbyn. Home: 26 S Middletown Rd Georgian Ct Pearl River NY 10965 Office: William Paterson Coll of NJ Wayne NJ 07470

HARTMAN, DELLA RUTH LOOPER (MRS. PAUL H. HARTMAN), dentist; b. Shelbyville, Tenn., Aug. 18, 1937; d. Bailey S. and Margaret (Allen) Looper; B.A., Longwood Coll., 1959; D.D.S., U. Md. Balt. Coll. Dental Surgery, 1963; m. Paul H. Hartman, Mar. 30, 1961; children—Virginia Ruth, Della Joyce. Gen. practice dentistry, Ellicott City, Md., 1963-70, Pelzer, S.C., 1970—. Swimming instr. YMCA of Howard County, 1967. Mem. Am., Md., S.C., Anderson County dental assns., Western Shore Dental Soc., Md. Soc. Dentistry for Children, Longwood Library League. Republican. Baptist. Clubs: Spanish, H20 (Farmville, Va.); Tom Thumb Squares (Ellicott City), Zonta (pres. 1974) (Greenville). Home: Rt 3 Old Georgia Rd Pelzer SC 29669

HARTMAN, ELIZABETH, actress; b. Youngstown, O., Dec. 1943; ed. Carnegie Inst. Tech. Motion pictures include Patch of Blue, The Group, You're A Big Boy Now, The Fixer, The Beguiled, Walking Tall. Address: care Blake Agy Ltd 409 N Camden Beverly Hills CA 90210

HARTMAN, ELIZABETH ROSE, music librarian; b. East Lansdowne, Pa., Apr. 13, 1910; d. Clarence F. and Mary Speedy (Braid) Hartman; B.A., Pa. State U., 1931; M.Sacred Music, Union Theol. Sem., 1943; B.S. in L.S., Drexel U., 1948. Investigator, Phila. Dept. Welfare, 1933-36; library asst. Drexel U. Library, Phila., 1943-46; librarian Curtis Inst. Music, Phila., 1946-53; asst. head music dept. Free Library of Phila., 1953-65, head music dept., 1965—. Recipient Distinguished Alumnus award Drexel Library Sch. Alumni Assn., 1971. Mem. Am., Pa. (chmn. orgn. and bylaws com. 1971) library assns., Phila. Library Pub. Relations Assn., Music Library Assn., Internat. Assn. Music Libraries (mem. pub. library commn. 1969—), Drexel Library Sch. Alumni Assn (pres. 1965-67), Assn. for Recorded Sound Coll. (chmn. membership com. 1967-71). Republican. Presbyn. Office: Free Library Phila Logan Sq Philadelphia PA 19103

HARTMAN, JOAN EDNA, educator; b. Bklyn., Oct. 5, 1930; d. H. Graham and Edna (Kuebler) H.; A.B., Mt. Holyoke Coll., 1951; A.M., Duke, 1952; postgrad. (Am. Assn. U. Women N.Y. State fellow), St. Anne's Coll., Oxford (Eng.) U., 1958-59; Ph.D., Radcliffe Coll., 1960. Instr. English, Washington Coll., Chestertown, Md., 1952-54; instr. English, Wellesley (Mass.) Coll., 1959-62, asst. prof., 1962-63; asst. prof. English, Conn. Coll., New London, 1963-66; asst. prof. English, Queens Coll., City U. N.Y., 1967-70; asst. prof. English, S.I. Community Coll., City U. N.Y., 1970-72, asso. prof., 1972—. Scholar, Radcliffe Inst., 1966-67. Mem. Modern Lang. Assn. (mem. commn. status women, co-chairperson 1974—), Women's Caucus Modern Langs., Nat. Council Tchrs. English, Coll. English Assn. (mem. com. undergrad. curriculum 1971—, chairperson 1973-74), Phi Beta Kappa. Home: 201 E 21st St New York City NY 10010 Office: 715 Ocean Terrace Staten Island NY 10301

HARTMAN, PAULINE, city ofcl.; b. Fostoria, O., Mar. 18, 1912; d. Ora Raymond and Minnie Rachel (Miller) Wade; grad. high sch.; m. Harold Cuyler Hartman, Apr. 20, 1932 (dec. Sept. 1969); 1 dau., Marilyn Sue (Mrs. Terry Dale Mills). Owner Tri-County Abstract Co., Fostoria, 1934-50; clk. Kaubisch Meml. Pub. Library, Fostoria, 1969-71; sec. to mayor, service dir. City of Fostoria, 1972-76. Home: 522 Gray Park Dr Fostoria OH 44830 Office: Municipal Bldg Fostoria OH 44830

HARTMAN, ROBERTA ANN, veterinarian; b. La Junta, Colo., July 25, 1928; d. Theodore and Eugenia Luoella (Munson) Hartman; med. tech. degree Colo. State Hosp., 1952; B.S., Colo. State U., 1952, M.S. in Clin. Pathology, 1954, D.V.M., 1961. Tchr. lab. Colo. State Hosp., Pueblo, 1951-52; researcher Colo. State U., 1957-60; pvt. vet. practice, North Vancouver, B.C., Can., 1969—. Cons. veterinarian in medicine and surgery Vancouver Pub. Aquarium, 1967-71; dir. Cove Animal Clinic, North Vancouver, 1969—; cons. North Vancouver Pollution Bd., 1974. Mem. Women's Vet. Med. Assn. (treas. 1963-65), P.E.O., Beta Sigma Phi. Research on whale cardiology; pioneer abdominal surgery on crocodiles. Home: 331 W 27th St North Vancouver BC V7N 2H5 Canada Office: 165 Riverside Dr North Vancouver BC Canada

HARTMANN, SISTER MARIA MERCEDES, educator; b. Ebensburg, Pa., Mar. 17, 1915; d. Francis Joseph and Edna (Lynch) Hartmann; B.A., Coll. Notre Dame of Md., 1936; M.S.W. (Barbara Seidenburg scholar), Loyola U., Chgo., 1940; postgrad. (scholar) St. Louis U., 1954. Caseworker, Catholic Charities, Syracuse, N.Y., 1937-39; exec. sec., Johnstown, Pa., 1939-41; joined Congregation of Sch. Sisters of Notre Dame, 1941; instr. to prof., chmn. dept. sociology Coll. Notre Dame Md., Balt., 1943-66, prof. sociology, 1970—; dir. research and information Nat. Conf. Catholic Charities, Washington, 1966-70; dir. health and retirement Balt. Province, Sch. Sisters of Notre Dame. Faculty, Human Relations Workshops St. Louis U., summers 1955-57; faculty Loyola U. Human Relations, Los Angeles, summers 1963-64, dir., summer 1965; cons. Nat. Migrant Worker Council, Balt. Archdiocesan Census Com., Nat. Council Catholic Men, Diocese Rochester. Mem. ad hoc com. to form Council on Higher Edn. in Urban Affairs, 1965; mem. edn. com. Nat. Conf. Christians and Jews, 1949—; mem. Balt. Tutorial Council, 1965-67; bd. mgrs. Montrose State Sch. for Girls, Balt. Archdiocesan Commn. on Aging. Mem. Nat. Assn. Social Workers (Md. chpt.), Acad. Certified Social Workers, Nat. Council Crime and Delinquency, Assn. Sociology Religion, Delta Epsilon Sigma. Author: Youth Reaches Youth: A Study of College Volunteers Working with Antisocial Adolescents, 1959; Unwed Parents, 1967; Catholic Maternity Residences: Characteristics and Trends in Facilities and Services. Contbr. articles to profl. jours. Home: 6401 N Charles St Baltimore MD 21212

HARTMANN, MARTHA CONSUELO (MRS. JAMES E. HARTMANN), mus. ofcl.; b. Mount Holly, N.J.; d. John Earnest and Estelle Miller (Cozine) Nelson; B.A., U. Colo., 1961, tchrs.' certificate, 1970; m. James E. Hartmann, June 12, 1971. Asst., jr. mus. dept. Newark Mus., 1961-63; with Denver Mus. Natural History, 1963—, curator edn., 1969—. Bd. dirs. Denver Children's Mus., Inc., 1973—. Mem. Am., Colo.-Wyo. (dir. 1973—) assns. of museums, Mountain Plains Mus. Conf., Nat. Wildlife Soc., Nat. Audubon Soc. Home: 7301 W Bowles Av Littleton CO 80123 Office: Denver Museum Natural History City Park Denver CO 80205

HARTNER, MIRIAM STURGEON (MRS. W. BRUCE HARTNER), child psychiatrist; b. Vandergrift, Pa., Dec. 22, 1936; d. Robert Harold and Ruth Miriam (Myers) Sturgeon; B.S., U. Pitts., 1958, M.D., 1962; m. W. Bruce Hartner, Aug. 4, 1962; 1 son, Robert Bruce. Intern Southside Hosp., Pitts., 1962-63; fellow gen. psychiatry Western Psychiat Inst. and Clinic, U. Pitts., 1963-65; fellow child psychiatry Emory U., Atlanta, 1965-67; research asso. U. Pitts. Grad. Sch. Pub. Health, 1967-68, lectr. mental health, 1968, adj. asst. prof. community mental health, 1968—; clin. instr. child psychiatry U. Pitts. Sch. Medicine, 1968—; practice child psychiatry, Pitts., 1968—. Dir. Vandergrift Fed. Savs. & Loan Assn. (Pa.). Co-recipient Lester N. Hofheimer prize research Am. Psychiat. Assn., 1973. Mem. Phi Beta Kappa, Alpha Omega Alpha. Contbr. articles to publs. Office: 121 University Pl Pittsburgh PA 15213

HARTOG, ELLIE MARIA, obstetrician and gynecologist; b. Haarlem, Netherlands, May 4, 1931; d. Frank H. and Ann E. (Sluyter) Hartog; came to U.S., 1958, naturalized, 1961; M.D., U. Miami (Fla.), 1964. Intern Lakeland Gen. Hosp. and Polk County Hosp., Bartow, Fla., 1965; staff physician Polk Gen. Hosp., Bartow, Fla., 1965-66; resident in obstetrics and gynecology Jackson Meml. Hosp., Miami, 1969; chief obstetrics and gynecology service Polk Gen. Hosp., Bartow, 1969—. Diplomate Am. Bd. Obstetrics and Gynecology. Fellow Am. Coll. Obstetrics and Gynecology; mem. Fla., Polk County Med. assns. Home: 520 Queens Loop Lakeland FL 33803 Office: Polk Gen Hosp Bartow FL 33830

HARTRIDGE, VIRGINIA BISHOP, physician; b. Milw., Mar. 29, 1919; d. Theodore Shears and Blanche (Bishop) Hartridge; B.A., Milw.-Downer Coll., 1941; M.S., U. Mich., 1942; M.D., Woman's Med. Coll. Pa., 1950. Intern, Hosp. Woman's Med. Coll., Phila., 1950-51; fellow anesthesiology Mayo Found., Rochester, Minn., 1953-56, cons. in anesthesiology, 1956—; asst. prof. anesthesiology Mayo Grad. Sch. Medicine, U. Minn., 1968—; dir. Mayo Clinic Sch. for Nurse Anesthetists, 1964—. Trustee Lawrence U. Served with Med. Specialist Corps, AUS, 1942-46. Diplomate Am. Bd. Anesthesiology, Nat. Bd. Med. Examiners. Fellow Am. Coll. Anesthesiology; mem. Am. Soc. Anesthesiologists, Internat. Anesthesia Research Soc., A.M.A., Zumbro Valley Med. Soc., N.Y. Acad. Scis., Nat. Audubon Soc., Izaak Walton League, Wis. Hist. Soc., Royal Soc. Medicine (fgn. asso.). Contbr. articles to profl. jours. Home: Hawkhurst Route 2 Rochester MN 55901 Office: 200 1st St SW Rochester MN 55901

HARTSOCK, LINDA SUE, assn. exec.; St. Joseph, Feb. 20, 1940; d. Waldo Emerson and Martha (Shelkop) Hartsock; B.S., Central Methodist Coll., Mo., 1962; M.Ed., Pa. State U., 1965, D.Ed., 1971. Tchr. jr. high sch. North Kansas City (Mo.) Sch. System, 1962-63; sr. resident Pa. State U., University Park, 1963-64, asst. coordinator residence halls, 1964-65, coordinator, 1965-66, asst. dean of women, 1966-68, asst. dean of students, 1968-71; researcher Center Study Higher Edn., 1970-71; dir. new student programs, 1971-72; dir. program Am. Assn. U. Women, Washington, 1972—. Mem. adv. bd. Off to College publ.; mem. adv. com. of nat. orgns. to Corp. for Pub. Broadcasting. Mem. Am. Acad. Polit. and Social Sci., Am. Assn. Higher Edn., Am. Assn. U. Women, Adminstrv. Women in Edn., Nat. Orientation Dirs. Assn., Pi Lambda Theta. Author: (monograph) Organizational Dynamics-A New Approach to Some Old Problems. Cons., contbr. articles on higher edn., organizational dynamics, women. Home: 403 Tennessee Av Alexandria VA 22305 Office: 2401 Virginia Av NW Washington DC 20037

HARTSOOK, MRS. FRANK M. (ELMA W. HARTSOOK), civic worker; b. Mt. Gilead, O.; d. Isaac W. and Maria (Ulrey) Wheeler; grad. pub. schs.; m. F.M. Hartsook, June 26, 1919 (dec. Jan. 1951). Treas. Crippled Children's Orgn., 1954—, Morrow County's Med. Aux., 1958—, Morrow County Mental Health, 1956—; bd. dirs. Central Ohio Mental Health Clinic, Delaware, O. Pres. Morrow County Republican Women's Orgn., 1954—; del. Rep. Nat. Conv., 1956. Mem. 40 and 8, Am. Legion Aux. Methodist (finance commn.) Mem. Ladies Oriental Shrine, Order White Shrine of Jerusalem, Order Eastern Star (past matron, past pres. dist.). Home: 133 E Main St Cardington OH 43315

HARTUNG, HAZEL JANE SPRINGER (MRS. DONALD NORMAN HARTUNG), hosp. ofcl.; b. Youngstown, O., Feb. 19, 1918; d. Homer Edward and Cora (Nichols) Springer; student pub. schs., Akron, O.; m. Donald Norman Hartung, July 18, 1937; children—Donald Glenn, Daniel Richard, James Lee. Newspaperwoman, Muskegon (Mich.) Chronicle, 1953-56; indsl. editor Muskegon Piston Ring Co., 1956-57; account exec. Studio 5 Advt. Agy., 1957-59; personnel and pub. realtions dir. Hardy-Herpolsheimer's Dept. Store, 1959-61; dir. advt. and pub. relations Nat. Lumberman's Bank, 1961-65; pub. relations dir. Farmers Nat. Bank & Trust Co., Ashtabula, O., 1965-66; mgr. advt. and promotion Fasson Products div. Avery Products Corp., Painesville, O., 1966-67; dir. pub. services McKay-Dee Hosp. Health Center, Ogden, Utah, 1967-69; dir. pub. relations Lima (O.) Meml. Hosp., 1969—. Free-lance writer for trade and religious mags., 1953—. Advt. and pub. relations dir. Greater Muskegon's Seaway Festival, 1963; mem. Juvenile Writer's Workshop; co-chmn. Red Cross Blood Fund Dr., 1972; mem. pub. relations com. United Fund, 1972-74. Bd. dirs. Child and Family Service, 1971-73, Marimor Workshop, 1971-73. Bd. dirs. West Ohio Kidney Found. Recipient Outdoor Advt. award for creation and execution billboards, 1963, Advt. Woman of Year award Advt. and Sales Club Western Mich., 1964, Layout and Editor award Intermountain Assn. Indsl. Editors, 1969. Mem. Greater Muskegon C. of C. (dir. women's div. 1961-64), Western Mich. Advt. and Sales Club (dir. 1962-64), Internat. Platform Assn. Mem. Reorganized Ch. of Jesus Christ of Latter-day Saints (women's leader 1961-63, 74). Clubs: Zonta (dir. 1962-63, treas. 1963-64), West State Press. (charter; dir. 1963-64). Home: 3139 Clifford Dr Lima OH 45805 Office: Linden and Mobel St Lima OH 45804

HARTWELL, PATRICIA LOCHRIDGE (MRS. DICKSON HARTWELL), journalist, educator; b. Austin, Tex., Sept. 22, 1916; d. Lloyd Pampell and Franklyn (Blocker) Lochridge; student U. Tex., 1933-34; B.A., Wellesley Coll., 1937; M.S., Columbia, 1938; m. Henry Nelson Bull, 1945 (div. 1953); children—Stephen Medaris, Jefferson Lochridge; m. 2d, Dickson Jay Hartwell, Aug. 6, 1953; children—Jay Craig, Ware Blocker. Asst. dir. news and spl. events CBS, N.Y.C., 1939-42; coordinator media OWI, Washington, 1942-43; asso. editor, Washington corr., war and fgn. corr. Woman's Home Companion, 1943-49; mag. dir. Carl Byoir & Assos., 1949-54; dir. pub. information Children's Fund UN, 1954-62; editor The Arizonian, Scottsdale, 1962-68; prof. internat. relations, history of Far East, Phoenix Coll., 1968—; lectr. mass communications Ariz. State U., 1970. Vice pres., trustee Corrs. Fund, 1952—; exec. dir. Scottsdale Fine Arts Commn., 1971—. Recipient certificate merit, USN, 1945. Mem. Soc. Mag. Writers. Clubs: Overseas Press (past v.p.), Newspaper Woman's (N.Y.C.). Home: 5301 N 77th St Scottsdale AZ 85253

HARTWIG, CLEO, sculptor; b. Webberville, Mich., Oct. 20, 1911; d. Albert and Julia (Klunzinger) Hartwig; A.B., Western Mich. U., 1932, D.F.A., 1973; student Internat. Sch. Art, Europe, 1935; m. Vincent Glinsky, 1951; 1 son, Albert. Tchr. pvt. schs., N.Y.C., 1935-42; instr. Cooper Union, 1945-46; sculpture instr. Montclair (N.J.) Art Mus., 1945-71. First one-man show, 1943; included group exhbns. Nat. Acad., Pa. Acad., Detroit Inst. Arts, Chgo. Art Inst., Met. Mus., Phila. Mus., Whitney Mus., others; rep. in collections Newark Mus., Detroit Inst. Arts, Pa. Acad., Montclair Art Mus., Mt. Holyoke Coll., Western Mich. U., Oswego (N.Y.) U., Norfolk Mus. Recipient Kamperman Haass prize Mich. Artists Assn., 1943, Anna Hyatt Huntington prize for sculpture, 1945, L. Reusch & Co. prize N.Y. Soc. Ceramic Arts, 1946, Nat. Assn. Women Artists 1st prize for sculpture, 1951, Audubon Artists prize for sculpture, 1952, 71, 72; award mural and sculpture competition Munson-Williams-Proctor Inst., 1958; Feist Meml. prize Nat. Assn. Women Artists, 1968, Salomone prize, 1972; silver medal Nat. Sculpture Soc., 1969. Mem. Audubon Artists, Sculptors Guild, Nat. Sculpture Soc., Nat. Assn. Women Artists (medal of honor 1967), Soc. Animal Artists, N.A.D. Home: 9 Patchin Pl New York City NY 10011 Studio: 5 W 16th St New York City NY 10011

HARTWIG, GRACE LOUISE BUCKLEY (MRS. MELVIN F. HARTWIG), therapist; b. Ft. Worth, May 16, 1930; d. Clarence Arthur and Ruby Pauline (Bryant) Buckley; B.S., Tex. State Coll. for Women, 1952; m. Melvin F. Hartwig, Dec. 24, 1956 (dec. 1958). Staff therapist psychiatry USPHS Hosp., Ft. Worth, 1952-56; tng. supr. mentally retarded Occupational Tng. Center, Ft. Worth, 1957-58; dir. occupational therapy chest div. Woodlawn Hosp., Dallas, 1959-65; dir. occupational therapy Convalescent Center, Dallas, 1965-67, Meth. Towers, Dallas, 1967-70; occupational therapist psychiatry Dallas County Hosp. Dist., 1970—. Cons. Meth. Towers Nursing Home, 1967, Colonial Acres Nursing Home, 1969. Recipient Superior Service award Dept. Health, Edn. and Welfare, 1956. Mem. Am., Tex. occupational therapy assns. Home: 1820 Robin Rd Irving TX 75061 Office: 5201 Harry Hines Blvd Dallas TX 75235

HARTY, MARGARET BROWN, coll. v.p.; b. Gloucester, Mass.; d. Harry J. and Mary (Walsh) Brown; B.A., with high honors, San Francisco State Coll., 1957; M.A., U. San Francisco, 1959; Ed.D., U. Cal. at Berkeley, 1965; children—Brian, Maureen, Elaine, Kevin. Asst. prof. nursing San Francisco State Coll., 1957-64; chmn. div. nursing and health scis. Chabot Coll., Cal., 1964-67; dir. nursing edn. Nat. League for Nursing, N.Y.C., 1967-69; dean Coll. Nursing, Tex. Woman's U., Denton, 1969-72, v.p. Inst. Health Scis., 1972—. Vis. lectr. continuing edn. U. Cal. Sch. Nursing, San Francisco, 1960-64; pres. Cal. League for Nursing, 1962-64; cons. to Surgeon Gen., U.S. Army, 1968-70; cons and lectr. at local, state and nat. level. Pres.,

Denton (Tex.) County Health Planning Council, 1970—. Mem. Am. Assn. U. Women, Nat. League for Nursing, Am. Nurses Assn., North Central Tex. Council of Govt. Health Planning Council (bd. dirs. 1970—), Tex. Nurses Assn. (dir. dist. 27, 1971-72), Western Regional Council League for Nursing (chmn. 1963-64), Sigma Theta Tau. Chmn. editorial adv. com. Internat. Nursing Index, 1971—. Contbr. articles to profl. pubs. Home: Box 22966 Denton TX 76204

HARVEY, CLARIE COLLINS (MRS. MARTIN L. HARVEY), mortuary exec.; b. Meridian, Miss.; d. Malachi C. and Mary Agusta (Rayford) Collins; B.A. in Econs., Spelman Coll., 1937; grad. Ind. Coll. Mortuary Sci., 1942; M.A. in Personnel Adminstrn., Columbia, 1950; postgrad. N.Y. U. Grad. Sch. Bus. Adminstrn., 1948-49, Union Theol. Sem., 1950; H.H.D., Rust Coll., 1971; m. Martin L. Harvey, Aug. 1, 1943. Owner, pres. Collins Funeral Home, Inc., Jackson, Miss., 1970—, Collins Ins. Co., Jackson, 1970—. Mem. Miss. Adv. Com. to U.S. Commn. on Civil Rights, 1964-71; mem. N.A.A.C.P.; chmn. Hinds County Community Service Assn., 1968-70; mem. White House Conf. on Human Relations, 1960, 66; del. 17th Nat. Disarmament Conf., Geneva, 1962; mem. City Jackson's Progressive Action Com., 1971—; nat. pres. Ch. Women United, 1971-74; chmn. new unit com. III: edn. and renewal cons. for Central Com. World Council Chs., 1972—; mem. exec. com. World Meth. Council, 1971—; mem. exec. com. Commn. on Structure United Meth. Ch., 1968-72; mem. Meth. Com. on Overseas Relief, 1964-68; mem. Gen. Bd. Christian Social Concerns, 1958-64, sec., 1960-64. Founder Womanpower Unltd., Jackson, Miss., 1961; founder, bd. dirs. State Mut. Savs. and Loan Assn. Jackson, 1958-69; trustee Martin Luther King, Jr. Center for Social Change, 1971—; mem. bd. So. Regional Council, Inc., 1963—, exec. com., 1966-68. Recipient citation for outstanding efforts for civil rights and peace Gen. Bd. Christian Social Concerns United Meth. Ch., 1963; Outstanding Alumnae award Spelman Coll., 1966; named Woman of Yr. Nat. Funeral Dirs. Assn., 1955; Outstanding Citizen Jackson City Jackson, 1971; Religious Heritage award as Churchwoman of Year, 1974; New Pittsburgh Courier Top Hat award, 1974. Mem. Nat. Council Negro Women (life), Miss. Funeral Dirs. and Morticians Assn. (pres. 1970-72, mem. nat. bd. 1970—), Epsilon Nu Delta, Alpha Kappa Alpha. Home: 415 N Farish St Jackson MS 39202

HARVEY, ELEANOR T.M. (MRS. BENSON HARVEY), church worker; b. Phila., Dec. 17, 1904; d. James and Eleanor (Thornton) Moss; B.A., Wellesley Coll., 1926; M.Sc., Western Res. U., 1931; grad. study econs. London U., 1934, N.Y. Sch. Social Work, 1938, Smith Coll., 1945-46; m. Rev. Benson Heale Harvey, Oct. 13, 1934; 1 dau., Eleanor Thornton (Mrs. Edward J. Tejirian). Case worker Phila. Family Soc., 1928-29; missionary Episcopal Ch. in Philippines, 1929-45, med. social worker St. Luke's Hosp., Manila, 1933-37; case worker A.R.C., mil. hosps., 1941-42; part-time news corr. Springfield (Mass.) Daily News, 1946-48; exec. dept. Christian social relations Diocese of Western Mass., 1949-67. Active Girl Scouts, past pres. Easthampton council. Chmn. Provincial Commn. Christian Social Relations, 1952-58; mem. bd. Hampshire County br. Mass. Soc. for Prevention Cruelty to Children, sec. 1956-68, pres., 1969—, also past sec. regional bd., mem. central bd.; v.p. bd. Worthington Health Center, 1970-71; mem. bd. Protestant Youth Center, v.p., 1966—; pres. Western Mass. Inst. Religion and Health, 1971—. Mem. Bus. and Profl. Woman's Club (past pres. Hampshire County, pres. state fedn. 1963-65, state parliamentarian 1967-69), Mass. (chmn. legislative com. 1959-64, 65-68, exec. bd. 1959-61, editor Social Relations Bull, 1959-68), Greater Springfield (exec. bd. 1952-61) councils chs., Ch. Women United Mass. (v.p. 1959-62), Episcopal Ch. Women, Nat. Assn. Social Workers (chpt. sec. 1961-63), Acad. Certified Social Workers, Am. Assn. U. Women, Acad. Religion and Mental Health (pres. Mass. br. 1972—). Episcopalian. Clubs: Tuesday Afternoon (past pres.), Springfield Wellesley (pres. 1971), Church Periodical (diocesan chmn. 1971—), Easthampton Women's (pres. 1966-68). Author: Sonnets from Captivity and Other Poems, 1949, 2d edit., 1973; (with others) Children of Tragedy, 1961. Editor: Diocesan Chronicle of Philippine Episcopal Ch., 1937-41, Massachusetts Church Woman, 1962—. Home: Ireland St West Chesterfield MA 01084

HARVEY, FLORENCE ELIZABETH (MRS. STEPHEN HARVEY), sorority exec.; b. Bklyn.; d. Frederick Charles and Alice Jennie (Kunkel) Hohnbaum; A.B., Bucknell U., 1939; M.S., N.Y. U., 1940; teaching certificate Montclair State Coll., 1941; m. Stephen Harvey, Aug. 4, 1951. Asst. prof. Washington Sq. Coll. N.Y. U., N.Y.C., 1940; tchr. Regional High Sch., Springfield, N.J., 1941; tchr.-coordinator High Sch., Bennington, Vt., 1941-42; county supr. distbv. edn. High Sch., Martinsburg, W.Va., 1942-43; interviewer, co. rep., personnel investigator Western Electric Co., Kearny, N.J., 1943-48; tchr., counselor Essex County (N.J.) Vocational High Sch., Newark, 1949-51; nat. judiciary chmn. Delta Zeta, 1967-70, nat. dir. house Corps., 1970-73, province II collegiate dir., 1972-73, nat. pres., 1973—. Leader Greater Essex council Girl Scouts U.S.A., 1934-35; mem. Community Players, 1964—. Recipient Martha Washington award N.J. soc. S.A.R., 1973; named to Am. Bicentennial Research Inst. Library Human Resources. Mem. Bucknell U. Alumni Assn. No. N.J., N.Y. U. Alumni Assn., Panhellenic Conf. (Westfield area, pres.), Woman's Aux. Lafayette Coll. YWCA, Newark Mus., So. Ocean County (N.J.) Hosp. Aux., N.J. Hist. Soc., Kappa Delta Epsilon, Delta Zeta (pres. No. N.J. Alumnae chpt. 1948-52). Republican. Presbyn. Mem. Order Eastern Star. Clubs: Bison (Lewisburg, Pa.); College Woman's (Westfield, N.J.); Beach Haven Park (N.J.) Yacht. Home: PO Box 456 Westfield NJ 07091

HARVEY, HARRIETTE ELIZABETH, museum ofcl.; b. Corpus Christi, Tex., Aug. 23, 1939; d. T.G. and Elizabeth Evans (Erwin) Allen; B.F.A., U. Tex. at Austin, 1970, postgrad.; m. John Rodque Agee, Sept. 5, 1959 (div. 1973); children—Julianne, John Marque, Jennifer Anne; m. 2d, Charles Minor Harvey, Jan. 20, 1973. Registrar, U. Tex. at Austin Art Mus., 1971-73; art curator, ednl. dir., head Slide Library U. Tex. at San Antonio, 1973—. Mem. N.Am., Mid Am. coll. art assns., Art Library Soc. Club: Weed N'Wish Garden (pres. Dickinson, Tex. 1969). Home: 116 Cottonwood St Boerne TX 78006 Office: 4242 Piedras Dr East San Antonio TX 78284

HARVEY, LYNNE COOPER (MRS. PAUL HARVEY), broadcasting exec., civic worker; b. nr. St. Louis; d. William A. and Margaret (Kehr) Cooper; A.B., Washington U., St. Louis, 1939, M.A., 1940; m. Paul Harvey, June 4, 1940; 1 son, Paul. Broadcaster ednl. program KXOK, St. Louis, 1940; broadcaster-writer women's news and WAC Variety Show, Fort Custer, Mich., 1941-43; gen. mgr. Paul Harvey News, ABC, 1944—; pres. Paulynne Prodns., Ltd., Chgo., 1968—, exec. producer Paul Harvey Comments, 1968—. Pres. woman's bd. Mental Health Assn. Greater Chgo., 1967—, v.p. bd. dirs., 1966—; pres. woman's aux. Infant Welfare Soc. Chgo., 1969—; nominating chmn. Salvation Army Woman's Adv. Bd., 1967-69; reception chmn. Community Lectures. Bd., Oak Park-River Forest, Ill., 1963-69; pres. Mothers Council, River Forest, 1961-62; charter bd. mem. Gottlieb Meml. Hosp., Melrose Park, Ill.; mem. adv. bd. Nat. Christian Heritage Found., 1964—. Mem. McGraw's Wildlife Found., Phi Beta Kappa, Kappa Delta Pi, Phi Sigma Iota, Eta Sigma Phi. Clubs: Chicago Golf, Woman's Athletic, Nineteenth Century Woman's, Press (Chgo.); Oak Park Country. Home: 1035 Park Av River Forest IL 60305 also Reveille Ranch Imperial MO 63052 also Carefree AZ 85331 Office: Box 77 River Forest IL 60305

HARVEY, MAYME LEE SUITT (MRS. WARREN ALBERT HARVEY), civic worker; b. Lake Village, Ark., Apr. 24, 1926; d. James Edward and May Ladelle (Pitts) Suitt; grad. high sch.; m. Warren Albert Harvey, Mar. 28, 1947. Fingerprint analyst and classifier War Dead File, FBI, Washington, 1943-46; reporter Am. Credit Bur., New Orleans, 1946-47. Mem. Gov.'s Com. on UN, 1966-69, Gov.'s Commn. on Vocational Rehab., 1968-69; chmn. sub-com. Work of State Library with State Agys., 1971-72; treas. Settlement Assn. N.H., 1968—; asst. sec. Manchester Vis. Nurses Assn., 1971-72, 2d v.p., 1972—; mem. nominating com. N.H. Heart Assn., 1971—, dir., 1972; mem. Hill Burton Adv. Council, N.H., 1969—; incorporator N.H. Charitable Fund, 1970—; mem. program com. Am. Bapt. Conv., 1970-72; mem. gen. bd. Am. Bapt. Chs. U.S.A., 1972—, mem. credentials and caucus com., mem. Am. Bapt. Assembly Bd. Dirs. Mem. town budget com. Town of Hooksett, N.H., 1970—; treas. Hooksett Republican Town Com. Trustee Arah W. Prescott Library, Hooksett, 1961-72; chmn. bd. dirs. Green Meadows Center of Learning for Children. Mem. N.H. Fedn. Women's Club (pres. 1966-68), Am. Bapt. Women N.H. (pres. 1970-74), N.H. Library Trustees Assn. (1st v.p. 1972, pres. 1974—), N.H. Bible Soc., N.H. Council Chs. (exec. com., trustee 1974—, dir. 1972—). Baptist (moderator 1970-74). Clubs: Hooksett Woman's, Christian Women's (vice-chmn.). Home: 25 Birch Hill Dr Hooksett NH 03106

HARVEY, VIRGINIA PEASELEY (MRS. E. W. HARVEY), educator; b. Richmond, Va.; d. Gabriel B. and Florence V. (White) Peaseley; B.S. in Chemistry, U. Md., 1929; M.S. in Phys. Edn., U. Wis., 1932; Ed.D. in Ednl. Psychology, Western Res. U., 1963; postgrad. Temple U., 1966-67; m. E. W. Harvey, Apr. 8, 1939 (div. 1958); 1 dau., Virginia Lynn. Instr. U. Mich., 1932-38; asst. prof. Kent (O.) State U., 1938-42, 44-46-54, asso. prof., 1954-64, prof., 1964—, faculty senate chairperson, 1973-74. Vis. prof. group dynamics Temple U., summer 1967; mem. Nat. Tng. Lab. Inst. Applied Behavioral Sci. Recipient Distinguished Tchr. award Kent State U., 1971, Service award Phi Delta Kappa, 1972. Amy Morris Homans fellow, 1962-63. Mem. Am. Assn. U. Profs., Am. Assn. Higher Edn., Am. Personnel and Guidance Assn., Assn. Counselor Educators, Kappa Kappa Gamma, Alpha Psi Omega, Delta Psi Kappa. Mem. Disciples of Christ Ch. Home: 1315 Greenwood Av Kent OH 44240

HARVEY, WESSIE MARGUERITE (MRS. JAMES EDWIN HARVEY), librarian; b. Porterville, Miss., Oct. 26, 1918; d. Lee Roy and Mary Bessie (Hall) Caraway; A.A., E. Miss. Jr. Coll., 1938; B.S., U. So. Miss., 1941, M.S., 1971; m. James Edwin Harvey, May 22, 1945; children—James Edwin, Rita (Mrs. Ross Lamberson). Tchr. English, Bassfield (Miss.) High Sch., 1939-41, Woodville (Miss.) High Sch., 1941-44, Poplarville (Miss.) High Sch., 1957-69; head librarian Pearl River Jr. Coll., Poplarville, 1969—. Bd. dirs. A.R.C., 1973—, co-chmn. fund dr. 1973. Mem. Miss. Library Assn. (regional officer 1972-73), Miss. Edn. Assn., Miss. Jr. Coll. Assn., Delta Kappa Gamma. Baptist. Home: 1023 S Maxwell St Poplarville MS 39470

HARVILL, ELEANOR K., pub. relations exec.; b. Yonkers, N.Y., Dec. 31, 1919; d. Peter K. and Anna (Rodak) Harvill; B.A., Barnard Coll., Columbia, 1941; M.A., Tchrs. Coll., Columbia, 1942. Sec., researcher Hill & Knowlton, Inc., N.Y.C., 1946-48, research asst., 1948-49, research supr., 1949-52, research dir., 1952-56; research asst. U.S. Steel Corp., N.Y.C., 1956-68, Pitts., 1969; mgr. corporate research pub. relations dept. Gulf & Western Industries, Inc., N.Y.C., 1970—. Tchr., Riverdale (N.Y.) Country Sch. for Boys, 1942-43. Served with WACS, 1943-46. Mem. Pub. Relations Soc. Am. (chpt. dir. 1967-68, chmn. research com. 1966-68, editor Reflections 1966-68, contbg. editor Pub. Relations Jour. 1968-70). Contbr. articles to profl. jours., chpt. to The Handbook of Public Relations, 1971. Home: 5552 Netherland Av Riverdale NY 10471

HARVIN, JANICE MARIE, univ. librarian; b. Alto, Tex., May 5, 1924; d. Roy Richard and Ruth Gertrude (Liles) Harvin; B.A., Stephen F. Austin State U., 1943; B.S. in L.S., George Peabody Coll., 1945; postgrad. (Med. Library Assn. scholar) Columbia, 1955, U.S. Dept. Agr., 1957-58, Little Rock U., 1962-65. Catalog librarian U. Md. Sch. Medicine, Balt., 1949-55; reference librarian Vanderbilt Sch. Medicine, Nashville, 1945-49, 56-57; U. Neb. Coll. Medicine, Omaha, 1955-56; reference librarian, head loan and stack sect. Nat. Library Medicine, Washington, 1957-60; head librarian U. Ark. Med. Center, asst. prof. library sci. U. Ark., Little Rock, 1960-66; research med. librarian U. Tex.-M.D. Anderson Hosp., prof. library sci. U. Tex., Houston, 1966—. Mem. Spl. Libraries Assn., Med. Library Assn. (sec. 1971-72, asso. editor Bull. 1949-50). Home: 3515 Deal St Houston TX 77025

HARWAY, VIVIAN IRENE (MRS. NORMAN I. HARWAY), psychologist, educator; b. N.Y.C., May 27, 1925; d. Joseph Raymond and Florence Victoria (Robinson) Thackaberry; B.A., Queens Coll., 1947; Ph.D., U. Rochester, 1952; m. Norman I. Harway, Nov. 27, 1951; children—Maura, Judith. Asso. prof. spl. edn. Eastern Mich. U., Ypsilanti, 1952-54; clin. asso. psychiatry U. Rochester (N.Y.), 1954-68; adj. prof. psychology U. Pitts., 1968—, clin. asso. prof. psychiatry, 1969—; pvt. practice clin. child psychology, Pitts. Cons. United Cerebral Palsy Assn., 1956-68, Eastman Dental Dispensary, 1962-68, Allegheny County Child Welfare Services, 1974—. Chmn. profl. adv. bd. Allegheny County Assn. for Children with Learning Disabilities, 1969—. Mem. Am. Psychol. Assn., Sigma Xi. Author: Psychological Assessment of the Learning Disabled Child: A Guide for Parents, 1971. Contbr. articles and chpts. to profl. jours. and books. Home: 1270 Bellerock St Pittsburgh PA 15217 Office: 201 DeSoto St Pittsburgh PA 15213

HARWELL, HELON BALDWIN (MRS. JOHN EARL HARWELL), educator; b. Center, Tex., Jan. 6, 1921; d. Aaron F. and Bernice (Gibson) Baldwin; B.S., Stephen F. Austin State Coll., 1948; M.R.E., S.W. Bapt. Theol. Sem., 1949, D.R.E., 1955; M.A., N.E. Mo. State Tchrs. Coll., 1962; Ph.D., East Tex. State U., 1967; m. John Earl Harwell, Aug. 22, 1953. Instr., Tex. Christian U., Ft. Worth, 1950-52; tchr. St. Joseph Acad., Tucson, 1953-54; asst. prof. psychology East Tex. Bapt. Coll., Marshall, 1954-56, 62-65; asso. prof. childhood edn. New Orleans Bapt. Theol. Sem., 1956-61; prof. elementary edn. S.W. Bapt. Coll., Bolivar, Mo., 1965-67; prof. edn. Nicholls State U., Thibodaux, La., 1967—, now also acting head dept. spl. edn. Cons. kindergarten edn., spl. edn. Mem. Assn. Childhood Edn. Internat., Assn. Tchr. Edn., La. Tchrs. Assn., Alpha Chi. Baptist. Home: Route 1 Box 220 Supercharge Dr Thibodaux LA 70301

HARWOOD, C. THERESA, govt. ofcl.; b. New Bedford, Mass., Apr. 5, 1920; d. James Vincent and Clara V. (Howarth) Harwood; B.A., Seton Hill Coll., 1941; M.S., Georgetown U., 1952, Ph.D., 1955; M.A. in Religious Edn., Catholic U., 1967. Technician hematology Goodyear Corp., New Bedford, 1941-42; jr. chemist U.S. Naval Torpedo Sta., Newport, R.I., 1942-45; chemist Army Chem. Center, Edgewood, Md., 1948-51; biochemist Walter Reed Army Inst., Washington, 1951-58, Nat. Inst. Mental Health, Washington, 1958-60; pharmacologist FDA, Washington, 1960-61, sr. pharmacologist Office Asso. Commr. Sci., 1966-68; chief pharmacology and biochemistry labs. Georgetown Clin. Research Inst. Office Aviation Medicine FAA, Washington, 1961-66; dep. chief div. drug scis. Bur. Narcotics and Dangerous Drugs, Dept. Justice, Washington, 1968-70, acting chief, 1970-71, chief biol. research br., 1971-73, chief pharmacologist Drug Enforcement Adminstrn., 1973—; sci. tchr. New Bedford Textile Inst., 1943-45; instr. sci. Union Hosp. Sch. Nursing, Fall River, Mass., 1946-47; clin. asst. prof. pharmacology Georgetown Med. Sch., 1956-61, asst. prof., 1961-65; asst. prof. pastoral tng. program Oblate Coll., Washington, 1970-72; lectr. pharmacology Sch. Nursing, Catholic U. Am., Washington, 1973—. Mem. Am. Chem. Soc., Am. Soc. Pharmacology and Exptl. Therapeutics, Sigma Xi, Sigma Delta Epsilon. Contbr. articles to profl. jours. Home: 700 Butternut St Washington DC 20012 Office: Drug Enforcement Adminstrn Dept Justice 1405 I St NW Washington DC 20537

HARWOOD, ELEANOR CASH, librarian; b. Buckfield, Me., May 29, 1921; d. Leon Eugene and Ruth (Chick) Cash; B.A., Am. Internat. Coll., 1943; B.S., New Haven State Tchrs. Coll., 1955; m. Burton H. Harwood, Jr., June 21, 1944 (div. 1953); children—Ruth (Mrs. William R. Cline), Eleanor, James Burton. Librarian, Rathbun Meml. Library, East Haddam, Conn., 1955-56; asst. librarian Kent (Conn.) Sch., 1956-63; cons. to Chester (Conn.) Pub. Library, 1965-71. Served from ensign to lt. (j.g.) USNR, 1944-46. Mem. Am., Conn. library assns., Chester Hist. Soc. (trustee 1970-72), D.A.V., Am. Legion, Aux. Mem. United Ch. Author: (with John G. Park) The Independent School Library and the Gifted Child, 1956; The Age of Samuel Johnson, LL.D., 1959. Home: Maple St Chester CT 06412

HARWOOD, HARRIET SIFLIN, advt. agy. exec.; b. Cleve., Sept. 27, 1923; d. Nathan and Clara Irene (Kangisser) Siflin; student Fenn Coll., 1941, Cleve. Coll., 1942; m. Elkan Harwood, June 10, 1944; children—Bobette, Richard G. Wilson. Office mgr. John P. Witt & Co., Cleve., 1942-47; with Harwood Advt. Inc., Tucson, 1950—, sec., treas., 1962—. Chmn. Tucson Festival Soc. Arts and Crafts Fair, 1968. Bd. dirs. Tucson Opera Co., 1973—. Mem. Women in Communications. Club: Soroptomist of Tucson. Home: 1122 E Via Lucerna St Tucson AZ 85718 Office: 1507 Tucson Federal Tower Tucson AZ 85701

HARWOOD, MADELINE BAILEY (MRS. CLIFFORD B. HARWOOD), Republican nat. committeewoman; b. Newbury, Vt., July 7, 1914; d. George A. and Maude (Smith) Bailey; R.N., Mary Fletcher Sch. Nursing, 1936; m. Clifford Burr Harwood, July 4, 1936; children—Clifford Burr, Catherine Harwood (Mrs. Robert Shepard), Richard David, Roger Bailey. Night supr. Mary Fletcher Hosp., Burlington, Vt., 1943-44; mem. Vt. Senate, 1968, 70-72; Rep. nat. committeewoman, 1973—. Regional legislative chmn. Aux. A.M.A., 1960-64; pres. Aux. Vt. Med. Soc., 1961-63; del. Am. Heart Assn., 1968-69; sec. Vt. Heart Assn., 1966-68; Sec. Vt. Republican State Com., 1961-67, vice-chmn., 1967-72; mem. drafting bd. Vt. Rep. Platform, 1964-70, chmn. platform com., 1972; del. Rep. Nat. Conv., 1964, 68, 72, sec. Nat. Rep. Platform Com., 1968; pres. Vt. Fedn. Rep. Women, 1965-67. Bd. dirs. Mt. Laurel Mentally Retarded Sch., Bennington Councty A.R.C., Vt. Tb Assn.; trustee Champlain Coll., Burlington, U. Vt., 1971—. Mem. D.A.R. (chmn. nat. def., mem. resolutions com. 1969). Address: Village View Rd Manchester Center VT 05255

HARWOOD, MARY AGNES (NINA), newspaperwoman; b. Orange, Tex., Apr. 25, 1906; d. Ernest and Georgia Ann (Brown) Holotik; student Our Lady of Lake Coll., San Antonio, 1922-23, 27-28, 57-58, U. Tex., 1927-31, 34-36, U. Cal. at Los Angeles, 1948; m. William Edmund Harwood, July 29, 1961. Tchr. pub. schs., Yoakum, Tex., 1924-25, Nordheim, Tex., 1926-27, 31-37, Cabeza, Tex., 1927-31, Crestonio, Tex., 1937-41, Pearsall, Tex., 1947-49, Westhoff, Tex., 1957-59; with Cuero (Tex.) Record, 1950-57, 60-66; staff writer Kerrville (Tex.) Daily Times, 1966-73, city editor, 1973—. Bd. dirs. Animal Welfare Soc. Kerr County. Recipient Honorable Mention award Tex. U.P.I. Editors Assn., 1965; 1st place award for front page column Tex. Press Assn., 1971. Mem. Tex. Press Women's Assn., Catholic Daus. Am. Roman Catholic (altar soc.). Home: 623 Elm St Kerrville TX 78028 Office: 327 Earl Garrett St Kerrville TX 78028

HARWOOD, RUTH, educator; b. Boston; d. Richard G. and Grace A. (Knight) Harwood; B.A., Wellesley Coll., 1940; M.A., Columbia, 1950, Ph.D., 1963. With Fgn. Service, Dept. State, Am. embassy, Panama, 1944-46, Am. consulate gen., Tientsin, China, 1946-47. Vol., Am. Friends Service Com., Community Devel. Project, El Salvador, 1956-58; instr., counselor Womans Coll., U. N.C. at Greensboro, 1953-55; asst. in anthropology U. N.C. at Chapel Hill, 1955-56; research asso. AID Project, Columbia, 1963-65; asst. prof. anthropology L.I. U., Bklyn., 1965-71, asso. prof., 1971—. Fellow Am. Anthrop. Assn., Soc. for Applied Anthropology; mem. Latin Am. Studies Assn., Am. Assn. U. Profs. Home: 400 W 119th St New York City NY 10027 Office: Zeckendorf Campus Long Island University Brooklyn NY 11201

HARY, EDITH LYDIA, librarian; b. Woonsocket, R.I., Sept. 18, 1922; d. Louis Jacob and Lucile Dodd (Perry) Hary; B.A., Bates Coll., 1947; M.S., Simmons Coll., 1950. Apprentice course Me. State Library, Augusta, 1941-42, circulation asst., 1942-43, various library jobs summers, 1944, 45, 46, law and legislative reference librarian, 1947-71, dir. state law library 1971—; mem. library staff Bates Coll., 1943-47; library cons. U. Me. Sch. Law, 1961-62; lectr. legal bibliography. Research cons., sec. Citizens Com. Survey of Me. Govt., 1956-59; lay mem. Me. Jud. Council, 1959—; exec. com. Nat. Legislative Conf., 1963-65; mem. Me. Archives Adv. Bd., 1965—; mem. Me. Criminal Law Revision Commn., 1972—. Trustee Hubbard Free Library, Hallowell, 1964—. Mem. Me. Bar Assn. (hon.), Pemaquid Point Assn., Inc. (sec. 1952-62), Me., New Eng. (sec., Me. rep. 1956-57) library assns., Am. Assn. Law Libraries, Law Librarians N.E. (pres. 1956-58), Me. (standing com.), Kennebec hist. socs., Me. League Hist. Socs. and Museums, English-Speaking Union. Clubs: Bates Key; Kennebec Valley Bates. Discoverer, pub. Nash's History of Augusta, 1961. Contbr. articles to profl. pubs. Home: 8 Middle St Hallowell ME 04347 Office: State Law Library State House Augusta ME 04330

HARZMAN, BARBARA KATHERYN (MRS. LEONARD ALVIN HARZMAN), home economist; b. Concordia, Kan., Dec. 4, 1943; d. Carl August and Erma Vera (Austin) Richard; student Kan. State U., 1963-66, M.S., 1973; m. Leonard Alvin Harzman, Dec. 27, 1969; children—Brent Austin, Jenny Marie. Home economist Clay County (Kan.) Extension Service, Clay Center, 1966-69, Dickinson County Extension Council, Abilene, 1969-74. Mem. adv. com. Abilene Meals on Wheels Program, 1970-74; adviser Abilene Young Farm Wives Orgn.; v.p. Clay Center Welcome Wagon, 1967; internat. Farm Youth exchangee to Australia, 1968. Mem. bd. edn. St. Andrew's Sch., 1974—. Named Young Career Woman, Clay Center Bus. and Profl. Women. Mem. Nat., Kan. home econs. assns., Kan. Extension Home Econs. Assn. (chmn. profl. improvement com.), Kan. Internat. Farm Youth Exchangee Alumni (sec. 1970), Internat. Farm Youth Exchangee Alumni (life mem.), Dickinson County Rural Life Orgn. Home: 321 NE 10th St Abilene KS 67410

HASCALL, JEAN TEAGUE (MRS. CARLETON CHANDLER HASCALL, JR.), artist; b. Shepherd, Mich.; d. Cassius Homer and Helen (Winegar) Teague; A.B., Wayne State U., 1940, Ph.D. (hon.), 1973; m. Carleton Chandler Hascall, Jr., Jan. 23, 1943; children—Carleton Chandler III, John T., Mary Elizabeth. Indsl. designer George W. Walker Co., 1940; fashion illustrator Detroit Newspaper, 1941; engring. draftsman Chrysler Corp., 1942; one-man shows Wayne State U. Gallery, Women's City Club Gallery, Grosse Ile Gallery; exhibited in group shows Detroit Mus. Arts, Scarab Club Gallery, Detroit Artists' Market; represented in permanent collections Ann Arbor Mus. Arts, Marquette Library, Grosse Ile Schs.; also pvt. collections. Reader, taper textbooks Recording for Blind, Inc. Bd. dirs., pres. Community Theatre Grosse Ile (Mich.); bd. dirs. Archives of Am. Art. Mem. Detroit Soc. Women Painters and Sculptors (pres. 1950), Mich. Watercolor Soc., Internat. Platform Soc., Grosse Ile Musicale, Classical Guitar Soc. Mich. Clubs: Grosse Ile Book (pres. 1963, 65), Grosse Ile Golf and Country. Home: 28273 Elba Dr Grosse Ile MI 48138

HASELDEN, ELIZABETH LEE (MRS. KYLE HASELDEN), civic and religious worker; b. Charleston, S.C., Sept. 13, 1913; d. Thomas Oswald and Mary E. (Pettigrew) Lee; Mus.B., Meredith Coll., 1935; student Columbia, summer 1935, Colgate-Rochester Div. Sch., 1936-37; m. Kyle E. Haselden, Sept. 8, 1936; children—Kyle Haselden II, Alice, Thomas Lee. Tchr. English, music high sch., Florence, S.C., 1935-36; tchr. piano prep. dept. Morris Harvey Coll., Charleston, W.Va., 1959-60. Vice pres. United Ch. Women, Mpls., 1947-49, infer-faith chmn., Charleston, 1958-60, mem. nat. Christian social relations adv. com. of triennium, 1961-64; nat. chmn. Christian social relations Ch. Women United, 1964-67, nat. v.p., 1967-71; nat. dir. urban ministries Ch. Women United, 1971—; mem. Bapt. Joint Com. Pub. Affairs, 1962-63; mem. div. Christian social concern Am. Baptist Conv., 1963-69; mem. commn. on Christian unity, mem. gen. council Am. Bapt. Chs. U.S.A., 1970—. Mem. Citizen's Council for Better Schs., Charleston, 1958-60; mem. Mayor's Council on Human Relations, Mpls., 1947-50; pres. Women's Conf. on Human Relations, Mpls., 1946-50, Council on Human Relations, Rochester, N.Y., 1952-54, Charleston, W.Va., 1959-60; mem. Mayor's Community Relations Commn. Evanston. Mem. women's planning com. Japan Internat. Christian U., 1959—. Mem. Am. Assn. U. Women. Author study guide, articles. Home: 1507 Lincoln St Evanston IL 60201

HASENPLAUGH, DOROTHY VIRGINIA BURGER (MRS. GAYLE WILLIAM HASENPLAUGH), realtor; b. Baxter Springs, Kan., Sept. 23, 1923; d. Clarence Emerson and Lela Angeline (Rhodes) Burger; B.S. (Eastern Star scholar 1941-42), Kan. State Tchrs. Coll., 1945; m. Gayle William Hasenplaugh, Jan. 31, 1946; children—William Arthur, Jeffrey Gayle. With personnel dept. Chiksan Co., Brea, Cal., 1946-47; pub. relations Sears, Santa Ana, Cal., 1951-52; real estate salesman Walter A. Diehl, Anaheim, Cal., 1967-71; broker Hasenplaugh, Realtors, Anaheim, 1971—. Mem. Anaheim Bd. Realtors, Alumni Assn. Kan., Am. Assn. U. Women, Psynetics, Nat. Assn. Female Execs., Pi Omega Pi, Alpha Gamma Delta, Theta Sigma Upsilon. Home: 200 N Ladera Vista Dr Fullerton CA 92631 Office: 1731 S Euclid Av Anaheim CA 92802

HASH, VIRGINIA, lawyer; b. Flagstaff, Ariz.; d. Edgar and Mary (Funston) Hash; B.A., Tex. Tech. Coll., 1934; J.D., U. Ariz., 1949. Admitted to Ariz. bar, 1949, U.S. Supreme Ct. bar, 1962; law clk., 1949; law practice with V.L. Hash, Phoenix, 1953; sr. partner firm Hash, Cantor & Tomanek, Phoenix, 1969—. Spl. hearing officer for selective service appeals U.S. Dept. Justice; referee Juvenile Ct. Chmn. air transp. sub-com. Phoenix Forward, 1969-70; mem. women's adv. bd. on aviation FAA, vice chmn., 1971-72; mem. Joint City and County Airport Zoning Bd., Phoenix, 1958. Bd. dirs. YWCA. Served with Woman's Airforce Service Pilots, 1944. Mem. Am., Lawyer-Pilots (past pres.) bar assns., State Bar Ariz., Bus. and Profl. Women's Assn., Nat. Assn. Women Lawyers, Nat. Pilots Assn., Aircraft Owners and Pilots Assn., 99's, Ariz. Acad., Kappa Beta Pi. Clubs: Arizona, Soroptimist (Phoenix). Home: 340 E Earll Dr Phoenix AZ 85012 Office: 1504 Ariz Title Bldg Phoenix AZ 85003

HASKELL, BARBARA, museum dir., b. San Diego, Nov. 13, 1946; d. John N. and Barbara (Freeman) Haskell; B.A., U. Cal. at Los Angeles, 1964-69. Dir. Exptl. Arts Festival U. Cal. at Los Angeles, 1966; asst. registrar Pasadena (Cal.) Museum Modern Art, 1969, curatorial asst., 1970, asst. curator, 1970, asso. currator, 1970-72, curator painting and sculpture, 1972-74, dir. exhbns., collections, 1974—. Home: 3725 Arbolada Rd Los Angeles CA 90027 Office: Pasadena Mus Modern Ar Colorado and Orange Grove Blvds Pasadena CA 91105

HASKEW, NANCY STONE (MRS. BALLARD LEE HASKEW), banker; b. Johnsonville, S.C., Mar. 18, 1939; d. William Austin and Pearline (McDaniel) Stone; student Mt. Olive Coll., 1956-57, Northwestern U., 1970, Sch. Bus. Adminstrn., U. S.C., 1972, Sch. Journalism, U. S.C., 1972; m. Ballard Lee Haskew, Sept. 30, 1970; children (by previous marriage)—William Wallace Altman III, Angela Nan Altman. With C & S Nat. Bank, Charleston, S.C., 1957-59; with Bankers Trust, Cola, S.C., 1962-65; with Southern Bank & Trust Co., Greenville, S.C., 1961-62; with Pamplico (S.C.) Bank & Trust, 1967-68; with Rogers, Newman & Cauthen, Inc., advt., pub. relations and marketing, Columbia, S.C., 1968-70, adminstrv. asst. to pres., 1968-70; dir. marketing The Nat. Bank of S.C. (Sumter), 1970—. Asst. dir. Carillon Ball, 1968-70; pub. chmn. United Fund, 1970-71. Mem. S.C. Bankers Assn., Nat. Assn. Bank Women (chmn. S.E. regional pub. relations com. 1973-74), Bank Marketing Assn. (S.C. chmn. nat. membership devel. com. 1973), Bank Adminstrn. Inst., Am. Fedn. Advertisers (membership com. 1972—), Am. Inst. Banking, Am. Women in Radio & TV (membership com. 1972—). Clubs: Taiwan Internat., U.S. Officers Wives, Air Force Officers Wives (Republic of China). Home: 516 N Hampton St Sumter SC 29150 also F108 Ya Ming Shan Republic of China Office: 207 N Main St Sumter SC 29150

HASKIN, DOROTHY CLARK (MRS. ROY A. HASKIN), author; b. Boston, Mar. 19, 1905; d. William and Evelyn (Howard) Clark; student Biola Coll., 1938; m. Roy A. Haskin, Feb. 13, 1932. Profl. actress and dancer, 1909-27; free-lance writer, 1940—. Moderator radio program Mission to Children on 20 stas. Founder Friendship Ministry Internat. Author books including God in My Kitchen, 1958; God in My Home, 1964; God in My Family, 1970; Let's Plan a Banquet, 1972. Home: 2573 Glen Green Hollywood CA 90068

HASKIN, MYRA RUTH, physician; b. Phila., Feb. 12, 1935; d. Phillip and Rose Cecilio (Frost) Singer; B.A., U. Pa.; M.D., Temple U.; children—Phyllis Dianna, Kenneth Geoffrey. Intern, Presbyn. Hosp. of U. Pa., 1960-61; resident phys. medicine and rehab. Hosp. of U. Pa., Phila., 1961-64, then mem. staff; practice medicine, Phila., 1965—; mem. staff VA Hosp., Phila. Home: 514 Ballytore Rd Wynnewood PA 19096 Office: VA Hosp University and Woodland Avs Philadelphia PA 19104

HASKIN, SUSAN MYRNETTE, librarian; b. Atlanta; d. Donald Raymond and Ruth Susan (Abbott) Haskin; B.A., Mich. State U., 1961; M.A., Western Mich. U., 1964. Tchr., Lansing (Mich.) Sch. Dist., 1961-62; with State Library Mich. Dept. Edn., Lansing, 1963—, order librarian, 1964-66, head librarian Blind and Physically Handicapped Library, 1966—. Mem. adv. council Mich. Braille Transcribing Service; mem. steering com. Radio Talking Book Service WKAR-FM. Mem. Am. (treas. round table on library service to blind 1967-69, chmn., 1972-73), Mich. (Walter H. Kaiser Meml. award 1973) library assns., Am. Assn. Workers for Blind, Beta Phi Mu. Home: 610 W Ottawa St Lansing MI 48933 Office: 735 E Michigan Av Lansing MI 48913

HASLBAUER, ANNA MARIE, psychologist; b. Miami, Fla., Nov. 11, 1941; d. Otto Frank and Phelma Marie (Andersen) Haslbauer; student Inst. Tech. y de Estudios Superiores de Monterrey, Mexico, 1959; A.B., U. Tenn., 1963; postgrad. U. Quito, Ecuador, 1964, U. Vienna, Austria, 1961; M.Ed., U. Ga., 1967, Ed.S., 1968. Tchr., German and Spanish, Dekalb County Bd. Edn., Decatur, Ga., 1963-66; teaching asst. U. Ga., Athens, 1967-68; sch. psychologist Atlanta Bd. Edn., 1968—. Cons., P.T.A., Atlanta, 1963-66, Nat. Orgn. for Women, 1972—. Active YWCA. Mem. Nat. Orgn. Women (dir., co-chmn. edn. com. 1973-74), Am., southeastern psychol. assns., Nat., Ga. assns. sch. psychologists, Safari Woods Civic Club, Atlanta Mental Health Assn., Delta Kappa Gamma, Sigma Delta Pi. Democrat. Episcopalian. Home: 573 Safari Circle Stone Mountain GA 30083 Office: Area IV Office Atlanta Pub Schs 2531 Gordon Rd Atlanta GA 30311

HASLEM, JANE NEHF (MRS. JOHN ARTHUR HASLEM), art gallery exec.; b. Knoxville, Tenn., Dec. 26, 1934; d. Andrew James and Carolyn (Anderson) Nehf; B.A., De Pauw U., 1956; postgrad. Ind. State U., 1956; m. John Arthur Haslem, Aug. 5, 1955; children—John Arthur, James Robert, Jeffrey Andrew. Tchr. art E. Mecklenburg and S. Mecklenburg High Schs., Charlotte, N.C., 1958-59; dir. Jane Haslem Gallery, Chapel Hill, N.C., 1960-65, Madison, Wis., 1965-69, exec. dir., 1969-71, Washington, 1969-71; pres., dir. Haslem Fine Arts, Inc., Washington, 1971—. Trustee, Md. Sch. Art and Design, Silver Spring, Md., 1973; bd. advisers Washington Printmaker Workshop. Mem. Art League No. Va., Washington Print Club, Alpha Phi. Home: 7006 Lovell Dr Hyattsville MD 20782 Office: 2121 P St NW Washington DC 20037

HASPEL, ELEANOR HARRIET COHEN, clin. psychologist; b. Bklyn., Dec. 11, 1944; d. Charles Issac and Gertrude (Takce) Cohen; B.A. cum laude (Regents scholar), City U. N.Y., 1965; M.A. (univ. fellow), U. Chgo., 1967, Ph.D. (univ. fellow), 1971; m. Lawrence Haspel, Aug. 15, 1965 (div. Dec. 1973); children—Charles Edward, Dyan Clarise. Instr. dept. psychology City U. N.Y., Bklyn., 1967-68, Roosevelt U., Chgo., 1968-70; advanced fellow clin. psychology Rush-Presbyn. St. Luke's Hosp., Chgo., 1972-73; freelance lectr., 1973—; individual practice clin. psychology. Mem. Am., Ill. psychol. assns., Analytical Psychology Club Chgo., Ill. Group Psychotherapy Soc., Effectiveness Tng. Assos. (orgnl. tng. div.). Author: Marriage in Trouble, 1975. Home: 1555 N Sandburg Terrace Chicago IL 60610 Office: 5 S Wabash Av Suite 1418 Chicago IL 60603

HASSELMEYER, EILEEN GRACE, health service adminstr.; b. Bklyn., May 23, 1924; d. Edwin Allen and Margaret Grace (Cody) Hasselmeyer; R.N. Bellevue Sch. Nursing, 1946; B.S., N.Y. U., 1954, M.S., 1956, Ph.D. (NIH Spl. fellow, Commonwealth fellow), 1963. Dir. Perinatal Biology and Infant Mortality br. Nat. Inst. Child Health and Human Devel., Bethesda, Md., 1969—. Goodrich vis. prof. Yale Sch. Nursing, 1968-69. Bd. dirs. USPHS, 1956—. Mem. Am. Nursing Assn. (mem. com. fetus and newborn 1968—), Am. Acad. Pediatrics, Sigma Theta Tau, Pi Lambda Theta. Author: Behavior Patterns of Premature Infanta, 1962; Horizons in Perinatal Research, 1974. Office: National Inst Child Health and Human Devel Bethesda MD 20014

HASSEMER, MARGUERITE CLAIRE, ednl. adminstr.; b. Bloomer, Wis., Dec. 17, 1916; d. Anton Valentine and Mary Theresa (Kramschuster) Hassemer; B.S., Mt. Mary Coll., Milw., 1950; M.A., Notre Dame U., 1957; M.S., Fordham U., 1962; Ph.D., U. Wis., 1968. Tchr. Sioux Indian Elementary Schs., Sisseton, S.D., 1936-48; tchr., Milw., 1948-49; tchr., asst. prin. Divine Savior High Sch., Milw., 1950-57; tchr. scis., maths., registrar and admissions Divine Savior Jr. Coll., 1958-59, 60-64; asst. prof. Mt. St. Paul Coll., Waukesha, Wis., 1964-65; grad. student, research asst. dept. entomology U. Wis.-Madison, 1965-68; project asso., 1968-70; head. div. edn. Notre Dame U., Nelson, B.C., Can., after 1970, now dir. Sch. Edn. Mem. Entomol. Soc. Am., A.A.A.S., Assn. Midwestern Coll. Biology Tchrs., Am. Inst. Biol. Scis., Sigma Xi, Phi Sigma. Contbr. articles to profl. pubs. Home: 514 Victoria St Nelson BC Canada Office: 820 10th St Nelson BC Canada

HASSENFELD, BARBARA L., state ofcl.; b. New Haven; student Conn. Coll. Women; A.B., Brandeis U., 1962; J.D., Boston Coll., 1965; m. Merrill I. Hassenfeld; 1 child. Admitted to Mass. bar, 1965, Fed. bar, 1966; since practiced in Boston; past. asst. dist. atty., Middlesex County, Mass.; commr. Mass. Dept. Pub. Utilities, Boston, 1973—; lectr. in field. Precinct capt. United Fund. Sec. adv. bd. Middlesex Community coll., 1972-73; bd. dirs. Women Concerned with Criminal Justice; incorporator Dial Help, Natick, Mass. Mem. Mass. (del. 1973-74, criminal law com. 1973-74), Boston (family law com. 1972-74), South Middlesex (legal aid com., vol. atty.), bar assns., Mass. Assn. Women Lawyers (pres. 1973-74, chmn. seminars), Internat. Fedn. Women Lawyers, Am. Arbitration Assn. (arbitrator). Address: 185 Devonshire St Boston MA 02110

HASTINGS, ANN JAMESON, real estate broker; b. Putnam, Conn., Aug. 18, 1934; d. Victor John and Jane Abbie (Seaver) Jameson; student Boston Mus. Sch. Fine Arts, 1953-54, Mass. Realtors Inst., 1968, 69, 70—; m. Elliot P. Hastings, May 8 (div. 1967); children—Deborah, Kimball, Andrea. Broker, Town & Country Real Estate, Amherst, Mass., 1968-70, sales mgr., broker, 1970-72, pres., 1972—; vice-chmn. Multiple Listing Service, 1973. Mem. Mass. Assn. Real Estate Bds. (edn. com. 1972), Hampshire County Bd. Realtors (chmn. edn. com. 1972), Nat. Inst. Real Estate Brokers, League Women Voters (mem. financial adv. com. 1973-74). Home: 132 High St Amherst MA 01002 Office: 79 S Pleasant St Amherst MA 01002

HASTINGS, DORTHY MARIE HAYES, educator, ednl. adminstr.; b. Bluemound, Kan., June 18, 1925; d. Earl Henry and Myrtle Marie (DeGraffenreid) Hayes; B.A., San Francisco State Coll., 1958 M.A., 1960; postgrad. U. Cal. at Berkeley, U. Pacific, Azusa Pacific Coll., Fresno State Coll., East Coast U., San Francisco State Coll.; m. Harold Clayton Hastings, Aug. 30, 1953 (div.); 1 dau., Lydia Joy. Youth and welfare worker Salvation Army, 1945-47; rural children's evangelist, Colo., 1948-50; reading specialist, psychometrist charge testing, audio-visual coordinator Pacifica High Sch., Pittsburg, Cal., 1962-65, sch. psychologist, reading co-ordinator, 1965-68; sch. psychologist Modesto (Cal.) City Schs., 1968-71; sch. psychologist El Dorado County office edn., Placerville, Cal., 1971—; pvt. practice, 1971—; dir. Sierra Counseling Services, 1972—. Instr., Workshop for Educationally Handicapped, San Francisco sch. dist., summer 1968; instr. U. Pacific, summer 1969. Speaker reading confs.; reading cons. Jr. High and High Sch.; ednl. and psychol. advisor to Berean Mission, Inc.; cons. Teen Challenge, Lodi, Cal. Served with WAC, 1951-53. Mem. Am. Personnel and Guidance Assn., Internat. Reading Assn., Nat., Central Cal. councils tchrs. English, No. Cal. Guidance Assn., Cal. Tchrs. Assn., Cal. Council for Adult Edn., D.A.V. (charter Sparks, Nev. chpt.), Cal. Assn. Sch. Psychologists and Psychometrists, Council for Exceptional Children, Nat. Educators Fellowship, Assn. Cal. Sch. Adminstrs., Cal. Psychol. Assn. (charter), Nat. Assn. Sch. Psychologists, Am. Assn. Marriage and Family Counselors (clin. mem.) Republican. Mem. Salvation Army. Contbr. articles to profl. jours. Home: PO Box 546 Placerville CA 95667 Office: 337 Placerville Dr Placerville CA 95667

HASTINGS, SYBIL BUTLER (MRS. MILO HASTINGS), business exec.; b. Farmington, Kan.; d. Charles Pardee and Mary (Wright) Butler; student pub. schs., Effingham, Kan.; m. Milo Hastings, Dec. 9, 1916 (dec. Feb. 1957); children—Edith (Mrs. John Charles Callahan Jr.), Warren. Sec., Dept. Labor, Washington, 1918; asst. to editor True Story Mag., 1919; sec. to prodn. mgr., reader, editor Dodd, Mead & Co., 1919-33; book cloth salesman, color cons., advt. mgr. Holliston Mills, N.Y.C., 1934-54; art dir., author, designer Color Notes, Columbia Mills, Inc., N.Y.C., 1954—. Mem. Am. Inst. Graphic Arts, Women's Nat. Book Assn. Contbr. articles to profl. pubs. Pioneer offset and silk screen book covers. Home: White Plains Rd Tarrytown NY 10591 Office: Columbia Mills Inc 101 Park Av New York City NY 10017

HASTY, SHIRLEY ANN FURY (MRS. JAMES L. HASTY), county ofcl.; b. Cortez, Colo., May 28, 1941; d. Paul and Mary Elizabeth (Winslow) Fury; student Western State Coll., 1959-60; m. James L. Hasty, Aug. 22, 1961; 1 dau., Lori Ann. Clk. Youngs Grocery, Dove Creek, Colo., 1955-56; legal sec. Guy B. Dyer, Jr., Atty., Dove Creek, 1957-59; pvt. sec. Union Carbide Corp., Dove Creek, 1960-63; bookkeeper Texaco, Inc., Dove Creek, 1963-65; dep. county clk. Dolores County, Dove Creek, 1965-69, dep. county treas., 1969-70, county treas., 1970—. Sec., treas. Dolores County Dem. Central Com., 1968—. Home: Dove St Dove Creek CO 81324 Office: Courthouse Dove Creek CO 81324

HATCH, ALLENE GATY (MRS. ALDEN R. HATCH), artist, author; b. Morristown, N.J., Jan. , 1926; d. Theodore Emmett and Jean (Gardner) Gaty; student Bard Coll., 1941-42, Fashion Acad., 1944-45, Columbia, 1945, Art Student's League, 1963-64; m. Alden R. Hatch, Sept. 9, 1950. Asst. art dir. Allied Display Corp., 1945-47; artist N.Y. Daily News, 1947, Edwin Freed Advt. Agy., 1948-50; illustrator books Henry Holt & Co., Prentice Hall, Inc., Am. Heritage mag., Doubleday & Co., Inc., Crown Pubs., Inc., 1950—; articles and cartoons for Barrytown Explorer; painter portraits in U.S., Europe. Com. mem. Windham Children's Service. Mem. Colonial Dames Am. Republican. Episcopalian. Author, illustrator: Menopause Can Be Fun, 1972. Home: Quartermile Germantown NY 12526

HATCH, LUCILE, librarian, educator; b. Walla Walla, Wash., Mar. 25, 1913; d. Arthur Davis and Blanche (Craft) Hatch; B.A. in Fgn. Langs., State Coll. Wash., 1935; B.S. in L.S., U. Denver, 1946; M.Ed., U. Ore., 1954; postgrad. advanced study program Columbia U. Grad. Sch. Library Service, 1969-70. Tchr., librarian Dayton (Wash.) High Sch., 1935-42; tchr. fgn. langs. Wapato (Wash.) High Sch., 1942-43; librarian Shumway Jr. High Sch., Vancouver, Wash., 1943-51, Lincoln High Sch., Tacoma, 1951-52, Sharples Jr. High Sch., Seattle, 1952-54, 55-56; vis. prof. U. Wash. Sch. Librarianship, 1954-55; asso. prof. Grad. Sch. Librarianship U. Denver, 1956-65, prof., 1965—, acting dean, 1966-68; vis. instr. U. Ore., summers 1949-51; cons. Sch. Library Jour., 1954-62; mem. library com. Field Enterprises Edn. Corp., 1965-73. Mem. Colo., Mountain Plains library assns. (chmn. young people's div. 1957-58), A.L.A. (life, chmn. mag. evaluation com. young adults services div. 1957-62, pres. 1962-63, mem. council, 1962-63, commn. on nat. plan for library edn. 1962-67, vice chmn., chmn. elect tchrs. sect., library edn. div. 1969-70, chmn. 1970-71), N.E.A. (life), Am. (dir. region, 1960-62, chmn. nominating com. 1967-68, chmn. Distinguished Library Service award for sch. adminstrs. jury 1968-69), Colo. assns. sch. librarians, Am. Assn. Library Schs., Phi Beta Kappa, Phi Kappa Phi, Pi Lambda Theta. Mem. Christian Ch. Club: Women's Faculty. Contbr. articles to profl. jours. Home: 2350 E Iliff Av Denver CO 80210

HATCH, MARY GIES (MRS. DAVID LINCOLN HATCH), educator; b. Omaha, Feb. 17, 1913; d. Charles George and Jane Elizabeth (Sturman) Gies; A.B., Vassar Coll., 1935; postgrad. (Vassar fellow) U. Heidelberg, 1935; M.A., U. Mich., 1937; Ph.D. (univ. scholar), Syracuse U., 1952; m. David Lincoln Hatch, Aug. 24, 1940; children—Charles Winthrop, Mary Abby (Mrs. Joel Cleland), Faith (Mrs. William Mann), Elizabeth Ann. Tchr., Detroit pub. schs., 1937-38, Montclair (N.J.) High Sch., 1938-40, Dana Hall, Wellesley, Mass., 1940-42; prof. German, Columbia Coll., Columbia, S.C., 1960—, chmn. German dept., 1963—. Columbia Coll. Research grantee, 1964; So. Assn. Research grantee, 1968. Mem. Modern Lang. Assn., Am. Assn. Tchrs. German, Am. Sociol. Assn., Phi Beta Kappa. Contbr. articles to profl. jours. Home: 2420 Terrace Way Columbia SC 29205

HATCH, PHYLLIS J., social worker; b. Rochester, N.Y., Nov. 8, 1927; d. Charles J. and Jennie (Brooks) Hatch; B.A., Middlebury Coll., 1949; M.S.S., Fordham U., 1958. With YWCA, 1949-57, teen age and adult program dir., Pottsville, Pa., 1949-52, Holyoke, Mass., 1952-53, health edn., recreation and camping adminstr., Reading, Pa., 1953-54, camp dir., Scranton, Pa., 1955-57; county office supr. Catholic Home Bur. for Dependent Children, Newburgh, N.Y., 1954-72; psychotherapist Orange County Mental Health Clinic, 1968-69; pvt. practice psychotherapy, Newburgh, N.Y., 1969—. Instr. field work Fordham U., 1961-62, Russell Sage U., 1964, 66. Mem. Newburgh Bd. Edn., 1961-66; youth work and health clinic vol. Community Workers Assn., 1958-60; mem. Newburgh Council for Community Affairs, 1955—, dir., 1956-66, 68-70, pres. 1958-60, 68-69; mem. Orange County Council for Social Services, 1955-66. Mem. Nat. Assn. Social Workers (pres. Hudson Valley chpt. 1962-66, del. Nat. Assembly on Human Rights 1964-65, Nat. Del. Assembly 1967-71), Acad. Certified Social Workers, Orange County Social Workers Club, Soc. Clin. Social Workers. Democrat. Roman Catholic. Home: 1 Paffendorf Dr Newburgh NY 12550

HATCHER, MARTHA OLIVIA TAYLOR (MRS. FRANK PRIDGEN HATCHER, SR.), educator; b. Birmingham, Ala., Feb. 17, 1920; d. Sanford Allia and Mary (McCullough) Taylor; B.S., Howard Coll., 1936-40; M.Ed. in Sci. Edn., U. Ga., 1966, Ed.D., 1973; tchrs. certificate Breanu Coll., 1964; m. Frank Pridgen Hatcher, Sr., Nov. 7, 1941; children—Frank Pridgen, Martha Elizabeth, Nancy Louise. Chief bacteriologist vet. div. Ga. Dept. Agr., Atlanta, 1943-45; supr. surg. pathology lab. Jefferson Hillman Hosp., Med. Coll. Ala., Birmingham, 1945-46, research asst. in pathology, 1945-46; mgr. offices Fran Mar Farms, Inc., Gainesville, Ga., 1957-66; instr. biology Gainesville Jr. Coll., 1966-67, asso. prof. biology, 1967, acting chmn. div. natural scis. and maths., 1968-74, chmn., 1974—; accompanist music dept. Brenau Coll., Gainesville, 1959-61. Chmn. Gray Ladies Vol. Services, Gainesville chpt. A.R.C., 1957-62; sec. Yohah Council Girl Scouts Am., 1959-61. Bd. dirs. Community Concert Assn. Gainesville, 1968-70. NSF Sci. Faculty fellow in microbiology, 1970-71. Mem. Am. Assn. U. Profs., A.A.A.S., Am. Guild Organists, Am. Inst. Biol. Scis., Nat., Ga. edn. assns., Nat. Assn. Biology Tchrs., Assn. S.E. Biologists, Nat. Assn. Research Sci. Teaching, Ga. Acad. Sci. Nat. Sci. Tchrs. Assn., Am. Legion Aux. (pres. 1948-50), Am.

Soc. Zoologists, U.D.C. (chpt. pres. 1949-51), Nat. Faculty Assn. Community and Jr. Colls., Am. Soc. Microbiology, Am. Assn. U. Women, Kappa Delta Pi, Alpha Epsilon Delta, Delta Kappa Gamma, Delta Zeta. Clubs: Music (pres. 1950-52), Federated Music (sec. 1957-58) (Gainesville), Phoenix Soc. Home: 840 Memorial Dr NE Gainesville GA 30501 Office: PO Box 1358 Gainesville Jr Coll Gainesville GA 30501

HATCHER, MILDRED (OBERA), educator; b. Murray, Ky.; d. William Thomas and Lorena (Taylor) Hatcher; B.S. magna cum laude, Murray State U., 1927; M.A., George Peabody Coll. Tchrs., 1930, postgrad., summers 1932, 48; postgrad. Vanderbilt U., 1930, U. Wis., summer, 1947, Ind. U., summer 1964; D. Litt., Protestant Episcopal U., 1966. Asst. prin., head English dept. Hardin (Ky.) High Sch., 1927-29; tchr. math. city pub. schs., Paducah, Ky., 1930-34; tchr. English, Paducah Tilghman High Sch., 1934-48; critic tchr. Murray State U., summer 1946, asst. prof. English, 1960-61, asso. prof. English, 1961—; asst. prof., then asso. prof. English Austin Peay State U., Clarkville, Tenn., 1948-60. Commd. Ky. col., 1967; recipient St. Andrews Ecumenical research fellowship intercollegiate, London, Eng., 1967. Mem. Marquis Biog. soc. (adv. bd. 1969), South Atlantic Modern Lang. Assn. (folklore div.), Conf. Coll. Composition and Communication, Nat. Council Tchrs. English (del. 1958-69, spl. pub. relations rep. golden anniversary 1960, dir. 1958-72, judge ann. awards 1961, 62, 63, mem. pub. relations com., program participant, liaison officer 1960-72), Ky. (dir. 1966-67, v.p. 1968-70, pres. 1970-72), Tenn. (pres. 1958-60, v.p. 1967), Miss. folklore socs., Ky. Hist. Soc., Middle Tenn. English Assn. (v.p. 1959, pres. 1960, liaison officer 1959-60), U.D.C. (pres. 1955-57), D.A.R. (chpt. regent 1953-54), Murray State U. Alumni Assn. (life; v.p. 1945-46), Kappa Delta Pi, Delta Kappa Gamma, Chi Alpha Pi. Baptist. Clubs: Murray Woman's, National Writers. Author articles and poems in profl. jours. Poems included in ann. Nat. Poetry Anthology, 1953-60. Collector of folklore. Home: 1305 Olive Blvd Murray KY 42071 Address: Box 1281 Murray State U Murray KY 42071

HATCHER, SHERRY LYNN (MRS. ROBERT LESLIE HATCHER), clin. psychologist; b. N.Y.C., July 13, 1944; d. Henry and Pearl (Olitsky) Marcus; B.A., City U. N.Y., 1965; M.A. (Woodrow Wilson fellow), U. Mich., 1966, Ph.D., 1972; m. Robert Leslie Hatcher, May 17, 1970; 1 dau., Jessamyn Anne. Clin. intern U. Mich. Psychol. Clinic, Ann Arbor, 1967-69, 71, research intern neuropsychiat. inst., 1970, staff psychologist student health service, 1972—; lectr. dept. clin. psychology U. Mich., Ann Arbor, 1974—. Mem. Am. Psychol. Assn., Phi Beta Kappa. Home: 3534 Frederick Dr Ann Arbor MI 48105 Office: U Mich Mental Health Clinic Student Health Service 207 Fletcher St Ann Arbor MI 48104

HATCHETT, EDITH RUBY, ret. banker; b. Stephenville, Tex., Jan. 17, 1902; d. John B. and Martha Christina (Preston) Hatchett; grad. high sch. Sec., State Nat. Bank, Big Spring, Tex., 1923-26, teller, 1926-29, asst. cashier, 1929-44, cashier, 1944-50, asst. v.p., 1950, v.p.-cashier, 1950-51, v.p., 1951-74. Baptist. Home: 1303 Johnson St Big Spring TX 79720 Office: Box 1271 Big Spring TX 79720

HATCHETT, META RUTH, ret. educator; b. nr. Durant, Okla., Oct. 20, 1905; d. Jesse Mercer and Meta Belle (Yarborough) Hatchett; B.A., U. Okla., 1926, M.A., 1940, postgrad., 1952-53; B.S., Southeastern State Coll., 1927; postgrad. Okla. State U., 1954, 57. In pvt. bus., 1927-36; chmn. dept. English, Atoka (Okla.) High Sch., 1936-43, Durant (Okla.) High Sch., 1943-46; asst. prof. English, Southeastern State Coll., Durant, 1946-71, asst. prof. emeritus, 1971—, also prof. logic and philosophy. Owner and operator farm, Durant, 1945—. Named Tchr. of Year, Southeastern State Coll., 1967. Mem. Modern Lang. Assn., Coll. English Assn., Nat. Council Tchrs. English, Okla. Edn. Assn., Am. Assn. U. Profs., Am. Assn. U. Women (pres. Durant 1952-54), D.A.R., Delta Kappa Gamma, Phi Alpha Theta, Theta Sigma Phi, Pi Kappa Delta. Democrat. Baptist. Home: Box 334 Star Route Durant OK 74701

HATFIELD, ANTOINETTE KUZMANICH (MRS. MARK ODOM HATFIELD), wife of U.S. Senator from Ore.; b. Portland, Ore., Jan. 17, 1929; d. Vincent and Josephine (Leovich) Kuzmanich; B.S., U. Ore., 1950; M.A., Stanford, 1955; m. Mark Odom Hatfield, July 8, 1958; children—Elizabeth, Mark Odom, Theresa, Charles Vincent. Tchr., counselor J. L. Parrish, Jr. High Sch., Salem, Ore., 1950-54; resident asst. Stanford, 1954-55, asst. dir. Roble Hall, 1955-56; tchr., counselor Grant High Sch., Portland State Coll., 1957-58. Mem. Assistance League, Salem, 1962—. Mem. Ore. Fedn. Republican Women, 1957—. Mem. N.E.A., Daus. of Nile, Am. Newspaper Women's Club (asso.), Delta Kappa Gamma, Alpha Phi. Author: Remarkable Recipes, 1966; More Remarkable Recipes, 1970; Food for Fellowship, 1972; co-author: Help! My Child Won't Eat Right, 1973. Address: PO Box 630 Newport OR 97365

HATFIELD, CAROL SUTHERLAND (MRS. THOMAS MARVIN HATFIELD), writer; b. McCamey, Tex., Apr. 10, 1935; d. Thomas Shelton and Lois Peyton (Hartley) Sutherland; B.J., U. Tex., Austin, 1956, postgrad., 1962-64, 73—; m. Thomas Marvin Hatfield, Oct. 24, 1959; children—Thomas Sutherland, Alice Elizabeth, Sara Carol. Editorial asst. Nat. Geog. Soc., 1957-59; ednl. writer News Service, U. Tex., 1964-66; pub. information dir. John Tyler Coll., Chester, Va., 1967-69; information dir. bd. trustees workshop U. Cal. at Los Angeles, 1970; ednl. writer S.W. Ednl. Devel. Lab., Austin, 1971-73, coordinator children's folklore program, 1973—. Bd. dirs. Austin Mental Health Assn. Mem. Women in Communication (pres. Austin profl. chpt., mem. task force long-range planning, nat. chmn. advancement fund). Author articles and research documents in field. Home: 408 W 32d St Austin TX 78705 Office: 211 E 7th St Austin TX 78701

HATFIELD, FRANCES STOKES, ednl. adminstr.; b. Tennille, Ga., Feb. 2, 1922; d. Lee P. and Frances M. (Murchison) Hatfield; B.S., Fla. State Coll. for Women, 1943; M.A., Fla. State U., 1949. Tchr., Ft. Lauderdale High Sch., 1943-47; dir. instructional materials Broward County Schs., Ft. Lauderdale, 1947—. Cons. Nat. Def. Edn. Act Insts. Sch. Librarians, 1960-65. Mem. N.E.A., Assn. Supervision and Curriculum Devel., Am., Fla. library assns., Am. (pres. 1971-72), Fla. (pres. 1966-67) assns. sch. librarians, Fla. Audio-Visual Assn. (pres. 1955-56), Delta Kappa Gamma, Beta Phi Mu, Alpha Xi Delta. Democrat. Baptist. Club: Soroptimist (pres. 1961-62) (Ft. Lauderdale). Contbr. articles to profl. jours. Home: 2601 Clematis Pl Fort Lauderdale FL 33301 Office: 1320 SW 4th St Fort Lauderdale FL 33312

HATHAWAY, FRANCES HILL, writer; b. Cleve., July 28, 1937; d. John David and Margaret Frances (Goldberg) Hill; B.S., Northwestern U., 1959, M.S., 1960; m. Harvey R. Hathaway, June 11, 1960; children—Wendy, Julia, Eric. Editorial staff Together mag., Chgo., 1960, Personnel World mag., Chgo., 1961, World Book Ency., Chgo., 1963; free lance writer Saturday Evening Post, 1962, Today newspaper, Cocoa, Fla., 1968; staff writer Palm Beach Times, West Palm Beach, 1969-74, Palm Beach Post, 1974—. Treas., Alcohol and Drug Abuse Council, 1972. Bd. dirs. United Way of Palm Beach County, 1974—. Mem. Women in Communications, Women's Aux. Palm Beach County Med. Soc. (dir. 1970-72), Jr. League Palm Beaches (chmn. grants com. 1973—, dir. 1974-75), League Women Voters, Fla. Press Club, Alpha Delta Pi. Methodist. Home: 4143 Hickory Dr Palm Beach Gardens FL 33410 Office: 2751 S Dixie Hwy West Palm Beach FL 33402

HATLER, MARY ESTHER RIDENOUR (MRS. CALEB GAYLORD HATLER), coll. dean; b. Tunis, Mont., Sept. 30, 1914; d. Vitallis Elmore and Bertha Esther (White) Ridenour; student No. Mont. Coll., 1931-32, 67, Eastern Mt. Coll., 1968, Nat. Tng. Inst., Carroll Coll., Ore. State U., Eastern Wash. State Coll., 1969, N.W. Christian Coll., 1970, 71, U. Ore., Stanford, 1973; m. Caleb Gaylord Hatler, Aug. 4, 1935; children—Gaylord Eugene, Russell Keith, Donald Wayne, Gerald Oval. Tchr., Chouteau County, Mont., 1932-35, Ft. Belknap Indian Reservation, 1936-38, 39-40; sales clk. Woolworth Dept. Store, Havre, Mont., 1938-39; br. librarian, Great Falls, Mont., 1950-51; sales clk., dept. mgr. Sears Roebuck & Co., Great Falls, 1951-56, toy dept. mgr., 1959-60, 63; collections clk. Electrolux Co., 1959; tchr., Hill County, Mont., 1966-69; dean women N.W. Christian Coll., Eugene, Ore., 1970—. Pres., Jr. High W., P.T.A., Great Falls, 1953-54, pres. council, 1954-55; chmn. spiritual and family life com. Mont. State P.T.A., 1964-66. Mem. N.E.A., Mont. Edn. Assn., Smithsonian Instn., Christian Deans Assn. Republican. Mem. Christian Ch. Address: PO Box 10814 Eugene OR 97401

HATTERER, MYRA SCHATZBERG (MRS. LAWRENCE J. HATTERER), psychiatrist; b. Vienna, Austria, Aug. 11, 1934; came to U.S., 1940, naturalized, 1945; d. Emanuel and Cila (Diamond) Schatzberg; B.A., N.Y. U., 1955; M.D., N.Y. Med. Coll., 1959; m. Lawrence John Hatterer, June 9, 1957; children—Julie Anne, Jane Paula. Intern Lenox Hill Hosp., N.Y.C., 1959-60; resident in psychiatry N.Y. Psychiat. Inst., 1960-63, Presbyn. Hosp.; practice medicine specializing in adolescent and adult psychiatry, N.Y.C., 1963—; asst. to dir. adolescent service N.Y. Psychiatric Inst., 1963-65, asso. attending psychiatrist, 1963; research asso. St. Lukes Hosp., 1965-70; psychiat. cons. Riverdale Sch. for Girls, 1964—; instr. Columbia U. Med. Sch., 1963. Nat. Inst. Mental Health grantee, 1965-70. Mem. Am. Psychiat. Assn., Soc. for Adolescent Psychiatry, Phi Beta Kappa, Mu Chi Sigma, Beta Lambda Sigma, Alpha Omega Alpha. Hostess (with Lawrence J. Hatterer) TV show Freely Speaking, 1971. Home: 167 E 79th St New York City NY 10021

HAUCK, HELEN GIFFIN, librarian; b. Springfield, O., Mar. 6, 1911; d. Charles Frederick and Myrl Middleton (Giffin) Hauck; A.B., Wittenberg Coll., 1933; B.S. in L.S., Western Res. U., 1933; M.A., U. Mich., 1943. Cataloger, Wittenberg Coll., Springfield, 1933-35; periodical librarian U. Cin., 1935-37; librarian Blackburn Coll., Carlinville, Ill., 1937-41, Westminster (Pa.) Coll., 1941-43, USAAF, 1944-46; reference librarian Rensselaer Poly. Inst., Troy, N.Y., 1947-49, research labs. Westinghouse Electric Corp., Pitts., 1950-52, Lewis Research Center, NACA-NASA, Cleve., 1954-60; head sci. and tech. dept. Cleve. Pub. Library, 1960—. Mem. A.L.A., Spl. Libraries Assn. Editor (with Allan S. Quinn) Business and Technology Sources, 1965—. Home: 11820 Lake Av Lakewood OH 44107 Office: 325 Superior Av Cleveland OH 44114

HAUENSTEIN, MARGARET LENA, librarian; b. Wooster, O., Dec. 14, 1913; d. Edward Harry and Sylvia (Frazier) Hauenstein; B.A., Coll. Wooster, 1935; B.S. in L.S., Western Res. U., 1938; postgrad. (Quarrie Library fellow), U. Chgo., 1941-42. Librarian, Wooster High Sch., 1936-40; reference asst. Cleve. Pub. Library, 1940-51, head Stevenson room for young people, 1952-54, asst. pub. relations, 1954-57, asst. head philosophy, psychology and religion dept., 1958-66; head Berea br. Cuyahoga County (O.) Pub. Library, 1968; dir. Wayne County Pub. Library, Wooster, 1969—. Mem. Am., Ohio (intellectual freedom com. 1969-70, nominating com. 1971-72) library assns., Phi Beta Kappa. Mem. United Ch. of Christ. Clubs: Quota, Wednesday Women's (Wooster). Home: 506 E Beverly Rd Wooster OH 44691 Office: 304 N Market St Wooster OH 44691

HAUGEN, BETTY M. CHILDRESS (MRS. ELMER NOLAN HAUGEN), nurse, educator; b. Hamilton, Mont.; d. Walter Louis and Bessie (Chapman) Childress; B.S., U. Ore., 1948, M.S., 1962; m. Elmer Nolan Haugen, Feb. 14, 1942; children—Mark Alan, Jon Thomas. Asst. supr. surg. dept. Emanual Hosp., Portland, Ore., 1941-42; office nurse Drs. Phillips, Boyd, Staats, Portland, 1942; supr. surg. dept. Emanuel Hosp., Portland, 1942-45, Santa Barbara (Cal.) Cottage Hosp., 1945; evening supr. Walker Clinic and Hosp., Eugene, Ore., 1945-46; supr. operating room VA Hosp., Portland, 1948-59; instr. U. Ore. Sch. Nursing, Portland, 1962-65, asst. prof., 1965-67; chmn. nursing dept. So. Ore. Coll., Ashland, 1967—. Mem. Ore. State Health Commn. Mem. exec. com. Jackson County Lung Assn., 1968—; pres. Ore. Bd. Nursing. Bd. dirs. Ore. Bd. Nursing. Mem. Am. (chmn. operating room forum 1968-70), Ore. nurses assns., Nat., Ore. leagues for nursing, Bus. and Profl. Womens Club (pres. 1970-71), Beta Sigma Phi. Club: Altrusa (Medford, Ore.). Home: 205 Granite St Ashland OR 97520 Office: 1250 Siskiyou Blvd Ashland OR 97520

HAUGEN, CHRISTINE MARIE (MRS. EDMUND EARL HAUGEN), occupational therapist; b. Colorado Springs, Colo., May 30, 1948; d. Wesley Neil and Mary Ellen (Howard) Pettigrew; student, Kan. Wesleyan U., 1966-67; B.S., U. Washington, 1971; m. Edmund Earl Haugen, Aug. 19, 1968. Research asst. Dept. Occupational Therapy, U. Wash., Seattle, 1969; clin. student supr. for occupational therapy students and interns Lake Wash. Spl. Edn. Center, Lake Wash. Sch. Dist. #414, Kirkland, 1971—. Mem. Wash. Supt. of Pub. Instructions Standing Com. for Revision of House Bill 90, 1973-74. Mem. Am., Wash. (treas. 1973—) occupational therapy assns., Nat. (mem. rep. assembly 1973-74), Wash. (mem. rep. assembly 1974), Lake Wash. (mem. exec. com. 1973-74) edn. assns., Soc. for Exceptional Children, Wash. Assn. for Retarded Children. Home: 13393 SE 137th Pl Renton WA 98055 Office: 11133 NE 65th St Kirkland WA 98033

HAUGH, DOLORES NORMA GEORGE (MRS. ROBERT WARREN HAUGH), editor; b. Chgo., Oct. 2, 1923; d. Sanford Orville and Norma Lucille (Leonard) George; A.A., Wright Jr. Coll., 1943; student Chgo. Art Inst., 1943-45; m. Robert Warren Haugh, Aug. 24, 1946 (dec. 1972); children—Cheryl Eileen, Sandra Alison. Feature writer Paddock Publs., Arlington Heights, Ill., 1958-66; woman's editor Day Publs., Field Enterprises, Arlington Heights, 1966-70; Woman's editor Mt. Prospect Times, 1970-73, mng. editor, 1972-73; news editor Mt. Prospect Topics, Shepherd Pub., Palatine, Ill., 1973; pub. relations dir. Village of Mt. Prospect, 1974—. Founder Mt. Prospect Art League, 1961, Mt. Prospect TOPS, 1962 (pres. 1963), Mt. Prospect Hist. Soc., 1968 (dir. 1968—), Mt. Prospect Craft Artistes, 1968 (pres. 1968—). Recipient awards including Pioneer Founders award medal, 1968; Ill. Sesquicentennial award, 1969; Environmental award U.S. Brewer's Assn., 1971, Shell Oil, 1972; Distinguished Service award Mt. Prospect Jr. C. of C., 1973; Mate E. Palmer award Ill. Woman's Press Assn., 1968, 70, 71, 72, also Silver Feather award, 1968, 70, 71; Nat. Fedn. Press Women award, 1971; Service award Harper Coll., 1972. Mem. Nat. Fedn. Bus. and Profl. Women's Club, Art Inst. Alumni Assn., Women in Communication, Ill. Press Photographers Assn., Izaak Walton League Am. (founder Mt. Prospect chpt., pres. 1972-74), Questers, Inc. (founder Scrimshaw chpt., pres. 1970-72). Author: (with Fern Schneider) Mount Prospect Pioneer Cook Book, 1969. Home: 7 S Edward St Mount Propect IL 60056 Office: 112 E Northwest Hwy Mount Prospect IL 60056

HAUGHTON, CAROLYN DIANE LANDSEM, logging supply co. exec.; b. Lebanon, Ore., Mar. 16, 1941; d. Theodore Norman and Helen (Beard) Landsem; student Edison Tech. Sch., 1958-59, Murphy Bus. Coll., 1958-59; children—Debra R., Craig A. With Molalla Iron Works, Inc. (Ore.), 1959—, pres., 1966—; pres. T. & C. Investment Corp., 1966—. Mem. Molalla C. of C. Lutheran. Home: Route 2 Box 168 Molalla OR 97038 Office: PO Box 121 Molalla OR 97038

HAUK, PATRICIA GERTRUDE, coll. adminstr.; b. Altoona, Pa., Nov. 6, 1928; d. James Walter and Anna Beatrice (Nugent) Hauk; B.A., Seton Hill Coll., 1956; M.A., Cath. U. Am., 1958, Ph.D., 1968. Instr. psychology lab. Seton Hill Coll., Greensburg, Pa., 1953-56, asst. prof. psychology, 1957-61, asso. prof., 1962-68; asso. prof. psychology Marillac Coll., St. Louis, 1968-69; prof. psychology, dean student acad. affairs Bowie (Md.) State Coll., 1969—. Mem. Nat. Assn. of Coll. Deans, Registrars and Admissions Officers (mem. exec. com. 1973—), Am., Md. psychol. assns., Am. Conf. Acad. Deans, Md. Assn. Higher Edn. Home: 1780 Crofton Pkwy Crofton MD 21113 Office: Bowie State College Bowie MD 20715

HAUN, ANN LYNN ESSLINGER, educator; b. Huntsville, Ala., Sept. 4, 1935; d. William Francis and Anna Mae (Linthicum) Esslinger; student Auburn U., 1953-54, U. Miami, Coral Gables, Fla., 1954; B.S. cum laude, S.W. Mo. State Coll., 1959; M.Ed., U. Mo., 1961, Ph.D., 1968; m. Cosmo L. Haun, Aug. 19, 1962 (div. Feb. 1969); 1 son, Gregory C. Tchr. home econs., 1958-59; tchr. English, Springfield, Mo., 1959-60; head personnel asst. U. Mo., 1960-61; grad. asst. U. Mo., 1961-62, research asst., 1962, Gregory fellow, 1962-63, research asst., 1964; elementary sch. counselor, Smyrna, Ga., 1965-67; asst. prof. Ga. State Coll., Atlanta, 1968-69; asst. prof. edn. Cal. State U., Sacramento, 1969-73, asso. prof., 1973—, chairperson dept. Counselor edn., 1973—. Mem. profl. adv. com. Suicide Prevention Service, 1970-71. Mem. Am. Personnel and Guidance Assn. (chairperson commn. women 1972-74), Am. Psychol. Assn., Assn. for Counselor Edn. and Supervision, Western Assn. Counselor Edn. and Supervision, Sacramento Area Sch. Psychologists and Psychometrists, Western Psychol. Assn., Sacramento Community Commn. for Women, Faculty Women's Assn. (pres. 1973-74), Nat. Orgn. Women. Home: 8335 Caribbean Way Sacramento CA 95826 Office: 6000 J St Sacramento CA 95819

HAUPT, ENID ANNENBERG, mag. editor-pub.; b. Chgo.; d. Moses Louis and Sadie (Friedman) Annenberg; student Mt. Ida Sem., Newton, Mass.; m. Ira Haupt, Aug. 11, 1936. Spl. corr. Phila. Inquirer, 1942-53, asst. to pub., 1953-54; pub., editor-in-chief Seventeen mag., N.Y.C., 1954—; author nationally syndicated column, Young Living, 1958-65. Recipient awards from French Republic, Govt. of Netherlands, Pan Am. Union, U.S. Com. for UNICEF, Ladies Aux. V.F.W. for work with young people. Author: The Seventeen Book of Young Living, 1957; The Seventeen Book of Etiquette and Entertaining, 1963; The Seventeen Guide to Your Widening World, 1965. Office: 320 Park Av New York City NY 10022

HAUSER, HELEN CATHERINE KNAPP (MRS. JAMES JULIUS HAUSER), realtor; b. Los Angeles, Jan. 28, 1921; d. Byron McDonald and Helen Catherine (Kegley) Knapp; B.S. in Home Econs., Ia. State U., 1943; M.S. in Higher Edn., U. So. Cal., 1952; m. James Julius Hauser, Sept. 14, 1945; children—Catherine Ann (Mrs. Gregory P. Woodson), Charles Knapp. Home economist So. Counties Gas Co., Los Angeles, 1943-45; instr. foods Purdue U., Lafayette, Ind., 1945-46; instr. home econs. Los Angeles City Coll., 1948-52, 54-56; instr. Cal. State Coll., Los Angeles, 1954-56; salesman real estate Arcadia, Cal., 1958-62; broker real estate, mgr. Beach & Flaaten, Inc., Arcadia, 1962—. Mem. women's aux. Meth. Hosp. of So. Cal., 1955-60, Huntington Meml. Hosp., 1968-70. Mem. Cal. Home Econs. Assn. (past dir.), Cal. Real Estate Assn. (dir. 1970—), Nat. Assn. Real Estate Bds. (womens council Arcadia chpt. 1962—), Arcadia Realty Bd. (bd. govs. 1968—), Arcadia Bd. Realtors (1st v.p.; Salesman of Year 1972), Pi Lamba Theta, P.E.O. (pres. chpt. 1965-67), Pi Beta Phi (pres. Pasadena alumnae 1967-69). Home: 1910 Highland Oaks Dr Arcadia CA 91006 Office: 150 N Santa Anita Dr Arcadia CA 91006

HAUSER, RITA ELEANORE ABRAMS (MRS. GUSTAVE M. HAUSER), lawyer, UN ofcl.; b. N.Y.C., July 12, 1934; d. Nathan and Frieda (Lit) Abrams; A.B., Hunter Coll., 1954; Dr. Polit. Economy (Fulbright grantee), U. Strasbourg (France), 1955; LL.B., Harvard, 1956, N.Y. U., 1958, licence en droit, U. Paris (France), 1956; LL.D., Seton Hall U., 1969, Finch Coll., 1969, U. Miami, 1971; m. Gustave M. Hauser, June 10, 1956; children—Glenvil, Patricia. Admitted to D.C. bar, 1959, N.Y. bar, 1961; practice law specializing in internat. law, N.Y.C., 1961—; partner firm Stroock & Stroock & Lavan, 1972—; dir. First Empire Bank, N.Y.C. U.S. rep. UN Commn. on Human Rights, 1969-73; mem. U.S. delegation to gen. assembly UN, 1969; mem. U.S. Adv. Commn. Internat. Ednl. and Cultural Affairs. Mem. N.Y. City Bd. Higher Edn. Trustee Inst. Internat. Edn.; bd. dirs. Legal Aid Soc. N.Y. Mem. Am. Soc. Internat. Law (mem. bd.), Am. Arbitration Assn., Legal Aid Soc. N.Y., Inst. Internat. Edn., Council Fgn. Relation, Phi Beta Kappa Assos. Republican. Contbr. articles on internat. law to profl. jours. Home: 130 East End Av New York City NY 10028 Office: 61 Broadway New York City NY 10006

HAUSERMAN, JOAN WEAVER (MRS. DANIEL MARTIN HAUSERMAN), realtor; b. Kansas City, Mo., July 15, 1928; d. Eli Milton and Halsene Adelaide (Eckert) Weaver; student U. Ark., 1946, U. Cal. at Los Angeles, 1948; A.B. in Drama, Immaculate Heart Coll., Los Angeles, 1949; m. Daniel Martin Hauserman, June 19, 1948; children—Susan (Mrs. David Bellomy), Julia (Mrs. Frank Perachiotti), Mary (Mrs. John Carnell), Daniel Martin, Timothy, Heidi. Real estate salesman Tahoe Assos., Tahoe City, Cal., 1962-66; co-owner, broker Hauserman Real Estate, brokerage and devel. firm, Tahoe City, 1966—. Pres., St. Raymond's Mothers' Club, Menlo Park, Cal., 1959; active Children's Theater, San Francisco, 1958-61, Sierra Winter Stock Co., Tahoe, 1962—; mem. Lake Tahoe Archtl. Rev. Com. Mem. Tahoe Sierra Bd. Realtors (sec. 1973). Republican. Roman Catholic (pres. ch. guild 1963, pres. women's community service group 1971-72). Clubs: Lake Tahoe Ski, Lake Tahoe Yacht. Home: 3180 Edgewater Dr Tahoe City CA 95730 Office: PO Box 907 Tahoe City CA 95730

HAUVER, CONSTANCE CARVER LONGSHORE (MRS. ARTHUR RONALD HAUVER), lawyer; b. Abington, Pa., Oct. 9, 1938; d. Malcolm Rettew and Margaret Evans (Lyon) Longshore; student Wellesley Coll., 1956-58; B.A. magna cum laude, Swarthmore Coll., 1960; M.A. (Nat. Def. Fgn. Lang. fellow), U. Cal. at Los Angeles, 1962; J.D. magna cum laude, U. Denver, 1967; m. Arthur Ronald Hauver, Sept. 1, 1962; 1 dau., Sian. Researcher Friends Com. on Nat. Legislation, Washington, 1960-61; lectr. polit. sci. U. Hawaii Coll. Gen. Studies, 1963-64; admitted to Colo. bar, 1968; since practiced in Denver; asso., Dawson, Nagel, Sherman & Howard, Denver, 1968-73, partner, 1973—. Mem. alumni council Swarthmore Coll., 1971-74. Mem. Am., Colo., Denver (1st v.p. 1974-75) bar assns., Rocky Mountain Estate Planning Council (treas. 1973-74), Order St. Ives. Asso. editor Denver Law Jour., 1966-67. Home: 5825

Bell Flower Dr Littleton CO 80123 Office: First Nat Bank Bldg Denver CO 80202

HAVEL, SISTER FRANCES ANN, hosp. adminstr.; b. Milligan, Neb., July 6, 1925; d. Emil A. and Antonie (Laun) Havel; R.N., St. Elizabeth Hosp. Sch. Nursing, 1946; B.S. in Nursing, Loretto Heights Coll., 1962; M. Hosp. Adminstrn., St. Louis U., 1964. Joined Sisters of St. Francis Order, 1947; operating room supr. various hosps. of Sisters of St. Francis, 1948-61; asst. adminstr. St. Elizabeth Hosp., Lincoln, Neb., 1964, adminstr., 1965-68; adminstr. St. Francis Hosp., Grand Island, Neb., 1968—. Bd. dirs. Hall County chpt. A.R.C., United Way, Grand Island. Mem. Am. Coll. Hosp. Adminstrs., Neb. Cath. Hosp. Assn. (exec. bd.), Altrusa Internat. Home and office: 1310 W Charles Grand Island NE 68801

HAVELOCK, CHRISTINE MITCHELL (MRS. ERIC A. HAVELOCK), coll. adminstr.; b. Cochrane, Ont., Can., June 2, 1924 (came to U.S. 1948); d. William Waterson and Annie Margaret (Graham) Mitchell; B.S., U. Toronto (Ont.), 1946; Ph.D. (Charles Eliot Norton fellow), Harvard, 1958; m. Eric A. Havelock, Nov. 21, 1962. Mem. faculty Vassar Coll., Poughkeepsie, N.Y., 1953—, chmn. art dept., 1968-71, asst. to pres., 1972-73. Mem. mng. com. Am. Sch. Classical Studies, Athens, Greece. Mem. Am. Inst. Archeology, Coll. Art Assn., Am. Assn. U. Women. Author: Hellenistic Art, 1971. Home and office: Vassar Coll Poughkeepsie NY 12601

HAVEMAN, JOSEPHA, educator; b. The Netherlands, Mar. 19, 1931; d. Aloysius Alphonsus Ostendorf and June Wyndham-Smeets; B.A. in Art with honors, San Francisco State Coll., 1956, M.A. in Fine Arts, 1966; postgrad. anthropology U. Cal. at Berkeley, 1957-61; m. Douglas Havemann, Oct. 23, 1954 (div.). Mus. artist, photographer U. Cal. Mus. Anthropology, Berkeley, 1958-61; crafts dir. U.S. Spl. Services, Heidelberg and Würzburg, Germany, 1962-64; instr. U. Cal. at Berkeley, 1965-66; pres., exec. dir. Image Circle, Inc., Berkeley, 1967—; asso. prof. photography Cal. Coll. Arts and Crafts, Oakland, 1968—. Free-lance photographer, writer, 1965—. Mem. Am. Assn. U. Profs., Soc. Photog. Edn., Friends of Photography, Internat. Mus. Photography, San Francisco Women Artists. Author: Workbook in Creative Photography, 1971. Address: Box 9063 Berkeley CA 94709

HAVEMEYER, RUTH NAOMI (MRS. R. NEIL FOLEY), pharm. co. exec.; b. N.Y.C., July 28, 1932; d. Gustav Adolph and Ida (Aufmkolk) Havemeyer; B.S., Columbia, 1953; M.S., Purdue U., 1955; Ph.D., U. Wis., 1960; m. R. Neil Foley, Aug. 17, 1968. Research scientist Squibb Inst. for Med. Research, New Brunswick, N.J., 1960-66; group leader Syntex Corp., Palo Alto, Cal., 1966-72, product devel. mgr., 1972—. Fellow A.A.A.S.; mem. Sigma Xi, Sigma Delta Epsilon. Patentee in field. Office: 3401 Hillview Av Palo Alto CA 94304

HAVENS, ISABELLE, microbiologist; b. McGill, Nev.; d. George Walter and Helen (Campbell) Havens; A.B., Western Coll., Oxford, O., 1935; M.S., U. Chgo., 1956. Asso. dir. clin. microbiology labs. Minn. State Sanatorium, Ah-gwah-ching, Minn., 1937, Litchfield County Hosp., Winsted, Conn., 1938-41, Station Hosp., Baer Field, Ft. Wayne, Ind., 1941-42, Charleroi-Monessen Hosp., Charleroi, Pa., 1942-44; with dept. microbiology U. Chgo., 1944-48, research asst. dept. medicine, 1948-58, research asso., 1958-69; microbiologist St. Joseph Mercy Hosp., Pontiac, Mich., 1969—; clin. instr. med. tech. Coll. Human Medicine Mich. State U. Recipient Hillkowitz Meml. award, Am. Soc. Med. Technologists, 1957; gold award Ill. State Med. Soc., 1956; named Employee of Yr., U. Chgo. Clinics, 1961, Ill. Med. Technologist of Yr., 1963; Corning award Am. Soc. Med. Technologists, 1964. Fellow Royal Soc. Health; mem. A.A.A.S., Am., Mich. pub. health assns., Am., Mich. soc. microbiology, Mich., Pontiac Soc. Med. Technologists, Ill. Acad. Sci., Am. Soc. Med. Technologists (editorial bd. Am. Jour. Med. Tech.), Ill. Med. Technologists Assn. (past pres.), Sigma Xi, Sigma Delta Epsilon. Research on immunity to cholera, Endamoeba histolytica, surg. infections, and respiratory flora. Home: 323 N Eton St Birmingham MI 48008 Office: 900 Woodward Av Pontiac MI 48053

HAVENS, JEANETTE LYNN, ednl. adminstr.; b. Jamestown, N.Y., Aug. 31, 1948; d. Ira Tull and Mae (Thompson) Havens; B.A. (N.Y. State Regents scholar, Seneca Nation Ednl. Found. grantee), Syracuse U., 1970. Asst. camp troop leader Girl Scout U.S.A. council Buffalo and Erie County, Holland, N.Y., 1966-67; copy editor Syracuse U. Daily Orange, 1969-70; free-lance journalist various publs., 1970-71; home-sch. liaison, ednl. counselor Seneca Nation Indians Edn. Program, Irving, N.Y., 1973—. Co-adviser Silver Creek Central Sch., Am. Indian Youth Orgn., 1973—; mem. Appalachian Trail Conf., 1972-73. Active Girl Scouts U.S.A. Mem. Women in Communications, Recreation Equipment, Soc. Profl. Journalists, Iroquois Seneca Archaeol. Soc., Mensa. Home: RD 1 Box 135 Gowanda NY 14070 Office: Saylor Bldg Irving NY 14081

HAVENS, SHIRLEY ELISE, editor; b. N.Y.C., Nov. 19, 1925; d. A. Barton and Eva Elizabeth (Havens) Havens; B.A. cum laude, Hunter Coll., 1947; postgrad. Columbia, 1947-52. Sec. to exec. sec. Mental Health Film Bd., N.Y.C., 1952-54; asst. to librarian Carnegie Endowment for Internat. Peace, N.Y.C., 1954-57; editorial asst. Library Jour., N.Y.C., 1957-59, mng. editor, 1959-66, asst. editor, 1966, asso. editor, 1967—, editor ann. archtl. issue, 1962-66. Mem. library com. Pres.'s Com. on Employment of Handicapped, 1963—. Mem. A.L.A., Phi Beta Kappa. Club: New York Library (editor bull. 1965-67). Contbr. articles to library jours. Office: 1180 Av of Americas New York City NY 10036

HAVERSTICK, MARTHA J., educator; b. Lititz, Pa., Dec. 23, 1921; d. Clayton Dietrich and Margaret (Heiss) Haverstick; B.S., Pa. State Coll., 1943; M.S., U. Wis., 1950; Ed.D., Boston U., 1962. Tchr., Sheffield (Pa.) Sch. Dist., 1943-44, Kendall (N.Y.) Central Sch., 1944-48; part-time instr. YWCA, Madison, Wis., 1948-50; instr., asst. prof. U. Md., College Park, 1950-62; asso. prof. Slippery Rock (Pa.) State Coll., 1962-63, prof. phys. edn., 1963—, coordinator womens program in phys. edn., 1962-71, asst. chmn. dept. phys. edn., 1973—. Counselor, head counselor Summer Girls Camps, summers 1940-59. Mem. A.A.H.P.E.R., Pa. Assn. for Health, Phys. Edn. and Recreation, Eastern Assn. for Phys. Edn. Coll. Women, Assn. Supervision and Curriculum Devel., Pa. Edn. Assn., N.E.A., Am. Bus. Women's Assn. (chpt. pres., One of Top 10 Women of Year 1971). Asso. editor Research Quar., 1965-68. Home: RD 1 Slippery Rock PA 16057

HAVERSTOCK, MARY SAYRE (MRS. NATHAN ALFRED HAVERSTOCK), writer; b. Cambridge, Mass., June 24, 1932; d. Daniel Clemens and Rosamond (Foster) Sayre; A.B., Radcliffe Coll., 1954; m. Nathan Alfred Haverstock, May 22, 1954; children—Rosamond, Daniel, Julia, Jonathan, Gwendolyn. Contbg. editor Art in Am. Mag., 1963-68; art critic Washington Post, 1964; free lance writer, 1965—. Author: Indian Gallery: The Story of George Catlin, 1973. Home and office: 1122 S 22nd St Arlington VA 22202

HAVICE, SHIRLEY L., social worker; b. Kalamazoo, Dec. 10, 1935; d. Owen Walter and Anna (Endres) Havice; student U. Mich., 1953-54; B.A., Western Mich. U., 1957; M.S.W., U. Mich., 1960. Social worker VA Hosp., Buffalo, 1960—. Mem. Nat. Assn. Social Workers (past pres., chmn. Northeastern Regional Inst. 1968), Acad. Certified Social Workers, Bus. and Profl. Womens Club (past pres.), 99s Internat., Zonta Internat. Methodist. Home: 4733 Bailey Av Buffalo NY 14226 Office: 3495 Bailey Av Buffalo NY 14215

HAVILAND, CAMILLA KLEIN (MRS. JOHN BODMAN HAVILAND), judge; b. Dodge City, Kan., Sept. 13, 1926; d. Robert Godfrey Haviland and Lelah (Luther) Haviland Klein; A.A., Monticello Coll., 1946; B.A., Radcliffe Coll., 1948; LL.B., Kan. U. Sch. Law, 1955, J.D., 1968; m. John Bodman Haviland, Sept. 13, 1926. Admitted to Kan. bar, 1955, Fed. bar, 1955; pvt. practice law, Wichita, Kan., 1955-56, Dodge City, Kan., 1956-57; judge Probate County and Juvenile Cts., Ford County, Kan., 1957—. Mem. Kan. Atty. Gen's. Youth Com., 1962-66, Kan. Jud. Council Probate Law Study Com., 1973. Nat. committeewoman Young Democrats of Kan., 1948-54; v.p. Young Dem. Clubs Am., 1953-55. Mem. president's council St. Mary of Plains Coll., 1961-67; bd. dirs. Cascade (Colo.) Property Owners Assn., 1964-70, mem. adv. bd. Salvation Army, Dodge City, 1966—; mem. adv. council Kan. U. Sch. Religion, 1970—, Kan. U. Sch. Social Welfare, 1972—. Recipient Nathan Burkan Meml. award in copyright law A.S.C.A.P., 1955; certificate of recognition Nat. Council Juvenile Ct. Judges, 1966. Mem. Am. (mem. probate and real estate com. 1967—), Kan., Southwest Kan. (sec., treas. 1957-70, 1971-73; pres. 1970-71, Ford-Gray County bar assns., Kan. Probate Judges Assn. (pres. 1963-64), P.E.O., D.A.R., Am. Legion. Club: Soroptimist (Dodge City). Author: Poems by Camilla, 1948; also articles in Kan. Law Rev. Home: 203 W LaMesa Dr Dodge City KS 67801 Office: 705 1st Av Dodge City KS 67801

HAVILAND, LEONA, librarian; b. Stamford, Conn., Nov. 10, 1916; d. Howard Brush and Ada Grace (Jewell) Haviland; B.S., U. Ala., 1940; M.S., U. Ill., 1951; postgrad. Columbia U., 1943, 56-60; m. Warren John Burke, Sept. 10, 1973. Jr. asst. Ferguson Library, Stamford, Conn., 1936-37, summers 1938-39, sr. asst., 1940-44; student asst. U. Ala., 1937-40; asst. to cataloguer U.S. Nat. Mus. Library, Washington, 1944-48; librarian Arts and Industries Mus., Smithsonian Instn. Washington, 1948-50; reference librarian U.S. Mcht. Marine Acad., Kings Point, N.Y., 1952—. Mem. council YWCA, Washington, 1945-47. Mem. A.L.A., Spl. Libraries Assn. (past group membership chmn.), L.I. Hist. Soc., N.Y. Geneal. and Biog. Soc., Smithsonian Assos., South Street Seaport Mus., Alpha Beta Alpha, Alpha Lambda Delta. Office: US Mcht Marine Acad Library Kings Point NY 11024 Home: 286 West Lane Revonah Woods Stamford CT 06905

HAVILAND, VIRGINIA, librarian; b. Rochester, N.Y., May 21, 1911; d. William J. and Bertha M. (Esten) Haviland; B.A., Cornell U., 1933. With Boston Pub. Library, 1934-63, successively children's librarian, br. librarian, 1934-52, reader's adviser for children, 1952-63; lectr. in library services to children Simmons Coll. Sch. Library Service, 1957-63; head children's book sect. Library of Congress, Washington, 1963—; profl. reviewer children's books Horn Book Mag., 1952—; lectr. children's lit. Trinity Coll., 1969—. Mem. Newbery-Caldecott award com., 1951-63, chmn., 1953-54; judge N.Y. Herald Tribune Spring Book Festival awards, 1955, 57, Spring Book Festival, Book World, 1968, Nat. Book award for children's books, 1969; mem. jury Hans Christian Andersen internat. children's book award, 1959-68, pres., 1971-74. U.S. del., conf. Internat. Bd. on Books for Young People, Vienna, 1955, Florence, Italy, 1958, Luxembourg, 1960, Hamburg, 1962, Madrid, 1964, Ljubljana, 1966, Amriswil, Switzerland, 1968, Bologna, 1970, Nice, 1972, Rio de Janeiro, 1974, Internat. Fedn. Library Assns., Belgium, 1955, Sweden, 1960, Scotland, 1962, Bulgaria, 1963, Italy, 1964, Finland, 1965, Netherlands, 1966, Can., 1967, Germany, 1968, Denmark, 1969, USSR, 1970, Eng., 1971, Hungary, 1972, working congress children's librarians in Scheveningen, Holland, 1959, Grenoble, France, 1973. Mem. A.L.A., Children's Library Assn. (chmn. 1954-55), Soc. Women Geographers, Pi Lambda Theta. Author: The Travelogue Storybook of the Nineteenth Century, 1950; William Penn, Founder and Friend, 1952; Favorite Fairy Tales Told in England, 1959; Favorite Fairy Tales Told in Germany, 1959; Favorite Fairy Tales Told in France, 1959. Compiler 100 Best Books for Children, 1956; Favorite Fairy Tales Told in Russia, 1961; Favorite Fairy Tales Told in Norway, 1961; Favorite Fairy Tales Told in Ireland, 1961; Favorite Fairy Tales Told in Scotland, 1963; Favorite Fairy Tales Told in Spain, 1963; Favorite Fairy Tales Told in Poland, 1963; Ruth Sawyer, 1965; Favorite Fairy Tales Told in Italy, 1965; Favorite Fairy Tales Told in Czechoslovakia, 1966; Favorite Fairy Tales Told in Sweden, 1966; Favorite Fairy Tales Told in Japan, 1967; Favorite Fairy Tales Told in Greece, 1969; (with William J. Smith) Children and Poetry, 1969; Favorite Fairy Tales Told in Denmark, 1971; The Wide World of Children's Books, 1972; A Fairy Tale Treasury, 1972; Favorite Fairy Tales Told in India, 1973. Editor: Children's Literature: A Guide to Reference Sources, 1966, 1st supplement, 1972; Books in Search of Children, 1969; Children's Books of Internat. Interest, 1972; Children and Literature, 1973; Yankee Doodle's Literary Sampler, 1974. Home: Harbour Sq 520 N St SW Washington DC 20024 Office: Library of Congress Washington DC 20540

HAVIR, EVELYN ANN, biochemist; b. Scranton, Pa., Sept. 5, 1933; d. Thomas and Ann (Pohonish) Havir; B.A., Beaver Coll., 1955; M.A., Temple U., 1957; Ph.D., Cornell U., 1962. Postdoctoral fellow N.Y. Pub. Health Research Inst., 1962-64; research asso. dept. biochemistry Conn. Expt. Sta., New Haven, 1965—. Mem. Am. Soc. Biol. Chemists, Am. Soc. Plant Physiologists, Sigma Xi. Contbr. articles to profl. jours. Home: 545 Whitney Av New Haven CT 06511 Office: Box 1106 New Haven CT 06504

HAWES, CAROLYN LORING, ednl. adminstr.; b. Providence, R.I.; d. Willard Maitland and Veronica Francis (Walsh) Hawes; B.S., U. R.I., 1950; M.A., Columbia U., 1952. Vocational counselor Cornell U., Ithaca, N.Y., 1952-57; asst. dean, office of dean of women Boston U., 1957-63; with R.I. Sch. of Design, Providence, 1963—, dir. career planning and placement and equal opportunity, 1973—. Cons. on placement functions Union of Ind. Colleges of Art, 1970—. Chmn. personnel com. Girl Scouts of R.I., Providence, 1965-70; mem. subcom. on employment policies and practices R.I. Permanent Adv. Commn. on Women, Providence, 1971—. Bd. dirs. Big Sisters Assn. of R.I., 1972—. Mem. Nat. Assn. Women Deans and Counselors, Am. Personnel and Guidance Assn., Am. Assn. U. Women, Eastern Coll. Personnel Officers (chmn. pub. relations com. 1972—). Clubs: Providence Art, Turks Head (Providence). Home: 22 Luzon Av Providence RI 02906

HAWES, EVELYN JOHNSON (MRS. NAT H. HAWES), author; b. Colville, Wash.; d. W. Lon and Iva (Dickey) Johnson; student U. Wash., 1932-33, 35-36, 37, Wash. State U., 1933-34; postgrad. U. Cin., 1948-49, Purdue U., 1950-51, State U. N.Y. at Buffalo, 1957-58; m. Nat H. Hawes, July 25, 1937; 1 dau., Linda (Mrs. James Alexander Clever). Faculty speech U. Wash., 1941-47; faculty world lit. U. Cin., 1950; mem. faculty State U. N.Y. at Buffalo, 1972. Mem. Service League, Michigan City, Ind., 1952. Bd. dirs. Friends of Library, Wash. State U. Recipient certificate Achievement, Buffalo and Erie County Hist. Soc., 1970. Mem. Am. Assn. U. Women, Nat. League Am. Pen Women (Founders medal for writing Western N.Y. br. 1955, past pres. Western N.Y. br.; mem. nat. letters bd. 1968-70, chmn. nat. letters bd. 1970—, 5th v.p. 1972-74), Women Aux. Meyer Meml. Hosp. Buffalo, Buffalo and Erie County Med. Hist. Soc., Salvation Army Assn., World Hospitality Assn., YMCA, Nat. Assn. Pub. Sch. Educators, U. Wash. Alumni Assn., Chi Omega. Author: Proud Vision, The History of Buffalo General Hospital: The First Hundred Years, 1964; The Happy Land, 1965; A Madras-Type Jacket, 1967; The Twentieth Century Club of Buffalo: 1894-1969, 1969; Six Nights a Week, 1971. Contbr. short stories, articles to mags. Home: Northside Apts Apt D 10550 NE 29th St Bellevue WA 98004

HAWES, LILLA KENNERLY MILLS (MRS. FOREMAN MCCONNELL HAWES), librarian; b. Camden, S.C., Feb. 1, 1908; d. Laurens Tenney and Margaret (Johnstone) Mills; A.B., Agnes Scott Coll., 1928; B.S. in L.S., George Peabody Coll., 1939; m. Foreman McConnell Hawes, May 29, 1936. Sec. chemistry dept. Ga. Inst. Tech., 1930-36; gen. asst. Savannah (Ga.) Pub. Library, 1937-40, reference asst., 1941-43, br. librarian, 1943-48; dir. Ga. Hist. Soc., 1948—. Mem. Savannah-Chatham County Historic Site and Monument Commn., 1954-67, sec., 1955-67. Rec. sec. Youth Mus. Savannah, 1954-56, corr. sec., 1962-64, trustee, 1954-66; bd. dirs. Friends of the Library, 1950-65, v.p., 1950-52; bd. dirs. Historic Savannah Found., 1955-59, 67—, award of merit, 1967. Mem. Am. Assn. U. Women (sec. Ga. div. 1943-45, dir. local br. 1954-58), Savannah Hist. Research Assn. (pres. 1946-48), Nat. Soc. Colonial Dames Am. (dir. 1961-64, chmn. Savannah regional com. 1962-64), So. Hist. Assn., Am. Assn. State and Local History, Soc. Am. Archivists, Southeastern, Ga. library assns., League Women Voters, Telfair Acad. Arts and Scis., Pi Gamma Mu, Delta Kappa Gamma. Presbyn. Editor: Collections of Ga. Hist. Soc., 1952, 64. Home: 1134 E 49th St Savannah GA 31404 Office: 501 Whitaker St Savannah GA 31401

HAWES, NANCYE ELIZABETH (MRS. GEORGE JASON HAWES), newspaperwoman; b. Somerset, Ky., Mar. 10, 1932; d. William Henderson and Ava Agnes (Foster) Smith; grad. high sch.; m. George Jason Hawes, Feb. 11, 1950; children—George Kelly, William Kevin, Kimberly Ellen. With Anderson (Ind.) Herald, 1965—, bridal editor, 1967-68, women's editor, 1968-72, editor Accent on Living, 1972-74, asst. news editor, 1974—. Chmn., Mental Health Blue Bell Ball Com., 1965; asst. leader Wapehani council Girl Scouts U.S.A., 1971; pub. relations dir. Kikthawenund council Boy Scouts Am., 1966-70. Del., Republican State Conv., 1970, 72; dir. Madison County Women's Rep. Club, 1970-72; mem. Hoosiers for Equal Rights Amendment. Bd. dirs. Madison County Assn. for Mental Health, 1965-73, Planned Parenthood Madison County, A.R.C. Recipient Unknown Scout award, 1957; award Women's Press Club Ind., 1969, 71, 72; certificate of merit Heart Fund Ind., 1971. Mem. Women's Orch. Guild, YWCA, N.A.A.C.P., Urban League, Indpls. Press Club, Lady Elks, Women of Moose, Women in Communications, Women's Press Club Ind. (editor state newsletter), Nat. Fedn. Press Women, Sigma Delta Chi. Beta Sigma Phi (Girl of Year award 1964), Sigma Delta Chi. Mem. Christian Ch. Clubs: Exchangettes (v.p. 1970-72) Soroptimist (pres. 1970-72). Home: 5122 Pearl St Anderson IN 46014 Office: PO Box 1090 Anderson IN 46015

HAWIRKO, ROMA ZENOVEA, educator; b. Winnipeg, Man., Can., July 27, 1919; d. John and Anna (Juba) Hawirko; B.S., U. Man., 1940; M.S., McGill U., 1949, Ph.D., 1951. Med. technician Deer Lodge Mil. Hosp., Winnipeg, 1942-47; asst. prof. dept. microbiology U. Man., Winnipeg, 1951-61, asso. prof., 1961-72, prof., 1972—. Mem. senate U. Man., 1966-69. Nat. Research Council of Can. operating grantee, 1971—, Canadian Fed. Fisheries Research grantee, 1966-73. Mem. Canadian Soc. Microbiologists, Am. Soc. Microbiology, Soc. for Gen. Microbiology, World Fedn. for Culture Collections, A.A.A.S. Clubs: University Women's, Altrusa (pres. 1969-71) (Winnipeg). Home: 5-185 Spence St Winnipeg MB R3C 1Y5 Canada Office: Dept Microbiology U Manitoba Winnipeg MB R3T 2N2 Canada

HAWK, ELEANOR DOROTHY, educator; b. Phillipsburg, N.J., Jan. 29, 1914; d. Frank L. and Leila (Carey) Hawk; B.A., Wilson Coll., 1935; M.Ed., Rutgers U., 1949; postgrad. Muhlenberg Coll., Trenton State Coll., Newark State Coll. Tchr. Latin and English, Matawan (N.J.) High Sch., 1937-47; guidance counselor New Brunswick (N.J.) High Sch., 1947-71, chmn. guidance dept., 1971—. Treas. New Brunswick YWCA, 1963-64. Recipient distinguished service award Middlesex County Guidance Council, 1966, Alumni Assn. Sch. Edn., Rutgers U., 1967. Mem. Am. Sch. Counselors Assn. (treas. 1964-67, bd. govs. 1968-71), Am. (meals and interests coordinator 1971 conv.), N.J. (v.p. 1954-56, bd. govs. 1967-70) personnel and guidance assns., N.E.A., Nat. Vocational Guidance Assn., N.J., New Brunswick (exec. com. 1959-71) edn. assns., Middlesex County Edn. Assn. (scholarship chmn. 1955-66), Middlesex County Council P.T.A.'s (bd. mgrs. 1967-69, 72-74), Middlesex County Guidance Council (pres. 1963-64), Alumni Assn. Sch. Edn. Rutgers U. (v.p. 1962-64), N.J. Schoolwomen's Club (exec. bd. 1971-73), Zonta (corr. sec. 1972-73, rec. sec. 1973-74), Kappa Delta Pi. Club: Raritan Valley Women's (charter, 1st sec. 1970). Home: 1153 Livingston Av North Brunswick NJ 08002 Office: 1125 Livingston Av New Brunswick NJ 08902

HAWKES, ARLYS JEAN (MRS. DENNIS LITCHFIELD HAWKES), newspaper exec.; b. Menomonie, Wis., Nov. 5, 1933; d. Guy Lymann and Mildred Elsie (Rasmusson) Hamann; B.S. in Home Econs., U. Wis.-Stout, 1955; m. Dennis Litchfield Hawkes, Oct. 15, 1954; children—Stephen Guy, Thomas Lester. Dietician, South Chgo. Community Hosp., 1955; asst. chemistry control lab. Malt & Barley Lab., Madison, Wis., 1956; co-owner, editor, bookkeeper Leader Printing Co., Lake Mills, Wis., 1965—. Mem. Wis. Press Assn., Lake Mills C. of C., Alpha Sigma Alpha. Club: Lake Mills Dance (pres. 1974). Home: 312 W Prospect St Lake Mills WI 53551 Office: 316 N Main St Lake Mills WI 53551

HAWKINS, CORNELIA FRANCES (MRS. FRANCIS CLAIBORNE HAWKINS II), librarian; b. Porterville, Cal., Jan. 5, 1916; d. Cornelius Francicus and Maude Eleanor (Porter) Keuzenkamp; A.B., E. Carolina U., 1942; M.A., George Peabody Coll., 1950; m. Francis Claiborne Hawkins II, Dec. 28, 1950; children—Francis, John, James. High sch. tchr., N.C., 1942-49, librarian, 1950-60; head librarian Sch. of the Ozarks, Point Lookout, Mo., 1960-64, Westark Coll., Ft. Smith, Ark., 1964-65, Cottey Coll., Nevada, Mo., 1965—. Home: 620 S Olive St Nevada MO 64772 Office: Cottey College Nevada MO 64772

HAWKINS, ELINOR DIXON (MRS. CARROLL WOODARD HAWKINS), librarian; b. Masontown, W.Va., Sept. 25, 1927; d. Thomas Fitchie and Susan (Reed) Dixon; A.B., Fairmont State Coll., 1949; B.S., U. N.C., 1950; m. Carroll Woodard Hawkins, June 24, 1951; 1 son, John Carroll. Children's librarian Enoch Pratt Free Library, Balt., 1950-51; head circulation dept. Greensboro (N.C.) Pub. Library, 1951-56; librarian Craven-Pamlico Library Service, New Bern, N.C., 1958-62; dir. Craven-Pamlico-Carteret Regional Library, New Bern, 1962—. Storyteller children's TV program Tele-Story Time, Greensboro, New Bern, 1952-58, 63—. Mem. New Bern-Craven County Bicentennial Commn., 1973—. Mem. N.C. Assn. for Retarded Children, N.C. Library Assn., Friends of Library. Baptist. Club: Pilot Internat. (pres. Greensboro 1957-58). Home: PO

Box 57 Cove City NC 28523 Office: 400 Johnson St New Bern NC 28560

HAWKINS, JULIA MAE YOUNG (MRS. CHARLES C. HAWKINS), social worker, state ofcl.; b. St. Augustine, Fla.; d. Abraham L. and Ida (Pappy) Young; A.B., Talladega Coll., 1931; grad. (Urban League fellow 1931-33) N.Y. Sch. Social Work, 1933; m. Charles Clinton Hawkins, May 31, 1932; children—Charles Clinton III, Homer C. Case worker, St. Louis, 1933-35; sr. med. social worker N.Y. State Dept. Welfare, N.Y.C., 1938; med. social work supr. N.Y.C. Dept. Welfare, 1935-46; dist. case supr. W.Va. Dept. Welfare, 1954-57, dist. casework supr. I, 1957-59, tng. supr., 1959-63, asst. dir. staff devel., Charleston, 1963-66; dir. foster grandparents program W.Va. Dept. Mental Health, Charleston, 1966—. Active civic and community affairs. Mem. Nat. Assn. Social Workers, Acad. Certified Social Workers, Am. Pub. Welfare Assn. (com. on social work edn. and personnel 1963-65), Columbia U. Sch. Social Work Alumni (dir. 1964-66), Delta Sigma Theta. Roman Catholic. Club: Links (charter mem. pres. 1952-54) (Charleston). Home: 219 Brookhaven Dr Nitro WV 25143 Office: WVa Dept Mental Health State Capitol Bldg Charleston WV 25305

HAWKINS, LUCY ELLA ROGERS (MRS. ANDREW BRYAN HAWKINS), editor; b. Kimball, Wis., June 19, 1896; d. Jay Philip and Mary Emma (Newberry) Rogers; B.A., U. Wis., 1918, M.A. 1921; m. Andrew Bryan Hawkins, Dec. 24, 1922. Asst. editor U. Wis. Press Bur., 1918-20; publicity sec. Detroit YWCA, 1920-22; editorial asst. Christian Century, Chgo., 1922-23; sec., publicity writer Northland Coll., Ashland, Wis., 1925-27; feature, editorial writer Evanston (Ill.) News-Index, 1927-29, 1932-33; asst. sec. City Club, Milw., 1929-32; free lance writer, 1933-44, 1961-66; mng. editor Jour. Am. Oil Chemists, Soc., 1944-61, exec. sec., 1947-61. Lectr. Medill Sch. Journalism, Northwestern U., 1938-57. Bd. dirs. U. Wis. Alumni Assn., 1939-55, Mary Thompson Hosp., Chgo., 1951-63. Mem. D.A.R., Am. Assn. U. Women, English-Speaking Union, Walker Art Center, Mpls. Soc. Fine Arts, Art Inst. Chgo., Wis., Minn. hist. socs., Women in Communications. Conglist. Address: Calhoun Beach Hotel 2925 Dean Blvd Minneapolis MN 55416

HAWKINS, PAULA, mem. Republican Nat. Com., state ofcl.; b. Salt Lake City; d. Paul B. and Leoan (Staley) Fickes; student Utah State U.; m. Walter Eugene Hawkins, Sept. 5, 1947; children—Genean, Kevin Brent, Kelley Ann. Pub. service commr. State of Fla., Tallahassee, 1972—. Republican precinct committeewoman Orange County, Fla., 1965—; speakers chmn. Fla. Rep. Exec. Com., 1967-69; mem. Fla. Rep. Nat. Conv., 1968, Nat. Fedn. Rep. Women, 1965—; bd. dirs. Fla. Fedn. Rep. Women, 1968—; mem. Rep. Nat. Com. for Fla., 1968—; mem. adv. council Nat. Young Rep. Fedn., 1971—; chmn. host com., mem. rules com. Rep. Nat. Conv., 1972; So. regional rep. Rep. Nat. Com., 1972—. Mem. Maitland Civic Center, 1965—; charter mem. bd. dirs. Fla. Ams. Constl. Action Com. of 100, 1966—, sec.-treas., 1966—; mem. Central Fla. Museum Speakers Bur., 1967-68; mem. Gov. Fla. Commn. Status Women, 1968-71; chmn. legislative com. Orange County Drug Abuse Council, 1970; co-chmn. Orange County March of Dimes, 1970. Recipient citation for service Fla. Rep. Party, 1966-67; Above and Beyond award as outstanding woman in Fla. politics, 1968; nominated Orange County Woman of Year, Maitland Womans Club, 1969. Mem. Maitland C. of C. (chmn. congl. action com. 1969). Mem. Ch. of Jesus Christ of Latter-day Saints (pres. Relief Soc., Orlando Stake 1963-64, sunday sch. tchr. 1964—). Clubs: Winter Park (Fla.) Racquet; Maitland Woman's. Home: 241 Dommerich Dr Maitland FL 32751 Office: Fla Pub Service Commn 700 S Adams St Tallahassee FL 32301

HAWKINS, ROBBIE FITE (MRS. JONATHAN HAWKINS), clubwoman; b. Early Grove, Miss., Jan. 12, 1905; d. William Robert and Cara Arnold (Davis) Fite; certificate in piano, classical diploma Miss. Synodical Coll., 1922; A.B., U. Miss., 1924, postgrad., summers 1928-63; postgrad. U. Tenn., 1930-31, Academia Americana, Rome, Italy, summer 1930, Memphis State U., 1963-64; m. Jonathan Dean Hawkins, Oct. 19, 1935; 1 son, Jonathan Dean. Tchr. English, Latin, Napoleonville (La.) High Sch., 1924-27, Snowden Jr. High Sch., Memphis, 1928-35; tchr. conversational French, The Hutchison Sch. for Girls, Memphis, 1952-54; tchr. English, Latin, 1956-64. D.A.R. rep. City Beautiful Com., Memphis, 1965-66; mem. steering com. Yellow Fever Meml. Monument, 1965; mem. Mayor's Citizens' Com. to Aid the Blind, Memphis, 1970—; mem. Memphis in May Internat. Festival, Inc. Bd. dirs. Mid South Eye Bank for Sight Restoration, Meth. Hosp., Memphis, 1970—. Ky. Col. Recipient citation and medal Memphis Soc. S.A.R., 1970; certificate of appreciation Sr. Citizens, Inc., Memphis, 1969, 70. Mem. Nat. Soc. So. Dames Am. (nat. v.p. for Tenn. 1965-67, nat. meml. scholarship chmn., 1965-67, nat. edn. chmn., 1967-69, nat. chaplain, 1969-70, nat. pres., 1970-72), Am. Assn. U. Women, Brooks Art Gallery League, D.A.R. (regent 1964-68; chmn. regents council 1965-66), Assn. for Preservation of Tenn. Antiquities, U.D.C., Internat. Group, Memphis, Inc., Memphis Symphony League, Colonial Dames Seventeenth Century (chpt. nat. def. chmn. 1970-72, pres. chpt., state chmn.), Delta Zeta, Delta Kappa Gamma (corr. sec. 1964-66). Presbyn. Lions Aux. (v.p. 1969-70). Clubs: Delta Study (recording sec. 1969-71); Tenn. Woman's Press and Authors (sec. 1964-65). Editor: Southern Dames of America Journal, 1970-72. Home: 1966 Snowden Av Memphis TN 38107

HAWLEY, CARLOTTA AUGUSTA (MRS. HORACE ELWELL JOHNSTON), orthodontist; b. Washington, Dec. 11, 1913; d. Charles Augustus and Evelyn S. (Frank) Hawley; student George Washington U., 1931; D.D.S., U. Md., 1936; grad. study Harvard, 1937-38; m. Horace Elwell Johnston, Sept. 2, 1944. Intern Forsyth Dental Infirmary for Children, Boston, 1936-37; practicing orthodontist, Washington, 1940—. Diplomate Am. Bd. Orthodontics. Mem. Am. Assn. Orthodontists, Northeastern, Middle-Atlantic, Washington-Balt. socs. orthodontists, Internat. Acad. Dentistry, Am. Dental Assn., D.C. Dental Society, Am. Assn. Women Dentists, Potomac Rose Soc., Omicron Kappa Upsilon. Address: 5016 Wyandot Ct Washington DC 20016

HAWLEY, ROSE DAMARIS HORNE, mus. ofcl.; b. Auburn, Mich., Nov. 12, 1889; d. Charles and Elizabeth (Moore) Horne; student Bay City (Mich.) Bus. Coll., 1907-08; m. Guy W. Hawley, Dec. 21, 1910 (dec. Feb. 1952); 1 son, Willard L. Sec., Bay County Abstract, Bay City, 1907; gen. office clk., sec., bookkeeper Cook Bros. Dept. Store, Akron, Mich., 1908-10; club editor Ludington (Mich.) Daily News, 1921-25; free lance writer history Mason County Enterprise, Scottville, Mich., 1925-30, Grand Rapids (Mich.) Herald, 1953-55; founder, dir. Rose Hawley Mus. (formerly Mason County Mus.), Ludington, 1951—. Chmn. Jr. Red Cross, Mason County, 1916-19; chmn. adult edn. Young Women's Club, 1921-24; pres. Mason County Garden Club, 1944-45. Recipient Pub. Service pin A.R.C., 1925; plaque City Ludington, 1970; citations Hist. Soc., 1970, Optimists Club Ludington, 1970, Mason County Hist. Soc., 1970. Mem. Woman's Lit. Club (hon.). Republican. Mem. Ch. of Christ (tchr. religious edn. 1910-68). Author: Old House Remembers, 1968. Home: 409 E Filer St Ludington MI 49431 Office: 305 E Filer St Ludington MI 49431

HAWTHORN, AUDREY ENGLE (MRS. HARRY B. HAWTHORN), educator; b. Neb., Nov. 25, 1917; d. Earl Theron and Mirth (Richardson) Engle; B.A., Columbia, 1939, M.A., 1940; postgrad. Yale, 1940-42; m. Harry B. Hawthorn, Jan. 18, 1941; children—Margaret Louise Currie, Henry Gilbert John. With Inst. Human Relations, Yale, 1941-42; joint fellow HBH Research for Inter-Am. Affairs, S.Am., 1941-42; with Family Agy., Yonkers, N.Y., 1945-46; asst. curator Mus. Anthropology, U. B.C., Vancouver, 1947-56, curator, 1956-72, prof. anthropology, 1969—. Can. Council grantee for research and publ., 1964-66, Univ. research grantee, 1970, L. & T. Koerner Found. grantee, 1956—, Vancouver Found. grantee for research and publ., 1972-74. Author: People of the Potlatch, 1956; Art of the Kwakiutl and Other Tribes of the Northwest Coast, 1967. Home: 4411 W3 Vancouver BC Canada Office: Museum of Anthropology U BC Vancouver BC Canada

HAWTHORN, SUE, home economist; b. Timpson, Tex., July 9, 1919; d. Otis Homer and Mabel (Harrison) Hawthorn; B.S., Tex. Woman's U., 1950; postgrad. U. Colo., 1958, Purdue U., 1962. Sch. lunch supr., Clarksville, Tex., 1941-44; county home demonstration agt., Kerr County, Kerrville, Tex., 1944-47, Angelina County, Lufkin, Tex., 1947-50, Nolan County, Sweetwater, Tex., 1950-66, Hidalgo County, Edinburg, Tex., 1966-71, Victoria County, Victoria, Tex., 1972—. Recipient Distinguished Service award Nat. Assn. Extension Home Economists, 1962. Mem. Am., Tex. home econs. assns., Am. Assn. U.. Women (sec. 1963), Tex. County Home Demonstration Agts. Assn. (v.p. 1968-69), Bus. and Profl. Women's Club (treas. 1953). Presbyn. (deacon 1971-74). Club: Victoria Music (sec. 1973-74). Home: 401 N Av E Victoria TX 77901 Office: 101 N Bridge Victoria TX 77901

HAWTHORNE, ANNA CARMELL, educator; b. New London, Conn., Apr. 15, 1908; d. Frederick A. and Bridget E. (Sullivan) Hawthorne; Ed.B., R.I. Coll., Edn., 1930, Ed.M., 1940; postgrad. Brown U., 1935-36, Providence Coll., 1948-50, Coll. Pacific, 1951, U. Havana, 1953; certificate advanced grad. studies Boston U., 1966. Tchr., Nathanael Greene Jr. High Sch., Providence, 1931-51, Esek Hopkins Jr. High Sch., 1951-56; tchr. Mt. Pleasant High Sch., 1956-71, head social studies dept. 1964-71; prof. edn., supr. student tchrs. R.I. Coll., Providence, 1972—. Orginator, dir. model legislature for high sch. students, 1946; tchr. TV series on world affairs, 1955; state cons. Future Tchrs. Am., 1958—, Student N.E.A., 1966—; chmn. R.I. Tchr. Edn. and Profl. Standards Commn., 1949—. Recipient Leaders key Future Tchrs. Am., 1960, Thanks badge Providence Girl Scouts, 1938. Mem. R.I. Social Studies Assn. (pres. 1949-51), New Eng. History Tchrs. Assn. (pres. 1955-57), R.I. Edn. Assn. (pres. 1965-66), Cath. Tchrs. Conclave (pres. 1945-47), Cath. Woman's Club (pres. 1952-53), Providence Tchrs. Assn., N.E.A., R.I. Assn. Curriculum Devel., Delta Kappa Gamma. Contbr. articles in field to profl. jours. Home: Field Hill Rd Clayville RI 02815 Office: Mann Hall Rhode Island Coll Providence RI 02908

HAWTHORNE, MARY ELIZABETH, biologist, assn. exec.; b. New London, Conn.; d. Frederick Alexander and Bridget (Sullivan) Hawthorne; B.S., U. R.I., 1937; M.S., Pa. State U., 1940; postgrad. U. Minn., 1948-49; Ph.D., Mich. State U., 1951. Instr. botany and zoology Pa. State U., 1940-44, 46-48, asst. prof. botany, 1952-55; grad. teaching asst. gen. botany and biology U. Minn., 1948-49; grad. teaching program basic biology Mich. State U., 1949-51; instr. botany U. R.I., 1951-52; asst. prof. biology Boston U., 1955-57, asso. prof., 1957-61, prof., 1961-65; asst. head acad. dept. U.S. Naval Med. Sch., Nat. Naval Med. Center, Bethesda, Md., 1965-67, head acad. dept., 1967-71; ednl. adviser to comdr. USAF Sch. of Health Care Scis., Sheppard AFB, Tex., 1971-73; staff specialist Am. Assn. Community and Jr. Colls., Washington, 1973—. Cons. design biol. projectuals Technifax Corp., Holyoke, Mass., 1960—; cons. biol. illustrations Kendall/Hunt Pub. Co., Dubuque, Ia., 1960—; mem. Mass. Sci. Fair Com., 1961—. Bd. dirs. Pa. Jr. Acad. Sci., 1942-44. Served to lt. (j.g.) USNR 1944-46; comdr. Res. Mem. Bot. Soc. Am., Genetics Soc. Am., Ecol. Soc. Am., Genetics Soc. Can., Assn. Mil. Surgeons, Sigma Xi, Phi Kappa Phi, Delta Kappa Gamma, Sigma Delta Epsilon, Chi Omega. Author: (with others) Laboratory Manual for General Biology, 1960. Contbr. articles to profl. jours. Research on cytogenetics. Home: Field Hill Rd Clayville RI 02815 Office: Am Assn Community and Jr Colls Nat Center Higher Edn One DuPont Circle Washington DC 20036

HAY, ALEXANDRA, actress; b. Los Angeles, 1947; d. Alexander and Allie (Rydalch) Hay. Appeared in motion pictures, 1966—; movies include Guess Who's Coming to Dinner, 1967, Skidoo, 1968, Model Shop, 1968, The Greatest Mother of 'Em All, 1969, The Love Machine, Fun and Games, 1970, The Screaming Woman, 1971, A Place to Die, 1972, How to Seduce a Woman, 1973; co-star Shadow Game on CBS Playhouse, 1969. Home: 20910 Bandera St Woodland Hills CA 91364

HAYCOCK, CHRISTINE E. (MRS. SAM MOSKOWITZ), physician; b. Mt. Vernon, N.Y., Jan. 7, 1924; d. John B. and Madeline (Sears) Haycock; Ph.B., U. Chgo., 1947, B.S., 1948; M.D., State U. N.Y., 1952; postgrad. N.Y.U., 1955; grad. Army Command and Staff Coll., 1973; m. Sam Moskowitz, July 6, 1958. Intern Walter Reed Army Med. Center, Washington, 1952-53; resident St. Barnabas Med. Center, Newark, 1954-58, St. John's Episcopal Hosp., Bklyn., 1958-59; practice medicine specializing in gen. surgery, Newark, 1959—; asst. prof. surgery, chief surg. trauma service N.J. Coll. Medicine and Dentistry, Newark; mem. staff St. Barnabas Med. Center, Presbyn. Hosp., Martland Med. Center. Dir. Automated Data Assos., Rahway, N.J. Bd. dirs. Newark YM-YWCA; state med. del. Essex County chpt. Am. Cancer Soc. Served as capt. M.C., AUS, 1952-54; now col. Res. Recipient Outstanding Alumni award Bloomfield Coll., 1971. Diplomate Am. Bd. Surgery. Fellow A.C.S., N.J. Acad. Medicine; mem. Essex County, N.J. State med. socs., A.M.A., Am. Med. Women's Assn. (pres. N.J. br. 1967, named Woman of Year, N.J. br. 1970), Assn. Mil. Surgeons, Am. Coll. Emergency Physicians (charter), Univ. Assn. Emergency Med. Services (founding), Am. Burn Soc., Res. Officers Assn., Photog. Soc. Am., Bus. and Profl. Women's Club, Amateur Radio Relay League. Clubs: Zonta; Vailsburg Camera. Address: 361 Roseville Av Newark NJ 07107

HAYDEN, FRANCES JEAN (MRS. MILFORD DUDLEY HAYDEN), civic worker; b. Remsen, Ia., Apr. 5, 1925; d. James Albert and Margaret (Case) Harman; student Westmar Coll., 1942-43, U. Ia., 1943-44; m. Milford Dudley Hayden, Dec. 16, 1944; children—Mary C. (Mrs. George Cundy), Patricia Ehrich (Mrs. Neal Ehrich), Linda (Mrs. Terry Burkhart), Michael Dudley. Pres. women's aux. Ia. Med. Soc.; mem. women's aux. A.M.A.; mem. Ia. Med. Polit. Action Com. Bd. dirs. Ia. Assn. Mental Health. Named Mother of Year, U. Ia., 1971. Republican. Methodist. Mem. P.E.O., Order Eastern Star (past matron). Home: 1125 W Willow St Cherokee IA 51012

HAYDEN, MELISSA (MILDRED HERMAN), ballerina; b. Toronto, Ont., Can., Apr. 25, 1928; d. Jacob and Kate (Weinberg) Herman; student Boris Volkoff Ballet Sch., Sch. Am. Ballet, Vilzak-Shollar; m. Donald Hugh Coleman, Jr., Feb. 1954; children—Stuart, Jennifer. Mem. corps de Ballet, Radio City, N.Y.C., 1945, then soloist Ballet Theatre, tours of U.S. and Europe, 1946-55, prima ballerina on tour, 1953; toured S.Am. with Ballet Alicia Alonso; with N.Y.C. Ballet, 1949-53, 55—; now artist in residence, Saratoga Spring N.Y., appeared in ballet Pas de Trois, The Cage, The Duel, Agon, Medea, Still Point, Miraculous Mandarin, Firebird, Ivesiana; appeared in motion picture Limelight; appeared as prima ballerina Nat. Ballet Can., Am. Ballet Theatre, Royal Ballet London, Chgo. Opera Ballet. Recipient merit award Mademoiselle, 1952; Dance Educators Albert Einstein Woman of Achievement award, Dance mag., 1962, Handel medallion, N.Y.C. Address: Skidmore Coll Saratoga Springs NY 12866

HAYDEN, ST. CLAIRE OKIE (MRS. WILLIAM FREDERICK HAYDEN), mining co. exec.; b. Washington, Dec. 26, 1898; d. John Brognard and Jeannette (Anderson) Okie; student St. Marys Coll., Notre Dame, Ind.; m. William Frederick Hayden, Oct. 22, 1916; children—John Brognard Okie. Pres., Hayden Realty Co., Denver, 1937—, Seaton Hayden Mines Co., 1930—, Colorontt Coal Co., Colo., 1937—, Charter Oak Coal Co., 1937—, Hayden Enterprises, 1960—, Hayden Farms, Denver, 1961—. Mem. D.A.R., Alliance Francaise. Club: Surf (mem. debutante ball com. 1972) (Miami Beach, Fla.). Home: 1029 E 8th Av Denver CO 80218 also 5750 Collins Av Miami Beach FL 33140

HAYENGA, LOIS E. WELLS, editor, pub.; b. Redwood Falls, Minn., Jan. 16, 1931; d. Fred Glenn and Helen (Champion) Wells; grad. pub. high sch.; m. Lester Hayenga, Mar. 10, 1950 (div. Oct. 1973); children—Keith Lester, Julie (Mrs. Edward Gallagher); m. 2d, Delbert Noetzelman, Sept. 27, 1974. Typesetter, Eagle Bend (Minn.) News, 1951-56, asst. editor, 1956, editor, 1959—, owner, pub., 1970—; typesetter Clarissa (Minn.) Ind., 1956. Vice chairwoman Todd County (Minn.) Republican Party, 1969—. Bd. dirs. St. John's Blood Bank. Mem. Nat., Minn. (recipient 3rd place Advt. Vigor 1960) newspaper assns., Nat. Fedn. Ind. Bus., Eagle Bend Commercial Club. Home and office: PO Box 144 Miltona MN 56354

HAYER, MYRTLE VENNETTE MATTSON (MRS. WILLIAM L. HAYER), educator; b. Cambridge, Minn., Apr. 11, 1918; d. Alfred and Hulda Mary (Paulson) Mattson; B.S. in Edn., Home Econs., U. Minn., 1942; certificate Phila. Sch. Occupational Therapy, 1945; postgrad. Mankato State Coll., 1974—; m. William L. Hayer, July 11, 1947; 1 dau., Susan (Mrs. Robert D. Brown). Tchr. Delavan (Minn.) High Sch., 1942, Buffalo Lake (Minn.) High Sch., 1943; occupational therapist U.S. Army Hosp., Rome, Ga., 1945, Memphis, 1945, Vets. Hosp., Jefferson Barracks, St. Louis, 1945-46, Vets. Hosp., Mpls., 1946-47; tchr. Mpls. pub. schs., 1951-54, St. Paul pub. schs., 1954—. Gen. Electric Found. fellow, 1973; Edn. Professions Devel. Act Inst. grantee, 1969. Mem. Am., Minn. home econs. assns., Am., Minn. vocational assns., Am. Occupational Therapy Assn., Alpha Delta Kappa, Delta Kappa Gamma. Club: St. Paul Home Economics. Home: 5833 Pleasant Av So Minneapolis MN 55419 Office: Central High School 275 N Lexington Parkway St Paul MN 55104

HAYES, ALBERTA PHYLLIS WILDRICK (MRS. GLENMORE BURTON HAYES), health service exec.; b. Blakeslee, Pa., May 31, 1918; d. William and Maude (Robbins) Wildrick; Diploma Wilkes Barre Gen. Hosp. Sch. Nursing, 1938-41; student Wilkes Coll., 1953-54, Pa. State U., 1969—; m. Glenmore Burton Hayes, Oct. 9, 1942; children—Glenmore Rolland, William Bruce. Nurse, Monroe County Gen. Hosp., East Stroudsburg, Pa., 1941-44; pvt. duty nurse, 1944-56; with White Haven (Pa.) State Sch. and Hosp., 1956—, asst. dir. nursing edn., 1966—. Pres. Tobyhanna Twp. Sch., P.T.A., 1948-49; v.p. To-o-Pocona Women of Rotary, 1973-74; nurse A.R.C., 1955. Mem. Am. Legion Aux. (unit pres. 1946-47). Club: Pocono Mountains Women's (Blakeslee). Home: Blakeslee PA 18610 Office: White Haven State Sch and Hosp White Haven PA 18661

HAYES, ANNA ELIZABETH, educator; b. Rockcreek, Ida., July 23, 1886; d. John Frederick and Anna Elizabeth (Peterson-Nyman) Hansen; B.S., Ida. State Normal Sch., 1904; B.Ed. (hon.), U. Ida., 1950, Litt.D., 1950; H.H.D., Coll. Ida., 1950; m. John E. Hayes, Dec. 25, 1905; children—Winifred Wilde (Mrs. Robert Kent Maddock), John H., William (dec.), Ruthann Hayes LeBaron. Tchr., Ida. State Normal Sch., Albion, 1904-05; tchr. pvt. schs., Denver, 1933-62; lectr. U.S., Can., Cuba, Japan and Mexico, 1933-68. Active various offices P.T.A., 1930-58, adviser Democratic use of P.T.A., Japan, 1950, nat. pres. Nat. Congress Parents and Tchrs., 1950-52. Active welfare, social service, health orgns., 1938-52; mem. exec. com. White House Mid Century Com., 1950; mem. Sylvania Award Com., 1953-57; mem. nat. bd. Women's Med. Coll., Pa., 1953—. Recipient U.S. Treasury Dept. medal, 1953; nat. awards Boy Scouts Am., 1952-53. Mem. Ida. Writers League, Am. Assn. U. Women (life), League Women Voters, U.S. Nat. Com. Childhood Edn., Episcopal Guild, Delta Kappa Gamma, (hon. life), Beta Sigma Phi (hon. life). Author: Lure of the Trail (poetry), 1918; Stepping Stones (poetry), 1950; Adventures of Hedvig and Lollie, 1960; Buckskin and Smoke, 1972. Adviser, Highlights for Children, 1954—. Contbr. poems to mags. and newspapers, articles to ednl. publs. Home: 343 Blue Lakes Blvd N Lynwood Manor Twin Falls ID 83301

HAYES, ANNIE R. DIAZ (MRS. PAUL HAYES), ednl. adminstr.; b. Reina Mercedes, Isabela, Philippines, July 26, 1932; d. Manuel Tominez Respicio and Guadalupe Gatan Palogan; B.S., St. Theresa's Coll., 1954; M.A., U. Philippines, 1960; Ed.D., George Washington U., 1968, postdoctoral work, 1968; m. Paul Hayes, Feb. 12, 1973. Tchr. math. Northeastern Coll., Isabela, Philippines, 1954-55; tchr. elementary grades St. Theresa's Coll., Manila, 1956-57; research asst. Statis. Center, U. Philippines, Manila, 1957-60, research instr. Grad. Coll. Edn., Quezon City, 1961-62, sr. research asso. Asian Labor Edn. Center, Quezon City, 1965-67; prof. statistics Grad. Sch., U. Santo Tomas, Manila, Philippines, 1965-66; research asst. Surveys and Research Corp., Washington, 1962-64, research asso., 1967-70; sr. research coordinator Volt Information Scis., Inc., Washington, 1970-71; dep. dir. instnl. research Fed. City Coll., Washington, 1971—. UN fellow, 1960-61; WHO-FAO fellow, 1964; Social Sci. Research Council grantee, 1964-66, Labor Research Council grantee, 1965-66. Mem. Am. Statis. Assn., Am. Ednl. Research Assn., Assn. Instnl. Researchers, Internat. Soc. Ednl. Accountability, Internat. Assn. Survey Researchers, Pi Lambda Theta. Home: 7505 Dolce Dr Annandale VA 22003 Office: Federal City Coll Washington DC 20005

HAYES, BETTINE J. (MRS. M. VINSON HAYES), investment mgr.; b. Boston, Sept. 6, 1928; d. Reginald W. P. and Ethel (Thomas) Brown; B.A., Wellesley Coll., 1950; m. M. Vinson Hayes, June 10, 1961; children—M. Vinson III, Juliet Dorothy. Security analyst Merrill Lynch, Pierce, Fenner & Smith, Inc., N.Y.C., 1950-60, portfolio analyst, 1960-73, Canadian research coordinator, 1967-69; mgr. N.Y. Wellesley Club, 1973—. Mem. D.A.R. (chpt. treas. 1958-59, historian 1961-62, rec. sec. Colonielles, 1961-71, treas. Colonielles 1971-73), N.Y. Soc. Security Analysts. Home: 39 Gramercy Park New York City NY 10010 also 11 Spring Close Lane East Hampton NY 11937 Office: 21 E 52d St New York City NY 10022

HAYES, DORA KRUSE (MRS. JOHN CLIFFORD HAYES), biochemist; b. Kindred, N.D., June 19, 1931; d. Martin George and Dorothy Ruth (Strehlow) Kruse; B.S., Hamline U., 1952; M.S., U. Wis., 1953; Ph.D., U. Minn., 1961; m. John Clifford Hayes, Nov. 27, 1953; children—Robert Martin, John Wallace. Instr. biology dept. Hamline U., St. Paul, summers 1952, 53; chemist Gen. Mills, Mpls., 1953-54; jr. scientist U. Minn., Mpls., 1954-57, teaching asst., 1957-61; research biochemist U.S. Army, Dugway, Utah, 1961-65, U.S. Dept. Agr., Beltsville, Md., 1965—. Pres., Fairhill Elementary P.T.A., 1969-70; sec. Briarwood Citizens Assn., 1970—. Mem. Federally Employed Women (pres. 1974—), Am. Soc. Biochemists, Entomol. Soc. Am., Internat. Soc. Chronobiology, A.A.A.S., Am. Soc. Microbiology, Am. Chem. Soc., Nat. Fedn. Bus. and Profl. Women, Grad. Women in Sci., Sigma Xi, Iota Sigma Pi. Lutheran. Home: 9105 Shasta Ct Fairfax VA 22030 Office: 110 Bldg 307 ARC Beltsville MD 20705

HAYES, DOROTHY TOOHEY, educator; b. Milw., Oct. 24, 1905; d. Michael Henry and Margaret (Hake) Toohey; B.A., U. Wis., 1926; M.A., U. Chgo., 1935, Ph.D., 1950; m. Birchard Platt Hayes, June 24, 1927 (dec. 1958); children—Jonathan, Carolyn (Mrs. Charles Pangborn), Margaret (Mrs. Malcolm Taylor), Richard, Libby (Mrs. Chester Sass), James Birchard. Elementary and secondary sch. tchr., West Bend, Wis., Clearwater, Fla., 1926-30; faculty U. Chgo., 1931-42; guidance dir., Western Springs, Ill., 1943-46; dir. early childhood edn. Syracuse U., 1946-48; prof., dir. early childhood edn. State U. Coll., Oswego, N.Y., 1948-50; prof., dir. edn., chmn. div. edn., dir. Mental Health Workstudy Program, State U. Coll., New Paltz, N.Y., 1950—; mem. Middle States Evaluation Teams, N.Y. State Congress Parents and Tchrs. Mem. Foster Parents Plan, 1966—; dir. Nursing Edn. Workshop, WHO, Taiwan, 1952. Mem. N.E.A., Assn. for Higher Edn., N.Y. State Assn. Tchr. Educators, Assn. for Supervision and Curriculum Devel., N.Y. State Assn. for Childhood Edn. (pres. 1952-54), Council for Children (chmn. 1955), Pi Lambda Theta, Delta Kappa Gamma, Kappa Delta Pi. Contbr. articles to profl. jours. Home: PO Box 584 New Paltz NY 12561

HAYES, ELIZABETH ROTHS, educator; b. Ithaca, N.Y., July 3, 1911; d. Leslie David and Emilie Roths (Hayes) Hayes; A.B. in Botany, W.Va. U., 1932; M.S. in Dance, U. Wis., 1935; Ed.D. in Edn., Stanford, 1949. Instr. phys. edn. Fairmont (W.Va.) State Tchrs.' Coll., 1936-38; instr. dance Rockford (Ill.) Coll., 1939-40; asst. prof. dance dept. ballet and modern dance U. Utah, Salt Lake City, 1941-44, 46, 47, 49, asso. prof., 1950-54, prof., 1954—; vis. asst. prof. U. Wis.-Madison, 1945. Dance adviser Arts IMPACT Project, U.S. Office Edn., 1970, 71. Named Woman of Distinction, U. Utah Faculty Women, 1968; recipient Honor award Utah Assn. for Health, Phys. Edn. and Recreation, 1971. Mem. Am. Acad. Phys. Edn., A.A.H.P.E.R. (chmn. nat. dance sect. 1954-56, chmn. dance edn. sect. 1967, v.p., chmn. dance div. 1970-72), Am. Assn. U. Profs., Am. Dance Guild, Com. on Research Dance, Mortar Bd., Phi Beta Kappa, Alpha Phi. Author: Dance Composition and Production, 1955; An Introduction to the Teaching of Dance, 1964. Home: 227 S 13th E St Salt Lake City UT 84102

HAYES, ELOISE DELAY, educator; b. Sharon, Kan.; d. Earle Roland and Leah Pearl (Griffith) DeLay; B.Ed., St. Cloud State Coll., 1939; M.A., U. N.C., 1951, Ph.D., 1953; divorced. Tchr. elementary schs. Minn., Alaska, Germany, 1936-44, 46-48; dir. Girl Scouts, Albuquerque and Amarillo, Tex., 1944-46; prof., head dept. elementary edn. Cedar Crest Coll., Allentown, Pa., 1953-55; prof. edn. U. Hawaii, Honolulu, 1955—. Dir. creative teaching projects, deprived areas Waimanalo, Molokai, Hana-Maui, Kalihi-Uka; cons. and workshops in creative drama, throughout U.S.; condr. seminars East-West Center Culture and Learning Inst. Mem. English Speaking Union (scholarship com. 1966-68), Creative Edn. Assn., Nat. Council Tchrs. English (nat. com. creative drama 1969-71), Am. Ednl. Theatre Assn., Assn. Childhood Edn. Internat., Ednl. Drama Assn. England, Jane Austen Soc., Internat. Communication Assn., Am. Assn. U. Women. Contbr. profl. jours. Home: The Ilika Apt 735 Honolulu HI 96815

HAYES, GRACE PERSON (MRS. ROBERT CARY HAYES), historian; b. Ware, Mass., Feb. 11, 1919; d. Flynn Russell and Effie Martha (Spencer) Person; B.A., Wellesley Coll., 1940; A.M., Columbia, 1941; m. Robert Cary Hayes, Oct. 21, 1950; children—Martha Anne, Benjamin Russell. Commd. ensign USN, 1943, advanced through grades to lt., ret. 1953; with Bur. Nat. Affairs, Washington, 1962-63; with Hist. Evaluation & Research Orgn., Dunn Loring, Va., 1963—, dir. research, 1969—; with T.N. Dupuy Assos., Dunn Loring, 1967—. Mem. Archeol. Inst. Am., Phi Beta Kappa. Author: The War Against Japan, 1953; (with Trevor N. Dupuy) The Campaigns on the Turkish Fronts, 1967, Naval and Overseas War, 1916-1918, 1967, The Military History of Revolutionary War Naval Battles, 1970; World War I: A Compact History, 1972. Editor: (with Paul Martell) World Military Leaders. Home: 5425 Harwood Rd Bethesda MD 20014 Office: Box 157 Dunn Loring VA 22027

HAYES, HELEN (MRS. CHARLES MACARTHUR), actress; b. Washington, Oct. 10, 1900; d. Francis Van Arnum and Catherine Estelle (Hayes) Brown; grad. Sacred Heart Acad., Washington, 1917; L.H.D., Hamilton Coll., Clinton, N.Y., 1939, Smith Coll., 1940; L.H.D., Elmira Coll., Elmira, N.Y.; Litt.D. Columbia, 1949, U. Denver, 1952, N.Y.U., Brandeis U., Brown U.; A.F.D., Princeton, St. Mary's Coll.; m. Charles McArthur, Aug. 17, 1928 (dec. Apr. 21, 1956); 2 children. First appeared on stage at 6 yrs. of age; mem. Columbia Players, Washington, 4 seasons; later toured with Lew Fields and John Drew; played in Old Dutch, Prodigal Husband, Pollyanna, Penrod; with William Gillette in Dear Brutus; 1 season Clarence; 2 seasons in Bab; 2 seasons in To the Ladies, We Moderns, Dancing Mothers, Caesar and Cleopatra, What Every Woman Knows, Coquette, Mr. Gilhooley; Mary of Scotland, 1934; Victoria Regina, 1937-38; Ladies and Gentlemen, 1939-40; Twelfth Night, 1940-41; Candle in the Wind, 1941-42; Harriet, 1943-45; Happy Birthday; appeared in motion pictures The Sin of Madelon Claudet, Arrowsmith; The Glass Menagerie (London), 1948; Farewell to Arms; Vanessa; The Wisteria Trees, 1950; My Son John (film), 1951; Mrs. McThing, 1952; Mainstreet to Broadway, 1953; Skin of Our Teeth (Europe and U.S.), 1955; Anastasia; appeared as Mrs. Derth in TV revival of Barrie's Dear Brutus, 1956, in TV series The Snoop Sisters. Awarded gold statuette Motion Picture Acad. Arts and Scis., 1932, as outstanding actress for previous year, based upon play, The Sin of Madelon Claudet; Emmy award, TV 1954. Hon. pres. Am. Theatre Wing; mem. N.Y. Council on Arts; bd. dirs. N.Y.C. Center for Music and Drama; bd. visitors N.Y. State Rehab. Hosp., Women's activities Nat. Found. for Infantile Paralysis. Republican. Roman Catholic. Home: Nyack NY 10960

HAYES, ISABELLA MALLORY (MRS. WALTER HAROLD HAYES), civic worker; b. Kewanee, Ill., Mar. 27, 1908; d. George Adelbert and Ella Bowie (Swayze) Mallory; B.A., Knox Coll., 1930, B.L.S., U. Wis., 1931; postgrad. U. Md., 1953; m. Walter Harold Hayes, Nov. 9, 1935; 1 dau., Anne (Mrs. Henry George Michel). With Kewanee Pub. Library, 1926-30; head reference dept., pub. library, Roanoke, Va., 1931-43; instr., asst. reference librarian U. Md. Library, College Park, 1949-58, head Md. and rare book room, also in charge displays and pub. relations, 1958-69, editor Library News, 1952-69. Exec. dir. Nat. Library Week in Md., 1962; chmn. First Citizens Conf. on Libraries in Md., 1965. Mem. State Adv. Com. on Day Care to Md. Dept. Social Services, 1962-72; chmn. Health and Welfare Council Prince Georges County, 1965-68. Bd. dirs. Health and Welfare Council Nat. Capital Area, Washington, 1964-68, Md. Com. for Day Care of Children, Balt., 1964-69, Prince George's County Retarded Day Care Center, 1962-69. Recipient Community Service award Health and Welfare Council Nat. Capital Area, Washington, 1968. Mem. League Women Voters (county pres. 1957-58, mem. state bd. 1958-62), Am. Assn. U. Women (2d v.p. br. 1972—), Mothers Club Kappa Alpha Theta, Alpha Delta Pi (patroness). Author: Ethics of Advertising: a Selected Bibliography, 1931; Financing Presidential Campaigns, A Selected Bibliography, 1953. Home: 70 Willow Dr St Augustine FL 32084

HAYES, MARGARET OTTENHEIMER, jewelry designer; b. Balt., Dec. 5, 1925; d. Jack Lewis and Clara (Bussy) Ottenheimer; student Johns Hopkins Tchrs. Coll., Md. Inst. Art; m. Herbert B. Swope, Oct. 11, 1947 (div. Sept. 1973); children—Herbert Byard III, Tracy Brooks. Actress numerous motion pictures including Black Bd. Jungle, 1956, Violent Saturday, others; actress various TV and theatre prodns., 1970; jewelry designer, Palm Beach, Fla., 1973—. Active United Cerebral Palsy Assn. Mem. Worth Av. Assn. Club: Poncianna (Palm Beach). Author: Maggie Hayes Jewelry Book, 1973. Home: 335 Worth Av Palm Beach FL 33480 Office: 242 Worth Av Palm Beach FL 33480 also 225 Worth Av Palm Beach FL 33480

HAYES, MARION ANGELA, business exec.; b. Phila.; d. Patrick Joseph and Josephine (Sullivan) Hayes; student pvt. schs., Phila. Owner, operator Hayes Personnel Service, Phila., 1962—. Active Hospitality Center, Phila., 1962-63; co-chmn. gray ladies A.R.C., Jefferson Hosp., 1956-57, 63—; mem. women's bd. Jefferson Hosp.; mem. Play and Players 17th and Delancey St., mem. box com. Phila. Horse Show; mem. Women's Com. Am. Revolution Bicentennial. Recipient award Jefferson Hosp. Gray Ladies, 1957. Republican committeewoman. Mem. Phila. Mus. Art., Hannah Penn House, Am. Flag Day Assn., Pan Am. Assn. (dir.), C. of C. Greater Phila. Soroptomist. Home: The Dorchester 226 W Rittenhouse Sq Philadelphia PA 19103 Office: 259 S 17th St Philadelphia PA 19103

HAYES, MARRIJANE JOHNSTON (MRS. JOSEPH A. HAYES), author, civic worker; b. Indpls., Feb. 18, 1920; d. Joseph Drake and Erna (Wessel) Johnston; student (scholar) Butler U., 1938, Ind. U., 1939-41; m. Joseph A. Hayes, Feb. 5, 1938; children—Gregory, Jason, Daniel. Co-author plays: And Came the Spring, Too Many Dates, Quiet Summer, Penny, Life of the Party, A Woman's Privilege, June Wedding, Come Over to our House, Come Rain or Shine, The Bridegroom Waits, Head in the Clouds, One in Every Family, other plays; author novel (with Joseph A. Hayes) Bon Voyage!, 1958, also movie script for Bon Voyage! for Universal-Internat., Hollywood, Cal., (screen-plays) So Long at the Fair; Ghost of a Witch; v.p. Hayes Prodns., Inc. Sec., P.T.A., Brookfield Centre, Conn.; mem. Women's Internat. League for Peace and Freedom, Brookfield Centre Library Com.; mem. Sane Nuclear Policy Com.; mem. parents com. Gunnery Sch., also Oakwood Friends Prep. Sch.; active Foster Parent Plans, Fresh Air Camp (both N.Y.C.), Cardiac Soc. (Washington), Sarasota County (Fla.) Civic League, United Appeal Fund, Sarasota, Women's Internat. League for Peace, Community Child Welfare Assn. Bd. dirs. Sarasota Library, Community Theatre, Brookfield, Conn., Am. Civil Liberties Union, Nat. Conf. Christians and Jews, Opera Guild, Ringling Art Mus. Mem. Am. Craftsmen's Council, Writers Guild Am., Nat. League Am. Pen Women (bd.), Sarasota Art Assn. (bd.), Authors League Am. (bd.), League Women Voters, Danberry Music Soc., Fine Arts Soc. Sarasota. Clubs: Nat. Travel, Bird Key Yacht. Inventor children's games. Home: Obtuse Hill Brookfield Centre CT 06805 also 1168 Westway Dr Lido Shores Sarasota FL 33577

HAYES, MARY ALMA, librarian; b. Oakland, Cal., Dec. 30, 1912; d. Michael Joseph and Catherine Gertrude (Burke) Hayes; A.B. in English, San Francisco Coll. Women, 1947; M.A. in L.S., Rosary Coll., River Forest, Ill., 1952. Joined Sisters of the Presentation of the Blessed Virgin Mary, Roman Catholic Ch., 1936; tchr., librarian schs. in San Francisco, 1938-56; coordinator workshops and insts. U. San Francisco, 1954-71, dir. library sci. program, 1958-62, 63—, asst. prof. library sci., 1968—; cons., lectr., condr. workshops and insts. in field. Mem. exec. bd., v.p. Book Bank U.S.A., 1973—. Adv. bd. Marin Assn. Gifted Children, 1970. Recipient Nat. Book award Library Binding Inst., 1961; Sister Alma Circulating Library named at St. Joseph Hosp., San Francisco, 1971. Mem. Nat. Council Tchrs. English, Cal. Assn. Tchrs. English (exec. bd. 1968—), Cal. Central Council Tchrs. English (exec. bd. 1963-67), Cath. Audio-Visual Educators Assn. (exec. bd. 1968-69, 70—), N.E.A., Audio-Visual Educators Assn. Cal., Nat. Assn. Ednl. Broadcasters, Am., Cal. (chmn. profl. edn. com. 1966-67, mem. council 1975—, vice chmn. com. continuing edn. 1975—), Cath. (co-founder, chmn. No. Cal. sect. chmn. sch. library cons. sect.) library assns., Cal. Assn. Sch. Librarians (rep. 1969—), Am. Assn. Higher Edn. Author: Teacher-Librarian Processing Manual, 3d edit.; Master Order List for Elementary School Libraries, 1964; also articles. Home: 2340 Turk Dr San Francisco CA 94118

HAYES, MARY ANNE OLSON, psychologist; b. Mpls., Dec. 18, 1923; d. Willard Clifford and Violet (Pickard) Olson; A.B. in Edn., U. Mich., 1944, M.A., 1962, postgrad., 1962-66; children—Karen (Mrs. Peter Scott Smyth), Colleen (Mrs. James Samanen), Anne, John Jr., Laurie. Typist U. Mich., Ann Arbor, 1942, teaching asst. Sch. Edn., 1945, research asst. Inst. for Human Adjustment Bur. Psychol. Services, Evaluations and Examinations Div., 1962-63, research asst. Univ. Sch. Research Project, 1963-65; tchr. Ann Arbor Pub. Schs., 1945-46; head psychol. services Devel. Evaluation Clinic Pediatrics Bowman Gray Sch. Medicine, Winston-Salem, N.C., 1967—, mem. staff Inst. Pediatrics, 1972—; asst. dir. Developmental Evaluation Clinic, 1974—. Cons., pvt. counselor. Bd. dirs., dir. tng., CONTACT crisis phone, Winston-Salem, 1972—. USPHS grantee. Mem. Am. (asso.), N.C. (asso.) psychol. assns., Am., N.C. assns. marriage and family counselors, Soc. Pediatric Psychology, Groves Conf. on Marriage and Family, Nat. Council Family Relations, N.C. Family Life Council, N.C. Group Behavior Soc. Home: 3441 York Road Winston-Salem NC 27104 Office: Developmental Evaluation Clinic Dept Pediatrics Graylyn Estates Winston-Salem NC 27106

HAYES, MARY DIANNE WIXTED (MRS. PAUL P. HAYES, JR.), lawyer; b. Danbury, Conn., Jan. 4, 1942; d. Francis J. and Mary Josephine (Zwyner) Wixted; student Trinity Coll., 1959-60; A.B. in Econs., Regis Coll., 1964; LL.B., Suffolk U., 1968, LL.M., 1970; m. Paul P. Hayes, Jr., June 18, 1966. Admitted to Mass. bar, 1970, since practiced in Quincy; partner Hayes and Hayes, 1970—. Vol. atty. Greater Brockton (Mass.) Neighborhood Legal Services, Inc., 1970; Mass. notary public, 1970—; real estate broker, Mass., 1972—. Bd. dirs. Quincy chpt. Mass. Citizens for Life, Inc. Mem. Mass. Assn. Women Lawyers, Mass., Boston (probate law com. 1973-74), Plymouth County, Quincy bar assns., Mass. Trial Lawyers Assn., Jr. Guild of Infant Saviour. Club: South Shore Regis (Pres. 1973-75). Home: 630 Adams St Milton MA 02186 Office: 31 Newcomb St Quincy MA 02169

HAYES, MARY PHYLLIS, savs. and loan exec.; b. New Castle, Ind., Apr. 30, 1921; d. Clarence Edward and Edna Gertrude (Burgess) Scott; student Ball State U., Ind. Extension, Earlham Coll.; grad. Am. Savs. and Loan Inst.; m. John Clifford Hayes, Jan. 1, 1942 (div. Oct. 1952); 1 son, R. Scott. Teller, Henry County Savs. & Loan Assn., New Castle, 1939-41, 50-51, loan officer, 1951-62, asst. sec.-treas., 1962-69, sec.-treas., 1969—; with Am. Nat. Bank, Nashville, 1943-44. Nurses aide A.R.C., 1942-45; treas. Henry County Heart Assn., 1965-67, 74—. Recipient Gold medallion Am. Heart Assn., 1973. Mem. Am. Savs. and Loan Inst. (permanent sec.-treas., dir. E. Central chpt.), Ind. Hist. Soc., New Castle C. of C. (dir. women's council), P.E.O., Altrusa Internat. (chpt. dir.), Psi Iota Xi. Mem. Christian Ch. (Sunday sch. tchr.; active children's choir). Home: 1405 H Av New Castle IN 47362 Office: 2118 Bundy Av New Castle IN 47362

HAYES, PATRICIA ANNE, govt. ofcl.; b. Chgo., Jan. 26, 1921; d. Frank Ambrose and Annabel (Fanning) Hayes; A.B., Coll. St. Teresa, 1942; B.S., U. Md., 1956; M.Ed., Coll. William and Mary, 1961; M.A., George Washington U., 1961; certificate in meteorology, U. Chgo., 1945. Tchr. pub. schs., Chgo., 1942-44; meteorologist U.S. Weather Bur., Washington, 1945-49, climatologist U.S. Dept. Army, 1949-52; commd. 1st lt. U.S. Air Force, 1951, advanced through grades to maj., 1966; meteorologist A.F. Cambridge Research Center, Boston, 1952-54; base weather officer, Molesworth, Eng., 1954-57; team chief Forecast Center, Langley AFB, Va., 1957-58, asst. chief climatology div. hdqrs. 2d weather group, 1958-64; weather officer European Theater Forecast Center, 1964-67, aerospace scis. officer 6th Weather Squadron, Westover AFB, Mass., 1967-70, S.E. Asia Weather Center, 1970-71; wing climatologist 4th Weather Wing Ent AFB, Colo., 1971-72; claims rep. Dept. Health, Edn. and Welfare, 1972—. Mem. Am. Meteorol. Soc., Am. Assn. U. Women, Air Force Assn., Res. Officers Assn., Kappa Gamma Pi. Home: 8145 N Harding St Skokie IL 60076

HAYES, PHOEBE FRANK, librarian; b. Cleve., Aug. 12, 1915; d. Calvin William and Hannah (Frank) Hayes; B.A., U. Wis., 1937, diploma Library Sch., 1937; M.A., U. Denver, 1965; postgrad. U. Chgo., U. Wis. With Joint Reference Library, Pub. Adminstrn. Clearing House, Chgo., 1937-41, U.S. Bur. Budget, Washington, 1942-44, Am. Fedn. State, County, and Municipal Employees, AFL, Madison, Wis., 1944-50, Nat. Farmers Union, Denver, 1950-61; dir. Bibliog. Center for Research, Denver, 1961-74; supr. library devel. services Colo. State Library, 1974—. Home: 4955 S Inca Dr Englewood CO 80110 Office: 1357 Broadway Denver CO 80203

HAYGOOD, BECKY CAVARNOS (MRS. ERVIN EUGENE HAYGOOD), lawyer; b. High Point, N.C., Nov. 9, 1930; d. Peter Basil and Margaret Almena (Griffin) Cavarnos; B.S., Stetson U., 1952; J.D., Stetson U. Coll. Law, 1968; m. Ervin Eugene Haygood, Jan. 21, 1952; children—Curtis Gray, Susan Lane. Admitted to Fla. bar, 1968; individual practice law, Clearwater, Fla., 1968-69; partner Haygood & Haygood, Clearwater, 1970-72, Haygood, Haygood & Locke, Clearwater, 1972—. Mem. parents com. St. Paul's Sch., Clearwater, 1968-69; cub leader Boy Scouts Am., Clearwater, 1965-67; Brownie leader, Girl Scouts Am., Clearwater, 1966-68; neighborhood rep. Heart Fund Drive, Clearwater, 1967-73. Sec. Gifted Assn. of Pinellas, Inc., Clearwater, 1973-74, dir., 1973-74, legal aid counselor, 1969-70. Bd. dirs. Guilford Sch., Clearwater, 1973-74. Mem. Fla. (mem. com. 1973-74), Clearwater bar assns., Nat., Fla. Assns. women lawyers, Am. Assn. U. Women, Zeta Tau Alpha (pres. 1961), Nu Beta Epsilon (treas. 1967-68), Kappa Delta Pi. Club: Carlouel Yacht (Clearwater). Home: 822 Keene Rd Clearwater FL 33516 Office: 501 S Ft Harrison Av Clearwater FL 33516

HAYLETT, CLARICE HELM (MRS. WARREN T. VAUGHAN), psychiatrist; b. Beloit, Wis., July 22, 1922; d. Robert Everett and Alice Mildred (Helm) Haylett; B.A. magna cum laude, Stanford, 1943, M.D., 1949; m. Warren T. Vaughan, Aug. 16, 1960; children—Richard H., Jennifer A. Health officer Marin County Health Dept., 1949-54; fellow in psychiatry Mayo Clinic, 1954-56; resident child psychiatry Mt. Zion Psychiat. Clinic, 1956-58; child psychiatrist San Mateo County Mental Health, 1958—; asst. prof. clin. psychiatry Stanford, 1958—. Trustee Common Coll. Mem. Am. Acad. Child Psychiatry. Episcopalian (mem. futures planning council Cal. Diocese). Club: Pennin Golf and Country (San Mateo, Cal.). Home: 1684 Lexington St San Mateo CA 94402 Office: 225 37th St San Mateo CA 94403

HAY-MESSICK, VELMA E. (MRS. BEN MESSICK), artist; b. Bloomington, Ill.; d. Peter Pinckney and Adeline (Oldham) Hay; art student with Julydia Artzt, 1938-40, Dong Kingman, 1944, Emil Bisttram, 1945, Otis Art Inst., 1947, Chouinard Art Inst., 1948-49; m. Benjamin Newton Messick, Nov. 24, 1949; 1 dau., Caroljean McDowell (Mrs. Eugene Richard Cambridge). One-man shows Magnolia Theatre Gallery, Long Beach, Cal., North Long Beach Woman's Club, San Pedro (Cal.) Art Assn., Long Beach Art Assn., Pacific Coast Club Galleria, Long Beach Community Theatre Gallery, Buffum's Long Beach Gallery, E. B. Crocker City Gallery, Sacramento, Messick-Hay Studio Gallery, Long Beach, Pacific Coast Club Galleria, Long Beach; exhibited widely in group shows in U.S.; represented in permanent collections M. Grumbacher Travel-Loan Collections, Seton Hall U., Newark. Sec., Brawley (Cal.) P.T.A., 1938-40, mem. earthquake emergency bd., 1938-39; fiesta chmn. children's div. Brawley C. of C., 1940; art chmn. Brawley Woman's Club, 1940-41; dir. Messick-Hay Studio Gallery, Long Beach. Recipient Key award Seton Hall U., 1958; 1st award Long Beach br. Nat. League Am. Pen Women, 1971. Mem. Long Beach Art Assn., Cultural Art Center Assn., Nat. Artists and Art Patrons Soc., Nat League Am. Pen Women (rec. sec. Long Beach 1968-69, bd. S.W. regional conv. 1969, historian 1970-71 co-chmn. state art com. 1972-74, art chmn. Long Beach br. 1972-74), D.A.R., (pub. relations chmn. Gaviota chpt. 1972-73), Colonial Dames XVIII Century (chmn. press, radio, TV, pub. relations com. Roanoke County chpt. 1972—), Nat. Soc. Magna Charta Dames, Soc. Mayflower Descs., Women Descs. Ancient and Honorable Arty Co. Republican. Baptist. Home: 133 St Joseph Av Long Beach CA 90803

HAYNES, DOROTHY FRANCES (DOROTHY F. BEVERLY-HAYNES), artist, advt. exec.; b. Hartford, Conn.; d. Henry Robinson and Hattie Elizabeth (Blake) Haynes; student Hartford Art Sch., pvt. instrn. portrait painting under Stanislav Rembski, Joseph Cummings Chase, N.Y.C., marine painting with Howard Hall Darnell, Phila., advt. art with Lou Kimmel and Paula Hutchison, N.Y.C. Illustrator My Psalm, 1939; asst. art dir. Robotham & Co., Hartford, 1943-48; one man shows, N.Y.C., Hartford; exhibited group shows Chgo., Topeka, Laguna Beach, Cal., Sarasota, Fla., Washington, Boston, Meriden, Naugatuck, Conn., Ogunquit, Me., Am. Victory poster traveling exhibit; works in U.S.S. Campbell, Conn. State Capitol. Recipient 1st prize Hartford Soc. Women Painters, 1953; gold award hon. mention Nat. Exhibit, Ogunquit, 1951, 52; 1st prizes N.Y. Advt. Show, 1940, 45; hon. mention Meriden Arts and Crafts, 1955; 2d prize in advt. and Conn. State Art Exhibit, Nat. League Am. Pen Women, 1959; 1st prize Meriden Arts and Crafts, 1965; others. Organizer evening div. Woman's Rep. Club, Hartford, 1953, pres., 1954-57; mem. pub. relations com. Conn. Soc. Crippled Children and Adults, 1960-62; exec. dir., pub. relations dir. Hartford County Citizens for Eisenhower and Youth for Eisenhower,

1956; dir. pub. relations Greater Hartford Easter Seal Campaign 1957, 60; dir. pub. information Conn. Inst. for Blind, 1958—; mem. bd. dirs. Citizen's Charter Com., Hartford, 1958-61; mem. Citizen's Com. Conn. Med. Dental Sch., mem. women's aux. Hartford Rehab. Center; bd. dirs., art chmn. Women's Assn. U. Hartford, 1960-62; bd. advisers Ogunquit (Me.) Art Center, 1968—. Dir., state extension chmn. Republican Workshops Conn., 1959-61; mem. Conn. Rep. Citizens Com., 1959-62. Mem. Nat. League Am. Pen Women (art chmn. 1957, pres. 1962-64 Greater Hartford br., state pres. 1970-72, North Atlantic regional mem. Commemorative Endowment Fund 1971-72), Children's Mus. Hartford, Hartford Hosp. Assn., Meriden Arts and Crafts Soc., Conn. Soc. Women Painters (v.p. 1956-58). Home: 1256-D Farmington Av West Hartford CT 06107

HAYNES, HILDA MOCILE LASHLEY, actress; b. N.Y.C.; d. Charles C. and Leonora (Alkins) Lashley; diploma Braithwaite Bus. Sch., 1934; postgrad., Am. Negro Theatre, 1941, Am. Theatre Wing, 1950, Am. Shakespeare Festival Acad., 1959; 1 son, Christopher C. Actress, appearances on Broadway (N.Y.C.) include Deep are the Roots, 1946, Anna Lucasta, 1947, A Streetcar Named Desire, 1948, King of Hearts, Wisteria Trees, 1954, Lost in the Stars, 1956, The Long Dream, 1959, The Irregular Verb To Love, 1963, Blues for Mr. Charlie, 1964; appeared in off-Broadway prodns., summer stock, Blues for Mr. Charlie, World Theatre Festival, London, 1965, The Great White Hope, Washington, 1967, Golden Boy, Chgo., London (Eng.), 1968, The Great White Hope, Broadway, 1968, Seattle Repertory Theatre, 1971, Mourning in a Funny Hat, 1972, Wedding Band, 1972, The River Niger, nat. tour, 1973; appearances on television, including commls., daytime serials, lead in Frontiers of Faith, Light in the Southern Sky, also appeared on Car 54, The Nurses, Phil Silvers Show, Studio One, Hallmark Hall of Fame, The Defenders, The Ed Sullivan Show, The Hawk, All My Children, Sanford and Son, others; appeared in motion pictures, including co-star of Purlie Victorious, 1963, Home From The Hill, Keywitness, Taxie, A Face in the Crowd, Stage Struck, The Pawnbroker, Across 110th St., Diary of a Mad Housewife, Supr., dir. Title II Cultural Enrichment Program, Virgin Islands, 1966. Mem. N.A.A.C.P., Negro Actors' Guild, Actors' Equity Assn. (councillor), Screen Actors' Guild, Am. Fedn. Radio and Television Artists. Mem. 1st Ch. Religious Sci. Address: 173 W 151st St New York City NY 10039

HAYNES, IRENE WHITFORD (MRS. EVAN HAYNES), lawyer; b. Tempe, Ariz., Apr. 17, 1901; d. William Thomas and Lena Irene (Champion) Whitford; A.B., U. Cal. at Berkeley, 1922; J.D., U. Cal. at Berkeley, 1924; m. Evan Haynes, July 23, 1928; children—Diana (Mrs. Robert H. Romer), Duncan Evan. Admitted to Cal. bar, 1924; librarian Fresno County (Cal.) Law Library, 1924-26; with real estate loan dept. Am. Bank, Alameda, Cal., 1926-29; with Sun Maid Raisin Growers, Fresno, Cal., 1925-29; indexer of office research material Morrison, Hohfeld, Foerster, Shumann & Clark, San Francisco, 1930-31. Coordinator adult edn. classes Napa Coll. and City of Calistoga, Cal., 1969-72. Sec. North Bay council A.R.C., Calistoga, 1966-67; mem. Calistoga Park and Recreation Commn., 1967—. Sec. bd. trustees Calistoga Pub. Library, 1969-73. Mem. State Bar Cal., San Francisco, Napa, Queens Bench bar assns., Napa Valley Wine Library Assn. (dir. 1970-73, sec. 1973-74), Upper Napa Valley Assos. (dir. 1960-65, vice-chmn. 1971-74).

HAYNES, JANE DOWLING (MRS. RICHARD WAYNE HAYNES), ednl. adminstr.; b. McCook, Neb., Sept. 29, 1947; d. Arthur James Dowling and Vivian Mae (Landau) Van Vleet; B.A. in Elementary Edn. cum laude, Ariz. State U., 1970, M.A. in Edn., 1971; m. Richard Wayne Haynes, Nov. 25, 1971. Tchr., program developer Valley of the Sun Sch. for Mentally Retarded, Phoenix, 1968-71; tchr. Hubert Wheeler State Sch. for Retarded, St. Louis, 1971-72; head tchr. Mesa (Ariz.) Assn. for Retarded Children Sch., 1972-73; asst. dir. in charge ednl. services Perry Rehab. Center, Phoenix, 1973—. Guest speaker spl. edn. classes various univs. Recipient certificate of appreciation Boy Scouts Am., 1969. Mem. Am. Assn. Mental Deficiency, Council for Exceptional Children, Nat. Rehab. Assn., Mesa Assn. Retarded Children Aux., Nat. Assn. for Retarded Citizens, Kappa Delta Pi. Democrat. Presbyn. Author: A Language Program for Mentally Retarded, 1970. Home: 1824 E Julie Dr Tempe AZ 85283 Office: 3146 E Windsor Av Phoenix AZ 85008

HAYNES, MARGARET ELIZABETH, nurse, educator; b. Hopkinsville, Ky., Feb. 25, 1919; d. Philip E. and Marion (Bell) Haynes; A.A., Bethel Woman's Coll., 1939; B.S. in Nursing, Vanderbilt U., 1942; M.P.H., U. N.C., 1954. Staff pediatric nurse Vanderbilt U. Hosp., Nashville, 1942-45; head pediatric nurse John Sealy Hosp., Galveston, Tex., 1943-45, U. Colo., Colo. Gen. Hosp., 1947-48, U. Colo., Denver Gen. Hosp., 1948-52; asst. instr. obstet. nursing Vanderbilt U. Sch. Nursing, 1946-47; pub. health staff nurse Dist. Health Dept., Chapel Hill, N.C., 1954-58; asst. prof. U. N.C. Sch. Nursing, Chapel Hill, 1958-65; asst. prof. U. Tenn. Coll. Nursing, Memphis, 1967-69, asso. prof., 1969—, nursing cons. Child Devel. Center, U. Tenn. Med. Units, 1967-71. Nursing cons. Arlington (Tenn.) Hosp. and Sch. for Retarded, 1970—; dir. Coop. Community Health Nursing Edn. Project, 1972—. Recipient Faculty award U. N.C. Sch. Nursing Class of 1965. Mem. Am. Nurses Assn., Nat. League for Nursing, Am. Pub. Health Assn., Am. Assn. on Mental Deficiency, Vanderilt U., U. N.C. Nursing alumnae assns., Sigma Theta Tau. Baptist. Contbr. articles to profl. jours. Home: 152 N McLean Blvd Apt 4 Memphis TN 38104

HAYNES, SOPHY PELLEGRINI-QUARANTOTTI, ednl. adminstr.; b. Rome, Italy, Feb. 28, 1928; d. Lelio and Anne Langdon (Townsend) Pellegrini-Quarantotti; came to U.S., 1938, naturalized, 1946; B.A., Barnard Coll., 1949; M.A., Columbia, 1952, M.A. in Edn., 1964; m. Robert Bontecou Haynes, Dec. 15, 1962; children—Schuyler B., Sophy Townsend, Robert Van Rensselaer. Tchr., Grace Ch. Sch., N.Y.C., 1952-56, Calhoun Sch., N.Y.C., 1956-60; tchr., adminstr. Barnard Sch. for Girls, N.Y.C., 1960-62; prin. Columbia Grammar Lower Sch., N.Y.C., 1962-63; chmn. Lower Sch., Profl. Children's Sch., N.Y.C., 1965-68; head Lower Sch., Buckley Sch., N.Y.C., 1968-69; asst. dean Juilliard Sch., N.Y.C., 1970—. Mem. steering com. Ind. Schs. Opportunity Project, 1967-68. Mem. pres.'s council Mus. City N.Y., 1973—; v.p. Southampton Home for Crippled Children. Mem. Assn. Tchrs. in Ind. Schs. (exec. bd. 1967-72), Nat. Soc. Colonial Dames. Club: Colony. Home: 300 West End Av New York City NY 10023 Office: Juilliard School Lincoln Center New York City NY 10023

HAYS, CAROLE ANN, therapist; b. Detroit, May 30, 1938; d. Ruby Edward and Dorothy Margaret (Wilcox) Hays; B.S., Eastern Mich. U., 1960; M.A., 1970; children (adopted)—Ancie, Vickie. Staff therapist Kalamazoo State Hosp., 1960-63; staff therapist U. Mich. Med. Center, Ann Arbor, 1963-65, dir. occupational therapy, 1970—; organizer, dir. occupational therapy depts. Peoples Community Hosp. and Authority of Mich., Wayne, 1965-69; asst. prof. div. allied health Wayne State U., Detroit, 1969-70. Mem. grad. adv. com. Western Mich. U., Kalamazoo, 1972—, Schoolcraft Community Coll., Livonia, Mich., 1972—, Wayne State U., 1973—. Mem. Superior Twp. Citizens Adv. Com., Mich., 1969-71; chmn. task force childrens service Washtenaw County Child and Family Service Agy., Ann Arbor, Mich., 1970-71; mem. dirs. com. Inst. for Study of Mental Retardation and Related Disabilities, 1971—. Bd. dirs. Child and Family Service. Recipient Mich. Minuteman citation of honor Mich. Dept. State, 1972. Mem. Am. (del. 1973—), Mich. (Outstanding Occupational Therapist of Mich. 1971, chmn. legislative com. 1972—) occupational therapy assns., World Fedn. Occupational Therapists. Home: 1738 Stephens Dr Ypsilanti MI 48197 Office: U Mich Med Center Ann Arbor MI 48104

HAYS, ELINOR RICE, author; b. N.Y.C., Oct. 12, 1904; d. Jacques B. and Rose (Frankfield) Rice; A.B., Barnard Coll., 1923; m. Paul R. Hays, Nov. 19, 1949. Author: (novels-under pen name Elinor Rice) The Best Butter, 1938; Action in Havana, 1940; Mirror, Mirror, 1946; Take the Cash, 1952; (biographies) Morning Star, A Biography of Lucy Stone, 1961; Those Amazing Blackwells, 1967; translator (Ferenc Molnar) Farewell My Heart, 1945; contbr. stories, articles to nat. mags. Mem. Authors Guild, P.E.N. Club. Club: Cosmopolitan. Home: 276 Riverside Dr New York City NY 10025

HAYS, ESTHER MARGARET FINCHER (MRS. DANIEL M. HAYS), educator, physician; b. Lexington, Ky., Apr. 18, 1927; d. Myron Gustin and Evelyn Nancy (Davis) Fincher; B.A., Cornell U., 1948; M.D., Cornell U. Med. Coll., 1951; m. Daniel M. Hays, Sept. 15, 1951; children—Sarah, Jonathan, Elizabeth, Margaret. Intern, N.Y. Hosp., N.Y.C., 1951-52, resident, 1952-54; mem. staff U. Cal. Hosp., Los Angeles; mem. faculty U. Cal., Los Angeles, 1972—, prof. medicine, 1972—. Research physician Lab. Nuclear Medicine and Radiation Biology, U. Cal., Los Angeles, 1955—. Mem. Am. Assn. Cancer Research, Am. Soc. Hematology, Western Soc. Clin. Research, A.C.P. Contbr. articles to profl. jours. Home: 181 S Las Palmas Av Los Angeles CA 90004 Office: 900 Veteran Av Los Angeles CA 90024

HAYS, IDA MAE, missionary; b. nr. West Plains, Mo., Feb. 2, 1940; d. Vernon Edward and Clarice S. (Highfill) (dec.) Hays; A.A., S.W. Bapt. Coll., 1960; B.A., Union U., 1965; M.R.E., Southwestern Bapt. Theol. Sem., 1968; diploma Escola de Portugues e Orientacao, Campinas, Sao Paulo, Brazil, 1972. Sec. to dean, registrar S.W Bapt. Coll., Bolivar, Mo., 1961-63; sec. to head music dept. Union U., Jackson, Tenn., 1963-65; sec. to Dr. L. Jack Gray, Southwestern Bapt. Theol. Sem., Ft. Worth, Tex., 1965-69; dir. young woman's aux. Woman's Missionary Union Okla., Oklahoma City, 1969-71; missionary to Brazil Fgn. Mission Bd., So. Bapt. Conv., Richmond, Va., 1971—. Home: Rua Rosa e Silva 537B Apt 707 Recife Pernambuco Brazil Office: Caixa Postal 1352 50000 Recife Pernambuco Brazil

HAYS, MARY KATHERINE JACKSON (MRS. DONALD OSBORNE HAYS), civic worker; b. Flora, Miss.; d. Rufus Lafayette and Ada (Collum) Jackson; student U. Miss., 1925-26, Millsaps Coll., 1926-27, 43-44; grad. Clark Bus. Sch., 1934; student Columbia U., 1935, Strayer Bus. Coll., 1951; m. Halbert Puffer Oliver, Aug. 9, 1927 (dec. 1934); m. 2d, Donald Osborne Hays, Aug. 30, 1937. Sec. to pres. McCullough Box and Crate Co., Pharr, Tex., 1934-36; sec. to field supr. Miss. Unemployment Compensation, 1936-37; rep. Homes of Tomorrow, 1940 N.Y. World's Fair; sec. to head interior design Lord & Taylor, N.Y.C., 1940; sales dept. Knabe Piano Co., N.Y.C., 1941-43. Active Little Theatre, Wilkes Barre, Pa., 1937-39; charter mem. and incorporator Conf. State Socs., Washington, 1952; vol. worker Am. Cancer Soc., Washington, 1956—; mem. women's com. Nat. Symphony Assn., vol. worker on symphony sustaining com. drives, 1957-66; mem. women's com. Corcoran Gallery Art, Washington, 1957-62; charter mem. Pierce-Warwick Adoption Assn. of Washington Home for Foundlings; vol. Washington Heart Assn., 1959-66; mem. Nat. Capital Area chpt. United Ch. Women, 1957—; mem. D.C. Episcopal Home for Children, 1961—; mem. D.C. Salvation Army Aux., 1962—. Mem. Miss. State Soc. D.C. (sec. 1950-53), Nat. Ballet Soc., Nat. Trust for Historic Preservation, Miss. Women's Club D.C., D.A.R. (vice regent chpt. 1970-72, regent chpt. 1972-74, vice chmn. D.C. com. celebration Washington's birthday 1973, 74, state librarian 1974—), U. D.C. Episcopalian. Club: Washington. Home: 4000 Massachusetts Av NW Washington DC 20016

HAYS, MAXINE RUTH (MRS. KENNETH ROBERT HAYS), ins. agy. exec.; b. Spokane, Wash., Nov. 18, 1927; d. Edward Herbert and Ollie Edna (Ronen) Jamieson; student U. Ore., 1945-48; m. Kenneth Robert Hays, July 24, 1948; children—Charlotte Ann (Mrs. Jerald F. Guscette), Eric Alan, Michael Lee. Co-owner Ken Hays Ins. Agy., Junction City, Ore., 1969—; tchr. ins. courses., mgmt. seminars. Area chmn. Cancer Prevention Study, Junction City, 1960-65; mem. troop coms. Ore. Trail council Boy Scouts Am. and Three Rivers council Girl Scouts Am., 1957-65; chmn. United Appeal, Junction City, 1967; mem. Dist. 5 Gov.'s Commn. Youth, 1969-71; mem. Gov.'s Com. Status of Women, 1971-74. Mem. Lane County (Ore.) Republican central com., 1964—; mem. budget com. City of Junction City, 1969—. Trustee Bus. and Profl. Women's Found.; bd. dirs. Lane Meml. Blood Bank, Am. Cancer Soc. Mem. Nat. Assn. Ins. Women, Nat. Assn. Women Hwy. Safety Leaders, P.T.A., Am. Field Service Com., Nat. (treas. 1971-72, nat. 2d v.p. 1972-73, 1st nat. v.p. 1973-74), Ore. (pres. 1968-69) fedns. bus. and profl. women's clubs, Junction City C. of C. (treas. 1969-71), Alpha Chi Omega. Methodist (youth counselor). Soroptimist. Clubs: Shadow Hills Country, Investment (Junction City). Home: 655 Laurel St Junction City OR 97448 Office: 620 Holly St Junction City OR 97448

HAYS, SUSAN JANE WALLACE (MRS. FORBES BROCK HAYS), editor; b. Indpls., Mar. 19, 1933; d. Leon Harry and Anna Ruth (Haworth) Wallace; B.A., Ind. U., 1955; M.A., Columbia, 1969; m. Forbes Brock Hays, Apr. 14, 1957 (dec. 1967); children—Martha, Forbes. Researcher Time Mag., Time, Inc., N.Y.C., 1956-59; asst. to dir. spl. summer program Carleton Coll., Northfield, Minn., 1967-68; reporter, asst. to editor Northfield (Minn.) News, 1968-69; copy editor, state editor Bloomington (Ind.) Courier-Tribune, 1969-70; edn. editor Ind. U. News Bur., Bloomington, 1970—. Mem. adv. com. to dean for women's affairs Ind. U., 1973—. Mem. Am. Polit. Sci. Assn., Edn. Writers Assn., Kappa Kappa Kappa, Theta Sigma Phi (chpt. pres. 1972-73). Democrat. Methodist. Club: University, Altrusa (chpt. rec. sec. 1971-72) (Bloomington). Home: 1631 Pickwick Pl Bloomington IN 47401 Office: 106 N Union St Bloomington IN 47401

HAYS, WILMA PITCHFORD (MRS. VERNON HAYS), author; b. Nance County, Neb., Nov. 22, 1909; d. Clarence Franklin and Grace Belle (Lull) Pitchford; student U. Neb., 1927-32; m. R. Vernon Hays, Mar. 17, 1928; 1 dau., Grace Ann (Mrs. Elliott Kone). Mem. staff Cape Cod Writers Conf., 1963-64, 73-74. Author numerous children's books including: Pilgrim Thanksgiving, 1955; Christmas On The Mayflower, 1956; Story of Valentine, 1956; Fourth Of July Raid, 1959; Easter Fires, 1959; Abe Lincoln's Birthday, 1961; George Washington's Birthday, 1963; Highland Halloween, 1962; Noko Captive of Columbus, 1967; May Day For Samoset, 1968; Patrick Of Ireland, 1970; The Open Gate (New Years 1813), 1970; Cape Cod Adventure, 1964; Little Horse That Raced A Train, 1959; The Burro Who Ran Away, 1969; Drummer Boy For Montcalm, 1959; Samuel Morse And The Electronic Age, 1966; Eli Whitney Founder Of Industry, 1965; The Scarlet Badge, 1963; Pontiac (biography), 1965; (novel) The Apricot Tree, 1968; Naughty Little Pilgrim, 1969; Circus Girl Without A Name, 1970; The Long Blond Wig, 1971; Rebel Pilgrim (biography of William Bradford), 1969; For Ma and Pa, 1972; (with R. Vernon Hays) Foods The Indians Gave Us, 1973; Little Yellow Fur, 1973; others. Conglist. Home: 1660 La Gorce Dr Venice FL 33595

HAYTER, DORIS LILLIAN SHEA, psychologist; b. N.J., May 2, 1942; d. James Norman and Doris Lillian (La Prade) Shea; B.A. in Edn., R.I. Coll., 1965; M.S. in Psychology, U. R.I., 1969; div.; children—Sean, Devin; m. 2d, Mr. Hayter. Substitute tchr. Providence Sch. Dist., 1965-67; clin. trainee R.I. Med. Center, 1967-69, R.I. Hosp., 1969; clin. intern Cranston (R.I.) Sch. Dept., 1969; sch. psychologist Warren (R.I.) Sch. Dist., 1969—. Cons. in field. Mem. Nat. Assn. Sch. Psychologists; mem. Am. (asso.) R.I. (asso.) psychol. assns. Home: 140 Lauriston St Providence RI 02906 Office: Hugh Cole School Asylum Rd Warren RI 02885

HAYTER, JEAN MARIE, educator; b. Washington County, Va., Mar. 19, 1921; d. Milton Augustus and Florence Olivia (Cunningham) Hayter; B.S., Med. Coll. Va., 1951; M.A., Columbia, 1958, Ed.D., 1961. Staff nurse Milligan Clinic, Jefferson City, Tenn., 1949-51, S. Plains Hosp., Amherst, Tex., 1951; instr. nursing Med. Coll. Va., Richmond, 1951-52, asst. prof., 1952-58, asso. prof., 1958-65; faculty U. Ky., Lexington, 1965—, prof. nursing, 1967—. Cons. Emory U., 1967, Am. U., 1968, VA Hosp., 1969, So. Missionary Coll., 1968, Henderson Community Coll., 1969-70, Midway Jr. Coll., 1971. Nat. League for Nursing fellow, 1960-61. Fellow Am. Acad. Nursing; mem. Nat. (v.p. 1956-67), Va. leagues for nursing, Ky. Nurses Assn., Council of Nurse Researchers, Kappa Delta Pi, Pi Lambda Theta. Contbr. articles to profl. jours. Home: 1340 Royalty Ct Lexington KY 40504

HAYWARD, WILHELMINA, educator; b. Chgo., Feb. 10, 1945; d. Thomas Zander and Wilhelmina (White) Hayward; A.A., Christian Coll., 1965; B.A., U. Denver, 1967, 5th year degree, 1968; M.S. (State of Ill. fellow, Fed. fellow 1969-71), No. Ill. U., 1971; certificate French, U. Geneva (Switzerland), 1971. Instr. dept. spl. edn. No. Ill. U., DeKalb, 1968-70; tchr. spl. edn. DeKalb County Sch. System, 1970-71; self-employed as spl. edn. cons., Geneva, 1971-73; ednl. specialist Office Pub. Instrn., Springfield, Ill., 1973—. Instr. trainer nat. aquatic sch. A.R.C., 1964-71; leader Boy Scouts Am., 1970-71, 72-73. Mem. Am. Assn. Mental Deficiency, Council for Exceptional Children. Clubs: Woman's Athletic (Chgo.); Jr. League (Springfield). Home: W County Line Rd Barrington Hills IL 60010 Office: 1020 S Spring St Springfield IL 62704

HAYWOOD, MARGARET A., judge; b. Knoxville, Tenn., Oct. 8, 1912; d. Jonathan W. M. and Mayme (Fain) Austin; LL.B., Robert H. Terrell Law Sch., 1940. 1 dau., Geraldine H. (Mrs. Porter). Admitted to D.C. bar, 1942; practiced in D.C., 1942-72; mem. D.C. Council, 1967-72; judge Superior Ct. of D.C., 1972—. Real estate broker, 1950-67. Mem. D.C. Commn. on Status of Women, 1968-72; dir. Nat. Capital council Girl Scouts U.S., 1968-72. Bd. dirs. Council Chs. Greater Washington, 1950-70. Mem. Fedn. Bus. and Profl. Womens Clubs, Lambda Kappa Mu (mem. nat. exec. bd.). Republican. Mem. United Ch. of Christ (moderator). Home: 4424 Hunt Pl NE Washington DC 20019 Office: Superior Ct DC 440 G St NW Washington DC 20001

HAZARD, HELEN HUTCHINSON (MRS. CLAUDE JACK HAZARD), realty exec.; b. Balt., Aug. 13, 1916; d. David William and Fennie S. (Swanson) Hutchinson; B.S., Johns Hopkins, 1938; m. Claude Jack Hazard, Sept. 29, 1947; children—Linda Wells (Mrs. Joseph Vincent Delaney III), Claudia Jane Saunders. Tchr. secondary edn. Balt. City Sch. System; instr. English dept. Morgan State Coll., Balt.; pres. Helen Hazard Realtors, Stamford, Conn., 1957—. Chmn. by-laws com. Stamford Bd. Realtors, 1974-75. Mem. Nat., Conn. assns. real estate bds., Women's Council Realtors, Johns Hopkins Alumni Assn. Clubs: Stamford Duplicate Bridge, Midday. Home: 82 Boxwood Dr Stamford CT 06906 Office: 140 Hoyt St Stamford CT 06905

HAZARD, KATHARINE ELIZABETH, educator; b. Lafayette, Ind., July 15, 1915; d. Clifton Terrell and Mabel Florence (Starbuck) Hazard; B.S., Purdue U., 1936, M.S., 1937; Ph.D. (fellow 1939-40), U. Chgo., 1940. Instr., Winthrop Coll., 1940-41, Wellesley Coll., 1941-45; mem. faculty Douglass Coll., New Brunswick, N.J., 1945—, prof. math., 1965—. Mem. Am. Assn. U. Profs., Math. Assn. Am., Am. Math. Soc. Sigma Xi., Kappa Alpha Theta, Pi Mu Epsilon, Kappa Delta Pi. Home: 2 Chester Circle New Brunswick NJ 08901 Office: Douglass Coll New Brunswick NJ 08901

HAZARD, MARY (MRS. LELAND HAZARD), civic worker; b. Kansas City, Mo., June 24, 1900; d. Samuel K. and Jane Hasseltine (Garnett) Chorn; A.B., U. Mo., 1921; M.A., U. Kan., 1929; LL.D., Carnegie-Mellon U., 1970; postgrad. U. Chgo., U. Pitts.; m. Leland Hazard, Dec. 22, 1923. Tchr. pub. and pvt. schs. Kansas City, 1921-39, headmistress Sunset Hill Sch., Kansas City, Mo., 1931-39; asst. prof. psychology U. Pitts., 1949-53; mem. Pitts. Bd. Pub. Edn., 1954-69, Vanguard Theater Support Group, 1962—, Women's com. Mus. Art, Carnegie Inst., 1957—; vis. com. Harvard Grad. Sch. Edn., 1957-62, Margaret Morrison Carnegie Coll., 1962-68; personnel practices com. Family and Children's Service, 1960-67; exec. com. United Mental Health Services, 1960-67; mem. Adv. Council on Library Devel. in Pa., 1961-64, chmn., 1964-68. Recipient citation of merit U. Mo., 1966, women's centennial honor award, 1968; named Distinguished Dau. Pa., 1973. Mem. Phi Beta Kappa, Kappa Kappa Gamma. Home: 5023 Frew Av Pittsburgh PA 15213

HAZELL, LOIS ADDISON SPRIGG (MRS. JOSEPH WILLIAM HAZELL), civic worker; b. Washington, June 5, 1896; d. William Mercer and Lucy Derby (Page) Sprigg; student Parsons Sch. Fine and Applied Arts, N.Y.C., 1914, New Sch. for Social Research, N.Y.C., 1938, Am. U., 1955; m. Joseph William Hazell, Nov. 28, 1923 (dec. Dec. 1950); 1 son, Joseph William. Asst., then mgr. Elsie Cobb Wilson Decorating Firm, Washington, 1915-17; occupational therapist Walter Reed Gen. Hosp., Washington, 1917-19; free-lance writer and photog. illustrator, 1938-39; employee Project Harbor Civil Def. Plan, Nat. Acad. Scis., 1964; illustrator Sound, Science and the Sea, U.S. Navy Underwater Lab., New London, Conn., 1966; illustrator Washington story Fair Lady mag., Johannesburg, South Africa, 1967. Bd. dirs. Friendship House, Washington, 1922-24; organizer A.R.C. arts and skills Walter Reed Hosp., 1943; vice chmn. to prepare civil def. plan for Montgomery County, Md., 1953-61; mem. exec. com. Montgomery County Civil Def. Adv. Bd., 1953-61; chmn. organizer Citizens Shelter Com. of Washington Met. Area, 1940-63; hostess daily radio program Woman's Angle, 1967, hostess weekly radio program Internat. Tea Time, 1965—; bd. dirs. Welcome to Washington Internat. Club, 1963—, pres., 1966-68. Recipient awards for civil def. work. Mem. English-Speaking Union, Montgomery County Press Assn., African Am. Women's Council. Club: Capital Speakers (mem. governing bd. 1963-64, pres.-elect 1970-71). Home: 37 Quincy St Chevy Chase MD 20015

HAZZARD, SHIRLEY, author; b. Sydney, Australia, Jan. 30, 1931; d. Reginald and Catherine (Stein) Hazzard; ed. Queenwood Sch., Sydney until 1946; m. Francis Steegmuller, Dec. 22, 1963. With Combined Services Intelligence, Hong Kong, 1947-48, U.K. High

Commnrs. Office Wellington, New Zealand, 1949-51, UN Secretariat (gen. service category), N.Y.C., 1952-62. Nat. Inst. Arts and Letters grantee in lit., 1966. Author: Cliffs of Fall and Other Stories, 1963; (novel) The Evening of the Holiday, 1966; (fiction) People in Glass Houses, 1967; (novel) The Bay of Noon, 1970; (hist. study) Defeat of an Ideal: A Study of the Self-Destruction of the United Nations, 1973. Contbr. short stories to New Yorker mag. Address: 200 E 66th St New York City NY 10021

HEAD, AGNES KASTNER (MRS. J.C. HEAD), newspaper co. exec.; b. Dexter, Mo., Jan. 31, 1904; d. Herman W. and Mary C. (Wise) Kastner; student S.E. Mo. State Coll.; m. J.C. Head, Sept. 1, 1923; children—Carol J., Rosemary (Mrs. Joe Gallegas), Genee (Mrs. George Schubert). Operator, Lovington (N.M.) Daily Leader, 1944-58; editor, pub., owner Hobbs (N.M.) Flare, 1948—. Chmn. Young Rep., 1940; del. N.M. Constl. Conv., 1969. Mem. Bus. and Profl. Women's Club, Am. Legion Aux. Home: 1826 N Jefferson Hobbs NM 88240 Office: PO Box 1095 114 E Dunnam Hobbs NM 88240

HEAD, JUDITH (MRS. THOMAS W. HEAD), civic worker; b. Decatur, Ill., Dec. 2, 1924; d. Maurice S. and June Walker (Moore) Sly; B.A., Wellesley Coll., 1947; m. Thomas W. Head, Aug. 14, 1948; children—Eric Richard, Molly Ann, Carol Elizabeth, Mary Julia. Profl. social worker, Peoria, Ill., 1949-52, Columbus, Ind., 65-68. Founder United Fund, 1968, Family Service, 1968 and Community Day Care, Columbus, 1969; founder, mem. exec. com. Ind. Forum, 1970; chmn. adv. com. Ind. Dept. Pub. Welfare Bd., 1970—; pres. Hoosiers for Equal Rights Amendment, 1973—; pres. Children, Inc.; mem. Columbus Housing Authority. Recipient Woodrow Wilson award Wellesley Coll., 1947. Mem. League Women Voters (mem. Ill. state bd. 1958-64; Ind. state bd. 1967-69; Ind. pres. 1969-73; nat. dir. 1974—). Presbyn. (council ch. and soc.).

HEAD, NANCY WINTERBOTTOM (MRS. WILLIAM E. HEAD), ednl. adminstr.; b. Laconia, N.H., Jan. 9, 1948; d. Frederick William and Guennlyn (Simpson) Winterbottom; student Mary Washington Coll., 1966-67; B.S., U. N.H., 1970; m. William E. Head, Aug. 22, 1970. Program coordinator N.H. Office Econ. Opportunity, Concord, 1970; admissions rep., dir. admissions Newton (Mass.) Coll., 1970-73; asst. dir. admissions U. N.H., Durham, 1973—. Mem. Coll. Entrance Exam. Bd., New Eng. Assn. Coll. Registrars and Admission Officers, New Eng. Personnel and Guidance Assn., Phi Kappa Phi. Author: Summer Recreation Manual, 1970. Home: 90 Mount Vernon St Dover NH 03820 Office: Admissions Office University of New Hampshire Durham NH 03824

HEADLEE, PATRICIA ELAINE, coll. dean; b. Pismo Beach, Cal., Apr. 24, 1942; d. Maurice Murl and Zela Beatrice (Wingo) Headlee; B.A., Cal. State U. at Fresno, 1963; M.A., Cal. State U. at Northridge, 1967; postgrad. U. Cal. at Los Angeles, 1968-72, U. Cal. at Irvine, 1972, U.S. Internat. U., 1973—. Tchr., Oxnard (Cal.) Unified Sch. Dist., 1963-66, Culver City (Cal.) Unified Sch. Dist., 1966-69; dean of women, counselor Simi (Cal.) Valley Unified Sch. Dist., 1969-71; dean of women, asso. dean students Santa Ana (Cal.) Coll., 1971—. Mem. Cal., Cal. Jr. Coll. assns. women adminstrs. Office: 17th at Bristol Santa Ana Coll Santa Ana CA 92706

HEADLEY, ANNE RENOUF (MRS. JOHN MILES HEADLEY), educator; b. N.Y.C., Apr. 3, 1937; d. Henry Charles and Helen (Donovan) Renouf; grad. Emma Willard Sch., 1954; A.B., Barnard Coll., 1959; M.A., Yale, 1962, Ph.D., 1966; postgrad. Sch. Law, Duke, 1970-71, Am. U., Washington Coll. Law, 1974—; m. John Miles Headley, July 27, 1965. Asst. prof. dept. polit. sci. U. N.C. at Chapel Hill, 1966-71; sr. profl. cons. U.S. Environmental Protection Agy., Washington, 1973-74, Fed. Power Commn., 1974—. Sr. faculty fellow U.S. Dept. State, 1967; sr. staff mem., vis. research scholar Carnegie Endowment for Internat. Peace, 1968-69; mem. Nat. Adv. Council on Grad. Edn., 1969-71. Mem. Nat. Com. for the Sanger Meml., 1969—. Woodrow Wilson fellow, 1958. Mem. Am. Bar Assn., Am. Polit. Sci. Assn., Am. Soc. Internat. Law, Internat. Studies Assn., The Innovation Group, Am. Acad. Consultants, Tech. and Communication, Phi Beta Kappa. Democrat. Home: 700 New Hampshire Av NW Washington DC 20037

HEADSPETH, DOROTHY WHITE (MRS. CLARENCE HEADSPETH), librarian; b. Navasota, Tex., July 22, 1926; d. Commodore H. and Lela Mae (Gaines) White; student, Houston Coll., 1943-45, Springfield Coll., 1968; m. Clarence Headspeth, Oct. 21, 1961; 1 dau., Stephanie. Release clk. adj. gen's. office U.S. Dept. Army, Washington, 1945-50; statis. clk. U.S. Continental Army Command, Ft. Monroe, Va., 1950-60; foreclosure clk. VA, N.Y.C., 1960-61; librarian Conn. State Dept. Edn., Hartford, 1964—. Recipient Meritorious award Conn. State Dept. Edn., 1970. Mem. Nat. Soc. for the Study of Edn., Central Office Edn. Assn., Parent Tchr. Assn. Home: 1631 Westover Rd Chicopee MA 01020 Office: Room 350 165 Capitol Av Hartford CT 06115

HEADY, ELEANOR BUTLER (MRS. HAROLD FRANKLIN HEADY), author; b. Bliss, Ida., Mar. 13, 1917; d. Arthur Harrison and Effie Marie (Carrico) Butler; B.A., U. Ida., 1939; m. Harold Franklin Heady, June 12, 1940; children—Carol (Mrs. Donald Richard DeMaria), Kent Arthur. Tchr. English, Rockland (Ida.) High Sch., 1939-40; radio broadcaster KRBM (KXIQ), Bozeman, Mont., 1943-45; free lance writer childrens books, 1960—. Pres., Thousand Oaks (Cal.) P.T.A., 1956; v.p. Berkeley-Albany P.T.A. Council, 1957. Mem. Berkeley (Cal.) Republican Womans Club, 1970—. Bd. dirs. Concerned Berkeley Citizens. Mem. Cal. Writers Club (pres. 1971-73), League Am. Penwomen, Authors Guild. Conglist. (mem. bd. of arts and communications 1970-73). Club: Berkeley City. Author: Jambo Sungura, 1965; Coat of the Earth, 1967; When the Stones Were Soft, 1968; Brave Johnny O'Hare, 1969; (with Harold F. Heady), High Meadow, 1970; Tales of the Nimipoo, 1970; Safiri the Singer, 1971; The Soil That Feeds Us, 1971; Sage Smoke, 1973; Make Your Own Dolls, 1974. Home: 1864 Capistrano Av Berkeley CA 94707

HEAL, FLORENCE LIPPINCOTT DARNELL (MRS. SIDNEY K. HEAL), educator; b. Camden, N.J., Dec. 5; d. J. Clifton and Hannah (Roberts) Darnell; B.S., Drexel Inst. Tech., 1936, M.S., 1946, postgrad., 1954-56; postgrad. Rutgers U., 1950-63, Temple U., 1954-55, Glassboro State Coll., 1961-63; m. Sidney K. Heal, Nov. 25, 1937; children—Martha Elizabeth (Mrs. Dean Everett Bekken), Joanne Darnell. Tchr. pub. schs., Riverton, N.J., 1936-39, Camden, 1940-44, Friend Sch., Moorestown, N.J., 1944-46; chmn. dept., tchr. Moorestown Pub. Schs., 1945-63; supr. home econs. State Dept. Edn., Trenton, N.J., 1963-72; cons. Div. Vocational Edn., N.J. Dept. Edn., Sewell, 1972—. Asst. state adviser Future Homemakers Am., 1950-63, state adviser, 1963-72. Mem. exec. com. Tri-State Council on Family Relations, 1958—; chmn. bd. mgrs. Greenleaf home. Mem. N.J. Personnel and Guidance Assn., Am., N.J. assns. for curriculum devel., Nat. Council in Family Relations, Am., N.J. home econs. assns., Am. Vocational Assn. (sec. exec. sec. 1966—), N.E.A., N.J. Edn. Assn., N.J. Assn. Adult Edn., Nat. Pub. Sch. Adult Sch. Educators, Am. Assn. U. Women, League Women Voters, Delta Kappa Gamma. Club: Soroptimist (Trenton, N.J.). Contbr. articles to profl. jours. Home: 149 E Main St Moorestown NJ 08057 Office: Tanyard and Salina Rds Sewell NJ 08080

HEALD, EMILY EASTHAM, civic worker; b. Lawrence, Mass., July 14, 1917; d. Ernest Eugene and Elsie (Eastham) Heald; grad. Katharine Gibbs Sch., Boston, 1935. With Mass. Electric Co., 1935—, now adminstrv. asst. marketing dept., North Andover. Mem. Girl Scout council Greater Lawrence, Inc., 1935-63, pres. leaders assn., 1938-42, adviser sr. Girl Scouts planning bd., 1949-51, dir., 1951-63, sec. bd. dirs., 1952-53, v.p., 1957-61, pres., 1961-63, nat. council mem. 1949-51, 63-69, dir., pres. Merrimack River Girl Scout Council, Inc., 1963-70; dir. Methuen chpt. A.R.C., 1952-54, chmn., 1953-54, dir. Greater Lawrence chpt., 1954—, sec., 1957-60, 1st vice chmn., 1961-63, chmn., 1963-65; sec. dist. 1 Mass. regional blood program, 1960-63, exec. com., 1963-66; chmn. Methuen div. Community Chest Drive, 1951; mem. budget com. United Fund, Lawrence, 1954-56, chmn. spl. gifts, Methuen, 1960; chmn. social action com. Greater Lawrence Council of Chs., 1959-61. Sec. bd. dirs. Greater Lawrence Guidance Center; trustee Methuen Meml. Music Hall, Inc., 1949—, sec., 1949-53, 55-56, 60-63, clk., 1951-55, 60-66, v.p., 1966-69, pres., 1969-73. Episcopalian (dir. choir mothers 1956-67, pres. Eureka club 1957-59, vestryman 1972—). Clubs: Quota (Lawrence); Appalachian Mountain (Boston). Home: 38 High St Methuen MA 01844 Office: 1101 Turnpike St North Andover MA 01845

HEALEY, BARBARA ANN OCHONICKY (MRS. LEO T. HEALEY), radiol. technologist; b. Herkimer, N.Y.; d. Paul and Catherine (Zeman) Ochonicky; student Ilion Sch. Bus.; grad. Albany Med. Sch. X-ray Tech., 1950; m. Leo T. Healey, Aug. 2, 1932 (dec.); children—Marsha (Mrs. Raymond D. Wheeler). Med. sec. Pine Crest County Lab., Herkimer, N.Y., 1947; med. lab. technician Herkimer County Clinic, N.Y., 1948-54, radiologic technologist, 1948-54; chief technologist dir. dept. radiology Little Falls Hosp., 1954—, mem. disaster team, 1965-74. Mem. Utica Soc. Radiologic Technologists, N.Y.C. Roentgen Ray Technicians, X-ray Technicians Soc. N.Y., Am. Soc. Radiologic Technicians, Am. Registry of Radiologic Technicians, Internat. Platform Assn. Home: 10 Whited St Little Falls NY 13365 Office: 114 Burwell St Little Falls NY 13365

HEALY, FRANCES PATRICIA, educator; b. Cleve., Nov. 20, 1923; d. Thomas Fitzgerald and Marie (Bruner) Healy; B.A., Flora Stone Mather Coll., 1946; M.A., Ohio State U., 1956, Ph.D., 1967. Editor, Employee Publs., Am. Greetings Corp., Cleve., 1951-53; asst. to dean of women Ohio State U., Columbus, 1953-60; asso. dean students Douglass Coll., Rutgers U., New Brunswick, N.J., 1960-69; dean students Russell Sage Coll., Troy N.Y., 1969-71, prof. edn., 1969—. Mem. Nat. Assn. Womens Deans and Counselors (com. on profl. standards and ethics 1970-72), Am. Assn. U. Women, Am. Assn. U. Profs., Am. Assn. for State and Local History, Rensselaer County Hist. Soc., Early Am. Soc., Council for Basic Edn., Pi Lambda Theta. Home: RD 2 Schaghticoke NY 12154

HEALY, MADELYN MEIER, educator; b. Buffalo, Oct. 3, 1932; d. Frank Michael and Madelyn Mary (Doyle) Meier; B.A., State U. N.Y. at Albany, 1954; M.A., Columbia, 1955, Ed.D., 1972; m. Thomas J. Healy, Jr., Aug. 25, 1956; children—Madelyn, Sharon, Thomas, Patrick. Guidance asso. Tchrs. Coll., Columbia, 1954-55; tchr. math. Kearny (N.J.) Schs., 1955-57, guidance counselor, 1972; asso. prof. guidance and student personnel services Newark State Coll., Union, N.J., 1972—, mem. adv. com. Inst. Child Study, 1972—. Adv. com., financial sec. Family Service Bur., West Hudson, N.J., 1971—; com. mgmt. YM-YWCA, West Hudson, 1972—; exec. com. West Hudson Community Council, 1973—. N.Y. State Regent's scholar, 1951-54; Pendleton Dudley scholar, 1969-70; Heft scholar, 1970-71. Mem. Am. Personnel and Guidance Assn., N.J. Assn. Counselor Educators and Suprs. (charter), Kappa Delta Pi, Pi Lambda Theta. Club: Arlington Women's (financial sec.). Home: 91 Park Pl Kearny NJ 07032 Office: White House Newark State College Union NJ 07083

HEALY, MARGARET TURNER (MRS. JAMES WILLIAM HEALY), newspaper editor; b. West Grove, Pa., Apr. 18, 1944; d. Robert Futhey and Sara Elizabeth (Kidd) Turner; B.A., Pa. State U., 1966; postgrad. West Chester State Coll., 1971—; m. James William Healy, Jan. 18, 1969. Reporter, Cecil Whig, Elkton, Md., 1966-68, news editor, 1968-69; editor Cecil Democrat, Elkton, Md., 1968; editor Chester County Press, Oxford, Pa., 1969-73, mng. editor, 1973—. Mem. Chester County Draft Bd., Oxford, Pa., 1972—. Mem. Friends of Oxford Library, V.F.W. Aux. Democrat. Presbyn. (trustee 1970). Clubs: Soroptimist, Oxford. Home: Rural Route 1 Box 349 West Grove PA 19390 Office: 107 S 3rd St Oxford PA 19363

HEALY, MARTINA B., innkeeper; b. St. Louis, Sept. 1, 1927; d. Martin Hamilton and Mary Elizabeth (Strahl) Lyvers; student Monterey Peninsula Jr. Coll., 1948-50; m. Paul Laverne Healy, Oct. 20, 1951; children—Bryan Joseph, Christopher Kenneth, Paula Diane. Music tchr., St. Louis, 1942, Monterey, Cal., 1947-51; receptionist Parsons Co., Newton, Ia., 1961-63, radio sta. KCOB, Newton, 1964; with Holiday Inn, Newton, 1968—, innkeeper-mgr., 1970—. Dist. pres. Diocesan Council Catholic Women. Mem. Newton C. of C. (bd. dirs., com. mem.), Sacred Heart Soc. (pres.), 99's (pres. Ia. 1960-62), Soroptimists Internat. Home: 1300 S 3d Av W Newton IA 50208 Office: I-80 and Hwy 14 Newton IA 50208

HEALY, SISTER MARY IMMACULATE, hosp. adminstr.; b. Bklyn., Oct. 13, 1927; d. Peter J. and Mary T. (Flanagan) Healy; B.A., St. Mary of Plains Coll., 1966; M.A., Xavier U., 1966. Bus. mgr. Bob Wilson Meml. Hosp., Ulysses, Kan., 1952-57, Ponca City (Okla.) Hosp., 1957-61; adminstr. Bob Wilson Meml. Hosp., 1961-63, St. Anthony Hosp., Dodge City, Kan., 1966-73, Mt. Carmel Med. Center, Pittsburg, Kan., 1973—. Cons., S.W. Plains Region Health Planning Council, Dodge City, Kan.; pres. Kan. Conf. Cath. Hosps., 1973. Bd. dirs. Congregation Sisters of St. Joseph, Wichita, Kan., St. Rose Hosp., Hayward, Cal., Western Kan. Regional Hosp., Dodge City, Kan., Conf. Cath. Hosps. Mem. Am., Kan., Cath. hosp. assns., Am. Coll. Hosp. Adminstrs., Hosp. Financial Mgmt. Assn., Dodge City C. of C. Address: Mt Carmel Med Center Pittsburg KS 66762

HEAP, VIRGINIA SKINKLE, interior designer; b. Chgo., July 29, 1907; d. George Elliot and Blanche (Randolph) Skinkle; student Sorbonne, Paris, France, 1925-27; m. Sydney Heyworth Heap, Nov. 12, 1932; 1 son, Randolph Heyworth. Owner Virginia Heap Interiors, Los Angeles, 1940—. Precinct capt. Pro. Am. Club, 1945—, Rep. Club, Los Angeles, 1945—. Mem. Nat. Soc. Interior Designers, Jr. League. Author column In One Ear, 1933-35, Urban Phenomena, monthly mag. page, 1930-32. Address: 435 S Curson Av Los Angeles CA 90036

HEARRON, MARTHA LUCILLE SOMMERFELD (MRS. ARTHUR E. HEARRON JR.), biostatistician; b. Highland Park, Ill., Apr. 4, 1943; d. Roy E. and Emma (Kedney) Sommerfeld; student Woman's Coll., U. N.C., 1960-62; B.S., U. Mich., 1964, M.P.H., 1966; m. Arthur E. Hearron, Jr., Mar. 8, 1969. Biostatistician Upjohn Co., Kalamazoo, 1966—. Costume chmn. Kalamazoo Civic Players, 1968-69. NIH fellow, 1964-66. Mem. Am. Statis. Assn. (sec. biopharm. subsect. 1972, 73, 74), Am. Pub. Health Assn., Biometric Soc. Methodist. Home: 5200 Whippoorwill Kalamazoo MI 49002 Office: Upjohn Co Kalamazoo MI 49001

HEARST, AUSTINE MCDONNELL, publishing co. exec.; b. Boston, Nov. 22, 1928; d. Austin and Mary (Belt) McDonnell; student King-Smith Jr. Coll.; m. William Randolph Hearst, Jr., July 29, 1948; children—William Randolph III, John Augustine Chilton. Reporter, columnist Washington Times Herald, 1949-54; syndicated columnist King Features Syndicate, 1949-54; radio Commentator CBS Mut. network; editor-in-chief Hearst Corp., N.Y.C. Active Lenox Hill Neighborhood Assn., N.Y.C., Parents Com. St. Davids Sch., Musicians Emergency Fund, North Salem Hist. Soc. Mem. Daus. Soc. Cincinnati, Nat. Soc. Barons of Runnemede, Soc. Descs. King William I the Conqueror and His Companions at Arm. Clubs: Sulgrave (Washington); American Fox Hound. Home: 810 Fifth Av New York City NY 10020

HEARST, BELLA RACHAEL, physician, artist; b. Pitts.; d. Aba and Bertha (Alpern) Hearst; B.M., Chgo. Med. Sch., 1949, M.D., 1950; postgrad. Johns Hopkins, 1952-53, Art Inst. Chgo., 1958-68. Rotating intern Norwegian Am. Hosp., Chgo., 1949-50; jr. asst. pathologist Cook County Hosp., Chgo., 1950-52; fellow med. legal pathology U. Md., 1953-54; sr. pathology resident Charity Hosp., New Orleans, 1955-56; spl. cardiac research Armed Forces Inst. Pathology, Washington, 1956-57; dir., coordinator pathology dept. Hosp. O'Horan, Merida, Yucatan, Mexico, 1957-58; founder Bertha Hearst Found., Inc., 1958, exec. dir., 1958-63; founder Diabetic Inst. Am., Inc., Chgo., 1959, exec. dir., 1959-63; founder Internat. Diabetic Inst., Inc., Chgo., 1963, exec. dir., 1963—; dist. med. dir. compensation U.S. Dept. Labor, Chgo., 1968—; research dir. Fed. Safety and Fire Council, Chgo.; research asso. microbiology Stritch Sch. Medicine, Loyola U., Chgo.; staff physician Western Ill. U., 1971-72, asso. prof., 1971-72. Founder Health Crusade, condr. radio programs. Art exhibit Shuster Art Gallery, N.Y., 1966, Internat. Dermatology Congress, Munich, 1967. Recipient 3d prize for art exhibit A.M.A. Conv., Chgo., 1962; testimonial plaque for work sr. citizens Chelsea House, Chgo. Fellow Am. Geriatric Soc., Royal Soc. Pub. Health; mem. Internat. Acad. Pathology, Am. Women's Med. Assn., Am. Soc. Microbiology Am. Assn. for Study Neoplastic Diseases, Reticuloendothelial Soc. Author: Diabetes and Juvenile Delinquency, 1964; Diabetes, Early Detection, Prevention and Eradication, 1964; Diabetes and Fitness, 1964; Diabetic Statistical Research Survey, 1961-65; Diabetes and Blood Groups, 1965; Diabetes and Aging, 1965; Diabetes and Newborns. Contbr. articles related to diabetes, tumors, reticuloendothelioses to med. publs. Editor: Archives of Diabetes, 1963—. Contbr. articles on blood groups, geog., phys., genetic, allergic, surg., congenital aspects, geog. groups in health and disease of blood. Pioneer in early mass detection, cure, prevention, eradication of diabetes. Address: 514 W Jefferson St Macomb IL 61455

HEARST, GLADYS WHITLEY HENDERSON (MRS. CHARLES JOSEPH HEARST), writer; b. Wolfe City, Tex.; d. William Henry and Helen (Butler) Whitley; student Trinity U., 1924-26; B.A., U. Tex., 1928, M. Journalism, 1928, postgrad., 1938-40; m. Robert David Henderson, May 17, 1933 (dec. 1941); m. 2d, Charles Joseph Hearst, Oct. 30, 1943. Editor, Future Farmer News, Austin, Tex., 1930-33; dir. Service Bur., Tex. Congress Parents and Tchrs., Austin, 1933-36; dir. Student Union, U. Tex., 1939-42; free lance writer, 1945—. Instr. writing Waterloo YWCA, 1966-69. Vice chmn. Black Hawk County Democratic party, 1945-57. Mem. County Extension Program Planning Com., 1965-68. Served to lt. WAVES, 1942-45. Mem. Am. Assn. U. Women (life, Ia. chmn. Status of Women 1954-56, past pres. Cedar Falls br.), Women in Communications (nat. pres., Distinguished Service award 1962, 73, nat. chmn. by laws 1969—, nat. citation 1969, Task Force Long Range Planning Com. 1973—), P.E.O., Zeta Tau Alpha, Kappa Tau Delta, Sigma Delta Chi. Mem. United Ch. of Christ (past deaconess). Club: Capital Gains Investment (past pres., treas. 1970-73) (Cedar Falls). A writer Cedar Falls (Ia.) Centennial Pageant, 1952; writer, editor hist. book Cedar Falls Naval Station 1942-45. Address: 2511 Ashland Av Cedar Falls IA 50613

HEARTT, CHARLOTTE BEEBE, univ. adminstr.; b. N.Y.C., Nov. 12, 1933; d. Stacey Kile and Charlotte Josephine (Wustl) Beebe; B.A., Wellesley Coll., 1954; m. William Hollis Peirce, June 19, 1954; children—Daniel Converse, William Kile; m. 2d, Stephen Heartt, May 26, 1962; children—Thomas Beebe, Sarah Lincoln. Intern, Office of the V.P., Richard Nixon, Washington, 1953; asst. in computing numerical analysis lab., U. Wis.-Madison, 1954-56; sec. to dir. corporate fund raising Boston Arts Festival, 1961; sec. to dean coll. relations Radcliffe Coll., Cambridge, Mass., 1961-62; sec. to chmn. dept. city planning Harvard, Cambridge, 1962; Fulbright Program adviser, study abroad adviser Brandeis U., 1966-71, dir. office internat. programs, 1971—. Cons. to Wellesley Coll., Wellesley, Mass., 1971—. Mem. Commonwealth Task Force on the Open Univ., 1973. Bd. dirs. Council on Internat. Edn. Exchange, 1973, Boston Area Seminar for Internat. Students, 1973. Mem. Sect. on U.S. Study Abroad (nat. sec., regional rep. 1972-74), Nat. Assn. Fgn. Student Affairs (Nat. Commn. Liaison). Nat. Assn. Women Deans, Adminstrs. and Counselors. Home: Old County Rd Lincoln MA 01773 Office: Office of International Programs Brandeis University Waltham MA 02154

HEATH, ARLINE C. (MRS. MAYO S. HEATH), social worker; b. Turkey, Sept. 29, 1925; student Franklin (Ind.) Coll., 1939-41; B.S., U. Pitts., 1943; postgrad. Western Res. U., 1947-49, U. Conn., 1955, U. Pitts.; m. Mayo S. Heath (dec.); 1 dau. Asst. psychologist Psychology for Industry, Cleve., 1947-49; occupational therapist Sta. Hosp., Fort Bragg, N.C., 1949; research asst. psychology Pitts. Plate Glass Co., Springdale, Pa., 1954-55; area dir. YWCA, Wilkinsburg, Pa., 1955-56; rehab. therapist VA Hosp., Pitts., 1956-60; admissions officer, registrar Grad. Sch. Pub. and Internat. Affairs, U. Pitts., 1960-64, asst. campus coordinator Ecuador Project, 1964-65, staff asso. Internat. Programs, 1965-66; operations asso. Health Planning and Devel. Commn., The Welfare Fedn., Cleve., 1967—. Mem. U. Pitts. Alumni Assn. (past pres.), Am. Assn. U. Women, Pitts. Council for Internat. Visitors. Baptist. Clubs: Edgewood Country; College. Home: Apt 303 12024 Shaker Blvd Cleveland OH 44120

HEATH, FLORENCE IRENE BROOKS (MRS. EDWARD NEWELL HEATH), bank exec.; b. Sidney, N.Y., July 15, 1923; d. William Morris and Mable Clara (Elliott) Brooks; grad. Lowell Sch. Bus., 1939; student IBM Sch., 1942-48, Broome Community Coll., 1965; m. Edward Newell Heath, Oct. 9, 1948. Legal sec. Samuel Feldman, Atty., Binghamton, N.Y., 1940-42, IBM Corp., Endicott, N.Y., 1942-48; with Binghamton (N.Y.) Savs. Bank, 1952—, corporate sec., 1970—. Secretarial tchr. Binghamton State Hosp., 1959-65, cons. family care patients, 1959—, mem. Vol. Council, 1959—, pres., 1966-69, pres. aux., 1974. Asst. sec. Conrad and Va. Klee Found., Inc., Binghamton, N.Y., 1971—. Bd. dirs. Broome County Mental Health Assn., 1973-74, Broome County chpt. Am. Cancer Soc., 1973-74. Recipient citation for Community Service in Mental Health Lane Bryant Internat. Award Soc. Mem. Broome County C. of C., Am. Inst. Banking, Nat. Secs. Assn. (pres. 1956, div. officer 1961-62), Chenango Shores Assn. (v.p. 1971-72). Methodist. Home: 4 Jameson Rd Binghamton NY 13905 Office: 62-68 Exchange St Binghamton NY 13902

HEATHMAN, ANN ELLA (MRS. FREDERICK STANLEY HEATHMAN), broadcasting co. exec.; b. Phila., Jan. 30, 1920; d. Mark Anthony and Lenora (Northey) Fisher; student, Carroll Coll., 1938-39; m. Frederick Stanley Heathman, Feb. 5, 1943; children—Judy (Mrs. Judy Foy), Linda (Mrs. John Wallace), William. With Mitchell Broadcasting Co., Grinnell, Ia., 1964—, condr. Ann's Clipboard, 1965—, sta. mgr., 1973—. Mem. Bus. and Profl. Women (pres. 1973—). Home: 1214 Broad St Grinnell IA 50112 Office: 909 1/2 Main St Grinnell IA 50112

HEATLEY, EVE SOLOMON, clin. social worker; b. St. Joseph, Mo., June 8, 1922; d. Arthur and Velma (Percyfield) Hancock; B.A., U. Mo., 1948; M.S.W., U. Kan., 1962; m. Hob C. Solomon, Aug. 6, 1946 (div. Mar. 1958); children—Marcia (Mrs. Ronald Barker), Colanne (Mrs. Eddie Burkett), Dale, Phillip; m. 2d, Robert L. Heatley, Sept. 2, 1962 (div. 1968); 1 dau., Brenda Renee. Med. technologist dept. bacteriology U. Mo. Med. Sch., 1948; research dept. pathology Kan. U. Med. Center, 1955; bacteriologist Stormont Vail Hosp., Topeka, Kan., 1955; clin. social worker in alcoholism VA Hosp., Houston, Tex., 1962-70; pvt. practice social work, Houston, 1966—; out patient psychiat. social worker VA Hosp., Houston, 1970—; clin. instr. psychiatry Baylor Med. Coll., Houston, 1970—; mem. faculty Inst. on Alcoholism, extension field div. U. Tex., 1972. Mem. Am. Soc. Clin. Pathologists, Nat. Assn. Social Workers, Am. Group Psychotherapy Assn., S.W. Regional Group Psychotherapy Soc., Tex. Soc. Clin. Social Workers. Home: 4709 Redstart St Houston TX 77035 Office: Doctor's Center 7000 Fannin St Suite 750 Houston TX 77025

HEATON, ELOISE KLOTZ (MRS. CHARLES TOLL HEATON), educator, composer; b. Baldwinsville, N.Y., June 1, 1909; d. John Adam and Lena (Parry) Klotz; B.Mus., Syracuse U., 1933, M.A., 1960; postgrad. New Eng. Conservatory Music, summers 1945, 46, 48, Boston U., summer 1952, Eastman Sch. Music, U. Rochester, summer 1969, 72; certificate in choir tng. Royal Conservatory Music, U. Toronto, summer 1950; m. Charles Toll Heaton, Aug. 29, 1934. Pvt. piano tchr., Syracuse, N.Y., 1933—; instr. music Peterboro (N.Y.) Union Sch., 1936-38; instr. piano, voice, chorus Itawamba Jr. Coll., Fulton, Miss., 1950-51; substitute tchr. Syracuse Pub. Schs., 1952-54, 55-60; instr. N.W. Miss. Jr. Coll., Senatobia, 1954-55; Mem. Music Tchrs. Nat. Assn., Am. Musicol. Soc., Music Educators Nat. Conf., N.Y. State Sch. Music Assn., Composers and Authors Assn. Am., Poetry Soc. Va., Am. Assn. U. Women, Am. Assn. U. Profs., Am. Soc. for Aesthetics, Am. Guild Organists, Internat. Musicol. Soc. Republican. Episcopalian. Composer sacred songs The Lord is Merciful, 1937, One Prayer, 1946, My Soul is Athirst for God, 1948, Hear Me When I Call, O Lord, 1965, 91st Psalm, 1962; sacred cantatas Christ in Gethsemane, 1944, Law of the Harvest, 1946; secular songs Lady at the Harpsichord, 1945, The Springtime Is My Mother, 1930; children's study pieces Play-time Music for Kindergarten, 1953; First Piano Duets, 1961; violin solo, Invocation, 1956; operetta The Queen's Garden, 1938. Author: Around the Sun, 1948. Contbr. to anthology American Lyricists, 1954. Home and studio: 135 Kensington Pl Syracuse NY 13210

HEATON, JANE, religious ofcl.; b. Centralia, Ill., Nov. 23, 1931; d. Wilbur Estle and Nina (Huddleston) Heaton; B.Music Edn., DePauw U., 1953; M.Religious Edn., Christian Theol. Sem., 1968. Sec., Div. Overseas Ministries, Christian Ch., Indpls., 1953-58, deptl. asso., 1958-61, dir. curriculum and edn., dept. ch. women Div. Homeland Ministries, 1961-72, dir. leadership devel., dept. ch. women, 1972—; missionary in Zaire, 1959-60; ordained to ministry Christian Ch., 1970; tchr. Mindolo Ecumenical Centre, Kitwe, Zambia, 1973. Sec.-treas. Irvington Community Council, Indpls., 1972—. Mem. Indpls. Radio Club, Theta Phi. Author: And What of Ourselves, Bible study guide on Hebrews, 1968. Home: 5126 Atherton N Dr Indianapolis IN 46219 Office: Box 1986 222 S Downey Indianapolis IN 46206

HEATON, SONJA RAE, assn. exec.; b. Red Oak, Ia., May 1, 1942; d. Harold Hill and Viola Margaret (Hendrickson) Heaton; B.S., U. Neb. at Omaha, 1964. Dist. dir. Omaha council Camp Fire Girls, 1964-69, exec. dir. Red River Valley council, Fargo, N.D., 1969—. Cons. recreation class Moorhead State Coll., 1973. Mem. Am. Camping Assn. (pres. Omaha sect. 1969), Quota Club of Fargo-Moorhead. Methodist. Home: 1809 S 13 1/2 St Fargo ND 58102 Office: 305 S 11th St Fargo ND 58102

HEBALD, EDITH LIPSIG, civic worker; b. N.Y.C., Jan. 18, 1920; d. Irving A. and Bertha (Evans) Lipsig; student Radcliffe Coll., 1937-39; LL.B., St. Lawrence U., 1943; m. Selian Hebald, June 28, 1940 (dec. Feb. 1959); children—Anne, Selian; m. 2d, Sidney Freidberg, June 11, 1962 (div. 1973). Pres., Forest Knolls Corp., N.Y.C., 1960—, Norman Homes Corp., N.Y.C., 1968—; cataloguer Nat. Collection Fine Arts, Smithsonian Instn., 1969—. Nat. sec. Women's Am. Orgn. for Rehab. through Tng., 1950; pres. Radcliffe Club of Washington, 1969; pres. Radcliffe Club N.Y., 1959, 63, bd. sponsors, 1974—; chmn. clubs Radcliffe Alumnae Assn., 1966; mem. founders com. Am. Symphony Orch. N.Y., 1962. Trustee Allergy Found. Am. Fellow Pierpont Morgan Library, N.Y. Home: 860 UN Plaza New York City NY 10017

HEBELER, JEAN RUTH, educator; b. Lockport, N.Y., Dec. 21, 1931; d. Richard Edward and Madeline Mary (May) Hebeler; B.S., State U. N.Y., 1953; M.S., U. Ill., 1956; Ed.D., Syracuse U., 1960. Tchr., Elba (N.Y.) Central Sch., 1953-54, Jacksonville (Ill.) Pub. Schs., 1954-55; instr. U. Utah, Salt Lake City, 1955-57, Syracuse (N.Y.) U., 1957-60; prof. spl. edn., chmn. dept. U. Md., College Park, 1960—; dir., sec. Washington Ear, Inc., 1973—. Lectr. U. Denver, 1966, U. Ida., 1966; on-going cons. Teaching Resources, Boston, 1969—. Vice chmn. Md. State Adv. Council on Vocational and Tech. Edn., 1968—. Bd. dirs. United Cerebral Palsy Prince Georges County, Prince Georges County Day Care Center. Named College Park Woman of Year, Bus. and Profl. Women, 1968. Mem. Council Exceptional Children (pres. 1971-72), Am. Psychol. Assn., Am. Ednl. Research Assn., Assn. Supervision and Curriculum Devel. Home: 6010 Westchester Park Dr College Park MD 20740

HEBENSTREIT, JEAN ESTILL STARK (MRS. WILLIAM J. HEBENSTREIT), Christian Sci. tchr. and practitioner; d.; Charles Dickey and Blanche (Hervey) Stark; student Conservatory of Music, U. Mo. at Kansas City, 1933-34; A.B., U. Kan., 1936; C.S.B., Mass. Metaphys. Coll., 1964; m. William J. Hebenstreit, Sept. 4, 1942; children—James B., Mark W. Authorized C.S. practitioner, Kansas City, 1955—; chmn. bd., pres. 3d Ch., Kansas City, 1953-54, reader, 1959-62; authorized C.S. tchr., Kansas City, 1964—. Mem. Art of Assembly Parliamentarians (charter, 1st pres.), Internat. Platform Assn., Pi Epsilon Delta, Alpha Chi Omega (past pres.). Clubs: Carriage, Kansas City Athletic. Contbr. articles to C.S. lit. Home: Wornall Plaza Kansas City MO 64112 Office: Skelly Bldg 605 W 47th Kansas City MO 64112

HEBERLIG, SUSAN LENORA, ret. banker; b. Shippensburg, Pa., Feb. 8, 1907; d. Benjamin Mervin and Mary Blanche (Killian) Heberlig; grad. Carlisle Comml. Coll., 1927. Bookkeeper Nat. Soc. for Broader Edn., Carlisle, Pa., 1928-29; bookkeeper First Nat. Bank, Shippensburg, 1929-54, asst. trust officer, 1954-70, trust officer, 1970-74. Mem. Shippensburg Bus. and Profl. Women's Club (chmn. finance com. 1973-74), Shippensburg Hist. Soc. Office: 1 W King St Shippensburg PA 17257

HECHT, LUCILLE, editor; b. Rockford, Ill.; d. Robert W. and Anna (Crowther) Hecht; A.B., U. Wis., 1937. Mng. editor Internat. Altrusan, 1943—. Del. Nat. Health Council Forum, Miami Beach, Fla., 1960, White House Conf. on Internat. Cooperation, Washington, 1965, World Conf. on Refugees, Washington, 1969. Chmn. Lincoln Sr. Center citizens com. 1956-58; bd. dirs. Sr. Citizens Met. Chgo., 1959-61; v.p. Sr. Centers Met. Chgo., 1961-63, chmn. benefit com., 1962, mem. bd., 1965—; exec. com. Div. Recreation and Informal Edn., Welfare Council Met. Chgo., 1962; com. nat. orgns. Nat. Com. Aging, 1960, mem. Community Fund reviewing com. budgets of Homes for the Aged, 1954-59, mem. art sch. com. Old Town Art Center, chmn., 1959-60, mem. bd., 1962; 1st v.p. Old Town Triangle Assn., 1960-61, pres., 1964-65; publicity chmn. Old Town Art Fair, 1960; Chgo. chmn. subcom. on accreditation vol. experience project Council Nat. Orgns. for Adult Edn. Mem. exec. com., bd. Lincoln Park Conservation Assn. Recipient numerous awards Ill. Women's Press Assn. and Nat. Fedn. Press Women, 1946—, Citation, OAS, 1970, Mem. Ill. Woman's Press Assn. (pres. 1973—, recipient 2 1st place awards, Woman of Year 1973), Chgo. Council Fgn. Relations, Women in Communications. Clubs: Altrusa (spl. rep. to Internat. Dist. Conf., Nottingham, Eng., 1966); Chicago Press. Author: (with Dr. George Lawton) Women Go To Work At Any Age, 1947. Contbr. articles to Internat. Altrusan. Home: 1915 N Lincoln Av Chicago IL 60614 Office: 332 S Michigan Av Chicago IL 60604

HECHT, MARIE BERGENFELD, educator, author; b. N.Y.C., Oct. 21, 1918; d. Frank Falle and Marie (Trommer) Bergenfeld; B.A., Goucher Coll., 1939; M.A., New Sch. for Social Research, 1971; m. Morton Hecht, Jr., Dec. 17, 1937 (div.); children—Ann (Mrs. David Bloomfield), Margaret (Mrs. Jason Crum), Laurence, Andrew. Tchr. Am. history Mineola High Sch., Garden City Park, N.Y., 1960—. Mem. Am. Hist. Assn., Orgn. Am. Historians. Author (with Herbert S. Parmet): Aaron Burr: Portrait of an Ambitious Man, 1967; Never Again: A President Runs for a Third Term, 1968; John Quincy Adams: A Personal History of An Independent Man, 1972; The Women, Yes, 1973. Address: 5 Hewlett Pl Great Neck NY 11024

HECHT, PATSY ANN (MRS. LAURENCE KARL HECHT), educator; b. Miami, Fla., Sept. 23, 1935; d. Harry and Detta Leola (Hart) Clark; B.A., U. Miami, 1957; postgrad. U. Cal. at Los Angeles, 1960-61; M.A., Cath. U. of Am., 1967; Ph.D., Wayne State U., 1971; m. Laurence Karl Hecht, Dec. 15, 1961 (dec.). Profl. actress performing with cos. including Kennebunkport Playouse, Coconut Grove Playhouse, Olney Theatre and Hilberry Theatre, 1958-60, 65-66, 67-71; recreation dir. U.S. Air Force, Evreux, France, 1962-64; asso. prof. theatre arts Stockton State Coll., Pomona, N.J., 1971—. Instr. Miami (Fla.) Dade Jr. Coll., 1968, U. Detroit Sch. Dentistry, 1968, Oak Park (Mich.) Recreation System, 1970-71. Fulbright scholar, 1957-58; Woodrow Wilson fellow, 1957-58. Mem. Actors' Equity, Screen Actors Guild, Phi Kappa Phi, Pi Delta Phi, Chi Omega. Home: 28 Donna Dr Pomona NJ 08240 Office: Studies in the Arts Stockton State College Pomona NJ 08240

HECHTENTHAL, SIBYL (MRS. JOE HECHTENTHAL), artist; b. Chgo; d. William and Bess (Zemon) Goodwin; student Chgo. Acad. Art, 1938-39; m. Joe Hechtenthal, Aug. 18, 1940; children—Barry, Carol. Exhibited in one man shows at Monroe Gallery, Chgo., 1958; John M. Smyth Gallery, Chgo., 1960, Chgo. Pub. Library, 1962, Sherman Hotel Gallery, 1962, Hollywood Beach (Fla.) Gallery, 1962, Diplomat Gallery, Fla., 1963, Miami (Fla.) Art Center, 1964, Mchts. and Mfrs. Club Gallery, 1963, Pick Gallery, Winnetka, Ill., 1963, Grosse Point (Mich.) Gallery, 1964, Esquire Theatre Gallery, 1964, Bonwit Teller Gallery, Chgo., 1972, Jordan Marsh Internat. Gallery, Miami, Fla., 1973; exhibited in group shows at Roosevelt U., 1961, Sun Times Exhibit, 1962, Union League Club, 1964, New Trier High Sch., 1960, 61, Miami Art Center, 1961, Artist Guild Chgo. Fine Art Ann., 1960-70, Evanston (Ill.) Art Center, Suburban Art Municipal Art League, 1968, Art Rental Gallery Art Inst. Chgo., 1971, Old Town Art Fair, 1958-72; represented in permanent collections at Springfield (Ill.) Hist. Soc., Livingston Oil Co., Tulsa, Plastic Contact Lens Co., Chgo., Soonges Optik Co., Frankfurt, Germany, Campanili Co., Bologna, Italy, Albertson & Co., Sioux City, Ia., Brass Builders Works, Cal., Mullers Co., Mexico, LaSalle Casualty Co., Chgo., Sunbeam Corp., Chgo., Adult Edn. Council of Chgo., City Bank & Trust Co., Boston, McDonald Plaza, Oakbrook, Ill., others, also pvt. collections; tchr. art YMCA, 1959-61, pvt. studio, 1961-67; lectr. on television shows Jim Conway Show, Today Show, Lee Phillip Show; demonstrated collage at Schiller Park Library, U. Ill. Sec. Gerry Freeman Fund for Cancer Care, 1950—, RCA pavilion N.Y. World's Fair, 1966; lectured, demonstrated collage Northwestern U., 1970; bull. editor, artist Jessie Werthamer Service Club, 1946-66; mem. Louis Weiss Meml. Hosp. Aux., 1956—; sec. Old Wells Assn., 1964. Recipient 2d prize North Shore Art League, 1966, 2d prize Suburban Art League, 1968, Merit award Artists Guild Chgo., 1963-66, Artist Guild Chgo. award Invitational Show Ill. State Mus., 1969. Mem. Artist Equity, Artist Guild Chgo., Adult Edn. Council Chgo. (Speakers Bur.), North Shore Art League, Municipal Art League. Home: 2650 Lakeview Chicago IL 60614 Office: 1526 N Wells St Chicago IL 60610

HECKART, EILEEN, actress; b. Columbus, O., Mar. 29, 1919; d. Leo Herbert and Esther (Stark) Purcell; B.A., Ohio State U., 1942; student Am. Theatre Wing, 1944-48; LL.D., Sacred Heart U., Bridgeport, Conn.; m. John Harrison Yankee, Jr., June 26, 1943; children—Mark Kelly, Philip Craig, Luke Brian. Actress Broadway plays, Voice of the Turtle, 1944, Brighten the Corner, 1946, They Knew What They Wanted, 1948, Stars Weep, 1949, The Traitor, 1950, Hilda Crane, 1951, In Any Language, 1953, Picnic, 1953, Bad Seed, 1955, A View From the Bridge, 1956, Dark at the Top of the Stairs, 1958, Invitation to a March, 1960, Everybody Loves Opal, 1961, Pal Joey (City Center revival), 1961, A Family Affair, 1962, Too True to be Good, 1963, Barefoot in the Park, 1965, And Things That Go Bump in the Night, 1965, You Know I Can't Hear You When the Water's Running, 1967, The Mother Lover, 1969, Butterflies Are Free, 1970, Veronica's Room, 1973; Children at Play, 1974; motion pictures include The Tree, Miracle in the Rain, Bad Seed, Somebody Up There Likes Me, Bus Stop, Hot Spell, Heller in Pink Tights, My Six Loves, 1962, Up the Down Staircase, 1967, No Way to Treat a Lady, 1968, Butterflies Are Free, 1972, Zande's Bride, 1973; The Hiding Place, 1974; actress television, N.Y.C., 1947—. Recipient Outer Circle award, 1953, Daniel Blum award, 1953, Sylvania TV award, 1954, Donaldson award, 1955, Oscar nomination, 1956, Hollywood Fgn. Press award, 1956, Film Daily citation, 1956, Variety Poll award, 1958, Emmy award for Save Me a Place at Forest Lawn, 1966; Aegis award, 1970, March of Dimes award, 1970, Ohio State U. Centennial award, 1970, Acad. award for Butterflies are Free, 1973, Straw Hat best actress award for Remember Me, 1973. Mem. Pi Beta Phi (chpt. pres. 1941). Home: 135 Comstock Hill Rd New Canaan CT 06840 Office: care Milton Goldman at Internat Famous Artists 1301 Av of Americas New York City NY 10019

HECKER, ANNE, pub. relations ofcl.; b. Dallas, Ore., July 6, 1924; d. Elwyn Gordon and Dorothy Ida (Dick) Craven; B.A. in Journalism, U. Ore., 1945; postgrad. U. Wis., 1946; m. Robert Hecker, Sept. 28, 1946; children—Sandra (Mrs. Glenn Biggerstaff), Barbara (Mrs. James Chatters), Nancy (Mrs. David Fox). Staff corr. U.P.I., Portland, Ore., 1945, Madison, Wis., 1946; publs. editor Nat. Aero. Assn., Washington, 1947; dept. editor Pacific Builder & Engr. publs., Seattle, 1951-53, 54-61; mng. editor N.W. Medicine mag., Seattle, 1953-54; contbg. editor Argus, polit. weekly, Seattle, 1961-65; pub. relations dir. Wash. State Dental Assn., Seattle, 1965—. Pub. relations cons. Seattle Urban League, 1967-68, continuing dental edn. dept. U. Wash., 1970-72. Recipient award for investigative reporting Wash. Press Women, 1962. Mem. Women in Communications, Inc. (pres. Seattle profl. chpt. 1971-72, nat. continuing studies and resolutions chmn. 1971-72, nat. treas. and dir. 1972—). Home: 13065 15th Av NE Seattle WA 98125 Office: 417 Grosvenor House Seattle WA 98121

HECKERT, CLARICE MARY UPSON (MRS. WINFIELD W. HECKERT), state legislator; b. Marion, Conn., Nov. 11, 1910; d. Robert Ellsworth and Helen (Nickerson) Upson; student Geneva (Switzerland) Sch. Internat. Studies, 1931; A.B., Wheaton Coll., 1932; m. Winfield W. Heckert, Sept. 9, 1933; children—John Upson, Frances Eleanor (Mrs. Michael A. Pane IV), Rowena Louise (Mrs. Thomas J. Gasser), Clark Webster. Mem. Del. Ho. of Reps., Dover, 1964—, chmn. edn. com., 1967—. Dir., mem. exec. com. Greater Wilmington Devel. Council, 1961-64; dir. Del. Citizens Crime Commn., 1962-64. Asst. sec. Del. State Republican Com., 1964. Mem. Am. Assn. U. Women (nat. legislative com.). Unitarian. Home: 16 Ravine Rd Wilmington DE 19810

HECKLER, MARGARET M. O'SHAUGHNESSY (MRS. JOHN M. HECKLER), congresswoman; b. Flushing, N.Y., June 21, 1931; d. John and Bridget (McKeown) O'Shaughnessy; B.A. (scholar), Albertus Magnus Coll., 1953, LL.D., 1972; LL.B. (scholar), Boston Coll., 1956; postgrad. U. Leiden (Holland), 1953; L.H.D., Northeastern U., 1970, Emanuel Coll., 1969; D. Law and Letters, Stonehill Coll., 1969; LL.D. honoris causa, Regis Coll.; m. John M. Heckler, Aug. 29, 1953; children—Belinda West, Alison Anne, John M. Admitted to Mass. bar, 1956; mem. Mass. Gov.'s Council, 1962-66; mem. 90th to 93d congresses from 10th Dist. Mass.; mem. Banking Com., Vets. Com. Keynote speaker Nat. Women's Republican Conv., 1967. Mem. pres.'s adv. com. Wheaton Coll.; mem. corp. Madeira Sch.; mem. nat. adv. com. Hampshire Coll. Bd. dirs. March Dimes; hon. bd. dirs. Epilepsy Found. Am., Kiddie Kamp; trustee Heart Research Found.; hon. trustee Newton Wellesley Hosp. Recipient numerous civic and profl. awards. Mem. Am. Bar Assn. (com. on govt., legislation and pub. interest of food, drug and cosmetic law div.), Boston Bar Assn., Mass. Trial Lawyers, Mass. Women Lawyers, Catholic Women's Coll. Alumnae Assn. (past pres.). Club: Ninetieth (v.p.) (Washington). Home: 30 Colburn Rd Wellesley Hills MA 02181 Office: House Office Bldg Washington DC 20510

HEDAHL, BEULAH MINERVA, psychologist, educator; b. Bismarck, N.D., Sept. 12, 1920; d. Edwin N. and Clara (Berge) Hedahl; A.A., Bismarck Jr. Coll., 1941; B.A., Concordia Coll., 1946; M.A., Wash. State U., 1948; M.A., U. Minn., 1953, Ph.D., 1958. Dean women, asst. prof. Pacific Lutheran U., 1948-51; instr. counseling center Mich. State U., 1956-59, asst. prof., 1959-63, asso. prof., 1963-64; asso. prof. psychology U. N.D. Counseling Center, Grand Forks, 1964-72, prof., 1972—, dir. counseling center, 1964—. Mem. Am. Psychol. Assn., Am., N.D. personnel and guidance assns., Am. Coll. Personnel Assn., Am. Assn. for Higher Edn., Nat. Vocational Guidance Assn., N.D. Psychol. Assn., Assn. Measurement and Evaluation in Guidance. Home: 424 28th Av S Grand Forks ND 58201

HEDDEN-SELLMAN, ZELDA LOUISE (MRS. WAYNE SELLMAN), painter, educator; b. Farmington, Ill., May 19, 1928; d. Clyde Francis and Iva Natalie (Taylor) Hedden; B.S., Bradley U., 1950, M.A., 1952; postgrad. Ohio U., 1953, Harvard, 1954, Western Res. U., 1955; m. Wayne Sellman, Mar. 16, 1956; children—James, Thomas, David, Daniel, Jonathan. Instr. art Ind. State U., Terre Haute, 1952-54, Ill. Central Coll., Peoria, 1969-71, Spoon River Coll., Canton, Ill., 1966—; one-woman shows at Demanes Gallery, Peoria, 1957, Caterpillar Tractor Adminstrn., Peoria, 1973, Ill. Prairie Dist. Library, Metamora, 1974; exhibited in group shows at Kottler Gallery, N.Y.C., 1973, Rotunda Gallery, London, Eng., 1973, Graham Hosp. Gallery, Canton, Ill., 1973; represented in permanent collection Spoon River Coll. Bd. dirs. Peoria Art Center Sch., 1954-56. Recipient Central Ill. Artists award, 1950-52. Mem. Am. Fedn. Arts. Mem. Soc. of Friends. Author: Treasures in the Snow, 1966. Address: 241 Timberlane Metamora IL 61548

HEDDING, SUSAN VIRGINIA LEBLANC (MRS. STEVEN LEO HEDDING), editor; b. Houston, Dec. 9, 1946; d. Raymond Marce and Hylda Mae (Doucet) LeBlanc; B.A. in Journalism, U. Houston, 1970; m. Steven Leo Hedding, June 13, 1970. Pub. relations writer Tex. Eastern Transmission Corp., Houston, 1970-73; editor Rowan Cos., Inc., Houston, 1973—. Editor monthly mag. Nat. Orgn. for Women, Houston, 1972-73; organizer Houston Self-Help Clinics, 1972-73. Recipient Community Service award Houston mayor, 1970. Mem. Internat. Assn. Bus. Communicators, Women in Communications, Harris County Women's Polit. Caucus. Home: 8850 Chimney Rock Houston TX 77035 Office: 5051 Westheimer Houston TX 77027

HEDLUND, MARILOU MCCARTHY (MRS. REUBEN L. HEDLUND), city ofcl.; b. Chgo., Dec. 16, 1937; d. James Wade and Louise (Cuprea) McCarthy; student Newton Coll., 1955-56; B.A., Barat Coll., 1959; m. Reuben L. Hedlund, Dec. 28, 1963; children—James Wade, Justine Marie. Newspaper writer Chgo. Tribune, 1961-66; alderman Chgo. City Council, 1971—. Free-lance writer, 1966-70. Home: 930 Castelwood St Chicago IL 60640 Office: City Hall Chicago IL 60602

HEDRICK, ADDIE MAE, poet; b. Black Rock, Ark., Aug. 22, 1903; d. William Henry and Mary Elizabeth (Lunsford) Underwood; student pub. schs.; m. Joseph A. Hedrick, Nov. 21, 1920; children—Louise (Mrs. Leonard Caranna), Joseph A. Author collections of poetry Sentient Dust, 1952; Mumbaloo, and other Poems, 1957; A Cup of Stars, 1969; contbr. numerous poems to various publs. Mem. Nat. League Am. Pen Women, Poetry Soc. Tenn., Ark. Authors and Composers, World Poetry Soc. Intercontinental. Baptist. Home: 1109 Weible St Pocahontas AR 72455

HEDSTROM, KRISTI LYN HAWKINSON (MRS. DEAN KARL HEDSTROM), mag. editor; b. St. Paul, Apr. 2, 1947; d. Roy Wilford and Marguerite Francis (Lampman) Hawkinson; B.A., Macalester Coll., 1969; m. Dean Karl Hedstrom, Apr. 29, 1972. Asst. to dir. Nat. Scholastic Press Assn. and Asso. Collegiate Press U. Minn., Mpls., 1969-70, asst. dir., 1970-74, dir. yearbook critical service, 1970—, editor Scholastic Editor Graphics/Communications, 1970—; dir. Gopher Machine & Engring. Co., Mpls. Recipient Journalism award North Central Pub. Co., 1969. Home: 784 2d Av NW New Brighton MN 55112 Office: U Minn 720 Washington Av SE Minneapolis MN 55455

HEE, VIOLET LEE (MRS. HONG MIN HEE), ednl. adminstr.; b. Honolulu, Mar. 25, 1917; d. Charles Y. and Ivy (Yap) Lee; grad. pvt. high sch.; m. Hong Min Hee, Aug. 15, 1942; children—Stephen, Bob, Randy. Tchr., Kauai (Hawaii) pub. schs., 1948-65, curriculum specialist lang. arts, 1965—. Sec., Kauai County YWCA, 1952-59. Pres., Kauai League Republican Women, 1971-73; mem. exec. bd. County Kauai Republican Party, 1971-73; committeewoman Kauai, Kekaha Precinct, 1972—; chmn. registration and credentials Hawaii Rep. party, 1973; dir. Rep. status women com., 1973-74. Mem. adv. bd. Kauai Mus. Hawaii State Found. Culture and Arts. English Inst. fellow, U. Hawaii, 1961. Mem. Kauai (pres. 1959, v.p. 1958), Hawaii (dir. 1959-61) edn. assns., Zonta Club (treas. 1969-71, corr. sec. 1973, 74, editor Ka Leo Holomu 1973), Kauai Chinese Heritage Club, Hawaii Chinese History Center, Friends of Library, Hui O Leka, Delta Kappa Gamma (pres. Eta chpt. 1961-64, first v.p., state chpt. 1969-71, dir. 1961-64, 69-71). Home: Box 313 Kekaha Kauai HI 96752 Office: Box 1307 Lihue Kauai HI 96766

HEEBNER, GLORIA DAWN MOORE (MRS. ROBERT ARTHUR HEEBNER), civic worker; b. Pasadena, Cal.; d. George Vinson and Hildagarde (Mountjoy) Moore; student Pasadena City Coll., U. Cal. at Los Angeles, 1947-50, U. So. Cal., 1950-51; m. Frederick William de Graaf (div. May 1950); 1 dau., Dana Victoria (Mrs. Thomas Knight McAteer); m. 2d, Robert Arthur Heebner, Apr. 19, 1952. Interior designer, decorator, 1954—. Bd. dirs. Long Beach (Cal.) Campfire Council, 1955—, group leader, 1954-59; founder Dominguez Valley Hosp. League, 1961; chmn. Greater Los Angeles Mardi Gras, 1963, 65; historian Woman's Aux. to Los Angeles County Med. Assn., 1958-59, chmn. various coms.; financial sec. St. Francis Hosp. of Lynwood Guild, 1953—, 2d v.p. membership, 1954, also chmn. various coms.; chmn. fashion show Ebell of Los Angeles, 1962; adviser on bd. Mary and Joseph League, 1961-69, membership chmn., 1961. Mem. Ninety Nines Inc., Los Angeles World Affairs Council, Mary and Joseph League, Ladies Charity, Opera Guild of So. Cal., Women's Aux. to Los Angeles County Med. Assn., Los Angeles Area C. of C. (women's div.), St. Francis Hosp. of Lynwood Guild, Los Angeles Orphanage Guild, Lifelighters, San Francisco Opera Guild, San Francisco Ballet Assn., Oceanic Soc., San Francisco Zool. Soc., Cal. Hist. Soc., Sierra Club, Internat. Orgn. Women Pilots. Republican. Roman Catholic. Club: Les Mages Investment. Home: 1126 Greenwich St San Francisco CA 94109

HEENEY, MARY ELLEN (MRS. DAVID GEELIN HEENEY), editor; b. Portland, Kan., Oct. 17, 1903; d. John Joseph and Fannie Alberta (Aker) Burger; student Colo. U., 1924, Phillips U., 1926-27, Kan. State Tchrs. Coll., 1929; m. David Geeslin Heeney, Sept. 2, 1931; children—Marylou (Mrs. William H. Boettcher), John David, Patricia Ann (Mrs. Bruce Reigh). Tchr., rural schs., Kan., 1924-28, elementary sch., South Hwy., Kan., 1929-31; corr. Sumner County (Kan.) News, 1939, Wellington (Kan.) Daily News, Kan., 1945-47; editor South Haven (Kan.) New Era, 1947-74. Bd. dirs. Wheatland Lodge, South Haven, 1970-74. Mem. Sumner County Hist. Soc. (historian 1971-73), Kan. (chmn. 1936-44), Sumner County (chmn. 1955-63) Fedns. women's Clubs, Kan. Authors Club (pub. chmn. Kan. 1962-64, fifth dist. 1954-55), Kan. Press Women. Mem. Order Eastern Star. Address: PO Box 98 South Haven KS 67140

HEER, NANCY WHITTIER (MRS. DAVID MACALPINE HEER), educator; b. Swampscott, Mass., June 23, 1927; d. Philip Page and Gladys Adele (Reid) Whittier; B.A., Syracuse U., 1954; M.A. (Ford Found. fellow), Radcliff Coll., 1956; Ph.D., Harvard, 1968; m. David MacAlpine Heer, June 29, 1957; children—Douglas (dec.), Laura Page, Catherine Reid. Polit. researcher U.S. Govt., Washington, 1956-59; teaching fellow govt. dept. Harvard, 1965-67; instr. govt. dept. Wellesley (Mass.) Coll., 1967-68; asst. prof., then asso. prof. govt. dept. Wheaton Coll., Norton, Mass., 1968-72, prof. govt., dean Coll., 1974—; lectr. U. Cal. at Riverside, 1973-74; asso. Russian Research Center, Harvard, 1974—. Mem. Am. Polit. Sci. Assn., Am. Assn. for Advancement Slavic Studies, Phi Beta Kappa, Phi Kappa Phi. Author: Politics and History in the Soviet Union, 1971. Editorial bd. Studies in Comparative Communism, 1973—. Home: 28 Elm St Norton MA 02766

HEFFRON, ALICE MARY (MRS. WILLIAM G. HEFFRON), civic worker; b. Buffalo; d. William P. and Alice A. (Costello) Dolan; A.B., U. Chgo., 1931; postgrad. Canisius Coll., Buffalo, 1932-33, U. Buffalo, 1934-35, Gregg Coll., Chgo., 1935; m. William G. Heffron, June 28, 1937; children—Jean (Mrs. W. Charles Gordon), William G., Alice Mary (Mrs. David L. Luce). Tchr. Latin, English, South Park High Sch., East High Sch., Buffalo, 1932-34; tchr. Bryant and Stratton Bus. Inst., Buffalo, 1934-38, 40-41; substitute tchr. St. Ambrose Sch., Buffalo, 1952-57. Mem. Nat. Council Cath. Women, nat. dir., Province, N.Y., 1964-68, treas., 1964-68; courtesies chmn. ann. conf. Diocesan Council, 1962, chmn. coordinating com. for Council Days, 1963, pres., 1963-65, mem. Speakers Bur., 1965-66, chmn. Orgn. Services Commn., 1970-71, bd. dirs., 1970—; office interviewer Buffalo Women in Community Service, 1965, project dir., 1966-67, asst. project dir., 1967-68; pres. Buffalo South Dist. Deanery Council, 1961-63; rec. sec. St. Ambrose Mothers Club, 1954-55, mem. exec. bd., 1955-56, del. Fedn. Home Sch. Assns., 1954-56, chmn. League Sacred Heart, 1955-56, chmn. Ann. Installation Dinner, 1956; chmn. baked goods sale, card parties St. Ambrose Rosary and Altar Soc., 1959-63, bd. mem., 1959-64, pres., 1961-62, 70-71, chmn. installation dinner, 1965-66; del. St. Ambrose Parish to Nat. Conv. Nat. Council Cath. Women, Detroit, 1962; adult sponsor St. Ambrose Cath. Youth Orgn., 1950-60, debate coach, 1952-57, chmn. Ann. Crystal Beach Day, 1953-61; co-chmn. Ann. Cath. Charities drive St. Ambrose Parish, 1950-63; co-chmn. St. Ambrose Ladies of Charity, 1961-62, chmn., 1962-63; bd. mem. Mt. Mercy Acad. Mothers Guild, 1958-60, chmn. installation banquet, 1958, chmn. Christmas Party, 1959, del. Buffalo Fedn. Womens Clubs, 1958-59, program chmn., 1958-59, chmn. constn. revision com., 1959; bd. mem. Daemen Mothers Club Rosary Hill Coll., 1957-61, corr. sec., 1958-59, chmn. spring luncheon, card party, fashion show, 1959, pres., 1959-60, publicity chmn., 1961-62, chmn. constn. revision com., 1966; mem. exec. bd. Nat. Found.-March of Dimes, Buffalo and Erie County chpt., 1962-68, Mothers March chmn., Buffalo, 1963-65, Mothers March chmn., Buffalo and Erie County, 1965-67, sec. to exec. bd., 1967-71, hon. bd. dirs., 1971—; pres. bd. dirs., mem., vol. Food and Nutrition Services, Inc.; mem. ednl. com. Priests-Lay Steering Com., Diocese Buffalo. Bd. dirs. Bishop McNulty's Latin Am. AID Com. Recipient Pro Deo et Juventute medal, 1957; Cross Pro Ecclesia et Pontifice, Pope Paul VI, 1968. Mem. Western N.Y. Fedn. Women's Clubs (past v.p., mem. exec. bd., com. chmn. ch. ann. conv. 1964), Nat. Assn. Women Hwy. Safety Leaders (dir. region II 1970—). Home: 121 Ridgewood Rd Buffalo NY 14220

HEFLIN, THELMA ELIZABETH CADE (MRS. GAILLARD HEFLIN), journalist, civic worker; b. Grafton, Neb., May 18, 1913; d. Clifford C. and Elizabeth (Mehaffey) Cade; grad. high sch.; m. Gaillard Heflin, June 2, 1931; children—Kenneth Lee, Mary Elizabeth (Mrs. John Higbie), Dennis Ray. Columist, feature writer Harlan (Ia.) Newspapers, 1964—; corr. Atlantic Farm Monthly, 1965-67; news writer Omaha World Herald, 1969—; on daily radio program KJAN, Atlantic, Ia., 1971—. Mem. County 4-H Girls Com., 1939-55, counselor state camp, 1956-61; chmn. Shelby County Family Living Com., 1955; women's chmn. Shelby County Farm Bur., 1954-55; sec. Bapt. Meml. Home Activities Group, 1961—; active County Assn. for Retarded Children, 1962—, bd. mem., 1964-65, v.p., 1966-67; mem. adv. com. Ia. State Extension, 1958-61; edn. chmn. Rural Area Devel. Commn., 1962-65; mem. sch. bd., Harlan, Ia., 1958-65, pres., 1962. Bd. curators Ia. Hist. Soc. Recipient Shelby County Extension Service Farm Homemaker award, 1952; Leadership award Harlan C. of C., 1965. Mem. Farm Bur., Nat., Ia. press women, Shelby County Art Guild, Shelby County Hist. Soc., Ia. Geneal. Soc., Am., Ia. mothers assns., Ch. Women United (exec. com. 1953-56, pres. 1955), Harlan Concert Assn. (membership chmn. 1967). Republican. Methodist (chmn. commn. on missions 1964-72). Clubs: Harlan Literary, Shelby County Saddle (Harlan). Home: RFD 4 Harlan IA 51537

HEGEMAN, SISTER MARY THEODORE, pub. relations ofcl.; b. Burlington, Wis., Mar. 8, 1907; d. Theodore Joseph and Mary Catherine (Harter) Hegeman; B.S. in Edn., Catholic Sisters Coll., Washington, 1939; M.A. in Psychology, Cath. U. Am., 1940; postgrad. U. Salzburg (Austria), 1957. Tchr. parochial sch., Jefferson, Wis., 1926-30; tchr. spl. education St. Coletta Sch., Jefferson, 1930-37, 40-64, supt., 1964-70, dir. pub. relations, 1970—; mem. grad. faculty Cardinal Stritch Coll., Milw., 1956—. Mem. Wis. Adv. Council on Spl. Edn., 1971—. Bd. dirs. Lt. Joseph P. Kennedy, Jr. Sch., Palos Park, Ill. Recipient Woman of Year award V.F.W. Aux., 1960. Fellow Am. Assn. Mental Deficiency; mem. Nat. Cath. Edn. Assn. (exec. com. spl. edn. dept. 1964—), Sisters of St. Francis of Assisi. Author: The Challenge of the Retarded Child, 1959. Home: St Coletta School Jefferson WI 53549

HEGHINIAN, ELIZABETH ALBAN TRUMBOWER, artist, educator; b. N.Y.C., Jan. 11, 1917; d. Eli Cadwallader and Maria Lucas (Coyle) Trumbower; certificate dept. indsl. design Pratt Inst., 1938; B.S. magna cum laude, N.Y. U., 1950, M.A., 1952, Ph.D., 1957; postgrad. Bklyn. Inst. Arts and Scis., 1963-66, Bklyn. Mus. Art Sch., L.I. U., 1963-66, Fairleigh Dickinson U., 1970; studied under Richard Mayhew, Georgiana Brown Harbeson, Edith Fetterolf, Katheryn I. Young, Howard W. Arnold, I.-Ching Ku; m. Aram Lincoln Heighinian, Aug. 24, 1957; children—Elizabeth Alban, Marie Hunazant. Indsl. designer Belle Kogan Assos., 1938-40; art dir. Norcross Pubs., 1940-42; buyer for battle damaged U.S. naval vessels and equipment Arma Corp., 1942-45; dir. arts and crafts YWCA Camp Program, 1946; designer Cosmopolitan Crafts, Camp Fire Outfitting Co., 1946-47; faculty N.Y. U., 1947-61, asst. prof. edn., 1957-61; specialist consultation services nat. arts and crafts com. Boys' Clubs Am., 1949-65; research and practicum in remedial reading techniques N.Y.C. Pub. Sch., Bklyn., 1966-68. Exhibited in group shows Pratt Inst., 1936-38, N.Y. U., 1948-52, represented in permanent collection Bklyn. Mus. Art Sch., pvt. collections. Mem. nat. adv. com. on recreation programs and activities arts and crafts sect. Nat. Recreation Assn., 1958-62; pres. Camp Jefferson, Inc., N.Y.C., dir. Camp Jefferson, Palisades Interstate Park, N.Y., 1945—; active town wide camping and sch. year program Girl Scouts U.S.A., 1969-73; mem. N.Y. Assn. for Brain Injured Children, 1963—. Recipient Founders Day certificate N.Y. U., 1950. Mem. Am. Watercolor Soc. (asso.), Am. Assn. U. Women, Nat. Congress Parents and Tchrs., Tenafly Nature Center Assn., Palisades Interstate Park Camp Dirs.' Assn., Pi Lambda Theta, Kappa Delta Pi, Epsilon Pi Tau. Author: The Contribution of Craft Activities to the Philosophy and Objectives of Boys Clubs of America, 1957; (monograph) Crafts in Boys' Clubs, 1958. Address: 52 Howard Park Dr Tenafly NJ 07670

HEGYELI, RUTH INGEBORG ELISABETH JOHNSSON (MRS. ANDREW FRANCIS HEGYELI), pathologist; b. Stockholm, Sweden, Aug. 14, 1931; d. John Alfred and Elsa Ingeborg (Sjogren) Johnsson; B.A., U. Toronto (Can.) 1958, M.D., 1962; postgrad. U. Wis., U. So. Cal.; m. Andrew Francis Hegyeli, July 2, 1966. Came to U.S., 1963. Intern, Queen Charlotte Islands (B.C.) Gen. Hosp., 1961; rotating intern Toronto (Ont., Can.) Gen. Hosp., 1962-63; research asso. in charge cell culture lab. Inst. for Muscle Research, Marine Biol. Lab., Woods Hole, Mass., 1963-65; research pathologist in charge cell culture lab. Battelle Meml. Inst., Columbus, O., 1965-67, sr. research pathologist, 1967-69; med. officer artificial heart program Nat. Heart and Lung Inst. NIH, Bethesda, Md., 1969-70, med. officer program planning and evaluation, office of the dir., 1970-73, chief program devel. and evaluation br., 1973—. Lederle Research scholar Dept. Anatomy U. Toronto, 1959; recipient Outstanding Sci. award life scis. Battelle Meml. Inst., 1966. Fellow Acad. Medicine; mem. A.A.A.S., Canadian Med. Assn., Ohio, N.Y. acads. scis., Tissue Culture Assn., Am. Soc. Artificial Internal Organs. Editor: Proceedings Artificial Heart Program Conf., 1969. Home: 10824 Middleboro Dr Damascus MD 20750 Office: Bldg 31 NIH Bethesda MD 20014

HEHMEYER, CAROL MARLIAVE (MRS. ALEXANDER MILLAR HEHMEYER), lawyer; b. Salt Lake City, June 30, 1941; d. Burton Hampton and Doris (Dodge) Marliave; B.A. with distinction (Kraft scholar), U. Cal. at Berkeley, 1963; J.D., 1967; m. Alexander Millar Hehmeyer, Mar. 15, 1969. Legal clk. Office Dist. Atty., Contra Costa County, Cal., 1967, West Long Beach Legal Aid, 1968; probation officer, Orange County, Cal., 1968; admitted to Cal. bar, 1969; asst. dist. atty. Office Dist. Atty., San Francisco, 1969—. Coro Found. fellow, 1963-64. Mem. Nat. Orgn. Women, Women's Equity Action League, Am., Cal., San Francisco bar assns., San Francisco Women Attys. (Queen's Bench, sec. 1963), San Francisco Bus. and Profl. Women's Club, Bay Area Prosecutors Assn., San Francisco Jr. C. of C., Phi Beta Kappa, Alpha Gamma Delta. Republican. Conglist. Home: 3340 Clay St San Francisco CA 94118 Office: 850 Bryant St 3d San Francisco CA 94103

HEIDE, CHARLOTTE ELLA DALE (MRS. PAUL G. HEIDE), ch. worker; b. Stafford, Kan., Apr. 29, 1915; d. Elmer L. and Ella Frances (Rusco) Dale; student Emporia State Tchrs. Coll., summers 1935-39, Midland Coll., 1940; Friends U., 1970, Oklahoma City U., summers 1970, 72; m. Paul G. Heide, June 16, 1940; children—Charlotte Ann (Mrs. Knut Aagaard), Paul Joe, Paula Jean (Mrs. Roland Hirsch), Jan Fredrick. Tchr., Hill Sch., Hudson, Kan., 1933-35; prin., tchr. Zenith (Kan.) Sch., 1935-38, Antrim Sch., St. John, Kan., 1938-40. Lay dir. religious edn. Pilgrim United Ch. of Christ, 1964-69, leader Y-Teens, 1958-62, ch. sch. tchr., 1941—, pres. Women's Fellowship Pilgrim, 1973-74, Kan.-Okla. Conf. Women's Fellowship study chmn., 1964-68, pres., 1970-72, chmn. ch. library, 1966-73, treas. Ch. Women United, Wichita, 1966-70, v.p., 1970-73, pres., 1973—. Pres. local P.T.A., 1955-56, 58-59; leader Camp Fire Girls, 1953-56, Horizon Club, 1957-59; den mother Cub Scouts Am., 1963-65; mem. exec. bd. YWCA, 1966; pres. Childrens Workers Council, 1963. Recipient Wakon award Camp Fire Girls, 1960. Mem. Assn. for Childhood Edn. (pres. local br. 1961-62, co-organizer Children's Traveling Mus. 1964—), Kan. Assn. for Childhood Edn. (pres. 1969-71). Club: Book Explorers (pres. 1960-61, 67-68). Contbr. articles to profl. jours. Home: 746 S Rutan St Wichita KS 67218

HEIDEMAN, KATHERINE GRAYSON GRAHAM (MRS. BERT M. HEIDEMAN), educator; b. Audubon, Ia., Apr. 11, 1910; d. James Melville and Katherine (Brown) Graham; student Northwestern U., 1927-28, U. Cal. at Berkeley, summer 1939; B.A., U. Cal. at Los Angeles, 1931; M.A., U. So. Cal., 1934; m. Bert M. Heideman, July 6, 1934; children—Eric Ronald (dec.), Bert Lawrence Karl, Eric Melville Bert. Writer, Collier's New Ency., N.Y.C., 1931-32; tchr. Enterprise Jr. High Sch., Compton, Cal., 1932-34; tchr., head English dept., coordinator dramatics and assembly programs John D. Pierce Jr. High Sch., Grosse Pointe, Mich., 1934-42, 44-46; tchr. English, Kramer Jr. High Sch., Washington, 1943-44; county supt. schs., Houghton County, Hancock, Mich., 1958-63; supt. Houghton County Intermediate Sch. Dist., Hancock, 1963-64, Houghton-Baraga and Keweenaw Counties Intermediate Sch. Dist., Hancock, 1964-65, Copper Country Intermediate Sch. Dist., Hancock, 1965—. Sec., Upper Peninsula com. on Mental Retardation, 1967; mem. Com. of 23 advisers Mich. Bd. Edn., 1972-74. Mem. Mich. Assn. Intermediate Sch. Adminstrs., Mich. Assn. Sch. Adminstrs., Mich. Assn. Sch. Bds., N.E.A., Mich. Edn. Assn., Mich. Assn. for Emotionally Disturbed Children, Nat. Rehab. Assn., Copper Country Assn. for Retarded Children, Am. Assn. U. Women, Mich. Alumni Acad., Houghton County Hist. Assn., Internat. Platform Assn., Copper Country Supts. Round Table, Mich. Tech. Faculty Women, U. Cal. at Los Angeles Alumni Assn., D.A.R., Alpha Delta Kappa, Chi Omega, Phi Beta, Chi Delta Phi. Clubs: Hancock Civic, Hancock Home Study. Home: 204 Montezuma St Hancock MI 49930 Office: 302 Front St Hancock MI 49930

HEIDEN, BARBARA, city ofcl.; b. Bklyn., June 20, 1930; d. Emanuel M. and Jennie (Shulsky) Heiden; B.S., N.Y. U., 1952. Recreation leader N.Y.C. Dept. Recreation, Parks, Recreation and Cultural Affairs Adminstrn., 1952-58, asst. supr., 1958-71, supr., 1971-73, adminstrv. dir. recreation, Bronx, N.Y., 1973—. Life mem. Am. Theater Assn. Office: Bronx Park E and Birchall Av Bronx NY 10462

HEIDEPRIEM, EVELYNN IRENE (MRS. GLEN HEIDEPRIEM), coll. adminstr.; b. Lead, S.D., Nov. 20, 1926; d. Albert and Wilmet Irene (Odgers) Hebert; student Colo. Nurses Tng., Denver Gen. Hosp., 1944-46, Boulder (Colo.) C. of C. Mgmt. Inst., 1968; m. Glen Heidepriem, Jan. 22, 1971; 1 son, Richard Alan Van Heuvelen. Owner, Evelynn Van Pine Cone Pottery Co., Deadwood, S.D., 1955-65; bookkeeper Deadwood (S.D.) C. of C., 1966-70, exec. sec. and mgr., 1966-70; travel devel. coordinator Old West Trail Found., West Berlin, Germany, 1970-71; spl. asst. to pres. Nat. Coll. Bus., Rapid City, S.D., 1971, placement dir., 1971—. Chmn., S.D. Heart Fund, 1955-57; sec. Deadwood United Fund, 1958-68, Attention Center, Rapid City, 1972—. Mem. Rapid City Med. Aux., Black Hills Art Assn. (curator 1964—), Beta Sigma Phi (pres. Deadwood 1963), Republican. Episcopalian. Home: PO Box 70 Rapid City SD 57701 Office: 321 Kansas City St Rapid City SD 57701

HEIDKE, FLORITA LAUGHLIN (MRS. ROY ALBERT HEIDKE), civic worker; b. Chgo., Mar. 22, 1927; d. John Thomas and Florence (Hilb) Laughlin; B.E., Chgo. Tchrs. Coll., 1948; M.A., Northwestern U., 1952; student Chgo. Acad. Fine Arts, 1950; m. Roy Albert Heidke, June 23, 1951; children—Michel Marie (Mrs. Lawrence McKown Wettermark), Patricia Ann, William Geoffrey, II, Amanda Jon. Tchr. pub. schs., Chgo., 1948-52; prof. muralist, 1955—; treas. Look & Heidke, Inc., Oak Lawn, Ill., 1958; featured columnist Southtown Economist Newspaper, 1959-63; supr. art Blue Island (Ill.) high schs.; head ceramics sch. adult edn. Blue Island. Founder, Oak Lawn Youth Commn., 1955, sec. 1955-57, v.p. 1957-59; founder Ranch Manor Homeowners Aux., 1954, v.p. 1955-58, pres. 1965-67; pres. Lawn Manor P.T.A., chmn. gov.'s commn. on Day Care Centers, 1970—. Bd. dirs. Nat. Found., 1960—, Ill. Animal Welfare; social chmn. Christ Community Hosp. Aux., 1971-73. Mem. Northwestern U. Alumni Assn., Chgo. Tchrs. Coll. Alumni Assn., Chgo. Tchrs. Union (social sec. to pres. 1951-62), Am. Assn. U. Women, Christ Community Hosp. Aux. (v.p. 1968-71, social chmn. 1970-71). Home: 11024 S Keeler Av Oak Lawn IL 60453 also 4800 N 68th St Scottsdale AZ 85251 Office: 5210 W 95th St Oak Lawn IL 60453

HEIFETZ, SONIA, pharmacist; b. Rowne, Poland; d. Zise and Toiba (Ehrlich) Heifetz; came to U.S., 1929, naturalized, 1934; Ph.G., Temple U., 1933. Asst. chief pharmacist Grad. Hosp. U. Pa., Phila., 1937-49, dir. pharmacy services, 1949—. Certified tchr. of Russian, Phila. Bd. of Edn. div. sch. extension. Mem. Am. Pharm. Assn., Am. Soc. Hosp. Pharmacists, Phila. Guild Hosp. Pharmacists (v.p. 1966), N.E.A., Am. Jewish Congress. Home: 2665 Willits Rd Philadelphia PA 19114 Office: 19th and Lombard Sts Philadelphia PA 19146

HEIKENEN, PATRICIA SMITH, editor museum publs.; b. Mpls., June 3, 1920; d. Earl Leslie and Alma Helen (Wigand) Smith; B.A. in Journalism, U. Minn., 1942, certificate interior design, Extension, 1962; m. Harry Wilbur Heikenen, Sept. 23, 1949 (div. June 1958). Chief copywriter Softlines advt. dept. Gamble-Skogmo, Inc., Mpls., 1943-45; program analyst NBC, N.Y.C., 1945; staff asst. club program A.R.C., Manila, P.I., Zama, Japan, Osaka, Japan, 1945-47; with decorating studio Dayton's, Mpls., 1957-63; sec. to pres. Bemis Co., Mpls., 1964-65; dir. program div. editor catalogs, publs. Minn. Museum Art, 1965—. Bd. dirs. Minn. UN Assn., 1965-67, v.p., 1966-67, editor Newsletter, 1964-67. Mem. Internat. Platform Assn., Women in Communication, Alpha Chi Omega. Episcopalian. Home: 3007 Atwood Dr Minnetonka MN 55343 Office: 305 St Peter St St Paul MN 55102

HEILMAN, JOAN RATTNER (MRS. MORTON HEILMAN), writer; b. N.Y.C.; d. Louis E. and Erna (Schneider) Rattner; B.A., Smith Coll., 1944; m. Morton Heilman, Aug. 12, 1956; children—Katherine, Julia, David. With press dept. UN, N.Y.C., 1946-48; with This Week Mag., N.Y.C., 1948-69; freelance writer, 1969—. Mem. Soc. Mag. Writers. Co-author: The Story of Weight Watchers, 1970, Kenneth's Complete Book on Hair, 1972; Growing Up Thin, 1975. Contbr. articles to various mags. Home: 812 Stuart Av Mamaroneck NY 10543

HEILMANN, MARTHA GERRY WHEELER, pub. co. exec.; b. Natick, Mass., Oct. 18, 1921; d. Sidney Watson and Mae F. (Holden) Wheeler; A.A., Stephens Coll., 1940; postgrad. N.Y. U., 1942-43, Fairleigh Dickinson U., 1949-51; m. Philip Eugene Heilmann, Apr. 12, 1946 (div. Feb. 1958); children—Geoffrey Clarke, Frank Eugene. Free lance writer, 1956—; genealogist, 1960—; adminstrv. staff U. Mass., Amherst, 1963-66; owner Heritage Studios, Hartshorne, Okla., 1964—; editor New Eng. Homestead, Mag., Springfield, Mass., 1968-70; house dir. Chamberlayne Jr. Coll., Boston, 1970-71; editorial dir. Bicentennial Publs., Inc., Cambridge, Mass., 1971—, now v.p. Sec., dir. Durham Park Civic League, Piscataway Twp., N.J., 1952-56. Mem. election bd. Piscataway Twp., N.J., 1952-56; sec. Hampshire County (Mass.) Republican Club, 1959-62; v.p. Women's Rep. Club Mass., 1967-72. Trustee North Am. Bapt. Alliance Ednl. Trust, N.Y.C., 1972—; bd. dirs. Holden Family Assn., 1969—. Served with WAC, 1943. Mem. New Eng. Historic Geneal. Soc., D.A.R. (chpt. regent 1968-70), Daus. Am. Colonists, Children of Am. Revolution (sr. soc. pres. 1967-73), Descs. of Minutemen of 1775 (nat. v.p. 1972—), Am. Legion (post comdr. 1954-55), Mass. Ex-Regents Club D.A.R. (sec. 1973—). Author: Heraldry for Everyone, 1967; Women in the American Revolution, 1974. Editor: New England Homestead Magazine, 1968-70; The Patriot, 1972—. Contbr. articles to profl. jours. Home: USWV Colony RFD 3 Wilburton OK 74578 also PO Box 604 Boston MA 02117 Office: Bicentennial Publs Suite 704 678 Massachusetts Av Cambridge MA 02138

HEIMBURGER, ELIZABETH MORGAN, psychiatrist; b. Atlanta, Apr. 23, 1932; d. Henry Durand and Elizabeth (Palmour) Morgan; B.S. with honors, Ga. State U., 1964; M.D., Med. Coll. Ga., 1967; m. Richard Ames Heimburger, Dec. 23, 1964; children—Elizabeth (Mrs. Alan Bowles), Aggie Whitaker III, Margaret Diane, Richard Ames, Katherine Durand. Intern internal medicine Med. Coll. Ga. Hosp., 1967-68, resident gen. psychiatry, 1968-69; resident psychiatry and neurology U. Tex. Med. Br., Galveston, 1969-70, fellow child and adolescent psychiatry, 1970-72, asst. prof. child and adolescent psychiatry, dir. adolescent psychiatry, 1972-73; asst. prof. psychiatry, asst. prof. community health and med. practice U. Mo. Sch. Medicine, Columbia, 1973—. Diplomate Am. Bd. Psychiatry and Neurology. Mem. Am. Acad. Child Psychiatry, Am. Psychiat. Assn., Am. Orthopsychiat. Assn., Am. Soc. Adolescent Psychiatry. Episcopalian. Home: 2713 Surfside Ct Columbia MO 65201

HEIN, MARGARET GILL (MRS. WILLIAM J. HEIN), educator; b. Arkadelphia, Ark., June 25, 1921; d. Joseph Mote and Lula (Helms) Gill; B.A., Henderson State Coll., 1943; M.A., So Meth. U., 1950; Ph.D., U. Tex., 1956; m. William J. Hein, June 25, 1969. Tchr. pub. schs., Arkadelphia, Okolona, 1944-46; tchr. So. Meth. U., Dallas, 1950-57; asso. sec. Assn. for Supervision and Curriculum Devel., Washington, 1957-59, exec. sec., 1959-65; prof. edn., head dept. tchr. edn. Mills Coll., Oakland, Cal., 1965-73; vis. prof. Lehigh U., Bethlehem, Pa., 1973-74, asso. dean Sch. Edn., 1974—. Mem. adv. com. Bay Area Learning Center, Oakland, 1972-73. Served with WAC, 1944-46. Mem. Nat. Council Tchrs. English, Am. Assn. for Higher Edn., Am. Assn. Sch. Adminstrs. (resolutions com. 1973), Nat. Assn. Secondary Sch. Prins., Am. Assn. U. Profs., Zonta, Kappa Delta Pi, Pi Lambda Theta. Contbr. articles to profl. publs. Home: 241 Braeside Av East Stroudsburg PA 18301 Office: 524 Brodhead Bethlehem PA 18015

HEIN, ROSEMARY RUTH, educator; b. Chgo., Sept. 12, 1924; s. Peter Leo and Alice Myrtle (Martin) Hein; B.A., Carleton Coll., 1946; M.S., George Washington U., 1951; Ph.D. (USPHS fellow), Northwestern U., 1954. Biologist, USPHS, Nat. Cancer Inst., 1946-50; asst. prof. biology Keuka Coll., 1954-58, asso. prof., 1958-62; asso. prof. biology Winthrop Coll., 1962-65; asso. prof. to prof. biology Upsala Coll., East Orange, N.J., 1965—, acting dean, 1972-73. Mem. Madison Meml. Park Com., 1971—. Recipient Lindbeck award for distinguished teaching Upsala Coll., 1967. Hon. fellow Am. Assn. U. Women; mem. Am. Soc. Zoologists, Am. Inst. Biol. Scis., Linnean Soc., N.J. Acad. Scis., Sigma Xi, Sigma Delta Epsilon, Phi Kappa Phi. Office: Dept Biology Upsala Coll East Orange NJ 07019

HEINE, DONNA MAE BURBANK (MRS. MICHAEL VICTOR HEINE), occupational therapist; b. Kalamazoo, July 25, 1947; d. Wendell Theodore and Cleo Mae (Wyman) Burbank; B.S., Western Mich. U., 1969; m. Michael Victor Heine, Sept. 27, 1969. Staff activity therapist Ill. State Psychiat. Inst., Chgo., 1969-70, staff therapist, 1971-73; staff therapist Kalamazoo State Hosp., 1970; occupational therapist supr. Neuro-Psychiat. Inst., U. Mich., Ann Arbor, 1973—. Cons. Cheng Hsin Rehab. Center, Taipei, Taiwan, 1970-71. Mem. Am. Occupational Therapy Assn., Pi Theta Epsilon. Lutheran. Home: 3815 Green Brier Blvd Ann Arbor MI 48105 Office: Neuro-Psychiat Inst Ann Arbor MI 48104

HEINE, URSULA INGRID, microbiologist; b. Berlin, Germany, Feb. 19, 1926; d. Georg Friedrich and Alice Frieda (Gunhold) Heine; Diplom Biologe, Humboldt U., Berlin, 1950, Ph.D., 1953. Came to U.S., 1959, naturalized, 1965. Asso., Inst. Exptl. Cancer Research, German Acad. Sci., Berlin, 1950-59, Duke Med. Center, Durham, N.C., 1959-68; microbiologist, head virus studies sect. Nat. Cancer Inst., NIH, Bethesda, Md., 1968—. Mem. German Soc. Electron Microscopy, Electron Microscopy Soc. Am., Am. Assn. Cancer Research, A.A.A.S., Sigma Xi. Home: 18712 Willow Grove Rd Olney MD 20832 Office: Nat Cancer Inst Bethesda MD 20014

HEINEY, ZELDA ELIZABETH, pediatrician; b. Farmersville, O., Jan. 31, 1912; d. Joseph Raymond and Pearl Augusta (Linebaugh) Heiney; B.S., Heidelberg Coll., 1934; M.D., U. Cin. Sch. Med., 1941. Resident Cin. Gen. Hosp., 1941-42; pediatric resident Bellevue Hosp., N.Y.C., 1942-43; obstetrics and gynecology resident Bellevue Hosp., 1943, pediatric resident Cal. Babies and Children Hosp., Los Angeles, 1944; pediatric staff No. Permante Hosp., Vancouver, Wash., 1945; practice medicine specializing in pediatrics, Dayton, O., 1946—; mem. active staff Children's Med. Center; cons. staff Miami Valley, Good Samaritan hosps.; courtesy staff Kettering Meml., St. Elizabeth hosps. Trustee Heidelberg Coll., Tiffin, O., 1974—. Mem. A.M.A., Southwest Ohio Pediatric Soc., Montgomery County Med. Soc., Internat. Platform Assn. Clubs: Altrusa, Dayton Executive. Home: 1947 Philadelphia Dr Dayton OH 45406 Office: 446 Forest Av Dayton OH 45405

HEINL, ELIZABETH (BETTY) LOUISE, editor; b. Yakima, Wash., Apr. 1, 1917; d. William and Katherine Ida (Taylor) Jenkins; grad. high sch.; m. Darwin Agustus Wood, May 6, 1943 (dec. 1947); m. 2d, Lawrence Fredrick Heinl, Nov. 15, 1947 (dec. 1955); children—Dorothy Louise (Mrs. Paul George Lambertsen), Douglas Findley, Barbara Shanon (Mrs. Thomas Grant Coles), David Lawrence, Sandra Louise (Mrs. Arnie Pomerinke), Richard Frederick. With various govt. agys., 1938-43; editor Wapato (Wash.) Ind. Newspaper, 1967—. Mem. C. of C. Christian Scientist. Office: PO Box 67 Wapato WA 98951

HEINLE, BEVERLY DIANE HOFFMAN, pub. co. exec.; b. Danville, Pa., May 18, 1940; d. Charles William and Beryl Dorothy (Ferree) Hoffman; student Pa. State U., 1959-61; B.A., W.Va. U., 1964, M.A., 1966; married. Editorial sec. Ginn & Co., Boston, 1966-67; asst. to editor in chief Blaisdell Pub. Co., Waltham, Mass., 1967; dir. distbn. Center for Curriculum Devel., Inc., Phila., 1967-72; marketing devel. mgr. F.W. Faxon Co., Inc., Westwood, Mass., 1973—. Mem. Thoreau Lyceum, Thoreau Soc., Sales and Marketing Execs. New Eng., Pa. State Players, W.Va. U. Alumnae, Assn. Home: 1095 Main St Concord MA 01742 Office: 15 Southwest Park Westwood MA 02090

HEINTZ, MARY ANNE, educator; b. Boston, May 24, 1924; d. H. Walter and Kathryn Elizabeth (Baker) Heintz; B.S., Boston U., 1946; M.S., U. Tenn., 1958; Ph.D., U. Ia., 1967. Tchr. Farmington (Conn.) High Sch., 1946-57; asst. prof. U. Tenn., 1959-62; mem. faculty Longwood Coll., Farmville, Va., 1962-66, prof. health and physical edn., 1967-73, asso. dean students, 1970-73, dean students, 1973—, v.p. student affairs, 1974—. Teaching grad. asst. U. Tenn., 1957-58; research asst. U. Ia., 1958-59, teaching grad. asst., 1966-67. Mem. Nat. Assn. Women Deans and Counselors, Regional Assn. Women Deans and Counselors, A.A.H.P.E.R., So., Nat. assns. phys. edn. for coll. women, Am. Personnel and Guidance Assn., Va. Edn. Assn., Va. Assn. for Health, Physical Edn. and Recreation. Home: PO Box 12 Longwood Av Farmville VA 23901 Office: Longwood Coll Farmville VA 23901

HEINTZ, SISTER MARY LAMBERT, librarian; b. Milw., Aug. 18, 1913; d. Alfred J. and Louise A. (Diederich) Heintz; B.A., Mundelein Coll., 1952; M.S., Cath. U. Am., 1962; postgrad. U. Ia., 1957, U. Ill., 1967. Entered Sisters of Charity, Dubuque, Ia., 1942; research librarian Mundelein Coll., Chgo., 1944-60; asst. librarian Clarke Coll., Dubuque, 1960-65; librarian Our Lady of Peace High Sch., St. Paul, 1965-72, librarian Carmel High Sch. for Girls, Mundelein, Ill., 1972-73; librarian Xavier High Sch., Phoenix, 1973—. Com. mem. Cath. Periodical and Lit. Index, 1969. Recipient Nat. Def. Edn. Act fellowship U. Ill., 1967. Mem. Am., Cath. (chmn. Minn.-Dakota unit 1970-72, mem. scholarship com. 1967-69) library assns., Ariz. State Librarians Assn., Minn. Assn. Sch. Librarians. Home: 4712 N 3d St Phoenix AZ 85012 Office: 4710 N 5th St Phoenix AZ 85012

HEINZ, CATHARINE FRANCES, librarian; b. Anaheim, Cal.; d. William J. M. and Genevieve (Rolling) Heinz; B.A., Rosary Coll., 1941; M.S., Columbia, 1952. Librarian, tchr. St. Vincent's Coll. and Acad., Shreveport, La., 1941-42; sch. dept. librarian Orange County Free Library, Santa Ana, Cal., 1942-43; served from ensign to lt. (j.g.) USNR, 1943-46; newspaper classifier Journalism Library, Columbia U., 1946-47; crew and med. librarian U.S. Naval Hosp., Bklyn., 1947; asst. dir. Hosp. Library Bur., United Hosp. Fund N.Y., N.Y.C., 1947-48, dir., 1948-56; librarian Mut. of N.Y.C., 1956-59, TV Information Office, N.Y.C., 1959-71; dir. Broadcast Pioneers Library, Washington, 1971—. Mem. A.L.A. (pres. hosp. libraries div. 1950-51, chmn. awards com. 1966-67, chmn. library adminstrn. div. pub. relations services to libraries radio-TV-film festival 1966-67), Am. Women in Radio and TV (chmn. industry information com. 1964-66, chmn. N.Y.C. chpt. membership com. 1968-69), Spl. Libraries Assn. (chmn. com. on standards for hosp. libraries, 1949-52, chmn. pub. relations com. 1959-61, chmn. hosp. group N.Y. chpt. 1947-48, exec. editor Greater N.Y. directory, 1963, sec. 1962-63), Columbia U. Sch. Library Service Alumni Assn. (pres. 1967-68). Club: Nat. Broadcasters (gov. 1972—, v.p. 1973—, sec. 1973—). Home: 730 24th St NW Washington DC 20037 Office: 1771 N St NW Washington DC 20036

HEISE, MARGARET ANN IRONS (MRS. REINALD CHRISTIAN HEISE), educator; b. Cin., Apr. 24, 1934; d. Roland Earl and Ruth Nadia (Wilsey) Irons; B.S., U. Minn., 1957; M.A., Cal. State U. at Long Beach, 1969; m. Reinald Christian Heise, July 13, 1957; children—Diane Christine, Elizabeth Ann. Tchr., Edison Jr. High Sch., Sioux Falls, S.D., 1957-58, Ocean View Sch. Dist., Huntington Beach, Cal., 1958—; sec.-treas. Colo.-Cal. Corp., 1967—. Guardian, Camp Fire Girls, 1970-73. Mem. Am. Assn. U. Women, N.E.A., Internat. Reading Assn., Cal. Tchrs. Assn., Cal., Orange County reading assns., West Orange County Educators (dir., sec. 1969-70), Ocean View Tchrs. Assn. (pres. 1969-70, treas. 1972-73), Kappa Delta Pi. Mem. Ch. of Christ. Mem. Job Daus. Home: 6771 Lawn Haven Dr Huntington Beach CA 92648 Office: 7972 Warner Av Huntington Beach CA 92647

HEISER, MARIAN ROWE (MRS. WALLACE B. HEISER), social orgn. officer; b. Milford, Mich., Jan. 22, 1901; d. Grant Squire and Carrie Maria (Jackson) Rowe; Ph.B., Denison U., 1925; m. Wallace B. Heiser, Sept. 8, 1928; children—David, Patricia Ann (Mrs. Patricia Ann Brooke), Joan Margaret (Mrs. Joseph Perry Kramer III). Mem. Ohio Am. Revolution Bicentennial Adv. Commn., 1970—. Chpt. regent D.A.R., 1952-54, state chmn. honor roll, 1956-59, state chmn. D.A.R. schs., 1959-62, state dir., 1962-65, state vice-regent, 1965-68, state regent, 1968-71, nat. organizing sec. gen., 1971-74. Mem. Phi Beta Kappa. Clubs: Cleve. Denison Alumnae, Lakewood College (pres. 1961-62). Home: 1112 Maplecliffe Dr Lakewood OH 44107

HEISER, RUTH BISHOP (MRS. KARL FLORIEN HEISER), cons. psychologist; b. Tipton, Ind., June 13, 1909; d. George William and Margaret Myrtle (Cochran) Bishop; A.B., Northwestern U., 1929; S.M., U. Chgo., 1936, Ph.D. (fellow), 1939; m. Karl Florien Heiser, July 9, 1954. With Coll. Entrance Exam. Bd., Princeton, N.J., 1939-40; state cons. Social Security Bd., Washington, 1940-42; acting dir. test devel. U.S. Civil Service Commn., 1942-43; civilian dir. ASTP Test Devel., War Dept., N.Y.C., 1943-45; supr. data evaluation unit Elmo Roper, N.Y.C., 1945-48; asst. prof. U. Tenn., Knoxville, 1948-49; research asst. U. Mich., Ann Arbor, 1949-50; dir. evaluation services Nat. League for Nursing, N.Y.C., 1950-54; research asso. Sch. Pub. Health Columbia, 1955-60; cons. psychologist, Glendale, O., 1960-74. Fellow A.A.A.S., Am. Psychol. Assn. (editor div. newsletter 1965-70); mem. Am. Statis. Assn., Psychometric Soc. Address: Cundy's Harbor ME 04011

HEISLER, OLGA KARLOVNA (MRS. MICHAEL ARTHUR HEISLER), librarian; b. Moscow, USSR, Jan. 16, 1929 (father Am. citizen); d. Harry Vincent and Irene Vlasta (Kratochvil) Phillips; A.B., U. Sask. (Can.), 1952; B.L.S., U. Toronto (Ont., Can.), 1958; m. Michael Arthur Heisler, July 31, 1964. Asst. librarian, govt. documents and serials Dalhousie U., Halifax, N.S., 1955-57; sci. librarian McMaster U., Hamilton, Ont., 1958-61; asst. sci. reference librarian Queens Coll., N.Y.C., 1961-64; asst. librarian N.Y. U. Coll. Dentistry, 1964-68, head librarian, 1968—. Mem. heritage com. Bicentennial Com. Planning Bd., Bklyn. Mem. A.L.A., Am. Assn. U. Profs., Spl. Libraries Assn. Home: 196 Greene Av Brooklyn NY 11238 Office: Library 421 First Av New York City NY 10010

HEISLER, VERDA THIMAS (MRS. WILLIAM WILBERT HEISLER), clin. psychologist; b. Lorenzo, Ida., Jan. 24, 1919; d. Michael Anton and Myrtle (Fisher) Thimas; B.A., U. Utah, 1942; Ph.D. (USPHS fellow), Stanford, 1951; m. William Wilbert Heisler, June 13, 1941. Caseworker, U.S.O.-Travelers Aid Service, Ogden, Utah, 1944-46; research aide dept. psychology Stanford U., Palo Alto, Cal., 1946, research asst., 1947, intern Stanford-Lane Hosp., 1949-50; intern Agnews State Hosp., Cal., 1950-51; pvt. practice clin. psychology, San Diego, 1951—; instr. psychology extension div. San Diego State Coll., 1955-56, San Diego extension div. U. Cal., 1958; cons. United Cerebral Palsy San Diego, 1963-64, 74—, bd. govs., 1966—; research grantee United Cerebral Palsy Research and Ednl. Found., 1964-65, 66-67; part-time faculty Cal. Sch. Profl. Psychology, San Diego, 1972—. Recipient 4 awards from Cerebral Palsy Assns. Diplomate Am. Bd. Profl. Psychology. Fellow Am. Psychol. Assn.; mem. Cal., San Diego County (pres. 1963) psychol. assns., Am. Acad. Psychotherapists (sec.-treas. western regional chpt. 1960-62), Soc. for Personality Assessment, Group Psychotherapy Soc. So. Cal., Acad. Religion and Mental Health (steering com. San Diego 1959-63), San Diego Acad. Behavioral Scis. (sec. bd. 1963), Insts. Religion and Health, Am. Assn. Marriage and Family Counselors, Phi Beta Kappa, Sigma Xi, Phi Kappa Phi. Author: A Handicapped Child in the Family - A Guide for Parents, 1972. Author articles profl. jours. Home: 3304 Brant St San Diego CA 92103 Office: 3636 1st Av San Diego CA 92103

HEISTER, MARGARET WALTON (MRS. ROBERT J. HEISTER), therapist; b. Cleve., May 2, 1923; d. Owen McKinley and Betty Lee (Van Voohris) Walton; student DePauw U., 1941-43; B.S., Ohio State U., 1946; postgrad. U. Pitts., 1972; m. Robert J. Heister, Aug. 18, 1951; children—Robert J., Marcia Elaine. Occupational therapist VA Hosps., Augusta, Ga., 1946-48, Aspinwall, Pa., 1948-53; occupational therapist psychiat. unit Columbia Hosp., Wilkinsburg, Pa., 1963-67; dir. occupational therapy asst. program Mt. Aloysius Jr. Coll., Cresson, Pa., 1964-65, mem. adv. bd. of program, 1965-72; with Community Mental Health Center, St. Francis Gen. Hosp., Pitts., 1967—, dir. occupational and recreational therapy, dept. psychiatry 1967—. Mem. Nat. Therapeutic Recreation Soc., Am. Occupational Therapy Assn., Am. Assn. U. Women. Home: 59 Woodland Farms Rd Pittsburgh PA 15238 Office: 45th St and Penn Av Pittsburgh PA 15201

HEITMAN, SISTER M. CLARA, hosp. adminstr.; b. Maryville, Mo., June 6, 1915; d. Herman J. and Catherine P. (Meyer) Heitman; R.N., St. Anthony's Sch. Nursing, Oklahoma City, 1939; B.A. in Psychology and Philosophy, Quincy Coll., 1965. Joined Order of St. Francis, 1933; nursing supr. St. Francis Hosp., Maryville, Mo., 1939-44; lab. supr. St. Mary's Hosp., Nebraska City, Neb., 1944-56; admitting officer St. Anthony's Hosp., Oklahoma City, 1956-62; dir. nursing service St. Joseph's Hosp., Southern Pines, N.C., 1965-67; instr. Sch. Nursing, St. Anthony's Hosp., Oklahoma City, 1967-69; asst. adminstr. St. Francis Hosp., Maryville, 1969-70; adminstr., pres. bd. dirs. St. Mary's Hosp., Nebraska City, 1970—. Bd. dirs. St. Francis Hosp., Maryville, 1969-70. Named Optimist Honoree of Year, 1973. Mem. Neb. Hosp. Assn., Am. Nurses Assn. Home: Sisters Residence 1320 4th Av Nebraska City NE 68410 Office: St Mary's Hospital Nebraska City NE 68410

HEITMANN, MARGUERITE MICHEL (MRS. WILLIAM ARTHUR HEITMANN), librarian; b. Dayton, O.; d. John William and Cora Elizabeth (Leonard) Michel; A.B., Miami U., Oxford, O., 1935; B.L.S., Emory U., 1936; M.A. in Edn., George Washington U., 1965; m. William Arthur Heitmann, Sept. 16, 1939; children—Helen Elizabeth (Mrs. Robert Loyal Ives), Melinda Carolyn (Mrs. Thomas Arthur Hinners). Adult asst. Pub. Library Cin. and Hamilton County, O., 1936-37; departmental sr. and br. librarian Pub. Library, Dayton, Montgomery County, O., 1937-39; tchr. Masonic Home Sch., Louisville, 1952; tchr., tutor Louisville Country Day Sch., 1953-55; tchr. Jeffersonville (Ind.) Pub. Schs., 1955-56; sch. librarian Arlington County (Va.) Pub. Schs., 1956-60; head librarian George C. Marshall High Sch., Fairfax County (Va.) Pub. Schs., 1960-67; learning resources specialist Marymount Coll. of Va., Arlington, 1967—. Life mem. Friends of Gettysburg (Pa.) Pub. Library. Mem. Am. Personnel and Guidance Assn., Am. Assn. U. Profs., Am. Assn. U. Women, N.E. Area Two Yr. Coll. Reading Assn. Home: 21 Rye Ct Gaithersburg MD 20760 also Bilmarmelen Carroll Valley Fairfield PA 17320

HEITSMAN, THELMA MAURINE, banker; b. Sully, Ia., May 19, 1908; d. Lester C. and Terry M. (Wood) Tice; grad. high sch.; m. Tracy L. Heitsman, Sept. 27, 1934 (dec. 1947). With Citizens State Bank, New Sharon, Ia., 1926-31, Ia. State Banking Dept., Oskaloosa, 1931-36; asst. cashier Hedrick (Ia.) Savs. Bank, 1936-46, v.p., 1946-50, dir., 1946-50; cashier Okey Vernon Nat. Bank, Corning, Ia., 1950—, v.p., 1950—, dir., 1950—; commr. Ia. Merit Employment Commn., 1971—. Active March of Dimes Fund drive, 1962—; commr. Corning Housing Commn., 1962—. Named Woman of the Year Bus. and Profl. Women's Club, 1957, 68. Mem. Nat. Assn. Bank Women, Ia. Fedn. (state pres., 1968-69), Corning bus. and profl. women's clubs, Am. Legion Aux., P.E.O. Methodist (pres. service guild, 1970-72, conf. del. 1971). Mem. Order Eastern Star. Club: Corning (Ia.) Departmental Woman's (pres. 1957-59). Home: 701 Davis St Corning IA 50841 Office: Box 109 Corning IA 50841

HEIZER, PHYLLIS SCHULER (MRS. EUGENE HEIZER), telephone co. exec.; b. Louisville, Dec. 5, 1925; d. Harry James and Louise (Ziegler) Schuler; student U. Cin.; m. Eugene Heizer, May 14, 1955. With Cin. Bell Inc., 1947—, woman's editor, pub. relations, 1954-61, lecture supr., 1961-63, pub. information supr., 1963-67, sch. relations supr., 1967-73, comml. supr.-tng., 1973—. Mem. Ohio Audio Visual Council. Mem. Cin. Indsl. Editors (treas. 1956-57). Episcopalian. Club: Zonta (bd. 1965-67, 70-71, editor Zontalk 1965-66). Office: 309 Vine St Cincinnati OH 45202

HELBERG, MELESSIA PIOR (MRS. DON L. HELBERG), state ofcl.; b. Commerce, Tex., Sept. 7, 1939; d. Herbert Travis and Virginia (Hastings) Pior; student N.M. State U., 1957-59, Eastern N.M. U., 1961-62; m. Harvey Gordon Brande, June 9, 1960; 1 son, Gregory Michael; m. 2d, Don L. Helberg, Aug. 6, 1972. Various clerical and secretarial positions, 1959-67; town clk., treas. Town of Tatum (N.M.), 1967-73; auditor charge municipalities local govt. div. N.M. Dept. Finance and Adminstrn., 1973; adminstrv. sec. N.M. Municipal League, Santa Fe, 1974—. Mem. Commn. on Aging, 1971-72, Gov.'s Statehood Commemoration Com., 1972-73. Mem. Ward B Democratic Com., sec., 1971—; mem. Lea County Dem. Central Com., 1971—; mem. N.M. Municipal League, Clks. and Finance Officers Assn. N.M. Methodist (youth dir.). Mem. Order Eastern Star. Home: 90 Country Club Gardens Santa Fe NM 87501

HELBERT, SYLVIA MARIE (MRS. CHARLES NICC HELBERT), home economist; b. Buffalo, Jan. 31, 1925; d. Milton Russell and Isabelle Lewis (Johnson) Mayer; B.S., Cornell U., 1946; M.Ed., State U. N.Y. at Buffalo, 1971; Registered Dietitian Binghamton City Hosp., 1950; m. Charles Nicc Helbert, July 13, 1946; children—Claudia Nicki, Charles Nicc, Russell Lewis. Sch. lunch adminstr. pub. schs., Binghamton, N.Y., 1946-48; adminstrv. dietitian Binghamton City Hosp., 1948-50; teaching dietitian Deaconess Hosp., Buffalo, 1953-54; extension home economist Coop. Extension Assn., Erie County, Buffalo, 1962-71, leader home econs. div., 1971—. Mem. Am., N.Y., Western N.Y. dietetic assns., Nat., N.Y., Western N.Y. assns. extension home economists, Sigma Kappa, Omicron Nu. Club: Zonta (Buffalo). Home: 152 Zimmerman Blvd Kenmore NY 14223 Office: 238 Main St Buffalo NY 14202

HELD, JUDITH JEAN KIDD (MRS. FRANCIS B. HELD), physician; b. Fort Collins, Colo., Mar. 13, 1940; d. Thomas William and Nilah Faye (Williford) Kidd; B.A., Hastings Coll., 1962; postgrad. Internat. Christian U., Mitaka, Japan, 1960-61, Colo. U., 1962-64; M.D., Ohio State U., 1966; m. Francis B. Held, Mar. 26, 1969; stepchildren—Nancy Haynes, Mary Bontecou. Intern, Mt. Carmel Hosp., Columbus, O., 1966-67, resident internal medicine, 1967-70, chief resident, 1970, now mem. staff; practice medicine specializing in internal medicine, Delaware, O., 1970—; mem. active staff Grady Meml. Hosp., chief medicine, head cardio pulmonary dept., 1973—; cons. staff mem. Marysville (O.) Union Meml. Hosp.; v.p., med. adv. Delaware County Heart Assn., 1971—, pres., 1973—; bd. dirs. Delaware County Cancer Assn., 1970-72, profl. edn. chmn., 1970-71; bd. dirs. Delaware County A.R.C., 1970-72. Mem. Delaware area C. of C., Central Ohio Heart Assn. (edn. commn.), Central Ohio Lung Assn. (edn. com.), Am. Coll. Chest Physicians (asso.), Am. Women's Med. Assn., Am., Ohio med. assns., Delaware County, Franklin County med. socs., Mid Ohio Council of Med. Staffs, Ohio State U. Alumni Assn., Japan Internat. Christian U. (women's com. 1972—). Home: 144 W Fountain St Delaware OH 43015 Office: 26 Troy Rd Shopping Center Delaware OH 43015

HELD, MARGARET JENNINGS DUNKLEY (MRS. EMIL C. HELD), realtor; b. Washington, Sept. 11, 1911; d. Randolph Lee and Susie (Engelke) Jennings; student Am. U., 1946, Southeastern U., 1944-47; m. Charles W. Dunkley, Aug. 30, 1937 (dec. July 1954); m. 2d, Emil C. Held, Aug. 20, 1955. Real estate broker Md., D.C., Va., 1936—; owner, pres. Margaret J. Dunkley Realtor, Bethesda, Md., owner, dir. Margaret J. Dunkley, Interior Designers, 1953—, Margaret J. Dunkley Ins. Agy., Inc., 1961—; v.p. Fed. Supply Co., Inc., Washington, 1955-70, pres., gen. mgr., 1970—. Mem. women's fitness bd. YMCA, Bethesda, 1968—; trustee Montgomery County Crippled Childrens Soc., 1956-58; mem. com. United Givers Fund, 1961—; realtor chmn. Montgomery County Heart Assn. Named Realtor of Year, Montgomery County, 1956, 57. Mem. Montgomery County (Md.) Bd. Realtors (pres. 1954-55), Bethesda-Chevy Chase C. of C. (v.p. 1956), Montgomery County C. of C. (past v.p.), Nat. Assn. Real Estate Bds. (past pres. Md. women's council), Nat. Inst. Brokers (gov. 1957-59), Md. Real Estate Assn. (gov. 1957-60), Internat. Real Estate Fedn. (del. to internat. congress Geneva, Switzerland, Vienna, Austria, 1954). Clubs: Congl. Country (Bethesda); Mid-Ocean (Bermuda); Pinehurst (N.C.) Country. Home: 8613 Fenway Dr Bethesda MD 20034 Office: 7613 Wisconsin Av Bethesda MD 20014 also 1108 K St NW Washington DC 20005

HELDER, JUDITH ANN, sch. adminstr.; b. Cin., Jan. 10, 1935; d. A.N. and Dorothy M. (DeRuyter) Hallerman; B.F.A., Coll. of Mus., Cin., 1956; M.A., Temple U., 1966; postgrad. Loyola U., 1972—; m. Richard L. Helder, May 5, 1956 (dec.). Dir. radio-TV dept. Coll.-Conservatory of the U. Cin., 1964-65; asso. dir. devel. Girl Scouts, Chgo., 1967-70; chmn. admissions and aid Sch. of the Art Inst., Chgo., 1970-73, asso. dean for adminstrn., 1973—. Mem. Midwestern Assn. of Financial Aid Officers, Nat. Assn. Coll. Admissions Counselors. Mem. Ch. of Christ (mem. ch. council 1972-73). Home: 852 W Wolfram Chicago IL 60657 Office: School of the Art Inst of Chicago IL 60603

HELEM, BEUELARESS KING (MRS. HORACE WILLIAM HELEM, JR.), club woman; b. Augusta, Ga.; d. Archie Samuel and Bess (Coffey) King; student pub. schs.; m. Horace William Helem, Jr., Apr. 29, 1942. Mem. Daus. of 1812 (state sec. 1961-62), D.A.R. (chmn. advt. nat. mag., chmn. spl. events), U.D.C. (chpt. historian), Fla. Soc. U.S. Daus. 1812 (chmn. chpt. rehab. work vets. hosp., chmn. approved schs. and Bacone College), Fla. Soc. Daus. of Am. Colonists, Nat. Soc. Colonial Dames, 17th Century, Orlando Day Nursery Assn., Fla. United Numismatists, Central Fla. Execs. Club, Orange Meml. Hosp. Aux., Fla. Symphony Orch. (women's com.), Orlando Humane Soc. Clubs: Marlando, Sorosis, Rio Pinar Country, Dubsdread Country, Country of Orlando. Mem. Marshall Com. Continental Congress, 1961—. Home: 1206 41st St Orlando FL 32805

HELLER, ANN WILLIAMS (MRS. WALTER L. HELLER), nutritionist, writer; b. Vienna, Austria, Aug. 25, 1904; d. Friedrich C. and Elsa (Spitzer) Wilhelm; came to U.S., 1938, naturalized, 1944; student U. Vienna, 1933-34, Tchrs. Coll., Columbia, 1938-39; m. Walter L. Heller, Dec. 27, 1933 (dec. Sept. 1966). Food and equipment editor Everywoman's mag., N.Y.C., 1955-57; writer feature articles various mags., including Better Homes & Gardens, Glamour, Harpers Bazaar, House & Garden, House Beautiful, Living for Young Homemakers, Parents' Mag., Redbook, Seventeen, Readers' Digest, Town & Country, Vogue, Woman's Day; articles in newspapers, trade jours. and syndicate features, including Am. Weekly, Christian Sci. Monitor, N.Y. Herald Tribune, Parade, Park East, Retailing Daily, This Week, Toronto Star, all major syndicates; writer several consumer product books. Lectr. to profl. and women's groups throughout U.S.; judge nat. recipe contests; radio and TV appearances. Author: Soybeans from Soup to Nuts, 1944; Cooked to Your Taste, 1945; It's A Sin To Be Fat, 1947; Reducers Cookbook, 1948; The Busy Woman's Cookbook, 1948; Thrifty Gourmet's Meat Cookbook, 1971; Eat & Get Slim Cookbook, 1973; Nature's Own Vegetables' Cookbook, 1973. Mem. Greater New York Dietetic Assn., Soc. Mag. Writers, Food and Nutrition Council Greater N.Y. Address: 1100 Madison Av New York City NY 10028

HELLER, DOROTHY (MRS. JOSEPH GRUNIG), artist; b. N.Y.C.; d. Samuel and Rebecca (Cohen) Heller; scholarship student of Hans Hofmann; m. Joseph Grunig, Dec. 10, 1949. One man shows Tibor De Nagy Gallery, N.Y.C., 1953, Galerie Facchetti, Paris, France, 1955, Poindexter Gallery, N.Y.C., 1956, 57, East Hampton Gallery, N.Y.C., 1963, Betty Parsons Gallery, 1972; represented by Betty Parsons Gallery; exhibited in numerous group shows including Denver Art Mus., 1953, Stable Gallery, 1953, Galerie Prismes, Paris, France, 1955, Walker Art Center, 1955, Whitney Mus., 1956, Allen Meml. Art Mus., 1956, Carnegie Endowment Internat. Center, 1958, Carnegie Internat., 1959, Mus. Modern Art Travel Exhibit, 1963, Wadsworth Atheneum, Conn., 1964, Picadilly Gallery, London, Eng., 1967; represented in permanent collections U. Cal. Art Mus. at Berkeley, Allen Meml. Art Mus., Oberlin, O., Mus. Modern Art, Haifa, Israel, Greenville County (S.C.) Mus. Art. Address: 8 W 13th St New York City NY 10011

HELLER, JEAN SHIRLEY (MRS. PRESTON R. STEPHENS), journalist; b. Warren, O., Oct. 14, 1942; d. Robert Newman and Dorothy V. (Schetzer) Heller; student U. Mich., 1960-62; B.A., Ohio State U., 1964; m. Preston R. Stephens, May 2, 1971. Gen. assignment reporter Asso. Press, N.Y.C., 1964-67, investigative reporter, Washington, 1967-74; investigative reporter Cox Newspapers, Washington, 1974—. Recipient Worth Bingham prize, 1968, Polk award L.I. U., 1972, Raymond Clapper award, 1972, Robert F. Kennedy award, 1972. Home: 1733 Corcoran St NW Washington DC 20009 Office: 1901 Pennsylvania St NW Washington DC 20006

HELLER, JEANETTE JUNE (MRS. S.L. NEMZOFF), psychiatrist; b. N.Y.C., July 4, 1924; d. Samuel and Sara (Schwartz) Heller; B.S., Columbia, 1948; M.D., U. Leiden (Netherlands), 1954; m. S.L. Nemzoff, July 29, 1950; children—Deborah, Joshua, Gabrielle. Intern St. Luke's Hosp., Bethlehem, Pa., 1955-56; resident Phila. State Hosp., 1956-58, Phila. Gen. Hosp., 1958-59; practice medicine specializing in psychiatry, Phila.; mem. staff Mental Health Clinic, Abington Meml. Hosp., Pa., 1964—; pvt. practice, Jenkintown, Pa., 1965—. Mem. A.M.A. (mem. fellowship commn. 1969-72). Office: Benson East Suite 207C Jenkintown PA 19046

HELLER, KAREN SUE, journalist; b. Chgo., Mar. 23, 1945; d. Joseph T. and Maxine Jean (Nieberg) Heller; B.J., U. Mo., 1966. Reporter, U.P.I., Indpls., 1969; criminal justice reporter Cin. Enquirer, 1969-74; free-lance writer, 1974—. Washington Journalism fellow, 1973. Mem. Sierra Club, Women in Communications, Inc. Address: 410 S Hauser Blvd Apt 3H Los Angeles CA 90036

HELLER, MARY MCGRUER (MRS. JOHN DESMOND HELLER), librarian; b. Ogdensburg, N.Y., July 24, 1913; d. Charles Baldwin and Carolyn May (Joyce) McGruer; A.B., St. Lawrence U., 1934; M.S., L.I. U., 1962; m. John Desmond Heller, June 30, 1939; 1 son, John Duncan. Tchr. Latin, Adams High Sch. (N.Y.), 1934-39; librarian, tchr. Latin, Southampton High Sch. (N.Y.), 1953-58; reference asst. C.W. Post Coll., Greenvale, N.Y., summer 1963; head librarian Friends Acad., Locust Valley, N.Y., 1958—; adj. asst. prof. Grad. Library Sch., L.I. U., Greenvale, 1965—. Mem. evaluation coms. Middle States Assn. Colleges and Secondary Schs., 1965, 67. Trustee Mattituck (N.Y.) Pub. Library, 1945-49, pres. 1949; mem. women's com. Bridgehampton (N.Y.) Pub. Library, 1949-58. Mem. Am., N.Y., Nassau Suffolk Sch. (treas. 1961-62, corr. sec. 1972-73), Nassau, Hudson Valley library assns., L.I. Edn. Communications Council, Palmer Grad. Library Sch. Alumni Assn. (1st pres. 1965), Beta Pi Theta, Delta Kappa Gamma, Pi Beta Phi. Episcopalian. Mem. adv. com. McGraw-Hill Ency. World Biography, 1968-71. Home: 15 Todd Dr Glen Head NY 11545 Office: Friends Academy Locust Valley NY 11560

HELLERSTEIN, ELINOR GARELY (MRS. WILLIAM E. HELLERSTEIN), pub. relations exec.; b. Jersey City, May 10, 1941; d. Abraham and Etta (Eig) Garely; B.S., Lesley Coll., 1962; postgrad. Rutgers U. Grad. Sch. Fine Arts, 1963, George Washington U. Grad. Sch. Fine Arts, 1965, Howard U. Sch. Law, 1965, N.Y. U. Grad. Sch. Bus., 1975. Adminstr. bus. and pub. information Odyssey House, Inc., N.Y.C., 1968-70; account exec., cons. Sidney W. Green & Assos., N.Y.C., 1972—; Bd. dirs. Nat. Pub. Relations Council of Health and Welfare Agys., Soc. for Prevention of Drug Addiction. Mem. Pub. Relations Soc. Am., Women's Career Forum (founding mem., resource dir.). Home: 152 E 94th St New York City NY 10028

HELLINGER, EVELYN MARY (MRS. JOSEPH W. HELLINGER), ednl. adminstr.; b. Milford, Mass., Oct. 30, 1921; d. Martin J. and Lillian S. (Jablon) Bukowski; B.A., N.Y. U., 1955; M.Rehab. and Counseling, U. Fla., 1960, Ed.D., 1963; m. Joseph W. Hellinger, Mar. 2, 1944; children—Nadya (Mrs. John S. Schmeder), Frederich Joseph. Research asst. U. Fla., Gainesville, 1961-62; coordinator Spl. Tng. Center, Sunland Tng. Center, Gainesville, 1962-63; cons. spl. edn. Norfolk (Va.) City Sch. System, 1963-66; founder, dir. Diagnostic Spl. Edn. Sch., Tidewater Rehab. Inst., Norfolk, Va., 1966—. Vis. prof. U. Va., Charlottesville, 1965, Old Dominion U., Norfolk, 1964-73, Norfolk State Coll., 1966—; adviser on needs of handicapped Va. Legislative Council, 1970-71; adviser Gov.'s Regulation Implementation Com. for White House Conf. on Children and Youth, 1971-73. Mem. Norfolk Com. for Improvement of Edn., 1972. Recipient Outstanding Citizen award B'nai B'rith, 1973. Mem. Am. Assn. Mental Deficiency, Va. Assn. for Children with Learning Disabilities (adv. bd. 1971-72), Tidewater Assn. for Retarded Children (adviser day care center 1970-73), Tidewater Assn. for Mental Health (v.p. 1972—), Council for Exceptional Children. Home: 5239 Powhatan Av Norfolk VA 23508 Office: Tidewater Rehab Inst 855 W Brambleton Av Norfolk VA 23510

HELLMAN, RHONA PHYLLIS (MRS. WILLIAM S. HELLMAN), psychologist; b. N.Y.C., May 22, 1935; d. David and Florence (Schlesinger) Rosenberg; B.A. cum laude, Bklyn. Coll., 1955; M.S., Syracuse U., 1960; m. William S. Hellman, Nov. 4, 1954; children—Ronald Bruce, Adrian David. Research asst. Syracuse (N.Y.) U., 1957-61; research audiologist VA, Washington, 1963-64; research asst. Northeastern U., Boston, 1965-66; with Harvard, Cambridge, Mass., 1967—, sr. research asst. Lab. of Psychophysics, 1967—. Mem. A.A.A.S., Acoustical Soc. Am., Common Cause, Am. Civil Liberties Union. Home: 31 Longfellow Rd Arlington MA 02174 Office: William James Hall 9th Floor Harvard Cambridge MA 02138

HELLMANN, SISTER KATHRYN, hosp. exec.; b. Terre Haute, Ind., Sept. 25, 1921; d. John Henry and Philomena Gertrude (Bockhold) Hellmann; student St. Mary's Jr. Coll., 1941-44, Ind. U., 1962-64; B.S., Coll. of Mount St. Joseph, 1966; M.H.A., St. Louis, U., 1969. Joined Sisters of St. Joseph, 1941; nursing supr. surgery dept. St. Joseph Hosp., Kokomo, Ind., 1951-62, asst. adminstr., 1962-64; pres., chief exec. officer St. Charles Meml. Hosp., Bend. Ore., 1969—. Pres., Sisters Council of Diocese, Baker, Ore., 1973. Trustee Central Ore. Hosp. Planning Commn., Med. Found., Bend. Mem. Am. Coll. Hosp. Adminstrs., Cath. Hosp. Assn. (pres. Ore. conf. 1970-72, trustee). Address: 700 Lava Rd Bend OR 97701

HELM, MARY JANE (MRS. FRITZ E. HELM), univ. ofcl.; b. Loyal, Wis., Oct. 28, 1923; d. William F. and Mae (Reif) Theisen; grad. Eau Claire Bus. Coll., 1942; bus. degree Layton Sch. Art, 1945-55; student Marquette U., U. Wis.; m. Fritz E. Helm, May 4, 1963; 1 son, Erik. With U.S. Employment Service, Eau Claire, Wis., and Milw., 1942-44; sec. M.A. Lemkuhl Advt. Agy., Milw., 1944-53; adminstrv. sec. Cramer-Krasselt Advt., Milw., 1953-65; with U. Wis., Milw., 1967—, dir. Union Art Gallery and Sales Gallery, 1972—. Exhibited in major local competitions and invitationals. Recipient awards from major local exhibits. Home: 3018 N Downer Av Milwaukee WI 53211 Office: 2200 E Kenwood Blvd Milwaukee WI 53201

HELMBRECK, ADA BARR (MRS. EARL JAMES HELMBRECK), social orgn. officer; b. Elkton, Md.; d. George Boulden and Hannah Elizabeth (McCool) Barr; B.S., U. Del., 1941; postgrad. Columbia, 1948-49, U. N.H., 1956-57; m. Earl James Helmbreck, Nov. 29, 1924; 1 son, Earl James. Tchr. phys. edn., social studies, English, various schs., Md., 1922-25, Del., 1926-55, Me., 1955-70. Pub. speaking coach. Chpt. regent D.A.R., 1958-62, state curator, 1962-65, state chaplain, 1965-68, state vice regent, Me., 1968-71, state regent, Me., 1971-74, nat. curator gen., 1974—, hon. state regent, state bicentennial chmn., 1974—; state v.p. Dames Ct. Honor; pres. Am. Assn. U. Women, 1970-71, 1st v.p. Woman's League of York, 1965-71; mem. N.E.A., Nat. Officers Club, also Nat. Execs. Club, D.A.R., State Vice Regents Club D.A.R., Nat. Bd. Mgmt., Daus. Am. Colonists. Episcopalian (pres. church women 1968-74, lay reader). Home: Box 71 Nubble Rd York Beach ME 03910 also 3000 Tilden St NW Washington DC

HELMER, FRANCIS HOPE WILSON (MRS. EDWARD ROBERT HELMER), sch. psychologist; b. Rock Springs, Tex., July 5, 1923; d. Frank Kevin and Annie (Hope) Wilson; student North Tex. State U., 1941-42; B.A., Whittier Coll., 1961; postgrad. U. Cal., 1961-67, Claremont Coll., 1963, La Sierra Coll., 1964, San Diego State Coll., 1966; M.S., Cal. State Coll., 1971; m. Edward Robert Helmer, Dec. 19, 1942; children—Edward Robert, Russel Lee, Richard Alan, Wendy Ann. Trainee fingerprint identification FBI, Washington, 1942; nursery sch. tchr. Trinity Lutheran Nursery Sch., Hemet, Cal., 1961; tchr. Hemet Jr. High Sch., 1961-63; counselor, tchr., 1963-65, counselor, title I coordinator, 1966-68; elementary dist. counselor Hemet Unified Sch. Dist., 1968-69; counselor, sch. psychologist Hemet Jr. High Sch., 1969—; dist. sch. psychologist Hemet Unified Schs., 1970—. Chmn. P.T.A., East Whittier Schs., 1950-60; area chmn. United Fund, Whittier, Cal., 1955; Cub Scout den mother, Whittier, Cal., 1950-57; leader 4-H Club, 1968, 70. Bd. dirs. Trinity Luth. Nursery Sch., 1960-63. Mem. Cal. Assn. Sch. Psychologists and Psychometrists, Cal., Hemet Valley tchrs. assns., League Women Voters. Home: 28310 Vista del Valle Dr Hemet CA 92343 Office: 2350 W Latham Av Hemet CA 92343

HELMERICKS, CONSTANCE, author, explorer, lectr.; b. Binghamton, N.Y., Jan. 4, 1918; d. Arthur Smith and Winifred (Browning) Chittenden; student U. Ariz., 1937-40, B.A. in Sociology, 1954; m. Harmon Robert Helmericks, Apr. 27, 1941 (div. May 1956); children—Constance Jean, Carol Ann; m. Gilbert Doyle Bertie Kitchner Barrett, 1969 (div. 1970). Comprehensive study (with Harmon Helmericks) Arctic populations and animals, Can. and Alaska, prin. studies including diet. interpretation primitive life to civilized man; field researcher in sociology for U. Ariz., 1962-63; lectr. Founding mem. Arctic Inst. N.A. Co-author travel books (with Harmon Helmericks): We Live in the Arctic, 1947; Our Summer With the Eskimos, 1948; Our Alaskan Winter, 1949; The Flight of the Arctic Tern, 1951. Author: We Live in Alaska, 1944; Hunting in North America, 1957; Down the Wild River North, 1968; Australian Adventure, 1972; also articles. Lectr. tour of U.S. on subjects of Alaska, Mexico, 1958. Home: Newport Towers #1001 1931 Nelson St Vancouver BC V66 1N5 Canada

HELMKAY, NELLIE EDITH, housing adminstr.; b. Estevan, Sask., Can., Sept. 25, 1910; d. Fredrick and Lucy Ellen (Barton) Woodward; student U. Sask.; m. Frederick Lloyd Melmkay, Oct. 11, 1933 (dec. Nov. 1967); children—Robert Lloyd, Frederick William, Gene Albert, Kenneth Wayne, Marilyn Joan (Mrs. Kenneth Stobbe), Sydney Dennis, Harold Earle. Matron, adminstr. Eaglestone Lodge, Kamsack, Sask., 1968—. Recipient Bronze medal, Regina Musical Festival, 1930. Mem. United Ch. of Can. (elder). Mem. Order of Eastern Star, Rebekah Lodge. Home and office: Box 1330 Kamsack SA Canada

HELPER, ROSE, educator; b. Port Arthur, Ont., Can.; d. Aaron and Fanny Leah (Strejevsky) Helper; M.A. in Sociology, U. Toronto (Ont.), 1945; Ph.D. in Sociology, U. Chgo., 1958. Teaching asst. Conn. Coll. for Women, New London, 1947-48; research asso. N.Y. U. Research Center for Human Relations, 1951-52; faculty Ind. State Tchrs. Coll., Terre Haute, 1959; asst. prof. sociology U. Toledo, 1959-66, asso. prof., 1966-71, prof., 1971—. Cons. in race relations and housing. Research fellow Fisk U., Nashville, 1945-47; research grantee Commn. on Race and Housing of Fund for the Republic of the Ford Found., 1955-56. Mem. Soc. for Study Social Problems, Internat., North Central, Am. sociol. assns., Soc. for Psychol. Study Social Issues, Pi Gamma Mu, Alpha Kappa Delta (nat. sec.-treas. 1968-70), Phi Kappa Phi. Author: Racial Policies and Practices of Real Estate Brokers, 1969. Editor: Sociological Focus on Sociology and Social Issues, 1970-71. Contbr. articles to profl. jours. Home: 2565 W Bancroft St Toledo OH 43607

HELPERN, BEATRICE LIEBOVITZ NIGHTINGALE, civic worker; b. N.Y.C., July 23, 1907; d. Abraham L. and Hannah (Weinberg) Liebovitz; B.A. summa cum laude, N.J. Coll. for Women, 1928; m. 2d, Lester M. Nightingale, Dec. 1, 1935 (dec. 1951); children—William L., Stuart L.; m. 3d, Milton Helpern, Jan. 1, 1955; stepchildren—Nancy H. (Mrs. Edward Moldover), Susan H. (Mrs. Paul Nettler), Alice. Vol. sec. to chief med. examiner City of N.Y., 1960-74; vol. sec. Milton Helpern Library of Legal Medicine, N.Y.C., 1962—, Inst. Forensic Medicine, N.Y. U. and City N.Y., dept. forensic medicine N.Y. U., 1960-72. Mem. ladies organizing com. Internat. Meetings Forensic Medicine, N.Y.C., 1960, London, 1963; hon. chmn. women's com. 1st World Meeting Med. Law, Belgium, 1967; chmn. 2d World Meeting, Washington, 1970; hospitality com. Internat. Assn. Accident and Traffic Medicine, chmn., 1967-69; chmn. hospitality com. Symposia on Forensic Medicine, N.Y.C., 1972-74. Bd. dirs. N.Y. chpt. Am. Jewish Com., 1950—, League for Emotionally Disturbed Children, Hemophilia Found., 1961-63, Womens Aux. Med. Soc. County of N.Y., 1973—. Mem. Phi Beta Kappa. Home: 303 E 57th St New York City NY 10022

HELVIE, JANICE BENHAM (MRS. JAMES CLIFFORD HELVIE), physician; b. Kokomo, Ind., Sept. 16, 1941; d. Durward Laverne and Marche Jeanette (Goldman) Benham; A.B., Asbury Coll., 1963; M.D., Ind. U., 1967; m. James Clifford Helvie, Nov. 24, 1964; children—Kirstin Noelle, Lana Lynn, Laura Jean. Intern St. Vincent's Hosp., Indpls., 1967-68; physician, Student Health Service Ind. U., Bloomington, 1968—; chmn. med. staff 1971; lectr. sex edn. to coll. groups. Home: Rural Route 1 Nashville IN 47448 Office: 600 N Jordan Bloomington IN 47401

HELWICK, PATRICIA ANN, educator, actress; b. Yonkers, N.Y.; d. Edward C. and Nellie (Schoonmaker) Helwick; B.A., Vassar Coll., 1954; M.F.A., Yale, 1965; pvt. study dance, voice; m. Arthur H. Ackerman, June 5, 1953 (div. Jan. 1966); children—William James, Jonathan Emzy; m. 2d, John Edward Carey, Nov. 25, 1967 (div. 1971). Real estate and ins. salesman Walhimer Real Estate Agy., New Haven, 1958-62; producer Clinton (Conn.) Playhouse, 1964; producer-actress weekly radio interview show, WLIS, Old Saybrook, 1964; head of drama Chapin Sch., N.Y.C., 1966—; lectr. speech, communications and theatre arts dept. City U. N.Y. Appeared in prodns. including Come Back Little Sheba, 1963, The Hostage, 1964, Present Laughter, 1964, Dark Light in May, 1965; head tchr. John Robert Powers Sch., N.Y.C., 1967; tchr. pvt. lessons acting and speech. Recipient Carol Dye Acting award, 1964. Mem. Yale Drama Sch. Alumni Assn. (pres. ex officio), Actors Equity. Home: 14 Sutton Pl South New York City NY 10022 Office: 100 East End Av New York City NY 10028

HEMENWAY, ILA JOHNSON (MRS. HAROLD ALGERNON HEMENWAY), music educator; b. Judsonia, Ark.; d. Jacob Theodore and Mary (McCauley) Johnson; grad. diploma Galloway Coll., 1924; postgrad. Ouachita Coll., 1926; student H. Levy, Am. Conservatory Chgo., 1923, H.D. Tovey, U. Ark., 1927, V. Stefanelli, N.Y.C., summer 1943; m. Harold Algernon Hemenway, June 3, 1934. Tchr. piano, harmony, musical history Russellville (Ark.) pub. schs., 1924-25, Holly Grove (Ark.) High Sch., 1927-30; asst. tchr. Ouachita Coll., 1925-27; tchr. music Little Rock Pub. Schs., 1930-34; tchr. piano, harmony, musical history DeWitt (Ark.) High Sch., 1935-49; pvt. tchr., Little Rock, 1951—. Mem. Ark. Authors and Composers Soc. (pres. 1950-52), Little Rock Musical Coterie (hon., pres. 1952-54), Nat. Soc. Arts and Letters (local chpt. pres. 1957-59), Bay View Study Club (pres. 1965), Nat., Ark. music tchrs. assns., Nat. Fedn. Music Clubs (life). Clubs: Woman's City, Community Culture. Author articles and poetry. Home: 1310 Summit St Little Rock AR 72202

HEMENWAY, NANCY WHITTEN (MRS. ROBERT BARTON), artist; b. Boothbay Harbor, Me., June 19, 1920; d. Robinson Sawyer and Marion Frances (Dix) Whitten; A.B., Wheaton Coll., 1941; M.A., Columbia, 1964; certificate U. Madrid (Spain), 1956; postgrad. Art Students League N.Y., 1957-60; m. Robert Durrie Barton, Sept. 26, 1942; children—Robert Bradford, William Emerson, Frederick Durrie. Exhibited in one-man shows Madrid, 1955, Watson Gallery Art, Wheaton Coll., Norton, Mass., 1963, Nat. Gallery Art, Bolivia, 1968, Municipal Gallery Art, Guadalajara, Mexico, 1972, Neiman-Marcus, Dallas, 1971, Woodmere Gallery, Phila., 1971, Copley Soc., Boston, 1972; group shows Smithsonian Mus., Washington, 1969, Pan Am. Union, 1971-72, Sci. and Art Found., Oklahoma City, 1974, McNay Art Inst., San Antonio, 1974, Fine Arts Mus., Santa Fe, 1974; represented in numerous collections. Dir., Hemenway Designs, Washington, 1970—; cons. Neiman-Marcus, 1970-71, Priscilla of Boston, 1971-73. Bd. dirs. Internat. Inst., Spain, 1964-66, San Esteban Martir Sch., Mexico, 1970—. Mem. Smithsonian Inst., Corcoran Gallery Art, Me. Hist. and Cultural Soc., Art Students League N.Y., Am. Craftsman's Council. Club: Boothbay Harbor Yacht. Inventor Bayetage art form. Address: 1524 30th St NW Washington DC 20007 summer West Boothbay Harbor ME 01575

HEMLOW, JOYCE, educator, author; b. Liscomb, N.S., Can., July 30, 1906; d. William and Rosalinda (Redmond) Hemlow; B.A., Queen's Coll., Kingston, Can., 1941, M.A., 1942; A.M., Radcliffe Coll., 1944. Ph.D., 1948; LL.D., Queen's, 1967, Dalhousie U., 1972. Faculty, McGill U., 1945—, Greenshields prof. English lit. and lang., 1965—. Guggenheim fellow, 1951-52, 66-67; recipient James Tait Black Meml. book prize for best biography in U.K., The History of Fanny Burney, 1958; Gov. Gen. Can. medal for acad. non-fiction,

1958; Rose Mary Crawshay prize, British Acad., 1960; Distinguished Achievement medal Radcliffe Coll., 1969. Fellow Royal Soc. Can.; mem. Johnsonians, Phi Beta Kappa. Author: A Catalogue of the Burney Family Correspondence, 1749-1878, 1971. Author chpt. in book. Editor: Journals and Letters of Fanny Burney (Madame d'Arblay). Home: 3555 Atwater Av Montreal 25 PQ Canada

HEMMERLING, GERALDINE STEIN (MRS. CLIFFORD A. HEMMERLING), lawyer; b. Los Angeles, Oct. 4, 1928; d. Louis and Ida (Minick) Stein; B.S., U. Cal. at Los Angeles, 1949, J.D., 1952; postgrad. U. Cal. at Berkeley, 1949-50; m. Clifford A. Hemmerling, Apr. 7, 1951; children—Keith Alan, Karen Lynn. Admitted to Cal. bar, 1953, U.S. Supreme Ct. bar, 1960; pvt. practice law, Los Angeles, 1952-57, asso. law firm Richards, Watson & Hemmerling, 1958-65; individual practice, Los Angeles, 1965-71; of counsel Abbott & Crahan, 1971—. Mem. dean's counsel U. Cal. at Los Angeles Law Sch.; cons. Cal. Continuing Edn. of Bar; lectr. various taxation insts., forums, seminars; chmn. Cal. Continuing Edn. Bar Seminar on Trusts and Estates, Los Angeles and San Francisco, 1972. Mem. Am., Los Angeles bar assns., State Bar Cal. (continuing edn. com.), Los Angeles C. of C. (bd. dirs. women's div.), U. Cal. at Los Angeles Law Alumni Assn. (pres. 1974). Sigma Delta Tau. Author: Multi-State Trusts: Tax and Conflict Problems, 1973; 1973, 74 supplements to California Will Drafting; contbg. author Supplement to Drafting California Irrevocable Trusts, 1973, California Decedent Estate Administration, 1974; Supplement to Drafting California Revocable Trusts, 1974. Contbr. profl. articles and papers. Home: 369 Homewood Rd Los Angeles CA 90049 Office: 10889 Wilshire Blvd Los Angeles CA 90024

HEMPHILL, BERNICE MONAHAN (MRS. CHARLES D. HEMPHILL), blood bank exec.; b. San Francisco; d. Thomas E. and Anne J. (McGinerty) Monahan; ed. U. Cal.; m. Charles D. Hemphill, June 30, 1939. Supervising technologist Honolulu Blood Plasma Bank, 1941-43; exec. dir., sec. Irwin Meml. Blood Bank, San Francisco Med. Soc., 1944—. Treas. Am. Assn. Blood Banks, 1949—, chmn. nat. com. on clearinghouse program, 1953—, com. on govt. liaison; sec. Cal. Blood Bank System, 1951-57; mem. state adv. com. on blood and blood derivatives Cal. State Dept. Pub. Health, 1964—; cons. on blood banking projects. Mem. nat. adv. communicable disease council U.S. Dept. Health, Edn. and Welfare, 1969-72; pres. Am. Women for Internat. Understanding, 1973—. Active United Community Fund San Francisco; mem. Mayor's Citizens Com. for Centennial Golden Gate Park, 1969. Bd. dirs. Catholic Social Service San Francisco, 1957-62. Mem. Women for Nixon-Agnew Com., 1968; co-chmn. Com. to Re-elect Pres., 1972. Recipient John Elliott award Am. Assn. Blood Banks, 1960, commendation Ft. Miley VA Hosp., San Francisco, 1961, award of merit Catholic Charities San Francisco, 1962, Lane Bryant citation, 1965, 66, 67, 68, Key of Guild award Medico-Dental Study Guild Cal., 1973; named Distinguished Woman, San Francisco Examiner, 1960, U.S. Lady-of-Month, U.S. Lady publ., 1963. Mem. U. Cal. Hosp. Aux., U. Cal. Doctor's Wives Club, St. Francis Hosp. Aux., Laguna Honda Home Aux., San Francisco Assn. Mental Health, Little Children's Aid Aux., World Affairs Council No. Cal., Internat. Soc. Blood Transfusion, Women's Aux. San Francisco Dental Soc., Pan Am. Fedn. Vol. Blood Donations (hon.). Conceived and created 1st blood bank clearinghouse, 1951. Clubs: Francisca, Commonwealth (San Francisco); Capitol Hill (Washington). Home: 1070 Green St Apt 1301 San Francisco CA 94133 Office: 270 Masonic Av San Francisco CA 94118

HEMSWORTH, MARIAN JEAN MACINNES (MRS. JOHN HEMSWORTH), hosp. adminstr.; b. Glace Bay, N.S., Can., Oct. 2, 1922; d. Thomas Charles and Sarah Jane (Mackenzie) Macinnes. Registered Nurse, Glace Bay Gen. Hosp. Sch. Nursing, 1945; student U. Toronto, 1947; m. John Hemsworth, Dec. 28, 1954; 1 dau., Morah Jane. Gen. staff head nurse Glace Bay Gen. Hosp., (N.S., Can.), 1945-46, instr. chief, 1947-55, dir. Sch. Nursing, 1956-63, adminstr., 1963—; asst. supt. nursing Point Edward Tb Hosp., 1955-56. Mem. com. Cape Breton Regional Health Planning Project, 1971-72; mem. continuing com. Cape Breton Health Services, 1972-73. Mem. Am. Coll. Hosp. Adminstrs., Canadian Coll. Health Service Execs., Cape Breton Regional Hosp. Assn. (pres. 1969-72), Registered Nurses Assn. N.S. Home: 9 Catherine St Glace Bay NS Canada Office: Brookside St Glace Bay NS Canada

HENAULT, MARIE JOSEPHINE (MRS. ROBERT JOSEPH HENAULT), educator; b. Oakville, Wash., July 16, 1921; d. Ernst Carl and Amanda Sophia (Anderson) Philipsen; B.A., U. Wash., 1945, M.A., 1946; Ph.D., U. Md., 1952; m. Robert Joseph Henault, Aug. 16, 1952; 1 son, Martial Ernst. Instr. English, U. Utah, Salt Lake City, 1949-52; instr. U. Md., College Park, 1950-52; instr. St. Joseph Coll., Emmitsburg, Md., 1961-62; prof. English, St. Michael's Coll., Winooski, Vt., 1962—. Am. Assn. U. Profs., Phi Kappa Phi. Author: Peter Viereck, 1969; Guide to Ezra Pound, 1970; Checklist of Ezra Pound, 1970, The Merrill Studies in The Cantos, 1971. Contbr. articles to profl. jours. Home: Route 1 Essex Junction VT 05452 Office: English Dept St Michael's College Winooski VT 05404

HENCKLER, MARGUERITE LUCILLE (MRS. GENE HENCKLER), savs. and loan assn. exec.; b. Columbia, Ill., Nov. 28, 1921; d. Theodore and Ida Caroline (Wilde) Ludwig; student Browns Bus. Coll., 1939-40; m. Gene F. Henckler, Apr. 20, 1946; children—Gene F., Martha Marguerite (dec.). Payroll clerk, sec. Greyhound Lines, St. Louis, 1940-46; mng. officer, dir. Columbia Savs. & Loan Assn., 1955—. Mem. mothers' aux. Okaw Valley council Boy Scouts Am., 1956-70. Mem. Ch. of Christ. Mem. Order Eastern Star. Home: 124 S Metter St Columbia IL 62236 Office: 238 N Main St Columbia IL 62236

HENDERSON, ADAMAE PARTIN, librarian; b. Meridian, Miss., Nov. 8, 1912; d. Charles Frederick and Ada (Edgar) Partin; student Miss. State Coll. Women, 1929-31; B.A. in English Lit., Millsaps Coll., 1933; M.L.S., Fla. State U., 1965; m. Roy Pitchford Henderson, June 18, 1937; children—David Christopher, Pamela Jane. Tchr. pub. schs. Meridian, 1933-37, 44-45, 52-57, 62-64, also librarian, 1962-64; dir. Kendalwood Playschool, Meridian, 1950-51; acting coordinator children's services Meridian Pub. Library, 1957-58, dep. dir., coordinator children's services, 1965-68; asst. to curator childhood poetry collection Strozier Library, Fla. State U., Tallahassee, 1964-65; sr. children's librarian N.Y. Pub. Library, N.Y.C., 1968-70, asst. regional librarian Regional Library Blind and Physically Handicapped, 1970-73, also acting regional librarian, 1971-73; asso. librarian N.Y. State Library, regional librarian State Library for Blind, Albany, 1973—. State pres. Miss. chpt. League Women Voters, 1958-62, publs. chmn., N.Y.C., 1969-71; state chmn. U.S. Com. for UN, 1958-64; dir. pub. relations Lauderdale County Mental Health Assn., 1960-64; women's dir. civ. def. Lauderdale County, 1962-64; dir. pub. relations Meridian Symphony Orch., 1962-64; cons. Headstart program East Central Miss., 1965-68; cons. on orgn. and publs. League Women Voters Miss., 1962-68; cons. publs. com. Library Congress Div. for Blind and Physically Handicapped, 1971—; writer-producer program series Family Reading Together, WTOK-TV, Meridian, 1965-68. Bd. dirs. N.Y. State Fedn. Workers for Blind. Mem. Am., N.Y. library assns., N.Y. Library Club, Library Pub. Relations Council. Editor Miss. Voters Guide, 1962. Home: 303 State St Albany NY 12210 Office: 226 Elm St Albany NY 12202

HENDERSON, AILEEN RICHMOND (MRS. LOUIS C. HENDERSON), ret. educator; b. Tillar, Ark., Oct. 31, 1905; d. Aquila Carr and Alice (Tillar) Richmond; A.A., Central Coll., 1924; A.B. cum laude, Hendrix Coll., 1926; M.A. with highest honors, U. Ark., 1956; m. Louis C. Henderson, June 6, 1931; 1 son, Louis C. Tchr. English Conway (Ark.) High Sch., 1926-31, Harlan (Ky.) High Sch., 1941-48, Central High Sch,, Little Rock, 1948-57; tchr. English, Hall High Sch., 1957-71, chmn. dept.; tutor Coll. Entrance Exams. Mem. Ark. Adv. Council Secondary Edn.; cons. Southwestern br. Coll. Entrance Exam. Bd., Austin, Tex. Named Ky. col. Mem. Am. Assn. U. Women, N.E.A., Classroom Tchrs. Assn., Ark. Edn. Assn., Nat. Council Tchrs. English (co-editor The Lit. Mag.), Coll. Tchrs. English, Ark. Council English Tchrs., Soc. Gen. Semantics, Internat. Platform Assn., Delta Kappa Gamma, Kappa Delta Pi. Contbr. chpt. to Successful Practices in Teaching English, 1967, also Ark. Jour. Edn. Book reviewer. Home: 506 N Martin St Little Rock AR 72205

HENDERSON, BONNIE CLIFTON (MRS. DONALD E. V. HENDERSON), editor, writer; b. Kansas City, Kan., Jan. 28, 1916; d. R. Aldine and Truett (Davis) Clifton; student Baylor U., 1932-35, U. Ala., 1940-41; B.A., Am. U., 1961; m. Donald E.V. Henderson, Aug. 19, 1935; children—Ruth Herrera, Rosemary Haley. Program dir. Noyes Camp, Portland, Conn., 1947-53; research asst. Nat. Acad. Sci., Washington, 1950-53; supr. earth sci. sect. Nat. Register of Sci. and Tech. Personnel, Am. Geol. Inst., Washington, 1954-66, editor, directory of geosci. depts., 1960—; manpower specialist writer on manpower analyses, Washington, 1966—. Commr., Sci. Manpower Commn., A.A.A.S., Washington, 1970—. Mem. Manpower Analysis and Planning Soc., Washington. Editor: Manpower Supply and Demand in Earth Science 1970-1975, 1971. Contbr. articles in field to profl. jours. Office: 5205 Leesburg Pike Falls Church VA 22041

HENDERSON, FREDA MAY, sch. adminstr.; b. Hereford, Md., Mar. 16, 1914; d. Charles Ernest and Caroline (Leyshon-Rees) Henderson; student Md. State Normal Coll., 1932; B.S., George Peabody Coll. Tchrs., 1952, M.A., 1959, Ed.S., 1967. Tchr., vice prin. pub. schs. Baltimore County, Md., 1932-45; (became blind 1945); mem. faculty, adminstrn. Tenn. Sch. Blind, 1952—, reading specialist, 1964-67, elementary supr., 1967—; instr. George Peabody Coll. Tchrs., Nashville, 1958—. Mem. nat. braille authority com. Assn. for Edn. Visually Handicapped and Am. Assn. Workers with Blind, 1967-72. Mem. Internat. Reading Assn. (mem. com. reading visually handicapped), Nat., Tenn. (local pres.-elect) edn. assns., Council Exceptional Children, Assn. Edn. Visually Handicapped (regional rep. to nat. bd. dirs.), Nat. Braille Assn., Nat. Council Tchrs. English, Found. for Exceptional Children, Kappa Delta Phi, Delta Kappa Gamma. Baptist. Author: (with Sam Ashcroft) Programmed Instruction in Braille, 1963. Contbg. author (Berthold Lowenfeld editor) The Visually Handicapped Child in School, 1972. Home: 2323 Sweetwood Rd Nashville TN 37214 Office: 115 Stewarts Ferry Nashville TN 37214

HENDERSON, JEAN CAROLYN GLIDDEN (MRS. ALGO D. HENDERSON), writer; b. N.Y.C., May 22, 1916; d. Edgar and Mary (Fischer) Glidden; B.S., N.Y.U., 1951, M.A., 1954; Ph.D., U. Mich., 1967; m. Algo D. Henderson, Apr. 6, 1963; children—Carol (Mrs. Armand Viole), Philip, Joanne (Mrs. James Pratt). Dir. admissions, registrar C. W. Post Coll., Brookville, N.Y., 1955-59; dean women Finch Coll., 1961-63; asso. prof. psychology, counselor, dir. research on student characteristics Cal. Coll. Arts and Crafts, Oakland, 1969-71. Mem. Internat. Hospitality Center of Bay Area, 1968—; mem. council U. Cal. Art Mus., 1968—. Bd. dirs. Kennedy-King Scholarship Fund, Ltd. Mem. Am. Assn. for Higher Edn., Am. Assn. U. Women, Am. Personnel and Guidance Assn., Am. Civil Liberties Union, Nat. Orgn. Women, Kappa Delta Pi, Pi Lambda Theta, Pi Omega Pi. Author: Women as College Teachers, 1967; co-author: Ms. Goes to College, 1974; Higher Education in America, 1974. Contbr. articles to profl. jours. Home: 239 Glorietta Blvd Orinda CA 94563

HENDERSON, JO ANN, ednl. adminstr.; b. Decatur, Ill., June 28, 1931; d. Orval Owen and Ruth Margaret (Alexander) Henderson; B.S., Ill. State U., Normal, 1953; M.S., Roosevelt U., 1963. Tchr. pub. schs., Decatur, Ill., 1953-60; supr. elementary phys. edn. pub. schs., Forest Park, Ill., 1960-64, tchr., 1964-69, asst. prin., 1969-70, prin., dir. pub. relations, 1970-74, bus. coordinator, dir. pub. relations, 1974—. Publicity chmn. Forest Park Oktoberfest, Inc., 1969, 73; mem. Forest Park Youth Commn., 1971—. Mem. Ill. Edn. Assn. (legislative chmn. 1968), Am. Assn. Sch. Adminstrs., Ill. Elementary Sch. Prins. Assn. (exec. bd. sect. 5, 1970-73), Nat. Assn. Elementary Sch. Prins., Lake Shore Prins. Assn. (exec. bd., chmn. sect. 1973-74), Supts. Roundtable No. Ill., Delta Kappa Gamma. Lutheran. Home: 7735 Monroe St Forest Park IL 60130 Office: 930 Beloit Av Forest Park IL 60130

HENDERSON, JUDITH HILL (MRS. STEPHEN JOHN HENDERSON), govt. ofcl.; b. Yakima, Wash., Mar. 1, 1947; d. Noble Grey and Lois Elizabeth (Van Meter) Hill; B.A. cum laude (Raitt Meml. scholar), U. Wash., 1969; m. Stephen John Henderson, Feb. 14, 1970. Consumer specialist Wash. Dept. Agr., Olympia, 1970—. Publicity chmn. Gov's. Festival of the Arts, Olympia, 1972-73, POSSCA, Olympia, 1972. Mem. Am. (mem. com. on consumer interests Wash. chpt. 1970-74), Wash. (state v.p. 1971-73) home econs. assns., Wash. Food and Nutrition Council (state pres. 1973), Mortar Bd., Alpha Phi, Omicron Nu, Alpha Lambda Delta. Home: 7130 Timberlake Dr Olympia WA 98503 Office: 406 General Administration Bldg Olympia WA 98504

HENDERSON, MARION LOUISE MARSHALL (MRS. JAMES GILCHRIST HENDERSON), social worker; b. Chgo.; d. Norman Stephen and Marjorie (Miles) Marshall; B.A., Hunter Coll., 1941; M.S.W., Columbia, 1943; m. James Gilchrist Henderson, Sept. 16, 1944; children—Marion W. (Mrs. James H. Waller), Christy Lee (Mrs. Frans M. leRoij), James Gilchrist. Caseworker, Salvation Army, Phila. Family Service, N.Y. Booth Meml. Hosp., 1943-45, instr. social work Sch. for Officers Tng., 1944-48, 68-70, camp dir. Blue Horizon, 1944-48, Ashford Hills, 1948-54, Saddle Lake, 1956-59, Star Lake Camps, 1962—, sec. League of Mercy, Yonkers, N.Y., Albany, N.Y., Hartford, Conn., 1948-61, dir. toy collection program Greater N.Y Unified Command, N.Y.C., 1962—. Cons. summer camp reading program N.Y.C. Bd. Edn., 1968-71; com. mem. camp sect. Community Council Greater N.Y., 1962—, Fedn. Protestant Welfare Agcys., 1962—. Mem. Nat. Assn. Social Workers, Acad. Certified Social Workers, Nat. Wildlife Assn., Am. Camping Assn. (pres. N.Y. sect. 1971-73, nat. dir., Nat. Honor award 1973). Home: 17 Brinkerhoff Av Teaneck NJ 07666 Office: 546 Av of Americas New York City NY 10011

HENDERSON, MARY EMMA (MRS. WARREN JASPER HENDERSON), librarian; b. Ashton, Ga., Apr. 16, 1923; d. Arlie and Myra Lee (Poole) Shultz; A.B., Ga. State Coll. for Women, 1943; M.S. in L.S., Fla. State U., 1966; m. Warren Jasper Henderson, June 19, 1949; children—Warren Jasper, Joseph Shultz. Circulation clk. Rotary Internat., Chgo., 1944-45; photograph editor Sci. Research Assos., Chgo., 1945-46; advt. prodn. clk. Nat. Co-ops. Inc., Chgo., 1946-47; librarian Irwin County High Sch., Ocilla, Ga., 1958-67; librarian Abraham Baldwin Agrl. Coll., Tifton, Ga., 1967—, head librarian, 1969—. Mem. Am. Ga. Library assns., S. Ga. Asso. Libraries (vice chmn., 1972-73, chmn. 1973-74), Ga., Tift assns. educators, Beta Phi Mu. Methodist. Home: 110 S Apple St Ocilla GA 31774 Office: Abraham Baldwin Agrl Coll Tifton GA 31794

HENDERSON, MAXINE OLIVE BOOK (MRS. WILLIAM HENDERSON III), ednl. cons.; b. Rush, Colo., Apr. 22, 1924; d. Jesse Frank and Olive (Booth) Book; B.A., U. Colo., 1945; m. William Henderson III, Apr. 10, 1948; children—William IV, Meredith. Personnel adminstr. Gen. Electric Co., Schenectady, N.Y.C., 1945-54; asst. dir. placement Katherine Gibbs Sch., N.Y.C., 1967-70; v.p., dir. William Henderson Cons., Inc., N.Y.C., 1969—; dir. recruitment Girl Scouts U.S.A., N.Y.C., 1973—. Pres., Goddard-Riverside-Trinity Sch. Thrift Shop, N.Y.C., 1964-65, Trinity Sch. Mothers' Orgn., N.Y.C., 1965-66; treas. Brearley Sch. Parents Assn., N.Y.C., 1966-67. Mem. Pan-Pacific-S.E. Asian Women's Assn. Episcopalian. Clubs: North Suffolk Garden, Nissequogue Beach, Nissequogue Golf, Nissequogue Platform Tennis Assn. (St. James, L.I., N.Y.). Home: 606 W 116th St New York City NY 10027 also Nissequogue River Rd St James NY 11780 Office: 830 3d Av New York City NY 10022

HENDERSON, METTA LOU, pharmacist; b. Battle Creek, Mich., Sept. 11, 1938; d. Hugh Robeson and Marie (Richards) Henderson; B.S., U. Ariz., 1961, M.S., 1966. Intern pharmacy Tucson Med. Center, 1959-60, Jims Pill Box, Tucson, 1960-61, U. Mich. Hosp., Ann Arbor, 1961-62; pharmacist Speakers Prescription Apothecary, Battle Creek, 1962-63; pharmacist Community Hosp., Battle Creek, 1963-65, 66-68, dir. pharmacy, 1968-73, dir. Poison Control Center, 1968-73; grad. asso. teaching in pharmacy U. Ariz., 1965-66; instr. Kellogg Community Coll., Battle Creek, 1967-74; adj. instr. clin. pharmacy Ferris State Coll., Big Rapids, Mich., 1973-74, asst. prof., 1974—. Mem. Am., Mich., Calhoun County (sec. 1970-71, v.p. 1971-72, pres. 1972-73) pharm. assns., Am. Soc. Hosp. Pharmacists, Am. Bus. Womens Assn. (chpt. sec. 1963), Am. Assn. Poison Control Centers, Western Mich. Soc. Hosp. Pharmacists, Profl. Panhellenic Assn. (treas. 1969-71, mem. at large 1973—), Beta Beta Beta, Rho Chi, Kappa Epsilon (grand pres. 1965-73). Methodist. Home: Rural Route 1 Box 24 Reed City MI 49677 Office: Ferris State Coll Sch Pharmacy Big Rapids MI 49307

HENDERSON, SANDRA RUSSELL (MRS. W. ELLIOTT HENDERSON), educator; b. N.Y.C., Apr. 1, 1936; d. Charles B. and Agnes (Brow) Russell; B.B.A. magna cum laude, U. Pitts., 1958, M.A., 1960; m. W. Elliott Henderson, Sept. 6, 1958; children—Allison, Kevin R. Instr., W.Va. U., Morgantown, 1964-66; asst. prof. W.Va. Inst. Tech., Montgomery, 1966-67; asst. prof. econs. W.Va. State Coll., Institute, 1967—, chmn. dept. econs., 1969—. Mem. Am. Assn. U. Profs. (exec. com. local chpt. 1970-72), Am. Econ. Assn., Phi Theta Kappa, Beta Gamma Sigma. Home: 1034 Valley Rd Charleston WV 25302 Office: Dept Econs West Virginia State Coll 307A Bldg institute WV 25112

HENDERSON, SHARON WARD (MRS. LOUIS CLIFTON HENDERSON, JR.), artist; b. Mobile, Ala., Dec. 18, 1938; d. Gordon Bert and Mary Caroline (Nash) Ward; student Lindenwood Coll. for Women, 1956-57, U. Ark., 1957-58; m. Louis Clifton Henderson, Jr., Jan. 24, 1959; children—Lisa Ward, Ann Richmond. One-woman shows Vestavia Country Club, Tavern Gallery, Cobb Lane Gallery, Downtown Club; exhibited in group shows Studio One Painters, Circle Painters, Birmingham Festival of Arts; represented in permanent collections So. Natural Gas Co., Birmingham Trust Nat. Bank, Vestavia Country Club; mem. Studio One, Birmingham, 1970-71; founder, Cobb Lane Gallery, Birmingham, 1971-72; mem. Circle Painters, Birmingham, 1973-74; owner Terrace Gallery, Birmingham. Pvt. art tchr., Birmingham, 1972-73. Chmn. Cobb Lane Christmas Open House, 1971-72. Recipient first prize Still Life Realists Tuscaloosa, 1973. Mem. Nat. Audubon Soc., Birmingham, Vestavia art assns., Birmingham Mus. Art, Bluff Park Art Assn. Clubs: Vestavia Country (pres. art com. 1972); Christian Women's (pres. 1970), Alea Literary (pres. 1974—) (Birmingham). Home: 3032 Westmoreland Dr Birmingham AL 35223 Office: Terrace Gallery 1 Cobb Lane Birmingham AL 35223

HENDERSON, VIOLETTE BREAZEALE (MRS. DON J. HENDERSON), coll. adminstr.; b. Lenoir City, Tenn., Oct. 30, 1922; d. Benjamin Franklin and Ethel Lee (Jenkins) Breazeale; student Lenoir City Bus. Sch., 1944; m. Don J. Henderson, Aug. 22, 1946. Sec. Alcoa Aluminum Co. (Tenn.), 1940-42; sec. Union Carbide-Carbon Co., Oak Ridge, 1942-44; asst. bursar Mars Hill (N.C.) Coll., 1954-70, bus. mgr., 1970—. Mem. Am. Assn. Higher Edn., So. Assn. Coll. and Univ. Bus. Officers. Baptist. Club: Woman's (pres. 1962-66, 68-70) (Mars Hill, N.C.). Home: 123 Mountainview Rd Mars Hill NC 28754

HENDERSON, VIRGINIA COWEN (MRS. JARVIS RICHARD HENDERSON), hosp. adminstr.; b. Waverly, Tenn., Sept. 9; d. Cardinal Woolsey and Minnie Delta (Harris) Cowen; student San Bernardino Valley Coll., 1930-31; m. Jarvis Richard Henderson, June 12, 1935. Office mgr. Valley Typewriter Co., 1931-38, B & H Food Products, 1938-40, Montgomery Tire Co., 1940-41; bus. mgr. San Bernardino Community Hosp., 1943-55, adminstr., 1955— (all San Bernardino, Cal.). Mem. spl. events com. San Bernardino Nat. Orange Show, 1964; mem. personnel commn. San Bernardino City Unified Sch. Dist.; mem. bd. councillors to Cal. State Coll., Dept. Adminstrn., San Bernardino. Bd. dirs. Health Found., Arrowhead United Fund, San Bernardino Vis. Nurses Assn., Children's Home Soc., Cal. Regional Med. Program, San Bernardino County Comprehensive Health Planning. Mem. Western Hosp. Assn., Hosp. Planning Assn. So. Cal. (dir. inland area), Hosp. Council So. Cal. (pub. relations com., dir., chmn. inland area hosps.), San Bernardino C. of C. (dir.), P.E.O. Presbyn. Home: 4758 Olivewood Lane North Woods Estates San Bernardino CA 92407 Office: 1500 W 17th St San Bernardino CA 92405

HENDLEY, EDITH DIPASQUALE, educator; b. N.Y.C., Sept. 5, 1927; d. Michael and Rose (Parillo) Dipasquale; A.B., Hunter Coll., 1948; M.Sc. (Univ. fellow), Ohio State U., 1950; Ph.D., U. Ill., 1954; m. Daniel Dees Hendley, Apr. 21, 1952; children—Jane, Joyce, Paul. Research asso. dept. physiology U. Chgo., 1954-56; asst. lectr. dept. physiology U. Sheffield, Eng., 1956-57; instr. dept. ophthalmology Johns Hopkins Sch. Medicine, 1963-66, research asso. dept. pharmacology, 1966-71; sr. investigator Friends Med. Sci. Research Center, Balt., 1972-73; asso. prof. dept. physiology U. Vt. Coll. Medicine, Burlington, 1973—. Mem. Assn. Women in Sci. (treas. 1972-74), Am. Physiol. Soc., Am. Soc. Pharmacology and Exptl. Therapeutics, Soc. Neuroscis., A.A.A.S., Phi Beta Kappa, Phi Sigma, Sigma Delta Epsilon. Home: 402 Dalton Dr Winooski VT 05404 Office: Dept Physiology U Vt Given Bldg Burlington VT 05401

HENDRICK, ZELWANDA, educator; b. Rusk, Tex., Nov. 28, 1925; d. Lloyd Irvin and Viola Alice (McGuire) Hendrick; A.A., Lon Morris Coll., 1945; B.S., N. Tex. U., 1947; M.A., So. Meth. U., 1958. Tchr. theatre arts Overton (Tex.) High Sch., 1947-49, Nacogdoches (Tex.) High Sch., 1949-50, Boude Storey Sch., Dallas, 1950-53, Kimball High Sch., Dallas, 1953-62; tchr. theatre arts H. Grady Spruce High

Sch., Dallas, 1962—, chmn. fine arts dept., 1963—; part time tchr. John Robert Powers Finishing Sch., 1951—; teaching fellow North Tex. U., 1964-65. Active Tyler (Tex.) Civic Symphony, 1949-50, Tyler Civic Theatre, 1949-50, Dallas Theatre Center, 1960-61. Mem. Internat. Thespians (state dir.), Tex. Speech Assn. (sec. 1973—), Am. Assn. Ednl. Theatre, Tex. Tchrs. Assn., Nat. Forensic League, Am. Assn. U. Women, Classroom Tchrs. Dallas, Internat. Platform Assn., Delta Kappa Gamma. Mem. Order Eastern Star. Contbr. to A Guide to Student Teaching in Music, 1968-70. Home: 3016 Westminster St Dallas TX 75205 Office: 9733 Old Seagoville Rd Dallas TX 75217

HENDRICKS, BETTY IMOGENE, banker; b. East Peoria, Ill., Aug. 13, 1926; d. Lloyd E. and Anna E. (Peak) Hendricks; grad. high sch. With 1st Nat. Bank, East Peoria, 1945-52, bank teller, 1945-47, bookkeeper, 1948-52; cashier Wilts Super Market, Elkhart, Ind., 1952-56; with St. Joseph Valley Bank, Elkhart, 1956—, savs. teller, comml. adminstrv. loan teller, bookkeeping clk., mortgage loan clk., now officer mortgage dept. Mem. Nat. Assn. Bank Women. Home: 2210 Necedah Dr Elkhart IN 46514 Office: Franklin at 2d Elkhart IN 46514

HENDRICKS, HARRIETT ELIZABETH, librarian; b. Richland Center, Wis., July 20, 1943; d. Clifford Lyle and Erna Abalone (Shaw) Hendricks; B.S., Wis. State U., 1965. Librarian, Weston Sch. Dist., Cazenovia, Wis., 1965—. Mem. Richland County Assn. for Retarded Children, 1970—, treas. 1971-72; vol. worker Adult Retarded Activity Group of Richland County, 1969—. Bd. dirs. Wis. Assn. for Retarded Children, 1972-73. Recipient Carol award, citation for achievement and recognition for outstanding leadership, 1968; named Wis.'s Handicapped Person of Year, 1973. Methodist. Home: 798 N Church St Richland Center WI 53581 Office: Weston High Sch Cazenovia WI 53924

HENDRICKS, MARY ELIZABETH, pub. relations exec.; b. Martinsville, Ind., Mar. 5, 1920; d. Thomas A. and Mary Elizabeth (Matthews) Hendricks; B.S., Ind. U., 1942. With Eli Lilly & Co., Indpls., 1942—, mgr. pub. relations services, 1969—. Mem. Women in Communications, Kappa Kappa Gamma. Club: Martinsville (Ind.) Country. Home: 7370 Lions Head Dr Indianapolis IN 46260 Office: 307 E McCarty St Indianapolis IN 46206

HENDRICKSON, NOREJANE JOHNSTON (MRS. ANDREW HENDRICKSON), educator; b. Coudersport, Pa., Mar. 6, 1919; d. Joseph F. and Caroline (Sanford) Johnston; B.S., Mansfield State Coll., 1943; M.A., Mich. State U., 1951; Ph.D. (scholar), Ohio State U., 1958; m. Andrew Hendrickson, Sept. 6, 1953; 1 dau., Dorothy Ann. Tchr., Northeast (Pa.) Joint High Sch., 1943-48; grad. asst. Mich. State U., Lansing, 1948-49; instr. home mgmt.-child devel. Simmons Coll., Boston, 1949-50; instr. family life and child devel. Ohio State U., Columbus, 1950-53, asso. prof., 1958-65, prof., also chmn. dept., 1966-68; prof. home and Family life Fla. State U., 1968—. Recipient Diamond Anniversary award distinguished alumna Ohio State U. Sch. Home Econs., 1971. Mem. Am. Home Econs. Assn., Soc. Research Child Devel., Internat. Platform Assn., Nat. Assn. Edn. Young Children, Childhood Edn. Assn. Internat., Nat. Council Marriage and Family Living, So., Fla. assns. children under six, Omicron Nu (nat. v.p. 1973—), Kappa Delta Pi. Contbr. articles to profl. jours. Tech. adviser Jour. Home Econs.; audiovisual rep. Young Children. Collaborator on films. Home: 1121 Mercer Dr Tallahassee FL 32303 Office: Fla State U Tallahassee FL 32306

HENDRICKSON, VIVIAN ECKERT (MRS. MORTIMER HENDRICKSON), hosp. adminstr.; b. Kutztown, Pa., June 2, 1914; d. Walter S. and Jennie (Smith) Eckert; grad. Cooper Hosp. Nurses Tng. Sch., Camden, N.J., 1936; R.N., U. Pa., 1941; m. Mortimer Hendrickson, Oct. 4, 1941; children—Verna Zoe, Vincent Mort. With Camden County Psychiat. Hosp., Lakeland, N.J., 1936—, supt. 1951—; owner and pub. relation program for radio sta. WDVL, Vineland, N.J.; co-dir. Fed. sponsored program In-Services Tng. Hosp. Nursing Personnel; dir. Fed. sponsored program of Day Care. Mem. profl. adv. com. Camden County Mental Health Assn., 1956-59; mem. Camden County Mental Health Planning Com., 1962-67; mem. Social Welfare Assn. Camden County, 1954—. Mem. Am. Coll. Hosp. Adminstrs., Am., N.J. hosp. assns., Am. Nurses Assn., Royal Soc. Health (Eng.). Address: Blackwood P O Lakeland NJ 08012

HENDRYSON, ELIZABETH SHIRES STAYER (MRS. IRVIN E. HENDRYSON), librarian; b. Pitts., Dec. 30, 1913; d. William Bechtel and Edna (Shires) Stayer; A.B., Wesleyan Coll., 1935; B.S. in L.S., Carnegie Inst. Tech., 1941; postgrad. Columbia; m. Frederick Winburn New, Dec. 15, 1933 (div. 1940); children—Peter, Elizabeth (Mrs. Philip S. Weld, Jr.); m. 2d, Aaron Edwin Margulis, Oct. 20, 1944 (dec. Dec. 1960); m. 3d, Irvin E. Hendryson, Sept. 25, 1965. Woman's page editor Augusta (Ga.) Chronicle, 1937-38; children's librarian Bklyn. Pub. Library, 1941-43; asso. librarian Rockefeller Inst. Med. Research, N.Y., 1943-44; librarian N.Y. Post-Grad. Med. Sch., Columbia, 1944-47; children's and young people's librarian N.M. Extension Library, 1948-49; children's librarian Santa Fe Pub. Library, 1958-62; coordinator children's World Library 21, Seattle World's Fair, 1962; mem. field service staff Am. Med. Assn., 1962-65; librarian Navajo Health Authority, Window Rock, Ariz., 1973—; mem. N.M. State Library Commn., 1955-62; exec. com. N.M. Schs. Study Council; mem. U.S. nat. commn. UNESCO.; mem. adv. com. on venereal disease control USPHS; edn. chmn. Aux. to Presbyn. Hosp., 1972—. Bd. dirs. Planned Parenthood Assn., Albuquerque Community Council. Recipient award of merit N.M. Sch. Bds. Assn., 1957; alumnae award Wesleyan Coll., 1968. Mem. Woman's Aux. to N.M. Med. Soc. (past pres.), Santa Fe County TB Assn. (past pres.), Nat. (pres. 1967-69, chmn. endowment fund), N.M. (past pres.) parents and tchrs. assns., A.L.A., Women's Aux. A.M.A. (nat. dir. 1960-62), Friends of Albuquerque Library (pres. 1972—), Community Concerts Assn. (dir.), Delta Kappa Gamma. Contbg. editor MD's Wife. Home: 6303 Indian School Rd NE Albuquerque NM 87110 also PO Box 647 Fort Defiance AZ 86504

HENEGAR, MARTHA LUCILE, pub. relations dir.; b. McMinnville, Tenn., July 9, 1937; d. Ulric Shaw and Lucile (Angel) Henegar; B.A., George Peabody Coll., 1959, M.A., 1960. Tchr., Met. Nashville Pub. Schs., 1959-68; promotion dir. WMCV-TV, Nashville, 1968-70; dir. pub. relations Nashville State Tech. Inst., 1970—. Mem. Internat. Assn. Bus. Communicators, Am. Women in Radio and TV (chpt. pres. 1973—), Pub. Relations Soc. Am. Club: Middle Tenn. Bus. Press (Nashville). Editor: Print-Out Mag., 1970—. Home: P 3 1900 Richard Jones Rd Nashville TN 37215 Office: 120 White Bridge Rd Nashville TN 37209

HENG, CATHERINE MARIE LUNDON (MRS. OWEN ALBERT HENG), journalist; b. Cedar Rapids, Ia., June 22, 1943; d. Frank Edward and Velma Catherine (Anderson) Lundon; B.S., Ia. State U., 1965; M.A., Central Mich. U., 1969; m. Owen Albert Heng, July 24, 1965; children—Melissa Catherine, Kathleen Marie. Reporter, Midland (Mich.) Daily News, 1965-71; pub. information dir. Midland Hosp. Assn. Fund Drive, 1970; free-lance journalist, Midland, Mich., 1970—. Publicity dir. Harbour House, 1970—. Bd. dirs. Vols. Youth Midland County. Recipient Program Devel. Chmn. of Year award Am. Assn. U. Women, Mich. State div., 1973. Mem. Am. Assn. U. Women (del. at large 1973-74), Women in Communications, Inc., League Women Voters. Home: 3713 McKeith Rd Midland MI 48640

HENKE, ESTHER MAE, librarian; b. Orlando, Okla., Apr. 4, 1925; d. Emil and Marie Edna (Weber) Henke; student St. John's Jr. Coll., 1943-44; B.A., U. Okla., 1947, M.A., in History, 1953. Bookmobile librarian, Ray County Library, Richmond, Mo., 1947-48, head librarian, 1948-51; reference librarian Okla. State Library, 1953-54, field librarian, 1954-55, extension librarian, 1955-67; asso. dir. for library services, Okla. Dept. Libraries, Oklahoma City, 1967—. Recipient Outstanding Woman of Year in field of library services Theta-Sigma Phi, 1966; Distinguished Service award Okla. Library Assn., 1971. Mem. Am. (mem. council 1961-65, com. nat. library week 1959—), Okla. (2nd v.p. 1962-63, sec. 1957-58, fed. coordinator 1958—), Southwestern library assns., Assn. State Library Agys. (exec. bd. 1973—, fed. relations coordinator 1958—), Okla. Women's Posse of Westerners. Lutheran. Clubs: Soroptimist (pres. 1973-74) (Oklahoma City). Home: 4316 Woodland Dr Oklahoma City OK 73105 Office: Oklahoma Dept Libraries Oklahoma City OK 73105

HENKEL, BARBARA MONROE OSBORN (MRS. WILLIAM HENRY HENKEL), educator; b. Oakland, Cal., Mar. 14, 1921; d. Russell Jerome and Ruth (Watson) Monroe; B.S., U. Cal., Berkeley, 1943; M.A., Cal. State, Los Angeles, 1956; Ed.D., U. Cal., Los Angeles, 1960; m. Robert W. Osborn, July 27, 1941 (div. Apr. 1951); children—Robert Stephen, Patricia J. (Mrs. James McClean); m. 2d, William H. Henkel, Sept. 14, 1968. Head nurse U. Cal. Hosp., San Francisco, 1943-44; dir., asst. dir. nursing and Sch. Nursing, Franklin Hosp., San Francisco, 1944-47; supr. nurses Cal. Physicians Service, Los Angeles, 1950-52; dir. nursing services Pasadena Am. Nat. Red Cross, 1952-55; instr. East Los Angeles Community Coll., 1955-56; prof. health edn. Cal. State U., Los Angeles, 1956—, Chmn. nursing services Los Angeles Am. Nat. Red Cross, 1966—. Mem. Lung Assn., Los Angeles, Sch. Health Activities com., 1962—. Outstanding Service award Los Angeles chpt. A.R.C., 1968. Fellow Am. Sch. Health Assn.; mem. Am. Pub. Health Assn., So. Cal. Pub. Health Assn. Republican. Author: Introduction to Community Health, 2d edit., 1970; Foundations of Health Science, 2d edit., 1971. Home: 1341 San Marino Av San Marino CA 91108 Office: 5151 State University Dr Los Angeles CA 90032

HENKEL, MARY ELIZABETH, univ. dean; b. Toledo, Oct. 15, 1936; d. Louis Gerald and Elizabeth (Rump) Henkel; B.E., U. Toledo, 1958; M.A., U. Tulsa, 1964; ednl. specialist degree U. Toledo, 1974. Women and girl's sec. YMCA, Findlay, O., 1958-62; grad. counselor Kappa Delta, U. Tulsa, 1962-64; resident counselor, coordinator women's housing U. Toledo, 1964-68, asst. dean students, 1968—. Mem. youth com. A.R.C., Toledo chpt., 1969—; alumnae adv. bd. chmn., rush adviser Kappa Delta, Bowling Green U., 1960-62, 64-70; alumnae asst. del. to City Panhellenic Council, 1964-69. Trustee YWCA, 1971, v.p. for personnel, 1973-74; bd. mgrs. YMCA, 1973—. Mem. Nat., Ohio assns. women deans and counselors, U. Toledo, U. Tulsa alumnae assns., Kappa Delta (nat. conv. mgr. 1965-73, nat. asst. conv. dir. 1974—), Pi Lambda Theta, Pi Gamma Mu. Clubs: University (sec., dir.), University Women's. Home: 3120 E Lincolnshire Blvd Toledo OH 43606 Office: 2801 W Bancroft St Toledo OH 43606

HENKER, BARBARA ANNE, psychologist, educator; b. LaCrosse, Wis.; d. Herbert T. and Mabel O. (Anderson) Henker; A.B., San Francisco State Coll., 1957; M.A., Sacramento State Coll., 1960; Ph.D., Ohio State U., 1963; postgrad. Harvard, 1964-65. Asst. personnel analyst Cal. State Personnel Bd., 1957-59; research asst. Ohio State U., 1959-61; intern Columbus Psychiat. Clinic, 1961; teaching asst. Ohio State U., Columbus, 1961-62, teaching fellow, 1962, asst. prof. psychology, 1964; asst. prof. psychology U. Cal. at Los Angeles, 1965-71, asso. prof., 1972—. Mem. Am. Psychol. Assn., Am. Assn. Mental Deficiency. Contbr. articles to profl. jours. Office: Dept Psychology U Cal Los Angeles CA 90024

HENLE, GERTRUDE, virologist; b. Mannheim, Germany, Apr. 3, 1912; d. Theophil and Elenore (Baumgart) Szpingier; M.D., U. Heidelberg (Germany), 1936; m. Werner Henle, Mar. 13, 1937. Came to U.S., 1937, naturalized, 1943. Intern, Inst. Hygiene, U. Heidelberg (Germany), 1936-37; faculty U. Pa., 1937—, instr. in bacteriology to prof. virology in pediatrics Sch. Medicine, 1940—; research staff Children's Hosp. of Phila., 1940—. Recipient Mead-Johnson award Am. Acad. Pediatrics, 1950; Variety of Heart award Phila., 1970, Smith, Kline & French award for excellence in research, 1971; Robert-Koch medaille and Robert-Koch Preis, Robert-Koch-Stiftung, 1971. Mem. Am. Acad. Microbiology, Tissue Culture Assn. Contbr. numerous articles on influenza, mumps, hepatitis, infectious mononucleosis and tumor viruses to sci. jours. Home: 533 Ott Rd Bala-Cynwyd PA 19004 Office: 1740 Bainbridge St Philadelphia PA 19146

HENLEY, ATHA LOUISE, univ. librarian; b. Marshall, Mo., May 17, 1927; d. Joseph Wheeler and Grace Marie (Allen) Henley; B.A., Missouri Valley Coll., 1949; M.L.S., U. Cal. at Berkeley, 1956. Librarian pharmacy bacteriology library Ohio State U., 1955-60; sci. librarian U. Fla., 1960-66; librarian div. plant industry Fla. Dept. Agr., 1966-70; librarian vet. med. library Auburn (Ala.) U., 1970—. Mem. Spl. Libraries Assn., Ala. Library Assn., Med. Library Assn. (chmn. vet. med. library group 1974—), Am. Assn. U. Women, Alpha Xi Delta. Mem. Disciples of Christ. Home: 65 Woodland Terrace Auburn AL 36830 Office: Vet Med Library Basic Science Bldg Auburn U Auburn AL 36830

HENLEY, ELAINE DIMITMAN (MRS. ERNEST MARK HENLEY), physician; b. Bridgeton, N.J., Jan. 19, 1926; d. Isaac O. and Rose (Moss) Dimitman; B.A., U. Cal. at Los Angeles, 1947; M.D., U. Cal. San Francisco, 1951; m. Ernest Mark Henley, Aug. 21, 1948; children—M. Bradford, Karen M. Intern U. Cal. Hosp., 1951-52; resident Bellevue Hosp., N.Y.C., 1952-53; fellow N.Y. Hosp., Cornell Med. Center, N.Y.C., 1953-54; fellow U. Wash., 1954-56, asst. in medicine, 1956-58, physician Health Center, 1956—, asso. med. dir., 1970—, clin. instr., 1958-61, clin. asst. prof., 1961-69, clin. asso. prof., 1969—; vis. research asso. Brookhaven Nat. Labs., Upton, N.Y., 1957, 65; research asso. Connective Tissue Research Inst., Copenhagen, Denmark, 1958-59; active attending physician Univ. Hosp., Seattle, 1959—, med. dir. occupational health, 1961—. Diplomate Am. Bd. Internal Medicine. Fellow A.C.P.; mem. Am. Fedn. Clin. Research, Endocrine Soc., Am. Diabetes Assn., European Assn. Study of Diabetes, Am. Soc. Internal Medicine, Phi Beta Kappa, Alpha Omega Alpha. Contbr. papers to profl. publs. Home: 4408 55th Av NE Seattle WA 98105 Office: Health Center GS10 U Wash Seattle WA 98195

HENLEY, HELEN MCTAGGERT (MRS. W. BALLENTINE HENLEY), rancher; b. Pawnee, Ill., Mar. 20, 1910; d. Albert Thomas and Edith L. (Fallenstein) McTaggart; student Washington U., St. Louis, 1935-38; m. William Ballentine Henley, Dec. 15, 1942. Co-owner, mgr. Delmar Farm, Momence, Ill., 1943-58, Creston Circle Ranch, Paso Robles, Cal., 1958—; income property owner devel. and mgmt., 1955—. Mem. Am. Saddle Horse Assn., Am. Aberdeen-Angus Assn., Cal. Saddle Horse Breeder's Futurity (dir. 1945-48, 58-71). Home: 1224 Geneva St Glendale CA 91207 Office: Creston Circle Ranch Creston Star Route Paso Robles CA 93446

HENLINE, FLORENCE, pianist; b. Ft. Wayne, Ind.; d. Samuel and Caroline Dorothy (Mollet) Henline; B.M., Chgo. Mus. Coll., 1928; m. Milson Jezek, Sept. 2, 1936. Made first concert appearance at age of 13; appeared with Ill. Symphony and Grant Park Orch., Chgo., Women's Symphony (ofcl. pianist); accompanist; staff pianist NBC network, 1930-32; pianist, soloist Chgo. Symphony String Ensemble, 1946-56, Chgo. Pops Symphonette; soloist Indpls. Symphony String Ensemble Symphonette, 1970; solo concert engagements throughout U.S.; faculty mem. Chgo. Conservatory, 1959. Judge auditions piano solo contest 35th ann. Chicagoland Music Festival, 1964, ann. competition soloists Young Judea Symphony Orch. Chgo., 1965, 67. Fellow Internat. Inst. Arts and Letters (life); mem. Lake View Mus. Soc., Musicians' Club Women, Alliance Francaise (Chgo.), Ill. Opera Guild, Chgo. Artists Assn., Mu Phi Epsilon (soloist at internat. conv. 1972). Club: Cordon. Home: 9715 S Vanderpoel Chicago IL 60643

HENN, SHIRLEY EMILY, librarian; b. Cleve., May 26, 1919; d. Albert Edwin and Florence Ely (Miller) Henn; A.B., Hollins Coll., 1941; M.S., U. N.C., 1966; m. John Van Bruggen, July 14, 1944 (div. May 1947); 1 son, Peter Albert (dec.). Library asst. Hollins (Va.) Coll., 1943-44, 61-64, reference librarian, 1965—; advt. mgr. R.M. Kellogg Co., Three Rivers, Mich., 1946-47; exec. sec. Hollins Coll. Alumnae Assn., 1947-55; real estate salesman Fowlkes & Kefauver, Roanoke, Va., 1955-61. Pres. Soc. for Prevention Cruelty to Animals, 1959-61, 69-72, bd. dirs., 1972—. Mem. Am. Alumni Council (dir. 1952-54, dir. women's activities 1952-54), Am., Va. (membership chmn. coll. and univ. sect. 1969—) library assns., Collie Club Am., Roanoke Bird Club, Roanoke Kennel Club. Clubs: Quota (chpt. pres. 1958-60) (Roanoke). Author and illustrator: Adventures of Hooty Owl and His Friends, 1953. Editor: Hollins Alumnae Bull., 1947-56. Home: 6915 Tinkerdale Hollins VA 24019 Office: Fishburn Library Hollins College VA 24020

HENNE, FRANCES ELIZABETH, educator; b. Springfield, Ill., Oct. 11, 1906; d. J. Z. and Laura (Taylor) Henne; A.B., U. Ill., 1929, M.A., 1934; B.S., Columbia, 1935; Ph.D., U. Chgo., 1949. Mem. library staff Springfield (Ill.) Pub. Library, 1930-34, N.Y. Pub. Library, 1935, N.Y. State Tchrs. Coll., Albany, 1935-38; librarian U. High Sch., U. Chgo., 1939-42; instr. N.Y. State Coll. for Tchrs., 1937-38, 39; instr. Grad. Library Sch., U. Chgo., 1939-46, asst. prof., 1946-49, asso. dean, dean of students, 1947-50, acting dean, 1951-52; became asso. prof. Sch. Library Service, Columbia, N.Y.C., 1954, now prof. library scis.; vis. prof. U. Minn., summer 1950, Rutgers U., summer 1954. Exec. adv. council Ednl. Media Selection Centers Project, 1968—; mem. N.Y. Regents Adv. Council on Libraries, 1964—. Carnegie fellow, 1938; recipient Lippincott award, 1963. Mem. A.L.A., Am. Assn. U. Profs., Am. Assn. Sch. Librarians (nat. pres. 1948-49). Author: Youth, Communication, and Libraries, 1949; Planning Guide for the High School Library Program, 1951; also numerous articles in field. Home: 345 E 50th St New York City NY 10022

HENNEMAN, CAROL ELIZABETH, physician; b. Eden Valley, Minn., Feb. 24, 1926; d. David Joseph and Kathryn Mary (Rothstein) Henneman; R.N., U. Minn., 1946; A.A., U. Cal. at Los Angeles, 1968; M.D., U. So. Cal., 1962. Intern, Los Angeles County Hosp., 1962-63, resident, 1963-67; practice medicine, specializing in obstetrics and gynecology, Los Angeles, 1967—; mem. staffs Los Angeles County-U. So. Cal. Med. Center, John Wesley County Hosp., Good Samaritan Hosp., Cal. Hosp. Med. Center, Cedars-Sinai Med. Center; dir. family planning John Wesley Hosp., Los Angeles, 1970—; instr. obstetrics and gynecology U. So. Cal., 1967-74, asst. prof., 1974—. Diplomate Am. Bd. Obstetrics and Gynecology. Fellow Am. Coll. of Obstetricians and Gynecologists; mem. Los Angeles Obstetrics and Gynecological Soc., Am., Cal., Los Angeles County med. assns., Am., Pacific Coast fertility socs., Alpha Omega Alpha. Home: 2024 Holly Vista Av Los Angeles CA 90027 Office: 2826 S Hope St Los Angeles CA 90007

HENNEMAN, DOROTHY HUGHES, physician; b. Sao Paulo, Brazil, Sept. 3, 1923; d. Reynold King and Edna Margaret (Geyer) Hughes (parents Am. citizens); B.A. (scholar), Wellesley Coll., 1945; postgrad. Radcliffe Coll., 1945-46; M.D. in Medicine, Johns Hopkins Med. Sch., 1949; m. Philip H. Henneman, Aug. 25, 1945 (div. 1963); children—Carolyn Hughes (Mrs. Michael Sternschein), Sally Edna (Mrs. Robert Linder), Philip Lee, Diane Gail. Intern McClean Hosp., Waltham, Mass., 1949-51; resident Mass. Gen. Hosp., 1951-53, fellow in anesthesia, 1954-55, research asso. in anesthesia, 1955-56; research asst. McLean Hosp., Waverly, Mass., 1950-54; research asso. anesthesia, asst. surgery Peter Bent Brigham Hosp., Boston, 1956-58, now cons. bone metabolism; asst. attending physician Jersey City Med. Center, 1958-66; spl. isotope trainee Columbia, N.Y.C., 1961; asso., cons. New Eng. Deaconess Hosp., Boston, 1970-73; research fellow anesthesia Harvard Med. Sch., Boston, 1954-55, research asso. anesthesia, 1955-58, asst. in surgery, 1956-58, asst. prof., 1971-73, instr. medicine Seton Hall Coll. Medicine, Jersey City, 1958-62; instr. bacteriology Rutgers U., New Brunswick, N.J., 1963; sr. scientist Inst. for Med. Research. E.R. Squibb, New Brunswick, 1963-66; sr. scientist Ortho Research Found., Raritan, N.J., 1966-67, Ortho Research fellow, 1967-71; sr. research asso. Cancer Research Inst., New Eng. Deaconess Hosp., Boston, 1971-73; asso. prof. health sci., coordinator clin. studies U. Del., Newark, 1973—. Cons. Nat. Heart and Lung Inst., NIH, Bethesda, Md., 1969—, mem. research panel Nat. Inst. Child Health and Devel., 1972—. Mem. team to reorganize Med. Sch. Nat. U. Iran, 1974. Acad. Arts and Sci. fellow, 1949-50; Postdoctoral fellow USPHS, 1950-54; Sr. Research fellowship NIH, 1961-63; recipient Distinguished medal A.M.A., 1970. Mem. Endocrine Soc., New Eng. Diabetes Assn., Am. Fedn. for Clin. Research, Am. Physiol. Soc., Nat. Am. Diabetes Assn., A.A.A.S., N.Y. Acad. Scis., Phi Beta Kappa, Alpha Omega Alpha. Home: Calvert Rd Calvert MD Office: 103 Willard Hall U Del Newark DE

HENNEN, MALINDA ANN, coll. ofcl.; b. Lawrenceville, Ga., July 1, 1944; d. William Franklin and Edna (Nix) Hennen; B.S., U. Ga., 1966, M.Ed., 1968, Ph.D., 1973. U.S. Office Edn. research fellow in sch. psychology, 1966-69; dir. psychol. services 9th dist. Coop. Ednl. Service Agy., NSF, Cleveland, Ga., 1971-73; asst. dir. Antioch Coll., Columbia, Md., 1973—. Mem. Am. Psychol. Assn. Author: Identifying Handicapped Children for Child Development Programs, 1973. Home: 9002 Watchlight Ct Columbia MD 21045

HENNES, JOANNE BETTE (MRS. WAYNE WALTER HENNES), artist; b. Rockford, Ill., Jan. 30, 1936; d. Paul Stegman and Minnie Martha (Kruse) Jackson; student Burpee Gallery of Art, Rockford, 1959, Academie de la Grande Chaumiere, Paris, France, 1963; m. Wayne Walter Hennes, Aug. 7, 1954. Exhibited one man shows Mont. Hist. Soc., 1967, Desert S.W. Art Gallery, Palm Desert, Cal., 1968; spl. exhibit at Grand Opening of Buffalo Bill Hist. Center, Cody, Wyo., 1969; spl. show Polynesian paintings Trailside Galleries, Jackson, Wyo., 1974; exhibited group shows Burpee Gallery Art, 1959-66, U. Ill., 1965, Trailside Galleries, Jackson, 1965-74, Saddleback Galleries, Santa Ana, Cal. and Phoenix, 1967-69, Main Trail Galleries, Scottsdale, Ariz., 1971-72, Village Art Gallery, Lahaina, Maui, Hawaii, 1972-74; represented in permanent collections Trailside Galleries, Main Trail Galleries, Fine Arts Center, Rock Springs, Wyo., East High Sch. Art Collection, Rockford. Recipient Popular Award winner, Jackson, Wyo., 1965. Illustrator: Teton Sketches of Summer, 1969; also various articles In Wyoming Magazine, 1969-71. Home and studio: Box 151 Jackson WY 83001

HENNESSEY, SISTER MARY AGNES, coll. pres.; b. Monticello, Ia., May 11, 1908; d. John David and Anna Josephine (DeLay) Hennessey; B.A., Loras Coll., 1939; M.A., St. Louis U., 1941, Ph.D., 1958. Elementary tchr. Marion, Oelwein and Cedar Rapids, Ia., 1931-40; secondary tchr. Immaculate Conception Sch., Cedar Rapids, 1941-42; faculty Mt. Mercy Coll., Cedar Rapids, 1942-43; supr. elementary and secondary schs., Cedar Rapids, 1943-55; academic dean Mount Mercy Coll., 1958-61, pres., 1961—. Bd. dirs., mem. edn. commn. Sisters of Mercy, 1947-53, 59-71. Bd. govs. Ia. Coll. Found., 1961—; bd. dirs. Cedar Rapids Art Assn., 1969—, Ia. Assn. Pvt. Colls., 1961—. Mem. Nat. Soc. for Study Edn., Ia. Assn. Coll. Presidents (pres. 1964-65), Am. Assn. Higher Edn., Common Cause, C. of C. (mem. edn. commn. 1971—). Democrat. Home and office: 1330 Elmhurst Dr NE Cedar Rapids IA 52402

HENNESSY, MARY MARILYN, govt. ofcl.; b. Bloomington, Ill., Nov. 20, 1936; d. Harry Jerome and Mary Catherine (O'Connor) Hennessy; B.S., Mount Mary Coll., 1954; postgrad. De Paul U., 1956, U. Wis., 1958, U. Chgo., 1970. Occupational therapist VA Hosp., Hines, Ill., 1956, supr. occupational therapy, 1957; asst. dir. occupational therapy Curative Workshop, Milw., 1958-60; cons. chronic disease and aging Wis. Bd. Health, Madison, 1961-66; program cons. Nat. Easter Seal Soc. for Crippled Children and Adults, Chgo., 1966-67, dir. care and treatment services, 1967-73; planning specialist Regional Bur. Supplemental Security Income, Dept. Health, Edn. and Welfare, Chgo., 1973-74. Recipient Alumni award Mt. Mary Coll., 1970. Mem. Am. Pub. Health Assn., Am., Ill. (accreditation com. 1965-67) occupational therapy assns., Easter Seal Execs. Assn., Common Cause, Delta Epsilon Sigma. Roman Catholic. Home: 1360 N Sandburg Terrace Chicago IL 60610 Office: 300 S Wacker Dr Chicago IL 60600

HENNEY, DAGMAR RENATE (MRS. ALAN G. HENNEY), educator; b. Berlin, Germany; d. G. Albert and Murgot (Philipp) Kirchner; came to U.S., 1951, naturalized, 1956; B.S., U. Miami, 1954, M.S., 1956; Ph.D., U. Md., 1965; m. Alan G. Henney, Aug. 16, 1953; 1 son, Alan Gilbert. Faculty, George Washington U., Washington, 1964—, prof. math., 1967—. Mem. Nat. Assn. Sci. Writers, Nat. Council Math. (hon.), Am. Math. Assn., Am. Math. Soc., Washington, N.Y. acads. sci., Nat. Fedn. Bus. and Profl. Women, Am. Phys. Soc., Phi Beta Kappa, Sigam Xi. Club: Capital Hill (Washington). Contbr. articles to profl. jours. Home: 6912 Prince Georges Av Takoma Park MD 20012 Office: Dept Math George Washington U Washington DC 20006

HENNIG, HANNA MARTHA, real estate broker; b. Germany, Nov. 4, 1911; d. Johannes Fredrich and Hanna Martha (Kelting) Alsleben; Citrus Coll., Azusa, Cal., 1963-64, Mt. Sac Coll., Walnut, Cal., 1969, U. Cal. at Los Angeles, 1961-62, 66; m. Carl F. Fischer, July 24, 1936 (div. 1949); children—J. Siegfried, Ingrid Martha (Mrs. Charles Neiswender); m. 2d, Carl Friedrich Hennig, Dec. 20, 1951 (div. 1966). Came to U.S., 1950, naturalized, 1955. Owner, salesman Hanna Hennig Real Estate, Duarte, Cal., 1952-55, real estate broker, 1955—. Commr. City of Duarte, Cal., 1968—. Mem. Monrovia Bd. Realtors (pres. 1962), C. of C. (dir. 1958-63, 66-72, pres. 1964-65). Office: 2318 E Huntington Dr Duarte CA 91010

HENNING, ALICE FOSNIGHT (MRS. JAMES DONALD HENNING), pub. relations cons.; b. Niagara Falls, N.Y., May 8, 1933; d. John Lawrence and Irene (Dougherty) Fosnight; ed. U. Toledo, 1951-54; m. James Donald Henning, July 10, 1954; children—A. Cathleen, James John, Michael, Matthew, Christopher. Pub. relations for Pacific N.W. Arts and Crafts Fair, Bellevue, Wash., 1962-65, Panaca Gallery, Bellevue, 1962-65, Am. Cancer Soc., King County, Wash.; 1963-65, Medina Children's Service, Seattle, 1965, Bellevue (Wash.) Montessori Sch., 1973; editor Toledo Jewish News, 1954. Human relations chmn. Chinook Jr. High Sch., Bellevue, 1971-72; active Sacred Heart Parents Club, Chinook Parents Club, Bellevue High Booster Club. Mem. Am. Women in Radio and TV (dir. 1972), Wash. Press Women, Women in Communication, Seattle Free Lances (v.p. 1972), Delta Delta Delta. Contbr. articles to religious mags. Home: 9045 NE 22d Pl Bellevue WA 98004

HENNING, EVELYN MARTIN (MRS. GERALD FRANKLIN HENNING), city ofcl.; b. Lynchburg, Va., Aug. 14, 1920; d. Walter Scott and Myra Elizabeth (Higginbotham) Martin; grad. high sch.; m. Gerald Franklin Henning, June 25, 1945; children—David Scott, Michael Craig, James Patrick. With Blue Buckle Overall Factory, Lynchburg, Va., 1938-42; statis. clk. U.S. Govt., Ordnance Dept., Washington, 1942; statis. clk. U.S. Govt., Phila. Ordnance, 1942-45; payroll clk. U.S. Govt., Pub. Bldgs. Adminstrn., Chgo., 1946-48; with Village of Hanover Park, Ill., 1961—, asst. village treas., 1964—, office mgr., 1969—. Sec. Ontarioville Sch. P.T.A., Hanover Park, 1964-66, chmn. ways and means com., 1960-62. Mem. Ill. Municipal Finance Officers Assn. Methodist. Home: 2180 Elm Av Hanover Park IL 60103 Office: 2121 W Lake St Hanover Park IL 60103

HENNING, PATRICIA ANN, librarian; b. Easton, Pa., July 10, 1933; d. Augustus John and Mary (Horvath) Henning; B.S., West Chester State Coll., 1956; M.S., Simmons Coll., 1960. Tchr., Parkland Sch. Dist., Orefield, Pa., 1956-58, Kauai High Sch., Lihue, Kauai, Hawaii, 1958-59; reference librarian, instr. library sci. W.Va. U. Library, Morgantown, 1960-62; reference librarian Van Pelt Library, U. Pa., Phila., 1962-68; head reference dept. Drexel U. Libraries, Phila., 1968-73, adj. asst. prof. Grad. Sch. Library Sci., 1969—; information specialist Research for Better Schs., Inc., Phila., 1973—. Mem. Am., Pa. (exec. bd. coll. and research div. 1970-73) library assns. Co-editor issues Drexel Library Quar., 1971-72. Editorial bd. Drexel Library Quar., 1972-73. Home: 325 W Durham St Philadelphia PA 19119 Office: 1700 Market St Philadelphia PA 19103

HENNINGS, JOSEPHINE SILVA (HALPIN), govt. ofcl.; b. St. Louis; d. Francois P. and Mary Josephine (Barrick) Silva; B.A., Washington U., polit. sci. George Washington U.; m. Breen Halpin; children—Breen, Joan; m. 2d, Thomas C. Hennings, Jr. (dec.). News analyst Sta. KMOX, St. Louis; news analyst, dir. radio Civil Def., P.R., V.I.; news analyst Sta. KGU, Honolulu; fgn. corr. St. Louis Globe-Democrat, CBS, Caribbean, Pacific; columnist, feature writer Honolulu Advertiser; feature editor, columnist St. Louis Star Times; editor Inter-Am. Affairs, USIA, State Dept.; sr. radio officer UN; news analyst Sta. WINS, N.Y.C.; news analyst, TV panelist ABC; dir. pub. relations, publicity V.I. Hotel, St. Thomas; editor U.S. Comptrollers Office, St. Thomas; now fed. govt. liaison officer Dept. of Def., Washington. Named top Am. woman broadcaster in internat. field UN, U.S. Dept. Labor. Clubs: Am. Women in Radio and TV, Washington Press, Nat. Press, Federal Editors (Washington); Overseas Press (N.Y.C.). Home: 2501 Calvert St NW Washington DC 20008 also 300 E 57th St New York City NY Office: Pentagon Washington DC 20301

HENNUM, SUSANNA SHELLY (MRS. PAUL ROGER HENNUM), mus. ofcl.; b. Iquique, Chile, Jan. 14, 1928 (parents Am. citizens); d. William Austin and Geneva Ellen (Lewis) Shelly; A.B., DePauw U., 1950; M.A., Wichita State U., 1970; m. Paul Roger Hennum, May 14, 1955; children—Ruth Eileen, Eric Lawrence. Travel cons. Travel Service of Ind. Nat. Bank, Indpls., 1952-55; artist, editor Heath Co., St. Joseph, Mich., 1955-57; exhibited one-man show Coloma, Mich., 1963; lectr. art history Wichita State U., 1969-70, Tabor Coll., Hillsboro, Kan., 1970; curatorial asst. to dir. Wichita (Kan.) Art Mus., 1970-73, registrar, dir. docents, 1973-74. Mem. Am. Assn. U. Women, Am. Assn. Museums, Kappa Pi, Pi Beta Phi. Home: 601 Comanche Dr Mount Vernon WA 98273

HENRIKSEN, JOAN FELICIA (MRS. EINAR HENRIKSEN), pub. relations ofcl.; b. Phila., Dec. 31, 1931; d. John Hibbard and Isabelle Etheline (Anderson) Stellwagen; B.J., U. Mo., 1955; m. Einar Henriksen, Dec. 31, 1966; children—Wendy, Dara, Sharon. Reporter, Progress-Index, Petersburg, Va., 1953-54; dir. pub. relations Jewish Community Centers Assn., St. Louis, 1963-66; pub. relations mgr. Cardinal Glennon Hosp. for Children, St. Louis, 1966-71, dir. pub. relations, 1971—; tchr. creative writing for adult continuing edn. Univ. City Sch., 1968-73; tchr. writing Pkwy. Adult Edn. Sch., 1969-71; lectr. St. Louis U., 1974—; free lance writer, corr. trade mags. Mem. publicity com. Journalism Found. St. Louis, 1973. Mem. Pub. Relations Soc. Am. (chmn. pub. service com. St. Louis chpt. 1973), Internat. Assn. Bus. Communicators Am., St. Louis socs. hosp. pub. relations dirs., Women in Communications (pres. St. Louis chpt. 1961-62), League Women Voters, Nat. Orgn. Women. Democrat. Episcopalian (lay reader). Home: 7335 Shaftesbury Blvd St Louis MO 63130 Office: 1465 S Grand Blvd St Louis MO 63104

HENRIKSEN, RUTH ANN, biochemist; b. Lewiston, Ida., Dec. 28, 1938; d. George B. and Margaret (Millay) Henriksen; B.S., Seattle Pacific Coll., 1961; M.S., U. Wash. 1964; postgrad. U. Neb., 1969-71. Research asst. dept. medicine Case Western Res. U., Cleve., 1964-65; tchr., chmn. sci. dept. Aldersgate Coll., Moose Jaw, Sask., Can., 1965-67; asst. prof. chemistry Neb. Wesleyan U., Lincoln, 1967-72; biochemist Washington U. Med. Sch., St. Louis, 1972—. Mem. Am. Chem. Soc., Neb. Acad. Sci. Am. Assn. U. Profs., Inter-Varsity Christian Fellowship (mem. Neb. local com. 1968-71). Home: Apt 7 2507 Bellevue Maplewood MO 63143

HENRIOT, ZOAUNNE MARLAENA LEROY, actress; b. Olympia, Wash.; d. Ernest Paul and Dorothea Zoanna (Michalson) LeRoy; B.A. (Weyerhaeuser Timber Found. Scholar), U. Wash., 1956; m. Rex Edward Henriot, Aug. 11, 1956 (div. Feb. 1974); children—Sam, Josh. Appeared in theater prodns. Balance, Atlanta, 1969, Red, White and Maddox, nat. tour, 1969, Six Characters in Search of an Author, The Threepenny Opera, The Lady's Not for Burning, Syracuse, N.Y., 1969, Alive and Well in Argentina, Syracuse, N.Y., 1970; appeared in Syracuse Repertory Theatre prodns. of Indians, The Time of Your Life, The Tavern, Room Service, The House of Blue Leaves, Happy Birthday, Wanda June, others; appeared in One Flew Over the Cuckoos Nest, A Conflict of Interest, The Hot L Baltimore, Streetcar Named Desire, A Contemporary Theatre, Seattle; Rendezvous, Tartuffe, Actors Theatre of Louisville; also film and radio work, Seattle. Dir. theatre St. Paul Children's Theatre, 1958-66. Mem. Am. Fedn. Astrologers, Nat. Legal Secs. Assn., A.F.T.R.A., Actors Equity, Author, dir., costumer Alice Through the Looking Glass, Gulliver's Travels. Author: Zo-ology. Home: 9611 Linden Av N Seattle WA 98115

HENRY, HARRIET PUTNAM (MRS. MERTON G. HENRY), judge; b. Ashland, Ky., Sept. 28, 1923; d. Donald Hardie and Hannah Sheldon (Russell) Putnam; B.A., Smith Coll., 1945; J.D., George Washington U., 1954; m. Merton G. Henry, Dec. 20, 1954; children—Donald, Douglas, Martha. With Nat. Security Agy., Washington, 1946-56; admitted to Va. bar, 1954, D.C. bar, 1955, Me. bar, 1955; practice law, Portland, Me., 1958-68; research dir. Sea Grant project U. Me. Law Sch., 1968-70; practice law, Portland, 1970-73; judge at large Me. Dist. Ct., Portland, 1973—. Corporator, Portland Savs. Bank. Mem. Me. Status of Women Commn., 1964-65, Portland Housing Authority, 1965-73; chmn. joint action commn. on univ. goals and directions U. Me. at Portland-Gorham, 1972-73; vice chmn. library council Smith Coll., 1972. Bd. dirs. United Community Services, 1968-73. Mem. Me., Cumberland County bar assns., League Women Voters (pres. Portland 1963-65). Republican. Episcopalian. Author: Maine Law Affecting Marine Resources, vols. 1-4, 1969-70; also articles in field. Home: 174 Prospect St Portland ME 04103 Office: 142 Federal St Portland ME 04111

HENRY, HENRIETTA SURRATT, hosp. adminstr.; b. Waco, Tex., June 9, 1909; d. Lawrence Seymore and Anna Sloan (Ingram) Henry; student Baylor U.; A.A., McLennan Community Coll., 1968; postgrad. U. Tex., 1970—. Office mgr. L.S. Henry Printer and Stationery, Waco, Tex., 1927-32; operator, owner Henrietta Henry Shop, 1932-42; adminstrv. clk. U.S. Civil Service, 1942-44; A.R.C. Hosp. Service, South Pacific, 1944-45; adminstr. VA Hosp., Waco, Tex., 1945—. Mem. steering com. McLellan Community Coll., Waco, Tex., 1965; organizer Tex. Old Missions and Forts Restoration Assn., 1962, pres., 1969—. Editor, El Campanario, 1972—. Home: 524 N 22d St Waco TX 76707 Office: VA Hosp Waco TX 76703

HENRY, JEANNE PEARLSON, economist; b. Cambridge, Mass., Aug. 26, 1919; d. Samuel and Eva (Kornfeld) Pearlson; B.S. in Math., Mass. Inst. Tech., 1940; postgrad. in econs. Columbia, 1944-45; M.A. in Econs., Harvard, 1947, Ph.D., 1953; m. Warren Elliott Henry, Apr. 6, 1957; 1 dau., Eva Ruth. Research statistician Fed. Milk Market Adminstrn., Boston, 1941-44; instr. econs. U. Conn., New London, 1947-48; lectr. bus. statistics Suffolk U., Boston, 1949; instr. bus. statistics Pa. State U., 1950-51; dir. research Ben Sackheim Advt. Agy., N.Y.C., 1953-54; research analyst Internat. Statis. Bur., Inc., N.Y.C., 1954-55; sr. economist Allied Chem. Corp., Morriston, N.J., 1955-57; asst. prof. econs. Am. U., 1957-58; lectr. econs. Trinity Coll., Washington, 1958-59; asso. prof. bur. Cal. State U., San Jose, 1964-69; prof., chmn. dept. bus. econs. and finance Sch. Bus. and Pub. Mgmt., Fed. City Coll., Washington, 1970—. Treas., Parents Nursery Sch., Palo Alto, Cal., 1963-64; program chmn. Women's Alliance, Palo Alto Unitarian Ch., 1963-64, pres., 1964-65, ch. trustee, 1964-65. Trustee Bayshore Employment Service, Inc., East Palo Alto, Cal., 1969. Mem. Am. Econ. Assn., Am. Statis. Assn., Am. Assn. U. Profs., Am. Assn. U. Women (chmn. com. on status women Washington br. 1959-60). Home: 4427 Springdale St NW Washington DC 20005

HENRY, MARGARET, physician, surgeon; b. Endicott, Wash., May 18, 1914; d. Daniel Webster and Ethel (Person) Henry; B.S., Wash. State Coll., 1935; M.D., U. Ore., 1939; postgrad. in ophthalmology U. Pa., 1941-42. Rotating intern Children's Hosp., San Francisco, 1939-40; asst. resident in opthalmology Stanford Hosp., 1942-43, resident, 1943-44; resident San Francisco City and County hosps., 1943-44; resident in ophthalmology U. Cal. Hosp., 1944-45; pvt. practice, San Francisco, 1944—; asso. clin. prof. opthalmology U. Cal. Sch. Medicine, 1961-71, clin. prof., 1971—; past chief ophthalmology Children's Hosp. Bd. dirs. No. Cal. Soc. for Prevention Blindness. Diplomate Am. Bd. Ophthalmology. Fellow A.C.S.; mem. Women Physicians Soc. (treas. 1954), Cal. (del. 1956-59), San Francisco (v.p. 1955, dir. 1956-58) med. socs., A.M.A., Pacific Coast Oto-Ophthalmologic Soc., Am. Acad. Ophthalmology and Otolaryngology, Nat. Soc. for Prevention of Blindness, Assn. for Research in Ophthalmology, Pan-Am. Assn. Ophthalmology, Pub. Health League of Cal., Mortar Board, Spurs, Kappa Kappa Gamma. Home: 640 Mason St San Francisco CA 94108 Office: 490 Post St San Francisco CA 94102

HENRY, MARGARET BREWER (MRS. JOHN ROBERTSON HENRY), pub. relations ofcl.; b. Miami, Fla., Oct. 29, 1927; d. William Bryan and Helen Rita (Toomey) Brewer; student Palm Beach (Fla.) Jr. Coll., 1945-46, Emory U., 1947-49; B.A., Agnes Scott Coll., 1949; postgrad. Atlanta div. U. Ga., 1950; m. John Robertson Henry, May 14, 1955; children—John Robertson, Taylor, Margaret Mary, Bryan. Asst. news editor Atlanta Suburban Reporter, 1949-50; staff corr., White House corr. Internat. News Service, Atlanta and Washington, 1950-54; copywriter radio sta. WGST, Atlanta, 1954; woman's editor Jackson (Miss.) State Times, 1955; news columnist, feature writer Birmingham (Ala.) News, 1957-63; spl. writer pub. relations Miss. U. for Women, Columbus, 1970—; guest script writer, master of ceremonies WCBI-TV, Columbus, 1971. Publicity chmn. Nat. Assn. Jr. Auxs., 1962-63. Mem. Nat. Fedn. Press Women (nat., state winner writing contests), Am. Assn. U. Women (pres. Columbus br. 1960-62), Miss. Press Women (v.p. 1972—), Women in Communications, Inc. (sponsor Miss. U. for Women chpt. 1972—), Am. Coll. Pub. Relations Assn., English-Speaking Union, Soroptimists (charter mem., dir. Columbus 1973—). Home: 624 2d Av N Columbus MS 39701

HENRY, MARGUERITE, author; b. Milw.; d. Louis and Anna (Kaurup) Breithaupt; ed. U. Wis.-Milw.; m. Sidney Crocker Henry. Author: King of the Wind (Newbery award 1950); Sea Star: Orphan of Chincoteague (Young Reader's Choice award Pacific N.W. Library Assn. 1950); Misty of Chincoteague (Boys' Clubs Am. award, Lewis Carroll Shelf award, Jr. Lit. Guild selection; film 1961) Justin Morgan Had a Horse (Jr. Lit. Guild selection, Friends of Lit. award, film 1972); Brighty of the Grand Canyon (William Allen White award, Jr. Lit. Guild selection 1956, film 1967); Black Gold (Sequoyah Children's Book award 1957); Gaudenzia: Pride of the Palio (Clara Ingram Judson award 1961); Mustang: Wild Spirit of the West (Sequoyah Children's Book award 1966; Western Heritage award 1966); San Domingo: The Medicine Hat Stallion (Soc. Midland Authors award 1973); Five O'Clock Charlie (Weekly Reader Children's Book Club selection); The Little Fellow (Jr. Lit. Guild selection); Album of Horses (Jr. Lit. Guild selection). Recipient So. Cal. Council Lit. for Children award for contbn. lasting value, 1973. Home: Rancho Santa Fe CA

HENRY, RACHEL IMOGENE SAUNDERS (MRS. HERMANN R. HENRY), civic worker; b. nr. Franklin, Ind., Mar. 24, 1920; d. Arland R. and Imogene (Stewart) Saunders; student Franklin Coll., 1939, Purdue U., 1940; m. Hermann R. Henry, Sept. 28, 1940; children—Pamela (Mrs. Norman E. Stucker), Diane (Mrs. Ralph W. Burford), David S. Author children's stories Johnson County News, Greenwood, Ind., 1952; curator Johnson County Mus., 1972—. Mem. Johnson County Sch. Reorgn. Com., 1961-62. Bd. dirs. United Fund, Johnson County, 1961-65, Gateway Sch. for Retarded Children, 1967-71. Recipient Matrix Table award Franklin Coll., 1969, Rural Life award Kiwanis Club, 1969. Mem. Ind. Soc. Mayflower Descs. (sec., rec. sec. 1971-73), Johnson County Hist. Soc. (pres. 1969-71), Delta Delta Delta (pres.), Psi Iota Xi (pres.). Conglist. (evangelism and devotional chmn. for state bd. 1957-59). Clubs: Women's Study (pres. 1963-64) (Franklin); State Assembly Women's (sec. 1969-71, pres. 1971—) (Indpls.). Author: Childrens Stories, 1952; Saunders Genealogy, 1966. Home: Route 2 Box 57 Franklin IN 46131

HENRY, VIRGINIA DEXTER (MRS. JAY E. HENRY), civic worker; b. Lone Rock, Wis., June 5, 1908; d. Forrester L. and Rosetta (Zimmerman) Dexter; B.A., U. Wis. (Panhellenic Council scholar 1932-33), 1934; m. Jay Everett Henry, Sept. 29, 1934; children—Terry Jay, Steven Dexter. Nat. editor Phi Chi Theta, 1934-48; social worker Wis. Gen. Hosp., Madison, 1930-36. Mem. spl. housing com., City of Wheeling, 1958-59; pres. Wheeling YWCA, 1957-60, dir., 1954-61; nat. rep. nat. support com., nat. bd. YWCA, 1962-64, mem. nat. bd., 1964-73; bd. dirs. Charleston YWCA, pres., 1970-71; pres. Charleston Aux. Profl. Engrs. Soc., 1967-69; chmn. state council W.Va. Soc. Profl. Engrs., 1970-72; mem. Meals-on-Wheels, Inc.; pres. United Ch. Women of Greater Wheeling Council of Chs., 1955-57, Women's Assn. First Presbyn. Ch., Wheeling, 1951-55, Wheeling Presbyterial, 1959-62; sec. Human Rights Commn. Wheeling; v.p. Synodical W.Va., 1968-70 U.P. Ch. in U.S.A. Life mem. Phi Chi Theta. Mem. Charleston Meml. Hosp. Aux. Club: Charleston Women's (chmn. pub. affairs dept. 1970-72, chmn. conservation 1972—). Home: 116 McGovran Rd South Hills Charleston WV 25314

HENS, CLARICE ROSE FELDER (MRS. RUSSELL JAMES HENS), lawyer; b. Peoria, Ill., Oct. 1, 1926; d. Edwin Herbert and Opal (Havens) Felder; A.B., George Washington U., 1956; LL.B., 1960; student U. Md., 1950-52; m. Russell James Hens, Aug. 7, 1965; children—Cynthia Leigh, Stephen James. Personnel officer Dept. of Army, Nancy, France, 1954-55; personnel specialist Dept. of Navy, Washington, 1957-59; personnel mgmt. specialist U.S. Civil Service Commn., Washington, 1959-62; head legislative coordination Office Indsl. Relations Navy Dept., Washington, 1962-67, dep. counsel Office Civilian Manpower Mgmt., 1968-73, counsel, 1973—, admitted to D.C. bar, 1961, Fed. bar, 1961, U.S. Supreme Ct. bar, 1969. Mem. Fed. Bar Assn., Bar Assn. D.C., Women's Bar Assn. (dir. 1965-71), League Women Voters, Kappa Beta Pi. Democrat. Club: Nat. Lawyers. Contbr. articles to profl. jours. Home: 6305 Winston Dr Bethesda MD 20034 Office: Civilian Manpower Mgmt Washington DC 20390

HENSCHEL, BEVERLY JEAN SMITH, educator; b. Boise, Ida., Nov. 1, 1927; d. Theodore and Laura (Brooks) Smith; B.A. (Episcopalian scholar), U. Wyo., 1949; M.F.A., U. Utah, 1952, Ed.D. with honors (univ. research grantee), 1964; Certificate of Achievement, U. Heidleberg, Germany, 1958; m. William E. Henschel, Sept. 5, 1954; children—Laura Jane, Karl Bruce, Linda Jean, Lisa Margaret. Tchr. English, art high schs., Roswell, N.M., 1949-51; art cons. ednl. div., dir. workshops Binney and Smith, Inc., N.Y.C., 1952-54; tchr., Deerfield, Ill., 1955-56; tchr. English, math. Army Edn. Center, Mannheim, Germany, 1957; free-lance TV producer, painter, writer, Lawton, Okla., 1959-61; founder art dept., tchr. Cameron Coll., Lawton, evenings, 1961; producer TV program Creative Art with Jean Henschel, Salt Lake City, 1963-66; dir. fine arts, also materials center Wyo. Dept. Edn., Cheyenne, 1966-67; asst. dir. Ednl. Service Unit 17, Alliance, Neb., 1967-68; conf. evaluator Nat. Dept. Audio-Visual Conf., Portland, 1969; cons. Cal. Dept. Edn., Sacramento, 1969-71; program analyst Occupational Safety and Health Adminstrn., Office of Field Performance Evaluation, U.S. Dept. Labor, Washington, 1972—; cons. Chadron (Neb.) State Coll., Epilepsy Found. Am. Judge, Lawton (Okla.) Art Show, 1959; leader Utah Conf. on Status of Women, 1963; speaker, cons. Nat. Instructional Materials Conf., Austin, Texas, 1966, participant art edn. series, Chgo. ednl. television, 1956; mem. nat. adv. bd. Oddo Pub. Co., Mankato, Minn.; cons. Craig Corp., Compton, Cal., Los Angeles County Fair Schs. Div., Coca Cola Bottling Co., Kiplinger

Washington Editors; art cons. Pomona Unified Sch. Dist.; tchr. extension div. U. Cal. at Riverside. A founder, art dir. Lawton Art and Lang. Sch., 1959; art dir. Lawton Youth Center program, 1959; area ednl. TV coordinator Project Asert, Lincoln, Neb. Recipient honors for community activities N.Am. Air Def. Command Officers' Wives Club, 1965; writing award Wyo. Press Women, 1968. Mem. Wyo. Edn. Assn. (chmn. library sect. 1966), Nat. Assn. Chief State Sch. Audio-Visual Officers (Wyo. rep. 1966), Nat. Assn. State Dept. Art Educators (Wyo. rep. 1966), Cheyenne C. of C., Am. Assn. U. Women (chmn. community problems Wyo. bd. 1966), Internat. Platform Assn., Phi Kappa Phi, Chi Omega, Exec. Club. Designer, painter mural for Hudson Bay Fur Co., Salt Lake City, 1963; writer, illustrator booklet Fun With Art, Deerfield, Ill., 1956; designer, painter children's murals, Baumholder, Germany, 1958. Book reviewer McGraw Hill Pub. Co., Hammond Inc., Watson-Guptill Pub. Co.; author bilingual, bicultural booklet for Cal. Dept. Edn., 1972; adviser Lakota Primer, 1971. Address: 12701 Epping Terrace Wheaton MD 20906

HENSEL, ISABEL SPROUL (MRS. H. STRUVE HENSEL), social worker; b. N.Y.C., Apr. 14, 1904; d. William C. and Maude (Gardiner) Sproul; student Wellesley Coll., 1924-26; m. H. Struve Hensel, June 9, 1948; 1 son, Albert Spaulding Howe III. Stylist R. H. Macy, 1932-42; asst. dir. personnel A.R.C., 1943-44, club dir. Australia, 1944, Philippines, 1945; tech. asst. U.S. High Commr. P.I., 1945-46; buyer Lord & Taylor, 1947-49. Vice pres. Home for Incurables; active Red Cross Motor Corps, N.Y.C., 1939-42, Community Chest, Nat. Symphony Orchestra Assn.; mem. women's com. Corcoran Gallery Art, House of Mercy; mem. Com. of 100 of Fed. City; trustee Am. Cancer Soc. Mem. Friends Am. Mus. (Bath, Eng.), English Ceramic Circle London, Union Interalliee Paris. Episcopalian. Clubs: Chevy Chase (Md.), Rolling Rock (Pa.); Tuxedo (Tuxedo Park, N.Y.); Sulgrave (Washington). Home: 322 E 57th St New York City NY 10022 also Route de Roches Brosville-sur-Iton France

HENSELMAN, FRANCES LORAINE WOOD (MRS. EDWARD RODDY HENSELMAN), librarian; b. Emmett, Ida., Sept. 2, 1916; d. Cartee and Dorothy Inger (Selby) Wood; student Boise Jr. Coll., 1936; B.A., U. Cal. at Los Angeles, 1939, M.Pub. Adminstrn., 1966; B.S. in L.S., U. So. Cal., 1943; postgrad. U. Chgo., 1946, Western Tng. Lab. in Human Relations, 1954; m. Edward Roddy Henselman, July 2, 1939. Mem. staff Long Beach (Cal.) Pub. Library, 1937—, head adminstrv. div., 1951-53, asst. librarian, 1953-69, city librarian, 1969—. Vis. lectr. U. So. Cal. Sch. Library Sci., 1968, 74, mem. adv. council, 1969-73. Mem. region IX Fed. Adv. Council on U.S. Archives, 1971—. Bd. dirs. Long Beach Regional Arts Council. Mem. U. So. Cal. Sch. Library Sci. Alumni (life, pres. 1943, 70), Am. (chmn. pub. relations sect. 1966, chmn. personnel adminstrn. sect. 1972-73), So. Dist. Cal. (pres. 1970), Cal., Pub. (sec. 1969) library assns., Spl. Libraries Assn., Pub. Library Execs. Assn. So. Cal., Am. Soc. Pub. Adminstrn., Libraria Sodalitas, UN Assn. U.S.A., Hist. Soc. Long Beach, Adult Edn. Assn. U.S., Freedom to Read Found., Long Beach C. of C., Long Beach Pub. Library Staff Assn. (pres. 1941), Long Beach City Employees Assn. (v.p. 1951-52), League Women Voters, Long Beach Civic League, Pi Sigma Alpha. Club: Soroptimist. Contbr. articles to profl. jours. Home: 270 Roswell Av Long Beach CA 90803 Office: Ocean at Pacific Av Long Beach CA 90802

HENSHAW, BETTY RUNALS (MRS. PAUL C. HENSHAW), civic worker; b. Ripon, Wis., Feb. 12, 1916; d. Guy Warner and Laura (Cunningham) Runals; student Scripps Coll., 1933-34, A.B., U. Cal. at Los Angeles, 1937; m. Paul Carrington Henshaw, May 25, 1939; children—Sydney Parker (Mrs. Paul W. Nordt III), Guy Runals, Paul Carrington. Vice chmn. No. Cal. sect. Women's Aux. to Am. Inst. Mining, Metall. and Petroleum Engrs., 1956, chmn., 1957, chmn. round table nat. conv., 1967, sec. No. Cal., 1967, chmn. nat. conv., 1972; co-chmn. Women Am. Mining Congress San Francisco Conv., 1958; chmn. pub. relations Alta Bates Community Hosp. Vol. Assn., 1954-67, pres., 1960, editorial adv. bd., 1962—, chmn. Red and White Ball, 1968; bd. mem. Alameda County Tb and Health Assn., 1960-66, chmn. Christmas Seal Campaign, 1964, 65; active Girl Scouts, De Young Mus. Assn., San Francisco Mus. Modern Art, San Francisco Symphony Found., World Affairs Council of No. Cal., Bay Area Ednl. TV Assn., Berkeley Civil Def. Disaster Orgn., Alameda County Council Social Planning, U. Art Mus. Council (U. Cal.), 1969—. Mem. Gamma Phi Beta. Republican. Episcopalian. Club: Town and Gown. Home: 875 Arlington Av Berkeley CA 94707

HENSLER, MARY CLINGER (MRS. HAROLD DORMIRE HENSLER), club woman; b. Carey, O., Oct. 29; d. Harry Edward and Sylvia (Frederick) Clinger; A.B., Wittenberg U., 1930; postgrad. Ohio State U., 1940-41; m. Harold Dormire Hensler, Aug. 14, 1935. Tchr., Cable (O.) High Sch., 1930-33, North Lewisburg (O.) High Sch., 1933-35; travelling tchr. Piqua (O.) High Sch., 1936-40; substitute tchr. Piqua Jr. and Sr. High Schs., 1940-42. Sec., YWCA, Piqua, 1940-42; treas. Newcomers' Club, Joliet, Ill., 1944-45, pres., 1945-46; organizer, pres. Newcomer's Alumnae, Joliet, 1948, now hon. mem. organizer Sanservis Guild Aux., parliamentarian, 1970—, trustee, 1970—; organizer Sunnyhill Sanatorium Will County, Joliet, 1948, pres. 1948-49, chmn. pub. relations com., 1949-50, membership com., 1958, nominating com., 1956, 61, chmn. properties com., 1954, 61, co-chmn. library com., 1961-62, chmn. 1962-63, revisions chmn. parliamentarian, 1965-69, corr. sec. 1969-70, hospitality chmn., 1966-67, purchasing chmn., 1967-68, membership chmn., 1968-69; rec. sec. Joliet Artists' League, 1951-52, chmn. membership com., 1954-55, parliamentarian, 1958-63, 64-65, v.p., 1961-62, 1st v.p., 1965-67, dir. pub. relations, 1967; Trailways council Girl Scouts U.S.A., Joliet, 1948-54, area camp chmn., 1948-49, parliamentarian, 1952-54, co-chmn. publicity com., 1947, revisions chmn., 1948-54, 61-62, program cons., 1961-62; youth conservation chmn. Joliet Woman's Club, 1949-50, chmn. pub. relations dept., 1950-52, art dept. 1952-53, corr. sec., 1953-54, chmn. civil def., 1954-56, 1st v.p. publicity, 1957-58, pres., 1958-60, house chmn., 1970-72; registrar Will County Fedn. Women's Clubs, 1956, scholarship com., 1957, 2d v.p., 1956-58, extension chmn., 1956-58, mag. chmn., 1960-62; chmn. radio and television dept. 11th Dist. Fedn. Women's Clubs, 1954-55, chmn. edn. dept. 1955-56, press and publicity com. 1960-61, 3d v.p., extension chmn., 1967-70; conv. door chmn. Ill. Fedn. Women's Club, 1961, dir., 1962-69, 70-72, chmn., 1962-64, press and publicity chmn., 1962-64, rep. to Nat. Safety Council, 1962-64, historian, 1964-66, asso. editor Ill. Clubwoman, 1966-67, sec., 1967-69, chmn. internat. affairs dept., 1970-72; door chmn. Joliet Woman's Club, 1970-72; hostess, chaperone Joliet Youth Center, 1952; mem. funds com. Easter Seal Center, Joliet, 1957-59; mem. welfare com. Lutheran Children's Home, 1960-61; mem. ways and means com. Family Service Agy. Will County, 1958-60; fund raiser Trinity Sch. Mentally Retarded Children, 1957-60; mem. hospitality com. Manteno State Hosp., 1959-60; active fund drives March of Dimes, Tb Assn., Community Chest, A.R.C., Cancer Dr., Heart Assn., Joliet, 1946—; organizer traffic safety com. Will County Citizens' for Action, Joliet, 1958, steering com., 1958-60; bd. dirs. Will County chpt. A.R.C., 1956-62, mem. exec. com., 1960-62, mem. fund drive adv. com., 1960-62, nominating com., revisions com., 1961-62; mem. Will County Panhellenic Council; bd. dirs. Sao Paulo-Ill. Partners of Am., 1970—; organizer Joliet Women's Cancer Crusade, 1959; hostess com. Citizenship Council Met. Chgo., 1965-67. Recipient citations for outstanding work Trailways council Girl Scouts U.S.A., 1953, 57, 25 year service award, 1972; award of merit for outstanding work in fund campaign Will County chpt. A.R.C., 1956; commendation for organizing traffic safety com. Ill. Gov., 1958; awards Gen. Fedn. Women's Clubs; awards Ill. Fedn. Women's Clubs; award recognition Sao Paulo Woman's Club; recognized in Ill. Lives, sesquicentennial publ., 1968. Mem. Am. Assn. U. Women (organizer Piqua chpt. 1939, v.p. 1941-42, chmn. publicity Joliet 1946-47, chmn. fellowship 1947-48), Kappa Delta Alumnae Assn. (parliamentarian 1962-63, Panhellenic rep. 1963-64, treas. 1970-72). Presbyn. (dir. Women's Assn., Matrons Club, Couples' Club). Mem. Order Eastern Star. Home: 605 Western Av Joliet IL 60435

HENSLEY, ATHENE MARJORIE (MRS. GLEN HENSLEY), banker; b. Grants Pass, Ore., Nov. 6, 1913; d. Alex Ransome and Marjorie Pauline (Wilcox) Orme; grad. So. Coll. Edn., 1935, Rutherford Bus. Coll., Dallas, 1946, Am. Inst. Banking, San Diego, 1964; m. Glen Hensley, Feb. 8, 1936. Tchr. schs., Grants Pass, 1935-40, Naguabo, P.R., 1941-43; exec. sec. United Cal. Bank, Los Angeles, 1947-52; sec. to exec. v.p. U.S. Nat. Bank, San Diego, 1952-59, asst. dir. advt. and pub. relations, 1959-61, pub. relations officer, 1961-62, indsl. relations officer, 1961-62, v.p., 1962-73; v.p. Crocker Nat. Bank, San Diego, 1973—. Bd. dirs. San Diego Evening College, Sister Cities of San Diego-Yokohama Soc., San Diego Bus. Industry Edn. Council, San Diego County Arthritis Found. Served with USNR, 1943-45. Recipient certificates of appreciation and Spl. awards USMC, 1964-66, 69, San Diego County Bd. Suprs., 1968, San Diego County Sheriff Dept., 1969, Arthritis Found., 1973, Asso. Coll. Students, 1973, 74, Pres.'s Council of Service Clubs, 1973; named Woman of Achievement San Diego County, 1964, 65, 69. Mem. Nat. Assn. Bank Women (regional v.p.), Bank Mgmt. Inst., Am. Inst. Banking, Urban League, San Diego C. of C. (v.p.), Fine Arts Soc., Opera Guild, Navy League. Club: Propeller. Home: 6763 Eldridge St San Diego CA 92120 Office: Crocker Nat Bank 190 Broadway San Diego CA 92112

HENSON, LUCY THERESA (MRS. EDWIN NOTT HENSON), bank exec.; b. Wilmington, Del., Apr. 16, 1926; d. Emmanuele and Theresa (DeVito) Benedetto; A.A., George Washington U., 1949, LL.B., 1953; B.S., Wilson Tchrs. Coll., 1950; spl. certificate Northwestern U., 1968; m. Edwin Nott Henson, June 12, 1949; 1 dau., Tracey L. Admitted to D.C. bar, 1954, Del. bar, 1958; mem. firm Rosenthal & Henson, Washington, 1954-56, Logan, Marvel, Boggs & Thiesen, Wilmington, 1958; trust rep., estate planner Bank of Del., Wilmington, 1959-63; asst. trust officer, estate planner Equitable Trust Co., Balt., 1963-66; with Md. Nat. Bank, Balt., 1966—, v.p. trust dept., 1971—. Lectr., speaker estate planning and drafting legal instruments. Mem. estate planning com. Md. Province Devel. Council of Jesuit Sem. and Mission Bur., Balt., 1973-74; mem. Springlake Community Assn., Timonium, Md., 1964—. Bd. dirs. Brandywine Estates Civic Assn., 1958-60, legal counsel, 1957-59; bd. dirs. Notre Dame Preparatory Sch. Mem. Nat. Assn. Bank Women (group chmn. 1968-69), Balt. Estate Planning Council, Women's Bar Assn. of D.C., Del., Md. bar assns., Bus. and Profl. Women's Club; Am. Bankers Assn. Club: Pilot (Balt.). Home: 2444 Springlake Dr Timonium MD 21093 Office: 10 Light St Baltimore MD 21202

HERBERT, ANTONIA RAGO (MRS. JACK D. HERBERT), judge; b. Chgo., Apr. 3, 1918; d. Samuel Francis and Isabella Maria (Adduccie) Rago; grad. Chgo. Tchrs. Coll., 1934; J.D., DePaul U., 1938, B.S., 1940; m. Jack D. Herbert, Dec. 18, 1948; children—Jade (Mrs. Jeffris Malcolm Warfield III), Barry. Admitted to U.S. Supreme Ct. bar, 1942, Ill. bar, 1938; since practiced in Chgo.; judge arbitrator Ill. Indsl. Commn., Chgo., 1963-74. Coordinator Civilian Def., Wilmette Village, Ill., 1950-55; pres. P.T.A., 1952; pres. Community Aid Counsel, 1972-73. Mem. corporate com. DePaul U., 1966-69. Recipient Franklin Roosevelt award, 1944. Mem. Internat. (v.p. 1961-65), Women's (dir. 1947-51) bar assns. Clubs: University Women's, Woman's (Chgo.). Author: Latin America's Model Prison, 1955; Cuba's Divorce Law, 1957. Home: 1209 Sheridan Rd Wilmette IL 60091 Office: 10 N LaSalle St Chicago IL 60602

HERBITTER, FRANCINE ELAYNE (MRS. JON ALAN HERBITTER), therapist; b. N.Y.C., Nov. 13, 1940; d. Aaron Bezalel and Frieda (Cohen) Provda; B.S., U. Fla., 1965; m. Jon Alan Herbitter, May 25, 1969; 1 dau., Arianne Gabrielle. Dir. children's occupational therapy Grasslands Hosp., White Plains, N.Y., 1966; adolescent program occupational therapist Payne Whitney Clinic, N.Y.C., 1966-70; with Bernstein Inst., Beth Israel Med. Center, N.Y.C., 1971—, dir. occupational therapy dept., 1971—. Instr. N.Y. U., 1973—; cons. Workmen's Circle Home for Aged, 1966. Mem. Am. Occupational Therapy Assn., Met. N.Y. Dist. State Occupational Therapy Assn. Home: 1225 Park Av New York City NY 10028 Office: New York U Barney Bldg New York City NY 10003

HERBOLSHEIMER, HENRIETTA, physician, educator; b. Peru, Ill., Feb. 10, 1913; d. George L. and Catherine Caroline (Neureuther) Herbolsheimer; S.B., U. Chgo., 1936, M.D., 1938; M.P.H., Johns Hopkins, 1948. Intern, Los Angeles County Gen. Hosp., 1938-40, resident, 1940-41; with Ill. Dept. Pub. Health, 1942-51; faculty U. Chgo., 1951—, asso. prof. medicine, 1955—. Bd. dirs. Vis. Nurse Assn. Chgo. WHO travel fellow, 1962. Diplomate Am. Bd. Preventive Medicine. Mem. Am. Pub. Health Assn., Am. Coll. Preventive Medicine, A.M.A., Ill. (del. 1960—), Chgo. (sec. 1973—, trustee, 1973—, mem. council 1968—, br. pres. 1969-70) med. socs. Club: Quadrangle (Chgo.). Contbr. articles to profl. jours. Home: 5528 Hyde Park Blvd Chicago IL 60637 Office: 950 E 59th St Chicago IL 60637

HERBST, BERNADETTE ANN, neurologist, educator; b. Phila., May 20, 1938; d. Edward Joseph and Anna May (Taylor) Herbst; A.B., Immaculata Coll., 1959; M.S., St. John's U., 1961; M.D., Med. Coll. Pa., 1967. Intern, Meyer Meml. Hosp., Buffalo, 1967-68, resident neurology, 1968-71; practice medicine specializing in neurology, Phila., 1971—; mem. staff Med. Coll. Pa., Eastern Pa. Psychiat. Inst.; asst. prof. neurology Med. Coll. Pa., Phila., 1973—, neurologic cons. Eastern Pa. Psychiat. Inst., 1971—, Inglis House, Phila., 1971—, Phila. VA Hosp.; med. dir. Happy Horsemanship for Handicapped, 1970—. Recipient award Army-Navy Union, 1968. Mem. Phila. Neurol. Soc., Phila. County Med. Soc. Home: 1459 E Cheltenham Av Philadelphia PA 19124

HERBST, CORNELIA LEDIG CARNAHAN, civic worker; b. New Orleans, Aug. 17, 1906; d. Frank Edmiston and Elise (Ledig) Carnahan; B. Oratory, New Orleans Coll. Oratory, 1925; B.Design, Newcomb Coll. Tulane U., 1929; m. Charles Thiel Govan, June 14, 1929 (div. Feb. 1936); 1 son, Charles Carnahan King; m. 2d, John Edward King, Jr., Mar. 7, 1936 (dec. June 1949); m. 3d, Edwin Winter Herbst, Aug. 9, 1951 (dec. Apr. 1961). Jr. exec. R.H. Macy, N.Y.C., 1940-44; mgr. exclusive handmades Louise, New Orleans, 1945-46; owner, mgr., tung and cattle farm, Folsom, La., 1947-49; with advt. dept. New Orleans Item, 1949-50; pvt. sec. La. Trade Sch., New Orleans, 1950-52. Dramatic readings, book revs. for ch. and sch. affairs, N.Y.C., 1937-38, ch. and local clubs, New Orleans, 1948-54; ednl. dir. study Women of Ch., New Orleans, 1957-58; financial sec. New Orleans Art Assn., 1959-60, 1st v.p., 1963-64, 1965-66; mem. various coms. Women's Aux. C. of C. of New Orleans Area, Crippled Children's Hosp. Guild, New Orleans Spring Fiesta Assn., Eye, Ear, Nose and Throat Hosp. Aux.; membership chmn. Goodwill Industries; mem. New Orleans Opera House Assn., financial sec. Women's Guild of New Orleans Opera House Assn., 1967, 5th v.p., 1968, 3d v.p., 1969, 2d v.p., 1970, guild home chmn., 1972-74, co-chmn. donors div. fund dr., 1973-74, 5th v.p., 1974—; pres. Sara Mayo Hosp. Guild, 1963-65, hon. life v.p., 1967, vice chmn. fashion show, 1969, ticket chmn., 1969, adv. chmn., 1969-70; active Julien Poydras Home for Aged, various community drives. Mem. Am. Assn. U. Women (life; organizer, charter mem. Crescent City br., br. pres. 1961-63, mem. state bd. 1963-64, adviser to br. bd. 1968, 70), U.D.C., Assn. Former Delphians. Club: Fine Arts New Orleans (program com. 1972-74, historian 1973-74). Presbyn. Home: 2204 Calhoun St New Orleans LA 70118

HERCEG, DIANE LYNNE (MRS. FRED PETER HERCEG), therapist; b. Rapid City, S.D., Apr. 10, 1941; d. Bernard William and Ferne Adele (Hofer) Payne; student, U. Wyo., 1959-60; B.S., Colo. State U., 1963, postgrad., 1973—; m. Fred Peter Herceg, Sept. 15, 1962; children—Todd Payne, Selena Sarah. With Colo. State Hosp., Pueblo, 1964-70, dir. occupational therapy, 1965-70; psychiat. occupational therapist Denver Gen. Hosp., 1971—. Instr. sr. psychiat. course Colo. State U., Ft. Collins, 1971—. Leader, LaLeche League, Denver, 1969—. Mem. Colo. Occupational Therapy Assn. (dir. 1968-69, bd. mgr. 1970-71). Home: 465 Yukon St Lakewood CO 80226 Office: 8th and Cherokee Denver CO 80202

HERD, CHARMIAN JUNE, educator, singer, actress; b. Waterville, Me., June 1, 1930; d. Samuel Braid and Jennie (Lang) Herd; B.A., Colby Coll., 1950; M.Ed., U. Me., 1964; postgrad. Boston U., 1951; ednl. certificate No. Conservatory, Bangor, Me., 1954; also study voice with Roger A. Nye. Dir. music State Sch. for Girls, Hallowell, Me., 1950-51; head English, French, dramatics dept. St. George High Sch., Tenants Harbor, Me., 1951-52; dir. music pub. schs. Albion, Unity, Me., 1952-54, Troy, Freedom, Me., 1953-54; dir. music pub. sch. system Belgrade, Me., Waterville Jr. High Sch., 1954-55; dir. vocal music Waterville Jr. and Sr. high schs., 1954-58; head English and dramatics depts. Besse High Sch., Albion, 1959-62; tchr. French, Adult Edn. Sch., 1963—; dir. dramatic arts program Skowhegan Sch. Adult Edn., 1966-69; instr. French, Lawrence Sr. High Sch., Fairfield, Me., 1969-71, chmn. dept. drama and speech, 1972—; dramatics instr. Farmington State Coll., U. Me., 1969-70; soloist various chs., Me., 1951—; soloist numerous club, ch., conv., coll. concerts, oratorios. 1st pres., performing mem. Waterville Theatre Guild, music dir., 1967—; performing mem. Theatre at Monmouth (Me.), Portland Lyric Theatre, Augusta Players, Camden Civic Theatre; mem. Titipu Choral Soc., Program chmn. Albion P.T.A. Mem. Waterville Friends Music, D.A.R. (music chmn. Winslow Me., 1955-57, sec. 1957-59, vice regent 1959-61, regent 1961-62, Me. advt. chmn. 1958-60); Actors' Equity, Ednl. Speech and Theatre Assn. of Me. (state pres. 1972-74), Waterville Bus. and Profl. Women's Club (program chmn. 1957-58, v.p. 1958-59, pres. 1959-61, chmn. drama dept. 1961), Albion-Burnham Tchrs. Club. (sec. 1960-61), Internat. Platform Assn., N.E.A., Me. Tchrs. Assn., Theatre Assn. Me. (exec. bd. 1972-74, 2d v.p. 1973-74), Actors Equity. Club: Cecilia (Augusta, Me.). Composer sacred music: Babylon, 1959, The Greatest of These is Love, 1961; Pan, 1963; Keep Not Thy Silence, O God; Remember Now Thy Creator; Slow, Slow, Fresh Fount; A Witch's Charm; Hymn to God The Father. Home: 62 Benton Av Winslow ME 04901 Office: Lawrence Sr High Sch Fairfield ME 04937

HERDLISKA, PHYLLIS ANN, musician; b. Ia. City, Ia., Feb. 17, 1948; d. Robert Henry and Barbara Jean (Williamson) Herdliska; student Eastman Sch. of Music, 1966-67; student of Lillian Fuchs, Manhattan Sch. of Music, 1967-70; student of William Lincer, Julliard Sch., 1970-71. Violist, Houston Symphony Orch., 1971. Mem. Aspen (Colo.) Festival Orch., summer 1967, 1968, 69. Home: 14423 Alkay St Houston TX 77045 Office: Houston Symphony Soc 615 Louisiana St Houston TX 77002

HERDRICH, RITA CECELIA POBLOCKI (MRS. RALPH C. HERDRICH), steel warehouse co. exec.; b. Chgo., Apr. 6, 1922; d. Leo C. and Cecelia E. (Kirschbaum) Poblocki; student DePaul U., 1941; m. Ralph C. Herdrich, Oct. 4, 1950; children—Ann E., Roger C. Sec., Inland Steel Co., 1941-50, Marvel Engring., 1964; sec.-treas. Tollway Steel & Storage Corp., Melrose Park, Ill., 1964—. Home: 5005 Flanders St McHenry IL 60050 Office: 25th and Main Sts Melrose Park IL 60160

HEREFORD, EULA FRANCES, poet, ret. rancher; b. Bluffton, Tex., Feb. 4, 1900; d. James Perry and Sophronia Ellen (Huddleston) Shaw; student Tex. A. and I. Coll., 1958; grad. N.Y. corr. Sch. of Writing, 1965; m. Leslie R. Hereford, Sept. 30, 1920 (dec. Sept. 1962); children—Leslie R., Annetta (Mrs. Herford H. Bridges), Rose (Mrs. Edwin E. Denson), Fay (Mrs. Kenneth W. Staggs). Rancher Llano and Lampasas, Tex., 1916-69. Fellow Internat. Poetry Soc.; mem. Tex. Poetry Soc. (First prize 1971), Acad. Am. Poets. Contbr. poems to lit. mags. Address: 12010 W Cow Path Austin TX 78759

HERENDEEN, MARY ANITA BLANCHARD, retail store exec.; b. Westbury, L.I., Dec. 27, 1930; d. John H. and Hannah (Olson) Blanchard; student Blackstone Coll., 1948-50, Katharine Gibbs Sch., 1950-51; 1 son, Mark Blanchard. Merchandising coordinator, mdse. editor Seventeen mag., N.Y.C., 1951-61, merchandising dir., 1962-67; spl. events, pub. relations dir. Jordan Marsh-Fla., 1968-72; fashion/activities dir. S. Fla. group, Sears, Roebuck & Co., Miami, 1972—. Mem. Fashion Group Miami, Women in Communications, Nat. Home Fashions League. Home: 1233 Aduana Av Coral Gables FL 33146 Office: 1300 Biscayne Blvd Miami FL 33132

HERING, BARBARA GORDON (MRS. LOUIS HERING), lawyer; b. N.Y.C., June 30, 1923; d. Alexander and Gertrude (Hackner) Gordon; B.B.A., City Coll., 1952; LL.B., Columbia, 1955; m. Louis Hering, Nov. 21, 1956; children—Janet, Louis, James. Law clk. Honorable Harold R. Medina, 1955-56; admitted to N.Y. bar, 1955; practiced in N.Y.C.; asso. Cravath, Swaine & Moore, 1956-57, Phillips, Nizer, Benjamin & Krim, 1957-59; asso. Prof. Charles M. Haar, cons. and legal writing for publ., 1959-64; counsel Nat. Broadcasting Co., N.Y.C., 1969—. Mem. Assn. Bar City N.Y. Home: 103 E 86th St New York City NY 10028 Office: 30 Rockefeller Plaza New York City NY 10020

HERING, MILLICENT BLAND (MRS. DONALD M. HERING), librarian, educator; b. Springfield, Colo., Nov. 28, 1921; d. Lester L. and Nora (Hawthorne) Bland; A.B., Colo. State Coll., 1946; M.A., U. Denver, 1965; postgrad. U. Alaska, 1964; m. Lloyd T. Reynolds, Feb. 17, 1943 (div.); m. Donald M. Hering, May 26, 1957; children—Lloyd Lester, Gregory Bruce. Tchr. high schs., Eureka, Utah, Jackson, Wyo., Carbondale, Colo., Granby, Colo., Grants Pass, Ore., Fairbanks, Alaska, 1945-62; librarian Lathrop High Sch., Fairbanks, 1963-66; head librarian reader services dept. U. Alaska, Fairbanks, 1966-71, asst. prof. library sci., 1966-74, coordinator library instrn. program, 1971—. Cons. on drug laws, 1969—. State chmn. Marijuana Law Reform Fund, Am. Civil Liberties Union, 1973-74. Mem. Am., Pacific N.W., Alaska library assns., Alaska Civil Liberties Union (bd. 1969—, sec. Fairbanks chpt. 1969—). Compiler: Library Skills, 1971. Contbr. articles to profl. jours. Home: 1041 Pedre

St Fairbanks AK 99701 Office: Rasmuson Library University of Alaska Fairbanks AK 99701

HERIOT, RUTH ANNE, museum curator; b. Pitts., July 11, 1948; d. James Fairgrieve and Mary Louise (Kloss) Heriot; A.B., Wheeling Coll., 1970. With Nat. Park Service, Dept. of Interior, 1970—, curator Lincoln's Home, Springfield, Ill., 1972—. Mem. Eastern Nat. Parks and Monuments Assn. Episcopalian. Home: 17 Memminger Av Wheeling WV 26003 Office: 413 S 8th St Springfield IL 62701

HERJANIC, BARBARA LOUISE MOSS (MRS. MARIJAN HERJANIC), child psychiatrist; b. Mt. Vernon, Ill., Mar. 22, 1922; d. Norman McAnally and Ethel (Adams) Moss; B.A., Northwestern U., 1943; B.S., Western Mich. Coll., 1946; M.D., U. Mich., 1950; m. Marijan Herjanic, June 8, 1963. Intern Sydenham Hosp., N.Y.C., 1950-51, asst. resident surgery, 1951-52; resident obstetrics and gynecology Bellevue Hosp., N.Y.C., 1958-61; resident psychiatry Barnes Hosp., St. Louis, 1961-64; practice gen. medicine, Inchon, Korea, 1953-58; community psychiatrist, Weyburn, Sask., Can., 1964-67; fellow child psychiatry Malcolm Bliss Mental Health Center, St. Louis, 1969-71; staff psychiatrist Children's Unit, Malcolm Bliss Mental Health Center, St. Louis, 1967-69, 71-72; asst. prof. Washington U. Sch. Medicine, 1972—; dir. child psychiatry Children's Hosp., 1972—. Recipient Outstanding Alumnae award Kendall Jr. Coll., 1964. Diplomate Nat. Bd. Med. Examiners, psychiatry and child psychiatry Am. Bd. Psychiatry and Neurology. Home: 9 Danfield Rd St Louis MO 63124 Office: St Louis Children's Hosp 500 S Kingshwy St Louis MO 63110

HERLIHY, JOANNE JAAP, fashion industry exec.; b. Kansas City, Mo., Sept. 23, 1925; d. Nelan Herbert and Virginia (Springer) Jaap; student pub. schs.; m. John Edward Herlihy, Jr., Sept. 20, 1956 (div. Jan. 1959). With Zeigfield Follies, 1943; toured for U.S.O. in Dough Girls, 1944; model Harry Conover, N.Y.C., 1945; featured in stage plays Duchess Misbehaves, 1946, Sweet Bye and Bye, 1946, Angel Street, summer 1947; sales/fashion coordinator Sam Freidlander, N.Y.C., 1950-51, Ben Zuckerman, N.Y.C., 1951-54, 56-59; asst. sales mgr. Christian Dior, N.Y.C., 1954-56, sales mgr., 1959-64, v.p., 1964-68; mng. dir. Design-Thai for U.S. div. Internat. Basic Economy Corp., 1969-73; exec. v.p. Design Thai (U.S.A.) Inc., N.Y.C., 1973—. Mem. Fashion Group of N.Y. Home: 41 E 68th St New York City NY 10021 Office: 550 7th Av New York City NY 10018

HERMAN, EDITH CAROL, journalist; b. Edgewood, Md., July 1, 1944; d. Herbert R. and Thirza E. (Simmons) Herman; B.A., Purdue U., 1966; m. Leonard Wiener. News reporter Hollister Publs., Wilmette, Ill., 1966-68; chief edn. writer, reporter Chgo. Tribune, 1968—. Recipient Edn. Writing award Ill. Edn. Assn., 1968. Mem. Sigma Delta Chi. Office: 435 N Michigan Av Chicago IL 60611

HERMAN, FLORENCE LANDRY (MRS. ROBERT K. HERMAN), editor; b. New Orleans, Aug. 9, 1940; d. Julian Hamilton and Helen Francis (Philips) Landry; student Loyola U., New Orleans, 1958-60; m. Robert K. Herman, Apr. 16, 1966. Exec. sec. Nat. Cath. Conf. Interracial Justices, So. Field Service, New Orleans, 1963-65; coordinator, Bur. Information, Archdiocese New Orleans, 1965-66; columnist, women's editor Clarion Herald Newspaper, New Orleans, 1966—. Recipient Writing awards Press Club New Orleans, 1969, 71-73, La. Press Women, 1972-74, Nat. Fedn. Press Women, 1972, 73. Mem. Women in Communications (v.p. New Orleans chpt. 1972), Press Club New Orleans (1st v.p. 1970-71). Roman Catholic. Home: 6807 Vicksburg St New Orleans LA 70124 Office: 523 Natchez St New Orleans LA 70130

HERMAN, MARY MARGARET (MRS. LUCIEN J. RUBINSTEIN), educator, neuropathologist; b. Plymouth, Wis., July 26, 1935; d. Elmer Frederick and Esther Lydia (Bross) Herman; B.S. (Regents' scholar), U. Wis., 1957, M.D., 1960; m. Lucien J. Rubinstein, Jan. 31, 1969. Intern, Mary Hitchcock Hosp., Hanover, N.H., 1960-61; resident in neurology U. Wis. Hosps., Madison, 1961-62; intern pathology Yale, 1962-63, resident pathology, 1963-64, fellow neuropathology, 1964-65; fellow, acting instr. pathology Stanford, 1965-67, asst. prof. pathology, 1967—. Hazel Duling scholar; Johnson Found. scholar; Mary Putnam Jacobi scholar; spl. fellow Nat. Inst. Neurol. Diseases and Stroke, NIH, 1964-67, research grantee, 1969-72, recipient Research Career Devel. award, 1967-72. Recipient Merck Faculty Devel. award, 1969. Diplomate Am. Bd. Pathology (anatomic pathology, neuropathology). Mem. Am. Acad. Neurology, A.A.A.S., Am. Assn. Neuropathologists, Am. Assn. Pathology and Bacteriology, Am. Assn. U. Women, Am. Assn. U. Profs., Am. Soc. Cell Biology, Internat. Acad. Pathology, Soc. Devel. Biology, Soc. Invertebrae Pathology, Soc. Neurosci., Phi Kappa Phi. Home: 101 Alma St Palo Alto CA 94301 Office: Dept Pathology Stanford U Med Sch Stanford CA 94305

HERMAN, PHYLLIS ANN COMBS (MRS. MICHAEL CHARLES HERMAN), pub. relations; b. Hazard, Ky., Aug. 13, 1944; d. Carter F. and Nancy (Shepherd) Combs; B.A., U. Ky., 1967; m. Michael Charles Herman, Aug. 20, 1966. Reporter, State Jour., Frankfort, Ky., 1966-68; asst. to pub. relations dir. Ky. State Coll., Frankfort, 1967-68; sr. publicity specialist Ky. Dept. Pub. Information, Frankfort, 1968, news bur. chief, 1968-70; exec. asst. Ky. Sec. State, Frankfort, 1970-71; pub. information officer Ga. Ho. of Reps., Atlanta, 1971-74. Freelance writer articles to various mags., 1967—. Chmn., Frankfort-Franklin County Beautification Com., 1969. State bd. publicity chmn. Ky. Fedn. Republican Women, 1968-71. Bd. dirs. Franklin County Lincoln Club, 1971. Mem. Women in Communications (pres. elect 1974), Eta Sigma Phi. Club: Press (Atlanta). Mem. Ch. of Jesus Christ of Latter-day Saints. Home: 3014 San Jose Dr Decatur GA 30032 Office: 401 E State Capitol Atlanta GA 30034

HERMAN, RUTH MARIE THORUP (MRS. MALVIN F. HERMAN), ednl. adminstr., counselor; b. Omaha, Dec. 24, 1920; d. Marinus and Mathilde (Pedersen) Thorup; B.A., U. Omaha, 1942; M.A., U. Cin., 1947; postgrad. U. Ia., 1947, U. Wyo., 1959, U. Omaha, 1960, U. Mich. and Ind. U., summer 1973; m. Malvin F. Herman, June 8, 1952. Tchr., Outstate Secondary Schs., Ulysses and Oakland, Neb., 1942-45, Luther Inst., Chgo., 1946-47; instr. Grandview Coll., Des Moines, 1947-49; tchr., counselor, dean, head counselor Omaha Pub. Schs., 1949-69, supr. guidance, 1969—. Profl. cons. counselor Omaha Job Corps. summer 1965. Taft Meml. scholar, U. Cin., 1945-46. Named Woman of Year, Bus. and Profl. Woman's Club, 1967. Mem. Bus. and Profl. Women, Neb. Women Deans and Counselors (pres. 1959), Neb. Personnel and Guidance Assn. (dist. pres. 1960), Nat. Assn. Women Deans and Counselors, Neb., Omaha edn. assns., N.E.A., Neb. Classroom Tchrs., Daus. of Nile, Phi Delta Gamma (nat. v.p. 1966-68, nat. pres. 1968-70). Lutheran. Mem. Order Eastern Star. Home: 6707 N 52nd St Omaha NE 68152 Office: 3819 Jones St Omaha NE 68105

HERMAN, SONDRA RENEE, educator; b. N.Y.C., Mar. 10, 1932; d. Irving and Dorothy (Rosenthal) Kleinman; A.B., Barnard Coll., 1953; M.A. (scholar), Rutgers U., 1956, Ph.D.; m. Frank Herman, Feb. 1, 1953; children—Laura, Valerie, Andrea. Research asst. John Higham, New Brunswick, N.J., 1956-57; asso. prof. Foothill Coll., Los Altos, Cal., 1966-71; acting prof. history U. Cal. at Santa Cruz, 1972—; now prof. history De Anza Coll., Cupertino, Cal. Author: Eleven Against War: Studies in American Internationalist Thought, 1969. Contbr. articles to mags. and jours. Home: 15 Anderson Way Menlo Park CA 94025 Office: De Anza Coll Cupertino CA 95814

HERMANN, MILDRED MARIE, financial assn. adminstr.; b. N.Y.C., July 22, 1924; d. John E. and Mildred L. (Erbe) Hermann; A.B. summa cum laude, Hunter Coll., 1946; M.A., Columbia, 1947; B.D., Union Theol. Sem., 1967. Dir. Christian edn. U.P. Bd. Nat. Missions, N.Y.C., 1948-53, gen. writer, curriculum specialist, 1953-60, dir. press relations, 1960-66, spl. asst. to gen. sec., 1966-70, asst. gen. sec., 1970-73; dir. adminstrv. services, sec. Financial Analysts Fedn., N.Y.C., 1973—. Mem. Pub. Relations Soc. Am., Phi Beta Kappa, Eta Sigma Phi. Presbyn. (elder). Author: Affluence and Poverty: A Guide to Study and Action, 1966. Contbr. numerous articles to religious jours. Home: 10 Mitchell Pl New York City NY 10017 Office: 219 E 42d St New York City NY 10017

HERNANDEZ, AILEEN CLARKE, pub. affairs cons., orgn. exec.; b. Bklyn.; d. Charles and Ethel Clarke; B.A. magna cum laude in Sociology and Polit. Sci., Howard U., 1947; postgrad. U. Oslo, summer 1947, N.Y. U., 1949-50, U.S. Cal., U. Cal. at Los Angeles; M.S. in Govt., Los Angeles State Coll., 1961; grad. Internat. Ladies Garment Workers Union Tng. Inst., 1951; divorced. Journalist, Washington, 1945-47; research asst. dept. of govt. Howard U., 1948; asst. edn. dir., organizer Pacific Coast region Internat. Ladies Garment Workers Union, 1951-59, edn. and pub. relations dir., 1959-61; asst. chief Cal. Div. Fair Employment Practices, 1962-65; commr. U.S. Equal Employment Opportunity Commn., 1965-66; now cons., lectr. urban affairs, pub. relations. Instr. adult edn. U. Cal. at Los Angeles Extension, 1958-60; lectr. tour of S. Am., representing U.S. State Dept., 1960; lectr. in social sci. San Francisco State Coll., 1968; frequent TV, radio, pub. appearances. Mem. Democratic Nat. Policy Council. Bd. dirs., sec. Mt. Zion Hosp.; bd. dirs., Western rep. Nat. Com. Against Discrimination in Housing, 1969-74; bd. dirs. Westside Mental Health Center, others. Recipient Distinguished Postgrad. Achievement award Bay Area Alumni Club, Howard U., 1967, Charter Day Alumni award for distinguished postgrad. achievement in labor and public service Howard U., 1968; others. Mem. Nat. Orgn. Women (past nat. pres., chmn. nat. adv. com.), Nat. Urban Coalition (exec., steering coms.), Nat. Black Caucus. Address: 4444 A Geary Blvd San Francisco CA 94118

HERNDON, ALAMAE NAN (MRS. LEO L. HERNDON), bus. exec.; b. Elmdale, Tex., Nov. 12, 1924; d. William Gober and Analou (Estes) Black; grad. Draughon's Bus. Coll., 1940; postgrad. Abilene Christian Coll., 1941-43, 69; m. Leo L. Herndon, Dec. 18, 1943; children—Patrick Leo, Cynthia Ann, Gina Kathryn. Bookkeeper doctor's office, 1940-43; with Tip Top Bakery, St. Louis, 1944; sec., Tex. State Hwy. Dept., Abilene, 1944-45; accountant, sec., dir. Grisham-Hunter Corp., Abilene, Tex., 1945-57; with Del. Basin Properties, Inc., Abilene, Tex., 1957—, office mgr., sec.-treas., dir., 1957-71, dir., 1957—, office mgr., v.p., sec.-treas., 1971—. Mem. Abilene Woman's Club (scholarship com. 1970—), Altrusa Club Abilene (sec. 1971-72, dir. 1971-72). Mem. Ch. Christ. Republican. Home: 526 E N 21st St Abilene TX 79601 Office: 520 Citizens Nat Bank Bldg Abilene TX 79601

HERNDON, JUDITH ANN, lawyer; b. Wheeling, W.Va., June 5, 1941; d. Richard G. and Virginia Ann (Holler) Herndon; student Mary Washington Coll. Va., 1959-61; A.B. in Econs., Duke, 1963; postgrad. Northwestern U. Law, 1964-65; J.D., W.Va. U., 1967. Price economist Bur. Labor Statistics U.S. Dept. Labor, Cleve. and Chgo., 1963-64; admitted to W.Va. bar, 1967; mem. firm Herndon, Morton & Herndon, Wheeling, W.Va., 1967—. Mem. W.Va. Gov.'s Commn. on Alcoholism and Drug Abuse. Mem. W.Va. Ho. of Dels., 1970-74, W.Va. Senate, 1974—; sec. Ohio County Republican Exec. Com., Wheeling, 1968-72; Rep. committeewoman Ohio County, 1968-72. Bd. dirs. Wheeling Coll., Russell Nesbitt Sch. for Crippled Children, Wheeling. Recipient Distinguished West Virginian award Gov. W.Va., 1971. Mem. W.Va. Bar Assn. (v.p.), Soroptimist Club, Delta Delta Delta. Republican. Roman Catholic. Home: 27 Elmwood Pl Wheeling WV 26003 Office: 84 15th St Wheeling WV 26003

HERNDON, MARY DAY (MRS. JOHN LARKIN HERNDON, JR.), state ofcl.; b. Marion, La., Mar. 1, 1931; d. James and Lucille (Murray) McVicker; student N.E. State U., La., 1957-59, U. Ark., 1968; m. John Larkin Herndon, Jr., Apr. 17, 1965; 1 son (by previous marriage), Stuart Randall Day. Gen. office sec. Bagpak div. Internat. Paper Co., Bastrop, La., 1951-57, exec. sec. Single Service div., 1957-59; copysetter, proofreader Bastrop Daily Enterprise, 1959-61; with Ark. Hwy. Dept., Little Rock, 1961—, asst. pub. relations officer, 1965—, editor employees mag., 1967—. Musician, active mem. Little Rock Community Theatre, 1961—; mem. Saxon Singers, profl. choral group, Little Rock, 1962-69. Baptist. Home: 1308 Kavanaugh St Little Rock AR 72205 Office: PO Box 2261 Little Rock AR 72203

HERNDON, MYRTIS ELIZABETH, educator; b. Miami, Fla., July 5, 1932; d. Burton J. and Evelyn D. (Thompson) Herndon; B.S., Fla. State U., 1954; M.S., No. Ill., U., 1959; postgrad. Kent State U., 1958-59, Tex. Women's U., summer 1960, Mich. State U., summer 1961, U. Mich., summer 1962, Ohio State U., 1969—. Instr., chmn. womens phys. edn. Nautilus Jr. High Sch., North Miami Jr. High Sch., Dade County Pub. Sch. System, Miami, 1954-57; grad. teaching asst. phys. edn. No. Ill. U., 1957-58; instr. phys. edn. Hiram (O.) Coll., 1958-60, asst. prof., 1960-62, asso. prof., chmn. womens phys. edn., 1966—. Peace Corps vol., prof. and cons. phys. edn. Chulalongkorn U., Bangkok, Thailand, 1962-64; interim asst. prof. edn. U. South Fla., Tampa, 1965-66; recreation dir. City and Sch. Summer Recreational Programs; phys. therapist McLean Leprosy Hosp., Chaingmai, Thailand; mem. U.S. Olympic Com., Internat. Olympic Acad. Swimming instr. A.R.C.; ballroom dance dir. adult community groups; coach youth and adult recreational sports leagues; adviser Sigil of Phi Sigma social club, Orchesis modern dance club, Starfish aquatic club at Hiram Coll. Recipient Spl. Membership award Phi Delta Pi, 1968. Mem. Am. (com. chmn.), Ohio (past sect. chmn.) assns. health, phys. edn. and recreation, Internat. Council Health, Phys. Edn. and Recreation, Nat. (com. chmn.), Midwest (com. chmn.) assns. phys. edn. for coll. women, Ohio Coll. Assn. (com. chmn. womens phys. edn. sect.), Midwest (commr., historian), Ohio (commr., historian-archivist) assns. for intercollegiate sports for women, N.Am. Soc. Sport History, Am., Internat. Assn. for Phys. Edn. and Sports for Girls and Women, Council Anthropology and Edn., Kent Tri-County Bd. Women Ofcls. (past chmn., sec.), Phi Delta Pi, Delta Psi Kappa. Author: Selected Fencing Articles, 1971; Selected Basketball Articles, 1971; Comparative Physical Education and International Sport: A Bibliographic Guide, Vols. I, II, 1972. Contbr. articles to profl. jours. Home: PO Box 12 Hiram OH 44234

HEROLD, FLORENCE RUTH (MRS. HOWARD F. HEROLD), radio broadcaster; b. Watertown, Wis., Oct. 13, 1926; d. Elmer Albert and Esther Leona (Degner) Nell; grad. pvt. sch.; m. Howard F. Herold, June 14, 1947; children—Gail (Mrs. Brian Thiede), Glenn E., Lynn Ellen (Mrs. Mark Langenfeld). Broadcaster, Watertown Radio Inc., Watertown, Wis., 1953—, women's program dir., 1953—. Recipient Recognition for Meritorious Service award, 4-H Clubs, 1963. Mem. Watertown Vocational and Tech. Sch. Homemakers Club (pres. 1957-59), Am. Women in Radio & TV (pres. Badger chpt. 1959-61). Lutheran. Home: 608 Elm St Watertown WI 53094 Office: 104 W Main St Watertown WI 53094

HERON, JEANETTE HELEN RICKETTS (MRS. HARRY HERON), realtor; b. Detroit, Oct. 19, 1915; d. James Henry and Lydia Ann (Norstrom) Ricketts; grad. high sch.; m. Harry Heron, Sept. 22, 1935; children—Robert Dale, H. Edward, Frederick. Partner, Gallery of Homes, Realtors, Santa Barbara, Cal., 1950—. Named Santa Barbara Realtor of Year, So. Santa Barbara County Bd. Realtors, 1962. Mem. Nat. Assn. Realtors (pres. Cal. state chpt. women's council 1973), Cal. Real Estate Assn., Santa Barbara Bd. Realtors (awards com. 1963-73). Republican. Presbyn. Mem. Order Eastern Star. Home: 426 Stanley Dr Santa Barbara CA 93105 Office: 3400 State St Santa Barbara CA 93105

HERPST, MARTHA JANE, artist, art educator; b. Titusville, Pa.; d. Henry Howard and Lou (Cupler) Herpst; student Pa. Acad. Fine Arts, Phila., 1931, Grand Central Sch. Art, N.Y.C. (medalist 1932), 1931-33; studied with Guy Pene DuBois, 1941. Began painting in oils at age of 9 yrs; sold first portrait at 12 yrs.; specializes in portraits; exhibited Nat. Arts Club, N.Y.C., 1933—, Butler Art. Inst., Youngstown, O., 1938, Ogunquit (Me.) Art Assn. Summer Show, 1951, 53, Catherine Lorillard Wolfe Art Club, 1954, 57, Am. Artist Profl. League, 1953—; represented in permanent collection Nat. Arts Club. Titusville (Pa.) Masonic Lodge, with portrait of Charles T. Evans, Titusville Woman's Club with portrait of Laura W. Luce, Titusville YWCA with portrait of Mrs. Fred B. Howland, USMC League with portrait of Capt. Robert Lee Green, Titusville Recreation Center with portrait of Mrs. Charles Burgess, Gannon Coll. with portrait of Archbishop John Mark Gannon, St. Benedict's Convent, Erie, Pa. with portraits of Sisters. Tchr. art St. Joseph Acad. High Sch., Titusville, 1955-69; portrait of Martha McKinney Fleming, McKinney Hall U. Pitts. Titusville Campus. Mem. Am. Artists Profl. League, Titusville Bus. and Profl. Women's Club. Clubs: Nat. Arts, Woman's Titusville Country. Republican. Roman Catholic. Home: 118 W Main St Titusville PA 16354

HERR, HELEN, state senator; ed. N.D. State Tchrs. Coll. Formerly real estate agt.; chmn. Town Bd., Whitney; state assemblywoman; mem. Nev. Senate, 1967—. Pres. Boulder Hwy. Assn.; sec. State Hwy. Adv. Bd. Mem. Soroptimists (past pres.). Address: 846 E Sahara St Las Vegas NV 89104*

HERR, MARILYN JEAN (MRS. EDMUND DAVIS HERR), TV performer; b. Watertown, N.Y.; d. Amos Clifford and Anita Estelle (Persons) Hubbard; student Am. Acad. Dramatic Art, 1946; student Syracuse U.; m. Edmund Davis Herr, Nov. 26, 1953; children—Corliss Alexandra, Charles Haskel. Played summer stock theatre, Thousand Islands, 1947; tour with Clare Tree Major's Children's Theatre, 1948-49; continuity dir. WHEN-TV, Syracuse, 1954-56, moderator, dir. Magic Toyshop program, 1955—, also Toyshop Jamboree, 1955-59. Regional auditioner Am. Acad. Dramatic Arts. Recipient Gabriel award outstanding children's program, 1973; Nat. Assn. TV Programming Execs., 1974. Home: 135 Sunnyside Park Rd Syracuse NY 13214 Office: 980 James St Syracuse NY 13203

HERRELL, SOPHIA, newspaper exec.; b. Clinton, Tenn., Jan. 6, 1914; d. Josiah B. and Nannie (Hamblen) Herrell; student U. Md., 1932-33, George Washington U., 1934, Washington Sch. Secs., 1934. Sec. to Ia. congressman, 1935-38; sec., asst. to dept. head, sec. to exec. v.p. U.S.C. of C., Washington, 1938-50; sec. to exec. editor, v.p., gen. mgr. St. Petersburg (Fla.) Times, 1951-58; asst. to operating head Savannah (Ga.) News-Press, Inc., 1958-66; personnel mgr., purchasing agt. Savannah News Press, 1966-73; corporate personnel coordinator Morris Communications Corp., Augusta, Ga., 1973—; sec. Savannah Newspapers, Inc., 1960-63. Sec. 1st dist. Ga. Heart Assn., 1967-72. Bd. dirs. Savannah Symphony Soc., Inc., 1959-71, treas., 1959-67. Mem. Am. Soc. Personnel Adminstrn., Bus. and Profl. Women's Club (local pres., dist. dir., chmn. Fla., pres. Savannah 1962-63), Newspaper Personnel Relations Assn., Friends of Library (pres. 1967-69, adv. bd. 1969-73), Kappa Delta. Baptist. Home: 3211 Wrightsboro Rd Augusta GA 30904 Office: News Bldg 725 Broad St Augusta GA 30903

HERRERA, CLARITA EVANGELISTA (MRS. THOMAS GEORGE ARGYROS), physician; b. Manila, P.I., Sept. 15, 1936; d. Crescencio and Arsenia Padilla (Evangelista) Herrera; A.A., U. Santo Tomas, Manila, P.I., 1954, M.D., 1961; m. Thomas George Argyros, Mar. 26, 1966; children—George C., Anthony D. Came to U.S., 1961, naturalized, 1971. Rotating intern N.Y.C. Infirmary, 1961-62; med. resident Lenox Hill Hosp., N.Y.C., 1964-66, fellow cardiopulmonary disease, 1966-67; fellow cardiopulmonary diseases Long Island Jewish Hosp., L.I., N.Y., 1963-64; resident pulmonary disease VA Hosp., N.Y.C., 1968-69, asso. research and edn. pulmonary circulation, 1969-72, med. dir. Drug and Alcohol Dependency Treatment program, 1973—; practice medicine, specializing in pulmonary physiology, N.Y.C., 1961—; mem. staff VA Hosp., N.Y.C. Contbr. articles to profl. pubs. Home: 340 Spring Av Ridgewood NJ 07450 Office: 122 E 76th St New York City NY 10021

HERRERA, PATSY GUSTAMANTES (MRS. JOSE DELFIN HERRERA), therapist; b. Roswell, N.M., Nov. 13, 1942; d. Richard Moya and Genevieve (Trujillo) Gustamantes; B.S. (Gates Found. scholar 1961-65, March of Dimes scholar 1961-65), Colo. State U., 1965; m. Jose Delfin Herrera, July 17, 1965; children—Genevieve, Jose Delfin. Staff occupational therapist Colo. State Hosp., 1966-68, sr. occupational therapist, 1968-73, acting dir. occupational therapy, 1973—. Cons. St. Charles Sr. Citizens Center, Pueblo, Colo., 1971-74. Mem. Am., Colo. (mem. legislative com. 1971-73) occupational therapy assns. Roman Catholic. Home: 1713 E 8th St Pueblo CO 81001 Office: 1600 W 24th St Pueblo CO 81003

HERRIDGE, FRANCES, drama and movie editor, dance critic; b. Troy, N.Y.; d. Frederick Thomas and Elizabeth (Osgood) Herridge; B.A., Smith Coll., 1933; postgrad. N.Y. U., New Sch. Social Research; m. John Tull Baker, 1947; (div.); 1 son, George Henry; m. 2d, Adna H. Karns, 1964. Asst. to Max Lerner, dance critic for PM, 1945-48; beauty and children's editor N.Y. Post, 1949-54, drama editor, dance critic, 1954—, movie editor, 1964—. Home: 305 W 28th St New York City NY 10001 Office: NY Post 210 South St New York City NY 10002

HERRING, MARJORIE JEAN BETHKE, occupational therapist; b. Milw., Feb. 3, 1924; d. Herman Frederick and Anna Leona (Kellner) Bethke; B.S., Milw. Downer Coll., 1953; postgrad. U. Wis., 1957-58; M.B.A., Rollins Coll., 1962; m. Luby Franklin Herring, Feb. 5, 1946. Staff occupational therapist VA Hosp., Woods, Wis., 1955-57, Columbia Hosp., Milw., 1958-60; supr. occupational therapy Muirdale Sanatorium, Milw. County Inst., 1963-66; dir. occupational therapy dept. Univ. Hosp., Cleve., 1968—. Mem. occupational therapy curriculum com. Cleve. State U., 1968—. Served with WAC, 1944-46. NIH grantee, 1958-59. Mem. Am., Ohio (chmn. conf. 1969) occupational therapy assns. Club: Zonta (Cleve.). Home: 1939 Green Rd Cleveland OH 44121 Office: Occupational Therapy Dept U Hosp Cleve University Circle Cleveland OH 44106

HERRING, ROYAL ELAINE HOUSE (MRS. PETER WAYNE HERRING), savs. and loan assn. exec.; b. nr. Washington, Oct. 2, 1941; d. John Royall and Elsie Gladys (Gough) House; student Carolina U., 1960-61, Ind. U., 1971—; m. Peter Wayne Herring, Sept. 27, 1961; children—Debra Marie, Denise Marie. Legal sec. James P. Davenport, Atty., Manassas, Va., 1962-67; mgr. Commonwealth Savs. & Loan Assn., Manassas, 1967-69, exec. v.p., 1969—. Mem. Am. Savs. and Loan Inst. (pres. study chpt. 1969-72), Bd. Realtors, Manassas C. of C., No. Va. Savs. and Loan League Council. Home: 13521 Carriage Ford Rd Nokesville VA 22123 Office: 9201 Church St Manassas VA 22110

HERRINGTON, DOROTHY EVANGELINE MEANS, educator; b. Moberly, Mo, Jan. 17, 1920; d. Lewis Manning and Evangeline (Boggs) Means; student Central Meth. Coll., 1937-39; B.A. in Polit. Sci., U. Mo., 1941, B.S. in Edn., 1961, M.Ed. in Guidance and Counseling, 1961; postgrad. U. Ind., summer 1964, U. Tex., 1964-65, U. Mo-Columbia, 1972-73; m. Frank Dwight Waddell, Aug. 1, 1942 (dec. July 1943); 1 son, Frank Dwight; m. 2d, William Palmer Oliver, Jr., Jan. 13, 1945 (div. Oct. 1946); 1 son, Thomas Means (dec.); m. 3d, Kenneth Frank Herrington, Jr., Feb. 1, 1950 (div. June 1961); children—Kenneth Frank III, Dorothy Evangeline, Martha Diane, Nancy Katherine (dec.), Lewis Gaylord, Geoffrey Royal. Sec. Mo. Dept. Edn., Jefferson City, 1940, 41; adminstr. asst. to comdg. gen. Mo. State Guard, Jefferson City, 1941-42; finance clk. VA, St. Louis, 1946-47, jr. adminstrv. asst. to dir. personnel Army Finance Center, 1947-49; tchr. pub. schs., Fayette, Mo., 1949-50; tchr. U.S. Air Force Acad., Colorado Springs, Colo., 1961-62; guidance counselor Ritenour Sr. High Sch., St. Louis, 1962-64; mgr. children's dining room Mayfair-Lenox Inn, St. Louis, 1963-64; counselor Gary Job Corps Tng. Center, San Marcos, Tex., 1965-66; counselor specialist, sch. psychologist Psychol. Services and Ednl. Research div. Milw. Pub. Schs., 1967-70; substitute tchr., counselor Columbia (Mo.) Pub. Schs., 1973—. Mem. Am., Mo., Wis. personnel and guidance assns., Internat. Assn. Ednl. and Vocational Counselors Assn., N.E.A., Nat. Council Social Studies, Am. Psychol. Assn., Am. Sch. Counselor Assn., Assn. Counselor Edn. Supervision, Mo. Assn. Realtors, U. Mo. Alumni Assn., Nat. Vocational Counselors Assn., Pilots Internat. Assn., UN Assn. U.S.A., Kappa Alpha Theta, Phi Beta Internat., Alpha Phi Zeta. Home: 504 N Linn Av Fayette MO 65248 also 2205 Country Lane Columbia MO 65201

HERRINGTON, GAYE WEBER, lawyer; b. Hays, Kan., Sept. 6, 1938; d. Ernest William and Grace Esther (Renner) Weber; A.B., Washburn U., 1960; J.D., U. So. Cal., 1970; 1 dau., Theresa Lynne. Admitted to Cal. bar, 1971; practiced in dep. atty. gen. Dept. Justice, State Cal., 1970-73; dep. dist. atty. County Los Angeles, 1973—. Mem. Los Angeles County Bar Assn., Kappa Alpha Theta. Republican. Methodist. Home: 6605 Green Valley Circle No 113 Culver City CA 90230 Office: 210 W Temple St Los Angeles CA 90012

HERRMANN, RONEE ISOBEL, psychiatrist; b. N.Y.C., Sept. 20, 1929; d. Julian Bertram and Marion Sylvia (Hecht) Herrmann; A.B., Stanford, 1950; M.D., Columbia, 1954; m. Norman Bank, Sept. 1, 1954; children—David Eugene, Susan Jeanne. Intern, Mt. Sinai Hosp., N.Y.C., 1954-55, attending physician in psychiatry, 1962-64; resident psychiatry Mass. Mental Health Center, Boston, 1955-57; fellow child psychiatry Judge Baker Guidance Center, Boston, 1957-59; practice adult and adolescent psychiatry, N.Y.C., 1959—. Cons. psychiatrist Jewish Bd. Guardians, 1959-60; adv. cons. Hudson Guild Mental Health Clinic, N.Y.C., 1965—. Mem. Am. Psychiat. Assn., Am. Orthopsychiat. Assn., Am. Soc. Adolescent Psychiatry, N.Y. Council Child Psychiatry. Home: 34 Fenimore Rd Scarsdale NY 10583 Office: 983 Park Av New York City NY 10028

HERRNSTEIN, BARBARA HARNESS (MRS. JOHN ELLETT HERRNSTEIN), occupational therapist; b. Chillicothe, O., June 12, 1935; d. Daniel R. and Margaret J. (Smith) Harness; B.S. in Occupational Therapy, Ohio State U., 1957; postgrad. Ohio U.; m. John Ellett Herrnstein, Jan. 4, 1957; children—John M., Susan E., Karen A., Seth A., Kristin S. Sr. occupational therapist VA Hosp., Chillicothe, 1970—. Active Girl Scouts Am., 1967-72, Boy Scouts Am., 1967-72, Jr. Civic League Chillicothe, 1967-70, Chillicothe Art League, 1968—. Mem. Am. Occupational Therapy Assn. Democrat. Roman Catholic. Home: 603 Seminole Rd Chillicothe OH 45601 Office: VA Hospital Chillicothe OH 45601

HERROLD, JOYCE NAZOR, physician, pharm. co. exec.; b. Lancaster, O., Feb. 18, 1933; d. Gordon William and Lucille (Nazor) Herrold; B.A., Ohio U., 1954; M.D., U. Cin., 1958; M.S., Ohio State U., 1970. Intern Gorgas Hosp., C.Z., Panama, 1958-59; U.S. Govt., S. Am., 1959-60; resident internal medicine Baylor U. Coll. Medicine, Houston, 1960-61, Queen's Hosp., Honolulu, 1961-62, VA Hosp., Long Beach, Cal., 1962-63; with Student Health Service, Ohio State U., Columbus, 1963-67; NIH fellow, div. endocrinology and metabolism Ohio State U. Hosp., Columbus, 1967-70; asst. dir. clin. research Hoechst Pharm. Co., Somerville, N.J., 1970-72, dir. clin. research (endocrinology), 1972-73; dir. med. research (immunology) Ortho Research Center, Raritan, N.J., 1973—. Mem. N.Y. Acad. Scis., Am. Diabetic Assn., Nat. Pharm. Council, A.A.A.S., Am. Fedn. Clin. Research, Pi Beta Phi. Presbyn. Contbr. articles to profl. jours. Home: 57 Bainbridge St Princeton NJ 08540 Office: Rte 202 Raritan NJ 08876

HERRON, DOROTHEA NANCY DECAROUSO, civic worker; b. Oakland, Cal.; d. Victor Harold and Nina Simone (Mitchell) deCarouso; student Sacramento Coll., 1943, Marin Coll., 1944; B.A., U. Cal., 1946; postgrad. Laney Coll., 1966; m. Joseph Baxter Herron, Jr., Apr. 5, 1947; children—Victor Joseph, Kathy Jo. Licenced hearing specialist. Cons., 1973—. Art lectr. Oakland Art Museum, Cal., sec. Art Docent Council, 1971, supr. Docents, 1968-73. Various Oakland Symphony Assn., 1960-73. sec., mem. bd. Symphony Guild, 1966-68; active East Bay Opera League, San Francisco Opera Guild, Holy Name's Symphony, Oakland Museum Assn., Sister City Fukuoka; sponsor Camp Fire Girls, 1965-70; mem. bd. P.T.A., 1957-70; various offices U.S. Officer's Wives bd., 1956-60. Mem. Nat. Hearing Soc., Garden Club, Queen of Spades (sec.), Pot and Trowel Club, Marines Meml. Club., Sigma Phi Omega. Republican. Episcopalian (devotional chmn. Women's Guild; mem. alter guild). Club: Northwood Golf (Guerneville, Cal.). Home: 3667 Redwood Rd Oakland CA 94619 also 15320 Paradise Lane Guerneville CA Office: 109 Geary St San Francisco CA 94108

HERRON, ELLEN PATRICIA, lawyer; b. Auburn, N.Y., July 30, 1927; d. David Martin and Grace Josephine (Berner) Herron; A.B., Trinity Coll., 1949; M.A., Cath. U. Am., 1954; J.D., U. Cal. at Berkeley, 1964. Asst. dean Cath. U. Am., 1952-54; instr. East High Sch., Auburn, 1955-57; asst. dean Wells Coll., Aurora, N.Y., 1957-58; instr. psychology and history Contra Costa Coll., 1958-60; dir. row Stanford, 1960-61; asso. firm Knox & Kretzmer, Richmond, Cal., 1964-65; admitted to Cal. bar, 1965; partner firm Knox & Herron, Richmond, 1965—. Gen. partner Real Estate Syndicates, Cal., 1967—. Active numerous civic orgns.; mem. Coordinating Council on Developmental Disabilities. Bd. dirs. Rhonoh Sch., Richmond. Mem. Am., Contra Costa (exec. com. 1969—), Richmond bar assns., Cal. Bar, Cal. Trial Lawyers, Applicants Atty.'s Assn., Queen's Bench. Democrat. Home: 51 Western Dr Point Richmond CA 94801 Office: 2566 McDonald Av Richmond CA 94804

HERSETH, LORNA B., state ofcl.; b. Columbia, S.D.; ed. No. State Coll.; m. Ralph Herseth; children—Karen H. Wee, Constance Stenseth, Ralph Lars. Dep. county supt. schs., N.D., 1932-36, county supt. schs., 1936-38; sec. state S.D., Pierre, 1972—. Past treas. Shelby Sch. Bd. Bd. dirs. Easter Seal Soc. Crippled Children and Adults. Democrat. Lutheran (supt. Sunday sch.). Address: 1100 E Church St Pierre SD 57501*

HERSEY, VIRGINIA STARR, real estate broker; b. Atlanta, Jan. 11, 1919; d. Francis Elisha and Lona Elisha (Tucker) Davis; A.A., Citrus Coll., 1961; B.S. in Bus. Adminstrn., Cal. State Poly. U., 1963; m., Dec. 27, 1935; children—Clifford Baker, Richard Starr, Virginia Diane, Miriam Ruth, Frances Rebecca. Office mgr. Hersey Paving Co., Ventura and Glendora, Cal., 1945-73; with Sears Roebuck, Ventura, 1963-70, installation mgr., Ventura, 1970-73; real estate broker own firm, Ventura, 1972—. Alumni dir. Cal. State Poly. U., San Luis Obispo, Cal., 1968-70. Pink Lady Community Hosp., Ventura, 1969-70; mem. council Jobs Daus., Ventura, 1969-71. Mem. Ventura Bd. Realtors (dir. 1974-76). Brethern. Home: 5472 Queens St Ventura CA 93003 Office: Suite 103 3200 Telegraph Rd Ventura CA 93003

HERSHAN, STELLA KREIDL, author; b. Vienna, Austria, Feb. 7, 1915; d. Felix and Lucy (Pick) Kreidl; came to U.S., 1939, naturalized, 1944; certificate liberal arts N.Y. U., 1962; certificate human relations New Sch. for Social Research, 1968; m. Rudolf Hershan, Nov. 19, 1933 (dec.); 1 dau., Lisa (Mrs. Allan Grabell). Publicity dir. Am. Council Emigres in the Professions, Inc., N.Y.C. Mem. P.E.N. Author: A Woman of Quality: Eleanor Roosevelt, 1970; The Naked Angel, A Historical Novel about the Times of Metternich and the Congress of Vienna, 1972. Editor, publicity dir. Talent Newsletter, 1971. Address: 2 Fifth Av New York City NY 10011

HERSHMAN, LYNN CAROLE LESTER (MRS. LAWRENCE C. HERSHMAN), artist; b. Cleve., June 17, 1941; d. Samuel Lester and Stella (Schwartz) Lester; student Ohio U., 1959-60, Cleve. Inst. Art, 1960-63; B.S., Western Res. U., 1963; postgrad. Cal. Coll. Arts and Crafts, 1963-64; Otis Art Inst., 1964-65; M.A., San Francisco State U., 1972; m. Lawrence C. Hershman, June 23, 1963; 1 dau., Dawn Lauryn. Exhibited one man shows Feingarten Gallery, Los Angeles, 1966, Santa Barbara (Cal.) Mus. Art, 1967, Richmond (Cal.) Art Center, 1970, William Sawyer Gallery, San Francisco, 1970, Graphics Gallery, San Francisco, 1970, Gallery Del Sol, Santa Barbara, 1971, DeSaisset Mus., Santa Clara, Cal., 1972, Mills Coll., 1972, Univ. Art Mus., Berkeley, Cal., Jody Scully Gallery, Los Angeles, 1973, U. Nev., 1974, others; exhibited in group shows at Mus. of Art, San Francisco, 1965-1970, Purdue U., Fry Mus. Art, Seattle, Laguna (Cal.) Mus. Art, Los Angeles Art Assn., Los Angeles County Mus. Art, La Jolla (Cal.) Mus. Art, Ankurm Gallery, Los Angeles, Art in the Embassies Program (Prague, Czechoslovakia), Butler Inst. Am. Art, Youngstown, O., Ohio U., all 1966, Bucknell U., Dulin Gallery, Knoxville, Tenn., Cleve. Mus. Art, Dache Gallery, N.Y.C., Tucson Art Gallery, all 1967, No. Ill. U., Ball State U., Cleve. Mus. Art, all 1968, Oakland Mus. Art, 1969, Comara Gallery, Los Angeles, 1969, William Sawyer Gallery, San Francisco, 1969, Graphics Gallery, San Francisco, 1969, Richard Demarco Gallery, Edinburgh, Scotland, 1973, San Francisco Art Inst., 1973, Laguna Mus. Art, 1973, Univ. Art Mus., Berkeley, 1973, 74, Richmond (Cal.) Art Center, 1973; exhibited in sculpture shows San Diego State Coll., Del Mar Coll. (Tex.); represented in permanent collections Santa Barbara Mus. Art, Univ. Art Mus., Berkeley, Nat. Collection Fine Arts, Smithsonian Instn., Cleve. Inst. Art., Cal. State Colls. Collection, Long Beach, City of San Francisco Collection, Richmond Art Center, Oakland Mus. Art, Jayell Pub. Co.; tchr. Cleve. Mus. Art, 1961-63; art critic San Francisco Progress, 1971-72; editor Artweek, 1971-73; sr. curator Mus. Conceptual Art; coordinator Insights, San Francisco Mus. Art; writer Studio Internat.; instr. Melville Coll., Edinburgh, summer 1973; tchr. Cal. Coll. Art, Oakland; vis. curator Walnut Creek Civic Arts Gallery, 1974. Recipient Bates and Springer award, Mary Suggett Ranney award Western Res. U., 1962; purchase prize San Francisco Art Festival, 1969; purchase prize Olive Nyde Art Center, 1972. Mem. Internat. Platform Assn., Los Angeles Art Assn. Home: 3595 Clay St San Francisco CA 94118

HERTZ, BARBARA VALENTINE (MRS. DAVID BENDEL HERTZ), coll. ofcl.; b. N.Y.C., Mar. 1, 1921; d. Herbert I. and Helen (Lachman) Valentine; student Swarthmore Coll., 1939-40; B.A., Barnard Coll., 1943; m. David Bendel Hertz, Dec. 20, 1941; children—Barbara Bendel, Valentine. Comml. continuity WOXR, 1945-46; free lance writing and publicity, 1947-51; asso. editor Parents' mag., 1951-56, mng. editor, 1956-68; dir. devel. Barnard Coll., 1968—. Mem. Alumni Assn. Friends Sem. (pres. 1954-56), Woman's Conf. Group N.Y.C. (exec. com., chmn. 1959-62), Class of 1943 Barnard Coll. (pres. 1953-58). Club: Cosmopolitan. Home: 225 E 74th St New York City NY 10021 Office: Barnard Coll 606 W 120th St New York City NY 10027

HERWIG, BARBARA LYNN, lawyer; b. Los Angeles, Nov. 1, 1944; d. Karl Edmund and Gertrude Dorothy (Ernst) Herwig; B.A., Stanford U., 1967; J.D., U. Cal. at Berkeley, 1970. Admitted to Cal. bar, 1971; atty. civil div. Dept. Justice, Washington, 1970-72, spl. asst. to asst. atty. gen., 1971-72, atty. civil div., 1973—; spl. asst. to acting dir. FBI, Washington, 1972-73. Mem. State Bar Cal., Am., Fed. bar assns. Home: 520 N St SW Washington DC 20024 Office: Dept of Justice Washington DC 20530

HERWIG, THELMA LANGE (MRS. THEODOR FREDRICK HERWIG), physician; b. Toledo, June 22, 1932; d. Edward Henry and Oleva Henrietta (Edler) Lange; B.S., U. Toledo, 1953; M.D., Ohio State U., 1958; m. Theodor Fredrick Herwig, June 10, 1956; children—Theodor Thomas, Nathaniel Christopher, David Edward. Intern, Mt. Carmel Hosp., Columbus, O., 1958-59; family practice medicine, Dublin, O., 1963-67, Columbus, 1967—; staff Riverside Meth. Hosp., Columbus. Mem. A.M.A., Am. Med. Womens Assn., Acad. Medicine Franklin County. Home: 2090 Cheltenham St Columbus OH 43220 Office: 3720 Olentangy River Rd Columbus OH 43214

HERWITZ, CARLA BARRON (MRS. DAVID HERWITZ), lawyer; b. N.Y.C., June 1, 1932; d. Harry C. and Ruth (Antell) Barron; A.B., Radcliffe Coll., 1952; LL.B., Harvard, 1955; m. David R. Herwitz, Jan. 22, 1960; children—Juliet Florence, Andrew Barron. Admitted to Mass. bar, 1955, N.Y. bar, 1959; asso. firm Winthrop, Stimson, Putnam & Roberts, N.Y.C., 1957-60; asso. firm Choate Hall & Stewart, Boston, 1960-70, partner, 1971—. Vice pres. bd. trustees Tower Sch., Marblehead, Mass. Home: Littles Point Swampscott MA 01907 Office: 28 State St Boston MA 02109

HERZ, ANNA PIRSCENOK (MRS. JULIUS M. HERZ), educator; b. Bethlehem, Pa., Mar. 15, 1922; d. Anton G. and Mary (Femiak) Pirscenok; R.N., Hahnemann Med. Coll. and Hosp. Sch. Nursing, 1943; B.S., U. Pa., 1949, M.A., 1950, Ph.D., 1956; M.A., Columbia U., 1951; m. Julius M. Herz. Night supr. Hahnemann Hosp., Phila., 1943-45; instr., supr. Episcopal Hosp., and Sch. Nursing, Phila., 1948-50; dir. nurses Montgomery Hosp., Norristown, Pa., 1951-53; research linguist Inst. for Coop. Research, U. Pa., 1953-58, instr. Slavic lang., 1956-59, asst. prof. Slavic langs., 1959-66; asso. prof. Russian, Lehigh U., Bethlehem, 1966-70, prof. Russian, 1970—, chmn. modern fgn. langs., 1972—; fgn. lang. free-lance translator, 1952—; instr. continuation courses Am. Chem. Soc., 1958-60, 63-65, TV courses in Russian, WHYY-TV, 1958-60. Instr. A.R.C. home nursing courses, 1948-50; instr. in Russian for Abington Twp. Adult Sch., Assn., 1957-58; supr. div. sch. extension Phila. Bd. Edn., 1958-60; mem. Pa. Adv. Com. on Modern Fgn. Langs., 1960-62, 66-70. Served as 1st lt., Army Nurse Corps., 1945-47. Recipient award for excellence in teaching U. Pa., 1959; U. Pa. and U.S. Office Edn. travel grant, 1960; Fulbright-Hayes award, 1964. Mem. Modern Lang. Assn. (asso. bibliographer 1957—, sect. head Slavic linguistics 1973—), Am. Assn. Tchrs. Slavic and East European Langs., Comparative Edn. Soc., Am. Assn. U. Women. Home: Route 1 Box 96 Riegelsville PA 18077 Office: Lehigh U Bethlehem PA 18015

HERZENBERG, CAROLINE LITTLEJOHN (MRS. LEONARDO HERZENBERG), physicist, educator; b. East Orange, N.J., Mar. 25, 1932; d. Charles F. and Caroline (Schulze) Littlejohn; S.B., Mass. Inst. Tech., 1953; M.S., U. Chgo., 1955, Ph.D., 1958; m. Leonardo Herzenberg, July 29, 1961; 1 dau., Karen Ann. Research asso. U. Chgo., 1958-59, Argonne (Ill.) Nat. Lab., 1959-61; asst. prof. physics Ill. Inst. Tech., Chgo., 1961-67; research physicist IIT Research Inst., Chgo., 1967-70, sr. physicist, 1970-71; ind. cons., 1971-72; asso. prof. physics U. Ill. at Med. Center, Chgo., 1972—. Prin. investigator lunar sample analysis NASA, 1969-71. Mem. Am. Phys. Soc., Am. Geophys. Union, A.A.A.S., Fedn. Am. Scientists (past pres. Ill. Inst. Tech. br., past del. nat. council), Sigma Xi. Research and publs. in low energy nuclear physics and Mossbauer effect. Home: 1814 Valley View Dr Freeport IL 61032 Office: Dept Med Chemistry U Ill Med Center 833 S Wood St PO Box 6998 Chicago IL 60680

HERZOG, ANN ELIZABETH, pub. relations exec.; b. Lawrence, Mass., May 21, 1940; d. George Earnest and Elsie Louise (Meinhold) Herzog; B.S., Boston U., 1961, M.S., 1963. Partner, Pub. Relations Bd. New Eng., Brookline, Mass., 1962-63; dir. pub. relations Promotions, Inc., Boston, 1963-64; dir. pub. relations Boston Lying-in Hosp., 1964-66; pub. relations account exec. Jon-Carter & Co., Boston, 1966; mgr. Boston office Bill Doll & Co., N.Y.C., 1966-67; pub. relations cons. Polaroid Corp., Montreal, Que., Can., 1967, A.E. Herzog & Co., 1967-69; pub. relations mgr. Dunkin' Donuts, Inc., Randolph, Mass., 1969-70; pub. relations and advt. cons. A.E. Herzog & Co., Brookline, Mass., 1970—. Music dir. WBUR-FM, Boston, 1958-61; communications book critic Boston Globe, 1962—; English instr. Academie Moderne Sch. Fashion Careers, Boston, 1971—. Vice-pres. Buddy Dog Humane Soc., 1972—; mem. exec. council U.S.O. Trustee Mass., mem. internat. bd. Armed Services YMCA; bd. dirs. Save our Shores. Mem. Pub. Relations Soc. Am., Am. Women in Radio and Television, New Eng. Women's Press Assn., Friends Boston Symphony, Grasshopper Com., Publicity Club Boston (past pres.), Boston U. Alumni Assn. (v.p. 1973-74). Clubs: Boston University Women's, Women's City (Boston). Mng. editor The Bostonian, 1968-69; food editor Apt. Life. Address: 63 Selkirk Rd Brookline MA 02146

HESLEP, EMMA LEOTA GRIDER (MRS. CHARLES HESLEP), civic worker; b. Vallonia, Ind.; d. William Rudias and Gertrude (Jackson) Grider; grad. Western Wash. State Coll., 1928; postgrad. U. Wash., 1952; m. James Peyton Howell, Nov. 28, 1921 (dec. Aug. 1938); m. 2d, Charles Thomas Heslep, July 12, 1942. Tchr., Garden City Sch., Elma, Wash., 1921-24, prin., 1924-26, 28-31; tchr. White Star Sch., Whites, Wash., 1931-36, prin., 1936-44; tchr. McCleary (Wash.) Elementary Sch., 1944-57. Mem. Grays Harbor County Bd. of Edn., 1959-69; leader 4-H Club, 1938-42; committeewoman Girl Scouts U.S.A., 1950-53, leader, 1953-54. Bd. dirs. Mark E. Reed Hosp., 1958-60; trustee Grays Harbor County Library, 1956-66. Mem. Wash. Assn. County Bds. Edn. (state pres. 1963), Mark E. Reed Hosp. Aux. (pres. 1958-60), P.T.A. (life), Wash. P.T.A., V.F.W. Aux., Daus. Union Vets. (past pres.), N.E.A. (life), Nat. Ret. Tchrs. Assn., Internat. Platform Assn., Delta Kappa Gamma (past pres.). Mem. Order Eastern Star (past matron). Writer column Truly Yours, McCleary (Wash.) Author: (poetry) What Manner of Love, 1973. Home: Box 2 McCleary WA 98557

HESS, BONNITA JEAN (MRS. JACK B. HESS), pub. co. owner; b. Crossville, Ill., Feb. 14, 1938; d. Gerald Maurice and Lydia Mary (Crowder) Sturm; student So. Ill. U., 1955-56; m. Jack B. Hess, June 17, 1956; children—Gregg, Sherry. Officer mgr. R.E. Banta Bookseller and Publisher, Crawfordsville, Ind., 1958-69, co-owner, mgr., 1969—. Club: Zonta. Home: 1000 North Dr Crawfordsville IN 47933 Office: 211 E Pike St Crawfordsville IN 47933

HESS, CLARE MARIE CAMILLA, librarian; b. Guttenberg, N.J., Apr. 11, 1921; d. Lawrence J. and Clara J. (Moerler) Hess; student Drake's Bus. Coll., Union City, N.J., 1940-41. Various positions Oxford U. Press, N.Y.C., 1942-57, librarian, 1957—. Mem. St. Michael's Rosary Soc. (v.p. 1971-73, sec. 1973—). Odd Fellow. Home: 520A Broad Av Palisades Park NJ 07650 Office: 200 Madison Av New York City NY 10016

HESS, EVELYN VICTORINE (MRS. MICHAEL HOWETT), physician, educator; b. Dublin, Ireland, Nov. 8, 1926; d. Ernest Joseph and Mary (Hawkins) Hess; M.B., B.Ch., B.A.O., Univ. Coll., Dublin, 1949; m. Michael Howett, Apr. 27, 1954. Came to U.S., 1959. Research fellow in epidemiology of Tb, 1955; Royal Free Med. Sch. traveling fellow, Scandinavia, 1956; registrar rheumatic diseases unit Royal Free Hosp. and Med. Sch., 1956-57; Empire Rheumatism council traveling fellow, U.S.A., 1958-59; asst. prof. dept. internal medicine U. Tex. Southwestern Med. Sch., Dallas, 1961-64; asso. prof. dept. med. U. Cin. Coll. Medicine, 1964-69, prof., 1969—, dir. div. immunology, 1964—; attending physician, also chief clinician arthritis clinic Cin. Gen. Hosp.; attending physician VA Hosp., Holmes Hosp.; cons. Children's Hosp., Children's Convalescent Hosp. Sr. investigator Arthritis and Rheumatism Found., 1963-68. Fellow A.C.P., Am. Acad. Allergy; mem. Heberden Soc., Am. Rheumatism Assn., Am. Fedn. for Clin. Research, Central Soc. for Clin. Research, Am. Assn. Immunologists, Am. Soc. Nephrology, Transplantation Soc., Physicians Forum, Sydenham Soc., Nat. Parks Assn., Smithsonian Inst., Sigma Xi. Democrat. Contbr. articles on immunology, rheumatic diseases to profl. jours., also chpts. to books. Home: 2916 Grandin Rd Cincinnati OH 45208 Office: K-3 Cin Gen Hospital Burnet Av Cincinnati OH 45229*

HESS, HELEN H., physician; b. Clarksburg, W.Va., Aug. 26, 1923; d. William Henry and Ercel May (Knight) Hess; B.A., W.Va. U., 1946, B.S., 1948; M.D., Harvard, 1951. Asst. in neuropathology McLean Hosp., Belmont, Mass., 1953-56, asst. neuropathologist, 1956-57, asso. neuropathologist, 1957-71; asst. in neuropathology Harvard Med. Sch., 1953-56, instr. neuropathology, 1956-59, research asso. neuropathology, 1959-69, prin. research asso. neuropathology, 1969-70, asso. prof. nueropathology, 1970-71; research med. officer Nat. Eye Inst., NIH, Bethesda, Md., 1971—; prof. neurology and biochemistry George Washington U., Washington, 1971—. USPHS postdoctoral fellow, 1951-53. Mem. A.A.A.S., Am. Acad. Neurology, Am. Assn. Biol. Chemists, Am. Assn. Neuropathologists, Soc. for

Neurosci., Assn. for Research in Vision and Opthalmology, Am. Chem. Soc., Am., Internat. socs. neurochemistry, N.Y. Acad. Sci., Phi Beta Kappa, Alpha Epsilon Delta. Editorial bd. Jour. Neurochemistry. Contbr. articles to profl. jours. Home: 5102 Acacia Av Bethesda MD 20014 Office: Nat Eye Inst Lab Vision Research NIH Bethesda MD 20014

HESTER, MARY EDNA, ins. co. exec.; b. Roanoke, Ala., Dec. 17, 1923; d. Charles Jeremiah and Docia Belle (Hardy) Hester; A.S., So. Union Jr. Coll., 1943. With Liberty Nat. Life Ins. Co., Birmingham, Ala., 1943—, life ins. underwriting exec., 1968—. Mem. Inst. Home Office Underwriters, Ala. Assn. Home Office Underwriters. Democrat. Mem. United Ch. Christ. Home: 1833 Woodland Av SW Birmingham AL 35211 Office: PO Box 2612 Birmingham AL 35202

HESTON, JULIE LOU, psychiatrist; b. Columbus, O., Aug. 13, 1939; d. Joseph Carter and Martha Jane (Allen) Heston; B.A., DePauw U., 1961; M.D., U. Mich., 1965. Intern, Phila. Gen. Hosp., 1965-66; resident psychiatry Johns Hopkins, 1966-69; practice psychiatry, Balt., 1969-73; fellow neurology Mass. Gen. Hosp., 1973—. Instr. psychiatry John Hopkins Sch. Medicine, Balt., 1969-73. Mem. Md. Soc. Adolescent Psychiatry, Phi Beta Kappa, Alpha Omega Alpha. Home: Wadleigh Point Rd Kingston NH 03827 Office: Dept Neurology Mass Gen Hosp Boston MA 02114

HETHERINGTON, ELLEN JOAN (MRS. JOHN A. HETHERINGTON), city ofcl.; b. Terre Haute, Ind., Dec. 3, 1929; d. John William and Frances Josephine (Maher) Brentlinger; grad. high sch.; m. John A. Hetherington, Nov. 19, 1971. Chief dep. city clk. City of Terre Haute, 1951-58, chief dep. city controller, 1963-67, chief dep. county auditor, 1968-71, city controller, 1972—. Chmn. city govt. div. United Way campaign Terre Haute, 1973. Vice pres. 6th Dist. Young Dems., 1951-60. Mem. Ind. Controllers Assn. (sec. 1973—), Ind. Real Estate Brokers Assn., Womens Aux. Med. Soc. Home: 4430 Wabash Av Terre Haute IN 47803 Office: 17 Harding Av Terre Haute IN 47801

HETRICK, SUZANNE HOLLINGSWORTH (MRS. JOHN A. HETRICK), govt. ofcl., psychologist; b. Harrisburg, Pa., June 25, 1943; d. Harold C. and Anne M. (Zarfoss) Hollingsworth; A.B. cum laude, Lebanon Valley Coll., 1965; M.A., Kent State U., 1967, Ph.D. (Nat. Inst. Mental Health fellow), 1969; m. John A. Hetrick, Dec. 17, 1966; children—Brent H., Joel A. Counseling specialist Counseling and Group Research Center, Kent (O.) State U., 1969-71; exec. dir. Portage County Mental Health and Mental Retardation Bd., Kent, 1971—. Mem. Am., Ohio Psychol. assns., Portage County Council Health and Social Agys. (exec. bd. 1972), Bd. Staff Assns., League Women Voters, Sigma Xi. Mem. United Ch. of Christ (chmn. bd. Christian edn.). Home: 538 Green Meadow Dr Tallmadge OH 44278 Office: 154 N Water St Kent OH 44240

HETTS, JOYCE WEBSTER (MRS. WILLIAM ORLO HETTS), civic worker; b. Glendale, Cal., July 1, 1933; d. Paul Kimball and Harriet Lois (Boardman) Webster; student Whitman Coll., 1950-52; B.A. in Econs., Stanford, 1954; m. William Orlo Hetts, Sept. 9, 1955; children—Katharine Cecile, Steven William. Congressional sec. U.S. Ho. of Reps., Washington, 1953; market research analyst, econs. research analyst, Stanford Research Inst., 1955-57; portfolio analyst Schwabacher & Co., San Francisco, 1958-59; asst. investment counselor Loomis, Sayles & Co., Inc., San Francisco, 1960-63. Dir. Assn. Jr. Leagues, Inc., 1972-74; pres. Jr. League San Francisco, Inc., 1970-71; dir. Vol. Bur. San Mateo Co., 1964-68, 72-74; dir., asst. treas. San Mateo Co. Jr. Museum, 1972-73. Mem. Phi Beta Kappa. Home: 645 Woodstock Rd Hillsborough CA 94010

HETZNER, BERNICE MARTIN, librarian; b. Omaha; d. Frederick Alexander and Edna May (Petrie) Martin; student Creighton U., 1930-33, U. Chgo. Grad. Library Sch., 1950; A.B. in L.S., U. Denver, 1934; M.A. in Edn., Colo. State Coll. Edn., 1935; m. Ralph W. Hetzner, Jan. 23, 1943. Grad. fellow Colo. State Coll. Edn., 1934-35; supr. elementary sch. libraries, librarian profl. library Omaha Pub. Schs., 1935-38; instr. U. Omaha Extension Div., 1936-38; librarian grade 11, sr. Los Angeles County Pub. Library, 1938-43; asst. librarian Riverside br. N.Y. Pub. Library, 1943; cataloger St. Elizabeth Hosp. Sch. Nursing, Lincoln, Neb., 1944; adminstrv. asst. charge pub. service Lincoln City Library, 1944-46; asst. librarian U. Neb. Coll. Medicine, 1947, librarian, asso. prof., 1948-63, librarian, 1963-73, prof. library sci., 1963—; cons. VA Med. Library Service, 1957. Vice-pres., sec.-treas. exec. com. Central States Regional Med. Library Group, 1969-70. Mem. com. on med. sch. libraries Assn. Am. Med. Colls.-Med. Libraries Assn., 1963-64; dir. Midcontinental Regional Med. Library Program, 1970-73; mem. Neb. Adv. Council on Libraries, 1971-73; bd. regents Nat. Library of Medicine, 1971—; mem. library aide adv. com. Omaha Tech. Coll., 1972—. Recipient Gottlieb Prize Essay, 1958; Distinguished Service to Medicine award U. Neb. Coll. Medicine, 1974. Mem. Med. (hon.; pres. 1971-72), Am., Neb., Mountain Plains library assns., Spl. Libraries Assn., Midcontinental Regional Library Group (pres., exec. com. 1970-71), Omaha-Council Bluffs Librarians Club (pres. 1951), Am. Soc. Information Sci., Am. Assn. History of Medicine. Co-author: Guidelines on Medical School Libraries, 1965. Contbr. to profl. jours., chpts. in books. Co-editor: Moon Collection on Obstetrics and Gynecology. Home: 327 S 92d St Omaha NE 68114

HEUSCHER, RUTH BERTHA ISLER (MRS. JULIUS E. HEUSCHER), physician; b. Mollis, Switzerland, June 15, 1916; d. Ernest J. and Bertha (Burkhart) Isler; student U. Basle, 1936-37, U. Zurich, 1938-39; M.D., U. Lausanne, 1943; m. Julius E. Heuscher, May 4, 1946; children—Enno Francis, Dominic Julius. Came to U.S., 1949, naturalized, 1954. Practice medicine specializing in opthalmology, clin. research asso. dept. surgery, div. opthalmology Stanford U. Med. Sch., Palo Alto, Cal., 1958-74; intern Valley Med. Center, San Jose, Cal., 1974—; mem. citizen's com. for planning Saratoga High Sch. Las Gatos-Saratoga Joint Union High Sch. Dist., 1958-59, mem. citizen's com. for Sci-Library Bldg., 1962—; bd. mem. Los Gatos-Saratoga Symphony, 1962. Mem. Pennisula Eye Soc., Stanford U. Med. Women. Republican. Home: 18500 Hillview Dr Monte Sereno CA 95030 Office: 751 S Bascom Av San Jose CA 95128

HEVEL, JOYCE ANN, rehab. facility adminstr.; b. Angola, Ind., Nov. 9, 1942; d. Russell and Ruth (Wolf) Hevel; B.S., Western Mich. U., 1965; M.S., St. Francis Coll., 1973. Exec. dir. Community Sheltered Workshop Steuben County, Angola, 1965—. Tchr., Tri-State Coll., Angola, 1973—; occupational therapy cons. Ind. U. Med. Center, 1970-72; cons. United Cerebral Palsy, State Ind., 1973—. Vice-pres. Steuben County Mental Health Assn., 1973-74. Bd. dirs., pres. Steuben County Campfire Council, 1969. Recipient Steuben County Homemakers Citizenship award Steuben County Home Econs. Assn., 1973. Mem. Internat. Platform Assn., Am., Ind. occupation therapy assns., Ind. Assn. Retarded Children, Steuben County Bus. and Profl. Women (Young Career Woman award 1967), Council Execs. Assns. for Retarded Children, Beta Sigma Phi, Delta Kappa Gamma. Republican. Baptist. Mem. Women of Moose. Home: 408 N Washington St Angola IN 46703 Office: 502 Weatherhead St Angola IN 46703

HEWGLEY, OPAL DOROTHY, town ofcl.; b. Chappell, Neb., Feb. 27, 1919; d. George Francis and Daisy Laura (Maus) Kintz; certificate Northeastern Jr. Coll., Sterling, Colo., 1973; m. Lester Fredrich Hewgley, Aug. 27, 1938; children—Lora Lee (Mrs. James Bierman), William Bob. Benchman lab. Gt. Western Sugar Co., Ovid, Colo., 1944-54; head sch. lunch program Ovid Pub. Schs., 1954-60; town clk. Town of Sedgwick (Colo.), 1970—. Chmn. precinct Sedgwick County Democratic Com., 1972, 74. Mem. Royal Neighbors of Chappell (Neb.). V.F.W. Aux. (charter), Wesleyan Service Guild. Methodist. Mem. Rebekah Lodge. Home: 415 County Rd 59 Box 242 Ovid CO 80744 Office: 122 Main St Box 27 Sedgwick CO 80749

HEWITT, LINDA VANESSA, mus. ofcl.; b. Boston, June 14, 1939; d. John Dickson and Evelyn Gertrude (Gliesman) Hewitt; B.A., Pembroke Coll., Brown U., 1960; M.A., Northeastern U., 1967. Catalog asst. and map cataloger Boston U., 1960-61; sec. Devon Plans Corp., Boston, 1961-62; head clk. Govt. Center Commn. for New Boston City Hall, 1963-65; teaching fellow history Northeastern U., Boston, 1965-67, docent and curatorial asst. Isabella Stewart Gardner Mus., Boston, 1967-72, asst. to dir., 1972—. Mem. Town of Cohasset Historic Commn., 1974—. Mem. Cohasset Hist. Soc. (exec. com. 1972—), U.S. and Brit. Nat. Trusts for Hist. Preservation, Am. Assn. Museums, Phi Alpha Theta. Contbr. articles to popular and profl. jours. Home: Cohasset MA 02025 Office: 2 Palace Rd Boston MA 02115

HEWITT, MARY FRANCIS (MRS. ROBERT E. FOOTE), trade assn. exec.; b. Cleve., Nov. 8, 1944; d. Francis Robert and Nancy Lee (Russo) Davine; student Heidelberg Coll., Tiffin, O., 1962-63, Ohio State U., 1963-65; 1 dau. by previous marriage, Amy Catherine Hewitt; m. Robert E. Foote, Aug. 18, 1973; stepchildren—Robert Ashley, William Blair. Adminstrv. asst. Ohio Trucking Assn., Columbus, 1967—. Mem. Ohio Trade Assn. Execs., Internat. Assn. Bus. Communicators. Home: 9174 Carriage Lane Pickerington OH 43147 Office: 41 S High St Columbus OH 43215

HEWITT, PATRICIA WIMAN (MRS. WILLIAM ALEXANDER HEWITT), agriculturalist; b. Chgo., Jan. 17, 1925; d. Charles Deere and Pattie (Southall) Wiman; student Conn. Coll. For Women, 1942-44, U. Cal. at Santa Barbara, 1944-45, George Washington U., 1946-47; m. William Alexander Hewitt, Jan. 3, 1948; children—Anna Deere, Adrienne Deere, Alexander Southall. Asst. to mgr. Midvale Farms Corp., Tucson, 1945-47, dir., sec., 1945—, half owner, 1963—; owner, mgr. Friendship Farms, East Moline, Ill., 1955—; owner, joint mgr. Camelot Vineyards, Rutherford, Cal., 1960—; dir. Diagnostic Data Inc., Mountain View, Cal. Equestrian coach Japanese Self Def. Forces, 1967-68. Mem. Jr. League, San Francisco, 1951—; asst. to field dir. A.R.C., San Francisco, 1944-45, service cons., 1950-54; bd. dirs. YWCA, San Francisco, 1951-52, Moline Welfare Agy., 1959-69; governing mem. Arabian Horse Club Registry Am., 1963-64; trustee, pres.'s council Newman Coll., Davenport, Ia., 1969—, v.p. U.S. Modern Pentathlon Assn., 1971—; mem. U.S. Olympic Games Com.; mem. nat. bd. advisers Nat. Assn. for Retarded Children, 1967—; pres. Ill.-Ia. Assn. for Children with Specific Learning Problems, 1970—; mem. Ill. State Adv. Council Edn. Handicapped Children, 1973—; mem. exec. com. Nat. Reading Council, 1970-72; trustee Charles Deere Wiman Meml. Trust, Morris Animal Found., Lincoln Acad. of Ill., Rock Island Franciscan Hosp.; chmn. bd. trustees Butterworth Meml. Trust; trustee Arabian Horse Owners Found., 1961-73, mem. adv. bd., 1973—; mem. Women's Bd. Field Mus. Natural History, Chgo., 1972—; bd. dirs. Family YMCA, Rock Island; mem. service council United Way Rock Island, Ill. and Scott County, Ia.; 1973—. Mem. Internat. Arabian Horse Assn. (dir. 1964-67), Grayson Found., Arabian Horse Racing Assn., Am. Horse Show Assn. (life, judge Aragian div.), Ind. State Saddle Horse Judges Assn. Episcopalian. Club: Santa Barbara Yacht. Home: 38th St and Blackhawk Rd Rock Island IL 61201 Office: Friendship Farms Rural Route 2 Box 612 East Moline IL 61244

HEWITT, VIVIAN ANN DAVIDSON (MRS. JOHN HAMILTON HEWITT), librarian; b. New Castle, Pa., Feb. 17, 1925; d. Arthur Robert and Lela Luvada (Mauney) Davidson; A.B., Geneva Coll., 1943; B.S. in L.S., Carnegie Inst. Tech., 1944; m. John Hamilton Hewitt, Dec. 26, 1949; 1 son, John Hamilton III. Sr. asst. librarian Wylie Av. br., Homewood br. Carnegie Library of Pitts., 1944-49; instr., librarian Sch. Library Service, Atlanta U., 1949-51; researcher, asst. to dir. Readers' Reference Service, Crowell-Collier Co., 1953-55; librarian Rockefeller Found., 1955-63, Carnegie Endowment for Internat. Peace, N.Y.C., 1963—. Librarian, Rockefeller Found. Mexican Agrl. Program, Mexico City, Mexico, summer 1958; eastern regional dir. Jack & Jill of Am., Inc., 1967-69. Mem. aux. guild Sydenham Hosp. Bd. dirs. Windham Child Care Center, N.Y. Met. Reference and Research Library Agy. Recipient merit award United Fund Greater N.Y., 1965-72, Creative Writing award Geneva Coll. Mem. A.L.A., Spl. Libraries Assn. (pres. N.Y. chpt. 1970-71), Alpha Kappa Alpha. Democrat. Episcopalian. Club: Women's City (N.Y.C.). Contbr. articles to profl. jours. Home: 862 West End Av New York City NY 10025 Office: UN Plaza at 46th St New York City NY 10017

HEWLETT, CHRISTIE ANN, telephone co. exec.; b. Detroit, Aug. 2, 1942; d. Thomas Harry and Freda Ivy (Pepper) Hewlett; A.B. in Psychology, Randolph-Macon Woman's Coll., 1964; M.A., Wayne State U., 1966. With Mich. Bell Telephone Co., 1966—, statistician, 1966-70, staff supr. personnel research, 1970-72, personnel assessment dir., 1972—. Profl. chmn. Jr. League, Birmingham, Mich., 1972-73; vol. Consumer Protection Agy.; active New Horizons Women's Aux. Mem. Am. Psychol. Assn., Personnel Women Detroit, Founder's Soc. Detroit Inst. Arts, Randolph-Macon Woman's Coll. Alumnae Assn. (class agt.). Club: Women's City of Detroit. Home: 951 Twin Oaks Lane Birmingham MI 48008 Office: 19th Floor Detroit Hilton Hotel Detroit MI 48231

HEYCK, GERTRUDE PAINE DALY (MRS. THEODORE R. HEYCK), club woman; b. Houston, Nov. 30, 1910; d. David and Gertrude (Paine) Daly; student Wellesley Coll., 1929, Pembroke Coll., 1931-34; B.A., Brown U., 1934; m. Theodore R. Heyck, May 1, 1935; children—Jane Peel (Mrs. Donald H. Gaucher), Theodore Daly. Dir., Union Stock Yards, San Antonio, 1961-64. Mem. Jr. League. Clubs: Wellesley, Brown-Pembroke (v.p.). Home: 1907 Bolsover Rd Houston TX 77005

HEYDE, MARTHA BENNETT (MRS. ERNEST R. HEYDE), psychologist; b. New Bern, N.C., Jan. 31, 1920; d. George Spotswood and Katherine (McIntosh) Bennett; A.B., Barnard Coll., 1941; M.A., Columbia, 1949, Ph.D., 1959; m. Ernest R. Heyde, Aug. 17, 1946. Instr. psychol. founds. and services Tchrs. Coll., Columbia U., N.Y.C., 1953-60, research asst., career pattern study Horace Mann-Lincoln Inst., Tchrs. Coll. Columbia U., 1957-59, research asso., 1960-70, cons., 1970-73. Mem. Barnard Coll. Alumnae Council, 1956-61, 69—, pres. class 1956-61. Trustee, Barnard Coll., 1974—. Mem. Am. Psychol. Assn., Am. Personnel and Guidance Assn., Sigma Xi, Kappa Delta Pi, Pi Lambda Theta. Club: Barnard College (pres. 1969-71, dir.) (N.Y.C.). Contbr. to research monograph The Vocational Maturity of Ninth Grade Boys, 1960, Floundering and Trial After High Sch, 1967. Home: 140 Cabrini Blvd New York City NY 10033

HEYMAN, JUDITH ANN GREENBERG (MRS. GLENN R. HEYMAN), journalist; b. Chgo., Apr. 29, 1938; d. Ray Carl and Jeanette (Rosenblatt) Greenberg; student U. Mich., 1955-56; B.S., Northwestern U., 1961; m. Glenn R. Heyman, Dec. 18, 1960; children—Scott, Rachel, Joanne. Editorial asst. Golf Digest, 1961; reporter, Lerner Newspapers, Chgo., 1969—. Mem. Women in Communications, Alpha Lambda Delta. Home: 4401 Morse St Lincolnwood IL 60646 Office: 7519 N Ashland St Chicago IL 60626

HEYWARD, JEANNE, lawyer; b. Chgo.; d. Harry and Jeannette (Mowen) Heyward; B.A., U. Fla., 1952; LL.B. magna cum laude, U. Miami, 1955, J.D., 1967. Admitted to Fla. bar, 1955; since practiced in Miami; mem. firm Dean and Adams, 1959-66. Mem. Dade County Bar Assn., Fla. Bar, Chi Omega, Kappa Beta Pi. Home: 8225 SW 108th St Miami FL 33156 Office: Concord Bldg 66 W Flagler St Miami FL 33130

HEYWOOD, ANNE, actress; b. Birmingham, Eng., Dec. 11, 1937; d. Harold James and Edna Elizabeth (Heywood) Pretty; ed. schs. in Eng.; m. Raymond Stross, Feb. 11, 1960; 1 son, Mark. Came to U.S., 1965. Films include The Fox, 1967; The Midas Run, 1968; The Chairman, 1968; Lady of Monza, 1968; Novice, 1969; I Want What I Want, 1969. Recipient Baxendale award for art, 1957; United Critics award Berlin Film Festival, 1966. Address: care Artists Agy Corp 9229 Sunset Blvd Los Angeles CA 90069

HIATT, FRANCES LYONS MARGARET (MRS. NED LEE HIATT), social orgn. exec.; b. Odessa, Wash., Nov. 23, 1914; d. Burton J. and Grace Ellen (Patterson) Lyons; student Wheaton Coll., 1932-34; m. Ned Lee Hiatt, Apr. 4, 1946. Co-owner, mgr. Hiatts China Shop and Music Store, Seattle, Wash., 1954-68, Oak Harbor, Wash., 1969-70. Bd. dirs. Kate Duncan Smith Sch.; adv. bd. Tamasee Sch. Mem. D.A.R. (state regent Wash. 1970-72, nat. v.p. 1972—, v.p. Vice Pres.'s Gen. Club 1974—), Children Am. Revolution (sr. nat. v.p. Western region 1974—), Descs. Colonial Clergy, Huguenot Soc. (v.p. Western Wash. 1969-71), Colonial Soc., Colonial Dames 17th Century (state 2d v.p. 1966-68). Home: Route 1 Box 475 Anacortes WA 98221

HIATT, MAE DECK (MRS. CLARENCE WRIGHT HIATT), educator; b. Oskaloosa, Iowa, Mar. 10, 1893; d. Ulysses Grant and Minnie Helen (Tullis) Deck; student William Penn Coll., 1910-12, Columbia, 1917, Neb. U., 1940-41; m. Clarence Wright Hiatt, May 10, 1921; children—Ruth Ann (Mrs. Roger K. Phipps), Robert Deck. Tchr. high sch. English, in various Ia. and Neb. schs., 1914-17, 44-51; tchr. English N.E. and Lincoln high schs., Lincoln, Neb., 1951-57. Operator canteens U.S. Army, France and Eng., 1917-18. Mem. Neb. Writers Guild, Women's Overseas Service League, Am. Assn. U. Women, Am. Legion Aux. (nat. v.p. 1933-35). Republican. Mem. Order Eastern Star. Contbr. poems and articles to various mags. and anthologies. Home: 4300 Everett St Lincoln NE 68506

HIATT, MARGARET LOUISE, educator; b. Portland, Ore., July 17, 1922; d. Louis Eugene and Lottie Louise (Young) Hiatt; teaching certificate Maryhurst Coll., 1943; B.A., Western Wash. Coll., 1947; M.A., Columbia U., 1948; Ed.D., No. Colo. U., 1956. Tchr. elementary grades Powellhurst Sch. Dist. (Ore.), 1943-46; lab. sch. tchr., supr. Miami U., Oxford, O., 1948-49; tchr., supr. Ore. Coll. Edn., Monmouth, 1949-54, prof. elementary edn., 1956—; lab. sch. tchr., supr. N. Colo. U., Greeley, 1955-56. Cons. Northwest Region Edn. Lab., 1966-70. Delta Kappa Gamma fellow, 1954-55. Mem. Assn. Supervision and Curriculum Devel. (cons. interaction analysis 1967-68), Ore. Assn. for Supervision and Curriculum Devel. (pres. 1973-74), Nat. Council Accreditation of Tchr. Edn. (team mem. 1966—), Assn. Tchr. Edn., World Confedn. Orgns. of Teaching Professions (del. 1970, 73), Internat. Council Tchr. Edn., Delta Kappa Gamma, Pi Lambda Theta. Mem. Order Eastern Star. Author: English for Meaning 3, 1968, English for Meaning Practice 3, 1968, English for Meaning Practice 4, 1968. Home: 378 Walnut Dr Monmouth OR 97361 Office: Ed 157 Oregon Coll Edn Monmouth OR 97361

HIBEL, EDNA (MRS. THEODORE PLOTKIN), artist; b. Boston, Jan. 13, 1917; d. Abraham B. and Lena (Rubin) Hibel; student Boston Mus. Sch. Fine Arts, 1934-39; Ruth Sturtevant traveling fellow to Mexico, 1939; m. Theodore Plotkin, Jan. 7, 1940; children—Jon, Andrew, Richard. Exhibited Robert C. Vose Gallery, Boston, DeCordova Mus., Lincoln, Mass., Boston Mus. Fine Arts, Miami Beach Library Art Gallery, Mass. Sch. Art, Art Inst. Chgo., Boston Inst. Modern Arts, Am. Fedn. Art traveling exhbn., Pa. Acad. Art, Boston Mus. Modern Art, Logan Internat. Airport, Hall Art, N.Y.C., N.A.D.; works in permanent collections Boston Mus. Fine Arts, Norton Gallery Mus., West Palm Beach, Fla., Harvard, Boston U., U. N.H., Fleichman Coll., Cin., Detroit Art Inst., Milw. Mus. Art, Phoenix Art Mus., Flint Inst. Art, Springfield (Mass.) Mus. Fine Arts, de Saisset Mus., Santa Clara, Cal., Lowe Gallery, U. Miami (Fla.), La Jolla Mus. Cal., numerous pvt. collections; one-man shows Tanglewood, Lenox, Mass., 1962, Wenham (Mass.) Mus., 1962, Sally Maren Gallery, Marblehead, Mass., 1962, Hall of Art, N.Y.C., 1962, 66, 68, Constn. Gallery, Hartford, Conn., 1962, Marble Arch Gallery, Miami Beach, Fla., 1963, St. Armands Key, Sarasota, Fla., 1963, Oehlschlaeger Gallery, Sarasota, 1965-74, Chgo., 1965-73, Harmon Gallery, Naples, Fla. 1965-74, Galerie de Tours, Carmel, Cal., 1968-73, Guggenheim Gallery, London, Eng., 1971, Hammer Galleries, N.Y.C., 1971, Flint Inst. Art, 1973, Ft. Wayne (Ind.) Art Mus., 1974, others. Home: 2923 Lake Dr Riveria Beach FL 33404

HICKEY, DORALYN JOANNE, educator; b. Houston, Oct. 5, 1929; d. Thomas Earl and Ethel (Place) Hickey; B.A., Rice U., 1951; M.A., Presbyn. Sch. Christian Edn., 1953; M.L.S., Rutgers U., 1957; Ph.D., Duke, 1962. Asst. librarian Duke Div. Sch., 1954-56; asst. research specialist Rutgers U., Grad. Sch. Library Service, 1957-58; serials cataloger Rice U. Library, 1958-60; research asst., dept. religion Duke, Durham, N.C., 1960-62, spl. asst. serials dept., summer 1962-63; vis. instr. Sch. Library Sci., U. N.C. summer, 1962, asst. prof., 1962-68, asso. prof., 1968-74; prof. library sci., dir. Sch. Library Sci., U. Wis.-Milw., 1974—. spl. cons. Library Devel. Program, Am. Theol. Library Assn., 1964; vis. instr. Library Sch. U. Wis. summer, 1964; vis. asst. prof. Library Sch., U. Minn., summer 1966. Recipient Margaret Mann citation in cataloging and classification A.L.A., 1973. Mem. Spl. Libraries Assn., Am. (com. on accreditation 1970-74, chmn. serials sect. 1970-71, pres. resources and tech. services div. 1974—), Am. Soc. Information Sci., Am. Soc. Indexers, Southeastern, N.C. library assns., Am. Theol. Library Assn., Assn. Am. Library Schs., Am. Assn. U. Profs., Am. Assn. U. Women, Phi Beta Kappa, Sigma Xi (asso.), Delta Kappa Gamma, Beta Phi Mu. Author: Problems in Organizing Library Collections, 1972. Contbr. articles to profl. jours. Home: 2007 E Lake Bluff Blvd Shorewood WI 53211 Office: Sch Library Sci U Wis-Milw Milwaukee WI 53201

HICKEY, LOU ANN MARIE (MRS. WILLIAM A. HICKEY), civic worker; b. Miles City, Mont., Nov. 1, 1932; d. Louis Hodge and Anna (Rush) Rabun; B.A., Rosar Coll., 1954; m. William A. Hickey, Sept. 3, 1955; children—William L., Robert E., Thomas J. Tchr. lit. Nazareth Acad., La Grange, Ill., 1954-55; substitute tchr. various schs., 1959-60; dir., writer childrens shows for ch. groups, elementary schs., adult orgns., Minnetonka, Minn., 1966—; writer, producer, dir.

Lady of Liberty, 1971, Acentuate the Positive, 1972. Pres., Women's Club, YWCA, Minnetonka, 1971-73; jr. great books leader. Pres., St. Therese Deephaven Bd. Edn., Wayzata, Minn., 1968-73. Mem. League Women Voters, (dir. 1970-71, pres. alumni group 1970-73). Roman Catholic. Club: YWCA Woman (pres. Minnetonka 1971-73). Book reviewer, Mpls., 1968—. Home: 17014 Patricia Lane Minnetonka MN 55343

HICKEY, SISTER M. FELICE, educator; b. Scranton, Pa.; d. Richard F. and Anna (Flanagan) Hickey; B.A., Marywood Coll., 1948; M.A., St. Johns U., 1952, Ed.D., 1968. Entered Congregation of Sisters, Servants of Immaculate Heart of Mary; tchr. St. Rose Sch., Carbondale, Pa., 1938-44, St. Ephrem Sch., Bklyn., 1944-52, South Scranton Catholic High Sch., Scranton, Pa., 1952-56, Altoona (Pa.) Catholic High Sch., 1956-58; guidance counselor St. Mary High Sch., Manhasset, N.Y., 1958-64; asso. prof. edn., chmn. dept. counselor edn., dir. guidance Marywood Coll., Scranton, 1967—. Bd. dirs. Youth Counseling Service, Diocese of Scranton, 1969—; mem. Pa. State Adv. Com. for Counselor Edn., 1969-71. Mem. Am., Pa., Northeastern Pa. personnel and guidance assns., Assn. Counselor Edn. and Supervision, Pa. Sch. Counselors Assn., Assn. for Children with Learning Disabilities (dir. Pa. sch. dist.), Am. Assn. Higher Edn., N.E.A., Nat. Catholic Guidance Conf. Office: Marywood Coll Scranton PA 18509

HICKEY, MADELYN EASTLUND (MRS. JOSEPH V. HICKEY), editor; b. Bklyn., July 13, 1928; d. John Daniel and Madeline Elizabeth (Bailey) Eastlund; grad. high sch.; m. Joseph V. Hickey, June 28, 1969; children (by previous marriage)—Deborah (Mrs. Richard Tilford Simons), Daniel John Halstead. Pub., editor Twigs, 1961-64; instr. creative writing U. State N.Y., 1962-72; dir. L.I. Lit. Agy., 1965-68; pub., editor Verdure Publs., Panorama City, Cal., 1969—. Mem. Armed Forces Writers League (regional dir. 1963-66), Internat. Poetry Soc., Academia Internazionale Leonardo da Vinci, Western World Haiku Soc., Haiku Soc. Am., World Poetry Soc., Centro Studi E. Scambi, Internat. Platform Assn., Nat. Writers Club, Ill. State Poetry Soc., L.I. Writers Assn. (pres. 1968-70). Office: Box 2312 Sepulveda CA 91343

HICKEY, MARGARET (MRS. JOSEPH T. STRUBINGER), pub. affairs editor; b. Kansas City, Mo.; d. Charles and Elizabeth (Wynne) Hickey; J.D., U. Mo., 1928; LL.D., Cedarcrest Coll., 1952, MacMurray Coll., 1957, Wilson Coll., 1962; Litt.D., St. Mary's Coll.; Ed.D., Culver-Stockton Coll., 1966; m. Joseph T. Strubinger, Oct. 20, 1935 (dec. Oct. 1973). Founded Miss Hickey's Sch. Secs., St. Louis, 1933, dir.; pub. affairs editor Ladies Home Jour., 1946-52, 55—. Vice chmn. medico-social commn. Internat. Conf. Red Cross, Vienna, 1965; vice chmn. humanitarian law/commn. Internat. Red Cross Congress, Istanbul, Turkey, 1969, Tehran, Iran, 1973. Chmn. Social Devel. Commn.; chmn. women's policy com. War Manpower Commn., 1942-45; mem. Internat. Devel. Bd. (Point IV), 1950-52; mem. Pres.'s com. White House Conf. Edn., 1955; mem. Nat. Manpower Council; mem. Pres.'s Commn. on Status Women, 1962, chmn. citizens adv. council status of women; chmn. organizing com. Internat. Conf. Social Work, 1966; mem. commn. on social scis. NSF. Vis. com. Harvard Grad. Sch. Edn.; trustee Am. Youth Found., Tuskegee Inst., Brandeis U.; bd. govs. League of Red Cross, 1972—. Recipient Benjamin Franklin award, 1953. Mem. Mo. Bar, Nat. Conf. Social Welfare (pres. 1956-57), Nat. (pres. 1944-46, research and edn. com.), Internat. (v.p. 1946-48) fedns. bus. and profl. women's clubs, Jr. League Phila. (hon.), Kappa Beta Pi (hon.), Theta Sigma Phi. Clubs: Cosmopolitan (N.Y.C.); Soroptimist (St. Louis); Sulgrave (Washington); Am. Newspaper Women's. Home: 3940 E Timrod St Tucson AZ 85711 Office: care Ladies Home Journal 631 Lexington Av New York City NY 10022

HICKEY, ROSE VAN VRANKEN (MRS. ROBERT C. HICKEY), artist; b. Passaic, N.J.; d. Gilbert and Rose (Camwell) Van Vranken; B.A. cum laude, Pomona Coll., 1939; postgrad. N.Y.U., 1941-42; M.A., State U. Ia., 1943; study William Zorach, Robert Laurent, Art Students League N.Y., 1939-42; m. Robert C. Hickey, June 11, 1942; children—Kathryn, Robert, Stephen, Dennis, Sarah. One man shows Pasadena (Cal.) Mus. Art, 1945, Dreyer Galleries, Houston, 1963, Little Studio Gallery, Madison, Wis., 1963, U. Wis. Meml. Union, 1964, Nat. Design Center, N.Y.C., 1967, Madison Art Center, 1968, Inst. Texan Cultures, San Antonio, 1970, others; exhibitied group shows at Beloit Coll., Wis., 1964-66, Audubon Artists Nat. Ann., N.Y.C., 1965, San Diego Mus., 1945, Walker Art Center, Mpls., 1951, 54, Pasadena Art Mus., 1944-46, 62-63, Nat. Assn. Women Artists Travelling Graphic Shows, U.S., 1954, Europe, 1956, Madison Art Center, 1965-67, Little Studio Gallery, 1966; represented in permanent collections Monona Pub. Library, Madison U. Hosps., Madison, U. Ia., Smith Coll., numerous other pub., pvt. collections. Recipient 1st prize Los Angeles Mus. Fine Arts., 1944; Pasadena Art Mus., 1951; Des Moines Art Center, 1953; Ia. State Med. Assn., 1960; Madison Art Guild, 1964; purchase award Baytown (Tex.) Community Center, 1968; 1st prize etching Springfield (Mass.) Mus. Fine Arts, 1968; award for portrait sculpture C.L. Wolfe nat. ann. N.A.D., N.Y.C., 1969; 1st prize sculpture Houston Art League Ann., 1969; numerous others. Mem. Nat. Assn. Women Artists (medal honor 1952), Tex. Watercolor Soc., Pasadena Soc. Artists, Artists Equity, Acad. Artists Assn., Tex. Soc. Sculpture. Address: 435 Tallowood Houston TX 77024

HICKEY, SISTER RUTH CECELIA, hosp. adminstr.; b. Erie, Pa., July 28, 1914; d. Sherman Sylvester and Nell (McKinney) Hickey; grad. St. Vincent's Sch. Nursing, Toledo, 1936, B.S., d'Youville Coll., U. Montreal, 1949; postgrad. Cath. U., 1950, U. B.C.; M.A., Columbia, 1954. Head nurse medicine-surgery St. Vincent Hosp. and Med. Center, Toledo, 1936-38, nursing service and asst. adminstr., 1956-62, adminstr., 1962-69; nursing cons., 1969—; adminstr. St. Boniface Gen. Hosp., Man., Can., 1972—; nursing instr. St. Mary's Hosp., Montreal, 1940-42; supr. obstetrics, surgery St. Peter's Gen. Hosp., N.B., 1942-47, dir sch. nursing and nursing service Regina Grey Nuns Hosp., Regina, Sask., Can., 1955-56. Mem. Pres.'s Commn. on Employment Handicapped. Trustee Hosp. Planning Assn. Greater Toledo; vice chmn. bd. dirs. Tache Hosp., 1974—. Named Toledo Woman of Year, 1969. Fellow Am. Coll. Hosp. Adminstrs.; mem. Am. Acad. Med. Adminstrs. Am., Ohio hosp. nurses assns., Am. Cath. Psychol. Assn., Am., Ohio nurses assns. Nat. Council Cath. Nurses, Nat. Assembly Women Religious Edn., Man. Cath. Hosp. Assn. (pres. 1974—), Cath. Hosp. Assn. Can. (dir. 1973—). Address: 409 Tache Av Winnipeg MB R2H 2A6 Canada

HICKLIN, FANNIE FRAZIER, educator; b. Talladega, Ala.; d. Demus and Willie C. (Pulliam) Frazier; B.A., Talladega Coll., 1939; M.A., U. Mich., 1945; Ph.D. (E.B. Fred fellow), U. Wis., 1965, postgrad., 1970-71; 1 dau., Ariel Yvonne. Tchr. high schs., 1940-56; mem. faculty Ala. A. and M. Coll., 1956-61, U. Wis., Madison, 1961-64; mem. faculty U. Wis., Whitewater, 1964—, prof. speech and theatre, 1966—. Frequent high sch. cons. in theatre and oral interpretation; frequent speaker or reader for civic groups. Recipient Distinguished Tchr. award State U. Wis., Whitewater, 1970. Mem. Danforth Assos., Am. Assn. U. Profs., Am. Theater Assn., Speech Communication Assn., Am. Assn. U. Women, Phi Kappa Phi, Zeta Phi Eta (nat. v.p.), Alpha Kappa Alpha. Conglist. (deacon 1970—). Dir. numerous plays including children's plays touring elementary schs. Home: 3814 University Av Madison WI 53705 Office: 2078 Center of the Arts Whitewater WI 53190

HICKMAN, ELIZABETH PODESTA (MRS. FRANKLIN J. HICKMAN), educator; b. Livingston, Ill., Sept. 30, 1922; d. Louis and Della (Martin) Podesta; B.Ed., Eastern Ill. State U., 1943; M.A., George Washington U., 1966; postgrad. U. Chgo., 1945, U. Va., 1964-66, Northeastern U., 1967-68; m. Franklin J. Hickman, Mar. 17, 1944; children—Virginia (Mrs. Jorge R. Robert), Franklin J. Tchr. pub. sch., Ill., Ohio, Va., Naples, Italy, 1944-64; dir. coll. transfer guidance Marymount Coll., Arlington, Va., 1964-67; community counselor Div. Employment Security, Newton, Mass., 1968-69; tchr. English conversation, Fuchu, Japan, 1969-73; placement dir., career counselor Gt. Falls (Mont.) Coll., 1973-74; dir. counseling services Marymount Coll. Va., Arlington, 1974—; lectr. Far East div. U. Md., 1971-73. Spl. adviser Internat. Ranger Camps, Denmark, Switzerland, 1954—; spl. cons. Internat. Quaker Sch., English sect., Werkhoven, Netherlands, 1959-63. Vol., Red Cross, 1967—, Family Services, 1967—; leader Cub Scouts, Girl Scouts U.S.A., 1954-64. Served with WAVES, 1943-44. Mem. Am. Personnel and Guidance Assn., Nat. Vocational Guidance Assn., Am. Coll. Personnel Assn., Nat. Assn. Women Deans and Counselors, Sigma Sigma Sigma, Pi Lamba Theta. Roman Catholic. Address: 2807 N Glebe Rd Arlington VA 22207

HICKMAN, RUBY MILDRED, editor; b. Cedar Rapids, Ia., Feb. 28, 1906; d. William Alpheus and Alice May (Garretson) Hickman; B.A. magna cum laude, Coe Coll., 1930; M.A., State U. Ia., 1933, Ph.D., 1938. Abstractor, Linn County Abstract Co., Cedar Rapids, Ia., 1924-46, asst. sec., 1937-46; instr. Latin, English, Redfield (S.D.) High Sch., 1930-32; research asst. State U. Ia., 1933-37; editor Latin textbooks Scott Foresman & Co., Glenview, Ill., 1946-67, cons. editor, 1967—. Worker Am. Heart Assn. fund drives, 1959-68; mem. Phoenix Center Blind Aux. Contbg. mem. Chgo. Northside unit Rep. Women Vols., 1961-68. Named Woman of Week in Chgo., Chgo. Am. newspaper, 1955. Fellow Coe Alumni Assn. (Merit award 1956); mem. Am. Philol. Assn. (life mem.), Am. Classical League, Classical Assn. Middle West and So., Cal. Classical Assn., Ill. Classical Conf., Vergilian Soc., State U. Ia. Alumni Assn. (life), Quota Internat. (pres. Chgo. club 1959-60, treas. 1965-67, Woman of Year, Chgo., 1951, 59), Chgo. Classical Club (pres. 1959-61), Ariz. Zool. Soc., Christian Bus. and Profl. Women's Club, Phi Beta Kappa, Eta Sigma Phi, Phi Kappa Phi. Presbyn. (pres. Bus. Women's Club Chgo., 1950-51; vol. sec. Phoenix 1968—). Author: Ghostly Etiquette on the Classical Stage, 1938, 64. Home: 2506 N 22d Dr Phoenix AZ 85009 Office: 1900 E Lake Av Glenview IL 60025

HICKMAN, VERNA A. STRATTEN (MRS. PAUL E. HICKMAN), ret. ins. exec.; b. Oakhurst, Tex.; d. William and Rosetta (Nickerson) Wright; student U. Cal. at Los Angeles, 1941-42, U. So. Cal., 1944-45, 53-55; m. Paul E. Hickman, June 15, 1939. Adminstrv. sec. Golden State Mut. Life Ins. Co., Los Angeles, 1926-44, pub. relations officer, 1945-55, agy. adminstrn. officer, 1955-64; policyowners service officer, 1964-67, v.p., asst. treas., 1967-69, v.p., sec., 1969—, treas., 1970-74, ret., 1974. Fellow Life Office Mgmt. Assn.; mem. Pub. Relations Soc. Am. Office: 1999 W Adams Blvd Los Angeles CA 90051 also 4219 Don Alegre Pl Los Angeles CA 90008

HICKMAN, VIVIAN ELAINE TUTTLE (MRS. FORREST F. HICKMAN), librarian; b. Peterson, Ia., Mar. 22, 1920; d. David Dungan and Hedwig E.J. (Wolff) Tuttle; B.A., Buena Vista Coll., 1941; postgrad. U. No. Ia., summers 1959-62; M.A. in Librarianship, U. Denver, 1965; m. Forrest F. Hickman, June 3, 1944; children—David William, Iris Ellen (Mrs. Dean W. Baird), Stephanie Jean. Tchr. English and math. Maurice (Ia.) High Sch., 1941-42; tchr. math. Battle Creek (Ia.) High Sch., 1942-44; tchr. English and math. Highview Consol. Sch., Linn Grove, Ia., 1946-47; tchr. math. and German, librarian Geneseo Consol. Sch., Buckingham, Ia., 1959-64; librarian Bunger Jr. High Sch., Evansdale, Ia., 1964-65; catalog librarian U. Ia. Libraries, Iowa City, 1965—. Mem. Ia. Library Assn., Ia., Iowa City (pres. 1972, librarian 1973—) geneal. socs., Am. Legion Aux. Lutheran. Home: 1101 Essex St Iowa City IA 52240 Office: Catalog Dept U Ia Libraries Iowa City IA 52242

HICKOK, BEVERLY, librarian; b. San Francisco, Oct. 31, 1919; d. Clifton Ewing and Adelaide Valentine (Cutler) Hickok; A.B., U. Cal. at Berkeley, 1941, B.L.S., 1947; gen. secondary credential U. Cal. at Los Angeles, 1942. Mem. documents dept. staff Gen. Library, U. Cal., Berkeley, 1947-48, librarian Inst. Transp., U. Cal., Berkeley, 1948—. Served with WAVES, 1944-46. Mem. Spl. Libraries Assn. (chmn. nonserial pubs. com. 1965-66, 68-69, chmn. transp. div. 1956-57, chpt. pres. 1957-58, sec. pro tem transp. div., transp. research information services coordinating com. 1973—, chmn. nominating com. San Francisco Bay Area chpt. 1974, chmn. nominating com. transp. div. 1974—), U. Cal. Librarians Assn. (appointment, promotion and advancement com. 1974—). Contbr. articles to profl. pubs. Home: 1066 Creston Rd Berkeley CA 94708

HICKS, DONNA JEAN HAIR (MRS. KARL L. HICKS), home economist; b. Marion, O., Jan. 9, 1928; d. Lloyd Donald and B. Lucinda (Beard) Hair; B.S., Madison Coll., 1948; m. Karl L. Hicks, Dec. 21, 1951; 1 dau., Karen Lynn. Tchr. pub. schs., Va., 1948-59; home economist Va. Electric & Power Co., Warsaw, 1959-64; sr. home service adviser Fla. Power Corp., St. Petersburg, 1965-69, dir. home service, 1969-73, mgr. consumer information dept., 1973—. Mem. Am. Home Econs. Assn., Fla. Home Economists in Bus., Women's C. of C. of Greater Gulf Beaches, Inc. (pub. affairs com., pres.). Episcopalian. Home: 6746 9th Av N St Petersburg FL 33710 Office: Box 14042 St Petersburg FL 33733

HICKS, EDITH ADAMS (MRS. JAMES ADAMS), ednl. adminstr.; b. Barnwell, S.C., Sept. 6, 1939; d. Curtis L. and Lucille (Williams) Hicks; B.A., Antioch Coll., 1974; m. James Adams, Oct. 14, 1960; children—Ronald, Curtis, Craig, Paul, Paula, Kevin. Ednl. specialist Morrisania Community Corp., Bronx, N.Y., 1968-69; coordinator Community Research and Devel. Children's Circle Planning Corp., Bronx, 1969-70, exec. dir. Children's Circle Day Care, 1970—. Vice pres. Shardig Realty Corp., Bronx. Mem. Bronx Regional Mental Retardation Com.; del. to Nat. Black Assembly, 1974; mem. Community Sch. Bd., Bronx, 1970—; mem. chancellor's com. N.Y.C. Bd. Edn., 1973—. Recipient Distinguished Service award Morrisania Edn. Council, 1969, 72, 73; Community Service award Community Sch. Dist. 9, 1973; Dedication to Children plaque Community Elementary Sch., 1972; Outstanding Performance plaque Edn. Adv. Council, 1973. Mem. Nat. Day Care Council, Soc. for Advancement and Betterment of Children, N.Y. Assn. Black Educators, Afro-Am. Ethnic Orientation Soc. (sec. 1970-73). Home: 531 E 167th St New York City NY 10456 Office: 1275 Grand Concourse New York City NY 10452

HICKS, HELEN JENNIE HARVEY (MRS. LAWRENCE HICKS), bus. exec.; b. Granby, Que., Can., Feb. 13, 1914; d. Arthur H. and Jennie (Shorten) Harvey; teaching diploma Macdonald Coll., Ste. Anne de Bellevue, Que., 1933; student Notre Dame Bus. and Comml., Montreal; m. Lawrence Hicks, July 18, 1936; children—Lawrence Arthur, Helen Claudia (Mrs. Mervin L. Brownsberger). Sec. to advt. mgr. Ayerst, McKenna & Harrison, Montreal, Que., 1935-37; sec. to pres. Organics, Inc., Chgo., 1944-66, v.p., 1950—, sec.-treas., 1966—; v.p. Lagrange Labs., Chgo. and Fennville, Mich., 1969—. Home: 2215 Lunt Av Chicago IL 60645 Office: 7125 N Clark St Chicago IL 60626

HICKS, SISTER JEANNE ELLEN, physician; b. Montclair, N.J., Aug. 20, 1940; d. Alfred Mark and Mary Ellen (McManus) Hicks; B.A., Georgian Court Coll., 1962; M.D., U. Tenn., 1966. Profl. musician, organist, N.J., Tenn., N.C., 1959-69; tchr. biology and math. N.J. Pub. Schs. System, 1962-63; intern medicine Watts Hosp., Durham, N.C., 1966; rotating intern City Memphis Hosps., 1966-67; staff physician Duke VA Hosp., Durham, 1967-69; joined Dominican Sisters, 1969; asst. to pub. health commr. City of Columbus (O.), 1969-70; practice internal medicine and geriatrics, Cin., 1970-72; jr. resident internal medicine U. Cin. Med. Center, 1970-71, sr. resident internal medicine, 1971-72, resident instr. internal medicine, 1970-72; resident cons. medicine Cin. Gen. Hosp., VA Hosp., Cin.; fellow in internal medicine, instr. U. Conn. Med. Center, Hartford Hosp., 1972-73; instr. medicine, clin. fellow in infectious diseases, rheumatology and immunology Yale-New Haven Med. Center, 1973—. Cons., New Haven Health Dept., Albertus Magnus Coll. Mem. Cin. Acad. Medicine, A.C.P. (asso.), Conn., New Haven County med. socs. Democrat. Home: Albertus Magnus College 790 Prospect St New Haven CT 06511 Office: Yale-New Haven Hospital 333 Cedar St New Haven CT 06510

HICKS, KATHRYN KEATON, computer specialist; b. Cuthbert, Ga., June 28, 1932; d. James Madison and Edna Irene (Dunn) Keaton; A.B. in Math. and Biology, Ga. State Coll. for Women, 1952; various courses U. Chattanooga, U. Tenn. at Chattanooga; m. Lester Melvin Hicks, June 14, 1969. Statis. clk. TVA, Chattanooga, 1952-56, engrng. aide, 1956-59, mathematician, 1959-68, supr. systems programing services, 1968—. Tchr. computer course U. Chattanooga. Mem. Assn. Computing Machinery (com. mem.), TVA Engrs. Assn. (group rep., hon. mem.). Baptist. Home: 413 S Mission Ridge Rd Rossville GA 30741 Office: 116 Old Post Office Chattanooga TN 37401

HICKS, LINDA RUTH (MRS. TOMMY GEARLD HICKS), newspaper co. exec.; b. Jefferson, Tex., July 21, 1940; d. Thomas Wesley and Verna Exzine (Bramlett) Morris; grad. high sch.; m. Tommy Gearld Hicks, July 26, 1958; children—Tommy Gearld, Angela Jona, Buster Alan, Mathew Garth. Owner, editor Dublin Progress, Dublin, Tex., 1965—. Chmn. ways and means com. Dublin (Tex.) P.T.A., 1973-74, stage, parade, queen dir. fall fair, 1966—. Bd. dir. Dublin Hist. Soc., 1971—. Baptist. Home: Box R Dublin TX 76446 Office: 116 W Blackjack Dublin TX 76446

HICKS, MILDRED PHILLIPS (MRS. ABRAM BERTON HICKS), county ofcl.; b. Albany, Ga., Nov. 18, 1913; d. James Field and Rebecca (Powell) Phillips; B.S. magna cum laude, U. Houston, 1961; m. Abram Berton Hicks, July 30, 1933; children—James Berton, Donald Shelby. Adminstrv. asst. U. Houston, 1952-61; free lance feature writer Houston Chronicle, 1950-61; asst. health educator Memphis-Shelby County Health Dept., Memphis, 1962-65, information coordinator, 1965-68, information dir., library supr., 1969—. Vice pres. Memphis Alcohol and Drug Council, 1971-73. Mem. Women in Communications (pres. 1970-72), Assn. for the Preservation of Tenn. Antiquities, D.A.R., W. Tenn. Hist. Soc. Episcopalian. Co-editor, contbr. History of Medicine in Memphis, 1971. Home: 1746 Carr Av Memphis TN 38104 Office: 814 Jefferson Av Memphis TN 38105

HICKS, PATRICIA FAIN (MRS. THOMAS EDWARD HICKS), pub. relations exec.; b. Brownwood, Tex., Dec. 16, 1927; d. William Taylor and Kathryn Ellen (Anderson) Fain; B.A., U. Tex., 1947; B.A., Tex. Tech Coll., 1948, M.S., 1951, Ph.D., 1953; m. Thomas Edward Hicks, Mar. 12, 1966. Analytical chemist Mallinckrodt Chem. Works, St. Louis, 1948-50, editor, tech. writer, 1957-59, asst. to v.p., tech. dir., 1960-71, asst. to dir. pub. relations, 1971—; with Los Alamos Sci. Lab., 1953-55; asst. prof. chemistry Tex. Tech Coll., Lubbock, 1955-57. Robert Welch Found. grantee, 1956-57. Mem. Am. Chem. Soc., Sigma Xi, Delta Delta Delta. Office: 3600 N Second St St Louis MO 63147

HICKS, VIRGINIA SYBIL DRAKE (MRS. HERMAN J. HICKS), editor; b. Ft. Sumner, N.M., Mar. 17, 1920; d. Paul S. and Calley Fay (Bates) Drake; student U. Munich (Germany), 1954-56, U. Bordeaux (France), 1956-57, So. Meth. U., 1972-73; m. Herman J. Hicks, July 20, 1941; children—Patricia, Virginia, Ricky, Heidi. Editor, Protocall, Washington, 1959-60, Contact, St. Louis, 1962-63, Totem Topics, Anchorage, 1968-70, Kaleidiscope, Kansas City, Mo., 1970-71; research and final manuscript editor Nat. Capitol, Washington, 1964-68. Mem. Internat. Platform Assn., Nat., Kansas City, Dallas, Alaska (Top award for best mag. in Alaska 1970-71) press clubs, Women in Communication. Home: 4610 Holborn Av Annandale VA 22003

HIDUCHENKO, KATHERINE, physician; b. Ukraine, Aug. 13, 1929; d. Fedor M. and Paraska (Horoshko) Hiduchenko; came to U.S., 1950, naturalized, 1956; cand. med. Ludwig-Maximillian U., Munich, Germany, 1950; M.D., U. Minn., 1954; m. Jakiw Karpuk, Aug. 17, 1967; 1 dau., Oksana H. Karpuk. Intern, Chgo. Presbyn. Hosp., 1954-55; resident internal medicine U. Minn. Hosps., Mpls., 1955-56; resident internal medicine VA Hosp., Bklyn., 1956-58, research asst., 1958-59; practice medicine, specializing in internal medicine, Montclair and Newark, N.J., 1960-64, N.Y.C., 1964-70, Mpls., 1971—; mem. staffs Mt. Sinai Hosp., Luth.-Deaconess Hosp. (both Mpls.); instr. medicine N.Y. Med. Coll., 1964-69, asst. prof., 1970. Diplomate Am. Bd. Internal Medicine. Mem. A.M.A., Minn., Hennepin County med. socs., Am. Diabetes Assn. Home: 6232 Knoll Dr Edina MN 55436 Office: 2219 Chicago Av Minneapolis MN 55404

HIEATT, CONSTANCE BARTLETT (MRS. ALLAN KENT HIEATT), educator; b. Boston, Feb. 11, 1928; d. Arthur Charles and Eleonora (Very) Bartlett; student Smith Coll., 1945-47; B.A., Hunter Coll., 1953, M.A., 1957; Ph.D., Yale, 1959; m. Allen Kent Hieatt, Oct. 25, 1958. Lectr., City Coll. N.Y., 1959-60; asst. prof. Queensborough Community Coll., City U. N.Y., 1960-62, asso. prof., 1962-65; asso. prof. St. John's U., Jamaica, N.Y., 1965-67, prof., 1967-70; prof. dept. English U. Western Ont., 1970—. Recipient Can. Council Research Grant, 1971-72. Mem. Mediaeval Acad. Am., Modern Lang. Assn. Am., Internat. Arthurian Soc., Soc. Advancement Scandinavian Studies, Children's Lit. Assn., Authors Guild, Canadian Authors Assn., Assn. Canadian Univ. Tchrs. English. Anglican. Author: Beowulf and Other Old English Poems, 1967; Essentials of Old English, 1968; The Castle of Ladies, 1973; others. Mem. editorial bd. English Studies in Can., 1973—. Home: 191 St James St London ON Canada

HIEBERT, ELIZABETH BLAKE (MRS. HOMER L. HIEBERT), civic worker; b. Mpls., July 18, 1910; d. Henry Seavey and Grace (Riebeth) Blake; student Washburn U., 1926-30; B.S., U. Tex. 1933; m. Homer L. Hiebert, Aug. 29, 1935; children—Grace Elizabeth (Mrs. John E. Beam), Mary Sue (Mrs. Donald Wester), John Blake, Henry Leonard, David Mark. Sec. Topeka Regional Sci. Fair, 1958-60, bd. dirs., 1964—; bd. dirs. YMCA 1968—, Topeka

(Kan.) Friends of the 300; water safety instr. and swimming tchr. of handicapped. Hon. fellow Harry S. Truman Library. Mem. D.A.R., Daus. Am. Colonists, Am. Assn. U. Women (dir. 1944-62, 65—), N.E. Hist. and Geneal. Soc., Tex. U. Alumni, Am. Home Econs. Assn., Shawnee County Med. Aux. (past pres.), Nat. Audubon, Met. Mus. Art, P.E.O. (past local pres. cooperative bd.), Topeka Art Guild, Nat. Soc. Ancient and Hon. Arty., Nat. Trust Historic Preservation, Internat. Oceanographic Found., Nat. League Am. Pen Women (pres. 1970-72), Washburn Alumnae Assn. Am. Assn. State and Local History, Colo. Hist. Assn., Shawnee County Hist. Soc., Detroit Soc. Geneal. Research, Colo., Minn. hist. socs., Smithsonian Assos., Oceanic Soc., Internat. Platform Assn., Delta Kappa Gamma (hon.), Delta Gamma. Club: Topeka Knife and Fork. Editor children's page Household mag., 1934-39. Home: 1517 Randolph Topeka KS 66604

HIERS, MARGARET HANES (MRS. EMORY MITCHELL HIERS), educator; b. Jonesboro, Ga., Nov. 3, 1917; d. Orville Arlington and Martha Elizabeth (Adams) Hanes; B.S., Valdosta State Coll., 1960; Ed.M. (fellow), U. Ga., 1967, Ed.D., 1970; m. Emory Mitchell Hiers, May 23, 1938; children—Emory Mitchell, Emily (Mrs. Robin Thomas), John Turner, Alfred Adams. With Dept. Pub. Welfare, Atlanta, 1937-38; elementary tchr. Moultrie (Ga.) City Schs., 1955-59, 60-62, 62-65; tchr. educable mentally retarded, 1965-66, supervising tchr. for student tchrs., 1963-65; instr. spl. edn. U. Ga., Athens, 1967-70; asso. prof. spl. edn. Valdosta (Ga.) State Coll., 1970—. Reading tchr. Pilot Gifted Program, Moultrie, Ga., 1962-65; cons. to various pub. schs. and sheltered workshops, Tng. Centers for Handicapped. Mem. adv. bd. Tng. Centers for Handicapped, 1972—. Mem. N.E.A., Am. Assn. Mental Deficiency, Ga. Assn. for Retarded Children (chmn. edn. com. 1973-74), Ga. Assn. for Mental Health, Ga. Assn. Educators, Council for Exceptional Children, Found. for Exceptional Children, Ga. Assn. Tchr. Educators, Ga. Assn. Gifted Edn., D.A.R., Phi Kappa Phi, Delta Kappa Gamma, Kappa Delta Pi. Baptist. Home: 514 Third St Moultrie GA 31768 Office: Valdosta State College Valdosta GA 31601

HIGBEE, ANN GERMAN (MRS. JAMES HIGBEE), advt. agy. exec.; b. Newark, N.Y., May 6, 1942; d. Roger Harold and Charlotte Mae (Ryan) German; student Keuka Coll., 1960-61; B.S., U. Md., 1964; postgrad. U. Coll. Syracuse U., 1965-67; m. James Lyman Higbee, June 26, 1965; 1 son, Travis James. Nat. liaison Am. Field Service, N.Y.C., 1964-65; v.p., account exec. Rath Orgn., Syracuse, N.Y., 1965-71, T.A. Best, Inc., Skaneateles, N.Y., 1972—. Am. abroad chmn. Central N.Y. com. Am. Field Service, 1965-68, sec., 1971-73; spl. events publicity chmn. Jr. League Syracuse, 1969, corr. sec., 1971-72, spl. events chmn., 1971, v.p., 1973-74, pres., 1974—. Bd. dirs., mem. pub. relations com. Literacy Vols. Am., Inc., Central N.Y. A.R.C. Am. Field Service scholar, Istanbul, Turkey, 1959. Mem. Pub. Relations Soc. Am., Women in Communications (spl. events chmn. N.Y.C. chpt. 1969-71, pres. 1972—), Kappa Alpha Theta Alumnae (pres. 1968-70). Republican. Home: 112 Guilford Rd Syracuse NY 13224 Office: 42 E Genesee St Skaneateles NY 13152

HIGBEE, CHARLOTTE MARGARET, govt. ofcl.; b. Milw., Jan. 19, 1921; B.S., U. Wis., 1941, LL.B., 1948. Admitted to Wis. bar, 1948; employment coordinator, equal rights div. State of Wis., Milw., 1956-71; contract compliance officer Milw. dist. Dept. Def., 1971-73, chief Milw. operations Office of Contract Compliance, 1973—. Mem. League Women Voters (Wis. div. 1965-67), Order of Coif, Phi Beta Kappa, Zeta Phi Eta, Phi Kappa Phi, Delta Sigma Rho. Home: 9223 N 70th St Milwaukee WI 53223 Office: 744 N 4th St Milwaukee WI 53203

HIGBEE, FLORENCE SALICK, librarian; b. Milw.; d. Otto Thomas and Mary (Reiter) Salick; B.A., U. Wis., 1933; M.A. in L.S., Cath. U. Am., 1965; 1 dau., Joan Florence. Reference librarian Shirlington Br. of Arlington County Pub. Libraries, Arlington, Va., 1965-67; br. librarian Glencarlyn br. Arlington County Pub. Libraries, Arlington, 1967, Columbia Pike Br., 1967-73; translator, archivist. Mem. nominating com. Literacy Council No. Va., Inc. State of Va. Grad. fellow, 1964-65. Mem. A.L.A. Am. Malacological Union. Home: 13 N Bedford Arlington VA 22201

HIGDON, IDA JEAN DOUGLASS (MRS. WILFORD DAIN HIGDON), owner youth camp; b. McAlester, Okla., Oct. 17, 1919; d. Joseph and Della (Humphrey) Douglass; grad. So. Coll. Beauty Culture, 1938, U. Okla., 1957-58; m. Wilford Dain Higdon, Jan. 1, 1943; children—James, Noel, Albert Dain, Janice Jean. Owner, operator Jean's Beauty Shop, McAlester, Okla., 1939-44, Pleasanton, Tex., 1956-58, Camp Jada for Girls, San Antonio, 1969—. Coordinator Bapt. Student Union Weekly Free Luncheons, San Antonio Coll., 1969-73; dir. Rest Home Devotional Group, 1969-73; hostess numerous fgn. students various groups, intermittently, 1958-74. Leader Cub Scouts Am., Pleasanton, Tex., 1952-54, Little League, Pleasanton, 1956-58; planner, dir. World Assembly of Girls Aux., Hemisfair, 1968, Bd. dirs. Bapt. Girls, Bexar County, Tex., 1964-69. Mem. Am. Camping Assn. (program chmn. Tex. 1974), Am. Legion Aux. (dir. 1969-73), Bapt. Women's Missionary Union, Sigma Phi Epsilon Mothers. Rotary Ann (dist. gov. 1972-73). Home: 139 Knibbe Rd San Antonio TX 78209 Office: Star Route 2 Box 326 Fischer TX 78623

HIGGINBOTHAM, WILMA DODSON, newspaperwoman; b. Charleston, W.Va., July 14, 1912; d. James William and Tina (Rhodes) Dodson; student Marshall U., 1928-31; m. W. Murrell Higginbotham, June 10, 1937 (div. Sept. 1943); 1 dau., Cynthia Kaye (Mrs. C.K. Payne). Reporter, Charleston Gazette, 1933-40; with W.Va. Rev. mag., Charleston, 1943-48; women's editor Charleston Daily Mail, 1948—. Active A.R.C.; mem. Def. Adv. Com. on Women in Services, 1969-71. Recipient prize as best woman feature writer W.Va. Press Assn., 1958, 59, 60. Mem. Child Study League, Alpha Iota. Clubs: Pilot (pres. 1962-63), Army-Navy (Charleston). Home: 1831 Oak Ridge Dr Charleston WV 25311 Office: 1000 Virginia St E Charleston WV 25330

HIGGINS, ALOYCE HUBEL, needle art designer, polit. worker; d. Albert Anthony and V. DeLella (Hulian) Hubel; B.A., St. Olaf Coll., 1950; children—Charles Hubel, Paul Dudley. Needle art designer, 1970—; owner The Yarn House, Excelsior, Minn., 1972—; exhibited Minnetonka Centre Arts; tchr. music Cal. and Minn. Precinct commr.; chmn. 2d Dist. Com.; mgr. Glaeser for Senate campaign, 1972, Metcalf for Senate campaign, 1964-68, Hagedorn for Congress, 1974. Chmn. Laketown Planning Commn., Carver City, Minn., 1961; bd. dirs. YWCA, 1973—. Home: Rural Route 1 Box 573-B Excelsior MN 55331 Office: 429 2nd St Excelsior MN 55331

HIGGINS, CLELIA (MRS. CLARENCE B. HIGGINS), art gallery exec.; b. Meriden, Conn., 1927; d. Mario C. and Marjorie (Suzio) Petruceli; student Mary Washington Coll., 1943-44; m. Clarence B. Higgins, July 23, 1945; 1 dau., Holly Reid. Propr., dir. Galleria Clelia, 1965—, Gallery 19, Washington, 1972—. Lectr. modern art, 1965—. Bd. dirs. Rosslyn Art Gallery, Arlington, Va., Old Alexandria (Va.) Gallery, Inc. Clubs: Army-Navy, Fairfax Country. Home: 904 St Stephens Rd Alexandria VA Office: 2111 K St NW Washington DC 20037

HIGGINS, LOIS LUNDELL, criminologist; b. Omaha, Neb., Aug. 4, 1909; d. Alvin O. and Gertrude (Hogan) Lundell; A.B. cum laude, Mt. Mary Coll., Milw., 1931, LL.D., 1949; M.S.W., Loyola U., 1947; certificate in police adminstrn., So. Police Inst., U. Louisville, 1955; certificate in human behavior and human relations, Western Res. U., 1955; certificate in law enforcement, Inst., Youth and Crime, N.Y.U., 1955; m. Frank James Higgins, Oct. 12, 1935; children—Frank James, Mary Lois. Caseworker, United Charities Chgo., 1932; probation officer Juvenile Ct., Cook County, Ill., 1933-34; social service worker Municipal Ct., Chgo., 1934-35; Civil Service policewoman, City Chgo., 1937—; on leave of absence, acting as dir. Crime Prevention Bur., 1950-63, crime prevention coordinator Municipal Ct., 1949, dir. bur. (by virtue of this position rates as a chief of police), also coordinator representing the chief justice Municipal Ct., 1950-63; exec. sec. Crime Prevention, Inc., 1958—; cons. on crime prevention and allied fields; prof. criminology U. Seven Seas, 1963—, trustee, 1964—; lectr., writer numerous publs. in fields; editor, pub. Police Digest, 1963—; editorial dir. Valor, 1961-63. Mem. Pres.'s Com. Juvenile Delinquency and Youth Crime; del. 1st, 2nd and 3d congresses of Am. Women Leaders, Washington, 1962, 63, 64, 2d UN Congress on Prevention Crime and Treatment Offenders, London, 1960, 3d congress, Stockholm, Sweden, 1965. Bd. govs. Mt. Mary Coll., 1936—. Internat. chmn. family and youth Internat. Fedn. Cath. Alumnae, 1946—; mem. nat. commn. Nat. Conf. Christians and Jews, 1959; pres. Internat. Assn. Women Police, 1956—; nat. treas. Kappa Gamma Pi, 1936-38. Named woman of distinction Woman's Ad Club, Chgo., 1952; recipient sheriff's medal for civic accomplishment (Cook County), 1952, plaque Italian Coll. Club, 1952, citation in Congl. Record, 1954, citation Chgo. City Council, 1955, certificate of merit and gold star Nat. Police Officers Assn. Am., 1956, citation Ill. Assn. Chiefs Police for work in legislation (1st Police Acad. for Ill.); Decadary Merit Award, Am. Assn. Criminology, 1963, Sara R. Ehrmann Award, 1964; Golden Plate Salute to Excellence, Am. Acad. Achievement, 1964; medallion 100 Outstanding Citizens of Chgo., 1971; named to Nat. Police Hall of Fame, 1959. Mem. Am. Assn. U. Women, Chgo. (organizer, pres. 1949-52), Ill. (mem. bd.) Policewomen's assns., Fedn. Crime Prevention and Control (sec. 1950-51), Internat. (com. crime prevention 1957—), Ill. (chmn. com. crime prevention and youth problems; mem. legislation com. 1955) assns. chiefs police. Author: Policewoman's Manual, 1960; (with others) Criminology and Crime Prevention, 1959. Office: 6655 N Avandale St Chicago IL 60631

HIGGINS, MARJORIE JOAN (MRS. LESLIE GRANT HIGGINS), newspaperwoman; b. Somerset, Pa., Jan. 5, 1923; d. Paul Sheldon and Mary Elizabeth (Witt) Bell; B.A., Kent State U., 1944; m. Leslie Grant Higgins, July 9, 1944; children—Marc, Jill (Mrs. Wayne Wells), Linnell. Area corr. Record-Courier, Ravenna, O., 1962-66, gen. assignment reporter, asst. on county copy desk, 1966-67, county-area editor, 1967—. Recipient 1st place award for page edited regularly by a woman other than society page Ohio Press Women contest, 1969, 3d place award for page edited regularly by a woman other than society page Nat. Press Women contest, 1969. Mem. Nat., Ohio press women, Nat., Ohio newspaper women's assns., Kent State U. Alumni Assn., Women in Communications. Republican. Mem. United Ch. of Christ. Home: 1594 Waterloo Rd Suffield OH 44260 Office: Record-Courier Chestnut St Ravenna OH 44266

HIGGINS, RUTH ELLEN, theatre dir.; b. Streator, Ill., Jan. 23, 1945; d. Thomas Francis and Mary Madeline (Ahearn) Higgins; B.S., No. Ill. U., 1967; M.A., U. Neb., 1968. Tchr., Glenbrook (Ill.) North High Sch., 1968-69; dir., instr. theatre and speech Highland Community Theatre, Freeport, Ill., 1969—; asso. producer Dinglefest Theatre Co.; dir. nat. champion prodn. Jr. Coll. Readers Theatre, 1973. Sec. Am. Fedn. Tchrs. Local 1957, 1970-71, v.p., 1972-73. Bd. govs. Nat. Collegiate Players. Mem. Speech Communications Assn., Nat. Assn. Collegiate Players (pres.), Am. Ednl. Theatre Assn., Central States Speech Assn., Ill. Speech and Theatre Assn. Editor faculty newsletter Ill. Assn. Jr. and Community Colls., 1970-71. Home: Rural Route 2 Freeport IL 61032 Office: Pearl City Rd Freeport IL 61032

HIGGINS, RUTH LOVING, coll. dean emeritus, prof. history emeritus; b. Columbus, O., June 21, 1895; d. Charles and Jessie Hoover (Schatzman) Higgins; B.A., B.S. in Edn., Ohio State U., 1917, M.A. (scholarship), 1921, Ph.D. (2 fellowships), 1926; postgrad. U. Wis., summer 1922, Cambridge U., Eng., summer 1929; LL.D., Beaver Coll., 1953. Tchr. history and civics, Ohio high schs., 1917-20, 22-23, instr. history, polit. sci. Elmira (N.Y.) Coll., 1924-25; asst. prof. Earlham Coll., Richmond, Ind., 1925-26; prof., head dept. Huntingdon Coll. (formerly Woman's Coll. of Ala.), Montgomery, 1926-34; mem. history faculty U. Ala., summers 1930-31; dean of coll., prof. history Beaver Coll., Glenside, Pa., 1934-60, chmn. dept. history and govt., 1949-60, now dean, prof. history and govt. emeritus. Trustee Cheltenham Adult Sch., 1940-48 (pres. 1943-45); mem. women's com. Japan Internat. Christian U. Found.; Am. Conf. Acad. Deans (sec., treas., 1945-47, editor, 1946-48). Mem. League Women Voters, Am. Acad. Polit. and Social Sci., Am. Hist. Assn., Orgn. Am. Historians (mem. exec. com. 1936-39), Nat. (publs. com. 1935-37), Pa. (chmn. publs. 1938-41) assns. women deans and counselors, Ohio State U. Assn., Am. Assn. U. Women (Columbus bd. 1965-70), World Affairs Council Phila. (past mem. speakers bur.), D.A.R., Phi Alpha Theta, Delta Kappa Gamma (state founder Ala. and Pa.). Presbyn. (former deacon) Author: Expansion in New York, with Especial Reference to Eighteenth Century, 1931; American Conference of Academic Deans—Developments and Abstracts, 1945-1969, 1969; also articles, hist. revs. Home: 5155 N High St Apt 808 W Columbus OH 43214

HIGGINS, VERNA JESSIE, educator; b. Middle Musquodoboit, N.S., Can., Feb. 11, 1943; d. Gerald Moritimer and Jessie Elizabeth (Burnett) Higgins; B.S. (Henry Burton Dewolfe scholar), Acadia U., 1964; M.S., Cornell, 1966, Ph.D. (Allied Chem. and Dye Corp. fellow), 1969. Prof., dept. botany U. Toronto (Ont.), 1969—. Mem. Am., Canadian phytopathol. socs., Fedn. Ont. Naturalists, Canadian Nature Fedn., Toronto Field Naturalists, Sigma Xi, Phi Kappa Phi. Home: 77 Quebec Av Apt 932 Toronto ON M6P 2T4 Canada

HIGGINSON, MARGARET ANN VALLIANT (MRS. WILLIAM JOHN HIGGINSON III), editor; b. Georgetown, Del.; d. William Enos and Emma (Friedel) Valliant; B.S., U. N.M., 1947, M.A., 1949; m. William John Higginson III, June 22, 1960. Caseworker, Del. Bd. of Welfare, Dover, 1949; personnel asst. John H. Dulany & Sons, Inc., Fruitland, Md., 1950; exec. sec. Major A. P. de Seversky, N.Y.C., 1951-52; adminstrv. asst. Glover Assos., Inc., N.Y.C., 1953-58; corp. sec., dir. office mgr. Glover Assos. Ltd., Montreal, Que., Can., 1958-61; research mgr. Collier Books, N.Y.C., 1962; orgzn. specialist Girl Scouts U.S.A., N.Y.C., 1963; sr. research asso. Am. Mgmt. Assn., N.Y.C., 1964-70; editor Research Inst. Am., N.Y.C., 1970—. Mem. Am. Sociol. Assn., Acad. Mgmt. Author: Managing with EDP, 1965; Management Policies I, 1966; Management Policies II, 1966. Home: 2 Tudor Pl New York City NY 10017 Office: 589 Fifth Av New York City NY 10017

HIGGINSON, MURIEL JEAN, librarian; b. New Liskeard, Ont., Can., Sept. 17, 1937; d. Charles Gordon and Muriel Theresa (Maitland) Higginson; B.S. in Nursing, McMaster U., 1959; B.L.S., U. Toronto, 1963. Staff nurse Halton County Health Unit, Oakville, Ont., 1959-62; staff librarian acquisitions div. Nat. Library of Can., Ottawa, Ont., 1963-65, chief acquisitions div., 1965-71, chief serials div., 1971-73, spl. asst. to nat. librarian, 1973—. Mem. Am., Canadian (subcom. on prof. staff 1969-72, chmn. elections com. 1971-72), Ont. library assns., Profl. Inst. Pub. Service Can., Library Assn. (Gt. Britain), Fedn. Ont. Naturalists, Library Assn. Ottawa. Home: 70 McEwen Av Apt 605 Ottawa ON K2B SM3 Canada Office: 395 Wellington St Ottawa ON K1A ON4 Canada

HIGH, HARRIETT ANN BROADDUS (MRS. JACK EUGENE HIGH), educator; b. Muskogee, Okla., May 17, 1922; d. Bower Slack and Harriett Ann (Noland) Broaddus; student Muskogee Jr. Coll., 1939-40, Randolph Macon Women's Coll., 1940-41, U. Colo., summer 1944; A.B., U. Okla., 1943, LL.B., 1945; tchr.'s certificate Central State Coll., Edmond, Okla., 1967; m. Jack Eugene High, Oct. 12, 1946; children—Jack Michael, David Royce, Nathan Rainey. Admitted to Okla. bar, 1945; spl. atty. Dept. Justice, 1945; tchr. Heritage Hall High Sch., Oklahoma City, 1969-74. Active YWCA, Okla. Art Center; former capt. drive United Fund; mem. women's com. Oklahoma City Symphony, 1958-69. Bd. dirs. Oklahoma City Jr. Symphony, 1962-65, Oklahoma City Legal Aid Soc., 1965-68. Mem. Okla. Bar Assn., Okla. Edn. Assn., Kappa Alpha Theta (past nat. legislative chmn., pres. Okla. City chpt. alumnae assn. 1964-65, named Woman of Year 1969), Kappa Beta Pi. Democrat. Presbyn. (elder). Home: 418 NW 34th St Oklahoma City OK 73118

HIGH, JEAN SKOGLUND (MRS. LESLIE CRAMMOND HIGH), civic worker; b. St. Joseph, Mo., Feb. 4, 1920; d. Walter Leland and Challis (Wood) Skoglund; B.S. magna cum laude, Beaver Coll., 1941; m. Leslie Crammond High, Oct. 25, 1941; children—Leslie Crammond, Kathryn Morrison, Walter Dickerson. Asst. sec. Emergency Aid Pa., 1959-60, v.p., 1961-62, exec. v.p., 1963, pres., 1964-65, bd. dirs., 1954—; sec. social service com. Bryn Mawr (Pa.) Hosp., 1958-60, v.p., 1960-63, mem. women's bd., 1970—; bd. dirs. Council on Vols., 1965-69; chmn. womens com. Childrens Aid Soc., 1958-59. Bd. dirs. Com. of 1926-Strawberry Mansion, 1964-70, pres., 1970-73; bd. mgrs. Inglis House-Phila. Home for Incurables, 1966—, 2d v.p., 1972—. Mem. Zool. Soc. Phila. (life), Swedish Colonial Soc., Nat. Soc. Colonial Dames of Am. in Commonwealth of Pa., Phila. Mus. Art, Pa. Soc. New Eng. Women. Episcopalian. Club: Merion Cricket (Haverford, Pa.). Home: 912 Field Lane Villanova PA 19085

HIGH, LILLIAN EVA (MRS. RUSSELL E.D. HIGH), librarian; b. Bristol, Pa., Jan. 10, 1930; d. Ezra Magill and Eva Elizabeth (Hughes) Hellyer; B.A., Alma White Coll., 1953; M.L.S., Rutgers U., 1957; m. Russell E.D. High, June 15, 1957; children—David, Vernon, Constance. Librarian, Alma White Coll., Zarephath, N.J., 1955-59, asst. prof. English, world history, 1960-67, library cons., 1960-67; tchr. Latin, English, Belleview Prep Sch., Westminister, Colo., 1959-60; reference librarian Somerset County Library, Somerville, N.J., 1969—. Home: 75 Dayton Av Somerset NJ 08873 Office: Somerset County Library County Adminstrn Bldg Somerville NJ 08876

HIGHAM, EILEEN (MRS. JOHN HIGHAM), psychologist, educator; b. East Troy, Wis., Mar. 18, 1922; d. Francis and Alma (Nettesheim) Moss; B.A., U. Wis., 1945, M.A., 1946; Ph.D., U. Cal. at Los Angeles, 1952; m. John Higham, Oct. 26, 1948; children—Constance, Margaret, Jay, Daniel. Chief psychologist Huron Valley Child Guidance Clinic, Ypsilanti, Mich., 1961-67; clin. psychologist Counseling Center U. Mich. at Ann Arbor, 1968-73; clin. psychologist psychol. clinic Johns Hopkins, Balt., 1971-72; instr. med. psychology Johns Hopkins Med. Sch., 1973—; individual practice clin. psychology, Balt., 1962—. Mem. Am. Psychol. Assn. Home: 309 Tuscany Rd Baltimore MD 21210 Office: 600 Wyndhurst St Baltimore MD 21212

HIGHMAN, BARBARA, physician; b. Washington, Aug. 14, 1942; d. Benjamin and Helen (Wienshienk) Highman; student Northwestern U., 1960-63; M.D., U. Mich., 1967; m. Lawrence A. Goldman, June 22, 1969; 1 dau., Judy. Intern Baylor U. Affiliated Hosps., 1967-68; resident dermatology Henry Ford Hosp., Detroit, 1968-71; fellow dermatology Johns Hopkins, 1971-72; cons. in dermatology U.S. Army Andrew Rader Health Clinic, Ft. Myer, Va., 1972—, mem. staff North Charles Gen. Hosp., Balt. Mem. Med. and Chirurgical Faculty State Md. Recipient Physician's Recognition award A.M.A., 1971. Diplomate Am. Bd. Dermatology. Fellow Am. Acad. Dermatology; mem. Soc. Investigative Dermatology, Balt. City Med. Soc., Alpha Lambda Delta, Kappa Delta. Home: 3335 Old Line Av Laurel MD 20810 Office: U S Army Andrew Rader Health Clinic Ft Myer VA 22211 also North Charles Gen Hosp Baltimore MD 21218

HIGHSMITH, PATRICIA ANN, ednl. adminstr.; b. Fort Myers, Fla., Sept. 24, 1931; d. Charles Wilson and Christina (Chapman) Starnes; student Fla. State U., 1949-51; postgrad. Ga. State U., 1957; postgrad. N.W. Ga. Tchrs. In-Service, 1968-73; m. Norwood Howell Highsmith, May 17, 1958 (div.); children—Tracy, Michael, Susan. Tchr., Fort Hill Sch., Dalton, Ga., Friendship House Kindergarten, 1961-62; publicity dir. Whitfield County United Appeal, Dalton, 1963-65; adminstrv. dir. Cheerhaven Sch. for Retarded, Dalton, 1966—. Mem. City Park P.T.A., 1961-67, pres., 1965-66; pres. Dalton Jr. Woman's Club, 1961-62; treas. Elk's Aux., 1960-61; pres. bd. St. Mark's Ch. Kindergarten, 1966-67; leader Girl Scouts U.S.A., 1963-65; den mother Cub Scouts Am., 1961-63. Named Woman of Year Dalton News-Citizen, 1969; named Outstanding Dir. Tng. Centers for Retarded in Ga., 1973. Mem. Council for Exceptional Children, Am. Assn. Mental Deficiency, Nat., Ga., N.W. Ga. assns. retarded children. Home: 1502 W Crawford St Dalton GA 30720 Office: 201 Bryant Av Dalton GA 30720

HIGHTOWER, FLORENCE JOSEPHINE COLE (MRS. JAMES R. HIGHTOWER), author; b. Boston, June 9, 1916; d. George E. and Josephine (Sahr) Cole; A.B., Vassar Coll., 1937; m. James Robert Hightower, June 1, 1940; children—James Robert, Samuel Cole, Josephine, Thomas Denzil. Author: Mrs. Wappinger's Secret, 1956; The Ghost of Follonsbee's Folly, 1958; Dark Horse of Woodfield, 1962; Fayerweather Forecast, 1966; The Secret of The Crazy Quilt, 1972. Home: 321 Central St Auburndale MA 02166

HIGHTOWER, (MARY) GRACE, state ofcl.; b. Brundidge, Ala., Sept. 27, 1918; d. Marshall E. and Effie (Haisten) Hightower; B.S., Ga. State Coll., 1941; B.S. in L.S., George Peabody Coll., 1943, M.L.S., 1965. Tchr.-librarian Decatur County Schs., Bainbridge, Ga., 1938-41; tchr. Bainbridge City Schs., 1941-42; librarian Bainbridge High Sch., 1942-43; children's librarian Nashville Pub. Library, 1943-46; instr. Ga. State Coll., Milledgeville, 1946-48; cons. sch. library unit Ga. Dept. Edn., 1948-68; coordinator sch. library services unit Ga. Dept. Edn., Atlanta, 1968—. Vis. prof. So. Methodist U., summer 1948, George Peabody Coll., summers 1964, 1966. Mem. A.L.A., Am. Assn. Sch. Librarians, Southeastern, Ga. library assns., Ga. Assn. Educators, N.E.A., Delta Kappa Gamma. Author: School Library Programs in Rural Areas, 1966. Editor, Ga. Libraries New

Bull., 1948-63, Ga. Librarian, 1964—. Home: 3157 Leeland Rd Decatur GA 30032 Office: Sch Library Services Unit Ga Dept Edn Atlanta GA 30303

HIGHTOWER, SHARON JOAN WILEY (MRS. JAMES K. HIGHTOWER), urban planner; b. Kalamazoo, Oct. 13, 1937; d. Milo W. and Vera (King) Wiley; A.B., Kalamazoo Coll., 1959; M.A., Claremont Grad. Sch., 1966, postgrad., 1969—; m. James K. Hightower, Sept. 7, 1957; children—Matthew, Elizabeth. Tchr. Claremont High Sch., 1962-63; research cons. Richmond (Va.) City Planning Commn., 1966-67; asst. city planner, City of Claremont, Cal., 1967-69; pvt. practice as cons., Claremont, 1969-70; dir. planning and community devel. City of Claremont, 1970-74; dir. planning, asst. city mgr. Rancho Palos Verdes, Cal., 1974—. Mem. exec. bd. P.T.A., Claremont, 1969-70. Mem. Am. Inst. Planners (co-chmn. Cal. chpt. ann. conf. 1972, bd. So. sect. 1973), Inland Planners Assn. (adminstrv. chmn. 1970-71, vice chmn. 1970-72, dir. 1973, chmn. 1973), League Women Voters (dir. 1965-69), League Cal. Cities (2d v.p. planning dept. 1973-74). Address: 1740 Longwood Av Claremont CA 91711

HILBERG, ROSEMARY HELEN KROSS (MRS. ALBERT W. HILBERG), civic worker; b. Elmhurst, Ill., Feb. 28, 1922; d. Michael and Gertrude Helen (Heegard) Kross; student Am. Conservatory Music, 1940-41; B.S. (with high honors), Elmhurst Coll., 1944, LL.D., 1971; m. Albert William Hilberg, Aug. 22, 1943; children—Jeffrey, Eric, David, Kristin, Susan. Med. asst. Kegereis Med. Clinic, Elmhurst, Ill., 1945-47; substitute tchr. Montgomery County Pub. Schs., 1957-58, 65-66. Leader Girl Scouts U.S.A., 1947-48; 1st v.p. Montgomery County Council P.T.A., 1966, sec., 1964-65; mem. Community Health Adv. Com., 1967-68; chmn. League Women Voters Silver Spring unit, 1952-53, dir., voters service chmn., Montgomery County, 1953-54; mem. Montgomery County Bd. Edn., 1966—, v.p., 1968-69, pres., 1969-70. Trustee Montgomery Coll., 1966-68; bd. dirs. Md. Assn. Bds. Edn., 1969—, treas., 1972-73, 2d v.p., 1973-74. Recipient Appreciation Montgomery County Council P.T.A.'s, 1970. Unitarian. Home: 12512 Davan Dr Silver Spring MD 20904 Office: 850 N Washington Rockville MD 20850

HILDEBRAND, RUTH MOORHEAD (MRS. FRANCIS E. HILDEBRAND), civic worker; b. Kittanning, Pa.; d. Robert West and Elizabeth (Findley) Moorhead; B.S., Simmons Coll., 1922; postgrad. George Washington U., 1926-29; m. Francis Edwin Hildebrand, Apr. 20, 1935; children—Melissa Ann (Mrs. Robert D. Crawford). Trustee Young Women's Christian Home, Washington, 1940—, pres. bd. trustees, 1950-52; mem. Gray Lady service D.C. chapter A.R.C., 1943-50, chmn., 1950-56, chmn. vols., 1956-64, nat. vice chmn. vols., 1964-68, nat. chmn. vols., 1968-72, vol. cons., 1973—; bd. dirs., chmn. vols. Nat. Center Voluntary Action, 1972—. Mem. Am. Newspaper Women's Club. Phi Delta Delta. Republican. Methodist. Home: 4501 Cathedral Av NW Washington DC 20016

HILDEBRAND, VERNA LEE (MRS. JOHN R. HILDEBRAND), educator; b. Dodge City, Kan., Aug. 17, 1924; d. Carrell E. and Florence N. (Smyth) Butcher; B.S., Kan. State U., 1945, M.S., 1957; postgrad. U. Cal. at Berkeley, 1946-48, Tex. Tech. U., 1968; Ph.D., Tex. Woman's U., 1970; m. John R. Hildebrand, June 23, 1946; children—Carol (Mrs. Mitchell Young), Steve. Home econs. high sch. tchr., Chapman, Kan., 1945-46; grad. asst. Inst. Child Welfare, U. Cal. at Berkeley, 1947-48; kindergarten tchr., Albany, Cal., 1948-49; instr. Kan. State U., Manhattan, 1953-54, 59, Okla. State U., Stillwater, 1955-56; asst. prof. Tex. Technol. U., Lubbock, 1962-67; asso. prof. child devel. Mich. State U., East Lansing, 1967—. Mem. Nat. Assn. for Edn. Young Children, Am., Mich. home econs. assns., Assn. for Childhood Edn. Internat., World Orgn. for Early Childhood Edn. Author: Introduction to Early Childhood Education, 1971; A Workbook for Introduction to Early Childhood Education, 1971. Home: 724 Albert St East Lansing MI 48823

HILDRETH, JANE D(IBBLE), assn. adminstr.; b. Rochester, Sept. 16, 1917; d. Harold Edward and Mary (Parmele) Dibble; B.A., U. Rochester, 1939; m. Clifford T. Morgan, Sept. 3, 1938 (div. July 1946); 1 dau., Jacquelyn (Mrs. Joel P. Cocks); m. 2d, Harold M. Hildreth, Feb. 18, 1949 (dec. Nov. 1965). Asst. dir. Office Psychol. Personnel, NRC, Washington, 1943-46; asst. chief clin. psychologist VA Central Office, Washington, 1946-49; research officer CIA, Washington, 1949-50; head mem. dept. Am. Psychol. Assn., Washington, 1950—, legislative cons., 1955-70. Mem. D.C., Va., Southeastern psychol. assns., A.A.A.S. Home: 6230 Lakeview Dr Falls Church VA 22041 Office: Am Psychol Assn Central Office 1200 17th St NW Washington DC 20036

HILE, MARGARET JENKINSON (MRS. VERLIN G. HILE), editor; b. Fort Worth, Oct. 10, 1934; d. Joseph James and Beatrice (Barrett) Jenkinson; B.S., Ind. U., 1956; m. Verlin G. Hile, Jan. 29, 1956; children—Laura Elizabeth, Andrew Barrett, Jay Matthew. Tchr. English and journalism Indpls. pub. schs., 1956-58; editor Tri-County Truth, Churubusco, Ind., 1970—. Mem. Theta Sigma Phi, Delta Theta Tau, Zeta Tau Alpha. Home: Route 3 Columbia City IN 46725 Office: 209 S Main St Churubusco IN 46723

HILER, JEAN FARNSWORTH (MRS. RICHARD L. HILER), hosp. adminstr.; b. Syracuse, N.Y., Feb. 21, 1929; d. John Archibald and Edith Lucile (Beebe) Farnsworth; B.S., State U. N.Y. at Oswego, 1950; certificate occupational therapy U. Pa., 1954; m. Richard L. Hiler, Sept. 6, 1952. Vocational crafts instr. Woodrow Wilson Rehab. Center, Fishersville, Va., 1950-51; shop instr. Percy M. Hughes Sch., Syracuse, N.Y., 1951-52; with Harrisburg (Pa.) State Hosp., 1954—, dir. rehab. dept., 1971—. Dir. Jandi, Inc., Shiremanstown, Pa., 1970—. Mem. adv. com. occupational therapy dept. Elizabethtown (Pa.) Coll., 1973—. Mem. Nat. Rehab. Assn., Am. Occupational Therapy Assn., Tri-County Mental Health Assn. Home: 301 Reservoir Rd Mechanicsburg PA 17055 Office: Cameron and Maclay Sts Harrisburg PA 17105

HILES, PATRICIA ANN, lawyer; b. San Bernadino, Cal., Sept. 26, 1936; d. Karl Max and Myrtle Mae (Yeager) Kandler; A.A., Principia Coll., 1955; student (Pub. Service scholar), Harvard, 1954; B.A., Cal. State U., 1957; M.A., George Washington U., 1960; LL.B., La Salle U., 1968; m. E. Raymond Hiles, Dec. 21, 1958 (div. Feb. 1970); 1 dau., Heather Ann. Tchr., 1957-64; dep. probation officer Los Angeles County, 1965-67; admitted to Cal. bar, 1969; superior ct. clk., Los Angeles County, 1967-69; estate and gift tax atty. Internal Revenue Service, Los Angeles, 1969—. Mem. State Bar Cal. Home: 4555 Santa Barbara Av Los Angeles CA 90016 Office: PO Box 231 Los Angeles CA 90053

HILFERTY, SISTER MARY CECILIA, educator; b. Phila., Jan. 15, 1915; d. Daniel Joseph and Catharine Mary (Graham) Hilferty; B.S., Villanova U., 1940, postgrad., 1940-47; postgrad. La Salle Coll., 1944-45, Coll. William and Mary, 1948-50; Mus.B., Manhattanville Coll., 1959; M.A., Catholic U. Am., 1963, Ph.D., 1973. Joined Sisters of Mercy, 1932; tchr. elementary schs. Phila. Archdiocese, 1935-41; tchr. Mercy Acad., Phila., 1941-47, Walsingham Acad., Williamsburg, Va., 1947-48; faculty Gwynedd-Mercy Coll., Gwynedd Valley, Pa., 1948—, asso. prof. history, 1968-73, prof., 1973—, asst. in music dept., 1948—. Dir. Symphony Orch. of Sisters of Mercy, 1961-67; area chmn. Ch. Women for World Peace, 1970; mem. Music Commn., Archdiocese of Phila. Mem. Am. Ch. History Soc., Mediaeval Acad. Am., Ch. Music Assn. Am., Phi Alpha Theta. Contbr. articles to various publs. Address: Gwynedd-Mercy Coll Gwynedd Valley PA 19437

HILGARTNER, MARGARET WEHR, physician; b. Balt., Nov. 6, 1924; d. Andrew Henry and Margaret (Wehr) Hilgartner; A.B., Bryn Mawr Coll., 1946; M.A., Duke, 1951, M.D., 1955; m. Albert Milton Arky, Mar. 24, 1958; children—George, Elizabeth, John. Intern, Bellevue Hosp. Children's Service, 1955-56: resident dept. pediatrics N.Y. Hosp., 1956-58, fellow dept. pediatric hematology, 1958-60, instr. pediatric hematology, 1960-67, asst. prof., 1967-73, asso. prof., 1973—, head pediatric coagulation lab., 1961—, dir. hemophilia clinic. Med. dir. met. chpt. Nat. Hemophilia Found., N.Y.C., 1968—, nat. trustee, 1969—, nat. med. bd. 1973. Mem. Duke U. Med. Alumni Assn., Am. Women's Med. Assn., Harvey Soc., Soc. for Study Blood, Am. Soc. Hematology, Am. Acad. Pediatrics. Home: 73 Depeyster Av Tenafly NJ 07670 Office: 525 E 68th St New York City NY 10021

HILKERT, JEAN ELLEN, educator; b. Lucerne, Ind., Sept. 18, 1932; d. Eugene Earl and Helen Lucille (Berkshire) Hilkert; B.S., Ball State U., 1954; M.S., Purdue U., 1957, supr. guidance certificate, 1963. Library asst. Cass County Library, Logansport, Ind., 1950-51; park dir. Kokomo (Ind.) Recreation Dept., 1952-53; tchr. jr. high phys. edn., Battle Creek, Mich., 1954-55; tchr. phys. edn. Jefferson High Sch., Lafayette, Ind., 1955-63, guidance counselor, 1963-68, dean students, 1968-69, dean girls, student activities coordinator, 1969—. Fair chmn. Home Hosp. Assn., 1962; exec. bd. Jefferson High Sch. P.T.A., 1971-73, life mem. Mem. N.E.A., Ind. State Tchrs. Assn., Nat., Ind. assns. women deans, adminstrs. and counselors, Lafayette Edn. Assn. (past v.p., pres. 1962-63, negotiating team 1970-71), City Panhellenic Council (sec. 1961-62, treas. 1962-63), Lafayette Women's Bowling Assn. (pres. 1962-66), Ind. Golf League (pres. 1962), Lafayette Golf Assn. (sec. 1966), 600 Club (pres. 1963-65), Ind. Women's State Bowling Assn. (dir. 1965-70, dir. Lafayette chpt. 1969-72), Delta Kappa Gamma (v.p. 1963-66). Home: 2224 Huron Rd West Lafayette IN 47906

HILL, A(GNES) JEAN, ednl. adminstr.; b. Natrona Heights, Pa., Sept. 10, 1942; d. Charles Henry and Rebecca (Hudson) Hill; B.Music Edn., Ind. U., 1964, M.S. in Edn. 1965-66; postgrad. Xavier U., 1964; Ed. D., Wash. State U., 1972. Tchr. music Cin. (O.) Pub. Schs., 1964-65; grad. asst. in residence hall Ind. U., Bloomington, 1965-66; asst. dean students State U. N.Y., Coll., Cortland, 1966-68; asst. dean women U. Ida., Moscow, 1968-71, asst. prof. guidance, 1971—, dean of women, 1971-72, dean for student adv. services, 1972— Mem. Ida. Women's Commn., 1972-74. Mem. Am. Assn. U. Women, N.W. Coll. Personnel Assn. (editorial bd. 1972—, pres.-elect, program chmn. 1973-74, pres. 1974-75), Nat. Assn. Student Personnel Adminstrs. (chairperson Region V task force on women, mem. adv. bd. Region V), Sigma Alpha Iota, Mosaic, Pi Lambda Theta, Alpha Lambda Delta (hon.). Contbr. articles to profl. publs. Home: NW 1345 Kenny Dr Pullman WA 99163 Office: U Ida Moscow IA 83843

HILL, ANN GEDDES STAHLMAN (MRS. GEORGE DEROULHAC HILL), civic worker; b. Nashville, Apr. 15, 1921; d. James Geddes Stahlman and Mildred (Thornton) Rhett; B.A., Vanderbilt U., 1943; m. George deRoulhac Hill, Sept. 23, 1947; children—Mary Geddes, George deRoulhac, Margaret Thornton, Thomas Stahlman. Pres., Nashville Childrens Theatre, 1956-58; exec. v.p. Southeastern Theatre Conf., 1960-61, v.p., 1961-62, pres., 1962-63; regional chmn. Childrens Theatre Conf., Am. Ednl. Theatre Assn., 1960-62, comptroller, 1961-66, asst. dir., 1967-69, dir., 1969-71; v.p. adminstrn. Am. Theatre Assn., 1972-73, pres.-elect, 1974, pres., 1975; exec. sec.-treas. U.S. Center for ASSITEJ (Internat. Assn. of Theatre for Children and Youth), 1967-73; mem. bd. dirs. ANTA, 1962-65. Treas. Nashville Symphony Guild, 1957-58; sec. Nashville Arts Council, 1957-58. Bd. dirs. Jr. League Nashville, Tenn. Bot. Gardens, Fine Arts Center; trustee Childrens Theatre Found. Served to lt. (j.g.) USNR, 1943-46. Mem. Nat. Soc. Colonial Dames Am., Phi Beta Kappa, Delta Delta Delta. Episcopalian. Clubs: Garden of Nashville, Garden of America. Home: 201 Lynwood Blvd Nashville TN 37205 Office: Nashville Children's Theatre PO Box 7066 Nashville TN 37210

HILL, BARBARA MAE, librarian; b. Keene, N.H., Sept. 19, 1924; d. Gale Earl and Gertrude Wiseman (Reed) Hill; B.E., Keene Tchrs. Coll., 1946; M.S., Simmons Coll., 1952. Tchr. sci. and math. Thayer High Sch., Winchester, N.H., 1946-47; children's librarian Keene Pub. Library, 1947-52; asst. librarian Mass. Coll. Pharmacy, Boston, 1952-58, asso. librarian, 1958-69, librarian, 1969—. Mem. Am. Assn. Univ. Profs., Am. Soc. for Information Sci., Drug Information Assn., Am. Assn. Colls. Pharmacy, Med. Library Assn. (chmn. pharmacy group 1965-66), Spl. Libraries Assn. (vice chmn. pharm. div. 1972-73, chmn. 1973-74), Kappa Delta Pi, Rho Chi. Office: Massachusetts College of Pharmacy 179 Longwood Av Boston MA 02115

HILL, CAROL, educator; b. Oakland, Cal.; d. Preston Lewis and Melinda Mae (Cuillard) Hill; B.A., Bklyn. Coll., 1972, M.S., 1973; D. Social Pedagogy in Arts (hon.), Great China Arts Coll., Kowloon, Hong Kong, 1973; student Sch. Radio Technique, N.Y.C., Am. Acad. Dramatic Art, N.Y.C. Talent on weather show, disc jockey WGLV-TV, Easton, Pa., 1956-57; talent on interviews, weather WNHC-TV, New Haven, 1958; free-lance actress, spokeswoman Voice-Overs, N.Y.C., 1959-66; talent on news, weather, features Cable TV, Channel 6, N.Y.C., 1963-66; tchr. Announcer Tng. Studios, N.Y.C., 1960-72; tchr. Kingsborough Community Coll., Bklyn., 1972-73; instr. John Jay Coll. Criminal Justice, N.Y.C., 1973. Exec. sec. World Poets Resource Center, 1971-72, exec. dir., 1973—; sec. Eastern Centre, Poetry Soc., London, Eng., 1968-71. Recipient Distinguished Service award Announcer Tng. Studios, 1970. Mem. Internat. Platform Assn., Am. Women in Radio and TV, Speech Communication Assn. Home: 724 E 27th St Brooklyn NY 11210

HILL, CAROLYN GREGG (MRS. VICTOR G. HILL, JR.), lawyer; b. Boston, June 4, 1936; d. David Almus and Virginia (Thompson) Gregg; B.A., Wellesley Coll., 1958; J.D., Oklahoma City U., 1969; m. Richard Howland Rawls (dec.); children—Margaret Gregg, Richard Gregg; m. 2d, Victor Gerald Hill, Jr.; 1 son, Victor Gerald III. Treas., dir. Cardast Corp., 1958-62, dir., 1973—; customers broker N.Y. Stock Exchange firm, 1962-64; atty. Kerr-McGee Corp., Oklahoma City, 1969—. Dir. N.H. Bankshares, Inc., 1964-70. Finance adviser Swift Water council Girl Scouts U.S.A., Manchester, N.H., 1960-62; pres. Wilton Youth Center, 1961-64. Chmn., Wilton Republican Women, 1960; pres. Southegan Women's Rep. Club, 1961-62; del. N.H. Rep. Conv., 1960, 62, 64. Mem. Soc. Colonial Dames Am. in Okla. (sec.), Am., Okla. bar assns. Clubs: New Eng. Old English Sheepdog (sec. 1963-64), Old English Sheepdog Am., Appalachian Mountain, Oklahoma City Golf and Country. Home: 1606 Camden Way Oklahoma City OK 73116 Office: Kerr-McGee Center Oklahoma City OK 73125

HILL, CECILIA (MRS. JACK HILL), educator; b. Manchester, Eng., Aug. 12, 1928; d. Richard Lionel and Mary (Heyes) Dearman; came to U.S., 1963, naturalized, 1968; teaching certificate Coll. Notre Dame, Liverpool, Eng., 1948; B.A., Cal. State U. at Northridge, 1965, M.A., 1968; postgrad. U. Cal. at Los Angeles; m. Jack Hill, July 22, 1950; children—Margaret Mary (Mrs. Steven Harris), Christopher John. Tchr. elementary sch. vice prin., Manchester, 1948-63; elementary tchr., reading specialist, tchr.-coordinator early childhood edn. and reading Los Angeles City Schs., 1965—; instr. Pepperdine U., 1973. Founder mem., dir. newsletter, exec. bd. Reading Specialists of Cal., 1970—. Sec., Cienega Community Adv. Council, Los Angeles. Mem. Nat. Soc. Study Edn., N.E.A., Cal. Tchrs. Assn., Internat. Reading Assn. Roman Catholic. Home: 2008 Veteran Av Los Angeles CA 90025 Office: Cienega Sch 2611 S Orange St Los Angeles CA 90064

HILL, DORLA JEAN, educator; b. Storm Lake, Ia., Feb. 15, 1948; d. Dale L. and Alice M. (Stanzel) Hill; B.A., U. Ia., 1971. Teaching asst. for speech debate team U. Ia., Iowa City, 1970-71; student tchr. Cedar Rapids (Ia.) Jefferson High Sch., 1970-71; tchr. speech, English, Carroll (Ia.) High Sch., 1971—. Ia. oratory champion, 1968. Named Outstanding Innovative and Humanizing Tchr., 1973. Mem. Nat., Ia. edn. assns., Nat., Ia. councils of tchrs. English, Ia. High Sch. Speech Assn., Ia. Council of Tchrs. Speech, Speech Communication Assn., Carroll Edn. Assn., Kappa Phi. Home: 1308 Simon Av Carroll IA 51401 Office: 1026 N Adams St Carroll IA 51401

HILL, EVELYN FOSTER (MRS. KENNETH MILLER HILL), psychologist, educator; b. Boston, Oct. 10, 1910; d. Jacob and Fannie (Davis) Foster; B.A., Goucher Coll., 1960; M.A., Catholic U. Am., 1962, Ph.D., 1964; m. Kenneth Miller Hill, June 26, 1948; children—Joseph Daniel Cooper, Jane Ellen, Susan Deborah. Dir. Labor Relations Fed. Telecommunications Lab., Nutley, N.J., 1941-48; staff psychologist Spring Grove State Hosp., Catonsville, Md., 1964-66; prof. psychology Towson State Coll., Towson, Md., 1966—; pvt. practice clin. psychology, Balt. Cons. Adolescent Out-Patient Clinic, Johns Hopkins Hosp., 1964—; instr. med. psychology Johns Hopkins Sch. Medicine, Balt., 1964—; cons. U. Md., College Park, 1968—. Nat. Inst. Mental Health grantee, 1964-67. Fellow Soc. Personality Assessment; mem. Am., Md. (rep. at large 1973-75) psychol. assns., Balt. Assn. Cons. Psychologists (pres. 1969-71), Sigma Xi, Psi Chi. Author: The Holtzman Inkblot Technique: A Handbook for Clinical Application, 1972; (with Helen E. Peixotto) A Workbook for the Holtzman Inkblot Technique, 1974. Address: 604 Dunkirk Rd Baltimore MD 21212

HILL, HELEN COLLINS, educator, civic worker; b. Hot Springs, Ark., Nov. 2, 1922; d. Ernest Govan and Rebecca Frank (Ware) Collins; B.S., Tenn. State U., M.S., 1962; Ph.D., So. Ill. U., 1971; m. Carl McClellan Hill, Aug. 2, 1970; 1 son by previous marriage—Ernest Collins Rose. Pub. sch. tchr. Hot Springs (Ark.) Nat. Park System, 1943-49; office mgr. Bur. Pub. Relations, Tenn. State U., Nashville, 1950-55, adminstrv. asst. to coll. pres., 1955-62, instr. psychology, 1962-67; head resident, counselor to women students So. Ill. U. at Carbondale, 1967-69, asst. dean students 1969-71; asst. prof. edn. Ky. State U., Frankfort, 1972—. Mem. Ky. Heritage Commn.; vol., United Givers, Heart Fund, Am. Cancer Soc. Bd. dirs. Wilderness Rd. council Girl Scouts U.S., also chmn. service unit West Frankfort council; v.p. bd. dirs. Frankfort Housing Authority; bd. dirs. Frankfort Arts Found., Big Bros.-Big Sisters Frankfort. Recipient So. Fellowship award. Mem. Am. Assn. Higher Edn., Am. Assn. U. Women, Nat. Assn. Continuing and Adult Edn., Nat. Council Negro Women, Am. Personnel and Guidance Assn., Nat. Assn. Women Deans, Adminstrs. and Counselors, Kappa Delta Pi, Alpha Kappa Mu, Alpha Kappa Alpha. Home: The Hillcrest Cold Harbor Dr Frankfort KY 40601 Office: Ky State U Frankfort KY 40601

HILL, HELEN THACKER (MRS. WALLACE CHARLES HILL), coll. adminstr.; b. Pike County, Ky., Feb. 16, 1923; d. Avie and Ellen (Turner) Thacker; A.B., U. Ky., 1944, M.A., 1953; D.Ed., Okla. State U., 1970; postgrad. U. Ky., 1973; m. Wallace Charles Hill, Nov. 25, 1959 (dec. Oct. 1968). Tchr. high sch. math., Elkhorn and Belfry, Ky., 1944-53; head resident U. Fla., Gainesville, 1954-56; women's counselor U. Houston, 1956-59; dir. counseling-women's residence halls Purdue U., Lafayette, Ind., 1959-61; asst. dean women Okla. State U., Stillwater, 1962-66; dean women W.Va. Inst. Tech., Montgomery, 1970-71, asso. dean students, 1971-73; dir. resource center for non-resident students U. Mass., Amherst, 1973—. Mem. Am. Personnel and Guidance Assn., Am. Coll. Personnel Assn., Am. Assn. Women Deans, Counselors and Adminstrs., Kappa Delta Phi, Alpha Lambda Delta. Mem. Order Eastern Star. Home: 37 Wildwood Lane Amherst MA 01002

HILL, HELENE ZIMMERMANN (MRS. GEORGE JAMES HILL, II), educator; b. Phila., Apr. 10, 1929; d. Albert Walter and Barbara (Shoemaker) Zimmermann; A.B., Smith Coll., 1950; Ph.D., Brandeis U., 1964; m. George James Hill, II, July 16, 1960; children—James Warren, David Hedgcock, Sarah, Helena Rundall. Instr. biology Brandeis U., Waltham, Mass., 1963-64; fellow dept. bacteriology and immunology Harvard Med. Sch., Boston, 1964-66; instr. biophysics U. Colo. Med. Center, Denver, 1966-67, asst. prof. biophysics, 1967-72; asso. prof. radiology Washington U. Sch. Medicine, St. Louis, 1973—. USPHS fellow, 1960-68, grantee, 1971—. Mem. A.A.A.S., Am. Assn. U. Profs., Am. Inst. Biol. Scis., Am. Soc. Human Genetics, Biophys. Soc., Jr. League, Sigma Xi. Club: Smith (St. Louis). Home: 7006 Westmoreland Dr St Louis MO 63130

HILL, HYACINTHE (VIRGINIA ANDERSON), poet; b. N.Y.C., May 24, 1920; d. Joseph Thomas and Angela Virginia (Bradley-Bruen) Cronin; B.A. cum laude with honors in English, Bklyn. Coll., 1961; M.A. in English and Comparative Lit., Hunter Coll., 1965; postgrad. Fordham U., 1965-69; Ph.D. (hon.), No. Pontifical Acad., Sweden, 1969; D.Arts and Letters (hon.), Gt. China Arts Coll., 1969; D. Hum., Coll. Alfred the Great, Hull, Eng., 1970; m. Johan Anderson, July 15, 1940; children—John Luke Anderson, Matthew Mark Anderson (dec.). Tchr. English, James Monroe High Sch., Bronx, N.Y., 1969—. Author: Shoots of a Vagrant Vine (Avalon Nat. Sonnets prize 1950), 1950; Promethea (Cameo Press book award 1957), 1957; also numerous individual poems; co-editor Diamond Year Anthology, 1970; editor North Atlantic edit. Great Am. World Poets Anthology, 1973. Recipient Poetry Soc. Am. prizes, 1958—; N.Am. Chapbook award, 1966; 1st prize Eleanor Otto award N.Y. Poetry Forum, 1969, 70; 1st prize Internat. Inst., 1970; numerous other awards. Mem. Acad. Am. Poets, Poetry Soc. Am., League Am. Pen-Women, Alpha Delta Kappa. Home: 166 Hawthorne Av Yonkers NY 10705 Office: James Monroe High School Bronx NY 10472

HILL, JANE MARGARET, editor; b. Youngstown O., May 25, 1919; d. Joseph Hamilton and Edith (Lowry) Hill; B.S. with distinction in Edn., Ohio State U., 1940, M.A., 1948. Tchr., Claridon Twp. Sch., Marion County, O., 1940-42, Upper Sandusky (O.) High Sch., 1942-43, Washington Pub. Schs., 1943-61; asst. dir. dept. math. Washington Pub. Schs., 1961-64; exec. dir. Pi Lambda Theta, Washington, 1964-71; mng. editor The Arithmetic Tchr. jour. Nat. Council Tchrs. Math., 1971—. Content cons. ednl. TV series Sets and Systems, 1963—; vis. faculty George Washington U., 1956-57, U. Va., 1956-57, Montclair (N.J.) State Coll., summer, 1959, 61, Colo. State Coll. summer, 1959, 61, U. Md., 1961-63, 66—. Cons., Brookline Math. Project. Fellow A.A.A.S.; mem. N.E.A. (life), Nat. Council Tchrs. Math., Math. Assn. Am., Central Assn. Sci. and Math. Tchrs.,

A.A.A.S., Assn. Supervision and Curriculum Devel. (co-author math. bibliography), Am. Ednl. Research Assn., Pi Lambda Theta (nat. treas.), Phi Delta Gamma, Alpha Delta Kappa, Delta Kappa Gamma. Home: 3051 Harrison St NW Washington DC 20015 Office: 1906 Association Dr Reston VA 22091

HILL, SISTER JUSTINE, coll. dean; b. Louisville, Mar. 1, 1933; d. John James and Nellie Warren (Callahan) Hill; B.A. magna cum laude, Mary Manse Coll., 1955, M.A., 1969; postgrad. U. Toledo, 1968-72. Secondary tchr. St. Ursula Acad., 1955-58, 59-63, Central Cath. High Sch., Toledo, 1964-68; intern in higher edn. U. Toledo, 1968-72; dir. student personnel Mary Manse Coll., Toledo, 1972-73, acad. dean, 1973—. Mem. Pi Lambda Theta, Kappa Gamma Pi. Home: 2413 Collingwood Blvd Toledo OH 43620

HILL, LOIS WILLADENE, bank exec.; b. Whitley County, Ind., Oct. 17, 1923; d. Edwin Barnhart and Blanche Dulcena (Myers) Cornelius; grad. Am. Inst. Banking courses LaSalle Corr. Sch., 1950; m. Floyd Stephen Hill, July 6, 1946. With Farmers Loan & Trust Co., Columbia City, Ind., 1942-44, 46-48; with First Nat. Bank Warsaw (Ind.), 1946-68, asst. cashier, 1954-60, auditor, 1960-67; dir. customer relations, 1967; tng. dir. Peoples Trust Bank, Ft. Wayne, Ind., 1968, asst. sec., 1968-71, asst. v.p., 1972-73, personnel adminstr., 1973—. Served with WAVES, 1944-46. Mem. Warsaw Bus. and Profl. Women's Club (pres. 1960-61), Northeastern Ind. Safe Deposit Assn. (sec. treas. 1962-63, v.p. 1963-64, pres. 1964-65), Nat. Assn. Bank Women (sec. treas. Ind. group 1970-71, vice chmn. 1971-72, nat. bd., mem. exec. com. 1971-72), Ind. Bankers Assn. (women's com. 1969-70), Am. Soc. for Tng. Devel., Am. Bus. Women's Assn. (Woman of Year 1973), Am. Mgmt. Soc., Am. Soc. Personnel Adminstrn., Zonta Internat., Am. Legion. Contbr. articles to profl. jours. Continent Banker, Hoosier Banker. Home: 7132 Winnebago Dr Fort Wayne IN 46805 Office: 913 S Calhoun St Fort Wayne IN 46802

HILL, LORRAINE WILSON (MRS. JOHN W. HILL), home economist; b. Whitewell, Tenn., Sept. 13, 1917; d. Samuel Bennett and Vera (Shirley) Wilson; student Peabody Coll., 1936-38; B.S. in Home Econs., U. Tenn., 1940; m. John W. Hill, May 25, 1957. Home econs. tchr. Chattanooga Sch. System, 1941-46; home agt. U. Tenn. Extension, Nashville, 1946-49; home economist Corning Glass Works (N.Y.), 1949-53; regional home economist TVA, Knoxville, 1953-55; exec. dir. Dairy Council Knoxville, 1955—. Mem. adv. com. Salvation Army Youth Groups, Knoxville, 1955—, now chmn.; mem. nursing service com. A.R.C., Knoxville, 1964-65, chmn.; mem. Greater Knoxville Nutrition Council Bd. dirs. Knoxville YWCA. Named hon. mem. Tenn. Future Homemakers Am., 1964; recipient Citizen of Month award Northside Kiwanis Club, 1965. Adv. com. M.B.L.S. Mem. Am., Tenn. (dir.), Knox Area home econs. assns., Tenn. Home Economists in Bus. (pres. 1960, treas. 1965), Home Econs. Occupational Tng. Program, Am. Pub. Health Assn., 2d Dist. Dietetic Assn., Greater Knoxville Agr. Council (chmn. program com., chmn. June dairy month, mem. commodity study com.), 2d Dist. Dental Health Com., Greater Knoxville C. of C., Am. Bus. Women's Assn., Phi Mu. Episcopalian. Club: Quota. Home: 5413 Neilwoods Dr Knoxville TN 37919 Office: 7025 Kingston Pike Knoxville TN 37919

HILL, MARGARET CURLE (MRS. NAT U. HILL), Republican nat. committeewoman; b. Indpls., Feb. 23, 1924; d. Marvin Emmett and Florence (Rilling) Curle; student Skidmore Coll., 1941-43; A.B. in Econs., Ind. U., 1944; m. Nat U. Hill, June 8, 1946; children—Nat U., Philip C. Mem. staff personnel dept. Electronics Labs., 1944-46. Republican precinct vice-committeewoman, Bloomington, Ind., 1963-69; vice chmn. Monroe County, Ind. Rep. Com., 1963-69; vice chmn. Rep. Dist. Com., 1964—; mem. Rep. Nat. Com., 1972—. Bd. dirs. Boys' Club, United Fund, Bloomington; Recipient Woman and Boy award Boys' Club Bloomington. Mem. Boys' Club Aux. (founder), Women's Dept. Club, Psi Iota Xi (pres.). Mem. Christian Ch. (trustee). Home: Rural Route 11 Box 36 Kinser Pike Bloomington IN 47401

HILL, MARGARET DUERR (MRS. CARRINGTON W. HILL), mathematician; b. Melrose, Mass., Apr. 18, 1913; d. Otto Eugene and Florence M. (Wade) Duerr; A.B., Colby Coll., 1935; postgrad. Mass. Inst. Tech., 1948-50; M.Ed., State Coll. Boston, 1968; m. Carrington W. Hill, June 17, 1935; children—Thomas E., Peter D., John D., Nancy J. Mathematician, Cruft Lab. Harvard, 1942, Mass. Inst. Tech., 1942-52, Air Force Cambridge Research Labs., Bedford, Mass., 1952—. Sec., Asso. Scis. Research Found. Mem. Equal Employment Opportunity Adv. Com. Hanscom Field. Mem. Soc. Women Engrs., Bus. and Profl. Womens Club Greater Malden, Parapsychol. Assn., Nat. Fedn. Fed. Employees (pres.), Delta Delta Delta. Home: 11 Foster St Arlington MA 02174 Office: L G Hanscom Field Bedford MA 01730

HILL, MARGARET JEANNE, civic worker; b. Willow, Okla., Mar. 30, 1925; d. Jonathan Edward and Mary Alice (Lloyd) Culwell; student Okla. U., 1952-53, Western State Coll., Gunnison, Colo., 1961-63, Practical Nurse Sch., Durango, Colo., 1971; m. Thomas Walter Hill, Dec. 14, 1942 (dec. May 1974); children—Ronald, Richard, Donald, Beverly, Tracy. Office worker, Los Alamos, 1947; housing mgr. North Campus, U. Okla., 1951-55; tchr., Norwood, Colo., 1963-65; nurse trainee Mercy Hosp., Durango, Colo., 1971. Vice chmn. community improvement project Pine River Pow Wow, 1972-73. Vice chmn. Bayfield (Colo.) Town Planning Commn., 1971—; precinct committeewoman Democratic Party. Mem. Gen., Colo. (state chmn. crime prevention) fedn. womans clubs, Order Eastern Star (officer La Plata chpt.). Presbyn. (elder, mem. parish council). Contbr. articles on crime prevention to club publs. Home: 310 Church St Bayfield CO 81122

HILL, MARGARET OLIPHANT DONALD (MRS. LAWRENCE K. HILL), librarian; b. Asheville, N.C., Feb. 12, 1923; d. John Clinton and Elizabeth Oliphant (Robertson) Donald; B.A. in Econs., U. N.C., 1948; m. Orville B. Lomason, Jan. 12, 1943 (dec. Aug. 1945); m. 2d, Lawrence K. Hill, May 16, 1953; children—Lawrence, Jr., James W. Sales asst. Am. Air Lines, N.Y.C., 1948-49; adminstrv. asst. Mut. Life Ins. N.Y.C., Greenville, S.C., 1950-51; adminstrv. asst. to pres. Henderson Advt. Agy., Greenville, S.C., 1952-54, on leave, 1954-56, media buyer, 1958-65, media broadcast supr., 1966-70, market research librarian, 1971—. Mem. S.C., Southeastern library assns., Piedmont Spl. Libraries Assn., Am. Assn. Univ. Women. Home: 307 McCarter Av Greenville SC 29607 Office: 55 S Pleasantburg Dr Greenville SC 29606

HILL, MARION FOGARTIE, ednl. adminstr.; b. Brookhaven, Miss.; d. William Henderson and Mary (Fogartie) Hill; B.A., Belhaven Coll., 1937; postgrad. Presbyn. Sch. Christian Edn., 1944; M.A., George Peabody Coll. for Tchrs., 1966. Elementary sch. tchr., Walnut Grove, Miss., 1937-39, Canton, 1939-43, Brookhaven, 1943-44; dir. Christian edn. Presbyn. Ch., Monticello, Ark., 1944-47, Jackson, Miss., 1947-57, Spartanburg, S.C., 1957-64; dean of women Presbyn. Coll., Clinton, S.C., 1964—. Mem. Am. Assn. U. Women, Nat., S.C. (sec-treas. 1972-73) assns. women deans and counselors, Assn. Christian Educators Presbyn. Ch. U.S. (program chmn. ann. meeting 1960), S.C. Assn. Christian Educators (pres. 1961). Home: 300 Pine St Clinton SC 29325 Office: Presbyn Coll Clinton SC 29325

HILL, MARSHA LOU TURNER (MRS. VIRL LEE HILL), theatre dir.; b. Streator, Ill., Apr. 21, 1940; d. Perry Ian and Lucille Marilyn (Mueller) Turner; B.S., Ill. State U., 1962; m. Virl Lee Hill, Aug. 18, 1962; children—Virl Zinn, Virl Lee, Emily Anne. Faculty asst. in speech and creative dramatics Ill. State U., Normal, 1962-63; substitute tchr. Livingston and LaSalle Counties, Streator, Ill., 1963-64; actress, dir. Community Players, Streator, Ill., 1958-71, bd. dirs., 1962-65; actress, dir. Kankakee (Ill.) Valley Theater, 1964—. Bd. dirs., pub. relations chmn., children's theater dir. Jr. Service League Kankakee; active Kankakee Community Arts Council, Kankakee Symphony Guild; former mem. Riverside Hosp. Aux. Bd. dirs., pres. Kankakee Valley Theater, 1971—. Recipient Edwards Poetry medal Ill. State U., 1962, Theater Service award Ill. State U., 1962, Dir. awards Streator Community Players, 1969, 71. Mem. Am., Children's, Ill. theater assns., Ill. Community Theater Assn., Ill. High Sch. Speech Assn. (contest judge in speech, drama), Sigma Tau Delta, Theata Alpha Phi. Methodist. Clubs: Country, Book Review, Minerva Study (Kankakee). Home: 1170 S Wilson Av Kankakee IL 60901 Office: PO Box 744 Kankakee IL 60901

HILL, MARY MARGARET (MRS. CHARLES WESLEY HILL), ins. co. exec.; b. Conroe, Tex., Sept. 3, 1924; d. Joseph Carl and Lillian Beatrice (Madeley) Miller; student Massey Bus. Sch., Houston, 1941-42, also life office mgmt. courses; m. Charles Wesley Hill, June 13, 1964; children——(from a previous marriage) Patricia (Mrs. Horace Ray Rather), John Thomas Capps. Gen. office work Leon Finch Paint Co., Houston, 1942-43, Montgomery County Tax Office, 1943-47; with Great Nat. Life Ins. Co., Dallas, 1952-65, underwriter, 1953-65; asst. sec., underwriter Keystone Life Ins. Co., Dallas, 1965-67; chief underwriter Life Ins. Co. of Southwest, Dallas, 1967—. Mem. Tex. Home Office Underwriters (sec. 1962), Southwest Ins. Assn. (v.p. 1971-72, membership v.p. 1971-72, program v.p. 1972-73, pres. 1973-74), Oak Cliff Evening Lions Aux. (pres. 1969-70). Home: 3106 Tennessee St Dallas TX 75224 Office: PO Box 45106 Dallas TX 75235

HILL, SISTER MARY MECHTILDE, coll. dean; b. Bennett, Colo., Sept. 5, 1923; d. Howard Leighton and Nellie Jane (Brown) Hill; B.S., Colo. State U., 1945; M.S., Creighton U., 1953; Ph.D., St. Louis U., 1958. Analytical chemist Eastman Kodak, Rochester, N.Y., 1945-47; faculty chemistry dept. Coll. St. Mary, Omaha, 1957-71, prof., 1958-71, chmn. dept., 1971, acad. dean, 1970-72, v.p. acad. affairs, 1973—. Radiol. monitor Omaha Civil Def., 1965. Vice chmn. bd. dirs. Mercy High Sch., Omaha, 1972—. Fellow Am. Inst. Chemists; mem. Am. Chem. Soc. (chmn. Omaha sect. 1973), Sigma Xi. Home: 1901 S 72d St Omaha NE 68124

HILL, MARY RAE, geologist; b. Great Falls, Mont., Sept. 2, 1923; d. Raymond Ernest and Mary Caroline (Brantly) Hill; A.B., U. Colo., 1944; postgrad., 1947-48; postgrad. U. Ill., 1945-46; M.A., San Francisco State U., 1970. Jr. geologist Phillips Petroleum Co., Bartlesville, Okla., 1944-45; research asst. Ill. State Geol. Survey, Urbana, 1945-46; instr. extension div. U. Colo., 1947; with Cal. Div. Mines and Geology, San Francisco, Sacramento, 1949—, sr. geologist, 1970—. Mem. Assn. Earth Sci. Editors (chmn. ednl. com. 1970-72, vice chmn. 1972-73, assn. chmn. 1973-74), Am. Geol. Inst. (publs. com. 1969-72). Author: Where to Look for Uranium in California, 1955; Marin Indians, 1957; The Mojave of the Colorado, 1959; Guide to Virginia City and the Comstock Lode, 1959; Jade in California, 2d edit., 1960; Diving and Digging for Gold, 1960, 2d edit., 1974; Hunting Diamonds in California, 2d edit., 1972; Geology of the Sierra Nevada, 1974; others. Editor: Cal. Geology, 1955—; (with Wendell Cochran and Peter Fenner) Geowriting: A Guide to Writing, Editing and Publishing in Earth Science, 1973. Contbr. articles to tech. jours. Filmmaker, Barrier Beach, 1971. Home: 6069 Contra Costa Rd Oakland CA 94618 Office: 1416 9th St Sacramento CA 95814

HILL, MOZELLE CARLOCK (MRS. HOUSTON ERNEST HILL), gift shop owner, civic worker; b. Oklahoma City, Sept. 11, 1922; d. William Cummings and Laura Mec (Russell) Carlock; student Sullins Coll., 1940-42; B.S., U. Okla., 1944; m. Houston Ernest Hill, Feb. 23, 1947; children—Marilyn, William Franklin, Houston Ernest. Owner, buyer Red Fox, Ltd., splty. gift shop, Oklahoma City, 1963—. Area chmn. United Fund, Oklahoma City, 1955-58; active membership drives various orgns. including Art Center, 1958-61, Symphony, 1958-61, YWCA, 1958-61; pres. P.T.A., Edgemere Sch., 1958-59; admission counselor Sullins Coll., 1966-72; rep. Ozark Boys Camp, 1959-68. Mem. Opti-Mrs. (charter pres. 1947), Chi Omega. Democrat. Methodist. Home: 1405 Kenilworth Rd Oklahoma City OK 73120 Office: 6433 Avondale Dr Oklahoma City OK 73116

HILL, MYRTLE ELIZABETH HARKINS (MRS. JAMES MARTIN HILL), hosp. exec., city ofcl.; b. Quanah, Tex., May 23, 1915; d. Fred Agusta and Ida Mae (Scott) Harkins; food service certificate Adult Tng. Center, 1972; m. James Martin Hill, Dec. 6, 1952; children—Travis, Alvie (Mrs. Dickie Barton). Nurses aid Lockney (Tex.) Gen. Hosp., 1967-69, food supr., 1969—. Mem. Lockney City Council, 1971—. Coordinator Civil Def., 1971—, radio dispatcher, 1969—. Mem. Hosp. Instn. Ednl. Food Service Soc., Bus. and Profl. Women. Democrat. Baptist. Home: 220 SW 2d St Lockney TX 79241 Office: 320 N Main St Lockney TX 79241

HILL, NORMA JEAN WILLIAMSON, edn. writer, reporter; b. Tampa, Fla., Dec. 7, 1926; d. Tedford Stewart and Vera Lee (Morris) Williamson; student U. Mo., 1943-45; m. Robert W. Hill, Oct. 29, 1945 (div. June 1958); children—Cheryl Jo (Mrs. Peter Cimino), Christopher, Craig Morris. Reporter, St. Petersburg (Fla.) Times, 1955-59; bur. head Tampa Tribune, Bradenton, Fla., 1959-63, edn. writer, reporter, Tampa, 1963-66; edn. writer, reporter The Ledger, Cowles Communications, Inc., Lakeland, Fla., 1966-68; edn. writer Today, Cocoa, Fla., 1968-70; Capitol News Bur. chief, Gaunett, Fla., 1970-72; information officer Fla. Dept. Transp., Tallahassee, 1972-73; pub. information officer Alachua County Schs., Gainesville, Fla., 1973—. Mem. Nat. Sch. Pub. Relations Assn., Alpha Gamma Delta. Democrat. Presbyn. Home: 1810 NW 23d Blvd Apt 151 Gainesville FL 32605 Office: 1817 E University Av Gainesville FL 32601

HILL, PHYLLIS MALIE SITES (MRS. RALPH HILL), librarian; b. Indian Springs, Md., Nov. 30, 1923; d. George A. and Mamie (Funkhouser) Sites; student Frostburg State Tchrs. Coll., 1941-43; B.A. in Secondary Edn., Shepherd Coll., 1963; postgrad. U. Md., 1963; M.A. in English, Shippensburg State Coll., 1971; m. Ralph Hill, Oct. 3, 1943 (dec. 1961); children—Ronald Ancil, Christine Anne, Marshall Clifton, Samuel Alexander. Asst. librarian West Frederick Jr. High Sch., 1963; librarian Boonsboro (Md.) Sr. High Sch., 1963-67, Resource Center Library, Washington County Bd. Edn., Hagerstown, Md., 1967—, also coordinator sch. libraries. Recipient Dr. Christian award for play, 1950. Mem. A.L.A., Delta Kappa Gamma. Methodist. Author play: The Rainbow Trail, 1949. Co-author: Thirteen to One, 1969. Home: Route 2 Boonsboro MD 21713 Office: Washington County Bd Edn Hagerstown MD 21740

HILL, ROWENA JANET, retail store exec.; b. Defiance County, O., Oct. 13, 1916; d. Eras Walter and Laura Deette (Goddard) Snodgrass; grad. high sch.; m. William F. Hill, Jan. 26, 1934; 1 dau., Kathie L. Spicer. Clk., buyer Doenges Dept. Store, Ravenna, O., 1935-42; bookkeeper, cashier E.W. Uhlman Co., Defiance, O., 1942-49; with payroll dept. Gen. Motors, Defiance, 1950-51; sec., treas., store mgr. Williams Stores, Inc., West Unity, O., 1951—. Mem. Am. Legion Aux., Bus. and Profl. Womens Club (v.p. 1971-72). Methodist. Home: 709 E Jackson West Unity OH 43570 Office: 202-04 W Jackson West Unity OH 43570

HILL, RUTH DEANE (MRS. JOHN BERNARD HILL), librarian; b. Ingraham, Ill., Oct. 11, 1921; d. Everett C. and Ida H. (White) McCord; B.A., U. Ill., 1943, M.S., 1950; m. John Bernard Hill, June 2, 1945. Acquisitions and cataloging librarian U. Ill. Library, Urbana, 1950-58; librarian Unit Dist. #4, Champaign (Ill.) Pub. Schs., 1958-68; dir. library services Lincoln Land Community Coll., Springfield, Ill., 1968—. Instr. Nat. Defense Edn. Act Inst. for Sch. Librarians, U. Ill. Grad. Sch. Library Sci., 1965. Mem. Am. (Ill. councilor 1972—), Ill. (sec. 1971-72) library assns., Ill. Audio-Visual Assn., Freedom to Read Found. Home: 1721 Cherry Rd Springfield IL 62704 Office: 3865 S 6th St Springfield IL 62703

HILL, SHIRLEY ANN, educator; b. Kansas City, Mo., Aug. 26, 1927; d. George Haddon and Lena (Oberdiek) Hill; B.A., U. Mo., 1948; M.A., U. Kansas City, 1956; Ph.D., Stanford U., 1961. Elementary sch. tchr. Kansas City (Mo.) Pub. Schs., 1956-57, Jefferson Union Dist., Santa Clara, Cal., 1958-59; research asso. Stanford U., 1960-63; asso. prof. U. Mo., Kansas City, 1963-64; prof. edn. and math., 1965—, acting dean, Sch. Edn., 1964-65. Mem. Nat. Council Tchrs. Math. (bd. dirs. 1972-75), Math. Assn. Am. (bd. govs. 1972-74), Am. Math. Soc., Assn. Symbolic Logic, Philosophy Edn. Soc., Phi Beta Kappa, Phi Kappa Phi. Author: (with P. Suppes) First Course in Mathematical Logic, 1964, (with V. Haag and C. Hardgrove) Elementary Geometry, 1970. Home: 4820 W 76th St Prairie Village KS 66208 Office: 5100 Rockhill Rd Kansas City MO 64110

HILL, WATHINA SMITH, audiologist, educator; b. Mt. Ayr, Ia., Nov. 11, 1919; d. Orville Clarence and Electa Merle (Craft) Smith; B.S. in Edn., William Paterson Coll., 1959; M.A., Columbia, 1962, Ed.D., 1969; children by previous marriage—Jeffrey, Gregory. Prof. speech pathology William Paterson Coll., Wayne, N.J., 1962—; audiologist Bronx (N.Y.) VA Hosp., 1966—. Mem. Acoustical Soc. Am., Am. Speech and Hearing Assn. Home: 60-D Lakeview Av Leonia NJ 07605 Office: William Paterson Coll 300 Pompton Rd Wayne NJ 07470

HILLER, PHYLLIS LILLIAN, composer, publisher, author, musician; b. Petaluma, Cal., Aug. 5, 1927; d. Carl I. and Lily Florence (Riewerts) Unger; A.A., U. Cal. at Berkeley, 1946; B.A. in Music, San Francisco State Coll., 1949; m. Aaron Hiller, June 12, 1949; children—Julie, David, Daniel, Jonathan. Elementary sch. tchr., Cal., 1949-65; music curriculum specialist, Cal., 1965-67; composer, author, 1963—; dir. Creative Materials Library, Nashville, 1970—; owner Oak Hill Music Pub., also C & M Record Co., Nashville, 1970—. Lectr., cons. in music edn., edn. and human relations to schs., colls., child-oriented orgns. Mem. Nat. Acad. Rec. Arts and Scis., A.S.C.A.P., Am. Guild Authors and Composers, N.E.A., Music Educator's Nat. Conf., Assn. for Childhood Edn. Internat., Am. Assn. U. Women. Author, composer Ramo (song story), album and book, 1970. Composer, lyricist popular songs including Hole in the Sky, 1973, Parent Cycle Songs, Stages I, II, III, 1970, Dear Lord, Have I Stayed Away Too Long?, 1970, It's My Life, 1971, Songs for Children, 1973, Love Makes the Christmas, 1973, Give a Little Happiness for Christmas, 1973, Love is a Circle, 1970; Funny World, 1964. Office: PO Box 12068 Nashville TN 37212

HILLER, WENDY, actress; b. Stockport, Eng.; d. Frank and Marie (Stone) Hiller; ed. Winceby Sch.; m. Ronald Gow, Feb. 25, 1937; children—Ann, Anthony. Broadway debut in Love on the Dole, 1936; stage appearances in N.Y. include The Heiress, 1947; Moon for the Misbegotten, 1957; Flowering Cherry, 1959; Aspern Papers, 1961-62, Crown Matrimonial, 1973; motion pictures include Pygmalion, 1939, Major Barbara, 1941, I Know Where I'm Going, 1945, Separate Tables (Acad. award for best supporting actress 1958), 1958, Sons and Lovers, 1960; Toys in the Attic, 1963; A Man for All Seasons, 1966; David Copperfield, 1969. Decorated Order Brit. Empire.

HILLERY, MARY JANE LARATO (MRS. THOMAS H. HILLERY), editor; b. Boston, Sept. 15, 1931; d. Donato and Porzia (Avellis) Larato; Asso. Sci. (scholar), Northeastern U., 1950; m. Thomas H. Hillery, Feb. 25, 1961; 1 son, Thomas H. Sales agt., linguist Pan Am. Airways, Boston, 1955-61; interpreter Internat. Conf. Fire Chiefs, Boston, 1966; tchr. Spanish, YWCA, Natick, Mass., 1966-67; community relations cons., adv. bd. dirs., lectr. for migrant edn. project div. Mass. Dept. Community Affairs, Boston, 1967-69; editor-in-chief Sudbury (Mass.) Citizen, 1967—; area editorial adviser Beacon Pub. Co., Acton, Mass., 1970—. Mem. bus. adv. com. Town of Sudbury, Mass., 1972—; mem. Meml. Day Celebration Com., 1972—, mistress ceremonies, parade marshall, 1973, chmn., 1974. Bd. dirs., incorporator Sudbury Nonprofit Housing Corp., 1973—, chmn. Sudbury Town Report, 1969-72. Served with WAVES, 1950-54. Named Editor of Year, Beacon Pub. Co., 1970. Mem. Nat. Editorial Assn., Nat. Newspaper Assn., Internat. Platform Assn., New Eng. Press Assn., Bus. and Profl. Womens Club (1st v.p. 1973-74, pres. 1974), League Women Voters (dir. 1964-68), Nat. League Am. Pen Women (exec. bd. Boston 1974—), Omega Sigma. Home: 66 Willow Rd Sudbury MA 01776 Office: 369 Boston Post Rd Sudbury MA 01776

HILLERY, MARY RUTH ROMIG (MRS. VICTOR H. HILLERY), civic worker; b, Rochester, Ind., Dec. 7, 1915; d. Jesse Harrison and Lulu (Borden) Romig; grad. high sch.; m. Victor H. Hillery, Nov. 14, 1934; children—Phyllis (Mrs. Wayne Fribley), Kathleen (Mrs. Richard Goshert), David L., Steven L. Field mgr. cosmetic div. Fuller Brush Co., 1948-52; with Ward Jewelers, 1953-56; dist. rep. Internat. Com. State Extension Homemakers, 1969-70, pres. exec. bd., 1969, pres. county, 1969; treas. Ind. Extension Homemakers Assn., 1971-72. Staff aid A.R.C., 1945-55; bd. dirs. Civil Def. 1951-59, Trustee County Fair Bd., 1968-69, gen. supr. women's dept., 1970. Mem. Internat. Platform Assn., Farm Bus. (county sec. 1961-62), Beauceant. Republican. Methodist. Mem. Order Eastern Star. Home: Route 2 Warsaw IN 46580

HILLIS, MARGARET, musician; b. Kokomo, Ind., Oct. 1, 1921; d. Glen R. and Bernice (Haynes) Hillis; B.A., Ind. U., 1947, Mus.D. (hon.), 1972; grad. student choral conducting, Juilliard Sch. Music, 1947-49; Mus.D. (hon.), Temple U., 1967. Dir. Met. Youth Chorale, Bklyn., 1948-51; asst. condr. Collegiate Chorale, N.Y.C., 1952-53; mus. dir., condr. Am. Concert Choir, N.Y.C., 1950, Am. Concert Orch., 1950; condr., instr. Union Theol. Sem., 1950-60, Juilliard Sch. Music, 1951-53; dir. choral dept. Third St. Music Sch. Settlement, 1953-54; founder, mus. dir. Am. Choral Found., 1954; mus. dir. N.Y. Chamber Soloists, 1956-60; choral dir. N.Y.C. Opera Co., 1955-56; condr., choral dir. Chgo. Symphony Chorus, 1957—, Santa Fe Opera Co., 1958-59; choral dir. Chgo. Mus. Coll., 1961-62; condr. Kenosha (Wis.) Symphony Orch., 1961-68; resident condr. Chgo. Civic Orchestra, 1967—; chmn. dept. choral activities Sch. Music, Northwestern U., 1971—; mus. dir., condr. Elgin (Ill.) Symphony Orch., 1971—. Adviser Nat. Fedn. Music Clubs Youth Auditions, 1966-70; music dir. Choral Inst., 1968-70; asst. to mus. dir. Chgo.

Symphony Orch., 1966-68; dir. Cleve. Orch. Choruses, 1969-71; mem. adv. music panel Nat. Endowment for Arts, 1972—. Civilian flight instr., USN, CAA, WTS, World War II. Recipient Profl. Pan Hellenic Assn. award, 1964; Golden Plate award Am. Acad. Achievement, 1967; Steinway award for outstanding contbns. to cause of music, 1969; outstanding alumnus of yr. award Ind. U. Sch. Music Alumni Assn., 1969; Leader Luncheon I award Chgo. YWCA, 1972; Friends of Lit. award, 1973. Mem. Nat. Fedn. Music Clubs (hon.), Musicians Club of Women (hon.), P.E.O., Internat. Platform Assn., Am. Choral Dirs. Assn., Assn. Choral Dirs., Sigma Alpha Iota (hon.), Pi Kappa Lambda. Office: Am Choral Found Inc 130 W 56th St New York City NY 10019 also Chgo Symphony Orch 220 S Michigan Av Chicago IL 60604

HILLIS, MARY OLIVE, chemist, educator; b. Beardstown, Ill., Dec. 11, 1919; A.B., MacMurray Coll., 1941; M.S. (scholar), U. Ill., 1942, Ph.D. in Analytical Chemistry (fellow), 1944. Instr. chemistry Vassar Coll., Poughkeepsie, N.Y., 1944-49, asst. prof., 1949-55, asso. prof., 1955-62, prof., 1962—, chmn. dept. chemistry, 1961-63, 67-69, 71-73, sr. advisor office of dean of studies, 1967, Vassar faculty fellow, 1969-70. Mem. Am. Chem. Soc. (curriculum com. div. edn.). Research on complex ion formation, qualitative micro analysis, procedure for systematic micro analysis of cations, computer assisted instrn. Address: Dept of Chemistry Vassar College Poughkeepsie NY 12601

HILLMAN, BARBARA JANE, lawyer; b. Chgo., Aug. 11, 1942; d. James J. and Anita (Sager) Hillman; B.A., U. Chgo., 1963, J.D., 1966; m. Arnold Eugene Charnin, Oct. 2, 1967. Admitted to Ill. bar, 1967; partner firm Kleiman, Cornfield & Feldman, Chgo., 1966—. Mem. Am., Chgo. bar assns., Chgo. Council Lawyers. Home: 544 W Belden Av Chicago IL 60614 Office: 10 S LaSalle St Chicago IL 60603

HILLMAN, ELSIE HILLIARD (MRS. HENRY LEA HILLMAN), polit. worker; b. Pitts., Dec. 9, 1925; d. Thomas Jones and Marianna (Talbott) Hilliard; student Westminster Choir Coll., 1944-45; m. Henry Lea Hillman, May, 1945; children—Juliet (Mrs. J. Todd Simonds), Audrey (Mrs. Timothy O. Fisher), Henry Lea, William Talbott. Mem. adv. com. Woman's Bd. Carnegie Mus. Mem. 14th ward Republican Com., 1956, chmn. 1964—; mem. Rep. Finance Com., 1963; mem. Pa. State Adv. Com., 1963; mem. Rep. State Exec. Com., 1963; alternate del. Rep. Nat. Conv., 1964, del., 1968; chmn. Rep. Exec. Com. Allegheny County, 1967-70; co-chmn. Re-elect Nixon Dinner, 1971. Trustee Ellis Sch., Pitts., 1951-66, hon. bd. mem. 1966—; mem. bd. trustees Carlow Coll.; 1st v.p., dir. Hill House Assn., 1973—; bd. dirs. Pitts. Oratorio Soc., Pitts. Symphony Soc., Squirrel Hill Bd. Trade, bd. dirs. Squirrel Hill Urban Coalition, 1972, v.p. 1972—. Named Women of Year, Squirrel Hill Kiwanis, 1965; Humanitarian award Guardians of Greater Pitts., 1973; Nat. Brotherhood award (with husband) Nat. Conf. Christians and Jews, 1973. Mem. Urban League of Pitts. (dir., 1st v.p. 1970). Episcopalian (mem. vestry 1973). Home: Holyrood Rd Morewood Heights Pittsburgh PA 15213

HILLMAN, JUANITA JULIA (MRS. ALFRED ZEIKUS), chemist; b. LaSalle, Ill., Oct. 16, 1939; d. Otto John and Ann (Mentgen) Hillman; A.A., LaSalle-Peru Jr. Coll., 1959; B.S., U. Ill., 1961; M.S., U. Ia., 1964, Ph.D., 1967; m. Alfred Zeikus, Aug. 1, 1970; 1 son, John. Summer chemist Dow Chem. Soc., Midland, Mich., 1962, U.S. Dept. Agr., Peoria, Ill., 1963; research asst. med. research U.S. Vets. Hosp., Iowa City, Ia., 1964; research chemist Ill. Inst. Tech. Research Inst., Chgo., 1967-71, Research Triangle Inst., Raleigh, N.C., 1972-73, E.I. duPont de Nemours & Co., Kinston, N.C., 1973—. Recipient NSF Summer Grant, U. Ill., 1961. Mem. Am. Chem. Soc., A.A.A.S., N.Y. Acad. Scis., Sigma Xi, Iota Sigma Pi. Patentee in field. Home: 512 Middle St New Bern NC 28560 Office: Box 800 Kinston NC 28501

HILLPOT, MAUREEN TOOMEY (MRS. WILLIAM ARTHUR HILLPOT), advt. and marketing exec.; b. N.Y.C.; d. Timothy Hugh and Bina Honora (Sullivan) Toomey; B.S. magna cum laude, Coll. White Plains, 1959; postgrad. Columbia U., 1960-62; m. William Arthur Hillpot, Oct. 29, 1959. Head, creative group J. Walter Thompson, N.Y.C., 1962-68; dir. marketing and advt. Am. Express Co., N.Y.C., 1968-70; asst. to pres. S.S.C.&B.-Lintas, N.Y.C., 1971—; dir. Windsor Life Ins. Co.; cons. Vogue, Beauty Fashion. Mem. planning com. Coll. of White Plains (N.Y.), 1973—. Rep. county committeewoman, 1967—. Mem. Am. Irish Hist. Soc., Womens Rest Tour Assn. Boston, Phi Beta Kappa. Club: Rolls-Royce Bentley Owners. Author: An American Woman, 1968; Beauty and Travel, 1971. Home: 295 Central Park W New York City NY 10024 Office: 1 Dag Hammerskjold Plaza New York City NY 10017

HILLS, BARBARA BEHRENS (MRS. DAVID ALLEN HILLS), psychologist, educator; b. Oelwien, Ia., July 4, 1933; d. Karl Frederick and Pearl Olga (Webb) Behrens; B.A. with highest distinction, U. Ia., 1955, M.A., 1959, Ph.D., 1960; m. David Allen Hills, Dec. 28, 1958; children—Karen Jane, Kristin Joan, Stuart David. Chief psychologist Child Guidance Clinic of Forsyth County, Winston-Salem, N.C., 1960—; asst. prof. Salem Coll., Winston-Salem, 1960-65, asso. prof. psychology, 1965—, chmn. dept. psychology-edn., 1973—. Cons. psychology Full Year Headstart Child Devel. Program, 1965—, N.C. Advancement Sch., 1970—. Mem. Mental Health Task Force, 1969-70; v.p. Child Devel. Program, 1970-74; mem. steering com. Citizens Coalition Early Childhood Devel., 1973-74; mem. exec. com. Urban Coalition Day Care Assn., 1968-70; mem. Forsyth County Day Care Com., 1970-73. Trustee Children's Home of the South, 1963-66. N.C. Dept. Mental Health Research grantee, 1971-72. Mem. Am., N.C. psychol. assns., Phi Beta Kappa. Democrat. Lutheran. Home: 2160 Royall Dr Winston-Salem NC 27106 Office: 1200 Glade St Winston-Salem NC 27101

HILLS, CARLA ANDERSON (MRS. RODERICK M. HILLS), lawyer; b. Los Angeles, Jan. 3, 1934; d. Herman Carl and Edith Hume (Wagner) Anderson; student Oxford U., Eng., 1954; A.B. cum laude, Stanford, 1955; LL.B., Yale, 1958; m. Roderick Maltman Hills, Sept. 27, 1958; children—Laura Hume, Roderick Maltman, Megan Elizabeth, Alison Macbeth. Admitted to Cal. bar, 1959; asst. U.S. atty. Civil Div., Los Angeles, 1959-61; partner firm Munger, Tolles, Hills & Rickershauser, Los Angeles, 1962-74; asst. atty. gen. civil div. Dept. Justice, Washington, 1974—. Adj. prof. law U. Cal. at Los Angeles Law Sch., spring 1972. Mem. standing com. on discipline U.S. Dist. Ct., Central Dist. Cal., 1970; mem. corrections task force Los Angeles County Subregional Adv. Bd. Reporting to Cal. Council on Criminal Justice, 1969-71; mem. Adminstrv. Conf. U.S., 1972-74; mem.-at-large exec. com. Yale Law Sch., 1973—. Trustee, Pomona Coll., 1974—; bd. councilors U. So. Cal. Law Center. Mem. Am. (chmn. publs. com. antitrust Sect.), Fed. (pres. Los Angeles chpt. 1963), Los Angeles County (chmn. Law Day com. 1967, chmn. issues and survey com. 1970-72, fed. rules and practice com. 1963-72, jud. qualifications com. 1971-72, chmn. sub-com. for revision local rules for fed. cts. 1966-72, mem. exec. com. trial lawyers sect. 1970-74) bar assns., State Bar Cal. (exec. com.), Womens Lawyers Assn. (pres. 1965). Club: Yale (v.p., dir. Los Angeles). Author: (with others) Federal Civil Practice, 1961; editor, author (with others): Antitrust Adviser, 1971. Home: 3125 Chain Bridge Rd Washington DC 20016 Office: Dept Justice Civil Div 10th and Constitution Av NW Washington DC 20530

HILLS, FRANCES MARIE GRUNDY (MRS. JETHRO LEE HILLS), mathematician; b. El Paso, Tex., May 14, 1926; d. Sherman and Blanche Ethel (Henderson) Grundy; B.A., Talladega Coll., 1945; postgrad. U. N.M., 1948-49; m. Jethro Lee Hills, Dec. 28, 1949; children—Jethro Lee II, Patricia, William. Tchr., El Paso (Tex.) Pub. Schs., 1945-47; critic tchr. math. Drewry Practice High Sch., Talladega, Ala., 1947-48; program sec., summer replacement dir. USO, El Paso, Tex., 1949; ballistic computer Civil Service, Ft. Bliss, Tex., 1951-52, clk. typist, 1954, math. aid, 1954, mathematician, 1955-59, supr. math., chief data reduction and analysis, 1959-71, supr. mathematician, chief data systems analysis U.S. Army Air Def. Bd. Ft. Bliss, 1971—. Chmn. Fed. Women's Program Com., Ft. Bliss, Tex., 1971-73; chmn. social concerns El Paso council Campfire Girls, 1972—; leader Rio Grande council Girl Scouts Am., 1945-47; co-chmn. steering com. Fed. Women's Council, El Paso, 1973. Recipient Outstanding Local Dau. of Isis award, 1970; named Civilian Servant of Year, Fed. Bus. Assn., El Paso, 1969. Mem. Delta Sigma Theta (pres. El Paso chpt. 1965-67). Baptist (dir. youth mission 1968-70). Mem. Order Eastern Star. Clubs: Progressive Bridge; Toastmasters (pres. 1973). Home: 3029 E Missouri Av El Paso TX 79903 Office: US Army Air Defense Bd Fort Bliss TX 79916

HILLS, VIRGINIA LOUISE CARTER (MRS. BENJAMIN O. HILLS, JR.), librarian; b. Essexville, Mich., Apr. 23, 1920; d. Charles Frederick and Emma (Treiber) Carter; B.S., Radford Coll., 1942; B.S. in Library Sci., Cath. U. Am., 1951; m. Benjamin O. Hills, Jr., Mar. 2, 1957. With Nat. Geog. Soc., Washington, 1943—, librarian, 1965—. Mem. Spl. Libraries Assn. (cons. com.), D.C. Library Assn. (dir.), Assn. Am. Geographers, Am. Assn. U. Women, Am. Soc. Information Scis., Zonta Internat. (Washington sec. 1968-69, local dir. 1970—). Home: 4004 49th St NW Washington DC 20016 Office: Nat Geog Soc 16th and M Sts NW Washington DC 20036

HILLSMAN, GLADYS M. ZORMEIR, sch. psychologist, psychiat. center exec.; b. St. Joseph, Minn., July 5, 1921; d. John Henry and Mary (Foley) Zormeir; B.S., Coll. St. Scholastica, 1943; M.S., Boston U., 1960; postgrad. Ohio State U., 1968—; m. John Mathis Hillsman, June 7, 1949 (div. Mar. 1958); children—Edward Lloyd, Joseph Dwight. Instr., St. Josephs Hosp., St. Paul, 1943-44; civil service staff nurse Gen. Hosp., Cristobal, CZ 1944-46; pvt. duty and group nursing, 1946; instr. Jackson Meml. Hosp., Miami, Fla., 1946-48; dir. nursing edn. Hillcrest Med. Center, Tulsa, 1948-49; dir. nursing Childrens Med. Center, Tulsa, 1957-58, 60-62; nursing cons. Ohio Dept. Health, Columbus, 1962-67; dir. Childhood League Pre-Sch. Devel. Center, Columbus, 1967-72; research asst. Nisonger Center, Ohio State U., 1972-73; exec. dir. St. Vincent Children's Center, Columbus, 1973—. Mem. profl. services adv. bd. United Cerebral Palsy Ohio, 1964—, Childhood League Pre-Sch. for Slow Learners, 1965-67; mem. exec. bd. Council for Retarded Children, 1966-68, Hearing and Speech Center Columbus and Central Ohio, 1966-69; mem. Ohio Gov.'s Task Force on Mental Health and Mental Retardation, Ohio Developmental Disabilities Planning and Adv. Council. Mem. Am. Orthopsychiat. Assn., Ohio Rehab. Assn., Am. Nurses Assn., Am. Assn. Maternal and Child Health, Ohio Assn. Retarded Children, Ohio Sch. Psychologists Assn., Central Ohio Psychol. Assn., Assn. Early Childhood Edn. Contbr. articles to profl. jours. Home: 222 Deland Av Columbus OH 43214 Office: 1490 E Main St Columbus OH 43205

HILLSMITH, FANNIE, artist; b. Boston, Mar. 13, 1911; ed. Boston Mus. Sch. Exhibited in one-man shows Norlyst Gallery, N.Y.C., 1943, Charles Egan Gallery, 1949, 54, The Swetzoff Gallery, 1949, 50, 54, 57, 63, The Peridot Gallery, 1957, 58, 62, Colby Coll., 1950, Santa Barbara Mus. Art, 1950, Dayton Art Inst., 1954, Currier Gallery, Manchester, N.H., 1954, Milton Acad., 1952, Weeden Gallery, Boston, 1967, 69, Fitchburg (Mass.) Art Mus., 1969, Inst. Contemporary Art, Boston, 1969, Brockton (Mass.) Art Mus., 1971, Thorne Art Gallery, Keene (N.H.) State Coll., 1972, Bristol (R.I.) Art Mus., 1972; group shows Art of this Century, N.Y.C., Carnegie Internat., 1955, Chgo. Art Inst., 1947, 48, 54, Boston Mus. Fine Arts, Bklyn. Mus., U. Ill., Walker Art Center, Mpls., Guggenheim Mus., N.Y.C., Whitney Mus., N.Y.C., Mus. Modern Art, N.Y.C., Boston Arts Festival, Dayton Inst., others; works represented in numerous collections. Tchr. Black Mountain (N.C.) Coll., 1945; vis. critic Cornell U., 1963. Recipient First Prize, Boston Arts Festival, 1957, 63; First Prize, Portland (Me.) Mus. Art, 1958, others. Traveling scholar Boston Mus. Fine Arts. Address: 915 2d Av New York City NY 10017

HILLYARD, LUCILE DORSEY, journalist; b. Kirksville, Mo., Mar. 3, 1917; d. Clyde A. and Frances (Buck) Dorsey; grad. high sch.; m. John H. Hillyard, July 6, 1941; children—John, Martin, Mary (Mrs. Dwight Sanburn), Stephen, James, Mark, Lucy, Thomas, Michael, Philip, Marguerite, Teresa, Joseph. Sec., Coast Counties Land Title Co., Monterey, Cal., 1940-41; bookkeeper, J.H. Hillyard & Sons, San Mateo, Cal., 1956-74; feature writer Advance-Star, Burlingame, Cal., 1967-69, Redwood City (Cal.) Tribune, 1969—. Mem. Christian Family Movement, 1955-60; mem. Circle of Concern, 1969—. Home: 1541 Ralston Av Burlingame CA 94010 Office: 901 Marshall St Redwood City CA 94063

HILPERT, BRUNETTE KATHLEEN POWERS (MRS. ELMER ERNEST HILPERT), civic worker; b. Baton Rouge, Feb. 12, 1909; d. Edward Oliver and Orvilla (Nettles) Powers; A.B., La. State U., 1930, B.S. in L.S., 1933; postgrad. Columbia, 1937; m. Elmer Ernest Hilpert, Aug. 1, 1938; children—Margaret Ray (Mrs. L. Bryan Woolley), Elmer Ernest II. Cataloguer, La. State U. Library, Baton Rouge, 1930-36, La. State U. Law Sch. Library, 1936-38; librarian Washington U. Law Sch. Library, St. Louis, 1940-42; reference librarian Washington U. Library, St. Louis, 1952-54. Drive capt. United Fund, St. Louis, 1956; del. White House Conf. on Edn., St. Louis, 1962. Trustee John Burroughs Sch., 1959-63; dir. Grace Hill Settlement House, 1957-63, v.p., 1960-62; dir. Internat. Inst., 1964-68; dir. Neighborhood Health Center, 1964-67, sec., 1964-66; dir. Arts and Edn. Council, 1967—; pres., dir. Womens Assn. St. Louis Symphony Soc., 1969-71; exec. com., dir. St. Louis Symphony Soc., 1969—; dir. Miss. River Festival, 1969—; dir. Women's adv. bd. Continental Bank & Trust Co., 1970—; dir. St. Louis Inst. Music, 1971—, St. Louis String Quartet, 1971—, Community Music Sch., 1973—. Recipient Woman of Achievement award St. Louis Globe Democrat, 1967. Mem. Nat. Soc. Arts and Letters (dir. 1964-65), Delta Zeta. Republican. Presbyn. Club: Wednesday (recording sec. 1963-64). Home: 6321 Pershing Av St Louis MO 63130

HILTON, CAROL RUTH SPECHT (MRS. JOHN E. HILTON, II), editor; b. Los Angeles, Dec. 22, 1925; s. Joseph Alexander and Elsie Agnes (Herring) Specht; A.B., U. So. Cal., 1948; M.A., U. Wash., 1966; m. John E. Hilton, II, Mar. 26, 1949; 1 son, John E. III. News editor Northshore Citizen, Bothell, Wash., 1959-64; asst. to dir. Sch. of Communications, U. Wash., 1966-70; reporter Herald-Republic, Yakima, Wash., 1970-71, women's news editor, 1971—. Recipient 1st place nat. award for publicity and promotion Nat. Fedn. Press Women, 1961, numerous state awards. Mem. Nat. Fedn. Press Women, Washington Press Women (treas. 1963-64), Women in Communications, Chi Omega. Home: Route 3 Box 750 Yakima WA 98901 Office: 114 N 4th St Yakima WA 98901

HILTON, ERNESTINE ISADORA (MRS. EARL HILTON), civic worker; b. Asotin, Wash., Feb. 20, 1920; d. Ernest Franklin and Myrtle Mae (Marks) McMillan; B.A. with honors in Edn., Eastern Wash. State Coll., 1941; m. Earl Laverne Hilton, Sept. 13, 1942; children—Earl Laverne, Nancy (Mrs. William R. Odell), Richard Lester, Jerold Lauren. Tchr. elementary sch., Spangle, Wash., 1941-42; pres. Spokane County United Sch. Groups, 1959, Cheney Sch. Bd., 1956-65; Eastside v.p. Wash. State Sch. Dirs. Assn., 1963-65; pres. Wash. State P.T.A., 1968-70; mem. tchr. edn. adv. com. State Supt. Office, 1966-72; adv. com. Vocational Edn., 1970-72; N.W. Regional Task Force for Counselor Edn. U.S. Office Edn., 1968-70; mem. Nat. Commn. for Support Pub. Schs., 1963-72; mem. nat. council Camp Fire Girls, 1960-66; mem. Gov.'s Steering Com. for Tax Reform, 1970; Gov.'s Com. for White House Conf. on Children and Youth, 1969-70; reviewer Nat. Assessment Ednl. Progress, 1970—. Mem. bd., chmn. edn. commn. Nat. Congress Parents and Tchrs., 1971—. Recipient Outstanding Service award Wash. State P.T.A., 1971; Nat. Camp Fire Leaders award for service to youth, 1966. Life mem. Nat., Ore. (life), Wash. State, Mont. P.T.A.'s; mem. League Women Voters. Home: Route 3 Box 75 Cheney WA 99004

HILTON, HELEN LE BARON (MRS. J. H. HILTON), coll. dean; b. Morrisville, Vt., Feb. 28, 1910; d. W. Irving and Ida May (Norton) Le Baron; B.S., U. Vt., 1932, D. Sc., 1964; M.S., Cornell U., 1938; Ph.D., U. Chgo., 1946; m. J. H. Hilton, May 1970. Dietetic internship Peter Bent Brigham Hosp., Boston, 1933; nursery sch. tchr., Burlington, Vt., 1934; high sch. tchr. home econs., Enosburg Falls, Vt., 1934-37; asst. state supr. home econs. State Dept. Edn., Vt., 1938-41, state supr. home econs., 1941-46; instr. U. Vt., 1938-41, asst. prof. home econs., 1941-46; asst. dir. home econs. Penn State Coll., 1946-48, asst. dean home econs., 1948-52; dean Coll. Home Econs., Ia. State U., Ames, 1952—. Dir., Jewel Cos., Inc., S.C. Johnson and Son, Inc. Mem. Am., Ia. home econs. assns., Am. Assn. U. Women, League Women Voters, Mortar Bd., Omicron Nu, Phi Epsilon Omicron, Phi Beta Kappa, Pi Lambda Theta, Delta Kappa Gamma, Alpha Xi Delta, Phi Kappa Phi. Unitarian. Club: Altrusa. Home: 1020 Gaskill Dr Ames IA 50010

HILTON, MARY NELSON, govt. ofcl.; b. Junction City, Ore., Nov. 22, 1914; d. Charles R. and Della (Myhre) Nelson; student Willamette U., 1932-34; B.A., U. Ore., 1936, M.A., 1941; m. Howard J. Hilton, Apr. 22, 1943; children—Howard Nelson, Mary Alice, Richard Judd. Grad. asst. econs. U. Ore., 1936-38, research asst. Bur. Municipal Research, 1938-39; jr. economist Maritime Labor Bd., 1939-40; asst. economist wage and hour div. Dept. Labor, 1940-41; div. chief Nat. War Labor Bd., Washington, 1941-46; chief research div. Women's Bur., Dept. Labor, 1949-55, chief sect. area unemployment and labor force surveys Bur. Labor Statistics, 1955, br. chief div. fgn. labor conditions, 1960-62; spl. asst. President's Commn. on Status of Women, 1962-63; dep. dir. Women's Bur., Dept. Labor, 1965—. Chmn. Am. Women's Group, Bonn, Germany, 1958-60. Recipient President's Commn. on Status Women Distinguished Service award, 1963, Distinguished Career Service award Dept. Labor, 1972. Mem. Am. Econ. Assn., Phi Beta Kappa. Home: 5022 Reno Rd NW Washington DC 20008 Office: Dept of Labor Washington DC 20210

HILTON, MAXINE TATE CALFEE, radio news exec., buyer and fashion coordinator; b. Seven Mile Ford, Va., Apr. 2, 1920; d. Alvin Luther and Willie (Seldomridge) Calfee; student Mary Washington Coll., 1937-38; B.S., Madison Coll., 1941; m. Donald E. Hilton, July 17, 1943; children—Helen Calfee, Howard Schaffer. Dietitian Johnston Meml. Hosp., 1941-44; owner, mgr. (with husband) various stores, 1944—, Maxine's ladies' specialty shop, Abingdon, Va., 1946—, Wytheville, Va., 1949—. Dir. women's news WBBI radio, Abingdon, 1956—, narrator, interviewer, women's program, 1956—. chmn. Abingdon Bd. Archtl. Rev., 1972—; dist. chmn. Girl Scouts U.S.A., Va., Tenn., 1966, bd. dirs. Appalachian council, 1966-69, council v.p., 1970-73, council pres., 1974—; pres. William King Sch. P.T.A., 1965-67; mem. adv. bd. Sr. Services, Inc., 1972—. Bd. dirs. Holston Tb Assn., 1964-65, Johnston Meml. Hosp. Aux., 1964-66, Va. Highland Arts and Crafts Festival, 1964-66. Recipient First Place award Va. A.P., annually, 1958-62. Named Woman of Year Abingdon br. Am. Assn. U. Women, 1968. Mem. Abingdon Bus. and Profl. Womens Club (v.p. 1958-59, 62-63, pres. 1972-73), Washington County Hist. Soc., Va. Congress P.T.A., Alpha Sigma Alpha. Methodist (pres. service guild 1957-58, mem. com. missions 1963-68, mem. pastoral relations com. 1967-72). Booklovers. Home: 108 Court St Abingdon VA 24210 Office: 112 Court St Abingdon VA 24210

HILTON, NANNIE ALICE (MRS. RALPH HILTON), mus. ofcl.; b. Ellensburg, Wash., Feb. 27, 1905; d. Benjamin Meeks and Mary (Dennis) Shelton; student U. Wash., 1930-32; B.A., Central Wash. Coll., 1948; m. Ralph Hilton, June 2, 1937; children—Judith Ann (Mrs. Frank Weldin), Mary Frances. Tchr., Ellensburg, 1923-37, Thorp, Wash., 1941-48, Monticello Jr. High Sch., Longview, Wash., 1948-70; dir. Cowlitz County Hist. Mus., Kelso, Wash., 1970—. Leader, Camp Fire Girls, 1934-37. Recipient Sci. Tchr. award Ore. Mus. Sci. and Industry, 1965. Mem. N.E.A., Nat. Council Tchrs. Math., Western Assn. Museums, Bus. and Profl. Womens Clubs (pres. Kelso 1974—). Rebekah, Soroptimist. Home: 2915 Garfield St Longview WA 98632 Office: Court House Annex Kelso WA 98626

HILTON, SUZANNE MCLEAN (MRS. WARREN MITCHELL HILTON), author; b. Pitts., Sept. 3, 1922; d. Edwin Postlethwaite and Helen Fish (McFeely) McLean; student Pa. Coll. for Women (now Chatham Coll.), Pitts., 1940-42; B.A., Beaver Coll., Glenside, Pa., 1945; m. Warren Mitchell Hilton, June 15, 1946; children—E. Bruce, Diana Lester. Author: How Do They Get Rid of It, 1970; How Do They Cope With It, 1970; It's Smart to Use a Dummy, 1971; It's a Model World, 1972; Beat It, Burn It and Drown It, 1973; The Way It Was-1876, 1975; copywriter advt. dept. Westminster Press, 1969-73; dir. pub. relations Jenkintown (Pa.) Sch. Dist., 1970—. Active Girl Scouts U.S.A., Boy Scouts Am. Mem. Phila. Children's Reading Round Table, Jenkintown Newcomer's Club (pres.). Methodist. Home: 301 Runnymede Av Jenkintown PA 19046

HIMENS, SISTER MARY KATHRYN, coll. adminstr.; b. Antioch, Ill., Sept. 24, 1929; d. Mike and Lucy Josephine (Bolte) Himens; A.B., Coll. St. Francis, 1951; M.Ed., St. Louis U., 1960; Ednl. Specialist in Counseling, Western State Coll., 1970. Tchr. Holy Family Acad., Beaverville, Ill., 1951-65, asst. prin., 1955-59, prin., 1959-65; coordinator religious edn. St. Peter's Parish, Gunnison, Colo., 1965-74; coordinator student ednl. devel. Western State Coll., Gunnison, 1970—. Supt. schs., directress of studies Servants of the Holy Heart of Mary, Am. Province, 1959-68. Mem. Nat., Colo.-Wyo. assns. women deans and counselors, Nat. Assn. Women Deans, Adminstrs. and Counselors. Home: Our Lady of Peace PO Box 882 Gunnison CO 81230 Office: Western State College 108 Taylor Hall Gunnison CO 81230

HIMMELSTEIN, FANNIE, lawyer; b. Hartford, Conn., Mar. 5, 1908; d. Joseph Nathan and Gussie (Beresner) Himmelstein; grad. Hartford Coll. Law, 1931. Admitted to Conn. bar; practice law with firm Albrecht & Richman, Hartford, 1926-65; pvt. practice law,

Hartford, 1965—; legal aid dir. City of Hartford, 1946-53; asst. corp. counsel Town of West Hartford, 1969—. Counsel to United Synagogues of Greater Hartford, Hadassah, Jewish Children's Orgn., Zonta Club of Hartford Area. Sec., Jewish Children's Service Orgn., Hebrew Women's Home for Children. Mem. West Hartford Republican Town Com., 1960—, Conn. Rep. Central Com., 1966-72. Mem. Am., Conn., Hartford County bar assns., Zonta (past dist. treas.), Alumni Assn. Hartford Coll. Law (past pres.), Hadassah (past pres.). Mem. Conn. Human Rights Commn. Home: 68 Carlyle Rd West Hartford CT 06117 Office: 410 Asylum St Hartford CT 06103

HIMWICH, WILLIAMINA ARMSTRONG (MRS. HAROLD E. HIMWICH), biochemist; b. Spokane, Wash., Mar. 4, 1912; d. George Kilpatrick and Zoe (Brouillet) Armstrong; B.S., U. Ida., 1933, M.S., 1934; Ph.D., Ia. State U., 1939; m. Harold E. Himwich, Sept. 24, 1943; children—Alec, Hugh, Ed. Researcher home econs. U. Ill., Urbana, 1939-41; head house econs. research Okla. A. and M. U., Stillwater, 1941-43; researcher in physiology Albany Med. Coll. (N.Y.), 1943-46; toxicologist, Army Chem. Center, 1946-49; research scientist Johns Hopkins U., Balt., 1949-51; med. research asso. Thudichum Psychol. Research Lab., Galesburg, Ill., 1952-69, adminstrv. research scientist, 1969-72. Research prof. psychiatry, prof. biochemistry U. Neb. Coll. Medicine, 1972. Chmn. sci. adv. com. Cerebral Palsy Ill., 19—. Recipient Distinguished Service award Cerebral Palsy Ill., 1972; Distinguished Achievement citation Ia. State U., 1974. Mem. Internat. Soc. Devel. Psychobiology (pres. 1974-75), Soc. Biol. Psychology (pres. 1973-74), Soc. Neuroscis., Am. Acad. Neurology, Am. Chem. Soc., Am. Neurochem. Soc., Am. Physiol. Soc., Internat. Brain Research Orgn., Am. Soc. Pharmacology and Exptl. Therapeutics. Editor: Biochemistry of Developing Brain, Vol. I, 1973, Vol. 2, 1974; Developmental Neurobiology, 1970. Home: 907 Hackberry Ct No 1904 Bellevue NE 68005 Office: 602 S 45th St Omaha NE 68106

HINCHLIFFE, ETHEL KOSSWIG (MRS. JOHN C. HINCHLIFFE), nurse; b. New Britain, Conn., May 16, 1919; d. Walter George and Hilda Frances (Helm) Kosswig; R.N., New Britain Gen. Hosp., 1940; m. John C. Hinchliffe, June 16, 1941; children—Diane (Mrs. Leo J. Dufour), David John, John C. Operating room nurse, pvt. duty nurse, staff nurse New Britain Gen. Hosp., 1940-41, staff nurse, 1950-56; asst. head nurse Petersburg (Va.) Gen. Hosp., 1941; indsl. nurse Farnir Bearing Co., New Britain, 1942; vis. pub. health nurse, 1943-44; nurse urologists office, surgery asst., New Britain, 1944-45; sch. nurse Consol. Sch. Dist., New Britain, 1956—. Conn. adv. com. Sch. Nurse Certification. Active YWCA, mem. Handicap Swim club. Mem. Assn. Sch. Nurses Conn. (area chmn. 1964-67, v.p. 1966-68, pres. 1969-71), Conn., New Britain edn. assns., N.E.A. (Conn. dir. to dept. sch. nurses 1968-71, Conn. del. to dept. sch. nurses nat. convs. Phila. 1969, San Francisco 1970, Detroit 1971, 1st bd. dirs. dept. sch. nurses 1968-69), Alumnae New Britain Gen. Hosp. Club: Baldwin Yacht (Saybrook, Conn.). Lutheran (chorister choir 1935—, music and worship com. 1967—). Office: Sch Adminstrn Bldg Hillside Pl New Britain CT 06050

HINCKLEY, JOAN (MRS. CHARLES EDWARD HINCKLEY), city ofcl.; b. Waurika, Okla., Nov. 18, 1918; d. Otis Lawrence and Jimmie Vaude (Allen) Ratcliffe; student San Mateo Jr. Coll., 1936-37; m. Charles Edward Hinckley, June 24, 1939; children—Judy Michele, David Charles. Clerical positions City Clk's. Office, San Mateo, Cal., 1937-41, city clk. San Mateo, 1971—; legal sec. city atty., San Mateo, Cal., 1941-42; sec. Concrete Ship Builders, San Diego, 1942-45; sec. to city mgr., San Mateo, Cal., 1946-71. Mem. Internat. Inst. Municipal Clks., Cal. City Clks. Assn. Home: 666 Ventura Av San Mateo CA 94403 Office: 330 W 20th Av San Mateo CA 94403

HINCKS, MARCIA LOCKWOOD (MRS. JOHN WINSLOW HINCKS), lawyer; b. N.Y.C., July 3, 1935; d. John Salem and Dorothy Eleanor (Tufts) Lockwood; B.A. magna cum laude, Bryn Mawr Coll., 1956; LL.B. cum laude, Yale, 1959; m. John Winslow Hincks, June 14, 1958; children—Rebecca, Jennifer, John, Benjamin. Admitted to Conn. bar, 1960; atty. Aetna Life & Casualty Co., Hartford, Conn., 1961-64, 67-70, counsel, 1971—. Bd. dirs. Planned Parenthood League Conn.; trustee Hotchkiss Sch., Lakeville, Conn. Mem. Conn., Hartford County bar assns., Jr. League Hartford. Democrat. Club: Hartford Golf. Home: 26 Sycamore Rd West Hartford CT 06117 Office: 151 Farmington Av Hartford CT 06115

HINDLIN, PAULA LEE, TV broadcasting co. exec.; b. N.Y.C., Oct. 24, 1931; d. Norman H. and Rebecca (Ediss) Hindlin; student Bklyn. Coll., 1949-50; N.Y. U., 1951-52, Coll. City N.Y., 1955-56, New Sch. for Social Research, 1966-67. Sec., Met. Life Ins. Co., N.Y.C., 1949-52; sec. CBS Radio, N.Y.C., 1952-54, sec., prodn. asst. CBS-TV, 1954-55, asst. TV casting dir., 1955-59, casting dir., 1959—. Mem. Am. Assn. for U.N. Democrat. Home: 166 E 63d St New York City NY 10021 Office: 530 W 57th St New York City NY 10019

HINDMAN, JANE FERGUSON, assn. exec.; b. Phila.; d. William Neal and Mary Anna (Eslen) Hindman; Library Sci. Certificate, Drexel U., 1924; B.S., Temple U., 1929. Asst. librarian S. Phila. High Sch. Girls, 1924-30; librarian Theodore Roosevelt Jr. High Sch., Phila., 1930-40, Benjamin Franklin High Sch., 1940-52, Abraham Lincoln High Sch., 1950-60; asst. librarian Holy Family Coll., Phila., 1960-63; editor Catholic Library World, Haverford, Pa., 1963-73; unit coordinator Catholic Library Assn., 1973—. Mem. Church & Synagogue, Cath. (asst. to exec. dir. 1963-73) library assns., Library Pub. Relations Assn., Phila. Bookseller's Assn. Author: Mathew Carey, Pamphleteer for Freedom, 1960. Contbr. to profl. and religious jours. Home: The Mermont Bryn Mawr PA 19010

HINDS, JEAN, educator; b. Cresco, Ia., Sept. 28, 1924; d. Frederick Calvin and Genevieve (Engstrom) Hinds; B.S., Rockford Coll., 1946; M.A., Columbia, 1951, Ed.D., 1964. Jr. and high sch. sci. tchr. Mercer and McHenry County bds. edn., Ill., 1946-49; personnel dir. Campbell Hall, Ia. State Tchrs. Coll., Cedar Falls, 1951-54; grad. asst. Columbia, N.Y.C., 1954-55, asst. to dean Tchrs. Coll., 1955-59, asst. coordinator ICA projects abroad, 1959-60; prof., dean women Miami U., Oxford, O., 1960-61; asst. dir., later asso. dir. U. counseling service Howard U,, Washington, 1964-65; asst. dean students Stanford (Cal.) U., 1965-67; prof. ednl. psychology, also dean of student affairs Alverno College Milw., 1968-70; asso. dean of students Grinnell (Ia.) Coll., 1970-71; prof. psychology, dean students Coe (Ia.) Coll., 1971—. Vol., A.R.C., 1942-46. Mem. Am. Coll. Personnel Assn., Am. Assn. Higher Edn., N.E.A. (life), Nat. Soc. Study Edn., Am. Personnel and Guidance Assn. (life), Am. Assn. U. Profs., Am. Psychol. Assn., Nat. Assn. Women Deans and Counselors, Kappa Delta Pi. Home: 210 19th St NE Cedar Rapids IA 52402

HINDS, LILLIAN RUTH MILLER, educator; b. Cleve., Oct. 11, 1918; d. Alexander and Dora (Schneider) Miller; B.A., Case Western Res. U., 1941, M.A., 1951, Ph.D., 1966; postgrad. Ariz. State U., 1961-62; m. Leonard Harold Hinds, Aug. 9, 1940 (div. June 1973); children—Douglas Miller, Kathleen Anne, Alexander Thomas. Lang. arts supr., dir. vision screening Euclid (O.) Publ Schs., 1951-57; dir. Ariz. Reading Improvement Center, Phoenix, 1957-63; tchr. Phoenix Jr. Coll., 1960-63; asso. prof. edn. Cleve. State U. Coll. Edn., 1964-70, tchr. tng. prof., 1970—; vis. prof. Sch. Edn., U.S. Internat. U., San Diego, 1973. Cons. Ency. Brit., 1966-68; officer Edn. Dynamic Center Profs. and Tchrs. Aids, 1972; cons. Ohio Internat. Reading Assn., 1970-72, Ohio State Testing Div., 1969-71. Mem. Cleve. Mental Health Assn., 1970—, Friends of Jones Hosp., 1970—, Right to Read for Ohio Right To Read, 1970—. Mem. Nat. Soc. Study Edn. Assn., Internat. Reading Assn. (pres. Ohio unit 1955, pres. Ariz. unit, 1957), Internat. Platform Assn., Kappa Delta Pi. Club: Zonta (Cleve.). Author: (with M. Bergmann, M. Hain) Reading Time, 1968. Home: 3115 Coleridge Cleveland Heights OH 44118 Office: 22d and Euclid Av Cleveland OH 44115

HINERFELD, RUTH JEAN GORDON, civic worker; b. Boston, Sept. 18, 1930; d. Morris Joseph and Anna (Shoolman) Gordon; A.B., Vassar Coll., 1951; certificate Harvard-Radcliffe Program Bus. Adminstrn., 1952; m. Norman M. Hinerfeld, Dec. 25, 1952; children—Lee Ann, Thomas Benjamin, Joshua Gordon. With Filene's, Boston, 1952; v.p., dir. League Women Voters Los Angeles, 1960-64, League Women Voters Cal., 1964-67; nat. bd. dirs. League Women Voters U.S., 1972—, observer at UN, 1969-72, v.p., 1974—. Mem. exec. com. non-govtl. orgn. reps. accredited to UN Office Pub. Information, 1969-72, Conf. UN Reps. of UN Assn. U.S.A., 1969-72; mem. nat. com. on information and field services UN-U.S.A., 1971-73. Bd. dirs. East-West Trade Council, 1973—, UN Assn. U.S.A., 1973—, Overseas Edn. Fund League Women Voters, 1974—. Mem. Am. Arbitration Assn. (arbitrator). Home: 11 Oak Lane Larchmont NY 10538 Office: 1730 M St NW Washington DC 20036

HINKEL, HELEN MARY RYKOWSKI (MRS. JOSEPH LOYD HINKEL), librarian; b. Dayton, O., Oct. 28, 1911; d. John and Regina (Perzanowska) Rykowski; student U. Cal., at Berkeley, 1949, Mary Hardin Baylor Coll., 1959; m. Joseph Loyd Hinkel, Dec. 1, 1934; 1 son, Vossler Sigmund. Reference asst. Fort Meade, Md., 1950-51; library asst. Ft. Lewis, Wash., 1952-53, Fort Hood, Tex., 1957-58; head librarian Killeen Pub. Library, Killeen, 1959-70, library dir., 1970—. Mem. Bell County Council on Alcoholism. Mem. C. of C., Am., Tex. library assns., Tex. Municipal League Librarians Assn., Tex., Killeen friends of the library, Nat. Council Cath. Women, Am. Bus. Women's Assn. (program chmn. 1969-70), Civil Air Patrol, Tex. Geneal. Soc., Internat. Soc. for Heraldry and Family Trees, Bell County Hist. Soc. Clubs: Killeen Garden, Killeen Area Music (reporter, historian). Home: PO Box 141 Killeen TX 76541 Office: 711 North Gray Killeen TX 76541

HINSDALE, ROSEJEAN CLIFFORD, coll. dean; b. Plymouth, Ind.; d. Jack Carl and Pauline (Arndt) Clifford; student Northwestern U., 1942-44, U. N.M., 1950; B.A. with distinction, Ariz. State U., 1960, M.A., 1963, Ph.D., 1973; postgrad. Stanford, 1966, U. Cal., 1967; m. James G. Hinsdale, Oct. 3, 1947; children—James G., Rosejean Susan, Cynthia Anne. Asso. editor The Arizonian, Scottsdale, 1959-60; tchr. Arcadia High Sch., Phoenix, 1961-65; asso. dean students Phoenix Coll., 1965—. Reader Ariz. Found. Blind Children, 1963—; publicity chmn. Camp Fire Girls, 1961-63. Mem. Ariz. Press Women (central dist. v.p. 1967), Nat. Fedn. Press Women, Am. Personnel and Guidance Assn., Am. Coll. Personnel Assn., Nat., Ariz. (pres. 1971-73) assns. women deans and counselors, Assn. Women's Active Return to Edn. (pres. 1973), Altrusa, Nat. Assn. Adminstrv. Women in Edn., Alpha Xi Delta, Delta Kappa Gamma. Home: 4235 N 68th Pl Scottsdale AZ 85251 Office: 1202 W Thomas Rd Phoenix AZ 85013

HINTERBUCHNER, CATHERINE NICOLAIDES (MRS. LADISLAV HINTERBUCHNER), physician; b. Greece, Nov. 22, 1926; d. Alexandre and Vienna (Marangio) Nicholaidis; M.D., Nat. and Kapodistriakon U., Athens, 1951; m. Ladislav Hinterbuchner, Dec. 10, 1955. Came to U.S., 1953, naturalized, 1959. Rotating intern St. Luke's Hosp., N.Y.C., 1953-54; resident internal medicine French Hosp., N.Y.C., 1954-55; resident internal medicine Jewish Chronic Disease Hosp., N.Y.C., 1956, fellow phys. med. and rehab., 1956-57; fellow phys. medicine and rehab. Bird S. Coler Hosp., N.Y.C., 1959-60, chmn. rehab. medicine, 1971—; instr. rehab. medicine State U. N.Y. Downstate Med. Center, 1960-64; chief rehab. medicine Met. Hosp. Center, N.Y.C., 1964—; chmn. rehab. medicine Grasslands Hosp., Valhalla, N.Y., 1971—; faculty N.Y. Med. Coll., N.Y.C., 1964—, prof., chmn. rehab. medicine, 1971—. Fellow A.C.P., N.Y. Acad. Medicine; mem. A.M.A., N.Y. State, N.Y.C., Kings County med. socs., Am. Acad. Phys. Medicine and Rehab., Am. Congress Rehab. Medicine, Am. Assn. U. Profs., N.Y. Soc. Phys. Medicine and Rehab., N.Y. Acad. Sci. Home: 344 Warren Dr Woodmere NY 11598 Office: 1249 Fifth Av New York City NY 10029

HINTON, BETTY JEAN, educator; b. Ft. Smith, Ark., Dec. 20, 1927; d. Champ Clark and Juanita (Carroll) Hinton; A.A., Ft. Smith Jr. Coll., 1950; B.A., U. Ark., 1952, M.A., 1954; Ph.D., So. Ill. U., 1965; LL.D., Geneva Theol. Coll., 1968. Instr. Ft. Smith Jr. Coll., 1951-53, Springdale (Ark.) High Sch., 1954-55; therapist Wichita (Kan.) Pub. Schs., 1955-56; asst. prof. Upper Ia. U., Fayette, 1956-58; asst. prof. McNeese State Coll., Lake Charles, La., 1959-63; prof., dir. grad. study in speech, Dept. Communications, Murray (Ky.) State U., 1965-70; chancellor Phoenix Inst., Chula Vista, Cal., 1970-71; ind. writer and researcher, practicing astrologer, 1971—; exec. v.p. World Astrological Services, Inc., Murray, 1973—. Owner, pres. Spl. Occasion, Ltd., 1974—. Named Ky. col. Mem. Speech Assn. Am., Inst. Gen. Semantics, Assn. Research and Enlightenment, Am. Fedn. Astrologers, Internat. Soc. for Astrological Research, Ky. Acad. Astrology, Pi Kappa Delta, Pi Phi Delta, Delta Kappa Gamma, Kappa Delta Pi, Pi Epsilon Delta, Tau Kappa Alpha. Home: 701 S 16th St Murray KY 42071

HINTON, FRANCES, librarian; b. Atlanta, Mar. 19, 1922; d. James and Frances Williams (Warlick) Hinton; B.A., Agnes Scott Coll., 1942; B.S. in L.S., U. N.C., 1943. Young adult reference librarian N.Y. Pub. Library, 1943-45; head librarian Lowndes County Pub. Library, Valdosta, Ga., 1945-48; head young adult dept. South Bend (Ind.) Pub. Library, 1948-49; head catalog dept. Kauai Pub. Library, Lihue, Hawaii, 1949-53; head young adult dept. Free Library of Phila., 1953-55, cataloger, 1955-62, head catalog dept., 1962—, mem. decimal classification editorial policy com. 1966—, chmn. 1969—. Mem. A.L.A., Pa. Library Assn. Republican. Methodist. Home: 105 W Walnut Lane Philadelphia PA 19144 Office: 19th and Vine Sts Philadelphia PA 19103

HINTON, NELDA RUTH HAHN (MRS. BENNY RAY HINTON), county ofcl.; b. Millersville, Mo., Sept. 27, 1937; d. Roy Marshall and Bernice Rose (Jenkins) Hahn; grad. high sch.; m. Benny Ray Hinton, Feb. 10, 1973; 1 son by previous marriage, Mark Anthony; 2 step-sons, Anthony G. Hinton and Scott A. Ray Hinton. Dep. circuit clk. Cape Girardeau County (Mo.), 1959-65; legal sec. Buerkle & Lowes Law Offices, Jackson, Mo., 1965; fee agt. State License Bur., Jackson, 1965-72; dep. magistrate clk. Jackson, 1973—. Mem. Cape County Democratic Women's Club, 1959-74; Democratic committeewoman, 1968-74; sec. Democratic Central Com., 1970-74. Mem. Am. Legion Aux., Beta Sigma Phi. Mem. Order Eastern Star. Club: Suburban Garden (pres. 1974) (Jackson). Home: 1205 Hwy 72 W Jackson MO 63755 Office: Courthouse Jackson MO 63755

HINTON, PATRICIA FERN, med. technologist; b. Booneville, Miss., June 13, 1932; d. Milliard Carroll and Mattie (Peeler) Hinton; B.S., Miss. State Coll. for Women, 1954; M.S., U. Miss., 1971. Asst. chief Univ. Hosp. Clin. Bacteriology Lab., Jackson, Miss., 1955-60; blastomycosis research lab. VA Hosp., Jackson, 1960-69; med. research in respiratory diseases VA Center, Jackson, 1969—; instr. microbiology U. Miss. Sch. Medicine, Jackson, 1971—. Mem. Am. Assn. U. Women, Miss. Soc. Med. Technologists (pres. 1959-60, dir. 1963), Am. Soc. Microbiologists, Med. Mycol. Soc. Am., Am. Soc. Med. Tech., Central Dist. Soc. Med. Technologists (pres. 1958), Alpha Mu Tau. Mem. Christian Ch. Contbr. articles to profl. jours. Home: 4911 Old Canton Rd Jackson MS 39211 Office: VA Center Research Lab Jackson MS 39216

HINTZ, JOY ALICE (MRS. HOWARD WILLIAM HINTZ), mus. curator; b. Zanesville, O., Feb. 7, 1926; d. James Sherman and Lela Gladys (Zink) Posey; B.A. in Biology, B.S. in Edn., Ohio State U., 1947, postgrad., 1947-49; postgrad. Capital U., 1950-51, Heidelberg Coll., 1967-73; m. Howard William Hintz, June 15, 1952; children—Loren, Constance Joy (Mrs. Mark Nusbaum), Julia Kay. Tchr., Tiffin, O., 1955-60; mus. curator Heidelberg Coll., Tiffin, O., 1956—. Pres. Seneca County (O.) Family Planning Services, 1969-70, outreach worker, 1969-71, dir., 1969—; mem. Ohio Gov.'s Com. on Migrant Affairs, 1974. Elizabeth McGee Found. grantee, 1973. Mem. Midwest Fedn. Mineral Clubs, Firelands Geol. Club, Mansfield Mineral Club, Ohio Acad. Sci., Seneca County Ch. Women United (pres. 1965-68), Ch. Women United in O. (dir. 1971—), Am. Assn. U. Women, (chmn. sci. group 1966—), League Women Voters, Com. Migrant Relations (chmn. 1970—), La Raza Unida de Ohio (dir. 1971—), Christian Women's Fellowship (pres. local unit 1962-63), Pi Lambda Theta. Mem. Ch. Disciples of Christ. Mem. Order of Eastern Star. Editor: An Anthology of Ohio Mexican American Writers, 1974. Contbr. articles to sch. and geol. jours. Home: 500 E Perry St Tiffin OH 44883 Office: Jones Collection of Minerals Heidelberg College Tiffin OH 44883

HINZ, DOROTHY ELIZABETH, writer, editor, pub. relations exec.; b. N.Y.C., Nov. 28, 1926; d. Hans and Anna (Borell) Hinz; A.B., Hunter Coll., 1948; postgrad. Columbia. Copy editor Collier's Mag., 1948-53; asst. to dir. of devel. Columbia, N.Y.C., 1953-55; mng. editor Grace-Log, econs. research-analyst, writer speeches, white papers, com. reports Latin Am. affairs, pub. relations dept. W.R. Grace & Co., N.Y.C., 1955-64; staff writer Oil Progress, fgn. news media, speeches, films, internat. petroleum operations, pub. relations dept. Caltex Petroleum Corp., N.Y.C., 1964-68; financial editor Merrill Lynch, Pierce, Fenner & Smith, 1969-74; research-writer, editor speeches, spl. studies and reports dept. corporate communications mfrs. Hanover Trust Co., N.Y.C., 1974—. Mem. Inter-Am. Round Table, N.Y. Acad. Scis., A.A.A.S., Soc. Am. Med. Writers. Club: Overseas Press (inter-Am. affairs com., fgn. press liaison com.) (N.Y.C.). Contbr. articles on multinat. corps., devel. nations, trade and finance to various publs. Home: 600 W 115th St New York City NY 10025 Office: 350 Park Av New York City NY 10022

HIPPS, DONNA MARIE (MRS. ROBERT O. HIPPS), librarian; b. Waterloo, Ia., May 18, 1925; d. George Fred and Mamie Jean (Livingston) Westlic; B.S., Ia. State U., 1946; M.A., U. Minn., 1963; m. Robert O. Hipps, Aug. 9, 1946; children—Alan, Margaret (Mrs. Douglas A. Peters), James. Tchr. pub. schs., Ia., 1946-48; teaching asst. Univ. High Sch., U. Minn., Mpls., 1960-63; librarian Lincoln High Sch., Bloomington, Minn., 1963-70; library specialist Jefferson High Sch., Bloomington, 1970-74, dir. resource center, 1974—. Mem. N.E.A., A.L.A., League Women Voters (state treas. 1958-59, dir. Edina 1955-58), Sigma Kappa, Beta Phi Mu. Methodist. Home: 6604 Dakota Trail Edina MN 55435 Office: 4001 W 102d St Bloomington MN 55431

HIPSHER, JEANNE WISE SLEEPER (MRS. ALVA C. HIPSHER), occupational therapist; b. Decatur, Ill., Apr. 20, 1920; d. Nate A. and Nona L. (Mount) Wise; B.S., U. Ill., 1966; m. Alva C. Hipsher, May 24, 1970; 1 son by previous marriage, James Robert Sleeper. Sec., WPB Washington, 1942-44, USAF, Santa Ana, Cal., 1944-46; sec. Emerson Drug Co., Balt., 1946-48; dir. Easter Seal Center, Decatur, Ill., 1967-69; coordinator day care services, cons. shelter care and nursing homes Decatur Mental Health Center., 1969—. Mem. Am., Ill. occupational therapy assns., Bus. and Profl. Women. Methodist. Home: 2045 Woodbine Dr Decatur IL 62526 Office: 2300 N Edward St Decatur IL 62526

HIPSMAN, BARBARA JEAN, journalist; b. Berwyn, Ill., Jan. 1, 1951; d. John Richard and Theresa M. (Nendick) Hipsman; student Mundelein Coll., 1968-70; B.S., No. Ill. U., 1972. Reporter, Star-Tribune Publs., Tinley Park, Ill., 1972—. Recipient award for pub. service for investigative reporting Ill. Press Assn., 1973. Mem. Women in Communications, Ill. Women's Press Assn. (best news story, best edited page 1974), Mortar Bd. Home: 1017 Joliet Rd West Chicago IL 60185 Office: 17239 Oak Park Av Tinley Park IL 60477

HIRAI, BERNICE YAMAGATA (MRS. HENRY TETSUO HIRAI), educator; b. Hakalau, Hawaii, Nov. 2, 1924; d. Reio and Toshiko (Yamagata) Yamagata; B.Ed., U. Hawaii, 1946, M.Ed., 1961; Ph.D., Ind. U., 1974; m. Henry Tetsuo Hirai, Aug. 6, 1950; 1 dau., Anna Chitose. Tchr., Hawaii Pub. Schs., 1947-55; intern supr. U. Hawaii, Honolulu, 1957-58, instr. Japanese, 1961-68, adminstrv. asst. Nat. Def. Edn. Act Japanese Lang. Inst., 1965, prof., 1974—; supr., tchr. Japanese, Univ. Elementary and Secondary Schs., Honolulu, 1958-61. Mem. Hawaii Assn. Lang. Tchrs. (pres. 1962-63), Assn. Childhood Internat. (pres. 1961-62), Pi Lambda Theta (chpt. pres. 1963-64, corr. sec. alumnae chpt. 1974—). Co-author: Learn Japanese (secondary sch. texts), vols. I-VI, 1969. Home: 2526 Ferdinand Av Honolulu HI 96822

HIRES, CLARA S., bot. researcher; b. Merion, Pa., Apr. 8, 1897; d. Charles E. and Clara K. (Smith) Hires; student Wellesley Coll., 1916-18, Tchrs. Coll., Columbia, others, 1920-32; B.A., Cornell U., 1928. Tchr. sci. Edgewood Sch., Greenwich, Conn., 1920-25, Buxton Country Day Sch., Short Hills, N.J., 1929-32, Shore Rd. Acad., Bklyn., 1932-34; owner, research dir. Mistaire Labs., Milburn, N.J., 1929—. Mem. mgmt. com. Overlook Hosp., Summit, N.J., 1938-42. Mem. A.A.A.S., Am. Fern Soc. (regional exec. com.). Brit. Pteridological Soc., N.Y., N.J. acad. scis., Bot. Soc. Am., Am. Assn. U. Women, Wyo. Assn., League Women Voters, Torrey Bot. Club, Summit Scientists, N.Y. Micros. Soc., Internat. Orgn. Paleobotany, Paleontol. Soc., Am. Hort. Soc.; Internat. Soc. Stereology, Sigma Delta Epsilon. (past local and nat. offices). Clubs: Maplewood Garden, Summit Nature. Author: Spores—Ferns—Microscopic Illusions Analyzed, Vol. I, 1965; also articles profl. jours. Address: 152 Glen Av Millburn NJ 07041

HIRN, DORIS DREYER, health service adminstr.; b. N.Y.C., Dec. 3, 1933; d. James Howard and Dorothy Van Nostrand (Young) Dreyer; student Colby Jr. Coll., 1950-51, Hofstra U., 1953-56; m. John D. Hirn, Oct. 27, 1956; children—Deborah Lynn, Robert William. Owner, Dutchlands Farm, Albany, N.Y., 1957-62, Hickory Hill Farm, Galena, Ill., 1965—; adminstr. Home Health Service, Chgo., 1972-74, exec. dir. Suburban Home Health Service, 1974—, also bd. dirs. Bd. dirs. Fox Valley council Girl Scouts U.S.A. Served with WAVES, 1951-52. Mem. Am. (dir.), Chgo. (dir.) camping assns., Nat. Health Delivery Systems (v.p.). Contbr. articles to various periodicals. Home: 1 E Schiller Chicago IL 60610 Office: 2250 E Devon Av Des Plaines IL 60018

HIRSCH, AMY ANCHELL (MRS. LEONARD HIRSCH), mus. ofcl.; b. N.Y.C., Jan. 7, 1903; d. Amos and Janette (Blumenthal) Anchell; student Columbia Coll., 1921-24, Goodman Sch., 1939-40, Northwestern Coll. Sch. Speech; m. Leonard Hirsch, Jan. 1, 1925; 1 dau., Elane Janet (Mrs. Sam Farkas). Editor Nat. Retail Trade paper, Chgo., 1942-44; editor Irving Krewson, buyer, N.Y.C., 1945-48; ready to wear buyer Hollywood (Cal.) Shops, 1949-56; tchr. speech and drama Albany (Ga.) High Sch.; exec. dir. Albany Area Mus., 1960—. Pres., Albany Little Theatre, 1958-59. Mem. Hebrew Ladies Benevolent Soc. (parliamentarian), Kappa Kappa Kappa. Club: Albany Womans (chmn. pub. affairs dept.). Home: 911 3d Av Albany GA 31701 Office: 516 Flint Av Albany GA 31701

HIRSCH, BARBARA B., lawyer; b. Chgo., July 5, 1938; d. Maurice L. and Ruth (Hartman) Hirsch; student U. Ill., 1956-58, Northwestern U., 1959; LL.B., DePaul U., 1966. Admitted to Ill. bar, 1966; asso. firm Chadwell Keck Kayser & Ruggles (now Chadwell, Kayser, Ruggles, McGee, Hastings & McKinney), Chgo., 1966-70; pvt. practice, Chgo., 1970—. Lectr., DePaul U. Coll. Law, Chgo., 1971. Mem. exec. bd. Am. Jewish Com., 1971—. Mem. Am., Fed., Ill., Chgo. bar assns. Author: Divorce: What a Woman Needs to Know, 1973. Home: 535 N Michigan Av Chicago IL 60611 Office: 208 S LaSalle St Chicago IL 60604

HIRSCH, BETTY WURTH, museum dir.; b. N.Y.C., Sept. 30, 1929; d. Daniel and Teresa (Shelley) Wurth; B.A., Pa. State U., 1951; postgrad. U. Tex., 1969-71; m. Richard Teller Hirsch, July 10, 1954 (div. Mar. 1974). Sec. Erwin-Wasey Advt. Corp., N.Y.C., 1951-52; with CIA, Washington, 1952-53; adminstrv. asst. WEB Advt. Corp., Palm Beach, Fla., 1954-56; asst. dir. Pensacola (Fla.) Art Center, 1956-59; asso. dir. Allentown (Pa.) Art Museum, 1959-68; dir. Beaumont (Tex.) Art Mus., 1972—; designer graphics, 1960—. Bd. dirs. Southeast Tex. Arts Council, 1972—, Beaumont Sch. Vol. Program, 1973—. Mem. Am. Assn. Museums, Mountain Plains Mus. Conf., Tex. Mus. Assn., Western Assn. Art Museums, Alpha Omicron Pi. Republican. Lutheran. Editor, designer numerous art catalogues. Home: 6068 Afton Lane Beaumont TX 77706 Office: 1111 9th St Beaumont TX 77702

HIRSCH, ELIZABETH FEIST (MRS. FELIX HIRSCH), educator; b. Mainz, Germany, Nov. 2, 1904; d. Sigmund and Toni (Rawicz) Feist; student U. Freiburg, 1924, U. Berlin, 1924-29; Ph.D., Marburg U., 1930; m. Felix Hirsch, Nov. 6, 1938; children—Roland, Thomas. Came to U.S., 1938, naturalized, 1941. Asst. prof. philosophy Bard Coll., Annandale-on-Hudson, N.Y., 1949-54; asst. prof. Philosophy and modern langs. Trenton State Coll., 1956-64, asso. prof. philosophy, 1964-69, prof. philosophy, prof. emeritus, 1972—, chmn. dept. philosophy and religion, 1969-72. Rockefeller Found. award for studies in France, 1929-30; Sterling research fellow, Yale, 1937-38; Gulbenkian Found. fellow, Lisbon, Portugal, summer 1960; Guggenheim fellow, 1960-61; prize Portuguese Acad. Internat. Culture. Mem. Renaissance Soc. Am., Am. Soc. Reformation Research, Heidegger Conf., Am. Assn. U. Women (May Treat internat. fellow 1954-55). Author: Weltbild und Staatsidee bei Jean Bodin, 1930; Damiao de Gois, The Life and Thought of a Portuguese Humanist (1502-1574), 1967. Editor: De Arte Dubitandi et Confidendi, Ignorandi et Sciendi, 1937. Contbr. articles on history of ideas and philosophy of Martin Heidegger to scholarly and profl. jours. Home: 14 Pershing Av Trenton NJ 08618

HIRSCH, GLADYS ELKIN, lawyer; b. Bronx, N.Y., June 22, 1920; d. Harry and Sarah (Binder) Elkin; A.B., Hunter Coll., 1940; J.D., George Washington U., 1966; m. Arthur E. Hirsch, 1941; children—Evin (Mrs. Charles T. Phillips), Marla. Admitted to D.C. and Md. bars, 1967; atty. adviser Office Gen. Counsel, Dept. Health, Edn. and Welfare, Washington, 1967-70; gen. practice law, Rockville, Md., 1970—; staff counsel Am. Occupational Therapy Assn. Mem. Am., D.C., Montgomery County bar assns., Women's Bar D.C. Office: 30 Courthouse Sq Rockville MD 20850

HIRSCH, GLORIA TISHLER, counselor; b. Chgo., Mar. 18, 1928; d. Abraham and Sarah (Mintz) Tishler; B.S., Roosevelt U., Chgo., 1949; M.A., Cal. State U. at Northridge, 1968; postgrad. U. Cal. at Los Angeles, 1968-70; m. Ira Hirsch, May 21, 1950; children—Susan Dee, Lisa Ellen, Karen Barbara. Adult edn. instr. Beverly Hills (Cal.) High Sch., 1957-60; tchr., dir. early childhood edn. programs, Los Angeles, 1949-60; mental health and edn. cons. Project Head Start, Office Econ. Opportunity, Los Angeles County, 1965-70; clin. dir. Friends of Family, family counseling and child abuse prevention center, Van Nuys, Cal., 1972—. Coordinator, Pacoima Community Parent-Child Program; examiner Cal. Bd. Behavioral Sci. Examiners; participant profl. convs., seminars. Mem. exec. com. Los Angeles Mayor's Adv. Com. on Status of Women, chairperson Child Care Com. Mem. Nat. Council Family Relations, Cal. Assn. Marriage and Family Counselors (trustee), Am. Assn. Marriage and Family Counselors, Nat. Assn. Edn. Young Children, Nat. Orgn. Women, League Women Voters, Am. Civil Liberties Union. Contbr. articles to profl. jours. Home: 13121 Addison St Sherman Oaks CA 91423 Office: 14521 Gilmore St Van Nuys CA 91401

HIRSCH, HILDEGARD, physician; b. Berlin, Germany, May 2, 1912; d. Siegfried and Irma (Sturmthal) Moses; Physikum, U. Berlin (Germany), 1933; M.D., U. Pisa (Italy), 1937; m. Erich Hirsch, Dec. 26, 1933; children—Peter, Lillian (Mrs. Peter Stern). Came to U.S., 1938, naturalized, 1944. Intern, S. Chiara, Pisa, 1937-38, resident, 1938-39; practice medicine specializing in pediatrics, Geneva, N.Y., 1939—; attending pediatrician Geneva Gen. Hosp., 1939—; health officer bd. Ontario Day Care Center, Geneva; part-time sch. physician and pre-sch. clinic physician. Mem. A.M.A., Ontario County Med. Soc., Acad. Medicine, Am. Womens Med. Assn., League Women Voters. Mem. Hadassah (pres. Fingerlakes chpt. 1941—). Club: College (Geneva). Home: RD 1 Dwyer Dr Geneva NY 14456 Office: 35 Mason St Geneva NY 14456

HIRSCH, JUDITH, journalist; b. Buffalo, Aug. 17, 1944; d. Samuel Albert and Roseann (McCann) Hirsch; B.A., Bowling Green State U., 1966. News dir. WBGU-TV, Bowling Green (O.) State U., 1967-68; reporter Daily Sentinel Tribune, Bowling Green, 1968—. Cons. advt., pub. relations to various polit. campaigns, 1972-73. Sec., Citizens Adv. Council on Alcoholism and Drug Abuse, Wood County, O., 1973-74. Recipient certificate of appreciation Ohio State Hwy. Patrol, 1971. Mem. Women in Communications, Delta Zeta. Editor: Alumnae Newsletter, 1972-73. Home: 440 N Main St Bowling Green OH 43402 Office: PO Box 298 Bowling Green OH 43402

HIRSCH, LORE (MRS. EUGENE HESZ), physician; b. Mannheim, Germany, July 8, 1908; d. Erwin and Marie (Kiefe) Hirsch; M.D., Heidelberg U., 1937; m. Eugene Hesz, Jan. 25, 1958. (div. 1968). Came to U.S., 1940, naturalized 1946. Intern, Greenpoint Hosp., Bklyn., 1942-43; resident in psychiatry Bellevue Hosp., N.Y.C. 1943-46; sr. psychiatrist Dept. N.Y.C., 1946-49; sect. chief pschiat. div. VA Hosp., Bronx, N.Y., 1949-54; clin. dir. psychiatry Wayne County Gen. Hosp., Eloise, Mich., 1954-55; dir. out-patient dept. Northville (Mich.) State Hosp., 1955-58; practice medicine specializing in psychiatry, Dearborn, Mich., 1958—; staff mem. Oakwood Hosp., Dearborn; asst. prof. Wayne State U., 1954-55. Pres. Health Council, Dearborn, 1960; mem. Western Wayne County Bd. YWCA; adv. bd. League Women Voters. Diplomate Am. Bd. Psychiatry and Neurology. Fellow Am. Psychiat. Assn., Pan Am. Psychiat. Assn.; mem. A.M.A., Mich., Wayne County, Women's med. socs., Am. Assn. U. Women, Mich. Assn. for Neurology and Psychiatry. Unitarian. Contbr. articles to med. jours. Home: 212 S Melborn St Dearborn MI 48124 Office: 2021 Monroe St Dearborn MI 48124

HIRSCH, MARY ANNE (MRS. OTTO HIRSCH), occupational therapist, educator; b. Dallas, June 19, 1928; d. William Howard and Myrtle E. (Mahler) McGill; B.S., Western Mich. Coll., 1949; m. Otto Hirsch, May 2, 1959; children—Andrew Joseph, Martha Hedwig. Occupational therapist Dallas County Woodlawn Tb Hosp., Dallas, 1949-50; chief occupational therapist Dallas Soc. Crippled Children, 1950-55; occupational therapist Austin (Tex.) State Hosp., 1955; chief occupational therapist Ft. Worth Soc. Crippled Children, 1956-58; supr. occupational therapist Cal. State Dept. Pub. Health, Berkeley, 1958-60; cons. teaching films Alameda County (Cal.) Dept. Pub. Health, 1960-61; occupational therapist Sacramento Med. Center, 1970-73, U. Cal. at Davis Med. Center, Sacramento, 1973—. Tchr. parent edn. classes Sacramento City schs., 1970-73. Recipient Fulbright Lecturing award, 1955-56. Mem. Am. Occupational Therapy Assn. Mem. Unitarian Ch. Club: Fruitridge Democratic. Home: 1857 4th Av Sacramento CA 95818 Office: 9555 Kiefer Blvd Sacramento CA

HIRSCH, ROSEANN CONTE (MRS. BARRY J. HIRSCH), editor; b. N.Y.C., Feb. 5, 1941; d. Frank and Anna (Burzycki) Conte; B.F.A., Boston U., 1962; m. Barry J. Hirsch, Oct. 1, 1967; 1 son, Brian Christopher. Asst. editor Ency. Internat., Grolier Inc., N.Y.C., 1962-64; editor Ideal Pub. Co., N.Y.C., 1968—, TV Star Parade, 1968-71, Movie Stars, 1972-73, TV Dawn to Dusk, 1973—. Mem. Actors Equity Assn. Contbr. articles to popular and TV mags. Home: 205 3d Av New York City NY 10003 Office: 575 Madison Av New York City NY 10017

HIRSCH, SHARLENE PEARLMAN, b. Chgo., Aug. 17, 1939; d. Leonard and Lillian (Orenstein) Pearlman; B.S., U. Ill., 1962; Ed.M., Harvard, 1966, Ed.D., 1969. Tchr. social studies high sch., Hammondsport, N.Y., and Marblehead, Mass., 1964-66; edn. dir. Gen. Subcom. on Edn., U.S. Ho. Reps., Washington, 1967-70; dir. Office Ednl. Devel., Human Resources of N.Y.C., 1970-73; nat. dir. exec. high sch. internships of Am., Inst. for Ednl. Devel., N.Y.C., 1973—. Cons. Ford Found., George Washington U., Urban Center of Columbia U., Boston Cons. Group, Far West Lab. Regional Ednl. Devel.; visiting asst. prof. Washington U., St. Louis, 1969; mem. faculty Harvard Summer Sch., 1966; sr. nat. lectr. Nova U., 1972—. Research asst. Edward W. Brooke for Senator Campaign, 1966. Nat. Defense Edn. Act fellow, 1965-67; grantee Ford Found., 1968, New World Found., 1971-73, Rockefeller Found., 1973. Mem. Am. Polit. Sci. Assn., Harvard Grad. Sch. Edn. Alumni Assn. (exec. bd. 1972—), Phi Kappa Phi, Alpha Lambda Delta, Pi Lambda Theta. Author: (with Roman C. Pucinski) The Courage to Change, 1971; Resources for Improving Education, 1973. Editor: Educational Needs of the Seventies, 1970. Home: 410 W 24th St New York City NY 10011 Office: 680 Fifth Av New York City NY 10019

HIRSCH, WILLA COBERT, psychotherapist; b. N.Y.C., Oct. 6, 1940; d. Eugene O. and Mary Esther (Rosenzweig) Cobert; B.A. in Psychology magna cum laude, Boston U., 1961; Ph.D. in Clin. Psychology, Adelphi U., 1969; m. Irwin Hirsch, June 20, 1971; 1 dau., Cara Jennifer. Intern psychology N.Y. State Psychiat. Inst., 1968-69; research asso. psychology Hillside Hosp., N.Y.C., 1964-68, staff psychologist, 1969-73; coordinator psychol. services Day Hosp. of Hillside Hosp., 1973-74; pvt. practice, N.Y.C., 1970—. Mem. Am. Psychol. Assn., Phi Beta Kappa, Psi Chi. Address: 575 West End Av New York City NY 10024

HIRSCHBERG, BESSE BRYNA, social worker; b. N.Y.C.; d. Sigmund and Lottie (Popick) Hirschberg; B.A., Hunter Coll., 1932; postgrad. Fordham U. Sch. Social Work, 1935-36, Columbia Sch. Social Work, 1938-61, Yale Summer Sch. Alcohol Studies, 1948, Yale Inst. for Orgn. Mgmt., 1955, Hunter Coll. Sch. Social Work, 1961-62. Caseworker, intake interviewer N.Y.C. Dept. Welfare, 1938-48, supr. div. employment and rehab., 1948-52, asst. field pub. relations rep., 1957-59, specialist on alcoholism, 1959-60, dir. day center program for older people, 1961-64, field supr. anti-poverty project, 1965—. Cons., liaison officer Alcoholism Research and Treatment Center N.Y.C. Magistrate's Ct. System, 1953-57; supr. Mayor's Mobile Information Center, N.Y.C., 1960-61; cons. community services Office Pres. Borough of Bronx, N.Y.C., 1964-65; cons. work incentive program N.Y.C. Dept. Social Services. Pres. profl. chpt. young men and women's div. Am. Orgn. Rehab. through Tng., 1944-48. Bd. dirs. B'nai B'rith Youth Orgn. Recipient personal citation Pres. Bronx Borough, 1965. Mem. Nat. Assn. Social Workers, Acad. Certified Social Workers, N.Y. League Bus. and Profl. Women (chmn. Nat. Bus. Women's Week 1965-66, chmn. civic participation com.), Assn. Suprs. N.Y.C. Dept. Welfare (program chmn.), N.Y. State Welfare Conf., Am. Pub. Welfare Assn. (N.Y.C. membership chmn. 1957-60), Hunter Coll. Alumnae Assn., Columbia Sch. Social Work Alumnae, Yale Sch. Alcohol Studies Alumnae. Home: 2 Stuyvesant Oval New York City NY 10009 Office: 250 Church St New York City NY 10013

HIRSCHENSTEIN, EVA (MRS. JEROME APPELBAUM), physician; b. Zagreb, Yugoslavia, July 28, 1934; d. Leopold and Olga (Fuchs) Hirschenstein; M.D. cum laude, Rome U., 1960; m. Jerome Appelbaum, July 29, 1959; children—David, Irene, Joan. Came to U.S., 1959, naturalized, 1962. Intern, Unity Hosp., Bklyn., 1961-62; resident medicine Jewish Chronic Disease Hosp., Bklyn., 1963; resident neurology Boston VA Hosp., 1964-65; resident neurology N.Y. VA Hosp. and Bellevue Hosp., 1965-67; practice medicine specializing in neurology, Bklyn., 1967—; asst. neurologist Jewish Hosp. of Bklyn., St. Johns Episcopal, Jewish Chronic Disease hosps., 1967-69, Bklyn. Cumberland Med. Center, 1969—; clin. asst. prof. neurology Downstate Med. Sch., Bklyn., 1969—; physician VA Outpatient Clinic, Bklyn., 1967—. Diplomate Am. Bd. Psychiatry and Neurology. Mem. Am. Acad. Neurology, A.M.A., Kings County Med. Soc. Home: 196-75 McLaughlin Av Hollis NY 11423 Office: 36 Plaza St Brooklyn NY 11238

HIRST, WILMA ELIZABETH, ednl. psychologist; b. Shenandoah, Ia.; d. James H. and Lena (Donahue) Ellis; A.B. in Elementary Edn., Colo. State Coll., 1948, Ed.D. in Ednl. Psychology, 1954; M.A. in Psychology, U. Wyo., 1951; m. Clyde Henry Hirst (dec. 1969); 1 dau., Donna (Mrs. Alan R. Goss). Elementary tchr., Cheyenne, Wyo., 1945-49, remedial reading instr., 1949-54; asso. prof. edn., dir. campus sch. Neb. State Tchrs. Coll., Kearney, 1954-56; sch. psychologist, head dept. spl. edn. Cheyenne (Wyo.) pub. schs., 1956-57, sch. psychologist, guidance coordinator, 1957-66; dir. div. of research, pub. relations, Cheyenne Schs., 1966-71; prin. investigator Coop. Research Study, U.S. Office Edn. project, dir. div. research and spl. projects, 1971-74; dir. research, spl. projects, also pupil personnel Laramie County Sch. Dist. 1, 1974—. Vis. asst. prof. U. So. Cal., summer 1957, Omaha U., summer 1958; vis. lectr. U. Okla., summers 1959, 60, U. Neb., summer 1961, U. Wyo., 1962, summer, 1964; extension asso. prof., Kabul, Afghanistan, 1970. Mem. Wyo. Bd. Psychology Examiners, 1965—, sec.-treas., 1965-66, vice chmn., 1968-73. Mem. speakers bur., local mental health orgn.; active Little Theatre, 1936—, Girl Scout Leaders Assn., 1943-50; mem., past chmn. bd. social devel. Cheyenne Model Cities; pres. S.E. Wyo. Mental Health Bd., 1968-69; v.p., dir. Wyo. Mental Health Assn.; bd. dirs. Wyo. Children's Home Soc. Diplomate Am. Bd. Profl. Psychology. Fellow Internat. Council Psychologists; mem. Am. Assn. State Psychology Bds. (sec.-treas. 1970—), Wyo. Press Women, Am. Assn. U. Profs., Am., Wyo. (state sec.-treas. 1958-60, pres. 1962-63, exec. bd.) psychol. assns., Am. Personnel and Guidance Assn., N.E.A. (life), Am. Assn. U. Women, Assn. Supervision and Curriculum Devel., Cheyenne Assn. Prin. and Spl. Personnel (pres. 1964-65), Laramie County Council Social Agys. (sec.-treas. 1962), Nat. Assn. Gifted Children (state membership chmn., pres.), Internat. Platform Assn., Am. Ednl. Research Assn., D.A.R., Psi Chi, Kappa Delta Pi, Pi Lambda Theta, Alpha Delta Kappa (Wyo. pres. 1965-66). Presbyn. Mem. Order Eastern Star, Daus. of Nile. Club: Zonta (pres. Cheyenne 1965-66). Author: Know Your School Psychologist, 1963. Contbr. articles in field. Home: 3458 Green Valley Rd Cheyenne WY 82001 Office: Sch Adminstrn Bldg Cheyenne WY 82001

HISLOP, HELEN JEAN, phys. therapist, educator; b. Linden, N.J., Mar. 13, 1929; d. Thomas and Margaret (Macmillan) Hislop; B.A. cum laude, Central Coll., Pella, Ia., 1950; certificate in phys. therapy U. Ia., 1951, M.S. in Physiology, 1953, Ph.D. in Physiology, 1960. Instr. U. Minn. Sch. Phys. Therapy, Mpls., 1953-55; asst. dir. profl. edn. Nat. Found., N.Y.C., 1955-58; instr. U. Pitts. Sch. Medicine, 1960-61; also instr. D. T. Watson Sch. Physiatrics, Pitts., 1960-61; asst. mem. dept. physiology Albert Einstein Med. Center, Phila., 1961-62; lectr., div. phys. therapy U. Pa., Phila., 1961-63; editor Jour. Am. Phys. Therapy Assn., N.Y.C., 1962—; asst. editor Phys. Therapy Rev., 1952-58, cons. editor, 1958-62, editor, 1961-68; prof. phys. therapy, dir. grad. studies U. So. Cal. Med. Sch., Downey, 1968—; dir. phys. therapy div. research tng. in rehab. U. So. Cal., 1971—. Phys. therapy editor Paul Hoeber med. div. Harper & Row, pubs., 1963—; editor Chas. B. Slack, Inc., Pub., 1972—. Sr. research cons. Inst. for Rehab. Medicine, 1966-69; cons. phys. therapy to Surgeon gen. U.S. Army, 1966-69. National Found. fellow, 1958-60; USPHS fellow 1961. Fellow A.A.A.S., Am. Coll. Sports Medicine; mem. Am. Soc. Assn. Execs., Am. Phys. Therapy Assn. (dir. conf. services 1962-68, Am. Congress Rehab. Medicine, Sigma Xi, Alpha Psi Omega. Contbr. Phys. Therapy Rev., Jour. Applied Physiology, Jour. Am. Phys. Therapy Assn., Archives Phys. Medicine, monographs. Home: 12313 Brock Av Downey CA 90242

HISSONG, CECELIA FERNE, physician; b. Detroit, Oct. 16, 1939; d. Cloyd F. and Ruth Cecelia (McLaughlin) Hissong; B.S., Notre Dame Coll., 1961; M.D., Loyola U., Chgo., 1965. Intern, Mount Carmel Mercy Hosp., Detroit, 1965-66; resident family practice St. Joseph Hosp., Syracuse, N.Y., 1966-67; resident gen. practice Oakwood Hosp., Dearborn, Mich., 1967-68; practice family medicine, Dearborn, 1968—; staff Oakwood Hosp., Dearborn, 1968—. Tchr., Jeffries Clinic, Detroit, 1968-71; preceptor Wayne U. Sch. Medicine, 1970—. Diplomate Am. Bd. Family Practice. Mem. Mich. (sec. 1969-72, chmn. edn. commn. 1970-73, speaker House 1972-73, pres.-elect 1973—), Wayne (pres. 1973—) acads. family physicians, Mich. (del. 1972—), Wayne County (dir. 1972—) med. socs., Christian Life Community. Roman Catholic. Club: Skiwi Ski (Detroit). Home: 16165 Steel St Detroit MI 48235 Office: 4407 Roemer St Dearborn MI 48126

HISSONG, CELIA SOUTH (MRS. ARTHUR E. HISSONG), home economist; b. Ashland, Miss., Nov. 25, 1906; d. Edward William and Lillie Bell (Roach) South; B.S., David Lipscomb Jr. Coll., Nashville, 1929; B.S., George Peabody Coll. for Tchrs., Nashville, 1934; M.S., La. State U., 1948; postgrad. U. Ark., 1953, U. Tenn., 1956, Mich. State U., 1957; m. Arthur E. Hissong, Mar. 3, 1942. Tchr. home econs. Dodson (Tex.) High Sch., 1930-34; home demonstration agt. Neshaba County (Miss.), 1934-40; asst. food preservation specialist State of Miss., 1941; home demonstration agt. Jones County (Miss.), 1941-48; home demonstration agt. La. State U. Agrl. Extension Service, Baton Rouge, 1948-55, home mgmt. specialist, 1955—. Chmn. home and recreation sect. La. Safety Council, 1965-69, bd. dirs., 1966—, also sec.; program chmn. Bus. Womens Circle, Presbyn. Ch. Baton Rouge, 1965-67. Mem. Baton Rouge Bus. and Profl. Womens Club (past pres.), Am., La., Baton Rouge home econs. assns., Am. Assn. U. Women, Womans Faculty Club (past sec.), Am. Legion Aux., La. Home Demonstration Agts. Assn. (past v.p., chmn. family financial home mgmt. sect.), Epsilon Sigma Phi, Phi Lambda Pi (past nat. pres.), Gamma Sigma Delta. Mem. White Shrine, Order Eastern Star. Home: 2128 Hollydale St Baton Rouge LA 70808 Office: Knapp Hall La State U Baton Rouge LA 70803

HITCHCOCK, BARBARA MACVEY (MRS. JOHN EDWARD HITCHCOCK, JR.), civic worker; b. New England, N.D., Sept. 19, 1919; d. Charles Henry and Laura (Searight) MacVey; student Sch. Pub. Affairs, Am. U., 1940-41; A.B. cum laude with honors, U. Ky., 1940; m. John Edward Hitchcock, Jr., May 9, 1946; children—John Emerson, David Forest, Deborah Lee, Sarah Doane, Rebecca Ann. Free lance writer; weekly columnist Eagle Bull. DeWitt Times, Fayetteville, N.Y., 1966—; pub. relations work TransNational Credit Corp., Syracuse, N.Y., 1972—. Exec. sec., dir. Soc. Advancement Visual Environment, 1967-72; bd. dirs. Planned Parenthood Center of Syracuse, Consortium for Children; pres. Fayettee Free Library. Mem. Phi Beta Kappa. Presbyn. (trustee 1967—, nat. missions com. 1967-72). Author plays and articles in various mags. including Concern, Presbyn. Life, Empire. Home: 415 Franklin St Fayetteville NY 13066 Office: 678 W Onondaga St Syracuse NY 13201

HITCHCOCK, JOANNA (MRS. MARTYN JOHN HITCHCOCK), editor; b. London, Eng., July 20, 1938; d. Christopher Noel and Joan Allisoun (Whybrow) Goodman; B.A. with Honors, Lady Margaret Hall, Oxford (Eng.) U., 1960, M.A., 1965; m. Martyn John Hitchcock, Mar. 29, 1929. Came to U.S., 1966. Publicity asst. Oxford U. Press, 1962-66; asst. promotion mgr. Princeton U. Press, 1966-68, asst. mgr. advt. and exhibits, 1968-70, staff editor, 1970-72, mng. editor, 1972—. Home: 22 Church St Kingston NJ 08528 Office: Princeton U Press 41 William St Princeton NJ 08540

HITCHMAN, IRENE LINK, physician, state ofcl.; b. Hohenems, Austria, Nov. 5, 1908; d. Joseph and Helene (Stoessel) Link; M.D., U. Innsbruck (Austria), 1933; m. Max Wolfgang Hitchman, Aug. 12, 1938; 1 dau., Eva (Mrs. Joel Goldstein). Came to U.S., 1940, naturalized, 1945. Intern, Neurol. Clinic, U. Innsbruck, 1933; resident Maria Theresien Schloessel Hosp. for Nervous and Mental Diseases, Vienna, 1933-38; sr. physician, psychiatrist Springfield (Md.) Hosp., 1941-46; practice medicine specializing in psychiatry, Md., 1946—; dir. psychiat. edn. and tng. Springfield State Hosp., Sykesville, Md., 1953-54, clin. dir., 1954-62, dir. hosp. inspection and licensure, 1962-66; dep. commr. Md. Dept. Mental Hygiene, Balt., 1966—. Asso. psychiatry Med. Sch., U. Md. Diplomate Am. Bd. Psychiatry and Neurology. Fellow Am. Psychiat. Assn., Am. Coll. Psychiatrists; mem. Balt. Med. Soc., Med. and Chirurg. Faculty Md., A.M.A. Home: 7221 Prince George Rd Baltimore MD 21207 Office: 301 W Preston St Baltimore MD 21201

HITSKY, BARBARA GRIFFIN, journalist; b. Pontiac, Mich., Oct. 8, 1943; d. Glenn Henry and Doris Margaret (Blynn) Griffin; B.A., U. Mich., 1965; m. Brian Hitsky, May 11, 1968. Tchr. journalism and English, Garden City, Mich., 1965-67; women's editor Dearborn (Mich.) Press, 1967-68; edn. reporter Ypsilanti (Mich.) Press, 1968-69; reporter Detroit News, 1969-70, asst. editor, accent on living dept., 1971-74, editor, 1974—; asst. city editor, 1974. Recipient 1st place award for feature writing Asso. Press, Mich., 1970, Mich. Press Women's Club, 1970. Mem. Mich. Women's Press Club, Women in Communications, Sigma Delta Chi, Alpha Chi Omega. Home: 29620 Middlebelt Rd Farmington MI 48024 Office: 615 Lafayette St Detroit MI 48231

HITT, MRS. ROBERT J. (PATRICIA R. HITT), govt. ofcl.; b. Taft, Cal., Jan. 24, 1918; d. John Bernard and Vera (Hearle) Reilly; B.S., U. So. Cal., 1939, B.A., 1939; Ph.D. (hon.), Chapman Coll., 1969; Ph.D. (hon.), Whittier Coll., 1972; m. Robert James Hitt, Sept. 26, 1947; children—John William Hamilton, Patrick Terrance Hamilton. Partner, Miller-Hitt Co., Whittier, Cal., 1950—; asst. sec. Dept. Health, Edn. and Welfare, 1969-73; dir. Reilly Holdings, Whittier. Bd. dirs. Assistance League Orange, Cal., 1954-60; regional council Nat. Assistance League, 1954-60. Mem. Cal. State Rep. Central Com., 1957-72, exec. com., 1960-64; women's vice chmn. Orange County Central Rep. Com., 1958-60; pres. Orange County Fedn. Rep. Women, 1957-60; bd. mem. So. div. Cal. Fedn. Rep. Women, 1957-68; Rep. nat. committeewoman for Cal., 1960-64, mem. exec. com. Rep. Nat. Com.; nat. co-chmn., dir. women's activities Nixon for Pres. Campaign, 1968. Dir. Reilly Found., 1956—; trustee Chapman Coll., Orange, Cal., 1957—, Whittier (Cal.) Coll. Named Woman of Year, Los Angeles Times, 1968. Mem. P.E.O., Chapman Coll. Town and Gown (pres. 1968), Delta Gamma. Methodist. Home: 730 Temple Pl Laguna Beach CA 92651 Office: VJR Trust Properties PO Box 344 Brea CA 92621

HITTINGER, MARTHA ELIZABETH (MRS. WILLIAM FRANK HITTINGER), ret. educator; b. Bloomsburg, Pa., June 20, 1917; d. Myron Philip and Kathryn (Miller) Shuman; A.B., Whittier Coll., 1938; M.A., Long Beach State Coll., 1957; postgrad. N.Y.U., 1940-41, U. So. Cal., 1940-42, Whittier Coll., 1958-60, U. Cal. at Los Angeles, 1962-63; specialist curriculum certificate U. So. Cal., 1967; m. William Frank Hittinger, June 9, 1943 (dec.); 1 son, Myron Frederick. Tchr. pub. schs., Whittier, Cal., 1938-42, Burbank, Cal., 1942-43, Los Nietos, Cal., 1945-53, prin., 1953-60, dir. curriculum, 1960-65, adminstr. curriculum, 1965-66, asst. supt., 1966-72; spl. cons. Cal. Dept. Edn., Sacramento, 1972-74. Mem. Am., Cal. assns. sch. adminstrs., Assn. Childhood Edn., N.E.A. (adviser ednl. policies commn. 1959-61), Association for Supervision and Curriculum Development, Assn. for Gifted, Nat. Soc. Study. Edn., Am. Assn. U. Women, Assn. Childhood Edn. Internat., Delta Kappa Gamma. Author articles profl. jours. Home: 6233 S Comstock Whittier CA 90601

HITTLE, ELIZABETH JOYCE, educator; b. Dayton, O., Oct. 12, 1925; d. Luther Allen and Elizabeth (Shacklett) Hittle; B.S., U. Akron, 1947; M.A., Kent State U., 1949; Ed.D., Western Res. U., 1962. Primary tchr. Bd. Edn., Cleve., 1947-48; tchr. nursery sch. for deaf, Akron, O., 1948-50; instr. speech U. Akron, 1950-53, asst. prof. speech, 1953-64, asso. prof., 1964-66, prof., 1966—, head dept. speech pathology and audiology, 1966-74, dir. speech and hearing clinic, 1953-74, mem. operations group Ednl. Research and Devel. Center, 1971—; dir. Akron Child Devel. Center, 1957-63; speech cons. St. Joseph's Sch., Cuyahoga Falls, 1953-63. Mem. Summit County Bd. Mental Retardation; mem. exec. com., sec. Archbishop Hoban High Sch. Bd. Edn., 1972—; project dir. Comprehensive Services for Adult Deaf, 1970-74; project dir. Bur. Edn. Handicapped, Dept. Health, Edn. and Welfare, 1965-67, 70-74. Trustee Sheltered Workshop of Summit County; pres. bd. trustees Blick Clinic for Developmental Disabilities, 1972-73; trustee United Services for Handicapped Children and Adults, 1972—. Mem. Nat. Assn. Hearing and Speech Agys. (recruiting com. 1970), Am., Ohio, Summit County speech and hearing assns., Am. Assn. U. Profs. (chpt. exec. com. 1968-70), Pi Kappa Delta, Zeta Tau Alpha. Home: 874 Westgrove Rd Akron OH 44303

HITTLE, JUDITH ANNE, home economist; b. Lafayette, Ind., Dec. 19, 1931; d. Leslie Lee and Emma Lu (Curtner) Hittle; B.S., Okla. Coll. Liberal Arts, 1953; postgrad. Colo. State U., summer 1963, U. Okla., 1964, Okla. State U., 1965, U. Ark., 1972-73. Clk., Post Exchange System, Fort Sill, Okla., 1956-61; asst. home economist Okla. Extension Service, Anadarko, 1961-67; home economist Ark. Extension Service, U. Ark., Booneville, 1967—. Sec. local chpt. vols. A.R.C., 1969-71; active Girl Scouts U.S.A. Mem. Ark. Extension Home Economists (councilor dist. 1972—), Ark. Home Econs. Assn., Pilot Internat. (local pres. 1969-70, dist. chmn. 1971-73), Nat. Assn. Extension Home Economists, Am. Assn. Home Econs. Methodist. Home: 1107 E 7th St Booneville AR 72927 Office: Court House Broadway Booneville AR 72927

HIX, ELIZABETH (MRS. CLIFTON HIX), lawyer; b. Greer County, Okla., Apr. 7, 1913; d. Leonard Alvin and Mary Elizabeth (Lewis) Coleman; student Cameron State Jr. Coll., 1931-32, Southwestern State, 1932-34; R.N., Kansas City Gen. Hosp., 1937; LL.B., Southwestern U., 1950; m. Clifton A. Hix, Apr. 14, 1956; 1 dau., Mary Elizabeth (Mrs. John F. Delaplane IV). Registered nurse Good Samaritan Hosp., Los Angeles, 1938-42; indsl. nurse Lockheed Aircraft, Burbank, Cal., 1942-43; sch. nurse Los Angeles City Bd. Edn., 1945-47; admitted to Cal. bar, 1951; since practiced in Long Beach and San Pedro, 1951—. Tchr. Adult div. Long Beach City Schs., 1952-56. Mem. State Bar Cal., San Pedro C. of C. Republican. Home: 27 Crest Rd W Rolling Hills CA 90274 Office: Hix and Hix 413 W 7th St San Pedro CA 90731

HIX, PHYLLIS MARIE (MRS. ERNEST HARMON HIX, JR.), lawyer; b. Bloomfield, Ia., Mar. 28, 1936; d. Hyle Leon and Myrtle Marie (Teasdale) Houston; student U. Ia., 1954-56; B.S. in Occupational Therapy, U. So. Cal., 1958; J.D., U. Cal. at Los Angeles, 1962; m. Ernest Harmon Hix, Jr., Mar. 29, 1958; 1 son, Jeffrey David. Intern and registration occupational therapy U. So. Cal., 1958-59; practice occupational therapy Arcadia (Cal.) Meth. Hosp., 1959; admitted to Cal. bar, 1963; v.p. Hix Devel. Corp., Los Angeles, 1959—, also dir.; atty. firm Lawler, Felix & Hall, Los Angeles, 1963, Overton, Lyman & Prince, 1963-67, Dryden, Harrington & Swartz, Los Angeles, 1967-73. Mem. U. So. Cal. Coordinating Council, 1970-72; dir., mem. legislative com. Soc. Cal. Def. Counsel Assn., 1970—. Mem. Pasadena Tournament of Roses Assn. Mem. Pres. Nixon's $500 Dinner Com. Republican party, Los Angeles County, 1971. Mem. Los Angeles County Bar Assn. (del. 1969-72, chmn. medico-legal com. 1973-74), Cal. State Bar (ethics com. 1971-72, chmn. local adminstrv. com. 1972-74), Am. Arbitration Assn., Am. Bd. Trial Advocates (advocate). TV appearances include: The Advocates, 1971; Today, 1972; 60 Minutes, 1972; Ralph Story's Los Angeles, 1972. Home: 1365 St Albans Rd San Marino CA 91108

HLADKY, CATHERINE RAE LEWIS (MRS. GEORGE WESLEY HLADKY), newspaper pub.; b. Ia. City, Ia., Sept. 20, 1927; d. Raymond Llewellyn and Marjorie K. (Williams) Lewis; A.B., Drake U., 1950; m. George Wesley Hladky, Aug. 28, 1950; children—William George, Douglas James. Tchr. rural sch., Muscatine County, Ia., 1945-47; library clk. Ia. Wesleyan Coll., Mt. Pleasant, 1947-48, Drake U., Des Moines, 1948-49; receptionist Son de Regger Advt. Agy., Des Moines, 1950-51; corr. Cowles Publs., Des Moines, 1951; receptionist Hall & Co., Des Moines, 1954; asst. instr. philosophy and religion Simpson Coll., Indianola, Ia., 1955-57; copublisher, editor Indianola Reminder, shopper newspaper, 1959—; sec. to Ia. State Rep. James Lynch, 1965. Active worker local Dem. orgns. Bd. dirs. FISH, 1972—; trustee Central Ia. Regional Library System, 1973—. Mem. Women's Internat. League for Peace and Freedom (br. action chmn. 1973), Shoppers Guides Ia., Indianola C. of C. Methodist. Home: 709 N Howard St Indianola IA 50125 Office: 205 W 1st St Indianola IA 50125

HO, CLARA LIN (MRS. BOU-LOONG HO), marine chemist; b. Shantung, China, Jan. 16, 1932; d. Pu-Chan and Hui-Fan (Sun) Lin; came to U.S., 1955, naturalized, 1969; M.S. in Soil Chemistry, Ore. State U., 1956; Ph.D. in Soil Chemistry, N.C. State U., 1959; m. Bou-Loong Ho, Sept. 1, 1960; children—Ellen, Linus. Postdoctoral research in soil biochemistry and soil engring. Ia. State U., 1959-65; asst. prof. Coastal Studies Inst., La. State U., Baton Rouge, 1966-69, asso. prof. dept. marine sci., 1969—. Fellow Am. Inst. Chemists; mem. Internat. Assn. Geochimie et Cosmochimie, Clay Mineral Soc., Am. Geochem. Soc., Sigma Xi. Home: 1987 Columbine St Baton Rouge LA 70808

HOAD, GRACE HAMILTON (MRS. JOHN G. HOAD), cons. psychologist; b. Detroit, Dec. 8, 1908; d. James and Jane Ann (Colclough) Hamilton; A.B., U. Mich., 1937, M.S.W., 1942; m. John G. Hoad, Nov. 24, 1937. Supr. pub. welfare, Detroit, 1933-42, Childrens' Center Met. Detroit, 1947-49; caseworker Community Service, N.Y.C., 1943-45; became psychotherapist, bus. mgr. Birmingham (Mich.; Psychiat. Clinic, 1954—; pvt. practice psychotherapy. Dir., Lincoln Mining Co., Wallace, Ida., 1947-49; dir., v.p. Hoad Corp., Ypsilanti, Mich., 1957—; v.p. Environment Improvement Corp. Mem. of Nat. Assn. Social Workers, Am. Orthopsychiat. Assn., Am. Acad. Psychotherapists, Am. Assn. Marriage Counselors, Mich. Assn. Marriage Counselors (sec.-treas. 1969-70, sec. 1972, pres.-elect 1973, pres. 1974). Author: Self Damage and the Classroom. Home: 40 Shady Hollow Dearborn MI 48124 Office: 861 Monroe Av Dearborn MI 48124

HOAG, SISTER DOROTHY, coll. adminstr.; b. Buffalo, Aug. 20, 1925; d. Wilbur E. and Hazel I. (Joslyn) Hoag; B.S., Mt. St. Joseph Tchrs. Coll., 1948, B.A., 1951, M.A., 1953; Ph.D., Georgetown U., 1966. Elementary sch. tchr., Buffalo, 1947-52; high sch. tchr., Lackawanna, N.Y., 1952-61; faculty Medaille Coll., Buffalo, 1966—, prof. linguistics, 1967—, asst. dean, 1967-69, dean, 1969-72, v.p. academic affairs, 1972—. Vice pres. Checktowaga D'Youville Medaille Sloan Policy Bd., 1973-74. Nat. Defense Edn. Act fellow, 1962. Mem. Internat. Reading Assn., Linguistics Soc. Am., Niagara Frontier Council, Am. Assn. Elementary Kindergarten Nursery Educators. Home: 10324 Main St Clarence NY 14031 Office: 18 Agassiz Circle Buffalo NY 14214

HOAG, MARY ESTHER HOTCHKIN (MRS. WILLIAM HARVEY HOAG), banker, former educator; b. Pulteney, N.Y., Jan. 30, 1887; d. Francis Granger and Laura May (Dean) Hotchkin; grad. Geneseo State Normal Sch. (N.Y.), 1906; postgrad. Am. Coll., 1915-16, N.Y. U., 1935-36; m. William George Dean, Dec. 3, 1913 (dec. Mar. 1917); m. 2d, William Harvey Hoag, Aug. 30, 1922 (dec. Feb. 1972); 1 son, Harvey Hotchkin (dec.). Tchr. pub. schs., Millerton, N.Y., 1906-07, North Tonawanda, N.Y., 1907-09, Nutley, N.J., 1909-10, Bloomfield, N.J., 1910-12, Rochester, N.Y., 1912-13, 1919-22, Corning, N.Y., 1918-19; tchr. English, Prattsburg (N.Y.) Central Jr. High Sch., 1936-43; chmn. bd. Bath (N.Y.) Nat. Bank, 1963—, dir., 1929—; dir. Prattsburg State Bank, 1928-62; mem. adv. com. Central Trust Co., 1963—. Lectr. hist. subjects. Bd. dirs. Women's Hall of Fame, Inc. Mem. D.A.R. (regent 1926-29, 45-47, chaplain, 1965-68, state rec. sec. 1929-32), N.Y. State Officers Club D.A.R. (pres. 1950-53, bd. govs. 1953—, v.p. 1947-50, sec.-treas. 1941-47), D.A.R. Ex-Regents Assn. N.Y. State, Genesee Council Area Regents, Steuben County (pres. 1947-51), Yates County hist. socs., Genesee Country Hist. Fedn. (v.p. 1953-58), N.Y. State Hist. Assn., Nundawaga Soc., New Eng. Geneal. Soc., Am. Inst. Genealogy, Daus. Am. Colonists, Colonial Dames 17th Century, Franklin Acad. Literary Club. Presbyn. (trustee 1962-65, elder, 1957-62, 65-71, del. N.Y. Synod 1965). Mem. Order Eastern Star. Author booklet. Contbr. articles in hist. field to profl. jours. Home: 32 N Main St Prattsburg NY 14873

HOAGLAND, MARGARET MCDONAGH (MRS. EARL JONES HOAGLAND), pub. co. exec.; b. N.Y.C., Nov. 7, 1910; d. Edwin Bernard and Margaret (Anderson) McDonagh; student Cornell U., 1928-30; m. Earl Jones Hoagland, Aug. 27, 1931. Various clerical, secretarial positions, 1931-57; asst. research dept. Tech. Pub. Co., Barrington, Ill., 1957-59, head dept., 1959—. Mem. Am. Marketing Assn. Home: 615 Prairie Av Barrington IL 60010 Office: 1301 S Grove St Barrington IL 60010

HOBBS, A. JANETTE WILLIAMSON (MRS. GEORGE E. HOBBS), med. technologist; b. Milford, Del., Jan. 2, 1932; d. Howard E. and Mary J. (Anderson) Williamson; grad. Franklin Sch. Sci. and Arts, 1951; m. George E. Hobbs, Apr. 12, 1952. Med. lab. technician Milford Meml. Hosp., Inc., 1951—. Cons. staff, lab. technicians program Georgetown Community Coll., Georgetown, Del., 1974—. Bd. dirs. Blood Bank of Del. Mem. Am. Assn. Blood Banks, Am. Soc. Med. Technologists, Am. Med. Technologists. Home: RD 3 Box 273 Harrington DE 19952 Office: Milford Meml Hosp Milford DE 19963

HOBBS, NOLA ANN, librarian; b. nr. McKenzie, Tenn., Nov. 5, 1937; d. William Thomas and Myrtle Alice (Edwards) Hobbs; student U. Tenn., 1957; B.A., Bethel Coll., 1959; M.A. in L.S., George Peabody Coll., 1960. Library asst. Memphis Pub. Library, 1960; med. librarian St. Jude Hosp., Memphis, 1961-63; cataloger Va. Poly. Inst., Blacksburg, Va., 1963-64, U. Ark. Med. Center, Little Rock, 1964-66; cataloger U. Tenn., Martin, 1966-70, acquisitions librarian, 1970—. Mem. Am. (sec.-treas. Tenn. tech. services librarians 1969-71), W. Tenn. (sec. 1970-71), Tenn. library assns., Phi Kappa Phi. Home: 311 Oxford St Martin TN 38237 Office: Paul Meek Library University of Tennessee Martin TN 38238

HOBBY, GLADYS LOUNSBURY, microbiologist, educator; b. N.Y.C., Nov. 19, 1910; d. Theodore Y. and Flora R. (Lounsbury) Hobby; B.A., Vassar Coll., 1931; M.A., Columbia, 1932, Ph.D., 1935. Research asso. Columbia U. Coll. Physicians and Surgeons, 1934-44; research microbiologist Pfizer, Inc., N.Y.C., 1944-59; chief spl. research lab. VA Hosp., East Orange, N.J., 1959—; sci. dir. Infectious Disease Research Inst., Livingston, N.J., 1959—; clin. asst. prof. pub. health Cornell U. Med. Coll., N.Y.C., 1959—. Bd. dirs. N.Y. Lung Assn., 1957—. Fellow Am. Acad. Microbiology, N.Y. Acad. Scis., Am. Pub. Health Assn., A.A.A.S.; mem. Am. Soc. Microbiologists, Am. Assn. Immunologists, Soc. Exptl. Biology and Medicine, Am. Thoracic Soc., N.Y. Trudeau Soc., Internat. Union Against Tb, Infectious Diseases Soc. Am., Reticuloendothelial Soc., Assn. Gnotobiologists, Council Biology Editors. Presbyn. Contbr. articles to profl. jours. Home: 315 E 72d St New York City NY 10021 Office: VA Hosp East Orange NJ 07019

HOBBY, GRETCHEN CLARK (MRS. WILLIAM M. HOBBY III), civic worker; b. Washington, D.C., Apr. 22, 1939; d. Bruce Edmund and Phyllis Bryans (Wilson) Clark; B.A., Mary Baldwin Coll., 1960; m. William M. Hobby III, Oct. 12, 1962; children—Amy, William. Asst. to slide librarian, pubs. supr., asst. chief pubs. Nat. Gallery Art, summers, 1957-59, 60-65; with art dept. Orlando (Fla.) Pub. Library 1967-68; mgr. Loch Haven Art Center Shop, Orlando, Fla., 1969—, docent, 1966-67. Chmn. teenage vols. Orange Meml. Hosp. Aux., 1968-70; mem. Jr. Sorosis, 1968-70, Orlando Opera Gala Guild, 1967-72, Orlando Civic Theatre Guild, 1971—; dir., recording sec. Loch Haven Art Center, 1970-71, mem. council of 101, commn. and corr. sec. Winter Park Sidewalk Art Festival Assn., 1970—. Mem. Orange County Bar Assn. Aux., Am. Assn. Mus.'s, Mus. Stores Assn. (chmn. conv. 1972, v.p. 1973—, editor Newsletter 1973—, exec. com. 1973—), Alumnae Assn. Mary Baldwin Coll. (dir. 1974—). Republican. Unitarian. Home: 749 Lake Davis Dr Orlando FL 32806 Office: Art Center Shop 2416 N Mills Av Orlando FL 32803

HOBBY, OVETA CULP (MRS. WILLIAM P. HOBBY), newspaper pub.; b. Killeen, Tex., Jan. 19, 1905; d. I.W. and Emma (Hoover) Culp; student Mary Hardin Baylor Coll., H.H.D., 1956; LL.D., Baylor U., Sam Houston State Tchrs. Coll., U. Chattanooga, 1943, Bryant Coll., Ohio Wesleyan U., 1953, Columbia, Smith Coll., Middlebury Coll., 1954, U. Pa., Colby Coll., 1955, Fairleigh Dickinson, Western Coll., 1956; D.Litt., Colo. Women's Coll., 1947, C.W. Post Coll., 1962; L.H.D., Bard Coll., Annandale, N.Y., 1950; L.H.D. LaFayette Coll., 1954; m. William P. Hobby, Feb. 23, 1931; children—William, Jessica (Mrs. Henry E. Catto, Jr.). Parliamentarian, Tex. Ho. of Reps., 1926-31, incomplete terms, 1939, 41; joined Houston Post as research editor, 1931, lit. editor, asst. editor, v.p., exec. v.p., editor, 1931-52, editor, pub., 1952-53, pres., editor, 1955-65, editor, chmn. bd., 1965—; chmn. bd. sta. KPRC, Channel II TV; chief women's interest sect. War Dept. Bur. Pub. Relations, 1941-42; apptd. dir. WAAC, 1942; col. AUS, dir. Wac, 1943-45; fed. security adminstr., 1953; sec. Dept. Health, Edn. and Welfare, 1953-55; dir. Gen. Foods Corp. Mem. Com. of 75 U. Tex., 1957-58, White House Conf. Edn., 1954-55; gov. A.R.C., 1950-55; nat. vice chmn. Am. Cancer Soc. campaign, 1949; pres. So. Newspaper Pubs. Assn., 1949; mem. Am. Design Awards com.; mem. nat. com. Am. Mus. Immigration, 1956; bd. dirs. Tex. Heart Assn.; trustee People to People. Nat. adv. com. Citizens for Eisenhower, 1956; sponsor Clark Sch. for Deaf; mem. Coll. Commn. Diocese of Tex., 1956; trustee Eisenhower Birthplace Meml. Park, 1966; bd. dirs. Com. Econ. Development, 1956—; mem. Carnegie Commn. on Ednl. Television; mem. Nat. Adv. Commn. on Selective Service; mem. Pres.'s coms. on Employment Physically Handicapped, Civilian Nat. Honors; trustee Eisenhower Exchange Fellowship; dir. Houston Symphony Soc.; mem. So. Regional Com. for Marshall Scholarships, 1957—; nat. bd. devel. Sam Rayburn Found.; nat. council Eleanor Roosevelt Meml. Found.; adv. commn. fund campaign A.R.C., 1950; nat. council Met. Opera; mem. corp. Crusade for Freedom; trustee Am. Assembly, Soc. for Rehab. Facially Disfigured, Rice U.; vis. com. Grad. Sch. Edn., Harvard, 1961-67; adv. bd. George C. Marshall Research Found.; mem. Cuban Freedom Com.; mem. Bus. Com. for Arts; mem. spl. studies project Rockefeller Bros. Spl. Fund. Recipient Pub. of Year award, 1960; Living Hist. award Research Inst. Am., 1960; Honor award Nat. Jewish Hosp.; award Carnegie Corp., 1967. Mem. Gamma Chi Alpha (hon. vice chmn.). Episcopalian. Clubs: Houston, Bayou, Ramada, Junior League (Houston); 1925 F Street, Headliners (Washington). Author: Mr. Chairman (parliamentary law textbook); also syndicated column same title. Office: The Houston Post 4747 Southwest Freeway Houston TX 77001

HOBLIT, ANNABELLE LORE (MRS. GORDON EDWARD HOBLIT), rancher; b. Alliance, Neb., Dec. 3, 1910; d. Arthur Henry and Bertha Etta (Ross) Lore; student Elizabeth Kay Bumpas, cosmetology, 1928; m. James Donald Hoblit, Jan. 15, 1942 (dec. Apr. 1959); m. 2d, Gordon Edward Hoblit, Sept. 14, 1962. Cosmetologist, Alliance, Neb., 1928-30, Mae Day Shop, Casper, Wyo., 1934-36, Annabelle Beauty Shop, Lusk, Wyo., 1936-42; partner Hoblit Ranch, C. & H. Refinery, 1959—. Family genealogist. Curator Stage Coach Mus., 1970—, bd. dirs. Hist. Soc., 1970—. Mem. Neb., Wyo., Niobrara County (pres. 1969-71) hist. socs. Conglist. Mem. Order Eastern Star.

HOBSON, ANN STEVENS, harpist; b. Phila., Nov. 6, 1943; d. Harrison Dennis and Grace (Stevens) Hobson; student Phila. Mus. Acad., 1961-64; B.Mus., Mus., Cleve. Inst. Music, 1966. Second harpist Pitts. Symphony Orch., 1965-66; prin. harpist Washington Nat. Symphony, 1966-69; asso. prin. harpist Boston Symphony Orch., 1969—; prin. harpist Boston Pops, 1969—; mem. New Eng. Harp Trio, 1971—; tchr. Phila. Mus. Acad., 1967-69, Temple U. Music Festival at Ambler, 1968, 69; now mem. faculty New Eng. Conservatory Music, Boston; soloist Boston Symphony Orch., Boston Pops, Washington Nat. Symphony, Phila. Concert Orch., Cleve. Women's Symphony, North Shore (Mass.) Philharmonic, Cape Cod Symphony. Recipient talent award Shriners, 1961. Mem. Am. Harp Soc. Recs. include Debussy Trio, Sonata for Flute, Viola and Harp (Deutsche Grammophone Gessellshaft). Home: 33 Pond Av Brookline MA 02146 Office: Symphony Hall Boston MA 02115

HOBSON, DONNA SUE (MRS. RICKEY J. THOMAS), editor; b. Amory, Miss., Sept. 11, 1945; d. Arthur Audell and Minnie Sue (Anderson) Hobson; A.A., N.E. Miss. Jr. Coll., 1965; B.A., U. Miss., 1968. Sec. to dean Blue Mountain (Miss.) Coll., 1968-70; editor Miss. Adult Edn. News, Itawamba Jr. Coll., Tupelo, Miss., 1970—. Col. on staff Gov. Miss., 1972—. Mem. Adult Edn. Assn. Miss., Miss. Editors and Dirs. Information Assn., Am. Assn. U. Women, Women in Communications, Inc. Club: Pilot. Home: 216 Glade St New Albany MS 38652 Office: PO Drawer 1588 Tupelo MS 38801

HOBSON, KATHERINE THAYER, sculptress, poet; b. Denver, Apr. 11, 1889; d. Henry Wise and Katherine S. (Thayer) Hobson; student law U. Leipzig, Koenigsberg, Goettingen, sculpture Dresden, Paris, Athens; m. Herbert Kraus, Dec. 2, 1911 (div. Nov. 1938); m. 2d, Diether Thimme, Feb. 21, 1939 (div. Dec. 1948). Exhibited in group shows galleries Berlin, Dresden, Hamburg, Koenigsberg, Paris Salon, Hudson Valley Art Assn., Nat. Acad. Design (N.Y.), Audubon Artists, Nat. Assn. Women Artists, Pen and Brush, Nat. Sculpture Soc., and others; important works include statue Bahnhofs Platz, Goettingen; busts Univs. Goettingen, Koenigsberg, Sch. Tech., Dresden; U. Library and Gymnasium Goettingen; 8 foot war meml. St. James Episcopal Ch., N.Y.C. Tchr. occupational therapy Halloran Gen. Hosp., World War II, Recipient awards Catherine Lorrillard Wolfe Club, 1953, 54, 68, 1st prize Womens Nat. Republican Club, 1964, medal Nat. Arts Club, 1967, Newington award Hudson Valley Art Assn., 1968, 73, 1st prize sculpture Cooperstown Art Assn. ann. exhbn., 1968, Anna Wyatt Huntington Meml. award Catherine Lorrillard Wolff Club, 1973. Fellow Nat. sculpture Soc. (mem. council); mem. Nat. Assn. Women Artists (past chmn. sculptor sect.), Pen and Brush (chmn. sculptor sect. 1953, 54, 62-64, 66; recipient Founders prize 1955, Gold medal, 1965, Silver medals, 1964, 66), Am. Artists Profl. League (v.p., asst. treas.; president's prize 1962, 66), Am. Artists Soc. (council), Fine Arts Fedn. N.Y. (sec. 1952-69),

Allied Artists Am., Hudson Valley Art Assn. (Gold medal 1963, Archer Milton Huntington award 1963, 64), Contemporary Arts Club, Woman Geographers, Poetry Soc. Am., Cath. Poetry Soc. Contbr. poems to newspapers, poetry mags. Address: 27 W 67th St New York City NY 10023

HOBSON, LAURA ZAMETKIN, author; b. N.Y.C.; d. Michael and Adella (Kean) Zametkin; A.B., Cornell; m. Thayer Hobson, July 23, 1930 (div. 1935); children—Michael and Christopher (adopted). Advt. writer until 1934, except for year as reporter N.Y. Eve. Post; promotion writer Time, Life, Fortune mags., 1934-40, becoming copy chief all Time, Inc. mag. promotion, then dir. promotion Time mag.; wrote 1st short story, 1935, continued with spare-time writing short stories, 1935-41; full time writing, 1941-56, 62—; promotion cons. Time, Sports Illustrated, Fortune, 1956-62; editorial cons. Sat. Rev./World, 1960—. Mem. Authors League Am., P.E.N., Am. Civil Liberties Union. Club: Regency Whist. Author: A Dog of His Own (juvenile), 1941; The Trespassers, 1943; Gentlemen's Agreement, 1947 (motion picture, winning Acad. Award as best picture 1947); The Other Father, 1950; The Celebrity, 1951; First Papers, 1964; I'm Going to Have a Baby (juvenile), 1967; The Tenth Month, 1971. Office: care Doubleday & Co 277 Park Av New York City NY 10017

HOBSON, PHYLLIS JOAN PURVIS (MRS. MAX B. HOBSON), newswoman; b. Kokomo, Ind., June 26, 1924; d. Marley Evan and Ethel (Tolley) Purvis; student pub. schs., Kokomo, Ind.; m. Max. B. Hobson, June 1, 1943; children—Richard, Charles, Jon, William, Elizabeth. Freelance writer to various mags. including Teen, St. Joseph mag., Ingenue, Teen Hit Parader; womens news editor Kokomo (Ind.) Tribune, 1963-68, desk asst., 1971-73, family news editor, 1973—; editor Howard County News, Greentown, Ind., 1970. Recipient nat. awards Nat. Fedn. Press Women, 1966-71. Home: Route 1 Greentown IN 46936 Office: 300 N Union St Kokomo IN 46901

HOBSON, VIVIAN CLAIRE, buyer; b. Blue Island, Ill., Mar. 27, 1925; d. Richard George and Paula (Kaiser) Moran; B.B.A, DePaul U.; m. Bernard E. Hobson, May 27, 1952 (div. July 2, 1955); 1 son, Bernard E. Exec. sec. United Airlines, Chgo., 1945-52; adminstrv. asst. to pres. Cluett Peabody Retail, Chgo., 1960-70; buyer Lytton's, Chgo., 1970—. Mem. Art Inst. Chgo. Club: Mid Town Tennis (Chgo.). Home: 1330 Estes Av Chicago IL 60626 Office: 235 S State St Chicago IL 60604

HOCH, EILEEN GLORIA (MRS. WENDEL JOSEPH HOCH), librarian; b. Oregon, Ill., Sept. 28, 1930; d. Alfred Herbert and Frieda Sophia (Benz) Anderson; B.S., U. Minn., 1952, postgrad., 1969—; m. Wendel Joseph Hoch, July 16, 1955; 1 son, John Wendel. Librarian Farmington (Minn.) pub. schs., 1952-56, St. Paul Park (Minn.) pub. schs., 1956-63; librarian, head dept. dist. secondary sch. libraries Park Sr. High Sch., Cottage Grove, Minn., 1966—; cons. in field. Sec.-Treas. P.T.A., 1952—. Mem. Farmington Pub. Library Bd. Mem. A.L.A., Nat., Minn., So. Washington County, Farmington (sec.-treas. 1953-54) edn. assns., Minn. Assn. Sch. Librarians. Conglist. Home: 7415 Harkness Av Cottage Grove MN 55016 Office: 8040 S 80th St Cottage Grove MN 55016

HOCH, MINNIE BELLE (MRS. MYRON L. HOCH), librarian; b. Pitts., Sept. 30, 1913; d. Nathan and Anna (Rieck) Belle; B.A., U. Pitts., 1934; B.S. in L.S., Carnegie Inst. Tech., 1935; M.S. (Carnegie Corp. fellow), Columbia, 1941; m. Myron L. Hoch, May 20, 1945 (dec. Feb. 1971); 1 dau., Susan. Librarian, Carnegie Library of Pitts., 1935-42, U.S. Office for Emergency Mgmt., Washington, 1942-43; information officer Australian War Supplies, Washington, 1943-45; research asst. U.S. Senate Small Bus. Com., Washington, 1945; librarian U.S. Office Tech. Services, Washington, 1945-47; research librarian Standard Brands, N.Y.C., 1947-48; sch. librarian, Balt., 1955-61; librarian, asst. dir. Community Coll. of Balt., 1961—. Mem. Am., Md. library assns., Am. Assn. U. Women Am. Assn. U. Profs., Md. Assn. Community and Jr. Colls. (dir.), Council on Library Tech., Beta Phi Mu. Author: Australia, The New Customer, 1946. Home: 3740 Oak Av Baltimore MD 21207 Office: 2901 Liberty Heights Av Baltimore MD 21215

HOCHMAN, SANDRA, poetess; b. N.Y.C., Sept. 11, 1936; d. Sidney and Mae Barnett (Schumer) Hochman; B.A., Bennington Coll.; postgrad. Columbia, Coll. de France, Paris; m. Harvey Leve (div.); 1 dau., Ariel. Author: (poems) Voyage Home, 1960, Manhattan Pastures (winner Yale Younger Poets award 1963), 1960, The Vaudeville Marriage, 1965, Love Letters From Asia, 1967, Earthworks (selected poems 1960-1970); (juvenile) The Magic Convention; (novel) Walking Papers; journalist N.Y. Times Mag., Look, Life, Cosmopolitan, Holiday, Esquire mags.; contbg. editor Harpers Bazaar. Poet-in-residence Fordham City Coll. Founder Hochman Scott Prodns., Womans Books; creator Gurilla Theatre. Recipient Mixed Media Workshop award for contbn. to feminist lit. Appeared on TV spl. Woman Poet And City. Home: 180 E 79th St New York City NY 10021

HOCHSTADT, JOY, biochemist, microbiologist; b. N.Y.C., May 6, 1939; d. Julius Louis and Edith (Tabatchnick) Hochstadt; A.B., Barnard Coll., 1960; A.M. in Biol. Scis., Stanford, 1963; Ph.D. in Microbiology, Georgetown U., 1968; m. Harvey L. Ozer, Feb. 3, 1960. Vis. fellow Karolinska Inst., Stockholm, Sweden, 1964-65; research fellow in biol. chemistry Harvard, 1965-66; NIH, USPHS postdoctoral fellow Nat. Heart and Lung Inst., Bethesda, Md., 1968-70; Am. Heart Assn. established investigator, 1970-75; sr. scientist Worcester Found. Exptl. Biology, Shrewsbury, Mass., 1972—. Mem. Am. Heart Assn. (basic sci. council 1970—), Am. Soc. Microbiology (com. on status of women 1970-73, sec. physiology div. 1971-73, nominating com. metabolism and physiology div. 1973—), Am. Acad. Microbiology, Genetic Soc. Am., Am. Soc. Biology Chemists, A.A.A.S., Assn. Women in Sci. (affirmative action rep. 1973—), Profl. Women's Caucus (nat. policy com. 1970-73), N.Y. Acad. Scis., Barnard Alumnae Assn. Contbr. numerous research articles to profl. lit. Home: 45 Flagg St Worcester MA 01602 Office: Worcester Found for Exptl Biology Shrewsbury MA 01545

HOCHSTETLER, RUTH, educator; b. Sullivan, Ind.; d. Perry and Ethel (Hurst) Hochstetler; B.S., Ind. State U., 1940, M.S., 1953; Ed.D., Ind. U., 1960. Tchr. elementary schs., Elkhart, Indpls., Bloomington, Ind., 1940-53; asst. prof. DePauw U., Greencastle, Ind., 1953-55; lectr. Ind. U., Bloomington, 1955-59; prof. elementary edn. Ball State U., Muncie, Ind., 1959—. Project dir. Regional Tng. Office, Headstart, 1969-70, Huffer Experience, 1973-74. Mem. Nat. Council Tchrs. English, Assn. for Supervision and Curriculum Devel. (pres. Ind. 1970-71, v.p. 1971-72), N.E.A., Ind. Tchrs. Assn., Delta Kappa Gamma, Pi Lambda Theta (pres. Alpha Tau chpt. 1972-74). Contbr. articles to profl. jours. Home: 3404 Mansfield St Muncie IN 47304

HOCHSTETTLER, PHYLLIS IRENE, educator, librarian; b. Aurora, Neb., July 2, 1915; d. Otto J. and Ethel A. (Beard) Hochstettler; B.A., Hastings Coll., 1937; M.A. in Librarianship, U. Denver, 1955. Tchr., Brule, Neb., Granada and Julesburg, Colo., 1937-47; sch. librarian, North Platte, Neb., 1947-59; cons. sch. libraries Ore. Dept. Edn., Salem, 1959-67; prof. librarianship Portland (Ore.) State U. Sch. Edn., 1967—. Instr., Rutgers U., summer 1967; Fulbright lectr. Australia Sch. Library Assn., 1970; cons. library workshops, Tex., La., Ore., Cal., 1969—. Mem. Am. Assn. Sch. Librarians (v.p. 1967-68, pres. 1968-69), A.L.A. (mem. coms.), N.E.A., Ore. Edn. Assn., Ore., Pacific N.W. (v.p., pres.-elect 1973—) library assns., Assn. for Ednl. Communications and Tech., Ore. Ednl. Media Assn., Am. Assn. U. Profs., Delta Kappa Gamma, Pi Lambda Theta. Contbr. articles to library, ednl. jours. Home: 1335 SW 66th St Portland OR 97225

HOCKER, MARGARET LOUISE, librarian; b. South Carrollton, Ky.; d. Asbury Charles and Fannie (Brown) Hocker; A.B., Western Ky. State Coll., 1941; B.S. in L.S., U. Ky., 1946; A.M. in L.S., U. Mich., 1950, postgrad., summer 1961. Elementary sch. tchr., Muhlenburg County, Ky., 1933-41; librarian, high sch. English tchr. Bremen (Ky.) High Sch., 1941-43; high sch. librarian, Central City, Ky., 1943-47; reference librarian U. Cin., 1947-49; reference librarian, asst. prof. Wis. State U., LaCrosse, 1950-61, reference librarian, asso. prof., 1961-67, chmn. library sci. dept., 1967—, tchr. U. Ore., Eugene, summer 1958; vis. lectr. U. Wis., Madison, summer 1965-67. Mem. Am., Wis. (past mem. com. on library edn.) library assns., Am. Assn. U. Women (chmn. local scholarship com. 1961-68, fellowship com. 1969-72), Wis., Western Wis. edn. assns., Beta Phi Mu, Delta Kappa Gamma. Methodist (pres. Wesleyan Service Guild 1959-61). Home: 1225 Park Av LaCrosse WI 54601

HOCKETT, RUTH REYNOLDS (MRS. STACY HOWARD HOCKETT), civic worker; b. Carrier Mills, Ill., Dec. 30, 1901; d. Herbert W. and Fanny (Ozment) R.; B.S., diploma in piano Guilford Coll., 1923; postgrad. (Grad. scholar), Bryn Mawr Coll., 1923-24, U. N.C., summers 1952, 57, Fla. State U., summer 1960; m. Stacy Howard Hockett, June 29, 1927; children—Stacy Howard, Jane Elma (Mrs. Milton Ernest Reece). Tchr. math., librarian Guilford County Schs., 1924-25, 27-28, 35-52; math. tchr. Greensboro (N.C.) High Sch., 1925-27, Rock Ridge (N.C.) High Sch., 1934-35; librarian Clara J. Peck Elementary Sch., Greensboro, 1952-65; math. tchr. Guilford Coll., summers 1924-25. Leader, camp counsellor Girl Scouts U.S.A., 1942-52, zone rep. Internat. Girl Scout Leadership Conf., Edith Macy, N.Y., 1946; rec. and presiding clk. Western Quar. Meeting of Friends, 1948-60; rec. clk. N.C. Yearly Meetings of Friends, 1954, asst. presiding clk., 1965-70, presiding clk., 1970—, chmn. planning and promotional counsel, 1964-66; v.p. N.C. Yearly Meeting United Soc. Friends Women, 1958-59, pres., 1959-62; sec. missionary edn. for children Nat. United Soc. Friends Women, 1954-59, editor Friends Missionary Adv., 1964-69; mem. Am. Friends Bd. on Christian Edn., 1954-59, Friends United Meeting Bd. Missions, 1959-62, 64-69; presiding clk. Centre Friends Meeting, 1968-71; mem. wider ministries commn. Friends United Meeting, 1971—, mem. gen. bd., 1971—; life mem. United Soc. Friends Women, 1962—. Mem. N.C. Edn. Assn. (past pres. Guilford County), Guilford County Classroom Tchrs. Assn. (past pres.), Greensboro Library Club (past pres.), Bryn Mawr, Guilford Coll. (v.p. 50 yr. group 1973-74) alumni assns., P.T.A. (life). Clubs: Friendly Centre Garden (past pres.), Centre Extension Homemakers. Address: Route 1 Box 626 Pleasant Garden NC 27313

HODGE, BLANCHE MOORE, church woman; b. Arkansas City, Kan.; d. William S. and Susan Isabelle (Northern) Moore; student Va. Intermost Jr. Coll., Bristol, Va., 1922-23, Western Bapt. Theol. Sem., Portland, Ore., 1929-31, Reed Coll., Portland, 1947; L.H.D., Linfield Coll., 1958; m. Maurice B. Hodge, Feb. 17, 1923. Pres., Ore. Bapt. Conv., 1947-48; state dir. Baptist Girls Work, 1931-42; dir. Woman's Am. Bapt. Fgn. Mission Soc., 1941-51; pres. Nat. Council Am. Bapt. Women, 1951-55; exec. com. Bapt. World Alliance, 1955—, sec. women's dept., 1960-65; pres. N.A. Bapt. Women's Union, 1955-61; pres. Am. Bapt. Conv., 1958-59, mem. gen. council, 1960-63; chmn. editorial com. Crusader, 1955-63; exec. com. United Ch. Women, 1951-55; bd. Nat. Council Chs., 1955-58, 63-66, exec. com., 1965; bd. mgrs. Ore. Bapt. Conv., 1963—, exec. com., 1966—; study com. Berkeley Bapt. Div. Sch.; officer United Ch. Women Ore.; pres. Portland Council Chs., chmn. dept. Christian edn., 1972—; del. World Council Chs. Trustee Linfield Coll.; bd. regents Berkeley Bapt. Div. Sch., Ecumenical Ministries of Ore., 1973—; chmn. Urban Tng. and Research Center. Named Woman of Achievement, Portland chpt. Theta Sigma Phi, 1958, Woman of Accomplishment, Ore. Jour., 1963. Home: 5605 SW Edgemont Pl Portland OR 97201

HODGE, MARY JO (MRS. CHARLES CEDRIC HODGE), health service adminstr.; b. Talladega, Ala., June 15, 1935; d. John Bowling and Allene Martha (Royal) McKinney; B.S., Auburn U., 1956, M.S. (fellow), 1958; postgrad. N.Y. U., 1974—; m. Charles Cedric Hodge, Aug. 6, 1955. Psychologist, McGuffey Reading Clinic U. Va., Charlottesville, 1962-64, U. Va. Hosp., 1964-65; psychologist St. Lawrence State Hosp., Ogdensburg, N.Y., 1966-73, mental hygiene treatment leader, 1973—. Mem. Am., Eastern psychol. assns., Assn. for Advancement Behavior Therapy, Kappa Delta Pi, Chi Delta Phi, Pi Tau Chi. Home: PO Box 476 Canton NY 13617 Office: St Lawrence State Hosp Ogdensburg NY 13669

HODGE, SISTER PATRICIA ANDREA, librarian; b. Pitts., Jan. 16, 1930; d. James Cormack and Isabel Agnes (McAuley) Hodge; B.A., Mt. Mercy Coll., 1957; postgrad. McGill U., 1958; M.A., Duquesne U., 1964; postgrad. N.Y. U., 1965, U. Colo., 1965-67; M.S. in L.S., Villanova U., 1972. Elementary sch. tchr. Pitts. Diocesan sch. system; secondary sch. tchr. St. Elizabeth High Sch., Pitts., 1957-62, Our Lady of Mercy Acad., Pitts., 1962-63; faculty Carlow Coll., Pitts., 1963-67, coll. supr. English tchrs., 1964-70, acting chmn. English dept., 1967-71, acad. librarian, 1972—. Newspaper Fund fellow, 1965. Mem. Am., Pa., Cath. library assns., Villanova U. Library Sci. Alumni Assn., Tri-State Assn. Coll. and Research Libraries, Pitts. Council Higher Edn. (mem. com. on continuing edn. 1972—, del. to regional library center 1972—). Home: 3333 5th Av Pittsburgh PA 15213 Office: Grace Library Carlow College Pittsburgh PA 15213

HODGES, MARGARET ANN HAYNES (MRS. CECIL R. HODGES), journalist; b. McCamey, Tex., Sept. 7, 1928; d. Ernest Cornelius and Margaret Isabel (Wood) Haynes; student Nat. U. Mexico, 1943; B.J., U. Tex. at Austin, 1948; m. Cecil Ray Hodges, July 2, 1954; children—Craig McNeley, Elizabeth Ann. Gen. assignments reporter Houston Chronicle, 1948-50, reporter-TV editor, 1951-58, TV editor, 1962—; soc. editor Mexico City News, 1950-51. Episcopalian. Club: Press of Houston (charter, pres. 1972-73). Home: 8534 Stroud St Houston TX 77036 Office: 512 Travis St Houston TX 77002

HODGES, MARGARET MOORE (MRS. FLETCHER HODGES, JR.), educator, author; b. Indpls., July 26, 1911; d. Arthur Carlisle and Anna (Mason) Moore; B.A., Vassar Coll., 1932; M.L.S., Carnegie Inst. Tech., 1958; m. Fletcher Hodges, Jr., Sept. 10, 1932; children—Fletcher III, Arthur Carlisle, John Andrews. Librarian, Carnegie Library of Pitts., 1953-64; story specialist Pitts. Pub. Schs., 1964-68; asst. prof. children's lit. U. Pitts., 1968—, asso. prof. grad. studies in library sci., 1972—. Mem. Pitts. Hist. and Landmarks Found. Mem. A.L.A., Pa. Library Assn., Am. Assn. Library Schs., Distinguished Daus. Pa. Episcopalian. Clubs: Zonta Internat., Pittsburgh Vassar. Author: One Little Drum, 1958; What's For Lunch, Charley, 1961; A Club Against Keats, 1962; Tell It Again, 1963; The Secret in The Woods, 1963; The Wave, 1964; Constellation, 1967; The Hatching of Joshua Cobb, 1968; Sing Out, Charley, 1969; Lady Queen Anne, 1969; The Making of Joshua Cobb, 1971; The Gorgon's Head, 1972; The Fire Bringer, 1972; Hopkins of the Mayflower, 1972; The Other World, 1973; Persephone and the Springtime, 1973; Baldur and The Mistletoe, 1974. Editorial cons. Stories to Tell Children, 1974. Home: 5812 Kentucky Av Pittsburgh PA 15232

HODGES, MARY ALYCE, banker; b. Bakersfield, Cal., Aug. 4, 1936; d. Jesse Lee and Ruth Melvina (Coffey) Duke; student Bakersfield Jr. Coll., 1955—; m. Dale E. Hodges, July 15, 1956; 1 son, Eric D. Med. sec., stenographer to medical office, Bakersfield, Cal., 1955-60; with Cal. Republic Bank, Bakersfield, 1964—, asst. cashier, 1968-71, exec. sec. to pres., 1965-71, dir. personnel, 1971—, asst. v.p., 1972—. Mem. Am. Inst. Banking (bd. govs. 1967-70, sec. chpt. 1968-70). Am. Bus. Women's Assn. (publicity chmn. 1971-72). Office: Cal Republic Bank PO Box 2167 Bakersfield CA 93303 Home: 105 Haggin St Bakersfield CA 93309

HODGINS, PATRICIA ANN, ednl. adminstr.; b. St. Louis, Feb. 11, 1946; d. David Frank and Marion Elizabeth (Clark) Hodgins; student (Presdl. scholar 1964) Marycrest Coll., 1964-66; B.A., U. Wis., 1969; M.A. (Minority Group scholar), Columbia, 1973. Admission counselor U. Wis.-Madison, 1969-70; admission officer Brown U., Providence, 1970-72; intern in grad. admissions Columbia Tchrs. Coll., N.Y.C., 1972-73; asst. dir. admissions Adelphi U., Garden City, L.I., N.Y., 1973—. Mem. workshop faculty Nat. Assn. Coll. Admissions Counselors, 1973. Sponsor Addicts Rehab. Center, N.Y.C., 1973-74. Bd. dirs. Family Services, Providence. Mem. Nat. Assn. Women Deans, Adminstrs. and Counselors, Am., N.Y. State personnel and guidance assns., Nat. Assn. Student Personnel Adminstrs., Assn. of Black Admission and Financial Aid Officers (sec. 1971-72), Alpha Kappa Alpha. Home: 530 Riverside Dr 4G New York City NY 10027 Office: Levermore Hall Adelphi Univ Garden City LI NY 11530

HODGINS, VIRGINIA P. WELCH (MRS. ROBERT E. HODGINS), city ofcl.; b. Cleve.; d. Earl Sutton and Winifred (Page) Welch; student Dyke Bus. Coll., 1936-37; m. Ralph W. Edwards, Mar. 21, 1941 (dec. July 1947); children—Ralph, James; m. 2d, Robert E. Hodgins, Aug. 21, 1948; 1 dau., Virginia Anne. Stenographer, Nat. City Bank, Cleve., 1937-40; sec. Cleve. C. of C., 1940-43; enumerator U.S. Census, North Olmsted, O., 1960; interviewer Consumer Price Index, Cleve., 1961-62; ward II councilman North Olmstead City Council, 1963-71; clk. of commns. City of North Olmstead, 1972—. Vol. driver Cleve. Soc. for Blind, 1963-72; leader Campfire Girls, 1961-63, dist. chmn., 1972—. Mem. League Women Voters. Episcopalian. Republican. Club: North Olmstead Womens (sec., v.p. 1956-60, 73—). Home: 24893 Florence Av North Olmsted OH 44070

HODGKINS, BILLIE JEWEL SANDERS (MRS. VICTOR S. HODGKINS), home economist; b. Oak Grove, La., July 2, 1929; d. T. William and Jewel (Wicker) Sanders; B.S., La. Poly. Inst., 1949; postgrad. N.E. La. State Coll., La. State U.; m. Victor S. Hodgkins, Dec. 25, 1949; children—Vicki Jewel, William Edgar, Paula Jean. Tchr., West Carroll Parish Sch. Bd., Oak Grove, La., 1949-50, Franklin Parish Sch. Bd., Wisner High Sch., 1950-51; asso. home demonstration agt. La. State U., Franklin Parish Agr. Extension Service, Winnsboro, 1955-58; home service rep. La. Power & Light Co., Winnsboro, 1961—. Active 4-H, Future Homemakers Am. Mem. La. Home Econs. Assn. (chmn. housing and household equipment 1964-66), La. Home Economists in Bus. (sec.), Delta Kappa Gamma (2d v.p. 1972-74). Baptist. Home: PO Box 372 Winnsboro LA 71295 Office: 1707 Warren Winnsboro LA 71295

HODGMAN, JOAN ELIZABETH, pediatrician; b. Portland, Ore., Sept. 7, 1923; d. Kenneth E. and Ann (Vannet) Hodgman; B.A., Stanford, 1943; M.D., U. Cal. at San Francisco, 1946; m. Amos N. Schwartz, Jan. 30, 1949 (dec. May 1970); children—Ann, Susan. Intern, U. Cal. Hosp., San Francisco, 1946-47; resident Harbor Gen. Hosp., Torrance, Cal., 1947-48, Los Angeles County Gen. Hosp., 1948-50; practice medicine, specializing in pediatrics, South Pasadena, Cal., 1950-52; attending staff Los Angeles County-U So. Cal. Med. Center, Los Angeles, 1950—; cons. Cal. Health Dept., 1963—, Huntington Meml. Hosp., Pasadena, 1972—; instr. pediatrics U. So. Cal. Sch. Medicine, Los Angeles, 1951—, prof. pediatrics, 1969—. Recipient certificate of appreciation Am. Cancer Soc., 1964, Cameo of Committment award B'nai B'rith Women, 1969, 4th Ann. Health Baby Merit award Nat. Found., 1969; named woman of year, Muses of Cal. Mus. Sci. and Industry, 1974. Mem. Am. Pediatric Soc., Am. Thoracic Soc., Am., Cal. med. assns., Am. Acad. Pediatrics, Los Angeles Acad. Medicine. Contbr. to publs. in field. Home: 494 Stanford Dr Arcadia CA 91006 Office: 1240 Mission St Los Angeles CA 90033

HODGSON, BEULAH DUBLER (MRS. GEORGE W. HODGSON), editor; b. Butte, Mont., July 31, 1915; d. Jesse and Lizzie (McCartney) Dubler; grad. Mont. State Normal Coll., 1936; postgrad. U. Chile, Santiago, U. Beirut (Lebanon), Clark Coll.; m. George W. Hodgson, Mar. 22, 1961. Tchr. rural schs. Mont., 1937-40; mem. staff Mont. State Orphanage, 1940-43; tchr., Butte, 1943-44, 46-47; tchr. Anaconda Copper Co., Chile, 1947-52; tchr. Arabian Am. Oil Co., Saudi Arabia, 1952-65; editor Mag. Silver, Vancouver, Wash., 1968—. Served with USAAF, 1944-46. Home: 5420 NW Walnut St Vancouver WA 98663 Office: Box 1208 Vancouver WA 98660

HODGSON, JACQUELINE LOU, educator, univ. dean; b. Rock Springs, Wyo., Feb. 3, 1927; d. Louis Ludvig and Frances (Barto) Hodgson; B.S., U. of Puget Sound, 1951, M.A., 1952; Ph.D., U. Wis., 1966. Instr. econs. U. Fla., Gainsville, 1956-57, exchange prof., 1971-72; instr. U. Americas, Puebla, Mexico, 1957-59, asst. prof., 1959-65, asso. prof., 1965-66, prof. of econs., 1967—, chmn. dept. econs., 1967-70, 72-73, dean continuing edn. Centro de Estudios, Mexico City 1973—. Fulbright grantee, 1964, Earhart Found. grantee, 1972. Mem. Am. Econ. Assn., Assn. for Social Econs. Editor: Thatelolco Econ. Monographs, 1967—. Home: Hamburgo 250 Mexico 6 DF Mexico

HODGSON, JANE ELIZABETH, obstetrician and gynecologist; b. Crookston, Minn., Jan. 23, 1915; d. Herbert Heber and Adelaide (Marin) Hodgson; B.S., Carleton Coll., 1934; M.D., U. Minn., 1940, M.S. in Obstetrics and Gynecology, 1947; m. Frank W. Quattlebaum, Feb. 22, 1940; children—Gretchen, Nancy. Intern, Jersey City Med. Center, 1939-40, resident internal medicine, 1940-41; fellow obstetrics and gynecology Mayo Clinic, 1941-44; practice obstetrics and gynecology, St. Paul, 1944-72; med. dir. Preterm Clinic, Washington, 1972-74; mem. staff Charles T. Miller, St. Paul Ramsey hosps.; mem. cons. staff St. Luke's, St. Joseph's, Midway hosps.; asst. clin. prof. obstetrics and gynecology U. Minn. Med. Sch.; tchr. St. Paul Ramsey Hosp. Mem. med. adv. com. Met. Council, 1969-70; chmn. med. adv. bd. St. Paul Planned Parenthood, 1968-72; v.p. No. Assn. Med. Edn., 1960-70; tour of duty on Ship Hope, 1963, 64, 66. Bd. dirs. Met. St. Paul Hosp. Planning Council. Recipient Republican Care award, 1964; WCCO Good Neighbor award 1964; Hope certificate of merit People-to-People Found., 1969; Marshmann S. Wattson award Am. Civil Liberties Union, 1970. Diplomate Am. Bd. Obstetrics and Gynecology. Fellow Am. Coll. Obstetrics and Gynecology (founding); mem. A.M.A., So. Minn. Med. Soc. (medal

1952, Bus. and Profl. Woman's award 1958), Minn. (spl. com. to study abortion 1968-69), Ramsey County med. socs., Minn. Soc. Obstetricians and Gynecologists (pres. 1964), Internat. Fertility Assn., St. Paul Surg. Soc. Contbr. articles to med. jours. Home: 1537 N Fisk St St Paul MN 55117

HODGSON, LOIS NATALIE, educator; b. Colusa, Cal., Nov. 20, 1925; d. George and Ethel (Page) Hodgson; B.A., Park Coll., 1948; M.A., San Francisco State Coll., 1961; Ph.D., U. Ia., 1967. Tchr. Mt. Diablo Unified Sch. Dist., Cal., 1949-53; curriculum cons. Alameda County (Cal.), 1953-55; tchr.-prin., spl. edn. supr. U.S. Air Force Dep. Schs., Okinawa, P.I., France, Saudi Arabia, Eng., Germany, 1955-65; prof. U. Toledo, 1967—, chairwoman dept. spl. edn., 1973—. N.W. Ohio dir. Ohio Assn. for Retarded Citizens, 1971—. Recipient U. Toledo Outstanding Tchr. award, 1972. Mem. Ohio Fedn. Council for Exceptional Children (chmn. legislative com. 1971-72), Pi Lambda Theta, Delta Kappa Gamma. Club: Quota Internat. (1st v.p. 1972—). Home: 3515 Havenhurst Blvd Toledo OH 43614

HODSON, JEAN ELAINE TURNBAUGH, educator; b. Anthony, Kan., July 10, 1920; d. Ralph Milton and Mabel Helen (Hohner) Turnbaugh; B.S. in Dental Hygiene, U. Washington, 1952, M.S. in Engring. Ceramics, 1958. Mem. faculty U. Wash., Seattle, 1952—, asso. prof. operative dentistry, 1964-69, prof. operative dentistry, 1969-70, prof. restorative dentistry, Sch. Dentistry, 1970—. Instr. dental hygiene program Shoreline Communtiy Coll., Seattle, 1972—; cons. dental anatomy for dental aux. tng. programs, 1970—. Mem. Am. Dental Assn. (asso.), Am. Assn. Dental Schs., Internat. Assn. for Dental Research and Dental Materials Group, Am. Acad. Gold Foil Operators (hon.), Phi Beta Kappa, Sigma Xi, Keramos, Sigma Phi Alpha. Contbr. articles to various publs. Home: 4203 Brooklyn Av NE Seattle WA 98105

HODSON, KAY ETHEL, librarian; b. Ithaca, N.Y., June 19, 1940; d. Adrian Zachariah and Kathryn May (Traer) Hodson; B.S. in Elementary Edn., So. Ill. U., Carbondale, 1962; M.S. in Library Sci., U. Ill., 1965. Tchr. elementary grades pub. schs., Alton, Ill., 1962, Harmony-Emge Schs., Belleville, Ill., 1962-64; reference librarian Dayton and Montgomery County Pub. Library, Dayton, O., 1965—. Home: Apt B-3 425 Dayton Towers Ct Dayton OH 45410 Office: 215 E 3d St Dayton OH 45402

HODSON, NORMA GAUKER (MRS. EARL M. HODSON), educator; b. Bison, S.D., Sept. 9, 1909; d. Lewis F. and Grace V. (Hutchings) Shuttleworth; B.S. cum laude, Butler U., 1950; M.S., Fla. State U., 1960, Ph.D., 1963; m. Earl M. Hodson, Nov. 26, 1965; children by previous marriage—John E. Gauker, Alice (Mrs. Adams). Tchr., Indpls. Pub. Schs., 1950-56, Lakeland (Fla.) Pub. Schs., 1957-60; instr. Fla. State U., Tallahassee, 1960-63; intern fellow Merrill-Palmer, Detroit, 1963-64; faculty family and child devel. Auburn (Ala.) U., 1964—. Mem. Am. Assn. Marriage and Family Counselors, Am. Home Econs. Assn., Am., Ala. psychol. assns., Nat., Ala., Southeastern (treas. 1964-65, sec. 1972—) councils on family relations, Kappa Delta Pi, Omicron Nu, Alpha Kappa Delta. Home: 236 Carter St Auburn AL 36830

HOEBEL, OLGA HEDWIG LAUMANN (MRS. LOUIS HOEBEL), artist, educator; b. Moscow, Russia, Sept. 14, 1905; d. Karl Emil and Josepha (Grullenbeck) Laumann; came to U.S., 1923, naturalized, 1927; student Nassau Collegiate Center, L.I., 1935-36; m. Louis Hoebel, June 10, 1925. Exhibited in one man shows Calderone Theatre, Hempstead, N.Y., 1952, Center Creative Art, Baldwin, N.Y., 1959, Hicksville Free Pub. Library, 1960, East Nassau Med. Center, Hicksville, 1964, Rory Ann Art Gallery, Hicksville, 1966; exhibited in group shows Art League Nassau County, 1936-57, Womens Internat. Expn. Arts and Industries Madison Sq. Garden, N.Y.C., 1944, N.Y. State Art Show, 1968, Nat. League Am. Pen Women, 1970-72, Union Carbide Galleries, N.Y.C., 1972, Madison Square Garden Mus. Sport, N.Y.C., 1973, Lever House Gallery, N.Y.C., 1973, Seamens' Bank for Savings, 1968, 74; represented in permanent collections Holly Patterson Home for Aged, Uniondale, L.I., Soc. Friends, Old. Westbury, L.I., Hicksville Free Pub. Library, A.R.C. Hdqrs., Mineola, L.I.; owner ind. atelier, art instr., 1938—; corr. L.I. br. Am. Artist mag., 1969; tchr. Adult Edn. Program, Dist. Sch., Nassau County, 1948-55. Chmn. nurses aides A.R.C., 1943-45. Coordinator for art shows Central Fed. Savs. & Loan Assn., 1963. Trustee Gregory Mus., Hicksville, 1971-73, fine arts chmn. Spring Art Festival, 1971, 72, 73, membership chmn., 1970-71. Recipient numerous art awards, 1935—. Mem. Nat. League Am. Pen Women (pres. L.I. br. 1966-68, historian, 1968—, publicity chmn. 1968-70), Ind. Art Soc., Am. Legion Aux. (charter). Club: Friendship (Hicksville, N.Y.). Address: 30 Terrace Pl Hicksville NY 11801

HOEDEL, SISTER CELESTINE MARIE, educator; b. Wilkes-Barre, Pa.; d. Joseph and Mary (Blank) Hoedel; B.S., Seton Hall U., 1950; M.A., Catholic U., 1955; Ph.D., St. John's U., 1961. Joined Sisters of Christian Charity, Roman Catholic Ch., 1932; prin. St. Michael Sch., Netcong, N.J., 1955-57; prin. Cathedral High Sch., Branch, Ill., 1958-60; schs. Sisters of Christian Charity, 1951-54; vis. prof. Miles Coll., Brentwood Coll., summers 1968, 1969; lectr. edn. Seton Hall U., 1961-62; asst. prof. philosophy Assumption Coll., 1962-68; prof. edn. Xavier U., 1968-73, acad. counselor, 1968-73; mem. social action com. New Orleans Sisters Council, 1969-72. Atlanta U. grantee in Afro-Am. Studies, summer 1970; faculty fellow in East Asian Studies, Hamline U., summer 1971. Home: Camp Hill PA 17011 Office: Community Mental Health Center Camp Hill PA 17011

HOEFLING, SUSAN JOAN BRANTWEINER (MRS. CHARLES W. HOEFLING), author; b. Cleve., Nov. 10, 1909; d. John and Susanna (Winkler) Brantweiner; student Geneva Coll., 1943-46; Nurses Aid, City Sch. Nursing, 1929; D.H.L., Free U. Asia, 1969; grad. Famous Writers Sch., 1971; m. Charles W. Hoefling, Sept. 10, 1929; children—Robert Mathias (dec.), Charles W. Poet laureat, Beaver County, Pa., 1949—. Recipient Greatness and Leadership award UN Day, Philippines, 1967; named Elegiac Poet, United Poet Laureate Internat., 1966. Mem. Am. Poetry League, Beaver County Poetry Soc. (founder, charter pres. 1953-54), Pa. Poetry Soc., Acad. Am. Poets. Mem. Order Eastern Star. Author: For You - Dream Weaver Poems, 1949; For You - Melody of Life, 1962; For You - Along the Avenue, 1968. Poetry editor The Beat, 1964-67. Home: Box 592 Mercer Rd RD 2 Beaver Falls PA 15010

HOEFT, FERNE ELOISE (MRS. MERLIN JAMES HOEFT), educator; b. Holmes, N.D., Nov. 29, 1921; d. George Fredrick and Melvina Lazetta (Frey) Hack; B.A., North Central Coll., 1944; certificate St. Norbert Coll., 1965; postgrad. U. Wis., 1966, 70, 71, 72, U. Minn. (Newspaper Fund fellow), 1967; m. Merlin James Hoeft, Feb. 27, 1944; children—Meryl Lee (Mrs. Stewart E. Nelson), Michael, Marjean. Reporter, feature editor Naperville (Ill.) Sun, 1943-48; editor, publisher Fox Valley Farm News, Aurora, Ill., 1947-48; publicity chmn. Milw. County Council Chs., 1956-57; editor, publisher Badger Tidings, Bonduel, Wis., 1960-65; tchr. Tremper High Sch., Kenosha, Wis., 1965—. Mem. Women in Communications, Journalism Edn. Assn., Wis. Tchr.-Adviser Council, N.E.A., Wis., Kenosha edn. assns. Methodist (mem. women's group). Home: 5040 21st Av Kenosha WI 53140 Office: 8560 26th Av Kenosha WI 53140

HOEFT, PHYLLIS COOK GREELY (MRS. HARRY F. HOEFT), newspaper editor; b. Hartland, Minn., Jan. 1, 1914; d. Floyd Edwin and Sadie Eugenie (Marvin) Cook; B.A., Hamline U., 1935; m. Clayton B. Greely, June 12, 1939 (dec. Dec. 1970); children—Ronald C., Carol (Mrs. Jon A. Gripentrog), Jane (Mrs. Mitchell Gripentrog); m. Harry F. Hoeft, Apr. 12, 1972; stepchildren—James, Gerald, Kenneth. Tchr. Reliance (S.D.) High Sch., 1935-36, Kimball (Minn.) High Sch., 1936-39, 43-45; asso. editor Tri-County News, Kimball, 1949-70, editor, 1970—. Republican. Mem. Order Eastern Star (past worthy matron). Mem. Ch. of Christ. Home: Kimball MN 55353 Office: Tri-County News Kimball MN 55353

HOEHN, MARGARET M., neurologist; b. San Francisco, Nov. 24, 1930; d. Peter Paul and Eve (Till) Maier; B.A., U. Sask., 1950; M.D., U. B.C., 1954; m. Robert J. Hoehn, June 27, 1961; children—Robert Anthony Till, Margaret Eve. Intern Vancouver (B.C.) Gen. Hosp., 1954-55, then resident; resident Shaughnessy Hosp., to 1959; mem. staff Nat. Hosp. Nervous Disease, London, Eng., 1960, 62-63, Boston VA Hosp., 1961-62; asst. prof. neurology Coll. Physicians and Surgeons, Columbia, 1963-70, U. Colo., Denver, 1970—. Fellow Royal Coll. Physicians and Surgeons Can.; mem. Am. Acad. Neurology, Assn. Research in Nervous and Mental Diseases, N.Y. Neurol. Soc., Colo. Soc. Clin. Neurologists, Alpha Omega Alpha. Research and publs. in Parkinson's Disease, other diseases of basal ganglia. Home: 3851 S Xanthia St Denver CO 80237 Office: Box 116 U Colo Med Center 4200 E 9th Av Denver CO 80220

HOEKSEMA, BEATRICE, radio exec.; b. Cicero, Ill., Jan. 13, 1918; d. Harry Oris and Catherine (Huizinga) OptHolt; grad. high sch.; m. John Hoeksema, May 21, 1938 (dec. 1962); children—Janet (Mrs. Edward Aul), Carol (Mrs. Ralph Bennett), Catherine (Mrs. James Schoon), Deborah (Mrs. John Rouwenhorst). Stenographer, bookkeeper Midland Structural Steel Co., Cicero, Ill., 1936-40; women's program dir. Grand Canyon Broadcasters, Inc., Phoenix, 1960—; dir. Southwestern Constrn. Co., Phoenix. Pres. women's classical union conf. Ref. Ch., 1970-73; pres. women's Guild for Christian Service, 1969-70, sec. edn., 1972; active Girl Scouts U.S.A. Precinct committeewoman Republican Party, 1964. Mem. Ariz. Ref. Ch. Women (pres. 1974—), Am. Women Radio and TV (pres. Ariz. chpt. 1973—), Nat. Fedn. Bus. and Profl. Women's Clubs. Home: 4633 E Wilshire Dr Phoenix AZ 85008 Office: 3883 N 38th Av Phoenix AZ 85019

HOEY, EVELYN LEVINE (MRS. REID A. HOEY), librarian; b. Estill, S.C., Aug. 28, 1919; d. Hyman and Lena (Cantor) Levine; B.A., Meredith Coll., 1939; B.L.S., Simmons Coll., 1940; m. Reid A. Hoey, Apr. 14, 1960. Cataloger, Charlotte (N.C.) Pub. Library, 1941-43; br. librarian Savannah (Ga.) Pub. Library, 1943; librarian U.S. Office Postal Censorship, Chgo., 1943-44; librarian subsistence Research and Devel. Lab. U.S. Army Q.M.C., Chgo., 1944-46; librarian U.S. Army Spl. Services European Theatre, 1946-49; plant librarian Union Carbide Nuclear Co., Oak Ridge Gaseous Diffusion Plant, 1949-60; tech. librarian Rome (N.Y.) Air Devel. Center, Griffiss AFB, 1960, chief documents library, 1960-62; specialist lit. acquisitions-research Gen. Electric Co., Syracuse, N.Y., 1962-66; adminstrv. librarian State U. N.Y., Upstate Med. Center, Syracuse, 1966-69, acting dir., 1969-70, dir., 1970—. Mem. adv. com. State U. N.Y. Biomed. Communications Network, 1970—; mem. adv. com. N.Y. and No. N.J. Regional Med. Library Program, 1970. Mem. Med. Library Assn. (Upstate N.Y. chpt. dir. 1969, mem. legislative com. 1970—), Profl. Womens League (sec. 1967—). Club: Stonecrest Supper (Manlius, N.Y.). Contbr. articles in field to profl. jours. Home: 215 Wedgewood Terrace Dewitt NY 13214 Office: 766 Irving Av Syracuse NY 13210

HOFF, GLORIA THELMA ALBUERNE (MRS. RAMON B. HOFF), educator; b. Cienfuegos, Cuba, May 10, 1930; d. Severiano T. and Gloria J. (Rodriguez) Albuerne; came to U.S., 1958, naturalized, 1974; D.Sci., U. Havana, 1951; M.S., U. Chgo., 1957, Ph.D., 1965; m. Ramon Brewster Hoff, June 17, 1959; children—Erich Julian, Kevin Glade, Sharon Olivia. Asst. prof. physics Inst. of Secondary Edn., Las Villas, Cuba, 1951-54, Inst. of Secondary Edn., Havana, Cuba, 1954-58, U. of Villanueva, Marianao, Havana, Cuba, 1957-58; instr. physics U. Ill., Chgo., 1964-65, asst. prof., 1965-68, asso. prof., 1968—. Research asso. Argonne Nat. Lab., Argonne, Ill., 1966. Summer Faculty fellow U. Ill., 1965, 1973. Mem. N.Y. Acad. Scis., A.A.A.S., Am. Phys. Soc., Assn. Women in Sci. Contbr. articles on physics to sci. jours. Home: 5634 S Blackstone Av Chicago IL 60637 Office: Physics Dept University of Illinois at Chicago Circle Box 4348 Chicago IL 60680

HOFF, VIVIAN BEAUMONT (MRS. ARVILLE H. HOFF), composer; b. nr. Foutaintown, Ind., Dec. 17, 1911; d. Robert and Mary Eunice (Logan) Beaumont; student Butler U., Jordan Coll. Music; student piano with Bomar Cramer, Thelma Todd, voice with Elma Igleman, harmony and advanced composition with William Pelz; m. Arville H. Hoff, Apr. 6, 1935. Piano tchr., 1940-50. Chmn., City-Wide July 4th Celebration, Indpls., 1965. Recipient certificate meritorious personal service Indpls. canteen A.R.C., 1946, certificate for entertaining troops, Los Angeles, 1947. Mem. A.S.C.A.P., Nat. Assn. Am. Composers and Condrs., Nat. League Am. Pen Women (nat. music editor 1964-68, 72—, pres. Indpls. 1970-72), Nat. Soc. Arts and Letters, Nat. Fedn. Music Clubs (spl. mem.), Indpls. Matinee Musicale. Baptist. Mem. Order Eastern Star. Composer: Father in Heaven and Suite for Piano (7 pieces), 1953-56; Be of Good Courage, 1957; I Look To My Lord, 1960; Keep The Star-Spangled Banner Waving, 1962; also various piano pieces. Home: 7025 Warwick Rd Indianapolis IN 46220

HOFFBERG, JUDITH ANN, assn. exec.; b. Hartford, Conn., May 19, 1934; d. George and Miriam (Goldenberg) Hoffberg; student Brandeis U., 1951-52; B.A. cum laude, U. Cal. at Los Angeles, 1956, M.A., 1960, M.L.S., 1964. Tchr. Hebrew, Temple Beth Am. Los Angeles, 1953-56; teaching asst., dept. Italian, U. Cal. at Los Angeles, 1958-60; librarian Bologne (Italy) center Johns Hopkins U., 1964-65; librarian spl. recruit program Library of Congress, Washington, 1965-66, cataloger prints and photographs div., 1966-67; fine arts librarian U. Pa., Phila., 1967-69; bibliographer in lit., linguistics and art U. Cal. at San Diego, La Jolla, 1969-71; librarian Brand Art Center, Glendale, 1971-73; founder Art Libraries Soc./N.Am., Glendale, Cal., 1972, exec. dir., 1973—, also editor newsletter, 1972—. Coordinator inventory visual resources on Americana, Bicentennial Bibliography Am. Art, Archives Am. Art. Recipient grant Italian Govt., 1960-61, Kress Found., 1972. Mem. Internat. Council Museums, Am., Cal. library assns., Assn. Coll. and Research Libraries (sec. art subsect. 1969-71), Renaissance Soc. Am., Coll. Art Assn. (chmn. librarians sect. 1972), Friends of Photography, Los Angeles Inst. Contemporary Art, Nat. Trust for Historic Preservation, Mus. Modern Art, Soc. Archtl. Historians, Smithsonian Assos., Am. Civil Liberties Union, Phi Beta Kappa, Phi Sigma Alpha. Clubs: Washington Print; Print (Phila.); Sierra (So. Cal.); Touring Club Italiano (Italy). Home: 1341 5th St Apt 2 Glendale CA 91201 Office: PO Box 3692 Glendale CA 91201

HOFFER, JANICE ANN HILL, educator; b. Lapeer, Mich., Feb. 13, 1934; d. Harry Jarvis and Lena Margaret (Gatkie) Hill; B.S., Mich. State U., 1955, Ph.D., 1971; M.A., Siena Heights Coll., 1964; m. Lyle Duane Hoffer, June 30, 1956 (div. Aug. 1964); children—Richard James, Randal Harry, Edward Reid. Tchr. speech Lapeer (Mich.) pub. schs., 1955-60; owner, operator Dairy Isle, Lapeer, 1955-60; tchr. English, Waterford Twp. schs., Pontiac, Mich., 1960-61; tchr. speech Adrian (Mich.) pub. schs., 1961-67; dir. forensics Adrian Coll., 1967-69, part-time faculty, 1969-70; dir. student activities, asst. prin. Adrian Sr. High Sch., 1969-72; dir. dramatics and speech Drager Middle Sch., Adrian, 1972-74; telecommunications cons. Adrian Pub. Schs., 1974—; faculty Siena Heights Coll., Adrian, 1974—. Chmn. summer stock com. Crowell Opera House, 1967, 68, program chmn., 1967. Bd. dirs. Croswell Opera House and Fine Arts Assn., Adrian, 1968-73, v.p. bd., 1972-73, founding chmn. bd., 1967. Mem. Delta Kappa Gamma (service chmn. 1974-75), Theta Alpha Phi. Club: Zonta (dir. 1974-75) (Adrian). Home: 1120 Williams St Adrian MI 49221 Office: 785 Riverside Av Adrian MI 49221

HOFFER, ROSE LIEBMAN, lawyer; b. N.Y.C., June 14, 1911; d. David and Gussie (Kominski) Liebman; student N.Y. U., 1928-31, 50-51; LL.B., Bklyn. Law Sch., 1954; m. Philip Hoffer, Aug. 8, 1933; children—M. Mark, Paul B. Admitted to N.Y. bar, 1955, U.S. Supreme Ct. bar, 1960; practice law, N.Y.C., 1955—; partner firm Hoffer & Hoffer, N.Y.C., 1955—; gen. counsel Empire Mut. Ins. Co., N.Y.C., 1958—, also dir.; gen. counsel Allcity Ins. Co., N.Y.C., 1963—, also dir., asst. v.p., 1963—. Master in civil ct., N.Y.C., 1966-68; hearing officer N.Y.C. Parking Violations Bur., 1970—; arbitrator Am. Arbitration Assn. Mem. Am., N.Y. State, N.Y. Women's (dir.), Bronx Women's bar assns., Nat. Assn. Women Lawyers, Internat. Fedn. Women Lawyers (UN affiliate, del.), Bklyn. Law Sch. Alumni Assn. (editorial adv. bd. Veritas mag.; Distinguished Alumna of Year 1973). Home: 200 Central Park S New York City NY 10019 Office: 200 Central Park S New York City NY 10019 also 1965 Broadway New York City NY 10023

HOFFMAN, ARLENE FAUN, educator; b. N.Y.C., Nov. 23, 1941; d. Abraham S. and Pearl (Weiss) Hoffman; B.S., Queens Coll., 1962; Ph.D. (USPHS fellow), State U. N.Y. Downstate Med. Center at Bklyn., 1967; postgrad. (USPHS fellow), Stanford, 1966-67; D.P.M., Cal. Coll. Podiatric Medicine, 1976. Asso. prof. dept. basic scis. Cal. Coll. Podiatric Medicine, San Francisco, 1967-68, prof., 1969—, asst. dir. dept. basic scis., 1967-69, dir. dept., 1970—, asso. dean for curricular affairs, 1972—. Mem. physiology sect. Nat. Bd. Podiatry Examiners, 1967—. Mem. Am. Ednl. Research Assn., Am. Assn. U. Adminstrs., Am. Pub. Health Assn., Assn. Women in Science, Cal. Group on Health Professions Edn., Nat. Assn. of Research in Sci. Teaching. Contbg. author: The Podiatry Curriculum, 1970. Editorial adv. bd. Jour. Podiatric Edn., 1971—; spl. editor Basic Med. Scis., Jour. Am. Podiatry Soc., 1972—; podiatric medicine editor Health Professions Edn. Exchange Research, newsletter Am. Ednl. Research Assn., 1973—. Contbr. articles to profl. jours. Home: 215 Main St Sausalito CA 94965 Office: 1770 Eddy St San Francisco CA 94115

HOFFMAN, BARBARA RODAMER, state ofcl., health service adminstr.; b. White Plains, N.Y., Jan. 28, 1933; d. Frank George and Helen Marie (Suda) Rodamer; B.A., Radcliffe Coll., 1957; M.A., Boston U., 1963, Ph.D., 1973. Head dept. psychology Grafton (Mass.) State Hosp., 1966-71; area program dir. Dept. Mental Health, State of Mass., Linwood, 1971—. Bd. dirs. Homophile Community Health Service, Boston. Mem. Am., New Eng., Mass. psychol. assns., Phi Beta Kappa. Home: 199 W Springfield St Boston MA 02118 Office: 154 Linwood St Linwood MA 01525

HOFFMAN, BETTY L. MCCULLOUGH (MRS. HERBERT R. HOFFMAN), exec. sec., accountant; b. McPherson, Kan., Sept. 20, 1934; d. Purnel E. and Lucille (Spencer) McCullough; student pub. schs.; m. William G. Ketterman, Nov. 19, 1952 (div. Nov. 1968); children—Katherine E., Lorri Ann, Mark William; m. 2d, Herbert R. Hoffman, Sept. 25, 1971. Asst. sec. Robert McKinney, bookkeeper New Mexican, Inc., Santa Fe, 1957-67; pvt. sec. Robert McKinney, New Mexican, Inc., Santa Fe, 1967-71; exec. sec. S.E. Watkins, pres. New Mexican, Inc., Santa Fe, 1967-71; corp. sec. New Mexican, Inc., 1967-71, Taos Pub. Corp., 1967-71, El Nuevo Mexicano, Inc., 1967-71, New Mexican Distbg. Corp., 1967-71, Santa Fe Photo & Engraving Co., 1967-71, (all Santa Fe); corporate sec. Robert Moody Found., Inc., 1967-71; exec. sec., accountant Hallmark Homes & Devel. Co., Albuquerque, 1971—. Mem. Nat. Secs. Assn. (chpt. publicity chmn. 1969-70, Sec. of Year award Santa Fe chpt. 1970), Santa Fe Opera Guild. Democrat. Roman Catholic. Home: 644 Running Water Circle Albuquerque NM 87112 Office: PO Box 11334 Albuquerque NM 87112

HOFFMAN, CATHERINE FLORENCE, occupational therapist; b. Iroquois, S.D., Dec. 11, 1921; d. John Joseph and Katherine Margaret (Florent) Hoffman; B.E., No. Ill. U., 1943; diploma in Occupational Therapy, Western Mich. U., 1946; M.S., U. Conn., 1962. Instr. homemaking Stockton (Ill.) High Sch., 1943-45; asst. dir. occupational therapy Winfield (Ill.) Hosp., 1946-51, dir., clin. supr., 1951-60; asst. supr. occupational therapy, gen. medicine and surgery U. Ill. Med. Center, 1961-62, research asst., 1968; asst. prof. Colo. State U., 1962-67; coordinator, instr. Occupational Therapy Asst. Program, Anoka-Hennepin Area Vocational Tech. Inst., Minn., 1969—. Coordinator, participant program series on Take It Easy Homemaking, Channel 4, KOA-TV, Denver, For Women Only Program. Mem. Am. (conf. chmn. Chgo. 1959), Minn. (sec. 1971-72), Colo. (dir. 1965-67), Ill. (pres. 1955-57) occupational therapy assns., Delta Kappa Gamma (pres. chpt. 1974-76). Roman Catholic. Contbr. articles to profl. jours. Home: 209 River Pkwy Champlin MN 55316 Office: Box 191 Anoka MN 55303

HOFFMAN, DARLEANE CHRISTIAN (MRS. MARVIN M. HOFFMAN), nuclear chemist; b. Terril, Ia., Nov. 8, 1926; d. Carl Benjamin and Elverna Emma (Kuhlman) Christian; B.S., Ia. State U., 1948, Ph.D., 1951; m. Marvin Morrison Hoffman, Dec. 26, 1951; children—Maureane, Daryl. Research asso., asst. inst. for Atomic Research, Ames, Ia., 1947-51; chemist Oak Ridge Nat. Lab., 1952; mem. staff Los Alamos (N.M.) Sci. Lab., 1953—, asso. group leader, 1971—. NSF sr. postdoctoral fellow, Oslo, Norway, 1964-65. Fellow Am. Inst. Chemists; mem. Am. Phys. Soc., Am. Chem. Soc., A.A.A.S., Sigma Xi, Sigma Delta Epsilon, Phi Kappa Phi, Iota Sigma Pi, Pi Mu Epsilon. Home: 3 Acoma Lane Los Alamos NM 87544 Office: Los Alamos Sci Lab Group CNC-11 Box 1663 Los Alamos NM 87544

HOFFMAN, DIANTHA ANN (MRS. JOSEPH EDWARD HOFFMAN), mfg. co. exec.; b. Hudson, Wis., Jan. 16, 1915; d. Arthur Carr and Jeanette (Krogstadt) Robertson; grad. high sch.; m. Joseph Edward Hoffman, Sept. 1, 1934; children—Susan J. (Mrs. Ralph G. Lea), Mary C. (Mrs. David A. Chamberlin), Joseph Edward, John R., Michael C., Mary D. (Mrs. Robert B. Larson). Sec. to v.p. Kimball Piano Co., Chgo., 1933-36; sec. to pres. Automatic Burner Corp., Chgo., 1936-41; corporate sec., dir. J.E. Hoffman & Co., Mundelein, Ill., 1946—. Club: Farmington Country (Charlottesville, Va.). Home: Route 1 Box 63-A Grayslake IL 60030 Office: 739 N Lake St Mundelein IL 60060

HOFFMAN, EDNA VIRGINIA WIGHT (MRS. HENRY CARL HOFFMAN), educator; b. Toronto, Ont., Can., June 28, 1909; d. Cecil James and Margaret (Craig) Wight; came to U.S., 1910, naturalized, 1914; B.S., U. Ore., 1947, M.Ed., 1950; postgrad. U. Portland, 1964; Ed.D., Colo. State Christian Coll., 1973; m. Henry Carl Hoffman, June 1, 1931; children—Veda Virginia (Mrs. George Daniel Keels), Norman Douglas. Tchr. pub. schs., Washington County, Ore., 1928-31, McMinnville, Ore., 1935-36, Sheridan, Ore., 1941-42, Portland, Ore., 1943-74, now ret.; social service worker WPA, McMinnville, Ore., 1934-35. Cons. early childhood edn. Head Start Program, 1965. Fulbright scholar, 1952-53; Merrill-Palmer scholar, 1959. Mem. Assn. for Childhood Edn. Internat. (pub. affairs chmn. Ore., internat. interpreter for Ore.), Ore., Nat. edn. assns., Portland Classroom Tchrs. Assn., Portland Grade Tchrs. Assn., Am. Overseas Educators Orgn., Am. Assn. U. Women, Internat. Platform Assn., Delta Kappa Gamma. Democrat. Episcopalian. Home: 7625 N Willamette Blvd Portland OR 97203

HOFFMAN, ELAINE JANET (MRS. CARL RUDOLPH HOFFMAN, JR.), watercolor artist; b. Oak Park, Ill., Aug. 19, 1925; d. DeWitt Alexander and Magda Catherine (Christensen) Patterson; student Averett Coll., 1944-45, Portland Art Mus., 1964, Northwest Acad. of Watercolor, 1967-68; m. Carl Rudolph Hoffman, Jr., Sept. 7, 1951; children—Lynda Louise, Clayton Carl, Byron Bruce. One-woman shows at Classic Gallery, Oregon City, 1967, The Loft, Portland, Ore., 1967, Arrowhead City Club, Molalla, Ore., 1967, Golden Legend Gallery, Lake Oswego, Ore., 1968, Gallery-by-the-Sea, Lincoln City, Ore., 1969, Window Gallery, Salem, Ore., 1970, The Sketch Box, Portland, 1970, Woodburn Art League, Woodburn, Ore., 1971, Lake Oswego Library, 1972, Illahe Country Club, Salem, 1972, Willamette View Manor, Milwaukie, Ore., 1972, Am. Gallery, Mountain Park, Ore., 1972, Longview (Wash.) Library, 1973, Virginia Mason Hosp., Seattle, 1973, Community Bank, Beloit, Wis., 1974; exhibited in group shows at John Day Coll., McMinnville, Ore., 1972, 73, Coos Bay (Ore.) Art Mus., 1972, 73, Maryhill (Wash.) Mus., 1974; Three Generation Show, Lake Oswego, Portland Art Mus., Capitol Bldg., Santa Fe, N.M., 1969, Arts of Riverwoods, Deerfield, Ill., 1974; represented in permanent collections at La.-Pacific Corp., Portland; represented in numerous pvt. collections. Tchr. of art Home Studio, Lake Oswego, Ore., 1965—. Recipient Grand award Washington Art Exhibit, 1968, Garden Club Ecology award, 1971, Purchase award Coos Bay Art Mus., 1973. Fellow Am. Artist Profl. League of N.Y.; mem. Ore. Soc. of Artists, Ore. (1st prize 1969, honor award 1970), Tamarowean watercolor socs., Portland Fine Art Guild, Lake Oswego Art Guild (dir. 1964-68), Lake Area Artists of Lake Oswego (pres. 1967, 71), Pen and Brush of N.Y. Address: 16695 Glenwood Court Lake Oswego OR 97034

HOFFMAN, ELINOR GENE, author, actress; b. Los Angeles, Jan. 3, 1919; d. Thorkild R. and Valley (Filtzer) Knudsen; grad. Pasadena Playhouse Sch. Theatre, 1940; B.F.A., Cal. Inst. Arts, 1971; m. Raymond Boshco, Feb. 15, 1942 (div. 1948); children—Nikolas Knudsen, Valley Via; m. 2d Hallock Hoffman, July 18, 1948 (div. 1973); children—Paul Craig, Erik Thorkild, Kristian Robert, Nina-Kiriki, Kai Lathrop. Author, narrator radio program Stories Children Love, stas. KWSO, KTMS, KSMA, KOWN, So. Cal., 1941-67; founder, dir. Santa Barbara Night Counseling Center, Santa Barbara br., 1968-70, tchr. re-evaluation counseling, 1970—, now bd. dirs.; tchr. poetry creation Immaculate Heart Community Learning Center, 1972—; columnist Food for Thought, Los Angeles Times, 1944-55, Friends Jour., 1974—; narrator, producer records Sound Book Press Soc., Scarsdale, N.Y., 1950; drama critic Gazette-Citizen, Goleta, Cal., 1963-68; columnist Amsterdam News, 1959; plays—Return of Ulysses, 1944, The Ugly American, 1960, others. Mem. Mayor's Com. for Arts; adv. council Adult Edn.; program com. Casa da Maria. Bd. dirs. Re-Evaluation Found., Knudsen Found., Los Angeles. Mem. Fellowship Reconciliation, Am. Assn. for Humanistic Psychology, War Registers League. Democrat. Mem. Soc. Friends. Contbr. to Dialogue on Women, 1967; Dimensions of the Future, 1974; also religious and psychol. mags. Home: 1387 Schoolhouse Rd Santa Barbara CA 93108

HOFFMAN, ELIZABETH W. PARKINSON (MRS. JAMES WILLIAM HOFFMAN), librarian; b. Pitts.; d. William Sterrett and Elizabeth (Hill) Parkinson; A.B., Dickinson Coll., 1942; M.L.S., Drexel Inst. Tech., 1961; postgrad. N.Y. U., 1943, Temple U., 1966; m. James William Hoffman, Apr. 2, 1944; children—William Sterrett, Elizabeth Whedon, Charles Harran, Lloyd Abbott. Tchr. librarian Womelsdorf (Pa.) Sch. Dist., 1942-45; tchr., librarian Hartley Prodns., N.Y.C., 1943-45; film editor New Hope Solebury Sch. Dist., Pa., 1946-48; librarian, library coordinator Haverford (Pa.) Twp. Sch. Dist., 1958-66, night sch. instr., 1963-65; instr. Plymouth-Whitemarsh Night Sch., Pa., 1964; sch. library specialist Pa. Dept. Edn., Phila., 1966, dir. div. sch. libraries, 1966—; instr. Villanova (Pa.) U. Editor Childrens page Presbyn. Life, 1948-58. Mem. Main Line Council on Alcoholism, 1961-67. Bd. dirs. Parastudy, Chester Heights, Pa. Mem. Am. (council 1973—, legislative com. chmn. 1973-74), Pa. library assns., Phila., Delaware County (pres. 1963-65) sch. librarians assns., N.E.A., Pa. State, Haverford Twp. edn. assns., Assn. State Sch. Library Suprs., Am. Assn. Sch. Libraries (chmn. suprs. sect. 1971-72). Presbyn. Author: Palm Reading Made Easy, 1971. Contbr. articles to profl. jours. Home: 805 Beechwood Rd Havertown PA 19083 Office: Dept Edn Commonwealth Pa 13 N 4th St Harrisburg PA 17101

HOFFMAN, FAE ELIZABETH, psychologist; b. Hartford, Conn., June 6, 1944; d. Israel A. and Sylvia (Vershbow) Hoffman; B.A., So. Meth. U., 1965; M.A., Western Res. U., 1966; postgrad. Rutgers U., 1968, Ulpan Borochov, Israel, 1970. Vocational counselor Mass. Div. Employment Security, Boston, 1966-67; counseling psychologist B'nai B'rith Vocational Service, Union, N.J., 1967-70; sch. psychologist City of B'nai Berak, Israel, 1971; sr. vocational counselor Jewish Vocational Service, Montreal, Que., Can., 1971-72; dir. profl. field services B'nai B'rith Career and Counseling Services, Washington, 1972—, project dir. Adult Career Edn. Resources Survey, 1973—. Mem. Am. Psychol. Assn., Am. Personnel and Guidance Assn., Nat. Vocational Guidance Assn., Sweet Adelines, Psi Chi. Home: 1400 S Joyce St Arlington VA 22202 Office: 1640 Rhode Island Av NW Washington DC 20036

HOFFMAN, JEANETTE OLIVE ANDERSON (MRS. RICHARD LEIGH HOFFMAN), speech pathologist, educator; b. Rock Island, Ill., Feb. 1, 1916; d. John William and Lydia (Aspengren) Anderson; B.A., Rockford Coll., 1938; M.A., U. Wis., 1940, Ph.D. (Legislative scholar, coll. fellow in speech, Laird fellow), 1942; m. Richard Leigh Hoffman, June 1, 1949; children—Jean Elizabeth, John Arthur. Asst. prof. speech, acting dir. speech clinic Purdue U., 1942-44; asso. prof. speech, dir. speech clinic La. State U., 1944-46; asso. prof. speech, dir. speech clinic Rockford (Ill.) Coll., 1946-49, lectr. speech, 1962-63, prof., 1964-71; speech pathologist Swedish-Am. Hosp., Rockford, 1971—; pvt. practice speech pathology, Rockford, 1949—. Cons. Ind. Dept. Edn., 1942-44, La. Dept. Edn., State Bd. Health, 1944-46, Ill. div. Services for Crippled Children, 1946-49, No. Ill. Speech and Hearing Assn., 1969-70. Pres. bd. Forest Hall Home for Girls, Rockford, 1951-53; pres. Marsh Sch. Dist. Bd. Edn., 1961-65. Recipient Vilas medal in speech U. Wis., 1942. Fellow Am. Speech and Hearing Assn.; mem. Speech Communication Assn. Am., Phi Beta Kappa, Delta Sigma Rho, Psi Chi. Contbr. articles to profl. jours. Address: 4843 Spring Creek Rd Rockford IL 61111

HOFFMAN, KATHRYN ANDERSON (MRS. MICHAEL GEORGE HOFFMAN), physician; b. Balt., Aug. 14, 1937; d. Clair Sherill and Kathryn Ann (Plovanich) Anderson; student, Mt. St. Agnes Coll., 1958; M.D., George Washington U., 1962; m. Michael George Hoffman, Sept. 6, 1960; 1 son, Douglas Michael. Intern, Good Samaritan Hosp., Phoenix, 1962-63; trainee surg. pathology Med. Center, Columbus, Ga., physician, 1963-64, physician, out patient dept., 1964-65; resident in phys. med. and rehab., Warm Springs (Ga.) Found., 1967-70. Active The Arthritis Found. Diplomate Nat. Bd. Med. Examiners, Am. Bd. Phys. Medicine and Rehab. Mem. A.M.A., Med. Assn. of Ga., So. Soc. Phys. Medicine and Rehab., Ga. Rheumatism Soc., Nat. Rehab. Assn. Address: Box 408 Warm Springs Foundation Warm Springs GA 31820

HOFFMAN, LISA, journalist; b. Essen/Ruhr, Germany, May 19, 1919; d. Otto and Elsa (Weis) Hoffmann; ed. Real Gymnasium, Frankfurt/Main, Germany. Came to U.S., 1946, naturalized, 1951. Free lance journalist and photographer, N.Y.C., 1948—; U.S. corr. Schweizer Illustrierte, Zurich, Switzerland, and Jasmin, Germany, 1966—; publicist Prentice-Hall, 1971—; translator subtitles for film cos. Mem. Fgn. Press Assn. (chmn. cultural affairs). Club: Overseas Press. Author: Reigning Cats and Dogs, 1964; (with Lucy Freeman) The Ordeal of Stephen Dennison, 1970. Contbr. articles to newspapers and mags. Home: 445 W 23d St New York City NY 10011

HOFFMAN, LOIS WLADIS (MRS. MARTIN LEON HOFFMAN), psychologist; b. Elmira, N.Y., Mar. 25, 1929; d. Gustave and Etta (Wladis) Wladis; B.A. cum laude, U. Buffalo, 1951; M.S., Purdue U., 1953; Ph.D., U. Mich., 1958; m. Martin Leon Hoffman, June 24, 1951; children—Amy Gabrielle, Jill Adrienne. Research fellow dept. sociology Purdue U., 1951-53; Flint Met. research fellow dept. sociology U. Mich., Ann Arbor, 1953-54, asst. study dir. Survey Research Center, 1954-55, research asst. Research Center for Group Dynamics, 1955-56, research asso., 1956-60, cons. Psychol. Clinic, 1959-60; co-editor Rev. Child Devel. Research, Soc. for Research in Child Devel., Ann Arbor, 1962-66; lectr. dept. psychology U. Mich., 1967-72, asso. prof. dept. psychology and dept. population planning, 1972—. Cons., Office Econ. Opportunity, 1968-70. Named Outstanding Woman Student, U. Buffalo, 1950. Mem. Am. Psychol. Assn., Am. Sociol. Assn., Soc. for Research in Child Devel., Soc. for Psychol. Study Social Issues, Population Assn. Am., Phi Beta Kappa, Phi Kappa Phi. Author: (with F. Ivan Nye) The Employed Mother in America, 1963. Editor (with Martin L. Hoffman) Review of Child Development Research, Vol. 1 (Family Life Book award Child Study Assn. Am. 1965), 1964, Vol. 2, 1966. Contbr. articles to profl. jours. Address: 1307 Baldwin Av Ann Arbor MI 48104

HOFFMAN, MARIAN J., orgn. exec.; b. Franklin, Pa., Feb. 24; d. John George and Ella M. (Haggarty) Hoffman; student Franklin Comml. Coll., 1935-36. Sec., office mgr. Fed. Deposit Ins. Corp., Franklin, 1941-50; sec., bookkeeper Jones-Laughlin Steel Corp., Oil City, Pa., 1951-54; office mgr., sec. Venango County Sesquicentennial Assn., Franklin, 1955, Franklin Area C. of C., 1955-71. Bus. mgr., dir. Venango County Mus. Corp., 1963-70, exec. dir., 1970—, sec. Franklin Retail Assn., 1961—. Gen. chmn., dir. Franklin Frontier Festival promotion, 1964—; co-chmn., dir. ann. Venango County Sportsmens Show, 1965—; mem. Mayors Citizens Adv. Com., 1967—, Allegheny Regional Adv. Bd., 1963—; exec. dir. Franklin Pub. Housing Authority, 1971—; founder Franklin Civic Operetta Assn., 1958, dir., finance chmn., 1958-70, pres., also dir., 1970—; co-chmn., sec. Community Concert Assn., Franklin, 1941-43; chmn. Tri-City Arts Council, 1967—; mem. Venango County Am. Revolution Bicentennial Com., 1973—. Bd. dirs. N.W. Pa. Regional Devel. and Planning Commn., Franklin Centennial Assn. Mem. Republican Women's Assn.; mem. publicity and pub. relations com. Rep. Women Venango County. Mem. Pa. Tourist Promotion Agys. Assn. (dir.), Pa. Retailers' Assn. (asso.), Nat. Secs. Assn. (chpt. pres. 1948-49), Bus. and Profl. Womens Club, Pa. C. of C. Execs. (asso.), Tourists Assn. Promotion Execs., Venango County Hist. Soc. Lutheran. Club: Franklin. Home: 1102 Elk St Franklin PA 16323 Office: 11 Dale Av Franklin PA 16323

HOFFMAN, MARIAN KASABIAN (MRS. WILLIAM JOHN HOFFMAN), educator; b. Andover, Mass., Mar. 7, 1919; d. Charles Aaron and Helen Charles (Tashian) Kasabian; B.S., Boston U., 1952; M.A., Columbia, 1955; Ph.D. (NIH fellow), Ohio State U., 1968; m. William John Hoffman, Sept. 1, 1956. Staff nurse Bklyn. Vis. Nurse Assn., 1952-56; asso. dir. St. Joseph's Sch. Nursing, Parkersburg, W.Va., 1957-64; asso. prof. W.Va. Wesleyan Coll., Buckhannon, 1964-65; asso. prof. State U. N.Y. at Buffalo, 1969-71; asso. prof. pub. health nursing U. Ill., Chgo., 1971—, research asso. Center Ednl. Devel., Coll. Medicine. Cons. nursing edn. Chgo. State U.; evaluation cons. Midsouth Health Planning Orgn. Oral bd. mem. City Chgo. Civil Service Commn. Trustee St. Joseph's Hosp., Parkersburg, 1962-64. Mem. Am., Ill. (program planning, rev. com. del. conf. Mid-South Health Planning Orgn.) nurses assns., Am. Pub. Health Assn., Nat. League Nursing, Council Nurse Researchers, Sigma Theta Tau. Episcopalian.

HOFFMAN, MARILYN FRIEDMAN, mus. ofcl.; b. Yonkers, N.Y., Jan. 27, 1946; d. Harris L. and Beatrice (Kassell) Friedman; B.A. with honors, Brown U., 1967, M.A., 1971; m. Alan R. Hoffman, Sept. 19, 1971. Asst. curator of edn. Mus. of Art, R.I. Sch. Design, Providence, 1967-68; grad. asst. Met. Mus. Art, N.Y.C., 1969; adj. lectr. Mus. Fine Arts, Boston, 1972; curator Brockton (Mass.) Art Center, 1971-73, dir., 1973—. Mem. Am. Assn. Museums, Coll. Art Assn. Office: Oak St Brockton MA 02401

HOFFMAN, RUTH STERLING (MRS. ELBERT LEE HOFFMAN), physician; b. Shreveport, La., Mar. 25, 1924; d. William Woodson and Hilda Eureka (Ellis) Sterling; B.A., Blue Mountain Coll., 1947; R.N., So. Baptist Hosp. Sch. Nursing, 1951; B.S. in Nursing, Tulane U., 1954, M.D., 1958, M.Med. Sci., 1965; m. Elbert Lee Hoffman, Dec. 20, 1958; 1 son, David Lee. Rotating intern So. Bapt. Hosp., New Orleans, 1958-59, resident in internal medicine, 1959-60; fellow internal medicine Tulane U. Sch. Medicine-Charity Hosp. La., 1960-62, USPHS fellow, 1962-65; dir. Hutchinson Meml. Clinic, chief med. center student health, asso. dir. univ. health service Tulane U., 1965—, asso. prof. medicine Med. Sch., 1970—, mem. staff So. Baptist Hosp., New Orleans. Rep. Tulane U. on Community Services Council Inc. Mem. Am. Med. Women's Assn., Orleans Parish Med. Soc., Am. Assn. U. Profs., Am. Coll. Health Assn., Am. Soc. Internal Medicine, Soc. Adolescent Medicine (charter). Baptist. Author med. articles. Home: 5880 Marcia Av New Orleans LA 70124 Office: 1430 Tulane Av New Orleans LA 70112

HOFFMANN, FRANCES C. (MRS. ALBERT THEODORE HOFFMANN), educator; b. Dunblane, Sask., Can., July 24, 1921; d. George Percy and Clara (Amerud) Carey; student Neb. State Tchrs. Coll., 1943, 51-53; B.S., Ia. State U., 1955, M.S., 1956; m. Albert Theodore Hoffman, Oct. 21, 1943 (dec. July 1951); children—Gerald Theodore, Thomas Gene. Library asst. Central High Sch., Sioux City, Ia., 1938-39; dining room asst. St. Joseph's Hosp., 1940-41; underphotographer Elko Photo Co., Sioux City, 1941-42, U.S. Civil Service, 1943-44; grad. research asst. Ia. State U., 1955-56; home econs. instr. Whittier (Cal.) Coll., 1957-66, asst. prof., 1966—, chmn. dept. home econs., 1971-72; home econs. dir. Saturday Programs and Summer Day Camps, Found. for the Jr. Blind, Los Angeles, 1964—, cons. bldg. addition, 1966-68. Am. Home Econs. Assn.-Rehab. Services Adminstrn. fellow, 1969-70. Mem. Am. Assn. U. Women, Am. (mem. rehab. com. 1970-72, com. on coms. 1971), Cal. (adviser coll. chpts. 1968); profl. sect. chmn. coll. chpt. 1968-70) home econs. assns., Am. Assn. U. Profs., Cal. Tchrs. Assn., Am. Textile Chemists and Colorists, Kappa Omicron Phi (chpt. adviser 1973). Methodist. Participant audio-visual documentary Out of Darkness-Light, 1971. Home: 5518 S Adele Av Whittier CA 90601

HOFFMANN, NORINE DALKERT KREISCHER (MRS. ARNOLD FRED HOFFMANN), newspaper editor; b. Monroe County, Ill., Aug. 20, 1917; d. George and Louise Pauline (Meyer) Kreischer; grad. high sch.; m. Herman John Dalkert, Apr. 16, 1936; children—Joanne (Mrs. Robert C. Kettler), Charles Herbert; m. 2d, Arnold Fred Hoffmann, Apr. 29, 1969. Press operator Waterloo (Ill.) Times, 1950-63, editor, 1966—, also photographer, photoengraver, pres. Mem. citizens com. Waterloo Community Schs., 1968. Bd. dirs. Waterloo Indsl. League, 1967. Recipient award for outstanding achievement and service Theta Sigma Phi (now Women in Communications), 1967. Mem. Ill. Press Assn., So. Ill. Editorial Assn. (v.p.). Mem. Order Eastern Star (past matron). Home: 120a N Main St Waterloo IL 62298 Office: 120 N Main St Waterloo IL 62298

HOFFNER, MARILYN, art dir.; b. N.Y.C., Nov. 16, 1927; d. Daniel and Elsie (Schulz) H.; grad. Cooper Union; m. Albert Greenberg, May 29, 1949. Art dir. Printers' Ink mag., N.Y.C., 1953-63; art dir. Print mag., N.Y.C., 1960-62; corporate art dir. Vision, Inc., N.Y.C., 1963—. Bd. dirs. Art Dirs. Club N.Y. Scholarship Fund, 1963-74, exec. treas., 1971-74, exec. sec. bd., 1973-75. Named Alumnus of Year Cooper Union, 1968. Mem. Cooper Union Alumni Assn. (editor-in-chief 1971-74, 1st v.p. 1974-75), Art Dirs. Club N.Y. (exec. bd. 1973-74, recipient numerous awards) Type Dirs. Club, N.Y. Art Dirs. Club (dir.). Contbg. editor Print mag., 1960-62, Art Direction, 1959-64, Graphic mag., 1959-65; designer children's books. Home: 51 Fifth Av New York City NY 10003 Office: 641 Lexington Av New York City NY 10022

HOFFNER, MARY MARGARET MILLER (MRS. LARRY WILLIAM HOFFNER), physician; b. Greeley, Colo., Dec. 21, 1937; d. David Jacob and Lydia (Alles) Miller; student Wellesley Coll., 1955-57; student U. Colo., Boulder, 1957-58; M.D., U. Colo., Denver, 1962; m. Larry William Hoffner, June 26, 1960; children—William Alexander, Katherine Margaret, Sarah Jane. Intern Weld County Hosp., Greeley, 1962-63; Maytag Cancer fellowship Poudre Valley Meml. Hosp., Ft. Collins, Colo., 1963-64, mem. staff, 1963—; practice medicine specializing in family practice, Ft. Collins, 1966—; mem. staff Colo. State U. Health Center, 1964-66. Recipient Physician's Recognition award, A.M.A., 1969, 73. Diplomate Am. Bd. Family Practice (charter). Fellow Am. Acad. Family Practice; mem. Colo., Larimer County med. scos., A.M.A., Am. Med. Women's Assn., Aux. Am. Veterinary Med. Assn., Waring Soc., Sigma Xi, Iota Sigma Pi, Gamma Phi Beta. Methodist. Contbr. articles to profl. jours. Home: 4409 E Prospect St Fort Collins CO 80521 Office: 1217 E Elizabeth St Fort Collins CO 80521

HOFMAN, DOROTHY LARSEN, home economist; b. Culbertson, Mont., Dec. 30, 1920; d. Willie and Isabella Elvina (Fryhling) Larsen; B.A. in Home Econs., Mont. State U., 1943, M.S. in Agrl. Edn., 1970; m. Frederick Peter Hofman, June 9, 1946; children—Gregory Fred, Dean Alvin, Cheryl Jean, Jerry Craig. Tchr. home econs. Sidney (Mont.) High Sch., 1943-46, sch. dist. 17, Culbertson, 1959; Ft. Peck Reservation extension agt. Mont. State U., 1963-71, county extension agt., Culbertson, 1971—. Cons. in field. Mem. Nat., Mont. (treas. 1970-72, v.p. 1972-74) assns. extension home economists, Extension Homemaker Club (pres. 1953), Mont. Coop. Extension Assn. (dir. 1972—). Contbr. papers to profl. jours. Address: PO Box 416 Culbertson MT 59218

HOFMANN, ADELE DELLENBAUGH, physician; b. Boston, Oct. 12, 1926; d. Frederick Samuel and Anne Celestine (Goddard) Dellenbaugh; B.A., Smith Coll., 1948; M.D., U. Rochester, 1952; m. Frederick G. Hofmann, July 28, 1956; children—Peter, Anne. Intern pediatrics U. Minn. Hosps., 1952-53; resident pediatrics Babies Hosp., N.Y.C., 1953-55; Nat. Found. fellow Presbyn. Hosp., N.Y.C., 1955-57; chief pediatric out-patient services St. Luke's Hosp., N.Y.C., 1957-59; asst. dir. teen-age service Beth Israel Hosp., N.Y.C., 1963-70; dir. adolescent med. unit N.Y. U. Med. Center-Bellevue Hosp., N.Y.C., 1970—; asst. clin. prof. pediatrics Mt. Sinai Sch. Medicine, 1969-70; asst. prof. clin. pediatrics N.Y. U. Sch. Medicine, 1970—. Cons., lectr. in field. Diplomate Am. Bd. Pediatrics. Fellow Am. Acad. Pediatrics (chmn. regional chpt. com. on youth, mem. nat. youth com.); mem. Soc. Adolescent Medicine (charter, exec. council 1970-73, chmn. N.Y. chpt. 1968-70), Am. Pub. Health Assn., Ambulatory Pediatric Assn., N.Y. State Com. on Children, Sigma Xi, Alpha Omega Alpha. Home: 85 Mayflower Dr Tenafly NJ 07670 Office: 550 1st Av New York City NY 10016

HOFMANN, CORRIS MABELLE, chemist; b. Plainville, Mass., Sept. 18, 1915; d. Edward Ferdinand and Mabelle Eaton (Fuller) Hofmann; B.S., U. Ill., 1937; Ph.D., Bryn Mawr Coll., 1941. Research chemist Am. Cyanamid, Pearl River, N.Y., 1941—. Fellow Am. Inst. Chemists; mem. Am. Chem. Soc., N.Y. Acad. Sci., Am. Assn. U. Women, Sigma Delta Epsilon. Methodist (bd. trustees 1974—). Home: 258 Ackerman St Ho-Hokus NJ 07423 Office: American Cyanamid Co Pearl River NY 10965

HOFMANN, PATREA CAROLINE (MRS. AUGUST A. HOFMANN), mag. editor; b. Cheyenne, Wyo., July 8, 1941; d. Owen Neils and Dora May (Henrie) Jensen; student Ida. State Coll., 1963; B.A., U. Colo., 1964; Reporter/editor Blackfoot (Ida.) News, 1959-63; editor Martin Co., Denver, 1963-65, Rocky Mountain and West Coast Druggist mags., Denver, 1966-68, Hoofs and Horns mag., Denver, 1968-73, Western Wear & Equipment mag., Denver, 1973—. Recipient photography award Asso. Press, 1961. Mem. Colo. Press Assn. Home: 2001 W 90th Av Denver CO 80221 Office: 2403 Champa St Denver CO 80205

HOFSCHULTE, RUTH ANNABEL, state health adminstr.; b. Greeley, Colo., Oct. 25, 1922; d. Joseph John and Martha (Rucker) Hofschulte; B.A., Cardinal Stritch Coll., Milw., 1949; M.A., Cath. U. Am., 1952. Tchr. mentally retarded St. Coletta Sch., Jefferson, Wis., 1942-56; dir. St. Coletta Day Sch. for Mentally Retarded, Milw., 1956-62; dir. Day Care Centers for Mentally Retarded, New Orleans, 1962-64; mental retardation program coordinator La. Health Dept., New Orleans, 1964-73; adminstr. div. maternal and child health La. Health and Human Resources Adminstrn., New Orleans, 1973—. Instr. spl. edn. Cardinal Stritch Coll., 1952-62. Chmn. health com. La. Adv. Council Developmental Disabilities, 1971—. Bd. dirs. La. Assn. Retarded Children, New Orleans Assn. Retarded Children, United

Cerebral Palsy Assn. Recipient Outstanding Pub. Ofcl. award La. Assn. Retarded Children, 1971; Pres.'s Cup for service to La. mentally retarded, 1972. Mem. Confrat. Christian Doctrine (dir. New Orleans 1964-67). Office: State Office Bldg Civic Center New Orleans LA 70130

HOFSTATTER, JUNE MARIE EICHENBERG (MRS. FRANK FOX HOFSTATTER), advt. agy. exec.; b. Cleve., Jan. 27, 1925; d. Arthur Conrad and Mattie (Kadlejack) Eichenberg; student Fenn Coll., 1942-43, Baldwin-Wallace Coll., 1943-44; m. Frank Fox Hofstatter, Aug. 22, 1945; children—Caren Lee, Linda Jean, Robert Alan. Exec. sec. Cleve. Graphite Bronze Co., Cleve., 1944-45; v.p. Stahl Assos., 1962—; partner Hofstal Co., Bellevue and Bryan, O., 1959—; co-owner Countyline, shoppers newspaper, Bryan, 1965-67. Mem. Nat. Fedn. Advt. Agys., Am. Advt. Fedn., Internat. Platform Assn., Women's Advt. Club Toledo, Federated Women's Clubs Bryan (pres. 1966-67). Republican. Presbyn. Clubs: Sorosis (publicity and program chmn. Bellevue 1960-61); Claire Newcomer (pres. 1966-67), Orchard Hills Country (Bryan). Home: 615 Circle Dr Bryan OH 43506 Office: 1002 Buffalo Rd Bryan OH 43506

HOFSTETTER, ELEANORE OTTILIA, librarian; b. Camden, N.J., May 16, 1939; d. George and Anna Ottilia (Kneissl) Hofstetter; B.S., Marywood Coll., 1961; M.S. in L.S., Drexel U., 1963; M.A., U. Del., 1967. Instr. history and sociology Trinity Coll., Burlington, Vt., 1961-62; reference librarian U. Del., Newark, 1963-66; head pub. service Towson (Md.) State Coll., 1966—. Book reviewer Library Jour., 1968—; editor Crab, newsletter Md. Library Assn., 1971-72. Home: 7725 Greenview Terrace Apt 273 Baltimore MD 21204 Office: Albert S Cook Library Towson State Coll Baltimore MD 21204

HOGAN, ALICE HAMILTON, author, educator, editor; b. New Haven; d. John Joseph and Mary (Gormley) Hogan; B.S., Tchrs. Coll. Columbia, 1932; M.A., Radcliffe Coll., 1942; spl. student Yale. Free-lance short story writer nat. mags., anthologies, 1950—; teacher English, James E. Hillhouse High Sch., New Haven, 1938-61, chmn. dept. English, 1961-71; lectr. So. Conn. State Coll., 1971—. Writer paperback introductions Airmont Pub. Co. Recipient Christopher Lit. award, 1956. Mem. Nat., Conn. edn. assns., Am. Assn. U. Women, N.E. Assn. English Tchrs., League Women Voters, Authors League Am., Platform Assn. Roman Catholic. Club: Radcliffe College of New Haven. Editor: The War of The Worlds. Home: 49 Osborn Av New Haven CT 06511 Office: 965 Dixwell Av New Haven CT 06511

HOGAN, BARBARA KARLSON (MRS. PETER DONELIN HOGAN), health service adminstr., psychotherapist; b. Montclair, N.J., Sept. 4, 1942; d. Vincent R. and Lucille M. (Tafaro) Ciccone; B.A., Cedar Crest Coll., 1964; M.A., N.Y. U., 1970; Ph.D., Union Grad. Sch., 1974; m. Peter Donelin Hogan, Mar. 17, 1970. Tchr. elementary schs., Los Angeles, 1964-65, South Orange-Maplewood, N.J., 1965-67; high sch. and elementary sch., N.Y.C., 1967-69; tchr. Mt. Sinai Hosp., N.Y.C., Psychiat. Inst., N.Y.C., 1967-69; psychotherapist, sex therapist, group psychotherapist, N.Y.C., 1970—; asst. dir. sex therapy and edn. program N.Y. Hosp., Cornell U. Med. Coll., N.Y.C., 1973—. Mem. Adv. Bd. Consultation Center for Women. Mem. Am. Psychol. Assn., Am. Assn. Marriage and Family Counselors, Soc. Sci. Study Sex, Am. Assn. U. Women, SIECUS, Assn. Women in Psychology, Easter Assn. Sex Therapists. Author: The Woman is Victim, 1974; The Masks of Anger, 1974; The Flight From Liberation, 1974. Home: 262 Central Park West New York City NY 10024 Office: 10 West 66th St New York City NY 10023

HOGAN, CARILEE ANN, educator, univ. adminstr.; b. Oklahoma City, Dec. 5, 1943; d. Stephen Lee and Carrie (Daniel) Hogan; B.Mus. Edn., U. Okla., 1965, M.Ed., 1966; Ph.D., St. Louis U., 1972. Asst. counselor housing, counselor, tower unit dir., tower unit coordinator, gen. counselor Office Student Affairs U. Okla., 1963-66; housing dir., social dir. Monticello Coll., Godfrey, Ill., 1966-67, asst. dean students, social dir., 1967-68; dir. Rogers Residence Hall, St. Louis U., 1968-69, dir. student personnel Sch. Nursing and Allied Health Professions, instr. edn., 1969-71, asso. dean Office Freshman Studies, 1971-73. Mem. Am. Personnel and Guidance Assn., Am. Coll. Personnel Assn., Nat. Assn. Student Personnel Adminstrs., Nat. Assn. Women Deans, Adminstrs. and Counselors, Mortar Bd., Alpha Chi Omega, Mu Phi Epsilon, Alpha Sigma Nu. Home: 7243 Southwest Av St Louis MO 63143

HOGAN, ELISABETH WOODBRIDGE MORRIS, editor, cons., lectr.; b. New Haven, Sept. 11, 1932; d. Charles Lester and Alice (Oviatt) Morris; B.A., Vassar Coll., 1953; m. 1953 (div. 1957); children—Michele Elisabeth, Pamela Joan. Copywriter, broadcaster Radio Sta. WSTC, Stamford, Conn., 1958-61; copywriter John C. Dowd, Inc., Boston, 1961-62; publicity dir. Kenyon & Eckhardt, Inc., Boston, 1962-64; creative dir. 1st Financial Advt. Group, Brookline, Mass., 1964-65; asst. advt. mgr. G.K. Hall & Co., Boston, 1965-67; writer, group leader, mgmt. cons. Harbridge House, Inc., Boston, 1967-72; owner Betsy Hogan Assos., pub., editor Womanpower, 1972—; dir. Women's Yellow Pages, Boston. Cons. employment task force Mass. Gov.'s Commn. on Status Women; speaker on fair employment practices for women. Mem. Publicity Club Boston (sec. 1963-64), Nat. Orgn. Women (state dir. 1972). Republican. Conglist. Author: Step-by-Step: Affirmative Action for Women. Home: 222 Rawson Rd Brookline MA 02146

HOGAN, GLORIA JERETTA CHERNE (MRS. DENNIS E. HOGAN, III), pub. relations and marketing exec.; b. Warroad, Minn., Aug. 1, 1922; d. Anthony G. and Emily (Cugnet) Cherne; grad. Va. Jr. Coll., 1942; B.A. in English and Theatre, U. Minn., 1944; m. Dennis E. Hogan, III, Oct. 23, 1948; children—Dennis IV and Diane (twins). Mpls. bur. chief of N.Y. Headquartered Fairchild Publs., Inc., 1945-70; partner Siegel-Hogan Enterprises Co., Mpls., 1970—. Dir. St. Paul-Mpls. Fashion Group, Inc., 1974-75. Mem. Pub. Relations Soc. Am. Clubs: Interlachen Country; Minn. Press (sec. 1965-67). Home: 6204 Belmore Lane Hopkins MN 55343 Office: Suite 321 920 Nicollet Mall MN 55402

HOGAN, JANE, pub. relations exec.; b. West Plains, Mo., Dec. 23, 1912; d. Jack Evans and Juanita (Stebbins) Hogan; B.J., U. Mo., 1935, postgrad., 1934-35. Employed with various newspapers, Okla., 1945-50; reporter, editor Marshall County News, Maryville, Kan., 1950-64; informational writer Kan. Dept. Health, Topeka, 1964-67; informational counsel, community mental health services Kan. Dept. Social Welfare, Topeka, 1967-71; informational writer Kan. Hwy. Commn., Topeka, 1972—. Mem. Women in Communications, Nat., Kan., Topeka press women, Topeka Pub. Relations Soc., Bus. and Profl. Women's Club (1st v.p. Topeka 1974—, editor state publ. 1961-62), D.A.R. (past chpt. regent). Mem. Daus. of Isabella (chpt. regent). Home: 635 Harrison St Topeka KS 66603 Office: 7th Floor State Office Bldg Topeka KS 66612

HOGAN, MARGARET ROSE, librarian; b. Little Rock, Jan. 23, 1932; d. Joseph Robert and Mayme Elizabeth (Corn) Hogan; B.S., St. Louis U., 1954; M.S., U. Ark., 1959. Research asst. in biochemistry U. Ark., Little Rock, 1956-59, reference librarian Health Sci. Library, 1962-66, dir., 1966—, prof., 1966—; research asst. VA Hosp., Little Rock, 1960-62. Mem. Med., Spl., Southwestern, Ark. (pres. 1970), library assns., Am. Assn. Colls. of Pharmacy (librarians sect.), Ozark Soc., Sierra Club, Sigma Xi. Contbr. articles to profl. jours. Home: 212 Vernon W St Little Rock AR 72205 Office: 4301 W Markham St Little Rock AR 72201

HOGAN, MARTHA WYRICK, pediatrician; b. Texarkana, Tex., Dec. 22, 1942; d. John Calhoun and Nelwyn Bates (Roach) Wyrick; B.A. in Biology, Tex. Christian U., 1964; M.D., Georgetown U., 1968; m. Thomas Francis Hogan, July 16, 1966. Intern, Georgetown U. Hosp., 1968-69, resident pediatrics, 1969-70, chief resident pediatrics, 1970-71; pediatrician with Boyer, Knox, Young, Hogan and Pfeffer, Springfield, Va., 1971—; staff hosp., clin. instr. pediatrics Georgetown U. Med. Sch., 1971—; mem. active staff Fairfax Hosp., Falls Church, Va. Named Outstanding Young Woman of Am., 1973. Diplomate Am. Bd. Pediatrics. Fellow Am. Acad. Pediatrics; mem. Am. Women's Med. Assn., Va., Fairfax County med. socs., Am. Acad. Pediatrics, No. Va. Pediatric Soc. Home: 514 New Mark Esplanade Rockville MD 20850 Office: 6828 Commerce St Springfield VA 22150 also 6116 Rolling Rd Springfield VA 22152

HOGAN, MILDRED ELINOR, librarian; b. Pine Bluff, Ark., July 30, 1911; d. Elmer Ellsworth and Margaret Jessie (Davis) Hogan; B.A., Centenary Coll., 1930; B.S. in L.S., La. State U., 1934; postgrad. Columbia, summer 1941. Tchr.-librarian Mooringsport (La.) High Sch., 1930-33; sec. to state supr. sch. libraries La. Dept. Edn., Baton Rouge, 1934-41, research librarian, 1941-44; asst. to dir. libraries La. State U., Baton Rouge, 1944-45; research librarian La. Dept. Commerce and Industry, Baton Rouge, 1945-51; librarian Transcontinental Gas Pipe Line Corp., Houston, 1951—. Spl. lectr. U. Tex. Grad. Sch. Library Sci., summers 1960, 61. Mem. Spl. Libraries Assn. (chpt. pres. 1947-48), Republican. Methodist. Home: 6544 Brompton Rd Houston TX 77005 Office: PO Box 1396 Houston TX 77001

HOGAN, RUTH S., city ofcl.; b. Accident, Md., June 13, 1925; d. Arthur D. and Marie (Coblentz) Scrogum; B.S. in Music Edn., Bridgewater Coll., 1946; certificate Internat. City Mgrs. Assn., 1956; 1 son, Ronald Ward. Music supr. Allegany County Schs., Cumberland, Md., 1946-47; sec. Gen. Brotherhood Bd., Ch. of Brethren, Elgin, Ill., 1947-48; dep. city clk. La Verne, Cal., 1949-53, city clk., 1953—, adminstrv. asst. to city mgr., 1970—. Mem. Internat. Inst. Municipal clks., So. Cal. City Clks. Assn., Municipal Mgmt. Assts. So. Cal. Home: 3530 Damien Av La Verne CA 91750 Office: 2061 3d St City Hall La Verne CA 91750

HOGARTH, FRANCES HARRIS (MRS. CHARLES P. HOGARTH), clubwoman; b. Pensacola, Fla., July 12, 1913; d. Edward Payne and Eva (Joiner) Harris; student Freemans Bus. Coll., U. Mich.; m. Charles P. Hogarth, Dec. 14, 1940; children—Nancy Eva, Charles P. Pres.'s wife, ofcl. hostess, interior decorator cons. Gulf Park Coll., Gulfport, Miss., 1950-52; Miss. State Coll. for Women, Columbus, 1952—. Mem. Hosp. Jr. League, Albany, Ga., 1934-38; sec. Music Civic Assn., 1938; social worker A.R.C., Detroit, 1941, Nashville, 1942-44; pres. Young Women's Bible Class, West End Meth. Ch., Nashville, 1945; corr. sec. Woman's Soc. Christian Service, Nashville, 1945; pres. Ward-Belmont Jr. Coll. Woman's Club, Nashville, 1945; Columbus Pilgrimage Homes, 1952—; den mother Cub Scouts Am., Columbus, 1959-61; patroness Delta Debutante Assembly, Greenville, 1966-67, Debutante Assembly N.Y., 1967-68, Internat. Debutante Ball, 1967-68. Recipient letter appreciation Miss. State Coll. Women, 1965, 69, named Queen of Hearts Faculty Wives Club, 1969. Past mem. Fannie Battle Social Workers, Fla. State U. Faculty Wives Club, Tallahassee, Gulf Coast Garden Club, Gulfport, Miss., Merry Maskers Dance Club, Epsilon Sigma Alpha, 20th Century Study Club, Gulfport Yacht Club, Gulfport Jr. Aux., now mem. Miss. Assn. for Preservation Antiquities, Met. Dinner Club, Miss. Ofcl. Women's Clubs, Jackson, Miss. State Coll. for Women Faculty Wives Club, Columbus Country Club; Queen's Cove Club, Ltd., Freeport, Grand Bahamas (charter). Home: 1217 College Av Columbus MS 39701

HOGARTH, GRACE W. ALLEN (MRS. PHILIP L. SAYLES), publisher, author; b. Newton, Mass., Nov. 5, 1905; d. John Weston and Caroline (Hills) Allen; student U. Cal. at Berkeley, 1924-25; A.B., Vassar Coll., 1927; postgrad. Mass. Sch. Art, 1927-28, Yale, 1928-29; m. William David Hogarth, Aug. 22, 1936 (dec. Sept. 1965); children—David Allen, Caroline Mary (Mrs. John Barron); m. 2d, Philip Livermore Sayles, May 22, 1971. With Oxford U. Press, N.Y.C. and London, Eng., 1929-38; editor childrens books Chatto and Windus, London, 1938-39; with Houghton Mifflin, Boston, 1940-43, scout, London, 1943-47; scout, various publishers, 1947-56; editor childrens books Constable & Co., Ltd., London, 1956-63; mng. dir. Constable Young Books, London, 1963-68, chmn., 1966-68; mng. dir. Longman Young Books, London, 1968, dir., 1968-73; editor-in-chief Lifetime Library, My Weekly Reader Family Book Service, Am. Edn. Publs., Middletown, Conn., 1968-71; gen. editor Classics for Today, Lifetime Library, William Collins, London, 1971—. Gov., North London Collegiate Sch., 1965-71, Camden Sch. for Girls, 1965-71. Mem. Delta Gamma, Childrens Book Circle London (hon.). Clubs: Vassar (N.Y.C.); Womens City (Boston); United Oxford and Cambridge (London). Author: A Bible A B C, 1940; Lucy's League, 1950; John's Journey, 1952; The Funny Guy, 1955; As a May Morning, 1958; This to be Love, 1949; The End of Summer, 1951; Children of this World, 1953. Home: Box 23 South Freeport ME 04078

HOGG, BEULAH JEAN, occupational therapist; b. Gibsonia, Pa., Sept. 27, 1918; d. Willis Edwin and Beulah Bessie (Boulden) Hogg; registered radiol. technician U. Ia., 1941; B.S. cum laude, Western Mich. U., 1954. Radiol. technician Percy Jones Army Hosp., Battle Creek, Mich., 1948-51; mem. staff Harold Upjohn Sch. of Spl. Edn., Kalamazoo, 1954—; occupational therapist Kalamazoo Pub. Schs., 1954—. Served with WAVES, 1944-46. Recipient scholarship Nat. Soc. for Crippled Children and Adults, 1956, Constance Brown Soc. for Better Hearing, Kalamazoo, 1958. Mem. Am. Occupational Therapy Assn., Mich., Kalamazoo City edn. assns., Alpha Delta Kappa. Office: 3400 Lovers Lane Kalamazoo MI 49001

HOGG, HELEN SAWYER (MRS. FRANK HOGG), astronomer; b. Lowell, Mass., Aug. 1, 1905; d. Edward Everett and Carrie (Sprague) Sawyer; A.B., Mt. Holyoke Coll., 1926, D.Sc. (hon.), 1958; M.A., Radcliffe Coll., 1928, Ph.D., 1931; D.S. (hon.), U. Waterloo, 1962; m. Frank Scott Hogg, Sept. 6, 1930; children—Sarah Longley (Mrs. Sarah MacDonald), David Edward, James Scott. Lectr., Smith Coll., 1927, Mt. Holyoke, 1930-31, asst. prof., acting chmn. dept., 1940-41; research asst. Dominion Astrophys. Obs., 1931-35; research asst. U. Toronto, 1936-41, lectr. 1941-50, asst. prof., 1951-55, asso. prof., 1955-57, prof. 1957—; program dir. astronomy NSF, Washington, 1955-56; astronomy columnist Toronto Daily Star, 1951—; research asso. David Dunlap Obs., Richmond Hill, Ont. Can., 1941—. Dir. Bell Can. Recipient citation Mt. Holyoke Coll., 1952; Rittenhouse Astron. Soc. medal, 1967, Centennial medal, 1967; medal of service Order of Can., 1968. Fellow Royal Soc. Can. (pres. sect. 3, 1960); mem. Internat. Astron. Union (past pres. sub-commn.), Royal Astron. Soc. Can. (past pres., Service medal 1967), Am. (Annie J. Cannon prize 1950), Canadian (pres. 1971-72) astron. socs., Am. Assn. Variable Star Observers (past pres.), Women's Press Club, Royal Canadian Inst. (pres. 1964-65), Fedn. Ont. Naturalists, Phi Beta Kappa, Sigma Xi. Club: University Women's (Toronto). Contbr. numerous research papers, articles to profl. lit. Home: 98 Richmond St Richmond Hill ON Canada Office: David Dunlap Obs Richmond Hill ON Canada

HOGGARD, OMA BLANCHARD (MRS. AMOS W. HOGGARD), real estate broker; b. Harrisburg, Ill., June 21, 1908; d. James Lafayette and Myrtle Ann (Allen) Blanchard; elementary tchrs. certificate S.E. Mo. State Tchrs. Coll., 1928; student Sacramento City Coll., 1958-59; m. Amos W. Hoggard, May 29, 1931; children—Betty Ann (Mrs. Ernst Jarke), Amos William. Tchr., New Liberty Sch., Blytheville, Ark., 1928-30; owner, mfr. fruit cakes So. Belle, Sacramento, 1942-52; producer, actress local theater groups, 1950-60; owner Oma Hoggard Realty, Sacramento, 1956—, Roman Prodns. Co., Sacramento, 1959—. Mem. Nat. Assn. Real Estate Bds., Sacramento Bd. Realtors (mem. publicity com. 1964-65), Delta Psi Omega. Address: 856 51st St Sacramento CA 95819

HOGUE, LINNIE ELLINGTON (MRS. JACOB J. HOGUE), univ. dean; b. Texarkana, Tex., Aug. 2, 1923; d. Harry Pickard and Martha Lee (Stewart) Ellington; B.S., U. Ark., 1960, postgrad., 1963; M.S., Henderson State Coll., 1965; m. Jacob Jefferson Hogue, June 1, 1941; children—Sherry Lynn (Mrs. Ashton Stuckey), Jacob Jefferson. Faculty, Monticello (Ark.) Pub. Schs., 1960-63; dean women U. Ark., Monticello, 1963—. Univ. coordinator Easter Seal Soc., 1963-70; mem. Ark. Coll. and Univ. Council on Status of Women. Mem. Ark. Personnel and Guidance Assn., Ark. Assn. Women Deans, Alpha Chi. Presbyn. (chmn. circle 1972-73). Address: U Ark at Monticello Monticello AR 71655

HOHL, ELIZABETH MASON, physician, surgeon; b. Beaver City, Neb., Aug. 8, 1890; d. William Henry and Nellie Lavina (Booth) Mason; B.S., U. Neb., 1913; M.D., U. Neb., 1915; m. Harrison L. Hohl, 1916 (div. 1934); 1 son, Mason. Intern Neb. Meth. Hosp., Omaha, 1915-16; in gen. practice, McCook, Neb., 1916-24, Hollywood, Cal., 1924—; cons. surgeon Los Angeles City Receiving Hosp.; mem. staff Hollywood Presbyn., Hollywood West, Los Angeles County General hosps.; chief of staff Good Shepherd Convent Sch., Mothers clinics; mem. bd. Clark Residence for Girls, YWCA; co-founder and chief of staff of Cancer Prevention Soc. and Clinic, 1944—. Founder and pres. Los Angeles Physicians Aid Assn., Career Women and Pan Am. Med. Women's Alliance. Recipient Distinguished Service award U. Neb., 1960; named Woman Physician of the Year, 1954, 55; Woman of The Year, Los Angeles Times, 1956. Member Am. Med. Woman's Assn. (past pres.; historian; editor in chief Jour. 1942—), World (founder mem.), Am., Cal., Los Angeles Co. (mem. council) med. assns., Internat. and Los Angeles Co. (mem. council) med. assns., Internat. and Los Angeles med. woman's assns., Hollywood Acad. Medicine, Pub. Health League, Am. Geriatrics Soc., Barlow Soc. for History Medicine (past pres.), Nu Sigma Phi, Mortar Bd. Republican. Author: World Around by Plane and Elephant, 1957. Translator: Diseases of Women (Tortula of Salerno), 1940. Contbr. to Ency. Brit., 1944. Home: 10401 Wilshire Blvd Los Angeles CA 90024 Office: 303 Loma Dr Los Angeles CA 90017

HOIHJELLE, ANNE LORRAINE BEENINGA (MRS. ALBERT L. HOIHJELLE), educator; b. Monroe, S.D.; d. Herman H. and Edith (Smith) Beeninga; teaching certificate Tchrs. Tng. Program Minn., 1939; B.A., Moorhead State Coll., 1949; M.A., U. Minn., 1952; Ed.D., U. Cal. at Berkeley, 1961; postgrad. Oxford U., 1972, U. London, 1972, U. Paris, 1972; m. Albert L. Hoihjelle, July 5, 1941. Elementary tchr. LacQui Parle County, Minn., 1939-41; civil service instr. radio communications Sioux Falls Air Base, S.D., 1942-43; elementary supr. Moorhead (Minn.) State Coll., 1948-51; curriculum coordinator dept. edn. San Diego County, Cal., 1952-60, audio-visual coordinator, 1960—. Served with WAC, 1943-45. Mem. N.E.A. (life), U. Cal. Alumni Assn. (life), Nat. Council Adminstrv. Women in Edn. (pres. San Diego council), Cal. Assn. Sch. Adminstrs. (communications com.), Cal. Assn. for Media and Tech., Assn. for Ednl. Communication and Tech., Nat. Educators Fellowship, Delta Kappa Gamma. Lutheran. Home: 1137 Savoy St San Diego CA 92107 Office: 6401 Linda Vista Rd San Diego CA 92111

HOISTAD, LOUISE MARIE CHARLOTTE CLARK (MRS. ARTHUR OWEN HOISTAD), mgmt. exec.; b. St. Paul, Mar. 23, 1915; d. Albert Hoefield and Louise Marie Charlotte (Potthoff) Clark; grad. Sch. Nursing, U. Minn., 1939; m. Arthur Owen Hoistad, Dec. 24, 1942; children—Maradeth (Mrs. R. Searle), Jonathan, Karen (Mrs. P. Averback), Barbara (Mrs. R. Polland), Gerald, Ronald, Charles. Vis. nurse St. Paul Nursing Service, 1939-40; sch. nurse, dietitian Snead Jr. Coll., 1940-41; sch. nurse Alexandria (Minn.) Sch. System, 1942; vol. nurse Red Cross Bloodmobile, Arlington, Va., 1942-43; night supr. St. Paul Nursing Home, 1971; v.p., sec., Indsl. Enterprises, Inc., St. Paul, 1966-74; now mgmt., sales exec. Mem. exec. com. Urban Coalition, 1969-72; mem. bd. Inter Club Council, 1970-71; chmn. United Fund Sch. Com., St. Paul, 1969-71; mem. State Edn. Task Force Integrated Edn., 1969; pres. Minn. Council Chs., 1972-74; chmn. ecumenical bd., v.p. St. Paul Council Chs., 1966-68; U.S. del. World Meth. Council, London, 1966, Denver, 1971; del. World Youth Conf. Amsterdam, 1939. Bd. dirs. St. Paul Parent Tchr. Student Assn. Council, 1962-74, pres., 1968-70. Mem. Church Women United (v.p. Minn., 1970-76), P.E.O., League Women Voters, Minn. Nurses Alumni Assn. Methodist (lay speaker 1973—). Mem. Order Eastern Star (past matron). Home: 1484 Clarmar Lane St Paul MN 55113

HOKE, ZONA MEADE (MRS. VIRGIL H. HOKE), educator; b. Kermit, W.Va., Sept. 5, 1907; d. William T, and Estella (Sammons) Meade; A.B., Marshall U., 1957; m. Virgil H. Hoke, June 17, 1939; children—Joyce Roselle (Mrs. Robert Lee Deskins III), William Brent and Hilton Kent (twins). Tchr. elementary sch., Stepptown, W.Va., 1930-32; prin. Lowney (W.Va.) Sch., 1932-34; tchr., Marrowbone Sch., Kermit, W.Va., 1935-42, Kermit Grade Sch., 1943-45; prin. Burning Creek Sch., Kermit, 1945-48, Naugatuck (W.Va.) Sch., 1949-53; tchr. Lenore (W.Va.) Sch., 1953-72. Tchr. adult edn., 1966-68; tchr. Head Start program, summers 1965-66; tchr. elementary grades Dingess Sch., summers, 1969, 70; tchr. sci. Kermit High Sch., summer, 1971. Active in numerous community affairs including Heart Assn., Crippled Children, United Fund, Am. Cancer Soc., Kermit Fall Festival; co-chmn. Antique Show, Kermit, W.Va., 1970-71; vol. for tutoring disadvantaged children; sponsor Am. Folk Song Festival, 1958-65; mem. W.Va. Centennial Commn., 1960-63, Black Diamond Jubilee Commn., 1969. Recipient award 4-H Club, 1950. Mem. Nat., W.Va. edn. assns., Class Room Tchrs., P.T.A., Appalachian Poetry Guild, Am. Assn. U. Women, Women's Soc. Christian Service (charter), D.A.R. (charter mem. Jennie Wiley chpt., regent 1958-60, 72-74), Kermit Area Women's Club. Democrat. Methodist. Mem. Order Eastern Star (past worthy matron), Rebekah (past noble grand, dist. deputy pres. 1964-66, treas. 1962-72). Home: 10 Collier St Kermit WV 25674

HOLBROOK, LEONA, educator; b. Lehi, Utah, Apr. 7, 1909; d. Horace Cook and Leona (Garn) Holbrook; B.S., U. Utah, 1929; M.S., Columbia, 1935, Ed.D., 1950. Recreation dir. Kaysville, Utah, summer 1927; recreation leader Salt Lake City, summer 1928-29; recreation dir. MIA Home, Brighton, Utah, summers 1930-31; tchr. Salt Lake City schs., 1929-36; with Brigham Young U., 1936—, successively instr., asst. prof., asso. prof., 1936-42, prof., chmn. dept. phys. edn., women, 1942—. Mem. adv. bd. Nat. Folk Festival, 1958-68, mem. exec. com. 1960; state chmn. Theodore Roosevelt Centennial Commn., 1957-58. Del. World Confedn. Orgns. Teaching Professions, Rio de Janeiro, 1963, Paris, 1964, UNESCO, Chgo., 1964, Hartford, Conn., 1967, Vancouver, B.C., Can., 1967, Abidjan, 1969; chmn. UNESCO-ICHPER study in ednl. planning also dir. pilot project, Chile, 1967-68; mem.-at-large, bd. dirs. U.S. Olympic Com., 1969-73. Chmn. Provo River Park Devel. Commn., 1972—, Bi-Nat. Commn. for Profl. Exchange, U.S.A.-Mexico, 1972—; mem. tech. adv. com. Provo-Jordon River Pkwy. Authority, chmn. Provo div.; mem. planning com. Utah Gov.'s Conf. on Libraries, 1973—. Trustee, Provo Library, 1970—, chmn., 1972-73, 74—. Recipient Utah Assn. Health, Phys. Edn. and Recreation Honor award 1964. Mem. Am. Acad. Phys. Edn. (chmn. internat. relations, historian, pres. elect 1974), A.A.H.P.E.R. (pres. 1966-67, honor fellow award 1968; received S.W. Honor award 1963, McKenzie award 1969, chmn. ethics com. 1969—, Gulick award 1974), Nat., Utah edn. assns., Am. Assn. U. Women, (Distinguished Woman of Utah 1970), Am. Camping Assn., Nat. Assn. Phys. Edn. Coll. Women (pres. 1963-65, panel meetings 1965—), Western Soc. Phys. Edn. Coll. Women (pres. 1959-62), Utah Recreation and Parks Assn. (Distinguished Service award 1962; legislative com. 1964-66), Intermountain Assn. Phys. Edn. Coll. Women, Brigham Young U. Edn. Assn., Am. Acad. Sports Medicine, Internat. Assn. Phys. Edn. and Sports Girls and Women, Utah Library Trustees Assn. (chmn.-elect 1973—), Delta Kappa Gamma (chmn. membership com. 1942-63), Delta Psi Kappa (research awards com. 1960, patroness 1962—), Kappa Delta Pi. Contbr. articles to profl. publs. and jours. Home: 1314 N Jordan Av RFD 1 Provo UT 84601

HOLCOMB, ALICE KRIGSMAN MCCAFFERY (MRS. H. LAWRENCE HOLCOMB), artist; b. N.Y.C., Oct. 7, 1906; d. Leo and Lettie (Pressfield) Krigsman; B.A., Smith Coll., 1927; m. Richard S. McCaffery, Jr., Dec. 7, 1929 (div. 1949); m. 2d, H. Lawrence Holcomb, Nov. 29, 1949. One-man shows Berzansky Galleries, N.Y.C., 1962, All-Souls Unitarian Ch., N.Y.C., 1963, Copley Soc., Boston, 1966; 1st Ch., Boston, 1968, Longboat Key Art Center, Sarasota, Fla., 1971; exhibited group shows Nat. Arts Club, N.Y.C., 1962-71, Nat. Acad., N.Y.C., 1962, 68, Rockport (Mass.) Art Assn., 1966-74, North Shore Arts Assn., Gloucester, Mass., 1966-74, invitational at Copley Gallery, Boston, 1968, Allied Arts Am., N.Y.C., 1967, Am. Artists Profl. League, N.Y.C., 1968, 70-72, Acad. Artists Assn., Springfield, Mass., 1967-74, Cambridge Art Assn., 1968-70, Sarasota (Fla.) Art Assn., 1971-74, Cape Coral Nat. Art Show, 1974, Butler Inst. Am. Art, Cleve., 1974, Nat. Assn. Women Artists, N.Y.C., 1962-74; exhibiting mem. Harbor Gallery, Rockport, Mass.; represented permanent collections Smith Coll. Mus. Art, Emerson Coll., Boston, also pvt. collections. Mem. governing bd. Rockport Art Assn., 1969-73. Recipient Nat. Arts Club Grumbacher prize, 1963, Sam Flex award, 1964, hon. mention, 1965, Catherine Lorillard Wolfe Art Club gold medal, 1963; Westchester Art Soc. award of merit, 1963; featured Prize-Winning Paintings, Book IV. Mem. Nat. Assn. Women Artists, Am. Artists Profl. League, Sarasota Art Assn., Catherine Lorillard Wolfe Art Club (dir. 1964, v.p. 1965), Royal Soc. Arts, London, Hudson Valley Art Assn. Unitarian (chmn. art com. 1963). Address: 101 Benjamin Franklin Dr Sarasota FL 33577 (summer) 11 Main St Rockport MA 01966

HOLCOMB, BEVERLY J., social anthropologist, educator; b. Springdale, Ark.; d. Joe Latimer and Elva M. (McKeown) Holcomb; B.A. summa cum laude, John Brown U., 1950; M.Ed., U. Ark., 1957; M.A., Brandeis U., 1965; Ed.D., U. Ark., 1970. Tchr. pub. schs., Spring Creek, Ark., 1945-48; radio announcer John Brown U., Radio Sta. KUOA, Sidoam Springs, Ark., 1945-50; descriptive linguist Mexican br. Summer Inst. Linguistics, Chiapas, 1950-51, Peruvian br., Puerto Isango, 1951-55; co-dir. Peruvian Ministry Edn., Inst. for Bilingual Indian Tchr. Trainees Peruvian Jungle, Lima and Pucallpa, 1955-60; field anthropologist Brandeis U., Montserrat, B.W.I., 1963; area field anthropologist Research Inst. for Study of Man, Sorata, Bolivia, S.Am., 1965-66; dir. counseling Opportunities Industrialization Center, Little Rock, 1966-68; specialist gerontology U. Ark. Extension Service, 1969—. Mem. sec. exec. com. Wycliffe Bible Translators-Summer Inst. Linguistics, 1955-57. Mem. Ark. Gov.'s Adv. Com. Handicapped, 1972—, Adv. Com. on Aging, 1972—. Mem. Sr. Advs. Internat., Am. Gerontol. Soc., Am. Home Econs. Assn., Ark. Wildlife Fedn. Author: Problems of the Aged in Craighead County, Ark.; Project Concern-A Call to Coordinators; Happiness-A-Do-It-Yourself Guide; Annotated Bibliography for Training the Disadvantaged; Course of Study Guides for Bilingual Indian Teachers. Home: 2 Yaqui Point North Little Rock AR 72116 Office: PO Box 391 Little Rock AR 72203

HOLCOMB, CAROLYN JENSEN (MRS. THOMAS JOEL HOLCOMB), journalist; b. Davenport, Ia., Nov. 18, 1940; d. Charles Howard and Catherine Mary (Cooper) Jensen; B.A., U. Ia., 1962; m. Thomas Joel Holcomb, May 5, 1962; children—Scott, Kellie. With Waterloo (Ia.) Daily Courier, 1964-72, reporter, columnist, 1964-72. Mem. P.E.O. (treas. 1968), Phi Beta Kappa, Gamma Phi Beta, Alpha Lambda Delta, Theta Sigma Phi. Presbyn. Home: 5 Timothy Sirkl Coal Valley IL 61240

HOLCOMB, DOROTHY TURNER, pub. relations exec.; b. Roanoke, Va., June 15, 1924; d. Wiley Bryant and Lena Mae (Gray) Turner; student Coronet Bus. Sch., Roanoke, 1943; interior decorator certificate N.Y. Sch. Interior Design, 1953; student U. Miami, 1962-63; m. Joseph E. Baxter, Aug. 1, 1944 (dec. Nov. 1944); m. 2d, G. William Holcomb, May 8, 1948 (div. 1962). Exec. sec. Am.'s Jr. Miss Pageant, Mobile, Ala., 1962; exec. asst. to pres. Gilbert Marketing Group, Inc., N.Y.C., 1963-65; br. dirs. Heart Assn., Miami, Fla., 1965-66; publicist in charge on-air promotion Screen Gems, Hollywood, Cal., 1966-68; publicity dir. Mus. of Sci./Planetarium, Miami, 1968-71, Bryna Cosmetics, Inc., Miami, 1973-74; free-lance publicist, 1971-73; pub. relations/communications ECKANKAR, Sri Darwin Gross, Las Vegas, Nev., 1974—. Mem. Publicists Guild, Internat. Alliance Theatrical Stage Employees, Moving Picture Machine Operators, Women in Communications. Home: 2619 Sherwood Las Vegas NV 89109 Office: PO Box 5325 Las Vegas NV 89102

HOLCOMBE, MAXINE BOGGAN (MRS. THOMPSON A. HOLCOMBE, JR.), educator; b. Memphis; d. Marvin Brooks and Josephine (Shea) Boggan; B.S., Delta State Coll., 1932; M.A., George Peabody Coll., 1933; m. Nathan House, 1937 (dec. 1947); m. 2d Thompson A. Holcombe, Jr., Apr. 22, 1950. Faculty art Delta State Coll., Cleveland, Miss., 1933-35, 60—, asso. prof., 1968—; comml. artist, advt. mgr., Memphis, 1935-39; art agt. Am. Authors and Artists, N.Y.C., 1939-43; dir. art Greenville (Miss.) City Schs., 1944-60. Designer, dir. Greenville Christmas parade, 1952-60; cons. Christmas parades Cleveland C. of C., 1966, Leland, Miss., 1967; mem. summer staff Miss. State U., 1949, state sch. systems evaluation com., 1960—; participant First Conf. on Adminstrn. Fine Arts sponsored by Ohio State U. at N.Y. U., 1967; state chmn. Youth Art Month, 1968-70; mem. Cleveland Arts Council. Bd. dirs. Cleveland Crosstie Arts Council. Exhibited one man show Miss. Art Assn., Jackson, Capitol Savs. & Loan, Jackson, 1972; exhibited Delta State Coll. Shows, McCarty Art Gallery, Monteagle, Tenn., Crosstie Art Festival, Cleveland, U. Miss. Recipient Nat. 3d pl. award for promotion Am. Art Week Miss., Am. Artists Profl. League, 1966; Outstanding Alumnus award Delta State Coll., 1969; named Outstanding Civic Contbr., Miss. Federated Women's Clubs, 1972; Distinguished Pub. Service award Cleveland Jr. C. of C., 1973. Research grantee to study art appreciation for elementary schs., 1969-70. Mem. Nat. League Am. Pen Women (br. pres. 1968-69), Nat., Miss. (pres. 1968-69, Miss. youth art month chmn.) art edn. assns., Southeastern Art Assn., Whistle Stop Theatre, Miss. Classroom Tchrs. Assn., Miss. Edn. Assn., Kappa Delta, Delta Kappa Gamma, Kappa Pi. Designer, supr. booth assembly for Miss., Miami Nat. Conv. N.E.A., 1965; illustrator (with Nathan House): Games the World Around, 1941; designer, dir. Children's Circus Studio, Miss. Arts Festival, 1972. Contbr. illustrations: Nat. Edn. Jour., Miss. Edn. Advance; contbg. author, cons. Handbook on Elementary Art for Mississippi Schools, 1961. Home: 209 S First Av Cleveland MS 38732

HOLDEN, GEORGIE ELIZABETH HOUGH, writer; b. nr. Lucketts, Va.; d. John Wesley and Mary (Barrett) Hough; student Blue Ridge Coll.; B.A., Bridgewater Coll.; postgrad. summer schs. U. Md., Madison Coll.; A.A. with high honors, Prince George's Community Coll., 1973; m. John Hopkins Holden; (dec. July 1961); children—Patricia (Mrs. Vincent (Squitieri), Mary (Mrs. Harold J. Domich). Tchr. pub. schs., Montgomery County, Md.; tchr. English, Wicomico High Sch., Wicomico Church, Va.; sec. Am. Legion, Washington; clerical asst. Higher Edn. div., Dept. Health, Edn. and Welfare, Washington; sec. Gallaudet Coll., Washington; pub. relations officer; dir. pub. relations, 1960-69, ret.; free-lance writer, 1970—; former asst. Stars and Stripes-The Nat. Tribune. Publicity dir. 5th Internat. Congress Philosophy, Washington, 1957; pub. relations chmn. Workshop Identification Researchable Vocational Rehab. Problems of Deaf, Washington, 1960, Workshop for Catholic Personnel for Deaf, Washington, 1961, Workshop for Episcopal Workers for Deaf, Washington, 1961; co-chmn. pub. relations Internat. Congress Edn. of Deaf, Washington, 1963; publicity chmn. Workshop for Luths. on Deafness and Rehab., Washington, 1963; mem. nat. adv. bd. Am. Security Council, 1970—. Mem. Am. Assn. Ret. Persons, Smithsonian Assos., Am. Legion Aux. Clubs: Republican Congressional (charter), Police and Fire Unit 29, Nat. Capital Aux. Vets. World War I (sr. v.p. 1968, group v.p. 1973-74). Hon. citizen Boys Town, Recipient award of merit Gallaudet Coll., 1969, Congl. award for vol. assistance, dedicated service and commitment Republicans of 93d Congress, 1973. Mem. Internat. Platform Assn., Nat. Assn. of the Deaf, Nat. Trust for Historic Preservation, Am. College Pub. Relations Assn. (mem. hospitality com. nat. conv. 1960, publicity chmn. Mason-Dixon dist. conf. Washington 1961, idea cons. dist. conf. Williamsburg, Va. 1964; dist. sec. 1964-66, planning com. mem. dist. sec. 1964-66, planning com. mem. dist. confs. 1964-66, registrar dist. conf. 1965, nominating com. 1968), Am. Newspaper Women's Club, Inc. (publicity com. 1966-67, ad hoc membership com. 1967-68), English-Speaking Union, Lancaster-Northumberland Edn. Assn. (chmn. pub. relations com. 1946-48), Nat. Religious Publicity Council, Ednl. Press Assn. Am. (steering com. Washington chpt. 1962-63, 66-67, sec.-publicity chmn., editor Edpress Notes 1967-68), Coll. Sports Information Dirs. Am., Prince George's County Mental Health Soc., Md. Park Improvement Area Assn. (sec. 1963), English-Speaking Union of Commonwealth, Delta Zeta (publicity co-chmn. scholarship benefits Gallaudet Coll., 1964-69). Republican. Baptist (pres. adult women's class 1963-66, pres. faith workers class 1963-68). Club: U.S. Senatorial (founding). Mem. adv. editorial bd. The Bridgewater Alumnus, 1960-66; editor Gallaudet Record, 1963-69. Contbr. articles to profl. publs. Home: 6402 A St Capitol Heights MD 20027

HOLDEN, MARY ANN, educator; b. Syracuse, N.Y., May 1, 1934; d. James Phillip and Emma Josephine (Kunkel) Holden; B.A., Cal. State U., 1956, postgrad., 1957-74; postgrad. Coll. Notre Dame, 1962-66. Tchr. speech and English, dir. forensics Jefferson Union High Sch. Dist., Daly City, Cal., 1957—, Westmoor High Sch., since 1957—. Mem. Dist. Certificated Employee Council, 1968-74, chmn., 1971-74. Mem. Am. Assn. U. Women, Nat. Council Tchrs. English, N.E.A., Cal., Westmoor (chmn. 1959-60, 62-63, 68-69, 72-74) tchrs. assns., San Mateo County Tchrs. Assn., Jefferson Union High Sch. Dist. Tchrs. Assn. (pres. 1970-71, 74-75), Speech Communication Assn. (mem. legislative council 1972—), Western Speech Communication Assn. (mem. legislative assembly 1970, 71, 72—), Cal. Speech Assn. (charter mem.), Cal. High Sch. Speech Assn., Golden Gate Speech Assn. (pres. 1963-64, sec. 1961-62, 68-69, 69-70, 72-74), Smithsonian Assos., Internat. Platform Assn. Home: 434 Firecrest Av Pacifica CA 94044 Office: Westmoor High Sch 131 Westmoor Av Daly City CA 94015

HOLDER, ANGELA RODDEY, lawyer, educator; b. Rock Hill, S.C., Mar. 13, 1938; d. John T. and Angela M. (Fisher) Roddey; student Radcliffe Coll., 1955-56; B.A., Newcomb Coll., 1958; postgrad. Faculty of Laws, King's Coll., London, Eng., 1957-58; J.D., Tulane U., 1960; div.; 1 son, John Thomas Roddey Holder. Admitted to La. and S.C. bars, 1960; counsel Roddey, Sumwalt & Carpenter, Rock Hill, 1960—; atty. criminal div. New Orleans Legal Aid Bur., 1961-62; counsel York County (S.C.) Family Ct., 1962-64; instr. polit. sci. Winthrop Coll., Rock Hill, 1964—. Mem. Rock Hill Sch. Bd., 1967-68. Bd. dirs. Family Planning Clinic, chmn., 1970-73. Mem. Am., S.C. (medico-legal com. 1973—), La. bar assns. Democrat. Episcopalian. Author: The Meaning of the Constitution, 1968; Principles of Medical Malpractice Law, 1974. Contbg. editor Prism mag. A.M.A. Home: 741 Schuyler Dr Rock Hill SC 29730 Office: 235 E Main St Rock Hill SC 29730

HOLDER, MARYLYNN JEANETTE, editor; b. Owensboro, Ky., Sept. 22; d. Cicero N. and Willie Jane (Talbott) Moorman; student Los Angeles City Coll., 1959, 60, W. Cal. at Los Angeles, 1969, 70. With So. Cal. Gas Co. (formerly Pacific Lighting Service), 1956—, editor employee newspaper, 1967-72, asst. publs. supr. employee publs., 1972—; feature writer Rodger McDonald Newspapers, 1960-71; women's editor Cal. Eagle, 1960; stringer Johnson Publs., 1959-70. Exec.; sec. San Diego br. N.A.A.C.P., 1956-57; mem. pub. relations bd. Far Western Regional Urban League, Los Angeles, 1960-63. Vol. John F. Kennedy campaigns; exec. sec. San Diego Jimmy Roosevelt Democratic Club, 1956. Recipient resolutions Urban League, 1959, Los Angeles City Council, 1967, Cal. State Assembly, 1971; spl. honors achievement in journalism Nat. Council Negro Women, 1961; named Woman of Year for journalism Nat. Council Bus. and Profl. Women, 1970. Mem. So. Cal. Indsl. Editor's Assn. (officer-at-large 1969-71), Nat. Fedn. Press Women (treas. 1970-72, 2d v.p. 1972-74), Cal. Press Women (treas. 1968-69, publs. dir. 1973-74). Home: 1457 Miller Way Hollywood CA 90069 Office: 720 W 8th St Los Angeles CA 90017

HOLDRIDGE, BARBARA (MRS. LAWRENCE B. HOLDRIDGE), phonograph record co. exec.; b. N.Y.C., July 26, 1929; d. Herbert L. and Bertha (Gold) Cohen; A.B., Hunter Coll., 1950; m. Lawrence B. Holdridge, Oct. 9, 1959; 2 children. Asst. editor Liveright Pub. Corp., N.Y.C., 1950-52; co-founder Caedmon Records, Inc., N.Y.C., 1952, partner, 1952-60, pres., 1960-62, treas., 1962-70; pres. Caedmon Records, 1970—. Co-founder v.p. Shakespeare Rec. Soc., Inc., N.Y.C., 1960—, Theatre Rec. Soc., Inc., N.Y.C., 1964—; co-founder History Rec. Soc., Inc., N.Y.C., 1964, pres., 1964-70. Lectr. on Ammi Phillips, 1959—. Recipient Am. Shakespeare Festival award, 1962, certificate of appreciation Mayor of N.Y.C., 1972; named to Hunter Coll. Hall of Fame, 1972. Mem. Phi Beta Kappa Assos. Contbr. articles to Antiques, Art in Am. Home: Stemmer House Caves Rd Owings Mills MD 21117 Office: 505 8th Av New York City NY 10018

HOLIFIELD, BETTY LOU, librarian; b. Forest, Miss., Mar. 15, 1939; d. Mallou and Curlee (Houston) Holifield; B.S., Fla. A. and M. U., 1962; postgrad. Drexel Inst. Tech., 1965; M.S., U. Mich., 1967. Head librarian Utica (Miss.) Jr. Coll., 1962-63; law librarian Genesee County Law Library, Flint, Mich., 1963-67; tech. services librarian Gen. Motors Inst., Flint, 1967—. Cons. Genesee Meml. Hosp. Med. Library, also Walter Winchester Hosp., Flint, 1964. Mem. Am., Mich. (mem. newcomers com. 1965) library assns., Spl. Libraries Assn. (mem. recruitment com., engring. div. 1973), Bus. and Profl. Women's Club, Indsl. Bus. Girls, Urban League (mem. planning com. 1973-74), Democrat. Episcopalian. Mem. Alpha Beta Alpha. Clubs: Flint Industrial Executives, Flint Library. Home: 6825 Orange Lane Flint MI 48505 Office: 1700 W 3d Av Flint MI 48502

HOLLAND, DOROTHY ANDERSON, editor, writer; b. Cordova, Tenn., Dec. 29, 1922; d. William Robert and Eddie Blanche (Hamner) Anderson; B.S., B.A. in Journalism, Tex. Woman's U., 1944; M.Ed., Tex. A. and M. U., 1968; m. Curtis R. Holland, Feb. 24, 1945; 1 dau., Cheryl Anne. Publs. editor Tex. Agrl. Extension Service, co-editor Tex. Agrl. Progress, 1958—; free-lance writing, advt. Mem. Am. Assn. Agrl. Coll. Editors, Tex. Woman's U. Alumnae Assn. (pres. 1972—), Phi Kappa Phi, Epsilon Sigma Phi. Contbr. numerous articles to farm mags. Home: 514 Kyle St College Station TX 77840 Office: Services Bldg College Station TX 77840

HOLLAND, EDNA OLIVE, housekeeping hosp. adminstr.; b. Perth, Ont., Can., Apr. 6, 1908; d. John Edmund and Jane M. (Morrison) Newell; student Canadian Hosp. Deptl. Mgmt. Course, 1967, courses in supervision Ottawa U., 1970-71, teaching and exec. housekeeping courses George Brown Coll., Toronto, 1972; m. John Harold Watt, June 29, 1929 (dec.); children—John Clifford Watt, Joel Harold Watt; m. 2d, Kenneth Blackmore Holland, May 21, 1949 (dec.). Mgr. splty. shop, 1942-43; with Canadian Treasury Dept., 1945-47; dept. mgr. Robert Bruce & Co., 1947-49; dist. mgr. Spirella Co., Kingston and Ottawa, 1952-55, div. mgr., 1956-58; dir. housekeeping services Kingston Psychiat. Hosp., 1958—. Mem. Canadian Adminstrv. Housekeepers Assn., Nat. Exec. Housekeepers Assn., Ont. Hosp. Housekeepers Assn., Kingston Bus. and Profl. Women's Club (past pres.). Home: 23 Algonquin Terrace Kingston ON Canada

HOLLAND, EVELYN FAUCETTE (MRS. SHERMAN W. HOLLAND, JR.), printing, advt. and pub. relations firm exec.; b. Lillington, N.C., Sept. 11, 1927; d. Henry Bethune and Virgina McRorie (Stegall) Faucette; student Charron-Williams Comml. Coll., 1946, U. Miami, 1947; m. Sherman William Holland, Jr., Apr. 28, 1946; children—Karen (Mrs. Charles W. Shaffer, Sr.), Sherman William Jr., Michael Edward. With Falco Printing, Inc., Miami, Fla., 1962—, Falco & Assos., Inc., Miami, 1968—. Commr., Hialeah Housing Authority, 1968-72; mem. Fla. Commn. on Status of Women, 1972—; chmn. Dade County Personnel Adv. Bd., 1970—, Model Cities Released Employment Bd., 1972-73; pres. local 11, Graphic Arts Internat. Union, 1965-67. Mem. Dade County Dem. Exec. Com., 1970—, treas., 1971—; mem. Dade County Dem. Com., 1970—. Recipient service award VA Hosp., Miami, Fla., 1970, pub. service award for sr. citizen service State Vets, Service Office, Hialeah, 1972; Holland Hall sr. citizens' housing project named in her honor, 1972. Home: 330 W 54th St Hialeah FL 33012 Office: 675 NW 90th St Miami FL 33150

HOLLAND, HARRIET ELAINE, journalist; b. Camden, S.C., Jan. 8, 1943; d. Edward English and Ida Elizabeth (McCaskill) Holland; student Winthrop Coll., 1961-63; B.A., U. S.C., 1965, M.A., 1967. City reporter Camden (S.C.) Chronicle, 1964-66; press sec. to U.S. Senator Strom Thurmond, 1967-70; asst. editorial dir. U.S. Senate Internal Security Subcom., Washington, 1970—. Recipient Scholarship, Winthrop Coll., 1961-62; Am. Newspaper Fund fellow, 1967. Mem. Women in Communication, Am. Newspapers Women's Club, U.S. Senate Press Secs. Assn., Theta Sigma Phi. Episcopalian. Home: 128 C St NE Washington DC 20002 Office: 3224 New Senate Office Bldg Washington DC 20510

HOLLAND, JIMMIE C.B., psychiatrist; b. Forney, Tex., Apr. 9, 1928; d. Clifford C. and Velma (Cox) Coker; B.A., Baylor U., 1948, M.D., 1952; m. James F. Holland, July 7, 1956; children—Steven M., Mary S., Sally A., Peter A., David C. Intern St. Louis City Hosp., 1952; psychiat. resident Malcolm Bliss Mental Health Center, Washington U. Sch. Medicine, 1953-54, Mass. Gen. Hosp., 1954-55; asso. clin. prof. dept. psychiatry State U. N.Y. at Buffalo Sch. Medicine, 1958-69, asso. prof., 1970-73; clin. dir. E.J. Meyer Meml. Hosp., Buffalo, 1968, dir., 1970-72; Nat. Inst. Mental Health cons., USSR, 1972-73; asso. clin. prof. psychiatry Montefiore Hosp., Albert Einstein Sch. Medicine, Bronx, N.Y., 1973—. Diplomate Am. Bd. Neurology and Psychiatry. Fellow Am. Psychiat. Assn. (pres. Western N.Y. Dist. br. 1968), Alpha Omega Alpha. Contbr. articles to profl. lit. Home: 31 Mamaroneck Rd Scarsdale NY 10583 Office: 211 E 210th St Bronx NY 10467

HOLLAND, LEILA DUNPHY (MRS. ROBERT HOLLAND), advt., pub. relations exec., free lance writer; b. Seattle; d. Rudolph and Lilly (Miller) Hansson; student U. Wash., 1953, 1955-56; m. Fred Dunphy, June 1942 (dec.); children—Kurtis Frederick, Lawrence Michael; m. 2d, Robert Holland, Aug. 5, 1972; children—Robert Victor, Victoria Anne, Kathleen Marie, Mary Therese, Francene Johanna. With The Taskett Agy., Seattle, 1952-56; copywriter, asst. account exec. Cole & Weber, Seattle, 1956-57; pub. information cons., editor Seattle Transit System, 1957-60; owner, editor publs. Northwest Advt. Agy., Seattle, also Bellevue, 1960-72; free lance writer, 1952—. Pub. relations cons. to bd. St. Nicholas Sch., Seattle, 1966-70. Bd. dirs. Totem council Girl Scouts U.S.A., 1955-57; neighborhood chmn. United Good Neighbors, Seattle, 1962—; mem. pub. relations com. Wash. Heart Assn., 1961-62, com. chmn., 1962-64. Recipient numerous awards including Sugar Plum award Wash. Press Women, 1961, Hon. Mention, Seattle Copy Club, 1968, Certificate of Merit, Los Angeles Advt. Women, 1965, Complete Campaign award, 1966. Mem. Pacific Northwest Indsl. Editors Assn. (pres. 1961), Seattle Advt. Club, Pub. Relations Round Table Seattle, World Affairs Council, UN Assn., Am. Woman in Radio and TV, Nat. Acad. TV Arts and Scis., Wash. Press Women, Nat. Fedn. Press Women. Club: Seattle Tennis. Home: 2854 116th NE Bellevue WA 98004

HOLLAND, MARION LUCEINE GAINES (MRS. WILLIAM FLETCHER HOLLAND), educator; b. Columbia, S.C., Sept. 21, 1925; d. Marion Little and Eloise (Cave) Gaines; student U. S.C., 1941-43, M.B.A., 1964; B.S., U. N.C. 1945; m. Thomas Clark Firzgerald, Jr., June 7, 1947; children—Thomas Clark III, Gaines Marion, Carolyn Sarah; m. 2d. John Thomas Rice, June 19, 1963 (dec. July 1969); m. 3d, William Fletcher Holland, Nov. 26, 1970. Staff accountant Peat Marwick Mitchell Co., Greensboro, N.C., 1943-47, Darmody Todd & Co., Boston, 1947-48; accountant J.P. Stevens &

Co., Greensboro, 1948-51; partner Fitzgerald & Co., C.P.A.'s, Columbia, 1951-63; controller Cardinal Chemical Co., Columbia, 1964-66; head accounting dept. Palmer Coll., Columbia, 1966-70; head accounting dept. Midlands Tech. Edn. Center, 1970—. Chmn. finance com. Girl Scouts Am., Columbia, 1960-63. Nominated Young Woman of Year, Jr. C. of C., 1960. C.P.A., S.C., N.C. Mem. Nat. Assn. Accountants (dir.), Nat. Assn. Security Dealers, Am. Inst. C.P.A.'s, S.C. Assn. C.P.A.'s, Phi Beta Kappa, Beta Gamma Sigma. Episcopalian. Club: Zonta (treas. 1965-67, mem. bd. dirs. Columbia chpt. 1965-68). Home: 4300 Chicora St Columbia SC 29206

HOLLAND, MARJORIE LEE DILDY (MRS. KENNETH A. HOLLAND), educator; b. Hope, Ark.; d. Clell A. and Lucille (King) Dildy; student Lindenwood Coll., 1941; B.S. in Edn., U. Ark., 1945, M.S., 1948, Ed.D., 1963; m. Kenneth A. Holland, July 11, 1948; 1 son, Michael William. Tchr. English, E. High Sch., Memphis, 1948-54, 56-59; instr. English, Ark. A. and M. Coll., Monticello, 1959-61; grad. asst. U. Ark., Fayetteville, 1961-63; faculty Northeastern State Coll., Tahlequah, Okla., 1963—, prof. English, 1966—, acting chmn. div. communications, 1971-72. Mem. Modern Lang. Assn., Am. Assn. U. Women (br. v.p. 1967-68), Okla. Edn. Assn. (sec. local unit 1969-70), Nat. Okla. councils tchrs. English, Conf. English Edn., Pi Beta Phi, Kappa Delta Pi (chpt. pres. 1962-63), Delta Kappa Gamma (chpt. pres. 1973—), Phi Delta Kappa. Episcopalian. Clubs: Fortnightly Study (v.p. 1966-68), Muskogee Pi Beta Phi Alumnae. Home: 407 Janet St Tahlequah OK 74464

HOLLAND, NANCY HINKLE (MRS. C. PHILLIP HOLLAND), physician, educator; b. Paris, Ky.; d. Charles Thomas and Susan (Buckner) Hinkle; B.S., U. Denver, 1949; M.D., U. Louisville, 1954; m. C. Phillip Holland, July 3, 1961. Intern, Kings County Hosp., Bklyn., 1954-55; resident in pediatrics Cin. Children's Hosp., 1955-57; fellow Children's Hosp. Research Found., Cin., 1957-60, sr. research asst., 1960-62, research asso., 1962-64; asst. prof. pediatrics U. Cin. Coll. Medicine, 1962-64; asst. prof. pediatrics U. Cin. Coll. Medicine, 1962-64; asst. prof. U. Ky. Med. Center, Lexington, Ky., 1964-67, asso. prof., 1967-72, prof., 1972—. Cons., Ky. Kidney Disease Inst., 1972—; mem. bacteriuria com. Nat. Kidney Found., 1973. Fellow Am. Acad. Pediatrics; mem. Soc. for Pediatric Research, Am. Soc. Nephrology, Am. Soc. Pediatric Nephrology (pediatric hemodialysis and transplantation com. 1973), Am. Pediatric Soc. Contbr. articles to med. and sci. publs. Home: Route 5 Paris KY 40361

HOLLANDER, HELEN CORNELIA ESKESEN (MRS. RICHARD I. HOLLANDER), author, artist; b. Perth Amboy, N.J.; d. Thoge Reinberg and Kate (Kjeldsen) Eskesen; B.A., Skidmore Coll., 1935-37; student Art Students League, 1935, Rutgers, 1937, Columbia, 1937-38, Chgo. Art Inst., 1939, Am. U., 1962, D.C. Tchrs. Coll., 1963; m. Richard I. Hollander, Mar. 7, 1953; 1 son, Jackson R. Chief med. artist Inter-Am. Affairs, Washington, 1943-45; visual aids specialist Rural Electrification, Washington, 1945-48; editorial asst. Am. Statis. Assn., Washington, 1948-49; chief artist A.R.C., Washington, 1949-51; woman's editor Washington Daily News, 1952-54; pvt. art tchr., Washington, 1954-61; roving art supr. D.C. Pub. Schs., 1963-64; head start project dir. Office Equal Opportunity, N.Y.C., 1964-65; dir. Cleveland Park Creative Action Center, Washington, 1969-70. Author: Portable Workshop for Pre-School Teachers, 1966; Creative Opportunities for the Mentally Retarded, 1971. Exhibited in one-man shows Dyer Gallery, 1962, S St. Gallery, Washington, 1963, Allen Gallery, Washington, 1964, Hollander Gallery, Washington, 1969; exhibited in group shows including Smithsonian Instn., Nat. Gallery Fine Arts, D.C. Arts Club, Artists Mart, also Skidmore Coll., Saratoga Springs, N.Y. Mem. Am. Assn. U. Women, League Women Voters, Soc. Washington Artists, Artists Equity. Home: 3502 Macomb St NW Washington DC 20016 Office: 3614 Newark St NW Washington DC 20016

HOLLEMAN, MARIAN ARNOTT PATTERSON (MRS. W. ROY HOLLEMAN), univ. librarian; b. Toronto, Ont., Can.; d. Arnott Martin and Etta (Freeman) Patterson; came to U.S., 1961; B.A., Victoria U., 1945; M.L.S., U. Toronto, 1946, M.A., 1948; m. W. Roy Holleman, June 27, 1961 (dec. Nov. 1969). Asst. librarian Acad. Medicine, Toronto, 1946-50, chief librarian, 1951-61; reference librarian U. So. Cal. Doheny Library, 1961-62; librarian U. Cal. at Los Angeles Biomed. Library, 1962-63; librarian Bishop's Sch., La Jolla, Cal., 1963-66; asst. librarian San Diego Coll. for Women, 1966-69, asst. prof. library sci., 1970-74, asso. prof., 1974—, librarian, 1970-73, univ. librarian James S. Copley Library, 1973—. Recipient Murray Gottlieb prize essay award Med. Library Assn., 1957. Mem. Cal. Library Assn., Am. Assn. U. Profs., Spl. Libraries Assn. (pres. San Diego chpt. 1969, editor chpt. bull.), Victoria Coll. Alumnae Assn., Delta Epsilon Sigma, Phi Delta Pi, Phi Alpha Theta. Editor: Sci. Meetings. Contbr. articles to profl. publs. Home: 2069 Sea View Av Del Mar CA 92014 Office: U San Diego James S Copley Library Alcala Park San Diego CA 92110

HOLLERORTH, BARBARA ELIZABETH (MRS. HUGO J. HOLLERORTH), clergywoman; b. Cedar Falls, Ia., Sept. 21, 1926; d. Winfield and Elizabeth (Moulton) Scott; student U. Ia., 1944-46, U. Chgo., 1948; B.D., Chgo. Theol. Sem., 1952; D.Ministry, Andover-Newton Theol. Sem., 1974—; m. Hugo John Hollerorth, Sept. 15, 1948; children—Rebecca, Rachel. Dir. week-day nursery sch.-family life program Plymouth Congl. Ch., Maywood, Ill., 1951-53; ordained to ministry Congl. Ch., 1952; accepted as minister in asso. fellowship Unitarian Universalist Assn., 1972; minister (with husband) Christian edn. Hinsdale (Ill.) Union Ch., 1953-56; asst. minister First Parish Ch. Unitarian-Universalist, Lexington, Mass., 1969-72; practicing psychotherapist, marriage counselor Boston Psychiat. Assos., 1972—; pastoral counselor Middleton (Mass.) Pastoral Counseling Center, 1974—. Mem. Clergymen's Consultation Service for Problem Pregnancies, 1969-71, bd. dirs., 1971. Bd. dirs. Homophile Community Health Service, Boston. Mem. Liberal Religious Edn. Dirs. Assn. (chmn. profl. concerns com. 1971-72), Phi Beta Kappa. Author: The Haunting House, 1974. Asso. editor Respond mag., 1968. Home: 3 Patton Dr Natick MA 01760

HOLLEY, BETTY BROOKS, home economist; b. Martin, Tenn., Oct. 29, 1944; d. Benjamin Franklin and Wilma Leon (Crittendon) Brooks; B.S. in Home Econs. (Farm Bur. scholar) U. Tenn., 1966; M.A. in Counseling, U. Ala., 1968; m. William Henry Holley, May 28, 1967. Extension home agt. Coop. Extension Service, Centreville, Ala., 1966-67; rehab. counselor Partlow State Sch. and Hosp., Tuscaloosa, Ala., 1968-69; specialist ednl. methods Coop. Extension Service, Auburn, (Ala.) U., 1969—. Chmn. of day Auburn U. Newcomers and Campus Club, 1971. Dairy princess and spokesman Am. Dairy Assn., 1965. Mem. Nat., Ala. edn. assns., Am., Ala. home econs. assns., Ala. Consumer Assn. Republican. Baptist. (mem. women's missionary union). Home: 1020 Rustic Ridge Rd Auburn AL 36830

HOLLIDAY, VIVIAN LOYREA, educator; b. Manning, S.C., Feb. 25, 1935; d. Louis Arlo and Ellen Loyrea (Brewer) Holliday; B.A. (fellow), Winthrop Coll., 1957; M.A. (fellow), U. Mo., 1959; Ph.D. (fellow), U. N.C., 1961. Instr. Coll. Wooster (O.), 1961-63, asst. prof., 1963-66, asso. prof., 1966-69, prof., 1969-70, Aylesworth prof. Latin, 1970—, chmn. dept. Greek and Latin, 1967—. Mem. personnel com. Am. Sch. Classical Studies, Athens, Greece. Fulbright fellow, Italy, summer 1965; Nat. Endowment Humanities grantee, summer 1970. Mem. Am. Philol. Assn., Classical Assn. Mid-West and South, Modern Greek Studies Assn. Author: Pompey in Cicero's Correspondence and Lucan's Civil War, 1969. Home: 236 Spring St Wooster OH 44691

HOLLIHAN, M(ATILDA) RAMONA GRAIEWSKI, bus. exec.; b. Hurley, Wis.; d. Stanley John and Theresa (Sloma) Graiewski; R.N., St. Mary's Sch. Nursing, Duluth, Minn., 1934; student Coll. St. Scholastica, Duluth, 1934; B.S., U. Minn., 1937; m. John Philip Hollihan, Jr., Nov. 30, 1939; children—Mary Kathleen (Mrs. Francois Marie Rolland), Mary Sheila (Mrs. John Elliot), John Philip III. Asst. supt. nurses U. Minn. Hosps., instr. U. Minn. Sch. Medicine, 1937-40; mgr. to mng. dir. Chem. Trade Internat., Passaic, N.J., 1962-67; pres. Chemtrade Internat., Inc., Passaic, 1967—; owner Casa Ramona Imports; dir. Chems. Venture Analysis (Guatemala), Textile Venture Analysis (El Salvador and Venezuela). Mem. India, Pakistan, Ceylon and Burma Shipping Conf.; adviser Corporacion Costarricense de Financiamiento Industrial S.A. (Costa Rica), 1964-65. Mem. Am. Nurses Assn., Nat. League Nursing Edn., Choate Sch. Mothers Assn., Vassar, U. Pa. parents coms., Alpha Tau Delta. Patentee in field. Home: 523 Old Woods Rd Wyckoff NJ 07481 Office: 40 Passaic Av Passaic NJ 07055

HOLLINGER, HELEN WETHERBEE, artist; b. Indpls., Oct. 12, 1913; d. Frederic and Madalyn (Brooks) Wetherbee; grad. Herron Sch. Art, Indpls., 1935; m. Harry Mills Hollinger, Oct. 9, 1937 (div. Mar. 1963); 1 son, Drew. Fashion dir. display dept. L.S. Ayres & Co., Indpls., 1935-37; field rep. Merchandising Group, N.Y.C., 1964-66; exhibited one man shows Chase Gallery, Miami Shores, Fla., 1967, Bacardi Gallery, Miami, 1968, Burdine's, Miami, 1969-70, exhibited in group shows Granville Gallery, 1964, Mirell Gallery, Coconut Grove, Fla., 1967, 68, 69, Bacardi Gallery, 1967, 68, Lever House, N.Y.C., 1970-72; represented in permanent collections Herron Sch. Art, Meth. Hosp., Indpls., Hist. Assn. S. Fla., Miami, 1st Fed. Savs. & Loan Assn., Coral Gables, Fla. Indpls. Marmon scholar, 1930, Art Assn. scholar, 1931-33, 35. Recipient James Whitcomb Riley medal, 1930; 1st Portrait award Palette Club Miami, 1962; 1st prize Fla. State Art Exhibit, Nat. League Am. Pen Women, 1969, 1st prize Wometco's 2d Ann. Art Competition, 1971. Mem. Miami Art League (pres., dir.), Nat. League Am. Pen Women (state art chmn. 1968, 72-73, pres. Miami br. 1970-72, nat. biennial art exhibit chmn., nat. art bd. 1972-74), Blue Dome Art Fellowship, Am. Artists Profl. League (award merit Miami chpt., Miami chpt. pres. 1969-71). Republican. Clubs: Miami Shores Woman's, Miami Shores Country. Address: 80 NE 97th St Miami FL 33138

HOLLINGSWORTH, ERMA INA CATION (MRS. IRVIN C. HOLLINGSWORTH), librarian; b. Savonburg, Kan.; d. John W. and Hannah (Jones) Cation; B.S., Pitts. State Coll., 1950, M.S., 1959; M.S., Kan. State Tchrs. Coll. Emporia, 1966; m. Irvin C. Hollingsworth, Aug. 10, 1930; children—Gene Irvin, Earl Lee. Tchr. pub. schs., Kan., 1927; tchr., librarian Fredonia (Kan.) Jr. High Sch., 1956-61; Librarian Central Jr. High Sch., Hutchinson, Kan., 1961-67; supr. library services Hutchinson Pub. Schs., 1967—. Mem. Kan. William Allen White Book Award Selection Com., 1972-73. Mem. Kan. Assn. Sch. Libraries (dist. dir. 1966-67, local arrangements chmn.), A.L.A. (state recruitment chmn.), Kan. Library Coordinators (pres.), Kan. Library Assn. (chmn. children and sch. sect. 1974—), Delta Kappa Gamma (chpt. treas. 1960-61). Mem. Christian Ch. (pres. guild 1971—). Home: 303 E 16th St Hutchinson KS 67501 Office: 1520 N Plum St Hutchinson KS 67501

HOLLIS, JEANNE, librarian; b. Phenix City, Ala., Dec. 13, 1915; d. Grady Miller and Anah Maude (Booker) H.; A.B., Ga. Coll., 1937; postgrad. Auburn U., 1938, 43; B.S. in Library Sci., Peabody Coll., 1945, M.A., 1958; postgrad. U. Ga., 1962, Columbus Coll., 1969. Tchr., Phenix City (Ala.) Elementary Sch., 1937-38; tchr. English, Central High Sch., Phenix City, 1938-40, librarian, 1940-45; librarian Jordan High Sch., Columbus, Ga., 1945-48; reference librarian W.C. Bradley Meml. Library, Columbus, 1948—. Mem. Southeastern, Ga. library assns., English-Speaking Union. Office: Bradley Dr Columbus GA 31906

HOLLISTER, CHARLOTTE ANN, computer research scientist; b. Santa Fe, N.M., Jan. 2, 1940; d. Bertram Keats and Sara (Vaughn) Hollister; A.B., Vassar Coll., 1961; Ph.D., Yale, 1965; m. Donald Carl Clagett, June 22, 1968; 1 dau., Jennifer Alison. Adj. asst. prof. N.Y. U., 1965-68; research asso. Mass. Inst. Tech., 1968, Harvard Obs., 1968-69; sr. research scientist Bolt, Beranek & Newman, Cambridge, Mass., 1969—. Mem. Am. Phys. Soc., Am. Chem. Soc. (mem. edn. com. N.E. sect., chmn. Newell award com.). Contbr. articles to profl. jours. Home: Sunnyside Lane Lincoln MA 01773 Office: 50 Moulton St Cambridge MA 02138

HOLLMAN, EMILY ELLSWORTH JENNINGS (MRS. ELWARD DERBY HOLLMAN), editor; b. Findlay, O., May 17, 1925; d. Lloyd Earle and Dorothy (Robertson) Jennings; B.A., U. Conn., 1948; M.A., Syracuse U., 1949; m. Elward Derby Hollman, Aug. 6, 1949; children—Patricia Archer, Sarah Derby. With pub. information dept. Eastern area hdqrs. A.R.C., Alexandria, Va., 1949-52; editor home office weekly Life in General, also monthly field clerical publ. Sampler, Conn. Gen. Ins. Co., Hartford, 1968-71, employment interviewer, 1971-72, sr. interviewer, coordinator, 1972-73, supr. employment services, 1973—. Bd. dirs. Windsor br. A.R.C., 1962-68, chmn. br., 1965-68. Mem. Pi Lambda Theta, Pi Beta Phi. Home: 301 Broad St Windsor CT 06095 Office: Conn Gen Ins Co Hartford Ct 06115

HOLLOWAY, ERNESTINE, coll. dean; b. Clyde, Miss., May 23, 1930; d. Dock and Blanche (Lee) Holloway; B.S., Tougaloo Coll., 1952; M.A. (A.M.A., United Ch. Christ grantee), N.Y. U., 1963; certificate (Nat. Def. Edn. Act fellow), Mich. State U., 1967. Tchr., Coleman Jr., Sr. High Sch., Greenville, Miss., 1952-53; sec. to pres. Tougaloo (Miss.) Coll., 1953-63, asst. dean students, 1963-65, dean students, 1965—. Cons. to counselors in Jackson (Miss.) Schs., 1965—. Bd. dirs. Crossroads Services Inc., Jackson, 1973—, sec. bd., 1973—. Mem. So. Assn. Colls. and Schs. (mem. com. evaluators for commn. on colls. 1969—), Nat. Assn. Student Personnel Adminstrs. (mem. exec. com. 1973—), Alpha Kappa Alpha (S.E. regional dir. 1970—). Home: 510 Beaverbrook Dr Jackson MS 39206 Office: Tougaloo College Tougaloo MS 39174

HOLLOWAY, SISTER MARCELLA MARIE, educator; b. St. Louis, Dec. 1, 1913; d. John James and Mary Maud (Kopp) Holloway; B.A., Fontbonne Coll., 1938; M.A., U. Mo., 1943; Ph.D., Catholic U. Am., 1947. Tchr. secondary schs., Atlanta, 1938-43; joined Sisters of St. Joseph of Carondelet, 1932; instr. English, head dept. St. Teresa Coll., Kansas City, Mo., 1943-62; prof. English, Fontbonne Coll., St. Louis, 1963—, dir. writing program, 1963—. Mem. faculty Catholic U. Am., Washington, summers, 1948-70; Nat. Endowment for Humanities grantee Yale, summer 1973. Mem. Nat. Pen Women Am., Hopkins Soc. (London). Author: Prosodic Theory of G.M. Hopkins, 1964; (plays) Last of Leprechauns, 1958, The Little Juggler, 1966. Address: Fontbonne College St Louis MO 63105

HOLLOWAY, MARY KATHERINE, editor univ. press; b. Knoxville, Tenn., Aug. 15, 1924; d. Sherman Walter and Katherine (Bourne) Holloway; B.A., U. Tenn., 1947. Clk., Matheny's, trade bookshop, Knoxville, 1941-46, mgr., 1946-51; asst. editor U. Tenn. Press and Pubs., 1952-57, asso. editor, 1957-62, sr. editor, 1963—. Home: 1726 Emoriland Blvd Knoxville TN 37917 Office: Communications Bldg University of Tenn Knoxville TN 37916

HOLLOWAY, TERESA FLOYD BRAGUNIER, author; b. Apalachicola, Fla., Jan. 17, 1906; d. David Ralph and Mordina (Floyd) Bragunier; grad. Fla. State Coll. Women, 1925; postgrad. U. Fla., 1930; m. John Calvin Holloway, Oct. 21, 1926; 1 son John (dec.). Office mgr., publicity writer Fla. C. of C., Jacksonville, 1928-35; polit. campaign office mgr., speech writer, West Palm Beach, Fla., 1935-36; owner, operator wholesale mfg. bus., Jacksonville, 1936-43; attache Fla. Senate, 1947-69, instr. creative writing Fla. Jr. Coll., Jacksonville, 1966-67, 73—, Jacksonville U., 1970-72. Cons. to pres. Fla. Tech. U., 1965-66; spl. corr. documentary scripts WFGA-TV, Jacksonville, 1955—. Mem. Friends of Library, 1960-63, Friends of Jacksonville U. Library, 1972-73. Recipient various certificates of recognition Gov. P.R., 1933, SSS, 1948, Pres. Harry Truman, 1951, U. Fla. Journalism Conf., 1959, Fla. Jr. Coll., 1966, Jacksonville U., 1971, Sears Found. Regional award for writing, 33 Intramural awards for writing and photography, Outstanding Lit. Contbn. award Nat. League Am. Penwomen, 1966, 1st Pl. unpub. novel, 2d pl. paid lectr. biennial competition, 1968; finalist Eve award Fla. Pub. Co., 1972. Mem. Nat. League Am. Penwomen (past pres. Jacksonville br., editor Southeastern region 1964-68), Mystery Writers Am. Author numerous novels including Girl In Studio B, 1967; Murder at Auction, 1961; Lady Lawyer, 1964; Nurse on Dark Island, 1969; Roses for Paula, 1969; River Nurse, 1969; Nurse to Remember, 1970; Campaign for Pam, 1970; Nurse Transplanted, 1971; Nurse Paige's Triumph, 1972; Tomorrow's Nurse, 1973. Spl. contbr. Jacksonville U. Compass mag., 1968-69; contbr. articles, columns, newspaper features. Address: 4349 Irvington Av Jacksonville FL 32210

HOLM, HELEN STRIHO (MRS. GEORGE A. HOLM), aero. engr.; b. Detroit, Nov. 22, 1926; d. Steven and Susan (Kupecz) Striho; B.S. in Aero. Engring., U. Mich., 1950; m. John D. Marble, June 26, 1952 (dec. Dec. 1952); m. 2d, George A. Holm, Aug. 2, 1956. Research asst. Engring. Research Inst., U. Mich., Ann Arbor, 1948-49; asso. aero. engr. Cornell Aero. Lab., Inc., Buffalo, 1950-60; asst. prof. mathematics and mech. tech. Erie Community Coll., Buffalo, 1960-62; propulsion analyst Bell Aerosystems Co., Buffalo, 1962-68; sr. propulsion engr. Lockheed-Cal. Co., Burbank, 1968-71, sr. flight test analysis engr., 1971-72; sr. research engr. Lockheed Missiles & Space Co., Sunnyvale, Cal., 1972—. Mem. Nat. Mgmt. Assn. Contbr. articles to profl. publs. Home: 887 Helena Dr Sunnyvale CA 94087 Office: Lockheed Missiles & Space Co PO 504 Box Sunnyvale CA 94088

HOLM, JEANNE MARJORIE, air force officer; b. Portland, Ore., June 23, 1921; d. John E. and Marjorie (Hammond) Holm; B.A., Lewis and Clark Coll., 1957; Commd. 2d lt. U.S. Army, 1942, advanced through grades to maj. gen. USAF, 1973; comdr. basic tng. regt., Fort Oglethorpe, Ga., 1943-46; co. comdr. WAC Tng. Co., Fort Lee, Va., 1948-49; wing plans officer Erding Air Depot, 1949-51, Air Command and Staff Coll., 1951; personnel plans officer Hdqrs. USAF, 1952-56; chief manpower and mgmt. Allied Air Forces So. Europe, NATO, Naples, Italy, 1957-61; congr. liaison officer Hdqrs. USAF, Washington, 1961-65, dir. Women in Air Force, 1965-73, dir. Air Force Personnel Council, 1973—. Trustee Air Force Hist. Found.; bd. dirs. Pentagon Fed. Credit Union, Campfire Girls, Inc. Decorated D.S.M., Legion of Merit, Medal Human Action; recipient Distinguished Achievement award Lewis and Clark Coll. Home: 807 S Fairfax St Alexandria VA 22314 Office: USAF Hdqrs Pentagon Washington DC 20330

HOLM, VANJA ADELE HOLM (MRS. CARL HOLM), pediatrician; b. Kiruna, Sweden, Oct. 5, 1928; d. C. V. Hjalmar and Elma Adele (Nystrom) Holm; M.D., Karolinska Inst. (Stockholm, Sweden), 1954; m. Carl Holm, June 15, 1952; children—Ingrid Adele, Erik Carl Anders. Came to U.S., 1955, naturalized, 1958. Intern, Swedish Hosp., Seattle, 1955-56; resident U. Wash. Med. Sch., Seattle, 1956, 62-64; fellow mental retardation, 1964-65; practice medicine specializing in pediatrics, Seattle, 1957—; mem. staff Univ., Childrens Orthopedic hosps., Harborview Med. Center; instr. pediatrics U. Wash. Sch. Medicine, 1965-69, asst. prof. pediatrics, 1969—. Fellow Am. Acad. Pediatrics; mem. Wash. State Soc. Pediatrics, North Pacific Pediatric Soc., A.M.A., Wash. State Med. Assn., Am. Assn. Mental Deficiency, Am. Women Med. Assn. Contbr. articles to profl. jours. Home: 16746 37th St NE Seattle WA 98155 Office: Clin Tng Unit Child Devel and Mental Retardation Center U Wash Seattle WA 98195

HOLMAN, DOROTHY ESTELLE (MRS. BASIL W. HOLMAN), med. assn. adminstr.; b. Balt., Apr. 2, 1918; d. Oscar Guy and Florence Estelle (Griffith) Fuhrman; student Coll. of Commerce, Balt., 1936-39; m. Basil W. Holman, Sept. 16, 1939. Adminstr. to supt. Bon Secours Hosp., Balt., 1941-45; sec. and asst. to physician, Balt., 1945-66; exec. dir. Balt. County Med. Assn., Timonium, 1960—, Md. Acad. Family Physicians, Timonium, 1966—. Mem. Bus. and Profl. Women (pres. 1950-52), Balt. Assn. Med. Assts. (pres.), Internat. Order Job's Daughters (grand treas. 1969—). Mem. Christian Ch. Home: 7609 Hillsway Av Baltimore MD 21234 Office: 10 Gerard Av Timonium MD 21093

HOLMAN, FELICE, author; b. N.Y.C., Oct. 24, 1919; d. Jac C. and Celia (Hotchner) Holman; student Drew Sem., 1936-37, Columbia, 1940; B.A., Syracuse U., 1941; m. Herbert Valen, Apr. 13, 1941; 1 dau., Nanine. Author: Elisabeth, the Bird Watcher, 1963; Elizabeth the Treasure Hunter (Jr. Lit. Guild selection), 1964; Silently, the Cat, and Miss Theodosia (N.Y. Times Best Books of Year selection), 1965; Victoria's Castle, 1966; Elisabeth and the Marsh Mystery, 1966; The Witch on the Corner (Jr. Book of Month selection), 1966; Professor Diggins' Dragons, 1966; The Cricket Winter (Jr. Book of Month, N.Y. Times Best Books of Year selection), 1967; The Blackmail Machine, 1968; A Year to Grow, 1968; The Holiday Rat and the Utmost Mouse, 1969; At the Top of My Voice and Other Poems, 1970; Solomon's Search, 1970; The Future of Hooper Toote, 1972; I Hear You Smiling and Other Poems, 1973; The Escape of the Giant Hogstalk, 1974; Slake's Limbo, 1974. Home: Westport CT 06880

HOLMAN, MARGARET GERTRUDE (MRS. WILLIAM HOLMAN), bank exec.; b. Libby, Mont., July 20, 1920; d. Raymond Paul and Andrea (Flugekvam) Holzknecht; student U. Cal. at Berkeley, 1938-39, Merritt Bus. Sch., 1939-40; m. William F. Holman, Sept. 12, 1942; 1 son, William F. With Central Bank Oakland (now United Cal. Bank), 1940-42, Mountain View office, 1954-61; escrow officer Western Title Guaranty Co., Palo Alto, Cal., 1961-63; with Barclays Bank (formerly First Valley Bank), Menlo Park, Cal., 1963—, asst. mgr., 1967-70, mgr., 1970-74, asst. v.p., mgr., 1974—. Mem. Assn. Profl. Mortgage Women, Nat. Assn. Bank Women, Soroptomist Club. Home: 674 Lee Nines Way Los Altos CA 94022

HOLMAN, MARY ALIDA, educator; b. West Point, N.Y., June 26, 1933; d. Jonathan Lane and Anna Alida (Johnson) Holman; B.A., George Washington U., 1955, M.A., 1957, Ph.D. in Econs., 1963; m. Theodore Suranyi-Unger, Jr., Dec. 15, 1962. Economist, U.S. Dept. Agr., 1958-59, Resources for the Future, Washington, 1960-61; asst. prof. econs. George Washington U., Washington, 1963-64, dir. Natural Resources Policy Center, 1971—, asso. prof. econs., 1964—. Econ. cons. Pres.'s Cost of Living Council, 1971-73, Asso. Adminstrn., NASA, 1966-68; professorial lectr. Indsl. Coll. of Armed Forces, 1965-74, Nat. War Coll., 1966-71. Thomas Alva Edison fellow McGraw Found., 1961-62; recipient Robert C. Watson award Am. Patent Law Assn., 1964. Mem. Am. Econs. Assn. Author: The Political Economy of the Space Program, 1974; also articles. Home: 940 Spring Hill Rd McLean VA 22101 Office: Dept Econs George Washington U Washington DC 20006

HOLMAN, NANCY ANN GATTUSO (MRS. JAMES A. HOLMAN), judge; b. Adams, Mass.; d. Henry A. and Helen A. (Sliwa) Gattuso; A.B. magna cum laude, Wheaton Coll., Mass., 1956; LL.B., Boston Coll., 1959; spl. student Harvard Law Sch., 1959, Middlebury Coll.; grad. Nat. Coll. State Judiciary, Reno, 1971; m. James A. Holman, June 29, 1957; children—Carrol Edwards, Andrew James, Hilary Alexandra. Admitted to Mass. bar, 1959; asso. Crane, Inker & Oteri, Boston, 1959-60; asso. Elliott, Lee, Carney, Thomas & Smart, 1960-64, jr. partner, 1964-70; partner Thomas, Holman, Holman & Dawson, 1970; judge Superior Ct. King County, Seattle, 1970—. Trustee Wheaton Coll. Mem. Nat. Conf. State Trial Judges, Wash. State Jud. Conf. (chmn. family law com. 1972—), King County Superior Ct. Judges (chmn. family law and mental illness com. 1971—), Am. Assn. U. Women, Wheaton Coll. Alumnae Assn., Am., Wash. bar assns., Phi Beta Kappa, Kappa Beta Phi. Home: 1608 Federal Av E Seattle WA 98102 Office: King County Superior Ct Seattle WA 98104

HOLMANN, ANNE SHARPE (MRS. E. J. HOLMANN), wholesale drug exec., bottling exec., civic worker; b. Bainbridge, Ga., Nov. 7, 1900; d. John Greenleaf and Anne Elizabeth (Sharpe) Garrett; student Salem Acad. and Coll., 1916-19; A.B., Vanderbilt U., 1922; m. Joseph Lee Brown, June 13, 1923 (dec. Apr. 1931); children—Anne Poindexter (Mrs. Anne Brown Helvenston), Joseph Lee, John Garrett, Stephen Glenmore; m. 2d, Ernest McClelland Archer, June 22, 1933 (dec. Jan. 1951); m. 3d, Edward Jacob Holmann, Mar. 29, 1952 (dec. Feb. 1972). Former sec. Jonesboro Coca-Cola Bottling Co., also Statesboro (Ga.) Coca-Coca Bottling Co., pres., treas. both cos., 1951—; former v.p. Archer Drug Co., Little Rock, now pres., treas.; mem. bd. Davis Wholesale Drug Co., Shreveport, La., 1951—. Mem. health subcom. Model Cities. Bd. dirs. Little Rock Unlimited Progress, City Beautiful Commn.; patron mem. Musical Coterie. Chosen Little Rock Woman of Week, Jan. 1948, Jan. 1949; Little Rock Citizen of Week, Feb. 1949; Ark. Woman Year, 1948; Elizabeth Wyman Alumnae award Alpha Omicron Pi, 1951; Mother of Year, Little Rock, 1971, Ark., 1972. Mem. Am. Assn. U. Women (former v.p., pres. Ark. div., past legislative chmn. Little Rock br.), YWCA, Nat. Cathedral Assn. (past state chmn.), Little Rock C. of C. (cultural affairs and edn. coms.), Women's Little Rock C.'s of C., Arkansas Drug Travelers, U.D.C., Dames Ct. of Honor (past pres.), Daus. Am. Colonists (treas.), Daus. Colonial Wars, Bus. and Prof. Women's Club, Colonial Dames Am., Delta Kappa Gamma, Alpha Omicron Pi (ex-alumnae dir. Ark., Tenn.). Methodist (bd. stewards). Clubs: Fine Arts of Ark. (past pres.), Little Rock Garden (past pres.), Woman's City, Altrusa, Aesthetic, Little Rock Country, Little Rock. Home: 3518 Hill Rd Little Rock AR 72205 Office: 107 E Markham Little Rock AR 72201

HOLMBERG, MATHA LOUISE (MRS. VINCENT V. HOLMBERG), clubwoman; b. Brookfield, Mo., Dec. 11, 1912; d. Edward Alexander and Mattie Beulah (Riley) Reno; student Mo. U.; m. Vincent Virgil Holmberg, Aug. 3, 1935; children—JoAnn (Mrs. James Edward Myers), Rodney R., William W. Cashier, Kansas City (Mo.), Power & Light Co., 1933-35, Wieboldt's, Chgo., 1937-43; mem. Ill. Fedn. Women's Clubs, Chgo., 1942—, pres., 1972—; pres. Leukemia Research Found., 1950-54; pres. League Women Voters, 1954-64; leader Girl Scouts, 1945-54; pres. Women's Lit. Club Chgo., 1963—; mem. Better Bus. Bur., 1971-72; mem. Brainerd Garden Club, 1950-72, Fernwood Evening Woman's Club, 1950—, Chgo. Women's Club, 1971—, Drama League, 1963-72; organizer Literary Forum 3d Dist., 1965—. Bd. dirs. Brain Research Found., 1972—. Mem. Beta Sigma Phi. Methodist. Home: 9025 S Claremont Av Chicago IL 60620 Office: 30 W Washington St Chicago IL 60602

HOLMBERG, RUTH SULZBERGER (MRS. ALBERT W. HOLMBERG, JR.), newspaper co. exec.; b. N.Y.C., Mar. 12, 1921; d. Arthur Hays and Iphigene (Ochs) Sulzberger; A.B., Smith Coll., 1943; m. Ben H. Golden, June 1, 1946 (div.); children—Stephen Arthur Ochs, Michael Davis, Lynn Iphigene (Mrs. Dolnick), Arthur Sulzberger; m. 2d, Albert William Holmberg, Jr., May 26, 1972. Reporter N.Y. Times, summers 1939-45; music critic Chattanooga Times, 1946-57; became asst. sec. Times Printing Co., Chattanooga 1950; pres., pub. Chattanooga Times, 1964-70, chmn. bd., 1970-72, pub., 1964—, dir. spl. activities; dir. N.Y. Times. Pres. Chattanooga Symphony, 1959-60; served with A.R.C., 1943-45; sustaining Jr. League. Bd. dirs. N.Y. Times Found.; trustee U. Tenn. at Chattanooga Found. Mem. Chattanooga Art Assn. (bd.). Home: 919 Scenic Hwy Lookout Mountain TN 37350 Office: 117 E 10th St Chattanooga TN 37402

HOLMES, DOROTHY BEHNER (MRS. OLIVER WENDELL HOLMES), ophthalmologist; b. Newton, Ia., May 25, 1902; d. Charles Edward and Maude Clark (Venables) Behner; student Carleton Coll., 1921-22; A.B., U. Missoula, 1925; M.A., N.Y. U., 1929, Ph.D., 1933; M.D. U. Pa., 1941; m. Oliver Wendell Holmes, Sept. 14, 1927; children—Benson Venables Holmes, Helena Victoria Holmes (Mrs. Charles E. Morrison). Instr. Montana U., Missoula, 1924-25; asst. in bacteriology City N.Y., 1926-27; instr. N.Y. U., N.Y.C., 1927-31; instr. in biology and bacteriology N.Y. State Commn. for the Blind, 1933-35; orthoptist, N.Y. State Health Dept., 1935-36; intern Wilmer Ophth. Inst. Johns Hopkins Hosp., 1941-42; resident Johns Hopkins Hosp., Balt., 1942-44; practice medicine, specializing in ophthalmology, Washington, 1944-74; mem. staff Washington Hosp. Center, Children's Hosp., Washington. Vol. Physician for Vietnam, 1969. Mem. Assn. for Research in Ophthalmology, Pan Am. Assn. Ophthalmologists, A.M.A., Women's Med. Soc. Contbr. articles to med. jours. Home: 3422 Fulton St Washington DC 20009

HOLMES, GLORIA MAUDE HENDREN (MRS. RICHARD L. HOLMES), educator; b. Newark, Ohio, Nov. 5, 1930; d. Walter Ebert and Corinne (Tope) Hendren; B.Ed., Ohio State U., 1952, M.Ed., 1957, postgrad., 1958—; m. Richard Lewis Holmes, July 19, 1959; children—Kimberly, Sally, Kathy, Jeffery, Nancy, David. Tchr. Newark (Ohio) Pub. Schs., 1952-56; asso. prof. elementary edn. Ashland Coll., also supr. elementary student teaching, acad. counselor, 1956—, founder, dir., supr. Ashland Coll. Kindergarten, 1960-63; cons., lectr. Hosp. vol. A.R.C., 1956-59; active United Appeal, Ohio State U. Devel. Fund, Ashland Coll. Devel. Fund. Jennings research scholar, 1974—. Mem. Ohio, Nat. edn. assns., Internat. Reading Assn., Ashland Symphony League, Ohio State U. Alumni Assn., Northeastern Ohio Tchrs. Assn., Guidance Assn., Ohio, Nat. assns. for higher edn., Ohio Assn. for Tchr. Educators, Altrusa Internat., Am. Assn. U. Women, Assn. Exceptional Children, Adminstrs. Assn., Nursery-Kindergarten-Primary Assn., Assn. for Supervision and Curriculum Devel., Ashland Bus. and Profl. Women's Club, Children's Lit. Club, Assn. for Childhood Edn., Beta Sigma Phi (pres. Delta Gamma chpt. 1969-70), Xi Iota Alpha, Phi Delta Kappa (hon.), Kappa Delta Pi, Sigma Phi Gamma, Alpha Delta Kappa. Mem. Park Street Brethren Ch. (v.p. Women's Missionary Soc. group III 1970-71). Mem. Order Eastern Star, White Shrine of Jerusalem. Club: Ashland Coll. Faculty, Ashland Christian Women's, Ashland Coll. Faculty Women's (pres. 1959-60). Author (with Richard L. Holmes) Innovations in Church School Teacher-Education Program, 1972. Home: 452 Hillcrest Dr Ashland OH 44805

HOLMES, GRACE ELINOR (MRS. FREDERICK FRANKLIN HOLMES), physician; b. Crookston, Minn., Mar. 27, 1932; d. William August and Erika Annie (Ermisch) Foege; B.A., Pacific Luth. U., 1953; M.D., U. Wash., 1957; m. Frederick Franklin Holmes, June 26, 1955; children—Heidi, Cynthia, Lisa, Theodore, Julia, Andrew. Intern, U. Kan. Med. Center, Kansas City, 1957-58, fellow children's rehab. dept. pediatrics, 1963-67, physician Birth Defects Center, 1965-70, instr. pediatrics, 1967-69, asst. prof. pediatrics, 1969-70, 72—; physician Lutheran Ch. Clinics, Malaysia, 1959-63; cons. pediatrics Kilimanjaro Christian Med. Centre. Moshi, Tanzania, East Africa, 1970-72; pediatric cons. Infant Devel. Center, Shawnee Mission, Kan., 1973—. Fellow Am. Acad. Cerebral Palsy; mem. A.M.A., Kan. Wyandotte County med. socs., Assn. Physicians of East Africa. Contbr. articles to profl. pubs. Home: 4701 Black Swan Dr Shawnee KS 66216 Office: Dept Pediatrics Univ Kan Med Center 39th and Rainbow Sts Kansas City KS 66103

HOLMES, JEANNE MAIDEN, librarian; b. Dayton, O., Feb. 10, 1922; d. Arthur Lee and Minnie Virginia (Coleman) Maiden; B.A., George Washington U., 1943; M.S. in L.S., Columbia, 1952; m. Robert Reynolds Holmes, July 27, 1946. Visa editorial asst. Dept. Agr., 1943-47; sec. internat. documents service Columbia U. Press, 1947-49; supr. periodical reading room Columbia, 1949-52; with Nat. Agrl. Library, Beltsville, Md., 1952—, chief analysis div., 1971—, acting coordinator agrl. vocabulary project, 1965-68. Mem. subpanel descriptive cataloging Com. Sci. and Tech. Information, 1965-67; chmn. various working groups Nat. Libraries Task Force, 1967—, mem. tech. liaison com. Nat. Serials Data Program, 1973—. Recipient Spl. Merit award Dept. Agr., 1966, Superior Service awards, 1968, 74. Mem. Am. (chmn. various coms. 1952—), D.C. library assns., Spl. Libraries Assn., Potomac Tech. Processing Librarians, Am. Soc. Information Sci., Internat. Assn. Agrl. Librarians and Documentalists, Beta Phi Mu. Home: 9727 Mt Pisgah Rd Silver Spring MD 20903 Office: Nat Agrl Library Beltsville MD 20705

HOLMES, MARJORIE ROSE (MRS. LYNN MIGHELL), author; b. Storm Lake, Ia.; d. Samuel Arthur and Rosa (Griffith) Holmes; student Buena Vista Coll., 1927-29; B.A., Cornell Coll., 1931; m. Lynn Mighell, Apr. 9, 1932; children—Marjorie (Mrs. Stanley Croner), Mark, Mallory, Melanie. Free-lance writer short stories, articles, verse for mags. including Ladies Home Jour., McCall's, Red Book, This Week, Parents, Reader's Digest, Better Homes and Gardens, Today's Health, Nation's Bus., Family Circle, Woman's Day, Glamour, 1931—. Writer weekly column Love and Laughter, Washington Evening Star, 1959—; monthly columnist Woman's Day, 1971—; tchr. writing Cath. U., 1964-65, Md. U., 1967-68; mem. staff Georgetown Writers Conf., 1959-70. Recipient Honor Iowans award Buena Vista Coll., 1966, Alumni Achievement award Cornell Coll., 1963; Woman of Achievement award Nat. Fedn. Press Women, 1972. Mem. Am. Newspaper Women's Club, Va. Press Women, Washington Nat. Press Club, Children's Book Guild, Delta Phi Beta. Author: World By the Tail, 1943; Ten O'Clock Scholar, 1946; Saturday Night, 1959; Cherry Blossom Princess, 1960; Follow Your Dream, 1961; Love is a Hopscotch Thing, 1963; Senior Trip, 1962; Love and Laughter, 1967; I've Got to Talk to Somebody, God, 1969; Writing the Creative Article, 1969; Who Am I, God?, 1971; To Treasure Our Days, 1971; Two From Galilee, 1972; Nobody Else Will Listen, 1973; You and I and Yesterday, 1973; As Tall as My Heart, 1974. Home: 1110 Shipman Lane McLean VA 22101 Office: 2d and Virginia Avs SE Washington DC 20003

HOLMES, MARY ALYCE, home economist; b. Lima, O., Mar. 10, 1930; d. Carl L. and Ruth E. (Arnold) Holmes; B.S. in Edn., Otterbein Coll., 1953; M.Sc., Ohio State U., 1956; postgrad. Fuller Theol. Sem., 1959-61. Research asst. Ohio Agrl. Expt. Sta., Ohio State U., 1953-54; tchr. Risingsun (O.) Sch., 1954-55, Springfield (O.) High Sch., 1955-59; vocal rec. and pre-sch. teaching, vol. missionary with youth, Los Angeles, 1959-61; counselor Youth for Christ, Columbus, O., 1961-63; instr. Otterbein Coll., 1962-64; tchr. Miami (Fla.) Christian Sch., 1964-65; extension home economist Coop. Extension Service, U. Fla., Miami, 1966—. Mem. home econs. curriculum adv. com. Fla. Internat. U.; mem. Greater Miami Dietetic Program Adv. Bd. Adviser, sec. Billy Graham Film Crusade, Miami; vol. Drug Rehab. Center; mem. adv. bd. Am. Christian Coll., Tulsa. Mem. Nat., Fla. assns. extension home economists, Am., Fla., So. Fla. home econs. assns., Nat. Educators Fellowship, Am. Bus. Women's Assn., Home Econs. Alumni Assn. Ohio State U., Epsilon Sigma Phi. Writer ednl. bulls. Office: 2690 NW 7th Av Miami FL 33127

HOLMES, OPAL LAUREL, author; b. Laurens, Ia., Oct. 14, 1913; d. Ila Laurel and Jessie Merle (Hesselgrave) Holmes; ed. pub. and pvt. schs.; m. Vardis Fisher, Apr. 16, 1940. Author: Gold Rushes and Mining Camps of the Early American West. Recipient Golden Spur award, 1969. Mem. Authors Guild, Inc., Authors League Am., Inc. Address: 1605 Promontory Rd Boise ID 83702

HOLMES, SANDRA GLENDALIN, TV broadcasting co. exec.; b. Bklyn.; d. William Bernard and Almeida (Taylor) Holmes; B.S., N.Y. U., 1963. Free lance editing, N.Y.C., 1963-64; with NBC, N.Y.C., 1964—, film editor, 1964—. Recipient Edward L. Kingsley's award, 1963. Mem. Am. Film Inst. Office: 30 Rockefeller Plaza New York NY 10020

HOLMGREN, PATRICIA KERN, bot. taxonomist; b. Athens, Ind., Jan. 21, 1940; d. Robert Evan and Ruth Eleanor (Beaudoin) Kern; B.S., Ind. U., 1962; M.S., U. Wash., 1964, Ph.D., 1968; m. Noel H. Holmgren, Nov. 25, 1969. Herbarium specialist N.Y. Bot. Garden, 1968-69, asso. curator, herbarium adminstr., 1969-73, herbarium supr., adminstr. phanerogamic herbarium, 1973—. Mem. Am. Soc. Plant Taxonomists, Bot. Soc. Am., Cal. Bot. Soc., Am. Inst. Biol. Scis., A.A.A.S., Sigma Xi. Home: 304 Woodland Hills White Plains NY 10603 Office: NY Bot Garden Bronx NY 10458

HOLMQUIST, K. JUNE DRENNING (MRS. DONALD C. HOLMQUIST), assn. exec.; b. Bedford, Pa., Sept. 29, 1924; d. DeLoss B. and Bertha M. (Ritchey) Drenning; student U. Pa., 1945-47; B.A. with honors, U. Minn., 1949; m. Donald C. Holmquist, Nov. 24, 1949. Sec. Am. Tel. & Tel. Co., Bedford, 1943-45; editorial asst. Classical Weekly, Phila., 1945-47; research and teaching asst. in classical langs. U. Minn., 1948-49; editorial asst. Minn. Hist. Soc., St. Paul, 1949-56, acting editor Minn. History mag., 1956-58, asso. editor Minn. Hist. Soc., 1956-60, mng. editor, head publs. dept., 1960-73, asst. dir., 1973—. McKnight Found. research fellow, 1967. Mem. Western History Assn., Phi Beta Kappa. Author six books. Contbr. articles to profl. jours. Home: 2197 Knapp St St Paul MN 55108 Office: Minn Hist Soc 690 Cedar St St Paul MN 55101

HOLMQUIST, KAY, journalist; b. Ft. Worth, Tex., Dec. 13, 1939; d. Huey Otis and Bonnie Lea (Langdon) Northcut; B.A. in Journalism and English, Harding Coll., 1964; m. Thomas Elvington Torrans, Dec. 12, 1969; 1 son, Joaquin. Advt. copywriter, copy chief Tandy Leather Co., Ft. Worth, 1963-65; advt. copywriter Sears, Roebuck & Co., Troy, Mich., 1965-67; with Ft. Worth Star-Telegram, 1967—, women's editor, 1968—. Recipient hon. mention Tex. A.P. Mng. Editors, 1968, 70, 1st pl., 1969. Mem. Women in Communications. Home: 3855 Medford Rd Fort Worth TX 76103 Office: 400 W 7th St Fort Worth TX 76102

HOLOUBEK, ALICE E. BAKER (MRS. JOE E. HOLOUBEK), physician; b. Paragould, Ark., Nov. 9, 1914; d. Erasmus B. and Effie (Wiseman) Baker; B.S., La. State U., 1937, M.D., 1938; m. Joe E. Holoubek, July 18, 1939; children—Mary Josephine (Mrs. James O'Rear), Brian Baker, Robert Joseph, Martha Alice (Mrs. T.P. Fitzgerald III). Intern, Charity Hosp., New Orleans, 1938-39; fellow internal medicine La. State U. Sch. Medicine, New Orleans, 1939-43, instr. medicine, 1943-68; practice medicine specializing in internal medicine, Shreveport, La., 1947—; instr. medicine La. State U., Shreveport, 1968—. Mem. Nat. Com. Health Care of Religious and Clergy, 1958-62. Bd. dirs. Shreveport chpt. Am. Tb Assn., 1960-68, Shreveport Child Guidance Center, 1960-64, St. Joseph's Collegium, 1962-68, Shreveport Community Council, 1962-68, Council on Alcoholism, 1964-68, Council on Human Relations. Fellow Acad. Psychosomatic Medicine, A.C.P. (asso.); mem. A.M.A., La. State, Shreveport med. assns., Am., La. heart assns., Nat. Fedn. Catholic Physicians Guilds, La., Nat. socs. internal medicine, Delta Delta Delta. Home: 6032 River Rd Shreveport LA 71105 Office: 1513 Line Av Shreveport LA 71101

HOLPP, MARYAN WEBER (MRS. JAMES R. HOLPP), educator; b. Lynch, Neb.; d. Edward J. and Alice (Hammerlun) Weber; B.A., U. Denver, 1953; M.A., U. N.M., 1956; postgrad. Stanford, 1964; m. Robert D. Moyer, Aug. 29, 1953 (div. Jan. 1965); m. 2d, James R. Holpp, Aug. 17, 1971. Speech therapist Sewall Rehab. Center, Denver, 1953-54; founder, dir. presch. for hearing handicapped children N.M. Hearing Soc., Albuquerque, 1955-65; exec. dir. Albuquerque Hearing and Speech Center, 1965—; model Flair Modeling Agy., Albuquerque, 1960-65. Mem. Jr. Womans Club, Albuquerque, 1956-59, v.p. Jr. C. of C. Wives Club, Albuquerque, 1960-61. Mem. Govs. Adv. Bd. Vocational Rehab., 1966—; mem. Govs. Com. on Hire the Handicapped, 1967—, sec.-treas., 1966—; mem. N.M. Commn. on Aging; mem. med. adv. com. Headstart. Bd. dirs. Spl. Edn. Center, Albuquerque; mem. policy bd. Child Devel. Centers, Econ. Opportunity Bd., Healthstart Program; bd. dirs. Middle Rio Grande Council on Comprehensive Health Planning. Mem. N.M. Speech and Hearing Assn. (honors award 1963), Nat. Assn. Execs. Speech and Hearing Centers (sec. 1967), Albuquerque City Panhellenic Council (Greek of month 1966), Am. Speech and Hearing Assn., N.M. Hearing Soc. (life, dir.), N.M. Rehab. Center Bd. (sec., dir.), Zeta Phi Eta, Sigma Alpha Eta, Gamma Phi Beta (Carnation award 1974). Democrat. Roman Catholic. Home: 2913 Alcazar NE Albuquerque NM 87110 Office: 1011 Buena Vista SE Albuquerque NM 87106

HOLSEY, JOYCE EDLINE (MRS. WILLIAM F. HOLSEY II), lawyer; b. N.Y.C., Jan. 7, 1927; d. Herbert and Emma (Ramsey) Chambers; B.A., Hunter Coll., 1946, M.A., 1951; J.D., U. Ariz., 1971; m. William F. Holsey II, Dec. 26, 1948; children—Denise, Dorine, William F. III. Elementary sch. tchr., N.Y.C., 1948-53; admitted to Ariz. bar, 1971; staff atty. Pima County Legal Aid Soc., Tucson, 1971—. Precinct committeeman Democratic party, 1970-72. Bd. dirs. Pima County Med. Aux., 1962-63, Tucson br. YWCA, 1971-74, Tucson Girls Club, 1973-76. Mem. N.A.A.C.P., Delta Sigma Theta (sec. Tucson alumni chpt.). Home: 6501 N Camino Arturo Tucson AZ 85718 Office: 30 N Church Av Tucson AZ 85701

HOLST, MARTHA IRENE, home economist; b. Bruceville, Ind., Feb. 19, 1920; d. Thomas Alva and Edith (Marsh) Cullop; B.S. in Home Econs., Purdue U., 1942; M.S. in Adult Edn., U. Chgo., 1954; m. John Richard Holst, Oct. 22, 1961; children—Richard Allen, Donna Lynn (Mrs. Bruce B. Scott). Vocational home econs. and phys. edn. tchr., Widner Twp., Knox County, Freelandville, Ind., 1942-46; with Ind. Coop. Extension Service, Purdue U., 1946—, extension specialist in programs, 1967—. Ford Found. scholar, 1954; Farm Found. scholar, 1954. Mem. Am. (vice chmn. extension sect. 1958), Ind. (mem. bd., chmn. mgmt. sect.) home econs. assns., Adult Edn. Assn., Co-op. Extension Specialists Assn. (dir. 1966-69), Ind. Farm Safety Council, Bus. and Profl. Women's Club (treas. Princeton, Ind. 1947), Internat. Ninety-Nines (treas. Ind. chpt. 1972-74), Purdue U. Alumni Assn., Purdue U. Sch. Home Econs. Assn. (chmn. 1973-74), Purdue Pilots (faculty adviser 1959-74), Internat. Flying Farmers, Epsilon Sigma Phi. Home: 127 Sylvia St West Lafayette IN 47906

HOLSTEIN, LILLIAN SOLOW (MRS. NATHAN HOLSTEIN), assn. exec.; b. N.Y.C., Mar. 1, 1914; d. Ralph and Rose (Pickus) Solow; student Jamaica Tchrs. Coll., 1930-32; teaching certificate Hunter Coll., 1933; m. Nathan Holstein, June 16, 1935; children—Stephen Arthur, Russell Marc, Bruce Jay. Pres., Menorah chpt. B'nai B'rith Women, Pitts., 1943-45, pres. Greater Pitts. Council, 1945-46, pres. Dist. 3 (Pa., Del., W.Va., N.J.), 1955-56, internat. pres., 1971-74, chmn. internat. affairs, 1974—; bd. govs. B'nai B'rith Supreme Lodge, 1968—. Mem. Pitts. United Jewish Fedn. Coll. Study Com., 1970-71, B'nai B'rith-Hillel-United Jewish Fedn. Bd., 1971—. Mem. Ladies Hosp. Aid Soc. Pitts., Am.-Israel Pub. Affairs Com., Hadassah, Nat. Council Jewish Women, Temple Sinai Sisterhood Pitts. (pres. 1948-50). Jewish religion. Home: 262 N Dithridge St Pittsburgh PA 15213

HOLT, CATHERINE ELIZABETH, home economist; b. Marion Center, Pa., Aug. 28, 1917; d. Verner Alexander and Eva Jane (Walker) Holt; B.S. in Home Econs., Indiana (Pa.) U., 1939; M.Ed. in Home Econs., Pa. State U., 1962. Tchr. home econs. Marion Center Joint High Sch., 1940-58; coop. tchr. Indiana U., 1953-58; extension home economist Indiana County, Pa. State U., 1958-60, asst. state leader N.W. Pa., 1960-73, asst. dir. North Central region Coop. extension service, 1973—, former chmn. consumer edn. com. and coordinator coop. extension service with visually handicapped of univ. Recipient hon. degree Pa. chpt. Future Homemakers Am., 1958; plaque Pa. Govt., 1966. Mem. Am. Homes Econs. Assn. (membership chmn. Pa. 1966-67), Am. Council Consumer Interest, Nat. Safety Council, Pa. State U., Indiana U. alumni assns., Bus. and Profl. Women's Club, Epsilon Sigma Phi, Omicron Nu, Delta Kappa Gamma (1st v.p. 1958-60). Methodist (administrv. bd.). Author articles in field. Home: 611 E Beaver Av Apt 2 State College PA 16801 Office: 325 Agrl Adminstrn Bldg University Park PA 16802

HOLT, CHARLOTTE SINCLAIR, med. illustrator, sculptor; b. Springfield, Mass., June 11, 1914; d. Horace Sinclair and Marion (Rowe) Holt; student Mass. Normal Art Sch., Boston Mus. Fine Arts, 1929-32, Child-Walker Sch. Fine Arts and Crafts, 1932-34, Boston U.

Coll. Liberal Arts, 1933-34, Coll. Med., 1934-35; postgrad. in med. art U. Ill. Coll. Med., 1935-37; studied portrait painting Bernard Keyes, Boston, sculpture with Malvina Hoffman, N.Y.C., 1939-68, water color with Elliot O'Hare, Me., 1941, 43; Ph.D. (hon.), 1972. Staff med. illustrator Ill. Dept. Pub. Health, Bur. Health Edn., 1935-71; dir. med audio-visual communications Akron (O.) Gen. Med. Center, 1972—, free lance illustrator and sculptor, 1935—; instr. U. Illinois College Medicine, 1937-45; profl. med. illustrator, sculptor, graphics display artist. Sec. Inst. Visual Med. and Health Edn., Inc., 1964—. Permanent lay exhibit (Miracle of Growth Sculptures) Mus. Sci. and Industry, 1950, 63. Recipient Beaux Arts gold medal, stained glass design and interior decorating, 1934-35, 1st award for most outstanding exhibit A.M.A. Med. Assembly, Chgo., 1962. Fellow Med. Artists Assn. Gt. Britain, Internat. Biog. Assn.; mem. Asso. Med. Illustrators (charter mem.; chmn. internat. liaison com. 1952-71, v.p. 1960-61, pres. 1970-71, editorial bd. orgn. jour. 1959—, editor membership directory 1969-70, gov. 1961-66, 71—, corr. sec. 1965-69, chmn. biog. reference com. 1965-70, chmn. editorial bd. and publs. com. 1970-72, distinguished service awards 1966, 70), Internat. Platform Assn., Inst. Med. and Biol. Illustration (charter mem., founder asso., Allied Artists Assn. Am., Council Med. TV, Med. Secs. Assn., Midwest Pharm. Advt. Club, M.B.L.S., Biol. Photographers Assn., Royal Photog. Soc. London, Am. Inst. Biol. Scis., Am. Forestry Assn., Nat. Wildlife Fedn. Conglist. Club: Airways. Co-author, illustrator: (with Frederick H. Falls) Obstetric and Gynecologic Nursing, 1937, rev. edit., 1945, The Use of Latex and Hydrocal in Casting, 1942, Atlas of Obstetric Complications, 1962. Address: 738 Keystone Av River Forest IL 60305

HOLT, ELIZABETH MANNERS, x-ray crystallographer; b. Montclair, N.J., Aug. 2, 1939; d. Theodore Roland and Helen (Whitenack) M.; B.A. cum laude, Smith Coll., 1961; Ph.D., Brown U., 1965; m. Smith Lewis Holt, Jr., Aug. 24, 1963; children—Alexandra, Smith Lewis III. Research asso. Poly. Laereanstalt, Copenhagen, Denmark, 1965-66; research asso., lectr. Bklyn. Poly. Inst., 1966-69; research asso. chemistry dept. U. Wyo., Laramie, 1969—. Mem. Sigma Xi. Research in structures of sulphur nitrogen compounds, iron-amino acid complexes. Home: Box 1311 Laramie WY 82070 Office: Chemistry Dept U Wyo Laramie WY 82070

HOLT, GLORIA WATSON (MRS. MILES HOLT), assn. exec.; b. Salt Lake City, Sept. 14, 1922; d. Richard Farnell and Joan Hazel (Milan) Watson; student Orange Coast Coll., 1965-66; m. Miles Robb Holt, Aug. 5, 1947; children—Diane (Mrs. Max Johnson), Mila A. (Mrs. James Albert). Fashion model, Seattle, 1940-44; sec. to operations mgr. KOMO Radio, Seattle, 1946-47; active in establishing mental health clinics for emotionally disturbed children, 1954-67; exec. sec. C. of C., Big Bear Lake, Cal., 1967—. Mem. Glendale Assistance League, 1948-55, Los Floristas, 1950-56. Mem. So. Cal. Assn. C. of C. Execs., South Coast Child Guidance Aux., Las Candelas. Republican. Presbyn. Home: PO Box 524 Big Bear City CA 92314 Office: PO Box 2860 Big Bear Lake CA 92315

HOLT, GRACE BUCKINGHAM, author; b. B.C., Can.; d. James E. and Phoebe Alice (Nicholls) Morden; student Phoenix Coll., 1923-25; summer study Columbia, U. Cal., U. Utah, Denver U., U. Colo.; m. George E. Buckingham, Sept. 13, 1912 (dec.); 1 son, Harry Earl; m. 2d, E. Lee Holt, July 31, 1926. Sec., Alderson & McIntyre, attys., 1914, Phoenix Flour Mills, 1917-23; sec. and research Phoenix Union High Schs., Phoenix Coll., 1923-59. Mem. Nat. Assn. Ednl. Secs., Ednl. Secs. Ariz. (past pres.), Bus. and Profl. Womens Clubs, Nat. League Am. Pen Women (past local and state pres.), Eugene Field Soc. Conglist. Clubs: Democratic Women's, Ballot Battalion Musicians. Author: Confessions (verse), 1937; (songs) Soldier Boy of Mine, 1921; I Remember Brown Eyes, 1926. Contbr. poems pub. in anthologies, mags., articles to mags. Home: Medicenter 531 W Thomas St Phoenix AZ 85013

HOLT, HELEN ELIZABETH (MRS. EDWIN CLAIR MUNRO), psychiatrist; b. Denver, Aug. 2, 1922; d. Robert Graves and Mabel Fredericka (Soper) Holt; B.A., U. Denver, 1944; M.D., U. Colo., 1946; m. Edwin Clair Munro, Mar. 17, 1946; children—William Clair, Frederick Graves, Stephen James. Intern, U. Ia., 1946-47; resident psychiatry Albany VA Hosp., (N.Y.), 1954-57; fellow psychiatry Albany Med. Center Hosp., 1957-58; practice medicine, specializing in psychiatry, Albany, part-time 1958—; mem. faculty Albany Med. Coll., 1958—, asso. prof. psychiatry, 1968—, dir. staff devel. Capital Dist. Psychiat. Center, 1972. Cons. Albany Home for Children, 1958-72. Home: Star Route Altamont NY 12009 Office: K 205 Albany Medical Center Albany NY 12208

HOLT, MARJORIE SEWELL, congresswoman; b. Birmingham, Ala., Sept. 17, 1920; d. Edward Roland and Alice Juanita (Felts) Sewell; B.A., Jacksonville (Fla.) U., 1945; J.D., U. Fla., 1949; m. Duncan McKay Holt, Dec. 26, 1946; children—Rachel (Mrs. Kenneth Hall Tschantre), Edward, Victoria. Admitted to bar, 1949; practice law, Annapolis, Md., 1949-66; clk. Anne Arundel Circuit Ct., Annapolis, 1966-72; mem. 93d Congress from 4th Md. dist. Supr. elections, Anne Arundel County, 1963-65; mem. housing com. Anne Arundel County Human Relations Commn., 1964-67; mem. Md. Gov.'s Commn. Law Enforcement and Adminstrn. Justice, 1970-73. Mem. Am., Md., Anne Arundel bar assns., League Women Voters, Bus. and Profl. Women's Club, Phi Kappa Phi, Phi Delta Delta. Presbyn. (elder). Mem. staff Fla. Law Rev., 1947-49. Office: 1510 Longworth Bldg Washington DC 20515

HOLT, ROBERTA L. CHANTLER, social worker; b. Pitts., Dec. 24, 1910; d. Thomas John and Sinah (Roberts) Chantler; B.A., Bethany Coll., 1932; M.S.W., U. Pitts., 1964; m. Donald Holt, July 18, 1935 (div. July 1945); children—Dawn (Mrs. Larry W. Anderson), Roberta (Mrs. John B. Buchanan). Recreation worker Fedn. Social Agys. Pitts., 1932-33; supr. Beaver County Mothers Assistance, Beaver, Pa., 1933-38, Beaver County Housing Authority, Beaver, 1941-61; caseworker Childrens Aid & Family Service, Beaver, 1961; dir. Beaver County Child Welfare Services, 1964—; therapist Beaver County Mental Health Center, Rochester, Pa., 1969—. Mem. Beaver County Health and Welfare Bd., 1965-67, Pa. Task Force for Foster Parent Tng., 1973—, Pa. Regional Com. for Social Work Staff Tng., 1973—; dir., sec. Tamaqui Village, 1955-57, 72—. Mem. Nat. Assn. Social Workers, Acad. Certified Social Workers, Profl. Social Workers Beaver County (treas. 1965-68), Conf. Agy. Execs., Pa. Assn. Child Welfare Execs., Human Services Forum, Am. Assn. U. Women. Republican. Mem. Christian Ch. Clubs: Beaver Century, Quota, Tamaqui Village Womans. Home: 124 Tamaqui Village Beaver PA 15009 Office: Allencrest Beaver PA 15009

HOLT, VICTORIA (PSEUDONYM OF ELEANOR BURFORD HIBBERT), author; b. London, Eng., 1906; d. Joseph and Alice (Tate) Burford; ed. privately; m. G.P. Hibbert. Author: (under pseudonym of Eleanor Burford) House at Cupid's Cross, 1949, Passionate Witness, 1949, Believe the Heart, 1950, Love Child, 1950, Saint or Sinner?, 1951, Dear Delusion, 1952, Bright Tomorrow, 1952, Leave Me My Love, 1953, When We Are Married, 1953, Castles in Spain, 1954, Heart's Afire, 1954, When Other Hearts, 1955, Two Loves in Her Life, 1955, Begin to Live, 1956, Married in Haste, 1956, To Meet A Stranger, 1957, Pride of the Morning, 1958, Dawn Chorus, 1959, Red Sky at Night, 1959, Blaze of Noon, 1960, Night of the Stars, 1960, Now That April's Gone, 1961, Who's Calling?, 1962; (under pseudonym Elbur Ford) Poison in Pimlico, 1950, Flesh and the Devil, 1950, Bed Disturbed, 1952, Such Bitter Business, 1953 (pub. in U.S. as Evil in the House, 1954); (under pseudonym Victoria Holt) Mistress of Mellyn, 1960, Kirkland Revels, 1962, Bride of Pendorric, 1963, The Legend of the Seventh Virgin, 1965, Manfreya in the Morning, 1966, The King of the Castle, 1967, The Queen's Confession, 1968, The Shivering Sands, 1969; (under pseudonym of Kathleen Kellow) Danse Macabre, 1952, Rooms at Mrs. Olivers', 1953, Lilith, 1954, It Began in Vauxhall Gardens, 1955, Call of the Blood, 1956, Rochester, The Mad Earl, 1957, Milady Charlotte, 1959, The World's A Stage, 1960; (under pseudonym of Jean Plaidy) Beyond the Blue Mountains, 1947, King's Pleasure, 1949 (pub. in Eng. as Murder Most Royal, 1949); Goldsmith's Wife, 1950, Madame Serpent, 1951, Italian Woman, 1952, Queen Jezebel, 1953, Daughter of Satan, 1952, Spanish Bridegroom, 1953, St. Thomas' Eve, 1954, Sixth Wife, 1954, Gay Lord Robert, 1955, Royal Road to Fotheringay, 1955, Wandering Prince, 1956, Health Unto His Majesty, 1956, Flaunting Extravagant Queen, 1957, Here Lies Our Sovereign Lord, 1957, Madonna of the Seven Hills, 1958, Triptych of Poisoners, 1958, Light on Lucrezia, 1958, Louis, The Well-Beloved, 1959, Rise of the Spanish Inquisition, 1959, Road to Compiegne, 1959, Castile for Isabella, 1960, Growth of the Spanish Inquisition, 1960, Spain for the Sovereigns, 1960, The Young Elizabeth, 1961, Meg Roper: Daughter of Sir Thomas More, 1961, The End of the Spanish Inquisition, 1961, Katherine, The Virgin Widow, 1961, The King's Secret, 1962, The Shadow of the Pomegranate, 1962, The Captive Queen of Scots, 1963, The Thistle and the Rose, 1963, The Young Mary Queen of Scots, 1962, Mary, Queen of France, 1964, The Murder on the Tower, 1964, Evergreen Gallant, 1965, The Three Clowns, 1965, The Haunted Sisters, 1966, The Queen's Favourites, 1966, The Spanish Inquisition: Its Rise, Growth and End, 1967, Caroline The Queen, 1968, Katharine of Aragon, 1968, The Prince and the Quakeress, 1968, The Third George, 1969, Catherine de Medici, 1969, Perdita's Prince, 1969, Sweet Lass of Richmond Hill, 1970; Indiscretions of the Queen, 1970; The Regent's Daughter, 1971; Goddess of the Green Room, 1971; Victoria in the Wings, 1972; Captive of Kensington Palace, 1972; The Queen and Lord M, 1973; The Queen's Husband, 1973; The Widow of Windsor, 1974; (under pseudonym of Ellaice Tate) Defenders of the Faith, 1956, Scarlet Cloak, 1957, Queen of Diamonds, 1958, Madame du Barry, 1959, This Was a Man, 1961. Contbr. to newspapers, mags. Home: 84 Kingston Hduse S Ennismore Gardens London SW 7 England Office: care A M Heath & Co Ltd 35 Dover St London WI England

HOLT, VIRGINIA RAYE, educator; b. Albany, Ga., Oct. 5, 1932; d. Clifford Raymond and Rosa Virginia (Jones) Holt; jr. coll. diploma Ga. Southwestern Coll., 1951; B.S., Ga. State Coll. for Women, 1953; M.S., Baylor U., 1959; Ed.D., U. Tenn., 1970. Tchr. phys. edn. Glynn Acad., Brunswick, Ga., 1953-58, supr. student tchrs., 1956; grad. asst. phys. edn. Baylor U., Waco, Tex., 1958-59; instr. phys. edn. Bonham Jr. High Sch., Odessa, Tex., 1959-61, instr. phys. edn. Odessa (Tex.) Jr. Coll., 1961-64, chmn. phys. edn. dept., 1963-67; grad. asst. phys. edn. U. Tenn., Knoxville, 1967-70, instr., 1970-71; dir. women's program, asso. prof. U. N.C., Chapel Hill, 1971-74, dir. women's intercollegiate program, 1971—, also mem. univ. com. on scholarships, awards and student aid, 1973—. Mem. Am., N.C. (chmn. required phys. edn. sect. 1974) assns. for health, phys. edn. and recreation, Nat. (mem. pres.'s adv. bd. 1971-73), So. (necrology com. 1974—) assns. for phys. edn. of coll. women, U.S. Lawn Tennis Assn., Am. Coll. Sports Medicine. Home: 1901 Fountainridge Rd Chapel Hill NC 27514

HOLTEN, VIRGINIA LOIS ZEWE (MRS. DAROLD DUANE HOLTEN), educator; b. McKeesport, Pa., Mar. 29, 1938; d. Albert Jacob and Virginia Kathryn (Minnick) Zewe; B.A. in Chemistry, Carlow Coll., Pitts., 1960; M.S. in Biochemistry, U. N.D., 1962, Ph.D., 1965; m. Darold Duane Holten, Dec. 29, 1962; 1 dau., Margaret. Research scientist Oak Ridge Asso. Univs., 1965; postdoctoral fellow Oak Ridge Nat. Lab., 1965-67; asst. prof. biology Roosevelt U., Chgo., 1967-68; postdoctoral fellow U. Cal. at Riverside, 1968-69; asst. prof. chemistry Riverside City Coll., 1969—, chmn. dept. chemistry, 1972—. Nat. Def. Edn. Act fellow, 1960-63; USPHS fellow, 1963-66; Am. Cancer Soc. fellow, 1966-67. Mem. Am. Chem. Soc., A.A.A.S., Sigma Xi. Author research publs. Home: 4928 Rockledge Dr Riverside CA 92506 Office: 4800 Magnolia Av Riverside CA 92506

HOLTER, CHARLOTTE SHEFFER (MRS. CECIL K. HOLTER, JR.), library adminstr.; b. Frederick, Md., June 24, 1925; d. George Washington and Ida Susan (Cline) Sheffer; A.B., Hood Coll., 1946; M.Ed. (grad. fellow), U. Md., 1972; m. Cecil K. Holter, Jr., Aug. 4, 1946; children—C. Kurt, G. Eric. With Frederick County (Md.) pub. schs., 1946—, tchr. Middletown High Sch., 1946-47, Elm St. Sch., Frederick, 1947-52; sch. librarian Frederick High Sch., 1963-64, New Midway Sch., Keymar, Md., 1964-66; library dept. chmn. Gov. Thomas Johnson High Sch., Frederick, 1966-71; supr. Instructional Materials Centers, Frederick County Bd. Edn., 1972—. Participant U. Md. Program for Adminstrs. in Curriculum Tech., 1970-72; mem. Middle States evaluation teams, 1966, 70, 73. Mem. N.E.A., Frederick County Sch. Librarians Assn. (past pres.) Md. State, Frederick County tchrs. assns., Assn. Ednl. Communications and Tech. Assn. Supervision and Curriculum Devel., Md. Ednl. Communications and Tech. Assn. Ednl. Media Assn. Md., Mortar Bd., Delta Kappa Gamma, Kappa Kappa Iota. Home: Route 1 Jefferson MD 21755 Office: Bd Edn Frederick County Annex Box 16A Route 1 Frederick MD 21701

HOLTER, JOANNE CLAIRE MINARD (MRS. ANDREW JACKSON RECTOR), social worker; b. Plattsburgh, N.Y., Nov. 15, 1929; d. Dalton Arthur and Arlene R. (Antes) Minard; student U. Rochester, 1947-50; B.A., Vanderbilt U., 1955; postgrad. Sch. Social Work, Bryn Mawr Coll., 1957-58; M.S.W., Smith Coll., 1963; m. Frank Robert Holter, Sept. 9, 1950 (div. Sept. 1962); 1 son, Peter Marcus; m. 2d, Andrew Jackson Rector, Aug. 10, 1973. With med. social service dept. U. Rochester Med. Center, 1963-65, pediatric research social worker, asst. in pediatrics and preventive medicine, 1965-67; pediatric social worker med. social service dept. Albany (N.Y.) Med. Center Hosp., 1969-70; adminstr., therapist, children's div. York County Mental Health Center, York, Pa., 1970-74; cons. dept. pediatrics U. Md. Sch. Medicine, Balt., 1974—. Mem. joint legislative com. on child care needs N.Y. State Subcom. on Health Services and Protective Services, 1968-69; mem. regional com. for protection children Pa. Dept. Pub. Welfare, inst. chmn., 1972-74; cons. to local agys., 1970-74; chmn. York County Com. for Protection Children, 1973-74, mem., 1974—. Mem. Nat. Assn. Social Workers, Acad. Certified Social Workers. Republican. Research and publs. in pediatrics. Home: 2299 Sycamore Rd York PA 17404 Office: 501A Grantley Rd York PA 17403

HOLTHAUS, ALICE MARION FESKO (MRS. JAMES J. HOLTHAUS), town ofcl.; b. Holyoke, Mass., Aug. 26, 1917; d. John and Barbara (Lokay) Fesko; grad. Coll. Practical Arts and Letters, Boston U., 1949; m. James Joseph Holthaus, June 14, 1952; 1 son, James Joseph. Sec., Highland Mfg. Co., Holyoke, 1936-40, Am. Bosch Corp., Springfield, Mass., 1940-41; sec. WPB, Washington, 1941-42, Springfield, 1942-43; exec. sec., auditor VA, Boston, 1945-53; asst. town clk., Rockland, Mass., 1962-67, town clk., 1967—. Served with USMCWR, 1943-45. Mem. Rockland C. of C. (dir., sec.), New Eng. Assn. City and Town Clks., Mass. Town Clks. Assn., Town and City Clks. Assn. Plymouth, Bristol and Norfolk Counties. Home: 38 Blossom St Rockland MA 02370 Office: Town Hall Rockland MA 02370

HOLTHOUSE, MARY MARGARET, journalist; educator; b. Portland, Ore., Dec. 13, 1911; d. Anthony Aloysius and Pearl Estelle (Fales) Holthouse; B.S., Ore. State U., 1937, M. in Home Econs., 1967; postgrad. Tchrs. Coll., Columbia, 1937. Food marketing specialist Ore. State U. Extension Service, Corvallis, 1965-66, extension communication specialist, newswriter dept. information, asst. prof., 1966—. Served to 1st lt. USAAF, 1943-46. Recipient Ore. State U. Found. grant to attend U. Wyo., 1968. Mem. Ore. Press Women (sec.), Nat. Fedn. Press Women, Ore. State U. Faculty Womens Club (past sec., chmn.), Omicron Nu, Gamma Phi Beta. Republican. Presbyn. Writer newspaper column Consumer Service, 1967. Editor columns Food Facts, 1971—, Speaking to the Consumer, 1971—. Contbr. articles to profl. publs. Home: 3407 NW Polk Av Corvallis OR 97330

HOLTON, CHARLENE POLAND (MRS. DECLAN J. O'DONNELL), physician; b. Memhis, Mar. 2, 1938; d. Clifford H. and Juanita (Smith) Poland; B.S., Fla. So. Coll., 1959; M.D., U. Miami, 1963; m. Rudolphus Holton, Jan. 29, 1960 (div. 1966); children—Stephanie, Dana; m. Declan J. O'Donnell, Sept. 18, 1971. Biology lab. asst. Fla. So. Coll., Lakeland, 1954-57; research asst., dept. clin. pathology U. Miami (Fla.), 1960-61, summer fellow, dept. pediatrics, 1961-62; intern Bapt. Meml. Hosp., Memphis, 1963-64; resident John Gaston Hosp., Memphis, 1964-65; research trainee chemotherapy St. Jude Childrens Research Hosp., Memphis, 1965, 66-67; chief resident Bapt. Meml. Hosp., Memphis, 1965-66; instr. pediatrics U. Tenn. Sch. Medicine, Memphis, 1966-67, asst. prof., 1968-69; asst. clin. pediatrician St. Jude Childrens Research Hosp., 1967-69; dir. pediatric oncology center Childrens Hosp., Denver, 1969—; clin. asst. prof. pediatrics U. Colo., 1969—. Mem. adv. bd. Colo. chpt. Leukemia Soc. Am., 1969-70; mem. new chemotherapeutic agts. liaison com. Nat. Cancer Inst., mem. nat. adv. com. Cancer Control. Mem. Colo. Gov.'s Commn. on Status of Women. Bd. govs. planning Cancer Center Rocky Mountain States; mem. adv. bd. Cancer Center No. Rockies. Diplomate Nat. Bd. Med. Examiners, Am. Bd. Pediatrics. Mem. Am. Womans Med. Soc., Western Soc. Pediatric Research, Internat. Soc Lymphology, Soc. Adolescent Medicine, Am. Assn. Cancer Research, Am. Assn. Cancer Edn., Am. Soc. Clin. Oncology. Contbr. articles to profl. jours. Home: Route 2 Box 289 Parker CO 80134 Office: 1056 E 19th Av Denver CO 80218

HOLTON, HILMA BERYL, editor; b. Northfield, Vt., Mar. 27, 1918; d. Edward Mayo and Anna May (Denny) Holton; A.B., Tufts U., 1941. With ins. dept. Mchts. Coop. Bank, Boston, 1941-43; Sec. Ark. Les Switch Corp., Watertown, Mass., 1943-44; with Harvard Bus. Sch., Boston, 1944—, asst. editor Business History Rev., 1950-62, adminstrn. asst., exec. sec. alumni office, 1962-66, asso. editor div. research, 1966—. Mem. Bookbuilders of Boston, Chi Omega. Conglist. (various coms.). Home: 58 Jacqueline Rd Waltham MA 02154 Office: Harvard Bus Sch 230 Morgan Hall Soldiers Field Boston MA 02163

HOLT-PAMOVSKIS, AINA JAUTRITE, psychiatrist; b. Ligatne, Latvia, May 29, 1919; d. Eduards Voldemars and Rozalija (Grinvalds) Zvaigzne; M.D., U. Latvia, Riga, 1943; postgrad. West London (Eng.) Med. Sch., 1957; m. William George Holt, July 29, 1953 (dec. Nov. 1971); m. 2d, Voldemars Pamovskis, Oct. 6, 1973. Came to U.S., 1961, naturalized, 1967. Practice medicine Latvia, 1945, Germany, 1945-49; capt. Pakistan Army Med. Corps, 1950-55; practice medicine, Eng., 1957-61; resident obstetrics and gynecology, Epsom Dist. Hosp., Surrey, Eng., 1959-61; practice medicine, U.S., 1961—; resident psychiatry U. Ore. Med. Sch., 1968-71; staff psychiatrist Dammasch Hosp., 1971—. Recipient Physicians Recognition award A.M.A., 1971. Mem. Am. Psychiat. Assn., Brit., Latvian med. assns. Office: Dammasch Hosp Wilsonville OR 97070

HOLTZMAN, ELIZABETH, congresswoman; b. Bklyn., Aug. 11, 1941; d. Sidney and Filla (Ravitz) Holtzman; B.A. magna cum laude, Radcliffe Coll., 1962; J.D., Harvard, 1965. Admitted to N.Y. bar, 1965; asso. firm Wachtell, Lipton, Rosen, Katz and Kern, N.Y.C., 1965-67; asst. to mayor N.Y.C., 1967-70; asso. firm Paul, Weiss, Rifkind, Wharton and Garrison, N.Y.C., 1970-72; mem. 93d congress from 16th dist. N.Y. Democratic state committeewoman, dist. leader, Bklyn., 1970; del. Dem. Nat. Conv., 1972; founder Bklyn. Women's Polit. Caucus, 1971. Mem. nat. adv. council Hampshire (Mass.) Coll. Named 1 of 10 Women of Yr. Mademoiselle mag., 1973; recipient Alumnae Recognition award Radcliffe Coll. Alumnae Assn., 1973. Mem. Bar Assn. City N.Y. Democrat. Jewish religion. Office: Longworth House Office Bldg Room 1009 Washington DC 20215

HOLVERSON, GEORGIA HELEN IDA, educator, therapist; b. Marshfield, Wis., May 13, 1942; d. Henry John and Helen Jewel (Carpenter) Holverson; A.A., Kendall Coll., 1961; B.S., U. Ill., 1964, M.A. (Office of Edn. fellow), 1969. Office of Vocational Rehab. trainee Dept. Health, Edn. and Welfare, Urbana, Chgo., 1961-64; asst. in occupational therapy U. Ill. Hosp., Chgo., 1964-66, acting supr., 1966-67; learning disabilities specialist cons. sch. dist. unit 5, Normal, Ill., 1969-70; supr. diagnostic clinic, dept. spl. edn. Ill. State U., Normal, 1970—; occupational therapy supr. Cook County Children's Hosp., Chgo., 1973—; asst. prof. occupational therapy U. Ill., Chgo., 1970—. Docent Chgo. Sch. Architecture Found., 1973—. Mem. Am., Ill. occupational therapy assns., Council for Exceptional Children, Orton Soc., Kappa Delta Pi, Phi Theta Kappa. Home: 1934 N Hudson St Chicago IL 60614 Office: Cook County Children's Hosp 700 S Wood Chicago IL 60612

HOLYER, ERNA MARIA (MRS. GENE WALLACE HOLYER), writer, artist; b. Weilheim, Bavaria, Germany, Mar. 15, 1925; d. Mathias and Anna Maria (Goldhofer) Schretter; came to U.S. 1956; naturalized, 1961; A.A., San Jose Evening Coll., 1964; student San Mateo Coll., San Jose State U., 1964-69; m. Gene Wallace Holyer, Aug. 24, 1957. Free lance writer under pseudonym Ernie Holyer, San Jose, 1960—; tchr. creative writing San Jose Met. Adult Edn., 1968—; one man shows, Saratoga, Cal., 1963, Los Gatos, Cal., 1964, Santa Clara, Cal., 1966. Recipient Lefoli award for excellence in adult edn. instr. San Jose Met. Adult Edn. Program, 1972; named Woman of Achievement, San Jose Mercury-News, 1973. Mem. Cal. Writers Club. Author: Rescue at Sunrise, 1965; Steve's Night of Silence, 1966; A Cow for Hansel, 1967; Lone Brown Gull, 1971; Song of Courage, 1970; Shoes for Daniel, 1974. Home: 6893 Campisi Ct San Jose CA 95120 Office: 6893 Campisi Ct San Jose CA 95120

HOLZBERG, BETTE CAROL, sch. psychologist; b. N.Y.C., Apr. 11, 1932; d. Paul and Gertrude (Dunay) Landsman; B.A., Hunter Coll., 1953; M.A., N.Y. U., 1954, M.A. in Edn. (U.S. Dept. Health, Edn. and Welfare grantee), 1964; m. Robert Holzberg, July 7, 1957; children—Lauren, Lisa, Leslie. Faculty dept. psychology Vassar Coll., 1954-56; staff psychologist Payne-Whitney Clinic, N.Y. Hosp., 1957; sch. psychologist Larchmont (N.Y.) Sch. System, 1958-59; dir.

guidance Westchester Children's Remedial Center, Yonkers, N.Y., 1959-71; dir. testing services Ednl. Center of Westchester, Yonkers, 1972—. Ednl. cons. Xerox Corp., 1971-73. Mem. Am. Psychol. Assn., Am. Personnel and Guidance Assn. Co-author: The I Don't Want to Read Workbook. Home: 27 Meadowood Path New Rochelle NY 10804 Office: Ednl Center Westchester Upper Mall Cross County Center Yonkers NY 10704

HOLZBERG, MARYLIN TELL (MRS. MARK HOLZBERG), merchant; b. Bronx, N.Y., Mar. 7, 1932; d. Louis and Ida R. (Holzberg) Tell; B.A., Brandeis U., 1953; m. Mark Holzberg, Sept. 5, 1954; children—Harris, Randy. Owner (with husband) Tells Originals, North Miami, Fla., 1961—. Treas. Greater Miami chpt. Brandeis U. Nat. Women's Com. Mem. Dade County Women's Polit. Caucus. Bd. dirs. Keystone Point Homeowner's Assn. Home: 13195 Biscayne Bay Dr North Miami FL 33161 Office: 12800 Biscayne Blvd North Miami FL 33161

HOLZINGER, MARGALITH, educator; b. Regensburg, Germany, Nov. 12, 1916; d. Ottmar and Daniela (Neuburger) Holzinger; teaching certificate Tchrs. Tng. Coll., Israel, 1939; M.A. (Nat. Council Jewish Women scholar), U. Minn., 1959, Ph.D. (Delta Kappa Gamma fellow, Merrill Palmer fellow), 1967. Tchr. in kibbutz movement, Israel, 1946-49; dir. curriculum lab. Tchrs. Coll., Tel Aviv, Israel, 1949-57; clinician, Israel, 1959-63; supr. U. Minn., Mpls., 1964-66, research fellow, 1966-67, coordinator psychology, 1967-69, asst. prof. ednl. psychology, 1969-70; asso. prof., program coordinator, dept. spl. edn. and rehab. Hofstra U., Hempstead, N.Y., 1970—. Cons. to adv. bd. Little Village Sch. for Handicapped Children, Merrick, N.Y., 1972—, South Shore Learning Center, Lynbrook, N.Y., 1973—; pvt. practice psychology, 1969—. Mem. Am. Psychol. Assn., Council for Exceptional Children, Am. Orthopsychiat. Assn., Internat. Reading Assn., Am. Assn. Univ. Profs., Pi Lambda Theta. Contbr. articles to profl. jours. Home: 150 Washington St Hempstead NY 11550

HOLZMAN, ELEANORE MARIENNE GRUSHLAW (MRS. ROBERT STUART HOLZMAN), psychologist; b. N.Y.C., Nov. 22, 1912; d. Israel and Isabelle (Feinberg) Grushlaw; B.A., Barnard Coll., 1933; M.A., Columbia, 1934; Ph.D., N.Y. U., 1950; m. Robert Stuart Holzman, May 27, 1938. Research psychologist House of Detention for Women, N.Y.C., 1935-40; co-founder, supr. psychol. clinic Exptl. Ct. for Wayward Minors, N.Y.C., 1937; staff psychologist N.Y.C. Dept. Correction, 1940-45, cons. psychologist, 1950-56, mem. med. adv. bd., 1957-61; lectr. dept. psychology Queens Coll., 1950, 51; acting asst. prof. dept. psychology Bklyn. Coll., 1952; cons. psychologist Bentley Schs., N.Y.C., 1951—, Eisman Day Nurseries, N.Y.C., 1965-73, Headstart Program for Handicapped, Conn., 1973—; pvt. practice children and adolescent clin. psychology, 1951—. Fellow Am. Psychol. Assn.; mem. Eastern, N.Y. State, Conn. psychol. assns., N.Y. Soc. Clin. Psychologists, N.Y. Soc. Freudian Psychologists (chmn. tng. com. 1967-69, corr. sec., dir. 1966—), Soc. Pediatric Psychologists, Phi Beta Kappa. Office: 35 Tamarack Av Danbury CT 06810 also 45 E 89th St New York City NY 10028

HOLZWORTH, DOROTHY CATHERINE, physician; b. Washington, Apr. 27, 1923; d. Fred R. and Catherine M. (Thomas) Holzworth; A.B., Coll. Notre Dame Md., 1944; M.A. (Peabody scholar 1944-46) Cath. U. America, 1946; M.D., George Washington U., 1950. Intern Emergency Hosp., Washington, 1950-51, resident 1951-54; resident Doctors' Hosp., Washington, 1954-55; instr. anesthesia U. Med. Hosp., Balt., 1955-57; staff anesthesiologist Md. Gen. Hosp., Balt., 1957-71, v.p. med. staff (1st woman), 1963-64; chief anesthesiology VA Hosp., Balt., 1971-73; gen. practice family medicine, Snow Hill, Md., 1973—. Diplomate Nat. Bd. Med. Examiners. Fellow Am. Coll. Anesthesiology; mem. Internat. Soc. Anesthesiologists, N.Y. Acad. Scis., Am. Soc. Anesthesiologists, Md. Soc. Anesthesiologists, A.M.A., Md. Soc. Med. Research, Worcester County, Balt. med. socs., Sigma Xi, Beta Beta Beta. Home: 203 Snow St Snow Hill MD 21863

HOMAN, DOROTHE LOUISE TARRENCE (MRS. DELMAR CHARLES HOMAN), librarian; b. Lincoln, Kan., Dec. 10, 1915; d. Harry Leslie and Lydia Augusta (Meinhartz) Tarrence; B.S. in Edn., Kan. State Tchrs. Coll., Emporia, 1939; m. Delmar Charles Homan, June 30, 1968. Elementary sch. tchr., Lincoln, 1939-43, Wichita, 1944-46; supt. sch. Lincoln County, Kan., 1947-67; head librarian Bethany Coll., Lindsborg, Kan., 1966—, also asst. prof. library sci. Mem. Kan. Study Com. for Educator's Handbook on Mental Health, 1961. Pres. Lincoln County Republican Women's Club, 1958-60; mem. sch. bd. United Sch. Dist. 400, Lindsborg, 1971—. Pres. bd. Lincoln-Carnegie Library, 1950-65. Mem. Am., Kan. library assns., Kan. Folklore Soc., Bus. and Profl. Women's Club (pres. Lincoln 1958-59), Federated Women's Club. Methodist. Club: Faculty Women's (Lindsborg). Editor Lincoln County Sch. Jours., 1947-66. Home: 705 W State St Lindsborg KS 67456

HOMET, MEREDITH ABELL MORGAN (MRS. ROLAND S. HOMET, JR.), urban affairs cons.; b. Tulsa; d. Dudley Digges and Rosalind (Hollow) Morgan; student Briarcliff Jr. Coll., 1949; B.A., Am. U., 1968, M.A., 1970; m. James Eliot Cross, Nov. 28, 1958 (div. 1971); children—Rosalind M., Daniel C.; m. 2d, Roland S. Homet, Sept. 18, 1971. Fashion coordinator Seidenbachs Dept. Store, Tulsa, 1950-52, head bridal dept., 1953; TV actress, producer KOTV, Tulsa, 1951-53; dir. nat. promotion Glenworth Corp., N.Y.C., 1952; producer Kids Kount, Am. U., 1968; cons. pub. affairs U.S. Office Econ. Opportunity, 1968-69; cons. audio visual dept. Doubleday & Co., N.Y.C., 1968-73; cons. pub. relations Smithsonian Instn., 1973—. Lectr. John Herron Art Mus., Indpls., 1954-55; chmn. children's awards Hollywood Bowl Com., 1957; lectr. Nat. Gallery, Washington, 1959-63; vice chmn. Presdl. Inaugural Medal Com., 1964; pres. Washington Area Tennis Patrons Found., 1964-67; chmn. Bal du Futur, 1966. Bd. dirs. D.C. Assn. Mental Health. Recipient award, D.C. Recreation and Park Soc., 1967, Community Action Vol. Service award United Planning Orgn., 1969. Hon. mem. Delta Sigma Theta. Home: 2950 University Terrace NW Washington DC 20016

HONEA, ELIZABETH ELMYRA FOX (MRS. JAMES TAYLOR HONEA), sch. adminstr.; b. Birmingham, Ala.; d. Chester Melton and Ida May (Jeff) Fox; student Howard Coll., U. Ala.; m. James Taylor Honea, Mar. 14, 1925; children—Jacqueline Elizabeth (Mrs. Prentiss Dean Wright), Joy Marie (Mrs. Roderick Theodore Hughes), James Taylor. Dir. Honea Pvt. Sch., Birmingham, 1943-53, Mountain Brook, Ala., 1953—; editor Honea Sch. Art Projects, 1964—. Mem. Birmingham Mus. Art (charter), Birmingham, Vestavia Hills art assns., Ala. Art League. Methodist (div. supt. children's depts.). Clubs: Vestavia Country; Executives, Metropolitan Dinner (Birmingham); Zonta (rec. sec. 1963-64, 69-70). Home: 1969 Hickory Rd Birmingham AL 36216 Office: 2102 Cahaba Rd English Village Mountain Brook AL 35223

HONEYCUTT, FLORA DIANE, ednl. ofcl.; b. Anson County, N.C., Apr. 26, 1947; d. Jack J. and Alma Ross (Kelly) Kendall; B.S., Appalachian State U., 1969; M.Ed., N.C. State U., 1974. Learning lab. coordinator Richmond Tech. Inst., Hamlet, N.C., 1969-70, registrar, 1970—. Sec., Hamlet Municipal Bd. Elections, 1973-74. Mem. Am., N.C. personnel and guidance assns., N.C. Student Personnel Services Assn. (sec. 1971-72), Carolinas Assn. Collegiate Registrars and Admissions Officers, Am. Personnel and Guidance Assn., Phi Alpha Theta. Home: 514 McDonald Av Hamlet NC 28345 Office: Box 1189 Hamlet NC 28345

HONG, EDNA HATLESTAD (MRS. HOWARD VINCENT HONG), author, translator; b. Thorpe, Wis., Jan. 28, 1913; d. Otto and Ida (Nordby) Hatlestad; B.A., St. Olaf Coll., 1938; m. Howard Vincent Hong, June 8, 1938; children—Irena (Mrs. Roy Elveton), Erik, Peder, Rolf, Mary (Mrs. Thomas Loe), Judith (Mrs. Patrick O'Sullivan), Theodore, Nathaniel. Recipient Nat. Book award Nat. Book Com., 1968, Nat. Endowment for the Humanities, 1972-73. Lutheran. Author: Muskego Boy, 1944, The Boy Who Fought with Kings, 1946, Clues to the Kingdom, 1968, Turn Over Any Stone, 1970, The Book of a Century, 1968, Gayety of Grace, 1972; From This Good Ground, 1974. Translator: (with Howard V. Hong) For Self Examination (S. Kierkegaard), 1944, Works of Love, 1962, Journals and Papers, I, II--, 1967, 70, Armed Neutrality, 1968, Kierkegaard's Thought (G. Malantschuk), 1972. Contbr. to Growing Up in Minnesota, 1974. Home: RFD 1 Northfield MN 55057

HONHOLT, EDITH MAY, editor; b. Charlotte, Mich., Mar. 3, 1928; d. Herman John and Lillian May (Bradley) Honholt; B.A., Cornell Coll., 1951; postgrad. Syracuse U., 1952-53. Asst. editor New Yorker mag., N.Y.C., 1953-57; with Houston Post, 1957—, asst. TV editor, 1957-60, TV editor, 1960-64, asst. to Sunday editor, 1964, women's reporter, 1964-65, women's editor, 1965-69, asst. to Sunday mag. editor, 1969-70, copy editor, 1970-71, day asst. news editor, 1971-72, day news editor, 1973—. Mem. Women in Communications. Home: 5529 Beverly Hill No 1 Houston TX 77027 Office: 4747 Southwest Freeway Houston TX 77001

HONIGMAN, HINDA LEBO (MRS. MAURICE HONIGMAN), club woman, music leader; b. Gastonia, N.C., July 17, 1903; d. David and Lena (Schultz) Lebo; student Peabody Conservatory Music, Balt.; studied voice with pvt. tchrs. in N.Y., Charlotte, N.C., Greenville, S.C.; Litt.D. (hon.), Catawba Coll., 1964; m. Maurice Honigman, June 19, 1923 (dec.); 1 dau., Shirley Aleen (Mrs. Ralph Sarlin). Pres. Gastonia Music Club, 1935-37, now hon. pres.; pres. N.C. Fedn. Music Clubs, 1940-44, mem. bd. dirs., 1929—, state treas., state v.p. 1932-40, N.C. rep. on bd. dirs. nat. fedn. 1943—, nat. extension chmn., 1947-51, v.p. Southeastern Region 1951-55, mem. nat. exec. com., 1954-56, chmn. bd. trustees Found. for Advancement of Music, hon. pres. N.C. Fedn., 1944—, hon. mem. and/or hon. pres. many state fedns., founder Mid-Week at Transylvania Music Camp, 1948; 1st v.p. Nat. Fedn. Music Clubs, 1965-67, nat. pres., 1967-71, chmn. finance dept., mem. nat. exec. com.; patroness mem. Sigma Alpha Iota. Mem. adv. com. N.C. Recreation Commn., 1941-62, vice chmn. adv. com., 1959-62; mem. U.S. Com. to Further Am. Contemporary Music; mem. Nat. Council Arts and Govt.; nat. adv. council Inst. Studies Am. Music, U. Mo.; 1st v.p. Nat. Music Council, 1967-71. Founder Gastonia Community Concert Assn., 1937; founder, pres. Gastonia Music Edn. Found.; founder Oglebay Midweek at Oglebay Inst., Wheeling, W.Va., 1953; bd. dirs. Gaston County Mental Health Assn., Am. Symphony Orch. League; rep. John F. Kennedy Center for Performing Arts, 1967—; trustee Brevard (N.C.) Music Center; mem. found. bd. Sigma Alpha Iota. First N.C. woman elected fellow Internat. Inst. Arts and Letters, 1961; Hinda Honigman ann. scholarship to Brevard Music Center named in her honor by Nat. Fedn. Music Clubs, 1949; recipient spl. citation for contbn. through music to recreation N.C. Recreation Soc., 1957; Distinguished Citizens award Gov. N.C.; named to Exec. and Profl. Hall of Fame. Pres. N.C. Assn. Jewish Women, 1938-40. A library bldg. valued at $20,000.00 erected at Transylvania Music Camp, Brevard, N.C., in 1959 through funds from 14 states in Southeastern Region of Nat. Fedn. Music Clubs called Hinda Honigman Music Library; Hinda Honigman dance scholarship established by Brevard Music Center, 1969; $500 ann. scholarship for blind in her name given by Nat. Fedn. Music Clubs, 1971; originator Am. Music Month (ann. observance), 1958. Home: 1660 Westbrook Circle Wesley Park Gastonia NC 28052

HOOD, JANET (MRS. PHILIP VAN ORDEN), physician; b. Cambridge, Mass., Apr. 17, 1916; d. Thurman Los and Ida Smith (Irving) Hood; A.B., Tufts U., 1936, M.S., 1937; M.D., Yale, 1941; m. Philip Stanley Van Orden, July 17, 1943; children—John Van Orden, Wendy (Mrs. Donald Kellogg), Kate. Intern, Albany Hosp., (N.Y.), 1941-42; resident Lakeside Hosp., Cleve., 1942-43; clin. asst. Albany Med. Sch., (N.Y.), 1945—; student health physician State U. N.Y., Albany, 1955-65, dir. student health service, 1965—; mem. staff Albany Med. Center. Active Planned Parenthood Clinics, Cleve. and Albany, N.Y., 1942-45; pres. N.Y. State Coll. Health Assn., 1968; chmn. med. adv. bd. Planned Parenthood, 1962, mem. exec. bd., 1963—. Fellow Am. Coll. Health Assn.; mem. Phi Beta Kappa, Chi Omega. Presbyn. Club: University (Albany, N.Y.). Home: 261 State St Albany NY 12210 Office: 1400 Washington Av Albany NY 12222

HOOD, JOAN HOLMAN, home economist; b. Milw.; d. John A. and Myrtle (Salter) Holman; B.S., U. Wis., 1956, M.S., 1958; certificate Chinese Cooking Sch., Tokyo, Japan, 1966; m. Robert G. Hood, Apr. 11, 1953 (div. 1967). Dir., Wis. Apple Inst., Madison, 1954; demonstrator home service Potomoc Electric Power Co., Washington, 1956-58; nutritionist Wis. Dept. Agr., 1958-60; free lance home economist cons., travel cons., Mukwonago, Wis., 1961—; producer womans spl. programs WISC-TV, 1961-67; writer food column Milw. Jour., 1961-63; first world food demonstrations for World Food Expn., Madison, 1967; home economist Far East Trade Fairs for Fgn. Agrl. Service, 1966; series of programs for Internat. Cookbook program over Nat. Ednl. tv, 1968-69; mgr. Diners-Fugazy travel, Milw., 1970-71; coordinator fed. projects Waukesha County Tech. Inst., 1971—; cons. West Bend Co., 1961-63; instr. fgn. cooking course Milw. Inst. Tech., 1967-69; mem. Milw. Internat. Inst.; hon. mem. Wis. Ednl. Broadcasters Council; cons. MODOC programming co. Co-chmn. twp. drive Am. Heart Soc., 1960; dir. drive Easter Seals, active drive for Waukesha County Hosp., 1958; supt. jr. div. Wis. State Fair, 1959-60; acting dir. women's com. June Dairy Month, 1960. Chmn. Republican Twp. drive, 1966. Recipient Wis. Jaycette C.A.R.O.L. State award, 1964. Mem. Am. Women in Radio and TV (past state program chmn.), Wis. Home Econs. Assn. (nat. meeting del.), Home Economists in Bus. (past membership and promotional dir.), Women in Communications, Phi Upsilon Omicron, Delta Delta Delta. Address: 2524 N 45th St Milwaukee WI 53208

HOOD, MARILYN GILBERTSON (MRS. KENNETH JAMES HOOD), editor; b. Chgo., Dec. 29, 1927; d. Gynter Nicholas and Anna Matilda (Quarfot) Gilbertson; B.A., Winona State Coll., 1949; m. Kenneth James Hood, June 20, 1953. Reporter, ch. editor Winona (Minn.) Daily News, 1949-53; ch. editor, reporter Watsonville (Cal.) Register-Pajaronian, 1953-54; newswriter Coll. Wooster (O.), 1959-63; book editor Doubleday & Co., N.Y.C., 1963, Ednl. Devel. Labs., Huntington, N.Y., 1964-65; editor spl. publs., author, editor Echoes monthly newsmag. Ohio Hist. Soc., Columbus, 1968—. Mem. Ohio Commn. Status of Women. Recipient James O. Supple award Religious Newswriters Assn., 1953; named Franklin County Author, Ohioana Library, 1970. Mem. Women in Communications, Nat. Acad. TV Arts and Scis., League Women Voters, Am. Assn. U. Women, Women's Polit. Caucus, Ohio Designer Craftsmen, Am. Craftsmens Council, Mensa, Sigma Delta Chi. Author: Canals of Ohio, 1825-1913, 1969, rev. edit., 1971; The First Ladies of Ohio and the Executive Mansions, 1970. Contbr. articles to profl. jours. Home: 3310 Somerford Rd Columbus OH 43221 Office: 1982 Velma Av Columbus OH 43211

HOOD, VIRGINIA FORD (MRS. FREDERICK REDDING HOOD), civic worker; b. Vinita, Okla., May 1, 1905; d. William Thomas and Demmeria (Byrd) Ford; student Northeastern State Tchrs. Coll., 1920-21, 21-22; A.B., Okla. U., 1924; m. Frederick Redding Hood, Dec. 7, 1924; children—Frederick Redding, William Richard, Virginia Carol (Mrs. Kenneth Lee Pierce). Pres., Ladies Aux. Oklahoma County Med. Soc., 1937, co-chmn. Oklahoma City conv. So. Med. Conv., 1938, chmn. state conv. Okla. Med. Soc., 1950. Dist. chmn. Big One Dr., United Fund, Oklahoma City, 1953; chmn. Okla. Art Center Dr., 1957; capt. spl. gifts div. United Appeal, 1960-69, gen. chmn. Kappa Alpha Theta Found. Drive, 1964-65; chmn. Heritage Hills Hist. Home Tour, 1970-72; pres. Mothers Assn. U. Okla., 1957-58, Okla. Art League, 1960-61, Heritage Hills Aux., 1972-73; mem. Modern Classics, Oklahoma City; dir. YWCA, 1939-41, 66-72, met. bd. dirs., 1969-72, v.p., 1966-69, chmn. personnel com. 1966-68, 70-72, mem. dept. campus Christian life Okla. Assn. Christian Chs., 1964-68; pres. Heritage Hills Women's Com. of Hist. Preservation, 1973—. Mem. Kappa Alpha Theta (Okla. chmn. 1928-31, pres. Oklahoma City alumnae chpt. 1948-51, corp. bd. Alpha Omicron chpt. at U. Okla. 1954-57, alumnae dist. pres. 1957-60, grand council 1960-64, v.p. service 1966-70, mem. bd. trustees found. 1966-70). Mem. Christian Ch. (deaconess bd. Oklahoma City 1954-57, 65-68, 72—, past chmn.; pres. Christian Women's fellowship 1960-61, 61-62, tchr. bus. women's class, sponsor young married class). Club: Coterie Study (Oklahoma City). Home: 300 19th St NW Oklahoma City OK 73103

HOOD-ADAMS, REBECCA CAROLYN, pub. relations exec.; b. Gernada, Miss., Oct. 15, 1949; d. Tildon Willie and Rose Marie (Couch) Hood; student David Lipscomb Coll., 1967-68, U. So. Miss., 1969; B.A. cum laude, Memphis State U., 1971; m. Michael Oliver Adams, July 17, 1972. Copywriter, Pat Martin Advt. Agy., Clarksdale, Miss., 1967; reporter, columnist Clarksdale (Miss.) Press Register, 1968-69; reporter, Today's News, Harriman, Tenn., 1971; pub. relations and mag. editor Malone & Hyde, Inc., Memphis, Tenn., 1972; talent coordinator Holiday Inns, Inc., Memphis, Tenn., 1972; asst. dir. pub. relations United Way Greater Memphis, 1973-74; senate communications coordinator State of Tenn., Memphis, 1974—; pres. Rivertown Enterprises, 1973—, Levee Side Pub. Co., 1973—. Recipient award Freedoms Found., 1966; named Outstanding Staffer in Mid-South, Memphis Comml. Appeal, 1967, Most Promising Young Poet in Miss., Miss. Penwomen, 1965-67. Mem. Internat. Assn. Bus. Communications, Women in Communication, Vol. Women's Roundtable (chmn. communications com. 1973-74), Sigma Delta Chi, Sigma Phi. Mem. Ch. of Christ. Clubs: Capitol (Nashville), Memphis Press, Nashville Press. Author: Dry Creek Lovers, 1973. Editor: Tiger Rag, 1970-71. Contbr. articles to profl. jours. Home: 531 Prescott St S Memphis TN 38111 Office: War Memorial Bldg Memphis TN 38101

HOOGENAKKER, VIRGINIA RUTH, educator, violinist; b. Des Moines, Apr. 8, 1921; d. Timothy and Bertha (Kaldenberg) Hoogenakker; Mus.B. cum laude, Belhaven Coll., 1943; Mus.M., Chgo. Mus. Coll., 1947. Tchr. instrumental music Jackson Pub. Schs., 1943-47; mem. faculty Belhaven Coll., Jackson, Miss., 1947—, asso. prof. violin and music theory, 1947—, chmn. div. I, 1964—, chmn. dept. music, 1964—. Prin. 2d violin Jackson Symphony Orch., 1944—; mem. bd., 1958—. Bd. mem., sec. Jackson Opera Guild, 1948—; mem. worship and music com. Southeastern Synod, Luth. Ch. Am., 1966—. Named Alumnus of Year, Belhaven Coll., 1963. Mem. Miss. (mem. bd. 1965—, v.p. 1971-72, pres.), Jackson (pres. 1948) music tchrs. assns., Mu Phi Epsilon (nat. v.p. 1962—, Southeastern province gov. 1962—). Club: Chaminade (pres. 1958—), Belhaven College Faculty (pres. 1959). Home: 2020 Plantation Blvd Jackson MS 39211

HOOK, ALICE PALO, librarian; b. Superior, Wis., Feb. 4, 1909; d. Elmer George and Helen (Payne) Palo; B.S., U. Minn., 1930; m. Norris M. Hook, June 21, 1945 (dec. Oct. 1946). Asst. in order dept. U. Minn., 1930; Taft order librarian U. Cin., 1931-37, head acquisition dept., 1943-46; order librarian Temple U., Phila., 1937-43; librarian Hist. and Philos. Soc. of Ohio, Cin., 1947-63, Cin. Art Mus., 1964-74. Mem. vol. canteen corps A.R.C., 1941-63. Bd. dirs. Cin. Met. YWCA, 1957-70, rec. sec. bd., 1959-61, pub. relations chmn., 1961-64, centennial chmn., 1968; women's bd. dirs. Clovernook Home for the Blind, 1974—. Mem. Am., Ohio library assns., Spl. Libraries Assn. (past pres. Cin., past chmn. nat. com. pub. relations, chmn. picture div. 1958-60, chmn. mus. div. 1964-66), Alpha Xi Delta. Clubs: Cincinnati Woman's (dir. 1974—), College (dir. Cin. 1967-74), Altrusa (gov. 5th dist. 1956-58). Contbr. articles to profl. publs. Home: 359 Resor Av Cincinnati OH 45220

HOOKS, ELEANOR WRIGHT (MRS. JONATHAN T. HOOKS), librarian; b. Raleigh, N.C., June 5, 1914; d. William Booker and Jennie (Ellis) Wright; B.A., Brenau Coll., 1935; profl. librarian certificate U. N.C., 1966; m. Jonathan Thel Hooks, Oct. 7, 1939; children—Jonathan Thel, William Robert, Ellis Wright. Mem. staff Smithfield (N.C.) Pub. Library, 1954-57, chief librarian, 1954-60; chief librarian Johnston County (N.C.) Library System, 1961—. Mem. exec. com. Johnston County Forum, 1973-74; v.p. Johnston County Arts Council, 1973-74, pres., 1974-75. Mem. Southeastern, N.C. library assns., Johnston County Hist. Soc., Johnston County Geneal. Soc., Hastings House Assn., N.C. Fedn. Woman's Clubs. Democrat. Methodist. Home: 108 Johnston St Smithfield NC 27577 Office: 305 Market St Smithfield NC 27577

HOOPER, ANNE CAROLINE DODGE (MRS. WILLIAM DALE HOOPER), physician; b. Groton, Mass., July 16, 1926; d. Carroll William and Bertha (Wiener) Dodge; A.B., Washington U., St. Louis, 1947, M.D., 1952; m. William Dale Hooper, June 17, 1952; children—Elizabeth Anne, Joan Elaine, Caroline Mae. Rotating intern Va. Mason Hosp., Seattle, 1952-53; resident internal medicine St. Francis Hosp., Hartford, Conn., 1953-54; resident pathology New Britain Gen. Hosp., 1954-57, Presbyn. Hosp., Phila., 1957-58; asst. med. examiner, Phila., 1958-60; regional med. examiner, Vt., St. Albans, 1968-71; dir. radioisotope lab. Coatesville (Pa.) Hosp., 1963; cons. pathology VA Hosp., Coatesville, 1964-66, acting chief lab., 1966; cons. pathology VA Hosp., Phila., 1964; dir. labs. St. Albans Hosp., 1966-69, Kerbs Hosp., St. Albans, 1966-71, Williamson (W.Va.), Mongan County (Ky.), McDowell (Ky.), 1971-74, Beckley (W.Va.) Appalachian regional hosps., 1974—; asst. pathology U. Pa., 1957-58; instr. dept. pathology U. Vt. Coll. Medicine, 1967-71. Vis. lectr. forensic pathology Jefferson Med. Coll., Phila., 1958-60. Pres., Fairfield St. P.T.A., St. Albans, 1967-68. Recipient Borden award Washington U. Sch. Medicine, 1952. Diplomate in path. anatomy, clin. pathology, forensic pathology Am. Bd. Pathology. Fellow Coll. Am. Pathologists, Am. Soc. Clin. Pathologists, Am. Acad. Forensic Scis.; mem. A.M.A., Internat. Acad. Pathology, W.Va., Raleigh County med. socs., Phi Beta Kappa, Sigma Xi. Home: 104 Elmridge Ct Beckley WV 25801 Office: Beckley Appalachian Regional Hosp Beckley WV 25801

HOOPER, DIXIE FAY LEECH (MRS. ROBERT DONALD HOOPER), city ofcl.; b. Charlotte, Tenn., Aug. 22, 1910; d. Willie L. and Eva B. (Underhill) Leech; diploma Byrne Comml. Coll., Dallas, 1930; m. Robert Donald Hooper, Dec. 26, 1947. Asst. cashier Bank Charlotte, Tenn., 1930-37, Dickson County Bank, Charlotte, 1937-52; bookkeeper, sec. Hamilton Ins. Agy., Charlotte, 1955—; sec. Judge W.M. Leech, Chancery Ct., 1960—; librarian Pub. Library, Charlotte, 1955—. City clk. City Charlotte, 1968—. Treas. Charlotte (Tenn.) Home Demonstration, 1967—. Mem. Am. Legion (treas. 1959—). Home: PO Box 213 Charlotte TN 37036 Office: PO Box 187 Charlotte TN 37036

HOOPER, IRENE UPSHAW, environmental edn. center adminstr.; b. Miami, Sept. 26, 1935; d. Len William and Florence Akin (Akin) Upshaw; A.A., Mars Hill Coll., 1955; B.A., Hardin-Simmons U., 1957; M.S., Barry Coll., 1972; m. Jackson Holloway Hooper, Sept. 2, 1960 (dec. Oct. 1970). Classroom tchr., Miami, Fla., 1958-60; guidance counselor, journalism tchr., Miami, 1961-69; camp dir. Seacamp, Big Pine Key, Fla., 1964—; exec. dir. Newfound Harbor Marine Inst., Big Pine Key, Fla., 1970—, site adminstr. San Francisco State U. project. Camp dir. Miami Bapt. Assn., 1960; mem. Big Pine Key Civic Assn., 1968—. Mem. Am. Personnel and Guidance Assn., Fla. Edn. Assn., Dade County Classroom Tchrs. Assn. (bldg. rep. 1960-69), Am. Camping Assn. (dir. Fla. sect.). Home: 750 NE 61st St Miami FL 33137 Office: Route 1 Box 170 Big Pine Key FL 33043

HOOPER, VIRGINIA FITE (MRS. JAMES F. HOOPER III), Republican nat. committeewoman; b. Byhalia, Miss., Sept. 23, 1917; d. Pleasant LaFayette and Nell (Brooks) Fite; student Southwestern U. at Memphis, 1936-37, U. Miss., 1937-39, U. Ala., 1939-41, U. Ga., 1941-42; m. James F. Hooper III, Jan. 29, 1943; children—Cynthia Merriman (Mrs. Ralph Rood), James Fullerton IV, Pleasant Fite. Pres., City Garden Council, 1961-63; mem. City Beautification Council, 1962; pres. P.T.A., Columbus, Miss., 1949-50; mem. Cherokee Garden Club, pres., 1955, Lowndes County Chowder and Marching Club; permanent meml. gifts chmn. Lowndes County Heart Assn.; adv. bd. Debutante Assembly; mem. membership com. Miss. State Heart Assn., 1969—. Bd. dirs. Lowndes County Kidney Found. Nat. del. States Rights Conv., 1948; del. Rep. Nat. Conv., 1960, 64; Miss. vice chmn. Miss. Rep. Com., 1960-62; mem. Rep. Nat. Com. from Miss., 1962—, mem. exec. com., 1969—. Bd. dirs. Natchez Trace Pkwy. Assn., 1971-73. Named GOP Woman of Year from Miss., 1969, Lowndes County Woman of Year, 1972. Mem. Nat. Assn. Parliamentarians, Nat. Assn. Jr. Auxs. (pres. Columbus 1957-58, nat. pres. 1959-60), D.A.R. (regent 1954-56), U.D.C. (pres. 1973), Am. Legion Aux., Five Crown, Lowndes County Hist. Soc., Lowndes County Soc. for Preservation of Antiquities, Historic Columbus, Inc. Delta Beta Sigma (nat. v.p. 1938-39), Chi Omega (pres. Nu Beta chpt. 1940, pres. Miss. alumnae 1972-73, Most Outstanding Miss. Alumnae award 1968). Mem. Order Eastern Star. Episcopalian. Clubs: Columbus Country; Lowndes County Chowder and Marching, Magowa Hunt (Lowndes County); Mary McCarty (Miss. State U.) (pres. 1972-73). Address: 800 8th St N Columbus MS 39701

HOOPER-SPEAR, EMILY FRANCIS, interior designer; b. Hamilton, Can., Sept. 3, 1891; d. Francis William and Mary Evelyn (Twizell) Hooper; B.A., Columbia, 1920; m. Alexander Spear, July 26, 1920. Advt. rep. Furniture World, N.Y.C., 1920-23; account exec. Blumenthal Bros., N.Y.C., 1923-35, Hyman & Co., N.Y.C., 1935-39, Fellows Davis, N.Y.C., 1939-42, all members N.Y. Stock Exchange; pvt. practice as interior designer. Mem. Nat. Soc. Interior Designers, Designers and Decorators Guild Miami, Miami Shores C. of C. (Miami), Internat. Platform Assn. Clubs: De La Casserole (Paris, France); La Gorce Country (Miami Beach, Fla.); Miami Shores Country (Miami, Fla.); Jockey. Home: 10659 E 10th Pl Miami FL 33138

HOOPES, JANET L., educator. Prof. edn. and child devel., dir. Child Study Inst., Bryn Mawr Coll. Office: Dept Edn Bryn Mawr Coll Bryn Mawr PA 19010

HOOSE, IDABELLE KARIN PETERSON (MRS. KENNETH A. HOOSE), lawyer; b. Akron, O.; d. Klaus and Karin (Anderson) Peterson; student U. Akron, 1930-33, J.D., 1969; B.S., Kent State U., 1938, M.A., 1938; m. Kenneth A. Hoose, May 18, 1934; children—Kenneth A., Frederick R. Instr. psychology Kent (O.) State U., 1947-53, asst. prof., 1953-69, asso. prof., 1969-71, mem. honors council, 1961-71, cons. teaching machines and programming, 1958-71, rep. Am. Assn. Colls. for Tchr. Edn., 1962-71; cons. self instrn. project Earlham Coll., 1959—; admitted to Fla. bar, 1970, Ohio bar, 1970; pvt. practice law, Ohio and Fla., 1970—; asst. law dir., pros. atty. City of Kent, 1971—. Mem. Kent Little Theatre, 1937-40; orgn. com. One Health Fund Drive, Kent, 1959. Bd. dirs. Portage County Mental Health Assn., pres., 1957-59; bd. dirs. Portage County Cancer Soc., 1958-61; mem. Portage County Mental Health and Retardation Bd., 1972—. Mem. Am. Acad. Polit. and Social Sci., Am., Midwestern, Ohio psychol. assns., Am. Assn. U. Profs. (acting v.p. 1962—), Am., Ohio, Fla., Portage County, Akron bar assns., Faculty Women Profl. Club, N.Y. Acad. Scis., Kappa Delta Gamma, Kappa Delta Pi, Psi Chi, Kappa Kappa Gamma, Phi Delta Delta. Mem. Order Eastern Star. Research in ednl. machine design. Home: Box 74 Kent OH 44240 also 631 16th Av S Naples FL 33940

HOOST, MURIEL SHANLEY, antique dealer; b. Bklyn., Feb. 11, 1915; d. Joseph Aloysius and Camilla Helamar (Doerner) Shanley; B.S. in Bus. Adminstrn., Adelphi-Suffolk Coll., Garden City, N.Y., 1962; m. Allen John Hoost, Apr. 14, 1934; children—Joan (Mrs. Lauren L. McMaster III), Wendy (Mrs. John Gagliotti). Pvt. exec. sec. to pub. accountant, Sayville, N.Y., 1946—; propr. Crown Antiques, Sayville, 1966—; lectr. in field, 1967—. Active local A.R.C., South Side Hosp., Bay Shore, N.Y.; chmn. publicity antique shows Suffolk Heart Assn. Mem. Am. Assn. U. Women (chpt. treas. 1965-67), East Hampton Property Owners Assn., Nat. Assn. Dealers in Antiques, Alpha Omicron Pi. Episcopalian. Club: Skytop. Home: 63 Benson Av Sayville NY 11782 Office: Box 266 Sayville NY 11782

HOOVER, HELEN D. (MRS. ADRIAN E. HOOVER), author; b. Greenfield, O., Jan. 20, 1910; d. Thomas Franklin and Hannah (Gomersall) Blackburn; student Ohio U., 1927-29, De Paul U., U. Chgo., 1943-49; m. Adrian Everett Hoover, Feb. 13, 1937. Proofreader, Audit Bur. Circulations, Chgo., 1931-43; chemist Pitts. Testing Lab., Chgo., 1943-45; prodn. metallurgist Ahlberg Bearing Co., Chgo., 1945-48; research metallurgist Internat. Harvester Co., Chgo., 1948-54; free-lance writer contbg. to gen., nature and juvenile mags., Minn., also N.M., 1954—. Recipient Ann. Achievement award Metal Treating Inst., 1959, Blue Flame Ecology Salute, 1973, Zia award N.M. Press Women, 1973. Mem. Authors Guild, Internat. Platform Assn., Authors League Am., Nat. Fedn. Press Women, Wilderness Soc., Defenders of Wildlife, Jersey Wildlife Preservation Trust, Internat. Council Bird Preservation, Internat. Union Conservation Nature, Nat. Audubon Soc., Nat. Wildlife Fedn., Mpls. Audubon Soc., Nat. Cath. Soc. Animal Welfare, Com. Preservation Tule Elk, Fauna Preservation Soc., Minn. Ornithologists Union, Friends of Sea Otter, Save-the-Redwoods League, Nature Conservancy, World Wildlife Fund, Humane Soc. U.S., Mystery Writers Am., Marquis Library Soc., Sierra Club and Found. Author: The Long-Shadowed Forest, 1963; Animals at My Doorstep, 1966; The Gift of the Deer, 1966; Great Wolf and the Good Woodsman, 1967; A Place in The Woods, 1969; Animals Near and Far, 1970; The Years of the Forest, 1973. Patentee agrl. implement disks. Address: Brandt & Brandt 101 Park Av New York City NY 10017

HOOVER, LILLIAN PEART (MRS. DONALD EDWARD HOOVER), occupational therapist; b. Los Banos, Cal., Sept. 9, 1930; d. Richard Harry and Christine L. (White) Peart; A.A., Monterey Peninsula Coll., 1952; B.A., San Jose State Coll., 1954; m. Donald Edward Hoover, Apr. 1, 1964. Staff occupational therapist Naval Hosp., Portsmouth, Va., 1955-57, Oakland, Cal., 1957-62, San Diego, 1962-65; head occupational therapist Naval Hosp., Bethesda, Md., 1965-71; head occupational therapy dept. Naval Hosp., Portsmouth, Va., 1971—. Mem. Assn. Mil. Surgeons (chmn. specialists sect. 1970-71), Am., Va., Washington (pres. 1969-71) occupational therapy assns. Toastmistress (pres. 1974-75). Clubs: Shrine Cruise, Elizabeth Manor Golf and Country (Portsmouth). Home: 207 Snead Fairway Portsmouth VA 23701 Office: Naval Hosp Portsmouth VA 23708

HOOVER, ROSALIE MARY (MRS. RAYMOND HOOVER), paper products mfg. co. exec.; b. Jersey City, Oct. 29, 1911; d. Bernard J. and Elizabeth (O'Callaghan) Quinn; ed. pub. schs.; m. Raymond Hoover, Sept. 18, 1935; children—Raymond, Rosalie (Mrs. Edward J. Dingler III), Kenneth C. Part-time personnel cons. Arvey Corp., Jersey City, 1948-49, dir. personnel, 1950—, also equal opportunity coordinator. Trustee Hudson County Tb Assn., 1963-64. Mem. Hudson County Personnel Assn. (sec. 1969-70), Hudson County Women's Grand Jury Assn., St. Aloysius Rosary Soc. Home: PO Box 470 Jersey City NJ 07304 Office: 300 Communipaw Av Jersey City NJ 07304

HOPE, CATHARINE MARGARET, clubwoman; b. Jefferson City, Mo., Oct. 26, 1898; d. George and Lily (Williams) Hope; B.S. in Edn., U. Mo., 1923. Tchr. Central Sch., Jefferson City, 1923-32; cashier Home Savs. & Loan Assn., Jefferson City, 1935-48; tchr. East Sch., Jefferson City, 1948-63. Vol. worker Meml. Community Hosp., Jefferson City, 1969-71. Mem. Cole County Hist. Soc. (historian 1963-69), Am. Bus. Women's Assn. (Woman of Year 1971), Alpha Gamma Delta Alumnae Club (treas. 1966—). Mem. Order Eastern Star. Clubs: Art (pres. 1968-70), Capital City Woman's (corr. sec. 1973). Address: 318 E McCarty St Jefferson City MO 65101

HOPE, ELIZA MILFORD TATUM (MRS. ROBERT HERVEY HOPE), sch. adminstr.; b. Walhalla, S.C., Mar. 20, 1908; d. Thomas Hubert and Bess McClair (Mann) Tatum; A.B., Goucher Coll., 1928; m. Robert Hervey Hope, June 10, 1933; children—Sara McClair (Mrs. James Emmanuel Bostic), Mary Tatum. Prin. pvt. sch., Ft. Bragg, N.C., 1928-29; tchr., dir. kindergarten Erlanger Sch., Lexington, N.C., 1930-33; owner, dir. Pvt. Pre-Sch., Honea Path, S.C., 1955-69; dir. Reading Clinic for Remedial Reading, 1960-63. Bd. dirs. Jennie Ervin Library, 1969—. Mem. Am. Assn. U. Women, D.A.R. (regent 1966-69), U.D.C. Episcopalian. Home: 210 Hampton Av Honea Path SC 29654

HOPF, ALICE MARTHA LIGHTNER, author; b. Detroit, Oct. 11, 1904; d. Clarence A. and Frances (McGraw) Lightner; grad. Westover Sch., 1923; A.B., Vassar Coll., 1927; m. Ernest J. Hopf, Apr. 29, 1935; 1 son, Christopher. Author fiction, sci. fiction, natural sci. and nature stories; contbr. articles and stories to Argosy, Audubon, Boys Life, Hitchcock Mystery, Man from Uncle, If, Scholastics mags., Nat. Humane Review, N.Y. Daily News. Mem. Authors Guild, Sci. Fiction Writers Am., Xerxes Soc., N.Y. Entomol. Soc. Author: The Rock of Three Planets, 1963; The Planet Poachers, 1965; The Space Ark, 1968; The Walking Zoo of Darwin Dingle, 1969; Doctor to the Galaxy, 1965; The Galactic Troubadours, 1965; The Space Plague, 1966; The Space Olympics, 1967; The Day of the Drones, 1969; Monarch Butterflies, 1965; Wild Traveler, the Story of a Coyote, 1967; Earth's Bug-Eyed Monsters, 1968; Butterfly and Moth, 1969; Carab, The Trap-Door Spider, 1970; Biography of an Octopus, 1971; The Thursday Toads, 1971; Biography of a Rhino, 1972 (Nat. Assn. Sci. Tchrs. award 1972); Wild Cousins of the Dog, 1973; Star Dog, 1973; Misunderstood Animals, 1973 (Nat. Assn. Sci. Tchrs. award 1973); Gods or Demons, 1973; Biography of An Ant, 1974; The Space Gypsies, 1974. Home: 136 W 16th St New York City NY 10011

HOPKINS, ANNE D. (MRS. SAMUEL HOPKINS), civic and polit. worker; b. Balt., Oct. 22, 1929; d. Theodore Rognald and Anne (Burrier) Dankmeyer; A.B., Goucher Coll., 1950; M.A., Pa. State U., 1952; m. Samuel Hopkins, Oct. 20, 1955; children—Robert Brooke, Frederick Matson. Chmn. unit legislation Women's Civic League, 1958-64; chmn. Goucher County Fair, 1960; pres. Legislative Clearing House, Balt. 1967-71, also bd. dirs.; bd. dirs. Md. Childrens Aid Soc., sec., 1970-72, v.p., 1972—; mem. Nat. Adv. Council on Adult Edn., 1970—, vice chmn., 1973; mem. Md. Commn. on the Status of Women. Exec. sec. Republican State Central Com. of Md., Balt., 1953-55, sec., 1956-62; Rep. Precinct exec., 1952—; treas. Md. Fedn. Young Reps., 1954-55; pres. Young Reps., 1955-56; alternate del. Rep. Nat. Conv., 1960, 72. del. Constl. Conv. Md., 1967. Mem. League Women Voters, Md. Hist. Soc., Goucher Coll. Alumni Assn. (dir. 1958-61), Women's Civic League (dir. 1961-69), Balt. Alumni Kappa Alpha Theta (pres. 1955-56). Republican. Episcopalian. Club: Gibson Island (Md.). Home: 4302 Wendover Rd Baltimore MD 21218

HOPKINS, CECILIA ANN (MRS. HENRY E. HOPKINS), educator; b. Havre, Mont., Feb. 17, 1922; d. Kost L. and Mary (Manaras) Sofos; B.S., Mont. State Coll., 1944; M.A., San Francisco State Coll., 1958, M.A., 1967; postgrad. Stanford; m. Henry E. Hopkins, Sept. 7, 1944. Bus. tchr. Havre (Mont.) High Sch., 1942-44; sec. George P. Gorham, realtor, San Mateo, Cal., 1944-45; escrow sec. Fox & Carskadon, realtors, 1945-50; escrow officer Cal. Pacific Title Ins. Co., 1950-57; bus. tchr. Westmoor High Sch., Daly City, Cal., 1958-59; bus. tchr. Coll. San Mateo, 1959—, chmn. real estate-ins. dept., 1963. Cons. to commr. Cal. Div. Real Estate, 1963—. Vice chmn. Community Coll. Adv. Com., 1970-71, chmn., 1971-72. Mem. Am. Assn. U. Women, Cal. Assn. Real Estate Tchrs. (state pres. 1964-65, hon. dir. 1962—); Real Estate Certificate Inst., Cal. Bus. Edn. Assn., San Francisco State Coll. Guidance and Counseling Alumni, Theta Alpha Delta, Pi Lambda Theta, Delta Pi Epsilon (nat. dir. interchpt. relations 1962-65, nat. historian 1966-67, nat. sec. 1968-69), Alpha Gamma Delta. Contbr. articles to profl. jours. Home: 504 Colgate Way San Mateo CA 94402

HOPKINS, ESTHER ARVILLA HARRISON (MRS. THOMAS EWELL HOPKINS), chemist; b. Stamford, Conn., Sept. 18, 1926; d. George Burgess and Esther (Smalls) Harrison; A.B., Boston U., 1947; M.S., Howard U., 1949; M.S., Yale, 1962, Ph.D., 1967; m. John Payne Mitchell, 1952; 1 dau., Susan; m. 2d, Thomas Ewell Hopkins, Jan. 21, 1959; 1 son, Thomas Ewell. Instr., Va. State Coll., Petersburg, 1949-52; research asst. biophysics New Eng. Inst. for Med. Research, Ridgefield, Conn., 1955-59; research chemist Am. Cyanamid Co., Stamford, 1959-61; scientist Polaroid Corp., Cambridge, Mass., 1967—, bd. dirs. Polaroid Employees Fed. Credit Union, 1969—, pres., 1970-71. Bd. assessors First Parish Unitarian-Universalist Ch., Framingham, Mass., 1970—, chmn., 1973-75; corporator Framingham Union Hosp., 1972—. USPHS training grantee 1962-66; Nat. Assn. Coll. Women scholar. Mem. Am. Chem. Soc. (nat. councilor 1972—), Biophysics Soc., Soc. Photog. Scientists and Engrs., Unitarian-Universalist Womens Fedn., Sci. Research Soc. Am., Scarlet Key, Sigma Xi, Beta Kappa Chi, Sigma Pi Sigma, Alpha Kappa Alpha. Mem. Order Eastern Star. Contbr. articles to profl. jours. Home: 72 Higgins Rd Framingham MA 01701 Office: Polaroid Corp Cambridge MA 02139

HOPKINS, HELEN LOUISE, educator; b. Allentown, Pa., Jan. 15, 1921; d. Charles William and Mildred Etta (Graffin) Hopkins; B.S., State Coll., West Chester, Pa., 1942; M.A., N.Y. U., 1958; certificate occupational therapy U. Pa., 1947; postgrad. Temple U., 1971. Tchr., Allentown Pub. Schs., 1942-45; occupational therapist Friends Hosp., Phila., 1947, Ind. U. Med. Center, Indpls., 1948-54; dir. occupational therapy Rehab. Services, Inc., Binghamton, N.Y., 1955; asst. spl. services div. Inst. Rehab. Medicine, N.Y.C., 1956-59; instr., adminstrv. asst. U. Pa., Phila., 1959-60; dir. occupational therapy St. Francis Gen. Hosp., Pitts., 1960-67; asso. prof. occupational therapy Temple U. Coll. Allied Health Professions, Phila., 1967—, rep. univ. faculty senate, 1968—, sec., 1973—. Mem. adv. bd. for occupational therapy assts. Mt. Aloysius Jr. Coll., Cresson, Pa., 1963-67, Lehigh County Community Coll., Schnecksville, Pa., 1969-73; cons. occupational therapy Stephen Smith Geriatric Center, Phila., 1970-72. Mem. stroke task force N. Met. area wide com. Greater Del. Valley Regional Med. Program, Phila., 1968-73. Recipient Bronze plaque St. Francis Gen. Hosp., 1967; citation Lehigh County Community Coll., 1970. Fellow Royal Soc. Health, Am. Occupational Therapy Assn. (council on finance 1970-73, mem. del. assembly 1970-74, chmn. dues and fees com. 1970-73, mem. scholarship com. 1971—); mem. World Fedn. Occupational Therapists, Eastern Pa. Occupational Therapy Assn. (del. exec. bd. 1968—), Am. Assn. U. Profs., Soc. for Behavioral Kinesiology. Delta Kappa Gamma. Methodist. Contbr. articles to profl. jours. Home: 5427 Houghton Place Philadelphia PA 19128

HOPKINS, JANET E. HINES, civic worker; b. Cin.; d. Harry Hayes and Luella (Kaufmann) Hines; student Wellesley Coll., 1943-45; m. Edwin B. Hopkins, Jr., Mar. 1, 1946 (div. Aug. 1962); children—Andrew Delmar II, Christopher Brent. Mem. Jr. League Abilene, Tex., 1956—; vol. worker W. Tex. Rehab. Center, 1953-60; mem. Abilene Community Theater; sponsor Abilene Philharmonic Orch., 1960—; patroness Children's Theater; dir. Abilene Philharmonic Assn., 1961-62; co-founder, chmn. Golden Horse Shoe Club for Crippled Children, 1970; chmn. Royal Lipizzan Stallion benefit for West Tex. Rehab. Center, 1970; mem. Abilene Fine Arts Mus., co-chmn. antique show, 1971; mem. Abilene Philharmonic Guild. Republican. Episcopalian. Clubs: Abilene Country, Allegro, Overture, First Nighters, Los Aficionados, Westwood. Home: 1441 Sylvan Dr Abilene TX 79605

HOPKINS, MARGARET LAIL (MRS. GARLAND EVANS HOPKINS), librarian; b. Schoolfield, Va., Oct. 19, 1910; d. David Arthur and Hattie (Hollie) Lail; grad. Scarritt Coll., 1933; M.S. in L.S., Cath. U. Am., 1957; postgrad. Am. U., Beirut, Lebanon, 1956; m. Garland Evans Hopkins, Dec. 23, 1935; children—Nancy (Mrs. William K. Phillips), Edward Christopher David, Peter Evans. Librarian, instr. Ferrum (Va.) Jr. Coll., 1933-34; recreational dir. Va. Meth. Children's Home, Richmond, 1934-35; librarian Clearbrook (Va.) High Sch., 1943-44; librarian Marymount Coll., Arlington, Va., 1957-58, 59-62, Herndon (Va.) High Sch., 1958-59; br. librarian Fairfax County (Va.) Pub. Library, 1962-65; Fulbright library cons. to U. Tehran (Iran), 1965-67; coordinator library services John Tyler Community Coll., Chester, Va., 1967-69; librarian Lynchburg (Va.) Coll., 1969—. Mem. Am., Va. library assns., Iranian Library Assn. Democrat. Methodist. Author: A History of the American University of Beirut Library, 1956. Home: 2317 Atherholt Rd Lynchburg VA 24501 Office: Lynchburg Coll Library Lynchburg VA 24504

HOPKINS, MARGARET MOORE (MRS. HARRY HOPKINS), coll. adminstr.; b. Fruitland, Md., Feb. 1, 1916; d. William Sidney and Lavinia Victoria (Acworth) Moore; B.S., Mary Washington Coll., 1936; m. Harry Hopkins, June 16, 1937; children—William Boyd, Harriet Sydney. High sch. tchr. Frederick (Md.) High Sch., 1936-37; sec. to pres., acting registrar Salisbury (Md.) State Coll., 1938-44, asst. dir. admissions and registrar, 1966-69, dir. admissions, 1969—; social worker Dept. Social Services, Salisbury, Md., 1960-66. Pres. Wicomico Womens Dem. Club, 1954; dist. chmn. United Womens Dem. Club, 1957-59. Pres. jr. bd. Peninsula Gen. Hosp., Salisbury, Md., 1959; mem. bd. visitors Salisbury (Md.) State Coll., 1973—. Mem. Nat. Assn. Coll. Admissions Counselors, Am. Personnel and Guidance Assn., Am., Middle States assns. collegiate registrars and admissions officers, D.A.R., (vice regent 1958). Home: 1013 Smith St Salisbury MD 21801

HOPKINS, MARGARETE WOLF, educator; b. Milw., Nov. 3, 1911; d. John Theodore and Caroline (Kupperian) Wolf; B.S., U. Wis., 1932, M.A., 1933, Ph.D., 1935; m. Edward John Hopkins, Aug. 31, 1941; children—Edward John, Margaret Louise. Instr., research asst. U. Wis., 1932-38; instr. Wayne U., 1938-41; instr. Hunter Coll., 1942-45; asst. prof. St. Joseph's Coll., 1958-64, asso. prof., 1965-68, prof. math., 1969—. Mem. Am. Math. Soc., Assn. Tchrs. of Math, Phi Beta Kappa, Sigma Xi. Home: 153-14 32d Av Flushing NY 11354 Office: 245 Clinton Av Brooklyn NY 11205

HOPKINS, MARY LOU PERKINS (MRS. WILLIAM J. HOPKINS), editor; b. Monrovia, Cal., July 1, 1915; d. William Narcome and Marie Bulah (Mitchell) Perkins; student Mt. St. Mary's Coll., 1934-36; m. William J. Hopkins, Nov. 29, 1941; children—William James II, Robert Lee. Reporter, Mirror News, Los Angeles, 1958; women's editor San Fernando Valley sect. Los Angeles Times, 1961-67, women's editor Orange County edit., Costa Mesa, 1967—. Active Assistance League So. Cal., Boys Club Am. Mem. Women in Communications, Orange County Press Club. Home: 413 Via Lido Saud Newport Beach CA 92660 Office: 1375 Sunflower St Costa Mesa CA 92626

HOPKINS, PAULENE A. (MRS. MACK HOPKINS), educator; b. Chambers County, Tex.; d. Elbert and Fannie (Patterson) Lewis; B.A., Wiley Coll., 1941, M.A., Columbia Tchrs.' Coll., 1943; postgrad. U. Cal. at Los Angeles, 1950-53. Tchr. elementary sch. Willowbrook Sch. Dist., 1951-56; remedial reading tchr., grade counselor Compton Union High Dist., 1956-58; tchr., psychometrist, counselor Los Angeles Secondary Schs., 1958-65, research and devel. specialist, 1965-66, community relations specialist, 1966-67, asst. dir. Demonstration Sch. for Adults, 1968-69, vice prin., 1969—. Sec., Los Angeles City Schs.' Council Human Relations, 1960-66; bd. dirs. Affiliated Tchrs. Los Angeles, 1961-65, v.p., 1964—; pres. Los Angeles sect. Nat. Council Negro Women, 1966-68, chmn. nat. conv., 1968, regional treas., 1967-69; corr. sec. Los Angeles County Fedn. Coordinating Councils, 1966-67, treas., 1967-68, adminstrv. asst., 1969—; mem. Women's Coalition for Community Action, 1968—; bd. dirs. S.W. Los Angeles YMCA, 1958-66; mem. bd. Westminister Neighborhood Assn., 1960-65; mem. Los Angeles area Fedn. Settlements and Neighborhood Centers, 1961-65; mem. San Fernando Valley Fair Housing Council, 1965-67. Named Industry-Edn. Council's Outstanding Tchr., 1964; recipient Regional Educator of Year award Nat. Council Negro Women, 1965,

Outstanding Community Leader award, 1968; Community Relations award Citizens Adv. Coms. Los Angeles City Schs., 1968. Home: 5127 Parkglen Av Los Angeles CA 90043 Office: 4600 W Olympic Blvd Los Angeles CA 90019

HOPKINS, VIVIAN CONSTANCE, educator, gravel co. exec.; b. Troy, N.Y., Sept. 2, 1909; d. Richard and Josephine (Brown) Hopkins; B.A., Wellesley Coll., 1930; M.A., U. Mich., 1931, Ph.D., 1943; M.A., Radcliffe Coll., 1939. Tchr., Stafford Springs, Conn., 1931-32, Clinton, N.Y., 1932-34, Russell Sage Coll. and Emma Willard Sch., 1935-36, Medina Collegiate Center, 1936-37, Pine Manor Jr. Coll., 1937-38; instr. English, State U. N.Y., Albany, 1941-48, asst. prof., asso. prof., 1948-53, prof., 1953-71, emeritus prof., 1971—; acting pres. Albany Gravel Co., 1972—. Recipient fellowship Am. Assn. U. Women, 1948-49; Guggenheim fellow, 1956-57; summer research fellowships State U. N.Y. Research Found., 1958, 60, 62. Mem. Am. Assn. U. Women, Am. Studies Assn., Modern Lang. Assn., N.Y. State Hist. Assn., Rensselaer County Hist. Soc. Club: Albany Wellesley. Author: Spires of Form: A Study of Emerson's Aesthetic Theory, 1951; Prodigal Puritan: A Life of Delia Bacon, 1959. Contbr. articles to profl. jours. Home: 824 2d Av Troy NY 12182

HOPKINSON, NORMA ELIZABETH JOYCE COOK (MRS. MERVYN HOPKINSON), physician; b. Hensall, Ont., Can., Oct. 25, 1923; d. Norman Elmer and Elizabeth (Thompson) Cook; M.D., U. Western Ont., 1946; m. Mervyn Alexander Hopkinson, Aug. 12, 1949; children—Joan, Bruce, Mary. Intern, St. Michael's Hosp., Toronto, Ont., 1946-47, Women's Coll. Hosp., Toronto, 1947-48; research fellow Queen's U., 1949-50; practice gen. medicine, Orillia, Ont., Lion's Head, Ont., mem. staff Bruce Peninsula Hosp., Wharton, Ont., Red Cross Hosp., Lion's Head; mem. courtesy staff Owen Sound Hosp.; coroner County of Bruce, Ont., 1962-74. Med. student preceptor U. Western Ont., 1969-73. Mem. sch. bd., Lion's Head, 1963-68; mem. town council, Lion's Head, 1957-61. Recipient award Can. Council Research, 1949, Scholarship award Upjohn Co., 1962. Mem. Coll. Family Physicians (pres. Bruce-Grey chpt. 1972-74). Address: Lion's Head ON Canada

HOPKINSON, SHIRLEY LOIS, educator; b. Boone, Ia., Aug. 25, 1924; d. Arthur Perry and Zora (Smith) Hopkinson; student Coe Coll., 1942-43; B.A. cum laude (Phi Beta Kappa scholar 1944), U. Colo., 1945; B.L.S., U. Cal., 1949; M.A. (Honnold Honor scholar 1945-46) Claremont Grad. Sch., 1951; Ed.M., U. Okla., 1952, Ed.D., 1957. Tchr. pub. sch. Stigler, Okla., 1946-47, Palo Verde High Jr. Coll., Blythe, Cal., 1947-48; asst. librarian Modesto (Cal.) Jr. Coll., 1949-51; tchr., librarian Fresno, Cal., 1951-52, La Mesa, Cal., 1953-55; asst. prof. librarianship, instructional materials dir. Chaffey Coll., Ontario, Cal., 1955-58; with Edn. Library San Jose (Cal.) State Coll., 1958-59, asst. prof. librarianship, 1959-64, asso. prof., 1964-69, prof., 1969—, dir. NDEA Inst. for Sch. Library Personnel, 1966. Mem. Am., Cal., library assns., Audio-Visual Assn. Cal., N.E.A., Sch. Librarians Assn. Cal. (com. mem., treas. No. sect. 1951-52), San Diego County Sch. Librarians Assn. (sec. 1945-55), Cal. Tchrs. Assn., League Women Voters (dir. 1950-51, publs. chmn.), Am. Assn. U. Women (social studies chmn., dir. 1957-58), Bus. and Profl. Women's Club (attendance chmn. 1957-58), Alpha Beta Alpha, Phi Beta Kappa, Alpha Lambda Delta, Delta Kappa Pi, Phi Kappa Phi, Delta Kappa Gamma. Author: Descriptive Cataloging of Library Materials, 1963; Instructional Materials for Teaching the Use of the Library, 1966. Editor: Sch. Librarians Assn. Cal. Bull., 1961-64. Contbr. articles to profl. jours. Home: 231 E San Fernando St San Jose CA 95112

HOPPER, AGNES WILHELM, guidance counselor; b. Gilpin, Ky.; d. Lewis and Ethel (Godbey) Wilhelm; B.S., Union Coll., Barbourville, Ky., 1953; M.A., Eastern Ky. U., 1960; postgrad. U. Ky.; children—E.R., Billie Jean (Mrs. Jerry Lee Poynter). Elementary tchr. Casey County Bd. Edn., Liberty, Ky., 1943-45; elementary and secondary tchr. Whitley County, Williamsburg, Ky., 1953-59, guidance counselor, 1959—; part-time tchr. Cumberland Coll., also Eastern Ky. U., 1963-68; unit dir. sch. social work services Ky. Dept. Edn., Frankfort, 1969—. Exec. dir., co-chmn. Midwest Sch. Social Work Conf., 1972, also bd. dirs. Mem. Tri-County Bus. and Profl. Women (pres. 1965-66), Tri-County Bus. and Profl. Women's Club (treas. 1968-69), Am., Ky. personnel and guidance assns., N.E.A., Ky. Edn. Assn., Am. Sch. Counselors, Ky. Sch. Adminstrs. Assn., Midwest Sch. Social Work Conf. (dir.), Assn. State Cons. Sch. Social Workers, Delta Kappa Gamma. Mem. Order of Eastern Star. Home: Scuffletown Rd Corbin KY 40701 Office: State Department of Education Frankfort KY 40601

HOPPER, JANICE WINIFRED HARRIS (MRS. REX D. HOPPER), govt. cons.; b. Fairfield, Con.; d. Edward and Esther (Kormansky) Harris; B.A. (class of '78 fellow), Hunter Coll., 1939; postgrad. U. Chgo., 1939-41; Ph.D. (Halle fellow), New Sch. for Social Research, 1956; m. Rex D. Hopper, June 10, 1961 (dec. June 1966). Tchr., asst. to exec. sec. U.S. State Dept. Cultural Center, Rio de Janeiro, Brazil, 1942-48; with readers' research bur. Crowell-Collier's Ency., N.Y.C., 1948-52; grad. faculty research asst. New Sch. for Social Research, N.Y.C., 1952-55; instr. sociology Hobart and William Smith Colls., Geneva, N.Y., 1955-56, community research Am. Found. for Blind, N.Y.C., 1956-59; lectr. dept. polit. sci. Bklyn. Coll., 1959-60; adminstrv. officer Am. Sociol. Assn., N.Y.U., N.Y.C., 1960-63; dir. Project Nat. Register, Am. Sociol. Assn., Washington, 1963-66; sr. research asso. Inst. Cross-cultural Research, Operations and Policy Research, Inc., Washington, 1966-69; sr. research asso. Human Scis. Research, Inc., McLean, Va., 1969-71; adviser Inst. Pub. Adminstrn., Nat. Inst. Pub. Adminstrn., Saigon, 1971-73; cons. Inst. Pub. Adminstrn., Washington, 1973—. Instr. dept. sociology N.Y.U., 1960-63; lectr. Latin Am. studies program Georgetown U. Fellow Am. Sociol. Assn.; mem. Eastern Sociol. Soc., Soc. for Study of Social Problems, A.A.A.S., Alpha Kappa Delta. Contbr. Perspectives on the Social Order, 1963. Address: Inst Public Adminstrn 1619 Massachusetts Av NW Washington DC 20036

HOPPIN, RUTH FIERMAN (MRS. STUART B. HOPPIN, JR.), writer; b. N.Y.C., Nov. 14, 1928; d. Jack and Sophie (Mindell) Fierman; B.A., Bklyn. Coll., 1949; m. Stuart B. Hoppin, Jr., Jan. 30, 1960; children—June Rosamond, Ralph Frederick. Writer, lectr. on scriptural status of women, especially mistranslations of scripture related to women's status, 1969—; lectr. many ch. and cultural groups San Francisco Bay area, including Grad. Theol. Union, Berkeley. Mem. Nat. Orgn. for Women (mem. ecumenical task force on women and religion 1971—), Internat. Assn. Women Ministers (asso.), Cal. Writers Club. Democrat. Episcopalian. Author: Priscilla: Author of the Epistle to the Hebrews, 1969. Contbr. articles to mags. Home: 15 Portola Av Daly City CA 94015

HOPPING, ANN, librarian, govt. ofcl.; b. Hollywood, Cal., Dec. 2, 1931; d. Forrest deGrasse and Louise (Bernal) Hopping; B.A. in Anthropology, Cal. State U., Fresno, 1962; M.L.S., U. Cal. at Los Angeles, 1963. Asst. to librarian Visalia (Cal.) Pub. Library, 1953-62; sr. reference librarian Cal. State U., Fresno Library, 1963-72; Country librarian USIS, Brasilia, Brazil, 1972—. Vis. librarian Chapman Coll. World Campus Afloat, spring 1970. Writer book reviews Choice mag. Mem. Cal. Library Assn. (pres. Yosemite dist. 1969, councilor at large 1971-72, U. Cal. Library Schs. Alumni Assn. (regional rep. Central Cal. 1965-66), Am. Fgn. Service Assn. Home: 5656 N Indianola Av Clovis CA 93612 Office: American Embassy USIS Brasilia APO New York City NY 09676

HOPSON, PEGGY RIDDLE (MRS. CHARLES LUTHER HOPSON, JR.), museum sec.; b. Raleigh, N.C., Feb. 23, 1938; d. Hubert Eugene and Helen Vaughn (Lewis) Riddle; ed. pub. schs.; m. Charles Luther Hopson, Jr., Apr. 4, 1959; children—Charles Luther III, Helen Vaughn, Vaughn Lewis. Various secretarial positions, 1956-63; with historic sites and museums sect., div. archives and history N.C. Dept. Cultural Resources, Raleigh, 1963—, exec. sec. to chief sect., 1963-73, sec. to chief archaeology sect., 1973—. Leader troop Girl Scouts, 1972—. Mem. N.C. Museums Council (sec.-treas. 1968—), N.C. Skin Diving Council (sec. 1971—), Raleigh Diving Assn. (v.p. 1968-69, 73, sec. 1971-72, pres. 1973—), Southeastern Museums Conf. (membership comn. 1969—). Home: 3807 Memory Lane Raleigh NC 27604 Office: 109 E Jones St Raleigh NC 27611

HORACEK, THELMA FRANCES WILLIAMS (MRS. GODFREY JERRY HORACEK), assn. exec.; b. Dalton, Ga., Mar. 18, 1914; d. Arie Henderson and Mabel Ann (Smith) Williams; A.B., Ga. Coll., 1935; M.S. (Rosenwald fellow) U. Ga., 1947; postgrad. Tulane U., 1950, U. Md., 1964, 66, U. Tenn., 1952, 53, 57, 58, Peabody Coll., 1954, George Washington U., 1965, Columbia, 1968, U. Me., 1970; m. Godfrey Jerry Horacek, July 8, 1938; children—Mona Marie. Elementary, high sch. and coll. tchr., Ga., 1935-46; prin., sch. social worker, supr., dir. spl. services Chattanooga Pub. Schs., 1946-62; prin., supr. instrn. Prince George's County (Md.) Bd. Edn., 1962-67; program coordinator, profl. devel. and instructional services N.E.A., Washington, 1967—. Cons. U.S. Office Edn., 1959. Chmn. pub. sch. div., Council Community Forces, Chattanooga, 1952-53. Bd. dirs. Goodwill Industries, United Cerebral Palsy Assn., Big Bros. Assn., Jr. League Reading Center, Chattanooga. Mem. N.E.A. (life), Nat. Assn. Supervision and Curriculum Devel., Acad. Certified Social Workers (charter), Nat. Elementary Prins. Assn., Adminstrs. and Suprs. Assn. (pres. 1951-52), Chattanooga and Hamilton County Social Workers Club (pres. 1951-52), Md. Congress Parents and Tchrs. (life). Home: 8109 River Bond Ct Oxon Hill MD 20022 Office: 1201 NW 16TH St Washington DC 20036

HORAK, ELAINE DOROTHEA LIMPERT (MRS. ALEXANDER HORAK), pub. relations exec., found. exec.; b. Bklyn., Feb. 22, 1927; d. John Harold and Sophia (Douropoulos) Limpert; B.A. cum laude, Radcliffe Coll., 1948; postgrad. Sorbonne, Paris, 1948-50; m. Alexander Horak, Apr. 16, 1961; 1 son, Philip Alexander. Columnist Nat. Herald newspaper, N.Y.C., 1951-52; publicist, fund-raiser, lectr. Theatre Guild, Inc., Stratford, Conn., 1952-53; publicity asst. to head firm Roy Pubs., N.Y.C., 1953-54; free-lance publicity work Schrafft's and Theatre Assos., 1956-57; pub. relations asst. to dir. devel. Pace Coll., 1959-60; publicity mgr. Green Mountain Theatre, Vt., summer 1960; asst. to pub. relations dir. Am. Nurses Assn., 1961-62; dir. publicity Mills Coll. Edn., 1963-66; founder-dir. Ednl. Pub. Relations Service, N.Y.C., 1966—; founder, exec. dir. Profl. Theatre Wing, Inc., 1963—; editorial researcher edn. dept. Time mag., 1957-58; asso. producer Broadway prodns., Red Roses for Me., 1955, The Innkeepers, 1956, Wake Up Darling, 1956; featured in plays including Alice-in-Wonderland, Othello, The Cretan Woman, Suddenly Last Summer, others; TV shows including Hellenic Am. TV Hour, 1956, Alan Jeffries Show, 1953. Founding mem. Independents for Lefkowitz, 1961; co-chmn. Schola Cantorum Concert, 1962; mem. Met. Coll. Pub. Relations Assn., Internat. Platform Assn., Am. Soc. Psychical Research. Clubs: Nat. Arts, Harvard, Radcliffe. Home: 120 Windermere Rd Staten Island NY 10305 Office: Profl Theatre Wing 201 E 17th St 5G New York City NY 10003

HORAN, SISTER BARBARA, coll. adminstr.; b. Buffalo, Jan. 16, 1927; d. John Joseph and Esther Marie (Christ) Horan; B.S., Mt. St. Joseph Coll., 1950, postgrad., 1961-62; postgrad. Albright Art Sch., 1955-56, N.Y. State Coll. at Buffalo, 1949, St. Francis Sch. Art, 1948, (Cardinal Spellman scholar), Pius XII Inst., Florence, Italy, 1964. Elementary tchr., Buffalo, 1950-51; faculty Medaille Coll., Buffalo, 1951—, prof. art, 1951—, chmn. humanities div., asst. dean and dir. summer and evening sessions, 1969—. Trustee St. Marys Sch. for the Deaf, 1973—. Recipient Ohio State award for weekly TV series, WNED-TV, Buffalo, 1967. Mem. Nat. Art Edn. Assn., Buffalo Fine Arts Acad., Sisters of St. Joseph (adminstrv. council mem. 1973—). Home: 1 Agassiz Circle Buffalo NY 14214 Office: 18 Agassiz Circle Buffalo NY 14214

HORIE, NANCY BOSWORTH SEWARD (MRS. TSUKASA HORIE), physician; b. Lewiston, Me., Aug. 11, 1932; d. Robert Douglass and Barbara Lloyd (Bosworth) Seward; B.S., U. Rochester, 1954; M.S., Wayne U., Detroit, 1956; M.D., Tufts U., 1960; m. Tsukasa Horie, May 5, 1962; 1 dau., Ayumi Cynthia. Intern, Detroit Receiving Hosp., 1960-61, resident internal medicine, 1961-62; resident anesthesiology Henry Ford Hosp., 1962-64; mem. staff St. Lukes Internat. Hosp., Tokyo, Japan, 1964-67, 70-71, Me. Med. Center, Portland, 1967-68, St. Mary's Hosp., Lewiston, 1968—, Central Me. Gen. Hosp., 1971—. Diplomate Am. Bd. Anesthesiology. Mem. Am., Me. socs. anesthesiologists, Me., Androscoggin County med. assns., Phi Beta Kappa. Home: 9 Arch Av Lewiston ME 04240 Office: Central Maine General Hosp Lewiston ME 04240

HORMANN, AIKO MIYASHITA (MRS. JERRY LEE HORMANN), sci. cons.; b. Yokohama, Japan; d. Tokizo and Umyeo (Yamaji) Miyashita; came to U.S., 1951, naturalized, 1958; B.S., State Coll. S.E. Mo., 1954; M.A., U. Mo., 1956; postgrad. U. Pitts., 1957-59; m. Jerry Lee Hormann, Aug. 21, 1954. Instr. math. U. Mo., Columbia, 1954-56; mathematician Westinghouse Research Labs., Pitts., 1956-59; mathematician, research scientist cybernetics System Devel. Corp., Santa Monica, Cal., 1959-69, sr. research scientist, 1969-71; ind. researcher, cons. to govt. agys. and industry on information sci., computer tech., mgmt. planning and decision-making methodologies, tech. assessment, 1971—. Participant sci. affairs div. NATO confs. Mem. Math. Assn. Am., SDC Br. Sci. Research Soc. Am. (pres. 1967), Assn. for Computing Machinery, A.A.A.S., Am. Soc. Cybernetics, Pi Mu Epsilon. Contbr. articles to profl. jours. Patentee in field. Home: 1008 2d St Santa Monica CA 90403

HORN, GLENERA THORNTON (MRS. RAYMOND J. HORN), antique dealer; b. Beeville, Tex., Sept. 18, 1916; d. George Glen and Ray (Quinn) Thornton; pvt. study art and painting, 1933-35, 41-42, 59; student U. Houston, 1939-42, Birmingham So. Coll., 1957-59; m. Raymond J. Horn, Sept. 22, 1942; children—Nancy Carolyn, Anthony W. Owner, Alley Antiques, Birmingham, Ala., 1968—. Exhibitor, lectr. rare glass. Mem. Ala. Antique Dealers Assn., Va. Hist. Soc. Home: 524 Tuscaloosa Av SW Birmingham AL 35211 Office: 528 Tuscaloosa Av SW Birmingham AL 35211

HORN, SOLVEIG WALD (MRS. JOHN CHISOLM HORN), found. exec., civic worker; b. Phila., Oct. 14, 1914; d. John Royal and Emma (Gulbrandson) Wald; A.B., Cornell U., 1936; m. John Chisolm Horn, June 22, 1938; children—Phyllis Downing, John Chisolm, Stephen Lunde (dec.), Eric Robert Gregg (dec.), Thomas, Dorothy Traill, James Melchior. Asso. Prismo Safety Corp., Huntingdon, Pa., 1943; asso. Wald Industries, Inc., John R. Wald Co., Inc., 1952, dir. Wald Industries, Inc.; treas. Ch. Mgmt. Service, Inc., 1970—. Active Region III, Girl Scouts Am., 1934—, camp unit leader, 1934-35, Girl Guide trainee, Waddow, England, 1936, leader trainer, 1936-52, chmn. tng., personnel Huntington council Girl Scouts, 1938-43, chmn. lone troops com., Alexandria, Pa., 1945-48, Brownie troop leader, 1960—, mem. bd. Hemlock council, 1966-69, field v.p., 1967; mem. Nat. Cub Scouting Com., 1970—; women's res. Boy Scouts Am., Civil Def., P.T.A. Bd. dirs. Blair Hosp. Aux., Skills of Central Pa., Huntingdon Developmental Workshop, Wald Found., Huntingdon, Pa. Recipient Golden Eaglet award Girl Scouts U.S.A., 1932, Silver Fawn award Boy Scouts Am., 1971. Mem. J.C. Blair Meml. Hosp. Aux. (dir.), Allegheny Luth. Home Aux., Susquehanna U. Aux., Alexandria Library Aux., Audubon Soc., Delta Gamma. Republican. Lutheran (chmn. campus ministry). Clubs: Alexandria Garden (Pa.); Huntington (Pa.) Country. Home: Kilmarnock Hall Alexandria PA 16611

HORNBROOK, CECELIA, librarian; b. Pleasantville, N.J., Sept. 15, 1915; d. Charles Philbrick and Clara (Hill) Hornbrook; A.B., Marshall U., 1936, M.A., 1939; B.S., Cath. U. Am., 1953, postgrad., 1965. Tchr. pub. schs., Wood County, W.Va., 1940-45; circulation asst. U.S. Dept. Agr. Library, Washington, 1947-50; head circulation unit, library and information div. U.S. Dept. Housing and Urban Devel., Washington, 1950-53, reference librarian, 1953-57, head reference unit, 1957-66, chief information service, 1966—. Mem. Spl. Libraries Assn., Urban Studies Libraries of Washington, United Meth. Women, Kappa Delta Pi. Methodist (librarian 1950—). Club: Toastmistress (pres. 1964) (Washington). Home: 8421 11th Av Silver Spring MD 20903 Office: 7th and D Sts SW Washington DC 20410

HORNE, JUDITH RAE ANDERSON (MRS. TIMOTHY PARMLEY HORNE), educator; b. San Francisco, Feb. 14, 1941; d. Harry Davey and Audrey (Garman) Anderson; A.B., Vassar Coll., 1962; M.A. in Teaching of English, Stanford, 1965; M.Ed., Boston U., 1972, Ed.D., 1974; m. Timothy Parmley Horne, Nov. 11, 1965; 1 stepdau., Tara Victoria. Tchr. English, drama, pub. speaking various schs., 1962-64; resident asst. for dean of women Stanford U., 1964-65; tchr. English, Abbot Acad., Andover, Mass., 1966-71, counselor, 1967-71, mem. exec. council, 1969-71; staff psychologist Lawrence Mental Health Center, 1972-73; counselor Salem State Coll., 1973-74. Benefit chmn. Boston Pops Benefit for Vassar Scholarships, 1967. Episcopalian. Clubs: Boston Vassar (area chmn. 1966-68, 69-70, mem. spl. gifts com. 1969). Home: 82 Porter Rd Andover MA 01810

HORNE, MARILYN, mezzo-soprano; m. Henry Lewis. Made operatic debut in Los Angeles as Hata in Smetana's The Bartered Bride; later appearances have included Venice Festival (at invitation of Igor Stravinsky); San Francisco Opera (as Marie in Berg's Wozzeck); with Am. Opera Soc., N.Y.C., several seasons (including roles in Gluck's Iphegenie en Tauride, Rossini's Semiramide); Vancouver Opera (as Adalgisa in Bellini's Norma); Philharmonic Hall, N.Y.C.; Covent Garden, London (in Wozzeck); concert performance of Donizetti's Lucrezia Borgia in N.Y.C.; appeared in Norma as Adalgisa, Met. Opera, 1970, as Carmen, 1972, in L'Italiana in Algeri, 1973; opened Chgo. Lyric Opera season in Semiramide, 1971. Sent (with husband) on European tour by U.S. State Dept., 1963. Recorded for London Records (often with Joan Sutherland) 'The Age of Bel Canto"; also recorded by Columbia in works by Gesualdo, Resphigi, Schutz, Stravinsky. A leading exponent of the florid vocal style. Address: care Herbert H Breslin Inc 119 W 57th St New York City NY 10019

HORNE, NANCY OALENE, sociologist, research co. exec.; b. Norton, Va., Aug. 25, 1931; d. Hoke Irvine and Alice Oalene (Beverly) Horne; A.A., Stephens Coll., 1952; A.B., U. N.C., 1954; M.A., Syracuse U., 1956; M.A., Columbia, 1956, Ph.D., 1969. Bus. mgr. Home Land & Investment Co., Inc., Norton, 1961-63; research asst. Bur. Applied Social Research, Columbia, N.Y.C., 1963-65, project dir. Tchrs. Coll. Columbia, 1965-67; asst. prof. sociology and family devel. U. Mo., Columbia, 1971-72; program asso. Nat. Lab. for Higher Edn., Durham, N.C., 1972—. Mem. adv. bd. YWCA, 1961-62. U.S. Office of Edn. grantee, 1965-67. Mem. Am. Psychol. Assn., Am. Sociol. Assn., Assn. for Instl. Research, Am. Ednl. Research Assn., Am. Assn. for Higher Edn., Midwest Sociol. Soc., A.A.A.S., D.A.R., Am. Mgmt. Assns., Epsilon Alpha (chmn. exec. council 1971, house adviser 1972), Pi Lambda Theta, Kappa Delta Pi. Presbyn. Asst. editor Sociol. Quar., 1971-73. Home: 17 Balmoray Ct Durham NC 27707 Office: Nat Lab for Higher Edn Mutual Plaza Durham NC 27701

HORNE, PHYLLIS GOODWIN, librarian; b. Somerville, Mass., Feb. 10, 1917; d. Garfield Wilmont and Edith May (Goodwin) Horne; B.S. in Home Econs., R.I. State Coll., 1939; B.S. in Library Sci., Simmons Coll., 1944; M.A., Trinity Coll., Hartford, 1950; postgrad. Hillyer Coll., Hartford, 1955-58, U. Conn., Central Conn. State Coll., U. Hartford. Tchr. home econs. jr. high schs., Norwich, Conn., 1939-43; librarian John Fitch High Sch., Windsor, Conn., 1944-46; asst. librarian Bulkeley High Sch., Hartford, 1946-55, librarian, 1956—. Mem. N.E.A., Conn., Hartford edn. assns., Conn. Sch. Library Assn. Republican. Methodist. Home: 18 Elm St Wethersfield CT 06109 Office: 470 Maple Av Hartford CT 06114

HORNER, ALTHEA JANE GREENWALD (MRS. DAVID R. DOROFF), psychologist; b. Hartford, Conn., Jan. 13, 1926; d. Louis and Celia (Newmark) Greenwald; student U. Cal. at Berkeley, 1945-46; B.S. in Psychology, U. Chgo., 1952; Ph.D. in Clin. Psychology, U. So. Cal., 1965; m. Edward N. Horner, June 12, 1945 (div. 1970); children—Martha June, Anne Louise, David Alfred, Kenneth Robert; m. 2d, David R. Doroff, Oct. 22, 1972. USPHS fellow Los Angeles Psychiat. Service, also Psychol. Service Center, U. So. Cal., Pasadena, 1962-64; staff psychologist Pasadena Child Guidance Clinic, 1964-66, mem. profl. adv. com., 1968-69; tchr. Pasadena City Coll., 1966-67; pvt. practice clin. psychology, Arcadia, Cal., 1965-70, N.Y.C., 1970—; asso. prof. psychology Los Angeles Coll. Optometry, 1967-70; supervising psychologist dept. child psychiatry Beth Israel Hosp., N.Y.C., 1972—. Mem., discussion leader Pasadena Area Liberal Arts Center, 1960-70. Mem. Am. Psychol. Assn., Am. Assn. Women in Sci., Am. Acad. Psychotherapists, Am. Group Psychotherapy Assn., Eastern Group Psycotherapy Soc., A.A.A.S. Contbr. to publs. in field. Home: Route 23 Great Barrington MA 01230 Office: 276 Riverside Dr New York City NY 10025

HORNER, B. ELIZABETH, zoologist, educator; b. Merchantville, N.J., Apr. 29, 1916; B.S., Rutgers U., 1938; M.A., Smith Coll., 1940; Ph.D. in Zoology (Wilder and Whipple fellow, Rackham fellow), U. Mich., 1948. Asst. in zoology Smith Coll., 1940-41, instr., 1941-44, 46-48, asst. prof., 1948-57, asso. prof., 1957, now Myra Sampson prof. biol. scis. Am. Assn. U. Women fellow U. Sydney (Australia), 1954-55. Mem. A.A.A.S., Am. Soc. Zoology, Ecol. Soc. Am., Soc. Mammals, Soc. for Study Evolution, Australian Mammal Soc. Research on postnatal skeletal devel. of carnivores and rodents, animal ecology, behavior of rodents and marsupials. Address: Dept Biol Scis Smith College Northampton MA 01060

HORNER, ESTHER EMMA BERGFELD (MRS. CLAY HORNER), mus. curator; b. Moscow Mills, Mo., Apr. 10, 1914; d. Henry C. and Louise A. (Ludwig) Bergfeld; student pub. schs.; m. Clay

Horner, Jan. 21, 1947; 1 dau., Karen. Curator, Stevens County Gas and Hist. Museum, Hugoton, Kan., 1966—. Mem. decorating com. Pioneer Manor Nursing Home, Hugoton, 1959. Mem. V.F.W. Aux. Republican. Mem. Ch. of God (mem. ch. bd. 1955-59, pres. missionary bd. 1971, missionary historian 1972-73). Home: 711 S Van Buren St Hugoton KS 67951 Office: 911 S Adams St Hugoton KS 67951

HORNER, MATINA SOURETIS (MRS. JOSEPH LEFEURE HORNER), coll. pres., dean; b. Boston, July 28, 1939; d. Demetre John and Christine (Antonopoulos) Souretis; A.B., Bryn Mawr Coll., 1961; M.S., U. Mich., 1963, Ph.D., 1968; m. Joseph LeFeure Horner, June 25, 1961; children—Tia Andrea, John Anton, Christopher Demetre. Lectr. dept. psychology U. Mich.; lectr. dept. social relations Harvard, asst. prof. to asso. prof. dept. psychology, and social relations; now pres., dean Radcliffe Coll., Cambridge, Mass., 1972—. Mem. Phi Beta Kappa, Phi Kappa Phi. Contbr. numerous articles to profl. jours. chpts to books. Home: 76 Brattle St Cambridge MA 02138

HORNER, ROSEMARY LESTER (MRS. JAMES TRUMAN HORNER), coll. adminstr.; b. Independence, Mo., Oct. 28, 1930; d. John A. and Florence Faye (Alley) Lester; A.A., Christian Coll., 1950; B.S., U. Mo., 1951, Ed.M., 1955; postgrad. Mich. State U., 1964-65; Ph.D., U. Neb., 1969; m. James Truman Horner, Aug. 22, 1950; children—Pamela Ann, James Lester, Paula Faye. Vocational home econs. instr. Fairfield (Ia.) Jr.-Sr. High Sch., 1954-55; instr. human devel. and family dept. U. Neb., Lincoln, 1967-68; asst. prof. edn. Neb. Wesleyan U., Lincoln, 1968-71; dir. student personnel services Southeastern Neb. Tech. Community Coll., Lincoln, 1971—. State dir. People to People Student Ambassador Program, Lincoln, 1969—. Bd. dirs. Community Concerts Assn. Lincoln, 1969—, treas., 1971-73; bd. dirs. Lincoln Found., 1971—. Mem. Nat. Edn. Assn., Neb. Adminstrs. Student Financial Aids Assn. (mem. exec. com. 1972—), Neb. Admissions Counselors and Coll. Registrars (mem. ad hoc com. 1973—), Am., Neb. (pub. relations chmn., dir. 1973—) personnel and guidance assns., Coll. Student Personnel Assn., Mo. Valley Adult Edn. Assn., P.E.O., Pi Lambda Theta, Phi Delta Gamma, Kappa Delta Pi, Phi Upsilon Omicron, Phi Theta Kappa, Delta Eta Chi, Delta Zeta. Methodist. Club: Altrusa (Lincoln). Home: 441 Hazelwood Dr Lincoln NE 68510

HORNICK, LITA ROTHBARD (MRS. MORTON J. HORNICK), publisher; b. Newark, Feb. 9, 1927; d. Samuel L. and Celia M. (Meltz) Rothbard; B.A., Barnard, 1948; M.A., Columbia, 1949, Ph.D., 1958; m. Morton J. Hornick, June 2, 1949; children—Louis, Blake. Pres., Kulchur Press, N.Y.C., 1961—. Pres., Kulchur Found., 1970—. Author: The Intricate Image, 1972. Address: 888 Park Av New York City NY 10021

HORNIG, LILLI SCHWENK (MRS. DONALD F. HORNIG), educator; b. Aussig, Czechoslovakia, Mar. 22, 1921; d. Erwin and Rascha (Schapiro) Schwenk; came to U.S., 1933, naturalized, 1939; A.B., Bryn Mawr, 1942; M.A., Harvard, 1943, Ph.D., 1950; m. Donald F. Hornig, July 17, 1943; children—Joanna Gail (Mrs. Ronald Forrest Fox), Ellen Constance (Mrs. J. Douglas Deal, III), Christopher Wayne, Leslie Elizabeth. Research asst. Harvard U., 1943-44; staff scientist, sect. leader Los Alamos (N.M.) Lab., 1944-46; teaching asst., instr., research asso. Brown U., Providence, R.I., 1946-52, exec. dir. higher edn. resource services, 1972—; asst. prof. chemistry Trinity Coll., Washington, 1964-66, asso. prof., chmn. dept., 1966-69. Dir. sci. div. Catalyst for Women, N.Y.C., 1966-69. Bd. dirs. Rochester (N.Y.) Assn. for UN, 1969-70, R.I. Hosp., Providence; trustee Woods Hole (Mass.) Oceanographic Instn., 1972—, mem. exec. com., 1973—; trustee Mary C. Wheeler Sch., 1972—. Fellow Am. Inst. Chemists; mem. A.A.A.S., Am. Assn. U. Profs., Am. Assn. U. Women. Contbr. articles to profl. pubs. Home: 55 Power St Providence RI 02906

HORNING, LEORA NORLENE, educator; b. Brooklyn, Mich., Oct. 19, 1916; d. Eben Foster and Belvia (Waters) Horning; B.S., Mich. State U., 1939, M.A., 1946; postgrad. U. Colo., U. Neb., U. Cal. at Los Angeles. Homemaking tchr. Onsted (Mich.) High Sch., 1939-41; cafeteria mgr., tchr. Eastern High Sch., Lansing, Mich., 1941-44; head dietitian Dow Chem. Co., Midland, Mich., 1944-45; instr. Mich. State U., 1945-49; head homemaking dept. Saginaw (Mich.) High Sch., 1949-53; homemaking supr., tchr., student tchr. supr. Lakeview Schs., Battle Creek, Mich., 1953-58; asst. prof. vocational edn. U. Neb., Lincoln, 1958-61, asso. prof., 1961-62, acting chmn. home econs. edn. dept., 1962-63, asso. prof. home econ. edn., 1963—. Recipient Pub. Relations award Mich. Home Econs. Assn., 1952, Achievement award for Neb., Mo. Valley Adult Edn. Assn., 1971; named Bus. Woman of Year, Am. Bus. Womens Assn., for Mich., 1958, for Neb., 1970. Mem. Neb. Home Econs. Assn. (pres. 1972-73), other profl. orgns., Sigma Kappa. Presbyn. Club: Toastmistress. Asso. editor: Adult Leadership, 1964-66, 72—. Home: 10 Gramercy Pl 7111 Old Post Rd Lincoln NE 68520

HORNING, MARJORIE GROOTHUIS (MRS. EVAN C. HORNING), educator; b. Detroit, Aug. 23, 1917; d. Herman and Nina Jane (Potter) Groothuis; B.A., Goucher Coll., 1938; M.S., U. Mich., 1940, Ph.D., 1943; m. Evan C. Horning, Sept. 25, 1942. Research chemist Nat. Heart Inst., Bethesda, Md., 1951-61; research asso. prof. Baylor Coll. Medicine, Houston, 1961-63, asso. prof., 1963-69, prof. biochemistry, 1969—. Mem. Am. Soc. Pharmacology and Exptl. Therapeutics, Am. Soc. Mass Spectrometry, Am. Chem. Soc., A.A.A.S., N.Y. Acad. Scis., Phi Beta Kappa, Sigma Xi. Mem. editorial bd. Drug Metabolism and Disposition, 1972—. Contbr. articles to profl. jours. Home: 11610 Starwood Dr Houston TX 77024

HORNSTEIN, LUSIA, pediatrician; b. Lvov, Poland, Feb. 24, 1925; d. Norbert and Frieda (Meier) Schwarzwald; M.D., U. Heidelberg (Germany), 1952; m. Stephen Hornstein, May 9, 1948; children—Mark, Frank, Ruth. Came to U.S., 1952; naturalized, 1957. Intern, Beth Israel Hosp., Newark, 1952-53; resident pediatrics Communicable Disease Hosp., Belleville, N.J., 1953, Beth El Hosp., N.Y.C., 1954, Children's Hosp., Cin., 1958-59; asst. dir. outpatient dept. Children's Hosp., Cin., 1959-60; asso. dir. pediatric diagnostic services Cin. Center for Developmental Disorders, Cin., asso. clin. prof. pediatrics U. Cin. Coll. Medicine, 1971—. Fellow Am. Acad. Pediatrics; mem. Cin. Pediatric Soc., Nat. Council Jewish Women, Hadassah, Am. Women's ORT. Office: 3300 Elland Av Cincinnati OH 45229

HOROWITZ, MARJORIE BRAILOVE (MRS. IRVIN MILTON HOROWITZ), librarian; b. Phila., Oct. 7, 1927; d. Sascha Alexander and Mathilda (Feder) Brailove; B.A., Wellesley Coll., 1949; M.L.S., Columbia, 1966; m. Irvin Milton Horowitz, June 19, 1949; children—Michal Ann (Mrs. Adoniram Bowen), Benjamin David, Rachel Jane, Ruth Alice. Publicity asst. Save the Children Fedn., N.Y.C., 1949-51; librarian Watchung Sch., Montclair, N.J., 1966-70, Nishuane Sch., Montclair, 1970-72, Hillside Middle Sch., Montclair, 1972—. Publicity chmn. Citizens Com. for Ednl. Planning, Montclair, 1970-72. N.J. Dept. Edn. mini-grantee, 1972-73. Mem. A.L.A., Nat., N.J., Montclair (counselor 1973—) edn. assns., Essex County Sch. Library Assn. (v.p. 1971—), N.J. Sch. Media Assn. (mem. nominating com. 1974—), Beta Phi Mu. Democrat. Jewish religion. Club: N.J. Wellesley. Home: 10 Prospect Av Montclair NJ 07042 Office: 54 Orange Rd Montclair NJ 07042

HOROWITZ, ROSLYN HAMMER (MRS. MURRAY HOROWITZ), psychologist; b. N.Y.C., June 1, 1926; d. Benjamin and Minnie (Halpern) Hammer; B.S., City U. N.Y., 1947; M.Ed., U. Miami, 1967, Ph.D., 1973; m. Murray Horowitz, Jan. 31, 1948; children—Judith Ellen, Seth Charles. Writer radio, TV commls., 1947-49; editor-in-chief Treasure Island News, North Bay Village, Fla., 1952-57; tchr. U. Miami, Coral Gables, Fla., 1970-71; pvt. practice psychologist. Mem. Am., Dade County psychol. assns. Home: 7540 Cutlass Av Treasure Island Miami Beach FL 33141 Office: 633 NE 167th St North Miami Beach FL 33162

HOROWITZ, RUTH HYLA LEVY, marriage, family therapist; b. Elizabeth, N.J., Dec. 1, 1910; d. Emmanuel and Ethel (Natelson) Levy; B.A., Cornell U., 1931; M.A., Drew U., 1957; certificate advanced marriage counseling U. Pa. Sch. Medicine, 1958; m. Harry Horowitz, June 5, 1935; children—Peter, Elizabeth, Paul. Staff marriage counselor Phila. Marriage Council, div. family studies, dept. psychiatry U. Pa. Sch. Medicine, 1958-59; individual practice, Summit, N.J., 1959—; lectr. Montclair (N.J.) State Tchrs. Coll., 1970—. Bd. dirs. Child Study Assn. Am., Family Service Assn., Mental Health Assn., Summit, Vis. Nurse Assn. Eastern Union County, Egenolf Day Nursery, Elizabeth. Tchr. first aid A.R.C. Home Service Corps, World War II. Past mem. N.J. Bd. Marriage Counselor Examiners. Mem. Nat. Council Jewish Women, Am. (clin.), N.J. assns. marriage and family counselors, Am. Jewish Congress (pres. Elizabeth women's div. 1946-47), Hadassah. Jewish religion (pres. temple sisterhood 1942-43). Club: Madison (N.J.) Golf. Home: 138 Hillcrest Av Summit NJ 07901 Office: 382 Springfield Av Summit NJ 07901

HORRY, RUTH NAOMI, educator; b. Bryan, S.C.; d. Albert F.B. and Sarah (Woodbury) Horry; A.B., Talladega Coll., 1936; M.A., Howard U., 1937; Ph.D., N.Y. U., 1948; postdoctoral student U. Chgo., U. Paris, U. Pa., U. Minn., Duke, 1964-65. Prof. French, Rust Coll., Holly Springs, Miss., 1938, Allen U., Columbia, S.C., 1939-49; N.C. Central U., 1949—; asso. dir. Nat. Defense Edn. Act Lang. Inst., N.C. Coll., summer 1964. Mem. N.C. Curriculum Study, 1959-61; vol. Durham United Fund, Cancer Crusade, others. Bd dirs. Durham YWCA, 1957-59. Recipient Ford Found. fellowship, 1953, Danforth grant, 1962. Mem. Modern Lang. Assn. Am., S. Atlantic Modern Lang. Assn., Coll. Lang. Assn. (pres. 1971-73), Am. Assn. Tchrs. French. Author: Paul Claudel and Saint John Perse: Parallels and Contrasts, 1971. Delta Sigma Theta, Pi Delta Phi. Methodist. Home: 211 Pekoe Av Durham NC 27707

HORSEMAN, JEAN MARY, librarian; b. Balt., July 31, 1932; d. Ezard Hamilton and Anna Elsie (Curry) Horseman; B.S., Towson State Coll., 1953; M.S., Johns Hopkins, 1958; M.S. in L.S., Cath. U., 1964. Tchr. William Paca Sch., Balt., 1953-54, Montebello Sch., 1954-58; librarian Glenmount Sch., Balt., 1958-65, Roland Park Sch., Balt., 1965-68, Herring Run Sch., Balt., 1968—. Mem. Phi Delta Gamma, Beta Phi Mu, Pi Lambda Theta. Home: 7915 Roseland Av Baltimore MD 21237 Office: 5001 Sinclair Lane Baltimore MD 21206

HORSLEY, IMOGENE, educator; b. Seattle, Oct. 31, 1919; d. William Henry and Lucille (Thompson) Horsley; B.A., U. Wash., 1943; M.A., Mills Coll., 1949; Ph.D., Radcliffe Coll., 1954. Faculty, Carleton Coll., Northfield, Minn., 1954-68, U. Wash., 1961-62; asso. prof. music Stanford, 1969—. Sr. fellow Nat. Endowment for Hunanities, 1968-69. Mem. Phi Beta Kappa, Mu Phi Epsilon. Author: Fugue: History and Practice, 1966. Contbr. articles to profl. jours. Home: 4047 Manzana Lane Palo Alto CA 94306 Office: Music Dept Stanford U Stanford CA 94305

HORST, ELEANOR, interior designer; b. N.Y.C., Aug. 3, 1892; d. Charles and Elizabeth (Freeman) Goulding; B.A. Hunter Coll., 1912; M.A., Columbia, 1916; student Art Students League, 1913, Parson's Sch. Interior Design, 1935-36; m. Amos Long Horst, June 20, 1920 (div. Nov. 1938); 1 dau., Nancy (Mrs. Alexander Buel Trowbridge, Jr.). Tchr., N.Y.C. sch. system, 1912-17; canteen worker World War I, France, 1918; exec. asst. to pub. Arts and Decoration Mag., 1919-20; art editor Women's Jour., 1920-23; designer interiors, N.Y.C., 1925—. Mem. Am. Inst. Interior Designers (nat. exam. bd.), Archtl. League, Nat. Soc. Historic Preservation, Greenwich Taxpayers Assn., Irish Georgian Soc., Conn. Conservation Assn., Friends of Greenwich Library, Met. Mus. Art of N.Y.C., Modern Art Mus. Republican. Club: N.Y. Decorators (v.p. 1940-42, 67-72, chmn. historic com. 1972-73, mem. numerous coms.). Home: 47 Putnam Park Greenwich CT 06830 Office: 40 E 54th St New York City NY 10022

HORTER, ELIZABETH BRADY (MRS. PHILIP C. HORTER), banker; b. West Orange, N.J., Mar. 30, 1910; d. Michael Joseph and Anna Rebecca (Boud) Brady; student various courses Am. Inst. Banking, N.Y.U.; m. Philip C. Horter, Oct. 5, 1956. Stenographer, N.J. Title & Mortgage Co., Newark, 1928-29, Fidelity Title & Mortgage Co., 1929-34; with Bankers Trust Co., N.Y.C., 1934—, asst. treas., 1953-61, asst. v.p., 1961-67, v.p., 1967—. Bd. dirs. Spence Chapin Adoption Service, N.Y.C. Mem. N.Y. League Bus. and Profl. Women (past pres.), Nat. Assn. Bank Women, Inc. (met. group chmn. N.Y.C. chpt. 1955-56). Home: 17 W View Rd West Orange NJ 07052 Office: 16 Wall St New York NY 10005

HORTIN, MELLIE BROWN SCOTT (MRS. LOREN JOSEPH HORTIN), author; b. Paducah, Ky., Aug. 5, 1908; d. George Winfield and Ada Richmond (Harris) Scott; B.S., Murray State U., 1932, postgrad., 1933-34, 72-73; m. Loren Joseph Hortin, Nov. 26, 1930. Tchr., Fisher Elementary Sch., McCracken County, Ky., 1927-28, 29-30, 30-31. Mem. Nat. League Am. Pen Women, Nat. Fedn. State Poetry Socs., Inc., P.E.O. (publicity chmn. 1968—), Ky. State Poetry Soc., Ky. Hist. Soc., Murray Mag. Club (pres. 1969-73), Theta Sigma Phi, Kappa Delta Pi. Democrat. Methodist (mem. bd. stewards 1950-54). Club: Woman's (publicity chmn. garden dept. 1969-70) (Murray, Ky.). Contbr. articles and poetry to profl. jours. Home: 1803 Lincoln Av Box 3126 University Sta Murray KY 42071

HORTON, JANET ELIZABETH (MRS. MARVIN DEAN HORTON), artist, TV script author; b. Tecumseh, Neb., Nov. 4, 1930; d. Charles Arthur and Eva Mae (Morton) Hunt; B.F.A., U. Neb., 1953; certificate Millsaps Coll., 1963; m. Marvin Dean Horton, Aug. 28, 1950; children—James Marvin, Anne Marie. Instr. Sch. Fine Arts Miss. Coll., Clinton, 1961-63; instr. fine arts Murrah High Sch., Jackson, Miss., 1966-68; script writer, TV producer Miss. Authority for Ednl. TV, Jackson, 1970-73; free lance TV script writer, New Orleans, 1973—; exhibited paintings in group shows Biloxi, Miss., 1968, Shreveport (La.) Art Club, 1968, Cross-Tie Arts Festival, Cleveland, Miss., 1970, 74, Miss. Art Assn., 1970, Chevron Art Competition, New Orleans, 1973, Edgewater Exhibit, Biloxi, 1974; dir. Two Plus Two, Ltd. Gallery, New Orleans, 1973—. Mem. Am. Assn. U. Women (com. chmn. 1960-65), Art Study Club (com. chmn. 1962-72), Kappa Delta. Episcopalian. Home: 3965 Peach Tree Ct New Orleans LA 70114 Office: 3906 General De Gaulle Dr New Orleans LA 70114

HORTON, LENA MARY, bus. exec.; b. Maryville, Mo., Feb. 22, 1903; d. George P. and Margaret (Bays) Horton; B.A. cum laude, Parsons Coll., 1928; M.A., U. Ia., 1933. Elementary tchr. Fairfield, Ia., 1921-29; elementary supr. Dowagiac, Mich., 1929-30, Ironwood, Mich., 1930-32; dir. curriculum and instr., Rock Island, Ill., 1933-36; dir. research Silver Burdett Co., N.Y., 1936-47; editorial curriculum cons. Scott Foresman and Co., Chgo., 1947-55, directing editor basic social studies program, 1955-62, directing editor basic reading and lang. programs, 1962-63, gen. editor, 1964-66; asst. v.p. Scott Foresman and Co., Glenview, Ill., 1966-70, v.p., 1971—. Mut. Security Adminstrn. curriculum specialist to Philippines, 1952-54. Bd. dirs. Dyslexia Meml. Found.; trustee Parsons Coll.; women's bd. Nat. Conf. Christians and Jews. Mem. Am. Acad. Social Scis., Am. Edn. Research Assn., N.E.A. (life), Internat. Reading Assn., English Speaking Union, Phi Kappa Phi, Pi Lambda Theta, Delta Kappa Gamma, P.E.O. Episcopalian. Clubs: Michigan Shores; The Neighbors (Kenilworth, Ill.). Home: 1440 Sheridan Rd Wilmette IL 60091 Office: 1900 E Lake Av Glenview IL 60025

HORTON, YVONNE, home economist, writer; b. Orwell, O.; d. Edmund Earl and Stella (Jenks) Horton; B.S. in Edn., Kent State U., 1943; vocational home econs. certification Ohio State U., 1944; M.S. in Home Econs., Syracuse U., 1950; postgrad. in edn. U. Nev., 1963-64; m. Stanley Kolsan, Dec. 29, 1951 (div. 1963); children—Vera Suzanne, Helen Jane. Home econs. tchr., secondary schs., No. Ohio, 1944-48; teaching asst. Syracuse U., 1948-50; asst. dir. Hoover Home Inst., North Canton, O., 1950-51; asst. home econs. editor Plain Dealer, Cleve., 1952-54; lang. arts tchr. secondary schs., Clark County, Nev., 1963-66; staff home economist Christian Sci. Monitor, Boston, 1966-70, writer Candid Consumer column, 1967-70; home econs. tchr. secondary schs., Mass., 1970-72; editor, writer Co-ed mag., N.Y.C., 1973. Mem. Frontier council Girl Scouts U.S.A., 1964, 65; mem. Boston Mus. Fine Arts, 1967—, Friends Old Sturbridge Village, 1968—. Recipient Alma award Assn. Home Appliance Mfrs., 1967, 68, 69. Mem. Nat. Council Tchrs. English (life), Am., Mass. home econs. assn., Friends of Concord Free Pub. Library (life). Address: 1784 Wedgewood Common Concord MA 01742

HOSEPIAN, CLAUDIA CANDYCE, automobile co. exec.; b. Fresno, Cal., Nov. 24, 1949; d. Ernest Karl and Alice Vanoosh (Karoglanian) Hosepian; B.A. summa cum laude Cal. State U. at Fresno, 1972. Editor hist. booklet Fresno Creamery Employees Union, Local 517, 1971; mem. KJEO news team, Fresno, Cal., 1972; asso. editor Autoweek, Reno, 1972-73; pub. relations specialist Toyota Motor Sales, Torrance, Cal., 1973—. Recipient William Randolph Hearst Found. award, 1970. Mem. ADS, Fresno Ad Club, Women in Communications, Kappa Alpha Theta, Phi Kappa Phi, Alpha Phi Gamma. Home: 211 Yacht Club Way 226 Redondo Beach CA 90277 Office: 2055 W 190th St Torrance CA 90509

HOSKINS, JANINA WANDA EWA KOZLOWSKI (MRS. HALFORD L. HOSKINS), librarian, historian; b. Latvia; d. Michael K. and Jadwiga (Bielska) Kozlowski; came to U.S., 1949, naturalized, 1956; student U. Paris, 1933-34, U. Warsaw (Poland); M.A., U. Cracow (Poland), 1946, Ph.D. in history, 1947; postgrad. Cath. U. Am., 1955-59; m. Francis Wojcicki, Jan. 3, 1931; children—Andrew, Stanley; m. 2d, Halford Lancaster Hoskins, May 9, 1960. Asst. prof. history U. Cracow, 1946-48; research history, Sweden, 1949; researcher history Mid-European Study Center, N.Y.C., 1950-54; part-time specialist Polish affairs Library of Congress, Washington, 1951-55, area specialist Poland and East Europe, 1955—. Mem. Am. Hist. Assn., Medieval Acad. Am., Assn. Advancement Slavic Studies, A.L.A. (vice chmn. Slavic and East European Subsect. 1970—), Kosciuszko Found. Author: Early and Rare Polonica in American Libraries, 1973, Polish Books in English, 1974. Contbr. articles to profl. jours. Home: 4807 Quebec St NW Washington DC 20016 Office: Library of Congress Washington DC 20540

HOSMER, BARBARA JEAN, journalist; b. San Francisco, July 24, 1935; d. Matthew Newell and Lillian (Roberts) Hosmer; B.A. in Journalism and English, U. Cal. at Berkeley, 1958; M.A., Columbia, 1959; postgrad. A. Press Inst., 1969. With San Francisco Call-Bull., 1955-56, Santa Barbara (Cal.) News-Press, 1959-61; with San Rafael (Cal.) Ind.-Jour., 1961—, reporter, feature writer, women's sect. editor, 1964—. Commr., Marin County (Cal.) Human Rights Commn., 1971—, chmn. com. equal opportunity, 1971—. Mem. Nat. Orgn. Women (pres. Marin County 1971-72), Prytanean. Author: African Travels, 1966; also articles series. Home: 312 Via Hidalgo San Rafael CA 94904 Office: Box 330 San Rafael CA 94902

HOSTETLER, MARGARET ANNE, home economist; b. Smithville, O., Mar. 30, 1937; d. Ralph William and Leona E. (Amstutz) Hostetler; B.S., Wittenberg U., 1960; M.A., Ohio State U., 1964, postgrad., 1969, 72. Home econs. tchr. Rittman (O.) High Sch., 1960-63, 64-65; grad. asst. Ohio State U., Columbus, 1963-64, county extension agt. home econs. Holmes County, Millersburg, O., 1965—. Mem. Am., Ohio home econs. assns., Nat. Assn. Extension Home Economists, Ohio Coop Extension Agts. Assn., Holmes County Hist. Soc., Delta Kappa Gamma (chpt. sec. 1968-72), Epsilon Sigma Phi, Alpha Eta. Clubs: Millersburg Business and Professional Women's (sec. 1967-70). Home: 3 1/2 E Clinton St Millersburg OH 44654 Office: Box 287 Millersburg OH 44654

HOSTETTER, MARY SPARKS (MRS. JOHN I. HOSTETTER), physician; b. Burkburnette, Tex., Mar. 19, 1920; d. Jared and Mary Ellen (Truman) Sparks; student Central Coll., 1939; A.A., Lindenwood Coll., 1940; B.A., U. Ia., 1943, M.D., 1950; m. John I. Hostetter, Sept. 6, 1949; children—Maryellen, Kathryn, Sarah, John, Jeffrey, Jesse. Intern, Broadlawns Hosp., Des Moines, 1951-52; practice medicine, Des Moines, 1952—; physician Des Moines Health Center, 1960-61; coordinator Drake U. Health Services, 1960—; med. cons. Social Security Disability Determination, 1967—. Mem. Polk County Med. Soc., Chi Omega, Alpha Omega Alpha. Home: 1045 19th St West Des Moines IA 50265 Office: American Republic Student Health Service Drake U Des Moines IA 50311

HOSTLER, SHARON LEE (MRS. ALAN DUANE DIMOCK), physician; b. Rutland, Vt., Oct. 24, 1939; d. John Gerald and Irene (Whitney) Hostler; A.B., Middlebury Coll., 1961; M.D., U. Vt., 1965; m. Alan Duane Dimock, Dec. 29, 1965; children—Kathleen Ann, Dylan Alan. Pediatric intern, U. Va. Hosp., Charlottesville, 1965-66, resident pediatrics, 1966-67, fellow pediatric hematology, 1967-69; practice medicine specializing in pediatrics, Charlottesville, Va., 1969—; mem. staff U. Va. Hosp.; asst. prof. Med. Sch., U. Va., 1969—; med. dir. Dept. Pediatrics, Comprehensive Care for Children and Youth, 1969-73; co-med. dir. Children's Rehab. Center U. Va. Med. Center, 1973—, med. dir. Handicapped Children's Clinic, 1973—, dir. Muscular Dystrophy Clinic, 1973—, dir. Learning Disabilities Clinic, 1973—. Established satellite clinics Dept. Pediatrics, Albemarle County, Va. Adv. bd. F.O.C.U.S. Gould Scholar. Diplomate Nat. Bd. Med. Examiners, Am. Bd. Pediatrics. Fellow Am. Acad. Pediatrics; mem. Va., Albermarle County med. socs., Ambulatory Pediatrics Assn., Am. Pub. Health Assn., So. Soc. Pediatric Research, Am. Med. Womens Assn., Am. Assn. U. Profs., Ambulatory Pediatric Soc., Am. Assn. Sex Educators and Counselors, Central Va. Child Devel. Assn. (dir.). Contbr. articles to profl. jours. Home: PO Box 65 North Garden

VA 22959 Office: Dept Pediatrics U Va Hosp Jefferson Park Av Charlottesville VA 22901

HOUDESHELDT, MINNETTE JEANNE, journalist; b. Hebron, Neb., Oct. 31, 1937; d. Nelson Lynn and Erline Marie (Walters) Taylor; B.S., U. Neb., 1959; m. Robert Marion Houdesheldt, Oct; 21, 1960; children—Dianne, Michael, Gregory. Reporter, Western Neb. Observer, Kimball, 1959-66, North Platte (Neb.) Telegraph, 1966-72; news editor Lincoln (Neb.) Sun Newspapers, 1973—. Recipient Top 10 award Nat. Press Women's writing contest, 1970; Service to Agr. award Neb. Press Assn., 1971. Mem. Neb. Press Women. Democrat. Methodist. Home: 4535 Hillside St Lincoln NE 68501 Office: Cotner and Garland Sts Lincoln NE 68501

HOUGHTON, RUTH ANNE MORTENSEN (MRS. EVANS FRANKLYN HOUGHTON), hosp. exec.; b. East Orange, N.J., Nov. 8, 1918; d. Richard Andreas and Maude Violet (Lyle) Mortensen; A.A., Centenary Coll. for Women, 1937; B.A., Radcliffe Coll., 1939; m. Evans Franklyn Houghton, May 27, 1949 (dec. May 1974); children—Stanley Allen, Charles Evans, Eleanore Louise, John Norris, Richard Henry. Dir. pub. relations Elm Farm Foods Co., Boston, 1960-65; dir. pub. information Mass. Heart Assn., Boston, 1966-67, Andover Newton Theol. Sch., Newton, Mass., 1968-73; dir. vol. and information services Concord (N.H.) Hosp., 1973—. Free lance writer, cons., 1950-60. Mem. Pub. Relations Soc. Am., New Eng. Hosp. Pub. Relations Assn. Democrat. Episcopalian. Club: Appalachian Mountain (Boston). Home: Box 42 Warner NH 03278 Office: 250 Pleasant St Concord NH 03301

HOUK, JUDITH ANN, research co. exec., librarian; b. Muncie, Ind., Feb. 2, 1935; d. William Harrison and Allie (Allen) Houk; student Western Coll. for Women, 1953-54, Ball State Tchrs. Coll., 1954-56; A.B. (with honors), Indiana U., 1958, M.A., 1959. Reference asst. Dayton & Montgomery County Pub. Library, Dayton, O., 1959-63; reference librarian USAF Inst. Tech., Wright-Patterson AFB, Dayton, 1963-64; head librarian Westminster (Colo.) Pub. Library, 1964-67; regional librarian Inter-County Regional Planning Commn., Denver, 1967-68; system librarian Central Colo. Pub. Library System, 1968-72; pres., exec. dir. Library Reports & Research Service, Inc., spl. research, tech. writing, library cons., Westminster, Colo., 1972—. Mem. Am. (councilor-at-large 1972—), Mountain Plains, Colo. (1st v.p. 1966-67, pres., 1967-68, exec. sec. 1970-72) library assns., Spl. Libraries Assn., Am. Soc. for Information Sci., Phi Beta Kappa, Beta Phi Mu. Roman Catholic. Author: Classification System for Ohio State Documents, 1962; Public Libraries in the Denver Metropolitan Area: A Plan and Program for Public Library Development to 1985, 1968. Contbr. articles to profl. publs., encys., newspapers. Address: 4140 W 80th Pl Westminster CO 80030

HOUP, DEBORAH DALEHITE (MRS. KENNETH EUGENE HOUP, JR.), ednl. adminstr.; b. Starkville, Miss., May 16, 1945; d. Thomas Hiram and Catherine Florence (Green) Dalehite; B.A., U. Fla., 1966, B.S., 1967; m. Kenneth Eugene Houp, Jr., Aug. 26, 1967. Editor, Friendly Flame mag. Tex. LP-Gas Assn., Austin, 1968-71, editor Tex. LP-Gas News mag., 1968-71; free-lance editor, 1971-74; job placement coordinator Office of Student Financial Aid, U. Tex., Austin, 1974—. Mem. Phi Mu. Club: Austin (Tex.) Lawyers' Wives' (pub. relations dir. 1972, 73). Home: 607-B Thrush Av Austin TX 78753

HOUSE, IRIS ELIZABETH FORD (MRS. MILLARD B. HOUSE), nursing home adminstr.; b. Schoepke, Wis., Apr. 10, 1919; d. Lucius Augustus and Lillian Mae (Flanery) Taylor; grad. high sch.; m. Floyd Ford, June 5, 1937 (dec. Nov. 1971); children—Sandra (Mrs. Charles F. Toms III), Carolee (Mrs. Carolee Josheff), Jill (Mrs. Gordon E. Sickler); m. 2d, Millard B. House, Sept. 25, 1972. Dorcas welfare worker, Rhinelander, Wis., 1942-52; adminstr. Oneida County Nursing Home, Rhinelander, 1947—; corp. pres. Friendly Village, Inc., Rhinelander, 1966—. Cons., lectr. on aging, 1956-60; lectr. on retarded programs Royal Soc. Medicine, London, 1970, Berkshire Coll., Eng., 1971, European Assn. Spl. Edn., Norrkopping, Sweden, 1971. Residential chmn. A.R.C., Rhinelander, 1971-73, organizer fund drive for retarded, 1971—; charter mem. Rhinelander Arts Council; co-chmn. Rhinelander Sch. Arts, 1963-68. Republican precinct committeewoman, 1962-63. Recipient Woman of Year award Am. Legion, 1968; Plaque award Rhinelander C. of C., 1969. Mem. Nat. Geriatrics Soc. (bd. govs. 1955-56), Nat. Gerontological Soc. (area rep. 1957-61), Am. Assn. Nursing Homes (governing council 1954-55), Am. Assn. Mental Deficiency (Wis. chpt. sec. 1972-74, mem. legislative com. 1972—), Wis. Nursing Home Assn. (pres. 1953-54), Wis. State Rehab. Assn. Seventh-day Adventist. Club: Woman's (Rhinelander). Home: Big Bearskin Lake RFD #1 Harshaw WI 54529 Office: 900 Boyce Dr Rhinelander WI 54501

HOUSE, JEAN JOHNSON (MRS. ROBERT H. HOUSE), physician; b. St. Louis, Aug. 6, 1941; d. Dale Riley and Helen (Bryan) Johnson; B.A., Oberlin Coll., 1963; M.D., U. Wis., 1968; m. Robert H. House, June 15, 1963; children—Laurie Jean, Daniel Robert. Intern family practice St. Joseph's Hosp., Syracuse, N.Y., 1968-69, resident, 1969-71; practice medicine, Ripon, Wis., 1971—; mem. staff Ripon Meml. Hosp., sec., 1971-72. Bd. dirs DAY (Drug Awareness and You), Ripon. Diplomate Am. Bd. Family Practice. Mem. Wis. Acad. Family Practice, Fox Valley Acad. Medicine, Fox Valley Perinatal Assn., Nat. Orgn. for Women, Am. Assn. U. Women. Home: Sunset Circle Ripon WI 54971 Office: 669 Thorne St Ripon WI 54971

HOUSE, LINDA MUSSER (MRS. CHARLES LYTLE HOUSE), occupational therapist; b. Kansas City, Mo., Mar. 3, 1943; d. Monod Blair and Thelma Grace (Bedford) Musser; B.S. with distinction in Occupational Therapy (Watkins scholar, Watkins-Berger scholar), U. Kan., 1965; m. Charles Lytle House, June 4, 1966; 1 dau., Kimberly Jean. Staff therapist U. Kan. Med. Center, Kansas City, 1965-67; chief occupational therapy Trinity Luth. Hosp., Kansas City, Mo., 1967-70; supr. psychiat. occupational therapy Menorah Med. Center, Kansas City, Mo., 1972—; clin. supr. staff U. Mo., 1969-70; clin. supr. U. Kan., 1965-70. Vol. worker United campaign, 1965-68, capt., 1970. Bd. dirs. Belles of Am. Royal, 1969, hospitality chmn., 1970. Mem. Am., Kan. (sec. 1966-69) occupational therapy assns., Kappa Alpha Theta. Home: 301 S Silver Top Raymore MO 64083 Office: 4949 Rockhill Kansas City MO 64113

HOUSE, RUBY DELL GRIFFIN, occupational therapist; b. Cameron, Tex., Apr. 17, 1944; d. Robert Nick and Lillian Lee (Stephen) Griffin; B.S., Tex. Woman's U., 1966; m. Willard Elijah House, Jr., May 31, 1966; 1 son, Nicholas Ryan. Staff occupational therapist VA, Dayton, O., 1966-67, Children's Med. Center, Dayton, 1967-74; dir. occupational therapy United Cerebral Palsy Met. Dayton, 1971—; cons. Crawford Convalescent Center, Dayton, 1966-67. Sec. Shaftesbury Block Club, Dayton, 1971-73. Mem. Am., Dayton Dist., Ohio (asst. treas. 1971-73, placement chmn. 1973) occupational therapy assns., Zeta Phi Beta. Baptist. Home: 3121 W Riverview Av Dayton OH 45406 Office: 1735 Chapel St Dayton OH 45401

HOUSER, MRS. GEORGE CROUSE, club woman; d.; Frank Herbert and Ursula F. (Handy) Hillman; student Boston U., 1918-21; m. George Crouse Houser, Oct. 8, 1925; children—George Crouse, Horace Milton. Pres. Garden Club of Brookline, 1946-48, program chmn., 1958-60; v.p. Garden Club Fedn. of Mass., 1953-55; sr. state pres. Children Am. Revolution, 1959-61, sr. nat. chaplain, 1962-64, hon. sr. nat. v.p., 1964-70, pres. sr. nat. officers' club, 1969-71, sr. nat. v.p. New Eng. region, 1972-74, life promoter; state historian D.A.R., 1953-56, regent Paul Revere chpt., 1967-68, state vice regent, 1968-70, state regent, 1970-74, hon. state regent, 1974—, nat. v.p. gen., 1974—; state corr. sec. Daus. Colonial Wars, 1959-62, state v.p., 1962-65, chaplain, 1965-68; 2d v.p., Mass. Huguenot Soc., 1962-65, 1st v.p., 1970—; state corr. sec. Daus. Founders and Patriots Am., 1964-67, chaplain, 1967-70. Recipient citation for good citizenship Freedom, Inc., 1958, George Washington Honor medal Freedoms Found., 1960. Mem. Soc. Mayflower Descs., New Eng. Historic Geneal. Soc., Soc. Descs. Colonial Clergy, Dutch Settlers Soc. Albany, Mass. Ct. Assts., Women Descs. Ancient and Hon. Arty. Co., Daus. Am. Colonists (state corr. sec. 1967-70, 2d vice regent 1971-73, 1st vice regent 1973—), Soc. Preservation New Eng. Antiquities, Bunker Hill Monument Assn., Boston Browning Soc., Mass. Soc. U. Edn. Women, New Eng. Farm and Garden Assn., English-Speaking Union. Clubs: College (Boston); China Student's (past dir.). Home: 220 Clyde St Chestnut Hill MA 02167

HOUSHOLDER, DORIS HARTMAN, lawyer; b. Pitts., Nov. 7, 1923; d. Robert N. and Emma (Kelly) Hartman; student Stetson U., 1940-43, George Washington U., summer 1943; J.D., U. Fla., 1946; m. Karlyle F. Housholder, June 1, 1945 (dec.); children—Melissa, Wayne, Mark. Admitted to Fla. bar, 1946; asso. Adkins & Adkins, Gainesville, Fla., 1946-47; pvt. practice, Sanford, 1947-58; atty. Workmen's Compensation div. Fla. Indsl. Commn., 1958-69, Legislative Service Bur., 1969-72; judge Indsl. Claims Ct., 1972—. Bd. dirs. Dist. Mental Health Assn. Mem. Am., Volusia County bar assns., Fla. Bar, Fla. Govt. Bar Assn. (pres. 1967), Am. Assn. U. Women, League Women Voters, Mental Health Assn. Democrat. Episcopalian. Club: Pilot Internat. Home: 1476 N Peninsula Dr Daytona Beach FL 32018 Office: 218 Seabreeze Blvd Daytona Beach FL 32018

HOUSNER, JILL PATON, food co. exec.; b. N.Y.C., Aug. 25, 1936; d. John Hezekiah and Millicent Alice Ora (Ford) Paton; student Bradford Jr. Coll., 1956; Asso. B.A., Tobe Coburn Sch. Fashion Merchandising, 1959; m. William Henry Housner, Dec. 2, 1961 (div.). Vice pres. Golden Blossom Honey, N.Y.C., 1970-71; chmn. bd. John Paton, Inc., N.Y.C., 1971—. Home: 169 E 78th St New York City NY 10021 Office: 630 5th Av New York City NY 10020

HOUSTON, EVELYN FRANCES DORSEY (MRS. JAMES D. HOUSTON), educator, librarian; b. Atlanta, May 3, 1925; d. Charlie George and Sallie Mae (Clemmons) Dorsey; B.S., Spelman Coll., 1946; M.S. in L.S., Atlanta U., 1959; m. James Daniel Houston, Sept. 8, 1946; children—Kenneth Vincent, Kazetta Victoria, Laura Ellen, Karen Yolanda. Lab. asst. foods dept. Spelman Coll., 1947-50; librarian's asst. Talladega (Ala.) Coll., 1951-53; librarian Westside High Sch., Talladega, 1954-64; tchr. fifth grade Eastside Sch., Talladega, 1963-69; tchr.-librarian Talladega High Sch., 1969—. Mem. N.E.A., Ala., Talladega City edn. assns. Baptist. Home: 208 S 25th St Talladega AL 35160 Office: 1177 McMillian St Talladega AL 35160

HOUSTON, LAURA PIRES (MRS. LAWRENCE R. HOUSTON), ednl. adminstr., social worker; b. Wareham, Mass., May 11, 1939; d. John P. and Adeline (Pereira) Pires; B.A., Smith Coll., 1961; M.S.W., Columbia U., 1963; m. Lawrence R. Houston, July 5, 1969. Program/research asst., group work cons. Harlem Youth Opportunities Unltd., Inc., 1963-64, program analyst, asst. chief employment, acting dir. Community Action Inst. HARYOU-ACT, Inc., N.Y.C., 1964-66; with Women's Talent Corps, Coll. for Human Services, N.Y.C., 1966—, field dir., 1966-68, dep. dir., 1968-69, v.p., 1970—; various positions in social work, N.Y.C., 1959-63. Field instr. N.Y. U., 1968-69, Columbia U. Schs. of Social Work, 1968-70; cons. Urban Coalition, 1971, Dept. Housing and Devel. Adminstrn., 1971. Mem. N.Y. State Adv. Council for Vocational Edn., 1969-72. Mem. adv. bds. Hale House, N.Y.C., 1972—, N.Y. Careerist Assn., 1971—. Recipient award Vocational Rehabilitation Office, 1962. Mem. Nat., N.Y. (1st. v.p. 1968) assns. of black social workers, Nat. Assn. Social Workers, Am. Soc. for Tng. and Devel. Editorial bd. New Generation Mag., 1972—. Home: 392 Central Park New York City NY 10025 Office: 201 Varick St College for Human Services New York City NY 10014

HOUSTON, MARTHA PETERSON (MRS. MAX S. HOUSTON), librarian; b. Kansas City, Mo., Oct. 17, 1924; d. Carl Adolph and Louise Virginia (Taylor) Peterson; student MacMurray Women's Coll., 1941-42; B.S., Kan. State Coll., 1945; postgrad. U. Wichita, 1958-74; M. Librarianship, Kan. State Tchrs. Coll., 1968; m. Max S. Houston, Sept. 23, 1944; children—Phillip Samuel, Tasker Louise, Sara Lyn. Med. librarian St. Francis Hosp., Wichita, Kan., 1964-67; biomed. librarian Wichita State U., 1968—. Mem. Am., Med. library assns., Spl. Libraries Assn., Kappa Kappa Gamma. Home: 403 N Fountain St Wichita KS 67208 Office: Library Wichita State U Wichita KS 67208

HOUSTON, ROSE PIK SIU CHAN, curator; b. Hong Kong, Nov. 3, 1935; d. Kwan Chiu and Hap Hing (Chung) Chan; came to U.S., 1955, naturalized, 1972; B.A. (Coll. scholar), Marian Coll., 1959; M.A. (grad. fellow), Fordham U., 1961, Ph.D., 1971; m. Douglas William Houston, Sept. 11, 1970; 1 son, Alan K.M. Library asst. Fordham U. Library, N.Y.C., 1961-65; instr. history Yeshiva U., N.Y.C., 1968-69; researcher history John H. Secondari Prodns., N.Y.C., 1970; asso. curator Far Eastern coins Am. Numis. Soc., N.Y.C., 1971—. Chinese abstractor for Am. Bibliographical Center, Clio Press, Santa Barbara, Cal., 1972—. Mem. Am. Hist. Assn., Am. Oriental Soc., N.Y. Oriental Club, Delta Epsilon Sigma. Home: 2431 Webb Av Apt 9C Bronx NY 10468 Office: American Numismatic Society Broadway and 155th St New York City NY 10032

HOUTZ, PATRICIA, univ. adminstr.; b. Sunbury, Pa.; d. William Wallace and Loretta (Maginnis) Houtz; B.S., Susquehanna U., 1950; M.S., Pa. State U., 1957, Ed.D., 1964; postgrad. Mich. State U., 1967-69, Wayne State U., 1972—. Instr. Ottomwa Heights Acad., 1950, Northumberland High Sch., 1950-51, Sunbury High Sch., 1952-57, Hanover Park High Sch., 1957-58; asst. prof. bus. edn. Bloomsburg State Coll., 1958-60; asst. dean women Pa. State U., 1960-65; asso. dean students Oakland U., Rochester, Mich., 1965-70, asst. v.p. for student affairs, 1970—. Bd. dirs. A.R.C., Southeastern Mich., 1966-71; mem. pub. adv. bd. Upward Bound Project, 1967-69. Mem. Nat. Assn. Women Deans and Counselors, N.E.A., Am. Personnel and Guidance Assn., Mich. Assn. Women Deans and Counselors (mem. exec. bd. 1967-69, treas. 1970-72), Mich. Assn. Higher Edn., Am. (mem.-at-large exec. council 1972—), Mich. (pres. 1970-71) coll. personnel assns., Assn. for Higher Edn., Bus. and Profl. Women (chpt. pres. 1954-55), Susquehanna Valley Alumni Assn. (past pres.), Pi Gamma Mu, Iota Alpha Delta. Home: 500 Romeo Rd Rochester MI 48063

HOVDA, MARY LOU, librarian; b. Tyler, Minn., Aug. 8, 1927; d. Lloyd Ellsworth and Grace Jerusha (Combes) Haburn; B.A., Northwestern Coll., 1953; B.A., Macalester Coll., 1962; M.A., U. Minn., 1965; m. Wilford Murrel Hovda, July 6, 1968. Asst. librarian Northwestern Coll., Mpls., 1954-59, 64-67; student acquisitions asst. Macalester Coll., St. Paul, 1959-64; adminstrv. librarian Met. Community Coll., Mpls., 1967-72, Northwestern Coll., Roseville, Minn., 1972—. Vis. lectr. Faith Mission Tng. Sch., Edinburgh, Scotland, summer 1966. Mem. Minn. Library Assn. (chmn. reference sect. 1964-65), Christian Librarian's Fellowship, Pioneer Girls Internat. Baptist. Home: 339 N Finn St St Paul MN 55104 Office: 3003 N Snelling St Roseville MN 55113

HOVERMALE, RUTH LENORE, coll. dean; b. Dayton, Va., Apr. 28, 1927; d. Ulsie Perkins and Jennie (Thompson) Hovermale; B.A., Otterbein Coll., 1949; M.S., Ohio State U., 1954, Ph.D., 1962. Tchr., West Carrolton (O.) High Sch., 1949-54; instr. U. Louisville, 1954-60; grad. asst. Ohio State U., 1960-61, Gen. Foods Grad. fellow, 1961-62; asso. prof. Winthrop Coll., Rock Hill, S.C., 1962-64, prof., 1964-66, prof., dean, 1966—; mem. sales personnel The Rike Kumler Co., Dayton, O., summers, 1955, 57. Adv. council Am. Dietetic Assn., 1971-74; consumer adv. panel Springs Mills, 1972-74. Recipient Diamond Anniversary award Ohio State U., 1971. Mem. Assn. Adminstrs. Home Econs. (mem. ad hoc com. on bylaws 1973-74, chmn. elect 1974), Nat. Council Home Econs. Adminstrs., So. Regional Home Econs. Adminstrs. (chmn. 1972), Am., S.C. home econs. assn. (pres. elect 1972-73, pres. 1973—), Assn. Coll. Profs. Textiles and Clothing, Eastern Regional Coll. Profs. Textiles and Clothing, Am. Council Consumer Interests, Fashion Group Inc., Am. Assn. U. Women (pres. Rock Hill br. 1971—), Am. Assn. U. Profs., Omicron Nu, Pi Lambda Theta, Phi Upsilon Omicron, Phi Kappa Phi (pres. Winthrop Coll. br. 1971-72), Delta Kappa Phi. Methodist (mem. adminstrv. bd.). Home: 1547 Clarendon Pl Rock Hill SC 29730

HOVEY, BETTE ANN (MRS. JOHN MICHAEL HOVEY), extension home economist; b. Rupert, Ida., Jan. 14, 1946; d. Franklin V. and Doris Louise (Stone) Meuleman; B.S. in Home Econs. Edn., Ida. State U., 1968; postgrad. U. No. Colo., 1973—; m. John Michael Hovey, Jan. 1, 1968. Home economist trainee U. Ida. Coop. Extension Service for Bingham County, Blackfoot, 1967, asst. extension prof., home economist for Power County, American Falls, 1968—. Mem. Nat., Ida. (dist. councilor 1970, treas. 1971-73) assns. extension home economists, Am., Ida (Southeastern dist. chmn.-elect 1971, chmn. 1972) home econs. assns., Epsilon Sigma Phi. Methodist. Home: Falls Av American Falls ID 83211 Office: Box 97 American Falls ID 83211

HOVEY, MARCIA JOHNSON, mag. editor; b. Warren, Pa., July 1, 1928; d. Harry Carl and Grace (Saunders) Johnson; B.A., Allegheny Coll., 1950; M.A., U. Pa., 1954; m. Richard B. Hovey, Aug. 20, 1955; 1 son, Daniel. Editorial asst. Am. Philos. Soc., Phila., 1953, Saturday Evening Post, Phila., 1953-55; instr. English, Western Md. Coll., Westminster, 1955-60; writer Women's Bur., Dept. Labor, Washington, 1969-71, chief publs., editor Job Safety and Health mag. Occupational Safety and Health Adminstrn., Dept. Labor, Washington, 1971—. Home: 4320 Van Buren St Hyattsville MD 20782 Office: 1726 M St NW Washington DC 20036

HOWARD, ANN SLOAN, physician; b. Rumford, Me., Aug. 10, 1925; d. Henry Marshall and Teresa Marie (Sloan) Howard; B.A., Regis Coll., 1947; M.D., Georgetown U., 1952. Intern, Me. Med. Center, Portland, 1952-53, resident, 1953-55; practice medicine, specializing in anesthesiology, Greenfield, Mass., 1955—; chief anesthesia service Franklin County Pub. Hosp., 1965—, med. dir. inhalation therapy, 1966—. Mem. A.M.A., Mass., Franklin Dist. med. socs., Am., Mass. socs. anesthesiologists, Mass. Fedn. Physicians, Western Mass. Heart Assn. Home: 39 Sunrise Av Greenfield MA 01301 Office: 486 Main St Greenfield MA 01301

HOWARD, ANNE BAIL (MRS. WILLIAM VAUGHAN HOWARD), educator; b. Albuquerque, Nov. 19, 1927; d. Ernest Benjamin and Effie (Barron) Bail; B.A. magna cum laude, U. Colo., 1949; M.A., U. N.M., 1954, Ph.D., 1966; m. William Vaughan Howard, Feb. 25, 1950; children—Jason, Emily. Asst., U. N.M., 1953-55; tchr. pub. schs., Espanola, N.M., 1954-55, Albuquerque, 1955-57; dir. English A, U. N.M., Albuquerque, 1959-63; instr. U. Nev., Reno, 1963-66, asst. prof. English, 1966-71, asso. prof., 1971—; instr. composition Nev. Inst. English, summer 1967, dir. freshman composition, 1970—. Mem. adv. bd. U. Nev. Student YWCA, 1964-72; mem. Pacific S.W. regional adv. bd. Nat. Student YWCA, 1965—. Mem. Modern Lang. Assn., Rocky Mountain Modern Lang. Assn., Women's Caucus for Modern Langs. (chmn. Rocky Mount region 1970-72), Am. Assn. U. Profs. (chpt. v.p. 1967-68, 70-71, pres. 1972-73), Nat. Council Tchrs. English, Nat. Soc. Profs., No. Nev. Women's Polit. Caucus. Democrat. Home: 860 Bowman Dr Reno NV 89503

HOWARD, BARBARA BYERS (MRS. RICHARD W. HOWARD), educator; b. Seattle, Mar. 9, 1930; d. Orva Oliver and Florence (Soderback) Byers; B.A. in Journalism, U. Wash., 1950; Ph.D., Ind. U., 1964; m. Richard W. Howard, Aug. 15, 1959 (dec. Dec. 1970). Mem. staff Bainbridge Rev., Winslow, Wash., 1950-51; dir. publs. Wash. Assn. County Commrs., 1951-56; grad. asst. dept. of govt. Ind. U. at Bloomington, 1956-58, instr., 1962-64, asst. prof., 1964-66; research cons. Bur. Govtl. Research and Services, U. Wash. at Seattle, 1966-69; cons. govt. and pub. affairs, Seattle, 1969-71; research analyst Wash. State Legislative Joint Com. on Higher Edn., Olympia, 1971-73; sr. research analyst Wash. State Senate Research Center, 1973—. Sec. Ind. Community Resources Assn., 1961-65. Mem. Am. Polit. Sci. Assn., Am. Soc. Pub. Adminstrn., Theta Sigma Phi, Pi Alpha Sigma, Pi Sigma Alpha. Author: County Government in Washington State, 1957; monograph County Road Adminstration in Illinois, 1957, Bond Mgmt.-Higher Edn., 1972, Tchr. Edn. Programs, 1973, Faculty Retirement Systems, 1973. Editor, contbr. Ind. Pub. Affairs Notes, 1959-66; contbr. Collier's Ency. Yearbook, 1960-66. Home: 1710 Villa Capri 600 Black Lake Blvd Olympia WA 98502

HOWARD, BETTY JO KINNEY, assn. exec.; b. Methuen, Mass., Jan. 17, 1938; d. Raymond B. and Alice M. (Wilson) Kinney; B.A., Bates Coll., 1959. Program dir. YWCA, Washington, Pa., 1959-60, Lewiston, Me., 1960-62; instr. phys. edn., coach Deering High Sch., Portland, Me., 1962-68; health, phys. edn., recreation and camp dir. YWCA Hartford (Conn.) region, 1968—. Mem. Am. Assn. Health, Phys. Edn. and Recreation, Am., New Eng. (dir. 1972-75) camping assns. Home: 1 Candlewood Dr South Windsor CT 06074 Office: 135 Broad St Hartford CT 06105

HOWARD, CAROLE MARGARET MUNROE (MRS. ROBERT WILLIAM HOWARD), pub. relations exec.; b. Halifax, N.S., Can., Mar. 5, 1945; d. Frederick Craig and Dorothy Margaret (Crimes) Munroe; came to U.S., 1965; B.A., U. Cal. at Berkeley, 1967; m. Robert William Howard, May 15, 1965. Reporter, Vancouver (B.C., Can.) Sun newspaper, 1965; with pub. relations dept. Pacific N.W. Bell Telephone Co., Seattle, 1967—, employee information supr., 1970-72, advt. supr., 1972, project mgr. for equal employment opportunity, 1972-73, information mgr., 1973—. Dir. Seattle Savs. and Loan Assn. Mem. membership com. Pacific Sci. Center, Seattle. Editor newsletters Wash. State Republican Central Com., 1973—. Mem. Women in Communications (bd. dirs.), Internat. Assn. Indsl. Communicators, Pub. Relations Soc. Am., Nat., Wash. press women,

Pi Beta Phi. Home: 1226 McGilvra Blvd E Seattle WA 98112 Office: Room 1429 Exchange Bldg Seattle WA 98104

HOWARD, CAROLYN MARIE ADAMS (MRS. ALDACE NEWTON HOWARD), univ. dean; b. Colorado Springs, Colo., Sept. 10, 1944; d. Charley F. and Julia S. (Werner) Adams; B.S., Colo. State U., 1966; M.Ed., Western Wash. State Coll., 1968; m. Aldace Newton Howard, Aug. 16, 1969; 1 son, Aldace McIntyre. Dean of women Pacific U., Forest Grove, Ore., 1968—. Sec.-treas. Forest Grove Recycling Com., 1972-73. Mem. Am. Personnel and Guidance Assn., Nat. Assn. Women Deans and Counsellors, Am., N.W. coll. personnel assns. Office: UC Box 697 Pacific U Forest Grove OR 97116

HOWARD, DICKEE MELVON (MRS. PHILIP H. GOODMAN), lawyer; b. Balt., Apr. 3, 1934; d. George Samuel and Anna May (Smith) Howard; A.A., U. Balt., 1956; LL.B., U. Balt., 1959; m. Philip H. Goodman, Sept. 7, 1971. Admitted to Md. bar, 1959; since practiced in Balt.; dep. securities commr. State of Md., 1962-64, asst. atty. gen. criminal div., 1965-68, asst. atty. gen. civil div., 1968—; asso. firm Goodman, Meagher & Enoch, Balt., 1973—. Bd. govs. U. Balt. Home: York Rd Parkton MD 21120 Office: 1507 1 S Calvert St Baltimore MD 21202

HOWARD, JANE OSBURN (MRS. ROLLINS STANLEY HOWARD), educator; b. Morris, Ill., Aug. 12, 1926; d. Everett Hooker and Bernice Otilda (Olson) Osburn; B.A., U. Ariz., 1948; M.A., U. N.M., 1966, Ph.D., 1969; m. Rollins Stanley Howard, June 5, 1948; children—Ellen Elizabeth, Susan (Mrs. John Karl Nuttall). Instr. U. N.M. Sch. Medicine, Sante Fe, 1968-70, mem. staff pediatrics, deaf blind children's program, Albuquerque, 1971-72, asst. dir. N.M. programs for deaf blind children, 1972—, instr. psychiatry, instr. pediatrics, coordinator deaf-blind children's program, 1972—. Cons. Mountain-Plains Regional Center for Services to Deaf-Blind Children, Denver, 1971-74, Bur. Indian Affairs, 1974. Active Cystic Fibrosis, Mother's March, Heart Fund, Arthritis Found., Easter Seal-Crippled Children. Trustee Harwood Sch. Recipient fellowships U. N.M., 1965, 66, 66-67, 67-68, U. So. Cal. John Tracy Clinic, 1973. Fellow Royal Soc. Health; mem. Council Exceptional Children, Am. Assn. Mental Deficiency, Nat. Assn. Retarded Children, Am. Assn. U. Women, Pi Lambda Theta, Zeta Phi Eta, Alpha Epsilon Rho, Republican. Methodist. Home: 615 Valencia Dr SE Albuquerque NM 87108

HOWARD, JOANNE LEE KAHME (MRS. ROY WILLIAM HOWARD), investment co. exec.; b. Akron, O., Jan. 19, 1942; d. Lawrence and Helen Frances (Nordell) Kahme; B.B.A, U. Wis., 1962, M.B.A., 1963; m. Roy Wiliam Howard, Aug. 20, 1961; children—Daniel, Dawn. Accountant, Wis. Dept. Taxation, Madison, 1962-64; jr. security analyst First Nat. Bank of Chgo., 1964-66; security analyst CNA Financial, Chgo., 1966-68; sr. security analyst, dir. research ISI Corp., investment co., San Francisco, 1968-72; portfolio mgr. Am. Express Investment Mgmt. Co., San Francisco, 1972—. Chartered financial analyst. Mem. Womens Am. ORT (treas. Oceana chpt. 1973), Phi Beta Kappa. Club: The Financial Women's (pres. 1972) (San Francisco). Home: 8199 Hansom Dr Oakland CA 94605 Office: 550 Laurel St San Francisco CA 94120

HOWARD, LINDA DURIAN NEEDLER, artist; b. Evanston, Ill., Oct. 21, 1934; d. Lowell Q. and Doris (Glidden) Needler; student U. Colo., 1953, Art Inst. Chgo., 1954, Northwestern U., 1955; B.A., U. Denver, 1957; postgrad. Pratt Inst., 1963, Art Students League, 1964; M.A., Hunter Coll., 1970; m. Phil Durian, 1953; 1 dau., Bonnie; m. 2d, Lloyd Howard, Feb. 15, 1964 (div. 1974). One-man shows at Silvermine, Conn.; exhibited in group shows at Katonah Gallery (N.Y.), Am. Women: 20th Century, Peoria, Ill., A.I.R. Gallery N.Y., Aldrich Mus., Ridgefield Conn., Sculptors Symposium Show, N.Y.C., Phila. Mus. Civic Center, New Britain (Conn.) Mus., Hudson River Mus., Yonkers, N.Y., Sculpture Now Gallery, N.Y.C., others. Tchr., Hunter Coll., 1969-72; guest artist Colo. Coll., 1973, Lehman Coll., 1974. Mem. Coll. Art Assn., Sculptors Symposium, Women in Arts, Ad Hoc Artist Group. Home: 130 Greene St New York City NY 10012

HOWARD, LORRAINE HARRIS, coll. dean; b. Laine, Ore., Dec. 17, 1921; d. Sidney D. and Judith (Donahue) Harris; student Linfield Coll., 1941-42; B.S., Ore. State U., 1945, Ed.M., 1961, Ph.D., 1964; postgrad. Portland State U., 1959, U. Ore., 1961-62; m. William Howard, 1944 (div.); children—Joseph S., Daniel W., William W. Asst. buyer Meier & Frank Co., Portland, Ore., 1944-45; asst. chemist Hawley Pulp & Paper Mill, Oregon City, Ore., 1946-47; dental asst., Portland, 1948-49; asst. to dir. Fruit Flower Day Nursery, Portland, 1949-50; juvenile caseworker, counselor, grad. asst. Ore. State U., 1963; instr. Cuesta Coll., San Luis Obispo, Cal., 1967—; asso. dean women Cal. State Poly. Coll., San Luis Obispo, 1964—. Active Emanuel Hosp. Gray Ladies, A.R.C., Portland Rehab. Center, Community Chest. Mem. Am. Personnel and Guidance Assn., Am. Psychol. Assn., Cal. Assn. Marriage and Family Counselors, Cal. State Employees Assn. (chpt. pres. 1969-70), Am. Assn. U. Women, Exec. Club San Luis Obispo, Panhellenic, Phi Kappa Phi (chpt. pres. 1971-72), Kappa Delta Pi, Omicron Nu. Home: 1724 Lee Ann Ct San Luis Obispo CA 93401

HOWARD, MARGUERITE EVANGELINE BARKER (MRS. JOSEPH D. HOWARD), bus. exec., civic worker; b. Victoria, B.C., Can., July 30, 1921; d. Reuel Harold and Frances Penelope (Garnham) Barker; brought to U.S., 1924, naturalized, 1945; B.A., U. Wash., 1943; m. Joseph D. Howard, June 16, 1952; children—Wendy Doreen Frances, Bradford Reuel. Vice pres., dir. Howard Tours, Inc., Oakland, Cal., 1953—; co-owner, gen. mgr. Howard Travel Service, Oakland, Cal., 1956—, mng. dir. Howard Hall, Berkeley, Cal., 1964—; co-owner, asst. mgr. Howard Investments, Oakland, Cal., 1960—. Bd. dirs. Piedmont Council Campfire Girls, 1969—, nat. council, 1972—; bd. dirs. Oakland Symphony Guild, 1969-72, pres., 1972—; bd. dirs. Oakland Symphony Orch., 1972—, mem. exec. bd., 1972—; bd. dirs. Piedmont Jr. High Sch. Mothers Club, 1968-69. Mem. Oakland Mus. Assn., Chi Omega Alumni Seattle, Chi Omega East Bay Alumni, Berkeley. Republican. Clubs: Womens University (Seattle); Womens Athletic (Oakland, Cal.). Home: 146 Bell Av Piedmont CA 94611 Office: 526 Grand Av Oakland CA 94610

HOWARD, MARJORIE ELLEN, physician; b. Pasadena, Cal., Dec. 11, 1940; d. Everett James and Mary Frances (Scott) Howard; B.A., LaSierra Coll., 1962; M.D., Loma Linda U., 1966. Intern, Pontiac (Mich.) Gen. Hosp., 1966-67, resident pediatrics, 1967-69; practice medicine specializing in pediatrics, Orchard Lake, Mich., 1969-70, Pontiac, 1970—; mem. staffs Pontiac Gen. Hosp., sec.-treas. pediatrics dept., 1972; also mem. staff St. Joseph's Hosp., Pontiac. Recipient fine arts award Bank of Am., 1958, physician's recognition award A.M.A., 1969. Diplomate Nat. Bd. Med. Examiners, Am. Bd. Pediatrics. Fellow Am. Acad. Pediatrics; mem. Am., Mich. med. assns., Oakland County Med. Assn. Seventh day Adventist. Office: 2157 Orchard Lake Rd Pontiac MI 48053

HOWARD, MARJORIE M., ret. nursing adminstr.; b. Basile, La., Jan. 10, 1914; d. Frank J. and Inez (McCrary) Howard; diploma Baylor Hosp. Sch. Nursing, Dallas, 1936; B.S., Vanderbilt U., 1951; M.S. in Nursing Edn., Ind. U., 1954. Head nurse, clin. instr. Baylor U. Hosp., Dallas, 1936-38; pvt. duty nurse, Dallas, 1938-41; supr. student health service Northwestern State Coll., Natchitoches, La., 1948-49; ednl. dir. Central State Hosp., Lakeland, Ky., 1951-52; mem. staff Larue D. Carter Hosp., Indpls., 1952-54; asst. chief nursing edn. VA Hosp., Waco, Tex., 1954-57; nursing specialist, edn. and tng. VA Central Office, Washington, 1957-63, chief edn. and tng. div., 1963-65, nurse adminstr., chief nursing VA Hosp., New Orleans, 1965-70; asso. chief nursing edn. VA Hosp., Alexandria, La., 1970-74. Expert com. on selection and tng. aux. workers WHO, Geneva, Switzerland, 1960, mem. adv. panel on nursing, 1960—. Served with Nurse Corps, AUS, 1941-48. Recipient Chief Med. Dir.'s Commendation, VA, 1965, Hosp. Dir.'s Commendation, New Orleans, 1970, Alexandria, 1974. Mem. Am. Nurses Assn., Am. Assn. U. Women, Nat. Soc. Study Edn., Sigma Theta Tau. Co-author: Inservice Education Activities in Nursing Service, 1963. Home: 122 Fairmount St Pineville LA 71360

HOWARD, MARY LOU (MRS. RICE MILFORD HOWARD), editor; b. Lafayette, Ala., Aug. 14, 1898; d. Robert Montgomery and Mary Elizabeth (Jones) Boazman; A.B., Woman's Coll. Ala., 1922; m. Rice Milford Howard, Sept. 30, 1923; 1 dau., Molly (Mrs. Calvin Coolidge Ryan). Reporter, The So. Democrat, Oneonta, Ala., 1945-64, bookkeeper, 1945-72, proofreader, 1945—, editor, pub., 1964—, pres., 1969—. Tchr. Blount County High Sch., Oneonta, 1922-25, 30-33, Oneonta Grammar Sch., 1933-43. Mem. Ala. Press Assn., Blount County Hist. Soc., Oneonta Bus. and Profl. Women's Club. Baptist. Editor: Genealogy of the Bynum Family, 1958. Home: 406 3d St N Oneonta AL 35121 Office: Washington Av and 3d St Oneonta AL 35121

HOWARD, NENA BELL (MRS. JOHN W. HOWARD), ret. tchr., civic worker; b. Cleve., Dec. 3, 1900; d. Henry and Elizabeth (Pugh) Bunch; student Tenn. State Normal Sch., 1924; B.S., Agrl. and Indsl. State U., 1952; M.A., Columbia, 1954; certificate U. Tenn., 1964; m. John W. Howard, July 26, 1924; children—Nena (Mrs. William M. Magowan), Johnnie (Mrs. William Posey). Tchr., Cook High Sch., Athens, Tenn., 1927-29, adult sch., Cleve., 1934-35, nursery sch., Cleveland, Tenn., 1942-44, Park City Sch., Madisonville, Tenn., 1948-55, College Hill High Sch., Cleveland, 1959-66. Active Girl Scouts Am., 1954-64; vol. A.R.C. Mem. Cleve. Sch. Bd., 1970-73. Mem. Afro-Am. Heritage Group, Cleveland-Bradley C. of C., Nat. Ret. Tchrs. Assn., N.A.A.C.P. Baptist. Mem. Order Eastern Star (past matron). Home: 230 East St SE Cleveland TN 37311

HOWARD, RUTH MARGUERITE, museum ofcl.; b. Ionia, Mich., Oct. 5, 1917; d. Frederick Bennajah and Flora Belle (Smith) Howard; A.B., Grinnell Coll., 1940; M.A., U. Mich., 1948. Tchr. County Farm Sch., Ionia County, Mich., 1944-45, Oak Grove Sch., Saranac, Mich., 1945-46; curator edn. Kalamazoo Pub. Museum, 1949—. Cons. Saginaw Pub. Schs., 1966. Recipient grant Nat. Sci.-Am. Assn. Museums, 1963. Mem. Nat., Mich., Kalamazoo City ednl. assns., Am. Assn. Museums, Midwest Museums Conf., Mich. Museums Assn., Gt. Lakes Planetarium Assn., Internat. Soc. Planetarium Educators, Handweavers Guild Am., Kalamazoo Weavers Guild. Home: 208 Allen Blvd Kalamazoo MI 49007 Office: 315 S Rose St Kalamazoo MI 49006

HOWARD, SANDRA ROBERTSON, coll. counselor; b. Chgo., June 12, 1937; d. Earl Van Buren and Bennette Hazel (Gilham) Robertson; B.S., Tenn. Arts and Industry State U., 1960; div.; 1 son, Deonn Earle. Group worker Hull House Assn., Chgo., 1960-65; youth counselor Cook County Pub. Aid Dept., Chgo., 1967-68; group work supr. Chgo. Bd. Edn., YMCA Bd. Edn., Chgo., 1968-70; spl. services counselor Central YMCA Community Coll., Chgo., 1970—. Ednl. cons., 1970—. Mem. Sassy Sensations, Theta Phi Epsilon. Home: 7611 S Indiana Av Chicago IL 60619

HOWARD, VIRGINIA CLARE WHITE (MRS. HAL W. HOWARD), lawyer; b. Bend, Ore., Oct. 12, 1923; d. Clyde Clinton and Clara Regina (Bellinger) White; B.A., Lewis and Clark Coll., 1949; M.A., No. Ariz. U., 1964; J.D., U. Ariz., 1971; m. Hal W. Howard, Aug. 14, 1949; children—Stephen Charles, Victoria Lee, Alison Clare. Purchasing agt. British Ministry War Transport, Portland, Ore., 1943-45; adminstrv. asst. Navajo Tribe, Window Rock, Ariz., 1952-53; instr. English dept. No. Ariz. U., Flagstaff, 1958-65; admitted to Ariz. bar, 1971; asst. prosecutor City of Tucson, 1971-73, asst. city atty., 1973—. Lectr. law U. Ariz. Law Sch., 1970-73; legal adviser Tucson Consumer Council, 1973; tchr., legal adviser Unitarian Sex Edn. Program, 1971-73. Recipient Am. Jurisprudence Book award Lawyers Coop. Pub. Co., 1969. Mem. Am. Civil Liberties Union, Ariz. State Bar, Phi Delta Phi. Unitarian Universalist (trustee 1967-69, legal adviser 1973). Democrat. Home: 2345 E Waverly St Tucson AZ 85719 Office: 250 W Alameda St Tucson AZ 85703

HOWARD, WILMA JANETTA, educator; b. Tompkinsville, Ky., Aug. 12, 1934; d. William Harmon and Chloe (Miller) Howard; A.B. in Edn., U. Ky., 1953, M.A., 1960; postgrad. U. Louisville, 1971—; m. Henry Joseph Klein, June 12, 1974. Tchr. elementary sch., Jefferson County Schs., Louisville, 1953-57; faculty U. Ky.; TV instr. Kentuckiana ETV, Louisville, 1957—. Pioneered 1st ednl. telecast in Ky. Named Ky. col. Mem. N.E.A., Ky., Jefferson County edn. assns., Nat. Assn. Ednl. Broadcasters, Hamilton House Alumnae Assn. (pres. 1966-68), Delta Kappa Gamma (state memberships chmn. 1963-65, chpt. pres. 1966-68, state expansion chmn. 1971-73), Ky. Sci. Tchrs. (v.p. 1966-67), Ky. Audio-Visual Assn. (mem. bd. 1966-67), Assn. Childhood Edn. (pres. Jefferson County 1959-61, nat. interpreter, v.p. Ky. 1963-65, pres. 1967-69), Ky. Elementary-Kindergarten-Nursery Educators (pres. 1972-73), Am. Women in Radio and TV (bd. mem. local chpt. 1971-72), Kappa Delta Pi. Baptist. Home: 2222 Manchester Rd Louisville KY 40205 Office: 4309 Bishop Lane Louisville KY 40218

HOWDON, ARLINE KAYE (MRS. WILLIAM MARTIN HOWDON), cytologist; b. N.Y.C.; d. Harry A. and Billie (Thompson) Kaye; B.A. summa cum laude, U. Miami, 1957; postgrad. Johns Hopkins, 1960-61; m. William Martin Howdon, July 19, 1941; children—William Martin, Andrea Leslie (Mrs. William Dixon Shay, Jr.). Sr. asso. cytotechnologist, teaching asst. Johns Hopkins Hosp., Balt., 1961-63, asso. teaching supr., instr., 1963-67, chief cytotechnologist, 1967—; field cons. cytotechnology Nat. Com. Careers in Med. Tech., Washington, 1964-66; cons. cytotechnology Nat. Council Med. Techn. Edn., Memphis, 1967-68. Cons. WHO, Iran, 1965, 66, 69, Profl. Exam. Service, 1973—; ednl. coordinator Internat. Acad. Cytology, 1971—; mem. Citizens Com. for Conquest Cancer, 1972—. Trustee, Grace and St. Peter's Episcopal Ch. Sch., 1973—. Fellow Royal Soc. Health; mem. Am. Soc. Cytology (past chmn. cytotech. adv. com.), Internat. Acad. Cytology, Am. Soc. Med. Technologists (Md. del. 1967, profl. achievement award in cytology 1972), Nat. Com. Careers in Med. Tech., Md. Soc. Med. Technologists, Md. Assn. Cytotechnologists, Phi Kappa Phi. Episcopalian. Club: Coral Gables Jr. Woman's. Contbr. articles to profl. jours. Home: 230 Stony Run Lane Baltimore MD 21210 Office: Johns Hopkins Hospital Baltimore MD 21205

HOWE, EDITH L. MILLER (MRS. W. ASQUITH HOWE), bus. exec.; b. Bowling Green, O., Apr. 29, 1913; d. Christie and Alta (Clark) Miller; B.S., Bowling Green State U., 1945; M.A., U. Toledo, 1948; student Ohio State U., 1949, Temple U., 1965-66; m. W. Asquith Howe, Feb. 2, 1936. Tchr. pub. schs., Wood County, O., 1941-47; tchr. dept. psychology U. Toledo, 1947-48; pres., mgr. Howe Real Estate Investments, Ohio, Pa., Fla. and N.J., 1948—, Howe Enterprises, Cheltenham, Pa. Mem. Intercontinental Biog. Assn. (life), Internat. Platform Assn. Home: 7812 Haines Rd Cheltenham PA 19012 also 538 W Shore Dr Brigantine NJ 08203

HOWE, EUNICE SIMM (MRS. HENRY DUNSTER HOWE), lawyer, nat. Republican Committeewoman; b. Belmont, Mass., Apr. 24, 1918; d. Glenn and Mary Eliza Simm; student Geneva Coll. (Switzerland), 1936-37; A.B., Mt. Holyoke Coll., 1938; LL.B., Boston U., 1941; postgrad. George Washington U.; m. Henry Dunster Howe, Feb. 9, 1946; children—Eunice Dunster, Maryalice Boardman. Admitted to Mass. bar, 1941; practiced in Boston, 1941—; asst. atty. gen. Mass., 1941-44; counsel Mass. Div. Employment Security, 1946-47; mem. Mass. Consumers Council, 1965—; chmn. Nat. Consumer Adv. Council, 1970—. Chmn. bequest and annuities com. Mt. Holyoke Coll., 1960—, chmn. alumnae fund com., 1961-63; mem. Adv. Com. Brookline, 1965—. Chmn. Republican Town Com. Brookline, 1967—; mem. bd. Mass. Fedn. Rep. Women, 1965—; nat. Rep. Committeewoman for Mass., 1968—. Bd. dirs. Mass. Council on Crime and Correction, 1968—; v.p. bd. dirs. New Eng. Citizens Crime Commn., 1968—; pres. Mass. Gen. Hosp. Service League; bd. dirs. Brookline Taxpayers Assn., Brookline Citizens Com.; trustee Beaver County Day Sch., Mt. Holyoke Coll., Eliot-Pearson Sch. Tufts U. Served to lt. (j.g.) USNR, World War II. Mem. Boston Bar Assn. Episcopalian. Home: 6 Woodbine Rd Belmont MA 02178

HOWE, MARIE ELIZABETH, state legislator; b. Somerville, Mass., June 13, 1944; d. William Andrew and Amelia Gertrude (McCauley) Howe; J.D., New Eng. Sch. of Law, 1969. Mem. Mass. Ho. of Reps., 1965—, asst. majority leader, 1973—. Mem. Somerville Sch. Com., 1964-67. Mem. Zonta. Home: 19 Pembroke St Somerville MA 02145 Office: State House Boston MA 02133

HOWE, MARION RITA, editor; b. Philipsburg, Pa., Mar. 15, 1936; d. Thomas Ambrose and Marion Priscilla (Bailey) Howe; B.A., Pa. State U., 1958, M.A., 1960. Editorial asst. Am. Hist. Review, Washington, 1960-65, asst. editor, 1965-70, asso. editor, 1970; editor Harvard U. Press, Cambridge, Ma., 1970-73; editor McCutchan Pub. Corp., Berkeley, Cal., 1973—. Mem. Phi Alpha Theta. Home: 1350 Balboa St San Francisco CA 94118 Office: 2526 Grove St Berkeley CA 94704

HOWE, SUZANNE ADELE LOUISE, physician; b. Chgo., Mar. 30, 1914; d. Willard Clay and Susan Adele (Plant) Howe; student Sweet Briar Coll., 1931-33; B.A., Barnard Coll., 1936; M.D., Cornell U., 1940; M.P.H., Columbia U., 1966. Med. intern, Letchworth Village, 1941-42; intern, asst. resident, resident in surgery (otolaryngology) N.Y. Hosp., 1942-44; asst. resident Meml. Hosp. for Cancer, N.Y., 1944-45; gen. practice otolaryngology, N.Y.C., 1945-65; asst. dir. Ambulatory Services and Community Medicine Long Island Jewish Hosp.-Queens Hosp. Center Affiliation Jamaica, N.Y., 1967-68; asst. attending surgeon N.Y. Hosp., 1954-69, asso. attending otorhinolaryngologist, 1969—; med. dir. Sunset Park Health Center, attending in medicine Luth. Med. Center, Brooklyn, N.Y., 1968—; instr. surgery (otolaryngology) Cornell U. Med. Coll., 1947-71, clin. asst. prof. otolaryngology, 1971—, clin. asst. prof. pub. health, 1971-73, clin. asso. prof. pub. health, 1973—. Diplomate Am. Bd. Otolaryngology. Fellow Am. Acad. Ophthalmology and Otolaryngology, N.Y. Acad. Scis.; mem. A.M.A., N.Y. State, New York County med. socs., Am. Med. Women's Assn. Home: 345 E 56th St New York City NY 10022 Office: 514 49th St Brooklyn NY 11220

HOWELL, BARBARA FERN FENNEMA (MRS. WILBUR A. HOWELL), phys. chemist, educator; b. Chgo., Dec. 18, 1924; d. Nick and Fern (First) Fennema; B.A., U. Minn., 1946; M.S., Kan. State U., 1949; Ph.D., U. Mo., 1964; m. Wilbur A. Howell, June 29, 1946; children—Susan, Gary, Michael. Instr. chemistry Kan. State U. at Manhattan, 1946-49, U. Tex. at Arlington, 1957-61; asst. prof. chemistry Kan. State Tchrs. Coll., Emporia, 1964-69; research asso. U. Mo. at Rolla, 1969-71; research chemist inorganic glass sect. Nat. Bur. Standards, U.S. Dept. Commerce, Washington, 1971-72, research chemist biorganic standards sect., 1972—. Mem. Am. Chem. Soc., A.A.A.S., Am. Assn. Clin. Chemists, Am. Assn. U. Women. Methodist. Contbr. articles to profl. jours. Home: 13405 Accent Way Germantown MD 20767 Office: Biorganic Standards Sect Nat Bur Standards US Dept Commerce Washington DC 20234

HOWELL, DEBORAH CAROLYN, editor; b. San Antonio, Jan. 15, 1941; d. Henry G. and Mary Delorah (Williams) Howell; B.J., U. Tex., 1962. Reporter sta. KZTV, Corpus Christi, Tex., 1962-63; reporter Corpus Christi Caller-Times, 1963-65; reporter, editor Mpls. Star, 1965—. Unit chmn., mem. exec. bd. local #2 The Newspaper Guild. Recipient Minn. Edn. Assn. awards edn. writing, Front Page writing awards. Mem. Sigma Delta Chi, Gamma Phi Beta. Home: 4651 Lyndale Av South Minneapolis MN 55409 Office: 425 Portland Av Minneapolis MN 55415

HOWELL, LAURIE ANN, pub. relations exec.; b. Monroe, Mich., Aug. 18, 1945; d. Alvin John and Florence Julia (Lowrey) Kohler; B.J., U. Mo., 1967; m. Edward Leslie Howell, Aug. 27, 1966 (div. Mar. 1974). Reporter, Monroe Evening News, summers 1962-65; reporter-staff writer Copley Newspapers, Los Angeles, 1967-69; account exec. Furman Assos., Inc., pub. relations, Los Angeles, 1969-71, v.p., 1971-74; with Bob Thomas & Assos., 1974—. Mem. Cal. Press Women (v.p. Los Angeles chpt. 1972, recipient writing award 1969), Women in Communications (past historian, sec. and v.p. Los Angeles chpt. 1969-72, chpt. dir. 1969-72, regional v.p. 1973). Home: 11500 Moorpark St Penthouse 304 Los Angeles CA 91602 Office: 835 Hopkins Way Redondo Beach CA 90277

HOWELL, LEISLA MORAN, clin. psychologist; b. Cin.; d. William T. and Edna (Brodt) Moran; B.S., U. Ky., 1941, M.A., 1947; postgrad. U. Cin., U. Cal. at Los Angeles, Claremont Grad. Sch. Psychologist, Cal. State Polytech. Coll., San Luis Obispo, 1948-49; clin. psychologist Atascadero (Cal.) State Hosp., 1954-58, Fairview State Hosp., Costa Mesa, 1959, 60, Guidance Center, Cal. Instn. for Men, Chino, 1961—; pvt. practice, Pomona, Cal.; psychologist Family Service, Anaheim, Cal. Mem. Am., Western psychol. assns., Phi Beta. Home: PO Box 364 Chino CA 91710 Office: CIM-RGC PO Box 441 Chino CA 91710

HOWELL, MABEL GREY, lawyer; b. Hillsboro, Tex., Feb. 10, 1910; d. Robert Edward and Josephine (Glover) H.; B.A., U. Tex., 1930; LL.B., Baylor U., 1933. Admitted to Tex. bar, 1933, practiced in Waco, 1933-38, 41-46; asst. city atty., City of Waco, 1938-41; asso. atty. Pioneer Savs. Assn., Waco, 1946-51; asso. Helm, Jones, McDermott & Pletcher, Houston, 1951-61; individual practice, 1961—; substitute judge Corp. Ct. City Houston; spl. justice Ct. Civil Appeals for 10th Supreme Ct. Tex. Pres. United Cerebral Assn., Inc., 1959, rep. dir. nat. and southwestern region, 1959-61, v.p. United

Cerebral Palsy Tex. Inc., 1961. Mem. State Bar Tex., Am., Houston (chmn. women's sect. 1959) bar assns., Am. Assn. U. Women, Bus. Women's Assn., Soroptimist Fedn. of Americas, Inc. Episcopalian. Club: Soroptimist (pres. 1958-59, dir. 1960). Home: 38 Bash Pl Houston TX 77027

HOWELL, MABLE SMITH (MRS. BRUCE INMAN HOWELL), coll. librarian; b. Chocowinity, N.C., Sept. 21, 1942; d. Hyman L. and Thelma (Evans) Smith; B.S., East Carolina U., 1964, M.Ed. in L.S., 1967; postgrad. Duke, 1970; m. Bruce Inman Howell, Aug. 22, 1965; 1 son, Bruce Inman. Librarian, Lenoir Community Coll., Kinston, N.C., 1964—, dir. Learning Center, 1968—, also instr., library tech. asst. for curriculum 1970—. Mem. N.C. State accreditation teams, 1969, 1972, mem. N.C. Com. for Edn. Librarianship, 1971. Mem. Ednl. Media Assn. (treas. dept. community colls. N.C. 1968-69, pres. 1969-71; dir. Eastern region N.C. 1967-68), N.C. Library Assn. (scholarship com. 1971-76), Am. Assn. U. Women (rec. sec. Kinston br. 1969-71), Lenoir County Hist. Assn., Librarians Lenoir County (pres. 1974-75). Home: 3012 Englewood Dr Kinston NC 28501 Office: PO Box 188 Kinston NC 28501

HOWELL, MARGARET ANDERSON (MRS. BENJAMIN HERBERT HOWELL), librarian; b. Penrose, Colo., Jan. 16, 1936; d. Earl and Gertrude Lee (Knowles) Anderson; B.S. (P.T.A. scholar), S.W. Mo. State U., 1957; M.S. (Mo. State Library fellow), U. Ill., 1959; m. Benjamin Herbert Howell, Dec. 31, 1961; children—Donald Herbert, Charles Daniel. Extension librarian Daniel Boone Regional Library, Columbia, Mo., 1959-62; library sci. librarian U. Mo., Columbia, 1968-74, spl. materials librarian, 1974—. Active Boy Scouts Am. Trustee Daniel Boone Regional Library. Mem. Am. Assn. Univ. Women, Spl. Libraries Assn., Am., Mo. library assns. Methodist. Club: Federated Women's (Armstrong, Mo.). Home: 17 E Craig St Columbia MO 65201

HOWELL, MARY GERTRUDE (MRS. CHARLES FREDERICK HOWELL), tech. information adminstr.; b. Wenona, Ill., May 25, 1932; d. Michael Joseph and Kathryn Harriet (Sennett) Danaher; B.S. with highest honors in Chemistry, U. Ill., 1954; Ph.D. in Organic Chemistry, Mass. Inst. Tech., 1959; m. Charles Frederick Howell, Dec. 27, 1954; children—William, Elizabeth. Research asst. E.I. du Pont de Nemours & Co., Inc., Wilmington, Del., 1954, Commonwealth Sci. and Indsl. Research Orgn., Canberra, Australia, 1959; research scientist Lederle Labs. div. Am. Cyanamid Co., Pearl River, N.Y., 1959-64, sr. research scientist, 1964-67, head lit. services dept., 1967-70, dir. tech. information services, 1971—. Mem. com. on chem. lit. Nat. Acad. Sci.-NRC, 1972—. Mem. Am. Chem. Soc., Drug Information Assn., Am. Soc. Information Sci., Sigma Xi, Iota Sigma Pi, Alpha Lambda Delta, Mortar Bd. Editor: (with others) Formula Index to NMR Literature Data, vol. I, 1965, vol. 2, 1966. Contbr. articles to profl. jours. Home: 28 Drake Lane Upper Saddle River NJ 07458 Office: Lederle Labs Pearl River NY 10965

HOWELL, MARY MARGARET, editor; b. Alliance, Neb., June 28, 1941; d. William Llewellyn and Thelma Margaret (Farnsworth) Howell; B.S., St. Louis U., 1964. Chemistry technologist Firmin Desloge Hosp., St. Louis, 1964-67; chemistry technologist Beth-Israel Hosp., N.Y.C., 1967-69; editor Med. Lab. mag., N.Y.C., 1969—. Cons., moderator N.Y. state med. tech. activities. Home: 18 Reed St Jersey City NJ 07304 Office: 750 3d Av New York City NY 10017

HOWELL, PATRICIA MARGARET, business exec.; b. Denver, Oct. 14, 1926; d. George W. and Daisy (Lawton) Howell; student Little Rock Jr. Coll., 1944, George Washington U., 1944-46, Am. Inst. Banking, 1946-47; certificate award Bur. Bus. Practice, New London, Conn., 1957. Sec., F.E.A., Washington, 1944-46; sec. to exec. v.p. Nat. Bank Commerce, Houston, 1946-47; sr. sec. Hughes Tool Co., Houston, 1947-62; pres., owner Quick Print div. Exec. Secs., Inc., Chattanooga, 1962—. Chmn. Tex. State Conv., 1959. Mem. Sales and Marketing Execs. Assn. (exec. sec. 1964-73), Houston C. of C. (life), Houston Assn. Legal Secs. (pres. 1958), Bus. Editors Assn. (pres. 1963), Dayton Boulevard Bus. Assn. (pres. 1973-74). Editor: The Nals Docket, 1959-62. Home: 5359 Hunter Trail Hixson TN 37343 Office: 1724 Dayton Blvd Chattanooga TN 37405

HOWELLS, MURIEL GURDON SEABURY (MRS. WILLIAM WHITE HOWELLS), civic worker; b. White Plains, N.Y., May 3, 1910; d. William Marston and Katharine Emerson (Hovey) Seabury; student Chapin Sch., 1928; m. William White Howells, June 15, 1929; children—Muriel Gurdon (Mrs. Richard E. Metz), William Dean. Founder Brit. War Relief Soc., Madison, Wis., 1941, pres., 1941-43; apptd. visitor Dept. Decorative Arts and Sculpture Boston Mus. Fine Arts, 1955-72, Dept. Am. Decorative Arts, 1972—; ladies com. Inst. Contemporary Art, Boston, 1955-65, 67-68, asso., 1965-67; bd. dirs. Boston br. English-Speaking Union, 1955—, v.p., 1973—. A founder, trustee Strawbery Banke, Inc., Portsmouth, N.H., 1958—, mem. steering com. Guild, 1959—; bd. dirs. Garden Club Am., 1959-62, nat. chmn. medal award com., 1962-65, judge flower arrangements; pres. Piscataqua Garden Club, 1952-54; chmn. Boston chpt. Venice Com., Internat. Fund for Monuments, 1970-71; vice chmn. Boston chpt. Save Venice Inc., 1971—. Recipient The King's medal for Service in the Cause of Freedom (Brit.). Mem. Nat. Soc. Colonial Dames N.H. Clubs: Women's Travel (pres. 1967-69), Vincent, Chilton (Boston); Colony (N.Y.C.). Home: 274 Beacon St Boston MA 02116 also Kittery Point ME 03905

HOWEY, MARY LOU (MRS. JACK EUGENE HOWEY), editor; b. Moravia, Ia., May 28, 1929; d. Jasper Noble and Arlyss LaFawn (Main) Cunningham; A.B. in Journalism and English, Ind. U., 1950; m. Jack Eugene Howey, Aug. 11, 1951; children—Ellen Elisa, Brian Andrew, Sara Melissa. Women's page editor Anderson (Ind.) Herald, 1950, Michigan City (Ind.) News-Dispatch, 1950-54; state editor Peru (Ind.) Daily Tribune, 1969—. Mem. PEO (past pres. chpts. BA, CQ), Theta Sigma Phi, Kappa Kappa Kappa. Republican. Methodist. Home: 948 Orchid Pl Peru IN 46970 Office: 24-26 W 3d St Peru IN 46970

HOWIE, MILDRED EVELYN CARTER, pub. relations exec.; b. San Francisco, June 13, 1922; d. John Bernard and Blanche Lydiard (Roddick) Carter; student U. Cal. at Berkeley, 1939-40; children—Linda Ann, Jann. Writer KJBS, San Francisco, 1942-44, traffic mgr., 1944-47; gen. asst. Drennan Advt., San Francisco, 1947-49; writer KGO-KGO-TV, San Francisco, 1949-58; pub. relations account exec. Lennen & Newell Advt., San Francisco, 1962-68; pub. relations div. S&W Fine Foods, San Francisco, 1968-71; owner Mildred Howie Pub. Relations, Corte Madera, Cal., 1971—. Bd. dirs. Sickle Cell Anemia Research and Edn., 1972-73, sec., 1972-73; bd. dirs. San Francisco Soc. Communicating Arts, 1973—; trustee Animal Med. Care Found. Marin, 1973—. Named Advt. Woman of Yr., San Francisco Advt. Club, 1968. Mem. Nat. Acad. TV Arts and Scis., Am. Women in Radio and TV (pres. 1969), Cal. Press Women, San Francisco Advt. Club (sec. 1969), San Francisco Publicity Club. Address: 212 Granada Dr Corte Madera CA 94925

HOWISON, EDNA MOORE, bank exec.; b. Bogata, Tex., Dec. 10, 1895; d. Neil MacCoul and Mary Frances (Clatterbuck) Howison; ed. pub. schs. Ins. agt. Howison and Howison, Bogata, 1923-70; dir. First Nat. Bank Bogata, 1969—, chmn. bd., 1970—. Presbyn. Address: 305 3d St NW Bogata TX 75417

HOWISON, JUANITA CARMACK (MRS. CLAUDE F. HOWISON), educator, artist; b. nr. Bristol, Va.; d. Alexander Watson and Lillie (Craig) Carmack; student U. Va., summer 1939, George Washington U., 1945-46, summer 1948, Corcoran Sch. Art, 1951; B.S. in Edn., Madison Coll., 1959; m. Claude Frederick Howison, May 1, 1948. Tchr., Konnarock (Va.) Sch,, 1929-36, Highland View Sch., Washington County, Va., 1936-41, Central Sch., Abington, Va., 1941-42, Herndon (Va.) Elementary Sch., 1942-46, Primary Day Sch., Washington, 1946-50, Fairlington (Va.) Elementary Sch., 1950; private tutor, 1950-56; remedial reading tchr., supr. Ft. Myer Elementary Sch., 1957-59; tchr. Potomac Elementary Sch., McLean, Va., 1960-67, tchr. spl. edn. Markham Sch., Ft. Belvoir, Va., 1967—; tchr. Haycock Elementary Sch., Falls Church, Va. Exhibited group shows Smithsonian Instn., 1952, 53, 62, Arts Club, D.C., 1966, 67, No. Va. Artists 1961-68, U. Va., 1966-68, Reston (Va.) Gallery, 1967, others. Mem. Nat. League Am. Pen Women (nat. biennial art exhibit chmn. 1954-56, Va. pres. 1963-64, state art chmn. 1965-66, nat. librarian 1965-66, nat. research chmn. 1966-67, mem. nat. art bd.), N.E.A., Internat. Reading Assn., Greater Washington Reading Council, Arlington Council Spl. Edn., Am. Arts League Washington, McLean Art League, Art Club Washington, No. Va. Art League, Fine Arts Center Roanoke, Delta Kappa Gamma. Presbyn. Home: 1512 Hardwood Lane McLean VA 22101

HOWLETT, MAEME MARLENE DAVIS (MRS. JOHN E. HOWLETT, JR.), sch. supt.; b. Louisville, Oct. 31, 1932; d. Robert and Mattie (Woods) Davis; student Howard U., 1949-50, Fisk U., 1951; B.A., Lane Coll., 1957; M.A., Tenn. State U., 1967; m. John E. Howlett, Jr., Aug. 18, 1967. Tchr., Crockett County Bd. Edn., 1957-65; grad. asst., dean Sch. Edn., Tenn. State U., 1966-67; supt. Tenn. Vocational Sch. for Girls, Nashville, 1968-71; v.p. J.E. Howlett, Jr. Enterprises, Inc., 1971—; sec.-treas. United Assn. Econ. Devel., Inc. Sec.-treas., dir. John E. Howlett, Jr. Constrn. Co. Vice pres. Tenn. Employees Credit Union, 1969-71; bd. dirs. Sons and Daughters of Charity Corp. Mem. Am. Soc. Pub. Adminstrn., Nat. Congress Parents and Tchrs., Urban League, N.A.A.C.P., Alpha Kappa Alpha. Democrat. Baptist (tchr. Sunday sch.). Elk. Address: PO Box 5705 Nashville TN 37208

HOWORTH, LUCY (SOMERVILLE), lawyer, internat. trade exec.; b. Greenville, Miss., July 1, 1895; d. Robert and Nellie (Nugent) Somerville; A.B., Randolph-Macon Woman's Coll., 1916; postgrad. Columbia, 1918; J.D., summa cum laude, U. Miss., 1922; m. Joseph Marion Howorth, Feb. 16, 1928. Asst. in psychology Randolph-Macon Woman's Coll., 1916-17; gauge insp. Allied Bur. Air Prodn., N.Y.C., 1918; indsl. research nat. bd. YWCA, 1919-20; admitted to Miss. bar, 1922; gen. practice Howorth & Howorth, Cleve., Greenville, Jackson, Miss,, 1922-34; U.S. commd. So. Jud. Dist. Miss., 1927-31; asso. mem. Bd. Vet. Appeals, Washington, 1934-43; legislative atty. VA, 1943-49, v.p., dir. VA Employees Credit Union, 1937-49; asso. gen. counsel War Claims Commn., 1949-52, dep. gen. counsel, 1952-53, gen. counsel, 1953-54; partner James Somerville & Assos., overseas trade and devel., 1954-56; pvt. law practice, Cleve., 1958—; atty. Commn. on Govt. Security, 1956-58. Chmn. Miss. State Bd. Law Examiners, 1924-28; treas. com. for econ. survey, 1928-30; mem. Research Commn. Miss., 1930-34; mem. com. on fed. employment policies and practices President's Commn. on Status of Women, 1962-63; initiator oral history program Delta State Coll., 1973. Mem. Ho. of Reps., Miss Legislature, Hinds County, 1932-36, chmn. com. pub. lands. Keynote speaker White House Conf. on Women in Post-war Policy Making, 1944; at conf. on opening 81st Congress. Mem. nat. bd. cons. Women's Archives, Radcliffe Coll.; mem. lay adv. com. study profl. nursing Carnegie Corp. N.Y., 1947-48; pres. trustee Monteagle Sunday Sch. Assembly, 1963—; dir. Monteagle Assembly Endowment Fund. Mem. Am. Assn. U. Women (nat. bd. dirs.; 2d. v.p., 1951-55, fellowship named in her honor 1973), Fed. Bar Assn., Nat. Assn. Women Lawyers, Am. Soc. Internat. Law (exec. council 1951-54), Am. Bar Assn., D.A.R., Daus. Am. Colonists, Am. Legion Auxiliary (past sec. Miss. dept.), Assembly Women's Orgns. for Nat. Security (chmn. 1951-52), Nat. Fedn. Bus. and Profl. Women's (nat. bd. dirs.; rep. Internat. Fedn., Trondheim, Norway, 1939; chmn. internat. conf., N.Y.C., 1946), Phi Beta Kappa, Pi Gamma Mu, Phi Delta Delta, Alpha Omicron Pi, Delta Kappa Gamma (hon.). Democrat (del. nat. conv., 1932). Methodist. Clubs: Woman's Nat. Democratic; Soroptimist (Washington). Editor: Fed. Bar Assn. News, 1944; asso. editor Fed. Bar Assn. Jour., 1943-44. Contbr. articles to profl. jours. Address: 515 S Victoria Av Cleveland MS 38732

HOWRY, CHERIE LEE BUTTS (MRS. REX R. HOWRY), physician; b. Belle Fourche, S.D., Dec. 18, 1930; d. Wallace Helm and Lucille (Youmans) Butts; B.S., U. Wash., 1952, M.D., 1957; m. Rex R. Howry, Dec. 27, 1952; children—Kurt Michael, Jennifer Jeanne, David Christopher. Intern, U. Wash. Sch. Medicine, Seattle, 1957-58, resident, 1958-60; practice medicine specializing in pediatrics, Bellevue, Wash., 1960—; pediatrician Rainier State Sch., 1960-64, Retarded Childrens Clinic, Childrens Orthopedic Hosp., Seattle, 1964-68; sch. physician Seattle-King County Health Dept., 1965-70; cons. Div. Vocational Rehab., 1965-70; med. clin. dir. Yakima Valley Sch., Selah, Wash., 1970—. Clin. instr. dept. pediatrics U. Wash., 1960—. Mem. adv. bd. Seattle King County Activity Center, 1967-70, Fish, 1968-70. Mem. Yakima County Med. Soc., Wash. Pediatric Soc., Alpha Omega Alpha, Pi Beta Phi (alumni treas. 1964-65). Episcopalian. Home: 113 Gilbert Dr Yakima WA 98902

HOWSE, DORIS KATHRYN (MRS. CECIL B. HOWSE), ins. co. exec.; b. Cass City, Mich., Jan. 1, 1912; d. Frank A. and Rose Lynn (Moore) Bliss; student Cleary Coll., Ypsilanti, Mich., 1929-30; m. Cecil B. Howse, Oct. 7, 1947. Sec., Pillsbury Flour Co., Croswell, Mich., 1931-32; with statis. and investment dept. N.Am. Benefit Assn., Port Huron, Mich., 1932-45, sec. to pres., 1945-65, sec.-treas., 1965-70, pres., 1970—, editor Review mag., 1970—; dir. Mich. Nat. Bank of Port Huron. Charter mem. Mercy Hosp. Aux.; organizer, charter mem. Vivians, Port Huron lodge Elks. Mem. adv. bd. Mercy Hosp. Named Sec. of Year, Blue Water chpt. Nat. Secs. Assn., 1965. Mem. Nat. Fraternal Congress Am. (exec. com. 1972), Canadian Fraternal Assn. (dir. 1972), League Catholic Women. Club: Quota. Home: 2655 10th St Port Huron MI 48060 Office: 1338 Military St Port Huron MI 48060

HOWTON, GEORGIA MARIANNE ZAKONYI-RADO, librarian; b. Budapest, Hungary; d. Joseph and Lilla (von Freund) von Zakonyi; B.A., Manhattanville Coll., 1956; B.S., U. Cal. at Los Angeles, 1958, M.L.S., 1961; m. David Ronald Howton, Nov. 23, 1973. Asst. librarian RCA, 1961-62; head Electronic Properties Information Center, Hughes Aircraft Co., Los Angeles, 1962-65; head librarian U.S. AEC Lab. Nuclear Medicine, U. Cal., Los Angeles, 1966—. Mem. Spl. Libraries Assn., Am. Soc. Information Scis., U. Cal. at Los Angeles Library Assn., Smithsonian Assos. Office: 900 Veteran Av Los Angeles CA 90024

HOY, DOROTHY H., state edn. cons.; b. Harrisburg, Pa., Sept. 27, 1919; d. William Ferguson and Clara (Voll) Hoy; A.B., Dickinson Coll., 1941; M.Ed., Pa. State U., 1950; M.A., State U. N.Y. at Buffalo, 1964; postgrad. Bryn Mawr Coll., 1941-42, Rensselaer Poly. Inst. summer 1952; m. George Wasdovich, Mar. 21, 1974. Tchr., Jamesburg (N.J.) High Sch., 1942-43, Highspire (Pa.) High Sch., 1943-45, Harrisburg (Pa.) Sch. Dist., 1945-69; adviser math. edn. Commonwealth of Pa., Harrisburg, 1969—; cons. tchr. edn. Columbia U. Contract Team in India, 1965; mem. staff N.S. Province Summer Sch., summer 1967. Mem. Math. Assn. Am., Nat. Council Tchrs. Math., Pa. Council Tchrs. Math., Am. Assn. U. Women, Phi Beta Kappa, Delta Kappa Gamma, Zeta Tau Alpha. Home: 1021 S Progress Av Harrisburg PA 17111 Office: Pa Dept Edn Box 911 Harrisburg PA 17126

HOYER, MILDRED NAEHER (MRS. NILS GUNTHER HOYER), poet; b. Bklyn.; d. Herman and Cora (Merritt) Naeher; student pub. schs., N.Y.C.; m. Nils Gunther Hoyer, June 1, 1930. Pres. Noon-Time Group, YWCA, Bklyn., 1946-58. Committeewoman, Kings County Republican Com., 1947-59. Recipient Edwin Markham award, 1964; Lady Beatrice Graham Poetry award, 1968, 69, 70, 71; World Poetry Day award Imprints Quar. 1969; citation Rochester Festival Religious Arts, 1966. Mem. Poetry Soc. Am., Nat. League Am. Pen Women (dir. and dir. poetry workshop N.Y.C. br., past v.p. N.Y.C. br., Louise Crittenden Moseley award 1955, 57, 58, 59, Marie Schroeder-Devrient award 1956, 61, Anna Hempstead Br. award 1957, 60, 1st place award Ruth Mason Rice contest 1959, 71, Marie-Louise d'Esternaux award 1961, 2 awards Midwest Regional contest, 1965, citation for 1st pub. book 1968, citation service, 1971) Bklyn. Poetry Circle (past v.p., pres. 1968-72, 1st pl. ann. book award, 1963, asso. critic 1964—, gold medal award 1968), Women Poets of N.Y. (pres. 1973—, Anne Lloyd Meml. award 1971), Haiku Soc. Am. Author: The Master Key, 1965. Asso. editor religious monthly. Contbr. poetry to mags. and newspapers. Address: 352 85th St Brooklyn NY 11209

HOYLAND, JANET LOUISE, govt. ofcl.; b. Kansas City, Mo., July 21, 1940; d. Robert J. and Dora Louise (Worley) Hoyland; B.A., Carleton Coll., 1962; postgrad. in music (Mu Phi Epsilon scholar 1966) U. Mo. at Kansas City, 1964-67. Policy writer Lynn Ins. Co., Kansas City, 1963-64; music librarian U. Mo. at Kansas City, 1966-68; benefit authorizer Social Security Adminstrn., Kansas City, Mo., 1969—. Piano tchr. Leta Wallace Piano Studio, Kansas City, 1963, 68; piano accompanist Barn Players, Overland Park, Kan., 1972-73, Off Broadway Dinner Playhouse, Inc., Kansas City, 1973. Co-chmn. Project Equality work area, 1971; work area chmn. on ecumenism Council on Ministries, 1969-70; sec. fair housing action com. Council on Religion and Race, Kansas City, 1968. Active ward and precinct work Democratic Com. for County Progress, 1968. Mem. Am. Fedn. Govt. Employees, Fellowship House Assn. Kansas City, New Dem. Coalition, Kansas City Mus. Club (chmn. composition dept. 1967-68), Mu Phi Epsilon (v.p. Kansas City 1968, sec. 1971), Pi Kappa Lambda. Methodist. Home: 610 W 46th St Kansas City MO 64112 Office: Social Security Administration 601 E 12th St Kansas City MO 64106

HOYLE, JANET CARR (MRS. J. RICHARD HOYLE), advt. agy. exec.; b. Vincent, Ala., Dec. 6, 1940; d. Woodrow W. and Mary Virginia (Lambert) Carr; student Birmingham Bus. Coll., 1960; m. J. Richard Hoyle, June 6, 1959; 1 dau., Barrie Creed. Supr., Realty Mortgage Co., Birmingham, Ala., 1960-69; media dir. Frank M. Taylor, Advt., Birmingham, 1969-73; v.p., Perry-Hoyle Advt., Birmingham, 1973—. Mem. Am. Women in Radio and TV (dir. 1973), Am. Marketing Assn., Vincent Study Club (v.p. 1970-71), Birmingham C. of C. Home: PO Box 165 Vincent AL 35178 Office: PO Box 31233 Birmingham AL 35222

HOYT, ELIZABETH ELLIS, educator; b. Augusta, Me., Jan. 27, 1893; d. William Adams and Fannie Hackelton (Ellis) Hoyt; A.B., Boston U., 1913; A.M., Radcliffe Coll., 1924, Ph.D., 1925. Research worker Nat. Indsl. Conf. Bd., N.Y.C., 1917-21; instr. Wellesley (Mass.) Coll., 1921-23; asso. prof. econs. Ia. State U., Ames, 1925-28, prof. econs., 1928—. Sec., exec. dir. La Verna Found., 1950—. Fulbright fellow to East Africa, 1950-51; Ford Found. fellow to Jamaica, 1957-58. Mem. Am. Econ. Assn., Am. Assn. U. Profs. Author: Primitive Trade, 1928, 68; Consumption of Wealth, 1928; Consumption in our Society, 1938; Income of Society, 1950; Choice and the Destiny of Nations, 1969; sr. author: Am. Income and its Use, 1954. Contbr. articles to Am., fgn. publs. Home: 3425 Woodland St Ames IA 50010

HOYT, MARGARET EDITH, lawyer; b. Berkeley, Cal., Oct. 22, 1927; d. Werner Fletcher and Grace Bodel (Larson) Hoyt; A.B., U. Cal. at Berkeley, 1949, J.D., 1952. Admitted to Cal. bar, 1953; practice law, Mt. Shasta, Cal., 1953-60, Lafayette, Cal., 1960-64, Davis, Cal., 1964—. Mem. Davis. (pres. 1975), Yolo County (dir.), chambers commerce, Bus. and Profl. Women's Clubs (past pres. Davis), Toastmistresses (past pres. Davis), Phi Beta Kappa, Sigma Kappa. Home: 1435 Wake Forest Dr Davis CA 95616 Office: 227 E St Davis CA 95616

HOYT, NELLY NOEMIE SCHARGO (MRS. N. DEMING HOYT), educator; b. Nicoleef, Russia, Jan. 15, 1920; d. Simon S. and Vera (Rivkind) Shargo; student Sorbonne, 1939-40; B.A., Smith Coll., 1943; M.A., Columbia, 1944, Ph.D., 1946; m. N. Deming Hoyt, Sept. 7, 1946; 1 son, Victor. Reference analyst U.S. Mission to UN, N.Y.C., 1946-48; research in contemporary culture Columbia U., 1948-53; cons. dept. history Smith Coll., Achilles prof. history, 1974—. Mem. Societe du XVIII Siecle, Alumnae Assn. Smith Coll. (spl. dir., chmn. edn. com. 1972—). Author: History in the Encyclopedie, 1947; co-author: The French Family in the Civil Code, 1952; Selections from Encyclopedia of Diderot and d'Alembert, 1965; Smith College Studies in History, 1964-68. Home: 89 Maynard Rd Northampton MA 01060

HOYT, OLGA GRUHZIT (MRS. EDWIN PALMER HOYT III), author; b. Columbus, Ga., Nov. 16, 1922; d. Oswald Martin and Elfriede Victoria (Nerica) Gruhzit; B.A., U. Mich., 1943; m. Edwin Palmer Hoyt III, May 24, 1947; children—Diana, Helga (Mrs. Benjamin Berliner), Christopher. Instr., insp. airplane wing factory Chrysler Corp., Detroit, 1943; with US. news div. OWI, N.Y.C., 1944-45, asst. news editor, Beirut, Lebanon, 1945; researcher Time mag., N.Y.C., 1945-47; free lance corr. N.Am. Newspaper Alliance, Europe, 1947-48; columnist, book reviewer Denver Post, 1949-50; book editor, columnist Colorado Springs, (Colo.) Free Press, 1951-55; stringer Time, Colorado Springs, 1951-54; children's book reviewer N.Y. Times, 1957-64; researcher Edwin Palmer Hoyt, author, 1959—. Mem. Alpha Phi. Author juvenile books including: If You Want a Horse, 1965; Witches, 1969; The Bedouins, 1969; Aborigines of Australia, 1969; (with Edwin Palmer Hoyt) Censorship in America, 1969; American Indians Today, 1972; (with Edwin Palmer Hoyt) Freedom of the News Media, 1973. Contbr. to Saturday Rev., Balt. Sun. Home: Bat Mansion Bomoseen VT 05732

HOYT, ROSALIE CHASE, physicist, educator; b. N.Y.C., May 20, 1914; B.A., Columbia, 1940; M.A., Bryn Mawr Coll., 1941, Ph.D. in Physics, 1945. Instr. physics U. Rochester, 1945-48; instr. physics Bryn Mawr (Pa.) Coll., 1941-45, asst. prof., 1948-52, asso. prof., 1952, now prof. Mem. Am. Phys. Soc. Research on bioelectric instrumentation, nerve models, counters and detectors for nuclear research. Address: Physics Dept Bryn Mawr Coll Bryn Mawr PA 19010*

HOYT-BROWN, A. ELIZABETH, lawyer; b. St. John, N.B., Can., May 30, 1925; B.A., McGill U., 1946; B.C.L., U. N.B., 1950. Admitted to N.B. bar, 1950, since practiced in St. John, mem. firm McKelvey, Macaulay, Machum & Fairweather. Mem. St. John Law Soc., N.B. Barristers' Soc., Canadian Bar Assn. Home: 61 Kennebecasis Dr St John NB Canada Office: McKelvey Macaulay Machum & Fairweather Brunswick House 44 Prince William St St John NB Canada

HOYTE, LENON HOLDER (MRS. LEWIS P. HOYTE), curator; b. N.Y.C., July 4, 1905; d. Moses Emanuel and Rose Pari (Best) Holder; diploma N.Y. Tng. Sch. for Tchrs., 1930; B.S. in Edn., Coll. City N.Y., 1937, postgrad. to 1959; postgrad. Columbia, 1937-40; m. Lewis P. Hoyte, Sept. 1, 1938. Tchr., N.Y.C. Pub. Sch. Systems, 1930-70; established Aunt Len's Doll and Toy Mus., N.Y.C., 1970—. Mem. Nat. Doll and Toy Collectors, L.I. Doll Hobby and Craft Club, Hamilton Terrace Block Assn., Upper Q Soc. Democrat. Episcopalian. Address: 6 Hamilton Terrace New York City NY 10031

HRNCIRIK, MARIE EMILY RAISPIS (MRS. JOSEPH F. HRNCIRIK), pharmacist; b. Chgo., Nov. 25, 1914; d. Joseph T. and Emilie (Louda) Raispis; student DePaul U., 1933-34; B.S., U. Ill., 1938; m. Joseph F. Hrncirik, May 25, 1940 (dec. May 1962); 1 son, Joseph J. With family pharmacy, Chgo., 1935-39, pharmacist Mercy Hosp. Clinic, Chgo., 1939-41; staff pharmacist Augustana Hosp., Chgo., 1942-43; chief pharmacist St. Joseph's Hosp., Chgo., 1944-45; part-time hosp., retail pharmacist, nursing home cons., 1946-54; chief pharmacist, organizer pharmacy MacNeal Meml. Hosp., Berwyn, Ill., 1954-66; chief pharmacist Martha Washington Hosp., Chgo., 1966-71, dir. pharmacy services, 1971—; mem. pharmacy preceptorship program U. Ill. Coll. Pharmacy. Mem. polio program Berwyn Health Dept., 1964; mem. fund raising com. Parents Assn. Loyola U., Chgo., 1966-68, high sch. student recruitment com. 1967. Mem. Am., Ill. pharm. assns., Am., No. Ill. socs. hosp. pharmacists, Am. Coll. Apothecaries, A.M.A. (asso.), Sacred Heart Acad. Alumna Assn., Lambda Kappa Sigma. Home: 6519 W Sinclair Av Berwyn IL 60402 Office: 4055 N Western Av Chicago IL 60618

HRUSKA, DOROTHY IRENE GARTAMAKER (MRS. JAMES EMIL HRUSKA), curator; b. Worthington, Minn., Jan. 20, 1924; d. Ward K. and Mildred Ann (Coon) Gartamaker; student pub. schs., Reading, Minn.; m. James Emil Hruska, Sept. 20, 1941; 1 son, David Kent. Co-dir., curator, guide LeSueur County Hist. Soc. Mus., Elysian, Minn., 1965—. Bd. dirs. Gish Families of the World, 1969-71. Mem. Assn. Hist. Adminstrs. (dir. Minn. 1969-71), Minn. Territorial Pioneers (life), Minn. State, LeSueur County (life, dir. 1970-73) hist. socs. Roman Catholic. Home: 306 West Lake St Waterville MN 56096 Office: PO Box 557 Elysian MN 56028

HRUSKA, VICTORIA ELIZABETH KUNCL (MRS. ROMAN LEE HRUSKA), wife U.S. senator; b. Omaha, Aug. 27; d. Vaclac Frank and Frantiska Anna (Bulicek) Kuncl; student U. Neb., 1924-26, Neb. Coll. Medicine, 1926-27; m. Roman Lee Hruska, Sept. 24, 1930; children—Roman Lee II, Quentin Jerold, Jana Lynn. Home: 2139 S 38th St Omaha NE 68105

HSU, SHU YING LI (MRS. H.F. HSU), educator; b. Peking, China, Aug. 16, 1920; d. Chiao Ping and Hsin Fu (Chen) Li; B.S., Nat. Peking Normal U., 1940; Ph.D., U. Ia., 1957; m. H.F. Hsu, Apr. 18, 1954; came to U.S., 1952, naturalized, 1961. Research asso. Harvard Sch. Pub. Health, Boston, 1953-54; faculty U. Ia., Iowa City, 1957—, prof. dept. preventive medicine and environmental health, 1973—. Mem. Am. Assn. Immunologists, Am. Soc. Tropical Medicine and Hygiene, Am. Soc. Parasitologists, Soc. for Experimental Biology and Medicine, Royal Soc. Tropical Medicine and Hygiene. Home: 1512 Derwen Dr Iowa City IA 52240

HU, SHIU-YING, botanist; b. Suchow, Kiangsu, China, Feb. 22, 1910; d. Fang-i and Niang (Chuan) Hu; B.A., Ginling Coll., Nanking, China, 1933; M.Sc., Lingnan U., Canton, China, 1937; Ph.D., Radcliffe Coll., 1949; m. Ming Yuan Hsu, July 30, 1949. Came to U.S., 1946, naturalized, 1956. Teaching fellow Lingnan U., 1934-37; instr. West China U., Chengtu, 1938-40, asst. prof., 1940-43, asso. prof., 1943-46; with Arnold Arboretum, Harvard U., Cambridge, Mass., 1949—, asst. in herbarium, 1949-53, chief botanist charge flora China project, 1953-57, botanist arboretum, 1957—. Mem. Com. Univ. Student Relief Work, Chengtu, 1939-46; adviser Sino-Tibetan Border Service Corps, 1940-45; mem. nat. com., labor dept. YWCA, 1941-46. Mem. A.A.A.S., Am. Inst. Biol. Scis., Am. Holly Soc., Am. Assn. Plant Taxonomists, Pacific Sci. Assn. (standing com. botany), N.Y. Acad. Scis., Internat. Dendrology Soc., Internat. Assn. Plant Taxonomists, Exec. and Profl. Hall of Fame, Conservation Soc. Hong Kong (exec. bd. 1969—), Phi Beta Kappa, Sigma Xi, Ginling Assn. (chmn. Boston chpt. 1963—, chmn. Thurston Meml. Fund 1960—). Conglist. (chmn. local mission bd. 1955-60, trustee). Research and publs. in field. Discoverer many new species Chinese plants; new genus Shiuyinghua named in her honor, 1962. Home: 11 Manchester Rd Brookline MA 02146 Office: 22 Divinity Av Cambridge MA 02138

HUANG, JANE SHAO CHEN WU (MRS. PAO CHYUAN HUANG), civil engr.; b. China; d. Sze Yuan and Fong (Cheng) Wu; B.S., Nat. Yunnan U. China, 1943; M.S., U. Mich., 1949; m. Pao Chyuan Huang, Feb. 10, 1946; children—David Da-wei, Diana Da-ann, Donald Da-jen. Came to U.S., 1948, naturalized, 1954. Jr. engr. Sze-Chuan Kunming Railway Bur., China, 1943-44; engr. Hwa Fu Engring. Constrn. Co., China, 1944-45; instr. civil engring. dept. Nat. Yunnan U., 1945-48; structural designer J. L. Faisant & Assos., cons. engr., Balt., 1956-58, Green Assos., Inc., Balt., cons. engr., 1958-68, chief computer sect., 1968—. Mem. Md. Soc. Profl. Engrs., Soc. Women Engrs. Presbyn. Home: 709 E Seminary Av Baltimore MD 21204 Office: 32 West Rd Towson MD 21204

HUANG, LENA LIU (MRS. CHIN TANG HUANG), pediatric cardiologist; b. Shanghai, China, July 7, 1934; d. Chieh Loh and Yu En (Foo) Liu; M.D., Nat. Taiwan U., 1957; m. Chin Tang Huang, Oct. 20, 1962; children—Laurence, Andrew, Cheryl. Intern, Nat. Taiwan U. Hosp., 1958; Kings County Hosp., N.Y.C., 1962; resident Kings County Hosp., 1962-64; practice medicine specializing in pediatrics, dir. pediatric cardiology Bklyn.-Cumberland Med. Center, Bklyn., 1967-74, St. Vincent Hosp., N.Y.C., 1974—; asst. prof. pediatrics dept. N.Y. U., N.Y.C. 1974—. Diplomate Am. Bd. Pediatrics, Spl. Bd. Pediatric Cardiology. Home: 2740 Whitman Dr Brooklyn NY 11234 Office: 121 DeKalbe Av Brooklyn NY 11201

HUANG, SOPHIA CHANG (MRS. YUN PENG HUANG), psychologist; b. Taiwan, Republic of China, July 20, 1934; d. Symonds Tung-Lang and Grace Yun-Huei (Chen) Chang; came to U.S., 1958, naturalized, 1973; B.S., Nat. Taiwan U., 1957; M.A., Ohio State U., 1959, Ph.D., 1962; m. Yun Peng Huang, Sept. 23, 1960; children—Jim Jui Jen, Christina Jui-Chun. Chief psychologist Mount Carmel Guild Inst., Union City, N.J., 1969-72; staff psychologist N.Y. Foundling Hosp., N.Y.C., 1973—. Coop. psychologist Bur. Children's Service State of N.J., 1972—. Chinese Cultural and National Sci. scholar, 1954-56, Li fellow, 1958. Mem. Am., N.J. psychol. assns. Home: 66 N Virginia Court Englewood Cliffs NJ 07632 Office: 1175 3d Av New York City NY

HUANG, SYLVIA SHU-FUNG LEE (MRS. HENRY HUANG), educator; b. Shanghai, China, July 14, 1930; d. Ho-Ming and An-Fu (Wang) Lee; B.S., Nat. Taiwan U., 1952; M.S. (Research fellow), U. Ida., 1957; postgrad. U. Wis., 1956-57; Ph.D., U. Pitts., 1961; m. Henry Huang, June 20, 1957; children—Peter, Paul, Philip. Came to U.S., 1955, naturalized, 1965. Grad. student research asst. U. Pitts., 1958-61; NIH postdoctoral fellow dept. microbiology U. Pitts. Sch. Medicine, 1961-62; research asso. Sloan-Kettering Inst., N.Y.C., 1962-64; instr. Cornell U. Med. Coll., N.Y.C., 1964-66; research scientist dept. biochemistry N.Y. U. Sch. Medicine, N.Y.C., 1966-67, instr. dept. biochemistry, 1967-69, research asst. prof., 1969-70, research asso. prof., 1970-71, asso. prof. dept. biochemistry, 1971—. Mem. Biophys. Soc., Harvey Soc., N.Y. Acad. Sci., A.A.A.S., Sigma Xi. Contbr. articles to profl. jours. Home: 345 E 69th St New York City NY 10021 Office: 550 1st Av New York City NY 10016

HUBBARD, CAROL ANN RESINGER, ednl. adminstr.; b. Ironton, Mo., Aug. 25, 1942; d. Clifton E. and Lorinne I. (Harris) Resinger; B. in Journalism, U. Mo. Sch. Journalism, 1964. Newspaper reporter Kansas City Star, 1964, Columbia (Mo.) Daily Tribune, 1966-70; editor Denver C. of C., 1971-73; pub. information officer City Aurora, Colo., 1973-74; staff asst. pub. relations dept. U. New Haven, 1974—. Communicators (treas. 1973), Colo. Press Women. Home: 100 State St North Haven CT 06473 Office: U New Haven 300 Orange Av West Haven CT 06516

HUBBARD, DORTHY STUART (MRS. RICHARD GLENN HUBBARD), polit. worker; b. Hannibal, Mo., Aug. 14, 1928; d. Grover Cleveland and Hattie Jane (Garver) Stuart; grad. high sch.; m. Richard Glenn Hubbard, Mar. 14, 1947; 1 dau., Kyle Jean. Mem. Mayor's Com. for Mark Twain Regional Planning Bd., 1974—. Sec., Marion County (Mo.) Young Democrats, 1958-59; adminstrv. v.p. Mo. Young Dems., 1961, nat. committeewoman, 1964-66, chmn. 9th Dist. Com., 1962; pres., Marion County Women's Dem. Club, 1969—, corr. sec., 1972-73; 4th v.p. 9th Dist. Women's Dem. Clubs, 1970-71, 2d v.p., 1971-72, 1st v.p., 1972—; mem. Mo. Dem. State Com., 1970—; sec.-treas. Mo. Dem. Days Exec. Bd., 1971—; mem. speakers bur. Mo. Federated Women's Dem. Club, 1972-73; mem. Marion County Dem. Central Com., 1974—. Methodist (sec. com. archives and history Mo. E. Conf. 1968—, lay speaker 1969—, asst. lay leader 1974—). Mem. Order Eastern Star. Clubs: Hannibal (Mo.) Study (pres. 1974-75), Parliamentary Law Federated (Hannibal). Home: 1406 Viley St Hannibal MO 63401

HUBBARD, FRANCES JOYCE (MRS. EDWIN S. HUBBARD), librarian; b. East Orange, N.J., Apr. 21, 1918; d. Sidney Wardell and Frances Louise (Cox) Peloubet; A.B., Radcliffe, 1940; postgrad. Newark Mus., 1941; M.S., Simmons Coll. Sch. L.S., 1968; m. Edwin S. Hubbard, Apr. 11, 1942; children—Benton S., Francis A. II, Thomas M., Candace L., Martha B., Peter M. Asst. curator Robert Hull Fleming Mus., Burlington, Vt., 1941-42; supr. elementary sch. libraries, Summit, N.J., 1942-43; tchr. modern dance, creative drama, phys. fitness Salem Coll., Winston Salem, N.C., 1953-55, Stamford, Conn., 1956-63; research asst. musicology N.Y. U., part-time 1960-63; research librarian Croft Ednl. Services, New London, Conn., 1964-65; spl. librarian Harbridge House, Boston, 1966-67; children's librarian Dedham (Mass.) Pub. Library, 1967-68; dir. children's services Nashua (N.H.) Pub. Library, 1968-71; asst. to coordinator of work with children Enoch Pratt Free Library, Balt., 1971-72; children's librarian Perrot Meml. Library, Old Greenwich, Conn., 1972-73; dir. Southington (Conn.) Pub. Library, 1973—. Tchr. children's lit. course Regional Center for Ednl. Tng., Dartmouth, 1970-71. Mem. Am., New Eng., Conn. library assns., New Eng. Roundtable of Children's Librarians (vice chmn. 1970-71), Puppeteers of Am., Assn. Children with Learning Disabilities, Am. Assn. U. Women. Home: 24 Clubhouse Dr Woodbury CT 06489 Office: Southington Pub Library Main St Southington CT 06489

HUBBARD, M. GAY FETROW, educator; b. Cedar, Kan., Mar. 16, 1931; d. Horace B. and Aurolyn (Weiser) Fetrow; B.A., Ft. Hays Kan. State Coll., 1959, M.A., 1961; Ph.D., U. Pitts., 1971; m. Joseph E. Hubbard, May 25, 1951; (div. Apr. 1964). Tchr., Zurich (Kan.) Elementary Sch., 1950-52; instr. dept. English, Ft. Hays Kan. State Coll., 1959-61; free lance editor, text book div. Charles Merril Pub., Columbus, O., 1961; prin., tchr. Columbus (O.) Childrens Psychiatric Hosp., 1961-66; practicum supr., area emotionally disturbed U. Pitts., 1967-68; coordinator, dept. emotionally disturbed, spl. sch. dist. St. Louis County, Mo., 1968-70; instr. Wright State U., Dayton, O., 1971; asst. prof. dir. child psychiatry Coll. Medicine, Ohio State U., Columbus, 1971—, asst. prof. Coll. Edn., 1971—. Vol. worker Audy Home for Children, Cook County, Ill., 1956-57. Mem. Am. Orthopsychiat. Assn., Council for Exceptional Children, N.E.A., Nat. Assn. Adminstrv. Women. Home: 4069 E Livingston Av Columbus OH 43227

HUBBARD, MARCIA JUNE, marketing/sales exec.; b. Bridgeport, Conn., June 13, 1938; d. Thomas Taylor and Hazel Austin (Hall) Hubbard; B.A., U. Mass., 1960. Personnel asst. Empire State Bldg. Corp., N.Y.C., 1960-61; sales rep. Nat. Car Rental, N.Y.C., 1962-65; sr. sales rep. Eastern Airlines, N.Y.C., 1965-69; sales rep. Am. Airlines, N.Y.C., 1969-72, mgr. women's market sales, 1972—. Recipient Scholarship, Rotary Club, 1956, Good Citizen award D.A.R., 1956. Mem. Chi Omega. Republican. Episcopalian. Club: U. Mass. Alumni (sec. 1965-67) (N.Y.C.). Home: 251 E 32d St New York City NY 10016 Office: 633 3d Av New York City NY 10017

HUBER, SISTER ALBERTA, coll. pres.; b. Rock Island, Ill., 1917; d. Albert and Lydia (Hofer) Huber; B.A., Coll. of St. Catherine, 1939; M.A., U. Minn., 1945; Ph.D., U. Notre Dame, 1954. Joined Sisters of St. Joseph of Carondelet, 1936; instr. high schs., 1938-40; faculty Coll. of St. Catherine, St. Paul, 1940—, prof. English, 1953—, chmn. dept., 1959-63, acad. dean, 1963-64, pres. Coll., 1964—. Trustee Fontbonne Coll., St. Louis, St. Joseph's Hosp., St. Paul; bd. dirs. St. Paul Opera Assn., Minn. Internat. Center; hon. mem. bd. dirs. Minn. Symphony Orch. Mem. Pi Gamma Mu, Delta Phi Lambda, Kappa Gamma Pi. Address: 2004 Randolph Av St Paul MN 55105

HUBER, SISTER ALICE M., coll. pres.; b. Buffalo; d. Charles J. and Margaret Rose (Haslow) Huber; M.S. in Edn., Mt. St. Joseph Coll.; M.A., Canisius Coll.; Ed.D., U. Buffalo. Entered Congregation of Sisters of St. Joseph; tchr. math. and sci. elementary and secondary schs., Buffalo, 1940-52; vice prin. secondary sch., Buffalo, 1952-58; dir. grad. div. Medaille Coll., Buffalo, 1958-63, pres. coll., 1963—. Trustee Sisters of St. Joseph; exec. com. Western N.Y. Consortium. Mem. Am. Assn. Coll. Tchrs. Edn. (exec. com. N.Y. State), Math. Assn. Am., Am. Assn. Higher Edn., Middle States Assn. Philosophy of Edn., Pi Lambda Theta. Author: The New Mathematics and How to Understand It, 1963; Getting Set With Sets, 1965. Contbr. articles to profl. jours. Home: 18 Agassiz Circle Buffalo NY 14214

HUBER, MARY SUMNER (MRS. ALFRED LEO HUBER), librarian; b. Ludlow, Vt., July 24, 1921; d. Floyd Taylor and Gladys Elinor (Armstrong) Sumner; A.B., U. Vt., 1943; M.L.S., Rutgers U., 1965; m. Alfred Leo Huber, Jan. 29, 1944; children—Jane (Mrs. James Arthur Wallace), Holly (Mrs. Douglas Manson Eddy). Chemist Gen. Chem. Co., Edgewater, N.J., 1943-44; librarian Am. Smelting & Refining Co., S. Plainfield, N.J., 1963-64, Coll. St. Elizabeth, Convent Sta., N.J., 1964—. Sec. Florham Park (N.J.) Planning Bd., 1953-54. Mem. Am., N.J. Library assns., Am. Soc. for Information Sci., Sierra Club, Appalachian Mountain Club. Republican. Presbyn. Home: 139 Summit Rd Florham Park NJ 07932 Office: Mahoney Library College of St Elizabeth Convent Station NJ 07961

HUBLITZ, SUSAN, occupational therapist; b. N.Y.C., June 6, 1940; d. Lincoln and Katherine Mary (Daly) Hublitz; B.A., Hofstra U., 1962; advanced standing certificate, Columbia, 1967. Speech therapist Bay Shore Pub. Schs., L.I., N.Y., 1962-64; speech therapist Columbia Presbyn. Hosp., N.Y.C., 1964-65, occupational therapist, 1967-69; occupational therapist Blythedale Childrens Hosp., Valhalla, N.Y., 1969-70, Med. Center Hosp. of Vt., Burlington, 1970-71; dir. occupational therapy, childrens unit St. Agnes Hosp., White Plains, N.Y., 1971—. Mem. Am. Occupational Therapy Assn. Home: 3 David Lane Yonkers NY 10701 Office: St Agnes Hosp North St White Plains NY 10605

HUCK, CHARLOTTE STEPHENA, educator; b. Evanston, Ill., Oct. 6, 1922; d. Carl Marshall and Mildred Adelaide (Bridges) Huck; student Wellesley Coll., 1940-41; B.S. with distinction, Northwestern U., 1944, M.A., 1951, Ph.D., 1955. Tchr. elementary sch., Ladue, Mo., 1944-45, Lake Forest, Ill., 1945-46, Kenilworth, Ill., 1946-51; instr., Northwestern U., Evanston, Ill., 1951-55; asst. prof. Ohio State U., Columbus, 1955-58, asso. prof., 1958-62, prof. elementary edn., 1962—. Vis. prof. U. Denver, 1964, U. Hawaii, 1965; co-dir. Experienced Tchr. Fellowship Program, 1968-69, 69-70; dir. Ed-Professions Devel. Act In-Service Project for Reading and Lang. Arts, 1970-71. Recipient Distinguished Tchr. award Ohio State Alumni Assn., 1972. Mem. Nat. Council Tchrs. English (mem. lit. commn. 1966-72, chmn. elementary sect. 1967-69, chmn. joint com. with Children's Book Council, editorial com. 1972-75, pres. elect 1975), Nat. Council Research in English (mem. exec. com. 1967-68), A.L.A. (chmn. May Hill Arbuthnot Honor Lectr. com.), Mortar Board, Delta Kappa Gamma. Author: (with Doris Young Kuhn) Children's Literature in the Elementary School, 1968; (with Willavene Wolf and Martha L. King) Critical Reading Ability of Elementary School Children. Home: 348 Gudrun Rd Columbus OH 43202 Office: 29 W Woodruff St Columbus OH 43210

HUCKABAY, REBA NEEL, educator; b. Converse, La., Aug. 3, 1920; d. Oliver Fulton and Lenora (McDonald) Neel; B.S., Northwestern State U., 1941; M.B.A., U. Tex., 1954; Ph.D., Ind. U., 1961; postgrad. U. Wis., summer 1957; m. Houston Keller Huckabay, Aug. 12, 1967. Tchr., Singer (La.) High Sch., 1941; ins. clk. United Gas Pipe Line Co., Shreveport, La., 1942-52; instr. bus. Lee Jr. Coll., 1954-58; instr. bus. adminstrn. Tex. Woman's U., 1961-63; asso. prof. office adminstrn. La. Tech. U., Ruston, 1963-65, prof., head dept. office adminstrn. and bus. edn., 1965—; apptd. Inst. for Certifying Profl. Secs., 1972—. Recipient Outstanding Faculty Woman award Asso. Women Students, 1972. Mem. Am. Bus. Writing Assn., Southwestern Social Sci. Assn., Nat. Bus. Edn. Assn., Nat. Collegiate Assn. for Secs. (nat. pres. 1968-70), Nat. Secs. Assn. (hon.), Beta Gamma Sigma, Pi Lambda Theta, Sigma Iota Epsilon. Contbr. chpt. on Business Education: An Evaluative Inventory to Nat. Bus. Edn. Assn. Yearbook No. 6, 1968. Home: 1505 Roosevelt Dr Ruston LA 71270 Office: La Tech U Ruston LA 71270

HUCKABEE, MARTHA CAROLYN, pharmacist; b. Uniontown, Ala., Oct. 13, 1926; d. Thomas Fendley and Carolyn (Blakeney) Huckabee; B.S., Ala. Poly. Inst., 1947. Pharmacist, Jones Drug Co., Anniston, Ala., 1948-49, Bradford Drug Co., 1949-65; owner, pharmacist Huckabee Drugs, Uniontown, 1965—. Instr. first aid A.R.C., 1960—; dir. med. services Civil Def., Perry County, 1961—; hon. dep. sheriff Perry County, 1962-71. Bd. dirs. Uniontown Community Chest, Perry County Hist. Preservation Soc. Recipient Outstanding Pharmacy Grad. award Ala. Pharm. Assn., 1947. Mem. Uniontown Mchts. Assn., Nat. Assn. Retail Druggists, Am., Ala. (county dir. 1967-71), Perry County pharm. assns., Nat. C. of C., Auburn, Auburn Pharmacy alumni assns., Ala., Central Ala. geneal. socs., D.A.R. (regent), U.D.C., Phi Kappa Phi. Republican. Baptist. Mem. Order of Eastern Star. Home: 101 Front St Uniontown AL 36786 Office: 300 Water St Uniontown AL 36786

HUCKE, DOROTHY MARIE, mfg. co. exec.; b. Bklyn., Jan. 14, 1927; d. Charles Vincent and Ida Marie (Deneke) Hucke; B.A., St. Joseph's Coll., 1949; M.S. in Biostatistics, Columbia, 1958; M.S. in Math., N.Y. U., 1963. Lab. Tech. Pfizer Inc., Bklyn., 1950-51, supr. microbiol. testing lab., 1951-54, statistician, 1954-60, supr. statistics, 1960-67, mgr. spl. services, 1967-72, adminstrv. asst., 1972-73, mgr. systems and planning, N.Y.C., 1973—; cons. on statis. problems, 1956-67. Mem. Am. Soc. Quality Control, Biometrics Soc., Am. Statis. Assn., Met. Girls Basketball Assn. (pres. 1953-55), Delta Epsilon Sigma, Kappa Gamma Pi, Sigma Iota Chi. Home: 82-44 63d Av New York City NY 11379 Office: 42d St New York City NY 10017

HUDAK, JULIA STEPHANIA, med. technologist; b. Shenandoah, Pa., Feb. 20, 1930; d. Louis T. and Stephania (Patrik) Hudak; grad. St. Joseph Hosp. Sch. X-Ray, Stamford, Conn., 1957; postgrad. isotope program Bellevue Hosp., 1961. Bookkeeper, Westport Bank & Trust Co. (Conn.), 1948-55; x-ray technologist St. Joseph Hosp., Stamford, 1957-60, asst. supr., part-time tchr. x-ray, technologist nuclear medicine, 1961-65; chief technologist nuclear medicine Norwalk (Conn.) Hosp., 1965—. Mem. Am. Registry X-Ray Technologists, Am. Registry Nuclear Medicine, Soc. Nuclear Med. Technologists, Soc. Nuclear Medicine. Author: Handbook for Technologists of Nuclear Medicine, 1971. Roman Catholic. Home: 55 W Parish Rd Westport CT 06880

HUDAK, MARTHA JOSEPHINE, coll. adminstr.; b. Chgo., Sept. 15, 1948; d. Raymond J. and Maryan Jean (More) Hudak; B.A. in Edn., Central State U., Okla., 1969; postgrad U. Okla., 1971—. Tchr. journalism Okla. City. pub. schs., 1969-70; pub. information officer Okla. Health Dept., Oklahoma City, 1970; coordinator pub. information Oscar Rose Jr. Coll., Midwest City, Okla., 1970—. Sec. Tinker County Bicentennial Com., 1973—; mem. Okla. Bicentennial Commn., 1972—. Named to Okla. Jour. Hall of Fame, 1968, Outstanding Young Women Am., 1973. Mem. Okla. Pub. Relations Assn. (mem. TV task force 1972—), Nat. (pub. relations dir. 1972—), Okla. (editor newsletter 1973—, pres. 1972-73) jr. coll. journalism assns., Okla. Collegiate Press Assn. (adviser, dir. 1971-73), Am. Coll. Pub. Relations Assn., Sigma Delta Chi. Home: 1519 NW 30 Oklahoma City OK 73118 Office: 6420 SE 15 Midwest City OK 73110

HUDAK, PATRICIA ANN (MRS. LOUIS DELUCA), banker; b. Wall, Pa., Dec. 20, 1938; d. Michael and Ann (Ramich) Hudak; B.A. in Psychology and Edn. Waynesburg Coll., 1960; M.S. in Indsl. Relations, W.Va. U., 1964; m. Louis DeLuca, Sept. 17, 1966. With Western Pa. Nat. Bank, Pitts., 1962—, br. mgr. Gateway Office, 1971—. Chmn. dist. 62 United Fund, 1965; bus. chmn. United Fund, 1969. Mem. Home Rule Commn. Mem. Nat. Assn. Bank Women,

Am. Inst. Banking, Am. Saluki Assn., Midwest, Pitts. hound assns., Western Pa. Kennel Assn., Sigma Kappa. Clubs: Greater Pitts. Afghan Hound (treas., dir.), Bradford Woods (Pa.) Women's (treas.). Home: Cedar Rd Box 361 Bradford Woods PA 15015 Office: Penn and Stanwix Sts Pittsburgh PA 15222

HUDDLESON, MARY TAEUSCH, civic worker; b. Cambridge, Mass., Nov. 29, 1917; d. Carl F. and Mary (Haman) Taeusch; B.A., Vassar Coll., 1939; M.A., U. Cal., 1969; m. Edwin E. Huddleson, Jr., July 21, 1941; children—Michael (dec.), Edwin E. III, Mary Catherine. Mem. Oakland Redevel. Agy., 1956-66, chmn., 1959, 66; exec. dir. Oakland Citizens Com. for Urban Renewal, 1970-71, pres., 1972-73. Mem. Oakland League Women Voters (pres. 1958), Amateur Fencers League Am. (nat. dir. 1959, 61, 62, 65-73, nat. v.p. for Pacific Coast 1965-69). Address: 2201 Bywood Dr Oakland CA 94602

HUDDLESTON, EDITH MARY, govt. ofcl.; b. Washington, Jan. 3, 1918; d. James Edgar and Edith (Bouis) Huddleston; B.A., George Washington U., 1939, M.A., 1940; Ph.D., N.Y. U., 1952. Test devel. specialist Coll. Entrance Exam. Bd. and Ednl. Testing Service, Princeton, N.J., 1942-58; edn. program specialist U.S. Office Edn., Washington, 1958-64, 70—; psychologist Nat. Inst. Mental Health, Bethesda, Md., 1964-70. Mem. Nat. Council Administrv. Women in Edn., Am. Psychol. Assn., Psychometric Soc., Am. Ednl. Research Assn., Internat. Council Psychologists, Nat. Council Measurement in Edn., Am. Assn. U. Women. Editor Yearbook, Nat. Council Measurement in Edn., 1955-61. Home: 5013 Elm St Bethesda MD 20014 Office: NCES Office Edn 400 Maryland Av SW Washington DC 20202

HUDGINS, CATHERINE HARDING (MRS. ROBERT SCOTT HUDGINS, IV), business exec.; b. Raleigh, N.C., June 25, 1913; d. William Thomas and Mary Alice (Timberlake) Harding; B.S., N.C. State U., 1929-33; grad. tchr. N.C. Sch. for Deaf, 1933-34; m. Robert Scott Hudgins, IV, Aug. 20, 1938; children—Catherine Harding, Deborah Ghiselin, Robert Scott V. Tchr., N.C. Sch. for Deaf, Morganton, 1934-36; sec. Dr. A. S. Oliver, Raleigh, 1937; tchr. N.J. Sch. for Deaf, Trenton, 1937-39; sec. Robert S. Hudgins Co., Charlotte, N.C., 1949-60, v.p., sec., treas., 1960—, also dir. Mem. Jr. Service League, Easton, Pa., 1939; project chmn. ladies aux. Profl. Engrs. N.C., 1954-55, pres., 1956-57; pres. Christian High Sch. P.T.A., 1963; program chmn. Charlotte Opera Guild, 1959-61, sec., 1961-63; sec. bd. Hezekiah Alexander House Restoration, 1949-52. Mem. N.C. Hist. Assn., English Speaking Union, Mint Mus. Arts (pres. drama guild 1967-69), Daus. Am. Colonists (N.C. chmn. nat. def. 1973—), D.A.R. (chpt. regent 1957-59, N.C. program chmn. 1961-63, N.C. chmn. nat. def. 1973—, N.C. chmn., N.C. sr. pres. Children Am. Revolution 1963-66, nat. bd. mgmt. 1963—, sr. nat. corr. sec. 1966-68, sr. nat. 1st v.p. 1968-70, sr. nat. pres. 1970-72). Presbyn. (past chmn. home missions, annuities and relief Women of Ch., past pres. Sunday Sch. class). Club: Carmel Country (Charlotte). Home: 1514 Wendover Rd Charlotte NC 28211 Office: PO Box 17217 Charlotte NC 28209

HUDGINS, MARY DENGLER, writer; b. Hot Springs National Park, Ark., Nov. 24, 1901; d. Jackson Wharton and Ida (Dengler) Hudgins; B.A., U. Ark., 1924; student U. Wis., 1941, U. Chgo., 1940, Emory U., 1952, Rice Sch. of Spoken Word, 1925. Tchr., Waldo (Ark.) High Sch., 1924-25; free-lance writer, 1925-39, 60—; librarian Hot Springs Pub. Library, 1939-43; med. and gen. librarian Army and Navy Gen. Hosp., Hot Springs, 1943-59; articles pub. in encys., hist., lit., profl. and popular publs., radio, TV. Dir., Hot Springs Writer's Workshop, 1960-61, rep. to Fine Arts Council, Hot Springs, 1960—. Historian YWCA, Hot Springs. Mem. Ark. Hist. Assn. (dir. 1964-71, v.p. 1971—), Ark. Geneal. Soc. (dir. 1965-73), D.A.R., Garland County Hist. Soc. (pres. 1962-63, program chmn. 1960, 61), Am. (sec. spl. libraries div. 1959-60), Med., S.W. (Ark. reporter 1955) library assns., Ark. Folklore Assn. (1st v.p. 1958-59), Am. Assn. U. Women (Ark. 1st v.p. 1929-30, pres. Hot Springs br. 1927, Ark. fellowship chmn. 1957-61, rep. to Fine Arts Council 1961-62), Med. Library Assn., Fine Arts Center (dir., incorporator 1961). Presbyn. Clubs: Altrusa Internat., Sabina (pres. 1935), Current Book (pres. Hot Springs, 1952, 64, 68, 74). Author numerous mag. articles in field of Ark. composers and lyricists. Address: 1030 Park Av Hot Springs AR 71901

HUDON, SISTER MARY OLIVER, ednl. adminstr.; b. Rochester, N.Y., Sept. 22, 1932; d. Oliver Joseph and Mary Rose (Yahn) Hudon; B.A., Coll. Notre Dame, 1966; M.L.S., U. Md., 1969, Ph.D., 1973. Joined Sch. Sisters of Notre Dame, 1950; tchr., librarian St. Marks Sch., Balt., 1965-67; dir. library-media services Archdiocese of Balt. Schs., 1967-73; dir. curriculum, devel. Coll. Notre Dame, Balt., 1974—. Adj. lectr. U. Md.; adj. prof. Coll. Notre Dame. Lobbyist, Com. for Full Edn. Funding, 1971; corr. sec. Locust Point Civic Assn. Mem. A.L.A., Catholic Library Assn., Assn. Supervision and Curriculum Devel., Assn. Edn. and Communication Tech., League of Women Voters, Beta Phi Mu. Home: 1424 Hull St Baltimore MD 21230 Office: 4701 N Charles St Baltimore MD 21210

HUDSON, BARBARA WILLIAMS (MRS. WALTER HUDSON), pediatrician; b. Bklyn., Sept. 12, 1926; d. Alun Sylvanus and Ada (Wallace) Williams; A.B., Cornell U., 1949; M.D., Columbia, 1956;; m. Walter Hudson, Feb. 25, 1961; children—Kevin, Scott. Intern, Yale, New Haven, 1956-57; resident Babies Hosp., N.Y.C., 1957-59; practice medicine specializing in pediatrics, Easton, Md., 1960-61; asst. dir. Central Evaluation Clinic for Children U. Md., Balt., 1966-73; med. dir. Rosewood Hosp. Center, Owings Mills, Md., 1973—; asso. prof. pd. U. Md., Balt.; past mem. Md. Sch. for Blind. Mem. Am. Acad. Pediatrics, Med. and Chirugal Faculty Md. Home: 319 Windsor Mill Rd Extended Baltimore MD 21207 Office: Rosewood Hospital Owings Mills MD 21117

HUDSON, EVA STEWART, social worker; b. Sedalia, Mo.; d. William R. and Jane (Gustine) Stewart; A.B., U. Cal. at Los Angeles, 1940; postgrad. U. So. Cal. Sch. Social Work, 1942-44; m. Frank E. Hudson, Oct. 1, 1921; children—Marjorie Hudson (Mrs. Richard A. Gunn), Grace (Mrs. Richard F. Inman). Grade tchr., Phoenix, 1918, 21, Morenci, Ariz., 1920; substitute tchr., Fresno, Cal., 1922; social worker, intake worker Children's Home Soc., Los Angeles, 1940-51; social caseworker Adoption Inst., Los Angeles, 1951-52; social worker Los Angeles County Bur. Adoptions, 1952-54, social casework supr., 1954-62; part time intake worker Childrens Home Soc. of Cal., 1964-68. Pres., Horace Mann P.T.A., Glendale, Cal., 1934-36, pres. Past Pres.'s Club, 1971-73; mem. Childrens Home Soc. Cal., Florence Crittenton Services, Los Angeles. Named one of 5 outstanding employees Los Angeles County, 1962. Registered social worker, Cal. Mem. Acad. Certified Social Workers, Nat. Congress Parents and Tchrs. State of Cal. (life), Nat. Assn. Social Workers, Los Angeles County Employees Assn. (life), Alumni Assn. Sch. Social Work of U. So. Cal., U. Cal. at Los Angeles Alumni Assn. (life), Am. Assn. U. Women, YWCA (life), Zeta Tau Alpha (life, pres. So. Cal. Fedn. 1973-74). Methodist (mem. W.S.C.S., circle chmn.). Home: 809 S Adams St Glendale CA 91205

HUDSON, FLEETA CAIN (MRS. DONALD HUDSON), ednl. adminstr.; b. Mocksville, N.C., Feb. 7, 1935; d. Arthur Reece and Ella (Eaton) Cain; student Knoxville Coll., 1953-55; m. Donald Hudson, Dec. 8, 1956; children—Robin, Vickie. Reading asst. Madison and Shelton schs., Bridgeport, Conn., 1966-73; ednl. counselor Youth Service Center, Bridgeport, 1973-74, community relations specialist Greater Bridgeport Mental Health Center, 1974—. Ednl. counselor Chessmen Found. Mem. Democratic Town Com., del. state conv., 1974. Mem. Bridgeport Bd. Edn., 1973—. Recipient Merit award Community Devel. Action Plan Agy. Commn., 1970. Mem. N.A.A.C.P. (mem. exec. com. 1968-74), Fedn. of Democratic Women, Conn. Fedn. Black Democrats (sec. 1972-74), League of Women Voters. Address: 1592 Stratford Av Bridgeport CT 06607

HUDSON, FLOREINE HERRON (MRS. JAMES HOOD HUDSON), educator; b. Columbus, Ga., July 5, 1916; d. William Francis and Laura Belle (Battley) Herron; B.S. in Gen. Sci., Ga. Coll., 1936; M.Ed., Auburn U., 1945, Ed.D., 1957; m. Luther P. Ray, Dec. 24, 1940 (dec. Nov. 1943); m. 2d, James Hood Hudson, June 8, 1947. Tchr., Harris County, Ga., 1936-40; tchr. Muscogee County, Ga., 1940-43, teaching prin., 1943-45, tchr. high sch., 1945-49, supervising prin., 1949-56; prin. DeKalb County, Ga., 1957-58, instructional supr., 1958-64, asst. prof., 1964-71, prof., 1971—; curriculum, instruction Ga. State Coll., Atlanta, 1964—. Life mem. Ga. P.T.A.; treas. Georgians for Quality Pub. Edn., 1971-73. Mem. Am. Assn. U. Women (exec. bd. 1967—), Assn. Childhood Edn. Internat., Ga. Assn. Supervision and Curriculum Devel. (state dir. 1967—; pres. 1971-72), Nat. Elementary Prins. Assn., Nat., Ga. math. councils, Am. Assn. U. Profs., N.E.A. (life), Assn. Student Teaching, Student Ga. Ednl. Assn. (pres. elect 1967-68, pres. 1968), Atlanta Assn. U. Women (pres. 1969-71), Delta Kappa Gamma (corr. sec. Ga. chpt. 1967—), Kappa Delta Pi, Kappa Delta Epsilon, Phi Delta Kappa. Methodist (tchr. adult Sunday Sch., past mem. ofcl. bd. stewards, past chmn. commn. on social concerns). Club: Quota (pres. 1973—) (Atlanta). Home: 2084 Beaver Rd NE Atlanta GA 30345

HUDSON, GLADYS WATTS (MRS. JACK WILSON HUDSON), business exec.; b. McKinney, Tex., July 23, 1926; s. Robert Andrew and Mary Gertrude (Rickerson) W.; B.A., E. Tex. Bapt. Coll., 1947; postgrad. Southwestern Bapt. Theol. Sem., 1947-49; M.A., Baylor U., 1964; m. Thomas Earl Waden, Dec. 23, 1945 (dec. 1962); children—Thomas Earl, Andrew Franklin; m. 2d, Jackson Wilson Hudson, Nov. 25, 1964. Tchr., pub. schs., S.C., 1958-62; instr. E. Tex. Bapt. Coll., Marshall, 1964-65; instr. English, Baylor U., Waco, Tex., 1965-74; asst. dir. product devel. Success Motivation, Inc., 1974—. Mem. Modern Lang. Assn., Coll. English Assn., Conf. Coll. Tchrs. English. Baptist. Mem. Order Eastern Star. Compiler: Paradise Lost: A Concordance, 1971; An Elizabeth Barrett Browning Concordance, 1973. Home: 3030 Lasker St Waco TX 76707

HUDSON, HARRIET DUFRESNE, coll. dean; b. Kirby, Pa., July 14, 1912; d. William Mestrezat and Florence Ronald (Barclay) Hudson; student Blackburn Coll., 1929-30, LL.D., 1957; A.B., Wellesley Coll., 1933; M.A., U. Chgo., 1936, Ph.D., 1950. Grader Harvard Grad. Sch. Bus. Adminstrn., 1937-39; instr. econs. and sociology Pine Manor Jr. Coll., 1939-42, Mt. Holyoke Coll, 1942-47; asst. prof. econs. U. Ill., Urbana, 1948-53; prof. econs., dean coll. Randolph-Macon Woman's Coll., Lynchburg, Va., 1953—. Mem. regional selection com. Woodrow Wilson Nat. Fellowship Found., 1959-70; mem. exec. council Commn. on Colls. Bd. dirs. Tuition Exchange, 1957-68; trustee Coll. Entrance Examination Bd., 1963-66, Common Fund, 1973—. Mem. Am., So., Western econ. assns., Indsl. Relations Research Assn., Am. Assn. U. Women, Am. Council on Edn. (com. on coll. teaching 1959-61, commn. on accreditation service experience 1972—), Assn. for Higher Edn. (exec. com. 1958-61), Am. Conf. Acad. Deans (dir.), So. Assn. Colls. and Schs. (com. on standards and reports 1960-70, exec. council commn. on colls. 1971—), Alliance Francaise, P.E.O. Presbyn. Home: 232 Norfolk Av Lynchburg VA 24503

HUDSON, JACQUELINE, artist; b. Cambridge, Mass.; d. Eric and Gertrude (Dunton) Hudson; student Columbia, Art Students League. One-man shows at Burr Gallery, N.Y.C., Rockport (Mass.) Art Assn., Present Day Club, Princeton, N.J.; exhibited in group shows at Nat. Acad., Pa. Acad. Fine Arts, Library of Congress, Cin. Mus., Riverside Mus., Portland (Me.) Mus. Art, Dayton Art Inst., Bixler Mus., Colby Coll., Me. Art Gallery, Wiscasset, many others; represented permanent collection Library of Congress; pvt. collections. Com. mem. Monhegan (Me.) Museum. Recipient Pennell purchase prize Library of Congress, 1951; Allen Kander Found. award Rockport Art Assn., 1957, Edith Wengenroth prize, 1971; Alice Standish Buell Meml. prize, Nat. Assn. Women Artists, 1968. Mem. Art Students League, Nat. Assn. Women Artists, Rockport Art Assn., Print Council Am., Lincoln County Cultural and Hist. Assn., Monhegan (Me.) Assos. (chmn. mus. com. 1963-67). Home: Rockport MA 01966 also Monhegan Island ME 04852 Studio: 220 Sullivan St New York City NY 10012

HUDSON, PAMELA SUE, psychiatric social worker; b. Sacramento, Aug. 2, 1934; d. Abram Clement and Doris Sue (Pearl) Penner; B.A., Mills Coll., 1956; M.S. in Social Work, Columbia, 1960; m. Jack Hudson, Oct. 31, 1957 (dec. Feb. 1970). Psychiat. social worker, N.Y.C., 1960-62, Redwood City, Cal., 1963-65; sr. psychiat. social worker Langley Porter Neuropsychiat. Inst., San Francisco, 1965-69; psychiatric social worker Mendocino County Mental Health Dept., Ft. Bragg, Cal., 1969—; pvt. practice, Mendocino, Cal., 1969—. Lectr. in social work U. Cal. Med. Center at San Francisco, 1969—. Founder, chmn. bd. dirs. Health Center of Mendocino Coast; chmn. bd. dirs. North Coast Opportunities, Inc. Mem. Nat. Assn. Social Workers, Acad. Certified Social Workers, Nat. Free Clinic Council. Democrat. Presbyn. Contbr. articles to profl. jours. Home: PO Box 807 Mendocino CA 95460 Office: Route 1 Box 3A Fort Bragg CA 95437

HUDSON, PHOEBE, physician; b. Wilmington, O., Feb. 7, 1922; d. Howard Garner and Georgiana (Barrett) Hudson; B.S., Wilmington Coll., 1944; M.D., Western Res. U., 1948. Intern pediatrics Bellevue Hosp., N.Y.C., 1948-49; intern pediatric pathology Columbia Babies Hosp., N.Y.C., 1949-50, asst. resident, 1951-53; fgn. asst. Hosp. for Sick Children, Paris, France, 1950-51; practice medicine specializing in pediatrics, Westwood, N.J., 1955-65; dir. child Evaluation Center, Hackensack Hosp., Hackensack, N.J., 1965—; mem. staff Hackensack Hosp. Mem. bd. Sch. Spl. Edn., Bergen County, N.J., 1972—. Fellow Am. Acad. Pediatrics (chpt. pres. 1966-67). Office: 251 Atlantic St Hackensack NJ 07601

HUDSON, WILMA JONES (MRS. MARION B. HUDSON), librarian; b. Walnut Grove, Mo., Jan. 29, 1916; d. William Henry and Myrtle Omega (McLemore) Jones; A.B., Drury Coll., 1936; M.A., Washington U., 1937; postgrad. S.W. Mo. State Tchrs'. Coll., 1937, U. Ill., 1941, Butler U., 1966-67; m. Marion B. Hudson, Dec. 25, 1941; children—Jack Alan, Tom Scott, Janet Sue. Tchr., English and speech Edwardsville (Ill.) High Sch., 1937-42; instr. Butler U., Indpls., 1942-43; tchr. English, Shortridge High Sch., Indpls., 1943-47, 63-65, Northview High Sch., 1965-66; librarian, audio visual coordinator Eagle Twp. Elementary Sch., Zionsville, Ind., 1966-68, Zionsville Jr. High Sch., 1968—. Editor, Bobbs-Merrill Co., Indpls., 1959-63. Mem. Ind. Sch. Librarians Assn. (mem. archives com. 1970—, area bd. mem. 1970, 71, 72), Nat. Council Tchrs. English, Mortar Bd., Psi Iota Xi (pres. 1955, v.p. 1956, corr. sec. 1954), Delta Delta Delta. Author: Dwight D. Eisenhower: Young Military Leader, 1970; J.C. Penney: Golden Rule Boy, 1972; Harry S. Truman: Missouri Farm Boy, 1973. Home: 10550 Zionsville Rd Zionsville IN 46077 Office: Zionsville Junior High School 5th and Walnut Sts Zionsville IN 46077

HUEBNER, GERTRUDE VENEKLASEN (MRS. GEORGE J. HUEBNER), univ. regent; b. Cheyenne, Wyo., Jan. 23, 1915; d. Egbert and Anna K. (Mannel) Veneklasen; grad. Grand Rapids Jr. Coll., 1934; A.B. summa cum laude, certificate in Journalism, U. Mich., 1936; m. Louis J. De Lamarter, Jr., Sept. 4, 1940 (div. 1959); children—Louis J. III and Lawrence K. (twins); m. 2d, George J. Huebner, Oct. 7, 1960. Copywriter, Maxon, Inc., Detroit, Chgo., N.Y.C., 1936-65; regent U. Mich., 1966—. Mem. adv. council Internat. Movement for Atlantic Union, 1968—; mem. scholarship com. Oakland U., Rochester, Mich., 1960-65; mem. women's com. United Found., 1962-66. Bd. govs. Mich. League. Recipient Distinguished Alumnus award Grand Rapids Jr. Coll., 1965. Mem. Jr. League Birmingham, Ladies' Aux. Engring. Soc. Detroit, U. Mich. Alumnae Club Birmingham, Detroit Hist. Soc. (dir.), Phi Beta Kappa, Phi Kappa Phi, Theta Sigma Phi. Republican. Clubs: Presidents' (U. Mich.); Detroit Athletic; Bloomfield Open Hunt. Home: 275 Guilford Rd Bloomfield Hills MI 48013

HUEBNER, LILLIAN MAE GROOMS (MRS. WALTER J. HUEBNER), artist, civic worker; b. Ottumwa, Ia.; d. Thomas Ausbury and Clara Jane (Chidester) Grooms; student Lockwood Art Sch., Kalamazoo, 1913-14, Ia. Wesleyan Coll., summers 1915-16, Cummings Sch. Art (Des Moines), 1916-18; m. Walter J. Huebner, Sept. 24, 1913; 1 dau., Gloria Jane. Paintings exhibited Santa Barbara Mus. Fine Art, De Young Mus. Art San Francisco, U. Cal. at Santa Cruz, Oakland Art Mus., fairs, festivals. Chmn. flood control commn., Santa Cruz, 1949-57, City Beautification Commn., 1945-52; pres. Cal. State Council T.T.T., 1956-57, state chpt. pres. 1959-61; area chmn. ann. Madonna Festival, Los Angeles, 1949-53; state dir. Penny Art Program, Gen. Fedn. Women's Clubs, 1950-51. Dir. Santa Cruz Art League, intermittently 1930—, pres. 1950-51, 62-64. Mem. Santa Cruz County Federated Art Club (founder, pres. 1958). Methodist. Mem. Order Eastern Star (past worthy matron), White Shrine of Jerusalem (past worthy high priestess). Club: Santa Cruz Woman's (pres. 1950-51, fine arts chmn. 1963-66). Home: 811 Broadway Santa Cruz CA 95060

HUEBNER, MILDRED HARRIET, educator; b. Buffalo, Dec. 6, 1913; d. Harrington Warner and Gertrude (Weber) Huebner; B.S., Edinboro State Tchrs. Coll., 1939; M.A., Western Res. U., 1947, Ed.D., 1955. Tchr. pub. schs., Girard Twp., Pa., 1937-41, Erie, Pa., 1941-51; asst. prin. various schs., Erie, 1951-53; asst. prof. edn. Western Res. U., Cleve., 1953-59; asso. prof. edn. So. Conn. State Coll., New Haven, 1959-61, prof. edn., 1961—, dir. Reading Center, 1959—, chmn. reading dept., 1971—. Dir. Nat. Def. Edn. Act. Spl. Reading Insts., summers 1965-67. Mem. Internat., N.E. reading assns., N.E.A., Nat. Soc. for Study Edn., Conn. Assn. Reading Research, Am. Assn. U. Women. Author: (with Mary C. Austin and Clifford L. Bush) Reading Evaluation 1961; (with C. L. Bush) Strategies for Reading, 1970. Contbr. articles to profl. jours. Home: 15 Santa Fe Av Hamden CT 06517

HUERTA, VIOLET FRANCES (MRS. ELISEO HUERTA), occupational therapist; b. LaCrosse, Wis., Apr. 10, 1924; d. William John and Edith Estella (Austin) Maas: Registered Occupational Therapist (Elks scholar), U. So. Cal., 1947, B.S., 1956, sch. psychometrist credential, 1956; m. Robert McCarty, Aug. 26, 1948 (div. Mar. 1951); 1 son, Paul; m. 2d, Eliseo Huerta, Dec. 22, 1956; children—Janet, David. Sr. occupational therapist Cal. Dept. Pub. Health, El Monte Cerebral Palsy Sch., 1951-56; chief occupational therapist Physically Handicapped Children's Program, Los Angeles County, 1956-58; pvt. practice occupational therapy, 1965—; occupational therapist El Monte (Cal.) Rehab. Hosp., 1966, Convalescent Hosp., Oakland, Cal., 1967-69; occupational therapist, cons. Three Oaks Hosp., Walnut Creek, Cal., Children's Hosp. and Med. Center, Oakland, Cal., Orinda and Walnut Creek Sch. Dists., 1968-74; occupational therapist, cons., sch. psychometrist Piedmont (Cal.) Sch. Dist., 1969—; occupational therapist, cons. Las Trampas Sch. for Mentally Retarded, Lafayette, Cal., 1969-71; lectr. Cal. Assn. for Neurologically Handicapped Children, 1968—; instr. in learning disabilities and sensory integrative dysfunction Cal. State U., San Jose and Hayward, St. Mary's Coll., Moraga, Cal., U. Hawaii Hilo campus, U. Cal. at Davis and Santa Cruz, 1973—; cons. United Cerebral Palsy projects, 1973—; cons. Alameda County Developmental Center for Retarded, Piedmont, Cal., 1971—, Contra Costa County Schs. Aphasic and Orthopedically Handicapped programs, 1972—. Served as 2d lt. Women's Med. Specialist Corps, U.S. Army Res., 1947-49. Fellow Am. Occupational Therapy Assn. (mem. pres.'s com. 1968-70); mem. No. Cal. Occupational Therapy Assn. (pres. 1968-70), Cal. Assn. for Neurologically Handicapped Children. Home and office: 101 Whitethorne Dr Moraga CA 94556

HUEY, BETTY ANN, ednl. cons.; b. Elizabeth, N.J., July 16, 1946; d. John Eugene and Elizabeth (Telofski) Huey; B.A., Jersey City State Coll., 1968; M.A. (Dept. Health, Edn. and Welfare fellow), Newark State Coll., 1969. Instructional materials coordinator Spl. Edn. Instructional Materials Center, Newark State Coll., Union, N.J., 1970-73; ednl. cons. Union County Day Tng. Center, Scotch Plains, N.J., 1973—. Mem. Am. Assn. Mental Deficiency, Council for Exceptional Children, Jersey City State Coll. Alumni Assn. (homecoming chmn. 1970, 71). Presbyterian (elder 1972—). Home: 27 North Hill Rd Colonia NJ 07067 Office: 1524 Terrill Rd Scotch Plains NJ 07076

HUEY, JOAN MARGARET SILL (MRS. DENNIS MICHAEL HUEY), educator; b. Medina, N.Y., July 12, 1944; d. John Edwin and Melba Aileen (Fuller) Sill; A.B., Wittenberg U., 1966; M.S., Ohio State U., 1968, Ph.D., 1973; m. Dennis Michael Huey, Aug. 20, 1966; children—Brian Michael, Kara Sill. Grad. teaching asst. Ohio State U., Columbus, 1966-68, grad. teaching asso. dept. botany, 1968-72; asst. prof. biology Atlantic Comm. Coll., Mays Landing, N.J., 1972—. Mem. Am. Bryological and Lichen Soc., Mycological Soc. Am., Bot. Soc. Am., Torrey Bot. Club, O. Acad. Sci., N.J. Acad. Sci., Sigma Xi, Sigma Delta Epsilon. Home: 1545 Shore Rd Linwood NJ 08221 Office: Atlantic Comm Coll Black Horse Pike Mays Landing NJ 08330

HUFF, BARBARA A., editor; b. Los Angeles, July 2, 1929; d. Robert H. and Irene Ruth (Lawton) Huff; B.A., U. Cal. at Los Angeles, 1952. With Doubleday & Co., N.Y.C., 1954—, mng. editor Jr. Lit. Guild, 1970—. Vol., Village Green Recycling Team, N.Y.C., 1973—. Contbr. poems to popular mags. Home: 1 Christopher St New York City NY 10014 Office: 245 Park Av New York City NY 10017

HUFF, BARBARA ANNE SIMPSON (MRS. ROGER E. HUFF), educator; b. Rochester, N.Y., May 22, 1947; d. Raymond Reid and Margaret (Wood) Simpson; B.S., State U. Coll. at Brockport, 1970; extension of teaching certificate State U. Coll. at Geneseo, 1972; m. Roger E. Huff, Oct. 9, 1971. Tchr., edn. dir. Gra-Mar Hall, Sch. for

His Spl. Child, Churchville, N.Y., 1966—. Mem. Am. Assn. Mental Deficiency, N.Y. State Assn. Tchrs. Mentally Handicapped. Mem. Nazarene Ch. (ch. sch. bd. 1973—). Home: 4 Elmwood Circle Scottsville NY 14546 Office: 99 S Main St Churchville NY 14428

HUFF, ELIZABETH, physician; b. Louisville, Oct. 2, 1907; d. Harrie L. and Clara L. (Hauser) Huff; B.S., U. Louisville, 1935; M.D., U. Chgo., 1937; postgrad. U. Pa., 1938-39. Gen. intern Saskatoon City Hosp., Can., 1936-37; gen. resident Myers Clinic Hosp., W.Va., 1937-38; resident dermatology Goldwater Hosp., N.Y.C., 1939-40; intern medicine Bellevue Hosp., N.Y.C., 1941-42; resident medicine, asst. in medicine Charity Hosp., New Orleans, 1942-43; resident medicine Queen's Hosp., Honolulu, 1943-44; employees' physician Met. Life Ins. Co., N.Y.C., 1944-46; physician med. out-patient dept. Bronx Vets. Hosp., N.Y.C., 1946-47, resident psychiatry, 1947-50; clin. asst. adult psychiatry Mt. Sinai Hosp., N.Y.C., 1949-51, clin. asst. child psychiatry. 1951-54; asst. psychiatrist Jewish Community Service L.I., N.Y., 1951-56; supervising psychiatrist Adolescent Pavilion Hillside Hosp., L.I., N.Y., 1954-55; supervising psychiatrist in charge Bklyn. Day Hosp., 1955-57; asst. attending child psychiatrist N.Y. State Psychiat. Inst. and Presbyn. Hosp., N.Y.C., 1957-63; instr. child psychiatry Columbia U. Coll. Phys. and Surg., N.Y.C., 1957-63; panel psychiatrist Jewish Family Service, N.Y.C., 1960-63; dir. East Bay Activity Center for Emotionally Disturbed Children, Oakland, Cal., 1964-65; staff mem. Alameda County Mental Health Services, 1967—; cons. Piedmont Schs., 1967-69, Albany Schs., 1967-70, cons. Cath. Schs. of Oakland Diocese, 1968-71, Devel. Center for Handicapped Minors, Oakland Pub. Schs., 1969-70, 28th Dist. P.T.A., Oakland, Cal., 1967-68, East Oakland-Fruitvale Planning Council, 1969-70, Cal. Sch. for Blind, Berkeley, 1970-72; psychiatrist Child Psychiat. Crippled Children Services, Oakland, Cal., 1967—; practice medicine specializing in psychiatry, child psychiatry, N.Y.C., 1950-63, Oakland, 1965—; mem. staff Children's Hosp. Med. Center East Bay, Herrick, Gladman, Highland, Brookdale hosps., Oakland, Diplomate Am. Bd. Internal Medicine, Am. Bd. Psychiatry and Neurology. Mem. A.M.A., Am. Assn. U. Women (area rep. for edn., chmn. com. on edn. 1969-70), Am., No. Cal., East Bay psychiat. assns., Cal. Assn. for Neuro Handicapped Children, Nat. Soc. Autistic Children, Alameda County Med. Assn. (mem. child welfare com. 1969—). Home: 4816 Gordon St Oakland CA 94601 Office: 2628 26th Av Oakland CA 94601

HUFF, MARGARET JOAN FARRIS (MRS. FRANK ROUSE HUFF), librarian; b. Danville, Ky., Oct. 23, 1925; d. Maurice Joseph and Irene Drixcoll (Kennedy) Farris; student Mary Baldwin Coll., 1943-45; A.B., U. N.C., 1947, B.S. in L.S., 1948; m. Frank Rouse Huff, Nov. 7, 1948; children—Frank Rouse, Tom, Anne. Asst. librarian VA Hosp., Columbia, S.C., 1948-49; high sch. tchr. Cameron (S.C.) High Sch., 1960-63: asst. librarian Calhoun County Pub. Library, St. Matthews, 1967-68; librarian Orangeburg-Calhoun Tech. Edn. Center, Orangeburg, S.C., 1968—. Active A.R.C. youth group. Mem. Am., Southeastern, S.C. library assns., Phi Beta Kappa, Alpha Delta Pi. Home: 111 Dantzler Av St Matthews SC 29135 Office: PO Drawer 1767 Orangeburg SC 29115

HUFFMAN, EDITH DEETTE (MRS. RICHARD E. HUFFMAN), occupational therapist; b. Jamestown, N.Y., Dec. 24, 1922; d. Allan William and Lillian Ethel (Middleton) Firth; B.S. in Occupational Therapy, U. Kan., 1963; M.Ed. in Ednl. Psychology, Wichita State U., 1973; m. Richard E. Huffman, June 28, 1968; children by previous marriage—Stephen R. Page, Lynne D. (Mrs. Michael J. Worthington), Thomas R. Page, Deborah Louise Page. Dir. occupational therapy Capper Found. for Crippled Children, Topeka, 1963-66, Wesley Med. Center, Wichita, Kan., 1966—. Cons., Elks Job Tng. Center, Wichita, 1971, N.E. Nursing Center, Wichita, 1972. Vol. probation officer Sedgwick County (Kan.) Juvenile Ct., 1972—. Bd. dirs. Kan. Health Consortium, 1972. Mem. Am., Kan. (alternate del. 1973) occupational therapy assns., Am. Assn. Univ. Women, Nat. Rehab. Assn., Am. Pub. Health Assn., Kan. U. Alumni Assn., Wichita State U. Alumni Assn., Fairfield Bay Community Club. Office: 550 N Hillside St Wichita KS 67214

HUFFMAN, PHYLLIS JEAN, pediatric allergist; b. Aberdeen, S.D., Apr. 1, 1925; d. R. Earl and Ione Swartz (Gilkey) Huffman; student U. Minn., 1943; B.A., U. S.D., 1947; M.D., Southwestern Med. Sch. U. Tex., 1953; M.S., U. Colo., 1957. Intern, Colo. Gen. Hosp., Denver, 1953-54; resident pediatrics U. Colo. Med. Center, Denver, 1954-57, chief resident, 1957, postdoctoral fellow in pediatric allergy and immunology, 1966-68; practice medicine specializing in pediatrics, Midland, Tex., 1958-66, pediatric allergy, 1968—; chief respiratory care unit Midland Meml. Hosp., 1968—; mem. staff Parkview Hosp., Midland; courtesy staff Odessa (Tex.) Med. Center Hosp.; asso. clin. prof. pediatrics Tex. Technol. U. Sch. Medicine, Lubbock. Bd. dirs. Midland Tb Assn., High Sky Girls' Ranch; trustee community Day Center. Fellow Am. Acad. Pediatrics (pediatric allergy sub-bd.); mem. Am. Assn. Certified Allergists, Am. Heart Assn. (cardiopulmonary council), Am. Acad. Allergy, Am. Coll. Allergy, Tex. Med. Assn., Am. Med. Soc., Tex. Pediatric Soc., Midland C. of C. (chmn. div. health), Pi Beta Phi. Republican. Presbyn. Home: 1504 Humble Av Midland TX 79701 Office: 606 Kent St Midland TX 79701

HUFFORD, MARY ANN UNCAPHER (MRS. PAUL WILLIAM HUFFORD, JR.), speech therapist; b. Blairsville, Pa., Dec. 18, 1943; d. Chester Paul and Lillian Doris (Ondrizek) Uncapher; B.S. in Speech Pathology and Audiology, Ind. U. Pa., 1967, M.Ed. in Speech Pathology and Audiology, 1971; m. Paul William Hufford, Jr., Dec. 2, 1967. With Cresson (Pa.) State Sch., 1967—, dir. Speech and Hearing Clinic, 1971—. Sec. Cresson (Pa.) Improvement Assn., 1972. Mem. Cresson Area Jaycettes (pres. 1972-73), Pa. Speech and Hearing Assn., Am. Assn. Mental Deficiency, Cresson State Sch. Assn., Kappa Delta Pi, Sigma Alpha Eta. Home: 144 Summer St Cresson PA 16630 Office: Cresson State Sch Cresson PA 16630

HUFFSTUTLER, JOAN BURNS (MRS. JAMES KENO HUFFSTUTLER), state ofcl.; b. Lincoln, Ala., Nov. 2, 1929; d. Harry Clay and Maudie (Phillips) Burns; B.A., U. Ala., 1951; m. James Keno Huffstutler, Apr. 27, 1952; children—Angela Joan, James Keno, Jr., Shannon Burns. Social worker St. Clair County (Ala.) Dept. Pensions and Security, 1951-52; mem. Ala. State Bd. Pensions and Security, Montgomery, 1968—, Licensure Adv. Bd. Ala., 1972—. Exec. dir. Planned Parenthood Assn., Mobile, Ala., 1970-71; health edn. cons. Mobile County Bd. Health, 1971; vol. adviser Nat. Found., March of Dimes, 1964—; co-founder Federated Jr. Woman's Club, Mobile, 1965; pres. Art Patron's League, Mobile, 1968-69; mem. Florence Crittenton Sr. Bd., 1972—. Bd. dirs. Mobile Art Gallery, 1968-72. Recipient M.O. Beale Scroll of Merit, Mobile Press Register, 1966; Ala. Sesquicentennial award State Ala., 1969; Recognition award Mobile Med. Soc., 1962; citation Ala. Fedn. Women's Clubs, 1966; named Club Woman of Year, Mobile, 1968; Beautiful Activist, Ala. Jr. C. of C., 1974. Mem. Am. Assn. U. Women (sec. 1956-57); Mobile Jaycettes, Colonial Dames XVII Century, Mobile Opera Guild Aux., Ala. Pub. Health Assn. Episcopalian. Home: 54 Kingswood Dr West Mobile AL 36608

HUFFSTUTTER, MARY IMOGENE (MRS. WHITE ELMORE HUFFSTUTTER), librarian; b. Trenton, Tenn., Nov. 26, 1914; d. Joseph Daniel and Jessie Delaney (Moore) Smith; A.B., Union U., 1932; M.A., George Peabody Coll., 1936, B.S. in Library Sci., 1941; m. White Elmore Huffstutter, Jan. 30, 1949; children—Paul James, William Maurice, Joseph Eugene. Elementary sch. tchr. Dyer County, Tenn., 1932-39; tchr., librarian Newbern (Tenn.) Grammar Sch., 1939-46; librarian Newbern City Schs., 1946-49, 54-55; librarian Dyersburg (Tenn.) High Sch., 1959—. Mem. Nat., Tenn., West Tenn., Dyersburg edn. assns., Am., Tenn., West Tenn., Southeastern library assns., Pi Gamma Mu, Alpha Delta Kappa. Mem. Ch. of Christ. Contbr. articles in field to profl. jours. Home: 5015 Ditmore Rd Newbern TN 38059 Office: Hwy 51 By-Pass Dyersburg TN 38024

HUFLER, DOROTHY RUTH, nurse, educator; b. Cleve., Mar. 1, 1931; d. Edmund S. and Florence (Affolter) Hufler; R.N., St. Alexis Sch. Nursing, Cleve., 1952; postgrad. Marymount Coll., Salina, Kan., 1956, U. Md., 1957-58; B.S., St. Louis U., 1960; M.S., U. Colo., 1964. Staff nurse St. Alexis Hosp., 1952-53; indsl. nurse Ford Motor Co., Canton, O., 1953-55; staff nurse to supr. USAF, 1955-59; nursing instr. St. Mary's Sch. Nursing, Galveston, Tex., 1960-61; unit supr., house supr. Santa Rosa Hosp., San Antonio, 1961-62; nursing instr. St. Joseph's Sch. Nursing, Denver, 1963; asst. prof. nursing Catherine Spalding Coll., Louisville, 1964-68; asst. prof. nursing U. Akron, O., 1969-70; asst. prof. nursing, sect. chmn. St. Louis U., 1970-71; asso. dir. nursing, clin. specialist Incarnate Word Hosp., St. Louis, 1971-73; clin. specialist coordinator Aultman Hosp., Canton, O., 1973—. Asst. A.B.C. Program, Louisville, 1967-68; adviser Med. Explorer Program. Mem. Am. Nurses Assn. (chmn. dist. edn. com.), Nat. League for Nursing, Am. Assn. U. Profs. (past chpt. sec.). Democrat. Roman Catholic. Home: 3217 9th St NW Canton OH 44708

HUFSTEDLER, SHIRLEY MOUNT (MRS. SETH M. HUFSTEDLER), judge; b. Denver, Aug. 24, 1925; d. Earl Stanley and Eva (Von Behren) Mount; B.B.A., U. N.M., 1945; LL.B., Stanford U., 1949; LL.D., U. Wyo., 1970, Gonzaga U., 1970, Occidental Coll., 1971, U. N.M., 1972, Tufts U., 1974; m. Seth Martin Hufstedler, Aug. 16, 1949; 1 son, Steven Mark. Admitted to Cal. bar, 1950, pvt. practice Los Angeles, 1961; mem. firm of Beardsley, Hufstedler & Kemble, Los Angeles, 1951-61; mem. staff Stanford Law Rev., 1947-49, article and book rev. editor, 1948-49, judge Superior Ct., County Los Angeles, 1961-66; justice Cal. Ct. Appeal 2nd dist., 1966-68; circuit judge U.S. Ct. Appeals, 9th Circuit, 1968—. Mem. Adv. Council Appellate Justice. Bd. councilors Law Center U. So. Cal. Trustee Inst. for Ct. Mgmt., Occidental Coll., Aspen Inst. Humanistic Studies. Named Woman of Year, Los Angeles Times, 1968. Mem. Am., Los Angeles bar assns., Women Lawyers Assn. (pres. 1957-58), Am. Judicature Soc., Am. Law Inst., Inst. Jud. Adminstrn., Town Hall, Order of Coif. Home: 720 W Inverness Dr Pasadena CA 91103 Office: US Ct House 312 N Spring St Los Angeles CA 90012

HUGHES, ANITA LILLIAN, educator; b. French Lick, Ind., Feb. 16, 1938; d. George Thomas Taggart and Sysomby (Willis) Hughes, Sr.; student (honor scholar) Drake U., 1955-56; B.S., Ind. U., 1959, M.S., 1961, Ed.D., 1967. Tchr. sci., English, Lincoln High Sch., Evansville, Ind., 1959-60; grad. asst., grad. counselor edn. dept. Ind. U., Bloomington, 1961-63, asst. dir. counseling services Northwest campus, Gary, 1963-66, counselor Counseling Center, Bloomington, 1966-67; asst. prof. edn., sr. counselor Howard U., 1967-68; mem. faculty Fed. City Coll., Washington, 1968—, prof. counseling psychology, chmn. dept., 1969—, dean Grad. Sch., 1970-73. Cons. U.S. Dept. Health Edn. and Welfare, 1969—, Social Invervention Systems, 1969-70, Indian Health Service, 1971-72, Nat. Inst. Edn., 1973—; sensitivity trainer Urban Tchr. Corp., 1969-70, Annapolis (Md.) High Sch. staff, 1969-70; Adviser health welfare council Neighborhood Youth Corp., 1968-69; mem. lectr. U. Md. Grad. Sch., 1973—. city-wide testing com. Washington (D.C.) Pub. Schs., 1969-70. Trustee Inst. Ednl. Mgmt., Harvard. Recipient Outstanding Educator's award Fed. City Coll. Student Govt. Assn., 1973. Mem. Am. Coll. Personnel Assn. (membership chmn. D.C., mem. nat. membership com., mem. task force on minority recruiting and acad. model devel. 1971—), Black Psychologists, Am. Personnel and Guidance Assn. (archivist 1970—), Council Adminstrv. Women in Edn., Assn. Counselor Edn. and Supervision, Assn. Non-White Concerns, Pi Lambda Theta. Contbr. articles to profl. publs. Mailing Address: 1250 4th St SW Washington DC 20024 Address: Fed City Coll 724 9th St NW Washington DC 20001

HUGHES, ANN HANSZEN (MRS. JOHN KINROSS-WRIGHT), physician; b. Dallas, Sept. 3, 1929; d. Eugene and Gillie May (Whitman) Hanszen; B.A., So. Meth. U., 1955; M.D., U. Tex. Southwestern Med. Sch., 1959; m. John Kinross-Wright, July 2, 1971; children—Robert Hughes, Ann Louise Hughes. Intern Baylor Med. Center, Dallas, 1959-60; resident in psychiatry Timberlawn Psychiat. Center, Dallas, 1960-62; practice medicine specializing in psychiatry, Dallas, 1964-69; mem. staff Parkland Meml. Hosp., Children's Med. Center; asst. prof. child psychiatry U. Tex. Southwestern Med. Sch., 1964—, dir. Childrens Psychiat. Clinic, 1966-69; dir. child and adolescent programs Tex. Dept. Mental Health and Mental Retardation, Austin, 1969-71; clin. dir. Central Brazos Valley Mental Health Center, 1972—, Discovery Land, Inc., 1972—. Cons. child welfare Hope Cottage Childrens Bur., Shadybrook Sch. Trustee, Ednl. Opportunities, Inc.; dir. Dallas United Community Center, Dallas Assn. Mental Health, Parents without Partners. Diplomate Am. Bd. Neurology and Psychiatry. Mem. A.M.A., Tex., Dallas County med. socs., Tex. Psychiatry Soc., Am. Psychiatric Assn., Tex. Soc. Child Psychiatry, Am. Acad. Child Psychiatry, Pi Beta Phi, Psi Chi, Alpha Epsilon Iota. Address: PO Box 813 Bryan TX 77801

HUGHES, ANNE FINKS, occupational therapy adminstr.; b. San Angelo, Tex., Aug. 8, 1934; d. Robert M. and Mary Elizabeth (Huffman) Finks; student Tex. Tech. U., 1953-54, So. Meth. U., 1959-60; m. William Jerome Hughes, Apr. 14, 1970; children by previous marriage—Elizabeth Anne, Randal Lee and Robert Donald Roberson. Dir. programs YMCA, San Angelo, 1967-71; exec. dir. Chimney House, BMH Prodns., 1972—; dir. occupational therapy dept. San Angelo Center, Tex. Mental Health and Mental Retardation Div., 1972—. Bd. dirs. San Angelo Civic Theatre, 1973—, sec., 1973-74. Mem. Tex. Pub. Employees Assn. (chpt. pres. 1973—, pres. regional council 1974—, sec.-treas. 1973-74). Home: 2609 Hemlock Dr San Angelo TX 76901 Office: San Angelo Center Carlsbad TX 76901

HUGHES, BARBARA JEAN SCHINDLER (MRS. ROBERT JAMES HUGHES), civic worker; b. Syracuse, N.Y., May 18, 1932; d. Clarence M. and Mary G. (Argersinger) Schindler; B.S., St. Mary's Coll., 1954; M.S., Syracuse U., 1958; m. Robert James Hughes, Sept. 11, 1964; children—John Christopher, William Patrick; stepchildren—Catherine Jankowsky, Robert James, Daniel, Joseph, Ellen. Bus. office rep. N.Y. Telephone Co., Syracuse, 1954-58; tchr. 5th grade Chittenango (N.Y.) Central Sch., 1958-62, guidance counselor, 1962-65. Mem. St. Joseph Hosp. Aux., Syracuse, 1964—. Recipient Cotter Cup award St. Mary's Coll., 1960. Club: Twins and Triplets (Syracuse). Home: 605 Lake St Chittenango NY 13037

HUGHES, CAROLINE ERICKSON (MRS. HUGH ROBERT HUGHES), civic worker; b. Drumright, Okla.; d. Christian Conrad and Caroline (Prewett) Erickson; student Blue Mountain Coll., 1937-39; B.S., Okla. State U., 1943; student U. Miss., summer 1943, Okla. State U., 1960; m. Hugh Robert Hughes, Oct. 19, 1941; 1 dau., Christine Louise. Tchr. Cushing (Okla.) High Sch., 1943-46; now cons. career edn. and vocational guidance. Mem. Bd. Edn., Cushing, Okla., 1961-66, pres. bd., 1964; mem. bd. edn. Central Okla. Area Vocational-Tech. Sch., 1967—, clk., bd. edn., 1967—, mem. nat. adv. commn. criminal justice, standards and goals, nat. adv. council vocational edn.; mem. Okla. Adv. Council on Vocational Edn., 1969—, chmn., 1969-70, sec., mem. exec. bd., 1971—. Mem. D.A.R. (state chmn. D.A.R. schs. 1966-68), C. of C. (dir. 1968), Pi Beta Phi (province pres. 1967-71. Presbyn. (elder 1962—). Clubs: Cushing Country, Womens Golf Assn., Geographic (pres. 1961-63). Home: 1000 S Howerton St Cushing OK 74023

HUGHES, CAROLYN SUE, ednl. cons.; b. Peoria, Ill., Mar. 20, 1938; d. Eldon Eugene and Bernadine Vivian (Thompson) Houghton; B.S., Miami U., Oxford, O., 1961, M.Ed., 1964; Ph.D., Kent State U., 1971; student Ohio State U., 1956, 57, Lincoln (Ill.) Christian Coll., 1956-58, U. Ill., 1958-60; m. J. Edward Hughes, Nov. 29, 1957; children—Laura Beth, Ronald, Lisa Kay. Tchr., Dayton, O., 1961, Eaton, O., 1962-63, Wooster, O., 1967-68; asst. prof., co-ordinator grad. reading program Youngstown State U., 1971-73; elementary cons. Parma (O.) City Schs., 1973—. Program chmn. P.T.A., 1970-71; leader Girl Scouts, 1971-73. Mem. Am. Assn. U. Women, League Women Voters (dir. Wooster 1965-67, publs. chmn. 1967-68), Assn. Supervision and Curriculum Devel., Internat. Reading Assn., Ohio Assn. Supervision and Curriculum Devel. (treas. 1973-74), Nat. Soc. Study Edn., Delta Kappa Gamma, Phi Kappa Phi. Mem. Christian Ch. (Bible sch. and camp tchr.). Home: 9705 Boundary Lane Parma OH 44130 Office: 6726 Ridge Rd Parma OH 44129

HUGHES, CATHERINE WERNER (MRS. THOMAS PATRICK HUGHES), librarian; b. N.Y.C., Apr. 12, 1920; d. Joseph George and Adelaide Theresa (Collins) Werner; B.S. in Edn., Fordham U., 1941; M.S. in L.S., Simmons Coll., 1967; m. Thomas Patrick Hughes, Sept. 16, 1940; children—Justin, Christine, Gregory. Library asst. Raytheon Co., Wayland, Mass., 1961-64; dir. library Framingham (Mass.) Union Hosp., 1967—. Mem.faculty New Eng. Regional Med. Library Service, 1973-74, mem. adv. com., 1973-75. Mem. Spl. Libraries Assn., New Eng. Library Assn. (treas. hosp. sect. 1973-74, chmn. nominating com. hosp. sect. 1971-73). Home: 87 Glen Rd Wellesley Hills MA 02181 Office: Framingham Union Hospital Framingham MA 01701

HUGHES, CLAIRE FINUCANE (MRS. MICHAEL J. HUGHES), pub. co. exec.; b. N.Y.C., May 6, 1920; d. Peter and Mary Ellen (Brew) Finucane; student Katharine Gibbs Sch., 1938, Fordham U., 1940-41, N.Y. U., 1945-46; m. Michael J. Hughes, June 28, 1947; children—Michael III, June Ellen. Women's editor Screen Guide, Movie-Radio Guide and Stardom, 1941-43; Women's editor Screenland, Silver Screen, Movie Show, 1945-48; asso. editor Levittown Eagle, 1951-54; editor, Harrison Independent, 1962-72; adminstrv. asst. to pub. Rutledge Books, N.Y.C., 1973—; free lance writer for trade and realty publs., fiction. Pub. information officer Eastchester Civil Def., 1969-74. Home: 2 Huntley Rd Eastchester NY 10707 Office: 25 W 43d St New York City NY 10036

HUGHES, ELINOR L(AMBERT), drama editor, critic; b. Cambridge, Mass., Mar. 3, 1906; d. Hector James and Elinor (Lambert) H.; ed. Buckingham Sch., Cambridge, 1915-20; May Sch., Boston, 1920-23; A.B., Radcliffe Coll., 1927; m. David D. Jacobus, July 14, 1957; stepchildren—David P. Jacobus, John H. Jacobus. Asst. in drama dept. Boston Herald-Traveler, 1929-34, drama and film editor and critic, 1934-66; lectr. on drama and film criticism. Mem. Soc. Preservation N.E. Antiquities, Inst. Contemporary Art. Republican. Unitarian. Clubs: Women's City (Boston). Author: Famous Stars of Filmdom (Men) and Famous Stars of Filmdom (Women), 1932, Passing Through to Broadway, 1948. Blank verse rev. of Shakespearean prodns. included in Best News Stories of 1937-38, article on Gielgud's Hamlet included in Hamlet, Enter Critic, 1960. Home: 24 Academy Lane Bellport NY 11713

HUGHES, GERALDINE (MRS. ROBERT DEAN HUGHES), real estate broker; b. Pella, Ia., Mar. 16, 1931; d. Bert and Hilda (De Cook) Van Haaften; student pub. schs., Pella; m. Robert Dean Hughes, Dec. 20, 1951; children—Douglas Craig, Thomas Lee. Bookkeeper, office mgr. Farmer's Union Co-op., Pella, 1948-51; teller Bank of Am., Upland, Ontario and Cucamonga, Cal., 1953-55, 56-58; real estate salesman, Upland, 1960—, broker, 1963—. Mem. budget com. United Fund, 1971-72; patroness Assistance League of Upland, 1971-73. Mem. Ontario-Upland-Chino Bd. Realtors (activities chmn. 1969, dir. 1970-71, ticket chmn. 1972-73, pres. women's council 1971, membership chmn. 1971; Salesman award 1972), Cal., Nat. real estate assns. Baptist (mem. stewardship com., chmn. and financial sec.). Home: 9548 Carrillo St Montclair CA 91763 Office: 732 N Mountain St Upland CA 91786

HUGHES, HELEN MARION (MRS. LESTER H. EMPEY), concrete co. exec.; b. Oakland, Cal., July 25, 1910; d. Robert Henry and Marion (Paschold) Hughes; B.A., U. Cal., 1932; m. Lester H. Empey, Jan. 27, 1934; children—Peter Hughes, Michael Robert. Dir. Pacific Ready-Mix, Inc., San Mateo, Cal., 1949—. Mem. Pro-Am.; pres. San Mateo City Panhellenic, 1951. Mem. friendly vis. adv. bd. dirs. Assistance League San Mateo County, 1960—, sec. 1965, vice chmn. 1966, chmn. 1967; bd. dirs. Assistance League San Mateo County, 1958-70, pres. 1960-61; bd. dirs. Hillbarn Theatre League, 1967-72, pres., 1968. Mem. Alpha Chi Omega. Home: 734 Parrott Dr San Mateo CA 94402 Office: Pacific Ready-Mix Inc 850 San Mateo Dr San Mateo CA 94401

HUGHES, INEZ HATLEY (MRS. SOLON GREENE HUGHES), museum ofcl.; b. Halleville, Tex., Jan. 29, 1903; s. Tapley Bynum and Daisy (McPherson) Hatley; A.A., Coll. Marshall, 1921; B.A., Baylor U., 1924; M.A., U. Tex., 1936; m. Solon Greene Hughes, Aug. 1, 1939. Tchr. elementary sch., Terlingua, Tex., 1921-23; tchr. high sch. English, Karnes City, Tex., 1924-27, Marshall (Tex.) High Sch., 1927-64; tchr. Coll. Marshall, summer 1933, Sul Ross State Coll., Alpine, Tex., summer 1938; dir. Harrison County Hist. Mus., Marshall, 1967—. Mem. Harrison County Hist. Survey Com., Tex. Hist. Commn. Mem. Am. Assn. U. Women, Soc. S.W. Archivists (charter), Tex. Geneal. Soc., Nat. Geneal. Soc., Nat. Trust for Historic Preservation, Tex. Hist. Assn., East Tex., Harrison County (1st v.p. 1964-67, 2d v.p. 1967—) hist. socs., Delta Kappa Gamma. Home: PO Box 23 Marshall TX 75670 Office: Peter Whetstone Square Marshall TX 75670

HUGHES, JOAN KIRKBY (MRS. WILLIAM E. HUGHES), author; b. Chgo., May 14, 1936; d. Raymond J. and Eleanor C. (Horsey) Kirkby; B.A., U. Cal. at Los Angeles, 1959; m. William E. Hughes, Feb. 15, 1964; children—John William, Jennifer Lynn. Asst. editor Woodland Hills Reporter, 1959-61; tchr., Las Virgenes Unified Sch. Dist., 1961-62; programmer, Bunker Rand Corp., Canoga Park, Cal., 1962-65; systems engr. IBM, 1965-70. Cons., IBM, 1970—, Gen. Telephone and Electric Data Services, 1973. Mem. community adv.

bd. Citrus Coll., Azusa, Cal., 1970-73, Pierce Coll., Woodland Hills, Cal., 1971-72; conf. leader Indsl. Relations Center, Cal. Inst. Tech., Pasadena, 1973—. Mem. Los Angeles Women's C. of C., Theta Sigma Phi. Author: Programming the IBM, 1969; PL/I Programming, 1973. Home: 13906 Wyandotte St Van Nuys CA 91405

HUGHES, JOSEPHINE ANN (MRS. JOHN C. HUGHES), ednl. adminstr.; b. Leavenworth, Kan.; d. John L. and Elsie Elizabeth (Watson) Hamilton; student Ryan Sch. Bus., 1936-37, Huff Bus. Coll., 1941-42, U. Kansas City, 1947-48; U. Mo., 1963-65, U. Neb., 1966; m. John C. Hughes, Mar. 15, 1941. Asst. and office mgr. T.J. Boone, Leavenworth, 1937-41; civil service auditor U.S. Army, Kansas City, Mo., 1942-46; bus. mgr. Kansas City Art Inst., Kansas City, Mo., 1948-70, v.p. finance, 1970—. Mem. Nat., Central assns. coll. and u. bus. officers, Union Ind. Colls. Art, Kansas City Regional Council Higher Edn., Women's C. of C., Am. Bus. Women's Assn., Altrusa, Lambda Tau Delta (pres. Delta Pi chpt. 1971-72, first v.p. Kansas City br. 1972-74, pres. 1974-76, chmn. philanthropic com. Kansas City br. 1972-74). Presbyn. Home: 8503 Overhill Rd Leawood KS 66206 Office: 4415 Warwick Blvd Kansas City MO 64111

HUGHES, JOYCE A., lawyer, educator; b. Gadsden, Ala., Feb. 7, 1940; d. Solomon and Bessie (Cunningham) Hughes; B.A. magna cum laude, Carleton Coll., 1961; postgrad. (Fulbright scholar), U. Madrid, 1961-62; J.D. cum laude (John Hay Whitney fellow) U. Minn., 1965. Admitted to Minn bar, 1965; law clk. to U.S. dist. judge, Mpls., 1965-67; asso. firm Howard, Lefevere, Lefler, Hamilton & Pearson, Mpls., 1967-71; cons. Auerbach Corp., Phila., 1970-71, Peterson & Holtze, attys., Mpls., 1971—, Ford Found., 1972; asso. prof. law U. Minn., Mpls., 1971—. Dir. Community Electronics Corp., Mpls, 1st Plymouth Nat. Bank, Mpls. Mayor's rep. Mpls. Com. on Urban Environment, 1968-69; mem. Minn. Selective Service Appeal Bd., 1971-72, Minn. Constl. Study Commn., 1971—; mem. com. to rev. Afro-Am. studies dept. Harvard, 1971—. Bd. dirs. Legal Aid Soc. Mpls., Girl Scouts U.S.A., N.Y.C.; trustee Carleton Coll., Nat. Urban League, N.Y.C. Named Outstanding Young Woman of Am., 1967, 70; recipient Alumni Achievement award Carleton Coll., 1969, Achievement award Minn. Afro-Am. Lawyers, 1972; Community Service award Miss Black Minn. pageant, 1972. Mem. Nat. (law profs. sect.), Minn. (housing and urban devel. law com.), Hennepin County (pub. relations com.) bar assns., Nat. Conf. Black Lawyers, Am. Judicature Soc., Minn. Civil Liberties Union, Jr. League Mpls., Order of Coif, Phi Beta Kappa. Office: Fraser Hall University Minn Law Sch Minneapolis MN 55455

HUGHES, LEAH STAPLES (MRS. FRANK M. HUGHES), librarian; b. Roopville, Ga., Feb. 28, 1911; d. Pelham Porter and Ola Idella (McDonald) Staples; A.B. in Edn., W. Ga. Coll., 1929; certificate in piano, Atlanta Conservatory Music, 1935; M.L.S., Emory U., 1962; m. Frank Monroe Hughes, June 8, 1935; children—Emily (Mrs. Roy B. Campbell), Frank Monroe, Staples Stilwell. Tchr. history, English and French secondary schs., Carroll, Paulding and Gwinnett Counties (all Ga.), 1931-37, Cook County, Ga., 1956-58; librarian Cook County secondary sch., 1943, Campbell High Sch., Fairburn, Ga., 1958-59, Lakeshore High Sch., College Park, Ga., 1959—. Mem. Lakeshore Library Club (dir. 1960—), Ga. Assn. Library Assts. (sponsor finance com. 1966—), Ga. Assn. Educators, Ga. Library Assn., Delta Kappa Gamma. Baptist (tchr. Sunday Sch. 1948—; youth leader missionary edn. 1940—). Home: 2619 Colonial Dr College Park GA 30337 Office: 2134 Lakeshore Dr College Park GA 30337

HUGHES, MAMIE CURRIE (MRS. LEONARD SHERMAN HUGHES, JR.), county legislator; b. Jacksonville, Fla., May 3, 1929; d. James Samuel and Amy Ramsey (Stewart) Currie; B.A., Fisk U., 1949; m. Leonard Sherman Hughes, Jr., Sept. 1, 1949; children—Leonard Sherman III, Kevin Samuel, Stefan Christopher, Patrick Shawn, Amy Evalen. Tchr. pub. schs., Kansas City, Mo., 1951-52, 57-62, Washington County (Miss.) Pub. Sch., 1954-55; mem. County (Mo.) Legislature, 1973—. Mem. Freedom Inc., Jack and Jill Am., Links. Democrat. Roman Catholic. Home: 1763 Woodland St Kansas City MO 64108 Office: 415 E 12th St Kansas City MO 64106

HUGHES MARCIA GOLD, psychiatrist; b. Chgo., Dec. 8, 1925; d. Morris Aaron and Esther (Yampolsky) Gold; B.S., U. Chgo., 1946, M.D., 1951; m. Robert James Hughes, Jan. 25, 1955 (div. Apr. 1963); children—Robert James, William Morris; m. 2d, George W. Farrell, June 11, 1971 (div. 1974). Rotating intern Michael Reese Hosp., Chgo., 1951-52; tng. adult and child psychiatry U. Ill. and Inst. for Juvenile Research, 1952-59; practice medicine specializing in child and adult psychiatry, Chgo., 1955-59, 63—, Crystal Lake, Ill., 1971—; staff Devereaux Sch., Santa Barbara, Cal., 1961, Cassel Hosp., Kingston-on-Thames, Eng., 1962-63; asst. clin. prof. Northwestern U., Chgo., 1963-65; asst. prof. U. Ill. at Chgo., 1965—; supr. Ill. State Psychiat. Inst., Chgo., 1963-68; coordinator, supr. group psychotherapy Rush-Presbyn.-St. Luke's Med. Center, Chgo., 1968-71; mem. staff McHenry Mental Health Center, McHenry, Ill., McHenry Hosp. Mem. Ill. Legislative Commn. on Sex Edn., 1970-71; mem. com. on sex. edn. Ill. Dept. Edn., 1971—. Diplomate Am. Bd. Psychiatry and Neurology. Mem. A.M.A., Am. Psychiat. Assn., Ill. Psychiat. Soc., Chgo. Psychiat. Soc. for Adolescents, Chgo. Council Child Psychiatry, McHenry County Med. Soc. Home: 2080 Broadway Crystal Lake IL 60014

HUGHES, MARGARET CYRENA, assn. exec.; b. Springfield, Ill.; d. Thomas Patrick and Elizabeth (Donelan) Hughes; student Springfield Jr. Coll., U. Ill. Campaign chmn. Community Fund Assn., 1947-51; exec. dir. Sangamon County Tb Assn., Springfield, 1951-70; exec. dir. Lincoln Land Tb and Respiratory Disease Assn., 1970—. Pres. Friends of Library, 1956. Exec. com. Sangamon County Council Social Agys., 1940-41; pres. Ill. State Assn. Women's Divs. Chambers of Commerce; bd. dirs., past sec. Springfield Safety Council; bd. dirs. Sangamon County Mental Health, 1948-53; Cath. adv. com. Girl Scouts, 1946-51, nat. resettlement adv. com. 1948-53; bd. dirs. St. John's Sanitorium Aux. Recipient Pro Ecclesia at Pontifice medal. Mem. Assn. Commerce and Industry (pres. women's div. 1961-62), Ill. C. of C. (v.p. women's div.), Ill. Conf. Tb Workers (pres. 1961-62), Dioceasen Council Cath. Women (past pres.; dir.), Nat. Council Cath. Women (past provincial dir.; chmn. youth com. 1944-51), Louise de Marillac Guild, Sacred Heart Acad. Alumni Assn. (past pres.), Cathedral Altar Soc. (pres. 1956-57). Clubs: Zonta (pres. Springfield 1962, area dist. dir. 1963-64); Cotarle (dir. 1943-44); Springfield Women's (dir., chmn. safety com., v.p. 1971—, pres. 1973-75). Home: 417 E Canedy St Springfield IL 62703 Office: 325 S New St Springfield IL 62704

HUGHES, MARGARET ELIZABETH, librarian; b. Grimsby, Ont., Can., June 22, 1911; d. Robert Henry and Elizabeth Emily (VanBuskirk) Hughes; came to U.S., 1937, naturalized, 1942; B.S., U. Minn., 1935. Faculty, U. Ore. Med. Sch., Portland, 1937—, prof., librarian, 1965—. Bd. dirs. Good Samaritan Hosp., Portland, Ore., 1973—. Mem. Am. Assn. U. Women, Portland Acad. Medicine (hon.), Am., Pacific N.W., Ore., Med. (dir. 1972—), Spl. (chmn. biol. scis. div. 1959-60) library assns. Club: University (Portland). Home: 1070 SW Gaines St Portland OR 97201 Office: 3181 SW Sam Jackson Park Rd Portland OR 97201

HUGHES, MARIJA MATICH, law librarian; b. Belgrade, Yugoslavia, Oct. 2, 1939; d. Zarija and Antonija (Hudowsky) Matich; B.A. in Music, Mokranjac, Belgrade, 1960; B.A. in English, U. Belgrade and Cal. State U. Sacramento, 1967; M.L.S., U. Md., 1968; student McGeorge Sch. Law, 1968-69. Counselor, gen. mgr. Career Counselling Service, Sacramento, 1963-64; sec. to mgr. Sacramento State Coll. Food Service, 1965-66; student librarian "High John", program U. Md., Fairmont Heights, 1967-68; reference librarian Cal. State Law Library, Sacramento, 1968-69; head reference, library-faculty liaison librarian Hastings Coll. Law U. Cal at San Francisco, 1969-72; head law librarian Am. Tel. & Tel. Corp., Washington, 1972-73; chief law librarian Nat. Clearinghouse Library, U.S. Commn. on Civil Rights, Washington, 1973—. Mem. Assn. Am. Law Libraries, A.L.A., Nat. Women's Polit. Caucas, Federally Employed Women, Profl. Women's Caucus, Soc. for Internat. Devel., Advs. for Women (dir. 1972), Spl. Libraries Assn., Assn. Internat. Law Libraries, Women in Legal Edn., Nat. Orgn. Women, Women's Equity Action League (sec.). Author, compiler: The Sexual Barrier: Legal and Economic Aspects of Employment, 1970-73. Contbr. articles to profl. jours. Home: 2116 F St NW Apt 702 Washington DC 20037 Office: Nat Clearinghouse Library US Commn on Civil Rights 1121 Vermont Av NW Washington DC 20425

HUGHES, MARION ROE CLOUD (MRS. EDWARD L. HUGHES), state ofcl.; b. Wichita, Kan., June 1, 1917; d. Henry and Elizabeth Georgian (Bender) Roe Cloud; B.A., Wellesley Coll., 1938; postgrad. U. Chgo., 1938-39; m. Edward L. Hughes, June 14, 1939; children—Edward R., Mark A. Staff asso. Friendly House, Inc., Portland, Ore., 1958-69; coordinator Ore. State Program on Aging div. Human Resources, Salem, 1969—. Pres., bd. dirs. League Women Voters of Portland, 1953-57; bd. dirs., state legislative chmn. League Women Voters of Ore., 1957-59; mem. adv. com. Housing Authority of Portland, 1959-62; chmn. Tri-County Community Council Com. on Aging, 1965-69; chmn. Gov.'s Com. on Aging, 1968-69. Mem. Am. Pub. Welfare Assn., Nat. Gerontological Soc. Author: History of Child Welfare in Oregon, 1949. Editor: Conf. Procs. on Protective Services for Older Adults, 1968. Home: 3120 SW Scholls Ferry Rd Portland OR 97221 Office: Public Service Bldg Salem OR 97310

HUGHES, MARY MARGARET FORTNER, editor; b. Butler, Mo., Sept. 2, 1924; d. Joseph Allen and Helen Frances (Prescott) Fortner; student U. Okla., 1942-44, U. Chgo., 1945; m. Edwin Lawson Hughes, Dec. 24, 1949 (div. Oct. 1960); children—John Lawson, James Prescott. Sales corr. Adams-Rite Mfg. Co., Glendale, Cal., 1958-61; pub. relations Marquardt Corp., 1961-63; asst. to pub., editor, editor-in-chief, now editor-in-chief Security World Books div., columnist, v.p. Security World Pub. Co., Inc., Los Angeles, 1964—. Mem. Cal. Democratic Central Com., 1966-67. Editor: (anthology) Successful Retail Security. Contbr. articles to periodicals. Home: 3717 Bagley Av Los Angeles CA 90034 Office: 2639 S LaCienega St Los Angeles CA 90034

HUGHES, MARY RUTH BROWNE (MRS. GEORGE A. HUGHES), librarian; b. Detroit; d. Michael O. and Victoria C. (Soloski) Browne; B.A., Wayne State U., 1940; B.S. in L.S., Simmons Coll., 1943; m. George A. Hughes, Aug. 7, 1948; 1 dau., Mary Christina. Librarian, Chrysler Corp. Engring., Highland Park, Mich., 1943-47, Fisher Body, Detroit, 1947-48, Ross Roy, Detroit, 1948-49, Detroit Inst. Arts, 1950-51; librarian U. Mich., Detroit, 1951—; on loan to Community Task Force of New Detroit Com. Bibliog. research H. A. Montgomery Chem. Co., Detroit, 1952—. Exec. bd. Mayor's Registration and Vote Com., Detroit, 1965-69, vice chmn., 1969; v.p. Detroit Area Council World Affairs, 1969-70, pres., 1970-72; vice chmn. Coordinating Council on Human Relations, 1969-71, chmn., 1972—; mem. Mayor's Task Force City Financing, 1967-69, Mayor's Citizen Study Team Consumer Protection, Citizens Action Com. Sch. Financing, 1969-71; police sub-com. Commn. Community Relations 1967—, mem. women's com., 1973—; sec. Mich. Assembly Omubdsman, 1969—; mem. New Detroit-Community Services sub-com., 1967—, mem. pub. safety com., 1973—; mem. women's com. Mich. United Negro Coll. Fund, 1968—, chmn., 1974—; chmn. Library Citizens Action Com., 1969-72. Dir. Friends Detroit Pub. Library, 1969-72; steering com. Keep Improving Detroit's Schs.; adv. com. Wayne County Community Coll.; council Heart of Gold Award. Bd. dirs. Neighborhood Service Orgn., 1973—. Named 1 of top 10 working women Met. Detroit, 1968; recipient Human Rights award, 1970; certificate of recognition Detroit Pub. Schs., 1972. Mem. Engring. Soc. Detroit, A.L.A., League Women Voters Detroit (dir. 1961-63, pres. 1965-69), Spl. Libraries Assn., Am. Assn. U. Profs., N.A.A.C.P., Women's Econ. Club Detroit, Am. Civil Liberties Union (dir. Mich. chpt. 1973—, Detroit chpt. 1973—), Nat. Orgn. Women. Home: 5751 Yorkshire Detroit MI 48224 Office: 60 Farnsworth St Detroit MI 48302

HUGHES, OLGA MARTHA, museum dir.; b. Ft. Montgomery, N.Y.; d. Julius Ernst and Olga (Vogelbach) Jargstorff; B.A. in Art History, Barnard Coll., 1951; postgrad. Universita Internazionale dell-Arte, Florence, Italy, 1973-74; m. George W. Hughes, Aug. 17, 1957; children—Gareth B., Mark L. With market research dept. J. Walter Thompson, N.Y.C., 1951-52; asst. Gibbons & Heidtmann, architects, N.Y.C., 1952-55, Archtl. Forum, N.Y.C., 1955-56; museum asst. Hayden Gallery, Mass. Inst. Tech., Cambridge, 1956-58; dir. Lafayette (Ind.) Art Center, 1970—. Dir. Interior Objects, Inc., Lafayette. Mem. restoration com. Tippecanoe County Courthouse, 1972-73. Mem. Am. Assn. Museums (v.p. Ind. chpt. Midwest Museums Council 1972-73), Assn. Ind. Museums (dir. 1972-73), Coll. Art Assn. Contbr. articles to profl. jours. Home: 520 Terry Lane West Lafayette IN 47906 Office: 101 S 9th St Lafayette IN 47901

HUGHES, PAULA DEMENNA (MRS. WILLIAM K. HUGHES), investment co. exec.; b. N.Y.C., Sept. 25, 1931; d. Louis M. and Alice Roosevelt (Agate) Rothenberg; student N.Y. Inst. Finance, 1961-62; m. William K. Hughes, July 27, 1956; 1 dau., Catherine (Mrs. Ronald Benton). With Brown & Bigelow, N.Y.C., 1953-61; account exec. Shields & Co., N.Y.C., 1961-72; v.p. Thomson & McKinnon Auchincloss Inc., N.Y.C., 1972—, dir. risk capital mgmt. program. Lectr., writer on investing. Bd. dirs. Rye (N.Y.) Art Center, WAIF/childrens div. Internat. Social Service; bd. dirs. Greenwich House, 1971—, mem. finance com., 1974—; bd. dirs. Franklin Book Programs, 1973—, mem. exec. com., 1974-75; trustee Carnegie Mellon U. Mem. Sales Execs. Club of N.Y., Women Investment Brokers (dir.). Home: 406 Grace Church St Rye NY 10580 Office: 299 Park Av New York City NY 10017

HUGHES, RUTH O'BRIEN, physician; b. Chgo., Feb. 22, 1909; B.S., U. Chgo., 1929, student medicine, 1929-31; M.D., Rush Med. Coll., 1934; m. Dr. Charles W. Hughes, Sept. 14, 1935; children—Brien D., Laurel (Mrs. Hollis Michael Wilson). Intern Los Angeles County Gen. Hosp., 1933-34; house physician Women's Hosp., Flint, Mich., 1935-36; resident anesthesiology Chgo. Lying-In Hosp., 1936-38, obstet. intern, 1939-40; practice gen. medicine, 1941-45, specializing in care of women and infants, Oak Park, Ill., 1945—; mem. obstet. and gynecol. staff West Suburban Hosp. Community chmn. River Forest area Girl Scouts, 1952-53. Mem. A.M.A., Am. Med. Women's Assn., Am. Acad. Family Practice, Chgo. Med. Soc. (treas. Aux. Plaines br.), Oak Park-River Forest Physicians Club. Home: 230 Keystone St River Forest IL 60305 Office: 1011 Lake St Oak Park IL 60301

HUGHEY, ELIZABETH HOUSE (MRS. ALBERT M. HUGHEY), librarian; b. Robersonville, N.C., Feb. 2, 1916; d. Thomas L. and Susan Elizabeth (Mizell) House; A.B., Atlantic Christian Coll., 1936, Litt.D. (hon.), 1961; B.S. in L.S., George Peabody Coll. for Tchrs., 1938; m. Albert Miles Hughey, Oct. 31, 1953. Tchr. Hookerton (N.C.) High Sch., 1936-37; librarian Simpsonville (S.C.) High Sch., 1938-39, Cool Springs High Sch., Forest City, N.C., 1939-41; organizer, adminstr. BHM Regional Library, Washington, N.C., 1941-46; field librarian N.C. Library Commn., Raleigh, 1946-50, sec., dir., 1950-56; state librarian N.C. State Library, Raleigh, 1956-65; adminstrv. librarian, div. library programs U.S. Office of Edn., Washington, 1965—. Mem. adv. com. N.C. Recreation Commn., 1956-65; mem. Gov.'s Coordinating Com. on Aging, 1958-65. Mem. A.L.A., N.C. (pres. 1959-61) Southeastern library assns., Delta Kappa Gamma. Home: 8013 Greeley Blvd Springfield VA 22152 Office: Room 5919 ROB 3 7th and D Sts SW Washington DC 20202

HUIZENGA, ANN HARRIET, pub. health cons.; b. Englewood, N.J., June 6, 1913; d. Lee Sjoerdt and Matilda (Van Dyken) Huizenga; A.B., Calvin Coll., 1933; M.D., Rush Med. Coll. U. Chgo., 1937; M.S.P.H., U. N.C., 1969; M.A., U. Conn., 1973. Intern Presbyn. Hosp., Chgo., 1937, Chgo. Municipal Contagious Disease Hosp., 1938, Children's Hosp., 1938-39; resident Margaret Hague Hosp., Jersey City, 1944-45, Women's Coll. Pa. Hosp., 1945, Evang. Deaconess Hosp., Detroit, 1957; missionary med. practice, China, N.M. and Ariz., 1939-50; practice medicine, specializing in obstetrics and gynecology, Greenville, N.C., 1950-62; cons. in maternal health and family planning N.C. Bd. Health, Raleigh, 1962—. Mem. Am. Coll. Obstetrics and Gynecology, N.C. Med. Soc., Nat. Council Family Relations, N.C. Pub. Health Assn., N.C. Family Life Council. Home: 2474 32d St SE Grand Rapids MI 49508 Office: State Bd Health Raleigh NC 27602

HUK, STEFANIE MICHALINA (MRS. WLADIMIR HUK), physician; b. Lwiw, Poland; d. Stefan and Tekla (Kostewych) Zwir; student U. Lwiw, 1939-44, U. Graz, 1944; M.D., U. Vienna (Austria), 1946; m. Wladimir Huk, May 2, 1942; children—Jerome, Larissa. Came to U.S., 1948, naturalized, 1954. Intern, East Orange (N.J.) Gen. Hosp., 1950-51, resident, 1951-54, asso. pathologist, supr. pathology lab., 1950-58; pvt. practice medicine, Newark, 1956—; staff physician in charge pulmonary ward East Orange VA Hosp., 1966-70; attending physician Essex County Blood Bank, East Orange, 1964-71; asst. med. dir. Seratec Biols., North Brunswick, N.J., 1969—; faculty N.J. Coll. Medicine and Dentistry, 1968-70; med. cons. Essex County Local Med. Assistance Unit, State of N.J. div. Med. Assistance and Health Services, 1970—. Mem. A.M.A., N.J., Essex County med. socs., Ukranian Med. Assn. Club: East Orange Tennis. Home: 55 Glenview Rd South Orange NJ 07079 Office: 90 Lenox St Vailsburg Newark NJ 07106

HUKILL, JANE ELLET (MRS. ROBERT P. HUKILL, SR.), librarian; b. Benton Harbor, Mich., Feb. 12, 1933; d. William Clinton and Helene Rene (Carmichael) Ellet; B.A., U. Mich., 1954; M.S., Villanova U., 1973; m. Robert P. Hukill, Sr., Nov. 25, 1954; children—Peverley, Robert Peverley, Elizabeth, Timothy. Librarian, dir. library services Brandywine Coll. Library, Wilmington, Del., 1967—. Mem. Am. Assn. U. Profs., Del. Library Assn. (sec. 1972-74, v.p. 1974-75), Panhellenic, Delta Delta Delta. Episcopalian. Club: Kennett Square (Pa.) Country. Home: RD 2 56 Deer Path Kennett Square PA 19348 Office: Box 7139 Concord Pike Wilmington DE 19803

HULBERT, JEWEL GENTRY (MRS. JAMES ALEXANDER HULBERT), educator; b. Trinidad, Colo.; d. James F. and Gertrude (Johnson) Gentry; student Tenn. State U., Nashville, 1936-37; A.B., Lemoyne Coll., 1941; postgrad. U. Chgo., 1947-51, So. U., Baton Rouge, summers 1965-66; m. James Alexander Hulbert, May 24, 1963; stepchildren—Marilyn, Marquerite. Tchr. history Manassas High Sch., Memphis, 1942—; soc. editor Memphis World newspaper, 1947—. So. U. grantee in sociology, 1965-66. Mem. Alpha Kappa Alpha. Clubs: Links (sec., chmn. publicity), International of Memphis. Home: 1032 S Lauderdale St Memphis TN 38126 Office: 1254 Mississippi Blvd Memphis TN 38126 also Manassas High Sch 781 Firestone St Memphis TN 38107

HULCE, CAROL JONES (MRS. J.T. HULCE), pub. relations agy. exec.; b. Lancaster, Pa., May 6, 1943; d. James Victor and Beatrice Carolyn (Beal) Jones; B.S., Northwestern U., 1965; m. J.T. Hulce, Nov. 27, 1964; 1 dau., Hillary M. Pub. relations/advt. dir. Am. Med. Affiliates, Inc., 1970-72; account exec. William Kostka & Assos., Denver, 1972; sr. account exec. Henderson, Bucknum, Inc., Denver, 1972-73; pres. Ball & Hulce, Inc., Denver, 1973—. Trustee Florence Crittenton Home, Denver. Mem. Pub. Relations Soc. Am., Jr. League Denver, Pi Beta Phi. Home: 1111 Race St Denver CO 80206 Office: 655 Grant St Denver CO 80203

HULICKA, IRENE MACKINTOSH (MRS. KAREL HULICKA), psychologist, educator; b. Gull Lake, Sask., Can.; d. George A. and Violet (Rose) Mackintosh; B.A., U. Sask., 1947, Honours Degree, 1948, M.A., 1949; B. Ed., U. Alta., 1952; Ph.D., U. Neb., 1954; m. Karel Hulicka, May 27, 1957; 1 son, Charles Mackintosh. Asst. prof. U. Okla., 1955-59; clin. and research psychologist VA Hosp., 1959-65; prof. psychology and chmn. dept. D'Youville Coll., 1965-67; prof. psychology State U. Coll., Buffalo, 1967—, chmn. dept., 1967-72; mem. grad. faculty State U. N.Y. at Buffalo. Cons., Cornell Aero. Labs., 1969-71, Standford Research Inst., 1970-71, IberoAm. Congress on Med. Rehab., Madrid, Spain, 1970; asso. dir. Center for Psychopathology and Rehab., Madrid, 1970—. Fellow Gerontol. Assn.; mem. Am., Eastern psychol. assns., Iberoam. Assn. for Rehab. (named Mem. of Honor 1973). Author: (with Karel Hulicka) Soviet Institutions, the Individual and Society, 1967; numerous others. Contbr. articles to profl. jours. Home: 98 University Av Buffalo NY 14214

HULKA, BARBARA SORENSON (MRS. JAROSLAV F. HULKA), epidemiologist, educator; b. Mpls., Mar. 1, 1931; d. Herbert Fritchof and Mabel Adelia (Alquist) Sorenson; B.A. (regional scholar), Radcliff Coll., 1952; M.S., Juilliard Sch. Music, 1954; M.D., Columbia, 1959, M.P.H. (USPHS fellow), 1961; m. Jaroslav F. Hulka, Nov. 13, 1954; children—Carol Ann, Gregory, Bryan. Intern, USPHS, S.I., N.Y., 1959-60; asst. pub. health physician Pa. State Health Dept., Pitts., 1961-62; research instr. dept. obstetrics and gynecology U. Pitts., 1962-65, research asst. prof., 1966-67; project dir. Cervical Cancer Detection Program, Pitts., 1962-67; asst. prof. dept. epidemiology U. N.C. Sch. Pub. Health, Chapel Hill, 1967-72, asso. prof., 1972—, research asso. dept. preventive medicine Sch. Medicine, 1967-68, asst. prof. dept. family medicine, 1968—, project dir. Study on Orgn., Utilization and Assessment Primary Health Care, 1967—, research asso. U. N.C. Internat. Fertility Research Program, 1971—, Health Services Research Center, 1971—. Cons. health manpower div. Nat. Center Health Services Research and Devel., 1971—. USPHS grantee, 1962—, Am. Cancer Soc. grantee, 1970-71. Diplomate Med. Bd. Preventive Medicine. Mem. Am. Pub. Health

Assn. (council epidemiology sect.), A.A.A.S., Soc. for Epidemiological Research (exec. com.). Contbr. articles to med., pub. health jours. Home: 2317 Honeysuckle Rd Chapel Hill NC 27514

HULL, ANN REMINGTON (MRS. GORDON CRITTENDEN HULL), state legislator; b. Seattle, Feb. 24, 1925; d. Arthur Ernest and Marian Ruby (Knowlton) Remington; B.A., U. Wash., 1945; M.A., Syracuse U., 1948; m. Gordon Crittenden Hull, Apr. 16, 1949; children—Suzanne, Peter Crittenden. Geographer, U.S. Govt., 1948-54; mem. Md. Ho. of Dels., 1967—. Pres. League Women Voters, Prince Georges County, Md., 1962-65. Mem. Assn. Am. Geographers, Phi Beta Kappa. Democrat. Home: 1629 Drexel St Takoma Park MD 20012 Office: 4811 Riverdale Rd Riverdale MD 20840

HULL, DIANNE LEE, actress; d. John Calkins and S. Loraine (Boos) Hull; student U. Cal. at Los Angeles, 1968-71; student Lee Strasberg Theatre Inst., Los Angeles, 1969-72, Actors Studio, Los Angeles, 1968—, Lee Strasberg, N.Y.C., 1966, Herbert Berghof's, 1966, Aaron Frankel's, N.Y.C. Appeared in motion pictures including The Arrangement, 1969, Man On a Swing, 1974; lead roles in The Magic Garden of Stanley Sweetheart, 1970, Hot Summer Week, 1972, Sundrops, 1972, Girls on the Road, 1973, Bobbie and Rose, 1974; TV appearances include The Betsey Palmer Show, 1969, Playhouse 90, 1970, Hawaii-Five-O, 1971, Medical Center, 1971, 72; Cannon, 1972, All in the Family, 1972, The FBI, 1972, Honeymoon Suite (ABC Spl.), 1972, Police Story (NBC Movie), 1973, Search, 1973; performed with Fond du Lac (Wis.) Community Theatre, 1962-67; performed summer stock, Baraboo, Wis., 1965. Govt. intern Congressman William Steiger, 1970; mem. Gov.'s Com. on Children and Youth, Wis., 1966-68; del. Nat. Conf. Christians & Jews, Miami, 1967; del. Nat. Conf. Children and Youth, Washington, 1968; mem. Wis. Youth Com., 1965-68; Am. Field Service exchange student to Germany, summer, 1967. Recipient scholarship Outstanding Americans Found., 1968, scholarship Elk's Club, acting award Wis. Community Theatre, 1964, 67; Young Am. award Gov. Wis., 1967; D.A.R. Good Citizen state winner, 1968; named Outstanding Teen-Age Girl Am., 1968, Miss Fond du Lac, 1968. Mem. Ecology Action Group, Current Issues Orgn., Bruin Belles (AFS chpt.), Sophomore Sweethearts, Little Sister of Sigma Alpha Epsilon, Alpha Phi. Author: Introduction to Outstanding Teenagers of America, 1973. Home: 2308 Takodah Dr Fond du Lac WI 54935 Office: Creative Management Associates 8899 Beverly Bvld Los Angeles CA 90048

HULL, ELEANOR MEANS (MRS. ANGUS CLIFTON HULL), author; b. Denver, Aug. 19, 1913; d. Carleton Bell and Florence (Crannell) Means; B.A., U. Redlands, 1932; B.F.A., U. Denver, 1934; m. Angus Clifton Hull, Jan. 9, 1938; children—Mary Margaret (Mrs. Joseph Philip Hammer), Angus Crannell, Stephen Carleton, Peter Henrich, Jeremy Robert. Social case worker, Bronx, N.Y. and Westchester County, 1964-69; author Tumbleweed Boy, 1940; The Third Wish, 1951; Papi, 1953; The Turquoise Horse, 1955; Suddenly the Sun, 1960; In the Time of the Condor, 1962; Moncho and the Dukes, 1964; Everybody's Somebody, 1957; Through the Secret Door, 1958; The Sling and the Swallow, 1958; The Church Not Made with Hands, 1965; A Trainful of Strangers, 1968; The Second Heart, 1973; also stories and articles. Home: 595 Baseline Rd Boulder CO 80302

HULL, JOAN CAROL, assn. exec.; b. Newark, Apr. 13, 1932; d. Milton O. and Amelia M. (Molitor) Hull; B.A., St. Lawrence U., 1954; M.A., Montclair State Coll., 1962. Copy reader Martindale Hubbell, law directory, Summit, N.J., 1955; tchr. social studies Butler (N.J.) High Sch., 1957-63; dir. jr. hist. socs. N.J. Hist. Soc., Newark, 1963-67, asst. dir. of soc., 1967—. Del. Council Social Agys. Newark, 1970-73. Mem. adv. com. Newark Curriculum, 1970-72; mem. Newark Curriculum Revision Com., 1971—; mem. exec. council N.J. Council for Social Studies, 1969-72. Mem. Sch. and local programs com. N.J. Hist. Commn., 1973—; mem. bicentennial steering com. Montclair State Coll., 1974—; mem. festival com. Newark Bicentennial Celebration, 1974—. Trustee Noyes Scholarship Found., 1972—. Mem. Am. Assn. U. Women (v.p. Essex County br.), Nat. Trust for Historic Preservation (mem. edn. com. 1971—), League Hist. Socs. N.J. (trustee 1969—), Alumni Assn. Pi Beta Phi. Clubs: Soroptimist (pres. 1968-70, dist. vice chmn. 1970—) (Newark); Columbia University; Skytop (Pa.); Editor Cockpit, history mag. for history students, 1963, Crossroads, history bull. for students club, 1963—. Home: 140 Hepburn Rd Apt 3F Clifton NJ 07012 Office: NJ Historical Soc 230 Broadway Newark NJ 07104

HULL, SUZANNE WHITE (MRS. GEORGE I. HULL), library ofcl.; b. Orange, N.J., Aug. 24, 1921; d. Gordon Stowe and Lillian (Siegling) White; B.A. with honors, Swarthmore Coll., 1943; M.S. in L.S., U. So. Cal., 1967; m. George I. Hull, Feb. 20, 1943; children—George Gordon, James Rutledge, Anne Elizabeth. News stringer Los Angeles Times, 1953-55; substitute librarian Los Angeles Pub. Library System, 1967-68; asst. head dept. reader services Huntington Library, San Marino, Cal., 1969-70; dir. programs Huntington Library Art Gallery and Bot. Gardens, San Marino, 1971-72, dir. pub. services, officer, 1972-74, dir. adminstrn. and pub. services, officer, 1974—. Charter pres. Portola Jr. High Sch. P.T.A., Los Angeles, 1960-62; mem. Swarthmore Alumni Council, 1959-62; mem. Swarthmore Centennial Campaign Com., 1964; pres. Children's Service League, Los Angeles, 1963-64; mem. community adv. council Los Angeles Job Corps Center for Women, 1972—. Bd. dirs. U.S.O., Los Angeles and Hollywood, Cal., 1967-70, Welfare Planning Council San Fernando Valley, 1963-68, Recreation and Youth Services Planning Council Los Angeles, 1968-69; co-founder, mem. bd. dirs. Friends of Los Angeles YWCA, 1968-72; bd. dirs. YWCA Los Angeles, 1963-69, 70-73, pres., 1967-69. Mem. Cal. Congress Parents and Tchrs. (hon. life), A.L.A., Beta Phi Mu. Home: 1465 El Mirador Dr Pasadena CA 91103 Office: 1151 Oxford Rd San Marino CA 91108

HULL, VIRGINIA TRACY (MRS. JOSEPH WILLIAM HULL), travel agy. exec.; b. Chgo.; d. Joseph Platt and Ada (Morris) Tracy; B.A., Occidental Coll.; m. Joseph William Hull, Nov. 26, 1938 (dec. Apr. 1953). Exec. sec. Alphonzo E. Bell Corp., 1928-38; pres. Bel-Air Travel, Inc., Los Angeles, 1953—. Chmn., Westwood area advanced gifts com. Los Angeles Community Chest and United Way; mem. Los Angeles Mayor's Community Adv. Com.; mem. Cal. Atty. Gen.'s Vol. Adv. Com., 1971—. Bd. dirs. Los Angeles chpt. A.R.C., 1966-71, 73—, Univ. Affiliates U. Cal. at Los Angeles, 1966-69. Mem. Am. Soc. Travel Agts. (sec. So. Cal. chpt. 1960-62, dir. 1963—), Westwood C. of C. (sec. 1960-72, v.p. charge legislation and pub. affairs 1972-74), Bus. and Profl. Women's Clubs (Los Angeles pres. 1965; pres. Sunset dist. 1969-70), Inst. Certified Travel Agts. (founder), D.A.R. (regent chpt. 1971—, mag. advt. vice chmn. 1972-73), Cal. State Soc. of Nat. Soc. D.A.R., Cal. Fedn. Bus. and Profl. Women's Clubs (world affairs chmn. 1970-71, chmn. women in appointive office 1971-72), Town Hall, Soc. Mayflower Descs. State Cal., Los Angeles Travellarians (pres. 1960), P.E.O. Clubs: Soroptimist (pres. Los Angeles West 1957). Home: 850 Moraga Dr Bel Air Los Angeles CA 90049 Office: 600 N Sepulveda Blvd Bel Air Los Angeles CA 90049

HULME, KATHRYN, author; b. San Francisco, Jan. 6, 1900; d. Edwin Page and Julia Frances (Cavarly) Hulme; student U. Cal., 1918-21; spl. courses Columbia Sch. Journalism, 1922, Hunter Coll., N.Y.C., 1923. Publicity dir. Ask Mr. Foster, travel service, 1935-43; dep. dir. UNRRA, U.S. Zone, Germany, 1945-47; U.S. Zone chief Emigration of Displaced Persons with IRO, 1947-51. Mem. Delta Kappa Gamma (hon.). Roman Catholic. Author: Arab Interlude, 1931; Desert Night, 1933; We Lived as Children, 1939; The Wild Place (Atlantic non-fiction award for 1953), 1953; The Nun's Story, 1956 (Commonwealth Club of Cal. lit. award 1956, Nat. Council Women U.S. award, 1957, Rupert Hughes award Authors Club of Los Angeles, 1957, Brotherhood award, Nat. Conf. Christians and Jews, 1957); Annie's Captain (biography), 1961; Undiscovered Country (autobiography), 1966; Look A Lion in the Eye: On Safari Through Africa, 1974. Home: Route 1 Kapaa Kauai HI 96746

HULSEY, LORETTA ETHEL DALE (MRS. GLEN HULSEY), data processing corp. exec.; b. Galveston, Tex., May 15, 1932; d. Jim Kenny and Loretta Amelia (Holland) Dale; B.A., Southwestern U., 1952; M.Ed., U. Houston, 1961; m. Glen Hulsey, June 24, 1952. Programmer Am. Oil Co., Texas City, Tex., 1952-62; mgr. Central Data Processing, Inc., Texas City, 1962-64, mgr., 1970—; head data processing dept. Alvin (Tex.) Jr. Coll., 1964-70. Tchr. Data Processing Vocational Tech. Program Coll. Mainland, Texas City, 1971. Adviser Coll. Mainland, 1971—. Mem. Am. Assn. U. Women, Bus. and Profl. Women (pres. 1969-70), Data Processing Mgmt. Assn. (chpt. dir. 1972-73). Methodist. Home: 1110 17th Av N Texas City TX 77590 Office: 2709 Texas Av Texas City TX 77590

HULSHIZER, NELLIE BLANCHE (MRS. ROY HULSHIZER), curator; b. Meadville, Neb., Feb. 19, 1897; d. William Parrin and Blanche May (Mead) Slenecker; student pub. schs.; m. Roy Hulshizer, Feb. 25, 1914; children—Gwenda (Mrs. Harvey Morter), Elvin Edwin, William Corneilus. Tchr. rural schs., Brown County, Neb., 1912-13; curator Sellors Meml. Mus., Ainsworth, Neb., 1964—; corr. Norfolk (Neb.) Daily News, 1961—. Mem. Royal Neighbors of America (recorder 1965), Woman's Relief Corps (state pres. 1951-52), V.F.W. Aux., Am. Legion Aux., Brown County Hist. Soc. Republican. Mem. Reorganized Ch. of Jesus Christ of Latter-day Saints. Club: Federated Woman's (pres. 1948-49, 64-65) (Ainsworth, Neb.). Home: 312 N Elm St Ainsworth NE 69210 Office: Sellors Meml Mus 4th and Main Sts Ainsworth NE 69210

HUMBERT, PAMELA ZUCKERMANN, drug rehab. cons.; b. N.Y.C., Oct. 28, 1941; d. Bernhard and Helen (Jobin) Zuckermann; B.S., Columbia, 1965, M.A. in Developmental Psychology, Tchrs. Coll., 1967, M.Ed. in Vocational and Rehab. Counseling, 1969. Vocational rehab. counselor Greenwich House Counseling Center, N.Y.C., 1967-69; narcotic rehab. counselor N.Y. State Narcotic Addiction Control Commn., 1970-71; dir. drug rehab. center Irene Byron Hosp., Ft. Wayne, Ind., 1971-72; dir. mobile drug abuse treatment unit Am. Tech. Assistance Corp., McLean, Va., 1973-74, cons., 1974—. Mem. Am. Psychol. Assn. (asso.). Republican. Episcopalian. Home: 84 Warwick Rd Bronxville NY 10708 Office: 7655 Old Springhouse Rd McLean VA 22101

HUMBRECHT, MARY, physician; b. Bellevue, Ky., Apr. 25, 1922; d. Joseph M. and Josephine A. (Niermann) Humbrecht; R.N., Good Samaritan Sch. Nursing, Cin., 1943; A.B., Ohio State U., 1948; M.D., U. Cin., 1952. Intern, Charity Hosp. of La., New Orleans, 1952-53, sr. vis. physician, 1957—; resident internal medicine Tulane-So. Bapt. Hosp., New Orleans, 1953-56, fellow internal medicine, 1956-57; practice medicine specializing in internal medicine, New Orleans, 1957—; dir. clinic New Orleans Bapt. Theol. Sem., 1964—; sr. vis. physician So. Bapt., Sara Mayo, Meth. hosps., New Orleans; clin. asso. prof. medicine Tulane U., New Orleans, 1957—. Served with Army Nurse Corps, 1944-46; lt. col. Res. Mem. Phi Beta Kappa, Alpha Omega Alpha. Home: 6618 Gen Diaz St New Orleans LA 70124 Office: 4426 Chef Menteur Hwy New Orleans LA 70126

HUMBY, ALICE FRANTZ (MRS. ROBERT HUMBY), educator; b. Iola, Kan., Nov. 19, 1946; d. Wayne E. and Dorothy Annette (Pereau) Frantz; student Iola Jr. Coll., 1964-65; B.S., Kan. State Coll., 1968; M.A., U. Mo., 1969, postgrad., 1972; postgrad. U. Fla., 1973—; m. Robert Humby, June 5, 1969. News broadcaster, interviewer radio sta. KSEK, Pittsburg, Kan., 1967; tchr. Dade County Public Schs., Miami Fla., 1969-70, charge media resources, adminstrv. offices, 1970-71; grad. asst. dept. speech U. Fla., Gainesville, 1973-74. Mem. Am. Ednl. Theatre Assn., Internat. Assn. Theatre for Children and Youth, Theta Alpha Phi, Kappa Delta Pi. Democrat. Roman Catholic (human devel. group sec. 1971-72, pres. 1972-73). Home: 3301 SW 13th St Apt R-256 Gainesville FL 32601

HUME, MARGARET MAE WILLIAMS (MRS. DAVID HUME), hosp. adminstr.; b. San Antonio, Feb. 2, 1921; d. Homer Talmage and Mae (Sumner) Williams; B.A., Tex. State Coll. for Women, 1942; Med. Technologist, Scott and White Sch. Tech., 1943; postgrad. Our Lady of the Lake, 1939, U. Okla., 1946, Tex. Agrl. and Indsl. U., 1961-62; m. David Hume, June 19, 1966; 1 dau., Margeann Hume. Dept. dir. bacteriology, serology Scott & White Hosp., Oklahoma City, 1945-47; hosp. adminstr. Meml. Hosp., Goliad, Tex., 1950-55, Meml. Hosp., Eagle Pass, Tex., 1965-67, hosp. cons., 1967—. Tech. cons., 1956-62; hosp. adminstrn. cons., 1963-65. Pres. P.T.A., Freer, Tex., 1963; dir. Tri-County P.T.A., 1964; leader Gulf Coast council Girl Scouts Am., 1957-62; sec., variety show dir. Band Booster, 1959-65. Mem. Am. Assn. U. Women, Am. Soc. Med. Technologists, Pan-Am. Round Table, International Good Neighbors Forum Round Table (sec. 1941), Tex. Hosp. Assn., Alumni Assn. (v.p. 1950), Delian, Beta Beta Beta. Presbyn. Mem. Order Eastern Sta. Home: Margarita Ranch Box 1212 Eagle Pass TX 78852 Office: 503 Quarry St Eagle Pass TX 78852

HUMEL, DOROTHY SONIA, constrn. co. exec., civic worker, musician; b. Cleve.; d. James and Sonia (Lanik) Humel; piano study with Jose Iturbi, Authur Loesser, Theodore Lettvin, Charles Rychlik. Concert career, including soloist Cleve. Orch., 1945-59; sec., treas. dir. Humel Constrn., Inc., Cleve., 1946—; dir. Union Savs. Assn. Pres. women's com. Cleve. Orch., 1959-61; pres. Assn. Women Coms. for Symphony Orchs., 1961-63. Trustee, Mus. Arts Assn., 1959—, mem. exec. com., 1968—, sec., 1968-71, chmn. pub. relations com., 1963—, mem. devel. com. Blossom Music Center; pres., trustee Lake Erie Opera Theatre, 1964—; trustee Cleve. Mus. Sch. Settlement, 1960—, pres., 1972—, v.p. 1962-66; trustee University Circle, Inc., 1970—, mem. finance com., 1971—; trustee Maison Francaise de Cleve., 1971—, Cleve. Women's Orch., 1961—, Cleve. Inst. Music, 1962-68, Cleve. Summer Arts Festival, 1967-70; mem. adv. council Cleve. Meml. Soc., 1965—; mem. vis. com. for humanities and arts Case-Western Res. U., 1973—. Mem. Nat. Council Met. Opera Assn., Cleve. Soc. Contemporary Art, Cleve. Playhouse Corp., Am. Symphony Orch League. Clubs: Cleve. Skating, Women's City (mem. fine arts prize com.), Music and Drama (pres. 1957-59). Home: 2764 Landon Rd Cleveland OH 44122 Office: 17706 Miles Av Cleveland OH 44128

HUMMEL, BARBARA JEAN, educator; b. Grand Rapids, Mich., May 11, 1938; d. Eugene Leonard and Anna (Van Dyke) Hummel; B.A., Albion Coll., 1960; M.A., Mich. State U., 1967. Tchr. L.C. Mohr High Sch., South Haven, Mich., 1960-63, Waukegan (Ill.) High Sch., 1967—. Directorial and tech. work Sister Lakes (Mich.) Playhouse, 1963-64, Circle Theatre, Grand Rapids, 1965-67. Mem. Am. Theatre Assn., Speech Communication Assn., Ill. Speech and Theatre Assn. Home: 419 Hickory St Waukegan IL 60085 Office: 1011 Washington St Waukegan IL 60085

HUMMEL, MARIE EMMA LIESE (MRS. HOMER H. HUMMEL), real estate broker; b. Corder, Mo., Apr. 28, 1913; d. Edward Amel and Amelia Louise (Schaeperkoetter) Liese; B.S., Washington U., St. Louis, 1950; postgrad. U. Cal. at Los Angeles, 1958; m. Homer H. Hummel, Nov. 27, 1935; children—Joan (Mrs. James C. Randall), Janice (Mrs. Stanley C. Sandell, Jr.), Homer H. Tchr. elementary sch., Warrenton, Mo., 1948-58, jr. high sch., Pasadena, Cal., 1958-61, jr. high sch., La Canada, Cal., 1961-64; real estate broker Reliable Realty, Glendale, Cal., 1964—. Pres. P.T.A., Warrenton, Mo., 1948; mem. Presidents Adv. Council of Glendale, 1974; mem. Women's Civic League of Glendale, 1973—. Named Asso. of Year, Glendale Bd. Realtors, 1970; recipient Diamond Pin award, women's council Nat. Assn. Realtors, 1970. Mem. Glendale Bd. Realtors (pres. women's council 1970, 74), Nat., Cal. assn. realtors, Nat. Notary Assn. Mem. Ch. of Religious Sci. (pres. Empatheians 1973—). Columnist for Glendale Bd. Realtors monthly mag., 1970—. Home: 1618 Kenneth Rd Glendale CA 91201 Office: 516 N Brand Blvd Glendale CA 91203

HUMMEL, RUTH SHARP (MRS. ROBERT HUMMEL), retail floral shop mgr.; b. Springfield, Mass., May 30, 1930; d. Edward Alexander and Ruth Marion (Blight) Sharp; m. Robert Hummel, Feb. 18, 1953; 1 son, Michael Bruce. Profl. floral designer, mgr. Flowers by Sharp, Plainville, Conn., 1950—; hist. writer column Plainville's Heritage, Plainville News and New Britain Herald, 1969—. Sec., Farmington Canal Corridor Assn., 1973—; mem. Plainville Conservation Commn., 1970—, chmn., 1972-73. Recipient Award of Merit, Conn. League Hist. Socs., 1970. Mem. Sterms, Plainville Hist. Soc. (pres. 1969—). Author: Story of Farmington Canal, Plainville, Connecticut, 1971. Home: 41 Ledge Rd Plainville CT 06062 Office: 75 East St Plainville CT 06062

HUMMEL, TYYNI MIRIAM NIEMI (MRS. MERLE CLARK HUMMEL), home economist; b. Atlantic Mine, Mich., Oct. 2, 1909; d. Isaai Emil and Anna Katarina (Niskanen) Niemi; B.S., No. Mich. U., 1933; postgrad. Mich. State U., 1937-38; M.S., Ohio State U., 1949; postgrad. U. Wis., 1958, U. Ariz., 1972; m. Merle Clark Hummel, Oct. 14, 1951 (dec.); children—Paul Rahmer, Carolyn (Mrs. Dale Laykun). Tchr. home econs., history and English, Felch (Mich.) Twp. Schs., 1934-36; tchr. home econs. and English, Gould City Sch., 1936-37; tchr. vocational home econs. L'Anse Twp. Schs., 1937-41; home mgmt. supr. Farm Security Adminstrn., 1941-43, 45-47; asst. Home Mgmt. House, conducted housing survey for regional housing study Coop. Extension Service, Ohio State U., Wauseon, 1948-49, county extension agt., asst. extension prof. home econs., 1949—. Served with USNR, 1943-45. Recipient Meritorious Service award County 4-H Council, 1964, 73; County Extension Homemakers Service award, 1969. Far Eastern Studies scholar Ohio State U., 1955, Farm Found. scholar, 1959, Grace Frysinger fellow Nat. Assn. Extension Home Economists, 1960. Mem. Am., Ohio, Ohio State U. home econs. assns., Nat. Assn. Extension Home Economists (Distinguished Service award 1971), Ohio County Extension Agts. Assn. (past dir.), Greater Toledo Nutrition Council, Ohio State U. Assn., Am. Legion, Bus. and Profl. Womens Club (past pres.). Presbyn. Address: Box 471 West Unity OH 43570

HUMPHREY, BOBBYE JEANNE, educator; b. Muskogee, Okla., Dec. 14, 1927; d. Hubert and Lola (Abrams) Humphrey; student Lincoln U., 1946-47; A.B., Friends' U., 1948; Wichita State U., intermittently 1948-53; M.S.W., U. Kan., 1964. Asst. exec. dir. Memphis Urban League, 1955-56; social worker Sedgwick County (Kan.) Social Welfare Bd., 1956-62, supr., 1964-67; instr. Grambling (La.) Coll., 1967-68; coordinator social services Wichita (Kan.) Bd. Edn. Head Start, 1968; asst. prof. social work Wichita State U., 1968—, asst. dean faculties for Personnel, 1972—. Cons. coop. urban tchr. edn. program Mid-Continent Regional Ednl. Lab., 1969-73; mem. Wichita-Butler and Sedgwick Counties Manpower Area Planning Council. Bd. mem., adv. bd. Starkey Developmental Center for Retarded, 1972—; bd. dirs. Wichita Urban League, 1968—, St. Paul Day Care Center, 1971-73. Mem. Acad. Certified Social Workers, Kan. Soc. Clin. Workers, Nat. Assn. Social Workers, Am. Assn. U. Profs., Nat. Conf. on Social Welfare, Nat. Council Negro Women (commn. on higher edn.), League of Women Voters, Alpha Kappa Delta, Alpha Kappa Alpha. Home: 1041 Indiana Av Wichita KS 67214

HUMPHREY, ELEANOR NICHOLSON (MRS. PAUL HUMPHREY), physician; b. Rochester, N.Y., Mar. 12, 1916; d. Albert and Lela Mae (Howard) Nicholson; A.B., U. Rochester, 1937, M.D., 1941; m. Paul Humphrey, Feb. 22, 1941; children—Paula (Mrs. Kim), Paul Nicholson, Joel William. Rotating intern New Eng. Hosp. for Women and Children, 1941-42, chief resident, 1942-43; house officer Boston Lying-In Hosp., 1943; with med. dept. Eastman Kodak Co., Rochester, 1944; practice medicine specializing in obstetrics and gynecology, Rochester, 1944—; tchr. anatomy, physiology Rochester Dental Dispensary, 1944-50; asst. attending obstetrics and gynecology U. Rochester, 1944-55, Highland Hosp., 1945-59, St. Mary's Hosp., 1946-58; physician Maternal Consultation Center, Rochester, 1945-64; mem. staffs Rochester Gen., Park Av., Monroe County Med. hosps.; mem. courtesy staff Genesee Hosp., Rochester. Mem. A.M.A., N.Y. Med. Soc. Clubs: Antique Automobile, Spencerport Garden (pres. 1966). Home: 2329 S Union St Spencerport NY 14559 Office: 277 Alexander St Rochester NY 14607

HUMPHREY, ESTHER LOUISA GREEN (MRS. HARRY F. HUMPHREY), theatrical printing co. exec.; b. nr. Shelby, Ia.; d. Charles Boyer and Christina Louisa (Kreimeier) Green; m. Harry F. Humphrey, Dec. 24, 1957. Meter record clk. Met. Utilities; owner Film Exhibitors Printing Co., Omaha, 1950—. Recipient Presdl. citation for Nat. Youth Opportunity campaign, 1966, recognition for portrait painting Joslyn Meml. Mem. Nat. Theatre Owners Am., U.S. Figure Skating Assn., Omaha Organ Soc., Phi Sigma Alpha. Episcopalian. Clubs: Happy Hollow, 66 Formal Dancing, Qui Vive Formal Dancing (Omaha). Home: 412 N 96th St Omaha NE 68114 Office: 416 S 14th St Omaha NE 68102

HUMPHREY, KATHRYN BRITT, histologist; b. Champaign, Ill., Jan. 24, 1923; d. Jessie James and Vennie (Johnson) Britt; student U. Ill., 1959-60, Parkland Jr. Coll., 1968-69; m. John C. Humphrey, Aug. 5, 1943 (dec. June, 1960); 1 child, Juanel Edward. Histologist Coll. of Vet. Medicine U. Ill. Urbana, 1955—. Active Champaign County Opportunities Industrialization Center, 1969-74. Mem. Bd. Champaign Community Sch. Dist., sec., 1970—. Recipient numerous civic awards. Mem. Nat. Caucus Black Sch. Bd. Mems. (dir. 1972—), Urban League (dir. 1964-70, five year service award 1969), Les Femmes Social Sorority. Baptist (trustee 19—, pres. dist. women's conv., statistician state women's conv.). Home: 716 Tawney Court Champaign IL 61820 Office: College of Veterinary Medicine University of Illinois Urbana IL 61801

HUMPHREY, LOUISE IRELAND (MRS. GILBERT W. HUMPHREY), civic worker, horsewoman; b. Morehead City, N.C., Nov. 1, 1918; d. R. Livingston and Margaret (Allen) Ireland; ed. pvt. schs.; m. Gilbert W. Humphrey, Dec. 27, 1939; children—Margaret (Mrs. J. Moffat Dunlap), George M. III, Gilbert Watts. Nurse's aide A.R.C., 1944—; chmn. children's council Welfare Fedn. Cleve., 1959-60, trustee Musical Arts Assn., mem. exec. com.; trustee vis. Nurse Assn., past pres., trustee, pres. No. Ohio Opera Assn.; trustee Lake Erie Coll., Ballet Guild Greater Cleve., Cleve. Zool. Soc., Greater Cleve. Arts Council, Case Western Res. U., Citizen's Adv. Bd. Juvenile Ct., Health Fund Cleve.; mem. Health Planning and Devel. Commn., Briarcliff Coll., Briarcliff Manor, N.Y., Archbold Hosp., Thomasville, Ga.; bd. dirs. Thomas County (Ga.) Hist. Soc. Mem. Cuyahoga and Lake County Republican Exec. Com. Mem. Jr. League, Met. Opera Assn. Master foxhounds Chagrin Valley Hunt, Gates Mills, O.; dir. U.S. Equestrian Team, Inc., zone v.p. Home: Hunting Hill Chagrin Falls OH 44022

HUMPHREY, LUCIE KING, mem. Republican Nat. Com.; b. Mokelumne Hills, Cal., Feb. 23, 1911; d. Ralph Mower and Mabel (Plumb) King; A.B., U. Nev., 1931; m. Marvin Bender Humphrey, Sept. 14, 1932; children—Joseph, Barbara (Mrs. F.E. Redman), Sarah, (Mrs. Robert H. White), Ellen. Sch. tchr., 1931-32; mem. Nev. Fedn. Rep. Women 1950—, pres., 1950-53; pres. Reno Rep. Women's Club, 1963-67; mem. Rep. Nat. Com. for Nev., 1968—. Bd. dirs. Sierra Nev. Reno Girl Scouts, 1944-66, pres., 1946-48; pres. Nev. Campus YWCA, bd., 1950-51. Mem. Nev. Hist. Soc., Nev. Hort. Soc., Gamma Phi Beta (local alumnae pres. 1933, house corp. pres. 1958-60). Episcopalian. Club: Monday (pres. 1946—) (Reno). Home: 30 Suda Way Reno NV 89502

HUMPHREYS, BARBARA ELIZABETH, educator; b. Wilmington, Del., June 24, 1932; d. Albert Orgain and Florence Anna (Lyons) Humphreys; B.S., U. Del., 1958, M.Ed., 1969. Gen. duty nurse Wilmington Gen. Hosp., 1953-54, evening supr., 1954-58, pediatric supr., 1960-63; gen. duty nurse Shriner's Hosp., Honolulu, 1958-60; sch. nurse Meadowood Sch. Trainables, Newark, 1963-67; supervising nurse Daytime Care Centers for Retarded Children, New Castle, Del., 1967-70, state supr., 1970—. Cons. U. Del. St. Francis Sch. Nursing, Westchester State Tchrs. Coll. nurses workshop on mental retardation. Methodist (mem. adminstrv. bd.). Home: 17 Henderson Hill Rd Newark DE 19711 Office: care Del State Hosp New Castle DE 19720

HUMPHREYS, PRISCILLA COBB (MRS. IRVIN WENDELL HUMPHREYS), Republican nat. committeewoman; b. Huntington, W.Va., Apr. 28, 1912; d. James Edward and Bertie Mae (Esque) Cobb; student Marshall U., 1930-33; m. Irvin Wendell Humphreys, Feb. 9, 1936; children—David Wendell, Bertie Anne, John Edward. Troop leader Girl Scouts U.S.A., 1952-56; pres. Alpha Xi Delta Mother's Club, 1962; vice chmn. art dept., bd. dirs. art dept. Huntington Woman's Club. Second v.p. Cabell County Republican Woman's Club, 1958-60, pres., 1960-62; vice chmn., committeewoman-at-large Cabell County Rep. Exec. Com., 1963—, mem. finance com., 1965; Rep. nat. committeewoman for W.Va., 1964—; bd. dirs. Rep. Youth Tng. Camp, 1965. Baptist. Address: 1546 16th St Huntington WV 25701

HUMPHRIES, BEVERLY NELL (MRS. DONALD R. HUMPHRIES), librarian; b. Gatesville, Tex., July 3, 1930; d. E.B. and Nora H. (Nelson) Harris; A.A., Clifton Jr. Coll., 1946-48; B.S., N. Tex. State U., 1950; M.S., So. Ill. U., 1971; m. Donald R. Humphries, May 27, 1951; children—Brett, Joel. Elementary tchr. Balmorhea (Tex.) Pub. Schs., 1948-49; res. librarian Tex. Technol. U., Lubbock, 1950-51; elementary tchr. Fairbanks (Alaska) Sch. Dist., 1952-54; serials and documents librarian Tex. A. and M. U., College Station, 1954-57; periodicals librarian Davenport (Ia.) Pub. Library, 1957-59; librarian Monticello Coll., Godfrey, Ill., 1965-71; librarian Lewis and Clark Community Coll., Godfrey, 1971—. Bd. dirs. Greater Alton Concert Assn., 1968—. Mem. Am., Ill. library assns. Home: 4810 Chateau Dr Godfrey IL 62035 Office: Lewis and Clark Community College Godfrey IL 62035

HUMPHRIES, NANCY EUGENIA COLVIN (MRS. JULIAN MAXWELL HUMPHRIES, JR.), orgn. exec.; b. Jacksonville, Fla., Oct. 22, 1949; d. John Ensley and Gladys Eugenia (Poole) Colvin; student Fla. State U., 1967-69; B.S. with honors, U. Fla., 1970; m. Julian Maxwell Humphries, Jr., Sept. 4, 1970. With Duval County Family Planning Project, Jacksonville, Fla., 1970-71; youth dir. Fist Ch., New Orleans, 1971-72; with CTI-Container Transp. Internat., New Orleans, 1972-73; asst. dir. pub. affairs Youth for Understanding, Ann Arbor, Mich., 1973-74; asst. to controller Med. Data Systems, Detroit, 1974—. Mem. Women in Communications, Phi Kappa Phi, Sigma Delta Chi, Kappa Tau Alpha. Methodist. Democrat. Home: 520 Cherry St Ann Arbor MI 48103 Office: 7375 Woodward Av Detroit MI 48202

HUMPHRIES, PAULINE HUTTON (MRS. ROBERT L. HUMPHRIES), city ofcl.; b. Strong City, Okla., Jan. 8, 1916; d. George W. and Lula J. (Howerton) Hutton; grad. high sch.; m. Robert L. Humphries; children—Polly (Mrs. Henry), Shirley (Mrs. John M. Dudley), Robert L. Tax assessor-collector Stockdale Ind. Sch. Dist., 1962—; city sec., Stockdale, Tex., 1969—; owner The Attic, dept. store, Stockdale, 1973—. Mem. Stockdale C. of C. (sec.-treas.). Baptist (Sunday sch. tchr.). Contbr. articles to newspapers. Home: Box 271 Stockdale TX 78160 Office: Box 446 Stockdale TX 78160

HUNER, BARBARA JOYCE, city traffic engr.; b. Napoleon, O., Nov. 3, 1948; d. Henry August and Henrietta (Behrman) Huner; B.S. in Civil Engring., U. Wis.-Platteville, 1971. Draftsman, Henry County, Napoleon, 1967, 68; asst. to campus planner U. Wis.-Platteville, 1970-71; civil engr. City of Dubuque (Ia.), 1970, 71-72; traffic engr. City of Greeley (Colo.), 1972—. Mem. Am. Soc. C.E., Am. Pub. Works Assn., Chi Epsilon (sec. 1970), Tau Kappa Phi. Lutheran. Home: 623 37th St Greeley CO 80631 Office: 919 7th St Greeley CO 80631

HUNGERFORD, MARY JANE (MRS. CHARLES H. LAWRANCE), marriage counselor; b. Chgo., Aug. 30, 1913; d. Ethelbert Arthur and Mary Jane (Walker) Hungerford; student Sargent Coll. of Boston U., 1930-32; M.A., New Coll., Columbia, 1937; Ph.D., Columbia, 1947; m. Charles H. Lawrance, Nov. 22, 1947; children—Kenneth Arthur, Lois Ruth, Robert Jefferson. Tchr. phys. edn., specializing in dance U. Ore., Columbia, U. So. Cal., La. State U., B.C. Summer Sch. Edn., Mary Washington Coll. U. Va., 1933-53; appeared, with own choreography, in various dance prodns., including Virginia Hall Johnson group, 1936-38, Lester Horton Dance Group, Los Angeles, 1938-40; instr. hygiene U. Wash., Seattle, 1945-46; mem. faculty Montclair (N.J.) State Tchrs. Coll., 1946-47; head, dept. edn., dir. South Bay br. Am. Inst. Family Relations, Redondo Beach, Cal., 1954—. Engaged in counselor tng. Am. Inst. Family Relations, Hollywood, Cal., 1958—; instr. marriage and family East Los Angeles Jr. Coll., 1968—; frequent lectr. for civic orgns., P.T.A.'s, chs.; appearances on radio and TV. Mem. Am., Cal. (officer), So. Cal. (treas. 1967) assns. marriage counselors, Internat. Coll. Applied Nutrition (past officer), Nat. Council on Family Relations (chmn. So. Cal. br.), Internat. Childbirth Edn. Assn. (a founder; past pres.; life mem.), Internat. Platform Assn., Childbirth Edn. Assn. Los Angeles (founder, past pres.), Soc. Sci. Study Sex, Am. Assn. Sex Educators and Counselors, League Women Voters. Author: Childbirth Education, 1972. Editor: Preparation for Parenthood News, 1958—. Contbr. articles to profl. publs. Home: 503 Camino De Encanto Redondo Beach CA 90277 Offices: 5287 Sunset Blvd Hollywood CA 90027 also 1840 S Elena St Redondo Beach CA 90277

HUNHOFF, SISTER GLADYS, pub. relations ofcl.; b. Utica, S.D., Aug. 21, 1918; d. Herman and Mary Martha (Huber) Hunhoff; B.S. in Bus. Edn., Coll. St. Scholastica, 1942; M.Ed., U. S.D., 1964; M.A. in Mgmt. and Communication, U. Ia., 1969. Instr., prin., supr. music edn. elementary and secondary schs., 1938-65; exec. sec. Walter L. Darling Corp., Yankton, S.D., 1965-69; asst. adminstr. St. Thomas More Hosp., Canon City, Colo., 1969-72; v.p. pub. relations Fremont Nat. Bank, Canon City, 1973—. Adult edn. instr. calligraphic and seriographic script. Sec., March of Dimes; coordinator Fremont County Health Careers Assn.; Fremont County coordinator Colo. Emergency Med. Technicians Tng. Program. Bd. dirs. Madonna Profl. Care Center, Lincoln, Neb., Fremont County United Single Fund. Mem. Am. Soc. Hosp. Pub. Relations Assns., Health Careers Assn., Zonta. Home: 725 Macon Av Canon City CO 81212 Office: 532 Main St Canon City CO 81212

HUNN, BERNICE ELEANOR, educator; b. nr. El Dorado, Kan., Oct. 20, 1909; d. Clyde Vrooman and Irene (Parsons) Hunn; B.S., Kan. State Coll., 1950; M.A., U. No. Colo., 1957, Ed.D., 1963. Tchr. pub. elementary sch. Butler County, Kan., 1927-41, Towanda, Kan., 1941-46, El Dorado, 1946-57; prof. elementary edn. U. No. Col., Greeley, 1957—. Exchange tchr. Fairweather Green Infant Sch., Bradford, Eng., 1948-49; del. regional meeting Ednl. and Sci. Orgn., UN, Denver, 1947, organizer Edn., Sci. Orgn. Council, Butler County, 1948, state v.p., 1951-53. Vol. worker Selective Service System, El Dorado, 1942. Named hon. citizen Beaugency, France, 1948, Outstanding Elementary Tchr. of Am., 1973. Mem. Kan. Tchrs. Assn. (dept. chmn. 1947), N.E.A. (life), Internat. Reading Assn., Gold Key, Kappa Delta Pi, Pi Lambda Theta, Delta Kappa Gamma (pres. Delta chpt. 1970-72). Conglist. Club: Knife and Fork. Home: 819 19th St Greeley CO 80631

HUNNEWELL, GERALDINE GROSVENOR, poet; b. Oakland, Cal., Aug. 21, 1918; d. William Bennett and Lavinia Ruth (Lay) Grosvenor; student El Camino Jr. Coll., 1956; m. Lester Arthur Hunnewell, Mar. 8, 1940; children—Larry Dennis, Richard Lynn. Sec. Richard & Dion Neutra & Assos., architects, Los Angeles. Mem. numerous profl., polit., geneal., and conservation orgns. Contbr. poetry to mags. and anthologies. Address: Oakdale Mobile Park 10799 Sherman Grove Av Space 39 Sunland CA 91040

HUNT, ALMA FAY, missions exec.; b. Roanoke, Va., Oct. 5, 1909; d. William Otis and Mary Myrtle (Wertz) Hunt; B.S., Va. State Tchrs. Coll., 1941; A.M., Columbia, 1947; D.H.L., William Jewell Coll., 1958. Tchr., Roanoke County (Va.) Schs., 1929-31, prin., 1931-32; tchr. Roanoke City Sch., 1932-44; dean women William Jewell Coll., Liberty, Mo., 1944-48; exec. sec. Woman's Missionary Union, Aux. So. Bapt. Conv., Birmingham, Ala., 1948-74, trustee, 1953-56; sec. bd. trustees Carver Sch. Missions and Social Work, 1948-57; mem. exec. com. Bapt. World Alliance Women's Dept., 1950-60, 65-67; mem. N.Am. Bapt. Women's Union Exec. Com., 1951—, pres., 1965-67; mem. relief com. Bapt. World Alliance, 1950-60; mem. Commn. Religious Liberty, 1961-65; mem. Commn. on Evangelism and Missions, 1965—, co-chmn., 1970-75; mem. Bapt. Joint Com. Pub. Affairs, 1958-73, 1st vice-chmn., 1970-72; v.p. Bapt. World Alliance, 1970—; mem. N.Am. Bapt. Fellowship, 1971—. Mem. exec. bd. Ala. chpt. Nat. Multiple Sclerosis Soc., 1953-58. Bd. dirs. So. Bapt. Found., 1970—. Mem. Nat. Assn. Deans Women, Kappa Delta Pi. Clubs: Kenilworth, Bibs Book Review. Author: Woman's Missionary Union, 1960; History of Woman's Missionary Union, 1964. Home: 3402 D Primm Lane Apt I Birmingham AL 35216 Office: 600 N 20th St Birmingham AL 35203

HUNT, ARLINE PAT BRUSH (MRS. PAUL HENRY HUNT), journalist, state ofcl.; b. N.Y.C., Jan. 23, 1928; d. Donald Linsley and Arline (Camp) Brush; A.B., U. Vt., 1949; m. Paul Henry Hunt, Aug. 20, 1949; children—Stuart Gerald, Donald Porter, Andrew Loren. Tchr., Kensington, Conn., 1949-51; reporter Burlington (Vt.) Free Press, Newport (Vt.) Daily Express, Caledonian Record, St. Johnsbury, Vt., 1956-68; editor Co-op Life, 1972—. Free lance writer, 1960—. Mem. Vt. Bd. Edn., 1969—, Vt. Edn. Conf. Bd., 1967, pres. Tri-County School Dirs., 1967-69; sch. dir., Brighton, Vt., 1961-69, No. Country Union High Sch., 1969—; mem. Vt. Bd. Historic Sites, 1960-63; mem. bd. Vt. council Nat. Endowment for Humanities. Mem. Republican State Com., 1966-67, Edn. Platform Com., 1968; alternate del. Rep. Nat. Conv., Miami, Fla., 1968; mem. county and town Rep. coms.; Young Rep. nat. committeewoman, 1964-66; Young Rep. state chmn., vice chmn., 1960-64. Trustee North region United Fund; mem. bd. New Eng. Program Tchr. Edn. Recipient Vt. Edn. Layman's award, 1966; named Mrs. Vt., 1964, Mrs. Am. Pageant, 1964. Mem. Vt. Fedn. Women's Clubs (pub. relations chmn., Creative Writing award 1966, 68), Vt. State Sch. Dirs. Assn. (mem. bd., legislative chmn. 1967-69), Nat. Assn. State Bds. Edn. (area v.p. 1973—), Greater Vt. Assn. (dir.), Kappa Alpha Theta. Mem. United Ch. of Christ. Club: Island Pond (Vt.) Women's (past pres.). Home: Morgan VT 05853

HUNT, AUDREY GEITZ (MRS. SAMUEL A. HUNT, JR.), radio-TV broadcaster; b. Topeka, May 6, 1925; d. Homer Nelson and Helen Albertine (Rehnquist) Geitz; m. Samuel Arthur Hunt, Jr., May 24, 1947; children—Samuel David, Andrew Franklin, Steven Richard. Broadcaster, continuity writer sta. WAIM, Anderson, S.C., 1946-47, sta. WESC, Greenville, S.C., 1947-48; broadcaster sta WMRC, Greenville, 1951-52; TV spl. features Sta. WIS-TV, Columbia, S.C., 1954-72, radio-broadcaster Sta. WIS, writer, 1958-72; freelance talent and writer; asst. to pres. State Telecasting Co., Inc., 1973—. Honored by Gov. S.C., 1972; recipient Best Actress award Town Theatre, Columbia, 1968-69 season; numerous honors and recognition for civic, pub. service activities. Mem. Am. Women in Radio and TV (pres. Palmetto chpt. 1966-68, nat. bd. dirs. 1969-72, trustee-at-large, treas. Ednl. Found. 1974—, So. area v.p. 1969-72, nat. research chmn. 1972—). Methodist. Home: 6821 Crosfield Rd Columbia SC 29206 Office: PO Box 1333 Columbia SC 29202

HUNT, BETTY EVANS (MRS. HAROLD TAFT HUNT), civic worker; b. Raleigh, N.C., Nov. 9, 1933; d. William E. and Lillian (McCraw) Evans; student Spartanburg Jr. Coll., 1951-52; m. Jesse Boyd Davis, Nov. 15, 1952; 1 dau., Carol Suzanne; m. 2d, Harold Taft Hunt, Oct. 5, 1973. Women and girls dir. YMCA Family Center, Spartanburg, S.C., 1954-55; pvt. sec. August W. Smith Co., 1952-53; office mgr. Spartanburg Country Club, 1956-57, Y. C. Balenger Elec. Contractor, 1958-64; owner, operator B. Davis Ltd., 1968-73. Sec., Spartanburg Crime Prevention Council, 1963-65; mem. S.C. Status of Women Commn., 1964—, S.C. Council for Common Good, Spartanburg bd. Nat. Found., 1958—; vol. A.R.C. S.C. bd. Nat. Found., 1961-65, state women's adviser 1961; mem. Council for Spartanburg County, 1960-65; P.T.A., 1961-68; S.C. Traffic Safety Com., S.C. Mental Health Com.; mem. adv. bd. Mental Health Social Club, 1964-65; state chmn. S.C. Women for Hwy. Safety. Mem. bd. dirs. YWCA Family Center. Mem. Gen. Fedn. Women's Clubs (nat. jr. sec. 1962-64, chmn. pub. affairs 1964-66, 2d v.p. S.E. council 1966-68), S.C. Fedn. Women's Clubs (dir. 1958-68, jr. dir. 1960-62, dist. pres. 1963-68), pub. affairs chmn. 1966-68), Spartanburg Federated Clubs (dir. 1963-68), Jay-C-Ettes (treas., sec., v.p. 1958-61), Spartansburg Bus. and Profl. Women's Club (chmn.). Baptist. Clubs: Nat. S.S. (pres. 1964-66), Piedmont Jr. Woman's (hon. life, pres. 1958—), Camellia Garden (pres. 1959-60), Toastmistress, Zonta. Home: 298 Heathwood Dr Spartanburg SC 29302

HUNT, EDITH JOAN, psychologist, educator; b. Pomona, Cal., Sept. 1, 1932; d. Philip S. and C. Mae (Weeden) Hunt; B.A., U. Redlands, 1954; M.A., Claremont Grad. Sch., 1964; Ph.D., U. Md., 1967. Tchr. elementary sch., Tulare and San Rafael, Cal., 1954-62; sch. psychologist, Tulare, 1962-65; prof. Inst. Child Study, U. Md., 1967—. Pvt. practice psychology. Mem. Am., Md. psychol. assns., N.E.A., Md. Tchrs. Assn., Am. Ednl. Research Assn., Council for Exceptional Children, Assn. Supervision and Curriculum Devel., Am. Assn. U. Profs., Delta Kappa Gamma. Author publs. Address: Institute for Child Study University of Maryland College Park MD 20742

HUNT, MARGARET CECILLE (MRS. JACK EDWARD HUNT), librarian; b. Madison, Wis., Apr. 2, 1923; d. Earl Clayton and Mary Lucretia (Harris) Flatman; B.S., Black Hills State Coll., 1968, M.Ed., 1970; postgrad. U. Wis., 1969; m. Jack Edward Hunt, Aug. 19, 1945 (dec. Dec. 1964); children—Pamela Kay, Debra Lynn, Traci Ann, Jack Edward. Faculty, Nat. Coll. Bus., Rapid City, S.D., 1968—, head librarian, 1971—. Mem. Rapid City Flood Com., 1972—. Recipient Grant, S.D. Library Assn., 1969. Mem. Am. Assn. U. Women, S.D., Mountain Plains, Rapid City (pres. 1969) library assns., Tau Sigma Phi. Presbyn. (elder 1960-64, trustee 1960-64). Moose. Home: 806 E Tallent Rapid City SD 57701 Office: National College Business Box 1780 Rapid City SD 57701

HUNT, MARJORIE CHILDS (MRS. LAWRENCE WESLEY HUNT), curator; b. Waltham, Mass., Sept. 4, 1902; d. Arthur Garland and Isabella (Westwood) Childs; B.S., Simmons Coll., 1924; m. Lawrence Wesley Hunt (dec. Apr. 1971). Cataloger, Mus. Fine Arts, Boston, 1924-51; librarian, 1952-68; sec., treas. Waltham (Mass.) Hist. Soc., 1956-57, curator, 1958—. Mem. Gore Place Soc., Soc. for Preservation New Eng. Antiquities, Nat. Trust for Historic Preservation, A.L.A. Home: 131-D North St Newtonville MA 02160 Office: 185 Lyman St Waltham MA 02154

HUNT, MARY LOUISE ROBINSON (MRS. VERNESS STEPHEN HUNT), univ. ofcl.; b. Indpls., June 11, 1924; d. Emitte and Irene Georgia (Anderson) Robinson; B.S. summa cum laude, Howard U., 1945, M.S. (fellow), 1946; m. Verness Stephen Hunt, May 23, 1947. Instr. Howard U., Washington, 1947-49, psychometrist-counselor, 1950-60, research asso., 1962-67, sr. research asso., dir. coll. research, 1967—. Mem. Am. Psychol. Assn., A.A.A.S., Delta Sigma Theta. Home: 2116 Branch Av SE Washington DC 20020

HUNT, PATRICIA A. (MRS. R.R. WESSON), physician; b. Omaha; d. Kenneth L. and Lois (Rice) Hunt; B.A., Goucher Coll., 1948; M.D., U. Neb., 1952; M.P.H., Columbia, 1959; m. R. Randolph Wesson, June 10, 1956; 1 dau., Alynne Rhys. Intern Grace Meml. Hosp., Detroit, 1952-53; resident U. Neb., 1953-54; coll. physician, asst. prof. health, phys. edn. Smith Coll., Northampton, Mass., 1954-55; dir. Amherst-Nelson Counties (Va.) Health Dist., 1955-58; dep. dir. Alexandria (Va.) Health Dept., 1959-66; fellow pediatric neurology Childrens Hosp., Washington, 1966-67; dir. Bur. Child Health, Va. Dept. Health, Richmond, 1967—. Fellow Am. Bd. Pub. Health and Preventive Medicine. Fellow Am. Acad. Pediatrics (affiliate); mem. Am. Assn. Pub. Health Physicians, Med. Soc. Va., Am. (affiliate), Va. acads. pediatrics, Va. Assn. Pub. Health Physicians, Richmond Acad. Medicine, Richmond Pediatric Soc. Contbr. articles to profl. jours. Home: 2956 Hathaway Rd Richmond VA 23225 Office: 109 Governor St Richmond VA 23219

HUNT, RUTH CECELIA, writer, editor, educator; b. Chgo., Apr. 5, 1923; d. Leslie Edward and Gladys Esther (Pratt) Hunt; B.S., Loyola U., Chgo., 1943, M.A., 1969, postgrad., 1969. Asst. editor Am. Osteo. Assn., Chgo., 1946-48; acting editor, 1948-51; advt. coordinator J.B. Roerig Co., Chgo., 1951-52; Copy editor Jordan-Sieber and Assos., Chgo., 1952-53; sci. editor Am. People's Ency., Chgo., 1953-57; mng. editor, 1957-59; editor-in-chief, 1959-63; editorial dir. LaSalle Extension U., Chgo., 1963-65; free lance writer, editor, Chgo., 1965—; lectr. edn. Loyola U., Chgo., 1969—. Cons. in psychometrics Am. Coll. Obstetricians and Gynecologists. Mem. A.A.A.S., Am. Statis. Assn., Am. Ednl. Research Assn., Nat. Council Measurement in Edn., Ill. Acad. Sci., N.Y. Acad. Scis. Home: 6874 N Northwest Hwy Chicago IL 60631 Office: 820 N Michigan Av Chicago IL 60611

HUNTER, BEATRICE TRUM (MRS. JOHN F. HUNTER), author; b. N.Y.C., Dec. 16, 1918; d. Gabriel and Martha (Engle) Trum; B.A., Bklyn. Coll., 1940; M.A., Columbia, 1942; postgrad. Harvard, 1940-41, Buffalo State Tchrs. Coll., summers 1941-42, N.Y. U., 1943-44, others; m. John F. Hunter, Aug. 2, 1943. Free lance writer; lectr., demonstrator natural foods, natural gardening, consumer problems, 1958—; hon. asso. Price-Pottenger Nutrition Found., 1973; Martha R. Jones lectr. in nutrition Asbury Theol. Sem., 1973, 74; television series Beatrice Trum Hunter's Natural Foods, WGBH, Boston, 1974. Recipient award for educating pub. on pesticide hazards Friends of Nature, 1961. Mem. Am. Acad. Applied Nutrition (hon. v.p. 1963-64), Fedn. Homemakers (hon. mem. bd. 1961—). Author: The Natural Foods Cookbook, 1961; Gardening Without Poisons, 1964; Consumer Beware, 1971; The Natural Foods Primer, 1972 (R.T. French Co. Tastemaker award 1972); Beatrice Trum Hunter's Whole-Grain Baking Sampler, 1972; Food Additives and Your Health, 1972; Yogurt, Kefir and Other Milk Cultures, 1973; Fermented Foods and Beverages, 1973. Home: RFD 1 Hillsboro NH 03244

HUNTER, DARLENE LOUCKS (MRS. THOMAS REMEGIUS HUNTER, JR.), physician; b. Hutchinson, Kan., Dec. 24, 1924; d. Harry Dayton and Mary Elizabeth (Wilson) Loucks; student Rollins Coll., 1942-44, U. Tex., 1944-45; M.D., Southwestern Med. Sch., 1949; m. Thomas Remegius Hunter, Jr., June 30, 1948; children—Thomas Remegius III, Elizabeth Gail. Intern, Parkland Hosp., Dallas, 1949-50, resident in anesthesiology, 1950; anesthesiologist St. Joseph's Hosp., Wellington, Tex., 1951-54; anesthesiologist McKnight State Tb Hosp., Carlsbad, Tex., 1954-69; dir. Angelo State U. Health Clinic, 1969—; mem. staff Shannon West Tex. Meml. Hosp. Bd. dirs. El Camino council Girl Scouts U.S., 1966-72, 1st v.p., 1970-72; bd. dirs. Concho Valley Home for Girls, 1969-72, v.p., 1971-72, pres., 1973—; bd. dirs. Status of Women Commn., San Angelo, Tex., 1972—. Mem. Am. Soc. Anesthesiologists, Tex. Soc. Anesthesiologists, Tex. Med. Assn., Tom Green County Med. Soc., Assn. Coll. Health Physicians. Home: 2602 Lindenwood St San Angelo TX 76901 Office: Box 11019 Angelo State U San Angelo TX 76901

HUNTER, DORIS MAY, psychiatrist; b. Hubbard Woods, Ill., Dec. 29, 1915; d. Paul Laubie and May Henrietta (Ackerman) Hunter; student Rockford Coll., 1933-34; B.S., U. Chgo., 1937; M.D., U. Ill., 1951. Intern, U. Chgo. Clinics, 1951-52; resident psychiatry Western Psychiat. Inst. and Clinic, Pitts., 1952-56, Phila. Psychoanalytic Inst., 1953-59; clin. asst. prof. psychiatry U. Pitts. Sch. Medicine, 1959-64, clin. asso. prof. dept. psychiatry, 1964—; part time pvt. practice psychiatry and psychoanalysis, Pitts., 1959—; mem. staff Western Psychiat. Inst. and Clinic, asst. to the dir. teaching analyst Pitts. Psychoanalytic Inst. Dept. Psychiatry, 1960—, asst. to dir., 1961—, tng. analyst, 1964—; teaching cons. Juvenile Court, Pitts., 1959-60; cons. Southeast Community Guidance Assn., 1960-61, Technoma Workshop for Disturbed Adolescents, 1961—, Community Psychiatry Sect. Hazelwood, Pitts., 1965-67, Mem. Am. Psychiat. Assn., Am., Pitts. psychoanalytic assns., Pitts. Neuropsychiatric Soc., A.M.A., Pa., Allegheny County med. socs., Phila. Psychoanalytic Soc., A.A.A.S. Contbr. papers to profl. pubs. Home: 154 N Bellefield Av Pittsburgh PA 15213 Office: 121 University Place Pittsburgh PA 15213

HUNTER, FRANCES EILEEN FULLER (MRS. CHARLES E. HUNTER), writer, lectr.; b. Anna, Ill., May 8, 1916; d. Fred and Dessie Bradilla (Pyles) Fuller; grad. high sch.; m. Lawrence Steder, Sept. 19, 1942 (dec. Mar. 1951); 1 son, Thomas Lawrence; m. 2d, Walter E. Gardner, Oct. 11, 1952 (div. Sept. 1957); 1 dau., Joan Eileen; m. 3d, Charles E. Hunter. Secretarial positions So. Bell Tel. & Tel. Co., St. Louis, 1936-41, Bauer & Black, 1941-44; with Peggy Newton Cosmetics, Newark, N.Y., 1946-47, regional mgr., 1947-51; owner Suniland Secretarial and Letter Service, Miami, Fla., 1956. Founder Alpha/Omega, Christian youth movement, 1966; active Campus Crusade for Christ, Youth for Christ; a founder Suniland Youth Center, Miami. Author: God is Fabulous, 1968; God is Fabulous; Go Man Go!; Hot Line to Heaven; My Love Affair With Charles, 1971; Hang Loose with Jesus, P.T.L.A. (Praise the Lord Anyway), 1972; How to Make Your Marriage Exciting, 1972; The Two Sides of a Coin, 1972; Since Jesus Passed By, 1973. Home: 10420 Memorial Dr Houston TX 77024

HUNTER, HELEN MANNING (MRS. HOLLAND HUNTER), educator; b. New Haven, Oct. 5, 1921; d. Frederick Johnson and Helen (Taft) Manning; A.B., Smith Coll., 1943; M.A., Radcliffe Coll., 1947, Ph.D., 1952; m. Holland Hunter, Jan. 31, 1946; children—Ann, Barbara (Mrs. John Chaffee), Christine, Timothy. Instr. Bryn Mawr (Pa.) Coll., part-time, 1949-51; lectr. Swarthmore (Pa.) Coll., part-time, 1952-71, asso. prof. econs., 1971-72; asso. prof. econs. Bryn Mawr Coll., 1972—. Mem. Am. Econ. Assn., Econometric Soc., League Women Voters, Phi Beta Kappa. Home: Featherbed Lane Haverford PA 19041 Office: Bryn Mawr Coll Bryn Mawr PA 19010

HUNTER, JOHNNIE PEARL DE BRUCE (MRS. NATHAN HUNTER), librarian; b. Enterprise, Miss., Jan. 30, 1910; d. John Henry and Susie (Thomas) DeBruce; B.S. in Elementary Edn., Jackson State Coll., 1958; postgrad. (Nat. Def. Edn. Act advanced librarianship scholar) U. Ariz., 1966, U. So. Miss., 1968-69; m. Nathan Hunter, Apr. 9, 1939; children—Nathan, Martha (Mrs. Alfred Ross), Mary E., Carrie P. Tchr., Enterprise pub. schs., 1937-39, 49-60; librarian Central High Sch., Enterprise, 1960-70; elementary librarian Enterprise West Campus, 1970-71; jr. high librarian Enterprise East Campus, 1971-74. Cub pack den mother Choctaw Area council Boy Scouts Am., 1970-71, troop leader Girl Scouts Am., 1969-74. Democratic primary election clk. Enterprise precinct, 1971. Named Mother of Year Jackson State Coll. Alumni Assn., 1972. Mem. A.L.A., Miss., Southeastern library assns., N.E.A., Miss. Tchrs. Assn., Clarke County Tchrs. Assn. (sec. 1972-74). Baptist (ch. financial sec. 1962-74. Sunday sch. tchr. 1960-74). Home: PO Box 97 Enterprise MS 39330 Office: Enterprise East Campus Library Enterprise MS 39330

HUNTER, JUDY ANN, assn. ofcl.; b. Louisville, July 23, 1940; d. Howard Samuel and Ann LaVerne (Stiles) Hunter; B.S., U. Louisville, 1966. Tchr. phys. edn. Harvey (Ill.) Sch. Dist., 1966-70; field dir., dir. resident camp, now dir. camping services Kentuckiana council Girl Scouts, Louisville, 1970—. Mem. Am. Camping Assn. (membership chmn. Ky. sect.; pres. elect 1973). Home: 1935 Gardiner Lane Louisville KY 40205 Office: 1268 Cherokee Rd Louisville KY 40204

HUNTER, KATHERINE MORTON (MRS. EDWARD OWEN HUNTER, JR.), microbiologist; b. Birmingham, Ala., Sept. 16, 1939; d. Jesse Thomas and Rosa Lorene (Hughes) Morton; B.S., U. Montevallo, 1959; Med. Technologist, Emory U., 1960; M.A., Vanderbilt U., 1962, Ph.D., 1968; m. Edward Owen Hunter, Jr., Sept. 23, 1967; children—Diane Leigh and Susan Marie (twins). Microbiologist, ednl. coordinator Bapt. Med. Centers, Birmingham, 1967—. Instr., U. Ala., 1967. NIH fellow, 1965-67. Mem. Am. Soc. Clin. Pathologists, Am. Pub. Health Assn., Am. Soc. Microbiology, Am. Acad. Microbiologists, Sigma Xi. Methodist (sec. covenant class 1973—). Contbr. articles to profl. jours. Home: 4605 Pine Mountain Rd Birmingham AL 35213 Office: 800 Montclair Rd Birmingham AL 35213

HUNTER, KRISTIN ELAINE EGGLESTON (MRS. JOHN I. LATTANY), author; b. Phila., Sept. 12, 1931; d. George L. and Mabel L. (Manigault) Eggleston; B.S., U. Pa., 1951; m. Joseph E. Hunter, Feb. 29, 1952 (div. Jan. 1962); m. 2d, John I. Lattany, June 22, 1968. Advt. copywriter Lavenson Bur. Advt., Phila., 1952-59; John Hay Whitney fellow, 1959-60; advt. copywriter Wermen & Schorr, Phila., 1961-62; information officer City of Phila., 1963-64, 66. Recipient Phila. Athenaeum Lit. award, 1964. Author: God Bless the Child, 1964; The Landlord, 1966; The Soul Brothers and Sister Lou (award Council on Interracial Books for Children), 1968. Author TV play Minority of One (prize Fund for Republic script competition 1955. Mailing Address: Broad St Philadelphia PA

HUNTER, M. SUSAN, univ. adminstr.; b. Fresno, Cal., Apr. 3, 1944; d. Bertram Harry and Virginia Hawes (MacCracken) Hunter; B.A. summa cum laude, Cal. State U., Fresno, 1966; postgrad. Cal. State U., Northridge, 1967, Cal. State U., Los Angeles, 1968-69; M.S. (Pi Mu Found. scholar), Ore. State U., 1971. Elementary tchr. Los Angeles City Schs., 1967-69; grad. asst. Ore. State U., 1969-71; dean women, instr. edn. Boise (Ida.) State Coll., 1971-72; adminstrv. asst. to dean students Cal. State U., Humboldt, Arcata, 1972; asst. dean students Cal. State U., Northridge, 1972—. Chmn. so. region Gov.'s State Youth Council, 1965-69; mem. Los Angeles Youth Goals Commn., 1967-69; mem. Ida. Commn. on Women's Programs, 1971-72; mem. community relations bd. West Valley Community Hosp., 1973; mem. Mayor's San Fernando Valley Adv. Com., 1973—; active Girl Scouts U.S.A. Bd. dirs. San Fernando Valley chpt. A.R.C. Recipient citation Los Angeles Mayor, 1969. Mem. Nat. Assn. Student Personnel Adminstrs. (mem. regional exec. bd. 1972—, also regional placement coordinator), Women's Equity Action League (Ida. pres. 1971-72), Town Hall, Municipal Mgmt. Assns. So. Cal., Student Personnel Assn. Cal. State Univs. and Colls., Nat. Assn. Women Deans, Adminstrs. and Counselors, Am. Personnel and Guidance Assn., League Women Voters, Am. Assn. Univ. Women, Council State Univ. and Colls. Child Care Centers (exec. com.), Cal. Women in Higher Edn. (steering com.), Am., N.W. coll. personnel assns., Phi Kappa Phi, Kappa Delta Pi, Phi Mu. Home: 9585 Reseda Blvd No 335 Northridge CA 91324

HUNTER, MABEL ALDEN, ret. coll. trustee; b. Waterbury, Vt., Nov. 6, 1901; d. Arthur Henry and Frances (Smith) Alden; diploma Sargent Sch. Phys. Edn., 1924; B.S., Columbia, 1929, M.A. in Edn., 1932; m. Ivor Eric Godfrey Hunter, June 3, 1933; 1 dau., Nancy (dec.). Tchr. YWCA, Buffalo, 1924-27; instr. phys. edn. Wash. State Tchrs. Coll., Ellensburg, 1929-31; instr. Women's Christian Coll., also YWCA, Tokyo, Japan, 1932-33. Pres. League Women Voters, Groton, Conn., 1957-59, state sec., 1959-63. Trustee, sec. bd. Mitchell Coll., New London, Conn., 1956-74. Pres. Am. Women's Club, Shanghai, China, 1937-38; chmn. joint com. Shanghai Women's Orgns., 1937-39. Mem. Am. Assn. U. Women (Shanghai pres. 1935-37, state sec. 1952-54, 1st v.p. 1954-57, state parliamentarian 1960-62, state pres. 1962-66), Garden Club Groton (sec.; librarian 1957-59), N.Y.C. Hort. Soc. Republican. Clubs: Town and County (Hartford); Highland Park (Lake Wales, Fla.). Home: Inchcliffe Dr Gales Ferry CT 06335

HUNTER, MARGARET KING, architect; b. Balt., May 13, 1919; d. Talmage Damron and Margaret Julie (Greenough) King; A.B., Wheaton Coll., 1941; postgrad. Smith Coll. Sch. Architecture, 1941-42, Harvard Grad. Sch. Design, 1942-45; m. Edgar Hayes Hunter, May 8, 1943; children—Christopher King, Margaret Greenough. Draftsman, H.V. Lawrence, landscape architect, Mass., 1940, Antonin Raymond, architect, N.Y.C., 1942-43; designer Raymond Loewy, N.Y.C., 1943; partner E.H. & M.K. Hunter, architects-planners, Hanover, N.H., 1945-66, Raleigh, N.C., 1969—; instr. design N.C. State U., 1968; owner Heritage Antiques. Chmn. soils com. N.C. Land Use Congress. Traveling exhibit of work, 1963, 66. Chmn., Hanover Dance Com., 1964-66. Recipient Progressive Architecture award, 1946, 47; award N.H. State Office Bldg. Competition, 1950. Mem. A.I.A., Soc. Women Engrs., Soil Conservation Soc., Constrn. Specifications Inst., N.C. Land Use Congress. Baptist. Club: North Hills (Raleigh). Important works include Laconia State Sch. Dormitories, 1955, Children's Study Home, N.H. State Hosp., 1954, N.H. Toll Rd Structures, 1955, House for Life mag., 1956, Dartmouth apts. and classroom bldg., 1960, Colby Jr. Coll. Art Center and Sci. Bldg., New London, N.H., 1962, classroom bldg., dormitories Bridgton Acad., Me., 1964, dormitory Conn. Coll., New London, 1965, Loon Mountain ski area, Lincoln, N.H., 1966, twenty year campus plan N.C. Central U., Durham, 1971, Student Internat. Meditation Soc. Acad., Santa Barbara, Cal., 1970. Home: 3808 Tall Tree Pl Raleigh NC 27612 Office: 4224 Six Forks Rd Raleigh NC 27609

HUNTER, MIRIAM EILEEN, educator, artist; b. Cin., June 6, 1929; d. James R. and Bertha (Oberlin) Hunter; B.S., Ball State Tchrs. Coll., 1951, M.A. in Art, 1957; M.A. in Christian Edn., Wheaton Coll., 1958. Tchr. art and English, Madison-Marion Consol. Sch., 1951-52; tchr. art Wheaton Coll., 1952—, chmn. art dept., 1969-70; asst. prof. art Fine Arts Gallery, Chgo., then asso. prof., 1971—; free lance art cons. Vol. Cook County Hosp., Chgo., 1955-58; mem. Wheaton Human Relations Orgn., 1965-67. Recipient Ingersol award for paintings, 1946, 47, 2d place award DuPage Sesquecentennial, 1968. Mem. Ill. Art Edn. Assn., Midwest Art Conf., Around Chgo. Art Educators, Delta Phi Delta, Sigma Tau Delta, Kappa Delta Pi. Home: 530 Aurora Way Wheaton IL 60187

HUNTER, RUBY SUE (MRS. CHARLES FORCE HUNTER), publishing co. exec.; b. Hico, Tex., Aug. 21, 1921; d. David Henry and Beulah (Boatwright) Persons; B.A., U. Tex., 1942; m. Charles Force Hunter; children—Shelley (Mrs. Roy Rudolph Richardson), Mary (Mrs. Jack McMasters Stone), Margaret. Air traffic controller CAA (now FAA), San Antonio and Houston, 1942-52; writer Bissonet Plaza News, 1969-72; coordinator Goals for La., 1971-74; adminstrv. dir. Jeff Publs. Inc., 1974—. Pres. United Ch. Women East Jefferson (La.), 1958-59, League Women Voters Jefferson Parish, La., 1961-64; pres. League Women Voters La., 1967-71, also bd. dirs., 1962-67; mem. probation services com. Community Services Council, Jefferson, 1966-73, v.p., 1970-72; mem. Library Devel. Com. La., 1967-71, Nat. Com. for Support of Pub. Schs., 1967-72; mem. Goals Found. Council Met. New Orleans, 1969—, sec. 1970, 72; mem. Goals La. Task Force State and Local Govt., 1969-70; pres. MMM Investment Club, 1969-72; bd. mem. New Orleans Area Health Planning Council, 1969—; mem. adv. council La. State Health Planning, 1971—; title I adv. council La. State Dept. Edn., 1970-72; mem. La. Citizens Ednl. Found. for Criminal Justice. Recipient Outstanding Citizens award Rotary Club, Metairie, La., 1962. Mem. New Orleans Panhellenic (pres. 1956-57), Lamar Soc., La. Civil Service League, Alpha Xi Delta. Presbyn. (elder). Home: 210 Stewart Av River Ridge LA 70123

HUNTER, TOMMIE LOU, extension program leader; b. Elmer, Okla., Mar. 2, 1927; d. Troy A. and Wilma (Holmes) Hunter; student Edinburg Jr. Coll., 1945-46; B.S., Southeastern State Coll. at Weatherford, Okla., 1949; M.S., Okla. State U., 1962, postgrad., 1967; postgrad. U. Ariz., 1971. Dietician West Okla. State Hosp., Weatherford, 1949; home demonstration agt. Extension Service, Duncan, Okla., 1949-68; program leader home econs. Va. Poly. Inst. Extension, Luray, 1968—. Program leader family resources County Mental Health, 1955-59. Bd. dirs. County Civil Def., 1964-68, local A.R.C., 1952-62. Extension Homemakers Council scholar, 1960. Mem. Okla. Assn. Extension Home Economists (pres. 1960), Okla., Va., Am. home econs. assns., Va. Extension Service Assn., C. of C., Nat. Assn. Extension Home Economists (Distinguished Service award, 1963), Bus. and Profl. Women Assn., Epsilon Sigma Phi. Home: 1125 E Main St Luray VA 22835 Office: 218 Page St Luray VA 22835

HUNTER BLAIR, PAULINE CLARKE (MRS. PETER HUNTER BLAIR), author; b. Kirkby-in-Ashfield, Eng., May 19, 1921; d. Charles Leopold and Dorothy Kathleen (Milum) Clarke; B.A. with honors, Somerville, Coll., Oxford, Eng.; m. Peter Hunter Blair, Feb. 1969. Free-lance writer, 1948—; lectr. Mem. Brit. Soc. Authors, Nat. Book League. Author: (under name Pauline Clarke) (juveniles) The Pekinese Princess, 1948, The Great Can, 1952, The White Elephant, 1952, Smith's Hoard, 1955 (reissued as The Golden Collar 1967), Sandy, the Sailor, 1956, The Boy with the Erpingham Hood, 1956. Hidden Gold, 1957, James, the Policeman, 1957, James and the Robbers, 1959, Torolv the Fatherless, 1959, The Lord of the Castle, 1960, James and the Smugglers, 1961, Keep the Pot Boiling, 1961, The Twelve and the Genii (pub. in U.S. as The Return of the Twelves 1963) (Library Assn. Carnegie medal 1962, Lewis Carroll Shelf award, Deutsche Jugend Buchpreis 1968), James and the Black Van, 1963, Crowds of Creatures, 1964, The Bonfire Party, 1966, The Two Faces of Silenus, 1972; (under pseudonym Helen Clare) (juveniles) Five Dolls in a House, 1953, Merlin's Magic, 1953, Bel, the Giant, and Other Stories, 1956, Five Dolls and the Monkey, 1956, Five Dolls in the Snow, 1957, Five Dolls and Their Friends, 1959, Seven White Pebbles, 1960, Five Dolls and the Duke, 1963, The Cat and the Fiddle, and Other Stories from Bel, the Giant, 1968; also author short stories and plays for adults. Contbr. to Eastern Daily Press; book reviewer for Times Lit. Supplement. Home: 62 Highsett Hills Rd Cambridge England Office: care Curtis Brown Ltd 1 Craven Hill London W 2 3EW England also care John Cushman Assos Inc 24 E 38th St New York City NY 10016

HUNTINGTON, MARTHA CRALLEY, coll. dean; b. E. St. Louis, Ill., Dec. 28, 1933; d. Lawrence William and Dorothy May (Howard) Cralley; student So. Ill. U., 1951-53; B.S., U. Ill., 1960; postgrad. U. Md., 1962; M.S., George Washington U., 1968; m. William Roy Huntington, July 8, 1956 (dec. May 1971); children—Lisa, Jeffrey, Michael. Faculty, Mount Vernon Coll., Washington, 1960-69, dept. chmn., 1965-69, dean of students, 1969-71, dean student affairs, 1971-75; dean students Agnes Scott Coll., Decatur, Ga., 1975—. Mem. Nat. Assn. Women Deans and Counselors, Am. Personnel and Guidance Assn., Am. Assn. U. Profs., Am. Assn. Community and Jr. Colls. Home: 206 S Candler St Decatur GA 30030

HUNTLEY, HELEN LOU, rehab. cons.; b. Scottdale, Pa., Nov. 8, 1925; d. Issac Newton and Josie Louisa (Hellein) Huntley; B.A., Muskingum Coll., 1946; M.A., U. Hawaii, 1951; Ed.D. (Dept. Health, Edn. and Welfare scholar), U. Ariz., 1972; certificate occupational therapy Tex. Womens' U., 1957; certificate sheltered workshop adminstrn. (Dept. Health, Edn. and Welfare scholar), U. San Francisco, 1968. Apprentice machinist Altec Lansing Radio Corp., Los Angeles, 1947-49; dir. Central Command Craft Shops, Japan, 1953-55; dir. occupational therapy dept. Mahelona Hosp., Kapaa, Kauai, Hawaii, 1957-67; project dir. Statewide Planning Rehab., Guam, 1968-69; project dir. Planning for New Vocational Rehab. Services Program, Trust Territory of the Pacific Islands, 1971-73; cons. Nat. Iranian Soc. for Rehab. of the Disabled, Iran, 1974—. Cons. Pub. Health Service, Kauai, Hawaii, 1965-67, also various hosps. on the Island of Kauai. State dir. at-large Hawaii Tb. Assn., 1966-69; charter mem., pres., sec. Rehab. Unltd., Kauai, 1957-67. Mem. World Fedn. Occupational Therapists, Rehab. Internat., Nat. Rehab. Assn., Am. Occupational Therapy Assn., U. Hawaii Alumni Assn., U. Ariz. Alumni Assn. Home: 5393 Pooia St Honolulu HI 96821 also 3000 Silverleaf Dr Austin TX 78757

HUNTLEY, JILL PERRY (MRS. HOWARD R. HUNTLEY), librarian; b. Black River Falls, Wis., July 6, 1934; d. Howard Ephraim and Frances Edna (Roberts) Perry; student U. Wis., 1952-54; B.S., No. Ill. U., 1958; M.S., in L.S., U. N.C., 1968; m. Howard Robert Huntley, June 13, 1953; children—Eve and Rhea (twins). Librarian, Stoughton (Wis.) Pub. Schs., 1958-62; order asst. Preston Library, Va. Mil. Inst., Lexington, 1962-64, reference librarian, 1965-66; law librarian Washington and Lee U., Lexington, 1967-68, acquisition librarian McCormick Library, 1968-70; librarian So. Sem., Buena Vista, Va., 1971—. Mem. League of Women Voters. Home: Route 1 Lexington VA 24450 Office: Southern Sem Buena Vista VA 24416

HUPALO, MEREDITH TOPLIFF (MRS. NICHOLAS HUPALO), artist, illustrator; b. Tarpon Springs, Fla., Apr. 28, 1917; d. Walter and Maurine (Martin) Topliff; certificate in design Pratt Inst., 1938; m. Nicholas Hupalo, July 13, 1940; children—Walter Topliff, John Nicholas. One man shows, Tarpon Springs Pub. Library, 1945, Valley Stream (N.Y.) Mus., 1962, Contemporary Arts, Inc., N.Y.C., 1966, Jet Clubs Internat., N.Y.C.; represented in permanent collection Valley Stream Pub. Library, Tarpon Springs (Fla.) Pub. Library, Eastern Airlines Exec. Offices, N.Y.C. Tchr. printmaking Nassau County (N.Y.) Home Extension Service; art adviser Valley Stream Mus., 1962-64; illustrator Eastern Airlines, 1964-68; artist Shell Oil Co., 1968-70; designer Continental Can Co., N.Y.C., 1970-73. Recipient spl. award oil painting 34th Nat. Spring Exhbn. Art League L.I., 1964; gold medal in oil painting 35th Membership Show Art League L.I., 1965. Mem. Nat. Art League L.I. (treas. 1959-60), Am. Mus. Natural History (asso.), Mus. Modern Art, N.Y.C. Methodist. Works included Paintings with Markers, 1972. Home: 55 Forest Rd Valley Stream NY 11581

HURAVITCH, MILDRED MARGARET (MRS. VERNON FREDRICK HURAVITCH), city ofcl.; b. Gillette, Wyo., Aug. 17, 1934; d. Howard Lewis and Margaret Janice (Hamaker) Bundy; student U. Wyo., 1952-53; m. Gary Del Sylvester, July 14, 1953 (dec. May 1961); children—Ricky, Howard, Tammy Jo; m. 2d, Vernon Fredrick Huravitch, Feb. 23, 1963. With, U.S. Dept. Agr., Campbell County Agrl. Stblzn. Conservation Com., Gillette, 1955-67; dep. assessor Campbell County, Gillette, 1968-70; city clk., Gillette, 1970—. Recipient Work Improvement award U.S. Dept. Agr., 1960, 64. Mem. Wyo. Assn. County Office Employees (sec. 1963-64). Home: PO Box 666 Gillette WY 82716 Office: PO Box 540 Gillette WY 82716

HURD, SUZANNE SHELDON, health sci. adminstr.; b. Elmira, N.Y., Dec. 17, 1939; d. Victor S. and Eleanor O. (O'Donnell) Hurd; B.S., Bates Coll., 1961; M.S., U. Wash., 1963, Ph.D., 1965. Fellow U. Cal., Berkeley, 1967-69; health scientist adminstr. Nat. Inst. Health, Bethesda, Md., 1969—. Home: 10513 Weymouth St Bethesda MD 20014 Office: Nat Inst Health Nat Heart and Lung Inst Bethesda MD 20014

HURLBURT, EVELYN M. (MRS. EVERETT H. HURLBURT), educator; b. Marion, O., Dec. 15, 1916; d. Randolph and Florence (Boblenz) McClelland; B.S., Ohio State U., 1938, M.A., 1939; Ph.D., U. Md., 1967; postgrad. Catholic U. Am., Syracuse U.; m. Everett H. Hurlburt, Sept. 2, 1939; children—Douglas, Diane, Donna Jean. Instr. dept. sci. edn. Ohio State U., Columbus, 1938-40; sci. cons. D.C. Pub. Schs., Washington, 1947-48; instr. biology Montgomery Coll., Takoma Park, Md., 1953-56, asso. prof. microbiology and radiation sci., 1956-67, prof. microbiology and radiation sci., 1967-71, prof. biology, 1971—; bacteriologist clin. labs. Children's Hosp. of D.C., Washington, part-time, 1957-58; founder, dir. Radiation Lab., under AEC Grant, 1960-64; co-dir. AEC Insts. in Radiation Biology, 1969-70; co-dir. NSF Coll. Sci. Improvement Program with Md. Community Colls., 1972—; prin. investigator survey teaching applications of nuclear energy Atomic Indsl. Forum and Nat. Sci. Tchrs. Assn., 1973. Mem. A.A.A.S., Am. Assn. U. Profs., Nat. Sci. Tchrs. Assn. (sci. materials review com. 1969-72), Nat. Assn. Biology Tchrs., Am. Soc. for Microbiology, Am. Inst. Biol. Scis. (chmn. nat. task force 2 yr. coll. biologists 1969-71; vis. radiation biologist Office Biol. Edn. 1968-73), Radiation Research Soc., N.E.A., Pi Lambda Theta, Phi Delta Gamma. Author: Tracing Life Processes with Radioisotopes, 1967. Contbr. articles in field to profl. jours. Home: 9522 Bruce Dr Silver Spring MD 20901 Office: Montgomery Coll Takoma Park MD 20012

HURLEY, LOUISE BRADLEY (MRS. ANDREW J. HURLEY), realtor; b. Monterey Park, Cal., Apr. 6, 1930; d. Charles A. and Alice J. (Boney) Bradley; grad. Sawyers Bus. Coll., 1948; m. William White, Feb. 15, 1949; children—Ronald Bradley, Carrie, Kelley, Alyson (Mrs. Ron Montgomery); m. 2d, Andrew J. Hurley, Oct. 16, 1970. Realtor, Spindrift Village, Shell Beach, Cal.; pres. San Luis Bay Realty, Avila Beach, Cal., 1968-71, Santos Land Co., Shell Beach, 1970—. Agt., San Luis Bay Club, Avila Beach, Cal., 1968-71. Pres., San Luis Obispo Real Estate Bd., 1961. Vol., St. Marys Hosp., Reno, 1967; sec. Natoma council Campfire Girls, 1970. Mem. Nat. Inst. Farm and Land Brokers, Nat. Inst. Real Estate Bds., Cal. Real Estate Assn. (regional v.p. 1971, dir.), Internat. Fedn. Real Estate Brokers. Methodist. Home: 2395 Shell Beach Rd Shell Beach CA 93449

HURLEY, MARIE V., librarian; b. Elmira, N.Y., Dec. 25, 1910; d. Daniel Joseph and Olga (Hauenstein) Hurley; B.S., Elmira Coll., 1932; B.S. in L.S., Columbia, 1933. Sch. and reference librarian N.Y.C. Pub. Library, 1933-42; librarian Riverdale (N.Y.) Neighborhood and Library Assn., 1942-46; asst. librarian U.S. Information Library, Sydney, Australia, 1946-47; librarian South Euclid-Lyndhurst (O.) Pub. Library, 1948-52; br. librarian Cuyahoga County (O.) Pub. Library, 1952-54; asst. dir. Ferguson Library, Stamford, Conn., 1954-65, dir., 1965—. Bd. dirs. Stamford Forum World Affairs. Mem. Am., New Eng., Conn. (pres. 1967-68) library assns. Home: 154 Cold Spring Rd Stamford CT 06905 Office: 96 Broad St Stamford CT 06901

HURLEY, SHIREEN MARY TWOGOOD (MRS. KENNETH DUANE HURLEY), newspaper editor; b. Berkeley, Cal., Sept. 17, 1917; d. Archie James and Dorothy Adelaid (Pierce) Twogood; student Riverside Jr. Coll., 1936-37; student Salem Coll., 1937-38, 59-61, B.A., 1961; student U. Cal. at Berkeley, 1938-39; m. Kenneth Duane Hurley, Aug. 14, 1937; children—Terry Anne (Mrs. Carroll D. Van Horn), Catherine Sue (Mrs. Richard L. Dixon), Rebecca Marie (Mrs. Gary D. Martin), Penelope Louise. Pvt. tchr. voice, piano, organ, 1942-70; instr. voice, piano, organ, Salem (W.Va.) Coll., 1963-72; tchr. voice, art, Johnson High Sch., Salem, 1963-64; pres. Salem Press, 1969—; editor, mgr., Salem Herald, 1969—. Pres. Salem High Sch. P.T.A., 1958-60, 65-66; mem. adv. council Foster Grandparent program Commn. on Aging, 1972-73. Bd. mgmt. Seventh Day Bapt. Housing Corp., 1968—. Mem. W.C.T.U., Madrigal Singers of Clarksburg, Salem Coll. Aux. Baptist (chmn. council on ecumenical affairs 1969-71). Club: Women's (Salem, W.Va.). Home: 1 Sylvan Heights Salem WV 26426 Office: 58 High St Salem WV 26426

HURRY, NANCY CAROLYN, educator; b. Granite City, Ill., Aug. 15, 1938; d. Elmer Alvin and Loretta (Krohne) Hurry; student U. Ill., 1956-59; B.S., Eastern Ill. U., 1961; M.A., U. Colo., 1966. Tchr. phys. edn. Morris (Ill.) High Sch., 1961-65; counselor Glenbrook North High Sch., Northbrook, Ill., 1966-67, Hinsdale (Ill.) Twp. High Sch. South, 1967—. Leader Trailways council Girl Scouts U.S., 1961-63. Mem. N.E.A., Am. Personnel and Guidance Assn., Am. Sch. Counselors Assn., Ill. Assn. Women Deans and Counselors (program com. 1972-74, chmn. 1973, pres. 1974—), Suburban Women Deans and Counselors (v.p. 1970-71), Ill. Edn. Assn., Hinsdale High Sch. Tchrs. Assn. (ethics chmn. 1969-70, sec. 1970-71, negotiator 1972-73). Home: 19W232 Winwood Way Downers Grove IL 60515 Office: 7300 Clarendon Hills Rd Clarendon Hills IL 60514

HURSCH, HELEN BLANCHARD, psychologist; b. Lincoln, Neb., July 29, 1929; d. Earl Gordon and Isabel (Krebs) Blanchard; B.A., U. Denver, 1950, M.A., 1952, postgrad. 1950-53, 64, 68, U. Colo., 1961, Adams State Coll., 1973; children by previous marriage—M. Charles, James A. Clin., sch. psychologist, Saratoga Springs, N.Y., 1953-54; sch. psychologist San Francisco Unified Sch. Dist., 1955-57, Marin County Schs., San Rafael, Cal., 1957-58, Adams County Dist., Denver, 1966-69, Colo. Div. of Youth Services, Denver, 1970—. Pres. Blanchard Ranch, Inc., Bridgeport, Neb. Mem. Am., Colo. psychol. assns., Colo. Soc. Sch. Psychologists, Colo. Juvenile Council. Democrat. Office: 3900 South Carr Denver CO 80235

HURSH, HESTER JO (MRS. DONALD M. DYRDA), surgeon; b. Macoun, Sask., Can., Oct. 31, 1935; d. Benjamin B. and Hester Maud (Bicknell) Hursh (parents Am. citizens); B.S., George Williams Coll., 1958; M.D., U. Ill., 1964; m. Donald M. Dyrda, Aug. 24, 1968; children—Donald, Susan, Chris, Cindy. Intern Cook County Hosp., Chgo., 1964-65, resident in gen. surgery, 1965-69, head surgery fellow, 1969-71; practice medicine specializing in hand surgery Northeastern Ill., 1970—; attending hand surgeon MacNeal Hosp., Berwyn, Ill., 1970—; instr. hand surgery Hinsdale (Ill.) Hosp. 1971—; cons. surgeon Downers Grove, Ill., Joliet, Ill., 1972-73; indsl. surgeon and cons. Sears Roebuck Nat. Office, Chgo., 1951—. Mem. DuPage County Med. Soc., Suburban Surg. Soc. Episcopalian. Home: 432 Rockhurst Rd Bolingbrook IL 60439 Office: Dept 708 Sears Tower Chicago IL 60684

HURST, ELAINE LANCIA (MRS. WILLIAM J. HURST), educator; b. Paterson, N.J., Jan. 10, 1946; d. Ugo Victor and Lillian Joan (Kopec) Lancia; B.A., Manhattanville Coll., 1966; M.A., N.Y. U., 1968; postgrad. Fordham U., 1968—; m. William James Hurst, Jan. 20, 1974. Instr. philosophy Dominican Coll., Blauvelt, N.Y., 1969-70, N.Y. Inst. Tech., Old Westbury and N.Y.C., 1970—. Mem. Am. Philos. Assn., L.I. Philos. Soc., Soc. for Philosophy and Pub. Affairs, Am. Catholic Philos. Assn. Home: 305 E 72d St Apt 5G-N New York City NY 10021

HURST, FRANCES ETHEL (MRS. HENRY O. HURST), librarian; b. Birmingham, Ala., Feb. 27, 1919; d. Harold Hudson and Nota Leigh (Windham) Weekley; B.A., U. Ala., 1941; B.A. in L.S., Emory U., 1945; m. Henry Odessa Hurst, Sept. 8, 1947 (dec. Feb. 1962); children—Rosalind Frances (Mrs. Charles Douglas Minderhout), Walter Henry. Tchr. pub. schs., Ala., 1941-44, 50-52, 58-62; librarian TVA, Wilson Dam, 1945-46; librarian U. Ala., Tuscaloosa, 1946-50, 62-69; caseworker Talladega County Dept. Pensions and Security, 1952-54; librarian Jefferson State Jr. Coll., Birmingham, 1969—. Mem. Kappa Delta Pi, Pi Tau Chi. Home: 1641 5th St NW Birmingham AL 35215 Office: 2601 Carson Rd Birmingham AL 35215

HURST, PAMELA BALDWIN (MRS. GREGORY SQUIRE HURST), social worker; b. Maui, Hawaii, July 2, 1947; d. Henry James and Helen (Johnson) Baldwin; B.A., Western Coll., Oxford, O., 1969; M.A., U. Wis., 1973; m. Gregory Squire Hurst, June 21, 1969. Tchr., Horicon (Wis.) Schs., 1969-70; counselor Wayland Acad., Beaver Dam, Wis., 1969-70, dean girls, 1970-73; dir., chief police social worker Human Services, Chapel Hill, N.C., 1973—. Cons. Community Youth Programs, 1973, Child Abuse/Neglect Team, 1973, also Police Rape Crisis Team, Alternative Rehab. Com. Co-chmn. amnesty com. Chapel Hill Peace Center, 1973-74; mem. New Hope Rescue Unit Ambulance Crew, 1973; resource cons. N.C. League Women Voters Juvenile Corrections Study, 1973. Mem. Internat. Thespian Soc., Am. Personnel and Guidance Assn., Nat. Assn. Women Deans and Counselors, Concerned, N.C. Assn. Communited-Based Programs for Youth, N.C. Juvenile Correction Assn. Home: 104 Stateside Dr Chapel Hill NC 27514 Office: 100 W Rosemary St Chapel Hill NC 27514

HURST, PATRICIA WITWER (MRS. ROBERT HURST), librarian; b. Danville, Ill., Sept. 18, 1923; d. Frederic Minor and Otha (Horning) Witwer; B.S., U. Ill., 1945; M.S., U. So. Cal., 1966; m. Robert Hurst, Mar. 6, 1948; children—Fred, Elizabeth. Chemist, Edwal Chem. Labs., Chgo., 1945-47; patent asst. Corn Products Refining Corp., Chgo., 1947-48; with Ventura County Library (Cal.), 1963—, supervising librarian, 1972—. Mem. Am., Cal. library assns., Beta Phi Mu. Democrat. Unitarian. Home: 3550 Willowick Dr Ventura CA 93003 Office: 651 Main St Ventura CA 93001

HURST, PEGGY, educator; b. Abington, Pa., May 15, 1925; d. Thomas Wesley and Norma Louise (Morison) Hurst; A.B., Wilson Coll., 1946; M.A., U. Wis., 1948, Ph.D., 1956. Instr. chemistry Bowling Green State U. (O.), 1955-59, asst. prof., 1959-63, asso. prof., 1963-72, prof., 1972—. Chemist, Am. Cyanamid Co., 1946, 47. Mem. Am. Chem. Soc., A.A.A.S., Sigma Xi, Phi Kappa Phi. Mem. Soc. Friends. Home: 125 Crim St Bowling Green OH 43402

HURST, VELMA POPLIN (MRS. KENNETH BURNAP HURST), ret. educator; b. nr. Norwood, N.C., Sept. 16, 1902; d. Samuel Austin and Lucy (Lowder) Poplin; B.S., Meredith Coll., 1925; postgrad. U. N.C., summer 1930, N.C. State Coll. Extension, 1935-36, East Carolina U. Extension, 1960-61; m. Kenneth Burnap Hurst, May 21, 1938; 1 dau., Sara Lowder (Mrs. James Christopher Thomas). Tchr., N.C. State Sch. for Blind, Raleigh, 1925-38, Camp Lejeune (N.C.) Dependent's Sch., 1947-70; tchr. remedial reading Stone Street School, Camp Lejeune, 1970-72. Mem. N.C. Edn. Assn., N.C. Lit. and Hist. Assn., Onslow County Hist. Soc. (sec.), N.C. Ret. Sch. Personnel, Delta Kappa Gamma (pres. chpt. 1952-54; treas. 1964-70). Democrat. Baptist. Home: 9 Ruth St Jacksonville NC 28540

HURT, SARAH MAY MINER (MRS. ROBERT C. HURT), artist; b. Fort Wayne, Ind., July 13, 1907; d. Charles W. and Mary S. (Criswell) Miner; student Fort Wayne Art Sch., 1925-27, John Herron Art Sch., 1927-28, Indpls. Art League Found., 1955-64; m. Robert C. Hurt, May 26, 1934; children—Robert M. (dec.), Stanley C. Exhibited art in one-woman shows at Jewish Community Center, 1963, Art House, Cin., 1965-67, Ind. Central Coll., 1969, Left Bank Gallery, Marion, Ind., 1970, Franklin Coll., 1973, Fort Wayne Art Mus. Gallery, 1973, Washington Gallery, Frankfort, Ind., 1973; exhibited art in group shows including Indpls. Art League, Ind. Artists Exhbn., Fifty Ind. Print Exhbn., Ind. State Fair, Mid-State Art Exhbn., Ann. Art for Religion, Wabash Valley Exhbn., Muncie Art Assn., Carver Ann. Art Show, Nat. Assn. Women Artists, Cin. Biennial, Les Semaines Internationales de la Femme, Cannes, France, Anderson Winter Show, Nat. Assn. Women Artists Italian Exhibit, Pallazzo, Vecchio, Florence, Italy, others; represented in permanent collections Indpls. Mus. Art Rental Gallery, Washington Gallery, Frankfort, Ind., Jeanne Gallery, Carmel, Ind., Left Bank Gallery, Marion, Ind., Ft. Wayne Art Mus. Gallery. Recipient numerous awards including Silver medal Les Semaines Internat. de la Femme; I.A.L.F. Fellows award 500 Fine Arts Exhibit, 1972; 2d oil painting prize Ind. State Fair, 1972; DeBoest Purchase award Ind. Artists Club, 1972; Bd. Dirs. prize Tippecanoe Regional Exhibit, 1973. Mem. Nat. Assn. Women Artists, Ind. Artist Club (Lilly Endowment prize 1971), Indpls. Art League, Assn. Profl. Artists, Contemporary Art Soc. Address: 6464 N Sherman Dr Indianapolis IN 46220

HURT, SUSANNE MORRIS (MRS. MARSHALL HURT), artist; b. N.Y.C.; d. Harold Cecil and Cosby Meriwether (Dansby) Morris; student, Duke U., 1941-42, Corcoran Gallery Sch., 1952-53; pvt. study with Wayman Adams and A. Ginsburg; m. Marshall Hurt, Nov. 6, 1942. Exhibited one-man show at Cayuga Mus. of History and Art, Auburn, N.Y., 1971; exhibited in group Shows at N.A.D., N.Y.C., 1971-72, Lever House, N.Y.C., 1972-74; represented in Douglas Gallery, Westport, Conn.; pvt. instr. art, N.Y.C., 1969—. Recipient Anna Hyatt Huntington first prize Catharine Lorillard Wolfe Art Club, 1970; first prize Composers, Authors and Artists of Am., 1972, Nat. Biennial Composers, Authors and Artists of Am. Conv., 1973. Mem. Am. Artists Profl. League, Catharine Lorillard Wolfe Art Club (corr. sec. 1971—), Hudson Valley Art Assn., Composers, Authors and Artists of Am. (nat. rec. sec. 1971—), Acad. Artists Assn., Art Students League. Home: 299 Riverside Dr New York City NY 10025 Office: 30 E 20th St New York City NY 10003

HURWITZ, JANICE, educator; b. Salem, Mass., Aug. 19, 1918; d. Barnet and Dora (Cushing) Hurwitz; diploma Perry Kindergarten Normal Sch., 1941; B.S. in Edn., Boston U., 1942, M.Ed., 1946; diploma Columbia, 1951. Tchr. elementary sch. Salem pub. schs., 1941-46, prin. Juniper Sch., 1946-50, prin. Endicott Sch., 1950-69, prin. Bentley Sch., 1969—, dir. summer sch., 1953-71; coordinator, dir. Head Start, Salem, 1965-69; coordinator, dir. Elementary and Secondary Edn. Act Title I, Salem, 1966—. Mem. Mass. Elementary Sch. Prins. Assn., North Shore Prins. Assn., Mass. Sch. Psychologists Assn. (charter), Salem Tchrs. Union, N.E.A. Contbr. articles to profl. jours.

HUSAK, LILLIAN GREIVE (MRS. CHARLES ALFRED HUSAK), ednl. adminstr.; b. Cleve., June 24, 1915; d. John Gerhardt and Lillie (Ruessman) Greive; Mus. B., Cleve. Inst. Music, 1936; m. Charles Alfred Husak, Dec. 19, 1936; children—Charles A., Douglas N. Faculty, Cleve. Inst. Music, 1936—, dir. preparatory and adult edn. dept., 1969—, asst. musical prodns. Karamu House, Cleve., 1950-51, Cleve. Play-house, 1951-52. Mem. Mu Phi Epsilon. Home: 2050 Clague Rd Westlake OH 44145 Office: 11021 E Blvd Cleveland OH 44106

HUSCHKE, VIRGINIA KINCAID (MRS. RALPH E. HUSCHKE), ednl. adminstr.; b. Washington, July 21, 1927; d. Earle Hill and Virginia Dorothea (Morris) Kincaid; B.A., Mt. Holyoke Coll., 1948; M.S., U. So. Cal., 1968, postgrad., 1968—; m. Ralph E. Huschke, Aug. 28, 1948; children—Peter Charles, Lisa Earle. Tchr. pub. schs., Mass., Conn., Washington, 1949-60; elementary tchr. Torrance (Cal.) Unified Sch. Dist., 1960-64, spl. edn. tchr., 1964-68, adminstr., cons., asst. coordinator spl. edn., 1968-71; cons. spl. edn. Escondido (Cal.) Union Sch. Dist., 1972—. Tchr. extension course for tchrs. ednl. handicapped Pepperdine Coll., Los Angeles, 1968-71. Co-founder Human Relations Council of Palos Verdes Peninsula, 1968; co-chmn. Intercoms 68-69-70, intercommunity forum and fairs on human relations, Palos Verdes, Cal., 1968-70. Mem. exec. bd., charge awards South Bay Mayors Com. on Employment of the Handicapped. Recipient Pointer award Assn. Spl. Classroom Tchrs. and Parents of Handicapped, 1968. Mem. League of Women Voters, Hon. Assn. Women in Edn. Methodist. (chmn. social concerns commn. 1970-71). Home: 6 Admiralty Cross Coronado Cays CA 92118 Office: 5th and Maple Sts Escondido CA 92025

HUSE, MARTHA RUTH (MRS. LOUIS D. HUSE), coll. librarian; b. Weimar, Tex., Dec. 15, 1925; d. Chester Allen and Viola Rosina (Voitle) Grobe; A.A., Weatherford Jr. Coll., 1966; B.A., Tex. Womans U., 1967, M.L.S., 1969; m. Louis D. Huse, June 2, 1944; 1 dau., Connie Sue. Sec., M.G. Feeds, Weimar, 1942-45; clerical positions Weatherford (Tex.) Jr. Coll. Library, 1962-66, asst. librarian, 1967-69, head librarian, 1969—. Mem. Bus. and Profl. Womens Club (treas. 1972-74, 2d v.p. 1974—), Delta Kappa Gamma. Lutheran. Home: Rural Route 6 Box 67 Weatherford TX 76086

HUSK, MARY JO, elementary sch. supr.; b. Scipioville, N.Y., Mar. 5, 1916; d. Thomas Robert and Ola (Orr) Husk; B.A., Maryville Coll., 1939; M.S., U. Tenn., 1953. Tchr. Smith County Schs., Raleigh, Miss., 1939-41, Everett Sch., Maryville, Tenn., 1941-42, West Side Sch., Maryville, 1943-52, Sam Houston Sch., Maryville, 1952-55, U.S. Air Force Dependent Schs., Tachikawa, Japan, 1955-57, Etain, France, 1957-58, Wiesbaden, Germany, 1958-60, Bearden Elementary Sch., Knoxville, Tenn., 1960-62; elem. supr. Knox County Schs., Knoxville, Tenn., 1962—. Mem. N.E.A., Internat. Reading Assn. (sec., treas. 1965-66, v.p. 1966-67, pres. 1967-68), Elementary Kindergarten Nursery Edn., Tenn., East Tenn., Knox County edn. assns., Assn. Childhood Edn. Internat. (v.p. 1968-70), Delta Kappa Gamma (state 1st v.p. 1965-67, state pres. 1971-73). Democrat. Presbyn. Home: 311 Cates St Maryville TN 37801 Office: 400 W Hill Av Knoxville TN 37902

HUSKETH, ALMA ORMOND (MRS. EDWARD THOMAS HUSKETH, JR.), librarian; b. Dover, N.C., Aug. 17, 1918; d. William Henry and Ella Carrie (White) Ormond; B.A. in English, Woman's Coll. U. N.C., 1939; M.S. in L.S., U. N.C. at Chapel Hill, 1966; m. Edward Thomas Husketh, Jr., June 12, 1943; children—Edward Thomas III, William Ormond, Craig Moss. Tchr., Wilton (N.C.) High Sch., 1939-44, 46-51, 57-61; tchr. Lenoir County (N.C.) Schs., 1944-46; librarian South Granville High Sch., Creedmoor, N.C., 1962—. Cons. rev. panel N.C. Emergency Sch. Assistance Program, 1971; rev. panelist office Edn. Dept. Health, Edn. and Welfare, 1973—. Mem. scholarship com. U. N.C. at Greensboro, 1969-73; Granville county dir. N.C. P.T.A., 1970-72. Bd. dirs. Richard H. Thornton Pub. Library, Oxford, N.C. Mem. N.C. Edn. Assn. (sec. East Central dist. 1965), N.C. Classroom Tchrs. Assn. (pres. Granville County unit 1951-52), N.C. High Sch. Library Assn. (dir. East Central dist. 1969—), Nat. Grange, Alpha Delta Kappa (pres. Rho chpt. 1972-74). Methodist (Sunday sch. tchr. 1940—; dir. youth activities 1962-73; active Women's Soc. Christian Service). Home: Box 198 Brassfield Rd Creedmoor NC 27522 Office: PO Box 395 South Granville High School Creedmoor NC 27522

HUSMAN, GRAYCE BURKHAM (MRS. JAMES EBBESEN HUSMAN), hosp. adminstr.; b. Bowie, Tex., May 23, 1920; d. John Thomas and May Belle (Simpson) Burkham; R.N., St. Francis Hosp. Sch. Nursing, 1941; postgrad. U. Cal. at Los Angeles, 1971-72; m. James Ebbesen Husman, Mar. 20, 1955; children—John Page, Dana (Mrs. Michael Rasmussen), Rebecca May. Operating room supr. West Side Community Hosp., Newman, Cal., 1941-42, operating room supr., asst. head nurse, 1948-68, hosp. adminstr., 1968—; dir. nurses Mohave Gen. Hosp., Kingman, Ariz., 1943-45; county pub. health nurse Lassen County, Cal., 1946-47. Mem. Democratic Central Com., 1971-72. Mem. Assn. Operating Room Nurses (pres. 1971-73), V.F.W. Aux. Democrat. Methodist. Club: Gustin (Cal.) Community. Home: 29175 W Sullivan St Gustine CA 95322 Office: Box 151 S Hwy 33 Newman CA 95360

HUSSELBEE, MARGARET VANYS STONE (MRS. JOHN WILLIAM HUSSELBEE), educator; b. London, Eng., Nov. 1, 1918; d. Albert Edward and Kathleen (Holland) Stone; B.S., Tex. Woman's U., 1951; M.S. in L.S., U. N.C., 1962; m. John William Husselbee, Jr., Jan. 26, 1939 (dec. Feb. 1944); 1 dau., Sandra (Mrs. Henry Adams). Tchr., librarian, elementary and secondary sch., Miami Beach, Fla., 1951—. Instr., U. Miami, 1970. Mem. Pi Lambda Theta, Phi Alpha Theta. Home: 710 NW 93d Terrace Pembroke Pines FL 33024

HUSSER, GERTRUDE MARIE IRWIN (MRS. GEORGE D. HUSSER), real estate broker; b. San Francisco, May 1; d. Edward H. and Gertrude G. (Holland) Irwin; B.A., U. Cal., 1932; m. Clarence L. Hamberlin, Oct. 17, 1936 (dec. 1966); children—James E., William L., Sally Ann (Mrs. Robert Belshe); m. 2d, George D. Husser, Aug. 27, 1971. With State C. of C., San Francisco, 1934-35, real estate dept. Pacific Savs. & Loan Co., San Francisco, 1936; salesman Ednah Standish, Berkeley, Cal., 1956-58, Owen Quinton Realty, El Cerrito, Cal., 1958-61, Thousand Oaks Realty, Berkeley, 1961-64; owner, broker Hamberlin Realty, El Cerrito, Cal., 1964-73. Mem. Sheriffs' Ladies Posse, Contra Costa County, Cal., 1960-72, Womens Council, Berkeley, Cal., 1956-73, West Contra Costa Council, Richmond, Cal., 1959-73. Bd. dirs. Nat. Real Estate Assos., Berkeley, West Contra Costa, 1967-70, 71-72. Mem. Bus. and Profl. Womens Club, C. of C. (dir. 1967-72), Alpha Delta Pi. Home: 1557 Douglas Dr El Cerrito CA 94530

HUSSEY, MAE GRACE (MRS. JOSEPH MICHAEL HUSSEY), physician; b. Toledo, May 30, 1913; d. Charles Edward and Kathryn Bessie (Yarlot) Schissler; B.S., U. Toledo, 1934; M.B., M.D., U. Cin., 1938; M.P.H., Harvard, 1952; m. Joseph Michael Hussey, Apr. 10, 1940; children—Daniel S., Kathryn S. (Mrs. Peter Evers). Intern, Cin., 1938-39; resident Mass. Meml. Hosp., Boston, 1939-40; practice medicine, Quincy, Mass., 1940-51; epidemiologist Mass. Dept. Pub. Health, Boston, 1951-53, asst. dir. div. cancer and chronic disease, 1953-59, dir. div. maternal and child health services, 1960—; asso. in medicine, child health div. Children's Hosp. Med. Center, Boston, 1965—. Diplomate Am. Bd. Preventive Medicine. Home: 121 Shore Av Quincy MA 02169 Office: 39 Boylston St Boston MA 02110

HUSSMAN, JULIA EL ATTRACHE (MRS. LOTHAR HUSSMAN), physician; b. Djebel Druse, Syria, Feb. 15, 1931; d. Emir Fawzi and Samra Al (Hannawe) El Attrache; B.Philosophie, Lycée Francais of Beyruth, Lebanon, 1950; M.D., French U. of Beyruth, Lebanon, 1956; m. Lothar Hussman, Apr. 15, 1958; children—Karl, Mark, John. Came to U.S., 1957, naturalized, 1961. Intern, St. Mary's Hosp., Wasau, Wis., 1956-57; resident Ill. Masonic Hosp., Chgo., 1957-58, Children's Meml. Hosp., Chgo., 1958-59; practice medicine specializing in pediatrics, Elk Grove, Ill., 1959—; mem. staff Holy Family Hosp., Des Plaines, Ill., 1962—; Alexian Bros. Hosp., Elk Grove, 1966—, Loyola Med. Sch., Maywood, Ill., 1972—. Diplomate Am. Bd. Pediatrics. Fellow Am. Acad. Pediatrics, Royal Soc. Health; mem. Am. Med. Soc. Club: Lake Shore Athletic. Office: 15 Park Lane Elk Grove IL 60007

HUSTACE, BETTY JEAN CHAMPION (MRS. EDWARD C. HUSTACE), civic worker; b. Milw. Aug. 19, 1919; d. Iden Charles and Irene Elizabeth (Nelson) Champion; student Monticello Prep. Sch., 1935-37, Lawrence Coll., 1937-38, Monticello Coll., 1938-39; A.A., Mt. Mary Coll., 1941; m. Edward Clarence Hustace, May 3, 1941; children—Margaret Jean (Mrs. Charles Joseph Pietsch III), James Jeffery. Co-chmn., Kukala, 1966, Pucci Fashion Benefit, 1972; chmn. Muumuu Mania, 1961, Crescendo, 1971; v.p. Women's Assn. for Honolulu Symphony Soc., 1965-67, pres., 1967-69, Danny Kaye benefit, 1969, Concert in Fashion, 1973; organized Jr. Guild for Honolulu Symphony, 1967; active San Francisco Opera auditions, 1969-73; pres. Punahou Sch. P.T.A., 1960-63; chmn. carnival, 1960; leader Brownies, 1951-54; leader Girl Scouts U.S.A., 1954-56; vol. Honolulu Acad. Arts; guide Spalding House. Bd. dirs. YWCA, Punahou Sch., Hawaii Opera Theatre, Honolulu Symphony Soc. (exec. com. 1972-73), Found. Study Hawaii and Abroad, Hawaii Performing Arts Co. Mem. Bishop Mus. Assn., Hawaiian Hist. Soc., Hawaiian Humane Soc., Queens Hosp. Aux., Kauikeolani Children's Hosp. and Rehab. Center Aux., Sea Life Park Assn., P.E.O. (chpt. pres. 1970-71), Friends of East-West Center, Jr. League Honolulu. Home: 4715 Aukai Av Honolulu HI 96816

HUSTED, BERNIECE FRANCIS GRENVILLE, social worker, polit. scientist; b. Toledo; d. Edward G. and Isabel Ann (Diemer) Husted; student Price, Besancion, U. Toledo, 1936-39; B.A., U. Mich., 1939, M.A., 1941, M.S.W., 1956; postgrad. Washington U., 1946, U. Mexico, 1950, Temple U., 1963—. Social worker govtl. agys., Washington, 1940-41; supr. social service A.R.C., Washington, St. Louis, 1941-45, field rep., 1945-50; supr. child welfare Lucas County (O.) Child Welfare Bd., 1950-64; cons. child welfare Ohio Dept. Welfare, Toledo, 1964—; lectr. Penta Tech. Coll., Rossford, O., 1970. Mem. Gov.'s Com. White House Conf. on Aging, 1960; mem. Phys. Fitness Com. Study European Nations, 1962; participant Internat. Council Health Phys. Edn. and Recreation, Stockholm, Sweden,

1962; observer Internat. Congress Bus. and Profl. Women, Oslo, Norway, 1962, del. nat. conv., 1970; vol. A.R.C., 1940—; vol. worker, team capt. Community Chest and Council, 1960—; active Jr. League; membership drs. worker Zool. Soc., 1950—; rep. at large women's div. Lucas County Safety Council, 1960—; adv. council Penta County Tech. Sch. and Coll., 1967-68; participant Psychol. Study Conf., Leningrad, Vienna, 1972. Bd. dirs. Internat. Inst., 1962, 70—, exec. com., sec. bd., 1964—, mem. adv. com. to exec. bd., 1969—, rep. to Spain-Africa, 1969, chmn. vols. com., 1970; chmn. Toledo Internat. Ethnic-Cultural Festival, 1973-74. Trustee Daisy Scott Scholarship Fund for Girls. Recipient Honors key U. Toledo; Service award A.R.C., 1947; Service to Mankind award Sertoma, 1965. Mem. Acad. Certified Social Workers, Nat. Assn. Social Workers (chmn. social action com. 1960-62), Polit, Sci. Assn., Council on World Affairs, Royal Soc, for Health, Eng., Am. Assn. U. Women, Toledo Legal Aid Soc., Nat. (platform com. 1964, del. nat. conv. 1970), Ohio (legislation adv. chmm. 1963, dist. dir., mem. state bd. 1963—). Toledo (pres. 1961-62) fedns. bus. and profl. women's clubs, Child Welfare Assn., Child Welfare League Am. (program com.), Zeta Tau Alpha. Club: Maumee Sailing-Boating (Toledo). Research, pubIs. in field. Home: 2340 Ottawa River Rd Toledo OH 43611

HUSTON, ANNIE LAURA COTTEN, educator; b. Oxford, N.C., Nov. 18, 1923; d. Leonard F. and Laura Estelle (Spencer) Cotten; A.B., Duke, 1945; M.Ed., U. Hartford, 1965; postgrad. Hartford Sem. Found., 1963-65; U. N.C., 1971—; m. Hollis W. Huston, Sept. 8, 1945 (div. June 1970); children—Hollis W., Rebecca Ann, Laura Cotten. Counseling intern Hartford (Conn.) Hosp., 1962-64; acting dir. dept. social service Greater Hartford Council Chs., 1964-67; faculty dept. psychology Central Conn. State Coll., New Britain, 1967—, asst. prof., 1972—. Mem. Ministerial standing and credentials com. Hartford Assn. United Ch. Christ, 1965-73; sec. Conn. Council on Family, 1972-74. Mem. Am. Assn. Marriage and Family Counselors, Nat. Council Family Relations, Am. Personnel and Guidance Assn., Conn. Psychol. Assn. Mem. United Ch. Christ (mem. bd. Christian edn. 1970-73). Contbg. editor The Family Coordinator, 1974. Home: 193 Westland Av West Hartford CT 06107 Office: Central Conn State Coll 1615 Stanley St New Britain Ct 06050

HUSTON, BEATRICE FAE (MRS. JOHNNIE W. HUSTON), educator; b. Granbury, Tex., Oct. 7, 1926; d. Charles Wolfton and Clara (Hembright) Moore; A.A., Weatherford Jr. Coll., 1945; B.B.A., North Tex. State U., 1947; M.A., Stephen F. Austin State U., 1952; D.Ed., Baylor U., 1967; m. Johnnie Weldon Huston, June 5, 1948; 1 son, Schulyn Medzell. Tchr. bus. Granbury (Tex.) High Sch., 1947-48, Canton (Tex.) High Sch., 1948-51; tchr. bus. and lang. arts Nacogdoches (Tex.) Jr. High Sch., 1951-52; tchr. bus. Nacogdoches (Tex.) High Sch., 1952; instr. Stephen F. Austin State U., 1952; tchr. English Belton (Tex.) Jr. High Sch., 1955; tchr. bus. and edn. Mary Hardin-Baylor Coll., 1956-72, instr., 1956-60, asst. prof., 1960-63, asso. prof., 1963-67, prof., 1967—. Treas. Belton P.T.A., 1965-66; mem. citizens adv. bd. Mary Hardin-Baylor Coll. Named Distinguished Prof., Mary Hardin-Baylor Coll., 1972; recipient Achievement award Phi Beta Lambda, 1973. Mem. Am. Econ. Assn., Tex. Tchrs. Assn., S.W. Acad. Mgmt., Belton Bus. and Profl. Women's Club (rec. sec. 1958-60), Am. Assn. U. Women (v.p. 1958-60, pres. Wesleyan Service Guild 1949), Nat., Tex. (state edn. com.) bus. edn. assns., Internat. Platform Assn., Tex. Soc. Coll. Tchrs. Edn., Am. Security Council, Pi Omega Pi, Delta Kappa Gamma (charter pres. Eta Theta chpt. 1963-65). Mem. Order Eastern Star (worthy matron 1958, chpt. treas., Tex. home endowment edn. com.). Home: 203 E 23d Av Belton TX 76513 Office: Box 308 MH-B Station Belton TX 76513

HUSTON, LUCILLE LEVINE (MRS. JAMES I. HUSTON), lawyer; b. N.Y.C., June 27, 1929; d. Martin and Rose (Adler) LeVine; student Hofstra U., 1946-47; A.B., U. Mich., 1950, J.D., 1952; m. James I. Huston, Aug. 14, 1951; children—Daniel, Margaret, Paul, Joseph. Admitted to Ohio bar, 1953; practiced in Chagrin Falls, O., 1961-66; mem. firm Davis & Young, att.-at law, Cleve., 1971-73, Ulmer, Berne, Laronge, Glickman & Curtis, Cleve., 1973—; mem. faculty Cleve. State U., 1966-68, Cleve. Marshall Law Sch., 1968, Oberlin (O.) Coll., 1969-72, Heidelberg U., Tiffin, O., 1969-72, Hiram (O.) Coll., 1969-72, Coll. of Wooster (O.), 1969-72. Councilman City of Cleveland Heights (O.), 1972—; commr. State of Ohio Local Govt. Services Commn., 1971—. Mem. Cleve. Bar Assn., Greater Cleve. Citizens League, Am. Civil Liberties Union (bd. dirs. Cleve. chpt. 1973—). Democrat. Unitarian. Home: 2812 Fairmount Blvd Cleveland Heights OH 44118 Office: 1100 Keith Bldg Cleveland OH 44115

HUSZAGH, ELENIE KOSTOPOULOS (MRS. RICHARD W. HUSZAGH), lawyer; b. Portland, Ore., May 1, 1937; d. Peter V. and Mary C. (Birou) Kostopoulos; A.B., U. Chgo., 1957; J.D., John Marshall Law Sch., 1963; m. Richard W. Huszagh, July 1, 1962; 1 son, Peter. Admitted to Ill. bar, 1963; house counsel Liberty Loan Corp., Chgo., 1964; asso. A.J. Geokaris, atty., Zion, Ill., 1965; partner Huszagh & Huszagh, Glenview, Ill., 1965-70; pres. Miller & Huszagh, Ltd., attys., Glenview, 1970—. Mem. caucus com. Village of Northbrook (Ill.), 1971. Mem. Chgo. Bar Assn. (uniform comml. code com., financial instns. com., sec. consumer credit com.), Womens Bar Assn. Ill., Hellenic Bar Assn. (dir.), U. Chgo. Alumni Assn. Mem. Greek Orthodox Ch. (pres. bd. trustees 1973). Home: 1951 Redwood Lane Northbrook IL 60062 Office: 800 Waukegan Rd Glenview IL 60025

HUTCHEON, JACQUELINE KENYON (MRS. WILLIAM RICHMOND HUTCHEON, JR.), tchrs. assn. adminstr.; b. Wakefield, R.I., Dec. 5, 1930; d. Lloyd Hoxie and Anna Marion (Fortune) Kenyon; B.A., U. R.I., 1952; m. William Richmond Hutcheon, Jr., June 27, 1953. Tchr., R.I., Conn., Wash., 1953-71; pres. Bellevue (Wash.) Edn. Assn., 1966-67, Wash. Edn. Assn., Seattle, 1970-71; cons. Issaquah (Wash.) Edn. Assn., 1971-72; exec. dir. Pilchuck Uni-Serv Council, Everett, Wash., 1972—. Mem. N.E.A. (life), Wash. Edn. Assn. Home: 3441 92d St NE Bellevue WA 98004 Office: 824 S Broadway St Everett WA 98204

HUTCHIN, MAXINE ELAINE, chemist; b. Kansas City, Mo., Dec. 11, 1922; d. William Lawrence and Flora May (Curry) Hutchin; student Kansas City Jr. Coll., 1939-40; A.A., San Francisco Jr. Coll., 1941; B.A., U. Cal. at Berkeley, 1943; postgrad. Stanford, 1945; m. William H. Hutchin, Oct. 12, 1946 (div. 1973); children—Kristine, Heidi. Supervisory biochemist Clin. Investigation Center, Naval Hosp., Oakland, Cal., 1950-62; research chemist Naval Radiol. Def. Lab., San Francisco, 1962-69; asst. toxicologist San Mateo County Coroners Lab., Redwood City, Cal., 1970—. Mem. A.A.A.S., Am. Chem. Soc., Cal. Assn. Toxicologists. Contbr. articles to profl. jours. Home: 5407 Greenridge Rd Castro Valley CA 94546 Office: 200 Edmonds Rd Redwood City CA 94062

HUTCHINGS, DIMPLE EDWARDS (MRS. J.W. HUTCHINGS), educator; b. Fort Worth; d. Anthony Gideon and Myrtie Mae (Parrish) Edwards; B.A., Austin Coll., 1934; M.A., U. Tex., 1954; m. J.W. Hutchings, Dec. 23, 1944. Tchr., Shreiner Inst., 1933, Spring Hill Elementary Sch., Gregg County, Tex., 1934-41, Alamo Heights Ind. Sch., San Antonio, 1941-45; elementary sch. tchr. Longview (Tex.) Ind. Sch. Dist., 1945-46, 58—; high sch. tchr. English, journalism White Oak Ind. Sch. Dist., Gregg County, Tex., 1947-58. Fellow, Coll. Entrance Exam. Bd., 1960, Wall St. Jour., 1963, Nat. Def. Edn. Act, 1965. Mem. N.E.A., Nat. Assn. Tchrs. English, Am. Assn. U. Women (Tex. div. and br. officer 1965-74). Women in Communications, Bus. and Profl. Women, Tex. Council Tchrs. English (dist. pres. 1961-62, 73-74), Journalism Edn. Assn., Tex. Classroom Tchrs. Assn., Tex. Press Assn., Tex. Assn. Journalism Dirs., Delta Kappa Gamma, Beta Sigma Phi. Mem. Order Eastern Star.

HUTCHINS, INEZ CRANFILL NICKSON (MRS. ALFRED F. HUTCHINS), city ofcl.; b. Loco, Okla., Apr. 28, 1909; d. John Wesley and Leah Maude (Cranfill) Nickson; student Okla. Bapt. U., 1942-43, Amarillo Coll., 1949-50; m. Thomas Charles Wyatt, Jr., May 8, 1931 (dec. 1943); children—Thomas Charles, Laurence Cranfill; m. 2d, Alfred F. Hutchins, May 29, 1948 (dec. 1968). Machine bookkeeping operator City of Shawnee, Okla., 1943-45, city treas., 1945-48; sec. to city mgr. City of Amarillo, Tex., 1948-58, asst. city sec.-treas., 1958-71, city sec.-treas., 1972—. Mem. C. of C., Tex. Assn. Election Ofcls., Tex. Assn. City Secs. and Clks. Mem. Disciples of Christ. Home: 3516 Concord Rd Amarillo TX 79109 Office: Municipal Bldg PO Box 1971 Amarillo TX 79186

HUTCHINS, MARY IMOJEANE KEYS ALLEN (MRS. P.O. HUTCHINS), bus. exec.; b. Lockney, Tex., Aug. 12, 1911; d. Arthur Russell and Ruth Francis (Simpson) Keys; high sch. grad.; m. Ira Russell Allen, 1932 (dec. 1957); 1 son, Arthur Lewis; m. 2d, P.O. Hutchins, June 10, 1959 (dec. 1966). Nurse tng. Lubbock (Tex.) San., 1928-31; owner salons, W.Va., Va., 1932-62; organizer, sec., pres. Schs. Cosmetology, Inc., Richmond and Hampton, Va., 1961—, also dir. pres. Va. Sch. Hair Design, Inc. Mem. Registered Profl. Hairdressers Bd. Examiners, 1962—, chmn., 1965-66; regional v.p. Nat. Interstate Council of State Bds., 1969-71; mem. visitation teams Nat. Accrediting Cosmetology Commn.; mem. Indsl. Vocational Adv. Bd. Mem. Va. Hairdressers and Cosmetologists Assn. (v.p.), Peninsula Bus. and Profl. Club, Va. Allied Council Cosmetology (pres. 1969-70), Va. Hair Fashion Com. (charter mem., treas.), Peninsula C. of C. (edn. com. 1973), Va. Beauty Sch. Assn. (treas.). Baptist. Home: Box 14 Hampton VA 23669 Office: 9903 Warwick Blvd Newport News VA 23601

HUTCHINS, THELMA JEAN, librarian; b. Roanoke, Va., Aug. 14, 1940; d. Fred Dewey and Mary Myrtle (Parks) Hutchins; A.A., Mars Hill Coll., 1960; B.S., Wake Forest U., 1962; B.D., Southeastern Baptist Theol. Sem., 1965; M.S. in Library Sci., U. N.C., 1968. Social caseworker Warren County Welfare Dept., Front Royal, Va., 1965-66; reference librarian Campbell Coll., Buies Creek, N.C., 1966-67; asst. librarian for tech. services S. Ga. Coll., Douglas, 1968-70, acting librarian, 1970-73, head librarian, 1973—, supr. central duplicating services, records mgmt. officer, 1972—. Mem. Am. Assn. Univ. Profs., Ga., Southeastern library assns., Satilla Regional Librarian's Council (local pres. 1973—). Editor: Union List of Seaials of South Georgia Associated Libraries, 1970—; mng. editor Occasional Papers from South Georgia, 1971—. Home: PO Box 93 Douglas GA 31533 Office: William S Smith Library South Georgia College Douglas GA 31533

HUTCHINSON, JANET LOIS, mus. ofcl.; b. Washington, May 2, 1917; d. Lewis Orrin and Gertrude Elizabeth (Hutchinson) Hutchinson; student Northfield Sem., 1933-34, Drew Sem., 1934-35, So. Sem., 1934-36, Blackstone Coll., 1936-38; 1 son, Jefferson Siebert. Free lance writer, N.Y.C., 1936-56; owner Hutchinson Assos., N.Y.C., Me., 1957-64, Broadlawn Art Gallery, Camden, Me., 1965—; dir. House of Refuge Mus., Stuart, Fla., 1965—, Elliott Mus., Stuart, 1964—, Martin County Hist. Soc., Stuart, 1964—. Asst. adviser publicity Fla. Inst. Tech., Jensen Beach, 1973—; mem. adv. bd. Environmental Studies Center, Jensen Beach, 1973—. Trustee Pioneer Occupational Center for Handicap. Republican. Author: Tiny Timids Christmas Wish, 1954. Home: 109 N Spruce Ridge Trail Stuart FL 33494 Office: Elliott Museum 888 NE MacArthur Blvd Stuart FL 33494

HUTCHINSON, PEGGYANN, journalist; b. Swan Lake, Mont., Sept. 29, 1928; d. Ansley Eugene and Ellen (Davies) Hutchinson; student Stephens Coll., 1946-47; B.A., U. N.M., 1950; postgrad. U. Denver, 1955-56. Radio copywriter Radio Sta. KGGM, Albuquerque, 1950-51; editor Navy Reporter, U.S. Navy, Great Lakes, Ill., 1952-53, pub. information journalist WAVE Recruit Training Regiment, asst. co. comdr., Bainbridge, Md., 1954-55; reporter, ch. news editor, Medford (Ore.) Mail Tribune, 1956-64, asst. news editor, 1964—. Treas. Jackson County Bd. Christian Edn., 1958-60. Fellow, Religious Pub. Relations Council, Inc.; mem. Ore. Press Women (Emmy award 1970, pres. 1971-73), Nat. Fedn. Press Women (rec. sec. 1973—), Nat. Newspaper Assn., Am. Assn. Univ. Women, Medford Bus. and Profl. Women's Club. Presbyn. (financial adv. com. '1964—, elder, 1964-66, 1968-70, 73—). Home: 912 S Holly St Medford OR 97501 Office: 33 N Fir St Medford OR 97501

HUTCHISON, ELIZABETH BREWER (MRS. JAMES D. HUTCHISON), librarian; b. Muncie, Ind., June 23, 1912; B.A., Whittier (Cal.) Coll., 1934; M.S. in L.S. with honors, U. So. Cal., 1954; m. James D. Hutchison, Sept. 21, 1939; children—Mary (Mrs. Donald Pedder), Alice (Mrs. Wayne L. Pryor). Lab. technologist Children's Hosp., Los Angeles, 1935-41, Pacific Mut. Life Ins. Co., Los Angeles, 1941-43; reference librarian Ventura (Cal.) County and City Library, 1949-50, head tech. services, 1950-65, asst. dir., 1965—. Mem. A.L.A., Cal. Library Assn. (pres. Black Gold dist. 1965-66), Bus. and Profl. Women's Club, P.E.O. (chaplain), Beta Phi Mu. Contbr. articles to profl. jours. Home: 1119 Via Cielito Ventura CA 93003 Office: PO Box 771 Ventura CA 93001

HUTCHISON, ELIZABETH SHIMER, physician; b. Ravenna, O., Feb. 8, 1909; d. William J. and Elizabeth (Shimer) Hutchison; A.B., Western Res. U., 1929, M.D. 1932. Intern Cleve. City Hosp., 1932-33; resident Western Res. U. Hosps., 1933-35. Practice medicine specializing in internal medicine, Cleve., 1935-44; concurrently instr. Western Res. U. and St. Luke's Hosp., staff physician, lectr. Cleve. Central YWCA; practice medicine, Dallas, instr. medicine Southwestern Med. Sch., 1944-49; practice, Corona Del Mar, Cal., 1949-58; practice specializing in internal medicine and endocrinology, Los Angeles, 1958—; instr. medicine U. So. Cal., 1960—. Recipient prizes in local and nat. art competition. Mem. Am., Cal., Los Angeles med. assns., Women Painters of West (pres.), Cal. Nat. Watercolor Soc. (dir.; pres. 1971-72, juror 1972-73, award 1973-74), Los Angeles Art Assn., Pasadena Soc. Artists, Alpha Omega Alpha. Home: 3611 Sapphire Dr Encino CA 91316

HUTCHISON, JANE CAMPBELL, educator; b. Washington, 1932; d. James Paul and Leone (Warrick) Hutchison; B.A. cum laude, Western Md. Coll., 1954; M.A., Oberlin Coll., 1958; Ph.D., U. Wis., 1964; Fulbright scholar, U. Utrecht (Netherlands), 1960-61. Tech. illustrator U.S. Navy Dept., David Taylor Model Basin, Washington, 1954-55; library asst. Toledo Mus. of Art, 1957-58; teaching asst., univ. fellow, acting instr. U. Wis., 1959-60, 61-63; asst. prof. art history U. Wis. at Madison 1964-69, asso. prof., 1969-74, prof., 1974—, summer chmn. dept. art history, 1972. Vis. prof. art history Temple U., summer 1967. Sec. Midwest Coll. Art Conf., 1970; cons. Nat. Endowment Humanities, 1971-74. Mem. Coll. Art Assn. Am., Mediaeval Acad. Am., Am. Assn. U. Profs. (dir. Madison chpt.), Am. Assn. U. Women. Club: University (dir.) (U. Wis.). Author: The Master of the Housebook, 1972; Dutch and Flemish Paintings from Private Collections, 1974. Home: 2410 Kendall Av Madison WI 53705

HUTH, MARY JO, educator; b. South Bend, Ind., Apr. 2, 1929; d. Edward A. and Margaret (Emonds) Huth; B.S., U. Dayton, 1950; M.A., U. Ind., 1951; Ph.D., St. Louis U., 1955. Chmn. sociology dept. St. Mary's Dominican Coll., New Orleans, 1954-55; asso. prof. social scis. St. Mary's Coll., Notre Dame, Ind., 1955-62; asso. prof. sociology U. Dayton (O.), 1962—, chmn. dept., 1965-70. Staff mem. human relations workshop Mexico City Coll., summer 1958, U. Detroit, summers 1959-63; v.p. Internat. Relations Council St. Joseph County, Ind., 1961-62; chmn. program com. Council Community Services, South Bend, 1960-61; mem. ednl. adv. com. Ohio Civil Rights Commn., 1969—. Bd. dirs. Family and Children's Center, Mishawaka, Ind., 1956-61, South Bend Civic Music Assn., 1960-62; bd. dirs. Dayton Catholic Charities, 1963-69, Dayton Urban League, 1965-68; v.p., dir. Dayton Civic Music Association, 1966—; bd. dirs. Travelers' Aid Soc., Dayton. Named outstanding woman grad. U. Dayton, Miami Valley chpt. Alumni Assn., 1950. Dept. Housing and Urban Devel. grantee, 1972-73. Mem. Am., Am. Catholic (v.p. 1961-62, exec. council 1957-59, 69-71) sociol. assns., Am. Assn. U. Women (v.p. South Bend chpt. 1960-62, chmn. com. status women Ind. 1958-60), Gamma Pi Epsilon, Alpha Kappa Delta, Alpha Sigma Tau. Roman Catholic. Author pamphlets. Contbr. articles to profl. publs. Home: 4841 Far Hills Av Apt B-2 Dayton OH 45429

HUTH, PATRICIA KATHLEEN (MRS. STEPHEN ANTHONY HUTH), psychologist; b. Sacramento, Oct. 5, 1948; d. Robert Francis and Cleo Marie (Stanifer) Boland; B.S., St. Louis U., 1969; M.A., U. Ill., Chgo., 1973; m. Stephen Anthony Huth, Aug. 29, 1970. Asst. psychologist Ark. Children's Colony, Conway, Ark., 1969-70; clin. psychology intern VA Hosp., Chgo., 1973—. Mem. 44th ward assembly, Chgo., 1973—. Mem. . Psychol. Assn. (student), Am. Assn. on Mental Deficiency, Phi Beta Kappa. Home: 3736 North Magnolia Chicago IL 60613

HUTINGER, PATRICIA LOU (MRS. PAUL W. HUTINGER), psychologist, educator; b. Iowa Falls, Nov. 24, 1932; d. Charles O. and Phyllis Lucille (McLeod) Barnes; B.A., U. Mo., 1962, M.A., 1965; Ed.D., Ind. U., 1971; m. Paul W. Hutinger, June 5, 1952; children—P. Charles, Scott Reed. Tchr. kindergarten, Raytown, Mo., 1954-64; tchr. first grade pub. schs., Macomb, Ill., 1965-66; headstart tchr., cons. Western Ill. U., Macomb, summer 1966, 67, asst. prof. early childhood edn., 1966-72, asso. prof., 1972—. Cons. early childhood. Chmn. White House Conf. on Children McDonough County, 1971—. Bd. dirs. McDonough County Council on Child Devel., vice chmn., 1971-74, chmn., 1974—. Mem. Am. Psychol. Assn., Am. Ednl. Research Assn., Assn. for Childhood Edn. Internat. (v.p. Ill. 1971-73), Am. Assn. U. Women, Pi Lambda Theta. Club: Western Illinois Masters Swimming. Home: 815 N Charles Macomb IL 61455 Office: 18 Horrabin Hall Western Ill Univ Macomb IL 61455

HUTMAN, NORMA LOUISE, educator; b. Buffalo, Sept. 7, 1935; d. George Albert and Florence (McLaughlin) Hutman; B.A. summa cum laude (N.Y. State scholar), D'Youille Coll., 1956; M.A. (grad. fellow), Western Res. U., 1957; Certificado, U. Madrid, 1959; Ph.D., U. Pitts., 1961. Instr. Spanish, Chatham Coll., Pitts., 1957-60; lectr. Spanish, U. Pitts., 1960, Andrew Melton predoctoral fellow, 1960-61; asst. prof. Spanish, Wilson Coll., Chamberburg, Pa., 1961-64; prof. comparative lit. Hartwick Coll., Oneonta, N.Y., 1964—, chmn. div. humanities, 1966—. Recipient award acad. achievement Cleve. Spanish Soc., 1957. Warfield research travel grantee, summer 1962, Coll. Center Finger Lakes research grantee, 1971. Mem. Modern Lang. Assn., Nat. Council Catholic Women (parish pres. 1963-64, dir. deanery 1963-64), Confraternity Christian Doctrine (dir.), Am. Comparative Lit. Assn., Sigma Delta Pi. Democrat. Roman Catholic. Author: Machado: A Dialogue With Time, 1969. Contbr. articles to profl. publs. Home: 395 Main St Oneonta NY 13820

HUTSON, RITA PATRICIA DOHERTY (MRS. ROBERT D. HUTSON), pub. relations exec.; b. Corpus Christi, Tex., Aug. 22, 1943; d. Edward Bernard and Alice (Morton) Doherty; B.S., U. Fla., 1964; M.A., So. Meth. U., 1973; m. Robert D. Hutson, Jan. 20, 1967. Copywriter WTVT, Tampa, Fla., 1967-68; gen. mgr. BC Advt., Dallas, 1968-70; acct. exec. Evans Young Wyatt, Dallas, 1970-72; advt. mgr. Mostek Corp., Dallas, 1972; advt. and pub. relations mgr. Moore Group Inc., Atlanta, 1973—. Corporate sec. Sign of the Zodiac, Dallas, 1968-70. Mem. Women In Communications, Zeta Phi Eta, Beta Sigma Phi (treas. 1973-74). Home: 3409 Moravia Dr Lithonia GA 30058 Office: 1100 Spring St NW Atlanta GA 30309

HUTTO, EDITH (MRS. JOEL CECIL HOLT), dermatologist; b. Winnsboro, S.C., Jan. 17, 1929; d. Darlin Lee and Maybelle (Williamson) Hutto; A.B., Greensboro Coll., 1953; M.D., Med. Coll. S.C., 1958; m. Joel Cecil Holt, Apr. 18, 1964; children—Joel Matthew, Jason Jerome. Intern, Greenville (S.C.) Gen. Hosp., 1958-59; resident in dermatology Duke U. Med. Center, Durham, N.C., 1959-62, chief resident, 1961-62; practice medicine specializing in dermatology, Asheville, N.C., 1963—; mem. staffs, also cons. St. Joseph Hosp., Ashville, Meml. Mission Hosp., Asheville, Highland Hosp., Asheville. Lectr. schs. and med. socs. Active A.R.C. Mem. A.M.A., So., N.C., S.C., Asheville med. socs. Home: 9 Frith Dr Asheville NC 28803 Office: 160 W Annex Doctors Bldg Asheville NC 28801

HUTTON, ELEANOR HALL (MRS. THOMAS LEE HUTTON, JR.), educator; b. Abingdon, Va., Nov. 27, 1936; d. George Avery and Mildred Louise (Fortune) Hall; student Va. Intermont Coll., 1953-54; A.B., Duke, 1957; M.Ed., U. Va., 1965; m. Thomas Lee Hutton, Jr., Aug. 26, 1966. Tchr., Englewood, N.J., 1957-59, Abingdon (Va.) High Sch., 1959-62, Collier Jr. High Sch., San Diego, 1963; tchr., coach, chmn. health and phys. edn. dept. Emory and Henry Coll., Emory, Va., 1964—. Mem. Recreation Commn., 1971—. Recipient Excellence in Teaching award Students of Emory and Henry Coll., 1972, 74. Mem. Am. Assn. U. Women, Am. Assn. U. Profs., A.A.H.P.E.R. Presbyn. (mem. choir). Home: Glenview Av Abingdon VA 24210 Office: Box AAA Emory VA 24327

HUTTON, LOUISE PHILLIPS (MRS. HAMPTON HUTTON), investor; b. Los Angeles, Aug. 19, 1918; d. Edwin Roscoe and Blanche (Wakeham) Phillips; B.A., Mills Coll., 1940; m. Hampton Hutton, Feb. 15, 1941; children—James Hampton, John Phillips. Owner, L.P. Hutton & Assos., South Pasadena, Cal., 1951—. Pres., South Pasadena Republican Women's Club, 1954-55, Huntington Harbour Rep. Women's Club, 1965, Orange County Fedn. Reps., 1966; campaign chmn. so. div. State Fedn. Rep. Women, 1965-70; vice-chmn. Los Angeles County Rep. Central Com., 1956-68; mem. Rep. State Central Com., 1954-72, chmn. edn., and promotion, 1964-66, asst. sec., 1968-70; mem. Electral Coll., Rep. Nat. Conv., 1956, alternate del., 1964, 68. Mem. First Century Families. Clubs: Huntington Harbour Yacht. East Beach, Huntington Harbour Beach (Cal.). Home: 16622 Somerset Lane Huntington Beach CA 92649 also

2190 N Cerritos Rd Palm Springs CA Office: PO Box 425 South Pasadena CA 91030

HUTTON, MARGARET MACSTEVEN, physician; b. Owensound, Ont., Can.; d. Arthur Ernest and Helen (MacSteven) Hutton; B.A., U. Alta., 1937, M.D., 1942. Intern Royal Jubilee Hosp., Victoria, B.C. and U. Alta. Hosp., Edmonton; specialist in obstetrics and gynecology. Fellow A.C.S., Royal Soc. Arts, Royal Coll. Surgeons of Can., Am. Coll. Obstetricians and Gynecologists; mem. Soc. Obstetricians and Gynecologists Can., Delta Kappa Gamma, Pi Beta Phi. Address: 4551 Parry Rd Rural Route 1 Victoria BC V8X 3W9 Canada

HUTTON, MARY MAGDELENE BOONE (MRS. RICHARD HUTTON), educator; b. Brownsville, Tenn., Nov. 1, 1925; d. George Alexander and Helen (Jones) Boone; student Wayne U., 1945-49, Tenn. Agrl. and Indsl. State Coll., 1946, Territorial Coll. Guam, 1954; A.A., Merritt Coll., 1962; student Laney Coll., 1967-68; B.A., Cal. State Coll. at Hayward, 1969; M.A. (Grad. Minority Program grantee), U. Cal. at Berkeley, 1971; Ph.D., Ind. U., 1974; m. Richard Hutton, Aug. 28, 1951; children—Cozzette (Mrs. Richard Davis), Larry Keith, Jacqueline Yvonne. Timekeeper, Govt. Service, Agana, Guam, 1955-56; clk. typist Health Dept., Oakland, Cal., 1957-58, clk. III, 1958-59; clk.-typist Oakland (Cal.) Police Dept., 1960-64, div. sec. to capt. police, 1964-69; prof. speech Ind. U., Bloomington, 1971-74; prof. Afro-Am. Studies, Milw., 1974—. Bd. dirs. Rose St. Child Care Center, Berkeley, Cal., 1970-71. Served with WAVES, 1950-51. Econ. Opportunity fellow, 1971-72; Ford Found. fellow, 1973-74. Mem. Pi Kappa Delta, Pi Lambda Theta. Mem. Disciples of Christ. Home: 832 Indian Rock Av Berkeley CA 94707 Office: Afro-Am Studies Dept Milwaukee WI 53202

HUUS, HELEN, educator; b. Northwood, Ia., Nov. 1, 1913; d. Jacob H. and Mary Belle (Tiffany) Huus; B.A., U. No. Ia., 1940; M.A., U. Chgo., 1941; Ph.D. (Walgreen Found. scholar), 1944; postgrad. (Fulbright scholar), U. Oslo, 1950-51. Tchr., Worth County Schs., Northwood, Ia., 1933-35, Mediapolis, Ia., 1936-38; faculty U. No. Ia., Cedar Falls, 1938-40, Wayne State U., Detroit, 1945-47, U. Pa., Phila., 1947-67; prof. edn. U. Mo., Kansas City, 1967—. Lectr. various ednl. groups at state, regional, nat. and internat. levels. Served with WAVES, 1944-45; now comdr. Res. Mem. Nat. Council Tchrs. English, Internat. Reading Assn. (pres. 1969-70), Nat. Conf. Research in English (pres. 1966-67), Am. Assn. U. Profs., Am. Assn. U. Women, Pi Lambda Theta. Author: Education of Children and Youth in Norway, 1961; Children's Books to Enrich the Social Studies, 1961, rev. edit., 1966; co-author field lit. series for grades kindergarten through eight. Contbr. articles in field to profl. jours. Home: 5000 Oak St Kansas City MO 64112

HUXTABLE, ADA LOUISE LANDMAN (MRS. L. GARTH HUXTABLE), archtl. critic; b. N.Y.C.; d. Michael Louis and Leah (Rosenthal) Landman; A.B. magna cum laude, Hunter Coll.; postgrad., Inst. Fine Arts, N.Y. U.; L.H.D. (hon.), Smith Coll., Skidmore Coll., Md. Inst., Mt. Holyoke Coll., Yale, Oberlin Coll., Trinity Coll., LaSalle Coll., Williams Coll., Colgate U., Pace Coll., Pratt Inst. Tech., Rutgers U., Finch Coll.; m. Garth Huxtable. Asst. curator architecture and design Mus. Modern Art, N.Y.C., 1946-50; free-lance contbr., contbg. editor to profl. and other mags., 1950-63; archtl. critic N.Y. Times, N.Y.C., 1963-73, mem. editorial bd., Sunday archtl. critic, 1973—. Bd. dirs. Municipal Art Soc. N.Y.; mem. corp. vis. com. Sch. Architecture and Planning, Mass. Inst. Tech.; mem. assos. La Salle Coll., Phila. Recipient Gold medal Phila. YWCA, 1970, Elsie de Wolfe award Am. Inst. Interior Designers, 1969, Finlandia Found., N.Y. chpt. Arts and Letters award, 1968, Frank Jewett Mather award Coll. Art Assn. for Art Criticism, 1967, Municipal Art Soc. N.Y. award, Kaufmann Internat. Design award for critical writing, citation L.I. Soc. chpt. A.I.A., 1964, N.Y. State Council on Arts award, 1967, Front Page award Newspaper Women's Club N.Y., 1965, 70, Bard citation Citizens' Union N.Y., Architecture Critic's medal A.I.A., 1969, Pulitzer prize for distinguished ciriticism, 1970; Strauss Meml. award N.Y. Soc. Architects, 1970; Diamond Jubilee medallion City of N.Y., 1973; Woman of Year award Am. Assn. U. Women, 1974. Fulbright scholar, Italy, 1950; Guggenheim fellow, 1958. Fellow Am. Acad. Arts and Scis.; mem. Soc. Archtl. Historians (dir.), Nat. Trust for Historic Preservation, Victorian Soc. Am. (adv. bd.), A.I.A. (hon. mem.), Phi Beta Kappa. Author: Pier Luigi Nervi, 1960; Classic New York, 1964, Will They Ever Finish Bruckner Boulevard?, 1970. Office: NY Times 229 W 43d St New York City NY 10036

HUXTABLE, KATHRYN ANNE (MRS. SAMUEL T. LEWIS III), pediatrician, educator; b. Lakewood, O., July 23, 1934; d. Harold Stafford and Ottilie Louise (May) Huxtable; student Cornell U., 1952-55; M.D., Yale, 1959; M.P.H., Johns Hopkins, 1964; m. Samuel T. Lewis III, Apr. 8, 1967; children—Samuel Theodore, Stephen Alexander Brown, Anne Elizabeth. Intern, U. Hosps. Cleve., 1959-60, resident pediatrics, 1961-63; resident Children's Hosp. Phila., 1960-61; practice medicine specializing in pediatrics, Cleve., 1965-67, Pitts., 1967—; dir. pediatric out patient dept. Cleve. Met. Gen. Hosp., 1966-67; asst. dir. Ambulatory Care Center Childrens Hosp., Pitts., 1967—; asst. clin. prof. dept. pediatrics, dept. community medicine U. Pitts., 1967—. Mem. Johns Hopkins Research Team in Family Planning, 1964-65; Ford Found. Project asso., Lahore, West Pakistan, 1964-65. Diplomate Am. Bd. Pediatrics. Fellow Am. Acad. Pediatrics, Am. Pub. Health Assn., Phi Beta Kappa. Presbyn. (Sunday sch. tchr.). Home: 101 Cherry Av Houston PA 15342 Office: Childrens Hosp Pitts 125 DeSoto St Pittsburgh PA 15312

HUYCK, MARGARET HELLIE (MRS. WILLIAM THOMAS HUYCK), educator; b. Waterloo, Ia., Apr. 14, 1939; d. Ole I. and Mary (Larsen) Hellie; A.B., Vassar Coll., 1961; M.A., U. Chgo., 1963, Ph.D., 1970; m. William Thomas Huyck, June 24, 1961; children—Elizabeth, Karen. Asst. prof. Ill. Inst. Tech., 1969—. Pres. Newstyles Inc., Chgo., 1972—. USPHS trainee in adult devel.; USPHS trainee in survey research. Mem. Am. Psychol. Assn., Am. Sociol. Assn., Gerontological Soc., Am. Assn. U. Profs., Nat. Orgn. Women. Author: Growing Older, 1974. Home: 1718 E 55th St Chicago IL 60615

HYATT, ESTELLE (MRS. JULIUS HYATT), govt. ofcl.; b. Bklyn., Apr. 9, 1921; d. Abraham and Eva (Wasserman) Karenetsky; grad. high sch.; m. Julius Hyatt, May 1, 1945; children—Alan, Robin. Sec., Bd. Econ. Warfare, Washington, 1941-45; analyst Merc. Metal & Ore Co., N.Y.C., 1945-46; supr. U.S. Census, N.Y.C., 1957, 60; with U.S. Dept. Labor Bur. Labor Statistics, N.Y.C., 1960—, councilmanic aide, 1972—. Mem. steering com. Flatbush Community for Youth, Bklyn., 1970; active in various youth activities. County Dem. committeewoman 44th Assembly Dist., 1970—. Mem. Bus. and Profl. Womens Club. Home: 1820 Cortelyou Rd Brooklyn NY 11226

HYDE, BEVERLY DEAN ERICKSON (MRS. SHELDON F. HYDE), social worker; b. Hoisington, Kan., Jan. 10, 1916; d. Andrew B. and Helen Dean (Butler) Erickson; student nurse Ida. Bannock County Gen. Hosp., 1934; B.S. in Secondary Edn., U. Utah, 1939, M.S.W., 1962, postgrad., 1964-65; postgrad. Columbia, 1965; m. Sheldon F. Hyde, Mar. 7, 1939; children—Jan Orson, Shelley Jeannette (Mrs. Russell S. Harlow). Social worker A.R.C. Home Service, Salt Lake City, 1944-47; with VA Hosp., Salt Lake City, 1953-61, sec., recreation technician and asst. technician neurophysiology research, 1958-61; with Utah Div. Family Services, Salt Lake City, 1962—, tng. specialist Bur. Staff Devel., 1966—. Field instr. grad. students U. Utah Grad. Sch. Social Work, 1967—. Mem. Nat. Assn. Social Workers, Utah State Conf. Social Welfare (sec. 1967—, exec. bd. mem. 1963-69). Home: 1566 Sunnyside Av Salt Lake City UT 84105 Office: 888 S 2d East Salt Lake City UT 84111

HYDE, NINA SOLOMON (MRS. LLOYD S. HYDE), fashion editor; b. N.Y.C., Sept. 17, 1932; d. Harry Aaron and Ruth (Wulfsohn) Solomon; B.A., Smith Coll., 1954; m. Lloyd S. Hyde, Feb. 23, 1961; children—Jennifer, Andrea. Research project dir. McCann Erickson, advt. agy., N.Y.C., 1954-57; reporter Women's Wear Daily, N.Y.C., 1957-58; researcher, writer Tobe & Assos., N.Y.C., 1959-61; fashion editor Washington Daily News, Washington, 1962-72, Washington Post, 1972—. Bd. advisers Freedmen's Hosp., Washington. Bd. dirs. Workshop for Careers in Arts, D.C. Black Reperatory Dance Co. Mem. Fashion Group (regional dir. 1966-68). Club: Washington Press. Home: 3505 Macomb St NW Washington DC 20016 Office: 1150 15th St NW Washington DC 20005

HYDER, GRACE MARY, computer programmer; b. Lawrence, Mass., Aug. 6, 1928; d. Henry K. and Nabeeha M. (Kouri) Hyder; B.S. in Math., U. Mass., 1950; postgrad. Boston U., 1957-58. Asst. scientist Avco Corp., Wilmington, Mass., 1956-61; mem. asso. tech. staff Mitre Corp., Bedford, Mass., 1962—. Mem. Assn. for Computing Machinery, Aiding Leukemia Stricken Am. Children. Mem. Order Eastern Star. Home: 651 Prospect St Methoen MA Office: Route 62 Bedford MA 01730

HYER, MARTHA (MRS. HAL WALLIS), actress; b. Ft. Worth, Aug. 10; d. Julien C. and Agnes (Barnhart) Hyer; student Fairfax Hall Jr. Coll., 1943-45; B.A., Northwestern U., 1947; m. Hal Wallis, Dec. 31, 1966. Featured in movies with RKO Studios, Hollywood, Cal., 1950-55, Universal Studios 1955-60; starred in movies including Some Came Running, Carpetbaggers, Sons of Katie Elder, The Happening, The Chase, others. Nominated for Acad. award, 1959. Mem. Pi Beta Phi. Home: 515 S Mapleton Dr Los Angeles CA 90024 Office: Universal Studios Universal City CA 91608

HYLAND, DONNA GAYE PETERSON (MRS. BRIAN BORU HYLAND), heavy equipment mfg. co. exec.; b. Jersey City, Feb. 22, 1945; d. Russell and Doris Edith Weichler (Martin) Peterson; student Rutgers U., 1970-71, Katharine Gibbs Sch., N.Y.C., 1970; m. Brian Boru Hyland, June 20, 1964; 1 dau., Elizabeth. Exec. sec., Temeco Chems., Piscataway, N.J., 1965-67; sec. specialist IBM Corp., Princeton, N.J., 1968-70; sec. to pres., office mgr. Procedyne Corp., New Brunswick, N.J., 1970—. Mem. Women's Equity Action League. Home: 15 Pine Ridge Dr East Brunswick NJ 08816 Office: 221 Somerset St New Brunswick NJ 08903

HYLAND, MARY ROSE, educator; b. Kenosha, Wis., June 18, 1930; d. Ambrose William and Dora Anne (Durocher) Hyland; B.S., Rosary Coll., 1952; M.S., U. Ia., 1958. Instr. nutrition and dietetics Mercy Hosp., Chgo., 1953-56; instr. nutrition and dietetics Marquette U., Milw., 1956-57; dir. Union Food Service, Stanford, 1958-62; quality control dietitian Walgreen Co., Chgo., 1962-63; instl. home economist Kraft Foods Co., Chgo., 1963-64; prof., instl. mgmt. specialist Coop. Extension Service, Purdue U., Lafayette, Ind., 1964-74; dietitian Eurest Internat., Paris, France, 1974—. Mem. adv. com. Wabash Center for Mentally Retarded; cons. food service Head Start Program, Lafayette. Sec., bd. dirs. Campus Employees Fed. Credit Union, Purdue U. Named Educator of Year, Purdue chpt. Food Service Execs. Assn., 1966. Mem. Am. (past del.), Ind. (past pres.) dietetic assns., Am. Home Econs. Assn., Inst. Food Technologists, Am. Sch. Food Service Assn., Ind. Extension Specialists Assn., Council Hotel and Restaurant Instl. Educators, Omicron Nu. Roman Catholic. Home: 6 Rue Quentin-Bauchart Paris 8 France

HYMAN, CAROLINE GRIGGS, occupational therapist; b. Waterbury, Conn., May 29, 1937; d. Robert Foote and Anne (Tranker) Griggs; student Simmons Coll., 1955-57; B.S., Tufts U.-Boston Sch. Occupational Therapy, 1960; M.S. in Edn., Syracuse U., 1963; m. Gerold Frederick Hyman, Oct. 24, 1965; children—William Morris, Alice Elizabeth. Occupational therapist Sunnyview Rehab. Center, Schenectady, 1960-62, United Cerebral Palsy Cin., 1963-66; occupational therapist children's unit New Haven Rehab. Center, 1966-67; occupational therapist Suffolk County Rehab. Center, Melville, N.Y., 1973—; cons. in field. Office Vocational Rehab. tuition grantee, 1962-63. Mem. Am., N.Y. State, L.I. Dist. occupational therapy assns. Home: 145 Ecker Av West Babylon NY 11704 Office: BOCES III-Bldg 30 Suffolk Developmental Center Melville NY 11746

HYMAN, ISABELLE MILLER (MRS. JEROME E. HYMAN), educator; b. N.Y.C., Apr. 19, 1930; d. Benjamin J. and Rachel (Tandick) Miller; B.A., Vassar Coll., 1951; M.A., Columbia, 1955; M.A., N.Y. U., 1965, Ph.D., 1968; m. Jerome E. Hyman, July 1, 1960. Instr. dept. fine arts N.Y. U., N.Y.C., 1963-68, asst. prof., 1968-71, asso. prof., 1971—. Sr. fellow I Tatti (Harvard Center Italian Renaissance Studies), Florence, Italy, 1972-73. Mem. Soc. Archtl. Historians, Renaissance Soc. Am., Coll. Art Assn. Home: 1125 Park Av New York City NY 10028

HYMEL, FRANCES M., physician; b. White Castle, La., Dec. 3, 1914; d. Lulovic Paul and Agnes (LeGlue) Hymel; M.D., La. State U., 1949. Head nurse Charity Hosp., New Orleans, 1935-36; staff nurse La. State Dept. Health, New Roads and Franklin, 1936-42; intern Charity Hosp., New Orleans, 1949-50, resident, 1950-51; practice gen. medicine, New Orleans, 1951—; mem. staff of Hotel Dieu, New Orleans, Mercy Hosp., New Orleans. Charter fellow Am. Acad. Family Physicians; mem. New Orleans Grad. Med. Assembly, Am. Acad. Gen. Practice, Am., Canadian med. women's assns., Orleans Parish, La. med. socs., Am., Gulf Coast camellia socs., Am. Assn. U. Women, Alpha Epsilon Iota. Home: 1241 N Hagan St New Orleans LA 70119 Office: 1239 N Hagan St New Orleans LA 70119

HYROOP, MURIEL EVADNE HALL (MRS. GILBERT L. HYROOP), psychiatrist; b. Toronto, Ont., Can., Oct. 1, 1900; d. Robert Pettigrew and Melissa (Craig) Hall; B.A., U. Toronto, 1926, M.D., 1928; m. Gilbert L. Hyroop, Aug. 3, 1930; children—Gilbert Hall, Craig Wensler. Intern pediatric dept. Hosp. for Sick Children, Toronto, 1928-29; obtetrics St. Francis Hosp., San Francisco, 1929-30, practice medicine specializing in psychiatry, Oklahoma City, 1931—, Woodward, Okla., 1949-52; mem. staff Coyne Campbell Research Inst., Oklahoma City, 1935-40; asst. prof. dept. psychiatry U. Okla. Med. Sch., 1931-42, 43-49. Sec.-treas. King-Size Clothes, Inc., Oklahoma City, Dallas, Tulsa, Atlanta and Houston, 1958—. Mem. Oklahoma County Sanity Bd.; part-time. Fellow Am. Psychiat. Assn., Am. Group Therapy Assn., A.A.A.S.; mem. A.M.A., Okla. Med. Soc., Alpha Gamma Delta. Club: Pilot of Northwest Oklahoma City. Home: 8000 Glenwood Av Oklahoma City OK 73114 Office: 3141 NW Expressway Oklahoma City OK 73112

IACHETTI, ROSE MARIA ANNE, educator; b. Watervliet, N.Y., Sept. 22, 1931; d. Augustus and Rose Elizabeth Archer (Orciuolo) Iachetti; B.S., Coll. St. Rose, 1961; M.Ed., U. Ariz., 1969. Joined Sisters of Mercy, Albany, N.Y., 1949-66; tchr. various parochial schs. Albany (N.Y.) Diocese, 1952-66; tchr. Headstart Program, Troy, N.Y., 1966; tchr. Tombstone, Ariz., 1968-71, Colonel Johnston Sch., Ft. Huachuca, Ariz., 1971—. Ann. chmn. Ariz. Children's Home Assn., Tombstone, 1973-74. Trustees Tombstone Sch. Dist. #1, 1972-76. Mem. Ariz. (so. regional dir. 1971-73), Ft. Huachuca edn. assns., Ariz. Sch. Bd. Assn., N.E.A. (del. 1971-73), Ariz. Classroom Tchrs. Assn., Tombstone Bus. and Profl. Womens Club, Pi Lambda Theta, Delta Kappa Gamma. Home: Skyline Apts #3 Box 705 Tombstone AZ 85638 Office: Colonel Johnston School Fort Huachuca AZ 85613

IACONO, PAULINE JEAN, librarian; b. Mpls., Dec. 26, 1938; d. John and Jean (Copeland) Iacono; B.A., Coll. St. Catherine, St. Paul, 1960; M.A., U. Ia., 1969. Cataloger St. Mary's Coll., Notre Dame, Ind., 1960-64, Macalester Coll., St. Paul, 1964-68; tech. services librarian Coe Coll., Cedar Rapids, Ia., 1969—. Mem. A.L.A., Ia. Library Assn., Am. Recorder Soc. Home: 2021 Bever Av SE Cedar Rapids IA 52403 Office: Coe Coll Library Cedar Rapids IA 52402

IANNIELLO, LYNNE YOUNG (MRS. PAUL J. IANNIELLO), assn. exec.; b. N.Y.C., Oct. 27, 1927; d. Joseph Gary and Gertrude (Goodman) Young; B.S., N.Y. U., 1946; m. Paul J. Ianniello, Nov. 21, 1948; children—Geoffry Dean, Richard Gary. Dir. pub. relations Anti-Defamation League B'nai B'rith, N.Y.C., 1962—. Recipient Citizenship award Oceanside Lions Club, 1965. Author: Milestones Along The March, 1965. Editor: The Ax-Grinders: Critics of Our Public Schools, 1962; Anti-Defamation League Bull., 1963—. Office: 315 Lexington Av New York City NY 10016

IDDINS, MILDRED, librarian; b. Fountain City, Tenn.; d. Joseph Franklin and Lucy (Chandler) Iddins; A.B., Carson-Newman Coll., 1936; B.S., George Peabody Coll., 1941. Tchr., Bell House Sch., Knoxville, Tenn., 1936-37; tchr. Roane County High Sch., Kingston, 1937-41; librarian, Dandridge (Tenn.) High Sch., 1941-43; Army librarian, Ft. Oglethorpe, Ga., 1943-44; librarian Carson-Newman Coll., Jefferson City, Tenn., 1944—. Mem. Am., Southeastern, Tenn. library assns., Am. Assn. U. Women (br. treas. 1964-66). Baptist. Clubs: Monday Literary, Modern Literary. Home: 403 Russell St Jefferson City TN 37760

IDEN, SHIRLEE ROSE (MRS. JACK IDEN), journalist; b. Detroit, Jan. 10, 1931; d. Jacob and Blanche (Paluba) Rose; B.A. cum laude, Wayne State U., 1966, M.A., 1970; m. Jack Iden, Feb. 23, 1949; children—Linda (dec.), Robert (dec.), Lauren, Elaine, Bruce. Instr. history Macomb Community Coll., Warren, Mich., 1967-68; free lance writer, 1967-73; instr. history Oakland Community Coll., Oak Park, Mich., 1970-73; women's and news writer Southfield (Mich.) Eccentric, 1973—. Pres. Mich. ladies aux. Jewish War Veterans of the U.S.A., Detroit, 1964-65, nat. patriotic instr., 1973—; chaplain Allied Veterans Council of Met. Detroit, 1965-66. Mem. League Jewish Women (dir. met. Detroit 1965), Pioneer Women, Women in Communications. Democrat. Jewish religion (dir. congregation 1971-73). Contbr. articles in field to profl. jours. Editor Nat. Ladies Bull. of Jewish War Veterans Assn., 1967-70, Mich. Salute. Home: 10005 Elgin Huntington Woods MI 48070

IGNATIEFF, WANDA ANTOINETTE ZBIEC, govt. ofcl.; b. Latrobe, Pa., Jan. 26, 1914; d. Alexander Frank and Antonina Wanda (Boguta) Zbiec; B.A., Bethany (W.Va.) Coll., 1936; postgrad. Pa. State Coll., 1941-42, George Washington U., 1947-49, Am. U., 1965, 67, Md. U., 1958; m. Anatoly Ignatieff, June 22, 1965. Accountant, Latrobe Bank & Trust Co., 1940-41; tchr. Confluence (Pa.) High Sch., 1941-42; instr. math. Bethany Coll., 1942-44; adminstrv. asst. Polish Embassy, Washington, 1944-51; editor, translator Library of Congress, 1951-57; editor, abstractor sci. and tech. information Dept. of Air Force, 1957-59; mgr. tech. information processing Dept. Commerce, 1959-63; mgr. sci. information processing Def. Dept., 1963-73; mgr. sci. information process Interior Dept., 1973—. Recipient govt. awards. Mem. Am. Soc. Information Sci., Spl. Libraries Assn., Soc. Fed. Linguistics, Am. Math. Soc. Catholic. Author govt. publns. Home: 2207 Iverson St Hillcrest Heights MD 20031 Office: Dept Interior 18th and C St NW Washington DC 20240

IJAMS, CATHERINE ELIZABETH, educator; b. Ottawa, Kan., Jan. 28, 1923; d. William Marshall and Cora Alice (Kelsey) Johnson; student Ottawa U., 1941-42, Washburn U., Topeka, 1970-73, Kan. State U., Manhattan, 1973; m. Charles Vincent Ijams, Feb. 20, 1969; children—Nancy (Mrs. Michael Warren Tomlinson), Peggy (Mrs. Wallace Edward Fisher II). Kindergarten tchr. Lafayette Elementary Sch. Dist., Topeka, 1961-62, Avondale East Elementary Sch., Topeka, 1962-66; lang. devel. tchr. speech dept. Kan. Neurol. Inst., Topeka, 1966—. Girl Scout leader, Ottawa, 1958-59. Research grantee. Mem. Am. Assn. Mental Deficiency, Kan. Assn. Pub. Employees. Mem. Christian Ch. (organizer pre-sch. 1972, coordinator edn. bldg. 1971-72, nursery vol. coordinator 1973). Home: 2807 Fairway Dr Topeka KS 66611 Office: 3107 W 21st St Topeka KS 66604

IKERMAN, RUTH C. PERCIVAL (MRS. LAWRENCE HOWSER IKERMAN), author; b. Redlands, Cal., Sept. 4, 1910; d. Clarence Christopher and Sophie Henrietta (Doll) Percival; A.B., U. Redlands, 1931; m. Lawrence Howser Ikerman, Jan. 12, 1947. Sec. to supt. schs., Redlands, 1932-39; sec. to dir. religious edn., Los Angeles, 1939-42; sec. orange processing div. Real Gold, Redlands, 1942-46; co-owner Larry's Paint House, Redlands, 1955-71. Reviewer books Los Angeles Times, 1962—. Devotional chmn. Redlands YWCA, 1952-57. Recipient 3 George Washington Honor medals Freedom Found. at Valley Forge, Mem. U. Redlands Fellows, Nat. League Am. Pen Women. Conglist. Club: Cosmos. Author: Devotional Thoughts From the Holy Land, 1968; Womens Programs for Special Occasions, 1966; The Disciplined Heart, 1964; Cooking By Heart, 1962; Devotional Programs About People and Places, 1960; Devotional Programs for the Changing Seasons, 1958; Devotional Programs for Every Month, 1957; Prayers of a Homemaker, 1955; Golden Words for Every Day, 1969; Calendar of Faith and Flowers, 1970; Meditations for Bird Lovers, 1972; On Morning Trails, 1974. Home: 11 Panorama Dr Redlands CA 92373

ILANO-LOZADA, DIVINIA JARDIANIANO, pediatrician; b. Imus, Philippines, Oct. 15, 1939; d. Lazaro Ramos Ilano and Josefa Topacio (Jardininano); A.A., U. St. Tomas, 1956, M.D. cum laude, 1961; m. Eriberto Lozada, May 16, 1964; children—Eriberto, John, Philip Joseph. Med. resident Vets. Meml. Hosp., Quezon City, Philippines, 1962; resident pediatrics Lincoln Hosp., N.Y.C., 1963-66; fellow ambulatory pediatrics Harlem Hosp., N.Y.C., 1966-67; chief resident pediatrics Meml. Hosp., N.Y.C., 1967-70; part-time clinician Child Health Bur., N.Y.C., 1971-72; pvt. practice pediatrics, N.Y.C., 1971-72; pediatrician Sagamore Children's Center, 1972—. Mem. N.Y. State, Suffolk pediatric socs. Address: 16 Elkland Rd Dix Hills NY 11746

ILEM, PRISCILLA G. (MRS. LEN MADLANSACAY), physician; b. Imus, Cavite, Philippines; d. Narciso S. and Felisa (Guevarra) Ilem; M.D. benemeritus, U. Santo Tomas, 1954; postgrad. Syracuse Psychiat. Hosp., 1956-57, Yale Med. Sch., 1960, Polyclinic Med. Sch., 1969, N.Y. State Psychiat. Inst., 1969, Columbia, 1969, Letchworth Village, 1969; M.P.H. (U.S. Children's Bur. fellow), U. Cal. at Berkeley, 1971; m. Len Madlansacay, Mar. 3, 1957; children—Rey Thomas, Priscilla Joy, May Ann. Rotating intern U. Santo Tomas Hosp., Manila, 1953-54, Truesdale Hosp., Fall River, Mass., 1955; resident psychiatry, research asso. Marcy (N.Y.) State Hosp., 1956-59; sr. psychiatrist Monson State Hosp., Palmer, Mass., 1959-61; staff psychiatrist Twin Elms Hosp., Syracuse, N.Y., 1966-67; supervising psychiatrist Rome (N.Y.) State Sch., 1967-68; practice medicine specializing in psychiatry and neurology, Manila, 1962-66, Rome, N.Y., 1967—; chief service Rome (N.Y.) State Sch., 1971—; cons. mental retardation and psychiatry Cal. Dept. Mental Health, 1971—. Mem. Am. Psychiat. Assn., Am. Assn. Mental Deficiency, Assn. N.Y. State Mental Hygiene Physicians, New Eng. Soc. Psychiatry and Neurology. Contbr. articles to profl. jours. Address: Letchworth Village Thiells NY 10984

ILER, SHIRLEY ARLENE (MRS. CLETUS EVERETT ILER), mfg. co. exec.; b. Detroit, Dec. 24, 1920; d. George Monroe and Edith Irene (Gibb) Jenkyn; student Wayne U., 1939-40; m. Cletus Everett Iler, Sept. 17, 1944; children—Michael Ralph, Cynthia Suzanne, Sheryl Lynn. With orthoptic dept. Dr. Ralph Pino, Detroit, 1939-44; started Mass. Vision Program, 1941-46, working with bd. edn. and Saginaw (Mich.) Health dept., Saginaw schs., 1955-61; partner with husband C.E. Iler Co., mfr. orthotics and prosthetics, Saginaw, 1946—. Dir. United Way, Saginaw, 1971-74, v.p., exec. bd. 1972-74; mem. allocations and budget com., Mich. United Way, 1969-73; mem. adv. bd. Salvation Army, 1971-74; v.p. Saginaw Camp Fire Girl program; mem. bd. March Dimes, 1972-74; treas. Saginaw County Hist. Commn., 1973. Sec. Saginaw br. George Romney for gov. Mich. vols., 1972-73. Mem. Saginaw Women's Council (pres.), Zonta Internat. (pres. Saginaw, 1968-70, chmn. dist. pub. affairs, 1968-70). Home: 1902 Wilson Av Saginaw MI 48603 Office: 1504 N Michigan Av Saginaw MI 48602

ILLES, TERRY TERWILLIGER, educator, artist; b. Elwood, Ind.; d. William A. and Bess (Moore) Terwilliger; A.B., Ind. U., 1955, M.A., 1957; m. Stephen R. Illes, Apr. 17, 1942 (div. June 1952). Lectr., Ind. U. N.W. Campus, Gary, 1962-63; asst. prof. fine arts dept. Ind. U., Bloomington, 1963-71, asso. prof., 1971—; exhibited one man shows Stow-Davis Showrooms, Mdse. Mart., Chgo.; exhibited in group shows Smithsonian Coll. Fine Arts, Mus. Contemporary Crafts, N.Y.C., Turman Gallery, Art Inst. Chgo., Terre Haute, Ind., Newark Mus., Ball State U. Art Gallery, Media Galleries, Orange, Cal., St. Paul Art Center, Evansville (Ind.) Mus. Arts and Scis., Milw. Mus. Art, Speed Mus., Louisville, numerous others; represented in permanent collections at Art Inst. Chgo., Johnson Wax Co., Marshall Field & Co., St. Paul Art Center, Ind. U. Fine Arts Mus., U. Tenn., others. Recipient Ind. Artist Craftsmen award, 1967, 69; Nat. Merit award, 1966; others. Mem. World Crafts Council, Am. Craftsmens Council, Ind. Artist-Craftsmen, Am. Assn. U. Profs. Home: 321 E 14th St Bloomington IN 47401

IMHOFF, MYRTLE MARY ANN, educator; b. St. Louis, Oct. 7, 1910; d. Clyde C. and Laura E. (Asmuth) Imhoff; B.A., Harris Tchrs. Coll., St. Louis, 1931; M.A., St. Louis U., 1935; Ph.D., Washington U., 1952. Established and taught kindergarten pub. schs., Crystal City, Mo., 1932-34; elementary tchr. pub. sch., St. Louis, 1934-44; critic tchr. Neb. State Coll., 1944-45; fed. personnel and field rep. Navy Civilian Dept., Washington, 1945-46; critic tchr. Normal U., Ill., 1946-47; dir. edn. pub. schs. Brentwood, Mo., 1947-48; asso. prof. elementary edn., dir. summer in-service workshop and related demonstration schs. Adams State Coll., 1948-50; lect. edn., supr. student teaching, Washington U., 1950-53; asso. prof., head kindergarten primary program, supr. student teaching, Washington U., 1950-53; asso. prof., head kindergarten primary program, supr. student teaching Long Beach State Coll., 1953-56, 58-59; specialist early elementary edn. U.S. Office Edn., Dept. Health Edn. and Welfare, 1956-58; curriculum expert UNESCO, Ministry of Edn., Bangkok, Thailand, 1959-60; prof. edn. Cal. State U., Fullerton, 1960-68, Cal. State U., Los Angeles, 1968—. Delegate to Pacific Intercollegiate Assn. Coll. Council on Asian Studies, 1967—, Fulbright adviser, 1967-68, mem. Asian Studies Com. Del. to India H.E.W. Internat. Studies Project, 1965; mem. Ednl. Testing Service Com. for rev. and evaluation Early Childhood Edn. and Elementary Edn. Test Forms, summers 1965, 66, 67; active various other ednl. programs. Cons. series filmstrips for Coronet Instrnl. Films, 1967-68. Mem. adv. bd. World Explorer's Program, 1965—. Mem. Am. Ednl. Research Assn., Internat. Council of Psychologists, N.E.A. (exec. bd. dept. elementary Kindergarten nursery edn. 1961-64, chmn. publs. com. 1961-64), Am. Psychol. Assn., Nat. Soc. Study Edn., UN Assn. World Affairs Council Orange County, Am. Acad. Polit. and Social Sci., Comparative Edn. Soc., U.S. Com. Early Childhood Edn., Internat. Platform Assn., Assn. Higher Edn., Am. Mus. Natural History, Washington U., St. Louis U. alumni assns., Kappa Delta Pi. Author: Early Elementary Education, 1959; also chpts. in books, articles in profl. jours. Home: Park Tustin 14175 Paseo Corto Tustin CA 92680 Office: Cal State U Los Angeles CA 90032

IMMEL, SHIRLEY JEANNE (MRS. ROGER NORMAN IMMEL), psychologist, educator; b. Toledo, Dec. 13, 1934; d. Harold Samuel and Ruth Catherine (Bordeaux) Lezotte; B.S., Bowling Green State U., 1960, M.A., 1964; m. Roger Norman Immel, July 10, 1953. Tchr. Bucyrus (O.) city schs., 1960, Danbury Twp. Schs., Lakeside, O., 1960-64; counselor Sandusky (O.) city Schs., 1964-68; intern psychologist Fremont (O.) city schs., 1968-69; psychologist Bellevue (O.) city schs., 1969—. Mem. Adv. Council Regional Spl. Edn. Center, Milan, O., 1971—. Rep. to Co-ordinating Com. for Children and Youth, Huron County, (O.) Child Abuse and Neglect Inter-Agy. Team, Sandusky County, O., 1973-74; mem. governing bd. Erie-Ottawa Guidance Center, Sandusky, 1974—. Mem. Bellevue Edn. Assn., Nat. Assn. Sch. Psychologists (mem. program and legislative coms. 1972-74), Ohio Sch. Psychologists Assn., Maumee Valley Sch. Psychologists (treas. 1971-72), Ottawa County Mental Health Assn. (dir. 1974—). Mem. Order Eastern Star (matron 1965). Home: 4311 East Norma Dr Port Clinton OH 43452 Office: 125 North Av Bellevue OH 44811

IMPASTATO, FARA, educator; b. New Orleans, Aug. 20, 1920; d. James John and Cecilia Blanche (Asher) Impastato; B.A. magna cum laude, Loyola U. (New Orleans), 1949; Ph.D. summa cum laude, St. Marys Sch. Sacred Theology, 1952; postgrad. as vis. scholar Cath. U. Am., autumn 1971, Fordham U., spring 1972. Tchr. religion, small rural missions, Albany, Gueydan, Theriot, La., 1939-45; tchr. religion to retarded children Louise S. Davis Sch., New Orleans, 1945-47; novice mistress Inst. Eucharistic Missionaries of St. Dominic, Covington, La., 1952-63; asst. prof. theology St. Mary Coll., Xavier, Kan., 1965-66; asst. prof. theology Loyola U., New Orleans, 1966, now asso. prof. Home: 1101 Aline St New Orleans LA 70115

IMPELLIZZERI, IRENE HELEN, educator; b. Bklyn., N.Y.; d. Joseph and Lucy (Colson) Macroe; B.S., N.Y. U., 1941; M.A., Columbia, 1942; Ph.D., Fordham U., 1958. Tchr. pub. schs., N.Y.C., 1942-59; prof. ednl. psychology, Bklyn. Coll., 1961—, asso. dean dept. edn., 1968-71, dean dept. edn., 1971—; psychologist Hearing and Speech Clinic, Manhattan Eye and Ear Hosp., 1955-58. Research coordinator N.Y.C. Bd. Edn., 1959-65, research cons., 1960-61. Mem. Am., N.Y. State, Bklyn. (exec. com., sec. 1959-64) psychol. assns., Am., N.Y.C. (trustee 1963-67) personnel and guidance assns., N.Y. State Counselors Assn., Doctorate Assn. N.Y. Educators, Am. Assn. U. Profs., Am. Catholic Psychol. Assn., Nat. Catholic Guidance Conf., N.Y. Acad. Sci., Am. Ednl. Research Assn., Nat. Council on Measurement in Edn., Assn. for Measurement and Evaluation in Guidance. Contbr. articles in field to profl. jours. Home: 205 Clinton Av Brooklyn NY 11205

IMPERI, LILLIAN LOUISE, psychiatrist; b. Grand Rapids, Mich., Jan. 16, 1924; d. Eggidio L. and Mabel P. (McConnell) Imperi; B.S., Marygrove Coll., 1950; M.D., U. Mich., 1955; m. William J. Rumbos, 1954 (div.); 1 son, William J. Intern St. Joseph Mercy Hosp., Pontiac, Mich., 1955-56; resident in psychiatry Wayne County Gen. Hosp., Eloise, Mich., 1956-59; post-doctoral fellow dept. student mental hygiene Yale, 1965-67, Undercliff Mental Health Center, Meriden, Conn., 1967-69; psychiatrist Camarillo (Cal.) State Hosp., 1971— practice medicine specializing in psychiatry, Yuma, 1969-71. Mem. Am. Psychiat. Assn., Am. Med. Women's Assn., A.M.A., Marygrove Alumni Assn., Kappa Gamma Pi, Alpha Epsilon Iota. Club: Zonta. Home: Box A452 Camarillo CA 93010

INABU, HANAKO HANA, YMCA exec.; b. Lynndyl, Utah, July 5, 1928; d. Sadaichi Sam and Fute (Akai) Inabu; student Los Angeles City Coll., 1954-55. Office mgr., sec. for camping services YMCA Met. Los Angeles, 1946—, dir., program coordinator deaf camp, 1959—. Mem. Ch. of Jesus Christ of Latter-day Saints. Author deaf camp counselors manual. Home: PO Box 33194 Los Angeles CA 90033 Office: 510 S Spring St Room 517 Los Angeles CA 90013

INBODY, NINA HELEN (MRS. PAUL WAYNE INBODY), univ. dean; b. Tahequah, Okla., June 10, 1933; d. Albert Orn and Vona (Juanita) Smithee; B.A., Tulsa U., 1967, M.A., 1969; postgrad. Okla. U., 1967-68, Mich. State U., 1969, Tulsa U.; m. Paul Wayne Inbody, Mar. 25, 1950; children—Marcia Lynn, Paula Ann, Paul Wayne. Urban specialist Okla. U., 1967-68; dean women Oral Roberts U., Tulsa, 1968—, asso. dean students, 1970—. Cons. Fed. Summer Youth program, Evaluation Fed. Aging Project, 1968. Mem. edn. com. Planned Parenthood Assn. Bd. dirs. Tulsa YWCA. Mem. Nat. Assn. Women Deans and Counselors, Louisa May Alcott Literary Soc., Am. Sociol. Assn., Nat. Assn. Student Personnel Adminstrs., Am. Assn. U. Women, League Women Voters, Alpha Lambda Delta. Baptist (mem. scholarship-loan com. women's aux. 1955-70). Club: Pilot Internat. Home: 11762 S 76th E Av Bixby OK 74008 Office: 7777 S Lewis St Tulsa OK 74105

INGALLS, DOROTHY MAY, educator; b. Newark, Jan. 22, 1922; d. William Percy and Josephine (Bogle) Ingalls; B.S., Trenton State Coll., 1943; M.A., Columbia U. Tchrs. Coll., 1958, Ed.D., 1958. Tchr. Bridgewater Twp. (N.J.) Pub. Schs., 1943, Hamilton Twp. (N.J.) Pub. Schs., 1943-47, Trenton (N.J.) Pub. Schs., 1947-55; asst. prin. Demonstration Sch., Trenton State Coll., 1955-57; elem. prin. and social studies coordinator Pennsbury Schs., Fallsington, Pa., 1958-67; asso. prof. Trenton State Coll., 1967—; mem. off-campus staff Pa. State U. Ogantz Center; cons. Singer Pub. Co.; lectr. on India to civic orgns. Mem. Assn. Supervision and Curriculum Devel. (Bucks County exec. com. 1962-67), Nat., N.J. edn. assns., Nat. Higher Edn. Assn., Assn. Supervision and Curriculum and Devel., N.J. Assn. Supervision and Curriculum Devel., Am. Assn. U. Profs., Kappa Delta Phi, Pi Lambda Theta. Home: 120 W Farrell Av Trenton NJ 08618 Office: Trenton State Coll Hillwood Lakes NJ 08625

INGALLS, IOLANI, educator; b. Honolulu, Dec. 12, 1911; d. Arthur Burdett and Iola Emogene (Barber) Ingalls; B.A., Principia Coll., 1937; M.A., U. Ore., 1942; postgrad. Harvard, summer 1938, Breadloaf Sch. English, summer 1940, U. London, summer 1949, Harvard Div. Sch., 1963-64; M.A., Northwestern U., 1971. Cataloger Principia Coll. Library, Elsah, Ill., 1931-38, instr. English, 1938-43, asst. prof., 1943-49, asso. prof., 1949-56, acting dean women, 1956, dean women, 1957-63, prof. Bible, 1964—, chmn. dept. religion and philosophy, 1964-73. Tchr. in field First Ch. Christ, Scientist, Boston, 1972-75. Adv. bd. Opportunity Centers, Howalton Day Sch., Chgo., 1970—. Recipient letter and award for 40 yrs. service Principia, 1971. Mem. Am. Acad. Religion, Soc. Bibl. Lit., Nat. League Am. Pen Women (charter Cahokia Valley br., v.p. 1966-68, pres. 1966-64, state sec. 1970-72, program chmn. 1966-68, membership chmn. 1968-70), League Women Voters, Phi Alpha Eta. Christian Scientist. Home: Lilac Lane Elsah IL 62028

INGALSBE, LILLIAN CAROLINE (MRS. CHARLES KREIGER), real estate broker, judge; b. Donald, Washington, Mar. 27, 1932; d. Wiley Claude and Lillian (Graham) Close; student Centralia Jr. Coll., 1970—; m. Charles Kreiger, Sept. 22, 1947; children—Sherry, Charles E., Roger, Tony, Shane. Justice peace, Morton, Wash., 1961-67; police judge, 1963—; real estate salesman Rainier Real Estate, 1966-67; broker, br. mgr. Forrester Realty, Morton, after 1968; now owner, broker Mountain Realty, Morton. Sec., Eastern Lewis County Democratic Club. Mem. Women of Moose. Home: Box 122 Morton WA 98356 Office: 2d St and Airport Way Morton WA 98356

INGBAR, MARY LEE MACK (MRS. SIDNEY H. INGBAR), economist; b. N.Y.C., May 18, 1926; d. Edward C. and Ruth (Prince) Mack; S.B. cum laude, Radcliffe Coll., 1946, A.M. in Econs., 1948, Ph.D. in Econs., 1953; M.P.H. cum laude in Pub. Health Practice, Harvard, 1956; m. Sidney H. Ingbar, May 28, 1950; children—David, Eric, Jonathan. Asst. in econs. Tufts Coll., 1949-50; price economist Bur. Labor Statistics, U.S. Dept. Labor, 1951-52; bus. economist Office of Chief Economist, Bur. Mines, U.S. Dept. Interior, 1952-53; lectr. med. econs. Harvard Sch. Pub. Health, 1957-61, research asso. Grad. Sch. Pub. Adminstrn., 1961-66; dir. program devel. Dept. Health, Hosp., Welfare, Cambridge, 1968-69; cons. health econs., dir. research Office Comprehensive Health Planning, Exec. Office Administn. and Finance, Commonwealth of Mass., 1969-72; asso. prof. Health Policy Program and div. ambulatory and community medicine U. Cal. at San Francisco Sch. Medicine, 1972—. Pres. Friends of Boston City Hosp. Fellow Am. Pub. Health Assn. (co-chmn. med. care, maternal and child health sects. liaison com. 1959-61); mem. A.A.A.S., Am. Econ. Assn., Am. Hosp. Assn., Am. Statis. Assn., Mass. Pub. Health Assn. (chmn. med. care sect. 1965-66; rec. sec. 1966-68), Phi Beta Kappa, Delta Omega. Author (with L.D. Taylor) Hospital Costs in Massachusetts, 1968. Contbr. articles to profl. jours. Home: 300 Upper Toyon Dr Ross CA 94957 Office: Health Policy Program School Medicine University of Cal San Francisco CA 94143

INGE, ELMA SOLOMON (MRS. GEORGE THOMAS INGE), civic worker; b. Denver, Dec. 19, 1906; d. James Elmer and Amanda (Malmgren) Solomon; student Okla. Women's Coll., 1923-24; A.B., Oklahoma City U., 1926; m. George Thomas Inge, Sept. 22, 1931; children—Betty Jean (Mrs. William Howes Farwell), Sue Marilynn (Mrs. Leroy Clark Fergces). Math. faculty Colo. Women's Coll., Denver, 1929-31. Mem. women's com. Freedom's Found. Valley Forge, 1967—; mem. Hear Found., 1968—; bd. mem. Glendale (Cal.) com. So. Cal. Symphony, Hollywood Bowl Assn., 1953—. Bd. dirs. So. Cal. com. WHO; bd. govs. Glendale Symphony Assn. Mem. Opera Guild So. Cal., U. Cal. at Los Angeles Affiliates, Los Angeles County Mus. Sci., Los Angeles World Affairs Council, Los Angeles County Mus. Art, Brand Cultural Center, Nat. Charity League, P.E.O., Town Hall Los Angeles, Assistance League So. Cal., Ebell, Oakmont League Glendale, Little Theatre Verdugos. Republican. Methodist. Clubs: Oakmont Country (Glendale), Balboa Bay (Newport Beach, Cal.). Home: 1106 Rossneoyne Av Glendale CA 91207

INGENITO, ESTELLE FASOLINO, biochemist, toxicologist; b. Westerly, R.I., Oct. 31, 1919; d. Ludwig Guy and Anne Santa (Guarino) Fasolino; B.A., Conn. Coll. for Women, 1941; M.S., U. Conn., 1945; Ph.D., Boston U., 1951; m. Francis E. Ingenito, Aug. 19, 1950; 1 son, Mark Christopher. Faculty and research scientist Boston U., 1946-51, Harvard, 1951-57, U. Pa., 1957-66, Commonwealth of Pa., 1966-73, Gov.'s Council on Drug and Alcoholic Abuse, 1973—. Vol. councils on drugs and alcohol; lectr. in field. Mem. Phi Beta Kappa, various profl. and sci. orgns. Contbr. to profl. jours. Home: 6 Nancy Dr Havertown PA 19083 Office: 915 Corinthian Av Philadelphia PA 19130

INGERSOLL, HAZEL LUELLA, ret. educator, artist; b. Raymond, Neb., Mar. 3, 1908; d. C. C. and Mabel B. (Weller) Ingersoll; B.S., U. Neb., 1934, M.S., 1942; Ph.D., Cornell U., 1947; postgrad. Colo. State U., 1937-39. Tchr. pub. sch. systems, Neb., 1925-30, vocational home econs. high schs., Neb., 1934-40; asst. prof., dir. preschool lab U. Me., 1944-45; prof., supr. tchr. tng. in preschool labs N.Y. U. at Buffalo, 1945-48; prof. U. Tenn., 1948-50; faculty Okla. State U., Stillwater, 1950-73, prof. family studies, 1950-73, prof. emeritus, 1973—; artist, 1970—. Active various community drives. Named U. Tchr. of the Year for Home Econs., Okla. State U., 1969. Mem. Am. Assn. U. Women, Am. Home Econs. Assn., Nat. Council on Family Relations, Am. Psychol. Assn., Okla. Home Econs. Assn., Okla. Health and Welfare Assn., Okla. Ednl. Assn., Okla. Council on Family Relations (sec.-treas. 1966-74), Phi Kappa Phi, Omicron Nu, Phi Upsilon Omicron. Methodist. Home: 120 S Willis St Stillwater OK 74074

INGERSON, HELEN G. KNAPP (MRS. JOSEPH P. INGERSON), dietitian; b. West Winfield, N.Y., Oct. 24, 1922; d. Marion R. and Geraldine (Smith) Knapp; B.S., Cornell U., 1944; M.Ed., U. Rochester, 1969; m. Joseph P. Ingerson, Feb. 24, 1950; children—Terrence V., Charles Joseph, Joanne Carol. Dietetic intern Eastman Kodak Co., Rochester, N.Y., 1945, ednl. dir. for dietetic internship, asst. supr. nutrition services, 1951-71, supr. nutrition services, 1971-72, dir. dietic internship, 1971-72; asso. prof. dept. human nutrition and food ecology Coll. Human Ecology, Cornell U., 1972-74; asst. dir. dietetics for therapeutics and edn. U. Rochester Med. Center, 1974—; dietitian Strong Meml. Hosp., Rochester, 1944, Bausch Lomb Optical Co., Rochester, 1945-47, Western Electric Corp., Chgo., 1947; chief dietitian Rochester Gen. Hosp., 1947-51. Vice chmn. Rochester and Monroe County Nutrition Com., 1954-56, chmn., 1956-58; health chmn. Iron-dequoit Parent Tchrs. Council, 1958-60. Area E rep. women's N.Am. sailing com. N.Am. Yacht Racing Union, chmn., 1974—. Mem. Am. (sec. council 1963-66, chmn. pub. relations com. 1960-62, del.-at-large 1963-66, mem. adminstrv. com. dietetic internship council 1966-69, chmn. adminstrv. com. 1966-68, mem. ednl. practices com. 1969-71), N.Y. State (pres. 1958-59, editor bull., 1949-57), Genessee (pres. 1949-51) dietetic assns., Am. Home Econs. Assn., Food Service Exec. Assn. Home: 299 Rock Beach Rd Rochester NY 14617 Office: Dietary Dept U Rochester Med Center Rochester NY 14620

INGRAHAM, BARBARA JEAN (MRS. JAMES MARSHALL INGRAHAM), educator; b. Hanover, Ind., Dec. 28, 1937; d. Raymond and Erma Doris (Kyle) Wingham; student U. Ill., 1959-60; B.S. in Bus. with honors, Ind. U., 1970, M.S. in Edn. with honors, 1972; m. James Marshall Ingraham, Apr. 10, 1955; children—Sharon Renee, Susan Elaine, Sheila Marie. Adminstrv. intern Ind. U., Bloomington, 1971-72; instr. Army Prep. Tng. Center, Ft. Knox, Ky., 1972-73; instr. El Paso (Tex.) Residential Manpower Center, 1974—. Caseworker vol. A.R.C., 1970-72; asst. to social worker Army Community Services, 1970-72. Recipient Outstanding Community Services award, Ft. Knox, 1971. Mem. Assn. Women Deans, Adminstrs. and Counselors, Nat. Orgn. Women, Ind. Alumni Assn., Officers Wives Orgn., Beta Gamma Sigma. Home: 10129 Honolulu Dr El Paso TX 79925 Office: PO Box 119 El Paso TX 79941

INGRAHAM, MARY ELIZABETH LOBODY (MRS. R. RUPERT INGRAHAM), educator; b. Jeannette, Pa., Nov. 6, 1905; d. George Peter and Elizabeth (Archer) Lobody; A.B., Wilson Coll., 1926; M.A. U. Pitts., 1942, postgrad. (NSF fellow), summers 1961-63; postgrad. (Gen. Electric fellow) Rennselaer Poly. Inst., 1954; m. R. Rupert Ingraham, Oct. 16, 1942 (dec. Jan. 1964); children—Natalie Ann (Mrs. Charles Robert Youngstead), George Edward. Sec., Archer Sheet Metal Co., Jeannette, Pa., 1918-27; tchr. Jeannette Sr. High Sch., 1926-46, 51-53; bookkeeper Pa. Dept. Hwys. Traffic Survey, 1953; asst. prof. math. Boyce campus Community Coll. Allegheny County, Monroeville, Pa., 1966-68, asso. prof. math., 1968-70, prof., 1970—; tchr. in-service insts. for elementary and secondary tchrs. Nat. Def. Edn. Act, Allegheny County, 1960-63; cons., faculty mem. NSF Inst. Community Coll. Tchrs.-Carnegie-Mellon U., summer 1970. Co-founder P.T.A. brs. Jeannette Pub. Schs., pres. Ft. Pitt unit, 1949-51. Mem. Am. Assn. U. Profs., N.E.A., Nat. Council Tchrs. Math. (nominations and elections com. 1963-66, contbr. to 28th yearbook 1963), Pa. Council Tchrs. Math. (del. at large 1964-67), Western Pa. Math. Council (exec. bd. 1955—, pres. 1966-68), Pa. State Edn. Assn. (pres. Jeannette br. 1936-38), Am. Assn. U. Women, N.Y. State Assn. Tchrs. Math., Math. Assn. Am. Episcopalian (dir. Christian edn. 1948-54, mem. bd. Christian edn. Diocese Pitts. 1948-51). Club: Progressive Woman's of Jeannette (v.p. 1971—, pres. 1931-33, 38-40, 73-74). Home: 319 Margaret St Jeannette PA 15644 Office: Boyce Campus Community Coll Allegheny County 595 Beatty Rd Monroeville PA 15146

INGRAM, BETTY ELAM (MRS. BILL M. INGRAM), assn. exec.; b. Birmingham, Ala., May 9, 1937; d. James Walter and Bettie Viola (Bates) Elam; B.S., U. Tenn., 1958; m. Bill M. Ingram, June 9, 1966; 1 son, Jon Bavritt. Women's editor Kingsport (Tenn.) Times-News, 1958-59; asst. pub. relations dir. Jefferson County United Appeal, Birmingham, Ala., 1959-62; pub. relations dir. Birmingham chpt. A.R.C., 1962-68, asst. mgr., 1968-70, sr. asst. mgr., 1970—. Promotion chmn. Internat. Fair, 1965; mem. pub. relations com. U.S. Savs. Bond Campaign, 1963-64; mem. fund campaign pub. relations com. St. Vincent's Hosp., 1968-69; mem. pub. relations com. Birmingham Symphony, 1967-68; mem. Drug Abuse Coordinating Com., 1971-74; mem. Citizens for Equal Rights Amendment, 1972-73; mem. Birmingham Civic Ballet League; mem. Jr. Women's Symphony Com. Bd. dirs. Jefferson County Com. for Econ. Opportunity, 1971-72. Named Woman of Year, Birmingham chpt. Am. Bus. Women's Assn., 1969; recipient Jaycettes Distinguished award, 1969. Mem. Am. Women in Radio and TV (pres. 1969-70), Am. Bus. Women's Assn. (pres. 1968-69), Pub. Relations Council Ala., U. Tenn. Alumni Assn. (pres. 1969-70), Women in Communications (pres. 1967-68). Lutheran. Clubs: Zonta (dir. 1970, pres. 1972—); Birmingham Press (dir. 1969-70). Editor Red Cross mag. Salute, 1960-68. Home: 1780 Murray Hill Rd Birmingham AL 35216 Office: 2316 4th Av North Birmingham AL 35202

INGRAM, ERNAGENE FORTESCUE (MRS. LEWIS K. INGRAM), clinician; b. Seattle, Feb. 8, 1921; d. Ernest Henry P. and Anna Mary (Clark) Fortescue; B.S. in Bacteriology, U. Wash., 1942; M.Sc., Ohio State U., 1944, M.D., 1949; m. Lewis Karl Ingram, Sept. 12, 1944; children—Jefferson, Leslie Ann, Gordon, Robin Edward, Sheldon. Bacteriologist Wash. State Health Dept., Seattle, 1942, U. Hosp., Columbus, O., 1944-45; intern Ft. Sanders Hosp., Knoxville, Tenn., 1950; clinician Wise County Health Dept., Norton, Va., 1957—. Mem. Va., Wise County (pres. 1971) med. socs., Sigma Xi (asso.), Alpha Omega Alpha. Episcopalian. Home: 1035 Spruce St NW Norton VA 24273 Office: Wise County Health Dept Norton VA 24273

INMAN, FLORENCE ELSIE MACDONALD (MRS. GEORGE STRONG INMAN), Canadian govt. ofcl.; b. West River, P.E.I., Can.; d. Alexander and Florence (White) Macdonald; grad. high sch.; m. George Strong Inman, Sept. 26, 1910 (dec. Nov. 1937); children—W. Robert (dec.), George S. A., Wilfred N., R. Victor. Hotel owner, 1946-56; mem. Senate of Can., 1955—. Originator, pres. Womens Liberal Assn., P.E.I.; chmn. Mothers' Allowance Commn., P.E.I., 1949-55; pres. Montague (P.E.I.) Hosp. Aux. Trustee Montague Hosp. Mem. P.E.I. Tourist Assn. (hon. pres.), Bus. and Profl. Women's Club, Canadian Legion Aux., Ind. Order Daus. Empire (pres. 1920), P.E.I. Hist. Soc., Commonwealth Parliamentary Assn., Canadian Group Interparliamentary Union, Beta Sigma Phi (hon. internat. mem.). Clubs: Canadian (former P.E.I. v.p.), Zonta International, Charlottetown Zonta. Home: 130 Renfrew St Ottawa ON Canada Office: Senate of Can Ottawa ON Canada

INMAN, JULIA DAUGHERTY, communications editor; b. Fort Benning, Ga.; d. Joseph B. and Martha (Oliver) Daugherty; student Wheaton Coll., 1947-49; B.A., Coll. William and Mary, 1951. Mem. staff Petersburg (Va.) Progress-Index, 1953-54; radio-TV editor Indpls. Star, 1954—. Mem. Phi Beta Kappa, Theta Sigma Phi. Home: 8825 River Rd Indianapolis IN 46240 Office: Indianapolis Star 307 N Pennsylvania St Indianapolis IN 46206*

INMAN, JUNE FRANCIS, librarian; b. Birmingham, Ala., Jan. 31, 1925; d. William Baker and Mary Myrtle (Francis) Inman; A.B. in Edn., Fla. State U., 1946, M.A. in L.S., 1948; MA.. in Edn., U. Miami, 1969. Reference librarian U. Miami, 1947-50; librarian Miami Pub. Library, 1950-53, Dade County Sch. Bd., Miami, Fla., 1953—. Recipient Outstanding Educator award for outstanding civic service for Miss Universe Beauty Pageant, 1965. Mem. Nat. Assn. Pen Women, Miami Panhellenic Assn. (past pres.), Alpha Delta Kappa, Delta Kappa Gamma, Phi Mu. Club: Coral Gables Women's. Home: 200 SW 23d St Miami FL 33129

INMAN, MARY JANE, biologist; b. Grand Rapids, Mich., Aug. 1, 1928; d. Frederick Arthur and Opal Edith (Hover) Inman; student Grand Rapids Jr. Coll., 1946-48; B.S., U. Mich., 1950, M.S. in Biology, 1970; postgrad. U. Miami (Fla.), summer 1970. Med. technologist, 1955-67; ranger-naturalist Everglades Nat. Park, Nat. Park Service, 1967-71; resources mgmt. ranger Organ Pipe Cactus Nat. Monument, Ariz., 1971; vol. biologist Teton County (Wyo.) Planning Commn., Jackson, Hole, 1972-74, mem. impact subcom., 1972-74. Recipient Spl. Service award Nat. Park Service, 1970. Author: Mangrove Nature Trail, 1972. Home: Jackson Hole WY

INMAN, MARY LOU, towing co. exec.; b. Evanston, Ill., Nov. 23, 1925; d. Glen Arnold and Wilhelmina (Yocum) Barrer; student Ripon Coll., 1942-43; B.S., Northwestern U., 1946; M.S., So. Ill. U., 1973; m. Merle T. Inman, Oct. 18, 1957. Display dir. Mavrakos Candy Co., 1948-53; art dir. Victoria Printed Products, Inc., 1953-56; free lance artist Cassell & Paul Advt. Art Studio, 1956-57; comptroller Inman Marine Co., 1960—; substitute tchr., Calhoun High Sch., Hardin, Ill., 1964—. Mem. Ill. Republican Central Com. from 20th Dist., 1966—; 2d v.p. Ill. Fedn. Rep. Women, 1973—; chmn. Calhoun County Rep. Com., 1964—; pres. Calhoun Rep. Women, 1964-66, 74—; Calhoun County dir. Rep. congl. campaign, 1964—; chairwoman Ill. Rep. State Com., 1974—. Mem. Nat. Audubon Soc., Calhoun Homemakers Extension Assn. (pres. 1961-62, 67-68), Order Eastern Star (past matron), Delta Zeta. Home: Rural Route 1 Batchtown IL 62006

INMAN, PHYLLIS JEAN, educator; b. Battle Creek, Mich., Mar. 22, 1924; d. Martin and Lois Marie (Ginter) Inman; B.S. in Home Econs., U. Tenn., 1946, M.S., 1969; summer student Colo. State U., 1965, Arrowmont Sch. Arts and Crafts, 1965-74. Tchr. Knoxville (Tenn.) pub. schs., 1947-52; Wash. County Extension home economist Tenn. Agrl. Extension Service, Johnson City, 1952-68; asso. prof. interior design and crafts Agrl. Extension Service, U. Tenn., Knoxville, 1969—. Mem. Nat. Assn. Extension Home Econs. (Distinguished Service award 1967), Am. Crafts Council, Am. Home Econs. Assn., So. Highland Handicraft Guild, Tenn. Artist-Craftsmen's Assn., Handweavers Guild Am., Omicron Nu, Epsilon Sigma Phi. Home: 203 Taliwa Garden St Knoxville TN 37920

INMON, THELMA JOSEPHINE GRAY (MRS. ROY ELMORE INMON), rancher, civic worker; b. Mountain Grove, Mo., Dec. 17, 1909; d. Lewis William and Verona (Simpson) Gray; student pub. schs.; m. Roy Elmore Inmon, Mar. 14, 1927 (dec. May 1948);children—Jack, Iona (Mrs. Paul Gamertsfelder), Delia (Mrs. Tommy Perez). Owner, mgr. Inmon Ranch, Deming, N.M., 1927—. Dir. Western Farm Bur. Mut. Ins. Co., Las Cruces, N.M. State chmn. women's com. N.M. Farm and Livestock Bur., 1955-68; mem. Govs. Adv. Com. N.M. Schs., 1950-56; county and zone chmn. White House Conf. on Edn., 1952-56; mem. N.M. State Bd. Edn., 1960—, sec., 1971-72; pres. council Girl Scouts U.S.A., 1949-53, leader, 1949-53; chpt. chmn. fund chmn. Luna County chpt. A.R.C., 1952-55; sec.-treas. Luna County Fair Assn., 1954-60. Sec. Republican Women's Club, Luna County, 1974—. Bd. dirs., N.M. Farm and Livestock Bur. Recipient Southwesterner of Year award, 1960, Family of Year award, 1968. Mem. Luna County Farmers Home Adminstrn. (chmn. 1954-57), N.M. Cattle Growers, Luna County Farm Bur. (orgn. and information chmn. 1968-70), Deming-Luna C. of C. (dir. women's div. 1973-74). Columnist Deming newspapers, 1959—, N.M. Farm and Ranch mag., 1955-68. Address: Route 2 407 Yucca Dr Deming NM 88030

INNIS, PAULINE, author; b. Devon, Eng.; student U. Manchester, U. London; m. Bernard B. Coleman, Sept. 30, 1946 (dec. 1954); m. Walter Deane Innis, Aug. 1, 1959. Came to U.S., 1954. Author: Hurricane Fighters, 1962; Ernestine or the Pig in the Potting Shed, 1963; The Wild Swans Fly, 1964; The Ice Bird, 1965; Wind of the Pampas, 1967; Fire from the Fountains, 1968; Astronumerology, 1971; Gold in the Blue Ridge, 1973. Bd. dirs. Washington Goodwill Industries Guild, 1962-66; membership chmn. Welcome to Washington Club, 1961-64; co-chmn. Internat. Workshop Capital Speakers' Club, 1961-64; pres. Children's Book Guild, 1967-68; dir. Ednl. Communications. Named Hoosier Woman of Yr., 1966. Mem. Soc. Woman Geographers, English-Speaking Union (mem. bd.), Spanish-Portuguese Group of D.C. (pres. 1965-66), Opera Soc. Nat. Ballet Soc. (v.p. women's bd.). Clubs: Am. Newspaper Women's (pres. 1971-73), Soroptimist. Home: 2700 Virginia Av NW Washington DC 20037

INOUE, YOLANDE MARYA (MRS. TADAYOSHI INOUE), food co. exec.; b. Montreal, Que., Can., May 3, 1946; d. Adolph Joseph and Eugenia M. (Zoinitska) Noran; student, McGill U., 1963-64; B.A., U. Cal. at Los Angeles, 1969; m. Tadayoshi Inoue, Mar. 14, 1972. Came to U.S., 1965. With Carnation Co., Los Angeles, 1969—, research mgr., 1972—. Home: 7907 Yorktown Av Los Angeles CA 90045 Office: 5045 Wilshire Blvd Los Angeles CA 90036

INOUYE, MARGARET AWAMURA (MRS. DANIEL KEN INOUYE), wife U.S. senator; b. Wailuku, Maui, Hawaii, June 23, 1924; d. Tokuyoshi and Mitsu (Sugiyama) Awamura; B.Ed., U. Hawaii, 1946; M.A., Columbia, 1947; m. Daniel Ken Inouye, June 12, 1949; 1 son, Daniel Ken. Instr. speech U. Hawaii, 1947-50, instr. edn., 1954-59. Home: 469 Ena Rd Honolulu HI 96815

INSINGER, ANNE MCCREADY, pub. relations exec.; b. Greenville, Pa., Sept. 18, 1918; d. Charles Franklin William and Mabel Anne (Lynch) McCready; B.A. cum laude, Thiel Coll., 1940; M.L., U. Pitts., 1946; m. Thomas H. Insinger, Sept. 7, 1946; children—Wendy Anne, Thomas Christopher. Advt. fashion writer J. Horne Co., Pitts., 1941-43; advt. writer Russell Allen div. Grey Advt., N.Y.C., 1943-44; account exec. Hirsbon-Garfield, N.Y.C., 1944-45, Amos Parrish, N.Y.C., 1945-46; fashion writer Kaufman's, Pitts., 1946-48; dir. pub. relations Sewickley (Pa.) Valley Hosp., 1962-64, Med. Coll. Pa., Phila., 1964—; free-lance advt. writing, 1950-52; co-propr. Village Photos, 1960-62. Tchr. retailing U. Pitts., evenings 1946-47. Mem. bd. Sewickley Women's Club, 1961-62; treas. Child Health Assn. Sewickley, 1960-61, mem. bd., 1956-60; Brownie troop leader, 1956-58, Scout leader, 1958-61. Mem. Pub. Relations Soc. Am., Hosp. Assn. Pa., Delaware Valley Hosp. Assn., Am. Assn. U. Women, Common Cause, Soroptomists, Beta Beta Beta, Sigma Kappa. Episcopalian. Home: 3927 Henry Av Philadelphia PA 19129 Office: 3300 Henry Av Philadelphia PA 19129

INSKEEP, PATRICIA RUTH, life ins. co. exec.; b. Covington, Ky., Oct. 10, 1931; d. Norval Francis and Helen (Wilson) I.; student U. Ky., U. Cin. With Union Central Life Ins. Co., Cin., 1949—, sec., 1969; sec. Union Central Assurance Corp., 1972—. Mem. Printing Industries Cin., Altrusa Club Cin. Home: 1336 Dalton Ct Fairfield OH 45014 Office: Union Central Life Ins Co PO Box 179 Cincinnati OH 45201

IONESCU TULCEA, ALEXANDRA, educator; b. Bucharest, Rumania, Aug. 30, 1935; M.S. in Math., U. Bucharest, 1957; Ph.D. in Math, Yale, 1959; m. 1956. Research asso. math. Yale, 1959-61; research asso. U. Pa., 1961-62, asst. prof., 1962-64; asso. prof. U. Ill. at Urbana, 1964-67; prof. math. Northwestern U., Evanston, Ill., 1967—. Mem. Am. Math. Soc. Office: Dept Math Northwestern U Evanston IL 60201

IPCAR, DAHLOV (MRS. ADOLPH IPCAR), artist; b. Windsor, Vt., Nov. 12, 1917; d. William and Marguerite (Thompson) Zorach; student Oberlin Coll., 1933-34; m. Adolph Ipcar, Sept. 29, 1936; children—Robert William, Charles. Exhibited one man show Mus. Modern Art, N.Y.C., 1939, Bignou Gallery, N.Y.C., 1940, Passedoit Gallery, N.Y.C., 1943, Phila. Art Alliance, Phila., 1944, ACA Gallery, N.Y.C., 1946, Farnsworth Mus., Rockland, Me., 1949, 56, Wellons Gallery, N.Y.C., 1950, 52, Portland Art Mus., 1959, 63, 70, U. Me., 1965, 67, 68, 69, Bates Coll., Lewiston, Me., 1966, 70, Westbrook (Me.) Jr. Coll., 1966, Dalzell-Hatfield Galleries, Los Angeles, 1970; exhibited group shows Corcoran Biennial, Pa. and Detroit Ann., Art: USA, Boston Art Festival, Eastern States Exhibit, Silvermine Guild, Portland Art Festival; 5 paintings show 14 outstanding women artists Detroit Inst., 1943; represented pub. collections Met. Mus., Art, N.Y.C., Whitney Mus. Am. Art, N.Y.C., Newark Mus., Farleigh-Dickinson U., Colby Coll., Bates Coll., Westbrook Jr. Coll., U. Me. at Orono and Portland; executed murals for sect. fine arts Treasury Dept., Washington, U.S. P.O. LaFollette, Tenn. and Yukon, Okla. Recipient Me. State award Me. Commn. Arts and Humanities. Clara A. Haas award Silvermine Guild, 1957, Juror Merit Award Bridgeton, 1973. Author, illustrator: (children's books) Animal Hide And Seek, 1947; One Horse Farm, 1950; World Full Of Horses, 1955; The Wonderful Egg, 1958; Ten Big Farms, 1958; Brown Cow Farm, 1959; I Like Animals, 1960; Deep Sea Farm, 1961; Stripes And Spots, 1961; Wild And Tame Animals, 1962; Lobsterman, 1962; Black And White, 1963; I Love My Anteater With An A, 1964; Calico Jungle, 1965; Horses of Long Ago, 1965; Bright Barnyard, 1966; The Song Of The Day Birds And The Night Birds, 1967; Whisperings And Other Things, 1967; Wild Whirlwind, 1968; The Cat At Night, 1969; The Marvelous Merry-Go-Round, 1970; Sir Addlepate And The Unicorn, 1971; The Cat Came Back, 1971; The Biggest Fish in the Sea, 1972; A Flood of Creatures, 1973; The Land of Flowers, 1974. Author (teen-age novels) General Felice, 1967; The Warlock Of Night, 1969; The Queen of Spells, 1973. Illustrator: (children picture books) The Little Fisherman, 1945; Just Like You, 1946; Good Work, 1948. Contbr. adult short stories to Tex. Quar., Yankee Mag., Argosy. Home: Star Route 2 Bath ME 04530

IRELAND, MARILYN JEAN, educator, lawyer; b. Mariemont, O., Mar. 4, 1943; d. Carl M. and Fern A. (Helfrich) Schleue; B.A., Miami U., Oxford, O., 1966; J.D., U. Chgo., 1969; m. Thomas Ireland, June 27, 1964; children—Lee Tera, Deron Eric. Admitted to Ill. bar, 1969; mem. firm Friedman & Kovan, Chgo., 1969-72; asst. prof. law Washington U., St. Louis, 1972—, asso. dean law, 1973—. Exec. sec., dir. Social Policy Inst. Interim pres. Miami U. Young Republicans, 1964; sr. liason chmn. for Ohio, Midwest Young Rep. Fedn., 1964; parliamentarian Ill. Young Rep. Fedn., 1967; sec. 5th Ward Chgo. Young Rep. Club, 1968-69; sr. party liason chmn. U. Chgo. Young Reps., 1969. Mem. Am., Chgo., Ill., 7th Circuit bar assns., Am. Polit. Sci. Assn., Am. Econ. Assn., Phi Beta Kappa, Order of Coif. Contbr. articles to legal jours. Editorial bd. U. Chgo. Law Rev., 1968-69. Office: Washington U Sch Law St Louis MO 63130

IRISH, ELEANOR FRANCES, dept. store exec.; b. Cambridge, Mass., Sept. 6, 1921; d. George B. and Doris (Peirce) Irish; B.J., U. Mo., 1943. Advt. mgr. Timothy Smith Co., Boston, 1943-45; account exec. Daniel F. Sullivan Co., Boston, 1945-48; free-lance advt., Boston, 1948-52; advt. mgr. Sheridan's Inc., Quincy, Mass., 1952-69; advt. mgr. Emmons, Concord, N.H., Emmons, Norwich, Conn., 1964-69; asst. copy chief Zayre, Natick, Mass., 1969-70; asst. copy chief Bradlees div. Stop and Shop Cos., Inc., Braintree, Mass., 1971—. Chmn. newspaper advt. com. United Fund, Quincy, 1952-57. Asso. mem. Republican Town Com., 1965. Mem. Norwell Art Assn., Norwell Hist. Soc., Gamma Alpha Chi. Home: 23 Trout Brook Lane Norwell MA 02061 Office: Campanelli Industrial Park Braintree MA 02184

IRISH, MARIAN D(ORIS), educator; b. Scranton, Pa., May 29, 1909; d. William Stitt and Martha Ann (Williams) Irish; A.B., Barnard Coll., 1930; M.A., Bryn Mawr Coll., 1932; Ph.D., Yale, 1939. Research librarian in govt. and law Lafayette Coll., Easton, Pa., 1930-31; asso. prof. Fla. State Coll. for Women, 1933-40, prof. and head div. of polit. sci., 1940-47; prof., head dept. polit. sci. Fla. State U., 1947-63, prof. govt., 1963-66; Charles O. Lerche prof. internat. relations Sch. Internat. Service, Am. U., Washington, 1966—. Cons. Fla. Legislative Com. on Economy and Efficiency, 1945, Fla. Citizens Com. on Taxation, 1947, State Merit Council of Fla., 1948, Va. Commn. Status of Women, 1971. Ford Found. fellow Harvard, 1952-53; vis. scholar Brookings Instn., 1963-64; fellow Woodrow Wilson Internat. Center for Scholars, 1972. Mem. Am. Polit. Sci. Assn. (council, sec., v.p.), So. Polit. Sci. Assn. (pres.), Am. Assn. U. Women, Phi Beta Kappa, Phi Kappa Phi. Democrat. Author: The People Govern (with Laurence Paquin), 1953; (with James Prothro) The Politics of American Democracy, 1959, rev., 1965, 68, 71, State and Local Government, 1960. Editor: Jour. Politics, 1965-69; Continuing Crisis in American Government, 1963; (with Elke Frank) Twelve Nation States, 1972. Editor: World Pressures on American Foreign Policy, 1964, Political Science: Advance of the Discipline, 1968. Contbr. articles and book revs. polit. and ednl. jours. Home: Scientists Cliffs Port Republic MD 20676

IRONS, MAE-MARIE, educator; b. San Jose, Cal., Jan. 8, 1924; d. Rollin Henry and Mary Marguerite (Coburn) Irons; B.A., San Jose State Coll., 1945. Tchr. elementary sch. Garfield Sch., Redwood City, Cal., 1945-53, Goodwin Sch., Redwood City, Cal., 1954-57, Navy Dept.'s Sch., Subic Bay, Philippines, 1957-58, Kennedy Sch., Redwood City, Cal., 1958—. First aid instr. A.R.C., San Jose and Redwood City, 1943-58. Mem. N.E.A., Cal. Tchrs. Assn., San Mateo County Tchrs. Assn., Redwood City Tchrs. Assn., Womens Overseas Service League (pres. Peninsula unit 1970-71, nat. sec. 1971-72). Republican. Methodist. Home: 3015-185 Bayshore Blvd Redwood City CA 94063 Office: Kennedy School Goodwin at Connecticut Sts Redwood City CA 94062

IRRGANG, DOROTHY L., coll. adminstr.; b. Cleve., Oct. 28, 1939; d. William and Mildred (Klapka) Irrgang; student Skidmore Coll., 1957-59; B.A., Lake Erie Coll., 1962. Asst. to dean students Lake Erie Coll., Painesville, O., 1962-65, dir. financial aid, 1964-68, exec. deans staff, 1965-66, asst. to dean students, 1966-68; financial aid officer Wheaton Coll., Norton, Mass., 1968-71; dir. financial aid Rice U., Houston, 1971—. Mem. Coll. Entrance Examination Bd. and Coll. Scholarship Service, Mem. Southwest, Tex. assns. student financial aid adminstrs. Home: 6403 Ella Lee Lane Houston TX 77027 Office: Rice U Houston TX 77001

IRSHAY, PHYLLIS CAROLINE, librarian; b. Danville, Ill., July 29, 1924; d. Zoltan and Emily Caroline (Cardiff) Irshay; student Maryville Coll., 1941-44; B.S., Wayne State U., 1945, M.L.S., 1953. Sales dept. Doubleday & Co., 1945-47; school librarian Detroit Pub. Schs., 1947-61; editorial asst. Ginn & Co., summer 1958; children's librarian Anaheim (Cal.) Pub. Library, 1961-62, asst. dir., 1962-66; dir. A.K. Smiley Pub. Library, Redlands, Cal., 1967—. Mem. Cal. Library Assn., Pub. Library Exec. Assn. So. Cal., So. Cal. Archivists, So. Cal. Local History Council (pres.), Redlands Area Hist. Soc., Am. Assn. U. Women. Soroptimist (Redlands). Editor: Biblio-Cal Notes, 1968-72. Home: 615 Juniper Ct Redlands CA 92373 Office: 125 W Vine St Redlands CA 92373

IRVIN, ALISE REID (MRS. ABRAM VANN IRVIN), library ofcl.; b. Elizabeth City, N.C., Mar. 7, 1924; d. Horace Gates and Eunice Maude (Stanton) Reid; B.S. in Home Econs., U. N.C., 1945, secondary sch. library certificate, 1965; m. Abram Vann Irvin, Aug. 10, 1946; children—Addison Vann, Benjamin Reid. Tchr. pub. schs. Cleveland County, N.C., 1945-46, 48-49, 61-65, librarian, 1965-66; acting dir. East Albemarle Regional Library, Elizabeth City, 1966-72, asst. dir., 1972—. Mem. Nat., N.C. edn. assns., Nat., N.C. home econs. assns., N.C. Library Assn., Am. Assn. U. Women. Democrat. Baptist. Home: 1712 Crescent Dr Elizabeth City NC 27909 Office: 205 E Main St Elizabeth City NC 27909

IRVIN, MARI GRIFFITHS (MRS. BRUCE ELWELL IRVIN), ednl. adminstr.; b. Jamestown, N.D., Sept. 12, 1933; d. Calvin Lawrence and Bella Corine (Bollingberg) Griffiths; B.A. cum laude, St. Olaf Coll., 1955; M.S., U. Ore., 1957; Ed.D., No. Ill. U., 1974; m. Bruce Elwell Irvin, June 16, 1956; children—Brian William, Paul Griffiths. Counselor Lutheran students, also grad. asst. in philosophy U. Ore., 1956-57; tchr., counselor Clark County Sch. Dist., Las Vegas, 1960-63, San Jose (Cal.) Unified Sch. Dist., 1963-65; sch. psychologist Fremont (Cal.) Unified Sch. Dist., 1965-68, DeKalb County (Ill.) Spl. Edn. Assn., 1968-71; dir. spl. services DeKalb Community Unit Sch. Dist., 1973—. Asst. prof. in spl. edn. No. Ill. U., 1971—, psychol. cons. dept. communication disorders, 1969—; cons. St. Charles (Ill.) Community Unit Sch. Dist., 1972-73. Mem. Psi Chi. Research relating the self, mother, and tchr. perceptions of child to acad. readiness, sex, and sibling position in family, 1972-74. Home: 1118 Holmes Pl DeKalb IL 60115 Office: 145 Fisk St DeKalb IL 60115

IRVIN, VIRGINIA HENDRICKSON (MRS. CHARLES EDGAR IRVIN), artist; b. Chgo., Oct. 9, 1904; d. Forman Spencer and Edith Bell (Gray) Hendrickson; student Chgo. Art Inst., 1922-24; m. Charles Edgar Irvin, Aug. 16, 1924; 1 son, Charles Edgar. Exhibited in group shows at Met. Mus. Art, N.Y.C., Portraits, Inc., Corcoran Galleries, Washington, Smithsonian Inst., Pa. Acad. Fine Arts, Phila., Los Angeles, Am. Soc. Miniature Painters; represented in permanent collection (miniature) Phila. Mus. Art, Smithsonian Inst.; exhibited miniatures at Royal Soc. Miniature Painters, Sculptors and Gravers, London, Eng. Recipient Boardman medal Am. Soc. Miniature Painters, 1944; D.J. McCarthy award Pa. Soc. Miniature Painters, 1950; 1st award Cal. Soc. Miniature Painters, 1949, 2d award, 1947; prize Nat. Assn. Women Artists, 1958, Babs Closter Beller prize, 1969; 2d award Miniature Painters, Sculptors, and Gravers Soc., 1967, 71, 73, 3d award, 1972 1st award, 1968, Boardman award, 1970; 2d award, honorable mention Art Soc. N.J., 1971; and others. Mem. Am., Pa. socs. miniature painters, Ann Arbor Women Painters, Miniature Art Soc. N.J., Ann Arbor Art Assn., Miniature Painters, Sculptors, Gravers Soc., Nat. Assn. Women Artists. Home: 619 E University Av Ann Arbor MI 48104

IRVINE, HELEN BECRAFT (MRS. HARRY WINFREE IRVINE), interior designer; b. Washington Grove, Md., Oct. 16, 1934; d. Henry Willard and Grace Isabel (Coffman) Becraft; certificate Parsons Sch. Design, 1952-55; B.S., N.Y. U., 1956; m. Harry Winfree Irvine, Nov. 26, 1958; 1 dau., Carol Susan. Self employed interior designer Craft Shop, Gaithersburg, Md., 1952—. Adv. bd. Community Savs. and Loan, Gaithersburg, 1974. Mem. bd. realtors Montgomery (Md.) County, 1964—. Mem. Am. Inst. Interior Designers, Md. Hist. Soc., Nat. Early Am. Glass Club. Home: 9510 Walkers Mill Rd Gaithersburg MD 20760 Office: PO Box 248 405 S Frederick Av Gaithersburg MD 20760

IRWIN, DOROTHY JUNE, dermatologist; b. Cornwall, Ont., Can.; d. Thomas Albert and Gertrude (Youngs) Irwin; B.A. in Biochemistry with honors, Queen's U., 1957; M.D., McGill U., 1961; div. Intern Montreal (Que., Can.) Gen. Hosp., 1961-62, resident, 1963, 64-67; resident Queen Mary Vets. Hosp., Montreal, 1963-64; practice medicine specializing in dermatology, 1967—; mem. active staff Montreal Gen. Hosp., Lakeshore Gen. Hosp., Pointe Claire, Que., Lachine Gen. Hosp. (Que.); lectr. McGill U. Home: 5055 Cote St Luc Montreal PQ H3W 2H5 Canada Office: 175 Sillview Pointe Claire PQ H9R 2Y5 Canada

IRWIN, ELEANOR CYNTHIA (MRS. FLOYD W. IRWIN), museum ofcl.; b. Denver, Mar. 19, 1910; d. Henry F. and Cora L. Evans; m. Floyd W. Irwin, Apr. 8, 1934; children—Cynthia Irwin-Williams, Henry T. First ballerina Kosloff and Pavlova Ballet Cos., 1927-31; chief preparator, research archeologist Blackwater Draw Mus. and Paleo Indian Inst. Eastern N.M. U., Portales, 1966—. Cons., producer archeol. reprodns. U. Chgo., U. Bordeaux (France), U. Chile, U. Alta. (Can.), Cambridge U. (Eng.), U. B.C. (Can.), Ind. U., U. N.M., Denver Mus. Natural History, Princeton, Harvard, U. Wyo. Mem. Soc. for Am. Archeology, N.M. Archeol. Soc. Developed technique for reprodn., coloring archeol. specimens in epoxy resin. Home: 1300 Espanola NE Albuquerque NM 87110 Office: Blackwater Draw Museum Eastern New Mexico University Portales NM 88130

IRWIN, GRACE LILIAN, author; b. Toronto, Ont., Can., July 14, 1907; d. John and Martha (Fortune) Irwin; B.A., Victoria Coll., U. Toronto, 1929, M.A., 1932, high sch. teaching certificate Coll. Edn., 1930. Tchr., Humberside Collegiate Inst., Toronto, 1931-42, head Classics dept., 1942-69. Lectr. classical, religious, lit. topics. Bd. dirs. Book Soc. Can. Recipient Can. Centennial medal, 1968. Mem. Canadian Authors' Assn., Canadian Classical Soc. Author: Least of All Saints, 1952; Andrew Connington, 1954; In Little Place, 1957; Servant of Slaves, 1961; Contend with Horses, 1968. Address: 33 Glenwood Av Toronto ON Canada

IRWIN, KATHLEEN BERTHA (MRS. ROBERT T. IRWIN), editor; b. Hindsboro, Ill., July 22, 1922; d. John Thomas and Stella (Phelps) Evans; student U. Ill., 1946-47; m. Robert T. Irwin, Feb. 1, 1943; children—Jan C. (Mrs. Martin Sadd), Perry, Brian. Editor Mt. Zion (Ill.) Region News, 1959—, Lovington (Ill.) Reporter, 1960—. Lectr. Lovington High Sch., 1973. Recipient 2d place award Ill. Newspaper Editorial Contest, 1960. Mem. Mt. Zion Bus. Assn. (sec. 1961-63). Lutheran (editor newsletter, mem. choir). Home: 1812 Lynnwood Ct Decatur IL 62521 Office: Box C Mt Zion IL 62549

IRWIN, MARIE EMILY (MRS. ROY H. IRWIN), hosp. ofcl.; b. Timmins, Ont., Can., Sept. 23, 1938; d. Chesney Osborne and Reta (Kwekkeboom) Davison; R.N., Mack Sch. Nursing, 1959; m. Roy H. Irwin, Apr. 9, 1960; children—Kelley Jayne, Steven Douglas. Mem. nursing staff operating room St. Catharines (Ont.) Gen. Hosp., 1959-65; supr. operating room Hotel Dieu Hosp., St. Catharines, Ont., 1971—, mem. Hosp. Intensive Care Unit, Infection Control coms., Vice-pres. Briardale Pub. Sch. P.T.A., St. Catharines, 1967-68. Mem. United Ch. Christ (former Sunday sch. tchr.). Mem. Order Eastern Star (past matron). Home: 104 Village Rd St Catharines ON L2T 3C1 Canada Office: 155 Ontario St St Catharines ON Canada

IRWIN, RUTH ELIZABETH BECKEY (MRS. HARRY POWER IRWIN), educator; b. Linwood, Kan., Jan. 8, 1906; d. Earl Durwood and Ann Girton (Springer) Beckey; B.S., Kan. State Tchrs. Coll., 1929; M.A., State U. Ia., 1936; Ph.D., U. So. Cal., 1940; m. Harry Power Irwin, Aug. 12, 1940. Tchr. rural schs., Kan., 1924-26; instr. English, dramatics Fredonia (Kan.) High Sch., 1929-36; instr. speech William Penn Coll., Oskaloosa, Ia., 1936-37; instr. English and speech Kearney (Neb.) State Tchrs. Coll., 1937-38; instr., dir. clinic in speech Ohio U., Athens, 1940-42; state supr. speech and hearing therapy Ohio Dept. Edn., Columbus, 1945-49; prof. speech and hearing sci. Ohio State U., Columbus, 1949—. Fellow Am. Speech and Hearing Assn., Am., Ohio psychol. assns.; mem. Internat. Council for Exceptional Children (chpt. pres. 1955-56), Ohio Speech and Hearing Assn. (pres. 1951-52), Delta Kappa Gamma (editor bull. 1953-70). Author: Speech and Hearing Therapy, 1953; Speech Pathologist Talks to Parents and Teachers, 1963; Speech and Hearing Therapy, 1965; (with J.W. Black) Voice and Diction, 1969. Contbr. articles to profl. jours. Home: 2685 Henthorne Rd Columbus OH 43221

IRWIN, VERA RUSHFORTH (MRS. WILLIAM M. IRWIN), educator; b. Yonkers, N.Y., Nov. 4, 1913; d. Robert Roy and Elizabeth Catherine (Streb) Rushforth; B.S., N.Y. U., 1937, M.A., 1947; postgrad. Colo. U., 1942-43, U. Colo., 1940-41, Inst. Advanced Studies in Theatre Arts, N.Y.C., 1959-69; m. William Moore Irwin, Aug. 8, 1951. Tchr. Carmel (N.Y.) High Sch., 1933-37, Croton-Harmon High Sch., Croton-on-Hudson, N.Y., 1937-47; asst. prof. theatre arts and drama State U. N.Y. at New Paltz, 1947-51, asso. prof., 1951-69, prof., 1969—. Margaret Webster scholar, 1950; Ford fellow, 1955-56; Inst. for Advanced Studies in Theatre Arts fellow, 1960, 61. Mem. Am. Theatre Assn., Am. Nat. Theatre Assn., Am. Soc. for Theatre Research. Club: Garden of Am. Editor: Four Asian Classical Plays, 1970. Home: 51 Elting Av New Paltz NY 12561

IRWIN, VIRGINIA PULLIAM (MRS. PAUL R. IRWIN), librarian; b. Clarkson, Ky., Feb. 13, 1913; d. Richard Lambuth and Elizabeth Henson (Swindler) Pulliam; student Hamilton Coll., Lexington, Ky., 1929-31; A.B., U. Ky., 1933; B.S. in L.S., Columbia, 1938; postgrad. (Quarrie Corp. fellow) U. Chgo., 1939-40; m. Paul Ross Irwin, Oct. 26, 1940; children—Elizabeth (Mrs. James M. Cahalan), James Ross, Richard Elliott. Tchr., librarian pub. sch., Leitchfield, Ky., 1934-38; asst. librarian Lake Forest (Ill.) Pub. Schs., 1938-39; mem. staff reference library Quarrie Corp., Chgo., 1939-40; librarian Bexar County Library, San Antonio, 1941, Our Lady of the Lake Coll. Library, San Antonio, 1963—. Mem. A.L.A., Tex., Bexar County library assns., Am. Assn. U. Profs., League Women Voters, Local Voters Service (chmn., 1st v.p. 1956-62), Chi Delta Phi, Delta Delta Delta. Presbyn. Home: 114 Rosemary St San Antonio TX 78209 Office: 411 SW 24th St San Antonio TX 78285

ISAAC, MARGRETHE GLORIA, educator; b. Chgo., May 6, 1927; d. Merle J. and Margrethe D. (Lehmann) Isaac; B.Ed., Chgo. Tchrs. Coll., 1947; M.A., Northwestern U., 1950, Ph.D., 1962. Tchr. Chgo. Pub. Schs., 1947-58; instr. TV Tchrs. Coll., WGN-TV, Chgo., 1958-59; asst. prof. Chgo. Tchrs. Coll., 1959-61; asso. prof. Northeastern Ill. U., Chgo., 1961—, asso. chmn. dept. early childhood edn., 1968-71, 73—. Vis. faculty Northwestern U., summer 1964. Mem. exec. com. Elementary Sch. sect. Nat. Safety Council, 1972—; book reviewer Ill. Reading Service, 1971—. Mem. Chgo. Pub. Schs. Kindergarten-Primary Assn. (pres. 1954-56), Ill. Edn. Assn. (pres. Chgo. div. 1964-65), Ill. Assn. Higher Edn. (pres. 1968-69), Assn. Childhood Edn. Internat. (chmn. various coms. 1954—, v.p. Chgo. area br. 1973—), N.E.A., Am. Assn. U. Profs., Am. Assn. Elementary-Kindergarten-Nursery Educators, Alpha Delta Kappa (pres. Ill. chpt. 1957-59, Ill. rec. sec. 1964-66), Pi Lambda Theta (rec. sec. chpt. 1965-67, corr. sec. Chgo. alumnae 1973—), Delta Kappa Gamma (music chmn. chpt. 1972—). Research on profl. problems of beginning tchrs. Home: 854 N Drake Av Chicago IL 60651 Office: Dept Early Childhood Edn Northeastern Ill U Bryn Mawr at St Louis Av Chicago IL 60625

ISAACS, ANNABELLE, coll. adminstr.; b. Bowling Green, O., Mar. 8, 1929; d. Virgil Richard and Anna Margaret (Gates) Isaacs; B.S., Bowling Green State U., 1959, M.Ed., 1965. Clk., stenographer IV, U.S. Immigration and Naturalization Service, Toledo, 1948-56; tchr. bus. edn. Maumee (O.) High Sch., 1959; office mgr. dept. bldgs. and facilities Bowling Green (O.) State U., 1959-64; adminstrv. asst. bd. trustees Med. Coll. Ohio, Toledo, 1965-66, adminstrv. asst., pres. coll., 1966-70, acting treas., 1965-70, registrar, 1970—, acting dir. personnel, 1970-71; sec. Inter-Instl. Com. grad. Edn. Northwestern Ohio, 1973—. Mem. Adminstrv. Mgmt. Soc., Med. Coll. of Ohio Women, Kappa Delta Pi, Delta Pi Epsilon. Republican. Home: 17301 Carter Rd Bowling Green OH 43402 Office: Medical College Ohio PO Box 6190 Toledo OH 43614

ISAACS, HELEN COOLIDGE ADAMS (MRS. KENNETH L. ISAACS), artist; b. Flushing, N.Y., Jan. 17, 1917; d. Thomas Safford and Martha (Montgomery) Adams; student Miss Hewett's classes, N.Y.C., Miss Porter's Sch., Farmington, Conn., Fontainbleau (France) Sch. Art and Music, 1935, Art Students League, 1936; m. Kenneth L. Isaacs, Mar. 10, 1949; children—Kenneth Coolidge, Anne Carpenter Richards. One-man show Chilton Club, Boston; exhibited in group shows Allied Artists, N.Y., Boston Arts Festival; portraits of various prominent persons; murals in various pub. bldgs., Boston, Rochester, N.Y., Pittsfield, Mass., Daytona, Fla. Mem. Colonial Dames Am. Clubs: Colony, River (N.Y.C.); Chilton (Boston). Home: 68 Beacon St Boston MA 02108

ISAACS, MARY JO, educator; b. Winston-Salem, N.C., June 27, 1931; d. James Spurgeon and Era (Brookshire) Isaacs; student Mars Hill Jr. Coll., 1949-51; A.B. cum laude, Meredith Coll., 1953; M.Ed., U. N.C. at Greensboro, 1958. Tchr. Sedge Garden Elementary Sch., Winston-Salem/Forsyth County Schs., 1953-59, supr. elementary edn., 1959-71, prin. Diggs Intermediate Sch., 1971—. Tchr. Western Carolina. U., Cullowhee, N.C., summers 1964, 65. Pres. Winston-Salem Maids of Melody, 1957; v.p. Winston-Salem Altrusa Club, 1967-68, pres., 1968-69. Bd. dirs. Forsyth Singer's Guild, 1959, 60. Mem. Assn. for Childhood Edn., N.C. (pres. div. suprs. and dirs. instrn. N.C. 1970-71), Winston-Salem/Forsyth County (pres. 1959-61) edn. assns., Forsyth County Prins. Assn. (sec.-treas. 1973-74), N.C. Assn. Educators (dir. prins.), N.C. Assn. for Childhood Edn. (sec. 1965-67), Assn. Suprs. Curriculum Devel., Delta Kappa Gamma. Democrat. Baptist. Home: Mashie Dr Grandview Route 1 Pfafftown NC 27040 Office: Vargrave St Winston-Salem NC 27107

ISAACSON, PAULINE HELEN, educator; b. Spring Valley, Wis., July 1, 1911; d. Isaac and Edith Wilhelmine (Haas) Isaacson; B.Ed., U. Wis.-River Falls, 1932, M.A., Madison, 1946; Ph.D., U. Minn., 1956. Tchr. high schs. in Wis. and Minn., 1932-44; mem. faculty U. Wis.-Stevens Point, 1946—, prof. speech and drama, 1948—, chmn. dept., 1958-64; dir. internat. programs, 1968—; editor II, State Hist. Soc. Wis., 1946—. Head recreation worker Stevens Point chpt. A.R.C., 1945-46. Mem. Speech Communications Assn., Wis. Speech Assn. (past pres.), Am. Assn. U. Women, P.E.O., Zeta Phi Zeta. Republican, Conglist. Mem. Order Eastern Star. Home: 1649 Clark St Stevens Point WI 54481

ISAAK, AMY (MRS. PAUL GERHARD ISAAK), educator; b. Bryant, S.D., Sept. 12, 1922; d. Christ Olson and Amelia Carolyn (Christensen) Christensen; certificate Luth. Bible Inst., 1944; B.A., Augustana Coll., 1949; postgrad. Renai Community Coll., 1970; m. Paul Gerhard Isaak, June 6, 1949; children—Karen (Mrs. Richard Gregg Encelewski), Joan, Jane (Mrs. Larry Grover Webb), David, James. Sec. to pres. Augustana Coll., Sioux Falls, S.D., 1945-50; substitute tchr. Soldotna (Alaska) Elementary Sch., 1968-71. Pres. State Med. Aux. of Alaska, Soldotna, 1973—; pres. Soldotna P.T.A., 1965-67, Kenai Peninsula dir., mem. state bd. 1969-73. Lutheran (sec. ch. council 1973—). Home: Box 569 Soldotna AK 99669

ISARD, ELEANORE (MRS. BERTRAM ISARD), psychologist, educator; b. Phila., Feb. 27, 1923; d. Herman Penard and Rose (Rovner) Sternberg; B.S. with honors, Temple U., 1951, M.A., 1952, Ph.D., 1955. Instr. psychology Temple U., Phila., 1955-57, asst. prof., 1957-61, asso. prof., 1961-66, prof., 1966—, dir. univ. counseling center, 1964—. Cons. sch. and community groups. Adv. bd. Phila. Lyric Opera Guild. Fellow Pa. Psychol. Assn.; mem. Am., Eastern psychol. assns., Insts. Religion and Health, Am. Humanist Assn., Am. Assn. Sex Educators and Counselors, Sex Information and Edn. Council U.S. (asso.), Soc. Clin. Psychologists. Contbr. articles to profl. jours. Home: 523 Shoemaker Rd Elkins Park PA 19117 Office: Temple U Philadelphia PA 19122

ISBELL, DOROTHY MAE CARLISLE (MRS. JASON B. ISBELL), educator; b. Hillsdale, Mich., June 7, 1917; d. Merton and Vera (Carter) Carlisle; A.B., Hillsdale Coll., 1938; M.Ed., U. Miami, 1956; m. Jason B. Isbell; children—Susan Mae (Mrs. Gavin Wallace O'Brien), James Carlisle. Tchr. Hillsdale Schs., 1938-44, Central Beach Elementary, Miami Beach, Fla., 1945-46, Silver Bluff Elementary, Miami, 1946-54; curriculum coordinator Hialeah, Fla., 1954-56; tchr. Henry S. West Lab. Sch., U. Miami (Fla.), 1956-58; prin. Pinecrest Elementary, Miami, 1958-72; coordinator South Area Elementary Curriculum Devel. Center, Dade County Schs., 1972—; instr. U. Miami, Children's lit., 1956-62, 67-71; writer, field reader Office Edn., Washington; v.p. J.B. Isbell, builders; pres. Applied Concepts, edn. cons. firm. Mem. Fla. Plant Survey Staff, 1972—. Mem. Nat., Fla. edn. assns. (dir.), Fla. Council on Elementary Edn., Assn. for Childhood Edn., Dade County Elementary Prins.' Assn., So. Assn. Colls. and Secondary Schs., Internat. Platform Assn., Pi Beta Phi, Alpha Delta Kappa, Kappa Delta Pi. Republican. Club: Zonta Internat. (v.p. Greater Miami No. II club). Home: 6851 SW 73d Ct Miami FL 33156 also summer Chestnut Hill Howard's Creek Dr Boone NC and Oakwood Lake Front Dr Red Beach Lake Sebring FL Office: 10250 SW 57th Av Miami FL 33156

ISHAM, CHARLOTTE, educator; b. Waterbury, Conn., May 17, 1912; d. Austin and Sarah (Mattoon) Isham; B.Ed., Danbury Tchrs. Coll., 1940; M.A., Yale, 1967; Ed.D., Harvard, 1967. Tchr. Holt Sch., Plymouth, Conn., 1935-36, Campville Sch., Harwinton, Conn., 1936-39, Bantam Sch., Litchfield, Conn., 1939-43; tchr., prin. Sandy Hook Sch., Newtown, Conn., 1943-47; elem. supr. Regional Dist. 3, Newtown, Southbury Woodbury, Bethlehem, Conn., 1947-50; elem. supr. Woodbury, Southbury, Bethlehem, Conn., 1950-53; elem. supr. Woodbury, Bethlehem, Conn., 1953-54; supr. instrn. Woodbury, Conn., 1954-64; asst. prof. Western Conn. State Coll., 1964-71, asso. prof., 1967-71, prof., 1971—. Mem. Conn. Tchrs. Assn., N.E.A., Assn. for Supervision and Curriculum Devel., New Eng. Reading Assn., Conn. Dept. Higher Edn., New Eng., Conn. assns. supervision and curriculum devel. Author: Now We Are Six, 1955; Freddie, 1973. Home: Woodbury CT 06798 Office: Western Conn State College Danbury CT 06810

ISHERWOOD, EVELYN LOUISE, real estate broker; b. Overland Park, Kan., Sept. 12, 1934; d. Grady William and Lady Helen (Gordon) Turner; student Southwestern Inst. Econs., 1962; student Anthoney Schs. Real Estate, 1962, 1964, 1969, Mt. San Antonio Coll., 1963-65, Rio Hondo Coll., 1966-68, Citrus Coll., 1970-74; m. William Downs, (div.); children—William Glen, Donna Lynn (Mrs. Roy David Steward); m. 2d., George Isherwood (div.); children—George Leonard, Robert Gordon. Salesman real estate Teeples Real Estate, El Monte, Cal., 1962-64, Norwood Realty Co., El Monte, 1965, 67-69; office mgr. Viking Constrn. Co., Temple City, Cal., 1966; owner Isherwood Realty, El Monte, 1969-74; owner El Monte Mortgage Co., 1973-74. Mem. arbitration com. San Gabriel Bd. Realtors, 1972. Treas. El Monte Little League, 1969-73, sponsor two baseball leagues, 1969-75. Mem. sign com. El Monte City League, 1969-72. Recipient Outstanding Citizen award El Monte Little League, 1973. Mem. Nat. Assn. Real Estate Bds., Cal. Real Estate Assn., Los Angeles Historic Bottle Club. Republican. Methodist. Home: 4922 Peck Rd El Monte CA 91732 Office: 140 Glendora Blvd West Covina CA

ISOM, MARY AGNES SCOTT (MRS. ODELL C. ISOM), educator, univ. dean; b. nr. Lavonia, Ga., Feb. 26, 1934; d. Thomas A. and Orene (Reeder) Scott; B.S., Winston-Salem State U., 1957; M.S., U. N.C., 1961; postgrad. Wake Forest U., 1967—; m. Odell C. Isom, Feb. 22, 1958; 1 son, James Edward. Supr. Battey State Hosp., Rome, Ga., 1957, Floyd Hosp., Rome, 1957; instr. Winston-Salem (N.C.) State U., 1957-60, asst. prof., 1961-66, asso. prof., 1966-68, prof. med.-surg. nursing, 1968—, dean Sch. Nursing, 1967—. Instr. grad. nurses Kate Bitting Reynold Meml. Hosp., 1965; adv. bd. sch. nursing Forsyth Tech. Inst., 1970-73. Bd. dirs. Forsyth County unit A.R.C., 1968-69; mem. Forsyth County Citizens Planning Council's Com. on Nursing, 1968-73; co-chmn. Northwestern Tb and Respiratory Disease Assn., 1968-69; mem. adv. bd. Expt. in Self Reliance Kimberly Park Service Center, 1966-68. Mem. Am., N.C. nurses assns., Nat., N.C. State leagues for nursing, Am. Assn. U. Profs., Guys and Dolls, (pres. 1967-70), Winston-Salem State U. Alumni Assn., Delta Sigma Theta. Democrat. Methodist. Club: If's Bridge (pres. 1967-70) (Winston-Salem). Home: 5050 Shattalon Dr Winston-Salem NC 27106

ISON, GERTRUDE SUTTON (MRS. LOVELL ISON), educator; b. Vest, Ky., Apr. 21, 1913; d. Joseph David and Sarah (Coburn) Sutton; A.B., Morehead State U., 1943; M.S., U. Ky., 1965; m. Lovell Ison, Apr. 14, 1934; children—Virchel, Lowell, Evelyn (Mrs. Orville J. Doyle), Clinton. Tchr. Knott County Grade Sch., Pippa Passes, Ky., 1932-44, Knott County High Sch., Pippa Passes, 1944-58; mem. faculty Pikeville Coll., 1958—, chmn. math. dept., 1970—, dir. workshops for modern math. Treas. Opportunity Workshop, 1971-72. Recipient Community Leader of Am. award, 1969. Mem. Am. Assn. U. Women (treas. 1970-74), Am. Assn. U. Profs. (treas. 1972—), Pi Mu Epsilon, Delta Kappa Gamma. Democrat. Presbyn. Mem. Order Eastern Star. Home: Williamson Rd Pikeville KY 41501 Office: Pikeville Coll Box 25 Pikeville KY 41501

ISRAEL, LORRAINE BACKAL (MRS. JOSEPH S. ISRAEL), lawyer; b. Bklyn., June 11, 1926; d. Aziz and Mahiba (Lewis) Backal; certificate St. Johns U., 1948; LL.B., N.Y. Law Sch., 1953; m. Joseph S. Israel, May 28, 1949; children—Sinde, Arthur Franklin. Admitted to N.Y. bar, 1953, since practiced in N.Y.C. Organized Empire State Chpt. Bronco World for asthmatic children, 1974, Adoptees Liberty Movement Assn., 1972; active in Christian and Jewish groups. Mem. N.Y., Bklyn. women's bar assns., Family Ct. Lawyers Assn. Mem. Assyrian Eastern Orthodox Ch. Home: 25 Wenwood Dr Brookville NY 11545 Office: 299 Broadway New York City NY 10077

ISROFF, LOLA KOVENER (MRS. EMANUEL R. ISROFF), artist, writer; b. N.Y.C.; d. Wolf and Hannah (Levin) Kovner; student Hunter Coll., 1929-31, Columbia, 1933-35, N.Y.U., 1937-39, U. Cal. at Los Angeles, 1939-40; m. Emanuel R. Isroff, June 9, 1961. One man shows at Cushman and Wakefield, N.Y.C., Lord and Taylor, N.Y.C., Dime Bank for Savs., N.Y.C. Akron (O.) Jewish Center, Village Theatre Gallery, Akron, Akron Pub. Library, Summit County Hist. Soc., Akron, Packard Gallery, Akron, Massillon (O.) Mus. Art, Canton (O.) Art Inst., Caravan House Gallery, N.Y.C., Boston Safe Deposit & Trust Co., Mansfield (O.) Art Center; exhibited in group shows at Salmagundi Club, N.Y.C., Village Art Center, N.Y.C., Nat. Acad. Art, N.Y.C.; represented in pvt. collections, N.Y.C., Coral Gables, Fla., Milw. Beverly Hills, Cal., Lisbon, Portugal, Hawaii, Westport, Conn., Denver, Kent, Akron; mem. Rudolph Galleries, Coral Gables, also Woodstock, N.Y. Mem. exec. bd. Friends Akron (O.) U. Library; cultural arts chmn. Akron Jewish Center. Recipient Merit award Art News Nat. Amateur Painters, 1950. Mem. Authors League, Soc. Archtl. Historians. Author: Mama and Papa Livnok, 1949; A Different Kind of Saturday, 1950; Old Houses of New York, 1952; I'll Call You at 10, Doll, 1957; Christmas is a Gift, 1957; Tender Deception, 1957. Contbr. articles, illustrations to mags. Home: 275 N Portage Path Akron OH 44303

ITTELSON, MARTHA LANE (MRS. WILLIAM H. ITTELSON), occupational therapist, artist; b. Greeneville, Tenn., Mar. 29, 1918; d. James Franklin and Maude (Weems) Lane; B.A. in Fine Arts, U. N.M., 1940; B.S. in Occupational Therapy, Washington U., St. Louis, 1944; postgrad. Ohio State U., 1949; m. William H. Ittelson, Feb. 16, 1946; 1 son, Lane. Art and occupational therapist Hammond Gen. Hosp., Modesto, Cal. 1944-45, Psychiat. Inst., N.Y.C., 1945-46, Trenton (N.J.) State Hosp., 1947-48; art therapist, Princeton, N.J., 1948-55, Hillside Psychiat. Hosp., N.Y.C., 1959-61. One-woman shows of paintings at Princeton (N.J.) Group Arts, 1949, Greenwich St. Gallery, Hempstead, N.Y., 1964, Bklyn. Coll., 1967, Baldwin (N.Y.) High Sch., 1968; exhibited in group shows at U. N.M., Albuquerque, 1940, Harwood Found., Taos, N.M., 1941, Princeton Print Club, 1952, Iwataya Gallery, Fukuoka, Japan, 1962, Hofstra U., 1963, Adelphi U., 1965, Post Coll., 1973, Firehouse Gallery, 1972, Profl. Artists Guild, 1974, Naggar Community Coll., Garden City, N.Y., 1975; others. Mem. Am. Occupational Therapy Assn., Profl. Artists Guild. Address: 1585 Westervelt Av Baldwin NY 11510

ITTMANN, MARJORIE MCCULLOUGH (MRS. WILLIAM MCLEOD ITTMANN), civic worker, assn. exec.; b. Cin., July 12, 1923; d. Robert Stedman and Mildred (Rogers) McCullough; student U. Cin., 1941-43; m. William McLeod Ittmann, Mar. 17, 1972; children from previous marriage—Karen Lunken, (dec.), Kathryn Lunken Batteau, Margo Lunken. Mem. bd. Jr. League Cin., 1944-58, regional dir., 1958-60, nat. pres. Assn. Jr. Leagues Am., 1960-62; mem. Ohio Citizen's Council, 1956-58; mem. exec. com. Council Nat. Orgns. Children and Youth, 1960-62, 68-72; bd. dirs. United Way Am., 1962-67, sec., 1965-66, v.p., 1966-67; mem. Nat. Assembly Social Policy and Devel., 1968-71; mem. policy com. Center Vol. Soc.; bd. dirs. Cin. Speech and Hearing Center, 1955-66, pres. bd., 1963-66, trustee emeritus; bd. dirs. Hamilton County (O.) Research Found., 1963—, Cancer Family Care, 1971-72; mem. nat. bd. Girl Scouts U.S.A., 1962—, nat. 4th v.p., 1966-69, nat. 1st v.p., 1969-72, nat. pres., 1972—; del. conv. World Assn. Girl Guides and Girls Scouts, Finland, 1969, Toronto, Ont., Can., 1972. Mem. Kappa Alpha Theta. Home: 7 Melville Lane Cincinnati OH 45208 Office: 830 3d Av New York City NY 10022

IVANTCHO, BARBARA PORTEOUS (MRS. JOHN B. IVANTCHO), librarian; b. Newton, Mass., Feb. 23, 1915; d. Thomas Clifford and Bertha (Roberts) Porteous; B.A. Wellesley Coll., 1935; B.S. in L.S., Columbia, 1941; m. John B. Ivantcho, June 7, 1956. Reference librarian Enoch Pratt Free Library, Balt., 1937-40, 41-42; service club librarian U.S. War Dept., Richmond, Va. and Europe, 1943-46; librarian McGraw-Hill Pub. Co., N.Y.C., 1947-48; librarian USIS, Istanbul, Turkey, 1949-53, Karachi, Pakistan, 1954-56; chief tech. services, asst. mgr. library services Stanford Research Inst., Menlo Park, Cal., 1957—. Mem. Spl. Libraries Assn. (pres. San Francisco Bay chpt. 1968-69). Home: 783 27th St San Francisco CA 94131 Office: Stanford Research Inst Menlo Park CA 94025

IVENS, JESSIE LOREENA (MRS. RALPH WILSON IVENS), editor; b. Wabash County, Ill., Apr. 5, 1922; d. Elisher and Arletta Gertrude (McKibben) Moudy; B.S., U. Ill., 1945, M.S., 1947; m. Ralph Wilson Ivens, Sept. 30, 1950. Instr. rhetoric U. Ill., Champaign, 1947-48; instr. English, journalism Ill. State U., Normal, 1948-50; asst. editor U. Ill. Inst. Aviation, Champaign, 1950-51; newspaper editor, Chanute AFB, Ill., 1951-60; tech. editor Ill. State Water Survey, Champaign, 1960—. Served with WAVES, 1943-44. Mem. Soc. for Tech. Communications (sr.), A.A.A.S., Women in Communication, Nat. League Am. Pen Women. Club: Altrusa (Champaign-Urbana). Home: 802 S Busey Urbana IL 61801 Office: 605 E Springfield Champaign IL 61820

IVERSON, ELLINE JEANNETTE, librarian, mus. curator; b. Sioux Falls, S.D., Feb. 19, 1943; d. Philip Ernest and Jeannette Kaspara (Strand) Iverson; student No. State Coll., Aberdeen, S.D., 1960-62; B.A., U. S.D., 1965. Clk., Augustana Coll. Library, Sioux Falls, S.D., 1965-66; mgr. Courtney's Books & Things, Sioux Falls, 1967-69; head librarian Canton (S.D.) Carnegie Pub. Library, 1970—; curator Earl Boyce Mus., Canton, 1970—. Mem. Planning Com. Canton's Mobile Meals, 1973—. Mem. S.D. Library Assn. (exec. bd., pres. pub. library sect. 1973-74), Bus. and Profl. Women's Orgn. Canton (corr. sec. 1974), P.E.O. (pres. 1973, v.p. 1974). Lutheran. Home: 727 E 5th Canton SD 57013 Office: Carnegie Pub Library 221 E 4th Canton SD 57013

IVES, JOSEPHINE ANNE PIEKARZ (MRS. SUMNER A. IVES), educator; b. Colchester, Conn., Feb. 14, 1921; d. Joseph S. and Anna (Przybos) Piekarz; B.S., Tchrs. Coll. Conn., 1943; M.Ed., Boston U., 1947; Ph.D., U. Chgo., 1954; m. Sumner A. Ives, May 25, 1965; 1 stepson, Sumner W. Tchr. pub. schs., West Hartford, Conn., 1943-46; reading supr. pub. schs., Plainville, Conn., 1947-49; clinician Cath. Youth Orgn. Reading Service, Chgo., 1949-50; diagnostician, high sch. reading specialist, asst. dir. U. Chgo. Reading Clinic, 1950-53; instr. U. Chgo., 1953; asso. prof., dir. reading clinic U. S.C., 1954-57; vis. prof. Cornell U., Ithaca, N.Y., 1957; prof. ednl. psychology N.Y. U., N.Y.C., 1957—. Mem. Am. Psychol. Assn., Internat., Coll. reading assns., Nat. Council Tchrs. English, N.Y. Acad. Scis., Am. Assn. U. Profs., Nat. Soc. for Study Edn., Am. Edn. Research Assn., Pi Lambda Theta, Kappa Delta Pi, Delta Kappa Gamma. Author: (with M. F. W. Pollack) Reading Problems and Problem Readers, 1963. Home: 2 Washington Square Village New York City NY 10012

IVES, KRISTIN VICTORIA, phys. therapist; b. San Francisco, June 10, 1944; d. G. Jerome and Louise Victoria Ives; B.A. in Phys. Edn., San Francisco State Coll., 1970; B.S. in Phys. Therapy, U. Cal. at San Francisco, 1971. Staff phys. therapist Fairfax County Health Dept., Fairfax, Va., 1971-73, chief phys. therapist, 1973—. Med. spltys. cons. in phys. therapy No. Va. Tng. Center for Mentally Retarded Adults and Children, Fairfax; guest lectr. spl. edn. George Washington U. Mem. Am. Phys. Therapy Assn., Am. Assn. Mental Deficiency. Home: 4037 Majestic Lane Fairfax VA 22030 Office: Joseph Willard Health Center 3750 Old Lee Hwy Fairfax VA 22030

IVES, LIDA SKILTON (MRS. SHERMAN KIMBERLY IVES), ins. co. exec.; b. Morris, Conn., Nov. 22, 1902; d. Joel White and Ida Florilla (Camp) Skilton; student Northfield Sem., 1918-19, Waterbury Hosp. Sch. Nursing, 1922-23; m. Sherman Kimberly Ives, Aug. 14, 1924 (dec. Mar. 1970); children—Alden A., Virginia I. (Mrs. Jack Stephens), Bradford S., Carolyn E., Esther I. (Mrs. Jay Taylor). With Ives Inc., Morris, Conn., 1930—, pres., 1964—. Tchr. adult edn. Litchfield, Conn., 1956-58; treas. Morris Thrift Shop, Inc., 1973. Mem. Rep. Town Com., 1930-52. Mem., sec. town finance bd. Morris, 1969. Mem. Morris Hist. Soc. (pres. 1964), Morris Grange (master 1939-40). Mem. Order Eastern Star. Republican. Conglist. Author: The Grange in Connecticut, 1953; History of the Patrons Mutual Insurance, 1960. Home: Rural Route 1 Box 438 Morris CT 06763 Office: Morris CT 06763

IVES, ROSE ANN, ins. co. exec.; b. Topeka, July 15, 1910; d. Peter J. and Mary (Florence) Letuks; grad. pub. schs.; m. Wendell F. Ives, May 29, 1942 (div. 1965). With Security Benefit Life Ins. Co., Topeka, Kan., 1928—, agy. sec., 1952-64, sales conf. mgr., 1964—, 2d v.p., 1971-73, v.p., 1973—. Mem. Topeka Against Crime program, 1971. Mem. Am. Bus. Women's Assn. Home: 2225 W 29th St Terrace Topeka KS 66611 Office: 700 Harrison St Topeka KS 66603

IVEY, EVELYN PARKER (MRS. LEE R. IVEY), physician; b. Cienfuegos, Cuba, Nov. 14, 1914 (parents Am. citizens); d. Richard J. and Lottie Lee (Barnes) Parker; A.B., Duke, 1936; M.D., Johns Hopkins, 1940; m. Lee R. Ivey, Dec. 27, 1943; children—Roy R., Clare Jean Reynolds. Intern, Duke, 1940-41; resident psychiatry Henry Phipps Psychiat. Clinic, Johns Hopkins Hosp., 1941-43; indsl. psychiatrist Picatinny Arsenal, Dover, N.J., 1943-45; lectr. Rutgers U., 1944-47; psychiatrist treatment div. Manhattan Childrens Ct. Psychiat. Clinic, 1945-46; instr. psychiatry N.Y. Sch. Social Work, Columbia, 1946; practice medicine, specializing in psychiatry, Morristown, N.J., 1945-63; chmn. dept. neurology and psychiatry Morristown Meml. Hosp., 1959-63; med. dir. Tri-County Childrens Center, 1958-64; dir. planning comprehensive mental health services N.J. Dept. Instns. and Agys., 1963-65, cons. community psychiatry, 1965-67; dir. childrens services N.J. State Hosp., Greystone Park, 1965-67; med. dir., chief exec. officer Arthur Brisbane Child Treatment Center, Farmingdale, N.J., 1967—. Recipient E.B. Bowis award for outstanding leadership and contbn. to Am. Coll. Psychiatrists, 1966. Diplomate Am. Bd. Neurology and Psychiatry. Fellow Am. Psychiat. Assn. (past dist. pres., chmn. bd. tellers), Am. Orthopsychiat. Assn. (past pres. N.J. dist. br.); mem. N.J. Neuropsychiat. Assn. (past pres.), A.M.A., N.J. Med. Soc., N.J. (past dir., mem. exec. com., chmn. profl. adv. com.), Morris County (past pres., dir.) mental health assns., Am. Assn. Psychotherapy, Eastern Psychiat. Research Assn., Assn. For Research and Nervous Mental Diseases, Am. Coll. Psychiatrists (pres. 1967-68), Monmouth County Med. Soc. Home: Arthur Brisbane Child Treatment Center Allaire PO Box 625 Farmingdale NJ 07727

IVEY, EVELYN ROGERS (MRS. JAMES BURNETT IVEY), editor; b. Annapolis, Md., Mar. 29, 1926; d. Milton E. and Margaret Anne (Skinner) Rogers; student St. Petersburg Jr. Coll., 1945-47, Fla. State U., 1947, U. Fla., 1950, Fla. State U., 1950; m. James Burnett Ivey, Jan. 12, 1957; 1 son, Donald James. Edn. editor St. Petersburg (Fla.) Times, Times Pub. Co., 1950-56, feature writer, 1966-70; with St. Petersburg (Fla.) Ind., 1956-59; city govt. reporter Burlingame (Cal.) Advance-Star, 1960-61; copy editor Orlando (Fla.) Sentinel-Star, 1970—. Mem. Women in Communications. Home: 561 Obispo Av Orlando FL 32807 Office: 633 N Orange Av Orlando FL 32801

IVEY, JEAN EICHELBERGER (MRS. FREDERICK M. IVEY), composer; b. Washington, July 3, 1923; d. Joseph S. and Elizabeth (Pfeffer) Eichelberger; A.B. magna cum laude, Trinity Coll., 1944; Mus.M. in Piano, Peabody Conservatory, 1946; Mus.M. in Composition, Eastman Sch. Music, U. Rochester, 1956; Mus.D., U. Toronto, 1972; m. Frederick M. Ivey, Dec. 27, 1958. Dir. electronic music studio, tchr. composition Peabody Conservatory, 1969—; performed in piano recitals, on concert tours U.S., Mexico, Europe, including own compositions. Mem. Am. Soc. U. Composers (editor newsletter 1968-70), A.S.C.A.P., Internat. Soc. Contemporary Music (dir.), Coll. Music Soc. (council). Compositions include: Passacaglia for chamber orch., 1954; Sonata for piano, 1957; 6 Inventions for 2 Violins, 1959; (choral anthems) O Come Bless the Lord, Lord Hear My Prayer, 1960; Sonatina for Unaccompanied Clarinet, Dinsmoor Suite (wind and percussion), 1963; Enter Three Witches (electronic piece), 1964; Pinball (electronic piece, Folkways rec.), 1965; Tribute: Martin Luther King (baritone and orch.), 1969; Terminus (mezzo and tape), 1970; 3 Songs of Night (soprano, 5 instruments, tape), 1971; Forms in Motion (symphony), 1972; Hera, Hung from the Sky, 1973; also music for art films, TV. Contbr. articles to publs., to book Electronic Music a Listener's Guide, 1972. Recs. Folkway records, 1973, Composers Recs. Inc., 1974. Home: 83-33 Austin St Kew Gardens NY 11415 Office: Peabody Conservatory Baltimore MD 21202

IVY, ARAH VICTORIA (MRS. VARDIE LEE IVY), coll. ofcl.; b. Belmont, Miss., June 12, 1906; d. William Carroll and Georgia Alice (Harp) Wood; student Miss. State U., 1923-25, Florence State U., 1926-28; certificate Draughon's Bus. Coll., 1938; m. Vardie Lee Ivy, Apr. 30, 1926 (dec. July 1936); 1 dau., Maxine (Mrs. Harold Lloyd Storment). Tchr., Tishomingo Co. Consol. Schs., Belmont, 1923-28, 32-33; clk. soil conservation Tishomingo Co. Agts. Office, Iuka, 1938-44; bookkeeper L.P. Allen Hardware, Belmont, 1944-48; clk. circuit ct. Tishomingo County, Iuka, 1948-51; social worker Miss. Children's Home, Jackson, 1952; technician med. lab. Cosby Med. Clinic, Iuka, 1953-55; owner, operator Ivy's Ladies Dress Shop, Belmont, 1956-65; ward clk. Sts. Mary and Elizabeth Hosp., Louisville, 1966-68; dorm proctor N.E. Miss. Jr. Coll., Booneville, 1970—. Methodist. Woodman of World; mem. Order Eastern Star. Clubs: Tishomingo County Homemakers. Home: Box 412 Belmont MS 38827 Office: Murphy Hall NE Miss Jr Coll Booneville MS 38829

IWAMASA, FUMIKO, govt. ofcl.; b. Honolulu; d. W.G. and Sho (Muraoka) Kimura; B.A., U. Hawaii, 1933; m. Haruto W. Iwamasa, Apr. 2, 1937. Social work Dept. Social Services, Hilo, Hawaii, 1939-47, asst. supr., 1947-54, supr., 1954-62, Hawaii br. adminstr., 1962—. Adviser, Big Island Presch. Assn., 1965—. Mem. disaster council County of Hawaii, 1960—; mem. eviction com. Hawaii Housing Authority, 1962—; mem. county com. Children and Youth, 1954—; mem. Gov.'s Com. Mental Health, proceedings chmn., 1962-63, screening com. mem. Com. Aging, 1962—; mem. Big Island Council on Addiction, 1963—; mem. Big Island adv. com. Law Enforcement Adv. Agy., 1969—; exec. com. Hawaii County Comprehensive Health Planning Adv. Council, 1968—. Bd. dirs. A.R.C., Hilo, 1962—, Am. Cancer Soc., 1962-71, Salvation Army, Hilo, 1963—, YMCA, 1963-70, Hawaii County Econ. Opportunity Council, 1965—, Hawaii Fed. and State Employees Fed. Credit Union, 1966-71; mem. Hawaii County Rural Devel. Com., 1970—. Mem. Am. Pub. Welfare Assn. Club: Zonta. Home: 52 Puuoko St Hilo HI 96720 Office: Dept Social Services and Housing PO Box 1562 Hilo HI 96720

IWAMOTO, RANKO, pub. relations co. exec.; b. Tokyo, Japan, Nov. 6, 1930; d. Torajiro and Seiko (Kyogoku) Iwamoto; grad. Bunka Gakuin Jr. Coll., Tokyo, 1954-56; B.A. cum laude, Whitworth Coll., 1960; M.S., Boston U., 1963; came to U.S., 1956. Research asst. Boston U., 1961-63; with Ruder & Finn, Inc., N.Y.C., 1963—, v.p., 1971-74, sr. v.p., 1974—. Spl. corr. Fukuso, Japanese woman's nat. mag., Tokyo, Japan, 1967-71. Bd. dirs. Caravan de France, 1972—. Club: Publicity (N.Y.C.). Editor U.S.-Japan News Digest, 1971—. Contbr. articles and photographs to various newspapers and mags including Nihon Keizai Shimbun, Tokyo, Japan, Image, Boston, Fgn. Jour., Washington, Sat. Rev. World, Financial World, N.Y.C., World Port mag. Home: 330 E 33rd St New York City NY 10016 Office: Ruder & Finn Inc 110 E 59th St New York City NY 10022

IZARD, ANNE REBECCA, library cons.; b. Henderson, N.C., Apr. 22, 1916; d. Walter and Harriet Belle (MacIntyre) Izard; A.B. magna cum laude, Duke, 1937; B.S. in Library Sci., Simmons Coll., 1940. Children's librarian N.Y. Pub. Library, 1940-45; head children's dept. Greenwich (Conn.) Pub. Library, 1945-47; chief children's dept. Mt. Vernon (N.Y.) Pub. Library, 1947-54; adminstrv. asst. chief circulation N.Y. Pub. Library, 1954-59; children's services cons. Westchester Library System, White Plains, N.Y., 1959—. Condr. workshop U. Tenn.; speaker to various orgns. Recipient Grolier award. Mem. A.L.A., (pres. children's services div. 1972-73), Westchester Sch. and Children's Librarians Assn. (pres.), Westchester Assn. Edn. Young Children (dir.), Westchester Library Assn., N.Y. Library Club, Zonta, Audubon Soc. UN Assn. Contbr. articles to library periodicals. Home: 151 Clarence Rd Scarsdale NY 10583 Office: 285 Central Av White Plains NY 10606

IZARD, BARBARA SINQUEFIELD (MRS. CARROLL E. IZARD), educator; b. Gulfport, Miss., May 8, 1926; d. Fred Herbert and Camille Olivia (West) Sinquefield; Mus.B., Yale, 1948; Mus.M., Syracuse U., 1950; postgrad. drama Vanderbilt U., 1958-60, Paris, France, 1966-67, Moscow, USSR, 1974; m. Carroll E. Izard; children—Carroll E., Camille Sinquefield, Ellen Ashley. Instr. drama Belmont Coll., Nashville, 1960-62; dir. summer theater Vanderbilt U., Nashville, 1965; instr. drama, speech and music Aquinas Coll., Nashville, 1970—. Mem. A.S.C.A.P., D.A.R., Colonial Dames Am. Co-author: Requiem for a Nun-On Stage and Off, 1970. Composer: Merry Christmas Is the Nicest Hello, 1973; A Child's Christmas Prayer, 1973. Home: 1701 Graybar Lane Nashville TN 37215

IZZO, KATHERINE LIACOS, lawyer; b. Peabody, Mass., Apr. 6, 1928; d. James A. and Pitsa (Karis) Liacos; B.S., Simmons Coll., 1949; LL.B. cum laude, Boston U., 1960; m. Edmund S. Izzo, May 29, 1957 (dec. June 1972); children—Jonathan, Jennifer. Admitted to Mass. bar, 1960; atty. Paul J. Donaher, Boston, 1960-61; partner Liacos & Liacos, Peabody, Mass., 1961—. Mem. Dem. City Com., 1964-72. Bd. dir. Northshore Family Planning Council, 1970-72; trustee Edmund S. Izzo Scholarship of Justice Trust, 1972—. Mem. Mass., Essex County, Peabody bar assns., Mass. Women Lawyers Assn., Mass. Judicature Soc., Am. Trial Lawyers Assn., League Women Voters, U. Boston Law Sch. Alumni Assn. (mem. exec. com. 1973), Simmons Coll. Alumni Assn. (mem. alumnae coll. com. 1972-74). Editor Boston U. Law Review, 1958-60. Home: 18 Sparrow Lane Peabody MA 01960 Office: 9 Main St Peabody MA 01960

JABLONSKI, EDITH JACQUELINE GARSON (MRS. EDWARD JABLONSKI), mag. editor; b. Richmond, Va., Aug. 21, 1926; d. Max and Rose (Fisher) Garson; B.A., Bklyn. Coll., 1948; postgrad. New Sch. for Social Research, 1948-50; m. Edward Jablonski, Sept. 2, 1951; children—David, Carla, Emily. Editor Retail News Bur., N.Y.C., 1949-50; fur fashion editor Women's Wear Daily, N.Y.C., 1950-53; copywriter Essie Pinsker Assos., N.Y.C., 1963-65; feature editor Knitting Mill Mgmt., N.Y.C., 1965-68; editor Knit Directions, N.Y.C., 1968—. Contbg. author: George Gershwin: A Study in American Music, rev. edit., 1958. Home: 161 W 75th St New York City NY 10023 Office: 1440 Broadway New York City NY 10018

JABLONSKI, WANDA MARY, pub. co. exec.; b. Czechoslovakia; d. Eugene and Mary Jablonski; B.A., Cornell U., 1942; M.A., Columbia, 1943. Came to U.S., 1938, naturalized, 1945. Oil editor Jour. Commerce, N.Y.C., 1943-54; sr. editor Petroleum Week, McGraw-Hill, N.Y.C., 1954-61; founder, owner, editor, pub. Petroleum Intelligence Weekly, N.Y.C., 1961—. Recipient award of merit Asso. Bus. Publs., 1956, 1st award, 1957. Mem. Am. Acad. Polit. and Social Sci., Overseas Press Club, Newsletter Pubs. Assn., Middle East Inst., U.S. Arab C. of C., Am. Arab Assn. Commerce and Industry. Contbr. articles to Colliers, other mags. Home: Centre Island Oyster Bay NY 11771 also 930 Fifth Av New York City NY 10021 Office: care PIW 48 W 48th St New York City NY 10036

JACKER, CORINNE LITVIN (MRS. RICHARD JACKER), author; b. Chgo., June 29, 1933; d. Thomas Henry and Theresa (Bellak) Litvin; student Stanford, 1950-52; B.S. (Lovdedale scholar, Univ. scholar), Northwestern U., 1954, M.A., 1955, postgrad., 1955-56; m. Richard Jacker, July 1, 1956 (div. Apr. 1958). Asso. editor Liberal Arts Press, 1959-60, trade sci. dept. Macmillan Co., 1961-63; asst. editor sci. book dept. Charles Scribner's Sons, N.Y.C., 1963-65; writer, researcher NET Playhouse, WNET, 1971-73; story cons. CBS Playhouse 90, 1973-74; script editor Bicentennial Minutes, CBS, 1974—. Mem. Authors League, Dramatists Guild Writers Guild Am., Zeta Phi Eta. Author: (books) Man, Memory, and Machines, 1964; Window on the Unknown, 1966; Black Flag of Anarchy, 1968; The Biological Revolution, 1971; (off-Broadway and regionally produced plays) Pale Horse, Pale Rider, 1958; A Happy Ending, 1959; Terminal; Jennifer, Jemima and the Machine, 1970; Scientific Method, 1970; Project Omega, Lillian, 1971; Bits and Pieces, 1973; Travellers, 1974; Night Thoughts, 1974; Taking Care of Harry, 1974; (TV plays) Actors Choice Series, 1970; The Anatomy of Love; When This You See, Remember Me; A Singular Man; Brewsie and Willie, 1972; Boxes, 1972; Secrets, 1973; various poems published in Spectrum, Fiddlehead, Carleton Miscellany, Riverside Poetry III, Mutiny. Home: 110 W 86th New York City NY 10024

JACKLIN, KATHLEEN BESSIE, archivist; b. Sayre, Pa., Nov. 17, 1924; d. William Russell and Hazel (Kunzman) Jacklin; student Pa. State Coll. Extension Sch., 1946-47; B.A. summa cum laude, Elmira Coll., 1950; certificate in archives adminstrn., Am. U., 1953; M.A., Cornell U., 1958. Tchr. English and history, high sch., Angola, N.Y., 1950-51; asst. curator dept. manuscripts and univ. archives Cornell U., Ithaca, N.Y., 1952-58, asso. curator, archivist, 1958-69, archivist, 1969—. Lectr. on local history, genealogy, archival practice for coll. classes, hist. socs., women's clubs, Cornell campus, City of Ithaca, adjacent towns. Mem. Am. Hist. Assn., Am. Assn. for State and Local History, Soc. Am. Archivists, Internat. Council on Archives, Elmira Coll. Alumnae Assn., Historic Ithaca, Inc., Phi Beta Kappa (Pi of N.Y. chpt.). Mem. Methodist Episcopal Ch. Clubs: Elmira Coll. of Tompkins County (sec. 1954-56, 60-69, pres. 1956-59), Cornell Women's of Ithaca. Editor: Report of the Curator and Archivist, 1954-58, 62-66. Home: 507 E Buffalo St Ithaca NY 14850

JACKSON, AGNES MORELAND, educator; b. Pine Bluff, Ark.; d. Nathaniel Edmund and Rosa (Wood) Moreland; A.B. cum laude, U. Redlands, 1952; M.A., U. Wash., 1953; Ph.D, in English and Comparative Lit. (So. fellow, Danforth fellow), Columbia, 1960; m. Harold Andrew Jackson, Jr., July 18, 1964. Instr. in English, Spelman Coll., Atlanta, 1953-55, Atlanta U., summer 1955; instr. communications Boston U. Coll. Basic Studies, 1959-61, asst. prof. communications and Am. lit., 1961-63; asst. prof. English, Cal. State Coll., Los Angeles, 1963-69, asso. prof. English, 1969-70; asso. prof. English, Pitzer Coll., also Black Studies Center, Claremont (Cal.) Colls., 1969—; tchr. U. Redlands, summer 1963; chmn. bd. stewardship Congl. Ch. Christian Fellowship, United Ch. of Christ, Los Angeles, 1966-67. Informal ednl. and vocational counseling, 1959—; pub. speaker. Conf. speaker Western Interstate Conf. for Tchrs. English, Las Vegas, 1970. Mem. South Central Jr. Coll. Com.; neighborhood solicitor Heart Assn., 1970-72, Am. Cancer Soc., 1971-72, Muscular Dystrophy, 1970-72. Cross-Disciplinary Post-doctoral fellow Soc. for Religion in Higher Edn., 1970-71. Mem. Soc. Religion in Higher Edn., Modern Lang. Assn., Am. Assn. U. Women, Am. Assn. U. Profs., Danforth Assos., N.A.A.C.P., Cal. Assn. Tchrs. English (conf. speaker San Francisco 1970), So. Cal. Conf. Tchrs. English (panelist 1963, 68, 69), Nat. Council Negro Women, Delta Sigma Theta (chmn. scholarship com. Boston Alumnae chpt. 1961-63). Home: 1234 Douglas Dr Pomona CA 91768 Office: Pitzer Coll Claremont CA 91711

JACKSON, ANN LONG, pathologist; b. Vicksburg, Miss., Nov. 6, 1931; d. Horace Taggart and Mary Pearse (Guider) Long; student Webster Coll., 1949-52, Newcomb Coll., 1951-52; M.D., Tulane U., 1956; m. James William Jackson, Feb. 7, 1959; children—James William, John Guider, Stacy Ann, Edward R. II, Mary Zita, Courtney Carol. Intern, Charity Hosp., New Orleans, 1956-57; resident pathology U. Cal. at San Francisco, 1957-58; Tulane Service, New Orleans, 1959-60; asso. pathologist St. Joseph's Hosp., Thibodaux, La., 1962-67, pathologist, 1967—. Fellow Am. Soc. Clin. Pathologists, Coll. Am. Pathologists; mem. Am. Assn. Blood Banks, A.M.A., La., Lafourche Parish med. socs., Alpha Omega Alpha. Address: PO Box 161 Thibodaux LA 70301

JACKSON, ANNE (MRS. ELI WALLACH), actress; b. Allegheny, Pa.; d. John Ivan and Stella (Murry) Jackson; grad. Neighborhood Playhouse Sch.; studied with Herbert Berghoff, Sanford Meisner, Actors Studio; m. Eli Wallach; children—Peter Douglas, Roberta Katherine. Appeared Broadway plays Summer and Smoke, Magnolia Alley, Love Me Long, The Last Dance, Oh Men! Oh Women!, Middle of the Night, also appearing in Exercise, 1969—, and Inquest; appeared in films The Journey, Tall Story, Lovers and Other Strangers, Dirty Dingus McGee; appeared with husband in plays including This Property Was Condemned, several Am. Repertory Theatre prodns., Rhinoceros (Broadway), The Typists, The Tiger (off-Broadway and London), The Glass Menagerie (summer circuit), Lullaby (TV), Major Barbara (Broadway), Brecht on Brecht (ANTA), Luv. Recipient Tinker award Brighton (Eng.) Argus, 1964. Home: 90 Riverside Dr New York City NY 10024

JACKSON, ANN(I)E LOU STINGLEY (MRS. JOSEPH JACKSON), librarian; b. Blevins, Ark.; d. William Henry and Nina (Duke) Stingley; A.B., Henderson State Tchrs. Coll., 1951; M.L.S., Tex. State Coll. for Women, Denton, Tex., 1954; m. Joseph Jackson, Sept. 4, 1922; children—Joseph Lyle, Andrew Stingley, Kenneth Edwin. Tchr., librarian Washington (Ark.) High Sch., 1940-46; asst. librarian Ouachita Coll., Arkadelphia, summer 1944; head librarian Arkadelphia City and Clark County Library, 1946-53; cons. for high sch. and pub. libraries Arkansas Library Commn., 1953-65; state sch. library supr. Ark. Dept. Edn., 1965-72; library cons., 1972—; dir. Elementary and Secondary Edn. Act, Title II. Active Community Chest Bd., Arkadelphia, UN Speakers Bur. in Ark.; mem. adult edn. coordinating bd. YWCA. Mem. Commr. Edn.'s Adv. Com. on sch. libraries; chmn. State com. on sch. library study Southern States Work Conf. on Edn., 1957—; Sec. Pulaski County Chapter UN, 1964; exec. dir. Nat. Library Week for Ark., 1963. Recipient certificate merit, Ark. Jr. C. of C., 1956; certificate merit for distinguished service to library sci. Mem. Am. Assn. Sch. Libraries (state rep. for Nat. Library Week 1959-60), Am. (chmn. Ark. membership com. Audio-Visual div. 1956), Ark. Student (librarian's council), Ark. library assns., Nat. Adult Edn. Assn., Ark. Hist. Assn., Nat. Assn. State Sch. Library Suprs. (pres. 1972-73), Am. Assn. U. Women (1st v.p. 1970-72), Vets. World War I Aux. (state conductress 1973-74, chaplain 1974—), UN Assn. (pres. state div. USA for Ark. 1969-70), Clark County Hist. Soc., N.E.A., Ark. Edn. Assn., Nat. Soc. Arts and Letters (pres. Little Rock 1974—), Internat. Platform Assn., Women's Nat. Book Assn. (chmn. U. Ark. Personal Library Contest 1972-73), Greater Little Rock Fedn. Womens Clubs (sec. 1974—), Delta Kappa Gamma (2d v.p. Gamma chpt. 1966-68), Kappa Delta Pi, Alpha Chi, Alpha Beta Alpha. Democrat. Baptist. Mem. Order Eastern Star. Clubs: Altrusa (bd. dirs. Little Rock 1965—, 1st v.p. 1968-69, pres. 1971-72, internat. relations chmn. internat. dist. 8 1970-72), Fine Arts. Mem. A.L.A. editorial subcom., compiling Basic Book Collection for High Schs., 1957; adviser and assisted editing Handbook for the Student Assistant in the School Library, 1959; rev. bibliography Arkansiana for High Schools, 1960, 1964; editorial com. for bibliography Ethnic Groups: Their Cultures and Contbns.; chmn. com. compiling bibliography on Black Ams. Contbr. World Book Ency., 1960, 72. Home: 321 East 7th St Little Rock AR 72202 Office: State Dept Edn State Capitol Grounds Little Rock AR 72201

JACKSON, AUDREY NABOR, sch. librarian; b. New Orleans, July 10, 1926; d. Raymond and Beulah (Carney) Nabor; B.A., So. U., 1951, M.A., 1966; postgrad. La. State U., 1954, 68, 69, Chgo. Tchrs. Coll.; m. Freddie Jackson, July 26, 1946; children—Claudia Ann (Mrs. Freddie L. Fisher), Beverly Ann (Mrs. Wilbur James Franklin), Freddie (dec.). Librarian, J.S. Dawson High Sch., St. Francisville, La., 1951-54, Southdown High Sch., Houma, La., 1954-55, Chaneyville High Sch., Zachary, La., 1955—. Chmn. community advancement Adv. Com. Parish East Baton Rouge, 1970-72; mem. Baton Rouge Civic Center Commn., 1973—. Bd. dirs. Family Planning East Baton Rouge Parish, Community Advancement Advisers, Inc. Audio-visual grantee La. State U., 1968; urban geography grantee So. U., 1970. Mem. Am. Assn. Sch. Librarians (nat. library week com. 1972-74), Am. (state membership chmn. 1972—, outreach program young adult com. 1973—), Southwestern, La. library assns., La. Sch. Librarians, Nat., La., East Baton Rouge edn. assns., Baton Rouge Library club, Delta Sigma Theta. Club: Futurama, De Charmette. Home: Route 3 Box 143 Zachary LA 70791

JACKSON, BARBARA ANN GARVEY SEAGRAVE (MRS. KERN C. JACKSON), educator; b. Normal, Ill., Sept. 27, 1929; d. Neil Ford and Eva Glenola (Burkhart) Garvey; Mus.B. with highest honors, U. Ill., 1950; Mus.M. (Tri Delta fellow), U. Rochester, 1952; Ph.D., Stanford, 1959; m. Kern C. Jackson, Mar. 29, 1970; stepchildren—Kern, Ross, Bruce, Paul. Faculty, U. Ark., Fayetteville, 1954—, prof. music, 1971—; spl. music tchr. Los Angeles Pub. Schs., 1956-57; asst. prof. music Ark. Poly. Coll., Russellville, 1957-61; pvt. tchr. violin. So. Fellowship Fund post doctoral grantee, 1959; Grad. Research Council grantee, U. Ark., 1965-73. Mem. Am. Musicological Soc., Am. String Tchrs. Assn. (pubs. com. 1961-71), Coll. Music Soc. (mem. council 1971-73), Am. Music Tchrs. Assn., Wider Quaker Fellowship, Pi Kappa Lambda, Phi Kappa Phi, Sigma Alpha Iota. Author: (with Bruce Benward) Practical Beginning Theory, 1963; (with Wesley Thomas) The Songs of the Minnesingers, 1965; (with W. Thomas) The Songs of the Minnesinger, Wizlaw of Rugen, 1968; (with Joel Berman) The A.S.T.A. Dictionary of Bowing Terms for Stringed Instruments, 1968; The Violin Sonatas of Giovanni Antonio Piani, 1974. Home: 235 Baxter Lane Fayetteville AR 72701

JACKSON, BARBARA LOOMIS, educator; b. Detroit, May 23, 1928; d. Lloyd Albert and Katherine (Quaker) Loomis; B.A., Wellesley Coll., 1950; M.A., Tchrs. Coll. Columbia, 1967; Ed.D., Harvard, 1970; m. William Edward Jackson, Aug. 12, 1950 (div.); children—Caroline, Jackson, William Edward II. Exec. dir. Health and Welfare Council Bergen County, Hackensack, N.J., 1959-64; research asso. pub. schs. Englewood, N.J., 1964-67; asst. adminstr. edn. and tng. Boston Model City Adminstrn., 1969-72; dir. evaluation Nat. Urban League Exptl. Schs. Street Acad. Project, 1972-73; asso. prof. Sch. Edn., Atlanta U., 1973—. Cons. Abt Assos., Cambridge, Mass., 1969-70, U.S. Office Edn., 1971, Ford Found., 1972. Trustee Wellesley (Mass.) Coll. Mem. Am. Assn. Sch. Adminstrs., Am. Ednl. Research Assn., Delta Sigma Theta. Office: Sch Edn Atlanta U Atlanta GA 30314

JACKSON, BEATRICE (MRS. DAVID HUMPHREYS), artist; b. London, Eng., Dec. 7, 1905 (parents Am. citizens); d. Walter Montgomery and Eloise (Carpenter) Jackson; student Smith Coll., 1923-26; student Grand Central Art Sch., 1926-27, Art Students League, Colorossi Acad. (Paris), 1927-29; pvt. study with George Elmer Browne, 1927-28, Wayman Adams, 1926-27, Andre Lhote (Paris), 1932-33; m. David Humphreys, Feb. 16, 1927; children—Anita (Mrs. Arthur Woodruff Jones), Elaine (Mrs. William Collins Kohler). One man shows at Van Dieman-Lilienfeld Gallery, So. Vt. Art Center, Manchester, Grand Central Art Galleries, N.Y.C.; exhibited in group shows at Nat. Acad. Art, Conn. Acad. Fine Arts, Hartford, Mus. Fine Arts, Springfield, Mass., Nat. Arts Club, Grand Salon, Paris; represented in permanent collection at So. Vt. Art Center, numerous pvt. collections. Dir. W.M. Jackson, Inc., N.Y.C., 1950-70, Humphreys Medecine Corp., N.Y.C., 1970-74. Bd. dirs. Big Sisters, Inc., 1948-74, pres., 1970. Recipient awards Nat. Assn. Women Artists, 1953, 59, 70, Conn. Acad. Fine Arts, 1955, Allied Artists Am. medal, 1955, prizes, 58, 60, 73, Am. Artists Profl. League, 1967, others. Mem. Audubon Artists (mem. exec. bd. 1964-74, rec. sec. 1964—), Nat. Assn. Women Artists (dir. 1959—), So. Vt. Artists Inc. (trustee 1972—), Royal Soc. Arts (London), Societe National des Beaux-Arts (Paris), Grand Central Art Galleries. Clubs: National Arts, Cosmopolitan (N.Y.C.). Home: PO Box 277 Dorset VT 05251 Office: 450 E 63rd St New York City NY 10021

JACKSON, BETTINA ADELINE BUSH (MRS. DANIEL F. JACKSON), immunologist, educator; b. Woburn, Mass., Sept. 4, 1910; d. Arthur Dermont and Ethel Ursula (Brown) B.; student Agnes Scott Coll., 1925-27; A.B. with high distinction, U. Mich., 1929, M.S., 1945; Ph.D., U. Pitts., 1951; m. Hayden A. Carter, Nov. 5, 1929 (div. 1938); children—Bettina (Mrs. F.R.J. DeWeeger), Anthony A., Lawrence Q.; m. 2d, Daniel Francis Jackson, Dec. 15, 1951. Laboratorian, N.Y. State Dept. Health, Albany, 1937-40; trouble shooter in serology USPHS, 1940-44; research immunologist Inst. Pathology, Pitts., 1944-53; asst. prof. microbiology Coll. Medicine, State U. N.Y., 1953-55; asst. prof. biology Western Mich. U., Kalamazoo, 1955-58, asso. prof., 1958-59; research asso, pathology, asso. prof. natural scis. U. Louisville, 1959-63; asso. prof. bacteriology Syracuse (N.Y.) U., 1963-69, prof. bacteriology, 1969-70; prof. biology, chmn. sci. and math. Cazenovia (N.Y.) Coll., 1970-73; cons. immunohematologist, Miami, Fla., 1973—. Lectr. epidemiology Duquesne U., Pitts., 1945-48; serologist to dist. atty., Pitts., 1952-53; mem. Mich. Basic Scis. Bd., 1957-59. Recipient research grant NIH, 1946-48, Eli Lilly Pharm. Co., 1948-50, Sigma Xi, 1960, NSF, 1961-62; Gerber award in biochemistry, research award Gerber Baby Foods Co., 1956; research award Blood Reference Lab., Manitoba, 1962. Mem. A.A.A.S.; Am. Chem. Soc., N.Y. Acad. Sci., Phi Beta Kappa, Sigma Xi, Phi Kappa Phi, Beta Beta Beta, Delta Phi Alpha. Author: Experiences in Microbiology, 1965. Contbr. articles to profl. jours. Home: 5220 SW 60th Pl Miami FL 33155

JACKSON, CAROLYN GOSSETT (MRS. CHARLES CLIFTON JACKSON), women's editor; b. Taylor, Tex., Apr. 23, 1927; d. Charles Carroll and Izetta Lucille (Hargon) Gossett; B.F.A., U. Tex., 1948; grad. Northwestern NBC Inst., 1948; m. Charles Clifton Jackson, July 2, 1949; children—Cynthia, Carol. Dir. women's programs KTAE, Taylor, 1948; mem. research dept. Leo Burnett Advt. Agy., Chgo., 1949; tchr. pub. schs. San Antonio, 1961-64, Taylor, 1965; tv tchr. KLRN, Austin, Tex., 1966-68; women's editor KTBC, Austin, 1968—. Worker, Williamson County treatment center for crippled children and adults Jr. Women's Study Club; participant Taylor Library Bldg. Fund drive; mem. com. on nominations Lone Star council Girl Scouts U.S.A., mem. adv. bd. March of Dimes, Austin. Mem. Am. Women in Radio and TV, Alpha Chi Omega. Methodist (mem. choir, active youth work). Home: 2006 Lathan Lane Taylor TX 76574 Office: Box 2223 Austin TX 78767

JACKSON, CAROLYN JANE, librarian; b. Paris, Tex., May 2, 1937; d. Frank William and Sallie Belle (Towers) J.; B.A., Tex. Woman's U., 1959, M.L.S., 1960, postgrad., 1970; postgrad. Midwestern U., 1963. Acquisitions librarian Midwestern U., 1960-68; periodicals librarian Sul Ross State U., 1968-69; asst. librarian E. Tex. Bapt. Coll., Marshall, 1969—. Cons., Am. Security Council, 1971. Active United Fund. Mem. Am. Assn. U. Women, Nat. Assn. Commercial Travelers, Southwestern, Tex. library assns., Mary Ellen Breckenridge Social Lit. Club, Alpha Beta Alpha. Democrat. Baptist. Mem. Order Eastern Star. Club: Woman's (Marshall, Tex.). Home: 1502 N Grove St Marshall TX 75670

JACKSON, DELLA ROSETTA HAYDEN, educator; b. Mill Spring, N.C., Mar. 2, 1905; d. Robert Twitt and Amanda (Petty) Hayden; B.A., Johnson C. Smith U., 1948; M.A., N.C. Coll., 1956; m. G. Franklin Davenport, Sept. 28, 1930 (dec. Jan. 1936); children—Evelyn Frances (Mrs. Alonzo David Petty), Amanda Elizabeth (Mrs. Lourn Clinton Gray), Robert Franklin; m. 2d, Clarence Eugene Jackson, Oct. 30, 1943 (dec. Mar. 1951); children—Mae Carolyn (Mrs. Joseph Williams, Jr.), Clarence Stinson. Tchr. Stony Knoll Sch., Polk County, N.C., 1927-30, Tryon Sch., 1930-31, Pea Ridge Sch., 1932-39, Union Grove Sch., 1939-48, Edmund Embury Sch., 1949-51, Cobb Elementary Sch., Tryon, N.C., 1951-65; spl. edn. tchr. Polk Central High Sch., Mill Spring, N.C., 1966-69; librarian Stony Knoll Community Library, 1937—, pres., 1972—, also chmn. bd. trustees; tchr. adult basic edn., Stony Knoll and Mill Spring, 1971—. State chmn. status of women N.C. Woman's Missionary Conf., Christian Meth. Episcopal Ch.; mem. Polk County agrl. adv. bd. Dept. Community Devel. and Pub. Affairs, 1966—; 4-H Club leader; mem. Polk Central P.T.A.; mem. Central Highlands Health Council, 1968-70; 2d v.p. Polk County Homemakers Council, 1969-73, pres., 1974—; sec.-treas. Polk County Community Devel. Council, 1969—; mem. adv. com. Polk County Dept. Social Services, 1970—; mem. Polk County Emergency Med. Services Adv. Com., 1973—; bd. dirs. Isothermal Health Council, 1970-72, sec., 1972—; bd. dirs. Regional Health Council Eastern Appalachia, 1970—; mem. Polk County steering com. Gov.'s Beautification Program, 1970—; chmn. Child Care Com. Polk County, 1971—; v.p. Childrens Council Eastern Appalachia, 1971-73; adv. bd. Polk County Mental Health Council, 1972-73; bd. dirs. St. Lukes Hosp. Aux., Tyron, 1972—; mem. Region C Ancillary Manpower Planning Bd., 1972—. Named Mother of Yr., Afro, 1948, Polk County Home Extension Council and Western Dist. N.C., 1971; recipient certificate service N.C. Recreation Soc., 1962, certificate leadership for service Western N.C. Community Devel. Program Asheville Agrl. Devel. Council, 1962. Mem. N.C., Polk County tchrs. assns., Stony Knoll Recreation Soc., Nat. Recreation Assn., N.C., Polk County, Nat. edn. assns., Polk County Home Extenison Council (v.p. 1972-73), League Women Voters (dir. Tryon 1970—). Mem. C.M.E. Ch. (all offices). Club: Stoney Knoll Community (pres. 1959-62). Writer poetry. Home: PO Box 95 Mill Spring NC 28756

JACKSON, DORIS GRACE (MRS. ELMER M. JACKSON, JR.), ednl. adminstr.; b. Camden, Ark., Oct. 5, 1925; d. Henry Barney and Christine (Lane) Grace; B.A., So. Methodist U., 1949; M.A., Towson (Md.) State Coll., 1972; m. Raymond O. Blummer, Jr., July 12, 1942; children—Raymond O., III, Sharan (Mrs. Robert A. Sutton), David Allen; m. 2d, Elmer M. Jackson, Jr., Apr. 18, 1972. Govt. documents librarian No. Tex. State U., Denton, 1949-50; cataloguer So. Meth. U., Dallas, 1950-51; head library order dept. Tex. Christian U., Ft. Worth, 1955-57; dir. vols. Balt. Mental Health Assn., 1968-70; media specialist Anne Arundel County (Md.) Pub. Schs., Glen Burnie, 1970—; dir. Pocomoke City Pub. Co. (Md.), 1972—. Vice pres. Annapolis (Md.) Fine Arts Festival, 1965, chmn., 1966, activities chmn., 1967-68; tour guide Hist. Annapolis tour, 1965-71; chmn. Annapolis Jr. Mus., 1968-69; v.p. Anne Arundel County Red Cross, 1971—; leader Friends of Scouting, 1957—; sec. Citizens Com. to Study Schs., Annapolis, 1968-71. Past sec., trustee Anne Arundel Library Assn., 1968—. Mem. Am. Assn. U. Women (pres. Annapolis br. 1969-71), Ednl. Media Assn., Md. Library Assn., Anne Arundel Arts Assn., Annapolis Opera Guild, D.A.R., Daus. Republic Tex. Democrat. Episcopalian. Clubs: Army-Navy (Washington); Annapolis Yacht, Naval Academy Golf, Naval Academy Officers and Faculty (Annapolis). Contbr. articles to profl. publs. Home: 219 Claude St Wardour Annapolis MD 21401 Office: Quarterfield Rd Glen Burnie MD 21601

JACKSON, DOROTHY LOUISA GREENLEE (MRS. FRED KNOX JACKSON), ct. reporter; b. Hamburg, Ia., Feb. 19, 1911; d. Henry Oliver and Mattie (Landreth) Greenlee; student pub. schs.; m. Fred Knox Jackson, Oct. 3, 1944. Asst. county ct. reporter, Auburn, Neb., 1927-29; sec. local atty., 1927-29; sec. Berksons, Kansas City, Mo., 1929-33; corr. A.A.A., Washington, 1933-36; sec. Intelligence Unit, Kansas City, St. Louis, 1936-40; free-lance ct., conv. reporter, St. Louis, 1940-44; free-lance ct. reporter, Prattville, Ala., 1948—; contract reporter Ala. Pub. Service Commn., Montgomery. Co-owner, operator Prattville (Ala.) Quick Freeze, 1948-63. Chmn., Autauga County Operation Santa Claus, State Christmas Card, Bryce Mental Hosp., Tuscaloosa, Ala., 1963-70. Mem. Nat. League Am. Pen Women (br. pres. 1964-68, 72-74, state pres. 1972-74), Birmingham Opera Guild, Ala. Writers Conclave, Montgomery Press and Authors Club (pres. 1971-72), Ala. Shorthand Reporters Assn., Montgomery Assn. Legal Secs., Nat. Shorthand Reporters Assn., Internat. Platform Assn., Ala. Poetry Soc., Autauga County Bus. and Profl. Womens Club (County Woman of Achievement 1972). Author: (poetry) Fallen Leaves, 1968; Poody, 1970. Home: 856 Gillespie St Prattville AL 36067 Office: 132 Adams Av Montgomery AL 36104

JACKSON, EDITH BANFIELD, physician; b. Colorado Springs, Colo., Jan. 2, 1895; d. William and Helen Fiske (Banfield) Jackson; A.B., Vassar, 1916; M.D., Johns Hopkins, 1921; grad. student Inst. Psychoanalysis, Vienna, 1930-36. Interne U. Ia. Hosp., 1921-22; interne pediatrics Bellevue Hosp., N.Y.C., 1922-23; asst. physician U.S. Children's Bur., New Haven, 1923-28; asst. physician St. Elizabeth Hosp., Washington, 1928-29; asst. in pediatrics Yale Sch. of Medicine, 1924-25, instr., 1925-27, clin. instr., 1927-29, clin. instr. psychiatry and mental hygiene, 1936-39, asst. clin. prof., 1939-41, asst. clin. prof. pediatrics (psychiatry), 1941-45, asso. clin. prof., 1945-49, clin. prof. pediatrics and psychiatry, 1949-59, emeritus 1959; vis. prof. pediatrics and psychiatry U. Colo., 1960—; attending pediatrician (psychiatric cons.) Grace-New Haven Community Hosp. (unit service), 1936-59, dir. rooming-in project, 1946-53; dir. Sigmund Freud Archives, Inc. Recipient Agnes McGavin award for preventive psychiatry Am. Psychiat. Assn., 1964. Fellow Am. Psychiat. Assn., Am. Acad. Child Psychiatry; mem. Denver Psychoanalytic Soc., Am. Acad. Pediatrics (hon. asso. mem., recipient C. Anderson Aldrich award child devel. 1968), Am. Com. Maternal Welfare, Western New Eng. Psychoanalytic Soc., Am. Orthopsychiat. Assn., World Fedn. Mental Health (asso.), Am. Psychoanalytic Assn., Am. Psychosomatic Soc., Am. Pediatric Soc. Editor (with Genevieve Trainham); Family Centered Maternity and Infant Care, supplement to Problems of Infancy and Childhood Trans., 4th Conf., 1950, of Josiah Macy, Jr., Found. Contbr. articles on care of child in hosp., clinic aspects of learning and discipline, rooming-in, etc. Home: 380 Albion St Denver CO 80220

JACKSON, EILEEN LOIS, journalist; b. San Diego, Apr. 15, 1906; d. Edward and Vera B. (Morse) Dwyer; student San Diego State Coll., 1923-25, U. Ariz., 1925-26; m. Everett G. Jackson, July 21, 1926; 1 dau., Jerry (Mrs. Thomas Williamson). Society editor San Diego Sun, 1921-25, court reporter, 1925; society editor San Diego Union, 1930-48, columnist, travel feature writer, 1952—. Recipient plaque Comite Sinfonica, Tijuana, Mexico; Galley Slave award Theta Sigma Phi, 1969, award San Diego Mental Health Assn., 1971; named Woman of Valor in San Diego, 1959, Woman of Elegance, 1968. Mem. Gamma Phi Beta. Home: 1234 Franciscan Way San Diego CA 92116

JACKSON, ELEANOR GERTRUDE ALEXANDER, microbiologist; b. N.Y.C., July 1, 1904; d. Jerome and Gertrude E. (Hammerslough) Alexander; B.A., Wellesley Coll., 1925; M.A., Columbia U., 1928; Ph.D., N.Y.U., 1934; m. William R. Jackson, Nov. 1, 1934 (div. 1947); 1 son, Togwell A. Research asst. U. Mich. Hosp., 1928-30; lab. asst. Med. Coll. N.Y.U., 1935-36; research N.Y. State Br. Lab., 1936-39; research fellow Med. Coll., Cornell U., 1941-50; research bacteriologist Cancer Research Lab., 1950-54; ind. research, 1954-60; guest investigator Inst. Comparative Medicine, Columbia U., 1960-65; cons. research microbiologist, N.Y.C., 1965—; research asso. U. San Diego (Cal.), 1968-73. Recipient A. Cressy Morrison prize N.Y. Acad. Scis., 1944, Grant-in-aid award Sigma Delta Epsilon, 1965. Fellow A.A.A.S., N.Y. Micros. Soc., N.Y. Acad. Medicine (asso.); mem. Am. Soc. Microbiology, U.D.C., Sigma Xi, Sigma Delta Epsilon (pres. Kappa chpt.). Clubs: Altrusa, Women's City (N.Y.C.). Contbr. articles to profl. jours. Discovered L forms of Mycobacterium tuberculosis, 1944, M leprae, 1951; research on cancer and other proliferative diseases. Home: 390 Riverside Dr New York City NY 10025

JACKSON, ELIZABETH NOLAND (MRS. DONALD WARRICK JACKSON), social agy. exec.; b. Indpls., Feb. 17, 1916; d. Stephen C. and Teresa (Murray) Noland; A.B., Radcliffe Coll., 1937; postgrad. Merrill-Palmer Inst., 1960, Ind. U., 1961-62; m. Bruce Hunt Fernald, June 5, 1936 (div. Jan. 1945); 1 son, Stephen Bruce; m. 2d, Donald Warrick Jackson, Apr. 2, 1947 (dec. June 1955); children—Anthony Hargrove, Jill Noland. Free-lance writer, editor Marion County Mail, Indpls., 1954-59, exec. dir. Social Health Assn., 1959—. Mem. Ind. Council Family Relations (past pres.), Soc. Ind. Pioneers. Clubs: Indianapolis Press; Radcliffe (Ind.). Republican. Episcopalian. Author (with Cloyd J. Julian), Modern Sex Education, 1967; rev., 1972. Author articles on sex edn. for profl. mags. Home: 4838 Young Av Indianapolis IN 46201 Office: 615 N Alabama St Indianapolis IN 46204

JACKSON, ESTHER COOPER, mag. editor; b. Arlington, Va., Aug. 21, 1917; d. George Posea and Esther (Irving) Cooper; B.A., Oberlin Coll., 1938; M.A., Fisk U., 1940; m. James E. Jackson, May 7, 1941; children—Harriet (Mrs. Henry Scarupa), Kathryn (Mrs. Daniel Rosenberg). Exec. sec. So. Negro Youth Congress, 1941-47; area dir. for Bklyn. community Girl Scouts Greater N.Y., 1959-60; membership dir. N.Y. Urban League, 1957-58; mng. editor Freedomways mag., 1961—. Rosenwald fellow, 1948. Office: 799 Broadway New York City NY 10003

JACKSON, ETHEL CURRY (MRS. RAYMOND T. JACKSON), civic worker; b. Mineral Point, Wis.; d. William Jenkin and Adeline (Argall) Curry; student Northwestern U.; m. Raymond T. Jackson, Sept. 30, 1918. Adv. mem. Marquis Biol. Library Soc.; mem. Cleve. Council on World Affairs, Cleve. Museum Art, Cleve. Health Museum, Cleve. Mus. Natural History, Musical Arts Assn., Garden Center of Greater Cleve., Women's Com. Cleve. Orch., Cleve. Inst. Music, Playhouse Women's Com., Cleve. Zool. Soc., UN Assn. U.S.A., Friends of Cleve. Pub. Library, Smithsonian Assos., Met. Mus. Art, N.Y.C., Cleve. Hist. Soc., Shaker Heights Western Res. Women's Rep. Club. Mem. Northwestern U. Alumni Assn. Republican. Methodist. Clubs: Country, Union, Women's City. Home: 13901 Shaker Blvd Cleveland OH 44120

JACKSON, GAIL PATRICK, TV producer; b. Birmingham, Ala., June 20; d. Lawrence C. and LaValle (Smith) Fitzpatrick; A.B. with honors, Howard Coll., 1932; m. Cornwell Jackson, July 25, 1947 (div. 1970); children—Jennifer, Thomas. Actress, Parmount Studios, 1932-39; motion pictures include Mississippi, My Man Godfrey, Death Takes a Holiday, Stage Door; free lance actress, 1939-47, pictures include My Favorite Wife, Kathleen, Claudia and David; propr. Gail Patrick's Enchanted Cottage, children's shop, Beverly Hills, Cal., 1945-54, Gail Patrick's Enchanted Weavers, Beverly Hills, 1950-51; exec. producer Perry Mason Show, Paisano Prodns., Hollywood, Cal., 1957-66; pres. Paisano Prodns., Inc., 1966—. Sec. Los Angeles Sister City Exec. Com., 1964-65; co-chmn. Mayor's Celebrity Com.; treas. women's div. Los Angeles County chpt. Freedoms Found. at Valley Forge; nat. hon. Christmas Seal chmn. Nat. Tb and Respiratory Disease Assn., 1970-71; nat. bd. dirs. Am. Diabetes Assn., 1972—, chmn., 1972—; mem. nat. arthritis, metabolism and digestive diseases adv. council NIH, 1972—. Mem. Nat. Adv. Com. for Reelection Pres., 1972. Trustee Columbia Coll.; bd. regents Immaculate Heart Coll., Los Angeles. Recipient Woman of the Year award Woodbury Bus. Coll., Los Angeles, 1950, Howard Coll. Outstanding Achievement award, 1955, Nat. Assn. Women Lawyers Justicia award, 1960, Humanitarian award City of Hope, 1961, Radio and TV Woman of So. Cal. award, 1961, Eve award as one So. Cal. best-dressed women Mannequins of The Assistance League, 1961, Woman of the Year award Los Angeles Times, 1961, Businesswoman of the Year award Nat. Assn. Accountants, 1962, Raven award for Perry Mason series, 1962, Mother of the Year award Helping Hand of Los Angeles, 1962. Mem. Acad. TV Arts and Scis. (nat. trustee bd. govs. 1959-60, 60-61, 61-62, 62-63, nat. v.p. 1960-61, 61-62, pres. Hollywood chpt. 1960-61, 61-62), Delta Zeta (v.p. Found., 1961-62, dir. Found. 1961-65, 68—, Woman of the Year, 1962), Zeta Phi Eta. Address: 2003 LaBrea Terrace Hollywood CA 90046

JACKSON, GITTA WIESSNER, psychiatrist; b. Berlin, Germany, Sept. 26, 1932; d. Walter Bruno and Betty Emma (Sikora) Wiessner; M.D., Duke U., 1968; m. Albert C. Jackson, Aug. 13, 1956 (div. Aug. 1961). Med. technician Paulinenhospital, Germany, 1952-54; x-ray tech. Kantonspital Chur, Switzerland, 1954-56; research asst. lipid chemistry Duke, 1950-59; Health, Edn. Welfare fellow pediatric research U. Sind, Karachi, Pakistan, 1967; 68—, resident psychiatry Duke,

1968-70; fellow child psychiatry Childrens Psychiat. Inst., Murdoch, N.C., 1970-73; asso. in psychiatry, div. adolescent and child psychiatry Highland Hosp. div. Duke Med. Center, Asheville, N.C., 1973—; guest investigator Rockefeller U., 1967. Mem. A.M.A., Womans Med. Soc., Durham Orange County Med. Soc. Home: Biltmore Garden Apts Apt 313 Asheville NC 28803 Office: Highland Hosp Asheville NC 28803

JACKSON, INEZ HOLLON (MRS. ODIS L. JACKSON), bank exec.; b. Prattville, Ala.; d. Kirby Clifton and Mattie Pearl (Thorn) Hollon; grad. high sch.; student Am. Inst. Banking, 1971; m. Odis L. Jackson, Feb. 13, 1946; 1 son, Daniel Nicholas. With Bank Prattville, 1944—, head bookkeeper, 1956-63, asst. cashier, 1963-74, asst. v.p., 1974—. Mem. Am. Assn. Bank Woman (chmn. 1964), Ala. Forestry Assn. Baptist. Home: Route 1 Box 322 Prattville AL 36067 Office: 124 W Main St Prattville AL 36067

JACKSON, JEAN DOLORES, food co. exec.; b. Chgo., July 2, 1927; d. Joseph and Martha Jean (Moore) Ambrose; student Wright Jr. Coll., 1945-47, Northwestern U., 1947-50; div. Client service exec. Market Research Corp. Am., San Francisco, 1948-63; marketing analyst Del Monte Corp., San Francisco, 1963-64, project supr., 1964-65, asst. mgr. marketing research, 1965-66, mgr. marketing research, 1966-67, dir. marketing research, 1967—. Mem. Am. Marketing Assn. (v.p. chpt. devel. 1973-74), Am. Assn. Pub. Opinion Research. Democrat. Home: 6876 Pinehaven Rd Oakland CA 94611 Office: 215 Fremont St San Francisco CA 94119

JACKSON, JEAN TUCKER (MRS. EARL L. JACKSON), editor; b. Lincoln, Neb., July 3, 1915; d. Joe E. and Fay (Nichols) Tucker; B.S. in Edn., U. Neb., 1937; m. Earl L. Jackson, Aug. 23, 1944. Mem. Kappa Delta Sorority, 1935—, mem. nat. council, 1971—, editor The Angelos, 1971—. Mem. Order Eastern Star. Address: 3201 S 39th St Lincoln NE 68506

JACKSON, JO ANNE, dentist; b. Birmingham, Nov. 17, 1938; d. Virgil William and Lillian (Smith) Jackson; B.S., U. Ala., 1960, D.M.D., 1963. Intern, Children's Hosp., Birmingham, 1964, resident, 1965; practice dentistry specializing in pediatric dentistry, Birmingham, 1963—; mem. staff Children's Hosp. Clinician Jefferson County Bd. Pub. Health, 1965—; adviser Birmingham Dental Assistants Assn., 1970. Vol. worker Girl's Clubs Am., 1954-57; tchr., instr. YWCA, Birmingham, 1956-61; asst. leader Tuscaloosa council Girl Scouts U.S.A., 1957-59. Diplomate Am. Bd. Pedodontics, Fellow Am. Acad. Pedodontics; mem. Birmingham Dist. (chmn. dental health week 1960), Ala. dental socs., Am. Soc. Dentistry Children, Southeastern chpt., Birmingham, Ala. pedodontic socs., Internat. Assn. Orthodontics, Pierre Fauchard Acad., Am. Assn. Pedodontic Diplomates. Methodist. Home: 2901-D Columbiana Ct Birmingham AL 35216 Office: 1031 S 17th St Birmingham AL 35205

JACKSON, JOAN KATHERINE CURRIE (MRS. STANLEY W. JACKSON), alcoholism cons.; b. Parkhill, Ont., Can., Sept. 24, 1922; d. John Errol and Ruth Irene (Fenn) Currie; B.A., McGill U., 1945, M.A., 1947; Ph.D., U. Wash., 1955; m. Stanley W. Jackson, Aug. 12, 1946. Came to U.S., 1951, naturalized, 1958. Researcher vets. rehab. McGill U., Montreal, 1945-46, teaching and research asst. dept. sociology, 1944-51; researcher senility Provincial Mental Hosp., Essondale, B.C., Can., 1947; instr. dept. psychiatry U. Wash., Seattle, 1951-57, asst. prof., 1957-61, asso. prof., 1961-64; self-employed cons. on alcoholism, 1964—; cons. on alcoholism to instns., state and fed. agys., 1952—; lectr. Yale Sch. Alcohol Studies, 1958, 60. Mem. Mayor's Com. on Rehab. of Alcoholics, Seattle, 1961-62, Gov.'s Adv. Bd. on Alcoholism, 1957-64. Bd. dirs. Seattle Com. on Alcoholism, 1952-64, Anti-Tb League King County, 1958-60. Recipient Matrix award 1960. USPHS Sr. Research fellow, 1959-63, Research Career Devel. award, 1964. Mem. Am. Sociol. Soc., Am. Soc. for History of Medicine. Editorial bd. Jour. Health and Human Behavior, 1960-64. Contbr. articles to publs. in field. Home: 386 W River Rd Orange CT 06477

JACKSON, JOY JUANITA, educator; b. New Orleans, Oct. 8, 1928; d. Oliver Daniel and Oneida Christina (Drouant) Jackson; student La. State U., 1946-49; B.A., Tulane U., 1951, M.A., 1958, Ph.D., 1961. Feature writer New Orleans Times-Picayune, 1951-56; instr. Nicholls State Coll., Thibodaux, La., 1961-62, asst. prof., 1962-66; asst. prof. Southeastern La. U., Hammond, 1966-68, asso. prof., 1968-73, prof. history, 1973—. Corr. sec. S.E. La. Hist. Assn., Hammond, 1973-74. Recipient Irma E. Voight fellow Am. Assn. U. Women, 1960-61. Mem. Am., La. (dir. 1966-68), So. hist. assns., Oral History Assn. Author: New Orleans in the Gilded Age, 1969. Home: 1411 University Dr Hammond LA 70401

JACKSON, KATHRYN BOWMAN, author, editor, cons.; b. N.Y.C.; d. John H. and Virginia (Landy) Bowman; student Pratt Inst., 1927-30; m. Byron Hubbard Jackson, Jr., Feb. 3, 1934 (dec. Oct. 1949); children—Byron Hubbard III, Timothy Alan. Author with Byron Jackson many books for young children, 1945-49; author books, poems, for young children, 1949-55; sr. editor primary lang. arts Silver Burdett Co., Morristown, N.J., 1955-60; editor early childhood periodicals Scholastic Mags., Inc., N.Y.C., 1960-66, asso. editorial dir., 1966-70. Recipient prize for book Farm Stories, Herald Tribune, 1946, Best Textbooks award for book Homes Around the World, 1956. Mem. Forum Writers for Young People, Assn. Curriculum and Devel., Elementary-Kindergarten-Nursery Edn. Pratt Alumni Assn. Presbyn. Author: Around the World Storybook, 1971; Dinosaurs, 1972; The Story of Christmas, 1973; created Kindergarten periodical Let's Find Out, 1965. Home: 41 Elm St Morristown NJ 07960

JACKSON, LILLIE MAE MILLS (MRS. HENRY EDWARD JACKSON), savs. and loan assn. exec.; b. Copeland, Ala., Jan. 8, 1908; d. John William and Sarah Azaline (Copeland) Mills; student Mobile Bus. Coll., 1925-26, Boyd U., 1937-38; m. Henry Edward Jackson, Dec. 24, 1927 (div. 1956); children—Henry Edward, William Howard. Bookkeeper, Bank of Laurel (Miss.), 1926-27; owner Jackson's Grocery Store, Laurel, 1938-42; aircraft inspection officer Brookley Field AFB, Mobile, 1942-49; with Laurel Fed. Savings & Loan Assn. 1949—, treas.-controller, 1965—. Mem. Credit Women Internat. (pres. 1968-69), Jones County Women (associational dir. 1972—). Baptist (treas. 1958—, tchr. Sunday Sch. 1965—, dir. Women's Missionary Union 1971—). Home: Route 6 Box 429 Laurel MS 39440 Office: 317 N Magnolia St Laurel MS 39440

JACKSON, LYDIA OCTAVIA, poet; b. Grafton, N.D., Mar. 5, 1902; d. Karl Olaf and Inga (Schellstad) Svarte; student pub. schs., N.D.; m. Arthur F. Jackson, Dec. 20, 1920; 1 dau., Elizabeth Marjean (Mrs. Leonard Fagerholt). Author: Rhymes for Every Season, 1943; Selected Poems, 1962; Pardon My Gaff (book verse), 1965; also numerous poems in various publs. Publicity chmn. Poetry Day, 1950. Treas. Grafton Sch. Dist. 22, 1931-62. Recipient Nat. Writers award Farmers Union Ednl. Dept., 1950. Mem. Walsh County Sch. Officers Assn. (treas. 1945-62), Am. Poets Fellowship Soc., (Poet Laureate V), World Poetry Day Assn. (membership chmn. N.D. and S.D., 1963—), Centro Studie Scambi Internazionali, Rome (Bronze medal 1965, Silver medal 1967), Midwest Fedn. Chaparral Poets (state regent 1950-51), Nat. League Am. Pen. Women, Am. Poetry League, World Poetry Soc. Inter-continental, Poetry Soc. of London, Ida. Poets and Writers Guild. Presbyn. Mem. Order Eastern Star. Clubs: Riverside Woman's (v.p. 1957-59, sec. 1955-57, 59-61); Sigma Rho Study (sec.-treas. 1958—, pres. 1952-54). Home: Route 2 Grafton ND 58237

JACKSON, MARGARET ELLEN, educator; b. Zanesville, O., Sept. 2, 1928; d. Harvey A. and Marion Beulah (Dunn) Jackson; B.S., Muskingum Coll., 1950; M.S., Auburn U., 1958, Ph.D., 1964. Chemist, Dow Chem. Co., Midland, Mich., 1951-52, Calverton Chem. Co., Balt., 1953-56; grad. asst., instr. Auburn U., 1962-64; asst. prof. Delta State Coll., Cleveland, Miss., 1964-65; asso. prof. chemistry U.S. Ala., Mobile, 1965—. Recipient NSF Summer Fellowship, Kan. State U., 1964. Mem. Am. Chem. Soc., London Chem. Soc., Ala. Acad. Sci. Presbyn. (deacon 1971, adult edn. supr. 1969—). Home: 113 Vanderbilt Dr Mobile AL 36608 Office: University Blvd Mobile AL 36688

JACKSON, MARJORIE, coll. dean; b. Oakland, Cal.; d. Arthur Leslie and Mabel (Gohrman) Jackson; B.A., Mills Coll.; M.A. summa cum laude, U. Cal. at Berkeley; Ed.D., Columbia, 1962; postgrad. Juilliard Grad. Sch., U. Denver, 1963. Oboist with maj. symphonies and operas; mem. faculty U. Louisville, until 1960; instr. woodwind instruments Columbia, N.Y.C., 1960-62; asst. dean women U. Fla. at Gainesville, 1963-66; dean students Hollins (Va.) Coll., 1966-67; dean of coll., asso. prof. music Hobart and William Smith Colls., Geneva, N.Y., 1967-69; dean women Boise State Coll., (Ida.), 1969-71. Mem. Am. Personnel and Guidance Assn., Nat. Assn. Student Personnel Adminstrs., Nat. Assn. Women Deans and Counselors, Internat. Platform Assn., Alpha Mu, Kappa Delta Pi, Alpha Lambda Delta, Beta Sigma Omicron, Zeta Tau Alpha (hon., nat. music com. 1973). Clubs: Chautauqua Womens; Etude (Berkeley, Cal.). Address: care Proctor 976 34th St Oakland CA 94608

JACKSON, MARY BETHANY BLANKS (MRS. JOHN R. JACKSON), home economist; b. Meridian, Miss., Oct. 29, 1909; d. Robert L. and Mary (Dement) Blanks; B.S., Miss. State Coll. for Women, 1931; M.A., U. So. Miss., 1954; m. John R. Jackson, June 8, 1935 (dec. Nov. 1952); children—John R., Robert T. Tchr. home econs. Forrest County Agr. High Sch., Brooklyn, Miss., 1931-32, 53-55, Philadelphia (Miss.) High Sch., 1932-34, Bay St. Louis (Miss.) High Sch., 1934-35, Petal (Miss.) High Sch., 1943-45; sr. home economist Miss. Power Co., Hattiesburg, 1955—. Pres., Hattiesburg Jr. Aux., 1947-48. Bd. dirs. Forrest County Safety Council. Mem. Am., Miss. (chmn. 1969-70) home economists in bus. group, Am., Miss. (chmn. nominating com.) home econs. assns., Hattiesburg Area Consumer Assn. (v.p.). Presbyn. Home: 620 S 28th Av Hattiesburg MS 39401 Office: 112 W Pine St Hattiesburg MS 39401

JACKSON, NANCY WINSLOW (MRS. ALPHONSE VILLAMIL), artist; b. East Lynn, Mass., Feb. 23, 1913; d. Ernest Edward and Annie (Henderson) Jackson; student Farnsworth Sch. Art, Sarasota, Fla., North Truro, Mass., 1947-50, Amagansett Art Sch., Sarasota, 1950, Art Student's League, N.Y.C., 1952; m. Frederick Enos Woltman, Oct. 31, 1952 (div. Oct. 1959); m. 2d, Alphonse Villamil, Mar. 14, 1968. Exhibited numerous group shows in large cities U.S.; represented in collections in 10 states, Burr collection D. Brooks Gallery, N.Y.C. Recipient awards in nat. exhibits. Mem. Copley Soc., Painters and Sculptors N.J., Nat. Assn. Women Artists Equity, Burr Gallery, Woodstock Art Assn. Episcopalian. Address: RFD Barnstead NH 03218

JACKSON, NELL CECELIA, educator; b. Athens, Ga.; d. Burnett L. and Wilhelmina (Neal) Jackson; B.S., Tuskegee Inst., 1951; student Wellesley Coll., 1952; M.S., Springfield Coll., 1953; student U. Oslo, 1955; Ph.D., State U. Ia., 1962. Asst. prof. Tuskegee Inst., Tuskegee Institute, Ala., 1953-60, 62-63; research and teaching asst. U. Ia., Iowa City, 1960-62; asst. prof. Ill. State U. at Normal, 1963-65; asso. prof. U. Ill. at Urbana, 1965-73; prof. asst. athletic dir. Mich. State U., 1973—. Chmn. nat. women's track and field com. Amateur Athletic Union U.S., 1968-71; chmn. U.S. Women's Olympic Track and Field Com., 1969-72; bd. dirs. U.S. Olympic Com., 1969-72; head coach U.S. Women's Olympic Track and Field Team. Mem. Am. Acad. Sports Medicine, A.A.H.P.E.R., Altrusa Internat., Delta Kappa Gamma. Author: Track and Field for Girls and Women, 1968. Home: 3546 W Hiawatha Dr Okemos MI 48864 Office: Jenison Gym Mich State U East Lansing MI 48824

JACKSON, PATRICIA LEE (MRS. CLIFFORD L. JACKSON), psychologist; b. N.Y.C., May 6, 1916; d. Albert George and Lisbeth P. (Lee) Scharf; B.A., Barnard Coll., 1938; M.A., Tchrs. Coll. Columbia, 1939, Ph.D., 1950; m. Clifford L. Jackson, Feb. 14, 1942. Dir. psychol. testing R. H. Macy & Co., Inc., 1941-49; employment dir. Alexander's Dept. Stores, Inc., Bronx, N.Y., 1949-52; asst. prof. psychology Hunter Coll., N.Y.C., 1951-66, asso. prof., 1966—; coordinator of counseling services, 1959—; research dir. Klein Inst. for Aptitude Testing, Inc., N.Y.C., 1953-59, asst. v.p., 1957-59; also pvt. practice in psycho-therapy. Mem. A.A.A.S., Am. Personnel and Guidance Assn., Am. Psychol. Assn., Am. Statis. Assn., Am. Group Psychotherapy Assn., Psychometric Soc. Author articles in field. Home: 129 E 35th St New York City NY 10016

JACKSON, PAULINE MCDONALD, psychiatrist; b. Santa Barbara, Cal., Sept. 16, 1936; d. John Stanley and Erma Kathleen (Young) McDonald; B.A., Stanford, 1957, M.D., 1961; m. William Francis Jackson, Jan. 2, 1965. Intern, Charles T. Miller Hosp., St. Paul, 1961-62; resident Cleve. Psychiat. Inst., 1962-65; sr. psychiatrist Napa State Hosp., Imola, Cal., 1965-68; dir. consultation and edn. Fallsview Mental Health Center, Cuyahoga Falls, O., 1968-69, supt., 1969-72. Psychiat. cons. VA Hosp., Brecksville, O., 1970-72. Diplomate Am. Bd. Psychiatry and Neurology. Mem. Am., Wis. psychiat. assns., Am. Med. Women's Assn., Wis. Med. Assn., La Crosse County Med. Soc., Guild Cath. Psychiatrists, Sierra Club. Home: 2520 Sherwood Dr La Crosse WI 54601 Office: Gundersen Clinic La Crosse WI 54601

JACKSON, PHYLLIS CATHERINE FOREMAN (MRS. HAROLD B. JACKSON), educator; b. San Francisco, Apr. 24, 1918; d. Joseph A. and Elizabeth (Brown) Foreman; B.A., U. Cal. at Berkeley, 1939, M.A., 1940; postgrad. Nat. U. Mex., summer 1961, U. So. Cal., 1964-65; m. Thomas W. Nelson, May 16, 1942; children—Judith Elizabeth, Thomas Joseph; m. 2d, Harold B. Jackson, Oct. 21, 1971. Tchr., Berkeley Evening Schs., 1941-42, Pasadena (Cal.) City Schs., 1950-63; asst. prof. Spanish, Portuguese, Pasadena City Coll., 1963-70, asso. prof., 1970—, chmn. fgn. lang. dept., 1968-73, chmn. ethnic studies program, 1969-72, dean student activities, 1973—. Mem. Am. Assn. Tchrs. Spanish and Portuguese, Modern and Classical Lang. Assn. So. Cal., Faculty Assn. Cal. Community Colls., Cal. Assn. for Afro-Am. Edn., Black Faculty Assn. So. Cal., UN Assn. U.S.A. (chpt. exec. bd. 1962-69), Nat. Assn. Negro Bus. and Profl. Women's Clubs, Am. Assn. U. Profs., Delta Kappa Gamma, Pi Delta Phi, Phi Beta Kappa. Methodist. Home: 191 Sequoia Dr Pasadena CA 91105

JACKSON, PRISCILLA THOMSON (MRS. WALTER N. JACKSON), educator, adminstr.; b. Canton, China; d. Joseph Oscar and Ethel (Ramsey) Thomson; student Oberlin Coll., 1939-42; postgrad. U. Chgo., 1942; M.A., Mich. State U., 1971; m. Walter N. Jackson, June 17, 1942; children—Jennifer Agnes, Lillian Avis, Nathan Oscar. With Continuing Edn. div. Oakland U., Rochester, Mich., 1960-72, inst. co-ordinator, 1961-62, instr. creative writing, asst. dir. confs., 1962, dir. confs., 1963-68, asst. dir. Mott Center Community Affairs, 1964-66, founder and dir. Continuum Center for Women, 1965-69, asst. dean for developmental programs, 1969-72; program dir., div. mgmt. edn. Grad. Sch. Bus. Adminstrn., U. Mich., 1972-73, lectr., 1973; cons. programming for spl. projects Univ. Center for Adult Edn., U. Mich.-Wayne U., Detroit, 1973—; cons. Women-in-Mgmt., 1974—. Commr., Oakland County Bd. Social Welfare, 1961-64. Mem. Adult Edn. Assn.-U.S.A. (chmn. sect. on continuing edn. of women 1969-71, sec. Mich. br. 1972-73), Nat. U. Extension Assn. (bd. confs. inst. sect. 1964-68, resolutions com. 1972, chmn. resolutions com. 1973), Assn. Asian Studies, Interprofl. Assn. Marriage, Divorce and Family, League Women Voters (v.p. Birmingham, Mich. br. 1959-60), Am. Assn. U. Women, Detroit Women Writers (past prose workshop chmn., founder Oakland writers conf.), Mich. Partners of Alliance with Brit. Honduras and Dominican Republic (chmn. women's com. 1967-70, exec. bd. 1970-72). Conglist. Clubs: Women's Economic (Detroit); Village Woman's (Bloomfield Hills, Mich.). Contbr. articles profl. publs. Author: The Continuum Center, 1973. Contbg. editor Women Today (formerly Washington Newsletter on Women), 1968-71. Home: 927 Madison St Birmingham MI 48008 also North Chittenden Pittsford PO VT 05763

JACKSON, REBA JUNE (MRS. DAVID LEE JACKSON), librarian; b. Hazard, Ky., Jan. 15, 1935; d. Remine and Edna Mae (Feltner) Combs; B.S. Cumberland Coll., 1962; postgrad. Eastern Ky. U., 1966-67; m. David Lee Jackson, Mar. 14, 1957; children—Jimmy Lee, Lissa Lou, Becky Faye, Mickey Joe. Tchr. elementary schs. Perry County, Ky., 1957-67, librarian, 1967-73. Mem. Democratic Com., Hazard, 1968-70. Mem. Nat., Ky. Edn. assns., Ky., Ky. Sch. library assns. Baptist (youth leader 1969—). Home: 436-4688 Route 2 Box 96 Hazard KY 41701 Office: 436-5632 Avawam KY 41713

JACKSON, ROSEMARY KEATING (MRS. WILLIAM SPENCER JACKSON), newspaper editor; b. Nanticoke, Pa., Jan. 12, 1937; d. James Joseph and Mildred Louise (Woodeshick) Keating; B.S., Pa. State U., 1958; m. William Spencer Jackson, Sept. 3, 1960; children—William Kitson, Tracy Keating. Chief check stewardess Overseas Nat. Airways, N.Y.C., 1958-59; with pub. relations Borden Co., N.Y.C., 1959-60; publicist Corning (N.Y.) Glass Works, 1963-64; free lance cons., 1964-68; asso. editor, advt. mgr. Weekly The Sun, Hummelstown, Pa., 1970—. Cons. Wee Explorer Early Childhood Center, Hershey, Pa., 1973—. Mem. Women in Communications, Sigma Delta Chi. Home: 108 W Bradley Av Hummelstown PA 17036 Office: 115-117 S Water St Hummelstown PA 17036

JACKSON, RUBY G., physician; b. Three Rivers, Mass., Mar. 9, 1916; d. David and Ida (Anglin) Jackson; B.A., Mount Holyoke Coll., 1937; M.D., McGill U., Montreal, Can., 1950. Intern surgery Albany (N.Y.) Hosp., 1950-51; resident Free Hosp. for Women and Boston Lying-in Hosp., 1951-54; practice medicine, specializing in obstetrics and gynecology, Boston; obstetrician-gynecologist Boston Hosp. for Women; instr. Harvard Med. Sch. Fellow Am. Coll. Obstetricians and Gynecologists; mem. A.M.A., Mass. Med. Soc., Assn. Am. Physicians and Surgeons, Boston Obstet. Soc. Home: 55 Wareland Rd Wellesley Hills MA 02181 Office: 30 Colpitts Rd Weston MA 02193

JACKSON, RUTH BERTHA LAVENDER (MRS. HOWARD JAMES JACKSON), civic worker; b. Seney, Mich., Oct. 19, 1914; d. Edward John and Bertha (Knuth) Lavender; A.B., U. Mich., 1937, postgrad., 1958-63; postgrad. U. Ga., Va. Poly. Inst.; m. Howard James Jackson, June 29, 1939; 1 son, James Howard. Tchr., Newberry (Mich.) High Sch., 1937-39, Rutland (O.) High Sch., 1942-43; exec. sec. Valley Day Sch., Charleston, W. Va., 1950-52; tchr. courses landscape design W. Va. State Coll., 1967—. Sec., Kanawha County Planning and Zoning Commn., 1959-70; pres. League Women Voters W. Va., 1963-70; mem. Gov.'s Commn. on Status Women, 1963-70; Nat. Com. for Support Pub. Schs., 1963-70, Citizens Air Pollution Control Council, 1965-70; chmn. Vol. Service Bur., 1965-66; mem. Gov.'s Task Force on Surface Mining, 1966, Citizens Adv. Commn. W. Va. Legislature, 1967-70; State Adv. Com. on Mental Health, 1966-70; co-chmn. State Citizens for Constl. Conv., 1967-70; adv. mem. Charleston Municipal Planning Commn., 1967-70; mem. recreation planning com. Action for Appalachian Youth-Community Devel., 1967; mem. womans com. Charleston Symphony Orch.; mem. W. Va. Planning Assn. Bd. dirs. Sunrise Found., Community Council Kanawha Valley; trustee United Fund Kanawha Valley; incorporator W. Va. Cleanup, Inc. Recipient citation for Lane-Bryant Community Achievement Awards, 1967; named Top Clubwoman of Year Charleston Gazette-Mail, 1961. Mem. U.S. Figure Skating Assn. (chmn. program devel.), Charleston Rose Soc., Nat. Council State Garden Clubs, Greensboro Beautiful, Inc., Phi Beta Kappa, Phi Kappa Phi, Pi Lambda Theta. Clubs: Greensboro Figure Skating, Greensboro Garden (dir., vice chmn. judges council); Essex Skating (N.J.). Contbr. articles to profl. publs. Home: 701 Leawood Dr Greensboro NC 27410

JACKSON, TOMI LEE STEPHENS, broadcasting co. exec.; b. Dallas, Nov. 28, 1923; d. Thomas and Ida (Alexander) Stephens; student Wayne State U., 1945, Highland Park Jr. Coll., 1950; children—JoAnne, Linda Marlane (Mrs. Dave Craft). Writer, producer, talent documentary WJBK-TV-2, Detroit, 1962-64; disc-jockey WPON-AM, Pontiac, Mich., 1952-56, WCHD-FM, Detroit, 1956—; women's dir. WCHD-FM, WCHB-AM, Detroit, 1956—; pres., Tomi Jackson & Assos., 1972—. Bd. dirs. United Found.; bd. dirs., chmn. pub. relations com. Metropolitan YWCA; mem. speakers bur. Detroit United Found. Mem. Am. Women in Radio and Television (nat. v.p. 1967-70), Women in Communication, Detroit Press Club, Media Women, Women's Advt. Club Detroit (bd. mem. 1968-72). Home: 17300 Pontchartrain Dr Detroit MI 48203 Office: 2994 E Grand Blvd Detroit MI 48202

JACKSON, VIOLET AGATHA BURDEN (MRS. LEWIS ALBERT JACKSON), educator; b. Marion, Ind., Nov. 27, 1917; d. Harley Fremont and Carrie Adeline (Jones) Burden; B.S. in Edn. summa cum laude, Central State U., 1958; M.A., Ohio State U., 1960, Ph.D., 1962; m. Lewis Albert Jackson, Sept. 17, 1938; children—Joyce Harlene (Mrs. Joe E. Turner), Robert Lewis. Tchr. fourth grade O. Soldier's and Sailors' Orphans' Home, Xenia, 1958-59; supervising tchr. Cook Lab. Sch., Central State U., Wilberforce, O., 1961-62, instr. elementary edn., 1962-66, asst. prof. elementary edn., 1966-67, dir. student teaching, 1967-68, asst. prof. elementary edn., 1968-70, chmn. dept. elementary edn., 1970—, asso. prof., 1970-72, prof., 1972—. Cons. elementary sch. math. Clinton County, O., 1965; instr. In-Service Inst. Math., NSF, 1965-67. Mem. Am. Assn. U. Women (br. v.p. 1964-66), Assn. Tchr. Educators (unit sec.-treas. 1964-65), O. Assn. Higher Edn. (sec.-treas. 1970-71; mem. exec. com. 1968-72), Am. Edn. Research Assn., Internat. Reading Assn., Nat. Council Tchrs. Math., O. Edn. Assn., League Women Voters, Pi Lambda Theta, Alpha Kappa Alpha. Home: 733 Silvers Dr Xenia OH 45385 Office: Box 532 Central State U Wilberforce OH 45384

JACOB, CAROL G., physician; b. Hamburg, Germany, Mar. 27, 1921; d. Leo and Claire (Lewisohn) Jacob; R.N., Johns Hopkins Hosp. Sch. Nursing, 1946; B.S., Johns Hopkins, 1950; M.A., U. Chgo., 1951; postgrad. Roosevelt U., 1955-57; M.D. cum laude Woman's Med. Coll. Pa., 1961. Came to U.S., 1940, naturalized, 1945. Head nurse surg. pediatrics Johns Hopkins Hosp., Balt., 1946-48; head nurse med. pediatrics State U. Ia. Clinics, Iowa City, 1948-50, U. Chgo. Clinics, 1951-53; head nurse psychiat. nursing Psychosomatic and Psychiat. Inst. Research and Tng., Michael Reese Hosp., Chgo., 1953-55; supr. psychiat. nursing St. Luke's Hosp., Chgo., 1955-57; rotating intern Montefiore Hosp., Pitts., 1961-62; resident teaching fellow psychiatry U. Pitts. Sch. Medicine and Western Psychiat. Inst. and Clinic, Pitts., 1962-63; staff psychiatrist VA Hosp., Pitts., 1963-64; resident psychiatry Sheppard and Enoch Pratt Hosp., Towson, Md., 1964-65, St. Elizabeth's Hosp., Washington, 1965-67; practice of medicine specializing in psychiatry, Washington, 1967—; candidate Washington Psychoanalytic Inst., 1968—. Cons. pyschiatrist Group Health Assn., Washington, 1968-73. Mem. A.M.A., Am. Psychiat. Assn., Am. Psychoanalytic Assn., Washington Psychiat. Soc., Med. Soc. D.C., Mortar Bd., Alpha Omega Alpha. Jewish religion. Address: 309 N St SW Washington DC 20024

JACOBS, BARBARA BEAMAN, immunologist; b. Cambridge, Mass., July 23, 1929; d. Isadore Richard and Rae Edna (Rodman) Beaman; B.S., Mich. State U., 1950, M.S., 1952; Ph.D., Ind. U., 1956; children—Kenneth A., Michael L. Research asst. Ind. U., Bloomington, 1952-55; Am. Cancer Soc. fellow U. Colo. Sch. Medicine, 1956-58; Nat. Cancer Inst. fellow Dept. anatomy Downstate Med. Center, State U. N.Y. at Bklyn., 1958-59; sr. research scientist Roswell Park Meml. Inst., Buffalo, 1959-63; lecture cons., dept. biology State U. N.Y., Buffalo, 1963; asso. research scientist Am. Med. Center at Denver, 1963-69, dir. immunology, 1969—. Dem. precinct committeewoman Arapahoe County, 1970-72; charter mem. Colo. Dem. Women's Caucus, 1971—. Recipient Ruth Estrin Goldberg meml. grant, 1968, 69, 73; Nat. Cancer Inst. grant, 1971—. Mem. Am. Assn. Cancer Research, Transplantation Soc., Soc. Exptl. Biology and Medicine, Am. Assn. Immunologists, Tissue Culture Assn., Common Cause, Am. Civil Liberties Union. Contbr. articles to profl. jours. Home: 2433 S Dahlia Lane Denver CO 80222 Office: Am Med Center 6401 W Colfax Av Denver CO 80214

JACOBS, DIANA MARY, pub. relations exec.; b. N.Y.C., July 21, 1937; d. Edmund James and Ann Elizabeth (Shields) Jacobs; B.A., Coll. William and Mary, 1959; postgrad., Hunter Coll., 1961. Publicity mgr. Kendall Co., N.Y.C., 1959-61; asst. pub. relations dir. Consol. Products, N.Y.C., 1961-65; mgr. consumer information Monsanto Co., N.Y.C., 1965-70; pub. relations dir. Jr. Achievement, N.Y.C., 1970—. Mem. Women Execs. in Pub. Relations (dir. 1973-74), Am. Women in Radio and Television (dir. 1970), Nat. Pub. Relations Soc. Am., Nat. Pub. Relations Council. Home: 179 E 79th St New York City NY 10021 Office: 909 3d Av New York City NY 10022

JACOBS, ELEANOR ALICE, clin. psychologist; b. Royal Oak, Mich., Dec. 25, 1923; d. Roy Dana and Alice Ann (Keaton) Jacobs; B.A., U. Buffalo, 1949, M.A., 1952, Ph.D., 1955. Clin. psychologist VA Hosp., Buffalo, 1954—, equal employment opportunity counselor, 1962—, clin. psychologist research sect. psychology service, 1967—; clin. prof. State U. N.Y. at Buffalo, 1950—. Speaker on psychology to community orgns., clubs, 1952—. Mem. adult devel. and aging com. NICHD, Dept. Health, Edn. and Welfare. Recipient Outstanding Superior Performance award Buffalo VA Hosp., 1958, Spl. Recognition award State U. N.Y. at Buffalo, 1971. Mem. Am., Eastern, N.Y. State psychol. assns., Am. Group Psychotherapy Assn., Am. Soc. Group Psychotherapy and Psychodrama, Nat., Western N.Y. leagues nursing, Psychol. Assn., Western N.Y., Group Psychotherapy Assn. Western N.Y. Research and publs. on hyperbaric medicine, hyperoxygenation effect on cognitive functions in aged. Home: Pleasant Av Ridgeway ON Canada Office: VA Hosp 3495 Bailey Av Buffalo NY 14215

JACOBS, FLORA GILL (MRS. EPHRAIM JACOBS), author; b. Washington, Dec. 22, 1918; d. Morris Hilliard and Dora (Seidenman) Gill; George Washington U., 1936-40; m. Ephraim Jacobs, Sept. 8, 1940; 1 dau., Amanda Bolling. Asst. women's editor Washington Times-Herald, 1940-42, women's page and fashion editor, 1942-43; reporter women's dept. Washington Post, 1950-52; lectr. at various instns., orgns. Mem. Mystery Writers Am., Author's Guild, Children's Book Guild Washington (past pres.). Clubs: Washington Press; American Newspaper-Women's (Washington). Author: A History of Dolls' Houses, 1953, rev. edit., 1965; A Book of Dolls and Doll Houses (with Estrid Faurholt), 1967; The Doll House Mystery, 1958; The Toy Shop Mystery, 1960; The Haunted Birdhouse, 1970; A World of Doll Houses, 1965; Dolls' Houses in America, 1974. Address: 16 W Kirke St Chevy Chase MD 20015

JACOBS, LINDA JOAN (MRS. MARTIN HOWARD JACOBS), educator; b. Balt., Mar. 25, 1941; d. Bernard and Freda (Statter) White; B.A., U. Md., 1962, M.A., 1965, Ed.D., 1971; m. Martin Howard Jacobs, Aug. 3, 1963; Tchr., Baltimore County Pub. Schs., 1962-64; research teaching asst. U. Md., Balt., 1964-65, demonstration tchr., 1965, research asso., 1965-67, instr. spl. edn., 1968-71, asst. prof. 1971—. coordinator undergrad programs in spl. edn., 1971-73. Pres. Innovative Learning, Inc., Balt., 1972—; sec. Compar Chesapeake Electronics Representation, Pikesville, 1962—; coordinator spl. edn. pub. schs. Anne Arundel County Md., 1974—; ednl. cons. pub. sch. St. Clairsville, O., Cin., Bowling Green, O., Panama City, Fla., St. Mary's, Prince George's, Charles, Calvert, Balt., Baltimore County, Howard County, Harford County, Anne Arundel County, Kent County, Md., Md. Dept. Edn. Bd. dirs. Council for Exceptional Children, Baltimore County Gen. Hosp. Recipient Excellence in Teaching nomination Spl. Edn. Dept. U. Md., 1970. Mem. Council for Exceptional Children (state student coordinator 1966-73, v.p. Md. fedn. chpts. 1969-70, pres. Md. fedn. 1970-72, Md. rep. to Nat. Bd. Govs. 1973—, Md. del. to internat. conv. 1966, 69, 70, 71, 72, 74, chmn. nat. com. study exec. functions, 1972—). Author: Instructional TV Series for Md. Pub. TV, 1973. Columnist learning problems Northwest Star Newspaper. Research in cognitive model for diagnosing learning characteristics. Home: 8808 Sonya Rd Randallstown MD 21133 Office: 7501 Liberty Rd Baltimore MD 21207

JACOBS, LOUISE AMELIA DOHERTY, court adminstr.; b. Pitts., Mar. 5, 1931; d. Charles Vincent and Emma Elizabeth (Lager) Doherty; A.B. magna cum laude, Seton Hill Coll., 1952; J.D. (Centennial scholar), Seton Hall U., 1969; children—Robert, Alice, Jr. mgmt. asst. U.S. Civil Service Commn., Washington, 1952-54; news reporter, feature writer Somerset Messenger Gazette, Somerville, N.J., 1961-66; admitted to N.J. bar, 1969; judicial law clk. to Hon. Victor A. Rizzolo, Somerset County, N.J., 1969-70; mem. firm Ozzard, Rizzolo, Klein, Mauro and Savo, Somerville, 1970-71; sr. staff att. Adminstrv. Office of the Courts, Trenton, N.J., 1971-73; asst. court adminstr., Morristown, N.J., 1973—. Mem. Am., N.J. (mem. state bar com. on specialization in legal profession 1972—), Somerset (mem. county bar legislation com. 1973-74, law day com. 1970-72) bar assns. Roman Catholic. Home: 72 Meadowbrook Dr Somerville NJ 08876 Office: Washington St Morristown NJ 07960

JACOBS, MARIAN BECKMANN, geologist; b. Teaneck, N.J., Dec. 20, 1935; d. Frederick J. and Marguerite J. (Thoma) Beckmann; B.A. cum laude (Grace Potter Rice fellow), Barnard Coll., 1957; M.A. (Columbia scholar, Quincy Ward Boese fellow, James Furman Kemp fellow), Columbia, 1959, Ph.D., 1963; m. Warren R. Jacobs Jr., Sept. 5, 1959 (div. Aug. 1973); children—Laura Diane, Anita Michelle. Research asst. mineralogy dept. Columbia, N.Y.C., 1960-63; research asso. Lamont-Doherty Geol. Obs. of Columbia, Palisades, N.Y., 1963—; asst. prof. oceanography Rampo Coll. of N.J., Mahwah, 1974-75. NSF grantee, 1965-66, 66-67, 69-71, 71-72, 72-73. Mem. Am. Geophsy. Union, Am. A.A.A.S., Mineral. Soc. Am., Geol. Soc. Am., Clay Minerals Soc., N.J. Acad. Sci., Hudson River Environmental Soc., Phi Beta Kappa, Sigma Xi. Contbr. articles to profl. jours. Research X-ray diffractions and fluorescence studies deep-sea sediments and particulate matter in sea water. Home: 7 Robin Rd Mahwah NJ 07430 Office: 204 New Core Lab L-DGO Palisades NY 10964

JACOBS, RITA ANN GOLDMAN (MRS. DAVID JACK JACOBS), physician; b. N.Y.C., Jan. 15, 1927; d. Joseph and Miriam (Feinstein) Goldman; B.A., N.Y. U., 1947; M.D., Woman's Med. Coll. Pa., 1951; m. David Jack Jacobs, Nov. 28, 1952; children—Etta Miriam, Helen Alice. Intern Queens (N.Y.) Gen. Hosp., 1951-52; resident anesthesia Columbia Presbyn. Med. Center, N.Y.C., 1952-54, asst. attending anesthesiologist, 1954-58; clin. asst. dept. anesthesiology service N.Y.C. Meml. Hosp., 1958-59, asst. attending anesthesiologist 1959-63, asso. attending anesthesiologist, 1963-68, attending anesthesiologist, 1968-71; asst. vis. anesthesiologist James Ewing Hosp., N.Y.C., 1958-63, asso. vis. anesthesiologist, 1963-68, attending anesthesiologist James Ewing Pavilion, N.Y.C., 1968-71; cons. anesthesiologist Calvary Hosp.; asst. prof. Cornell Med. Coll., 1968-71; anesthesiologist Berkshire Med. Center, Pittsfield, Mass., 1971—. Recipient First prize sci. exhibit Postgrad. Assembly, N.Y. State Soc. Anesthesiologists, 1960. Diplomate Am. Bd. Anesthesiology. Fellow Am. Coll. Anesthesiology; mem. Am., Mass. socs. anesthesiologists, Mass., Berkshire County med. socs. Home: Goodrich Hollow Stephentown NY 12168 Office: 725 North St Pittsfield MA 01201

JACOBSEN, JOSEPHINE (MRS. ERIC JACOBSEN), author; b. Coburg, Can., Aug. 19, 1908 (parents Am. citizens); d. Joseph Edward and Octavia Bryan (Winder) Boylan; ed. pvt. tutors; D.H.L., Notre Dame of Md., 1974, Goucher Coll., 1974; m. Eric Jacobsen, Mar. 17, 1932; 1 son, Erland Ericsen. Author: (collected poetry) Marble Satyr, and other poems, 1928; Let Each Man Remember (Louise Imogen Clark award), 1940; For the Unlost (selected as 1 of Fifth Books of Yr. Am. Inst. Graphic Arts), 1946; The Human Climate, new poems, 1953; The Animal Inside, 1966; The Shade-Seller: New and Selected Poems, 1974; (criticism) (with William R. Mueller) The Testament of Samuel Beckett, 1964; The Testament of Samuel Beckett: a study, 1966; Ionesco and Genet; Playwrights of Silence, 1968; contbr. poems, short stories, essays to Poetry, New Yorker, N.Y. Times, Nation, New Republic, Saturday Rev., Commonweal, Prairie schooner, others; also book revs. Poetry cons. to Library Congress, Washington, 1971-73, hon. cons. Am. letters, 1973—. Home: 220 Stony Ford Rd Baltimore MD 21210

JACOBSEN, KIM, editor, pub.; b. Escanaba, Mich., Nov. 19, 1933; d. Arthur and Charlotte (Smith) Jacobsen; B.S., Mich. State Normal Coll., 1955. Editor, Hawaii Bus. Mag., 1961-67, publisher, editor, 1967—; v.p. parent co. Hawaii Bus. Pub. Corp. Home: 555 University St Honolulu HI 96808 Office: 825 Keeaumoku St Honolulu HI 96813

JACOBSON, EDNA FLORENCE, chemist; b. Boston; d. Alexander and Rae (Nathanson) Jacobson; student Boston U., 1956-59, 62-63, Boston Coll., 1960-61. Technician, Watertown Arsenal Labs. (Mass.), 1942-62; analytical chemist Army Materials and Mechanics Research Center, Watertown, 1962—. Mem. Am. Chem. Soc., Soc. Applied Spectroscopy, Am. Soc. for Testing and Materials (com. sec., Lundell-Bright Meml. award 1973), Am. Mus. Natural History (asso.), Smithsonian Instn. (charter). Recipient Performance award Dept. Army, 1956, Spl. Acts award, 1966, Outstanding Performance award, 1972. Home: 18 Royal Crest Dr Marlborough MA 01752 Office: Arsenal St Watertown MA 02172

JACOBSON, FLORENCE DORFMAN (MRS. NATHAN JACOBSON), educator; b. Chgo., Mar. 25, 1918; d. Aron and Anna (Schwartzman) Dorfman; B.S., U. Chgo., 1938, S.M., 1940, postgrad., 1940-42; m. Nathan Jacobson, Aug. 25, 1942; children—Michael Sidney, Pauline Ida. Instr. math. U. N.C., Chapel Hill, 1942-43; mem. faculty Albertus Magnus Coll., New Haven, 1955—, asso. prof., 1961-65, prof., 1965—. Cons. Sch. Math. Study Group, 1961-66, In-Service Insts. NSF, 1961-66; mem. exec. bd. Area Cooperative Ednl. Services, New Haven, 1969-72. NSF Sci. Faculty fellow, 1961-62. Mem. Am. Math. Soc., Math. Assn. Am., Nat. Council Tchrs. Math. Home: 2 Prospect Ct Hamden CT 06511 Office: Dept Math Albertus Magnus Coll New Haven CT 06511

JACOBSON, GAIL MORRIS, biochemist, educator; b. Bartlesville, Okla., Feb. 6, 1938; d. William Butler and Georgia (Dunseth) Morris; B.A., Mt. Holyoke Coll., 1960, M.A., 1962; Ph.D., Cornell U., 1966; postdoctoral study Cal. Inst. Tech., 1966-68; m. Ralph A. Jacobson, Aug. 27, 1963; children—David, Leif, Kirsten. Asst. prof. home econs. U. Okla., Norman, 1968-72, asst. prof. Health Sci. Center, 1972—; research asso. biochemistry Okla. Med. Research Found., 1968-73. Mem. Women's Polit. Caucus, 1971—; precinct co-chmn. Democratic party, 1973. Mem. Am. Assn. U. Profs. (chpt. sec.-treas. 1972-73), Sigma Xi. Contbr. articles to profl. jours. Home: 5 Bingham Pl Norman OK 73069 Office: Biochemistry Dept 800 NE 13th St OK 73112

JACOBSON, HELEN CHARLOTTE (MRS. RAYMOND C. JACOBSON), ednl. adminstr.; b. Cartwright, N.D., May 21, 1908; d. Hilmar Mandus and Clara Isabelle (Johnson) Theige; B.S., Minot State Coll., 1958; M.S., No. Ill. U., 1968; postgrad. N.D. State U., 1971—; m. Raymond C. Jacobson, Dec. 27, 1930 (dec. July 1963); 1 son, Gene A. Tchr. pub. schs., Williams County, N.D., 1926-49; dep. supt. county schs., Williams County, Williston, N.D., 1949-51, supt. county schs., 1951—. Counselor, cons. N.D. Dept. Pub. Instrn., 1970—; mem. N.D. Com. Elementary Sch. Guidance, 1968—. Named Outstanding Woman in Ednl. Adminstrn., N.D. Council Adminstrv. Women in Edn., 1961. Mem. Nat. Rural Edn. Assn. (dir. 1962—, reporter 1971—), N.D. Edn. Assn. (pres. 1961), County Supts. Assn. (pres. 1957), Delta Kappa Gamma, Sons of Norway, Kappa Delta Pi, Pi Lambda Theta. Home: PO Box 573 Williston ND 58801 Office: Box 1246 Williston ND 58801

JACOBSON, HELEN G. (MRS. DAVID JACOBSON), civic worker; b. San Antonio, Tex.; d. Jac Elton and Rosetta (Dreyfus) Gugenheim; B.A., Hollins Coll.; m. David Jacobson, Nov. 6, 1938; children—Elizabeth, Dorothy (Mrs. Sam Miller). News, spl. events staff NBC, N.Y.C., 1933-38. First v.p. San Antonio, Bexar County Council Girl Scouts, 1957-63; Tex. State rep. UNICEF, 1964-69. Bd. dirs. U.S. com. UNICEF, chmn. field services com.; bd. dirs. Nat. Fedn. Temple Sisterhoods, Temple Beth-El Sisterhood; bd. dirs. Community Guidance Center, chmn. bd., 1960-63; bd. dirs. Sunshine Cottage Sch. for Deaf Children, chmn. bd., 1952-54; pres. Community Welfare Council; pres. bd. trustees San Antonio Pub. Library, 1957-61; trustee Nat. Council Crime and Delinquency, 1964-70, San Antonio Mus. Assn., 1964-73; bd. dirs. Tex. United Community Services, San Antonio Urban Coalition, Tex. Council Crime and Delinquency; chmn. Mayor's Commn. on Status of Women; del. White House Conf. on Children, 1970; chmn. Foster Grandparent project Bexar County Hosp. Dist. chmn., 1968-69; sec. Nat. Assembly for Social Policy and Devel. Recipient Headliner award for civic work Theta Sigma Phi, San Antonio chpt., 1958; named Vol. Woman of Yr., Express-News, 1959; honoree San Antonio chpt. Nat. Conf. Christians and Jews, 1970. Mem. San Antonio Women's Fedn., Nat. Council Jewish Women, Symphony Soc. (women's com.). Club: Argyle. Home: 207 Beechwood Lane San Antonio TX 78216

JACOBSON, JOAN ELSINGA, educator; b. Hull, Ia., Apr. 26, 1924; d. Fred and Mary (Hoogschagen) Elsinga; B.A., Morningside Coll., 1944; M.A., Syracuse U., 1948, Ph.D., 1958; postgrad. U. Ill. extension, 1958-61, State U. Ia., summer 1962; m. John Jacobson, June 20, 1946 (div. 1951). Grad. instr. Syracuse U., N.Y., 1946-51; speech therapist Brookline (Mass.) pub. schs., 1951-58, Mass. Gen. Hosp., 1951-58; asso. prof. speech pathology Eastern Ill. U., Charleston, 1958-62; prof. speech pathology, head speech pathology and audiology training program St. Cloud State Coll., Minn., 1962-69. Mem. profl. adv. com. Easter Seal Soc., 1964—, Minn. Soc. for Crippled Children and Adults, 1964—; mem. govs. com. on Services for Hearing Impaired, 1964-66. Mem. Minn. Speech and Hearing Assn. (regional chmn. 1966-67), Am., Mpls. speech and hearing assns., Minn. Soc. for Hearing Impaired, Sigma Pi Sigma. Home: 412-1/2 7th Av S St Cloud MN 56301

JACOBSON, LILLIAN ESTHER (MRS. WILLIAM V. TENZEL), radiol. physicist; b. N.Y.C.; d. Lazar Benjamin and Betty (Blumberg) Jacobson; B.A., Cornell U., 1925; M.A., Columbia, 1932; m. William V. Tenzel, Oct. 26, 1933; children—Joan Louise (Mrs. Robert P. Davis), James Henry. Physicist, Crile Clinic, Cleve., 1925-28, physicist to Dr. Gustave Bucky, N.Y.C., 1928-31; radiation physicist Montefiore Hosp., Bronx, N.Y., 1931-55; biophysicist Presbyn Hosp. unit United Hosps. of Newark, 1956-66; radiation physicist L.I.J. Hosp., 1968—; cons. radiol. physicist; tchr. physics, N.Y.C. Mem. A.A.A.S., Am. Assn. Physicists in Medicine, Health Physics Soc. (pres. Greater N.Y. chpt. 1965-66), Radiation Research Soc., Biophys. Soc., Soc. Nuclear Medicine (founding mem., pres. N.Y. chpt. 1959-60), Radium Soc., Radiol. Soc. N. Am., Cornell Women's Club N.Y. (sec. 1934-35), Phi Beta Kappa. Contbr. papers to teach lit. Address: 3964 46th St Long Island City NY 11104

JACOBSON, LOUISE, psychiatrist; b. N.Y.C., Jan. 24, 1927; d. Larry and Jean (Goldstein) Jacobson; A.A., Bklyn. Coll., 1949; student Hunter Coll., part-time 1959-62; M.D., Woman's Med. Coll. Pa., 1966; postgrad. Phila. Psychoanalytic Inst., 1970—. Asst. art, prodn. editor Mus. Natural History, N.Y.C., 1950-54; pres. Louise Photog. Studios, Bklyn., 1946-53; mng. editor Surg. Bus., Inc., N.Y.C., 1954-62; intern Albert Einstein Med. Center, Phila., 1966-67; resident adult psychiatry Phila. Psychiat. Center, 1967-70; fellow child psychiatry Irving Schwartz Inst., Phila., 1970-72; pvt. practice psychiatry, Phila., 1970—; psychiatrist So. Home for Children, Phila., Montgomery County Community Mental Health. N.Y. U. fellow, 1953-54; A.M.A. fellow in med. journalism, 1963; Foreman Fleicher Found. fellow, 1963-66. Mem. Woman's Med. Coll. Alumnae Assn. (pres. chpt. 1970-71, editor nat. Alumnae News 1971-73), Am. Med. Women's Assn. (chpt. pres. 1972-73), Am. Psychiat. Assn., Am. Assn. Adolescent Psychiatry, Regional Council Child Psychiatry. Address: 13A Oak Hill Estates Narberth PA 19072

JACOBSON, MARGARET ESCHBACH (MRS. HERBERT JACOBSON), car rental co. exec.; b. Chgo., Aug. 11, 1944; d. Leon Christian and Kathleen Eileen (Brennan) Eschbach; B.S. in Advt., U. Ill., 1967; m. Herbert Jacobson, Dec. 8, 1973. Asst. to advt. mgr. Velsicol Chem. Co., Chgo., 1968-70; account exec. Gardner, Stein & Frank Inc., Chgo., 1970-74; dir. advt. Budget Rent-A-Car Corp., Chgo., 1974—. Mem. Women's Advt. Club, Profl. Women for Brain Research (treas. 1970-74, dir. 1970-74), Phi Mu. Office: 35 E Wacker Dr Chicago IL 60601

JACOBSON, MARION ELNA LOUISE, nutritionist, educator; b. Sacred Heart, Minn., May 21, 1911; d. Carl A. and Caroline (Nyman) Jacobson; B.A., Gustavus Adolphus Coll., 1932; M.S., U. Minn., 1947; Ph.D., Cornell U., 1954. Sci. tchr. Pub. Schs. Minn., 1932-41; instr. foods Syracuse (N.Y.) U., 1947-48; asst. prof. Carnegie Inst. Tech., Pitts., 1948-52; asso. prof. Purdue U., Lafayette, Ind., 1954-56; prof. Wash. State U., Pullman, 1956—. Mem. ednl. adv. council Nat. Livestock and Meat Bd., 1970—. Served with WAVES, 1943-46. Mem. Inst. Food Technologists, Am. Chem. Soc., Am. Home Econs. Assn., Audubon Soc., Phi Kappa Phi, Omicron Nu, Sigma Xi. Republican. Lutheran. Author: Food Principles, 1966. Contbr. articles to profl. jours. Home: NE 1210 McGee Way Pullman WA 99163

JACOBSON, NANCY ANN, librarian; b. Los Angeles, Feb. 9, 1931; d. Walter James and Bernice Mary (Kaun) Crown; A.B., U. Cal. at Berkeley, 1952; M.S., Simmons Coll., 1970; m. Larry L. Jacobson, Sept. 13, 1952; children—Michael Lloyd, Ann Katherine, Robin Sue. Librarian elementary sch., Andover, Mass., 1966-67, jr. high sch., 1967-71; asst. dir. Meml. Hall Library, Andover, 1971-74, dir., 1974—. Pres., League Women Voters, Bellevue, Wash., 1963-64. Mem. Am., New Eng., Mass. library assns. Author booklet. Home: 183 Woburn St Andover MA 01810 Office: Elm Sq Andover MA 01810

JACOBSON, NITA JEAN GROSSMAN (MRS. IRWIN ROBERT JACOBSON), educator; b. Boston; d. Joseph Arthur and Sadie (Feldberg) Grossman; student Syracuse U., 1948-49; B.S., Boston U., 1952; M.Ed., Northeastern U., 1965; m. Irwin Robert Jacobson, Mar. 20, 1955; children—Lisa Faye, Barry Steven. Tchr., Plympton Sch., Waltham, Mass., 1952-55; dean of women Emerson Coll., Boston, 1965-68; cons., dir. edn. research Spl. Legislative Commn. on Drug Abuse State Mass., Boston, 1968-70; pres. Nat. Ednl. Evaluation Services, Inc., 1971—. Mass. commr. Edn. Commn. of States, 1971-73. Mem. pub. relations com. Mass. Easter Seal Soc., 1972—. Trustee Parker Hill Med. Center, 1961—, rec. sec., 1963-64, asst. sec. bd. trustees 1969—; mem. exec. bd. Womens Scholarship, 1969-70; mem. exec. bd. Friends League Sch. Boston, 1968—. Mem. Nat., Mass. assns. women deans and counselors, N.E.A., Nat. Assn. Adminstrv. Women, Am. Ednl. Research Assn., Am. Assn. U. Women, Am., Mass., Boston personnel and guidance assns., Am. Assn. Higher Edn., Nat. Vocational Guidance Assn., Child Study Assn. Am., Am. Counselor Edn. Suprs., Brookline Mental Health Assn., Brookline Chamber Music Soc., Internat. Child Study Assn., Pi Lambda Theta, Kappa Delta Pi, Phi Kappa Phi. Mem. B'nai B'rith, Hadassah. Home: 152 Beverly Rd Chestnut Hill MA 02167

JACOBSON, ROVENA FURNIVALL (MRS. CALHOUN E. JACOBSON), educator, writer; b. Los Angeles, Oct. 21, 1918; d. Joseph Walter and Florence (Gieson) Furnivall; B.Ed., U. Cal. at Los Angeles, 1940; M.Ed., Loyola U., Los Angeles, 1965; Ed.D., U. So. Cal., 1969; m. Calhoun E. Jacobson, Aug. 6, 1941; children—Denise Rovena (Mrs. Jeremy Ferris), Eric Calhoun. Tchr. Mojave (Cal.) Elem. Sch., 1941-42; adult edn. classes in art and home econ.

Downey, Rivera, and Bellflower, Cal., 1944-52; tchr., counselor Santa Monica City, Cal., 1952—; psychol. cons. film Runaway, Runaway; producer Interchange, KCRW-FM radio sta., Los Angeles. Pres., chmn. bd. dirs. Assn. for Women's Active Return to Edn., 1965—. Mem. Nat. Assn. of Bus. and Profl. Women, Cal. Tchrs. Assn., Nat. Assn. Pub. Sch. Adult Edn., Am. Assn. U. Women (Status of Women award Santa Monica br. 1967), Cal. Coll. Personnel Assn. (sec. 1973-74), Cal. Personnel and Guidance Assn., Am. Women in Radio and TV, Phi Mu, Pi Lambda Theta. Presbyn. Club: Malibu Woman's. Author: (with Denise Ferris) It's Your Baby, Baby. Community coll. editor Open Channels quar. Home: 6804 Zumirez Dr Malibu CA 90265 Office: 1815 Pearl St Santa Monica CA 90403

JACOBSON, SUSAN LYNN, coll. dean; b. Hackensack, N.J., Nov. 30, 1942; d. Allan Churchill and Lucile Jeanne (LeMaitre) Jacobson; B.A., Wells Coll., 1964. Editorial asst. Ladies' Home Jour., N.Y.C., 1965-66, McCall's Mag., N.Y.C., 1966-67; asso. editor fiction Ladies Home Jour., 1967-70; dean students Wells Coll., Aurora, N.Y., 1970—. Mem. Am. Assn. Higher Edn., Nat. Assn. Women's Deans and Counselors, Am. Assn. U. Women. Democrat. Address: Wells College Aurora NY 13026

JACOBSON, SYLVIA ROSALIE, educator; b. N.Y.C., May 9, 1911; d. Albert Edward and Rosalie Henriette (Hartogensis) Jacobson; B.A., Hunter Coll., 1932; M.S., Columbia Sch. Social Work, 1941; postgrad. Smith Coll. Sch. Social Work, 1958. Caseworker, Foster Home Bur., N.Y.C., 1941-43; psychiat. social work Nat. A.R.C., Mil. Welfare Service U.S. Naval Hosps., Newport, R.I., Long Beach, Cal., 1943-46; chief psychiat. social worker Nat. Com. for Mental Hygiene, Can., also lectr. U. Toronto (Ont.), 1946-47; asso. prof. Sch. Social Work U. Louisville, 1947-49, U. B.C., Vancouver, 1950-51; research asso. therapist Clinic of E.W. Haertig, M.D., Seattle, 1951-55; asso. prof. dept. social work, W.Va. U., Morgantown, 1956-60; caseworker-supr. Jewish Family Service, also asso. prof., schs. social work and nursing Ohio State U., Columbus, 1964-66; asso. prof. Sch. of Social Work, Fla. State U., Tallahassee, 1966—. Field instr. Sch. of Social Work, U. So. Cal., Los Angeles, 1945-46; vis. asso. prof., schs. nursing and social work Ohio State U., 1960-61; med. field agt. Selective Service Bd., N.Y.C., 1941-43; cons. Family Service Orgn., Louisville, 1947-49, Nichols Gen. Hosp., Louisville, 1947-49, Shaughnessy Hosp., Vancouver, B.C., Can., 1950-51, Tacoma-Pierce County Health Dept., Tacoma, Wash., 1954, Ohio State Dept. Social Adminstrn., 1961-64. Bd. dirs. Planned Parenthood, Louisville, 1947-49. Nat. Inst. Mental Health grantee, 1947-48, 1956-60. Mem. Nat. Assn. Social Workers, Acad. Certified Social Workers, Internat. Commn. on Social Welfare, Am. Orthopsychiat. Assn., Council on Social Work Edn., Am. Assn. Univ. Profs., Asso. Charities of Leon County, Leon County Mental Health Assn., Sigma Tau Delta. Contbr. articles to profl. jours. Home: 2208 Escambia Dr Tallahassee FL 32306 Office: Florida State Univ School of Social Work Tallahassee FL 32306

JACOBY, KATHE SOLIS-COHEN, mgmt. cons.; b. Phila., July 15, 1926; d. Myer and Rosebud (Teschner) Solis-Cohen; B.A. with honors, Swarthmore Coll., 1946; M.A., U. Pa., 1948; children—David Alexander, Edith Sharon, Alice Louise (Mrs. Peter Scott Egan). Research asst. Moore Sch. Elec. Engring., U. Pa., Phila., 1947-48; with Philco Corp., 1956-64, engring. group supr., 1959-64; sr. research engr. Franklin Inst. Research Labs., Phila., 1964-65, 68; system analyst Elec. and Music Industries, Hayes, Middlesex, Eng., 1966-67; pvt. practice as cons., Ft. Washington, Pa., 1968-69; sr. cons. 1st Pa. Corp., Phila., 1969—. Lectr. computer tech. Grad. Sch. Elec. Engring., Drexel U., 1963-65, 68-69. Mem. Gov.'s Rev. of Govt. Mgmt., 1972; sec. Citizens Council Whitemarsh Twp., 1973—. Mem. I.E.E.E., Assn. Computing Machinery, Sigma Xi (asso.). Home: 7032 Lafayette Av Fort Washington PA 19034

JACOBY, PATRICIA JOHNSEN (MRS. ALFRED W. JACOBY), hosp. adminstr.; b. Pitts., Jan. 13, 1927; d. Rutherford Thompson and Orpha Marion (Emory) Johnstone; A.A., U. Cal. at Berkeley, 1946; B.J., U. Mo., 1948, M.A., 1949; m. Harold S. Johnsen, Mar. 13, 1950 (dec. Mar. 1963); children—Rutherford Scott, Julie Paige; m. Alfred W. JaCoby, Dec. 29, 1970. Reporter, U.P.I., Dallas, 1950-54; reporter Stockton Record, Stockton, Cal., 1954-60; editor, pub. Del Mar Surfcomber, Del Mar, Cal., 1960-63, staff writer San Diego Union, 1963-69; pub. information officer U. Cal. at San Diego, 1969—, dir. communications U. Cal. Hosp. at San Diego, 1969—. Mem. Planning Commn., Del Mar, 1969-72, Design Rev. Bd., Del Mar, 1972—. Bd. dirs. Aux. U. Hosp., San Diego, 1970—. Mem. Women in Communications (dir. 1968—), N. San Diego County Press Club (dir. 1969—), Am. Field Service, Assn. Am. Med. Coll., Alpha Phi. Home: PO Box 893 Del Mar CA 92014 Office: 225 W Dickinson St San Diego CA 92103

JACOX, MARILYN ESTHER, phys. chemist; b. Utica, N.Y., Apr. 26, 1929; d. Grant Burlingame and Mary Elizabeth (Dunn) Jacox; B.A. in Chemistry, Syracuse U., 1951; Ph.D. in Phys. Chemistry, Cornell U., 1956. Postdoctoral research asso. U. N.C., Chapel Hill, 1956-58; fellow in fundamental research Mellon Inst., Pitts., 1958-62; phys. chemist Nat. Bur. Standards, Washington, 1962—. Recipient, Outstanding Alumnus award Utica Coll. of Syracuse U., 1963, Washington Acad. of Sci. award in Phys. Scis., 1968; Gold Medal award for Distinguished Service, U.S. Dept. Commerce, 1970; Fed. Woman's award, 1973; Samuel Wesley Stratton award Nat. Bur. Standards, 1973. Mem. Am. Chem. Soc., Am. Phys. Soc., A.A.A.S., Washington Acad. Scis., Sigma Xi. Research on prodn. and molecular spectroscopy of reaction intermediates trapped in low-temperature solids. Home: 10203 Kindly Ct Gaithersburg MD 20760 Office: National Bureau of Standards Washington DC 20234

JACQUES, HELEN PATRICIA HARDY (MRS. RAOUL ADRIEN JACQUES), advt. agy. exec.; b. N.Y.C., Dec. 8, 1933; d. Thomas Edward and Helen (Chmela) Hardy; B.A., Swarthmore Coll., 1956; m. Raoul Adrien Jacques, June 27, 1970; stepchildren—Peter J., Ann (Mrs. Eric Lohmeyer), Timothy J. Asst. account exec. Chirurg & Cairns, Inc., N.Y.C., 1957-62; account exec. Kallir, Philips, Ross Inc., N.Y.C., 1963—. Mem. Pharm. Advt. Club, Early Am. Soc., Nat. Wildlife Assn. Republican. Unitarian. Home: 75 Sheridan Av Hohokus NJ 07423 Office: 919 3d Av New York City NY 10022

JAEGER, RITA C. (MRS. HANS G. HOTTENROTT), physician; b. Bklyn., Nov. 22, 1932; d. Henry W. and Helen V. (Staab) Jaeger; A.B., Vassar Coll., 1954; M.D., State U. N.Y., 1959; m. Hans G. Hottenrott, Apr. 28, 1962; children—Peter A., Carol A., Catherine E., Susan I. Intern St. Luke's Hosp., N.Y.C., 1959-60, resident, 1960-62; resident Babies Hosp., N.Y.C., 1961; practice medicine specializing in pediatrics, Poughkeepsie, N.Y., 1962—; mem. staff Vassar Bros. Hosp.; staff physician Dutchess County Health Dept., Poughkeepsie, 1962—; acting dep. health commr. Dutchess County, 1974—. Bd. dirs. Dutchess County chpt. Heart Assn., 1967—. Mem. Am. Acad. Pediatrics, Nat. Fedn. Catholic Physicians' Guilds, Phi Beta Kappa, Alpha Omega Alpha. Roman Catholic. Home: 7 Smoke Rise Lane Wappingers Falls NY 12590 Office: 22 Market St Poughkeepsie NY 12601

JAEGER, ROBERTA ALICE, psychiatrist; b. N.Y.C., Aug. 12, 1941; d. Benjamin and Minna (Kovadlo) Kinstler; A.B. magna cum laude, Barnard Coll., 1963; M.D., Columbia Coll. Phys. and Surgs., 1966; children—Adam James, Caroline Ann. Intern, Greenwich (Conn. Hosp., 1966-67; resident Columbia Presbyn. Hosp. and N.Y. State Psychiat. Inst., 1967-70, attending psychiatrist, 1971—; Psychoanalytic Clinic for Tng. and Research Columbia U., N.Y.C., 1971—; pvt. practice psychiatry, N.Y.C., 1970—; staff psychiatrist Beth Israel Hosp., N.Y.C., 1970-71; St. Luke's Hosp., 1971-72. Cons. Stuyvesant High Sch., N.Y.C., 1970-71. Mem. Am. Psychiat. Assn., Am. Psychoanalytic Assn., Assn. for Psychoanalytic Medicine, Phi Beta Kappa. Office: 829 Park Av New York City NY 10021

JAFFE, ESTHER COHEN (MRS. JULIUS C. JAFFE), nurse, counselor; b. Chgo., Dec. 1, 1913; d. Solomon and Fannie (Sapera) Cohen; diploma Cook County Sch. Nursing, 1939; B.S., Loyola U. (Chgo.), 1962; m. Julius C. Jaffe, Sept. 28, 1944; children—Edward A., Judith (Mrs. Ronald Freed). Pvt. duty nursing, Chgo., 1940-43; occupational health nurse Grand Sheet Metal Works, Melrose Park, Ill., 1943-45; counselor Dept. of Labor, Ill. State Employment Service, Chgo., 1967-71; ind. med. and patient care product market researcher, 1972—; Instr. first aid A.R.C., 1941-42, blood chmn., 1952-53. Bd. dirs. Cook County Sch. Nursing, 1962-67; bd. dirs. nat. women's com. Greater Chgo. chpt. Brandeis U., 1972—. Recipient Sealantic scholarship, 1960-61. Mem. Am. Nurses Assn., Nat. League Nursing, Am. Personnel and Guidance Assn., Nat. Employment Counselors Assn., Chgo. Guidance and Personnel Assn., Cook County Sch. Nursing Alumnae Assn. (bd. dirs. 1959-60, pres. 1960-62), Loyola U. Sch. Nursing Alumnae Assn. (treas. 1960). Home: 175 E Delaware Pl Chicago IL 60611

JAFFE, IRMA BLUMENTHAL (MRS. SAMUEL B. JAFFE), art historian, educator; b. New Orleans; d. Harry and Estelle (Blumenthal) Levy; m. Samuel B. Jaffe, June 12, 1941; 1 dau., Yvonne Schwartz. Research curator Whitney Mus. Am. Art, N.Y.C., 1963-65; prof. art history Fordham U., Bronx, N.Y., 1966—, chmn. Fine Arts dept., 1966—. Nat. Endowment for Humanities fellow, 1973-74; Am. Council of Learned Socs. grantee, 1968; Kress Found. grantee, 1972. Mem. Coll. Art Assn., Am. Studies Assn., Am. Assn. U. Profs., Phi Beta Kappa. Author: Joseph Stella. Editor: Baroque Art: The Jesuit Contribution. Contbr. to The Genius of American Painting; also articles on art history to scholarly publs. Home: 880 5th Av New York City NY 10021 Office: Fine Arts Dept Fordham Univ Bronx NY 10458

JAGIELLO, GEORGIANA MARY (MRS. ROBERT JAMES FAIRALL), physician, educator; b. Boston, Aug. 2, 1927; d. George Harold and Maryanna Helen (Mazur) Jagiello; A.B. (New Eng. scholar), Boston U., 1949; M.D. (Mass. Soc. U. Edn. Women scholar), Tufts U., 1955; m. Robert James Fairall, Aug. 13, 1957. Intern U. Ill. Hosps., Chgo., 1955-56; resident New Eng. Center Hosp., Boston, 1956-57, research fellow endocrinology, 1958-60; Stimson fellow biology Scripps Clinic, LaJolla, Cal., 1957-58; research fellow cytogenetics Guy's Hosp., London, Eng., 1960-61; attending physician U. Ill. Hosps., 1961-66; asst. prof. medicine U. Ill. Research and Edn. Hosp., Chgo., 1961-66, asso. prof., 1966; asso. Inst. for Advanced Studies, U. Ill. at Urbana, 1964-65; sr. lectr. cytogenetics Guy's Hosp., London, 1966-69; prof. pediatric research U. Ill. at Chgo., 1969-70; prof. human genetics and devel. Columbia, N.Y.C., 1970—, also prof. obstetrics and gynecology, 1970—. Rep. NIH Biology study sect., 1972-74, chmn., 1974-76. Mem. Soc. for Cell Biology, Environmental Mutagen Soc., Genetical Soc. of Gt. Britain, Teratology Soc. Am., Royal Soc. Medicine, Endocrinology Soc., Soc. for Study of Reprodn., Am. Fedn. Clin. Research. Home: 317 Old Sleepy Hollow Rd Pleasantville NY 10570 Office: 630 W 168 St New York City NY 10032

JAGNOW, NANETTE JENSEN (MRS. GEORGE T. JAGNOW), physician; b. Grand Rapids, Mich., Dec. 11, 1925; d. Raymond L.R. and Genevieve (Bannen) Jensen; B.A., U. Mich., 1951; M.D., Wayne State U., 1960; m. George T. Jagnow, Apr. 21, 1951; children—Pamela Dean, Lynn Bannen. Nurse U. Mich. Hosp., Ann Arbor, 1948-49, St. Joseph Hosp., Pontiac, Mich., 1948, William Beaumont Hosp., Royal Oak, Mich., 1955-56; intern, Wm. Beaumont Hosp., 1960-61; resident Henry Ford Hosp., Detroit, 1961-63; practice medicine specializing in pediatrics, Birmingham, Mich., 1964—; mem. staff William Beaumont Hosp. Mem. A.M.A., Mich. State, Oakland County med. assns., Henry Ford Hosp. Sch. Nursing Alumni Assn., Wayne State U. Med. Coll. Alumni Assn. Club: Altrusa. Home: 4480 Tarry Lane Bloomfield Hills MI 48013 Office: 525 Southfield Rd Birmingham MI 48009

JAHIEL, DEBORAH BERG (MRS. RENE JAHIEL), virologist; b. Bklyn., Feb. 28, 1929; d. Abraham and Martha (Dubinsky) Berg; B.A. Hunter Coll., 1949; postgrad. Columbia, 1952-56; m. Rene Jahiel, May 8, 1955; children—Abigail Ruth, Richard Moses, Beth Lillian. Virologist, Walter Reed Inst. Research, Washington, 1956-57, U. Colo. Sch. Medicine, Denver, 1957-59; asst. investigator tissue culture research dept. pathology Mt. Sinai Hosp., N.Y.C., 1959-61. Contbr. articles on immunology of Dextran, tissue culture to profl. jours. Home: 100 Bleecker St Apt 22D New York City NY 10012

JAHNSON, SHIRLEY MANOR JENSEN (MRS. JOHN CHARLES NACOS), psychologist; b. Mankato, Minn., Sept. 28, 1923; d. Arthur Dewey and I. Nina (Manor) Jensen; B.A., U. Minn., 1949, M.A., 1953, Ph.D., 1955; m. John Charles Nacos, Aug. 16, 1963; 1 son, Edward Stewart. Instr. U. Minn. Med. Sch., 1953-56, Devereux Schs., Santa Barbara, Cal., 1956-62; psychologist mental retardation tng. project U. Cal. Med. Sch., San Francisco, 1962-63, dir. tng. in clin. psychology, asst. prof. med. psychology Langley Porter Neuro-psychiat. Inst., 1963-69; regional supr. psychologist San Mateo Mental Health Center (Cal.) 1970—. Pvt. practice clin. psychology, 1954—; leader, organizer mental health, mental retardation workshops, 1957—; cons. Information and Referral Service for Mentally Retarded San Francisco, 1965-67. Fellow Am. Orthopsychiat. Assn.; Am. Psychol. Assn., Cal. Assn. Sch. Psychologists and Psychometrists, San Francisco (chmn. youth activities com. 1965-66, childhood mental health committee 1966-68), Cal. (program and planning com. 1968-70, vol. program advisor 1968—) assns. for mental health, Phi Beta Kappa, Psi Chi. Research on psychol. effects of temporal lobectomy, residential and ednl. treatment of emotionally disturbed and/or retarded children. Home: The Manor Belmont 1601 B Manzanita St Belmont CA 94002 Office: Child & Family Service 3700 Edison St San Mateo CA 94403

JAHODA, GLORIA LOVE (MRS. GERALD JAHODA), author; b. Chgo., Oct. 6, 1926; d. Chase Whitney and Adelaide Warren (Peterson) Love; B.A., Northwestern U., 1948, M.A., 1950; m. Gerald Jahoda, Aug. 25, 1952. Teaching and research fellow U. Wis., Madison, 1950-53; author; Annie, 1960, Delilah's Mountain, 1963, The Other Florida, 1967, The Road to Samarkand: Frederick Delius and His Music, 1969, River of the Golden Ibis, 1973; contbr. articles and poems to popular and lit. mags. Bd. dirs. Tallahassee Civic Ballet, Concert Bd., Tallahassee Sesquicentennial. Honored for contbrs. to lit. by Fla. Legislature, 1973; recipient Best History Book of 1973 award Soc. Midland Authors. Mem. Tallahassee Hist. Soc. (pres. 1966), Delius Assn. Fla., Audubon Soc., Humane Soc., Friends of Animals, Fla. Hist. Soc., Percy Grainger Library Soc. Home: 225 Westridge Dr Tallahassee FL 32304 Office: Julian Bach Literary Agy 3 E 48th St New York City NY 10017

JAKAB, IRENE, physician, educator; b. Oradea, Rumania; d. Odon and Rosa A. (Riedl) Jakab; came to U.S., 1961, naturalized, 1966; M.D., Ferencz Jozsef U., Kolozsvar, Hungary, 1944; license in psychology, paedagogy, philosophy cum laude Hungarian U., Kolozsvar, 1947; Ph.D. summa cum laude psychology, paedagogy, gen. lit., Pazmany Peter U., Budapest, 1948. Rotating intern Ferencz Jozsef U., Kolozsvar, 1943-44; resident psychiatry Univ. Hosp., Kolozsvar, 1944-47, resident in neurology, 1947-50; resident internal medicine Univ. Hosp. of Internal Medicine, Pecs, Hungary, 1950-51; chief physician Univ. Hosp. for Neurology and Psychiatry, Pecs, 1951-59; staff neuropathological research lab. Neurol. Univ. Clinic, Zurich, Switzerland, 1959-61; sect. chief Kan. Neurol. Inst., Topeka, 1961-63; dir. research and edn., 1966; resident psychiatry Topeka State Hosp., 1963-66; asst. psychiatrist McLean Hosp., Belmont, Mass., 1966-67, asso. psychiatrist, 1967-74; prof. psychiatry U. Pitts. Med. Sch., 1974—. Mem. faculty dept. psychiatry Med. Sch., Pecs, 1951-59; asst. Univ. Hosp. Neurology, Zurich, Switzerland, 1959-61; asso. in psychiatry Harvard Med. Sch., Boston, 1966-69, asst. prof. in psychiatry, 1969-74; dir. planning Children's Treatment and Ednl. Center, John Merck Found., 1970—; program dir. grad. course in mental retardation Nat. Inst. Mental Health, 1970—. Fellow Menninger Sch. Psychiatry, Topeka, 1963-66. Recipient Prinzhorn prize, 1967, Ernst Kris prize, 1973. Diplomate Am. Bd. Psychiatry. Mem. A.M.A., Am. Psychol. Assn., Am. Psychiat. Assn., Societe Medico Psychologique de Paris, Internat. Rorschach Soc., Internat. (v.p. 1959—), Am. (chmn. 1965—) socs. psychopathology of expression, Internat. Soc. Child Psychiatry and Allied Professions, Kansas City Neurol. Soc., Deutschsprachige Gesellschaft fur Psychopathologie des Ausdrucks (hon.). Author: Dessins et Peintures des Alienes, 1956; Zeichnungen und Gemalde der Geisteskranken, 1956. Editor: Art and Psychiatry, Proceedings of the Fourth International Colloquium of Psychopathology of Expression, 1968, Art Interpretation and Art Therapy, 1969; Conscious and Unconscious Expressive Art: Theories, Methodology and Pathographies, 1971; co-editor: Dynamische Psychiatrie (Berlin), 1968; mem. editorial bd. Confinia Psychiatrica (Basel), 1968. Reviewer Annales Medico-Psychologiques, 1957—, Acta Paedo Psychiatrica, 1963—, Bulletin of Art Therapy, 1968—. Contbr. articles to publs. Home: 228 Parkman Av Pittsburgh PA 15213 Office: 3811 O'Hara St Pittsburgh PA 15213

JAKOB, CAROL ANNE, pub. relations exec.; b. Phila., Oct. 27, 1944; d. Walter John and Genevieve Agnes (Higgins) Jakob; A.B., Chestnut Hill Coll., 1966. Asst. editor Food Engring. Mag., Chilton Co., Radnor, Pa., 1966-71; pub. relations dir. Selinger/Rambo, Inc., advt. and marketing, Bala-Cynwyd, Pa., 1971-72; asst. pub. relations dir., Phila. Zoo, 1972—. Mem. Women in Communications, Zool. Soc. Phila., Am. Assn. Zool. Parks and Aquariums. Home: 311 W Spencer St Philadelphia PA 19120 Office: 34th St and Girard Av Philadelphia PA 19104

JAKUBIAK, VICTORIA MARY, librarian; b. Newark, May 23, 1938; d. Charles Anthony and Kathryn Lee (Metarko) Jakubiak; B.A., Douglass Coll., 1960; M.A., Tchrs. Coll. Columbia, 1961; M.A. in History, N.Y. U., 1966; M.L.S., Pratt Inst., 1968. Tchr. social studies Hillside (N.J.) Av. Sch., 1961-62; tchr. English, Clinton Place Jr. high Sch., Newark, 1962-64; tchr. English and social studies John Adams Jr. High Sch., Edison, N.J., 1964-66; librarian Newark Sch. System, 1968—. Librarian Newark Pub. Library, part time, 1970-72. Mem. Am. Library Assn., Am. Assn. U. Women, Newark Sch. Librarians' Assn. (v.p. 1971-73, pres. 1973-75), N.J. Sch. Media Assn., Beta Phi Mu. Home: 51 Marsac Pl Newark NJ 07106

JAMES, ALICE, social worker; b. Los Angeles, Apr. 5, 1919; d. John Craigmiles and Reba (Brewster) James; A.B., U. Cal. at Berkeley, 1942; M.A., U. Chgo., 1947. Caseworker A.R.C., Chgo., 1945-46; supr. Evanston (Ill.) Hosp. Assn., 1946-49; supr. social work students U. Chgo. Clinics, 1949-53; asst. prof. U. Chgo. Sch. Social Service Adminstrn., 1953-62; chief social work Inst. for Juvenile Research, Chgo., 1962-69; dir. profl. services Ill. Children's Home and Aid Soc., Chgo., 1969—. Chmn. social work com. Am. Assn. Psychiat. Clinics for Children, 1967-69. Mem. Nat. Assn. Social Workers, Council Social Work Edn., League Women Voters, Ill. Welfare Assn., Ill. Child Care Assn. Home: 1374 E Madison Park Chicago IL 60615 Office: 1122 N Dearborn St Chicago IL 60610

JAMES, BETTY MATTAS, pres. toy co.; b. Altoona, Pa., Feb. 13, 1918; d. Clair Christian and Irene (Love) Mattas; student Pa. State Coll., 1937-39 (div.) children—Elysabethe (Mrs. Stephen Etzel), Richard T. II, Christopher, Susan, Peter, Rebekah. Sec.-treas. James Industries, Inc., Hollidaysburg, 1945-60, pres., owner, 1960—; owner, James Industries, Inc. of Ont., Scarboro, 1963—; pres. Siblings Real Estate Co., Hollidaysburg, 1964—. Mem. adv. com. Jr. Achievement, Altoona Symphony Soc. Bd. dirs. YWCA, 1967, Blair County Arts Found. Mem. C. of C., Toy Mfrs. Am., Bus. and Profl. Women (named Woman of Year 1965). Republican. Presbyn. Club: Blairmont Country. Home: Brushmeade Hollidaysburg PA 16648 Office: Box 230 Hollidaysburg PA 16648

JAMES, DOROTHY TURLEY (MRS. WILLIAM LOUIS JAMES, JR.), librarian; b. Rural Retreat, Va., Aug. 28, 1925; d. Thomas A. and Mae (Painter) Turley; B.S., Longwood Coll., 1946; postgrad. Va. Poly Inst., 1948, Va. Commonwealth U., 1964-68; M.Ed., Va. State Coll., 1974; m. William Louis James, Jr., Dec. 23, 1946; children—Mary, William Louis III. Teller, Nat. Bank, Blacksburg, Va., 1947; tchr. Blackburg High Sch., 1948, Rockingham County Schs., Harrisonburg, Va., 1949-52, librarian, 1951-52; librarian pub. schs., Richmond, Va., 1966, 70-71, Chesterfield, Va., 1967-70, Chesterfield County, Midlothian, Va., 1971—. Active P.T.A., Jr. and Sr. woman's clubs. Mem. A.L.A., Va. Edn. Assn., Va. Sch. Librarians, Chesterfield County Edn. Assn., Nat., Va. assns. for ednl. communications and tech., Friends of the Library, Alpha Sigma Alpha. Home: 7650 Whittington Dr Richmond VA 23225 Office: Salem Ch Jr High Sch 9700 Salem Church Rd Richmond VA 23234

JAMES, ESTELLE DINERSTEIN, educator; b. Bronx, N.Y., Dec. 1, 1935; d. Abraham and Lee (Zeichner) Dinerstein; B.S., Cornell U., 1956; Ph.D., Mass. Inst. Tech., 1961; m. Harry Lazer, June 27, 1971; children by previous marriage-Deborah Sue, David Micah. Lectr. U. Cal. at Berkeley, 1964-65; asst. prof. Stanford, 1965-67; asso. prof. econs. State U. N.Y. at Stony Brook, 1967-72, prof., 1972—. Mem. Am. Econs. Assn. Contbr. articles to profl. jours. Home: 8 University Dr Setauket NY 11733 Office: Dept Econs State U NY Stony Brook NY 11790

JAMES, FRANCES MARGARET, statistician; b. Laurinburg, N.C.; d. Arthur A. and Hattie Lee (McCauley) James; A.B., Randolph-Macon Women's Coll., 1925; M.A., U. N.C., 1933; student Am. U., 1937-38, Johns Hopkins, 1938. Tchr. high schs., Lumber Bridge and Wadesboro, N.C., 1925-34; computer audit div. Gen. Accounting Office, Washington, 1934-37; statis. clk. Children's Bur., Dept. Labor, Washington, 1937-42; jr. fiscal analyst, asst. statistician Bur. of the Budget, Exec. Office of Pres., Washington, 1942-46, statistician Council Econ. Advisers, Washington, 1946-53; statistician White House, Washington, 1953; statistician Council of Econ. Advisers, Exec. Office of Pres., Washington, 1953—. Recipient of 8th Annual Fed. Woman's award, 1968. Mem. Am. Statis. Assn. Democrat. Baptist. Home: 4000 Massachusetts Av NW Washington DC 20016 Office: Exec Office Bldg 17th and Pennsylvania Av NW Washington DC 20506

JAMES, JANET WILSON (MRS. EDWARD T. JAMES), historian; b. N.Y.C., Dec. 23, 1918; d. Willard Oliver and Helen (Peters) Wilson; A.B., Smith Coll., 1939; M.A., Bryn Mawr Coll., 1940; Ph.D., Radcliffe Coll., 1954; m. Edward Topping James, May 12, 1945; children—Edward Topping, Lucy Wilson. Instr. history, English, Mills Coll., 1950-53; instr. history Wellesley Coll., 1954-55; asst. editor Notable Am. Women, 1607-1950, Radcliffe Coll., 1961-63, asso. editor, 1963-71, dir. Arthur and Elizabeth Schlesinger Library on History of Women in Am., Radcliffe Coll., 1965-69; lectr. history Boston Coll., 1971-72, asso. prof., 1972—. Ellen C. Sabin fellow Am. Assn. U. Women, 1947-48. Mem. Am. Studies Assn., League Women Voters, Am. Hist. Assn. Contbr. articles and revs. to jours. Home: 62 Gorham St Cambridge MA 02138

JAMES, JONELL SCHUTZ, ednl. adminstr.; b. Luling, Tex., Mar. 2, 1941; d. Clifton G. and Theresa M. (Karnstadt) Schutz; B.A., U. Tex. at Austin, 1962, M.Ed., 1965, Ph.D., 1967; m. Lewis F. James, Apr. 30, 1966. Asst. prof. edn. Northwestern State U., Natchitoches, La., 1969-70; dir. personnel Houston Ind. Sch. Dist., 1971—. A.C. Ellis fellow, 1965-67. Home: 2807 Bissonnet Houston TX 77005 Office: 3830 Richmond Av Houston TX 77027

JAMES, JUDITH RAY VOGEL MUNRO (MRS. HOWARD ANTHONY JAMES, JR.), newspaper pub.; b. Wrentham, Mass.; d. Frank Chafee and Charlis Hugh (Fishback) Vogel; student Kalamazoo Coll., 1955-56; B.A., U. N.H., 1960; m. Stevenson Munro, Sr., Apr. 25, 1959 (dec. Apr. 1970); children—Mark Stevenson, Eric Burton, Katherine Charlis, Stevenson; m. 2d, Howard Anthony James, Jr., Jan. 1, 1972; 1 son, Jonathan Howard Chafee. Reporter, advt. saleswoman Westbrook (Me.) Am. Newspaper, 1960-65; originator, pub. Westbrook (Me.) Guide, 1964-65, Tri-County Shopper, Norway, Me., 1965-67; co-founder, pub. Northland News, Berlin, N.H., 1965—; co-owner Berlin Reporter, Munro Enterprises, Inc., 1965-70, owner, pub., 1970—, editor, 1973. Mem. N.H. Council for Humanities. Mem. Am. Assn. U. Women. Christian Scientist. Home: 4 Prospect Terrace Gorham NH 03581 Office: 151 Main St Berlin NH 03570

JAMES, M(ARIAN) LUCIA, educator; b. Camden, S.C., May 28, 1924; d. Sammie Walker and Ruth Lula (Johnson) James; A.B., N.C. Coll., 1945; M.S., U. Ill., 1949; Ph.D., U. Conn., 1963. Asst. prof. Sch. Library Sci., Atlanta U., 1949-53; asst. prof., 1953-56, asso. prof., dir. curriculum lab. Fla. A. and M. U., Tallahassee, 1956-59; 1962-65, acting librarian curriculum lab. U. Conn. at Storrs, 1962; asso. prof., dir. curriculum lab. U. Md., College Park, 1965-70, prof., 1970—. Cons., workshop dir. schs. Fla., 1958-65, Md., 1965—, Del. and Va., 1969-71, S.C. and N.C., 1969-70. Den mother Apalachicola council Boy Scouts Am., 1954-59. John Hay Whitney fellow, 1959-60; recipient Carnegie Research Grant, 1951; named Den Mother of Year Apalachicola Council, 1957. Mem. Assn. Supervision and Curriculum Devel. (editor Md. jour. and newsletter, 1968-69), A.L.A. (co-chmn. com. treatment of minorities in library materials 1967-72), Md. Sch. Library Assn. (chmn. scholarship com., 1968-70), Am. Assn. Sch. Librarians, Ednl. Media Assn. Md., Md. Tchrs. Assn., Md. Library Assn., N.E.A., Assn. Supervision and Curriculum Devel., Beta Phi Mu, Pi Gamma Mu, Kappa Delta Pi, Phi Delta Gamma (exec. bd. 1972-74), Delta Kappa Gamma, Delta Sigma Theta (exec. bd., nat. com. 1953-73). Presbyn. (elder). Home: 6700 Belcrest Rd Hyattsville MD 20782 Office: Coll Edn U Md College Park MD 20742

JAMES, SISTER MYRA, hosp. adminstr.; b. Cin., Feb. 1, 1924; d. John and Mary (McManus) Bradley; B.S. in Edn., Atheneum of Ohio, 1950; R.N., Good Samaritan Hosp., Dayton, O., 1954; M. Hosp. Adminstrn., St. Louis U., 1955. Joined Sisters of Charity, 1942; with Good Samaritan Hosp., Dayton, 1955-57; asst. adminstr. St. Mary Corwin Hosp., Pueblo, Colo., 1960, adminstr. St. Joseph Hosp., Mt. Clemens, Mich., 1960-65; adminstr. Penrose Hosp., Colorado Springs, Colo., 1965—. Instr., Dayton U., 1956; preceptor St. Louis U., 1965-73. Colo. U., Denver, 1970. Mem. Colo. (chmn. bd. 1973), Catholic (mem. legislative com. 1973, mem. ad hoc com. on legislative review 1973)., Regional (pres. South central dist. 1966), Am. hosp. assns. Home and office: 2215 N Cascade St Colorado Springs CO 80907

JAMES, NORMA WHITENER (MRS. JOHN WARREN JAMES), civic worker; b. Lincolnton, N.C., Feb. 14, 1903; d. John Roadman and Hattie (Hull) Whitener; student U. Fla., 1925; m. John Warren James, Sept. 13, 1937 (dec. Dec. 1943). Mem. Broward Hosp. Aux., 1950-55, Opera Guild, 1952-59, Civic Music Assn., 1956-58; chmn. Broward County unit Am. Cancer Soc., 1950-51, hon. life mem. bd. dirs. Mem. Internat. Platform Assn., Nova U. Assn. (charter). Club: Garden Hills Golf and Turf (Ocala, Fla.). Home: El Rancho Orange Springs FL 32682 Office: Box 38 Ft McCoy FL 32637

JAMES, ROWENA ASENATH, editor; b. Hastings, Ia., Aug. 6, 1915; d. Mearl Arthur and Ethelyn Leota (McKie) Gable; A.B., U. Ia., 1937; M.S., Ia. State U., 1959; div.; 1 dau., Margaret Elizabeth. Research asst. and writer, sec. to editor editorial page Des Moines Register & Tribune, 1949-52; writer, asst. producer sta. WOI-TV, Ames, Ia., 1954-55; instr. journalism Ia. State U., 1953-55, promotion mgr., asso. editor univ. press, 1958-63, mng. editor, 1963—. Mem. P.E.O., Women in Communications, Zeta Phi Eta, Delta Delta Delta. Democrat. Episcopalian (vestry). Club: Altrusa. Contbr. articles to profl. jours. Home: 2004 Greeley St Ames IA 50010

JAMES, VERDA INEZ, educator, state legislator; b. Stratford, Ont., Can., Sept. 27, 1905; d. William Henry and Sara Ann (Nice) James (father U.S. citizen); B.A., U. Ia., 1927; postgrad. U. Colo., 1937, N.Y.U., 1940; M.A., U. Denver, 1960. Tchr. English, Natrona County High Sch., Casper, Wyo., 1927-38: asst. state supt. schs., Cheyenne, Wyo., 1939-50; reading cons. Casper elementary schs., 1951-54; instr. Casper Jr. Coll., 1954-58; asst. supt. schs., Casper, 1958-68. Mem. Wyo. Community Coll. Commn., Wyo. Commn. Status of Women. Mem. Wyo. Ho. of Reps., 1953-71, speaker pro tem, 1967-69, speaker, 1969-71 (first woman elected to position in Wyo.). Recipient Carol Lane Certificate of Merit award Shell Oil Co., 1954. Mem. Bus. and Profl. Women (Woman of Yr. award 1973), Delta Zeta, Delta Kappa Gamma. Republican. Episcopalian. Mem. Order Eastern Star, P.E.O. Home: 314 E 10th St Casper WY 82601

JAMES, VIOLA SULLIVAN, veterinarian; b. Waco, Tex., Aug. 1, 1944; d. Godfrey Robert and Viola (Wallace) Sullivan; student Baylor U., 1962-65; B.S., Tex. A. and M., 1967, D.V.M., 1968; M.P.H., U. Tex., 1972. Pvt. vet. practice Winnsboro, Tex., 1968-71; veterinarian U.S. Dept. Agr., Harlingen, Tex., 1971; pub. health veterinarian, Houston, 1972-73; pvt. vet. practice, Houston, 1973—. Pres., Lone Star Aviation, Inc., Houston, 1973—. Mem. Am. Pub. Health Assn., Am., Tex., Harris County vet. med. assns. Address: 14526 Piping Rock Houston TX 77077

JAMESON, FLORENE BROWN, broadcasting exec.; b. Wayside, Tex., June 12, 1923; d. Carl O. and Zora (Wesley) Brown; student Amarilla Jr. Coll., 1940-42; m. John C. Jameson, Jan. 31, 1942 (div. 1970); children—Richard, Sue, Martha (Mrs. George Zamber), Janice (Mrs. Larry D. Erven). Bookkeeper, sec., traffic dir. KENS-TV, San Antonio, 1951-54; staff KONO Radio, San Antonio, 1954-57, traffic dir., 1963-65; traffic dir. KONO-TV, San Antonio, 1957-63; sales asst. KENS-TV, San Antonio, 1965-66; sales asst. WOAI-TV, San Antonio, 1966-69, traffic dir., 1969-74, account exec., 1974—. Mem. Am. Women in Radio and TV (chpt. pres. 1962-63, 71-72, mem. nat. electron com. 1969-70). Home: 13645 IH 35 North #66 San Antonio TX 78233 Office: 1031 Navarro St San Antonio TX 78299

JAMESON, GRACE KLEIN (MRS. HENRY E. JAMESON), psychiatrist, educator; b. Balt., Oct. 19, 1924; d. David B. and Rose (Schaffer) Klein; B.A., U. Tex., 1945, M.D., 1949; m. Henry E. Jameson, May 2, 1943; children—Elizabeth Ann, Alice, David, Philip. Intern, U. Tex. Med. Br. Hosps., Galveston, 1949-50, resident, 1950-53; instr. dept. neuropsychiatry, 1953-56, clin. asst. prof., 1956-67, clin. asso. prof., 1967—; practice medicine, specializing in psychiatry, Galveston, Tex., 1953—; mem. staff U. Tex. Med. Br. Hosps., St. Marys Infirmary. Cons. on multiple impact therapy project. Med. dir. Galveston Child Guidance Center, 1959-66, Youth Devel. Project, U. Tex. Med. Br., 1959-61; dir. Tex. Rehab. Center, 1958-61. Mem. A.M.A., Tex., Galveston County med. assns., Am. Med. Womens Assn., Am. Psychiatric Assn., Am., Southwestern group psychotherapy socs. Democrat. Jewish religion. Contbr. articles in field to profl. jours. Home: 121 Tarpon St Galveston TX 77550 Office: 200 University Blvd Galveston TX 77550

JAMESON, MARION KATHERINE (MRS. ROBERT J. JAMESON), antiquarian, appraiser; b. Mpls., Apr. 21, 1922; d. Charles William and Adalea Katherine (Ranis) Lee; grad. high sch.; m. Robert Joseph Jameson, Dec. 24, 1940; children—Carol Anne (Mrs. Johnson), David Robert, Suzanne Lorelei (Mrs. Paul J. Kramer). Partner Old Curiosity Book Shop, Excelsior, Minn., 1944-50; partner A.B.C. Antiques and Books, Mpls., 1950-65; owner A.B.C. Antiques and Books, Monticello, Minn., 1965—; condr. radio program local history sta. KRWC, 1971—; lectr. in field. Historian Wright County, Minn., 1973—. Chmn. Gov.'s Citizen Council on Aging, Wright County, 1974; co-chmn. Wright County Bicentennial Com., 1974. Bd. dirs. Citizens Club Settlement House, Mpls., 1952-58, Pillsbury Settlement House, Mpls., 1958-64. Mem. Minn. Archaeol. Soc. (dir. 1958-62), Minn., Wright County (dir. 1969—) hist. socs., D.A.V. Aux., Minn. Mycol. Soc. Unitarian. Home: Territorial Rd Route 2 Monticello MN 55362

JAMESON, MARY MARGARET, univ. dean; b. Anderson, S.C.; d. Lynn Otho and Ruth Idona (Garrison) Jameson; B.A., Winthrop Coll., 1941; postgrad. Duke, 1943-44; M.A., Syracuse U., 1948. High sch. tchr. math., Ellerbe, N.C., 1941-42, Oxford, N.C., 1942-43; engrng. aide Pratt & Whitney Aircraft Co., East Hartford, Conn., 1944-46; asst. dean women Vanderbilt U., 1948-52; dean women Tex. Western Coll., El Paso, 1952-55; asso. dean women U. Md., 1955-60; dean students Miss. State Coll. for Women, Columbus, 1960-66; dean women La. State U., Baton Rouge, 1966—. Mem. 41st Joint Civilian Orientation Conf., 1972. Active Baton Rouge Mental Health Assn., 1966—, A.R.C., 1960—. Mem. Am. Assn. U. Women, Nat. Assn. Women Deans, Adminstrs. and Counselors (chmn. liaison com. 1971-72), Nat. Assn. Student Personnel Adminstrs., Delta Kappa Gamma. Clubs: Pilot, Womans (Baton Rouge). Home: 2508 McGrath Av Baton Rouge LA 70806

JAMESON, PATRICIA MADOLINE, microbiologist; b. Rhinelander, Wis., Mar. 17, 1939; d. Errol Donald and Mary Maxine (Shields) Jameson; B.S. (coll. scholar), Carrol Coll., 1961; M.S. (USPHS grantee), Ind. U., 1963, Ph.D., 1965. Microbiologist U.S. Dept. Def. Ft. Detrick, Frederick, Md., 1965-69; instr. microbiology Med. Coll. Wis., Milw., 1969-70, asst. prof., 1970—. Cons., P-L Biochems., 1969-70. Mem. Am. Soc. Microbiology, A.A.A.S., Soc. Gen. Microbiology. Mem. Order of Eastern Star. Office: Microbiology Dept Medical College of Wisconsin 561 N 15th St Milwaukee WI 53233

JAMIESON, ADDIE MAE, religious worker; b. Ripley, Miss., May 9, 1919; d. Jesse Darnel and Frances Ardena (Moore) Jamieson; A.B., Blue Mountain Coll., 1943; M.A., Scarritt Coll., 1949; postgrad. Emory U., summers, 1953, 58. Tchr. Dry Creek Elementary Sch., Booneville, Miss., 1939-43, Slate Spring (Miss.) High Sch., 1944, Wilkinson County, 1945, Ripley High Sch., 1945-47; rural worker Fla. Conf., Tallahasse Dist., 1949-55; coordinator Ga. Coop. Rural Work, North and South Ga. Confs. Methodist Ch., Macon, 1955-60; dir. Christian edn. Mulberry St. Meth. Ch., Macon, Ga., 1960-65, coordinator in Holston Meth. Conf., Johnson City, Tenn., 1965-72, North Miss. Conf., 1973—; sec. North Miss. Conf. Enlistment Ch. Occupations, 1973—. County dir. Cancer Drive, Liberty County, Fla., 1951; charter mem. Ga. Meth. Federal Credit Union, 1960—, v.p. bd. dirs. 1963-65; mem. hosp. aux. Winston County Hosp., Louisville, Miss. Bd. dirs. Wesley Found., Ga. So. Coll., Statesboro, 1963-64. Mem. South Ga. Conf. Meth. Ch. (exec. com. 1955-60, Holston conf. 1965-72, bd. edn. 1955-63, exec. com. 1960-63, pres. deaconess bd., 1957-59, interconf. com. Meth. student work 1960-64, fellowship Christian edn. 1962-63 South Ga. 1962-63, Holston Conf. 1965-72, North Miss. 1973—). United Meth. Deaconess Home Missionary Service (com. 1964-72, rep., chmn. by-laws jurisdiction assn. 1964-72). Home: PO Box 127 Louisville MS 39339

JAMIESON, FRANCES JEAN KENTOR (MRS. ROBERT HOWARD JAMIESON), psychologist; b. Denver, Apr. 8, 1922; d. Charles and Hazel (Dietrich) Kentor; A.B., U. Denver, 1943; M.A., Stanford, 1950; postgrad. U. Cal. at Berkeley, 1959-60; Ph.D. (hon.), Hamilton State U., Tucson, 1973; m. Robert Howard Jamieson, Nov. 2, 1946 (dec. June 1953); 1 dau., Nancy Rose. Supr. attendance Office Edn., Modesto, Cal., 1944-46; tchr. pub. schs., Stockton, Cal., 1943-44, 48-49, prin., 1949-50, supr. guidance, Richmond, Cal., 1949-50; tchr., Sacramento, 1950-58; dean girls, Crockett, Cal., 1958-60, head English dept., 1958-60; coordinator psychol. services Monterey County Office Edn., Salinas, Cal., 1960-64; pvt. practice as psychologist, Sacramento, 1956-58, Salinas, 1963-68; psychologist Diagnostic Sch. for Neurologically Handicapped No. Cal., San Francisco, 1968-70, dir. ednl. and psychol. services, 1970—. Sec. Monterey County Democratic Central Com.; mem. Dem. state com., 1966-68. Mem. Am. Personnel and Guidance Assn., N.E.A., M.M.S., Nat., Cal. assns. parliamentarians, Cal. Employees Assn., Cal. Fedn. Bus. and Profl. Women's Clubs (pres. 1973-74), San Francisco Bus. and Profl. Women's Club, Phi Lambda Theta. Presbyn. (deacon). Club: Zonta Internat. Mem. Order Eastern Star, White Shrine. Home: 45 Poncetta Dr Apt 331 Daly City CA 94015

JAMISON, DOROTHY JANE, civic worker; b. Alexandria, S.D., June 9, 1925; d. Frank Marion and Maude Grace (Albertson) Harper; grad. high sch.; m. Maurice Edward Jamison, Dec. 23, 1946; children—Sandra Sue, Jacqueline Jean. Pres., P.T.A., Litchfield, Mitchell, S.D., 1955-57, council pres., 1958-60, state pres., 1968-70, state membership chmn., 1970-72, state culture arts chmn., 1966-68, life mem. state, nat. P.T.A.'s; mem. adv. council State Coll., Brookings, S.D., 1970-73, Title III Dept. Edn., 1970-73. Mem. V.F.W. Aux. (membership chmn. 1971; pres. 1972), Women's Fellowship, Epsilon Sigma Alpha. Conglist. (Sunday sch. tchr. 1950-66; youth dir. 1966-68). Died Sept. 7, 1973. Home: S Harmon Dr Mitchell SD 57301

JAMISON, JOAN ASPINWALL, educator, theatrical producer; b. Providence, Apr. 1, 1931; d. Everett Hamilton and Ruth Agnes (Pierce) Aspinwall; B.S., U. R.I., 1953; m. George Hill Jamison, Jr., Sept. 12, 1953; children—George Hill III, Ruth Margaret. Exec. sec. Albany (N.Y.) League Arts, 1971-73; feature writer KITE, arts newspaper, Schenectady, 1971-72; chmn. drama dept. St. Agnes Sch., Loudonville, N.Y., 1971—; producer, dir. Playwright's Theatre, Albany, 1971—; a founder, now exec. producer, mem. bd. dirs. Playwrights Prodn. Co., Inc., 1973—. Cons. in field; rec. sec., corr. sec., season subsciption chmn. Slingerlands Community Players, 1961-68, pub. relations dir., 1968-71. Sec. Guilderland Woman's Republican Club, 1964. Grantee N.Y. State Council Arts, 1972. Mem. Alpha Xi Delta. Author: (play) No Quarter for the Better Half, 1964; (play) Humpty Dumpty Had a Great Fall, 1969. (play) The Adventures of Nicholas, 1971; (play) Bar the Door with a Feather, 1975. Home: 13 Glenwood St Albany NY 12203 Office: 216 Loudonville Rd Albany NY 12211

JAMISON, MARY LLOYD (MRS. LARRY R. JAMISON), journalist; b. Evansville, Ind., Nov. 27, 1946; d. Edward Lloyd and Margaret (Harding) Engelbrecht; B.A. in Journalism, Ind. U., 1969; m. Larry R. Jamison, Feb. 1, 1969. Work measurement analyst Mellon Nat. Bank, Pitts., 1969-70; editorial asst. Jacques Cattel Press, Tempe, Ariz., 1970-71; pub. asst. Rialto Unified Sch. Dist., Cal., 1971—. Mem. Women in Communications, Cal. Sch. Employees Assn., Ind. U. Alumni Assn., Sigma Kappa. Home: 683 E Margarita St Rialto CA 92376 Office: 182 E Walnut Av Rialto CA 92376

JAMISON, OLLIE FRANCES, lawyer; b. Dossville, Miss., June 4, 1926; d. Samuel Boggan and Mary Jane (Smith) Jamison; student Univs. Night Sch., 1965-69; J.D., Jackson Sch. Law, 1970. With So. Bell Tel. & Tel. Co., Jackson, Miss., 1952-54, Magnolia Petroleum Co., Jackson, 1954-60, Univ. Hosp., Jackson, 1960, Standard Oil Co., Jackson, 1961; with VA Hosp., Jackson, 1962—; admitted to Miss. bar, practiced in Jackson and Kosciusko, Miss. Mem. Attala County Hist. Soc., Bus. and Profl. Womens Club, Am., Miss., Hinds County bar assns., Nat. Hist. Soc., D.A.R. Baptist. Mem. Order Eastern Star. Address: 827 N State St Apt 9A Jackson MS 39201

JAMISON, SARA MOYNE TUSTIN (MRS. LLOYD D. JAMISON), psychologist, counselor; b. Gove, Kan.; d. Elmo L. and Etta Jane (McKinney) Tustin; student Kan. Wesleyan U., Colo. U., East Los Angeles Jr. Coll.; A.A., Phoenix Jr. College; B.S., M.S., Ariz. State U.; postgrad. (Nat. Def. Edn. Act scholar, Family Finance Workshop scholar) U. Cal. at Los Angeles, also postgrad. (Am. Inst. Family Relations fellow) Pepperdine U.; m. Lloyd D. Jamison; children—Kendall, Nolya (Mrs. Quentin Augsperger), Jarrol. Tchr. music pub. schs.; timekeeper Sawyer Electric Co., Los Angeles; counselor West High Sch., Phoenix, 1954-62, sch.-community counselor, 1963-67; counselor Westminster High Sch., Huntington Beach, Cal., 1962-63; counselor West High School, 1965-74; operator Progress Counseling, Phoenix, 1974—. Mem. Ariz. Counselor Certification Com., 1955-60. Adviser Ariz. Anytown, 1957-58, 60, 67, co-dir. Ariz. Anytown, Teenage Workshop in Human Relations, 1965-66; adviser Phoenix Inter-High Sch. Brotherhood Council, 1960—; program planning com. N.W. br. Phoenix YMCA, 1957-65; resource mentor Ariz. Youth Confs. Human Relations, 1955—. Recipient Certificate of Leadership, Nat. Conf. Christians and Jews, 1960, 70. Mem. Ariz. Personnel and Guidance Assn. (sec., corr. sec. 1956-58, historian, 1959-61, state profl. counselor certificates coordinator 1967-69, del. to nat. convs. 1969, 70), Nat. Assn. Sch. Counselors (regional coordinator 1971—), Marguis Biog. Library Soc. (adv. com.), Ariz. Edn. Assn. (coordinating com. allied orgns. 1973-74), Psi Chi, Kappa Delta Pi. Office: 4647 N 16th St Phoenix AZ 85016

JAMME, SUSAN HAMLIN (MRS. LOUIS THEODORE JAMME), social worker; b. N.Y.C., Nov. 26, 1915; d. Francis B. and Clara (Danforth) Hamlin; B.A., U. N.C., 1937; M.S., Columbia, 1955; m. Louis Theodore Jamme, May 3, 1941 (dec. Mar. 1949); 1 dau., Frances (Mrs. Stephen Carlson). Caseworker, Nassau County (N.Y.) Dept. Pub. Welfare, Mineola, 1938-41, Nassau County chpt. A.R.C., Mineola, 1943-44, Nassau County Dept. Social Services, Mineola, 1949-66; supr., asst. dir. Childrens Services, Social Service, 1953-66; sch. social worker Bd. Coop. Ednl. Services, Dix Hills, N.Y., 1966—; instr. sociology Molloy Catholic Coll. for Women, 1964-66. Zone chmn. Garden City Community Fund, 1973. Mem. Nat. Assn. Social Workers (vice chmn. 1966-68), N.Y. State Sch. Social Workers Assn., Acad. Certified Social Workers, N.Y. State Welfare Conf., N.Y., State Tchrs. Assn., Nature Conservancy. Episcopalian. Home: 365 Stewart Av Garden City NY 11530 Office: 507 Deer Park Rd Dix Hills NY 11746

JANCSO, LIVIA, librarian; b. Nagyvarad, Hungary; d. Charles and Ilona (Csak) Nemethy; baccalaureate State Gymnasium, Budapest; nursing degree Red Cross, Hungary, B.A., L'Alliance Francaise; M.S. in L.S., Cath. U. Am., 1965; m. V. Jancso (div.). Came to U.S., 1962, naturalized, 1967. Head nurse St. John's Hosp., Budapest, 1949-55; translator Am. legation, Budapest, 1955-60; cataloger Columbia, 1965-66; librarian Inst. Sino-Soviet Studies George Washington U., Washington, 1966—. Cons. library affairs Am. Hungarian Studies Found., 1970—. Vol. heritage groups div. Republican Party, 1971—. Mem. Am., Med., D.C. library assns., Am. Hungarian Studies Found., Smithsonian Assos., Nat. Geog. Soc., Nat. Wildlife Fedn., Am. Transylvanian Fedn., Hungarian Freedom Fighters Fedn. Rep. Hungarian Reformed Ch. Home: 2117 E St NW Apt 316 Washington DC 20037 Office: Inst Sino-Soviet Studies George Washington U Library Washington DC 20006

JANE, SISTER MARY, librarian; b. Worcester, Mass.; d. Alexander and Julia (Zarzecka) Menzenski; A.B., Marywood Coll., 1938; B.S. in L.S., St. John's U., 1946; M.S. in L.S., Drexel Inst. Tech., 1958; postgrad. Columbia, 1971-72. Tchr. Holy Cross Sch., Maspeth, N.Y., 1933-34: tchr. Nazareth Acad., Phila., 1938-39, tchr., librarian, 1946-55; tchr. Little Flower Catholic Girls High Sch., Phila., 1939-43, St. Stanislaus Kostka Sch., Bklyn., 1943-46; librarian Holy Family Tchr. Tng. Sch., 1946-55, Holy Family Coll., Torresdale, Phila., 1955-73, coll. archivist, 1974—. Pres., Tri-State Coll. Library Coop., 1970-72. Mem. Am., Catholic, Pa. library assns., Assn. Coll. and Reference Libraries (dir.-at-large Delaware Valley chpt. 1969-70), Soc. Am. Archivists, Beta Phi Mu. Author: Archives and Other Special Collections: A Library Staff Handbook, 1973. Contbr. articles to profl. jours. Home: Grant and Frankford Avs Torresdale Philadelphia PA 19114

JANES, BARBARA BECKETT, hosp. devel. dir.; b. Boonville, Mo., Nov. 5, 1930; d. Theodore Cooper and Gladys G. (Watson) Beckett; A.B. in Eng., U. Mo., 1952; div.; children—Sally, Lisa, Susan. Spl. services recreation dir. USAF, Germany, 1952-55; pub. relations asst. Alcoa Corp., Cleve., 1955-56; writer, producer TV sta. WIIC, Pitts., 1961-62, writer, producer KMOX Radio, St. Louis, 1962-64, Condor Film, KTVI, 1962-64; dir. devel. and community relations Jewish

Hosp. of St. Louis, 1964—. Cons. on fund raising. Mem. pub. relations com. Mayor's Council on Aging, St. Louis, 1972—, Mayor's Council on Youth, 1971—. Recipient Pulse on Patient Relations award Jewish Hosp. St. Louis, 1966, 67, 68, MacEachern award Jewish Hosp. St. Louis, 1969, 72. Mem. Nat. Assn. Hosp. Devel. (Harold J. Seymour Nat. Honors award 1971, Spl. Projects award 1972), Nat. Soc. Fund Raisers (Golden Owl award 1969), Pa. Press (Golden Quill award 1962), Pub. Relations Soc. Am., Women in Communications, Press Club St. Louis, Phi Beta Kappa. Club: St. Louis Ski (pub. dir. 1972-73, sec. 1973-74). Home: 1103 Rue La Chelle St St Louis MO 63141 Office: 216 S Kingshighway St Louis MO 63110

JANES, MARONEE FLEMING (MRS. ROBERT GLENN JANES), civic worker; b. Fairmont, W.Va., Jan. 22, 1929; d. David Phillips and Evalena (Ford) Fleming; A.B., Fairmont State Coll., 1963; postgrad. W.Va. U., 1963; m. Robert Glenn Janes, June 5, 1948; children—Pamela, David, Robert Glenn, Anne, Thomas. Pres. Jr. League Fairmont, Inc., 1968-70; neighborhood chmn. Vandalia council Girl Scouts U.S.A., 1964-66, pres., 1973-74, v.p. Black Diamont council, 1974—; mem. Marion County Humanities Council, 1972-74, Gov.'s Commn. on Drug Abuse, 1971—, Gov.'s Critical Issues Com., 1971. Mem. adv. bd. Town and Gown Theater, 1967—. Mem. Woman's Aux. W.Va. Med. Assn. (pres. 1972-73), Woman's Aux. Marion County Med. Aux. (pres. 1965-66), Gamma Chi Chi. Republican. Episcopalian (pres. Episcopal Ch. Women 1974—, vice directress Altar Guild 1971-73, co-chmn. parish homecoming 1974). Club: Green Hills Garden (mem. bd. gardeners 1972-74) (Fairmont). Home: 1707 Country Club Rd Fairmont WV 26554

JANEWAY, ELIZABETH (HALL), author; b. Bklyn., Oct. 7, 1913; d. Charles H. and Jeannette F. (Searle) Hall; student Swarthmore Coll.; A.B., Barnard Coll., 1935; D. Litt., Simpson Coll., 1972, Cedar Crest Coll., 1974; m. Eliot Janeway; children-Michael, William. Author: The Walsh Girls, 1943; Dairy Kenyon, 1945; The Question of Gregory, 1949; The Vikings, 1951; Leaving Home, 1953; Early Days of the Automobile, 1956; The Third Choice, 1959; Angry Kate, 1963; Accident, 1964; Ivanov Seven, 1967; Man's World, Woman's Place, 1971; Between Myth and Meaning, 1974; also short stories and critical writing in periodicals and newspapers. Judge, Nat. Book Award, 1955, Pulitzer Prize Com., 1971. Trustee Barnard Coll.; bd. dirs. MacDowell Colony. Berkeley fellow Yale. Mem. Authors Guild Inc., PEN. Editor: Women's Changing Roles vol. N.Y. Times Series; bd. editors Civil Liberties Rev., Exec. Woman; contbr. sect. on women Comprehensive Textbook of Psychiatry, 1974. Home: 15 E 80th St New York City NY 10021

JANICKI, HAZEL (MRS. WILLIAM SCHOCK), artist; b. London, Eng., Feb. 9, 1918; d. Herbert Paul and Madeleine Emily (Faulkner) Middleton; came to U.S., 1928; diploma (Ranney scholar), Cleve. Inst. Art, 1941, postgrad., 1942; m. William Schock, Apr. 6, 1952. One-man shows Durlacher Bros. Gallery, N.Y.C., 1952, 54, 58, 62, 67; exhibited in group shows Fairweather Hardin Gallery, Chgo., 1970, Am. Painting and Sculpture, 1948-69, U. Ill., 1971, Cleve. Inst. Art, 1971, Ohio State U. Art Gallery, 1974, Am. Art Exhbn., Butler Art Inst., Whitney Mus. Am. Art, N.Y.C., Nat. Acad. Design, N.Y.C., Pa. Acad. Art, Phila., Cleve. Mus. Art, Akron (O.) Art Inst., Mansfield (O.) Fine Arts Center, La. State U., Childe Hassam Fund Purchase Exhbn., 1965; represented in permanent collections Akron (O.) Art Inst., Canton (O.) Art Inst., Cleve. Mus. Art, Cleve., Chgo. Art Inst., Chgo., Detroit Inst. Fine Arts, Detroit, Melbourne (Australia) Art Inst., Butler Inst. Am. Art, Youngstown, O., U. Ill., Urbana, Columbus (O.) Mus. Art, Akron (O.) Pub. Library, Kansas City (Kan.) Art Inst., Munson-Proctor Williams Inst., James Michener Collection, Kent (O.) State U., numerous pvt. collections. Lectr. sch. art Kent (O.) State U. Recipient Purchase prize U. Ill., 1948, Clarke prize Nat. Acad. Design, 1950, Nat. Inst. Arts and Letters award, 1955, Butler Inst. Am. Art Merit award, 1972, Jury award Cleve. Mus. Art, 1973. Louis Comfort Tiffany Found. grantee, 1949. Mem. Artists Equity Assn. Home: 3390 Verner Rd Kent OH 44240

JANIS, JUEL MILLER MENDELSOHN (MRS. JAY JANIS), educator, b. Los Angeles, May 17, 1934; d. Leonard T. and Ida (Miller) Mendelsohn; A.B., George Washington U., 1956; M.S., U. Miami, 1966; Ph.D., U. Md., 1971; m. Jay Janis, Sept. 7, 1954; children—Laura Ann, Jeffrey Andrew. Feature editor North Shore Jour., Bay Harbor-Surfside, Fla., 1956-57; research asso. Evaluation of an In-Service Program for Sch. Desegregation, Washington, 1967; instr. dept. ednl. psychology U. Miami, 1970; Head Start coordinator Dade County, Fla., 1971-73; asso. prof., acting chairperson health scis. dept. Fla. Internat. U., 1973—. Grant Found. fellow, 1968-69. Mem. Am. Psychol. Assn., Phi Kappa Phi. Author: Black Image: Studies of the Negro in Materials for Elementary and Secondary School Students, 1972. Contbr. articles to profl. jours. Home: 1021 N Greenway Dr Coral Gables FL 33134

JANIS, ROSAMOND, physician; b. N.Y.C., Apr. 6, 1930; d. David and Melia (Spaiser) Pomerantz; A.B., Hunter Coll., 1951; M.D., N.Y. U., 1955; m. Michel Janis, Dec. 24, 1953; children—Juliane, Marc, Lynn. Intern, Bronx (N.Y.) Municipal Hosp. Center, 1955-56; resident Hosp. U. Pa., Phila., 1956-57, Bronx VA Hosp., 1958-60; faculty Albert Einstein Coll. Medicine, Bronx, 1960—, asso. prof. pathology, 1969—, pathologist hosp., 1967—; pathologist Bronx Municipal Hosp. Center, 1961—. Mem. Phi Beta Kappa, Alpha Omega Alpha. Home: 4 Floral Dr Hastings-On-Hudson NY 10706 Office: 1300 Morris Park Av Bronx NY 10461

JANISH, JEANNE RUSSELL (MRS. CARL F. JANISH), sci. illustrator; b. Marshalltown, Ia., Oct. 20, 1902; d. Francis Wayland and Lucile (Cross) Russell; A.B., Vassar Coll., 1924; M.A., Stanford, 1925; m. Carl F. Janish, Oct. 5, 1929. Instr. sci. illustration Stanford, 1936-42; sci. illustrator numerous books, including The Life Story of the Fish, 1938; Marine Algae of the Monterey Peninsula (Dr. Gilbert M. Smith); 1944; Vascular Plants of the Pacific Northwest, 4 vols., 1959-69; Illustrated Flora of the Pacific States, 3 vols., 1944-66; Island Life, 1965; California Shore Wildflowers, 1964; Hawaii, a Natural History, 1970; Flora of the Galapagos Islands, 1971; Intermountain Flora, vol. 1, 1972; Flora of the Pacific, 1973; Death Valley Wildflowers; Ethnobotany of Western Washington, 1973; many others. Presbyn. Home: PO Box 12208 Las Vegas NV 89112

JANJIGIAN, HANNAH M. (MRS. EDWARD R. JANJIGIAN), broadcasting exec., civic worker; b. Edinburg, Ind., Dec. 7, 1911; d. W. Alfred and Elsie (Meier) McEwen; student (Am. Assn. U. Women scholar), Franklin Coll., 1930-31; B.S. in Home Econs. (4-H scholar 1931-34), Purdue U., 1934; postgrad. U. Chgo., 1933-34, Ohio State U., 1934-35, Coll. Misericorida, 1964, Pa. State U., 1965-66, Mansfield State Coll., 1968; m. Edward R. Janjigian, Aug. 22, 1937; children—Jessie, Hannah, Edward R. Instn. mgmt. work U. Chgo., 1933-34, Carson, Pirie Scott & Co., Chgo., 1934, Ohio State U., 1934-35; nat. range home economist Westinghouse Electric Co., Mansfield, O., 1935-36; home demonstration agt. U.S. Dept. Agr., 1936-37; owner, mfr. Feather Brand Cakes, Kingston, Pa., 1947-54; originator med. TV series sta. WILK-TV, Luzerne County Med. Soc., Kingston, 1956, co-producer Safeguard Your Health series, 1956—. Pres. Nebbitt Hosp. Aux., Kingston, 1951-53, fund raiser, 1958-68; conferee Working with Disadvantaged Youth, Dept. Health, Edn. and Welfare, 1965; publicity chmn. Luzerne County Nutrition Com. Dept. Agr., 1965-66; vol. dir. YWCA Tutorial, Wilkes-Barre, Pa., 1969—; mem. adv. com. Upward Bound Wilkes Coll., Wilkes-Barre, 1972—. Recipient Governor's award for safety Commonwealth of Pa., 1965; citation Nat. Safety Council, 1965; Benjamin Rush award Luzerne County Med. Soc., 1972. Mem. Woman's Aux. Luzerne County Med. Soc. (TV-radio-press chmn. 1959-65, pres. 1955-56, 64-65) Woman's Aux. Pa. Med. Soc. (pub. relations chmn. 1956-58, mental health chmn. 1958-59; editor newsletter 1961-63), V.F.W. Aux., Aux. Am. Acad. Neurology, D.A.R. (treas. Wyoming Valley 1956—). Methodist. Club: Wyoming Valley Women's. Home: 22 Pierce St Kingston PA 18704

JANKA, KATHERINE ELISE CHADDOCK (MRS. LESLIE ALLAN JANKA), writer, pub. relations cons.; b. Wilmington, Del., Sept. 11, 1945; d. Richard Eastman and Katherine Anna (Massfeller) Chaddock; B.S., Northwestern U., 1967; postgrad. George Washington U., 1970-71; m. Leslie Allan Janka, July 6, 1968. Writer, USIA, Washington, 1967-69; mag. editor U.S. Dept. Agr., Washington, 1969-71; editorial cons. Nat. Commn. on Criminal Justice, U.S. Dept. Justice Washington, 1971-72; communications cons. Nat. Tng. and Devel. Service, mgmt. tng., Washington, 1972—; freelance mag. writer, 1972—. Exec. bd. Foggy Bottom Citizens Assn., Washington, 1971; v.p. Forest Hills Citizens Assn., Washington, 1973. Mem. Women in Communications. Home: 2510 Upton St NW Washington DC 20008 Office: Room 320 5020 Wisconsin Av NW Washington DC 20016

JANKO, MAY, educator, artist; b. N.Y.C., Feb. 27, 1926; d. Jacob and Clara (Schupler) Janko; B.A., Hunter Coll., 1946, M.A., 1952; student Art Students League, 1949-53. Tchr. art pub. schs. N.Y.C., 1953-60. Exhibited graphics, Pa. Acad., Soc. Am. Graphic Artists, Inc., Cin. Art Museum, Portland Mus., Phila. Print Club, 1955, Library of Congress, 1956, 63, Whitney Mus., Nat. Gallery, Washington, Walker Collection, 1959, Print Council of Am., Bklyn. Mus., 1960, Nat. Acad. Fine Arts, Boston Mus. (all 1965), Audubon Artists, 1965, 70, Bklyn. Mus. Print Exhbn., 1966, Am. Color Print Soc., 1968; represented permanent graphics collection Met. Mus. Art, N.Y.C. Recipient Henry B. Shope award Soc. Am. Graphic Artists, Inc., 1954; Achievement award Hunter Coll., 1956; Louis Comfort Tiffany Found. fellowship in graphic arts, 1959-60; graphic prizes Audubon Artists, 1961, N.W. Printmakers, 1965, U. Potsdam, 1965, Pratt Graphic Art Center Miniature Exhbn., 1966, Patrons of Art prize Painters and Sculptors Soc. N.J., 1972, Am.-Scandinavian Found., 1973. Home and studio: 2914 Jerome Av New York City NY 10468

JANNEY, KATE ELIZABETH PRINT (MRS. FREDERICK GEORGE JANNEY), educator; b. Cleve., June 22, 1938; d. Walter James and Zenza Rita (Williams) Print; student Western Coll. for Women, 1955-56; B.A. cum laude, Western Reserve U., 1959, M.A., 1962; m. Frederick George Janney, Feb. 6, 1960; children—Brooke Hopkins, Eric Matthew, Catherine Marie. Tchr., pub. schs. Cleve. area, 1959-65; dir., Huntington Playhouse, Manakiki Playhouse, Lakewood Shakespeare Festivals, Greater Cleve. Area, dir. Children's Theatre, Shaker Heights, O., 1960-62; chmn. speech and theatre dept. Berea High Sch., Berea, O., 1962-65; instr. speech communication U. Conn. Storrs, 1967-70, instr. dramatic arts, Groton, 1971—, dir. drama br. campus, 1971—. Mem. Speech Assn. Am., Am. Theatre Assn., Eastern Communication Assn., New Eng. Theatre Conf. Presbyn. (choir dir. 1972). Home: 154 Clift St Mystic CT 06355 Office: University of Connecticut South East Branch Groton CT 06340

JANOWSKI, BARBARA EDGECOMBE RAY (BARBARA RAY), photographer, writer, lectr.; b. East Liverpool, O., Jan. 14, 1912; d. Arthur Elmore and Elizabeth Birney (Ripley) Edgecombe; high sch. grad.; m. Joseph Earnest Janowski, Aug. 1, 1946; children—Jan Joel, Joel Justin. Prof., editor, cost estimator, copywriter, layout, design Hawkins & Loomis, Chgo., 1929-32, McCormick & Henderson, Chgo., 1932-37, Ill. Typesetters, Chgo., 1938-40, LaSalle St. Press, Chgo., 1940-43; owner, operator Barbara Ray Portrait Studio, Gary, Ind., 1943-52; camera page editor Gary Post-Tribune, 1956-70; free-lance writer. Mem. Gary C. of C. Speakers' Bur., 1960-69. Recipient Good Citizenship medal, Ind. Soc. Sons Am. Revolution, 1963. Mem. Gen. Soc. Mayflower Descs. (corr. sec. 1963-64), Ind., Nat. socs. daus. founders and patriots Am., Colonial Dames 17th Century, Nat. Soc. D.A.R. (Ind. state chmn. pub. relations 1961-64, nat. vice chmn. pub. relations East-Central div. 1962-65, regent local chpt. 1964-66), Nat. League Am. Pen Women, Profl. Photographers Am., Gary Women's Press Club (sec. 1963-64), Nat. Soc. Magna Charta Dames, Nat. Soc. Women Descs. Ancient and Hon. Arty. Co., Nat. Soc. Descs. Knights Most Noble Order Garter, Sovereign Colonial Soc., Ams. Royal Descent, Plantagenet Soc., Order of Washington, Order Three Crusades 1096-1192. Home: 149 Morningside Av Gary IN 46408

JANSEN, AMANDA ROHDE, clin. psychologist; b. Davenport, Ia.; d. Hans J. and Anna (Staack) Rohde; student Ia. State Tchrs. Coll., 1914-15; A.B., U. Colo., 1919; student New Sch. Social Research, N.Y.C., 1927-28, Harvard, summers 1930, 31, 32, Radcliffe Coll., 1935-36; A.M., Columbia, 1942; m. Frederick W. Jansen, Feb. 27, 1957. Tchr., coordinator N.Y.C. Bd. Edn., 1925-28; dir. vocational edn. Bd. Edn., Sioux City, Ia., 1929-35; case-work Psycho-Ednl. Clinic, Harvard, 1936-38; pvt. practice psychology, N.Y.C., 1938-43; chief clin. psychologist Nat. Hosp. for Speech Disorders, N.Y.C., 1943-48; clin. psychologist VA Mental Hygiene Clinic, N.Y. Regional Office, 1948-51; sr. clin. psychologist Camarillo State Hosp., 1953-57; pvt. practice, Long Beach, Cal., 1957—. Diplomate in clin. psychology Am. Bd. Examiners in Profl. Psychology. Mem. Am., Cal. State, Los Angeles County, Long Beach psychol. assns., Internat. Platform Assn., Long Beach Writers Club. Author: Rohde Sentence Completion Test, 1940; Manual for Sentence Completion Test, 1947; The Sentence Completion Method: Its Diagnostic and Clinical Application to Mental Disorders, 1957; also articles psychol. jours. Address: 82 Lime Av Long Beach CA 90802

JANSEN, RUTH LEONA KRAMER (MRS. ALLEN R. JANSEN), psychiatrist; b. Waukegan, Ill., Sept. 15, 1920; d. John and Leona Bell (Wilmington) Kramer; B.A., U. Ill., 1941, M.D., 1950; m. Allen R. Jansen, May 3, 1952; children—Patricia Ann, Mary Beth, Susan Jean. Intern, Milwaukee County Gen. Hosp., 1950-51; resident psychiatry Milwaukee County Hosp. for Mental Diseases, 1951-53; practice medicine specializing in psychiatry, Milw., 1956—; sch. physician City of Milw., 1953-56; psychiat. physician Milwaukee County Mental Health Center, 1956-68, psychiatry fellow, 1968-70, staff psychiatrist So. div., 1970—; pres. Developmental Tng. Center, Inc., 1964—. Mem. Am. Psychiat. Assn., A.M.A., Am. Assn. Mental Deficiency. Home: 2924 S 56th St Milwaukee WI 53219 Office: 5232 W Oklahoma St Milwaukee WI 53219

JANSKY, JEANNETTE JEFFERSON, speech therapist, clinic dir.; b. Urbana, Ill., Nov. 27, 1927; d. Bernard Levi and Irma Nicholson (Williams) Jefferson; B.S. cum laude, U. Ill., 1949; M.S., Coll. City N.Y., 1960; Ph.D., Columbia U., 1970; m. Curtis Moreau Jansky, Aug. 14, 1949; 1 son, Matthew Jefferson. Speech therapist Bythedale Convalescent Home, Valhalla, N.Y., 1950-51; therapist Lang. Disorder Clinic, Columbia Presbyn. Med. Center, N.Y.C., 1950-57, 65-72, dir., 1972—; asso. with Katrina de Hirsch in pvt. practice diagnosis and treatment lang. disabilities and learning, N.Y.C., 1951—. Asst. dept. pediatrics Coll. Phys. and Surg., Columbia U., N.Y.C., 1966—. Health Research Council grantee, 1962-64, 66-68. Mem. Am. Speech and Hearing Assn., Am. Orthopsychiat. Assn., Am. Psychol. Assn., Internat. Reading Assn., Orton Soc. (dir. 1972—), Am. Youth Hostels, Sigma Xi, Psi Chi, Gamma Phi Beta, Presbyn. Author: (with de Hirsch and Langford) Predicting Reading Failure, 1966; Preventing Reading Failure, 1972. Home: 120 E 89th St New York City NY 10028 Office: Language Disorder Clinic Babies Hospital Co-Presbyterian Medical Center 168th and Broadway New York City NY 10028

JANSONS, VILMA KARINA (MRS. ANSIS JANSONS), microbiologist, educator; b. Riga, Latvia, Sept. 21, 1926; d. Alexander K. and Pauline (Sprogis) Lasmanis; came to U.S., 1957; naturalized, 1965; B.A., Bklyn. Coll., 1961; Ph.D., Rutgers U., 1967; m. Ansis Jansons, Sept. 10, 1944; 1 dau., Mara Donis. Research asso. lectr. Princeton (N.J.) U., 1967-71; asst. prof. N.J. Sch. Medicine and Dentistry, Newark, 1972—. Mem. N.Y. Acad. Sci., Am. Soc. Microbiology, A.A.A.S., Am. Latvian Assn. in U.S., Latvian Soc. Am. Contbr. articles to profl. jours. Home: 22 Lawrence Brook Dr East Brunswick NJ 08816 Office: 100 Bergen St Newark NJ 07103

JANZEN, MARTHA, accountant; b. Koldiez, Germany, Sept. 11, 1925; d. Jacob and Catherine (Quiring) Janzen; student Bible Sch., Virgil, Ont., Can., 1943-44, Bible Coll., Winnipeg, Man., Can., 1951. Clk.-typist Canadian Wood Products, Grimsby, Ont., 1946-51; bookkeeping machine operator Lowry Fuels, Hamilton, Ont., 1952-57, DeFehr & Sons, Winnipeg, 1957-58; bookkeeper, accountant Bethesda Home, Vineland, Ont., 1959—. Home: 22 Glenview Rd Vineland ON Canada Office: Box 1000 Vineland ON Canada

JANZEN, NORINE MADELYN QUINLAN (MRS. DOUGLAS MACARTHUR JANZEN), med. technologist; b. Fond du Lac, Wis., Feb. 9, 1943; d. Joseph Wesley and Norma Edith (Gustin) Quinlan; B.S., Marion Coll., 1965; med. technologist St. Agnes Sch. Med. Tech., Fond du Lac, 1966; m. Douglas MacArthur Janzen, July 18, 1970. Med. technologist Mayfair Med. Lab., Wauwatosa, Wis., 1966-69, Dr.'s Mason, Chamberlain, Franke, Klink & Kamper, Milw., 1969—. Substitute poll worker Democratic com., Fond du Lac, 1964-65; mem. Dem. Nat. Com., 1973—. Mem. Nat., Wis., Milw. (pres., 1971-72; dir. 1972-73) socs. med. technologists, Alpha Delta Theta (nat. dist. chmn., 1967-69; nat. alumnae dir. 1969-71). Methodist. Home: N 98 W 17298 Dotty Way Germantown WI 53022 Office: 324 E Wisconsin Av Milwaukee WI 53202

JARAMILLO, VIRGINIA, artist, author; b. El Paso, Tex., Mar. 21, 1939; d. Louis and Lupe (Carrillo) Jaramillo; student Otis Art Inst., 1959-61; m. Daniel Larue Johnson, July 1, 1960; children—Daniel Aaron, Marc Rothko. Exhibited in group shows Los Angeles County Mus. Art Annual, 1959, 61, Southwest Regionial Painting and Sculpture Show, Houston (Tex.) Mus. Fine Arts, 1962, 71, Whitney Mus. Am. Art Ann., N.Y.C., 1972, Aldrich Mus. Contemporary Art, Ridgefield, Conn., 1972; represented in permanent collections Long Beach (Cal.) Mus. Art, Pasadena (Cal.) Art Mus., Aldrich Mus. Contemporary Art, Ridgefield. Dir. Hybrid Arts Inc. Ford Found. grantee, 1962, Nat. Endowment for the Arts and N.Y. State Council Arts grantee, 1971-73, Creative Artists Pub. Service grantee, 1974-75. Mem. Internat. Platform Assn., Nat. Soc. Lit. and Arts. Author: Religious Architecture Throughout Europe, 1965. Office: PO Box 101 Prince St Sta New York City NY 10012

JARBOE, PATRICIA ANN, home economist; b. Evansville, Ind., Feb. 20, 1940; d. Wilford Andrew and Josephine R. (Kraft) Jarboe; B.S., Purdue U., 1962; M.S., U. Mo., 1970. Tchr. home econs. Bruceville (Ind.) Sch., 1962-63; extension agt. Ind. Agrl. Extension Service, Jasper, Ind., 1963-64; extension home economist U. Mo. Extension Service, St. Joseph, 1964—. Recipient Grace Frysinger fellowship Nat. Assn. Extension Home Economists, 1971. Mem. Nat. Assn. Extension Home Economists (dir. 1973—), Am. (extension sec. 1973—), Mo. (extension chmn. 1972—), Northwest Mo. (pres. 1973—) home econs. assns., St. Joseph C. of C. (pres. women's div. 1971), U. Mo. Extension Assn. (bd. dirs. 1969-72, pres. 1974), Beta Sigma Phi, Sigma Kappa, Epsilon Sigma Phi. Club: Altrusa (v.p. 1972) (St. Joseph). Home: 3102 N 36th Terrace St Joseph MO 64506 Office: 4525 Downs St St Joseph MO 64507

JARED, GRACE EVA HEMINGER, author; b. Cerro Gordo, Ill.; d. Adam P. and Josephine Eva (Upshaw) Heminger; student Eastern Ill. State Normal, Charleston, 1907; m. Ray V. Jared, June 28, 1910; children—Mildred (Mrs. Ernest Johnson), Milfrieda Bower, Leland H. Founder, Double R Hatcheries, Olney, Ill., 1921-47; owner farms, bus. mgr., Vermilion, Douglas, Edgar counties (Ill.), 1962—. Reporter AP, 1940-42; columnist The Hatchery Tribune, Mount Morris, Ill., 1936-47. Mem. Ill. Poultry Improvement Assn. (organizer, charter officer 1934), D.A.R. (librarian 1961-69), Nat. Soc. Daus. Am. Colonists. Clubs: Olney Woman's (founder 1937), Author: They Met Challenges . . . With Memoirs, 1968. Genealogist, contbr., editor The Upshaw Family Journal, 1974. Contbr. articles and editorials to various newspapers. Home and office: 503 S Fair St Olney IL 62450

JARKOWSKI, STEFANIA AGNES DOBROWOLSKA (MRS. BOLESLAW ZENON JARKOWSKI), artist, educator; b. Gdansk, Poland, Dec. 19, 1914; d. Julian and Jadwiga (Weyher) Dobrowolski; Humanistic Coll. Diploma, Torun, Poland, 1934; studied Acad. Arts, Hamilton, Can., 1952, Kalamazoo Art Inst., 1959-61, Coll. Art Study Abroad, Paris, 1966, Nat. Mus., Warsaw, Poland, 1969; m. Boleslaw Zenon Jarkowski, Dec. 11, 1948. Came to U.S., 1959, naturalized, 1964. Dir. art gallery Carver Mus., Tuskegee (Ala.) Inst., 1962—, faculty Coll. Arts and Scis., 1962—. One man shows Carver Mus., 1963-66, Polish Artists Assn. Zacheta, Warsaw, Poland, 1965; group shows Kalamazoo Art Inst., Kalamazoo Art Festivals, 1961-62, Nat. Festivals Beaux Arts Guild, Tuskegee, 1962-66, Ala. Art Faculty Exhbn., Birmingham Art Gallery, 1966, Nat. Art Gallery Warsaw, 1965, Nat. Traveling Exhbn., Ala. Watercolor Soc., 1968, 73; represented in permanent collections Carver Mus., Sch. No. 1000 Art Gallery, Warsaw. Mem. Polish Resistance Orgn., Warsaw Uprising, 1939-45. Mgr. YMCA, Sloan Sq., London, Eng., 1946-47. Recipient awards Nat. Festival Beaux Arts Guild, Tuskegee, 1964-66. Mem. Am. Artists Assn., Am. Assn. Museums, Beaux Arts Guild (art dir. 1962—), Polish Artists Assn. Zacheta. Restored 70 x 40-inch canvas Yucca Gloriosa by George Washington Carver, damaged in fire, 1947. Home: 410 Parker Av Tuskegee Institute AL 36088

JARRATT, VIRGINIA R., univ. adminstr.; B.S., Ph.D., U. Tex.; M. Nursing Adminstrn., U. Minn. Dean, Harris Coll. Nursing, Tex. Christian U., 1967—, also prof. nursing. Address: Harris Coll of Nursing Fort Worth TX 76129

JARVIE, JEAN OBERLE, educator; b. Pittsfield, Mass., Mar. 13, 1932; d. James Grant and Cecile (Oberle) Jarvie; B. Music Edn., Oberlin Coll., 1954; Mus. M., Boston U., 1959; postgrad. in theatre edn. N.Y. U., summers 1963-66. Tchr. music Pub. Sch. Dept., Pittsfield, Mass., 1954-59; mem. faculty Pittsfield Community Music

Sch., 1955-59; tchr. music and drama Masconomet Regional Sch. Dist., Boxford, Mass., 1959—. Bd. dirs. Village Players, Topsfield, Mass., 1971-73. Mem. Music Educator Nat. Conf. (sec. Mass. N.E. dist. 1968), Am. Theater Assn., Mass. Tchrs. Assn. Home: 2 Park St Topsfield MA 01983 Office: Masconomet Regional High Sch Boxford MA 01921

JARVIK, LISSY F. (MRS. MURRAY E. JARVIK), physician, educator; b. The Hague, Netherlands;; d. Leo and Regina (Engelart) Feingold; came to U.S., 1941, naturalized, 1947; A.B. cum laude, Hunter Coll., 1946; M.A., Columbia, 1947, Ph.D., 1950; M.D., Western Res. U., 1954; m. Murray E. Jarvik, Dec. 19, 1954; children—Laurence A., Jeffrey G. Research asst., research asso. dept. psychiatry N.Y. State Psychiat. Inst., N.Y.C., 1946-50; teaching asst. Western Res. U., Cleve., 1953; rotating intern Mt. Sinai Hosp., N.Y.C., 1954-55; pediatric resident Babies Hosp., Columbia-Presbyn. Med. Center, N.Y.C., 1955-56; pediatric fellow Vanderbilt Clinic, 1957-58, asst. attending psychiatrist, 1962-63, asso. attending psychiatrist, 1963-72; practice medicine, specializing in psychiatry, N.Y.C., 1959-62; sr. research scientist dept. med. genetics N.Y. State Psychiat. Inst., 1955-62, radiation safety officer, 1962-72, asso. research scientist, 1963-69, psychiatrist II, 1969-72; research asso. dept. psychiatry Coll. Phys. and Surg. Columbia, 1956-62, asst. clin. prof., 1962-70, asso. prof., 1970-72; chief psychogenetics unit VA Hosp., Los Angeles, 1972—; vis. asso. prof. U. Cal. at Los Angeles, 1970-71, prof. dept. psychiatry, 1972—. Recipient R. Thornton Wilson award, 1967; NSF travel fellow, 1956. Diplomate Am. Bd. Pediatrics. Fellow A.A.A.S., Gerontol. Soc., Am. Geriatric Soc. (founding fellow Western div.), Am. Acad. Pediatrics, Am. Psychol. Assn. (div. sec.-treas., pres.); mem. A.M.A., Am. Soc. Human Genetics, Environmental Mutagen Soc., Am. Eugenics Soc., Eastern Psychiat. Research Assn., Am. Psychopath. Assn., Am. Psychiat. Assn., Sigma Xi. Editorial bd. Behavior Genetics. Contbr. articles to profl. jours. Office: 760 Westwood Plaza Los Angeles CA 90024

JARVIS, BARBARA ANNE, mem. Democratic nat. com., lab. technologist; b. Kansas City, Mo., Apr. 14, 1934; d. Herman Edward and Marjorie Maude (Graber) Spitzenfeil; A.A., Kansas City Jr. Coll., 1953; student Ariz. State U.; m. Thomas B. Jarvis, Sept. 9, 1965; 1 son, Kenneth Mark. Technologist Menorah Med. Center, Kansas City, Mo., 1955-56, Ariz. State U. Student Health Service, 1960-62, Scottsdale (Ariz.) Bapt. Hosp., 1962-65; chief technologist Skyline Lab., Globe, Ariz., 1967-72. Sec. Globe Planning and Zoning Commn., 1970—; asso. coordinator Women's Polit. Caucus Ariz.; 1st vice chairperson Ariz. Dem. party; mem. Dem. nat. com. from Ariz. Bd. dirs. Salvation Army, Globe, Gila Pueblo campus Eastern Ariz. Coll., Gila County Guidance Clinic. Address: 1266 Skyline Dr Globe AZ 85501

JARVIS, CATHY CLAIRE (MRS. WILLIAM DAVID COLLARD), physician; b. Evansville, Ind., July 21, 1942; d. Phares Hayden and Mildred Elizabeth (Timberlake) Jarvis; A.B., U. Mo., 1964, M.D., 1969; m. William David Collard, Apr. 30, 1971. Research asst. Washington U., summers 1960-63, camp counselor, summers, 1964-65; personnel asst. residents hall U. Mo., winters 1963-66; extern Ellis Fischel Cancer Hosp. and U. Mo. Med. Center, 1968; intern St. John's Mercy Med. Center, St. Louis, 1969-70, resident internal medicine, 1970-73, mem. patient care com., 1971-73; med. dir. rehab. center St. John's Mercy Med. Center, St. Louis, 1974—. Recipient award U. Mo. Curators, 1960. Diplomate Nat. Bd. Med. Examiners, Am. Bd. Internal Medicine. Mem. U. Mo. Alumni Assn., Beta Sigma Phi (pres. 1973-74). Home: 845 Glen Elm Glendale MO 63122 Office: 493 St Francois St Florissant MO 63031 also 164 W Clayton Rd Ballwin MO 63011

JARVIS, ELIZABETH ORYSIA BURDENY (MRS. JOSEPH CHARLES JARVIS), ednl. cons.; b. Ethelbert, Man., Can., Mar. 8, 1931; d. Michael Peter and Mary (Soroka) Burdeny; B.A., McMaster U. (Can.), 1960; B.Ed., U. Toronto (Ont., Can.), 1962, M.Ed., 1966, Ph.D., 1973; m. Joseph Charles Jarvis, Jan. 1, 1956; children—Joy Ann, Jaye Kim. Tchr. Sch. dist. Winnipeg, Man., 1949-56, Waterdown (Ont.) pub. schs., 1959, Burlington (Ont.) Bd. Edn., 1960-66; grad. asst. Ont. Inst. for Studies in Edn., Toronto, 1966-68; program cons. Ont. Ministry of Edn., St. Catherines, 1968—. Cons. early childhood edn., asst. dir. swimming program for handicapped. Fed. Women Tchrs. Assn. of Ont. fellow, 1967; Ont. Inst. Studies in Edn., 1966-68. Mem. Assn. Supervision Curriculum Devel., Nat. Soc. Study Edn., N.E.A., Assn. Childhood Edn. Internat., Nat. Assn. Edn. Young Children, Ont. Edn. Assn., Ont. Assn. Curriculum Devel., Fedn. Women Tchrs. Assns. Ont., Ont. Tchrs. Fedn., Internat. Reading Assn., Canadian Coll. Tchrs. (v.p. chpt. 1974-75), Ont. Ednl. Research Council, Ont. Municipal and Provincial Edn. Officers, Canadian Assn. Sch. Adminstrs., Delta Kappa Gamma. Home: Bayview House Rural Route 2 Hamilton ON L8N 2Z7 Canada Office: Box 906 15 Church St St Catherines ON L2R 7A1 Canada

JARVIS, LUCY HOWARD (MRS. SERGE JARVIS), TV producer; b. N.Y.C.; d. Herman M. and Sophie (Kirsch) Howard; B.S., Cornell U., 1938, M.S., 1941; postgrad. New Sch., 1942; m. Serge Jarvis, July 18, 1940; children—Barbara Ann, Peter Leslie. Dietitian, N.Y. Hosp., 1938-39; dir. spl. promotion Beechnut Foods Co., 1939-40; asso. food editor McCall's mag., 1940-43; vol. instr. A.R.C., 1943-45; nat. v.p. Women's Am. Orgn. for Rehab. through Tng., 1944-51, mem. profl. staff, producer radio-TV, 1951-55; asst. to producer Talent Assos., 1955-56; women's TV editor Pathe News, 1956-57; co-producer Capitol Close-Up, WOR-Mut. Daily, 1957-60; TV producer news and public affairs NBC, N.Y.C., 1960—, produced shows including The Nation's Future, White Paper and Du Pont series, The Kremlin documentary (Emmy award, Golden Mike award 1963), Mus. Without Walls, Louvre Mus. award-winning film, 1964, Who Shall Live, 1965, Mary Martin: Hello Dolly! Around the World, 1965, Dr. Barnard's Heart Transplant Operations, 1968, 2 NBC white papers on youth, 1970, others. Frequent lectr. Bd. dirs., officer Am. Israel Cultural Found., 1954-64; dir. Presbyn. World Ch. Service, 1956. Recipient Bronze medal Pan Am. Soc., 1953; McCall's mag. Golden award, Am. Woman of Year in Radio and TV, 1963; Internat. Guardianship award Orgn. for Rehab. Through Tng.; named Producer of Year in Am. Newspapermen's Poll, Radio and TV Daily decorated chevalier Order Arts and Letters. Mem. Cornell Alumni Assn. (centennial campaign 1964-65), Sigma Delta Tau. Author: Enjoyment of Wines, 1957. Home: 116 Central Park South New York City NY 10019 Office: NBC 30 Rockefeller Plaza New York City NY 10020

JAUNISKIS, RUTA ORLAUSKAITE (MRS. MECYS JAUNISKIS), psychiatrist; b. Kirshach, USSR, Aug. 30, 1917; d. Juozas and Marija (Eidrigeviciute) Orlauskis; M.D., U. Kaunas, Lithuania Sch. Medicine, 1942; m. Mecys Jauniskis, May 31, 1948; 1 dau., Egle (Mrs. Valdas Casimer Duoba). Came to U.S., 1948; naturalized, 1954. Intern obstetrics and gynecology Red Cross Hosp. and Women's Clinic, Kaunas, Lithuania, 1942-43, resident, 1943-44; intern Mounds Park and Midway hosps., St. Paul, 1950-52, resident, 1952-55; resident psychiatry VA Hosp., Perry Point, Md., 1958-61; house physician several hosps., Germany, 1944-48; Mounds Park and Midway hosps., St. Paul, 1950-57; staff psychiatrist State Hosp., Fergus Falls, Minn., 1957-58, VA hosps., Perry Point, Md., 1958-61, Danville, Ill., 1961-63, Northport, N.Y., 1963-67; asst. dir. Suffolk Psychiat. Hosp., Central Islip, N.Y., 1967-72. Psychiatrist Mental Health Center, Manhasset, N.Y., 1969—; chief unit Kings Park (N.Y.) State Hosp., 1972—. Diplomate Am. Bd. Psychiatry and Neurology. Mem. A.M.A., Am. Psychiat. Assn., Lithuanian Med. Assn. Home: 1114 5th Av East Northport NY 11731 Office: Kings Park State Hosp Kings Park NY 11754 also Mental Health Center 1691 Northern Blvd Manhasset NY 11030

JAVELLAS, INA JUNE, social worker; b. Pawhuska, Okla., June 15, 1934; d. Tom D. and Grace E. (Hyde) Javellas; B.A., U. Okla., 1956, M.S.W., 1958. Social work asst. Central State Griffin Meml. Hosp., Norman, Okla., 1957-58, psychiat. social worker, 1958-62; social work supr. Enid State Sch., 1962-63; social work supr. Eastern State Hosp., Vinita, Okla., 1963; psychiat. social worker Community Services Project, Tulsa, 1963-65; coordinator community mental health div. Dept. Mental Health, Oklahoma City, 1965—. Participant teaching program for student nurses Central State Griffin Meml. Hosp., Norman, Okla., 1960-62, psychiat. residency teaching program, 1961-62; cons. tng. headstart program trainees Okla. State U., 1966. Vista workers tng. program, 1966; mem. Gov.'s Adv. Com. for Planning Vocational Rehab. Services and Sheltered Workshops and Facilities, chmn. task force on sheltered workshops and rehab. services, 1966-68; cons. tng. seminar Urban League, U.S. Dept. Labor, Neighborhood Program Trainees, 1968; mem. health edn. com. Interagy. Tech. Panel for Study of Health Edn. of Children and Youth in Okla., 1969-70; mem. Gov.'s. Adv. Com. on Employment of Handicapped, 1969-70; participant Project Hope, Internat. Social Service Project, 1964-69; cons. Nat. Inst. Mental Health, 1972—. Grad. Counselor scholar Phi Mu, Memphis 1956-57. Bd. dirs. Okla. Health and Welfare Assn., 1972—. Recipient citation Tulsa County Mental Health Assn., 1966; named Outstanding Young Woman in Am., 1965. Mem. Nat. Assn. Social Workers (psychiat. council 1958—, sec. ad hoc com. on grad. edn. Western Okla. chpt. 1969-71, named social worker of year 1970), Conf. Social Workers in State and Territorial Mental Health Programs (editor Newsletter 1967—, chmn.-elect 1973—), Am. Assn. U. Women, Acad. Certified Social Workers, Nat. Conf. on Social Welfare, Phi Mu. Republican. Episcopalian. Home: 3447 SE 44th St Del City OK 73135 Office: PO Box 53277 Capitol Station Oklahoma City OK 73105

JAWETZ, ILSE KAULBACH, psychiatrist; b. Vienna, Austria, Oct. 11, 1915; d. Richard and Sofie (Fuchs) Kaulbach; candidate medicine U. Vienna, 1938; M.D., Stanford, 1949; grad. San Francisco Psychoanalytic Inst., 1958; m. Allen B. Wheelis, Apr. 19, 1954. Came to U.S., 1938, naturalized, 1944. Intern, Stanford Hosp., San Francisco, 1948-49; resident Longley Porter Clinic, San Francisco, 1949-51; fellow psychiatry Austen Riggs Center, Stockbridge, Mass., 1951-53; pvt. practice psychiatry and psychoanalysis, San Francisco, 1953—; instr. San Francisco Psychoanalytic Inst., 1956—; asst. chief Mt. Zion Psychiat. Clinic, San Francisco, 1962—; asst. clin. prof. U. Cal. Sch. Medicine, 1971—. Fellow Am. Psychiat. Assn.; mem. San Francisco Med. Soc., Cal. Med. Assn., A.M.A., No. Cal. Psychiat. Soc., San Francisco Psychoanalytic Inst. and Soc., Am. Psychoanalytic Assn., Alpha Omega Alpha. Office: 3731 Jackson St San Francisco CA 94118

JAY, FLORENCE ETHEL, ret. social worker; b. Jonesboro, Ind., Oct. 1, 1903; d. Charles A. and Blanche A. (Thomas) Jay; A.B., Chatham Coll., 1924; M.A., U. Pitts., 1948, Ph.D., 1956. Tchr. Pa. high schs., 1924-29; caseworker Dept. Pub. Welfare, Greensburg, Pa., 1934-72. Recipient Chi Omega Alumnae award, U. Pitts. Mem. Am., Eastern sociol. socs., Alpha Kappa Delta. Methodist. Home: 1711 Kenneth Av Arnold New Kensington PA 15068

JAY, IRNA STEIN MOORE (MRS. PETER A. JAY), editor; b. N.Y.C., July 27, 1944; d. Samuel H. and Esther I. (Goodman) Stein; B.A. in English, U. Wis., 1965; M.S. in Journalism, Columbia, 1966; m. Michael F. Moore, June 5, 1966 (div.); m. 2d, Peter A. Jay, Dec. 28, 1963. Reporter, Capital Times, Madison, Wis., 1966-67; reporter, editor Washington Post, 1967-74; asso. editor, pub. Record, Havre de Grace, Md., 1974—. Woodrow Wilson fellow, 1965. Mem. Am. Newspaper Guild, Phi Beta Kappa. Home: Box 206 Churchville MD 21028 Office: The Record 357 Green St Havre de Grace MD 21078

JAYNE, LOUISE MARGARET (MRS. CHESTER S. KURZET), lawyer; b. Pitts., June 30, 1927; d. Reuel Curtis and Margaret May (Fry) Jayne; B.A., U. Pa., 1948; LL.B., Yale, 1951; m. Chester S. Kurzet, June 30, 1951; children—Reuel, Jay. Admitted to N.Y. bar, 1951, Ore. bar, 1953, U.S. Supreme Ct. bar, 1970; atty. Sullivan & Cromwell, N.Y.C., 1951-53; dep. dist. atty., Multnomah County, Ore., 1954; practiced in Portland, Ore., 1954—. Vice pres., dir. Woodland Acres Acad., Inc., Beaverton, Ore., 1964—, legal counsel, 1962—, mem. Queen's Bench Ore., 1954—, 1973—. Legal counsel, dir. Metro Women's Club, Portland, 1973—; vice chmn., dir. Alcoholic Counseling and Rehab. Program, Greater Portland, 1973—. Mem. Am., Ore., Multnomah County (chmn. jud. adminstrn. com. 1971-72) bar assns., Phi Beta Kappa, Pi Gamma Mu. Home: 1265 SW Cardinell Dr Portland OR 97201 Office: Am Bank Bldg Portland OR 97205

JAYNES, RUTH MARGARET, author; b. Santa Ana, Cal., Oct. 17, 1899; d. William Henry and Addie May (Boxley) Barry; student U. So. Cal., U. Cal. at Los Angeles; B.A., M.A., Los Angeles State Coll.; m. Joseph Alva Jaynes, Mar. 2, 1920; 1 dau., AlVerta (Mrs. Paul Garland Williamson). Tchr. elementary sch. Los Angeles, then elementary supr. Author: Yo-Ho and Kim series; Do You Know What; Friends! Friends! Friends!; Benny's Four Hats; What is a Birthday Child; What Me Outdoors; The Biggest House; My Tricycle and I; Watch Me Indoors; Melinda's Christmas Stocking; Box Tied With a Red Ribbon; Tell Me, Please! What's That?; That's What It Is!; Three Baby Chicks; Where Is Whiffen?; Amy the Cat-Sitter; Mamá Grande Is Like That!; It Happened to Henry; Justin's Hill. Home: 1140 E Ocean Blvd Unit 115 Long Beach CA 90802 Office: 7120 Hayvenhurst St Van Nuys CA

JEANE, BONNIE ANN, assn. adminstr., city ofcl.; b. Perry, Ga., Oct. 11, 1944; d. Carlton Clark and Frances Marie (Miller) Homan; student U. Tex., 1962-65, Lindenwood Coll., 1965-66; B.S., So. Methodist U., 1967; m. Charles Donald, May 29, 1965; 1 dau., Corrie. Tchr. math. Dallas Ind. Sch. Dist., 1967-68; sales rep. Mcht.'s Greeter Service, Dallas, 1973—. City chmn. United Fund, 1972; program chmn. Collin County Mayor's Assn., 1973-74. Mem. Plano C. of C., Tex. Municipal League (utility adv. council 1973), North Central Tex. Council Govts. (mem. nat. transp. study com. 1973), Zeta Tau Alpha (Dallas met. historian 1972). Home: 8 Eastlane Plano TX 75074 Office: 921 Peek Dallas TX

JEANES, ALLENE ROSALIND, chemist; b. Waco, Tex., July 19, 1906; d. Lonnie E. and Viola (Herring) Jeanes; B.A., Baylor U., 1928; M.A., U. Cal. at Berkeley, 1929; Ph.D. in Organic Chemistry, U. Ill., 1938. Instr. math. and physics high sch., 1930; head sci. dept. Athens (Ala.) Coll., 1930-35; instr. chemistry U. Ill., 1936-37; Chem. Found. fellow, 1937-38; Corn Industries Research Found. fellow Nat. Inst. Health, USPHS, 1938-40; research chemist Starch and Dextrose div. No. Regional Research Lab., U.S. Dept. Agr., Peoria, Ill., 1941—. Recipient Distinguished Service award U.S. Dept. Agr. 1953, Superior Service award, 1968, Garvan medal, 1956; Fed. Woman's award U.S. Civil Service Commn., 1962. Mem. Am. Chem. Soc., Sigma Xi, Iota Sigma Pi. Contbr. articles in field to profl. jours. Patentee in field. Home: 5021 N University St Peoria IL 61614 Office: 1815 N University St Peoria IL 61604

JECT-KEY, ELSIE (MRS. D. WU JECT-KEY), artist; b. Koge, Denmark; d. Peter Kjarsgaard; student N.A.D., Art Students League, Beaux Arts Inst.; m. D. Wu Ject-Key (dec. Apr. 1968). One man shows at Argent Gallery, Creative Gallery, Crespl Gallery; represented in permanent collections Butler Inst. Am. Art, Youngstown, O., Norfolk (Va.) Mus. Art, various pvt. collections; exhibited in numerous group shows. Recipient Knickerbocker Artists prize, 1960, 65; Allied Artists award, 1964; Salmagundi Club prize Allied Artists, 1967; Purchase prize Butler Inst., 1967; award Nat. Assn. Women Artists, 1968, medal of honor, 1971; William Church Osborne Meml. award Am. Watercolor Soc., 1972. Mem. Am. Watercolor Soc. (treas. 1969—), Allied Artists (corr. sec. 1961-64, treas. 1966-67), Nat. Assn. Women Artists (dir., 1st v.p. 1966-68, award 1968, Woodbury Meml. award 1974), Nat. Soc. Painters in Casein and Acrylic (Frank Monaghan Meml. award 1973, treas. 1973—), Knickerbocker Artists (dir., corr. sec., rec. sec. 1973). Home: 333 E 41st St New York City NY 10017

JEDEIKIN, LILLIAN ANN, psychoanalyst; b. N.Y.C., July 25, 1917; d. Nathan and Mollie (Levine) Jedeikin; B.A., Hunter Coll., 1939; M.S., N.Y. U., 1945; Ph.D., Temple U., 1954. Research asst. prof. physiology Albert Einstein Coll. Medicine, N.Y.C., 1955-68; tng. Nat. Psychol. Assn. Psychoanalysis, N.Y.C., 1968-72; pvt. practice as psychoanalyst, N.Y.C., 1969—; adj. asst. prof. dept. guidance L.I. U., 1971—; faculty Center for Modern Psychoanalytic Studies, N.Y.C., 1973—. Recipient various fellowships and grants. Mem. Nat. Psychol. Assn. Psychoanalysis, Center Modern Psychoanalytic Studies, Am. Heart Assn., Am. Cancer Soc., Am. Chem. Soc., Biochem. Soc., Sigma Xi, Delta Epsilon Sigma. Contbr. articles to profl. jours. Home: 205 West End Av New York City NY 10023 Office: 350 Central Park W New York City NY 10025

JEDLICKA, PHYLLIS LOUISE IGO, advt. agy. exec.; b. Mpls., Oct. 8, 1934; d. Lewis Schee and Phyllis (Aeschliman) Igo; student St. Cloud State Coll., 1952-53; B.A., U. Minn., 1957; m. Philip A. Jedlicka, May 17, 1958 (div. Nov. 1965); 1 dau., Wendy Louise. Copywriter radio sta. KSTP, 1957-58; adminstrv. asst. Gile Letter Service, 1959-60, 62-65; prodn. mgr. Pidgeon, Savage, Lewis, 1960-62; account exec. Kaufman, Spicer & Co., Mpls., 1966-70; owner Communications Et Cetera, Mpls., 1969—. Founding mem. Edina-Morningside Community Theater, 1960—, dir., 1961-64, appeared in Little Foxes, 1962, Rapunzel, 1963, Three Penny Opera, 1966, author, dir. Tales of Sheherazade, 1966; dir., sec. Mpls. Council Civic Clubs, 1963-65; mem. econ. opportunity com. Task Force Edn. and Tng., 1963-65; chmn. gift fair com. Women's Assn. Mpls. Symphony Orch., chmn. luncheon Mpls. Aquatennial Queen's Rev. Luncheon, vol. staff asst. to exec. sec. Nat. Gov.'s Conf., 1965. Bd. dirs. Friends of Mpls. Library. Mem. Twin Cities Mail Advt. Service Assn. (sec., treas. 1963-65), Mpls. Soc. Fine Arts, Mpls. C. of C. (chmn. publicity women's div. 1963—), Alpha Epsilon Rho. Clubs: Upper Midwest Direct Mail (dir., treas. 1964-65), Women's Advertising of Minneapolis (dir. 1963-65), Advertising of Minn. Co-author: Scentuous Cookery, 1971. Home: 1322 W 32d St Minneapolis MN 55408 Office: Communications Et Cetera Minneapolis MN 55402

JEFFERDS, MARY LEE, environmental edn. assn. exec.; b. Seattle, July 16, 1921; d. Amos Osgood and Vera Margaret (Percival) Jefferds; A.B., U. Cal. at Berkeley, 1943, gen. secondary teaching certificate, 1951; M.A., Columbia, 1947; certificate Washington and Lee U., 1945. Sec., Fair Play Com. Am. Citizens Japanese Ancestry, 1943-44; adminstrv. asst. U.C. Alumni Assn. book Students at Berkeley, 1949; dir. Student Union Monterey Jr. Coll., 1949-50; mgr. Nat. Audubon Soc. Conservation Resource Center, Berkeley, 1951-66; dir. Nat. Audubon Soc. Bay Area Ednl. Services, 1966-71; curriculum cons. Project WEY, U. Cal. Demonstration Lab. Sch., Berkeley, 1972—. Cons. Berkeley Sch. Dist., Alameda County Schs. Mem. land use com., environmental edn. com. East Bay Municipal Utility Dist., 1968—; mem. steering com. Nat. Sci. Guild, Oakland Mus., 1971—; community adviser Jr. League of Oakland, 1973—. Mem. Berkeley Women's Town Council, 1970—. Bd. dirs. East Bay Regional Park Dist., 1972—, Save San Francisco Bay Assn., 1969—, Cal. Natural Areas Coordinating Council, 1968—. Served with USAAF, 1944-46. Recipient merit award Cal. Conservation Council, 1953. Mem. Prytanean Alumnae, Inc. (pres. 1969-71, chmn. adv. council 1971-73), Am. Assn. U. Women (mem. Cal. com. 1970-73), Nature Conservancy (chmn. no. Cal. chpt. 1970-71), League Women Voters, U. Cal. Class of 1943 (permanent sec.), Regional Parks Assn., Golden Gate Audubon Soc., Urban Care, Stiles Hall, U. Cal. Art Council, U. C. Alumni Assn., Inst. Cal. Man in Nature, N.A.A.C.P., Mortar Board, Gavel (pres.). Democrat. Home: 2932 Pine Av Berkeley CA 94705

JEFFERS, FLORICE STRIPLING, writer; b. Bullard, Tex.; d. James Carl and Mary Evie (Shipp) Stripling; m. Frank Grover Jeffers; children—Mary Allyne (Mrs. Wallace B. Landrum), Gordon Frank. Bookkeeper, Jeffers Oil Co., Jeffers Drilling Co. Judge, critic, poetry contests; condr. programs on poetry, other lit.; contbr. to anthologies, poetry mags. Mem. Nat. Fedn. State Poetry Socs., Acad. Am. Poets (founder), Poetry Soc. Tex. (awards and prizes, mem. council), Wichita Falls Poetry Soc. (pres.), Tex. Fedn. Women's Clubs (poet laureate 1960), Current Lit. Club (past pres.), Woman's Forum Wichita Falls (past pres. writers dept.). Baptist. Home: 608 Meadow Dr Burkburnett TX 76354 Office: PO Box 638 Burkburnett TX 76354

JEFFERSON, DEBRAH HILL (MRS. NICKEY L. JEFFERSON), educator; b. Kansas City, Kan., July 14, 1947; d. Clarence and Arthie Mae (Carter) Hill; B.J., U. Mo., 1969, M.A., 1972, postgrad., 1972—; m. Nickey L. Jefferson, Nov. 20, 1973. Advt. sales promotion copywriter Successful Farming and Better Homes & Garden Mags., Meredith Corp., Des Moines, 1969-70, asso. editor Imprint Mag., 1970-71; communications grad. asst. Agr. Editor's Office, U. Mo., Columbia, 1971-72; instr., asst. editor, extension information specialist, 1972—. Mem. Columbia's Project Equality, Columbia, Mo., 1973—. Mem. Am. Assn. U. Women, Women in Communications, Omicron Nu, Alpha Kappa Alpha. Office: 1-98 Agriculture Bldg Univ of Mo Columbia MO 65201

JEFFERSON, LILLIAN FRANCIS HINTON, city ofcl.; b. Corona, N.Y., Nov. 12, 1923; d. George Warren and Sarah Foster (Hunt) Hinton; B.A., Morgan State Coll., 1944; postgrad. Fordham U., 1944-45, Loyola U., Chgo., 1952-53, U. Chgo., 1953; m. Lawrence R. Jefferson, Feb. 14, 1944 (div. Oct. 1952). Clk. Jewish Welfare, Chgo., 1946-49; with Chgo. Dept. Pub. Aid, 1949-52; with Cook County Dept. Pub. Aid, Chgo., 1952—, asst. dist. office supr., 1955—; adminstrv. assn. for Chgo. Plan, 1967-68. Mem. N.A.A.C.P., Urban League, Ill. Welfare Assn., Alpha Kappa Alpha. Home: 8258 S Vernon St Chicago IL 60619 Office: 6125 S Halsted St Chicago IL 60621

JEFFRESS, J. ELIZABETH, psychiatrist, educator, assn. exec.; b. Va.; M.D., Woman's Med. Coll. Pa., 1949. Intern Meth. Hosp., Gary, Ind.; resident Phila. Psychiat. Hosp. Successively asst. prof. psychiatry Woman's Med. Coll. Pa.; staff psychiatrist Haverford (Pa.) State Hosp.

Outpatient Clinic; now chief profl. edn. Napa State Hosp., Imola, Cal.; clin. asst. prof. U. Cal. Med. Sch., San Francisco; asst. clin. prof. Stanford. Fellow Am. Psychiat. Assn.; mem. Am. Med. Women's Assn. (nat. corr. sec. to med. women's internat. assn. 1969-72), Santa Clara County (pres. 1970-71), No. Cal. (v.p. 1971-72) psychiat. socs., Pan Am. Med. Women's Alliance (pres. elect 1973). Editor: Psychosomatic Medicine: Current Journal Articles, 1971. Home: 470 Maple Way Woodside CA 94062

JELKS, MARY LARSON (MRS. ALLEN N. JELKS), pediatrician; b. Galva, Ill., May 23, 1929; d. Henry G. and Nelle F. (Johnson) Larson; A.B. cum laude, U. Neb., 1950, M.D., 1955; m. Allen N. Jelks, June 16, 1957; children—Helen Irene, Allen Nathaniel, Howard L., Alice C. Intern Johns Hopkins Hosp., 1955-56, jr. asst. resident, 1956-57, asst. resident, 1958-59; jr. asst. resident Grace New Haven Hosp., 1957-58; research asso. outpatient dept. U. Fla. Teaching Hosp., Gainesville, 1959-61; practice medicine specializing in pediatrics, allergy, Sarasota, Fla., 1961—. Diplomate Am. Bd. Pediatrics. Fellow Am. Acad. Pediatrics; mem. Am. Acad. Allergy (pollen and mold com.). Address: 1700 S Osprey St Sarasota FL 33579

JENCICK, MARIAN ANNA, civic worker; b. N.Y.C., June 24, 1904; d. Stephen Kalman and Emilie Marguerite (Stoeckicht) Jencick; A.B., Mather Coll., 1925; M.A. in Eng., Western Reserve U., 1942. Tchr., English, Cleve. pub. schs., 1925-60, dept. chmn., 1938-60. Curator, Chagrin Hist. Soc., Chagrin Falls, O., 1965—; vol. worker Western Res. Hist. Soc., Cleve., 1961—. Mem. Nat., Ohio ret. tchrs. assns., Cleve. Ret. Tchrs., Delta Kappa Gamma. Republican. Mem. United Ch. Christ. Mem. Order Eastern Star. Club: Woman's of Chagrin Falls. Home: 250 N Main St Chagrin Falls OH 44022 Office: Chagrin Falls Hist Soc 21 Walnut St Chagrin Falls OH 44022

JENG, HELENE WU (MRS. BIH-JING JENG), librarian; b. Taipei, Taiwan, Republic of China, July 23, 1938; d. Shou-Li and Mei-Tze H. (Huang) Wu; B.A., Soochow U., 1962; M.L.S., Appalachian State U., 1968, M.A. in L.S., 1968; m. Bih-Jing Jeng, Nov. 27, 1971. Came to U.S., 1966. Asst. to dir. Nat. Taiwan Sci. Mus., Taipei, 1962-64; exec. sec. Taiwan Power Co., Taipei, 1964-66; head librarian U. S.C. at Lancaster, 1968-73; library dir. Villa Julie Coll., Stevenson, Md., 1973—. Mem. Southeastern Md. library assns. Club: Evening Garden (Lancaster, S.C.). Home: 4108 Paran Rd Randallstown MD 21133 Office: Greenspring Valley Rd Stevenson MD 21153

JENICKE, ALICE ELIZABETH (MRS. LAWRENCE OLIVER JENICKE), univ. librarian; b. Natrona Heights, Pa., Nov. 9, 1943; d. Laurence Albert and Ruth Marion (Edwards) Keim; B.A., Alma Coll., 1965; M.L.S., U. Mich., 1966; m. Lawrence Oliver Jenicke, Aug. 21, 1971. Librarian, Dayton and Montgomery County Pub. Library, Dayton, O., 1966-68, Mich. State U. Engring. Library, East Lansing, 1968—. Mem. A.L.A., Spl. Libraries Assn. Home: 559 Stoddard St East Lansing MI 48823

JENKINS, CLARA BARNES, educator; b. Franklinton, N.C.; d. Walter and Stella (Griffin) Barnes; B.S., Winston-Salem State U., 1939; postgrad. N.Y.U., 1947-48, U.N.C., 1963; M.A., N.C. Central U., 1947; Ed.D., U. Pitts., 1965; postgrad. N.C. Agrl. and State U., summer 1971; m. Hugh Jenkins, Dec. 24, 1949 (div. Feb. 1955). Tchr. pub. schs., Wendell, N.C., 1939-43, Wise N.C., 1943-45; faculty Fayetteville State U., 1945-53; faculty Rust Coll., Holly Spring, Miss., 1953-58; asst. prof. Shaw U., 1958-64; prof. edn. and psychology St. Paul's Coll., Lawrenceville, Va., 1964—; vis. prof. edn. Friendship Jr. Coll., Rock Hill, S.C., summer 1947, N.C. Agrl. and Tech. State U., 1966-73. United Negro Coll. Fund Faculty fellow, 1963-64; recipient grant Am. Bapt. Conv., 1963-64. Mem. Am. Assn. U. Profs., Nat. Soc. for Study Edn., N.E.A., Am. Assn. U. Women, Am. Hist. Assn., Va. Edn. Assn., Am. Acad. Polit. and Social Sci., A.A.A.S., Internat. Platform Assn., Assn. Tchr. Educators, History Edn. Soc., Doctoral Assn. Educators, Am. Assn. Higher Edn., Acad. Polit. Sci., Am. Psychol. Assn., Marquis Biog. Library Soc., Phi Eta Kappa, Zeta Phi Beta. Episcopalian. Home: 920 Bridges St Henderson NC 27536 Office: St Paul's Coll Lawrenceville VA 23868

JENKINS, ELLA L., folk singer; b. St. Louis, Aug. 6, 1924; B.A., San Francisco State Coll. Dir. teenage program YWCA, Chgo., 1952-56; folk singer, 1956—; formerly hostess folk music radio show Meetin House, also other TV appearances; condr. workshops in Austria, Montreal and Toronto; worked with children in Switzerland; numerous recs. Mem. A.S.C.A.P., Internat. Platform Assn., Am. Fedn. Musicians, Music Educators Nat. Conf. Author: This is Rhythm; The Ella Jenkins Song Book for Children. Author, arranger, singer film series Themetooshow. Address: care Folkways Records 701 7th Av New York City NY 10036*

JENKINS, ESTHER CALL, educator; b. New Cumberland, W.Va., Mar. 17, 1910; d. William Edward and Margaret May (Lyons) Call; A.B., Alderson Broaddus Coll., 1931; M.A., Ohio State U., 1947, Ph.D., 1962; m. Harold Otis Jenkins, Aug. 8, 1934 (div. Sept. 1941); 1 dau., Carol Ann. Tchr. elementary sch., Clarksburg, W.Va., 1931-35, Warren O., 1941-47; critic tchr. lab. sch. U. Hawaii, Honolulu, 1948-55, dir. aux. tchr. tng. program, 1955-60, instr. tchr. edn., 1955— now prof. edn., chmn. masters program elementary edn. Vis. prof. U. So. Cal., summer 1958, U. Ill., summers 1955, 68, O. State U., 1951-52, 60-62; cons. elementary edn., pub. and pvt. schs. Hawaii. U.S. Office Edn. grantee, 1964; Delta Kappa Gamma Internat. scholar, 1960. Mem. Hawaii Council Tchrs. English, Nat. Council Tchrs. English, Hawaii Edn. Assn., N.E.A., Pi Lambda Theta. Democrat. Conglist. Club: Zonta (pres.). Home: 1634 Makiki St #606 Honolulu HI 96822 Office: 1776 University St Honolulu HI 96822

JENKINS, E(THEL) VALERIE, librarian; b. Amherst, O., Sept. 7, 1913; d. Frank A. and Ethel E. (Dute) Eppley; student Hiram Coll., 1932; B.A., Baldwin-Wallace Coll., 1936; postgrad. Western Res. U., 1936, 41, 66, State U. Ia., 1938-39, Ohio State U., 1960; M.A., Kent State U., 1962; m. William J. Jenkins, Aug. 13, 1944 (div. May 1964). Dir. dramatics Baldwin-Wallace Coll., Berea, O., 1936-38; tchr. English and speech St. Elmo (Ill.) High Sch., 1939-42; tchr. English, speech, dir. dramatics Clearview-Loraine (O.) High Sch., 1942-57, librarian, 1949-57; librarian Amherst (O.) Pub. Schs., 1957—. Instr. Kent State U., 1963-66; instr. speech Cleve. State U., 1966-70; lectr. costumes for theatre; owner, operator children's theatre, also costume rental; cons. Amherst Pub. Library Bldg. Program, 1972-73. Founder Workshop Players, Inc., 1948, trustee, 1948—, pres., 1948-49, 56-58, 60; mem. bd. Amherst Pub. Library, 1962—, pres., 1963-65. Mem. Nat., Ohio (life) edn. assns., Am. Theatre Assn., A.L.A., Ohio Assn. Sch. Librarians, Amherst Tchrs. Assn. (pres. 1962-64), Internat. Platform Assn., Delta Kappa Gamma, Phi Mu. Republican. Conglist. Home: 439 Shupe Av Amherst OH 44001 Office: 450 Washington St Amherst OH 44001

JENKINS, JOAN VIRGINIA WILLIAMS (MRS. RAMON BARTON JENKINS), psychologist; b. Detroit, Dec. 4, 1929; d. Joseph Henry and Ella (Wyse) Williams; B.A., Bryn Mawr Coll., 1951; M.A., U. Mich., 1953, Ph.D., 1959; m. Ramon Barton Jenkins, May 6, 1961; children—Matthew Barton, David Andrew. Research asst. dept. psychology U. Mich., Ann Arbor, 1955-58; research asso. U. N.C., Chapel Hill, 1958-64, asst. prof., 1959-64; research psychologist Nat. Inst. Mental Health, Rockville, Md., 1966—. Mem. Am. Psychol. Assn. Contbr. chpt. to book. Home: 6016 Highboro Dr Bethesda MD 20034 Office: Nat Inst Mental Health 5600 Fishers Lane Rockville MD 20852

JENKINS, MARGARET QUANTE (MRS. LOUIE BOYD JENKINS), physician; b. Savannah, Ga., Feb. 6, 1923; d. Frederick H. and Dorothea G. (Siem) Quante; B.S. magna cum laude, Newberry Coll., 1949; M.D., Med. Coll. Ga., 1949; m. Louie Boyd Jenkins, Jan. 30, 1950; children—Margaret Lucinda, Dorothea Denise, Pamela Cullie, Karen Louise, Amelia Elizabeth. Intern, Roper Hosp., Charleston, S.C., 1949-50, resident, 1950-52; teaching fellow Roper Hosp. and Med. Coll. S.C., Charleston, 1952-53; mem. faculty Med. U. S.C., Charleston, 1954—, asst. prof. pediatrics, 1956-68, asst. clin. prof., 1968—. Lectr., Tech. Edn. Center, 1972; co-dir. Charleston Poison Prevention Project, 1961-65; chmn. community-wide mass polio immunization campaign, 1963; dir. S.C. Cystic Fibrosis Clinic, 1966—, Charleston Rheumatic Fever Clinic, 1958-66, Charleston Poison Control Center, 1958—; co-ordinator S.C. Crippled Children's Program, 1966—. Chmn. bd. mgmt. YMCA, James Island, 1973—; bd. mgmt. Met. YMCA, 1973. Recipient citation for contbn. to poison prevention project HEW, 1965. Diplomate Am. Bd. Pediatrics. Mem. Am. Acad. Pediatrics, Charleston County Med. Soc., S.C. Med. Assn., A.M.A., Assn. Poison Control Centers, Charleston County Pediatric Soc., S.C. Pediatric Soc. (chmn. accident prevention com. 1967—), So. Soc. Pediatric Research, Alpha Epsilon Iota. Lutheran (ch. council). Home: 699 North Shore Dr Charleston SC 29412 Office: Med U Hosp 80 Barre St Charleston SC 29402

JENKINS, MARIE MAGDALEN, educator; b. Eldorado, Ill., Sept. 26, 1909; d. B. Robert and Clara Ann (Rhine) Jenkins; A.B., Phillips U., 1929; M.S., Catholic U. Am., 1951; Ph.D., U. Okla., 1961. Tchr. schs., Jet, Okla., 1931-32, Okeene, Okla., 1934-36, Tishomingo, Okla., 1936-40, Edmond, Okla., 1940-41, Monte Cassino Sch., Tulsa, 1941-42, St. Joseph's Convent, Guthrie, Okla., 1942-44, Marquette High Sch., Tulsa, 1944-48, 49-52; tchr. Benedictine Heights Coll., Guthrie, 1952-55, Tulsa, 1955-57, registrar, 1954-57; instr. zoology U. Okla., Norman, 1960-62; prof. biology Madison Coll., Harrisonburg, Va., 1962—. Recipient grants So. Fellowships Fund, 1959, Sigma Xi-Research Soc. Am., 1963, 64, Va. Acad. Scis., 1963, NIH, 1966-69. Mem. A.A.A.S., Am. Soc. Zoology, Am. Micros. Soc., Southwestern Assn. Naturalists, Va. Acad. Sci., Sigma Xi, Phi Sigma. Author: Moon Jelly Swims through the Sea (ages 6-10), 1969; Animals Without Parents (ages 10-17), 1970; The Curious Mollusks, 1972. Contbr. articles to profl. jours. Home: Route 1 Box 113 Hinton VA 22831

JENKINS, MYRA ELLEN, archivist; b. Elizabeth, Colo., Sept. 26, 1916; d. Lewis Harlan and Minnie (Ackroyd) Jenkins; B.A. cum laude, U. Colo., 1937, M.A., 1938; Ph.D., U. N.M., 1953. Instr. pub. schs., Climax, Colo., 1939-41, Granada, Colo., 1941-43, Pueblo, Colo., 1943-50; fellow U. N.M., 1950-52, asst., 1952-53; free-lance historian and hist. cons., Albuquerque, 1953-59; archivist Hist. Soc. N.M., Santa Fe, 1959-60; sr. archivist N.M. Records Center and Archives, 1960—; instr. Coll. Santa Fe. Mem. Soc. Am. Archivists, Western History Assn., Hist. Soc. N.M., Phi Beta Kappa, Phi Kappa Phi, Phi Alpha Theta, Kappa Delta Pi. Democrat. Episcopalian. Author: The Baltazar Baca Grant, History of an Encroachment, 1961; Guide and Calendar to the Spanish Archives of New Mexico, 1968; Guide and Calendar to the Mexican Archives of New Mexico, 1970; also articles profl. jours. and book reviews. Home: 1022 Don Cubero St Santa Fe NM 87501

JENKINS, ROSE DEMOLL (MRS. GEORGE LORENZO MALLORY), child psychiatrist; b. Rocky Mount, N.C., Dec. 24, 1925; d. Addison D. and Rose (Cherry) Jenkins; B.S., Agrl. and Tech. Coll., 1944; M.D., Howard U., 1952; m. John M. Hamilton, Aug. 10, 1950 (div. Oct. 1961); children—Marsha Gayle, Karen Rose; m. 2d, Geroge Lorenzo Mallory, Oct. 16, 1961; 1 son, Lloyd David. Intern Freedmen's Hosp., Washington, 1952-53, resident psychiatry, 1954-56; resident pediatrics Norfolk (Va.) Community Hosp., 1953-54; resident psychiatry Crownsville (Md.) State Hosp., 1956-57; staff psychiatrist Pacific State Hosp., Pomona, Cal., 1957-60; psychiatrist Child Guidance Clinic, Los Angeles, 1958-60; practice medicine specializing in adult and child psychiatry, Los Angeles, 1960—; dir. children's psychiat. outpatient clinic Los Angeles County Hosp., 1961-65, dir. child psychiat. admitting, 1968-69; asst. clin. prof. child psychiatry U. So. Cal., Los Angeles, 1961-71; chief div. child psychiatry M.L. King Gen. Hosp., 1971-73; regional chief S.E. Mental Health Service County Los Angeles, 1973—; co-chmn. psychiatry search com. Charles R. Drew Postgrad. Med. Sch., Los Angeles, 1969-70, asso. prof., 1971—; cons. Cal. Vocational Rehab. Service, 1961—. Bd. dirs. YWCA, Pasadena, 1967-70, corr. sec. bd. dirs., 1969-71, 1st v.p., 1971-72; bd. dirs. nursing services Pasadena chpt. A.R.C., 1967—, bd. dirs. youth services, 1967-69; rep. to Pasadena Commn. Human Need and Opportunity, 1969-70; mem. Bishop's Commn. on Marriage, Los Angeles Diocese, 1963—; pres. Vilia Esperanza Aux., 1970; mem. Gov.'s Developmental Disabilities Adv. Council, 1972—. Nat. Inst. Mental Health fellow, 1965-67, Ida L. Jackson award Alpha Kappa Alpha, 1970; named Woman of Achievement in medicine Nat. Council Negro Women, Los Angeles, 1964; Tribute award Los Angeles County Head Start, 1969. Diplomate Am. Bd. Psychiatry and Neurology in psychiatry and subsplty. child psychiatry. Fellow Am. Psychiat. Assn. (mem. task force community mental health services poverty areas); mem. Los Angeles Soc. Child Psychiatry (treas. 1969-70), Black Psychiatrists Am., N.Y. Acad. Scis., Charles Drew Med. Soc., Los Angeles Soc. Child Psychiatry, A.M.A., Nat., Los Angeles County med. assns., Links Inc. (gen. chmn. Western area conf. 1970), Alpha Kappa Alpha. Democrat. Episcopalian. Home: 2021 N Arroyo Blvd Pasadena CA 91103 Office: 1828 S Western Av Los Angeles CA 90006

JENKINS, RUTH ELIZABETH, investment counselor; b. Bethlehem, Pa.; d. Thomas and Mary (Weiser) Jenkins; A.B. cum laude, Radcliffe Coll. 1947. Vice pres., investment counselor Loomis, Sayles & Co., Inc., Phila., 1951—. Mem. D.A.R., Financial Analysts Phila. (past sec., dir.), Nat. Soc. Colonial Dames Am. Presbyn. Clubs: Acorn; Waynesborough Country. Home: Ardglen Gardens 16 W Montgomery Av Ardmore PA 19003 Office: Fidelity Bldg 123 S Broad St Philadelphia PA 19109

JENKINS, VICTORIA WILLIAMS, librarian; b. Walterboro, S.C., Feb. 1, 1931; d. Wesley Mims and Helen (Simmons) Williams; B.S., Morris Brown Coll., 1951; M.S., Atlanta U., 1968; m. Luther Jenkins, Feb. 25, 1955; children—Tyna Yvette, Tammye Yvonne. Tchr. Whitman St. Sch., Toccoa, Ga., 1951-52; tchr.-librarian Carver High Sch., Hamilton, Ga., 1952-57; tchr. base schs. Fort Richardson, Alaska, 1957-59; librarian D.H. Stanton Sch., Atlanta, 1959-68; head librarian Morris Brown Coll., Atlanta, 1968—. Instr. children's lit. Morris Brown Coll., Atlanta, 1969—. Active United Negro Coll. Fund, 1972—, N.A.A.C.P., 1971—, Nat. Negro Women's Bus. League, 1972—. Nat. Def. Edn. Act grantee, 1965, 66, 71, HEW grantee, 1971. Mem. N.E.A., Am., So. library assns., Delta Sigma Theta. African Meth. Episcopalian. Club: Sparker's Bridge. Home: 205 Rockmart Dr SW Atlanta GA 30314 Office: 643 Hunter St Atlanta GA 30314

JENKS, MARY ELLEN (MRS. DOUGLAS RAYMOND JORDAL), food co. exec.; b. Milw., Oct. 4, 1933; d. Frank George and Emma Augusta (Sweitzer) Jenks; B.S., U. Wis., 1956, M.S., 1957; m. Douglas Raymond Jordal, Feb. 9, 1963; children—Joyellyn Jenks, Jared Brent. Dir. speech dept. Monona Grove (Wis.) High Sch., 1957; dir. home services Salada Foods, Toronto, Ont., Can., 1957-59. Boston, 1959-61; editorial writer Am. Dairy Assn., Chgo., 1961-62; dir. home services dept. Green Giant Co., Mpls., 1962—. Mem. Foremost Women in Communication, Grocery Mfrs. Am. (chmn. consumer services com. 1968-70), Am. Frozen Food Inst. (chmn. home econs. council 1969-70), Am. Women in Radio and TV, Instl. Food Editorial Council, Am. Home Econs. Assn., Twin Cities Home Economists in Bus., Mpls. Inst. Art, Friends of the Inst., Women's Assn. Minn. Symphony Orch. Home: 6405 Cherokee Trail Edina MN 55435 Office: Green Giant Co Hazeltine Gates Office Park Jonathon MN 55318

JENNINGS, AMY REBECCA, librarian; b. Murfreesboro, Tenn., May 17, 1907; d. E. Bertram and Lillian Lee (Jordan) Jennings; student Middle Tenn. State Tchrs. Coll., 1929-33; A.B., Cumberland U., 1940; B.S. in L.S., George Peabody Coll. Tchrs., 1942. Tchr., prin. pub. schs., Wilson County, Tenn., 1927-39; librarian city sch. systems Tenn. and Miss., 1939-42; reference librarian Law Library, Social Security Bd., Washington, 1943, Law Library, U.S. Dept. Agr., Washington, 1943-44; chief librarian NLRB, Washington, 1944-47; chief librarian FTC, Washington, 1947-72, librarian, adviser to exec. dir. for adminstrn., 1972-73). Trustee Falls Church (Va.) Pub. Library. Mem. Law Librarians' Soc. D.C. (sec. 1946-48), Spl. Libraries Assn. (Washington chpt. chmn. legislative reference sect. 1946-48), D.A.R., Nat. Trust Historic Preservation, Va. Library Assn. (trustee sect.), Va. Hist. Soc. Episcopalian. Contbr. articles to profl. jours. Home: 417 Poplar Dr Falls Church VA 22046

JENNINGS, ANNE HEISE (MRS. BLANDFORD JENNINGS), educator, author; b. Milw.; d. Paul Edgar and Dora (Tyre) Heise; B.A., U. Wis., 1917, M.A., 1919; postgrad. St. Louis U., 1930-33; m. Blandford Jennings, Sept. 2, 1919; children—James Blandford, Paul George. Asso. prof. French, Spanish various univs., 1918-32; instr. German Lindenwood Coll., 1931-32; feature writer, play reviewer Webster-News-Times, Webster Groves, Watchman-Adv., Clayton, Mo., 1932-42; asst. prof. Webster Coll., Webster Groves, Mo., 1945-56, dir. depts. French and German, 1952-56; pvt. tchr. langs., Maplewood, Mo., 1956—. Writer, actress Art in St. Louis, KFUO for City Art Mus., 1944-58. Mem. Am. Assn. Tchrs. French, Am. Assn. Tchrs. German (sec.-treas. 1961-63), Internat. League Childrens Poets, Soc. Children's Book Writers, Theta Sigma Phi, Phi Beta Kappa, Pi Delta Phi, Alpha Xi Delta. Author: Los Amantes sordos (play), 1918; The Clock Struck One (play), 1928, Armchair Land, 1950; Arcadia Revisited, 1965; The Little Evergreen Tree (play), 1969; The Visit of Mother Cloud (play), 1969; poems and translations in various anthologies. Home: 7746 Rannells Av Maplewood MO 63143

JENNINGS, ETHLYN CLARIBEL, physician; b. Mpls., Feb. 10, 1917; d. Edwin C. and Anna Ethlyn (Jennings) Weybe; M.D., U. Kan., 1949; m. Abdelali Khodadad, June 1, 1951 (dec. Nov. 1968); children—Behroo, Behram. Intern Research Hosp., Kansas City, Mo., 1950; practice medicine, Kansas City, Mo., 1950-61; instr. Pahlavl U., Shiraz, Iran, 1962-63; resident radiology Roswell Park Meml. Inst., Buffalo, N.Y., 1964-67; staff radiologist, 1967-71, chief diagnostic radiology dept., 1971—. Home: 336 Woodgate St Tonawonda NY 14150 Office: 666 Elm St Buffalo NY 14223

JENNINGS, MARGUERITE NAEGLE (MRS. RUSSELL JENNINGS), lawyer; b. Benson, Ariz., Jan. 31, 1916; d. Marion Beck and Hattie (Davis) Naegle; B.A., Ariz. State U., 1936; postgrad. Northwestern U., summer, 1936; J.D., U. Ariz., 1968; m. Russell Jennings, 1941; children—James Russell, Robert Alan, Jeanne Marie, William Warren. Admitted to Ariz. bar, 1968, since practiced in Benson; pres. Benson Econ. Enterprises, Inc., 1969—; pres., gen. mgr. Cochise Gardens of Rest, 1963—; real estate broker Strout Realty, Benson, 1957—; asst. v.p., state mgr. E.A. Strout Western Realty, Arcadia, Cal., 1970—; gen. ins. agt. Jones-Wilson Ins. and Investments, Benson, 1957—. Sec., Cochise County Adv. Council on Air Pollution, 1967-70, Benson Youth Culture, Inc.; pres. San Pedro Artists; pres. Benson Festival Com., 1974. Bd. dirs. Benson Hosp., sec., 1970-73; pres. Cochise County Alcoholism Council, 1974—. Mem. Cochise County Health Planning council, 1974—. Mem. Cochise County Bar Assn. (pres. 1974—), Benson C. of C. (centennial chmn. 1972—), Cochise County Hosp. Assn. (dir. 1973—). Editor, pub. Valley Sun, 1951-58. Home: 303 Orr Av Benson AZ 85602 Office: 800 W 4th Box 2 Benson AZ 85602

JENNINGS, SHIRLEY KATHRYN LAWRENCE (MRS. WARREN DAVID JENNINGS), ednl. cons.; b. Nipawin, Sask., Can., Feb. 28, 1931; d. William Warren and Kathryn Ruth (Gunness) Lawrence; B.A. with honors in Psychology, Notre Dame U., 1967; M.A., U. Toronto, 1970; m. Warren David Jennings, Dec. 27, 1952; children—Gregory, Timothy, Gail. Research asst. Ont. Inst. for Studies in Edn., Toronto, 1967-68; sch. psychologist Metro Toronto Sch. Bd., 1968-69; diagnostician, cons., counsellor Madame Vaniers Children's Services, London, Ont., 1970-74; supr. pre-sch. unit Mental Health Services Clinic, Edmonton, Alta., 1974—. Coordinator learning disabilities course Fanshawe Coll., London, 1971-73, also mem. adv. com. Mem. adv. com. Ministry Edn., Province of Ont., Toronto. Recipient Gov. Gen.'s medal, 1967. Mem. Council for Exceptional Children, Assn. for Children with Learning Disabilities. Mem. Anglican Ch. Club: University Women's (London). Home: 104 Brander Village Edmonton AB T6H 5C9 Canada Office: 10010 105th St Edmonton AB Canada

JENNRICH, LYNNE HARVEL (MRS. JOHN HAROLD JENNRICH), editor; b. Durham, N.C., Dec. 22, 1945; d. Paul W. and Rose Wade (Scroggs) Harvel, Jr.; B.A. in Journalism, U. N.C., 1968; m. John Harold Jennrich, Sept. 11, 1971. Reporter, Richmond (Va.) News Leader, 1968-69, Burlington (N.C.) Daily Times News, 1969-71; women's editor Md. Gazette, Glen Burnie, 1972; publs. editor Am. Newspaper Pubs. Assn., Reston, Va., 1973—; free lance writer, 1973—. Mem. Women in Communications, Am. Assn. Univ. Women. Home: 11573 North Shore Dr Apt 21 C Reston VA 22090 Office: PO Box 17407 Dulles International Airport Washington DC 20041

JENS, ELIZABETH LEE SHAFER (MRS. ARTHUR M. JENS, JR.), civic worker; b. Monroe, Mich., Jan. 25, 1915; d. Frank Lee and Mary (Bogard) Shafer; student Kalamazoo Coll., 1932-34, U. Wis., summer 1935; B.S., Northwestern U., 1936; postgrad. Wheaton Coll., summer 1965; L.P.N., Triton Coll., 1969; m. Arthur M. Jens, Jr., Aug. 14, 1937; children—Timothy V., Christopher E., Jeffrey A. Gray Lady, Hines, (Ill.) Hosp., 1948-49, 51-53; vol. Elgin (Ill.) State Hosp., 1958-72; writer Newsletter Vol. Planning Council, 1960-62; mem. Family Service Assn. Du Page County; vol. coordinator for social center for recovering mental patients Du Page County, 1966—; weekly vol. FISH orgn., 1973—. Bd. dirs. Du Page County Mental Health Soc., 1962-68, sec., 1963-64, 65-68, chmn. forgotten patient com., 1963-68, chmn. new projects, 1965-68; co-chmn. Glen Ellyn unit Central Du Page Hosp. Assn. Women's Aux., 1959-60; bd. dirs., chmn. com. on pesticides, Ill. Audubon Soc., 1963—; mem. Ill. Pesticide Control Com., 1963—, Citizens Com. Dutch Elm Disease, Glen Ellyn, 1960; bd. dirs. Natural Resources Council Ill., 1961-67, sec., 1961-64; bd. dirs. Du Page Art League, 1958-68, chmn. bd., 1961-63, bldg. and grounds, paint-out and spl. memberships chmn., 1963-68, chmn. new bldg. com., 1968—; bd. dirs., mem. planning com., publicity chmn., Du Page Fine Arts Assn., 1965-67; bd. dirs. Friends Library Glen Ellyn, 1967-68, Rachel Carson Trust for Living Environment, 1971-74; bd. dirs. sec. DuPage unit Mental Health Assn. Greater Chgo., 1973—. Hon. mention in Nat. Sonnet contest, 1967. Mem. Wilderness Soc., Du Page County Humane Soc., Du Page County Hist. Soc., Nat., Du Page Audubon socs., Nat. Writers Conf. (monthly meeting chmn. Midwest chpt.), Defenders of Wildlife, Theosophical Soc. Am., Nature Conservancy Ill., N.A.A.C.P., Chgo. Art Inst. (life), Ill. Assn. Mental Health (dir. 1971—), Pi Beta Phi. Writer column Mental Health and You for Press Publs., 1969—. Home: 22 W 210 Stanton Rd Glen Ellyn IL 60137

JENSEN, EDYTHE RUTH (MRS. JOHN JENSEN), editor; b. Bklyn., July 5, 1948; d. Robert Benjamin and Betty M. (Farber) Edgar; B.A. in Journalism, Ariz. State U., 1970; m. John Jensen, June 13, 1970. Copy editor Phoenix Gazette, summer 1969, reporter, 1969-70, editor youth sec., 1970—; also free lance writer. Pres. Phoenix chpt. Nat. Orgn. for Women, 1972-74; mem. Ariz. Women's Polit. Caucus, 1972—. Mem. Sigma Delta Chi (treas. 1972-74). Club: Ariz. Press. Home: 601 E Palo Verde Dr Phoenix AZ 85012 Office: 120 E VanBuren St Phoenix AZ 85001

JENSEN, GLORIA JEAN, horse trainer; b. Libertyville, Ill., June 23, 1941; d. Russell Charles and Irene Martha (Blach) Boehm; grad. high sch.; m. Rudolph Walter Jensen, Jr., Oct. 1, 1960 (div. Dec. 1972); children—Debra Ann, Robert Allen. Owner, mgr. Gold-D-An Horse Farm, Gurnee, Ill., 1959—. Mem. Wadsworth Wranglers, Sheriff's Posse, Libertyville Lariettes (pres. 1959-62). Address: 5555 Washington St Gurnee IL 60031

JENSEN, IDA-MARIE (MRS. LYMAN JENSEN), librarian; b. Logan, Utah; d. Samuel E. and Ida (Andersen) Clark; M.S., Utah State U., 1956; M.A., U. Denver, 1960; m. Stanley H. Logan, Sept, 8, 1939 (dec. 1946); m. 2d, Lyman Jensen. Asso. prof., asso. librarian Utah State U. Library, Logan, 1947—. Bd. dirs. No. Utah Safety Council, 1959—. Recipient Jasper award Bibliographic Center Research Denver; certificate of recognition Utah State U., 1967. Mem. A.A.A.S., Am. Assn. U. Women, Utah Acad. Scis., Arts, Letters, Am. (councilor rep. Utah 1970—), Utah (sect. pres. 1962-63, exec. bd. 1970—), Mountain Plains (sect. pres. 1963-65) library assns., Internat. Platform Assn., Alpha Chi Omega, Phi Kappa Phi, Delta Kappa Gamma, Alpha Lambda Delta, Pi Gamma Mu. Clubs: Logan Literary, A.C. Woman's, Knife and Fork (bd. dirs. 1958-61). Mem. Ch. of Jesus Christ of Latter-day Saints (mem. youth com. All Ch. Coordinating Council). Home: 1461 Sumac Dr Logan UT 84321

JENSEN, ROSALIE SEYMOUR (MRS. RICHARD ALAN JENSEN), educator; b. Elberton, Ga., Feb. 25, 1938; d. William Lloyd and Bertha (Maxwell) Seymour; B.A., Shorter Coll., 1960; M.A., U. Ga., 1962; Ph.D. (U. fellow), Fla. State U., 1966; m. Richard Alan Jensen, Dec. 22, 1963; 1 dau., Karen Irene. Instr. math. West Ga. Coll., Carrollton, 1962-63; asst. prof., chmn. dept. math. Shorter Coll., Rome, Ga., 1966-68; asso. prof. edn., math. and urban life Ga. State U., 1968-74, prof. curriculum and instrn., 1974—. Dir. Day Camp, Atlanta Girl's Club, 1961; treas. Rome Newcomers Club, 1968. Nat. Def. Edn. Act fellow, 1960. Mem. Math. Assn. Am., Nat. Council Tchrs. Math., Ga. Edn. Assn. (pres. local chpt.), Atlanta Math. Club (pres. 1973-74), Pi Mu Epsilon, Pi Sigma Alpha. Author: Developing Mathematical Concepts for the Young Child, 1970; Developing Mathematical Concepts and Skills for Children, 1972; Exploring Mathematical Concepts and Skills in the Elementary School, 1973; contbg. author Concept Learning: Designs for Instruction, 1972. Home: 1369 Emory Rd NE Atlanta GA 30306

JENSEN, WILMA MARY WESTBURG (MRS. EMMANUEL T. JENSEN), assn. exec.; b. Hopkins, Minn., June 11, 1916; d. Andrew Herman and Ida (Anderson) Westburg; B.A., Gustavus Adolphus Coll., 1938; B.L.S., U. Minn., 1940; m. Emmanuel T. Jensen, Aug. 15, 1947. Asst. librarian reference library, U. Minn., Mpls., 1940-43; counsellor for students Nat. Lutheran Council, U. Cal., Berkeley, 1943-47, Ia. State U., Ames, 1947-48; librarian, sec. Donovan-Lovering-Boyle, Contractors, Pickstown, S.D., 1951-56; sec. Lutheran World Fedn., Mpls., 1957; sec. bd. Am. missions, Augustana Lutheran Ch., Mpls., 1957-62; exec. sec. Lutheran Ch. Library Assn., Mpls., 1963—. Nat. del. Lutheran Ch. Am., 1966; nat. adv. Lutheran Student Assn. Am., 1946-47; mem. Minn. Adv. Council on Library Scis., 1973—. Bd. dirs. Com. Am. Missions, Minn., Lutheran Ch. in Am., Minnetonka (Minn.) Music Assn. Named World Brother, World Brotherhood Exchange, 1962; recipient Distinguished Alumni citation Gustavus Adolphus Coll., 1974. Mem. Lutheran Ch. Library Assn. (nat. v.p., 1962, nat. pres., 1963), Ch. and Synagogue Library Assn. (nat. dir. 1967—, v.p. 1970-71, pres. 1971-72), Am., Minn. library assns., United Lutheran Ch. Women (life), Alpha Phi Gamma, Iota Beta. Republican. Lutheran. Home: 3620 Fairlawn Dr Minnetonka MN 55343 Office: 122 W Franklin Av Minneapolis MN 55404

JERDONE, CLARE RICHARDSON GOLDEN (MRS. FRANK H. JERDONE), social worker; b. Jackson, Mich.; d. James Andrew and Laura (Richardson) Golden; A.B., Nazareth Coll., 1937, M.Sc. Western Reserve U. Sch. Applied Social Sci.; m. Frank H. Jerdone, June 8, 1962. Caseworker Mich. Ann Arbor, 1946-54, supr., 1950-57; foster family care, also adoptions specialist Children's Bur., Dept. of Health, Edn. and Welfare, Washington, 1957-60; child welfare specialist Bur. Indian Affairs, Dept. of Interior, Washington, 1960-68, prin. child welfare specialist, 1968—. Mem. Nat. Assn. Social Workers, Acad. Certified Social Workers, Am. Pub. Welfare Assn. Club: Farmington Country (Charlottesville, Va.); Kent Island Yacht (Chester, Md.). Address: 11444 Orchard Lane Reston VA 22090

JERGER, EMILY REMINGTON, pub. relations exec.; b. Thomasville, Ga., Dec. 24, 1921; d. Edward Remington and Emily Neilson (Hatch) Jerger; student Mary Baldwin Coll., 1939-41, U. Wis., 1941-43. News editor Thomasville (Ga.) Times Enterprise, 1943-44, wire editor, reporter, feature writer, 1946-56, women's editor, 1956-64; pub. relations dir., coordinator vol. services Archbold Meml. Hosp., Thomasville, 1964—. Pres. Thomasville Entertainment Found., 1960-62, Jr. Service League, 1953-54; chmn. Thomasville Community Chest, 1952-53. Served with WAC, 1943-45. Mem. Am. Hosp. Assn. Soc. for Pub. Relations Dirs. (area rep. 1965-66), Ga. Hosp. Assn. Soc. for Pub. Relations (dir. 1970-74), Colonial Dames Am. (pres. town com. 1960-61), Chi Omega. Home: 319 N Dawson St Thomasville GA 31792 Office: Archbold Hospital Gordon Av Thomasville GA 31792

JERNIGAN, SARA STAFF, educator; b. Lakewood, O.; d. Otto Karl and Elsie (Walther) Staff; B.S., Stetson U., 1935; M.A., 1937; m. Harvey Jordon Jernigan, Dec. 16, 1942. Prof., dir. dept. phys. edn. women Stetson U., DeLand, Fla., 1937—. Chmn. bd. dirs. Nat. Inst. Girls Sports, 1963-69, dir. nat. insts., 1963, 66, 68, 69; chmn. women's bd. U.S. Olympic Devel. Com., 1960-68, mem.-at-large U.S. Olympic Devel. Com., 1966—; lectr. Internat. Olympic Acad., Olympia, Greece, 1965, 66, 70, 72; mem. bd. cons. U.S. Olympic Com., 1969—; U.S. State Dept. grant to teach in Greece, 1966. Recipient Dist. Honor award A.A.H.P.E.R., 1960, Fla. Honor award, 1958, Nat. Honor fellow award, 1971; Woman of Year award Central Fla. So. Assn. Phys. Edn. Coll. Women, 1963; service award Internat. Olympic Acad., 1970, Distinguished Alumni award Stetson U., 1972. Fellow Am. Coll. Sports Medicine; mem. Am. (v.p. 1960-61, chmn. div. for girls and sports 1960-61, chmn. internat. relations sect. 1968, chmn. internat. relations So. dist. 1957-59), Fla. (v.p. 1962-63) assns. health, phys. edn. and recreation, Am. Acad. Phys. Edn., Am. Recreation Soc., N.E.A., Nat. Recreation and Parks Assn., Nat., So. (v.p. 1955-57, pres. 1958-61) assns. phys. edn. coll. women, Am. Assn. U. Profs., Country Dance Soc. Am., U.S. Lawn Tennis Assn., Internat. Assn. Phys. Edn. and Sports Girls and Women, Nat. League Am. Pen Women, Internat. Olympic Acad. (hon. life), Delta Delta Delta, Delta Kappa Gamma. Clubs: International Relations (pres. 1967-69) (Volusia County), Ikebana Internat. Sr. author: Playtime: A World Recreation Handbook, 1972. Contbr. to nat. and internat. mags. Home: 623 N Cherokee St DeLand FL 32720

JESMER, JEAN BEEMAN (MRS. JOHN H. JESMER), banker; b. Lake Placid, N.Y., Nov. 4, 1925; d. Loyal Anson and Alma Agnes (LaMountain) Beeman; grad. high sch.; m. John H. Jesmer, July 12, 1945. Bookkeeper, proof supr. Bank of Lake Placid, 1945-58, asst. cashier, 1959-62, cashier, 1962—, v.p., 1970-72, exec. v.p., 1972—, also dir. Treas. Lake Placid Service unit Salvation Army, 1962—. Bd. dirs. Lake Placid Pub. Library, 1972—. Mem. Lake Placid C. of C. (dir. 1968-71), Am. Legion Aux. Republican. Home: 22 West Valley Rd Lake Placid NY 12946 Office: 81 Main St Lake Placid NY 12946

JESSEN, ARDELE LAURAINE, editor, poet; b. Chgo., Oct. 13, 1916; d. Robert Laurence and Rose Marie (Freiboth) Jessen; student Northwestern U., 1941-42. With Watson Publs., Inc., Chgo., 1955-71, asst. to publisher, 1960-71; asso. editor Murphy-Richter Pub. Co., Chgo., 1971—. Mem. Am. Poets Fellowship Soc., Centro Studi e Scambi Internazionali, Ill. Poetry Soc., Maj. Poets, World Poetry Soc. Intercontinental. Contbr. poetry to many quarterlies and anthologies, also mags. and newspapers, including Chgo. Tribune, Kansas City Star, Houston Post, Reader's Digest. Home: 104 S Craig Pl Lombard IL 60148 Office: 20 N Wacker Dr Chicago IL 60606

JESSNER, LUCIE NEY, psychiatrist; b. Frankfurt am Main, Germany, Sept. 15, 1896; d. Emanuel and Rose (Lowenhaar) Ney; Ph.D., Frankfurt U., Germany, 1921; M.D., Koenigsberg, Germany, 1926; m. Frederic Jessner, 1928 (dec.); stepchildren—Mrs. Anne Laufer, Mrs. Eva Sampson. Intern Charite Berlin, Germany, 1926-27; asst. psychiatry U. Koenigsberg, 1928-33; psychiatrist Sanatorium Muenchenbuchsee, Switzerland, 1933-37; res. psychiatrist McLean Hosp., Waverly, Mass., Baldpate, Georgetown, Mass., 1938-41; acting dir. Habit Clinic for Child Guidance, Boston, asst. psychiatrist, Mass. Gen. Hosp., Boston, 1943-46; instr. psychiatry Harvard, 1944—, also clin. asso. Harvard Med. Sch.; dir. pychiatric service for children Mass. Gen. Hosp., 1947-55; prof. psychiatry, sch. medicine U. N.C., 1955-63, Georgetown U. Med. Center, 1963-73, prof. emeritus, 1973—; tng. analyst Washington Psychoanalytic Inst. Mem. A.M.A., N.E. Med. Soc., Boston Psychoanalytic Soc. Author: (with Gerald Ryan) Shock Treatment in Psychiatry, 1941; (with Eleanor Pavenstedt) Dynamic Psychopathology in Childhood, 1959. Home: 3640 Appleton St NW Washington DC 20008

JESSOP, NANCY JANE MEYER (MRS. RAYMOND E. JESSOP), educator; b. Pasadena, Cal., Dec. 24, 1926; d. William J. and Juanita (Gindling) Meyer; B.A., U. Redlands, 1945; M.A., U. Ore., 1947; Ph.D. (E.B. Scripps fellow 1948-50), U. Cal. at Berkeley, 1953; m. Raymond E. Jessop, Aug. 31, 1947; children—Christina, Laurel. Tchr. sci. Oceanside (Cal.)-Carlsbad Union High Sch., 1953-55, asst. prof. U.S. Internat. U., San Diego, 1960-63, asso. prof., 1964-72, prof. biology, 1972—, chmn. dept. biology, 1965-73. Mem. Animal Behavior Soc. (sec. 1972-74), Am. Soc. Zoologists. Author: Biosphere: A Study of Life, 1970; Biosphere Laboratory and Field Studies, 1971. Home: 839 Regal Rd Encinitas CA 92024 Office: Daley Hall Sci US Internat Univ San Diego CA 92131

JESTER, DOROTHY, coll. adminstr.; b. Lynchburg, Va., Jan. 18, 1916; d. Royston and Lucie (Withers) Jester; A.B., Agnes Scott Coll., 1937. With Pacific Mut. Life Ins. Co., 1939-45; asst. to dean students Randolph-Macon Woman's Coll., 1946-47; acting dir. admission Sweet Briar (Va.) Coll., 1953-54, dean students, 1955—; asst. dean women Coll. William and Mary, 1954-55. Dir. handicrafts Jr. Camp, Camp Alleghany, W.Va., summers 1946, 47. Exhibited ceramics works gen. art exhibit, Lynchburg, 1953. Presbyn. Home: 4715 Boonsboro Rd Lynchburg VA 24503 Office: Sweet Briar Coll Sweet Briar VA 24595

JESTER, MARY GEORGE, educator; b. Montgomery, Ala., Nov. 4, 1946; d. George Henry and Elizabeth Mae (Dees) Jester; student La. State U., 1964-65, U. Ala., 1966; B.A. cum laude, Huntingdon Coll., 1968; M.A., U. N.C., 1971, postgrad., 1971-72; postgrad. Troy State U., 1971-72. Tchr., Jefferson Parish Schs., Metairie, La., 1968; copywriter, also prodn. asst. Leavell & Wise Assos., Montgomery, 1969; asst. to dir. new projects Fuller & Dees Marketing Group, Montgomery, 1969-70; tchr. English, speech, drama Montgomery County Schs., 1971—. Mem. Supt.'s Commn. on Effectively Selling Edn., Montgomery, 1971-72; mem. community relations bd. sta. WKAB-TV, 1973—. Named Outstanding Tchr., Floyd Jr. High Sch. Community Center Council, 1971-72. Mem. Ala. (mem. pub. relations commn. 1972), Montgomery (dir. pub. relations 1971—) edn. assns., Ala. Assn. Classroom Tchrs. (dist. VII dir. 1973—), Ala. Speech and Theatre Assn. (mem. steering com. Trumbauer Drama Festival 1971—), Nat. Edn. Assn., Montgomery Little Theatre, Pi Beta Phi, Baptist. Creative editor; Outdoor Cooking, 1970; University Women's Cookbook, 1971; Lutheran Ladies Cookbook, 1971; Eastern Star Women's Cookbook, 1971. Home: 3423 Wilmington Rd Montgomery AL 36105 Office: Lanier High School 1756 S Court St Montgomery AL 36104

JETER, AGNES MORGAN, camp dir.; b. Union, S.C., Feb. 22, 1908; d. Robert Russell and Agnes Morgan (Coleman) Jeter; A.B., Winthrop Coll., 1929; M.A., Peabody Coll., 1950. Tchr., Whitmire Elementary Sch., Whitmire, S.C., 1930, Wilmington, N.C., 1930-34; dir. phys. edn. Greensboro (N.C.) Coll., 1934-44; dir. phys. edn. The Out-Of-Door Sch., Sarasota, Fla., 1944-49; camp counselor, 1926-50; asst. dir. Camp Kiwanis Augusta (Ga.) YMCA; owner, dir. Camp Yonahlossee, Blowing Rock, N.C., 1955—. Mem. Am. Camping Assn. (sec. south eastern sect.). Methodist. Home: 413 E Main St Union SC 29379 Office: Camp Yonahlossee Blowing Rock NC 28605

JETER, KATHERINE LESLIE BRASH (MRS. ROBERT MCLEAN JETER, JR.), lawyer; b. Gulfport, Miss., July 24, 1921; d. Ralph Edward and Rosa Meta (Jacobs) Brash; B.A., Tulane U., 1943, J.D., 1945; m. Robert McLean Jeter, Jr., May 11, 1946. Admitted to La. bar, 1945; asso. mem. Montgomery, Fenner & Brown, New Orleans, 1945-46, Tucker, Martin, Holder, Jeter & Jackson (and predecessor firms), Shreveport, La., 1947—. Pres., Little Threatre Shreveport, 1966-67, YWCA, 1963, League of Women Voters, 1950-51; treas. Am. Nat. Theatre and Acad., Shreveport, 1963; 1st v.p. Shreveport Art Guild, 1973-74. Mem. Am., La., Shreveport bar assns., Nat. Assn. Women Lawyers, La. State Law Inst. (jr.), Jr. League Shreveport, Order Coif, Phi Beta Kappa. Editor Tulane Law Rev., 1945. Home: 3959 Maryland Av Shreveport LA 71106 Office: 1300 Beck Bldg 400 Travis St Shreveport LA 71101

JETT, PEARL MAUREEN, county ofcl.; b. West Union, W.Va., Apr. 9, 1919; d. Joseph and Lucy (Smith) Jett; student W.Va. U., 1937-38; B.S. in Bus. Adminstrn., Salem Coll., 1958, postgrad., 1959; postgrad. W.Va. U., 1960. Office employee Doddridge County Agrl. Conservation Assn., 1939-42, prin. clk., 1942-53; county exec. dir. Doddridge County Stablzn. and Conservation Service, West Union, 1953—, also exec. dir. Chmn. Doddridge County Library Bd.; chmn. Doddridge County Def. Com., U.S. Dept. Agr., mem. Gov.'s Commn. Status of Women, 1964-68; mem. Community Action Assn., Rural Area Devel. Com. Doddridge County; mem. Farming for Better Living Council; mem. area. adv. council Salem Coll.; bd. dirs. Doddridge County Tb Assn., Crippled Children's Assn., Nat. Found., W.Va. Heart Assn., West Union chpt. A.R.C., Community Action Assn. Recipient Outstanding Performance award U.S. Dept. Agr., 1959, Superior Performance award, 1960; High Quality Performance award State Agrl. Stablzn. and Conservation Service Office, 1963; named outstanding woman in pub. affairs of Western dist. W.Va., Gen. Fedn. Women's Clubs. Mem. Bus. and Profl. Women's Clubs (nat. dir., pres. West Union 1951-53, chmn. W.Va. radio and TV com. 1953-55, chmn. health and safety com. 1955-58, state pres. 1962-64), D.A.R. (chpt. regent 1958-60), W.Va. Assn. County Agrl. Stablzn. and Conservation Service Office Employees (exec. com.), Salem Coll. Alumni Assn. (nat. pres. 1967-69), Internat. Platform Assn. Mem. Christian Ch. (clk.). Clubs: West Union Woman's (parliamentarian); Laudati (past pres.) (Salem Coll.). State editor W.Va. D.A.R. News, 1972-74. Home: 306 Main St West Union WV 26456 Office: Box 365 Columbia West Union WV 26456

JEWETT, MARY JANE MCCALL (MRS. DAVID FRANCIS JEWETT, JR.), educator; b. Milford, Mich., Aug. 29, 1922; d. Samuel Leonard and Bessie Jane (Fisher) McCall; B.A., Mich. State Coll., 1944; M.A., U. Mich., 1949; certificate as reading specialist State U. N.Y., 1973; m. David Francis Jewett, Jr., June 25, 1952; children—Jennifer, Heidi and Cynthia (twins). Tchr. pub. schs., Birmingham, Mich., 1944-47; supr. Campus Sch., State U. N.Y. at New Paltz, 1950—, asst. prin., 1969-71, reading specialist, 1971—, tchr. grad. courses in reading, 1968—. Adv. dir. First Nat. Bank of Highland, New Paltz, 1970—. Republican committeewoman 1957—. Trustee Elting Meml. Library, New Paltz, 1956-58. Mem. Am. Assn. U. Women, N.E.A., N.Y. Tchrs. Assn., N.Y. Council for Reading, Internat. Reading Assn., Kappa Delta Pi, Pi Lambda Theta, Phi Delta Kappa, Delta Kappa Gamma. Club: Locust Tree Country (bd. govs. 1972-74) (New Paltz). Home: 9 Lincoln Pl New Paltz NY 12561

JICK, HELEN, educator; b. N.Y.C., Dec. 19, 1922; d. Hyman Joseph and Esther Malka (Schorr) Kahana; B.A., Hunter Coll., 1945; M.A., Columbia, 1949, postgrad., 1953-55, Ed.D., 1969; postgrad. Yeshiva U., 1955-65; m. Jerome Jick, Oct. 11, 1947; children—Esther (Mrs. Edward Turkel), Phyllis, Sandra (Mrs. Alan Kasnett), Linda (Mrs. Zvi Fisher). Research mathematician, meteorologist Signal Corps U.S. Army, Eatonton, N.J., 1942-45; tchr. math. Yeshiva Chaim Ozer, N.Y.C., 1945-49, Westchester Day Sch., Mamaroneck, N.Y., 1955-59; prof. math. faculty Bronx Community Coll. City U. N.Y., 1959—. Nat. bd. dirs. Am. Mizrachi Women. NSF Faculty fellow, 1964-65. Mem. Math. Assn. Am., Assn. Math Tchrs. N.Y. State, Nat. Council Tchrs. Math., Am. Assn. U. Profs., Assn. Math Tchrs. N.Y.C., Kappa Delta Pi. Contbr. profl. jours. Home: 2726 Lurting Av New York City NY 10469 Office: Dept Math Bronx Community Coll 181st St and University Av New York City NY 10453

JINNETTE, ZELMA NADINE CONN (MRS. WILLIAM SAUNDERS JINNETTE), dietitian; b. Kirbyville, Tex., Nov. 21, 1913; d. James Amos and Martha Louise (Howell) Conn; B.S., Kan. State U., 1934; postgrad. Duke, 1935; m. William Saunders Jinnette, Dec. 27, 1936; 1 son, James S. Dietitian Duke Hosp., Durham, N.C., 1935-37; lunchroom supr. Kirbyville (Tex.) Consol. Ind. Sch., 1953-55; dietary cons. Max Mixson Meml. Clinic, Kirbyville, Tex., 1965—. Pres. Kirbyville P.T.A., 1950-52; pres. South Jasper County unit Am. Cancer Soc., 1972-73; pres. Woman's Civic Club, Kirbyville, 1959-61. City councilwoman, Kirbyville, 1971—. Bd. dirs. Kirbyville Pub. Library, 1964—, Deep East Tex. Council of Govts., 1972—. Recipient Outstanding Citizen award Kirbyville C. of C., 1971. Mem. Kirbyville C. of C. (dir. 1971-73), Chi Omega. Baptist (departmental supt. 1948-62). Home: Box 26 Kirbyville TX 75956 Office: Max Mixson Meml Clin Drawer 580 Kirbyville TX 75956

JIONGCO-AVES, AGNES MARCELO (MRS. RENATO B. AVES), physician; b. Manilla, P.I., Jan. 21, 1938; d. Pedro A. and Florencia P. (Marcelo) Jiongco; M.D., U. Santo Tomas, 1959; m. Renato B. Aves, May 5, 1962; children—Irene, Teodulo, Sylvia, Renato. Intern, Western Pa. Hosp., Pitts., 1965-66; resident 1966-68, VA Hosp., East Orange, N.J., 1968-69; clin. researcher cancer Roswell Park Meml. Inst., Buffalo, 1969-71; practice medicine, Mt. Pleasant, Mich., 1971-72; mem. staff Mt. Pleasant Hosp., Labette County Med. Center, Parsons, Kan.; practice medicine, Parsons Clinic, 1972—. Mem. Am. Soc. Internal Medicine. Home: 3300 Dirr St Parsons KS 67357 Office: Parsons Clinic 1509 Main St Parsons KS 67357

JIRAUCH, SISTER MARY THOMAS, hosp. adminstr.; b. St. Louis; d. Milton and Margaret (Thomas) Jirauch; B.S. summa cum laude in Nursing, St. Louis U., 1958, M.H.A., 1960. Joined Order of Sisters of Divine Providence, 1946; tchr. St. Mark's Sch., Venice, Ill., 1950-52; tchr., Tipton, Mo., 1952-54; dir. nursing service St. Elizabeth Hosp., Granite City, Ill., 1960-62, asst. adminstr., 1960-62, adminstr., 1962—. Fellow Am. Coll. Hosp. Adminstrs.; mem. Ill. Hosp. Assn. (trustee 1968-72, dist. pres. 1967-68), Ill. Conf. Cath. Hosps. (pres. 1963), Springfield Diocesan Conf. Cath. Hosps. (pres. 1964)., Tri-State Hosp. Assembly (trustee 1971-73). Contbr. articles to profl. jours. Address: 2100 Madison Av Granite City IL 62040

JIROUDEK, ELLEN, physician; b. N.Y.C., Oct. 1, 1920; d. Stanley and Antionette (Bazata) Jiroudek; B.A., Barnard Coll., 1941; M.D., N.Y. U., 1945; m. 1951 (dec.). Intern, Queens Gen. Hosp., L.I., N.Y., 1945-46; resident Jersey City Med. Center, 1946-47; prof. health Mt. Holyoke Coll., South Hadley, Mass., 1948-49; pvt. practice family medicine, S.I., 1950—; mem. staff Sea View Hosp., S.I., N.Y.C. Health Dept. Diplomate Am. Bd. Family Practice. Mem. Power Squadron S.I. Club: Raritan Yacht (Perth Amboy, N.J.). Address: 34 Rose Av Staten Island NY 10306

JOACHIM, SISTER ANN, educator, lawyer, lectr., author; b. Cologne, Germany, Oct. 15, 1901; d. August A. and Johanna (Fuhrkotter) Joachim; LL.B., Detroit Coll. Law, 1923, J.D. (hon.), 1959; LL.M., U. Detroit, 1924; A.B., Siena Heights Coll., 1930; M.A., Loyola U., Chgo., 1933; Ph.D., Internat. Cath. U. Fribourg (Switzerland), 1936; J.D. (hon.), Detroit Coll. Law, 1959. Joined Congregation Sisters of St. Dominic, 1928; chmn. history dept., prof. econs., polit. sci., bus. law Siena Heights Coll., Adrian, Mich. 1936—. Admitted to U.S. Supreme Ct. bar. Mem. Adrian City Commn., 1971—. Bd. dirs., legal adviser Lenawee County Commn. on Econ.

Opportunity, 1965—. Sec. gen., treas. Assn. Cath. Colls., Mich., 1945-55. Mem. Mich. State Fulbright Com., 1950—, Adrian Mayor's Com. on Human Relations. Del., Mich. Democratic Conv.; mem. Adrian City Commn., 1972—. Recipient Woman of Year award Alumnae Assn. U. Detroit, 1951, Certificate of Merit, DIP, London, Eng. Mem. Am., Mich., Lewanee County bar assns., Am., Cath. hist. assns., Am. Econ. Assn., Nat. Women Lawyers Assn. (hon.), Am. Inst. Parliamentarians, Nat. Assn. Parliamentarians, Nat. Assn. Authors and Journalists, Kappa Beta Pi (former grand chancellor), Delta Kappa Gamma (v.p. 1972—, chmn. fgn. affairs com.). Contbr. articles profl. jours. Home: Dominican Motherhouse Adrian Siena Heights Coll Adrian MI 49221

JOB, AMY GRACE SEGEAR (MRS. KENNETH ALVIN JOB), librarian; b. Orange, N.J., Mar. 8, 1942; d. George Calvert and Amy Clark (Barrett) Segear; B.A., Montclair State Coll., 1964; M.L.S., Rutgers U., 1966; postgrad. Potsdam State U., 1966, Paterson State Coll., 1968; m. Kenneth Alvin Job, Nov. 8, 1968. Library asst. Livingston (N.J.) Pub. Library, 1958-64; asst. dormitory dir.-counselor Douglass Coll., New Brunswick, N.J., 1964-65; asst. librarian Potsdam (N.Y.) State U. Coll., 1965-67, William Paterson Coll., Wayne, N.J., 1968—. Library cons. Long Branch (N.J.) Pub. Sch., 1968, Brielle Pub. Schs., 1971-72; judge history fair Butler (N.J.) High Sch., 1970—. Recipient Scholarship, Am. Assn. U. Women, 1960-64, Grad. Fellowship, Rutgers U., 1965-66. Mem. N.E.A., Am. Assn. U. Women, Nat. Council Social Studies, N.J. Library Assn., William Paterson Coll. Faculty Assn. (sec., v.p. 1970—), Gamma Theta Upsilon, Pi Lambda Theta. Home: 5 Navajo Trail West Milford NJ 08848 also Box 588 RD 2 Butler NJ 07405 Office: 300 Pompton Rd Wayne NJ 07470

JOBE, JOYCE JOSEPHINE, univ. adminstr.; b. Trinidad, West Indies, Oct. 20, 1936; d. Monroe and Mary Elizabeth (Baptiste) Jobe; B.S. in Bus. Adminstrn., Southeastern U., 1970; M.A., Cath. U. Am., 1973, postgrad., 1973—. Came to U.S., 1964, naturalized, 1971. Asst. bus. mgr. Southeastern U., Washington, 1967-68, bus. mgr., bursar, 1968-73, dir. adminstrn., 1974—. Student rep. Fgn. Student Service Council Adv. Bd., 1967-69. Ednl. Professions Devel. Act fellow, 1972-73. Recipient Jr. Class Meritorious Service award Southeastern U. Am., 1969, Gold Key, 1970, Alumni Assn. award, 1970, SGA Appreciation of Services award, 1974. Mem. Nat. Assn. Coll. and U. Bus. Officers, Am. Assn. Higher Edn., Internat. Personnel Mgmt. Assn., Del.-D.C.-Md. Assn. Financial Aid Adminstrs., Caribbean-Am. Intercultural Assn. Home: 1723 Swann St NW Washington DC 20009 Office: 501 Eye St SW Washington DC 20024

JOBSON, MARIAN, pub. relations exec.; b. Chgo.; d. George Baigrie and Almira (Giddings) Jobson; A.B., Chatham Coll. Began career as field sec., asst. to pres. Chatham Coll., Pitts.; former asso. Tamblyn & Brown, N.Y.C., Harold F. Strong Corp., N.Y.C.; founder, partner Hartwell, Jobson & Kibbee, pub. relations, N.Y.C., 1937—; chmn. bd. Jobson Assos., Inc., Pub. Relations Counsel, N.Y.C., 1960—. Vice pres. Seeing Eye, Inc., 1942—. Mem. Pub. Relations Soc. Am. (accredited), Am. Assn. Workers for Blind, N.Y. Chatham Coll. Alumae Assn. (treas. 1967). Home: 253 E 49th St New York City NY 10017 Office: 1 Rockefeller Plaza New York City NY 10020

JOCHUM, VERONICA (MRS. WILHELM V. VON MOLTKE), pianist; b. Berlin, Germany; d. Eugen and Maria (Montz) Jochum; M.A., Staatliche Musikhochschule, Munich, 1955, Concert Diploma, 1957; pvt. study with Edwin Fischer, Josef Benvenuti, 1958-59, Rudolf Serkin, Phila., 1959-61; m. Wilhelm V. von Moltke, Nov. 15, 1961. First pub. concerts in Germany, 1954; numerous tours throughout N. and S.Am., Europe and Africa as soloist with world renowned orchs., 1961—, including Boston Symphony, Berlin Philharmonic, Hamburg and Munich Philharmonics, Bavarian and Bamberg Symphonies, Munich Chamber Orch., Radio Orchs. of Hamburg, Munich and Frankfurt, Mpls. and Denver Symphonies, Orch. Maggio Musicale, Florence, La Fenice Orch., Venice, RAI-Orch., Naples, Mozarteum Orch., Salzburg, Concertgebouw Orch., Amsterdam, The Hague Philharmonic, Venezuelan Symphony, Caracas, others; appearances on radio and television, recitals in numerous countries in Europe, N. and S.Am. and Africa; participant Marlboro Music Festival, 1959-60; artist in residence Eastern Music Festival, 1967-72; faculty Settlement Sch. Music, Phila., 1959-61, New Eng. Conservatory Music, Boston, 1965—, Berkshire Music Center, Tanglewood, 1974. Recordings with Deutsche Grammophon, Philips, Golden Crest. Home: 14 Gray Gardens W Cambridge MA 02138 Office: New Eng Conservatory of Music 290 Huntington Av Boston MA 02115

JOE, SHIRLEY (MRS. HENRY A. POY), ophthalmologist; b. San Diego, Aug. 1, 1930; B.A., U. Cal. at Berkeley, 1952; M.D., Woman's Med. Coll. Pa., 1956. Intern Highland Hosp., Oakland, Cal., 1956-57, resident ophthalmology, 1957-60, clin. staff dept. ophthalmology, 1962—; NIH fellow ophthalmic pathology, dept. ophthalmology U. Cal. Med. Center, San Francisco, 1960-62, clin. asso. dept. ophthalmology U. Cal., 1962-65, asst. clin. prof., 1965—; practice medicine specializing in ophthalmology, Permanente Med. Group, Oakland, Cal., 1962-70; pvt. practice, Oakland, 1970—. Diplomate Am. Bd. Ophthalmology. Fellow Am. Acad. Ophthalmology and Otolaryngology; mem. Am., Cal., Alameda-Contra Costa med. assns., East Bay Ophthalmology Soc., Frederick C. Cordes Eye Soc., Zeta Phi. Home and office: 47 Truitt Lane Oakland CA 94618

JOFFE, JULIA ELIZABETH SCHUELKE (MRS. LESTER L. JOFFE), social worker; b. Denver, Feb. 7, 1927; d. Max Norman and Mary Nalle (Sheldon) Schuelke; B.A., U. Tex., 1945; diploma in social work Our Lady of Lake Sch. Social Work, 1946; M.S.W., Columbia, 1949; m. Lester L. Jeffe, Sept. 5, 1949; children—Barbara, Susan, Paul, Elizabeth. Caseworker, Charity Assn., San Antonio, 1946; pediatric caseworker U. Tex. Med. Br., Galveston, 1947-48; sr. social worker Dallas Community Guidance, 1949; program and social work cons. N.Y. State Assn. for Crippled Children, N.Y.C., 1949-53; caseworker Abbott House, Irvington, N.Y., 1965-66; asst. dir. mental health clinic White Plains (N.Y.) Hosp., 1966—. Bd. dirs. P.T.A., Irvington, 1958, 64. Mem. Nat. Assn. Social Workers, Am. Orthopsychiat. Assn., Am. Group Psychotherapy Assn., League Women Voters (pres. Irvington 1964-65). Home: 499 Broadway White Plains NY 10603 Office: 41 E Post Rd White Plains NY 10601

JOHANSEN, MARY JANET MALONE (MRS. HARRY BARNES JOHANSEN), bus. exec.; b. Mobile, Ala., Dec. 28, 1930; d. Price William and Anna Louise (Delahunty) Malone; student U. Ala., 1948-49, Sorbonne, 1952; certificate in marketing research, N.Y. U., 1968, A.A., 1972; B.A. in Psychology, Fordham U., 1974; m. Harry Barnes Johansen, Oct. 4, 1958 (dec. Oct. 1959). With House & Garden mag., N.Y.C., 1952-59; self-employed and pres. Hadox, Inc., Chattanooga and N.Y.C., 1959-62; research and promotion dir. Am. Legion mag., N.Y.C., 1962-64; research dir. Parent's Mag. Enterprises, N.Y.C., 1964—. Mem. Media Research Dirs. Assn. (pres. 1973-74), Internat. Platform Assn., Advt. Women New York. Roman Catholic. Home: 315 E 69th St New York City NY 10021 Office: 52 Vanderbilt Av New York City NY 10017

JOHANSON, EDNA JOSEPHINE LOUISE (MRS. JOHN E. JOHANSON), elec. products co. exec.; b. Union City, N.J., May 12, 1917; d. Joseph and Bertha Olivia (Peterson) Christiansen; grad. Sch. Comptometry, Newark, 1935; student N.Y. U., 1960, Summit Secretary Sch. (N.J.), 1950; m. John E. Johanson, June 18, 1938; children—Eric N., Nancy E. (Mrs. Gerald Krawczyk). With Johanson Mfg. Corp., Boonton, N.J., 1945—, exec. v.p., 1969—. Active Girl Scouts Am., 1944-52. Vice-pres. John E. Johanson Found., 1969—. Lutheran. Club: Rockaway Valley Garden. Home: Split Rock Rd Boonton NJ 07005 Office: PO Box 329 Boonton NJ 07005

JOHANSON, GWYNNE JUSTICE, banker; b. Amesville, La., Mar. 30, 1908; d. William Marion and Clara (Wall) Justice; secretarial diploma Fowler's Bus. Coll., 1928; certificate Am. Inst. Banking, 1955, grad. certificate 1961; m. August Johanson, June 4, 1949 (dec. Dec. 1961). Card clk. Underwood Corp., New Orleans, 1927-28, bill clk., 1928-31; clk. Fed. Res. Banks of Atlanta, New Orleans, 1932-42, supr., 1942-50; personal loans teller First Nat. Bank of Jefferson Parish, Gretna, La., 1951-53, loans and discounts teller, Westwego, La., 1953-56, asst. mgr., Westwego, 1956-65, asst. cashier, mgr. Westwego office, 1965-72, asst. v.p., mgr., 1972—. Charter mem. Women's Aux. West Jefferson Gen. Hosp. Named Woman of Year, Westside Bus. and Profl. Women's Club, 1965. Mem. Am. Inst. Banking (chmn. women's com. 1945-46, nat. women's com. 1949-50, vice-chmn. 1956), Nat. Assn. Bank Women (chmn. 1960-61), Westside Bus. and Profl. Women's Club (charter mem., pres. 1968-69). Mem. United Ch. of Christ. Mem. Order Eastern Star. Home: PO Box 22 Marrero LA 70072 Office: PO Box 218 Westwego LA 70094

JOHANSON, PATRICIA MAUREEN, artist, design cons.; b. N.Y.C., Sept. 8, 1940; d. Alvar Einar and Elizabeth (Deane) J.; student Art Students League; A.B., Bennington Coll., 1962; M.A., Hunter Coll., 1964; postgrad. City Coll. Sch. Architecture, 1971-73; m. E.C. Goossen; 1 son, Alvar Deane. Exhibited one-man shows Tibor de Nagy Gallery, N.Y.C., 1967, State U. N.Y. at Albany, 1969; retrospective, Bennington Coll., 1973; exhibited group shows Hudson River Mus., Yonkers, 1964, Bennington Coll., 1964, Stable Gallery, N.Y.C., 1966, Tibor de Nagy Gallery, N.Y.C., 1966, 68, Larry Aldrich Mus., Ridgefield, Conn., 1968, Mus. Modern Art, N.Y.C., 1968, Grand Palais, Paris, 1968, Kunsthaus, Zurich, 1969, Tate Gallery, London, 1969, Vassar Coll., 1969, Finch Coll. Mus., 1971, Everson Mus., Syracuse, N.Y., 1971, Detroit Inst. Arts, 1973, Mass. Inst. Tech., 1974; represented in permanent collections Detroit Inst. Arts, N.Y. State Council on Arts Film Collection, Syracuse, N.Y.; films: The Art of the Real, USIA, 1968; Stephen Long, CBS-TV, 1968; vis. prof. art State U. N.Y. at Albany, 1969; vis. artist Mass. Inst. Tech., 1974, Oberlin Coll. (O.), 1974, Alfred U. (N.Y.), 1974; cons. Mitchell Giurgola Assos. Architects, N.Y.C. also Phila., 1972—; works include sculpture, landscape sculpture, street furniture, pavement designs, site planning for Consol. Edison Co., Yale U., Columbus East High Sch. (Ind.), Montclair State Coll. (N.J.), others. Guggenheim fellow, 1970. Home: RFD 1 Buskirk NY 12028 Office: 795 Lexington Av New York City NY 10021

JOHENGEN, DORIS VALENTINE (MRS. CHARLES A. JOHENGEN), investment banker; b. Buffalo, May 2, 1913; d. George G. and Emma (Smith) Valentine; student Bryant & Stratton Bus. Inst., 1928-30; m. Charles A. Johengen, Feb. 14, 1945 (dec. Dec. 1968). Underwriter, Columbia Casualty Co., Buffalo, 1931-41; sec.-dir. Geo. E. Keiser & Co., N.Y.C., 1942-45; sec. to pres. B. Wolff & Co., Chgo., 1945-47; office mgr. H. K. Heussler, Buffalo, 1948-55; dept. mgr. Harold D. Farber, Buffalo, 1955-61; v.p., office mgr. E. P. Agy., Inc., Buffalo, 1961-64; dept. mgr. Internat. Life Ins. Co., Buffalo, 1964—; v.p., mng. prin. Ilicob Sales Corp., Buffalo, 1970—. Mem. Order Eastern Star. Clubs: Buffalo Kennel; Tonawandas Sportsmen's (North Tonawanda, N.Y.). Office: 120 Delaware Av Buffalo NY 14202

JOHNS, ALICE DELORES, lawyer; b. Tulsa, May 5, 1920; d. James A. and Birdie (Hart) Johns; B.S., Tuskegee Inst., 1940; LL.B., John Marshall Law Sch., 1956, J.D., 1970; student U. Chgo., 1943-44. Admitted to Ill. bar, 1958; claim processor and adjuster Packinghouse Workers Welfare Fund, Chgo., 1954-59; sec. to exec. dir. Mayor's Com. on Race Relations, Chgo., 1943-44; pvt. practice law, Chgo., 1959-73; apptd. dep. license commnr. City Chgo., 1973—. Vice-pres. 20th Ward Regular Democratic Orgn., 1966-68. Office: 127 N Dearborn St Chicago IL 60602

JOHNS, FRANCES WALKER MANSELLE, social work educator; b. Easley, S.C.; d. Eugene G. and Hattie (Davis) Manselle; student Va. State Coll., 1939-41, 44-45, A.B., 1950; M.S.W., Coll. William and Mary, 1958; postgrad. Hampton Inst., 1965, Cath. U. Am., 1966; m. Reginald R. Johns, Oct. 28, 1952; children—Benjamin Leon Walker, Reginald R., Harriette F. Playground leader City of Norfolk, Va., 1945-48; pub. assistance caseworker Social Service Bur., Norfolk, 1950-51, child welfare caseworker, 1951-53; child welfare caseworker Social Service Bur., Portsmouth, 1954; casework counselor Peninsula Family Service and Travelers Aid, Newport News, 1956-63; asst. prof. sociology Va. State Coll., 1963-68; dir. undergrad. social welfare edn. Hampton Inst., 1970-72; now asst. prof. sociology Thomas Nelson Community Coll., Hampton, Va.; ordained deacon Presbyn. Ch., 1974. Cons. to commr. youth affairs City of Hampton. Troop leader Girl Scouts Am., Va., 1946-48; spl. cons. Phyllis Wheatley YWCA Y-Teens, 1956-65; dir. Peninsula Coordinating Com., 1965-66; dir. Peninsula Jr. Women's League, 1962-65; chmn. family life edn. com., P.T.A., 1962-66. Bd. dirs. Community Action Agy., Emergency Sch. Assn. Program, Girls Club Hampton, Penninsula Planned Parenthood Assn. Mem. Acad. Certified Social Workers, Nat. Assn. Social Workers, Va. Council Social Welfare (dir. 1970—), Am. Assn. U. Women (community area problems rep. 1963-65), Am. Assn. U. Profs., Am. Sociol. Assn., Va. Tchrs. Assn., Nat. Council Negro Women (chmn. social welfare com. 1956-64), N.E.A., Va. Social Sci. Assn. (state office auditor 1970—), Council Social Work Edn. (ho. dels. 1970-72), Black Educators Council Human Services (charter dir. 1971—), So. Assn. Undergrad. Social Welfare Workers (state rep.), Jack and Jill Am. (pres. Newport News chpt.), Altruists, Inc., Delta Sigma Theta, Alpha Kappa Delta, Iota Phi Lambda (past chpt. pres.). Home: 22 Lynnhaven Dr Hampton VA 23366 Office: Mechanical Bldg Thomas Nelson Community Coll Hampton VA 23568

JOHNS, GLYNIS, actress; b. Durban, South Africa, Oct. 5, 1923; d. Mervyn and Alya (Steele) J. Appeared in London stage prodns. Buckie's Bears, The Children's Hour, A Kiss for Cinderella, Quiet Weekend; Broadway prodn. Gertie, 1952, Major Barbara, 1956-57; motion pictures include: South Riding, Murder in the Family, Prison Without Bars, Mr. Brigg's Family, 49th Parallel, Adventures of Tartu, Half-Way House, Perfect Strangers, This Man is Mine, Frieda, An Ideal Husband, Miranda, Third Time, Lucky Mr. Proback, The Great Manhunt, Flesh and Blood, No Highway in the Sky, Appointment with Venus, Encore, The Card, The Sword and the Rose, Rob Roy, Personal Affair, The Weak and the Wicked, The Seekers, The Beachcomber, Mad About Men, Court Jester, Josephine and Men, Loser Takes All, Day They Gave Babies Away, Another Time Another Place, Shake Hands With the Devil, The Sundowners, The Spiders Web, The Chapman Report, Mary Poppins, Dear Brigette, Don't Just Stand There, Lock Up Your Daughters; TV series Glynis; guest TV appearances include Dr. Kildare, Roaring Twenties, Naked City, The Defenders, Danny Kaye Show, Noel Coward's Star Quality. Address: care Chartwell Artists Ltd 9720 Wilshire Blvd Beverly Hills CA 90212*

JOHNS, MARISOL GRIMAL (MRS. HOWARD OLIVER JOHNS), univ. dean; b. Tampa, Fla., May 1, 1930; d. Angel Solano and Marie Dulce (Franquiz) Grimal; student Fla. State U., 1947-50, Northwestern U., 1959-60; B.A., U. Tampa, 1963; M.A., U. South Fla., 1967; m. Howard Oliver Johns, June 6, 1950; children—Mariella, Marcia. Concert pianist, piano tchr., 1947-60; chief dispatcher, interpreter Cuban Airlines, 1950-52; tchr. modern langs., chmn. lang. dept. Acad. Holy Names, Tampa, 1960-65; teaching asst. guidance dept. U. S. Fla., Tampa, 1965-67, counselor Counseling Center, instr. Honduras project, 1967-69; counselor Fla. Presbyn. Coll., 1967; dean women U. Tampa, 1969-73, dean student devel., 1973—. Mem. Nat. Assn. Women Deans, Adminstrs. and Counselors, Am., Fla. personnel and guidance assns., Modern Lang. Assn., Nat. Assn. Student Personnel Adminstrs., Am., So., Fla. coll. personnel assns., Am. Assn. U. Women, Delta Kappa Gamma, Tau Beta Sigma, Kappa Delta Pi, Sigma Alpha Iota, Pi Delta Phi, Omicron Delta Kappa. Home: 5101 Poe Av Tampa FL 33609

JOHNS, VERONICA PARKER, mcht.; b. N.Y.C., Dec. 28, 1907; d. Ashton and Ethel Irving (Barker) Parker; student Columbia Sch. Journalism, 1925-26; m. Richard Johns, Apr. 8, 1935 (dec.). Owner, operator Seashells Unltd., Inc., N.Y.C., 1964—. Mem. Mystery Writers of Am. (v.p. N.Y. region 1958), Am. Malacological Union, Conchologists of Am., New York Shell Club, Am. Mus. Natural History. Author: Hush, Gabriel, 1940; The Singing Widow, 1941; Shady Doings, 1941; Murder By The Day, 1953; Servant's Problem, 1958; She Sells Seashells, 1968. Contbr. short stories to anthologies. Home: 155 E 38th St New York City NY 10016 Office: 590 3d Av New York City NY 10016

JOHNSEN, MADALYN LINNETTA, physician; b. Sioux Falls, S.D., Nov. 26, 1913; d. Julius Albert and Eva Elizabeth (Kissel) Johnsen; B.A., Lawrence Coll., Appleton, Wis., 1937; M.D., U. Wis., 1943. Intern, U. Chgo.-Billings Hosp. and U. Chgo. Clinics, 1943-44; asst. resident surgery New Haven Hosp., 1944-46; mem. staff Laurel Heights Sanitarium, Shelton, Conn., 1946-48; mem. staff N.C. Sanitarium, McCain, 1948-57, chief Negro div., 1954-57; cons. USPHS in 1950s; pvt. practice medicine, specializing in internal medicine, Fayetteville, N.C., 1958—; former chief medicine Cape Fear Valley Hosp., Highsmith Rainey Hosp.; mem. adv. com. to comdg. gen., Ft. Bragg, 1970—; mem. Def. Adv. Com. on Women in Services, 1972—. Mem. Fayetteville Area Indsl. Corp. Pres. Better Health Found.; bd. dirs. Fayetteville Little Theatre, Fayetteville Symphony. Mem. A.M.A., N.C., Cumberland County (past pres.), Dist. med. socs., N.C. (dir., past com. chmn.), Fayetteville Area (pres. 1973—) chambers commerce. Episcopalian. Club: Highland and Green Valley Country. Home: 1060 Stamper Rd Fayetteville NC 28303 Office: 524 Beaumont Rd Fayetteville NC 28304

JOHNSEN, MAY ANN COLANGELO (MRS. DAVID S. JOHNSEN), artist; b. Port Chester, N.Y.; d. Michael and Mary A. (Viscionti) Colangelo; grad. high sch.; m. David S. Johnsen, Nov. 6, 1949; 1 son, David Mark. One-man shows at Squillaci Gallery, Schnectady, Little Gallery, Warrensburg, N.Y.; exhibited in group shows at Drawing Internat., Barcelona, Spain, Knickerbocker Nat., N.Y.C., Catherine Lorrilac Wolfe Nat., N.Y.C., N.M. Nat. Show, Albuquerque, Hudson Valley Nat. Show, Smithsonian Inst., Washington, Berkshire Museum, Pittsfield, Mass. Recipient marine award Silvermine Guild, miniature painting marine award Ohio Miniature Soc., Hamilton, 1st prize Columbia County Fair, Nassau spl. award marine painting. Mem. Miniature Soc. N.J. Home: Box 5 Brainard NY 12024

JOHNSON, ADNA AMOS, sch. counselor; b. Butler, Ga., Dec. 28, 1910; d. Thomas J. and Dorothy (Willis) Amos; B.S., Ga. State Coll. for Women, 1935; M.Ed., U. Ga., 1962, postgrad. (Union Bag scholar), 1964; m. Olen V. Johnson, Feb. 18, 1931; 1 dau., Constance. Tchr., Bacon County, Ga., 1930-32, 36-39, Tift County, Ga., 1932-36, Ware County, 1939-41, Taylor County, 1941-42, Chatham County, 1943-62; sch. counselor, Savannah, Ga., 1962—. Cons. tutorial program; mem. adv. com. Div. Exceptional Children; participant pilot program for elementary counselors Ga. Dept. Edn., 1965-68. Recipient Delke award as outstanding dist. counselor, 1971. Mem. Nat., Ga., Chatham edn. assns., Ga. Assn. Sch. Counselors, Nat. Congress Parents and Tchrs. (life), Am. Assn. U. Women, Alpha Delta Kappa. Methodist (adminstrv. bd.). Home: 6 Pinewood Av Savannah GA 31406 Office: 220 E 49th St Savannah GA 31401

JOHNSON, AGNES DORAN, coll. adminstr.; b. Johnsons Cross Roads, W.Va., June 14, 1916; d. Frank P. and Frances (Broadfield) Johnson; Licentate of Instn., Fla. So. Coll., 1936, B.S., 1950; Ed.M., U. Fla., 1954. Elementary tchr., Mascotte, Fla., 1936-38, Clermont-Minneola Sch., Clermont, Fla., 1938-50, Lee and Skeen schs., Leesburg, Fla., 1950-54, Palm Springs Sch., Hialeah, Fla., 1954-55; field rep. Fla. Assn.; dean women Fla. So. Coll., Lakeland, now dir. alumni relations. Pres. Clermont Welfare League, 1943-44; cons. Fla. Future Tchrs. Am., 1956-67; treas. Fla. Council on Elementary Edn., 1955—; adv. council on tchr. edn., Fla., 1954-59. Mem. So. Scholarship and Research Found. Bd., 1962—. Recipient Alumni Distinguished Service award Fla. So. Coll., 1964. Mem. Fla. So. Coll. Alumni Assn. (past v.p., pres.), N.E.A., Lake County Edn. Assn. (pres. 1947-48), Lake County Classroom Tchrs. Assn. (pres. 1943-45), Fla. Edn. Assn. (pres. dept. classroom tchrs. 1954-55, dir. 1951-53), Nat. Edn. Field Service Assn. (exec. com. 1959-60), Adminstrv. Women in Edn. (pres. Fla. br. 1970-72, nat. bd.), Tallahassee Hammond Organ Soc. (pres. 1959), Am. Assn. U. Women (pres. Tallahassee br. 1965-67), Phi Chi Theta, Delta Kappa Gamma, Kappa Delta Pi, Alpha Chi Omega (pres. alumnae 1971), P.E.O. Ch. organist and choir dir. 20 yrs. Home: 620 E Park St Lakeland FL 33803

JOHNSON, ALBERTA HELYN DIXON (MRS. WILLIAM BYRD JOHNSON), city ofcl.; b. Tampa, Fla., Sept. 11, 1942; d. Charles Delano and Mary Lee (Collins) Dixon; student (United Negro Coll. Fund scholar), Talladega Coll., 1958-62; B.A., U. Wyo., 1974; m. William Byrd Johnson, Sept. 23, 1963; children—Felicia Daika. Tchr. pub. schs., Tampa, Fla., 1962-63; interviewer, job corps recruiter Wyo. Employment Service, Cheyenne, 1965-68. Precinct committeewoman Laramie County Democratic Com. 1972—; mem. city council, City of Cheyenne, 1974—. Chmn. Laramie County Legal Services, 1970—. Mem. N.A.A.C.P. (pres. Cheyenne chpt. 1971—), League Women Voters, Nat. Black Caucus Local Elected Ofcls. Methodist. Home: 211 McComb Av Cheyenne WY 82001 Office: PO Box 961 City of Cheyenne Cheyenne WY 82001

JOHNSON, ALFREDA JUANITA ASKEW (MRS. RICHARD W. JOHNSON), ednl. adminstr.; b. St. Petersburg, Fla., Jan. 24, 1935; d. Hiram M. and Weltha M. (Bryandt) Askew; B.A., Fisk U., 1956; M.Ed., Shippensburg State Coll., 1964; m. Richard W. Johnson, Apr. 12, 1957; 1 son, Richard Williams. Tchr. math. Harrisburg (Pa.) Pub. Schs., 1958-64, counselor, chmn. counseling Camp Curtin Jr. High Sch., 1964-69, counselor, 1969-71, transfer placement counselor, 1972-73, asso. dean, 1973—. Ednl. cons. Dept. Edn.

Commonwealth Pa., 1968-74. Trustee Harrisburg Acad. Gen. Electric fellow Boston U., 1967. Mem. Am., Pa. personnel and guidance assns., Pa. Coll. Counselors Assn., Pa. Sch. Counselors Assn., Am. Coll. Testing Program Council Pa. (mem. exec. com. 1972—), Delta Sigma Theta. Home: 1608 North St Harrisburg PA 17103 Office: 3300 Cameron St Rd Harrisburg PA 17110

JOHNSON, ANNA ELIZABETH BOOTHE (MRS. ERNEST LEWIS JOHNSON, JR.), librarian; b. Victoria, Va., Aug. 25, 1913; d. James Witten and Nannie Wilson (Booth) Boothe; student Pan-Am. Bus. Sch., Richmond, Va., 1936; diploma Kennedy's Comml. Sch., Durham, N.C., 1940; B.S., Longwood Coll., Farmville, Va., 1956; m. Ernest Lewis Johnson, Jr., Feb. 20, 1937; children—Ernest Lewis III, Kaye (Mrs. Robert Paul Wolf). Piano and violin tchr., pvt. lessons, Victoria, 1931-33, 47-50; violin tchr., choral dir. WPA, Lunenburg County, Va., 1934-36; sec., receptionist Dr. H.E. Whaley, Victoria, 1937-40; sec., sr. clk. Universal Credit Co., Durham, 1940-42; elementary sch. tchr., Victoria, 1950-52; librarian Victoria High Sch., 1953-59; law librarian Marshall-Wythe Sch. of Law, Coll. William and Mary, Williamsburg, Va., 1959-71, asso. law librarian, 1971—. Mem. evaluating com. Va. Bd. Edn., 1956, 58. Mem. Nat., Va. (sec. librarians sect. Dist. D 1958-59), Lunenburg County (chmn. program com. 1953-54, pres. 1955) edn. assns., Am., Southeastern Am. assns. law libraries, Delta Kappa Gamma. Baptist. Home: 116 Oak Rd Williamsburg VA 23185

JOHNSON, ANNE BRADSTREET, neuropathologist; b. Boston, Mar. 5, 1927; d. Stafford F. and Catherine (Tyler) Johnson; A.B., Cornell, 1948, M.D., 1951; m. Jack Minkoff, June 19, 1948; children—Ellen Louise, Paul Andrew. Intern, Mt. Sinai Hosp., Cleve., 1951-52, resident internal medicine, 1952-53; resident Cleve. City Hosp., 1953-54; teaching fellow U. Hosp., Cleve. 1954-55; pvt. practice internal medicine, Cleve., 1955-57; med. researcher Coll. Phys. and Surgs. Columbia, N.Y.C., 1957-59; researcher Albert Einstein Coll. Medicine, Bronx, 1959—, asst. prof. pathology, 1970—. Am. Cancer Soc. research fellow, 1959-61; research grantee NIH, 1967-70, Nat. Multiple Sclerosis Soc., 1970—. Diplomate Am. Bd. Internal Medicine. Mem. Am. Assn. Neuropathologists, Histo-chem. Soc., Am. Soc. Cell Biology, A.A.A.S. Contbr. articles to profl. jours. Office: Dept Pathology Albert Einstein Coll Medicine Bronx NY 10461

JOHNSON, A(ROLYN) ROBERTA, assn. exec.; b. Portland, Me., Mar. 19, 1927; d. Harold Dearing and Arolyn (White) Johnson; B.A., U. Me., 1949; student Drew U., 1950-51, Columbia, 1952, N.Y.U., 1952, 68. Women's and girls dir. YMCA, Morristown, N.J., 1950-53, Torrington, Conn., 1953-57; adult program dir. YM-YWCA, Newark, N.J., 1957-63; program dir. YMCA, Montclair, N.J., 1963-70; exec. dir. YMCA-YWCA, Logansport, Ind., 1971-73; exec. dir. Howard County br. YMCA Greater Balt., 1973. Chmn. Nat. YMCA Commn. on Younger Girls Work, 1953-54; mem. Conf. on Assn. Profession, 1959, 60, 69, 70; mem. nat. adv. com. Work with Women and Girls, 1964-67, Nat. YMCA Camp Standards Revision Com., 1965-67. Mem. Assn. Profl. Dirs. YMCA (v.p. program dirs. sect. 1960-63, career devel. bd. 1970-71, area bd. dirs. 1966-69, regional bd. dirs. 1969-71, exec. com. adminstrv. sect. 1972—), Womens Soc. Christian Service, Am. Assn. U. Women, Delta Zeta. Methodist. Club: Altrusa (sec. 1966-68). Home: 8876-D Town & Country Blvd Ellicott City MD 21043 Office: 4331 Montgomery Rd Ellicott City MD 21043

JOHNSON, AUDREY EILEEN ARONSON (MRS. BRADFORD V. H. JOHNSON), mfg. co. exec.; b. Mpls., Feb. 27, 1937; d. Leo and Lillian (Thompson) Aronson; B.A., St. Olaf Coll., 1959; M.A., U. Minn., 1969; student Harvard-Radcliffe U., 1960; m. Bradford V. H. Johnson, June 8, 1963; children—Anne Aronson, Bradford V.H. Tchr. high sch., Osseo, Minn., 1960-61; personnel asst. U. Minn. at Mpls., 1961-63, personnel rep., 1966-69; employee relations mgr. Gillette Co., St. Paul, 1969-73; partner, v.p. Lakeville Devel. Co. (Minn.), real estate developers, 1974—. Dakota county chairwoman Young Republicans, 1960. Mem. Twin City Personnel Assn. (sec.-treas. 1971-72), Minn. Hist. Soc., Hennepin County Hist. Soc., Iota Rho Chi. Home: Box Y Lakeville MN 55044 Office: 5th at Broadway St Paul MN 55101

JOHNSON, AUDREY ST. DENYS (MRS. EUGENE M. JOHNSON), journalist; b. Toronto, Ont., Can., Dec. 21, 1915; d. Sidney and Florence May (Chipp) Wood; tchr.'s diploma, Asso. Royal Schs. Music, London, Eng., 1931; m. Eugene Maurice Johnson, June 28, 1941. Tchr. music and music appreciation courses, 1933-38; free-lance journalist, 1939-56; mem. staff Victoria (B.C.) Daily Times, 1956—, columnist, 1944—, music and drama critic, 1942—; dir. 1st prodn. Amahl and the Night Visitors in Canadian catherdeal, 1959, accredited adjudicator for drama B.C. Govt. Community Programmes Br. Mem. Community Arts Council Greater Victoria, Art Gallery Greater Victoria, Victoria Conservatory Music (guarantor), Internat. Theatre Inst., Music Critics Assn. Inc. Author poetry. Home: 2229 Arbutus Rd Victoria BC Canada Office: 2631 Douglas St Victoria BC Canada

JOHNSON, BARBARA COE, med. librarian; b. Detroit, Jan. 19, 1923; d. Harrison Thomas and Ann (Mack) Coe; B.A., Bryn Mawr Coll., 1944; B.S. in L.S., U. Cal. at Berkeley, 1951. Patient's librarian VA Hosp., Palo Alto, Cal., 1951-53, med. librarian 1953-56; dir. libraries Harper Hosp., Detroit, 1956—. Mem. Med. Library Assn. (bd. dirs. 1968-71), Spl. Libraries Assn. (profl. cons. 1959—). Mem. Soc. of Friends. Contbr. articles to profl. jours. Home: 2075 Hyde Park Rd Detroit MI 48207 Office: 3990 John R St Detroit MI 48201

JOHNSON, BARBIE PRITCHARD, editor; b. Chgo., Jan. 11, 1945; d. Irving Henry and Virginia (Baker) Pritchard; B.J., U. Mo., 1967, M.A., 1969; m. P. J. Johnson, Aug. 20, 1966. Asso. editor Advt. Age, N.Y.C., 1969-70; editor Braniff Internat. (inflight mag.), N.Y.C., 1970-71; editor Chef mag., Culinary Review, Inc., N.Y.C., 1971—, asso. pub., 1973—; exec. editor Tube Talk mag. A Children's Guide to the Best in TV, Young Communications, Inc., N.Y.C., 1973—; contbg. editor: Indsl. Marketing mag., 1971—. Vol. Environmental Action Coalition, N.Y.C., 1972. Frank Luther Mott fellow, 1968; named Foremost Women in Communication, Foremost Am. Pub. Corp., 1971. Mem. Theta Sigma Phi, Kappa Tau Alpha, Delta Delta Delta. Author: What Florida Holds for You, 1972. Freelance writer for numerous consumer and trade mags. Home: 333 E 75th St New York City NY 10021

JOHNSON, BEVERLEY BEAUCHAMP BROWN, ednl. adminstr.; b. Atlanta, Oct. 9, 1917; d. Carl Lewis and Carolyn Beatrice (Bird) Brown; A.B., Fla. State U., 1938; M.A., Columbia, 1947; Ph.D., U. N.C., 1959; m. Victor Bernhard Johnson, Dec. 24, 1966 (dec. Sept. 1968); 1 dau., Carolyn S. Parlato. Residence counselor Fla. State U., 1943-45; personnel interviewer A.R.C., 1945-46; asst. personnel dir. N.A.M., 1948-49; asst. dean women U. Miami, 1952-53; dist. dir. Girl Scouts U.S.A., 1954-57; tchr. preparation program U. N.C., 1957-59; cons. for guidance and sch. psychology Fla. State Dept. Edn., 1959-67; dir. Occupational Information Center for Edn.-Industry, Atlanta, 1967-72; dir. career guidance Atlanta pub. schs., 1972—. Mem. nat. adv. council Manpower Inst. Mem. Am. Psychol. Assn., Am. Personnel and Guidance Assn., Assn. for Counselor Edn. and Supervision, Nat. Vocational Guidance Assn., Assn. for Measurement in Guidance, So. Assn. Counselor Edn. and Supervision (pres. 1973-74), Am. Soc. Personnel Adminstrn. Contbr. articles to profl. jours., encys. Home: 3488 Paces Pl NW Atlanta GA 30327 Office: 2960 Forrest Hill Dr SW Atlanta GA 30315

JOHNSON, BEVERLY EDNA, writer; b. Los Angeles, Mar. 31, 1920; d. Hugh Edgar and Jessie Elvira (Smith) Johnson; B.A. cum laude, U. So. Cal., 1942; m. Anthony Agbe-Davies, May 16, 1961, (div. Mar. 1964). Reporter, feature writer Santa Barbara (Cal.) News-Press, 1942-46; free-lance writing and promotion Santa Barbara, 1946-56; dir. pub. relations Daniel, Mann, Johnson & Mendenhall, Los Angeles, 1956; free-lance writing and promotion of architecture, 1956-59; editor, arts and crafts Los Angeles Times, Home Mag., 1959—; editor Equestrian Trails mag., 1971; Los Angeles corr. Craft Horizons, 1965-67; cons. for galleries and sponsors of art and craft exhbns.; freelance design of interiors, jewelry, dress, ceramics; freelance photographer. Vol. promotional writing for Santa Barbara Humane Soc. and Hillside House, Santa Barbara, 1946-50. Bd. dirs. Santa Barbara Humane Soc., 1946-50; founder, pres. Fauna Found., 1973—. Mem. So. Cal. Designer-Craftsmen, Theta Sigma Phi. Home: 7017 Senalda Rd Los Angeles CA 90028 Office: Home Mag Los Angeles Times Times-Mirror Square Los Angeles CA 90053

JOHNSON, BONNIE JEAN MCKECHNIE (MRS. EMSLEY W. JOHNSON, JR.), bank ofcl., civic worker; b. Stanford, Ky., May 26, 1917; d. Robert L. and Fionnie C. (Hammond) McKechnie; A.B., Butler U., 1938; m. Emsley Wright Johnson, Jr., Oct. 8, 1938; children—Martha Susan (Mrs. William George Batt), Gracia Elizabeth (Mrs. Charles Rutherford Meyer). Piano tchr., 1935-45; substitute high sch. English tchr., 1938-42. Dir. First Bank & Trust Co., Indpls., 1965—, vice chmn. bd., 1972—. Bd. dirs. Indpls. Day Nursery Assn., 1953-59, 71—, sec., 1955; pres. Aux. Indpls. Day Nursery, 1965-66, v.p., 1973—; mem. adv. council Conner Prairie Pioneer Settlement, 1972—; mem. Northside bd. Indpls. Symphony, 1957-63; mem. alumni bd. dirs. Butler U., 1970—, trustee, 1972—. Bd. dirs. Marion County Hist. Soc. (dir. 1970—). Mem. D.A.R. (regent 1959-61), Alliance Indpls. Mus. Art, Kappa Alpha Theta (chpt. adv. bd. 1959-67, chpt. financial adviser 1959-66). Clubs: Fortnightly Literary (pres. 1964-65), Indianapolis Alumnae (v.p. 1946-47); Contemporary; The Propylaeum. Home: 9508 Holliday Circle Indianapolis IN 46260

JOHNSON, BURDETTA FAYE BEEBE, author; b. Marshall, Okla., Feb. 4, 1920; d. Alfred Khlar and Beulah Blondina (Thurlow) Beebe; grad. high sch.; m. James Ralph Johnson, Oct. 11, 1961. Conv. mgr. Nat. Food Brokers Assn., Washington, 1957-65; writer, 1964—. Author: Run, Light Buck, Run (chosen as Jr. Lit. Guild selection and Walt Disney film), 1962; Appalachian Elk, 1962; Coyote, Come Home (Walt Disney film), 1963; Chestnut Cub, 1963; American Lions and Cats, 1963; American Wolves, Coyotes and Foxes, 1964; Coyote for Keeps, 1965; Assateague Deer, 1965; American Desert Animals, 1966; Ocelot (Jr. Lit. Guild selection), 1966; Little Red, 1966; Yucatan Monkey (Walt Disney film), 1967; Animals South of the Border, 1968; African Elephants, 1968; African Lions and Cats, 1969; African Apes, 1969; Little Dickens, Jaguar Cub, 1970. Address: Box 5295 Santa Fe NM 87501

JOHNSON, CAROLYN BAKER (MRS. WILLIAM ROY JOHNSON), civic worker; b. Frankfort, Ind.; d. Earl Quincy and Maud (Johnson) Baker; student pub. schs., Detroit; m. William Roy Johnson, May 19, 1930; children—Jacqueline (Mrs. Edward James Twiford), Doris Johnson. Sec., Pere Marquette R.R., Detroit, 1922-24; sec. U.S. Customs, Fort St., Detroit, 1925-30. Pan Am. Liaison Com. Womens Orgns., Washington, 1958—, 3d v.p., 1966-68, 68-70, rec. sec. 1960-66; rec. sec. Salvation Army Aux., Washington, 1968-69; mem. Woman's Guild Swartzell Meth. Home for Children, pres., 1956-60. Bd. dirs. Barkers Home, Falls Church, Va., 1966-68. Mem. Womans Soc. Christian Service (life), Internat. Platform Assn. Methodist. Clubs: Capital Speakers (governing bd. 1969-70), Metropolitan Womens Bridge (pres. 1968-70), Welcome to Washington Internat. Home: 4234 42d St NW Washington DC 20016

JOHNSON, CAROLYN ELNA, educator; b. Parkers Prairie, Minn., Aug. 9, 1941; d. Clarence Leonard and Edith Florence (Wahlin) Johnson; B.A. in English (freshman scholar, Lutheran Brotherhood scholar, Amity Among Nations scholar), Augsburg Coll., 1963; M.A. in Journalism (dept. fellow), Am. U., Washington, 1968. Asst. librarian Edina-Morningside (Minn.) High Sch., 1963-65; tchr. English Sr. High Sch., Helena, Mont., 1965-67; tchr. english and journalism Wheaton (Md.) High Sch., 1968-72; asst. prof. journalism Cal. State U. at Fullerton, 1972—. Instr. Communications Arts Inst. U. N.M., Las Cruces, summer 1970, 71. Mem. Soc. for Profl. Journalists, Women In Communications, Am. Swedish Inst. Am. Assn. U. Women (v.p. 1970-72). Lutheran. Contbr. articles to publs. Home: 1257 Kraemer Blvd Placentia CA 92670 Office: 800 N State College Blvd Fullerton CA 92634

JOHNSON, CAROLYN LAURAETTA COLTER, ednl. adminstr.; b. Leesburg, Fla., Feb. 11, 1945; d. Curtis and Laura Elizabeth (Barnhill) Colter; B.A., Bethune Cookman Coll., 1966; M.S., East Tex. State U., 1971; 1 dau., Debria. Tchr. primary grades, Groveland, Fla., 1966-68; dir. County Central Developmental Center, Dallas, 1968—. Cons. Montessori Sch., Allen, Tex., 1973-74. Mem. adv. bd. human service East Field Coll., 1973-74. Recipient Ednl. Service award East Field Coll., 1973. Mem. Assn. Black Social Workers, Am. Assn. Mental Deficiency. Democrat. Methodist. Home: 3128 Larkspur Lane Dallas TX 75233 Office: 2910 S Beckley Dallas TX 75224

JOHNSON, CAROLYN NEAL (MRS. WILBERT WILSON JOHNSON), librarian; b. Ft. Smith, Ark., July 6, 1926; d. Benjamin Franklin and Lillie Mae (Curry) Neal; B.S. in Gen. Sci., St. Augustine's Coll., Raleigh, N.C., 1953; M.L.S., N.C. Central U., 1956; m. Wilbert Wilson Johnson, Apr. 22, 1946; children—Wilbert B., Jerome, Dwight W., Benjamin W., Gregory J. Tchr., librarian St. Anges Sch. Nursing, Raleigh, 1954-57; circulation librarian St. Bonaventure U., 1957-62; librarian Garner (N.C.) Consol. High Sch., 1963-67; catalogue librarian Shaw U., 1969, media specialist, 1969-71, acting dir. Learning Resources Center, 1971-72; asst. state librarian div. state library N.C. Dept. Cultural Resources, Raleigh, 1971—. Trustee, sec. Carolina Readers Theatre. Mem. A.L.A., Southeastern, N.C. library assns., Internat. Personnel Mgmt. Assn., Audio-Visual Edn. and Communication Technicians, N.A.A.C.P., Catholic Daus. Am., Guys and Dolls, Alpha Kappa Alpha. Democrat. Roman Catholic. Club: Interstate Bridge. Home: 2133 Lyndhurst Dr Raleigh NC 27610 Office: 109 E Jones St Raleigh NC 27611

JOHNSON, CATHERINE COMMON, newspaper, radio, TV exec.; b. Watertown, N.Y., Feb. 12, 1914; d. James Allison and Minna (Anthony) Common; B.A., St. Lawrence U., 1935; M.S. in Journalism, Columbia, 1937; m. John Brayton Johnson, June 21, 1941; children—John Brayton, Ann Catherine, Deborah Jane, Harold Bowtell. Reporter, editor Watertown Daily Times, 1937-41, editorial and spl. features writer, 1950—; v.p., sec. Brockway Co., owners Watertown Daily Times, WWNY-TV, Carthage-Watertown, radio sta. WWNY, Watertown, WMSA, Massena, N.Y., 1951—. Treas. Thousand Islands State Park Commn. Mem. Nat. League Am. Pen Women. Watertown Artists Guild (dir.). Presbyn. Club: College Women of Jefferson County (pres. 1954-56). Home: 221 Flower Av Watertown NY 13601 Office: 260 Washington St Watertown NY 13601

JOHNSON, CATHRYNE CHRISTINE LALIM (MRS. KENT ALLAN JOHNSON), editor; b. Williston, N.D., May 9, 1947; d. Lester Earl and Lila Marion (Hove) Lalim; B.A. summa cum laude, U. N.D., 1969, M.A., 1971; student U. Oslo (Norway), 1968; m. Kent Allan Johnson, Nov. 25, 1972. Teaching asst. Am. history U. N.D., Grand Forks, 1969-71; mng. editor, manuscripts curator S.D. State Hist. Soc., Pierre, 1971-72; editor State Hist. Soc. Colo., Denver, 1972—. Sons of Norway scholar, Grand Forks, N.D., 1968, Arneberg scholar U. N.D., 1968. Mem. Sons of Norway, Norwegian-Am. Hist. Assn., Westerners, Western History Assn., Phi Beta Kappa, Phi Alpha Theta. Lutheran. Home: 6916 S Knolls Way Littleton CO 80122 Office: 200 14th Av Denver CO 80203

JOHNSON, CECILE RYDEN (MRS. PHILIP JOHNSON), artist; b. Jamestown, N.Y.; d. Ernest Edwin and Agnes E. (Johnson) Ryden; A.B., Augustana Coll.; postgrad. Am. Acad. Fine Arts, Art Inst. Chgo., U. Wis., U. Colo., Pa. Acad. Fine Art, Scripps Coll.; m. Philip Arthur Johnson; children—Pamela Cecile, Stevan Philip. One-man shows Woman's Club, Chgo., Swedish Club, Chgo., 1953, Augustana Coll., Rock Island, Ill., 1953, Davenport Municipal Gallery, 1954, Am. Swedish Inst., Mpls., 1956, Burpee Art Gallery, Rockford, Ill., 1957, Chgo. Galleries, 1957, J. Walter Thompson, N.Y., 1958, Hudson River Mus. 1960, N.W. Ayer, Phila., 1960, Charter Gallery, Scarsdale, N.Y., 1960, N.Y. Grand Central Gallery, 1965, 67, 69, 71, 73, Paris, 1973, sponsored by Fifth Army, central and western U.S., 1955; 67, 69, 71, 72; solo traveling exhibit exhibited in group shows Am. Watercolor Soc., Washington Watercolor Soc., Artist Guild of Chgo., Art Dirs. Annual, Hudson Valley Shows; featured designer Am. Artists, Group, Inc.; 11 paintings for U.S. Naval Art Collection of Women Marines, 1964; 12 paintings of Bermuda for collection Bank of Bermuda, 1964; traveling solo exhibit, Am. Univs., 1964, 65, 66; designed covers Ford Times, Chgo. Tribune Sunday Mag., others; designed Am. UNICEF Christmas card (design of Rockefeller Center Skating Rink) for 1968; illustration in Motor Boating, Ford Times, Lincoln Mercury Times; designed and executed stained glass windows for Nursery Chapel, Augustana, Chgo., series of 16 prints for TWA, 1973; represented in permanent collections Augustana Coll., Ford Motor Co., Nat. Safety Council, Garcia Corp., Wagner Coll., Skiing mag., Davenport Municipal Art Gallery, others; mural for Regatta Room, Bermuda Airport, 1966; affiliation Grand Central Galleries, N.Y.C. Recipient awards for paintings All Ill. Watercolor, 1953, Ill. Fedn. Music Clubs, 1955, Larchmont Art Fair, 1960, Scarsdale Watercolor, 1960; Outstanding Achievement award Alumni Assn. Augustana Coll., 1962; Woman of Achievement award in Art Nat. League Pen Women, 1962, named 1st Woman Artist by USN and NACAL com. Salmagundi Club; Catherine Lorillard Wolffe gold medal for watercolor, 1965. Mem. Am. Watercolor Soc., Hudson Valley Art Assn., Scarsdale Art Assn., Nat. Arts Soc. Lutheran. Home: 340 Riverside Dr New York City NY also 48 The Quadrangle London W2 England

JOHNSON, CONSTANCE RUTH WORSLEY (MRS. BERT W. JOHNSON), counselor; b. N.Y.C., Jan. 23, 1914; d. John Edgeley and Ruth (Bixton) Worsley; student Rice U., 1931-34; A.B., Washburn U., 1935; M.A., Roosevelt U., 1966; m. Bert W. Johnson, Oct. 19, 1935 (dec. Jan. 1973); 1 dau., Roberta Liane (Mrs. T. Michael Garrison). Classroom tchr., 1942-44, 50-59; counselor jr. high sch., 1959-67; guidance dir. Lockport (Ill.) Dist. 96, Park View Sch., 1967-70; asst. prof. edn. Coll. St. Francis, 1970-72, chmn. dept. edn., 1972—; dir. State of Ill. Elementary Guidance Demonstration Center, 1967-69; cons. State of Ill. Elementary Guidance Insts. Mem. Am., Ill. personnel and guidance assns., Am., Ill. sch. counselors assns., Nat. Vocational Guidance Assns., N.E.A. (life), Am. Fedn. Tchrs., Menninger Found., Assn. Measurement Evaluation in Guidance, Ill. Elementary Sch. Counselors Assn., Am. Assn. U. Profs., Assn. for Humanistic Psychology. Contbr. articles profl. jours. Home: 8 Hunter Av Joliet IL 60436 Office: Edn Dept Coll St Francis Joliet IL 60435

JOHNSON, CYNTHIA SENN (MRS. ROBERT W. JOHNSON), ednl. adminstr.; b. Milw., Nov. 15, 1932; d. Charles L. and Mary Isola (Ewing) Senn; B.A., Cal. State U., 1954, postgrad., 1954-57; postgrad. Pacific Oak Coll., 1965; m. Robert W. Johnson, Apr. 5, 1952; children—Jeffrey Alan, Jodi Ann, Jay Austin. Adminstr., Cal. State U., Los Angeles, 1954-57; pre-sch. dir. Pasadena (Cal.) City Schs., 1965-67; child devel. supr. Headstart Program, Pasadena, 1965-68; adminstr. U. Cal. at Irvine, 1968—, now dir. career planning and placement. Cons., lectr. Pacific Oaks Coll., 1966-67, Pasadena City Schs., 1966, Cal. State U. at Los Angeles, 1967. Mem. ednl. adv. bd. Pasadena Commn. Human Needs and Opportunities, 1966-69. Mem. Am. (exec. council 1973—), Cal. (pres. 1973-74) coll. personnel assns., Cal. State U. at Los Angeles Alumni Assn. (dir. 1956-72), Pi Lambda Theta. Home: 502 Emerald Bay Laguna Beach CA 92651 Office: Career Planning and Placement U Cal Irvine CA 92664

JOHNSON, DANESSA VERNA WISE, educator; b. Phila., Mar. 22, 1933; d. Benjamin Earl and Mabel Lavinia (McCauley) Wise; B.A., Chestnut Hill Coll., 1954; M.Ed., Temple U., 1969, Ed.D., 1974; 1 son, Quinn. Student/staff occupational therapist Army Med. Service Corps, Ft. Sam Houston, Tex., 1954-55, Walter Reed Hosp., Washington, 1955-56, Letterman Gen. Hosp., San Francisco, 1956-57; recreational leader service clubs Spl. Services, Ulm, Germany, Schwabish Gemund, Germany, 1957-58; mem. staff Army Med. Service Corps Walter Reed Hosp., Washington, 1960-63, Valley Forge Hosp., Phoenixville, Pa., 1963-65, Walson Army Hosp., Ft. Dix, N.J., 1965-66, supr., 1963-65, chief occupational therapist, 1965-66; asst. prof. Boston U., 1973—. Recipient fellowships Rehab. Services Adminstrn., 1969. Mem. Am., D.C. (co-chmn. ways and means com. 1960-62) occupational therapy assns., Council Exceptional Children, Burlington County N.J. Assn. Brain-Injured Children (mem. profl. adv. bd. 1966-67). Home: 175 Freeman St No 221 Brookline MA 02146

JOHNSON, DIANA JORJORIAN (MRS. RICHARD GORDON JOHNSON), librarian; b. Worcester, Mass., Sept. 16, 1932; d. Arthur Eleazer and Isabel Marie (Calusdian) Jorjorian; A.B., Radcliffe Coll., 1954; M.S., Simmons Coll., 1957; m. Richard Gordon Johnson, July 11, 1959; children—Eric Christian, Dana Harald. Earth scis. librarian Mass. Inst. Tech., 1958-59; art and music librarian Providence Pub. Library, 1959-60; reference librarian Worcester (Mass.) Poly. Inst., 1961—. Republican. Episcopalian. Clubs: Radcliffe, Worcester Polytechnic Institute Business Women's. Home: 9 Wetherell St Worcester MA 01602 Office: Institute Rd Worcester MA 01609

JOHNSON, DOLORES MICHELL (MRS. C.E. JOHNSON), personnel exec.; b. Little Rock, July 17, 1923; d. Moreau Edwin and Eleanor D. (Harlin) Michell; student Little Rock U., 1952-53; m. C.E. Johnson, Sept. 4, 1939; 1 son, Allen E. Personnel officer U. Ark. Med. Center, Little Rock, 1948—. Mem. Personnel Assn. Ark. (sec. 1968). Mem. Christian Ch. (mem. bd. 1961-62). Club: Altrusa (bd. mem. Little Rock 1961-67). Home: 12 Delray Dr Little Rock AR 72207

JOHNSON, DORIS, dietitian; b. Woodstock, Ill., Sept. 18, 1910; d. Alfred E. and Flora (Longanecker) Johnson; B.S., U. Wis., 1932, M.S., 1938, Ph.D., 1951. Dietetic intern Johns Hopkins Hosp., 1933; dietitian St. Joseph's Hosp., Milw., 1934-36, Wis. State Sanatorium, 1938-40, Hines Hosp., 1940, Columbia-Presbyn. Med. Center, N.Y.C., 1941-48; asst. prof. U. Wis., 1951-52; dir. dietetics, asst. prof. pub. health Yale-New Haven Med. Center, 1952—. Fellow Am. Pub. Health Assn.; mem. Am. Dietetic Assn. (treas. 1956-58, pres. 1959-61, treas. found. 1966-69; Marjorie Hulsizer Copher award 1967), Am. Bd. Nutrition, Am. Home Econs. Assn., Am. Soc. Clin. Nutrition, Am. Heart Assn., Sigma Xi, Sigma Delta Epsilon, Omicron Nu, Phi Upsilon Omicron, Phi Kappa Phi. Club: Quota. Author: Modern Dietetics, 1951; Laboratory Manual in Cookery, 1948; Overweight is Curable. Home: 5 Cole Rd Hamden CT 06518 Office: 789 Howard Av New Haven CT 06504

JOHNSON, DORIS CAPRA (MRS. ROBERT NEIL JOHNSON), librarian; b. N.Y.C.; d. Ottavio Araldo and Amneris Aida (Tonegatti) Capra; Certificate in L.S., Pratt Inst., 1948; postgrad. Queens Coll., 1951-53, Columbia, 1961-62; m. Robert Neil Johnson, Dec. 27, 1969. Librarian Queens Boro Pub. Library, Jamaica, N.Y., 1943-47, Hempstead (N.Y.) Pub. Library, 1948-49; head reference research Adelphi U. Library, Garden City, N.Y., 1950—. Mem. Am., N.Y. State, Nassau County library assns., Am. Civil Liberties Union, Am. Assn. U. Profs. Home: 58 St Paul's Rd N Hempstead NY 11550 Office: South Av Garden City NY 11530

JOHNSON, DORIS THERESSA HOLT (MRS. CHARLES EDWIN JOHNSON), coll. librarian; b. Bethany, La., June 26, 1934; d. George and Marie (Jackson) Holt; B.A., Tex. Coll., 1960; M.L.S., E. Tex. State U., 1968; m. Charles Edwin Johnson, Dec. 24, 1960; children—Ardwin Bertram, Gary Lafayette. Bus. instr. Southwestern Christian Coll., 1960-67, librarian, 1967—. Mem. South Terrell Action Group, 1973—. Mem. A.L.A., Tex. Library Assn., Tex. Jr. Coll. Tchrs. Assn. Club: 22 Marechal Niel. Home: 803 S Rockwall St Terrell TX 75160

JOHNSON, DOROTHY ELOISE, educator; b. Savannah, Ga., Aug. 21, 1919; d. Charles Leroy and Annie (Bryce) Johnson; A.A., Armstrong Jr. Coll., 1938; B.S., Vanderbilt U., 1942; M.P.H., Harvard, 1948. Instr. Vanderbilt U., 1942-43, 44-47, asst. prof. pediatric nursing, 1948-49; staff nurse Chatham-Savannah Health Council, 1943-44; asst. prof. nursing U. Cal. at Los Angeles, 1949-53, asso. prof., 1953-63, prof., 1963—. Vis. prof. U. Wash., State U. Ia., others; cons. 1955—; tech. asst. U.S. State Dept., India, 1955-56. Recipient Founder's medal Vanderbilt U., 1942, Distinguished Teaching award U. Cal. at Los Angeles, 1969. Mem. Am. Nurses' Assn., Nat. League for Nursing, Am. Pub. Health Assn., Delta Omega, Sigma Theta Tau. Contbr. articles to profl. jours. Home: 1975 Linda Flora Dr Los Angeles CA 90024

JOHNSON, DOROTHY LOU, state ofcl.; b. Sioux Falls, S.D., June 13, 1924; d. Melvin M. and Minnie C. (Aasen) Johnson; B.A., Augustana Coll., 1946. Merchandising exec. Foote, Cone & Belding, advt. agy., Chgo., 1947-61; merchandising account exec. Edward H. Weiss & Co., advt. agy., Chgo., 1962; owner advt. and sales promotion firm, Chgo., 1963-64; mgr. pub. relations Ill. Soc. C.P.A.'s, Chgo., 1965-67; mgr. Chgo. br. Crossroads of Sport, 1968; asst. to publs. mgr. Touche, Ross & Co., accountants, Chgo., 1969-72; occupational program coordinator Ill. Dept. Mental Health, Chgo., 1973—; owner and mfg. firm, Chgo., 1964—. Mem. Assn. Labor-Mgmt. Adminstrs. and Cons. on Alcoholism, Ill. Alcohol and Drug Dependency Assn., Occupational Program Cons. Assn. Home: 1460 Sandburg Terrace Chicago IL 60610 Office: 188 W Randolph St Chicago IL 60601

JOHNSON, EDDIE BERNICE, state polit. party ofcl.; b. Waco, Tex., Dec. 3, 1934; d. Edward Johnson; student St. Mary's Coll. Holy Cross Central Sch. Nursing, South Bend, Ind., 1953-55; B.S., Tex. Christian U., 1968; 1 son, Dawrence Kirk. Chief psychiat. nurse psychotherapist VA Hosp., Dallas, 1956-72; exec. asst. personnel div. Neiman-Marcus, Inc., Dallas, 1972—. Cons to student nurses Baylor U., Tex. Woman's U.; mem. Equal Employment Opportunities com. VA Hosp., 1966. Vice chmn. Tex. Democratic Conv., 1972; mem. Tex. Dem. Exec. Com., 1972-74; mem. credentials com. Nat. Dem. Conv., 1972. Recipient Sustained Superior Performance award VA Hosp., 1971; Woman of Year award Greyhound Corp., 1972; Woman of Year award Kappa Zeta Chpt. Zeta Amicae, 1973; Outstanding Black Achievement award Alpha Rho chpt. Phi Delta Kappa, 1973. Mem. Nat. Council Negro Women (pres. 1963-66), Women for Change (dir.), YWCA, League Women Voters, Progressive Voter's League, Bus. and Profl. Women's Club (Trailblazer of Year award S. Dallas chpt. 1973), Jack and Jill Am. (nat. v.p.), Alpha Kappa Alpha. Home: 2107 Lanark Dallas TX 75203 Office: PO Box 25 Dallas TX 75203

JOHNSON, EDITH LINE, city ofcl.; b. Junction City, Kan., May 22, 1911; d. Fred Amos and Mabel Amelia (Allen) Line; student Woodbury Coll., 1936-37, extension courses U. Ariz., 1955, Phoenix Coll., 1956; m. William S. Johnson, Mar. 15, 1948 (dec.). Adminstrv. asst. Phoenix Urban League, 1957-60; part owner printing bus., Phoenix, 1960-64; asst. dir. pub. relations Ameco, Phoenix, 1964-65; dir. pub. relations Kaiser-Cox, Phoenix, 1965-66; reporter News Bur. Ariz. State U., Tempe, 1966-67; pub. information specialist Operation LEAP, Phoenix, 1967-73; pub. information specialist Phoenix Parks and Recreation Dept., 1973—. Lectr. race relations, integration to schs., chs., govt. seminars, So. Cal., 1957-60. Chmn. interrracial housing project Phoenix, 1957-60; mem. Phoenix Urban League Guild, 1957-60. Recipient Silver Medal award Phoenix Art Dir.'s Club, 1966. Mem. Pub. Relations Soc. Am. Author: Indians in Arizona, 1962. Editor The Phoenician, 1965-66, South Phoenix Round-Up newspaper, 1962-63, LEAP News, 1967—. Contbr. articles to nat. mags. Home: 1528 W Campbell St Phoenix AZ 85018 Office: 2300 N Central St Phoenix AZ 85004

JOHNSON, EDNA DECOURSEY (MRS. LAURENCE H. JOHNSON), orgn. adminstr.; b. Balt., June 1, 1922; d. Jacob Garfield and Rosa Felicia (Wilson) De Coursey; B.S., Coppin State Coll., 1944; postgrad. Rutgers U., 1950, 56, Johns Hopkins, 1952, U. Md., 1959-63, U. Wis., 1966; m. Laurence Harry Johnson, Sept. 30, 1956. Tchr. pub. schs., Balt., 1944-63; asso. dir. Family Life Project Balt. Urban League, 1963-65, project dir. consumer protection program Community Action Agy., 1965-68, dir. consumer services, 1968—. Mem. faculty U. Dayton, 1967; cons. Sears, Roebuck and Co. Treas. Md. Council on Family Relations, 1970—; mem. Commn. on Status Women, 1968—, Pres.'s Consumer Adv. Council, 1974—, Md. Gov.'s Energy Adv. Commn., 1974—. Bd. dirs. Balt. Area Council on Alcoholism, Voluntary Action Center Central Md., Consumers Union U.S.A., Md. Assn. Adult Edn.; adv. council Am. Bankers Assn. Named Tchr. of Week Afro-Am. Newspapers, 1947; recipient outstanding community service awards Pi Beta Sigma, 1958, Balt. Club Nat. Assn. Negro Bus. and Profl. Women's Clubs, 1968, Nat. Negro Coll. Fund, 1970, Tau Gamma Delta, 1971, Lambda Kappa Mu, 1972. Mem. Nat. Assn. Negro Bus. and Profl. Women's Clubs (Mid-Atlantic gov. 1973—, nat. corr. sec. 1971-73; pres. Balt. Club 1970-73), Am. Council on Consumer Interests, Md. Conf. Social Concerns, Citizens Housing and Planning Assn., Coppin State Coll. Alumni Assn., Zeta Phi Beta, Pi Beta Sigma. Mem. United Ch. of Christ. Home: 3655 Wabash Av Baltimore MD 21215 Office: Balt Urban League 1150 Mondawmin Concourse Baltimore MD 21215

JOHNSON, EDNA FAY HOGAN (MRS. LANDON CARTER JOHNSON), data processor; b. Tennyson, Tex., Aug. 23, 1923; d. Eddie H. and Mary Elizabeth (Hodges) Hogan; student San Angelo Coll., 1940-41; B.A., Howard Payne Coll., 1944; M.A., U. Tex., 1948; m. Landon Carter Johnson, Jr., Aug. 23, 1945; children—Robert Eugene, William Luke, John Michael. Prin. Tennyson Pub. Sch., 1942-43; instr. math. Ranger (Tex.) Jr. Coll., 1943-44; tchr. math. Brownwood, Tex., 1944-45; asst. prof. math. Howard Payne Coll., Brownwood, 1945-54; data processing analyst Continental Oil Col., Ponca City, Okla., 1955-63, sr. analyst, operations research, 1965—; instr. data processing No. Okla. Coll., Tonka, 1963-65. Mem. math. programming mixed integer com. SHARE, Inc. Pres. Mothers Club Ponca City Future Farmers Am., 1968-69. Mem. Math. Assn. Am., Am. Assn. U. Women, Assn. for Computing Machinery, Alpha Chi. Democrat. Baptist. Home: 8 Woodlands St Ponca City OK 74601 Office: Drawer 1267 Ponca City OK 74601

JOHNSON, ELEANOR ANTOINNETTE, coll. adminstr.; b. Jersey City; d. Richard S. and Della A. (Howard) Johnson; B.A. cum laude, Va. Union U., 1948; postgrad. U. Conn., 1963; M.A., Jersey City State Coll., 1966. Asst. dean of women Va. State Coll., Petersburg, 1960-67; now with Jersey City State Coll., asso. dir. grad. div., 1969—; asst. dir. nat. bd. YWCA, Jersey City, 1967-69. Mem. Nat. Assn. Women Deans and Counselors, Nat. Assn. Fgn. Student Affairs, Am. Assn. U. Women, League Women Voters (mem. pub. relations com. 1971-73), Alpha Kappa Alpha. Office: Jersey City State Coll Office of Grad Studies 2039 Kennedy Blvd Jersey City NJ 07305

JOHNSON, ELEANOR M., banker; b. N.Y.C., May 9, 1920; d. James and Hilda (Thompson) Johnson; B.A., Barnard Coll., 1941; postgrad. N.Y. U., 1942-46. Research asst. Tax Inst., Phila., 1940-42; asst. v.p. Irving Trust Co., N.Y.C., 1942—. Mem. Am. Finance Assn., Am. Statis. Assn., Nat. Econs. Club, N.Y. Assn. Bus. Economists, Women's Bond Club, Sons Norway. Club: Barnard (Bklyn.). Home: 608 E 17th St Brooklyn NY 11226 Office: 1 Wall St New York City NY 10015

JOHNSON, ELIZABETH MOSIER (MRS. RONALD LEE JOHNSON), coll. adminstr.; b. Nacozari, Mex., Feb. 2, 1914; d. McHenry and Louise (Laurance) Mosier; B.A., Scripps Coll., 1935; M.A., Claremont U., 1939; m. Ronald Lee Johnson, Aug. 14, 1936 (dec. May 1967); children—William Laurance, Ann (Mrs. Raymond Hertel). Asst. in humanities Scripps Coll., Claremont, Cal., 1936-44, trustee, 1945-50, dir. financial aid, 1968—; dist. bookkeeper Thermal (Cal.) Union Sch. Dist., 1947-63; tchr. Desert Sun Sch., Mecca, Cal., 1944-46. Mem. Western regional exec. com. Coll. Entrance Exam. Bd. Chpt. pres. Am. Field Service, 1967. Mem. Western Assn. Student Financial Aid Adminstrs., Cal. Assn. Student Financial Aid Adminstrs. (panel financial aid cons., state scholarship need analysis team). Home: 440 B Vista Dr Claremont CA 91711 Office: Scripps Coll Claremont CA 91711

JOHNSON, ELSIE CARLSON (MRS. ROBERT DAVID JOHNSON), educator; b. Chillicothe, Ill., Jan 1, 1922; d. George Arthur and Carrie (Ohlman) Carlson; B.S., Ill. State U., 1944; M.S., U. Ill., 1945; certificate advanced study, No. Ill. U., 1969; m. Robert David Johnson, Sept. 16, 1945; children—Jeffrey E., Jay E. Asst. supr. bacteriology Ill. Health Dept., Chgo., 1945-54; tchr. Dist. 41 Sch., Glen Ellyn, Ill., 1954-56, Dist. 93 Sch., Carol Stream, Ill., 1957-59; supt. schs. Dist. 93, Cloverdale Consol. Schs., Carol Stream, Ill., 1959—; prin. Cloverdale Sch. for Trainable Mentally Retarded, 1966-70. Mem. bd. Coop. Assn. Spl. Edn., Audio-Visual Inst. (both DuPage County). Recipient Distinguished Service award Carol Stream Jr. C. of C., 1966, Service and Achievement award Wheaton Coll., 1970. Mem. Ill. Assn. Elementary Prins. (div. sec.-treas. 1962-63, div. pres. 1964-65), Ill., Am. (Profl. Devel. award 1973) assns. sch. adminstrs., N.E.A. (life), Ill. Assn. for Supervision and Curriculum Devel., Ill. Assn. Sch., Coll., U. Staffing, Ill. Congress of Parents and Tchrs. (charter mem. 5 local units Dist. 32), Council for Exceptional Children, Delta Kappa Gamma (sec. 1967-68, chpt. pres. 1968-70, state program chmn. 1973—). Clubs: Glen Ellyn Countryside Garden (pres. 1973), Carol Stream Woman's (hon.). Home: 558 Lee St Glen Ellyn IL 60137 Office: 393 Illini Dr Carol Stream IL 60187

JOHNSON, EMILY BRAWNER, govt. ofcl.; b. Honolulu, Dec. 27, 1920; d. Maxwell Oscar and Emily (Hetfield) Johnson; B.A., U. Hawaii, 1941; LL.B., J.D., Hastings Coll. of Law, 1951. Admitted to Cal. bar, 1952; pvt. practice law, San Francisco, 1952-56; atty. State of Cal., San Francisco, 1956-61; referee Workmen's Compensation Appeals Bd., San Francisco, 1961-74, referee in charge, San Francisco, 1974—. Served with USAAF, 1941-44, AUS, 1944-48. Mem. Amateur Fencers League Am. (v.p. 1973—). Home: 1250 Ellis St San Francisco CA 94109 Office: 455 Golden Gate Av San Francisco CA 94102

JOHNSON, ESTELLA SCOTT (MRS. RUFUS C. JOHNSON), educator; b. Harrisburg, Pa., July 17, 1910; d. John Paul and Estella (Harris) Scott; B.S., Cheyney State Coll., 1934; M.S., U. Pa., 1936, postgrad.; m. Rufus C. Johnson, Aug. 7, 1945. Elementary pub. sch. tchr., Harrisburg, Pa., 1928-30; research fellow, head resident Fisk U., Nashville, 1936-39, sociology prof., adminstrv. asst. to head social sci. dept., 1939-43; adminstrv. asst. to pres. Cheyney (Pa.) State Coll., 1943-53, asso. prof. social sci. 1957-66, prof., 1966—, acting dean Arts and Scis., 1969-70; dir. World Cultures Center, Pub. relations, fashion coordinator Peg Connor Modiste, Phila., 1965-66; host, coordinator TV series Afro-Am. Experience, KYW-TV, Phila. Field reader U.S. Office of Edn., 1973—. Mem. evaluation panel, ad hoc com. higher edn. act U.S. Office Edn. Recipient fashion award Nat. Assn. Fashion and Accessory Designers, 1959; Gold medallion Cheyney State Coll., 1972; named Outstanding Educator in Am., 1970. Gen. Edn. fellow, Julius Rosenwald fellow, 1941-42. Fellow Am. Sociol. Assn.; mem. Nat., Pa. State edn. assns., Nat., Pa. (pres. 1972—), councils for social studies, African Studies Assn., Am. Assn. U. Women, A.A.A.S., Internat. Studies Assn., Smithsonian Assos., M.M.S. Address: Cheyney State Coll Cheyney PA 19319

JOHNSON, ESTHER F., ret. labor leader; b. Springville, Ia., Dec. 30, 1904; d. Clinton A. and Carrie (Gregg) Shanklin; student Coe Coll., 1923; m. Arthur J. Johnson, Oct. 13, 1923 (dec. Feb. 1940); 1 son, Warren A. Tchr. pub. schs., Ia., 1923-24; chief clk. Norton AFB, San Bernardino, Cal., 1943-46. U.S. Army, Aberdeen Proving Grounds, Md., 1946-47; ofcl. hostess V.I.P. Quarters Hickam AFB, Honolulu, 1948-49; Supply Corps clk. USN Constrn. Bn. Center, Port Hueneme, 1950-53; supply requirements and distbn. officer stock control div. Navy Yards and Docks Supply Office, 1953-56; active Am. Fedn. Govt. Employees, 1950—, sec.-treas. Pacific S.W. Dist. council, 1953-54, del. Pub. Employee Confs., 1952-54, floor leader Cal. delegation 1952 conv., del. nat. convs., 1952—, nat. sec.-treas., 1956-70, nat. sec.-treas. emeritus, 1970—; mem. indsl. adv. com. to Asst. to Sec. Labor. Mem. Sec.-Treas.'s Conf. all AFL-CIO unions. Mem. adult program activities com. YWCA, Washington; mem. com. fed. employment Pres. Kennedy's Commn. on Status Women, 1961-63; active Civilian Blood Bank. Home: Apt 102 5773 Encina Rd Goleta CA 93017

JOHNSON, ETHEL MARIE, educator; b. Jamestown, Kan.; d. Frank E. and Frida M. (Gustafson) Johnson; B.A., Bethany Coll., 1935; M.A., U. Kan., 1941; postgrad. U. Colo., 1946, U. Uppsala (Sweden), 1959. Tchr. English high schs., Olsburg, Kan., 1935-37, Burden, Kan., 1937-39, Salina, Kan., 1941-46; dean of women Bethany Coll., Lindsborg, Kan., 1946-49, Neb. Wesleyan U., Lincoln, 1950—. Bd. dirs. Lincoln (Neb.) YWCA, 1964-70. Mem. Am. Assn. U. Women (state bd. dirs. 1964-71), Neb. Assn. Deans of Women (treas. 1970-71), Nat. Assn. Women Deans and Counsellors, Cardinal Key, Delta Kappa Gamma. Home: 5340 Walker Av Lincoln NE 68504

JOHNSON, EVA MAYNE, educator, psychologist; b. Balt.; A.B., George Washington U., 1949, M.A., 1951, Ph.D., 1957; m. Edwin Joseph Johnson, June 2, 1935. Prof. psychology George Washington U.; lectr.; creator daily radio program Psychologically Speaking, WTOP Radio; creator weekly program WAMU-FM. Active UNRRA, Near East, Egypt, Greece and Italy, World War II; clin. psychologist D.C. Health Dept., Center for Psychol. Service, D.C. Vocational and Rehab. Service. Adviser on children's TV programs WRC, Washington. Pres., D.C. Assn. for Retarded Children, Inc., 1964—. Bd. dirs. Nat. Assn. for Retarded Citizens. Author: A Code for Behavior for Parents and Youth, 1966. Research on effects of brain damage upon mental functioning in children, motivational factors related to acad. achievement. Home: 3800 52d St NW Washington DC 20016

JOHNSON, EVELYN ALICE STEIL (MRS. THRUSTON JOHNSON), pub. co. exec.; b. N.Y.C., June 11, 1921; d. William George and Martha Anna (Roehm) Steil; B.A. in Music and English cum laude, Hunter Coll., 1945; M.F.A. in Mass Communications, Columbia, 1963; m. Thruston Johnson, Apr. 5, 1953; Registrar, N.Y. Coll. Music, N.Y.C., 1945-50; fund campaign asst. Metropolitan Opera Guild, N.Y.C., 1950-51; program dir. WABF-FM, N.Y.C., 1952-54; dir. Records from Abroad, 1954-57; advt. mgr. Harvey Famous Name Comics, N.Y.C., 1957-72, v.p. advt. and merchandising, 1973—. Mem. Advt. Club N.Y., Phi Beta Kappa. Home: 600 W 116th St New York City NY 10027 Office: Harvey Famous Name Comics Inc 15 Columbus Circle New York City NY 10023

JOHNSON, FATIMA NUNES, chemist; b. Makati, Philippines, Jan. 1, 1939; d. Carlos da Luz and Maria da Pureza (d'Eca) N.; B.S., Adamson U., 1959; M.S., Boston Coll., 1961, Ph.D., 1964; m. Edgar McCarthy Johnson, Sept. 9, 1967. Came to U.S., 1959, naturalized, 1971. Research asst. NSF, 1962-64; sr. staff chemist Arthur D. Little Inc., Cambridge, Mass., 1964-69; research chemist Edgewood Arsenal, Md., 1969-70; sr. scientific asso. U.S. Pharmacopeia, Rockville, Md., 1971—. Mem. Am. Chem. Soc., Sigma Xi. Contbr. articles to profl. jours. Patentee drugs useful as central nervous system depressants. Home: 5314 Dunleer Lane Burke VA 22015 Office: 12601 Twinbrook Pkwy Rockville MD 20852

JOHNSON, (FLORENCE) DEBORAH (MRS. CHARLES HARRISON EID), physician; b. Lake Nebagamon, Wis., June 7, 1928; d. John Carl and Ida Josephine (Anderson) Johnson; B.S., U. Wis., 1950, M.D., 1953; m. Charles Harrison Eid, Feb. 23, 1957; children—Jeffrey, Tom, Jennifer. Intern, King County Hosp., Seattle, 1953-54; resident internal medicine U. Mich., Ann Arbor, 1954-59, fellow med. oncology, 1959-60; asst. research physician, cancer research unit U. Cal. at San Francisco, 1962-67, asst. clin. prof., 1967-74, asso. prof., 1974—; practice internal medicine, specializing in oncology, San Francisco, San Mateo and Burlingame, Cal., 1967—; mem. staff Mills Meml. Hosp., San Mateo, Peninsula Hosp., Burlingame, H.C. Moffitt Hosp., San Francisco. Mem. San Francisco Bay Area Cancer Epidemiology Bd., 1972—. Vice pres. San Mateo County Jr. Mus., 1967-68, membership chmn., 1968. Bd. dirs. San Mateo County Bd. Health and Welfare, 1973—, San Mateo County unit Am. Cancer Soc., 1973—. Mem. Am., Cal., San Mateo County Med. assns., A.C.P. (life), Am. Assn. U. Women, League Women Voters, Am. Fedn. Clin. Research, Western Cancer Study Group, No. Cal. Clin. Oncology, Am. Women for Internat. Understanding (charter). Contbr. articles to profl. jours. Home: 321 W Bellevue Av San Mateo CA 94402 Office: 1201 HC Moffitt Hosp U Cal Med Center 3d and Parnassus San Francisco CA 94122

JOHNSON, FRANCES ELLIOTT LAMBERT (MRS. BOYD LYNN JOHNSON), educator; b. Ashland, Ky., Apr. 21, 1938; d. Elliott and Katherine Margaret (Hetzel) Lambert; B.A., Centre Coll. Ky., 1959; M.A., U. Ky., 1963; m. Boyd Lynn Johnson, Sept. 4, 1959. Free lance artist and dance instr., 1959-60; program dir. YWCA, Lexington, Ky., 1960-61; profl. dist. adviser Girl Scouts, Lexington, Ky., 1961-63; tchr. English jr. high sch., Orlando, Fla., 1963-64; asst. prof. speech and theatre Coll. of Orlando, 1964-70; mem. faculty Fla. Tech. U., Orlando, 1968—, instr. speech and theatre, 1970—. Producer, dir. Miss Fla. Pageant, 1970. Mem. Fla. Speech Communication Assn., Orlando Dog Tng. Club, Delta Kappa Gamma, Alpha Psi Omega, Delta Psi Omega, Phi Rho Pi. Republican. Presbyn. Home: Rural Route 8 Box 726 Kamelot Orlando FL 32807

JOHNSON, FRANCES NELSON, registrar; b. Asheville, N.C., May 15, 1921; d. Clarence Rex and Bertha (Puryear) Nelson; ed. Biltmore Jr. Coll., Cecil's Bus. Coll., Capitol Radio Engring. Inst., Asheville-Buncombe Tech. Inst.; B.A. in Psychology, U. N.C.; M.A. in Edn., Appalachian State U., 1974; m. Walter A. Johnson, Oct. 24, 1965. Radio engr. Radio Sta. WWNC, Asheville, 1942-65, also sec.-treas. Creasman Radio TV, Inc., 1951-61; equipment coordinator Asheville-Buncombe Tech. Inst., 1961-67, registrar, 1967—; dir. Creasman Radio-TV. Recipient recognition as 2d woman radio engr. in U.S., Broadcast Mag., 1942. Mem. Student Services Personnel Assn. (exec. com. dept. community colls.), Am., N.C. vocational assns. Democrat. Baptist. Club: Asheville Quota (sec.-treas. 19th dist. internat. 1964-65). Home: 101 Riverview Dr Asheville NC 28806 Office: 340 Victoria Rd Asheville NC 28801

JOHNSON, FREDA JANE SANDERS (MRS. E. MACK JOHNSON), ins. agt.; b. Lebanon, Ind., June 14, 1926; d. Fred I. and Mamye (Gwin) Sanders; A.B., MacMurray Coll., 1947; m. E. Mack Johnson, June 14, 1969; step-children—Myra Jo, Melinda Jill. With radio sta. WIBC, Indpls., summers 1945, 46; traffic mgr. sta. WTHI, Terre Haute, Ind., 1947-49, Sta. WPDQ, Jacksonville, Fla., 1949-51, WRHC, Jacksonville, Fla., 1951-53; staff writer Prudential Ins. Co. of Am., Jacksonville, Fla., 1953-54, editor, 1954-68, spl. agt. Jacksonville Ordinary Agy., 1968—. Publicity chmn. N.E. Fla. Heart Assn., 1967, sec., 1968; mem. womens div. Duval County Safety Council, 1963-65. C.L.U. Fellow Life Office Mgmt. Inst.; mem. Nat., Jacksonville assns. life underwriters, N.E. Fla. Bus. and Indsl. Editors (pres. 1959), So. Council Indsl. Editors (sec. 1966-67), C. of C., Am. Soc. Chartered Life Underwriters, Nat. Assn. Life Underwriters (life mem. women's leaders round table). Episcopalian. Mem. Order Eastern Star. Club: Pilot (pres. 1959-61). Home: 1319 Monticello Rd Jacksonville FL 32207 Office: Prudential Bldg Jacksonville FL 33027

JOHNSON, GENEVA FRANCIS RICHARD (MRS. EUGENE BARTOLETT JOHNSON), ednl. cons.; b. Eunice, La.; d. Ollie Peter and Pearl (Darbonne) Richard; B.S., U. Southwestern La., 1942; M.A., U. S.C., 1959; Ph.D., U. Pitts., 1971; m. Eugene Bartolett Johnson, Feb. 3, 1950. Staff physical therapist Beaumont Army Hosp., El Paso, 1946-48; emergency assignments Nat. Found. for Infantile Paralysis, Raleigh, Monroe and Charlotte, N.C., 1948-49; staff phys. therapist State U. Ia., Mercy Hosp., Iowa City, 1949-51, Fitzsimons Army Hosp., Brooke Army Hosp., San Antonio, 1951-54; coordinator therapies, supr. phys. therapy Baylor U. Coll. of Medicine, 1954-57; coordinator therapies Med. Coll. Ga., 1957-59; cons. rehab. teaching program Case-Western Res. U., 1959-60, dir. grad. phys. therapy curriculum, 1960-71, asst. dean for gen. adminstrn. Frances Payne Bolton Sch. Nursing, 1972-74. Cons. USPHS, 1966, chmn. subcom. NRC-Nat. Acad. Scis., 1967. Mem. Am. Physical Therapy Assn. (Ohio chpt. pres. 1963-65, chief del. 1965-68), M.M.S., Council Phys. Therapy Sch. Dirs. (sec. 1964-66, v.p. 1966-68, program chmn.), Northeastern O. Rehab. Assn. (dir. 1963, sec. 1965), Soc. for Behavioral Kinesiology (pres. 1972—), Alpha Sigma Alpha, Democrat. Roman Catholic. Contbr. articles in field to profl. jours. Home: 3430 Sylvanhurst Rd Cleveland OH 44112

JOHNSON, GENEVA LYNN BOLTON (MRS. RICHARD G. JOHNSON), social worker; b. nr. Bath, S.C., Mar. 21, 1929; d. Pierce and Lillie Mae (Hightower) Bolton; B.S., Albright Coll., 1951; M.S. in Social Adminstrn., Western Res. U., 1957; m. Richard G. Johnson, Nov. 2, 1957 (div. 1972). Program dir. YWCA, Houston, 1951-55; psychiat. social worker Wernersville (Pa.) State Hosp., 1957-59; supr. Children's Aid Soc., Reading, Pa., 1959-65; community planning dir. United Community Service, Reading, 1965-69, asst. exec. dir., 1969—; dir. planning United Fund and Council of Del., Wilmington, 1970-72, Community Chest of Rochester and Monroe County, N.Y., 1972—. Dir. Hutchins/Darcy, Rochester, N.Y., 1973—. Tech. cons. motion picture The Neglected, Mental Health Film Bd., N.Y.C., 1965; program dir. teen-age radio show, Houston, 1954-55; human relations cons. Wilmington Pub. Schs.; guest lectr. U. Del.; cons. Ednl. Change, Inc. Sec., dir. Econ. Opportunity Council, 1965; charter mem., dir. Threshold, Inc., 1965-66; dir. Camp Fire Girls of Berks County, 1965-66; group work cons. Jewish Community Center of Reading, Berks County Mental Health Assn., YWCA, 1963-64; resource person on human relations for youth confs. and insts., 1960-66; mem. Gov.'s Task Force Com. Comprehensive Mental Health Mental Retardation Study, 1964-66, asst. exec. dir., 1966—; chmn. Mental Health/Mental Retardation Bd. Berks County, 1967—; mem. Del. Council for Women, 1971—, Del. Agy. to Reduce Crime, 1972—, Del. Health Authority, 1970—, Del. Com. for Community Coordinated Child Care, 1970—, Gov.'s Task Force for Fed. Funding, 1970—, Del. Manpower Planning Council, 1972—; mem. neighborhood council Wilmington Model Cities, 1971—; exec. com. Eastern regional conf. United Way of Am.; sec.-treas. Urban Coalition of Met. Wilmington; mem. steering com. Rochester Inst. Tech. Urbanarium, 1973; mem. social services adv. com. County of Monroe, 1973—. Mem. Afro Am. Culture Center Reading and Berks County. Trustee Fgn. Affairs Councils Reading. Mem. Nat. Assn. Social Workers (local v.p. 1963; social action and legislation chmn. 1965, mem. Pa. council 1964), Acad. Certified Social Workers, Mid-Atlantic Child Welfare League Conf. (planning com.), Child Welfare League Am. (exec. com. Eastern regional conf.), N.A.A.C.P. (pub. relations chmn. 1963-65), M.M.S., Albright Coll. Alumni (sec. 1968), Am. Acad. Polit. and Social Sci., Pi Alpha Tau. Mem. United Ch. of Christ. Home: 15B Pamela Lane Rochester NY 14618 Office: 70 N Water St Rochester NY 14604

JOHNSON, GENEVIEVE ELOISE LOOFBORO (MRS. ROGER H. JOHNSON), educator; b. Lost Nation, Ia., Jan. 30, 1914; d. Lewis Lester and Bertha (Reyelts) Loofboro; B.A., Milton Coll., 1935; M.A., U. Wis., 1936; Specialist in Edn., Kan. State Tchrs. Coll., 1969; postgrad. Kan. State Coll., 1956, 57, 62; m. Roger H. Johnson, June 20, 1938; children—Mary Ann, Jerry Warren, Gene Douglas. Tchr. English, Linden (Wis.) High Sch., 1936-38; children's librarian Parsons (Kan.) Pub. Library, 1956-58; faculty Parsons (Kan.) Jr. Coll., 1958-62; faculty Coll. of Emporia (Kan.), 1962-74, prof. English, 1962-74, dean of women, 1963-72; English tchr. Parsons High Sch., 1974—. Mem. Nat., Kan. (pres. 1967-70) assns. women deans and counselors, Nat. Council Tchrs. English, Kan. Assn. Tchrs. English, Am. Assn. U. Women. Republican. Mem. Seventh Day Baptist Ch. Home: 705 Creek Av Parsons KS 67357

JOHNSON, GERTRUDE PEARL WIENCKE (MRS. CHARLES WILFORD JOHNSON), univ. librarian; b. Grand Island, Neb., May 24, 1918; d. Gustav Karl and Patty Frances (Matthews) Wiencke; B.A. summa cum laude (Mona M. Diehl fellow), Midland Luth. Coll., 1940; M.A., cum laude, U. Chgo., 1945; M.L.S., U. Wash., 1960; m. Charles Wilford Johnson, Apr. 2, 1945; children—Carolyn (Mrs. L. Kendal Ryan), Peter, Timothy, Gaynor. Asst. librarian Westminster Coll., Salt Lake City, 1957-60; serials librarian U. Utah, 1960-61; reference librarian Ore. Coll. Edn., 1961-63; dir. readers' services Willamette U. Library, Salem, Ore., 1963—. Mem. Am. Assn. U. Profs., Audubon Soc., Pacific N.W. (vice-chmn. reference div. 1973-75), Ore. library assns., Friends Willamette U. Library. Contbr. articles to profl. jours. Home: Route 1 Box 943 Salem OR 97304

JOHNSON, GERTRUDE SHANKS (MRS. JAMES IRVING JOHNSON), law librarian; b. Danville, Ill., Dec. 30, 1910; d. Roy Newton and Hedwig Erinstine (Prackel) Shanks; B.A., Case-Western Res. U., 1933, J.D., 1935; M.L.S., Kent State U., 1964; m. James Irving Johnson, Sept. 23, 1939; children—Eric Johnson, Elsa (Mrs. William A. LeFaiver). Admitted to Ohio bar, 1935; practiced in Cleve., 1935-42, Twinsburg, O., 1955-64; law librarian, asso. prof. law U. Akron (O.), 1964-73; law librarian Akron Law Library Assn., 1973—. Clk. Twinsburg Twp., 1955-64; chmn. citizens com. Improvement of Law Enforcement and Corrective Facilities, Akron, 1960-62. Recipient Womans Orgn. for Nat. Prohibition fellowship, 1935. Mem. Am. Assn. Law Libraries, Am. Assn. U. Profs., Ohio, Akron bar assns. Home: 9372 Liberty Rd Twinsburg OH 44087 Office: Summit County Court House Akron OH 44308

JOHNSON, HALLIEN HICKMAN (MRS. GARDNER HERRICK JOHNSON), coll. dean; b. Centerville, Ia.; d. Charles Stephen and Maude (Hicks) Hickman; B.A., Stanford U., 1932; M.Ed., Whitworth U., 1971; m. Gardner Herrick Johnson, Sept. 11, 1937; children—Carolyn (Mrs. Gerald Allen), Stephen, Mary Beth. Counselor, tchr. West Valley Sr. High Sch., Spokane, Wash., 1961-64; English instr. Spokane (Wash.) Community Coll., 1964-67; dean of women Spokane Falls Community Coll., Spokane, Wash., 1967—. Dir. womens programs Wash. Community Coll. Dist. 17, Spokane, 1971—. Mem. Spokane (Wash.) Sch. Adv. Com., 1953-55. Recipient Golden Key award Wash. Bus. and Profl. Womens Club, 1973. Mem. Nat. Assn. for Women Deans, Adminstrs. and Counselors (community coll. rep. on state exec. bd. 1970—), Am. Assn. Jr. Colls. (womens council 1973—), Am. Personnel and Guidance Assn., Am. Coll. Personnel Assn., Am. Assn. U. Women (pres. Spokane br. 1959-61), Pi Lambda Theta, Theta Sigma Phi, Delta Delta Delta. Episcopalian. Club: Altrusa (Spokane). Home: 927 W 27th Av Spokane WA 99203 Office: W 3410 Fort George Wright Dr Spokane WA 99204

JOHNSON, HAZEL MARIE, univ. librarian; b. Sylvania, O.; d. Otto Harrison and Caroline Alma (Lamley) Johnson; A.B., U. Mich., 1942, A.B. in L.S., 1943, M.A. in L.S., 1950. Circulation librarian U. N.M., Albuquerque, 1943-44; forestry librarian Colo. State U., Fort Collins, 1944-47; cataloger U. Denver, 1947-50; asst. librarian U. Mich. Bur. Govt. Library, Ann Arbor, 1951-54; asso. reference librarian Ohio State U., Columbus, 1955-60; reference librarian U. Pitts., 1960-68, social scis. bibliographer, 1968—, lectr. Grad. Sch. Library and Information Scis., 1962—. Mem. Commn. on Documentation in Anthropol. Scis. Mem. Am., Pa. library assns., Tri-State Assn. Coll. and Research Libraries, Am. Assn. Library Schs., Am. Assn. U. Profs., Ch. and Synagogue Library Assn., Pitts. Bibliophiles, Phi Delta Gamma, Beta Phi Mu. Republican. Episcopalian. Home: 4628 Bayard St Pittsburgh PA 15213

JOHNSON, HELEN MARIE (MRS. BERNARD G. JOHNSON), ednl. adminstr.; b. Bklyn., Sept. 19, 1915; d. Louis Jonas and Marie Helen (Aneser) Fischer; B.A., Hunter Coll., 1937; M.Ed., U. Md., 1948; m. Bernard G. Johnson, Sept. 5, 1936; children—Helen (Mrs. David E. Dodson), Gail (Mrs. Leonard S. Ricketts). Tchr. bus. math., tng. dept. Sperry Gyroscope Co., Lake Success, N.Y., 1942-45; tchr. Montgomery County Pub. Schs., Silver Spring, Md., 1948-51, prin. Four Corners Elementary Sch., 1951-57, sup. elementary edn., 1957-58, dir. staff devel., 1958-64, area dir., 1964-71, area asst. supt., 1971—. Vis. prof. U. Md., Western Md. Coll., Md. State Coll.; cons. Row Publishers, 1955-57, Md. State Com. Schs., 1959-61, Nat. Def. Edn. Act. workshop Omaha Pub. Schs., summers, 1965-66, Mid Continent Regional Ednl. Lab., Kansas City, Mo., 1966-68, U. Guam, summer, 1968. Mem. Assn. Supervision and Curriculum Devel., N.E.A., Am. Assn. Sch. Adminstrn., Am. Childhood Edn. Internat., Assn. Montgomery County Adminstrs., Nat. Council Adminstrv. Women Edn., Pub. Sch. Supts. Assn. Md., Delta Kappa Gamma, Delta Zeta. Contbr. articles to profl. jours. Home: 4401 Sunflower Dr Rockville MD 20853 Office: 14811 Notley Rd Silver Spring MD 20904

JOHNSON, HELEN WHEELER (MRS. WILLIAM BERT JOHNSON), sociologist; b. Oshkosh, Wis., Apr. 17, 1910; d. William Philander and Nina Helen (Wallen) Wheeler; student Milw.-Downer Coll., 1927-29; Ed.B., Wis. State U., 1932; M.A., Am. U., 1960; m. William Bert Johnson, May 10, 1940; children—Margaret Wheeler (Mrs. Joseph Edward Herman), Stephen Wheeler. With U.S. Dept. Agr., Washington, 1935-42, 65—, research sociologist, 1965-69, asst. to dir. research div., 1969—; with Nat. Planning Assn., Washington, 1952-56; with Ford Found., Arlington, Va., 1958-61, New Delhi, India, 1961-65, writer, editor Ford Found. Post Report, India, 1965. Recipient certificate of merit U.S. Dept. Agr., 1968, superior service award, 1971. Mem. Rural Sociol. Soc., Nat. Planning Assn. Author: India's Roots of Democracy, 1965; also U.S. Dept. Agr. research reports. Editor Am. Women's Club mag., News Circle, New Delhi, India, 1965. Home: 1310 N Abingdon St Arlington VA 22207 Office: 500 12th St SW Washington DC 20250

JOHNSON, INDIA ROSE RHODES (MRS. REEDIE EARL JOHNSON), coll. adminstr.; b. Kinston, N.C., Oct. 13, 1935; d. Thad and Myrtle Lavane (Bryant) Rhodes; B.S., Shaw U., 1967; postgrad. U. So. Miss., 1971—; m. Reedie Earl Johnson, Oct. 14, 1969. Dormitory counselor Shaw U., Raleigh, N.C., 1965-67, dir. women's residence, 1967-70, instl. research asst., 1970-71; bus. mgr. Natchez (Miss.) Jr. Coll., 1972—. Co-dir. Project Sunflower County, 1969. Named Mother of Year, Shaw U., 1969; Tchr. of Year, Natchez Jr. Coll., 1973. Mem. Women's Personnel Council (pres. 1966-67), Pyramid, Delta Sigma Theta. Baptist. Home: 644 1/2 E Stiers Lane Natchez MS 39120

JOHNSON, IRENE VIVIAN (MRS. FRANK JOHNSON, JR.), extension home economist; b. Crockett, Tex., Dec. 24, 1912; d. Peter and Roxie (Jones) Hopkins; student Mary Allen Sem., 1930-34; B.S., Prairie View A. and M. Coll., 1941, M.S., 1970; postgrad. Tex. Tech. U., 1964; m. Frank Johnson, Jr., May 7, 1953. Tchr. elementary sch., Crockett, Tex., 1930-40, high sch., 1940-44; home demonstration agt. Tex. Agrl. Extension Service, Lufkin, Tex., 1944-73, dist. dir., county extension agt., 1973—. Mem. Lone Star Home Demonstration Assn. (pres. 1964-66, recipient Distinguished Service award 1965), Internat. Fedn. Home Econs., Nat. County Home Demonstration Agts' Assn. (recipient citation 1965), Am. Home Econs. Assn., Nat. Assn. Extension Home Economists, County Home Demonstration Agts. Tex., Angelina County C. of C., So. Agrl. Assn., Epsilon Sigma Phi, Am. Woodman. Home: 311 Booker St Lufkin TX 75901 Office: County Courthouse Lufkin TX 75901

JOHNSON, IRMA LYDIA, extension home economist; b. Eveleth, Minn., May 3, 1914; d. Karl Vitalis and Ida Maria (Salakka) Saven; B.S., Pratt Inst., 1950; M.S., Mich. State U., 1961; m. Gordon Roy Johnson, June 1, 1957. Supr. children Clarke Sch. for Deaf, Northampton, Mass., 1944-46; extension home economist Mich. State U., East Lansing, 1950—. Mem. Mich. Council Family Relations. Human Devel. Workshop scholar, Cornell, 1955. Recipient Distinguished Service award Nat. Home Demonstration Agts. Assn., 1963, Presdl. citation 4-H Agts. Assn., 1966. Mem. Nat., Mich. (Distinguished Service award 1972) extension home economists assns., Am., Mich. home economists assns., Am. Assn. U. Women, Epsilon Sigma Phi. Lutheran. Home: Star Route 1 Box 179 Iron Mountain MI 49801 Office: Armory Bldg Kingsford MI 49801

JOHNSON, JACQUELINE YVONNE, coll. adminstr.; b. Plainfield, N.J., May 10, 1949; d. George Russell and Ruby Helena (Burke) Johnson; B.A., Keuka Coll., 1971; M.Ed., Springfield Coll., 1972. Grad. admissions asst. Springfield (Mass.) Coll., 1971-72, asst. dir. admissions, 1973—; admissions counselor Russell Sage Coll., Troy, N.Y., 1972-73. Co-founder Afro-Am. Soc., Keuka Coll., 1968; co-leader Y-Teens, Corliss Park, N.Y., 1972. Mem. Nat. (chmn. task force on concerns of minorities 1974-75), Mass. assns. for women deans, adminstrs. and counselors, Nat. Assn. Coll. Admissions Counselors, N.Y., Capital Dist. personnel and guidance assns., Mass. Assn. Coll. Minority Adminstrs. Home: Norfield Commons #20 Agawam MA 01001 Office: Box 1758 Springfield Coll Springfield MA 01109

JOHNSON, JAN VOSS (MRS. CONRAD LOREN JOHNSON), ednl. adminstr.; b. Exira, Ia., Nov. 18, 1922; d. George Carl and Evelyn Hope (Rendleman) Voss; grad. high sch., 1941; m. Conrad Loren Johnson, Jan. 8, 1955; children—Dawn (Mrs. Norman Bissell), Lisa (Mrs. L. Lewis), Scott; stepchildren—Joyce (Mrs. Edward Arbuckle), Harry, Paul Douglas, David. Traffic mgr., continuity dir. radio sta. KJAN, Atlantic, Ia., 1952-53; dir. women's activities KVTV, Sioux City, Ia., 1953-57; asso. producer WMT radio and WMT-TV, Cedar Rapids, Ia., 1957-64; dir. nat. consumer affairs Schaper Mfg. Co., Mpls., 1964-65; dir., producer WMT-TV, Cedar Rapids, 1965-70; dir. publs., community relations Joint County Sch. System, Cedar Rapids, 1970—. Writer, Better Homes & Gardens, Meredith Pub. Co., Des Moines, 1965-69. Mem. exec. bd. Am. Cancer Soc. Ia. div., Ia. chmn. pub. edn. and information com., 1966—; active Muscular Dystrophy Assn., 1967-69, Easter Seal Soc., 1966-69, La. Field Alcoholism, 1967-69. Mem. Am. Women in Radio and TV (nat. v.p. 1967-69), Nat. Sch. Pub. Relations Assn., Women in Communications, Beethoven Club. Democrat. Lutheran. Mem. Order of Eastern Star. Author: Poems My Mother Taught Me, 1970; Quo Fata Vocant, 1972. Contbr. to Fairland Papers, 1968. Home: 1300 O Av NW Cedar Rapids IA 52405 Office: 4401 6th St SW Cedar Rapids IA 52406

JOHNSON, JANE GAULT (MRS. JAMES D. JOHNSON), librarian; b. Union, S.C., Sept. 28, 1935; d. James William and Louise (Patterson) Gault; student Mary Washington Coll., 1953-54; A.B., Converse Coll., 1957; student U. S.C., 1954-56, 1962-63, 1965-67, 1968; student Wofford Coll. summers 1954, 55, Queens Coll. (Nat. Def. Edn. Act fellow 1965), 1965; M.S. in L.S., La. State U., 1968; m. James Delane Johnson, Sept. 29, 1954; children—James Delane II, William David. Instr. Spanish, Spartanburg (S.C.) High Sch., 1960-61; asst. librarian Greenville (S.C.) Sr. High Sch., 1961-62; librarian Spartanburg Day Sch., 1962-63; librarian Fremont Elementary Sch., Spartanburg, 1963-68; head librarian Spartanburg Regional Campus U. S.C., 1968—. Mem. S.C., Am., Southeastern library assns., Am. Assn. U. Women (br. rec. sec. 1964-66, br. treas. 1970-72), Spartanburg County Hist. Soc. University Women's Club (treas. 1971-72), Mortar Board, Delta Kappa Gamma. Episcopalian. Home: 150 Woodhaven Dr Spartanburg SC 29302 Office: Spartanburg Regional Campus U SC Spartanburg SC 29303

JOHNSON, JANE MILLER (MRS. NAPOLEON B. JOHNSON), social worker; b. Welch, W. Va.; d. Leon P. and Mildred (Foster) Miller; A.B., Fisk U.; M.S.W., Atlanta U.; m. Napoleon B. Johnson, Aug. 29, 1953; children—Napoleon B. III, Patrelle E. Asst. to dir. social service Tuskegee (Ala.) Inst., 1953-54; caseworker Traveler's Aid Soc., Atlanta, 1955, Bur. Child Welfare, Atlanta, 1955-59; caseworker, instr. sch. nursing U. Okla. Med. Center, 1959-61; supr. Milw. County Welfare Dept., 1961-63; supr. social service dept. Milw. County Hosp., 1961-64; supr. social service Columbia-Presbyn. Med. Center, N.Y.C., 1964-69; coordinator direct services Planned Parenthood N.Y., 1969-72, asso. exec. dir., 1972—. Lectr. human relations Herman Lehman Coll., Coll. City N.Y. Home: 225 Voorhees St Teaneck NJ 07666 Office: 300 Park Av S New York City NY 10010

JOHNSON, JANET (MRS. KENNETH ROGER JOHNSON), occupational therapist; b. Cleve., Nov. 6, 1939; d. Charles Adam and Frances Helen (Dunham) Haas; student Miami U., Oxford, O., 1957-59; B.S. cum laude, Ohio State U., 1961, M.S., 1969; m. Kenneth Roger Johnson, Apr. 8, 1961; children—Steven Alan, Laura. Chmn. occupational therapy dept. Riverside Meth. Hosp., Columbus, 1963-64; staff therapist Columbus Childrens Hosp., 1965-67; asst. prof. occupational therapy Ohio State U., Columbus, 1969-72; occupational therapist Columbus (O.) Pub. Schs., 1972—. Adj. tchr. Worthington Alternative High Sch. Program, cons. pvt. clinic for learning disabled children. Recipient grant Dept. Health, Edn. and Welfare, 1961. Mem. Am., Ohio (state legislation chmn. 1970-72) occupational therapy assns., Delta Gamma. Office: 2571 Neil Av Columbus OH 43202

JOHNSON, JANICE MARY, govt. ofcl., educator; b. Omaha, Aug. 1, 1925; d. Walter Richard and Mary (Burt) Johnson; B.S. in Edn., U. Neb., 1947; postgrad. George Washington U., 1950-52, 59, U. Colo., 1951, Am. U., 1963-64; M.A. in Internat., Comparative and Edn./Asian Studies, Columbia, 1966. Tchr., Topeka pub. schs., 1947-49, Washington pub. schs., 1949-51, Arlington (Va.) Forest Pre-Sch., 1951-52; edn. specialist schs. br. FCDA, 1953; instr. Nat. Civil Def. Staff Coll., 1953-55, asst. dir. women's activities, 1955-56; civil def. edn. specialist Office Edn., Dept. Health, Edn. and Welfare, Washington, 1956-57, program specialist Far East and Southeast Asia area Bur. Internat. Edn. (now Inst. for Internat. studies), 1957-72; specialist edn. and social devel. U.S. Terrs., Dept. Interior, Washington, 1972—; cons., lectr. Asian Cultures seminar U. Minn. summer, 1963. Exec. sec. Internat. Conf. on World Crisis in Edn., 1967. Nat. committeewoman D.C. Young Republicans, 1953. Bd. govs. Neb. State Soc. Recipient Service award U. Neb., 1963. Mem. Comparative Edn. Soc., Assn. Asian Studies, Nat. Assn. Fgn. Student Affairs, U. Neb. Alumni Assn. (pres. Washington 1961-62), D.C. Council Adminstrv. Women in Edn., Am. Assn. U. Women, Alpha Phi, Pi Lambda Theta, Kappa Delta Pi (commn. internat. edn., co-dir. Western European Study Seminar 1971). Lutheran (vice chmn. edn. bd.; deaconess, chmn. evangelism com.; chmn. interchurch apt. ministry program). Club: Internat. (Washington). Home: 1405 44th St NW Washington DC 20007

JOHNSON, JANICE PLATT, artist; b. N.Y.C., Mar. 9, 1918; d. Simon M. and Alma Louise (Broaker) Platt; student Pratt Inst., 1938; B.A., Eckerd Coll., 1971; m. E. Ashby Johnson, July 27, 1963; 1 dau., Marjorie J. Clarke. With Norcross Co., N.Y.C., 1938-42; artist Shawl, Nyeland and Seavey, San Francisco, 1942-45; art dir. Fla. Sun, Miami Beach, Fla., 1945-50; owner, operator Jan Platt Advt. Agy., Coral Gables, Fla., 1950-63; advt. dir., artist Shoe Villa, Pinellas Park, Fla., 1971-73; tchr. perceptual impressionism Art Club St. Petersburg, also Suntan Art Club, 1965-72, Arts Center, 1973-74; one and two man exhbns., 1964—. Adv. bd. Developmental Center, St. Petersburg, 1971—. Mem. Arts Center Assn. Club: St. Petersburg Art (past pres., dir.), Weavers Guild Pinellas County, League Women Voters. Home: 134 23d Av S St Petersburg FL 33705

JOHNSON, JEANNE LOUISE, data processing co. exec.; b. Kenosha, Wis., Nov. 14, 1928; d. Byron Simpson and Amanda (Zeitler) Knight; B.S. cum laude U. Dubuque, 1949; m. Roger H. Johnson, Jan. 29, 1954. Head editing dept. Film Prodn. unit Ia. State U., 1954-56; head Continuity dept. WICS-NBC TV, Springfield, Ill., 1958-59; home service adv. Central Ill. Light Co., Springfield, 1959-61; instr. home economics Centralia (Ill.) City Schs., 1962-66; v.p. Tallman Robbins & Co., Springfield, 1967—; v.p. Delta Business Forms, Cairo, Ill., 1971—. Mem. Data Processing Mgmt. Assn., Zeta Phi. Home: 20 Villa Grove Springfield IL 62707 Office: 2171 S 9th St Springfield IL 62703

JOHNSON, JENNIFER CALENE, physician; b. Holdenville, Okla., Sept. 30, 1939; d. Willie D. and Bertha (Trevathan) Johnson; B.S. cum laude, Lambuth Coll., 1961; M.D., U. Tenn., 1964. Intern, City Memphis Hosps., 1965, asst. resident, 1966-67; staff physician West Tenn. Tb Hosp., Memphis, 1966; fellow infectious diseases and immunology U. Tenn. Coll. Medicine, Memphis, 1967-68; instr. medicine Med. Coll. of Ga. at Augusta, 1968-70, chief resident in medicine, 1968-69, asst. prof., 1970-73, dir. tng. program dept. medicine, 1972-73; research and edn. asso. in cardiology VA Hosp., Augusta, 1969-71, asst. chief medicine, 1971-73, asso. chief staff edn., 1972-73; chief medicine VA Hosp., Louisville, 1974—; asso. chmn., vice-chmn. dept. U. Louisville Sch. Medicine, 1974—. Named Outstanding Young Woman of Am., 1965. Mem. A.M.A. Contbr. articles to profl. jours. Home: 3805 Benje Way Louisville KY 40222 Office: VA Hosp Louisville KY 40202

JOHNSON, JERRY A., occupational therapist, coll. dean; b. Lubbock, Tex., Sept. 21, 1931; d. Weldon F. Johnson and Geraldine (Buckner) Mallory; B.S., Tex. Womans U., 1953; postgrad. Washington U. (St. Louis), Radcliffe Coll., 1959-60; M.B.A., Harvard, 1961; Ed.D., Boston U., 1970. Staff occupational therapist USN, Oakland, Cal., 1954-56; dir. occupational therapy Easter Seal Soc., Alton, Ill., 1956, exec. dir., 1957-59; asst. hosp. adminstr. USN,

Newport, R.I., 1961-62; legal counsel for party Phys. Evaluation Bd., USN, Chelsea, Mass., 1962-70; asso. prof., chmn. div. occupational therapy Sargent Coll. Allied Health Professions, Boston, 1963-69, acting exec. dir. Rehab. Council, Boston U., 1969-70; prof., chmn. Center for Allied Instrnl. Personnel, U. Fla., 1971-72; prof., chmn. div. grad. studies Sargent Coll. Allied Health Professions, Boston, 1972-73, asso. dean acad. affairs, 1973-74; dir. grad. studies and research dept. occupational therapy Colo. State U., Ft. Collins, 1974—. Project dir., ednl. cons. Am. Occupational Therapy Assn., Detroit, Chgo., 1966-67, 69-70, mem. exec. bd., 1967-72, pres. elect, 1972-73, pres., 1973—; ednl. cons. U. Ala., 1968, Eastern Mich. U., 1972-73, mem. U. Puget Sound, 1974; panel cons. to adv. com. on edn. Allied Health Professions, Council on Med. Edn. A.M.A., 1969-73; cons. Hebrew U., Jerusalem, 1971-74; vis. scholar Western Mich. U., 1974. Mem. med. adv. com. Bay State Soc. for Crippled, 1969-73. Mem. Govs. Task Force on Tng. and Manpower in Mental Health, Boston, 1964-66. Mem. Mass. Assn. Occupational Therapy, (pres. 1964-66), Nat. Rehab. Assn., Internat. Soc. Rehab. Disabled, World Fedn. Occupational Therapists, Assn. Sch. Allied Health Professions, Harvard Bus. Sch. Assn., Am. Occupational Therapy Assn. (chmn. task force on social issues), Common Cause, Nat. Wildlife Fedn., Mass. Audubon Soc., Smithsonian Assos. Democrat. Episcopalian. Club: Radcliffe College. Contbr. articles to profl. jours. Home: 33 Wachusetts Dr Lexington MA 02173

JOHNSON, JO ANNE ETHEL MCGARY THOMPSON, editor; b. Weslaco, Tex., Mar. 16, 1932; d. Gilbert James and Donna Eloise (Buckels) McGary; B.A., George Washington U., 1964; M.A., Colo. U., 1966; m. Robert Crawford Thompson, Sept. 13, 1952 (div. Oct. 1962); m. 2d, Robert Murray Johnson, Apr. 13, 1974. Asso. editor Nat. Assn. Bus. and Ednl. Radio, Washington, 1966-69; editor Nat. Def. Transp. Assn. Jour., Washington, 1969-73; editor Security Mgmt., publs. dir. Am. Soc. for Indsl. Security, Washington, 1973—. Mem. Nat. Press Club. Unitarian (pres. women's alliance 1971-72). Home: 6252 Columbia Pike Falls Church VA 22041 Office: 2000 K St NW Washington DC 20006

JOHNSON, JOAN D., educator; b. Wyandotte, Mich., Oct. 10, 1929; d. Joel C. and Emily (Timm) Johnson; student Western Mich. Coll., 1947-49; B.S., U. Wis., 1951; M.S., U. So. Cal., 1955, Ph.D., 1965; student U. Mich., 1958. Instr., Bloom Twp. High Sch., Chicago Heights, Ill., 1951-53; asst. prof. Cal. State U., Los Angeles, 1955-65, asso. prof., 1965-70, prof. phys. edn., 1970—, asso. chmn. dept. phys. edn. and athletics, 1969—; vis. prof. U. So. Cal., 1960. Recipient Women's Tennis Leadership award U.S. Lawn Tennis Assn., 1970. Mem. Cal. Assn. Health, Phys. Edn., Recreation, A.A.H.P.E.R., Western Soc. Phys. Edn. Coll. Women (sec. 1967-68, treas. 1972—), Nat. Assn. Phys. Edn. Coll. Women, Phi Kappa Phi. Author: (with Paul Xanthos) Tennis, 2d edit., 1972; (with David L. Kelley), A Work book for Tests and Measurements in Physical Education, 1967. Office: 5151 State University Dr Los Angeles CA 90032 Mailing address: 3341 Balzac St Alhambra CA 91803

JOHNSON, JUANITA IRENE (MRS. PAUL R. JOHNSON), home economist; b. Edna, Kan., Mar. 14, 1923; d. Howard and Ethel (Houck) Billington; B.S., Kan. State U., 1945; m. Paul R. Johnson, Dec. 21, 1952. Extension home economist, Girard, Kan., 1948—. Sec. Crawford County Mental Health Assn., 1959. Mem. Kan. Home Econs. Assn. (pres. 1972—), Bus. and Profl. Women. Presbyn. Home: 708 N Summit St Girard KS 66743 Office: Courthouse Girard KS 66743

JOHNSON, JUANITA (MRS. RAY JOHNSON), librarian; b. Bethel, Okla., May 11, 1922; d. John Emmett and Ethel (Daniels) Green; B.S., Southeastern State Coll., 1940, M. Teaching, 1964; M.L.S., U. Okla., 1970; m. Ray Johnson, May 23, 1944; children—John Charles, Deborah Ann (Mrs. Dwayne Williams), La Donna Raye. Tchr. pub. schs., Nanichito, Okla., 1942, Smithville, Okla., 1943-44, Oklahoma City, 1945-46, Idabel (Okla.) High Sch., 1947-51, Panola (Okla.) pub. schs., 1958-65; librarian Eastern Okla. State Coll., Wilburton, 1966—. Mem. Okla. Library Assn., Higher Edn. Alumni Council Okla., Am. Assn. U. Women (1st v.p. 1972-74), Choctaw Nation Hist. Soc. Baptist (tchr.). Home: Box 422 Wilburton OK 74578

JOHNSON, JUDY LENORE, librarian; b. Marshalltown, Ia., Oct. 16, 1944; d. James Benjamin and Neta (Richards) Johnson; B.A., Ft. Hays State Coll., 1962-66; M.L.S., Kan. State Tchrs. Coll., 1968; postgrad. Austin Peay State U., 1973—. Librarian, Hays (Kan.) Sr. High Sch., 1967-70, U.S. Dept. Defense, Zama (Japan) Am. High Sch., 1970-71; cataloging librarian asst. Austin Peay State U., Felix G. Woodward Library, Clarksville, Tenn., 1971-74, U. Neb., Lincoln, 1974—. Kan. Library Assn. scholar, 1966. Mem. Am. Assn. U. Women (br. treas. 1972-74), N.E.A., Am., Southeastern, Tenn. library assns., Delta Kappa Gamma. Home: PO Box 82 Hays KS 67601 Office: Love Library U Neb Lincoln NE

JOHNSON, JULIA LAVONNE LAWRENCE (MRS. GEORGE WILHELM JOHNSON), coll. adminstr.; b. Harvey, Ia., Aug. 28, 1919; d. Kenneth Alfonso and Erma Christina (Norquist) Lawrence; grad. Knapps Bus. Coll., 1938; m. George Wilhelm Johnson, Feb. 8, 1969; 1 dau., Denise Christine. Personnel office mgr. Clover Park Sch. Dist. 400, Tacoma, Wash., 1960-66; dir. personnel and mgmt. services Community Coll. Dist. 11, Tacoma, 1966—. Mem. Pacific N.W. Personnel Mgmt. Assn., Am. Soc. for Personnel Adminstrn. Mem. Order Eastern Star (grand Ruth 1970-71), Order of Amaranth. Home: 7211 Onyx Dr SW Tacoma WA 98498 Office: Ft Steilacoom Community College PO Box 99186 Tacoma WA 98499

JOHNSON, JUNE BEVERLY LOMBARD, librarian; b. Galesburg, Ill., Oct. 10, 1930; d. Elmer Clifford and Violet Bernice (Sampson) Lombard; A.A., So. Colo. State Coll., 1950; B.A., U. No. Colo., 1952; M.A. (Maleam Wyer Fund scholar), U. Denver, 1960; children—Deanna K., Marlena B. Asso. librarian Iliff Sch. Theology, Denver, 1955-57; head librarian, mgr. bookstore, prof. English, Lamar (Colo.) Community Coll., 1960-62; high sch. librarian Pueblo (Colo.) Pub. Sch. System, 1962-69, elementary sch. media specialist, 1969—. Mem. Nat., Colo., Pueblo edn. assns., Colo. Assn. Sch. Librarians, Parents without Partners. Republican. Methodist. Home: 1506 Horseshoe Dr Pueblo CO 81001 Office: 916 N Fountain St Pueblo CO 81001

JOHNSON, KATHARYN PRICE (MRS. EDWARD F. JOHNSON), civic worker; b. Smyrna, Del., Mar. 24, 1897; d. Lewis M. and Jennie Cairl (Smithers) Price; grad. Centenary Coll., 1915; student Goucher Coll., 1915-18; m. Edward F. Johnson, Nov. 16, 1920; children—Edward A., Jane Cairl (Mrs. Warner W. Kent, Jr.). With Liberty Loan Com. for Md. and Liberty Loan Assn. of Balt., 1918-20; pres. Women's Guild Hitchcock Meml. Ch., 1930-32; dir. Scarsdale Woman's Club, 1933-36; dir. White Plains Thrift Shop, 1930-43, pres. 1936-43; mem. exec. com. Scarsdale Community Fund, 1934-38; active Scarsdale council Girl Scouts, 1937-53, commr., 1939-41, now hon. mem. Scarsdale-Hartsdale council, 1953-69; mem. region 2 com. Girl Scouts U.S.A., 1942-56, mem. nat. bd., exec. com., 1947-55, chmn. orgn. and mgmt. dept., 1952-55, mem. nat. field com., 1943-55, mem. equipment service com. 1956-69, mem. internat. com., 1956-60; mem. Bd. Edn., Scarsdale, N.Y., 1943-46; disaster chmn. Scarsdale chpt. A.R.C., 1942-45. Rep. World Assn. Girl Guides and Girl Scouts to UN, 1957-71, mem. NGO com. on UNICEF, 1965-72, sec., 1968-70; participant World Confs., World Assn. Girl Guides and Girl Scouts, Greece, 1960, Denmark, 1963, Japan, 1966, Finland, 1969, Can., 1972. Mem. Nat. Council Women U.S., Pi Beta Phi. Republican. Presbyn. Clubs: Scarsdale Woman's (life); Nat. Women's Republican. Home: 165 Brewster Rd Scarsdale NY 10583

JOHNSON, KATHERINE M. KING (MRS. NORMAN F. JOHNSON), artist, real estate exec.; b. Lincoln, Neb., 1906; d. John Ray and Clara (Plamondon) King; student U. Neb. Coll. Fine Arts, 1923-24, U. Vt. Extension, 1941-42, Coll. of Desert, 1965-66; m. Norman F. Johnson, Sept. 4, 1925; children—Raymond E., Lyman W., Carlene King (Mrs. Don C. Holloway) (dec.). Land devel. designer, contractor Eastridge Acres, Piedmont Devels., Rutland, Vt., 1957—; one man show Chester (Vt.) Art Guild, 1970; participant in three man art show, Shadow Mountain Club, Palm Desert, Cal., 1964; exhibited with So. Vt. Artists in major U.S. cities, 1950, N.Y. World's Fair with Mid Vt. Artists, 1964; exhibited one man show Chaffee Art Gallery, Rutland, 1967, 74, Weston (Vt.) Playhouse, 1969; represented in permanent collections; displayed painting 1967 Nat. Christmas Tree from Vt. in Washington, 1967, painting now in Lyndon B. Johnson collections, L.B.J. Ranch Center, Johnson City, Tex. Co-chmn. Vt. Com. for Nat. Art Week, 1940; dir. bicentennial exhibit Rutland (Vt.) Mus. Arts, 1961; founder Chaffee Art Gallery, Rutland, pres. bd. dirs., 1962—; mem. Vt. Council on Arts 1963—, art com. Manchester (Vt.) Art Center, 1961-66, Rutland Hosp. Aux., 1958-72. Bd. dirs. Desert Art Center, Palm Springs, Cal., 1963. Mem. Mid Vt. Artists (pres. 1941-49), Rutland Area Art Assn., Inc. (pres. 1962—), Nat. League Am. Pen Women (pres. So. Vt. br., state art chmn. 1964-65, state pres. 1972-73), Shadow Mountain Palette Club, Sigma Kappa. Conglist. Home: summer—40 Piedmont Pkwy Rutland VT also winter—36505 Florida Av Hemet West 255 Hemet CA 92343 Office: Chaffee Art Center 16 S Main St Rutland VT 05701 Mailing Address: 40 Piedmont Pkwy Rutland VT 05701

JOHNSON, KORDILLIA CHRISTEEN, librarian; b. Valley Springs, S.D.; d. Adolph C. M. and Otillia (Sognesand) Johnson; B.A., Augustana Coll., 1934; B.L.S., U. Wis. at Madison, 1947, postgrad., spring 1968; M.L.S., U. Ill. at Urbana, 1960. Tchr., Willow Lakes, S.D., 1934-35; teacher Sand Creek High Sch., Wessington, S.D., 1935-37, Glenham (S.D.) High Sch., 1937-39, Ashton (S.D.) High Sch., 1939-42; tchr. Morse Code, tactical procedure USAAF Tech. Coll., Sioux Falls, S.D., 1942-45; asso. prof., librarian Augustana Coll., 1947-68; asst. prof., divisional librarian U. Wis. at Platteville, 1968—. Mem. S.D. (pres. 1963-64, sec.-treas. 1950-51, v.p. 1953-54), Mountain Plains, Am., Wis. library assns., S.D. Ornithol. Union, Am. Assn. U. Women, Sons of Norway, Norwegian Am. Hist. Assn., Eagle Valley Environmentalists, Oral History Assn. Republican. Lutheran. Club: Soroptimist Club of Sioux Falls (past pres.). Home: 885 Stonebridge Platteville WI 53818 Office: Karrmann Library U Wis Platteville WI 53818

JOHNSON, LADY BIRD (CLAUDIA ALTA) (MRS. LYNDON BAINES JOHNSON), wife former pres. U.S.; b. Karnack, Tex., Dec. 22, 1912; d. Thomas Jefferson Taylor; B.A., U. Tex., 1933, B.Journalism, 1934, D.Letters, 1964; LL.D., Tex. Woman's U., 1964; D.Letters, Middlebury Coll., 1967; L.H.D., Williams Coll., 1967; H.H.D., Southwestern U., 1967; m. Lyndon Baines Johnson (36th Pres. U.S.), Nov. 17, 1934 (died Jan. 22, 1973); children—Lynda Bird (Mrs. Charles Robb), Luci Baines (Mrs. Patrick Nugent). Mgr. husband's congl. office, Washington, 1941-42; owner, operator radio-TV sta. KTBC, Austin, Tex., 1942-63, cattle ranches, Tex., 1943—. Hon. chmn. Nat. Headstart Program, 1963-68, Town Lake Beautification Project. also cotton and timberlands, Ala. Mem. Adv. council Nat. Parks, Historic Sites, Bldgs. and Monuments; bd. regents U. Tex., 1971—, mem. internat. conf. steering com., 1969; trustee Jackson Hole Preserve, Am. Conservation Assn., Nat. Geog. Soc. Recipient Togetherness award Marge Champion, 1958; Humanitarian award B'nai B'rith, 1961; Businesswoman's award Bus. and Profl. Women's Club, 1961; Theta Sigma Phi citation, 1962; Distinguished Achievement award Washington Heart Assn., 1962; Industry citation Am. Women in Radio and Television, 1963; Humanitarian citation Vols. of Am., 1963; Peabody award for White House TV visit, 1966; Eleanor Roosevelt Golden Candlestick award Women's Nat. Press Club. Life mem. U. Tex. Ex-Students Assn. Episcopalian. Author: A White House Diary, 1970. Address: LBJ Ranch Stonewall TX 78671

JOHNSON, LAURA ALICE, coll. pres.; b. Clarendon, Vt., Nov. 21, 1910; d. Bertram A. and Alice (Greene) Johnson; B.S., U. Vt., 1933, M.A., 1935; M.A., Radcliffe Coll., 1937; L.H.D., U. Hartford, 1965. Student supr. apprentice tchrs. in English, Harvard, 1939-40; resident head Simmons Coll., 1939-40; tchr. English, Concord (Mass.) Acad., 1940-42; tchr. English, Bancroft Sch., Worcester (Mass.), 1942-43; dean Hartford (Conn.) Coll., 1943-57, pres., 1957—. Dir. Phoenix Mut. Life Ins. Co. Past sec. New Eng. Jr. Coll. Council. Corporator Hartford Conservatory Music, Hartford Hosp. Trustee Hartford Pub. Library, Loomis and Chaffee Schs.; asso. trustee St. Joseph Coll. Mem. Bd. of State Colls.; mem. scholarship bd. Heublin, Inc. Recipient Woman of Year award B'nai Brith, 1970, Distinguished Alumni award U. Vt., 1972. Mem. Conn. Conf. Ind. Colls. (sec.), Radcliffe, U. Vt. alumnae assns., League Women Voters, Conn. Hort. Soc., Wadsworth Atheneum, Farm Bur. Vt., Greater Hartford C. of C. (dir., Charter Oak Leadership medal 1973). Clubs: Hartford, College (Hartford). Address: 1265 Asylum Av Hartford CT 06105

JOHNSON, LAURA MYERS, educator, civic worker; b. Omaha, Dec. 7, 1899; d. Hugh A. and Maybelle (Ittner) Myers; student Hillsdale Coll.; A.B., U. Mich., 1917; M.A., Creighton U., 1933, U. Neb., 1940; m. Leslie F. Johnson, Apr. 25, 1918 (dec. Apr. 1963); children—Leslie H., Grove C., Richard Lee. Staff dept. English, U. Omaha, 1923-53, ret.; cons., acting prin. Pratt School Individual Instrn., 1961-62, then prin., now prin. high sch. div., lectr. in field. Appeared on Today TV Show, 1967. Mem. state com. accreditation of high schs., 1949; mem. Gov.'s Conf. Youth. Chmn. staffing vol. Red Cross blood bank Canteen Service, Omaha, 1949-50, chmn. Phoenix Found. Fund in Omaha. Mem. Douglas County Central Republican Com., 1958; del. Douglas County Republican Conv. Mem. Nat. Radio Council, Am. Assn. U. Women (v.p. Omaha br. 1948-49). D.A.R. (del. nat. congress 1954, 60, nominated to charter conv. Omaha, 1956), League Women Voters, Pi Beta Phi, Sigma Tau Delta. Episcopalian. Clubs: Nebraska Writer's Guild and Press (Omaha); Republican Women's of Douglas County (pres. 1956). Author: Modern Treatment of Medieval Themes and Subject Matter, 1940. Contbr. articles to profl. jours. Home: 8405 Indian Hills Rd Omaha NE 68114

JOHNSON, LILA RUTH JONES (MRS. LEONARD E. JOHNSON, JR.), trade assn. exec.; b. Mattoon, Ill., Nov. 5, 1926; d. Robert Gerald and Ruth Erma (Pinkard) Jones; B.S., U. Ill., 1948; postgrad. Detroit Soc. Arts and Crafts, 1961-62, Wayne State U., 1968-70; m. Leonard E. Johnson, Jr., July 17, 1948; children—Douglas, Steven, Paul, Susan. Accounting personnel asst. Mich. Bell Telephone Co., 1949-50; self-employed in pub. relations, 1959-64; editor, publicity dir. Women's City Club Detroit, 1964-69; communications and legislative coordinator Nat. Hearing Aid Soc., Detroit, 1969—. Pub. relations dir. Bekley Council Better Schs., 1958—; chmn. Huntington Woods Community League, 1960-61. Trustee Oakland Community Coll., 1964—. Mem. Pub. Relations Soc. Am., Zeta Tau Alpha, Shi Ai, Shorter Board. Editor: Mag. Women's City Club Detroit, 1964-69; asst. editor Audecibel, 1970—. Home: 12726 LaSalle St Huntington Woods MI 48070 Office: 24261 Grand River St Detroit MI 48219

JOHNSON, LINDA ELIZABETH (MRS. JOHN ERIC JOHNSON), librarian; b. Kansas City, Mo., Feb. 9, 1940; d. Chester E. and Kathryn F. (Huntington) Lee; B.A., Kansas State U., 1961, M.A., 1963; M.A., U. Minn., 1967; m. John Eric Johnson, June 17, 1967. Grad. asst. Kan. State U., Manhattan, 1961-63; adult edn. instr. Mainz, Germany, 1963-64; tchr. English Shawnee Mission, Kan., 1964-66; adult edn. instr., Mpls., 1966-67; serials librarian No. Ill. U., DeKalb, 1967—. Mem. Gamma Phi Beta. Episcopalian. Home: 303 Bush DeKalb IL 60115 Office: Universities Library Northern Illinois University DeKalb IL 60115

JOHNSON, LOIS BOSWELL, physician; b. Chgo., Dec. 13, 1930; d. Louis R. and Inez (White) Shirky; B.A., Manchester Coll., 1952; B.S. U. Ill. Coll. Medicine, 1955, M.D., 1956, M.S. in Physiology, 1958; m. William R. Johnson, Jr., Aug. 2, 1966; children—David, Diane, Dan, Dawn, Billy. Intern, U. Ill. Hosps., Chgo., 1956-57; resident Mercy Hosp-Loyola U., Chgo., 1958-60; practice medicine specializing in pediatrics, Dayton, O., 1960-66; asso. dir. adolescent clinic Cin. Gen. Hosp., 1967—, mem. staff Children's Hosp., Cin. Fellow Am. Acad. Pediatrics; mem. Adolescent Soc. (charter mem.). Home: 12 Cypress Garden Cincinnati OH 25220 Office: Children's Hosp Med Center Pavilion Bldg Eland and Bethesda Avs Cincinnati OH 45229

JOHNSON, LORNA DRUMMOND, physician; b. Liverpool, Eng., Nov. 26, 1920; d. Peter Minto and Anna Grace Clare (Gregg) Drummond; B.A., Barnard Coll., 1941; M.D., N.Y. U., 1944; m. Robert Edmond Johnson, Dec. 28, 1946; children—Laurel (Mrs. Gerald Lyons), Amy, Robert, Samuel (dec. 1971). Came to U.S., 1926, naturalized, 1948. Intern, resident Bellevue Hosp. 1st Med. Div., N.Y.C., 1944-46, asst. clin. attending physician, 1948-50; research asst., asso. Boston Hosp. for Women, 1955—; research asso. pathology Harvard Med. Sch., 1957-69, prin. asso. pathology, 1969—; research asso. virology Boston U. Sch. Medicine; vis. scientist New Eng. Regional Primate Center. Mem. adv. bd. Framingham Union Hosp. Sch. Nursing. 1958—; chmn. med. library constrn. com. Framingham Union Hosp., 1960. Mem. Framingham Sch. Com., 1967—, chmn., 1970-71, mem. permanent sch. bldg. constrn. com., 1972—. Nat. Cancer Inst. grantee, 1958-70, 72—. Recipient Woman of Year award, Framingham, 1972. Mem. Am., Mass. med. assns., Mass. Cytologic Soc., Obstet. Soc. Boston, League Women Voters. Republican. Episcopalian. Contbr. articles to profl. jours. Home: 151 Edgell Rd Framingham MA 01701 Office: 221 Longwood Av Boston MA 02115

JOHNSON, LOUISE BULLOCK (MRS. EDWARD ALDEN JOHNSON), real estate exec.; b. Mehoopany, Pa., Sept. 2, 1926; d. J. Myron and Elsie Irene (Haines) Bullock; grad. high sch., 1943; m. Edward Alden Johnson, Oct. 30, 1948; children—Diana Jean (Mrs. Donald M. Brigham), Boyd, Steven Bruce, James Elliot. Freight clk. N.Y., N.H. & H. R.R., Hyannis, Mass., 1943-48; with Tax Collector Office, South Yarmouth, Mass., 1948-49; clerk Barnstable Registry of Deeds, Barnstable, Mass., 1959-61; teller savs. dept. Barnstable County Nat. Bank, Hyannis, 1961-65; with Cape Realty, real estate broker, South Yarmouth, 1965-66; adminstr., supr. personnel and real estate brokers L.B.J. Realty, Bass River, Mass., 1966—. Mem. Bd. Realtors (program com. 1969-70), Yarmouth C. of C. (dir. 1967-74). Baptist (youth adv. 1961-66). Club: Quote (Hyannis). Home: 11 Crosby St S Yarmouth MA 02664 Office: 909 Route 28 Bass River MA 02664

JOHNSON, LOUISE CLAYTON, educator; b. Kansas City, Mo., June 15, 1923; d. John Richard and Susan (Thresher) Clayton; student Kan. State U., 1940-43; A.B., Syracuse U., 1958; M.S.W., U. Conn., 1962; m. Charles F. Johnson, Jan. 23, 1943 (div. Sept. 1956); children—Nancy (Mrs. Gilbert A. Emmert), Charlotte (Mrs. Steven P. Vanderlinden). Social group worker Neighborhood Center, Utica, N.Y., 1958-60; exec. dir. Waterbury (Conn.) Girls Club, 1962-64; supervising psychiat. social worker Conn. Valley Hosp., Middletown, 1964-68; asst. prof. social work U. Ia., Iowa City, 1968-74; dir. social work program U. S.D., Vermillion, 1974—. Field work instr. U. Conn. Sch. Social Work, 1965-68; group work cons. Hillcrest Children Services Ia., 1968-69, Johnson County Dept. Social Services, 1969; group work cons. State Juvenile Home, Toledo. Active Girl Scouts U.S. Sec. bd. dirs., mem. provisional com. Community Pastoral Counseling Service. Mem. Am. Assn. U. Women (sec. local br. 1966-68), Acad. Certified Social Workers, Nat. Assn. Social Workers (sec. group work sect. 1964-65), Delta Delta Delta. Baptist (pres. women's group 1961-62, 67-68, chmn. bd. Christian edn. 1971—). Club: Altrusa (bd. mem. at large 1963-64) (Waterbury, Conn.). Home: 220 Sycamore St Parkview Ct Vermillion SD 57069

JOHNSON, LYDIA MARGARET, educator; b. St. Louis, Oct. 20, 1932; d. Wilford A. and Dorothy Clare (Egbert) Johnson; student Centre Coll., Danville, Ky., 1950-52; B.S. magna cum laude in Home Econs., U. Ky., 1955, J.D., 1973; M.R.E., So. Bapt. Theol. Sem., 1960; profl. diploma Columbia, 1961, Ed.D., 1965. Home demonstration agt. U. Ky., Lexington, 1955-58; ednl. researcher Inst. of Life Ins., N.Y.C., 1961-63; chmn. home econs. dept. Western Ill. U., Macomb, 1965-69. Mem. Nat. Council Adminstrs. of Home Econs. (mem. exec. bd. 1967-69), Am., Ill. (mem. exec. bd 1968-69) home econs. assns., N.E.A., Nat., Ill. councils family relations, Kappa Omicron Phi, Omicron Nu (chpt. v.p. 1962-63), Phi Upsilon Omicron, Kappa Delta Pi, Pi Lambda Theta, Phi Delta Phi. Baptist. Author: Handbook of the National Council of Administrators of Home Economics, 1969; (with Mary Ruth Swope) Facts about Curricula in Home Economics in Institutions of Higher Education, 1970. Home: Rt 3 Box 206 Frankfort KY 40601

JOHNSON, MARCIA WALKER (MRS. RAYMOND MARSHALL JOHNSON), merchandising co. exec.; b. Griffin, Ga., July 2, 1936; d. George Leonard and Gladys (Duplessis) Walker; B.A., Vanderbilt U., 1957; Fulbright scholar U. Paris, 1957-58; M.S., Northwestern U., 1966; m. Raymond Marshall Johnson, Dec. 10, 1960; children—Erik, Kristin, Linnea. Systems engr. IBM, Chattanooga and Knoxville, Tenn., 1959-62; research engr., lectr. math., systems programmer Northwestern U., Evanston, Ill., 1967-68; operations research analyst Montgomery Ward & Co., Chgo., 1968-69, operations research project mgr., 1969-73, marketing research mgr., 1973—. Mem. Operations Research Soc. Am. (chmn. Chgo. sect. 1971-72, sec.-treas. bus. applications sect. 1973-74), Am. Statis. Assn., Inst. Mgmt. Sci., Am. Marketing Assn., League Women Voters. Presbyn. Editor Proc. Operations Research/Mgmt. Sci. in Chgo., 1972. Home: 2330 Park Pl Evanston IL 60201 Office: 619 W Chicago Av Chicago IL 60607

JOHNSON, MARGARET A., sch. adminstr.; b. Washington, Sept. 30, 1919; d. John D. and Janet (Harmon) Johnson; B.A., Radcliffe Coll., 1941, M.A., 1949. Tchr., Mary C. Wheeler Sch., Providence, 1941-44, Winsor Sch., Boston, 1944-48; prin. Girls' Sch., Milton

(Mass.) Acad., 1950—. Home: 123 Center St Milton MA 02186 Office: Milton Acad Milton MA 02168

JOHNSON, MARGARET FORBUSH (MRS. HERBERT F. JOHNSON, JR.), newspaperwoman; b. Fredericksburg, Va., Feb. 12, 1933; d. Charles S. and Anne (Oliver) McWhirt; student Mary Washington Coll., 1929-30, U. Tenn., 1941-42; m. Herbert F. Johnson, Jr., Sept. 17, 1970; 1 son, Charles S. Forbush. Woman's editor Bristol (Va.) Herald Courier, 1952—. Mem. exec. bd. Bristol ristol Meml. Hosp. Aux., 1959-69. Recipient 1st Pl. awards Va. Press, 1965. Clubs: Altrusa (v.p. Bristol 1966-67); Virginia Presswomen (exec. bd. 1958-70); Country. Home: Route 4 PO Box 208 Bristol TN 37620 Office: 300 Pierce St Bristol VA 24201

JOHNSON, MARGUIRETTE GEORGE (MRS. FRED THOMAS JOHNSON), sch. adminstr.; b. Albemarle, N.C., Sept. 2, 1917; d. William Clarence and Myrtle (Hendrick) George; diploma Brevard Jr. Coll., 1937; A.B., U. N.C. at Greensboro, 1937-39; M.A. East Carolina U., 1962, postgrad., 1966-67; postgrad. Appalachian State U., 1968-72; m. Fred Thomas Johnson, Nov. 11, 1944; children—Fred Thomas, William George. Tchr. home econs. Gaston County Schs., Gastonia, N.C., 1940-41; tchr. Spanish Newton Conover City Schs., Newton, N.C., 1941-43; tchr. Spanish Raleigh (N.C.) City Schs., 1943-44; tchr. high sch. history, jr. high and mentally retarded New Bern (N.C.) City Schs., 1948-61; counselor Craven County Schs., New Bern, N.C., 1961-68; dir. guidance and spl. edn. Burke County Pub. Schs., Morganton, N.C., 1968-70; asst. prof. spl. edn. Winthrop Coll., Rock Hill, S.C., 1970-72; dir. tng. Habilitation Services, Inc., Gaffney, S.C., 1972-73; counselor Kings Mountain (N.C.) Dist. Schs., 1973—. Cons. to upgrade spl. edn. programs to various S.C. Sch. Dists., 1970-72. Active with Girl Scouts U.S.A., Gastonia, 1939-41, Boy Scouts Am., New Bern, 1952-56, 62-63; program and social sec. YWCA, Durham, 1944. Recipient N.C. Alpha Delta Kappa scholarship grant, 1970. Mem. Nat. Assn. for Retarded Children, Am., N.C. personnel and guidance assns., Am. Assn. on Mental Deficiency, Am. Assn. U. Profs., Council of Exceptional Children, State Edn. Assn. (state dist. pres. of romance langs. 1943-44, state dist. pres. spl. edn. 1959-60, state dist. pres. guidance services 1969-70), N.E.A., Assn. Classroom Tchrs., Alpha Delta Kappa. Mem. Order Eastern Star. Club: Pilot (internat. relations chmn. 1969-70) (Morganton). Home: 509 Beaumond Terrace Shelby NC 28150 Office: Kings Mountain High Kings Mountain NC 28086

JOHNSON, MARIE CORNELIA, govt. ofcl.; b. Boley, Okla., Nov. 25, 1911; d. Louis Cecil and Bertha (Watson) Taylor; LL.B., John Marshall Law Sch., 1947, J.D., 1970; m. Wesley Maurice Johnson, Aug. 17, 1944; children—Harold, Viola Cecile, Marie Christine. Admitted to Ill. bar, 1948; practice law, Chgo., 1948-58; atty. Internal Revenue Service U.S. Treasury, Chgo., 1958-62; hearings referee Unemployment Compensation div. Ill. State Dept. Labor, Chgo., 1971-73. Bd. dirs. Phyllis Wheatley Home for Girls. em. Ill. State, Am., Nat. bar assns., Nat. Assn. Women Lawyers, Women's Bar Assn. of Ill. Mem. Order Eastern Star. Home: PO Box A 3257 Chicago IL 60690 Office: 540 W Randolph St Chicago IL 60606

JOHNSON, SISTER MARIE INEZ, librarian; b. Mitchell, S.D., June 2, 1909; d. Charles and Inez L. (Williams) Johnson; B.A. in English, Coll. St. Catherine, 1929, B.S. in L.S., 1939; M.S. in L.S., Columbia, 1940; postgrad. U. Denver, 1951-52, U. So. Cal., 1953-54. Joined Sisters St. Joseph Carondolet, 1926; tchr. elementary schs. St. Paul, 1930-38; librarian Coll. St. Catherine, St. Paul, 1940-42, head librarian, 1942—. Mem. steering com. U. Minn. Workshop for Librarians, 1956; library cons. survey Mt. Mercy Coll., Cedar Rapids, Ia., 1963-64; bldg. cons. Fontbonne Coll., St. Louis, 1964—. Mem. Conf. Am. Folklore for Youth, St. Paul Speakers Bur., com. standard catalog for high sch. Cath. Support, Children's Lit. TV Series. Butler Fgn. Study fellow Coll. St. Catherine, 1958. Named Minn. Librarian of Year, 1967. Mem. Am. (various coms.), Cath. (various coms.) library assns. Editor column Cath. Library World, 1954—. Contbr. articles to profl. jours. Address: Coll St Catherine St Paul MN 55116

JOHNSON, MARJORIE CARROLL (MRS. OWEN M. JOHNSON), lawyer, clubwoman; b. Iroquois, S.D., Dec. 7, 1903; d. Philip Gregory and Olive (Scales) Carroll; student Huron Coll., 1921-23, U. So. Cal., 1923-24; Ph.B., U. Chgo., 1925, J.D., 1927; m. Owen M. Johnson, Dec. 31, 1928; children—Phyllis (Mrs. William Bruce Warfel), Owen M., David Gregory. Admitted to Ill. bar, 1929; law clk. Judge Evan A. Evans of U.S. Circuit Ct. of Appeals, 7th Circuit, 1927-30; law clk. Judge of 7th Circuit, 1933-36; individual practice, Belvidere, Ill., 1936-73. Pres., Boone County Health Council 1946-50. Bd. dirs. Highland Hosp., 1943-74, Ida. Pub. Library. Recipient Doctor of Civic Betterment award Belvidere C. of C., 1970. Mem. Ill. Bar Assn., Boone County Fedn. Women's Clubs (past pres.), D.A.R., Delta Sigma. Methodist (ch. trustee). Clubs: Belvidere Woman's (past pres.), New Century. Home: 704 Kishwaukee St Belvidere IL 61008

JOHNSON, MARJORIE SEDDON (MRS. WILLIAM EVERITT JOHNSON), educator; b. Flourtown, Pa., Nov. 28, 1918; d. Alfred Morris and Elsie Catherine (Mowrey) Seddon; B.S., Temple U., 1939, M.Ed., 1948, Ed.D., 1954; m. William Everitt Johnson, Mar. 23, 1944 (dec. Dec. 1944). Tchr. Springfield Twp. High Sch., Erdenheim, Pa., 1939-48; supr. lab. sch. of reading clinic Temple U., Phila., 1948-65, acting dir. reading clinic, 1960-63, asso. dir. reading clinic, 1965-70, dir. reading clinic, 1970—, lectr. psychology, 1948-63, asso. prof., 1963-64, asso. prof. psychology and ednl. psychology, 1964-66, prof., 1966-70, chmn. psychology of reading dept., 1970—. Vis. prof. U. Ore., summers, 1958, 59; cons. various schs. and ednl. agys. Mem. Internat. Reading Assn. (dir.), Am. Assn. U. Profs., A.A.A.S., Am., Pa. psychol. assns., Am. Ednl. Research Assn., Nat. Soc. for Study of Edn., Nat. Conf. on Research in English, Nat. Council Tchrs. English, Delaware Valley Reading Assn., Phila. Soc. Clin. Psychologists, Phila. Soc. Projective Techniques, Sigma Pi. Contbr. to publs. in field. Home: 61 Grove Av Flourtown PA 19031 Office: Temple U Broad and Montgomery Sts Philadelphia PA 19122

JOHNSON, MARTIE, TV newswomen; b. St. Petersburg, Fla., Apr. 24, 1928; d. Alfred Carl and Pauline (Lyon) Krayer; A.A., St. Petersburg Jr. Coll., 1947; A.B., Duke, 1949; m. Cecil Simmons Johnson, June 3, 1952; children—Sherron Patricia, Jana Lynne, Cecil Simmons. Tchr. English, Durham (N.C.) High Sch., 1949-56, 1959-60; dir. pub. information Anti-Poverty Program, Durham, 1965-66; reporter, anchorwoman WTVD-TV, Durham, 1966—. Commentator fashion shows, pub. speaker, lectr. Chmn., Durham County March of Dimes, 1966; pres. Club Boulevard Sch. P.T.A., 1969-70, Durham High Sch. P.T.A., 1970-71; adv. bd. Duke U. Hosp. Mem. Am. Women in Radio and TV, Alpha Phi. Republican. Methodist. Home: 2609 Glendale Av Durham NC 27704 Office: WTVD Box 2009 Durham NC 27702

JOHNSON, (MARY) ANITA, physician, med. service adminstr.; b. Clarksburg, W.Va., Oct. 18, 1926; d. Paul F. and Mary Elizabeth (Harris) Johnson; B.S., North Tex. U., 1946; M.D., Woman's Med. Coll. of Pa., 1950; m. Lawrence J. Ciessau, Aug. 22, 1959 (div. 1974); children—Mathew A., Susan E., Sharon L., Mark A. Intern, Baylor U. Hosp., Dallas, 1950-51, resident, 1951-54; practice medicine specializing in internal medicine, Dallas, 1954-58, Chgo., 1958—; instr. internal medicine Southwestern Med. Coll., U. Tex., Dallas, 1954-58; med. dir. YWCA, Dallas, 1955-58; physician infant welfare Chgo. Bd. Health, 1960-63; house physician, emergency physician St. Mary of Nazareth Hosp. Center, Chgo., 1963—, instr. for nurses intensive care unit, 1963—, asst. cardiologist, 1963—; cons. internal medicine to Lisbon VA Hosp., Dallas, 1955-56. Lectr. to community elementary sch. students on opportunities in health field, 1967—. Named Med. Woman of Year, St. Mary of Nazareth Hosp. Center, 1973. Mem. A.M.A., Am. Med. Woman's Assn. (regional dir. 1955-58), Ill., Chgo. med. socs., Zeta Phi. Home: 1146 N Ashland Av River Forest IL 60305 Office: 4301 W Foster Av Chicago IL 60630

JOHNSON, MARY ANN (MRS. H. MAX LANDEY), psychiatrist; b. Memphis, Aug. 26, 1933; d. Ora Dennis and Ruth (Russell) Johnson; student Rice U., 1951-54; M.D., La. State U., 1958; m. H. Max Landey, Jan. 11, 1958; children—Carl David, Valerie Lynn, Alana Ruth. Intern U. So. Cal.-Los Angeles County Med. Center, 1958-59, resident psychiatry, 1960-63; staff psychiatrist Hathaway Home for Children, Los Angeles, 1963; organizer, dir. Humboldt Mental Health Clinic, Eureka, Cal., 1964-65; pvt. practice as psychiatrist, Eureka, 1965-67, San Jose, Cal., 1968-69, Marion, Va., 1970—; staff psychiatrist Adult and Child Guidance Clinic, San Jose, Cal., 1968-69; cons. psychiatrist, Marion, Va., 1970—; cons. Blue Ridge Job Corps, Southwestern State Hosp., Smyth County Community Hosp. (all Marion). Diplomate Am. Bd. Psychiatry and Neurology. Mem. Am. Psychiat. Assn., Neuropsychiat. Assn. Va., Southwest Va. Med. Soc., Smyth County Med. Soc. (sec.-treas. 1973—). Adress: 392 Panorama Dr Marion VA 24354

JOHNSON, MARY ELIZABETH, librarian, educator; b. Warsaw, Ind., May 3, 1916; d. William Bina and Edith Miona (Connell) Johnson; A.B., Butler U., 1937; M.S., Purdue U., 1945; M.L.S., Columbia, 1960. Tchr. math. and English, librarian Batesville High Sch., 1937-39; librarian, tchr. math. Marion (Ind.) High Sch., 1939-49; librarian, asso. prof. Burris Lab. Sch., Ball State U., Muncie, Ind., 1949—; librarian reference dept. Denver Pub. Library, summer 1946; librarian First Bapt. Ch., Muncie. Mem. A.L.A., Ind. Library Assn., Ind. Sch. Librarians Assn., N.E.A., Ind. Tchrs. Assn., Kappa Delta Pi, Delta Zeta. Am. Baptist. Mem. Order Eastern Star. Home: 224 N Talley St Muncie IN 47303

JOHNSON, MARY FRANCES KENNON (MRS. LEONARD L. JOHNSON), librarian; b. Columbia, S.C., Nov. 1, 1928; d. Robert Lewis and Frances (Lofton) Kennon; student Wesleyan Coll., Macon, Ga., 1945-46; A.B., U. S.C., 1949; M.S.L., U. N.C., 1954; m. Leonard L. Johnson, Aug. 1962. Tchr. South Fork High Sch., Winston-Salem, N.C., 1949-50; librarian Charlotte (N.C.) pub. schs., 1950-54; library specialist Balt. City Schs., 1954-56; instr. Sch. Library Sci. U. N.C., 1956; asso. supr. Sch. Library Services, N.C. Dept. Pub. Instrn., Raleigh, 1956-61; instr. dept. library sci. Appalachian State Tchrs. Coll., Boone, N.C., 1954, 58; dir. Sch. Library Devel. Project A.L.A., Chgo., 1961-62; instr. library edn. U.N.C., Greensboro, 1962-66; asst. prof. library edn., 1966-71, asso. prof., 1971—. Mem. N.C. Lit. and Hist. Assn., Am. (chmn. editorial com. 1966-69), Southeastern, N.C. library assns., Nat., N.C. edn. assns., Assn. for Supervision Curriculum Devel., Assn. Ednl. Communications and Tech., Am. Assn. U. Profs., Phi Beta Kappa, Beta Phi Mu, Delta Kappa Gamma. Democrat. Conglist. Editor: Sch. Libraries, 1969-72. Contbr. articles to library, edn. periodicals. Home: 109 Falkener Dr Greensboro NC 27410

JOHNSON, MARY LEE CLARE (MRS. RALPH A. JOHNSON), real estate broker; b. Wann, Neb., Feb. 21, 1934; d. Harry Peter and Clara Anna (Heldt) Schlesiger; student Cabrillo Coll., 1970-72; m. Ralph A. Johnson, Sept. 2, 1950; children—Christopher, Christine, Curtiss, Candace. Music tchr., Omaha, 1948-50; office mgr. Logging Co., Eureka, Cal., 1957-60; with Hansen Real Estate, Watsonville, Cal., 1969—, mgr., real estate broker, 1971—. Pres., E.A. Hall Jr. High Sch. and H.A. Hyde Sch. P.T.A., Watsonville, 1965-66, 67-68; leader Girl Scouts U.S.A., Watsonville, 1965-67; leader Cub Scouts Am., Eureka, 1961-63; sec. Southbay Union Sch., Eureka, 1961-62; mem. Vol. Service Watsonville. Mem. Watsonville Bd. Realtors (dir.). Lutheran. Mem. Order Eastern Star. Home: 407 Tuttle St Watsonville CA 95076 Office: 1393 Freedom Blvd Watsonville CA 95076

JOHNSON, MARY LYNN MILLER (MRS. JAMES JEFFERSON JOHNSON, JR.), educator; b. Pampa, Tex., Mar. 12, 1938; d. Emmitt Ray and Ladye Hortense (Allison) Miller; student W. Tex. State U., 1955-57; B.S., U. Tex., 1958; M.S. (Dept. Health Edn. and Welfare fellow), N.M. State U., 1961; Ph.D. (Dept. Health, Edn. and Welfare fellow), Pa. State U., 1970; m. James Jefferson Johnson, Jr., Aug. 17, 1957; children—Melinda Ann, James Jefferson III. Air pollution chemist El Paso City-County Health Unit, 1959-60, 61-63; chemist Tex. Pub. Health Dept., El Paso, 1963-64; asst. prof. chemistry U. Tex., Arlington, 1968—. Indsl. cons. air pollution and combustion, 1966—. Mem. Am. Chem. Soc., A.A.A.S., Air Pollution Control Assn., Combustion Inst., Tex. Assn. Coll. Tchrs., Iota Sigma Pi, Alpha Chi. Presbyn. Home: 3004 Croydon St Denton TX 76201 Office: 201C Science Hall U Texas at Arlington Arlington TX 76010

JOHNSON, MARY RITZ (MRS. JOHN JOHNSON), fashion tchr.; b. Szatmar, Hungary, Mar. 15, 1904; d. George and Mary (Zaharia) Ritz; student Booth & Bayliss Comml. Sch., 1918-20, Ecole Guerre-Lavigne, Paris, 1954; m. John Johnson, June 24, 1925; 1 dau., Marilyn (Mrs. Martin Thomas Mannion). Came to U.S., 1911, naturalized, 1942. Owner, dir. Town and Country Clothes by Mary Johnson, 1925-42; instr., cons. sewing D. M. Read & Co., Bridgeport, Conn., 1948; tchr. fashion sewing and designing Fashion Edn. Sch., Bridgeport, Conn., 1948—. Mem. Internat. Platform Assn. Club: Quota (Bridgeport, Conn.). Author: Sewing the Easy Way, 1958, rev. edit., 1966; Sew for Your Children, 1961; Mary Johnson's Guide to Altering and Re-styling Ready Made Clothes, 1963; Easier Way to Sew for Your Family, 1972. Contbg. sewing editor Woman's Day Mag., 1958—. Home: 291 Grovers Av Bridgeport CT 06605

JOHNSON, MARY WITKOWSKI (MRS. SHELTON WARNER JOHNSON), lawyer; b. N.Y.C., July 26, 1915; d. Casimir Felix and Caroline Virginia (Stewart) Witkowski; B.S., Loyola Coll. Balt., 1965; LL.B., Eastern Coll., Balt., 1968; J.D., U. Balt., 1970; m. Shelton Warner Johnson, July 22, 1933; children—Shelton Warner, Suzan Mary, Felicia (Mrs. James Parker). Admitted to Md. bar, 1969; asst. states atty. Baltimore City, 1970-71; mem. firm Holniker & Johnson, Balt., 1971—. Asst. prof. bus. law evening div. Loyola Coll., Balt., 1971—, faculty adviser Daniel Cavanaugh Scholarship Fund, 1973—. Bd. dirs. Charles Village Civic Assn., 1968-71. Mem. Am., Md., Baltimore City (mem. grievance com. 1971—), Md. Women's (v.p.) bar assns. Home: Box 22 Monkton MD 21111 Office: 416 E 25th St Baltimore MD 21218

JOHNSON, MARYALYCE, psychiat. social worker; b. Youngstown, O., Sept. 20, 1933; d. Arthur Wherry and Elizabeth (Campbell) Johnson; A.B., Birmingham-So. Coll., 1956; M.S. S.W., U. Tenn., 1959; m. Robert J. Bartelt, Nov. 9, 1967. (div. 1970). Clin. social worker VA Regional Office, Nashville, 1959-62; instr. U. Tenn. Coll. Medicine, Memphis, 1962-64; adminstrv. asst. Mental Health Center, Morristown, Tenn., 1964-65; supr. Fla. State Hosp., Chattahoochie, 1965-66; community placement social worker VA Hosp., Downey, Ill., 1966-68; cons. Dade County Criminal Ct., Miami, Fla., 1969-70; pvt. practice psychiat. social work, Miami and Largo, Fla., 1968-70; social work cons. in med. aging and mental health, St. Petersburg, 1970—, field instr. Fla. State U., Sch. Social Work, 1974—. Mem. Nat. Assn. Social Workers, Acad. Certified Social Workers, Gerontol. Soc. Episcopalian. Address: 7875 2d Av S St Petersburg FL 33707

JOHNSON, MAXINE CHAMPAGNE, educator; b. Oketo, Kan., Mar. 30, 1925; d. Cedric Boyd and Victoria A. (Keck) Champagne; B.A. in Econs., Wash. State U., 1948; M.A. in Econs., U. Mont., 1952; m. Manford Elwood Johnson, Dec. 27, 1947; 1 son, Kurt Boyd. Faculty, U. Mont., 1960—, prof. Sch. Bus. Adminstrn., 1974—; dir. Bur. Bus. and Econ. Research, 1972—. Dir. Mountain Supply Co., Western Mont. Nat. Bank. Mem. Sec. Agr. Adv. Com. on Multiple Use of Nat. Forests, 1967-68; Mont. Bd. Investments, 1971—, Gov. Mont. Commn. on Status Women, 1969—. Mem. Am. Assn. U. Women (chmn. resolutions con. nat. conv. 1971), Assn. Univ. Bus. and Econ. Research (pres. 1972), Phi Beta Kappa. Contbr. numerous articles, monographs to profl. lit. Home: 3717 Creekwood Rd Missoula MT 59801

JOHNSON, MILDRED LOIS SWANSON, civic leader, univ. trustee; b. Flint, Mich., Oct. 8, 1924; d. Herbert Carl Morton and Regina Alfrida Naomi (Rosenberg) Swanson; B.A., Augustana Coll., 1946; postgrad. Western Mich. U.; m. Conrad Eugene Johnson, June 20, 1947. Tchr. social studies Durant (Ia.) Sr. High Sch., 1946-47; tchr. English, Am. and Mich. history Angell Jr. High Sch., Muskegon, Mich., 1948-53. Mem. Mich. Coordinating Council Pub. Higher Edn., 1964-66; mem. Gov. Mich. Citizens Com. Higher Edn., 1963-66; mem. Gov. Mich. Commn. Status Women, 1962-66, 67-68, chmn. com. edn., 1962-66, 67-68; mem. adv. com. Mich. State Coop. Extension. First v.p. Muskegon YWCA, 1958, bd. dirs., 1956-58; mem. adult program com. YMCA, 1969-71; pres. coordinating council Women's Clubs Muskegon County, 1954-55; pres. Muskegon br. Am. Assn. U. Women, 1950-52, Mich. div., 1961-63, editor Mich. div. News Bull., publicity chmn. div. 1957-61, div. named Internat. fellowship for her, 1963, Muskegon br. named fellowship for her, 1962. Bd. dirs. Muskegon Community Concert Assn., pres., 1968-70; trustee Western Mich. U., 1964—; bd. dirs. Young Family Christian Assn. Greater Muskegon, 1972—, v.p., 1973—. Recipient Augustana Coll. Alumni Assn. Outstanding Achievement award, 1971. Mem. Hist. Soc. Mich., Muskegon County (v.p. 1971, 72-73, pres. 1973—), Augustana hist. socs., Mich. Archaeol. Soc., Adult Edn. Assn. Greater Muskegon (pres. 1969-70), Western Mich. U. Alumni Assn. (dir. 1973—, v.p. 1973—), Mich. Heritage Assn. (steering com.), Geneal. Soc. Muskegon County, Vasa Order Am. Lutheran. Author: (with Bertha Freye) The Hackley House, 1961. Address: 1670 Langeland Av Muskegon MI 49442

JOHNSON, MINA FIELDS (MRS. STEWART JOHNSON), educator; b. Amarillo, Tex., May 5, 1935; d. Madison F. and Minnie S. (Seelbach) Fields; B.A., Baylor U., 1956; M.A., Hardin-Simmons U., 1962; m. Charles Stewart Johnson, Feb. 1, 1960; children—Elisabeth, Matthew, Catherine, Rebecca. Tchr., Ketchikan, Alaska, 1956-58; lectr. Hunter Coll., N.Y.C., 1970-71; tchr. Rye (N.Y.) Pub. Schs., 1972-73; asst. prof. English, Shelby State Community Coll., Memphis, 1973—. Bd. dirs. July-O-Rama Day Camp, New Rochelle, N.Y., 1970-72. Mem. Am. Assn. Univ. Women (dir. 1964), League Women Voters (dir. 1970-72), Kappa Alpha Theta. Home: 1756 Central Av Memphis TN 38104 Office: 4166 Park Av Memphis TN 38111

JOHNSON, MYRA ANN CRAWFORD, writer; b. Birmingham, Ala., July 10, 1937; d. John Raymond and Ressie Lorene (Quinn) Crawford; B.A., Samford U., 1958; M.A., U. Ala., 1969; postgrad., U. Ia., 1970—; m. John Henry Johnson, Apr. 6, 1965; children—Crystal Mikel, Shaun Hill-Ford. Account exec., media dir. Pub. Relations and Advt. Assos., Inc., Birmingham, 1960-63; co-owner, sec.-treas. United Advt., Inc., Atlanta and Birmingham, 1963-68; free lance writer, 1968—; instr. English, U. Ala., Birmingham, 1970—; editor Folio, lit., mag., 1968—; editorial asso. Birmingham Mag., 1973—. Cons. to pres. U. Ala., Tuscaloosa, 1973—. Bd. dirs. Crawford's Day Care Center, Birmingham, 1973—. Bd. dirs. Birmingham Festival of Arts, 1969—, chmn. Hackney Lit. awards, 1969—. Recipient 1st prize short story div. Ala. Festival of Arts, 1965, 68, grant-in-aid Ind. U. Found., 1971, silver bowl Birmingham Festival of Arts, 1972; winter Ala. Prize Stories Contest, 1970. Mem. Women in Communications (1st v.p. 1970-72), Ala. Conservancy. Address: 4650 Old Looney Mill Rd Birmingham AL 35243

JOHNSON, NANCY EBERSOLE (MRS. ROBERT L. JOHNSON), educator; b. Sioux Falls, S.D., Dec. 12, 1925; d. Paul F. and Mildred (Nelson) Ebersole; B.S., Ia. State U., 1947, M.S., 1949; Ph.D., U. Wis., 1969; m. Robert L. Johnson, June 14, 1951; children—Christopher, Jeffrey, Brian. Research asst. Ia. State U., Ames, 1948-49, research asso., 1949-50, instr., 1950-51; instr. Chgo. Tchrs. Coll., 1952; clin. nutritionist Chgo. Maternity Center, 1952-53; pub. health nutritionist City of Milw., 1953-54; instr. dept. foods and nutrition U. Wis., Madison, 1965-66, research asst., 1966-69, asst. prof. dept. nutrition scis., extension specialist, 1969-73, asso. prof., 1973—. Mem. Am., Wis. dietetics assns., Soc. for Nutrition Edn., Wis. Assn. Perinatal Care, Sigma Xi, Sigma Delta Epsilon. Home: 105 Quarterback Dr Madison WI 53705

JOHNSON, OLIVE LUCILLE HARDING (MRS. STANLEY FRANK JOHNSON), educator; b. Trivoli, Ill., Jan. 1, 1904; d. Adoniram Judson and Eva Cecelia (Kellogg) Harding; student Bradley U., 1918-20; B. Ed., Nat. Coll. Edn., 1958; M.A., Northwestern U., 1960; m. Stanley Frank Johnson, June 21, 1924; children—Shirley (Mrs. Milton E. Libby), Roger Frank, Stanley David. Tchr. Latin and history Trivoli (Ill.) Community High Sch., 1923-24; tchr. guidance center Nat. Coll. Edn., Evanston, Ill., 1958-60; tchr. Avoca Jr. High Sch., Wilmette, Ill., 1960-72; individual therapist learning disabilities, Wilmette, 1969—. Mem. Kappa Delta Pi. Conglist (pres. Women's Soc. 1953—). Club: Woman's (sec.-treas. 1938-48) (Wilmette). Author: The Church for One World, 1951; The Church for Today's World, 1959. Home: 1925 Thornwood St Wilmette IL 60091

JOHNSON, PAMELA HANSFORD (LADY C. P. SNOW), writer; b. London, Eng., May 29, 1912; d. Reginald Kenneth and Amy Clotilda (Howson) Johnson; ed. Clapham County Sch., London; D.Litt. (hon.), Temple U., York U., Toronto, Widener Coll., Chester, Pa.; m. Gordon Neil Stewart, Dec. 15, 1936; children—Andrew Morven, Lindsay Jean; m. 2d, Charles Percy Snow, July 15, 1950; 1 son, Philip Charles Hansford. Novelist, critic and broadcaster, 1945; mem. panel Brains Trust on BBC, 1956—, Critics on BBC, 1953—. Fellow Centre Advanced Studies, Wesleyan U., Middletown, Conn., 1961, Timothy Dwight Coll., Founders Coll. York U.; Timothy Dwight fellow arts and letters Yale, 1961. Fellow Royal Soc. Literature; mem. Societé Européene de Culture. Author: (novels) This Bed Thy Centre, 1935; Too Dear for My Possessing, 1940; An Avenue of Stone, 1947; A Summer to Decide, 1948; Catherine Carter, 1952; An Impossible Marriage, 1954; The Last Resort (in U.S., The Sea and The Wedding), 1956; The Unspeakable Skipton, 1959; The Humbler Creation, 1959; An Error of Judgement, 1962; Night and Silence Who is Here?, 1963; Cork Street, Next to The Hatter's, 1965; The Survival of the Fittest, 1967; The Honours Board, 1970; The Holiday Friend, 1972; The Good Listener, 1975; (criticism) Thomas Wolfe, a Critical Study, 1947 (in U.S. as The Art of Thomas Wolfe, 1963), I. Compton-Burnett, 1953; On Iniquity (social criticism), 1967; (essays) Important to Me, 1974; (play) Corinth House, 1948; (radio series) Six Proust Reconstructions, 1948. Translator: (with Kitty Black) Anouilh's The Rehearsal, 1962. Address: care MacMillan Ltd Little Essex St Strand London WC2 England

JOHNSON, PATRICIA CARLEY (MRS. RUFUS WILLIAM RAUCH, JR.), educator; b. Bklyn., Mar. 2, 1934; d. Herbert Lyman and Frances (Carley) Johnson; A.B., CHestnut Hill Coll., 1955; Ph.D., U. Rochester, 1964; m. Rufus William Rauch, Jr., Aug. 11, 1962. Teaching asst. U. Rochester (N.Y.), 1955-59; instr. Temple U., 1959-64, asst. prof., 1964-66; asso. prof. West Chester (Pa.) State Coll., 1966-69, prof., 1969—, chmn. Departmental Procedures and Orgn. Com., 1970-71, chmn. history dept., 1971—; vis. asst. prof. U. Del., summer 1966. Vice pres. Assn. Pa. State Coll. and Univ. Faculties, 1972-73, pres., 1973. Faculty sponsor Women's Student Service Orgn., Temple U., 1964-66; mem. Pa. State Coll. Planning Commn., 1973—. Mem. aux. Childrens' Hosp. Phila. Mem. Am., Pa. hist. assns., Nat., Pa. edn. assns., Orgn. Am. Historians, M.M.S., Nat. Trust For Historic Preservation, Nat. Trust For Places of Historic Interest or Natural Beauty. Republican. Roman Catholic. Home: 914 Valley Forge Rd Devon PA 19333 Office: Main Hall West Chester State Coll West Chester PA 19380

JOHNSON, PATRICIA LARRANE HAHN (MRS. JERALD A. JOHNSON), co-owner advt. agy.; b. Gt. Falls, Mont., Oct. 6, 1945; d. Raymond Kennly and Elizabeth Mary (Lanky) Hahn; student Mont. State U., 1963-65; m. Jerald A. Johnson, Sept. 5, 1964; children—Michael Ray, Brenda Denise. Free-lance comml. artist, 1964-66; owner Tamareck Letter Art, Missoula, Mont., 1966-69; co-owner Jacobson Agy., advt. agy., Missoula, 1969—. Creator advt. and pub. relations campaign Mont. Constl. Conv. Chmn. com. to organize a safety com. in Missoula, 1971-74. Bd. dirs., exec. com. Missoula YMCA. Mem. Missoula C. of C., Missoula Downtown Bus. Assn. (pub. relations 1973—), Missoula Red Coats (charter, vice-chmn. 1974-75). Club: Altrusa (pres. 1972—) (Missoula). Dist. editor Altrusan, 1973-75. Home: 31 Willowbrook Lane Missoula MT 59801 Office: 219 E Main St Missoula MT 59801

JOHNSON, PAULA GAY, assn. exec.; b. Carbondale, Ill., Jan. 16, 1936; d. Edgar Nash and Bernice Elsie (Moulic) Johnson; student Ind. U., summer 1956; B.A., Principia Coll., 1959. Editor, asst. pub. relations dept. Allstate Ins. Cos., Northbrook, Ill., 1959-62, asst. dir. women's div., Washington, 1968-70; staff writer, editor, women's rep. consumer relations program Amoco Oil Co., Chgo., 1962-68; information specialist FTC, Washington, 1970-71; account exec. Robert R. Mullen & Co., Washington, 1971-73; staff exec. Assn. Nat. Advertisers, Washington, 1974—. Recipient Christian Science Monitor Journalism award Principia Coll., 1959; Co. and Trade Publs. award Jr. Achievement Chgo., 1961. Mem. Indsl. Editors Assn. Chgo. (4th v.p. 1965, 1st v.p. 1966, pres. 1967), Pub. Relations Soc. Am. (dir. Washington chpt. 1974), Am. Newspaper Women's Club (2d v.p. 1974-75). Contbr. articles to profl. and popular publs. Home: 4501 Arlington Blvd Arlington VA 22203 Office: 1725 K St NW Washington DC 20006

JOHNSON, PAULA STEEN (MRS. ROGER L. JOHNSON), veterinarian; b. Salinas, Cal., Mar. 28, 1945; d. Paul Oscar and Eva May (Hockenjos) Steen; B.S., U. Ill., 1967, D.V.M., 1969; m. Roger L. Johnson, June 12, 1966; 1 dau., Jennifer Lea. Veterinarian, Decatur (Ill.) Animal Clinic, 1969-72; pvt. practice vet. medicine, Monticello, Ill., 1974—. Mem. Am., Ill., Women's vet. med. assns. Club: Zonta (Decatur). Address: 706 Jackson St Monticello IL 61856

JOHNSON, PEARL ANTOINETTE (MRS. JAMES E. JOHNSON), librarian; b. Zion, Ill., Dec. 2, 1918; d. William David and Sarah (Dolan) Connell; B.A., U. Ill., 1939, B.L.S., 1947; m. James Edward Johnson, June 5, 1943. Tchr. social sci. Zion-Benton-Twp. High Sch., Zion, 1939-43, librarian, 1943-51; young adult librarian Waukegan (Ill.) Pub. Library, 1955—. Mem. N.E.A., Am., Ill. library assns., Victory Meml. Hosp. Assn., Phi Beta Kappa, Beta Phi Mu. Methodist. Home: 829 N Baldwin St Waukegan IL 60085 Office: 128 N County St Waukegan IL 60085

JOHNSON, PHYLLIS AUDREY, pub. relations exec.; b. Pitts., Dec. 24, 1929; d. Sam and Ida Goldie (Goldman) Weiss; B.S in Home Econs. Journalism, Pa. State U., 1951. Free lance writer of advt. copy, feature articles Pitts. Post Gazette, Pitts. Press, Squirrel Hill News, Squirrel Hill Gazette, East Liberty Gazette, Pittsburg Forum, Pitts., 1953-69; pub. relations mgr. Buhl Planetarium and Inst., Pitts., 1969—. Mem. Women in Communications, Pitts. Indsl. Communicators Assn., Pitts. Advt. Club. Home: 5731 Bartlett St Pittsburgh PA 15217 Office: Buhl Planetarium and Inst Allegheny Square Pittsburgh PA 15212

JOHNSON, PHYLLIS CONNER (MRS. PAUL ALBERT JOHNSON), writer; b. Wheeling. W.Va., Oct. 24, 1928; d. Guy O. and Lulu M. (Jackson) Conner; student Fenn Coll., 1947-48, San Diego State Coll., 1965, San Diego City Coll., 1970; m. Paul Albert Johnson, Aug. 28, 1948; children—Gaye (Mrs. Michael Kennedy, Paula (Mrs. Stephen Cokenour), Kristin. Free-lance writer fiction, gen. interest articles pub. Am. Home, Cal. Garden, Scholastic Adventure, others, 1960—; travel cons. Stinnett Travel, LaMesa, Cal., 1972-73, Travel House, San Diego, 1973-74. Republican. Lutheran. Home: 9360 Monona Dr LaMesa CA 92041

JOHNSON, RACHEL RAMIREZ (MRS. THOMAS J. JOHNSON), coll. adminstr.; b. Malakoff, Tex., June 10, 1937; d. Pedro F. Ramirez and Felicitas Brune; B.A., Tex. Christian U., 1959, M.A., 1960; postgrad., U. Wis., 1960-62; m. Thomas J. Johnson, Aug. 27, 1960; 1 son, Thomas Jeffrey. Adminstrv. asst. world extension div. Credit Union Nat. Assn., U. Wis., Madison, 1964-67, internat. program coordinator Office for Fgn. Students and Faculty, 1967-68; dir. career opportunities program Ft. Worth Ind. Sch. Dist., 1970-72; dir. financial aid Tarrant County Jr. Coll., Ft. Worth, 1972—. Mem. Mayor's Com. on the Status of Women, Ft. Worth, 1972-73; cons. Ft. Worth Human Relations Commn., 1972; mem. personal and social adjustment priority study com. United Way, Ft. Worth, 1973—. Bd. dirs. Tarrant County YWCA, 1972—, Wesley Community Center, 1973—; trustee Ft. Worth Mus. of Sci. and History, 1971—, sec. 1972-73; trustee Nat. Mexican Am. Scholarship Fund, 1971-74. Recipient So. fellowship, 1959-62. Mem. Council Adminstrv. Women in Edn., Tex. Assn. Financial Aid Adminstrs., Southwestern Assn. Student Financial Aid Adminstrs., Nat. Assn. Financial Aid Adminstrs., Delta Kappa Gamma. Home: Rural Route 3 Box 14350 Westherford TX 76086 Office: Tarrant County Junior College 5301 Campus Dr Fort Worth TX 76019

JOHNSON, RITA B. (VOLKMAN) (MRS. STUART RICHARD JOHNSON), educator; b. N.Y.C., July 19, 1933; d. William and Anna (Kasten) Blaustein; A.A., U. Cal. at Los Angeles, 1954, B.A., 1957, M.A., 1963, Ed.D., 1966; m. Stuart Richard Johnson, Dec. 7, 1964. Coordinator student teaching U. Cal. at Los Angeles, 1963-66, instr. edn., 1960-66; asso. prof. edn. Cal. State Coll. at Los Angeles, 1966-69; coordinator ednl. improvement Nat. Lab. Higher Edn., Durham, N.C., 1969-71; tng. coordinator, asso. prof. Sch. Medicine, U. N.C. at Chapel Hill, 1971-73; asso. dir. self-instructional materials project Health Scis. Consortium, 1973—. Cons. Group Ten for the 70's, Miami, Fla., 1965-67, Instructional Systems Group, Inc., Long Beach, Cal., 1965-72, Parents Without Partners, Los Angeles, 1963-68, Indio (Cal.) Med. Center, 1963-68. Alumni scholar, 1952-54; Helen Matthewson award, 1955. Mem. Internat. Platform Assn., Am. Edn. Research Assn., Nat. Soc. Programmed Instruction, Am. Assn. Med. Colls., Phi Beta Kappa, Pi Lambda Theta. Author: Instructional Reorganization series, 1969; Developing Individualized Instructional Material, 1970; Humanizing Instruction, 1972; Assuring Learning, 1971. Contbr. to profl. jours. Home: 3711 Cambridge Rd Durham NC 27705 Office: Sch Medicine U NC Chapel Hill NC 27514

JOHNSON, RUTH CARTER (MRS. J. LEE JOHNSON III), civic worker; b. Ft. Worth, Oct. 19, 1923; d. Amon Giles and Nenetta (Wiess) Carter; B.A., Sarah Lawrence Coll., 1945; m. J. Lee Johnson III, June 8, 1946; children—Sheila Broderick, J. Lee IV, Karen Carter, Catherine Lehane, Mark Lehane. Pres. Ft. Worth Jr. League, 1954-55, chmn. bd. Amon Carter Mus. Western Art, Ft. Worth, 1961—; pres. Arts Council Greater Ft. Worth, 1963-64; bd. regents U. Tex. at Austin, 1963-69; v.p. internat. council Mus. Modern Art, 1966-72; trustee Nat. Trust Historic Preservation, 1968—; mem. Nat. Council on Arts, 1969-70. Roman Catholic. Home: 1200 Broad Av Ft Worth TX 76107

JOHNSON, RUTH ELAINE, librarian; b. Cleve., Jan. 30, 1935; d. Carl Robert and Ruth Mildred (Bergner) Johnson; A.B. cum laude, Western Reserve U., 1958, M.S., 1959. Head librarian Anchorage Community Coll., 1965-69; sr. cataloger in charge serials Cleve. State U., 1969-71; librarian Borromeo Coll., Wickliffe, O., 1972—. Mem. Beta Phi Mu. Club: Newcomers (sec. 1973—) (Cleve.). Home: 29055 Weber Av Wickliffe OH 44092 Office: 28700 Euclid Av Wickliffe OH 44092

JOHNSON, RUTH LYNN (MRS. WALTER F. JOHNSON), civic worker; b. Salt Lake City, May 14, 1900; d. William Penn and Lily Emma Anna (Duke) Lynn; grad. high sch.; m. Walter F. Johnson, June 18, 1921; children—Walter L., Jacquelynn Ruth (Mrs. Hugh Kyle), Scott Stewart. Chpt. chmn. North Bay March of Dimes, 1961—. Recipient certificate of appreciation A.R.C., 1941-45, certificate of recognition March of Dimes, 1957, capt. wings Ground Observers Corps, 1936, citation San Anselmo C. of C., 1965, Luther Gulich award Nat. Camp Fire Girls, 1947, trophies State of Cal. chpt. 8 and 40, 1958, and 1959, award merit A.R.C, 1951, award of accomplishment Cancer Soc., 1956, medal and citation Am. Heart Assn., 1961, sterling silver bracelet and charms March of Dimes, 1968, 2 plaques March of Dimes, 1965, sterling silver bowl, March of Dimes, 1964, sterling silver tray, March of Dimes, 1967, citation, silver medal Am. Legion Aux. Mem. Nat. Found. March of Dimes, Am. Legion Aux., 8 and 40. Republican. Home: 200 Montura Way Novato CA 94947

JOHNSON, SALLY THOMPSON (MRS. ROBERT JOHNSON), banker; b. Clanton, Ala., Oct. 26, 1912; d. b. Dudley and Elizabeth G. (Goodgame) Thompson; student U. Ala., 1965, 67, Samford U., 1971; m. Robert Johnson, June 18, 1938; 1 son, Jay Robert. With First Nat. Bank, Montgomery, Ala., 1942-46; teller Birmingham (Ala.) Trust Nat. Bank, 1952-53, supt. installment loans, 1953-60, asst. cashier 1960-65, asst. v.p. 1965-72, mgr. proof and transit dept. 1967—, v.p., 1972—. Active Nixon for President campaign, 1968. Mem. Birmingham Mgmt. Assn., Am. Inst. Banking, Bus. and Profl. Women Club. (pres. 1972). Club: Quota of Birmingham (pres. 1971, 72), Nat. Assn. Bank Women. Baptist (tchr. sunday sch. 1942-46). Home: 3221 D Av S Birmingham AL 35208 Office: 112-118 N 20th St Birmingham AL 35290

JOHNSON, SELINA TETZLAFF, museologist, historian; b. N.Y.C., Sept. 7, 1906; d. John Victor and Augusta Bertha (Seidel) Tetzlaff; A.B. cum laude, Hunter Coll., 1925; postgrad. Harvard, 1926, Columbia, 1927; M.S. in Edn., Coll. City N.Y., 1954; Ph.D. in Museology, N.Y. U., 1962; m. H. Herbert Johnson, June 1, 1927 (dec.); children—Jacqueline (Mrs. Donald J. Horvath), Frank Wheeler. Instr. biology and comparative anatomy Hunter Coll., N.Y.C., 1925-26, Coll. City N.Y., 1926-32, N.Y. U., 1931-32. Chmn. Bergen County (N.J.) Cultural and Heritage Commn., 1972—; commr. Girl Scouts Am., 1949-51; founder, pres. Conservation Council N.J., 1953-56; chmn. cultural events Bergen Mall, 1957-68; cons. Hall History County, 1968—. Founding dir., trustee Youth Mus. Leonia (N.J.), 1950-56; co-dir. Nantucket Nat. Sci. Mus., 1959-65; bd. trustees Jersey Blues Armory Mus.; founding trustee North Jersey Opera Theatre, 1969—; founder, pres. Bergen Community Mus., 1956-70, trustee, 1970—. Mem. Nantucket Hist. Assn. (field archeologist 1973—), Leonia Home and Sch. Assn. (pres. 1943-47), English Neighborhood Hist. Soc. (charter trustee 1959—), Palisades Nature Assn. (dir. 1973—), Caduceus Soc. (hon.), Maria Mitchell Assn., N.J. State Fedn. Women's Clubs (recipient Silver Orchid award 1951), Mus. Council N.J. (chmn. standards com. 1965-67), Leonia Women's Club (chmn. art, garden and youth conservation depts. 1940-70), N.Y. Acad. Scis. (life), Nat. Hist. Soc. (founding asso.), Maria Mitchell Assn. (hon.), N.J. Cultural Council, Nat. Trust Historic Preservation, Phi Beta Kappa. Illustrator: Classification of Insects; Adventures With Living Things; Angina Pectoris; Hunt for the Mastodon. Author: Creating A Community Museum, 1954; Museums for Youth in the United States: Their Origins, Development and Cultural Contributions, 1962. Editor: Greater Light on Nantucket, 1973. Home: 24 Hawthorne Terrace Leonia NJ 07605

JOHNSON, SHIRLEY ANN, educator; b. Macon, Miss., Jan. 3, 1947; d. Albert Leroy and Ardell (Moore) Johnson; B.A. magna cum laude, Dillard U., 1968; M.Ed., Loyola U., Chgo., 1974. Clinic coordinator U. Chgo., 1968-69; tchr. Ill. State Pediatric Inst., Chgo., 1969—. Recipient Lucille E. Young award New Orleans chpt. Dillard U. Alumni Assn., 1966. Mem. Am. Assn. Mental Deficiency, Council for Exceptional Children, Dillard U. Alumni (Chgo. v.p. 1973-74), Alpha Kappa Alpha, Alpha Kappa Mu. Home: 3041 S Michigan Av Apt 304 Chicago IL 60616 Office: 1640 W Roosevelt Rd Chicago IL 60608

JOHNSON, SHIRLEY ZAISS, lawyer; b. Burlington, Ia., Mar. 6, 1940; d. Arthur Frank and Helen Martha (Nelson) Zaiss; B.A. summa cum laude (Falk Found. fellow 1961), U. Ia., 1962; J.D., U. Mich., 1965. Admitted to Cal. bar, 1966; trial atty. antitrust div. U.S. Dept. Justice, San Francisco, 1965-72; counsel antitrust subcom. U.S. Senate, Washington, 1973—. Bd. dirs. Inst. Criminal Justice, 1971-72. Mem. Am. (chmn. com. on prison reform 1971-72), San Francisco bar assns., State Bar Cal., Order of the Coif, Phi Beta Kappa. Home: 1608 33d St NW Washington DC 20007 Office: 203 Senate Annex Washington DC 20007

JOHNSON, SUE STORER (MRS. DONALD C. JOHNSON), operations research exec.; b. Indpls., Feb. 2, 1935; d. Horace Elbert and Billie Mae (Kreider) Storer; B.S., Purdue U., 1956; m. John C. Jamison, June 2, 1956 (div. Dec. 1963); m. 2d, Donald C. Johnson, Jan. 1964; children—Susan Storer, Anne Lucille, Alice Anne. Research engr. Convair div. Gen. Dynamics, San Diego, 1957-59; profl. staff mem. Arthur D. Little, Inc., Cambridge, Mass., 1960-63; research sect. head Sperry Gyroscope Co., Great Neck, N.Y., 1963-64; cons. Airborne Instruments Lab., Deer Park, N.Y., 1965-66; cons. Sci. and Tech. Task Force, Pres.'s Commn. on Law Enforcement and Adminstrn. of Justice, Washington, 1966-67; cons. Franklin Inst. Research Labs., Phila., 1968—; pres. Brookville (N.Y.) Systems Co., Inc., 1969—. Cons. U.S. Dept. Justice, 1969—, N.Y.C. Police Dept., 1971—, N.Y. State Jud. Conf., 1973—. Mem. Operations Research Soc. Am., Am. Judicature Soc., Am. Acad. Polit. and Social Sci., Transp. Assn. Am., Mortar Bd., Theta Delta Phi, Kappa Kappa Gamma. Republican. Episcopalian. Patentee in field. Home: 91 McCouns Lane Old Brookville NY 11545

JOHNSON, SUSAN BUCHWALD, state ofcl., educator; b. Gulfport, Miss., Dec. 17, 1947; d. Joseph Maurice and Maxine Odney (Mathisen) Buchwald; B.S., Memphis State U., 1969, M.S., 1973; m. Richard Carl Johnson, Dec. 19, 1970. Tchr., Oakhaven High Sch., Memphis, 1969-70, Hamilton High Sch., Memphis, 1970-72; faculty Christian Bros. Coll., Memphis, 1972-74, chmn. women's phys. edn. dept., 1972-74; coordinator elementary phys. edn. N.C. State Dept. Edn., 1974—. Traveling clinician, cons. Pres.'s Council on Phys. Fitness and Sports, 1970. Mem. A.A.H.P.E.R., Nat., So. assns. phys. edn. for coll. women. Office: State Dept Edn Raleigh NC

JOHNSON, VERNA CORINNE, ednl. adminstr.; b. Wakefield, Mass., May 22, 1920; d. Axel E. and Alfreda G. Johnson; S.B., Simmons Coll., 1940; A.M. (hon.), Harvard, 1971. Sec. to dean Faculty Arts and Scis., Harvard, 1940-56, adminstrv. asst. Office of Dean Faculty of Arts and Scis., 1956—. Home: 215 Massachusetts Av Arlington MA 02174 Office: 5 University Hall Harvard University Cambridge MA 02138

JOHNSON, VIRGINIA E. (MRS. WILLIAM H. MASTERS), psychologist; b. Springfield, Mo., Feb. 11, 1925; d. Hershel and Edna (Evans) Eshelman; student music Drury Coll., Springfield, 1940-42, U. Mo., 1944-47; Washington U., St. Louis, 1964; m. George Johnson, June 13, 1950 (div. Sept. 1956); children—Scott Forstall, Lisa Evans; m. 2d, William H. Masters, Jan. 7, 1971. With St. Louis Daily Record, 1947-50, radio sta. KMOX, St. Louis, 1950-51; with div. reproductive biology, dept. obstetrics and gynecology Washington U. Sch. Medicine, 1957-63, research instr., 1962-64; research asso. Reproductive Biology Research Found., St. Louis, 1964-69, asst. dir., 1969-73, co-dir., 1973—. Bd. dirs. Sex. Information and Edn. Council U.S.; adv. bd. Homosexual Community Counseling Center. Fellow Soc. Sci. Study Sex, Soc. Study Reproduction; mem. Internat. Soc. for Research in Biology of Reprodn., A.A.A.S., Authors Guild, Internat. Platform Assn., Eastern Mo. Psychiat. Soc. (hon.). Episcopalian. Author: (with Dr. William H. Masters) Human Sexual Response, 1966, Human Sexual Inadequacy, 1970. Home: 2221 S Warson Rd St Louis MO 63124 Office: 4910 Forest Park St Louis MO 63108

JOHNSON, VIVIAN ANNABELLE, physicist, educator; b. Portland, Ore., July 1, 1912; d. Albert Godfrey and Ada (Stanley) Johnson; B.A., Reed Coll., 1932; M.S., Purdue U., 1934, Ph.D., 1937. Grad. asst. Purdue U., Lafayette, Ind., 1932-37, instr. physics, 1937-44, asst. prof., 1944-47, asso. prof., 1947-56, prof., 1956—, asst. head dept. physics, 1973—. Fellow Am. Phys. Soc.; mem. A.A.A.S., Am. Assn. Physics Tchrs., Sigma Xi, Sigma Pi Sigma. Author: Karl Lark-Horovitz, Pioneer in Solid State Physics, 1969. Editor: Methods of Experimental Physics, Vols. 6A, 6B, 1959. Contbr. numerous articles on solid state physics, elementary semiconductors and thermoelectricity to profl. jours. Home: 1100 Hillcrest Rd West Lafayette IN 47906 Office: Dept Physics Purdue U Lafayette IN 47907

JOHNSON, VIVIAN KATHLEEN, hosp. adminstr.; b. nr. Helena, Mont.; d. George and Maximilan (Barron) Johnson; B.A., U. So. Cal., 1948. Youth dir. Salvation Army, Wenatchee, Wash., 1934-38, Gt. Falls, Mont., 1938-39, Aberdeen, Wash., 1940-41; program dir. White Shield Home, 1949-50; asst. adminstr. Oakland Booth Meml. Home and Hosp., 1950; adminstr. Door of Hope Home, San Diego, 1950-56, Booth Meml. Home and Hosp., Los Angeles, 1956—. Mem. Salvation Army Nat. Commn. on Women's and Children's Services, 1955—, womens and childrens social service sec. Western ty., 1967—. Mem. Cal. Assn. Health and Welfare (mem. bd.), Acad. Certified Social Workers, Nat. Assn. Social Workers. Clubs: Commonwealth of Cal., Soroptimist (mem. bd. 1963-64, alternate del. 1965). Address: 310 Arballo Dr 4G San Francisco CA 94132

JOHNSTON, SISTER ANDREA, educator; b. Mpls., Mar. 13, 1921; d. Charles R. and Susan E. (Berres) Johnston; B.A., St. Mary Coll., 1948; M.S., Cath. U. Am., 1952, Ph.D., 1954. Joined Sisters of Charity of Leavenworth, 1942; head math. dept. St. Mary Coll., Leavenworth, Kan., 1954—, prof., 1968—; instr. math Kan. State Penitentiary, part-time, 1969—. Address: St Mary Coll Leavenworth KS 66048

JOHNSTON, BARBARA, physician; b. Bklyn., Nov. 27, 1921; d. John Wesley and Blanche (Stoney) Johnston; B.A., William Smith Coll., 1943; M.D., N.Y.U., 1951; D.Sc., Hobart Coll., 1967. Intern, resident, fellow N.Y.U. Post Grad. Med. Sch., 1951-54, instr. medicine, 1953-54, asst. prof., 1954-60, dir. cancer research lab., 1954-60; dir. cancer cytogenetic lab. St. Luke Hosp. Women's Div., N.Y.C., 1960-69; chief med. oncology service St. Vincents Hosp., 1969—. Fellow Nat. Bd. Med. Examiners, Am. Coll. Angiology, A.C.P.; mem. Harvey Soc., Am. Soc. Clin. Oncology, N.Y. Cancer Soc., A.A.A.S., Am. Soc. Human Genetics, Am. Soc. Cytology, Am. Assn. U. Women, A.M.A., N.Y. State, N.Y. County med socs., World Med. Assn., Royal Soc. Medicine, Am. Assn. U. Profs. Home: 10 Lenox Rd Rockville Centre NY 11570 Office: 142 E 16th St New York City NY 10003

JOHNSTON, CHARLOTTE MARIE (MRS. HOWARD F. JOHNSTON), city clk.; b. Port Edwards, Wis., Nov. 13, 1919; d. Carl Albert and Iva Blon (Lewis) Enerson; grad. high sch.; m. Howard F. Johnston, Sept. 3, 1939; children—Marie B. (Mrs. C. Larry Stapleton), Jack D. Sec., A.F. Billmeyer & Son, architects and builders, Wisconsin Rapids, Wis., 1937-42; cashier J.C. Penney Co., 1941; bookkeeper Prodn. Credit Assn., 1941; bookkeeper, typist C.E. Boles Ins./Abstract Agy., 1942-43; bookkeeper Consol. Water Power & Paper Co., 1943-44; receptionist, personnel, sec. U.S. Civil Service, Army Air Force Hdqrs., Amarillo, Tex., Las Vegas, Nev., Gulfport, Miss., Tampa, Fla., 1944-46; bookkeeper Howard's Tobacco & Candy Subjobbing, Wisconsin Rapids, 1946-52; escrow sec. 1st Nat. Bank, Orange, Cal., 1957-58; bookkeeper C.N. Jensen, C.P.A., 1960-63; steno-clk., City of Orange, 1963-68; dep. city clk., Orange, 1968-72, city clk., elections clk., 1972—; bookkeeper Howards Barber Shop, 1963—. Leader, Girl Scouts Am., Boy Scouts Am., 1955-60; Sunshine chmn., sec., program chmn., council auditor, treas. elementary, jr. high, sr. high sch. level P.T.A., 1951-66; hon. life mem. Palmyra Elementary Sch. P.T.A., Orange, 1960—. Mem. Cal., So. Cal. city clks. assns., Internat. Inst. Municipal Clks., Cal. Assn. Local Elected Ofcls., Womens Aux. Am. Master Barber and Beauticians, Orange C. of C. Methodist (ch. youth adviser). Club: Soroptimist (Orange). Office: 300 E Chapman Av Orange CA 92666

JOHNSTON, DOLORES MAE MASCIK (MRS. ROBERT EDGAR JOHNSTON), clubwoman; b. Conneaut, O., May 26, 1927; d. Michael Morris and Roberta Mary (Jacobs) Mascik; B.S., Ohio State U., 1949; m. Robert Edgar Johnston, Mar. 19, 1950; children—Kirk, Christine, Mark. Researcher, hematology Ohio State U., Columbus, 1949-54; med. technologist Youngstown (O.) Hosp. Assn., 1954-55, Eli Lilly Clin. Research Labs., Indpls., 1955-57, Green Bay, Wis., 1958-60. Mem. Green Bay Community Chorus, 1966-70, Bach Choir of Green Bay, 1970—; pack officer Boy Scouts Am., 1970-71; co-chmn. A.R.C. Blood Bank, 1970-72, mem. Lakeland chpt. steering com., 1974—; vol. worker Mobile Meals, 1971—. Mem. Brown County Republican Women's Club, 1969—. Bd. dirs. Wis. Polit. Action Com., 1972-73. Recipient Brown County Med. Aux. outstanding mem. award, 1973-74. Mem. Woman's Aux. State Med. Soc. Wis. (pres. 1973-74), A.M.A. Aux. (N.C. regional family council 1974-75), Aesculapian Soc. (charter), P.E.O. (chpt. treas. 1970-72), Alpha Lambda Delta, Alpha Chi Omega. Lutheran. Mem. Order Eastern Star. Clubs: Federated Women's, Junior Women's. Home: 3285 Waubenoor Dr Green Bay WI 54301

JOHNSTON, ELIZABETH, physician; b. Bristol, Va., Jan. 17, 1917; d. William Henry and Eva (Deal) Johnston; student Berea Coll., 1949-52, U. Tenn., 1952; M.D., U. Tenn., 1955; m. David Mililani Bray, Nov. 17, 1956 (div. Apr. 1959). Intern, Queen's Hosp., Honolulu, 1955-56; practice medicine, Honolulu, 1956-58, El Sobrante, Cal., 1961—; resident gen. surgery Kaiser Found. Hosp., San Francisco, 1958-61; active staff Brookside Hosp., San Pablo, Cal., Richmond (Cal.) Hosp., Doctor's Hosp., Pinole, Cal. Sec. bd. dirs. Contra Costa Workshop, 1967-73. Mem. Am. Acad. Family Physicians, Am., Cal., Alameda-Contra Costa County med. assn., Am. Soc. Hypnosis, Am. Soc. for Acupuncture Research, El Sobrante Bus. and Profl. Women's Club, El Sobrante C. of C., Berea Coll. Alumni Assn., Tenn. Alumni Assn. Republican. Methodist. Home: 5929 Harbor View Av Richmond CA 94806 Office: 4450 San Pablo Dam Rd El Sobrante CA 94803

JOHNSTON, EMMA GRACE, real estate broker; b. Plainview, Ark., Jan. 26, 1920; d. Birk Jefferson and Alice Damon (Walker) Ward; student Anthony Real Estate Sch., 1968, San Jose State Coll., 1969, Modesto Jr. Coll., 1971-73; m. Victor Allen Johnston, Mar. 16, 1940; children—Doyle W., Rita La June (Mrs. Rodney D. Grove), Ferrel D. Broker, Johnston Real Estate, Turlock, Cal., 1962—. Sec., Turlock Bd. Realtors, 1973, also com. mem. for budget and finance chmn.; mem. com. for polit. affairs and legis. Turlock Real Estate Bd., 1973. Mem. entertainment com. Hilmar (Cal.) Sr. Citizens. Mem. Turlock C. of C., Home Builders Assn. Central Cal. Rebekah Lodge. Club: Hilmar Over 50. Home: 2213 Briar Rd Turlock CA 95380 Office: 223 5th St Turlock CA 95380

JOHNSTON, HELEN, advt. agy. exec.; b. N.Y.C., Sept. 17, 1934; d. Dominick and Bridget (Carroll) Johnston; B.A., Hunter Coll., 1962. With Grey Advt., Inc., N.Y.C., 1957—, v.p., 1970—. Mem. Agy. Media Research Council, Radio TV Research Council (pres. elect 1973-74). Office: 777 3d Av New York City NY 10017

JOHNSTON, HELEN ELIZABETH HUGHES, physician; b. Eston, Sask., Can.; d. Thomas John and Mary Lillian (Smith) Johnston; came to U.S. 1957, naturalized, 1969; B.A. certificate in medicine, U. Sask., 1944; M.D., U. Toronto, 1946; m. John Alder Hunter, Mar. 22, 1947 (div. May 1949). Intern Vancouver (B.C.) Gen. Hosp., 1946-47, resident, 1951-52, 54-55; resident St. Paul's Hosp., Vancouver, 1947-49, U. Ore., 1949, Royal Jubilee Hosp., Victoria, 1951, B.C. Cancer Inst., 1956; Vanderveer fellow, teaching fellow Banting Inst., Toronto, Ont., 1952-53; instr. U. B.C., 1955-57; asso. pathologist New Westminster, B.C., Can., 1956-57, Meml. Hosp., Johnstown, Pa., 1957-58, St. Johns Hosp. and Ohio Valley Hosp., Pitts., 1958-65; dir. pathology and clin. labs. Passavant Hosp. and North Hills Passavant Hosp., Pitts., 1961—. Diplomate Am. Bd. Pathology. Mem. A.M.A., Pa., Allegheny County med. socs., Coll. Am. Pathologists, Pa., Pitts. pathol. socs., Am. Soc. Clin. Pathologists, Am., Pa. blood bank socs., Am. Assn. Clin. Scientists, Vancouver Br. Coll. Physicians and Surgeons Can. Club: Oakmont Country. Home: Chatham Center Apt Tower Pittsburgh PA 15219 Office: North Hills Passavant Hosp 9100 Babcock Blvd Pittsburgh PA 15237

JOHNSTON, HELEN EWING (MRS. DOUGLAS ANDREWS JOHNSTON), clubwoman, civic worker; b. Paotingfu, China, Feb. 28, 1895; d. George Henry and Sarah (Porter) Ewing; student Wellesley Coll., 1914-15; grad. Pratt Inst., Sch. Kindergarten Tng., 1917; summer study Columbia; m. Douglas Andrews Johnston, June 10, 1922; children—David Endicott, Richard Ewing. Kindergarten dir., Franklin, N.J., Hagerstown, Md., Glen Cove, N.Y., 1917-22. Pres. Coll. Club New Britain, 1924-26; dir. New Britain YWCA, 1923-29; organizer, pres. New Britain Council Internat. Relations, 1931-33; pres. Conn. Council Internat. Relations, 1933-34; registrar D.A.R., New Britain, 1933-36; dir. Newington Red Cross bd., 1945-47; mem. nat. com. Community Relations Girl Scouts U.S.A., 1950-60; mem. women's planning com. Japan Internat. Christian U. Found., 1958—. Rec. sec. Woman's Club of New Britain, 1928-31, v.p., 1931-33, pres., 1945-47; pres. Woman's Club of Newington, 1942-44; chmn. various depts. Conn. Fedn. Women's Clubs, 1930-38, rec. sec., 1938-41, dir., parliamentarian, 1941-43, chmn. dept. legislation, 1943-45, editor Conn. Clubwoman, 1945-51, 3d v.p., 1947-49; 1st v.p., 1949-51, pres., 1951-53; mem. bd. Gen. Fedn. Women's Clubs, 1951-53, chmn. youth div., 1956-58, editor News Bull of it's Council Internat. Clubs, 1960-64, chmn. Internat. Clubs, 1964-66, international hostess, 1966—; v.p. New Eng. Conf. State Fedns., 1955-57. Mem. New Britain Gen. Hosp. Aux., Conn. Mental Health Assn., Planned Parenthood Conn., Nat. Assn. Parliamentarians (Conn. chmn. 1951-57, 68-71, mem. finance com. 1959-65, vice chmn. 1960-64). Republicans. Conglist. Clubs: Hartford Wellesley, Newington Garden, Travelers' Century. World traveller and lectr. Co-author: World Travels with the Johnstons, 1949-73. Home: 31 Frederick St Newington CT 06111

JOHNSTON, JANE, broadcasting exec.; b. Anderson, Ind., 1922; d. George and Irene (Gustin) Johnston; student U. Louisville, 1939-41. With WAVE radio, Louisville, 1939-42; performer WDAY Radio-TV, 1954-60, various TV stas., Mpls., 1960-63; dir. women's activities KSTP Radio-TV, Mpls., 1963—. Author: Scentuous Cookery, 1971. Home: 1300 Mt Curve Av Minneapolis MN 55403 Office: 3415 University Av Minneapolis MN 55414*

JOHNSTON, JANET JOAN, music tchr., polit. party exec.; b. Woodland, Cal., Aug. 25, 1939; d. Henry Harold and Margaret Grace (Chulick) Johnston; grad. Am. River Coll., 1960. Pvt. tchr. accordion and piano, composer, performer, 1958—. Leader, 4-H Clubs, 1969-72. Vice-pres. Winters Republican Women Federated, 1968; asso. mem. Rep. Central Com., Yolo County, Cal., 1969-71, regular mem., 1971—, treas., 1971, vice-chmn., 1972; Yolo County campaign chmn. for re-election of Ivy Baker Priest, Cal. State Treas., 1970; asso. mem. Rep. State Central Com. of Cal., 1971-72; mem. Cal. Delegation to Rep. Nat. Conv., 1972; Rep. Nat. Committeewoman from Cal., 1972—; co-chmn. Rep. Nat. Com., 1973—; mem. Rep. Coordinating Com., 1973—. Mem. Winters Dist. C. of C. (pres. 1967, mgr. 1968-70), Cal. Farm Bur. Fedn., Cal. Fedn. Womens Clubs, Yolo County C. of C. (dir.), Native Daus. of Golden West, Internat. Arabian Horse Assn., Cal. Arts Soc.; life mem. Internat. Order of Rainbow for Girls. Presbyn. Club: Winters Fortnightly. Patentee emergency warning system for automobiles, 1967. Home: Winters CA 95694

JOHNSTON, KATHERINE WALLECK, newspaper editor; b. Ganado, Tex., June 23, 1933; d. Joe and Helen (Scheel) Walleck; grad. high sch.; div.; children—Brenda Kay, Glen Robert. Editor, Ganado Tribune, 1954—. Pres. Jackson County Heart div. Tex. Heart Assn., 1966-73. Bd. dirs. Jackson County Hist. Mus., Edna, Tex., 1967-69. Home: 312 S 2d St Ganado TX 77962 Office: 315 W Putnam St Ganado TX 77962

JOHNSTON, LILLIAN BEATRICE (MRS. CHARLES L. JOHNSTON), ednl. cons.; b. Appleton, Minn.; d. Michael and Elizabeth (Birkbeck) Spinner; A.B., Colo. State Tchrs. Coll., 1930; M.A., U. Ariz., 1936; D.Ed., U. So. Cal., 1947; postgrad. extension classes Ariz. State U., 1954-63; m. Charles L. Johnston; 1 son, Charles L. Tchr., Gadsen, Ariz., 1930-38, prin., 1938-48, state dir. elementary edn., State Ariz., Phoenix, 1948-51, asst. state sch. supt. pub. instrn., 1951-55, state dir. secondary edn., 1957-59; dir. spl. edn. Maricopa County Schs., Phoenix, 1959-63; ednl.-guidance cons., Phoenix, 1964-65. Instr. for tchrs. learning Laubach method teaching adult illiterates, 1969—. Mem. aux. Hope Manor, 1969—; bd. dirs. Valley Sun Sch. for Retarded Children, 1947-65; bd. dirs. Alexander's Home for Girls, mem. adv. bd. 1970—; 1st v.p. bd. dirs. Ariz. Mus., 1971—, program chmn. ednl. series, 1972; mem. Girls' Ranch. Mem. N.E.A. (state dir. rural edn. 1945-55, council exceptional children 1950-64, life mem:) Ariz. Reading Assn. (dir. 1958-64), Maricopa County Council Retarded Children, Internat. Reading Assn. (state orgn. chmn. 1959-61), Am. Assn. U. Women, Nat. Wildlife Fedn. (asso.), Ariz. Zool. Soc., Am. Legion Aux., Delta Kappa Gamma (chpt. pres. 1946-47). Mem. Order Eastern Star (worthy matron 1939); Rebekah. Clubs: Business and Profl. Women of Phoenix (pres. 1961-62, rep. inter-club council 1962-64, 70, 71, chmn.-fellowship 1963), Soroptimist, Phoenix Writer's (pres. 1965-66). Contbr articles profl. jours. Home: 538 W Vernon Av Phoenix AZ 85003

JOHNSTON, MARGARET MIMS, educator, journalist; b. Chester, S.C., Oct. 3, 1933; d. John K. and Anna Edith (Mims) Johnston; A.A., Mars Hill Coll., 1953; B.A. magna cum laude, Furman U., 1955; M.A. in Journalism, Syracuse U., 1965, postgrad., 1965—. Editorial asst. America's Textile Reporter, Greenville, S.C., 1959, So. Baptist Fgn. Mission Bd., Richmond, Va., 1955-59, 60-64, 65, 66; tchr. Goochland County (Va.) pub. schs., 1966-67, Henrico County (Va.) pub. schs., 1967-68; instr. pub. relations U. Ga., Athens, 1968—, also coordinator Ga. Scholastic Press Assn., 1969—. Editor newsletter Athens-Clarke County Mental Health Assn., Athens, Ga., 1969-72, dir., 1969-72. Mem. Assn. for Edn. in Journalism, Women in Communications, Journalism Edn. Assn., Ga. Assn. Journalism Dirs. (treas. 1970—), Pub. Relations Soc. Am. (asso.). So. Baptist. Home: 235 Sycamore Dr Apt K-1 Athens GA 30601 Office: School of Journalism University of Georgia Athens GA 30602

JOHNSTON, MARGUERITE (MRS. CHARLES WYNN BARNES), journalist, author, lectr.; b. Birmingham, Ala., Aug. 7, 1917; d. Robert C. and Marguerite (Spradling) Johnston; A.B., Birmingham-So. Coll., 1938; m. Charles Wynn Barnes, Aug. 31, 1946; children—Susan, Patricia, Steven, Polly. Reporter, Birmingham News, 1939-44; Washington corr. Birmingham News, Birmingham Age-Herald and London Daily Mirror, 1945-46; columnist Houston Post, 1947-69, fgn. news editor, mem. editorial bd., 1969—, asso. editor editorial page, 1972—. Lectr., 1947—; instr. creative writing U. Houston, 1946-47, lectr. feature writing, 1965-66. Del. Asian-Am. Women Journalists Conf., Honolulu, 1965, 1st World Conf. Women Journalists, Mexico City, 1969. Bd. dirs. Tex. Bill of Rights Found., 1962-64; mem. bd. Planned Parenthood, 1953-55; bd. Homes St. Mark, 1962-63. Recipient Theta Sigma Phi Headliner award, 1954; 1st ann. award of merit Houston Com. Alcoholism, 1956; Am. Soc. Safety Engrs. certificate of merit Gulf Coast chpt., 1960; Agnese Carter Nelms award Planned Parenthood, 1968; Sch. Bell award Tex. State Tchrs. Assn., 1974. Mem. Mortar Bd., Phi Beta Kappa, Pi Beta Phi, Theta Sigma Phi (hon.). Club: Houston Press. Author: Public Manners, 1957; A Happy Worldly Abode, 1964. Home: 5319 Cherokee St Houston TX 77005 also Box 4 Round Top TX 78954 Office: Houston Post Houston TX 77001

JOHNSTON, MARIA, real estate broker; b. Rotterdam, Netherlands, May 22, 1913; d. Reinier Martinus and Elizabeth (Helders) Smulders; degree bus. adminstrn. Pont's Coll., Rotterdam, 1931; postgrad. Kaiser's Coll., 1951, real estate, Lumbleau Sch. Real Estate, 1967; m. William Johnston, May 10, 1959 (dec. July 1962). Came to U.S., 1949, naturalized, 1955. Mgr. accounting dept. Argo Electric Supply Co., Vernon, Cal., 1952-65; real estate sales person Don K. Nakajima, Gardena, Cal., 1965-68; real estate broker Imperial Realty, Torrance, Cal., 1968—. Mem. Torrance-Lomita, Gardena (sec. women's council 1967-68), bds. realtors. Mem. Order Eastern Star, White Shrine Jerusalem. Clubs: Brittania (Inglewood, Cal.); Avio (Buena Park, Cal.); South Bay Internat. (Hermosa Beach, Cal.). Office: 18010 Crenshaw Blvd Torrance CA 90504

JOHNSTON, MARY E(LIZABETH), journalist; b. Austin, Tex., July 24; d. Harry M. and Winifred (Graham) Johnston; B.A., Rice U., 1941. Reporter Houston Post, 1942-49; Houston corr. Christian Sci. Monitor, 1947-49; researcher Time mag. 1949-51; researcher Fortune mag., 1951-52; asst. chief of research, 1952-55, chief of research, 1955, mem. bd. editors, 1956—. Mem. council Rice U. Fund; mem. exec. bd. Rice U. Alumni Assn., 1970-73. Home: 249 E 48th St New York City NY 10017 Office: Time Inc Rockfeller Center New York City NY 10020

JOHNSTON, MYRNA MORNINGSTAR (MRS. WARREN ERIC JOHNSTON), foods cons.; b. Des Moines; d. Edward R. and Ella (Kimball) Morningstar; B.S., Drake U., 1923; student U. Chgo., 1921; m. Warren Eric Johnston, Mar. 13, 1926; 1 dau., Joed Elender (Mrs. Roger Steinberg). Foods and equipment editor Better Homes and Gardens, 1937-66, foods cons. 1966—; editorial content published in the Better Homes & Gardens Cook Book, 1940, Jr. Cook Book, 1955, Barbecue Book, 1956, Salad Book, 1958, Meat Cook Book, 1959, Holiday Cook Book, 1959, Famous Foods from Famous Places, 1965. Mem. Des Moines Bd. Edn., 1946-49. Recipient Drake U. Distinguished Service Alumni award, 1959. Mem. Am. Home Econs. Assn., Home Econs. in Bus., Elec. Women's Round Table, P.E.O., Theta Sigma Phi, Delta Phi Delta, Kappa Delta Pi. Clubs: Washington Press, Des Moines Women's. Home: 3450 SW 31st St Des Moines IA 50321 Office: Meredith Pub Co Des Moines IA 50303

JOHNSTON, NELDA YVONNE MARSH (MRS. CLARENCE KNIGHT JOHNSTON), accountant; b. Abilene, Tex., Feb. 8, 1933; d. Virgil P. and Ruby Lee (Mitchell) Marsh; grad. high sch.; m. Clarence Knight Johnston, Aug. 16, 1958; 1 son, Clarence Keith. Accountant, Charles Parker Music Co., Inc., Houston, 1952—, exec. sec., 1961—, also dir. Home: 8157 Wier Dr Houston TX 77017 Office: 5005 Gulf Freewy St Houston TX 77023

JOHNSTON, VERNA RUTH, educator; b. Berwyn, Ill., Apr. 27, 1918; s. John F. and Mabel Jane (Anderson) Johnston; B.S., U. Ill., 1939, M.S., 1941; postgrad. U. Colo., 1941, U. Pacific, 1948, Ariz. State U., 1963. Biology instr. Cerro Gordo (Ill.) High Sch., 1939-42; tchr. sci. Thornton (Ill.) High Sch. and Jr. Coll., 1942-44; field ecologist U. Ill. Ecology Expdns., U.S. and Mexico, 1943-44; tchr. biology Live Oak (Cal.) High Sch., 1944-45; prof. biology and ecology San Joaquin Delta Coll., Stockton, Cal., 1945—. Freelance writer and photographer on conservation subjects in Europe, Hawaii, and U.S., 1959-62. Recipient merit award Cal. Conservation Council, 1961; Nat. Wildlife Fedn. fellow, 1960, NSF fellow, 1963. Mem. No. Cal. Nature Conservancy (chpt. bd. dirs. 1965-69), Nat. Audubon Soc., Wilderness Soc., The Nature Conservancy, Ecol. Soc. Am., Friends of the Earth, Author's Guild, Sierra Club. Democrat. Author: Sierra Nevada, 1970. Contbr. articles, chpts., photographs to various biol. mags. Home: 1812 W Sonoma Av Stockton CA 95204

JOHNSTONE, JEAN LILLIAS, owner floral and gift shop; b. N.Y.C., Mar. 4, 1919; d. Hector and N. Haven (Street) Johnstone; student Am. Banking Inst., 1939-41, N.Y. U., 1944-45, Coll. City of N.Y., 1959-61. Asst. to personnel dir. Bank of N.Y., N.Y.C., 1936-43; asst. personnel supr. Am. Can Co., N.Y.C., 1943-45, sec. to pres., 1952-55, asst. treas., asst. gen. mgr. pub. relations, 1955-60; asst. club dir. A.R.C., MTO, also ETO, 1945-47; asst. to pres. Clinton Foods, Inc., N.Y.C., 1948-51; asst. to pres. Parsons & Whittemore, N.Y.C., 1962-69; owner Thomas Flowers & Gifts, Hoquiam, Wash., 1969—. Mem. Planning Commn. Hoquiam, 1973—. Mem. Pub. Relations Soc. Am., Seraphic Secs. of Am., Am. Overseas Assn., Grays Harbor C. of C. (dir. 1973—), Hoquiam Retail Trade Bd., Bus. and Profl. Women's Club. Episcopalian (vestryman). Home: 2314 N Highland Dr Hoquiam WA 98550 Office: Haven Pauzé Bldg 714 J St Hoquiam WA 98550

JOHNSTONE, LOUISE MOFFIT (MRS. JAMES GEORGE JOHNSTONE), ednl. cons.; b. Morganfield, Ky., May 10, 1921; d. James William and Daisy (Spear) Moffit; B.S., Western Ky. State Coll., 1942; M.S., Purdue U., 1953; m. James George Johnstone, Aug. 24, 1946; 1 dau., Nancy Louise. Home econs. tchr. Taylorsville High Sch., Ky., 1942-44, Morganfield High Sch., 1944-46, Arvada (Colo.) High Sch., 1946-48; adult edn. tchr. home econs. Jefferson High Sch., Lafayette, Ind., 1950-55; home econs. tchr. Dayton (Ind.) High Sch., 1955-56; county supt. schs. Jefferson County, Colo., 1965-67, coordinator Jefferson County Community for Retarded, 1967—. Mem. Nat. Adv. Com. on Handicapped. Bonus mem. Colo. Rep. Central Com., 1967-72; pres. Jefferson County Woman's Rep. Club, 1967-71. Mem. Am. Soc. C.E., Aux. to Profl. Engrs. of Colo. (chmn. 1965-67), Colo. Sch. Mines Faculty Wives, Nat. Assn. Parliamentarians, M.M.S., Republican. Methodist. Home: 6535 W 26th Av Denver CO 80214 Office: 5628 Kendall Ct Arvada CO 80002

JOHNSTONE, ROSE MAMELAK (MRS. DOUGLAS JOHNSTONE), educator; b. Lodz, Poland, May 14, 1928; d. Jacob Shea and Esther (Rotholz) Mamelak; B.Sc., McGill U., 1950, Ph.D., 1953; m. Douglas Johnstone, Aug. 9, 1953; children—Michael, Eric. Nat. Cancer Inst. of Can. fellow Nat. Inst. for Med. Research and Strangeway Research Lab., Cambridge, England, 1954-56; research asso. McGill-Montreal Gen. Hosp. Research Inst., 1956-60; faculty McGill U., Montreal, Que., Can., 1961—, asso. prof. biochemistry, 1967—. Mem. Senate, McGill U., 1970-72. Recipient Nat. Cancer Inst. of Can. grant, 1965-68; Med. Research Council of Can. grant, 1965—. Mem. McGill Assn. U. Tchrs. (treas., membership sec. 1967-70), Biol. Chemists Am., Canadian Soc. Biochemistry, Biochem. Soc. London. Contbr. articles to profl. jours. Home: 4064 Oxford Montreal PQ Canada Office: McGill University Dept Biochemistry 3655 Drummond Montreal PQ Canada

JOKI, JEANNE MARIE BACKSTROM (MRS. LEO JOHN JOKI), equipment co. exec.; b. Butte, Mont., Jan. 16, 1925; d. Leonard Manual and Anne Cecilia (Kinsella) Backstrom; student Butte Bus. Coll., 1945; m. Leo John Joki, Aug. 28, 1949; children—Kristine Ann, Laura Jeanne, Leah Marie, J. Michael, Kathleen Ellen. Accountant, Wilson Motors, Butte, 1947-50, Barclay Motors, Butte, 1950-54; accountant Roberts Rocky Mountain Equipment Co., Butte, 1956-60, office mgr., 1960-64, corporate sec., 1964—; owner J.J.'s Klothes Kloset, Inc., Butte, 1972. Sec., treas. local council Boy Scouts Am., 1970-73. Named sec. of yr. Nat. Secs. Assn., 1971. Mem. Bus. and Profl. Women, Elk Ladies. Democrat. Roman Catholic. Home: 2040 Adams Av Butte MT 59701 Office: 505 Centennial Av Butte MT 59701

JOLLEY, FLORENCE WERNER, educator, composer; b. Kingsburg, Cal., July 11, 1917; d. August and Betty (Akeson) Werner; A.B. in Pub. Sch. Music, Cal. State U. at Fresno, 1939; postgrad. composition and theory Eastman Sch. Music, 1941-42; M.A., U. So. Cal., 1957; m. Truman M. Jolley, Dec. 21, 1940 (div. 1965); children—Truman M., David Clayton, Mark C. Chmn. dept. piano Los Angeles Community Colls., 1962—; asso. prof. music Los Angeles City Coll., 1962—; founder, owner Innovative Music Studies, Santa Monica, Cal., 1972; composer choral works. Mem. A.S.C.A.P., Am. Univ. Composers, Am. Aesthetic Soc., Sigma Alpha Iota. Author: Florence Jolley Piano Method with recorded instrn., 1972; Quick, Easy Ways to Write Your Own Songs (text and rec.). Home: 1122 10th St Santa Monica CA 90403 Office: 855 N Vermont St Los Angeles CA 90029

JOLLEY, JOY BATES (MRS. LEWIS RAY JOLLEY), social worker; b. Grinnell, Ia., June 30, 1924; d. Roy E. end Katherine Belle (Buchanan) B.; student Ia. State U., 1942-44; B.A., State U. Ia., 1947; m. Lewis Ray Jolley, Dec. 10, 1949; 1 dau., Barbara (Mrs. Robert Barnhouse, Jr.). With dept. social services U. Hosp., Iowa City, Ia., 1947-49; social welfare worker County Dept. Social Services, Grinnell, Ia., 1949-50; child welfare worker County Dept. Social Services, Oskaloosa, 1955-69; mental retardation specialist Ia. Dept. Social Services, Des Moines, 1970—. Cons. for establishment Ia. S. Central Mental Health Center, 1959-62, sec. bd. dirs., 1963-66. County organizer Big Buddy System, 1967. Organizer Oskaloosa Child Guidance Council, 1960-61, pres., 1961-64; co-chmn. youth council YW-YMCA, 1966-68; mem. Gov.'s Task Force on Mental Retardation, 1966-67. Bd. dirs. Mahaska County Assn. Retarded Children, 1971—. Mem. Am. Assn. Mental Deficiency, Ia. Welfare Assn., P.E.O., Alpha Xi Delta. Mem. Disciples of Christ (deaconess 1965-68). Clubs: Oskaloosa Women's, Altrusa (Oskaloosa). Home: 464 N 10th St Oskaloosa IA 52577 Office: Bur Mental Retardation Dept Social Services 6th Floor Lucas Bldg Des Moines IA 50319

JONA, MARJORIE HELEN PUGH, county ofcl.; b. Mansfield, O., July 18, 1917; d. Walter C. and Hasel (Kennedy) Pugh; student Richland County Jr. Coll., 1934-35, Mansfield Bus. Coll., 1935-36. div. 1956; 1 son, Robert P. K. Clk., Reese Optical Co., Mansfield, O., 1936-43; sec. P & E. Tile Co., Los Angeles, 1953-54, Hamilton Realty, Mansfield, 1951-52, 55; sales rep. Mid-Ohio Realty, Mansfield, 1955-56; X-ray technologist Mansfield Gen. Hosp., 1956-57, registered X-ray technologist Madison Hosp., Mansfield, 1957-60; with Richland County Welfare Dept., 1960-69, social worker intake dept., food stamp dept., 1967-69; probation officer Domestic Relations div. Richland County Ct. Common Pleas, 1969—. Sec. adv. bd. Richland County Welfare. Treas., Malabar Music Parents Club,

1967-68. Mem. Am. Registry Radiol. Technologists. Methodist. Mem. Order Eastern Star, Rebekah Lodge. Home: 207 S Mulbery St Mansfield OH 44903 Office: Richland County Adminstrn Bldg 50 Park Av E Mansfield OH 44902

JONASON, PAULINE MARIE, art educator; b. N.Y.C., Jan. 26, 1928; d. Mario and Concetta (Ruggio) Barbara; B.A. in Art Edn., Queens Coll., 1948; M.A., Coll. City N.Y., 1950; postgrad. Columbia, 1949, Adelphia U., 1960; m. Charles Ray Jonason, July 8, 1950; children—Raymond Charles, Ruthellen, Randall Paul. Opaquer for Famous Studios, 1944; teenage program dir. Queens YWCA, 1948; tchr. art Hicksville (N.Y.) Jr. High Sch., 1949, Hicksville Elementary Sch., 1955; tchr. art Hicksville Sr. High Sch., 1961—, acting chmn. art dept. Historian Woodlands P.T.A., 1956—. Recipient St. Gaudens medal of art Thomas Jefferson High Sch., 1944. Mem. Nat. Art Edn. Assn., Eastern Arts Assn., N.Y., L.I. art tchrs. assns., Nat. Congress P.T.A., Nassau Agrl. Inst. Home: 978 Little Whaleneck Rd North Merrick NY 11561 Office: Hicksville Sr High Sch Division Av Hicksville NY 11801

JONES, ADRIENNE APPLEWHITE (MRS. RICHARD MORRIS JONES), writer; b. Atlanta, July 28, 1915; d. Arthur Washington and Orieanna (Mason) Applewhite; student pub. schs.; m. Richard Morris Jones, Aug. 18, 1939; children—Gregory Lee, Gwen. Short stores pub. in text book anthologies; speaker at libraries, schs., writers confs. Mem. P.E.N., Cal. Writers Guild, Newport Writers Group, So. Cal. Council on Lit. for Children and Young People, Am. Civil Liberties Union, N.A.A.C.P., So. Christian Leadership Conf. Democrat. Unitarian. Author: Thunderbird Pass, 1952; Where Eagles Fly, 1957, German edit., 1958; Ride The Far Wind, 1964; Wild Voyageur, 1966; Sail Calypso! (U. Cal. at Irving award, 1968), 1968, Danish edit., 1970, Italian, 1972; Another Place, Another Spring (U. Cal. at Irvine award 1972, Notable Book award So. Cal. Council on Lit. for Children and Young People 1972), 1971, Dutch edit., 1972; The Mural Master, 1974; So, Nothing Is Forever, 1974. Address: 24491 Los Serranos Dr Laguna Niguel CA 92677

JONES, ALICE CABLE HANSON (MRS. HOMER JONES), educator; b. Seattle, Nov. 7, 1904; d. Olof and Agatha (Tiegel) Hanson; A.B., U. Wash., 1925, M.A., 1928; Ph.D., U. Chgo., 1968; m. Homer Jones, Apr. 21, 1930; children—Robert Hanson, Richard John, Douglas Coulthurst. Teaching fellow U. Wash., 1927-28; fellow, research asst. dept. econ. U. Chgo., 1928-29, 1932-34; asst. editor Ency. Social Scis., N.Y.C., 1930; researcher, writer, President's Com. on Social Trends, N.Y.C., 1931; economist, asst. chief Cost of Living div. U.S. Bur. Labor Statistics, Washington, 1934-44; economist div. Statis. Standards U.S. Bur. Budget, Washington, 1945-48; sec. com. on nat. accounts Nat. Bur. Econ. Research, Washington, 1957; supervising economist, cons. U.S. Dept. Agr., Washington, 1958-61; lectr. dept. econs. Wash. U., 1963-68, asst. prof., 1968-71, asso. prof., 1971-73, adj. prof., 1973—, prin. investigator Social Sci. Inst., 1969—; adj. prof. dept. econs. Claremont Men's Coll., 1973-74; econ. adviser Bank of Korea, U.S. AID, 1967-68. NSF research grantee, 1969—, Nat. Endowment for Humanities grantee, 1970—. Mem. Am. Econ. Assn., Econ. History Assn., Assn. for Evolutionary Econs., Internat. Assn. for Research in Income and Wealth, Phi Beta Kappa, Omicron Delta Epsilon, Mortar Board, Delta Zeta. Home: 404 Yorkshire Pl Webster Groves MO 63119 Office: Dept Econ Wash U St Louis MO 63130

JONES, ALICE PALACHE (MRS. RUSSELL KENNEDY JONES), banking exec.; b. Cambridge, Mass., Apr. 12, 1907; d. Charles and Helen (Markham) Palache; A.B. cum laude, Bryn Mawr Coll., 1928; m. Russell Kennedy Jones, Dec. 21, 1954. With Fiduciary Trust Co. N.Y., N.Y.C., 1933—, sr. v.p., 1968—. Bd. dirs. Bryn Mawr Coll. Club: Cosmopolitan. Home: Keeler Lane North Salem NY 10560 Office: 2 World Trade Center New York City NY 10048

JONES, ALMA WEST (MRS. ANDREW GRAHAM JONES), banker; b. Johnston County, N.C., Oct. 28, 1923; d. Joseph Franklin and Amelia Frances (Pope) West; diploma Kings' Bus. Coll., 1941; m. Andrew Graham Jones, Apr. 26, 1947; children—Annie Frances (Mrs. Howard Landis Whitley), Andrew Graham, Amelia Claudette. Legal sec., 1941-42; sec. to pres. First-Citizens Bank & Trust Co., Smithfield, N.C., 1947-58, sec. investment dept., 1958, sec., also adminstrv. asst. to pres., v.p., 1958-70, sec., 1970—. Laubach Literacy Tutor, 1973; vol., com. chmn. Contact Teleministry. Adminstr. First-Citizens Found., Inc., Robert P. Holding Found., Inc. Active Girl Scouts U.S. Mem. Bus. Profl. Women's Club (past dist. sec.), Smithfield P.T.A. (exec. bd., 3 yrs.). Democrat. Presbyn. (financial sec., 1964—). Home: 510 S 4th St Smithfield NC 27577 Office: 614 E Market St Smithfield NC 27577

JONES, AMY, artist; b. Buffalo, Apr. 4, 1899; d. Squire and Clara Alberta (Hammond) W.; student Pratt Inst., 1918-20; m. D. Blair Jones, Dec. 19, 1920 (dec. 1955); m. 2d, Owen Phelps Frisbie, May 13, 1961 (dec. 1963); 1 dau., Lucy (Mrs. Berk). Painter, art tchr., lectr., printmaker, sculptor; tchr. Greenwich Art Center, Bedford Art Center; tchr. graphics Westchester Art Workshop, White Plains, N.Y., 1971, Coll. of New Rochelle, 1972; one man shows, Venice, Italy, 1958, 72, 74, N.Y.C., Buffalo, N.Y., Annapolis, Md., La Grange, Ill., Katonah Gallery, N.Y., 1950, 70, Okla. Art Center, 1959, Phila. Art Alliance, 1961, Village Art Center, 1963, New Britain Mus. Am. Art, 1963—, Ruth White Gallery, N.Y.C., 1963, 69, Lycenum Club, Women's Art Assn. Can., 1965, Mus. on St. Croix, U.S. Virgin Islands, 1966, Norfolk (Va.) Mus. Arts and Scis., 1967, Hastings Gallery of Harvey Sch., 1969, Council of the Arts for Westchester, 1970; Byram Hills Sch., 1970, Bankers Trust of N.Y., 1970, Galleria Santo Stefano, Venice, 1972; exhibited in group shows Leicester 1963-64, 65, 66, nat. exhbns. N.A.D., Nat. Gallery, London, Eng., Norfolk Mus. Arts and Scis., 1963, 65, 67; exhibited travelling exhbn., Gallery, Pa. Acad., Balt. Mus. Art, Carnegie Inst., Mus. in Brighton, Eng., Phila. Watercolor Club, 1970-72, Audubon Artists ann., Kendall Galleries, Wellfleet, Mass., Katonah (N.Y.) Gallery, numerous others; invited to London by Royal Soc. Painters in Watercolor, 1962; murals executed for post offices at Winsted, Conn., Painted Post N.Y., Scotia, N.Y.; watercolors in collection of Carville Leprosorium; represented in pvt. collections, also Wharton Sch. of Finance, Briarly Sch. Phila., N.Y. Hosp., New Britain Mus. Am. Art, Hudson River Mus., Rental collection Katonah Gallery, Norfolk (Va.) Mus. Mem. adv. council Village Art Center; dir. Katonah Gallery. Dir. Planned Parenthood Council Mt. Kisco, 1945-46, Mt. Kisco A.R.C., 1951-52; active Mt. Kisco Boys Club. Recipient Fellowship award Buffalo Soc. Artists, 1930; purchase prize Nat. Acad. Design, Ranger Fund, 57; Balt. Watercolor Club, 1940, Hirchberg prize, 1954; watercolor prize Village Art Center, 1951, 59, 60, oil prize, 1954, 57-60; Roaring Brook prize N. Westchester County, 1955; 1st prize watercolor Mahopac Art Assn., 1957; Grumbacher prize Balt. Watercolor Club, 1958; watercolor prize Washington County Mus. Art, Hagerstown, Md., 1959; prizewinner oils, graphics, Village Art Center, 1960, etching, 1961; 1st prize Graphics No. Westchester Artists, 1962; hon. mention for graphics No. Westchester Artists, 1967. Mem. Silvermine Guild Artists, Am. Water Color Soc., Phila. Watercolor Club, Artists Equity, Audubon Artists, Portraits, Inc., Yonkers Art Assn. (bd. dirs. 1972), Leicester Galleries, London, Eng. Episcopalian. Home: Byram Lake Rd Mount Kisco NY 10549

JONES, ANNA BELLE KELSO (MRS. WILLIAM N. JONES), lawyer; b. Mercer, Pa., Feb. 21, 1924; d. George Wesley and Ethel Margaret (Anderson) Kelso; B.S., Grove City Coll., 1945; m. William N. Jones, Oct. 12, 1946; 1 son, James J. Admitted to Pa. bar, 1965; sec. to law firm Stranahan & Stranahan, Mercer, 1945-65, mem. firm, 1965—. Pres. Mercer Community's Brandy Springs Park, 1968—. Home: Rural Delivery 4 Mercer PA 16137 Office: Stranahan Bldg Mercer PA 16137

JONES, ANNE PRIOLEAU, educator; b. Urbana, Ill., Aug. 22, 1911; d. Harry Stuart Vedder and Margaret (Walker) Jones; B.A., U. Ill., 1932, M.A., 1934; postgrad. Sorbonne, Paris, 1932-33, U. Munich (Germany), Columbia. Tchr. French, Knox Sch., Cooperstown, N.Y., 1935-37; from instr. to prof. French, Lawrence U., Appleton, Wis., 1937—; Bergstrom prof. French, 1960—, chmn. modern fgn. lang. dept., 1954-62, chmn. freshman studies, 1948-53, 63-65, chmn. French dept., 1965-68. Fellow Fund for Advancement Edn., 1953-54. Recipient Urhig Found. prize for excellence in teaching, 1963; Ordre des Palmes Academiques French Govt., 1967. Mem. Modern Lang. Assn. Am., Am. Assn. Tchrs. French, Phi Beta Kappa. Author: (with Germaine Bree) Hier et Aujourd'hui, 1958; Andre Malraux: Lectures Choisies, 1965; also profl. articles. Home: 620 N Owaissa St Appleton WI 54911

JONES, ANNIE LOU, banker; b. Adairsville, Ga., Sept. 5, 1919; d. Fred Obsorne and Annie May (Hardeman) Maynor; student Rome (Ga.) Bus. Coll., 1945, Manatee Jr. Coll., 1959-62, 65-69, Bank Adminstrv. Inst. U. Richmond, 1968; certificate Am. Inst. Banking, 1957, 65, Dale Carnegie, 1959; m. Rufus E. Jones, Aug. 27, 1938. Sec., Rome Provision Co., Inc. (Ga.), 1945-51; with Manatee Nat. Bank, Bradenton, Fla., 1951—, asst. cashier, 1961-66, asst. v.p., 1966-72, v.p., 1972-73, v.p., cashier, 1973—. Sec., Bradenton Charitable Solicitation Bd., 1970-72. Mem. Am. Inst. Banking (bd. govs. 1962-65, pres. 1966-67), Manatee County C. of C., Nat. Assn. Bank Women (nat. com. 1970-71, group chmn. 1969-70, Fla. regional v.p. 1973-74, nat. membership com. 1971-72), Data Processing Mgmt. Assn. Democrat. Baptist. Club: Pilot. Home: 3012 17th Av W Bradenton FL 33505 Office: 920 Manatee Av W Bradenton FL 33505

JONES, AVALENE, govt. ofcl.; b. Russell Springs, Ky., Apr. 4, 1934; d. Lewis Wade and Martha Catherine (Roy) Chumbley; student U. Ill., 1961-62; m. James T. Jones, Apr. 8, 1966; children—Steven, Christi, Alan Carmack. Sec., USAF, Chanute AFB, Ill., 1952-66; personal sec. to pres. Miss. Steel Corp., Jackson, 1966; exec. sec. Krueger Metal Products Co., Tupelo, Miss., 1968-70; co-owner Therix, Inc., Tupelo, 1970—; mgmt. asst. Columbus AFB, Miss., 1972—. Capt., mem. state adv. council Civil Air Patrol, 1968—, information officer, 1968-70, adj. composite squadron, 1970-72, adminstrn. officer, 1972. Recipient awards D.A.R., 1952. Sustained Superior Performance award USAF, 1963. Mem. Ch. of Christ. Club: Altrusa (pres. 1971-72). Home: Route 2 Box 186 Tupelo MS 38801 Office: PO Box 1202 Tupelo MS 38801

JONES, B. CORINE, bank exec.; b. Statesboro, Ga., Jan. 28, 1925; d. Mallie C. and Maude (Gay) Jones; grad. high sch. Clk. Western Auto Supply Co., Savannah, Ga., 1943-46; teller Carolina Nat. Bank, Anderson, S.C., 1950-51; with Liberty Nat. Bank & Trust Co., Savannah, 1946-50, 59—, clk., 1959-69, asst. cashier, 1969-72, banking officer, 1972—. Active United Community Services, March of Dimes, Cancer Soc. Mem. Inter City Credit Council (named outstanding credit women 1965, 71), Savannah Credit Womens Club (pres. 1959-60), Ga. Assn. Credit Women (pres. 1970-71), Credit Women Internat., Certified Consumer Credit Exec. Soc., Nat. Assn. Bank Women, Am. Inst. Banking. Home: 3605 E Gate Dr Savannah GA 31404 Office: PO Box 8668 Savannah GA 31402

JONES, BARBARA, pediatric hematologist; b. Salt Lake City, Feb. 8, 1928; d. George Merrell and Helen (Skeen) Jones; A.B., Stanford, 1949; M.D., U. Utah, 1952. Intern, St. Louis Children's Hosp., 1952-53, resident, 1953-55; instr. pediatrics Washington U. Sch. Medicine, St. Louis, 1955-58, asst. prof. pediatrics, 1958-61; asst. prof. W.Va. U. Sch. Medicine, Morgantown, 1961-63, asso. prof., 1963-68, prof., 1968—, asst. chmn. dept., 1970—. Med. cons. Head Start Program, Parkersburg, Fairmont and Clarksburg, W.Va., 1968—. Chmn. campus ministry com. Episcopal Diocese W.Va., 1968-73. Mem. Am. Soc. Hematology, Am. Acad. Pediatrics (chmn. W.Va. 1970—), Am. Cancer Soc. (sec. Monongalia County unity 1966-68), Am. Pediatric Soc., Soc. Pediatrics Research, Am. Assn. Cancer Research, Sigma Xi, Alpha Omega Alpha. Contbr. articles to profl. jours. Home: 667 Bellaire Dr Morgantown WV 26505 Office: WVA U Med Center Morgantown WV 26506

JONES, BARBARA ANN (MRS. MACK H. JONES), educator; b. Oklahoma City, Okla., June 23, 1943; d. Weldon Burnett and Alma (Inglemon) Posey; A.B., U. Okla., 1963; M.A., U. Ill., 1966; Ph.D., Ga. State U., 1972; m. Mack Henry Jones, Apr. 1, 1964; children—Patrice Lumumba, Tayari Acio. Instr. econs. Tex. So. U., 1966-67, Atlanta U., 1968-69; asso. prof., chmn. dept. econs. Clark Coll., Atlanta, 1971—. Recipient Eleanor Roosevelt Research award, 1967; So. fellowships Fund, 1969-71; Ford Found. Dissertation Year grant, 1970-71. Mem. Assn. Social and Behavioral Scientists, Am. Econs. Assn., Caucus of Black Economists. Home: 739 Lynn Valley Rd SW Atlanta GA 30311 Office: Clark Coll Atlanta GA 30314

JONES, BESS SPRINGFIELD, sem. administr.; b. Vernon, Ala.; d. Claudius D. and Beatrice (Hicks) Springfield; student George Washington U., 1953-56; B.S., Am. U., 1970, M.B.A., 1973; m. Stewart D. Jones, Mar. 20, 1943; 1 son, Wayne Rogers. Office mgr. Consol. Grocers, Inc., Washington, 1945-50; comptroller Harper's, Inc., Alexandria, Va., 1950-58; asst. to pres. Wesley Theol. Sem., Washington, 1958-65, dir. devel., 1965—; tchr. bus. adminstrn. Am. U. Mem. adminstrv. bd., chmn. commn. ecumenical affairs Arlington Meth. Ch.; trustee No. Va. Bd. Missions; mem. Nat. Religious Publicity Council. Mem. Nat. Assn. Ednl. Buyers, Am. U. Alumni Assn. (pres. ch. mgmt. chpt.), Am. Coll. Pub. Relations Assn., Soc. Religious Instn. Mgmt. (award for outstanding adminstrn. in religious instns. 1969, treas., trustee). Home: 4201 Massachusetts Av NW Washington DC 20016 Office: 4400 Massachusetts Av NW Washington DC 20016

JONES, BETTY, dancer, educator; b. Meadville, Pa.; studied dance with Jose Limon, Ted Shawn, Alicia Markova. Mem. tour Oklahoma, Bloomer Girl; mem. Jose Limon Co., 1947-70; tours of Europe, Far East, C.Am., S.Am.; faculty Conn. Coll. Sch. Dance, 1948-67, Fresno State Coll., summer session 1968-69, Long Beach Summer Sch. Dance Cal. State Coll., 1968-70, 72; mem. dance faculty Juilliard Sch., N.Y.C., 1953-71; dir. dance summer session U. Hawaii, 1970, 72, lectr. in residence, 1972; artist in residence Centre International de la Danse et Rencontre Internationales de Danse Contemporaine, Paris, 1970, 71, 73, Fedn. Francaise de Danse et Rencontres Internationales de Danse Contemporaine, Vichy, 1971, 73, Etudés et Rencontres Artistiques, Geneva. Dir. lectr.-concert Dances We Dance, 1963—. Home: 31 West 69th St New York City NY 10023

JONES, BETTY MATILDA LOMBARD (MRS. ROBERT EDWARD JONES), librarian; b. Grand Rapids, Mich., Dec. 25, 1919; d. George LeGrande and Lelia Jane (Carlisle) Lombard; student, Albion Coll., 1937-38; A.B. cum laude, U. Mich., 1941, M.A., 1960; m. Robert Edward Jones, May 26, 1945; children—Jeffrey, Kathryn (Mrs. John Schoenherr), Lawrence, Robert. Head, Creston Br., Grand Rapids (Mich.) Pub. Library, 1957-58, head, bus. and tech. dept., 1959-60; librarian Ridgeview Jr. High Sch., Grand Rapids (Mich.) Pub. Schs., 1960-65, coordinator library services Grand Rapids (Mich.) Pub. Schs., 1965-68; reference librarian Grand Valley State Colls., Allendale, Mich., 1968—. Lectr. sch. library adminstrn. U. Mich., Ann Arbor, 1971, 73. Recipient Grand Rapids Found. fellowship, 1959-60. Mem. Am. Assn. U. Profs., Women's Nat. Book Assn. (v.p. 1972—), Mortar Bd., Phi Kappa Phi, Pi Lambda Theta, Beta Phi Mu, Delta Kappa Gamma. Episcopalian. Clubs: Women's City (Grand Rapids); Grand Rapids (Mich.) Librarians (v.p. 1972-73). Home: 2230 Skyline Dr NW Grand Rapids MI 49504 Office: Grand Valley State Colleges Allendale MI 49401

JONES, BETTY MULLINS (MRS. ALEXANDER ELVIN JONES), fraternity exec.; b. Greencastle, Ind., Aug. 17, 1921; d. Raleigh P. and Montie (Folck) Mullins; A.A., William Woods Coll., 1940; A.B., DePauw U., 1942, M.A., 1944; postgrad. MacMurray Coll., 1959; Litt.D., William Woods Coll., 1971; m. Alexander Elvin Jones, Jan. 16, 1946; children—Jo Ellen, Sara Elisabeth. Instr. English, DePauw U., 1942-44, U. Minn., 1946-50, MacMurray Coll., 1959; pres., mem. exec. bd. Alpha Phi Internat. Frat., Evanston, Ill., 1970—. Del. Nat. Panhellenic Conf., 1970—. Bd. dirs. Hoosier Capitol Girl Scouts Am., 1953-70, Flanner House, Alpha Phi Found. Mem. Mortar Bd., Delta Kappa Gamma. Club: Woman's (chmn. exec. com. 1969-70) (Indpls.). Author: A Code for the Coed, 1962. Editor: Music as Therapy, 1959. Home: 530 W Hampton Dr Indianapolis IN 46208

JONES, CAMILLA DELORES (MRS. ADAM O. TATEM), pediatrician; b. N.Y.C., Oct. 15, 1936; d. Joseph Henry Noble and Edna (White) Jones; B.A., Bryn Mawr Coll., 1958; M.D., Med. Coll. Pa., 1962; m. Adam Oliver Tatem, Nov. 24, 1962; children—Adam Oliver, Lawrence Paul, Caryl Edna. Intern L.I. Coll. Hosp., Bklyn., 1962-63, asst. pediatric resident, 1963-64, chief pediatric resident, 1964-65; pediatrician Columbia Presbyn. Med. Center, N.Y.C., 1965-68, N.Y.U., 1969-70; med. specialist, pediatrician Queens State Sch., Howard Beach, N.Y., 1970—; asst. in pediatrics Columbia U., 1966-68; instr. pediatrics Columbia U., 1968-69; instr. pediatrics N.Y.U., 1969-70. Diplomate Am. Bd. Pediatrics. Mem. Am. Assn. Mental Deficiency, Am. Pub. Health Assn., Am. Profl. Practice Assn. Home: 10 South Rd Harrison NY 10528 Office: Queens State Sch 155-55 Cross Bay Blvd Howard Beach NY 11414

JONES, CAROL LEE MOCKEL, accountant; b. Bozeman, Mont., Sept. 10, 1937; d. Clifford Phillip and Jessie Amanda (Rasmussen) Mockel; B.S., Mont. State U., 1959; m. Marvin R. Jones, Feb. 7, 1970 (div. Apr. 1972). Audit supr. Touche Ross & Co., C.P.A.'s, Fresno, Cal., 1959-70, Wolf & Co., C.P.A.'s, Portland, 1971—. Treas. Fresno Ballet Assn., 1970. C.P.A., Cal., Ore. Mem. Cal. Soc. C.P.A.'s (chpt. dir. 1970-71, mem. state savs. and loan com. 1969-71, mem. state cooperation with students com. 1968-69), Ore. Soc. C.P.A.'s (chmn. municipal accounting and auditing com. 1974-75), P.E.O. (chpt. pres. 1968-69). Home: 1035 SW Perfecta Av Beaverton OR 97005 Office: 1901 Georgia Pacific Bldg Portland OR 97204

JONES, CAROL YVONNE (MRS. DANIEL JONES), librarian; b. Mpls., Aug. 2, 1937; d. Elmer Victor and Caroline (Thoe) Erickson; B.A., U. Minn., 1959, student, 1960-61; m. Daniel Jones, Aug. 9, 1959; 1 dau., Dana Wavalynn. Shelver, jr. library aid Mpls. Pub. Library, 1953-59; grad. library asst. Mpls. Pub. Library, 1960-61; asst. librarian Electronics div. Gen. Mills, Mpls., 1961-65; librarian Northwestern Coll. Chiropractic Found. Inc., Mpls., 1966—. Mem. Seventh-day Adventist Ch. (music librarian 1959—). Home: 2940 35th Av S Minneapolis MN 55406 Office: Northwestern Coll Chiropractic Found Inc 1834 S Mississippi River Blvd St Paul MN 55116

JONES, CATHERINE ANN (MRS. THOMAS MICHAEL JONES), librarian; b. Conneaut, O., Apr. 30, 1936; d. Leo Joseph and Mary Louise (McGinty) Delanty; B.A., U. Ala., 1965; M.S., Cath. U. Am., 1969; m. Thomas Michael Jones, May 18, 1957. Reference librarian U.S. Office of Mgmt. and Budget Library, Exec. Office of the Pres., Washington, 1968-72; head of reference and loan, 1972; asso. dir. Am. Library Assn., Washington, 1972-73; asst. librarian George Washington U. Library, Washington, 1973—. Mem. Am., Spl. library assns., Law Librarians Assn. Washington. Home: 217 Wolfe St Alexandria VA 22314 Office: George Washington University Library 2130 H St NW Washington DC 10006

JONES, CLARA ARAMINTA STANTON (MRS. ALBERT D. JONES), librarian; b. St. Louis, May 14, 1913; d. Ralph Herbert and Etta (James) Stanton; student Milw. State Tchrs. Coll., 1929-30; A.B., Spelman Coll., Atlanta, Ga., 1934; A.B. in L.S., U. Mich., 1938; m. Albert D. Jones, June 25, 1938; children—Stanton William, Vinetta Claire (Mrs. Albert W. Black, Jr.), Kenneth Albert. Asst. librarian Dillard U. Library, New Orleans, 1938-39; library sci. instr. So. U., Baton Rouge, La. summer, 1940, asst. librarian, 1940-41; with Detroit Pub. Library, 1944—, successively youth librarian, adult librarian, chief div., 1951-63 chief dept., 1963-68, neighborhood cons., 1968-70, dir., 1970—. Trustee YWCA Met. Detroit, New Detroit Inc., Met. Fund., Inc.; adv. bd. Sch. L.S. Western Mich. U. Recipient Distinguished Alumnus award U. Mich. Sch. L.S., 1971. Mem. N.A.A.C.P., A.L.A. (Black Caucus award 1970, council), Mich. Library Assn., Am. Civil Liberties Union, Internat. Afro-Am. Mus., Detroit, Assn. for Study of Afro-Am. Life and History, Women's Internat. League Peace and Freedom. Presbyn. Home: 16631 Princeton Av Detroit MI 48221 Office: 5201 Woodward Av Detroit MI 48202

JONES, CONSTANCE JAUCHLER, mathematician; b. Jefferson City, Mo., Jan. 24, 1922; d. Thomas Griffith and Miriam Maude (Jauchler) Jones; B.A., Incarnate Word Coll., 1943; M.A., U. Tex., 1950; postgrad. Harvard, 1943-44, Mass. Inst. Tech., 1944, Clark U., summer 1959, Rutgers State U., summer 1960, U. Tex. at Austin, part time, 1962-68. Instr. sci. Incarnate Word Coll., San Antonio, 1946-47; analytical chemist Tex. Pharmacal Co., San Antonio, 1951-57; asst. prof. math. San Antonio Coll., 1957-62; teaching asst. U. Tex., Austin, 1962-66; asst. prof. math. Trinity U. San Antonio, 1966-69; cons. mathematician, San Antonio, 1969-71; mathematician Office Mgmt. Analysis, Lackland AFB, Tex., 1971-72; asst. prof. math. Incarnate Word Coll., 1972-73. Mem. League Women Voters, 1955—, San Antonio Conservation Soc., 1955—; judge Alamo Dist. Sci. Fair, 1957-59, 67, 72, Navy award Internat. Sci. Fair, Dallas, 1966, Fort Worth, 1969. Served with USNR, 1944-46. Named Hon. adm. Tex. Navy. Mem. Am. Chem. Soc. (treas. 1960), Res. Officer Assn., A.A.A.S., Tex. Acad. Sci., Math. Assn. Am., Am. Math. Soc., U.S. Naval Inst., Daus. Republic Tex. (v.p. 1957-59, 71-73), Incarnate Word Coll. Alumnae Assn. (pres., 1952-54), Sigma Xi. Home: 148 E Elsmere St San Antonio TX 78212

JONES, DEE WALKER (MRS. WARREN WORTH JONES), pub. relations exec.; b. Chgo., Dec. 15, 1921; d. Francis John and Dessie (Lawes) Walker; B.A., La. State U., 1943; m. Warren Worth Jones, Dec. 8, 1944; children—Christopher, Philip and Stephen (twins). With United Press, Washington, 1945, San Juan (P.R.) World Jour., 1944-45, Time-Life, San Juan, 1945, Pensacola (Fla.) News-Jour., 1946-47, Young America, Washington, 1954, Seattle Times, 1961-62; owner Dee Jones Pub. Relations, Seattle, 1962-72; pub. relations coordinator Regional Med. Program, Seattle, 1973—. instr. Highline Coll., Des Moines, Wash., 1973—. Mem. Women in Communications (regional v.p. 1972-73), Mortar Bd., Alpha Xi Delta. Home: 19095 35th Av NE Seattle WA 98195 Office: 500 University District Bldg Seattle WA 98105

JONES, DEZIE DELL (MRS. ROBERT ELROY JONES), coll. adminstr.; b. Ruston, La., Nov. 11, 1941; d. Roy Mayfield and Tena (Lowery) Woods; student Fresno City Coll., 1959-61, Fresno State Coll., 1962-64, U. Cal. at Berkeley, 1971; m. Robert Elroy Jones, Apr. 1, 1968; 1 son, Robert Elroy. Supr. for community relations and spl. community task force Park Job Corps Center, Pleasanton, Cal., 1964-66; dir. Merrit Coll. North Oakland (Cal.) Devel. Center, 1968-70; coordinator community services North Perlata Community Coll., Oakland, 1970—. Community organizer Congress Racial Equality, San Francisco, 1964-67; nat. fund raising chmn., community organizer Student Nonviolent Coordinating Com., Atlanta, 1966-69; chmn. coll. campus United Crusade campaign, Oakland, 1972-73. Active numerous polit. campaigns. Mem. N.A.A.C.P. (pres. 1957-59), Cal. Tchrs. Assn., Perlata Community Coll. Assn., Cal. Community Coll. Community Services Assn., Black Bus. and Profl. Women Assn., Cal. Assn. for Higher Edn. Democrat. Club: Charm Unlimited Health (Oakland). Home: 10966 Cliffland Av Oakland CA 94605

JONES, DORIS PEAKS (MRS. WALTER GARFIELD JONES), ednl. orgn. adminstr.; b. Salisbury, N.C., Dec. 7, 1933; d. Moses and Zellie Lee (Alexander) Peaks; A.B., Livingstone Coll., 1953; M.A., N.C. Central U., 1965; postgrad. N.C. Agrl. and Tech. State U., 1957-58, 60-61, U. Pitts., 1959, Hampton Inst., 1961, Rutgers U., 1968; m. Walter Garfield Jones, Aug. 28, 1955; children—Joycelyn Dorene, Jennifer Dennecia. Tchr., Monroe Street Sch., Salisbury, 1954-57; tchr. Price High Sch., Salisbury, 1957-59, guidance counselor, 1959-68; placement dir. Livingstone Coll., Salisbury, 1968-71, dir. counseling and testing services, 1971-73; asso. dir. Coll. Placement Services, Inc., Bethlehem, Pa., 1973—. Counselor Upward Bound program U. N.C., Greensboro, also N.C. Agrl. and Tech. State U., summers, 1966, 67; cons. counseling, also career placement. Youth service dir. Nat. Conf. Christians and Jews, 1968-73. Adv. bd. on black adoptions Children's Home Soc. N.C.; founder mem. bd. dirs. DIAL Help Telephone Ministry, 1970-72. Recipient Brotherhood award Nat. Conf. Christians and Jews, 1971. Mem. N.C. Tchrs. Assn. (local pres. 1966-67), N.C. Placement Assn. (sec. 1969-70), So. Coll. Placement Assn., Am. Assn. for Coll. and Univ. Staffing, Jack and Jill Club Am., Salisbury Bus. and Profl. Women's Club (young careerist chmn. 1972-73), Salisbury-Rowan Ch. Women United (treas. 1971-72), Salisbury-Rowan League Women Voters (a founder, bull. editor 1969-72), Delta Sigma Theta. Club: Merry Matrons Social (Salisbury). Home: 1124 Crestview Dr Salisbury NC 28144 Office: 64 E Elizabeth Av Bethlehem PA 18001

JONES, DOROTHY KIRBY (MRS. CALVIN LEGETTE JONES), librarian; b. Charlotte, N.C., Nov. 30, 1917; d. Thomas Pinckney and Willie Beatrice (Moss) Kirby; B.A., Columbia Coll., 1938, B.A. in L.S., 1962; M.Ed., U. S.C., 1958; m. Calvin Legette Jones, Apr. 24, 1944; children—Harriet Anne (Mrs. Jim I. Price), Leonard Kirby, Robert Thomas. Tchr. pub. schs., Mt. Croghan, S.C., 1938-39, Nichols, S.C., 1940-43, Georgetown, S.C., 1943-44, Blaney, S.C., 1947-48, Monticello High Sch., Strother, S.C., 1948-50, Dentsville High Sch., Columbia, S.C., 1951-56, Lower Richland High Sch., Columbia, 1957-59; test scorer, reception center Army Dept., Ft. Jackson, S.C., 1950-51, library asst., 1959-61; librarian VA Hosp., Columbia, 1961-63; librarian VA Hosp., Augusta, Ga., 1963-64, chief library service, 1965—. Mem. Southeastern, S.C. (chmn. spl. library sect. 1971-73), Central Savannah River Area (sec. 1968-69) library assns., Columbia Coll. Alumnae Augusta-North Augusta (pres. 1969-71), Women's Missionary Union. Baptist. Club: Pilot (sec. North Augusta S.C. 1971-73, 1st v.p. 1973-74, pres. 1974—). Home: 681 Lorraine Dr North Augusta SC 29841 Office: VA Hosp Augusta GA 30904

JONES, EDITH AUGUSTA, dietitian; b. Muscle Shoals, Ala.; d. Leonidas and Ora (Phillips) Jones; B.S., U. Ala., 1941; M.S., U. Tenn., 1949. Dietetic intern Johns Hopkins Hosp., 1941-42, staff dietitian, 1942-43, dir. student curriculum, sch. dietetics, 1946-49; nutritionist Nutrition div., Bur. State Services USPHS, 1950-51, dietitian cons. Hosp. Facilities div. Bur. Med. Service 1951-52; chief nutrition dept. Clin. Center, NIH, Bethesda, 1952—. Gen. chmn. 5th Internat. Congress Dietetics, Washington, 1969. Recipient Distinguished Service award U. Ala., 1956; McLester award Assn. Mil. Surgeons U.S., 1957; award of achievement Alpha Chi Omega, 1962, Meritorious Service medal USPHS, 1971. Fellow Am. Pub. Health Assn.; mem. Am. (coordinating council and cabinet, pres. 1962-63, chmn. internat. com. 1965-69, (Marjorie Hulsizer Copher award 1971), D.C. (rep. ho. dels. Am. assn., chmn. internat. congress 1969, certificate of distinction 1972) dietetic assns., Am. Home Econs. Assn., Mortar Bd., Alpha Chi Omega, Phi Kappa Phi, Phi Upsilon Omicron, Alpha Lambda Delta, Omicron Nu. Author articles in field. Home: 4977 Battery Lane Bethesda MD 20014 Office: Clin Center NIH Bethesda MD 20014

JONES, EDITH BUCHANAN, retail store exec.; b. Albertville, Ala., Jan. 3, 1919; d. John Wyeth and Alma Annie (Jackson) Buchanan; grad. high sch.; m. William Homer Jones, Nov. 18, 1937; children—Julia Marie (Mrs. Woodie N. Tully), John William. Organizer Jones Lamplighter, Inc., 1965, then Candle Cabin & Paper Palace, 1968; organizer, 1969, since pres.; chief exec. officer Candle Cabin Am., Inc., Mobile, Old South Candle Makers, Inc., Mobile, 1971—, Candle Cabin Tex., Inc., 1971—. Bd. dirs. Christian Booksellers Assn., 1963-67, sec., 1966-67, dir. seminars, 1967-71; bd. dirs. Bel Air Mall, Mobile, 1968-71. Mem. Mobile Area C. of C. Republican. Baptist. Author: Establishing Bridal Department in Retail Stores, 1966; also articles. Home: 13710 Hambleton Circle Houston TX 77069 Office: PO Box 40307 Houston TX 77040

JONES, EDITH IRBY (MRS. JAMES BEAUREGARD JONES), physician; b. Conway, Ark.; d. Robert and Mattie (Buice) Irby; B.S., Knoxville Coll., 1948; B.S., U. Ark., 1952, M.D., 1952; postgrad. W. Va. Coll., 1965, Chgo. Sch. Medicine, 1966, Northwestern U., summer 1948; m. James Beauregard Jones, Apr. 16, 1950; children—Gary, Myra, Keith. Intern, Univ. Hosp., Little Rock, Ark., 1952-53; resident Baylor Affiliated Hosps., Houston, 1962—; practice medicine, Hot Springs, Ark., 1953-59; asst. prof. medicine Baylor Coll., Houston, 1962—. Bd. dirs. Sudan Corp., Afro-Am. Book Distbrs., Mercy Hosp., Houston Met. Ministries, Harris County Leukemia Soc., Houston chpt. Am. Heart Assn.; sec. Mercy Hosp. Comprehensive Health Care, Inc.; mem. med. adv. bd. Planned Parenthood of Houston, Houston Council on Alcoholism, Family Service Bur., Prospect Med. Lab.; mem. exec. bd. St. Elizabeth Hosp. Bd. dirs. Houston Epilepsy Assn., Houston chpt. Am. Heart Assn.; trustee Knoxville Coll. Mem. Am., Nat. (commn. on hypertension), Tex., Lone Star, Harris County med. assns., Am. Med. Womens Assn., Links, Alpha Kappa Mu, Delta Sigma Theta, Eta Phi Beta, Baptist. Home: 3402 S Parkwood Dr Houston TX 77021 Office: 2601 Prospect St Houston TX 77004

JONES, EDNA MAE, educator; b. Cin.; d. James Oliver and Elmina (Luechauer) Jones; student St. Petersburg Jr. Coll., 1938; diploma Gordon Keller Sch. Nursing, 1941; B.S. in Nursing, Fla. State U., 1949; M.S. in Nursing, U. Ala., 1957. Staff nurse U.S. Vets. Hosp., Bay Pines, Fla., 1942-47; instr. Sch. Nursing, Shannon Meml. Hosp., San Angelo, Tex., 1949-56; asst. prof. nursing U. Fla. at Gainesville, 1957-65; asst. prof. nursing Jacksonville (Fla.) U., 1965-68; prof., dir. div. nursing Valdosta (Ga.) State Coll., 1968-71; instr. Fla. Jr. Coll., Jacksonville, 1973—. Mem. nursing edn. com. Am. Cancer Soc., Fla. Div., Inc., 1973—. Mem. Sigma Theta Tau. Club: Mandarin Garden. Home: 10248 Scott Mill Rd Jacksonville FL 32217

JONES, ELEANOR GREEN DAWLEY, mathematician; b. Norfolk, Va., Aug. 10, 1929; d. George Hebert and Lillian (Vaughn) Green; B.S. cum laude, Howard U., 1949, M.S., 1950; postgrad. N.Y.U., summer 1957, U. So. Cal., summers 1959-60; Ph.D., Syracuse U., 1966; m. Edward Armistead Dawley, Jr., Sept. 1, 1951 (div.); children—Edward Armistead III, Herbert Green; m. 2d, Everette Benjamin Jones, June 27, 1967; 1 son, Everette Benjamin. Tchr. sci. and math. Norfolk High Sch., 1950-53; asst. prof. math. Hampton (Va.) Inst., 1955-65, asso. prof. math., 1965-67; prof. math. Norfolk State Coll., 1967—. Va. vice chmn. Congress of Racial Equality, 1958-60. Recipient commendation for aid in compiling curriculum guide for math. program Norfolk secondary schs., 1953. Mem. Math. Assn. Am., Nat. Tech. Assn., Am. Math. Soc., Nat. Assn. Mathematicians (Va. rep. 1971—), Am. Assn. U. Women, Sigma Xi, Pi Mu Epsilon, Delta Sigma Theta. Roman Catholic. Home: 6301 Bucknell Circle Virginia Beach VA 23462 Office: Math Dept Norfolk State Coll Norfolk VA 23504

JONES, ELISE CECIL, editor; b. Starke, Fla., Feb. 6, 1910; d. DeWitt Cecil and Ada Viola (Darby) Jones; A.B., Agnes Scott Coll., 1931; student U. Fla., 1933, 52-53. Asso. with family bus., 1932-45; elementary sch. tchr., Gainesville, Fla., 1933-36; head project payroll unit Resettlement Adminstrn., Welaka, Fla., 1938; acting supr. Service Club, dir. Spl. Services div. MidPac Hdqrs., Honolulu, 1946; asst. staff Service Club adviser, Spl. Services div. Hdqrs. Far East Command, Tokyo, 1947-49; mem. staff Bur. Econ. and Bus. Research, U. Fla., 1953-72, research instr., editor Fla. Statis. Abstract, 1967-72. Vice pres. Starke Coca-Cola Bottling Co., 1931-35, 40-42, DeWitt C. Jones Co., 1931-35, 49-55, 51-59; sec.-treas. DeWitt C. Jones Services, 1963-71. Chmn. Alachua County (Fla.) chpt. Jr. Red. Cross, 1944-45; pres. Jr. Welfare League Gainesville, 1939-40; sec.-treas. Fla. Council Aging, 1961-62; pres. Altrusa Club Gainesville, 1968-69, Jr. Welfare Sustaining Group, 1967-68. Mem. Am. Statis. Assn., So. Econs. Assn., Phi Chi Theta (hon. mem. Alpha Omicron chpt.). Democrat. Baptist. Co-author: Florida's Older People, A Chart Book, 1955; Florida's Commercial Fisheries; Markets, Operations, Outlook, 1955; Older People in Florida, a Chart Book, 1963. Author leaflets, chpts. in books. Home: 545 NE 10th Av Gainesville FL 32601

JONES, ELIZABETH BOOTH, coll. dean; b. Portsmouth, Va., June 8, 1917; d. Charles I. and Alma Elizabeth (King) Booth; B.S., Longwood Coll., 1937; postgrad. Old Dominion U., 1963-64; M.Ed., Coll. William and Mary, 1970; postgrad. N.C. State U., 1970-71; m. James Eldridge Jones, Apr. 27, 1940 (div. 1968); children—Eva Elizabeth (Mrs. Nathaniel Reuben Williams), James Eldridge. Tchr. pub. schs., Portsmouth, Va., 1937-40, Holland, Va., 1958-63; dir. guidance Holland High Sch., 1963-65; asst. dean students Meredith Coll., Raleigh, N.C., 1965-70, dean students, summers, 1966-69; edn. coordinator Raleigh City Schs., 1971-72; asso. dean students St. Mary's Coll., Raleigh, 1972-73, dean students, 1973—. Pres. Holland P.T.A. Mem. Am. Personnel and Guidance Assn., Nat. Assn. Women Deans, Adminstrs. and Counselors, N.C. Personnel and Guidance, N.C. Women Deans and Counselors, N.C. Assn. Coll. Personnel, N.C. Coll. Personnel Assn. (mem. exec. council 1973-74), Vocational Guidance Assn., Am. Assn. Univ. Women. Baptist. Home: 3939 Glenwood Av Raleigh NC 27612 Office: 900 Hillsborough St Raleigh NC 27611

JONES, ELIZABETH ELEANORE JONES (MRS. HERBERT LEA JONES, SR.), assn. sec.; b. Delaware, O., Sept. 28, 1916; d. Charles Aubrey and Ireta (Lowe) Jones; student Ohio State U., 1937; m. Herbert Lea Jones, Feb. 5, 1938; children—Nancy (Mrs. Thomas Pfahler, Jr.), Donald, Elizabeth Carr, Charles Allen, Herbert Lea. Sec. Bristol (Va.) C. of C., 1962-71. Active Appalachian council Girl Scouts U.S., 1939-52, mem. orgn. com. Camp Sky-Wa-Mo, 1945-52; mem. exec. com., bd. dirs. Bristol United Fund, 1950-65; chmn. housing com. Southeastern Band Fest., 1950—, also asst. sec. bd. dirs.; sec., v.p. Bristol Meml. Hosp. Aux., 1963-64; active Girl Scouts U.S., 1923-73; rep. Va. High Sch. P.T.A. to Bristol Sch. Bd., 1969—. Pres. Bristol Democratic Women, 1969-71; del. Bristol Dem. Central Com., 1972—. Bd. dirs. Bristol Boy's Club, 1953-68, Bristol Speech and Hearing Center, 1967—, Salvation Army, Bristol, 1971—. Recipient Man and Boy award Bristol Boys Club, 1963. Mem. D.A.R. Club: Altrusa Bristol, (Va.-Tenn.). Home: 959 Long Crescent Rd Bristol VA 24201

JONES, ELIZABETH RIEKE (MRS. WAYNE VAN LEER JONES), club woman; b. Chgo., Oct. 15, 1903; d. Henry Edward and Vina Genevieve (Coulter) Rieke; A.B., Northwestern U., 1925; m. Wayne Van Leer Jones, Jan. 14, 1926; 1 son, Wayne Van Leer II. Dir. Houston Grand Opera Assn. Charter mem. Assistance Guild Houston, 1966-68, Assistance League, 1968— (nat. finance com. 1970). Mem. Art Mus. Guild, Houston, U. Women's Alliance (pres. 1951-53, scholarship chmn. 1963-65, meml. scholarship chmn. 1965—), Houston Geol. Aux. (parliamentarian, 1950-51, 60-61, 63-64), Kappa Kappa Gamma, Theta Sigma Phi. Republican. Presbyn. Home: 5672 Longmont Dr Houston TX 77027

JONES, ELIZABETH SHIPPLETT (MRS. MARCUS CLEVELAND JONES), coll. adminstr.; b. Huntington, W.Va., Oct. 27, 1914; d. George Dinges and Jane Maude (Jenkins) Shipplett; grad. Longwood Coll., Farmville, Va., 1938; m. Marcus Cleveland Jones, July 1, 1947; children—Marcus Cleveland, Jane Elizabeth. With Appalachian Electric Power Co., 1938-47; exec. alumnae dir. Longwood Coll., Farmville, Va., 1957-74, ofcl. coll. hostess, 1974—, also mem. adminstrv. staff, editor Alumnae mag. Past pres. local P.T.A.; pres. Community Center, 1973—. Mem. Hermitage Guild Methodist Ch., Kappa Delta. Clubs: Wedgewood Country, Buckingham County Womans (founder, pres., dir.). Home: Sheppards Route 2 Box 198 Farmville VA 23901

JONES, ELSA VON RUECAU (MRS. THOMAS L. JONES), religious edn. adminstr.; b. Cripple Creek, Colo., May 11, 1896; d. Louis Hector Roloff and Georgina Margaretta (Morrin) von Ruecau; B.S., U. No. Colo., 1917; postgrad. Boston U., 1925; m. Thomas Lewis Jones, Dec. 27, 1932; 1 son, Thomas M. Tchr. pub. schs., Denver, 1918-22; dir. Christian edn. and parish work Presbytery of Denver, asso. dir. dept. ch. relations Presbyn. Bd. Ch. Edn., Phila., 1922-32; dir. Chirstian edn. St. John's Cathedral, Denver, 1949-58; dir. 75 collegiate chpts. Sigma Sigma Sigma, Woostock, Va., 1961-71. Mem. St. Luke's Hosp. Aux., 1960—. Recipient Silver Loving Cup for outstanding service Sigma Sigma Sigma, 1968, Council Ring, 1971, Golden Violet award, 1967. Religious Pub. Relations Council (charter), Welsh Nat. Gymanfa Gana Assn. (life). Episcopalian (columnist edn. Colo. Episcopalian 1950-60). Home: Crescent Arms 6K 909 Logan St Denver CO 80203

JONES, EMILY STRANGE, film cons.; b. Rochester, N.Y., June 24, 1919; d. Leonard Warburton and Helen (Stone) Jones; A.B., Vassar Coll., 1940. Asst. in children's room N.Y. Pub. Library, 1941-43; editorial asst. Trained Nurse Mag., 1943-44; film prodn. asst. Emerson Yorke Studio, 1944-46; adminstrv. dir. Ednl. Films Library Assn., 1946-69; now freelance prodn. cons., lectr.; partner Acorn Films, N.Y.C., 1973—. Exec. dir. Am. Film Festival; bd. dirs. Internat. Film Found.; mem. Ednl. Media Council; v.p. Council on Internat. Non-Theatrical Events; mem. internat. jury Teheran Children's Film Festival, 1970. Girl Scout leader, N.Y.C., 1944-49. Author: Films and People, 1951; (with Jessie Kiching) Index to Selected Film Lists, 1950; Manual on Film Evaluation, 1967; also articles mags. Supervisory editor Film Evaluation Guide, 1965; editor Sightlines Mag., 1965-69, College Film Library Collection, 1971. Home: 72-61 113th St Forest Hills New York City NY 11375

JONES, ETHEL BENGREE, educator; b. Camden, Ark., Sept. 14, 1930; d. Arthur Bengree and Ethel (Roberts) Jones; A.B., Vassar Coll., 1952; M.A., U. Chgo., 1954, Ph.D., 1961. Research asso. dept. econ. U. Chgo., 1958-59; instr. Roosevelt U., 1959-60, asso. indsl. specialist, 1960-62, sr. indsl. specialist, 1962-64; asst. dir. Indsl. Research and Ext. Center U. Ark., 1964-65; asso. prof. U. Ga., 1965-68, prof. dept. econs., 1968—; bd. editors So. Econ. Jour.; mem. U.S. Southwest Manpower Adv. Council, 1965; mem. econs. grants panel U.S. Nat. Inst. Edn., 1973. Ford Found. fellow on role of women in society, 1973-74. Mem. Am., So. econ. assns., Regional Sci. Assn. Home: 550 N Chase St Athens GA 30601 Office: Econ Dept U Ga Athens GA 30601

JONES, ETHEL GRACE (MRS. NOLAN E. JONES), realtor; b. Deepwater, Mo., June 29, 1923; d. William E. and T. Blanche (Tullis) Chiles; grad. high sch.; student Weaver Sch. Real Estate, Jefferson City, Mo., 1967; m. Nolan E. Jones, Dec. 27, 1941; children—Nolan E., Mary Lou (Mrs. James R. Clary), Michael L. Mailwoman, U.S. Govt., Brownington, Mo., 1953-54; owner, operator Redwood, Sunrise Beach, Mo., 1955-58; ennumerator U.S. Census, Sunrise Beach, 1959-67; with Willmore Real Estate, Sunrise Beach, 1968; mgr. Willmore Co., Shawnee Bend br., Sunrise Beach, 1967-69; owner Ethel Jones, realtor, Sunrise Beach, 1970—. Mem. steering com. Lake of Ozarks Hosp. Rep. committee woman, Henry County, Mo., 1948-54, Camden County, 1960-64; vice chmn. Rep. Com., 1964-72. Mem. Nat., Mo. real estate assns. Lutheran. Club: Business and Professional Women (chaplain 1972—, treas. 1973-74) (Sunrise Beach). Home: Lake Rd 5-35 Sunrise Beach MO 65079 Office: Junction 5 & F Sts Sunrise Beach MO 65079

JONES, EUGENIA EDWINA BYRD, govt. ofcl.; b. nr. Brookhaven, Miss., Jan. 15, 1923; d. Ellis Eugene and Virgie Edwina (Beacham) Byrd; student Millsaps Coll., 1941-43, Jackson Comml. Coll., 1944-45; m. Marvin Harold Jones, Dec. 22, 1951 (dec. Nov. 1958); 1 dau., Virgie Ann; m. 2d, Cameron Stokes, Aug. 7, 1965 (div.). Sec., Shell Oil Co., Jackson, Miss., 1945-47, United Gas Corp., Jackson, 1947-51; dep. chancery clk. Franklin County, Meadville, Miss., 1952-58, chancery clk., 1958-72; now finance officer Office Miss. Atty. Gen., Jackson, Miss. Methodist (past steward). Home: 5730 Sedgwick Dr Jackson MS 39211 Office: 5th Floor Carroll Gartin Justice Bldg Jackson MS 39205

JONES, FLORENCE EVELINE (MRS. JOHN DURWARD MIMS), physician; b. Chgo., June 21, 1932; d. Charles John and Florence Marie (Schmidt) Jones; pre-med. student Tulane U., 1956-59, M.D., 1963; m. John Durward Mims, July 2, 1966; children—Judith (Mrs. Robert E. DuBose, Jr.), Rebecca Orin Dean, Daniel Orin Dean (dec.). Intern, then resident So. Bapt. Hosp.; resident Touro Infirmary, VA Hosp.; practice gen. surgery with Clinic Indsl. Medicine and Surgery, New Orleans, 1967-69, Uptown Med. Center, New Orleans, 1969—; mem. staff Saro Mayo Hosp., East Jefferson Hosp., Metairie Hosp., Hotel Dieu, Lakeside Hosp. for Women; asst. in surgery Tulane U. Med. Sch. Fellow gen. surgery Alton Ochsner Med. Found., 1966-67. Mem. Am. Med. Women's Assn. (pres. br. 8, 1972, 2d v.p. 1974), La. Surg. Soc., Am. Soc. Abdominal Surgeons, So. Med. Assn., La., Orleans Parish (gov.) med. socs., New Orleans Grad. Med. Assembly, Tulane U. Women's Assn., Theone, Inc. Republican. Episcopalian. Home: 1427 8th St New Orleans LA 70115 Office: Suite 320 2100 Perdido St New Orleans LA 70112

JONES, FRANCES CLARISSA, concrete co. exec.; b. Glenside, Pa., June 29, 1918; d. Herbert and Rosa A. (Messinger) Muffley; grad. high sch.; m. Melvin M. Jones, Nov. 25, 1967; 1 dau., Rosalie (Mrs. Joseph H. Mitchell, Jr.). Bookkeeper, pvt. sec. Messinger Mfg. Co., 1936-46; bookkeeper Rock Hill Materials Co., Quakertown, Pa., 1947-66, treas., 1966—, also trustee pension plan. Bd. dirs. Quakertown Hosp. Gray Ladies, 1955-65. Mem. Am. Legion Aux., Pa. Ready-Mixed Concrete, Sand and Gravel Assn. (dir. 1973—). Mem. United Ch. of Christ. Clubs: Quakertown Soroptimist; Indian Valley Country (Telford); Country of Northampton County (Easton, Pa.); Womens. Home: 221 N Penrose St Quakertown PA 18951 Office: 223 N Penrose St Quakertown PA 18951

JONES, FRANCES FOLLIN, museum curator; b. N.Y.C., Sept. 8, 1913; d. T. Carlyle and Rosalie (Warner) Jones; A.B., Bryn Mawr Coll., 1934, M.A., 1936, Ph.D., 1952; postgrad. Am. Sch. Classical Studies, Athens, Greece, 1937-38. Research asst. Inst. for Advanced Study, Princeton, 1939-46; sec., asst. curator classical art Art Mus., Princeton, 1943-46, asst. to dir., curator classical art, 1946-65, chief curator, curator classical art, 1965-71, curator of collections, 1971—. Mem. Museums Council N.J. (past chmn.), Archaeol. Inst. Am., Am. Assn. Museums, Rei Cretariae Romanae Fautores. Contbr. to profl. publs. Author: Ancient Art in the Art Museum, Princeton Univ., 1960. Home: 1041 Kingston Rd Princeton NJ 08540

JONES, GERDA ANNEMARIE (MRS. ELMER DAVID JONES), librarian; b. Gera, East Germany, July 7, 1923; d. Vinzenz and Louise Anna (Haase-Ackermann) Plaretka; came to U.S., 1948, naturalized, 1951; A.A. with honors, Long Beach City Coll., 1955; B.A., U. Cal. at Riverside, 1962; M.S., U. So. Cal., 1966; m. Elmer David Jones, Oct. 7, 1948. Interpreter, translator U.S. Occupation Forces, Germany, 1946-48; with U. Cal. at Riverside, 1966—, asso. librarian monographs dept., 1973—. Mem. selection com. U. Cal. Edn. Abroad Program, 1967-73. Mem. Am., Cal. library assns., Libraria Sodalitas, Librarians Assn. U. Cal. Riverside (exec. bd. 1973-74, treas. 1968-71, 73—), U. So. Cal., U. Cal. at Riverside alumni assns., Town and Gown, World Affairs Council, Alpha Mu Gamma. Republican. Clubs: Am. Continental, Faculty (Riverside). Home: 484 Glenhill Dr Riverside CA 92507

JONES, GLADYS HURT, educator; b. Selma, Ala., Dec. 13, 1920; d. Naxie and Osceola (Martin) Hurt; student Talladega Coll., 1937-39; B.S., Tenn. A. and I. Coll., 1941; postgrad. (Gen. Edn. Bd. fellow) U. Mich., 1950-51; M.S., Atlanta U., 1947; m. Herbert Whittier Jones, Sept. 14, 1953; 1 dau., Brenda Elaine. Tchr. math., chemistry Center High Sch., Waycross, Ga., 1941-46; instr. math Morehouse Coll., Atlanta, 1947-53; research asst. U. Mich., Ann Arbor, 1953-57; asst. prof. math. Fla. A. and M. U., Tallahassee, 1957—. Mem. Math. Assn. Am., Nat. Council Tchrs. Math., Nat. Assn. Math., Delta Sigma Theta, Beta Kappa Chi. Mem. A.M.E. Ch. Democrat. Home: 308 Barbourville Dr Tallahassee FL 32301

JONES, GRETCHEN PAGE (MRS. SAMUEL ARCHIE JONES), poet, artist; b. Ninock, La., July 30, 1908; d. John Franklin and Lelia Virginia (Cabaniss) Page; student Centenary Coll., La., 1936-37, 50-51, 55-56; m. Samuel Archie Jones, Sept. 14, 1924; children—Marilyn (Mrs. B. Lester Bogan), Beverly (Mrs. Harlan O'Neal Washington). Exhibited paintings in group shows at ann. spring, fall exhbns. La. State Mus., Pierremont Mall, Barnwell Art Center, 1958-74, Centenary Coll., Shreveport, La., Panola Coll., Carthage, Tex., 1969; free lance writer, 1963-74. Recipient 1st prize Interstate Art Exhibit, Panola Coll., 1969; various awards for poetry. Mem. La. State, Shreveport poetry socs., U. D.C. (pres. 1968-69, v.p. 1970-74), Shreveport Writers Club, Shreveport Art Club, Shreveport Artists and Writers Guild (chmn. 1954-58), Hoover Watercolor Soc., Am. Legion Aux. Methodist. Contbr. poems to popular mags. Died Oct. 9, 1974. Address: 1624 Claiborne Av Shreveport LA 71103

JONES, GWENDOLA M. MITCHELL (MRS. JIM ARTHUR JONES), social worker; b. Jacksonville, Fla., Jan. 21, 1936; d. David A. and Merca (Judge) Mitchell; student Hampton Inst., 1952-53; B.S., Tuskegee Inst., 1957; M.A., U. Chgo., 1965; m. Jim Arthur Jones, Apr. 9, 1959; children—Gwendola Evon, Murray Charles. Tchr., Duval County Bd. Pub. Inst., Jacksonville, 1957-58; social worker Fla. Dept. Pub. Welfare, Jacksonville, 1958-63, state welfare cons., 1965-66, family and childrens supr., 1966-67, orientation tng. supr., 1967-68, casework supr., 1968-70, welfare program supr., 1970-72; clin. social services dir. div. health Fla. Dept. Health and Rehab. Services, 1970—. Mem. policy adv. bd. Jacksonville Urban Missions of United Methodist Ch., 1969; mem. Fair Housing Council, Jacksonville, 1969-71; mem. policy adv. bd. Parent Child Center, 1969-70, Summer Head Start, 1969-70; mem. State-wide Family Planning Task Force, 1970-71; agy. adv. com. social work edn. project U. Fla., 1972—. Mem. Nat. Assn. Social Workers (chpt. sec. 1967-69), Fla. Fedn. Social Workers (v.p. 1968-71), Am. Assn. U. Women, Nat. Council Negro Women, Womens Soc. Christian Service, Delta Sigma Theta. Democrat. Methodist. Home: 6526 Manhattan Dr Jacksonville FL 32208 Office: PO Box 210 Jacksonville FL 32201

JONES, GWYNETH, opera singer; b. Pontnewynydd, Wales, Nov. 7, 1936; d. Edward and Violet (Webster) Jones; Degree, Royal Coll. Music, London, Eng., 1960; student Accademia Chicigina Siena, 1960, Internationales Opernstudio Zurich, 1961-62; m. Till Haberfeld, Mar. 4, 1969; 1 dau., Susanne Daphne. Mem. Royal Opera, Covent Garden, London, 1963—, State Opera Vienna (Austria), 1966—, Bayreuth Festival, 1966—; guest appearances La Scala, Milan, Italy, Rome (Italy) Opera, Met. Opera, N.Y.C., San Francisco, Dallas, Paris, France, Munich, West Germany, Hamburg, West Germany, Berlin, Germany, also Japan, South Am., rec. CBS, Decca/London, Deutsche Grammophone, Polydor EMI. Fellow Royal Coll. Music, London. Home: PO Box 8040 Zurich Switzerland

JONES, HAZEL LUCILE JAMES, coll. adminstr.; b. nr. Eckert, Colo., Feb. 3, 1915; d. Robert Phelps and Ethel (Hart) James; B.A., Western State Coll., 1937; M.A., U. So. Cal., 1958, Ed.D., 1963; 1 dau., Annette. Tchr. English, high schs., Colo., 1938-50, Cal. High Schs., 1950-59; prof. edn. Los Angeles State Coll., 1959-60; prof. English Cal. State Coll., Fullerton, 1960—, asso. dean Sch. Letters, Arts and Scis., 1967-70, dean, 1970-74; v.p. acad. affairs Cal. Poly. State U., San Luis Obispo, 1974—. Mem. exec. bd. Whittier (Cal.) Library, 1956-59. Cons. Cal. sch. dists. jr. colls., and univs., 1955-70. Chmn. Cal. Com. Tchr. Preparation in English, 1969-70. Delta Kappa Gamma fellow, 1961-62. Mem. Cal. Assn. Tchrs. English (pres. 1965-66), Cal. Assn. Econ. Edn. (mem. exec. bd. 1965—), Nat. Council Tchrs. English, Coll. English Edn. Home: 121 Wawona Av Shell Beach CA 93449

JONES, HELEN HINCKLEY (PEN NAME HELEN HINCKLEY), author; b. Provo, Utah, Apr. 12, 1903; d. Samuel Ernest and Ida Lenore (Cheever) Hinckley; B.S., Brigham Young U., 1924, M.S., 1928; postgrad. Stanford, Columbia, Cambridge, Utah State U., U. Cal. at Berkeley, U. Colo.; m. Ivan Charles Jones, June 29, 1938; children—Jacqueline (Mrs. Gary Gene Ballard), Samellyn (Mrs. Harold Wayne Wood). Author: The Mountains Are Mine, 1946; Persia Is My Heart, 1953; Reveille for a Persian Village, 1958; (with Najmeh Najafi) Wall and Three Willows, 1967; Over the Mormon Trail, 1963; Land and People of Iran; 1964; Rails from the West, 1969; The Opossum's Table, 1973; also numerous stories, articles, translations. Instr. writing for publ. Pasadena (Cal.) City Coll.; dir. Writer's Week, Pasadena. Recipient Distinguished Service award Brigham Young U., 1972. Mem. Cal. Writers Guild, Authors Guild, Western History Assn., Pasadena Writer's Club, Los Angeles Women's Press Club (hon.). Home: 1191 E Mendocino St Altadena CA 91001

JONES, HELEN JEAN, pub. relations exec.; b. Butte, Mont., Apr. 18, 1931; d. John Johnstone and Helen Elizabeth (Kolemaine) Jones; B.A., U. Ore., 1953. News editor Baker (Ore.) Democrat-Herald, 1953-55; adminstrv. asst. U.S. Fgn. Service, Athens, Greece, and Kobe, Japan, 1955-59; copy editor Cal. Farmer, San Francisco, 1959-62; with Am. Lung Assn., N.Y.C., 1962—, asso. dir. pub. relations, 1970—. Mem. Nat. Assn. Sci. Writers, Women in Communications, Phi Beta Kappa. Home: 150 West End Av New York City NY 10023 Office: 1740 Broadway New York City NY 10019

JONES, HELEN JEANE, coll. dean; b. Idaho Falls, Ida., Apr. 17, 1924; d. Lyman Dick and Sarah Mabel (Evans) Jones; A.A., Albion State Normal Sch., 1945; B.S., U. Ore., 1948; M.S., U. Utah, 1958; Ed.D., Wash. State U., 1964. Tchr. high sch., Lava Hot Springs, 1945-48, Marsh Valley High Sch., Arimo, Ida., 1950-54; dir. guidance, dean women Grays Harbor Coll., Aberdeen, Wash., 1957—. Cons., Twin Harbors and Thurston County high sch. counselors; mem. Certification Com. for Counselors of Twin Harbors and Thurston County. Mem. Wash. Higher Edn. State Legislative Com., 1960-72, Cosmopolis Planning Commn., 1972—, Health Planning Commn. for Grays Harbor and Pacific counties, 1973—. Mem. Nat., Wash. edn. assns., Assn. Higher Edn., Am. Assn. Women in Community and Jr. Colls., Wash. Dirs. Guidance, Grays Harbor Coll. Faculty Assn. (chmn. legislative com.), Am. Legion Aux., Phi Lambda Theta, Delta Psi Omega. Democrat. Eagle Aux. Club: Altrusa International (dir., past pres.) (Aberdeen). Home: 1208 Franklin Dr Cosmopolis WA 98537 Office: Grays Harbor Coll Aberdeen WA 98520

JONES, IRENE BYRON (MRS. JAMES ARTHUR JONES, SR.), coll. adminstr.; b. Macon, Ga., Dec. 29, 1931; d. Edward and Susie (Allen) Byron; B.A. cum laude, Morris Brown Coll., 1954; postgrad. Atlanta U., summer 1958; m. James Arthur Jones, June 6, 1952; children—James Arthur, Sheree, Kevin. Sec. to bus. mgr. Morris Brown Coll., Atlanta, 1954-66, student financial aid dir., 1966—. Mem. Nat., So., Ga. assns. student financial aid adminstrs. Home: 2718 Canova St Atlanta GA 30311 Office: Morris Brown Coll Atlanta GA 30314

JONES, IRENE STEVENS (MRS. FRANK C. JONES), banker; b. Charlotte, N.C., Jan. 8, 1928; d. Peter Alexander and Anna Belle (Autry) Stevens; certificate Am. Inst. Banking, 1960; m. Frank C. Jones, Oct. 1, 1946; 1 son, Steven Frank. With Morris Plan Bank Va. (now Bank Va.), Richmond, 1944-45; with Exchange Nat. Bank Tampa, (Fla.), 1945-50, 53—, exec. sec., 1953-65, asst. cashier, 1965-73, marketing officer, 1973—. Named 1st Citizen of Tampa, 1959. Mem. Am. Inst. Banking (sec. Tampa chpt. 1968-69, treas. 1969-70, 2d v.p. pres. 1972-73, nat. sec. 1959-60), Beta Sigma Phi. Home: 4206 Obispo Tampa FL 33609 Office: PO Box 1809 Tampa FL 33601

JONES, ISABELLA JENKS, orgn. exec.; b. Connellsville, Pa.; d. John Stanley and Mary (Stewart) Jenks; grad. Nat. Park Coll., 1924; A.B., Columbia, 1927; m. Evan Jones, Oct. 20, 1927 (dec. July 1945); children—Johns Jenks, Memory Stewart (Mrs. Charles Edwin Smith). Dir. pub. relations Pa. exhibit N.Y. World Fair, 1939-40; mem. staff U.S. Senator James J. Davis, 1941-45; editor Mt. Lebanon News, Pitts., 1945-47, North Pittsburgh Times, 1947-50, part owner, 1949—; exec. asst. charge information and legislation Dept. Welfare of Pa., 1950-51; dep. sec. Welfare of Pa., 1951-55; editor East Liberty Tribune, Pitts., 1955-56; spl. asst. to asst. sec. for legislation U.S. Dept. Health, Edn. and Welfare, Washington, 1956-58; asso. dir. Golden Anniversary White House Conf. Children and Youth, 1958-60, dir., 1960; exec. dir. Nat. Com. for Children and Youth, 1960-71; exec. v.p. Nat. Consultants for Children and Youth, 1971—. Mem. Freedmen's Hosp. Study Commn., 1955, study commn. on pub. welfare invited to tour Fed. Republic of Germany, 1953; sec. Ednl. Leadership Council Am., 1972—. Bd. dirs. United Cerebral Palsy of Pa., 1950-56, Pa. Welfare Forum, 1952-61. Active Republican Party, sec. Pa. state com., 1950-56, Pa. del. nat. conv., 1952, presdl. elector, 1952, mem. Pa. state platform com., 1942-54. Mem. nat. bd. Med. Coll. Pa. (formerly Woman's Med. Coll. Pa.), 1952—, chmn. commonwealth com., 1954; trustee P.R. Jr. Coll. Named Woman of Yr., Bus. and Profl. Women's Club Pitts., 1954, Pa., 1958. Mem. Nat. Fedn. Bus. and Profl. Women's Clubs (mem. nat. bd. 1952-60, pres. Pa. fedn. 1956-58, nat. career advancement chmn. 1958-60), Nat. Park Coll. Alumnae Assn. (pres. 1938-39). Clubs: Woman's City (Pitts.); Capitol Hill (Washington). Home: 3700 Massachusetts Av NW Washington DC 20016

JONES, JANE HARDY (MRS. JOHN ROBERT JONES), psychologist; b. St. Louis, May 9, 1927; d. Charles Merton and Lois (Lavery) Hardy; B.A., U. Colo., 1947; M.Ed., Auburn U., 1965, Ed.D., 1967; m. John Robert Jones, Aug. 24, 1947; children—Leslie, Robert. Tchr. Arvada (Colo.) High Sch., 1947-51, Warwick (Va.) High Sch., 1951-52; editor Dept. Army, Ft. Eustis, Va., 1952-54; tchr. Giessen (Germany) Am. Sch., 1961-63; tchr., counselor Columbus (Ga.) High Sch., 1963-65; counseling psychologist, intern supr. Counseling and Testing Center, U. Hawaii, Honolulu, 1967—. Mem. Am., Hawaii psychol. assns., Am. Assn. U. Profs., Am., Hawaii personnel and guidance assns., Phi Beta Kappa (treas. chpt. 1970, pres. 1972), Phi Sigma Iota, Alpha Omicron Pi. Home: 7019 Nuimalu Lp Honolulu HI 96825 Office: Counseling and Testing Center 1615 East-West Rd Honolulu HI 98622

JONES, JANE SADLER (MRS. DONALD W. JONES), librarian; b. Phila., Oct. 26, 1919; d. Milton and Kathryn (Bientzle) Sadler; B.S. in Edn., Temple U., 1940; M.S. in L.S., Drexel U., 1941; m. Donald W. Jones, May 30, 1953. Librarian, Free Library Phila., 1941-42, Bartlett Jr. High Sch., Phila., 1942-54, Fels Jr. High Sch., Phila., 1954—. Mem. Assn. Sch. Librarians Phila., Pa. Library Assn., Chapel of 4 Chaplains, Am. Radio Relay League, Pa.-Jersey Radio Club, Phi Sigma Delta. Home: 19 Edgemoor Rd Cheltenham PA 19012 Office: Devereaux and Langdon Sts Philadelphia PA 19111

JONES, JEAN BOSWELL (MRS. EDWARD S. JONES), polit. worker; b. Baxter Springs, Kan., June 27, 1920; d. James Henry and Maud Cramer (Cramer) Boswell; A.B., U. Kan., 1941; m. Edward S. Jones, Aug. 31, 1941; children—Stephen Edward, Pamela (Mrs. Gene Spinelli), Bradley Boswell. Clk., Skelly Oil Co., Kansas City, Mo., 1942-44. Mem. Mo. Gov.'s Adv. Council Aging; mem. Mo. Bicentennial Commn. Pres. Cass County Meml. Hosp. Aux., 1963-65; mem. Met. Council March Dimes. Chmn. Cass County Republican party, 1964-72; mem. Rep. State Com., 1968-73, vice chmn., 1968-70; del. Rep. Nat. Conv., 1972; pres. 4th Congl. Dist. Federated Rep. Women, 1973—. Bd. dirs. Youth and Civic Assn., Harrisonville, Mo., 1963. Mem. P.E.O., Cass County Hist. Soc., Chi Omega. Episcopalian. Home: 301 N Price Av Harrisonville MO 64701

JONES, JEAN CLARK, librarian; b. Youngstown, O., Dec. 6, 1913; d. Colin Reed and Jean Beatrice (Small) Clark; student Wells Coll., 1933-34; B.A., Western Res. U., 1937; B.L.S., Carnegie Library Sch., 1939; Tchrs. certificate, Fairmont State Coll., 1953; m. John H. Jones (div.); children—David Colin, Philip C., Michael J., Laura (Mrs. John Phillips). Cataloger, Fairmont (W.Va.) State Coll., 1953-58; librarian Linmoor Jr. High Sch., Columbus, O., 1958-61; med. librarian Ross Labs., Columbus, 1961-63; med. librarian Am. Psychiat. Assn., Washington, 1963—. Mem. Med. Library Assn., Spl. Libraries Assn., A.L.A., Soc. Am. Archivists, Am. Assn. for History Medicine. Home: 3701 Massachusetts Av NW Washington DC 20009 Office: 1700 18th St NW Washington DC 20009

JONES, JEAN LENORE MCCLARIN, educator; b. Norfolk, Va., June 2, 1927; d. Donald Stokes and Caroline (Blanks) McClarin; B.S., Mary Washington Coll., U. Va., 1948; M.R.E., Emory U., 1950; Th.D., Boston U., 1968; m. Randolph Lee Jones, June 11, 1948 (div. Apr. 1969); children—Randolph Lee, Caroline Blanks, Lenore Jean, Catherine Wylie. Missionary tchr. Bd. of Missions of Meth. Ch., 1952-67; instr. Kwansei Gakuin U., Japan, 1954-64; asst. prof. Seiwa Coll. for Women, Japan, 1963-64; dean of students, asst. prof. psychology Brenau Coll., Gainesville, Ga., 1968-73; asso. dean students, asst. prof. psychology Pfeiffer Coll., 1973—. Vol. instr. water safety and first aid, chmn. safety com. Lake Nojiri chpt. A.R.C., Japan, 1955-64; vol. leader, trainer, day camp trainer, Far East council, Wellesley Council Girl Scouts U.S., 1955-68. Trustee Canadian Acad., Kobe, Japan, 1959-64. Mem. Am. Assn. U. Women, Nat., Ga. (pres. 1971-73) assns. women deans and counselors, Am., So. coll. personnel assns., Am. Personnel and Guidance Assn., Chi Beta Phi, Mu Phi Epsilon, Alpha Phi Sigma, Phi Alpha Theta. Address: Box 913 Misenheimer NC 28109

JONES, JESSIE ELISE, physician, educator; b. Independence, Miss., June 2, 1922; d. Elmer H. and Mary E. (McKinnon) Jones; B.A., U. Miss., 1944, B.S., 1944; M.D., U. Tenn., 1947. Intern Bapt. Hosp., Little Rock, 1947-48; resident Meth. Hosp., Memphis, 1948-49, Kennedy-VA Hosp. Memphis, 1951-53, U. Tenn., 1953-55; gen. practice medicine, obstetrics and gynecology, also minor surgery, Senatobia, Miss., 1950-51; mem. faculty, dept. pathology U. Tenn. Sch. Medicine, Memphis, 1953—, asst. prof. pathology, 1956—; pathologist Oakville Meml. Hosp., 1959—; staff City of Memphis Hosps., 1957—. Diplomate Am. Bd. Pathology. Mem Am. Soc. Clin. Pathologists, Am. Assn. U. Women, Memphis and Shelby County Soc. Pathologists, Memphis and Shelby County Med. Soc., A.M.A., Coll. Am. Pathologists, Am. Assn. U. Profs. Contbr. articles to profl. jours. Home: 57 N Somerville St Memphis TN 38104 Office: 858 Madison St Memphis TN 38103

JONES, JOYCE GILSTRAP, musician; b. Taylor, Tex., Feb. 13, 1933; d. Johnnie Cavitt and Jessie Lee (Stiles) Gilstrap; Mus.B., U. Tex., 1952, Mus.M., 1953; M. Sacred Music, Southwestern Bapt. Theol. Sem., 1957; D.Mus. Arts, U. Tex. at Austin, 1970; asso. Am. Guild Organists, 1956; m. Robert Carmon Jones, Aug. 28, 1953; children—Robin Lisette, Janet Carol and Jeffrey Carr (twins). Teaching fellow U. Tex., 1952; Tex. Wesleyan Coll., 1953; mem. music faculty Mary Hardin-Baylor Coll., 1957-59; organist First Meth. Ch., Austin, Tex., 1952-53; organist, choir dir. Richland Hills Meth. Ch., Ft. Worth, 1955-57; organ concertizing 1958—; faculty U. Tex., 1966-67; artist-in-residence Huston-Tillotson Coll., 1966-67; mem. faculty Baylor U., Waco, Tex., 1969—. Recipient first prize Julia Heusinger McCall Piano Contest, San Antonio, 1952; 1st place organ winner state, dist., nat. student auditions Nat. Fedn. Music Clubs, 1953; 2d place winner G. B. Dealey Meml. Award, Dallas, 1957, 1st place, 1958; semi-finalist J. S. Bach Competition, Ghent, Belgium, 1964. Fellow Am. Guild Organists; mem. Mu Phi Epsilon (past pres. Ft. Worth Alumnae chpt.), Pi Kappa Lambda, Alpha Lambda Delta. Address: Box 502 George West TX 78022

JONES, JUNE KRAUSE (MRS. HERMAN DOUGLAS JONES), toxicologist; b. Akron, O., June 7, 1918; d. Dwight Adam and Gertrude (Dearsom) Krause; student John B. Stetson U., 1935-38; B.S. in Chemistry, Auburn U., 1939, M.S. in Biochemistry, 1940; postgrad. Walter B. Jones Law Sch. Montgomery, Ala., 1939-40; m. Herman Douglas Jones, Sept. 30, 1942; children—Herman Douglas, Dwight Maxwell. Tchr. sci. Valley Vocational High Sch., Fairfax, Ala., 1940-41; dye chemist Ciba Co., N.Y.C., 1941-42; instr. biochemistry Oglethorpe U. Med. Sch., Atlanta, 1942-44, instr. dept. chemistry, 1945-47; toxicologist Ga. Crime Lab., Atlanta, 1952-61, sr. toxicologist, 1961-73, chief toxicologist, 1973—. Lectr., Ga. Police Acad., 1968—. First sec. Dykes High Sch. P.T.A., Atlanta, 1961. Trustee Herman D. Jones Meml. Found. Fellow Am. Acad. Forensic Scis. (program chmn. toxicology sect. 1967, 68, sec. toxicology sect. 1969, 70, chmn. 1970-72, exec. com. 1972—); mem. Internat. Assn. Forensic Toxicologists, So. Assn. Forensic Scientists (sec. 1966-71), Atlanta Assn. Instrumental Analysts, Peace Officers Assn. Ga. (pres. Ladies Aux. 1963), Atlanta Soc. Hammond Organists, Mortar Bd., Phi Kappa Phi, Gamma Sigma Epsilon, Alpha Xi Delta (pres. Atlanta alumnae 1947-48, Ga. membership chmn. 1957-60, v.p. Omega province 1966-72). Lutheran. Research on effect of trauma on insulin-glucose mechanism of partially, completely hypophysectomized albino rats. Home: 80 Interlochen Dr NE Atlanta GA 30342 Office: 959 E Confederate Av SE Atlanta GA 30316

JONES, KATHRYN NAOMI, social worker; b. Gallup, N.M., Mar. 1, 1921; d. Manson and Eunice (Jenkins) Jones; student Amarillo Jr. Coll., 1938-42; B.B.A., W.Tex. State Coll., 1943; postgrad. U. Okla., 1949-50; M.S.W., U. So. Cal., 1955. Teen-age program dir. YWCA, Amarillo, Tex., 1946; young adult program asst. YWCA, Wichita, Kan., 1946-49; social worker Bur. Indian Affairs, Ft. Defiance, Ariz. 1950; social worker Bur. Adoptions County Los Angeles, 1955; child welfare worker N.M. Dept. Pub. Welfare, Gallup, Albuquerque, Farmington (all N.M.), 1950-62; exec. dir. McKinley County Family Consultation Service, Inc., Gallup, 1962-67; Community Social Worker McKinley County Dept. Pub. Welfare, N.M.; tchr. sociology, social problems, social work Gallup Community Coll., 1962-67; social worker McKinley County Community Planning Project, Health and Social Services Dept., 1967-69; social worker Eastern Navajo Agy. Bur. Indian Affairs, Crownpoint, N.M., 1969—. Chmn. com. children and youth McKinley County White House Conf., 1960-66; mem. program adv. com. Gallup Indian Community Center, 1961-64; program chmn. McKinley County Assn. Retarded Children, 1965-66; mem. McKinley County Com. on Aging, 1965—; v.p. N.W., N.M. Econ. Opportunity Council, 1965-67; v.p. McKinley County Econ. Opportunity Council, 1965—; mem. Community Coordinating Council, 1966—. Named Gallup Bus. Woman of Year Gallup Bus. and Profl. Women's Club, 1963. Mem. Nat. Assn. Social Workers, Acad. Certified Social Workers, Gallup Bus. and Profl. Women's Club (past pres.) League of Women Voters. Democrat. Methodist. Soroptimist (v.p., past treas., com. chmn., past pres.). Home: 613 E Coal Av Gallup NM 87301 Office: Eastern Navajo Agy Bur Indian Affairs Crownpoint NM

JONES, LEAH ALBERTA, ret. educator; b. Ridgeland, S.C., Oct. 4, 1903; d. Paul Wesley and Fannie (Malphrus) Jones; B.S., U. Ga., 1947; M.A., George Peabody Coll. for Tchrs., 1951. Tchr. elementary sch. Ridgeland, 1928-51, prin., 1951-69; elementary supr. Title I program Jasper County Schs., 1969-71. Sec., S.C. Tchr. Edn. and Profl. Standards Commn., 1966-67. Asso. chmn. Jasper County Centennial Commn., 1961-62; mem. civil def. teaching staff; chmn. Jasper County Tricentennial Schs. Participation Program. Chmn. bd. trustees Frederic R. Pratt Meml. Library, 1970—. Named Jasper County Woman Year, 1962-63, 69-70; 1970 S.C. Career Woman of Yr., S.C. Fedn. Bus. and Profl. Women's Clubs, also Silver Tray award. Mem. Jasper County Edn. Assn. (past pres.), Dist. Elementary Prins. (past pres.), Ridgeland Bus. and Profl. Women's Club, N.E.A. (life), S.C. Edn. Assn., Nat. Ret. Tchrs. Assn., Sr. Citizens Am., Delta Kappa Gamma. Baptist. Mem. Order Eastern Star. Address: Great Swamp Rd Ridgeland SC 29936

JONES, LEOTTA WILKINSON, educator; b. N.Y.C., Aug. 26, 1934; d. Marcus and Winifred (Bushell) Wilkinson; B.A., Bklyn. Coll., 1957; M.A., N.Y. U., 1964; m. Russel Jones, June 16, 1956 (div. May 1963); 1 son, Russel Brian (dec.); m. 2d, Winthrop Jones Boulware, Dec. 29, 1973. With Met. Life Ins. Co., N.Y.C., 1952-55; tchr. N.Y.C. Bd. Edn., 1957—. Guidance counselor Adult Basic Edn. Title III, N.Y.C., 1969—. Mem. Met. Sinfoniatta Soc., N.Y.C. Mem. United Fedn. Tchrs., Am., N.Y. State personnel and guidance assns., Am. Assn. Sch. Adminstrs., Assn. N.Y. State Educators of Emotionally Disturbed, Am. Sch. Counselor Assn. Home: 140 Cadman Plaza W Brooklyn NY 11201

JONES, LILY ANN, educator; b. Montevideo, Minn., July 6, 1938; d. Chester Malcolm and Leona (Maus) Jones; B.A., U. Minn., 1960, M.S., 1963, Ph.D., 1964; m. Gerald Domasicwicz, Aug. 2, 1966 (div. 1970); children—Lynne Audrey, Laura Antoinette. Lab. attendant dept. bacteriology U. Minn., 1956; lab. animal attendant dept. bacteriology U. Minn., 1956-60, sr. lab. technician dept. microbiology, 1960-64; instr. dept. microbiology Wayne State U., Detroit, 1964-67, asst. prof., 1967—. Mem. A.A.A.S., Am. Soc. Microbiology, Japanese Soc. Plant Physiologists, Soc. for Indsl. Microbiology, Am. Inst. for Biol. Scis., Genetics Soc. Am., N.Y. Acad. Scis. Contbr. articles in field to profl. jours. Home: 14217 Alma Detroit MI 48205 Office: 540 E Canfield Rd Detroit MI 48201

JONES, LINDA J., univ. adminstr.; b. Denver, Oct. 17, 1949; m. Robert L. and Jual (Haas) Jones; B.A., Emory U., 1970; M.Ed., Ga. State U., 1972; postgrad. U. Minn. Asst. dean women, dir. Oliver Hall, asst. dir. Oliver Coll., U. Kan., Lawrence, 1972-73, asst. dean women, Panhellenic and Cwens adviser, 1973-74; dir. career planning office Coll. Liberal Arts, U. Minn., Mpls., 1974—. Mem. Nat. Assn. for Women Deans, Adminstrs. and Counselors (pub. relations chmn. nat.

conv. 1974), Nat. Assn. Student Personnel Adminstrs., Am. Assn. U. Women, Nat. Orgn. for Women, Women's Equity Action League, Kappa Alpha Theta. Home: 1640 9th St Apt 302 White Bear Lake MN 55110

JONES, LOIS MAILOU (MRS. VERGNIAUD PIERRE-NOEL), artist, educator; b. Boston; d. Thomas Vreeland and Carolyn (Adams) Jones; diploma, Boston Mus. Sch., 1927; certificate, Boston Normal Art Sch., 1928; certificate, Designers Art Sch., 1928; certificate Academie Julian, Paris, France, 1938; A.B. magna cum laude, Howard U., 1945; student Harvard, 1927, Columbia, 1934-36; m. Vergniaud Pierre-Noel, Aug. 18, 1953. Exhibited one man shows Vose Galleries, Boston, Whyte Gallery, Washington, Barnett Aden Gallery, Washington, Howard U. Gallery Art, Washington, UN Club, Washington, Dupont Theater Art Gallery, Pan Am. Union, Centre d'Art, Port au-Prince, Haiti, Gallery Internationale, N.Y.C., Artist's Mart, Lincoln U., Pa., Hampton Inst., Va., Cornell U., Ithaca, N.Y., Del. State Coll., Galerie Soulanges, Paris, France; retrospective exhbn. Howard U. Gallery Art, 1972, Boston Mus. Fine Arts, 1973, Acts of Art Gallery, N.Y.C., 1973; exhibited group shows Salon des Artistes Francais, 1938, 39, 66, Biennial exhbn. Corcoran Gallery Art, Nat. Acad. Design, N.Y.C., Nat. Mus., Pa. Acad., Balt. Mus., Oakland Art Mus. (Cal.), Seatle Mus., Wash. State, A.C.A. Galleries, N.Y.C., Grand Central Art Galleries, San Francisco Mus. Art, Inst. Modern Art, Boston, Galerie Jean Charpentier, Paris, Galerie de Paris, Salon des Independents, Paris, Rhodes Nat. Gallery, S. Rhodesia, King George VI Gallery, Port Elizabeth, Republic S. Africa, Smith Coll., Harman Found., Pa. U. Mus., Am. Embassy, Tanzania; represented permanent collections; Phillips Collection, IBM Corp. Palais Nationale, Haiti, Howard U. Gallery Art, Atlanta U., Barnett Aden Gallery, Bklyn. Mus., 135th St. Pub. Library, Rosenwald Found., Retreat for Fgn. Missionaries, Washington, U. Panjab, Pakistan, Internat. Fair Gallery, Izmir, Turkey, Walker Art Mus., Am. Embassy, Luxembourg, Ebony hdqrs., Chgo. Prof. design and watercolor painting Coll. Fine Arts Howard U., Washington; lectr. Afro-Am. Artists, Contemporary Haitian Artists. Conducted 5 week Around the World Tour, summers 1966, 67, study tour 11 African countries, 1970, 71. Recipient many awards and prizes, including Robert Woods Bliss award, 1st Luban award, 1958; Franz Bader award, 1962; 1st hon. mention for oil painting Societe des Artistes Francais, Paris, 1966; diplome and decoration de l'Ordre Nat. D'Honneur et Merite Haitian Govt., 1954. Fellow Royal Soc. Arts; mem. Nat. Art Dirs. Club, Washington Soc. Artists, Am. Watercolor Assn. (asso.), Washington Watercolor Assn., Alumni Assn. Boston Mus. Sch., Artists Equity, Nat. Conf. of Artists (1st v.p.), Blenfalteur, Foyer Montparnasse, Paris, Alpha Kappa Alpha. Author: Peintures, Lois Mailou Jones, 1937-51, 1952. Home: 4706 17th St NW Washington DC 20011

JONES, LOUISE HINRICHSEN, educator; b. Ames, Ia., Dec. 24, 1930; d. John J.L. and Helen A. (Barnard) Hinrichsen; A.B., Radcliffe Coll., 1952, M.A., 1953; M.A., U. Del., 1968, Ph.D., 1970. Physicist, E.I. duPont de Nemours & Co., Inc., Wilmington, Del., 1953-59, research physicist, 1959-66; asst. prof. statistics and computer sci. U. Del., Newark, 1969—. NSF fellow, 1952-53. Mem. Soc. Indsl. and Applied Math., Am. Math. Soc., Assn. Computing Machinery, Phi Beta Kappa. Home: 233 Cheltenham Rd Newark DE 19711

JONES, MARGARET EILEEN ZEE, physician, educator; b. Swedesboro, N.J., June 24, 1936; d. Wilmer and Elsie (Schober) Zee; B.A., U. Pa., 1957; M.D., Med. Coll. Va., 1961; m. John Walker Jones, Aug. 29, 1959; children—John Stewart, Mary Cassaday, Amanda Worthington. Intern, U. Wash., Seattle, 1962-63, resident in pathology and neuropathology, 1963-65; resident in pathology Med. Coll. Va., Richmond, 1966-67, instr. pathology, 1967-68, acting dir. div. neuropathology, 1967, 68-69, asst. prof. 1968-69; asst. prof. pathology Mich. State U., East Lansing, 1969-73, asso. prof., 1973—. Lectr. neurosurgery Med. Sch., Yale, 1969—. A.D. Williams summer fellow, 1959, 60; Nat. Inst. Neurol. Diseases and Blindness-NIH fellow, 1970-71. Mem. Am. Assn. Neuropathologists, Am. Fedn. for Clin. Research, Nat. Soc. for Programmed Instruction (pres. Mich. chpt. 1973), Am. Soc. Clin. Pathology, Soc. for Neurosci. (pres. Mich. chpt. 1974—). Methodist (tchr. ch. sch. 1952, 61—). Contbr. articles to tech. jours. Home: 599 Pebblebrook St East Lansing MI 48823

JONES, MARGARET PENELOPE HUFF (MRS. HENRY MIKELL JONES), banker; b. Rome, Ga., July 16, 1944; d. Robert Wheeler and Emma Jean (Grant) Huff; student Mary Baldwin Coll., 1962-64; B.B.A., Emory U., 1966; m. Henry Mikell Jones, Oct. 5, 1968. With Trust Co. Ga., Atlanta, 1966-72, comml. banking rep., 1967-68, comml. officer, asst. br. mgr., 1968-72; v.p., cashier First Nat. Bank Tucker, 1972—. Vol. Cancer Soc., United Appeal, Heart Fund. Mem. Nat. Assn. Bank Women. Episcopalian. Home: 4211 Steinhaur Rd NE Marietta GA 30060 Office: PO Box 446 Tucker GA 30084

JONES, MARIAN ABEL (MRS. EDWARD CORNELUIS JONES), assn. exec.; b. Columbia, S.C., June 29, 1926; d. Jepsie Thomas and Ira Beatrice (Bookhart) Abel; B.A., Bennett Coll., 1946; M.A., S.C. State Coll., 1957; postgrad. U. S.C., 1965-71; m. Edward Corneluis Jones, Dec. 25, 1948 (dec.); children—Aurelia Marvene, Edward Corneluis III, Beatrice Lorraine. Tchr. Columbia (S.C.) City Schs., 1946-48, Sumter (S.C.) City Schs., 1948-73; asso. dir. age level ministries S.C. United Meth. Conf. Council on Ministries, Columbia, 1973—, youth coordinator, 1972. Program dir. S.C. Orthopedic Camps, 1947-48; alumna counselor Bennett Coll., Greensboro, N.C., 1950. Leader, Girl Scouts, Sumter, 1960-62. Bd. dirs. Killingsworth Home for Women, 1973—; mem. adv. bd. Boylan-Havan-Mather Acad., 1971—. Named Mother of Year, Black Youth of Sumter, 1971. Mem. N.A.A.C.P., League Women Voters. Home: 40 S Washington St Sumter SC 29150 Office: 1420 Lady St Columbia SC 29201

JONES, MARTHA DABNEY, ret. ednl. adminstr.; b. Williamsburg, Va., Jan. 15, 1910; d. Edmund Ruffin and Jane Bell (Dabney) Jones; B.A., Sweet Briar Coll., 1929; M.A., U. N.C., 1935. Tchr. pub. schs., 1929-31; religious edn. worker, 1932-34; tchr. Hannah More Acad., 1935-37; tchr., adminstr. St. Mary's Jr. Coll., 1937-55; headmistress Stuart Hall, Staunton, Va., 1955-72, dir. devel., 1972-73. Served with WAC, 1943-45. Decorated Croix de Guerre avec Etoile. Home: 405 DuPont Av Staunton VA 24401

JONES, MARY ALICE, editor, author; b. Dallas, June 23, 1899; d. Paul and Mamie (Henderson) Jones; B.A., U. Tex., 1917; M.A., Northwestern U., 1923; Ph.D., Yale, 1934. Tchr. Chattanooga High Sch., 1920-22; editor Children's Publs., The Methodist Ch., Nashville, 1923-25; dir. Children's Work Nat. Council Chs., Chgo., 1926-46; children's book editor Rand McNally Co., Chgo., 1946-52, religious book editor, Chgo., 1965—; dir. Children's work The Methodist Ch., Nashville, 1952-65; vis. prof. Northwestern U., Yale Div. Sch., Union Theol. Sem., Pacific Sch. Religion. Mem. gen. bd. Nat. Council Chs., 1952-65; adminstrv. com. World Council Christian Edn. Mem. UN Assn., League of Women Voters, Am. Assn. U. Women, Sigma Theta Phi, Pi Beta Phi. Methodist. Author: The Faith of Our Children, 1940; The Christian Faith Speaks to Children, 1956; Tell Me About God, 1942; Tell Me About Jesus, 1944; Tell Me About the Bible, 1946; Tell Me About Prayer, 1946; Tell Me About Heaven, 1948; Tell Me About Christmas, 1954; Know Your Bible, 1960; God Speaks to Me, 1963; God's Plan for Growing Things, 1966; Friends Are For Loving, 1970; Bible Stories, 1973. Home: 3415 West End Apt 908 Nashville TN 37203

JONES, MARY DAILEY (MRS. HARVEY BRADLEY JONES), club woman; b. Billings Mont.; d. Leroy Nathaniel and Janet (Currie) Dailey; student Carleton Coll., 1943-44, U. Mont., 1944-46, U. Cal. at Los Angeles, 1959; m. Harvey Bradley Jones, Nov. 15, 1952; children—Dailey, Janet Currie, Ellis Bradley. Founder Jr. Art Council, Los Angeles County Mus., treas., 1953-55, v.p., 1955-56, mem. Pasadena (Cal.) Philharmonic com., Costume Council, co-founder Art Rental Gallery, 1953, chmn. art and architecture tour, 1955; founder mem. Art Alliance, Pasadena Art Mus., sec., 1955-56; benefit chmn. Pasadena Girls Club, 1959, bd. dirs., 1958-60; chmn. Los Angeles Tennis Patron's Assn. Benefit, 1965; sustaining Jr. League Pasadena; mem. docent council Los Angeles County Mus.; mem. costume council Los Angeles County Mus. Art., program chmn. 20th Century Greatest Designers; mem. blue ribbon com. Los Angeles Music Center; benefit chmn. Venice com. Internat. Fund for Monuments, 1971. Interior decorator Mary Jones Interiors. Mem. Kappa Alpha Theta. Clubs: Valley Hunt (Pasadena); California (Los Angeles). Home: 260 Hillside Rd South Pasadena CA 91030

JONES, MARY GARDINER, lawyer, educator; b. N.Y.C., Dec. 10, 1920; d. Charles Herbert and Anna Livingston (Short) Jones; B.A., Wellesley Coll., 1943; J.D., Yale, 1948. Intern tchr. George Sch., Newtown, Pa., 1943-44; research analyst research and analysis br. Internat. Law sect. OSS, Washington, 1944-46; admitted to N.Y. State bar, 1949; admitted to D.C. bar, U.S. Supreme Ct. bar; asso. firm Donovan, Leisure, Newton & Irvine, N.Y.C., 1948-53; chief trial atty. N.Y. Office, Antitrust div. Dept. of Justice, N.Y.C., 1953-61; asso. firm Webster, Sheffield, Fleischmann, Hitchcock & Chrystie, N.Y.C., 1961-64; commr. FTC, Washington, 1964-73; prof. Coll. Law, Coll. Commerce and Bus. Adminstrn., U. Ill., Champaign-Urbana, 1974—. Former adj. mem. Interdisciplinary Council on Communications Smithsonian Instn.; mem. com. on sci. and tech. information Fed. Council Sci. and Tech.; mem. nat. adv. council Hampshire Coll.; adv. council Assn. for Consumer Research. Dir. Alcon Labs., Inc., Ft. Worth. Trustee Nat. Consumer Law Center, Boston, Wellesley Coll., Colgate U., Suomi Coll.; bd. dirs. Nat. Consumers League, Washington, NTL Labs., Washington. Mem. Am. (antitrust sect., subcom. on patents, trademarks and knowhow, chmn. consumer protection com. adminstrv. law sect., Fed. (trade regulation com.; former mem. nat. com. for equal opportunity in bus. Nat. Bus. League Council on Community Affairs in D.C.) bar assns., Am. Assn. U. Women (2d v.p. Washington br. 1968, 69; cons. to Nat. Com. Studying Human Use Urban Space nat. orgn.), Yale Law Sch. Assn. (v.p. 1969-70; v.p. exec. com. 1971—). Contbr. articles to law jours. and bus. and financial periodicals. Home: 603 W Illinois Av Urbana IL 61801 Office: Coll Law U Ill Champaign IL 61820

JONES, (MARY) MARGUERITE RUNYAN (MRS. CARL JONES), realtor; b. Knightstown, Ind., Apr. 8, 1914; d. Jesse C. and Lena B. (Hudelson) Runyan; grad. high sch.; m. Carl Jones, Aug. 25, 1934; 1 dau., Mary Louise (Mrs. Donald L. Bisch). Real estate saleswoman, 1949-53; owner Marguerite Jones Realty Co., Dayton, O., 1953—. First woman dir. Dayton Real Estate Bd. Mem. Ohio Assn. Real Estate Bds. (pres. women's council Dayton 1967; state trustee 1959-63, 68—, alternate trustee 1965-67), Dayton Area C. of C., Dayton Area Bd. Realtors (dir. 1968-70), Ohio Assn. Realtors (trustee, Make Ohio Better com.), Dayton Traders Club (sec. 1961-65), Builders Assn., Dayton Soc. Painters and Sculptors, Women's Council Nat. Assn. Realty Bds. (sec. 1970). Club: Quota (Dayton). Home: 8 Napoleon Dr Dayton OH 45429

JONES, MILDRED LOUISE LOVING (MRS. LUCIEN N. JONES), educator; b. Bluefield, W.Va., Dec. 13, 1904; d. William Porcher and Helen Dell (Lamborn) Loving; student Med. Coll. Va., 1936-44, 50-52, Harvard, 1959; m. Lucien N. Jones, Oct. 31, 1925; children—Jo-Lo (Mrs. Willie Fergusson), Lucien N. Technician dept. anatomy Med. Coll. Va., Richmond, 1940-41, teaching asst., 1941-47, instr., 1947-52, asst. prof., 1952-60, asso. prof., 1960—. Consultation lectures to psychiat. staff; tutor splty. bds. in surgery, neurology, psychiatry. Recipient Distinguished Service award Graduating Class in medicine Med. Coll. Va., 1966. Mem. Pan Am. Congress Anatomy, So. Soc. Anatomy, Va. Acad. Sci., Alpha Sigma Chi. Clubs: Altrusa (com. chmn. 1960), Country of Va., Willow Oaks Country; Cajal. Research and publs. on staining and embedding brain slices in plastic, central nervous system stimulation in animals. Home: 7025 Riverside Dr Richmond VA 23225

JONES, MURIEL ELLENOR, physician; b. Washington, Mar. 23, 1943; d. Milton Ankers and Fannie (Ferris) Jones; A.B., Randolph-Macon Women's Coll., 1965; M.D., Med. Coll. Va., 1969; student Va. Poly. Inst., summer 1964. Intern Virginia Mason Hosp., Seattle, 1969-70; mem. temporary staff Johnston Meml. Hosp., Abingdon, Va., summer 1970; med. staff mem. Group Health Coop., Seattle, 1970—. NSF Undergrad. Research grantee, 1964. Baptist (trustee ch. 1971—). Home: 819 W Galer St Seattle WA 98199 Office: 200 15th East Seattle WA 98122

JONES, NANCY CAROL, educator, journalist; b. Pitts., June 15, 1934; d. Eugene E. and Mary Jane (Cassilly) Jones; B.A. magna cum laude, U. Pitts., 1956; M.S. in Journalism, Northwestern U., 1959; Ph.D., U. Mo., 1967. Reporter, Williamsburg Bur., teen page editor main bur. Newport News (Va.) Daily Press, 1956-58; city hall reporter Hollywood bur., chief Melbourne bur. Miami (Fla.) Herald, 1959-61; editor A.P., Louisville bur., 1961-65; faculty Pa. State U., Sch. Journalism, University Park, 1967-71; asso. prof. Duquesne U., Pitts., 1971—. Recipient Nationality Rooms Hostess award U. Pitts., 1955. Mem. Women in Communications (chmn. nat. scholarship com. 1972-73, faculty adviser Duquesne U. student chpt. 1972—, 2d v.p. Pitts. chpt. 1973-74), Sigma Delta Chi (rec. sec. Pitts. chpt. 1973-74. Methodist. Contbr. articles to profl. jours. Home: 117 Georgetown Av Pittsburgh PA 15229

JONES, NANCY HERMINE DOERMANN, educator; b. Chgo., Feb. 20, 1931; d. Gerhard Herman and Mary (Mesarvey) Doermann; B.A., Capital U., 1953; m. William Oberst Jones, June 8, 1954; children—William Bradley, Gwyn Elizabeth, Douglas Gerhard. Tchr. English, Ashville (O.) High Sch., 1953-54; sec., pres.'s office Columbia Tchrs. Coll., 1954-55, asst. to personnel dir., 1957-58; instr. speech U. R.I., 1965-66; travel services Plasma Physics Lab., Princeton, 1974—. Pres., League Women Voters, South Kingstown, 1960-62, pres., R.I., 1969-72; pres. South County Jr. Women's Club, 1965-66; div. chmn. R.I. State Fedn. Women's Clubs, 1968-70; active Planned Parenthood R.I., Children's Friend and Service; mem. Gov.'s Commn. Subcom. on Legal Rights of Women. Trustee Nat. Assembly for Social Policy and Devel. Named Outstanding Young Woman in Am., 1965. Mem. Pi Epsilon Delta, Phi Beta. Lutheran. Home: Northgate Apts Cranbury NJ 08512

JONES, NINA FLEMISTER (MRS. WILLIAM M. JONES), sch. adminstr.; b. Madison, Ga., July 30, 1918; d. Sumner Lewis and Hallie (Hall) Flemister; A.B., Central YMCA Coll., 1938; M.Ed., Chgo. Tchrs. Coll., 1942; student U. Chgo., 1940-58; Loyola U., 1971—; m. William M. Jones, Sept. 21, 1940; children—William M. Jr., Steven L. Tchr. Chgo. Bd. Edn., 1942-65, prin. 1966-69, dist. supt. Dist. 2, Chgo., 1969—. Active Ill. Children's Home and Aid Soc.; mem. Friends of the New Provident Hosp., 1971—. Mem. Am. Assn. U. Women, Adminstrv. Women in Edn., Alpha Kappa Alpha, Alpha Gamma Pi. Club: Ella Flagg Young. Home: 9156 S Constance Chicago IL 60617 Office: 6110 N Fairfield St Chicago IL 60659

JONES, NORMA JOY HOPSON (MRS. S. MURRAY JONES), club woman; b. Ft. Atkinson, Wis.; d. Edgar DeLos and Mary (Colwell) Hopson; B.S., Boston U.; student Radcliffe Coll., Katherine Gibbs Secretarial Sch., Harvard; m. S. Murray Jones, May 2, 1931 (dec.); children—Claire Joyce (Mrs. Richard H. Royston), Malcolm Murray. Personal dir., N.Y.C., 1929-31. Leader Girl Scouts Am., Scarsdale, N.Y., 1942-45. Mem. bldg. fund com. YWCA, Boston, 1951; mem. Bunker Hill Monument Assn. Mem. Nat. League Am. Pen Women (rec. sec. Boston br. 1966-68, v.p. 1968-70), D.A.R. (regent 1963-65, librarian 1964-68, vice regent 1968-70, historian 1967—, pub. relations chmn. 1963-70), Nat. Soc. Daus. of 1812 (state rec. sec. 1965-67, historian 1967-70, state pres. 1970-71, nat. resolutions com. 1971-73), Hereditary Order Descs. Colonial Govs. Daus. Founders and Patriots of Am. (state councillor 1966-67, state pres. 1967-70, state historian 1970-73), Nat. Soc. Women Descs. Ancient and Honorable Arty. Co. (state color bearer 1965-68, state dep. 1971-74, v.p. 1974—), Soc. Daus of Colonial Wars (state historian 1968-71, state custodian 1971-74), Nat. Soc. Old Plymouth Colony Descs. (v.p. gen. 1969-72, pres. gen. 1972—), Soc. Daus. of Barons of Runnemede, Soc. of Descs. of Colonial Clergy (mem. council 1969—), Living Descs. Blood Royal, Merrimac Valley Colony Nat. Soc. New Eng. Women, Huguenot Soc. Mass. and N.H. (mem. council 1971-73, pres. 1973—), Piscataqua Pioneers, Magna Charta Dames, Nat. Soc. Dames Ct. of Honor (organizing pres. and pres. Mass. 1970-74, nat. trustee 1974—), Soc. Descs. Knights Most Noble Order of the Garter, Order Ams. of Armorial Ancestry, Order Three Crusades, Nat. Gavel Club, Colonial Dames Vt., Flagon and Trencher, Doolittles of Am., Conn. Soc. Genealogists, Stamford Geneal. Soc., Hereditary Register U.S.A., Pi Beta Phi. Author poems Boston Pops, Skywalk, others. Home: 14 Concord Av Cambridge MA 02138

JONES, NORMA LOUISE, educator; b. Poplar, Wis.; d. George Elmer and Hilma June (Wiberg) Jones; B.E., U. Wis.; M.A., U. Minn., 1952; postgrad. U. Ill., 1957; Ph.D., U. Mich., 1965. Librarian, Grand Rapids (Mich.) pub. schs., 1947-62; Grand Rapids (Mich.) Pub. Library, 1948-49; instr. Central Mich. U., Mt. Pleasant, 1954, 55; librarian Benton Harbor (Mich.) pub. schs., 1962-63; lectr. U. Mich., Ann Arbor, 1954, 55, 61, 63-65, asst. prof., 1966-68; asst. prof. dept. library sci. U. Wis.-Oshkosh, 1968-70, asso. prof., 1970—. Mem. com. on certification of sch. librarians State of Wis., 1972—. Mem. Am. (mem. reference awards com. 1973—), Wis. library assns., Am. Assn. Sch. Librarians, Phi Beta Kappa, Phi Kappa Phi, Pi Lambda Theta, Beta Phi Mu, Sigma Pi Epsilon. Home: 1220 Maricopa Dr Oshkosh WI 54901

JONES, NORMA MARY CATHARINE, nurse educator; b. LaFleche, Sask., Can., Dec. 26, 1929; d. Samuel and Florence Ada (Scott) Jones; R.N., Hamilton Gen. Hosp., 1952; B.A., Seattle Pacific Coll., 1956; diploma midwifery Simpson Meml. Maternity Pavilion, Edinburgh (Scotland), 1959; diploma clin. instr. Coll. Nurses, Edinburgh, 1963-64. Staff nurse Tillsonburg (Ont., Can.) Dist. Meml. Hosp., 1952-53, dir. inservice edn., 1968—; instr. Missionary Health Inst., Toronto, Ont., 1956-58; midwife Nazareth Hosp., Israel, 1960-62, instr. student nurses, 1964-67. Mem. adv. com. Fanshawe Community Coll., 1970-74; chmn. Community Services Com., 1973—. Mem. R.N. Assn. Ont. Home: Rural Route 1 Springford ON NOJ 1XO Canada Office: 167 Rolph St Tillsonburg ON N4G 4H3 Canada

JONES, PATRICIA, govt. computer analyst; b. Algood, Tenn., Mar. 5, 1939; d. Mayhew Pettus and Sara Josephine (Currin) Jones; B.S., George Peabody Coll. for Tchrs., 1960, M.A., 1971; Ed.D. (hon.) U.S. U. Am., 1974. Ednl. sec. First Bapt. Ch., Alexandria, Va., 1967-68; data processing supr. So. Bapt. Fgn. Mission Bd., Richmond, Va., 1968-70; asst. coordinator women's residence halls Western Carolina U., Cullowhee, N.C., 1971-72; asso. dean students, asst. prof. math. W.Va. Wesleyan Coll., Buckhannon, 1972-74; computer systems analyst Va. State Police, Richmond, 1974—. Served as officer USNR, 1960-66. Mem. Nat. Assn. Women Deans, Adminstrs. and Counselors (mem. com. 1973-74), Am. Assn. U. Women (exec. bd. 1972-74), Am. Assn. U. Profs., W.Va. Student Personnel Adminstrs. Republican. Baptist. Home: 1201 Claxton Rd Richmond VA 23233 Office: Va State Police Hdqrs Richmond VA 23261

JONES, QUINCETTE COTTING (MRS. ROBERT ALLAN JONES), psychologist; b. Los Angeles; d. Quincy and Kathryn (McLaughlin) Cotting; B.A., U. So. Cal., 1939, M.A., 1965; postgrad. U. Cal., Los Angeles, 1950-66, Immaculate Heart Coll., 1958-59, Loyola U., Los Angeles, 1960-61; m. Robert Allan Jones, Sept. 27, 1940; 1 son, Robert Cotting. Counselor Los Angeles City Schs., 1940—, sch. psychologist, 1965—, sch. psychometrist, 1950—. Mem. Assistance League, Delta Kappa Gamma, Delta Delta Delta. Home: 1008 N Sepulveda Blvd Los Angeles CA 90049

JONES, REBA LOYCE BROUGHTON (MRS. ROSS EDWARD JONES), psychologist; b. Lamesa, Tex.; d. James Thomas and Florence (Jordan) Broughton; student Tex. Tech. Coll., 1935-36; B.A., Tex. Christian U., 1954, M.A., 1958; m. Ross Edward Jones, June 12, 1937. Comml. pilot, self-employed, Albuquerque, 1943-45; psychologist Tex. Christian U., Testing Center, Ft. Worth, 1952-54; psychologist pub. schs., Ft. Worth, 1954—; cons. psychol. services dept. Ft. Worth Pub. Schs. Individual practice psychology, Ft. Worth, summers 1958—; mem. writing com. Guidance in Tex. Schs. for Tex. Edn. Agy., 1960. Bd. dirs. Tex. Assn. Mental Health; past pres. Tarrant County Assn. Mental Health. Mem. Am., Southwestern, Tex. (pres., dir. div. sch. psychology) psychol. assns., Tex. Guidance and Personnel Assn., Am. Assn. U. Women (bd. dirs.), Internat. Platform Assn., Delta Kappa Gamma. Author: Handbook for Diagnosing and Developing Learning Skills, 1971. Home: 4617 Hildring Dr E Ft Worth TX 76109 Office: 3210 W Lancaster St Ft Worth TX 76107

JONES, SISTER ROSANNE, educator; b. Tampa, Fla., Jan. 27, 1924; d. Hafford Coke and Jane Teresa (Semmes) Jones; secretarial diploma Bus. U. Tampa, 1942; B.S. magna cum laude, St. Bonaventure U., 1954, M.A., 1964; postgrad. St. Bonaventure U., Siena Coll., U. Fla. Joined Sisters of St. Francis of Allegany, N.Y., 1946; tchr., counselor St. Paul's Sch., St. Petersburg, Fla., 1945-55, St. Mary's Sch., Rome, N.Y., 1956-57. St. Patrick St., Catskill, N.Y., 1958-59, Corpus Christi Sch., Miami, Fla., 1960-61, Verot Sch., Ft. Myers, Fla., 1962-65; instr. U. Tampa, 1965-66, St. Elizabeth Coll., Allegany, N.Y., 1966-68; prof., coordinator human devel. center, success program Hillsborough Community Coll., Tampa, Fla., 1968—; chief price control panel OPA, Hillsboro County, Fla., 1942-44. Mem. Am. Social. Assn., Am. Personnel and Guidance Assn., Nat. Vocational Guidance Assn., Assn. for Measurement in Edn. and Guidance, Am. Coll. Personnel Assn., Tampa Hist. Soc., D.A.R., U.D.C., Urban League. Author: Introduction to Sociology-an Individualized Program, 1970. Home: 2812 Central St Tampa FL 33602

JONES, ROSEMARY LYONS (MRS. ISAAC HARDEMAN JONES), educator, writer; b. N.Y.C., Aug. 3, 1902; d. Michael and Harriet Carol (Levey) Lyons; ed. U. Wis.; m. Isaac Hardeman Jones, June 19, 1923; children—June Carol (Mrs. Samuel Bradshaw Morgan Jr.), Michael Hardeman, Gerald Lyons. Editor Fashion Acad., N.Y.C.; feature writer Bklyn. Daily Eagle; corr. Christian Sci. Monitor, Macon, Ga., 1934-38; weekly column writer Macon (Ga.) Telegraph & News, 1934-37; creator, writer various radio shows for WMAZ and WBML, Macon, 1938-45; dir. women's activities, dir. publicity WBML, Macon, 1938-45; dir. Radio Rich's Atlanta, 1945-50; corr. Automotive News Mag., Detroit, 1965—, Modern Beauty Shop Mag., Chgo. 1971—; tchr. profl. non-fiction Community Edn. Services, Emory U., Atlanta, 1970—; dir. pub. relations office Macon (Ga.) Pretressed Concrete, Inc., 1973—. Mem. Nat. League Am. Pen Women (pres. Atlanta br. 1974-76), Ga. Writers Assn., Dixie Council Authors and Journalists, Women in Communications. Christian Scientist. Editor Atlanta br. Nat. League of Am. Penwomen's Pengraphs; founding editor First Ch. of Christ Scientist Newsletter, Decatur, 1973—. Home and office: 423 Clairmont Av Decatur GA 30030

JONES, RUBY AILEEN HIDAY (MRS. HARRY PAUL JONES), educator, author; b. Fortville, Ind., 1908; d. James W. and Ora C. (James) Hiday; A.B., Earlham Coll., 1930; student Butler U., 1928-29, U. Ind. Ext., 1929-30; postgrad. Ball State U., 1960; m. Harry Paul Jones, Sept. 26, 1934; children—James Dennis, David Meredith, Jon Stuart. Tchr. English, history McCordsville (Ind.) High Sch., 1930-34; mem. English, journalism faculty Madison Heights Sr. High Sch., Anderson, Ind., 1959-74. Columnist As I See It, Middletown (Ind.) News, 1958—, Alexandria (Ind.) Times Tribune, 1964-71; guest columnist Anderson (Ind.) Bulletin. Recipient Nat. Poetry Anthology Contest for poems, 1961, 63, 64, 65, 66, 70, 71, 72, 73, 74; Poetry award Poets Ind., Inc., 1963; Hoosier State Press Assn. award, 1973. M.M.S. Methodist (tchr., youth worker). Author: The Searching Wind, 1964; Notes of a Journey (serial) 1965-66; Westward Ho! (serial travelogue), 1969; Steamboat Round the Bend (travelogue serial), 1971. Contbr. articles to religious, profl. publs., nat. mags. Home: Maplestone Farm RR 1 Box 53 Daleville IN 47334 Office: 4610 Madison Av Anderson IN 46013

JONES, RUTH BERNIECE (MRS. FRED M. JONES), savs. and loan assn. exec.; b. Urbana, Ill., Jan. 22, 1910; d. Rodney R. and Cora Belle (Johnson) Smith; student U. Ill., 1927-28; m. Fred Mitchell Jones, June 18, 1932; 1 dau., Ruth Ellen (Mrs. Charles M. Clark). Joined Citizens Bldg. Assn., Urbana, 1929, pres., 1961—, also dir.; owner, operator Ruth B. Jones Ins. Agy., Urbana, 1937—; dir. Busey First Nat. Bank. Mem. Champaign County Pub. Aid Adv. Bd., 1961—. Mem. Champaign-Urbana Bus. and Profl. Women's Club (pres. 1935-37), Ill. Fedn. Bus. and Profl. Women's Club (pres. 1948-50, trustee state-wide fellowship), D.A.R. (regent Alliance chpt. 1957-61; state chmn. 1961-63), Ill. Savs. and Loan League, Phi Mu (adviser 1965—). Home: 202 E Washington St Urbana IL 61801 Office: 107 S Race St Urbana IL 61801

JONES, RUTH ELIZABETH KNOCH (MRS. EDWIN C. JONES), ret. educator; b. Stanleyville, O., Nov. 14, 1914; d. George Henry and Laura (Best) Knoch; B.S., Ohio U., 1935, M.S., 1937; student Cornell U., 1946, U. Okla., 1958, W.Va. U., 1965; m. Edwin C. Jones, July 2, 1961. Dietitian Ohio U., 1935-38; home demonstration agt. Morgan County, O., 1938-41; home demonstration agt. Upshur County, W.Va., 1941-46; state extension specialist in clothing and textiles, asst. prof. W.Va. U., 1946-70. Mem. Am., W.Va. Home econs. assns., Elec. Woman's Round Table, Phi Upsilon Omicron, Epsilon Sigma Phi (sec. 1968-70), Gamma Sigma Delta. Home: 1380 Western Av Morgantown WV 26505

JONES, RUTHANNE MARR (MRS. KEITH D. JONES), phys. therapist, motel exec., clubwoman; b. Warrensburg, Mo., Oct. 19, 1935; d. J. Kenneth and Ruth A. (Noble) Marr; student U. Mo., 1953-54, U. Colo., 1954; B.A. in Psychology, U. So. Cal., 1956, B.S. in Phys. Therapy, 1958, grad. student London Sch. Econs., 1956-57; M.A. in English, Central Mo. State U., 1962; m. Keith D. Jones, Jan. 31, 1964; children—Brian Kent, Stephen Dennis. Phys. therapist Cerebral Palsy Nursery Sch., U. Cal. at Los Angeles, 1958-59; chief phys. therapist Warrensburg (Mo.) Nursing and Med. Center, 1966—. Vice pres. Holiday Inn, Warrensburg, 1968—, asst. sec., 1968—. Vol. therapist Johnson County Meml. Hosp., Warrensburg, 1964-66; vol. instr. in phys. therapy, cons. Jordan for Medico, 1962-63; pres. Johnson County Med. Aux., 1965-66, 6th dist. dir., 1968-70; 3d v.p. Mo. State Med. Aux., 1970-71; Mo. councilor to So. Med. Assn., 1967-69, historian, 1973-74; founder Johnson County Meml. Hosp. Guild, 1967. Mem. Am. Assn. Phys. Therapy, Nat. Assn. Parliamentarians, Woman's Aux. to A.M.A., Woman's Aux. to Mo. State Med. Assn. (pres. 1972-73), Am. Contract Bridge League, League Women Voters, Chi Omega. Presbyn. Mem. Order Eastern Star. Clubs: Secunda Study (Federated, pres. 1966-67), Johnson County Parliamentarian (sec. 1969, historian 1970-71, pres. 1971-72), Arts Book and Craft. Home: 711 S Holden St Warrensburg MO 64093 Office: 122 E Market St Warrensburg MO 64093

JONES, SALLY MESSER (MRS. JOHN RAYMOND JONES), banker; b. Los Angeles, Aug. 2, 1939; d. John G. and Laura (Gregg) Messer; B.S. in Bus. Adminstrn., U. So. Cal., 1961, M.B.A., 1974; m. John Raymond Jones, Apr. 2, 1964 (div. June 1969); 1 son, Christopher Eric. Tchr., Los Angeles City Schs., 1961-62; with Erwin Wasey, Ruthrauff & Ryan, Inc., Los Angeles, 1963-64, Internat. Prodns. Inc., Los Angeles, 1964-67; accountant, financial analyst Winkast Film Prodns., 1965-73; loan officer Security Pacific Nat. Bank, Los Angeles, 1974—. Mem. Pi Beta Phi. Home: 513 N Arden Blvd Los Angeles CA 90004

JONES, SARA RODDIS (MRS. HENRY STEWART JONES), club woman; b. Marshfield, Wis., May 14, 1909; d. Hamilton and Catherine (Prindle) Roddis; student Sophie Newcomb Coll., 1925-28; m. Henry Stewart Jones, Apr. 16, 1929; children—Roddis Stewart, David Stewart, Jarl Hamilton. Vice chmn. Republican Party Wis., 1951-61; Wis. chmn. campaign activities Wis. Fedn. Rep. Women, 1954-60. Pres. Hamilton Roddis Found., Marshfield, 1953—; bd. dirs. Tamassee Sch. Mem. D.A.R. (Wis. chmn. nat. def. 1953-62, vice chmn. nat. resolutions com. 1961-65; nat. chmn. def. com. 1962-65, 68—, treas. gen. nat. soc. 1965-68, 1st v.p. gen. 1968-71, pres. gen. 1974—), Wis. Fedn. Women's Clubs (7th dist. legislative chmn. 1956-62), P.E.O. Episcopalian. Home: 303 Park St Marshfield WI 54449

JONES, SARAH DOWLIN, librarian; b. Media, Pa., Sept. 20, 1916; d. William Dowlin and Elsie May (Lutton) Jones; A.B., U. Pa., 1937, M.A., 1939, Ph.D., 1954; B.L.S. Pratt Inst. Library Sch., 1944. Reference asst. Pratt Inst. Library, 1944-45; reference librarian Am. Library, London, 1945-47; head math. physics library U. Pa., 1947-49, head reference dept. U. Pa. Library, 1949-52; librarian Goucher Coll., 1952—. Mem. Modern Lang. Assn., Md. Library Assn., A.L.A. (council 1969-71), Assn. Coll. and Reference Libraries, Women's Internat. League, Am. Assn. U. Women, Mortar Bd., Phi Beta Kappa. Home: 24 E Aylesbury Rd Timonium MD 21093

JONES, SHIRLEY BRANNOCK (MRS. WILLIAM L. JONES), judge; b. Cambridge, Md., June 27, 1925; d. Linwood U. and Edith (Lake) Brannock; A.A., U. Balt., 1944, LL.B., with honors, 1946; m. William L. Jones, Aug. 29, 1953. Admitted to Md. bar, Supreme Bench Balt. City, 1947, U.S. Dist. Ct. Md., 1952; atty. Md. Dept. Employment Security, 1946-52; gen. practice law, Balt., 1952-61; asst. city solicitor, Balt., 1952-58; asst. atty. gen. Md., 1958; served on Orphans' Ct., Balt., 1959-61; apptd. to Supreme Bench Balt., 1961, elected asso. judge, 1962—. Mem. Savs. and Loan Study Commn., 1960, Commn. to Study Criminal Sentencing, 1962-65, Commn. to Study Md. Correctional Systems, 1966-67; former lectr. U. Balt. Sch. Law. Trustee U. Balt. Named Alumna of Year U. Balt., 1970, Woman of Year Balt. Bus. and Profl. Women's Club, 1961. Mem. Am., Md. bar assns., Bar Assn. Balt. City, Md. Hist. Soc., Iota Tau Tau. Methodist. Home: 8 Charles Plaza Baltimore MD 21201 Office: Court House Baltimore MD 21202

JONES, SHIRLEY MAXWELL, ednl. adminstr.; b. Dellrose, Tenn., Dec. 4, 1935; d. Elerson Butler and Alice Marie (Zwally) Jones; B.A. with distinction U. Ky., 1966; M.A., George Peabody Coll., 1969; m. Robert Louis Jones; children—Melinda Kay, Randall Eugene. Exec. sec. to v.p. financial affairs La. State U., Baton Rouge, 1957-58; tchr. and guidance counselor Met. Nashville Sch. Bd., 1967-68; asst. dean students Vanderbilt U., Nashville, after 1969. Mem. Am., So. (sec. 1972-74) coll. personnel assns., Tenn. Women Deans and Counselors Assn., Nat. Assn. Women Deans, Adminstrs., Counselors, Am. Guidance Personnel Assn., Nashville Ballet Soc. (exec. v.p. 1971-73), Shreveport Jr. C. of C. Aux. (pres. 1960-61). Home: Box 92 Mississippi State MS 39762

JONES, SHIRLEY R. DOUGLAS (MRS. DAVID B. JONES), mdse. exec.; b. Milw.; d. Edward P. and Sarah (Carr) Douglas; m. David B. Jones, Feb. 10, 1951. Exec. editor Midwest, Charm mag., Chgo., 1950-58; pres. Shirley Douglas Jones Assos., Florence, Italy, 1958-66; mdse. editor McCall's Fashion News, N.Y.C., 1966-67; mdse. dir. McCall's Pattern Publs., N.Y.C., 1967-71; market relations dir. McCall Pattern Co., 1971—. Mem. Fashion Group, Womens Fashion Fabrics Assn. Home: 60 E 8th St New York City NY 10003 Office: 230 Park Av New York City NY 10018

JONES, STELLA MARGUERITE, librarian; b. Waukon, Ia., Apr. 11, 1906; d. Arthur Albert and Nancy Belle (McShane) Jones; A.A., Upper Ia. U., 1927, B.A., 1933; M.A., U. Denver, 1962. Rural grade sch. tchr., Allamakee County, Ia., 1924-27; tchr. English Jr. High Sch., Garner, Ia., 1928-31; normal tng. supr., Shell Rock, 1935-44; tchr. English, Decorah, Ia., 1944-47; instr. Am. history Arlington Heights Jr. High Sch., 1947-49; instr. English, librarian DeWitt High Sch., 1953-61; librarian Camanche High Sch., 1961-71. Mem. A.L.A., N.E.A., Ia. Edn. Assn., Nat., Ia. ret. tchrs. assns., Am. Assn. U. Women, D.A.R., Daus. Am. Colonists, Wa tan Ye, Delta Kappa Gamma, Pi Kappa Delta, Sigma Tau Delta. Methodist. Home: 2385 Chancy St Clinton IA 52732

JONES, SUZANNE (TAFFY) (MRS. DONALD S. JONES), writer; b. Binghamton, N.Y., Sept. 27, 1922; d. Frank W. and Villo (Latcher) Taft; student Finch Coll., N.Y.C., 1942, Am. Acad. Dramatic Arts, N.Y.C., 1942, Bread Loaf, Writer's Conf., Vt., 1966; m. Donald S. Jones, June 22, 1944; children—Ronald, Laurie. Photographer's model Anscofilm, 1935-41; fashion model, 1940-62; dancing and drama tchr. Knox Sch. for Girls, Cooperstown, N.Y., 1943-44; dir. Aquacades and Ballets Sidney Recreation Center, 1959-69; writer, commentator TV show Show Window, WNBF-TV, 1953-55; syndicated column Frazzles, 1966-68. Lectr. on writing Bloomfield Hill Lasher High Sch. Pres. Sidney Service Council, 1961-67; active Youth Centers, 1956—; bd. dirs. Camp Brace, Masonville, N.Y. Mem. Nat. Assn. Penwomen, Fashion Group Detroit Inc. Mem. Women's Nat. Book Assn. (editor The Bookwoman). Presbyn. Author childrens books; writer, dir. children's plays; syndicated columnist Grandma's Delite, 1974; contbr. articles in field to profl. jours. Designer Taffy doll. Home: 4852 Malibu Dr Bloomfield Hills MI 48013

JONES, VIRGINIA RIDDLE, social worker, educator; b. Birmingham, Ala.; d. Thomas Watkins and Lula (Hendricks) Riddle; student U. Montevallo, 1938-40; B.A., U. Ala., 1942; M.S.W., Tulane U., 1944; postgrad. Columbia, 1963, Western Res. U., 1965; m. Thomas Ward Jones (div. June 1963); children—Thomas Robert, Hal Dale. Med. social worker A.R.C., New Orleans, 1944-45, Travelers Aid, USO., Battle Creek, Mich., 1945-46, State Crippled Childrens Service, Birmingham, Ala., 1946-47, Muskogee City-County Health Dept., Columbus, Ga., 1947-49; social worker Childrens Aid Soc., Birmingham, 1949-51; med. social worker, supr., asso. dir. social service dept. Univ. Hosp., Birmingham, 1961-64; asst. dir. Community Service Council Jefferson County, Inc., Birmingham, 1964-69; social work asso. prof. social sci. dept., dir. social work program U. Montevallo (Ala.), 1969-73 chmn. social work dept., 1973—; panel mem. Research Group, Inc., Atlanta, 1966—. Instr. sociology dept. U. Ala., Birmingham, 1966-68, Grad. Sch. Social Welfare, Fla. State U., Tallahassee, 1963-64, sociology dept. Samford U., Birmingham, 1966-68, Grad. Sch. Social Work, U. Ala., University, 1968-69. Chmn., Vestavia-Cherokee United Appeal, 1956-57; mem. Council Social Work Edn., 1968—; treas. Ala. Commn. for Social Welfare Manpower, 1969-73; mem. adv. bd. Family Ct. of Jefferson County, 1965-71, Parent Child Center, Birmingham, 1967-70, Chilton and Shelby County Mental Health, 1973—. Mem. Nat. Assn. Social Workers (chpt. pres. 1968-70), Birmingham Dist. Dental Aux., Ala. Conf. Social Workers (pres. 1973-74), Social Workers Club, Delta Zeta (alumni chpt. pres., coll. chpt. adviser 1951-58, Woman of Yr. Birmingham 1973). Methodist. Club: Vestavia Country. Home: 2117 Vestavia Lake Dr Birmingham AL 35222 Office: U Montevallo Montevallo AL 35115

JONES, WILMA JOYCE KROUTIL, home economist; b. Oklahoma City, Oct. 15, 1929; d. Frank and Ida (Holman) Kroutil; B.S., Okla. State U., 1950; postgrad. Okla. State U., 1952-64, Okla. U., 1951-53; m. Sol P. Jones, Mar. 18, 1955 (div. Apr. 1961); children—Odis Duty, Gerald Philip. Tchr. home econs. Crescent (Okla.) High Sch., 1951-52, Stroud (Okla.) High Sch., 1952-55, Oklahoma City Schs., 1960-68; tchr. seventh grade Stevenson (Wash.) Sch., 1955-58; northwest dist. dir. for Extension Home Economists, 1971-73, Okla. State U., Alva, 1968—. Recipient Norma Brumbaugh scholarship, 1971. Mem. Delta Kappa Gamma, Am. Assn. U. Women (v.p. 1970-71), Delta Zeta Alumnae (pres. 1971-73). Methodist (sec. of ofcl. bd. 1971—). Home: 1132 Flynn St Alva OK 73717 Office: Box 743 Courthouse Alva OK 73717

JONTZ, PAULINE PRATHER (MRS. LELAND D. JONTZ), museum ofcl.; b. Akron, O., Oct. 26, 1928; d. Clinton Charner and Lora Elizabeth (Hunter) P.; A.B., Ind. U., 1949; m. Leland D. Jontz, June 25, 1950; children—James Prather, Mary Lee. Dir. pub. relations Children's Museum of Indpls., 1963—. Pres. Children's Museum Guild, 1962-63. Recipient 1st place awards for brochure and use of multi-media Ind. Women's Press Club, 1972, 73, 2d pl. awards Nat. Fedn. Press Women, 1972, 73. Mem. Pub. Relations Soc. Am. (Ind. sec. 1973-74), Nat. Fedn. Press Women, Women in Communications (Indpls. pres. 1973-74), Women's Press Club Ind., Ind. Bus. Communicators (v.p. 1973-74), Am. Assn. Museums, Kappa Kappa Gamma (pres. Indpls. 1972-73). Methodist. Club: Indianapolis Press. Home: 8702 Pemberton Circle Indianapolis IN 46260 Office: 3010 N Meridian St Indianapolis IN 46208

JORDAN, ALICE YOST (MRS. FRANK B. JORDAN), composer; b. Davenport, Ia., Dec. 31, 1916; d. J. Frank and Anna (Mock) Yost; B.S.M., Drake U., 1938, grad. work in composition, 1955-57, 1967; student Union Theol. Sch. Sacred Music, 1965; m. Frank B. Jordan, Nov. 3, 1944. Composer: The Beatitudes, 1965; God Who Touchest Earth with Beauty, 1960; Prayer is the Soul's Sincere Desire, 1961; Late Have I Loved Thee, 1956; See the Land, 1972; Only a Manger, 1963; All Things are Thine, 1959; God of Mercy, God of Blessing, 1957; Song of Praise, 1959; Joyfully We Hymn Thy Praise, 1964; God is Here on Every Hand, 1966; Prayer in Winter, 1958; The Time for Singing Has Come, 1969; As Joseph Was A Walking, 1962; Hymn of Praise, 1972; Hymn to Spring, 1973; Touch My Life, 1972; Sing Praises, 1973; Beloved Night, 1960; In Spring, 1957; God's Lark at Morning, 1960; Psalm 103 - Bless the Lord O My Soul, 1970, For Organ: Cantabile on Hyfrydol, Meditation on Penitentia, 1974, others. Pres. Des Moines Civic Music Assn., 1961-63, dir., 1970—; mem. speakers bur. also area chmn. United Campaign, 1950-55. Recipient Alumni Distinguished Service award Drake U., 1970. Mem. Des Moines Symphony Assn., Drake Alumnae Assn., Ia. Fedn. Music Clubs, Pi Kappa Lambda, Mortar Board, Kappa Alpha Theta, Mu Phi Epsilon. Methodist. Home: 4106 Ovid Av Des Moines IA 50310

JORDAN, ANNA JOYCE (MRS. SAMUEL EUGENE JORDAN), park ofcl.; b. Cedar Run, Va., Dec. 15, 1935; d. Elbert Gordon and Catherine Alice (Bailey) Bettis; grad. high sch.; m. Samuel Eugene Jordan, Apr. 25, 1970; 1 son, Gregory Allen. With C & P Telephone Co., Washington, 1954-59; sec. Dept. Interior, Washington, 1959-61; with Carolina Home Life Ins. Co., Jacksonville, Fla., 1962-63; fiscal accounting clk. Navy Finance Office, Dept. Navy, Jacksonville, 1963-70; admissions clk. Pender Meml. Hosp., Burgaw, N.C., 1971-72; adminstrv. clk. Moores Creek Nat. Mil. Park, Nat. Park Service, Dept. Interior, Currie, N.C., 1972—. Mem. Tarheel Appaloosa Assn. (treas. 1971—). Clubs: Buccaneer Country, Cotillion (Burgaw). Home: Hwy 53 PO Box 925 Burgaw NC 28425 Office: Moores Creek National Military Park PO Box 69 Currie NC 28435

JORDAN, BARBARA C., congresswoman; b. Houston, Feb. 21, 1936; d. Arlyne Jordan; B.A., Tex. So. U., 1956; LL.B., Boston U., 1959, then LL.D.; LL.D., Tufts U., Howard U. Admitted to Tex. bar; adminstrv. asst. to county judge, Harris County; mem. Tex. Senate, 1966-72, pres. pro tem, chmn. labor and Mgmt. Relations Com. and Urban Affairs Study Com.; mem. 93d Congress from 18th Dist. Tex. Mem. compliance and rev. commn., charter commn. Dem. Nat. Com.; vice chmn. Tex. Dem. party. Named One of 10 Most Influential Women in Tex., One of 100 Women in Touch With Our Time, Harpers Bazaar mag. Mem. Am., Tex., Houston, Mass. bar assns., Tex. Trial Lawyers Assn., N.A.A.C.P., So. Regional Council. Julia C. Hester House Found. Office: 1725 Longworth House Office Bldg Washington DC 20575

JORDAN, BARBARA MOORE (MRS. HARMON GEIGER JORDAN), psychiatrist; b. Petersburg, Va., June 5, 1928; d. Carlisle Seward and Edna (Beasley) Moore; A.B., U. N.C. at Greensboro, 1949; M.D., U. N.C. at Chapel Hill, 1954; m. Harmon Geiger Jordan, Oct. 28, 1960; children—Jon David, Lisa Anne, Monica Leigh, Robert Bruce. Research asst. dept. pathology U. N.C. Med. Sch. at Chapel Hill, 1949-50; intern Queens Hosp., Honolulu, 1954-55; resident psychiatry U. N.C. Hosp. at Chapel Hill, 1955-57; resident psychiatry Dorothea Dix Hosp., Raleigh, 1957-58, chief female service, 1958-60, clin. dir., 1966-71, asst. supt., 1971-73, med. cons. Vocational Rehab. Facility; mem. attending staff Rex Hosp., Raleigh, 1961-66; now practice medicine specializing in psychiatry, Lumberton, N.C. med. cons. div. disability determination N.C. Dept. Pub. Welfare, 1961-66; project physician, psycho-pharmacology collaborative study Nat. Inst. Mental Health, 1965-66, Diplomate Am. Bd. Psychiatry and Neurology. Fellow Am. Psychiat. Assn.; mem. A.M.A., N.C., Robeson County med. assns., N.C. Neuro-psychiat. Assn. Home: 302 Highland Av Lumberton NC 28358 Office: Southwestern Regional Mental Health Center 209 W 28th St Lumberton NC 28358

JORDAN, CAROLYN JOYCE SNYDER (MRS. DUANE PAUL JORDAN), city ofcl.; b. Los Angeles, Feb. 23, 1936; d. Lloyd H. and Grace R. (Miller) Snyder; B.S., Stanford U., 1957, M.A., 1959; m. Duane Paul Jordan, June 22, 1957; children—Charlotte Elizabeth, Catherine Michelle. Data processor, tech. writer Hiller Helicopter, Palo Alto, Cal., 1957; asso. engr. data processing Lockheed, Sunnyvale, Cal., 1958-59. Active Campfire Girls, Lubbock, Tex., 1966—. Mem. city council City of Lubbock, 1972—. Chmn. steering com. Livermore (Cal.) Symphony Orch., 1963-64. Mem. League Women Voters (pres. Lubbock chpt. 1969-72), Am. Assn. U. Women (pres. Livermore chpt. 1964, v.p. Lubbock chpt. 1965-68). Methodist (mem. adminstrv. bd. 1970-72, 74). Home: 3419 62nd St Lubbock TX 79413 Office: Box 2000 Lubbock TX 79457

JORDAN, CONSTANCE BRINE, educator; b. Newton, Mass., Dec. 26, 1919; d. Edward David and Elizabeth (Morrisey) Brine; B.S., Framingham State Coll., 1941; M.P.H., Harvard U., 1948; Ph.D. (Anna Cora Smith fellow 1951-53), Cornell U., 1954; m. John Q. Jordan, Aug. 14, 1957 (dec. Nov. 1970); children—John Q., Kirk E., Kathleen A., Elizabeth A., Mary L. Chief dietitian Newton-Wellesley Hosp., Newton, 1942-45; asst. in nutrition Harvard Sch. Pub. Health, Boston, 1946-48; asso. prof. U. R.I., 1948-56; prof., chmn. dept. home econs. Framingham State Coll., 1956—, grad. dean, 1973—; cons. Elm Hill Nursing Home, Arthur D. Little, Inc. Named Outstanding Alumna, Framingham State Coll., 1961. Mem. Am. Dietetic Assn. (chmn. awards fellowship bd. 1973—, state pres. 1967), Am. Home Econs. Assn., Pi Lambda Theta, Kappa Delta Pi, Omicron Nu, Phi Upsilon Omicron. Contbr. articles calcium metabolism to profl. jours. Home: 14 Adams Rd Framingham MA 01701

JORDAN, ELIZABETH COOKE (MRS. CLAUDE WEAVER JORDAN), ret. psychiat. social worker; b. Phila.; d. John William and Ella Jane (Hahn) Cooke; B.S., U. Pa., 1925, M.S.W., 1955; m. Joseph Oliver Barnes, June 26, 1926 (div. Apr. 1940); m. 2d, Claude Weaver Jordan, May 20, 1957. Tchr., Upper Darby (Pa.) High Sch., 1925-28; acting dean girls High Sch., Lansdowne, Pa., 1938-39; home and sch. visitor Ambler (Pa.) Sch. Dist., 1940-43; personnel dir. Croasdale and deAngelis, Inc., Oakmont, Pa., 1943-47; counselor Pa. Bur. Vocational Rehab., Phila., 1947, Pa. Dept. Welfare Children's Services, Harrisburg, 1948; exec. dir. Phila. Planned Parenthood Assn., 1948-50; psychiat. social worker Embreeville (Pa.) State Hosp., 1950-56, Norristown (Pa.) State Hosp., 1956-58, Devereux Found., Devon, Pa., 1959-69. Vol. instr. 1st aid Southeastern Pa. chpt. A.R.C., 1943-57. Fellow Am. Orthopsychiat. Assn.; mem. Bus. and Profl. Women's Club (pres. 1954-56), Chester County Health and Social Workers Club (pres. 1953-55), Nat. Assn. Social Workers, Acad. Certified Social Workers, D.A.R., Alpha Xi Delta, Mortar Bd., Pi Lambda Theta, Theta Alpha Phi. Home: PO Box 535 Paoli PA 19301

JORDAN, GRACE HARTLEY EDGINGTON (MRS. LEONARD BECK JORDAN), author; b. Wasco, Ore.; d. Jesse and Martha Ann (Hartley) Edgington; B.A., U. Ore., 1916; m. Leonard Beck Jordan, Dec. 30, 1924; children—Patricia Jean (Mrs. Charles F. Story), Joseph Leonard, Stephen Edgington. Faculty, U. Wash., 1917-20; faculty U. Ore., editor Old Oregon, 1920-24; tchr. pub. schs., Grangeville, Ida., 1943-46; faculty Boise Coll., 1961-62; condr. Creative Writing Workshop Womens Congl. Club, 1963-72. Instr. night writing classes Boise YWCA, 1959-62. Mem. League Am. Pen Women, Am. Assn. U. Women, Phi Beta Kappa, Theta Sigma Phi, Pi Beta Phi, Beta Sigma Phi. Republican. Methodist. Author: Home Below Hell's Canyon, 1954; Canyon Boy, 1958; The King's Pines, 1961; Idaho Reader, 1963; The Unintentional Senator, 1972. Polit. columnist Where Rolls the Potomac, 1963-72. Home: 3110 Crescent Rim Dr Boise ID 83704

JORDAN, JEWELL (MRS. JACK JORDAN), banker; b. Monticello, Ark., Jan. 28, 1917; d. T. J. and Rena Julia (Bordeaux) Johnson; student Ark. A. and M., 1936-37, Northwestern U., 1962-63; m. Jack Jordan, June 3, 1937; children—Julia Ann (Mrs. Robert C. McWilliams III), H.J. Asst. v.p. pub. relations and bus. devel. Citizens Bank, Jonesboro, Ark., 1961—. Corr. sec. Jonesboro Jr. Aux., 1959-60. Bd. dirs. Abilities Unltd. Mem. Nat. Assn. Bank Women (pres. Ark. group 1968-69), Ark. Jr. Bankers (historian 1965-66), Jonesboro C. of C. (chmn. city beautiful 1964-65), Downtown Bus. and Profl. Womens Club (pres. 1970-71), P.E.O. Home: 705 W Washington St Jonesboro AR 72401 Office: Main and Washington Sts Jonesboro AR 72401

JORDAN, JUNE MEYER, author; b. N.Y.C., July 9, 1936; d. Granville Ivanhoe and Mildred Maude (Fisher) Jordan; student Barnard Coll., 1953-57; m. Michael Meyer, Aug. 5, 1955 (div. Apr. 1966); 1 son, Christopher David. Instr. English, Coll. City N.Y., 1967-68, Conn. Coll., New London, 1968-69; instr. Sarah Lawrence Coll., 1969-70, instr. lit., 1973-74; vis. lectr. English and Afro-Am. studies Yale, 1974-75. Co-founder The Voice of the Children, Inc., N.Y.C., 1968-71; co-founder Afro-Americans Against the Famine, N.Y.C., 1973—. Recipient Prix de Rome in environmental design, 1970-71. Rockefeller grantee in creative writing, 1969-70. Author: Who Look At Me, 1969; Some Changes, 1970; Soulscript, 1970; His Own Where, 1971; The Voice of the Children, 1971; Dry Victories, 1972; Fannie Lou Hamer, 1972; New Days, 1974; I Love You, 1974. Address: care Wendy Weil Julian Bach Literary Agy 3 E 48th St New York City NY 10017

JORDAN, LAURA JOSEPHINE, educator; b. Champaign, Ill., May 6, 1926; d. Theodore Nelson and Josephine (Giertz) Jordan; B.A., U. Ill., 1948, M.S., 1950, Ph.D., 1961. Tchr. mentally handicapped pub. schs. Danville, Ill., 1950-52, Galveston, Tex., 1952-56; research asst. U. Ill., Urbana, 1956-57, 58-59, research asso., 1959-60, mem. faculty, 1960—, prof. spl. edn., 1970—. Vis. prof. Tex. Tech. Inst., Lubbock, summer, 1969. U. Ill. fellow, 1957-58. Fellow Am. Assn. Mental Deficiency; mem. Am. Assn. U. Profs., Council for Exceptional Children. Lutheran. Office: 1005 W Nevada St Urbana IL 61801

JORDAN, MARGARET WILKINSON, state govt. ofcl.; b. Madison, N.J., July 1, 1922; d. Harry Rockerfellow and Mary (Wolf) Wilkinson; B.S. in Elec. Engring., Rutgers U., 1948, B.S. in Mech. Engring., 1949; J.D., U. Mo.-Kansas City, 1965; m. Ben B. Jordan, Sept. 17, 1944; children—Brad, Marsha. Engring. asst. Western Electric Co., 1941-44; archtl. designer David Ludlow, A.I.A., Summit, N.J., 1954-57; admitted to Kan. bar, 1965; practiced in Johnson County, 1965-73; dist. atty. 10th Jud. Dist. Kan., Olathe, 1973—. Mem. Mid-Am. Drug Forum, Region I Kan. Drug Abuse Council; mem. nat. adv. com. Rape Treatment and Prevention, Kan. Com. Criminal Justice Standards and Goals. Councilman, Leawood, Kan., 1969-71, mayor, 1971-72. Bd. dirs., regional rep. Johnson County Drug Abuse Council. Recipient Community Leadership award U. Mo.-Kansas City, 1971. Mem. Am., Kan., Johnson County (treas. 1972-73) bar assns., Nat. Dist. Attys. Assn., Kansas County and Dist. Attys. Assn., Met. Chiefs and Sheriffs Assn. (asso.), Johnson County Chiefs of Police (asso.), Phi Alpha Delta. Club: Perry Yacht (gov.). Home: 2515 W 91st St Leawood KS 66206 Office: PO Box 728 Olathe KS 66061

JORDAN, MARION EVELYN MYERS (MRS. T. HURLEY JORDAN, JR.), ct. reporter, lawyer; b. Lawton, Okla., Sept. 2, 1925; d. Marion Calvin and Lovie Jewel (Watkins) Myers: LL.B., Oklahoma City U., 1949; m. T. Hurley Jordan, Jr., July 5, 1968; 1 son (by previous marriage), Philip C. Wise. Sec., ct. reporter, Ft. Sill, Okla., 1943-44; ct. reporter State Indsl. Ct., Oklahoma City, 1944-53, 59-67; admitted to Okla. bar, 1949; individual practice law, also atty. Okla. Dept. Pub. Welfare and Commrs. Land Office, 1953-59; dist. ct. reporter 7th Jud. Dist. Oklahoma, Oklahoma City, 1967—. Mem. Okla. Bd. Examiners Ofcl. Shorthand Reporters, 1971—. Chmn. Women's Civic Clubs Council, Oklahoma City, 1971-72; mem., vice chmn. Gov.'s Com. on Status of Women, 1972—. Mem. Nat. Shorthand Reporters Assn., Okla. Assn. Shorthand Reporters, Okla. Bar Assn., Nat. (mem. nat. legislation com. 1973-74), Okla. (state pres. 1972-73) fedns. bus. and profl. women's clubs, Oklahoma City Bus. and Profl. Women's Club (pres. 1970-71), Equal Rights Assn. (pres. 1973), Iota Tau Tau (internat. supreme dean 1963-65). Democrat. Baptist. Club: Jefferson Bryan. Home: 710 NE 19th St Oklahoma City OK 73105 Office: 805 Oklahoma County Courthouse Oklahoma City OK 73102

JORDAN, MARION NUCKOLLS, sch. librarian; b. Toone, Tenn., Aug. 25, 1910; d. James Madison and Kate (Thompson) Nuckolls; A.B., Union U., 1930; student George Peabody Coll., 1949-52; m. Charles Marvin Jordan, June 8, 1932; children—Charles Marvin Jr., James Thomas, John Nuckolls. Tchr.-librarian Hardeman County, Tenn., 1930-51; librarian White Station High Sch., Memphis, 1951-64; supr. library services Memphis City Schs., 1964—; cons. library service Am. Sch., Guatemala, 1966; cons. NDEA Inst. Elem. Sch. Librarians, Middle Tenn. State U., 1967, Austin Peay State U., 1967, U. Ga., 1970. Mem. Am., Tenn. Southeastern library assns., Nat., Tenn. edn. assns., West Tenn. Edn. Assn., Tenn. Supervising Tchrs., Am. Assn. U. Women, Delta Kappa Gamma. Home: 3646 Mimosa St Memphis TN 38111 Office: 2597 Avery St Memphis TN 38112

JORDAN, MARY AGNES, aerospace co. exec.; b. West Pittston, Pa., Dec. 7, 1937; d. Joseph Thomas and Agnes Margaret (Granahan) Jordan; B.A., Marywood Coll., 1964; Ph.D. (scholar), U. Notre Dame, 1970. Tchr. East Rockaway, N.Y., 1958-64, St. Rose High Sch., Carbondale, Pa., 1964-66; dean Coll. Continuing Edn. Lewis U., Lockport, Ill., 1970-73; project adminstr., mgmt. and organizational devel. Gen. Motors Inst., Flint, Mich., 1973-74; mgr. Orgn. Devel. Martin Marietta Aerospace Corp., Orlando, Fla., 1974—; Lectr. U. Mich., 1974. Cons. Nat. Secs. Assn., 1972-74. Mem. adv. council Joliet (Ill.) Jr. Coll., 1972-74; adviser Ill. Dept. Corrections, Chgo., 1972-73; coordinator of tutoring neighborhood study help program, Community Action Program, South Bend, Ind., 1967-68; adviser upward mobility of women Dept. Health, Edn. and Welfare, Chgo. region, 1972-73. Mem. Nat. Orgn. for Women, Am. Assn. U. Women, League Women Voters. Home: 897 S Wymore Rd Altamonte Springs FL 32701 Office: PO Box 5837 Sand Lake Rd Orlando FL 32805

JORDAN, SISTER MARY LUKE, educator; b. New Orleans, Mar. 1, 1914; d. Joseph Alphonse and Dolores (Meza) J.; student Notre Dame Jr. Coll., 1932-35; A.B., St. Louis U., 1937; M.A., Notre Dame U., 1959, M.F.A., 1965. Mem. Order Sch. Sisters of Notre Dame, Roman Catholic Ch., 1935—; in charge art dept. St. Mary of the Pines, Chatawa, Miss., 1937-48; head art dept. Le Clerc Coll., Belleville, Ill., 1948-49; head art dept. Notre Dame Acad., Belleville, 1949-58, tchr. art Notre Dame Jr. Coll., 1950-54; dir. art dept. Notre Dame Coll., 1959-66; diocesan art cons. Catholic Schs. of Miss., 1966-69; dir. art dept. St. Mary's U., 1969—; commd. sculptor and mosaics for art and sci. bldgs. Notre Dame Coll., 1963; commd. to erect pedement of the Holy Family for St. Joseph's Ch., Cottelville, Mo., 1964-65; exhibited one-man shows East St. Louis Pub. Library, San Antonio Pub. Library, 1973; exhibited group shows Miss. Art Assn. Municipal Art Gallery, Jackson, Miss., 1947, Soc. Ind. Artists South Center Mall, St. Louis, 1965; 2d annual Outdoor Festival of Art, Webster Groves, Mo., 1965; Bon Marche Nat. Art Gallery, 1962; Nat. Liturgical Conv., St. Louis, 1964; Liturgical Art Exhibit St. John Cantius Sem., St. Louis, 1964; Monticello Coll., 1964; Jewish Community Center, St. Louis, 1966; Trinity Baptist Ch., San Antonio, 1970; Starving Artist Show and Art Jamboree, San Antonio, 1970, 1971. Mem. Nat., Tex. art edn. assns., San Antonio Art League. Home: 159 Camino Santa Maria San Antonio TX 78228 Office: 2700 Cincinnati Av San Antonio TX 78284

JORDAN, VIRGINIA GENERZIA GEISEL (MRS. PAUL HARTLEY JORDAN), psychiat. social worker; b. Hawarden, Ia., Jan. 9, 1909; d. George and Madge V. (Davis) Geisel; Ph.B., U. Chgo., 1934, M.A., 1943; m. Paul H. Jordan, July 12, 1947; 1 son, Paul Geisel. With Inst. for Juvenile Research, Chgo., 1943-45, A.R.C. Overseas Hosp. Service, 1945-47; chief psychiat. social worker Mental Hygiene Clinic for Woman and Children, Women and Children's Hosp., 1947-49; individual practice psychiat. social work, Flint, Mich., 1949, Grand Blanc, Mich., 1959—; instr. psychology and sociology Washtenaw Community Coll., Ann Arbor, Mich., 1967—. State chmn. internat. affairs League Women Voters, 1954-56, also mem. local and state bds. Recipient Lawrence Mayers Peace award L. & C. Mayers Co., 1954; 1st prize Midwestern Writers Conf., 1947. Fellow Am. Orthopsychiat. Assn., Conf. for Advancement Pvt. Practice in Social Work (editor Proc. 1965—); mem. Am. Assn. for UN (state pres. 1955-57), UN Assn. U.S.A., Nat. Assn. Social Workers, Acad. Certified Social Workers. Contbr. articles to profl. jours.Home: 1125 Jordan Lane Grand Blanc MI 48439 Office: Box 345 Ann Arbor MI 48106

JORDEN, ELEANOR HARZ, linguist, educator; b. N.Y.C.; d. William George and Eleanor (Funk) Harz; A.B., Bryn Mawr Coll., 1942; M.A., Yale, 1943, Ph.D., 1950; m. William J. Jorden, Mar. 3, 1944 (div.); children—William Temple, Eleanor Harz, Marion Telva. Instr. Japanese, Yale, 1943-46, 47-48; dir. Japanese lang. program and Fgn. Service Inst. Lang. Sch., Am. Embassy, Tokyo, Japan, 1950-55; sci. linguist Fgn. Service Inst., Dept. State, Washington, 1959-69, acting head dept. Far Eastern langs., 1961-64, chmn., 1964-67, 69, chmn. Vietnamese lang. div., 1967-69; vis. prof. linguistics Cornell U., 1969-70, prof., 1970—, Mary Donlon Alger prof. linguistics, 1974—, dir. Japanese FALCON program, 1972—; examiner for Japanese, Critical Lang. Program. Mem. Fulbright-Hays Com. on Internat. Exchange Scholars, 1972—; area adv. com. for East Asia, CIES, 1972—. Recipient Superior Service award Dept. State, 1965. Mem. Linguistic Soc. Am., Assn. for Asian Studies, Assn. Tchrs. Japanese. Author: (with Bernard Bloch) Spoken Japanese 1945; Syntax of Modern Colloquial Japanese, 1955; Gateway to Russian, 1961; Beginning Japanese, Part 1, 1962, Part 2, 1963; (with Sheehan, Quang and others) Basic Vietnamese, vols. I, II, 1965; (with Quang) Vietnamese Familiarization Course, 1969. Home: 333 N Sunset Dr Ithaca NY 14850

JORDY, SARAH STOUGHTON SPOCK (MRS. WILLIAM H. JORDY), documentalist; b. New Haven, Aug. 28, 1917; d. Benjamin Ives and Mildred L. (Stoughton) Spock; A.B., Vassar Coll., 1939; student City Coll. N.Y., 1943-44; m. Homer L. Trueblood, July 30, 1938 (div. Aug. 1941); m. 2d, William H. Jordy, July 25, 1942. Market research and pub. opinion polling Elmo Roper, N.Y.C., 1941-42; statis. research, dept. data and trends Nat. Bd. YWCA, N.Y.C., 1942-44; research asso. in documentation Yale Center Alcohol Studies, New Haven, 1945-62, Rutgers Center Alcohol Studies, New Brunswick, N.J., 1962—. Author: International Bibliography of Studies on Alcohol. Editor: (asst.) Quarterly Jour. Studies on Alcohol, 1959—. Contbr. articles in field to profl. jours. Home: 55 Bond Rd Riverside RI 02915 Office: Rutgers U Center Alcohol Studies New Brunswick NJ 08903

JORGENSEN, JOYCE ORABELLE, newspaper editor; b. Newell, Ia., Feb. 26, 1928; d. James G. and Elsie C. (Haahr) Andersen; pvt. art study with Arthur Schweider, 1945-46; m. John G. Jorgensen, Apr. 27, 1949 (dec. Dec. 1958); children—Richard, Kirsten, John (dec.), Brian; 2d. m. L.A. Johnson, Jan. 1, 1965 (div. Jan. 11, 1968). Profl. free lance artist, writer, also co-publisher and editor Orleans (Neb.) Chronicle, 1949-53; with Ouray (Colo.) County Herald, 1954-56; operator Little Studio and Gallery, Ouray, 1954-56; pvt. sec., office mgr. Atty. Gen., Juneau, Alaska, 1957-58; free lance artist, instr., operator Jorgensen Studio and Gallery J., Ouray, Colo., 1959-68; editor Ouray County Plaindealer, 1967-70, publisher, editor Ouray County Plaindealer and Herald, 1970—. Artist represented in permanent collection Okla. State U. Bd. mem., sec. Ouray City Planning and Zoning Commn., 1969-70; chmn. Ouray Bd. of Zoning Appeals, 1971—. Bd. dirs., creator Ouray County Arts Council and Artists Alpine Holiday, 1961-62. Mem. Nat. Newspaper Assn., Colo. Press Assn., Colo. Presswomen's Assn., Ouray County Hist. Soc., Ouray C. of C. Home and Office: 540 8th Av Ouray CO 81427

JORGENSEN, LAVERNIA MAE, educator; b. Luck, Wis., Mar. 2, 1918; d. George and Alice (Christensen) Jorgensen; B.S., U. Wis. at River Falls, 1939; M.Ed., U. Minn., 1950; Dir. P.E., Ind. U., 1955, P.E.D., 1960. Tchr. English and phys. edn., Plummer, Minn., 1941-43, history, phys. edn. Sleepy Eye, Minn., 1943-46; girls' phys. edn., Detroit Lakes, Minn., 1946-49; teaching asst. U. Minn., Mpls., 1949-50; health and phys. edn. Manchester Coll., 1950-55, Ind. U., Bloomington, 1955-56; tchr. health and phys. edn. Eastern Mich., 1956-58, U.S.D., 1958-61, Augustana Coll., 1961-63; mem. faculty U. N.D., Grand Forks, 1963—, now asso. prof.; lectr. in field. Fellow Am. Sch. Health Assn., A.A.H.P.E.R., Soc. Park and Recreation Educators; mem. Am. Assn. U. Profs., Am. Corrective Therapy Assn., Am. Assn. U. Women, N.D. Health, Phys. Edn., Recreation and Coaches Assn., Nat., N.D. assns. for phys. edn. coll. women, Nat. Recreation and Parks Assn., Am. Camping Assn., N.D. Park and Recreation Assn. Nat. Found. for Health, Phys. Edn., and Recreation, Am. Acad. Sports Medicine, Am. Numismatic Assn., Ind. U. Alumni Assn., Internat. Platform Assn., Internat. Recreation Assn. Delta Psi Kappa. Republican. Lutheran (deacon). Club: River Bend Country. Contbr. articles in field to profl. jours. Home: 2007 2d Av North Grand Forks ND 58201

JORGENSEN, NORMA ANDERSON (MRS. ALBERT NELS JORGENSEN, JR.), coll. adminstr.; b. Hartford, Conn., Dec. 12, 1920; d. Carl Ernest and Anna Maria (Johnson) Anderson; B.S., U. Conn., 1943; m. Albert Nels Jorgensen, Jr., Oct. 30, 1943; children—Catherine Anne (Mrs. Richard Phillips), Albert Nels III. Commr. for Higher Edn., State of Conn., 1972—. Mem. adv. com. Burritt Mutual Savs. Bank, New Britain, Conn., 1973. Trustee, U. Conn., Storrs, 1971—. Mem. Nat. Assn. Women Deans, Adminstrs. and Counselors, Nat. Rifle Assn., Nat. Wildlife Fedn., Nat. Audubon Soc., Wilderness Soc., Am. Forestry Assn., U. Conn. Alumni Assn. (dir. 1967—), Kappa Alpha Theta (nat. pres. 1968-72). Home: 295 E Cedar St Newington CT 06111

JORGENSEN, VALERIE, physician; b. Tacoma, Wash., July 30, 1940; d. Harry William and Vera (Maybo) Jorgensen; B.S., Wash. State U., 1962; M.D., U. Wash., 1966. Intern Pa. Hosp., Phila., 1966-67, resident, 1967-70, asso. obstetrics and gynecology, 1971; pvt. practice medicine, specializing in obstetrics and gynecology, Phila., 1971—; psychosomatic obstetrics and gynecology cons. U. Pa. Hosp., mem. teaching staff U. Pa. Hosp., Pa. Hosp., 1970—; asst. prof. obstetrics and gynecology U. Pa., 1971—. Ford Found. Endocrinology grantee, 1963-64; Mead Johnson Obstetrics and Gynecology award, 1970. Fellow Am. Coll. Obstetrics and Gynecology; mem. Phila. Soc. Obstetrics and Gynecology, Am. Infertility Soc., Am. Obstetrics and Gynecology Soc., Am. Women's Med. Assn. Home: 210 Locust St Philadelphia PA 19107 Office: 807 Spruce St Philadelphia PA 19107

JORGENSEN, VIRGINIA TRIEST (MRS. ERIC JORGENSEN), psychiatrist; b. New Orleans, Mar. 22, 1923; d. Kenneth G. and Luise (Schiele) Triest; B.A. cum laude, Hofstra U., 1951; M.D., U. Copenhagen (Denmark), 1957; postgrad. N.Y. Sch. Psychiatry, 1963; m. Eric Jorgensen, Aug. 5, 1951; children—Ellen Verena, Nina. Intern, Flushing (N.Y.) Hosp., 1957-58; resident Creedmore State Hosp., Queens, N.Y., 1959-62, sr. psychiatrist, 1962-64; practice medicine specializing in psychiatry, Garden City, N.Y., 1964—; psychiat. cons. Sch. for Emotionally Disturbed Children, Nassau County, N.Y., 1962-71, Childrens Village, Dobbs Ferry, N.Y., 1964-65. Mem. med. adv. bd. Planned Parenthood of Nassau County, 1966—. Diplomate Am. Bd. Psychiatry. Mem. Am. Psychiat. Assn., Am. Med. Women's Assn., Nassau County Psychiat. Soc. Club: Garden City Ski Club. Office: 520 Franklin Av Garden City NY 11530

JORSTAD, DOROTHY LEAH PHINNEY (MRS. MELVIN E. JORSTAD), librarian; b. Dooley, Mont., Apr. 18, 1914; d. Herbert Lee and Theckla Rose (Keller) Phinney; B.A. in Hist., U. Minn., 1939, B.S. in L.S., 1940; m. Melvin E. Jorstad, Oct. 4, 1940; children—Augusta (Mrs. Richard E. Gorell), Herbert Lee. Tchr., Vesta, Minn., 1934-35; librarian U. Minn., St. Paul, 1941-42, 43-46; head librarian pub. library South St. Paul, Minn., 1950-62; circulation and reference librarian No. Ill. U., DeKalb, 1963-70; reference librarian Kishwaukee Coll., Malta, Ill., 1970-74, dir., 1974—. Pres. Lincoln Sch. P.T.A., South St. Paul, 1949-50; sec. South St. Paul Mayor's Youth Com., 1958. Mem. Bus. and Profl. Women's Club (chmn. dist. 6 1973-74), Ill. Fedn. Bus. and Profl. Women. Contbr. to profl. jours. Home: 219 Phyllis Av Rochelle IL 61068 Office: Library Kishwaukee College Malta IL 60150

JOSCELYN, VERLA NESBITT (MRS. DOUGLAS JOSCELYN), bottling co. exec.; b. Marquette, Kan., Feb. 14, 1905; d. Olin Charles and Daisy (McHenry) Baird; student Bethany Coll., 1923-25, Emporia State Tchrs. Coll., 1923-25; m. Rowland Nesbitt, June 5, 1930, (dec. Aug. 1945); m. 2d, Douglass Joscelyn, Apr. 4, 1957. Tchr. pub. schs., Eudora, Kan., Hamilton, Kan., 1925-30; owner, pres., mgr. Pepsi-Cola Bottling Co. of Salina, (Kan.), 1945—; dir. First Nat. Bank & Trust Co. of Salina. Bd. dirs. St. John's Hosp., YMCA. Mem. Kan. Bottlers Assn. (pres. 1956, dir. 1969—), Salina C. of C., Mgmt. Devel. Council, Nat. Soft Drink Assn. Presbyn. (trustee 1970—). Clubs: Asbury Century, St. John's Club, Kan. Wesleyan. Home: 223 Channel Dr Salina KS 67401 Office: 604 N 9th St Salina KS 67401

JOSEPH, BARBARA BASCOM, athletic adminstr.; b. Cortland, N.Y., Apr. 18, 1939; d. Sidney George and E. Elizabeth (Waltermire) Bascom; A.S., Orange County Community Coll., 1957-59; B.S., Ithaca Coll., 1962, M.S., 1965; postgrad. Boston U.; m. Lidio A. Joseph, Aug. 25, 1973. Mem. staff Rockland Community Coll., Suffern, N.Y., 1962-65, Ursuline Acad., Ill., 1965-66, Western Conn. State Coll., Danbury, 1966-69; asso. prof., women's athletic coordinator Wesleyan U., Middletown, Conn., 1970—. Recreational therapist West Hartford United Cerebral Palsy Center. Mem. Am., Conn. assns. health, phys. edn. and recreation, U.S. Field Hockey Assn., Conn. Amateur Fencing Assn. Home: 4 Willow St Cromwell CT 06416 Office: Wesleyan U Middletown CT 06457

JOSEPH, EDNA WHITEHEAD (MRS. LAWRENCE J. JOSEPH), bank exec.; b. Everett, Mass., Feb. 4, 1924; d. Alfred Edward and Mary Kathleen (Butler) Whitehead; student Am. Inst. Banking; m. Lawrence James Joseph, May 30, 1958. With Nat. Shawmut Bank, Boston, 1941-55, 57—, asst. tax officer, 1965-69, tax officer, 1969—; income tax mgr. Sam C. Charlson, Manhattan, Kan., 1955-57. Bd. dirs. Found. of Hope, Boston. Mem. Fiduciary Tax Assos., Mass. Bankers Assn. (vice chmn. taxation com. 1971-72, chmn. 1972-73), Nat. Assn. Bank Women, Am. Inst. Banking, Nat. Early Am. Glass Club, Mus. Fine Arts. Club: Women's Republican of Essex County. Home: 8 Laurel Rd Lynnfield MA 01940 Office: Nat. Shawmut Bank 40 Water St Boston MA 02109

JOSEPH, ESTHER GRIFFING, social worker; b. Rhinebeck, N.Y.; d. Joseph and Ruth (Mang) Griffing; B.A., Skidmore Coll., 1949; M. Social Service (univ. scholar), Adelphi U., 1951; postgrad. Hunter Coll., 1958-59; m. Charles Edward Joseph, Jan. 3, 1964. Psychiat. social worker Pilgrim State Hosp. and After Care Clinic, Brentwood, N.Y., 1951-53; psychiat. social worker supr. Bellevue Hosp. and Mental Hygiene Clinic, N.Y.C., 1953-57; clinic supr. N.Y.C. Magistrates Ct. Adolescent Psychiat. Clinic, 1957-60; social worker cons. Mental Retardation Center, N.Y. Med. Coll., Flower Hosp., 1959—; chief psychiat. social worker N.Y. Alcoholism Vocational Rehab. Service, Nat. Council Alcoholism, N.Y.C., 1960-62; field worker supr., instr. Fordham U. Sch. Social Service, 1962-64; supr., group therapist N.Y. Council Alcoholism, ACCEPT, N.Y.C., 1965-70; dir. social service Columbus Hosp. and Mental Hygiene Clinic, 1966-68; social worker supr. Manhattan Sch. Seriously Disturbed Children, N.Y.C., 1969-70. Instr. field work Social Research Lab., Coll. City N.Y., 1963—; supr. field work Am. Council Emigrees in Professions, 1967-70; cons. social work Dutchess County Mental Health Clinic, 1968-69. Stage mgr. Gellendre Theatre, 1953-55; dir. adolescent group Hamilton Madison House, 1956-57; publicity dir. Hyde Park Playhouse, 1957; intake social worker Community Guidance Service, 1959-70; dir. social service Trafager Hosp. Alcoholism Project, 1962; music therapist coordinator, Grasslands M.R.I., 1972—; group therapist cons., Parent League for Edn., 1964, Bur. Child Guidance Clin. Services, 1966-67; sch. social worker Lower East Side Neighborhood Services Com., 1967-68; group therapy cons. Lower East Side Center Narcotic Addiction, 1968; coordinator Astor Home, 1970-71; group therapy Washington Sq. Inst., 1973—; therapist Blueberry Inc., 1974—. N.Y. State Mental

Health fellow Yeshiva U. Grad. Sch. Edn., 1959-60; Nat. Council Alcoholism fellow Yale Sch. Alcoholic Studies, 1960. Mem. Acad. Certified Social Workers, Nat. Assn. Social Workers (alcoholism com. N.Y.C., 1967—), Assn. for Help of Retarded Children, N.Y. State Certified Social Workers, Am. Group Psychotheraphy Assn. (sec. audio-visual com. 1964—), Am., Nat. assns. mental deficiency, Nat. Assn. Music Therapy, Internat. Assn. Social Work, Actors Equity Assn., Adelphi U. Sch. Social Work Alumni Assn. (exec. bd. 1969-70), Am. Assn. U. Women (rep., 1970—), Am. Soc. Group Psychotherapy and Psychodrama, N.Y.C. Med. Soc. Alcoholism. Contbr. articles to tech. lit. Research in alcoholism, psychotherapy and rehab. Home: Fiddlers Bridge Rd Staatsburg NY 12580

JOSEPH, JOAN JUDITH, author; b. Tel Aviv, Israel, July 13, 1937 (mother Am. citizen); d. Philip and Dena (Shapiro) Joseph; B.A., McGill U., 1959; student U. So. Cal., 1958, U. Aix-Marseille (France), 1963-64, Alliance Francaise (France), 1964; Sr. Dipl. U. Paris (France), 1964; postgrad. U. Miami, 1965; student New Sch. for Social Research, 1968-69; m. Morton H. Levy, Dec. 21, 1958 (div. Apr. 1965); 1 son, Robert Evan. Head information service Book of Knowledge Grolier Pub. Co., Montreal, Que., Can., 1959-61; tchr. French Miami Beach (Fla.) Sr. High Sch., 1964-65; research cons. La Jeunesse Ency. Grolier Pub. Co., 1965-66; French translator, Chinese transl. editor U.S. Dept. Commerce Joint Publs. Research Service, N.Y.C., 1966-68; research cons. nine langs.; reader history dept. U. So. Cal., 1958; reader history dept. Dr. Cyril James, Vice-Chancellor McGill U., 1959-61. Mem. The Authors Guild, Anglo-Jewish Hist. Soc., Am. Jewish Hist. Soc., Am. Hist. Soc., McGill Alumni Assn. Democrat. Jewish religion. Author: Peter the Great, 1958; South African Statesman, 1969; Folk Toys Around the World, 1972; Ancient Black Africa, 1973; Corruption in Politics, Prelude to Watergate, 1974; Henry Hudson, 1974; sole contbr. articles on French medieval drama McGraw Hill Encyclopedia of World Drama, 1972; contbr. Medical Encyclopedia, 1971; New American Bible, 1971; Encyclopedia of History, 1974; Time-Life Encyclopedia of Gardening, 1971. Home: 136 E 76th St New York City NY 10021 Office: 136 E 76th St New York City NY 10021

JOSEPH, JUDITH ROSE, chemist; b. Worcester, Mass., May 5, 1940; d. Albert A. and Elsey E. Joseph; ed. Charlotte Coll., Rutgers U., Hunter Coll., Center for Profl. Advancement. From lab. asst. to flavor chemist Internat. Flavors and Fragrances, N.Y.C., 1959-70; flavor chemist Warner Lambert-Am. Chicle, N.Y.C., 1970-73; flavor chemist Glidden-Durkee, Inc., Jacksonville, Fla., 1973-74; dir. flavor creation Aromatics Internat., Atlanta, 1974—. Mem. Republican Com., Staten Island, N.Y., 1968. Mem. Soc. Flavor Chemists (publicity chmn. 1971), Inst. Food Technologists, Soc. Soft Drink Technologists, Am. Assn. Candy Technologists, Mensa (editor newsletter 1966). Club: Jacksonville Shell. Contbr. numerous articles in field to profl. jours., articles on scrimshaw to craft mags. Home: 4253 Trout River Blvd Jacksonville FL 32208

JOSEPH, LENORE CLARK (MRS. MICHAEL J. JOSEPH), glass co. exec.; b. Hickory, Pa., Nov. 10, 1924; d. Ralph B. and Margaret E. (Stunkard) Retzer; B.S., Ind. State U., 1945; m. Michael J. Joseph, Dec. 27, 1972. Tchr., Somerset, Pa., 1945-50; home economist Columbia Gas Co., Pitts., 1950-55; pres. Ohio Valley Window Co., Wheeling, W.Va., 1969—. Dir. Morris Plan Bank, 1972—. Mem. Wheeling C. of C. (bd. dirs. 1972—). Club: Garden. Home: 27 Shawnee Hills St Wheeling WV 26003 Office: 2210 Water St Wheeling WV 26003

JOSEPH, MARGUERITE WILSON, state ofcl.; b. Camden, O., Mar. 26, 1919; d. Roeloff H. and Grace D. (Gilpin) Wilson; student Miami U., Oxford, O., 1936-37, 44-45, Baldwin-Wallace Coll., 1937-38; m. Kenneth L. Joseph, Sept. 9, 1938 (div. June 1948); 1 dau., Claudia F. (Mrs. Raymond Hampton). Social worker Ohio State Aid for Aged, Hamilton, 1945-47, Fla. Dept. Welfare, Jacksonville, 1947-48; mgr., owner West Side Drugs, St. Augustine, Fla., 1948-50; radiol. technician St. Joseph's Hosp., Mishawaka, Ind., 1954-56, McCullough-Hyde Hosp., Oxford, 1957-60, Christ Hosp., Cin., 1960-62; test examiner Ohio State Employment Service, Hamilton, 1962-69; WIN coordinator Butler County, 1969—. Mem. adv. bd. Miami Valley Tech. Sch., Hamilton, 1967—. Mem. Internat. Assn. Personnel in Employment Security, Nat. Wildlife Assn., Aircraft Owners and Pilots Assn., Soc. Radiol. Technologists, Ohio Civil Service Employees Assn. Mem. Order Eastern Star. Contbr. poems to anthologies, mags. including Etude, Silhouette, Am. Poetry, others. Home: 119 N Campus Av Oxford OH 45056 Office: 112 N 2d St Hamilton OH 45012

JOSEPH, MARJORY L. (MRS. WILLIAM D. JOSEPH), educator; b. Milan, O., Oct. 10, 1917; d. Ernest J. and Bertha (Allyn) Lockwood; B.S., Ohio State U., 1939, M.S., 1952; Ph.D., Pa. State U., 1962; m. William D. Joseph, Aug. 11, 1941; 1 dau., Nancy-Joyce. Supr. alternation dept. Collegienne Shop, Lazarus Dept. Store, Columbus, 1939-41; ind. designing and constrn. original designed clothing, 1941-44; supr. workrooms custom designing shop Ruth Harris, Inc., N.Y.C., 1944-46; mgr., co-owner MarJay Co., Milan, 1946-48; tchr. secondary schs., Ohio, 1948-51; teaching asst. textile div. Ohio State U. Sch. Home Econs., 1951-52; instr. to asso. prof. Juniata Coll., Huntingdon, Pa., 1952-62; part-time instr. in clothing and textiles research Pa. State U., 1957-62; head textiles and clothing asso. prof. Dept. of Home Econs., Cal. State U., Northridge, now prof., chmn. dept. Cons. textile fiber and fabric care So. Cal. Gas Co., Los Angeles, Springs Mills, Inc., Ft. Mill, S.C., U.S. Borax Co., Los Angeles. Recipient Distinguished Alumni award Ohio State U., 1972. Mem. Am. Assn. Textile Chemists and Colorists, Am. Soc. for Testing and Materials, Am. Home Econs. Assn., Electric Women's Round Table, Omicron Nu, Sigma Delta Epsilon. Author: Introductory Textile Science, 1966, 2d edit., 1972; Illustrated Guide to Textiles, 1973. Contbr. articles to profl. jours. Home: 10612 Collett Av Granada Hills CA 91344 Office: 18111 Nordhoff St Northridge CA 91324

JOSEPH, MARTHA, civic worker; b. Cleve., Oct. 21, 1917; d. Ralph Siegmund and Ray (Hahn) Joseph; student Smith Coll., 1935-37, U. Dijon (France), 1937, Sorbonne, Paris, France, 1938; m. Frank Emil Joseph, Feb. 24, 1938; children—Frank E., Maddy L., Adele (Mrs. Jack Dolin), William R., Cathy G. Pres. women's com. Cleve. Orch., 1950-52; pres. Blvd. Sch. P.T.A., 1953-54; pres. Cleve. Women's Orch., 1955-60; pres. women's com. Cleve. Inst. Music, pres. inst., 1965-70, chmn. bd., 1970—; mem. exec. com. Cleve. Area Arts Council, Nat. Partnership Arts, Maison Francaise Cleve. Bd. dirs. Cleve. Women's City Club Found.; trustee Cleve. Music Sch. Settlement, Univ. Circle, Inc. Mem. Assn. Ind. Colls. Music (sec.), Cleve. Mus. Art (council), No. Ohio Opera Assn. (women's com.). Clubs: Smith College, Women's City, Oakwood, Union, Clevelander, Play House. Home: 2886 W Park Blvd Shaker Heights OH 44120

JOSEPH, MARY TERRELL (MRS. CHENEY CLEVELAND JOSEPH, JR.), lawyer; b. Seymour, Ind., Sept. 30, 1944; d. John Searcy and Alexandrine (Querbes) Terrell; A.B., Hollins Coll., 1966; J.D., La. State U., 1970; m. Cheney Cleveland Joseph, Jr., Dec. 21, 1967; children—John Terrell, Allen Fort Colley. Admitted to La. bar, 1970; mem. firm Joseph & Joseph, Baton Rouge, 1970—. Precinct leader J. Bennett Johnston's campaign for gov. La., 1971, senatorial campaign, 1972. Mem. La., Baton Rouge bar assns., Baton Rouge Jr. League, La. Arts and Sci. Center. Club: Bocage Racquet (Baton Rouge). Address: 4859 Tulane Dr Baton Rouge LA 70808

JOSEPH, ROSALINE RESNICK (MRS. ROBERT J. JOSEPH), physician; b. N.Y.C., Aug. 21, 1929; d. Joseph and Malca (Rosenberg) Resnick; A.B., Cornell U., 1949; M.D., Woman's Med. Coll. Pa., 1953; M.S., Temple U., 1958; m. Robert J. Joseph, Jan. 2, 1954; children—Joy Sara, Nina Beth. Intern, Kings County Hosp., Bklyn., 1953-54; resident Phila. Gen. Hosp., 1954-55, Temple U. Hosp., Phila., 1955-57; instr. medicine Temple U. Health Scis. Center, 1958-60, asso. in medicine, 1960-63, asst. prof. medicine, 1963-69, asso. medicine, 1969—. Joel Wagman fellow in hematology, 1957-58. Diplomate Nat. Bd. Med. Examiners. Fellow A.C.P.; mem. Am. Fedn. Clin. Research, Am. Soc. Hematology, Coll. Physicians of Phila., Am. Rheumatism Assn., Phi Beta Kappa, Alpha Epsilon Delta. Home: 610 Arbutus St Philadelphia PA 19119 Office: 3401 N Broad St Philadelphia PA 19140

JOSEPHSON, JUDITH STERN (MRS. MILES J. JOSEPHSON), computer programmer; b. Newark, July 10, 1946; d. Charles and Elenor Irene (Rush) Stern; student Cedar Crest Coll., 1964-66; B.S., George Washington U., 1968; M.A., New Sch. for Social Research, 1972; m. Miles Jay Josephson, July 16, 1972. Asst. programmer Control Data Corp., N.Y.C., 1968-71; sr. programmer Chase Manhattan Bank, N.Y.C., 1971-73; software analyst Met. Life Ins. Co., N.Y.C., 1974—. Home: 17 Madison Av #32 Madison NJ 07940 Office: 1 Madison Av New York City NY 10004

JOSHEL, SUZANNE WOLF (MRS. LLOYD M. JOSHEL), civic leader; b. Berlin, Germany, Mar. 16, 1921; d. Richard and Yetta (Gerstle) Wolf; student Lyceum, Berlin, 1931-38, London (Eng.) Sch. of Econs., 1942-44; m. Lloyd M. Joshel, July 18, 1948. Came to U.S., 1946, naturalized, 1950. Student of Anna Freud in child devel., London, 1941-46; psychiat. social worker Children's Asthma Research Inst. and Hosp., Denver, 1946-50; exec. sec. Denver Inst. for Psychoanalysis, 1971—. Active League Women Voters, 1949—, pres. Denver, 1958-61, bd. dirs. Colo., 1961-70, 2d v.p. Colo., 1963-67, pres., 1967-70, bd. dirs. U.S., 1970-72. Mem. Gov.'s Commn. on Local Govt., 1964-66; mem. Colo. Jud. Nominating Commn., 1970—. Bd. dirs. Denver War on Poverty, 1965-66, Friends of Chamber Music, Denver, 1960—, Met. Denver Urban Coalition, 1968—. Recipient distinguished service award Ams. by Choice, 1959. Home: 220 S Dahlia St Denver CO 80222

JOSSELYN, IRENE DOROTHY MILLIKEN (MRS. EUGENE ENGELHARD), physician; b. LaGrange, Ill.; d. Orris J. and Hattie (Fagersten) Milliken; B.A., Rockford Coll., 1925; M. Social Sci., Smith Coll., 1926; M.D., U. Chgo., 1934; m. Livingston Josselyn, Aug. 29, 1931 (dec. Apr. 1957); 1 dau., Helen (Mrs. William Kennedy); m. 2d, Eugene Engelhard, Oct. 27, 1960. Intern at Women's and Children's Hosp., 1933-34; resident fellow Inst. Juvenile Research and Ill. Newropsychiat. Inst., 1935-36; postgrad. tng. in psychoanalysis Chgo. Inst. Psychoanalysis, 1941-45, staff, 1950-61, clin. prof. dept. psychiatry U. Ill. Coll. Medicine, 1957-61; cons. psychiatrist supr. psychiat. aspects of rheumatic fever Herrick House, 1941-59; cons. psychiatrist North Shore Mental Health Assn., 1952-54, Irene Josselyn Clinic (formerly North Shore Mental Health Clinic), 1955—, Ridge Farm, 1949-59; cons. child study Ariz. Dept. Health; pvt. practice, Chgo.; tng. and supervising analyst, 1950-61; tng. analyst So. Cal. Psychoanalytic Inst., 1962—; pvt. practice psychiatry and psychoanalysis, Phoenix, 1961—; cons. psychiatrist VA Hosp., Phoenix, 1961—; clin. prof. child psychiatry U. So. Cal. Diplomate in child psychiatry Am. Bd. Neurology and Psychiatry. Mem. A.M.A., Internat. Psychoanalytic Assn., Maricopa County Med. Soc., So. Cal. Psychoanalytic Soc., Am. Psychoanalytic Assn., Am. Psychiat. Assn., Am. Acad. Child Psychiatry. Author: Psychosocial Development of Children, 1948; The Adolescent and His World, 1952; The Happy Child, 1955; Adolescence, 1971. Editor: Jour. Am. Acad. Child Psychiatry, 1960-65. Home: 1515 N 11th Av Phoenix AZ 85007 Office: 1515 N 11th Av Phoenix AZ 85007

JOURDAIN, ALICE MARIE (MRS. DIETRICH VON HILDEBRAND), educator; b. Brussels, Belgium, Mar. 11, 1923; d. Henri M. and Martha (van de Vorst) Jourdain; came to U.S., 1940, naturalized, 1948; B.A., Manhattanville Coll., 1944; M.A., Fordham U., 1946, Ph.D., 1949; m. Dietrich von Hildebrand, July 16, 1959. Lectr. dept. philosophy Hunter Coll., City U. N.Y., 1947-57, instr., 1957-60, asst. prof., 1960-64, asso. prof., 1965-71, prof., 1971—. Recipient William O'Brien award Newman Club, 1963. Author: Graven Images-Substitutes for True Morality; 1957; Greek Culture: The Adventure of the Human Spirit, 1965; Philosophy of Religion, 1971; (with D. von Hildebrand) The Art of Living, 1965; Morality and Situation Ethics, 1966; On the Pseudo-Obvious, 1969. Home: 43 Calton Rd New Rochelle NY 10804 Office: Hunter Coll New York City NY 10021

JOWSEY, JENIFER (MRS. FENWICK CHARLES RILEY, JR.), med. research scientist; b. London, Eng., Mar. 14, 1930; d. Cyril and Aileen (French) Jowsey; B.A., Oxford U., 1952, M.A., Ph.D., 1955; m. Fenwick Charles Riley, Jr., Sept. 9, 1966; children—John Benjamin, Pamela Grace. Came to U.S., 1955. Brit.-Am. Cancer Soc. Exchange fellow U. Chgo., 1955-56; research asso. Argonne Nat. Lab., Chgo., 1956-58; research asso. Royal Nat. Orthopaedic Hosp., London, 1958-60; research asso. Albert Einstein Med. Center Research Lab., Phila., 1960-63; research asso. Mayo Clinic, Rochester, Minn., 1963-64, mem. staff, 1964—, also dir. orthopaedic research lab., tng. orthopedic residents, cons. orthopedic research problems; prof. Mayo Med. Sch., 1973—. Mem. Orthopedic Research Soc., Endocrine Soc., Bone and Tooth Soc. Contbr. articles to profl. jours. Home: Nether Wallop Route 2 Byron MN 55920 Office: 200 SW 1st St Rochester MN 55901

JOY, HELANE MARGARET—EKDAHL, real estate broker; b. Kansas City, Mo., Dec. 11, 1919; d. Vincent James and Irene Theresa (Stockstill) Murphy; grad. high sch.; m. Richard Dale Joy, Sept. 17, 1967; children—Vickie Ekdahl (Mrs. William Bernard Bisho), Dean Alden Ekdahl. Owner, Dean's Dress Shop, Santa Monica and Beverly Hills, Cal., 1941-43; office mgr. Cal. Ink Co., Phoenix, 1951-53; owner Helane's Dress Shop, Phoenix, 1953-63; rental mgr. Bay & Beach Realty, Newport Beach, Cal., 1964-68; mgr. Burr White Realty, Newport Beach, 1968-70; partner, mgr. Assos. Brokers Newport Beach, 1970—. Mem. C. of C. (dir. woman's div. 1972-74), Costa Mesa Bd. Realtors (sec., treas., dir.), Costa Mesa Woman's Council Realtors (pres. 1973), Polit. Action Commn., Common Sense Coalition. Toastmistress. Home: 2052 Tustin Av Newport Beach CA 92660 Office: 2025 W Balboa Blvd Newport Beach CA 92660

JOYCE, FLORENCE V. MIENERT (MRS. GEORGE T. JOYCE), civic worker; b. Fosston, Minn., Feb. 13, 1923; d. William P. A. and Clara (Lindfors) Mienert; R.N., Ancker Hosp. Sch. Nursing, St. Paul, 1944; student U. Minn., 1944-45; m. George T. Joyce, Aug. 8, 1946; children—Roberta Eileen, Elizabeth Anne. Bd. dirs. N. Central Ia. chpt. A.R.C., 1960-66, 67-73, nursing services chmn., 1967—; pres. Vols. Service League, St. Joseph Mercy Hosp., Mason City, Ia., 1959-61; leader Girl Scouts U.S.A., 1948-66; bd. dirs YWCA, 1963-66. Mem. Nat. Trust for Historic Preservation, League Women Voters, Cerro Gordo County Med. Aux., Ancker (Hosp.) Alumni Assn., Charles H. MacNider Art Guild (pres. 1972-73). Club: Mason City Womans (dir. 1965—, pres. 1969-70). Roman Catholic. Home: 259 N Crescent Dr Mason City IA 50401

JOYCE, MARGARET ELIZABETH, physician; b. Birmingham, Ala., July 23, 1916; d. Gail Harry and Willie Ellen (Burdette) Joyce; B.S., Ala. Coll., 1937; postgrad. Med. Coll. Ala., 1942-45; M.D., U. Ala., 1949. Intern Jefferson-Hillman Hosp., Birmingham, 1949-50; resident Kans. U. Hosp., 1951-53, St. Francis Hosp., Wichita, 1953-54; practice of medicine, specializing in obstetrics and gynecology, Knoxville, Tenn., 1954—; mem. staffs E. Tenn. Bapt. Hosp., U. Tenn. Meml. Hosp., Ft. Sanders Presbyn. Hosp., St. Mary's Hosp. Fellow Am. Coll. Obstetrics and Gynecology; mem. Am. Bd. Obstetrics and Gynecology, Am. Fertility Soc., A.M.A., Knoxville Med. Soc. Home: 8708 Aragon Lane Knoxville TN 37919 Office: Blount Profl Bldg Knoxville TN 37920

JOYCE, MARY ROSERA (MRS. ROBERT E. JOYCE), writer; b. Coleman, Wis., June 20, 1930; d. Paul E. and Saba Minnie (Ausloos) Rosera; student Mt. Mary Coll., 1948-54; B.A., St. Xavier Coll., 1956-57; M.A., Loyola U., Chgo., 1959; postgrad. (fellow), St. Louis U., 1959-61; m. Robert E. Joyce, Aug. 12, 1961. Instr. philosophy Coll. St. Benedict, St. Joseph, Minn., 1963-65; instr. psychology and sociology St. Cloud (Minn.) Sch. Nursing, 1965-67. Supr. Shaklee, distbrs. consumer products, 1972—. Bd. dirs. Minn. Citizens Concerned for Life, 1968—, central Minn. regional coordinator, 1970-73. Recipient Lumen Gentium award Thomas More Inst., Tucson, 1972. Mem. Assn. for Human Sexual Devel. (dir. 1973). Author: (with Robert E. Joyce) New Dynamics in Sexual Love, 1970, Let Us Be Born, 1970; The Meaning of Contraception, 1970; Love Responds to Life, 1971. Contbr. to publs. in field. Address: 1248 13th Av N St Cloud MN 56301

JOYNER, JUDITH REBECCA, educator; b. Meggetts, S.C., Aug. 14, 1920; d. Ernest Luther and Rebecca (Butler) Joyner; student Martha Berry Coll., 1938-40; B.S., Appalachian State U., 1942, M.A., 1957; postgrad. U. N.C., Temple U.; Ph.D., U. S.C., 1960. Tchr., High Sch., Tabor City, N.C., 1942-43; dir. clubs and programs Am. Nat. Red Cross, Holland and Germany, 1945-47; coll. instr. Heidelberg and Berlin, 1947-48; employee relations chief, Berlin, 1948-50; employee utilization chief, Munich, 1950-52; mgmt. analyst Frankford Arsenal, Phila., 1952-54; tchr. High Sch., Loris, S.C., 1957-58; grad. instr. U. S.C., 1958-60, asst. prof., 1960-64, asso. prof., 1964-71, prof., 1971—, chmn. ednl. founds. Coll. Edn. Mem. state bd. League Women Voters S.C., 1966-67. Mem. South Atlantic Philosophy Edn. Soc. (pres. 1968-70), S.C. Edn. Assn., History Edn. Soc., Am. Assn. U. Profs., Nat. Soc. Study Edn., Nat. Soc. Am. Archivists, Delta Kappa Gamma. Contbr. articles to profl. jours. Home: 57 Churchill Circle Columbia SC 29206

JOYNER, MARY ABBAY LEATHERMAN (MRS. GUY EUGENE JOYNER), club woman; b. Tunica, Miss., Aug. 28, 1898; d. Samuel Richard and Ethel (Irwin) Leatherman; grad. Briarcliff Manor, 1916; m. Guy Eugene Joyner, Apr. 7, 1931 (dec. Aug. 1946); children—Guy Eugene, Mary Abbay (Mrs. M.A.J. Knox). Mem. Jr. League, Memphis; pres. Memphis Symphony Soc., 1942-43, Little Garden Club, Memphis, 1958-60; mem. Garden Club Am. Bd. dirs. James Lee Meml. Acad. Arts, Memphis, 1933-39, Memphis Acad. Arts, 1936-46, Memphis Open Air Theatre, 1939-50. Recipient certificate of award FSA, 1946, USPHS, 1946, Marine Hosp., Memphis, 1946, A.R.C., 1946. Mem. Colonial Dames Am. in Tenn. (chmn. Memphis 1952-53). Presbyn. Clubs: Memphis Hunt and Polo, Memphis Country. Contbr., editor, compiler: One Hundred Years of Delightful Indigestion, 1935. Home: 3550 Central Av Memphis TN 38111

JOYNER, VICTORIA KRIENKE (MRS. ALBERT ANDREW JOYNER), bus. exec., city ofcl.; b. Osseo, Minn., Sept. 29, 1904; d. Otto Carl and Pauline (Kottke) Krienke; student pub. schs.; m. Albert Andrew Joyner, June 4, 1924; children—Albert K., Orlyn D., Gwendolyn V. (Mrs. Elmer Christensen). With Joyners Silver & Electroplating, Osseo, 1941—, sec., 1953—; v.p. Joyners Bowling Lanes, Osseo, 1958—; pres. Lavco Corp., Osseo, 1957—, Bklyn. Park Oil Co., Osseo, 1960—, Joynerdale Golfcourse, Osseo, 1962—; sec. Silver Creek Golfcourse, Osseo, 1972—. Mem. Hennepin County Nursing Dist. Bd., Osseo, 1956—; chmn. Seven County Mosquito Control, 1958; 4-H leader Hennepin County, 1933-41. Mayor, City of Osseo, 1954—. Recipient Woman of Year award N. Hennepin Bus. and Profl. Womans Club, 1973; Minn. Woman of Year award Minn. Bus. and Profl. Women, 1973. Mem. N. Hennepin Pioneer Soc. (dir.), Hennepin County Farm Bur., League of Municipalities (v.p. 1968-70), Methodist. Club: Soropotimist (Mpls.). Home: 233 6th St NW Osseo MN 55369 Office: 7716 Lakeland PO Box 406 Osseo MN 55369

JUDAS, ILSE, physician; b. Freiburgi Br., Germany, May 5, 1924; d. Abraham and Ernestine (Kaufmann) Judas; came to U.S., 1938, naturalized, 1942; Ph.B., U. Wis., 1946, B.S., 1947. M.D. (Knapp scholar 1947), 1950; m. Jerome M. Grunes, Mar. 5, 1955; children—Allen Paul, Ernestine Mina. Teaching asst. zoology U. Wis., 1945-46; intern Michael Reese Hosp., Chgo., 1950-51, resident in psychiatry, 1951-54, asst. chief child psychiatry, 1954-55; certified in psychoanalysis Chgo. Inst. for Psychoanalysis, 1965; certified in child psychoanalysis, 1970; practice medicine specializing in psychiatry and psychoanalysis, Chgo., 1954—. Cons. for Mental Health Clinics, Family Service Agys., Child Welfare Depts., others; faculty child therapy program of Inst. for Psychoanalysis, 1962—, faculty child psychoanalytic program, 1971—; asso. clin. prof. psychiatry U. Ill. Med. Sch., 1970—. Diplomate in child psychiatry Am. Bd. Psychiatry and Neurology; certified Children's Clinic Am. Mem. Am. Psychiat. Assn., Am. Orthopsychiat. Assn., Am. Acad. Child Psychiatry, Chgo. Psychoanalytic Soc., M.M.S., Am. Psychoanalytic Assn., Phi Beta Kappa, Phi Kappa Phi. Contbr. articles profl. jours. Address: 5454 South Shore Dr Chicago IL 60615

JUDD, SALLY CLARK, owner art gallery; b. San Francisco, Dec. 29, 1930; student House in Pines Jr. Coll., 1948-49, Stanford, 1949-50. Owner Sally Judd Gallery, Portland, Ore., 1968—. Guide for children's museum tours and traveling exhbns., adult tours and orgns., lectr. Portland Art Assn., 1957-68; art coordinator, cons. Sun River (Ore.) Lodge, 1969—; juror art exhbns. Activities council Portland Art Mus., 1960-68; mem. Gov.'s Adv. Com. for Arts, 1971—. Trustee Contemporary Crafts Gallery, Portland. Home: 1311 NW 24th St Portland OR 97210 Office: 224 SW 1st Av Portland OR 97204

JUDSON, JEANNETTE ALEXANDER (MRS. HENRY JUDSON), artist; b. N.Y.C., Feb. 23, 1912; d. Phillip George and Gertrude (Leichter) Alexander; student N.A.D., 1956-59, Art Student League, N.Y.C., 1959-61; m. Henry Judson, Sept. 23, 1945; children—S. Robert Weltz, Jr., Pauline Flatto; 1 stepson, E. William Judson. Exhibited one-man shows Fairleigh Dickinson U., 1965, Bodley Gallery, N.Y.C., 1967, 69, 71, 73, N.Y. U., 1969, Pa. State U., 1969, Laura Musser Mus. Art, Muscatine, Ia., 1969; exhibited in group shows including anns. Nat. Assn. Women Artists, N.Y.C., France, Italy, 1965—, Audubon Artists, N.Y.C., 1962, 64, 65-67, Allied Artists, N.Y.C., 1966-67; represented in permanent collections Joseph H. Hirshhorn, N.Y. U., Norfolk (Va.) Mus. Arts and Scis.,

Brandeis U., Peabody Art Mus., Mus. of N.M., Sheldon Swope Art Mus., Syracuse U., Evansville Mus. Arts and Scis., Rutgers U., Colby Coll., Butler Inst. Am. Art, Laura Musser Mus., Fordham U., Lehigh U., Ga. Mus. Art, U. Ga., Fairleigh Dickinson U., Lowe Mus., U. Miami, Washington County (Md.) Mus. Fine Arts, Miami Mus. Modern Art, Bruce Mus., Greenwich, Conn., Bklyn. Mus., Hudson River Mus., Dartmouth Coll. Mus., Mus. Modern Art, Lending Service, also numerous pvt. collections. Mem. Nat. Assn. Women Artists, Artists Equity N.Y., Art Students League (life), Am. Soc. Contemporary Artists, League Present Day Artists, N.Y. Soc. Women Artists. Home: 1130 Park Av New York City NY 10028 Studio: 140 W 57th St New York City NY 10019

JUDSON, MARGARET ATWOOD, educator; b. Winsted, Conn., Nov. 5, 1899; d. George W. and Minnie (Atwood) Judson; B.A., Mt. Holyoke Coll., 1922, Litt.D., 1972; M.A., Radcliffe Coll., 1923, Ph.D., 1933; LL.D., Rutgers U., 1968. Instr. history Douglass Coll., Rutgers U., 1928-33, asst. prof., 1933-42, asso. prof., 1942-48, prof., 1948—, chmn. history and polit. sci. dept., 1954-63, acting dean Douglass Coll., 1966-67; Alice F. Palmer vis. prof. U. Mich., 1959. Guggenheim fellow, 1954-55. Fellow Royal Hist. Soc.; mem. Am. Hist. Assn., Am. Assn. U. Profs., Brit. Conf., Berkshire Hist. Conf. (pres. 1948-50), League Women Voters, Phi Beta Kappa. Author: The Crisis of the Constitution, 1949; The Political Thought of Sir Henry Vane The Younger, 1969. Home: 8 Redcliffe Av Highland Park NJ 08904

JUERGENSMEYER, ELIZABETH BOGART (MRS. JOHN ELI JUERGENSMEYER), educator; b. Columbia, Mo., May 28, 1940; d. Ralph and Frances (Warbritton) Bogart; B.S., Ore. State U., 1962; M.S. (NSF fellow), U. Ill., 1964, Ph.D., 1967; m. John Eli Juergensmeyer, Sept. 10, 1963; children—Margaret Ann, Frances Elizabeth. Teaching and research asst. U. Ill., Chgo. Circle, 1965-68; asst. prof. biology William Rainey Harper Coll., Palatine, Ill., 1968-69; asso. prof. biology Judson Coll., Elgin, Ill., 1969—. Mem. A.A.A.S., Am. Soc. Zoologists, Genetics Soc., Am. Soc. Protozoologists, Am. Inst. Biol. Sci., N.Y. Acad. Sci. Home: 401 Hazel Dr Elgin IL 60120

JUHASZ, ANNE MCCREARY, educator; b. Stratford, Ont., Can., Jan. 19, 1922; d. John Harold and Edythe Selina (Staines) Phillips; B.S., Cortland Coll., 1958; M.Ed., Cornell U., 1959, Ph.D., 1961; m. Stephen Eugene Juhasz, June 29, 1965. Asso. prof. edn. U. B.C., Vancouver, Can., 1962-67; asso. prof. edn. founds. Loyola U., Chgo., 1967-69, prof., 1969—. Canadian Scandinavian research fellow, 1961-62. Mem. Am. Psychol. Assn., Am. Sch. Health Assn., A.A.A.S., Am. Ednl. Research Assn., Nat. Council Family Relations. Author: Effective Study, 1965; (with E. Thorn) Language Experience Readers, 1965; (with G. Szasz) Adolescents in Society, 1970; Sexual Development And Behavior: Selected Readings, 1973. Home: 831 Belleforte Av Oak Park IL 60302 Office: 820 N Michigan Av Chicago IL 60611

JULIAN, HENRI-JANE SWEGMAN (MRS. FORREST L. JULIAN), psychiat. social worker; b. Red Oak, Ia., Aug. 12, 1925; d. Eugene Henry and Bertha Jane (Smith) Swegman; B.A., U. Wis. 1949, M.S. in Social Work, 1962; m. Forrest L. Julian, Nov. 20, 1942; 1 son, Bryan E. Social work therapist, dir. profl. services Family Service, Madison, Wis., 1962—; student supr. U. Wis.; pvt. practice psychotherapy. Mem. Nat. Assn. Social Workers, Acad. Certified Social Workers, Bus. and Profl. Womens Club, Nat. Orgn. Women, Am. Group Psychotherapy Assn. (asso.), Internat. Transactional Analysis Inst. Home and office: 2022 Wisconsin Av Sun Prairie WI 53590 Office: 2059 Atwood Av Madison WI 53704

JUMONVILLE, MARTHA ALINE HUNDEMER, advt., pub. relations exec.; b. Baton Rouge, Feb. 12, 1923; d. Charles Christian and Martha Louise (Dieckmann) Hundemer; B.Ed., La. State U., 1944; m. Frank Barker Jumonville, June 17, 1950; children—Martha Louise, Frank Barker, Jill Anne. Display sales Advt. dept. State Times Morning Advocate, Baton Rouge, 1944-46; asst. sales mgr., copywriter WLCS Radio Sta., Baton Rouge, 1946-50; account exec. Hundemer Assos., Advt. Agy., Baton Rouge, 1969-72; pub. relations dir. Safety Council Greater Baton Rouge, 1973-74; dir. edn./information sect. Gov.'s Office of Consumer Protection, State of La., 1974—. Pres. Service League of Plaquemine, 1969; Area Troop organizer Girl Scouts Am., 1968; bd. mem. Plaquemine Little Theatre, 1967; publicity chmn. Iberville Parish Heart Fund, 1973. Mem. Press Club Baton Rouge, Advt. Club Baton Rouge. Club: Krewe Du Roi Carnival Ball Assn. Home: 708 Canal St Plaquemine LA 70764 Office: Capitol Sta PO Box 44091 Baton Rouge LA 70804

JUNCK, MARY ELIZABETH, newspaper exec.; b. Jefferson, Ia., Sept. 2, 1947; d. Howard John and Elizabeth (Pearson) Junck; B.A., Valparaiso U., 1969; M.A. in Journalism, U. N.C., 1971. Research asso. Inst. for Research in Social Sci., U. N.C., 1970-72; mktg. research mgr. Charlotte (N.C.) Observer, 1972-74, asst. retail advt. mgr., 1974—. Cons. survey research. Research coordinator Charlotte Quality Edn. Com., 1973—; research coordinator McGovern Campaign in Mecklenburg, 1972. Mem. Women in Communication (sec. Charlotte chpt. 1972), Sigma Delta Chi, Kappa Tau Alpha. Author: Charlotte Retailing Guide, 1972. Home: 6107 Bent Tree Ct Charlotte NC 28212 Office: Knight Pub Co Box 2138 Charlotte NC 28202

JUNE, EVA M. (MRS. WILLIAM L. DEVRIES), mgmt. cons.; b. Budapest, Hungary, Sept. 17, 1935; d. Istvan and Edith (Teichner) Banyai; certificate in electronics Kando Coll., Budapest, 1952; m. William Lee Devries, Feb. 8, 1962; children—Marianne, Thomas, Gretchen. Came to U.S., 1957, naturalized, 1962. Sound engr., radio repair specialist Circle Rec. Studio, Washington, 1957-59; performer WXYZ-TV, Detroit, 1959-60, KPLR-TV, St. Louis, 1960-61; media analyst D'arcy Advt., St. Louis, 1960-61; treas. AABCO Employment Corp., Washington, 1961-63; v.p. Exec. Secs., Inc., Washington, 1963-64; pres., chief exec. officer Ability Search, Inc., Washington, 1964—; chmn. bd. Chem. Tech., Inc., Washington, 1973. Cons. Dept. Def. on career transition; cons. Environmental Protection Agy. Mem. U.S. Presdl. Inauguration Com., 1968. Mem. Operations Research Soc. Am. (membership chmn. bus. applications sect.), Washington Operations Research Council, Inst. Mgmt. Sci., Assn. Computing Machinery. Republican. Episcopalian. Pioneer in use of videotape interviews for exec. search and selection. Home: 6220 Goodview St Bethesda MD 20034 Office: 1629 K Street NW Suite 202 Washington DC 20006

JUNEAU, JOCELYNE BLAIN, librarian; b. Montreal, Que., Can., Apr. 22, 1923; d. Raynald and Adele (Vincent) Blain; B.A., Coll. Marie Anne, 1945; B.L.S., U. Montreal, 1964, M.L.S., 1975; m. Jean Juneau, Apr. 18, 1949; children—Danielle, Monique, Jean-Pierre, Nicole, Marie France, Jean Luc. With Papineau Smallware, importers, Montreal, Que., 1952-63; head tech. services Coll. St. Ignace Library, Montreal, 1964-66; librarian, serials and classification Coll. de Maisonneuve Library, Montreal, 1966-68, head library tech. sch., dept. dir., 1969-71, prof., 1969-73; librarian, catalog and classification U. Que. Library, Montreal, 1968-69; dir. med. library Hosp. de la Misericorde, Montreal, 1971—. Mem. Am., Canadian library assns., Que. Library Assn., Assn. Canadienne des Bibliothecaires de Langue Francaise, Assn. pour L'Avancement des Sciences et des Techniques de la Documentation. Home: 4003 Lacombe Av Montreal PQ H3T 1M7 Canada Office: 1051 St Hubert St Montreal PQ H2L 3Y5 Canada

JUNG, CHARLOTTE J., banker; b. Tipton, Ind., Apr. 24, 1924; d. John Simon and Dorothy K. (Howard) Jung; B.S., Internat. Bus. Coll., 1944. Sec., Wefel & Maxfield, Ft. Wayne, Ind., 1944-46; exec. sec. State Exchange Bank, Culver, Ind., 1946-57, dir., 1965—, v.p., 1967-74, trust officer, 1967—, sr. v.p., 1974—; sec. State Exchange Finance Co., Culver, 1957, v.p., 1974—; sr. v.p., dir. Farmers State Bank, LaPaz, Ind.; dir. State Exchange Finance Co., Culver, State Exchange Bank Bldg. Corp., Culver. Mem. Nat. Assn. Bank Women, Am. Legion Aux. (unit pres. 1956). Democrat. Methodist. Home: 200 W Williams St Argos IN 46501 Office: Main St Culver IN 46511

JUNGERMAN, NANCY LEE KIDWELL (MRS. JOHN ALBERT JUNGERMAN), counseling psychologist; b. San Francisco, Dec. 22, 1925; d. William Norman and Julia (Jorgensen) Kidwell; A.B. with honors, U. Cal. at Berkeley, 1946, M.A., 1949; m. John Albert Jungerman, Oct. 23, 1948; children—Mark Albert, Eric John, Roger Lee, Anne Marie. Teaching asst. U. Cal. at Berkeley, 1946-47, 48-49, psychometrist counseling center, 1947, psychometrist Oakland guidance center, 1947-48; supervising clin. psychologist, Syracuse Psychopathic Hosp., 1949-50; psychometrist U. Cal. at Davis, 1953-55, counseling psychologist, 1955—; pvt. practice as counseling psychologist, 1968—. Certified psychologist, Cal. Mem. United World Federalists, Am. Assn. UN, M.M.S., Davis Community Center Arts, Am. Personnel and Guidance Assn., Sacramento Valley Psychol. Assn., Assn. Higher Edn. Democrat. Unitarian. Home: 712 Elmwood Dr Davis CA 95616 Office: Counseling Center U Cal at Davis Davis CA also 241 B St Davis CA 95616

JUNGHANS, JOLINE KERN, occupational therapist; b. Montclair, N.J., July 2, 1930; d. John Babcock and Laurie Rohrer (Garber) Kern; student St. Lawrence U., 1947-48; certificate occupational therapy U. Pa., 1951; m. Max Junghans, Sept. 7, 1951 (div.); children—David Kern, Kathy Ann, Carol Sue, Jenny Lou. With Helen Hays Hosp., West Haverstraw, N.Y., 1951-53, occupational therapist in pediatric rehab., 1967—. Asst. leader Girl Scouts Am., Nanuet, N.Y., 1964. Mem. Kappa Delta. Methodist. Club: Woman's (Nanuet). Home: 17 Edsall Av Nanuet NY 10954

JUNGMAN, JEAN ANN, newspaperwoman; b. San Angelo, Tex., Sept. 12, 1950; d. Lawrence William and Flora Pauline (Shackleford) Jungman; B.A., N. Tex. State U., 1972. Soc. editor Athens (Tex.) Rev., 1972-73; gen. assignment reporter, youth editor Tyler (Tex.) Morning Telegraph, 1973-74, gen. assignment reporter, 1974—. Mem. Women in Communications (sec. 1971-72), Sigma Delta Chi (treas. 1971, sec. 1971-72). Home: 3100 New Kilgore Hwy Tyler TX 75701 Office: Tyler Morning Telegraph Tyler TX 75701

JUNGWIRTH, IRENE GAYAS, artist; b. McKee's Rocks, Pa.; d. Alexander and Berenice (Murawska) Gayas; B.A. in Fine Arts-Art Edn., Marygrove Coll., Detroit, 1935; postgrad. Wayne State U., 1937-38, Mich. State U., 1944-45; m. Leonard D. Jungwirth, Apr. 10, 1939 (dec. Aug. 1963); children—Alessandra Irene (Mrs. George Scott Ayers), Andrea Cecilia Jungwirth, M.D. (Mrs. H. Lams). Comml. artist, 1935-36; tchr. art Detroit pub. schs., 1937-40, Detroit Inst. Arts, 1938-40; exhibited in one-man shows Artists Market, 1947, Marygrove Coll., 1949; J. L. Hudson Co., 1950, Anna Werbe Gallery, Detroit, 1954, Mich. State U., 1958, Garelicks Gallery, Detroit, 1959, Grinnell's, 1963, Bloomfield Hills, Mich., 1966; exhibited in group shows Butler Art Inst., Youngstown, 1948, 52, 54, Detroit Art Inst. Annual, 1940, 50, 62, Va. Biennial, 1940, and others; represented in permanent collections Detroit Inst. Arts, Marygrove Coll., Marquette U., libraries, chs., many pvt. collections; designer stained glass windows, stage scenery, costumes, jewelry, 1945—; lectr. art, allied subjects, 1940—; spl. commns. include comml., religious, secular portraits. Address: Westwinds Studio Route 1 Box 153-A Mountain View Rd Emmitsburg MD 21727

JUNKER, GRACE KELLETT (MRS. WILLIAM OTTO JUNKER, JR.), banker; b. Laurens County, S.C., Feb. 3, 1929; d. Talmadge Milton and Minnie Mae (Vaughan) Kellett; A.B., Spartanburg Jr. Coll., 1947; pre-standard certificate Am. Inst. Banking, 1960, standard certificate, 1963; grad. certificate S.C. Bankers Sch., 1964; grad. Sch. Banking of South, La. State U., 1974; m. William Otto Junker, Jr., Sept. 13, 1947; children—Linda Charlene, William Otto III. With Citizens & So. Nat. Bank, Columbia, S.C., 1945-50, 54—, system operations officer, 1972—. Counselor Jr. Achievement, 1970, 71, 72. Bd. Dirs. S.C. Bankers Sch., United Fund, Piedmont area Girl Scouts Am. Named Career Woman of the Year, Profl. and Bus. Women's Club, 1971-72. Mem. Spartanburg C. of C., Nat. Assn. Bank Women, Inc. (chmn. S.C. group 1968; dir. Bank Adminstrv. Inst.), Adminstrv. Mgmt. Soc. Clubs: Altrusa (pres. 1968-69). Home: 204 Nottingham Rd Columbia SC 29210 Office: Greystone Blvd Columbia SC 29202

JUNKIN, ELAINE WALKER (MRS. JAMES H. JUNKIN), librarian; b. Pickens County, Ala., Aug. 28, 1927; d. Claude Neander and Maggie (McCool) Walker; diploma Birmingham Bus. Coll., 1947; B.S., Livingston U., 1949; M.A., U. Ala., 1969; m. James Hubert Junkin, Dec. 20, 1947; children—Stanley, Bridgett, Lance. Tchr. bus. edn. Palmetto High Sch., Reform, Ala., 1946-47, Fruitdale (Ala.) High Sch., 1949-51, Ala. Mills Inc., Birmingham, Ala., 1951-52, Brilliant (Ala.) High Sch., 1955-56; bookkeeper D. F. Mobley, Am. Oil Distbr., Guin, Ala., 1956-58; tchr. bus. edn. Hamilton (Ala.) High Sch., 1958-65; Winfield (Ala.) City Schs., 1966; librarian Marion County High Sch., Guin, Ala., 1966—. Mem. En Avant Study Club (pres. 1967, v.p. 1966, treas.-sec. 1964), Am. Edn. Assn., A.L.A., Ala. Instructional Media Assn., Marion County Tchrs. Assn., Delta Kappa Gamma. Baptist (tchr. adult women Sunday sch. 1955—). Mem. Order Eastern Star. Home: 601 12th Av Guin AL 35563 Office: Marion County High Sch Guin AL 35563

JUNKINS, IMA MAE VAN HOOK (MRS. JAMES HOWARD JUNKINS), librarian; b. Burnside, Ky., Mar. 28, 1914; d. John Gilbert and Rose Lee (McDonald) Van Hook; B.A., Ohio State U., 1935; B.S. in L.S., U. Ky., 1945; M.A., Columbia, 1946; m. James Howard Junkins, Sept. 7, 1946; 1 dau., Catherine Rose. Tchr. French, English, Eubank (Ky.) High Sch., 1935-37; librarian Somerset (Ky.) High Sch., 1939-46; supervising librarian Carnegie Pub. Library, Somerset, Ky., 1939-46; catalog reviser library sci. dept. U. Ky., Lexington, 1946-47; elementary librarian Oak Ridge Schs., 1947-50, 56—. Mem. Bus. and Profl. Women's Club (pres. 1941-42, state chmn. 1942-44), Am. Assn. U. Women, Phi Delta Gamma. Republican. Methodist. Mem. Order Eastern Star (worthy matron 1946-47). Home: 396 East Dr Oak Ridge TN 37830 Office: Woodland Sch Oak Ridge TN 37830

JURGENSEN, BARBARA (MRS. RICHARD JURGENSEN), author; b. Excelsior, Minn., Nov. 22, 1928; d. William Harold and Ethel Elisabeth (Nesbitt) Bitting; B.A., St. Olaf Coll., 1950; m. Richard Jurgensen, Aug. 28, 1949; children—Janet, Marie, Peter. Author numerous mag. articles, stories and poems, 1958—. Author: Leaping Upon the Mountains, 1960; All the Bandits of China, 1965; Oh, Please Not Bethlehem!, 1966; Men Who Dared, 1967; Parents, Ugh, 1968; Quit Bugging Me, 1968; The Lord is My Shepherd, 1969; You're Out of Date, 1971; Don't Bug Me, Preacher, 1972; Some Day We've Got to Get Organized, 1972; God Probably Doesn't Know I Exist, 1973; How to Live Better on Less, 1974; A Polluter's Garden of Verses, 1974. Home: 5135 S Kimbark Av Chicago IL 60615

JURINAC, (SREBRENKA) SENA, opera singer; b. Travnik, Yugoslavia, Oct. 24, 1921; d. Ludwig Jurinac and Christine Cerv; ed. high sch., Musical Academy; m. Josef Lederle, 1961. First appearance on stage as Mimi, with the Zagreb Opera, 1942; mem. Vienna State Opera, 1944—; numerous appearances Glyndebourne Festivals, 1949-56, also Salzburg Festivals; regular guest artist LaScala, also Covent Garden; prin. parts include Donna Elvira in Don Giovanni, Leonore in Fidelio, Elisabeth in Tannhauser, Tosca, Jenufa, Komponist in Ariadne auf Naxos, Marschallin in Der Rosenkavalier, Marie in Wozzeck, Elisabeth in Don Carlos, Desdemona in Othello. Kammersangerin award, 1951; recipient Mozart medal 1st class Austrian award Litteris et artibus. Her biography, by Ursula Tamussino, pub. 1971. Address: Sekretariat Wien Wehrgasse IIa Austria

JURKA, EDITH MILA, psychiatrist; b. N.Y.C., Dec. 4, 1915; d. Charles Anton and Edith Dorothy (Schevcik) Jurka; B.A., Smith Coll., 1936; B.A., Charles U., Prague, Czechoslovakia, 1936-38; M.D., Yale, 1944; postgrad. N.Y. Psychoanalytic Inst., 1956-62. Intern Children's Med. Service Bellevue Hosp., N.Y.C., 1944-45; rotating intern Gallinger Hosp., Washington, 1945-46; intern N.Y. State Psychiat. Inst., N.Y.C., 1946-47; asst. alienist Bellevue Psychiat. Hosp., N.Y.C., 1947-49; asst. psychiatrist out-patient dir. Mt. Sinai Hosp., N.Y.C., 1949-51; staff psychiatrist Pleasantville (N.Y.) Cottage Sch., 1951-54, chief psychiatrist, 1961-74, sr. cons. psychiatrist, 1974—; asst. psychiatrist Roosevelt Hosp., N.Y.C., 1954-56; cons. research project Jewish Guild for the Blind, N.Y.C., 1966-69. Mem. Assn. Yale Alumni Medicine (mem. exec. com. 1952-55, 73—, sec. 1974—), N.Y. State Med. Soc. (mem. mental hygiene com. 1971—). Home: 300 Albany Post Rd Croton-on-Hudson NY 10520 Office: 116 E 66th St New York City NY 10021

JURKOVICH, SYLVIA TERESE (MRS. ROGER CHARLES YANULE), ins. exec.; b. Joliet, Ill., Jan. 19, 1937; d. John Frank and Magdalen P. (Madarik) Jurkovich; A.A., Joliet Jr. Coll., 1956; B.A. in Journalism, Bradley U., 1958; m. Roger Charles Yanule, Apr. 15, 1972. Reporter, New World, Cath. newspaper, Chgo., 1958-59; with pub. relations dept. Zurich Ins. Co., Chgo., 1960-63, Am. Coll. Radiology, Chgo., 1964; dir. pub. relations La Salle Nat. Ins. Co., Chgo., 1964-69, N.Am. Co. of Life Ins., Chgo., 1970; dir. pub. relations Cath. Order of Foresters, Chgo., 1970—. Free-lance pub. relations for various small firms, 1969—. Bd. advisers Bradley U., Peoria, 1970-72. Mem. Pub. Relations Soc. Am., Windy City Life Advertisers Assn., Nat. Fraternal Congress (chmn. publicity com. 1973-74), Bradley U. Alumni Assn. (pres. 1967-68). Home: 1560 N Sandburg Terrace Chicago IL 60610 Office: 305 W Madison St Chicago IL 60606

JURMA, MALL KUNSIK, radio script writer; b. Estonia; d. Juhan and Pauline (Kaasik) Kuusik; Magister Philosophiae, U. Tartu, Estonia, 1927; m. Endel Jurma, Sept. 28, 1929 (dec. Oct. 1943). Came to U.S., 1949, naturalized, 1954. Sr. librarian Central Municipal Library, Tallinn, Estonia, 1926-42; insp. pub. libraries Ministry of Edn., Tallinn, 1942-44; radio information specialist, asst. editor Estonian Service, Voice of Am., Washington, 1951-71. Pres. Baltic Women's Council, N.Y.C., 1947—. Recipient Medal of Merits for cultural service Estonian Red Cross, 1936. mem. Estonian Arts and Letters Found., Estonian Learned Soc., P.E.N., Estonian Ednl. Soc. Lutheran. Home: 24 Central Av Ridgefield Park NJ 07660

JURNEY, DOROTHY MISENER, journalist; b. Michigan City, Ind., May 8, 1909; d. Herbert Roy and Mary Zeola (Hershey) Misener; student Western Coll. for Women, 1926-28; B.S. in Journalism, Northwestern U., 1930; m. Frank J. Jurney, Sept. 1940 (legally separated). Reporter, Michigan City News and News Dispatch, 1930-39; women's editor Gary (Ind.) Post-Tribune, 1939-41; asst. to press rep. Panama Canal, 1941-42; editor in women's dept. Miami (Fla.) News, 1943-44; 46-49; asst. city editor Washington News, 1944-46; women's editor Miami Herald, 1949-59; women's editor Detroit Free Press, 1959-72, asst. mng. editor, 1972-73; asst. mng. editor Phila. Inquirer, 1973—. Mem. Women in Communications, Am. Soc. Newspaper Editors, A.P. Mng. Editors (dir.). Clubs: Florida Women's Press (life); Detroit Press; Michigan Women's Press. Lectr., cons. in field. Home: 325 West Av Wayne PA 19087 Office: Phila Inquirer Philadelphia PA 19101

JUSSIM, ESTELLE, educator; b. N.Y.C., Mar. 18, 1927; d. Boris and Mollie (Glusker) Jussim; B.A., Queens Coll., 1947; M.S. in L.S., Columbia, 1963; D.Library Sci. (fellow), Columbia, 1970. Art dir. and graphic designer for communications industries, N.Y.C., 1950-62; exec. asst. to dir. ednl. resources Borough of Manhattan Community Coll., N.Y.C., 1965-66; asso. dir. media services, asst. prof. communications media Hampshire Coll., Amherst, Mass., 1969-72; asst. prof. film and communications media Simmons Coll. Grad. Sch. Library Sci., Boston, 1972—. Cons. utilization of media in higher edn., also cable TV in regional networks of schs. and libraries. Trustee State Library Commonwealth Mass. Mem. Assn. Ednl. Communications and Tech., Assn. Nat. Ednl. Broadcasters, Popular Culture Assn., Beta Phi Mu. Contbr. articles to profl. jours. Home: 8 Hubbard Dr Granby MA 01033 Office: Sch Library Sci Simmons Coll Boston MA 02115

JUST, BERNICE EVELYN, journalist; b. Concordia, Kan., Dec. 24, 1911; d. Gustav Theodore and Ella (Fogelberg) Palmquist; B.S. in Edn., U. Neb., 1932; M.Journalism, Northwestern U., 1939; m. William L. Just, Jan. 15, 1949 (dec. May 1, 1973); 1 dau., Shigeyo (Mrs. Ronald K. Kirkpatrick). Tchr. English, journalism, 1932-49; reporter, columnist Waukegan (Ill.) News-Sun, 1954—; dir. Keystone Printing Service. Mem. bd. 12th Congl. Republican Women's Club, 1964—. Bd. dirs. Lake County unit Am. Cancer Soc., 1968—, mem. state bd. Ill. unit, 1970—; bd. dirs. Barwell Settlement, Waukegan, Just Found., Ill. State Lung Assn.; hon. mem. bd. Grove Sch. Exceptional Children, Lake Forest. Mem. Chi Omega; hon. mem. Lake County Women's Mgmt. Assn., Delta Kappa Gamma. Baptist. Home: 2325 Corona Rd Waukegan IL 60085 Office: 100 Madison St Waukegan IL 60085

JUSTEN, KATHLEEN PETERS (MRS. FRANK CHARLES JUSTEN), educator; b. Mishawaka, Ind., Apr. 18, 1928; d. William Marvin and Minnie (Yawkey) Peters; B.S., Ind. U., 1949; M.Ed., U. Toledo, 1960; postgrad. U. Cin., 1951-56, U. Toledo, 1960-67; m. Frank Charles Justen, Dec. 9, 1961; step-children—Frank A., Diane Ruth (Mrs. James David Waltz). Tchr., Columbia City (Ind.) High Sch., 1949-51, Withrow High Sch., Cin., 1951-56; tchr. Scott High Sch., Toledo, 1956-59, counselor, Toledo, 1959-66; supr. pupil appraisal services Toledo Pub. Schs., 1966-67, dir. pupil evaluation services, 1967-70, dir. child services, 1970—. Grad. asst. U. Toledo, summers 1960, 61. Adv. mem. bd. dirs. Toledo Dental Dispensary, 1969-71; mem. ednl. adv. com. Toledo Hosp., 1968—. Bd. dirs. Toledo Mental Hygiene Clinic, pres.-elect, 1973. Mem. Am. Personnel and Guidance Assn., Am. Vocational Guidance Assn., Am. Sch. Counselors Assn., Assn. Counselor Edn. and Supervision, Assn. for Measurement and Evaluation in Guidance (sec. Ohio 1971-72),

Nat. Council Measurement in Edn., Council on Exceptional Children, Am. Assn. Sch. Adminstrs., Toledo Assn. Adminstrv. Personnel, Am. Assn. U. Women. Home: 2370 Parkwood Av Toledo OH 43620

JUSTICE, BARBARA ADELE, educator; b. Lawndale, N.C., July 30, 1923; d. Thomas Weldon and Bessie Burdell (Wray) J.; A.A., Gardner Webb Coll., 1942; B.S., Appalachian State U., 1948; M.A., 1963. Tchr. primary grades, pub. schs., Shelby, N.C., 1943-61; music supr. Charlotte-Mecklenburg Schs., 1962-66; asst. prof. music Appalachian State U., Boone, 1967—. Music cons. to academically talented, 1966; mem. guest faculty U. N.C., Charlotte, 1966-67. Dir. Women's Chorus, Cleveland County, N.C., 1954-57. Recipient outstanding alumnus citation Gardner Webb Coll., 1959, award Early Childhood Edn. Assn. Mem. Nat. Commn. for Music Spl. Edn., N.C. Vocational Music Assn. (state com. mem. 1972), Music Educators Nat. Assn., Alpha Delta Kappa, Sigma Alpha Iota, Pi Kappa Lambda. Home: 211 Faculty Apartments Appalachian State U Boone NC 28607

JUTKOWITZ, BERNICE EPSTEIN (MRS. DAVID JUTKOWITZ), civic worker; b. N.Y.C., June 3, 1919; d. Samuel and Ethel (Rosenblum) Epstein; B.B.A., Ohio State U., 1941; m. J. David Jutkowitz, June 15, 1947; children—Linda (Mrs. Richard Eric Meyers), John G. Organizer, chmn. Sr. Vol. Service, Yonkers, N.Y., 1965—; bd. dirs. Community Planning Council Yonkers, 1966—; trustee Yonkers Pub. Library, 1966—, treas., 1966-67, v.p., 1968, pres., 1969-70, treas., 1971—; bd. dirs. Nat. Council Jewish Women, 1949—, Gorton High Sch PTA, 1957-61, Riverdale Country Sch., 1957-61. Mem. Westchester Library Assn., A.L.A., Library Trustees Found. N.Y. State, Nat. Council Jewish Women, Yonkers Gen. Hosp. Aux., Jewish Community Center Aux. Jewish religion. Home: 112 Holls Terrace Yonkers NY 10701

JUVE, JANET MAY, occupational therapist; b. Washington, May 10, 1921; d. Oscar A. and Belinda Maria (Sanders) Juve; B.A., U. Wis., 1943; certificate Phila. Sch. Occupational Therapy, 1944-45. Asst. dir. Curative Workshop Phila. Sch. Occupational Therapy, 1946-48; supervising occupational therapist U. Cal. Sch. Cerebral Palsied Children, Redwood City, 1948-55; supervising cerebral palsy therapist Crippled Children's Services, Contra Costa County (Cal.) Health Dept., 1956—. Mem. Am., No. Cal. occupational therapy assns. Home: 1330 Grizzly Peak Blvd Berkeley CA 94708 Office: Health Dept Ward and Pine Sts Martinez CA 94553

JUVILER, AMY HERZ (MRS. MICHAEL JUVILER), lawyer; b. Paterson, N.J., Aug. 27, 1937; d. Robert and Isabel (Cannel) H.; A.B. with distinction, Mt. Holyoke Coll., 1958; LL.B., Yale, 1961; m. Michael Juviler, July 30, 1961; children—Adam Herz, Elizabeth Katherine. Admitted to N.Y. bar, 1961; asso. atty. Legal Aid Soc., N.Y.C., 1962-63; asst. atty. gen. State of N.Y., N.Y.C., 1964—. Trustee Bklyn. Heights Montessori Sch., 1970-73, pres., 1972-73. Mem. Assn. Bar. City N.Y. (chmn. subcom. on legislation of civil ct. com. 1973—). Home: 115 Willow St Brooklyn NY 11201 Office: 2 World Trade Center New York City NY 10047

JUZAK, TATANIA, psychologist; b. Willimantic, Conn.; d. Pafnuty and Constance (Krenichyn) Juzak; B.S., Willimantic State Tchrs. Coll., 1942; M.A., U. Minn., 1944; Ph.D., N.Y.U., 1953. Chief psychologist Grasslands Hosp., Valhalla, N.Y., 1960—. Psychol. cons. Health Ins. Plan of Greater N.Y., 1962—, Jewish Child Care Assn. N.Y., 1962—, Altro Health and Rehab. Services, N.Y.C., 1963—; asst. prof. psychiatry N.Y. Med. Coll., 1970—. Diplomate in clin. psychology Am. Bd. Profl. Psychology. Mem. N.Y. Soc. Clin. Psychologists (mem. exec. bd. 1962—, exec. sec. 1946-47, 53-54, charter mem.). N.Y. Acad. Sci., N.Y. State psychol. assn., Internat. Council Psychologists, Soc. Interam. Psychology. Office: 108 E 91st St New York City NY 10028

KAAPU, MYRTLE KING (MRS. DAVID MAKALIU KAAPU), educator, state ofcl.; b. Baker, Ore., Sept. 19, 1898; d. William Rufus and Elizabeth Myrtle (King); B.A., Goucher Coll., 1920; M.A., U. Hawaii, 1937; m. David Makaliu Kaapu, Oct. 3, 1935; children—Kekoa David, Kapua (Mrs. Herbert Kamaka Sproat). Tchr. Canby (Ore.) High Sch., 1921-22, Waianae (Oahu, Hawaii) Elementary Sch., 1922-23, Miyagi High Sch. and Coll., Sendai, Japan, 1923-24, Shantung Christian U., Tsinan, China, 1924-25, Meth. Sch. for Girls, Meerut, India, 1925-26, Am. Sch. for Boys, Baghdad, Iraq, 1926-27, Andrew E. Cox Jr. High Sch., Waialua, Hawaii, 1928-37, Kahuku High Sch., 1939-44, Farrington High Sch., Honolulu, 1944-62; mem. Hawaii State Bd. Edn., 1966—. Bd. dirs. Koolau Community Assn. Named Speech Tchr. of Year, Pacific Speech Assn., 1958. Mem. Pacific Speech Assn. (pres. 1954, dir. 1966—). Author: A Grammar for Hawaii, 1937; (with others) We Speak, A Handbook for the Bi-lingual American, 1953. Home: PO Box 269 Hauula HI 96717

KABAIVANSKA, RAINA, mezzo soprano; b. Burgas, Bulgaria, Dec. 15, 1935; d. Takim Kabaivanska; ed. Nat. Conservatory Sofia, Liceo Musicale Viotti, Vercelli, Italy, Teatro alla Scala Sch., Milan, Italy; m. Valerio Corsaletti, Jan. 12, 1963. Frequent appearances at La Scala, Teatro S. Carlo, Naples, Teatro Bellini, Catania Teatro Massimo, Palermo, Teatro Comunale, Genoa, Teatro Regio, Parma, Teatro Municipale, Reggio Emilia, Teatro Comunale, Modena, Teatro Comunale, Bologna, Teatro Regio, Turin-Arena, Verona Opera (all Italy), Sofia Opera, Budapest, Bolshoi, Moscow, Leningrad Opera, Covent Garden, London, Eng., Staatsoper, Vienna, Austria and Hamburg, Germany, Teatro Colon, Buenos Aires, Argentina, Teatro Municipal, Santiago, Chile, Met. Opera, N.Y.C., Lyric Opera, Chgo., Civic Opera, Bklt., Lisner Auditorium, Washington, Opera Theatre, Phila., New Orleans and San Francisco; repertoire includes leading roles in Beatrice di Tenda, Il Pirata, Benvenuto Cellini, Mefistofele, Turandot, Wally, Queen of Spades, Eugene Onegin, Adriana Lecouvreur, Andrea Chenier, I Pagliacci, Thais, Il Tabarro, Suor Angelica, Madame Butterfly, Manon Lescaut, Boheme, Tosca, Turandot, William Tell, Rienzi, La Forza del Distino, Don Carlos, Otello, Falstaff, Ernani, Trovatore, Vespri Siciliani, Faust, Francesca da Rimini. Recipient Premio Bellini, 1966, Viotti d'Oro, 1970. Home: Piazza Vesuvio 8 20144 Milan Italy also care Dr Dino Meucci V le Coni Zugna 57 20144 Milan Italy

KABEL, BARBARA (MRS. JEROME R. KABEL), curator; B.A., Northland Coll., 1953; postgrad. U. Wis.; m. Jerome R. Kabel. Former educator, librarian; curator Rhinelander (Wis.) Mus., 1961—. Com. mem. Am. Indian Fund of the Assn. on Am. Indian Affairs, 1967—. Trustee, Rhinelander Library Bd., 1964-66, Wis. Valley Library Assn., 1964-66. Mem. Wis. Geneal. Soc. (dir.), Wis. (award merit 1968), Northland (dir., pres.) hist. socs., Nat. Trust for Historic Preservation, Wis. Arts Found. and Council, Am. Assn. Museums, Am. Assn. State, Local History, Wis. State Old Cemetery Assn. (dir., charter mem.). Named Charter mem. Women's Hall of Fame, 1972. Mem. Order Eastern Star, White Shrine of Jerusalem. Author: Northwoods Anthology, 1970; History of the Rhinelander Logging Museum—1932 to 1972, 1971. Editor rev. edit. (original 1902): Fearsome Creatures of the Lumberwoods (Cox), 1968. Producer record Lumberjack Songs from Hodagland, 1969. Home: 28A Stevens St Rhinelander WI 54501 Office: Rhinelander Museum Rhinelander WI 54501

KABLE, JUNE PRENTICE, educator; b. Shreveport, La., June 22, 1928; d. George Warren and Elna (Petterson) Cowart; B.Mus., Baylor U., 1949; M.Ed., Sul Ross State Coll., 1959; Ed.D., N. Tex. State U., 1971; m. W.T. Kable, Jr., Jan. 12, 1974; children by previous marriage—Fred David, Junellen. Tchr. Wichita Falls (Tex.) Pub. Schs., 1962-64; faculty Midwestern U., Wichita Falls, 1968—, prof. speech and drama, 1973—, chmn. dept. speech and drama, 1973—. Clinic judge for various interscholastic league events. Mem. Tex. Speech Assn. (pres. 1967-68), So. Speech Communication Assn., Delta Kappa Gamma. Home: 4402 Montego Wichita Falls TX 76308

KACIR, BARBARA BRATTIN (MRS. CHARLES STEPHEN KACIR), lawyer; b. Buffalo, July 19, 1941; d. William James and Jean (Harrington) Brattin; B.A., Wellesley Coll., 1963; J.D., U. Mich., 1967; m. Charles Stephen Kacir, June 3, 1973. Admitted to Ohio bar, 1967; since practiced in Cleve.; asso. firm Arter & Hadden, Cleve., 1967-74, partner, 1974—. Mem. Mich. Law Sch. Nat. Fund Raising Com., 1973—. Mem. Am., Ohio (mem. counsel dels. 1972—), Cleve. (mem. continuing legal edn. com. 1969-74, trustee 1974—, vice chmn. 1973—; mem. young lawyers com. 1968-72, mem. arbitration com. 1971-74) bar assns., Am. Arbitration Assn. (mem. Cleve. Regional Counsel 1972—). Home: 3280 Ingleside Rd Shaker Heights OH 44122 Office: 1144 Union Commerce Bldg Cleveland OH 44115

KAEL, PAULINE, movie critic; b. Sonoma County, Cal., 1919; d. Isaac Paul and Judith (Friedman) Kael; ed. U. Cal. at Berkeley, 1936-40; LL.D., Georgetown U., 1972; D.Arts and Letters, Columbia Coll., Chgo., 1972; Litt.D., Smith Coll., 1973; L.H.D., Kalamazoo Coll., 1973; 1 dau., Gina James. Writer. for numerous mags., including Partisan Rev., Vogue, McCall's, Atlantic; included in many anthologies on film; movie critic New Republic, 1966-67; critic New Yorker, 1968—. Recipient George Polk Meml. award for criticism, 1970. Guggenheim fellow, 1964. Mem. Nat. Soc. Film Critics (chmn. 1970). Author: I Lost it at the Movies, 1965; Kiss Kiss Bang Bang, 1968; Going Steady, 1970; The Citizen Kane Book, 1971; Deeper into Movies, 1973 (Nat. Book award 1974). Address: care The New Yorker 25 W 43d St New York City NY 10036

KAEPPLER, ADRIENNE LOIS (MRS. PETER W. GATHERCOLE), anthropologist, educator; b. Milw., July 26, 1935; d. Bernard and Laura Leonora (Tews) Kaeppler; student U. Wis., 1956-58; B.A., U. Hawaii, 1959, M.A., 1961, Ph.D., 1967; m. Peter W. Gathercole, July 15, 1972. Asst. Bernice Pauahi Bishop Mus., Honolulu, 1962-67, anthropologist, 1967—; asst. prof. depts. music and anthropology U. Hawaii, Honolulu, 1967—. Area studies coordinator Peace Corps, Tonga II. Wenner-Gren Found. grantee, 1964, 67-70, Nat. Inst. Mental Health grantee, 1965-67, Am. Philos. Soc. grantee, 1972, Nat. Endowment for the Arts grantee, 1972. Fellow Am. Anthrop. Soc.; mem. Polynesian Soc., Soc. for Ethnomusicology (mem. council 1969-72, 2d v.p. 1974—), Internat. Folk Music Council, Phi Beta Kappa, Alpha Delta Kappa. Contbr. articles on social anthropology, ethnomusicology and dance ethnology to profl. jours. Home: 1550 Wilder Av Honolulu HI 96822 Office: Bishop Museum Box 6037 Honolulu HI 96818

KAFKA, ANNE GUDRUN, lawyer; b. Chgo., Oct. 25, 1920; d. Rudolf D. and Gertrude (Thomas) K.; A.B., Oberlin Coll., 1941; LL.B. cum laude, St. John's U. Sch. Law, 1949. Admitted to N.Y. bar, 1949; asso. law firm J. D. Edwards, N.Y.C., 1950-60; asso. firm C. J. Jones Law Office, N.Y.C., 1960-68; partner law firm Jones & Kafka, Mineola, N.Y., 1968-74, Luiker & Kafka, Patchogue, N.Y., 1974—; cons. Workmen's Compensation to numerous ins. cos. Mem. N.Y. County Lawyers Assn., N.Y. State, Bklyn., Suffolk County, N.Y. Workmen's Compensation (dir.) bar assns., Oberlin Alumni Assn. (admissions rep. County Suffolk, N.Y.), U.S. Power Squadron. Legislation editor St. John's Law Review, 1947-49. Home: 55 Cedar Dr Miller Place NY 11764 Office: 39 Baker St Patchogue NY 11772

KAFKA, MARIAN ADELE STERN (MRS. JOHN S. KAFKA), scientist; b. Richmond, Va., Mar. 30, 1927; d. Henry S. and Adele (Lewit) Stern; B.A., Conn. Coll., 1948; Ph.D. (Marie J. Mergler fellow 1949-50), U. Chgo., 1952; m. John S. Kafka, Oct. 3, 1952; children—David Egon, Paul Henry, Alexander Charles. Research asst. dept. biol. chemistry Emory U., 1952-53; research asso. dept. psychiatry U. Ill., 1953-54; research asso. dept. medicine Yale, 1954-56; vis. scientist Nat. Heart Inst., NIH, Bethesda, Md., 1964, physiologist endocrinology br., 1968-74, physiologist Adult Psychiatry br., 1974—. USPHS postdoctoral fellow, 1965-68. Mem. Phi Beta Kappa, Sigma Xi. Home: 7834 Aberdeen Rd Bethesda MD 20014 Office: Adult Psychiatry BR Nat Inst Mental Health NIH Bethesda MD 20014

KAGAN, ESTHER HOROWITZ (MRS. LEON I. KAGAN), clin. psychologist; b. Luck, Russia; d. Nathan G. and Pearl Isabella (Assig) Horowitz; came to U.S., naturalized, 1921; student Lewis Inst., Chgo., 1921-24; B.A., Roosevelt U., 1955; M.A., U. Chgo., 1958; m. Leon I. Kagan, Nov. 6, 1926; children—Ralph Clyde, Paul Richard. Mem. research team Milieu Therapy Project, Chgo. State Hosp., 1957-58; intern Am. Inst. Family Relations, Los Angeles, 1958-59, asso. counselor, 1959-61; individual practice marriage and family counseling, Sherman Oaks, Cal., summers, 1959-63; social worker, psychologist Planned Parenthood Assn., Chgo., 1961-62; instr. sociology Wilson Jr. Coll., Chgo., 1961-62; asso. prof., creator discovery course for women Roosevelt U. Continuing Edn. and Extension, Chgo., 1963—, instr. human devel. courses grad. div., 1964; asso. prof. psychology and continuing edn. Park Forest (Ill.) Coll., 1965-66; divorce conciliator Divorce Conciliation Service, Circuit Ct. Cook County, Chgo., 1965—; dir. Potential, Greenerfields Unltd., Northfield, Ill., 1970—. Lectr. human devel. dept. edn. Chgo. Tchrs. Coll. North, 1964; asst. prof. psychology U. Ill., 1964; adviser, lectr., cons. to women's groups on continuing edn. for women, 1961—; participant radio and TV programs, Chgo. Mem. com. on edn. for Founders Guild Clinic for Emotionally Disturbed Children, San Fernando Valley, Cal., 1962-63. Recipient award Discovery Alumni Roosevelt U., 1963. Mem. Am. Assn. U. Profs., Am., Ill. psychol. assns., Ill. Group Psychotherapy Assn. Jewish religion (mem. temple bd.). Research in ednl. needs of mature women. Home: 3200 N Lake Shore Dr Chicago IL 60657 Office: care Divorce Conciliation Service Civic Center Chicago IL 60602

KAGEY, KAREN STEEL (MRS. RICHARD D. FRINK), physician; b. N.Y.C., Dec. 18, 1935; d. Rudolph Hornaday and Gladys Karen (Bleiman) Kagey; B.A., Vassar Coll., 1956; M.D., N.Y. U., 1960; m. Richard D. Frink, July 16, 1967. Rotating intern U. Okla. Hosps., 1960-61; resident in medicine Hartford (Conn.) Hosp., 1961-64, fellow cardio-respiratory lab., 1964-67; asst. in surgery, asso. dir. intensive care-dept. surgery Peter Bent Brigham Hosp., Boston, 1967—; clin. asst. in surgery Harvard Med. Sch., Boston, 1967—. Mem. Assn. for Advancement Med. Instrumentation, I.E.E.E., Mass. Hosp. Assn. (com. on hosp. safety 1972—). Home: 207 Sycamore Dr Westwood MA 02090 Office: 721 Huntington Av Boston MA 02115

KAHAN, LOIS M., ednl. adminstr.; b. Chgo., Aug. 6, 1930; d. Sheldon C. and Eleanor (Levin) Kahan; student U. Ill., 1948-50; B.A., Roosevelt U., 1952; M.S., Federal City Coll., 1974. Asst. registrar Roosevelt U., Chgo., 1957-64, registrar, 1965-67; registrar Albert Einstein Coll. Medicine, Bronx, N.Y., 1967-70, Federal City Coll., Washington, 1971—. Cons. records and registration, 1970—. Mem. Am. Assn. Collegiate Registrars and Admissions Officers, Am. Assn. for Higher Edn., Nat. Assn. Coll. Deans, Registrars and Admissions Officers, Nat. Assn. Women Deans, Adminstrs. and Counselors, UN Assn., Am. Civil Liberties Union. Home: 1545 18th St NW Washington DC 20036 Office: 929 E St NW Washington DC 20004

KAHANE, MILDRED DOROTHEA LOUGHLIN (MRS. ALBERT J. KAHANE), nurse adminstr.; b. Tarrytown, N.Y., Aug. 2, 1927; d. Harold F. and Ida (Lindsay) Loughlin; B.S., Adelphi U., Garden City, N.Y., 1949; postgrad. Columbia, 1958-60; M.S., U. Cal., San Francisco, 1965; m. Albert J. Kahane, Sept. 5, 1960. Staff nurse, head nurse Meadowbrook Hosp., East Meadow, N.Y., 1949-57; office nurse, Bay Shore, N.Y., 1957-58; dir. in-service edn. Jewish Chronic Disease Hosp., Bklyn., 1958-59; dir. nursing Evang. Deaconess Hosp., Bklyn., 1959-60; sch. nurse, Anchorage, 1960-61; exec. officer State Bd. Nursing, Anchorage, 1961-63; dir. nursing Presbyn. Community Hosp., Anchorage, 1963-64; asst. prof. nursing Sacramento State Coll., 1965-69, asso. prof., 1969-70, adviser Student Nurse Assn., 1967-70; project dir. nurse practitioner program Permanente Med. Group, Sacramento, 1970-74; asso. dir. nursing Sutter Community Hosps., Sacramento, 1974—; asst. clin. prof. U. Cal. at Davis Sch. Medicine, 1972—. Rep. Sacramento State Coll. to Western Interstate Commn. for Higher Edn. in Nursing, 1967; organizer TV presentation Home Health Care for Sick and Injured, Anchorage, 1963; instr. home health care A.R.C., Bklyn., 1958-60, dir. nursing services, Anchorage, 1962-64; mem. Cal. Bd. Nursing Edn. and Nurse Registration, 1969—, pres. bd., 1972-73, v.p., 1973—. Named Woman of Day Anchorage, 1963. Mem. Am., Cal. (dist. pres. 1968-70, dir. 1970-72, past conv. del., mem. state structure com. 1969-70) nurses assns., Nat., Cal. (past sec., com. chmn.) leagues nursing, Am. Assn. U. Women, Am. Pub. Health Assn., Sigma Theta Tau. Home: 1501 Menlo Av Carmichael CA 95608 Office: 2025 Morse Av Sacramento CA 95825

KAHLE, ANNE BETTINE, research geophysicist; b. Auburn, Wash., Mar. 30, 1934; d. Charles O. and Elfrida (Jenkins) Lewis; B.S., U. Alaska, 1955, M.S., 1962; student U. Cal. at Los Angeles, 1970—; m. James Kahle, May 8, 1957; children—Richard, Sheree, Vicki, Jeffrey. Research phys. scientist Rand Corp., Santa Monica, Cal., 1962-74, mem. internat. working group which selected the Internat. Geomagnetic Reference Field, 1969; sr. scientist Jet Propulsion Lab. Cal. Inst. Tech., 1974—. Leader Angeles council Girl Scouts Am., 1966-70. Mem. Am. Geophys. Union, Am. Meteorol. Soc. Contbr. numberous articles to sci. jours. Home: 19767 Grandview Topanga CA 90290 Office: Jet Propulsion Lab Cal Inst Tech Pasadena CA

KAHLER, ELIZABETH SARTOR (MRS. ERVIN NEWTON CHAPMAN), physician; b. Washington, Oct. 20, 1911; d. Armin Adolphus and Lenore Elome (Sartor) Kahler; B.S., George Washington U., 1933, M.A., 1935, M.D. with distinction, 1940; m. Ervin Newton Chapman, Feb. 24, 1942. Intern Gallinger Municipal Hosp. (now D.C. Gen. Hosp.), 1940-41; resident Children's Hosp., Washington, 1941-42; practice medicine, Washington, 1942—; asso. univ. physician George Washington U., 1942-50; examining physician YWCA, 1942-45; courtesy staff Washington Hosp. Center, Doctor's Hosp., George Washington U. Hosp.; alternate physician to Wards of Bd. Pub. Welfare, Dept. Human Resources, Govt. D.C., 1953—; sch. physician Burdick Vocational High Sch., 1959—. Trustee Wilson Coll., Chambersburg, Pa., 1956-66. Mem. Women's Med. Soc. D.C. (pres. 1950-51), Am. Med. Women's Assn. (pres. 1957-58), A.M.A., Med. Soc. D.C. (chmn. medicine and religion com. 1967-72), D.C. Assn. Mental Health, Am. Heart Assn., Camp Fire Girls Inc. (nat. program com.), Columbian Women George Washington U. (life), George Washington U. Alumnae Soc. (life). Home: 2600 36th St NW Washington DC 20007 Office: 3601 Davis St NW Washington DC 20007

KAHLER, MARY ELLIS, librarian; b. Santiago, Chile, Aug. 2, 1919; d. John William and Edna (Doan) Ellis; A.B., Swarthmore Coll., 1940; B.L.S., Drexel Inst. Tech., 1949; M.A., George Washington U., 1953; Ph.D. in History, Am. U., 1968; m. Joseph W. Darlington, Aug. 17, 1940 (dec. 1948); m. 2d, George W. Kahler, Feb. 11, 1950. Library asst. Post Library, Ft. Dix, N.J., 1944-48; with Library of Congress, 1949—, asst. chief serial record div., 1953-56, chief, 1957-66, asst. chief of union catalog div., 1966-70, asst. chief Latin Am., Portuguese and Spanish div., 1971-73, chief, 1973—. Mem. A.L.A. (chmn. serials sect. resources and tech. services div. 1959-60, mem. coms., dir. at large 1967-70), Latin Am. Studies Assn. (chmn. scholarly resources com. 1971—), Spl. Libraries Assn. (local chpt. corr. sec. 1963-64, state rep. A.L.A., Recruitment Network 1966-68, A.L.A. councilor 1969-72), D.C. Library Assn. (sec. 1964-65), Soc. Am. Archivists, Am. Hist. Assn., Am. Assn. U. Women, Phi Beta Kappa, Phi Alpha Theta. Home: 6395 Lakeview Dr Falls Church VA 22041 Office: Library of Congress Washington DC 20540

KAHN, ELAINE LOUISE SCHWARTZ, lawyer; b. Muncie, Ind., Mar. 3, 1926; d. Leo and Anna (Winick) Schwartz; B.A., Ind. U., 1947; J.D., George Washington U., 1957; m. Melville Joseph Kahn, June 22, 1947 (div. Aug. 1954); 1 dau., Lisa Ann. Admitted to D.C. bar, 1960; staff atty., legal assistance office Bar Assn. D.C., Washington, 1960-61; atty.-adviser, gen. counsel's staff NLRB, Washington, 1961-66; practice law, Washington, 1966—. Mem. Am., Fed. bar assns., Nat. Assn. Women Lawyers, Am. Judicature Soc., Bar Assn. D.C. (chmn. juvenile practice com. 1972-73), Women's Bar Assn. D.C. (pres. 1971-72, dir. 1973—), Chevy Chase Bus. and Profl. Women's Club (pres. 1973-74). Clubs: National Lawyers, Zonta (Washington). Home: 7712 Rocton Av Chevy Chase MD 20015 Office: 1730 Rhode Island Av NW Washington DC 20036

KAHN, ELAYNE JOYCE, psychotherapist; b. N.Y.C., Nov. 24, 1939; d. Philip and Leah (Berman) Kahn; B.A., Hunter Coll., 1959; M.Ed., Harvard, 1962; Ph.D., U. Ill., 1966; m. Umberto Assante, Sept. 15, 1968 (separated); 1 son, Victor S. Pvt. practice psychotherapy, N.Y.C., 1967—; chief psychologist Comprehensive Child Care Center, Brookdale Hosp., Bklyn., 1968-73; pres., dir. clin. services N.Y. Center for Sexual Guidance, N.Y.C., 1973—. Adj. asso. prof. Coll. City N.Y. Grad. Sch. Edn., 1972—; cons. Nutrition Inst. Am., N.Y.C., 1973—. N.Y. Acad. Medicine Research grantee, 1973. Mem. Am., N.Y. State psychol. assns., Assn. for Advancement Behavior Modification, N.Y. Soc. Clin. Psychologists, Psychologists in Pvt. Practice, Am. Soc. Group Psychotherapy. Contbr. articles to profl. jours. Address: 103 E 86th St New York City NY 10028

KAHN, LAURA JANE, lawyer; b. N.Y.C., Apr. 25, 1942; d. Samuel J. and Estelle M. (Miller) Kahn; B.A., Rutgers U., 1965, J.D., 1968. Admitted to N.J. bar, 1968, N.H. bar, 1972; staff atty. Newark Legal Services, 1968-70, Newark-Essex Joint Law Reform Project, 1970; gen. counsel Newark Community Devel. Adminstr., 1970-71; mng. atty. Nashau (N.H.) br. law office N.H. Legal Assistance, 1972—. Mem. Women's Information Service, 1973-74, Women's Program Adv. Council, 1974, Women United, 1974. Bd. dirs. Newark Legal Services, 1970-71, Ironbound Day Care Center, 1970-71. Recipient Am. Jurisprudence award for legal method and research and criminial law Am. Jurisprudence Year Book, 1965. Reginald Heber Smith Community Lawyer fellow, 1972-74. Mem. N.H., Nashua bar assns.

Home: Shore Dr Merrimack NH 03054 Office: 3 Water St Nashau NH 03060

KAHN, MERCIA LETON (MRS. BERNARD KAHN), govt. ofcl.; b. Portland, Ore., July 15, 1910; d. Natan and Lena (Blecker) Leton; J.D., Northwestern Sch. Law at Lewis and Clark Coll., 1933; m. Bernard Kahn, Sept. 23, 1938; children—Noreen (Mrs. Michael Moiseff), Carolyn. Admitted to Ore. bar, 1933; atty. P.R. Reconstrn. Adminstrn., 1936-37; jr. atty., gen. counsel's office A.A.A., Washington, 1934-35; with Social Security Adminstrn., 1937-65; regional rep. Bur. Health Ins., San Francisco, 1965—. Lectr. San Francisco State Coll., 1958-62. Chmn. Mgrs. Regional Adv. Com. on Aging, 1957; del. Cal. Gov.'s Conf., 1960; mem. exec. bd. San Francisco Program on Aging, 1955-65; chmn. pub. relations Fifth Internat. Congress Gerontology, 1960; coordinator White House Conf. on Aging, 1961; mem. ad hoc com. San Francisco Heart Assn., 1965; mem. program com. San Francisco Hearing Soc., 1965-67. Recipient Phoebe Apperson Hearst gold medallion San Francisco Examiner, 1965, Distinguished Service award Dept. Health, Edn. and Welfare, 1968, Geri award Los Angeles County Council Nursing Home Assn., 1969, Ewell T. Bartlett Meml. award humanity in govt. Social Security Adminstrn. Fellow Nat. Gerontological Soc.; mem. Nat. Assn. Social Workers, Nat. Rehab. Assn. (exec. com. 1961). Home: 175 Miraloma Dr San Francisco CA 94127 Office: 50 Fulton St San Francisco CA 94102

KAHN, SUSAN BETH (MRS. JOSEPH KAHN), artist; b. N.Y.C., Aug. 26, 1924; d. Jesse B. and Jenny Carol (Peshkin) Cohen; student Parsons Sch. Design, 1945; pupil Moses Soyer, 1950-57; m. Joseph Kahn, Sept. 15, 1946. One-man shows at Sagittarius Gallery, 1960, A.C.A., Galleries, 1964, 68, 71, Charles B. Goddard Art Center, Ardmore, Okla., 1973, Albrecht Gallery Museum Art, St. Joseph, Mo., 1974, N.Y. Cultural Center, N.Y.C., 1974; exhibited in group shows at Audubon Artists, N.Y.C., Nat. Acad., N.Y.C., Springfield (Mass.) Mus., City Center, N.Y.C., A.C.A. Galleries, N.Y.C., Nat. Arts Club, N.Y.C., Butler Inst., Youngstown, O.; represented in permanent collections at Tyler (Tex.) Mus., St. Lawrence U. Mus., Canton, N.Y., Fairleigh Dickinson U. Mus., Rutherford, N.J., Syracuse U. Mus., Sheldon Swope Gallery, Terre Haute, Ind., Montclair (N.J.) Mus. Fine Arts, Butler Inst. Am. Art, Youngstown, O., Reading (Pa.) Mus., Albrecht Gallery Mus. Art, St. Joseph, Cedar Rapids (Ia.) Art Center, N.Y. Cultural Center, N.Y.C. Recipient Knickerbocker prize for best religious painting, 1956, Edith Lehman award Nat. Assn. Women Artists, 1958, Knickerbocker Artists award, 1961, Simmons award Nat. Assn. Women Artists, 1961, Nat. Arts Club award, 1967, Knickerbocker Medal of Honor, 1964, Famous Artists Sch. award, 1967. Mem. Nat. Assn. Women Artists, Artists Equity, Knickerbocker Artists, Met. Mus., Mus. Modern Art, Whitney Mus. Art. Home: 870 United Nations Plaza New York City NY 10017

KAHRS, MARY VIOLA, educator; b. Ft. Collins, Colo., Dec. 23, 1927; d. Alfred James and Ruth (Hageman) Kahrs; B.A., U. No. Ia., 1951; M.A., U. Ia., 1954, Ph.D., 1960. Tchr., Clayton County, Ia., 1945-47, Colesburg, Ia., 1948-50, Cedar Rapids, Ia., 1951-59; mem. faculty Mankato (Minn.) State Coll., 1960—, prof., chmn. dept. elementary edn., 1964—. Cons. elementary sch. math. edn., 1960—. Mem. N.E.A., Am. Ednl. Research Assn., Nat. Council Tchrs. Math., Nat. Soc. Study Edn., Pi Lambda Theta, Delta Kappa Gamma, Kappa Delta Pi. Author: (with Spitzer, Banks, Burns & Folsom) Elementary Mathematics: Concepts, Properties, and Operations, 1968. Home: 112 E Glencrest Dr Mankato MN 56001

KAIN, IDA JEAN (MRS. FRED F. BEACH), author; b. Port Huron, Mich.; d. Andrew and Adeline (Smith) Kain; B.S., Battle Creek Coll., 1925; postgrad. U. Pa., 1926; M.A., Columbia, 1935; m. Fred F. Beach, June 17, 1938. Columnist, St. Louis Globe Democrat, 1931; syndicated columnist King Features Syndicate, 1937-69. Author: Prescription for Slimming, 1940; Get in Shape, 1942; (with Mildred Gibson) Stay Slim for Life, 1958, 66. Recipient award of achievement Alpha Chi, 1957; D.C. Home Econs. award, 1969. Mem. Am. Dietetic Assn., Am. Home Econs. Assn., Am. Newspaper Women's Club, Women in Communications. Club: Washington Press. Home: 6696 Glenbrook Rd Chevy Chase MD 20015

KAINS, MIRDZA, counselor; b. Riga, Latvia, Apr. 14, 1942; d. Peteris and Irma (Ruska) Kains; B.Sc., U. New South Wales (Australia), 1966. Came to U.S., 1966. With Neb. Div. Rehab. Services, 1967—, counselor Lancaster Office Mental Retardation, Lincoln, 1972—. Mem. Am. Assn. Mental Deficiency, Neb., Am. rehab. assns., Lincoln Community Services (mem. budget com. agy. relations div. 1973—). Club: Soroptimist Club of Lincoln (dir. 1973-74, corr. sec. 1973-74). Home: 930 Rutland Dr Lincoln NE 68512 Office: 2202 S 11th St Lincoln NE 68502

KAINSKI, MERCEDES LENORE HUNSADER (MRS. JOHN M. KAINSKI), educator; b. Algoma, Wis., Jan. 26, 1923; d. Joseph J. and Mary (Alt) Hunsader; B.S., U. Wis., 1944, M.S., 1955, Ph.D., 1957; m. John M. Kainski, Nov. 26, 1964. Technician, Carnation Research Lab., Milw., 1945-48, Wilson Research Lab., Chgo., 1944; tchr. Sturgeon Bay (Wis.) High Sch., 1948-51, Crivitz High Sch., 1951-52, Sheboygan (Wis.) pub. schs., 1952-53; asso. prof. Kan. State U., 1957-65, Bowling Green State U., 1965-67; prof. food and nutrition U. Wis.-Stout, Menomonie, 1967—. Mem. Am. Home Econs. Assn., Inst. Food Technologists, Am. Dietetic Assn., Sigma Xi, Omicron Nu, Gamma Sigma Delta, Sigma Delta Epsilon. Home: 1712 5th St W Menomonie WI 54751

KAISER, EDREA, pub. relations writer, b. Orange, N.J., Oct. 27, 1949; d. Solomon and Claire Alberta (Schonfeld) Kaiser; B.A., U. Miami, 1971. Feature writer Coral Gables (Fla.) Times, 1970; writer Miami (Fla.) Met. Dept. of Publicity and Tourism, 1971; writer-econ. feasibility studies for exec. office Nat. Motel Chain, Dutch Inns of Am., Inc., Coral Gables, 1971-72; writer-public relations and publicity Milt Roth Asso., Inc., Miami, 1972—. Mem. Women in Communications. Home: 2629 S Bayshore Dr A33 Coconut Grove FL 33133 Office: 1175 NE 125th St Miami FL 33161

KAISER, JOHANNA, psychotherapist; b. Konstanz, Germany; d. Emil and Mathilde (Model) Frank; B.S., U. Bonn (Germany), 1932; M.A., Columbia U. Teachers Coll., 1964; Ph.D., N.Y. U., 1971; m. Hans Kaiser, Oct. 4, 1934; children—Richard S., Ann E. (Mrs. Morton Julius). Came to U.S., 1938, naturalized, 1945. Vocational rehab. counselor Inst. Crippled and Disabled, N.Y.C., 1962-63; sr. counselor YMCA Counseling & Testing Service, N.Y.C., 1964—; pvt. practice psychotherapy, also marriage counseling, N.Y.C., 1972—; affiliated Am. Inst. Psychotherapy and Psychoanalysis, Recipient N.Y.U. Founders Day award, 1972. Mem. Am. Psychol. Assn., Am. Personnel and Guidance Assn., Am. Assn. Marriage and Family Counselors, Nat. Rehabilitation Counseling Assn. Home: 100 Thayer St New York City NY 10040 Office: 420 9th Av New York City NY 10001

KAISER, OPHELIA THERESE REHAGEN (MRS. GEORGE R. KAISER), real estate broker; b. St. Louis, Aug. 29, 1901; d. John J. and Kathryn (Sting) Rehagen; trained as nurse; m. George R. Kaiser, July 2, 1932; children—Kathryn Rose (Mrs. George C. Lindenau), Judith Ann (Mrs. LeRoy B. Dunkelberger). Chorus girl, 1st prodn. St. Louis Municipal Opera, 1919; pvt. duty nurse St. John's Hosp., 1923-25; pub. health nurse City of St. Louis Municipal Clinics, 1925-33; floor duty nurse Barnes and St. Louis County hosps., St. Louis, 1942-46; hostess, Welcome Wagon Internat., San Carlos, Cal., 1953-55; rep. World Book Ency., San Carlos, 1957-67; real estate salesman Kaufman Realty Co., San Francisco, 1961-63, Kaiser Realty, Mountain View, Cal., 1963—. Mem. Mountain View Bd. Realtors (sec.-treas. 1969, v.p. 1970), Cal. Real Estate Assn., Nat. Assn. Real Estate Bds. (women's council 1966—). Home and office: 3380 Lubich Dr Mountain View CA 94040

KAISER, RUTH HARTER (MRS. ROBERT M. KAISER), sociologist; b. Perryton, Ill.; d. Harold M. and Winifred (Osborn) Harter; B.A., U. Cal. at Berkeley, 1943; postgrad. fellow Stanford, 1960-61; M.S., San Jose State Coll., 1968; m. Robert M. Kaiser, Dec. 15, 1945. Exec. sec. Newman Hall, U. Cal. at Berkeley, 1943-44; program dir. U.S.O. Club, Nat. Catholic Community Services, Bremerton, Wash., 1944-45; exec. dir. Cal. Fedn. Civic Unity, 1948-52, Cal. Assn. Health and Welfare, San Francisco, 1953-59, Santa Clara County Assn. Mental Health, San Jose, 1961-65; project dir. Comprehensive Mental Health Planning Com., San Jose, 1965-68; exec. dir. Comprehensive Health Planning Assn. Santa Clara County, San Jose, 1968—; mem. nat. expectations study group Comprehensive Health Planning Services, Health Services and Mental Health Adminstrn., Dept. Health, Edn. and Welfare, 1971-72. Mem. Regional Med. Programs Area Adv. Council, 1971. Bd. dirs. Social Planning Council Santa Clara County, 1968-71; v.p. Mexican-Am. Community Services Agy., San Jose, 1968, bd. dirs., 1967-72. Mem. Nat. Assn. Social Workers (chmn. grad. sch. social work 1968-72, mem. Bay area commn. mental health 1968-69), Acad. Certified Social Workers, Am. Assn. U. Women, Santa Clara County Med. Soc. (mental health com. 1968—), No. Cal. Pub. Health Assn., Lawyer's Wives of Santa Clara County, Alpha Kappa Delta. Home: 1989 Adele Pl San Jose CA 95125 Office: 1600 Willow St San Jose CA 95125

KALES, JOYCE DANIELSKI (MRS. ANTHONY KALES), psychiatrist; b. Detroit, Sept. 22, 1934; d. Julius S. and Helen (Kasprick) Danielski; B.S., Wayne State U., 1956, M.D., 1960; m. Anthony Kales, Aug. 22, 1960; children—Stephen Nicholas, Helen Christine, James Peter. Intern Santa Monica (Cal.) Hosp., 1960-61; resident Brentwood VA Hosp., Los Angeles, 1961-66; research fellow dept. anatomy U. Cal. at Los Angeles, 1967-69, asst. research anatomist, 1969-71; asst. prof. dept. psychiatry Pa. State U. Hershey Med. Center, Hershey, 1971—. Diplomate in psychiatry Am. Bd. Psychiatry and Neurology. Mem. Am. Psychiat. Assn., Assn. for Psychophys. Study of Sleep, Pa. Psychiat. Soc., Dauphin County Med. Assn., Am. Med. Women's Assn. Contbr. numerous articles to profl. jours. Office: Dept Psychiatry Pa State U Hershey Med Center Hershey PA 17033

KALES, SHIRLEY MCBRIDE (MRS. ROBERT GRAY KALES), investment co. ofcl., club woman; b. Detroit, Feb. 18, 1927; d. George L. and Elsie J. (Storey) McBride; student Wayne State U., 1946-48; student Detroit Conservatory Music, 1948-50; m. Robert Gray Kales, Feb. 14, 1961; children—John Gray, Nancy Davis. Mem. advt. staff Detroit Evening News Assn., 1949-55; mem. advt. and publicity staff Bielfield Agy., Detroit, 1955-59; mem. advt. and sales dept. Mich. Bell Telephone Co., Detroit, 1959-60; mem. sales promotion and advt. staff Mich. Consol. Gas Co., Detroit, 1960-61; personnel dir. Kales Kramer Investment Co., Detroit, 1967—; dir. Automotive Bin Service Co., Detroit. Mem. Detroit Mus. Art Founders Soc., Fine Arts Soc. Detroit, Navy League U.S. (pres. women's council). Clubs: Review (pres.), Women's City (dir.), Country (Detroit); Grosse Pointe (Mich.) Yacht. Home: 87 Cloverly Rd Grosse Pointe Farms MI 48236 Office: Kales Bldg Detroit MI 48226

KALIL, MARGARET, singer; b. Monroe, La.; d. Fred and Anna (Shamis) Kalil; B.S., Columbia, 1949, M.A., 1950; postgrad. Julliard Sch. Music, 1956-60. Soloist, N.Y. Philharmonic, Boston Symphony orchs., Dallas, Detroit symphonies, 1959-64; resident artist North Tex. State U., 1960-64; mem. faculty Columbia Tchrs. Coll., 1964—; operatic performer, debut in Donna Anna, Chautauqua Opera Co., 1959, Town Hall, N.Y.C., 1963, Met. Opera in Celestial Voice, 1965, European opera debut in Barcelona (Spain) Teatrode Liceo, 1972; mem. Met. Opera Assn. Recipient Aid to Music award Martha Baird Rockefeller, 1957, Concert Artists Guild award, 1963, James Loeb Meml. hon. award Julliard Sch. Music, 1959-60. Mem. Nat. Assn. Tchrs. Singing, Sigma Alpha Iota, Pi Kappa Lambda. Home: 600 W 111th St New York City NY 10025 Office: Met Opera Assn Lincoln Center New York City NY 10023

KALIL, MILLICENT LILLIAN, educator; b. Plainfield, N.J., Dec. 8, 1939; d. Frederick Albert and Millicent Lillian (Riley) Kalil; B.A., Wellesley Coll., 1961; postgrad. Ariz. State U., 1961-62; Ph.D., U. Wis., 1967. Fellow U. Wis. at Madison, 1967; asst. prof. dept. botany U. Wis. at Waukesha, 1967-72, asso. prof., 1972—. Mem. Comprehensive Health Planning Agy. of Southeastern Wis., 1973—; recycling chmn. Waukesha County (Wis.) Environmental Council, 1971, 72—, sec., 1973. Center System research grantee U. Wis., 1968, Grad. Sch. grantee, 1969, recipient Tchr. of Yr. award U. Wis., 1968-69, award for excellence in teaching Standard Oil, 1969. Mem. Bot. Soc. Am., Am. Inst. Biol. Scis., Nat. Assn. Biology Tchrs., Tissue Culture Assn., Sigma Xi, Sigma Delta Epsilon, Delta Delta Delta. Contbr. to publs. in field. Home: W287N8290 Dobbertin Rd Merton WI 53056 Office: 1500 University Dr Waukesha WI 53186

KALISKI, JUDITH PUTNAM (MRS. MARTIN EDWARD KALISKI), psychotherapist; b. Norristown, Pa., Aug. 7, 1946; d. Allan Ray and Marion Sara (Witmer) Putnam; B.A. in Psychology, Wellesley Coll., 1968; M.A., U. R.I., 1971; m. Martin Edward Kaliski, June 8, 1969. Social worker Cushing Hosp., Framingham, Mass., 1968-69, 70; clin. trainee R.I. Med. Center, Howard, 1970-71, City Hosp. Elmhurst, Flushing, N.Y., 1971-72; psychol. intern Catholic Charities Guidance Clinics, Bklyn., 1972-73; asst. psychology clinic U. R.I., Kingston, 1973—. Nat. Inst. Mental Health fellow, 1968-69. Asso. mem. Am. Psychol. Assn. Home: 83 Beach St Foxboro MA 02035 Office: 119 Chaffee Bldg Univ of Rhode Island Kingston RI 02881

KALMANOWITZ, LINDA, lawyer; b. N.Y.C., Jan. 19, 1943; d. Sam and Irene (Sirota) Kalmanowitz; B.A. cum laude, Smith Coll., 1964; J.D., N.Y. U., 1967; m. Jay A. Grunin, Aug. 17, 1969; 1 son, Jeremy David. Admitted to N.J. bar, 1967; practiced in Asbury Park, 1967-70, Toms River, 1970—; asso. firm Abraham R. Klitzman, Asbury Park, 1967-70. Gen. counsel Dover Twp. Young Republicans. Mem. Ocean County Bar Assn. Home: 857 Westminster Dr Toms River NJ 08753 Office: 189 Hwy 37 West Toms River NJ 08753

KALMANSOHN, KATHERINE WITLIN (MRS. ROBERT B. KALMANSOHN), physician; b. Jamaica, N.Y., Apr. 5, 1926; d. Alexander and Sadie (Schirtz) Witlin; student Queens Coll., 1941-42, Coll. City N.Y., 1942-43; B.A., U. Cal. at Los Angeles, 1945, M.D., 1949, postgrad., 1955-58; m. Robert B. Kalmansohn, Sept. 17, 1949; children—Jeanne, Mark, Alan. Intern Mt. Zion Hosp., San Francisco, 1949-50, Brentwood Hosp., 1955-58; resident psychiatry Reiss-Davis Children's Center, Los Angeles, 1957-58, Santelle VA Hosp., Los Angeles, 1956-57; practice medicine specializing in psychiatry, Los Angeles, 1958-66; staff psychiatrist Los Angeles Psychiat. Service, 1958-60; asso. psychiatrist U. Cal. Student Health Service, 1960—; research asso. child psychiatry U. Cal. at Los Angeles 1963-64; cons. to schs., adoption agys. Community Services div. Los Angeles County Mental Health Dept., 1965—; dep. regional chief West Central Community Health Service, 1966—; asst. clin. prof. psychiatry U. So. Cal. Med. Sch., 1971—; mem. staffs Westwood Hosp., Cedars-Sinai Hosp. Sec. Jewish War Vets., 1954-55; leader Girl Scouts U.S.A., 1958-60. Fellow Am. Psychiat. Assn.; mem. So. Cal. Psychiat. Soc., So. Cal. Soc. Adolescent Psychiatry, A.A.A.S., Internat. Platform Assn. Home: 1129 Maybrook Dr Beverly Hills CA 90210 Office: 1090 S La Brea Los Angeles CA 90019

KALNINS, ZELMA-ALVINE GRINFELDS (MRS. PETERIS KALNINS), cytopathologist; b. Riga, Latvia, Sept. 3, 1908; d. Roberts Andrejs and Katrine (Lode) Grinfelds; M.D., U. Latvia, Riga, 1932, postgrad., 1938; m. Peteris Kalnins, Dec. 24, 1949. Came to U.S., 1951, naturalized, 1957. Intern Univ. Hosp., Riga., 1932-33, resident, 1933-36; resident City Hosp., Liepaja, Latvia, 1936-38, doctor-ordinator dept. obstetrics and gynecology, 1938-44; practice medicine specializing in obstetrics and gynecology, Liepaja, 1938-44; secundarius County Hosp. dept. gynecology and obstetrics County Hosp., Leoben, Austria, 1944-46; health supr., physician Displaced Persons' Camp, Camp Ohmstede, Oldenburg, Germany, 1947-51; fellow in cytology dept. pathology Bowman Gray Sch. Medicine, Wake Forest U., Winston-Salem, N.C., 1952-55, instr. pathology, 1955-62, asst. prof. clin. cytology, 1962-69, asso. prof. clin. cytology, 1969—, dir. lab. exfoliative cytology, 1956-58, asso. dir. cytopathology lab., also Sch. Cytotech., 1962-69, dir. clin. cytology labs., also Sch. Cytotech., 1969—. Fellow Royal Soc. Health (London), Internat. Acad. Cytology; mem. Assn. Am. Med. Colls., Am. Soc. Cytology, Am. Med. Women's Assn., Latvian Med. and Dental Assn. in U.S. Contbr. articles to med. jours. Home: 184 N Hawthorne Rd Winston-Salem NC 27104 Office: 300 Hawthorne Rd SW Winston-Salem NC 27103

KALSEM, MILLIE E., investment co. exec.; b. Huxley, Ia., Dec. 12, 1896; d. Ole J. and Anna (Nelson) Kalsem; B.S., Ia. State Coll., 1921; dietetic study Michael Reese Hosp., Chgo., 1922-23; postgrad. U. Ill. Med. Sch., 1935-36. Tchr. home econs. and physiology Monticello (Ia.) High Sch., 1921-22; hosp. dietitian Beaver Valley Gen. Hosp., New Brighton, Pa., 1923, Ia. Meth. Hosp., Des Moines, 1923-27, Ill. Tng. Sch. for Nurses and Cook County Sch. of Nursing, 1927-38; chief exec. dietitian Cook County Hosp., 1938-62; v.p., dir., registered rep. Lorraine L. Blair, Inc., investment broker, Chgo. Selected by Carrie Chapman Catt as one of 100 Women, Women's Centennial Congress, 1940; recipient Alumni merit award, Ia. State Coll., 1946, alumni medal, 1956. Mem. Am. (v.p. 1946-47), Ill. (organizer and 1st pres.), Chgo. dietetic assns., Women's Finance Forum Am. (research chmn. 1954-57, regional dir. 1960—), Art Inst. Chgo. (life), Order of Knoll, Omicron Nu, Phi Kappa Phi, Chi Omega. Club: Altrusa (pres. Chgo. 1959-61). Home: 1350 Lake Shore Dr Chicago IL 60610 Office: 11 S N LaSalle St Chicago IL 60603

KAMAR, ASTRID ELAINE WENNERMARK (MRS. PASCAL M. KAMAR), toy mfg. co. exec.; b. Los Angeles, Nov. 29, 1934; d. Ernest and Emmy (Kraus) Wennermark; student Sawyer's Bus. Sch., 1952-53; m. Pascal M. Kamar, Feb. 14, 1958; children—Christopher, Jenny Lynn, Laurie Lynn. Secretarial position sta. KTTV, Hollywood, Cal., 1955-56; with fgn. service Dept. State, Washington and Kingston, Jamaica, 1956-57; co-founder Kamar, Inc., mfg. stuffed toys, Gardena, Cal., 1958, exec. v.p., nat. sales mgr., 1958—; dir. Kamar Internat., Kamar Internacional SA, Love Things and Kamar, Inc., Universal Motor Cars, Wennemark Investments, Moon Imports, Sun Imports; co-founder Jolimer, Briquedese Brindes Ltd., Lisbon, Portugal, 1972. Chmn., founder Los Angeles chpt. Valley Orthopedic Hosp. Com., 1969-72. Bd. dirs. Valley Orthopedic Clinic. Lutheran. Home: 1757 Paseo Del Mar Palos Verdes Estates CA 90274 Office: 2020 W 139th St Gardena CA 90249

KAMEN, VIOLET KELMENSON (MRS. DANIEL H. KAMEN), lawyer; b. N.Y.C., Aug. 16, 1913; d. Nathan and Esther (Keilson) Kelmenson; B.S., N.Y. U., 1933, J.D., 1935; m. Daniel H. Kamen, Oct. 8, 1940; children—Heather, Roxanne (Mrs. Steven Eldridge). Admitted to N.Y. bar, 1936; mem. firm Kelmenson & Kelmenson, N.Y.C., 1936—, sr. mem., 1960—. Dir. Rhinelander Assn., N.Y.C., 1050 Fifth Av. Corp., N.Y.C. Mem. law adv. council N.Y. U. Law Sch. Mem. N.Y. Women's Bar Assn. (dir., chmn. legislation 1966—, del. to jud. conv. 1965, mem. Bronx County com. 1964-65), Am. Bar Assn., N.Y. State Trial Lawyers. Contbr. articles on women's rights legislations to profl. jours. Home: 1050 Fifth Av New York City NY 10028 Office: 253 Broadway New York City NY 10007

KAMENSKE, GLORIA LEE CHEEK, psychologist; b. Battle Creek, Mich., Oct. 26, 1931; d. George W. and Edith (Olds) Cheek; A.B., U. Mich., 1953; M.A., Mich. State U., 1955, Ph.D., 1965; m. Bernard H. Kamenske, Dec. 19, 1960. Counselor women's dormitories Mich. State U., East Lansing, 1953-54, statis., teaching asst. psychology dept., 1954-56, research asst. Labor and Indsl. Relations Center, 1956-58; social psychology intern VA Hosp., Ann Arbor, Mich., 1958-59; research psychologist personnel research br. Adj. Gen.'s Office, Dept. Def., Washington, 1959-60; research asso. tng. methods div. Human Resources Research Office, Washington, 1960-62; manpower research analyst Office of Manpower, Automation and Tng. Dept. Labor, Washington, 1962-63; research asso. Bur. Social Sci. Research, Washington, 1963-65; research psychologist USPHS, 1965-70; social sci. adviser Office Internat. Health, Office of Sec., Dept. Health, Edn. and Welfare, Washington, 1970—. Cons. Dept. Labor, 1962-63, Union Theol. Sem., 1963-65; internat. cons. on psychology and population. Recipient award for service Psi Chi, 1957. Fellow Am. Pub. Health Assn.; mem. Am., Eastern, D.C. psychol. assns., Internat. Union Sci. Psychology, Am. Acad. Polit. and Social Sci., Internat., Am., D.C. sociol. assns., A.A.A.S., Internat. Council Psychologists, Inter Am. Soc. Psychology, D.A.R., Psi Chi. Contbr. numerous articles and speeches to profl. and trade jours. Home: One Buttonwood Lane Washington DC 20016 Office: Internat Health Office of Secretary Dept Health Education and Welfare 330 Independence Av SW Washington DC 20201

KAMERSCHEN, KAREN SUE, psychologist; b. Laurium, Mich., Sept. 27, 1943; d. Bernard Pearce and Julia Alvina (Picchiottino) Kamerschen; B.A. in Psychology magna cum laude, Mich. State U., 1964, M.A. in Psychology, 1965, Ph.D. in Clin. Psychology (USPHS fellow), 1969. Asst. prof., psychologist Mich. State U. Counseling Center, East Lansing, 1969-70; psychologist, outreach coordinator Counseling-Psychol. Services Center, U. Tex., Austin, 1970—. Pvt. practice psychology, Austin, 1971—. Mem. Am., S.W., Tex., Capital Area psychol. assns., Am. Personnel and Guidance Assn., Am. Coll. Personnel Assn. Home: 8100 Balcones St Apt 176 Austin TX 78759

KAMINKOWITZ, GRACE, cosmetics co. exec.; b. N.Y.C., May 23, 1935; d. Louis and Gertrude (Noachs) Kaminkowitz; B.A., U. Ia., 1955; postgrad. Northwestern U., 1956-58. Advt. copywriter Montgomery Ward & Co., Chgo., 1955-57, retail advt. mgr., major appliances, 1957-61; advt. copywriter May Co., dept. store, Los Angeles, 1957; advt. copy chief Helene Curtis Industries, Inc., Chgo.,

1961-70, dir. marketing, 1970-73, v.p. marketing, 1973—. Mem. Women in Communications (Chgo. pres. 1966-67, regional dir. 1968-69), Fashion Group. Home: 505 N Lake Shore Dr Chicago IL 60611 Office: 4401 W North Av Chicago IL 60639

KAMM, JANE ANN FANSLER, psychiat. social worker; b. Menominee, Mich., Feb. 7, 1918; d. Ralph L. and Ada Louise (Schwartz) Fansler; B.A. with high distinction, Wayne State U., 1939; Diploma in Social Work U. Melbourne, Australia, 1951; M.S.W., U. Mich., 1956, 1960-64; D.S.W., Tenn. Christian U., 1974; m. Robert L. Kamm, May 4, 1942 (div. Apr. 1966). Social worker Australian Immigration Dept., 1951-53; exec. sec. Melbourne Clinic for Psychotherapy, 1953-56; dir. edn. Cleve. Psychiat. Inst., 1956-58; asst. prof. Western Res. U., 1958-60; chief social worker Genesee div. Pontiac (Mich.) State Hosp., 1964-73; dir. Family Counselling Assos., 1973—. Clin. field instr. Wayne State U., 1964-71, U. Mich., 1967-71; pvt. practice social work Birmingham Psychiat. and Med. Assos., 1964-73. Mem. Nat. Assn. Social Workers, Acad. Certified Social Workers, Mich. Soc. Group Therapy, Am. Acad. Psychotherapists, Assn. Humanist Psychologists, Mich. Soc. Clin. Hypnosis (v.p.). Author: (with J. Butman) Social and Psychological World of the Teen-Age Girl, 1965; (with E. Thomas, R. Feldman) Introduction to Role Theory, 1964. Home: 920 Purdy St Birmingham MI 48009 Office: 250 Martin St Birmingham MI 48011

KAMMERMAN, SANDRA, physician; b. N.Y.C., Oct. 8, 1940; d. Irving and Nettie (Blank) Kammerman; B.S. with distinction (N.Y. State Regents scholar), Cornell U., 1962; M.D. (Pfizer scholar), N.Y. U., 1966; m. Sy Hyman, Feb. 25, 1973. Intern Beth Israel Hosp., Boston, 1966-67, resident medicine, 1967-68; teaching fellow medicine Harvard Med. Sch., 1967-68; fellow endocrinology Columbia Presbyn. Med. Center, N.Y.C., 1968-71; asst. prof. medicine N.Y. U. Sch. Medicine, N.Y.C., 1971—. Population Council of N.Y. grantee, 1971—. Diplomate Am. Bd. Internal Medicine with subsplt. in endocrinology. Asst. editor Am. Jour. Med. Scis., 1971—. Contbr. articles to profl. pubs. Home: 220 Central Park South New York City NY 11019

KAMMET, PAULINE H. (MRS. LAWRENCE KAMMET), psychiat. social worker; b. E. Hartford, Conn., Nov. 26, 1911; d. Samuel and Mary (Jaffee) Hurwitz; B.A., N.Y. U., 1933; certificate N.Y. Sch. Social Work, 1935; M.S., Columbia, 1942; m. Lawrence Kammet, Jan. 16, 1936; children—James (dec.), Paul, Richard. Supr., N.Y.C. Dept. Welfare, 1935-46; psychiat. social worker Bur. Child Guidance, N.Y.C. Bd. Edn., 1947—. Mem. Am. Orthopsychiat. Assn., Nat. Assn. Social Workers, United Fedn. Tchrs., Sigma Tau Delta. Contbr. articles to profl. and popular mags. Home: 1488 Carroll St Brooklyn NY 11213 Office: 362 Schermerhorn St Brooklyn NY 11217

KAMPA, SISTER MARY ARILDA, educator; b. Chgo., Jan. 1, 1907; d. Micael and Mary Ann (Szymanski) Kampa; student Ind. U., 1937, St. Louis U., 1955; B.S., St. Francis Coll., 1949, postgrad. 1950-57; M.A., Cardinal Stritch Coll., 1965. Joined Order of St. Francis, 1923; elementary tchr., Memphis and New Orleans, 1925-37; tchr. jr.-sr. high sch., Kentland, Ind., and Griffith, Ind., 1937-52; prin. St. John the Bapt. Sch., Earl Park, Ind., 1952-55; tchr. St. Casimir Sch., Hammond, Ind., 1955-57; prin. St. John (Ind.) Sch., 1957-63; instr. tchr. edn. St. Francis Coll., Ft. Wayne, Ind., 1963-68, prof. edn. and reading grad. sch., reading cons., dir. reading center, 1968—. Mem. Ind. State Reading Adv. Com., Ft. Wayne, 1968—; mem. Ind. Right-to-Read Com., 1969-71. Mem. Nat. Soc. for the Study of Edn., Internat. Reading Assn. (mem. standing com. 1969-72, pres. Ft. Wayne council 1974-75), Coll. Reading Assn., Ind. Reading Specialist, Ind. Profs. Reading, Assn. for the Study of Perception, Delta Epsilon Sigma. Home and office: 2701 Spring St Fort Wayne IN 46808

KAMPEN, IRENE BLANCHE TREPEL, writer, lectr.; b. Bklyn., Apr. 18, 1922; d. Jack and Mary (Harris) Trepel; B.A., U. Wis., 1943; m. Owen Kampen, Jan. 4, 1944 (div. Nov. 1956); 1 dau., Christine Guthrie. Lectr. on humorous topics for women's clubs, town halls, celebrity series, 1970—; guest lectr. Suffield Writers Conf., Litchfield, Conn., 1969-72. Fellow MacDowell Colony, 1971. Mem. P.E.N., Theta Sigma Phi. Author: Life Without George, 1961; We That Are Left, 1963; Europe Without George, 1965; The Ziegfelds Girl, 1964; Last Year at Sugarbush, 1966; Here Comes the Bride, 1967; Due to Lack of Interest Tomorrow Has Been Cancelled, 1969; Are You Carrying Any Gold or Living Relatives, 1970. Contbr. short stories and articles to various major mags., including Ladies Home Jour., Redbook, McCall's, Good Housekeeping. Home: 5 Rockwell Rd Ridgefield CT 06877

KAN, DIANA ARTEMIS MANN SHU (MRS. PAUL SCHWARTZ), artist; b. Hong Kong, Mar. 3, 1926; d. Kam Shek and Sun-Ying (Hong) Kan; student Art Students League, 1949-51, Beaux Arts, Paris, France 1951-52, Grande Chaumiere, Paris, 1951-52; m. Paul Schwartz, May 24, 1952, 1 son, Kan Martin Meyer Sing-Si. Came to U.S., 1949, naturalized, 1966. One-man shows, London, 1949, 63, 64, Paris, 1949, Hong Kong, 1937, 39, 41, 47, 48, 72, Shanghai, 1935, 37, 39, Nanking, 1936, 38, Macao, 1947, 48, Bangkok, 1947, Casblanca, 1951, 52, San Francisco, 1950, 67, N.Y.C., 50, 54, 59, 67, 71, 72, Naples, 1971, Elliot Mus., Fla., 1967, Bruce Mus., Conn., 1969, Nat. Hist. Mus., Taipei Taiwan, 1971, Hong Kong City Hall, 1972, N.Y. Cultural Center Mus., 1972, Galerie Barbarella, Palm Beach, Fla., 1972; exhibited in group shows at Royal Acad. Fine Arts, London, 1963, 64, Royal Soc. Painters, London, 1964, Am. Watercolor Soc., N.Y.C., 1966-69, N.A.D., N.Y.C., 1967, 69, 70, Nat. Arts Club, N.Y.C., 1964-71, Charles and Emma Frye Mus., Seattle, 1968, Willamette U., Salem, Ore., 1968, Columbia (S.C.) Mus. Art, S.C., 1969; represented in permanent collections at Elliot Mus., Fla., Bruce Mus., Dalhousie U., Nat. Hist. Mus., Taipei. Fgn. corr., city editor Cosmorama Pictorial Mag., Hong Kong, 1968; art reviewer Villager, N.Y.C., 1966; lectr. Birmingham-So. U., N.Y. U., Mills Coll. Edn., St. Joseph's Coll., Jenson Beach, Fla. Recipient N.Y.C. Summer Festival award, 1959; named Most Outstanding Profl. Woman of Year, Washington Square chpt. N.Y. League Bus. and Profl. Women's Club, 1971. Mem. Pen and Brush Club (dir. 1968, Brush Fund award 1968, Alice S. Buell Meml. award 1969), Am. Watercolor Soc. (traveling award 1968), Art Students League, Pen Women, Allied Artists Am. (Barbara Vassilieff Meml. award 1969), Catharine Lorillard Wolf Art Club (Anna Hyatt Huntington bronze medal 1970). Club: Overseas Press (N.Y.C.). Author: White Cloud, 1938; The How and Why of Chinese Painting, 1973. Home: 26 W 9th St New York City NY 10011

KANARIK, ROSELLA KANARIK (MRS. EMERY KANARIK), educator; b. Bartfa, Hungary, Feb. 7, 1909 (parents Am. citizens); d. Albert and Sarah (Schondorf) Kanarik; B.A., U. Pitts., 1930, M.A., 1931, Ph.D., 1934; m. Emery Kanarik, July 25, 1936; children—Richard, Susan Carol. Came to U.S., 1913. Tchr. math. high sch., Pitts., 1932-36; faculty U. Pitts., 1932-36; lectr. math. U. So. Cal., Los Angeles, 1946-52; instr. math. Los Angeles City Coll., 1953-61, asso. prof. 1961-67, prof., 1967—, counselor, 1953—. Mem. Math. Assn. Am., Am. Math. Soc., Sigma Xi, Pi Lambda Theta. Home: 238 S Mansfield Av Los Angeles CA 90036

KANAZAWA, SHIMEJI (MRS. KINJI KANAZAWA), state ofcl.; b. Kamuela, Hawaii, Dec. 29, 1915; d. Torazo and Saki (Harada) Ryusaki; certificate Chamberlain Sch. of Retailing, 1950; m. Kinji Kanazawa, Dec. 28, 1947; children—Sidney Kinji, Joni Sakiko. Sec. Kohala (Hawaii) High Sch., 1934-41; exec. sec. Swedish Vice-consulate, Honolulu, 1941-45; tchr.-coordinator retail tng. McKinley High Sch., Honolulu, 1951-52; buyer Liberty House, Honolulu, 1954-55; auditor Moiliili Hongwanji Mission, Honolulu, 1968—. Pres. Lawyers Wives Hawaii, 1961-62; chmn. study laws affecting family life and youth Commn. on Children and Youth, Honolulu, 1961-67. Mem. Hawaii State Commn. on Aging, chmn., 1972—; mem. Honolulu Home Care Service Adv. Com., 1973. Bd. dirs. Health and Community Services Council of Hawaii, 1973—, Aloha United Fund, 1966-71, 74—, Conf. on the Culture and Arts in Hawaii, 1973. Home: 2316 Oahu Av Honolulu HI 96822

KANE, KATHARINE FITZHUGH DANIELS (MRS. LOUIS I. KANE), civic worker, former state legislator; b. Indpls., Apr. 12, 1935; d. Joseph Johnston and Katharine (Holliday) Daniels; B.A. summa cum laude, Smith Coll., 1956; m. Louis I. Kane, Sept. 21, 1957; children—Elizabeth Holliday, Jennifer Johnston, Joseph Daniels. Research asst. Pres. Com. on Fgn. Aid Program, Washington, 1956; research asst. Dept. of State, Washington, 1957; research asst. Prof. Donald Morgan, Mt. Holyoke Coll. at Harvard, 1958-59; mem. Mass. Ho. of Reps., 1964-68; dir. Mayor's Office Cultural Affairs, Boston, 1968-72; dir. office Boston Bicentennial, 1972— Vice chmn. Com. on Pub. Welfare, 1965-68; founder Summerthing, Boston's Neighborhood Festival, 1968; chmn. Mass. Gov.'s Task Force Accessibility of the Arts. Bd. dirs. United Community Services, Boston; Boston Ballet Co.; corporator Inst. Contemporary Art, Boston; trustee Miss Porter's Sch., Farmington, Conn.; past trustee Charles Playhouse, Boston; bd. overseers Boston Symphony Orch.; charter dir. Boston com. Young Audiences, Inc. Mem. League Women Voters Boston (pres. 1961-64), Mass. Mental Health Assn., Smith Coll. Alumnae Assn. (dir.), Phi Beta Kappa Home: 10 Chestnut St Boston MA 02108

KANE, MARGARET BRASSLER, sculptor; b. East Orange, N.J., May 25, 1909; d. Hans and Mathilde (Trumpler) Brassler; student Packer Collegiate Inst., 1920-26, Syracuse U., 1927, Art Students League, 1927-29, N.Y. Coll. Music, 1928-29, John Hovannes Studio, 1932-34; Ph.D. (hon.), Colo. State Christian Coll., 1973; m. Arthur Ferris Kane, June 11, 1930; children—Jay Brassler, Gregory Ferris. Work has appeared at Jacques Seligmann Gallery, N.Y., Whitney Ann. Exhbns., All Sculptors Guild Museum and Outdoor Shows, Nat. Sculpture Soc. Ann. Bas-Relief Exhbn., 1938, Whitney Mus. Sculpture Festival, 1940, Bklyn. Mus. Sculptors Guild, 1938, Bklyn. Soc. Artists, 1942, Lawrence (Mass.) Art Mus., 1938, N.Y. World's Fair, 1939, Sculptors Guild World's Fair Exhbn., 1940, Robinson Gallery, N.Y., 1939, Traveling Museums and Instns., 1938, Lyman Allyn Mus., 1939, Met. Mus., Internat. Exhbns., 1940, 1949, Phila. Mus., N.Y. Archtl. League, Nat. Acad., Penn. Acad. Art Inst., Chgo., Am. Fedn. Arts, Riverside Mus., Montclair Mus., Grand Central Art Galleries (N.Y.C.), N.Y. Coliseum, N.Y.C, 1956, Sculptors Guild Ann., Roosevelt Art Center, Garden City, L.I., 1957, Silvermine Guild Artists Ann. N.E. Exhbns., 1957, Lever House, N.Y.C., 1959-75, 11th Ann. New Eng. Exhibit, 1960, Rye (N.Y.) Library, 1962-63; 70th Year N.J. State Mus. exhibit, 1961—, Montclair (N.J.) Art Mus., Awards Artists Exhbn., 1966, Mattatuck Mus., Waterbury, Conn., 1967, Lamont Gallery, Exeter, N.H., 1967; executed plaque for Burro Monument, Fairplay, Colo.; sculpture exhibit Friends of Greenwich Library, 1962; engaged in carving 3 limewood panels depicting history of mankind. Head craftsman for sculpture, arts and skills unit, A.R.C., Halloran Gen. Hosp., N.Y., 1942-43. Fellow Internat. Inst. Arts and Letters; mem. Sculptors Guild, (sec. to exec. bd. 1942-45, chmn. exhbn. com. 1942, 44), Nat. Assn. Women Artists (2d v.p. 1943-45), Artists Council, U.S.A., Bklyn. Soc. Artists, Greenwich Soc. Artists (council mem.), Pen and Brush, Silvermine Guild Artists. Recipient Ann Hyatt Huntington award, 1942; awards Am. Artists Profl. League, Montclair Art Assn., 1943; 1st Henry O. Avery prize, 1944; sculpture prize Bklyn. Soc. Artists, Bklyn. Mus., 1946, John Rogers award, 1951; Lawrence Hyder prize, 1952, 54; David Zell Meml. award, 1954-63; hon. mention U.S. Maritime Commn., 1941; A.C.A. Gallery Competition, 1944; medal of honor for sculpture, 1951, Nat. Assn. Women Artists, Nat. Acad. Galleries, N.Y.; prize for carved sculpture, 1955, animal sculpture, 1956, Ann. New Eng. Exhbns., Silvermine, Conn.; 1st award for sculpture Greenwich Art Soc., 1958, 60. Jury mem. Brooklyn Mus., 1948, Am. Machine & Foundry Co. Art Exhibit, Greenwich, Conn., 1957; com. mem. Am. Group, Inc. Slide lectr. and sculpture demonstrator for art socs. and orgns. Contbr. articles to mags. Home and studio: 30 Strickland Rd Cos Cob CT 06807

KANE, MARGARET O'SHEA (MRS. WILLIAM CHRISTOPHER KANE), educator; b. N.Y.C.; d. James Daniel and Delia (O'Shea) O'Shea; A.B., Hunter Coll., 1940; M.A., N.Y. U., 1942, Ed.D., 1954; m. William Christopher Kane, Sept. 9, 1944; 1 son, William Christopher. Mem. faculty bus. edn. Hunter Coll., N.Y.C., 1943—, instr., 1954-59, asst. prof., 1959-64, asso. prof., 1964-71, prof., 1971; officer in charge div. bus. edn. Herbert H. Lehman Coll., City U. N.Y., 1968—, counselor, Guidance Bur., 1954-59, exec. asst. dean of faculty, 1960-62, fgn. student adviser, 1959-68. U.S. Dept. State grantee, 1965; del. First World Conf. on Internat. Houses and Centers, Paris, 1961. Named Profl. Woman of Year Bus. and Profl. Women's Clubs N.Y. State, Inc. Mem. Bronx Council on the Arts (exec. bd.), Nat. Assn. Fgn. Student Affairs, Delta Pi Epsilon. Home: 1541 Metropolitan Av New York City NY 10462

KANE, NANCY ANN, educator; b. Omaha, Dec. 7, 1929; d. Leo Dale and Margaret Louise (Kastner) K.; B.A., Duchesne Coll., 1953; M.A., San Francisco Coll. Women, 1956; Ph.D., Stanford, 1958; postgrad. Hamline U., 1967, U. Wash., 1971, San Diego State U., 1972, Sophia U. (Japan), 1970. Tchr., Duchesne Acad., Omaha, 1951-56; faculty San Francisco Coll., 1957-58, Duchesne Coll., Omaha, 1958-62; asso. prof. history Barat Coll., Lake Forest, Ill., 1962—, dir. personnel, 1962-67, placement dir., 1968-72, grad. and fgn. study adviser, 1972—. Mem. Am. Hist. Assn., Am. Assn. U. Profs., Assn. Asian Studies. Democrat. Roman Catholic. Home: 730 E Westleigh Rd Lake Forest IL 60045

KANE, PATRICIA LOIS LANEGRAN (MRS. DONALD PATRICK KANE), educator; b. St. Paul, June 23, 1926; d. Walter B. and Lita E. (Wilson) Lanegran; B.A. cum laude, Macalester Coll., 1947; M.A., U. Minn., 1950, Ph.D., 1961; m. Donald Patrick Kane, Apr. 1, 1947; children—Laura Marie, Maura Leslie. Asst. prof. dept. English, Macalester Coll., St. Paul, 1947-67, asso. prof., 1967-71, prof., 1971—. Vis. lectr. U. Minn., spring 1961; cons. Mpls. Coll. Art, 1951; star radio program Critically Speaking, 1951-52; hostess TV series Faces of Perfection, 1960-61; co-dir. curricular guidance undergrad. women Region V Dept. Health, Edn. and Welfare, 1972-73; pub. speaker in field Am. and modern lit., 1957—; lectr. Minn. Humanities Commn., 1973. Mem. adv. bd. Macalester YWCA, 1955. Recipient Danforth Tchr. award, 1958. Mem. Modern Lang. Assn., Am. Studies Assn., Am. Assn. U. Profs. (chpt. v.p. 1961), Minn.-Dakotas Am. Studies Assn. (pres. 1967-68), Phi Beta Kappa (hon.), Pi Kappa Delta. Democrat. Unitarian. Contbr. articles to lit. jours. Home: 394 Macalester St St Paul MN 55105

KANG, ELLEN SOO SUN SONG (MRS. ANDREW HO KANG), physician; b. Wahiawa, Oahu, Hawaii, Feb. 17, 1929; d. Suk Soon and Bok Pil (Chun) Song; B.A., U. Hawaii, 1951; postgrad. Woman's Med. Coll. Pa., 1951-52; M.D., Stanford, 1955; m. Andrew Ho Kang, Sept. 6, 1958; children—Cynthia, Edith, Audrey. Intern Queen's Hosp., Hawaii, 1955-56; med. officer Schofield Barracks, Hawaii, 1956-57; pediatric resident Children's Med. Center, Boston, 1957-59; research fellow neurology, 1959-62, clin. fellow in neurology, 1962-64, dir. PKU and other Inborn Errors of Metabolism Clinic 1963-64, after 1967, asst. in clin. genetics, after 1970; asst. prof. pediatrics Harvard Med. Sch., after 1970; now asso. biochemistry St. Jude's Children's Research Hosp., Memphis; asso. prof. pediatrics U. Tenn. at Memphis. Med. cons. mental retardation br. div. chronic diseases Dept. Health, Edn. and Welfare, 1964, metabolic cons. Children's Bur., 1964—.; mem. staff group mental retardation and mental retardation abstracts com. NIH. Diplomate Am. Bd. Pediatrics. Mem. Sigma Xi. Contbr. articles to med. jours. Home: 2334 Massey Rd Memphis TN 38138 Office: Dept Biochemistry St Jude's Research Hosp 332 N Lauderdale St Memphis TN 38101

KANICK, VIRGINIA, physician; b. Coaldale, Pa., Nov. 10, 1925; d. Martin and Anna (Pisklak) Kanick; A.B., Barnard Coll., 1947; M.D., Columbia, 1951. Intern Western Res. U. Hosps., Cleve., 1951-52; asst. resident radiology St. Luke's Hosp., N.Y.C., 1952-54, chief resident, 1954-55, asst. attending radiology, 1955-58, asso. attending, 1958-62, sr. attending, 1962—, also asso. dir. radiology dept., 1962—, sec. med. bd., 1970—; practice medicine specializing in radiology, N.Y.C., 1955—; asso. prof. clin. radiology Columbia U. Coll. Phys. and Surg., N.Y.C. Fellow Am. Coll. Radiology; mem. Radiol. Soc. N.Am., N.Y. State Radiol. Soc., Am., N.Y.C. roentgen ray socs., A.M.A., Phi Beta Kappa, Alpha Omega Alpha. Contbr. articles to med. jours. Home: 501 W 113th St New York City NY 10025 also RD 2 Dawson Rd Hillsdale NY Office: St Luke's Hosp 114th St and Amsterdam Av New York City NY 10025

KANIN, DORIS MAY, Democratic nat. committeewoman; b. Somerville, Mass.; d. Sidney J. and Ida Gloria (Gelbsman) Small; B.A. in Govt., Boston U., 1966, M.A., 1970, now postgrad.; m. Irving Lynwood Kanin; children—Dennis, Erik, Lisa. Legislative and exec. asst. to Congressman Joe Moakley of Mass., 1973—; pres. Lynwood Labs. Inc.; Mem. Norwood (Mass.) Human Rights Steering Com. Mem. state steering com. Mass. PAX, 1970-73; mem. state exec. bd. Citizens for Participatory Politics, 1971-72; del. at large Dem. nat. conv., 1972; mem. presdl. campaign staff, 1962, coordinator urban ethics div., head Concerned Clergy for McGovern-Shriver, 1962; mem. Dem. nat. com. from Mass., 1972—; nat. legislation chmn. Ams. for Dem. Action, 1973—; mem. nat. legislation com. Nat. Women's Polit. Caucus, 1973—. Mem. Am. Polit. Sci. Assn., Dem. Nat. Committeewomen's Caucus, Capitol Hill Women Polit. Caucus, Federally-Employed Women, League Women Voters (pres. chpt. 1957-59). Patentee chem. products. Home: 2111 Jefferson Davis Apt 410N Arlington VA 22202 also 25 Buckingham Rd Norwood MA 21062 Office: Canon House Office Bldg 238 Washington DC

KANZLER, MAUREEN BYRNE (MRS. ROBERT LEE), psychologist, educator; b. Bklyn., Sept. 10, 1916; d. Richard Michael and Mary Agnes (Colligan) Byrne; B.A., Hunter Coll., 1938, M.S., 1960; M.A., N.Y. U., 1940; Ph.D., Fordham U., 1968; m. Ernest Kanzler, Feb. 3, 1945 (dec. June, 1965); m. 2d, Robert Lee, Oct. 21, 1972. Guidance counselor Yorktown Heights (N.Y.) High Sch., 1955-59; sr. research scientist dept. biol. psychiatry N.Y. State Psychiat. Inst., N.Y.C., 1966—; asst. prof. med. psychology Columbia Coll. Physicians and Surgeons, N.Y.C., 1971—; pvt. practice, 1968—. Mem. Am. Psychol. Assn., Sigma Xi, Kappa Delta Pi. Roman Catholic. Research in Psychopharmacology. Home: 35 Temple Rd Dobbs Ferry NY 10522 Office: 722 West 168 St New York City NY 10032

KAPFER, MIRIAM BIERBAUM (MRS. PHILIP G. KAPFER), ednl. research specialist; b. Atlantic, Ia., May 8, 1935; d. Roy Christopher and Alma (Bees) Bierbaum; B.Music Edn., Drake U., 1956; M. Music Edn., U. Kan., 1958; postgrad. Kings Coll., U. Aberdeen (Scotland), 1958-59; Ph.D., Ohio State U., 1964; m. Philip Gordon Kapfer, Aug. 21, 1960; children—Paul Christopher, Stephanie Anne. Instr. piano Concordia Tchrs. Coll., Seward, Neb., 1958, St. John's Coll., Winfield, Kan., 1959-61; tchr. pub. elementary schs. Franklin County, Columbus, O., 1962-64; mem. faculty, staff Clark County Sch. Dist., Las Vegas, Nev., 1964-70, librarian, 1966-67, research specialist, 1967-70; curriculum and publs. specialist Center to Improve Learning and Instrn., U. Utah, Salt Lake City, 1970-73, co-dir. Life-Involvement Model project Bur. Ednl. Research, 1973—. Reviewer arts Winfield Courier, 1959-61; mem. textbook selection com. pub. schs. Franklin County, O., Clark County, Nev., 1964-65; cons., writer Nev. Dept. Edn., 1968, Inter-Island Ednl. Program, San Juan Islands, Washington, 1971, Consortium of Profl. Assn. for Study Spl. Tchr. Improvement Programs, Washington, 1971; mem. music adv. bd. Las Vegas chpt. Young Audiences, Inc., 1967-70. Drake U. honor scholar, 1954-56, U. Kan. grad. scholar, 1956-57. Mem. Music Educators Nat. Conf. (life), Am. Ednl. Research Assn., Nev. Music Educators Assn. (state 2d v.p., state historian 1967-70), Mu Phi Epsilon (leadership award Des Moines Alumnae chpt. 1954), Alpha Lambda Delta, Pi Kappa Lambda. Lutheran (mem. nat. European study project 1955). Author: Toward the Life-Internship Curriculum, 1970; Behavioral Objectives in Curriculum Development, 1971; Learning Packages in American Education, 1972. Editor: Nevada Notes jour. Nev. Music Edn. Assn., 1965-70, Educational Progress Reports jour. Center to Improve Learning and Instrn., U. Utah, 1970-73; guest editor Ednl. Tech. mag., Sept. 1972. Contbr. profl. jours. Home: 4344 Pin Oak St Salt Lake City UT 84117 Office: 308W Milton Bennion Hall Univ Utah Salt Lake City UT 84112

KAPIT, HANNA ELIZABETH (MRS. MILTON E. KAPIT), psychoanalyst; b. Vienna, Austria, June 16, 1917; d. Herbert and Ilse Elizabeth (von Arnim) Elias; came to U.S., 1938, naturalized, 1944; student U. Vienna, 1936-38; B.E., U. Mich., 1943; Ph.D., Columbia, 1956; m. Eric Husserl, Sept. 1940 (dec.); 1 dau., Susan; m. 2d, Milton E. Kapit, Apr. 10, 1954; 1 son, Andrew. Psychology intern Headache Clinic Montefiore Hosp., Bronx, N.Y., 1952-53, VA Hosp., N.Y.C., 1953-56; asst. clin. prof. psychiatry Einstein Coll. of Medicine, Bronx, 1966—. Lectr. Columbia Med. Sch., N.Y.C., 1966—; lectr., supr. Postgrad. Center for Mental Health, N.Y.C., 1960—. Mem. Am. N.Y. State psychol. assns., Postgrad. Center for Mental Health, Hon. Ednl. Soc. Contbr. articles on psychotherapy to profl. jours. Address: 1 West 85th St New York City NY 10024

KAPITZKY, FRANCES HILDA, banker; b. Strasburg, O., Jan. 14, 1902; d. Emil Philip and Mary Ann (Koehler) Kapitzky; A.B., Western Res. U., 1924; H.H.D., Heidelburg Coll., 1958; LL.D., Hood Coll., 1962. Tchr. pub. schs., Beach City, O., 1926-29, Strasburg, O., 1929-30; with Strasburg Citizens Bank, 1959—, now pres. Mem. central com. World Council Chs., 1961-68; pres. Strasburg Bd. Edn., 1940-48. Bd. dirs. New Philadelphia-Tuscarawas County Library Bd. Mem. MacDowell Music Club, Delphian Study Club. Mem. United Ch. Christ (nat. moderator, 1959, 59-62). Mem. Eastern Star Order. Club: Women's. Home: 632 Oak Av NW Strasburg OH 44680 Office: 202 N Wooster Av Strasburg OH 44680

KAPLAN, ALINE, religious orgn. exec.; b. N.Y.C., June 23, 1923; d. Morris and Dora (Zeresky) Kaplan; B.A., Hunter Coll., 1943; LL.B., Columbia, 1946; postgrad. Grad. Sch. Edn., Yeshiva U., 1959-62. Admitted to N.Y. State bar, 1946, Fed. bar, 1948; practiced in N.Y.C., 1946-52; exec. dir. Jr. Hadassah, N.Y.C., 1952-64, asst. exec. dir. Hadassah, 1964-71, exec. dir., 1971—. Del. World Zionist Congress, Jerusalem, 1956, 64, 72. Bd. dirs. Am. Zionist Fedn., United Jewish Appeal. Mem. Delta Phi Epsilon. Jewish religion. Office: 65 E 52d St New York City NY 10022 Mailing address: 215 E 80th St New York City NY 10021

KAPLAN, ANN ESTHER, chemist; b. N.Y.C., Dec. 28, 1926; d. Julius Jacob and Vera Timothea (Deutschman) Kaplan; B.A., Hunter Coll., 1947; M.A., Mt. Holyoke Coll., 1949; Ph.D., U. Pa., 1959. Fellow, N.Y.U. Coll. Medicine, 1959-60; sr. fellow, instr. Albert Einstein Coll. Medicine, N.Y.C., 1960-63; research asso. Rockefeller U., N.Y.C., 1963-65; asst. prof., mem. grad. faculty City U. N.Y., 1965-67; sr. research asso. Salk Inst., La Jolla, Cal., 1967-72; chemist Nat. Cancer Inst., NIH, Bethesda, Md., 1972—. Mem. Am. Soc. Biol. Chemists (mem. com. on status of women in biochemistry 1972—), Am. Chem. Soc., Biophys. Soc., N.Y. Acad. Scis., Sigma Xi. Home: 3003 Van Ness St NW Washington DC 20008 Office: National Cancer Institute NIH Landow Bldg Room A-306 Bethesda MD 20014

KAPLAN, ELIZABETH ANN BREMNER (MRS. ALBERT J. KAPLAN), psychoanalyst, psychiatrist; b. Louisville, Jan. 27, 1910; d. George L. and Sue (Hamlett) Bremner; B.A., Ohio State U., 1935, M.D., 1935; m. Albert J. Kaplan, Aug. 4, 1956. Intern Toledo State Hosp., 1935-36, resident, 1936-40, clin. dir. women's div., 1940-44; Commonwealth Fund fellow child psychology Phila. Child Guidance Clinic, 1943-44; child psychiatrist, div. dir. Bur. Mental Hygiene, Conn. State Health Dept., Hartford, 1946-47; unit dir. Med. Coll. Western Res. U. and Univ. Hosps., Cleve., 1947-56; dir. Children's Psychiat. Clinic, 1947-56; asst. prof. psychiatry Western Res. Med. Sch., 1947-56; clin. prof., dir. tng. Hahnemann Med. Coll., Phila., 1964—, dir. residency tng. child psychiatry Peberdy Child Psychiatry Clinic, 1966—; practice medicine, specializing in adult and child psychiatry and psychonanlysis, Toledo, 1935-43, Phila., 1943-44, 56—, Hartford, 1946-47, Cleve., 1947-56; mem. staff Phila. Psychiat. Center. Dir. extension sch. Phila. Assn. Psychoanalysis, 1959; tng. analyst Inst. Phila. Assn. Psychoanalysis, 1960. Patron Doctor's Symphony, 1968—. Served to capt. M.C., AUS, 1944-46. Diplomate Am. Bd. Psychiatry and Neurology. Mem. Am. Acad. Child Psychiatry, Am. Assn. Child Psychoanalysts, Am. Psychoanalytic Assn. Author: (with others) A Handbook of Child Psychoanalysis, 1968; Symposium on Handicapped, Hospitalized Child, 1954; Psychoanalytic Study of Child, Vol. XX, 1965. Address: 1706 S Park Towne Place Philadelphia PA 19130 also Hahnemman Med Coll 210 N Broad St Philadelphia PA 19102

KAPLAN, EVE LINDA, educator; b. Vineland, N.J., Oct. 5, 1948; d. David Irving and Helen Judith (Cotler) Kaplan; B.S., West Liberty State Coll., 1970; postgrad. Villanova U., 1972; secondary certificate Glassboro State Coll., 1972; M.S., W.Va. U., 1973. Student asst. West Liberty (W.Va.) State Coll., 1967-70; grad. teaching asst. W.Va. U., Morgantown, 1970-71; tchr. math. Vineland Sr. High Sch., 1972—. Adviser, Vineland B'nai B'rith Girls, 1972—; sponsor Mu Alpha Theta, Vineland Sr. High Sch., 1973—; cons. S. Jersey B'nai B'rith Youth Orgn., 1973—. Recipient Midge Levy Meml. award, 1973; named Outstanding B'nai B'rith Girls adviser, 1973. N.J. State scholar, 1966-70, H.A. Davis Math. scholar, 1969-70. Mem. Math. Assn. Am., Assn. for Women in Math., N.E.A., Vineland Edn. Assn. (exec. com.), Nat. Council Tchrs. Math. (mem. conv. com.), B'nai B'rith Women, Chi Beta Phi, Alpha Delta Pi. Home: 33 Chestnut Av Vineland NJ 08360

KAPLAN, HELEN SINGER, psychiatrist; b. Vienna, Austria, Feb. 6,, 1929; d. Phillip Sigmund and Sophie (Lanzi) Singer; came to U.S., 1940, naturalized, 1947; B.F.A., Syracuse U., 1949; M.A., Columbia, 1951, Ph.D., 1955; M.D., N.Y. Med. Coll., 1959; m. Harold I. Kaplan, June 20, 1953 (div. 1970); children—Phillip, Peter, Jennifer. Intern Bronx (N.Y.) Hosp., 1960-61; resident N.Y. Med. Coll., 1961-64; practice medicine specializing in psychiatry, N.Y.C., 1964—; asso. vis. psychiatrist Met. Hosp.; asso. prof. psychiatry N.Y. Med. Coll.; asso. clin. prof. psychiatry Cornell U. Med. Coll.; head sexual treatment and study program, coordinator student teaching of psychiatry, asso. attending psychiatrist N.Y. Hosp., N.Y.C., Nat. Inst. Mental Health career teacher in psychiatry, 1964-66. Fellow Am. Psychiatric Assn., Am. Psychol. Assn., Acad. Psychoanalysis; mem. Sigma Xi, Alpha Omega Alpha. Co-editor: Progress in Group and Family Therapy, 1972. Asst. to editors: Comprehensive Textbook Psychiatry, 1967, New Sex Therapy, 1974. Co-editor Jour. Sex. and Marital Therapy. Contbr. articles to profl. jours. Home: 912 Fifth Av New York City NY 10021 Office: 65 E 76th St New York City NY 10021

KAPLAN, JUDITH HELENE (MRS. WARREN KAPLAN), investment co. exec.; b. N.Y.C., July 20, 1938; d. Abraham and Ruth (Kiffel) Letich; B.A., Hunter Coll., 1960; postgrad. New Sch. for Social Research, 1960-61; m. Warren Kaplan, Dec. 31, 1958; children—Ronald Scott, Elissa Ann. Registered rep. Herzfeld & Stern, N.Y.C., 1963; agt. N.Y. Life Ins. Co., N.Y.C., 1964-69; registered rep. Scheinman, Hochstin & Trotta, 1969-70; v.p. Alpha Capital Corp., N.Y.C., 1970—; pres. Tipex, Inc., N.Y.C., 1966—; v.p. Alpha Pub. Relations, N.Y.C., 1970-73; pres. Utopia Recreations Corp., 1971—, Howard Beach Recreation Corp., 1972—; chmn. bd. Alpha Exec. Planning Corp., 1970-72, Life Underwriters N.Y. Life, 1974—. Mem. Nat. Orgn. for Women, Women Leaders Round Table, Nat. Assn. Life Underwriters, Bus. and Profl. Women, Assn. Feminist Cons., Nat. Women's Polit. Caucus. Home: 86-55 Santiago St New York City NY 11423 Office: 61-17 190th St Fresh Meadows NY 11365

KAPLAN, MURIEL SHEERR (MRS. MURRAY S. KAPLAN), sculptor; b. Phila., Aug. 15, 1924; d. Maurice J. and Lillian J. (Jamison) Sheerr; B.A., Cornell U., 1946; postgrad. Sarah Lawrence Coll., 1958-60, U. Cal. at Oxford (Eng.) U., summer 1971 U. Florence (Italy), summer 1973; student Silvermine Art Guild, 1954-57, Norton Art Sch., 1950-51; m. Murray S. Kaplan, June 3, 1946; children—Janet, James, S. Jerrold, Amy. Exhibited sculpture in shows at Bklyn. Mus., 1968, Bergen (N.J.) Community Mus., 1973, Sculptor's Guild, N.Y.C.; created bust of John F. Kennedy in permanent collection U. Tex., 1966, Israel, 1967; portrait busts at Columbia, N.Y.C., Brandeis U., Waltham, Mass.; two 30 foot tall Cor-ten steel sculptures erected at Tarrytown, N.Y., 1972; pvt. tchr. sculpture, 1970—; art cons., interior designer, 1971—. Sec. com. to establish Art Mus., Westchester, N.Y., 1956; sec. Pleasant Ridge P.T.A., Harrison, 1957; chmn. WNET Channel 13 Art Auction, 1963; chmn. sculpture Brandeis U. Creative Arts Festival, Westchester, 1956; mem. various coms. Friends of Whitney Museum; mem. Museum Modern Art, Met. Mus., Guggenheim Mus. Chmn. Pvt. Sch. Students to Elect Johnson, 1964. Bd. dirs. Fedn. Jewish Philanthropies, 1951, Brandeis U. Women's Orgn. for Westchester, 1957. Recipient sculpture prize Westchester Women's Club, 1955, 56, Catherine Lorillard Wolfe Club, 1961, Nat. Assn. Women Artists, 1966, Allied Artists Am., 1969. Mem. Nat. Assn. Women Artists, Ethical Culture Soc., Artists and Engrs. in Tech. Democrat. Home: 150 E 69th St New York City NY 10021 Office: 1053 Lexington Av New York City NY 10021

KAPLAN, RHODA BURSTEIN, artist; b. Newark, June 23, 1921; d. Samuel C. and Paula B. (Rothman) Burstein; student Newark Sch. Fine and Indsl. Art, 1940-41, 55-58, Hull Art Sch., 1959-60; m. Philip A. Kaplan, Feb. 15, 1942; children—Carolyn K., A. Stephen. Exhibited one-man shows Paper Mill Playhouse, 1966, 68, Haib Gallery, 1974; exhibited in group shows at Newark Mus., Montclair Mus., N.J. State Mus., Expn. Inter-Continentale, Am. Artists Profl. League, Nat. Catherine Lorrilard Wolfe Club, N.A.D., Bamberger's Newark, Hudson Valley Art Assn., Westfield State Show, Art Centre of Oranges, Ringwood Manor State Show, Ramapo Coll., Drew U., Seton Hall U., Newark State Coll., Bergen Community Mus., Morris County Mus. Lectr. civic orgns., schs., clubs, profl. assns., 1962—; tchr. Sloan Sch., South Orange, N.J., 1963-64, YWCA, Summit, N.J., 1965—, YM-YWHA, West Orange, 1968—, Artmakers, N.J., Irvington (N.J.) Art Assn., 1973; also pvt. tchr. art. Mem. Am. Artists Profl. League, Artists Equity, Westfield Art Assn., Art Gallery South Orange and Maplewood (past pres.). Home: 10 Archbridge Lane Springfield NJ 07081

KAPPEL, R. ROSE, artist; b. Hartford, Conn., Sept. 23, 1910; d. Morris and Anna Evlyn (Superior) Kappel; student Pratt Inst., 1930; B.S., N.Y.U., 1947, M.A., 1950; student Wash. U., Wis. U., Yale; m. Irving Gould, Dec. 24, 1944. Art specialist Bur. Edn. Physically Handicapped Children, Bd. Edn., Bklyn., 1944—. Numerous one-man shows leading galleries, N.Y.C., 1935-50; exhibited Nat. Acad. Art, 1960-67, Washington Art Assn.; represented in permanent collections Fogg Mus., Cleve. Mus., Boston Mus., Orange Mus., Met. Mus. Art, Mattatuck Mus. Art, New Britain Mus. Am. Art, Mt. Holyoke Mus.; lithographs exhibited with Am. Graphics Art Soc., Kennedy Galleries, N.Y.C., 1955-60, others; art cons. Am. Assn. U. Women. Recipient Beth Creedy Hamm prize for water color Nat. Acad., 1960, prize for water color Nat. Assn. Women Artists, 62, Nat. Acad., 1961. Mem. Council Exceptional Children, Nat. Assn. Women Artists, Print Council Am., Internat. Platform Assn., Center for Am. Living, Assn. Council Arts, Am. Assn. U. Women (area rep. in cultural interests for N.Y. state, dir.-at-large, v.p. N.Y.C. br.). Illustrator: Ships and Sails, 1947. Home: 35-36 76th St Jackson Heights NY 11372

KAPPELL, JEAN LIGHTFOOT (MRS. LON C. KAPPELL), newspaper columnist; b. Springfield, Mo., Apr. 27, 1916; d. Murchison David and Gretchen (Gill) Lightfoot; B.J., U. Mo., 1936; M.Ed., Miami U., Oxford, O., 1963; m. Lon C. Kappell, Apr. 23, 1948; 1 dau., Melinda Lightfoot. Columnist, Springfield Leader-Press, 1936-37; women's and society editor Kansas City (Mo.) Jour., 1937-39; syndicated feature writer Scripps Howard-Newspaper Enterprise Assn., 1940-41; feature writer St. Louis Post-Dispatch, 1941-42, editorial and polit. writer, 1942-47; Washington corr. N.Y. Post, 1948; promotion mgr. Sta. KWTO, 1949; editorial writer Dayton (O.) Daily News, 1950-69, columnist, 1969—. Free-lance writer for mags., 1940—; lectr., instr. fgn. affairs, English lit., 1944—. Mem. Ohio Newspaper Women's Assn., Ohio Press Women's Assn., Nat. Fedn. Press Women, Pi Beta Phi. Episcopalian. Clubs: Dayton Garden, Miami Valley Hunt. Home: Wigslip House Swimming Pool Rd Yellow Springs OH 45387 Office: Dayton Daily News 4th at Ludlow St Dayton OH 45401

KAREM, MARY JANE, lawyer; b. Louisville, Oct. 27, 1908; d. Edmund Gibbs and Virginia (Allen) Mansfield; B.A., Nazareth Coll., 1931; J.D. magna cum laude, Jefferson Sch. Law, 1948; m. Fred J. Karem, Sept. 1, 1936 (dec.); children—Virginia C., James F., Edmund Peter, David Kevin, Jane Catherine. Admitted to Ky. bar, 1949; partner firm Karem & Karem, Louisville, 1949—. Committeewoman, Democratic Com., 1952—; mem. Louisville and Jefferson County Human Relations Commn. Sec. bd. counselors Catherine Spalding Coll.; mem. delegation Am. Women to USSR, Hungary and Rumania, 1971. Ky. col. Named Louisville Bus. Woman of Yr., 1967, Outstanding Woman Lawyer Council Women Presidents, 1972; recipient Spalding Coll. Alumni Caritas medal, 1968. Mem. Nat. Assn. Women Lawyers, Nat. Catholic Theatre Conf., Catholic Theatre Guild Louisville, Am., Ky., Louisville bar assns., Bellarmine Coll. Athletic Assn., Bellarmine Women's Council (exec. com.), Am. Assn. U. Women, Jefferson County Women Lawyers Assn. (pres.), Internat. Platform Assn., Catherine Spalding Alumnae (pres.), English Speaking Union. Clubs: Highland Woman's, Nazareth Luncheon. Home: 1857 Alfresco Pl Louisville KY 40205 Office: Lincoln Fed Bldg Louisville KY 40202

KAREN, RUTH (MRS. SHLOMO A. HAGAI), editor, author; b. Nuremberg, Germany, Feb. 18, 1922; d. David and Paula (Freudenthal) Karpf; student U. Jerusalem, London U., New Sch. Social Research; m. Shlomo A. Hagai, Mar. 1966. Fgn. corr. Toronto Star, Europe and Middle East, 1946-48, UN corr., N.Y.C., 1949-52, Far East war corr., fgn. corr. The Reporter mag., 1952-53; columnist, editor World Wide Press, N.Y.C., 1954-60; Central Am. fgn. corr. Latin Am. Times, Business Abroad, 1962-66; editor Bus. Internat. Corp., N.Y.C. and Latin Am., 1966-71, sr. editor, N.Y.C. and Asia, 1972—. Mem. Authors' League Am. Clubs: Town Tennis Club (N.Y.C.); Overseas Press. Author: The Land and People of Central America, 1965; Neighbors in a New World: The Organization of American States, 1966; The Seven Worlds of Peru, 1969; Hello Guatemala, 1970; Song of the Quail: The Wondrous World of the Maya, 1972; Brazil Today: A Case Study in Developmental Economics That Worked, 1974. Address: Care of Curtis Brown Ltd 60 E 56th St New York City NY 10022

KARESH, JANICE LEHRER, educator; b. N.Y.C., May 22, 1924; d. Maxwell E. and Lillian (Cohen) Lehrer; B.S., Douglass Coll., 1945; M.A., N.Y. U., 1946; m. Irwin Karesh, June 15, 1947 (dec. Jan. 1959); children—Sara, Hyman, Ann, Charles. Tchr. Charleston County, S.C., Pub. Schs., 1946-47, 65-66, counselor Drop Out Program, North Charleston, S.C., 1965-66; asso. coordinator Trident Forum for Handicapped, Charleston, S.C., 1966-69; supr. spl. edn. Beaufort County (S.C.), 1969—; cons. programs for emotionally disturbed, learning disabled, handicapped in rural counties. Chmn. Beaufort Assn. Retarded Child; vice-chmn. Beaufort Jasper Council for Handicapped. Recipient NSF grant, 1965. Mem. Nat. Council Jewish Women (pres. Charleston sect. 1952-53, state legislative chmn. 1953-73), League Women Voters of S.C., YWCA Greater Charleston, Council Exceptional Child, Am. Assn. Mental Deficiency, N.E.A. Democrat. Jewish religion. Home: Box 4391 Burton SC 29902 Office: Drawer 350 Beaufort SC 29902

KARK, NINA MARY MABEY (MRS. AUSTEN STEVEN KARK; PSEUDONYM NINA MARY BAWDEN), author; b. London, Eng., Jan. 19, 1925; d. Charles and Ellalaine Ursula May (Cushing) Mabey; student Somerville Coll., 1943-46; B.A. with honors, 1946, M.A., 1946; m. Austen Steven Kark, Aug. 5, 1954; children—Nicholas, Robert, Perdita. Justice of Peace, Surrey, Eng., 1968. Fellow Royal Lit. Soc.; mem. Internat. P.E.N. Author: Devil by the Sea, 1951; A Little Love, A Little Learning, 1968; Birds on the Trees, 1970; Tortoise by Candlelight, 1963; The Witch's Daughter, 1967; Anna Apparent; George Beneath A Paper Moon; (juveniles) Three on the Run, The Runaway Summer, A Handful of Thieves, Squib, Carrie's War. Address: 30 Hanger Hill St Weybridge Surrey England

KARL, JEAN EDNA, editor, publishing co. exec.; b. Chgo., July 29, 1927; d. William A. and Ruth (Anderson) Karl; B.A., Mt. Union Coll., 1949, LL.D., 1949. With Scott, Foresman & Co., Chgo., 1949-56; editor children's books Abingdon Press, 1956-61; dir. children's book dept. Atheneum Pubs., N.Y.C., 1961—, v.p., 1964—. Mem. joint com. A.L.A.-Children's Book Council, 1961-66, chmn., 1961-63; bd. dirs. Children's Book Council, 1963-66, 74—, pres., 1965; bd. dirs. Childrens Services div. A.L.A., 1971-74. Trustee Mt. Union Coll. Author: From Childhood to Childhood, 1970. Home: 300 E 33d St New York City NY 10016 Office: 122 E 42d St New York City NY 10017

KARL, VIRGINIA CATHERINE CARDONA (MRS. ERNEST ARNOLD KARL), social work adminstr.; b. Boston; d. Charles and Josephine (Martina) Cardona; B.S., Simmons Coll., 1938; M.A., U. Chgo., 1940; m. Ernest Arnold Karl, July 4, 1943. Social worker Boston City Hosp., 1938-39, Evanston (Ill.) Hosp. Assn., 1941-42, A.R.C., Walter Reed Hosp., Washington, 1942-43; with VA, 1944—, supr. regional office, Washington, 1946-49, chief adminstrn. standards and services Central Office Social Work Service, 1949—. Mem. Nat. Assn. Social Work, No. Va. Mental Health Assn. (dir. 1964-67), Arlington Health and Welfare Assn. (sec. 1966-67, nominating com. 1967-68), Council Social Work Edn., Acad. Certified Social Workers. Home: 2245 N Vermont St Arlington VA 22207 Office: 810 Vermont Av Washington DC 20420

KARLE, ISABELLA LUGOSKI, ofcl. Navy Dept.; b. Detroit, Dec. 2, 1921; B.S., U. Mich., 1941, M.S., 1942, Ph.D. in Phys. Chemistry (Rackham fellow 1942-43, Am. Assn. U. Women fellow 1943), 1944; m. 1942; 3 children. Asso. chemist U. Chgo., 1944; instr. U. Mich., 1944-46; physicist U.S. Naval Research Lab., Navy Dept., Washington, 1946-59, head X-ray analysis sect., 1959—. Civilian cons. AEC. Mem. U.S. Nat. Com. on Crystallography. Recipient Superior Civilian Service award Navy Dept., 1965, Annual Achievement award Soc. Women Engrs., 1968; Hillebrand award, 1970; Fed. Woman's award, 1973. Mem. Am. Phys. Soc., Am. Biophys. Soc., Am. Crystallography Assn., Am. Chem. Soc. Research in application electron and x-ray diffraction to structure problems in chemistry and biology. Office: Naval Research Lab Code 6030 Washington DC 20375

KARMAZIN, JOSEPHINE ROSE, realtor; b. N.Y.C., Feb. 9, 1922; d. John and Rose Marie (Mares) Karmazin; grad. Bradford Jr. Coll., 1941. Personnel mgr. Kline's Store, Detroit, 1945-53; asst. buyer and advt., Hutzel Store, Ann Arbor, Mich., 1953-55; v.p. personnel and labor relations Karmazin Products Corp., 1955-69; now salesman Lee H. Clark, realtor, Grosse Ile, Mich. Chmn. Downriver Bd. Mgmt., YMCA, 1970-73, chmn. Camp Cavell com. YMCA Met. Detroit; mem. bd. mgmt. Family Neighborhood Services, 1958-68. Presbyn. (deacon). Club: Grosse Ile Yacht. Home: 22085 Thorofare Grosse Ile MI 48138 Office: 8600 Macomb St Grosse Ile MI 48138

KARN, ETTA BERNICE, sch. adminstr.; b. Sioux City, Ia., Nov. 4, 1923; d. Samuel Edward and Della Bernice (Guyer) Benton; B.A., Bob Jones U., 1948; M.A., San Diego State U., 1963. Tchr. elementary sch., 1948-64; elementary prin. Mary Fay Pendleton Sch., Camp Pendleton, Cal., 1964—. Demonstration art teaching cons. San Diego County Schs., 1959-63. Recipient Commendation, Camp Pendleton, Cal. Mem. Internat. Reading Assn., Nat. Assn. Elementary Sch. Prins., Nat. Council of Adminstr. Women in Edn., Cal. Elementary Adminstrn. Assn., Cal. Assn. Elementary Prins., P.T.A. (hon., life), Delta Kappa Gamma. Club: Soroptimist (sec. 1971-72) (Fallbrook, Cal.). Home: 2125 Foster Oceanside CA 92054 Office: 110 Marine Dr Camp Pendleton CA 92055

KARN, GLORIA STOLL (MRS. FRED S. KARN, JR.), painter, educator; b. N.Y.C., Nov. 13, 1923; d. Charles Theophile and Anne Vera (Finamore) Stoll; student Eliot O'Hara Watercolor Sch., Me., 1945-46, Art Students League of N.Y., 1946-48; m. Fred S. Karn, Jr., Nov. 13, 1948; children—Vera Anita, Shari Marie, Keith Stoll. Free lance comml. artist with popular publs., N.Y.C., 1942-48; tchr. North Hills Art Center, Pitts., 1965—, Community Coll. of Allegheny County, Pitts., 1973—. Exhibited paintings in group shows Asso. Artists Pitts., 1949-68, Butler Inst., 1960-61, N.E. U.S. Art Rental Exchange, 1961, Three Rivers Art Festival of Pitts., 1960-67, 71-74; one woman shows Carnegie Inst. Mus. of Art, N.Y.C., 1966, Pitts. Plan for Art, 1965; represented in permanent collections Yale, Conn., Bklyn. Mus., Carnegie Inst., N.Y.C. Bd. dirs. Arts and Crafts Center of Pitts., 1969-71. Recipient Purchase prize Bklyn. Mus. Nat. Print Annual, 1949, Purchase prize Carnegie Inst., 1960. Mem. Asso. Artists of Pitts., Pa. Council Arts (mem. adv. bd. 1968-70). Presbyn. (deacon 1970-73). Address: 151 Louise Rd Pittsburgh PA 15237

KARNES, LUCIA ROONEY (MRS. THOMAS CAMPBELL KARNES), educator; b. Moncton, N.B., Can., Mar. 9, 1921; d. Charles William and Jean Waring (Robson) Rooney; B.S., Ga. State U., 1942; M.A., Emory U., 1947; Ph.D., U. N.C., 1968; m. Thomas Campbell Karnes, June 7, 1946; children—Eleanore Edith, Thomas Campbell III, Timothy Robson, Charles Waring. Tchr. pub. schs., 1942-46; tchr. pvt. sch., 1947; from instr. to prof. psychology Salem Coll., Winston-Salem, N.C., 1948—; vis. lectr. psychology Western Carolina U., 1968-70. Lang. therapist Bowman Gray Sch. Medicine; cons. Learning Disabilities Program. Trustee Forsyth Meml. Hosp.; bd. dirs. YWCA Arts Council. Mem. Am., N.C., Southeastern psychol. assns., Orton Soc., Am. Assn. U. Profs., N.C. Assn. Educators (pres. div. higher edn.), League Women Voters (dir.), Nat. Orgn. Women, Delta Kappa Gamma. Contbr. articles to profl. jours. Home: 438 Westover Av Winston-Salem NC 27104

KARNIOL, HILDA HUTTERER (MRS. FRANK KARNIOL), artist, educator; b. Vienna, Austria, Apr. 28, 1910; d. Simon and Josephine (Weisman) Hutterer; student Acad. for Women, Vienna, 1926-30, Mrs. Olga Konetzny-Maly and A. F. Seligman, Vienna, 1925-28; m. Frank Karniol, June 25, 1933; 1 son, William George. Over 100 one-man shows, including Susquehanna U., 1952, Pa. State Mus., Harrisburg, 1954, Neville Mus., Green Bay, Wis., 1958, Addha Artzt Gallery, N.Y.C., 1960, Cornell Library Gallery, Ithaca, N.Y., 1960, Drexel Inst. Tech., Phila., 1960, Farnsworth Mus., Rockland, Me., 1960, Mary Buie Mus., Oxford, Miss., 1960, Columbus (Ga.) Mus., 1962, Rutgers U., 1965-66, Laurel (Miss.) Rogers Mus., 1962; La Salle Coll., Phila., 1964; Hallmark Art Gallery, Kansas City, Mo., 1967, U. Ill., Urbana, 1968, U. Minn., St. Paul, 1969, U. Mich., 1969, U. Ky., Elizabethtown, 1970, La. State U., New Orleans, 1971, Kan State Coll. at Pittsburg, 1972, Purdue U., 1973; represented in permanent collections at St. Vincent Arch Abbey, Latrobe, Pa., Susquehanna U., Selinsgrove, Pa., Lincoln Sch., Honesdale, Pa., Del. Art Center, U.S. Govt. Dept. Health, Welfare and Edn., Lycoming Coll., Williamsport, Pa.; instr. fine arts Susquehanna U.; lectr., artist-in-residence Fed. Govt. Cultural Enrichment Program for Clearfield, Clinton, Centre and Lycoming counties, Pa., 1967; art adviser Sunbury Bicentennial Com., 1972. Recipient First prize in portraiture Berwick (Pa.) Arts Center, 1965. Mem. Mid-State Artists Pa., Nat. Forum Profl. Artists, Art Alliance Central Pa., Societé d'Honneure Française, Pi Delta Phi. Sigma Alpha Iota. Club:

Soroptimist (Sunbury, Pa.). Home: 960 Race St Sunbury PA 17801 Office: Susquehanna U Selinsgrove PA 17870

KARNITSCHNIG, ANN RUSSELL GADDUM (MRS. HEINZ H. KARNITSCHNIG), physician; b. London, Eng., Nov. 24, 1931; d. John and Iris Mary (Harmer) Gaddum; M.B., Ch. B., U. Edinburgh (Scotland), 1956, M.D., 1964; m. Heinz H. Karnitschnig, May 11, 1956; children—Sharon, Teresa, Leslie, Jennifer. Came to U.S., 1959, naturalized, 1967. Intern Royal Infirmary, Edinburgh, 1956-57, Kingston (Ont.) Gen. Hosp., 1957-58; house physician to Dr. J. K. Slater, Royal Infirmary, Edinburgh, 1956-57; house surgeon Sir Walter Mercer, 1957, research fellow internal medicine Queen's U., Kingston, Ont., 1957-58; dir. Physicians Pathology Lab., Norfolk, Va., 1967-70; dir. drug outreach center Virginia Beach Free Clinic, 1972—; mem. staffs Norfolk Gen. Hosp., Gen. Hosp. of Virginia Beach; cons. physician family planning, maternity, children and youth Va. State Health Dept., 1965—; med. dir. Tidewater Treatment Center, 1974—; mem. faculty dept. adolescent medicine Eastern Va. Med. Sch., 1974—. Vice pres. B. & K. Sailmakers, Inc., Virginia Beach, Va., 1968-70. Southeastern regional rep. Nat. Free Clinic Council, 1973. Mem. Va. Beach Med. Soc., Internat. Planned Parenthood Fedn., Nat. Free Clinic Council, Broad Bay Sailing Assn., Soc. Adolescent Medicine, Tidewater Psychiat. Assn., Chesapeake Bay Yacht Racing Union. Home: 1304 Starling Ct Virginia Beach VA 23451 Office: Virginia Beach Free Clinic 2022 Atlantic Av Virginia Beach VA 23451

KARO, ELSIE VIOLET COOPER (MRS. H. ARNOLD KARO), religious TV programs producer; b. Everett, Wash., Nov. 9, 1914; d. Frank L. and Lillian (Hillier) Cooper; A.B., U. Wash., 1936; m. H. Arnold Karo, Nov. 2, 1936; children—Douglas P., Kathryn R. Producer Bauman Bible Telecasts, WMAL-TV, Washington, 1958—; lectr. art appreciation courses. Mem. gen. council Presbyn. Ch. U.S., 1968-73; v.p. Council of Chs. Greater Washington, 1966-69; pres. Ch. Women United for Greater Washington, 1966-70; mem. exec. com. Ch. Women United in U.S.A., 1967-70, chmn. communications, 1966-69. Mem. Nat. Orgn. Women, Zeta Phi Eta. Home: 6307 Kirby Rd Bethesda MD 20034 Office: WMAL-TV 4461 Connecticut Av NW Washington DC 20008

KARP, MARY ARTAL, real estate cons.; b. Sunnyvale, Cal., Dec. 12, 1923; d. Cirilo Claberal and Maria (Medina) Artal; B.S., U. Cal. at Berkeley, 1944, postgrad., 1947-48; certificate Real Estate Inst. Cal. Real Estate Assn., grad. Realtors Inst.; m. Charles S. Karp, Apr. 2, 1947 (div. Oct. 1967); children—Richard, Robert, Maria. Tchr. pub. schs., Richmond, Cal., 1947-53; real estate broker William E. Doad Co., San Francisco, 1946, David Rockwell Assos., Concord, Cal., 1968, Mary Karp Real Estate Investments, 1969—. Instr. real estate investments Mt. Diablo Adult Coll., Concord, 1968-74, Los Medanos Community Coll., Antioch, Cal., 1974—. Vice pres. Concord Community Hosp., 1962, treas., 1963; vice chmn. Nat. Wildlife Found., Pleasant Hill, Cal., 1972—. Bd. dirs. Contra Costa County chpt. Am. Cancer Soc., 1956-60. Mem. Nat. Inst. Real Estate Brokers (certified comml. investment mem., v.p. No. Cal. chpt. 1, 1975), Nat. Assn. Real Estate Bds., Cal. Real Estate Assn. (faculty exchange div. 1971—, vice chmn. North indsl., comml. exchange div.), Contra Costa Bd. Realtors (edn. chmn., edn. chmn. women's council), Am. Assn. U. Women (treas. 1957, v.p. 1958), Cal. Assn. Health and Phys. Edn. (treas. 1952, pres. 1954). Home: 1166 Ridgewood Dr Concord CA 94518 Office: 3607 Clayton Rd Concord CA 94518

KARR, SHARON KAY STUDER (MRS. GERALD LEE KARR), psychologist; b. Beloit, Kan., Jan. 27, 1938; d. William V. and Fern Louise (Johnson) Studer; B.S. with honors, Kan. State U., 1959; M.S., So. Ill. U., 1962, Ph.D. (grad. fellow), 1970; m. Gerald Lee Karr, Oct. 18, 1959; children—Kevin Lee, Kelly Jolleen. Social work aide Topeka Kan. State Mental Hosp., summer, 1959; tchr. elementary sch., Freeburg, Ill., 1960, Crainville, Ill., 1960-61; researcher, Sierra Leone, West Africa, 1967-70; psychologist intern Urbana (Ill.) Sch. Dist. 116, 1971-72; psychologist Ohio Sch. Dist., Greenfield, 1972-73; psychologist, counselor Wilmington (O.) schs., 1973—; tchr. Wilmington Coll., 1973. Co-pres. P.T.A., King Sch., Urbana, 1971-72; pres. Van Zile Dorm, 1958-59; sec. Westminister Fellowship, 1957-58. Mem. Southwestern Ohio Sch. Psychologists Assn., Am. Psychol. Assn., Council for Exceptional Children, Ohio Tchrs. Assn., Nat. Edn. Assn., Phi Delta Kappa, Pi Lambda Theta, Phi Kappa Phi, Mortar Bd. Home: 337 Orchard Rd Wilmington OH 45177 Office: 576 W Main St Wilmington OH 45177

KARSEN, SONJA PETRA, educator; b. Berlin, Germany, Apr. 11, 1919; d. Fritz and Erna (Heidermann) Karsen; came to U.S., 1938; naturalized, 1945; Titulo de Bachiller, Colombia, 1937; student Nat. U., Bogota, Colombia, 1937-38; B.A., Carleton Coll., 1939; M.A. (scholar in French 1939-41), Bryn Mawr Coll., 1941; Ph.D., Columbia, 1950. Instr. Spanish, Lake Erie Coll., Painesville, O., 1943-45; instr. modern langs. U. P.R., 1945-46; instr Spanish, Syracuse U., 1947-50, Bklyn. Coll., 1950-51; asst. to dep. dir. gen. UNESCO, 1951-52, Latin Am. Desk, tech. asst. dept., 1952-53, mem. tech. assistance mission Costa Rica, 1954; asst. prof. Spanish, Sweet Briar Coll., 1955-57; asso. prof., chmn. dept. Romance langs., Skidmore Coll., Saratoga Springs, N.Y., 1957-61, prof. Spanish and chmn. dept. Romance langs., 1961-65, prof. Spanish, chmn. dept. modern langs. and lits., 1965—; Fulbright lectr. Free U. Berlin, 1968. Exchange student auspices Inst. Internat. Edn. at Carleton Coll., 1938-39. Decorated chevalier dans l'Ordre des Palmes Academiques, 1964; recipient Leadership award N.Y. State Assn. Fgn. Lang. Tchrs., 1973. Buenos Aires Conv. grantee for research in Colombia, S.A., 1946-47; faculty research grantee Skidmore Coll., summer 1959, 61, 63, 65, 67, 69, 70. Mem. Am. Assn. U. Profs., Modern Lang. Assn., Am. Assn. Tchrs. Spanish and Portuguese, Am. Assn. U. Women, Nat. Geog. Soc., Instituto Internacional De Literatura Iberoamericana, Asociacion Internacional De Hispanistas, UN Assn. of U.S.A. Club: Zonta. Author: Guillermo Valencia, Colombian Poet, 1951; Educational Development in Costa Rica with Unesco's Technical Assistance, 1951-54, 1954; Jaime Torres Bodet: A Poet in a Changing World, 1963; Selected Poems of Jaime Torres Bodet, 1964; Versos y prosas de Jaime Torres Bodet, 1966; Jaime Torres Bodet, 1971. Contbr. articles to profl. jours. Office: Skidmore Coll Saratoga Springs NY 12866

KARWOSKI, AGNES L. (MRS. ROBERT E. OLSEN), physician, surgeon; b. Chgo.; d. Albin and Anna (Tekeniewski) Karwoski; B.S.M., Loyola U., Chgo., 1937, M.D., 1939; m. Robert E. Olsen, Dec. 25, 1947; children—Rory R., Nancy C. Intern Oak Park (Ill.) Hosp., 1939-40; resident Columbia Hosp. for Women, 1940; practice medicine specializing in surgery, Washington, 1940-42; mem. staff St. Anthony Hosp. Mem. Am. Acad. Family Physicians, Am. Profl. Practice Assn., Assn. Am. Physicians and Surgeons, Ill. Catholic Women's Assn. Home: 6447 W Archer Av Chicago IL 60638 Office: 6447 West Archer Av Chicago IL 60638

KASHI, ALIZA, actress; b. Tel-Aviv, Israel, Apr. 5, 1940 (came to U.S. 1964); d. Ben and Sarah (Kaly) Kashi; ed. Ayanot Agr. Sch., Coll. of Jerusalem; m. Daniel H. Wolfe, Oct. 30, 1968 (div. Aug. 1973). Actress appearing in clubs, theatre, TV. Named Miss Ziegfield, 1968, Woman of Year, Variety Club, 1970; recipient award of merit United Cerebral Palsy, 1971, award of merit Anti-Defamation League, 1970. Served with Israeli Army, 1966-67. Office: 5 E 51st St New York City NY 10022

KASHIKI, ELAINE GAYLE, performing arts exec.; b. Yokohama, Japan, June 23, 1948; d. Akira and Misako (Takahaski) Kashiki; came to U.S., 1965; student U. Cal. at Los Angeles, 1966-69, Inner City Inst. for the Performing and Visual Arts, 1973—. Asst. to exec. dir. Inner City Cultural Center, Los Angeles, 1968—; instr. bus. skills Inner City Inst. for the Performing and Visual Arts, Los Angeles, 1972—, dir. Inner City Casting Service, 1972—, also personnel coordinator; actress East-West Players, 1966-71, Inner City Repertory Theatre Co., 1972—. Mem. minority adv. council KCOP-TV, Channel 13, 1973; bd. dirs. League of Los Angeles Theatres, 1973—. Office: 1308 S New Hampshire Av Los Angeles CA 90006

KASLOW, RUTH, veterinarian; b. Bklyn., June 26, 1914; d. Nathan and Bess (Berg) Kaslow; B.A., Bklyn. Coll., 1935; D.V.M., Kan. State U., 1947; m. Murray Zaret, June 20, 1948; children—Leona (Mrs. Leon Sherman), Joel. With med. lab. Trinity, Jewish hosps., Bklyn., 1935-43; veterinarian Jewish Hosp., 1947-67, Montefiore Hosp. and Med. Center, Bronx, N.Y., 1967—. Mem. Am., N.Y. State, N.Y.C. vet. med. assns., Phi Kappa Phi. Home: 3450 Wayne Av Bronx NY 10467 Office: 111 E 210th St Bronx NY 10467

KASMAR, JOYCE VIELHAUER (MRS. EDWARD GADDIS KASMAR), psychologist, educator; b. Oak Park, Ill., Nov. 26, 1935; d. Otto W. and Gladys (Carlson) Vielhauer; B.A., Northwestern U., 1958; M.A. (USPHS fellow), La. State U., 1962, Ph.D. (USPHS fellow), 1965; m. Edward Gaddis Kasmar, July 17, 1965; 1 dau., Anne Gaelyn. Asst. prof. dept. psychiatry Neuropsychiat. Inst., U. Cal. at Los Angeles, 1965-68; asst. prof. Western Conn. State Coll., Danbury, 1969-70; research asso. City U. N.Y. Grad. Center, 1970-71; postdoctoral scholar U. Cal. at Los Angeles, Sch. Architecture and Urban Planning, 1971-72. Publicity chmn. Friends of Brentwood Library, 1971-72. Mem. Am. Psychol. Assn., Environmental Design Research Assn., Am. Assn. U. Profs., Am. Assn. U. Women. Contbr. articles to profl. jours. Home: 503 S Westgate Av Los Angeles CA 90049

KASNIC, MAUREEN ROSE, librarian; b. Akron, O., Apr. 10, 1943; d. Nick James and Elizabeth Marie (Zupon) Kasnic; B.A., U. N.M., 1965; M.L.S., Ind. U., 1967. Grad. asst. Ind. U., 1966; young adult librarian Levittown (N.Y.) Pub. Library, 1967-68; br. librarian Denver Pub. Library, 1969-70, head young adult library, 1970—. Mem. McGraw-Hill cons. com. World Ency. Biography, 1968-69. Vol. Call for Action, Urban Coalition, 1969; sec. S.W. coordinating com. Denver Met. Council for Community Service, 1969-70; mem. Advocacy Children and Youth Colo. Coalition, 1973. Mem. Am. (social responsibilities roundtable), Colo. (roundtable co-chmn. 1971, chmn. Young Adult Services Roundtable 1973) library assns., Beta Phi Mu. Home: 1209 Elizabeth St Denver CO 80206 Office: Denver Public Library Denver CO 80204

KASPER, CAROL KATHERINE (MRS. HOWARD WINET), physician, educator; b. Long Beach, Cal., Apr. 22, 1936; d. Stephen Lawrence and Dorothy Geraldine (Saunders) Kasprzak; B.A., U. Chgo., 1954; M.D., U. Cal. at San Francisco, 1959; m. Howard Winet, Nov. 23, 1968; children—Evan and Heather (twins). Intern San Francisco Gen. Hosp., 1959-60; resident in internal medicine St. Mary's Hosp., San Francisco, 1960-62; resident in internal medicine Children's Hosp., San Francisco, 1960-62, fellow in hematology, 1962-65; staff hematologist City of Hope, Duarte, Cal., 1965-66; asst. prof. medicine U. So. Cal., Los Angeles, 1966—; hematologist Internat. Hemophilia Tng. Center, Orthopaedic Hosp., Los Angeles, 1966—, dir., 1968-69. Mem. med. adv. council World Fedn. for Hemophilia. Mem. Am. Soc. Hematology, Internat. Soc. for Thrombosis and Haemostasis. Contbr. articles to profl. jours. Office: 2400 S Flower St Los Angeles CA 90007

KASS, CAROLE MARIE (MRS. JOSEPH KASS), journalist; b. N.Y.C., Apr. 30, 1926; d. Leon and Helene Beatrice (Leopold) Gottlieb; student Mt. Holyoke Coll., 1943-45; m. Joseph Kass, Dec. 14, 1952; children—Nicholas Charles, Carrie Lee. With theatrical prodn. and publicity Jean Dalrymple, N.Y.C., 1947-49; TV prodn. asst. Kenyon & Eckhardt Advt., N.Y.C., 1949-51, NBC, N.Y.C., 1954-60; TV news reporter WWBT-TV, Richmond, Va., 1962-63; columnist, movie critic Richmond Times Dispatch, 1963—. Tchr. history motion pictures Va. Commonwealth U., 1970—. Bd. dirs. Richmond Pub. Forum, 1964-68. Mem. Nat., Va. press women, Sigma Delta Chi. Unitarian. Home: 1400 Chowan Rd Richmond VA 23229 Office: 333 E Grace St Richmond VA 23219

KASSELL, BEATRICE (MRS. HARRIS L. FRIEDMAN), educator; b. N.Y.C., Mar. 25, 1912; d. Daniel H. and Bertha (Jaret) Kassell; B.A., Barnard Coll., 1931; Ph.D., Columbia, 1938; m. Harris L. Friedman, Aug. 25, 1940; children—Neil, Marilyn (Mrs. Alan R. Hoffman). Research asst. Columbia U., N.Y.C., 1938-43; instr. Queens Coll., N.Y.C., 1944-45; research asso., Chem. Biol. Coordination Center, NRC, Washington, 1948-56; asso. biochemistry Marquette U. Sch. Medicine, Milw., 1956-64, asso. prof., 1965-71; prof. biochemistry Med. Coll. Wis., Milw., 1971—. Chmn. hospitality council Internat. Inst., Milw., 1958-59. Recipient award Milw. sect. Am. Chem. Soc., 1970. Research grantee USPHS, 1965—, NSF, 1967—, Patrick Cudahy Found., 1968-71, Herman Frasch Found., 1972—, Rockefeller Found., 1973—. Mem. Am. Soc. Biol. Chemists, Am. Chem. Soc., Biochem. Soc. Gt. Britain. Am. Women in Sci., Women's Equity Action League, Sigma Xi, Sigma Delta Epsilon. Contbr. articles to profl. jours. Home: 4043 N Larkin St Milwaukee WI 53211

KASTEN, ELIZABETH ANN, psychologist; b. Oak Park, Ill., July 2, 1918; d. Lloyd Anderson and Margaret Josephine (Prescott) Faxon; B.A., Drake U., Des Moines, 1961, M.A., 1967; m. Carl August Kasten, Oct. 12, 1940; children—Fritz, Katherine, Samuel. Psychometrist for psychologist Dr. Allan Frankle in pvt. practice, Des Moines, 1956-60; part-time clin. asst. psychiat. dept. Broadlawns Polk County Hosp., Des Moines, 1960-67, clin. psychologist, 1967—; cons. in field. Mem. exec. com. Polk County Alcoholism Service Center. Adv. bd. Pastoral Counseling Centers; bd. dirs. River Hills Day Care Center. Mem. Am., Ia., Central Ia. psychol. assns., Nat. Orgn. Women, Drake U. Faculty Wives, Alliance Francaise, Des Moines Symphony Guild. Club: Des Moines Racquet. Home: 405 49th St Des Moines IA 50312 Office: Broadlawns Polk County Hosp Hickman Rd Des Moines IA 50314

KATAJA, EVA IRENE, educator; b. N.Y.C., Sept. 28, 1936; d. Mauno and Aino (Wallin) K.; B.S., U. Rochester, 1957; M.S., U. Wis., 1960; Ph.D., Harvard U., 1966. Am. Cancer Soc. research fellow Mass. Inst. Tech., 1966-68; asst. prof. biology U. So. Cal., 1968—; ednl. adv. com. to Paul Bindrim, psychologist, 1972—. Recipient NSF Research grant, 1970-73. Mem. A.A.A.S., N.Y. Acad. Sci., Am. Soc. Microbiology, Assn. Humanistic Psychology. Home: 1208 Fernwood Pacific Dr Topanga CA 90290 Office: Student Health Center U So Cal Los Angeles CA 90007

KATCHER, PHYLLIS (MRS. MORRIS KATCHER), securities broker; b. Bklyn., June 13, 1929; d. Benny and Pauline (Darrow) Bakalchuck; grad. high sch.; m. Morris Katcher, Nov. 30, 1960; children—Hope Ilene, Marc Steven. With Crown Hill Realty Corp., Bklyn., 1961-71, v.p., 1965—; v.p. Katcher-Goldsmith Stable, Bklyn. and Monticello, N.Y., 1967-72; pres. Sparc Investment Group, N.Y.C., 1967—; registered rep. Mayflower Securities Co., Inc., N.Y.C., 1973—. Pres. elect Med. Students Aid Soc., Nat. Womans Aux., 1974—; pres. Bklyn. Alumni Club Woman's Aux., 1967-68; contbg. founder Hebrew U., Jerusalem, 1967—; mem. Am. Friends of the Hebrew U., 1967—, mem. Jr. League of Brookdale Hosp. Center, Bklyn., 1961—. Mem. Womans League for Israel, Physicians Wives League. Jewish religion. Home: 45 Parade Place Brooklyn NY 11226 Office: 1 State St Plaza New York NY 10004

KATES, SUSAN NINA PRENTKY, counseling psychologist; b. Providence, R.I., Sept. 19, 1944; d. Joseph and Henrietta (Meirowitz) Prentky; B.A. in Psychology, Russell Sage Coll., Troy, N.Y., 1965; M.A. in Personnel Techniques in Counseling, Columbia Tchrs. Coll., 1968; certificate sch. psychology, Seton Hall U., S. Orange, N.J., 1974; m. Steven Michael Kates, Nov. 4, 1970. Personnel officer Poly. Inst. Bklyn., 1967-69; adminstr., scorer and interpreter tests, counselor B'nai B'rith Career and Counseling Service, Union, N.J., 1969—; adj. instr. Union Coll., Cranford, N.J., 1973—; indsl. cons. Career Cons., Irvington, N.J., 1973—. Mem. Am. Psychol. Assn., Am. Personnel and Guidance Assn., N.J. Assn. Sch. Psychologists, Assn. Mentally Retarded, Camp Williams Assn. Underprivileged. Home: 22-24 Rosol Lane Saddle Brook NJ 07662 Office: 1767 Morris Av Union NJ 07083

KATKIN, LENORE SELF (MRS. BURTON KENNETH KATKIN), physician; b. Bronx, N.Y., Mar. 1, 1933; d. Lowell Harry and Estelle (Bloom) Self; B.A., Barnard Coll., 1954; M.D., State U. N.Y., 1958; m. Burton Kenneth Katkin, Dec. 26, 1954; children—Faith, Julie, Paula, Jonathan. Intern Bronx Municipal Hosp. Center, N.Y., 1958-59, resident 1959-61; practice medicine specializing in pediatrics, Bronx and N.Y.C., 1962—; Child Health fellow dept. pediatrics Albert Einstein Coll. Medicine, N.Y.C., 1961-62, instr., 1962-63, asso., 1963-65, asst. prof., 1965-73, asso. prof., 1973—; asst. dir. pediatric out patient dept. Bronx Municipal Hosp. Center, 1963-66, dir., 1966—, attending pediatrician, 1971—; v.p. med. bd., 1972, 73. Diplomate Am. Bd. Pediatrics. Fellow Am. Acad. Pediatrics; mem. Ambulatory Pediatric Assn. Home: 15 Deer Hill Lane Scarsdale NY 10583 Office: Bronx Municipal Hospital Center Bronx NY 10461

KATO, KAY, cartoonist, illustrator, columnist, lectr.; b. Budapest, Hungary, Dec. 11, 1926; d. Eugene and Irene (Nemet) Kato; student Pa. Acad. Fine Arts, Am. Acad. Dramatic Arts and Europe; m. George S. Szekely, June 2, 1945 (div. 1959); 1 dau., Jeanne Andrea. Contbr. to N.Y. Times, Newark Star Ledger, Sat. Eve. Post, N.Y. Herald Tribune (mag. covers), This Week, Nation's Bus., C.S. Monitor, Am. Weekly, Modern Baby, New York Times Mag. (illustrations), also others, 1943—; instr. Cambridge Center Adult Edn. Mass., 1944-47; guest cartoonist on TV, 1950—; cartoonist, painter 14th ann. White Mountains Festival of 7 Arts, 1963; cartoonist Am. Cyanamid Co., Nat. Assn. Home Economists Conv.; instr. South Orange and Maplewood Adult Sch., fall 1963; lectr.; illus. bookjacket The Television Radio Audience and Religion, 1955; one-man shows Boston Vose Galleries, Boston Pub. Library, 1945, N.J. Women's Clubs, others, 1955-57, Gallery of South Orange, Maplewood, 1962; exhibited Pa. Acad. Fine Arts, Am. Fine Arts Soc. Galleries, Montclair Art Mus., N.J. State Shows 1953, 56, Newark Pub. Library, 1957, 67, other N.J. Art shows, 1955—. Represented in Best Cartoons of the Year, 1943; mem. com. on war cartoons for O.W.I., 1944-45. Recipient 2d prize Am. Art Week, 1955, others. Mem. Essex Watercolor Club. Clubs: Overseas Press of Am. (chmn. graphic arts com., mem. bull. com.); Glen Ridge Women's. Illustrated talks, lectures women's and men's clubs, profl. socs., mag. article; also pictorial essay; cartoons in Pretty Witty, 1968. Address: 60 Chapman P Glen Ridge NJ 07028

KATSIGEANIS, AMALIA, surgeon; b. Calexico, Cal., Oct. 11, 1925; d. John and Mercedes (Lopez) Katsigeanis; A.B. in Zoology, U. So. Cal., 1946; M.D., Johns Hopkins, 1950. Intern Childrens Hosp., San Francisco, 1950-51; resident gen. surgery Bellevue Med. Center, N.Y. U., N.Y.C., 1951-55; practice medicine specializing in gen. surgery, Calexico, Cal., 1956—; chief staff Calexico Hosp., 1970—. Drug cons., Imperial County, Cal., 1971—. Founder, pres. We Help You, Calexico Community Drug Center, 1970—; mem. mental health adv. bd. Imperial County, Cal. Bd. dirs. Clinica de Salubridad de Campesinos, Brawley, Cal. Diplomate Am. Bd. Surgery. Mem. A.M.A., Cal. Med. Assn., Imperial County Med. Soc., Assn. for Advancement Med. Instrumentation, Instrument Soc. Am. Phi Beta Kappa, Phi Kappa Phi, Alpha Epsilon Delta. Home: 424 Washington St Calexico CA 92231 Office: 40 E 3rd St Calexico CA 92231

KATZ, DORIS BARRY (MRS. MORRIS KATZ), educator; b. Wrens, Ga., Dec. 20, 1920; d. Dixie Gerald and Rosa Lee (Farr) Barry; A.A., Middle Ga. Coll., 1939; postgrad. Ga. State Coll. for Women, 1940, 51-52, Bklyn. Coll., 1951, U. Va., 1956-60, 64-65, Coll. William and Mary, 1960-61; B.A., Am. U., 1963; postgrad. George Washington U., 1967-68, Madison Coll., Harrisonburg, Va., 1974—; m. Sidney Magelof, June 27, 1943 (div. 1963); children—Susan Gail (Mrs. Randolph Macon Gilbert), Barbara Ruth (Mrs. Lawrence Richard Parlee); m. 2d, Morris Katz, July 10, 1966; stepchildren—June Diane (Mrs. Paul Marvin Levine), Stephen Gary, Mark Allen, Lisa Beth. Elementary tchr. Reedy Creek Sch., Ocilla, Ga., 1939-41; tchr. Irwinville, Ga., 1941-42; telephone operator So. Bell Tel. and Tel. Co., Augusta, Ga., 1942-43; clk. Am. Tel. & Tel. Co., N.Y.C., 1943-44; tchr. Wrens (Ga.) High Sch., 1952-53; service rep. Chesapeake & Potomac Telephone Co., Falls Church and Arlington, Va., 1954-59; tchr. Tuckahoe Jr. High Sch., Richmond, Va., 1960-61; tchr. Fairfax (Va.) County Pub. Schs., 1961—, Herndon High Sch., 1972—. Tchr. word devel. Arlington County (Va.) Adult Edn. Program, 1962-66. Mem. Nat., Va. edn. assns., Fairfax County Ednl. Assn., Council for Exceptional Children. Jewish religion. Home: Route 2 Box 66A Stanley VA 22851 Office: Herndon High School Bennett St Herndon VA 22070

KATZ, ELLEN LOEB (MRS. MORT KATZ), hematologist, oncologist; b. Wuppertal-Elberfeld, Germany, Jan. 30, 1925; d. Julius and Dina (Meyer) Loeb; came to U.S., 1946, naturalized, 1952; student U. Amsterdam (Holland), 1945-46, So. Methodist U., 1946-47; M.D., Southwestern Med. Sch., U. Tex., 1952; m. Mort Katz, July 18, 1964. Intern VA Hosp., McKinney, Tex., 1952-53, resident, 1953-55; resident VA Hosp., Lisbon, Tex., 1955-56; practice medicine specializing in hematology and oncology, Wadley Insts. Molecular Medicine, 1956—; clin. hematologist, internist J.K. and Susie L. Wadley Research Inst., Dallas, 1956-69; clin. hematologist, oncologist Granville C. Morton Cancer and Research Hosp., Dallas, 1969—; asst. prof. clin. pathology Baylor U., Dallas, 1958-69. Mem. exec. com., med. adv. com. Greater Dallas chpt. Leukemia Soc. Am., mem. med. adv. com., 1969, patient service com. Leukemia Assn. N. Central Tex., 1970—; mem. Dallas Council World Affairs. 1968—. Recipient Americianism medal D.A.R., 1968. Mem. Am., Internat. socs. hematology, Am. Cancer Soc., Am., Tex., So., Dallas County med. assns., Dallas So. Clin. Soc., Am. Med. Women's Assn., Acad. Internal Medicine, Bus. and Profl. Women's Club (Dr. Minnie Maffett award 1966), Leukemia Assn. North Central Tex. (mem. com. med. adv. com. and patient service com. 1970—), Tex. Soc. Internal Medicine. Clubs: Dallas Ski, Internist (sec. 1963-64). Contbr. med. articles on hematology to profl. jours. Home: 4318 Briar Creek Dallas TX 75214 Office: 9000 Harry Hines Blvd Dallas TX 75235

KATZ, HILDA, artist; b. N.Y.C.; d. Max and Lena (Schwartz) Katz; student N.A.D. (New Sch. Social Research scholar), 1940-41. One-woman shows Bowdoin Coll. Art Mus., 1951, Cal. State Library, 1953, Print Club of Albany (N.Y.) Albany Inst., 1955, U. Me., 1955, 58, Jewish Mus. of N.Y., 1956, State Tchrs. Coll., Pa., 1956, Masillon (O.) Mus., 1957, Ball State Tchrs. Coll., 1957, Springfield Art Mus., 1957, U. Me., 1958, Miami Beach (Fla.) Art Center, 1958, Art Assn. Richmond (Ind.), 1959, Old State Capitol Mus. La., La. Art Commn., others; exhibited in group shows at Corcoran Bienniale Library Congress, Am. in the War (26 museums) Pa. Acad. Fine Arts, Soc. Am. Graphic Artists, Phila. Water Color Club, Audubon Artists, Print Club Albany, Albany Inst., Bklyn. Mus., Delgado Mus. Art-U.S.A., 1959, Jewish Mus., Boston Printmakers, Massillon Mus., Springfield Art Mus., N.A.D., Met. Mus. Art, Italian Fedn. Women in Art, Italy, Venice Biennial, Italy, Conn. Acad. Fine Arts, Congress for Jewish Culture, Cal. State Library, Bowdoin U., State Tchrs. Coll. Pa., Art Assn. Richmond, Boston, N.Y. pub. libraries, Miami Beach Art Center, Children's Mus., Hartford, Conn., Washington Printmakers, Miniature Painters, Engravers and Sculptors Soc., Peoria Art Center, Engrs. Club., Phila., La. Art Commn., also numerous others in U.S., Eng., France, Italy, Israel, S.Am., S.E. Asia, Middle East; represented in permanent collections Library of Congress, Balt. Mus. Art, Fogg Mus., Franklin D. Roosevelt Collection, Santa Barbara Art Mus., Colo. Springs Fine Arts Center, Soc. Am. Graphic Artists, U.S. Nat. Mus., Met. Mus. Art, Bezalel Nat. Mus., Jerusalem, Israel, Addison Gallery Am. Art, State Tchrs. Coll. Pa., Springfield (Mo.) Art Mus., Newark Pub. Library, N.Y. Pub. Library, Cal. State Library, Pa. State Library, U. Minn., Print Club Albany, Safed Mus., Bat Yam Museum (both Israel), Peoria (Ill.) Art Center, St. Margaret Mary Sch. Art, numerous others, including several colls. and univs.; pictures represented in spl. collections U.S. Nat. Mus., 1965, 72 U. Me., 1965, Library Congress, 1965, Met. Mus. Art, 1965, Nat. Gallery Art, 1965, Nat. Collection Fine Arts, 1966; Nat. Air and Space Mus., others. Recipient award graphic Nat. Assn. Women Artists, 1945, water color, 1947, Am. artists group prize Soc. Am. Graphic Artists, 1950; best painting in landscape Soc. Miniature Painters, Sculptors, Gravers, 1959, print award Peoria Art Center, 1960, Library of Congress Purchase Prizes; Purchase award Print Club of Albany, 1964, Peoria (Ill.) Art Center, 1964, U. Minn., Cal. State Library, Met. Mus. Art, State Tchrs. Coll. Pa., Art Assn. Richmond, N.Y. Pub. Library, Newark Pub. Library, St. Margaret Mary Sch. Art Coll., plaque of honor Hall Fame, 1966, also life mem.; life fellow Met. Mus.; named Dau. of Mark Twain. Mem. Nat. Assn. Women Artists, Soc. Washington Print-makers, Am. Color Print Soc., Audubon Artists, Soc. Am. Graphic Artists, Internat. Platform Assn., Hunterdon Art Center; Conn. Acad. Fine Arts, Phila. Watercolor Club, Boston Print-makers (award 1955), Hunterdon County Art Center, Print Club Albany, Print Council Am., Marquis Biog. Library Soc. (adv. mem.), Poetry Soc. Am. Author (under pen name Hulda Weber) poems included in numerous anthologies. Contbr. numerous poems and short stories to mags. Address: 915 West End Av Apt 5D New York City NY 10025

KATZ, JUDITH BARBARA KAPUSTIN (MRS. SOLOMON HERTZ KATZ), clin. psychologist; b. Phila., Apr. 22, 1939; d. David and Belle (Erfer) Kapustin; A.B., Temple U., 1960; M.A., U. Mich., 1961; Ed.D., U. Pa., 1974; m. Solomon Hertz Katz, June 21, 1964; children—Noah, Rachael. Research assistant engineering psychology laboratory University Michigan, Ann Arbor, 1960-61; clin. psychologist Norristown State Hosp., 1961-67; psychol. counselor Haverford (Pa.) Coll., 1965-70; dir. career counseling Swarthmore Coll., 1970—; counselor Westtown Sch., 1967-68; psychol. cons. and testing by referral. Mem. Am., Pa. psychol. assns., Nat. Assn. Women Deans, Adminstrs. and Counselors, Pa. Assn. Women Deans and Counselors, Mid-Atlantic Placement Assn. Psi Chi. Contbr. articles in field to profl. jours. Home: 519 N Wynnewood Av Narberth PA 19072 Office: Swarthmore Coll Swarthmore PA 19081

KATZ, LEE, research adminstr.; b. Bklyn., June 24, 1930; d. Mendle and Anna (Pearlman) Pankler; B.A. cum laude, U. Ill., 1951; M.S., Syracuse (N.Y.) U., 1961; Ph.D., U. Mich., 1973; m. Harold William Katz, Sept. 27, 1947; children—Rhonda, Stuart. Planning asso. edn. Syracuse Mayor's Commn. for Youth, 1963-65; program adminstr. pub. affairs Syracuse U., 1965; staff asst. to exploratory com. assessment ednl. progress U.S. Carnegie Corp., 1965-66; cons. Mich. State Office Econ. Opportunity, 1966-67; spl. cons., vis. lectr. Eastern Mich. U., Ypsilanti, 1965-67, acting dir. spl. projects and research devel., 1967-68, dir. spl. projects and research devel., 1968—, participant workshops and seminars; cons. in field. Mem. planning com., chmn. county-wide planning United Fund Ann Arbor, mem. budget com.; adv. com. Bd. Edn., also mem. Human Relations subcom.; chmn. Ann Arbor Symphony Ball.; mem. Mich. State Council Crime and Delinquency; mem. Coop. Area Manpower Program Washtenaw and Monre Counties, Mich.; mem. adv. com. evaluations fed. projects Ann Arbor Sch. System; mem. exec. com. Mich. State Council Humanities. Chmn. Washtenaw County Bd. Suprs., mem. ad hoc com. transition, mem. justice and planning bd., corrections subcom. Bd. dirs., chmn. nominating com. Ann Arbor Family Service; bd. dirs. Washtenaw County Office Econ. Opportunity; v.p. bd. dirs. Washtenaw County Child and Family Service Bd.; v.p. bd. dirs. St. Joseph's Mercy Hosp., Ann Arbor, chmn. community relations com. Travel grantee to USSR; recipient Pub. Service certificate Ann Arbor United Fund. Mem. Nat. Council Research Adminstrs. (chmn. commn. goals 1973, chairperson midwest region IV 1974), Zonta, Alpha Kappa Delta, Pi Lambda Theta, Psi Chi. Contbr. articles to profl. jours. Home: 1050 Wall St Ann Arbor MI 48104 Office: Eastern Mich U Ypsilanti MI 48197

KATZ, MOLLY SIMON, advt. co. exec.; b. N.Y.C., Jan. 12, 1943; d. Hubert Klein and Betty Pauline (Chuckrow) Simon; student, Boston U., 1961-63; m. Peter Joel Katz, Dec. 8, 1963 (div. 1974); children—Christopher Reuel and Terry Daniel (twins). Copywriter, WMEX Radio, Boston, 1963; editor Western New Eng. edit. TV Guide, Boston, 1963-65; asst. tech. assignments coordinator WOR-AM-FM-TV, N.Y.C., 1965-68; with H.K. Simon Co., Hastings-on-Hudson, N.Y., 1968—, exec. creative dir., 1970—. Press rep. Westchester Women for Peace, 1970—. Home: 300 Broadway Dobbs Ferry NY 10522 Office: Box 236 Hastings-on-Hudson NY 10706

KATZ, PHYLLIS ALBERTS (MRS. ARON B. KATZ), psychologist; b. N.Y.C., Apr. 9, 1938; d. Martin and Alice (Weiner) Alberts; A.B. summa cum laude, Syracuse U., 1957; Ph.D., Yale, 1961; m. Aron B. Katz, Mar. 25, 1961; children—Martin Jonathan, Margaret Elizabeth. Sr. research asso. N.Y. Med. Coll., 1961-62; asst. prof. N.Y.U., 1963-67, asso. prof., 1967-69; asso. prof. City U.N.Y., 1969-72, prof., 1972—, program head ednl. psychology, 1972—. Nat. Inst. Child Health and Human Devel. grantee, 1966-68, 68-72; Office Child Devel. grantee Dept. Health, Edn. and Welfare, 1972—, also cons. Mem. Am., Eastern psychol. assns., Soc. Research Child Devel., Am. Assn. U. Profs. Contbr. articles to profl. jours. Home: 815 Park Av New York City NY 10021 Office: 33 W 42d St New York City NY 10036

KATZ, VIRGINIA GABRIEL TEARE (MRS. ALBERT MICHAEL KATZ), educator; b. Cleve., Sept. 7, 1938; d. Wallace Gleed and Dorothy Gabriel (Schaefer) Teare; B.A., Wellesley Coll., 1960; M.A., Case Western Res. U., 1966, U. Mich., 1965; postgrad. Kent State U., 1972-73; m. Albert Michael Katz, Sept. 2, 1962; children—Rachel Susannah, Rebecca Meriam. Tchr., Columbia High Sch., Columbia Station, O., 1961-62, Wilson High Sch., St. Johns, Mich., 1962-63, Alma (Mich.) High Sch., 1963-65, Ypsilanti (Mich.) High Sch., 1965-66; instr. U. Minn., Duluth, 1966-70, asst. prof., 1970—; grad. asst., dept. secondary edn. Kent State U., 1972-73. Costume designer Alma (Mich.) Coll., 1963-65; guest costume designer U. Wis., Superior, 1967, 70, guest choreographer, 1968. County chmn. Citizens for Johnson-Humphrey, St. Louis County, Mich., 1964. Mem. Speech Communication Assn., Am., Wis. theater assns., Speech Assn. Minn., Am. Assn. U. Profs., Assn. for Supervision and Curriculum Devel. Home: 2105 Harvard St Duluth MN 55803

KATZEL, JEANINE ALMA, journalist; b. Chgo., Feb. 20, 1948; d. LeRoy Paul and Lia Mary (Arcuri) Katzel; B.A. in Journalism, U. Wis., 1970; M.S. in Journalism, Northwestern U., 1974. Publs. editor U. Wis. Sea Grant Program, Madison, 1969-72; editor research div. agrl. sch. U. Wis., Madison, 1972; research editor Prism mag. Am. Med. Assn., Chgo., 1972-73; free lance writer, 1974—. Recipient Elsie Bullard Morrison prize in Journalism, U. Wis., 1969. Mem. Women in Communications, Phi Kappa Phi. Home: 2453 N Oak Park Av Chicago IL 60635

KATZEN, LILA PELL (MRS. PHILIP KATZEN), sculptor; b. Bklyn.; d. Harry and Rose (Schultz) Pell; student Art Students League, 1946, Cooper Union Coll., 1950, Hans Hofmann Sch., 1952-53; m. Philip Katzen, June 6, 1948; children—Denize (Mrs. Milton Schwartz), Hal Zachary. Instr. Md. Inst. Coll. Art, Balt., 1962—; works exhibited Sao Paulo Bienniale, 1970; permanent exhibits include Max Hutchinson Gallery, N.Y.C., 1970—, Jacobs' Ladder Gallery, Washington, 1972—. Lectr., Balt. Mus., Kalamazoo Art Center, Archtl. League, N.Y.C., Cento Venezolano, Caracas, Santa Barbara (Cal.) Mus., Mass. Inst. Tech., Coll. Art Conf., N.Y.C., Art Students League, State U. N.Y. at Purchase, U. Mich., Cranbrook Acad. Tiffany Found. fellow, 1964; Archtl. League N.Y. grantee, 1968; Nat. Endowment grantee, 1973. Mem. Archtl. League N.Y., Coll. Art Assn., Am. Assn. U. Profs. Sculpted: Light-Floors, Archtl. League, N.Y.C., 1968; Universe As Environment, N.Y. U. and State U. N.Y. at Stonybrook, 1969; Laterna Magika Facade, Expo 70, Osaka, Japan, 1970; Liquid Tunnel, Sao Paulo Exhibit, 1970; Slipedge-Bis, Storm King Art Center, Mountainville, N.Y., 1972; Traho II, World Trade Center, N.Y.C., 1973. Office: 345 W Broadway St New York City NY 10013

KATZENTINE, UCOLA COLLIER (MRS. ARTHUR FRANK KATZENTINE), radio sta. exec.; b. Tonkawa, Okla., Aug 2, 1905; d. Clyde and Lula (Wills) Collier; student Central Mo. State Coll., 1923-25; m. Arthur Frank Katzentine, June 11, 1928 (dec. Mar. 1960). Vice pres. in charge women's programs sta. WKAT, Miami Beach, Fla., 1937-42, v.p., mng. dir., 1942-46, pres., 1960—. Mem. Sigma Sigma Sigma. Roman Catholic. Clubs: Surf, Miami Beach; Army and Navy (Washington). Home: 4745 Pine Tree Dr Miami Beach FL 33140 Office: 1759 Bay Rd Miami Beach FL 33139

KATZOWITZ, COLLEEN MAY, ednl. adminstr.; b. Wenatchee, Wash., Aug. 16, 1939; d. Kenneth Nicholas and Sara (Austin) Carmody; B.A., Vassar Coll., 1961; m. Saul Katzowitz, Nov. 11, 1962; children—Deborah, Andrea. Membership sec. Am. Civil Liberties Union, N.Y.C., 1961-64; asst. dir. financial aid Vassar Coll., 1967-68; dir. student services San Francisco Conservatory of Music, 1969—. Mem. Western Assn. Student Financial Aid Adminstrs., Nat. Assn. Coll. Admissions Counselors. Home: 333 Caselli St San Francisco CA 94114 Office: 1201 Ortega St San Francisco CA 94116

KAUDER, LOIS NASH (MRS. WARREN G. KAUDER), lawyer; b. Newark, May 18, 1924; d. Herman S. and Lillie (Newmann) Nash; B.A., Smith Coll., 1944; M.A., Columbia, 1946, Ph.D., 1950; J.D., Rutgers U., 1972; m. Warren G. Kauder, Sept. 10, 1949 (dec. Jan. 1971). Instr. chemistry Rutgers U., Newark, 1951-54, research asso., 1960-67; research asst. chemistry Columbia U., N.Y.C., 1954-60; vis. asst. prof. chemistry Rutgers U., 1963; admitted to N.J. bar, 1972; legal analyst City of Newark, 1973—. Mem. Am. Chem. Soc., Am. Bar Assn., Phi Beta Kappa, Sigma Xi. Contbr. articles to various jours. Home: 320 S Harrison St East Orange NJ 07018 Office: City Hall Newark NJ 07012

KAUDERS, SYLVIA WOLINSKY (MRS. RANDLE MORGAN KAUDERS), city ofcl.; b. Phila.; d. Morris and Sadie (Pincus) Wolinsky; A.B., U. Pa., 1942; m. Randle Morgan Kauders, Jan. 24, 1954. Asst. to dir. pub. relations Jewish Community Relations Council and Phila. Fellowship Commn., 1944-50; pub. information officer Commn. on Human Relations, Phila., 1950-55; pub. information officer City Reps. Office, Phila., 1955-57, spl. events coordinator, 1957-66, spl. events dir., 1966—, asst. exec. dir. Phila. area council tourism, 1968—. Producer, moderator Under Billy Penn's Hat sta. WHYY-TV; free-lance writer, fashion coordinator, commentator, radio, TV, stage actress, tchr., pub. relations cons. Mem. tourist com. Phila. Conv. and Tourist Bur., 1967—; mem. Phila. Com. Met. Opera, 1967—; Vol. Week Com., 1964—, Easter Promenade Com., 1963—, U. Pa. Com. Continuing Edn. for Women, 1967—; chmn. Vol. Week, Council Vols. Health and Welfare Council United Fund, 1965—. Bd. dirs. Phila. Area Council on Tourism, Council on Vols., Singing City, Chinese Cultural Center, Friends Civic Center, Women's Bicentennial Adv. Council. Recipient Freedoms Found. George Washington Medal award, 1960; Armed Forces Week award, 1963; citation USAF, 1966; Jr. C. of C. citation, 1963; Lit Bros. Good Neighbors award, 1963; Woman of Year Temple Israel, 1967. Mem. Phila. Pub. Relations Assn. (pres.), Phila. Fashion Group (sec.), Phila. Drama Guild, Women in Communications (pres. 1970, nat. conv. chmn. 1974). Home: 1901 Kennedy Blvd Philadelphia PA 19103 Office: Municipal Services Bldg Philadelphia PA 19107

KAUFFMAN, TREVA ERDINE, home economist; b. Osborne, O., Sept. 23, 1889; d. Theodore and Anna Laura (Hershey) Kauffman; B.S., Ohio State U., 1911; M.A., Columbia, 1931; postgrad U. Chgo., 1916. Tchr. Hamilton (O.) pub. schs., 1911, 13; instr. Ohio State U. Extension Service, 1913-15, asst. prof. home econs., 1917-20; organizer of sch. lunch program in rural and centralized schs. of Ohio, 1915-16; state leader 4-H Girls Clubs, 1916-17; state supr. home econs. edn., Ohio, 1918-20, N.Y. State Edn. Dept., 1920-59; coordinator grad. program Russel Sage Coll., evening div., 1960; now cons. home econs. edn.; acting chief Bur. Home Econs. Edn., 1944-47; sometime mem. faculties Syracuse U., Cornell U., Columbia, N.Y. U. and others. Mem. White House Conf. on Child Health and Protection, 1930, President's Conf. on Home Bldg. and Ownership, Washington, 1931; mem. nat. com. Household Employment, N.Y., 1933-35; dir., organizer N.Y. Fed. and State Temporary Emergency Relief Adminstrn. Adult Program Homemaking Edn., 1932-35; mem. adv. bd. Forecast mag., 1936-63, vis. lectr. Syracuse U., 1960; also lectr. and adviser on home econs. edn. Am. Women's Vol. Services, N.Y.C., 1941; mem. N.Y. State Coll. Home Econ. Council of Cornell U., 1944-47; asso. in edn. State U. N.Y., 1947-59; mem. food and nutrition com. Albany County chpt. A.R.C.; mem. Citzens Planning Com. Greater Albany, Inc.; mem. N.Y. State Women's Legislative Forum; asso. mem., mem. edn. and woman's coms. Saratoga Performing Arts Center. Hon. mem. N.Y. State Assn. Future Homemaker Am., 1944—, N.Y. State Nutrition Council, 1974—; patron Albany Symphony Orch., Capitol Hill Choral Soc.; charter mem. N.Y. Council Nutrition. Recipient citation for service N.Y. State Vocational Edn. Assn., citation 25 years service A.R.C., Civic citation Knickerbocker News, Albany, 1972. Mem. N.E.A., World Assn. for Adult Edn., Am. Home Econs. Assn. (life, certificate of recognition 1972), Am., N.Y. State (exec. sec.) sch. food service assns. Am. Assn. UN, Albany Inst. History and Art, Nature Conservancy, Ohio State U. Assn. (life), Nat. Trust for Historic Preservation, Center Square Assn., Lake Placid Club Edn. Found., N.Y. State Home Econs. Assn. (state chmn. legislative com. 1943-54, historian 1956-60, Eastern dist. chmn. legislation 1969-74), Am. Assn. Sch. Adminstrs., Nat. Council on Family Relations, Nat. Fedn. Bus. and Profl. Women, World Affairs Council, Acad. Polit. Sci., Nat. Geog. Soc., Albany County Hist. Assn., Internat. Fedn. Home Econs., Save Redwoods League, N.Y. State Legislative Forum, Columbia Alumni Assn., many other nat. state, local and related assns., Phi Upsilon Omicron, Kappa Delta Pi. Republican. Clubs: Nat. Travel (N.Y.C.); Woman's City (dir., vice chmn. civic affairs), Civic Music Assn., Mendelssohn, Monday Musical, Albany Girls' (Albany). Author: Teaching Problems in Home Economics, 1930; Young Folks at Home, 1948, 53; The Development and History of Home Economics in New York State, 1959; also textbooks and numerous articles and bulletins. Home: Knickerbocker Apts 175 Jay St Albany NY 12210 also 50 N Grand Av Fairborn OH 45324 Office: 175 Jay St Albany NY 12210

KAUFMAN, BEL, author, educator; b. Berlin, Germany; d. Michael J. and Lala (Rabinowitz) Kaufman; B.A. magna cum laude, Hunter Coll.; M.A. with highest honors, Columbia; LL.D., Nasson Coll., Me.; div.; children—Jonathan Goldstine, Thea Goldstine. Tchr. English, N.Y.C. high schs., also New Sch. Social Research; now asst. prof. English, Borough of Manhattan Community Coll.; lectr. throughout country, also appearances on TV and radio. Recipient plaque Anti-Defamation League; award and plaque United Jewish Appeal; named Woman of Yr., Women's League for Histadrut Scholarships; Paperback of Year award, Box Office Blue Ribbon award, Nat. Sch. Bell award. Mem. Author's Guild, Dramatists Guild, P.E.N. (exec. bd.), A.F.T.R.A., Internat. Platform Assn., English Grad. Union of Columbia, Phi Beta Kappa. Author: Up the Down Staircase, 1965; also short stories, mag. articles, TV play, translations of Russian, lyrics for musicals. Address: 1020 Park Av New York City NY 10028

KAUFMAN, EDNA RAMSEYER (MRS. EDMUND G. KAUFMAN), coll. dean; b. Smithville, O., Jan. 18, 1910; d. Alvin Conrad and Mary Ellen (Schrock) Ramseyer; A.B., Bluffton Coll., 1932; postgrad. Kent U., summer, 1932, U. Wis., summer 1936, U. Cal., summer 1937; A.M., Ohio State U., 1938, Ph.D., 1956; m. Edmund G. Kaufman, June 10, 1965; stepchildren—Gordon D., Karolyn K. (Mrs. Homer Zerger). Tchr. home econs. High Sch., Trenton, O., 1932-35; prof. home econs., dean women, Bluffton Coll. O., 1935-65; home sci. adviser Punjab Agrl. U., Ludhiana, India, 1965-67; prof. home econs., dean of women Bethel Coll., North Newton, Kan., 1967—; children refugee work, Marsailles, France, 1940. Recipient Spl. Diamond Anniversary Recognition award, Ohio State U., 1971; Outstanding Alumni award Bluffton Coll., 1971. Mem. Am. Assn. U. Women, Am. Home Econs. Assn., Womens Internat. League for Peace and Freedom, Dean of Women's Assn., Delta Kappa Gamma. Home: 211 E 25th St North Newton KS 67117

KAUFMAN, ELIZABETH SLOANE, educator; b. White Plains, N.Y., Feb. 3, 1925; d. Josiah A. and Anna (Sloane) Zoller; R.N., B.A., Stanford, 1947; P.H.N., U. Cal. Grad. Sch. Nursing, 1959, M.S., 1960; m. Peter H. Kaufman, July 22, 1950; children—Catherine Elizabeth, Robert Drew. Instr. U. Cal. at Los Angeles Sch. Nursing, 1961-63; prof. nursing Cal. State U. at Long Beach, 1963—; cons. Fairview State Hosp. Mem. adv. bd. Harbor Area Retardation Regional Center. Nat. Inst. Mental Health grantee, 1969—. Mem. Am. Nurses Assn., Nat. League for Nursing, Orthopsychiat. Assn. Home: 3441 Don Porfirio Dr Carlsbad CA 92008 Office: 6101 E 7th St Long Beach CA 90804

KAUFMAN, EVALYN DARROW (MRS. JOSEPH KAUFMAN), editor, writer; b. Jackson, Mich., Feb. 9, 1919; d. Maurice Edward and Lulu Eunice (Benham) Darrow; student N.Y. U., 1950-52, French Inst., 1961-65; m. Joseph Kaufman, Feb. 23, 1957. Editor, Mother's-to-Be and Infant Care, Dell Pub. Co., N.Y.C., 1962-63, sr. editor Hair Do Mag., 1965-66; editor Figure Beauty, Pyramid Pub. Co., N.Y.C., 1963-64; writer, editor Redbook Mag., N.Y.C., 1966—. Mem. French Inst. of N.Y.C., Mus. Modern Art of N.Y.C. Author: Figure Beauty, 1965; Top Secrets of Figure Beauty, rev. edit., 1967. Home: 18 W 70th St New York City NY 10023 Office: 230 Park Av New York City NY 10017

KAUFMAN, JANE A., artist; b. N.Y.C., May 26, 1938; d. Herbert and Roslyn (Lesser) Kaufman; student Cornell U., 1956-58; B.A., N.Y. U., 1960; M.A., Hunter Coll., 1965. One-man shows A.M. Sachs Gallery, N.Y.C., 1968, 70, Whitney Mus. Am. Art, N.Y.C., 1971, Paley & Lowe Gallery, N.Y.C., 1972, Henri Gallery, Washington, D.C., 1973; exhibited in group shows at Westerly Gallery, N.Y.C., 1966, Westmoreland County Mus., Greensburg, Pa., 1966, 69, Dallas Mus. Fine Arts, 1969, A.M. Sachs Gallery, 1969, Aldrich Mus., Ridgefield, Conn., 1970, Visual Arts Gallery, N.Y.C., 1970, Columbus (O.) Gallery Fine Arts, 1971, Whitney Mus. Am. Art, 1971, 73, Brouwersgracht 225, Amsterdam, The Netherlands, 1971, Paley & Lowe Gallery, 1971, Harcus Krakow Gallery, Boston, 1972, Corcoran Gallery Art, Washington, 1972, 73, Cin. Inst. Fine Arts, 1973; represented in permanent collections Whitney Mus. Am. Art, Aldrich Mus., Wooster (Mass.) Mus. Fine Arts, also pvt. collections. Tchr. fine arts N.Y.C. Pub. High Schs., 1960-69; instr. fine arts Lehman Coll., Bronx, N.Y., 1969-70, Bard Coll., Annandale-on-Hudson, N.Y., 1971-73, Bklyn. Mus. Art Sch., 1972-73; lectr. Queens (N.Y.) Coll., 1973—. Address: 262 Bowery St New York City NY 10012

KAUFMAN, JANICE NORTON (MRS. I. CHARLES KAUFMAN), physician; b. Denver, June 22, 1923; d. James Theodore and Esther (Collins) Norton; B.A., U. Utah, 1948, M.D., 1951; m. I. Charles Kaufman, May, 1972. Intern Strong Meml. Hosp., Rochester, N.Y., 1951-52, resident, 1952-55; instr. dept. psychiatry U. Colo. Med. Center, 1955-56, asst. prof., 1956-63, prof., 1963—; tng. and supervising analyst Chi Inst. Psychoanalysis, 1966; dir. Denver Inst. Psychoanalysis, 1969-72. USPHS Career Teaching fellow, 1956-58. Fellow Royal Soc. Medicine, Am. Psychiat. Assn; mem. Am. Psychoanalytic Assn., Alpha Omega Alpha. Home: 180A S Monaco Pkwy Denver CO 80222 Office: 4200 E 9th Av Denver CO 80220

KAUFMAN, JOANNE PAULA KLEIN (MRS. JAMES S. KAUFMAN), business exec.; b. Cleve.; d. Joseph E. and Martha (Ulmer) Klein; A.B. with honors, Western Res. U., 1958, M.A., 1963; m. Dr. James S. Kaufman, 1946; children—Martha Jo, Peter T., Thomas H. Pres., Urban Reports Corp., Cleve., 1966—. Manpower program analyst Anti-Poverty Programs of U.S. Govt., 1969; cons. manpower tng. and edn. U.S. Dept. Commerce, Econ. Devel. Adminstrn., 1967-68; cons. Cleve. Dept. Community Devel., 1966, Office of Econ. Opportunity, 1969—, Cleve. Commn. Higher Edn., 1972-73; cons., project dir. Office Edn. Dept. Health, Edn. and Welfare, 1973—. Mem. Heights Citizens for Human Rights; pres. Vital Information and Edn. for Women, 1972—. Mem. Nat. (convenor Cuyahoga chpt. 1971), Cuyahoga (co-chmn. steering com. 1972) women's polit. caucuses. Editor: Work and the Nature of Man (Frederick Herzberg), 1964. Home: 2676 E Overlook Rd Cleveland Heights OH 44106 Office: Lincoln Bldg Cleveland OH 44114

KAUFMAN, MARJORIE RUTH, educator; b. Milw., May 24, 1922; d. Nathan and Helen (Greenberg) Kaufman; student U. Wis., 1939-41; B.S., Wis. State Coll., Milw., 1944; M.A., U. Wash., 1947; Ph.D., U. Minn., 1954. Tchr. Wausau (Wis.) Sr. High Sch., 1944-46; teaching asst. U. Wash., 1946-47; instr. U. Minn., 1947-54; instr. Mt. Holyoke Coll., South Hadley, Mass., 1954-56, asst. prof., 1956-62, asso. prof., 1962-69, prof., 1969—, chmn. freshman English, 1965-68, fellow faculties grants com., 1968—. Lectr. grad. faculty U. Minn., 1964. Mem. exec. council Am. Civil Liberties Union Western Mass., 1955-61, sec. to bd., 1966—. Sec. to bd. Ind. Citizens for Stevenson, Minn., 1951-54. Gladys Murphy Graham fellow Am. Assn. U. Women, 1961-62, fellow in Japanese studies Four-Coll. Asian-African studies, 1964-65. Mem. Am. Assn. U. Profs. (past chpt. pres.), Modern Lang. Assn., Am. Studies Assn., Nat., Mass. Audubon socs. Author: Henry James's Comic Discipline, 1954. Editorial bd. Mass. Rev., 1959-65. Home: 51 Collegeview Heights South Hadley MA 01075

KAUFMAN, MAVIS ANDERSON, physician; b. Yonkers, N.Y., July 14, 1919; d. Percy S. and Betty (Kapferer) Kaufman; A.B., Radcliffe Coll., 1941; M.D., N.Y. Med. Coll., 1944. Intern, Flower-Fifth Av., Hosp., 1944; residencies in pathology N.Y. postgrad and Bronx VA Hosps., resident in psychiatry, Kings County Hosp. Bklyn., 1945-53; instr. neuropathology Coll. Phys. & Surgs., Columbia, 1953-56, asst. prof., 1956-69, asso. prof., 1969—; asso. research scientist N.Y. State Psychiat. Inst., 1956—. Diplomate in neuropathology Am. Bd. Pathology. Mem. Met. Mus. Art, Am. Assn. Neuropathologists, Am. Acad. Neurology (asso.), N.Y. Acad. Scis. Clubs: Radcliffe, N.Y. Physicians Art. Mem. adv. bd. Jour. Neuropathology and Exptl. Neurology, 1971—. Home: Tower 2 100 Haven Av New York City NY 10032 also Layton NJ Office: 722 W 168th St New York City NY 10032

KAUFMAN, ROSAMOND ARLEEN VAN POZNAK (MRS. WILLIAM I. KAUFMAN), travel exec., author, editor; b. Newark, July 23, 1923; d. Ira and Esther (Tepper) Van Poznak; B.A. magna cum laude, Upsala Coll. 1945; m. William I. Kaufman, Dec. 15, 1946; children—Iva Anne, Lazarus Seley. Singer, actress under name of Rosamond Vance, 1941-54; author, star Van and the Genie TV show, 1947-48; indexer Wonderful World of Cooking, Dell Pub. Co., N.Y.C., 1964-65; v.p. Food Photographers, Inc., N.Y.C., 1967—; exec. v.p., creative marketing dir. TC Internat. Inc.; dir. Simmons Student Holidays div. Strauss-Simmons-Sullivan, Inc. Dir. pub. information Chateaux Hotels of France; dir. creative marketing Travel Concepts Internat., St. Thomas, V.I. Substitute tchr. Hillside (N.J.) schs., 1947-48; interpreter Simmons Tours, 1967—; exec. sec. Edn. and Acquisition Fund, Jewish Mus., 1961-65. Parents bd. dirs. Park Av. Synagogue, N.Y.C., 1964—, chmn. Book Fair, 1966-67. Mem. Vols. of Shelter, Alliance Francaise, Met. Opera Guild, Lambda Sigma Alpha. Author: Checklist for Expectant Mothers, 1964; Free for Women, 1967; (with Sybil Leek) Astrological Guide to Sex and Love. Editor: Art of Creole Cooking (William I. Kaufman), Chocolate Cookbook (William I. Kaufman); Hot Dog Cookbook; Apple Cookbook and numerous others, 1949-67. Researcher and translator Cooking In a Castle, 1964; The Champagne Cookbook, 1969; Guide to French Hotels of Character. Home: 1361 Madison AV New York City NY 10028

KAUFMAN, YVONNE HECHLER (MRS. HARRY FOSTER KAUFMAN), broadcasting co. exec.; b. New Centerville, Pa., Sept. 15, 1918; d. Harry J. and Lucretia S. (Sechler) Hechler; student Ind. State Coll., 1939-40; m. Harry Foster Kaufman, Dec. 31, 1940; children—Lucretia Joan, Donna Lynne. Continuity writer WVSC radio, Somerset, Pa., 1953-74; broadcaster PGM Club News and Such, 1966—, program dir., 1969—, continuity dir. 1953—, pub. service and pub. relations dir., 1969—. Bd. dirs. Somerset County Cancer Soc., 1973—. Mem. Somerset Music Club, Soroptimist (pres. 1968-69, 71-72, v.p. 1965-68, rec. sec. 1957-60, dir. 1968-74). Methodist (trustee). Republican. Home: 134 Missoura St Somerset PA 15501 Office: Box 231 Somerset PA 15501

KAUFMANN, ELSA RAICHELSON (MRS. MALCOLM ALBERT KAUFMANN), lawyer; b. Springfield, Mass., Jan. 21, 1931; d. Israel Lawrence and Bessie (Robinson) Raichelson; B.A., Wellesley Coll., 1952; J.D. with honors, George Washington U., 1965; m. Malcolm Albert Kaufmann, Jan. 3, 1954; children—Lisa Lynn, Carol Beth. Admitted to Md. bar, 1966, D.C. bar, 1967; atty. appellate div. NLRB, Washington, 1966-67; asso. Pasternak and Kaufmann, Washington, 1967; partner Schwartz, Pasternak, Kaufmann, Kaufmann & Glosser, Washington, 1968—. Mem. D.C. Women's Commn. for Crime Prevention, 1973-74. Mem. Md. (mem. spl. com. to study lowering age of majority from 21 to 18), Montgomery County bar assns., Women's Bar Assn. D.C. (pres. 1973-74), Bar Assn. D.C., Nat. Assn. Women Lawyers, D.C. Fedn. Bus. and Profl. Women's Clubs (pres. Chevy Chase 1974-75), Kappa Beta Pi. Club: Zonta (Washington). Home: 7600 Winterberry Place Bethesda MD 20034 Office: 4400 Jenifer St NW Washington DC 20015

KAULILI, ALVINA NYE (MRS. LORD OLINOIKALANI KAULILI), ednl. adminstr., educator; b. Honolulu, Oct. 20, 1918; d. Henry Atkinson and Pearl Judith (Kekumano) Nye; Mus.B. in Mus. Edn., New Eng. Conservatory Music, 1942; M.A. in Music and Music Edn., Columbia, 1958; m. Lord Olinoikalani Kaulili, Apr. 21, 1947. Tchr. music Olaa (Hawaii) Intermediate Sch., 1942-43, Hilo Intermediate sch., 1943-44, Waialua High Sch., 1944-45, Farrington High Sch., 1945-50, Stevenson Intermediate Sch., 1950-51; chmn. music dept. Kaimuki High Sch., Honolulu, 1951-57, McKinley High Sch., Honolulu, 1958—. Dir. Honolulu Police choral group, various musicals for Honolulu Community Theatre. Sec. Aloha Week Hawaii, Inc., 1973—; mem. State Found. on Culture and Arts, 1966—; chmn. State Council on Hawaiian Heritage, 1969—. Spl. Internat. scholar Delta Kappa Gamma Soc., 1961. Mem. Hawaii Music Educators Assn. (sec. 1972-73, v.p. 1973-74), Musicians Assn., Beta Beta, Delta Kappa Gamma, Pi Lambda Theta, Mu Phi Epsilon. Republican. Roman Catholic. Home: 3817 Kaimuki Av Honolulu HI 96816 Office: 1039 S King St Honolulu HI 96814

KAUNITZ, RITA DAVIDSON (MRS. PAUL E. KAUNITZ), environmentalist and city planning ofcl., writer; b. N.Y.C., Apr. 18, 1922; d. David and Bessie (Golden) Davidson; B.A. magna cum laude, N.Y. U., 1942; M.A., Columbia, 1946; Ph.D., Radcliffe Coll., 1951; m. Dr. Paul E. Kaunitz, Aug. 10, 1947; children—Victoria Moss, Jonathan Davidson, Andrew Moss. Adminstrv. analyst OPA, Washington, 1943-44; columnist on planning and housing Progressive Agr. mag., N.Y.C., 1944-46; editor plan for rezoning First Year's Studies, N.Y.C., 1948-49; asso. editor Bull. Housing and Town and Country Planning, UN Secretariat, 1950-52; research asso. The Atlantic Urban Region Project Grad. Program in City Planning, Yale, 1955-57, cons. Centre for Housing, Bldg. and Planning, UN Secretariat, 1960-66, vis. lectr. Grad. Curriculum in Community Planning and Area Devel. U. R.I., Kingston, 1967-67, Harvard Grad. Sch. Design, 1975—. Mem., sec. Planning and Zoning Commn., Wesport, Conn., 1955-63, vice chmn., 1961-63; rep. Southwestern Regional Planning Agy., 1961-66, chmn. 1965-66; mem. commn. to study necessity and feasibility met. govt. Gen. Assembly Conn., chmn. sub-com. on state and regional planning, 1966-67; seminar associate Columbia U., 1966—; mem. Adv. Council on Community Affairs, Conn., 1967-74; mem. Clean Air Task Force, Conn., 1968-71; coordinator Urban Affairs Study, Fairfield U., 1968; vice chmn. legislative panel Conn. Gov.'s Com. Environmental Policy, 1970-71; mem. governing council Conn. Air Conservation Com., 1970—; mem. Conn. Gov.'s Task Force Housing, 1971—; sci. adviser L.I. Sound Study New Eng. River Basins Commn., 1972—. Mem. Am. Inst. Planners, Am. Soc. Planning Ofcls. (dir. 1973—). Clubs: Inc., Radcliffe of Lower Fairfield County. Author articles in field. Address: 14 Red Coat Rd Westport CT 06880

KAUSKAY, ROBERTA LAURA BORK (MRS. STANLEY STUART), librarian; b. Buffalo, July 14, 1916; d. Robert Allen and Emma Barbara (Keil) Bork; student Elmhurst Coll., 1933-35; B.A., Washington U., 1937; postgrad. U. Buffalo, 1938-40, Syracuse U., 1963-64; M.L.S., U. Okla., 1965; m. Stanley Stuart, Jan. 11, 1946; children—Karen Leola, Linda Christine. Caseworker Erie County (N.Y.) Dept. Social Welfare, Buffalo, 1939-42; adminstrv. asst. USAAF, Buffalo, 1942-47; tchr. Rome (N.Y.) pub. schs., 1957-63, Rome Free Acad., 1963-64; grad. asst. library sci. U. Okla., 1965, social sci. librarian, 1965-66, dir. U. Okla. Office of Research Adminstrn. Library Center, 1966—. Mem. A.L.A., Southwestern, Okla. library assns., Internat. Assn. Sch. Librarianship, Am. Assn. Sch. Librarians, Assn. Ednl. Communications and Tech., Am. Assn. U. Women, Am. Assn. U. Profs., N.E.A., Okla. Edn. Assn., Nat. Sch. Pub. Relations Assn., State Sch. Library/Media Suprs. Assn. Home: 1621 Chestnut Lane Norman OK 73069

KAUTZ, SANDRA ANN, youth orgn. adminstr.; b. Farmersville, Tex., Nov. 11, 1933; d. Harold Martin and Leata (Farrar) Kautz; B.A., North Tex. State U., 1955. Dist. adv. Rio Grande council Girl Scouts Am., El Paso, Tex., 1955-68, program services dir., 1968—, dir. resident camp, 1967—. Bd. dirs. Tex. United Community Services, 1973—. Mem. Assn. Girl Scout Profl. Workers (membership coordinator 1972—, mem. steering com. 1972—), Am. Camping Assn., El Paso Youth Workers Council, North Tex. State U. Alumni Assn. Home: 1306 St John's St El Paso TX 79903 Office: 3214 E Yandell St El Paso TX 79903

KAVALER, FLORENCE, physician; b. N.Y.C., Nov. 9, 1935; d. Samuel and Rose (Garfinkel) Kavaler; B.A., Barnard Coll., Columbia, 1955; M.D., State U. N.Y., 1961; M.S., Columbia, 1961, M.P.H., 1965. Biostatis. trainee Research Found. State U. N.Y., Downstate Med. Center, 1959-61; asst. project dir. N.Y. Cerebral Palsy Study, State U. N.Y., 1960-61; intern Beth El Hosp., Bklyn., 1962, admitting physician 1963-64; house staff physician Coney Island Hosp., Bklyn., 1963; resident, health officer-in-tng. N.Y.C. Dept. Health, 1964-66, project dir. narcotics register project 1965-68, dep. exec. med. dir. Medicaid program, 1968—, asst. commr., 1970-72; study dir. Milbank Meml. Commn. for Study Higher Edn. for Pub. Health, Chapel Hill, N.C., 1972—. Instr. N.Y.U., Columbia schs. pub. health, 1964—; adj. asst. prof. Grad. Sch. Health Adminstrn., Baruch Coll., 1970—, Sch. Pub. Health, Columbia U., 1968—; adj. asso. prof. pub. health U. N.C., 1972—; mem. adv. bd. N.Y.C. Population Health Survey, 1969—. Mem. Am., N.Y.C. pub. health assns, N.Y. State Downstate Med. Center, Brookdale Hosp., Barnard alumni assns. Contbr. articles to profl. jours. Home: Bolinwood Apts 500 Umstead Dr Chapel Hill NC 27514 Office: 140 1/2 E Franklin St Chapel Hill NC 27514

KAVALER, LUCY LYDIA ESTRIN (MRS. ARTHUR R. KAVALER), author; b. N.Y.C., Aug. 29, 1929; d. L.I. and Helen (Vishniac) Estrin; B.A., Oberlin Coll., 1948; fellow advanced sci. writing program Columbia Sch. Journalism, 1969-70; m. Arthur R. Kavaler, Nov. 9, 1947; children—Roger, Andrea. Mem. Soc. Mag. Writers, Nat. Assn. Sci. Writers, P.E.N. (exec. bd.), Authors Guild. Author: The Private World of High Society, 1960; Mushrooms Molds and Miracles, 1965; The Astors, 1966; Freezing Point, Cold As A Matter of Life and Death, 1970; (books for young readers) The Wonders of Algae, 1960; The Artificial World Around Us, 1963; The Wonders of Fungi, 1964; Dangerous Air, 1967; The Astors, an American Legend, 1968; Cold Against Disease, 1971; Life Battles Cold, 1973. Home: 103 E 86th St New York City NY 10028

KAVANAGH, ALICE PATRICIA, editor; b. Jersey City, Oct. 8, 1922; d. William Francis and Alice Josephine (Woods) Kavanagh; student St. Peter's Inst. Indsl. Relations, 1949-50, Fordham U., summers 1940, 41. Exec. sec. Irving Trust Co., N.Y.C., 1943-54; exec. sec., asso. editor Bldg. Contractors Assn. N.J., 1954-70, dir. pub. relations, editor, 1970—. Chmn., Com. to Preserve Historic Speer Cemetery, 1970-73; active A.R.C., U.S.O., Civic Theatre of Jersey City, Players Theatre. Recipient citation and plaque for civic leadership 29th Div. Assn., 1971; citation and good citizenship medal Old Bergen chpt. S.A.R., 1971. Mem. N.J. Press Assn., Am. Legion Aux. Republican. Roman Catholic. Home: 20 Highland Av Jersey City NJ 07306 Office: 500 Morris Av Springfield NJ 07081

KAVENA, JUANITA TIGER (MRS. WILMER R. KAVENA), home economist; b. Catoosa, Okla., Aug. 27, 1925; d. Cotsar and Maude (Bear) Tiger; student Bacone Jr. Coll., 1946; B.S., East Central State Coll., Ada, Okla., 1951; postgrad. No. Ariz. U., 1968, U. Ariz., 1970; m. Wilmer R. Kavena, Sept. 7, 1949; children—Cedric, Roderick, Alice Jane, Tracy Rene, Wilmer II. Adivser home econs. Bur. Indian Affairs, 1948, tchr., 1953; tchr., 1950; tchr. Polacca (Ariz.) Day Sch., 1950-53; extension home economist Keams Canyon (Ariz.) Boarding Sch., 1953-56; tchr. home econs. Hopi Indian Agy., Keams Canyon, 1956-69; home economist U.S. Dept. Agr., Keams Canyon, 1969—. Leader 4-H Club. Mem. Ariz. Assn. Extension Home Economists (pres. 1971.). Democrat. Baptist. Lioness. Address: PO Box 425 Keams Canyon AZ 86034

KAWA, FLORENCE KATHRYN, artist, painter; b. Weyerhauser, Wis., Feb. 24, 1912; d. John and Katherine (Czechalski) Kawa; student Mpls. Sch. Art, 1930-32; B.S., U. Wis.—Milw., 1940; M.A., La. State U., 1944; summer study Black Mountain Coll., 1944, Cranbrook, 1951, Columbia, 1946-48, Mass. Inst. Tech., 1956, Corcoran Summer Sch. Abroad, 1970. Asso. prof. art dept., Drake U., 1964—. One-man shows Contemporary Arts Gallery, N.Y., 1950, 53, 62, 64, Stockton, Cal., 1953, Fla. State U. Art Gallery, 1962, Contemporary Arts, 1962, Drake U. Gallery, 1969, Pacem In Terris Gallery UN Plaza, 1969; exhibited Bklyn. Mus. Internat. Biennial Water Color show, 1951, 55, 57, 59, 61, Whitney Mus. 1953, St. Paul Art Center, 1963, Le Moyne Art Found., Tallahassee, 1964-66, Des Moines Art Center, 1969, 70, 71; exhibited in numerous group shows in U.S., fgn. countries including Milw. Art Inst., Pa. Acad. Fine Arts, Met. Mus., larger mus. of France; represented in permanent collections U. Wis., La. Art Commn., S.S. United States, Des Moines Art Center, USIA in Am. embassies abroad, many pvt. collections. Recipient awards and purchase prizes Milw. Art Inst., U. Wis., Polish-Am. Show, Milw., Nat. Competition Pub. Bldgs. Adminstrn., Fla. Internat., Fla. Fedn. Art, Nat. Watercolor Show, Jackson, Miss.; Edith and Esther Younker award for creative painting, 1969; Edmundson award for best work in any medium, 1970. Home: 1545 29th St Des Moines IA 50311

KAY, HELEN (MRS. HERBERT GOLDFRANK), author; b. N.Y.C., Oct. 12, 1912; d. Hyman Coloony and Tessie (Herman) Kay; student Bank St. Coll., 1955-57, N.Y. U., 1957-58, Columbia, 1959; m. Herbert Goldfrank, Dec. 8, 1933; children—Lewis, Deborah, Joan. Researcher, Time-Fortune, N.Y.C., 1936-38, labor editor, 1939-44. Mem. Author's League, P.E.N. Am. Center, Child Study Assn. Author: Secrets of the Dolphins, 1964; Picasso's World of Children, 1965; Man and Mastiff, 1967, others. Address: 435 E 87 St New York City NY 10028

KAY, HERMA HILL, educator; b. Orangeburg, S.C., Aug. 18, 1934; d. Charles Esdorn and Herma Lee (Crawford) Hill; B.A., So. Meth. U., 1956; J.D., U. Chgo., 1959. Admitted to Cal. bar, 1960; law clk. to Justice Roger Traynor, Cal. Supreme Ct., 1959-60; asst. prof. law U. Cal. at Berkeley, 1960-62, asso. prof., 1962, prof., 1963—, dir. family law project, 1964-67, chairperson acad. senate, 1973-74. Co-reporter uniform marriage and divorce law, Nat. Conf. Commrs. on Uniform State Laws, 1968-70; vis. prof. U. Manchester (Eng.), 1972; mem. Gov.'s Commn. on Family, 1966. Trustee Russell Sage Found. Fellow Center for Advanced Study in Behavioral Scis., Palo Alto, 1963-64. Mem. Cal. State Bar Assn. (mem. family law com. 1964-67), Ninety-Nines, Order of Golden Bear. Democrat. Club: Zonta (sec. 1971-72) (Berkeley). Contbr. articles to profl. jours. Contbg. author: Law in Culture and Society, 1969; co-author Text, Cases and Materials on Sex-Based Discrimination, 1974. Office: Sch Law U Cal Berkeley CA 94720

KAY, JANICE ANNE, bus. cons.; b. Oakland, Cal., Sept. 23, 1939; d. Bernard Maxwell and Dorothy Lee (Cuthrell) Kassell; B.S., U. Md., 1961; postgrad. Holy Names Coll., 1968—. Recreation worker Red Cross, Korea and U.S., 1961-63, 64-65; employment counselor, interviewer State of Cal., Oakland and San Rafael, Cal., 1965-67; pres. Career Information, Oakland, 1968—; practice as career cons., Oakland, 1968—. Cons. to State Wash., U. Cal., Foremost McKesson, Stanford Assn. for Continuing Edn., Am. Inst. Banking, Fed. Civil Service Commn., USN, Sacramento County (Cal.) Office Edn., Levi Strauss, Inc., Kaiser Employee's Club, First Nat. Bank Ariz. Recipient Outstanding Career Woman award Bay Valley Dist. Bus. and Profl. Women's Club, 1972. Mem. Nat. Orgn. for Women (chmn. speakers bur. 1972-73), Bay Area Consortium on Continuing Edn. for Women (mem. exec. com. 1972-73), Am. Soc. Tng. Dirs., East Oakland Bus. and Profl. Women's Club (past pres. elect), Internat. Transactional Analysis Assn. Author: Career Information: Secretary, 1968; Public Service: Career Information, 1972; Self Directed Career Development for Women, 1974. Contbr. chpts. to books. Developed computerized career cross match system, 1968. Home: 4036 Everett Av Oakland CA 94602

KAY, M. JANE, personnel exec.; b. Detroit, Aug. 31, 1925; d. Albert A. and Celia R. (Betzing) Kay; B.S., U. Detroit, 1948; M.A., Wayne State U., 1952; M.B.A., U. Mich., 1963. Sr. personnel interviewer employment Detroit Edison Co., 1948-60, personnel coordinator for women, 1960-65, office employment adminstr., 1965-70, gen. employment adminstr., 1970-71, dir. personnel services, 1971-72, mgr. employee relations, 1972—. Tchr. U. Detroit Evening Coll. Bus. and Adminstrn., 1964—; seminar leader div. mgmt. edn. U. Mich., 1968-74. Mem. Mich. Employment Security Adv. Council, 1967—. Bd. dirs. Detroit Inst. Commerce. Recipient Alumni Tower award U. Detroit, 1967; Headliner award women Wayne State U., 1970, Wayne State U. Alumni Achievement award, 1974, Career Achievement award Profl. Panhellenic Assn., 1973; named one of Top Ten Women of Detroit, 1970. Mem. Internat. Assn. Personnel Women (pres. 1969-70), Women's Econ. Club (v.p. 1971-72, pres. 1972-73), Personnel Women Detroit (pres. 1960-61), U. Detroit Alumni Assn. (pres. 1964-66), Phi Gamma Nu (nat. v.p. 1955-57). Home: 471 Shelbourne Rd Grosse Point Farms MI 48236 Office: 2000 2d Av Detroit MI 48226

KAY, MAIRE WEIR, editor; b. Balt., July 10, 1912; d. Gilbert Byron Weir and Mary Eliza (Tresize) Kay; B.A., U. Kan., 1936; M.A., U. Utah, 1938; Ph.D., U. Wash., 1943; postgrad. (Muellhaupt scholar) Ohio State U., 1944-46; Instr. Wells Coll., Ithaca, N.Y., 1943-44; editorial staff G and C Merriam Co., Springfield, Mass., 1946—, asso. editor, 1957-72, sr. editor, 1972—. Office: 47 Federal St Springfield MA 01101

KAY, PATRICIA MCGOLDRICK (MRS. MORRIS I. KAY), educator; b. Bklyn., June 22, 1934; d. Lawrence Peter and Helena Frieda (Seifert) McGoldrick; B.S., Cornell U., 1956; Ed.D., Rutgers U., 1969; m. Morris I. Kay, Aug. 10, 1957; children—Mary Katherine, Andrew Stephen. Asst. prof. office tchr. edn. City U. N.Y., N.Y.C., 1969-73, asso. prof. edn. measurement Bernard Baruch Coll., 1973—, dir. competency based tchr. edn. project, 1972—. Mem. Metuchen (N.J.) Bd. Edn., 1971—, v.p., 1973-74. N.Y. State Bd. Regents grantee. Mem. Am. Ednl. Research Assn., Nat. Council on Measurement in Edn., Am. Psychol. Assn., Am. Statis. Assn., Nat. Soc. for Study Edn. Home: 5 Mark Circle Metuchen NJ 08840 Office: 17 Lexington Av New York City NY 10010

KAYDEN, MIMI RIGA, pub. co. exec.; b. N.Y.C., Oct. 19, 1933; d. Gustave Lawrence and Jean (Riga) Kayden; B.A. in Polit. Sci., Wellesley Coll., 1955. Sec. to editor Foreign Policy Assn., N.Y.C., 1955-57; sec. to pub. dir. Henry Holt & Co., N.Y.C., 1957; pub. dir. Criterion Books Inc., N.Y.C., 1957-58; pub. dir. children's books Harper & Bros., N.Y.C., 1958-59; dir. children's books promotion Thomas Y. Crowell Co., N.Y.C., 1960; dir. publicity Ivan Obolensky, Inc., N.Y.C., 1961; asst. dir. library and edn. dept. E.P. Dutton & Co., N.Y.C., 1961-62, dir. library and edn. dept., 1970—; coordinator library promotion Prentice-Hall, Inc., Englewood Cliffs, N.J., 1963-68; coordinator children's book promotion, Holt, Rinehart & Winston, Inc., N.Y.C., 1968-69. Mem. Am. Library Assn., Library Pub. Relations Council (dir. 1964), Children's Book Council (mem. Book Week com. 1967-68, vacation reading com. 1968-69, dir. 1973—, treas. 1974), Pubs. Library Promotion Group (bd. advisers 1972-73). Home: Richardsville Rd Rural Route 2 Carmel NY 10512 Office: 201 Park Av S New York City NY 10003

KAYE, CARMEN JIMENEZ (MRS. SIDNEY KAYE), physician; b. Loiza, P.R., Apr. 18, 1918; d. Julio and Elvira (Calzada) J.; B.S., U. P.R., 1938; M.P.H., U. Mich., 1945; M.D., Med. Coll. Va., 1952; m. Sidney Kaye, June 7, 1951; children—Cynthia S., Frederic J. Intern Med. Coll. Va. Hosp., Richmond, 1952-53, gen. practice medicine, out patient dept., 1956-60; resident VA Hosp., Richmond, 1953-54; clin. investigator A.H. Robins, Inc., Richmond, 1960-62; dir. geriatric program Rio Piedras (P.R.) Mental Health Center, 1963—. Instr. gerontology Sch. Pub. Health, U. P.R., 1969—. Bd. dirs. Sr. Citizens, Inc., 1966—. Fellow Am. Soc. Geriatrics; mem. Sigma Zeta, Alpha Omega Alpha, Delta Omega. Home: 116 Lilas Rio Piedras PR 00927 Office: Psychiatric Hospital Rio Piedras PR 00927

KAYE, CHERYLE THOMPSON (MRS. NORMAN KAYE), composer, recording artist; b. Jacksonville, Fla.; d. Warren Ferrell and Mary Genevieve (Brunson) Thompson; student U. So. Nev., 1963; m. Norman Kaye, Sept. 27, 1964; children—Richard Warren, Donald N., Alexander James. Entertainer nightclub, TV, charity orgn.; soloist, records, 1958; songwriter. Saleswoman, Norman Kaye Real Estate Co. Chosen Miss Las Vegas and Miss Nevada, 1963, semi-finalist, Miss Am. Contest, nominee Grammy award Nat. Acad. Recording Arts and Scis., 1966. Composer (recorded): Time to Pretend Again, Top Twenty, The Third Person, Mansion on the Hill, Something to Think About. Home: 1608 Raindance Las Vegas NV 89109 Office: Norman Kay & Assos 4813 Paradise Rd Las Vegas NV 89109

KAYE, JUDITH SMITH (MRS. STEPHEN RACKOW KAYE), lawyer; b. Monticello, N.Y., Aug. 4, 1938; d. Benjamin and Lena (Cohen) Smith; B.A., Barnard Coll., 1958; LL.B. cum laude, N.Y.U., 1962; m. Stephen Rackow Kaye, Feb. 11, 1964; children—Luisa Marian, Jonathan Mackey, Gordon Bernard. Admitted to N.Y. bar, 1963; mem. firm Sullivan & Cromwell, N.Y.C., 1962-64; staff atty. IBM, N.Y.C., 1964-65; atty. Olwine Connelly Chase O'Donnell & Wehher, N.Y.C., 1969—. Mem. N.Y. State Bar Assn. (mem. internat. law com. 1962-63), Assn. Bar City NY (mem. adminstrv. law com. 1972—). Home: 101 Central Park West New York City NY 10023 Office: 299 Park Av New York City NY 10017

KAYE, NORA, ballerina; b. N.Y.C.; d. Gregory and Lisa Koreff; m. 3d, Herbert Ross, Aug. 21, 1959. Prima ballerina Ballet Theatre, 1940-50; joined N.Y.C. Ballet Co., 1951; asst. dir. Am. Ballet Theatre, 1964. Home: 806 N Rexford Dr Beverly Hills CA 90210 Office: care Am Ballet Theatre 1790 Broadway New York City NY 10019

KAYE, PHYLLIS RITA (MRS. ROBERT KAYE), performing arts exec.; b. New Brunswick, N.J.; d. Harry Isadore and Jennie (Field) Johnson; student U. Conn., 1948-50; m. Robert Kaye, June 18, 1950; children—Steven, Amy. With O'Neill Theater Center, Waterford, Conn., 1965—, program coordinator, 1971—. Bd. dir. O'Neill Playwrights, 1972—. Editor Vol. II and III New Playwrights Catalogue, 1969-71. Home: 1050 Ocean Av New London CT 06320 Office: 305 Great Neck Rd Waterford CT 06385

KAYHART, MARION, educator; b. Kinnelon, N.J., Sept. 14, 1926; d. Lawrence and Beatrice (Ackerman) K.; B.A., Drew U., 1947; M.A., U. Pa., 1949, Ph.D., 1954. Lab. instr. biology Drew U., 1947-48; asst. prof. biology Roanoke Coll., 1949-52; asst. instr. zoology U. Pa., 1952-53, research asst. genetics, 1953-54; asst. prof. biology Cedar Crest Coll., 1954-56, asso. prof., 1956-57, prof., 1957—, chmn. dept. biology, 1957—. Trustee Cedar Crest Coll. AEC fellow, 1948-49. Recipient Drew U. Alumni Achievement award in Sci., 1970. Mem. Am. Inst. Biol. Sci., Am. Genetic Soc., Pa. Acad. Sci., Nat. Biology Tchrs. Assn., A.A.A.S., Sigma Xi. Home: 1521 Hamilton St Allentown PA 18102 Office: Cedar Crest Coll Allentown PA 18104

KAZANJIAN, ZABELLE NARGIZIAN (MRS. HAROLD G. KAZANJIAN), clubwoman; b. Bklyn; grad., Hofstra U., 1939; m. Harold G. Kazanjian; 3 daughters. Vol. sewing instr., pres., bd. dirs. Girls Clubs, Waterbury, Conn., 1956-68; regional chmn. Girls Clubs Conn., met. N.Y.C., 1962-65; bd. dirs., exec. com. Girls Clubs Am., 1962—, pres., 1970-74; former vice-chmn. Middlebury, Conn. A.R.C.; former chmn. Information Referral Service, Waterbury, Adult Edn. Council, Middlebury; mem. centennial com. Waterbury, 1963-64; vice-chmn. Vol. Action Center, Waterbury, 1973, chmn., 1974—. Bd. dirs. United Way Central Naugatuck Valley, Inc., 1962—, Keep Am. Beautiful, Inc., 1970-72; bd. dirs. Pearl St. Neighborhood House, Waterbury, 1964-70, pres., bd. dirs. Elisha Leavenworth Found., Waterbury; 1st vice chmn., mem. adv. bd. Salvation Army, Waterbury, 1st pres. women's aux., 1969. Home: 3 Mile Hill Rd Middlebury CT 06762

KAZICKAS, JURATE CATHERINE, journalist; b. Vilnius, Lithuania, Feb. 18, 1943; d. Joseph Peter and Alexandra (Kalvenas) Kazickas; student U. Exeter, 1962-63, U. Neuchatel, 1963; B.A., Trinity Coll., 1964; postgrad. Columbia Sch. Gen. Studies, 1965, New Sch. for Social Research, 1972. Came to U.S., 1947, naturalized, 1952. Vol. tchr. St. Cecilia's Tchr. Tng. Coll., Nyeri, Kenya, 1964-65; with Look mag., 1966-67; free-lance photojournalist, 1967-68; feature writer A.P., N.Y.C., 1969—. Free-lance TV producer, mag. writer, photographer, 1968. Named Outstanding Young Woman of Am., 1967; recipient award of merit Sports Illus., 1965, Headliner award N.Y. Newspaperwoman's Assn., 1973. Mem. Nat. Orgn. for Women. Co-author: The Liberated Woman's Appointment Calendar, 1971, 72, 73, 74, 75; The Liberated Woman's America, 1975. Home: 56 Lyncroft Rd New Rochelle NY 10804 Office: 50 Rockefeller Plaza New York City NY 10020

KAZMAIER, GERALDINE TERESA (MRS. MARTIN KAZMAIER), owner, breeder, trainer race horses; b. N.Y.C., Aug. 2, 1919; d. Jeremiah and Ann (Clifford) O'Connor; student Grace Inst., 1939; m. Martin Kazmaier, Sept. 2, 1940; children—Martin, Gerald T., Daniel J., Richard D. With Noble Farms, Far Hills, N.J., 1959—, pres. 1961—; with Saratoga Research Labs., Saratoga Springs, N.Y., 1960—; v.p. since 1967; sec., treas., Kazmaier Stable, Inc., Marina del Rey, Cal., 1973—. Pres. Costline Guild United Cerebral Palsy, Los Angeles, 1974—. Mem. U.S. Trotting Assn., Western Harness Horsemen, Marina del Ray C. of C. (parliamentarian 1973—). Home: 14016 Bora Bora Way Marina del Rey CA 90291

KEADLE, LUCIE TAYLOR, social worker; b. Delbarton, W.Va., Nov. 28, 1929; d. Roy Howard and Bertha (Taylor) Keadle; A.A., Stephens Coll., 1949; B.S., W. Va. U., 1951, certificate, 1964; M.S.W., Catholic U. Am., 1961; postgrad. No. Ariz. U., 1969, Ariz. State U., 1969-70. Child welfare worker, W.Va., 1951-59, Santa Cruz County, Ariz., 1959; psychiat. social worker Ariz. Children's Home, Tucson, 1961; caseworker Ariz. Welfare Dept., 1962-63, child welfare supr. adoption programs, 1963-64, psychiat. social worker Jane Wayland Child Guidance Center, 1965-69; social work cons. information and referral service Phoenix Community Council, 1970; coordinator staff devel. and tng. Ariz. Dept. Pub. Welfare, 1970-73, tng. office Dept. Econ. Security, 1973—. Cons. in field. Mem. W.Va. Conf. Social Welfare, 1951-59; dir. Mingo County (W.Va.) Crippled Children's Soc., 1952-57, Santa Cruz County Crippled Children's Soc., 1959-60; chmn. Social Work Everybody's Bus., Phoenix, 1966-67; mem. Steering Com. on Human Relations, Phoenix, 1969. Named Citizen of Week, KBUZ Broadcasting Co., 1970. Mem. Am. Bus. Women's Assn. (chpt. pres. 1968, Woman of Year award Cactus Wren chpt. 1970), Am. Pub. Welfare Assn., Nat. Assn. Social Workers, Ariz. Conf. Health and Welfare. Presbyn. (elder). Clubs: Tug Valley Jr. Women's Club (Williamson, W.Va.); Harmony Jr. Women's Club (Phoenix). Home: 1013 W Mission Lane Phoenix AZ 85021 Office: 1717 W Jefferson St Phoenix AZ 85007

KEAGLE, SUSAN JANE, univ. dean; b. Corning, N.Y., June 27, 1940; d. C. Roger and Mary Catherine (Lesky) Keagle; A.S. in Gen. Edn., Corning Community Coll., 1960; B.S., Elmira Coll., 1966; M.S. in Higher Edn., Ind. U., 1973. Tchr. elementary sch. Elmira (N.Y.) Sch. System, 1964-65; asst. dean students State U. Coll. at Oneonta, 1966-71, asso. dean students, 1971—. Mem. Copperstown Art Assn., Nat. Assn. Women Deans, Adminstrs. and Counselors, Am., N.Y. State personnel and guidance assns., Am. Coll. Personnel Adminstrn. Home: 79 River St Oneonta NY 13820

KEAN, DORIS EGBERT (MRS. JULIAN ARTHUR KEAN), comml. artist, civic worker; b. N.Y.C., May 13, 1911; d. Louis Morford and Winfred (Morgan) Egbert; student John Herron Art Inst., Indpls., 1929-30, Am. Lab. Sch. of Theatre, N.Y.C., 1930-31; m. Julian Arthur Kean, July 14, 1934 (dec. 1971); 1 son, Barret E. Advt. mgr., textbook designer Noble & Noble Pubs., N.Y.C., 1936-40; free-lance comml. artist., 1944-55; art dir., asso. editor Johnson Pub. Co., Richmond, Va., 1942-44; head art dept. Duplex Envelope Co., Richmond, 1955-74. Chmn. steering com. Inter-Organizational Com. on Status Women in Va., 1967; chmn. steering com. Citizens Com. on Status Women in Va., 1968; program chmn. First Statewide Conf. Citizens Com., 1968 chmn., 1968-69; chmn. Va. Commn. on Status Women, 1970—. Mem. Va. Fedn. Bus. and Profl. Womens Clubs (past pres.), Nat. Assn. Parliamentarians (unit pres. 1970-72) Nat. Fedn. Bus. and Profl. Womens Clubs (nat. resolutions com.), Interstate Assn. Commns. on Status of Women (S.E. region rep.), Va. Mus. Episcopalian. Mem. Order Eastern Star. Clubs: Parliamentary Law, Colony (both Richmond). Home: 3901 Kensington Av Richmond VA 23221

KEAN, LURAYN SNYDER (MRS. WILLARD JAMES KEAN), editorial cons.; b. Wilkinsburg, Pa., Oct. 16, 1918; d. Albert Powell and Esther Lurene (Kallmyer) Snyder; student Allegheny Community Coll., 1969; m. Willard James Kean, Feb. 7, 1942; children—Willard James, Esther L. (Mrs. Albert Ross Stewart). With Penn Hills (Pa.) Progress Newspaper, 1951-72, editor, 1970-72; editor Wilkinsburg (Pa.) Gazette, 1968-70; editorial cons. Forbes Hosp. System, Pitts., 1973—. Bd. dir. Penn Hills Library, 1967—, treas. 1974—. Mem. Beulah Hist. Soc. (recording sec. 1973—), Pa. Women's Press Assn. (S.W. dist. dir. 1970-72), Women in Communications. Home: 309 Duff Rd Pittsburgh PA 15235

KEANE, LEONTINE RITA, pub. relations exec.; b. Grosse Pointe, Mich., July 8, 1920; d. William Edward and Leontine (D'Haene) Keane; B.A., Manhattanville Coll., 1941; M.A., U. Detroit, 1951. Instr. English, U. Detroit, 1947-51; woman's editor WJLB, Detroit, 1951-53; broadcaster, writer, producer WDTR, Detroit, 1953-54; asst. to exec. sec. WTVS, Detroit, 1955-58; dir. radio-TV publicity Wayne State U., Detroit, 1958-66, dir. information Coll. Lifelong Learning, 1966—, instr. pub. relations Univ. Center for Adult Edn., 1963—. Mem. pub. relations adv. bd. United Found., 1973—; tribute fund bd. United Community Services, 1969—; trustee Detroit City Theatre Assn., 1969—. Recipient award for excellence in publs. Am. Coll. Pub. Relations Assn., 1968, award for contbns. to pub. relations Pub. Relations Soc. Am., 1972. Mem. Pub. Relations Soc. Am. (Detroit pres. 1973), Am. Women Radio and TV (Detroit pres. 1961-63), Women in Communications (Detroit pres. 1968-70), Detroit Women Writers, Detroit Hist. Soc. (dir. 1971—). Clubs: Detroit Press, Country, Manhattanville (Detroit). Home: 1007 Harvard Rd Grosse Pointe MI 48230 Office: 2978 W Grand Blvd Detroit MI 48202

KEANE, SISTER MARY CHARLES, social worker; b. Omaha, Nov. 4, 1907; d. Thomas and Rose (Harrigan) Keane; A.B., Creighton U., 1941; M.S., Catholic U. Am., 1944. Supt., St. James Home for Children, Omaha, 1944-63; mother provincial Sisters of Mercy, Province of Omaha, 1963-70, dir. dept. social services, 1970—. Recipient award in social service Catholic U. Am., 1967. Mem. Nat. Conf. Catholic Charities (pres. 1965-67), Neb. Assn. Child Care Instns. (pres. 1958-59), Nat. Assn. Social Workers Omaha (chpt. chmn. 1962-63), Child Welfare League of Am., Neb. Welfare Assn., Internat. Conf. Social Work. Contbr. articles to profl. jours. Home: Mercy Hospital 6th and University St Des Moines IA 50314

KEARBY, NORMA LOU, physician; b. Dallas, Nov. 14, 1930; d. John Gallatin and Julia Vivian (Drew) Kearby; student Rice U., 1948-49; B.S., Baylor U., 1952; M.D., U. Tex., 1955. Intern Hotel Dieu Hosp., New Orleans, 1955-56; resident otolaryngology Charity Hosp., New Orleans, 1956-59; fellow Ochsner Found. Hosp., 1957; practice medicine specializing in otolargyngology Browne-McHardy Clinic, New Orleans, 1959—; mem. exec. com Eye, Ear, Nose and Throat Hosp., 1967-71, v.p. staff, 1969-70, sec.-treas. staff, 1973—; chief dept. otolaryngology and mem. exec. com. East Jefferson Hosp., Metairie, La., 1973—; asso. prof. dept. otolaryngology La. State U. Med. Sch., 1968—. Bd. dirs. St. Marks Community Center, New Orleans Speech and Hearing Center. Diplomate Am. Bd. Otolaryngology. Fellow Am. Acad. Ophthalmology and Otolaryngology; mem. A.M.A., Pan-Am. Assn. Otolaryngology, So., Jefferson Parish med. assns., La. Med. Soc., La.-Miss. Ophthalmology and Otolaryngology Assn., Centurion Club Deafness Research, Am. Council Otolaryngology, Am. Assn. Phys. and Surg., D.A.R., La. Landmarks Soc., Vieux Carre Property Owners Assn. Methodist (mem. council on ministry 1970—). Home: 1235 Decatur St New Orleans LA 70116 Office: 4315 Houma Blvd Metairie LA 70002

KEARIN, ANITA MARCELLA, govt. ofcl.; b. Chgo., July 24, 1924; d. Dennis A. and Anne M. (Brophy) Kearin; grad. high sch. With Internal Revenue Service, Dept. Treasury, 1943-68, supervisory tax examiner, 1943-56, informants claims examiner, income tax technician, auditor 1957-67; pub. assistance specialist, dir. fed. information center Region V, Gen. Services Adminstrn., Chgo., 1968—. Dir. Clifford Peterson Tool Co., Chgo., 1968-71; sec., dir. Triangle Mfg. Co., Chgo., 1968-71. Mem. consumer issues com. Fed. Execs. Bd., 1973—. Mem. Chgo. Boosters League, 1968—; asso. mem. Chgo. Policemen's Benefit and Welfare Assn., 1967-68; mem. Mayors Com. for Cleaner Chgo., 1958—; exec. bd. Chgo. Beautiful Com., 1964—, mem. Riverfront Com., 1970—, Awards Com., 1971-72; chmn. Minipark program, 1973. Vice pres. Loretto Hosp. Women's Aux., 1965-66, membership chmn., 1965-66. Mem. Nat. Assn. Employees of Collector of Internal Revenue, Chgo. Boosters League (dir., sec. 1969—), Federally Employed Women's Program. Club: Cook County Women's (Chgo.). Home: 203 N Kenilworth Av Oak Park IL 60302 Office: 219 S Dearborn St Chicago IL 60604

KEARNES, MARY DELL BUDD (MRS. ROBERT ARNOLD KEARNES), banker; b. Chatham County, N.C., May 9, 1920; d. Walter Ivey and Anna Kirk (Stone) Budd; B.S., U. N.C. at Greensboro, 1940; m. Robert Arnold Kearnes, Feb. 10, 1946; children—Marilynn, Deborah, Larry B., Douglas, Ronald. Tchr. bus. edn. high schs., N.C., 1940-43; exec. sec. to employment mgr. Fairchild Aircraft Co., Burlington, N.C. div., 1943-45; exec. sec. to gen. mgr. Firestone Tire & Rubber Co., Burlington, 1945-46; with Trust Co. Ga. Group, 1946—; with 1st Nat. Bank & Trust Co., Macon, Ga., 1951—, exec. sec., 1951-62, adminstrv. asst. trust dept., 1962-66, asst. trust officer, 1966-72, supr. trust operations, 1966-67, account adminstr., 1967—, sr. trust officer, 1972—. Found. mgr. Porter Charitable Trust; sec. to pub. com. James H. Porter Charitable Trust, 1961—; sec. to bd. mgrs. Baconsfield, 1963-68. Mem. Am. Inst. Banking (women's com. 1966—, instr. 1972—), Macon Estate Planning Council, Nat. Assn. Bank Women. Home: 758 Lee Rd Macon GA 31204 Office: PO Box 4248 Macon GA 31208

KEARNEY, JUNE FRANCES, educator; b. Newburyport, Mass., July 15, 1940; d. James Francis and Rita June (Dorsey) Kearney; B.S., Taylor U., 1962; M.Ed., Wittenberg U., 1965; Ph.D., Ohio State U., 1973. Instr. health and phys. edn. Cedarville (O.) Coll., 1962-64, asst. prof., 1964-69, asso. prof., 1969-73, prof., 1973—. Resident dir. Camp Fire Girls Camp, Kiser Lake, O., 1969-71. Recipient Service award Cedarville Coll., 1972. Mem. Am., Ohio assns. health, phys. edn. and recreation, Nat., Midwest assns. phys. edn. coll. women, Ohio Coll. Assn., Southwestern Ohio Bd. Ofcls. Baptist. Home: 460 Lamplighter Pl Xenia OH 45385 Office: Cedarville Coll Cedarville OH 45314

KEARNEY, MAUREEN JOAN, counseling psychologist; b. Elizabeth, N.J., July 8, 1942; d. John R. and Loretta M. (Duffey) Foley; A.B. in Math., Marywood Coll., Scranton, Pa., 1964; M.Ed. in Counseling, Am. U., 1970, Ph.D., 1972; m. James F. Kearney, Aug. 14, 1965. Tchr., Binghamton (N.Y.) Pub. Schs., 1964-65, Charlottesville (Va.) Pub. Schs., 1965-68; program dir. Am. Found. Autistic Children, Chevy Chase, Md., 1973; counseling psychologist, career devel. splty., tchr. grad. course counseling U. Me., Portland, 1973—. Lectr., cons. in field. Vice pres. Rockville-Wheaton (Md.) Welcome Wagon Club, 1973. Grad. fellow Am. U., 1971-73. Mem. Am., Western, Me. psychol. assns. Home: 46 Mona Rd Portland ME 04103

KEARNS, DORIS HELEN, educator; b. Rockville Centre, N.Y., Jan. 4, 1943; d. Michael Alouisius and Helen Witt (Miller) Kearns; B.S. magna cum laude, Colby Coll., 1964; Ph.D. in Govt., Harvard, 1968. Intern, Dept. State, summer 1963, Ho. of Reps., summer 1965; research asso. Dept. Health, Edn. Welfare, summer 1966; White House fellow, also spl. asst. Dept. Labor, 1967; spl. asst. to Lyndon B. Johnson, 1968, spl. cons., 1969; asst. prof. govt. Harvard, 1969-71, asso. prof., also asst. dir. Inst. Politics, 1972—. Polit. analyst for news desk, WBZ, Boston. Mem. Democratic Party Platform Com., 1972, steering com. Women's Polit. Caucus in Mass., 1972—. Trustee Robert F. Kennedy Found., Wesleyan U., Colby Coll.; chmn. bd. advisers Women Involved, Boston. Named Outstanding Young Woman of the Year, 1966. Mem. Am. Polit. Sci. Assn., Council on Fgn. Relations (mem. nominating, reform coms.), Group for Applied Psychoanalysis, Harvard Faculty Council, Signet Soc., Phi Beta Kappa, Phi Sigma Iota. Home: 153A Mt Auburn St Cambridge MA 02138 Office: 78 Mt Auburn St Cambridge MA 02139*

KEARNS, NORA LYNCH, club woman; b. Greenville, Pa., 1902; d. William Halloran and Matilda Catherine (Hartman) Lynch; A.B., Thiel Coll., 1923; M.A., U. Pitts., 1935; student Am. Acad. Dramatic Arts, N.Y.C., 1927; m. Carroll D. Kearns, Aug. 30, 1933. Tchr. history, drama Penn High Sch., also Thiel Coll., Greenville, Pa., 1923-41; writer, prod. Greenville Centennial Pageant, 1939; dir. Greenville Theater Guild, 1931-36; author, producer Congl. Club 40th Anniversary Pageant, 1948; chmn. Mercer County (Pa.) chpt. Am. Jr. Red Cross, 1943-63; past mem. council Shenango Valley Girl Scouts; past mem. council women's com. Nat. Symphony Orch., Washington; v.p. bd. mgmt. Washington Home for Incurables, Arthritis and Rheumatism Found. of D.C.; spl. cons. Post Master Gen., Dept. Post Office, Washington, 1959-61. Trustee Thiel Coll. Named Republican Woman of Year, 1956. Mem. Nat. Fedn. Rep. Women (past pres., past nat. program chmn., editorial staff Washington News Letter), League Rep. Women (pres. D.C. 1949-53), Capitol Hill Asso., Inc., Bus. and Profl. Women's Club, Am. Legion Aux., Nat. Soc. Arts and Letters (life), Am. Soc. for Theatre Research, Phi Alpha Theta, Delta Kappa Gamma, Alpha Psi Omega, Sigma Kappa. Lutheran. Mem. Order Eastern Star, White Shrine of Jerusalem, Ladies Oriental Shrine of N.A., Order of Amaranth, Grange. Clubs: Congressional (1st v.p. 1951-53), Congressional Country, Newspaper Women's, Washington, Capitol Hill (Washington); College, Women's Quota (hon.) (Sharon, Pa.); Iroquois (Conneaut Lake, Pa.); Thiel's Women's (Meadville, Pa.). Home: RD 1 Conneaut Lake PA 16316 also 4010 Galt Ocean Dr Fort Lauderdale FL 33308

KEAS, JACQUELINE BILOTTI (MRS. WILLIAM O. KEAS), retail co. exec.; b. Buchanan, Mich., Aug. 22, 1924; d. Benedict Eugene and Frances (Roti) Bilotti; grad. high sch.; m. William O. Keas, Nov. 8, 1952; 1 stepson, William; 1 dau., Stephanie. Buyer for various dept. stores, South Bend, Ind., Chgo., Jackson, Mich., 1945-52; with Weinstocks Dept. Store, Sacramento, 1971—, depts. mgr., 1971—. Coordinator for state wide com. to secure maj. sch. finance legislation Citizens' Alliance for Reform Edn. Support, 1971—; adv. commn. Sacramento County (Cal.) Welfare, 1963-64; pres. San Juan P.T.A. Council, 1966-67; mem. steering com. San Juan Sch. Dist. Overide Election, 1967-68. Mem. Republican State Central Com. of Cal., 1962-70, state vice chmn. for state precinct com., 1964-67; vice chmn. Rep. State Central Com. for No. Cal., 1967, 69. Mem. Cal. Congress of Parents and Tchrs. (life). Episcopalian. Club: Am. River Patrons (Sacramento). Home: 4340 Figwood Way Sacramento CA 95825 Office: Weinstocks Country Club Plaza Sacramento CA 95821

KEATING, ANNE STEPHANIE, publishing exec.; b. N.Y.C., Apr. 17, 1931; d. William Aloysious and Anne Catherine (Clayton) Keating; student Barnard Coll., 1947-49; B.A., Hunter Coll., 1953. Asst. account exec. N.W. Ayer & Sons, Inc., N.Y.C., 1953-56; asst. promotion mgr. Natural History Mag., Am. Mus. Natural History, N.Y.C., 1956-57, promotion mgr. and advt. mgr., 1958-61, promotion dir., 1962-69; circulation dir. Smithsonian Mag., Smithsonian Instn., N.Y.C., 1969—. Cons., Change Mag., N.Y.C., 1973—, Doubleday & Co., Inc., N.Y.C., 1964-69, Interplay Mag., N.Y.C., 1966-68, Art News mag., N.Y.C., 1974—. Mem. Women's Direct Response Group (dir. 1972—, treas. 1973—), Direct Mail Marketing Assn. (recipient Direct Mail Leaders award 1963, 70), Nat. Assn. Direct Mail Writers, Hundred Million Club, Direct Mail Ideas Exchange, Fulfillment Mgrs. Assn. Office: 420 Lexington Av New York City NY 10017

KEATING, CHARLOTTE MATTHEWS (MRS. KENNETH LEE KEATING), civic worker; b. Peking, China, Sept. 9, 1927 (parents Am. citizens); d. Harold Shepard and Grace Hazel (Waters) Matthews; student Kalamazoo Coll., 1945-46, Simmons Coll., 1946-47, U. Mo., 1949-50; B.A., Stanford, 1954; postgrad. U. Ariz., 1965-68; m. Kenneth Lee Keating, June 15, 1947; children—Roger Lee, Kevin Jackson. Vol. Lehigh County (Pa.) Community Council and Lehigh County League Women Voters, Allentown, 1954-55; chmn. Unitarian Universalist Fellowship for Social Justice, Tucson, 1964-66; del. Tucson Community Council, 1964-66; vol. adult literacy tutor Holy Cross House, Tucson, 1966-71; mem. legislative com. Amphitheater Sch. Dist., Tucson, 1972-73, also Tucson Community Council; chmn. Canyon del Oro Community Sch. Council, Tucson, 1972—. Bd. dirs. Tucson League for Pub. Schs., 1964-66, Holy Cross House, 1966-71, Tucson Adult Literacy Vols., Inc., 1974—. Recipient Community Service award Lehigh County Community Council, 1955. Mem. N.A.A.C.P., League Women Voters (dir. 1955-57), Common Cause, Delta Kappa Gamma (hon.). Democrat. Mem. Unitarian Universalist Ch. Club: Stanford (Tucson). Author: Building Bridges of

Understanding, 1967; Building Bridges of Understanding Between Cultures, 1971. Home: 7054 N Magic Lane Tucson AZ 85704

KEATING, MAUD ELIZABETH, bank exec.; b. Holyoke, Mass., Dec. 21, 1903; d. William Patrick and Della (Mullins) Keating; student Holyoke Community Coll. 1954-57. Sec., White & Wyckoff Mfg. Co., Holyoke, 1928-47; pvt. sec. to chief engr. Worthington Corp., Holyoke, 1947-52; pvt. sec. to pres. Holyoke Nat. Bank, 1952—, also asst. cashier. Mem. Bank Women Officers Assn. (publicity chmn. Pioneer Valley chpt. 1968-69), Nat. Secs. Assn. (corr. sec. Holyoke chpt. 1954-58, rec. sec. 1959-65, publicity com. 1956-66), Am. Soc. Notaries, Exec. Secs. Seminar Group, P.S. for Private Secs., Friends of Holyoke Mus., Holyoke Speakers' Club, Nat. Council Catholic Women, Blessed Sacrament Women's Club. Home: 14 Charles St Holyoke MA 01040 Office: 225 High St Holyoke MA 01040

KEAVENY, JEAN DIXON (MRS. NORBERT J. KEAVENY), diversified industry exec.; b. Bangor, Wis., Jan. 30; d. Harvey Dixon and Doris (Esch) Kyhl; student U. Wis., 1930-32; m. Norbert J. Keaveny, Oct. 1, 1936 (dec. Jan. 1949). Editor, writer, Internat. Tel. and Tel. Corp., N.Y.C., 1946-60, adminstr. editorial services, 1960-65, exec. asst. to dir. corporate relations and advt., 1965—. Served with WAC, 1943-45. Mem. Pub. Relations Soc. Am. Home: 155 W 68th St New York City NY 10023 Office: 320 Park Av New York City NY 10022

KECK, CHRISTIANE E., educator; b. Jena, Germany, July 19, 1940; d. Paul H. and Johanna (Gonizianer) Keck; brought to U.S., 1948, naturalized, 1954; A.B. (Dante scholar), Coll. of New Rochelle, 1961; M.A., Columbia, 1962; Ph.D., U. Tex., 1966. Instr. German, Columbia, 1962; teaching asst. German, U. Tex. at Austin, 1962-63; instr. English to fgn. students U. Kan., summer 1963; asst. prof. German, Purdue U., Lafayette, Ind., 1964—, chmn. dept., 1973—. U. Tex. research grantee, 1963-64, Purdue U. postdoctoral research grantee, 1967, Mem. Modern Lang. Assn., Midwest Modern Lang. Assn., Am. Assn. Tchrs. German (sec. Ind. 1972—), Am. Assn. U. Profs. (campus sec. 1970—), Delta Phi Alpha. Home: 2711 Covington West Lafayette IN 47906

KEDDIE, FRANCES MARGARET (MRS. CHARLES D. O'MALLEY), dermatologist; b. Montreal, Que., Can., Mar. 10, 1907; d. Casper Haliburton and Margaret (Ham) Keddie; B.A., U. Cal. at Berkeley, 1928, M.D., 1938; m. Charles Donald O'Malley, Apr. 29, 1939. Intern San Francisco County Hosp., 1938-39; resident U. Cal. Med. Sch., San Francisco, 1939-42, clin. instr., 1942-49, asst. clin. prof., 1949-58, asso. clin. prof., 1958-59; asso. clin. prof. U. Cal. Med. Sch., Los Angeles, 1958-59, research asso. prof., 1958-68, research prof., 1968—. Cons. Stanford Health Service, 1949-59, Palo Alto Clinic, 1949-59, U. Cal. at Los Angeles, 1959—. Spl. fellow in electron microscopy U. Cal. at Los Angeles, 1964-66; NIH grantee in mycology, 1959-69. Diplomate Am. Bd. Dermatology. Fellow Royal Micros. Soc., mem. Los Angeles Med. Soc., Soc. Investigative Dermatology, Internat. Soc. Human and Animal Mycology. Home: 987 Somera Rd Los Angeles CA 90024

KEECH, ELIZABETH ANNE JUDSON (MRS. MICHAEL CARL KEECH), occupational therapist; b. Goshen, Ind., Oct. 3, 1946; d. Victor James and Charlotte Johanna (Lake) Judson; B.S., Ind. U., 1968; m. Michael Carl Keech, Apr. 15, 1967. Staff therapist Elkhart (Ind.) Gen. Hosp., 1968, head dept. occupational therapy, 1969—; occupational therapist Cochise County Health Dept., Bisbee, Ariz., 1969. Co-chmn. Beatty Hosp. Christmas Drive, Mental Health Assn., Elkhart (Ind.) County, 1971. Mem. Am., Ind., Mich. occupational therapy assns. Episcopalian. Club: Vette Set (Elkhart, Ind.). Home: Rural Route 7 Box 108B Goshen IN 46526 Office: PO Box 1329 Elkhart IN 46514

KEEFE, ALICE ELIZABETH, univ. dean; b. Meadville, Pa.; d. Frank Thomas and Pearl Margaret (McCullough) Keefe; A.B., Mercyhurst Coll., 1932; grad. Genesee Hosp. Sch. Nursing, 1935; M.A., N.Y. U., 1946, Ph.D., 1958. Instr. nursing Manhattanville Coll. of Sacred Heart, N.Y.C., 1945-47; asst. prof. nursing Seton Hall U., Newark, 1951-53, chmn. gen. nursing program, 1952-53; asso. prof. nursing St. Johns U., N.Y.C., 1953-64; nurse researcher testing and devel. service VA, Washington, 1964, chief div. nursing edn., 1965-67; nurse coordinator Fla. Nurses Assn., Manpower Devel. Tng. Adminstrn., USPHS, 1967; dean, prof. nursing U. S. Fla., Tampa, 1968—. Mem. so. regional edn. bd. Council on Collegiate Edn. Nursing, 1968—; mem. adv. com. Hillsborough Jr. Coll. Nursing Program, 1970—; cons. health facilities planning and constrn. services USPHS, Dept. Health, Edn. and Welfare, 1970-73. Served as commd. officer USPHS, 1947-51. Mem. Nat. League Nursing (mem. council baccalaureate and higher degree programs 1968—), Am., Fla. (mem. com. deans and dirs. nursing program colls. and univs. 1968) nurses assns., Fla. League Nursing (dir. 1968), Kappa Delta Pi, Pi Lambda Theta, Sigma Theta Tau. Club: Zonta (Tampa). Home: 3306 McFarland Rd Tampa FL 33618

KEEFE, CAROLYN BERGLUND (MRS. FREDERICK LAWRENCE KEEFE), educator; b. Grand Rapids, Mich., Oct. 2, 1928; d. Martin and Sigrid Elvera (Walstrom) Berglund; A.B., Oberlin Coll., 1950; M.A., Temple U., 1968; postgrad. Villanova U., 1970—; m. Frederick Lawrence Keefe, June 11, 1949; children—Cheryl, Larry. Tchr. elementary sch., East Millstone, N.J., Franklin Twp. Sch. System, 1951-53; tchr. Rutgers U., Camden N.J., 1965-69, debate coach, 1965-68, dir. debate, acting chmn. speech dept., 1968-69; asst. prof. speech, dir. forensics West Chester (Pa.) State Coll., 1969—. Recipient First Place poetry div. Evangelical Press Assn., 1972. Mem. Speech Communication Assn., Am. Forensic Assn., Collegiate Forensic Assn. (v.p. 1971), Pa. State Colls. Forensic Assn. (pres. 1970-71), Debating Assn. Pa. Colls. (exec. sec.-treas. 1973—), Pi Kappa Delta. Presbyn. (pres. dist. presbyterial 1954-56). Editor: C.S. Lewis: Speaker and Teacher, 1971. Contbr. poetry to profl. jours. Home: 12 S Pennock Av Upper Darby PA 19082 Office: Dept Speech Communication and Theatre West Chester State Coll West Chester PA 19380

KEEFER, BEVERLY ANN, Girl Scouts adminstr.; b. Sharon, Pa., July 31, 1945; d. Dale Starry and Edna (Spangler) Keefer; B.A., Hiram Coll., 1967; M.Ed., Kent State U., 1973. Field adviser Western Res. council Girl Scouts Am., Akron, O., 1967-68, asst. program services dir., 1968-71, program specialist, 1972—. Mem. Akron Recreation Com., 1972—; mem. com. on adminstrn. YWCA, 1973—; mem. YM-YW Joint Operating Com., Cuyahoga Falls, O., 1973—. Mem. Am. Camping Assn., Assn. Girl Scout Profl. Workers, Common Cause. Home: 4602 Fish Creek Rd Stow OH 44224 Office: 108 Fir Hill Akron OH 44309

KEEFER, JANET HILL (MRS. JOSEPH DEROY KEEFER), journalist; b. Knoxville, Tenn., Mar. 6, 1945; d. James Hubert and Sarah Hester (Harrison) Hill; B.S. (Tenn. Assn. Broadcasters scholar), U. Tenn., 1966; M.A., Ohio State U., 1968; m. Joseph DeRoy Keefer, June 13, 1970. Broadcasting teaching assistantship Ohio State U., 1967-68. Women's staff writer, religion editor Columbus (O.) Citizen Jour., 1968-69; reporter, photographer, producer WTVN-TV, Columbus, 1969-71; chief news reporter WBRC-TV, Birmingham, Ala., 1972—. Sec., Citizens for Equal Rights Amendment, 1973-74. Mem. Nat. Orgn. Women, Women in Communications, Soc. Profl. Journalists, Ala. Women's Polit. Caucus, Sigma Delta Chi (Excellence in Journalism awards 1972, 73), Kappa Tau Alpha, Beta Gamma Sigma. Home: 3422 Flintshire Dr Birmingham AL 35226 Office: PO Box 6 Birmingham AL 35220

KEEGAN, JANE CLAUDIA, educator; b. Ft. Lyon, Colo., July 30, 1922; d. John William and Mae Elizabeth (Cahill) Keegan; B.S., St. Mary Coll., 1954; M.A., U. Portland, 1966. Asso. librarian, St. Mary Coll., Leavenworth, Kan., 1958-65; asst. dean women U. Portland (Ore.), 1965-66; prof. library adminstrn. Lewis-Clark State Coll., Lewiston, Ida., 1966—, mem. adminstrv. council, dean's div. chmn. com., library adv. com., faculty rank and salary com. Mem. World Book Evaluation Com., 1964; cons. library service Regional Med. Task Force, 1968—. Mem. Ida. Gov.'s Commn. Libraries, 1969-71. Charter mem. Ida. Vote Rockers, 1969. Mem. Am., Catholic (chmn. Book Week 1962-65), Pacific N.W. (chmn. nominating com. 1970), Ida. (chmn. coll.-univ. div. 1968-69) library assns., Luna House Hist. Assn., Am. Assn. U. Profs., United Native Americans. Club: Soroptimist (rec. sec. 1968-70) (Lewiston, Clarkston, Wash.). Home: 1517 27th Av Apt 3 Lewiston ID 83501

KEEGAN, MARCIA KAY, photographer, writer; b. Tulsa, May 23, 1943; d. Otis Claire and Mary Elizabeth (Collar) Keegan; B.A., U. N.M., 1961. Editor, photographer Albuquerque Jour., 1961-65; free-lance photographer, writer, N.Y.C., 1965—. Grantee N.Y. State Council Photography, 1971. Mem. Am. Soc. Mag. Photographers. Illustrator: Only the Moon and Me, 1968; author, photographer: The Taos Indians and Their Sacred Blue Lake, 1971; Mother Earth, Father Sky, 1974; We Can Still Hear Them Clapping, 1975. Address: 140 E 46th St New York City NY 10017

KEEGAN, PATRICIA, coll. adminstr.; b. Rye, N.Y., May 18, 1937; d. Vincent L. and Eleanor (Cassidy) Keegan; S.B., Simmons Coll., 1958. Asst. dir. admissions Simmons Coll., Boston, 1959-70, dir. student financial aid, 1970—. Cons., Mass. State Scholarship Program, 1973-75. Mem. Neighborhood Assn. Back Bay, 1971—. Mem. Nat., Eastern, Mass. assns. student financial aid adminstrs., Alumnae Assn. Simmons Coll. Office: 300 The Fenway Boston MA 02115

KEEHAN, VIRGINIA R., ednl. adminstr. Tchr. schs. Cal., Tex., N.M., Chgo.; specialist program orgn., guidance, counseling, U.S. Dept. Health, Edn., Welfare; dir. program div. Job Corps; with City Colls. Chgo., 1967—, coordinator planning, devel., 1967-74, acting pres. Southwest Coll., 1971-72, pres., 1972—; developer of community coll. Columbus, Ind., 1971-72. Office: Southwest Coll 7500 S Pulaski Chicago IL 60652*

KEEL, ALICE ROSE HALJUN (MRS. SIMON KEEL), lawyer; b. Los Angeles, Jan. 9, 1924; d. Samuel Arthur and Mary Theresa (Dalton) Haljun; student Santa Monica City Coll., 1950-55; LL.B., LaSalle Extension U., 1958; m. Simon Keel, Dec. 10, 1944. Secretarial positions various govt. agys. and businesses, 1942-48; exec. sec. to v.p. Hughes Aircraft Co., Culver City, Cal., 1948-65; admitted to Cal. bar, 1964, So. Dist. Ct. bar, 1964, U.S. Supreme Ct. bar, 1969, U.S. Ct. Mil. Appeals, 1969; mem. firm Holtzman, Sager & Keel, West Los Angeles, 1965-72; individual practice, Los Angeles, 1972—. Republican candidates for Cal. Assembly, 1966. Mem. Cal. Trial Lawyers, Culver City Bar Assn. (pres. 1967-68), Los Angeles County Bar, Women Lawyers' Assn. Los Angeles, Cath. Daus. Club: Soroptimist (West Los Angeles).

KEELE, MARJORIE SUE HARSHBARGER (MRS. DOMAN KEELE), physician; b. Pottsboro, Tex., June 27, 1921; d. Grant Elmore and Willie Elmira (Goodpasture) Harshbarger; B.S., North Tex. State U., 1941, M.S., 1943; M.D., Southwestern Med. Sch., 1949; m. Doman Keele, June 19, 1953; children—Roger, Randy (dec.), Sheri. Tchr. secondary sch., Canton, Electra, Tex., 1941-43; tchr. sci. Abilene (Tex.) Christian Coll., 1943-45; intern Parkland Hosp., Dallas, 1949-50; resident Children's Med. Center, Dallas, 1950-53; tchr. Southwestern Med. Sch., 1954-56, Okla. U. Med. Sch., 1959-63; staff physician Denton State Sch. for Mentally Retarded, 1963-67; practice medicine specializing in pediatric neurology, Denton, Tex., Dallas, 1967—; asso. prof. allied health scis. Tex. Woman's U., Denton and Dallas; clin. instr. pediatrics Health Sci. Center U. Tex. at Dallas, 1973—; tchr. occupational therapy, 1971—. Cons. pvt. and pub. schs. local area. mem. adv. bd. Dean Meml. Learning Center, Dallas, Mid-Cities Learning Center, Euless, Tex. Mem. Alpha Omega Alpha. Mem. Ch. of Christ (active adoptive and foster care children's program 1967—). Home: 12512 Croydon Circle Dallas TX 75230 Office: Texas Woman's University Denton TX 76204

KEELY, ANN, marketing cons.; b. Milton, Pa.; d. Robert Russell and Mary Catherine (D'Angelo) Keely; student Dana Hall Sch., 1944-46, Principia Coll., 1946-48; B.F.A., Chgo. Art Inst., 1952; postgrad. N.Y. U., 1972—. Designer, artist for various theatre, TV, trade shows and interiors, 1952-63; interior decorator Armstrong Cork Co., Lancaster, Pa., 1956-58; partner Group Interviewing Services, N.Y.C., 1963-67; owner Ann Keely Ideational Research, N.Y.C., 1968—. Lectr. Columbia Coll., Chgo., 1959, Pa. State U., University Park, 1960. Mem. Am. Marketing Assn., United Scenic Artists, Allied Bd. Trade, Mensa. Contbr. article to profl. jour. Home: 140 E 81st St New York City NY 10028 Office: 133 E 56th St New York City NY 10022

KEELY, JANE BARTHOLOMAE (MRS. HARRY W. KEELY), home economist; b. Chgo., Apr. 1, 1922; d. Carl H. and Lucy (Brandt) Bartholomae; student MacMurray Coll., 1939-41; B.S., Cornell U., 1943; m. Harry W. Keely, June 30, 1961; 1 son, William D. Dietetian, Gen. Foods Corp., Hoboken, N.J., 1943-45, M & M Ltd., Newark, 1945-48; dir. appliances and home care Good Housekeeping mag., N.Y.C., 1948—. Mem. Am. Home Econs. Assn., Elec. Womens Round Table. Home: 1 Deepdale Dr Middletown NJ 07748 Office: 959 8th Av New York City NY 10019

KEENE, MARILYN ELLIS (MRS. JOHN ERNEST KEENE), educator, artist; b. Seattle, Sept. 30, 1919; d. W. Neil and Ellen (Johnson) Ellis; student Stephens Coll., 1937; B.S., U. Wash., 1940; m. John Ernest Keene, May 10, 1940; children—Laurel Elizabeth, Jennifer Ellis. Exhibited in group shows including Seattle Art Mus., Frye Art Mus., Seattle, Panaca Gallery, Bellevue, Wash., Seattle U., Woessner Gallery, Pacific N.W. Art Annual, Eugene, Ore.; represented in numerous pvt. collections; founder, tchr. creative art classes for deaf teenagers Seattle Hearing and Speech Center, 1966; pvt. art classes for tchrs. of deaf, 1967; owner pvt. studio for classes, paintings and hand screen designs, 1970—; conducted art workshops for Seattle Pub. Sch. Tchrs. of Deaf, 1967, for U. Wash. Tchrs. Mentally Retarded, 1971. Founder, pres., bd. dirs. Seattle Pre-Sch. for Deaf; founder, bd. dirs. Seattle Child Hearing League. Recipient citation Wash. Dept. Health, 1954, Stephens Coll. Alumni Achievement citation, 1959, Golden Lyre award for community service Alpha Chi Omega, 1966; named Woman of Achievement, Seattle Matrix Table, 1954, Seattle Quota Clubs, 1964. Mem. Child Hearing League, Hearing Ltd. (charter), N.W. Watercolor Soc., Artists Equity Assn., Seattle Pioneer's Assn., Soc. Western Artists, Women Painters Wash., Olympic Arts, Alpha Chi Omega. Conglist. Home: 6811 47th Av NE Seattle WA 98115

KEENER, MARILYN, educator; b. Freeport, Pa., May 8, 1933; d. Paul Cowan and Eleanor (Otterman) Keener; diploma Allegheny Gen. Hosp. Sch. Nursing, 1954; B.S., Millikin U., 1957; M.S., Boston U., 1965. Sch. nurse Millikin U., Decatur, Ill., 1954-57; staff nurse Decatur and Macon County Hosp., 1955-57, instr., 1957-59, clin. coordinator, 1959-66; dir. nursing edn. Black Hawk Coll., Moline, Ill., 1966—, established dept. nursing and related health fields, 1966. Examiner, cons. asso. North Central Assn. Colls. and Secondary Schs., 1969—. Chmn. nursing services A.R.C., 1967—, instr. home nursing and mother baby care, 1967—, instr., trainer, 1968—. Mem. adv. bd. St. Anthony's Hosp. Sch. Nursing, Rock Island, Ill., 1969-70. Mem. Ill. Nurses Assn. (dist. pres. 1968-70, dir. 1971—). Nat. League for Nursing, Am. Assn. U. Women (dir.); Child Care Assn. Ill. (co-chmn. short term courses 1968-73). Lutheran (Sunday sch. tchr. 1968—). Club: Zonta. Home: 4108 11th St East Moline IL 61244 Office: 6600 34th Av Moline IL 61265

KEENEY, VIRGINIA TRIPP (MRS. ARTHUR H. KEENEY), physician; b. Albany, N.Y., Mar. 23, 1920; d. Leon Lyle and Mabel (Tipping) Tripp; B.S., Coll. William and Mary, 1942; M.D., U. Louisville, 1954; m. Arthur H. Keeney, Dec. 27, 1942; children—Steven Harris, Martha Blackledge, L. Douglas. Intern Ky. Bapt. Hosp., Louisville, 1954-55; fellow Louisville Gen. Hosp., 1956-58; co-founder Ky. Eye Clinic in Childrens Hosp., Louisville, 1958; program dir. Sabin oral polio vaccine campaign, Louisville, 1962-63; dir. Nat. Conf. on Dyslexia, Phila., 1966; asst. prof. opthalmology Temple U. Sch. Medicine, Phila., 1970-73; asso. prof. family practice, coordinator med. ethics program U. La. Sch. Medicine, 1974—; cons. in ophthalmology Operation Head Start. Pres., trustee YWCA, Louisville; bd. dirs. women's com. Louisville Orch., Child Guidance Clinic Louisville, Shut-In Soc., Phila. Recipient Schering award, 1953; named Citizen Laureate, Louisville, 1964. Fellow Coll. Physicians of Phila. Presbyn. Editor: (with Arthur H. Keeney) Dyslexia (Transaction of Nat. Conf.), 1966. Home: 715 Alta Vista Rd Louisville KY 40206

KEES, BEVERLY ANN, editor; b. Mpls., June 4; d. Burton Joseph and Dorothy Ann (White) Kees; B.A., U. Minn., 1963. Reporter women's dept. Mpls. Star, 1963-66, reporter suburbs, 1966-67, reporter bus., 1967-69, editor taste sect., 1969-71, editor spl. sects., 1971-73, with research planning dept. Mpls. Stars' Tribune Co., 1973-74; asst. to the editor Mpls. Tribune, 1974—. Bd. dirs. Four Winds. Mem. Newspaper Guild, U. Minn. Alumnae Bd. Author: (with Donnie Flora) Fondue on the Menu, 1971, revised edit., 1972; Wonderful Ways with Chicken, 1972; Cook With Honey, 1973. Home: 15 S 1st St Minneapolis MN 55401 Office: 425 Portland Av Minneapolis MN 55415

KEESLING, KAREN RUTH, govt. ofcl.; b. Wichita, Kan., July 9, 1946; d. Paul W. and Ruth (Sharp) Keesling; B.S., Ariz. State U., 1968, M.A., 1970. Asst. dean women U. Kan., Lawrence, 1970-72; staff asst. vol. div. Com. to Re-Elect the Pres., Washington, 1972; exec. sec., sec.'s adv. com. on the rights and responsibilities of women Dept. Health, Edn. and Welfare, Washington, 1972—. Regional dir. Intercollegiate Assn. Women Students, Tempe, Ariz., 1968-69, exec. dir., 1969-71. Nat. Def. Act fellow, 1970-72. Mem. Nat. Assn. Women Deans, Adminstrs. and Counselors, Nat. Fedn. Bus. and Profl. Womens Clubs (chmn. nat. young careerist 1973—), Women's Equity Action League, Am. Assn. U. Women, P.E.O., Mortar Bd. Home: 3504 Stoneybrae Dr Falls Church VA 22044 Office: 330 Independence Av SW Washington DC 20201

KEEVER, RUTH CORNELIA, educator; b. Albuquerque, July 28, 1911; d. Charles Pinkston and Gussie (Barnett) Keever; A.B., Winthrop Coll., 1933; postgrad. Coll. Charleston, 1935, 37, Tchrs. Coll. Columbia, 1938; M.Ed., U. S.C., 1949, postgrad., 1958-59, 61-62; postgrad. Northwestern U., 1950, 55. Tchr. Charleston County (S.C.) schs., 1933-34; tchr. Charleston city schs., 1934-49, elementary prin., 1949-58, adminstrv. asst., 1958-59, coordinator fed. programs, 1966-68; with consolidation Charleston County Schs., 1968, asst. coordinator Charleston County Schs. Fed. Programs, 1968-73, asst. dir. fed. programs, 1973—; social dir. Coll. Charleston, summer 1941; tchr. Coll. Charleston Demonstration Sch., summer 1942; asst. librarian Med. Coll. S.C., summer 1944. Cons. handwriting specialist Zaner-Bloser Co., Columbus, O., 1959-66. Owner, dir. Reading and Writing Lab., Charleston, S.C., 1959—. Mem. S.C. Council Common Good, 1942-45; pres. womens div. U.S.O., Charleston, 1945. Mem. Am. Assn. U. Women (v.p. 1942-43, state v.p. 1944-47), Winthrop Alumnae (state v.p. 1943-45), S.C. Elementary Prins. Assn., N.E.A. (chmn. S.E. regional conf. 1955—), Elementary Tchrs. Charleston (pres. 1942), Central Council Charleston Tchrs. (past pres.), S.C., Charleston County edn. assns., S.C. Hist. Soc., Charleston County League Women Voters, Childhood Edn. Assn., Assn. Children Under Six, S.C. Sch. Adminstrs., S.C. Assn. Curriculum and Supervision, Charleston Preservation Soc., Internat. Platform Assn., Delta Kappa Gamma (sec. Beta chpt. 1948-49). Club: Zonta International (Charleston). Contbr. articles to profl. jours. Produced ETV-In-Service Tng. films Guiding Growth in Handwriting, for tchrs. S.C. Ednl. TV, 1964. Home: 273 Calhoun St Charleston SC 29401

KEGAN, ESTHER OSWIANZA (MRS. ALBERT I. KEGAN), lawyer; b. Chgo., June 29, 1913; d. Abraham and Ida (Segal) Oswianza; B.S., Northwestern U., 1933; J.D., 1936, M.A., 1953; m. Albert I. Kegan, Jan. 29, 1939 (dec.); children—Judith (Mrs. Richard Gardiner), Daniel, Franklin. Admitted to Ill. bar, 1936, U.S. Supreme Ct., 1943, U.S. Patent Office, 1947; mem. law dept. City of Chgo., 1936-41; mem. firm Kegan, Kegan & Berkman and predecessor firms, Chgo., 1943—. Dir. editing Municipal Code, Chgo., 1939; law lectr. patents and trademarks Northwestern U. Law Sch., Evanston, Ill., 1961-62. Mem. Ill. Food, Drug, Cosmetic and Pesticide Laws Study Commn., 1965-67; mem. adv. council Ill. and Met. Chgo. Comprehensive Health Planning, 1968-73. Mem. Internat. Assn. for Protection Indsl. Property, Inter-Am., Am. (chmn. com. on internat. trademark treaties and laws 1973—), Chgo. (chmn. food, drug and cosmetic laws com. 1973—), Women's bar assns., Decalogue Soc. Lawyers (dir.) Nat. Assn. Women Lawyers (dir.), Northwestern U. Law Alumni Assn. (dir.), Patent Law Assn. Chgo., Chgo. Council Lawyers, Order of Coif, Phi Beta Kappa. Contbr. articles in field to profl. jours. Home: 412 Ashland Av Evanston IL 60202 Office: 79 W Monroe St Chicago IL 60603

KEHOE, LETITIA ELAINE BELIVEAU, editor; b. Bklyn., July 15, 1921; d. George A. and Kathryn (McClintock) Beliveau; B.A., Vassar Coll., 1943; m. William J. Kehoe, Apr. 29, 1949 (div. 1967). Asst. editor, asso. editor Womans Home Companion, N.Y.C., 1944-49; asso. editor McCall's mag., N.Y.C., 1949-50, Woman's Day, N.Y.C., 1954-62, Reader's Digest Gen. Books, N.Y.C., 1962—. Home: 300 E 46th St New York City NY 10017 Office: 380 Madison Av New York City NY 10017

KEHOE, MONIKA, educator; b. Dayton, O., Sept. 11, 1909; d. Thomas Joseph and Josephine (Martin) Kehoe; A.B., Mary Manse Coll., 1932; Ph.D., Ohio State U., 1935. Dir. adult edn. Nat. Housing Authority, Detroit and Los Angeles, 1940-42, War Relocations

Authority, Gila River, Ariz., 1942-44; edn. specialist U.S. Mil. Govt., Korea, 1946-48; cons. to UN, N.Y.C. and Tokyo, 1948-52; edn. officer Bur. Adult Edn., N.Y. State Dept. Edn., Albany, 1952-54, Colombo Plan, Sydney, Australia, 1955-57; vis. prof. Russell Sage Coll., Troy, N.Y., 1957-58; dean of women Haile Sellassie U., Addis Ababa, Ethiopia, 1961-64; prof. English, Marianopolis Coll., Montreal, Que., Can., 1964-71; vis. prof. McGill U., 1969-71; prof. English, U. Guam, Agana, 1971—. Vis. scholar Tchrs. Coll., Columbia, 1961. Mem. Am. Assn. U. Women, Am. Assn. U. Profs., Modern Lang. Assn., Internat. Assn. U. Profs., Tchrs. English Speakers Other Langs., Canadian Linguistic Assn. Co-author: The Laurel and the Poppy, 1968. Editor: Applied Linguistics: A Survey for Language Teachers, 1968. Contbr. articles to profl. jours. Office: U Guam Box EK Agana GU 96910

KEHRER, BARBARA HOLTZ (MRS. KENNETH CARL KEHRER), health economist; b. N.Y.C., Feb. 22, 1943; d. Abraham and Charlotte (Leifer) Holtz; B.A., Barnard Coll., 1963; M.A. (Woodrow Wilson fellow), Yale, 1964, Ph.D. (U.S. Dept. Labor Manpower Devel. and Tng. Act grantee), 1970; m. Kenneth Carl Kehrer, Dec. 18, 1965. Research asso. Center for Health Care Research, Meharry Med. Coll., Nashville, 1969-71; asst. prof. econs. Fisk U., Nashville, 1968-71; dir. dept. econ. research Center for Health Services Research and Devel., A.M.A., Chgo., 1971—. Cons. Afro-Am. Assos. Nashville, 1969-70. Mem. Am. Econ. Assn., Phi Beta Kappa, Omicron Delta Epsilon. Editor: Yale Econ. Essays, 1965-67. Home: 5508 S Kenwood Av Chicago IL 60637 Office: American Medical Assn 535 N Dearborn St Chicago IL 60610

KEHRMAN, CAROL PHILLIPS, educator; b. Baton Rouge, Jan. 27, 1918; d. Robert Bowman and Sue Mary (Arbour) Phillips; B.S., La. State U., 1939; M.Ed., St. Louis U., 1965, Ph.D., 1972; m. Rolla F. Kehrman, Mar. 25, 1940; children—Rolla William, Robert F., J. Richard. Tchr., Lawtell (La.) High Sch., 1939-40, Istrouma Sr. High School, Baton Rouge, La., 1940-42, Omaha Pub. Schs., 1943-45, Balt. Pub. Schs., 1950-52, St. Peters Sch., Kirkwood, Mo., 1954-61, Spl. Sch. Dist. St. Louis (Mo.) County, 1961—; critic tchr. in practicum St. Louis U.; guest lectr. psychology of exceptional children, methods and materials Harris Teachers Coll., 1968; tchr. psychology of exceptional children U. Mo. at St. Louis, 1973. Permanent chmn. Harold C. Smith and Lucy C. Elliott Scholarship Fund, Harris Tchrs. Coll. Mem. Nat. Edn. Assn., Council Exceptional Children, Am. Assn. Mental Deficiency, Mo. Tchrs. Assn., Community Tchrs. Assn., Suburban Teachers Assn. St. Louis County, Alpha Delta Kappa, Phi Lambda Theta. Home: 1503 Starling Dr St Louis MO 63126 Office: Southview Sch 11660 Eddie and Park Rd St Louis MO 63126

KEHTEL, CARMEN HELENE, educator; b. Duluth, Minn., Sept. 30, 1933; d. William Richard and Gunvor (Kornstad) Kehtel; B.S., U. Minn., 1955; M.S. U. Colo., 1958; postgrad. U. Neb., 1961-62, U. Hawaii, 1967, U. Minn., 1971. Instr. swimming Camp Newaygo, 1953; small craft dir. Camp Nicolet, 1955-57, Eagle River, Wis., 1961-63; tchr. Denfeld High Sch., 1955-57; grad. asst. U. Colo., Boulder, 1957-58; asst. prof. U. Neb., Lincoln, 1958-63; asst. prof. phys. edn. Temple Buell Coll. (now Colo. Woman's Coll.), Denver, 1963—. Camp counselor YWCA Camp, Grand Rapids, Mich., 1952; waterfront dir. Jedcen Day Camp, Duluth, Minn., 1953-55; small craft dir. Camp Nicolet, Eagle River, Wis., 1956, 57, 62, 63; student asst. women's phys. edn. dept. U. Minn., Duluth, 1952-54; summer swimming program dir. Colo. Woman's Coll., 1965-67. Swimming instr. YWCA, Duluth, Minn., 1952-54; water safety trainer, first aid instr. A.R.C., Lincoln, Neb., Denver, 1958-70. Recipient Elizabeth Graybeal award Woman's Athletic Assn., 1955; named Outstanding Prof. of Year, Colo. Women's Coll., 1972. Mem. Am. (rep. assembly 1969), Colo. Central Dist. assns. health, phys. edn. and recreation, Nat. (mem. at large 1973-75), Central (chmn. girls and woman's sports 1967-69, chmn. spl. com. on intercollegiate sports 1968-71) assns. phys. edn. coll. women, Am. Coll. Sports Medicine, Colo. Bd. Ofcls. (chmn. 1967-69). Home: 1122 Grape St Denver CO 80220

KEIM, KATHIE MARIE, newspaper reporter; b. Orlando, Fla., Nov. 22, 1947; d. Frank Frederick and Althea (Leidy) Keim; B.S.J., U. Fla., 1969. Staff writer Women's dept. Pompano Beach (Fla.) Sun-Sentinel, 1969; reporter Boca Raton (Fla.) News, 1969-70; reporter Broward Times, 1970-71; courthouse reporter Hollywood (Fla.) Sun-Tattler, 1971-73; courthouse reporter, bur. reporter Ft. Lauderdale (Fla.) News, 1973—. Mem. Women in Communications Inc. Democrat. Presbyn. Home: 2281 NE 12th St Pompano Beach FL 33062 Office: 2501 N Federal Hwy Pompano Beach FL 33060

KEIMIG, MARY JANE, librarian, educator; b. Seattle, Aug. 18, 1945; d. Hans Max and Annie (Reid) Polack; B.A. in Anthropology, U. Wash., 1966, M.L.S., 1967; m. Alan Charles Keimig, May 13, 1973; children—Randall, Angela, Christina, John, Jené. Librarian, Highline Community Coll., Midway, Wash., 1967—; designer, planner Design by Keimig, Puyallup, Wash., 1973—; planner Chehalis and Muckleshoot Indian tribes, 1973—. Home: 4403 372d St Puyallup WA 98371 Office: Highline Community Coll Midway WA 98031

KEISTER, ETHEL MARKS WILLIAMS (MRS. ALBERT FRASER KEISTER), civic leader; b. West Newton, Pa.; d. Alfred Daniel and Martha (Marks) Williams; B.A., Chatham Coll., 1914; postgrad. Cornell U., 1914-16; Ph.D. in Music, Waynesburg (Pa.) Coll.; m. Albert Fraser Keister, Dec. 19, 1917 (dec. Mar. 1937); children—Jean Fraser (Mrs. George Wolff Ratcliffe), Phyllis Alberta (Mrs. Harton Singer Semple). High sch. tchr. Latin, botany, Wilkinsburg, Pa., 1925-26. Guarantor summer music camp Chatham Coll., 1955, dean's asst., 1928-29. Founder Pitts. (Pa.) Playhouse, 1935—, Opera Workshop, Pitts., 1949, Lyric Theater, Inc., Pitts., 1955, Operalogues, Pitts., 1951, Lab. Sch. Music, Pitts., 1953; pres. Women's Assn. of Pitts. Symphony Soc., 1951-53, bd. dirs., 1946—; v.p. Women's City Club, Pitts., 1935-36; chmn. music com. Twentieth Century Club, 1939-40; chmn. finance com. Coll. Club, Pitts., 1927; Pa. chmn. Ind. Coalition Am. Women, 1936—; bd. dirs. Pitts. Symphony Soc., Pitts. Opera, Inc., Pitts. Civic Light Opera Mendelssohn Choir, Pitts. Woodwind Soc.; adv. chmn. young artists group Musicians Club N.Y.C., 1969—. Recipient numerous awards including Distinguished Service award Pa. Fedn. Music Clubs, 1968, Chatham Coll. Centennial award, 1969; named Distinguished Dau. of Pa., 1971. Chmn. Western Pa. Hospitalized Vets. Assn. Mem. Dame of Mil. and Hospitaler Order of St. Lazarus, Met. Opera Nat. Council, Pitts. Arts Council, Chatham Coll. Alumni Assn. (pres. 1931-32), Pitts. Soc. Architects, Western Pa. Conservancy (hon. life), Nat. Fedn. Music Clubs (hon. life). Home: Rockledge Farm Sewickley PA 15143

KEITER, M. ROBERTA WARF (MRS. BLAIR E. KEITER), educator; b. Pitts., Apr. 22, 1918; d. Harry Lee and Lily J. (Davis) Warf; B.S., Shippensburg State Coll., 1940; M.A., U. Md., 1950, Ph.D., 1957; postgrad. Duke, summer 1941, George Washington U., Am. U., 1955-63; m. Blair E. Keiter, Feb. 7, 1942; 1 son, Robert Blair. Tchr. math. Williamstown (Pa.) High Sch., 1940-43, U. Md., summer 1951, Montgomery Blair High Sch., Silver Spring, Md., 1952-61; tchr. math. resource Montgomery County Schs., Rockville, Md., 1961-65, supr. pupil and program appraisal, after 1965, now asst. dir. dept. Councilwoman, Glen Echo, Md., 1966—; sec. Montgomery County Scholarship Com., 1964-67. Sec., Democratic Precinct, 1950. Sec. Montgomery County Scholarship Found., 1970—. Served to lt. USCG Womans Res. 1943-46. Mem. Montgomery County Edn. Assn. (mem. exec. com. 1959-67, pres. 1963-65), Nat. Council Urban Edn. Assns. (pres. 1964-65, mem. exec. bd. 1961-66), N.E.A., Md. State Tchrs. Assn. (pres. 1967-68, exec. bd. 1964-69), Math. Assn. Am., Assn. Edn. Data Systems, A.A.A.S., Nat. Council Math. Tchrs., Nat. Council on Measurement in Edn., Md. Assn. Measurement in Edn. (pres. elect), Delta Kappa Gamma (chpt. treas. 1960-67). Home: 6003 Bryn Mawr Av Glen Echo MD 20768 Office: 850 N Washington St Rockville MD 20850

KEITH, CAMILLE TIGERT, airlines pub. relations exec.; b. Ft. Worth, Tex., Feb. 27, 1945; d. Marvin and Catherine (Tuscany) Keith; B.A., Tex. Christian U., 1967. Asst. promotion mgr. Sta. WFAA TV, Dallas, 1967-71; dir. agy. Read-Poland Inc., Dallas, 1971-72; pub. relations, promotion dir. Southwest Airlines, Dallas, 1972—. Recipient excellence in pub. relations award Women In Communications, 1973. Mem. Tex. Soc. Daus. Am. Revolution, Tex. Soc. Children of Am. Revolution (adviser 1960-73), Freedom Found., Dallas chpt. The 500 Inc., The Assemblage, Women in Communications, Dallas Advtg. League. Mem. Christian Ch. (Sunday sch. teacher 1967-73). Club: Press (Dallas). Home: 4611 Amesbury Dr Dallas TX 75206 Office: 3300 Love Field Dr Dallas TX 75235

KEITH, CLARA MARGUERITTE, univ. dean.; b. Beresford, S.D.; d. Walter S. and Philura B. (Drey) Keith; B.S., No. Tchrs. Coll., 1955; M.A., Columbia, 1957. Placement dir. S.D. State Coll., 1952-56; dean of students Moore Inst. Art, Phila., 1957-58; asst. dean of women Colo. Coll., 1958-60; dean women and asso. dean of students State U. Coll. Edn., Brockport, N.Y., 1960-64; dean students Westhampton Coll., U. Richmond, 1964—; cons. student personnel. Mem. adv. bd. World U. Hon. mem. Father Flanagan's Home. Mem. Nat. Assn. Women Deans and Counselors, N.Y. State Tchrs. Assn., N.Y. Faculties Assn., Jr. Red Cross, Jr. Audubon Soc., S.D. Mental Health, Fine Arts Assn., Midwest Central Placement Assn., Am. Coll. Personnel Assn., Am. Assn. U. Women, Bus. and Profl. Women's Club, Am. Personnel Guidance Assn., Nat. Vocational Guidance, Wilderness Soc., Internat. Platform Assn., Internat. House, English-Speaking Union, Va. Mus. Art, Marquis Biog. Library Soc. (adv. mem.), Am. Acad. Polit. and Social Sci.; Kappa Delta Pi, Delta Kappa Gamma, Pi Gamma Mu. Clubs: Nat. Travel, Toastmistress, Colony. Office: Westhampton Coll U Richmond Richmond VA 23173

KEITH, JOCELYN SULLIVAN FREER, realty co. exec.; b. Boston, Sept. 24, 1927; d. Harold Wardsworth and Alice Elizabeth (Barry) Sullivan; student George Washington U., 1945-47; children—Quentin Barry, Jonathan Chilton, Jocelyn Deborah. Interviewer program Diplomatic Debs, radio sta. WBBC, 1947, 58; bd. dirs. Ch. Farm Sch., 1954-67, Children's Convalescent Hosp., 1958; asso. A.S. Gardiner & Co., Inc., Washington, 1968—. Clubs: Chevy Chase (Md); Sulgrave (Washington); Lyford Cay (Nassau, Bahamas). Home: 21 Farmington Ct Chevy Chase MD 20015 Office: 917 15th St NW Washington DC 20005

KEITH, SISTER JUDITH MARIE, hosp. adminstr.; b. Little Rock, Sept. 5, 1933; d. John Patrick and Johanna (Werner) Keith; B.S. in Nursing, St. Louis U., 1960; M.Hosp. Adminstrn., Xavier U., 1968. Adminstrv. resident Holy Cross Hosp., Salt Lake City, 1967-68; orthopedic nursing supr. St. Joseph Hosp., Hot Springs, Ark., 1958-60; obstet. nursing supr. Warner Brown Hosp., El Dorado, Ark., 1961-62; med. surg. nursing supr. Mercy Hosp., New Orleans, 1962-65; asst. adminstr. St. Edward Mercy Hosp., Ft. Smith, Ark., 1968-70, adminstr., 1970—, instr. Warner Brown Hosp., 1965-66. Mem. Ark. Gov.'s Hosp. Adv. Council, 1973—; exec. com. health planning council Western Ark. Econ. Devel. program. Mem. Am. Coll. Hosp. Adminstrs., Ark. Hosp. Assn. (trustee 1971-73, pres. elect 1973-74, trustee 1972-73). Contbr. articles to profl. jours. Address: 1411 Rogers Av Fort Smith AR 72901

KEITH, MARGARET DYCHE (MRS. LUKE KEITH JR.), publisher, editor; b. London, Ky., Jan. 9, 1943; d. Will Martin and Rubye Hazel (Boles) Dyche; student Fla. State U., 1960-62; Mus.B., U. Ky., 1965; m. Luke Keith Jr., Aug. 28, 1970; children—Kathryn Logan, Karlyle Martin. Tchr. music LaRue County (Ky.) Bd. Edn., 1966-69; minister music First Bapt. Ch., Hodgenville, Ky., 1968-69; pub., soc. editor, treas. Sentinel-Echo, London, 1969—, editor, 1974—. Pres., United AID Laurel County (Ky.), 1972-73, v.p., 1971-72, 73-74. Mem. Fine Arts Assn. Southeastern Ky. (sec. 1972—), Nat. Newspaper Assn., Ky. Press Assn., Co-op. Ch. Ministry (dir. 1973), Zeta Tau Alpha, Phi Beta. Republican. Baptist. Home: E 1st St London KY 40741 Office: 123 W 5th St London KY 40741

KEITH-SPIEGEL, PATRICIA COSETTE (MRS. DONALD E. SPIEGEL), educator, researcher, author; b. Glendale, Cal.; d. Boyd E. and Barbara (Halsey) Keith; B.A. cum laude, Occidental Coll., 1961; M.A. (Nat. Def. Edn. Act predoctoral fellow), Claremont Grad. Sch., 1964, Ph.D., 1968; m. Donald E. Spiegel, June 17, 1966; 1 son, Gary Brian. Psychology research asst. Brentwood VA Hosp., 1964-66, vol. research asso., 1966—; asst. prof. psychology Cal. State U. at Northridge, 1966-69, asso. prof. psychology, 1969-73, prof., chmn. dept. psychology, 1973—. Free-lance civic and indsl. cons., 1968—. Recipient Superior Performance award VA, 1965, Vol. Service awards, 1967-68. Mem. Am., Western, Cal. (chairperson com. social issues 1969—, women's role and status com. 1970—), Los Angeles (dir. 1971—) San Fernando Valley (membership chmn. 1970—, treas. 1972—) psychol. assns., A.A.A.S., Psi Chi (chpt. pres. 1960-61), Beta Phi Delta (chpt. pres. 1960-61). Author: Outsiders U.S.A., 1973. Contbr. articles to profl. jours. Home: 15374 Longbow Dr Sherman Oaks CA 91403 Office: Cal State University Northridge CA 91324

KELL, MARY POTTER (MRS. LAURENCE DEVINE KELL), writer, research cons.; b. Northville, Mich., May 8, 1928; d. Allen Victor and Margaret Eleanor (Van Houten) Potter; B.A., Wayne State U., 1951; m. Laurence Devine Kell, Oct. 1, 1955. Research asst. Saturday Evening Post, Detroit, 1951; continuity dir. WMRY Radio, New Orleans, 1952-54; informational rep. La. State Dept. Health, New Orleans, 1955-56; pub. relations dir. Goodwill Industries, New Orleans, 1961-63; founder, co-owner Kell Asso., New Orleans, 1963—; editor, co-founder Undercurrents Mag., New Orleans, 1968-71; free lance writer, researcher, 1956—. Pub. relations cons. to various commercial diving companies and undersea equipment mfrs., 1964—; research cons. Nat. Geog. Soc., 1971, 73, Wall Street Jour., 1970, Pelagic Sea Research, 1972—. Vice pres. Alliance for Good Govt. Exec. Session, New Orleans, 1972—; mem. French Quarter Residents Assn., New Orleans, 1973—. Recipient Writing award Internat. Council Indsl. Editors, 1970. Mem. Internat. Assn. Profl. Divers, Internat. Assn. Bus. Communicators (v.p. 1963), Marine Tech. Soc. (chmn. New Orleans sect. 1973-74), Audubon Zool. Soc., Friends of Cabildo. Democrat. Author: (with William A. Meyerer) Hurricane Betsy-The Nation's Greatest Natural Disaster, 1966. Contbr. articles in field to profl. jours. Home and office: PO Box 2383 New Orleans LA 70176

KELLAM, SHIRLEY YVONNE, physician; b. Brampton, Ont., Can., June 27, 1936; d. Percy Herbert Howard and Hazel Ellen (Watson) Kellam; B.A., U. Western Ont., 1958; M.D., U. Toronto (Ont.), 1962. Intern Toronto Western Hosp., 1962-63; gen. practice medicine, Brampton, Ont., 1963—; staff Peel Meml. Hosp., Brampton, 1963—. Mem. Canadian, Ont. med. assns. Presbyterian. Home: 24 Nanwood Dr Brampton ON Canada

KELLEHER, GRACE JAYNE WALKER, statistician, operations research analyst; b. Sarasota, Fla., Aug. 8, 1927; d. Harney Henry and Nella (Yarbrough) Walker; student Am. U., 1946-50, M.A. in Statistics, 1955; B.S. in Pub. Adminstrn. and Mil. Sci., U. Md., 1952, postgrad. in math. econs., 1965-68; postgrad. in econs. So. Methodist U., 1969-71; postgrad. engring. U. Tex. at Arlington, 1972-74; m. Frank J. Kelleher, 1951 (div. 1968); children—Eileen, Linda; m. 2d, John Edward Walsh, Sept. 18, 1969 (dec. Aug. 1972). Statistician, Dept. Navy, Washington, 1945-50; statistician, logistician Hdqrs. USAF, Washington, 1952-63; sr. research staff, econs. and systems analysis Inst. for Def. Analyses, Arlington, Va., 1964-69; lectr. econs. So. Meth. U., Dallas, 1969-70; asst. prof. mgmt. sci. U. Tex. at Arlington, 1970-72; sr. asso. Computer Aid Cos. Inc., Dallas, 1972-73; operations research analyst Def. Communications Engring. Center, Reston, Va., 1973—. Served to capt. USAF, 1951-52. Recipient Meritorious Civilian Service award USAF, 1957. Fellow A.A.A.S.; mem. Operations Research Soc. Am. (sects. com. 1967-68, long range planning com. 1967-69, A.A.A.S. liason com. 1970-72), Inst. Mgmt. Scis. (vice chmn. Washington chpt. 1968-69), Am. Statis. Assn. Co-author, editor: The Challenge to Systems Analysis: Public Policy and Social Change, 1970. Home: 9500 Tuba Ct Vienna VA 22180

KELLEHER, SISTER MARY ANNUNCIATA, hosp. adminstr.; b. Buffalo, Apr. 4, 1926; d. James J. and Julia Marie (Hyde) Kelleher; student Canisius Coll., 1945-46; R.N., Mercy Hosp. Sch. Nursing, 1948; B.S.N., D'Youville Coll., 1958; postgrad. State U. of N.Y. at Buffalo, 1966. Joined Religious Sisters of Mercy, 1949; staff nurse Mercy Hosp., Buffalo, 1948-49, asso. adminstr., dir. nursing service, 1966-68, adminstr., 1968—; nursing supr., head nurse St. Jerome Hosp., Batavia, N.Y., 1952-54; dir. nursing service, nursing supr. Kenmore (N.Y.) Mercy Hosp., 1954-66. Mem. adv. com. nursing curriculum Erie Community Coll., 1970—. Bd. dirs. Trocaire Coll., Mercy Hosp., Buffalo, Kenmore Mercy Hosp., St. Jerome Hosp., Comprehensive Health Planning Coll. Erie County. Mem. Am. Coll. Hosp. Adminstrs., Cath. Hosp. Assn. (pres. western N.Y. sect. 1969-71), Health Orgn. Western N.Y., Am., N.Y. State hosp. assns., Mental Health Assn. Erie County. Address: 565 Abbott Rd Buffalo NY 14220

KELLER, EDITH LIGHT, educator, poet; b. Watseka, Ill., Jan. 9, 1893; d. Samuel Emlin and Edith Frances (McDill) Light; A.B., Park Coll., Kansas City, Mo.; postgrad. U. Wyo., Ariz. U.; m. Albert William Keller, Feb. 26, 1925. Tchr., Yavapai County Schs., Prescott, Ariz., 1924-37, 39-57; prin. schs., Cave Creek, 1951-52, Yarnell, 1952-56. Mem. Gov.'s Bd. for Ariz. Curriculum, 1944-46; helped write course of study exptl. teaching in rural schs. No. Ariz. U. Organizer, Youngtown (Ariz.) Good Neighbor Policy; research worker Cancer Found., 1960-65; mem. aux. Alexander Home for Underprivileged Grils. Bd. dirs. Plus Sixty. Mem. Nat., Ariz. assns. ret. tchrs., Penwomen, World Poetry Club, Ariz. U. Women, Nat. State Poetry Soc., Writers Club, Delta Kappa Gamma. Presbyn. Clubs: Federated Women's (pres. 1960-61); Federated Garden (pres. 1959-61) (Youngtown). Contbr. poems to mags. Home: 1401 S 7th Av Phoenix AZ 85007

KELLER, FLORENCE, physician, educator; b. Bklyn. Sept. 6, 1912; d. Frederick and Edith (Mead) Keller; B.A., Adelphi Coll., 1934; M.D., L.I. Coll. of Medicine (now Downstate Med. Center of State U. N.Y.), 1943. Intern L.I. Coll. Hosp., 1943; med. fellow Cleve. Clinic Found., 1944; tng. Duke Hosp., 1945-47; resident Watts Hosp., Durham, N.C., 1947-48; attending physician, dept. obstetrics and gynecology Yale-New Haven Hosp., 1956—; mem. courtesy staff obstetrics and gynecology Hosp. of St. Raphael, New Haven; clin. prof. dept. obstetrics and gynecology Yale, 1949—. Mem. adv. com. New Haven Vis. Nurse Assn., 1971—. Named Woman of the Year, Bus. and Profl. Women's Club of New Haven, 1967. Diplomate Am. Bd. Obstetrics and Gynecology. Fellow A.C.S.; mem. New Haven County (bd. govs.), Conn. med. assns., A.M.A., New Haven Obstet. Soc. (pres. 1971), Quota Internat., Phi Mu. Home: 309 Old Tavern Rd Orange CT 06477 Office: 264 Amity Rd Woodbridge CT 06525

KELLER, JUDITH ADRIENNE (MRS. JUDAH ROHER), physician; b. Budapest, Hungary, Oct. 26, 1933 (parents Am. citizens); d. Nandor and Helen (Beck) Keller; B.S. cum laude, Bklyn. Coll., 1954; M.D., State U. N.Y. at Bklyn., 1958; M.P.H., Columbia, 1969; m. Judah Roher, Mar. 3, 1965;children—David, Dina, Alyssa. Intern, Maimonides Hosp., Bklyn., 1958-59, attending physician in medicine Coney Island div., 1962-67; resident Bklyn. VA Hosp., 1959-62; attending physician Brookdale Hosp., Bklyn., 1963-65; physician Bklyn. Coll., 1963-67; dep. commr. health Westchester County, White Plains, N.Y., 1969—. Mem. Am., N.Y. State socs. internal medicine, Westchester Med. Soc., Phi Beta Kappa. Home: 22 Idlewood Rd White Plains NY 10605 Office: 85 Court St White Plains NY 10601

KELLER, LOUISE JEAN, educator; b. Kansas City, Mo., May 27, 1928; d. Albert and Mary M. (Duden) Keller; B.S., Pitts. State Coll. (Kan.), 1953; M.S., Kan. Tchrs. Coll., Emporia, 1956; Ed.D., Mont. State U., 1968. Office edn. tchr., coordinator Wichita (Kan.) Pub. Sch. Systems, 1953-59, dept. head. bus. edn. Wichita South High Sch., 1959-64, city supr. bus. edn., area vocational edn., sch. planner adminstr., 1964-67; prof., dir. chmn. dept. vocational edn. U. No. Colo., Greeley, 1968—; editor Charles E. Merrill Pub. Co., 1970—. Speaker, cons., workshop instr., 1959—. Mem. N.E.A., Am. Vocational Assn., Assn. for Ednl. Communications and Tech., Nat. Bus. Edn. Assn., Nat. Council Local Adminstrs. and Practical Arts. Home: Box 172 North Fork Drake CO 80515 Office: University No Colo Greeley CO 80631

KELLER, MARGARET GILMER (MRS. GEORGE HENRY KELLER, III), educator; b. Harrisburg, Pa., July 11, 1911; d. Charles Greenwalt Gilmer and Mary Ellen (Sullivan) Gilmer; A.B., Trinity Coll., 1933; A.M., Columbia, 1934, certificate, 1942; certificate State Tchrs. Coll., Bloomsburg, Pa., 1934; m. George Henry Keller, III, July 13, 1940; children—Mary Ellen, Margaret Marie, George Henry, IV. Acting chmn. dept. history Trinity Coll., Washington, 1935-36; chmn. classical dept. Convent Sacred Heart, 1936-37, Steelton (Pa.) High Sch., 1937-41; lectr. English dept. U. Coll., Rutgers U., 1946—, mem. dean's adv. com. Univ. Coll., 1968—, also advisor to women's clubs Univ. Coll.; chmn. classical dept. Glen Rock (N.J.) High Sch., 1956-59, chmn. fgn. lang. dept., 1959—. Mem. Sch.-Community Adv. Com. to Ridgewood (N.J.) Pub. Sch., 1956—, TV adv. bd., 1955—. Active Am. Cancer Soc., Community Chest, A.R.C., Girl Scouts Am.; chmn. clinic com. jr. auxiliary Patterson (N.J.) Gen. Hosp., 1942—; mem. nominating bd. Ridgewood (N.J.) Nursing Service, 1959-60. Chmn. Trinity Coll. Devel. Fund Drive N.J.; trustee Trinity Coll., 1964—. Committeewoman, Republican County Com. Cited by Rutgers U., 1953, 61, 64, 65, 66, 71, by Newman Province of N.J., 1963; recipient Robert Ax award for distinguished teaching, 1971. Mem. N.E.A., N.J. Edn. Assn., Am. Classical Soc., Am. Assn. U. Women (former dir.), Met. Assn. Coll. Tchrs. English, Chaplain's Aid Assn., Trinity Coll., Alumnae Assn. (nat. pres.), Phi Chi Theta. Clubs: Newman (adv. Rutgers U.), Univ. Coll. Women (hon. Rutgers U.).

Home: 200 Phelps Rd Ridgewood NJ 07450 Office: Rutgers U New Brunswick NJ 08903

KELLER, MARGARET LEONA, real estate broker; b. Denver, Aug. 16, 1899; d. Ira Bird and Marie K. (Laird) Griffith; student Cottage Coll., 1915-16, Kings County Hosp. Nursing Sch., 1920; grad., Tex. Christian U., 1921; m. Edwin W. Keller, May 21, 1958 (dec. 1973); children by previous marriage—Elisa Marie (Mrs. Owen E. Wood), Herman Frederick Stute, William B. Stute (dec.). Registrar vital statistics, Tex., 1921; columnist S.W. mag., Ft. Worth, 1922-45; rancher, Tex., 1925-44; mgr. Ft. Worth Safety Council, 1942-48; owner, mgr. Gen. Store, Borrego Springs, Cal., 1951-54; hotel cashier Hollywood Knickerbocker (Cal.), 1954-58; Brisa Del Mar Motel, San Clemente, Cal., 1958-60; owner, real estate broker AActive Realty, Vista, Cal., 1960—. Mem. Soc. Safety Engrs., Bus. and Profl. Womans Club, Am., Cal., Vista real estate bds. Home: 1290 Cypress Vista CA 92083 Office: 114 Natal Way Vista CA 92083

KELLER, SISTER MARY KENNETH, educator; b. Cleve., Dec. 17, 1913; d. John Adam and Katherine Josephine (Sullivan) Keller; A.B., DePaul U., 1943, M.S., 1952; Ph.D., U. Wis., 1965; postgrad. Dartmouth, 1961, U. Mich., 1966, Tulane U., 1971. Educator, math. instr., cons. Ill-Ia. area, 1943-63; prof., chmn. computer scis. dept. Clarke Coll., Dubuque, Ia., 1965—. Cons. State Ill. Mgmt. Information Div., 1970-71; dir. NSF Summer Insts. in Computer, 1968-71; tech. adviser, City of Dubuque, 1969-70. NSF fellow, 1961-63. Mem. Assn. Computer Machinery. Author: Mathematical Logic and Probability, 1971. Home: Clarke Coll Dubuque IA 52001

KELLER, SUZANNE, sociologist; b. Vienna, Austria; Ph.D., Columbia, 1953. Interpreter and translator, Paris, 1952-53; postdoctoral fellow Princeton, 1953-54, vis. prof. sociology, 1967-68, prof., 1968—; research asso. Mass. Inst. Tech., 1954-57; asst. prof. Brandeis U., 1957-60; asso. prof. Vassar Coll., 1962-63; Fulbright lectr. Athens, Greece, 1963-65; lectr. and research analyst Athens Center of Ekistics, 1965-67; cons. to govt., bus. and profl. groups. Author: Beyond the Ruling Class, 1963; The Urban Neighborhood, 1968. Home: 59 College Rd Princeton NJ 08540

KELLERHOUSE, MURIEL ARLINE (MRS. KENNETH D. KELLERHOUSE), educator; b. Halcottsville, N.Y., May 20, 1927; d. William E. and Ethel A. (Dean) Griffin: B.A., State U. N.Y., 1947, M.A., 1954; postgrad. U. Colo., 1959, U. Mo., 1961; Ph.D., Ind. U., 1973; m. Kenneth D. Kellerhouse, Aug. 21, 1949; 1 son, Dean Kenneth. Tchr., Grand Gorge (N.Y.) Central Sch., 1947-60; faculty State U. Coll., Oneonta, N.Y., 1960—, prof. theatre, 1960—, actress, dir. summer theatre, 1965—. Actress, dir. Albany (N.Y.) Arena Theatre, 1953; actress U. Mo. Summer Theatre, Columbia, 1961-73. Mem. Am. Theatre Assn., Am. Theatre and Acad., Ind. U. Alumni Assn. Democrat. Methodist. Home: 1 Ravine Park N Oneonta NY 13820

KELLEY, ELLEN ABBOTT (MRS. JOHN CHARLES KELLEY), educator; b. Carbondale, Ill., Jan. 8, 1933; d. Talbert Ward and Hazel Esther (Ervin) Abbott; B.A., U. Ill., 1955; M.A., So. Ill. U., 1960; m. John Charles Kelley, May 4, 1966. Instr., curator collections Univ. Mus., supr. Univ. Mus. Research Labs., So. Ill. U., Carbondale, 1960-71, asst. prof. Univ. Mus., curator No. Mesoam. Archaeology U. Mus., supr. U. Mus. Mesoam. Research Lab., 1971—. Mem. Am. Anthropol. Assn., A.A.A.S., Soc. Am. Archaeology, Soc. Applied Anthropology, Central State Anthrop. Soc., Ill. State Acad. Sci., Pi Lambda Theta. Presbyn. Home: Rural Route 1 Makanda IL 62958 Office: U Mus So Ill U Carbondale IL 62901

KELLEY, FRANCES THERESE, computer programmer; b. Lawrence, Mass., Sept. 17, 1928; d. Hubert Joseph and Anna (Duggan) Kelley; A.B., Emmanuel Coll., 1949; postgrad. Worcester Poly. Inst., 1970—. Engring. asst. Gen. Electric Corp., Lynn, Mass., 1950-55; mem. staff Mass. Inst. Tech. Lincoln Lab., Lexington, Mass., 1955-57; sr. project mem. RCA, Burlington, Mass., 1957-71, engr., Moorestown, N.J., 1971—. Recipient RCA Tech. Excellence award, 1968; Tech. Excellence Team award, 1967, 1969. Mem. Assn. for Computing Machinery. Clubs: College Club of Lawrence, Emmanuel Coll. Club. Home: 11 Sheridan St Lawrence MA 01841 Office: RCA Moorestown NJ 08057

KELLEY, HELEN, coll. pres.; b. Cedar Rapids, Ia., May 21, 1925; d. William John and Frances (Heenan) Kelley; B.A., Immaculate Heart Coll., Los Angeles, 1949; M.A., St. Louis U., 1954, Ph.D., 1959. Tchr. grammar sch., Visalia, Cal., 1947-48; tchr. history Immaculate Heart High Sch., Los Angeles, 1948-55; tchr. sociology Immaculate Heart Coll., 1958-63, pres., 1963—, also trustee. Fellow Radcliffe Inst., 1963. Mem. Am. Sociol. Assn., Soc. Sci. Study Religion, Assn. Higher Edn., Nat. Catholic Ednl. Assn. Democrat. Roman Catholic. Contbr. articles to profl. jours. Home: 2120 E Live Oak St Los Angeles CA 90027

KELLEY, JEAN ANN JACOBS (MRS. CLARENCE BRECK KELLEY), educator; b. Vintondale, Pa., Nov. 16, 1930; d. John and Mary Ann (Kanich) Jacobs; diploma in nursing Mercy Central Sch. Nursing, Mich., 1951; B.S. in Nursing, U. Ala., 1956, Ed.D., 1969; M.A. in Edn., N.Y.U., 1958; m. Clarence Breck Kelley, Nov. 8, 1952; children—Mary L., Clarence Breck, Michael Steven. Staff nurse maternity Mercy Hosp., Bay City, Mich., 1951-52; asst. head nurse Univ. Hosp., 1956-57, supr. maternity Mt. Sinai Hosp., 1958-59 (both N.Y.C.); asst. prof. nursing U. Ala. at Birmingham, 1959-64, 65-67, prof. nursing, asst. dean, chmn. grad. program, 1969—; dir. ednl. program nursing of children St. Vincent, Druid City, Sylacauga Schs. Nursing, Birmingham, 1964-65. Mem. paramed. adv. com. Jefferson (Ala.) State Jr. Coll., 1970—; mem. adv. com. nursing program U. Ala. at Huntsville, 1970-71; faculty in-service cons. Sylacauga (Ala.) Sch. Nursing, 1970-72; nurse cons. Tuskegee (Ala.) VA Hosp., 1971-73, Birmingham VA Hosp., 1969-72; speaker universities, profl. orgns. in S.C., N.C., Tex., Mich., Ala. Served to 1st lt. Nurse Corps, AUS, 1952-54. Decorated UN Service medal, Nat. Def. Service medal, Korean Service medal. Spl. nurse research fellow USPHS, 1967-69. Mem. Am. Nurses Assn., Nat., Ala. (bd. dirs. 1961-63, 69-71, 71—), N.Ala. (chmn. nominating com. 1965-66) leagues nursing, Birmingham Bot. Soc., Women's Aux. Birmingham Bar Assn., V.F.W. Aux., Women's Aux. Sigma Delta Kappa., Sigma Theta Tau (nat. sec. 1965-69, 69-73), Kappa Delta Pi. Research in leadership behaviors of suprs. of nursing in gen. hosps. Ala. Home: 4766 Overwood Circle Birmingham AL 35222

KELLEY, MARION LIPPITT MURDOCK (MRS. W. D. KELLEY), civic worker; b. Providence, Mar. 17, 1921; d. Clarence T. and Helen G. (Lippitt) Murdock; A.B. summa cum laude, Brown U., 1942; M.A., Columbia, 1943; postgrad. U. N.M., 1950-54; m. Wilfrid D. Kelley, Feb. 22, 1946 (dec. June 6, 1973). With OSS and Dept. State, 1944-46; graduate asst. in history U. N.M., 1950-51. Mem. bd. League Women Voters, 1950-71, mem. nat. com. on U.S. Congress, 1970-72, pres., Albuquerque, 1960-61, Tucson, 1962-65, Ariz., 1965-71, mem. Ariz. legislative com., 1971—; mem. steering com. Tucson Municipal Capital Improvements Com., 1964-66; mem. Ariz. adv. council Taft Inst. Govt., 1971—; mem. Ariz. Statewide Com. on Child Day Care, 1972; mem. Tucson Charter Revision Com., 1965-70; bd. dirs. Tucson Regional Plan, Inc., 1966—, sec., 1971-73, exec. sec., 1973—; bd. dirs. Tucson Community Council, 1969-73, v.p., 1971-73, chmn. legislative com., 1971-73, co-chmn. united community campaign guidelines com., 1972; bd. dirs. Com. for Econ. Opportunity of Pima and Santa Cruz Counties, 1969-72, United Way of Tucson, 1973—; bd. dirs. Ariz. Acad. Pub. Affairs, 1965-73, mem. exec. com., 1966-72; mem. Ariz. Econ. Security Adv. Council, 1973-75, Ariz. Council Humanities and Pub. Policy, 1973—; mem. steering com. City-County Commn. on Improved Govtl. Mgmt., 1974—. Mem. Am. Assn. U. Women, UN Assn., Ariz. Civil Liberties Union, Nat. Municipal League, Phi Beta Kappa. Club: Brown (Tucson). Home: 2708 E 3d St Tucson AZ 85716 Office: Tucson Regional Plan 810 Lawyer's Title Bldg Tucson AZ 85701

KELLEY, MARY ELIZABETH, lawyer; b. Boston, Oct. 23, 1907; d. Daniel Cornelius and Johanna Josephine (Falvey) Kelley; spl. courses Boston U., 1930-33, 39; J.D., Northeastern U., 1937. Admitted to Mass. bar, 1937, U.S. Dist. Ct., 1938, U.S. Ct. Appeal bar, 1938, ICC bar, 1938; individual practice law, Boston, 1938-57; asso. Kaplan & Linsky, Boston, 1957-69; individual practice law, Medford, Mass., 1969—. Mem. Motor Carrier Lawyers Assn., ICC Practitioners Assn. (Mass. v.p. 1971-73), Mass., Middlesex County bar assns., Mass. Trial Lawyers Assn., Mass. Women Lawyers Assn. Clubs: Medford Catholic Women's, Sen Fu (Boston). Home: 22 Stearns Av Medford MA 02155 Office: 11 Riverside Av Medford MA 02155

KELLEY, SHEILA SEYMOUR (MRS. ROBERT M. KAUFMAN), pub. relations co. exec., polit. media specialist; b. Bronxville, N.Y., Feb. 3, 1928; d. William J. and Jane (Seymour) Kelley; B.A. magna cum laude, Syracuse U., 1949; m. Robert M. Kaufman, Nov. 1959. Reporter, Yonkers (N.Y.) Herald Statesman, 1950; reporter Close-Up column N.Y. Herald Tribune and Tribune Syndicate, 1950-52; editor Close-Up, 1952; producer, dir. Tex & Jinx McCrary radio and television programs WNBC, N.Y.C. and NBC Network, 1953-54; media cons. Rep. Jacob K. Javits, 1954; spl. asst. to Alfred Gwynne Vanderbilt, pub. relations dir. World Vets. Fund, 1955; media cons. to Atty. Gen. Javits in race for U.S. Senate, 1956; asst. and press sec. to Senator Javits, Washington, 1956-60; account exec., later supr., now v.p. Harshe-Rotman & Druck, Inc., N.Y.C., 1961—; media dir. Javits campaign for re-election, 1962, 68, Wachtler for N.Y. State Ct. Appeals, 1972. Founder, pres. VOTES Inc., specializing in polit. advt., 1973—. Mem. Pub. Relations Soc. Am., Phi Beta Kappa. Home: 345 E 52d St Apt 6D New York City NY 10022 Office: 300 E 44th St New York City NY 10017

KELLEY, VIOLETA REYES ANDRES, physician; b. Munoz, Philippines, June 9, 1941; d. Victoriano and Angelina (Reyes) Andres; M.D., U. St. Thomas, 1963; m. Russell Randolph Kelley, Aug. 10, 1968; children—Iris, Angela, Priscilla. Intern, Cambridge (Mass.) Hosp., 1964-65, resident obstetrics and gynecology, 1965-68; resident gynecol. pathology Boston Lying-In Hosp., 1968-69, resident anesthesiology, 1969-71; practice medicine specializing in obstetrics, gynecology and anesthesiology, Boston, 1971—; clin. instr. anesthesiology Tufts Med. Sch., 1971—. Mem. Am., Mass. socs. anesthesiologists. Home: 406 Broadway St Cambridge MA 92139 Office: VA Hosp South Huntington St Boston MA 02130

KELLNER, CLARA ELIZABETH BALINT (MRS. PAUL J. KELLNER), business exec.; b. Vienna, Austria, Sept. 1, 1921; d. Zoltan S. and Maria Gemma (Gombac) Balint; grad. Maria Theresia Coll., Budapest, Hungary, 1940; m. Paul J. Kellner, June 9, 1940; 1 son, George Andrew. Came to U.S., 1947, naturalized, 1952. Designer men's neckwear, 1947-51, prodn. cons., 1947-51; pres. Better Bows, Inc., N.Y.C., 1951—; v.p. Formal Fashions, Inc., N.Y.C., 1959—; owner, mgr. Mountain Range Farm, Germantown, N.Y. Active Hungarian Red Cross, 1941-43; head children's div. Internat. Red Cross, Budapest, 1944-45; active immigration div. UNRRA, 1946; mem. permanent scholarship fund raising com. Am. Hungarian Med. Assn., 1953—; mem. fund raising com. A.R.C., N.Y.C.; chmn. ann. George Washington awards dinner com. Am. Hungarian Studies Found., 1968, permanent mem. fund raising com.; member Nat. Council Women U.S. Trustee Columbia Meml. Hosp., Hudson, N.Y. Mem. Men's Tie Found., Bow Tie Mfrs. Assn. Am. (v.p.), Mgmt. Inst. Am. (mem. presidents council). Lutheran. Inventor trade patterns. Home: 25 E 86th St New York City NY 10028 Office: 740 Broadway New York City NY 10003

KELLNER, THEDA AILEEN BUTLER (MRS. HARVEY WILLIAM KELLNER), librarian; b. Farmington, Ill., Mar. 3, 1919; d. Lloyd Perry and Mabel Gertrude (Bennett) Butler; B.A., U. Colo., 1940; M.A., U. Denver, 1959; m. Harvey William Kellner, Dec. 20, 1940; 1 dau., Judith Ann (Mrs. John Thomas Hancock). Tchr., Cortez, Colo., 1940-42, Manzanola, Colo., 1946-48, Holly, Colo., 1948-51, La Junta, Colo., 1951-57; librarian, Swink, Colo., 1957-59, La Junta, Colo., 1959-67; library services coordinator Colo. State Library, Denver, 1967—. Mem. Am. (dir. at large health and rehab. library div. 1974—), Mountain Plains, Colo. library assns., Am. Hosp. and Instn. Libraries (chmn. audio visual com. 1969-74), Am. Correctional Assn. Colo. Bus. and Profl. Women's Club, Beta Phi Mu. Contbr. articles to profl. jours. Home: 1255 Ogden St #407 Denver CO 80218

KELLOGG, ANGEL IVEY (MRS. KARL BRITTAN KELLOGG), club woman; b. Seattle, Nov. 30, 1922; d. Joseph Nettles and Margaret (Armstrong) Ivey; B.S., U. Wash., 1948; m. Karl Brittan Kellogg, Aug. 12, 1955. Dietetic intern N.Y. Hosp., 1949; dietitian Providence Hosp., Seattle, 1953-55. Chmn. local affairs Baton Rouge chpt. League Women Voters, 1955-56, chmn. state affairs, 1956-57, chmn. finance, 1956-57, 1st v.p., 1958-59, bd. dirs. La., 1957-58; mem. bd. dirs. Baton Rouge YWCA, 1957-60, sec. bd. dirs., 1958-59, chmn. pub. relations, 1957-59, chmn. nominating com., 1959-60, mem. adult classes com., 1961—, mem. devel. com., 1961—; chmn. layouts for program advt. Baton Rouge Civic Symphony Women's Aux., 1957-58, editor newsletter, 1958-59. 1st v.p., 1958-59, pres., 1959-60; bd. dirs. Baton Rouge Civic Symphony Assn., 1957-60; capt. United Givers Fund, Baton Rouge, 1962-63, vice chmn., 1964; family investigation Goodfellows of Baton Rouge, 1962-63; vol. Cancer Soc. Greater Baton Rouge, 1963-64; fed. jury duty, 1963. Mem. edn. com. Commn. on Status of Women, 1965—. Precinct committeewoman 45th dist. Seattle Democratic Party, 1954-55. Mem. Baton Rouge Chamber Music Soc., La. Ornithol. Soc., Internat. Platform Assn., Nat. Orgn. Women. Methodist. Clubs: Baton Rouge Country, Bocage Racquet (Baton Rouge). Contbr. stories to local newspapers. Home: 2360 Fairway Dr Baton Rouge LA 70809

KELLOGG, JEAN DEFREES (MRS. JAMES H. KELLOGG), educator; b. Chgo., Dec. 28, 1916; d. Donald James and Florence (Baker) Defrees; B.A. with highest honors, Smith Coll., 1939; M.A., U. Chgo., 1965, Ph.D., 1968; m. James H. Kellogg, Nov. 4, 1939; children—Frances (Mrs. George P. Smith), James M. Editor, Henry Regnery Co., Chgo., 1947-64, asst. editor, 1947-50, asso. editor, 1950-60, editor-in-chief, 1960-64; prof. Mundelein (Ill.) Coll., 1968-70; prof. Rosary Coll. and Mundelein Grad. Sch. Religious Studies, 1970-73; prof. English, theology and lit. Rosary Coll., River Forest, Ill., 1971-73; prof. U. Chgo. Div. Sch., 1974—. Sculptress, designer Nancy China Co., Marshall Field & Co., 1940-47. Bd. dirs. Great Books Found., 1956-60. Mem. Am. Acad. Polit. and Social Sci., Am. Cath. Philos. Assn. Author: The Vital Tradition, 1970. Home: 179 E Lake Shore Dr Chicago IL 60611

KELLY, AGNES ALOYSIA, lawyer; b. Pitts., June 21, 1906; d. Anthony Andrew and Mary Ann (McGinty) K.; B.B.A., Western Res. U., 1956, LL.B., 1958; m. Norbert P. Kelly, Apr. 2, 1929. Admitted to Ohio bar, 1958, practice in Cleve., 1958—. Mem. Ohio, Cleve. bar assns., Phi Delta Delta. Home: 22350 Hilliard Blvd Rocky River OH 44116 Office: 13604 Lorain Av Cleveland OH 44111

KELLY, AUREL MAXEY, lawyer; b. Cleve., Apr. 24, 1923; d. Chester Collins and Elnora (Campbell) Maxey; A.B. cum laude, Whitman Coll., 1943; LL.B., Columbia, 1947; m. Thomas F. Kelly, May 29, 1943; children—Shannon, Keven. Continuity acceptance MBS, N.Y.C., 1947; asst. editor Baker-Voorhis Pub. Co., 1947-48; admitted to Wash. State bar, 1949, Colo. bar, 1961; practiced in Walla Walla, Wash., 1949-60; dep. pros. atty. Walla Walla County, 1955-56; justice of peace Walla Walla precinct, 1956-69; asso. firm Roepnack & Orahood, 1961-62; partner firm Kelly & Kelly 1962—; spl. asst. atty. gen. State of Colo., 1963-68, sr. asst. atty. gen., 1968—, chief criminal div., 1971-74; judge Colo. Ct. Appeals, 1974—. Vice pres. State Fedn. Young Republicans, 1952-54, nat. committeewoman, 1954-56; v.p. Walla Walla County Rep. Central Com. Mem. Wash., Walla Walla County, Colo., 1st Dist. bar assns., Nat. Bd. Arbitrators, Am. Arbitration Assn., Am. Acad. Polit. and Social Scis., Am. Judicature Soc., Kappa Kappa Gamma. Home: 8957 W 56th Pl Arvada CO 80002 Office: 8580 Ralston Rd Arvada CO 80002

KELLY, BELLA SHAFF, journalist; b. Miami, Fla., Aug. 12, 1924; d. Louis and Tillie (Rosenbloom) Shaff; student U. Miami, 1942-44; m. Herbert R. Kelly, Aug. 7, 1946. Reporter, Miami Daily News, 1945-47, edn. writer, 1947-53, news and spl. feature writer, 1953-63, spl. feature writer, 1966—; staff writer U. Miami News Bur., 1963-66. Grey Lady, A.R.C., 1957-66. Mem. mgmt. bd. Alley Legitimate Theater, Miami, 1957—. Recipient Civic Merit award for community service Miami Jr. C. of C., 1958. Mem. Women in Communications. Clubs: Vizcayans, Racquet, Miami Beach. Home: 498 SW 27th Rd Miami FL 33129 Office: Miami News 1 Herald Plaza Miami FL 33101

KELLY, BRENDA MARIE, physician; b. Winthrop, Mass.; d. Brendan A. and Eileen M. (McMullen) Kelly; B.S., Boston Coll., 1960; M.D., Boston U., 1964. Intern, U. Utah Affiliated Hosps., 1964-65; resident neurology Bronx N.Y. VA Hosp., 1965-68, acting asst. chief neurology, 1968-70; instr. clin. neurology, attending neurologist N.Y. Med. Coll., 1970-72; asso. dir. clin. investigation Lederle Labs., Pearl River, N.Y., 1972-73; asst. med. dir. Davis & Geck div. Am. Cyanamid Co., Pearl River, 1973—. Mem. Am. Acad. Neurology. Home: 85D Hawthorne Av Park Ridge NJ 07656 Office: Davis & Geck div. Am Cyanamid Co Pearl River NY 10965

KELLY, CATHERINE BURTON, judge; b. Washington, Dec. 12, 1917; d. William Francis and Catherine (Burton) Kelly; B.A., Smith Coll., 1939; J.D., George Washington U., 1951. Admitted to D.C. bar, 1951; practiced in Washington; asst. U.S. atty., 1953-57; asso. judge D.C. Ct. Gen. Sessions, 1957-67; asso. judge D.C. Ct. Appeals, 1967—. Recipient George Washington U. Alumni Achievement award, 1965. Mem. Am., D.C., D.C. Womens, Fed. bar assns., Nat. Assn. Women Lawyers, Am. Judicature Soc., Nat. Lawyers Club, Nat. Fedn. Bus. and Profl. Womens Clubs, Kappa Beta Pi. Home: 4501 Connecticut Av NW Washington DC 20008 Office: 400 F St NW Washington DC 20001

KELLY, CLEO BELL, librarian; b. Clearwater, Neb., Jan. 20, 1914; d. John L. and Anna Bell (Woodard) Kelly; B.A., Wayne (Neb.) State Coll., 1946; postgrad. U. Neb., summers 1951, 52; M.A. in L.S., U. Denver, 1953. Tchr. pub. schs. Neb., 1937-51; revisor, U. Denver Sch. Librarianship, summer 1953; asst. librarian Peru (Neb.) State Coll., 1953-57; reference librarian S.D. State U., 1957-60; cataloger Kan. State U., Manhattan, 1960-62; chmn. tech. processes dept. Kan. State Coll., Pittsburg, 1962-66; mem. staff Stephen F. Austin State U. Library, Nacogdoches, Tex., 1966—, asst. humanities librarian, 1973—; tchr. library sci. Peru State Coll., 1954-57, S.D. State U., 1958-59. Mem. Am., Mountain-Plains, Southwestern, Tex. (council 1971-72, chmn. dist. 8, 1972), library assns., Assn. Coll. and Research Libraries, Am. Assn. U. Profs., Tex. Assn. Coll. Tchrs., U. Denver Alumni Assn., Univ. Profl. Women, Pi Gamma Mu. Clubs: Women's Faculty, Camillia Soc. (Nacogdoches). Home: 315 Blount St Nacogdoches TX 75961

KELLY, DOROTHY ANN, coll. pres.; b. Bronx, July 26, 1929; d. Walter David and Sarah (McCauley) Kelly; B.A., Coll. New Rochelle, 1951; M.A., Catholic U., Washington, 1958; Ph.D., U. Notre Dame, 1970. Mem. faculty Coll. New Rochelle (N.Y.), 1957—, chmn. dept. history, 1965-67, acad. dean, 1967—, acting pres., 1970-71, pres., 1972—. Mem. com. New Rochell Hosp. Sch. Nursing, 1970—. Mem. Am. Assn. U. Profs., Am. Hist. Assn., Am. Assn. U. Women, Am. Assn. Higher Edn., Am. Assn. U. Adminstrs. Address: Coll New Rochelle New Rochelle NY 10801

KELLY, DOROTHY LIBBY, assn. exec.; b. Newfield, Me.; d. Eugene E. and Nellie (Thompson) Libby; B.S., U. N.H., 1938, postgrad., 1939-43. Tchr., Cushing Acad., Ashburnham, Mass., 1943-45, Lyman Hall Sch., Wallingford, Conn., 1945-49; legal sec., Washington, 1949-51; treas. Dairy Service Corp., Washington, 1949-51; mem. legal staff Johns Hopkins U. Applied Physics Lab., Balt., 1951-57; with Nat. Alcoholic Beverage Control Assn., 1957—, exec. v.p.-treas., 1967—. Sec.-treas. Joint Com. of States to Study Alcoholic Beverage Laws, 1967—. Mem. Am. Mgmt. Assn., Nat. Assn. Execs., U.S., Montgomery County chambers commerce, Washington Bd. Trade, Am. Soc. Assn. Execs. Home: 5007 Battery Lane Bethesda MD 20014 Office: Nat Alcoholic Beverage Control Assn Inc 5454 Wisconsin Av Washington DC 20015

KELLY, EILEEN MARY, state ofcl.; b. Binghamton, N.Y., Sept. 29, 1936; d. Robert Emmett and Mary (O'Neill) Kelly; A.B., Randolph-Macon Woman's Coll., 1958; M.A., State U. N.Y., Albany, 1963, Ed.D., 1971. 1 dau., Kathleen. Supr. market research dept. Procter & Gamble Co., Cin., 1958-61; tchr. English, City Sch. Dist., Binghamton, 1961-62; counselor VA Counseling Center, Albany, 1964-65; teaching fellow State U. N.Y., Albany, 1964-65; with N.Y. State Edn. Dept., Albany, 1965—, asso. in research, 1970—. Test cons. Mem. Am., N.Y. State personnel and guidance assns., Nat. Vocational Guidance Assn., Assn. for Measurement and Evaluation in Guidance, Nat. Council Measurement in Edn., Assn. Ednl. Data Systems, Am. Ednl. Research Assn., Nat. Orgn. for Women (pres. Albany area chpt. 1972, coordinator N.Y. 1973-74), Nat. Women's Polit. Caucus, Coalition For Free Choice. Democrat. Presbyn. Home: 98 S Pine Av Albany NY 12208 Office: NY State Bureau of Urban and Community Programs Evaluation Dept of Edn Albany NY 12224

KELLY, FREDDA JONI, psychologist; b. N.Y.C., July 7, 1943; d. Hyman and Gertrude (Star) Steckler; B.B.A., Coll. City N.Y., 1964; M.A., U. Conn., 1968, Ph.D., 1973; m. John Kelly, Feb. 5, 1967. Psychologist, West Haven (Conn.) VA Hosp., 1967-71; chief psychology Elmcrest Psychiat. Inst., Portland, Conn., 1971—; psychotherapist Psychotherapy Assos., New Haven, 1972—. N.Y. State Regents scholar, 1960-64; N.Y. State scholar children dec. vets., 1960-64; USPHS fellow, 1965-67. Mem. Am. Psychol. Assn., Beta

469 WHO'S WHO OF AMERICAN WOMEN

Gamma Sigma. Co-author article. Home: 175 Forest Rd Milford CT 06460 Office: 25 Marlborough St Portland CT 06480

KELLY, GENEVIEVE RUTH, librarian; b. West Hollywood, Cal., Apr. 12, 1927; d. James John and Bertha (Gilligan) Kelly; A.B., Westmont Coll., 1948; M.A., U. So. Cal., 1951, M.S. in L.S., 1953, Ph.D. (Am. Theol. Library Assn. research grant), 1965; B.D. (Hons.), U. London, 1966. Asst. librarian Am. Baptist Sem. of West, Covina, Cal., 1951-54, librarian, 1954—. Organist Holliston Av. United Meth. Ch. Mem. Am. (pres. 1971-72), Western (pres. 1962-63) theol. library assns., Am., Cal. library assns., Am. Baptist Hist. Soc. (bd. mgrs. 1970—), Mediaeval Acad. Am., Mediaeval Assn. Pacific, Am. Guild Organists. Baptist. Contbr. articles to profl. jours. Address: Seminary Knolls Covina CA 91724

KELLY, JOAN ELEANOR BRAND (MRS. PHILIP JOHN KELLY), banker; b. N.Y.C., Aug. 17, 1938; d. William Herman and Rosa (Werne) Brand; B.B.A., St. John's U., 1967; certificate basic banking Am. Inst. Banking, 1971; M.B.A., So. Meth. U., 1972; postgrad. Southwestern Grad. Sch. Banking (Nat. Assn. Bank Women scholar), 1974—; m. Philip John Kelly, Nov. 19, 1960. Research asst. to trust officer Fed. Bank and Trust Co., N.Y.C., 1958-67; research officer econ. research div. Republic Nat. Bank of Dallas, 1967—. Mem. League of Women Voters, Am. Marketing Assn., Am. Statis. Assn., Southwestern Social Sci. Orgn., Dallas Council on World Affairs, Nat. Assn. Bank Women, Am. Assn. U. Women, Bus. and Profl. Women's Club of Dallas, So. Meth. U., Alumni Assn., St. John's Alumni Assn., Alpha Beta Chi, Omicron Delta Epsilon. Roman Catholic. Club: Altrusa. Home: 767 Taft Dr Apt H Arlington TX 76012 Office: PO Box 5961 Dallas TX 75222

KELLY, JOAN FLEMING (MRS. FRANK KELLY), paper co. exec.; b. Washington, June 30, 1936; d. Henry J. and Thelma L. (Barrett) Fleming; B.S., U. Neb., 1959; M.B.A., Golden Gate U., 1972; m. Frank Kelly, Dec. 27, 1969. Tchr. Julesburg (Colo.) Jr. High Sch., 1959-60; market research field supr. Procter & Gamble, Cin., 1960-63; sr. marketing research analyst Crown Zellerach, San Francisco, 1965-73, asst. to sales mgr., 1973—. Lectr. M.B.A. program Golden Gate U., San Francisco, 1973—. Mem. Am. Marketing Assn. (chpt. pres. 1973-74). Home: PO Box 956 San Francisco CA 94101 Office: Crown Zellerbach Distbr Div #1 Bush St San Francisco CA 94119

KELLY, JOAN LARSON (MRS. THOMAS WYLIE KELLY), pub. relations exec.; b. Platteville, Wis., July 31, 1927; d. Irving Philip and Willah Marie (Johnson) Pross; B.S., U. Toledo, 1949; postgrad. Sophia U., 1956-58, U. Mo., 1967, Am. U., Washington, 1966-67, Georgetown U., 1969; m. Thomas Wylie Kelly, Sept. 8, 1973. Dir. community relations VISTA, 1964-68; dir. photography Peace Corps, 1968-70; dir. assn. relations Am. Assn. State Colls. and Univs., 1971-73; dir. pub. information Old Fed. Cts. Bldg., St. Paul, 1973—. Mem. Minn. Am. Bicentennial Commn. Mem. Washington Press Club, Am. Newspaper Womens Club, Am. Women in Radio and Television, Women in Communications, Directory Internat. Biography, Foremost Women in Communications. Author: Visit With Us in Japan, 1964; The Geisha Cookbook, 1973. Home: 56 Arundel Apt 12 St Paul MN 55102

KELLY, MARGARET EASLEY (MRS. EDWARD T. KELLY), home economist; b. Pitts., May 27, 1923; d. Thomas H. and Alice (Kenney) Easley; B.S., Seton Hill Coll., 1945; m. Edward T. Kelly. Tchr. home econs. Sacred Heart High Sch., Pitts., 1945-47; food supr. Statler Hotel, Washington, 1947-48; home service dir. Binghampton Gas Works (N.Y.), 1948-50; dir. cooking schs. Columbia Gas, Pitts. Group of Cos., 1950-56; asst. dir. home econs. Tappan Co., Mansfield, O., 1956-66, dir. home econs., 1966—. Mem. Am., Ohio home econs. assns., Home Economists in Bus., Assn. Home Appliance Mfrs. Conf., Elec. Womans Round Table, Mansfield Fedn. Women. Club: Mansfield Home Economics (chmn. 1965-66). Address: 450 Park Ave Mansfield OH 44906 Office: Tappan Park Mansfield OH 44901

KELLY, MARGARET RICAUD (MRS. THOMAS W. KELLY), educator; b. Dillon, S.C., Mar. 22, 1910; d. Robert Barry and Lulu Mowery (Crosland) Ricaud; A.B., Winthrop Coll., 1931; postgrad. Duke, 1931, U. Miami, 1937, U. Fla., 1938, U. N.C., 1950, 52, 53, U. S.C., 1954, Coker Coll., 1954-55; m. Thomas W. Kelly, Sept. 12, 1950. Tchr. high sch., Elizabethtown, N.C., 1931-32; prin. Ebenezer Sch., Bennettsville, S.C., 1932-35; tchr. pub. schs., Homestead, Fla., 1937-39; tchr. Fletcher Meml. Sch., McColl, S.C., 1940-46; 67-69; attendance tchr. Marlboro County Schs., Bennettsville, 1946-50; tchr. elementary Sch., Tabor City, N.C., 1950-51; tchr. pub. schs., Cordova, N.C., 1951-56, Society Hill, S.C., 1956-67; tchr. spl. edn. Blenheim (S.C.) primary schs., 1970-73; individual tutor, Bennettsville, 1973—. Mem. Nat., S.C. edn. assns., Marlboro County Tchrs. (chmn. pub. relations 1940-45), Colonial Dames 17th Century, Magna Charta Dames, Most Noble Order of Garter, Geneal. Soc. London, French Huguenot Soc., Colonial Order of Crown. Author: Jack and the Flying Saucer, 1973; Poems by Margaret Ricaud Kelly, 1974. Contbr. poetry to anthologies, articles to various local newspapers. Home: 402 Fayetteville Av Bennettsville SC 29512

KELLY, SISTER MARIE JOHN, hosp. adminstr.; b. N.Y.C., Feb. 28, 1936; d. John and Bridget (Lavelle) Kelly; student, Mercy Coll., 1957-60; B.S., Coll. of White Plains, 1962; M.B.A., Xavier U., 1971. Asst. treas. Mercy Coll., Dobbs Ferry, N.Y., 1962-63; instr. Our Lady of Victory Acad., Dobbs Ferry, N.Y., 1963-67; bus. office mgr. Mercy Gen. Hosp., Tupper Lake, N.Y., 1967-69, adminstr., 1969—. Instr. N. Country Coummunity Coll., Saranac Lake, N.Y., 1968-69; mem. Med. Scholarship Bd., Franklin County, Malone, N.Y., 1971—. Mem. Am., N.Y., No. N.Y. hosp. assns. Home: 106 Wawbeek Av Tupper Lake NY 12986 Office: 114 Wawbeek Av Tupper Lake NY 12986

KELLY, MARSHA SUSAN MAIN (MRS. JOSEPH J. KELLY), hotel exec.; b. Duluth, Minn., Apr. 15, 1949; d. Charles Aubrey and Barbara Jane (Beron) Main; B.S. magna cum laude, U. Minn., 1971; m. Joseph J. Kelly, Sept. 21, 1968; 1 son, Patrick John. Substitute tchr. Duluth Bd. Edn., 1971; copywriter, J.F.P. & Assos., Inc., Duluth, 1971-72, pub. relations account exec., 1972-74; sales mgr. Hotel Duluth, 1974—. Chmn. pub. relations Duluth Hall of Fame Com., 1972-73, We Love Ice Capades Com., 1973. Mem. Am. Women in Radio and TV, Speech Assn. Am., Am. Legion Aux., Twin Ports Press Club, Pi Kappa Delta. Club: Sweet Adelines (Duluth). Home: 4816 W 6th St Duluth MN 55807 Office: 231 E Superior St Duluth MN 55802

KELLY, MARY ANNETTE KLINESMITH, psychologist, educator; b. New Kensington, Penn., Aug. 19, 1922; d. Charles Francis and Olive Varco (Jenkins) Klinesmith; B.A., Mary Washington Coll. U. Va., 1944; M.A. (Ednl. Research scholar), Ohio State U., 1945; student (Fulbright scholar) Inst. Psychiatry U. London, 1950-51; m. Walter Butler Kelly, Dec. 27, 1952 (div. Feb. 1971); children—Kevin Oliver, Lisa Dodd, Walter Butler. Teaching fellow, Ohio State U., Columbus, 1945-46; asst. prof. psychology, dir. Children's Clinic, Mary Washington Coll., Fredericksburg, Va., 1951-58, asso. prof., 1959-68, dir. counseling center, 1965—, prof. psychology, 1974—; Cons. Disability Determination div., Va. Dept. Vocational Rehab., 1970—. Mem. Am. Psychol. Assn., Phi Beta Kappa, Mortar Bd. Presbyn. Home: 119 Lake Shore Dr Fredericksburg VA 22401

KELLY, SISTER MARY AQUINICE, ednl. adminstr.; b. Chgo., Jan. 5, 1910; d. John Joseph and Catherine (Casserly) Kelly; student U. Wis. at Milw., summers 1934-39; B.A., Rosary Coll., 1942; M.A., Cath. U. Am., 1951; postgrad. St. Louis U., summers 1952-57. Joined Dominican Order (Sinsinawa), 1928; tchr. schs., Bronx, N.Y., 1928-29, Holy Name Sch., Kansas City, Mo., 1929-33, St. Matthew Jr. High Sch., Milw., 1933-39; prin. St. Mary's Sch., Freeport, Ill., 1939-45; tchr. Annunciation Jr. High Sch., Green Bay, Wis., 1945-49; prin. St. Dominics Sch., Washington, 1949-50; supr. Community Schs., Washington, 1949-50; instr. sociology Rosary Coll., River Forest, Ill., 1950-55, asst. prof., 1955-59, asso. prof., 1960-68, dept. head, 1960-68; research dir. Dominican Edn. Center, Sinsinawa, Wis., 1968—; tchr. sociology Our Lady Lake Coll., San Antonio, summer 1959; mem. staff Human Relations Workshop, St. Louis, summer 1955. Cons. Religious Edn. Forum, Wis. and Ia., 1971. Mem. Am. Cath. Sociol. Soc. (exec. sec. 1959-66; citation 1966), Am. Sociol. Assn., Am. Acad. Polit. and Social Sci., Religious Research Assn., Nat. Family Assn. Office: Dominican Education Center Sinsinawa WI 53824

KELLY, MARY BURKE (MRS. JOSEPH THOMAS KELLY), librarian; b. Scranton, Pa., May 12, 1928; d. John Francis and Elsie Ann (Andren) Burke; A.B., Marywood Coll., 1950, B.S. in L.S., 1951, postgrad., 1954, 68, 73; postgrad. N.Y.U., 1953; m. Joseph Thomas Kelly, Aug. 28, 1954; children—Marilyn, Thomas. Jr. librarian Buffalo Pub. Library, 1951-52; tchr. elementary sch. Scranton (Pa.) Pub. Schs., 1952-58, librarian secondary sch., 1958-66; tchr. secondary sch., librarian Lourdesmont Pvt. Sch., Clarks Summit, 1956, 57; library supr. Scranton Pub. Schs., 1967—. Mem. Am., Pa. library assns., Assn. Ednl. Communication and Tech., Assn. Supervision and Curriculum Devel., Pa. Sch. Librarians Assn., Delta Kappa Gamma. Home: 315 5th Av Scranton PA 18505 Office: Scranton Sch. Dist Instrnl Materials Center Scranton PA 18503

KELLY, MATTIE CAROLINE MAY, business woman, educator; b. Vernon, Fla., Mar. 12, 1912; d. William W. and Mary Alice (Russ) May; student Rollins Coll., 1944-46, 48-49; A.B., Fla. State U., 1952, postgrad., 1970-71; m. Coleman Lee Kelly, Mar. 26, 1932 (div. June 1971); children—Carnera Lee, Lila Bernarr, Imogene (Mrs. J.J. Toole), Carol (Mrs. Robert Charles Adams), Cecelia (Mrs. Stephen W. Metz); m. 2d, Paul Sims, July 13, 1973. Tchr. pub. schs., Fla., 1928-33, 37; v.p. Kelly Boat Service, Inc., now pres.; sec., treas. Kelly Homes, Inc., Destin, Fla.; co-trustee, co-owner Kelly Enterprises. Mem. Okaloosa County Democratic Com., 1958—; mem. State Dem. Exec. Com., mem. adv. bd., 1966-70, del. nat. conv., 1968, 72. Bd. dirs. Destin Library, 1956—, Okaloosa County chpt. A.R.C., 1954-60, chmn., 1957-58; adv. bd. diversified cooperative tng. Choctawhatchee High Sch., 1960—; camp counsellor Senior Hi, Camp Weed, 1964; patron Stagecrafters. Mem. coordinating council for arts Okaloosa-Walton Jr. Coll., 1965—, rep. to Fla. Arts Council, 1966—; chmn. Historic Sites Commn., Okaloosa-Walton. Recipient of award A.R.C., 1960. Mem. Ft. Walton Beach C. of C. (edn. com.), Fla. Boatsmen's Assn. (sec. 1972—), Hist. Soc. Okaloosa and Walton Counties, Ft. Walton Beach Woman's Club (chmn. fine arts com. 1957-58), Woman's Club (v.p. 1958-59), Am. Assn. U. Women (legislative com. 1971—), Asso. Council Arts, Okaloosa County Community Concert Assn. Mem. P.E. Ch. (adminstr., supt. ch. sch. 1956-60, br. chmn. Christian edn. 1955-60, dist. chmn. Christian edn. 1958-61, del. adult conf. 1957, 59, del. religious TV programming workshop 1955-56; v.p. women of ch. 1956-57, 61—, dist. v.p. 1961—; pres. church-women Diocese Fla. 1965-68). Clubs: Officers Wives, Northwest Fla. Officers Wives. Author: Songs and Sonnets From the Sea (poetry), 1964. Address: PO Box 425 Indian Bayou Destin FL 32541

KELLY, PATRICIA MARIE, cytotechnologist, writer; b. San Francisco; d. Patrick J. and Mary J. (O'Rourke) Kelly; grad. exfoliative cytology U. Cal., 1949. Cytotechnologist U. Cal. Med. Center, San Francisco, 1948-60, Labs. Carl M. McCandless, Jr., M.D., and R. Eugene Tolls, M.D., San Francisco, 1960—. Author: Acta Cytologica, vol. IV, 1960; The Mighty Human Cell, 1967, 1970. Address: 476 Diamond St San Francisco CA 94114

KELLY, SALLY M(ARIE), physician; b. Bridgeport, Conn.; d. James F. and Elizabeth R. (Burke) Kelly; A.B., Conn. Coll., 1943; M.A., U. Wis., 1944, Ph.D., 1946; M.D., N.Y. U., 1963. Research fellow Bklyn. Botanic Garden, 1945-47; instr. Simmons Coll., Boston, 1947-48; research fellow Harvard U., 1947-48; asst. prof. Vassar Coll., Poughkeepsie, N.Y., 1948-51; sr. research scientist N.Y. State Dept. Health, Albany, 1951-64, asso. research scientist, 1964-67, research physician, 1967—; asst. prof. pediatrics Albany Med. Coll., 1967-74, asso. prof., 1974—; cons. pathology St. Peter's Hosp., Albany, 1968—. Lalor fellow, 1950-51, Brown-Hazen fellow, 1958-59, 60-63. Diplomate Am. Bd. Pathology. Fellow A.A.A.S.; mem. Am. Soc. Human Genetics, Soc. Exptl. Biology and Medicine, Grad. Women in Sci., Phi Beta Kappa, Sigma Xi. Contbr. articles to profl. jours. Office: 120 New Scotland Av Albany NY 12203

KELLY, VIRGINIA STUART, editor; b. N.Y.C., Feb. 18; d.; Walter and Florence (Stuart) Kelly; B.A., Manhattanville Coll. Sacred Heart, 1942; M.A., Fordham U., 1943. Asst. editor Robbins Pub. Co., N.Y.C., 1945; with Newsweek mag., N.Y.C., 1945-61, asso. editor, 1950-55, editor life and leisure sect., 1955-61, writer for books, art, music, dance, movies, theatre, edn., religion depts., Europe, Asia, Africa, S.Am., 1950-61; sr. editor Look mag. N.Y.C., 1961-65; asso. producer Universal Pictures, Hollywood, Cal., 1965-66; roving editor Reader's Digest, 1967—. Mem. fund raising com. Manhattanville Alumnae, 1961—. Bd. dirs. Caramoor music festival, Katonah, N.Y. Recipient essay medal French Ministry Fgn. Affairs, 1951; Belgian Westourism 1st prize for article on Bruges, 1972. Mem. Jr. League, Am. Portugese Cultural Soc. (exec. com., dir., v.p.). Roman Catholic. Co-editor: The Five Worlds of Our Lives, 1961. Contbr. articles to N.Y. Times, N. Am. Newspaper Alliance, Gentlemen's Quar., Reader's Digest. Home: 200 E 66th St New York City NY 10021 Office: Readers Digest 200 Park Av New York City NY 10017

KELLY-GADOL, JOAN M., educator; b. N.Y.C., Mar. 29, 1928; d. George V. and Ruth (Jacobsen) Kelly; B.A. summa cum laude, St. John's U. Coll., 1953; M.A. (Woodrow Wilson fellow), Columbia, 1954, Ph.D. (Danforth Found. fellow), 1963. Faculty, City Coll. N.Y., 1956—, asso. prof., 1968-72, prof., 1972—; prof. history Sarah Lawrence Coll., Bronxville, N.Y., 1971-74; vis. asst. prof. Columbia, 1963-64. Kent fellow 1954-56; Nat. Endowment for Humanities jr. fellow, 1967-68. Mem. Renaissance Soc. Am. (exec. bd. 1971—), Am. Hist. Assn., Am. Assn. U. Profs. Author: Leon Battista Alberti Universal Man of the Early Renaissance, 1969. Contbr. numerous articles to profl. jours. Home: 150 Claremont Av New York City NY 10027 Office: History Dept City Coll City U NY New York City NY 10031

KELSALL, ELVA SALOME NEWCOMBE, musician, educator; b. Toledo, Mar. 30, 1909; d. Joseph James and Ada Z. (Benton) Newcombe; student Marion Acad., 1924-25, Collingwood Conservatory of Music, Toledo, 1926-30, Ithaca Coll., 1932; Mus. B., Westminster Choir Coll., 1935; m. Joseph Kelsall, June 15, 1935; children—Jay Williams, John Benton. Mem. Toledo Choral Soc., soloist, 1929-31; pvt. voice; elementary piano tchr., 1940—; studied with Frederich Schorr, Met. Opera, 1939-41; debut as soloist with Cleve. Symphony, 1929; soloist Lake Placid Club, 1932-35, Phila. Symphony, 1947, 50, Cin. May Festival, 1946—; tchr. music Cranbury Pub. Schs., 1940-42, Princeton Theol. Sem., 1945-51, Hun Sch., Princeton, 1959-63, Columbus Boy Choir Sch., 1960-64; pvt. voice tchr., Princeton, 1940—. Founder Chamber Music Sch., Camp Solitude, Lake Placid, N.Y., 1952. Mem. Princeton Community Homemaker Service, 1968—. Mem. Mu Phi Epsilon. Republican. Presbyn. Club: Princeton Music. Home: 256 Varsity Av Princeton NJ 08540

KELSAY, DOROTHA BRADFORD, legislative reference librarian; b. Strawberry Point, Ia., Mar. 24, 1913; d. Lewis Addison and Ella Grace (Baker) Bradford; B.A., U. Wis., 1938, M.A., 1939; B.S. in L.S., U. Chgo., 1944; m. Omar Frank Kelsay, July 20, 1946; 1 son, Michael. Asst. librarian, instr. English, Baker U., Baldwin, Kan., 1940-43; librarian Roswell (N.M.) Army Air Force Base, 1944-45; librarian 7th Army, ETO, 1945-46; govt. research and legislative reference librarian Ore. State Library, Salem, 1962—. Mem. Pacific N.W., Ore. library assns. Home: 2660 5th St NE Salem OR 97303 Office: Ore State Library State Library Bldg Salem OR 97310

KELSEY, DORIS YVONNE SANDERS (MRS. WESTON M. KELSEY), pediatrician; b. Springfield, Tenn., Dec. 23, 1936; d. Paul M. and Evelyn Douglas (Sadler) Sanders; B.A., Austin Peay State Coll., 1958; M.D., Vanderbilt U., 1962; m. Weston M. Kelsey, Dec. 24, 1965. Intern, Vanderbilt Hosp., Nashville, 1962-63; resident N.C. Baptist Hosp., Winston-Salem, 1963-65; USPHS fellow in infectious disease and virology, instr. pediatrics Children's Hosp., Columbus, O., 1965-66; asst. prof. dept. pediatrics Bowman Gray Sch. Medicine, Winston-Salem, 1967-72, asso. prof., 1972—. Diplomate Am. Bd. Pediatrics. Mem. Am. Fedn. Clin. Research, So. Soc. Pediatric Research. Home: Route 11 Everidge Rd Winston Salem NC 27103

KELSEY, MARIAN JEAN (MRS. DARRYL M. KELSEY), theatre dir., educator; b. Cleve., Apr. 4, 1941; d. George Franklin and Marian Avis (Gamble) Mills; B.S. magna cum laude, Lake Erie Coll., 1963; M.A., Case Western Res. U., 1971; m. Darryl M. Kelsey, Aug. 18, 1962. Spl. tchr. Painesville (O.) City Schs., 1964-65; dir. family plays Lake Erie Coll., Painesville, 1966-70, staff dir., 1966—, instr. theatre arts, 1971—. Dir. summer youth theatre Guild Arts, Painesville, 1972, 73. Mem. Am., Children's, U. and Coll. theatre assns., Alpha Lambda Delta. Home: 8 E Walnut St Painesville OH 44077

KEMP, BETTY RUTH, librarian; b. Tishomingo, Okla., May 5, 1930; d. Raymond Herrell and Mamie Melvina (Hughes) Kemp; B.A., U. Okla., 1952; M.S., Fla. State U., 1965. Extramural loan librarian U. Tex. Library, Austin, 1952-55; reference librarian Dallas Pub. Library, 1955-56, head Oaklawn br., 1956-60, head Walnut Hill br., 1960-64; dir. Cherokee Regional Library, LaFayette, Ga., 1965—. Mem. Walker County Coordinating Council, 1965-74. Mem. Am., Southeastern, Ga., Chattanooga Area library assns., Library Pub. Relations Council, Wesleyan Service Guild (dist. vice chmn. 1971-72), United Meth. Women (dist. v.p. 1972-74), Beta Phi Mu. Methodist. Club: LaFayette Womans (historian 1969-71). Home: PO Box 1112 Lafayette GA 30728 Office: 305 S Duke St LaFayette GA 30728

KEMP, HELEN KOSUNEN (MRS. EDWARD K. KEMP), public health assn. exec.; b. N.Y.C., Feb. 4, 1914; d. Arvid Karlson and Anna Alexandria (Wuorinen) Kosunen; student Fla. State U., evenings, 1952-65; m. Edward K. Kemp, Jan. 27, 1939; children—Edward K., Judith (Mrs. Bobby Underhill). Pvt. sec. A. Schrader & Sons, Bklyn., 1933-39; personnel and purchasing mgr. Leon County Health Dept., Tallahassee, 1953—; co-owner Ed Kemp Real Estate, 1964—. Mem. Am., Fla. (treas. 1959-60, chmn. mgmt. sect. So. br. 1972-73) pub. health assns., Nat. Assn. Real Estate Bds. (womens council), Fla. Assn. Realtors, Tallahassee Bd. Realtors. Mem. Order Eastern Star. Club: Altrusa (pres. 1970-71) (Tallahassee). Home: 2726 N Monroe St Tallahassee FL 32303 Office: 2965 Municipal Way Tallahassee FL 32304

KEMP, MARCIA JEAN MILLER (MRS. DONALD EUGENE KEMP), mag. editor; b. Omaha, June 11, 1933; d. Ralph Franklin and Irma Aljoe (Broomhall) Miller; B.S. (Asso. Neb. Indsl. Editors scholar), U. Omaha, 1957; m. Donald Eugene Kemp, Dec. 27, 1957; children—Donald Matthew, Suzanne Elizebeth. Editorial asst. Criss Cross Currents, Mutual & United of Omaha, 1956-58; asst. dir. pub. relations U. Neb. Coll. of Medicine, Omaha, 1960-62; advt. mgr., asso. editor Forum Mag., Assn. Profl. Dirs. of YMCA, Arvada, Colo., 1969—. Republican. Methodist. Address: 12328 W 70th Av Arvada CO 80004

KEMP, ROSE BLYTH, coll. vice-pres.; b. Salem, Ohio, May 14, 1917; d. Robert Marye and Rose (Heilman) Modisette; student U. So. Cal., 1934-36; m. Myron Bradley Kemp, Mar. 20, 1965; children—Sheriden Bentley, Michaela (Mrs. Greg Ruggles), Andrew Blyth, Ian Blyth, Donna (Mrs. Dale Williams), Duncan Blyth, Susan (Mrs. Daniel de Anfrazio), Bradley. Dir. television and motion pictures Cal. Inst. Tech., 1955-62; founder, dir. community devel. KCET-Channel 28, Los Angeles, 1962-65; dir. television and motion pictures Cal. Inst. Tech., 1965-70; v.p. Columbia Coll., Los Angeles, 1970—. Mem. communications com. Los Angeles County Human Relations Commn., 1969-72; pres.'s com. Employment of Handicapped, 1972-73; mem. operating com. NATA-UCLA TV Library, 1973—. Mem. adv. bd. Los Angeles Free Clinic; trustee U. Film Found. Recipient Eastman award, 1964; Cine Golden Eagle award, 1968. Mem. Am. Women in Radio and Television (nat. pres. 1972-73), Nat. Acad. Television Arts and Scis. (gov. 1972-74), Nat. Assn. Broadcasters, Nat. Soc. Fund Raisers, Western Ednl. Soc. Telecommunications. Club: Lahaina Surf and Racket (Hawaii). Home: 4711 Cartwright Av North Hollywood CA 90612 Office: 925 N LaBrea Av Los Angeles CA 90038

KEMP, VIRGINIA JOANNE, reporter, editor; b. Cin., Ohio, Oct. 25, 1935; d. James Arnold and Frances (Brackett) Higginbotham; B.S. in Journalism, Ohio U., 1961; m. John William Kemp, Dec. 23, 1956; children—Deborah, John T., Andrew W., Rebecca Jo. Intern reporter Cin. Times-Star, summers, 1955, 1956, gen. reporter, 1957, edn. editor, 1957-58; reporter, news editor Milford (O.) Advertiser, 1959-65; asso. editor Clermont Courier, Batavia, O., 1973—; substitute elem. sch. teacher Milford Exempted Village Schs., 1967—. Publicity dir. Old Milford Area Inc.; newsletter editor Milford South PTA, 1972-73; publicity chmn., den leader coach Cub Scout Pack 120 Dan Beard council Boy Scouts Am., 1971-73; mem. publicity com. Milford Better Schs. Com., 1969. Recipient Old Milford Area Inc. award of Merit for Journalistic Services, 1973. Mem. Theta Sigma Phi, Alpha Lambda Delta, Kappa Tau Alpha. Mem. Ch. Christ (tchr. Bible sch. 1970—). Home: 25 Apple Lane Milford OH 45150 Office: 385 W Main St Batavia OH 45103

KEMPFER, HELEN FRIEND (MRS. HOMER H. KEMPFER), educator; b. nr. Troy, O.; d. W.R. and Lena O. (Shook) Friend; B.S., Bowling Green State U., 1945; postgrad. Am. U., 1950-52, Purdue U.,

1953-54; M.A., Columbia, 1955; m. Homer H. Kempfer, Dec. 31, 1955. Tchr. Champaign County (O.) Schs., 1940-42; research asst. N.E.A., Washington, 1952; asst. dir. Nat. Home Study Council, 1955-59; exec. sec. Accrediting Commn., Nat. Home Study Council, 1958-59; editor Indian Jour. Adult Edn., New Delhi, 1960-63; dir. research Indian Adult Edn. Assn., 1962-63; head, corr. program Grad. Sch., U.S. Dept. Agr., Washington, 1963-66; pres. Inst. Ind. Study, Inc., 1968; research analyst Wis. Dept. Health and Social Services, Madison, 1968-70; asso dir. Cosmetology Accrediting Commn., 1970, Nat. Study Accreditation Vocational Tech. Edn,, 1970-73; research supr. Va. Dept. Corrections, Richmond, 1973—. Mem. Am. Personnel and Guidance Assn., Indian Adult Edn. Assn., Adult Edn. Assn. U.S.A., Am. Vocational Assn., Internat. Council on Corr. Edn., Nat. Soc. Programmed Instrn., Am. Soc. Assn. Execs. Author numerous books, pamphlets, articles. Home: 11336 Orchard Lane Reston VA 22090 Office: 22 E Cary St Richmond VA 23219

KEMPNER, RUTH LYDIA (BENEDICTA MARIA) (MRS. ROBERT M. W, KEMPNER), author, social worker; b. Geislingen, Germany; d. Hermann and Marie-Luise (Spring) Hahn; diploma social work Sch. Social Work, Berlin, Germany, 1930; postgrad. Pa. Sch. Social Work, Phila., 1940-41; m. Robert M. W. Kempner; children—Lucian K., Andre K. Social worker City of Berlin, 1929-33; dean women Fiorenza Coll., Florence, Italy and Nice, France, 1936-39; social work agys. in Phila., 1941-45; M-project, Pres. F. D. Roosevelt, 1944-45; research analyst U.S. Army, Nuremberg War Crimes Trials, 1947-48; work on claims for health damage Catholic and Jewish Nazi victims, 1953-63; researcher martyr priests, 1963—, TV, radio documentations, Rome, Germany, U.S. Decorated Pro Ecclesia et Pontifice, Pope Paul VI; Cross of Merit, Govt. German Fed. Republic; recipient Golden Honor award Austrian Govt. Mem. Am. Assn. Social Workers, Am. Acad. Social Work, also Internat. Pen Club Am. Author: (under pen name Benedicta Maria) Women in Nazi Germany, 1944; Priester before Hitler's Tribunals, 1966. Contbr. to Catholic mags. Home: 112 Lansdowne Court Lansdowne PA 19050

KEMPTON, GRACE FICKLING ARRINGTON (MRS. WILLETT MAIN KEMPTON), journalist, realtor; b. Rome, Ga., June 26; d. Homer Newell and Grace (Fickling) Arrington; A.B., Shorter Coll.; B.A. in Journalism, U. Ga., 1940; m. Willett Main Kempton, Aug. 5, 1939 (dec. Nov. 1962); children—Willett Main, Grace Arrington (dec. May 1973), John Houston. Soc. columnist Athens (Ga.) Banner Herald, 1940-41; with Clark County Draft Bd., Athens, 1941; spl. writer Atlanta Constn., 1942; reporter Army Pub. Relations, Atlanta, 1942-43; owner, mgr. Embassy Service Bur., Washington, 1946-47; adminstrv. asst. Congressman Henderson Lanham, Ga., 1947-48; Washington soc. columnist Palm Beach (Fla.) Life, 1947; social news columnist Providence Jour., McLean, Va., 1952-53; columnist Courier of George Washington U. Med. Sch., 1952-57; owner, realtor Grace A. Kempton Realty Co., McLean, Va., 1955—. Mem. women's bd. George Washington U. Hosp., Washington, 1953—; life mem. Athens Jr. Assembly; dir. McLean Horse Show Assn., 1950-70. Served from 2d lt. to capt., WAC, 1943-45. Mem. Nat., No. Va. bds. realtors, Va. Real Estate Assn., Am. Newspaper Women's Club, Nat. Trust for Historic Preservation, Ga. State Soc. (v.p.), Women in Communications, Chi Omega. Methodist. Clubs: Capitol Speakers, Washington. Home: 1313 Rockland Terrace McLean VA 22101 Office: 8112 Old Dominion Dr McLean VA 22101

KENASTON, SARA JEAN, social worker; b. Sioux City, Ia.; d. Hampton Ray and Maurine (Bulow) Kenaston; B.A., U. S.D., 1952; M.S.W., Tulane U., 1962. With Fla. Dept. Pub. Welfare, 1952-69, social worker, Marianna, 1952-56, child welfare worker, Panama City, 1957-59, social work supr., Pensacola, 1960-61, Daytona Beach, 1962-64, social work cons., field rep., Jacksonville, 1964-70; community services dir. Community Planning Council Jacksonville Area, 1970-71; supr. instnl. program Fla. Div. Family Services, Jacksonville, 1971—. Program chmn. conf. Fla. Health and Welfare Council, 1971, bd. dirs., 1971— pres., 1972. Mem. Nat. Assn. Social Workers (pres. chpt. 1968-70), Am. Pub. Welfare Assn. (program com. S.E. area regional conf. 1965, 69, 70), Am. Assn. U. Women (dir. Daytona Beach br. 1963-64, Jacksonville br. 1969—, v.p. 1971-73, pres. 1973—, Duval County Community Services Assn. (dir. 1971-73), Jacksonville Urban League, League Women Voters, Fla. Pub. Health Assn., Pi Beta Phi. Roman Catholic. Home and office: 1200 Bretta St Jacksonville FL 32211

KENDALL, ALICE BROWN, editor; b. Cape Elizabeth, Me., Apr. 14, 1919; d. Gould Johnson and Alice (Howard) Brown: grad. Vesper George Sch. Art, Boston, 1941; m. Kenneth K. Kendall, Jr., Sept. 10, 1944; children—Kerry Linne, Kenneth K. III. Draftsman Firemen's Mut. Ins. Co., Boston, 1939-40; tech. illustrator Radiation Lab. Mass. Inst. Tech., 1941-44; poetry editor, critic Writer's Research Digest, Garden Grove, Cal., 1968-70; editor Feedback Jour., publ. of Glass Mountain Inn, Inc., non-profit corp. for severely orthopedically handicapped adults; artist traditional landscape; poetry pub. in numerous lit. jours. and anthologies. Mem. Writer's Workshop of Orange County (pres. 1968-70, treas. 1970-73), Chaparral Poets, So. Cal. Poetry Soc., Centro Studi E Scambi Internazionali, Anaheim Art Assn., Delphian Soc. (seminar bd. chmn. 1974). Home: 2105 W Forest Ln Anaheim CA 92804 Office: Glass Mountain Inn Inc 3401 Del Monte Dr #13 Anaheim CA 92804

KENDALL, DONNA JOYCE, coll. ofcl.; b. Milan, Ill., Jan. 15, 1929; d. Orville Daniel and Marie Grace (Hansen) Kendall; A.A., Stephens Coll., 1948; B.A., State U. Ia., 1950. Reporter, Milan (Ill.) Independent, 1950-56; pub. relations asst. Modern Woodmen of Am., Rock Island, Ill., 1956-57, publs. editor, 1957-60, asst. to pub. relations mgr., 1960-63; corporate pub. relations asst. Title Ins. & Trust Co., Los Angeles, 1963-69; marketing officer Comml. & Farmers Nat. Bank, Oxnard, Cal., 1969-71; pub. information dir. Western Ins. Information Service, Los Angeles, 1971-73; corporate relations mgr. 1st Western Bank, Los Angeles, 1973-74; pub. relations dir. Palmer Coll., Davenport, Ia., 1974—. Free-lance pub. relations cons. in areas of real estate and politics. Recipient Achievement award Los Angeles Advt. Women, 1968. Mem. Pub. Relations Soc. Am. (dir. Los Angeles 1966-67), Los Angeles Advt. Women (dir. 1967-69, rec. sec. 1972-73, 1st v.p. 1973-74), Los Angeles C. of C. (dir. women's div. 1967-69, 71-74), Cal. Assn. Real Estate Tchrs. (dir. 1965-69), Am. Advt. Fedn., D.A.R., Alpha Delta Pi, Gamma Alpha Chi. Republican. Methodist. Home: 512 W 14th Av Milan IL 61264 Office: 1000 Brady St Davenport IA 52803

KENDALL, ELEANOR EMELINE, coll. dean; b. Cheney, Wash., Oct. 8, 1913; d. Clark Ivan and Ina (Sperry) Jones; A.B., U. Cal. at Los Angeles, 1934; M.S., U. So. Cal., 1950; m. George Johnson Kendall, Mar. 8, 1942. Tchr. Escondido (Cal.) Union High Sch., 1937-43, Burbank (Cal.) High Sch., 1943-48; vice prin. Jordan Jr. High Sch., Burbank, 1948-52; tchr., counselor Mission Bay High Sch., San Diego, Cal., 1953-58; vice prin. Clairemont High Sch., San Diego, 1958-63; dean of students San Diego Mesa Coll., 1963—. 3d v.p. bd. dirs. YWCA, San Diego, 1967-70; mem. San Diego Homemakers Service Bd., 1964-70; mem. youth incentives com. San Diego Urban League, 1965-67; mem. ground obs. corps Air Def. Command, USAF, 1952-53; mem. Old Globe Theater of San Diego. Mem. San Diego Community Colls. Adminstrs. Assn. (sec. 1972), Pacific Assn. Coll. Registrars and Adminstrv. Officers, U. Cal. at Los Angeles Alumni Assn. (life), Cal. P.T.A. (life), Zool. Soc. San Diego, P.E.O., Delta Kappa Gamma (area dir. 1965-67). Club: San Diego Altrusa (corr. sec. 1967, dir. 1972). Home: 130 21st St Del Mar CA 92014 Office: 7250 Mesa Coll Dr San Diego CA 92111

KENDALL, PATRICIA LOUISE (MRS. PAUL F. LAZARSFELD), educator; b. Pueblo, Colo., June 12, 1921; d. David M. and Louise (Benjamin) Kendall; B.A. summa cum laude, Smith Coll., 1942; Ph.D., Columbia, 1954; m. Paul F. Lazarsfeld, Nov. 21, 1949; 1 son, Robert. Research asst., sr. research asso. Bur. Applied Social Research, Columbia, N.Y.C., 1942-65; instr. Columbia, 1946-51, sr. vis. lectr., 1968-69; prof. sociology Queens Coll. and Grad. Center, City U. N.Y., Flushing, 1965—. Cons NIH, Assn. Am. Med. Colls., A.M.A., others. Rockefeller fellow, 1943. Fellow Am. Sociol. Assn., N.Y. Acad. Med. (asso.); mem. Assn. Am. Med. Colls., Eastern Sociol. Soc., Am. Assn. for Pub. Opinion Research. Author: (with P.F. Lazarsfeld) Radio Listening in America, 1949; Conflict and Mood, 1954; (with R.K. Merton and M. Fiske) The Focused Interview, 1958; (with R.K. Merton and G.G. Reader) The Student-Physician, 1957; The Relationship between Medical Educators and Medical Practioners, 1965. Contbr. articles to profl. jours. Home: 50 W 96th St New York City NY 10025 Office: Queens Coll Dept Sociology Flushing NY 11367

KENDEL, DORLA DEAN (MRS. ROBERT LEWIS KENDEL), mfrs. rep. co. exec.; b. Los Angeles, Apr. 16, 1930; d. Thomas Weston and Lois May (Oliver) Hall; grad. high sch.; m. Robert Lewis Kendel, Aug. 13, 1949; children—Robert L., Michael L., Richard L. Tchr. oil painting, LaCrescenta, Cal., 1960-62; with Air Conditioning Specialties Co., Inc., mfrs. rep., LaCrescenta, 1962—, corp. sec.-treas., 1970—. Active Scouting, sch. and sport activities, 1956-70. Mem. Am. Soc. Heating Refrigerating and Air Conditioning Engrs. Address: 2926 Foothill Blvd LaCrescenta CA 91214

KENDER, DOROTHY, constrn. co. exec.; b. Bklyn., Feb. 12, 1928; d. Emil and Mary (Schenone) Perosio; B.S., Duquesne U., 1950; m. Joseph Kender, Apr. 15, 1948; children—Karen (Mrs. Robert H. Jones Jr.), Scott. Adminstr., Ring Engring., Pitts., 1950-53, Tom Mistick, Inc., Monroeville, Pa., 1953-57; with Bldg. Stone Inst., N.Y.C., 1958—, exec. asst., 1960—, researcher, producer Stone Catalog, 1962—, Stone Information Manual, 1974, editor Building Stone News, 1970—. Home: 65 Tappan Landing Tarrytown NY 10591 Office: 420 Lexington Av New York City NY 10017

KENDRICK, MILDRED A., biometrician; b. Haynesville, La.; d. William Alexander and Ruth (Shockley) Kendrick; B.A., La. State U., 1940; M.S.W., Catholic U. Am., 1944, Ph.D., 1956. Supr. intake sect. nat. hdqrs. A.R.C., Washington, 1942-44; cons. vital statistics div. Census Bur., Washington, 1944-47; statistician research and statistics div. VA, Washington, 1947-49; statistician Tb research div. USPHS, Muscogee County, Ga., 1949-59; instr. U. Ga. at Columbus, 1952-56; biometrician study on precursors of coronary artery disease Johns Hopkins Sch. Pub. Health, 1959-61; biometrician study on late effects of radiation div. radiol. health USPHS, Washington, 1961-63, occupational health, chief biometrics and social studies br., 1963-67; chief epidemiology and research br. fgn. quarantine program Communicable Disease Center, USPHS, Atlanta, 1967-73; research asso. in medicine U. So. Cal., Los Angeles, 1973—. Home: 800 W First St Los Angeles CA 90012

KENDRICK, VIRGINIA CATHERINE (MRS. W. DUDLEY KENDRICK), pianist, composer; b. Mpls., Apr. 8, 1910; d. Ralph and Lelia B. (Hall) Bachman; student music U. Minn., 1928-33; m. W. Dudley Kendrick, Nov. 28, 1934; children—Warren, Nancy (Mrs. Charles Ivey), James, Susan (Mrs. James Williamson), David. Organist, First Ch. of Christ Scientist, Excelsior, Minn., 1962-72; organ music cons. Schmitt Music Co., Mpls., 1958-74; pianist Andahazy Ballet Co., Mpls., 1958-74. Mem. Am. Guild of Organists, Nat. Fedn. Music Clubs, Sigma Kappa, Mu Phi Epsilon. Composer: Wealth of Mine, 1941; Little Red Hen, 1955; Little Old Train, 1955; Goody Two Shoes, 1956; From My Window, 1960; Green is the Willow, 1965; Little Miss Whuffit, 1962; White Sky, 1967; Music is Beauty, 1969; Tribute, 1970; Jade Summer, 1971; Before The World Was, 1973; Look Unto Me Saith Our God, 1974; composer musical settings to Mary Baker Eddy Hymns Love, also Mother's Evening Prayer, 1974. Home: 5800 Echo Rd Shorewood MN 55331 Office: 88 S 10th St Minneapolis MN 55403

KENEALLY, DOROTHY EVELYN O'DELL (MRS. HENRY JOHN KENEALLY, JR.), agy. exec.; b. Orient, Ia., Nov. 15, 1912; d. Oscar Seward and Besse Kate (Hunt) O'Dell; A.B., Mills Coll., 1934; m. Henry John Keneally, Jr., May 5, 1935; children—Patricia Jeanne, Michael O'Dell, Henry John III. Liason officer, pediatric sec. U. Cal. Med. Sch., San Francisco, 1950-52; exec. sec. Butte County Soc. for Crippled Children and Adults, Oroville, Cal., 1952-54; exec. dir. Epilepsy League Ore., Portland, 1954-56; exec. dir. Maricopa County Council for Retarded Children, Phoenix. 1959-67; exec. dir. Arthritis Found., Phoenix, 1967—. Pres., Le Conte Sch. P.T.A., San Francisco, 1950-51; active Girl Scouts U.S.A., 1946-54; pres. Girl Scout Leaders Assn., Butte County, 1953-54; active Boy Scouts Am. Mem. Conf. Execs. Assns. for Retarded Children (charter), Soc. Assn. Execs. Ariz. (sec. 1965—), Council for Exceptional Children, Nat. Rehab. Assn. Clubs: Soroptimist of Phoenix (program chmn. 1961-62), Wives (USPHS) (Phoenix). Home: 5815 N 22d Av Phoenix AZ 85015 Office: 100 W Osborn Rd Phoenix AZ 85013

KENNAN, CLARA BERNICE, writer; b. Rogers, Ark., Sept. 16, 1892; d. Alvero Alexander and Rosella Roxanice (Reeves) Kennan; B.S., U. Ark., 1924, M.S., 1927; postgrad. Columbia, summers 1937, 52; postgrad. So. Cal. U., 1934. Tchr. pub. schs. Benton County, Ark., 1910-20; faculty El Dorado (Ark.) Jr. Coll., 1927, Ark. A. and M. at Magnolia, 1928-30, Ark. A&M at Monticello, 1930-46, Little Rock Jr. Coll., 1946-51; asst. prof. Ouachita Bapt. Coll., Arkadelphia, Ark., 1952-55, reference librarian North Little Rock Pub. Library, 1955-56. Ford Found. grantee. Recipient short story award, Nat. League of Am. P.E.N. Women. Mem. Ark. Ret. Tchrs. Assn. (state dir.), Ark. Hist. Assn., Nat. League of Am. P.E.N. Women, Am. Assn. Univ. Women (state treas. 1937-41), Women's Nat. Book Assn., Kappa Delta Pi (chpt. pres. 1927), Lambda Tau. Democrat. Mem. Christian Ch. Author: (with Dr. T.M. Stinnett) All This and Tomorrow Too (The Hundred Year History of the Arkansas Education Assn.), 1969. Contbr. articles to mags. and newspapers including Ark. Hist. Quarterly, Chronicles of Okla., Christian Sci. Moniter, Ark. Gazette, Ark. Democrat, Jour. Ark. Edn., College English, others. Address: 1200 Commerce St Little Rock AR 72202

KENNEDY, ANN WHITE (MRS. JOHN HINES KENNEDY), dir. inst.; b. Cleve., July 7, 1920; d. Walter C. and Mary (Saunders) White; B.A., Vassar Coll., 1942; m. Robert S. Stockton, Jan. 1945 (dec. 1970); children—Virginia Saunders (Mrs. H. Lawrence Serra, Jr.), Christine Heron, Sarah Boudinot, Mary Evelyn; m. 2d, John Hines Kennedy, Jan. 2, 1972. Pres. Jr. council Cleve. Mus. Arts, 1959-60; bd. dirs. Cleve. Inst. Music, 1962—, Family Health Assn., 1955-70, Mus. Arts Soc., 1970—; bd. dirs. Cleveland Playhouse, 1960—, pres., 1971-72; chmn. 4 maj. charity balls, Cleve. Served to lt. (j.g.) USNR, 1942-45. Clubs: Chagrin Valley Hunt (Gates Mills, O.); Intown (Cleve.). Home: 7677 Sherman Rd Chesterland OH 44026 also 2215 Albans Rd Houston TX 77005

KENNEDY, ANNA HELEN, educator; b. Los Angeles, May 16, 1910; d. John Cunningham and Helen Lucile (Berkey) Kennedy; B.A., U. Cal. at Los Angeles, 1932; M.A., Claremont Grad. Sch., 1934; Ph.D., U. Chgo., 1941. Reading cons. Pasadena (Cal.) City Schs., 1934-38, tchr., 1940-42; sch. psychologist Long Beach (Cal.) City Schs., 1946-47, supr. spl. edn., 1947-49; faculty Cal. State U., Los Angeles, 1949-58, coordinator spl. edn., 1951-57, head dept. audiology, 1953-57; prof. edn. Cal. State U., Northridge, 1958-71, prof. emeritus, 1971—. Served with USNR, 1942-45. Mem. Retired Officers Assn., Pi Lambda Theta. Home: 101 N Grand Av Apt 7 Pasadena CA 91103

KENNEDY, ANNE MARTHA REYNOLDS (MRS. CORNELIUS BRYANT KENNEDY), civic worker; b. Evanston, Ill., Mar. 4, 1932; d. Frank George and Margaret (McMillan) Reynolds; B.S., Wheelock Coll., 1954; m. Cornelius Bryant Kennedy, June 20, 1959; children—Anne Talbot, Lauren Asher. Tchr., Bateman Sch., Chgo., 1955-56, Chgo. Latin Sch., 1956-59, dir. vols., 1960—, trustee, 1972—. Trustee St. John's Child Devel. Center, Washington, 1972—; chmn. hospitality Wolf Trap Assos. of Wolf Trap Farm for Performing Arts, 1973—. Mem. Jr. League Washington. Club: F Street (Washington); Gibson Island (Md.). Home: 7720 Old Georgetown Pike McLean VA 22101

KENNEDY, BERENICE CONNOR (MRS. JEFFERSON KENNEDY, JR.), mag. ofcl.; b. Phila.; d. William J. and Ethel N. (Waltman) Connor; A.B., U. Pa., 1947; m. Jefferson Kennedy, Jr., Oct., 1963. Account exec. Geare-Marston, Inc., advt., Phila., 1948-50; dir. radio and TV, Buckley Orgn., Phila., 1950-51; dir. editorial promotion Ladies' Home Jour., Phila., 1951-60, asso. editor, asst. to exec. editor, N.Y.C., 1961-62; sr. editor, editorial asst. to pres. McCall Corp., N.Y.C., 1962-66; pres. Feminine Forecast, Inc., 1966—; editor Girl Talk mag., 1969—; dir. Donovan Communications, Inc. Named Phila. Advt. Woman of the Year, Phila. Advt. Clubs, 1960; recipient award for creative design Phila. Art Dirs. Club, 1955, Salute to Women award Rep. Women in Bus. and Industry. Mem. Am. Soc. Mag. Editors, Phila. Club Advt. Women (dir. 1953-55), Fashion Group (dir. 1957-59), Advt. Women N.Y. (dir. 1962-64), Advt. Fedn. Am., Delta Delta Delta. Club: Overseas Press. Home: 200 E 66th St New York City NY 10021

KENNEDY, BERNICE E.; B.A., U. Tex., 1940; M.S.W., Washington U., St. Louis, 1957. Tchr. adminstr. Colegio Carlota Kemper Instituto Gammon, Lavras E. de Minas Gerais, Brazil, 1945-52; caseworker, child welfare supr. Fulton County Pub. Welfare Dept., Atlanta, 1952-59; caseworker Family and Children's Service Greater St. Louis, 1959-62; child welfare supr. El Paso County (Colo.) Dept. Pub. Welfare, Colorado Springs, 1962-64; dir. social services Presbyn. Children's Home and Service Agy., Dallas, 1964-66; foster care cons., Office Human Devel., chief Children's Bur., coordinator Office for Handicapped, Region VII, Dept. Health, Edn. and Welfare, Kansas City, Mo., 1966—. Mem. Nat. Assn. Social Workers, Acad. Certified Social Workers, Nat. Conf. Social Welfare, Nat. Council Family Relations, Kappa Delta. Home: 9519 Perry Lane Overland Park KS 66212 Office: 601 E 12th St Kansas City MO 64106

KENNEDY, BETTE IRENE, banker; b. Eustis, Fla., July 10, 1920; d. Isaac Newton and Stella Mae (Golding) Kennedy; student Fla. State U., 1939-40; certificate Am. Inst. Banking, 1955, 58. With Atlantic Bank of Eustis, 1944—, asst. v.p., 1961-73, v.p., 1973—. Precinct Democratic committeewoman Lake County, Fla., 1970. Trustee Central Fla. Lung Assn., 1948—, Waterman Meml. Hosp., 1966—; bd. dirs. A.R.C., 1964—. Named Woman of Year, Kiwanis, Rotary, Lions and Bus. and Profl. Womens Club, 1957; named Orange Queen of Eustis, 1971. Mem. Nat. Assn. Bank Women, Am. Inst. Banking, Lake County Gem and Mineral Soc., Bus. and Profl. Womens Club (pres. 1950-51), Eustis C. of C. (dir. 1969-70). Methodist (mem. adminstrv. bd. 1962—). Mem. Order Eastern Star, Order of Amaranth. Home: PO Box 841 802 Hill St Eustis FL 32726 Office: Atlantic Bank of Eustis PO Drawer A Eustis FL 32726

KENNEDY, CAROL SHANKLAND (MRS. STEPHEN L. KENNEDY), journalist; b. St. Louis, May 22, 1948; d. Wilbur Morse and Louise Erna (Warmbrodt) Shankland; B.J., U. Mo., 1971; student Georgetown (Ky.) Coll., 1966-68; m. Stephen L. Kennedy, Jan. 15, 1972. Advt. asst. Rawlings Sporting Goods Co., St. Louis, 1969-70; copywriter C.V. Mosby Co., St. Louis, 1971-73; freelance journalism, 1973—. Home: 213 Stoney View Ct St Louis MO 63141

KENNEDY, CORNELIA BLANCHE GROEFSEMA (MRS. CHARLES S. KENNEDY, JR.), judge; b. Detroit, Aug. 4, 1923; d. Elmer H. and M. Blanche (Gibbons) Groefsema; A.B., U. Mich., 1945, J.D., 1947; LL.D., No. Mich. U., 1971, Eastern Mich. U., 1971; m. Charles S. Kennedy, Jr., Mar. 5, 1960; 1 son, Charles S., III. Law clk. Harold M. Stephens, U.S. Ct. Appeals, Washington, 1947-48; admitted to Mich. bar, 1947; atty. Elmer H. Groefsema, Detroit, 1948-52; practiced in Detroit, 1952-54; mem. firm Markle & Markle, Detroit, 1954-66; judge Wayne County Circuit Ct., Detroit, 1967-70; U.S. dist. judge Eastern dist. Mich., 1970—. Fellow Am. Bar Found.; mem. Phi Beta Kappa. Office: 219 Fed Bldg Detroit MI 48226

KENNEDY, DOREEN ELIZABETH (MRS. GILBERT DUNSTAN KENNEDY), educator; b. Victoria, B.C., Can., June 12, 1922; d. Robert and Sara Elizabeth (Monteith) Jenkinson; B.A., U. B. C., 1943, M.A., 1948; m. Gilbert Dunstan Kennedy, Aug. 23, 1948; children—Mary Louise (Mrs. James M. Longridge), Gloria Beverly (Mrs. Gloria Beverly Senkler), Patricia (Mrs. Patricia Elizabeth Ross). Lectr. U. B.C., 1944-53, 54-57, Simmons Coll., Boston, 1953-54; lectr. U. Victoria, 1957-58, asst. prof., 1958-64, asso. prof., 1964—. Mem. sch. bd. Univ. Endowment Lands, 1954-57. Bd. dirs. Family and Children's Service, Victoria, 1964-71, pres., 1968-71; area commr. Girl Guides of Can., 1971-74; adv. bd. Capital Regional Hosp. Dist., 1974—. Mem. Math. Assn. Am., Can. Math. Congress. Home: 3145 Weald Rd Victoria BC Canada

KENNEDY, ELIZABETH LANE, state ofcl.; b. Washington, Mar. 28, 1920; d. Robert Eugene and Alice (Kent) Kennedy; A.B., Western Coll., 1941; postgrad. Johns Hopkins, 1947-51; spl. courses Am. Mgmt. Assn. High sch. tchr. Balt. County Bd. Edn., 1941-43; with Md. State Employment Service, Balt., 1943-73, state supr. indsl. services, 1960-63, state supr. employment service programs, 1963-68, chief employment service mgmt. services, 1968-73; mgmt. analyst Md. Dept. Employment and Social Services, 1973—. Mem. Internat. Assn. Personnel in Employment Security (chmn. internat. edn. com. 1968-70), Am. Personnel and Guidance Assn., Am. Assn. U. Women. Methodist (treas.). Home: 912 Belgian Av Baltimore MD 21218 Office: 1100 N Eutaw St Baltimore MD 21201

KENNEDY, ETHEL AGNES, educator; b. New Haven; d. William John and Agnes (Loveland) Kennedy; B.A., Albertus Magnus Coll., 1940; M.A., Columbia, 1945, Ed.D., 1964; postgrad, Yale, 1947-48, U. Pa., 1949, London Sch. Econs. in Eng., 1952, Stanford U., 1965, Fairfield U., 1969. Began career as reader econ. papers Wilson H. Lee Co., 1941-42; high sch. tchr. social scis., English, East Haven (Conn.)

High Sch., 1942-47, dean, 1947-53; dean and guidance head Lyman Hall High Sch., Wallingford, Conn., 1953-71; dir. pupil personnel services Wallingford Pub. Schs., 1971—. Tchr. St. Barnabas High Sch. Religion, 1964-69. Mem. adminstrv. council and steering com. Wallingford Sch. System, 1953—, chmn. testing curriculum com., 1967—; nursing council Meriden (Conn.) Hosp., 1953-60; chmn. Guidance Curriculum Com. Wallingford, 1957-65; ambassador chmn. Columbia U. Tchrs. Coll. Fund, 1965-70; mem. Gov.'s Task Force on Edn. Com. on Status Women, 1967. Adv. council Central Conn. State Coll., 1953-71; bd. dirs. Central Conn. Tb Assn., 1959-60, mem. Wallingford Drug Abuse Adminstrv. Com., 1969—. Recipient research grant to study mentally retarded Devereux Found. Camp, 1965. Mem. Nat. Soc. Daus. Founders and Patriots Am., Greater Hartford Guidance Dirs. Assn., Am. Ednl. Research Assn., Assn. Counselor Edn. and Supervision, Am. Rehab. Counseling Assn., A.A.A.S., Conn. Assn. Suprs. Instrn. Spl. Edn., Assn. for Children with Perceptual Learning Disabilities, Nat., Conn. (state pres. 1957-59) assns. women deans and counselors, Conn. Council Tchr. Edn. (dir. 1956-61), Am., Conn. personnel and guidance assns., Nat. Vocational Guidance Assn., N.E.A., Conn. (mem. bd. dept. adminstrn. 1958-60), Wallingford edn. assns., Mayflower Soc. North Haven, New Haven Guidance Dirs. Assn., Nat., Conn. assns. pupil personnel dirs., North Haven Hist. Soc., Albertus Magnus Alumnae Assn., D.A.R., Delta Kappa Gamma (regional pres. 1958-60, state chmn. 1959-63), Pi Lambda Theta. Roman Catholic. Clubs: North Haven Garden, Zonta (local sec. 1963-65, safety chmn. 1965-68, pres. 1967-70; internat. conv. del. 1966). Home: 98 Clintonville Rd North Haven CT 06473

KENNEDY, FAYE COLLIER (MRS. JOHN BRUCE KENNEDY), lawyer; b. Ardmore, Okla., Dec. 10, 1941; d. Marvin Merrill and Cora Alice (Bearden) Collier; Asso. Sci., Ricks Coll., 1962; LL.B., U. Ia., 1967; m. John Bruce Kennedy, May 3, 1970; 1 son, David Duff IV. Admitted to Wash. bar, 1967; law clk. Wash. Supreme Ct., Olympia, 1967-68; dep. prosecutor Office of Snohomish County Prosecutor, Everett, 1968-70; judge Everett Dist. Ct., 1971-73; now practice law, Everett. Mem. Snohomish County Mental Health Adminstrv. Bd., 1969-72; chmn. Snohomish County Mental Health Services Bd., 1972-73. Mem. Am., Wash. bar assns., Am. Judges Assn., Wash. Magistrates Assn. (mem. ethics com. 1972-73, mem. pub. relations com. 1972-73), Am. Judicature Soc.

KENNEDY, FRANCES, librarian; b. St. Louis, Dec. 2, 1907; d. William John and Maud (Gilhart) Kennedy; student Oklahoma City U., 1924-26; A.B., U. Okla., 1928; B.S. in L.S., U. Ill., 1931, M.S. in L.S., 1948. Br. librarian Muskogee (Okla.) Pub. Library, 1928-29; staff mem. State U. Ia., summer 1931; reference librarian Oklahoma City Pub. Library, 1931-47; librarian and prof. library sci. Oklahoma City U. Library, 1947-74; exec. sec. Okla. Library Assn., 1974—; instr. U. Okla. Library Sch., summers 1958, 59. Dir. Oklahoma County Health Assn., 1956-60; bd. dirs. Variety Health Center, 1960-64, pres., 1962-63. Mem. Am. (council 1956-60, 69-72), Southwestern (dir. 1955-56, exec. bd. 1960-62; editor newsletter 1959-64), Okla. (state pres. 1945-47, editor jour. 1954-57, Distinguished Service award 1965), library assns., Alpha Omicron Pi, Beta Phi Mu. Democrat. Episcopalian. Home: 1629 Camden Way Oklahoma City OK 73116 Office: Oklahoma City U Oklahoma City OK 73106

KENNEDY, JANET ALTERMAN (MRS. JAY RICHARD KENNEDY), psychoanalyst; b. N.Y.C., May 28, 1913; d. Louis L. and Rebecca (Cohen) Alterman; B.A., N.Y.U., 1935, M.D., 1939; m. Jay Richard Kennedy, May 21, 1943; 1 dau., Susan. Rotating intern Harlem Hosp., N.Y.C., 1939-41, resident in obstetrics and gynecology, 1940-41, Lucius N. Littauer fellow in infectious diseases, 1941-42; resident in psychiatry Manhattan State Hosp., N.Y.C., 1947-49; postgrad. tng. Psychoanalytic Clinic for Tng. and Research, Columbia Coll. Phys. and Surg., N.Y.C., 1947-50; practice medicine specializing in psychoanalysis, N.Y.C., 1950—; asso. attending in medicine and psychiatry Montefiore Hosp., Bronx, N.Y., 1957—, co-chief psychosomatic service, 1957—; adj. vis. psychiatry Bronx State Hosp., 1968—; asst. clin. prof. psychiatry Albert Einstein Coll. Medicine, Yeshiva U., Bklyn., 1957-72, asso. clin. prof., 1972—. Fellow Am. Psychiat. Assn.; mem. A.M.A., Am. Psychoanalytic Assn., Assn. for Psychoanalytic Medicine, Am. Psychosomatic Soc. Contbr. articles to profl. jours., chpts. to books. Address: 122 E 78th St New York City NY 10021

KENNEDY, JANICE MADIGAN (MRS. WILLIAM WILSON KENNEDY II), educator; b. nr. Towanda, Pa., Apr. 5, 1924; d. George William and Lura (Haight) Madigan; B.S., Mansfield (Pa.) State Tchrs. Coll., 1946; M.S., Cornell U., 1966, postgrad., 1969-70; postgrad. Pa. State U., 1971, Marywood Coll., 1971, 73; m. William Wilson Kennedy II, Aug. 2, 1947; children—Winifred (Mrs. Eric Ivan Evers), William Wilson III. Tchr. home making pub. high sch., Troy, Pa., 1946-69; asst. prof. textiles and clothing Mansfield State Coll., 1969—. Cons., coordinator N.Am. projects Council for Internat. Contact, London, Eng. Recipient hon. degree Pa. chpt. Future Homemakers Am., 1965. Mem. Am., Pa. (sec. treas. N.E. dist. 1971-72) home econs. assns., Internat. Fedn. Home Econs., Am. Assn. U. Women, Am. Assn. Coll. Profs. Textiles and Clothing, Assn. Profs. State Coll. Univ. Faculties, Pa. Assn. Higher Edn., Kappa Omicron Phi (conclave mgr. nat. council 1963-72), Omicron Nu, Pi Lambda Theta, Kappa Delta Pi. Home: RD 2 Box 184 Troy PA 16947 Office: Home Econ Center Mansfield State Coll Mansfield PA 16933

KENNEDY, JOYCE LAIN (MRS. WILLIAM A. KENNEDY), newspaper columnist; b. Louisiana, Mo.; d. Miller and J. Irma (Pitman) Lain; B.S. in Bus. Adminstrn., Washington U., St. Louis, 1953; m. William A. Kennedy, May 23, 1970. Air talent prodn. asst. Ed Wilson Show, Sta. KWK-TV, St. Louis, 1954-55; asst. to pub. Prom Mag., St. Louis, 1955-59; pub. relations cons. United Fund Greater St. Louis, 1959-63; creative dir. Civic Service, Inc., St. Louis, 1963; advt. and pub. relations dir. Mansion House Center, St. Louis, 1964-66; communications dir. Greater St. Louis council Girl Scouts U.S.A., 1966-68; columnist Career Corner, McNaught Syndicate, Inc., N.Y.C., 1968—, exec. editor Career World mag., 1972—. Mem. Youth Commn., St. Louis and St. Louis County, 1968-69. Author: Secrets of Finding Your First Job, 1970; Automotive Careers, 1972. Office: One W Deer Park Dr Gaithersburg MD 20760

KENNEDY, LEILA MAY (MRS. ROY KENNEDY), lawyer; b. Marysville, Ind., Nov. 9, 1895; d. John Conrad and Katharine Elizabeth (Reis) Hartling; LL.B., Benjamin Harrison Law Sch., 1936, Ind. U., 1944; m. Roy Kennedy, May 14, 1913 (dec.); children—Roy Albert, Dorothea Leila (Mrs. James W. Powers). Sec., Herbert Foltz & Son, Indpls., 1933-37; admitted to Ind. bar, 1940; registrar Ind. Law Sch., Indpls., 1937-44; law librarian Ind. Supreme Ct. Library, Indpls., 1944-50; referee Juvenile Ct., Indpls., 1950-53; real estate broker Irvington Realty Co., Indpls., 1953-60; pvt. practice law, Indpls., 1960—. Mem. Bus. and Profl. Womans Club, Ind. U. Alumni Assn., Ind. U. Women's Assn., Mutual Service Assn., Phi Alpha Delta. Club: Pilot (pres. Indpls. 1940) Presbyn. Mem. Order Eastern Star. Home and office: 1314 N Emerson Av Indianapolis IN 46219

KENNEDY, LINDA GAIL ANDRESS (MRS. MURDOCK M. KENNEDY, JR.), telephone co. exec.; b. Peterman, Ala., Aug. 19, 1941; d. William James and Ethel Naomi (Stevens) Andress; student U. So. Miss., 1959-60; m. Murdock M. Kennedy, Jr., July 11, 1959; children—Murdock M. III, Steven Andress. With Monroeville Telephone Co. (Ala.), 1960—, v.p., 1966—. Chmn. Mother's March of Dimes March, 1970. Mem. Monroeville Jaycettes (co-organizer 1964, pres. 1964-65). Baptist. Home: PO Box 96 Monroeville AL 36460

KENNEDY, MADELINE GILLILAND (MRS. ROBERT A. KENNEDY, JR.), home economist; b. Raymondville, Tex., Aug. 17, 1918; d. Cleo Dean and Beulah Myrtle (Caldwell) Gilliland; student Tex. Coll. Arts and Industries, 1936-37; B.S. in Home Econs., U. Tex., 1940; postgrad. Tex. A. & M. U.; m. Robert A. Kennedy, Jr., Sept. 9, 1943; children—Al Clifton, Robert A., III. Tchr. home econs. Raymondville (Tex.) High Sch., 1940-41; county home demonstration agt. Angelina County, Lufkin, Tex., 1941-43, Kleberg and Kenedy Counties, Kingsville, Tex., from 1956; now with Tex. Agrl. Extension Service, Tex. A & M. U., College Station. Co-owner Kennedy Ins. Agy., Lufkin, Kennedy Gift and Book Mart, Lufkin. Pres. Community Resource Council Kleberg County, 1973-74. Recipient Distinguished Service award Nat. Assn. Extension Home Economists, 1966, Outstanding Citizens award, 1967. Me. C. of C. (mem. com. 1965-71), Am., Tex. (sec. treas. 1964-65) home econs. assns., County Home Demonstration Agts. Assn. Tex. (state pres. 1964-65), Nat. Assn. Extension Home Economists (state del. 1963-65; So. region councelor 1966-67), Agrl. Workers Assn., Tex. Nutrition Council, Am. Assn. U. Women, P.E.O., Alpha Xi Delta. Methodist. Home: 530 S Wanda Dr Kingsville TX 78363 Office: PO Box 313 Kingsville TX 78363

KENNEDY, MARGARET SARAH, state ofcl.; b. New Orleans, June 1, 1917; d. Matthew James and Hazel (DeSilva) Kennedy; B.S., La. State U., 1942, M.A., 1944. With La. Dept. Employment Security, Baton Rouge, 1936—, sec., 1936-44, personnel officer, 1944-45, adminstrv. asst., 1945-46, time study analyst, 1946-49, test adminstr., 1949-55, state supr. testing, 1955-63, chief counseling and testing, 1963—. First aid instr. A.R.C., Baton Rouge, 1962—. Mem. Nat. Vocational and Guidance Assn., Am. Personnel and Guidance Assn., Nat. Employment Counselors Assn., Assn. for Counselor Edn. and Supervision, Assn. for Measurement and Evaluation in Guidance, Internat. Assn. Personnel in Employment Security, Am. Assn. U. Women, Mental Health Assn. Clubs: Woman's, Camelot (Baton Rouge). Home: 4646 Loyola Dr Baton Rouge LA 70808 Office: PO Box 44094 Baton Rouge LA 70804

KENNEDY, MARIE CATHERINE MATTICK, assn. exec.; b. Vancouver, B.C., Can., Jan. 15, 1910; d. Charles Joseph and Rose Marie (McSweeney) Mattick; came to U.S., 1910, naturalized, 1959; student U. Cal. Extension at San Francisco, 1946-47; m. John Henry Kennedy, Dec. 17, 1931 (dec. Sept. 1943); children—John J., Patricia Marie (Mrs. David J. Kott), Charles Lawrence. Sec., asst. credit mgr. Acme Breweries, 1945-54; mgr. Cal. Profl. Service Assn., 1954-59, pres., 1959—, editor house paper CPSA Asso., 1959—; mgr. Cal. Profl. Credit Union, 1954—. Tax cons. on income tax, San Francisco, 1954—. Mem. Nat. Notary Assn., Ret. Firemen's Assn. Denver. Author: 100 Years with the Denver Fire Department, 1967. Home: 2241 Lincoln Way San Francisco CA 94122 Office: Cal Profl Service Assn 323 Geary St San Francisco CA 94102

KENNEDY, MELANIE JANE SPROUL (MRS. BRUCE H. KENNEDY), physician; b. Lima, O., Oct. 21, 1942; d. James Wesley and Clellah Leola (Stotts) Sproul; B.A. cum laude (scholar) Ohio No. U. 1964; M.D., Ohio State U., 1968; m. Bruce H. Kennedy, Feb. 20, 1965; 1 dau., Melita Lucille. Intern, Mt. Carmel Hosp., Columbus, O., 1969-70; asst. dir. Central Ohio Red Cross Blood Center, 1969, acting dir., 1970-71, dir., Columbus, 1971—; resident clin. pathology, clin. instr. Ohio State U. Hosps., 1973—. Mem. Am., Ohio (dir. 1972—) assns. blood banks, Am. Med. Women's Assn. (v.p. br. 12, 1972, br. pres. 1973), A.M.A. (Recognition award 1972), Ohio State Med. Assn., Central Ohio Blood Bankers (co-chmn. 1971), Acad. Medicine Columbus and Franklin County. Contbr. articles to profl. jours. Office: 995 E Broad St Columbus OH 43205

KENNEDY, ROSE FITZGERALD (MRS. JOSEPH P. KENNEDY), b. Boston, 1890; m. Joseph P. Kennedy, 1914 (dec.); children—Joseph (dec.), John Fitzgerald (Pres. of U.S. 1961-63, dec.), Rosemary, Kathleen (dec.), Eunice (Mrs. Robert Sargent Shriver), Patricia, Robert Francis (dec.), Jean (Mrs. Stephen Smith), Edward M. Address: Hyannis Port MA 02647

KENNEDY, RUTH ANNA COURTRIGHT (MRS. GEORGE CASSIUS KENNEDY), civic worker; b. Elmwood, Neb., July 28, 1892; d. Clarance Lewis and Emma Elizabeth (Willcockson) Courtright; student Neb. State Tchrs. Coll., 1913-15; m. George Cassius Kennedy, July 28, 1920; children—Bond, Betty (Mrs. John F. Leeds), Clay. Rural sch. tchr., Furnas County, Neb., 1912-13, 40-43; jr. high sch. tchr., McCook, Neb., 1915-17, Moore, Mont., 1917-18; 5th grade tchr. Overseas Red Cross Canteen, Nantes, France, 1918-19; tchr. high sch., Bayard, Neb., 1919-20. Sec., Farm Bur. Orgn., Nemaha County, Neb., 1935-36; Nemaha County pres. Extension Work Neb., 1935-36. Named Honored Citizen, Peru (Neb.) Kiwanis Club, 1936, Neb. State Mother, Peru P.E.O. Sisterhood, 1969. Mem. P.E.O. (state pres. 1938-39). Mem. Order Eastern Star. Home: RFD Brownville NE 68321

KENNELLY, SISTER MARINA, educator; b. Chgo., Nov. 12, 1919; d. Patrick Joseph and Mary Josephine (McGuire) Kennelly; B.S., Mundelein Coll., 1942; M.S., U. Notre Dame, 1950, Ph.D., 1950; Entered Order Blessed Virgin Mary, Roman Catholic Ch., 1942; with Mundelein Coll., Chgo., 1947—, instr. chemistry, 1947-49, chmn. chemistry, 1950-56, prof. chemistry, 1961—. Coordinator Charismatic Prayer Groups, Chgo., 1970—. Recipient Ill. Acad. Sci. grantee 1950-54; NIH grantee, 1960-62; NSF grantee. Mem. Ill. Acad. Sci., Am. Chem. Soc., Am. Inst. Chemists. Home: 6363 Sheridan Rd Chicago IL 60660

KENNER, JOANNE (MRS. JOHN CATLETT ALLENSWORTH), physician; b. Abilene, Tex., Apr. 26, 1924; d. Claude William and Elizabeth (Kirby) Kenner; B.A., Hardin-Simmons U., 1947; M.D., Southwestern Med. Sch., 1947; m. John Catlett Allensworth, Oct. 15, 1955. Intern St. Joseph's Hosp., Ft. Worth, 1947-48, rotating resident gen. surgery, 1948-49; resident physician in obstetrics and gynecology Harris Hosp., Ft. Worth, 1949-50, Doctor's Hosp., N.Y.C., 1950-51, Woman's Hosp., N.Y.C., 1951-54; practice medicine specializing in obstetrics and gynecology, Ft. Worth, 1954-55, Mineral Wells, Tex., 1955—; mem. staff Palo Pinto Gen. Hosp., Mineral Wells. Civilian cons. Beach Army Hosp., Ft. Welters, Tex., 1956—; dir., physician Community Family Planning Center, Mineral Wells, 1967—. Diplomate Am. Bd. Obstetrics and Gynecology. Fellow A.C.S., Am. Coll. Obstetrics and Gynecology; mem. Am., Tex. med. assns., Tri-County Med. Soc., Tex. Soc. Obstetricians and Gynecologists. Office: 208 NW 2d St Mineral Wells TX 76067

KENNERLY, BILLIE WYRICK (MRS. IRL F. KENNERLY), club woman; b. Luttrell, Tenn., Oct. 11, 1909; d. Hamilton B. and Maryetta Frost (Needham) Wyrick; student music 1927-28; B.A., U. Houston, 1954; student Cath. Acad. grad. Palestine Bus. Coll., 1928; m. Irl F. Kennerly, Oct. 17, 1940 (dec. Dec. 1958). Legal sec., Refugio, Tex., 1928-29; postmaster, Refugio, 1930-40; pres. Kennerwyck Antiques, Inc., Houston, 1946-60. Mem. Democrat Woman's Club, rec. sec. 1955-56, program chmn. 1957-58, 61-62, 1st v.p. 1963-64, pres. 1965-67. Mem. Nat., Tex. (corr. sec. 1957-58) parliamentarians, Am. Assn. U. Women, Tex., City (chmn. health 1960-61) fedns. women's clubs, Houston Geneal. Forum (sec. 1963-64), D.A.R. (state chmn. advt.; chpt. sec. 1964-65, 1st vice regent Ann Poage chpt. 1967-68), Tex. Soc. Children Am. Revolution (patron), Friends of Houston Pub. Library, U.S. Daus. 1812 (sec.), Colonial Dames Am., English Speaking Union, Daus. Am. Colonists, Daus. Founders and Patriots of Am., Nat. Soc. Magna Charta Dames, Womens Aux. Houston Bar Assn., Phi Theta Kappa, Phi Kappa Phi. Baptist. Mem. Order Eastern Star. Clubs: Woman's Breakfast, Tennessee Birthday (organizer, pres. 1964-65). Author: Tennessee Grainger County Marriage Bonds and Licenses, 1796 to 1837, 1964; Tennessee Grainger County Marriage Bonds and Licenses, 1838 to 1866, 1968. Certified genealogist. Home: 1925 Richmond Av Houston TX 77006

KENNEY, VIRGINIA BANNING (MRS. FRANK D. KENNEY), polit. worker; b. Evanston, Ill., June 12, 1922; d. Thomas A. and Margery (Ames) Banning; A.B., U. Chgo., 1945; m. Frank D. Kenney, Feb. 12, 1944; children—Claudia, Pamela, Sarah, Stuart. Adminstrv. asst. to Congressman Robert McClary from 13th Dist. of Ill. Sec., Hyde Park-Kenwood Community Conf., 1951-52; treas. Countryside Sch. Mothers Club, 1964-65; sec. Fox Valley Pony Club, 1964-65; adv. board 29th Ward Family Center of Chgo., 1973—; mem. Def. Adv. Com. on Women in Services, 1970—. Vice chmn. Cook County Young Republicans, 1956; membership chmn. Ill. Fedn. Rep. Women, 1957-60, 1st v.p., 1962-64, pres., 1965-69; mem. at large Nat. Fedn. Republican Women, 1968-69, finance chmn., 1970—, community service chmn., 1972—; exec. com. Ill. Citizens for Nixon-Agnew, 1968; mem. action now com. Rep. Nat. Com.; sec. Ill. Rep. Citizens League, 1961-62; alternate del. Rep. Nat. Com., 1968. Unitarian. Club: Wyvern (U. Chgo.). Home: Route 2 Box 104 Barrington IL 60010 Office: 150 Dexter Ct Elgin IL 60120

KENNY, JANICE MARIE (MRS. BEN RICHARD KENNY), psychologist, health service adminstr.; b. Zanesville, O., Jan. 31, 1925; d. Joseph and Clara Catherine (Cervenka) Schmidt; student Ohio Wesleyan U., 1942-44; A.B. in Chemistry, U. N.C., 1946; B.A. in Psychology, St. Lawrence U., 1949; M.A. in Ednl. Psychology, Temple U., 1953; A.M. in Exptl. Psychology, U. Pa., 1955, Ph.D. in Clin. Psychology, 1957; m. Carl Hobkirk, June 12, 1946 (div. June 1954); children—Linda, Steven; m. 2d, Ben Richard Kenny, Feb. 21, 1959; children—Charlotte, Susan. Psychologist Phila. State Hosp., 1957-61; exec. dir. Northeast Psychol. Clinic, Phila., 1959—. Psychol. cons. to schs. in Levittown, N.J., Mt. Holly, N.J., Hainesport, N.J. Nat. Inst. Mental Health grantee, 1959. Mem. Am., Pa. psychol. assns., Phila. Soc. Clin. Psychologists, Common Cause. Home: 15 Hyacinth Rd Levittown PA 19056 Office: 1536 Pratt St Philadelphia PA 19124

KENSINGER, MARY RAY, librarian; b. Butler, Tenn., Jan. 6, 1914; d. Joseph Todd and Bessie Elizabeth (Trivett) Ray; Tchrs. certificate East Tenn. State U., 1934; m. James Cornelius Kensinger, Sept. 15, 1945. Office mgr., dist. tng. supr. Tenn. Dept. Employment Security, Johnson City, also Rogersville, 1935-56; asst. librarian H.B. Stamps Meml. Library, Rogersville, 1964-71, librarian, 1971—. Mem. Tenn., East Tenn. library assns., Bus. and Profl. Womens Club. Democrat. Presbyn. Author: Lion of the West, 1971. Home: Rt 3 Box 265 Rogersville TN 37857 Office: 415 W Main St Rogersville TN 37857

KENT, ELIZABETH LIPFORD (MRS. CECIL KENT), educator, nursing adminstr.; b. Cleve., Feb. 23, 1919; d. Charles Meshach and Cora (Wiggins) Lipford; A.B., Spelman Coll., 1942; B.S., Med. Coll. Va., 1945; M.P.H. (Rosenwald fellow), U. Mich., 1946; Ph.D., Rackham Sch. Grad. Studies, 1955; m. Cecil A. Kent, June 25, 1955; children—Cecil Alexander, Jane Elizabeth. Instr. med. surg. nursing Meharry Med. Coll., Nashville, 1946-47; instr. home nursing A.R.C. chpts., Atlanta, Tuskegee, Ala., Cleve., Detroit, 1945-57; adminstr. coll. health service, instr. Spelman Coll., Atlanta U., 1947-50; nurse, instr. psychiat. nursing VA Hosp., Tuskegee, Ala., 1950-51; staff nurse, clin. instr. Providence Hosp., Detroit, St. Joseph Hosp., U. Mich. Hosps., Ann Arbor, 1951-56; pub. health educator Detroit Dept. Health, 1953-57; asso. dir. nursing edn. Lafayette Clinic, Detroit, 1958-65, dir. nursing, 1965—; asst. prof. Coll. Nursing, Wayne State U., 1965—. Mem. Am., Mich., Detroit Dist. nurses assns., Am., Mich. pub. health assns., Am. Acad. Polit. and Social Sci., Nat., Mich. leagues for nursing, Mich. Soc. Mental Health, Mich. Assn. For Emotionally Disturbed Children, Pi Lambda Theta. Home: 19344 Stratford Rd Detroit MI 48221 Office: 951 E Lafayette St Detroit MI 48207

KENT, ELSA KURFURST, physician; b. Vienna, Austria; d. Sigmund and Charlotte (Wohlfeder) Kurfuerst; Dr. Univ. Med., Med. Sch. U. Vienna, 1935; M.D., N.Y. Dept. Edn., 1959. Came to U.S., 1940, naturalized, 1945. Intern, Vienna, 1935-38, Eng., 1939-40; house physician Nat. Jewish Hosp., Denver, 1941-46; chief resident Municipal Sanatorium, Otisville, N.Y., 1946-52; physician Kans. Sanatorium, Norton, 1954-55, dir. Hillrest div., Topeka, 1956; supervising Tb physician J.N. Adam Meml. Hosp., Perrysburg, N.Y., 1957-60, asso. physician, 1960-65, supervising psychiatrist, 1965-67; acting asst. dir. div. West Seneca State Sch., Perrysburg, 1967-70, psychiatrist in mental retardation, 1970—. Fellow Am. Coll. Chest Physicians; mem. A.M.A., N.Y. Med. Soc., Am. Psychiat. Assn., Cattaraugus County Med. Soc. Address: 111 Buffalo St Gowanda NY 14070

KENT, JEAN ELAINE, real estate broker; b. Bridgeport, Mich., Dec. 28, 1923; d. Stanley Kenneth and Hazel (Sloan) Sloan; B.A., U. Mich., 1944; m. Justin Fredrick Kent, Aug. 27, 1949, (div. Dec. 1969); children—Joni Elizabeth, Julie Elaine. Owner, broker Jean E. Kent Realty, Glendora, Arcadia also Big Bear Lake, Cal., 1971—. Mem. Glendora Bd. Realtors (1st v.p. 1974-75), San Gabriel Valley Symphony Assn. Club: Altrusa Internat. (dir. 1973-74). Home: 720 Lilac Lane Glendora CA 91740 Office: 1309 E Alosta Av Glendora CA 91740

KENT, JOAN GAY, bus. exec., editor; b. Mineola, L.I., N.Y.; d. William Lewis and Helen (Remsen) Gay; student Mills Coll.; B.A., Colby Coll., 1942-45. Editorial asst. nat. bd. YMCA's, 1949-51; asst. pub. relations dir. U.S.O., 1951-53; sales promotion mgr. Am. Aviation publs., 1953-56; v.p., mng. editor Missiles and Space, NATO Jour., Manhasset, N.Y., 1956-63; editor The Manhasset Mail, The Port Mail, Manhasset, 1964-66; editor United Tech. Publs., Garden City, N.Y., 1967, writer, editorial cons., 1968—. Pres. Friends of Port Washington Library. Mem. League Women Voters, Cowneck Hist. Soc. (trustee), Pi Gamma Mu, Sigma Kappa. Club: N.Y. Colby Coll. Alumni. Home: Sycamore Dr Sands Point NY 11050 Office: 305 Northern Blvd Great Neck NY 11021

KENT, JOAN LOUISE (MRS. ALAN FINKELSTEIN), geneticist; b. Poland, Nov. 25, 1936; d. George John and Nadine Lillian (Salomon) Kent; came to U.S., 1941, naturalized, 1946; B.A., Barnard Coll., 1958; Ph.D., Rockefeller U., 1963; m. Alan Finkelstein, Aug. 7, 1966; children—Jeffrey Adam, Amy Nadya. Guest investigator

Rockefeller U., N.Y.C., 1963-64; research asso., dept. molecular biology Albert Einstein Coll. Medicine, N.Y.C., 1964-66; guest lectr. bacterial genetics Flower-Fifth Av Hosp.-N.Y. Med. Coll., 1964-66; asso. in genetics Pub. Health Research Inst., N.Y.C., 1966—; research adj. asst. prof. microbiology N.Y. U. Sch. Medicine, N.Y.C., 1968—. Jane Coffin Childs Meml. Postgrad. fellow, 1964-66, research grantee. Mem. A.A.A.S., Sigma Xi. Home: 11 Riverside Dr New York City NY 10023 Office: Public Health Research Inst 455 1st Av New York City NY 10016

KENT, LOIS SCHOONOVER (MRS. LOUIS R. KENT), geologist; b. Marietta, O., Dec. 1, 1912; d. Draper Talman and May Haines (Bowen) Schoonover; student Marietta Coll., 1929-30; B.A., Oberlin Coll., 1934; M.A., Cornell U., 1936; Ph.D., Bryn Mawr Coll., 1940; m. Louis R. Kent, May 5, 1943; 1 dau., Katherine Louise (Mrs. James J. Kloss). Jr. geologist U.S. Geol. Survey, Washington, 1941-43, asst. geologist, 1943-45; editorial asst. Geol. Soc. Am., N.Y.C., 1946; instr. U. Ill., Urbana, 1953-54; asso. geologist Ill. State Geol. Survey, Urbana, 1956—. Mem. Paleontol. Soc. Am., Paleontol. Research Inst., Soc. Econ. Paleontologists and Mineralogists, Geol. Soc. Am., Sigma Xi. Home: 1003 Lincolnshire Dr Champaign IL 61820 Office: Illinois State Geological Survey 25 Natural Resource Bldg Urbana IL 61801

KENT, MARGUERITE ALICE KIRTSINGER, assn. exec.; b. Chgo., Sept. 10, 1905; d. Charles Martin and Maude (Fontaine) Kirtsinger; Ph.B., U. Chgo., 1947; m. Leonard Kent, Nov. 19, 1951 (div. May 1956). Exec. sec. Bus. Problems Bur., U. Chgo., 1943-47; exec. asst., advt. mgr. Am. Marketing Assn., Chgo., 1947—. Home: 3140 Sprucewood Dr Wilmette IL 60091 Office: 222 S Riverside Plaza Chicago IL 60606

KENT, MARY ANN, librarian; b. Mt. Judea, Ark., Mar. 3, 1943; d. William Howard and Mary Clara (Strong) Kent; B.S., S.W. Mo. State Coll., 1964; M.L.S., George Peabody Coll., 1965. Librarian, Vitro Corp. Am., Silver Spring, Md., 1965-66; library systems analyst Booz, Allen Applied Research, Inc., Bethesda, Md., 1966-69; librarian, dir. Nat. Emergency Med. Services Clearinghouse U.S. Dept. Health, Edn. and Welfare, Rockville, Md., 1969—; tchr. needlepoint Montgomery County (Md.), 1972—. Mem. Spl. Libraries Assn., Embroiderers Guild Am., Delta Phi Delta scholar, 1964. Home: 4977 Battery Lane Bethesda MD 20014 Office: 5600 Fishers Lane Rockville MD 20852

KENT, PAULA (MRS. STANLEY J. LLOYD), public relations exec., marketing cons.; b. N.Y.; d. John and Estelle (Frye) Smith; B.S., State Tchrs. Coll., Worcester, Mass., 1939; Master's degree, Grad. Sch., Coll. Bus. Adminstrn., Boston U., 1941; m. Stanley J. Lloyd, Jan. 23, 1943; children—Diane Adrienne Noel, Robin Michele Cheri, Kevin Christopher Kent, Gisele Nicolette Jolie. Methods engr. IBM, 1941-42; personnel dir. Daily Jour., San Diego, also Sta. KSDJ, 1946-48; fashion editor San Diego Union, 1949; promotion dir. San Diego Union and Evening Tribune, 1950-70; dir. ICC div. Bell and Howell Co., San Diego, 1970—; v.p. La Jolla Clin. Labs., Inc., 1972—. Pub. speaker in U.S., Paris, Brussels, Madrid, 1960—. Active A.R.C., Am. Cancer Soc., Gray Ladies, Med. Aux., San Diego, Fiesta Del Pacifico, U. San Diego Aux. Served as chmn. San Diego's Ann. Giant Sales Rally, 1953, 56, 65; chmn. Advt. Recognition Week Campaign, San Diego, 1953-54; dir. Bowl Down Cancer, 1963; dir. San Diego Ann. Boxing Tournament, 1961-68, San Diego Ann. Metro Tennis Championships, 1952-70, San Diego Ann. Model Yacht Regatta, 1952-70, San Diego Ann. Power Boat Regatta, 1950-62, San Diego Annual Investment Clinic, 1962-70, San Diego Ann. Hole-in-One Tournament, 1951-70; pub. relations cons. Mrs. Am. Pageant, San Diego, 1966, Unlimited Hydroplane Races, San Diego, 1964; producer Ann. Gentleman of Distinction awards, 1967, 68, 69, Woman of Year awards, 1967, 68, 69 (both San Diego). Commd. ensign, Women's Res., USNR, 1942, transferred USCG, served from ensign to lt., 1943-46. Recipient 158 awards 1950—, including 39 nat., 18 western states and Hawaii, 100 Cal. state awards, 1 local resulting from ann. competitions sponsored by Los Angeles Advt. Women's Club, Nat. Newspaper Assn. Mgrs., Cal. Newspaper Publs. Assn., California Press Women, Nat. Fedn. Press Women; named one of San Diego's Women Achievement, 1958, 59, 64, One San Diego's Women Valour, 1958, one of San Diego's Advt. Men of Distinction, 1972; recipient San Diego Outstanding Citizen award, 1961; Outstanding Service plaque Sales and Marketing Execs. Club, 1963, 66, 67, 68; San Diego Woman of Yr. award, Council Women's Service and Bus. Clubs, 1965; Los Angeles Man of Year award Sales Promotion Execs. Assn., 1965; Golden Spear award Twin Cities Sales Promotion Execs. Assn., Mpls., 1965; Woman of Achievement award Nat. Fedn. Bus and Profl. Women, 1966; Jeanne Hoffman Unique Coverage award, 1968, Don award Legion of Portola, 1968, Distinguished Service award Investment Edn. Inst., Detroit, 1969, many others. Mem. Sales Promotion Execs. Assn. Los Angeles, Advt. and Sales Club San Diego (dir., former editor monthly bull). Sales and Marketing Execs. Club San Diego (dir., bull. editor, pres. 1970-71), Internat. Newspaper Promotion Assn. (pres. western region 1965, Distinguished Service award 1971) Cal. Press Women, Cuyamaca, Nat. Fedn. Press Women, Sales and Marketing Execs. Internat. (internat. dir.-at-large 1971-73), Am. Advt. Fedn. (western states edn. chmn. 1970-71). Roman Catholic. Clubs: Kona Kal, San Diego. Home: 515 Bon Air St La Jolla CA 92037 Office: PO Box 2243 7847 Fay Av La Jolla CA 92037

KENT, RUTH, broadcasting exec. Dir. viewer relations Sta. WSB-TV, Atlanta. Bd. dirs. Atlanta Symphony Women's Assn., Alliance Theatre Guild, Nat. Found. March of Dimes, Better Infant Births, Cystic Fibrosis Research Found.; trustee Davison Sch. Speech; bd. sponsors Alliance Theatre Co. Mem. Profl. Panhellenic Assn., Nat. Acad. Television Arts and Scis., Zeta Phi Eta, Zeta Tau Alpha. Address: 1601 W Peachtree St NW Atlanta GA 30309

KENWORTHY, JOY ANNE, psychologist; b. Chgo., July 19, 1927; d. Walter Abraham and Gertrude Sarah (Cone) Bowers; B.A. (LaVerne Noyes scholar), U. Ia., 1949; M.A., Drake U., 1964; Ph.D., Ia. State U., 1968; m. James A. Kenworthy, Aug. 6, 1948 (div. May 1963); children—James A., David M., Peter A. Sch. psychologist Dallas County Sch. Bd., Ia., 1963-65; lectr. psychology Drake U., 1966-67; clin. and community psychologist Children's Cons. Service, Mendota Mental Health Inst., Madison, Wis., 1968—; clin., counseling and cons. psychologist Mental Health Assns. S.C. Service Center, Madison, 1969—, also counseling psychologist Organizational Cons. Service. Clin. instr. dept. psychiatry, psychology Women's Work Sci. Center, U. Wis. dept. psychiatry, Madison, 1971—, also cons. Briarpatch. Group co-leader Great Books, Inc., Des Moines, 1953-60; area chmn. United Fund, Des Moines, 1960; organizer Des Moines Child Guidance Center Vol. Orgn., 1958, bd. dirs., 1958-65, pres., 1959-60; organizer Plymouth Congl. Nursery Sch., 1955, bd. dirs., 1955-59, pres., 1956; organizer, group leader Police-Community Relations Project, Madison, 1968-69; co-organizer Women's Caucus, 1974. Bd. dirs. Des Moines Child Guidance Center, 1959-65, pres., 1962-63, recipient Outstanding Vol. award, 1965. Recipient Outstanding Vol. award Jr. League Des Moines, 1962, Day-Hosp. Pilot Project grantee, 1959. Am., Wis. psychol. assns., Dane County Assn. Clin. Psychologists (exec. com. 1970-71), Assn. Women in Psychology, Assn. Humanistic Psychology, Sierra Club, Sigma Xi, Psi Chi, Kappa Alpha Theta. Clubs: Hoofers, Wisconsin Union (U. Wis.). Home: 1314 Whenona Dr Madison WI 53711 Office: 301 Troy Dr Madison WI 53704 also 20 S Park Madison WI 53715

KENYON, EUNICE LENORA, psychologist; b. Corfu, N.Y., June 19, 1921; d. Orvis S. and Rachael (Smith) Kenyon; B.E., Brockport State Tchrs. Coll., 1942; M.A., City Coll. N.Y., 1952. Tchr. pub. schs., Ala., N.Y., 1942-49; asst. dir. testing and evaluation center Buffalo Assn. for the Blind, 1949-50; presch. psychologist, adminstrv. asst. Lighthouse Psychol. Guidance Service, 1950-52; exec. dir. Boston Center for Blind Children, 1952—. Mem. Am. Assn. Workers with Blind, Internat. Council Exceptional Children, Am., Mass. psychol. assns. Author: (with others) Understanding Your Blind Child, 1952; Problems of Adjustment of Handicapped Children, 1959. Home: 8 Highledge Av Wellesley Hills MA 02181 Office: 147 S Huntington Av Boston MA 02130

KENYON, LILLIAN HARRIETTE FENNEP (MRS. MAYNARD LEROY KENYON), social worker; b. Cleveland Heights, O., Jan. 1, 1909; d. Percy William and Harriette Lillian (Thrush) Fenner; A.B., Flora Stone Mather Coll. Case Western Res. U., 1931, M.S., 1945; m. Maynard L. Kenyon, Nov. 27, 1935. Child care cons. State of O., Cleve., 1942-45; intake supr., field instr. Jewish Children's Bur., Cleve., 1945-50; adoption supr. Luth. Children's Aid, Cleve., 1950; med. social worker Cleve. Metropolitan Gen. Hosp., 1951; Y-Teen dir. Central Cleve., 1952-54; dir. Friendly Visitors, 1955-59; med. social worker Cleve. Met. Gen. Hosp., 1960-63; dir. social work, dir. day care center Cleve. Christian Home, 1963-65; dir. social service, admissions dept. Cleve. Psychiat. Inst., Cleve., 1965-68; sr. psychiatric social worker El Paso (Tex.) Child Guidance, 1968—. Pvt. practice social work, 1945—; field instr. undergrad. students U. Tex., El Paso, 1970, 71. Treas. Co-op Credit Union, Lakewood, O., 1954-56; mem. Cleve. Council Camp Fire Girls, 1954-59, El Paso (Tex.) Council, 1969-72, chmn. personnel, 1969-72. Fellow Am. Orthopsychiat. Soc.; mem. El Paso Springer Spaniel Assn., League of Women Voters, Acad. Certified Social Workers (chmn. spl. awards com. 1946). Universalist (bd. dirs. 1959-67). Club: Women's City (Cleve.). Home: 225 Resler Dr El Paso TX 79912 Office: 1501 N Mesa St El Paso TX 79902

KEOGH, JEANNE MARIE, librarian; b. Toledo, Sept. 20, 1924; d. Thomas Leroy and Agnes Mary (Wenzler) Keogh; B.A., Mary Manse Coll., 1946; B.S. in L.S., Western Res. U., 1947. Asst. librarian tech. dept. Toledo Pub. Library, 1946-54; tech. librarian Libbey Owens Ford Co., Toledo, 1954—. Established library Riverside Hosp. Nursing Sch., Toledo, 1950-51; grey lady A.R.C., Toledo, 1966-70; chmn. Detroit Conf. Hospitality Com., Detroit, 1970; mem. Transp. Safety Information Com., N.Y.C., 1972—; mem. finance com. Mary Manse Coll., Toledo, 1972—. Mem. Ohio, Catholic librarians assn., Spl. Libraries Assn. (mem. scholarship com. 1968-74, chmn. 1969-70, 72-74), Mary Manse Coll. Alumni Assn. (dir. 1971—, pres. 1972-73). Club: Quota (Toledo). Home: 3634 Rugby Dr Toledo OH 43614 Office: 1701 E Broadway Toledo OH 43605

KEPLINGER, LORRAINE JOYCE MILLER (MRS. RICHARD ALAN KEPLINGER), book and music co. exec.; b. Lena, Ill., Apr. 9, 1931; d. Arthur Leroy and Elizabeth Maude (Baker) Miller; student Ill. Wesleyan Sch. Music, 1949-50, Kent State U., 1963-67; m. Richard Alan Keplinger, Aug. 20, 1950; children—Karen (Mrs. Thomas R. Kaufman) Marilyn, Joy. Sales clk. Gantt's Grocery, Lena, Ill., 1947-52; gen. operator Gospel Book Store, New Philadelphia, O., 1962-68; owner, operator Gospel Book & Music Co., New Philadelphia, 1969—. Tchr. Peniel Holiness Christian Day Sch., Beach City, O., 1968-71. Council pres. P.T.A., 1966-68; active Tusarawas County Philharmonic Orch. Mem. Am. Legion Aux. (unit treas. 1971), Music Study Club. Lutheran (asst. organist 1971—). Home: 144 3d St SW New Philadelphia OH 44663 Office: 127 Allen Lane SW New Philadelphia OH 44663

KERBIS LEMPP, GERTRUDE, architect; B.S., U. Ill.; M.A., Ill. Inst. Tech.; postgrad. Grad. Sch. Design, Harvard, 1949-50; m. Walter Peterhans (dec.); m. 2d, Donald Kerbis (div. 1972); children—Julian, Lisa, Kim. Archtl. designer Skidmore, Owings & Merrill, Chgo., 1954-59, C.F. Murphy Assos., Chgo., 1959-62, 65-67; pvt. practice architecture, Chgo., 1967—; lectr. U. Ill., 1969; asso. prof. William Rainey Harper Coll., 1970—; prin. works include: dining hall U.S. Air Force Acad. (Colo.), Skokie (Ill.) Pub. Library, 1959, Meadows Club, Lake Meadows, Chgo., 1959, Tennis Club, Highland Park, Ill., 1968, 7 Continents Bldg., O'Hare Internat. Airport, 1963. Lectr. Art Inst. of Chgo., U. N.M., Women's Archtl. League, Ill. Inst. Tech. Archtl. cons. Dept. Urban Renewal, City of Chgo.; mem. Northeastern Ill. Planning Commn., Open Land Project, Mid-North Community Orgn., Met. Housing and Planning Council Chgo., Mayor's Commn. Preservation Chgo. Hist. Architecture. Fellow A.I.A. (dir. Chgo. chpt. 1971—); mem. Assn. U. Profs., U. Ill., Ill. Inst. Tech. alumni assns., Art Inst. Chgo., Am. Civil Liberties Union, Chgo. Council Fgn. Relations, Planned Parenthood Assn., Lincoln Park Zool. Soc., Chgo. Arts Club. Home: 335 Belden Av Chicago IL 60614 Office: 664 N Michigan Av Chicago IL 60611

KERBY, GRACE PARDRIDGE, physician, educator; b. Syracuse, N.Y., June 24, 1912; d. Robert Edward and Francis Sprague (Cory) Kerby; B.S., Fla. State Coll. for Women, 1933; M.D., Duke, 1946. Intern, Duke Med. Sch., Durham, N.C., 1946-47, resident, 1947-51, faculty, 1951—, prof. medicine, 1962—. Home: 1108 Wells St Durham NC 27707

KERCHEVILLE, CHRISTINA JOHNSON, artist; b. Altus, Ark., Aug. 14, 1906; d. Robert Henry and Frances Ada (Gipson) Johnson; B.A. U.S.D., 1929; student U. N.M.; m. Francis Monroe Kercheville, Aug. 28, 1927 (dec. 1969); 1 dau., Francina (Mrs. Thomas Joseph Hall). One-man shows Mus. N.M. Art Gallery, 1947, 63, N.M. A. and M. Coll., 1947, Clovis, 1955, Guadalajara, Mexico, 1955, 58, 61, U. Mex. Student Union, 1966-67, Tex. Art and Industries U. Kingsville, 1967-69, First Am. Title Co. Gallery, 1974; 3-man show Albuquerque County Club, 1971; exhibited group shows ann. Las Artistas, Mus. N.M., N.M. Art League, Fez Club, Witte Memorial Mus., Artist Equity Shows, 1970-73, N.M. State Fair Gallery, 1970-72, Brandywine Galleries, 1972, 73. Exhibited at spl. shows over state; represented in Tex. Fine Arts Assn. Circuit, also pvt. collections throughout south and S.W. Mem. Contemporaries Gallery, Santa Fe, 1961-64. Recipient purchase recommended Am. exhbn. Mus. N.M. Traveling Show, 1954; with traveling shows State Mus., 1953-56; 1st purchase prize Mus. N.M., Santa Fe, 1959. Mem. N.M. Art League (1st v.p.), Tex. Watercolor Soc., Las Artistas, Artists Equity Assn. (chpt. v.p. 1961-63), South Tex. Art League (2d prize citation show 1967), Tex. Fine Arts Assn. (award winner 1967). Democrat. Mem. Ch. of Christ. Clubs: Woman's, Music, Faculty (Kingsville). Illustrator: Tierra Amarilla, 1971. Address: 8810 James St NE Albuquerque NM 87111

KERGER, MARY HELEN, bank exec.; b. Erie, Pa., July 27, 1948; d. John Marvin and Jean (Westfall) Kerger; B.A., Ohio State U., 1970; m. Robert Eugene Deavers, July 2, 1974. Reporter, photographer Ashtabula (O.) Star Beacon, 1967-69; dir. communications BancOhio Corp., Columbus, O., 1970—. Recipient Financial World mag. Merit award, 1970-71. Mem. Internat. Assn. Bus. Communicators (Peer award 1974), Women in Communications, Jewel Club, Alpha Gamma Delta (treas. 1967-68). Republican. Methodist. Club: Ohio State U. Alumni. Home: 6745 Red Fox Rd Reynoldsburg OH 43068 Office: 51 N High St Columbus OH 43216

KERLIN, GERALDINE YOUNG CAMPBELL (MRS. SHERMAN M. KERLIN), utility co. exec.; b. Emporium, Pa., Sept. 4, 1919; d. Walter S. and Edna A. (Casbeer) Campbell; grad. high sch.; m. Sherman M. Kerlin, June 12, 1962; 1 son, Robert; stepchildren—Robert L. Young, Lillian Jean Waller, Mary Catherine Feistner. With Western Auto Co., 1939-49, Wingate Ins. Agy., 1949-56; owner, mgr. Young Ins. Agy., 1956-60; pres. Wellsboro Electric Co., (Pa.), 1960—. Mem. Tioga County Planning Commn., 1970—. Bd. dirs. Grow. Mem. Bus. and Profl. Womens Club. Home: 59 Waln St Wellsboro PA 16901 Office: 19 Main St Wellsboro PA 16901

KERMEEN, DONNA C., marketing exec.; b. N.Y.C., Apr. 21, 1938; d. Leonard L. and Gertrude Iva (Jackson) Kermeen; B.A., Principia Coll., 1959. Writer, Planned Communications Services, Inc., N.Y.C., 1964-66; account exec. Rowland Co., pub. relations, N.Y.C., 1966-67; publicity mgr. Clairol, Inc., N.Y.C., 1967-73, bus. devel. asso., 1973—. Mem. Fashion Group. Democrat. Home: 50 E 73rd St New York City NY 10021 Office: 345 Park Av New York City NY 10022

KERN, ANN THOMPSON, editor; b. Wilmington, Del., Feb. 6, 1942; d. Friar Matthews and Annie Laurie (Hill) Thompson; B.A., Dickinson Coll., 1963; postgrad. (scholar) U. Bridgeport Shakespeare Inst., 1967; M.A., San Diego State U., 1970. Grad. teaching asst. speech arts San Diego State U., 1966-68; instr. speech and theatre arts U. San Diego, 1967-68; publs. asst. ESL/bilingual project San Diego City Schs., 1969-70, editorial coordinator materials acquisition project, 1970—. Instr. speech and theatre arts Southwestern Coll., Chula Vista, Cal., 1971—. Reporter, Alpha Omega Players, San Diego, 1970-72; mem. Chicano Fedn. Edn. Com., 1971—, Chula Vista (Cal.) Players, 1970, La Jolla (Cal.) Town Council, 1967—, Old Globe Theatre, San Diego, 1969—; rec. sec. Scripteasers Actors and Playwrights Orgn., San Diego, 1973—. Served with WAVES, 1964-66. Mem. Am. Assn. U. Profs., Am. Theatre Assn., Assn. Mexican Am. Educators, Alpha Psi Omega, Pi Delta Epsilon, Chi Omega. Democrat. Episcopalian. Originator, editor: Materials on the March, 1972-74. Home: 334 Playa del Norte La Jolla CA 92037 Office: 2950 National Av San Diego CA 92113

KERN, DALE ELLEN, editor; b. Camden, N.J., Apr. 12, 1946; d. Norman A. and Sylvia (Zonies) Kern; student Cal. State Polytech. U., 1966-70. Writer news and fashion Cal. Apparrel News, Los Angeles, 1971-72; editor Cal. Men's Stylist, Los Angeles, 1972; editor fashion and beauty Los Angeles Herald-Examiner, 1972—. Mem. Women in Communications (historian 1973-74), Sigma Delta Chi. Home: 1845 Fox Hills Dr Los Angeles CA 90025 Office: 1111 S Broadway St Los Angeles CA 90015

KERN, MARGUERITE ANN, physician; b. New Castle, Pa., July 25, 1937; d. John William and Marguerite (McMullen) Kern; student W.Va. U., 1955-60; M.D., Med. Coll. Va., 1962. Intern, Med. Coll. Va., Richmond, 1962-63, pediatric resident, 1963-64, clin. instr., 1965—; practice medicine specializing in pediatrics, Petersburg, Va., 1965-66, Richmond, 1966—; mem. staffs Richmond Meml. St. Mary's, Stuart Circle, Johnston-Willis hosps., Med. Coll. Va., Retreat for Sick. Diplomate Nat. Bd. Med. Examiners. Mem. A.M.A., Med. Soc. Va., Women's Soc. Christian Service, Woodman Civic Assn., Richmond Pediatric Soc., Med. Coll. Va., W.Va. U. Sch. Medicine alumni assns., Alpha Epsilon Delta, Alpha Xi Delta. Republican. Methodist. Mem. Order Eastern Star. Home: 9800 Thacker Lane Richmond VA 23228 Office: 2309 Hungary Rd Richmond VA 23228

KERN, RUTH ELLEN, lawyer; b. Chgo., Aug. 22, 1914; d. Fred and Ellen (Tollin) Olson; J.D., Chgo.-Kent Coll. Law, 1946; m. Robert Markman, Jan. 25, 1936 (div. 1938); 1 son, Peter; m. 2d, Martin Kern, Oct. 6, 1948 (div. 1967); children—David, Susan (Mrs. Scott McCoy). Admitted to Ill. bar, 1946, Tex. bar, 1967, U.S. Supreme Ct. bar, 1972; practice law, Chgo., 1946, El Paso, Tex., 1967—; mem. faculty U. Tex. at El Paso Sch. Bus., 1968-72. Chmn. El Paso com. Am. Friends Service Com., 1970-72; chmn. legal com. El Paso Civil Liberties Union, 1971-73. Bd. dirs. Group Against Smog and Pollution, Anti-Defamation League. Mem. El Paso, Tex. bar assns., Tex. Trial Lawyers Assn., El Paso Trial Lawyers Assn. (dir. 1973-74), El Paso Women's Polit. Caucus, Nat. Orgn. Women, Women's Exec. Council. Jewish religion (mem. social action com. 1973-74). Home: 505 Cincinnati St El Paso TX 79902 Office: 304 ABC Bldg El Paso TX 79901

KERPER, HAZEL BOWMAN (MRS. W. G. KERPER), lawyer, educator; b. Laramie, Wyo.; d. Elmer E. and Claribel (Colby) Bowman; B.A. with honor, U. Wyo., 1926, J.D. with honor, 1928; postgrad. Stanford Law Sch., 1926-27, Spanish Lang. Sch., San Jose, Costa Rica, 1960-63; certificate in corrections Fla. State U., 1964, M.S. in Criminology, 1965; m. W. G. Kerper June 17, 1927; children—Minabelle, Loujen, Janeen, Jill (Mrs. Johne M. Lennon). Admitted to Wyo. bar, 1928, Cal. bar, 1942, Fed. Ct. bar, 1944, Tex. bar, 1971; partner firm Kerper & Kerper, Cody, Wyo., 1928-40, 43-54; practiced in Los Angeles, 1940-43; ct. commr. Park County, Wyo., 5th Jud. Dist., 1930-59, asst. atty., 1928-30; mem. pub. relations and publicity staff Children's Orthopedic Hosp., Los Angeles, 1940-43; sec., mgr. Title Ins. and Trust Co., Cody, 1954-59; exec. sec. Avanza Industria, S.A., San Jose, 1959-64, also cons. Kativo, S.A. (Costa Rica, El Salvador, Nicaragua, Panama, Guatemala); asst. prof. sociology Sam Houston State Coll., Huntsville, Tex., 1966-67, asso. prof. sociology and criminal law, 1967-68, prof. criminal justice, 1968—. Mem. (Wyo.) Dist. 6 Sch. Bd., 1930-38, clk., 1932-38. Sec., Wyo. Republican Com., 1934-36. Recipient Distinguished Prof. award Sam Houston State Coll. 1967. Mem. Cody C. of C. (sec. 1928-55), P.E.O., Mortar Bd., Delta Delta Delta (finance dir., contbr. nat. publ. 1954-59), Phi Kappa Phi, Delta Sigma Rho, Phi Gamma Mu, Delta Tau Kappa Alpha Kappa Delta. Club: Quill. Author: Introduction To The Criminal Justice System, 1972; (with Janeen Kerper) Legal Rights of The Convicted. Editorial adv. bd. West Pub. Co. Home: 2018 Av S Huntsville TX 77340

KERR, ADELAIDE, journalist; b. Ottawa, Kan.; d. James Woods and Clara (Johnson) Kerr; ed. U. Kan., State U. Mont., N.Y. U. Mem. editorial staff A.P., 1949—, successively writer, N.Y.C., fgn. corr., Paris, France, features editor, Paris, spl. assignment writer, London, writer news features service, N.Y.C., editor Woman's Page, originator column These Women. Mem. Author's Guild, Author's League Am. Presbyn. Club: Overseas Press (gov.). Home: 130 E 39th St New York City NY 10016

KERR, ANN THOMAS (MRS. WILLIAM ERNEST KERR), civic worker, author; b. Pitts., June 3, 1911; d. Alfred Cyrus and Lucy Eliza (Forquer) Thomas; student pub. schs.; m. William Ernest Kerr, July 14, 1944; children—William David, John Alexander. Sec. to pres. J&L Steel Corp., Pitts., 1940-44; tchr. Pitts. Acad., 1938-43. Pres., Magee Womens Hosp. Aux., Pitts., 1968-71; mem. jr. com. West Pa. Hosp., Pitts., 1964-68; mem. Pitts. Opera, 1962—, Pitts. Symphony Soc., 1960—, Pitts. Music Guild, 1955-62, Civic Light Opera, 1958—,

Opera Workshop of Chatham Coll., Pitts., 1954—. Mem. Nat. Soc. Arts and Letters. Club: Twentieth Century (Pitts.). Author: My Trip to Europe, 1964; Around the World, 1968. Home: 927 Hulton Rd Oakmont PA 15139

KERR, CHARLOTTE ALICE HERMAN (MRS. JOHN E. KERR), physician; b. Champaign, Ill., May 25, 1920; d. Charles Everett and Gladys (Chaney) Herman; B.S., U. Ill., 1940; M.S., Ia. State U., 1944; M.D., U. Ill., 1948; m. John E. Kerr, Aug. 10, 1946; children—Patricia, Philip (dec.). Intern, Cook County Hosp., Chgo., 1948-50, resident obstetrics-gynecology, 1951-54; practice medicine specializing in obstetrics and gynecology, Chgo., 1954-60, Michigan City and LaPorte, Ind., 1958—; clin. instr. obstetrics and gynecology Northwestern U. Med. Sch., 1954-60; attending physician Passavant Hosp., Chgo., 1954-60; attending physician St. Anthony Hosp., Michigan City, 1958—; attending physician Meml. Hosp., Michigan City, 1958—, chmn. obstetrics and gynecology dept., 1970-71. Diplomate Am. Bd. Obstetrics and Gynecology. Fellow A.C.S., Am. Coll. Obstetricians and Gynecologists; mem. Am. Med. Women's Assn. (nat. treas. 1965, 72), Central Assn. Obstetrics and Gynecology, Pi Beta Phi. Home: 2618 Oriole Trail Michigan City IN 46360 Office: 1707 Buffalo St Michigan City IN 46360

KERR, DOROTHY MARIE BURMEISTER, advt. agy. exec.; b. Chgo., Oct. 1, 1935; d. Edwin Charles and Dorothy Gladys (Braithwaite) Burmeister; B.A., Cornell U., 1956; m. James Robert Kerr, Aug. 27, 1955 (div. Jan. 1970). 1 dau., Kathryn Elizabeth. Publicity dir. United Chaps. Phi Beta Kappa, Washington, 1957-62; dir. circulation, promotion The Am. Scholar, Washington, 1957-62; pres., creative dir. Dorothy Kerr & Assos., Inc., Washington, 1962—. Cons. Annenberg Sch. Communication, U. Pa., Phila., 1973—; lectr. George Washington U., 1974—. Bd. dirs. Florence Crittenton Home, Washington, 1968-71. Recipient Man of Year award, Mail Advt. Club, 1971. Mem. Direct Mail Marketing Assn. (mem. awards com. 1971—), Nat. Soc. Arts and Letters (lit. scholarship chmn. 1972—), Assn. Direct Marketing Agencies (bd. dirs. 1970-72), Kappa Delta. Clubs: Advt. (bd. dirs. 1972—), Soroptimist (Washington), Capital Speakers (v.p. 1971), Direct Marketing (pres. 1965) (Washington). Home: 3106 Cleveland Av NW Washington DC 20008 Office: 1211 Connecticut Av NW Washington DC 20036

KERR, FAITH FLORENCE (MRS. THOMAS M. KERR), ins. and stock broker; b. Bayonne, N.J., Apr. 27, 1930; d. Arthur G. and Elizabeth H. (Baron) Bintz; student Profl. Sch. of Bus., Denville, N.J., 1961; m. Thomas Murray Kerr, June 2, 1951; children—Karen, David. Head Bookkeeper First Nat. Bank, Washington, N.J., 1949-52; sec. N.J. dist. Assemblies of God, 1952-56; sec. Banks E. Moyer Agy., Washington, N.J., 1956-61, ins. broker, 1961—, investment broker and dealer, 1963—, exec. v.p., treas., 1967-73; commercial lines mgr. Bowers, Schuman & Welch, 1973—. Recipient Mut. Ins. Woman of the Year award, 1967. N.J. Assn. Mut. Ins. Agts. (bd. dirs. 1970—), Warren County Assn. Independent Ins. Agts. (sec.-treas. 1966-72). Mem. Assembly of God ch. (pres. women's missionary council 1967-68). Home: 45 Hillcrest Av Washington NJ 07882 Office: 21 W Washington Av Washington NJ 07882

KERR, FRANCES WILLARD, writer, editor; b. Independence, Mo.; d. Rector Monroe and Lucy (Whitney) Kerr; grad. Kansas City Jr. Coll.; student Columbia, N.Y. U. Advt. copywriter, radio continuity writer, pub. relations for YWCA, free-lance writer for Kansas City Star and Jour.-Post (all Kansas City, Mo), 1931-43; tech. writer, U.S. Signal Corps, Ft. Monmouth, N.J., 1943-46; econs. writer, U.S. Dept. Labor, Washington, 1946-47; feature writer Dept. State, Washington, 1947-53; supervising editor, writer, Far East publs. USIA, Washington, 1953—. Mem. Am. Newspaper Women's Club, Welcome to Washington Club, Bronte Soc. Club: Washington Press. Contbr. articles to various publs. Home: 4305 Murdock Mill Rd NW Washington DC 20016

KERR, JOAN PATERSON (MRS. CHESTER BROOKS KERR), art editor; b. Orange, N.J., Nov. 8, 1921; d. David Archibald and Marjorie (Sclater) Paterson; B.A., Vassar Coll., 1942; M.A., Mills Coll., 1943; m. Edwin S. Mills, Jr., July 14, 1946 (div. Aug. 1960); children—Edwin S. III, Hilary P., Alison; m. 2d, Chester Brooks Kerr, June 30, 1964. Researcher, Life mag., 1944-49; editorial asst. Picture Press, 1952-54; asst. editor Am. Heritage mag., N.Y.C., 1954-58, asso. editor, 1958-66, art editor, 1966-68, cons. editor, 1968—; picture editor Founding Fathers series Newsweek Book Div., 1972—. Mem. edn. com. New Haven Model Cities Program, 1968-69; bd. dirs. New Haven Human Relations Council, 1969-70; vice chmn. Friends of New Haven Pub. Library, 1973—. Mem. New Haven Colony Hist. Soc. (dir., program chmn. 1970—). Picture editor Am. Album, 1968. Home: 421 Humphrey St New Haven CT 06511 Office: 1221 Av of Americas New York City NY 10020

KERR, MABEL DOROTHEA, physician; b. Toronto, Ont., Can. (parents Am. citizens); d. George Houston and Mabel (Wark) Kerr; B.S., Ohio State U., 1944; M.D., Columbia, 1950. Intern dept. medicine St. Luke's Hosp., N.Y.C., 1950-51, resident, 1951-52; psychiat. resident Payne Whitney Clinic, N.Y. Hosp., 1952-57; practice medicine, specializing in psychiatry, N.Y.C., 1954—; asst. attending psychiatrist N.Y. Hosp.; clin. asst. prof. psychiatry Cornell U. Med. Coll., 1968—; asst. med. examiner, officer chief med. examiner City of N.Y., 1957-66, med. investigator, 1966—. Pres. Elmora Found. Fellow N.Y. Acad. Medicine; mem. A.M.A., Am. Psychiat. Assn., Am. Acad. Forensic Scis., Am. Acad. Compensation Medicine, Pan Am. Med. Assn., Women's Med. Soc. N.Y. State. Address: 20 E 68th St New York City NY 10021

KERR, NELLE THORBURN (NELLY DEACHMAN) (MRS. WILLIAM JOHN KERR), artist, educator; b. Prescott, Ark.; d. Frederick Robert and Gertrude (Brooks) Thorburn; student Ark. Tchrs. Coll., 1914-16, Peabody Coll., U. Chgo., summer 1921; B.F.A., Art Inst. Chgo., 1939, M.F.A., 1941; student De Paul U., 1939-41; m. Thomas Wilson Deachman, May 4, 1935 (dec. Mar. 1945); m. 2d, William John Kerr, Dec. 9, 1950. Tchr. Prescott pub. schs., 1918-22; art supr. Stuttgart (Ark.) schs., 1922-26; asst. art dir. fashion dept. Barns Crosby Co., Chgo., 1926-35; owner, mgr. Abbey Gallery, Chgo., 1952-70; numerous one-woman shows, Chgo., also Ark. Mus., Little Rock, Hendrix Coll., Conway, Ark., sta. KFPW, Ft. Smith, Ark., St. Louis; exhibited numerous group shows including Centro Studi E. Scambi Internat., Rome, Italy, Ark. Mus. anns., Ill. State Fair Profl. Exhibits; represented in numerous pvt. collections; tchr. Graver Park Water Color Club, Chgo., 1956-64, Casa Des Artes South Shore Country Club, Chgo., 1964-74; instr. water and oil Village Artists Flossmoor, Ill., 1970—. Recipient numerous awards for work. Mem. Am. Artist Profl. League, Cordon Centro Studi Escambi Internat., Alumnae Assn. Sch. Art Inst. Chgo., Nat. League Am. Pen Women, Ill. Soc. Fine Arts (pres. 1962-65). Works include portrait Gov. Terral, Ark. Capitol, Little Rock, 1947. Address: 2625 H Hawthorne Lane Flossmoor IL 60422

KERR, ROSE GLADYS HALL, home economist; b. San Francisco, June 20, 1913; d. Albert John and Orabelle Ann (DesChamps) Hall; B.S., U. Ida., 1936; m. John Harry Kerr, Mar. 1, 1941. Home econs. tchr. Blackfoot (Ida.) High Sch., 1936-37, Rupert (Ida.) High Sch., 1937-40; dir. home econs. Weiser (Ida.) Vocational Sch., 1940-41; home economist U.S. Dept. Agr., Washington, 1943; chief Nat. Home Econs. Research Center of U.S. Dept. Commerce, College Park, Md., 1944-72. Recipient certificate appreciation meritorious service U.S. Dept. Army, 1944; outstanding performance ratings Dept. Interior, 1946-61, sustained superior performance awards, 1961-65; Blue Pencil award Fed. Editors Assn., 1966; Bronze medal Superior Fed. Service Dept. Commerce, 1972. Mem. Am., D.C. home econs. assns. Author govt. publs. Home: 4522 Roxbury Dr Bethesda MD 20014

KERRUISH, SHIRLEY WELLS, artist; b. Toledo, Sept. 16, 1924; d. Clark E. and Rita (Bastin) Wells; ed. Ringling Sch. Art, Sarasota, Fla., Keene Sch. Art, Toledo; m. William H. Kerruish, June 5, 1948. One-man shows Toledo Mus. Art, 1960, Park Lane Hotel, Toledo, 1961, Larcada Gallery, N.Y.C., 1965, 67; exhibited group shows U.S.A. Drawing Show, St. Paul, 1961, 63, 66, Butler Art Inst., Youngstown, O., 1954, 63, Pa. Acad. Fine Arts, Phila., 1952-65, 69, N.A.D., N.Y.C., 1966, 68, Toledo Art Mus., 1956-59, 60, 63, 65, No. Ill. U., 1968, also others. Recipient Roulet Medal for achievement in art Toledo Mus. Art, 1963. Home: 121 Brinkerhoff Av Mansfield OH 44906 Office: Larcada Gallery 23 E 67th St New York City NY 10021

KERRY, GLORIA DIANE JAMES (MRS. ROBERT LEE KERRY), periodontist; b. Detroit, Apr. 14, 1931; d. Edgar and Gertrude Alice (Krafft) James; B.S., U. Mich., 1955, D.D.S. (Grad. women fellow), 1956, M.S. in Periodontics, 1966; m. Robert Lee Kerry, Aug. 21, 1954; children—Karen, Julie, Susan, Bob, Bruce. Individual practice gen. dentistry, Detroit, 1956-63; practice dentistry specializing in periodontics, Detroit, 1966—. Pres. Assn. Am. Women Dentists; past pres. R.W. Bunting Periodontal Study Club. Vice pres. Kerry Med. Found. Mem. Am. Acad. Periodontology, Mich. Dental Assn., Detroit Dist. Dental Soc., Midwest Soc. Periodontics, Fedn. Dentaire Internationale, Mich. Soc. Periodontists, Am. Soc. Preventive Dentistry, Kappa Kappa Gamma (Alumnae Achievement award). Contbr. articles to profl. jours. Home: 340 Barton North Dr Ann Arbor MI 48105 Office: 1427 David Whitney Bldg Detroit MI 48226

KERSAVAGE, CAROL JOAN, tech. writer, editor; b. Marquette, Mich., Apr. 23, 1934; d. L. John and Jen (Peterson) Larson; B.S., Mich. State U., 1956; M.A., Pa. State U., 1959; m. Paul C. Kersavage, Sept. 13, 1958; children—Jeffrey, Gregory, Bradley, Lisa. Asst. home econs. editor Pa. State Coop. Ext. Service, 1956-58, 1966; free lance writer, editor, 1967—; editor GROWTH-Coll. Agriculture Alumni Newsletter, 1968-70, editor other alumni mags.; publicity writer Coll. Edn., 1969-70; editor Pa. State U. Agrl. Corr. Course office, 1972—, editorial specialist Center for Study of Higher Edn., 1972—, asst. editor Rural Sociology, 1973—. Mem. Am. Assn. U. Women (recording sec. 1969-70), Pa. Assn. for Retarded Children (dir. State coll. chpt. 1968-70), Women in Communications. Lutheran. Home: 229 Oak Ln State College PA 16801 Office: 229 Oak Ln State College PA 16801

KERSHAW, BEULAH FRANCES (MRS. BRYAN IVESON KERSHAW), music tchr., poet; b. Cloride, Miss., Jan. 9, 1921; d. William Washington and Esther Matilda (Bone) Warren; student pub. schs.; m. Bryan Iveson Kershaw, July 10, 1965; children—Georgia (Mrs. W.D. Verdon), Sandra (Mrs. Tom Gentry). Tchr. piano, organ, guitar and drums, 1962—; writer poetry, 1942—; rec. artist. Vol. worker in rest homes. Mem. Republican Com., Evansville, Ind., Carmi, Ill., 1967—. Author: Poems by Beulah, Vol. I, 1968, Vol. II, 1973. Composer: It Hurts to be Hurt, 1939; Your Woman, 1964; Santa Kissed Me. Home: Route 1 Crossville IL 62827

KERSTEIN, PHYLLIS MARIE (MRS. MILTON S. NUSBAUM), pest control co. exec.; b. Chgo., Feb. 6, 1928; d. Harry and Yetta (Fishbein) Kerstein; B.A., Roosevelt U., 1948; m. Milton S. Nusbaum, Nov. 26, 1952; children—Howard C., Susan Lee, Andrea Lynn. Sec.-treas. Advanced Exterminating Service, Inc., Chgo., 1948—. Mem. planning bd. Purdue U. Pest Control Conf., 1966; mem. U. Ill. Pest Control Planning Bd., 1965-66. Recipient citation for outstanding service Ill. Pest Control Assn., 1965. Mem. Am., Royal entomol. assns., Nat. (dir. 1964-67), Ill. (sec. 1961-66, dir. 1968-70) pest control assns., Chgo. Real Estate Bd., South Shore C. of C. (pres. 1968-69), Alpha Epsilon Phi. Jewish religion (dir. 1968-70). Home: 4950 S Chicago Beach Dr Chicago IL 60615 Office: 1326 S Michigan Av Chicago IL 60605

KERTZ, ANNA MARGARET DONOVAN (MRS. VICTOR L. KERTZ), librarian; b. Jamestown, N.D., Nov. 5, 1925; d. Charles J. and Anna (Tschetter) Donovan; B.A. in Journalism, U. N.D., 1945; postgrad. Valley City State Coll., 1948; M.A. in L.S., U. Minn., 1966; m. Victor L. Kertz, May 29, 1948; children—Katherine, Camille. News editor Cavalier County Republican, Langdon, N.D., 1945-47; tchr. English, Langdon High Sch., 1949-52, librarian, 1958—; tchr. English and comml. subjects Osnabrock (N.D.) High Sch., 1953-56, prin., tchr., 1957-58; co-owner Nodak Hotel-Motel, Langdon, 1963—. Mem. N.E.A., N.D., Langdon edn. assns., Am. Assn. U. Women, N.D. Library Assn., Phi Beta Kappa, Theta Sigma Phi, Beta Phi Mu. Home: 612 3d St Langdon ND 58249 Office: Langdon High School Langdon ND 58249

KESICH, LYDIA, educator; A.B., Vassar Coll.; A.M., Ph.D., Columbia U. Prof. Russian, Sarah Lawrence Coll., 1969—. Office: Sarah Lawrence Coll Bronxville NY 10708*

KESSINGER, MARGARET ANNE (MRS. LOYD IRWIN ERNST WEGNER), oncologist; b. Beckley, W.Va., June 4, 1941; d. Clisby Theadore and Margaret Anne (Ellison) Kessinger; B.A., W.Va. U., 1963, M.D., 1967; m. Loyd Irwin Ernst Wegner, Nov. 27, 1971. Intern, U. Neb. Hosp., Omaha, 1967-68, resident internal medicine, 1968-70, fellow clin. oncology, 1970-72; asst. prof. dept. internal medicine U. Neb. Coll. Medicine, 1972—. Am. Cancer Soc. fellow, 1971-72. Diplomate Nat. Bd. Med. Examiners, Am. Bd. Internal Medicine. Mem. Am. Geriatrics Soc., Am. Coll. Physicians, Neb. Med. Soc., Omaha-Douglas County Med. Soc., Am. Soc. Clin. Oncology, Am. Fedn. Clin. Research, Alpha Epsilon Delta. Home: Route 1 Scribner NE 68057 Office: 42d and Dewey Sts Omaha NE 68105

KESSLER, MINUETTA SHUMIATCHER (MRS. MYER MICHAEL KESSLER), musician; b. Gomel, Russia; d. Abraham Isaac and Luba Hessia (Lubinskaya) Shumiatcher; grad. in piano Juilliard Sch. Music, 1934, postgrad. in piano, 1936; pvt. study with Ernest Hutcheson, Howard Brockway, Ania Dorfmann; pvt. study composition with Ivan Langstroth; m. Myer Michael Kessler, Sept. 14, 1952; children—Ronald, Jean. Pvt. piano tchr., 1934—; tchr. piano Juilliard Sch. Music, 1936-40; radio broadcasts throughout U.S., Latin Am. and Can.; solo pianist with Montreal, Toronto, Que. Regina and Calgary Symphonies, Boston Pops, N.Y.C. Symphony, Boston Civic Symphony. Faculty mem. Nat. Piano Tchrs. Guild, 1971—. Organizer Concerts in the Home, 1964-69. Bd. dirs. Belmont Community Center Music Com. Recipient awards Composers, Authors & Pubs. Assn. Can. Ltd., 1945, 46; Composition Prize, Brookline Library Music Assn., 1957-58; Golden Key, City of Calgary (Alta., Can.), 1948. Mem. Mass. Music Tchrs. Assn. (chmn. certification 1964-66), Mass. Fedn. Music Clubs (dir. 1969-71), Chromatic Club (program com. 1965—), New Eng. Pianoforte Tchrs. Assn. (pres. 1965-67), Boston Juilliard Alumni Assn. (founder, pres.), New Eng. Jewish Music Forum (a founder, program dir. 1958-60, 71-72, v.p. 1960-65, Composer: Piano Concerto The Alberta, 1947; Ballet Memories of Tevye, 1962; Cantata Brotherhood and Peace Through Music, 1966. Inventor music edn. game Staftonia, 1960. Home: 30 Hurley St Belmont MA 02178

KESSLER, SANDRA RUTH, pub. health adminstr.; b. Cuthbert, Ga., May 24, 1945; d. George Ferman and Sara (Sanders) Kessler; student Valdosta State Coll., 1963-65; A.B.J., U. Ga., 1967; postgrad. Fla. Atlantic U., 1971-73. Career devel. program trainee Am. Lung Assn., N.Y.C., 1967; dir. information Ga. Lung Assn., Atlanta, 1968; program adminstr. Am. Lung Assn. of Southeast Fla., West Palm Beach, Fla., 1969—, program cons., speaker Am. Lung Assn. Ann. Meeting, 1973; program cons., speaker Northeastern TB and Respiratory Disease Conf., 1973. Juvenile counselor, tutor Fla. Teen-Aid Vol. Program, 1972-73. Recipient Nat. Pub. Relations award Am. Lung Assn., 1973. Mem. Women in Communications, Community Services Council Palm Beach County (sec. 1970-72), Fla. Pub. Health Assn. (sec. health edn. sec. 1972-73), Fla. Respiratory Disease Conf. (mem. exec. com. 1970), Fla. Council for Clean Air, Am. Personnel and Guidance Assn. Club: Soroptimist (v.p. 1971). Home: 903 Lake Shore Dr 303 Lake Park FL 33403 Office: 2701 N Australian Av West Palm Beach FL 33407

KESSLER, SHIRLEY, artist; b. N.Y.C.; d. Isaac and Leah (Gross) Schwartz; student Art Students League, 1941-44, N.Y.U., 1940; m. William Kessler; 1 dau., Marian B. (Mrs. Seymour Baldash). One-man shows Barzansky Gallery, N.Y.C., 1949, 56, Upstairs Gallery, Toronto, 1959, Angeleski Gallery, N.Y.C., 1959, 60; thirty eight one-man traveling exhbns. U.S.A., 1959-67; exhibited in group shows Whitney Mus., Met. Mus. Art, N.A.D., Riverside Museum (all N.Y.C.); represented permanent collections Ia. State Mus., Iowa City, Nashville Mus., Norfolk (Va.) Mus., Asheville (N.C.) Mus.; represented European, S.Am., Mexico, Can. traveling exhibits. Mem. Charles Barzansky Gallery, N.Y.C., 1945-59. Angeleski Gallery, N.Y.C., 1959-63; art instr. adult edn., Bd. Edn. N.Y.C., 1946—. Recipient award, nat. ann. N.J. Painters and Sculptors Soc., 1966, Nat. Soc. Painters in Casein, 1970, Art Laureate, Rosette, Nat. medal honor Paris, France Soc. Encouragement au Progres, 1970. Mem. Nat. Assn. Women Artists (dir. 1959-71, finance chmn. 1959-61, chmn. U.S.A. traveling watercolor exhbn. 1961-65, chmn. Va. traveling watercolor exhbns. 1963-67, 1st v.p. 1965-67, pres. 1967-70, permanent adv. bd. 1971—, medal of honor 1970), Painters and Sculptors Soc. N.J., Art Students League (life), N.Y. Soc. Women Artists (dir. 1969—), Artists Equity, Pen and Brush, Am. Fedn. Arts, Internat. Platform Assn., Marquis Biog. Library Soc. (adv. bd. 1970—), Nat. Soc. Painters Polymer and Casein (dir. 1970—), Internat. Art Assn. (rep. 1970—). Microfilmed biography Archives of Am. Art Smithsonian Inst., 1971. Home: 185 E 85th St New York City NY 10028 Studio: 41 Union Sq New York City NY 10003

KESTEN, DOROTHY, publisher; b. Rochester, N.Y., Apr. 9, 1923; d. Hyman and Sara (Spetner) Kay; B.S., Cornell U., 1943; m. Arthur H. Kesten, July 8, 1946; children—Dale, Lynn (Mrs. John Rolfs). With Manhattan Project, Rochester, 1945-46; pub. Army Aviation mag., Westport, Conn., 1952—; pres. Ladd Agy., Inc., sec.-treas. The Kesten Agy., Inc. Mem. Aviation Writers Am., Internat. Soc. Aviation Writers, Am. Helicopter Soc., Army Aviation Assn. Am., Inc., Cornell Alumni Assn. (exec. com.), Assn. U.S. Army. Home: 1 Crestwood Rd Westport CT 06880 Office: Army Aviation Mag Westport CT 06880

KESTER, NANCY CONRAD, physician; b. Winston-Salem, N.C., June 22, 1928; d. Julius Curtis and Connie (Fowler) Kester; A.B., Duke U., 1949; M.S., Bowman Gray Sch. Medicine, Wake Forest Coll., 1951, M.D., 1955. Intern in pediatrics N.C. Bapt. Hosp., Winston-Salem, 1955-56; intern, internal medicine U. Cal. Hosp., San Francisco, 1956-57; research fellowship neurosurgery Bowman Gray Sch. Medicine, Winston-Salem, N.C., 1957-58; resident phys. medicine and rehab. N.Y.U. Med. Center, N.Y.C., 1958-61, acad. career tng. fellow, dept. phys. medicine and rehab., 1961-63; physiatrist on SS Hope in Peru, 1963; attending physician Inst. Rehab. Medicine, 1963—; coordinator rehab. medicine Univ. Hosp., N.Y.U. Med. Center, 1963—, instr. phys. medicine and rehab., 1964-65; asst. prof. rehab. medicine N.Y.U. Sch. Medicine, 1965-69, asso. prof., 1969—. Recipient Am. Women's Med. Assn. award, 1955. Mem. Am. Congress Rehab. Medicine, Am. Acad. Phys. Medicine and Rehab., N.Y. County, N.Y. State med. socs., A.M.A., Am. Heart Assn. (council cerebrovascular disease), Alpha Omega Alpha. Contbr. articles to profl. jours. Home: 200 East 66th St New York City NY 10021 Office: 400 E 34th St New York City NY 10016

KETCHAM, JOYCE PARKER (MRS. CHARLES BROWN KETCHAM), librarian; b. Erie, Pa., Nov. 24, 1929; d. Emmett Scott and Mame Birdella (Steva) Parker; B.S. in Edn., Mt. Union Coll., 1950; M.S. in L.S., Columbia, 1966; m. Charles Brown Ketcham, June 29, 1950; 1 son, Merrick Scott. Tchr., Mt. Freedom (N.J.) Elementary Sch., 1951-52; librarian First Dist., East End elementary schs., Meadville, Pa., 1964-65, Sr. High Sch., Meadville, 1966-67; librarian Edn. Dept. Library, Allegheny Coll., Meadville, 1967—, lectr. children's lit., 1967—. Bd. dirs. YWCA, 1961-63, French Creek Valley Conservancy, 1971; bd. dirs. Northwestern Pa. Heart Assn., 1969-71, mem. heart edn. council Meadville br., 1970—. Mem. Pa. Library Assn., League Women Voters (chmn. environmental quality 1970-72, Crawford County Guild Spinners & Weavers, Beta Phi Mu. Author: The Bibliomania of Reverend William Bentley, 1972. Home: 369 Henry St Meadville PA 16335

KETCHAM, MARY EVELYN, realtor; b. Indpls., Nov. 30, 1916; d. Francis Newton and Lola Mabel (Goodwin) Daniel; A.B., Butler U., 1938; grad. Office Mgmt. course, Nat. Inst. Real Estate Brokers, 1969, 70, Grad. Realtors' Inst. Mass., 1971; m. Leymon Wesley Ketcham, Dec. 27, 1942 (dec. Aug. 1966); children—Daniel Leymon, David Wesley, Wendell James. Tchr. English and speech, Thomas Carr Howe High Sch., Indpls., 1940-42; broker Robert Stone, Inc., Melrose, Mass., 1961, Bay Rd. Realty, Hamilton, Mass., 1961-64; founder Mary E. Ketcham Realty, South Hamilton, Mass., 1964—; lectr., speaker, 1938—. Substitute tchr., Del., 1954-55, N.Y., 1955-60. Mem. League Women Voters, 1962—, chmn. devel. human resources study, 1964. Mem. Nat., Mass. assns. real estate bds. Greater Salem Bd. Realtors, Women's Council Nat. Assn. Real Estate Bds., Beverly C. of C., Nat. Inst. Real Estate Brokers, Salem Multiple Listing Service, Delta Delta Delta (chpt. pres. 1936-38). Home and office: 5 Old Cart Rd South Hamilton MA 01982

KETOLA, HELEN, librarian; b. Lima, O., Mar. 9, 1915; d. Carl and Anna (Lindquist) Ketola; student Chgo. Tchrs. Coll., 1935-38; B.S., U. N.M., 1949; M.A., U. Denver, 1962. Spl. edn. tchr. Chgo. Pub. Schs., 1939-43; physics group sec. Los Alamos Sci. Lab., 1949-54, tech. processes librarian, 1970—; elementary tchr. Los Alamos Sch., 1954-59, jr. high sch. librarian, 1959-70; cons. Jr. High Sch. Library Catalog, H.W. Wilson Co. , 1965-68. Served with WAC, 1943-48. Mem. A.L.A., N.M. Library Assn., (treas. 1967, v.p. 1968, pres. 1969, chmn. intellectual freedom com. 1965). Home: 3811 Gold St Los Alamos NM 87544 Office: PO Box 1663 Los Alamos NM 87544

KETRON, MARY BETTY (MRS. HARRIS L. KETRON), ednl. adminstr.; b. Sheffield, Eng., June 27, 1927; d. Norman and Dorothy (Brierley) Laidlow; student Burridges Comml. Coll., Luton, Eng., 1941-44, Pacific Oaks Coll., 1973; m. Harris L. Ketron, July 14, 1955; children—Roger John, Susan Marie. Came to U.S., 1958; naturalized, 1961. Apprentice accountant Perks Ins., Luton, Eng., 1941-44; accountant, mgr. USAF Non-Commd. Officers Club, Sculthorpe, Eng., 1951-55; adminstrv. asst. Am. Dependents Sch., 1955-58; chief central accounting USAF Mountain Home, AFB, Ida., 1958-61, Chaumont, France, 1962-64; accountant U. Cal. at Los Angeles, 1964-66; dir. bus. and finance Pacific Oaks Coll., Pasadena, Cal., 1966-70, dir. devel., 1970-73, exec. dir. finance, planning and coll. affairs, 1973—. Bd. dirs. Red Cross Youth Com. Mem. Pasadena C. of C. (bus. devel. com. 1971—), Zonta Internat. (dir. Pasadena br.), Nat. Soc. Fund Raisers, Nat. Assn. Coll. and Univ. Bus. Officers, Am. Coll. Pub. Relations Assn., Am. Alumni Assn., Coll. and Univ. Personnel Assn. Club: Altadena Town and Country. Home: 2233 E Midwick Dr Altadena CA 91001 Office: 714 W California St Pasadena CA 91105

KETTER, SHIRLEY HELEN (MRS. ROBERT E. KETTER), electronics co. exec.; b. Chgo., Aug. 18, 1928; d. Rudolph F. and Martha L. (Lorenz) Renner; student Chgo. City Coll., 1967; m. Robert E. Ketter, June 3, 1950; 1 son, Barry. Sec. to major appliance buyer Wieboldt Stores, Inc., Chgo., 1946-50; sec. to pres. Maid O'Mist, Inc., plumbers, Chgo., 1951—; personnel dir. Bel-Tronics Corp., Addison, Ill., 1958—. Treas. Sch. Dists. 10, 20, 108 of DuPage County, 1968—; trustee Village of Itasca, 1973—. Mem. Bus. and Profl. Women of Ill. Methodist. Home: 418 S Home St Itasca IL 60143 Office: 344 Interstate Rd Addison IL 60101

KETTNER, DOROTHY HAGEN (MRS. CURTIS FRED KETTNER), librarian; b. Oakes, N.D., Mar. 23, 1943; d. Clifford Morris and Edith (Johnson) Hagen; Asso. Arts and Scis., N.D. State Sch. Sci., 1963; B.A., St. Cloud State Coll., 1965; M.A., U. Minn., 1966; m. Curtis Fred Kettner, Nov. 24, 1967. Cataloger S.W. Minn. State Coll. Library, Marshall, 1966, acquisitions librarian, 1967-69, adminstrv. asst., 1969-71, coordinator adminstrv. services, 1972—. Cons. establishment profl. library Western Mental Health Center, Marshall, Minn., 1971. Mem. S.W. Minn. State All-Coll. Budget and Finance Com., 1970-74, chmn., 1973-74. Grantee U. Minn. Library Sch., N.D. State Library Commn., 1965; U. Denver Sch. Librarianship grantee, 1974-75. Mem. Minn. Inter-Faculty Assn. (local sec. 1969-71), Minn. Library Assn. Home: 615 Thomas Av Marshall MN 56258

KEUSINK, POLLY WELLES (MRS. RICHARD W. KEUSINK), newspaper exec.; b. Milw., Mar. 19, 1930; d. Colin G. and Doris B. (Hursley) Welles; B.A., Stanford U., 1951; m. Richard W. Keusink, Dec. 27, 1948; children—Christopher, Deborah Ellen, Katherine. Free lance writer for various mags. including Am. Home, 1951-59; reporter Santa Monica (Cal.) Evening Outlook, 1959-62; owner, editor Brookings-Harbor Pilot Newspaper, Brookings, Ore., 1962—. Home: Box 700 Brookings OR 97415

KEWLEY-PORT, DIANE (MRS. ROBERT FREDERICK PORT), communications scientist; b. Cleve., Mar. 5, 1943; d. Norman Edward and Mary Ester (Beebower) Kewley; B.S. in Sci. Engring., U. Mich., 1964, M.S. in Communications Scis., 1968; postgrad. City U. N.Y. Grad. Sch., 1973—; m. Robert Frederick Port, June 11, 1967; 1 son, Nicholas F. Systems programmer Regnecentralen, Copenhagen, Denmark, 1965; research asst. neurocommunications lab. Johns Hopkins Sch. Medicine, Balt., 1967-68; communications scientist Hasking Labs., New Haven, 1969—. Recipient Marian Sarah Parker Meml. award U. Mich., 1963; NIH grantee, 1966-67. Mem. Mortar Bd., Acoustical Soc. Am., Tau Beta Pi. Home: 454 14th St Brooklyn NY 11215 Office: 270 Crown St New Haven CT 06510

KEYES, ELIZABETH D. (MRS. FENTON KEYES), ret. investment banker; b. Evanston, Ill., Oct. 17, 1914; d. George Evertson and Janet (Dortch) Dix; A.B., Vassar Coll., 1936; m. Fenton Keyes, Nov. 18, 1944; children—Charles Fenton, Janet Bayard. Sec. to dep. mgr. Am. Bankers Assn., N.Y.C., 1937-39; research asst. Nat. Planning Assn., Washington, 1942-46; stock broker (registered rep.) Courts & Co., 1967-68; sr. investment officer Provident Nat. Bank, Phila., 1971-74, ret., 1974. Bd. dirs., program chmn. Pee Dee area council Girl Scouts Am.; chmn. room reps. Thornwell Sch. P.T.A.; bd. dirs. Darlington County Cancer Soc., Friends Hartsville Meml. Library. Mem. Am. Assn. U. Women (program chmn. local br.), League Women Voters. Episcopalian (pres. women). Club: Spring Beauty Garden. Home: 643 Addison St Philadelphia PA 19147 summer Chelmsford North Litchfield Beach Box 221 Pawley's Island SC 29585

KEYES, MARGARET NAUMANN, educator; b. Mt. Vernon, Ia., Mar. 4, 1918; d. Charles Reuben and Sarah (Naumann) Keyes; B.A., Cornell Coll., Mt. Vernon, Ia., 1939; M.S., U. Wis., 1951; Ph.D. (Ellen H. Richards grad. fellow), Fla. State U., 1965. Tchr. home econs. Stanley (Ia.) High Sch., 1939-42, Washington Jr. High Sch., Clinton, Ia., 1942-44, Clinton High Sch., 1944-50; instr. related art U. Ia. Iowa City, 1951-57, asst. prof. related art dept. home econs., 1957-68, asso. prof., 1968—, research prof. U. Ia. Found., 1971-74. Mem. Terrace Hill Planning Commn. for Ia.; mem. design rev. bd. Iowa City Urban Renewal Commn.; dir. research Old Capitol Restoration Com. Mem. Am. (exec. bd., chmn. art sect.), Ia. home econs. assns., Am. Assn. U. Profs., Soc. Archtl. Historians, Am. Inst. Interior Designers, Interior Design Educators Council, Ia. Soc. for Preservation Hist. Landmarks (dir. 1970—), Cornell Coll. Alumni Assn. (dir. 1970-73), Iowa City Craft Guild, State Hist. Soc. Ia. (bd. curators 1973—), Nat. Trust for Hist. Preservation, Internat. Fedn. Home Econs. (individual mem.), P.E.O., Omicron Nu. Democrat. Presbyn. Club: Altrusa (pres. 1969-70). Author: Nineteenth Century Home Architecture Iowa City, 1967. Mem. editorial bd. Home Econs. Research Jour. Contbr. articles to periodicals. Home: 306 Ferson Av Iowa City IA 52240

KEYSERLING, POLLY LEAH JACOBSON (MRS. WILLIAM KING KEYSERLING), librarian; b. Winston-Salem, N.C., Aug. 31, 1916; d. Harry and Esther Malka (Hyatt) Jacobson; A.B., U. N.C., 1935, A.B. in L.S., 1936; m. Arthur Beane, Dec. 7, 1940; m. 2d, William King Keyserling, Feb. 19, 1950; children—Harry Leroy, William Monroe, Thomas Charles. With catalog dept. Duke U. Library, Durham, N.C., 1936; with U. Md. Dental Sch. Library, Balt., 1937; with catalog dept. Enoch Pratt Library, Balt., 1938-40; librarian various mil. libraries, Va., S.C., Fla., 1941-45; sales clk. book dept. Legerton's Bookstore, Charleston, S.C., 1946; librarian U. Miami (Fla.), 1947-50; librarian Marine Corps Air Sta., Beaufort, S.C., 1957—. Pres. P.T.A., 1962-63; chmn. Christmas Seal Sales, 1962; active Mother's March, Planned Parenthood, A.R.C., United Jewish Appeal, others. Mem. Am. Assn. U. Women (v.p. 1964-65), Am. (chmn. armed forces library achievement citation com. 1967-68), Southeastern, S.C. library assns., League Women Voters, Phi Beta Kappa. Democrat. Jewish religion. Home: Beaufort Arms Apt 11B Beaufort SC 29902 Office: Station Library Marine Corps Air Station Beaufort SC 29902

KHALOUF, SHIRLEY ANN THOMPSON (MRS. HERBERT CHARLES KHALOUF), physician; b. Paradise, Pa., Feb. 29, 1932; d. Ross Harold and Emma Susanna (Johnson) Thompson; A.B., Susquehanna U., 1954; M.D., Woman's Med. Coll. Pa., 1958; m. Herbert Charles Khalouf, July 9, 1960; children—Linda Sharlene, Stephanie Ann, Barbara Susanne, David Thompson. Intern, Harrisburg (Pa.) Hosp., 1958-59; resident phys. medicine and rehab. Cleve. Clinic Found., 1962-65; active staff Montefiore Hosp., Pitts., 1965-67; active staff Marion (Ind.) Gen. Hosp., 1967—, dir. phys. medicine and rehab, 1968—, chief medicine, 1973-74. Diplomate Am. Bd. Phys. Medicine and Rehab. Mem. Internat. Congress Rehab., Am. Congress Rehab. Medicine, A.M.A., Ind. Med. Assn., Grant County Med Soc. Home: 1204 Overlook Rd Marion IN 46952 Office: Marion Gen Hosp Wabash Av Marion IN 46952

KHAYAT, ELIZABETH (MRS. ALFRED N. BOUTON), pathologist; b. N.Y.C., Dec. 17, 1910; d. Azeez and Mary (Farah) Khayat; B.A., U. Cairo (Egypt) 1929; M.A., U. Paris (France), 1931, Ph.D., 1939; M.D., U. Paris and Toulouse (France), 1938; m. Alfred N. Bouton, June 3, 1946. Intern, Flower 5th Av Hosp., N.Y.C., 1941-42; fellow microbiology and parasitology Colonial Inst. Tropical Medicine, Marseilles, France, 1940-41; fellow basic scis. N.Y. Med. Coll., N.Y.C., 1942-43, instr. pathology, 1947-48; fellow and instr. pathology Flower Fifth Av Hosp., N.Y.C., 1946-47; asso. pathology Mary Immaculate Hosp. and Jamaica (N.Y.) Hosp., 1948-55; chmn. dept. Jamaica Hosp., 1956—, dir. residency tng. program in pathology, 1958—; cons. pathology Mary Immaculate, Creedmore State hosps.; cons. blood banking Intercounty Blood Bank Rockville Center. Served to maj. M.C. AUS, 1944-46. Diplomate Am. Bd. Pathology. Fellow Coll. Am. Pathologists, A.C.P., Am. Soc. Clin. Pathologists; mem. Am. Geriatrics Soc., A.A.A.S., Am. Assn. Blood Banks, A.M.A., A.C.P. Home: 100-20 210th St Queens Village NY 11429 Office: Jamaica Hosp Jamaica NY 11418

KIBRE, PEARL, ret. educator, historian; b. Phila.; d. Kenneth and Jane (du Plone) Kibre; student U. Cal. at Los Angeles, 1920-22; A.B., U. Cal. at Berkeley, 1924, M.A., 1925; Ph.D., Columbia, 1936. Instr. history Pasadena (Cal.) Jr. Coll., 1925-28; research asst. Columbia, 1929-37; instr. history Bklyn., 1937-38; mem. faculty Hunter Coll., N.Y.C., 1938—, prof. history, 1957—; doctoral faculty Grad. Center City U. N.Y., 1964-71, prof. emeritus, 1971—. Research fellow N.Y. Acad. Medicine, Nyon, Switzerland, 1938-39; Guggenheim fellow, 1950-51. Recipient Charles Homer Haskins medal 1964. Fellow Mediaeval Acad. Am. (v.p. 1964-67); mem. History Sci. Soc., Am. Assn. U. Profs., Medieval Club N.Y.C., Am. Hist. Assn., Acad. Internationale d'histoire des sciences (corr.), Phi Beta Kappa. Author: The Library of Pico della Mirandola, 1936; (with Lynn Thorndike) A Catalogue of Incipits of Mediaeval Scientific Writings in Latin; 2d edit., 1963; The Nations in the Mediaeval Universities, 1948; Scholarly Privileges in the Middle Ages, 1962. Co-editor: Osiris, vol. XI, 1954. Contbr. to New Catholic Ency., Dictionary Sci. Biography, also to books, profl. jours. Home: 1100 Madison Av New York City NY 10028

KIDD, RUBY PHILLIPS, artist, personnel worker; b. Rock Hill, S.C.; d. Stephen Horton and Ada (Robertson) Phillips; studied art under Miss Annie Dunn Winthrop Coll.; pvt. tchrs., Ina Olsen, 6 yrs., Chgo. Sch. Design, Southeastern U.; m. Frederic Eugene Kidd, Apr. 19, 1921 (dec. 1946); children—Esther Kidd Barto, Susan Jeanette. Tchr. art, designing and sewing in pvt. classes, also pvt. schs., assisted pub. sch. tchrs. planning lessons several years; bridal cons., 1930-44; personnel work Manhattan Project, Oak Ridge, Tenn., 1944-46; exhibited one-man show at St. John's Ch., Georgetown, 1963, Vitro Corp., Silver Spring, Md., 1963, Bethesda area every year; exhibited more than 100 paintings of Smokey Mountains, Chalker Portrait Co., Tenn., 1929; pvt. exhibits in home, tchr. art, Knoxville, Tenn., 1935—; exhibited at Silver Spring Library, 1959; have repertoire over 100 illustrations explaining Bible; tchr. classes creative arts, self-improvement, Charming Miss programs, YWCA; lectr. Bible classes, others. Trustee Montgomery County Soc. Crippled Children and Adults. Mem. League Am. Pen Women, Winthrop Coll. Alumni Assn. Episcopalian. Clubs: Probanata (Washington); Soroptimist (past pres. Montgomery County). Home: 701 Cedar Lane Apt 150 Knoxville TN 37912

KIDD, SARA WARREN (MRS. ARNETT LEE KIDD), home economist; b. Alderson, W.Va., Nov. 15, 1914; d. Everett Harlow and Grace Isabel (Shields) Warren; B.S., W.Va. U., 1940; postgrad. W.Va. Wesleyan U., 1956, Cornell U., 1962; m. Arnett Lee Kidd, Sept. 30, 1950; 1 son, Warren Lee. Home demonstration agt., Roan County, W.Va., 1940-45, Ohio County, W.Va., 1946; nutrition specialist Pa. State U., 1946-51; extension home economist Dinwiddie County, Va., 1957-66, Queen Anne's County, Centreville, Md., 1966—. Home econs. tchr. Buckhannon (W.Va.) Upshur High Sch., 1955-56; dietitian N.J. State 4-H Camp, Stokes Forest, 1951-55. Exec. bd. Heart Assn. Eastern Shore, 1969-70. Mem. Am. Home Econs. Assn. (exec. bd. 1969-72), Nat. Assn. Extension Home Economists Distinguished Service award Queen Annes County Hist. Soc., Bethany House Aux., Am. Assn. U. Women (br. treas. 1968-72), Delta Kappa Gamma (pres. Nu chpt. 1969-72). Home: 104 Turpins Lane Centreville MD 21617 Office: County Bldg Centreville MD 21617

KIDDER, GEORGINA GARRETT (MRS. FREDERICK ELWYN KIDDER), educator; b. Ponce, P.R., Sept. 14, 1933; d. Julio and Georgina (Pasarell) Garrett; B.S. magna cum laude, U. P.R., 1954; M.S., Fla. State U., 1957; postgrad. U. Ill. at Urbana, 1968-69; m. Frederick Elwyn Kidder, Aug. 10, 1957; children—Julio Wallace, Luis Andres. Mem. faculty dept. math. U. P.R. at Mayaguez, 1954-60, 61-68, U. South Fla. at Tampa, 1960-61; prof. math. U. P.R. Sch. Architecture at Rio Piedras, 1969—, acad. asst. to the dean, 1973—. Mem. Am. Statis Assn., Am. Assn. U. Women, Math Soc. Am., Nat. Council Tchrs. of Math., Asociacion de Graduadas de la U. P.R., Asociacion Puertorriquena de Maestros de Matematicas, Alpha Delta Kappa, Mu Alpha Phi. Episcopalian. Home: 103 Elemi St Alturas de Santa Maria Rio Piedras PR 00927

KIDNEY, JULIET ELIZABETH FISHER (MRS. DANIEL M. KIDNEY), economist; b. Richmond, Ind., Nov. 9, 1913; d. Edgar Andrew and Florence (Corwin) Fisher; student Oberlin Coll., 1930-31; B.A. cum laude, Mt. Holyoke Coll., 1934, M.A., 1937; M.A., Radcliffe Coll., 1943; m. Daniel M. Kidney, July 6, 1946; children—James Andrew, Stephen Corwin. Instr. econs. and sociology Mt. Holyoke Coll., 1937-40, 41-43; economist, OPA, Springfield Mass. dist. office, 1943, P.R. office, 1944-45, constrn. div., Washington, 1945-47; economist CIA, 1951-56; cons., Women's Bur., Dept. Labor, 1960, chief monograph br., Div. Fgn. Labor Conditions, Bur. Labor Statistics, 1961-67, economist office program planning, 1967-70, chief Div. Fgn. Labor Conditions, 1970-72, chief div. tng., 1972—. Instr. econs. night session U. P.R., 1944-45. Active P.T.A. Mem. Indsl. Relations Research Assn., Clubs: Mount Holyoke (pres. 1950-52) (Washington); Quota (pres. 1973-74) (Montgomery County, Md). Home: 7812 Marion Lane Bethesda MD 20014 Office: 441 G St NW Washington DC 20212

KIEFER, ROBERTA BLODWYN, psychologist, educator; b. Alta., Can.; d. Edward Max and Katherine Eleanor (Morris) Kiefer; A.T.C.M., Toronto Conservatory of Music, 1941; B.Ed., U. Alta., 1947, M.Ed., 1950; Ed.D., U. Va., 1966; m. W. Maddry Simmons, May 30, 1954 (div. Apr. 1963). Came to U.S., 1953. Chief clin. psychologist Oliver Mental Inst., Province of Alta., Edmonton, 1950-53; Fulbright exchange fellow Bowman Gray Sch. Medicine, Dept. Psychology, Winston-Salem, N.C., 1953-54; chief clin. psychologist Va. Dept. Mental Hygiene and Hosps., Norfolk, 1955-60; dir. psychol. services Hampton (Va.) City Schs., 1960-64; psychologist legal psychiat. services Dept. Pub. Health, Washington, 1966-67; asst. prof. clin. psychology dept. pediatrics U. Va. Sch. Medicine, Charlottesville, 1967-72; asst. prof. George Mason U., Fairfax, Va., 1972-73; pvt. practice clin. and ednl. psychology, Norfolk, 1955-64, Charlottesville, 1964-72, Fairfax, 1972—; staff psychologist St. Elizabeth Hosp., Washington, 1974—. Lectr. psychology Greensboro (N.C.) Coll., Bennett and Agrl. and Tech. colls., 1954-55, Sch. Gen. Studies, U. Va. Extension, 1956-59. Mem. Am., Va., D.C. psychol. assns., Internat. Council Applied Psychology, Internat. Council Psychologists (membership chmn. 1968-72), Orton Soc., Va. Acad. Sci., Interam. Soc., Kappa Delta Pi. Home: 10902 Maple St Fairfax VA 22030

KIEHL, ANNA KATHARINE (MRS. LESLIE G. RATHBUN, JR.), physician; b. Pittsburg, Kan., Aug. 27, 1918; d. Otto B. and Georgia Lee (Howard) Kiehl; B.A., U. Kan., 1939, M.D., 1943; m. Leslie G. Rathbun, Aug. 17, 1946; children—Kiehl, Katharine Cady. Intern Wis. Gen. Hosp., Madison, 1943-44; asst. resident Columbia Presbyn. Med. Center, Babies Hosp., 1944-46; sr. resident U. Kan. Med. Center, 1946; instr. pediatrics Harvard, Boston, 1947-50; chmn. dept. pediatrics Freeman Hosp., St. John's Hosp., Joplin, Mo., 1953-64; practice medicine, specializing in pediatrics, Joplin, 1953-64, South Houston, Tex., 1964-68, Seabrook, Tex., 1968-71, Detroit, 1971-72; staff Meml. Gen. Hosp. and Golden Clinic, Elkins, W.Va., 1972—; clin. asst. prof. U. Tex. Med. Branch, Galveston, 1965-71, Baylor U., Houston, 1968-71. Diplomate Am Bd. Pediatrics. Mem. A.M.A., Am. Acad. Pediatrics, Alpha Chi Omega. Home: 6 Park St Elkins WV 26241 Office: 1200 Harrison Av Elkins WV 26241

KIELSMEIER, META LENA, dairy exec.; b. Manitowoc, Wis., Oct. 17, 1906; d. Otto August and Clara Marie (Toepel) Kielsmeier; grad. Milw. Tchrs. Coll., 1927; postgrad. Northwestern U., Stout Inst., U. Wis. Tchr. pub. schs., Wausau, Wis., 1927-30, elementary sch. prin., 1931-39; with Crystal Dairy Products, Inc., Watseka, Ill., 1939—, pres., 1969—; pres. Watseka Dairy Products, Watseka Dry Milk, Crystal Food Products. Organizer, Watseka Youth Center, 1941-46; mem. Watseka Hosp. Aux., 1960-73. Mem. Watseka Republican Com., 1964-67, Rep. Women's Club, 1964-73. Mem. Watseka Profl. Women's Club (dir. 1944-50). Lutheran (Missionary Woman's Club). Clubs: Lake Shore, Lake Point Tower (Chgo.); Delray Beach, Hamlett Golf (Delray Beach, Fla.); Kankakee (Ill.) Country; Shewami Golf (Watseka, Ill.). Home: 332 East Oak St Watseka IL 60970 Office: Box 340 Watseka IL 60970

KIERNAT, JEAN MARIE CHAPMAN (MRS. WILLIAM KIERNAT), educator; b. Portage, Wis., Aug. 27, 1935; d. Gordon Charles and Edna Lucy (Lytle) Chapman; B.S., U. Wis., 1957, M.S., 1970; m. William Kiernat, June 29, 1963; children—Katherine, William, Carolyn. Dir. occupational therapy Kenosha County Instns., Kenosha, Wis., 1958-59; asst. supr. occupational therapy Curative Workshop Milw., 1959-62; supr. occupational therapy U. Wis. Hosps., 1962-64; asso. prof. occupational therapy U. Wis., Madison, 1970—. Co-chmn. patient edn. so. dist. Wis. Arthritis Found., 1973—; mem. Gov.'s Task Force on Problems of People with Phys. Disabilities, 1973-74, chmn. edn. and rehab. com., 1973-74. Bd. dirs. Madison Neighborhood Centers, 1968-71; bd. dirs., pres. Ind. Living, Inc. Mem. Am., Wis. (sec. 1958—) occupational therapy assns., League Women Voters. Democrat. Home: 1102 Harrison St Madison WI 53711 Office: 1308 W Dayton St Madison WI 53706

KIERSTEAD, KARIN DEIRDRE, violinist; b. Irvington, N.J., May 21, 1943; d. George Washington and Vera (Bondeson) Kierstead; Juilliard Scholarship scholar, Julliard Sch. Music, 1962-64. First violinist, librarian N.C. Symphony, 1965; 1st violinist Denver Symphony Orch., 1965-68; 1st violinist Oklahoma City Symphony, 1970-71; violinist Houston Symphony Orch., 1971—; mem. Marlboro (Mass.) Chamber Players, 1965-69, West Point Chamber Orch., 1968-70, Monteaux Chamber Players, 1968-70, Ionian String Quartet, 1972—; music instr., Newburgh, N.Y., 1969-70, Caldwell, N.J., 1969-70, Houston, 1971—. Recipient Fedn. of Music award, Bloomfield, N.J., 1961. Mem. Am. Symphony Orch. League. Home: 4713 Fleetwood St Bellaire TX 77401 Office: 615 Louisiana St Houston TX 77002

KIES, CONSTANCE VIRGINIA, educator; b. Blue River, Wis., Dec. 13, 1933; d. Guerdon Francis and Gertrude (Pitts) K.; B.S., Wis. State Coll. at Platteville, 1955; M.S. U. Wis. at Madison, 1960; Ph.D., 1963. Tchr. English, Rothchild-Scolfield (Wis.) Pub. Schs., 1955-56; tchr., librarian Portage (Wis.) High Sch., 1956-58; research asst. U. Wis. at Madison, 1960-63; with U. Neb., 1963—, asst. prof. nutrition, 1963-65, asso. prof., 1965-68, prof., 1968—. Recipient Borden award Am. Home Econ. Assn. for Nutrition Research, 1973. Mem. Am. Inst. Nutrition, Inst. Food Technologists, Am. Chem. Soc., Am. Dietetic Assn., Am. Home Econ. Assn., Am. Assn. Cereal Chemists, Sigma Xi, Omicron Nu. Contbr. numerous articles to profl. jours. Home: 46 Trendridge Rd Lincoln NE 68503

KIESEWETTER, EVELYN VAUGHT CUNDIFF (MRS. FRANK H. KIESEWETTER), educator; b. Meridian, Miss.; d. William E. and Neatie (Vaught) Cundiff; student Meridian (Miss.) Sch. Music, 1920-27, Cin. Conservatory of Music, 1931; A.B., U. Ky., 1938, M.A., 1953, postgrad., 1953—; m. Frank Howard Kiesewetter. Elementary sch. tchr., Lexington, Ky., 1930-57; ednl. cons. Houghton Mifflin Co., Boston, 1957-59; part time mem. faculty U. Ky., Lexington, 1954-60, Morehead State U., 1959; with Zaner-Bloser Co., Columbus, O., summers 1962-69; program dir. Lexington Recreation Dept., 1937. Mem. adv. com. Juvenile Ct., Lexington, 1955-57; mem. Henry Clay Meml. Found., 1955—, Blue Grass Trust for Historic Preservation, 1960—. Bd. dirs. Central Ky. Concert and Lecture Series. Mem. N.E.A., Nat. Assn. for Supervision and Curriculum Devel., Ky., Central Ky. edn. assns., Nat., Buckley Hills Audubon socs. Phi Beta, Kappa Delta Pi. Episcopalian. Club: Spindle Top Hall. Address: Merrick Pl 3520 Milam Lane Apt 409 Lexington KY 40502

KIESLER, ROSE SEGAL, educator; b. N.Y.C., May 11, 1912; d. Lucian and Mayme (Sobel) Segal; B.A., Hunter Coll., 1932; M.A., Columbia, 1933, postgrad., 1934-40; m. Harry I. Kiesler, Dec. 25, 1938; children—David, Lewis, Kenneth. Tutor, Hunter Coll., 1933-39, instr., 1940-56, asst. prof., 1956-69; asso. prof., 1970-73, chmn. dept. geology and geography Lehman Coll., City U. N.Y., Bronx, 1968-72. Co-dir. Nanuet (N.Y.) Country Day Camp, 1957-60; mem. nat. bd. Nat. Women's League Conservative Judaism, 1966—, pres. Westchester-Rockland br., 1966-68, editor Outlook quar., 1970—, v.p. nat. bd., 1972—. mem. nat. women's com. Brandeis U., 1973—; v.p. Nanuet Hebrew Center, 1973—. Mem. Assn. Am. Geographers, Hunter Coll. Alumni Assn. Mem. Hadassah. Home: 46 Hutton Av Nanuet NY 10954

KIESSLING, ALICE HEYL (MRS. OSCAR EDWARD KIESSLING), psychiatrist; b. Phila., May 8, 1903; d. Paul Renno and Lucy (Knight) Heyl; A.B., Cornell U., 1925; M.D., George Washington U., 1929; m. Oscar Edward Kiessling, Aug. 3, 1928; children—Julie Alice (Mrs. Jasper Warner Rothuizen) Peter Jonathan, Brenda Robin, Deborah Lynn, Douglas Oscar. Intern, Gallinger Municipal Hosp., Washington, 1929-30; resident St. Elizabeth's Hosp., Washington, 1930-34; practice gen. medicine, psychiatry, psychoanalysis, Washington, 1930-31, Falls Church, Va., 1931—; dir. Out Patient Psychiat. Clinic George Washington U. Hosp., 1930-36, clin. instr. psychiatry George Washington U., 1930-36; mem. staff George Washington U., Arlington (Va.), Fairfax (Va.), Emergency Hosp., Sibley, Garfield, Dr.'s hosps., Washington; physician Child Sch. Health, elementary schs., Fairfax County. Cons. Disability Determination sect. Social Security Adminstrn. Mem. Va. Adv. Legislative Council Com. on Care of Retarded Children, 1959—; active in obtaining Dept. Transp. grant for project treatment alcoholic drivers, Fairfax County, Va., 1970-71; organizer, chmn. No. Va. Physicians Mental Health Com., 1958; regional Va. rep. Physicians for Automotive Safety. Bd. dirs. No. Va. Mental Health Assn. Diplomate Nat. Bd. Med. Examiners. Founding fellow Am. Coll. Psychiatrists, Eastern Psychoanalytic Soc. (pres. 1968), Am. Coll. Psychoanalysts (charter); fellow Am. Psychiat. Assn.; mem. Va. Med. Soc., Med. Soc. D.C., Washington Psychiat. Soc. (chmn. com. psychiat. aspects automotive safety 1966-71), Fairfax County Med. Soc. (life; pres. 1946; chmn. com. to plan med. facilities for Fairfax Hosp. 1958, chmn. grievance com. 1950-60). Columnist: Med. Bull. No. Va. Contbr. articles to profl. jours. Home: 7048 Haycock Rd Falls Church VA 22043 Office: 7048 Haycock Rd Falls Church VA 22043

KIEVAT, IRENE MARIE, economist; b. Seattle, Nov. 27, 1940; d. Eugene Russell and Dorothy June (Taylor) Kievat; B.A., Wash. State U., 1962; postgrad. Mich. State U., 1963-65. Teaching asst. Wash. State U., 1962-63, Mich. State U., 1963-65; economist Mich. Dept. Commerce, Lansing, 1965-73; economist, chief market analyst Mich. State Housing Devel. Authority, 1974—. Cons. prodn. mag., 1968—. Mem. Gov.'s Task Force on Emergency Employment, 1971. Mem. Am. Econ. Assn., Am. Civil Liberties Union, Delta Delta Delta. Democrat. Unitarian (trustee). Home: 1410 Roxburgh East Lansing MI 48823 Office: Commerce Center Lansing MI 48913

KIEWITT, EVA LORENE, educator, librarian; b. Crothersville, Ind., Aug. 12, 1927; d. Henry Gerhart and Helena Fannie (Nehrt) Kiewitt; B.S., Ball State U., 1949; M.A., Ind. U., 1960, Ph.D., 1973. Tchr., Berne, Ind., 1949-54; tchr., librarian, Paradise, Cal., 1954-58; librarian, East Gary, Ind., 1958-60, Ulm, Germany, 1960-62, Bloomington, Ind., 1962-67; univ. librarian Ind. U. Sch. Edn., Bloomington, 1967-73, asst. prof., librarian Grad. Library Sch., 1973—, dir. project for Eric Computer Searches, 1971-73. Mem. N.E.A., Am. Assn. Sch. Librarians, Assn. Ednl. Communications and Tech., Assn. Coll. and Research Libraries, A.L.A., Am. Soc. Information Sci., Ind. Library Assn., Ind. Sch. Librarians Assn. (state pres. 1968-69), Pi Lambda Theta, Delta Kappa Gamma, Beta Phi Mu. Mem. United Ch. of Christ. Home: 4100 Cambridge Dr Bloomington IN 47401 Office: Grad Library Sch Ind U Bloomington IN 47401

KIFF, CAROLE JOYCE, bus. exec.; b. Attleboro, Mass., May 15, 1939; d. LeRoy and Lillian (Padelford) K.; grad. pub. schs. Exec. sec. Leach & Garner Co., Attleboro, 1958-64; exec. sec. Attleboro Area Mental Health Clinic, 1964-67; traffic mgr. Lyons Advtg. Inc., Attleboro Falls, Mass., 1967-74; pres., treas. C. J. K. Assos., Attleboro, 1973—. Publicity chmn. Attleboro Cancer Fund. Bd. dirs. Attleboro Area Mental Health Inc. Home: 38 Black Oak Dr Attleboro MA 02703 Office: 25 Cushman St Attleboro Falls MA 02763

KILANDER, ELLIE CHAFFEE (MRS. DONALD JOHN KILANDER), univ. dean; b. Detroit, June 24, 1944; d. William Henry and Ellen Earle (Douglas) Chaffee; B.A., U. Ky., 1966; M.S. (State Bd. Edn. scholar), N.D. State U., 1971; m. Donald John Kilander, Feb. 18, 1967; 1 dau., Kerry Lynn. Tchr. English, Hinsdale (Ill.) High Sch., 1966-67; writer, editor Inst. Ednl. Research, Downers Grove, Ill., 1967-69; English tchr. Moorhead (Minn.) High Sch., 1969-70; residence hall dir. N.D. State U., Fargo, 1970-71, asst. dean students, dean women, equal opportunity officer, Gov.'s 1971—. Pres. N.D. Commn. on Status Women, 1973-74, mem., 1972—; vol. supr. Ednl. TV Fund-raising Auction, 1974; state coordinator Equal Rights Amendment, 1973; mem. exec. bd. Fargo-Moorhead Found. Abuse Drugs, 1971-72; mem. exec. bd. N.D. Com. for Humanities and Pub. Issues, 1972-74. Mem. Am. Assn. Higher Edn., Am. Assn. U. Women, Nat. Assn. Women Deans, Adminstrs. and Counselors, Assn. Feminist Cons., N.D. Assn. Personnel Deans, Mortar Board, Kappa Alpha Theta. Presbyn. Home: 1338 7th St S Fargo ND 58102 Office: ND State U Fargo ND 58102

KILEY, MARY LOUISE, coll. dean; b. Boston, Aug. 24, 1934; d. Albert James and Grace Elizabeth (Judge) Kiley; grad. Boston Acad. Notre Dame, 1951; B.S., Framingham State Coll., 1955; Ed.M., Tufts U., 1961. Tchr., Stamford (Conn.) Pub. Schs., 1955-59; instr. Garland Jr. Coll., Boston, 1959-61, asst. acad. dean, 1961-67; dean students Westbrook Coll., Portland, Me., 1967—, also organizer Vol. on Aging Inst. Active United Fund; active sr. citizens program; corporator Boys Club Portland. Recipient Distinguished Alumni award Framingham State Coll., 1972. Mem. Nat. Assn. Women Deans, Adminstrs. and Counselors (pres. Me. chpt. 1971), Mass. Home Econs. Assn. (v.p. 1965-67).

KILGOUR, RUTH EDWARDS, collector of headgear, lectr., author; b. Worcester, Mass., Apr. 28, 1902; d. Victor E. and Janet (Gage) Edwards; ed. pvt. schs. Worcester and Paris, France; m. Vernon E. Kilgour, June 26, 1954. Reportedly has one of greatest collections of traditional headgear, collected over 20 years from 52 countries. Past pres. Jr. League, Friendly House (settlement house), YWCA (all Worcester). Club: Worcester Garden (sec.). Author: A Pageant of Hats, 1958; contbr. hat. sect. to Ency. Brit. Address: 66 Malden St West Boylston MA 01583

KILLEBREW, ELLEN JANE (MRS. EDWARD S. GRAVES), cardiologist; b. Tiffin, O., Oct. 8, 1937; d. Joseph Arthur and Stephanie (Beriont) Killebrew; B.S. in Biology, Bucknell U., 1959; M.D., N.J. Coll. Medicine, 1965; m. Edward S. Graves, Sept. 12, 1970. Intern, U. Colo., 1965-66, resident 1966-68; dir. coronary care, Permanent Med. Group, Richmond, Cal., 1970—; asst. prof. U. Cal. Med. Center at San Francisco. Pacific Med. Center San Francisco Cardiology fellow, 1968-70; recipient Robert C. Kirkwood Meml. scholarship award in Cardiology, 1970, Physician's recognition award continuing med. edn. Mem. Fedn. Clin. Research. Home: 450 E Strawberry Dr Mill Valley CA 94941 Office: 14th and Cutting Blvd Richmond CA 94804

KILLIAM, EVA KING, pharmacologist, educator; b. N.Y.C., Nov. 16, 1921; d. Charles H. and Louise King; A.B., Sarah Lawrence Coll., 1942; M.A., Mt. Holyoke Coll., 1944; Ph.D. (USPHS fellow in pharmacology), U. Ill., 1953; m. Keith F. Killam, Jr., May 12, 1955; children—Anne Louise, Paul Fenton, Melissa Helen. Instr. Sarah Lawrence Coll., 1944-46; research asso. N.Y.U. Med. Sch., 1947-49; pharmacologist Army Chem. Center, Md., 1949-51; asst., asso. research pharmacologist, anatomy dept. U. Cal. at Los Angeles, 1953-59; research asso. pharmacology dept. Stanford U. Sch. Medicine, 1960-68; prof. in residence pharmacology U. Cal. Sch. Medicine, Davis, 1968—. Recipient John J. Abel award in pharmacology, 1954. Mem. A.A.A.S., Soc. Exptl. Biology and Medicine, Am. Soc. Pharmacology and Exptl. Therapeutics, Am. Coll. Neuropsycho-pharmacology, Sigma XI. Home: 2225 Anza Av Davis CA 95616

KILLINGBECK, JANICE LYNELLE (MRS. VICTOR LEE KILLINGBECK), bank exec.; b. Flint, Mich., Nov. 11, 1948; d. Leonard Paul and Ina Marie (Harris) Johnson; B.A., Mich. State U., 1970; postgrad. Delta Coll., 1971-72; m. Victor Lee Killingbeck, Sept. 26, 1970. Tourist counselor Mich. Dept. State Hwys., Clare, 1969; copy editor Mich. State News, East Lansing, 1969-70; gen. reporter Midland (Mich.) Daily News, 1970; tchr. Saginaw (Mich.) Pub. Schs., 1971; pub. relations exec. 1st State Bank of Saginaw, 1971—. Mem. Women in Communications, Sigma Delta Chi. Methodist. Home: 4527 Wisner St Saginaw MI 48601 Office: 821 Court St Saginaw MI 48602

KILMER, ANNE ELIZABETH DRAFFKORN (MRS. HARLAN N. KILMER), educator; b. Chgo., June 1, 1931; d. August Theodore and Elsie (Seybert) Draffkorn; Ph.D., U. Pa., 1959; m. Harlan N. Kilmer, Sept. 5, 1959; 1 dau., Mary Brunton. Research asst. Oriental Inst., U. Chgo., 1957-61; research fellow Guggenheim Found., 1961-63; vis. lectr. Assyriology dept. Near Eastern studies U. Cal. at Berkeley, 1963-64, asst. prof., 1965-67, asso. prof., 1967-72, prof., 1972—, chmn. dept., 1970-72, divisional dean humanities, 1972—, also asso. curator Babylonian sect. Lowie Mus., 1967—; research fellow Am. Assn. U. Women, 1964-65. Dir. Near Eastern Lang. and Area Center, U.S. Office Edn., Berkeley, 1971-72. Mem. grad. council Grad. Theol. Union of Berkeley, 1971—. Contbr. articles to profl. jours. Home: 1414 Hawthorne Terrace Berkeley CA 94708

KILPATRICK, JULIA, educator; b. Van Buren County, Ia., Sept. 12, 1915; d. James Woodrow and Edna (Laughlin) Kilpatrick; B.S., U. Mo., 1937; M.S., Ia. State U., 1942; Ed.D., Pa. State U., 1960. High sch. tchr., Mo. 1937-42, Ill., 1944-46; instr. Ia. State U., 1942-44, 46-48; head home econs. dept. W.Va. Inst. Tech., Montgomery, 1948-50; asst. prof. home econs., coordinator student teaching Eastern Ill. U., Charleston, 1950-60; prof. home econs. No. Ill. U., DeKalb, 1960-67; dir. div. home econs. State U. Coll., Oneonta, N.Y., 1967-72, prof. home econs. Madison Coll., Harrisonburg, Va., 1973—. Mem. Ill. Vocational Homemaking Tchrs. Assn. (pres. 1964-65), Am. Assn. U. Women, Am., Ill. (pres. 1965-66) vocational assns., N.E.A., Va. Edn. Assn., Va. Home Econs. Tchrs. Assn., Nat. Council Home Econs. Adminstrs. (treas. 1972), Assn. Student Teaching, Am., Va. home econs. assns., Pi Lambda Theta, Delta Kappa Gamma (pres. Alpha chpt. 1966-68), Phi Upsilon Omicron, Kappa Omicron Phi. Club: Dames (pres. 1963-64). Home: 1384-B Central Av Harrisonburg VA 22801

KILPATRICK, MARY EDNA WILL (MRS. JACK JONES KILPATRICK), psychologist, cons.; b. Pomeroy, O., Jan. 29, 1915; d. William Allison and Edna Anne (Garen) Will; teaching certificate, Ohio U., 1935; B.S., Capital U., 1959; postgrad. Toledo U., 1962-63; Nat. Def. Edn. Act grantee, Wiesbaden, Germany, 1962; M.A., Ohio State U., 1966; m. Jack Jones Kilpatrick, Dec. 26, 1936; children—John Milton, Marianna (Mrs. Donald D. Mullen), Kathleen Ellen (Mrs. Arthur E. Schmidt), Christine K. (Mrs. John J. Altmaier) (dec.). Tchr. Chester (O.) Elementary Sch., Meigs County, 1935-37, Whitehall (O.) City Schs., 1946-48, 52-63; child study cons. Columbus (O.) Pub. Schs., 1963-66, counselor, 1966-69, counselor, psychologist Health Services, 1969—. Mem. Nat. Assn. Sch. Psychologists, Nat., Ohio, Columbus edn. assns., Ohio Counselors Assn., Franklin County Mental Health Assn. Presbyn. Mem. Order Eastern Star. Home: 958 Euclaire Av Columbus OH 43209 Office: 61 S Sixth St Columbus OH 43215

KILZER, SISTER LAETICIA, educator; b. Bentley, N.D., June 7, 1920; d. Frank and Clara (Gion) Kilzer; student Mt. Marty Coll., 1938-47; B.A., Coll. St. Benedict, 1948-50; M.A., U. S.D., 1954-55; Ph.D. (AEC grantee), U. Notre Dame, 1960; postgrad. U. Neb., 1951-52, U. Cal. at Berkeley (NSF grantee), summer 1961, Mich. State U. (NSF grantee), summer 1962. Elementary sch. tchr., various schs. and locations, 1940-47; tchr. Fairview Pub. High Sch., Polo, S.D., 1950-51, St. Mary's High Sch., Richardton, N.D., 1951-54, Trinity High Sch., Hartington, Neb., 1954-55, Mt. Marty High Sch., 1955-57; prof., head dept. organic chemistry Mt. Marty Coll., Yankton, S.D., 1960—; NASA Research fellow, summer 1970-71. Researcher Institut für Okologische Chemie, Bonn (Germany), 1972-73. Postdoctoral research U. Notre Dame, summer 1967-69. Mem. Am. Chem. Soc., Midwest Assn. Chemistry, Tchrs. Liberal Arts Colls., Sigma Xi, Delta Kappa Gamma, Delta Epsilon Sigma. Home: 1100 W 5th St Yankton SD 57078

KILZER, SISTER M. PHILOMENE, educator; b. Richardton, N.D., Oct. 25, 1916; d. Frank and Clara (Gion) Kilzer; jr. coll. diploma Mt. Marty Coll., 1940; Ph.B. cum laude, Marquette U., 1941; postgrad. U. Toronto (Ont., Can.), 1947-48; M.A., Creighton U., 1958; Ph.L., Cath. U., 1973. Tchr. elementary schs., S.D., 1938-41; prin. high schs., N.D. and S.D., 1943-65; tchr. high schs., Neb., 1948-49; asst. prof. Mt. Marty Coll., Yankton, S.D., 1966-68, asso. prof. philosophy, 1968—, chmn. dept. philosophy, 1966-70. Mem. ednl. com. Diocese of Sioux Falls, 1960-65; active local charitable orgns. Precinct chmn. Democratic party, Yankton, 1968-72. Mem. Am. Assn. U. Profs., Am. Benedictine Acad., Am. Cath. Philos. Assn. Home: Sacred Heart Convent Yankton SD 57078 Office: Mt Marty Coll Yankton SD 57078

KIMBALL, BARBARA STAPLES, coll. dean; b. Lynn, Mass., Mar. 26, 1920; d. Ralph Stillman and Mildred Helen (Longley) Staples; B.S. in Edn., State Tchrs. Coll., Salem, Mass., 1942; M.Ed., St. Lawrence U., Canton, N.Y., 1961; m. Dean Cushman Kimball, Oct. 2, 1945; 1 son, David Longley. Tchr., Howe-Manning Elementary Sch., Middleton, Mass., 1943-48; tchr. then prin. South Londonderry (Vt.) Central Sch., 1953-57; tchr. English, Potsdam (N.Y.) Central Sch., 1957-62; tchr. English, then guidance counselor Masconomet Regional High Sch., Boxford, Mass., 1962-69; dean student Vermont Coll., Montpelier, 1969-74. Served with WAVES, 1943-45. Mem. Am., Vt. personnel and guidance assns., Am. Coll. Personnel Assn., Am. Assn. U. Women, Norwich U. Parents Assn. (sec., dir. 1973-74), Am. Legion Aux. (past unit pres.), St. Lawrence U. Alumni Club, Bible-A-Month Club.

KIMBALL, CHRISTINA CHANGARIS (MRS. JOHN G. KIMBALL), ednl. adminstr.; b. Durham, N.C., Jan. 28, 1918; d. Steven and Helen (Crist) Changaris; B.A., U. N.C., 1940; certificate occupational therapy Richmond Profl. Inst., 1946; M.S., Barry Coll., 1962; m. John G. Kimball, Oct. 20, 1945; 1 son, Stephen John. Chief registered occupational therapist United Cerebral Palsy Miami, 1948-50; occupational therapist Dade County Pub. Schs., Miami, 1950-62, coordinator spl. edn., 1962-68, coordinator Center Emotionally Disturbed Children, 1968-69, asst. to cons. spl. edn., 1969-72, asst. elementary prin., 1972—. Recipient Occupational Therapy Traineeship, Office Surgeon Gen., 1945-46, Grad. Traineeship grant Office Vocational Rehab., 1961-62. Mem. Nat. (co-chmn. conf. 1965), Fla. (v.p. 1952-54, charter mem.), occupational therapy assns., Am. Assn. Univ. Women, Ceramic League Miami, Delta Kappa Gamma.

KIMBALL, FLORENCE PAGE, educator; b. Salt Lake City; vocal studies with George Hamlin, Clara Tippet, Genaro Papi, Marcella Sembrich, Povia Frisch, Sarah Robinson-Duff, Frank King Clark; piano studies with May Alport, Carlo Buonamici, Arthur Sheperd. Recital debut in Aeolian Hall, N.Y.C., numerous concerts and appearances in theatre; mem. voice faculty Juilliard Sch. Music, N.Y.C., 1927—. Address: Julliard School of Music 120 Claremount Av New York City NY 10027*

KIMBALL, MARGARET AGNES EVERETT (MRS. RAY ROBERSON KIMBALL), veterinarian; b. Newark, Nov. 18, 1924; d. Harmon Cary and Helen Inez (Cary) Everett; D.V.M., Mich. State U., 1949; m. Ray Roberson Kimball, June 27, 1953 (dec. 1968); children—Susan M., Ray M., Howard M., Helen M., Edith M. Veterinarian, Mich. Dept. Agr., 1949-51; individual practice as veterinarian, DeWitt, Mich., 1951-69; veterinarian animal pathology U. R.I., Kingston, 1969—. Mem. Am. Assn. Vet. Lab. Diagnosticians, Am. Assn. Equine Practitioners, Animal Rescue League, Am., Mich. vet. med. assns., Arabian Horse Assn. R.I. Baptist. Home: Lauri Dr Kenyon RI 02836 Office: U RI Kingston RI 20881

KIMBALL, VERA F., editor, writer; b. Seward, Alaska, Feb. 8, 1903; d. Irving L. and Della (Carpenter) Kimball; A.B., Columbia, 1929; m. William T. Castles, Jr., Dec. 2, 1942. On clerical staff Legislature of Ty. of Alaska, 1923; with Alaska R.R., Anchorage, 1923-24, N.A. Newspaper Alliance, Met. Mus. Art, Gen. Foods Corp., Todd-Robertson & Todd (all N.Y. City), part time 1924-29; asst. to sec. Am. Inst. Chemists, 1929-35; editor Chemist, N.Y.C., 1935-68, asso. editor, 1968-70; sec. S.C. Inst. Chemists, 1970—. Mem. N.Y. Acad. Scis., Am. Inst. Chemists (hon. life), A.A.A.S., Cook Inlet Hist. Soc., Alaska (charter), Chester County Hist. Soc. Club: Barnard College (N.Y. C.). Author: (with W. T. Castles) Firearms and Their Use, 1942; (with M. R. Bhagwat) Your Future in Chemistry, 1943. Contbr. to World Scope Ency. Ency. of Chemistry, year books, profl. and popular mags. Home: Magnolia Apts Chester SC 29706 Office: Route 2 Chester SC 29706*

KIMBLE, VESTA BAKER, co-owner oil co.; b. Metz, W.Va., Dec. 25, 1900; d. Jesse Ferris and Mollie Blanch (Hibbs) Baker; student pub. schs.; m. Miltom M. Kimble, Mar. 11, 1917; children—LaVerna (Mrs. James E. Cox Jr.), Ralph J. Co-owner Kimble Oil Co., Breckenridge, Tex., 1950—. Ofcl. poet Stephen County Hosp. Aux., 1965-73. Mem. Internat. Platform Assn., Breckenridge Poetry Soc. (v.p. 1971). Author: Gods Gift To Me (book of poems), 1959. Home: 701 W Hullum St Breckenridge TX 76024 Office: 124 W Walker St Breckenridge TX 76024

KIMMEL, ANNE ROSE, hosp. adminstr.; b. Cicero, Ill.; d. John R. and Marie (Kanera) Kimmel; grad. Presbyn. Hosp. Sch. Nursing, Chgo., 1945; B.S. in Nursing Edn., Loyola U., Chgo., 1953; M.A., U. Chgo., 1957. Nurse, Presbyn, Hosp., Chgo., 1945-47, head nurse, 1947-50, supr., 1954-56, instr. sch. of nursing, 1950-54; asst. dir. Presbyn St. Luke's Hosp., Chgo., 1956-69; asst. adminstr. for nursing Sherman Hosp., Elgin, Ill., 1959-69; asst. hosp. dir., dir. nursing Loyola U. Hosp., Maywood, Ill., 1969—; asso. dean Loyola U. Sch. Nursing, 1971—. Instr. Elgin Community Coll., 1967. Mem. Alumnae Assn. Presbyn. Hosp. Sch. Nursing (pres. 1956-60), Alumni Assn. Presbyn. St. Luke's Hosp. Sch. Nursing (pres. 1960-62), Chgo. and Northeastern League for Nursing (treas., dir. (1958-62), Ill. Nurses' Assn. (pres. dist. 2 1962-66, dir. 1966-68, assn. dir. 1966-69, chmn. nursing service adminstrs. sect. 1966-69), Am. Assn. U. Women (pres. Maywood-Proviso br. 1973—). Mem. Order Eastern Star. Club: Altrusa (pres. Elgin 1967-69). Home: 2230 S 19th St Broadview IL 60153 Office: Foster G McGaw Hosp Loyola U 2160 S 1st Av Maywood IL 60153

KIMZEY, ARDIS MESSICK (MRS. JAMES MORRIS KIMZEY), ednl. adminstr., poet; b. Washington, N.C., Feb. 10, 1937; d. Jesse Bradford and Cassie Elizabeth (Martin) Messick; B.A., Duke, 1959; postgrad. N.C. State U., 1971; m. James Morris Kimzey, Feb. 27, 1959; children—James, Bradford, Tabor. Book reviewer News and Observer, Raleigh, N.C., 1968—, poet-tchr. N.C. Poetry-in-the-schs. Program, 1972-74, state coordinator, 1973-74; dir. Raleigh Cultural Centers Writers-in-Residence Program, 1973—. Bd. dirs. Raleigh Cultural Center, Tenth Muse. Mem. N.C. Poetry Soc., N.C. Art Soc. Baptist (deacon 1973—). Asso. editor Southern Poetry Rev., 1970—; editor poetry anthologies: All I Have For Tenderness is Words, 1972; I Don't Need You, Rod McKuen, Goodbye, 1973. Contbr. poems to numerous lit. publs. Address: 2011 Stone St Raleigh NC 27608

KINCAID, DOROTHY LOUISE, editor; b. Mpls., Oct. 10, 1923; d. Watt Thomas and Dessie Edith (Huesman) Kincaid; B.A., U. Minn., 1949. Gen. reporter Dubuque (Ia.) Telegraph-Herald, 1949-57; soc. reporter Milw. Jour., 1957-62; soc. reporter, asst. women's editor Milw. Sentinel, 1962-66, women's editor, 1966—. Served with USMCR, 1943-45. Mem. Milw. Press Club, Women in Communications, Sigma Delta Chi. Home: 1822 N Cambridge Av Milwaukee WI 53202 Office: 918 N 4th St Milwaukee WI 53201

KIND, PHYLLIS (MRS. JOSHUA KIND), art gallery adminstr.; b. N.Y.C., Apr. 1, 1933; d. Harold P. and Dorothy H. (Weintraub) Cobin; A.B., U. Pa., 1954; M.A. with honors, U. Chgo., 1966; m. Joshua Kind, Mar. 18, 1956; children—Jonathan, Gabriel, Deborah, Rachel. Propr., mgr. Phyllis Kind Gallery, Chgo., 1967—. Home: 317 N East Av Oak Park IL 60302 Office: 226 E Ontario St Chicago IL 60611

KINDER, KATHERINE LOUISE, librarian; b. Rockford, O., Mar. 21, 1912; d. George R. and Nelle O. Kinder; B.A., Miami U., 1936; B.L.S., Columbia, 1936. Head circulation dept. Mt. Holyoke Coll. Library, 1938-43; chief librarian Johns-Manville Research & Devel. Center, Manville, N.J., 1946-72, Denver, 1972—. Served with USNR, 1943-46. Mem. Spl. Libraries Assn. (pres. 1956-57), A.L.A., Am. Soc. Information Sci., Soc. Am. Archivists. Home: 3 Par Circle Littleton CO 80123 Office: Johns-Manville Research and Devel Center Denver CO 80217

KINDIG, PAMELA MARIE, psychologist; b. Pitts., Feb. 2, 1947; d. Frederick Eugene and Marie Matilda (Doyle) Kindig; B.A., Miami U., Oxford, O., 1969; M.A., Ohio State U., 1970. Intern sch. psychologist Columbus (O.) Bd. Edn., 1970-71; sch. psychologist Madison County Bd. Edn., London, O., 1971—. Mem. Nat. Assn. Sch. Psychologists. Council Exceptional Children, Am. Civil Liberties Union, Smithsonian Assos., Ohio Sch. Psychol. Assn., Sch. Psychologists Central Ohio. Democrat. Home: 1949 Willoway Circle N Columbus OH 43220 Office: 63 N Main St London OH 43140

KINDLE, HELEN JOAN SWOVERLAND (MRS. PAUL EUGENE KINDLE), city ofcl.; b. Warsaw, Ind., Feb. 17, 1929; d. Howard Louis and Miriam Pauline (Yeager) Swoverland; student Manchester Coll., 1946-47; grad. Ft. Wayne Internat. Bus. Coll., 1949; m. Paul Eugene Kindle, Dec. 22, 1950; children—Jeffrey Eugene, Ken Eugene. With C. of C., Warsaw, Ind., 1949-56, office mgr., 1951-56; clk. to city clk.-treas., Warsaw, Ind., 1965-67, clk.-treas., 1968—. Mem. adv. bd. Salvation Army, 1973—. Treas., Warsaw-Wayne Twp. Library, 1968-71. Mem. Ind. League Municipal Clks. and Treas. (pres. 1971-72, chmn. edn.-tng. com. 1972—), Ind. Assn. Cities and Towns (mem. resolutions com., chmn. clk.-treas. forum 1971 conv.), D.A.R. (treas. 1973-76). Brethren. Mem. Order Eastern Star. Home: 1701 E Clark St Warsaw IN 46580 Office: City Bldg E Market St Warsaw IN 46580

KINDLE, MARY ETHEL SMYERS (MRS. CECIL HALDANE KINDLE), librarian; b. Aplin, Ark., Sept. 24, 1913; d. Dan Taylor and Ruby Robb (Neale) Smyers; B.S., U. Ark., 1936; M.S. in L.S., Columbia, 1941, postgrad., Tchrs. Coll., 1941, 54-57, 69—; postgrad. Fordham U., 1962-63; m. Cecil Haldane Kindle, Jan. 26, 1941; children—Mary Anne (Mrs. Roger Alan Stafford) (dec.), Elizabeth Lee (Mrs. Burke Baker III), Cecil Haldane, Millicent Robb. Asst. children's and adult depts. Little Rock Pub. Library, 1930-34; librarian elementary schs., Fort Smith, Ark., 1936-39, Liberty St. Elementary Sch., Nyack, N.Y., 1940-41; librarian young people's dept. Bloomingdale br. N.Y. Pub. Library, 1954, Nyack High Sch., 1954-57, Hilltop Jr. High Sch., Nyack, N.Y., 1957-68, Valley Cottage Elementary Sch., 1968—. Cons. Bethlehem (Conn.) Pub. Library, 1958. Mem. Vols. for Internat. Tech. Assistance, 1965-69. Recipient Martha Washington medal S.A.R., 1971. Mem. N.E.A. (co-chmn. membership Rockland County, N.Y., 1967-69), Am., N.Y. library assns., Rockland County Sch. Librarians Assn. (rec. sec. 1963), Am. Security Council, N.Y. State, Rockland County (rec. sec. 1968-72), Nyack tchrs. assns., Am. Assn. U. Women, Internat. Platform Assn., Little Rock Jr. Fedn. Women's Clubs, Kappa Delta Pi, Delta Kappa Gamma (chmn. publicity and publs. com. Alpha Eta chpt.). Editor: Authors of Rockland County, 1960. Home: 332 N Midland Av Upper Nyack NY 10960 Office: Elementary Sch Valley Cottage NY 10989

KINDRED, INGRID CAMILLE TARVER, newspaper reporter; b. Birmingham, Ala., Dec. 5, 1948; d. John W. and Ethel (Williams) Tarver; student Lane Coll., 1966-67; B.J., So. Ill. U., 1970; m. Fred Louis Kindred, Apr. 10, 1971; 1 son, Patrick O'Neill. Summer reporting intern Birmingham (Ala.) News, 1969; reporter Daily Egyptian, So. Ill. U., 1969-70; reporter Birmingham (Ala.) News, 1970—; jour. lectr. high sch. assemblies, jour. courses. Recipient William Randolph Hearst award, 1970; Ala. Asso. Press award, 1970. Mem. Women in Communications. Club: Club Feminique. Home: 2525 Princeton Av SW Birmingham AL 35211 Office: 2200 4th Av N Birmingham AL 35202

KINDRED, WENDY RUTH GOOD, artist, educator, author; b. Detroit, Dec. 19, 1937; d. Charles Roger and Ida Ruth (Berndt) Good; B.F.A., U. Chgo., 1959, M.F.A., 1963; m. Michael Jon Kindred, Dec. 27, 1960 (div. Nov. 1968); children—Audrey Lauren and Jessica Berit (twins). Tchr. Sch. Fine Arts, Addis Ababa, Ethiopia, 1965-69; free lance writer, N.Y.C., 1969-73; asst. prof. art U. Me., Fort Kent, 1973—; exhibited paintings one-woman shows at Addis Ababa, Ethiopia, 1966, 68, 69, Carmichael Hall, Ball State U., Muncie, Ind., 1970, Washington Gallery, Frankfort, Ind.; exhibited in group shows U. Chgo., 1963, Washington Gallery, 1973, U. Me. at Orono, 1974. Bd. govs. Children's Community Workshop Sch., N.Y.C., 1971. Recipient John B. Fehsenfeld award in painting Indpls. Mus., 1973; Weekly Reader Children's Book Club fellow Bread Loaf Writers' Conf., 1971. Author: Negatu in the Garden, 1971; Ida's Idea, 1972; Lucky Wilma, 1973. Office: Univ of Maine Fort Kent ME 04743

KING, ALICE BRONSON (MRS. LYMAN M. KING, JR.), community service; b. Los Angeles, Dec. 23, 1909; d. Edmond Butler and Olive (Banker) Bronson; ed. U. Cal. Los Angeles, Riverside U., U. Redlands; m. Lyman M. King, Jr., June 6, 1929 (dec. 1953); children—Edmond Bronson, Carolyn, Cynthia; m. 2d Frank Brewster Frye, Oct. 19, 1956 (div. December 1964). With the Assistance League, Redlands, California, 1932-62; mem. Exceptional Children's Found., Los Angeles; caseworker, counsellor Vol. bd. Family Service, Redlands, 1955-61; leader Girl Scouts Am., Redlands, 1932-49; mem. Childrens Home Founding Soc., Laguna Beach, Cal., since 1961—; active A.R.C.; bd. dirs. Family Service, 1962-63, Orange County, 1969-73; mem. S. Coast Child Guidance Clinic; mem. Friends U. Cal. Irvine library; mem. Friends Library Laguna Beach, Laguna Beach Art Mus., Assn. Gallery U. Cal. Irvine; docent council Newport Harbor Art Mus.; mem. Orange County Philharmonic. Republican. Episcopalian. Mem. Newport Harbor Panhellenic, Pi Beta Phi. Home: 2025 Avenida Chico Newport Beach CA 92660

KING, ANGIE LENA TURNER (MRS. ROBERT ELMORE KING), educator; b. Elkhorn, W.Va.; d. William and Laura (King) Turner; B.S., W.Va. State Coll., 1927; M.S., Cornell U., 1931; Ph.D., U. Pitts., 1955; m. Robert Elmore King, June 9, 1946 (dec. May 1958). Instr. math. and chemistry, supr. student tchrs. W.Va. State Coll. at Institute, 1927-46, prof. chemistry, 1948-71, emeritus, 1971, chmn. div. natural scis. and math., 1968-71. Treas. Institute Sewer Co. (W.Va.), 1966—. Chmn. W.Va. Commn. Status of Women, 1973—. Rec. sec., bd. dirs. Inst. Fed. Credit Union, 1958-72. Recipient awards including Distinguished Service award Beta Kappa Chi, 1966; named Outstanding Educator of Am., 1970. Mem. Am. Assn. U. Women (br. 1st v.p. 1966-68, div. 2d v.p. 1969-72, mem. assn. implementation com. 1971-73, pres. W.Va. div. 1973-75), Am. Chem. Soc., W.Va. Acad. Sci., Am. Assn. U. Profs., W.Va. State Coll. Alumni (editor bull. 1955-62), Beta Kappa Chi (regional v.p. 1956-61, editor bull. 1962-71). Presbyn. (elder, mem.-at-large world mission chmn.'s assn. 1969-70, chmn. ecumenical mission and relations com. 1968-70, sec. witness com. Guyandotte Prebytery 1970-73, bd. dirs. Davis-Stuart Sch. 1971—, mem. synod com. on instns. 1971-73, gen. assembly com. on inter-ch. relations 1972-74, gen. assembly council on evangelism and lay renewal 1972—, mem. com. gen. assembly operations 1973—, mem. synod pub. and higher edn. ministry group 1973—). Author: (with Paul J. Moore) A Laboratory Manual for College Chemistry, 1959. Home: 700 Washington Av Institute WV 25112

KING, ANNE TRUSCOTT, psychologist; b. Pasadena, Cal., May 23, 1938; d. Charles Robertson and Kathryn Maria (King) Dailey; B.A. with honors, U. Denver, 1968, M.A., 1972, Ph.D., 1975. Research psychologist Denver Research Inst., U. Denver, 1968-72, Human Resources Lab., Lowry AFB, Denver, 1972—. Mem. Am. Psychol. Assn., Phi Beta Kappa, Sigma Xi, Pi Gamma Mu, Psi Chi, Mu Phi Epsilon. Author publs. in field. Home: 1054 Revere St Aurora CO 80011 Office: Human Resources Lab Lowry AFB Denver CO 80230

KING, ANNIE GREENE (MRS. JAY BERNARD KING), librarian; b. Trenton, N.C., Jan. 19, 1922; d. Lott Thomas and Annie (Williams) Greene; A.B., N.C. Central U., 1942, B.L.S., 1947; M.L.S., U. Ill., 1952; m. Jay Bernard King, Mar. 19, 1950; children—Margaret Denise, Cheryl Louise, Jay Bernard, Wayne Maurice. Tchr. pub. schs. Jones County, N.C., 1942-46; librarian Jones High Sch., Washington, N.C., 1946-47; librarian Fla. Meml. Coll., St. Augustine, 1948-50; reference librarian Tuskegee Inst. Ala., 1951-66, librarian, 1966—. Mem. Am., Southeastern, Ala. library assns., Jack and Jill of Am., Delta Sigma Theta. Methodist. Home: 207 Johnson St Tuskegee Institute AL 36088

KING, BONNIE BUCHTEL (MRS. MARSHALL N. KING), musician, educator; b. Emporia, Kan., Nov. 8, 1929; d. Forrest Lawrence and Jessie Helene (MacDonald) Buchtel; Mus.B., Mich. State U., 1951; postgrad. Aspen Inst., summer 1951; Mus. M., DePaul U., 1966; m. Marshall M. King, Sept. 1, 1951; children—Marshall, Wanda, Randolph, Charles. Tchr. pub. schs., Lansing, Mich., 1953-55, Dist. 65 Schs., Evanston, Ill., 1960-67; profl. cellist Milw. Symphony, 1966-70, Houston Symphony, 1970—; solo cellist Evanston Symphony, 1960-66, Nat. Music Camp Chamber Music Festival, Interlochen, Mich., 1962-71, DePaul U. Symphony, 1966, Alverno Coll., 1969. Tchr. Mich. State U., summers 1953, 54, Wis. Coll.-Conservatory, Milw., 1966-70, Blue Lake Fine Arts Camp, Muskegon, Mich., 1971-72. Mem. Delta Omicron, Chi Omega. Home: Apt 101 3510 E Broadway Pearland TX 77581 Office: Houston Symphony Jones Hall 615 Louisiana St Houston TX 77002

KING, CAROLE (MRS. CHARLES LARKEY), composer; b. Feb. 9, 1941; d. Sidney Klein; m. Gerry Goffin (div.); children—Louise, Sherry; m. 2d, Charles Larkey, Sept., 1970; 1 dau., Molly. Composer since 1960; now composer, singer, rec. artist, 1968—. Recipient Grammy award for album Tapestry. Composer: (with G. Goffin) Will You Love Me Tomorrow?, Take Good Care of My Baby, Up on the Roof, Natural Woman, Heigh De Ho. Address: A & M Records 1416 North La Bera Hollywood CA 90028

KING, CORETTA SCOTT (MRS. MARTIN LUTHER KING JR.), lectr., writer, concert singer; b. Marion, Ala., Apr. 27, 1927; d. Obidiah and Bernice McMurray) Scott; A.B., Antioch Coll., 1951; Mus.B., New Eng. Conservatory Music, 1954; L.H.D., Boston U., 1969; m. Martin Luther King, Jr., June 18, 1953 (dec. Apr. 1968); children—Yolanda Denise, Martin Luther III, Dexter Scott, Bernice Albertine. Concert debut, Springfield, O., 1948, numerous concerts throughout U.S.; concerts India, 1959; performances Freedom Concert; voice instr. Morris Brown Coll., Atlanta, 1962; lectr., writer. Del. to White House Conf. on Children and Youth, 1960; Sponsor Sane Nuclear Policy, Com. on Responsibility, Inc., Moblzn. to End War in Viet Nam, 1966, 67, Margaret Sanger Meml. Found.; pres. Martin Luther King Jr. Meml. Center, active YWCA. Bd. dirs. So. Christian Leadership Conf., Martin Luther King Jr. Found. Gt. Britain; trustee Robert F. Kennedy Meml. Recipient Outstanding Citizenship award Montgomery (Ala.) Improvement Assn., 1959, Merit award St. Louis Argus, 1960, Woman of Year award Utility Club N.Y.C., 1962, Distinguished Achievement award Nat. Orgn. Colored Women's Clubs, 1962, Louise Waterman Wise award Am. Jewish Congress Women's Aux., 1963, Myrtle Wreath award Cleve. Hadassah, 1965, Wateler Peace prize, 1968, numerous others; named Woman of Year, Nat. Assn. Radio and TV Announcers, 1968. Mem. Nat. Council Negro Women (ann. Brotherhood award 1957), Women Strike for Peace (del. disarmament conf. Geneva, Switzerland 1962, citation for work in peace and freedom 1963), Women's Internat. League for Peace and Freedom, United Ch. Women (bd. mgrs.), Links, Inc (Human Dignity and Human Rights award Norfolk chpt. 1964), Alpha Kappa Alpha (hon). Baptist (mem. choir, guild adviser). Address: 234 Sunset Av NW Atlanta GA 30314

KING, EDITH WEISS (MRS. MARVIN M. KING), educator; b. Detroit, July 16, 1930; d. Otto A. and Fay (Eskay) Weiss; B.A., U. Mich., 1951; M.A., Wayne State U., 1961, Ed.D., 1966; m. Marvin M. King, Dec. 22, 1951; children—Melissa, Matthew. Tchr. elementary and kindergarten Mich. Pub. Schs., 1951-54; dir. Oak Park Coop. Nursery Sch., 1958-60; supr. student tchrs., curriculum cons. Mich. Pub. Schs., 1964-66; mem. faculty Sch. Edn., U. Denver, 1966—, asso. prof. ednl. sociology, 1969—, dir. Arts and humanities Fed. Inst., summer, 1968, dir. early childhood edn. workshop, 1971. Cons. early childhood edn. programs City of Denver, coop. nursery schs., pub. schs.; cons. social sci. projects Eng. Schs. Council, 1972-74. Mem. Colo. Commn. Status of Women, 1972-74. Assn. Supervision and Curriculum Devel., 1969-70; reader and cons. for various pub. cos.; dir. Worldmindedness Inst., Edn. Profs. Devel. Act, 1969-70; mem. adv. com. Coordination Program for Tng. of Early Childhood Workers, Denver Met. area, 1970-72. Mem. Am. Assn. U. Profs., Consortium on Peace, Research and Edn., Am. Sociol. Assn., Am. Ednl. Studies Assn., Nat. Council for the Social Studies (mem. com. early childhood edn. and the social studies 1971-72), Rocky Mountain Social Sci. Assn., Social Sci. Edn. Consortium, Sociologists for Women in Soc. Author: (with August Kerber) The Sociology of Early Childhood Education, 1968, Danish translation, 1972; The World: Context for Teaching in the Elementary School, 1971; Educating Young Children Sociological Interpretations, 1973. Contbr. articles to profl. jours. Home: 3734 S Niagara Way Denver CO 80237

KING, EILZABETH SOUDDER (MRS. WALLACE T. KING), statistician; b. Orange, N.J., July 1, 1930; d. George L. and Susan (Scudder) Hadden; A.B., U. Mich., 1952; postgrad N.Y. U., 1953-57; m. Wallace T. King, May 16, 1959. Staff statistician N.Y. Telephone Co., 1952-59; staff statistician Pacific Telephone Co., Los Angeles, 1959-69, statistician, 1969—. With sampling sect. Survey Research Center, U. Mich., part-time 1951-52; lectr. statistics U. Cal. at Los Angeles, Extension Sch., 1968. Mem. Am. Statis. Assn. (chpt. pres. 1968-69, mem. nat. com. on chpt., dist. and regional activities 1968-72, chmn. nat. com. corporate membership 1970-71, vice chmn. adv. com. to U.S. Bur. Census 1972—). Home: 8811 E Camino Real San Gabriel CA 91775 Office: 740 S Olive St Los Angeles CA 90014

KING, ELSIE VIOLA, counselor; b. Bailey, Okla., Nov. 9, 1911; d. Frances Hamilton and Florida Melda (Robinson) French; A.B. in Psychology, U. Cal. at Los Angeles, 1949, certificate in Social Welfare, 1950; M.A. in Edn., Cal. State Coll. at Los Angeles, 1956; Ph.D. in Sociology, U. So. Cal., 1961; m. Edmond Samuel King (div. Mar. 5, 1945); 1 son by previous marriage, Ronald Keith. Social case worker County of Los Angeles, 1952-56; marriage counselor and family therapist, Van Nuys, Cal., 1961—. Lectr. U. So. Cal., Los Angeles, 1960-61; asso. prof. Cal. State Coll., Los Angeles, 1961; lectr. U. Cal. at Irvine, summer 1973; mem. faculty Everywoman's Village, Van Nuys, 1965—, mem. exec. bd., 1972—. Bd. dirs. San Fernando Valley Counseling Center. Mem. Am., Western psychol. assns., Cal. Assn. Marriage and Family Counselers, Psi Chi, Alpha Kappa Delta. Author: Dear Smoker: With Love, 1973. Home: 16 Dudley Av Venice CA 90291 Office: 14411 Hamlin St Van Nuys CA 91401

KING, EMILY ELIZABETH, educator; b. St. Louis, Aug. 23, 1921; d. William Matthew and Maymie (Bolin) King; B.S. in Home Econs., U. Tenn., 1942; M.Ed., U. Fla., 1954; Ph.D. in Co-op. Extension Adminstrn. and Edn. (Kellog Found fellow), U. Wis., 1961. Mech. engring., tool die and spl. machine design, Detroit, 1942-46; asst. home demonstration agt., Plant City, Fla., 1946-53; state girls' 4-H Club agt. Fla. State U., 1953-63; state 4-H Club agt. U. Fla., 1964; extension home economist tng., prof. home econs. edn. Fla. State U., Tallahassee, 1964-69; home econs. resource devel. Inst. Food and Agrl. Scis., U. Fla., Gainesville, 1969-70, extension program specialist, 1971-74, extension program analyst, 1974—. Mem. So. Scholarship and Research Found.; founding mem. bd. dirs. Fla. 4-H Club Found., 1963, sec., 1963-65. Mem. Am., Fla. (chmn. colls., univs., research coms. 1965—, pres. 1970-72) home econs. assns., Am. Assn. U. Women (pres. Tallahassee 1967—), D.A.R., Fla. Extension Workers Assn., Pi Lambda Theta, Delta Kappa Gamma, Epsilon Sigma Pi, Alpha Omicron Pi (alumni chpt. adviser 1966-69. Baptist. Home: 2049 NW 9th Av Gainesville FL 32603

KING, ETHEL MARGUERITE, educator; b. Vancouver, B.C., Can., June 16, 1927; d. Walter and Mildred Laura (Mason) King; B.Ed., U. Alta., 1949; M.A., U. Ia., 1950, Ph.D., 1963. Tchr. pub. schs., Edmonton (Alta., Can.), 1950-53; asst. prof. Meml. U. Newfoundland, 1953-55; mem. faculty U. Calgary (Alta.), 1955—, lectr., 1955-57, asst. prof. curriculum and instrn., 1957-62, asso. prof., 1962-67, prof., 1967—. Fellow Canadian Coll. Tchrs.; mem. Internat. Reading Assn. (dir. 1968-71), Orgn. Mondiale Ecole Prescholaire, Assn. Childhood Edn. Internat., Am., Canadian ednl. research assns., Nat., Canadian councils tchrs. English, Early Childhood Edn. Council (dir. 1966-68), Canadian Assn. U. Tchrs., Nat. Conf. on Research in English. Club: Altrusa. Gen. editor: Canadian Tests of Basic Skills, Form 1, 1967, Form 2 and manuals, 1968. Contbr. articles to profl. publs. Home: 3620 6th St SW Calgary AB T2S 2M7 Canada

KING, GERALDINE BEATY (MRS. JACK B. KING), research cons.; b. Omaha, May 23, 1936; d. Richard Lawrence and Elizabeth Vernetta (Bell) Beaty; B.A., Grinnell Coll., 1958; M.A., U. Minn., 1962, Ph.D. (U.S. Office Edn. fellow), 1971; m. Jack B. King, Feb. 15, 1958. Reference librarian Cedar Rapids (Ia.) Pub. Library, 1962-63; librarian I. instr. U. Ia. Law Library, Iowa City, 1963-64; reference librarian, asso. dir. Coll. St. Thomas Library, St. Paul, 1964-67; lectr. U. Minn. Library Sch., Mpls., 1966-73, asst. prof., 1972-73; program dir. OMSIG, St. Paul, 1972—. Cons. Library div. Minn. State Dept. Edn. 1970, Ramsey County Pub. Library, 1972, 74, Hennepin County Pub. Library, 1972, Washington County Pub. Library, 1972, Hill Reference Library, 1972, St. Paul Pub. Schs., 1972, U. Minn. Library Reference Dept., 1973, Rapid City (S.D.) Pub. Library, 1973, Minn. Interlibrary Loan Network, 1973, U. Minn. Continuing Edn., 1974. Recipient Regents scholarships U. Neb., 1954, U. Omaha, 1954, 56 Honor scholarship Grinnell Coll., 1956-58, Loring Prize in English, Grinnell Coll., 1958. Mem. Assn. Spl. Librarians Gt. Britain, Speech Communication Assn., Am., Minn. (pres. 1973-74) library assns. Contbr. articles to profl. jours. Home: 387 Cretin Av S St Paul MN 55105 Office: Box 16314 Elway Sta St Paul MN 55116

KING, GLORIA JEAN, educator; b. Muskogee, Okla., Dec. 9, 1943; d. Albert Eugene and Buleah Faye (Sullins) King; B.A., Ouachita Bapt. U., 1965; M.A., U. Ark., 1971; postgrad. U. Ga., 1972, Eastern Ill. U., 1973. Tchr., Morrilton (Ark.) High Sch., 1965—. Mem. Ark. Arts Center, Little Rock. Mem. Internat. Thespian Soc. (Ark. dir. 1971-74), N.E.A., Ark., Conway County (pres. 1967-68), Morrilton edn. assns., Speech Communication Assn. Am., Speech Communication Assn. Ark., Am. Theatre Assn., So. Speech Communication Assn., Nat. Collegiate Players, Delta Kappa Gamma, Kappa Kappa Iota. Baptist. Home: 100 E Clifton St Morrilton AR 72110 Office: 701 E Harding St Morrilton AR 72110

KING, HELEN A. (MRS. ALVIN F. HATTORF), artist; b. Huntington, Ind., Feb. 12, 1900; d. Otto U. and Mayme (Beaver) King; B.A., Northwestern U., 1921; student art Inst. Chgo., Art Students League N.Y., Chgo. Normal Sch.; M.A., Columbia, 1950; studied art with Hans Hoffman, Morris Kantor, V. Uytlacil, Walter Plate; m. Alvin F. Hattorf, Apr. 22, 1935. Art tchr. high schs., Chgo., 1926-37, Richmond, Va., 1937-51; one-man shows Va. Mus. Fine Arts, 1960, 68, 70, oil paintings, 1968; exhibited Va. Artists biennial Va. Mus. Fine Arts, 1967, 69 (certificate distinction), Am. Painting Quadrennial, 1970; exhibited group shows Art Inst. Chgo., Pa. Acad. Fine Arts, Provincetown Art Assn., Corcoran Gallery Art, Washington Herron Gallery Art, Valentine Mus. (merit award 1968), Va. Mus. Fine Arts, Hoosier Salon, Chgo., Indpls., Va. Artists Biennial, 1957, 59, 61, 63, James River 5th Ann. Exhbn., 1971, 6th annual, 1972; painting in 2 yr. traveling exhibit of Va. Mus.; represented in permanent collection U. Va., Valentine Mus., Longwood Coll., Va. Mus. Fine Arts. Recipient Stewart prize Hoosier Salon, 1930; John McCutcheon prize, 1931; purchase award Valentine Museum, 1960; and many others. Mem. Richmond Artists Assn., Alpha Phi. Home and studio: 4313 Stuart Av Richmond VA 23221

KING, HELEN BLANCHE, educator; b. Logan, Utah, May 21, 1919; d. George Edward and Carolyn (Campbell) K.; A.S., Weber State Coll., 1939; Normal degree Utah State U., 1940; B.A., Cal. State Coll., 1957; M.A., Northridge State U., 1964; postgrad. U. So. Cal., 1966-72, U. Pacific, 1966-67, St. Mary's Coll., 1971-73. Tchr., Kenilworth (Utah) Sch., 1940-41; with Ogden Ordnance Depot, 1941-46, War Assets Adminstrn., 1946-48, VA, 1949, Transp. Corps, 1949-50, Hamilton AFB, 1950-53; tchr. Quartz Hill and Del Sur (Westside) Jr. High Sch., Lancaster, Cal., 1955-63, gen. studies instr. Jr. Coll., 1964-66; tchr. Westside Union Sch. Dist., Lancaster, 1954—; partner Pup 'n Kitten Dog Lodge, Palmdale, Cal., 1957—, handling, showing of Tinka Samoyeds (non profl.); show chmn. Antelope Valley Kennel Club, 1967, 1970—. Mem. Internat. Reading Assn. (past pres. A.V. local council), Alumni Assn. Northridge State U. (life), Am. Assn. U. Women, Antelope Valley Community Orch. Clubs: Antelope Valley Kennel (hon. life), Samoyed of Wash. State, So. Cal. Samoyed, No. Cal. Samoyeds Fanciers, Inc., Samoyed Club of Am., Orgn. Working Samoyeds, Cal. Sled Dog Assn. Office: 41820 N 50th St W Lancaster CA 93534 also 39846 N 18th St W Palmdale CA 93550

KING, JEAN DAVIS, lawyer; b. Des Moines, July 21, 1919; d. Charles L. and Stella (Moose) Davis; B.A., State U. Ia., 1941; J.D., U. Miami, 1951; LL.M., Boston U., 1953; m. Donald Y. King, Aug. 22, 1941 (dec.). Admitted to Fla. bar, 1951, U.S. Supreme Ct. bar; practiced in Miami, Fla., 1951-52, Coral Gables Fla., 1953-54; trial atty. gen. internal security div. Dept. Justice, Washington, 1954-66; atty.-adviser Office Legal Counsel, Regional Office, Dept. Housing and Urban Devel., San Francisco, Cal., 1966—. Served as lt. USNR, World War II; comdr. USNR. Mem. Inst. Contemporary Arts, Fla., Fed. bar assns., Naval Res. Assn., Corcoran Gallery Art, U. Ia. Alumni Assn., Fla. State Soc. Washington, Nat. Geog. Soc., San Francisco Maritime Mus., Friends of South Street, Nat. Trust for Historic Preservation, The de Young Mus. Soc., Marines Meml. Club, Queen's Beach, Kappa Beta Pi, Theta Sigma Phi. Clubs: Nat. Yacht; Pilot (Coral Gables); Commonwealth of California. Home: 2160 Leavenworth St Russian Hill San Francisco CA 94133 Office: Office Area Counsel US Dept Housing and Urban Devel 1 Embarcadero Center San Francisco CA 94111

KING, JOANNE, broadcasting exec.; b. San Antonio; d. Dunlap and Maelean (McGill) Johnson; m. Robert R. Herring; children—Beaufort E., Robert D. Fashion ambassadress to Europe World's Fair, 1968; women's dir. KPRC-TV, Houston. Home: 3195 Inwood Dr Houston TX 77019 Office: PO Box 2222 8181 Southwest Freeway Houston TX 77001

KING, JOYCE DEERING, lawyer; b. Onawa, Ia., Mar. 4, 1924; d. John Stewart and Hazel (Harnsburger) Deering; A.A., Cottey Coll., 1943; LL.B., U. Okla., 1961; m. Roy G. Brown, June 27, 1943 (div. 1949); 1 dau., Hallie Deering; m. 2d, Edmund E. Volts, Feb. 13, 1950 (dec. May 1956); m. 3d, Lester W. King, Aug. 5, 1967. Admitted to Ariz. bar, 1962; pvt. practice law, Phoenix, 1962-65; counsel to Ariz. Indsl. Commn., Phoenix, 1965-67; research atty. Continuing Edn. of Bar Extension U. Cal. at Berkeley, 1968—. Mem. Ariz. Bar Assn.,

P.E.O. Home: 892 Las Trampas Lafayette CA 94549 Office: 2150 Shattuck St Berkeley CA 94704

KING, LILLIAN SAARELA (MRS. CHARLES WILLIAM KING), realtor; b. St. Louis County, Minn.; d. Daniel and Hella (Kopponen) Saarela; B.S. with high distinction, U. Minn., 1951; M.A. with great distinction, Long Beach State Coll., 1958; postgrad. U. Cal. at Los Angeles, 1962-64; m. Charles William King, Sept. 4, 1937; children—Alice Lillian, Philip Richard. Tchr., Minnetonka Mills (Minn.) Pub. Schs., 1952-53, Prior Lake (Minn.) High Sch., 1954-55, Costa Mesa (Cal.) Pub. Schs., 1955-56; substitute tchr. Orange, and Los Angeles Counties Pub. Schs., 1958—; mem. Millie Coine Sanders Realty, Long Beach, Cal., 1960; real estate sales Raphael Realty, Long Beach, 1961, 63; owner King Realty, Garden Grove, Cal., 1963-71; asso. broker United Properties & Investments Co., Garden Grove, 1971—. Mem. Nat. Assn. Real Estate Bds., Cal. Real Estate Assn., West Orange County Bd. Realtors (chmn. by-laws com. 1965), Orange County Area Assn. for Gifted. Home: 12355 Pentagon St Garden Grove CA 92641 Office: 6062 Chapman St Garden Grove CA 92641

KING, LINDERSON, social worker; b. Bklyn., June 17, 1928; d. Carlton Leroy and Ena (Stoute) King; B.S., St. Paul's Coll., 1956; M.S.W., N.Y. U., 1963. With N.Y.C. Dept. Social Services, 1958—, supr. Bur. Child Welfare, Div. Services to Families, Child Protective Service Unit, 1969—. Bd. mgrs. N.Y.C. Mission Soc. Mem. Nat. Assn. Social Workers, Internat., Nat. confs. on social work, Acad. Certified Social Workers, N.A.A.C.P., St. Paul's Coll., N.Y. U. Gen., N.Y. U. Grad. Sch. Social Work alumni assns., Nat. Assn. Black Social Workers, N.Y.C. Dept. Social Services Assn. Suprs., Social Service Employees Union, Nat. Council Women, Nat. Assn. Exec. Female, UN Assn., Clinton Hill Tenant Assn., Wall Street Choral Soc., Nat. Council Women, Episcopal Ch. Women, Shelton Health Club, Delta Sigma Theta. Home: 185 Clinton Av Brooklyn NY 11205 Office: 80 Lafayette St New York City NY 11013

KING, LIS SONDER, pub. relations co. exec.; b. Roskilde, Denmark, Nov. 25, 1932; d. Carl Otto and Gerda Vohnsen (Soender) Petersen; grad. Roskilde Katedralskole, 1952; 1 dau., Dorte King. Came to U.S., 1956, naturalized, 1961. Feature writer Berlingske Tidende, Copenhagen, Denmark, 1956-58; reporter, editor Moreau Pub. Co., Bloomfield, N.J., 1957-59; author St. Thomas Directory, 1951; reporter, editor St. Thomas (V.I.) Daily News, Island Times, San Juan, P.R., 1962-63, Advance, Dover, N.J., 1963-64; v.p. pub. relations Keyes, Martin & Co., Springfield, N.J., 1964-69; pres. Lis King, Inc., pub. relations, Mahwah, N.J., 1969—. Mem. Pub. Relations Soc. Am., Internat. Platform Assn. Author: St. Thomas Directory, 1961. Contbr. articles to various pubs. Address: 30 Dundee Court Mahwah NJ 07430

KING, LUCILLE ALFREDA (MRS. ROY WHEATLEY KING), Democratic nat. committeewoman; b. New Haven, Feb. 17, 1937; d. William Lloyd and Eva Carol (Pierce) McAlpine; grad. high sch.; m. Roy Wheatley King, Feb. 25, 1961; children—Lisa Yvette, Ronald Warren, Rodmon Cedric. Clerk, typist Liberty Mut. Ins. Co., Bklyn., 1956-61; sales clk. Abraham & Strauss Dept. Store, Bklyn., 1959-60. Co-pres. P.T.A. Number 24 Sch., Rochester, 1972-73; vol. Rochester Sch. Dist., 1970—; mem. exec. council Parent Adv. Com., Rochester B. Edn., 1972-73; mem. exec. com., edn. com. S.E. Area Coalition, 1970-71. Sec. edn. com. Monroe County (N.Y.) Democratic Action Com., 1970-71; del. to Dem. Nat. Conv., Miami Beach, Fla., 1972; mem. Dem. Nat. Com., 1972—, mem. charter commn., 1973-74. Bd. dirs. Early Childhood Devel. Corp., 1973, A. Philip Randolph Inst., 1973—. Mem. Women's Aux. Monroe County Bar Assn., Syracuse U. Internat. Wives, Black Polit. Caucus (treas. No. region N.Y. 1974—). Club: Falcon Rod and Gun Auxiliary. Home: 369 Rockingham St Rochester NY 14620

KING, LUCY JANE, psychiatrist, educator; b. Vandalia, Ill., Dec. 23, 1932; d. Ira M. and Lucy (Harris) King; A.B., Washington U., St. Louis, 1954, M.D., 1958. Intern Butterworth Hosp., Grand Rapids, Mich., 1958-59; resident Washington U., St. Louis, 1959-62, research instr., 1962-63, instr., 1963-65, asst. prof. psychiatry, 1965-70, asso. prof., 1970-74; prof. Med. Coll. Va., 1974—; asst. psychiatrist Barnes and Renard Hosps., Washington U. Sch. Medicine, 1963—; mem. staff Renard Hosp., St. Louis. Cons. to mission physicians Med. Assistance Programs, Inc., 1964, 65, 67, 68, 69. Recipient Research Career Devel. award Nat. Inst. Mental Health, 1963-68, 1968-73. Diplomate in psychiatry Am. Bd. Psychiatry and Neurology. Fellow mem. Am. Psychiat. Assn.; mem. A.A.A.S., Psychiat. Research Soc., Internat. House of Japan, Phi Beta Kappa, Sigma Xi. Contbr. articles to profl. jours. Address: Dept Psychiatry Med Coll Va Va Commonwealth U Richmond VA 23219

KING, MAE ELIZABETH, librarian; b. Roanoke, Ind., Feb. 4, 1908; d. Frank Delbert and Winifred Rebecca (Welbaum) King; student Earlham Coll., 1927-29; A.B., Ind. U., 1931; B.L.S., U. Ill., 1943. Tchr., librarian Webster (Ind.) High Sch., 1932-36, Harrison Twp. High Sch., Union County, Ind., 1936-37, Driftwood Twp. High Sch., Jackson County, Ind., 1937-39, Test Jr. High Sch., Richmond, Ind., 1939-49; head librarian secondary schs., Richmond, 1949-57; periodicals librarian, asst. prof. Ball State U., Muncie, Ind., 1957-74, ret.; vis. librarian, instr. Lab. Sch., 1952. Mem. Ind. Sch. Librarians Council, 1949-50. Mem. Ind. Sch. Librarians Assn. (treas. 1951), Am., Ind. library assns., Am. Assn. U. Profs., Ind. Tchrs. Assn., N.E.A., Am. Assn. U. Women (treas. 1967-69, rec. sec. 1970-72, pres. 1972-74), Central Sect. Ind. Sch. Librarians (sec. treas. 1949), Friends of Muncie Pub. Library (pres. 1974—), Delta Kappa Gamma (pres. 1956-58). Republican. Methodist (ofcl. bd. 1965—, ch. librarian 1968—). Home: 2107 Linden St Muncie IN 47303

KING, MARGARET GIBSON, broadcasting co. exec.; b. Birmingham, Ala., Nov. 3, 1937; d. Cecil Franklin and Kathleen (Casey) Gibson; B.A., U. Ala., 1958. Traffic and continuity dir. radio sta. WBRC, Birmingham, 1959-60; partner, program mgr. radio sta. KTRY, Bastrop, La., 1961-68; traffic and continuity dir. radio sta. WYDE, Birmingham, 1968—. Lab. tchr. for broadcast students Jefferson State Jr. Coll., 1968-69. Home: 3401 8th Av S Birmingham AL 35222 Office: 2112 11th Av Birmingham AL 35205

KING, MARJORIE MELVILLE CAMERON (MRS. HARRY MOLYNEUX KING), author; b. Midland, Ont., Can., Sept. 3, 1909; d. Angus E. and Ada Isobel (Millar) Cameron; B.A., U. Toronto, 1932; postgrad. Ont. Coll. Edn., 1933; m. Harry Molyneux King, July 4, 1935; children—Patricia (Mrs. Clare Mullett), Garrison, Susan (Mrs. George Rabick). Came to U.S., 1935, naturalized, 1952. Recipient Headliner award Women in Communications, Detroit chpt. 1971; named Detroit Woman Author of Year Detroit Women Writers, 1970. Mem. Women in Communications, Inc. (nat. corr. 1971—), Women's Nat. Book Assn., Nat. League Am. Penwomen. Author: Ladies, Please Come to Order, 1968; Ladies, Let's Travel, 1970. Home: Box 413 Route 6 Winchester VA 22601

KING, MARNA JEANENE, educator; b. Middletown, O., Aug. 9, 1939; d. Lester James and Helen Katherine (Gebhart) King; B.S., Northwestern U., 1961; M.F.A., Yale, 1964. Staff costumer Yale Sch. Drama, New Haven, 1964-66; faculty costume designer Goodman Theatre, Art Inst. Chgo., 1966-67; resident costume designer, asso. prof. dept. theater and drama U. Wis., Madison, 1969—. Costume designer summer stock Dartmouth Repertory Co., Dartmouth Coll., 1965; designer, lectr. Northwestern U., 1966; costume designer The Eccentricities of a Nightingale, 1967, The Three Sisters, 1969. Research grantee U. Wis., summer 1973. Home: 5160 Brindisi Ct Middleton WI 53562 Office: 821 University Av Madison WI 53706

KING, SISTER MARY WILMA, ednl. adminstr.; b. Vallejo, Cal., Dec. 28, 1908; d. William Albert and Rose (Brady) King; B.A., Coll. of Holy Names, 1943; M.A., Catholic U. Am., 1959; postgrad. Seattle U., 1960-61, San Jose State U., 1967. Mem. Order Notre Dame de Namur, Roman Catholic Ch., 1909—. Tchr., prin. Mt. Carmel Sch., Redwood City, Cal., 1929-39; tchr., vice prin., dean students, supr., counselor Notre Dame high schs., 1939-59; tchr., chmn. dept. history, counselor, sr. coordinator Blanchet High Sch., Seattle, 1959-63; instr. history and Spanish, Coll. of Notre Dame, Belmont, Cal., 1966—, registrar, 1969—. Mem. Cal., San Mateo County, Nat. hist. assns., Smithsonian Assos., Am. Assn. U. Profs., Am., Pacific assns. coll. registrars and admissions officers, Alpha Mu Gamma. Author: Translator Ecumenical Projects in Latin America, Latin Am. Bur., Washington, 1971; book reviews on Cal. history, Catholic Hist. Review, 1968. Home: Ralston Rd Belmont CA 94002 Office: Ralston Rd Belmont CA 94002

KING, MARYDE FAHEY ORR (MRS. LAWRENCE KING), librarian; b. Walla Walla, Wash., Jan. 30, 1925; d. Reginald Michael and Mary (Duncan) Fahey; B.A., Whitman Coll., 1946; M.L., U. Wash., 1953; postgrad. U. Neb., 1953-55; m. John T. Orr, July 15, 1945 (div. 1955); 1 son, John Michael; m. 2d, Lawrence H. King, May 29, 1970. Instr. reference and cataloging, librarian sci. dept. U. Neb., 1953-55; specialist mgmt. information Gen. Electric Co., Richland, Wash., 1955-63, mgr. Whitney Library Research, Lab., Schenectady, 1963—. Lectr., Center for Grad. Study, Grad. Sch. Librarianship, U. Wash., Richland, 1961-63, State U. N.Y. at Albany, 1964—. Republican precinct committeewoman. Mem. Am. Assn. U. Women, A.L.A., A.A.A.S., Am. Chem. Soc., Spl. Libraries Assn. (chpt. pres. 1973-74), Columbia Sci. Fair Assn., Med. Library Assn., Am. Soc. Information Sci. Conglist. Clubs: Richland Internat. Folk Dance, Richard Women's Republican. Home: 1308 Myron St Schenectady NY 12309 Office: Gen Electric Co Research and Devel Center Whitney Library PO Box 8 The Knolls Schenectady NY 12301

KING, MONIQUE VIOLETTE WOLF (MRS. RICHARD CLYDE KING), psychiatrist, psychoanalyst; b. Paris, France, Apr. 20, 1932; d. Charles K. and Bertha (Simon) Wolf; B.A., Case-Western Res. U., 1954, Ph.D., (NSF fellow), 1959, M.D., 1965; m. Richard Clyde King, Dec. 19, 1950. Came to U.S., 1950, naturalized, 1954. Research chemist Union Carbide Research Lab., Cleve., 1958-61; resident psychiatry Univ. Hosps., Cleve., 1966-68; resident child psychiatry, 1968-70; sr. clin. instr. child psychiatry, 1970—; practice medicine specializing in adult psychoanalysis and child psychiatry, Cleve., 1970—; tchr. adult psychiatry Case Western Res. U. Sch. Social Applied Scis., 1971—, sr. clin. instr. psychiatry, 1972—. Mem. Am. Psychiatric Assn., Phi Beta Kappa, Sigma Xi. Home: 1481 Blackmore St Cleveland Heights OH 44118 Office: 11328 Euclid St Cleveland OH 44106

KING, PATRICIA ELAINE, lawyer; b. Chester, S.C., Jan. 16, 1943; d. William Robert and Ellen Louise (Nelson) King; B.S., Johnson C. Smith U., 1965; postgrad. Howard U., summer 1965. Funeral dir. King's Funeral Home, Chester, 1961—; tchr. Chester City sch. system, 1965-66; legal research firm Pearson, Malone, Johnson, De Jarmon, Durham, N.C., 1967-68, Jenkins, Perry & Pride, Columbia, S.C., 1968-69; admitted to N.C. bar, 1971; mem. firm Bell and King, Charlotte, 1971—. Active Girl Scouts. Candidate for Chester City Council, 1970. Recipient awards legal work Lawyers Coop. Pub. Co., 1968. Mem. Am., Nat., N.C., 26th Jud. bar assns., N.C. Bar Found., Black Lawyers Assn., S.C. Funeral Dirs. Assn., Delta Sigma Theta. Elk. First black female lawyer in N.C. Home: 129 Cemetery St Chester SC 29706 Office: 112 S Irwin Av Charlotte NC 28208

KING, ROSA IRENE (MRS. ARTHUR W. KING), librarian; b. Manson, Ia., Nov. 4, 1916; d. Howard Hillard and Hannah Marie (Dirks) Long; student library courses Utah State Agr. Coll., 1956-57, U. Nev., 1965, 67; m. Kenneth E. Peterson, July 14, 1934; children—Kenneth E., Elaine (Mrs. Robert LaMar Tyler); m. 2d, Arthur W. King, Feb. 16, 1945 (dec. Jan. 1962). Librarian, Babbitt (Nev.) Community Library, 1946-55, Mineral County Pub. Library, Hawthorne, 1955—. Counselor for merit badges Boy Scouts Am., 1969—. Mem. Am., Nev. (chmn. fed. relations com. 1963) library assns., Pub. Library Assn. Nev. (chmn. 1965), Mineral County Hist. Soc. (historian 1971, 72, 73). Club: Walker Lake Art (pres. Hawthorne, 1965), Soroptimist (pres. Hawthorne 1971-72). Home: 201 English St Hawthorne NV 89415 Office: Mineral County Pub. Library Hawthorne NV 89415

KING, RUBY THOMPSON (MRS. S. LARRY KING), educator, club woman, ch. worker; b. nr. Wrightsville, Ga.; d. Charles D. and Maude (Douglas) Thompson; student S. Ga. Coll.; B.A., Scarritt Coll., M.A.; postgrad. George Peabody Coll. Tchrs. U. Ga., Fla. State U., U. Edinburgh, Scotland; m. Seabron Larry King. Tchr. English, Brunswick, Ga.; tchr. Lowndes County Ga.; tchr. English, Coffee County, Ga. high schs., 1966—. Mem. Am. Security Council. Conf. sec. missionary personnel Woman's Soc. Christian Service; active numerous local fund drives; coordinator Wesleyan Service Guild; 8th Dist. Sci. Fair Committeewoman; sponsor Young Teens; adviser High Sch. Chemistry Club; charter mem. Tri-Hi-Y Internat., chmn. convocation; field rep. World Field Research, Inc.; editor Ga. Bull. Dir. Thompson-King Found.; trustee Florence Crittendon Home, Savannah, Ga.; mem. Pub. Library Bd.; White House appointment Nat. Traffic Safety Council, Washington; staff Am. Research Bur., Inc. state news reporter Atlanta Jour. Named Star Tchr., Ga. C. of C. Douglas Citizen of Year for distinguished community service. Albert Schweitzer fellow. Mem. Home Demonstration Council, So. Ga., Conf. Hist. Soc., Ga. Edn. Assn. (county chmn. pub. relations), N.E.A., Am. Soc. Psychical Research, Ga. Assn. Edn., Nat. Assn. English Tchrs., U.D.C., Internat. Platform Assn., Internat., Am. assns. U. women, D.A.R., Philharmonic Club, Nat. Heritage Commn. Preservation Hist. Shrines, Nat. Council Tchrs. English, Internat. Assn. U. Women, Scarritt Alumni Club. Methodist. Mem. Order Eastern Star. Clubs: Garden Study; Fine Arts, Woman's Garden Guild. Author poetry pub. in Am. Anthology of Verse, Nat. Anthology Poetry, Quaderni di Poesia, Anthology of Internat. Poetry. Address: Box 428 Douglas GA 31533

KING, SALLY TAYLOR (MRS. CHARLES ALBERT KING), coll. dean; b. Alhambra, Cal., Jan. 19, 1926; d. Ezra Felton and Margaret Cunningham (Rae) Taylor; B.A., Pomona Coll., 1948; M.A., Stanford, 1950; m. Charles Albert King, June 17, 1961 (div. Oct. 1964). Asst. prof. Pomona (Cal.) Coll., 1950-61; tchr., Tulare (Cal.) High Schs., 1961-63; dean girls Desert Sun (Cal.) Sch., 1963-64; dean students Bradford (Mass.) Jr. Coll., 1964-68; dean students Christian Nurses Tng. Sch., Chestnut Hill, Mass., 1969-71, Endicott Jr. Coll., Beverly, Mass., 1971—. Mem. Nat. (mem. nominating com. 1973-74), Mass. (membership chmn. 1972-74) assns. women deans, adminstrs., counselors. Christian Scientist. Home: 384 Summer St Manchester MA 01944 Office: 376 Hale St Beverly MA 01915

KING, SHARON LOUISE, lawyer; b. Ft. Wayne, Ind., Jan. 12, 1932; d. Frank W. and Edith (Brewer) King; A.B., Mt. Holyoke Coll., 1954; J.D., Valparaiso U., 1957; LL.M., Georgetown U., 1961. Admitted to Ind. bar, 1957, D.C. bar, 1958, Ill. bar, 1962; practiced in Washington, 1957-62, Chgo., 1962—; trial atty. U.S. Dept. Justice, 1957-62; asso. firm Isham, Lincoln & Beale, 1962-66, partner, 1966—. Lectr. Mid-Am. Tax Conf., 1973, seminars Ill. Inst. Continuing Legal Edn., Valparaiso U. Estate Planning Seminars for Women. Mem. YWCA McCormick Com., 1966-68, Real Estate Hearing Bd., Village of Winnetka; mem. university council Valparaiso U., also bd. visitors Law Sch. Mem. Am., Ill., Chgo. (bd. mgrs. 1973—) bar assns., Women's Bar Assn. Ill. (vice chmn. legislative com. 1968-69, chmn. internat. relations 1969-70, bd. dirs. Found. 1968—, chmn. subcom. personal holding cos., mem. com. corporate stockholder relationships). Club: Chicago Mt. Holyoke (treas., dir. 1965-69). Home: 724 Oak St Winnetka IL 60093 Office: One First Nat Plaza Chicago IL 60670

KING, VERNE LORENE (MRS. GERALD G. KING), apparel co. exec.; b. Danbury, Conn., Oct. 20, 1921; d. Vernon J. and Mildred M. (Roswell) Elsenboss; B.S. in Journalism, Boston U., 1943; m. Gerald G. King, Aug. 5, 1944 (dec. Feb. 1950); children—Gerald G., Susan V. Editor, Chance Vought Aircraft Co., Stratford, Conn., 1944-45, Columbia Record Co., Bridgeport, Conn., 1951-61; publs. editor Olin Co., New Haven, 1961-62; editor Warnaco Inc., Bridgeport, Conn., 1962—. Lectr. employee communication, 1965—. Chmn. employee publs. United Way, Bridgeport, 1958-73, mem. pub. relations com., 1958-73, chmn., 1974; mem. pub. information com. Bridgeport Mayor's Energy Adv. Commn., 1974. Bd. dirs. Bridgeport Child Care, Inner City Children's Center, Bridgeport. Mem. Barnum Festival Soc. (hist. 1972-73, gov. 1971-73), Conn. Assn. Profl. Communicators (pres. 1966-67), Internat. Assn. Bus. Communicators (dir. chpt. affairs 1967-69). Home: 1 Barrows St Stratford CT 06497 Office: 350 Lafayette St Bridgeport CT 06602

KINGKADE, MARY JANE WARD, chemist, educator, univ. dean; b. Salt Lake City, May 28, 1922; d. Walter James and Isabelle (Jarvis) Ward; B.S., Ia. State U., 1943, Ph.D. (fellow 1943-46); m. William Bruce Kingkade, Mar. 29, 1948; 1 son, William Ward. Chemist Lilly Research Labs., Eli Lilly & Co., Indpls., 1946-50; research asso. U. Minn., 1950-52, Harvard, 1952-53; instr. Hunter Coll., 1954-59, asst, prof. chemistry, 1960-63, asso. prof. chemistry, 1963-68, prof., 1968—, dep. chmn. dept. in Bronx, 1961—, chmn. dept. chemistry, 1965—, coordinator grad. studies, 1968—; prof., also asso. dean of faculties Herbert H. Lehman Coll., City U. N.Y., 1968-72; dean for univ. and spl. programs Grad. Sch. and Univ. Center, City U. N.Y., 1972—, prof. chemistry, 1972—. Mem. N.Y. Acad. Scis., Am. Chem. Soc., A.A.A.S., Phi Beta Kappa (hon.), Pi Mu Epsilon, Omicron Nu, Iota Sigma Pi, Sigma Delta Epsilon. Research on bio-organic chemistry and microbiology. Home: 48 Iselin Terrace Larchmont NY 10538 Office: Graduate School and University Center City U NY 33 W 42d St New York City NY 10001

KINGMAN, (MARY) LEE, author, editor, reviewer; b. Reading, Mass., Oct. 6, 1919; d. Leland W. and Genevieve (Bosson) Kingman; A.A., Colby Jr. Coll., 1938; B.A., Smith Coll., 1940; m. Robert H. Natti, Sept. 22, 1945; children—Susanna, Peter. Juvenile book editor Houghton Mifflin Co., Boston, 1944-46; editor Horn Book, Inc., Boston, 1957-66, now dir.; author numerous books for children; reviewer children's books newspaper media. Bd. dirs. Sawyer Free Library, Gloucester, Mass. Editor: Illustrators of Children's Books: 1957-66; Newberry and Caldecott Medal Books: 1956-65. Home: Blood Ledge Lanesville Gloucester MA 01930

KINGSLEY, ROSEMARY CECILE, irrigation systems co. exec.; b. Ft. Thomas, Ky., Feb. 12, 1923; d. John Thomas and Cora Mae (Smuck) Kingsley; grad. high sch.; m. Kermit Wayland Hall, July 27, 1949 (div. 1970); children—Cecile Ann, Kermit Kingsley, Cynthia, Dan, Kathleen, Kris, Gregory, Jeffrey, Marcia, Leslee, Stuart. Sec., Union Central Life Ins. Co., Cin., 1941-45; sec. Van Duesen Engring. Co., Escondido, Cal., 1948-51; sec.-treas. Portable Aluminum Irrigation Co., Inc., Vista, Cal., 1960-73; adminstrv. exec. Roberts Irrigation Products, Pauma Valley, Cal., 1973—. Sec.-treas. Metabolic Research Found. Republican. Roman Catholic. Home: 725 N Fig Apt 29 Escondido CA 92025 Office: Roberts Irrigation Products Pauma Valley CA 92061

KINGSMORE, LOTTIE LOUISE BURTON (MRS. HUGH H. KINGSMORE), educator; b. Ellen, Ky., Feb. 16, 1916; d. Samuel Worthington and Hattie Jane (Berry) Burton; A.B., U. Ky., 1940, M.L.S., 1958; m. Hugh H. Kingsmore, May 13, 1944; children—Samuel Stuart, Karen (Mrs. William Morrison Kennedy, Jr.), Janet (Mrs. David Clayton Kearns). Elementary sch. tchr. Lawrence County, Ky., 1934-40; tchr. English Louisa (Ky.) High Sch., 1940-41, librarian, 1946-69; tchr. social studies Ky. pub. schs., 1941-42, W.Va. high schs., 1942-43; with Bethlehem Steel Ship Yard, Balt., 1943; inspector Curtiss Wright Airplanes, Columbus, O., 1944. Treas. Lawrence County Pub. Library, 1960-62; election officer Lawrence County, Ky., 1937—. Republican. Methodist. Mem. Order Eastern Star. Home: Box 78 Rt 1 Louisa KY 41230

KINLEY, ELINOR REGINA, mag. editor; b. Morrisville, Pa., Apr. 9, 1918; d. George Rogers and Hannah Theresa (McElwee) Mild; A.B. in English, Chestnut Hill Coll., 1940; m. Martin Redmond Kinley, Sept. 24, 1949 (dec. Dec. 1953); children—Martin Andrew, Theresa Marie. Communications specialist Reliance Ins. Co., Phila., 1965-69; pub. relations and advt. mgr. First Investment Annuity Co., Phila., 1969-73; mng. editor Spectator, Chilton Publ., Radnor, Pa., 1973—. Coeditor Alumnae newspaper Chestnut Hill Coll., 1972—. Served with Women's Res., USMC, 1945. Mem. Pub. Relations Soc. Am., Women Marines Assn.

KINNANE, JANET ELEANOR (MRS. WILLIAM H. DEMPSTER), lawyer; b. Bay City, Mich., June 1, 1907; d. John E. and Maude M. (Crosbie) Kinnane; student Bay City Jr. Coll., 1925-26; A.B., U. Mich., 1928; m. William H. Dempster, Jan. 20, 1971. Admitted to Mich. bar, 1938; pvt. practice law in Bay City, 1938—; friend of ct., Bay County, 1942-43; justice of peace, Bay City, 1942-48; asst. U.S. atty. eastern dist. Mich., Bay City, 1945-53. Mem. Mich., Bay County Bar assns., Nat., Mich. Women Lawyers assns., Bay City Bus. and Profl. Women, Am. Assn. U. Women. Home: 837 S Linwood Beach Rd Linwood MI 48634 Office: 420 Shearer Bldg Bay City MI 48706

KINNE, KATHARINE (MRS. CHARLES E. SIGETY), home economist; b. Herkimer, N.Y., Nov. 23, 1921; d. Cornelius Harry and Katharine (Kinne) Snell; B.S., Cornell U., 1944; m. Charles Edward Sigety, July 17, 1948; children—Charles Birge, Katharine Kinne, Robert Griswold, Cornelius, Elizabeth. Tng. squad J.L. Hudson Co., Detroit, 1944; overseas recreation work A.R.C., 1945-46, nat. fund campaign speaker, 1947; publicity work Union Carbide and Carbon Corp., 1947-48; dist. sales mgr. Berger Bros., New Haven, 1948-50; European tour condr. Olson Travel Orgn., 1950; TV home economist Sally Smart's Kitchen, WOR-TV, 1951-53; on camera food editor,

Home Show, NBC-TV, 1953-56; owner, dir., gen. mgr. Video Vittles, Inc. N.Y.C., 1953—. Co-chmn. nat. parents com. Bates Coll., Lewiston, Me. Bd. dirs. Parents League N.Y., Trinity Sch. Mothers Orgn., Grace Ch. Sch. Parents Orgn., 1966-67. Recipient scholarships N.Y. State Fedn. Women's Clubs, D.A.R. Home Econ., Women in Bus., Mortar Bd., Delta Delta Delta. Mem. Am. Home Econs. Assn., Am. Women in Radio and TV, Am. Fedn. TV and Radio Artists, Screen Actors Guild. Presbyn. Address: 175 E 96th St New York City NY 10028 also Pipersville PA 18947

KINNEALEY, MOYA, occupational therapist; b. Boston, Dec. 18, 1943; d. Arthur J. and Eleanore (Wedberg) Kinnealey; B.S., Tufts U., 1965; M.S., Boston U., 1968; Staff therapist Lemual Shattuck Hosp., Jamaica Plains, Mass., 1965-67; trainer in occupational therapy Eunice Kennedy Shriver Center, W. E. Fernald Sch., Waltham, Mass., 1968-69, dir. occupational therapy tng., 1969-73; dir. Kindersch. United Cerebral Palsy Assn., Natick, Mass., 1973—. Clin. faculty Boston U., 1969—. Vets. Rehab. Adminstrn. grantee, 1964-65; Health Manpower Tng. grantee, 1968-69; grantee various maternal and child health training workshops, Dept. Health, Edn. and Welfare. Mem. Mass. Occupational Therapy Assn. (program chmn. 1971-72, legislative chmn. 1972-74), Am. Occupational Therapy Assn. (mem. council on practice 1970-73, chmn. spl. interest group in mental retardation 1970-73, legislative resource person in mental retardation 1972-74), Am. Pub. Health Assn., Am. Assn. Mental Deficiency, World Fed. Occupational Therapy (U.S.A. del. 1972, 76). Contbr. articles to profl. jours. Home: 396 Canton Av Milton MA 02186 Office: United Cerebral Palsy Assn Kinderschool Rt 16 Natick MA 01760

KINNEY, JILL CLAIRE, psychologist; b. Seattle, Mar. 27, 1944; d. James Kreuger and Lillian Anna (Nesheim) McCleave; B.S. with honors, U. Wash., 1965; M.S., Stanford, 1968, Ph.D., 1969; m. Barry Hall Kinney, July 18, 1969. Psychologist, evaluator spl. project Tacoma schs., 1970-71; staff psychologist, then children's services dir. Tacoma Comprehensive Mental Health Center, 1971—; asst. mgr. Tacoma Youth Services Bur., 1974—; cons. in field, 1969—. Mem. Pierce County Health Council, 1972—; exec. com. Sharing Our Caring, 1973-74; mem. bd. Panel Family Living, 1971—. Recipient Most Distinguished Sr. award U. Wash., 1965; Nat. Inst. Pub. Health fellow, 1965-67. Mem. Am., Wash. psychol. assns., Phi Beta Kappa, Sigma Xi. Author articles. Home: 1901 Markham St NE Tacoma WA 98422 Office: 1202 S K St Tacoma WA 98405

KINNEY, JO ANN SMITH, psychologist; b. Akron, O., Dec. 6, 1927; d. Harrison and Jane (Murphy) Smith; A.B. cum laude, Smith Coll., 1949; M.A., Cornell U., 1954; Ph.D., U. Conn., 1959; research psychologist Submarine Med. Research Lab., Naval Submarine Base, Groton, Conn., 1949-63, head vision br. Naval Submarine Med. Center, 1963—. Teaching and research asst. Cornell U., 1951-52; lectr. U. Conn., 1967—. Bd. dirs. U.S. nat. com. Commn. Internationale de l'Eclairage, 1969—. Recipient Fed. Woman's award, 1969. Fellow Optical Soc. Am., Am. Psychol. Assn.; mem. Eastern, Northeastern psychol. assns., Psychonomic Soc., A.A.A.S. Contbr. articles to profl. jours. Patentee in field. Home: RFD 1 Box 26-1-A North Stonington CT 06359 Office: Box 600 US Navy Submarine Base Groton CT 06340

KINNEY, JOANNE ELKIN (MRS. RICHARD R. KINNEY, JR.), graphic designer; b. Detroit, Apr. 8, 1932; d. Benjamin Kibbe and Rebecca (Hayman) Elkin; B.F.A., Wayne State U., 1954; m. Richard R. Kinney, Jr., Aug. 19, 1970; children by previous marriage—Joel Matthew Colman, Victor Jon Colman. Freelance graphic designer, 1960—; book designer Wayne State U. Press, 1966—. Mem. Mich. Watercolor Soc. Home and office: 21630 Cloverlawn Oak Park MI 48237

KINOSHITA, FLORENCE KEIKO, toxicologist; b. Salem, Ore., Aug. 6, 1941; d. Masato and Haruko (Satogata) Kinoshita; B.S., U. Chgo., 1963, M.S. (USPHS trainee), 1966, Ph.D., 1969. Instr. dept. pharmacology U. Chgo., 1969-71, research asso., asst. prof., 1971-73; toxicologist Indsl. Bio-Test Labs., Inc., Northbrook, Ill., 1973—. Cons. FDA Bur. Vet. Medicine, 1970, Bur. Drugs, 1972-73; mem. pesticide adv. com. U.S. Environmental Protection Agy., 1971-72. Mem. Am. Indsl. Hygiene Assn., A.A.A.S., Am. Chem. Soc., Soc. for Exptl. Biology and Medicine, Ill. State Acad. Sci., Soc. of Toxicology (chmn. ednl. com. 1973—), Sigma Xi. Contbr. articles to profl. jours. Home: 1510 Plymouth Pl Glenview IL 60025 Office: 1810 Frontage Rd Northbrook IL 60062

KINSER, HOLLY EDEN, retail exec.; b. Gorman, Tex., Feb. 9, 1941; d. Roy Andrew and Lovena (Porter) Kinser; student Tarleton State Coll., 1959-61; B.B.A., North Tex. State U., 1963. Asst. buyer Sanger Harris, Dallas, 1963-66; fashion distbr. J. C. Penney Co., Dallas, 1966-70, asst. buyer, 1970-72, buyer, 1972—. Mem. Fashion Group. Republican. Home: 9230 Flickering Shadow Dallas TX 75231 Office: 5217 Ross Av Dallas TX 75221

KINSEY, MATTIE (MRS. GLAUCUS E. KINSEY), club woman; b. Milan, Tenn.; d. Ezekiel Jessie W. and Martha M. (McGee) Armstrong; student pub. schs., Bonham, Tex.; m. Glaucus Edward Kinsey, May 10, 1917; children—Martha Dell (Mrs. Samuel L. Carpenter III), Margaret Louise (Mrs. Raymond C. Tay Brown). Asso. mem. Los Angeles Music Center for Performing Arts. Mem. Braille Inst. Aux. (life, exec. bd.), U. D.C., Opera Guild. Cal., Assistance League (life), Cal. Mus. Scis. and Industry (charter), Town and Gown (life). Clubs: Ebell (life), Los Angeles Country, Jonathan of Los Angeles (Los Angeles), Balboa Bay (Newport Beach). Home: 450 N Rossmore Av Los Angeles CA 90004

KINTNER, JANET IDE (MRS. CHARLES F. KINTNER), lawyer; b. Dayton, O., Feb. 25, 1944; d. Herbert Albert and Marian Gertrude (Hetzler) Ide; B.A., U. Ariz., 1966, J.D., 1968; m. Charles F. Kintner, Sept. 14, 1968. Admitted to Cal. bar, 1969; civil atty. Legal Aid Soc., San Diego, 1969-70; dep. city atty. City of San Diego, 1971-74. Tchr. law for laymen San Diego Coll., 1973—; guest speaker on consumer fraud San Diego TV, radio, and various seminars. Mem. So. Cal. Consumer Protection Com., 1972-73; mem. Cal. Atty. Gen's. Task Force for Consumer Protection, 1972—. Mem. State Bar Cal., State Bar Ariz. San Diego County Bar Assn. (dir. 1973—, del. state bar conv. 1973). Club: Lawyers (San Diego). Author monthly law column, 1972-73. Office: 202 C St City Adminstration Bldg 2d Floor San Diego CA 92101

KINZEL, MADELEINE CHAMBERS (MRS. OTTO KINZEL), artist; b. Paris, France, 1920; d. Robert N. and Suzanne (De LaSalle) Chambers; came to U.S., 1926; grad. Fox Hollow Sch., 1938; student Sch. Applied Design, 1940; m. Otto Kinzel, Sept. 2, 1944; children—Otto III, Robert. Exhibited in group shows at Audubon Artists, Allied Artists, Knickerbocker Artists, Silvermine Guild, Nat. Arts Club, Pepsi-Cola show, 1965, N.Y. World's Fair, 1964; represented in permanent collections. Mem. Nat. Assn. Women Artists (chmn. traveling oil exhbn., 1965-68), Cooperstown (N.Y.) Art Assn., East River Artists. Home: 333 E 69th St New York City NY 10021 Office: East River Artists 1700 York Av New York City NY 10028

KINZER, LYDIA GREENE (MRS. JOHN R. KINZER), mathematician; b. Bridgeton, Ind.; d. William Nenian and Lydia (Remington) Greene; A.B., Washburn Coll., 1930; M.A., U. Kan., 1931; m. John R. Kinzer, Jan. 18, 1936. Statistician dept. mathematics Ohio State U., 1947-62, Bell Aerosystems Co., Tucson, 1962-67; statistical analyst office county assessor, Orange County, Cal. Mem. Sigma Xi, Sigma Delta Epsilon. Contbr. articles to profl. jours. Home: 1001 Charwood Lane Santa Ana CA 92705

KINZIE, JEANNIE JONES (MRS. JOSEPH KINZIE), physician; b. Gt. Falls, Mont., Mar. 14, 1940; d. James Wayne and Lillian Alice (Young) Jones; B.S., Mont. State U., 1961; M.D., Washington U., St. Louis, 1965; m. Joseph Kinzie, Mar. 25, 1965; 1 son, Daniel Joseph. Intern surgery U. N.C., Chapel Hill, 1965-66; resident radiology (radiation therapy) Washington U. Sch. Medicine, St. Louis, 1968-71, instr. radiology, 1971-73; Am. Cancer Soc. advanced clin. fellow, 1971-74; asst. radiologist Barnes Hosp., St. Louis, 1971-73; cons. radiology Homer G. Phillips Hosp., St. Louis, 1971-73; mem. med. records com., asst. prof. radiology Med. Coll. Wis., 1973—; asso. attending Staff Milw. County Gen. Hosp., 1973—; head radiation therapy dept. Wood (Wis.) Vets. Hosp., 1973—; cons. in radiology Community Meml. Hosp., Menomonee Falls, Wis., 1974—; radiology staff West Allis (Wis.) Meml. Hosp., 1973—. N.I.H. grantee, 1974. Diplomate Am. Bd. Radiology. Mem. A.M.A., Am. Coll. Radiology, Mo. Med. Soc., Soc. Nuclear Medicine, Am. Soc. Therapeutic Radiologists, A.A.A.S., Wis. Soc. Therapeutic Radiologists, Am. Assn. U. Profs., Alpha Lambda Delta, Phi Kappa Phi, Mortar Bd. Republican. Lutheran. Home: 4162 N Lake Dr Shorewood WI 53211 Office: 8700 W Wisconsin Av Milwaukee WI 53226

KIPGEN, JOYCE EVELYN GUSTIN (MRS. DONALD J. KIPGEN), psychologist; b. Las Vegas, N.M., Dec. 25, 1925; d. Ray Irvin and Oma Anna (Coffey) Gustin; B.A., Eastern N.M. U., 1951, postgrad., 1967—; M.A., Highlands U., 1955; m. Donald J. Kipgen, Dec. 23, 1958; children—Paul, Anna. Tchr. elementary sch., Otero County, N.M., 1949-50, Cimarron, N.M., 1950-52, Dodge City, Kan., 1952-54, Lovington, N.M., 1954-57, 66-69, San Tome' Venezuela, 1957-59; psychol. asso. West Tex. Edn. Center, Midland, 1970—. Pvt. practice psychol. services, Odessa, Tex., 1973—. Mem. Tex. State Tchrs. Assn., N.E.A., Am. Psychol. Assn. Baptist. Home: Rural Route 1 Box 600 Odessa TX 79763 Office: West Tex Edn Center PO Box 6020 Midland TX 79701

KIRBER, MARIA WIENER (MRS. HERBERT PETER KIRBER), educator; b. Prague, Czechoslovakia, Feb. 19, 1917; d. Otto and Dora (Alberti) Wiener; Med. U. Cand., German U. of Prague, 1938; postgrad. Charles U., 1938-39; M.S., U. Pa., 1941, Ph.D., 1942; Sc.D. (hon.), Med. Coll. Pa., 1973; m. Herbert Peter Kirber, May 21, 1943; children—Michael Thomas, William Martin. Came to U.S., 1939, naturalized, 1945. Faculty, Med. Coll. Pa., Phila., 1941—, prof. virology and microbiology, 1962-72, prof. emeritus, 1972—. Recipient Zentmeyer award Coll. of Physicians Phila., 1954; Golden Apple award Student Body Med. Coll. Pa., 1971; Christian R. and Mary F. Lindback award, 1971; Research grants Nat. Soc. for Prevention of Blindness, 1968-70. Fellow Am. Acad. Microbiology (charter); mem. Am. Soc. Microbiology, Am. Assn. Immunologists, N.Y. Acad. Sci., Sigma Xi.

KIRBY, JUANITA FAY WERNER (MRS. LEONARD KIRBY), physician, psychiatrist; b. Royse City, Tex., Mar. 8, 1927; d. Garland Daniel and Velma (McCord) Werner; A.A., Amarillo Coll., 1953; postgrad. So. Meth. U., 1953-54; M.D., U. Tex. Southwestern Med. Sch., 1958; m. Richard O. Higginbotham, June 27, 1943 (div. Sept. 1963); children—LaNona Fay, Werner Lee; m. 2d, Leonard Kirby, Dec. 18, 1965; children—Michael Dale, David Russell. Intern St. Paul Hosp., Dallas, 1958-59; resident Timberlawn Psychiat. Center, U. Tex. Southwestern Med. Sch., 1959-62; practice medicine, specializing in psychiatry, Dallas, 1962—; dir. Dallas State Mental Health Clinic, 1962-73. Acting dir. Dist. VI Mental Health Center, 1969-70; clin. instr. U. Tex. Southwestern Med. Sch., 1962—. Mem. task force Goals for Dallas, 1967-69, N. Tex. Planning Council, 1968; mem. profl. adv. bd. Dallas County Mental Health and Mental Retardation Center, 1967-69; founder, med. dir. Turtle Creek Manor Rehab. House, 1968; founder Routh Street Center, 1972. Bd. dirs. Mental Health Assn. Dallas County, chmn. profl. adv. bd., 1969-72; bd. dirs. Suicide Prevention Inc., Center for Personnel Growth, 1968-73, Pastoral Councilling Center, Tng. and Therapy Insts. Diplomate Am. Bd. Psychiatry and Neurology. Fellow Am. Psychiat. Assn.; mem. Am., Southwestern (sec. 1966-68, pres. 1974-75), Dallas (pres. 1967-68) group psychotherapy socs., Tex., Dallas County med. socs., So. Med. Assn., Phi Theta Kappa. Home: 808 Danfield Ct Irving TX 75062 Office: 3605 Routh St Dallas TX 75219 also 3524 Fairmount St Dallas TX 75219

KIRBY, LINDA LOUISE, newspaper exec.; b. Winston-Salem, N.C., Oct. 31, 1940; d. Elmer Thomas and Lillian (Holder) K.; B.A., Meredith Coll., 1962. Asst. supr. comparison dept. Woodward & Lothrop, Inc., Washington, 1962-63, fashion training rep., 1963-64; mem. staff Corp. Research & Advanced Studies, Washington, 1964-67; presentation writer Washington Star-News, 1967-73, advt. marketing and research mgr., 1973—. Mem. Media Research Council Washington (newspaper chmn. print com. 1973—), Am. Marketing Assn. Home: 3244 S Utah St Arlington VA 22206 Office: 225 Virginia Av Washington DC 20003

KIRCHNER, JOANN EMILIE, computer co. exec.; b. East Orange, N.J., Apr. 5, 1935; d. Karl Frederick and Cornelia (Malloch) Kirchner; student U. Wis., 1953-54; B.S., Columbia, 1958. With Paul Klemtner & Co. (now Klemtner Advt., Inc.), N.Y.C., 1958-73, media dir., 1959-69, v.p., 1969-73; exec. v.p. PERQ Corp., Ridgefield, Conn., 1973—. Advt. agy. rep. to med. comparability com. Bus. Publs. Audit Circulation; mem. adv. bd. Health Media Buyer's Guide. Mem. Am. Assn. Advt. Agys. (panel chmn. pharm. adv. 1969-73), Assn. Indsl. Advertisers (mem. media data form com. 1969—), Pharm. Advt. Club (chmn. media com. 1967-68). Home: 3 Kumquat Lane Ridgefield CT 06877 Office: Yankee Ridge Bldg Ridgefield CT 06877

KIRK, BARBARA ANNE MAYER (MRS. LEOPOLD M. KIRK), psychologist; b. San Francisco, Nov. 26, 1906; d. Julius and Ida (Son) Mayer; A.B., Stanford, 1927, M.A., 1934; postgrad. U. Minn., 1936-37; m. Leopold M. Kirk, Feb. 17, 1945; 1 dau., Ann Elizabeth. Research asst. Stanford, 1927-36; supr. Nat. Youth Authority Counseling Service, Nat. Youth Adminstrn., San Francisco, 1937-46; dir. counseling center U. Cal. at Berkeley, 1946-73, dean counseling, 1972-73; lectr. edn., 1954-73; pvt. practice psychology, Berkeley, Cal., 1974—; man tech. research cons., 1973—. Vocational cons. Bur. Hearings and Appeals, Social Security Adminstrn., Dept. Health, Edn., Welfare, 1962—; cons. counseling psychology Dept. Vets. Benefits, Compensation, Pension and Edn. Service, Vocational Rehab. Bd., 1960—; mem. tech. adv. com. testing Cal. Employment Relations Agy., Fair Employment Practice Commn., San Francisco, 1965—. Diplomate Am. Bd. Examiners. Fellow Am. Psychol. Assn. (div. sec. 1969-72); mem. Am., Cal. (treas. 1967-69) personnel and guidance assns., Am. Coll. Personnel Assn. (pres. 1964-65), Cal., Western psychol. assns., No. Cal. Guidance Assn., Nat. Council Measurement in Edn., Phi Beta Kappa, Sigma Xi, Psi Chi, Tau Psi Epsilon. Contbr. numerous articles to profl. jours. Home: 580 Euclid Av Berkeley CA 94708 Office: 1898 Allston Way Berkeley CA 94701

KIRK, CHRISTINA (MRS. JOSEPH F. DEMUL), journalist; b. Gary, Ind., July 25, 1928; d. Peter and Mary Ann (Hotchkiss) Kirk; A.B., Ind. U., 1950; m. Joseph F. DeMul, July 22, 1967. Gen. reporter Hays (Kan.) Daily News, 1951-52; women's page reporter Gary Post-Tribune, 1952-54; European cable editor N.Y. bur. Internat. News Service, 1955-58; asso. editor Dun's Rev., N.Y.C., 1958-60; financial reporter N.Y. Herald-Tribune, 1960-63; feature writer N.Y. Daily News, 1963-73; Women's editor The Nat. Star, 1973—. Recipient Loeb Spl. Achievement award for bus. reporting, 1961; Paul Tobenkin citation, 1961; Cultural award Newspaper Reporters Assn. N.Y., 1964. Mem. Newswomen's Club N.Y. (Best series award 1961, Best News Story award 1966, treas., past pres.), Women in Communications. Club: N.Y. Press. Home: 235 E 22d St New York City NY 10010 Office: 730 Third Av New York City NY 10017

KIRK, CYNTHIA GRACE, newspaper reporter; b. Chgo., Mar. 5, 1949; d. Kenneth Burson and Helen (White) K.; B.S. in Journalism, Northwestern U., 1970, M.S. in Journalism, 1971. Reporter Evansville (Ind.) Press, 1971, entertainments reporter (editor), 1972-73; reporter, critic Hollywood Reporter, Los Angeles, 1973—. Recipient 1st Place award Hearst Feature Writing Competition, 1968. Mem. Women in Communications, Theta Sigma Phi, Kappa Tau Alpha. Democrat. Home: 8737 Wonderland Av Los Angeles CA 90046 Office: 6715 Sunset Blvd Los Angeles CA 90028

KIRK, HELEN WHITE (MRS. KENNETH BURSON KIRK), club woman; b. Detroit; d. William John and Grace (Ramsay) White; B.A., U. Mich.; m. Kenneth Burson Kirk; children—Cynthia Grace, Helen Victoria. Sec.-treas., dir. Kirk Dial Corp., Beverly Hills, Cal. Dir. Beverly Hills (Cal.) Women's Club, 1936-37, Palm Springs (Cal.) Women's Club, 1953-54; pres. Lifelighters, 1955-56, 71-72, Palm Springs chpt. W.A.I.F., 1958-59; chmn. Bookworms of Assistance League So. Cal., 1967-68; mem. adv. bd. Los Angeles Women's chpt. Freedom's Found., 1972-74; mem. women's com. Los Angeles Philharmonic Orch., Opera Guild Soc. Cal.; gen. chmn. ladies div. Rotary Internat. Conv., 1962; pres. Palm Springs chpt. Nat. Charity League, 1965; v.p. women's aux. Desert Hosp., 1965. Mem. Internat. Platform Assn. Home: 702 N Bedford Dr Beverly HIlls CA 90210 also 155 S Belardo Rd Palm Springs CA 92262 Office: 140 S Beverly Dr Beverly Hills CA 90212

KIRK, SISTER M. REGINA, educator; b. Pitts.; d. William Joseph and Regina (Carroll) Kirk; B.A., Canisius Coll., 1930, M.A., 1934; Ph.D., Niagara U., 1937; Litt.D., Gallaudet Coll., 1968. Tchr. of deaf, 1927-40; high sch. supr. St. Mary's Sch. for Deaf, Buffalo, 1940-60; dir. tchr. tng. coop. program U. Buffalo-St. Mary's Sch. for Deaf, 1960-62; dir. tchr. preparation, profl. experiences coop. program Canisius Coll. and St. Mary's Sch. for Deaf, 1963—. Mem. Conv. Am. Instrs. for Deaf, Alexander Graham Bell Assn. for Deaf, N.Y. State Assn. for Educators Deaf, Conf. Execs. Am. Schs. for Deaf (asso.). Home: 2253 Main St Buffalo NY 14214

KIRK, ORA LEE JOHNSON, coal co. exec.; b. Morgantown, W.Va.; d. Thomas J. and Nora Belle (Browning) Johnson; student Mountain State Bus. Coll., Parkersburg, W.Va., 1937, W.Va. U., 1947; m. Eugene P. Kirk, Dec. 6, 1947 (div. Nov. 1957); children—Eugene Phillip, Lisa Ann. Sec., treas. Rosedale Coal Co., Morgantown, 1947—; sec.-treas. Mon Valley Mining Co., Morgantown, 1958—; sec.-treas. Mon Valley Coal & Lumber Co. Treas., Gen. Hosp. Women's Aux., Morgantown, 1970-74, snack bar treas., 1953-57; pres. aux. Monongalia Gen. Hosp., 1974—; Mem. White Shrine of Jeruseleum, Delta Delta Delta (alumni assn. chpt. pres. 1960-62, house corp. treas. 1966—). Methodist. Mem. Order Eastern Star. Home: 940 Riverview Dr Morgantown WV 26505 Office: PO Box 676 Morgantown WV 26505

KIRK, RUTH ELEANOR KRATZ (MRS. LOUIS GLADWIN KIRK), writer, photographer; b. Los Angeles, May 7, 1925; d. Reginald Patrick and Esther Clarice (Cumberland) Kratz; student Occidental Coll., 1943-44, Tenn. State U., 1946; m. Louis Gladwin Kirk, Sept. 3, 1943; children—Bruce Gladwin, Wayne Louis. Co-producer films and filmstrips of natural history U. Wash. Press, Seattle, 1968—; writer, narrator films CBC-TV, Vancouver, B.C., Can., 1966—. Instr. creative photography Peninsula Coll., Port Angeles, Wash., 1962-65. Bd. mgrs. Wash. State Congress P.T.A., 1966-68; trustee Wash. State Nature Conservancy, 1970—. Recipient Gov.'s award State Festival Arts, 1967, 71; award Wash. Pen Women, 1969; Kenneth Boyle award Northwest Booksellers, 1967. Mem. Nat. Audubon Soc., Wilderness Soc., Delta Kappa Gamma. Author: Exploring Dealth Valley, 1956, rev. edit. 1965; The Olympic Rainforest, 1965; Japan: Crossroads of East and West, 1966; Exploring Yellowstone, 1972; Desert: The American Southwest, 1973, others.

KIRKBRIDE, VIRGINIA RANDOLPH, educator; b. Bostwick, Neb., Sept. 14, 1910; d. John Wesley and Mary (Chitwood) Kirkbride; A.B., U. Neb., 1941, M.A., 1942; Ed.D., George Washington U., 1959. Elementary tchr., 1927-32, jr. high sch., 1932-38, sr. high sch., 1941-43 instr. U. Neb., summer 1943; instr. George Washington U., Washington, 1943-44, dir. activities for women, 1944-61, dean of women, 1961-67, asso prof. psychology, 1967—. Mem. women's hosp. bd. George Washington U. Mem. Nat. (exec. bd. 1954-67), Regional (pres. 1958) assns. women deans and counselors, N.E.A., Am. Psychol. Assn., Am. Coll. Personnel Assn., Am. Personnel Guidance Assn., P.E.O., Am. Assn. U. Women, Mortar Bd., Pi Lambda Theta, Phi Delta Gamma, Sigma Kappa. Presbyn. Club: Altrusa. Home: 3016 Tilden St Washington DC 20008 Office: 2125 G St NW Washington DC 20006

KIRKBY, RUTH ALBERTA (MRS. SAMUEL E. KIRKBY), mus. ofcl.; b. Middlepoint, O., Jan. 27, 1914; d. Fred and Maude Augustine (Moore) Lybarger; student Wayne City Coll., 1934, Riverside City Coll., 1952-53, U. Cal. at Riverside; m. Samuel E. Kirkby, July 11, 1936; children—Martha Ann (Mrs. John Leibert), Paul David, Noel E., Carolyn R. (Mrs. Clyde Kegley). Geology cons. Riverside Municipal Mus., 1952-57; curator of earth sci. and dir. ednl. services San Bernardino County Mus., Bloomington, Cal., 1957-65; exec. dir. Jurupa Mountains Cultural Center, Riverside, 1965—. Mem. Jurupa Dist. Steering Com., Riverside, 1969-73; mem. Lake Perris Reservoir Citizens Com., 1971—. Recipient Richfield Conservation award, 1966; Riverside County Tchrs. Pub. Relations award, 1967; Jurupa Dist. C. of C. Civic award, 1968; Spl. Environmental award Assn. for Environmental and Outdoor Edn., 1973. Mem. Internat. Botanists, So. Cal. Acad. Scis., Paleobotanists of Am., Cal. Native Plant Soc., Bot. Soc. Am., San Bernardino County Mus. Assn. (dir. 1959-60), Zonta. Club: Glen Avon Womens (pres. 1950-51) (Riverside). Home: 7701 Mission Blvd Riverside CA 92509 Office: 7621 Hwy 60 Riverside CA 92509

KIRKHAM, JOAN, mathematician; b. Topeka, Dec. 21, 1926; d. Joseph Earl and Anna Leona (Hamill) Kirkham; A.B., U. Kan., 1948; M.A., U. Denver, 1960. Research mathematician U. Denver, 1954-65; sr. scientific programmer McDonnell Automation Co., St. Louis, 1965-67; mathematician Hdqrs. Aerospace Def. Command, Ent AFB, Colo., 1967—. Mem. assn. Computing Machinery, Soc. Indsl. and Applied Math., Sigma Xi, Pi Mu Epsilon. Office: XPXY Headquarters Aerospace Defense Command Ent AFB CO 80912

KIRKIEN-RZESZOTARSKI, ALICJA MARIA (MRS. WACLAW JANUSZ RZESZOTARSKI), educator; b. Lodz, Poland; d. Leszek Tadeusz and Francesca Irene (Mortkowicz) Kirkien; M.Sc., Polish U. Coll., 1951; Ph.D., London U., 1955; m. Waclaw Janusz Rzeszotarski, Dec. 14, 1971. Asso. prof. U. W.I., 1956-61, asst. prof., 1961-65; asso. prof. Trinity Coll., Washington, 1966-68, prof. chemistry, 1968—, chmn. dept. chemistry, 1969—. Fellow Royal Inst. Chemistry Gt. Britain, Royal Soc. Commonwealth Bursary; mem. Am. Assn. U.

Profs., Am. Chem. Soc., Chem. Soc. Gt. Britain. Contbr. articles to profl. jours. Home: 4607 Brandywine St NW Washington DC 20016

KIRKLAND, BERTHA THERESA (MRS. THORNTON CROWNS KIRKLAND, JR.), constrn. co. exec.; b. San Francisco, May 16, 1916; d. Lawrence and Theresa (Kanzler) Schmelzer; m. Thornton Crowns Kirkland, Jr., Dec. 27, 1937; (dec. July 1971); children—Kathryn Elizabeth (Mrs. Burr C. Passenheim), Francis Charles. Supr. hosp. operations Am. Potash & Chem. Corp., Trona, Cal., 1953-54; office mgr. T.C. Kirkland, elec. contractor, 1954-56; sec.-treas., dir. T.C. Kirkland, Inc., San Bernardino, Cal., 1958-74; design and build estimator Add-M Electric, Inc., San Bernardino, 1972-74, v.p., 1974—. Episcopalian. Home: 526 E Sonora St San Bernardino CA 92404

KIRKLAND, ELEANOR RUTH (MRS. HENRY F. KIRKLAND, SR.), educator; b. Phila., July 21, 1918; d. Thomas H.A. and Carrie M. (Hemmerle) Turner; B.S., State Tchrs. Coll., West Chester, Pa., 1940; postgrad. Temple U., 1953-56; B.A., Cal. State U. at Los Angeles, 1958, M.A., 1960; Ed.D., U. Cal. at Berkeley, 1967. Free lance artist, Reading, Pa., 1949-53; tchr. mentally retarded Tng. Sch., Vineland, N.J., 1940-41; substitute tchr. pub. schs., Berks County, Pa., 1950-53; tchr. pub. schs. Wyomissing, Pa., 1953-56, Covina, Cal., 1956-59; classroom tchr., resource tchr., remedial reading tchr., dir. reading research San Juan Unified Sch. Dist., Carmichael, Cal., 1959-67; tchr. part time Cal. State U., Sacramento, 1964-67; tchr. (Fulbright grant) Moray House Coll. Edn., Edinburgh, Scotland, 1965-66; prof. reading, lang. arts, lang. acquisition, lang. and learning, maths., early childhood edn. Cal. State U., Sacramento, 1967—. NSF Scholar, 1961-62; one of 20 U.S. profs. selected to attend Nat. Def. Edn. Act. Inst., U. Cal. at Berkeley, summer, 1968. Mem. Cal., Internat. reading assns., Cal. Math. Council, Assn. Supervision and Curriculum Devel., Assn. Overseas Educators, N.C. Tchrs. English, U. Cal. Ednl. Alumni Soc., Am. Assn. U. Profs., Cal. Tchrs. Assn., Alumni Assn. Los Angeles State U., Assn. for Edn. of Young Children, Am., Cal. edn. research assns., Pi Lambda Theta. Author: (with Henry Bamman) Kaleidoscope, 1969. Contbr. articles to profl. pubs. Home: 8707 Mohawk Way Fair Oaks CA 95628 Office: Sch Edn Cal State U 6000 Jay St Sacramento CA 95819

KIRKLAND, MARJORIE LOVE HAMAKER, social worker; b. Washington, Sept. 22, 1917; d. John Irvin and Ray (Parker) Hamaker; A.B., Randolph-Macon Woman's Coll., 1938; M.A. in Psychology, Syracuse U., 1939; M.S.S.W., Richmond Profl. Inst. Coll. William and Mary, 1957; m. Charles Henry Kirkland, May 11, 1940 (div. 1963); children—Archie Howard, Richard Gish, Ray Love. Asst. prof. Lynchburg (Va.) Coll., 1948-49; social worker Lynchburg Tng. Sch. and Hosp., 1951-54, chief psychiat. social service, 1954-63; dir. social work edn. mental retardation Grad. Sch. Social Work U. Tex., 1963-65; cons. social services mentally retarded children U.S. Children's Bur., Washington, 1965-67; cons. mental retardation Rehab. Services Adminstrn. Dept. Health, Edn. and Welfare, Dallas, 1967-69; social work cons., Washington, 1969—; dep. br. chief U. Affiliated Facilities, 1972—; lectr. in field. Mem. Am. Assn. Mental Deficiency, Nat. Assn. Social Workers, Acad. Certified Social Workers, Phi Beta Kappa, Psi Chi. Author: Retarded Children of the Poor, 1971. Home: 103 G St SW Washington DC 20024 Office: HEW South Bldg Washington DC 20201

KIRKLAND-CASGRAIN, MARIE CLAIRE (MRS. PHILIPPE KIRKLAND-CASGRAIN), lawyer, provincial judge; b. Palmer, Mass., Sept. 8; d. Charles Aime and Rose A. (Demers) Kirkland; B.A., McGill U., 1947, M.L.A., 1950; m. Philippe Casgrain, May 1, 1954 (div. 1972); children—Lynne-Marie, Marc, Kirkland. Provincial judge for Que.; pres. Minimum Wage Bd.; first woman elected to Que. (Can.) legislature, 1961-73; first woman cabinet minister in Que. Mem. Can., Montreal bar assns., Kappa Alpha Theta. Roman Catholic. Home: 1321 Sherbrooke St W Apt B71 Montreal PQ Canada

KIRKPATRICK, BARBARA LYNN KELLER (MRS. MARTIN SMITH KIRKPATRICK), educator; b. Orlando, Fla., June 7, 1943; d. Holly Martin and Alice Bernice (Colglazier) Keller, Jr.; B.A. in Edn., U. Fla., 1965, postgrad., 1965-66; m. Martin Smith Kirkpatrick, Aug. 5, 1968. Corr., Sentinel-Star, Orlando, 1959-61; tchr. Fla. Jr. Coll., Jacksonville, 1966-68; tchr. English, Santa Fe Community Coll., Gainesville, Fla., 1968—, pres. Faculty Assn., 1970-71, 73-74. Bd. dirs. Spring Arts Festival Gainesville. Nat. Endowment for Arts grantee, 1973, 74. Mem. Nat. Council Tchrs. English, Fla. Assn. Community Colls., S. Atlantic Modern Lang. Assn., Internat. Soc. for Gen. Semantics, Kappa Alpha Theta. Home: 1655 NW 10 Av Gainesville FL 32605

KIRKPATRICK, CAROL ANN (MRS. RICO FRANK SERBO), soprano; b. Saratoga Springs, N.Y., Jan. 6, 1942; d. Robert Johnstone and Dorothy Gretchen (Gottsche) Kirkpatrick; Mus.B., U. Ariz., 1965; m. Rico Frank Serbo, Feb. 11, 1967. Concert with San Francisco Symphony, 1965; appeared with Merola Tng. Program, 1965, Am. Opera Soc., N.Y.C., 1965, Am. Youth Performs concerts Mass., Cal., Ariz., 1965, Lincoln Sq. Opera Co., N.Y.C., 1965, Goldovsky Opera Theatre, Washington, 1966, San Francisco Spring Opera, 1966-67; concert So. Ariz. Opera Guild, 1966; appeared with San Francisco Fall Opera, 1966-67; recorded Army of Stars Christmas Album, Salvation Army, Los Angeles, 1966; appeared with Western Opera Theatre, 1966-67, 67-68; 2d soprano Redlands (Cal.) U. Symphony, 1967; joint recital Redlands Bowl Community Concert, 1967; soprano Fremont (Cal.) Symphony, 1967; soprano soloist Tucson Symphony, 1967; artist in residence Flagstaff (Ariz.) Summer Festival, 1968; appeared with Laguna Beach (Cal.) Opera Assn., 1968; joint recital San Francisco Opera Action, 1968. Named Woman of Year in field music Tucson, 1967. Mem. Sigma Alpha Iota. Home: 2025 Pine St San Francisco CA 94115*

KIRKPATRICK, JEANE DUANE JORDAN (MRS. EVRON M. KIRKPATRICK), educator; b. Duncan, Okla., Nov. 19, 1926; d. Welcher F. and Leona (Kile) Jordan; A.B., Barnard Coll., 1948; M.A., Columbia, 1950, Ph.D., 1967; postgrad (French govt. fellow) U. Paris, Inst. de Sci. Politique, 1952-53; m. Evron M. Kirkpatrick, Feb. 20, 1955; children—Douglas Jordan, John Evron, Stuart Alan. Research analyst Dept. State, 1951-53; research asso. George Washington U., 1954-56, Fund for the Republic, 1956-58; asst. prof. polit. sci. Trinity Coll., 1962-67; asso. prof. polit. sci. Georgetown U., Washington, 1967-73, prof., 1973—. Cons. Am. Council Learned Socs., Dept. State, Dept. Health, Edn. and Welfare, Dept. Def., intermittently, 1955-72. Earhart fellow, 1956-57. Mem. Am., D.C. polit. sci. assns. Democrat. Author: (with Harold C. Hunt, others) Perspectives, 1962; Foreign Students in the United States: A National Survey, 1966; Mass Behavior in Battle and Captivity, 1968; Leader and Vanguard in Mass Society: The Peronist Movement in Argentina, 1971; Political Woman, 1973. Editor, contbr.: Elections: USA, 1956; Strategy of Deception, 1963. Contbr. articles to profl. jours. Home: 6812 Granby St Bethesda MD 20034 Office: 284 Neville Bldg Georgetown U Washington DC 20007

KIRKPATRICK, JOANNA, educator; b. Los Angeles, Sept. 6, 1929; d. John Edwin and Mary Catherine (Huggins) Kirkpatrick; B.A., Stanford, 1951; M.A., Yale, 1954; Ph.D., U. Cal. at Berkeley, 1970; 1 son, John Dadabhay. Field researcher, Punjab, India, 1965-66; prof. anthropology Bennington (Vt.) Coll., 1967—. Nat. Defense Edn. fellow U. Cal. at Berkeley, 1962-64, NIH fellow, 1966-67. Fellow Am. Anthrop. Assn., Royal Anthrop. Inst. Gt. Britain and Ireland; mem. Soc. Applied Anthropology. Address: Bennington Coll Bennington VT 05201

KIRKPATRICK, MARTHA JEAN (MRS. SEYMOUR PASTRON), physician; b. Oxnard, Cal., Dec. 30, 1925; d. Leland and Marion (Brewer) K.; B.A., U. Mich., 1946; M.D., McGill U., 1950; m. Seymour Pastron, May 26, 1957; children—Willard, Charles. Intern, Hosp. Good Samaritan, Los Angeles, 1950-51; resident in psychiatry VA Hosp., Brentwood, Cal., 1952-55; practice medicine specializing in psychiatry, Beverly Hills, Cal., 1955—; asst. clin. prof. Med. Sch., U. Cal. at Los Angeles, 1955—; mem. vol. staff Children's Hosp., 1955-58, Mt. Sinai Hosp., 1959—; psychiat. cons. Los Angeles County Health Dept., 1966-69. Fellow Am. Psychiat. Assn.; mem. So. Cal. Soc. for Child Psychiatry (past pres.), So. Cal. Psychiat. Soc., Los Angeles Psychoanalytic Soc. and Inst. Home: 265 N Layton Dr Los Angeles CA 90049 Office: 1800 Fairburn Los Angeles CA 90025

KIRSCHSTEIN, RUTH LILLIAN (MRS. ALAN S. RABSON), physician; b. Bklyn., Oct. 12, 1926; d. Julius and Elizabeth (Berm) Kirschstein; B.S., L.I. U. 1947; M.D., Tulane U., 1951; m. Alan S. Rabson, June 11, 1950; 1 son, Arnold. Intern, Kings County Hosp., Bklyn., 1951-52; resident in pathology VA Hosp., Atlanta, 1952, Providence Hosp., Detroit, 1952-54; Nat. Heart Inst. fellow, instr. dept. pathology Tulane U. Sch. Medicine, New Orleans, 1954-55; resident Clin. Center, NIH, Bethesda, Md., 1956, pathologist div. biologics standards, 1957-64, chief lab. pathology, 1964-72, asst. div. dir., 1971-72; dep. dir. Bur. Biologics, Food and Drug Adminstrn., 1972-73, dep. asso. commr. sci., 1973—. Diplomate Am. Bd. Pathology. Mem. Am. Assn. Immunologists, Am. Pathologists and Bacteriologists, Research on pathogenesis of viral diseases, viral oncogenesis. Home: 4 West Dr Bethesda MD 20014 Office: FDA 5600 Fishers Lane Rockville MD 20582

KIRSHBLUM, HELEN FRIED (MRS. I. USHER KIRSHBLUM), educator, religious worker, pub. speaker; b. Port Chester, N.Y., Mar. 6; d. Joseph and Rose (Boehm) Feiner; B.C.S., N.Y.U., 1934, M.A., 1938; m. Albert Fried, June 30, 1935 (dec. Dec. 1967) children—Arthur William, J. Michael; m. 2d, I. Usher Kirshblum, May 21, 1972. Tchr. Rhodes Sch., N.Y.C., 1935-42; pub. speaker, 1956—; tchr., internat. pub. speaker, 1948—; asst. prof. speech, theatre Borough Manhattan Community Coll., 1967-68, Kingsborough Community Coll., 1968—. Del., Pres.'s Conf. Major Jewish Orgns., 1973—. Bd. dirs., mem. commn. Jewish Life Synagogue Council of Am., 1962—; dir., mem. bd. overseas Jewish Theol. Sem. of Am., 1960—; exec. com. Jewish Braille Inst., 1958—; mem. exec. com., dir. World Council of Synagogues, 1960—; dir. United Synagogue of Am. Active A.R.C., Braille Inst.; Israel Bonds, United Jewish Appeal. Participant in White House Conf. on Edn., 1965, White House Conf. on Civil Rights, 1966; N.G.O. del. to UN, 1966-72. County, committeeman Kings County Liberal party. Mem. bd. Jewish Theol. Sem., United Synagogue Am. Recipient Woman of Achievement award, Jewish Theol. Sem. Am.; Nat. Community Leadership award Jewish Theol. Sem., 1968; Community Leadership award United Jewish Appeal, 1970. Mem. Nat. Womens League United Synagogues (nat. pres. 1962-66, br. pres. 1950-52, hon. pres. Bklyn. br., nat. chmn. speakers training), Internat. Platform Assn., Am., Eastern States speech assns. Contbg. author Beacons of Light, 1965. Contbr. articles to profl. jours. Home: 135-12 72d Av Kew Gardens Hills NY 11367 also Copake Lake Estates Hillsdale NY 12529 Office: Kingsborough Community Coll Oriental Blvd Brooklyn NY 11235

KIRSHNER, GLORIA IFLAND, editor; b. N.Y.C.; d. Edward William and Lillian (Fineman) Ifland; B.A., Barnard Coll., 1953; M.A., Columbia Tchrs. Coll., 1958; div.; 1 son, Ralph. Guest editor Mademoiselle mag., 1953; tchr. elementary sch., N.Y.C., Network, 1955-62; ednl. cons., script writer, editor NBC Tchrs. Guides, NBC TV, 1962-65; ednl. cons. Robert Saudek Assos., N.Y.C., 1965-71; script writer, ednl. supt., asst. to exec. producer TV program Animal Secrets, 1967-68; editor, v.p. Tchrs. Guides to TV, N.Y.C., 1969—; tchr. spl. course in TV and film Columbia Tchrs. Coll., 1970-72; cons. in field. Recipient for series spl. award merit Nat. Soc. Med. Research, 1967, Thomas Alva Edison award, 1967, Cine Golden Eagle award, 1967, Ohio State award, 1967, Gran Premio Internat., Tecnica Cinematografica, 1967, Brotherhood award Nat. Conf. Christians and Jews, 1965, Freedoms Found. award, 1965, Distinguished Achievement award Ednl. Press Assn., 1973. Mem. Edn. Writers Assn., Ednl. Press Assn., Nat. Council Social Studies, Internat. Radio and TV Soc. Author: From Instinct to Intelligence: How Animals Learn, 1969; (TV and film scripts) Exploring, 1964-65, Animal Secrets, 1967-68, When Children Search for Themselves, 1971. Contbr. articles to profl. jours. Office: 145 E 69th St New York City NY 10021

KIRTLEY, MARJORIE ESTHER DUKE, librarian; b. Portsmouth, Va., Apr. 23, 1917; d. James M.C. and Margaret (Dempsey) Duke; grad. Thomas Jefferson High Sch., Richmond, Va., 1931-35; m. William Melton Kirtley, Aug. 9, 1941 (dec. Sept. 27, 1969); children—William Melton Jr., Richard Wayne, Thomas Alan (dec.). Library asst. U. Richmond Boatwight Meml. Library, 1962-67; asst. to librarian Va. State Law Library, Richmond, 1967-68, acting librarian, 1968, law librarian, 1968—. Active YWCA. Mem. Am. Assn. Law Libraries. Episcopalian. Club: Bon Air Woman's (sec. 1961-62). Home: 3002 Waddington Dr Richmond VA 23224 Office: Supreme Ct Bldg Richmond VA 23210

KIRTS, KATHERINE JEAN, educator; b. Dayton, O., July 25, 1945; d. Marvin O. and Elizabeth (Molter) Kirts; B.S., Lindenwood Coll., 1967; M.S., Ind. U., 1968. Teaching asso. Ind. U., Bloomington, 1967-68; asst. prof. women's phys. edn. McKendree Coll., Lebanon, Ill., 1968—, dir. women's athletics. Instr. summer horsemanship programs Jo-An Farms, Milan, Mo., 1962-64. Mem. Am., Ill. assns. health, phys. edn. and recreation, Midwest Assn. for Phys. Edn. for Coll. Women. Presbyn. Home: Rural Route 1 Box 166A Caseyville IL 62232 Office: McKendree Coll Lebanon IL 62254

KIRWAN, KATHARYN GRACE (MRS. GERALD BOURKE KIRWAN, JR.), clothing store exec.; b. Monroe, Wash., Dec. 1, 1913; d. Walter Samuel and Bertha Ella (Shrum) Camp; student U. Puget Sound, 1933-34; B.A., B.S., Tex. Woman's U., 1937; postgrad., U. Wash., 1941; m. Gerald Bourke Kirwan, Jr., Jan. 13, 1945. Librarian, Brady (Tex.) Sr. High Sch., 1937-38, McCamey (Tex.) Sr. High Sch., 1938-43; mgr. Milady's Frock Shop, Monroe, 1946-62, owner, mgr., 1962—. Meml. chmn. Monroe chpt. Am. Cancer Soc., 1961—; mem. Snohomish County Police Services Action Council, 1971; mem. Monroe Pub. Library Bd., 1950-65, pres. bd., 1964-65; mem. Monroe City Council, 1969—; mayor City of Monroe, 1974—; commr. Snohomish County Hosp. dist. 1, 1970—. Served with USNR, 1943-46. Mem. Am. Assn. U. Women, U.S. Naval Inst., Ret. Officers Assn., Naval Res. Assn., Snohomish County Pharm. Aux., C. of C. (pres. 1972). Episcopalian. Home: 538 S Blakely St Monroe WA 98272 Office: 102 W Main St Monroe WA 98272

KISER, LOLA FRANCES, educator; b. Selmer, Tenn., Dec. 6, 1930; d. Buel Theodore and Grace (Wood) Kiser; B.S., Memphis State U., 1952; M.A., U. Ga., 1954; Ph.D., U. Ala., 1971. Instr. math. U. Ga., 1954-55; asst. prof. math. Birmingham So. Coll., 1955-60, asso. prof., 1960-71, prof., 1971—; NSF trainee U. Ala., 1968-69. Mem. Math. Assn. Am., Ala. Assn. Coll. Tchrs. Math. Home: 816G 12th St W Birmingham AL 35208

KISER, THELMA SCOTT (MRS. ALAN BOYD KISER), govt. ofcl., poet; b. nr. Lexington, Ky., Dec. 25, 1916; d. Robert Moore and Mattie Wallace (Riddle) Scott; student Transylvania U., Ky., 1932-35, Ashland Community Coll., 1944-45; m. Alan Boyd Kiser, Aug. 21, 1955. Lab. technician Ashland Oil & Refining Co. (Ky.), 1942-47, chemist, 1947-50; chemist U. Ky. Agrl. Research, Lexington, 1950-55; food processing inspector U.S. Dept. Agr., Ashland, 1965—. Bd. dirs. State Poetry Library, Ashland, Ky., founder, 1966. Recipient Atlantic award, 1968, Jesse Stuart award, 1971, Pegasus award, 1972. Mem. Ky. State Poetry Soc. (dir. 1966—, v.p. 1971-72), Ky. Jr. Poets (founder 1967, dir. 1967—), W.Va., Eastern Ky. Poetry socs., Hon. Order Ky. Cols., Nat. League Am. Pen Women. Mem. Christian Ch. (librarian 1962-73, Bible sch. tchr. 1969—). Contbr. numerous poems to lit. publs. and mags. Editor: Pegasus, 1966-69, contbg. editor, 1969—; guest editor U.S. edit. World Poetry Mag., Poet, 1971; book editor Ashland Daily Ind., 1970—; weekly columnist Lookout mag., 1962-65. Home: 1508 Montgomery Av Ashland KY 41101 Office: 2209 Central Av Ashland KY 41101

KISH, MOTHER MARY OLGA, ednl. adminstr.; b. Phila., Mar. 13, 1912; d. Michael and Anna Kish; B.S., Cath. U. Am., 1946; M.S., Fordham U., 1953; M.A., Villanova U., 1963. Mem. Sisters of St. Basil, Phila., vice provincial, 1970—; tchr. St. Basil's Sch., Phila., 1929-50, prin., 1935-53; tchr. history and religion St. Basil Acad., Foxchase, Phila., 1953-57; acad. dean, instr. Manor Jr. Coll., Jenkintown, Pa., 1955-70, pres., 1971—. Mem. Fordham Personnel and Guidance Assn., Am. Assn. U. Adminstrs., Hist. Soc. Pa., Pa. Assn. Jr. Coll. (exec. bd.), Nat. Cath. Edn. Assn. Author: My Soul Doth Magnify the Lord. Address: Fox Chase Manor Jenkintown PA 19046

KISMARIC, CAROLE LEE (MRS.CHARLES MIKOLAYCAK), editor; b. Orange, N.J., Apr. 28, 1942; d. John Joseph and Alice Felicia (Bruskos) Kismaric; B.A., Pa. State U., 1964; m. Charles Mikolaycak, Oct. 1, 1970. Picture researcher, Time Life Books div. Time Inc., N.Y.C., 1964-66, picture editor, 1967—. Asst. dir. From the Picture Press, photography show Mus. Modern Art, 1973; photo researcher documentary film Let the Good Times Roll, 1973—. Author: Duel of the Ironclads, 1969; Charles Mikolaycak) The Boy Who Tried to Cheat Death, 1970; On Leadership, 1974. Home: 115 E 90th St New York City NY 10028 Office: Time-Life Bldg Rockefeller Center New York City NY 10020

KISROW, SUSAN E. CARLSON, psychologist; b. New Ulm, Minn.; d. Herbert Gustav and Pauline (Bryan) Carlson; B.A., U. Minn., 1959; M.S., Ind. U., 1970; m. Lowell Alan Kisrow, June 4, 1960. Research asst. U. Minn., Mpls., 1960-64; counselor Minn. Dept. Employment Security, St. Paul, 1964-66, counseling supr., 1966-69; psychologist, dir. Renlaar Experience Center, child guidance and tng., Mpls., 1969—. Mem. Am., Minn. personnel and guidance assns. Home: PO Box 88 St Michael MN 55376

KISS, MARY CLEMENT, newswriter; b. Johnson City, Tenn., July 28, 1928; d. Hugh Wilfred and Ruby (Sammons) Clement; student St. Mary-of-the-Woods Coll., 1946-47; B.J., U. Mich., 1950; m. Alvin Josef Kiss, Feb. 27, 1954; children—Anthony J., Stephen C., Mary Margaret. News reporter Kingsport (Tenn.) Times-News, 1950-55, staff writer, 1967—, environmental editor, 1973—; freelance mag. writer, 1970—. Mem. Women in Communications. Home: 100 Edmond Circle Kingsport TN 37663 Office: 701 Lynn Garden Dr Kingsport TN 37660

KISSANE, SHARON FLORENCE, dir. reading center; b. Chgo., July 2, 1940; d. William B. and Agnes (Payne) Mrotek; B.A., DePaul U., 1962; M.A., Northwestern U., 1963; Ph.D., Loyola U., 1970; m. James Q. Kissane, July 2, 1966; 1 dau., Laura Janine. Speech teacher Notre Dame High Sch., Chgo., 1960-61; speech teacher Our Lady of Solace Elem. Sch., Chgo., 1963; editor, writer Commerce Clearing Publishing Co., Chgo., 1963-66; instr. speech and communications Ill. Inst. Tech., 1963; instr. Columbia Coll. Communicative Arts, 1964; editorial writer Park Ridge (Ill.) Herald, 1967; instr. Ridgewood High Sch. Adult Edn. Program, 1968-70; asso. dir. Felician Coll. Reading Clinic, 1971; Learning Center dir. Stevenson Elementary Sch., Des Plaines, Ill., 1972; dir. Park Ridge (Ill.) Reading Center, 1972—; cons. spl. ednl. programs Children's World Montosorri Program, Park Ridge. Exhibited art one-man shows Stevenson Sch., Des Plaines, 1972, Tam-O-Shanter Tennis Club, Niles, Ill., 1974; exhibited group shows, McCormack Place, Chgo., 1972, Am. Soc. Artists, Chgo., 1972—, WTTW TV Art Auction, 1972, South Park Art Exhibit, Park Ridge, Ill., 1973, Water Tower Art Show, Chgo., 1972, Civic Center Art Exhbn., Chgo., 1973, Water Tower Art Show, Chgo., 1973, Civic Center Art Exhbn., Chgo., 1973, Raymond Duncan Gallery, Paris, France, 1973, Ligoa Duncan Gallery, N.Y.C., 1973, Rouge's Gallery, Allentown, Pa., 1974. Mem. Catholic Alumni Assn. (spl. events dir. 1964-65), Am. Soc. Artists, Chgo. Sketch Club, Nat. Edn. Assn. (treas. DePaul br. 1961), Central States Speech Assn. (registration com. 1963), Council Communication Socs., Northwest Suburban Audio-Visual Soc., Park Ridge Hist. Soc. (founding), Am. Assn. U. Women, Delta Sigma Pi, Kappa Gamma Pi. Home: 624 Seminary St Park Ridge IL 60068 Office: 303 Northwest Hwy Park Ridge IL 60068

KISTLER, ELLEN DOWNEY, librarian; b. Royal Center, Ind., Aug. 10, 1900; d. Oliver Perry and Alma Cora (Downey) Kistler; student Ind. U., 1917-18, U. Mich., 1919; A.B., U. Wis., 1930; Asst., Logansport (Ind.) Pub. Library, 1918-19, Peru (Ind.) Pub. Library, 1920-23; head cataloger Milw. Pub. Library, 1924-28; cataloger, Dante Collection, U. Notre Dame, South Bend, Ind., 1930-31, head catalog dept., 1931-47; head catalog dept. South Bend, Ind., 1930-31, head catlacatalog dept., 1931-47; head catalog dept. South Bend Pub. Library, 1947-65; cataloger rare books St. Mary's Coll., Notre Dame, Ind., 1966-69. Vol. cataloger Head Start, 1973, Temple Bethel, 1972—, Mental Health Assn., 1971—, First Christian Ch. Library, 1960—, Planned Parenthood, 1973, No. Ind. Hist. Soc., 1974—, Meml. Hosp., 1965—. Recipient George award Mishawaka Enterprise Record, 1971. Mem. Am., Ind. library assns. Club: Altrusa (pres. 1957-59) (South Bend). Home: 1214 E Madison St South Bend IN 46617

KISTNER, RUTH EMERSON, lectr.; b. Fitchburg, Mass., Jan. 18, 1907; d. Franklin Sawyer and Helen (Nelson) Davis; B.A., Boston U., 1929; M.A., Columbia U., 1934; m. Henry Magnus Kistner, Oct. 9, 1937. Lectr. countless garden and women's clubs, civic groups throughout nation; lectr. for French Govt., 1970; accredited judge Nat. Council State Garden Clubs; tchr. Nat. Council Judging Schs. Winner blue-ribbon, tri-color awards Internat. Flower Show, N.Y.C. Mem. Women's Aux. Littleton Hosp., 1968—. Mem. Bellerose Garden Club (pres. 1968-72), N.Y. Hort. Soc., Mass. Hort. Soc., White Mountain Garden Club, Jamaica Women's Club, Garden City Hempstead Community Club, Nat. Council State Garden Clubs (life). Author: (with Gladys Tabor) Flower Arranging for the American Home, 1930. Home: 7726 87th St Glendale NY 11227

KITAZUMI, MARIE NAKAMURA, religious assn. exec.; b. Sacramento, Feb. 5, 1921; d. Iwazo and Kishino (Yamamoto) Nakamura; student Merritt Sch. Bus., Oakland, Cal., 1939-41, Ind. U. Extension, 1944-46, U. Chgo. Extension, 1955-56, Northwestern U.

Extension, 1964-66; m. Tadasu Kitazumi, Dec. 12, 1942 (div. 1962); children—Anita Lin, Constance Marie, Lisa Kishino. Jr. relocation officer War Relocation Authority, Indpls., 1944-46; asst. to chief research analyst Nuermberg Trials, Germany, 1947; office mgr. Chgo. Pottery Co., Chgo., 1950-55; owner Kitazumi Ins. Agy., Waukegan, Ill., 1959-62; adminstrv. asst. Gen. Council on World Service and Finance, United Methodist Ch., Evanston, Ill., 1962-72, asst. gen. sec. Council on Finance and Adminstrn., 1973—. Sec. adminstrv. bd. 1st United Methodist Ch., Evanston, 1970-71. Home: 1711 Ridge St Evanston IL 60201 Office: 1200 Davis St Evanston IL 60201

KITCHEN, MILDRED (MRS. CHARLES TREUTER, JR.), food editor; b. San Antonio, Jan. 6, 1906; d. James Harry and Mary Nannie Laura (Nickelson) Owen; student Westmoreland Coll., 1922-24, U. Minn., 1950-51, U. Wis., 1951-52; m. Charles D. Treuter, Jr., Oct. 9, 1928. Reporter San Antonio Light, 1925-27, food editor, 1927-48, 53—; owner-pub. Comml. Recorder Legal Newspaper. Mem. Blue Bird Aux. Mem. Atlanta Humane Soc., Women in Communications. Methodist. Club: Quota (San Antonio chpt.). Home: 114 Hermosa Dr E Olmos Park Estates San Antonio TX 78212 Office: 420 Broadway St San Antonio TX 78206

KITCHEN, VALERIE EUSTELLE GAUTHIER, city ofcl.; b. Salem, Mass., Feb. 26, 1933; d. Joseph Aime and Irene Margaret (Bell) Gauthier; student pvt. schs., Royal Oak, Mich.; m. July 12, 1952 (div.); 1 son, Michael Paul. Sec., Chrysler MoPar, Centerline, Mich., 1955-59; office mgr. Fine Mfg. & Tool Co., Ferndale, Mich., 1959-63; city clk. City of Ferndale, 1964—. Mem. Ferndale Youth Assistance Com., 1973—. Mem. Internat. Inst. Municipal Clks., Municipal Clks. Assn. Mich., Oakland County Municipal Clks. Assn., Ferndale Bus. Women's Club. Home: 271 E Oakridge St Apt 105 Ferndale MI 48220 Office: 300 E Nine Mile Rd Ferndale MI 48220

KITCHIN, ROSEMARIE ATKIN, pub. relations exec.; b. Springfield, Ill., June 6, 1939; d. Bernard and L. Lucille (McCarty) Atkin; B.S. in Journalism, Northwestern U., 1961; m. K. Thomas Kitchin, Jr., Dec. 17, 1960 (div. 1974); children—Kraig Thomas, Kevin Thomas. TV prodn. asst. NBC-TV, Chgo., 1960; continuity and promotional writer WSJV-TV, Elkhart, Ind., 1961; public service and continuity writer WKBN, Youngstown, O., 1963; advt. copywriter Strouss-Hirshberg, Youngstown, 1964-66; free-lance writer and publicist, Detroit, Los Angeles and Boston, 1966-72; social worker Combined Jewish Philanthropies, Boston, 1971-72; dir. pub. relations Jewish Welfare Fedn. Detroit, 1972—. Mem. Women in Communications. Home: 1900 Coolidge Rd Apt 203 Troy MI 48084 Office: Jewish Welfare Fedn Detroit 163 Madison AV Detroit MI 48226

KITTINGER, IDA MAE LUCAS (MRS. JOSEPH WILLIAM KITTINGER), realtor; b. Screven County, Ga.; d. Robert Hamilton and Cora (Merritt) Lucas; student Richards Bus. Coll., Savannah, Ga., 1923; m. Joseph William Kittinger, Sr., Aug. 4, 1927; children—Joseph William, John Boyd. Agt., Ry. Express, Casselberry, Fla., office mgr. Casselbery Ferneries, 1937-44; owner, operator Kittinger Florist, Orlando, Fla., 1944-46. Ida Mae Kittinger, Realtor, 1946-72; now with Ormond Realtors, Inc., Ormond Beach, Fla. Vice pres. Women's Council Winter Park Bd. Realtors, 1972-73. Mem. Ormond Beach Hosp. Aux. Recipient Violet Dunham award, 1964. Mem. Orlando Winter Park Bd. Realtors (pres. womens council 1961, mem. exec. bd.), Nat. Assn. Real Estate Bds., Daytona Beach Area Bd. Realtors, Nat. Safety Council, Nat. Inst. Real Estate Brokers. Presbyn. Mem. Order Eastern Star. Clubs: Zonta Internat. (pres. 1966-68, v.p. 1972-73) Mothers of Demolay (pres. 1950), Does (sec. 1948, charter), Sorosis (Orlando); Azalea Garden (Ormond Beach). Home: 211 Lynnhurst Dr Ormond Beach FL 32074 Office: 2280 AIA Hwy Ormond Beach FL 32074

KITTRELL, FLEMMIE PANSY, educator; b. Henderson, N.C., Dec. 25, 1904; d. James Lee and Alice (Mills) Kittrell; grad. Acad. Hampton Inst., 1924; B.S., Coll. Hampton Inst., 1928; Ph.D. (Rosenwald scholar 1929; Gen. Edn. Bd. scholar 1933), Cornell U., 1936. Dean of students Bennett Coll., Greensboro, N.C., 1930-40; dean of women Hampton Inst., 1940-44; prof., head dept. home econs. Howard U., Washington, 1944-71; spl. assignment U.S. State Dept. to Liberia, West Africa, 1947-48; Fulbright prof. Baroda U., India, 1950, mem. bd. studies for faculty of home sci., 1956. Home econ. cons. ICA in Baroda, India under U.S. State Dept., 1953-55; cons. edn. program Leopoldville, Congo Republic, 1961-65, leader 22 Ind. women to Japan, U.S. State Dept. project, 1955; lecture tour East and West Africa for U.S. Dept. State, 1958. Del. Internat. Congress of Home Econs., Stockholm, Sweden, 1949; del. Meth. Ch. to Internat. Missionary Council in Willingen, Germany, 1952; del. UN Conf., Geneva, 1959; mem. nat. bd. YWCA, 1959; FAO nutrition assignment to India, 1960; State Dept. cultural exchange tour, West Africa, 1961; mem. group Airlift of Understanding to Bangladesh, 1972; U.S. observer Conf. on New Horizons for Women of Africa, Morocco, 1971; AID sponsored observer Zaire, 1972; convener Ph.D. nutrition exam. U. Madras (India), 1972. Trustee Sibly Hosp., Hampton Inst.; mem. home econ. council Cornell U., 1964; bd. dirs. Washington chpt. UN. Recipient Liberian (West Africa) award for outstanding service to country, 1948; Hampton Alumni award, 1955; Gold Key Award, Am. Tchrs. Assn., 1962; Internat. award Century Club Bus. and Profl. Women, 1965; Cornell U. Alumni award for contbn. to human devel., 1968; Hampton Inst. Centennial medal, 1968. Fellow A.A.A.S.; mem. Soc. Prodigal Son, N.C., Am. Assn. U. Women, Am. Dietetics Assn., Am. Home Econs. Assn., Women's Internat. League for Peace and Freedom, Sigma Xi, Sigma Delta Epsilon, Phi Kappa Phi, Pi Lambda Theta, Omicron Nu, Beta Kappa Chi. Home: 3200 Warder St NW Washington DC 20010

KIVI, ELSIE KAREN, librarian; b. Hibbing, Minn., Jan. 31, 1919; d. Toivo Nestor and Sophia (Talvinen) Kivi; A.A., Hibbing Jr. Coll., 1938; B.S., U. Minn., 1941; M.S., U. Ill., 1951, certificate, 1965; postgrad. U. Mich., 1955-56. Librarian pub. schs., Deer River, Minn., 1941-43, Aitkin, 1943-46, Bessemer, Mich., 1946-47; reference librarian, asso. prof. library sci. Moorhead (Minn.) State Coll., 1947—. Vis. prof. Tex. Woman's U., summers, 1959, 61, 63, 68; cons. Detroit Lake Pub. Library, 1956-58. Mem. Am. Minn. library assns., Nat., Minn. edn. assns., State Coll. Interfaculty Orgn. (local pres. 1959-60), Am. Assn. U. Profs. (local pres. 1963-64, 70-71, exec. bd.), Am. Assn. U. Women (local treas. 1949-50), League Women Voters, Am. Scandinavian Soc., Minn. Finnish Am. Soc., Folio Soc. (London), Pvt. Libraries Assn. (London), Red River Valley, Cuyuna Range hist. socs., Fargo Moorhead Unitarian Fellowship (dir. 1973-76), Moorhead Bus. and Prof. Woman's (pres. 1965-66), Beta Phi Mu (dir. 1971-73). Home: 1015 1/2 7th Av S Moorhead MN 56560

KIZER, BERNICE LICHTY (MRS. HARLAN D. KIZER), lawyer, state legislator; b. Fort Smith, Ark., Aug. 14, 1915; d. Ernest C. and Opal (Culler) Lichty; student Stephens Coll., 1935-36; J.D., U. Ark., 1946; m. James M. Parker, Oct. 6, 1939 (dec. Aug. 1955); children—James M., Shirley (Mrs. Jim C. Wilhite), Karolyn Kay (Mrs. Roger Sparkman); m. 2d, Harlan D. Kizer, Oct. 2, 1959. Admitted to Ark. bar, 1946; pvt. practice law Ft. Smith, 1956—. Mem. Ark. Ho. Reps., 1961—, chmn. labor com. Chmn. protective labor legislation for women Gov.'s Commn. Status Women, 1964; mem. Ark. Legislative Council, Gov.'s Adv. Council Aging; mem. Gov.'s Adv. Com. on Status Women, 1968. Bd. dirs. Ark. Assn. for Mental Health. Recipient Mother Ark. award 1964; Woman Achievement award S.W. Am. Times Record, 1969. Mem. Sebastian County, Ark. bar assns., Nat. Assn. Women Lawyers, Nat. Women Legislators Assn., Bus. and Profl. Women's Club, League Women Voters, Am. Assn. U. Women, Soroptimist Fedn. Americas, Delta Delta Delta. Episcopalian. Mem. P.E.O. Home: 221 May Av Fort Smith AR 72901 Office: 2714 Barry St Fort Smith AR 72901

KIZZIAR, JANET WRIGHT, psychologist; b. Independence, Kan.; d. John L. and Thelma V. Wright; B.A., U. Tulsa; m. Mark Kizziar. Tchr., sch. psychologist; individual practice psychology; lectr. colls. and univs. throughout U.S. Named Outstanding Woman of Okla., 1970, Outstanding Alumnae, U. Tulsa. Mem. Am., Tulsa (past pres.) psychol. assns. Author: Gemini: The Psychology and Phenomena of Twins. Home: 2416 Circle Dr Bartlesville OK 74003 Office: 2651 E 21st St Tulsa OK 74114

KJELGAARD, BETTY MARJORIE, writer; b. Marshlands, Pa., Sept. 1, 1926; d. Carl Winfield and Betty Henrietta (Hoffman) Kjelgaard; bus. diploma Elmira Bus. Inst., 1945. Adminstrv. asst. to dir. curriculum Ithaca (N.Y.) City Sch. Dist., 1969—; writer numerous stories pub. in mags. including Redbook, Woman's Day, McCall's, Ladies Home Jour., Good Housekeeping, Seventeen; novellas in McCall's; stories in Braille; travel articles in Ford Times; also stories in anthologies; TV story End of Night. Home: 310 E Tompkins St Ithaca NY 14850 Office: 400 Lake St Ithaca NY 14850

KLAGES, CONSTANCE WARNER, mgmt. cons. exec.; b. N.Y.C., May 29, 1934; d. Ernest Frederick and Elsie (Roedler) Klages; B.A., Dickinson Coll., 1956; certificate personnel mgmt. and indsl. relations N.Y. U., 1959. Asst. to personnel dir., personnel asst. Inst. Internat. Edn., N.Y.C., 1956-62; salary analyst, employment supr. Remington Rand div. Sperry Rand Corp., Univac Div., N.Y.C., 1962-65; research and survey mgr. Commerce and Industry Assn. N.Y., N.Y.C., 1965-66; asso. and research mgr. Battalia, Lotz, & Assos., Inc., N.Y.C., 1966-72, v.p., 1972—. Vol. Elmhurst (N.Y.) Gen. Hosp., 1957-62. Mem. N.Y. Personnel Mgmt. Assn., Dickinson Coll. Alumni Council, Phi Mu (pres. N.Y.C. alumni chpt. 1962-63). Presbyn. Office: 342 Madison Av New York City NY 10017

KLAGSBRUN, FRANCINE LIFTON (MRS. SAMUEL C. KLAGSBRUN), writer, editor; b. Bklyn.; d. Benjamin and Anna (Pike) Lifton; B.A., Bklyn. Coll. 1952; M.A., N.Y. U., 1959; B.H.L., Jewish Theol. Sem. Am., 1952; m. Samuel C. Klagsbrun, Jan. 23, 1955; 1 dau., Sarah Devora. Research asst. Jewish Theol. Sem. Am., N.Y.C., 1953-57; subject editor World Book Ency., Field Enterprises Ednl. Corp., Chgo., 1957-60, sr. editor, 1960-64, asso. editor, 1964; exec. editor Ency. Americana, Grolier, Inc., N.Y.C., 1964-65; mng. editor Hart Pub. Co., N.Y.C., 1965; mng. editor ednl. div. Cowles Communications, Inc., N.Y.C., 1965-66; exec. editor Cowles Book Co., 1966-68; creative dir. Ednl. Systems UEC, Inc., 1969-73; editorial cons., N.Y.C., 1973—. Bd. dirs. Melton Research Center of Jewish Theol. Sem. Mem. Bklyn. Coll., N.Y. U., Jewish Theol. Sem. alumni assns., Phi Beta Kappa, Author: Sigmund Freud, 1967; First Book of Spices, 1968; The Story of Moses, 1968; Psychiatry-A Book for Young People, 1969; Your Health: Nutrition, 1969; Read About the Teacher, 1970; Read About the Librarian, 1970; Read About the Parkman, 1971; Read About the Sanitation Man, 1972; Freedom Now! The Story of the Abolitionsts, 1972. Editor: Assassination: Robert F. Kennedy, 1968; The First Ms. Reader, 1973; Free to Be You and Me, 1974; What Women Say, 1974. Home and office: 1010 Fifth Av New York City NY 10028

KLAGSBRUNN, ELIZABETH RAMSEY (MRS. HANS A. KLAGSBRUNN), physician; b. N.Y.C., Feb. 17, 1906; d. Charles Cyrus and Grace (Keys) Ramsey; grad. The Bishop's Sch., LaJolla, Cal.; B.A., Mills Coll., 1928; fellow Inst. Internat. Edn., Hamburg, Germany, 1928-29; M.D., Yale, 1932; D.Sc., Med. Coll. Pa., 1965; m. Hans Alexander Klagsbrunn, Jan. 27, 1934. Intern, asst. resident New Haven Hosp., 1932-34; asst. pathology Yale, 1933-34; asso. pathology George Washington U., 1934-41, professorial lectr., 1941-55; asst. chief Office Med. Information, NRC, 1942-45; guest investigator dept. embryology Carnegie Inst., Washington, 1934-51, research asso. and pathologist, 1951-63, staff mem. placentalogy, pathology, 1963-71; Mamie A. Jessup vis. prof. obstetrics and gynecology U. Va. Sch. Medicine, 1972—, Bartholomew Mosse Meml. lectr. Rotunda Hosp., Dublin, Ireland, 1970. Bd. dirs. Nat. Symphony Orch., 1949—, 2d v.p., 1952-55, mem. exec. com., 1955-64, 67-68, 73—, chmn., 1955-61. Recipient Alumna of Year citation Bishop's Sch., 1960, Lewis prize Am. Philos. Soc., 1970, diplome d'Honneur, Federation Internationale de Gynecologie Infantile et Juvenile, 1972. Hon. fellow Chgo. Gynec. Soc. Mem. Audubon Naturalist Soc. Central Atlantic States (dir. 1961-64), Am. Assn. Anatomists (exec. com. 1963-66), Am. Coll. Obstetricians and Gynecologists (hon. asso.), Soc. Gynecologic Investigation (hon.), A.A.A.S., Phi Beta Kappa, Sigma Xi. Episcopalian. Club: City Tavern. Contbr. to profl. jours. Home: 3420 Que St NW Washington DC 20007 also Salem Farm Box 157 Route 1 Purcellville VA 22132 Office: Dept Obstetrics and Gynecology U Va Med Sch Charlottesville VA 22901

KLAPPMEIER, MARION MARIE, state ofcl.; b. Amsterdam, N.Y., Mar. 22, 1920; d. John H. and Alvine C. (Gerdom) Klappmeier; B.S., Russell Sage Coll., 1941; M.A., Columbia, 1952. Operating room supr. Albany (N.Y.) Hosp., 1941-47; operating room supr., instr. Am. U., Beirut, Lebanon, 1947-49; operating room nurse U. Va., 1950; asst. dir. nurses Waltham (Mass.) Hosp., 1950-51; Ohio Valley Gen. Hosp., Wheeling, W.Va., 1952-54; asso. exec. dir. N.Y. State Nurses Assn., Albany, 1954-63, exec. dir., 1963-69; exec. dir. Me. Bd. Nursing, Augusta, 1970—; pres. Am. Jour. Nursing Co., N.Y.C., 1958-72. Corporator Med. Care Devel., Inc. of Me., 1970—; mem. med. adv. com. Me. Dept. Health and Welfare, 1970-73. Mem. Am. Nurses Assn. (dir. 1964-72). Home: 52 S Chestnut St Augusta ME 04330 Office: 295 Water St Augusta ME 04330

KLAURENS, MARY KATHRYN, educator; b. Lincoln, Neb., Sept. 22, 1924; d. Roy L. and Ermal F. (Graff) Klaurens; B.S., U. Minn., 1959, M.A., 1965, Ph.D., 1967. Bookkeeper, Independent Gasoline Co., Mpls., 1946-52; mgmt. trainee Dayton's, dept. store, 1952-58; tchr. distributive edn. Tucson Pub. Schs., 1959-62, Mpls. Pub. Schs., 1962-64; mem. faculty U. Minn., 1964—, asso. prof. distributive tchr. edn., 1970-74, prof., 1974—. Chmn. Nat. Distributive Edn. Profl. Devel. Awards Com., 1971—. Recipient service awards Distributive Edn. Clubs Am., 1970-72, 74. Mem. Nat., Minn. edn. assns., Am., Minn. vocational assns., Nat. Council Distributive Tchr. Edn. (pres. 1974—). Author: (with Warren G. Meyer) Guide for Cooperative Vocational Education, 1969, Economics of Marketing, 1970. Cons. editor: Charles E. Merrill Pub. Co., 1970—. Contbr. articles to profl. jours. Home: 4948 Fremont Av S Minneapolis MN 55409

KLAUSMEIER, MARGUERITE SUE, pub. relations ofcl.; b. Indpls., Aug. 5, 1950; d. Donald Ray and Margaret (Mendenhall) Lash; B.A., Purdue U., 1972; m. Michael Douglas Klausmeier, June 18, 1972. Traffic sec. WRTV, Indpls., 1969-71; traffic sec. WIFE-AM, Indpls., 1972; media asst. Republican State Central Com., Indpls., 1972, press relations for Ind., 1972—; producer-dir. WFYI Pub. TV Sta., Indpls., 1972-74, announcer, camera opr., traffic-continuity dir., 1972-74; tng. supr. Community Services Program City of Indpls., 1973, dir.-producer Tourism show for Dept. Commerce; pub. relations dir. Marion County Rep. Central Com., Indpls., 1974—. Named Hon. Lt. Gov. State of Ind., 1973. Mem. Ind. Speech Assn., Gold Peppers, Purdue U. Alumnae, Zeta Tau Alpha. Office: 144 N Delaware St Indianapolis IN 46202

KLAW, BARBARA VAN DOREN (MRS. SPENCER KLAW), author, editor; b. N.Y.C., Sept. 17, 1920; d. Carl and Irita (Bradford) Van Doren; B.A., Vassar Coll., 1941; m. Spencer Klaw, July 5, 1941; children—Joanna (Mrs. Robert Schultz), Susan, Rebecca, Margaret. Writer-researcher OWI, Washington, 1942-43; reporter N.Y. Post, 1943-45; free lance editor, writer, 1945-63; editor Am. Heritage and Horizon mags., 1963—. Author: One Summer, 1936; One Winter, 1938; A Pony Named Nubbin, 1939; Joan and Michael, 1941 (all under pseudonym Martin Gale); (under pseudonym Eleanor Benton) The Complete Book of Etiquette, 1956; Camp Follower, 1944. Editor folklore anthology, 1960. Home: 24 Charlton St New York City NY 10014 Office: 1221 Av of Americas New York City NY 10020

KLEBANOW, SHEILA, psychiatrist; b. N.Y.C., Feb. 17, 1932; d. Irving and Ruth (Neufeld) Klebanow; B.A., Bklyn. Coll., 1953; M.A., Radcliffe Coll., 1954; M.D., N.Y. U., 1960 1 son, David. Intern Maimonides Hosp., Bklyn., 1960-61; resident Bellevue Hosp., N.Y.C.; 1961-64; practice of psychiatry, N.Y.C., 1964—; psychoanalytic tng. N.Y. Med. Coll., N.Y.C., 1964-69, clin. asst. prof. psychiatry, 1972—; asst. in psychiatry Mt. Sinai Sch. Medicine, N.Y.C., 1966-68, asso. in psychiatry, 1968-72; dir. adolescent psychiat. clinic Mt. Sinai Hosp., N.Y.C., 1968-72. Dir. 175 E. 74th St. Corp., N.Y.C. Co-recipient William V. Silverberg award in psychoanalysis N.Y. Med. Coll., 1967. Mem. Am. Acad. Psychoanalysis, Soc. Med. Psychoanalysts, Am. Psychiat. Assn., Phi Beta Kappa. Address: 175 E 74th St New York City NY 10021

KLEE, LUCILLE HOLLJES (MRS. JAMES BUTT KLEE), educator; b. Balt., Dec. 8, 1924; s. Henry Diedrich and Elizabeth Carin (Kennedy) Holljes; B.A., Bryn Mawr Coll., 1946, M.A., 1947, Ph.D., 1951; m. James Butt Klee, Sept. 20, 1959; children—Margaret Ann, Kathren Elizabeth. Chemist, Sloan-Kettering Found., N.Y.C., 1946; instr. chemistry Barnard Coll., Columbia U., N.Y.C., 1950-54, class adviser, 1954-56; research chemist Toni Co. div. Gillette Co., Chgo., 1956-57; asso. prof. chemistry Lowell (Mass.) State Coll., 1967-71; asso. prof. sci. edn. and environmental studies W. Ga. Coll., Carrollton, 1971—. Faculty mem. Sarah Lawrence Coll., Bronxville, N.Y., 1950-52; sci. supr. Douglas County Bd. Edn., Douglasville, Ga., 1969-70; dir. Merrimac Valley Elementary Sci. Project, Lowell, Mass., 1970-71; cons. Dracut (Mass.) Sch. System, 1971, Carroll County Early Childhood Devel. Center, 1974—. Active Carrollton P.T.A. Mem. Am. Chem. Soc., A.A.A.S., Nat. Sci. Tchrs. Assn., World Future Soc., Am. Inst. Chemists, D.A.R., League Women Voters, Ga. Conservancy, Ga. Mental Health Assn., Sigma Xi. Author: Laboratory Text in General Chemistry, 1957, rev. edit., 1959. Editor Merrimac Valley Elementary Sci. Newsletter, 1970-71. Home: 24 Forest Dr Carrollton GA 30117

KLEIN, ALICE MCGINNIS, assn. exec.; b. Ashland, Ky., Sept. 8, 1923; d. David Franklin and Anna Francis (Scott) McGinnis; bus. degree Ashland Sch. Bus., 1942; student Western Res. U., 1944-45, U. W.Va., 1945-46; m. Thomas W. Klein, Aug. 8, 1958 (div. July 1966); children—David, Stephen, Stephanie. Supr. Bur. Supplies and Accounts, U.S. Dept. Navy, Washington, 1942-45; buyer Sterling Faucet Co., Morgantown, W.Va., 1945-46; purchasing agt. E.I. duPont de Nemours & Co., Inc., Louisville, 1946-58; with Louisville Area C. of C., 1965—, mgr. econ. research dept., 1971—. Mem. Am. C. of C. Researchers Assn. (editor newsletter 1973—). Republican. Mem. Christian Ch. Contbr. articles to various publs. Home: 148 N Bayly St Louisville KY 40206 Office: 300 W Liberty St Louisville KY 40202

KLEIN, ANN ROSENSWEIG (MRS. ROBERT LAWRENCE KLEIN), state ofcl.; b. N.Y.C., July 23, 1923; d. Mack and Hilda (Barnett) Rosensweig; B.A., Barnard Coll., 1944; M.S., Columbia, 1945; m. Robert Lawrence Klein, Sept. 11, 1943; children—Mara Jayne (Mrs. Jeffery Miller), David Lawrence. Social case worker Worcester (Mass.) Child Guidance Clinic, 1945-47, Morris County Family Service, Morristown, N.J., 1957-59; pres. League Women Voters N.J., Montclair, 1967-71, bd. dirs., 1964-67; mem. N.J. Assembly, 1972-74; commr. Dept. Instns. and Agys., State of N.J., 1974—. Mem. N.J. State Tax Policy Com., 1970-73. Mem. Am. Assn. Social Workers. Home: 9 Woodlawn Dr Morristown NJ 07960 Office: 135 W Hanover St Trenton NJ 08625

KLEIN, EDITH IOLAMAY MILLER (MRS. SANDOR S. KLEIN), lawyer, state senator; b. Wallace, Ida., Aug. 4, 1915; d. Fred L. B. and Edith (Gallup) Miller; J.D., George Washington U., 1946, LL.M., 1954; B.S., U. Ida., 1935; grad. fellowship Washington State U., 1936; m. Sandor S. Klein, July 11, 1949 (dec. June 1970). Admitted to D.C. bar, 1946, Ida. bar, 1947, N.Y. bar, 1955, U.S. Supreme Ct. bar, 1954; partner Langroise, Sullivan & Smylie, Boise, Ida., 1957—; mem. Ida. Legislature, 1949-50, 65-68; mem. Ida. Senate, 1968—; judge Municipal Court, Boise, 1947-49; gen. practice law, Boise, 1946—; atty. FHA, N.Y.C., 1955-56, FCC, Washington, 1953-54, personnel specialist War Dept., 1943-46; dir. Sun Valley Music Camp, Inc., Boise and Sun Valley, Legislative mem. Ida. Law Enforcement Planning Commn.; mem. Gov.'s Adv. Council Comprehensive Health Planning; mem. Ida. Gov's commn. on women's programs, 1965—, chmn. 1965-71. Former pres. Ada County Republican Women's Club. Named Woman of Year Boise Altrusa Club, 1966, Greater Boise C. of C., 1970. Mem. Am., Fed., Ida., Inter-am. bar assns., Am. Judicature Soc., Am. Assn. U. Women, D.A.R., League Women Voters, Ida. State Conf. on Social Work (past pres.), Boise Altrusa (past pres.), Boise Toastmistress Club (past pres.), Ida. Mental Health Assn., Boise Art Assn., Boise Bus. and Profl. Women's Club, Kappa Beta Pi. Republican. Conglist. Home: 1732 Warm Springs Av Boise ID 83702 Office: Simplot Bldg 805 Idaho St Boise ID 83701

KLEIN, ELEANOR HASDAY, lawyer; b. Phila., June 13, 1927; d. Marco and Molly (Goodman) Hasday; B.S., Temple U., 1948; J.D., Rutgers U., 1966; m. Arthur S. Klein, Sept. 19, 1948; children—Jonathan E., Kenneth D., Sydria B. Admitted to N.J. bar, 1966; with firm Plone, Tomar, Parks & Seliger, Camden, 1966-68; individual practice law, Cherry Hill, 1968-73; mem. firm Forkin, Klein & Segal, matrimonial trial lawyers, Cherry Hill, 1973—; legal cons. Jewish Family Service. Fellow Am. Acad. Trial Lawyers; mem. Am., N.J., Camden County bar assns., Am. Arbitration Assn. (arbitrator), Rutgers U. Law Sch. Alumni Assn. (corr. sec. 1969-70, chancellor 1974; served award 1974), Camden County Mental Health Assn. Editor Rutgers U. Law Jour., 1966. Office: Suite 621 One Cherry Hill Blvd Cherry Hill NJ 08034

KLEIN, ESTHER MOYERMAN (MRS. PHILIP KLEIN), publisher; b. Phila., Nov. 3, 1907; d. Louis and Rebecca (Feldman) Moyerman; B.S., Temple U., 1929; student U. London, 1954; m. Philip Klein, Apr. 26, 1930; children—Arthur, Karen Louise (Mrs. Paul Mannes). Reporter Phila. Jewish Times, 1925, Atlantic City Times, 1927; feature writer Pub. Ledger Syndicate, 1928-29, Pub.

Ledger, Evening Bull., Phila. Record, 1929-32; pub. relations counsellor, editor Art Alliance Bull. 1945-49; commentator radio sta. WPEN, 1949-53; pub. Phila. Jewish Times, 1953—; lectr. Women's Clubs, 1951—. Del. Internat. Conf. of Residential Adult Edn., Holland, 1957, Germany, 1959; participant in first workshop of Residential Adult Edn. for Adult Edn. Assn. of U.S., 1954. Mem. Govs. Commn. on Charitable Orgns., 1969—; chmn. Rittenhouse Sq. Women's com. for Phila. Orch., 1957. Bd. dirs. Rittenhouse Found., Phila. Jewish Times Inst., also dir. ann. cooking festivals; exec. com. Long Beach Island Found. Arts and Scis., N.J. Named Distinguished Dau. Pa. Mem. Pa. Newspaper Pubs. Assn., Temple U. Alumni (honored at 80th anniversary, 1964), Phila. High Sch. for Girls Alumnae, Hannah Penn House, Emergency Aid of Pa., Chgo. Art Mus., Mus. Modern Art N.Y., Pan Am. Assn. Club: Print. Author: A Guidebook to Jewish Philadelphia, 1965; International House Celebrity Cookbook, 1965; History and Guidebook of Fairmount Park, 1974. Home: 1250 Spruce St Philadelphia PA 19102

KLEIN, FANNIE J. LICHTBLAU (MRS. SOL TUNICK), educator, lawyer; b. N.Y.C., Oct. 9, 1906; d. Elias and Anna (Knath) Lichtblau; LL.B., N.Y. U., 1928, LL.M., 1951; m. Albert J. Klein, June 14, 1929 (dec. 1955); children—Woody, Esther (Mrs. Malcolm R. Willson); m. 2d, Sol Tunick, Oct. 30, 1963. Admitted to N.Y. bar, 1928; asst. to George E. Ferris, trial counsel Ferris, Shepard, Joyce & McCoy, N.Y.C., 1929-32; pvt. practice law, N.Y.C., 1932-42; reference librarian, research coordinator N.Y. U. Sch. Law, N.Y.C., 1942-52, research coordinator, librarian Inst. Jud. Adminstrn., 1952-60, asst. dir., librarian, 1960-67, asso. dir., sec., 1967—, prof. law, 1965—. Cons. automobile ins. and compensation study, 1970-72; cons. on cts. to nat. criminal justice ref. service, 1971-72; cons. to criminal justice glossary project Auerbach, Phila., 1971—. Bd. dirs. Com. for Modern Cts., N.Y.C. Recipient Distinguished Achievement award Republican Women in Industry and Professions, 1967; Florence E. Allen award N.Y. U. Sch. of Law and N.Y. Women's Bar Assn., 1973; Grad. Achievement award for excellence in legal edn., N.Y. U., 1974. Mem. N.Y. Women's (pres. 1966-67), Am. (mem. com. 1960—) bar assns., Assn. Bar City N.Y. (mem. com. 1960—), N.Y. County Lawyers Assn. (mem. com. 1966-70), Fed. Bar Council (mem. com. 1966—), Am. Fgn. Law Assn., Am. Assn. U. Profs., Fed. Bar Council, Am. Assn. Law Librarians. Author: Judicial Administration and the Legal Profession Annotated Bibliography, 1963. Editor: (with Joel S. Lee) Arthur T. Vanderbilt, Selected Writings, 2 vols., 1965-67. Home: 3 Washington Square Village New York City NY 10012 Office: 40 Washington Sq S New York City NY 10012

KLEIN, FRANCES ANN WANG (MRS. ELVIN B. KLEIN), toy co. exec.; b. Bklyn., June 18, 1923; d. Philip and Sarah (Eckstein) Wang; B.S. with high honors, U. Ill., 1945; m. Elvin B. Klein, June 23, 1943; children—Michael, Bari (Mrs. Floyd Freiden), Philip. Pre-sch. tchr. Kansas City (Mo.) Co-op. Pre-Sch., 1952-59; co-founder U.S. Toy Co., Inc., Kansas City, Mo., 1952, exec. v.p., 1952—, founder Constructive Playthings div., 1954. Guest lectr. at tchr.-tng. instns., 1959—; mem. adv. council, spl. edn. dept. Shawnee-Mission Sch. Dist., 1972. Mem. Mo. (state sec. 1967-68), Kansas City (v.p. 1956-57) assns. for edn. young children, Johnson County Assn. for Children with Learning Disabilities (v.p. 1970-71), Council Jewish Women, Phi Sigma Sigma. Jewish religion. Hadassah. Club: Altrusa (Kansas City, Mo.). Home: 8301 Briar Lane Prairie Village KS 66207 Office: 1040 E 85th St Kansas City MO 64131

KLEIN, FREDA VINIKOW (MRS. JERRY J. KLEIN), state ofcl.; b. Seattle, May 17, 1920; d. Joseph and Julia (Caplan) Vinikow; B.A., U. Wash., 1942; M.S., U. Nev., 1969, postgrad., 1970—; m. Jerry J. Klein, Oct. 20, 1946; children—Jan Susan, Kerry Joseph, Robin Jo. With Parisian Candy Co., 1936-41, Asso. Shipbuilders, 1941-46; owner, mgr. retail bus., Provo, Utah, 1958-63, Las Vegas, Nev., 1963-66; counseling supr. State of Nev. Employment Security Dept., Las Vegas, 1966—. Mem. Clark County Council Social Agys.; mem. exec. com. Interagy. Council Alcoholism. Mem. Am., Nev. (treas. 1972) personnel and guidance assns., Nat. Vocational Guidance Assn., Nat. Employment Counselors Assn., Internat. Assn. Personnel in Employment Service, Am. Assn. U. Women, Phi Kappa Phi. Home: 2830 Phoenix St Las Vegas NV 89121 Office: 135 S 8th St Las Vegas NV 89101

KLEIN, JENNY WITKOWSKI (MRS. WILLIAM H. KLEIN), govt. ofcl.; b. Braunschweig, Germany, Dec. 14, 1921; d. Meir and Esther A. (Grajewski) Witkowski; came to U.S., 1938, naturalized, 1942; B.A., Boston U., 1945; M.Ed., U. Md., 1956, Ed.D. (fellow), 1969; m. William H. Klein, Dec. 26, 1942; children—Richard, David. Kindergarten and nursery sch. tchr., Greenbelt, Md., 1953-58; Md. dir. Marc Nursery Schs. for Retarded Children, Bethesda, 1958-68; supr. spl. edn. Montgomery County Schs., Rockville, Md., 1968-69; dir. ednl. services Office of Child Devel., Dept. Health, Edn. and Welfare, Washington, 1969—. Instr. U. Md., 1963-67; cons. Md. State Health Dept., 1964-67, Project Head Start, 1965-68, Coop. Nursery Schs., 1967-68. Pres. Greenbelt (Md.) P.T.A., 1956-57. Mem. Nat. Assn. for Edn. Young Children, Soc. Research in Child Devel. Contbr. articles to profl. jours. Home: 7921 Maryknoal Av Bethesda MD 20034 Office: Office of Child Development Box 1182 Washington DC 20013

KLEIN, JOAN DEMPSEY, judge; b., 1927; LL.B., U. Cal. Admitted to Cal. bar, 1955; now judge Municipal Ct., Los Angeles. Address: County Courthouse Los Angeles CA 90012*

KLEIN, LORRAINE ROSLYN, psychologist; b. N.Y.C., Sept. 2, 1939; d. Nathan and Sarah (Seidman) Gittler; B.A., Bklyn. Coll., 1961, postgrad., 1961-63; M.S., Coll. City N.Y., 1967; m. Leonard B. Klein, Apr. 6, 1963; 1 dau., Melanie Avi. Caseworker, Bur. of Child Welfare, N.Y.C., 1961-67, supr., 1967; psychologist Narcotics Addiction Control Commn., N.Y.C., 1967-73; pvt. practice psychotherapist, N.Y.C., 1971—. Mem.-in-tng. Nat. Psychol. Assn. for Psychoanalysis, 1970—. Mem. Nat. Health Fedn., Am. Orthopsychiat. Assn., N.Y. Soc. Clin. Psychologists, Joint Council for Mental Health Services, Inst. for Study Drug Addiction, Civil Liberties Union, Common Cause. Home: 172-42 133rd Av 12A Jamaica NY 11434 Office: 172-42 133d Av 12A Jamaica NY 11434

KLEIN, SISTER M. ROSALIE, ednl. adminstr.; b. Milw.; B.S. in Nursing, Marquette U., 1952, M.S. in Nursing, 1960; M. in Med. Sci., Tulane U., 1968, D.Sc., 1970. Nursing supr. St. Francis Hosp., Cape Girardeau, Mo., 1952-54; nursing supr. St. Michael Hosp., Milw., 1954-56, dir. nursing service, 1956-59; instr. Marquette U. Milw., 1959-62, asst. prof. 1962-67, coordinator, basic program in nursing, 1965-67, dean Coll. Nursing, 1970—. Mem. Wis., Milw., Nat. leagues for nursing, Am. Assn. Colls. Nursing, Milw. Deans of Nursing (coordinating councils), Assn. Allied Health, Southeastern Med. Center, Milw. Urban Observatory, Am. Nurses Assn. Home: 5000 W Chambers Milwaukee WI 53210 Office: Marquette U 3029 N 49th St Milwaukee WI 53210

KLEIN, SHIRLEY SNYDERMAN (MRS. RALPH LINCOLN KLEIN), partner retail store; b. Balt., Oct. 23, 1929; d. Julius Herman and Fannie (Dannenberg) Snyderman; B.A., Towson State Tchrs. Coll., 1951; m. Ralph Lincoln Klein, Jan. 4, 1953; children—Andrew P., Michael J., Howard S. Mem. office staff accounts receivable, jr. treas. Maurice Klein & Son, retail store, Forest Hill, Md., 1952-60, jr. buyer, 1960-70, partner, buyer Children's ladies, linens depts., 1970—; treas. Mortgage Service Co., Inc., 1956-64. Pres., Hadassah, Harford County, 1966-68; v.p. adv. bd. John Carroll Sch., Md. Diocese, 1967, bd. mem., 1971; chmn. Retinitis Peimentosa Found., Harford County, Md., 1971. Mem. League Women Votors (chpt. bd. dirs. 1968), Harford Artist Assn. Jewish religion. Home: 109 W Jarrettsville Rd Forest Hill MD 21050 Office: 2331 Rockspring Rd Forest Hill MD 21050

KLEINAU, MARION LORENE DAVIS (MRS. MARVIN D. KLEINAU), educator; b. Independence, Mo., Jan. 6, 1926; d. Lyle H. and Ruth E. (Jones) Davis; student Graceland Coll., 1946-48; B.A., Central Mo. Coll.; 1952; M.A., La. State U., 1956; Ph.D., U. Wis., 1959; m. Marvin D. Kleinau, Mar. 18, 1962. Mem. faculty dept. speech So. Ill. U., Carbondale, 1959—, prof., 1969—, dir. oral interpretation, 1959—, founder, dir. Calipre Stage, 1965—. Interpretation textbook cons. Prentice-Hall Co., 1968—. Nat. Endowment Humanities grantee, 1973-74. Mem. Speech Communication Assn., Ill. Speech and Theatre Assn., Central States Speech Assn., Nat. Interpretation Interest Assn. (editor jour. 1969). Contbr. articles to profl. jours. Home: Rural Route 1 Murphysboro IL 62966 Office: Dept of Speech Southern Ill University Carbondale IL 62901

KLEINDIENST, LINDA ELISE, journalist; b. Bklyn., Aug. 24, 1948; d. Harold Frederick and Frida (Palmer) Kleindienst; B.A., U. Miami, 1971. Staff writer Beach Sun, Miami Beach, Fla., 1971; staff writer Sun-Sentinel, Fort Lauderdale, Fla., 1971—. Recipient Broward County Community Relations Commn. Human Relations award, 1973. Mem. Women in Communications, Fla. Press Club, Sigma Delta Chi, Sigma Kappa. Home: 3240 Mary St Coconut Grove FL 33133 Office: 101 N New River Dr E Fort Lauderdale FL 33302

KLEINMAN, SUE (MRS. SAMUEL J. KLEINMAN), artist; b. N.Y.C., Nov. 12; d. Adolph and Sabina (Teitlebaum) Augustine; B.F.A., Pratt Inst. 1933; postgrad. Caton Rose Inst. Fine Arts, 1956, New Sch. Social Research, 1960; m. Samuel J. Kleinman, Aug. 17, 1940. Exhibited oils Crown Gallery, N.Y.C., 1962, Center Art Gallery, N.Y.C., 1969-72, Lord & Taylor Gallery, N.Y.C., 1973; represented in permanent collections at Fairleigh Dickinson Coll., Rutherford, N.J., Maimonides Hosp., Bklyn., Brown U., Providence; guide docent program Broward Art Guild, 1974. Pres., Bklyn. Hebrew Home and Hosp. for Aged, 1963-65; mem. nat. planning com. Nat. Multiple Sclorosis Soc., 1971-74; mem. women's com. Brandeis U., 1974—. Bd. dirs. Am. Cancer Soc., Met. Geriatric Center; bd. dirs. United Jewish Appeal, chmn. Queens div. 1960-63. Mem. Artists Equity, Kew Forest Art League (chmn. 1950-55), Nat. Council Jewish Women (chmn. 1950-56). Address: 405 N Ocean Blvd Pompano Beach FL 33062

KLEMA, VIRGINIA CARLOCK (MRS. ERNEST D. KLEMA), mathematician; b. Atlanta, Mar. 13, 1929; d. John A. and Mamie C. (Bugg) Carlock; A.B., LaGrange Coll., 1949; M.S., Auburn U., 1951; m. Ernest D. Klema, May 23, 1953; children—Donald David, Catherine Marion. Asst. mathematician Oak Ridge Nat. Lab., 1951, jr. mathematician, 1952-54, asso. mathematician, 1955-56; instr. math. Kendall Coll., Evanston, Ill., 1960, chmn. sci. div., 1961; lectr. math. Northwestern U., Evanston, 1962-68; research asso. Argonne (Ill.) Nat. Lab., 1967-69, cons., 1969—; research asso. Computer Research Center, Nat. Bur. Econ. Research, Cambridge, Mass., 1972—. Mem. Math. Assn. Am., Am. Math. Soc., Soc. Indsl. and Applied Math., Assn. for Computing Machinery, A.A.A.S., Am. Assn. U. Profs., Pi Mu Epsilon. Contbr. articles to profl. jours. Home: 53 Adams St Medford MA 02155 Office: NBER Computer Research Center 575 Technology Sq Cambridge MA 02139

KLEMESRUD, JUDY LEE, journalist; b. Forest City, Ia., June 11, 1939; d. Theordore S. and Glee C. (Florence) Klemesrud; B.A., U. Ia., 1961; M.S. in Journalism, Columbia, 1962. Gen. assignment reporter Chgo. Daily News, 1962-66; reporter, writer family style dept. N.Y. Times, N.Y.C., 1966—; contbg. editor Women Sports mag. Recipient Newspaperwoman's award best lifestyle feature, 1968, N.Y. Newspaper Guild award, 1973, numerous others. Mem. Am. Newspaper Guild (shop steward), Mortar Board, Zeta Tau Alpha. Democrat. Methodist. Contbr. numerous articles to mags. Home: 340 E 57th St New York City NY 10022 Office: 229 W 43d St New York City NY 10036

KLEPAK, RALLA DOLORES, lawyer; b. Chgo., Dec. 20, 1936; d. John J. and Dolores B. (Blumenthal) Klepak; B.S., Northwestern U., 1957, M.S., 1959; J.D., John Marshall Law Sch., 1964. Tchr. Chgo. Bd. Edn., 1957-64. Cons. lang. arts and reading skills, 1959-64; admitted to Ill. bar, 1964, since practiced in Chgo. Legal adviser Chgo. High Sch. Asst. Prins. Assn., 1973. Bd. dirs. Henry Horner Chgo. Boys Club, 1973, Lower North Mental Health Center Adv. Bd., 1973. Mem. Am., Ill., Chgo. bar assns., Women's Bar Assn. Ill. (dir. 1970-71). Cons., contbr. to encyclopedic dictionary. Office: 179 W Washington St Suite 520 Chicago IL 60602

KLEPP, AMELIA LOIS, ret. univ. dean; b. Elizabeth, N.J., Aug. 27, 1911; d. John Charles and Amelia (Klem) Fischer; B.A., Coll. St. Elizabeth, 1946; M.S., N.Y.U., 1948, M.B.A., 1960; m. Henry P. Klepp, June 12, 1938 (dec.). Dir. tng. Hahne & Co., Newark, 1934-43; mem. faculty N.Y.U., 1948-57, Coll. St. Elizabeth, 1960; dean of women Seton Hall U., 1960-73. Fellow Case Inst. Tech., 1960, N.Y.U., 1948-60. Mem. Nat. Assn. U. Women, Nat. Assn. Women Deans and Counselors, Newark Mus. Author articles, tng. manuals. Home: 60 Fairmount Av Morristown NJ 07960

KLEPPINGER, DOROTHEA BITTNER (MRS. RICHARD KUTZ KLEPPINGER), physician; b. Kutztown, Pa., Apr. 30, 1923; d. Jacob Webster and Carrie Amelia (Rauch) Bittner; B.S., Bucknell U., 1944; M.D., Hahnemann Med. Coll., 1948; m. Richard Kutz Kleppinger, Mar. 30, 1946; children—Trygve, Kimberly. Intern, Reading (Pa.) Hosp., 1948-49; gen. practice medicine, Kutztown, 1950-58; mem. staff Reading Hosp.; Planned Parenthood clinician, Reading, 1950—; lectr.; dir. health edn. center, Reading Hosp., 1964-72; health edn. coordinator Gov. Mifflin Sch. Dist., 1966—. Mem. Sch. Bd., Reading, 1962-66. Trustee Muhlenberg Coll., Lutheran Home of Topton. Mem. Physicians of Planned Parenthood World Fedn. (charter), A.M.A., Bucknell U. Gen. Alumni Assn. (bd. dirs. 1968-73, pres. 1972-73). Republican. Lutheran. Club: Bucknell Alumni (pres. 1966-74) (Reading). Address: 1300 Lancaster Pike West Reading PA 19607

KLIEBHAN, SISTER JOANNE MARIE, educator; b. Milw.; d. Alfred S. and Mary Eileen (McNamara) Kliebhan; student Cardinal Stritch Coll., 1947-52, Marquette U., 1951; B.S. magna cum laude, Loyola U., Chgo., 1954; M.A., Columbia, 1957; Ph.D., U. Ill., 1966. Spl. edn. tchr. of mentally handicapped Lt. J. P. Kennedy, Jr. Sch. for Exceptional Children, Palos Park, Ill., 1949-63, supervising tchr., 1952-63; instr. Cardinal Stritch Coll., Milw., part-time 1958-66, instr. grad. div., spl. edn. dept., 1966-68, asso. prof., supr. spl. edn., 1968—, chmn. spl. edn. dept., 1970—; dir. St. Francis Children's Activity and Achievement Center, 1969—. Cons. learning disabilities projects, St. Louis, Harrisburg, Pa., Pocatello, Ida., Balboa Heights, C.Z.; dir. St. Francis Children's Activity and Achievement Center. Mem. Am. Assn. Mental Deficiency, Council Exceptional Children, Nat. Cath. Edn. Assn., Assn. for Edn. Young Children, Assn. for Children with Learning Disabilities, Am. Psychol. Assn., Nat. Rehab. Assn., Pi Lambda Theta, Kappa Delta Pi. Address: 6801 N Yates Rd Milwaukee WI 53217

KLIEGMAN, PAULA GOLDEN, psychiat. social worker; b. Chgo., Mar. 23, 1937; d. Herman H. and Ethel (Kamfner) Golden; B.A., Northwestern U., 1958; A.M., U. Chgo., 1960; Child Therapy Tng. certificate Chgo. Inst. for Psychoanalysis, 1973. Med. social worker LaRabida Sanitarium, Chgo., 1960-66; child psychiatry intake supr., dept. psychiatry Michael Reese Hosp., Chgo., 1966—; pvt. practice as psychiat. social worker, Chgo., 1971—. Field work instr. U. Chgo., 1964-66, 72. Mem. Nat. Assn. Social Workers, Am. Orthopsychiat. Assn., Assn. Child Psychotherapists. Home: 1607 E 50th Pl Chicago IL 60615

KLINCKMANN, EVELYN MARIE, coll. dean; b. Oak Park, Ill., Mar. 18, 1926; d. Arthur and Alice Marie (Clauss) Klinckmann; B.S., U. Wis., 1946, M.S., 1950; Ph.D., U. Chgo., 1975. Teaching asst. U. Wis., Madison, 1948-50; research asst. Northwestern U. Med. Sch., 1950-51; claims adjuster Washington Nat. Life Ins. Co., 1951; instr. U. Wyo., 1951-54; asst. prof. physiology George Williams Coll., Chgo., 1954-57; research asst. U. Chgo. Family Study Center, 1957; substitute tchr. Chgo. pub. schs., 1958; lectr. U. Chgo., 1958-59; asst. prof. Loyola U., Chgo., 1958-60; mem. faculty Lone Mountain Coll., San Francisco, 1960—, asso. prof. philosophy and edn., 1972—, dean grad. and spl. programs, 1973-74, provost, 1974—; cons. in field. Initiator, mem. planning bd. coll.-community projects Arts and Culture of Black Americans, 1968-70; organizer, participant San Francisco-Mill Valley Workshop, 1970; mem. steering com., bd. dirs. Biol. Scis. Curriculum Study, 1968—, mem. exec. com., 1968—. Recipient Civic Service award Sta. KABL, San Francisco, 1968. Scholar U. Chgo., 1953, fellow, 1958-60. Mem. Am. Civil Liberties Union, Sierra Club, Center Study Democratic Instns., Nat. Soc. Study Edn. Contbg. editor Biology Tchrs. Handbook, 1970; others. Contbr. articles to pubfs. Home: 382 Monte Vista Mill Valley CA 94941 Office: 2800 Turk Blvd San Francisco CA 94118

KLINE, ALMA, sculptor; b. Nyack, N.Y.; d. Charles D. and Charita (Hall) Kline; A.B., Radcliffe Coll., 1929; student sculpture with Jose De Creeft, 1939-41. Exhibited one man shows Creative Gallery, 1952, Burr Gallery, 1963, Thomson Gallery, 1969 (all N.Y.C.); exhibited one-man shows museums throughout U.S., 1964-65; exhibited group shows U.S., 1947—, England, 1955—, Argentina also Mexico, 1963—; represented in permanent collections, including Cronkhite Grad. Center, Cambridge, Mass.; Norfolk Museum of Arts and Sci., Va.; St. Lawrence U. Recipient Graumbacher award, 1960; Knickerbocker Artists medal honor, 1964; Nat. Arts Club award, 1969; Patrons of Art award, Painters & Sculptors of N.J., 1969. Mem. Audubon Artists Inc., Nat. Assn. Women Artists, Soc. Animal Artists, Knickerbocker Artists, Silvermine Guild Artists. Club: Harvard Club of N.Y.C. Home: 225 E 74th St New York City NY 10021 Office: 225 E 74th St New York City NY 10021

KLINE, CECELIA ARMINDIA TILLEY (MRS. DOIL FRANKLIN KLINE), pub. relations, advt. agy. exec.; b. Columbus, O., Mar. 22; d. William Benjamin and Armindia Belle (Seel) Tilley; student Ohio State U., 1936, George Washington U., 1942-43, Ariz. State U., 1969—; A.A., Scottsdale Community Coll., 1974; m. Doil Franklin Kline, Nov. 12, 1944; 1 dau., Donna Cecelia. Dir. pub. relations, advt. Ebco Mfg., Columbus, 1947-50; pres. Cecelia Kline & Assos., Phoenix, 1960-67, Kline, Inc., Scottsdale, Ariz., 1967—. Tchr. Phoenix Coll., 1964-66; vis. lectr. U. Ariz., Tucson, 1966. Staff mem. Congressman John M. Vorys' Office, Washington, 1942-44; precinct committeeman, Phoenix, 1956-64, 72— mem. State Central Com. Ariz., 1956-58; bd. dirs. Ariz. Fedn. Rep. Women, 1971—; corr. sec. Central Rep. Women's Club, 1972-74. Chmn. Scottsdale Art Collection Com., 1968-71; chmn. Ariz. Poetry Day, 1973-74; mem. adv. com. Scottsdale Bapt. Hosp., 1970. Recipient numerous awards in advt. and pub. relations, Las Guias award Heard Mus. Anthropology, 1970. Mem. English Speaking Union (dir. 1972-74), Phoenix Press Club, Nat. Fedn. Press Women, Ariz. Press Women, Theta Sigma Phi, Phi Theta Kappa. Club: Soroptimist (pres. 1968) (Scottsdale). Feature writer, columnist Women's Pages Phoenix Gazette, 1956-58; Editor Ohio Jersey News, 1948-50, Timberline, Paper Clips, Mill Whistle and Timber Topics, 1960-61. Home: 4515 E Cheery Lynn Rd Phoenix AZ 85018 Office: Kline Inc PO Box 15012 Phoenix AZ 85060

KLINE, HARRIET (MRS. EUGENE MONROE KLINE), artist; b. N.Y.C., Sept. 25, 1916; d. James H. and Beatrice (Kheel) Meyer; B.A., Hunter Coll., 1938; pvt. study of oil painting with Isaac Soyer, Robert Phillip, Morris Kantor, 1945-59; pvt. study Chinese watercolor Y.C. Wang; m. Eugene Monroe Kline, July 2, 1939; children—Robert Andrew, Thomas Russell. Pvt. tchr. oil painting, Scarsdale, N.Y., 1959-68; exhibited in one-woman shows at Selected Artists Gallery, N.Y.C., 1960, 66, 68, 73, Little Gallery of Hudson Park Br. N.Y. Pub. Library, 1962; exhibited in group shows at Art U.S.A., 1958, Silvermine Nat. Exhbn., 1959, Riverside Mus. and Nat. Acad., N.Y.C., 1959—, Okla. Printmakers Soc., 1960, 61, Butler Inst. Am. Art, 1974; also Nat. Assn. Women Artists Traveling Shows, Europe, 1965, U.S.A., 1969, Europe and Can., 1969, in traveling graphics show U.S.A., 1973; Old Bergen Art Guild Traveling Graphics Shows in U.S.A., 1973; represented in permanent collections N.Y. U., State U. Coll. at Oswego, N.Y., Western New Eng. Coll., Springfield, Mass., I.B.M., and numerous pvt. collectors. Recipient numerous awards. Mem. Nat. Assn. Women Artists, Silvermine Guild of Artists, Art Students League, Yonkers Art Assn., Mamaroneck Artists Guild, Artists Equity Assn. of N.Y. Home: 390 Heathcote Rd Scarsdale NY 10583

KLINE, IRENE TABITHA, biochemist, educator; b. Harmony, N.Y., Dec. 18, 1909; d. Floyd Edwin and Dora (York) Kline; A.B., Oberlin Coll., 1931; M.A., Duke, 1941; Ph.D., Western Res. U., 1950; postgrad. U. Wis., 1933, Baldwin-Wallace Coll., 1943. Tchr. pub. schs., Connellsville, Pa., 1931-42, Scarsdale, N.Y., 1942-43; research technician in endocrinology Cleve. Clinic, 1943-46; pre-doctoral fellow, post-doctoral fellow in biochemistry Western Res. U. (now Case Western Res. U.), 1946-51, instr. biochemistry dept. obstetrics and gynecology, 1951-54, asst. prof., 1954-55, now asst. prof. biochemistry and reproductive biology; former research asso. dept. obstetrics and gynecology Cleve. Met. Gen. Hosp.; research asst., instr. dept. physiology Yale, 1951; head endocrinology research lab. Henry Ford Hosp., Detroit, 1955-60, also research asso. Edsel Ford Inst. for Med. Research; asso. prof. anatomy U. Tex., 1960-63; prof. biology, chmn. dept. Tex. Woman's U., Denton, 1963-65, grad. research prof. biology dept., 1965-67; research dept. physiology U. Ill., Urbana, summer 1967. Cons. endocrinology Kaman Nuclear, Colorado Springs, 1960-61. Woods Lauer fellow, 1948-49, Sigma Delta Epsilon fellow, 1949-50. Fellow A.A.A.S.; mem. Endocrine Soc., Am. Chem. Soc., N.Y. Acad. Scis., Soc. Exptl. Biology and Medicine, Sigma Xi. Republican. Research dynamics of intermediary metabolism of steroid hormones and feed back control especially in primate brain. Home: 13800 Fairhill Rd Shaker Heights OH 44120 Office: Mac Donald House Univ Hosps Cleveland OH 44106

KLINE, JOYCE CLAIRE (MRS. FLAVIO PULETTI), physician, educator; b. Madison, Wis., July 26, 1929; d. William James and Leta (Shipley) Kline; B.S., U. Wis., 1951, M.D., 1954; m. Flavio Puletti, June 1, 1957. Intern, Michael Reese Hosp., Chgo., 1954-55; resident internal medicine St. Mary's Hosp., Madison, Wis., 1955-56; resident radiology Univ. Hosps., Madison, 1956-59, NIH fellow radiation therapy, 1962-63; practice medicine specializing in radiology, Madison, 1959-62; instr. radiology U. Wis. at Madison, 1963-64, asst. prof. radiology, 1964-70, asso. prof., 1971—. Diplomate Am. Bd. Radiology. Mem. Am. Coll. Radiology, A.M.A., Dane County Med. soc., Radiol. Soc. No. Am., Wis. Radiologic Soc., Am. Soc. Clin. Oncologists, Am. Soc. Therapeutic Radiologists, Soc. Nuclear Medicine, Am. Radium Soc., A.A.A.S., Am. Assn. U. Profs., Am. Women's Med. Assn., Alpha Epsilon Iota. Home: 4806 Waukesha St Madison WI 53705

KLINGELE, DOROTHY ANN, geneticist; b. Yakima, Wash., Dec. 6, 1925; d. Joseph Edward and Agnes Barbara (Chott) Klingele; student Coll. Great Falls, 1943-45; B.S. chemistry, Seattle U., 1947, B.S. med. tech. 1949; M.S., U. Notre Dame, 1963, Ph.D., 1968. Clin. lab. supr. Providence Hosp., Everett, Wash., 1953-58; research asst. U. Notre Dame (Ind.), 1964-66; human cytogeneticist Sacred Heart Hosp., Spokane, Wash., 1969; research asso. lab. exptl. pathology Children's Hosp. of Phila., 1969-72; genetics fellow dept. human genetics U. Ore. Med. Sch., Portland, 1973—. Mem. Am. Genetics Assn., Am. Soc. Zoologists, A.A.A.S., Sigma Xi. Roman Catholic. Democrat. Contbr. articles in field to profl. jours. Home: 3575 SW 106th Av Beaverton OR 97005 Office: Dept Med Genetics Child Devel and Rehab Center U Ore Med Sch Portland OR 97201

KLINGENSMITH, THELMA HYDE (MRS. DON J. KLINGENSMITH), educator; b. Rauville, S.D., May 23, 1904; d. Eber Watson and Ida (Lebert) Hyde; B.A. magna cum laude, John Fletcher Coll., 1928; M.Ed., U. N.D., 1962; m. Don Joseph Klingensmith, Sept. 11, 1930; children—Merle Joseph, Eunice Victoria (Mrs. Hilary Evans). Tchr. rural schs., Almont, N.D., 1922-24; exec. sec. Young People's Gospel League, Chgo., 1928-30; asst. supt. Ponca Meth. Indian Mission, Ponca City, Okla., 1936-43; tchr. English, Almont (N.D.) High Sch., 1951-54; supt. schs. Morton County, Mandan, N.D., 1959-73. Dir. N.D. div. Am. Cancer Soc., 1958-72, chmn. pub. edn. com., 1958-60, sec., 1960-66; sr. v.p. N.D. Young Citizens League, 1959-63, sr. pres., 1963-65; legislative rep. N.D. Council County Supts. Assn., 1963-66; adviser Morton County Library Bd., 1960—; sec.-treas. Heart River Gospel Assn., 1950-66, dir., 1950—; dir., treas. N.D. Action Com. for Environmental Edn., 1968—. Mem. Am. Assn. Sch. Adminstrs. seminar to Russia, 1969. Bd. dirs. Dickinson Coll. Found. Named N.D. Mother of the Yr., 1965. Mem. Mandan Hospital Aux., N.D., Nat. edn. assns., Nat. Council Administrn. Women Edn., Am. Bible Soc, N.D. Library Assn., A.L.A., N.D. Library Trustees Assn. (v.p. 1967-68; sec. 1971-73). Methodist. Club: Zonta (dist. VII chmn. pub. affairs com. 1968-70; del. internat. convs. 1968, 70, 72). Editor: Almont Jubilee History Book, 1956. Home: 206 Collins Av Mandan ND 58554

KLINGHOFFER, JUNE FLORENCE, physician, educator; b. Phila., Feb. 12, 1921; d. Harry and Esther (Uram) Klinghoffer; B.A., U. Pa., 1941; M.D., Woman's Med. Coll. Pa., 1945; m. Sidney U. Wenger, June 24, 1947; 1 son, Robert Klinghoffer. Intern, Albert Einstein Med. Center, Phila., 1945, resident medicine, 1945-47; fellow pathology Woman's Med. Coll. Pa., Phila., 1947-48, dir. student health service, 1948-51, clin. instr. medicine, 1950-51, asso. in medicine, 1952-53, asst. prof., 1953-59, asso. prof., 1959-69; prof. medicine Med. Coll. Pa., Phila., 1969—. Recipient Lindback award for distinguished teaching Med. Coll. Pa., 1965, Commonwealth award, 1973. Diplomate Am. Bd. Internal Medicine. Fellow A.C.P., Phila. Coll. Physicians; mem. Assn. Am. Med. Colls., N.Y., Acad. Scis., Am. Heart Assn., Am. Assn. U. Profs., A.M.A., Pa., Phila. County med. socs., Phila. Rheumatism Soc., Am. Rheumatism Assn., Alpha Omega Alpha. Home: 356 Meadow Lane Merion Station PA 19066 Office: 3300 Henry Av Philadelphia PA 19129

KLINKHAMER, SISTER MARIE CAROLYN, educator; b. Detroit, Mar. 21, 1917; d. Maurice Peter and Marie (Dungan) Klinkhamer; student U. Detroit, 1935-38; A.B., Siena Heights Coll., 1939; M.A., Cath. U. Am., 1941, Ph.D., 1943, postgrad., 1953-55. Tchr., Dominican High Sch., Detroit, 1943-44; instr. Cath. U. Am., Washington, 1944-48, asst. prof., 1948-55, asso. prof., 1955-61, prof. history, 1961-64; prof. history, politics, chmn. grad. div. Barry Coll., Miami, Fla., 1964-67; pres. St. Dominic Coll., St. Charles, Ill., 1967-69; research fellow Yale Law Sch., 1969-70, Inst. So. History, Johns Hopkins, 1970-71; prof. history Norfolk (Va.) State Coll., 1971—. Mem. Am., Am. Cath. (2d v.p. 1966) hist. assns., Orgn. Am. Historians, Am. Polit. Sci. Assn., Am. Acad. Polit. Sci., Am. Acad. Polit. and Social Sci., Am. Assn. U. Profs., Am. Assn. U. Women, Phi Beta Kappa, Pi Kappa Delta, Pi Gamma Mu. Contbr. articles to profl. jours. Home: Pembroke Towers Apt 602 601 Pembroke Av Norfolk VA 23507

KLOCHKOFF, KATHLEEN ANITA LIVINGSTON (MRS. EUGENE KLOCHKOFF), physician; b. N.Y.C., Aug. 3, 1924; d. Stephen McKay and Anna Marie (Barry) Livingston; B.S., Fordham U., 1944; M.D., N.Y. Med. Coll., 1950; m. Eugene Klochkoff, Oct. 15, 1952; children—Eugene, Gregory. Intern, N.Y.C. Hosp., 1950-51, resident, 1951-52; practice medicine specializing in obstetrics and gynecology, N.Y.C., 1954—; dir. Strang Clinic, N.Y. Infirmary, 1961-66; exec. med. dir. N.Y. Infirmary, 1966-71. Mem. A.M.A., N.Y. State, N.Y.C. med. assns., N.Y. Acad. Scis., Am. Womens Med. Assn. Home: 105 E 67th St New York City NY 10021 Office: 20 E 74th St New York City NY 10021

KLONOWSKI, JOAN THERESA, psychiatrist; b. Chgo., Dec. 30, 1942; d. John Stanley and Mary Helen (Zagajewski) Klonowski; B.S., Loyola U., Chgo., 1964; M.D., U. Ill., 1968. Intern, Cook County Hosp., Chgo., 1968-69, Chgo. Wesley Meml. Hosp., 1969-70; resident psychiatry Northwestern U. Med. Sch., Chgo., 1970-73; practice medicine specializing in psychiatry, Chgo., 1973—; staff physician Hines (Ill.) VA Hosp., 1973—, Loyola Med. Sch., Chgo., 1973—, also instr., 1973—. Ill. State scholar, 1960. Diplomate Am. Bd. Psychiatry. Mem. Phi Sigma Tau. Roman Catholic (Sunday sch. tchr. 1963-64). Home: 505 N Lake Shore Dr Chicago IL 60611 Office: 5th and Roosevelt Hines IL 60141

KLOOZ, MARIE STUART, lawyer; b. Louisville, Dec. 29, 1901; d. Louis Frederick and Sankie Belle (Hudson) Klooz; B.A., Sweet Briar Coll., 1923; M.A., Columbia, 1939; J.D., George Washington U., 1960. Admitted to D.C. bar, 1961; pvt. practice law, Washington, 1961-65, Rockville, Md., 1970-73; staff atty. poverty law office Neighborhood Legal Services, Washington, 1965-70. Vol. atty. Legal Aid Soc., Washington, 1961-65. Bd. dirs. Sandy Spring Friends Center, Sandy Spring, Md., 1965-67. Mem. Md., Montgomery County bar assns., Montgomery County Criminal Def. Bar. Mem. Soc. of Friends. Editor: International Agencies in Which the United States Participates, 1946. Address: 17200 Quaker Lane Sandy Spring MD 20860

KLOSSNER, PATRICIA ANN MARKHAM, editor; b. Syracuse, N.Y., Apr. 15, 1937; d. Rudolf Markham and Evelyn Elizabeth (Dudden) Klossner; A.B., Vassar Coll., 1959; M.A., Yale, 1960. Counselor, Baldridge Reading Services, Greenwich, Conn., 1960-65; editor Am. Book Co., N.Y.C., 1966-69; Van Nostrand Reinhold Co., N.Y.C., 1969-72; sr. editor D. Van Nostrand Co., N.Y.C., 1972-73; editor, coll. dept., Random House, N.Y.C., 1973—. Mem. Am. Ednl. Research Assn., Am. Civil Liberties Union, Speech Communication Assn. Home: 255 Avenue of the Americas New York City NY 10014 Office: Random House 201 E 50th St New York City NY 10022

KLOTZMAN, DOROTHY ANN HILL, composer, educator; b. Seattle, Mar. 24, 1937; d. Henry and Irva (Graham) Hill; B.S., Juilliard Sch. Music, 1958, M.S., 1960; postgrad. U. Wash., 1969. Mem. faculty Bklyn. Coll., 1962—, prof. music, 1973—, chmn. music dept., 1971—, condr. Bklyn. Coll. Symphonic Band and Wind Ensemble, 1970—. Recipient N.Y. Philharmonic composition prizes, 1953-54, Fromn prize Aspen Music Sch., 1960, E. Harris Harbison award for gifted teaching Danforth Found., 1972. Mem. A.S.C.A.P., Am. Musicological Soc., Am. Music Center, Coll. Music Soc., Music Library Assn. Composer: (cantata) Good Day, Sir Christmas; Four Songs on Medieval Texts; Sonatine for Piano, others. Home: 543 E 24th St Brooklyn NY 11210

KLUCKHOHN, FLORENCE ROCKWOOD (MRS. GEORGE E. TAYLOR), educator; b. Ill., Jan. 14, 1905; d. Homer Garfield and Florence (McLaughlin) Rockwood; A.B., U. Wis., 1927; Ph.D., Radcliffe Coll., 1941; m. Clyde Kluckhohn, Oct. 15, 1932 (dec. 1960); 1 son, Richard Paul Rockwood; m. 2d, George E. Taylor, 1968. Tchr., Wellesley Coll., 1940-48; analyst OWI, Washington, 1944-45; lectr. dept. social relations, asso. in Lab. Social Relations, Harvard, 1948-68, ret. Mem. Am. Anthropology Assn., Am. Sociol. Assn., Am. Acad. Polit. and Social Scis., Soc. for Applied Anthropology, Phi Beta Kappa. Club: Radcliffe (Boston). Author: (with Fred L. Strodtbeck) Variations in Value Orientations, 1961; The American Family Past and Present and America's Women, 1952. Home: The Highlands Seattle WA 98177

KNAPP, DEANNE ERMA EVANDER (MRS. DAVID ALLAN KNAPP), researcher; b. N.Y.C., Jan. 12, 1941; d. Leonard Conrad and Sarah (Gdalin) Evander; B.S., Purdue U., 1962, M.S., 1963, Ph.D., 1964; m. David Allan Knapp, June 2, 1962; 1 dau., Wendy Kay. Asst. prof. Otterbein Coll., Westerville, O., 1964-65; research asso. Ohio State U. at Columbus, 1965-68, asst. prof. Coll. Pharmacy, 1968-70; vis. scholar, Nat. Center Health Services Research and Devel. spl. postdoctoral fellow U. Mich., Ann Arbor, 1970-71; pub. health analyst NIH, Bethesda, Md., 1971-72; tech. information specialist Food and Drug Adminstrn., 1972—. Home: 11318 Cushman Rd Rockville MD 20852

KNAPP, DOLORES MARIE, lawyer; b. Chgo., Sept. 15, 1928; d. Dennis Leo and Maude (Maxwell) Bresingham; B.S. cum laude Mundelein Coll., 1950; J.D. with honors John Marshall Law Sch., 1968; m. Keith Charles Knapp, Sept. 15, 1951, (div. July 1973); children—Nora, Keith, John, Patrick. Admitted to Ill. bar, 1968; tchr. St. Agnes Grammar Sch., Chgo., 1964-68; asst. pub. defender Cook County Pub. Defender's Office, Chgo., 1969-72; dist. counsel Equal Employment Opportunity Commn., Chgo., 1973—; instr. John Marshall Law Sch., Chgo., 1970—; speaker Chgo. Bar Assn. Continuing Legal Edn. Seminar on Juvenille Ct., 1970; speaker Social Service Workers Seminar on Child Abuse, 1971. Mem. Lyric Opera Guild; Art Inst. Chgo. Recipient Lawyers Inst. of John Marshall Law Sch. scholarship, 1968. Mem. Am. Bar Assn. (mem. gen. practice and legal edn. com. 1969-73), Ill. State, Chgo. (mem. juvenile delinquents and adolescent offenders com. 1973-74, adoption com. 1973-74) bar assns., Women's Bar Assn. Ill. (editor newsletter 1969-71, dir. 1970). Editor: John Marshall Jour., 1967-68. Home: 3016 S Lowe Av Chicago IL 60616 Office: 536 S Clark St Chicago IL 60605

KNAPP, DORIS CARLTON (MRS. GEORGE EDWIN KNAPP), lawyer; b. St. Peter, Minn., Oct. 21, 1911; d. Ernest Conrad and Lois Olive (Treadwell) Carlton; B.A., Gustavus Adolphus Coll., 1931; J.D., Washington Coll. Law, 1938; M.B.A., Am. U., 1955; postgrad., London Sch. Econs. and Polit. Sci., 1956; m. George Edwin Knapp, Mar. 16, 1957; children—Lois Estelle (Mrs. Alfred Karl Pfister), Lynn Doris Allan. Writer, Social Security Bd., Washington, 1935-41; with WPB, Supreme Comdr. Allied Powers, Washington, Tokyo and Okinawa, 1941-53; economist Bur. Outdoor Recreation, Nat. Park Service, 1953-73; admitted to D.C. bar, 1938, U.S. Supreme Court, 1965, U.S. Court of Mil. Appeals, 1953; practiced law, Washington, 1938—. Home: 1273 A-1-A Satellite Beach FL 32937 Office: 510 N St SW N-331 Washington DC 20024

KNAPP, ELAINE STUART (MRS. WILLIAM F. KNAPP, JR.), editor; b. Indpls., July 31, 1947; d. John Neil and Dorothy Marie (Murray) Stuart; B.A., U. Ky., 1969; m. William F. Knapp Jr., Aug. 17, 1968. Editor, State Govt. News and State Headlines, Council of State Govts., Lexington, Ky., 1969—. Mem. Women In Communications, Phi Beta Kappa. Democrat. Mem. Ch. of Christ. Home: 11 N Main St Dry Ridge KY 41035 Office: Iron Works Pike Lexington KY 40511

KNAPP, ELMA BONNER (MRS. WALTER LEE KNAPP), librarian; b. Zanesville, O., Aug. 29, 1909; d. Otto Herman and Elizabeth Grace (Gallagher) Bonner; student Western Res. U., Fenn Coll., John Huntington Poly. Inst.; m. Walter Lee Knapp, June 18, 1928. Formerly in advt. and sales promotion; head adult basic edn. class loans Cleve. Pub. Library, 1960—. Creative writer radio and TV commls., mag. advts., newspaper publicity. Mem. Am., Ohio library assns., Adult Edn. Council Greater Cleve., Council on Human Relations, Cleve. Art Mus., Friends of Cleve. Pub. Library, Women's Advt. Club Cleve. Compiler Platt's War-Oil Directories, 1943-44, List of Adult Basic Education Books by Subject With Grade Levels. Home: 28413 Wolf Rd Bay Village OH 44140 Office: Cleveland Public Library Cleveland OH 44114

KNAPP, HAZEL LOUISE QUINN (MRS. ANDREW STEPHEN KNAPP), club woman; b. St. Louis, Oct. 29, 1892; d. Louis James and Marie (Becker) Quinn; student Washington U., St. Louis, 1929-30; m. Andrew Stephen Knapp, Aug. 11, 1913; 1 son, Robert Stephen. Nurses aide A.R.C., St. Louis, 1944-46. Nat. program chmn., also mem. hdqrs. com. Nat. Council State Garden Clubs, Inc., also master flower show judge, landscape design critic, trustee; past dir. East-Central Dist. Federated Garden Clubs Mo., 1958-59, state bd. dirs., 1951—, chmn. awards; sec.-treas. hort. council Mo. Bot. Garden. Mem. St. Louis Hort. Soc., Mo., Natchez (Miss.) hist. socs., Nature Conservancy, Ikebana Internat. Club: Pilgrimage Garden (hon.) (Natchez). Home: 17 Midpark Lane St Louis MO 63124

KNAPP, S. MAGNET (MRS. GEORGE J. KNAPP), artist; b. N.Y.C., July 18, 1909; d. Louis and Annie Magnet; student N.Y. Tng. Sch. for Tchrs., Coll. City N.Y., Bklyn. Mus. Art Sch., Atelier 17; m. George J. Knapp, Aug. 23, 1934; 1 son, Malcolm Magnet; 1 stepson, David King. Artist, work exhibited Audubon Artists, Bklyn. Mus., Pa. Acad., Butler Art Inst., Balt. Mus., Library of Congress, Corcoran Mus., also others in U.S., Eng., Can., Japan, Mexico, France, India, Switzerland, Scotland, Italy, Argentina; traveling shows Am. Fedn. Arts, Library of Congress, Am. Jewish Tercentary; represented in collections Norfolk Mus., Ga. Mus. Art, Riverside Museum, N.Y.C., also in pvt. collections. Recipient prize for watercolor Balt. Mus., 1957, 58, 61, Living mag., 1957, Silvermine, 1965, Artists Craftsmen of N.Y., 1966, Nat. Acad., 1968. First v.p. Parents Assn. Forest Hills High Sch., 1957-58, adviser to bd. Mem. Nat. Assn. Women Artists (chmn. traveling watercolors 1958-64, 1st v.p. 1961-65, pres. 1965-67; permanent advisor to bd.), Am. Soc. Contemporary Artists, N.Y. Soc. Artists Craftsmen, Balt. Watercolor Club, Artists Equity, Nat. Soc. Painters in Casein (treas. 1960-63), Artists Guild Palm Beaches. Home: 162 Somerset H West Palm Beach FL 33401

KNAPP, VIRGINIA ESTELLA, educator; b. Washington, May 11, 1919; d. Bradford and Stella (White) Knapp; B.A., Tex. Tech. U., 1940; M.A., U. Tex. 1948; postgrad. Sul Ross Coll., 1950, Stephen F. Austin U., 1964-68. Tchr. journalism, high schs., Silverton, Tex., 1940-41, Electra, Tex., 1941-42, Joinerville, Tex., 1942-60, Carthage, Tex., 1961-69; tchr. history and journalism Longview (Tex.) High Sch., 1969—; instr. Trinity U., San Antonio, summer 1972; fellowship tchr. Wall St. Jour., Tex. A. and M. U., College Station, summers 1964-67. Recipient Wall St. Jour. award Outstanding Journalism Tchrs. of Year, 1965-66. Mem. Tex. State Tchrs. Assn., Classroom Tchrs. Assn., Tex. Assn. Jour. Dirs., Rusk County Heritage Assn., D.A.R., Rusk County Hist. Survey Com., Women in Communications (pres. Longview chpt. 1972-74), Tex. Press Women. Episcopalian. Contbr. hist. writing to Ala. Rev., Progressive Farmer, Rusk County C. of C. Brochure, Rusk County Heritage, numerous others. Home: 321 College Av Henderson TX 75652 Office: Longview High Sch 2d St at Whaley Longview TX 75601

KNAUER, VIRGINIA HARRINGTON WRIGHT (MRS. WILHELM F. KNAUER), govt. ofcl.; b. Phila., Mar. 28, 1915; d. Herman Winfield and Helen (Harrington) Wright; B.F.A., U. Pa., 1937; postgrad. Pa. Acad. Fine Arts, 1933-38, Royal Acad. Fine Arts, Florence, Italy, 1938-39; LL.D., U. Pa., Phila. Coll. Textiles and Sci., Allentown Coll. Saint Francis de Sales, Widener Coll., Litt. D., Drexel U.; L.H.D., Russell Sage Coll., Pa. Coll. Podiatric Medicine; m. Wilhelm F. Knauer, Jan. 27, 1940; children—Wilhelm F., Valerie H. (Mrs. I. Townsend Burden III). Dir. Pa. Bur. Consumer Protection, 1968-69; spl. asst. for consumer affairs to Pres. Richard Nixon, 1969—; dir. Fed. Office Consumer Affairs, 1971—. Mem. Cost of Living Council, Nat. Commn. Productivity, Domestic Council Com. on Right to Privacy. Councilman-at-large, Phila., 1959-68. Vice chmn. Phila. County Republican Com., 1958—; pres. Phila. Congress Rep. Councils, 1958—; dir. Pa. Council Rep. Women, 1963—; founder, pres. N.E. Council for Rep. Women, 1956-64. Bd. dirs. Hannah Penn House, 1956—, Baby Welfare, 1960—; co-founder Knauer Found. for Historic Preservation. Named Distinguished Dau. Pa., 1969. Mem. Nat. Trust Historic Preservation, Zeta Tau Alpha. Episcopalian. Club: Doberman Pinscher (nat. pres. 1957-58). Home: Morelton 9601 Milnor St Philadelphia PA 19114 Office: White House Washington DC 20500

KNEE, RUTH IRELAN (MRS. JUNIOR K. KNEE), social worker, health care cons.; b. Sapulpa, Okla., Mar. 21, 1920; d. Oren M. and Daisy (Daubin) Irelan; B.A., U. Okla., 1941, certificate social work, 1942; M.A., U. Chgo., 1945; m. Junior K. Knee, May 29, 1943. Psychiat. social worker, asst. supr. Ill. Psychiat. Inst., U. Ill. at Chgo., 1943-44; psychiat. social worker USPHS Employee Health Unit, Washington, 1944-46, chief psychiat. social worker, 1946-49; psychiat. social work asso. Army Med. Center, Walter Reed Army Hosp., Washington, 1949-54; psychiat. social work cons. Dept. Health, Edn, Welfare, Region III, Washington, 1955-56; with Nat. Inst. Mental Health, Chevy Chase, Md., 1956-72; chief mental health care adminstrn. br. USPHS, 1967-72, asso. dep. adminstr. Health Services and Mental Health Adminstrn., 1972-73, dep. dir. Office of Nursing Home Affairs, 1973-74. Fellow Am. Pub. Health Assn. (sec. mental health sect. 1968—, chmn. 1971-72), Am. Orthopsychiat. Assn.; mem. Am. Assn. Psychiat. Social Workers (pres. 1951-53), Nat. Conf. Social Welfare (nat. bd. 1968-71, 2d v.p. 1973-74), Council on Social Work Edn., Nat. Assn. Social Workers (chmn. competence study com., practice and knowledge com. 1963-71), Am. Pub. Welfare Assn., D.A.R., Phi Beta Kappa, Psi Chi. Address: 8809 Arlington Blvd Fairfax VA 22030

KNEELAND, JANE HOUGHTON, civic worker; b. Corning, N.Y., Nov. 28, 1930; d. Arthur Amory and Jane Olmsted (McMillan) Houghton; grad. Foxcroft Sch., 1948, Katherine Gibbs Sch., 1950; student Wells Coll., 1948-49; children—Susan, Jane, Hope, Peter Hadley. Mem. women's com. N.Y. Pub. Library, 1958-60; mem. adv. com. Sawtooth Nat. Forest, 1971; chmn. Sun Valley Village Hosp. Emergency Room Aux., 1969-71; mem. adv. bd. Exec. High Sch. Internships Am. Chmn., Vols. for Nixon-Lodge, Blaine County, Ida., 1960; Republican precinct committeeman Blaine County, 1968-73; del. Ida. State Rep. Conv., 1968, 70; chmn. Vols. for Nixon-Agnew, Blaine County, 1968; co-chmn. host com. Lt. Gov.'s Conv., 1971; Ida. chmn. Regional Women's Western States Conf., Phoenix, 1972. Trustee Blaine County Sch. Dist. 61; chmn. bd. trustees Corning (N.Y.) Pub. Library, 1957-60; bd. dirs Ketchum Community Library, 1965, chmn. bd. dirs., 1969, 70; trustee Sun Valley Ski Edn. Found., 1968-73, pres., 1969-73, African-Am. Inst. Club: Sun Valley (Ida.) Ski (gov. 1969-73). Home: Box 205 Sun Valley ID 83353 also 200 E 66th St New York City NY 10021

KNEITZ, MARGARET HOOKER, educator; b. New Willard, Tex., Apr. 8; d. Dewey Wallace and Ella Wheeler (Wharton) Hooker; A.A., Wharton County Jr. Coll., 1963; B.A., Sam Houston State U., 1965, M.A., 1967; Ed.D., U. Houston, 1969; children—Margaret K. (Mrs. John Francis Sissons), John W., Joel S., Jenny E. Tchr. math. Columbia-Brazeria Ind. Sch. Dist., West Columbia, Tex., 1965-67; teaching fellow U. Houston, 1967-69; asst. prof. math. Tex. So. U., 1969-70; prof., head dept. math. Dominican Coll., Houston, 1970—. Cons. Houston Chronicle, 1971—, Houston Community Coll., 1971-72; vis. lectr. U. Houston Coll. Edn., 1969-72. Organized and started 1st Needville (Tex.) Kindergarten, 1964. Mem. Math. Assn. Am., Nat. Council Tchrs. Math., Tex. Soc. Coll. Tchrs. Edn., Kappa Delta Pi, Kappa Epsilon. Presbyn. Clubs: Needville Band Booster's. Contbr. articles to profl. pubs. Home: 3206 Suffolk Houston TX 77027 Office: 2401 Holcombe St Houston TX 77021

KNIEF, LOTUS MAE, ednl. psychologist; b. Readlyn, Ia.; d. E. G. and Anita Knief; B.A. summa cum laude, Wartburg Coll., 1952; M.A., U. Ia., 1953, Ph.D., 1959. Asst. prof., dir. testing Wartburg Coll., 1959-61; prof. psychology Phoenix Coll., 1961-63; prof. ednl. psychology U. Ariz. at Tucson, 1963—. Mem. Am. Psychol. Assn., Am. Ednl. Research Assn., Nat. Council Measurement in Edn., Assn. Devel. Instructional Systems, Ariz. Assn. Ednl. Data Systems, Pi Lambda Theta. Office: Dept Educational Psychology U Ariz Tucson AZ 85721

KNIEF, URA MAE HARRELL (MRS. OSCAR LEE KNIEF), civic worker; b. Winters, Tex., Oct. 3, 1911; d. James Orange and Jo Pearl (White) Harrell; A.A., Mesa Coll., 1970; B.A., Cal. State U., San Diego, 1972; m. Oscar Lee Knief, Apr. 19, 1943; children—Roberta Susan (Mrs. Richard Lee Vermillion), Charles Lee. Mgr., Safeway Store, Los Angeles, 1943-44. Den mother Cub Scouts, 1955-58; pres. bd. dirs. San Diego post Vols. of Am., 1959; residential chmn. United

Fund, 1961; county chmn. Gt. Decisions by Fgn. Policy Assn., 1963-64; pub. relations chmn. UN Assn. San Diego, 1964; mem. Mayor's Com. for UN Week, 1964; co-chmn. San Diego region Nat. Conf. Christians and Jews, 1962-65, chmn. women's com., 1965-66; pres. San Diego Council United Ch. Women, 1961-62, v.p., 1963-64; sec. San Diego County Council Chs., 1962; mem. exec. com., dir., rep. Meth. denomination and San Diego County Council Chs. to Council Chs. So. Cal., 1963—, mem. radio-TV-film commn., 1964-68; mem. Assn. Coll. and U. Ministers of Meth. Ch., 1965-67; mem. nat. interbd. com. for campus ministries, 1965-68; sec. campus ministry Western jurisdiction Woman's Soc. Christian Service, 1964-68; mem. campus ministry and older youth com. So. Cal.-Ariz. Conf., 1960-64, lay del. conf., 1964-72; pres. work with sr. citizens adv. com. project Bd. Missions, Meth. Ch., 1964-67; community service rep. Cal. State Commn. on Aging, 1972; social worker Adult Protective Service, 1973-74. Bd. dirs. Wesley Found. of San Diego State Coll. (sec. 1960-68). United Methodist v.p. San Diego Dist. United Meth. Union 1972, pres. 1973). Editor Christian Progress, newspaper, 1964. Home: 4549 E Talmadge Dr San Diego CA 92116

KNIGHT, ALICE D. TIRRELL, state legislator; b. Manchester, N.H., July 14, 1903; d. Nathan Arthur and Clara (Stiles) Tirrell; B.A., U. N.H., 1925; postgrad. 1933; postgrad. Boston U., 1941-42; m. Norman Knight, Nov. 15, 1952. Tchr. Newton Falls (N.Y.) High Sch., 1925-26; prin. Oswegatchie (N.Y.) Union Sch., 1926-27; prin. Bartlett Sch., Goffstown, N.H., 1932-35; home lighting specialist Pub. Service Co. N.H., Manchester, 1935-39; tchr. merchandising Mt. Ida Jr. Coll., Newton Centre, Mass., 1939-45; home service dir. Boyd Corp., Portland, Me., 1945-47; dist. home economist Frigidaire Sales Corp., Boston, 1948-64; mem. N. H. Ho. of Reps., 1967—. Mem. budget com. Town of Goffstown, 1966-72; mem. Gov.'s Adv. Com. on Alcoholism, 1972-73, 74—. Past pres., bd. dirs. Hillsborough County North Cancer Soc.; bd. dirs. N.H. Cancer Soc. Recipient award N.H. Program on Alcohol and Drug Abuse, 1971. Mem. Am. Home Econs. Assn., Nat. Home Fashions League (pres. 1957-58), Nat. Soc. State Legislators, Am. Women in Radio and Television, League Women Voters, N.H. Council World Affairs, Nat. Grange, D.A.R. (regent 1974—), Nat. Order Women Legislators (treas. 1968-71), Manchester Bus. and Profl. Women (pres. 1972-74). Mem. Order Eastern Star. Clubs: Soroptimist (life mem.) (Boston); Goffstown Unity, Goffstown Garden (v.p. 1973-74), Goffstown Shirley. Home: Addison Rd RD 2 Goffstown NH 03045

KNIGHT, ERNESTINE WRIGHT, librarian; b. Norfolk County, Va., May 8, 1934; d. Linwood Alton and Helen Katherine (McDearmid) Wright; B.S., Madison Coll., 1963; M.Ed., Coll. William and Mary, 1971; m. John Thomas Knight, Dec. 31, 1953 (div. Feb. 1969); children—Barry Dean, Shannon Leigh, Susan Gale, Terry Lynn. Librarian, Thoroughgood Elementary Sch., Virginia Beach, Va., 1962-67; asst. librarian Kempsville High Sch., Virginia Beach, 1967-69; head librarian Kempsville Jr. High Sch., 1969-72; librarian Vocational-Tech. Center, Virginia Beach, 1972—. Mem. Nat., Va. (chmn. state conf. exhibits 1973), Virginia Beach (chmn. nominating com. 1969) edn. assns., Am., Va., Virginia Beach (pres. 1965, 66) library assns., Va. Assn. Ednl. Communications and Tech., Am. Assn. U. Women (treas. 1969, 70), Internat. Platform Assn., Women's Mission Union (pres. 1967, 68), Alpha Delta Kappa (historian), Kappa Delta Pi. Baptist. Clubs: Cavalier Junior Women's (2d v.p. 1964, 65), Toastmistress (pres. 1958, 59). Home: 1105 Burlington Rd Virginia Beach VA 23462 Office: 2925 N Landing Rd Virginia Beach VA 23456

KNIGHT, EVA GOFF (MRS. ROYAL E. KNIGHT), educator; b. Leesburg, Fla., May 23, 1933; d. Carlos Clyde and Dorothy (Shultz) Goff; B.A. (William Delches scholar, Goucher Coll. scholar), Goucher Coll., 1955; M.A. (Dean Van Meter Alumna fellow 1962-63), Columbia U., 1963, Ed.D., 1968; Certificate Advanced Studies Edn., Johns Hopkins, 1964; postgrad. (Gen. Electric Econs. fellow), Union Coll., summer, 1962, Stanford (H. Wilson summer fellow), summer 1963; m. Royal E. Knight, May 28, 1972. Tchr. history pub. schs., Balt., 1955-64; project asst. for Knapp Sch. Libraries project Columbia, 1964-65; ednl. cons. Silver Burdett Pub. Co., Morristown, N.J., 1965-67; asst. prof. edn. State U. Coll., Geneseo, N.Y., 1967-72; asso. prof. Oakland City (Ind.) Coll., 1972—. Stanford U. grantee, summer 1962; NSF fellow Purdue U., summer 1972. Mem. Assn. Ednl. Communications Tech., Nat. Council Social Studies, Assn. Tchr. Educators, Assn. Supervision Curriculum Devel., Pi Lambda Theta, Phi Delta Gamma, Kappa Delta Phi, Kappa Delta Gamma. Presbyn. Home: 2023 9th Av Greeley CO 80631

KNIGHT, EVA TURNER (MRS. STERLING LAFAYETTE KNIGHT), writer; b. Lynchburg, Va., Feb. 12, 1898; d. James Andrew and Alice May (Crater) Turner; student Massey Bus. Coll., 1920; m. William Lee Farrar, Jan. 22, 1916 (dec. Dec. 1930); children—William J., Robert Kelly; m. 2d, Sterling Lafayette Knight, Jan. 16, 1932; children—Shirley (Mrs. Frederick Hamill), Fay, (Mrs. Caroll O. Sandvig). Office sec. Lynchburg Shoe Co., 1926-28; sec. to judge Juvenile and Police Ct., Lynchburg, 1928-32; column writer Amherst (Va.) New-Era, 1926-30; staff writer Bedford (Va.) Democrat, 1950-73; staff Bristol (Tenn.) Tri-Cities Observer, 1970-72. Librarian Forest Library, Forest, Va. 1964—. Recipient various awards Progressive Farmer, Va. Press Assn. Mem. Episcopal Ch. Women. Episcopalian. Author: The Grandchildren's Book, 1963; The Farrars in Virginia, 1965; The Kettle and the Hearth in Old Virginia, 1966; Frontier Life in New River Valley, 1970; What's Cooking in Boonsboro?, 1967. Home: 5543 Boonsboro Rd Lynchburg VA 24503

KNIGHT, FRANCES (GLADYS), govt. ofcl.; b. Newport, R.I., July 22, 1905; d. Frederick and Fanni (Smolik) Knight; ed. in France, Czechoslovakia, Monaco; student N.Y.U., Columbia, Hunter Coll., N.Y.C.; Dr. Humanities (hon.), Mo. Valley Coll., 1963; m. Wayne W. Parrish, Sept. 15, 1935. Div. chief Nat. Indsl. Recovery Adminstrn., 1934-36; dep. dir. information program WPA, 1936-39; pub. relations cons. White House Conf. on Children, 1940; spl. asst. to commr. Nat. Def. Adv. Com., 1941-42; pub. relations dir. U.S. Office Civilian Def., 1942-45; dir. pub. relations Am. Retail Fedn., 1945-47; Congl. cons., 1947-48; information specialist; dep. adminstr. Security and Consular Affairs, Dept. State, 1948-55, dir. Passport Office, 1955—. Home: 2221 30th St NW Washington DC 20008 Office: Dept State Washington DC 20525

KNIGHT, GLADYS MARIA, vocalist, rec. artist; b. Atlanta, May 28, 1944; d. Merald and Elizabeth Knight; div.; children—Kenya, James. First pub. recital Mt. Mariah Bapt. Ch., Atlanta, 1948; winner Ted Mack's Amateur Hour TV, 1952; jazz vocalist Lloyd Terry Jazz Band, Atlanta, 1959-61; lead singer Gladys Knight and the Pips, 1953—; concert tours, Eng., 1967, 72, 73; appearances numerous TV shows, Eng., U.S.; rec. artist Brunswick Records, 1957-61, Fury Records, 1961-62, Motown Records, 1965-73, Buddah Records, 1973—. Performer Democratic Nat. Conv., Miami, Fla., 1972. Recipient numerous honors including: gold records Rec. Industry Assn. Am., 1967, 71, 72, 73, 74, gold album, 1973; Inspiration to Youth award Washington City Council, 1972; named Top Female Vocalist Blues & Soul mag., 1972, Soul Artist of Year, Rolling Stone mag., 1973, Entertainer of Year, Soul mag., 1973. Author lyrics songs including I Don't Want to Do Wrong, Do You Love Me Just a Little Honey, Daddy Don't Swear (I Declare), Me and My Family, Way Back Home. Address: Care SAS Inc 1414 Av of Americas New York City NY 10019

KNIGHT, GLENDA EVELYN, educator; b. N.Y.C., Jan. 2, 1947; d. W. Lee and Evelyn (Walton) Knight; B.A., Columbia, 1968; M.Ed., U. N.C., 1969; postgrad. State U. N.Y., Plattsburgh, 1972-73. Research asst. U. N.C. at Chapel Hill, 1969; owner, dir. Algonquin Sch. for Retarded Children, Saranac Lake, N.Y., 1969—. Mem. adv. bd. for mental health program N. Country Community Coll., 1972-73. Mem. Council Exceptional Children, Am. Assn. Mental Deficiency, Nat., N.Y. State assns. for pvt. residential facilities, Phi Beta Kappa, Kappa Delta Epsilon. Club: Women's College (sec. Saranac Lake 1971). Address: Box 629 Saranac Lake NY 12983

KNIGHT, GUYRENA JULIA, psychologist; b. St. Louis, July 27, 1923; d. James and Gladys Margaret (Hankins) Knight; A.B., Stowe Tchrs. Coll., 1945; A.M., U. Ill., 1951; postgrad. St. Louis U., Washington U., St. Louis, Fontbonne Coll., U. Mo., Harris Tchrs. Coll., U. Chgo., Drury Coll. Tchr. elementary sch. St. Louis Pub. Sch. System, 1945-63, psychol. examiner, 1963-68, sch. psychologist, 1968-74, cons. spl. edn., 1974—. Pvt. tutor, 1971-72; instr. Harris Tchrs. Coll., St. Louis, 1973-74. Mem. Nat. Assn. Sch. Psychologists, Mo. Assn. for Children with Learning Disabilities, United Teaching Profession Orgn., N.E.A., Mo., St. Louis tchrs. assn., Spl. Edn. Instructional Materials Center. Roman Catholic. Home: 5147 Northland St St Louis MO 63113 Office: Division of Spl Edn St Louis Pub Schs 1616 S Grand Blvd St Louis MO 63104

KNIGHT, JANE KRISTINE (MRS. WARREN STANLEY KNIGHT), pub. relations exec.; b. Salem, Ore., Dec. 13, 1946; d. George Jasper and Wilma Joan (Legernes) Harding; B.S., U. Ore., 1968; m. Warren Stanley Knight, May 29, 1971. With Olson-Skene Studio, Portland, Ore., 1968-70; with W.S. Myers Advt. Agy., Honolulu, 1970-71; promotion rep. TV Guide, Portland, 1972—. Mem. Women In Communications, Portland Advt. Fedn., Alpha Gamma Delta. Home: 20055 SW Newcastle Aloha OR 97005 Office: 707 SW Washington Portland OR 97205

KNIGHT, JEANNE ENID (MRS. REGINALD CAYWOOD KNIGHT), educator; b. Moretown, Vt., Dec. 6, 1923; d. Fred Moore and Jean Baird (Clark) Sellars; A.B., Hunter Coll., 1946; M.A., Columbia, 1948; m. Reginald Caywood Knight, Nov. 9, 1951; children—Jeanne Enid, Houghton Caywood, Eliot Holladay. Lectr. Wagner Coll., 1946-47, critic, 1940-42, instr. English lit., lit. criticism, creative writing, 1947-51; dramatics coach, Wagner Players, 1946, Dutch Reformed Players, S.I., N.Y., 1948-49, Island Players Exptl. Theater, S.I., 1950-51; charge nursery sch. Holy Trinity Parish Day Sch., Collington, Md., after 1967; mem. staff St. Peter and Paul, Miami, after 1968. Mem. Longboat Key (Fla.) Art Center, Sarasota, Manatee art assns., Women's League for Peace and Freedom, Sigma Tau Delta. Episcopalian. Home: Box 1524 Eugene OR 97401

KNIGHT, KAREN LINDA, lawyer; b. New Orleans, Mar. 19, 1940; d. Nathaniel Butler and Ada Emelda (Brunies) Knight; student Queen's Coll., London, 1958, Tulane U., 1959-67; J.D., Loyola U., New Orleans, 1968. Admitted to La. bar, 1968; partner Knight, D'Angelo & Knight, Gretna, 1968—; cashier, asst. sec., dir. Jefferson Savs. & Loan Assn., Gretna, 1973—. Mem. adv. bd. Eye Found. Am., 1969—. Mem. Am., La., Jefferson Parish bar assns., Phi Delta Delta. Home: 626 1st St Gretna LA 70053 Office: 1011 4th St Gretna LA 70053

KNIGHT, LEONA JOSEPHINE (LEE KNIGHT), broadcaster; b. Toledo, O.; d. Stanley F. and Rose (Cross) Knight; Ph.B., U. Toledo, 1943. Broadcaster, writer Allan Miller Agy., 1943-45; broadcaster Storer Broadcasting Co. WSPD, 1945—. Organized March of Dimes Train from Toledo to N.Y.C., 1956; mem. Lucas County chpt. Muscular Dystrophy Assns. of Am., Inc., 1953—, 1st v.p., 1957—, v.p. Greater Toledo chpt., 1968-69; organized Tricks or Treats for UNICEF, 1956; co-chmn. Advt. Recognition Week, 1961-68. Recipient certificate of merit Am. Cancer Soc., 1956, 57, 58; Friendship medal from Marshall Georgi Zhukov, 1957, Russian Minister of Agr., 1957; spl. recognition medal Prince Rainier of Monaco, 1958; named Advt. Woman of Yr., Toledo, 1962-63. Mem. Cath. Collegiate Assn. (program chmn. 1960; pres. 1967-68), Am. Assn. U. Women, Women's Advt. Club Toledo (co-chmn. nat. advt. week 1961; mem. bd. 1966-67), Am. Assn. U. Women (dir., publicity chmn. 1964—; mass media chmn. 1962-64), Am. Women in Radio and TV, City Mgrs. League, Toledo Theatre Assn. (v.p. Mimes 1960-62, 65-66). Clubs: Toledo Tennis, Toledo Woman's. Home: 133 Austin St Toledo OH 43608 Office: 136 Huron St Toledo OH 44839

KNIGHT, LYNETTE WILLIAMSON (MRS. THOMAS C. KNIGHT), educator; b. Springfield, Mo., Jan. 22, 1928; d. Irl and Lenna (Colley) Williamson; student Drury Coll., 1945-46, S.W. Mo. State Coll., 1946-47; B.S., U. Mo., 1949; M.Guidance and Counseling, Ariz. State U., 1966, Ph.D., 1973; m. Thomas C. Knight, Sept. 3, 1950; children—Lisa Lynette (dec.), Darin Casey. Tchr. Am. govt. Lebanon (Mo.) High Sch., 1949-50; chmn. counseling Coronado High Sch., Scottsdale, Ariz., 1965-71; tchr., adminstr. Ariz. State U., Tempe, 1971-73; prof. U.S. Internat. U., San Diego, 1973—. Mem. Nat. Bd. Am. Coll. Testing Program Secondary Sch. Counselors. Pres., Inter-Faith Counseling Service, Scottsdale, Ariz., 1970-73. Mem. Am. Assn. U. Women, Am. Personnel and Guidance Assn., Zeta Tau Alpha. Presbyn. (elder 1968—). Home: 8520 Via Mallorca Dr La Jolla CA 92037 Office: Sch Edn US Internat U San Diego CA 92131

KNIGHT, MARGARETT LEE, law editor; b. Newtown, Ind., Jan. 3, 1923; d. Charles Oscar and Edna (Pace) Smith; LL.B., Ind. U. Sch. Law, 1945, J.D., 1965; A.B., Mills Coll., 1953; LL.M., Yale Law Sch., 1955; m. Robert Cook Knight, June 20, 1961. Admitted to Ind. bar, 1945; law editor The Bobbs-Merrill Co. Inc., Indpls., 1970—. Home: 1318 Hoover Ln Indianapolis IN 46260 Office: 4300 W 62d St Indianapolis IN 46268

KNIGHT, PAULINE ELEANOR TETIRICK (MRS. CLARENCE ANDREW KNIGHT), educator; b. Blackwell, Okla., Oct. 4, 1913; d. James Willis and Blanche (Dix) Tetirick; student Keister's Dress Designing Sch., 1938-39, Compton Jr. Coll., 1944-45; A.A., Huntington Meml. Hosp. Sch. Nursing, 1948; B.S., U. Wash., 1951; M.A., Columbia U., 1959; postgrad. U. Cal. at San Francisco, 1964-65, Mental Research Inst., 1966, 67; m. Clarance Andrew Knight, July 2, 1960. With Mode O'Day Dress Mfr., Los Angeles, 1941-45; charge nurse Huntington Meml. Hosp., Pasadena, Cal., 1948-49; staff nurse Seattle-King County Hosp., part-time 1949-51, Seattle-King County Dept. Pub. Health, 1951-57; supr. pub. health nursing Tacoma-Pierce County Dept. Pub. Health, 1959-61, San Mateo County (Cal.) Dept. Health and Welfare, 1961-64; asst. prof. nursing San Francisco State Coll., 1965-68; asst. prof. Fresno (Cal.) State Coll. (now Cal. State U. at Fresno), 1968-70, asso. prof., 1970-73; asso. prof. Cal. State U., Chico, 1973—. Commd. Officer USPHS Res. Nat. Inst. Mental Health grantee, 1964-65. Mem. Am., Cal., San Mateo County (mem. legislative com. 1967-68) nurses assns., Cal. Employees Assn. Democrat. Mem. Ch. of Nazarene (Sunday sch. bd. mem. 1966—). Home: 10914 Wheeler Dr Lower Lake CA 95457

KNIGHT, VIRGINIA LUCINDA, interior designer; b. Cleve., Dec. 10, 1931; d. Vick Ralph and Janice (Higgins) Knight; student Los Angeles City Coll., 1951. Designer, Albert Van Luit Wallpaper Co., Los Angeles, 1955; interior designer W. & J. Sloane Co., Beverly Hills, Cal., 1955-62, Barnett Bros., Beverly Hills, 1962-69, Cannell & Chaffin, 1969—; resident designer West Atwood Yacht Club. Mem. bldg. and sites com. Los Angeles Epilepsy Soc. Corporate mem. Am. Inst. Interior Designers (bd. govs. 1969-71, 72—). Republican. Clubs: Altrusa (charter); South West Los Angeles (pres. 1967-69). Home: 1601 Sunset Plaza Dr Los Angeles CA 90069 Office: 3000 Wilshire Blvd Los Angeles CA 90005

KNISELY, SALLY, psychotherapist; b. Baraga, Mich., Mar. 17, 1917; d. Henry Samuel and Flora (Hagerman) Knisely; A.B., U. Mich., 1944; M.A., U. Chgo., 1946; Ed.D., Columbia U., 1964. Day nursery caseworker Bur. Family Service, Orange, N.J., 1946-49; caseworker to mentally ill vets. VA, N.Y.C., 1949-53; child psychotherapist Inter-Agy. Guidance Center, Yonkers, N.Y., 1953-58; child psychotherapist Monsey (N.Y.) Mental Health Clinic, 1957-58; child psychotherapist New Rochelle (N.Y.) Guidance Center, 1958-59; pvt. practice psychotherapy, Stamford, Conn., 1954—; cons. numerous nursery sch. and presch. programs. Mem. profl. adv. bd. Early Childhood Programs, Martha's Vineyard, Mass. Mem. Am. Orthopsychiat. Assn., Council Psychoanalytic Psychotherapists, Nat. Assn. Edn. Young Children, Conn. Soc. Clin. Social Workers, Nat. Assn. Social Workers. Home: 69 Jordan Ln Stamford CT 06903 Office: 69 Jordan Ln Stamford CT 06903

KNOBBE, MARY LOUISE SIEFER, librarian; b. Cherryvale, Kan., Aug. 26, 1918; d. Clarence E. and Lula (Funkhouser) Siefer; A.B., Washburn U. 1940; postgrad. Sch. Library Sci. and Information U. Md., 1965-67; m. Ray H. Knobbe, Jan. 23, 1946; children—Ann, Jane. Library asst. Washburn U., Topeka, 1941-42; librarian Dept. Research, Kansas City, Mo., 1944-46; reference librarian Carnegie Library, Steubenville, O., 1950-51; planning librarian Md. Nat. Capital Park and Planning Commn., Silver Spring, Md., 1961-67; librarian Met. Washington Council Govts., 1967—. Mem. Council Planning Librarians, Spl. Libraries Assn. (chmn. social sci. div. D.C. chpt. 1967-68, chpt. dir. 1968-70; mem. govt. information services com. 1971-75, chmn. elect urban affairs sect. 1974-75), Kan. Soc. Washington, Pi Gamma Mu. Episcopalian. Editor: Planning and Urban Affairs Library Manual, 3d edit., 1974; Planning, Building and Housing Libraries, 1969. Home: 2300 Eccleston St Silver Spring MD 20902 Office: 1225 Connecticut Av Washington DC 20036

KNOBLOCH, HILDA, physician; b. N.Y.C., Dec. 14, 1915; d. Philip J. and Minnie (Jacobson) Knobloch; B.A., Barnard Coll., 1936; M.D., N.Y.U. 1940; M.P.H., Johns Hopkins, 1951, Dr. P.H., 1955; m. Benjamin Pasamanick, May 1, 1942. Rotating intern Harlem Hosp., N.Y.C., 1941-42, resident in medicine, 1942; resident in contagious disease Willard Parker Hosp., N.Y.C., 1943; asst. clinic of child devel. Yale U. Sch. Medicine, 1945-46; asst. resident in pediatrics U. Hosp., Ann Arbor, Mich., 1946-47; practice medicine specializing in pediatrics, New Haven, 1944-45, N.Y.C., 1947-49; pediatric cons., bur. child hygiene Conn. Dept. Health, also pediatrician, well-baby clinics New Haven City Health Dept.; jr. attending pediatrician Grace Hosp., New Haven, 1944-45; asst. clin. vis. pediatrician Bellevue Hosp., N.Y.C., also clin. asst., child guidance clinic Mt. Sinai Hosp., N.Y.C., 1947-49; research in cerebral palsy Hosp. for Spl. Surgery, N.Y.C., 1948-50; pediatric cons. N.Y.C. Health Dept., 1949-50; research asso., maternal and child health div. Johns Hopkins Sch. Hygiene and Pub. Health, 1951-55, asst. prof., 1955; asso. prof. pediatrics Ohio State U. Coll. Medicine, 1955-62, prof. pediatrics, 1962-66, asst. prof. psychiatry, 1958-66; prof. pediatrics U. Ill. Coll. Medicine at Chgo., 1966-67; prof. pediatrics Mt. Sinai Sch. Medicine, 1967-70; dir. child devel. divs. Dept. Pediatrics Mt. Sinai Hosp., N.Y., 1967-70; prof. Albany Med. Coll., 1970—; med. specialist N.Y. Dept. Mental Hygiene, Albany, 1970—; dir. clinic child devel. Children's Hosp., Columbus, O., 1956-66. Mem. developmental and behavioral scis. study sect. NIH, 1971-75. Diplomate Am. Bd. Pediatrics, Am. Bd. Preventive Medicine. Fellow Am. Acad. Pediatrics, Am. Orthopsychiat. Assn., Soc. for Research in Child Devel.; mem. Am. Pediatric Soc., Am. Acad. Cerebral Palsy, Am. Psychiat. Assn., Phi Beta Kappa, Sigma Xi. Home: Feura Bush Rd Glenmont NY 12077 Office: Albany Med Coll Albany NY 12208

KNOCK, FRANCES ENGELMANN (MRS. THEODORE EMANUEL KNOCK), surgeon; b. Chgo., July 8, 1921; d. William Fred and Frances (Tietze) Engelmann; B.S., U. Chgo., 1940, Ph.D. (Swift fellow), 1943; M.D., U. Ill., 1954; m. Theodore Emanuel Knock, Oct. 23, 1943. Asso. organic chemist Armour Research Found., Chgo., 1943-46, organic chemist, 1946-49, chem. cons., 1950-51; dir. Nat. Registry Rare Chems., Chgo., 1945-50; chem. cons. Merck Sharp & Dohme, Rahway, N.J., 1954-56; intern Evanston (Ill.) Hosp., 1954-55; resident Presbyn. Hosp., Chgo., 1955-59; practice medicine specializing in surgery, Chgo., 1959—; dir. Knock Research Found., Chgo., 1955—; staff Augustana Hosp., Chgo., VA Hosp., Hines, Ill., 1961—; mem. faculty U. Ill., Chgo., 1959—, clin. asst. prof. surgery, 1962—; lectr. in pharmacology Loyola, Hines, 1972—. Cons., E.R. Squibb & Sons, New Brunswick, N.J., 1964-66. Diplomate Am. Bd. Surgery, Nat. Bd. Med. Examiners. Fellow A.A.A.S., Am. Inst. Chemists, Am. Geriatrics Soc., Royal Soc. Health, Internat. Coll. Angiology, Sci. Council, Internat. Coll. Surgeons, Am. Coll. Med. Hypnotists; mem. A.M.A., Am. Chem. Soc., N.Y. Acad. Scis., Am. Inst. Chemists, Am. Coll. Angiology, Phi Beta Kappa, Sigma Xi, Alpha Omega Alpha. Author: Anticancer Agents, 1967. Contbr. articles to chem. and med. jours. Patentee in field. Home: 416 Country Lane Glenview IL 60025 Office: 30 N Michigan Av Chicago IL 60602

KNOERLE, SISTER JEANNE, coll. pres.; b. Cleve., Feb. 24, 1928; d. Harold and Bernedine (Seufert) Knoerle; B.A., St. Mary-of-the-Woods Coll., 1949; M.A., Ind. U., 1961, Ph.D., 1966; LL.D., Rose Hulman Inst. Tech., 1971; LL.D., Ind. State U., 1972. Tchr. high schs., 1952-54; chmn. dept. journalism St. Mary-of-the-Woods Coll. (Ind.), 1954-63, asst. to pres., asso. prof. Asian studies, 1967-68, pres., prof., 1968—; vis. prof. Providence Coll., Taichung, Taiwan, 1966-67. Mem. Gov.'s Commn. Status of Women, 1973—; mem. instnl. relations com. Nat. Cath. Ednl. Assn.; pres. Ind. Conf. Higher Edn., 1973-74. Bd. dirs. Union Hosp., Terre Haute, Ind., United Way of the Wabash Valley, Mental Health Assn. Vigo County, Wabash Valley Goodwill Industries, Inc. Mem. The Asia Soc., Am. Soc. for Aesthetics, Assn. for Asian Studies, Am. Soc. Eastern Arts, Asso. Colls. Ind. (sec. 1970-72), Ind. Conf. Higher Edn. (exec. com. 1972-73), Vigo County Coordinating Council, Housewives Effort for Local Progress, Delta Kappa Gamma. Author: The Dream of the Red Chamber, a Critical Study, 1972. Contbr. articles to profl. jours. Address: St Mary-of-the-Woods Coll St Mary-of-the-Woods IN 47876

KNOOP, SISTER CATHERINE THERESE, educator; b. Los Angeles; d. Henry Louis and Katharine (Quinn) Knoop; B.A., Mt. St. Mary's Coll., 1953; M.A., St. Louis U., 1954; Ph.D., U. Cal. at Berkeley, 1957. Joined Sisters of St. Joseph of Carondelet, 1942; instr. Mt. St. Mary's Coll., Los Angeles, 1957-59, asst. prof., 1960-62, chmn. dept. bus. and econs., 1960-67, asso. prof. econs., 1963-67, prof. econs., 1968—, coordinator grad. studies, 1965-67, dir. instnl. research, 1967—. Mem. Western Econ. Assn., Assn. Social Econs.

(pres. 1971), Assn. Instl. Research. Contbr. to profl. jours. Address: 12001 Chalon Rd Los Angeles CA 90049

KNOPF, TERRY ANN, social scientist; b. N.Y.C., July 20, 1940; d. Albert A. and Irene (Kaufman) Knopf; B.A. cum laude, Queens Coll., 1962; M.A. in Teaching, Harvard, 1963. Curriculum specialist Ednl. Services, Inc., Cambridge, Mass., 1963-66; research coordinator for senatorial campaign Sen. Edward W. Brooke, 1966; research asso. Lemberg Center for Study of Violence, Brandeis U., Waltham, Mass., 1967-73; asso. producer WCVB-TV, Needham, Mass., 1973—. Mem. Phi Beta Kappa, Phi Alpha Theta. Author: Rumors, Race and Riots, 1973. Contbr. articles to profl. publs., chpts. to books. Office: WCVB TV Needham MA 02192

KNORR, BETTY JEWEL BENKERT (MRS. NEIL MCLEAN KNORR), naturalist; b. Summit, N.J., Aug. 10, 1928; d. William R. and Amelia (Kreutzer) Benkert; grad. high sch.; Ph.D. (hon.), Hamilton State U., 1973; m. Neil McLean Knorr, Dec. 13, 1946. Licensed bird bander Fish and Wildlife Service, U.S. Dept. Interior, 1957—; banded over 43,000 wild birds of 170 different species; spl. ornithol. research on shorebirds, hummingbirds and blackbirds; other varied research in bird banding; established extensive wildflower preserve and rhododendron gardens at home; engaged in propagation rare native wildflowers donating same to pub. arboretums, preserves and sanctuaries; vol. tchr., cons. on conservation and nature study, 1948—; active many local, state, nat. conservation issues; responsible for saving wilderness area threatened with destruction and now preserved as part of Cheesequake State Park. Active Girl Scouts U.S.A., 1938—; counselor, cons. Boy Scouts Am., 1960—. Mem. Am. Ornithologists' Union, Eastern, Northeastern, Western, Inland bird banding assns., Nat., N.J. Audubon socs., Torrey Bot. Club, Am. Rhododendron Soc., Shore, Monmouth organ socs. Home: 81 Hope Rd New Shrewsbury NJ 07724

KNOWLES, DOROTHY AILEEN, librarian; b. Toronto, Ont., Can., Mar. 15, 1918; d. Leonard James and Jessie Sisson (Lowe) K.; B. Household Sci., McGill U., 1940, B.L.S., 1953. Technician, munitions lab. Inspection Lab. of U.K. and Can., St. Paul L'Hermite, Que., 1941-42; lab. technician Canadian Army Lab. for Studies in Shock and Damage, Montreal, Que., 1942-43; food chemist Oxo Can., Ltd., Montreal, 1943-52; asso. reference librarian U. B.C., Vancouver, 1953-56; reference librarian, cataloger Albert R. Mann Library, Cornell U., Ithaca, N.Y., 1956-57; asst. librarian Govt. of Can. Dept. Fisheries, Ottawa, 1957-59; chief librarian Nat. Energy Bd., Govt. of Can., Ottawa, 1959—. Library Assn., Spl. Libraries Assn. (chmn. petroleum div. 1973-74), Profl. Inst. Pub. Service of Can. Mem. Anglican Ch. Home: 2060 Palmer Av Ottawa ON K1H 5Z4 Canada Office: Room 962 473 Albert St Ottawa ON K1A 0E5 Canada

KNOWLES, EDITH VAN CISE, clubwoman; b. Summit, N.J., June 13, 1913; s. William Marsh and Mary Winifred (Fritz) Van Cise; student Ga. State Coll. Women, 1930-31, Pratt Inst., 1931-32; m. Benjamin R.W. Knowles, Jan. 7, 1933; children—Benjamin R.W., Van Cise, Grace W. Designer Albany Floral Co. (Ga.), 1956-64, Pace Florist, Albany, 1964-68; chpt. pres., then dist. pres., now nat. pres. Gold Wives Am. Vol. A.R.C.; chmn. vols. U.S.O. Methodist (tchr., supt. jr. high sch. dept.). Club: Ministers' Wives. Home: 5106 Old Dawson Rd Albany GA 31702 Office: PO Box 1703 Albany GA 31702

KNOWLES, HELEN VALENTINE, ednl. adminstr.; b. Colorado Springs, Colo., Feb. 14, 1909; d. George and Annie (Fleming) Knowles; B.A., Colo. Coll., 1930; M.A., Columbia, 1942. Tchr., Ft. Collins (Colo.) High Sch., 1930-41, ednl. counselor for girls, 1939-40; tchr. Wellesley Hills (Mass.) Jr. High Sch., 1942-43; dean residence Salem Acad., Winston-Salem, N.C., 1943-45; dir. students Douglass Coll., Rutgers U., New Brunswick, N.J., 1945-48, dir. placement bur., 1956—; dir. recruiting for personnel dept. Nat. Bd. YWCA, 1948-56. Treas. bd. YWCA, New Brunswick, 1957-63; mem. bd. Urban League, New Brunswick, 1961-64; mem. bd. Protestant Fellowship Found., 1965-67, mem. bd. United Campus Ministry, 1967—; mem. exec. com. Coll.-Fed. Agy. Council, 1967-69. Mem. Council on Social Work Edn. (com. on recruiting for careers in social work 1963—), Am. Personnel and Guidance Assn., Eastern Coll. Personnel Officers (sec. 1964-66), Personnel Club N.Y.C., Met. N.Y. Placement Officers (mem., v.p. exec. com. 1965-67), Garden State Choral Soc. (sec. 1964-65), United Christian Fellowship (mem. bd. 1966—), Phi Beta Kappa, Pi Lambda Theta, Eta Sigma Phi. Mem. Reformed Ch. Club: Zonta (treas. 1964-66). Home: 101A Taylor Av East Brunswick NJ 08816

KNOWLES, JEAN TURNBULL (MRS. JAMES KNOWLES, JR.), artist; b. Cambridge, Mass.; d. Frederick Moncrieff and Alice E. (Hilton) Turnbull; grad. Wheelock Coll., 1919; student Boston Mus. Sch., Chgo. Art Inst., U. Cal. at Los Angeles, Washington U.; m. James Knowles, June 24, 1922; children—James Turnbull, John Hilton. Exhibited in one man shows at Belmont Hill Sch., Mass., St. Louis Artists Guild, Rockefeller Found.; exhibited in group shows at St. Louis Art Mus., Artists Guild, University City Library, St. Louis, others; paintings at W. J. Polk Gallery, St. Louis, also many pvt. collections. Mem. St. Louis Symphony Soc., Artists Guild St. Louis, Friends of St. Louis Art Mus. Home: 7025 Kingsbury Blvd University City MO 63130

KNOWLES, MARY GARDNER, librarian; b. Waltham, Mass., July 10, 1910; d. William E. and Annie (Mackin) Gardner; student Bates Coll., 1930-33; m. Clive D. Knowles, Apr. 1933 (div. 1948); 1 son, Jonathan. Children's librarian Watertown (Mass.) Free Pub. Library, 1935-38; br. librarian Morrill Meml. Library, Norwood, Mass., 1949-53; librarian William Jeanes Meml. Library, Lafayette Hill, Pa., 1954—. Home: 543 N Whitehall Rd Norristown PA 19401 Office: 4051 Joshua Rd Lafayette Hill PA 19444

KNOWLES, RUTHEA, social worker, educator; b. Chgo., Dec. 15, 1916; d. Paul Thomas and Ida (Natzke-Bowers) Knowles; B.S. summa cum laude, Central Mich. U., 1950; M.S.W., U. Mich., 1958. Adminstr. Luth. Community Services. Saginaw, Mich., 1941-57; social worker Midland (Mich.) Family Service, 1958-60; supr. casework Mich. Children's Aid Soc., 1960-66; psychiat. social worker Child Guidance Clinic of Kalamazoo, 1966—. Field instr. grad. students U. Mich., 1960—, Mich. State U., 1962—. Active Saginaw (Mich.) Council Community Services, 1943-58. Mem. Nat. Assn. Social Workers (charter mem.), Acad. Certified Social Workers. Home: 3707 Croyden Av Kalamazoo MI 49007 Office: 2615 Stadium Dr Kalamazoo MI 49001

KNOX, BEULAH CHRISTINA FEELHAVER (MRS. KNOX), electric line constrn. co. exec.; b. Hartington, Neb., May 3, 1916; d. Howard Homer and Tillie (Schmidt) Feelhaver; student Chillicothe Bus. Coll., 1934-35; m. Beryl Knox, Aug. 22, 1935 (dec. June 1973); children—Kenneth, James, Howard. Bookkeeper, Knox Constrn. Co., Grand Island, Neb., 1948-65, sec., 1965—, owner, 1973—. Bidding cons. rural electric and municipal electric lines exhibited art in group shows, Lincoln, Neb. Mem. Order Eastern Star. Office: 1220 E Capital St Grand Island NE 68801

KNOX, NANCY THERESE, internat. marketing cons.; b. Hollywood, Cal., Apr. 16, 1923; d. John Joseph and Anne Veronica (Taughran) Holland; student Regis Coll., 1941-42, Bryant Coll., 1943; m. James Whitworth Knox, Dec. 26, 1946 (div.). Asst. fashion dir. I. Miller Shoes, N.Y.C., 1953-55; partner fas,ion cons. firm Clark-Knox, N.Y.C., 1956-59; co-founder, sec. Jags Unltd. Inc., N.Y.C., 1959-63; co-founder, pres. Renegade Corp., N.Y.C., 1963—, designer Renegade line, 1963—. Mem. adv. com. Garland Coll. Recipient Caswell Massey design award Renegades, 1968, Creative Menswear design ann. mention, 1969, Coty award, 1971, Internat. award Playboy, 1971. Mem. Show Women's Execs. (v.p. 1967-68), Fashion Group, Internat. Platform Assn. Address: 2 Beekman Place New York City NY 10022

KNOX, PATTI JEANNE STEARNS (MRS. ROBERT D. KNOX), polit. worker; b. Detroit, Aug. 18, 1925; d. Dedrick F. and Amelia V. (Seanor) Stearns; student Mich. State U., 1946-48; m. Robert D. Knox, Nov. 27, 1946; 1 son, John. Vice chmn. Mich. Democratic State Central Com., 1967, pres. Mich. Fedn. Dem. Women, 1967—; sec. Dem. Midwest Conf., 1969, 71, 73; mem. Commn. on Party Structure and Del. Selection, Washington, 1969—; mem. Polit. Reform Commn., Detroit, 1969—; mem. Dem. Nat. Com. Charter Com., 1973—. Bd. dirs. Citizens for Better Care, 1973—. Mem. Trade Union Leadership Council, Mich. Ednl. Found., N.A.A.C.P., League Women Voters. Home: 2150 Iroquois Detroit MI 48214 Office: 918 Book Bldg Detroit MI 48226

KNOX, TRUDY, cons. psychologist; b. Cape Girardeau, Mo., Aug. 11, 1926; d. Raymond Kenneth and Gertrude Frances (McCann) Knox; B.S., Northwestern U., 1948; M.A., U. Fla., 1951; postgrad. Ohio State U., 1952-69; Ed.D., U. Ark., 1973. Psychologist, schs. for retarded and residential correctional sch. for delinquent girls State of Ohio, 1952-62; individual practice as cons. psychologist and group psychotherapist, Columbus, O., 1962—; adj. faculty Grad. Sch. Adminstrn. Capital U. Nat. Inst. Mental Health grantee, 1968, 69. Mem. Am. Psychol. Assn., Am. Group Psychotherapy Assn. Home: 112 E Kossuth St Columbus OH 43206

KNUDSEN, HELEN L(EONE), physician; b. Albert Lea, Minn., Oct. 10, 1911; d. Peter S. and Bessie T. (Peterson) Knudsen; B.S., U. Minn., 1934, B.A., 1942, M.B., 1943, M.D., 1944, M.P.H., 1947. Chief technologist, instr. med. tech. U. Minn. Hosps., 1934-40; intern U. Minn. Hosps., 1944; resident Minn. Dept. Health, Mpls., 1944-46, adminstr. emergency maternity and infant care program, 1944-46, dir. div. hosp. services, 1947-74, ret. Lectr. Sch. Pub. Health U. Minn., Mpls., 1950-74. Diplomate Am. Bd. Preventive Medicine. Fellow Am. Coll. Preventive Medicine; mem. Am. Hosp. Assn. (hon.), Am. Assn. Hosp. Planning (pres. 1961-62), A.M.A., Am., Minn. pub. health assns., Minn. State Med. Assn., Hennepin County Med. Soc., Alpha Epsilon Iota. Home: 2101 E River Rd Minneapolis MN 55414

KOBER, ARLETTA REFSHAUGE (MRS. KAY L. KOBER), civic worker; b. Cedar Falls, Ia., Oct. 31, 1919; d. Edward and Mary (Jensen) Refshauge; B.A., State Coll. Ia., 1940, postgrad.; m. Kay Leonard Kober, Feb. 14, 1944; children—Kay, Karilyn. Tchr. high schs., Soldier, Ia., 1940-41, Montezuma, Ia., 1941-43, Waterloo, Ia., 1943-50; tchr. East High Sch., Waterloo, Ia., 1966—; co-ordinator Office Edn., also Health Occupations Waterloo Community Schs., 1966—. Mem. Waterloo Sch. Health Council; nominating com. YWCA, Waterloo; Black Hawk County chmn. Tb Christmas Seals; ward chmn. A.R.C., Waterloo; co-chmn. Citizen's Com. for Sch. Bond Issue; pres. Waterloo P.T.A. Council, Waterloo Vis. Nursing Assn., 1956-57, Kingsley Sch. P.T.A, 1959-60; pres. Waterloo Women's Club, 1963-64, trustee bd. clubhouse dirs., 1957—; mem. Gen. Fedn. Women's Clubs, Nat. Congress Parents and Tchrs.; Presbyterial world service chmn. Presbyn. Women's Assn. Bd. dirs. Black Hawk County Republican Women, 1952-53. Bd. dirs. United Services of Black Hawk County, Broadway Theatre League (v.p. 1963-65). Mem. Am. Assn. U. Women (v.p. 1946-47), N.E.A., League Women Voters (dir. Waterloo 1951-52), Delta Pi Epsilon (charter mem. Alpha Delta chpt.). Club: Town (dir.) (Waterloo). Home: 1046 Prospect Blvd Waterloo IA 50702 Office: Baltimore and Ridgeway Waterloo IA 50702

KOBLENZER, CAROLINE SCOTT ADAMSON (MRS. PETER JOHANN KOBLENZER), physician; b. Bolton, Eng., Sept. 26, 1929; d. James Robertson and Caroline Peach (Scott) Adamson; M.B., U. London (Eng.), 1950; B.S. with honors, U. London, 1953; m. Peter Johann Koblenzer, May 12, 1951; children—Jonathan James, Frances Elizabeth, Graham Peter. House officer obstetrics Royal Free Hosp., London, 1953; lady med. officer gen. duties Sudan Med. Service, Kassala and Juba, Sudan, 1954-55; gen. practice medicine, Kudat and Tawau, Brit. North Borneo, 1955-57; rotating intern West Jersey Hosp., Camden, N.J., 1963; resident dermatology Temple U., Phila., 1964-65, chief resident, 1966; pvt. practice medicine specializing in dermatology, Moorestown and Blackwood, N.J., 1966—; asso. dermatologist W. Jersey Hosp., Camden, N.J., 1967—; attending dermatologist Temple U. Hosp., 1967—; clin. instr. Med. Coll. Pa., Phila., 1967—; asst. prof. clin. dermatology Temple U., 1967—; cons. dermatology Cherry Hill (N.J.) Med. Center, 1968—, John F. Kennedy Hosp., Strattford, N.J., 1968—, Underwood Meml. Hosp., Woodbury, N.J., 1968—. Fellow Am. Acad. Dermatology, Coll. Physicians Phila.; mem. Brit. Med. Assn., A.M.A., Phila. Dermatology Soc., Dermatology Found. Home: Pinetop PO Box 98 159 Warren St Edgewater Park NJ 08010 Office: 303 Chester Av Moorestown NJ 08057 also 141 Blackhorse Pike Blackwood NJ 08012

KOCH, ESTHER DOROTHY, librarian; b. Kansas City, Mo., June 9,, 1909; d. William Christian and Ella Susanna (Asling) Koch; B.A., U. Cal. at Berkeley, 1930, certificate in librarianship, 1931. Jr. librarian Oakland (Cal.) Pub. Library, 1935-37; cataloger U.S. Dept. Agr. Library, Washington, 1937-43, chief catalog dept., 1944-50; cataloger Library U. Cal. at Los Angeles, 1951-58, asst. head catalog dept., 1958-67, head catalog dept., 1967-70, head catalog div., tech. services dept., 1971—. Reorganizer Library of Escuela Nacional de Agricultura, Chapingo, Mex., 1947. Mem. Am. (chmn. nominating com., div. cataloging and classification 1956-57, chmn. cataloging and classification sect., resources and tech. services div. 1969-70), Cal. (pres. tech. services div. 1968) library assns., Am. Assn. U. Women (br. v.p. for membership 1961-62), Los Angeles Regional Group of Catalogers (chmn. 1953-54), So. Cal. Tech. Processes Group. Republican. Methodist. Home: 1510-D California Av Santa Monica CA 90403 Office: 405 Hilgard Av Los Angeles CA 90024

KOCH, HELEN LOIS, research psychologist; b. Blue Island, Ill., Aug. 26, 1895; d. Louis George and Sophia (Uhlich) Koch; Ph.B., U. Chgo., 1918, Ph.D., 1921. Instr. ednl. psychology U. Tex., 1921-23, asst. prof., 1923-25, asso. prof., 1925-27, prof., 1927-29; asso. prof. child psychology U. Chgo., 1929-42, prof. child psychology and human devel., 1942-60, prof. emeritus, 1960—, dir. Nursery Sch., 1934-48, coordinator, 1938-48. Vis. prof. Johann Wolfgang Goethe U., Frankfurt-Main, Germany, 1948-49, 58, Julius Maximilian U., Würzburg, Germany, 1948-49; lectr. U. So. Cal., summer 1962. Mem. Ill. Soc. Cons. Psychologists (pres. 1940-41), Chgo. Psychol. Club, Chgo. Assn. Child Study and Parent Edn., Am. Psychol. Assn. (G. Stanley Hall medal 1967), Soc. Research Child Devel., A.A.A.S., Phi Beta Kappa, Sigma Xi, Pi Lambda Theta, Delta Kappa Gamma (founder, mem. nat. adminstrv. bd. 1965-69). Author: Twins and Twin Relations, 1965; monographs. Contbr. articles to profl. jours. Mem. editorial bd. Child Development, 1968-70, Jour. Research in Child Devel., 1964-70. Home: 1130 S Michigan Av Chicago IL 60605 Office: U Chgo Chicago IL 60637

KOCH, MARCELLA M. HURLEY (MRS. LOREN M. KOCH), newspaper editor; b. Antigo, Wis., Dec. 4, 1914; d. Dan and Adele Rose (Moss) Hurley; grad. Langlade Tchrs. Coll., 1933; m. Loren M. Koch, Oct. 20, 1934; children—Marian (Mrs. Stephen Schleck), Daniel L., Michael J. Tchr. primary grades, Antigo, 1933-35; with Antigo Banner, German lang. newspaper, 1935-38; news editor Menomonee Falls (Wis.) News, 1952-56; editor Poynette (Wis.) Press, 1956—, editor Retail and Bus. Rev. Mag., 1966-72, editor Modern Schs. mag., 1966-72, editor Writer's Showcase, 1967—; pub. Poynette Printing Co. (Wis.), 1971—; sec. South Central Publs., Inc., Stoughton, Wis., 1964—. Recipient editorial award Wis. Press Assn., 1967, Wis. Press Women, 1968, 69, 70, Nat. Fedn. Press Women, 1969, Nat. Fisheries Inst., 1970, 71; named Madison chpt. Woman of Yr., Theta Sigma Phi. Mem. Wis. Press Assn., Wis. Press Women, Wis. Regional Writers (state dir. 1964-72), Poynette (dir. 1957-59, sec. 1958-59), Lake Wisconsin (dir. 1971—, treas. 1971—) chambers commerce, Castle Rock-Petenwell Lakes Assn. (pub. relations dir. 1969-71), Theta Sigma Phi. Clubs: Poynette Garden, Poynette-Arlington Woman's. Home: 307 N Howard St Poynette WI 53955 Office: 513 Highway St Poynette WI 53955

KOCH, SISTER MARY THERESE, hosp. adminstr.; b. Petersburg, Neb., Oct. 28, 1924; d. Frank J. and Elizabeth (Brachle) Koch; student Chadron State Tchrs. Coll., 1942, Creighton U., summer 1944, Coll. St. Mary, Omaha, 1944-45, St. Louis U., summer 1957, Columbia, 1960-61. Joined Internat. Congregation of Missionary Benedictine Sisters, 1940; accountant, receptionist Holy Trinity Hosp., Graceville, Minn., 1945-47; accountant, receptionist Our Lady of Lourdes Hosp., Norfolk, Neb., 1947-52, accountant, bus. mgr., 1952-60, asst. adminstr. 1960-62, adminstr., 1962—. Sec.-treas. Our Lady of Lourdes Hosp. Corp., 1947—. Tchr. shelter mgmt. courses Civil Def., 1969—; mem. Adv. Com. for Continuing Edn. of Nurses, 1973—; mem. Area 5 Emergency Med. Service Council, State of Neb., 1973—; mem. adv. bd. Norfolk Madison County Civil Def., 1970—. Recipient Nat. Pfizer award of merit Chas. Pfizer Co., Inc., 1970. Mem. Cath. Hosp. Assn. (pres. Neb. conf. 1969, 70, mem. exec. bd. Neb. conf. 1972-73), Neb. Assn. Alcoholism Counselors, Hosp. Financial Mgmt. Assn., Neb. Pub. Health Assn., Norfolk C. of C., Am. Acad. Med. Adminstrs., Internat. Platform Assn. Address: PO Box 1129 Norfolk NE 68701

KOCH, NANCY DODGE, city commr.; b. South Bend, Ind., Mar. 13, 1931; d. Nelson Edward and Pauline Marcella (Treesh) Dodge; B.A. cum laude, DePauw U., Greencastle, Ind., 1953; m. James A. Koch, Sept. 5, 1953; children—Martha, Steven, Carol. Psychol. testing personnel dept. Sears, Roebuck & Co., Chgo., 1953-54; dept. supr. Am. Hosp. Assn., Chgo., 1954-56; city commr., Albuquerque, 1972—, vice chmn., 1973—. Mem. Pub. Safety Steering Com. Nat. League Cities, 1973-74, mem. nominating com. Nat. League Cities Conf., 1973—. Chmn. nominating com., bd. dirs. Chaparral council Girl Scouts Am., 1968-71; pres. Jr. League, Albuquerque, 1970-71; div. chmn. United Community Fund, 1971; pres. N.M. Municipal League, 1973—. Bd. dirs. Albuquerque Hist. Soc.; trustee, publicity chmn. Kappa Alpha Theta Found. Republican. Home: 2901 Euclid Av NE Apt 21-A Albuquerque NM 87106 Office: City Hall Albuquerque NM 87103

KOCH, REGINA MARIE, coll. dean.; b. Long Branch, N.J., Sept. 23, 1926; d. Joseph and Eva (Rachor) Koch; B.A., Regis Coll., 1952; M.A., Boston Coll., 1956; Ph.D., Harvard, 1964. Prof. medieval German lit. Regis Coll., Weston, Mass., 1964-70, acad. dean, 1970-73; v.p. for acad. affairs U. Me., Presque Isle, 1973—. Prof. medieval German lit. Boston Coll., 1970, 72. Mem. Am. Assn. Tchrs. German, (pres. New Eng. council 1969-70), Modern Lang. Assn., Am. Assn. U. Women, Am. Assn. U. Profs., Phi Beta Kappa. Home: Presque Isle ME 04769 Office: 181 Main St Presque Isle ME 04769

KOCH, RUTH MARGUERITE, educator, artist; b. Hazleton, Pa., July 11, 1901; d. Henry George and Margaret (Zimmerman) Koch; grad. Bloomsburg State Tchrs. Coll., 1921; Ph.B., Muhlenberg Coll., 1931; M.A., Bucknell U., 1948; student Sch. Fine and Applied Arts, Chgo., 1923; postgrad. N.Y.U., 1925, 28, Pa. State U., 1935; visited art schs., galleries, Europe, 1952, 57, 65, 68. One-man shows at Penn State U. Center, 1937, Hazleton Art League, 1948; exhibited annually in group shows Lehigh Art Alliance, Lehigh U., Muhlenberg Coll., nat. shows Miniature Painters Soc., Smithsonian Instn., Corcoran Gallery, also N.Y., N.J., Pa., Kan., Washington; represented in permanent collections at Lehigh U. Art Gallery, Call Chronicle Newspaper Art Collection, Allentown, Pa., also pvt. collections in U.S., P.R., Eng. Art tchr. elementary sch., Hazleton, Pa., 1921-39, jr. high sch., 1939-40, sr. high sch., 1940-67; designed, painted children's stories on glass lantern slides, 1930-35; lectr., demonstrator of art various religious and civic groups, clubs, schs., colls. Recipient 1st place water color, Hazleton, 1938, 3d water color award, Harrisburg, 1940, 41. Mem. Pa. Edn. Assn. (pres. art group Scranton 1947) Nat., Pa., Luzerne County ret. tchrs. assns., Community Concert Assn., Lehigh Art Alliance, Hazleton Art League (purchase award 1968), Pa. Guild Craftsman, Internat. Platform Assn., Delta Kappa Gamma. Author articles in art and other periodicals. Lutheran. Home and Studio: 551 Lincoln St Hazleton PA 18201

KOCHANT, HELEN E. HOFFMANN (MRS. WILLIAM M. KOCHANT), educator; b. N.Y.C.; d. Edward J. and Violet I. (Randall) Hoffmann; B.S., Fordham U., 1951; M.S., 1956; M.A., Columbia U., 1960, Ed.D., 1968; m. William M. Kochant, July 9, 1960. Tchr. elementary sch. Villa Maria Acad., N.Y.C., 1951-55, N.Y.C. Pub. Sch. System, 1955-60; instr. Tchrs. Coll., Columbia U., N.Y.C., 1961-63, asst. instr. summer work conf., 1961-63; asst. prof. edn. State U. N.Y., Coll. New Paltz, N.Y., 1963-69, asso. prof., 1969-72, prof., 1972—. Tchr. summer reading N.Y.C. Pub. Sch., 1958; instr. fed. supported reading program, Hyde Park, N.Y., 1963; cons. and speaker children's lit. and reading Mid-Hudson Valley Area, N.Y., 1966—; active Children's Lit. Conf., summer, 1970, Children's Lit. Festival, spring 1972; co-dir. work conf., co-instr. in-service course, primary edn. Sch. for 70's, Kingston, N.Y., 1971. Mem. Nat. Council Tchrs. English, Internat. Reading Assn., N.E.A., Nat. Assn. Edn. Young Children, N.Y. State Tchrs. Assn. N.Y. State English Council, A.L.A. Author: (with Camp and Henry) Book 2, The World of Language, 1970. Editor (with Jane Vreeland) Individualizing Learning; (with others) Follett Elementary English Series. Home: PO Box 482 New Paltz NY 12561

KOCHER, MARJORIE ELEANOR BARTLE (MRS. JOHN WAYLAND KOCHER), sch. adminstr.; b. Oakland, Cal., Aug. 23, 1926; d. Henry Mitchell and Alma Valentine (Berntsen) Bartle; student Santa Rosa Jr. Coll., 1943-45; B.A., U. Cal. at Berkeley, 1948, postgrad., 1950-51; postgrad. U. Ore., 1963-64; internat. diploma in child devel. and edn. Maria Montessori Tng. Organization, London, Eng., 1966; m. John Wayland Kocher, Mar. 4, 1949; children—Cynthia, Jeffrey Bartle. Social welfare worker Sonoma

County and Oakland, Cal., 1948-50; nursery sch. tchr., dir. Presbyn. Ch., Eugene, Ore., 1961-64; tchr. Eugene Montessori Sch., 1970-72; founder Montessori Internat. Inc.; dir. Montessori Internat. Sch., Cottage Grove, Ore., 1972—. Pres. USAF Officers' Wives, 1960; Japanese-Am. relations chmn. USAF Wives, 1959. Mem. Ore. Assn. Nursery Edn. (pres. 1963), Ore. Assn. Edn. Young People (sec. 1971), Maude I. Kerns Art Center, Nat. League Am. Pen Women. Club: Toastmistress (pres. 1957-58) (Tokyo, Japan). Author: Montessori Manual of Cultural Subjects, 1972. Contbr. articles to jours. and mags. Home: 565 Kingswood Av Eugene OR 97405 Office: Montessori Internat 216 S 3d St Cottage Grove OR 97424

KOCHERTHALER, MINA, artist; b. Munich, Germany (came to U.S. 1940, naturalized 1946); d. Josef and Selma (Zeilberger) Kocherthaler; student Coll. City N.Y., Columbia, Art Students League, N.A.D.; m. Henry Moser, 1951 (div.). Exhibited in group shows with Allied Artists Am., N.Y.C., Audubon Artists, N.Y.C., Nat. Soc. Painters in Casein and Acrylic, N.Y.C., Am. Watercolor Soc., N.Y.C., Royal Watercolour Soc., London, Eng., 1962, Met. Mus., 1967, Museo de la Acuarela, Mexico City, 1968, Butler Inst., 1970, Canadian Soc. Painters, 1971-72, also mus. and colls. in U.S., Can.; represented in permanent collections. Recipient various awards Nat. Soc. Painters in Casein and Acrylic, Inc., Audubon Artists, Am. Watercolor Soc. Mem. Allied Artists Am., Audubon Artists, Nat. Soc. Painters in Casein and Acrylic, Inc. (v.p. 1962—), Fine Arts Fedn., Am. Watercolor Soc. (rec. sec. 1963—, coordinating chmn. 1962-72). Home: 124 W 79th St New York City NY 10024

KOCHTA, RUTH MARTHA (MRS. ALBERT EMIL KOCHTA), painter; b. N.Y.C., Jan. 5, 1924; d. Harry Joseph and Anna (Braun) Evers; student Art Students League, 1966-70; m. Albert Emil Kochta, Nov. 7, 1948; children—Alan, Carol. Exhibited in group shows N.A.D., 1969, Audubon Artists, 1970, Wadsworth Atheneum, 1970, Elizabet Ney Mus., 1971, New Britain Mus., 1972; represented in permanent collections Philathea Coll. Mus., Fine Arts Gallery Ardmore, Scarsdale Gallery Contemporary Art, Ruth Green's Gallery. Recipient numerous awards in various competitions. Mem. Conn. Acad. Fine Arts, Va. Mus. Home: 143-43 Poplar Av Flushing NY 11355 Office: 156-09 45th Av Flushing NY 11355

KOCH-WESER, SOPHIE CAROLINE SCHWENDER, architect; b. Shanghai, China, Apr. 3, 1930 (came to U.S. 1947, naturalized 1953); d. Carl G. J. and May M. (Fuchs) Schwender; student U. Utah, 1947-49; B.S., Ill. Inst. Tech., 1954; m. Dieter Koch-Weser, June 3, 1950; children—Carol-Ann, Suzanne. Archtl. apprenticeship Hermann & Saltzman, Architects and Engrs., Chgo., 1954-56; archtl. designer, job capt. Leon Gordon Miller & Assos., Cleve., 1957-64; architect Office of Max O. Urbahn, N.Y.C., 1964-67; partner firm Med. Facilities Planning Assos., Inc., 1970—. cons. to Dept. Hosps., N.Y.C., 1968—. Mem. Am. Soc. Indsl. Designers, Archtl. League N.Y., A.I.A. Home: 19 Standish Rd Wellesley MA 02181 Office: 1575 Tremont St Boston MA 02120

KOCK, VERA CALVO (MRS. WINSTON EDWARD KOCK, JR.), psychologist; b. Rio Negro, Argentina, Dec. 25, 1940; d. Alfonso Daniel and Juana (Lafuente) Calvo; M.A. in Clin. Psychology, U. Salvador, Buenos Aires, 1963, M.A. in Diplomacy, 1964; M.A. in Personnel and Indsl. Psychology, Columbia, 1968; m. Winston Edward Kock, Jr., Nov. 14, 1971. Came to U.S., 1964, naturalized, 1970. Tchr. elementary and secondary schs., Buenos Aires, Argentina, 1958-61, Buenos Aires, 1960-64; instr. John F. Kennedy U., Buenos Aires, 1963-64; psychometrician Puerto Rican Community Devel. Project, Inc., N.Y.C., 1969-71; chief psychometrician Bd. of Edn. Drug Program, Bklyn., 1971-72; psychologist Ct. Employment Project Criminal Ct., N.Y.C., 1972-74; asso. human rights analyst N.Y. State Div. Human Rights, 1974—. Mem. Am. Psychol. Assn. Home: 220 East 73rd St New York City NY 10021 Office: 346 Broadway New York City NY 10013

KOCOUREK, JUNE DOROTHY, antique dealer; b. Birmingham, Eng., June 9, 1928; d. Percy Richard and Ida Dorothy (Tranter) Wise; grad. Malvern (Eng.) Girls' Coll., 1946, Kerr-Sander Secretarial Sch., London, Eng., 1947; m. James F. Kocourek, Aug. 8, 1970. Came to U.S., 1955, naturalized, 1971. Hotel managerial positions in Eng., Scotland, Can., Jamaica and Nassau, 1952-61; office mgr. Bahamas Tourist Office, London, 1961-62; owner English Accent Antiques, Dania, Fla., 1965—. Mem. Dania Antique Dealers Assn. (pres. 1971-72), Malvern Coll. Assn. (life). Republican. Mem. Ch. of Eng. Club: British Floridian (Ft. Lauderdale). Home: 600 NE 2d St Dania FL 33004 Office: 57 N Federal Hwy Dania FL 33004

KOEBEL, SISTER CELESTIA, hosp. adminstr.; b. Chillicothe, O., Jan. 12, 1928; d. George Francis and Gertrude (Billian) Koebel; grad. Good Samaritan Hosp. Sch. Nursing, Cin., 1951; B.S., Coll. Mt. St. Joseph, 1958; M.H.A., St. Louis U., 1964. Joined Sisters of Charity of Cin., 1946; maternity nursing supr. Good Samaritan Hosp., Cin., 1952-55; med. and maternity nursing supr. St. Mary-Corwin Hosp., Pueblo, Colo., 1955-61; asst. dir. nursing service Good Samaritan Hosp., Dayton, O., 1961-62; hosp. adminstrv. resident Providence Hosp., Seattle, 1963-64; adminstr. St. Joseph Hosp., Albuquerque, 1964—. Bishop's rep. for hosps. Archdiocese of Santa Fe, 1969-73; mem. Denver Provincial Council of Sisters of Charity, 1967-69, 72-73. Mem. exec. com. Conf. Diocesan Coordinators Health Affairs, U.S. Catholic Conf., 1974. Bd. dirs. United Community Fund Albuquerque, 1974-76. Recipient award Nat. Fedn. Bus. and Profl. Womens Clubs, 1968. Fellow Am. Coll. Hosp. Adminstrs.; mem. Am., Catholic, N.M. (treas. 1968-70, v.p. 1970 pres. 1972), hosp. assns., Assn. Western Hosps., N.M. Conf. Cath. Hosps. (pres. 1966-67), Albuquerque Area Hosp. Council (pres. 1966-67), Mid Rio Grande Health Planning Council (treas. 1972-73), Greater Albuquerque C. of C. Home: 400 Walter St NE Albuquerque NM 87102 Office: 400 Walter St NE Albuquerque NM 87102

KOEHLER, BARBARA ANN COX (MRS. ROBERT EDMUNDS KOEHLER), physician; b. Jersey City, Oct. 4, 1943; d. George Joseph and Edna Frances (Thorsen) Cox; B.A. magna cum laude, Drew U., 1965; M.D., Cornell U., 1969; m. Robert Edmunds Koehler, June 8, 1968. With Reproductive Biology Research Found., St. Louis, 1969-70. Cons. Atlanta area family planning survey from Met. Atlanta Council for Health to family planning evaluation activity br. Center for Disease Control, 1971. Unitarian-Universalist. Home: 52 Gaviota Way San Francisco CA 94127

KOEHLER, ISABEL WINIFRED, writer, artist; b. Boston, Feb. 5, 1903; d. George Wallace and Mary Elizabeth (Strout) Goodwin; student art courses Harvard, Mass. Inst. Tech., others; m. Frederick Mills Koehler, Apr. 16, 1925; 1 son, Alden Goodwin. Contbr. articles to Boston Daily Post, Boston Herald-Traveler, poetry to Boston Daily Globe, Melrose Free Press, Everett Leader Herald, others; exhibited numerous galleries, festivals, ann. exhbns. Recipient commemorative medal for art achievement Leonardo da Vinci Accademia, Rome, 1973, other awards, prizes. Mem. Mass. Poetry Soc., New Eng. Women's Press Assn., Agnes Carr Writers Club (pres., exec. bd.), Internat. Poetry Soc., Nat. Writers Club, Internat. Platform Assn., Everett Art Assn., Old Boston Soc. Ind. Artists, Centro Studi e Scambi Internazionali. Address: 30 Fremont Av Everett MA 02149

KOEHLER, MARY JANE (MRS. FULTON KOEHLER), real estate exec.; b. Mpls., Sept. 8, 1914; d. Ogden Armour and Ruth (Palmer) Confer; B.A., U. Minn., 1935; m. Fulton Koehler, Mar. 26, 1940; children—George Fulton, Ruth (Mrs. John Frederick Bergerson), James Fulton, Thomas Edward. Corporate sec. Confer Bros., Inc., Mpls., 1945-63, pres., 1963—; dir. Hubbard Milling Co., Mankato, Minn. Bd. dirs. Pillsbury-Waite Neighborhood Services, 1964-70, hon. bd. dirs., 1970—. Mem. League Women Voters, Delta Gamma. Presbyn. Club: Woman's (Mpls.). Home: 4726 Girard Av S Minneapolis MN 55409 Office: Hubbard Milling Co 424 N Front St Mankato MN 56001

KOELBL, DOROTHY JUNE, librarian; b. Lancaster, Pa.; d. George Anthony and Florence (Walters) Koelbl; B.S., Millersville State Coll., 1963, M.Ed. in Elementary Edn., 1972; postgrad U. London, 1967, Temple U., 1973—. Librarian, Solanco Sch. dist., Quarryville, Pa., 1963-64, Lancaster Sch. dist., 1964—. Mem. Lancaster Unitarian Service Com., chmn. 1973—; mem. Will-Do Night Ministry, Community Alert Plan. Life fellow Intercontinental Biog. Assn.; mem. Philatelic Soc. Lancaster County (pres. 1972-74), Lancaster Hiking Club (treas. 1973-75), Am., Lancaster County library assns., Nat., Lancaster, Pa. edn. assns., Lancaster Lebanon Reading Assn., Am. Topical Assn., Pi Lambda Theta (chpt. corr. sec. 1973). Home: 407 N Cherry St Lancaster PA 17602 Office: Reservior St and Lehigh Av Lancaster PA 17602

KOENIG, GLORIA ELEANOR, lawyer; b. Bayonne, N.J., Oct. 8, 1926; d. Benjamin M.A. and Beatrice (Abramson) Kline; B.A., Washington Square Coll., 1946; M.S., N.Y. U., 1949, J.D., 1963, LL.M., 1967, J.S.D., 1972; m. Burton G. Koenig, June 27, 1954. Teacher math. Bayonne (N.J.) Tech. and Vocational High Sch., 1946-48; research chemist Vitro Labs., West Orange, N.J., 1948-57; admitted to N.J. bar, 1963; pvt. practice law, specializing in patent law, Bayonne, 1963—; dir. Mr. Liberty Industries Inc., Bayonne. Trustee Bayonne Community Mental Health Center. Recipient Frances Lewis Haymen award N.Y.U. Sch. Law, 1967. Mem. Am., N.J. State, Hudson County, Bayonne bar assns., N.J. Patent Law Assn., Nat. Council Jewish Women, Eclectic Honor Soc. (Washington Sq. Coll.), Hadassah, Orgn. for Rehab. Tng. Jewish religion. Author: Patent Invalidity: A Statistical and Substantive Analysis, 1974. Contbr. articles to profl. jours. Home: 807 Avenue C Bayonne NJ 07002 Office: 664 Broadway Bayonne NJ 07002

KOENIG, KATHRYN ELINOR, educator; b. St. Louis, Oct. 5, 1931; d. Ernest W. and Laura (Zenk) Koenig; A.B., Washington U., St. Louis, 1952, M.A., 1954; Ph.D., U. Mich., 1962. Mem. faculty Bennington (Vt.) Coll., 1962-63; lectr. Bryn Mawr (Pa.) Coll., 1963-65; asst. prof. psychology York U., Toronto, Ont., Can., 1965-68, asso. prof., 1968—, asso. dean Faculty of Arts, 1973—. Mem. Eastern, Am., Canadian psychol. assns., Soc. Psychol. Study Social Issues, Canadian Assn. U. Tchrs., Phi Beta Kappa, Sigma Xi. Author: (with T. M. Newcomb, R. Flacks, D. Warwick) Persistence and Change, 1967. Home: 19 Howard Dr Willowdale Ontario Canada Office: Department of Psychology York University Downsview Ontario Canada

KOENIG, LINDA MIRIN (MRS. GUNTER W. T. KOENIG), economist; b. N.Y.C., Feb. 22, 1939; d. Reuben Louis and Ethel Bloom (Lehrer) Mirin; B.A. summa cum laude, Radcliffe Coll., 1959; Ph.D., Harvard, 1964; postgrad. U. Paris, 1959-60; m. Gunter W. T. Koenig, June 20, 1968. Sr. economist Inter-Am. Devel. Bank, Washington, 1964-67, Internat. Monetary Fund, Washington, 1967-71, asst. div. chief, 1971-72, adviser, 1972-73, div. chief, 1973—. Mem. Am. Econ. Assn., Am. Polit. Sci. Assn. Home: 9411 Overlea Dr Potomac MD 20850 Office: Internat Monetary Fund Washington DC 20431

KOENIG, RACHEL HOPE, coll. adminstr.; b. Rochester, N.Y., Dec. 28, 1944; d. Fred and Laurena Myrtle (Stiles) Koenig; B.A., N. Central Bible Coll., Mpls., 1967; postgrad. U. Minn., 1967-68. Coll. recorder N. Central Bible Coll., Mpls., 1967-71, coll. registrar, 1971—. Mem. Upper-Midwest Assn. Collegiate Registrars and Admissions Counselors, Am. Assn. Higher Edn., Delta Epsilon Chi. Mem. Assembly of God Ch. (jr. high Sunday sch. supt. 1969—, childrens ch. coordinator 1973—). Home: 3806 Toledo Av N Robbinsdale MN 55422 Office: 910 Elliot Av S Minneapolis MN 55404

KOENIG, WILLA LISETTE, educator; b. Staplehurst, Neb., July 2, 1908; d. William H. and Lisette R. (Weller) Koenig; B.S., Concordia Tchrs. Coll., 1948; M.A., Omaha Municipal U., 1952; Ph.D. (state scholar), U. Mich., 1964. Faculty St. John Luth. Sch., White Lake, S.D., 1928-29, Zion Lutheran Sch., Bancroft, Neb., 1929-36; prin. Trinity Luth. Sch., Boone, Ia., 1936-43; faculty Cross Luth. Sch., Omaha, 1943-47; dean of women Concordia Tchrs. Coll., Seward, Neb., 1948-51, registrar, 1951-73, prof., 1972—. Mem. Gov.'s Commn. on Human Rights, 1964-66. Mem. Seward County Historical Soc. (co-founder 1967), Seward Bus. and Profl. Women's Club, Nat. Deans of Women Assn. (state pres. 1953-55), Am. Assn. Collegiate Registrars and Admissions Officers (state pres. 1956-57), Delta Kappa Gamma (state historian 1973—, internat. com. scholarship 1972—). Republican. Lutheran. Contbr. articles to profl. jours. Home: 310 E Hillcrest Dr Seward NE 68434

KOERBER, JANET P., lawyer; b. Milw., Nov. 22, 1933; d. Clarence F. and Isabelle (Arndt) Koerber; student U. Wis., 1952-53; B.A., Marquette U., 1963, J.D., 1966. Admitted to Wis. bar, 1966; pvt. gen. practice law, Milw., 1966—; sec., dir. Bay Point Enterprises Ltd., Bay Point Pharmacy Inc., Olympic Boxing Club Inc.; dir. Shelton Industries Ltd.; treas., dir. Design & Print Shop Inc., dir. Melody Ranch, Inc. Mem. Am., Wis., Milw. bar assns., Kappa Beta Pi. Home: 8235 N Mohawk Rd Fox Point WI 53217 Office: 152 W Wisconsin Av Milwaukee WI 53203

KOESTLER, FRANCES ADLERSTEIN (MRS. MILTON KOESTLER), writer, editor, pub. relations cons.; b. N.Y.C., Jan. 11, 1914; d. Louis and Minna (Rindner) Adlerstein; B.A., Bklyn. Coll., 1936; m. Milton Koestler, Aug. 2, 1954 (dec. Aug. 1969). Staff writer Am. Hebrew Mag., N.Y.C., 1930-35, editor, 1936-38; dir. publicity Am. Joint Distbn. Com., N.Y.C., 1938-43; dir. pub. relations Welfare Council N.Y., 1943-46; mgr. sales promotion Cornelius Products Co., N.Y.C., 1947-52; dir. pub. relations Nat. Travelers Aid Assn., N.Y.C., 1952-58; dir. community relations Jewish Child Care Assn., N.Y.C., 1958-63; pub. relations cons., 1963—. Editorial cons. N.Y.C. Regional Rehab. Commn., 1965-68, Am. Found. for Blind, 1964-66, Am. Occupational Therapy Assn., 1969, Indsl. Home for Blind, Bklyn., 1969; columnist Wonderful World Women, Nat. Jewish Monthly, Washington, 1960-70; dir. Kingsview Homes Inc., Bklyn., 1967-69. Mem. Nat. Pub. Relations Council (dir. 1965-71, v.p. 1972—), Nat. Social Welfare Assembly (chmn. com. on ednl. TV 1956-58), Nat. Conf. Social Welfare (mem. pub. relations com. 1962-70). Author: Careers in Social Work, 1964; Dealing With Controversy, 1963; Creative Annual Reports, 1970; The Unseen Minority: A Social History of Blindness, 1974. Editor: Joint Distribution Commn. Digest, 1940-43; Better Times, 1943-46; Shifting Scenes, 1952-58; Our Children, 1960-63; Comstac Report, 1966; Rehab. Workshop Reports, 1965-68; Continuing Edn. in Occupational Therapy, 1970; Out of the Shadows, 1970. Office: 135 Ashland Pl Brooklyn NY 11201

KOETHER, NATALIE IRIS SALKIND (MRS. PAUL OTTO KOETHER), constrn. co. exec.; b. Wilmington, Del., Dec. 16, 1939; d. Milton and Ruth (Pechter) Salkind; B.A., U. Pa., 1961, LL.B., 1965; m. Paul Otto Koether, May 11, 1971. Admitted to Pa. bar, 1966; law clk. Court of Common Pleas, Phila., 1965-67; asso. firm Morgan, Lewis & Bockius, Esqs., Phila., 1967-71; sec., gen. counsel, dir. Residex Corp., Far Hills, N.J., 1971-73, v.p., adminstrv. and legal affairs, 1973—. Mem. Am., Pa., Phila. bar assns. Address: Pennbrook Rd Far Hills NJ 07931

KOGER, MILDRED EMMELENE NICHOLS, educator; b. Jacksonville, Fla.; d. Hugh Huntley and Edna (Snell) Nichols; student Rollins Coll., 1945-46; B.A., Fla. State U., 1949; Mus.B., B. Mus. Edn., Jacksonville U., 1955; M. Ed., U. Fla., 1966, Ed.D., 1970. Tchr., Lakeshore Jr. High Sch., Jacksonville, Fla., 1949-56; choral dir., head music dept. Paxon Sr. High Sch., Jacksonville, 1956-65; lectr. voice Jacksonville U., 1955-66; grad. asst. music U. Fla., 1965-67; counselor, psychology faculty Fla. Jr. Coll., Jacksonville, 1967-68; staff psychologist Duval County Bd. Pub. Instrn., Jacksonville, 1968-69, chief psychologist, 1969, 70, counselor, psychologist, 1972—; resident coordinator student teaching Fla. State U., 1970-71; prof. Edward Waters Coll., 1971-72; lectr. Jacksonville U., 1973—. Mem. Nat. Assn. Tchrs. Singing, Am. Choral Dirs. Assn., Am. Personnel and Guidance Assn., Fla. Sch. Psychologists Assn., Council for Exceptional Children, Alpha Xi Delta, Sigma Alpha Iota. Democrat. Contbr. article to textbook. Home: 3629 Marianna Rd Jacksonville FL 32217

KOHIN, BARBARA CASTLE (MRS. ROGER P. KOHIN), educator, polit. worker; b. Providence, R.I., Dec. 11, 1932; d. William A. and Barbara Lucille (Valentine) Castle; B.S., Coll. William and Mary, 1953; M.S., U. Md., 1956, Ph.D., 1960; m. Roger P. Kohin, July 17, 1959; children—Margaret, Judith Ann, Suzanne. Boyle Found. fellow van der Waals Lab., U. Amsterdam (Netherlands), 1956-57; physicist Batelle Inst., Geneva, Switzerland, 1961-62; instr. State Coll. at Worcester, Mass., 1964-67; asst. prof. physics Clark U., Worcester, 1967-68, asst. prof. affiliate edn., 1973—; research asso. Mass. Inst. Tech., Cambridge, 1972-74. Chmn. community forums com. Community Services Planning Council, Worcester, Mass., 1972—; mem. Worcester Art Mus. Mem. Worcester Democratic City Com., 1972—; mem. Mass. State Democratic Platform Com., 1972—; city councillor City of Worcester, 1974—. Corporator Children's Friend Soc., 1972; mem. adv. bd. Marillac Manor, 1972. Mem. Am. Civil Liberties Union, Common Cause, League Women Voters (dir. 1965-66), C. of C. (mem. local govt. com. 1971). Contbr. articles in field to profl. jours. Home: 11 Berwick St Worcester MA 01602

KOHL, KATHLEEN ANN, museum curator; b. Milw., Oct. 5, 1943; d. Charles Edward and Ann Mary (Harley) Kohl; B.A., Mt. Mary Coll., 1965; postgrad. U. Edinburgh (Scotland), 1966-67, U. Wis., 1969-70. Instr., Meml. High Sch., Waukesha, Wis., 1965-66; research asst. Milw. Art Center, 1967-68; curator Birmingham (Ala.) Museum Art, 1968-69; curator, dir. art Stamford (Conn.) Museum, 1970—, cons. exhibit design and art program, 1970—. Free-lance graphic designer. Mem. Am. Assn. Museums, Delta Phi Delta. Office: 39 Scofieldtown Rd Stamford CT 06903

KOHLER, ANNE TRIMBLE (MRS. WILLIAM R. KOHLER), rehab. ofcl.; b. Ft. Worth, Sept. 4, 1925; d. Terrell Marshall and Elizabeth (Llewellyn) Trimble; B.S., U. Tex., 1948, M.A., 1952; m. William R. Kohler, Aug. 10, 1950 (dec. Feb. 1961); children—Robert Daniel, Raymond Llewellyn. Dir., Pease Elementary Child Care Center, Austin, Tex., 1948-55; psychiat. social worker Austin State Hosp., 1959-61, vocational rehab. counselor for mentally ill, 1961-69; research utilitzation specialist Tex. Rehab. Commn. and Region VI Dept. Health, Edn. and Welfare, Austin, 1969-72; program adminstr. research utilization Gov.'s Com. on Aging, 1972—. Mem. Am., Tex. personnel and guidance assns., Austin Social Welfare Assn. (pres. 1969), Tex. United Community Services, Nat. Rehab. Counseling Assn., Tex. Psychol. Assn. (exec. bd.), Mental Health Assn. Austin-Travis County, Austin Personnel Assn., Internat. Soc. Rehab. of Disabled, Nat. Gerontological Soc., Internat. Assn. Scholar and Profl. Guidance. Contbr. articles to profl. jours. Home: 3902 Idlewild St Austin TX 78731 Office: PO Box 12786 Capitol Station Austin TX 78711

KOHLER, CHARLOTTE, editor; b. Richmond, Va., Sept. 16, 1908; d. Edwin Charles and Augusta F. (Bromm) K.; B.A., Vassar Coll., 1929; M.A., U. Va., 1933, Ph.D., 1936; Litt.D., Smith Coll., 1971. Instr. English, Woman's Coll. of U. of N.C., 1936-41, asst. prof., 1941-42, mng. editor The Virginia Quarterly Review, 1942-46, editor, 1946—; asso. prof. English, U. Va., 1965-71, prof., 1971—. Mem. Am. Assn. Univ. Women, Phi Beta Kappa. Episcopalian. Home: 1900 Edgewood Lane Charlottesville VA 22903 Office: One West Range Charlottesville VA 22903

KOHLMAN, HELEN SLIPMAN (MRS. HERMAN SEIFERTH KOHLMAN), lawyer; b. New Orleans, June 22, 1932; d. Isadore and Fannie (Rosenzweiz) Slipman; student Sophie Newcomb Coll., 1949-52; J.D., Loyola U., New Orleans, 1968; m. Herman Seiferth Kohlman, June 22, 1963; children—Sandra, Marsha, Neil, Ira. Tchr. elementary sch., New Orleans, 1962-64; admitted to La. bar, 1968; law clk. Civil Dist. Court, New Orleans, 1968-69; mem. firm Kohlman & Kohlman, New Orleans, 1969—. Coordinator, Mayor's Juvenile Deliquency Task Force, New Orleans, 1972-73; co-chmn. Vol. Juvenile Court Probation Program, 1973—; mem. Mayor's Property Tax Revision Com., 1972; mem. steering com. Nat. Endowment for the Humanities, 1972-73. Mem. steering com. Democratic Women's Polit. Caucus, 1972. Bd. dirs. Ind. Women's Orgn., 1972—; mem. adv. bd. Juvenile Court, 1973—; bd. dirs. Youth Assistance Commn. of New Orleans, 1973—. Mem. La. Bar Assn., Nat. Women's Lawyers Assn., Nat. Council of Jewish Women (bd. dirs. New Orleans sect. 1970—), La. Law Inst., League Women Voters (legal adviser 1971-73, bd. dirs. 1971-72), Brandeis Women's Orgn. Mem. Hadassah (dir. 1966—). Home: 4325 State St Dr New Orleans LA 70125 Office: 1807 Pere Marquette Bldg New Orleans LA 70112

KOHLMEYER, IDA RITTENBERG (MRS. HUGH BERNARD KOHLMEYER), artist; b. New Orleans, Nov. 3, 1912; d. Joseph and Rebecca (Baron) Rittenberg; B.A., Tulane U., 1933, M.F.A., 1956; student Hans Hofmann Sch. Art, Provincetown, R.I., 1956; m. Hugh Bernard Kohlmeyer, Mar. 15, 1934; children—Jane Louise (Mrs. Henry Lowentritt), Jo Ellen (Mrs. Arthur Morris). One-man shows at Delgado Mus. Art, New Orleans, 1957, 66, 67, Tulane U., 1959, 64, Sheldon Meml. Art Gallery, Lincoln, Neb., 1967, Marion Koogler McNay Art Inst., San Antonio, 1968, Ft. Wayne (Ind.) Mus. Art, 1968, High Mus. Art, Atlanta, 1972; exhibited in group shows Knoedler Galleries, N.Y.C., Bertha Schaeffer Gallery, N.Y.C., Harvard, Yale, Toledo Mus. Fine Arts, Cleve. Inst. Art, Denver Art Mus., Va. Mus. Arts, Richmond, La Jolla (Cal.) Mus. Art; represented in permanent collections New Orleans Mus. Art, Rochester Meml. Art Gallery, Rochester, N.Y., Addison Gallery Am. Art, Phillips Acad., Andover, Mass., Oklahoma Art Center, Oklahoma City, Columbus (Ga.) Mus. Art, Tyler (Tex.) Art Inst., Centro-Artistico,

Baranquilla, Colombia, Mus. Fine Arts, Houston, High Mus. Art, Atlanta, Sheldon Meml. Art Gallery, Lincoln, Neb., Ind. State U., Terre Haute, Nat. Collection Fine Arts, Washington, Emory U., Atlanta, Marion Koogler McNay Art Inst., San Antonio, Ind. State U., Terre Haute, Corcoran Gallery Art, Washington; mem. faculty art dept. Newcomb Coll., Tulane U., New Orleans, 1956-64; vis. asso. prof. fine arts La. State U., New Orleans, 1973-74. Recipient award Artist's Ann., Delgado Mus., New Orleans, 1957, 58, 60, 65, 73, Chautauqua Nat. Exhb., 1962, 28th Corcoran Biennial of Am. Art, Washington, 1963, 67, Artists Ann., High Mus. Art, Atlanta, 1963, 66. Address: 11 Pelham Av Metairie LA 70005

KOHLS, FLORENCE CATHERINE, city ofcl.; b. Shepherd, Mich., July 29, 1918; d. Jerome and Elizabeth Mary (Erhart) Kohls; B.C.S., Cleary Bus. Coll., Ypsilanti, 1939. Dep. city treas., sec. to mayor City of Owosso (Mich.), 1953-62, city treas., 1962—, city clk., 1969—. Sec. or treas. Retirement System City of Owosso, 1969—; clk. Civil Service Bd., 1969—. Mem. Nat., Mich. municipal clks. assns., Am. Bus. Women's Assn., Municipal Finance Officers Assn. Mich., Altar Soc., Sacred Heart Guild, Palette and Brush Club. Roman Catholic. Home: 1307 W Main St Owosso MI 48867 Office: 301 W Main St Owosso MI 48867

KOHN, KATE HIRSCHBERG (MRS. HENRY L. KOHN), physician; b. Cinn., June 4, 1909; d. Sylvan and Alma (Yondorf) Hirschberg; A.B., Bryn Mawr Coll., 1930; M.D., Rush Med. Coll., 1935; m. Henry L. Kohn, Aug. 25, 1932; children—Henry L., Richard H. Intern Michael Reese Hosp., Chgo., 1934-35, resident, 1935-36; practice medicine specializing in rehab. medicine, Chgo., 1952—; physician Nursing Sch., Michael Reese Hosp., Chgo., 1938-50, attending staff, 1963—, acting dir. dept. rehab. medicine, 1970—; dir. med. services Schwab Rehab. Hosp., Chgo., 1952-67; clin. asso. prof. U. Ill. Abraham Lincoln Coll. Medicine, Chgo., 1961—; cons. Cook County Dept. Pub. Aid, 1963—. Induction physician WAC, 1942-45. Fellow Inst. of Medicine; mem. Am., Ill., Chgo. med. assns., Am., Chgo. (pres. 1970-71) heart assns., Am. Congress Rehab. Medicine, Ill. Soc. Rehab. Medicine, Multiple Sclerosis Soc. Home: 1225 E 50th St Chicago IL 60615 Office: 29th and Ellis Chicago IL 60616

KOHN, ZILLAH L. (MRS. SYLVAN H. KOHN), assn. exec.; b. Meridian, Miss.; d. Wolff and Fannie S. (Willner) Willner; B.A., Rice U., 1917; m. Sylvan H. Kohn, July 7, 1921; children—Joshua Kossy (dec.), Ezra. Tchr. English, Central High Sch., Houston, 1917-21. Vice pres. Maple Av. P.T.A., Newark, 1936-38; v.p. N.J. Women's League of United Synagogue of Am., No. N.J., 1942-46. Nat. bd. dirs. Women's League for Conservative Judaism, 1950, mem. exec. bd. 1954-68, editor nat. quar. Outlook, 1953-70, editor column nat. bull. Idea Exchange; nat. bd. dirs. Women's Orgn. Jewish Welfare Bd., 1952-69; bd. dirs. Newark sect. Women's div. Am. Jewish Congress, 1967—. Mem. Newark Hadassah (recording sec. 1922-29, corr. sec. 1929-33, mem. governing bd. 1922—). Home: 259 Reynolds Terrace Orange NJ 07050

KOHRING, HAZEL LOUISE ROBERTS (MRS. WALTER G. KOHRING), life ins. broker; b. Moberly, Mo.; d. Elmer P. and Ruby (Murphy) Roberts; student Moberly Comml. Coll.; m. Walter G. Kohring, Aug. 4, 1939; children—Dorothy (Mrs. Charles Chappell), William Halliburton. Gen. agt., Met. Life Ins. Co., 1942-46; fashion mgr. Sears Roebuck & Co., Alton, Ill., 1946-59; life ins. broker, 1959—; life ins. broker Gen. Am. Life Ins. Co., 1961—. Finance chmn., chmn. pub. edn., mem. exec. com. Mo. Heart Assn.; mem. com. to aid handicapped Triple V; mem. United Fund Speaker's Bur. Bd. dirs. St. Louis Heart Assn., 1965—, membership chmn., 1965-66, co-chmn. raising heart fund campaign, 1965; bd. dirs. St. Louis Met. YWCA. Recipient Man of Year award St. Louis Gen. Agts. and Mgrs. Assn., 1962-65, 68-69. Distinguished Salesman awards Sales and Marketing Execs. Assn.; award Heart Fund, 1965; named outstanding Woman in Bus. Achievements, Downtown St. Louis, 1968; named one of three outstanding women of Mo., Phi Chi Theta, 1968. Mem. Nat. Assn. Life Underwriters (nat. pres. womens roundtable 1971-72, I.H. Dublin Nat. award 1971, nat. pub. service chmn. 1973-74), Million Dollar Round Table (life, qualifying mem.), Mo. Fedn. Bus. and Profl. Women's Club (1st v.p. 1971, pres. 1974-75, Woman of Year dist. VIII 1973), Bus. and Profl. Women's Club St. Louis (pres. 1958-59, Top Hat award 1965). Republican. Methodist (dir.). Mem. Order Eastern Star. Club: Altrusa (dir. St. Louis, Woman of Distinction 1971). Home: 2955 Moniteau St Bel Nor MO 63121 Office: 11147 Olive Rd St Louis MO 63141

KOHTZ, JANET ELIZABETH (MRS. ROBERT S. NOLAND), optometrist; b. Los Angeles, Jan. 17, 1942; d. Wesley S. and Elizabeth (Chequer) Kohtz; student U. Cal. at Los Angeles, 1960-62; B.S., Los Angeles Coll. Optometry, 1966, D. Optometry, 1967; m. Robert S. Noland, Jan. 11, 1971. Clk., counselor juvenile halls County Los Angeles, 1962-67; optometrist with Dr. Larry Stevens, Ridgecrest, Cal., 1967, Dr. Ernest Ames, Downey, Cal., 1967; individual practice optometry, Torrance, Cal., 1968-71, Riverside, Cal., 1971—. Head, Center for Developmental Learning, Torrance, Cal., 1968-71; mem. panel specialists Crippled Children's Services, 1968-72; state dir. Coll. Vision Devel. So. Cal., 1974. Bd. dirs. Noland Research Found.; mem. adv. council Speech, Hearing and Lang. Rehab. Center, Loma Linda U. Mem. Am., Cal. optometric assns., South Bay Optometric Soc. (dir. 1970-71), Nat. Optometric Soc. for Developmental Vision Care (dir. 1970-71), Optometric Extension Program, South Bay Visual Tng. Study Group, Omega Epsilon Phi. Office: 1044 E La Cadena St Riverside CA 92501

KOISCH, MARLENE ANN WYNNE (MRS. ANTHONY J. KOISCH), city ofcl.; b. Newburgh, N.Y., Oct. 13, 1937; d. Joseph William and Kathryn (Hamill) Wynne; grad. high sch.; m. Anthony J. Koisch, Apr. 18, 1959; children—Marlayna, Nadina, Laurina. Sec., Newburgh (N.Y.) Urban Renewal Agy., 1968-69; sec. City Mgrs. Office, Newburgh, 1969-71; city clk., Newburgh, 1971—. Sec., Newburgh Planning Bd., 1969—, Newburgh Zoning Bd. Appeals, 1969—. Home: 26 City Terrace N Newburgh NY 12550 Office: 83 Broadway St Newburgh NY 12550

KOJANCIK, MARY LOU JOSEPHINE DEMOULLY (MRS. JOE JOHN KOJANCIK), educator; b. Milw., Nov. 19, 1917; d. Oliver M. and Rose Pearl (White) DeMoully; J.D., U. N.D., 1940; postgrad. U. Mont., summers 1948-50, Colo. State Coll. Edn., summer 1952, Eastern Mont Coll., summer 1961; m. Joe John Kojancik, Mar. 6, 1943. Admitted to N.D. bar, 1940, Mont. bar, 1950; practiced in Flasher, N.D., 1940-41; asso. C.L. Young, Bismarck, N.D., 1941-42; mem. N.D. Code Revision Commn., 1942-43, Wash. State Code Revision Commn., 1943-44; tchr., Ryegate (Mont.) High Sch., 1947-53, Fairview (Mont.) High Sch., 1954-65, Red Lodge, (Mont.) High Sch., 1968-70, Wibaux County (Mont.) High Sch., Wibaux 1965-67, 70—. Sec. Fairview P.T.A., 1957-58. Bd. dirs. Econ. Devel. Council Eastern Mont., 1971-73. Mem. Nat., Mont. (pres. Eastern dist. library sect. 1962-63) edn. assns., Mont. Bar Assn. Am. Federated Women's Club, Delta Delta Delta, Sigma Epsilon Sigma. Roman Catholic. Home: 314 W Nolan St Wibaux MT 59353

KOKAS, ESZTER BALINT (MRS. LAJOS BALINT), scientist; b. Hungary, Nov. 20, 1903; M.D., U. Debrecen, 1927; privat dozent U. Budapest, 1938; m. Lajos Balint, May 4, 1947 (dec.). Came to the U.S., 1960, naturalized, 1965. Prof. physiology U. N.C. Med. Sch., Chapel Hill, 1960—. Mem. Am. Physiol. Soc., Gnotobiotisc Assn. Contbr. articles to profl. jours. Home: 215A Hillsborough St Chapel Hill NC 27514

KOKOSKY, MARY JEAN, physician; b. Bethlehem, Pa., July 9, 1937; d. John J. and Mary (Evancho) Kokosky; B.A. with honors, U. Pa., 1959, M.S., 1961; M.D. with honors, Med. Coll. Pa., 1967. Intern Henry Ford Hosp., Detroit, 1967-68, pediatric resident, 1968-70; neonatology fellow Los Angeles County Hosp., U. So. Cal. Med. Sch., 1970-71; dir. nurseries, pediatric staff Henry Ford Hosp., Detroit, 1971-72; asst. dir. pediatrics Mt. Carmel Mercy Hosp. and Med. Center, 1972-73; asst. dir. pediatrics, neonatologist Northwest Detroit Met. Hosp. Assn., 1973—. Diplomate Am. Bd. Pediatrics. Fellow Am. Acad. Pediatrics; mem. A.M.A., Am. Assn. Med. Women, Mich. State, Wayne County med. socs., Detroit Pediatric Soc., Alpha Omega Alpha. Home: 1930 Golfview Dr Troy MI 48084 Office: 6071 W Outer Dr Detroit MI 48235

KOLARIK, MARGARET MILLER (MRS. DONALD GRANT KOLARIK), lawyer; b. Clinton, Ia., May 3, 1895; d. Carlyle Bartlet and Lena Ura (Young) Miller; student Cedar Falls (Ia.) Tchrs. Coll., 1914-15; m. Donald Grant Kolarik, Sept. 25, 1943; foster children—Marie (Mrs. LeRoy B. Rockrohr), Margaret (Mrs. Robert H. Shumake), Edison W. Miller, Ernest L. Miller; 1 adopted dau., Carol (Mrs. Jim Runquist). Tchr. rural schs., Clinton, 1914-17; sec., law office, Clinton, 1918-25; admitted to Ia. bar, 1925; mem. firm Miller & Claussen, Clinton, 1925-30, Miller, Miller & Cousins, Clinton, 1930-52; individual practice law, Clinton, 1952—. An organizer Clinton Humane Soc., 1941, pres., 1942-46; pres. Ia. Fedn. Humane Socs., 1958-60, now life mem. Mem. sch. bd. Ind. Sch. Dist. Clinton, 1951-57; pres. Clinton County Council Republican Women, 1954—; parliamentarian Second Dist. Council Ia. Rep. Women, 1954—. Bd. dirs. Clinton Council Girl Scouts, 1938-40, YWCA, 1952-54. Named one of Clinton's Outstanding Women, YWCA, 1973. Mem. C. of C. U.S., Ia., Clinton County (pres. 1962-63) bar assns., P.E.O. Conglist (trustee 1951-57). Clubs: Wa Tan Ye (pres. 1973—), Clinton Woman's (chmn. civic and pub. affairs com. 1963). Address: 2109 N 2d St Clinton IA 52732

KOLENDA, PAULINE SLOAN MOLLER (MRS. KONSTANTIN KOLENDA), social anthropologist; b. Manchester, N.H.; d. Fulton and Mary P. (Sloan) Moller; B.A., Wellesley Coll., 1949; Ph.D. (fellow 1953-54), Cornell U., 1955; m. James M. Mahar, Mar. 31, 1954 (div. Apr. 1961); m. 2d, Konstantin Kolenda, June 9, 1962; 1 son, Christopher. Prof. anthropology, research asst. depts. sociology, anthropology Cornell U., 1950-53, research asso. Stirling County Studies Psychiatry, 1956-57, research asso. dept. sociology and anthropology, 1957-58; post-doctoral fellow Cornell India Program, 1954-56; Irma Voight fellow Am. Assn. U. Women, 1958-59; instr. sociology, anthropology U. Ariz., 1959-61; asst. prof. sociology, anthropology Mich. State U., Oakland, 1961-62; asso. prof. U. Houston, 1963-69, prof. anthropology, 1969—. Fellow Am. Anthrop. Assn., Am. Sociol. Assn.; mem. Assn. Asian Studies (bd. dirs.), Soc. Sci. Study Religion, Am. Ethnol. Assn. Home: 2515 Glen Haven Blvd Houston TX 77025

KOLIN, SACHA, artist; b. Paris, France; d. Julius and Malvina (Slobodianiuk) Kolin; B.S., Realschule (Vienna, Austria), 1929; student Wiener Kunstgewerbeschule, Acad. Fine Arts, Societaire de la Societe Nat. Des Beaux Arts (Paris, France), 1934-35. Came to U.S., 1936, naturalized, 1943. One man shows Burliuk Gallery, 1953, Contemporary Arts, 1957, Condon Riley Gallery, 1959, 60, Easthampton Gallery, 1963, 65, U. Center, L.I. U., 1969, Southampton Coll. of L.I. U., 1972, Everson Mus., Syracuse, 1973, others; exhibited in group shows Smithsonian Instn., Bklyn. Mus., Boston Mus., Whitney Mus. Am. Art, Isaac Delgado Mus., Kunst Mus., Bern, Switzerland, many others; represented in permanent collections Parrish Mus., Finch Coll. Mus., Ohio State U., Brandeis U., Phoenix Art Mus., Chrysler Art Mus., Cooper Hewitt Mus. of Smithsonian Instn., Fordham U., Easthampton Guildhall, Southampton Coll., Wadsworth Atheneum, Hartford, Conn., Trinity Coll., Nat. Collection Fine Arts, Washington, Everson Mus., Cornell U., many others. Mem. Expts. in Art and Tech.Home: 1651 2d Av New York City NY 10028

KOLKER, SISTER MARY DELPHINE, educator, author; b. Dayton, O.; d. John James and Estella (Young) Kolker; B.A., U. Dayton, 1942; M.A., Cath. U. Am., 1945, Ph.D., 1952; postdoctoral studies Notre Dame U., 1953-54. Tchr. English, U. Dayton Extension, 1945-58; tchr. humanities St. Joseph Coll., Rensselaer, Ind., 1958-60; prof. English and philosophy St. John Coll., Cleve., 1960—; reviewer books on philosophy of art and literary criticism Choice mag., 1966—. Mem. sisters senate Diocese of Cleve., 1965-68, mem. exec. bd., rec. sec., 1966-69. Mem. adminstrv. bd. Sisters of the Precious Blood, Dayton, 1966-69. Mem. Modern Lang. Assn., Am. Cath. Philos. Assn., Council English Tchrs. Author: Aspects and Attitudes, 1965. Contbr. articles and translations periodicals, New Cath. Ency. Home: 2061 Cornell Rd Cleveland OH 44106 Office: St John College Cathedral Sq Cleveland OH 44114

KOLNICK, VIRGINIA TOWLES, rehab. counselor, nurse; b. Smelterville, Ida., Feb. 21, 1934; d. Dolph and Ruberta Rhoda (Hunt) Towles; A.A., Phoenix Jr. Coll., 1961; B.S., Ariz. State U., 1966, M.A., 1968, M. Counseling, 1971; m. Dec. 30, 1953 (div. Apr. 1963); children—JoAnn, Phyllis Ann, Betty Sue. Corrdinator student personnel service Good Samaritian Hosp. Sch. Nursing, Phoenix, 1968-69; registered nurse, pvt. duty coordinator Med. Personnel Pool, Phoenix, 1971-72; registered nurse interviewer Ariz. Health Plan, Phoenix, 1973; vocational rehab. counselor State Ariz., Phoenix, 1974—. Instr. nursing, evening continuing edn. program Maricopa County Jr. Coll., Phoenix, 1973-74. Mem. Nat. Assn. Women Deans and Counselors, Am. Nurses Assn., Am. Personnel and Guidance Assn., Nat. Rehab. Assn., Nat. Rehab. Counselors Assn., Kappa Delta Pi. Home: 3101 W McLellan Phoenix AZ 85017 Office: Ariz Dept Econ Security Vocational Rehab 438 W Adams St Phoenix AZ 85003

KOMAROVSKY, MIRRA (MRS. MARCUS A. HEYMAN), educator; b. Russia; d. Manuel and Anna (Steinberg) Komarovsky; A.B., Barnard Coll.; M.A., Columbia; Ph.D., 1940; m. Marcus A. Heyman, Oct. 2, 1940. Came to U.S., 1922, naturalized, 1933. Asst. prof. sociology Skidmore Coll., 1927-29; research asst., research asso. Yale Inst. Human Relations, Columbia U., 1931-32; instr. sociology Barnard Coll., 1936-45, asst. prof., 1945-47, asso. prof., 1948-53, prof., 1954-70, prof. emeritus, spl. lectr., 1970-74, chmn. dept., 1949-68. Buel G. Gallagher vis. prof. City Coll., City U. N.Y., 1965; vis. prof. New Sch. Social Research, grad. faculty Sch. Gen. Studies Columbia, 1974—. Mem. Am. (council 1967-69, v.p. 1971-72, pres. 1972-73), Eastern (pres. 1955-56) sociol. assns., Phi Beta Kappa. Author: Leisure, A Suburban Study (with Lundberg and McInerney), 1934; The Unemployed Man and His Family, 1940; Women in The Modern World: Their Education and Their Dilemmas, 1953. Editor: Common Frontiers of the Social Sciences, 1957; Blue Collar Marriage, 1964. Asso. editor: Am. Sociol. Review, 1957-60. Contbr. articles profl. jours. Home: 340 Riverside Dr New York City NY 10025

KOMECHAK, MARILYN GILBERT, psychologist; b. Wabash, Ind., Aug. 28, 1936; d. Russell and Evelyn Georgianna (Snyder) Gilbert; B.S., Purdue U., 1958; B.S., Tex. Christian U., 1966, M.Ed., 1968; Ph.D., N. Tex. State U., Denton, 1975; m. George Judy Komechak, Aug. 23, 1958; children—Kimberly Ann, Gilbert Matthew. Tchr. elementary sch., Huntsville, Ala., 1959-60; counselor, staff psychologist Child Study Center, Ft. Worth, 1968—; asso. dir. Center for Behavioral Studies, North Tex. State U., 1974—, mem. faculty, 1974—; cons. in behavioral therapy. Mem. adv. com. Tarrant County Day Care Assn. Chmn. bd. dirs. certified course child devel. Tex. Edn. Assn., 1972; profl. adv. bd. Easter Seal Center. Mem. Am., Tarrant County, Southwestern psychol. assns., Am., North Central Tex. (awards chmn.) personnel and guidance assns., Psi Chi, Delta Gamma. Episcopalian (vestryman). Contbr. to profl. jours. Home: 8109 Rush St Fort Worth TX 76116 Office: Box 13592 Center for Behavioral Studies North Tex State U Denton TX 76203

KOMP, DIANE MARILYN, pediatric hematologist, oncologist; b. Bklyn., Aug. 6, 1940; d. Richard Carrier and Anna Florence (Daly) Komp; B.S., Houghton Coll., 1961; M.D., State U. N.Y., Bklyn., 1965. Intern pediatrics Kings County Hosp., Bklyn., 1965-66, sr. resident pediatrics, 1966-67; USPHS fellow in pediatric hematology-oncology U. Va., Charlottesville, 1967-69, asst. prof. pediatrics, 1969-73, asso. prof., 1973—; practice medicine specializing in pediatric hematology-oncology, Charlottesville, 1969—; mem. staff Univ. Hosp., Charlottesville. Mem. S.W. Oncology Group, 1970-74; Nat. Cancer Inst. grantee, 1971. Mem. Soc. Pediatric Research, Am. Soc. Hematology, So. Soc. Pediatric Research, Am. Soc. Oncology, Am. Assn. Cancer Research, Internat. Soc. Hematology, Oratorio Soc. Charlottesville. Contbr. articles to profl. jours. Home: 799 Madison Av Charlottesville VA 22903 Office: University of VA Hospital Charlottesville VA 22901

KONER, SILVIA, magazine editor; b. Bklyn., Oct. 3, 1922; d. Louis and Pearl (Newmark) Topp; student Bklyn. Coll., 1939-41; m. Marvin Koner, July 2, 1943; 1 dau., Pamela Ivy. Asso. articles editor Redbook mag., N.Y.C., 1968—. Home: 345 E 56th St New York City NY 10022 Office: 230 Park Av New York City NY 10017

KONHEIM, BEATRICE GOLDSTEIN (MRS. HARVEY S. KONHEIM), educator; b. N.Y.C., Aug. 29, 1909; d. Sidney Emanuel and Susan E. (Sugarman) Goldstein; B.A., Hunter Coll., 1929; M.A., Columbia, 1931, Ph.D., 1939; m. Harvey S. Konheim, Nov. 29, 1933; children—Susan Eleanor, Jon Morton. Tutor, instr. Hunter Coll., 1929-31, 31-42, asst. prof., 1942-51, asso. prof., 1951-57, prof., 1958—, acad. dean Inst. Health Scis., 1968—. Dir. Ford Seminar on Coll. Teaching, 1955-56. Recipient research grant Am. Physiol. Soc., summer 1957, 58. Fellow Am. Pub. Health Assn., N.Y. Acad. Sci., A.A.A.S.; mem. Am. Assn. U. Profs. (Hunter pres. 1957-59, chmn. com. student acad. freedom 1962—, mem. nat. exec. council 1966-69, 72-75, exec. com. 1967-69, 72-74, 2d nat. v.p. 1972—), Assn. Higher Edn., Am. Civil Liberties Union, Sigma Xi. Author publs. on physiology and pub. health and higher edn. Frequent judge for awards and grants given by A.A.A.S., NSF, others. Home: 500 E 77th St New York City NY 10021 Office: 695 Park Av New York City NY 10021

KONIECKO, ALYSON KISTLER (MRS. FRANK KONIECKO), librarian; b. East Stroudsburg, Pa., Oct. 24, 1919; d. Herbert Allison and Olive Travis (Stone) Kistler; B.S. with highest honors, Stroudsburg State Coll., 1940; M.S., Drexel U, 1963; postgrad. Columbia U., 1941-42, Temple U., 1970-71; m. Frank Koniecko, Aug. 23, 1943; children—Anne (Mrs. John Powell), Scott. Tchr. jr. high sch., East Stroudsburg, Pa., 1940-41; librarian Roosevelt Jr. High Sch., West Orange, N.J., 1942-43, Kingspoint Acad., Kings Point, N.Y., 1943-44, Ithan Elementary Sch., Bryn Mawr, Pa., 1963—. Sch. library adviser div. sch. libraries Pa. Dept. Edn., 1968—; mem. selection adv. com. Elementary and Secondary Edn. Act, 1968-74; instr. children's lit. Eastern Coll., Wayne, Pa., 1972-74; cons. elementary sch. library collection, 1968—. Trustee Meml. Library Radnor Twp., 1966. Mem. Nat., Pa. edn. assns., Pa., Delaware County sch. librarians, Pa. Library Assn., Radnor Tchrs. Edn. Assn., Beta Phi Mu, Kappa Delta Pi, Alpha Delta Kappa. Home: 400 Maplewood Rd Wayne PA 19087 Office: Ithan Sch Library Bryn Mawr PA 19010

KONNER, JOAN WEINER, broadcasting exec.; b. Paterson, N.J., Feb. 24, 1931; d. Martin and Tillie (Frankel) Weiner; student Vassar Coll., 1948-49; B.A., Sarah Lawrence Coll., 1951; M.S., Columbia, 1961; children—Rosemary, Catherine. Editorial writer-columnist, asst. to editor The Record, Hackensack, N.J., 1961-63; producer, reporter WNDT Ednl. Broadcasting Corp., N.Y.C., 1963-65; writer, reporter NBC News, N.Y.C., 1965-68, producer, writer TV documentaries NBC, N.Y.C., 1968-73, dir. programs NBC Radio Network, N.Y.C., 1973—. Recipient Emmy award Nat. Acad. TV Arts and Scis., 1969, 71, award A.P. Broadcasting Assn., 1969, 70, 71, gold medal Atlanta Film Festival, 1970, 71, award N.Y. Film Festival, 1970, 71, 73, San Francisco Environmental Film Festival, 1970, Ohio State award Ohio State U., 1973 awards Cath. Broadcasters Assn., 1970, Council Chs., 1970, 72. Home: Snedens Landing Palisades NY 10964 Office: 30 Rockefeller Plaza New York City NY 10020

KONRAD, EVELYN, mgmt. cons. exec.; b. Vienna, Austria, Dec. 28, 1930; d. Eugene and Greta (Duekler-Breitner) Konrad; came to U.S., 1940, naturalized, 1949; B.A., Stanford U., 1949, M.A., 1950; postgrad. N.Y.U.; grad. N.Y. Sch. Interior Design, 1965; m. Bernard Jereski; children—Laura, Elizabeth, Richard and Robert (twins). Profl. free-lance translator German, French and Italian books and articles, 1950-57; columnist UN World mag., 1950-51; asso. editor Everybody's Digest, also World Digest, 1950-51; asst. to fiction editor Today's Woman mag., 1951-52; sr. editor Sponsor mag., 1952-58; propr. Evelyn Konrad, Pub. Relations, N.Y.C., 1958—, pres. The Computer in Marketing, Inc. Bd. govs. Parents' League N.Y., Yorkville Youth Council. Mem. Radio-Television Execs. Soc., Am. Pub. Relations Assn., Am. Women Radio and Television, Internat. Radio and Television Soc., Pub. Relations Soc. Am. Clubs: Stanford of N.Y., N.J. and Conn. (v.p. 1950-52); Overseas Press, Point O'Woods; Soroptomist (N.Y.C.). Author: (with Rod Erickson) Marketing Research: A Management Overview, 1966; Computer Innovations in Marketing, 1970. Contbr. articles to Pageant, Seventeen, Mag. Digest; TV scripts for The Hunter, Man Against Crime. Home: 955 Park Av New York City NY 10028 Office: 750 Park Av New York City NY 10021

KONRICK, VERA BISHOP (MRS. RUDOLPH JOSEPH KONRICK), poet, artist; b. Jasper, Tex., Mar. 4, 1900; d. George Walters and California (Blake) Bishop; ed. pvt. tchrs.; Dr. Literary Leadership (hon.), Internat. Acad. Leadership, Philippines, 1968; m. Rudolph Joseph Konrick, Sept. 19, 1922; 1 dau., Duverne (Mrs. Litterio Bernard Farsace). Exhibited Pirates Alley Art Shows, New Orleans, 1950-60; nat. councillor, sec. Avalon World Arts Acad., 1951-56; state chmn. Nat. Poetry Day Com., 1956—; historian, archivist Crescent City chpt. Am. Pen Women, 1955—; chmn. La. Poetry Day, 1956-63; Poet Laureate, 1954; asst. dir. World Poetry Day, 1963; chmn. Western N.Y. Nat. Poetry Day, 1963; adv. cons. Rochester World Poetry Day, 1965-69; appointed N.Y. state chmn. Nat. Poetry Day, Inc., 1970—. Recipient silver medal, also diploma merit Studi E Scampi Internat., 1968, medal for achievement Fla. Poetry Soc., Inc., 1970; numerous other awards for poetry. Mem. Nat.

Poetry Soc., Nat. Audubon Soc., American Poetry League, Composers, Authors and Artists Am. (chmn. La. 1953-57), Nat. League Am. Pen Women (treas. 1953-55), Sidney Lanier Poetry Soc. New Orleans (past pres.). Democrat. Roman Catholic. Author: (poems) Moon Flame, 1953; poems pub. in French and Greek newspapers and mags., Spanish lang. newspapers in Mexico, also anthologies, mags. Co-editor: The Golden Atom Poets of History, 1973. Home: 187 N Union St Rochester NY 14605

KONSTANS, DOROTHY JANICE HUME (MRS. CONSTANTINE KONSTANS), psychologist; b. Chgo., Apr. 21, 1936; d. James Theodore and Winnifred May (Hayhurst) Hume; A.B., Ripon Coll., 1958; M.A., U. Chgo., 1960; m. Constantine Konstans, Feb. 28, 1959; children—Chris Theodore, Randall James, Russell Douglas. Sch. psychologist intern Chicago Heights Pub. Sch., 1959-60; psychologist Silver Cross Sch. Nursing, 1961; sch. psychologist St. Charles Pub. Schs., 1964-73; pvt. practice as psychologist, Geneva, Ill., 1973—; sch. psychologist Central Sch. Dist., Burlington, Ill., 1970—. Bd. dirs. Tri-City Youth Project. Mem. Am., Ill. psychol. assns., Nat. Assn. Sch. Psychologists. Home: PO Box 527 St Charles IL 60174 Office: 1705 South St Geneva IL 60134

KONTRAS, STELLA BICOUVARIS (MRS. GUS N. KONTRAS), pediatrician; b. Newport News, Va., June 28, 1928; d. Gregory Andrew and Urania (Pondicas) Bicouvaris; B.A., Ohio State U., 1948, M.A., 1949, M.D., 1953; m. Gus N. Kontras, Dec. 31, 1947; children—Constance, Gregory, Katherine. Intern, Ohio State U. Hosp., Columbus, 1953-54; resident Children's Hosp., Columbus, 1954-57; prof. pediatrics Ohio State U., 1970; dir. med. genetics lab. Children's Hosp., Columbus, 1966—; cons. State Services for Crippled Children Ohio, 1968. Recipient Spl. fellowship Nat. Cancer Inst., NIH, 1964. Mem. Soc. Pediatric Research, Am. Soc. Human Genetics. Home: 2922 Belmar Rd Columbus OH 43209 Office: Children's Hosp 561 S 17th St Columbus OH 43205

KONWINSKI, SISTER MARIE PATRICE, hosp. adminstr.; b. Grand Rapids, Mich., Feb. 14, 1937; d. Bernard Floyd and Leocadia Mary (Przybysz) Konwinski; B.A., Aquinas Coll., 1961; postgrad. (corr.) Ind. U., 1963-68; M.B.A., Xavier U., 1971. Mem. Order Dominican Sisters, 1957—; bus. mgr. Nazareth Hosp., Albuquerque, 1963-69, adminstr., 1971—; cons., bd. govs. Nazareth, Grand Rapids, 1971—. Mem. Cath. Hosp. Assn. (pres. elect), Hosp. Finance Mgrs. Assn. (pres. elect), Am. Coll. Hosp. Adminstrs. Address: 501 Richfield Av NE Albuquerque NM 87113

KOO, DELIA (MRS. ANTHONY KOO), educator; b. Hankow, China, May 14, 1921; d. William H.T. and S.L. (Zung) Wei; B.A., St. John's U., 1941; A.M., Radcliffe Coll., 1942; Ph.D., 1947; M.A., Mich. State U., 1954; m. Anthony Koo, June 6, 1943; children—Victoria (Mrs. Anthony Hitchins), Margery (Mrs. James Bussey), Emily. Came to the U.S., 1941, naturalized, 1962. Instr. Mich. State U. East Lansing, 1955-56, 57-58; lectr. Douglass Coll., New Brunswick, N.J., 1956-57; faculty Eastern Mich. U., Ypsilanti, 1965—, asst. prof. math., 1965-67, asso. prof. math., 1967—. Organizer Chinese lang. class for children, Greater Lansing, Mich., 1969. Mem. Math. Assn. Am. (sec.-treas. Mich. sect. 1974—), Econometric Soc., Inst. Math. Statistics, Phi Beta Kappa, Sigma Xi, Phi Kappa Phi, Pi Mu Epsilon. Author: (with others) First Course in Modern Algebra, 1963. Office: Dept Math Eastern Michigan U Ypsilanti MI 48197

KOOB, THEODORA JOHANNA, educator; b. Jersey City, N.J., Sept. 16, 1913; d. George Frederick and Theodora Katherine (Schmidt) Foth; B.S., N.Y. U., 1941, M.A., 1944, Ph.D., 1946; m. Robert Anthony Koob, June 24, 1942, (div. Mar., 1973); children—George Frederick, Joseph E., Stephen Phillip, Katherine Rose. Teacher N.J. Elem., Jr. High Schs., 1935-43; teacher L.I. Jr., Sr. High Schs., 1943-45; prin., dir. Am. Dependent Sch. in Far East, Okinawa, 1946-47; prof. English, linguistics, semantics, lit. Shippensburg State Coll., 1964—; cons. linguistics, gen. semantics. Active Boy Scouts Am.; active Girl Scouts Am. Mem. Modern Language Assn., Pa. State, Nat. edn. assns., Am. Assn. U. Profs., Author's Guild, Authors' League, Nat. Catholic Women, Confraternity of Christian Doctrine, Chambersburg Hosp. Assn., Pi Lambda Theta. Author: Johann of the Trembling Hand, 1960; Surgeon's Apprentice, 1963; Benjy Brant, 1965; The Tacky Little Icicle Shack, 1966; The Green Goose, 1967; This Side of Victory, 1967; Hear a Different Drummer, 1968; The Deep Search, 1969; The Deep Search in paperback, 1969. Home: Box 307 Scotland PA 17254 Office: Box 464 Shippensburg State Coll Shippensburg PA 17257

KOONCE, DOLORES CHAPLINE (MRS. RICHARD PRESTON KOONCE), librarian; b. Clorendon, Ark., Dec. 5, 1912; d. George Fleming and Marion Dolores (Johnson) Chapline; B.S., Monticello A. and M. Coll., 1960; m. Richard Preston Koonce, June 24, 1929; children—James Fitzhugh, Marietta K. (Mrs. James Albert Spring). Librarian, Altheimer (Ark.) Sch., 1958-60; librarian Pine Bluff (Ark.) Pub. Sch., 1960—. Baptist. Mem. Order Eastern Star, Nat. Campers and Hikers Club (sec. 1972-73). Home: 1304 Avondale St Pine Bluff AR 71601 Office: 1301 Commerce St Pine Bluff AR 71601

KOONS, FLORENCE KARANSKY (MRS. WALTER B. KOONS), computer specialist; b. N.Y.C., Apr. 2, 1919; d. Nathan and Celia (Miller) Karansky; B.A. in Math., Bklyn. Coll., 1939; postgrad. Coll. City N.Y., 1939-40; m. Walter B. Koons, June 30, 1946; 1 son, Stephen Joel. Mathematician, Coast and Geodetic Survey, Washington, 1942-43; statistician War Dept., Washington, 1944-46; math. statistician U.S. Census Bur., 1946-47, chief electronic computer br., 1950-51; mathematician computer devel. br. U.S. Bur. Standards, 1947-50; self-employed as computer cons., 1951-64; chief research br., data processing div. Nat. Center for Health Statistics, Rockville, Md., 1964-70, spl. asst. computer tech. Office Statis. Methods, 1970—. Mem. Assn. Computing Machinery, Am. Statis. Assn. Home: 2406 Harmon Rd Silver Spring MD 20902 Office: Nat Center for Health Statistics 5600 Fishers Lane Rockville MD 20852

KOONTZ, ELIZABETH DUNCAN, state ofcl.; b. Salisbury, N.C., June 3, 1919; d. Samuel Edward and Lena (Jordan) Duncan; A.B., Livingstone Coll., 1938; M.A., Atlanta U., 1941; hon. degrees 24 univs. and colls.; m. Harry Lee Koontz, Nov. 26, 1947. Tchr. Harnett County Tng. Sch., Dunn, N.C., 1938-40, Aggrey Meml. Sch., Landis, N.C., 1940-41, Fourteenth St. Sch., Winston-Salem, N.C., 1941-45, Price High Sch., Salisbury, N.C., 1945-49, Monroe Sch., 1949-65, tchr. spl. edn. Price Jr. Sr. High Sch.; then dir. Women's Bur. Dept. Labor, Washington; now asst. sec. coordination nutrition programs N.C. Dept. Human Resources; Raleigh. Mem. Rowan County Negro Civic League, Salisbury, 1946—; mem. Youth Commn. of Rowan County, 1955-57. Trustee Atlanta U., Center Vocational Tech. Edn. Ohio State U., mem. nat. exec. bd. Girl Scouts U.S.; adv. Council N.C. Inst. Nutrition U. N.C. at Chapel Hill; adv. com. N.C. Inst. Politics. Woodrow Wilson Nat. Fellowship Found. sr. fellow. Mem. N.C. Assn. Classroom Tchrs. (pres. 1958-62), Nat. Edn. Assn. (pres. 1968-69), Zeta Phi Beta. Episcopalian (div. racial and urban affairs). Home: 1287-F Schaub Dr Driftwood Manor Raleigh NC 27606 Office: 325 N Salisbury St Raleigh NC 27611

KOPECKY, PAULINE WITTER, educator; b. Ballinger, Tex., Aug. 22, 1927; d. Everett and Florence Gertrude (Gray) Witter; student Tex. Tech. Coll., 1944-45, Colo. Women's Coll., 1946-47; B.B.A., Southwestern U., 1949; M.Ed., U. Tex. at Austin, 1957; Ph.D. in Econs., U. Houston, 1972; children—Paula, Jeff. Asst. prof. econs. San Houston State U., Huntsville, Tex., 1964-67; asst. prof. econs., acting dir. Center for Econ. Edn., Okla. State U., Stillwater, 1967-73, dir. affirmative action program, 1973—. Mem. Omicron Delta Epsilon, Pi Gamma Mu. Presbyn. Home: 2615 Quail Ridge Ct Stillwater OK 74074

KOPEL, DOLORES BLANKE (MRS. GERALD HENRY KOPEL), lawyer; b. Emmetsburg, Ia., Jan. 8, 1931; d. Cornelius and Bess Blanche (Oldfield) Blanke; student U. Colo., 1948-51; B.S., U. Denver, 1952, J.D. cum laude, 1954; m. Gerald Henry Kopel, June 16, 1952; children—David, Stephen. Admitted to Colo. bar, 1954; mem. firm Kopel & Kopel, Denver, 1958—. Mem. bd. mgrs. East Denver YMCA, 1972-73. Mem. Am., Colo., Denver bar assns., Order of St. Ives, Kappa Beta Pi. Home: 1755 Glencoe Denver CO 80220 Office: 1718 Security Life Bldg Denver CO 80202

KOPENHAVER, PATRICIA ELLSWORTH, podiatrist; b. N.Y.C., Aug. 18, 1928; A.B., George Washington U., 1954; M.A., Columbia U., 1956; Dr. Podiatric Medicine, U. State N.Y., 1963; Ph.D. (hon.), Hamilton State U., 1973; m. William C. Lydden, Feb. 26, 1970 (div. 1974). Practice podiatric medicine, Greenwich, Conn., 1964—; mem. staff Laurelton Convalescent Hosp., Greenwich. Mem. Greenwich Women's Club; v.p. Monmouth Opera Festival, 1964, trustee, 1966; mem. Greenwich Woman's Gardeners Club; publicity dir. Neighbors Club, YWCA, 1968—. Bd. dirs. Monmouth Opera Guild, 1965. Recipient Hosp. Fund award for med. research translations A.R.C. Diplomate Nat. Bd. Podiatric Medicine. Examiners. Mem. Am. (pres. 1970), Conn., Fairfield, Am. Woman's (pres. 1972—) podiatry assns., Acad. Podiatry, Am. Podiatry Council, Columbia U. Alumni Assn., UN Assn. U.S.A., George Washington U. Alumni Assn., Internat. Platform Assn., Nat. Assn. Professions, Am. Assn. U. Women, Nat. Orgn. for women. Clubs: Soroptomist, Greenwich Women's Republican. Home: 2 Sutton Pl S New York City NY 10022 also 8 Dearfield Dr Greenwich CT 06830

KOPLIN, NORMA JEAN, artist; b. Chgo., 1936; d. Harry and Hannah Ruth (Libman) Koplin; B.F.A., Yale, 1957; 1 dau., Yamina Marie-Claude. Illustrator A Piece of String Ivan Obolensky, 1964; works pub. Harper's mag.; exhibited in one-woman shows at David Herbert Gallery, N.Y.C., 1962, Kasha Herman Gallery, Chgo., 1963 Graham Gallery, N.Y.C., 1968, Benson Gallery, N.Y.C., 1971; exhibited in group shows at Yale, New Haven, 1959, Art Inst. of Chgo., 1963, Mus. of Modern Art, N.Y.C., 1962-71, Phila. Mus. Art; 1967, Finch Coll. Mus., N.Y.C., 1974; tchr. Columbia, 1967. Recipient Art Dirs. Club award, mem. Women in Arts, Artists Equity. Address: 525 East 86th St New York City NY 10028

KOPLOW, FREYDA PECK (MRS. IRVING KOPLOW), state ofcl.; b. Willimantic, Conn., Oct. 26, 1907; d. Nathan and Pauline (Applebaum) Peck; student Williams Meml. Inst., 1926; B.S. in Edn., Boston U., 1930; M.S. in Social Research, Simmons Coll., 1931; m. Irving Koplow, June 17, 1931;children—Richard A., Michael D., Kenneth P. Social worker Mass. Dept. Pub. Welfare Bur. Old Age Assistance, 1931-33; state rep. Mass. Gen. Ct., 1955-67; commr. banks State of Mass., 1967—. Mem. exec. com. Met. Area Planning Council, 1964-71, chmn. tech. adv. com. econ. devel.; chmn. women's adv. com. Regis Coll. Seminar Met. Problems, 1958-63; mem. adv. com. Sr. Living, Inc., 1965—, Mass. Mental Health Planning Project, 1965-67. Mem. Mass. Republican Com., 1952-55. Mem. Pi Lambda Theta. Home: 75 Grove St Apt 221 Wellesley MA 02108 Office: 100 Cambridge St Boston MA 02202

KOPP, ALICE ELEANOR, govt. ofcl.; b. Tuscarawas, O., Apr. 24, 1916; d. George John and Eunice Estelle (Crites) Kopp; ed. library sci., Syracuse U., 1947-51. With Tuscarawas County (O.) Library, 1937-42, 57-62; asst. librarian New Philadelphia (O.) Pub. Library, 1942-57; country librarian USIS, Brasilia, Brazil, 1962-63, library cons. Caribbean and S.Am., Washington, 1969—. Asst. cultural officer Am. Embassey, Rio de Janeiro, Brazil, 1963-69. Mem. Am. Soc. for Information Sci., A.L.A., Spl. Libraries Assn., Am. Soc. Rio de Janeiro, Am. Fgn. Service Assn. Lutheran. Clubs: Am. (Rio de Janeiro, Brazil), Press (Washington). Home: 2121 Virginia Av NW Washington DC 20037 Office: USIS Fgn Service Room 1776 Pennsylvania Av NW Washington DC 20547

KOPPELMAN, DOROTHY, artist; b. Bklyn., June 13, 1920; d. Harry Walter and May (Chalmers) Myers; student Bklyn. Coll., 1938-42; student Art Students League, 1942; Am. Artists Sch., 1940-42; student aesthetic realism with Eli Siegel, 1942—; m. Chaim Koppelman, Feb. 13, 1943; 1 dau., Ann. Exhibited one-man show Terrain Gallery, N.Y.C., 1961; exhibited group shows Riverside Mus., Bklyn. Mus., 1960, Mus. Modern Art, N.Y.C., 1962, Butler Art Inst., 1965, Walker Art Center, 1963, Balt. Mus., others; aesthetic realism cons. The Kindest Art, 1971; dir. Terrain Gallery. Mem. Com. of Professions, 1968; mem. Artists and Writers Protest, 1966; mem. Angry Arts for Life and Against the War in Vietnam, 1966. Exec. dir. Aesthetic Realism Found. Inc. Recipient 1st prize for painting City Center 1957, Bklyn. Soc. Artists, 1960; Tiffany grantee 1965. Mem. Soc. Aesthetic Realism, Art Workers Coalition. Author (with others): Aesthetic Realism: We Have Been There, 1969; illustrator Children's Guide for Parents, 1971; columnist New York Art Scene, Washington Independent, 1966-67. Home: 498 Broome St New York City NY 10012 Office: 141 Greene St New York City NY 10012

KOPPLER, VERA ELAINE, author; b. Martinsville, Ill., Jan. 16, 1914; d. Alfred and Ellen (Caffin) Haddix; grad. pub. schs.; m. Leon F. Koppler, Mar. 19, 1946; children—Jennifer (Mrs. Ron Clark), Dion, Joanne (Mrs. Mar Ciampi), Jerry, Terry. Author: Lilacs, 1968; Wild Harvest, 1969; Little Poems, Light Verse, 1973; contbg. author to Grit; Hyacinths and Biscuits; Poet's Roundtable; Journal Publications; Capper's Weekly; Inky Trails. Mem. Poets' Study Club of Terre Haute (Ind.) (librarian 1969—, publicity chmn. 1969-70, v.p. 1970-73, sec. 1973—, chmn. nat. contest 1973—), Acad. Am. Poets, Internat. Poetry Soc., Ill., Ind. State poetry socs., Western World Haiku Soc. (rep. 1973-74). Home: Rural Route 1 Box 243 Marshall IL 62441 Office: Rural Route 1 Box 243 Marshall IL 62441

KORBELAK, IRMINGARD KALTSCHMIDT (MRS. DANIEL KORBELAK), writer, photographer; b. Chgo., May 23, 1936; d. Eugene Henry and Hannelore (Keilig) Kaltschmidt; student Wright Jr. Coll., 1954-56; m. Daniel Korbelak, Apr. 19, 1958. Writer, Seng Co., Chgo., 1954-57; new products writer Modern Hosp. Pub. Co. (now subsidiary McGraw-Hill), Chgo., 1957-60; editor, communications mgr. R.R. Donnelley & Sons Co., Chgo., 1960-73; free lance writer, photographer, Chgo., 1974—. Recipient awards Internat., Am. indsl. editors assns., Publicity Club Chgo., Printing Industries Am. Mem. Chgo. Press Club, Mid-North Assn. (sec. 1962-63), Chgo. Hist. Soc., Art Inst. Address: 3629 N Greenview Av Chicago IL 60613

KOREMAN, DOROTHY PHYLLIS GOLDSTEIN (MRS. NEIL MICHAEL KOREMAN), physician; b. Bklyn., Nov. 1, 1940; d. Benjamin and Ida (Krenick) Goldstein; B.A. cum laude, Bklyn. Coll., 1961; M.D. magna cum laude, State U. N.Y., 1965; m. Neil Michael Koreman, Aug. 16, 1964; children—Elizabeth Ann, Robert Stephen. Intern straight pediatrics Kings County Hosp. Center, Bklyn., 1965-66; resident dept. dermatology and syphilology Wayne State U. Sch. Medicine, Detroit, 1966-69, instr. dept. dermatology and syphilology, 1969-71; practice medicine specializing in dermatology, Detroit, 1969-71; clin. asst. prof. dept. dermatology U. Miami Sch. Medicine, Hialeah, 1971—. Diplomate Am. Bd. Dermatology. Fellow Am. Acad. Dermatology; mem. Fla. State Med. Soc., Dade County Med. Soc., Phi Beta Kappa. Home: 6914 Bottle Brush Dr Miami Lakes FL 33014 Office: 1800 W 49th St Hialeah FL 33012

KOREY, LOIS BALK, advt. agy. exec.; b. N.Y.C., 1933; d. Samuel and Lillian Balk; student Barnard Coll., 1952-54; children—Susan, Christopher. Writer, Steve Allen Tonight show, Ernie Kovacs show, Sunday Night Comedy Hour, 1954-61, Andy Griffith show, Peter Lind Hayes-Mary Healy show, 1959-61; copywriter Jack Tinker and Partners, 1961-63; sr. v.p., creative supr. McCann-Erickson Advt., 1963-71; v.p., creative dir. Needham, Harper & Steers, Advt., N.Y.C., 1971-74; v.p., creative dir. advt. Revlon Corp., N.Y.C., 1974—. Mem. Advt. Club N.Y., Writers Guild. Home: 145 Central Park W New York City NY 10023 Office: 767 Fifth Av New York City NY 10017

KORJUS, VERONICA MARIA ELISABETH, portrait artist; b. Estonia, Feb. 2; d. Voldemar L. and Mary E. (Krusenberg) Korjus; student Higher State Acad. Art, Estonia, 1940-42, Stockholm U., 1943-45, Phoenix Sch. Art, 1953-56, Nat. Acad. N.Y., 1960-61; M.A., Columbia, 1952; pvt. studies Louvre, Paris, 1961, Nat. Mus., Stockholm, 1945-47, Stuttgart Staats Mus. (Germany), 1961, Acad. La Grande Chaumiere, Paris, France, 1961, Riiks Mus., Amsterdam, 1969. Came to U.S., 1949, naturalized, 1954. One-man shows including Poughkeepsie IBM Art Gallery, 1964, Center Art Gallery, N.Y.C., 1964, 65, Lucian Art Gallery, N.Y.C., 1965, 66, Hotel Loudres, Nice, France, 1966, Hotel Victoria, Maiorca, Spain, 1966, other hotels Italy, 1966, N.Y.C. Chem. Bank, 1967, Barbizon Hotel, N.Y.C., 1969; exhibited in group shows including Barnard Coll. Art Assn., N.Y.C., 1969, hotels Lisbon, Portugal, Tangier, Morocco, Paris, France, 1966; represented in permanent collections at World Council Chs., N.Y.C.; portrait commns. include Countess Maria Therese Perez de Cavanillas, Ambassador to UN Dr. Jan Papanek, Ingrid Bergman, Dr. Robert J. McCracken. Lectr. IBM Country Club, 1964-65, Riverside Arts, N.Y.C., 1965-67, Deer Hill Conf., Wappingers Falls, N.Y., 1968, Paris, France, 1970, Cape Coral (Fla.) Yacht Club, 1972; radio talks on painting, 1964; travel to Euorpe, Middle East and Far East, Africa, Exec. gen. sec. Council European Women in Exile, 1956-60. Mem. Am. Artists Profl. League, Fraternitas Artis, Internat. Platform Assn. Mem. Order of Eastern Star. Address: 5350 Del Monte Ct Cape Coral FL 33904

KORKMAS, SISTER MARGARET ANN, librarian; b. Tyler, Tex., Dec. 22, 1934; d. Joseph Kallel and Mary Agnes (Korkames) Korkmas; B.A., Notre Dame Coll., 1957; M.Ed., Our Lady of the Lake Coll., 1965; M.S. in L.S. La. State U., 1971. Elementary sch. tchr., 1957-61; secondary tchr., librarian, 1961-69; religious edn. coordinator, 1969-70; pre-sch. tch., 1970-71; literacy services librarian Dallas Pub. Library, 1971—. Mem. A.L.A., Cath., Tex. library assns., Nat. Assn. Edn. Young Children, Council Religious Women (pres. 1971-73), School Sisters Notre Dame. Republican. Office: 1954 Commerce St Dallas TX 75201

KORMAN, BARBARA, educator, sculptor; b. N.Y.C., Apr. 8, 1938; d. David and Rose (Katz) Korman; student U. Mich., 1955-56; B.F.A., Alfred U., 1959, M.F.A., 1960; postgrad. City U. N.Y., 1960-61. Teaching fellow N.Y. State Coll. Ceramics, 1959-60; tchr. fine arts and sculpture N.Y.C. Bd. Edn., 1961—; freelance sculpture studio, N.Y.C., 1960—; exhibited in group shows at Rochester Meml. Art Gallery, 1959, Albright Knox Art Gallery, 1960, Hartford Mus. Gallery Shop, 1961, Hudson River Mus., 1973, 74, Nat. Acad. Design, 1973, 74; represented in permanent collections. Guest lectr. art edn. dept. City Coll. N.Y., 1971-73. Recipient Heydenryk prize for sculpture Nat. Assn. Women Artists, 1974. Mem. Nat. Assn. Women Artists, Bronx Council Arts, Westchester Art Soc., Yonkers Art Assn. Address: 325 E 201 St New York City NY 10458

KORMAN, JOAN CHRISTINA DRUCKENMILLER (MRS. JOHN M. KORMAN), violinist; b. Johnstown, Pa., July 21, 1944; d. Lester Luther and Olive Christina (Bloom) Druckenmiller; ed. U. Cal. at Los Angeles; Los Angeles Conservatory Music; m. John Michael Korman, Jan. 26, 1963; children—Jean Elizabeth, John Christopher, Kathryn Louise. Violinist on radio, TV, in films, 1949-60; performed with Boston Pops, Boston Symphony, Boston Ballet, Boston Opera, San Francisco Ballet; others; presently asst. prin. violist St. Louis Symphony. Mem. faculty Webster Coll.; rep. of U. Cal. at Los Angeles to Ojai Music Festival. Protestant. Home: 7321 Westmoreland Dr University City MO 63130 Office: 718 N Grand Blvd St Louis MO 63103

KORMENDY, ELIZABETH (MRS. EUGENE KORMENDY), artist, sculptor; b. Budapest, Hungary; diploma, Acad. Beaux Arts, Budapest; student Acad. Collarossi, Paris, Acad. Julien, Paris; also studied in Rome, Vienna, Berlin; m. Eugene Kormendy. Came to U.S., 1939, naturalized, 1949. Art tchr. Dunbarton Coll., Washington; one man shows Art Inst. Milw., Renaissance Soc., Chgo., Herron Art Inst., Indpls., Norton Gallery, Palm Beach, Fla.; exhibited group shows in numerous European cities including Budapest, Paris, Vienna, the Hague, Arnheim, Stockholm, Oslo, Copenhagen, Nurenberg, Venice; also Milw., Chgo., Smithsonian Instn., Washington; represented pub. and pvt. collections including City Mus., Nurenberg, also Budapest; important works include aluminum reliefs Ch. of Father Flanagan's Boystown, stas. 14 of cross Immaculate Conception Ch., East Chicago, Ill., aluminum plaques St. Peter's Ch., Oshkosh, Wis., murals in St. Catherine's and St. Joseph's chs., St. Louis, murals Our Lady of Lake, Syracuse, Ind., Sculptures Holy Spirit Ch., Washington, mosaic outdoor shrine St. Marys Convent, Notre Dame, Ind. Mem. Artists Equity, Nat. League Pen Women. Clubs: Kiln; Arts of Washington. Address: 2943 Upton St NW Washington DC 20008

KORN, ELIZABETH P., artist, educator; b. Silesia, Germany; d. Martin and Rosa (Frankel) Friedlaend; came to U.S., 1939; naturalized, 1942; Ph.D., Berlin Mus. Fine and Applied Art; studied Rome, Italy, Madrid, Spain; postgrad. Columbia, N.Y. U., N.Y. Inst. Fine Art, N.Y. Art Students League; m. Arthur Korn (dec.). 1 child, Graninoa. Prof., chmn. dept. art Drew U., Madison, N.J., to 1967—; mem. faculty Summit (N.J.) Art Center, 1968—; vis. prof. Newark Coll. Engring., Sacred Heart Acad., others; lectr. in field; exhibited in one man shows in U.S. and 8 fgn. countries including Roko Gallery, N.Y.C., Drew U., Eckerd Coll., Emory and Henry Coll., King Coll., Genessee Community Coll., other schs., museums, exhibited in group shows Newark Mus., N.J. State Mus., Trenton, City Center Gallery, N.Y.C., N.A.D., N.Y.C., Nat. Gallery, Berlin, Germany, others; also travelling exhibits; represented in permanent collections Smithsonian Inst. Archives Am. Art, Washington, 1972—, also Columbia N.Y.C., Newark Mus., Scripta Mathematica N.Y., Grumbacher, N.Y.C., Prudential Ins. Co. Am., Stevens Inst. Tech., Hoboken, N.J., Posnam

(Poland) Mus., Drew U. Center. Adv. bd. Art in Context. Recipient Eastern Coll. exhibit Argus Gallery, Madison, N.J., Windsor and Newton award, Grumbacher award, Jersey City Mus. 1st prize, 1st prize Posnan Mus., others. Govt. grantee. Mem. Coll. Art Assn. Am., Am. Assn. U. Profs., Art Students League, Nat. Assn. Arts and Letters, Nat. Assn. Women Artists, Kappa Pi, Sigma Phi. Illustrator, co-author: At Home with Children; Skippy's Family; Portraits of Famous Physicists; Trailblazer to Television; Apple Pie for Lewis, Read Up on Life; Nando of the Beach; Christmas; others. Contbr. articles to profl. jours. and illustrations to popular and sci. mags. Home: 1500 Manhattan Av Union City NJ 07087

KORNBLUTH, FRANCES HELEN SCHACHTER (MRS. MARVIN HUBERT KORNBLUTH), artist; b. N.Y.C., July 26, 1920; d. Jacob and Sarah (Goodstone) Schachter; B.A., Bklyn. Coll., 1940; M.S., Pratt Inst., 1962; postgrad. Bklyn. Mus. Art Sch., 1955-59, Adelphi U., 1964-66, N.Y. U., 1940-41; m. Marvin Hubert Kornbluth, Nov. 21, 1942; children—Bruce Ian, Jane Allyse Cathy. Exhibited one man shows Bklyn. Mus. Art Sch., 1958, Rockville Centre (N.Y.) Pub. Library, 1960, Sunken Meadow Gallery Contemporary Art, King's Park, N.Y., 1961 Hofstra U., Hempstead, N.Y., 1961, Charcoal Gallery, Manhasset, N.Y., 1962, Pratt. Inst., Bklyn., 1962, Guild Gallery, Hempstead, 1963, Hicks St. Gallery, Bklyn., 1964, Dowling Coll., Oakdale, N.Y., 1965, Mineola (N.Y.) Pub. Library, 1965, Baiter Gallery, Huntington, N.Y., 1968, Art Works Gallery, N.Y.C., 1970, Annhurst Coll., Woodstock, Conn., 1971, Community Gallery, Livermore Falls, Me., 1972; exhibited in group shows at Heckscher Mus., 1957, 58, Bklyn. Mus., 1960, Hofstra U., 1960, 61, Riverside Mus., 1959, Nat. Mus., Washington, 1961, Nat. Acad., 1961-70, Pa. Acad. Fine Arts, 1963, Whitehall Galleries, London, Eng., 1962, Royal Scottish Acad. Galleries, Edinburgh, 1963, Royal Birmingham Soc. Artists, 1964, Adelphi U., 1965, Norfolk Mus., 1961, Molloy Coll., 1965, Nassau Community Coll., 1964, 67, 68, Lever House, 1963, 65, 66, 67, William and Mary Coll., 1966, Senate Office Bldg., Washington, 1966, Me. Art Gallery, 1967, Albuquerque Pub. Library Galleries, 1964, East Chicago Libraries, 1964, State Capitol, Albany, N.Y., 1963, Worcester Art Mus., 1970, Mystic Seaport Gallery, 1970, Sturbridge Art Assn., 1970; tchr. Mineola Pub. Schs., 1959-67, Mills Coll. Edn., 1967-68, Hofstra U., 1967-68, Dowling Coll., 1968, Adelphi U., 1968, U. Conn., 1970—. Recipient Medal of Honor and Catherine and Henry J. Gaisman prize for watercolor Nat. Assn. Women Artists Ann., 1961, Spl. Mention award Norfolk Mus. Am. Drawing Ann., 1961, first prize in graphics Hofstra Coll. 12th Ann. L.I. Artists Exhbn., 1961, Honorable Mention for oil North Shore Ann. L.I., 1961, Honorable Mention for watercolor North Shore Ann., 1962, Aileen O. Webb prize Nat. Assn. Women Artists, 1964, Medal of Honor and Elizabeth Ringius Fulda award in oil Nat. Assn. Women Artists Ann., 1968. Mem. Monhegan Assos., Lincoln Country Cultural and Hist. Soc., Nat. Assn. Women Artists (mem. oil jury, 1968—), Boston Visual Artists Union, Cambridge Art Assn. Home: Buckley Hill Rd Route 1 North Grosvenordale CT 06255

KORNER, ANNELIESE FRIEDE (MRS. SUMNER KALMAN), psychologist; b. Munich, Germany; d. Leopold and Jenny (Deutsch) Friedsam; diploma Inst. J. J. Rousseau, U. Geneva, Switzerland, 1938; M.A., Columbia, 1940, Ph.D., 1948; m. Sumner M. Kalman, Oct. 18, 1952; 1 dau., Susan. Research asso. Social Sci. Research Council, N.Y., 1942-43; instr. dept. psychiatry U. Chgo. Med. Sch., 1943-48; chief psychologist dept. psychiatry Mt. Zion Hosp., San Francisco, 1948-61, sr. psychologist 1961—; cons. San Mateo Mental Health Services, 1960-71; research asso. dept. of psychiatry Stanford U. Sch. Medicine, 1964-70, sr. scientist, 1970—. Fellow Am. Orthopsychiat. Assn., Am. Psychol. Assn., Soc. Projective Techniques; mem. San Francisco Psychoanalytic Soc. Author: Individual Differences at Birth: Implications for Early Experience and Later Development, 1971; also articles. Home: 2299 Tasso St Palo Alto CA 94301 Office: Dept Psychiatry Stanford U Sch Medicine Palo Alto CA 94305

KORNETZ, MITZI, pub. relations exec.; b. Boston; d. Max and Sarah (Crosby) Kornetz; B.S., Simmons Coll., 1939. Publicity dir. WTAG, Worcester, Mass., 1939-46; radio and TV dir. United Community Services Met. Boston, 1946-54; cons. Mass. Bay Telecasters, Cambridge, 1954-55; radio-TV dir. Boston U., 1957-60; dir. community relations Family Service Assn. Greater Boston, 1961-66; asst. to exec. dir. Med. Found., Boston, 1968—. Mem. health task force Mass. Commn., White House Conf. on Aging, 1971; mem. exec. com. Interdisciplinary Group on Aging, 1971. Writer, producer radio series Sex Guidance for Today's Youth (Variety award 1946); co-producer Portrait: Albert Schweitzer (Ohio State U. award 1959). Home: 60 Babcock St Brookline MA 02146 Office: 29 Commonwealth Av Boston MA 02116

KORNFELD, PHYLLIS LORRAINE SCHAUM (MRS. ARTHUR N. KORNFELD), educator; b. Bklyn.; d. Max and Gussie (Goldberg) Schaum; B.A., Bklyn. Coll., 1949, M.S., 1965; postgraduate Coll. City N.Y., 1959-62; Ed.D., Columbia, 1972; m. Arthur N. Kornfeld, Apr. 3, 1949; children—Keith D., Elise J. Tchr. pub. sch., Bklyn., 1949-53; reading clinician Bklyn. Community Counsel Center, 1961-63, N.Y. Infirmary, 1962-67; sr. lang. disabilities therapist Coney Island (N.Y.) Hosp., 1967-68; remedial edn. tchr. Children's Aid Soc., 1966-69; lectr. grad. div. Bklyn. Coll., 1969; asst. prof. lang. arts and reading Paterson Coll., Wayne, N.J., 1969-70, Bklyn. Coll., City U. N.Y., 1971-72; asst. prof., co-dir. Reading Center Ferkauf Grad. Sch. Yeshiva U., N.Y.C., 1972-74; asst. prof. Coll. New Rochelle, 1974—. Fellow Am. Orthopsychiat. Assn.; mem. Manhattan Council Internat. Reading Assn. (pres. 1969-70), Mensa, Am. Assn. U. Profs., Nat Council Tchrs. English, Coll. Reading Assn., Internat. Reading Assn. Home: 124 Laurel Rd New City NY 10956 Office: Coll New Rochelle New Rochelle NY 10801

KORNREICH, SONYA LEE KAPLAN (MRS. MELVIN KORNREICH), economist; b. Jersey City, Sept. 9, 1923; d. Bert and Sadye (Goodkin) Kaplan; B.A., Bklyn. Coll., 1942; M.A., Columbia, 1947; postgrad. New Sch. Social Research, 1947-50; m. Melvin Kornreich, Feb. 8, 1943; 1 son, Robert David. Economist, labor market analyst N.Y. State Div. Employment, L.I. dist office, Hicksville, 1961—. Mem. Am. Econs. Assn., Indsl. Relations Research Assn. Home: 8 Kay Av Jericho NY 11753 Office: 303 Old Country Rd Hicksville NY 11801

KOROS, AURELIA MARIE CARISSIMO (MRS. PETER J. KOROS), educator; b. Boston, Aug. 28, 1934; d. Nino and Josephine (Sciacca) Carissimo; A.B., Harvard, 1956; M.S., U. Pitts., 1960, Ph.D., 1965; m. Peter J. Koros, June 1, 1957; children—Nina Leslie, Alicia Jane, Sonya Marie. Research asst. Harvard U., Boston, 1956-58; teaching asst. U. Pitts. dept. biol. scis., 1958-60, research asst., 1960, fellow Dept. Microbiology Sch. Medicine, 1965, instr. microbiology, 1966-67, asst. prof. microbiology, 1967-73, research asst. prof., dept. obstetrics and gynecology Magee-Women's Hosp., U. Pitts., 1973—. NIH grantee 1966—; Health Research and Services Found. grant, 1968-70; Am. Cancer Soc. Instl. Research grant, 1966-67. Mem. Am. Assn. U. Profs., A.A.A.S., Am. Soc. for Microbiology, Am. Assn. Immunologists, N.Y. Acad. Scis., Reticuloendothelial Soc., Sigma Xi. Contbr. articles in field to profl. jours. Office: U Pitts Sch Medicine Pittsburgh PA

KORT, MARGARET ALEXANDER, educator; b. Jerusalem, Jan. 16, 1928; d. Alexander John and Mary Katrina Kort; B.S., Georgetown Coll., 1958; M.S., U. Louisville, 1960; Ed.D., U. No. Colo., 1968. Instr. biology Coe Coll., Cedar Rapids, Ia., 1961-64; teaching fellow U. No. Colo., Greeley, 1964-67; prof. biology Southwest Bapt. Coll., Bolivar, Mo., 1967—. Pres. Thursday Musicale, Bolivar, 1973. Mem. A.A.A.S., Nat. Sci. Tchrs. Assn., Sigma Xi, Lambda Sigma Tau. Home: Rural Route 2 Bolivar MO 65613

KORTAS, SISTER MAUREEN, educator; b. Chgo., July 17, 1911; d. Bernard and Anna Elizabeth (Monaghan) Kortas; Mus. B., Cardinal Stritch Coll., 1956; M.Ed., Wayne State U., 1960; Ph.D., U. Ill., 1969. Faculty, St. Coletta Sch., Jefferson, Wis., 1944-47; faculty Cardinal Cushing Sch., Hanover, Mass., 1947-53, adminstr. 1947-53; faculty Kennedy Sch., Palos Park, Ill., 1956-61; faculty Cardinal Stritch Coll., Milw., 1961—, asso. prof. spl. edn., 1968—, asso. prof. psychology, 1972—, chmn. dept., 1972—. Vis. prof. Coll. of St. Rose, Albany, N.Y., 1970-72. U.S. Office Edn. fellow, 1964. Mem. Am. Psychol. Assn., Council for Exceptional Children. Address: Cardinal Stritch College Milwaukee WI 53217

KORTE, ADELE DOROTHY JULIA, sch. psychologist; b. St. Louis, Dec. 21, 1922; d. Arthur Fred and Dorothy Agnes (Hammerle) Korte; B.A., Harris Tchrs. Coll., 1943; M.A., Washington U., St. Louis, 1953, postgrad., 1954-56; postgrad. U. Chgo., 1967-68, Mo. U., 1970—. Tchr. schs., St. Louis, 1944-64, psychol. examiner, 1964—. Lectr. to parent groups. Mem. Nat. Assn. Sch. Psychologists (charter), N.E.A. (life), Mo. Tchrs. Assn. Lutheran. Home: 4092 Haven St St Louis MO 63116 Office: 1520 S Grand St St Louis MO 63104

KORTH, EVELYN RUTH, stock broker; b. Fond du Lac, Wis., July 25, 1923; d. William Henry and Anna Clara (Hagenau) Korth; grad. high sch. Clk., Aid Assn. for Luths., Appleton, Wis., 1941-43; personnel and indsl. sec. Fred Rueping Leather Co., Fond du Lac, Wis., 1943-53; personnel Douglas Aircraft, Long Beach, Cal., 1953-55; advt. sec. Western Gear Corp., Lynwood, Cal., 1955-57; sales sec. Minn. Mining & Mfg. Co., Los Angeles, 1957-59; exec. sec. Cal. Investors, Long Beach, 1959-64; office mgr. DAC Investment Co., 1964-65; v.p. operations Diversified Securities, Inc., 1966—. Lutheran. Home: 179 E Louise St 4 Long Beach CA 90805 Office: 343 E San Antonio Dr Long Beach CA 90807

KORWIN-RHODES, MARTA LIPKOWSKI (MRS. H.G.E. RHODES), educator, writer; b. Wilno, Poland; d. Henry and Helen (Korwin-Milewski) Lipkowski; M.M., Krakow Conservatory (Poland), 1936; student London Sch. Econs. and Polit. Sci., Social Sci. and Adminstrn., 1944; postgrad. U. Toronto (Can.), 1952; M.S.W., U. Pa., 1956; m. H.G.E. Rhodes, Oct. 12, 1962. Came to U.S., 1955, naturalized, 1964. Concert pianist, Poland, U.S.A., Near East, 1937-39; in charge of hosps. and rescue teams during siege of Warsaw (Poland), 1939; lectr., Eng. and Scotland, 1940-45; prin Coll. of Arts, UNRRA, Hagen, Germany, 1945-48; engaged in survey of condition of sub-Arctic Circle, Can., 1951; researcher Psychiat. Inst. U. Md., Balt., 1956-58; asst. prof. Fla. State U. Grad. Sch. Social Work, Tallahassee, 1959-60; asso. prof. research Coll. William and Mary, Richmond, 1962-63; asso. prof. social work Coll. of Continuing Studies, George Washington U., Washington, 1968—. Cons. psychiat. social work and prevention of delinquency; founder Hosp. Maltanski, 1939. Served with Underground Polish Army, 1939-40. Decorated Polish Mil. Cross, Golden Cross of Valor, Soverign Order Knights of Malta Cross, 1st class. Mem. Polish-Am. Arts Assn. Washington (founder 1964, pres. 1964-66), Acad. Certified Social Workers, Polish Vets. Assn., Am. Assn. U. Profs., Polish Am. Congress, Council on Social Work Edn. Author: The Mask of Warriors. Editor in chief Perspectives, Polish-Am. ednl. and cultural quar., 1969—. Contbr. to sci. publs. Home: 700 7th St SW Washington DC 20024

KOSCIOLEK, SYLVIA MAY, radiologist; b. Hamtramck, Mich., May 5, 1937; d. Walter and Florence (Krawczyk) Kosciolek; B.A. with high distinction, Wayne State U., 1959; M.D., U. Mich., 1963. Intern, Wayne County Gen. Hosp., Eloise, Mich., 1963-64; resident in internal medicine Henry Ford Hosp., Detroit, 1964-65, resident in radiology, 1965-68; mem. staff St. Mary's Hosp., Grand Rapids, Mich., 1968-73, mem. staff Hurley Hosp., Flint, Mich., 1973—. Mem. A.M.A., Am. Coll. Radiology, Mich. State, Kent County med. socs., Mich. Radiol. Soc. Home: 11105 Woodbridge Dr Grand Blanc MI 48439 Office: Hurley Hosp Flint MI 48507

KOSEDNAR, SISTER FRANCINE, occupational therapist; b. Milw., Mar. 11, 1938; d. Louis Francis and Ann Frances (Sterzinger) Kosednar; B.S., Mt. Mary Coll., 1963. Joined Order Sisters of Divine Savior, 1956; organizer occupational therapy dept. Wausau (Wis.) Hosps., Inc., 1963, head dept. occupational therapy, 1963—; cons. Meml. Hosp. of Taylor County, Medford, 1971—, Colonial Manor Nursing Home, Wausau, 1974—. Recipient Carol award Wis. Jaycettes, 1973. Mem. Am., Wis. occupational therapy assns., Arthritis Found., Nat. Rehab. Assn., Neuro-Developmental Treatment Assn. Home: 1105 S 10th Av Wausau WI 54401 Office: Wausau Hospital Inc Wausau WI 54401

KOSKY, PATRICIA B., educator; b. Worcester, Mass.; d. William J. and Frances (Danilowicz) Kosky; A.B., Anna Maria Coll., 1961; M.Ed., Boston Coll.; postgrad. Johns Hopkins. Research asst. Worcester Found. for Exptl. Biology, Shrewsbury, 1957-58; guidance counselor Grafton (Mass.) High Sch., 1962, dir. guidance, 1962-64; counselor Catonsville (Md.) Community Coll., 1964-65; counselor Marlborough (Mass.) High Sch., 1965-69, Framingham North High Sch., 1969—. Coordinator, 10th ann. Mass. Sch. Counselors Conf., Deans of Women Nursing Edn. Recruitment Orgn.; coordinator Nat. Career Guidance Week, 1973-75. Active Worcester Civic Community Concert Series. Mem. Am., New Eng., Mass. (coordinator workshops, pres. elect), Greater Boston personnel and guidance assns., Mass. Counselors Assn., Assn. for Counselor Edn. and Supervision, South Central Guidance Assn., Mass. Tchrs. Assn., Nat. Vocational Guidance Assn., Mass. Sch. Counselors Assn. (treas.; coordinator workshops), Worcester Art Museum, Framingham Tchr. Assn., South Suburban Guidance Assn., Anna Maria Alumni Assn. Home: 2 Maxdale Rd Worcester MA 01602 Office: North High Sch A St Framingham MA 01701

KOSS, HELEN L., state legislator; b. N.Y.C., June 3, 1922; A.B., Bennington Coll., 1942; m. Mem. Md. Ho. of Dels., 1971—. Mem. Montgomery County Adv. Com. on Special Youth Needs, 1962-63, Montgomery County Commn. on Youth, 1959-61, Montgomery County Health and Welfare Council, 1958-61; chmn. Reapportionment, Constl. Studies Com., 1959-63. Del., Constl. Conv. of Md., 1967-68; chmn. Com. on Suffrage and Elections. Bd. visitors Bowie State Coll. Mem. League Women Voters of Md. (pres., 1963-67). Mem., Gov.'s Commn. on Reapportionment, Gov.'s Commn. on Crime, Delinquency. Address: 3416 Highview Ct Wheaton MD 20802

KOSS, ROSABEL STEINHAUER (MRS. FRANKLYN C. KOSS), educator; b. Phila., Sept. 3, 1913; d. Arthur H. and Agnes (Temple) Steinhauer; B.S., Trenton State Coll., 1935; M.A., Columbia, 1942, Ed.D., 1964; m. Franklyn C. Koss, July 6, 1946; children—Lynn, Susan, Carolyn, Rosalind. Supr. phys. edn., pub. schs., Flemington, N.J., 1935-37; instr. phys. edn. Ridgewood (N.J.) Jr. and Sr. High Schs., 1937-40; dir. phys. edn. for girls Passaic Valley Regional High Sch., Little Falls, N.J., 1940-47; asst. prof. Montclair State Coll., Upper Montclair, N.J., 1958-61; asst. prof. Upsala Coll., East Orange, N.J., 1964-71, also dir. phys. edn. also intramurals for women; prof., coordinator women's phys. activities Ramapo Coll. N.J., Mahwah, 1971—; study grant to Sweden, 1968, 70, 72. Chmn., N.J. Bd. Womens Rated Ofcls.; v.p. Little Falls, Bd. Edn., 1962-63; chmn. Laison Bds. Edn. Passaic Valley Dist., 1963-64; safety services chmn. Ramapo Valley Chpt. A.R.C. Recipient merit certificate A.R.C., 1949. Mem. N.E.A., Am., N.J. (sec.) assns. health, phys. edn. and recreation, Nat. and Eastern Assn. Phys. Edn. Coll. Women, Internat. Council Health, Phys. Edn. and Recreation (pres. state Coll. chpt.), Am. Coll. Sports Medicine Am. Assn. U. Profs., P.T.A., Kappa Delta Pi. Club: Federated Women's; Soroptomist. Editor: Soccer-Speedball Guide 1962, 64. Contbr. articles to profl. jours. Home: 35 Jacobus Av Little Falls NJ 07424

KOSTANICK, CELESTE BUDD (MRS. HUEY LOUIS KOSTANICK), geographer, educator; b. Terrell, Tex., Oct. 25, 1921; d. Harrell and Mae (Burbank) Budd; B.A., So. Meth. U., 1940; M.A. (geography scholar), Clark U., 1942; postgrad. U. Wis., 1948-49, U. Cal. Los Angeles, 1970; m. David H. Horne, Sept., 1942 (div. Feb. 1948); m. 2d, Huey Louis Kostanick, Feb. 4, 1950; 1 son, Christopher Harrell. Instr. geography Stephens Coll., Columbia, Mo., 1942-45, U. Mo. at Columbia, 1946-47, So. Meth. U., Dallas, 1947-48; asst. prof. geography Los Angeles State Coll., 1950-52; asso. prof. geography Pierce Coll., Woodland Hills, Cal., 1957-72, prof., 1972—. Tchr., summers So. Meth. U., Dallas, 1944, 47, 48, Los Angeles State Coll., 1951, Pierce Coll., 1958, 59, 64, 65, 69; tchr. eves. Los Angeles State Coll., 1952, San Fernando Valley (Cal.) State Coll., 1961-62; field worker in geography U. Colo. at Boulder, summer 1939 Europe, Greenland, 1969; grad. asst. in geography Mt. Holyoke Coll., South Hadley, Mass., 1941-42, U. Wis. at Madison, 1947-48; independent study, Europe and Middle East, 1952-53, 69; lectr. before profl. and community orgns., 1954—. Mem. Assn. Am. Geographers, Pacific Coast Geographers, Cal. Council Geography Tchrs., Los Angeles Geog. Soc. Contbr. articles to profl. jours. Home: 22338 Philiprimm St Woodland Hills CA 91364

KOSTER, KAREN GRACE, pediatric rheumatologist; b. N.Y.C., Sept. 18, 1941; d. Henry Milton and Grace Edna (Gourley) Koster; A.B., Vassar Coll., 1963; M.D., N.Y. Med. Coll., 1967. Intern Cedars Lebanon Hosp., Los Angeles, 1967-68; jr. resident in pediatrics Montefiore Hosp., N.Y.C., 1968-69; sr. resident in pediatrics Childrens Hosp. Los Angeles, 1969-70, fellow in pediatric rheumatology, 1970-72, courtesy staff, 1971—, full-time staff, 1972—; asst. in pediatrics U. So. Cal. Sch. Medicine, 1969-70, instr. pediatrics, 1971-74, asst. prof., 1974—. Diplomate Am. Bd. Pediatrics. Mem. Am. Rheumatism Assn., Am. Acad. Pediatrics, Los Angeles Pediatric Soc. Home: 1630 N Edgemont St Los Angeles CA 90027 Office: 4650 Sunset Blvd Los Angeles CA 90027

KOSTKA, DOROTHY GABRIELLE PARMENTER (MRS. WILLIAM KOSTKA), writer, civic worker; b. Ft. Smith, Ark., May 24, 1906; d. Robert Davis and Lillian (Bollinger) Parmenter; A.B. magna cum laude, Knox Coll., 1928; m. William Kostka, June 15, 1928; children—William James, Stefan Matthew. Copywriter, J. P. Lippencott Co., Chgo., 1929-33; free-lance writer fiction and articles on family relations, social problems, 1945—; columnist Freedom after Fifty, Denver Post, 1964—. Mem. Denver Area Library Adv. Com., 1961—, Gov.'s Commn. on Aging, 1970—. Bd. dirs. Littleton Pub. Library, 1957, chmn. bd., 1957-61; bd. dirs. Met. Council for Community Service, 1959-63, Littleton YMCA, 1956-61, Arapahoe County United Fund, 1955-61, Arapahoe County Library Council, 1961-63; alumnae trustee Knox Coll., 1959-62, bd. trustees, 1964—. Recipient numerous awards for writing and community service, most recent being: Layman's award Colo. Asso. Nursing Homes, 1964, 71, Alumni Achievement award Knox Coll., 1964; named Littleton's Most Valuable Citizen, Littleton, Ind. Citizen's Com., 1959. Mem. Colo. Authors' League (treas. 1961-62, recipient Top-Hand awards 1953, 59, 61, 62, 63, 65, 66, 72, mem. bd. 1970—), Mortar Bd., Theta Sigma Phi, Phi Mu, Sigma Delta Chi. Club: Denver Woman's Press (dir. 1956-58, 60-63, 70—). Author: (juvenile book) Climb to the Top (Boys' Clubs Am. Nat. award), 1962. Address: 1090 Lafayette St Denver CO 80218

KOSTROWSKI, JEAN KIMBALL (MRS. ROMAN KOSTROWSKI), mfg. co. exec.; b. Glen Ridge, N.J., Apr. 20, 1920; d. Robert Nathan and Irene Louise (Dusenbury) Kimball; student U. Richmond, 1938-39; m. Roman Kostrowski, Mar. 19, 1946; children—Edward Kimball, Paul Raymond. Med. asst., lab. technician, sec. John C. Cox, M.D., Maplewood, N.J., 1940-42; dental asst., lab. technician, sec. Pierce A. Cassedy, D.D.S., South Orange, N.J., 1942-53; with Robert N. Kimball & Son, Inc., Irvington, N.J., 1958—, sec., treas., 1958—, dir., 1958—. Den mother Cub Scouts, Florham Park, N.J., 1955-58. Presbyn. Home: 271 Shunpike Rd Chatham NJ 07928 Office: 80 Mill Rd Irvington NJ 07111

KOTARIDES, LUCY RITA CRESCENZO (MRS. ARTHUR KOTARIDES), educator; b. N.Y.C., Nov. 28, 1914; d. Alfred Fredrick and Rose (Fatterusso) Crescenzo; B.S., N.Y. U., 1940; LL.B., St. John's U., 1939, J.D., 1968; M.Ed., Loyola Coll., 1963; postgrad. U. Md., 1959, Cath. U. Am., 1964-66; m. Arthur Kotarides, Dec. 12, 1942 (dec. Aug. 1969); children—Arthur, Donna, Jude, Mark. Admitted to N.Y. bar, 1940; pvt. practice law, N.Y.C., 1940-46; tchr. exceptional children Baltimore County Pub. Schs., 1959-61; organizer pilot program spl. edn. Cath. Schs. Archdiocese Balt., 1961; tchr. Villa Maria, Towson, Md., 1961-64; prin. Inst. Children, State Psychiat. Hosp. for Emotionally Disturbed Children, Balt., 1964-65; instr. spl. edn. Loyola Coll., Balt., 1965-67, asst. prof. emotionally psychology of disturbed, dynamics of group behavior, 1967-68, asso. prof., 1968—, chmn. dept. reading and edn. exception child, 1969—. Legal adviser Children's Benevolent Assn., N.Y.C., 1940-45; ednl. cons. Day Care Center of Sheppard and Enoch Pratt Hosp., Towson 1968, mem. ednl. adv. bd. hosp., 1968—; ednl. cons. Inst. for Children, State Psychiat. Hosp. for Emotionally Disturbed Children, Dept. Mental Health Md., 1968-69; cons. to edn. workshops for tng. tchrs. pub. schs. Md., 1968—, Confrat. Christian Doctrine, Archdiocese Balt., 1968—; mem. adv. com. State Dept. Edn. Md. Certification and Accreditation Tchrs., 1969—; mem. adv. com. Md. Dept. Spl. Edn., 1969—; mem. edn. com. Children and Youth for 1970 White House Conf., 1969. Fellow Orthopsychiat. Assn., mem. Md. Assn. Mental Health (dir. 1969—), Nat., Baltimore County (parliamentarian 1965-67, mem. legal com. of exec. com. 1968—, co-chmn. legal action com.) councils exceptional children, Am. Assn. U. Profs. Home: 1506 Pickett Rd Lutherville MD 21093

KOTTAS, HELEN ROSE (MRS. WILLIAM JAMES KOTTAS), civic and polit. worker; b. Tobias, Neb., Jan. 4, 1924; d. Anton and Mary (Nadherny) Stejskal; grad. high sch.; m. William James Kottas, Oct. 27, 1942; children—Sharon (Mrs. Allen Brozovsky), Marylin (Mrs. Albert H. Ericksen), Janice Ann (Mrs. Mark Schweer), Douglas James. Tchr. rural sch. Fillmore County (Neb.), 1941-42, Saline County (Neb.), 1943-44; clk. F.W. Woolworth Co., Lincoln, Neb., 1945; clk. Tobias Locker & Grocery, 1952-66; distbr. Amway

Products, Tobias, 1971-73. Den mother Cub Scouts, Tobias, Neb., 1969-70; pres. Tobias (Neb.) Community Hist. Soc., 1968—. Pres. Saline County Democratic Women's Soc., 1971-72; chmn. Olive precinct Saline County Dem. Com., 1972—. Mem. Am. Legion Aux. (pres. 1963-64), St. Joseph's Altar Soc. (pres. 1968-69). Roman Catholic. Club: Tobias (Neb.) Extension (pres. 1956, historian 1967—). Home: Box 45 Tobias NE 68453

KOTTRA, LORRAINE LANG (MRS. JOHN JOSEPH KOTTRA), anesthesiologist; b. Chgo., Sept. 26, 1940; d. Louis and Anna (Mitzler) Lang; B.S. magna cum laude, Loyola U., 1962; M.D. (USPHS fellow), U. Chgo., 1965; m. John Joseph Kottra, June 29, 1963; children—Christopher Louis, Jennifer Jean, Jason Adam. Intern, U. Chgo. Hosp. and Clinics, 1965-66; gen. med. officer USPHS Alaska Native Med. Center, Anchorage, 1966-68, chief of anesthesia 1971-72; pvt. practice anesthesia, 1972—; cons.; resident anesthesia Stanford Med. Center, 1969-70; asst. prof. anesthesiology, Stanford. Mem. Am., Alaska socs. anesthesiologists, Alpha Omega Alpha. Home: 3300 Princeton Way Anchorage AK 99504

KOTWITZ, GENEVIEVE MARY (MRS. WALTER ALFRED KOTWITZ), real estate broker; b. Milw., Sept. 24, 1914; d. Leonard Webster and Anna Marie (Paulu) Ashley; student Solano Jr. Coll., 1962-64, U. Cal. at San Francisco, 1966; m. Walter Alfred Kotwitz, Feb. 14, 1959; children—Kay (Mrs. Phi Berger), Diane (Mrs. William Jordan), Marguerite. Saleswoman Arthur's Realty, San Francisco, 1952-55; broker, salesman 4 Leaf Clover Realty, Vallejo, Cal., 1963-65; owner, real estate broker Jean Kotwitz Realty Co., Vallejo, 1969—. Owner Kotwitz Resident Care Home for Elderly People, Vallejo, 1971-74. Recipient Woman of Year award Am. Bus. Women's Assn., 1973. Mem. Am. Bus. Women's Assn., Cal. Assn. Resident Care Homes (v.p. Napa chpt. 1971-74), Sons of Italy, Bus. and Profl. Women's Club, Nat. Assn. Real Estate Brokers, Nat. Inst. Real Estate Brokers, C. of C. (mem. legislative and edn. com. 1970-74), Solano County Property Owners Assn. (pres. 1970-72, dir. 1972-73). Mem. Ch. of Jesus Christ of Latter-day Saints. Home: 332 Indiana St Vallejo CA 94590 Office: 126 Tennessee St Vallejo CA 94590

KOUDELIK, HELEN, bakery exec.; b. Trenton, N.J.; d. Alois and Anna (Grajova) Koudelik; night student Rider Coll., Trenton. Various positions with Motor Parts & Ignition Co., Trenton. Del. River Joint Toll Bridge Commn., Morrisville, Pa., and Shadyside Hosp., Pitts., 1940-59; accountant Adams Rental and Sales Co., Trenton, 1962-63; social hostess Italian ship Riveria, 1963; office mgr. Italian Peoples Bakery, Inc., Trenton, 1963—. Treas. Yardley Players; rec. sec. Slovak Gymnastic Union Sokol. Club: Sokolettes (Trenton). Author publicity and advt. for bakery. Home: 1140 Lamberton St Trenton NJ 08611 Office: 63 Butler St Trenton NJ 08611

KOULIAS, ELIZABETH MERCIA, radiologic technologist, librarian; b. Lowell, Mass.; d. Nicholas George and Helen Maria (Dragataris) Koulias; grad. nursing course Georgetown U., 1961; student Lowell Technol. Inst., 1967—. Technologist trainee St. Josephs Hosp., Lowell, Lowell Gen. Hosp. for Deep Therapy, 1953-57; head med. records librarian Groton (Mass.) Community Hosp., St. Josephs Hosp., Nashua, N.H., 1957—, Mass. Hosp. Sch., Canton, 1965—; chief radiologic technologist St. Joseph's Hosp., Lowell, VA Clinic, Lowell, 1959—, Sancta Maria Hosp., Cambridge, Mass., 1963—, Lowell Gen. Hosp., 1963—, Indsl. Med. Clinic. Boston, Dr. A. Branca's Clinic, Boston; now librarian Govt. Documents and Publs. sect. Lowell Technol. Inst. Mem. Daus. of Penelope, Greek Orthodox Youth Assn., Am. Soc. Radiologic Technologists, Am. Registry Radiologic Technologists, Med. Records Librarian Assn., Am. Soc. Med. Technologists, Nat. Security Council, Smithsonian Assn. (nat. mem.). Playwright: The Mosquitoes of the Soul, 1955: The Orion Hill, 1960. Home: 56 Gilmore St Lowell MA 01854 Office: Lowell Technol Inst Textile Av Lowell MA 01854

KOURI, JOSEPHINE (MRS. RENE PELLEYA), physician; b. Havana, Cuba, Oct. 9, 1919; d. J.B. and Josefina (Barreto) Kouri; M.D., Havana U., 1943; m. Rene Pelleya, Aug. 15, 1945; children—Rene J. Josefina (Mrs. G. Pino), Maria, Roberto. Intern Univ. Hosp., Havana, 1943-44, Kendall Hosp., Miami, Fla., 1961-62; asst. prof. U. Havana, 1943-46; resident in psychiatry Jackson Meml. Hosp., Miami, 1963-66; practice medicine specializing in psychiatry, Miami, 1966—; mem. staff South Fla. State Hosp., Hollywood, 1966—. Mem. South Fla. Psychiat. Soc., Dade County Med. Assn., Am. Psychiat. Assn. Clubs: Cuban Women's, Big Five (Miami). Author: (with Pedro Kouri) Lecciones de Parasitologia, 1946. Home: 400 Como St Coral Gables FL 33146

KOURY, ALICE FRANCISCO E. (MRS. JORGE P. EL KOURY), civic worker, educator; b. San Juan, P.R., Oct. 12, 1919; d. Miguel Francisco and Matilde Azize (Frangle) Assanna; B.S., Notre Dame Coll., Balt., 1939; M.T., Sch. Tropical Medicine, San Juan, 1940; M.S., U. Pa., 1941; m. Jorge P. El Koury, Nov. 11, 1942; children—Jorge Miguel, Jaime Antonio. Lab. technician Sch. Tropical Medicine, San Juan, 1940; prof. U. P.R., 1943-47, asso. prof. biology dept., 1957—; head lab. San Juan Diagnostic Clinic, 1948-51. Bd. dirs. P.R. chpt. A.R.C., 1951-58, Assn. Infantile Paralysis, 1943-45; bd. regents Colegio Puertorioueno de Ninas; bd. academia Perpetuo Socorro. Recipient merit pin Boy Scouts Am., 1953, award for meritorious vol. work A.R.C., 1962. Mem. A.A.A.S., Am. Pub. Health Assn., Soc. Am. Microbiologists, Soc. Microbiologists P.R. (pres. 1964-66), Am. Soc. for Microbiology (mem. edn. com.), Latin Am. Assn. for Microbiology, Soc. Med. Technologists of P.R., Tissue Culture Assn., Cath. Daus. Am., U. Pa. Alumnae Soc., Union Mujeres Americanas, Royal Soc. for Promotion Health (Eng.), Soc. Cath. U. Women, Corte de Lourdes de P.R., Hermandad del Santo Cristo, Ntra. Senora de la Providencia Soc., Asociacion Salud Publica de P.R., Navy League, Beta Beta Beta, Nu Sigma Chi. Roman Catholic. Clubs: Pa. Cornell, Swimming and Tennis, U.S. Travel (San Juan); Caseno de P.R., Civicos de Damas. Contbr. articles to profl. jours. Home: Magnolia 2009 Monteflores Santurce PR 00915 Office: PO Box 1105 San Juan PR 00902

KOVACHEVICH, ELIZABETH ANNE, circuit judge; b. Canton, Ill. Dec. 14, 1936; d. Dan and Emilie (Kuchan) Kovachevich; A.A., St. Petersburg Jr. Coll., 1956; B.B.A. magna cum laude, U. Miami 1958; J.D., Stetson U., 1961. Admitted to Fla. bar, 1961, U.S. Supreme Ct. bar, 1968; research, adminstrv. aide Pinellas County legislative delegation Fla. Legislature, 1961; asso. DeVito & Speer, 1961-62; house counsel in credit dept. Rieck & Fleece Bldrs. Supplies, Inc., 1962; gen. practice, St. Petersburg, Fla., 1962—, now circuit judge; legal adviser for women's residence com. YWCA, St. Petersburg,. adv. bd., mem. ho. com. Chmn. St. Petersburg profl. legal project Days In Court, 1967; producer, coordinator TV prodn. A Race to Judgment; dir. Sheraton Inn, St. Petersburg. Vice chmn., Fla. conf. publicity chmn. 18th Nat. Republican Women's Conf., Atlanta, 1971. Mem. Def. Adv. Commn. on Women in the Services. Bd. regents State of Fla. Life, active mem. Children's Hosp. Guild, St. Petersburg. Recipient Appreciation award St. Petersburg Panhellenic Assn., 1964, award St. Petersburg Bus. and Profl. Women, 1967; named Woman of Year, St. Petersburg, chpt. Beta Sigma Phi, 1970, Distinguished Alumnae, Stetson U., 1970. Mem. Am., Fla., St. Petersburg (sec. 1969-70) bar assns., Fla. Assn. Women Lawyers, Am., Pinellas County trial lawyers assns., Am. Judicature Soc., Internat. Platform Assn., Am. Acad. Polit. and Social Sci., Smithsonian Instn. Nat. Assos., Phi Delta Delta, Delta Delta Delta, Alpha Sigma Epsilon, Phi Kappa Phi. Roman Catholic. Home: 2459 Woodlawn Circle East St Petersburg FL 33704 Office: 545 First Av N St Petersburg FL 33701

KOVACS, ARANKA EVE, educator; b. Eger, Hungary; d. Louis and Ethel (Nagy) Kovacs; B.A., McMaster U., 1955; M.A., U. Toronto, 1956; postgrad. London Sch. Econs. (Eng.), 1958-59; Ph.D., Bryn Mawr Coll., 1960. Lectr. McGill U., 1960-61; asst. prof. U. Windsor, Ont., 1961-64, asso. prof., 1964-69, prof. econs., 1969—. Exec. mem. U. Windsor Faculty Assn., 1963-65. Recipient numerous grad., post-doctoral fellowships for study and research; numerous Research grants Can. Council and Can. Dept. Labour. Mem. Am., Canadian (exec. mem. 1967-69) econs. assns., Am., Canadian (exec. mem. 1969-70) indsl. relations research insts., Canadian Faculty Assn. U. Tchrs. Editor: Readings in Canadian Labour Economics, 1961. Contbr. articles to profl. jours. Home: 2458 Mark Av Windsor 11 ON Canada

KOVACS, HELEN VON MAGYARY-KOSSA (MRS. LORAND KOVACS), former librarian, lectr.; b. Pecs, Hungary; d. Bela and Julianna (Ott)von Magyary-Kossa; student schs. in Eng., Belgium, Austria; m. Lorand Kovacs, July 10, 1941; 1 dau., Beatrice Helen. Periodicals and dental librarian U. Ala. Med. Center, Birmingham, 1948-53; head librarian, N.Y. U. Coll. Dentistry, N.Y.C., 1954-57; asso. librarian, State U. N.Y. Downstate Med. Center, Bklyn., 1957-61, dir., librarian Med. Research Library Bklyn.; 1961-74; lectr. Mem. Med. Library Assn. (chmn. N.Y. regional group 1955, chmn. membership com. 1959-60, dir. 1970-72). Home: 220 Reichelt Rd New Milford NJ 07646

KOVAL, ELIZABETH NORMA, pub. health nurse; b. Bklyn., Dec. 20, 1939; d. Charles Cedric and Mary (Middlebrook) Weirman; R.N., Ellis Hosp. Sch. Nursing, 1960; B.S. magna cum laude Syracuse U., 1973; student Russell Sage Coll., 1968; m. Stephen V. Koval, Nov. 10, 1965; children—Stephen Charles, Christopher John, Adam Paul. Operating room staff nurse Ellis Hosp., Schenectady, 1960-61; gen. duty nursing Saratoga Hosp., summers, 1972, 1973; staff nurse Saratoga County Pub. Health Nursing Service, Saratoga Springs, N.Y., 1963-66; substitute sch. nurse-tchr. Stillwater and Mechanicville Schs., N.Y., 1972-73; female interviewer Venereal Disease Clinic, Saratoga Springs, 1973—. Dir. Saratoga County Farm Bur., 1971-73, sec., dir., 1973—; bd. dirs. Saratoga County Economic Opportunity Council. Mem. Wagman's Ridge Homemakers (co-pres. 1972-73), Sigma Theta Tau. Republican. Methodist. Home: Burke Rd RFD 1 Stillwater NY 12170

KOVAL, MARY KOSKO (MRS. GEORGE KOVAL), sociologist; b. N.Y.C., Aug. 9, 1919; d. Alexander and Mary (Zaranchuk) Kosko; B.A., Hunter Coll., 1940; postgrad. N.Y. U., Hunter Coll., N.Y. Sch. Social Research; m. George Koval, Feb. 1, 1942; children—Georgia, Virginia, Kathryn. Econ. forecaster Inst. Applied Econometrics, N.Y.C., 1940-42; statistician Western Union Telegraph Co., N.Y.C., 1942-45; with N.Y.C. Youth Services Agy., 1954-68, asst. dir. research, 1960-68; chief epidemiol. and drug prevention research N.Y. State Drug Abuse Control Commn., N.Y.C., 1968—; research cons. Ralph Whelan Assos., N.Y.C., 1968—. Mem. Am. Sociol. Assn., Am. Statis. Assn., Am. Acad. Polit. and Social Scis., A.A.A.S., Am. Soc. Criminology, Ukrainian Nat. Women's League Am. Contbr. to publs. in field. Home: 14 Metropolitan Oval New York City NY 10462 Office: 2 World Trade Center New York City NY 10047

KOWALLIS, WINIFRED ANNIE, home economist; b. Los Angeles, June 6, 1913; d. Hermann Rudolph and Bertha Dorthea (Thompson) Kowallis; student Los Angeles Jr. Coll., 1932-34; B.E., U. Cal. at Los Angeles, 1937; M.A., Mills Coll., 1942; postgrad. Columbia, 1962. Asst. dept. home econs. Mills Coll., Oakland, Cal., 1937-38, 1941-42; tchr. home econs. Westwood (Cal.) Jr. Sr. High Sch., 1938-41, dean girls, 1940-41; home adviser U. Cal. Agrl. Extension Service, Butte County, 1942-69, Sacramento County, 1969—. Mem. Am., Cal. home econs. assns., Soc. Nutrition Edn., Sacramento County Inter Agy. Nutrition Com., Cal. Inter Agy. Nutrition Council, Omicron Nu. Mem. Ch. Jesus Christ of Latter-day Saints. Club: Soroptimist (Sacramento). Home: PO Box 628 Sacramento CA 95803 Office: 9645 Kiefer Blvd Sacramento CA 95826

KOZELKA, TRESSIE MASOCCO, ret. educator; b. Fiatt, Ill., Nov. 16, 1908; d. Angelo and Antonietta (Licini) Masocco; B.S., Eureka Coll., 1931; postgrad. U. Wis., 1932, U. Ill., 1935, Columbia, 1938, U. Colo., 1959, Fresno State Coll., 1962; M.A., U. Chgo., 1945; m. Robert Frank Kozelka, July 14, 1968. Instr. biology Eureka (Ill.) Coll., 1932-33; tchr. Fairview, Ill., 1933-35; tchr. biology and phys. edn., dean Rushville (Ill.) High Sch., 1935-42, Oakwood (Ill.) High Sch., 1942-43; tchr. phys. edn. Peoria (Ill.) High Schs., 1943-57, counselor, 1957-58, 69-71; counselor Rockford (Ill.) West High Sch., 1958-69, No. Ill. U., summer 1967. Case aide Ill. Emergency Relief Commn., summers 1933, 34; critic tchr. Bradley U., 1947-57. Mem. Ill. Curriculum Guide for Health Com., 1946-48. Trustee Eureka Coll., 1951-57. Recipient award of Merit Eureka Coll., 1968. Mem. Am., Ill. (v.p. 1962-63, state program chmn. 1961-62), guidance and personnel assns., Ill. (state chmn. nat. sect. on girls and women's sports 1952-54), Am. Assns. health, phys. edn. and recreation, Eureka Coll. Alumni Assn. (nat. pres. 1949-50), Pi Kappa Delta, Pi Lambda Theta. Contbr. articles to profl. jours. Home: 2520 W Downs Circle Peoria IL 61604

KOZIELL, SUZANNE SIMONDS (MRS. JOHN KOZIELL), occupational therapist; b. Waltham, Mass., Nov. 6. 1941; d. Lermond Fales and Helen Adelaide (Bosworth) Simonds; B.S. cum laude, U. N.H., 1963; m. John Koziell, June 22, 1963; children—Lisa Anne, Theresa Lynn, Cynthia Jeanne, Constance Marie. Occupational therapist Joseph P. Kennedy Meml. Hosp., Boston, 1962, St. Elizabeth's Hosp., Washington, 1964, Mt. Alto VA Hosp., Washington, 1964. Leader Girl Scouts U.S., Balboa, C.Z., 1966-67, St. Paul, 1968-69; welfare chmn. McCoy AFB Officers Wives Club, Orlando, Fla., 1970-73; office chmn. McCoy AFB Family Services, Orlando, 1972-73. Mem. Am. Occupational Therapy Assn., Phi Kappa Phi, Pi Theta Epsilon. Home: 17 Olsen Dr Mansfield Center CT 06250

KOZLOFF, JOYCE, painter, educator; b. Somerville, N.J., Dec. 14, 1942; d. Leonard and Adele (Rosenberg) Blumberg; B.F.A. Carnegie Inst. Tech., 1964; M.F.A., Columbia, 1967; m. Max Kozloff, July 2, 1967; 1 son, Nikolas. Exhibited one-woman shows at Tibor de Nagy Gallery, N.Y.C., 1970, 71-72, 73, 74, Douglass Coll. Library, New Brunswick, N.J., 1973, U. R.I., Kingston, 1974; exhibited in group shows Whitney Mus., N.Y.C., 1972, GEDOK Am. Woman Artists Show, Kunsthaus, Hamburg, Germany, 1972, Color Forum, U. Tex. at Austin, 1972, N.Y. Cultural Center, N.Y.C., 1973, Suffolk Mus., Stony Brook, N.Y., 1972, 73, Phila. Civic Center, 1974. Mus. Modern Art, N.Y.C.; represented in permanent collections Bklyn. Mus., Mus. Modern Art, Oberlin Coll., Vassar Coll.; tchr. Ox-Bow Summer Sch. of Painting, Saugstuck, Mich., 1972, Queens Coll. of City of N.Y., 1972-73, Sch. Visual Arts, N.Y.C., 1973-74. Tamarind Lithography Inst. grantee, 1972, Creative Artists Program grantee, 1973. Address: 152 Wooster St New York City NY 10025

KOZLOWSKI, LUCILLE KATHRYN, lawyer; b. Nashua, N.H., Feb. 22, 1926; d. Augustyn and Anna (Markar) Kozlowski; A.A., Northeastern U., 1954; J.D., Boston Coll. Law Sch., 1958. Admitted to N.H. bar, 1958; partner law firm Velishka and Kozlowski, Nashua, N.H., 1958—. Mem. Am., N.H., Nashua (sec.-treas. 1962—) bar assns., St. Stanislaus Ladies' Guild. Democrat. Roman Catholic. Home: 6 Bitirnas St Nashua NH 03060 Office: 1 E Hollis St Nashua NH 03060

KRAFFT, JULIA GERTRUDE CLARK, business exec.; b. Wheaton, Ill.; d. George Barnard and Rose (Austin) Clark; ed. pub. and bus. schs.; m. Walter A. Krafft, June 25, 1939 (dec.). Pres. Steven's Candy Kitchens, Inc., 1921-56; owner The Little Traveler, Inc., Geneva, Ill., 1953-63. Bd. dirs. Salvation Army, 1948, mem. woman's bd., 1947; mem. Ill. Youth Commn., 1961; chmn. Chgo. Beautiful Com., 1966—; mem. women's bd. Passavant Meml. Hosp., 1944. Bd. dirs. Lyric Opera, 1953; nat. dir. Hadley Sch. for Blind, 1956. Recipient award Vets. Fgn. Wars, 1944, Harding Coll., 1962, citations Am. Legion, 1944, 45, 46. Mem. Alliance Bus. and Profl. Women's Club, Woman's Advt. Club, Fashion Group, Inc. Republican. Clubs: Woman's Athletic, Arts (Chgo.); Lake Geneva Garden. Home: PO Box 228 Rancho Santa Fe CA 92067

KRAFT, ELISE RHODA (MRS. JOSEPH LEDMAN), chem. cons.; b. N.Y.C., Mar. 14, 1926; d. Samuel and Mildred Rita (Daum) Kraft; A.B. summa cum laude (Elizabeth Shippen scholar), Bryn Mawr Coll., 1946; Ph.D., Harvard-Radcliffe Coll., 1954; m. Joseph Ledman, Aug. 2, 1968; children (by previous marriage)—Alison McLamore, Amy McLamore. Sr. chemist Revlon, Inc., N.Y.C., 1954-62; sr. chemist, tech. service Nopco Chem. Co., North Arlington, N.J., 1962-66; sr. chemist Malstrom, Inc., Linden, N.J., 1968-71. Cons. Malmstrom div. Emery Industries, 1972; vol. faculty City U. N.Y., Manhattan Community Coll., 1971-72. Vol. adminstrv. asst. to late Congressman William Fitts Ryan, 1958-70; vol. dep. atty. gen. State of N.Y., 1972—. Fellow Am. Inst. Chemists; mem. Soc. Cosmetic Chemists, Soc. Plastics Industry, Sigma Xi. Jewish religion. Clubs: Radcliffe, Bryn Mawr (N.Y.C.). Democrat. Patentee in field. Home: 2109 Broadway New York City NY 10023

KRAFT, JESSICA EBBETS VAN AUSDALL (MRS. HAROLD R. KRAFT), museum curator; b. Cold Spring Harbor, N.Y., Jan. 2, 1909; d. Foster and Katherine Lawrence (Ebbets) Van Ausdall; grad. high sch.; m. Harold R. Kraft, June 12, 1928; children—Barbara (Mrs. Walter S. Comstock), Jane (Mrs. James J. Mills), Edith (Mrs. Donald J. Greeley). Adminstr., curator Sagamore Hill, Theodore Roosevelt Assn., Oyster Bay, N.Y., 1953-63; museum curator Sagamore Hill Nat. Historic Site, Nat. Park Service, U.S. Dept. Interior, Oyster Bay, 1963—. Pres. Oyster Bay P.T.A., 1948; sec. Oyster Bay Am. Revolution Bicentennial Commn., 1971—. Mem. Nassau County Rep. Com., 1957-63. Mem. D.A.R. (chpt. treas. 1970-71), Theodore Roosevelt Assn. (asst. treas. 1966—, trustee 1957—), Oyster Bay Hist. Soc. (trustee 1973—), Order Eastern Star. Home: 71 Burtis Av Oyster Bay NY 11771 Office: Sagamore Hill National Historic Site Mounted Route Box 304 Oyster Bay NY 11771

KRAFT, MARY (MRS. ERWIN M. FREY), editor; b. Canton, O., May 1, 1911; d. Leonard F. and Anna (Koch) Kraft; student Cleve. Sch. Art, 1929-31, John Huntington Poly. Inst., 1932-34; m. Erwin M. Frey, Sept. 14, 1956. Interior decorator Palmer & Riley Co., Cleve., 1940-46; dir. design studio Armstrong Cork Co., Lancaster, Pa., 1946-52; editor, dir. home bldg. and decorating dept. Good Housekeeping, N.Y.C., 1953—. Recipient 4 Dorothy Dawe awards Am. Furniture Mart; named to Writers Hall of Fame, So. Furniture Market, 1972. Mem. Am. Inst. Decorators, Nat. Home Fashion League (Trailblazer award 1973), Archtl. League, Nat. Soc. Interior Design, Environmental Design Inst., Nat. Assn. Home Builders. Author: Complete Book Decorating, 1971. Home: 220 Central Park S New York City NY 10019 Office: 959 8th Av New York City NY 10019

KRALL, VITA, clin. psychologist; b. New Haven, Conn., July 9, 1923; d. Moses Adams and Jennie Edith (Alper) Krall; B.A., Antioch Coll., 1944; M.A., State U. Ia., 1945; Ph.D., U. Rochester, 1951. Intern in clin. psychology Rockland State Hosp., Orangeburg, N.Y., 1945-47; teaching asst. U. Rochester (N.Y.), 1947-49, grad. instr., 1949-50, clin. asso., 1950-51; instr. Mich. State Coll., East Lansing, 1951-53; sr. clin. psychologist Topeka (Kan.) State Hosp., 1953-57; cons. Menninger Found., Topeka, 1957-58; acting dir. psychology dept. Kan. Neurol. Inst., Topeka, 1959-61; staff psychologist Child Guidance Clinic, Bridgeport, Conn., 1961-62; sr. clin. psychologist Michael Reese Hosp., Chgo., 1963—, chief child psychologist, dir. tng. in clin. psychology, 1969—. Cons., Michael Lane Inst., Chgo. Mem. Assn. Chgo. Clin. Tng. Centers in Psychology (sec. 1969-71), Soc. for Research in Child Devel., Soc. for Personality Assessment, Am., Ill., Kan., Conn. psychol. assns., Eastern, Midwestern, New Eng. psychol. assns., Am. Ortho-psychiat. Assn., Sigma Xi. Home: 1716 E 55th St Chicago IL 60615 Office: Michael Reese Hosp Chicago IL 60616

KRAMER, ALICE MARIE POULSEN, clin. psychologist; b. N.Y.C., Jan. 10, 1937; d. Carl M. and Ellen M. (Juliussen) Poulsen; B.A., Queens Coll., 1958; M.S. cum laude, L.I. U., 1961; Ph.D., St. John's U., 1973; m. Milton Kramer Jan. 9, 1960 (div. Nov. 1971); 1 dau., Karen. Lectr. psychology L.I. U., Bklyn, 1961-64; clin. psychologist St. Vincent's Hosp., N.Y.C., 1970—, Logan Meml. Hosp., N.Y.C., 1974—. Mem. Am. Psychol. Assn. (presented paper conv. 1972), N.Y. Soc. Clin. Psychologists. Home: 140 Cadman Plaza W Brooklyn NY 11201 Office: 60 W 10th St New York City NY 10011

KRAMER, ANITA MISSEN (MRS. BERNARD J. KRAMER), advt. co. exec.; b. Phila., June 8, 1917; d. Max W. and Sophia E. (Simkin) Nissenholtz; student (scholar), Emily Krider Norris Sch. Dramatics, 1935; student Temple U., 1938-40; m. Bernard J. Kramer, Mar.9, 1941; children—Karen (Mrs. Alain Lepere), Jill. With Gersh & Kramer, Inc., advt. agy., Phila., 1960—, corporate treas., 1960—; v.p., treas. Direct Response Broadcasting Network, Inc., Phila., 1972—. Cons. Office Psychiat. Cons. div. spl. edn. Bd. Edn., Phila., 1969-74; actress Neighborhood Players Repertory Theatre, Phila., 1934-41; drama tchr. West Oak Lane Community Center, Phila., 1954-56; actress, spokeswoman and narrator of various TV and radio commercials, 1961-74. Recipient Achievement award Phila. Assn. Retarded Children, 19—. Mem. Phila. Assn. Retarded Children (pres. council 1958-59, dir. 1958—). Mem. B'nai B'rith. Clubs: TV and Radio Advt.; Variety (Phila.). Home: The Philadelphian Apt 9B-33 2401 Pennsylvania Av Philadelphia PA 19130 Office: Direct Response Broadcasting Network Inc Parkway at 21st St Philadelphia PA 19103

KRAMER, BERTHA YABROFF, writer, social worker; d. Benjamin and Rose (Katznelson) Yabroff; B.A., U. Wis., 1919; postgrad. Columbia U., 1930, Western Res. U., 1928; m. Ben V. Kramer, Dec. 25, 1927; children—Carolyn (Mrs. Alan D. Greenberg), Baron David. Tchr., Waushara County Tng. Sch. for Tchrs., Wautoma, Wis.; tchr. English, editor sch. annual Green Bay (Wis.) High Sch.; tchr. English, dramatic coach Stevens Point (Wis.) High Sch.; tchr. Cleve. Pub. Schs.; substitute tchr. Columbus (Ohio) Pub. Schs., D.C. Pub. Schs.;

dist. dir. Girl Scouts U.S., D.C., Phila.; dir. Golden Age Program, Balt. Community Center. Mem. Nat. League Am. Pen Women (pres. Cleve. br. 1972—); Women in Communications, Cleve. Coll. Writers (pres. 1970). Contbr. articles to Cleve. Plain Dealer, Sunday Travel, Sunday Mag. Supplement, Women's Pages, Women's Club Mag., Washington, King Features Syndicate, Poetry, Blue Moon Mag., others. Home: 472 Karl Dr Richmond Heights OH 44143

KRAMER, EDNA ERNESTINE (MRS. BENEDICT TAXIER LASSAR), mathematician, educator; b. N.Y.C.; d. Joseph and Sabine (Elowitch) Kramer; A.B., Hunter Coll., 1929; Ph.D., Columbia U., 1936; postgrad. Courant Inst., 1939-40, 65-69, U. Chgo., 1941; m. Benedict Taxier Lassar, July 2, 1935. Asst. prof. math. N.J. State Tchrs. Coll., Montclair, 1935-39; instr. grad. div. Bklyn. Coll., 1936-40; adj. prof. Poly. Inst. Bklyn., 1948—; instr. grad. div. N.Y. U., 1949-50. Cons. math. Columbia U., 1943-45, U. Ore., 1963. Mem. Am. Math. Soc., Math. Assn. Am. Author: First Course in Statistics, 1936; Mathematics Takes Wings, 1942; The Main Stream of Mathematics, 1951; Nature and Growth of Modern Mathematics, 1970. Contbr. articles to profl. jours. and Dictionary Sci. Biography. Home: 360 W 22d St New York City NY 10011 Office: Polytechnic Inst New York City NY 11201

KRAMER, I. JANET PHILLIPS, med. adminstr.; b. Pottsville, Pa., Dec. 25, 1942; d. Earl Milton and Isabel (Price) Phillips; B.S., Pa. State U., 1964; M.D., Woman's Med. Coll. Pa., 1968; m. Brian D. Kramer, June 10, 1967. Intern T. M. Fitzgerald Mercy Hosp., Darby, Pa., 1968-69; resident internal medicine Wilmington Med. Center, 1969-71, fellow adolescent medicine, 1971-72; fellow adolescent medicine Children's Hosp., Washington, 1971; med. dir. Del. Drug Detoxification Program, Wilmington, 1972-73; med. dir. Del. Office Drug Abuse, 1972—; guest lectr. adolescent medicine, drug abuse U. Del. extension courses, 1971; lectr. drug abuse U. Del. Bur. Narcotics and Dangerous Drugs, 1971. Med. adviser State Drug Information Action Line, 1970—; chmn. profl. adv. com. Del. Mental Health Assn., 1971-73; mem. profl. adv. com. Del. Adolescent Program, 1971-73. Bd. dirs. Del. Mental Health Assn. Mem. Am. Med. Woman's Assn., New Castle County Med. Soc., Am. Soc. Internal Medicine, Adolescent Medicine Soc., Am. Acad. Clin. Toxicology, Alpha Epsilon Delta. Office: 1100 Gilpin Av Wilmington DE 19806

KRAMER, JEANNE MARTY (MRS. ARDATH DALE KRAMER), newspaper editor; b. Trinidad, Colo., May 9, 1921; d. Harlo U. and Mary B. (Marty) Bennett; student Trinidad Jr. Coll., 1940-41, U. Colo., 1939-40; m. Ardath Dale Kramer, Feb. 19, 1972; 1 dau. by previous marriage, Marion (Mrs. Douglas Cruger). Accountant Sta. WMBR-TV, Jacksonville, Fla., 1952-53; soc. editor, bookkeeper Dos Palos (Cal.) Star, 1954-56, bus. mgr., editor, 1961-74; bookkeeper, exec. sec. Roth Chevrolet, Merced, Cal., 1956-61. Mem. Nat. Sec. Assn. (charter pres. 1947), Central Newspaper Women's Assn. Club: Women's Improvement (Dos Palos). Home: 52083 Althea Rd Firebaugh CA 93622 Office: 1527 Center Av Dos Palos CA 93620

KRAMER, MARGARET MARY, educator; b. Bancroft, Ia., Nov. 10, 1932; d. Mathias C. and Mary B. (Rapp) Kramer; B.S., Briar Cliff Coll., 1955; M.S., Mankato State Coll., 1965; postgrad. U. S.D., 1955-56, U. Colo., 1961, U. Ia., 1970, U. N.M., 1971-72. Elementary and secondary tchr. Webster City Community Schs., 1955-56, Vinton Community Schs., 1956-65, St. Charles Sch., Albuquerque, 1971-72; asst. prof. phys. edn. Upper Ia. Coll., Fayette, 1965—, dir. women's intramurals, 1965-74, dir. women's intercollegiate sports, coach women's volleyball, basketball, softball and tennis, 1968-74. Grad. asst. U. S.D., 1955-56, Mankato State Coll., 1964-65. Mem. Coll. Assn. Phys. Edn. Women, Am., Ia. (sec. 1967-68) assns. health, phys. edn. and recreation, Delta Psi Kappa. Roman Catholic (sec. parish council 1970-71). Club: Big Rock Country (chmn. women's golf 1970-71). Home: 402 E Water St Fayette IA 52142

KRAMER, MARIA KRAUS (MRS. PAUL KRAMER), psychoanalyst; b. Vienna, Austria, Mar. 14, 1913; d. Rudolf and Maria (Terzer) Kraus; student U. Santiago (Chile), 1929-32, U. Vienna (Austria), 1933-37; M.D., Rush Med. Coll., Chgo., 1939; m. Paul Kramer, 1937. Came to U.S., 1937, naturalized, 1942. Intern Women's and Children's Hosp., Chgo.; resident Psychiat. Clinic, U. Vienna; practice medicine specializing in psychiatry, Palo Alto, Cal., 1968—. Mem. A.M.A., Chgo. Med. Soc., Chgo. Psychoanalytic Soc., Am. Psychoanalytic Assn., Am. Psychiat. Assn. Home: 855 Northampton Dr Palo Alto CA 94303

KRAMER, MARY RAINEY GASTON (MRS. ROBERT KRAMER), economist; b. Spokane, Wash., May 2, 1912; d. Herbert E. and Ethel (Bell) Gaston; A.B., Vassar Coll., 1933; postgrad. (Rockefeller fellow pub. adminstrn.) U. Minn., 1939-40; m. Robert Kramer, Mar. 22, 1941; children—Mary Elizabeth (Mrs. Howard Helsinger), Lucy Mapes (Mrs. Dorsey Gardner), Robert Gaston. Economist FCA, 1934-41; labor economist, women's br. Econ. Status and Opportunities div. U.S. Dept. of Labor, Washington, 1966—. Mem. women's bd. George Washington U. Hosp., Washington, 1961—. Mem. Women's Equity Action, Federally Employed Women. Democrat. Episcopalian. Clubs: George Washington University Faculty Women's, Washington Vassar (mem. adv. council 1969-73). Contbr. chpt. to book: Washington Opportunities for Women. Home: 4326 36th St NW Washington DC 20008 Office: US Dept Labor Women's Bur 14th and Constitution Sts NW Washington DC 20210

KRAMER, NORA, cons. on books for children and young people; b. Pendleton, Eng.; d. Harris and Rachel (Wolf) Atkins; student Beaux Arts Inst., N.Y. 1920-21, Mus. Sch., Boston, 1929-30, City Coll. N.Y., 1939-43; m. Sidney David Kramer, Oct. 27, 1917; (dec. June 1955); children—Karl Robert, Virginia I. (Mrs. Jerome David Stein, Jr.), Joan (Mrs. Arthur Philip Stoliar). Cons. (under name of Eleanor Brent) The Little Bookshop, Macy's, N.Y., 1943-53; creator The Bookplan, 1944, dir., 1944—; editorial cons. Scholastic's Arrow Book Club, 1958—; leader juvenile writing workshop Colo. U., 1955. Mem. children's book coms. Child Study Assn. of Am., 1934—, Nat. Conf., Christians and Jews, 1947—, English-Speaking Union Books-Across-the-Sea, 1953—. Judge for Herald Tribune spring book festival, 1947, 53. Mem. Woman's Nat. Book Assn., Author's Guild, English-Speaking Union, Child Study Assn. Am. Author: Nora Kramer's Storybook for Threes and Fours, 1955; Nora Kramer's Storybook for Fives and Sixes, 1956; The Cozy Hour Storybook, 1960; The Arrow Book of Ghost Stories, 1960; The Grandma Moses Storybook, 1961; Princess Tales, 1971; Tricky Tales, 1970; The Ghostly Hand and Other Haunting Stories, 1972. Co-author: (with K.R. Kramer) Coppercraft and Silver Made at Home, 1958, paperback edit., 1972. Editor-in-chief The Bookwoman, 1954-56. Editor: Grimms' Fairy Tales, 1962; (abridged editions) Swiss Family Robinson, 1960, Hans Brinker, 1967, Dracula, 1971, Ramona, 1972, Journey To The Center of The Earth, 1973. Address: 46 Jane St New York City NY 10014

KRAMER, SELMA (MRS. ERNEST WITKIN), psychoanalyst; b. Phila., Apr. 27, 1920; d. Morris and Jennie (Schneidman) Kramer; B.A., Temple U., 1940; M.D., Women's Med. Coll. Pa., 1944; m. Ernest Witkin, May 1, 1945; children—Karen (Mrs. John Berberian), James Bruce. Intern, St. Lukes Hosp., Phila., Children's Med. Center, Phila., 1944-45; trainee psychiatry Norristown (Pa.) State Hosp., 1945-47; trainee child Child Study Center, Inst. of Pa. Hosp., Phila., 1951-53; trainee child and adult analysis Phila. Psychoanalytic Inst., 1949-55; practice medicine, specializing in psychiatry, Phila., 1949—; asso. prof. clin. psychiatry St. Christ Hosp., Temple Med. Sch., 1961-65; clin. prof. child psychiatry Med. Coll. Pa., Phila., 1965-73, prof., 1973—; head sect., 1965—; cons. Norristown State Hosp., 1964-70, Family Service Phila., 1953-57. Fellow Am. Acad. Child Psychiatry, Am. Psychiat. Soc.; mem. Am. (asst. editor jour.), Phila. psychoanalysic socs., Assn. Child Analysis. Book review editor Jour. American Acad. Child Psychiatry, 1962-65. Contbr. articles to profl. jours. Home: 3902 Netherfield Rd Philadelphia PA 19129 Office: Medical Coll Pa Henry Av at Abbottsford Rd Philadelphia PA 19129

KRAMERSON, TOBY (MRS. JULIUS JACOBSON), psychotherapist; b. Balt., Mar. 8, 1919; d. Rachmiel Gedaliah and Frieda Liebe (Zuckerman) Zucker; B.S., Hunter Coll., 1941; M.S.S., Smith Sch. Social Work, 1944; m. Julius Jacobson, May 24, 1969; 1 son by previous marriage, Paul Kramerson. Caseworker, supr. Jewish Family Service, N.Y.C., 1946-61; psychotherapist, family counselor Arthur Lehman Counseling Service, N.Y.C., 1961-68; pvt. practice psychotherapist and family counselor, N.Y.C., 1968—. Mem. Nat. Assn. Social Work, Am. Orthopsychiat. Assn., Assn. for Applied Psychoanalysis, Am. Assn. Marriage and Family Counselors, Soc. Clin. Social Work. Asso. editor I mag. Home and office: 205 West End Av New York City NY 10023

KRAMRISCH, STELLA (MRS. LASZLO NEMENYI), museum curator, educator; b. Mikulov, Austria; d. Jacques and Berta Kramrisch; Ph.D., U. Vienna, 1919, hon. Ph.D., 1968; D.Litt. desiKottama (hon.), Visva-Bharati U.; m. Laszlo Nemenyi, Apr. 15, 1929. Came to U.S., 1950, naturalized, 1955. Prof. Indian art U. Calcutta (India), 1923-50; lectr. Indian art Courtaul Inst., U. London (Eng.), 1937-41; prof. art. of South Asia U. Pa., 1950-69; prof. Indian art Inst. of Fine Arts, N.Y. U., 1964—; curator Indian art Phila Museum of Art, 1954—. Bollingen Found. fellow, 1950-53; Am. Philos. Soc. grantee, Ford. Found. grantee, John D. Rockefeller III Found. grantee. Mem. Ecole Francoise d'Extreme Oriente (hon.); mem. Indian Soc. Oriental Art (v.p.), Am. Oriental Soc., Asia Soc. Author: Principles of Indian Art, 1924; Vishnudharmottara, 1924; History of Indian Art, 1929; Indian Sculpture, 1932; Asian Miniature Paintings, 1932; A Survey of Painting in the Deccan, 1937; Indian Terracottas, 1939; Kantha, 1939; The Hindu Temple, 1946; Arts and Crafts of Travancore, 1948; Dravida and Kerala, 1953; Art of India, 1954; Indian Sculpture in the Philadelphia Museum of Art, 1960; The Triple Structure of Creation, 1962; The Art of Nepal, 1964; Unknown India: Ritual Art in Tribe and Village, 1968. Editor Artibus Asiae, 1959—, Jour. India Soc. Oriental Art, 1932-50. Home: Rural Route 1 Box 111 Malvern PA 19355 Office: Philadelphia Museum of Art PO Box 7646 Philadelphia PA 19101 also Inst Fine Arts NY U 1 E 78th St New York City NY 10009

KRANIDAS, ELLEN ANTOINETTE (MRS. EVANS KRANIDAS), govt. ofcl.; b. Klitor, Greece, Sept. 23, 1933; d. Nicholas Theodore and Theodora Andrew Yanacopoulos; J.D., U. Athens, 1950; postgrad. (univ. fellow), Georgetown U. Sch. Fgn. Service, 1950-51, M.A., 1958; m. Evans Kranidas, Aug. 20, 1951; children—Van Theodore (dec.), Nicole Antoinette. Came to U.S., 1950, naturalized, 1955. With U.S. Govt., Washington, 1949—, free lance asst. corr. U.P.I., N.Am. Newspaper Alliance, 1949-50, program/policy analyst Dept. Housing and Urban Devel., 1965-69, div. dep. dir., 1969-71, spl. asst. to commr. FHA, 1971, dir. Office Mgmt. and Orgn., Dept. Housing and Urban Devel., 1972, dir. Office Regional Liaison, 1973—. Trustee, Pediatric Orthopedic Hosp., Home of Affection Found. for Orphan Boys. Home: 1409 Kingston Av Alexandria VA 22302 Office: Dept Housing and Urban Devel 451 7th St SW Washington DC 20410

KRANTZ, HAZEL NEWMAN (MRS. MICHAEL KRANTZ), editor, author; b. Bklyn., Jan. 29, 1920; d. Louis John and Eva (Newman) Newman; B.S., N.Y. U., 1942; M.S., Hofstra U., 1959; m. Michael Krantz, June 7, 1942; children—Laurence, Margaret, Vincent. Elementary tchr. Nassau County (N.Y.) Pub. Schs., 1957-68; editor True Frontier mag., Valley Stream, N.Y., 1969-72; copy editor db The Sound Engrng. Mag., Plainview, 1973—. Mem. Ontological Soc. Hadassah. Author: 100 Pounds of Popcorn, 1961; Freestyle for Michael, 1964; The Secret Raft, 1964; Tippy, 1968; A Pad of Your Own, 1973. Home: 875 Leeds Dr North Bellmore NY 11710 Office: 1120 Old Country Rd Plainview NY 11803

KRANTZ, MARILYN, editor; b. Phila., Jan. 31, 1927; d. Samuel and Ethel (Rosenthal) Rosen; B.S. in Bus. Adminstrn., Temple U., 1948; m. Barney Krantz, Oct. 10, 1948; children—Jane (Mrs. Fred Silverbook), Charles, Martin, Kathy. Editor Tri-County Newspapers, community weeklies, Phila., 1965—; columnist Jewish Exponent, weekly, Phila., 1974—. Condr. workshops for vols. Pres. Hilltop chpt. Women's Am. ORT, 1962-63, regional publns. chmn. Main Line-Suburban West region, 1960-62; pres. M.E. Kalish Folkshul, 1974—; mem. com. edn. Fedn. Jewish Agencies, 1970—, exec. bd. women's council, 1971—; mem. adult edn. com., adv. com. Gratz Coll., Phila., 1970—; publicist Phila. Jewish Archives Center, 1973—. Bd. dirs. Jewish Nat. Fund, Phila. Recipient Service award Lamberton Home and Sch. Assn., 1970; 1st prize poetry Phila. Regional Writers Conf., 1964. Mem. Pa. Poetry Soc. Author booklets, verse for greeting cards, ednl. materials, poetry and plays for children's theatre. Home: 1383 Kimberly Dr Philadelphia PA 19151

KRANZ, ERMA BERGMAN (MRS. ALAN Z. KRANZ), psychologist; b. Bklyn., Oct. 4, 1928; d. David and Sonia (Prager) Bergman; B.A., Hunter Coll., 1950; M.Ed., Temple U., 1966; m. Alan Z. Kranz, Dec. 25, 1954; children—David, Susan. Elementary sch. tchr., N.Y.C., 1950-55, Pitts., 1955-56, Princeton, 1956-57; cons. psychologist Wissahickson (Pa.) Sch. Dist., 1967-68; sch. psychologist Leonia Sch. Dist., 1968-70, Hackensack (N.J.) Sch. Dist., 1970—. Mem. Nat. Assn. Sch. Psychologists, Bergen County Sch. Psychologists Assn. (treas. 1970-73). Home: 821 Downing St Teaneck NJ 07666 Office: Broadway Sch Hackensack NJ 07601

KRASNER, JOAN DANZIG (MRS. JOSEPH KRASNER), editor; b. Elmira, N.Y.; d. George Hamilton and Estelle (Saqui) Danzig; student Elmira Coll.; m. Joseph Krasner, May 23, 1953; children—Susan, Karin. Reporter Athens (Pa.) Bur. Sayre Evening Times, 1948-50; soc. editor 1950-52; women's editor, fashion editor Buffalo Evening News, 1952—. Mem. publicity com. Buffalo Philharmonic Orch., 1958-60; sec. Bradford County (Pa.) Cancer Soc., 1948-49, pub. worker, 1949-50; mem. Athens (Pa.) Sch. Adv. Com., 1950; pub. information officer Civil Air Patrol, Tioga Point, Pa., 1951. Recipient Feature Writing award Pa. Women's Press Assn. 1949; Headlinewriting award Buffalo Newspaper Guild, 1957, Women's Page writing award, 1964. Mem. Am. Newspaper Guild, Bus. and Profl. Women's Club (Athens pres. 1948-50), Sigma Delta Chi. Office: 1 News Plaza Buffalo NY 14240

KRASNER, LEE, painter; b. Bklyn; ed. Cooper Union, City Coll. N.Y., N.A.D.; studied with Hans Hofmann; m. Jackson Pollock (dec.). Exhibited paintings at Palazzo Franeri, Turin, Italy, 1959, Galerie Beyeler, Basle, Switzerland, 1961, Laing Art Gallery, Newcastle-upon-Tyne. Eng., 1961, Marlborough Fine Art, London, Eng., 1961, Yale Art Gallery, 1961-62, Mt. Holyoke Coll., 1962, Wadsworth Atheneum, Hartford, Conn., 1962, Guild Hall, East Hampton, N.Y., 1962-64; Mary Washington Coll., U. Va., Fredericksburg 1962, Queens Coll., N.Y.C., 1962, Howard Wise Gallery, 1962, Guggenhelm Mus., N.Y.C., 1964, Gallery of Modern Art, N.Y.C., 1965, Southampton Coll. of L.I. U., 1965; exhibited with shows Hans Hofmann and His Students, 1963, 64, Abstract Watercolors by 14 Americans, 1963-65, White House traveling exhbn., 1967; Jewish Mus., N.Y.C., 1967, Mus. Modern Art, 1969, Palazzo Reale, Milan, 1971, Lakeview Center, Peoria, Ill., 1972; exhibited in one-man shows Betty Parsons Gallery, N.Y.C., 1951, Stable Gallery, N.Y.C., 1955, Martha Jackson Gallery, N.Y.C., 1958, Signa Gallery, East Hampton, 1959, Howard Wise Gallery, 1960, 62, Whitechapel Gallery, London, 1965, Arts Council of Gt. Britain, London, 1966, U. Ala. Gallery, 1967, Marlborough-Gerson Gallery, N.Y.C., 1968, 69, Reese Paley Gallery, San Francisco, 1969, Marlborough Gallery, N.Y.C., 1973, Whitney Mus. Am. Art, N.Y.C., 1973-74, Beaver Coll., Glenside, Pa., 1974; represented in numerous collections. Address: The Springs East Hampton NY 11937

KRASNOW, FRANCES (MRS. MARCUS THAU), cons. biochemist, educator; b. N.Y.C., Oct. 16, 1894; d. Raphael and Sara Rifka (Lubarsky) Krasnow; B.S. magna cum laude, Barnard Coll., 1917; A.M., Columbia, 1917, Ph.D., 1922; m. Marcus Thau, Dec. 25, 1930; 1 dau., Hudelle K. Mem. research and teaching staff dept. biochemistry Columbia U. Coll. Phys. and Surg., 1917-32, asst. dir., 1932-44; staff Guggenheim Dental Clinic, Sch. Dental Hygiene, N.Y.C., head dept. research, 1944-52; research dir. Universal Coatings, Inc., Newark, 1952-72; research cons., N.Y.C., 1972—. Cons. biochemistry, 1952—. Active P.T.A., also various community drives; area chmn. A.R.C., 1943-44. Recipient various awards civic and profl. orgns. Mem. Am. Chem. Soc., Soc. Exptl. Biology and Medicine, Am. Bd. Clin. Chemistry, A.A.A.S., N.Y. Acad. Medicine, A.M.A., Am. Assn. Clin. Chemists, Am. Soc. Microbiology, N.Y. Acad. Scis., Internat. Assn. Dental Research (pres. 1947-49, editor 1949-60), Am. Inst. Chemists, Am. Assn. Dental Editors, Alumni Assn. Tchrs. Inst.-Sem. Coll. (dir., pres. 1947-53, hon. pres. 1968—), N.Y. State (hon.) N.Y.C. (hon.) dental hygiene assns., Phi Beta Kappa, Sigma Xi. Home: 405 E 72d St New York City NY 10021 Office: 405 E 72d St New York City NY 10021

KRATZ, ELIZABETH ORR (MRS. DAVID L. KRATZ), church exec.; b. Belfast, Ireland, Jan. 6, 1902; d. Robert and Ellen (Gordon) Orr; student Reed Coll., 1919-21, Ore. Coll., 1922-23; m. David L. Kratz, Mar. 24, 1927 (dec. Nov. 1960); children—Phyllis E. (Mrs. Leon M. Hall), David G., Charles R., James S. Office sec. Meier & Frank Co., Portland, Ore., 1920-21; tchr. pub. schs., Condon, Ore., 1923-25, Portland, Ore., 1925-27; art supr. pub. schs., The Dalles, Ore., 1927-28; supr. Released Time Religious Edn., Vallejo, Cal., 1945-48; minister edn. 1st Christian Ch., Lincoln, Neb., 1960; v.p. Christian Chs., No. Cal. and Nev., Berkeley, Cal., 1962-70, acting pres.-bishop, 1970—, exec. sec. Christian Womens Fellowship, 1962—. Ordained to ministry Disciples Christ, 1965. Acting exec. dir. No. Cal. Ecumenical Council, 1972—; del. Ch. Leaders Consultation to Paris Peace Talks, 1971. Dir. Eskaton, Sacramento, Cal., Faith and Life Corp., Berkeley, Center for Environmental Action, Salem, Ore. Mem. adminstrv. com. Office Women's Affairs, Grad. Theol. Union, Berkeley; bd. dirs. No. Cal. Ecumenical Peace Inst., Western Acad. for Church Life and Mission, Oakland, Cal. Mem. Ch. Women United (nat. bd. mgrs. 1963-65; state chmn. citizen action 1972—), N. Cal. Council Chs. (dir. 1963—), Cal. Ch. Council, Cal. Migrant Ministry (pres. 1968—), P.E.O. Republican. Mem. Disciples of Christ (dir. disciples peace fellowship, fellowship of reconciliation, steering com. Disciples for Mission and Renewal 1969-72). Home: 904 Evelyn Av Albany CA 94706 Office: 1177 San Pablo Av Berkeley CA 94706

KRATZ, MILDRED SANDS (MRS. LOWELL FORREST KRATZ), artist; b. Pottstown, Pa., July 15, 1923; d. Matthew Stanley Quay and Anne (Hohl) Sands; grad. high sch.; m. Lowell Forrest Kratz, Oct. 18, 1947; children—Melissa Ann and Melinda Lou (twins). One-man shows Reading (Pa.) Pub. Mus., William Penn Museum, Harrisburg, Pa., Piccolo Mondo; Palm Beach, Fla., Hill Sch., Pottstown, Pa., Gallery Madison 90, N.Y.C., Camp Hill Acad., Harrisburg, Pa., others; exhibited in group shows at Pa. Acad. Fine Arts, Allied Artists, Am. Watercolor Soc., Audubon Artists, Knickerbocker Artists, Nat. Art Club, Nat. Acad., Catherine Lorillard Wolfe Pro Women, Nat. League Am. Pen Women, Acad. Artists, N.A.D., Nat. Art League, Hudson Valley Art League, Phila. Water Color Club, others; represented in permanent collections Reading Pub. Mus., Am. Fine Arts Collection, Cleve., Motorola, Chgo., also pvt. collections, U.S. and Europe. Judge juror, condr. critiques, 1963—. Pres., Hosp. Jr. Aux., 1953; organizer, co-founder Pottstown Area Artists Guild, 1960. Recipient numerous nat. regional and local awards including gold medal Catherine Lorillard Wolfe 72d, N.Y.C., 1969, 73; Gold medal A.A.P.L., 1973; Morse award for water color, 1968. Mem. Am. Watercolor Soc., Acad. Artists, Phila. Art Alliance, Phila. Water Color Club, Nat. League Am. Pen Women (award 1974), Nat. Forum Profl. Artists, Allied Artists, Am. Artists Group, Nat. Art League, Woodmere, Chester County art assns., Pottstown Area Artists Guild (founder 1960, pres. 1961, sec. 1962). Club: Doe (Pottstown). Contbr. to mags. Home: County Park Rd RD 2 Pottstown PA 19464 Office: Mildred Sands Kratz Gallery St Peters Village St Peters PA 19470

KRAUCH, VELMA ANN (MRS. WILLIAM HENRY KRAUCH), author; b. Los Angeles, Sept. 21, 1916; d. Frank Earl and Susie Velma (Stephens) McDonald; A.A., Santa Monica City Coll., 1955; student Cal. State U. at Northridge, 1964-65, U. Cal. at Los Angeles; m. William Henry Krauch, June 12, 1937; children—Bill, Nikki (Mrs. John Lee). Tchr., Tocaloma Nursery Sch., West Los Angeles, 1957-63; sec. to mystery writers, Encino, Cal., 1964-72; free lance writer, 1967—. Active Camp Fire Girls, 1953-69. Mem. Assn. for Women's Active Return to Edn. (v.p. 1973-74, Minerva award 1972). Author: Three Stacks and You're Out, 1971. Address: 1716 Roscomare Rd Los Angeles CA 90024

KRAUFT, VIRGINIA RAE HORAK (MRS. CONRAD CHESTER KRAUFT), sch. psychologist; b. Cedar Rapids, Ia., May 27, 1944; d. Edward A. and Marian C. (Sowers) Pospishil; B.A. cum laude, Coe Coll., 1966; M.S., So. Ill. U., 1968; Ed.D., U. Ark., 1973; m. Conrad Chester Krauft, June 8, 1968; 1 son, Jonathan Conrad. Rehab. counselor Ill. Dept. Mental Health, Carbondale, 1968-69; sch. psychologist intern Mt. Vernon (Ill.) Spl. Edn. Dist., 1969-70; psychol. examiner N.W. Ark. Supplementary Edn. Center, Fayetteville, 1970-71; dir. sch. service Ozark Guidance Center, Springdale, Ark., 1971—. Psychol. cons. The New Sch., sch. for gifted preschoolers, 1970—, asst. dir., bd. dirs., 1970—. Vol. probation officer, 1971—; mem. juvenile ct. adv. bd., Fayetteville, 1973—. Mem. Phi Kappa Delta. Home: 800 Pittman St Fayetteville AR 72701 Office: 712 Maple Av Springdale AR 72764

KRAUS, EVELYN GERDA LAUER (MRS. PETER KRAUS), librarian; b. Vienna, Austria, Sept. 15, 1938; d. Erwin Peter and Berta Margaret (Feyfarek) Lauer; B.A., State U. N.Y., Buffalo, 1960; M.S., Columbia, 1961; m. Peter Kraus, July 28, 1973. With reference dept. Columbia U. Libraries, N.Y.C., 1961-68, head library service, 1968—. Ford Found. grantee, 1966. Mem. New York Rug Soc., Friends

Columbia Libraries. Compiler: Index to Little Mags., 1966-67. Home: 970 Park Av New York City NY 10028 Office: 535 W 114th St New York City NY 10024

KRAUS, LILI, pianist, educator; b. Budapest, Mar. 4, 1908; d. Victor and Irene (Bak) Kraus; student of Zoltan Kodaly, Bela Bartok; studied at Royal Acad. Music, Budapest, 1915-22, tchrs. diploma, 1925; student of Steuermann, New Acad., Vienna, 1925-27, M.A., 1927; student Artur Schnabel, Berlin, Germany, 1930-34; Mus.D. (hon.), Roosevelt U., 1968; m. Otto Mandl, Oct. 31, 1930 (dec. Aug. 26, 1956); children—Ruth Maria (Mrs. Fergus Pope), Michael Otto Patrick. Pianist with orchestras in Europe, 1926—, Dutch East Indies, 1940; Japanese prisoner-of-war, 1941-45; pianist in Australia and New Zealand, 1945-49, Europe, N. and S. Am., Asia, 1949—; world tours, 1925—; made first recordings of Mozart, Fant, Sonata K475, K457, B minor adagio K540, 1936, Schubert, Sonata A minor opus 143, 1936, Bartok's 3 Rondos on Folk, also chamber music works with violinist Szymon Goldberg; recording integral works of Mozart, 1937—; commd. to record all 25 Mozart Concerti, 1965, 17 Mozart Sonatas, 1967; lectr. various univs., U.S. and Europe; head piano dept. Cape Town U., S. Africa; artist in residence Tex. Christian U., 1967—. Hon. mem. Music Tchrs. Assn. Cal., Sigma Alpha Iota. Office: care Alix Williamson 1860 Broadway New York City NY 10023

KRAUS, MARCIA DIANE BUCHMAN (MRS. I. MARTIN KRAUS), psychologist; b. Danbury, Conn., May 7, 1942; d. Jack Melvin and Lillian (Katzman) Buchman; B.A., U. Chgo., 1963, M.A., 1964; m. I. Martin Kraus, June 18, 1967. Sch. psychologist LaGrange (Ill.) Area Dept. Spl. Edn., 1964—. Recipient State Ill. Fellowship, 1965-66. Mem. Nat. Assn. Sch. Psychologist, Am. Orthopsychiat. Assn., Am., Ill. psychol. assns. Home: 1105 S Clarence Av Oak Park IL 60304 Office: Box 400 LaGrange IL 60525

KRAUS, MOZELLE DEWITTE BIGELOW (MRS. RUSSELL WARREN KRAUS), psychologist; b. Vicksburg, Miss., Sept. 29, 1929; d. Raymond Demar and Henrietta (DeWitte) Bigelow; B.S., D.C. Tchr's. Coll., 1952; M.A., George Washington U., 1954; Ed.D., Am. U., 1965; m. Russell Warren Kraus, Sept. 30, 1961. Instr., Dept. Def., Washington, 1952-54; tchr. Wheaton (Md.) High Sch., 1954-55; grad. asst. Am. U., 1955-56; research psychologist Dr. Leonard Carmichael, former sec. Smithsonian Instn., Washington, 1956-72, v.p. Nat. Geog. Mag.; pvt. practice, Washington, 1972—. Asso. prof. psychology George Washington U., 1965—; instr. psychology U.S. Dept. Agr. Grad. Sch., 1964—; vis. prof. Nat. Naval Sch. Hosp. Adminstrn., 1968-69. Mem. A.A.A.S., Am., D.C. psychol. assns., Smithsonian Soc. Assos., D.A.R., Salvation Army Aux., Phi Delta Gamma, Sigma Xi, Psi Chi, Kappa Delta Epsilon, Sigma Kappa. Episcopalian. Contbr. articles in field to profl. jours. Home: 4604 Chevy Chase Blvd Chevy Chase MD 20015 Office: Suite 818 LaSalle Bldg 1028 Connecticut Av NW Washington DC 20036

KRAUS, PANSY DAEGLING, editor; b. Santa Paula, Cal., Sept. 21, 1916; d. Arthur David and Elsie (Pardee) Daegling; A.A., San Bernardino Valley Jr. Coll., 1938; student Longmeyer's Bus. Coll., 1940; grad. gemologist diploma Gemological Inst. Am., 1966; m. Charles Frederick Kraus, Mar. 1, 1941 (div. Nov. 1961). Clk., Convair, San Diego, 1943-48; clk. San Diego County Schs. Publs., 1948-57; mgr. Rogers and Boblet-Art Craft, San Diego, 1958-64; part-time editorial asst. Lapidary Jour., San Diego, 1963-64, asso. editor, 1964-69, editor, 1970—; lectr. gems, gemology local gen., mineral groups; gem & mineral club bull. editor groups. Mem. San Diego Mineral & Gem Soc., Gemol. Soc. San Diego, Gemol. Assn. Great Britain, Mineral. Soc. Am., Epsilon Sigma Alpha. Editor, layout dir.: Gem Cutting Shop Helps, 1964; The Fundamentals of Gemstone Carving, 1967; Appalachian Mineral and Gem Trails, 1968; Practical Gem Knowlege for the Amateur, 1969; Southwest Mineral and Gem Trails, 1972. Home: 6127 Mohler St San Diego CA 92120 Office: 3564 Kettner Blvd San Diego CA 92101

KRAUS, SHIRLEY RUTH, educator; b. N.Y.C., Dec. 24, 1919; d. Michael Herbert and Hannah (Gordon) Dushkind; B.A., Hunter Coll., 1940; M.A., Cornell U., 1942; Ph.D., U. Ill., 1946; m. Jerome Kraus, Sept. 14, 1946; children—Terry (Mrs. Raymond Schwartz), Gordon. Physiologist Gastroenterology Lab., Mt. Sinai Hosp., N.Y.C., 1947-48; biochemist Cancer Research Found., Harlem Hosp., N.Y.C., 1948-50; lectr. physiology N.Y. U. Coll. Dentistry, N.Y.C., 1950-51; pharmacologist cancer research and metabolism unit Mt. Alto Hosp., Washington, 1951-63; instr. pharmacology Howard U. Med. Sch., 1955-56; asso. prof. pharmacology Bklyn. Coll. Pharmacy, 1957-65, prof. pharmacology, 1965—; prof. grad. faculties L.I. U., 1965—; asso. prof. internal medicine Downstate Med. Sch., 1969-70; item writer physiology Bur. Higher Profl. Ednl. Testing N.Y. State Edn. Dept., 1972—; reviewer Jour. Pharmaceut. Scis., 1968—; book reviewer Am. Jour. Pharm. Edn., 1961. Recipient Lederle Pharmacy Faculty Research award, 1963; NIH Research grants, 1956-57, 1956-62, NSF grants, 1963-66, Am. Tobacco Council Research grant, 1972—. Mem. Endocrine Soc., Soc. Exptl. Biology and Medicine, Am. Physiol. Soc., Am. Soc. Pharmacology and Exptl. Therapeutics, Internat. Soc. Biochem. Pharmacology, Sigma Xi, Iota Sigma Pi, Phi Sigma, Sigma Delta Epsilon, Rho Chi, Lambda Kappa Sigma. Contbr. numerous articles to profl. jours. Home: 139-01 Coolidge Av Jamaica NY 11435 Office: 600 Lafayette Av Brooklyn NY 11216

KRAUSE, EVELYN WOLFF (MRS. SYDNEY J. KRAUSE), occupational therapist; b. Berlin, Germany, Nov. 14, 1922; d. Max Karl and Lucie (Tichauer) Wolff; B.S., Shurtleff Coll., 1944; Occupational Therapist, Registered, Columbia, 1948; M.A., N.Y. U., 1955; m. Sydney J. Krause, June 18, 1952; children—Robert J., Catherine A. Dir. pediatric occupational therapy dept. N.Y. Hosp.-Cornell Med. Center, N.Y.C., 1948-53; instr. occupational therapy curriculum Ohio State U., Columbus, 1954-55; supr. occupational therapy dept., phys. medicine Ohio State U. Hosp., Columbus, 1953-55; chief occupational therapist United Cerebral Palsy of Akron, 1965-67; chief occupational therapist ambulatory patient center Children's Hosp., Akron, 1967-68; chief occupational therapist Children's Rehab. Center, Warren, O., 1970-74; asst. prof., clin. coordinator occupational therapy, dept. biology and health scis. Cleve. State U., 1974—. Fulbright lectr. Soc. and Home for Cripples, Copenhagen, Denmark, 1968-69; lectr. and cons., Lisbon, Portugal, 1969. Served with Hosp. Corps, USNR, 1944-46. Mem. Am. (bd. mem.), Ohio (chmn. Akron dist. 1972-74) occupational therapy assns. Home: 512 Harvey St Kent OH 44240 Office: Dept Biology and Health Scis Cleve State U Cleveland OH 44115

KRAUSE, MARCELLA ELIZABETH MASON (MRS. EUGENE FITCH KRAUSE), educator; b. Norfolk, Neb.; d. James Haskell and Elizabeth (Vader) Mason; B.S., U. Neb., 1934; M.A., Columbia, 1938; postgrad. summers U. Cal. at Berkeley, 1950, 51, 65, Stanford, 1964, Creighton U., 1966, Chico (Cal.) State Coll., 1967; m. Eugene Fitch Krause, June 1, 1945; 1 dau., Kathryn Elizabeth. Tchr., Royal (Neb.) Pub. Schs., 1930-32, Hardy (Neb.) Pub. Schs., 1933-35, Omaha Pub. Schs., 1935-37, Lincoln Sch. of Tchrs. Coll. Columbia, 1937-38, Florence (Ala.) State Tchrs. Coll., summer 1938, Tchrs. Coll. U. Neb., 1938-42, Corpus Christi (Tex.) Pub. Schs., 1942-45; head counselor, data processing coordinator Oakland (Cal.) Pub. Schs., 1945—. Bd. dirs. U. Neb. Womens Faculty Club, 1940-42; mem. Neb. State Tchrs. Conv. Panel, 1940; mem. U. Neb. Reading Inst., 1940; speaker Ia. State Tchrs. Conv., 1941; reading speaker Neb. State Tchrs. Conv., 1941; lectr. Johnson County Tchrs. Inst., 1942; chmn. Reading Survey Corpus Christi Pub. Schs., 1943; chmn. Inservice Reading Meetings Oakland Pub. Schs., 1948-57. Mem. Gov.'s Adv. Commn. on Status Women Conf., San Francisco, 1966; service worker A.R.C., Am. Cancer Soc., United Crusade, Oakland Civil Def. Republican precinct capt., 1964-66; active YWCA. Ford Found. Fund for Advancement Edn. fellow, 1955-56; scholar Stanford, 1964; Cal. Congress P.T.A. scholar U. Cal., 1965. Mem. Nat. Council Women, Am. Assn. U. Women (dir.), No. Cal., Oakland personnel and guidance assns., Nat., Oakland edn. assns., Cal. Tchrs. Assn., Am. Fedn. Tchrs., Ladies Grand Army Republic, 1960 Ruth Assn., D.A.R. Grand Lake Bus. and Profl. Women (pres.), No. Cal. Alumnae Pi Lambda Theta (past pres.), Alpha Delta Kappa. Methodist. Mem. Order Eastern Star (past matron). Contbr. articles to profl. jours. Home: 5615 Estates Dr Oakland CA 94618 Office: 2874 Florida Av Oakland CA 94602

KRAUSE, SONJA (MRS. WALTER W. GOODWIN), educator; b. St. Gall, Switzerland, Aug. 10, 1933; d. Friedrich and Rita Helene Delphine (Maas) Krause; came to U.S., 1939, naturalized, 1945; B.S., Rensselaer Poly. Inst., 1954; Ph.D. (NSF fellow), U. Cal. at Berkeley, 1957; m. Walter W. Goodwin, Nov. 27, 1970. Sr. phys. chemist Rohm & Haas Co., Phila., 1957-64; vol. U.S. Peace Corps, serving as jr. lectr. Lagos (Nigeria) U., 1964-65; asst. prof. Gondar (Ethiopia) Health Coll., 1965-66; vis. asst. prof. chemistry U. So. Cal., Los Angeles, 1966-67; asst. prof. phys. chemistry Rensselaer Poly. Inst., Troy, N.Y., 1967-72, asso. prof., 1972—. Mem. Am. Chem. Soc., Am. Phys. Soc., A.A.A.S., Am. Assn. U. Profs. (chpt. v.p. 1973-74). Contbr. articles to profl. jours. Office: Dept. Chemistry Rensselaer Poly Inst Troy NY 12181

KRAUSKOPF, JOAN MIDAY (MRS. CHARLES J. KRAUSKOPF), lawyer, educator; b. Canton, O., Apr. 24, 1932; d. Clement I. and Elizabeth (Bellinger) Miday; A.B., Ohio U., 1954; postgrad U. Cal. at Los Angeles, 1954-55; J.D. summa cum laude, Ohio State U., 1957; m. Charles J. Krauskopf, July 4, 1954; children—Timothy, David. Admitted to Ohio bar, 1958, Colo. bar, 1961, Mo. bar, 1969; instr. Ohio State U., Columbus, 1957-59, asst. prof., 1959-60; research asst. to dean U. Colo. Sch. Law, Boulder, 1961; pvt. practice law in Boulder, Colo., 1961-62; faculty U. Mo. Sch. Law, Columbia, 1963—, prof., 1973—. Mem. Mo. Adv. Com. to U.S. Civil Service Commn., 1974—. Mem. Mo. Gov.'s Com. Children and Youth, 1972—; vol. Butterfield Youth Services, Marshall, Mo., 1973-74; adviser Am. Civil Liberties Union, Columbia, 1969-72. Mem. Colo., Ohio, Mo. (mem. council family law com. 1970-74) bar assns., Am. Assn. U. Profs. (mem. com. women's status 1972-74), Phi Chi Theta. Unitarian (program chmn.). Contbr. articles on sex discrimination to profl. jours. Home: Rural Route 4 Columbia MO 65201

KRAUSS, RUTH FLORENCE, physician; b. Buffalo, N.Y., Apr. 5, 1920; d. Albert E. J. and Anna (Millheiser) Krauss; M.D., U. Buffalo Sch. Medicine, 1943; m. Russell Stewart Kidder, Jr., June 10, 1942. Intern, Meyer Meml. Hosp., Buffalo, 1943-44; resident Children's Hosp. Buffalo, 1944-47, pediatric neurology and EEG, 1947-51; practice medicine, specializing in pediatric neurology, pediatric electroencephalography, Buffalo, N.Y., 1950—; clin. asso. prof. pediatrics, clin. instr. neurology State U. N.Y. at Buffalo, 1964—; dir. EEG dept. Children's Hosp. of Buffalo, 1950—. Mem. Am. Acad. Pediatrics, Am. Acad. Neurology, Eastern Assn. Electroencephalographers, Med. Soc. State N.Y., Med. Soc. Erie County, Alpha Omega Alpha, Sigma Xi. Club: Park Country Club of Buffalo, Inc. Home: 111 Columbia Blvd Kenmore NY 14217 Office: 219 Bryant St Buffalo NY 14222

KRAUT, ROSE BAUM (MRS. IRVING DAVID KRAUT), lawyer; b. N.Y.C., Dec. 31, 1908; d. Abraham Joseph and Anna (Lichtenberg) Baum; B.S., N.Y.U., 1931, J.D., 1936; m. Irving David Kraut, Dec. 20, 1939; children—Richard Stephen, Nina Ellen. Admitted to N.Y. bar, 1936; practice law, N.Y.C., 1936-42, Poughkeepsie, N.Y., 1942—. Tax editor Research Inst. Am., 1936-40. Organizer Dutchess County Legal Aid Soc., 1954, gen. counsel, 1954-60; pres. Lung Assn. N.Y. State, 1964-69. Recipient award for def. of civil liberties Assn. Bar City of N.Y., N.Y. County Lawyers Assn. and N.Y. State Bar Assn., 1963. Mem. Am. (mem. legal edn., legal aid and lawyer referral coms.), N.Y. State, Dutchess County bar assns., Am. Assn. U. Women, Assn. Bar City N.Y., Internat. Fedn. Women Lawyers, Nat. Assn. Women Lawyers, League Women Voters. Democrat. Jewish religion (pres. temple sisterhood 1950-54). Co-author: Guide to Tax Economy, 1936, Legal Tax-Saving Methods, 1937, Social Security Coordinator, 1937-40, Tax Coordinator, 1937-39. Home: 6 Wilbur Ct Poughkeepsie NY 12601 Office: 11 Market St Poughkeepsie NY 12601

KRAVIS, LILLIAN PANZER (MRS. IRVING B. KRAVIS), physician; b. Phila., Dec. 8, 1920; d. Julius and Tillie (Markowitz) Panzer; B.A., U. Pa., 1940, M.D., 1943; m. Irving B. Kravis, June 22, 1941; children—Robert, Marcia (Mrs. David Reich), Ellen, Nathan. Intern, Garfield Meml. Hosp., Washington, 1944; resident Children's Hosp. of Phila., 1944-46, asso. physician, asso. allergist, 1949—; resident Lying-In Hosp. div. Pa. Hosp., 1950; practice medicine specializing in pediatrics, Phila., 1949—; asst. prof. clin. pediatrics U. Pa. Med. Sch., Phila., 1964—; cons. allergist Children's Seashore Home, Atlantic City, 1964—. Pa. Thoracic Soc. grantee, 1968-69. Mem. Am. Acad. Pediatrics, Am. Acad. Allergy, Phila. Allergy Soc., Phila. Pediatric Soc. Contbg. author: Practice of Pediatrics (Brenneman), 1968, Pediatric Clinics in North America (Hyde), 1969, Allergy and Immunology in Childhood (Speers, Dockhorn, Shira), 1972. Home: 438 Warick Rd Wynnewood PA 19096 Office: Children's Hospital of Philadelphia 1 Childrens Plaza 34th St and Civic Center Blvd Philadelphia PA 19174

KRAWCHICK, FAY BINENKORB (MRS. GEORGE KRAWCHICK), editor, psychologist; b. Buffalo, Nov. 27, 1928; d. Aaron Louis and Marion Betty (Coplon) Binenkorb; B.A., Cornell U., 1950, M.A., 1952; m. George Krawchick, Sept. 28, 1967; children by previous marriage—Anthony Lee Suchman, Nancy Ellen Suchman. Research sec. Cornell U., Ithaca, N.Y., 1952-53; research asst. Psychol. Corp., N.Y.C., 1965-67, sr. editor, 1967—. Mem. Am. Psychol. Assn. Author: Typing Test for Business, 1968. Home: 46 Colonial Av Larchmont NY 10538 Office: 757 3d Av New York City NY 10017

KREBS, MARGARET ELOISE, pub. co. exec.; b. Clearfield, Pa., Apr. 20, 1927; d. Henry Louis and Delia Louise (Beahan) Krebs; grad high sch. With Progressive Pub. Co., Inc., Clearfield, 1945—, bus. office mgr., 1956-60, bus. mgr., 1960-63, asst. to pub., 1963-69, dir., exec. v.p., 1969—. Dir., asst. sec. Radio Sta. WDAD-AM and QQMU-FM, Indiana, Pa., 1967—; dir. Niles Suburban Newspapers, Inc., Niles, O., 1970—; sec. Clearfield Broadcasters, Inc., 1965—, dir., 1971—; dir., exec. v.p. Danville (Pa.) News, 1969—. Mem. Clearfield Bus. and Profl. Women's Club (pres. 1952-53, dist. membership chmn. 1952-53). Home: 526 Ogden Av Clearfield PA 16830 Office: 206 E Locust St Clearfield PA 16830

KREBSBACH, RITA ANN, realtor; b. Mt. Clemens, Mich., May 25, 1930; d. Howard H. and Myrtle M. (Shay) Hatzenbuhler; adopted dau. of Clifford N. Devereaux; student Marygrove Coll., 1949-50; m. Dale T. Krebsbach, Apr. 11, 1953 (div.); children—Deborah J., Sue A., Fred, Chris, Ed. Comml. artist, Detroit, 1951-53; saleswoman Erb Realty, Flint, Mich., 1955-56; dist. mgr. State House Sterling, Flint, 1954-55; real estate broker Ed Rose & Son, Flint, 1965-67; self-employed K-Realty, Flint, 1967—, owner, pres. K-Realty, Inc., 1970—, owner, pres. K-Way Devel., Inc., 1970—; part-owner, sec. Davison Mgmt. Assos., Inc. Dir. pub. relations Kearsley-Holy Rosary Girl Scout Council, 1965-67; publicity chmn. Holy Rosary Parish, 1968-69. Mem. Urban League, Flint Bd. Realtors (publicity com. 1970-71), Flint C. of C., Mich. Real Estate Assn., Nat. Assn. Real Estate Bds., Mich. Assn. Children with Learning Disabilities (publicity chmn. 1972-73). Office: 1818 S Averill St Flint MI 48503

KREEK, MARY JEANNE, physician; b. Washington; d. Louis Francis and Esperance (Agee) Kreek; B.A., Wellesley Coll., 1958; M.D., Columbia, 1962; m. Dr. Robert A. Schaefer, Jan. 24, 1970; 1 son, Robert A. Med. research NIH, Bethesda, Md., 1957-62; intern, resident Cornell N.Y. Hosp. Med. Center, N.Y.C., 1962-65, fellow, 1965-67; instr. medicine Cornell Med. Coll., 1966-67; acad. medicine specializing in internal medicine, endocrinology, gastroenterology, N.Y.C., 1966—; mem. staff N.Y. Hosp.-Cornell U., now clin. asst. prof., asst. attending physician; asst. prof. Rockefeller U., 1967—, now sr. research asso. Recipient Borden Research award, 1962. Mem. Am. Fedn. for Clin. research, Shakespeare Soc. of Wellesley, Am. Gastroent. Assn., Endocrine Soc., Phi Beta Kappa, Sigma Xi. Home: 1161 York Av New York City NY 10021 Office: Rockefeller U New York City NY 10021

KREIN, CATHERINE MITCHELL, broadcasting exec.; b. N.Y.C.; d. Timothy Thomas and Catherine Agnes (Lavery) Mitchell; B.S., Fordham U., 1960; student Hunter Coll. Grad. Sch. Polit. Sci., 1961-62; film certificate N.Y. U., 1974; m. Robert Edward Krein, Apr. 18, 1970. With CBS, 1963—, polit. research, writer CBS News election unit, 1969-73, editorial dir., asso. producer spl. events unit, 1973—. Mem. Writers Guild Am. (shop steward 1971-73), Nat. Acad. TV Arts and Scis., Am. Acad. Polit. and Social Scis., Center Study Democratic Instns., Center Study Presidency, N.Y. Power Squadron. Catholic. Author bio-monthly CNB News polit. report, 1972, CBS News, polit. newsletters, 1974, also contbr. handbooks. Home: 151-31 88th St Howard Beach NY 11414 Office: CBS News Spl Events 518 W 57th St New York City NY 10019

KREINDLER, DORIS BARSKY (MRS. HARRY E. KREINDLER), artist; b. Passaic, N.J., Aug. 12, 1901; d. Jacob and Rebecca (Levitch) Barsky; student Nat. Acad., 1920, Art Students League, 1923, Hans Hofmann Sch. Abstraction, 1946; m. Harry E. Kreindler, Feb. 12, 1921; children—Lee S., Rosamond (Mrs. Harold S. Koffmon). One-man shows Bklyn. Mus. Art. Jacques, Seligmann Gallery, Research Studio, Maitland, Fla., Silvermine Guild, Santa Monica Art Library, Nan Rosequist Gallery, Tucson; exhibited in group shows Whitney Mus., N.A.D., Smithsonian Inst., Rutgers U., Notre Dame U., N.Y. Pub. Library, Pa. Acad. Fine Arts; represented in permanent collections Nat. Collection Art, Washington, Mus. Modern Art, N.Y.C., Met. Mus., N.Y.C., Fogg Mus., Boston Mus. Art, Art Inst. Chgo., Phila. Mus. Art, Norfolk Mus. Art, Butler Inst., Bklyn. Mus.; lectr. in field. Recipient prizes Bklyn. Soc. Artists, 1954, 59, 62, Nat. Soc. Painters in Casein, 1963, 70, Nat. Assn. Women Artists, 1965, Am. Soc. Contemporary Artist, 1970, Painters and Sculptors N.J., 1958, 59. Mem. Audubon Soc. Artists, Nat. Assn. Women Artists, Nat. Soc. Painters in Casein (gov. 1936-60), Am. Soc. Contemporary Artists (dir. 1929-60), Am. Soc. Graphic Artists. Address: 75 Central Park W New York City NY 10023

KREIS, BERNADINE (MRS. MAXWELL ELIOT MARSHALL), writer; b. Boston, June 26, 1915; d. Benjamin and Miriam (Igar) Mathan; student Cornell Coll., 1932-33, Fashion Acad., 1933-34, Archipenko Art Sch., 1938-40, Alvienne Drama Sch., 1938-39; m. Casriel Kreis, Apr. 18, 1934 (dec. 1964); children—Robert Brian, Peter Michael; m. 2d, Maxwell Eliot Marshall, May 11, 1973. Author: Up From Grief, 1968; Loneliness and The Search for Love, 1974; writer short stories and articles appearing in various newspapers and mags. including Ladies Home Jour., Redbook, Liberty, N.Y. Times, N.Y. Daily News, Phila. Inquirer, Toronto Star and True Story, 1945-64. Tchr., dir. Writer's Workshop, Riverside Ch., N.Y.C., 1966-73. Club: Creatives (pres. 1950-64) (N.Y.C.). Home: 40 Central Park New York City NY 10019

KREITLER, BONNIE JO BOHLING (MRS. ROBERT PHILIP KREITLER), govt. ofcl.; b. Chgo., June 11, 1947; d. Frank Nicholas and Lois Jane (Gordon) Bohling; B.S. magna cum laude, Mich. State U., 1969; m. Robert Philip Kreitler, Nov. 4, 1970. Technical editor Mich. State U. Coop. Extension Service, East Lansing, 1967-69; writer WILS Radio, Lansing, Mich., 1969-70; editor, research div. of bus. sch. Mich. State U., E. Lansing, 1969-70; editor, writer Office of Communication, U.S. Dept. Agr., Washington, 1970—. Mem. Am. Assn. of Agrl. Coll. Editors (sec. Washington chpt. 1973-74), Fed. Editors Assn., Women in Communications, Tower Guard, Alpha Lambda Delta. Office: Room 545-A US Dept Agriculture Washington DC 20250

KREMER, BARBARA GRAYBEAL (MRS. LEWIS N. KREMER), journalist; b. Mountain City, Tenn., Sept. 21, 1935; d. Claude Harold and Ruby Lucille (Hodge) Graybeal; B.A. magna cum laude, Marietta Coll., 1957; m. Lewis N. Kremer, June 7, 1958. With New Yorker mag., N.Y.C., 1957-58; asso. editor Sat. Eve. Post, Phila., 1958-62, Episcopalian mag., Phila., 1962-69; asst. editor Lutheran Mag., Phila., 1971-72; instr. journalism Temple U., Phila., 1972—. Mem. com. on interpretation and promotion, dept. overseas missions Nat. Council Chs., 1966-68. Mem. Phila. Dem. Com., 1968. Bd. dirs., sec. Friends of Free Library Phila. Mem. Women in Communications, Marietta Coll. Alumni Assn., Am. Assn. U. Women, Phi Beta Kappa, Alpha Xi Delta. Episcopalian. Contbr. articles, photography, poetry and book revs. to various publs. Home: Main St Old Chatham NY 12136

KRENIS, LINDA JOAN, editor, poet; b. N.Y.C., Aug. 5, 1940; d. Albert Morton and Sylvia Kyla (Rigerman) Gross; B.A., N.Y. U., 1961; postgrad. Brandeis U., 1961-62; m. Milan Potmesil, Apr. 5, 1974; 1 son by previous marriage, James Randall Krenis. Theatre critic Show Bus., newspaper publ., N.Y.C., 1968-69; lit. editor New York Quar., N.Y.C., 1970—. Guest lectr. New Sch. Social Research; tchr. World and Am. poetry N.Y. U., 1971. N.Y. State Regents scholar, 1957-61. Mem. Poetry Soc. Am., Phi Beta Kappa. Contbr. poems to lit. jours. Home: 345 E 80th St New York City NY 10021 Office: 4 West 43rd St Room 603 New York City NY 10036

KREPS, JUANITA MORRIS (MRS. CLIFTON H. KREPS, JR.), univ. adminstr.; b. Lynch, Ky., Jan. 21, 1921; A.B., Berea Coll., 1942; M.A. (fellow), Duke U., 1944, Ph.D., 1948; m. Clifton H. Kreps, Jr., 1944; 3 children. Instr. in econs. Denison U., Granville, O., 1945-46, asst. prof., 1947-50; lectr., Hofstra U., Hempstead, N.Y., 1952-54, Queens Coll., N.Y., 1954-55; vis. asst. prof., Duke U., Durham, N.C., asst. prof., 1958-61, asso. prof., 1962-67, prof., 1967—, dean Women's Coll., asst. provost, 1969-72, James B. Duke prof., 1972—, v.p.,

1973—. Dir. N.Y. Stock Exchange, 1972—, J.C. Penny, 1972—, N.C. Nat. Bank, Coll. Retirement Equities Fund, 1972—, N.C. Blue Cross, Blue Shield. Ford faculty fellow, 1963-64. Bd. dirs. Ednl. Testing Service, 1971—, Nat. Merit Scholarship Bd., 1972—, Am. Assn. Higher Edn., 1974—. Trustee Berea Coll. Co-author: Principles of Economics. Editor: Employment, Income and Retirement Problems of the Aged, 1963; Technology, Manpower and Retirement Policy, 1966; Lifetime Allocation of Work and Income, 1971; Sex in the Marketplace: American Women at Work, 1971. Office: Dept Economics Duke U Durham NC 27706*

KRESKY, BEATRICE GREENWALD (MRS. PHILIP J. KRESKY), physician; b. Bklyn., Mar. 26, 1916; d. Harry M. and Elizabeth (Holzman) Greenwald; B.A., Bryn Mawr Coll., 1936; M.P.H., Columbia U., 1938; M.D., N.Y.U., 1945; m. Philip J. Kresky, Oct. 10, 1938; children—Harry, Caroline (Mrs. Michael Bernstein). Intern, Bellevue Hosp., N.Y.C., 1945-46; practice medicine specializing in pediatrics, Rockville Centre, N.Y., 1952-66; dep. dir. task force Comprehensive Health Planning Agy. for N.Y.C., 1970-72; chmn. dept. ambulatory care Jamaica (N.Y.) Hosp., 1973—; project dir. Comprehensive Child Care Program Bookdale Hosp. Center, Bklyn., 1968-70; med. asso. Health and Hosp. Planning Council of So. N.Y., Inc., N.Y.C., 1965-68; cons. South Massau Communities Hosp., Oceanside, N.Y., 1952—; chmn. ad hoc com. narcotic addition Community Council Greater N.Y.C., 1969—; mem. health div. Community Council Greater N.Y., 1970—; chmn. adv. com. Community Health Inst., N.Y.C., 1970—. Fellow Am. Pub. Health Assn.; mem. N.Y. Assn. for Ambulatory Care (sec. 1971). Contbr. articles to profl. jours. Home: 61 Hempstead Av Rockville Centre NY 11570 Office: 89th Av and Van Wyck Expressway Jamaica NY

KRESS, LAURA MAE, govt. ofcl; b. Boston, Mar. 10, 1935 d. Albert Henry and Miriam (Hovey) Kress; A.B., Oberlin Coll., 1956; M.A., Cath. U. Am., 1968. Asst. to asso. dean women Oberlin (O.) Coll., 1956-58; dir. student activities, asst. to dean Mount Vernon Jr. Coll., Washington, 1958-63; specialist for profl. information Am. Personnel and Guidance Assn., Washington, 1963-67; information officer div. allied health manpower Bur. Health Resources Devel., Health Resources Adminstrn. U.S. Dept. Health, Edn. and Welfare, Bethesda, Md., 1967-73, spl. asst. to dir. div., 1973—. Alumni admissions rep. Oberlin Coll., 1969-70. Bd. dirs. Westmoreland Square Homes Assn., 1972-75, v.p., 1972-73. Mem. Am., Nat. Capitol (sec. 1968-69) personnel and guidance assns., Am. Coll. Personnel Assn., Nat. Vocational Guidance Assn. (sec. career information review service com. 1963-67, film review service com. 1966-67), Nat. Assn. Industry-Edn. Coop. (chpt. sec.-treas. 1966-68). Club: Washington Oberlin Alumni (alumni class v.p. 1966—). Editor reprint series Am. Personnel and Guidance Assn., 1968-71. Mem. editorial com. Career Opportunities for Health Technicians (Robert E. Kinsinger), 1970. Office: 9000 Rockville Pike Bethesda MD 20014

KRESSLER, AUGUSTA HOLMSTOCK (MRS. JACOB JAY KRESSLER), physician; b. Phila., Apr. 25, 1917; d. David and Ida Mollie (Hurwitz) Holmstock; B.A., U. Pa., 1937; M.D., Women's Med. Coll. Pa., 1941; m. Jacob Jay Kressler, Dec. 31, 1943;children—Steven A., Carolyn F. (Mrs. Stanley H. Greenberg), Charles C. Intern, Phila. Gen. Hosp., 1941-43; practice medicine, specializing in internal medicine, Worcester, Mass., 1944—; mem. staffs Jewish Home for the Aged, Meml., City, Fairlawn hosps; physician Vis. Nurses Soc., 1944—; examining physician Worcester Sch. Dept., 1946—; lectr. pediatrics Worcester City Hosp.; lectr. health edn. Clark U., 1960—; examining physician Worcester State Coll.; mem. health task force Gov. Sargent's Commn. Study Status Women in Mass., 1971-72; vol. physician A.R.C. Blood Program, 1960-72. Mem. Am., Mass., Worcester Dist. med. assns., Am. Assn. U. Women, Soroptimist, Hadassah, Pythian Sisters, Brandeis U. Womens Aux. Home: 14 Wetherell St worcester MA 01602 Office: 27 Elm St Worcester MA 01608

KRETZER, CAROLE LEIGH, state ofcl.; b. Lincoln, Ill., Aug. 25, 1933; d. Dan and Mary Louise (Mowrey) Kretzer; A.B., U. Ala., 1955. Editor, publicity, pub. relations work Am. Hosp. Supply Corp., Evanston, Ill., 1956-57; asso. editor Cal. Bank, Los Angeles, 1957-60; asso. editor FM and Fine Arts Guide, Los Angeles, 1960-62; asst. information officer Cal. Div. Hwys., 1962-66; information officer Cal. Pub. Utilities Commn., 1966—. Mem. Am. Contract Bridge League, Mortar Bd., Phi Beta Kappa, Kappa Kappa Gamma, Theta Sigma Phi. Contbr. articles to various publs. Home: 315 California Terrace Pasadena CA 91105 Office: 107 S Broadway Los Angeles CA 90012

KREYCHE, DOLORES ANN (MRS. ROBERT JOSEPH KREYCHE), librarian; b. Los Angeles, Jan. 5, 1928; d. Francis Herbert and Anna Still (Robings) Pritchard; B.A., U. Cal. at Los Angeles, 1959; M.L.S., U. Cal. at Berkeley, 1960; m. Robert Joseph Kreyche, Jan. 16, 1971; stepchildren—Michael, Thomas, John, Catherine, Andrew. Reference librarian U. Cal. at Santa Barbara, 1960-62, asst. head reference dept., 1965-70; librarian U.S. Army Spl. Services, Amberg, Germany, 1962-63; head cataloging dept. System Devel. Corp., Santa Monica, Cal., 1963-65; treas., librarian Thomas More Inst., Tucson, 1971—. Served with WAVES, 1951-55. Author: Sidney Hook, 1966; Micrea Eliade, 1968. Home and office: 2441 N Grannen Rd Tucson AZ 85705

KRGA, JOAN STUART GALLAGHER (MRS. JOSEPH KRGA), pub. relations exec.; b. Chgo., Sept. 15, 1943; d. John Francis and Dorothea Frances (Maynard) Gallagher; B.A., Drake U., 1965; m. Joseph Krga, July 20, 1968. Asst. editor Coop. News Service, Chgo., 1965-66; editor Arbogust Co., indsl. co. pub., Chgo., 1966-67; account exec. Daniel J. Edelman, Inc., pub. relations agy., Chgo., 1968-69; dir. pub. relations McCann-Erickson, Inc., advt. agy., Chgo., 1969-72; v.p. dialog div. J. Walter Thompson Co., Advt. Agy., Chgo., 1972—. Mem. Pub. Relations Soc. Am., Publicity Club of Chgo., Theta Sigma Phi. Home: 4224 Saratoga St Downers Grove IL 60515 Office: 875 N Michigan Av Chicago IL 60611

KRICHBAUM, ROLLYN GAY OSTERWEIS (MRS. DANIEL H. KRICHBAUM), editor; b. New Haven, Conn., Apr. 22, 1942; d. Rollin Gustav and Ruth Mildred (Loewenstein) Osterweis; B.A., Wellesley Coll., 1964; M.A. in Teaching, U. Chgo., 1966; m. Daniel H. Krichbaum, Nov. 22, 1972. Editor, Follett Pub. Co., Chgo., 1967-71, Detroit Inst. Arts, 1973—. Mem. Women in Communications. Home: 1343 Nicolet Pl Detroit MI 48207 Office: 5200 Woodward Av Detroit MI 48207

KRIDER, MARY ALTHEA WILSON (MRS. STEPHEN J. KRIDER), educator; b. Amy, Mo., May 14, 1906; d. Francis Shepard and Mary Alice (Gum) Wilson; A.B., U. Neb., 1927; Ed.M., U. Okla., 1939; Ed.D., Wayne State U., 1958; m. Stephen Joshua Krider, Feb. 15, 1941 (dec.); children—Velora (Mrs. Donald Claude Bonneau), Roberta (Mrs. William Henry Brumble), Edward Albert, Laveda Mae (dec.). Tchr., Central High Sch., Tulsa, 1939-44; asst. to cons. psychiatrist Tulsa Pub. Schs., 1944-51; asst. prof. Brigham Young U., 1954-56, 58-59, asso. prof., 1959-62; instr. sp. edn. Ore. State System Higher Edn., 1951-54; doctoral fellow Wayne State U., Detroit, 1956-58; asso. prof. ednl. psychology and measurements, U. Neb., 1962—, asst. dir. ednl-psychol. clinic, 1962—, Neb. Council on Tchr. Edn., 1965-68. Sec. Gov.'s Citizens com. for Mental Retardation, Neb., 1967-70; cons. Follow Through. Mem. Neb. Fedn. Council for Exceptional Children (pres. 1964-65), Internat. Council for Exceptional Children (sec. treas. div. tchr. edn. 1960-63), Am., Neb. psychol. assns., N.E.A., Alpha Xi Delta, Psi Chi, Kappa Delta Pi, Phi Lambda Theta. Recipient research grant to study progress of Head Start and non-Head Start Children in kindergarten, Office of Econ. Opportunity, 1965-66. Home: 4624 A St Lincoln NE 68510

KRIEBEL, MARY ELIZABETH, coll. adminstr.; b. Macungie, Pa., July 9, 1914; d. Elias Wilbur and Isabella Augusta (Lesser) Kriebel; B.A., Cedar Crest Coll., 1937, postgrad., 1937-38; postgrad. U. Pa., summers 1940-42; M.A., Lehigh U., 1964. Tchr., Terre Hill, Pa., 1938-39; tchr. Allentown (Pa.) High Sch., 1939-43; sec. to pres. and dir. placement Cedar Crest Coll., Allentown, 1943-67, dir. career planning, 1967—. Vol. worker Allentown Hosp., 1955—. Recipient Alumnae award Cedar Crest Coll., 1972. Mem. Middle Atlantic Placement Assn. (v.p. 1972-74), Mid-Atlantic Assn. Sch., Coll. and Univ. Staffing (pres. 1970-71), Bus. and Profl. Women's Club, League Women Voters (sec. 1958-60), Am. Assn. U. Women, Cedar Crest Coll. Alumnae Assn. (treas. 1945-55). Home: 6 N 17th St Allentown PA 18104

KRIEGER, DOLORES RUTH, educator; b. Paterson, N.J., Aug. 1, 1921; d. Maurice Herbert and Mary (Ezor) Krieger; B.S., N.Y. U., 1960, M.A., 1962, Ph.D. (Founders Day scholar), 1967. Profl. registered nurse, N.Y., 1955; grad. staff nurse Grasslands Hosp., Valhalla, N.Y., 1955-57; rehab. nurse, supr. Inst. of Rehab. Medicine, N.Y.C., 1957-59; instr. N.Y. U., 1963-67, asst. prof., 1967-70, asso. prof. nurse edn., 1971—. Cons. thermal balance, bone necrosis, hyperbaric environments Underseas Med. Soc., N.Y. U. Inst. of Rehab. Medicine, Harlem Hosp. Med. Center, 1969—; V.A., Nat. Acad. Sci., Boston U., U. Buffalo, others. Trustee Northeast Theosophical Found., 1964-74. Founders' Day scholar N.Y. U., 1967; Teaching and Traineeship grantee Rehab Service Adminstr., 1968—. Mem. Aerospace Med. Assn., Am. Assn. U. Profs., Am. Nurses Assn., Council of Nurse Researchers, Nat. League for Nursing, N.Y. Acad. Sci., Underseas Med. Soc. Editorial cons. C.V. Mosby. Contbr. numerous articles to profl. jours. Office: New York University Washington Square New York City NY 10003

KRIEGER, DOROTHY TERRACE (MRS. HOWARD P. KRIEGER), physician; b. N.Y.C., Feb. 7, 1927; d. Morris Abraham and Esther (Marsh) Terrace; A.B. summa cum laude, Barnard Coll., 1945; M.D., Columbia U., 1949; m. Howard P. Krieger, July 31, 1953; children—James, Nancy. Intern, Mt. Sinai Hosp., N.Y.C., 1949-50, asst. resident surgery, 1950-52, asst. resident medicine, 1952-53, chief resident medicine, 1954-55, now mem. staff; practice medicine, specializing in endocrinology, N.Y.C.; faculty Mt. Sinai Sch. Medicine, 1966—, prof. medicine, 1972—; dir. div. endocrinology Mt. Sinai Hosp., Endocrinology Lab., N.Y.C., 1973—. Prin. investigator USPHS grants, 1972—, Diplomate Nat. Bd. Med. Examiners. Fellow A.C.P.; mem. Am. Soc. Clin. Investigation, Assn. Am. Physicians, Endocrine Soc. (mem. publs. com. 1973-74, v.p. 1974-75). Editor: Peptide Hormone Assay and Action, 1973—. Contbr. articles in field to profl. jours. Home: 1148 Fifth Av New York City NY 10028 Office: Mount Sinai Hospital Endocrinology Laboratory 5th Av and 100th St New York City NY 10028

KRIEGER, MEDORA LOUISE HOOPER (MRS. PHILIP KRIEGER), geologist; b. Ticonderoga, N.Y., Sept. 29, 1905; d. Frank Cyrus and Medora (Higgins) Hooper; B.A., Vassar Coll., 1928; M.A., Columbia, 1931, Ph.D., 1943; m. Philip Krieger, Sept. 17, 1931 (dec. Aug. 1940); 1 dau., Katherine Elizabeth (Mrs. James S. Pessin). Asst. to C.P. Berkey, Columbia U., 1929-31; temporary field geologist N.Y. State Geol. Survey, summers, 1930-37; instr. geology Mt. Holyoke Coll., 1942-44; geologist U.S. Geol. Survey, Washington, 1944-49, Prescott, Ariz., 1949-57, Menlo Park, Cal., 1957—. Fellow Geol. Soc. Am.; mem. Geol. Soc. Washington, Peninsula, Ariz. geol. socs. Home: 743 Cornelia Ct Mountain View CA 94040 Office: 345 Middlefield Rd Menlo Park CA 94025

KRIEGER, MILDRED LEVITAN, lawyer; b. New Orleans, Dec. 23, 1923; d. Morris and Mamie (Robbins) Levitan; B.A., Newcomb Coll., 1944; J.D., Tulane U., 1962; m. I. Jay Krieger, Dec. 4, 1944; children—Terry M., Monty. Admitted to La. bar, 1962; mem. firm Krieger, Krieger and Tracy, New Orleans, 1962—, partner, 1966—; partner Empire Investment Co.; partner Panama Enterprises. Mem. community relations com. Jewish Welfare Fedn., 1970—, mem. budget planning com., 1973—; alternate del. Jewish Welfare Bd. Ann. Biennial. Bd. dirs. Jewish Community Center; mem. governing bd. La. Arthritis Found. Mem. La., Am. bar assns. Jewish religion. Office: 234 Loyola Bldg 234 Loyola Av New Orleans LA 70112

KRIGSMAN, NAOMI, psychologist; b. Haifa, Israel, Apr. 30, 1930; d. Bezalel and Regina (Yacobi) Goussinsky; came to U.S., 1953, naturalized, 1961; B.A., Hebrew U., Jerusalem, 1951; M.S., Coll. City N.Y., 1955; Ph.D. candidate Yeshiva U., 1967—; m. Ruben Krigsman, July 29, 1956; children—Michael W., Richard G., Jonathan H. Psychologist, Mental Retardation Clinic, Flower-Fifth Av. Hosp., N.Y.C., 1954-56, Children's Center, N.Y.C. Dept. Welfare, 1954-65, Rehab. Clinic, St. Barnabas Hosp., Newark, N.Y., 1956-57, United Cerebral Palsy Center, Roosevelt, N.Y., 1957-58, 63-65, Burke Rehab. Center, White Plains, N.Y., 1967-70, New Rochelle (N.Y.) City Sch. Dist., 1970—. Chmn. parent edn. com. Eastview Jr. High Sch. P.T.A., White Plains, N.Y., 1971-74; mem. human relations com. White Plains High Sch. P.T.A., 1973—. Fellow N.Y. State Mental Health Dept., 1958-59. Mem. Nat. Assn. Sch. Psychologists, Westchester County Psychol. Assn. Author article.

KRINER, WILMA H. LOHKAMP (MRS. WILLIAM ROBERT KRINER), advt. agy. exec.; b. Indpls., Aug. 24, 1927; d. Henry W. and Edna (Rosebrock) Lohkamp; student pub. schs., Indpls.; m. William Robert Kriner, Dec. 26, 1947. Sec. to gen. agt. Pacific Mutual Ins. Co., Indpls., 1945-48; sec. to dir. engring. div. Eli Lilly & Co., Indpls., 1949-57; media dir., exec. sec. W. M. Zemp & Assos., Inc., Advt. Agy., St. Petersburg, Fla., 1958-68, treas., 1968—, v.p., 1971—. Mem. Am. Women in Radio and Television (chpt. sec. 1962-64, treas. 1964-66, v.p. 1967, pres. 1968-69, nat. dir. at large So. area 1969-71, nat. v.p. So. area 1972-74, sec.-treas. 1974-76), Am. Bus. Womens Assn. Home: 8315 Robin Rd Seminole FL 33542 Office: 1213 16th St N St Petersburg FL 33705

KRINSKY, CAROL HERSELLE (MRS. ROBERT DANIEL KRINSKY), art historian, educator; b. Bklyn., June 2, 1937; d. David and Jane (Gartman) Herselle; B.A., Smith Coll., 1957; M.A., N.Y. U., 1960, Ph.D., 1965; m. Robert Daniel Krinsky, Jan. 25, 1959; children—Alice Elizabeth, John David. Asso. prof. art history N.Y. U., N.Y.C., 1965—, also co-dir. Urban Design Studies Program, 1973—. Mem. Soc. Archtl. Historians, Victorian Soc., Coll. Art Assn., Phi Beta Kappa. Editor: Vitruvius, De Architectura Como, 1521, 1969. Contbr. articles on history of art to profl. jours. Home: 370 1st Av New York City NY 10010 Office: 1007 Main Bldg New York Univ Washington Square New York City NY 10003

KRITCHMAN, MARILYN MIRIAM (MRS. BEN KRITCHMAN), physician, educator; b. N.Y.C., Jan. 26, 1928; d. George B. and Tillie (Levy) Sugarman; A.B., Washington Square Coll., N.Y. U., 1946; M.D., Yale, 1950; m. Ben Kritchman, May 4, 1950; children—Ellen, Brian, Tracy. Intern, Queens Gen. Hosp., Jamaica, N.Y., 1950-51; resident Presbyn. Med. Center, N.Y.C., 1951-53; asso. in anesthesiology Coll. Physicians and Surgeons, Columbia, N.Y.C., 1953-58; asst. prof. anesthesiology Albert Einstein Coll. Med., Bronx, N.Y., 1960-70; asso. prof. anesthesiology State U. N.Y. Med. Coll., Stonybrook, 1971—. Bd. trustees Great Neck Sch. Dist., 1973—. Fellow, Nassau Acad. Medicine (pres. sect. 1971-72), Am. Acad. Anesthesiologists; mem. Am., Am. Women (asst. editor jour. 1957-72) med. assns., N.Y. State (chmn. edn. com. 1968—), Am. Soc. Anesthesiologists, Am. Jewish Congress, Mizrachi Women, Am. Women's Orgn. for Rehab. and Tng., Yale Club Long Island. Mem. B'nai B'rith, Hadassah. Contbr. articles to profl. jours. Home: 13 Tain Dr Great Neck NY 11021 Office: Nassau County Medical Center East Meadow NY 11554

KRIVACKA, EDNA MAE (MRS. EDDIE A. KRIVACKA), nursing dir.; b. Ellinger, Tex., July 16, 1935; d. John and Sophie (Prihoda) Jasek; student Wharton Jr. Coll., 1953-54; R.N., Dominican Coll., 1954, B.S., 1958; m. Eddie A. Krivacka, May 24, 1959; 1 son, Mark. Dir. nurses Eagle Lake (Tex.) Community Hosp., 1959-71, 72—; pvt. duty nurse, county health relief nurse, Eagle Lake, Tex., 1971-72. Dir. Heritage House Convalescent Home, Eagle Lake. Mem. City Council Eagle Lake, 1971-73. Mem. Am., Tex. nurses assns., Tex. Soc. Hosp. Nursing Service Adminstrs. Home: 200 Fairway Dr Eagle Lake TX 77434 Office: 702 S McCarty Av Eagle Lake TX 77434

KRIZ, CAROLINE MARIE, editor; b. Chgo., Jan. 6, 1946; d. James Vaclav and Caroline Marie (Blazek) Kriz; B.S., Purdue U., 1967; M.S., Northwestern U., 1968. Asst. food editor, Chgo.'s American, 1968; mgr., asst. buyer Marshall Field & Co., Chgo., 1968-69; free lance writer also office mgr. MAI Corp., Chgo., 1969-70; acct. exec. Drucilla Handy Co., pub. relations, Chgo., 1970-72; free lance pub. relations cons. and writer, 1972; projects editor, dir. pub. relations Sphere, The Betty Crocker Mag., Chgo., 1972—. Mem. Women in Communications. Clubs: Purdue; Northwestern (Chgo.). Home: 111 E Chicago Av Chicago IL 60611 Office: 500 North Michigan Chicago IL 60611

KRODEL, VIVIAN FRANCES HAFNER (MRS. MASON V. KRODEL), real estate broker; b. St. Paul, Oct. 6, 1916; d. Frank Joseph and Catherine Barbara (Kramer) Hafner; student Our Lady of the Lake Coll., 1938; m. Mason V. Krodel, Dec. 24, 1941 (dec. 1970); children—Kathleen K. (Mrs. Kathleen K. Shaw), Gregory. Secretarial positions Coastal Sales Agy., Houston, 1935-37, Pub. Works Adminstrn., 1938-40; with State Dept. Washington, 1940, U.S. Engr., Honolulu, 1941-45; sec. to chief wage adminstrn., sec. San Antonio Gen. Depot, 1945-46; secretarial positions Ames Aero. Lab., Mountain View, Cal., 1954, Cal. Packing Corp., Sunnyvale, Cal., 1954-55, Wooldrige Mfg. Co., Sunnyvale, 1955-56, Petersen Engring. Co., Inc., Santa Clara, Cal., 1956-57; city clk. City of Sunnyvale, 1957-59; salesman Frank Bohannon and Paul Strassberger, 1959-66; owner Vivian Krodel & Son, Realtor, 1966—. Roman Catholic. Home: 1696 Quail Av Sunnyvale CA 94087 Office: 197 S Mathilda Av Sunnyvale CA 94086 also 1696 Quail Av Sunnyvale CA 94087

KROG, KARIN, singer; b. Oslo, Norway, May 15, 1937; d. Eilif and Ragnhild (Naess) Krog; pupil Anne Brown, 1960-68, Ivo Knesevic, 1968-71; m. Johs Bergh, Sept. 21, 1957; children—Cathrine, Dot Elisabeth. Appeared concerts at internat. jazz festivals, Antibes, France, 1964, Prague, Czechoslovakia, 1966, Warsaw, Poland, 1966, Berlin, Germany, 1967, Molde, Norway, 1961, 62, 65, 68, 70, 71, 73, Kongsberg, Norway, 1966, 67, 68, 72, 74, Ill., 1972, Osaka, Japan, 1970, at internat. art. festivals, Recklinghausen, Germany, 1967, Bergen, Norway, 1967, Harstad, Norway, 1968, Helsinki, Finland, 1969, Frankfurt, Germany, 1970, World Expo. Osaka, Japan, 1970; featured TV programs, Europe; recs. Don Ellis Orch., Los Angeles, 1967; State grant study tour, U.S., 1970. Mem. Norwegian Jazz Musicians Orgn. (founder 1965, chmn. 1965-66). Recs. include By Myself, 1964, Jazz Moments, 1966, Joy, 1968, Some other Spring, 1970, Gershwin Songs 1973, Popofoni, 1973, Sings Michael Legrand, 1974, You Must Believe in Spring, 1974, We Could Be Flying, 1974. Home: 35 Nobelsgt Oslo 2 Norway

KROHN, MILDRED IRENE SCHNEIDER (MRS. EDWIN F. KROHN), county ofcl.; b. nr. Cassville, Wis., Mar. 23, 1909; d. George E. and Jessie I. (Willmers) Schneider; student pub. schs., Lancaster, Wis.; m. Edwin F. Krohn, Feb. 2, 1932; children—Marcus E., Maurice L. Stenographer, Grant County, Lancaster 1932-66, adminstrv. asst., 1957-63, county clk., 1963—. Clk. sch. dist. 14 S. Lancaster Twp., 1945-62; clk. S. Lancaster Twp., 1949-63; sec. Wis. Rural Schs. Assn., Lancaster, 1950-60. Chmn. of women's com. Grant Electric Coop. Trustee, sec. Lancaster Meml. Hosp., 1954-60. Mem. Wis. Towns Assn. (sec. Grant County unit 1950-63), Farm Bur. (South Lancaster Women's leader 1945-48). Mem. Evang. and Ref. Ch. (supt. Sunday Sch. 1955-60). Mem. Order Eastern Star, Rebekah (past noble grand Lancaster). Clubs: West Grant Saddle (sec. 1952-61), Friendly Neighbors Homemakers (past pres.). Home: Route 1 Bagley WI 53801 Office: Box 191 Lancaster WI 53813

KRON, RITA GLYNN (MRS. WILLIAM KRON), writer; b. Paterson, N.J., Apr. 13, 1919; d. Patrick Burke and Mary Sheridan (Holland) Glynn; student Munson Bus. Coll., Coll. San Mateo; m. William Yung Kron, Apr. 11, 1942; children—William Delos, Mary Elise. Sec., Wells Fargo Bank, San Francisco, 1938-43; free-lance writer, contbr. to San Francisco mag. and Popular Handicraft. Recipient 25th award Writer's Digest Creative Writing Contest, 1973. Mem. Cal. Writers. Roman Catholic. Home: 3036 The Alameda San Mateo CA 94403

KRONE, IRENE BECKMANN (MRS. HELMUT KRONE), advt. co. exec.; b. N.Y.C., Oct. 12, 1940; d. Frederick Wilhelm and Gertrude Hedwig (Gottschlich) Beckmann; student U. Vienna, Austria, 1960-61; B.S., Chestnut Hill Coll., 1962; postgrad. N.Y. U., 1967-68, Sch. Visual Arts, 1962-64, N.Y. Sch. Interior Design, 1962-64; m. Helmut Krone, Nov. 14, 1970. Market research analyst Celanese Fibers Co., N.Y.C., 1962-63, supr., Brussels, Belgium, 1963-66, color coordinator, N.Y.C., 1966; product devel. asso. Doyle Dane Bernbach, N.Y.C., 1967-70, v.p., fashion dir., 1970—. Mem. Fashion Group, Nat. Home Fashions League. Home: 1 E 62d St New York City NY 10021 Office: 20 W 43rd St New York City NY 10036

KRONEGGER, MARIA ELISABETH, educator; b. Graz, Austria; Sept. 23, 1932; d. Karl and Josefine (Sparovitz) Kronegger; M.A., Graz U., 1960; M.E., Kan. U., 1957; Ph.D., Fla. State U., 1960. Came to U.S., 1962, naturalized, 1968. With Lycee de Jeunes Filles, Reims, France, 1955-56; instr. Fla. State U., 1957-60, Rosenberg Coll., Switzerland, 1961-62, Hollins Coll., Va., 1962-64; asst. prof. Romance languages and comparative lit. Mich. State U., East Lansing, 1964-67, asso. prof., 1967-70, prof., 1970—. French Govt. scholar, 1953-54, Italian Govt. scholar, 1954, 61, Fulbright scholar, 1956-60, Lisle fellow, 1954, 56-57, Am. Friends Service Com., grantee, 1952, 55, 57, Ford Found. grantee, 1965, 66. Mem. Am. Assn. U. Profs., Modern Lang. Assn., Am. Assn. Tchrs. French, Assn. Internationale des Etudes Francaises, Societe des Professeurs Francais en Amerique, Assn. Internationale de Litterature Comparee, Internat. Platform Soc., Alliance Francaise, Midwest Modern Lang. Assn., Société Paul

Claudel, Société Jean Giraudoux, Phi Sigma Iota. Author: James Joyce and Associated Image Makers, 1968; Impressionist Literature, 1972. Contbr. articles to profl. jours. Home: 351 Oakhill Av Apartment 307 East Lansing MI 48823

KRONENBITTER, ANN WILLIAMSON (MRS. ROBERT LEE KRONENBITTER), publishing co. exec.; b. Rich Hill, Mo., Jan. 20, 1930; d. James Russell and Ivonne Constance (Emerson) Williamson; A.A., Cottey Coll., 1949; A.B., Drury Coll., 1953; m. Robert Lee Kronenbitter, Feb. 25, 1967. Indsl. editor Bendix Corp., Kansas City, Mo., 1953-58; publicist Fred Kline & Assos., Los Angeles, 1958-60; asst. to staffers Carl Byoir & Assos., Los Angeles, 1960; publicity dir. Western Ins. Information Service, Los Angeles, 1960-71; resident mgr., writer, pub. relations rep. Underwriters' Report, Los Angeles, 1972—. Mem. Pub. Relations Soc. Am., Publicity Club of Los Angeles, Ins. Women Los Angeles, So. Cal. Indsl. Editors Assn., Wilshire Bus. and Profl. Women. Home: 405 S Old Ranch Rd Arcadia CA 91006 Office: 429 S Western Av Los Angeles CA 90005

KROOTH, DIANE MARIE (MRS. ROBERT SCHILD KROOTH), educator, psychologist; b. Sacramento, Mar. 7, 1941; d. Barrett Robert and Anita Louise (Burns) Powell; B.A., U. Cal. at Berkeley, 1962; M.A. (USPHS fellow), Mich. State U., 1965, Ph.D. (USPHS trainee), 1969; m. Robert Schild Krooth, Dec. 21, 1970. Instr., Lansing (Mich.) Community Coll., also staff psychologist Lansing Child Guidance Clinic, 1968-69; staff psychologist Midwest Mental Health Clinic, Dearborn, Mich., 1969-70; asst. prof. psychology U. Pitts., 1970-71; asst. prof. psychology Hofstra U., Hempstead, N.Y., 1971—. Individual practice psychology, N.Y.C., 1970—. NSF grantee, 1970-71. Mem. Am., N.Y. State psychol. assns., N.Y. Acad. Scis., Am. Assn. Univ. Profs. Contbr. articles to profl. jours. Home: 100 Haven Av New York City NY 10032 Office: Hofstra U Hempstead Turnpike Hempstead NY 11550

KROPF, ELEANOR A., bank officer; b. Chgo.; d. Oscar A. and Edith (Anderson) Kropf; B.S., Northwestern U., 1936. Sec., H. B. Le Quatte, advt., N.Y.C., 1942-44; trust dept. tax accountant tax accounting div. The Chase Manhattan Bank, 1944-48, trust rep. personal trust planning div., 1948-58, personal trust officer, 1958-65, 2d v.p., 1965—. Mem. bequest com. Vis. Nurse Service N.Y. Mem. Nat. Assn. Bank Women (pres. 1965-66), N.Y. State Bankers Assn., Am. Assn. U. Women (trustee endowment fund), N.Y. Woman's Council, Phi Gamma Nu. Clubs: Women's Bond, Zonta Northwestern University (N.Y.C.). Contbr. articles to profl. jours. Home: 200 E 57th St New York City NY 10022 Office: 1 Chase Manhattan Plaza New York City NY 10015

KROTZ, VIRLA ROPER (MRS. DONALD KROTZ), civic worker; b. Ashland, Ore., Mar. 23, 1905; d. Frederick L. and Rosetta (Chapman) Roper; B.S. cum laude, U. Cal. at Berkeley, 1926; m. Donald Philip Krotz, Oct. 12, 1929; 1 son, Douglas Roper. With stock and bond dept. Bank of Am., Oakland, Cal., 1927-28; cashier Manheim Dibbern Co., San Francisco, 1928-30; with Heald Bus. Coll., Oakland, Cal., 1931-36; chmn. bd. Far West Regional Lab. for Ednl. Research and Devel., 1974—. Mem. State Bd. Edn., 1968—; mem. Cal. Adv. Council on Venereal Disease, 1972—. Mem. Cal. Republican State Central Com., 1956-70, mem. exec. com., 1961-68; 1st v.p. Cal. Fedn. Rep. Women, 1959-61, pres., 1961—, state pres., 1965-67; del. nat. conv., 1964, alternate del., 1960, 68; sec. Contra Costa United Rep. Finance Com., 1954-60. Sec.-treas. Nat. Assn. State Bds. Edn., 1968-69, pres., 1972-73. Bd. dirs. Contra Costa Nat. Polio Found. Bd., Orinda Library; treas. bd. dirs. Mt. Diablo Therapy Center. Mem. Beta Gamma Sigma, Phi Mu, Phi Chi Theta, Delta Kappa Gamma. Conglist. Club: Orinda Country. Home: 44 Monte Vista Rd Orinda CA 94563

KROUWER, MARGOT (MRS. HENRI KROUWER), painter, poet; b. Goeppingen, Germany; d. Max and Mathilde (Noerdlinger) Gutmann; m. Henri Krouwer, Nov. 14, 1935; children—Tom Max, Peter John, Jan Steven. Came to U.S., 1940, naturalized, 1947. Exhibited paintings and drawings in one-woman shows Fairleigh Dickinson U., 1961; group shows include A.C.A. Gallery, City Center, Allied Artists, Nat. Arts Club and Carus Gallery, Westchester Art Soc. Graphic Show, others; represented in pvt. collections, U.S. and abroad. Free lance poet, 1968—. Recipient numerous painting awards, also poetry awards Pa. Poetry Soc., 1970, 71, Ariz. State Poetry Soc., 1971, Sharon Creative Arts Found. Mem. Artists Equity, Group Three, Poetry Soc. Am. Address: 15 Rhynas Dr Mount Vernon NY 10552

KRUCK, DONNA JEAN HAGEMEYER (MRS. MICHAEL ROY KRUCK JR.), ednl. adminstr.; b. Peoria, Ill., Jan. 26, 1930; d. Walter George and Lois Irene (Newburn) Hagemeyer; B.S., Ill. State U., 1962; M.Ed., U. Ill., 1968; m. Michael Roy Kruck, Jr., June 27, 1948; children—Pamela Ann (Mrs. Paul Robert Hokanson), Michael Roy III, Quentin Robert. Tchr. elementary sch., New Lenox, Ill., 1957-62, Lincolnway Area Joint Agreement, Lincolnway High Sch., 1962-67; chmn. spl. edn. dept. Joliet (Ill.) Twp. High Schs., 1967-69, coordinator high schs., 1969—. Mem. Nat., Ill., Joliet (v.p. 1972-73, pres. 1974-75) edn. assns., Am. Assn. Mental Deficiency, Council for Exceptional Children (membership chmn. 1969-71), Am. Bus. Women's Assn. (profl. affairs chmn. 1974-76), Kappa Delta Pi, Delta Kappa Gamma (research chmn. 1968-70, scholarship chmn. 1970-72, project chmn. 1972-74, parliamentarian 1970-72). Lutheran. Club: East Campus Women's. Home: 156 John St New Lenox IL 60451 Office: 1101 Mills Rd Joliet IL 60433

KRUEGER, KEATHA KATHRINE, govt. ofcl.; b. S.D., Nov. 15, 1921; d. Henry Frederick and Carrie Sydna (Smith) Krueger; B.A., U. S.D., 1943; M.S., U. Wis., 1945, Ph.D., 1948. Asst. prof. biochemistry U. S.D., 1948-56; editor biochem. sects. Chem. Abstracts Service, 1956-63; sci. communications officer Nat. Inst. Arthritis, Metabolism and Digestive Diseases, NIH, Bethesda, Md., 1963-74, diabetes program dir., 1974—. Fellow A.A.A.S., Sigma Xi; mem. Am. Chem. Soc., N.Y. Acad. Scis., Am. Soc. Information Scis. Home: 9325 E Parkhill Dr Bethesda MD 20014 Office: NIH Bethesda MD 20014

KRUEGER, VIRGINIA C., mus. exec.; B.S. in Edn., State U. N.Y. at Buffalo; postgrad. U. So. Cal., U. Cal. at San Diego, U. Cal. at Los Angeles extension; m. Robert Blair Krueger; children—Lisa Carmichael, Paula Leah, Robert Blair. Tchr., Batavia, N.Y., 1953-54, La Jolla, Cal., 1954-56, Los Angeles city schs., 1956-57, South Pasadena (Cal.) pub. schs., 1957-62, Poly. Sch., Pasadena, Cal., 1966; docent Los Angeles County Mus. Art, 1967—, chmn. docent council, 1974-75. Leader Girl Scouts Am., 1964-69; vol. Pasadena Art Mus. Jr. Workshop, 1964-65; chmn. WWW Tennis Tournament, 1966-67; active Center Theatre Group Vols., 1967-69. Bd. dirs. Vol. Bur. Pasadena, 1969-70, Los Angeles Jr. Tennis, 1971-72, Am. Field Service, 1973-74, Graphic Arts Council Los Angeles County Mus. Art. Mem. Pasadena Art mus., La Jolla Mus. Modern Art, Mus. Modern Art, Met. Mus. Art. Home: 501 Vallombrosa Dr Pasadena CA 91107 also 9822 La Jolla Farms Rd La Jolla CA 92027

KRUG, ADELE JENSEN (MRS. WALTER JOHN KRUG), educator; b. Thief River Falls, Minn., Mar. 30, 1908; d. Anton Martin Hulbert and Tillie Manspand (Johnson) Jensen; B.A., Gallaudet Coll., 1930; M.S., Cath. U. Am., 1961; m. Walter John Krug, June 18, 1932 (dec. May 1962); children—Janice (Mrs. Robert B. Riley III), Diana (Mrs. Robert F. Armstrong), Walter F., Warren J. Instr., R.I. Sch. for Deaf, 1930-32; instr. library sci. Gallaudet Coll., Washington, 1955-63, asst. prof., 1963-67, asso. prof., 1967—. Pres., Stuart Jr. High Sch. P.T.A., Washington, 1954-56, McKinley High Sch. P.T.A., 1956-57. Mem. Am. Assn. U. Profs., A.L.A., D.C. Library Assn., Conv. Am. Instrs. Deaf, Nat. Assn. of Deaf, D.C. Women's Aux., Nat. Luth. Home, Amos Kendall Soc., Phi Kappa Zeta (nat. alumnae pres. 1954-60). Contbr. to Am. Anns. of Deaf. Home: 1915 Gaither St Hillcrest Heights MD 20031 Office: Gallaudet College Washington DC 20002

KRUG, MARY ELLEN, lawyer; b. Oshkosh, Wis., Jan. 13, 1918; d. Ernest H. and Leo V. (Johns) Krug; student Macalester Coll., 1935-37; A.B., U. Wash., 1939, LL.B., 1943; m. John M. Case, Apr. 6, 1949. Admitted to Wash. bar, 1943; law clk. Wash. Supreme Ct., 1943-45; asso. McMicken, Rupp & Schweppe, Seattle, 1945-54; partner Schweppe, Doolittle, Krug, Tausend, Beezer & Beierle, Seattle, 1954—. Bd. dirs. Seattle YWCA, mem. financial adv. bd. Mem. Am. (mem. com. on antitrust and labor relations law 1969-73), Wash. State (mem. com. of bar examiners 1973—), Seattle-King County (chmn. sect. labor relations law 1966-67; Pacific Coast labor law conf. 1967) bar assns., Order of Coif, Phi Beta Kappa, Phi Alpha Delta. Co-author: West's Federal Forms, Vol. 1B, 1952, 63, 69. Home: 1604 NE Ravenna Blvd Seattle WA 98105 Office: 657 Colman Bldg Seattle WA 98104

KRUGER, NORMA BURTON, ednl. adminstr.; b. Nelsonville, O., Feb. 24, 1926; d. Roy C. and Lucille (Canter) Burton; grad. high sch.; m. Robert M. Kruger, May 30, 1947 (div. Oct. 1965); 1 dau., Linda. With W.M. Ritter Lumber Co., Columbus, O., 1946-52; with Harvey Mudd Coll., Claremont, Cal., 1960—, registrar, 1970—. Mem. Assn. Coll. Registrars and Admissions Officers, Pacific Assn. College Registrars and Admissions Officers, Cal. Assn. Women Adminstrs. and Counselors. Democrat. Home: 3049 Knollwood St LaVerne CA 91750 Office: Harvey Mudd Coll Claremont CA 91711

KRUGER, NORMA JANE, coll. adminstr.; b. Wisconsin Rapids, Wis., Oct. 31, 1924; d. Harrison Harland and Grace Helen (Staffon) Kruger; student Wis. State Coll. at Stevens Point, 1942-43; B.S., Wis. State Coll. at LaCrosse, 1946; M.S., U. Ore., 1966; postgrad. U. Mo., 1967-68. Owner, mgr. Kruger Cranberry Co., Wisconsin Rapids, 1948-65; pub. sch. tchr., Wis., 1946-58, 59-60, Ore., 1958-59, 63-64; tchr. Air Force Dependent Schs., Ankara, Turkey, 1960-61, Japan, 1961-62, Okinawa, 1968-69; counselor, instr. Central Ore. Community Coll., Bend, 1966-67; dir. tchr. placement U. Ore., Eugene, 1969-72; dir. career devel. placement Edmonds Community Coll., Lynnwood, Wash., 1972—. Nat. Def. Edn. Act fellow, 1967-68. Mem. Am. Assn. U. Women, Am. Assn. Higher Edn. (pres. chpt. 1973-74), Am. Personnel and Guidance Assn., N.W. Community Coll. Placement Assn. (pres. 1974-75), N.W. Personnel Mgrs. Assn. (v.p. chpt. 1974-75). Democrat. Conglist. Soroptomist. Office: 20000 W 68th St Edmonds Community College Lynnwood WA 98036

KRUGMAN, DOROTHY CAROL (MRS. HERBERT E. KRUGMAN), psychologist; b. New Bedford, Mass., Apr. 30, 1923; d. Isaac and Paula (Freund) Coleman; B.S., Coll. City N.Y., 1942; M.A., Columbia, 1942, Ph.D., 1950; m. Herbert E. Krugman, Dec. 26, 1942; children—Edward Paul, Laura Nan. Cons. psychologist Louise Wise Services, N.Y.C., 1948—, Jewish Child Care Assn., 1952—, Leake and Watts Childrens Home, 1960—. Chmn., Morningside Citizens Com., N.Y.C., 1959-64; sec. Central Harlem Sch. Bd., N.Y.C., 1960-63. Mem. Am. Psychol. Assn., Soc. Research Child Devel., Am. Orthopsychiat. Assn. Home: 7709 Courtland Av Stamford CT 06902

KRUGMAN, MARIAN GOLD, librarian; b. Union City, N.J., Dec. 13, 1923; d. Samuel and Bertha (Neiman) Gold; student Hunter Coll., 1940-43; B.A., L.I. U., 1948; postgrad. U. Ky., 1949-51; M.S., U. N.C., 1968; m. Arnold David Krugman, Dec. 14, 1947; children—Janet, Neil, Craig, Meredith. Librarian Durham Acad., 1968-69; librarian, also editor ESE Notes U. N.C., 1969—. Mem. USMC Women's Res. Mem. A.L.A. Home: 2605 Tanglewood Dr Durham NC 27705 Office: Dept Environmental Sciences University of North Carolina Chapel Hill NC 27715

KRUMEICH, DOROTHY MAHON, journalist; b. Peekskill, N.Y., Aug. 23, 1907; d. George and Emma (Anderson) Mahon; student Columbia, 1950-53; m. Edwin Anthony Krumeich, Apr. 23, 1928 (dec. Oct. 1961); children—Edwin Anthony, William Barry. Women's editor Peekskill Star Corp., 1949-68. Feature writer. spl. assignments columnist, 1968—. Feature writer USIA, 1959-60, Westchester-Rockland Newspapers, 1952-71. Mem. women's com. Brandeis U., 1966-67. Trustee Field Library, Peekskill. Recipient Guardsman award Depts. Army and Air Force N.G. Burs., 1962, service citation Peekskill Power Squadron USCG Aux., 1966. Mem. Norchester Hadassah (hon.). Clubs: Hudson Valley Yacht (hon.), Women's (exec. bd. 1952-54), Garden (exec. bd. 1960-68) (Peekskill). Home: Hudson View Estates Peekskill NY 10566 Office: 824 Main St Peekskill NY 10566

KRUMM, CAROL MAE RHODEBACK (MRS. DELBERT RUSSELL KRUMM), librarian; b. Pataskala, O., June 17, 1923; d. Donald F. and Ethel Irene (Stevenson) Rhodeback; B.A., Capital U., 1945; B.S. in L.S., Western Res. U., 1946; m. Delbert Russell Krumm, July 28, 1946; 1 dau., Carolyn (Mrs. Dennis Dean Heffner). Asst., Capital U. Library, Columbus, O., 1941-42, Bexley (O.) Pub. Library, 1941-45; asst. librarian Otterbein Coll. Library, Westerville, O., 1946-57; cataloger Ohio State U. Libraries, Columbus, 1952-53, 59-65, catalog maintenance librarian, 1965-71, asst. prof. library adminstrn., 1968—, head catalog maintenance and card prodn. div., 1971-72, head bibliog. records div., 1972—; cataloger Ohio Legislative Service Commn., 1953; serials cataloger Cleve. Pub. Library, 1957-58. Cons. Ohio State U. Christian Center Library, 1966-67; librarian E. Linden Evangelical United Brethren Ch. Library, 1965-68, Westgate United Meth. Ch. Library, 1970—; resource leader Children's Work Council, also cons. reading program Ohio S.E. Conf., Evangelical United Brethren Ch., 1960-64. Mem. Am., Ohio, Franklin County library assns., Ohio Valley Group Tech. Service Librarians, Inter-Univ. Library Council, Ch. and Synagogue Library Assn., Am. Assn. U. Profs. Methodist. Clubs: Faculty Women's; Kiwanikwee (chaplain 1972-73). Home: 53 S Powell Av Columbus OH 43204 Office: 1858 Neil Av Columbus OH 43210

KRUPANSKY, BLANCHE ETHEL, judge; b. Cleve., Dec. 10, 1925; d. Frank Albert and Anna (Lawrence) Krupansky; A.B., Flora Ston Mather Coll., 1947; J.D., Case Western Reserve U., 1948, LL.M., 1966; m. Frank William Vargo, Apr. 30, 1960. Admitted to Ohio bar, 1949; practiced in Cleve. and Columbus, O., 1949-61; asst. atty. gen. Ohio, Columbus, 1953-56; asst. chief counsel Bur. of Workmen's Compensation, Columbus and Cleve., 1957-59; judge Cleve. Municipal Ct., 1961-69; judge Common Pleas Ct. Cuyahoga County, 1969—. Recipient Supreme Ct. of Ohio honors for Outstanding Jud. Service, 1973. Mem. Ohio State, Cuyahoga County, Cleve. bar assns., Nat. Assn. Women Lawyers, Cleve. Women Lawyers, Common Pleas Judges Assn., Ohio Assn. Attys. Gen., League of Women Voters. Club: Women's City. Home: 18846 N Valley Dr Fairview Park OH 44126 Office: Common Pleas Court 1 Lakeside Av Cleveland OH 44113

KRUPP, IRIS MARIE, med. educator; b. New Orleans, May 1, 1928; d. Philip J. and Ione M. (White) Krupp; B.S., La. State U., 1948; M.S., Tulane U., 1955, Ph.D., 1958, M.D., 1971. Research asst. parasitology Tulane U., New Orleans, 1949-53, research and teaching asst., 1954-58, instr. parasitology, 1959-61, asst. prof., 1961-65, asso. prof., psychiatry and neurology, 1966-68, asso. prof. tropical medicine, 1966—; instr. vet. parasitology Mich. State U., East Lansing, 1953-54; intern USPHS Hosp., New Orleans, 1971-72; resident dermatology Charity Hosp., New Orleans, 1973; research and edn. asso. VA Hosp., New Orleans, 1972-73. Mem. adv. bd. parasitic diseases Dept. Army, 1973—. Research grantee USPHS, 1973-74. Mem. Fedn. Am. Socs. for Exptl. Biology, Am. Soc. Tropical Medicine and Hygiene, A.C.P., Am. Assn. Immunology, Am. Pub. Health Assn., Am. Med. Women's Assn., Reticuloendothelial Soc., La., Orleans Parish med. socs., Sigma Xi. Contbr. articles to profl. jours. Home: 111 Spencer Av New Orleans LA 70124 Office: Dept Tropical Medicine and Parasitology Tulane U 1430 Tulane Av New Orleans LA 70112

KRUPSAK, MARY ANNE (MRS. EDWIN MARGOLIS), state senator; b. Schenectady, Mar. 26, 1932; d. Ambrose Michael and Mamie (Wytrwal) Krupsak; B.S. in History, U. Rochester, 1953; M.S. in Pub. Communications, U. Boston, 1954; LL.D., U. Chgo., 1962; m. Edwin Margolis, June 30, 1969. Program asso. Gov. Averell Harriman, 1954-58; adminstrv. asst. to Congressman Samuel S. Stratton, 1958-59; admitted to N.Y. State bar, 1962; pvt. practice; asst. counsel Office of Temp. Pres., N.Y. State Senate, mem. staff Speaker N.Y. Assembly, until 1968; mem. N.Y. State Assembly, after 1968, now mem. N.Y. Senate. Co-chmn. N.Y. Delegation, Democratic Nat. Conv., Miami, Fla., 1972. Bd. dirs. Cornell U. Regional Adv. Council, Albany Med. Center, Bridge Center Rehab. Half-Way House, Schenectady; trustee Capitol Dist. Library Council. Recipient Amsterdam Bus. and Profl. Women's Columbian award, 1970, Outstanding Citizen award, 1971, Woman of Year Service award Polish-Am. Vets. World War II, 1971. Hon. chmn. Albany Internat. Center, Albany League of Arts, Internationally Famous Dancers from Poland, 1971. Mem. N.Y. State, Montgomery County bar assns., Am. Assn. U. Women, Bus. and Profl. Women Amsterdam, Assn. Bar City N.Y., Rosary Soc. Roman Catholic. Club: Emblem. Home: Shaper Av Extension Canajoharie NY 13317 Office: State Capitol Albany NY 12224

KRUSE, CATHERINE EMMA (MRS. ROBERT ROLAND KRUSE), hotel exec.; b. Lawrence, Kan., May 5, 1915; d. Frank Hugh and Leila Claire (Weidlein) Penner; A.B., U. Kan., 1936; m. Robert Roland Kruse, Sept. 3, 1938; children—Philip R., David V., Stephen D., Barbara Claire (Mrs. Michael Clell Todd). Bus. mgr. Radio stations KANU-KFKU, Lawrence, Kan., 1955-61; with Inn Operations, Inc. (name changed to Topeka Inn Mgmt., Inc. 1969), Topeka, 1961—, sec.-treas., 1967—; treas. Inn Operations Inc., 1969—; sec., treas., dir. Torrance Inn Mgmt., Inc., Cal. Inn Mgmt. Inc. Dir. Security Equity Fund, Inc., Security Investment Fund, Inc. Chmn., Kan. Civil Service Bd. Appeals, 1970; chmn. Adv. bd. St. Francis Hosp., 1970-72. Mem. P.E.O. (v.p. coop. bd. 1971, pres. 1972, del. conv. 1971), T.K. Ambassadors (Community Service award 1969), Greater Topeka C. of C. (Distinguished Service award 1972, chmn. women's div. 1968, chmn. new projects com. 1972, bd. dirs. women's div. 1967-69), D.A.R., Native Daus. Kan. (v.p. 1972), Women in Communications, Kappa Alpha Theta (pres. Mothers Club 1969). Mem. Conglist. Ch. (trustee 1969-73). Mem. Order Eastern Star. Club: Soroptimist (chmn pub. affairs com. 1971-72). Home: 2103 Burnett Rd PO Box 497 Topeka KS 66601 Office: 2209 W 29th St Topeka KS 66611

KRUSE, LORANE CHRISTINA, educator; b. Miles, Ia., Apr. 10, 1914; d. John and Christina (Hoop) Kruse; diploma Good Samaritan Hosp. Sch. Nursing, 1947; student Coll. Mt. St. Joseph, 1947; B.S., Ohio State U., 1953, postgrad., 1968; M.A., U. Chgo., 1958. Nurse obstet. dept. Good Samaritan Hosp., Cin., 1947; office nurse Dr. W.R. Griffin, Columbus, O., 1948-49; staff nurse Red Cross Blood Center, 1949-51, asst. chief nurse, 1951-54; staff nurse neurosurgery Ohio State U. Hosp., Columbus, 1954-56, asst. evening supr., 1956, faculty Univ., 1956-58, 59—, chmn. div. leadership and mgmt., 1966-68, asso. prof., 1968-69, asst. dir., asso. prof. continuing edn., 1969-72, acting dir., asso. prof., 1972-73, asst. dir., asso. prof., 1973—. Mem. adv. com. for disaster planning com. Acad. Medicine Columbus and Franklin County, 1966-73; Mem. sci. content com. med. micro-wave utilization study Ohio Valley Health Services Found., 1969-70; mem. adv. council continuing edn. project Video Nursing, Inc., 1971—. Mem. Am., Ohio (legislative com. 1965, chmn. legislative com. Mid-Ohio dist. 1966-67) nurses assns., Nat. League Nursing (pres. Ohio 1972-74), Nursing Coordinating Council Continuing Edn. (chmn. 1970-72), Nat. Soc. Programmed Instrn., Ohio State Regional Med. Program, Fayette County Profl. Nurses Assn., Sigma Theta Tau (chmn. nat. com. on nominations 1969-71). Presbyn. (deacon 1969-71, elder 1973, clk. of session 1974). Home: 1669 Elmwood St Columbus OH 43212 Office: 1585 Neil Av Columbus OH 43210

KRUSE, RHODA EMMA, librarian; b. Bklyn., Aug. 8, 1929; d. Harry Martin and Elsa Alvina (Rohde) Kruse; B.A., Bethany Coll., 1951; M.L.S., Pratt Inst., 1954. Tchr. library Girls' High Sch., N.Y.C., 1954-57; librarian San Diego Pub. Library, 1957-62; sr. librarian, extension div. San Diego Pub. Library, 1962-72, sr. librarian in charge Cal.-newspaper-genealogy spl. collections, 1972—. Mem. KleeWyk Soc. of San Diego Museum of Man. Mem. Pacific Beach Town Council, 1965—, dir., 1970-72. Recipient Status of Women award Pacific Beach Women's Club, 1965. Mem. San Diego Pub. Library Staff Assn. (pres. 1972), San Diego Hist. Soc. (treas. women's com. 1968), So. Cal. Local History Council, San Diego Council Congress of History (rec. sec. 1973—), Fremont-Kearny Historians (sec. 1973—), West Coast Assn. Women Historians. Republican. Mem. Christian Ch. (mem. gen. bd. 1970-73). Home: 876 Reed Av San Diego CA 92109 Office: 820 E St San Diego CA 92101

KRUSKAMP, JANET ELAINE KUNCL (MRS. HARDY KRUSKAMP), artist; b. Grants Pass, Ore., Dec. 10, 1934; d. Charles Jacob and Florence Elizabeth (Matye) Kuncl; student Chouinard Art Inst. Los Angeles, 1951-52; m. Hardy Kruskamp, June 20, 1953; children—Charles, Stephen, Jennifer. Exhibited one-woman shows at numerous galleries, museums including Villa Montalvo Center for Arts, Saratoga, Triton Mus. Art, Santa Clara, Rosicrucian Egyptian Mus. Gallery, San Jose, Cal., 1970, 73, Charles and Emma Frye Mus. Art Seattle, 1974; exhibited in numerous group shows including Long Beach Mus. Art Ann. Exhbn., Santa Clara County Hist. Soc. Exhibit, Soc. Western Artists San Francisco Exhbn., Soc. Western Artists De Saisset Exhibit, Santa Clara, Cal., Santa Cruz (Cal.) Statewide Exhbn., Cal. Expn. Fair, Sacramento, Artistes U.S.A. Galeries Raymond Duncan, Paris, N.Y.C., Prix De Paris, Galeries Raymond Duncan, Paris, France, Solon of 50 State, Ligoa Duncan Gallery, N.Y.C., Charles and Emma Frye Art Mus., M.H. De Young Mus. Art, San Francisco, Soc. Western Artists 1972, 74 Invitational, San Jose, Grand Galleria Nat. Exhbn., Seattle, 1972, 73, Catharine Lorillard Wolfe Art Club 76th Ann. Exhibit, N.Y.C., Am. Artists Profl. League Grand Nat. Exhbns., N.Y.C., 1972-74, Springfield (Utah) Mus. Art

50th Ann., 1974; represented in permanent collections including Rosicrucian Egyptian Mus., Triton Mus. Art, Santa Clara, Grand Galleria. Recipient numerous awards including First Grand prize and Andy trophy Grand Galleria Nat. Art Competition, 1973. Fellow Am. Artists Profl. League; mem. Soc. Western Artists, Los Gatos Art Assn. (pres. 1969). Home: 1627 Hyde Dr Los Gatos CA 95030

KRUUSE, ELSA, editor, translator; b. Catskill, N.Y.; d. Roscoe Platt and Grace (Hazard) Conkling; spl. student Smith Coll., 1926-27, Cass Tech., 1927-28, Sorbonne, Paris, 1930-32, U. Stockholm, 1942; m. Sigvard Kruuse de Verchou, Oct. 1932 (div.); children—Robin Christopher Nils, Sigrid Karen Kay Toye, Astrid Monica (Mrs. Douglas E. Mitchell). With OWI, Stockholm, London, and San Francisco, 1941-45; U.S. corr. Aftontidning, Sweden, 1945-47; corr. for Scandinavia and Finland, Christian Sci. Monitor, Stockholm, 1947-49, feature writer Christian Sci. Monitor, mem. editorial staff McFadden mags., Better Living mag., 1949-52; asst., then mng. editor Advance (Cong. Christian Chs.), N.Y.C., 1952-57; asst. editor, then editor Religious Newsweekly, news and feature writer Outlook, mng. editor Inter-Ch. News, publs. editor, asso. editor Tempo dept. information Nat. Council Chs., N.Y.C., 1957-70; book editor, mgr. N.Y. office A.L. Fierst Lit. Properties, chief instr. N.Y. Sch. Writing, 1970—; editor Ecumenical Courier, World Council Chs., N.Y.C., 1971—. Mem. Overseas Press Club, Ams. Democratic Action. Translator (from Swedish) We Dared the Andes (Gustaf Bolinder), 1959; Tariro (Arvid Albrektson), 1959; The Sudden Sun (Olav Hartman), 1964; Can Two Become One? (B. and L. Jonsson), 1965; Anna-Clara (Hasse Zetterstrom), 1970; No Roses Grow in Sawdust (Nicolas Fokker), 1973. Home: 334 Riverside Dr New York City NY 10025 Office: 630 9th Av Suite 208 New York City NY 10036

KRYN, JEANNETTE MIRIAM, educator; b. Louisville, May 23, 1913; d. Hyman and Mary (Kohnop) Kryn; B.A., U. Cin., 1934, B.Ed., 1935, M.A., 1944; Ph.D., U. Mich., 1952. Tchr. pub. schs., Cin., 1936-46; asst. prof. biology U. Buffalo, 1947-51; wood technologist, botanist US. Forest Products Lab., Madison, Wis., 1952-58; lectr. U. Wis.-Madison, 1955-58; tchr. Schenk Sch., Madison, 1959-66, Kennedy Sch., Madison, 1966—. Tchr. botany U. Wis. Summer Exptl. Sch., 1962; tchr. botany for gifted children, Madison, 1967—. Fellow A.A.A.S.; mem. Bot. Soc. Am.; mem. Sigma Xi, Phi Kappa Phi. Author: The Woods of Liberia, 1959. Home: 3710 Atwood Av Madison WI 53714 Office: Kennedy Sch 221 Meadowlark Dr Madison WI 53714

KUBIAK, TERESA WOJTASZEK (MRS. JANUSZ KUBIAK), soprano; b. Lodz, Poland, Dec. 26, 1937; d. Feliks and Janina (Witczak) Wojtaszek; B.A., Sch. of Music, 1960; M.A., State Coll. Music, Lodz, 1965; m. Janusz Kubiak, Feb. 24, 1962; children—Malgorzata, Dorota. Appeared at Grand Teater, Lodz, 1965, Carnegie Hall, N.Y.C., 1970, New York Philharmonic Orch., San Francisco Opera House, 1971-72, Chgo. Lyric Opera, 1971, Houston Grand Opera, 1971, Teatro La Fenice, Venezia, Italy, 1971, Miami Grand Opera, 1972, Covent Garden Opera, London, 1972, Ravinia Festival, Chgo., 1972, also in Vienna, Austria, France, Germany, Bulgaria, Russia, Czechoslovakia, Lisbon, Portugal. Recipient 2d prize Mus. Competition, Finland, 1961, 3d prize Internat. Mus. Competition, Tuluz, France, 1962, 2d prize, Munich, Germany, 1965. Mem. Assn. Polish Musician Artists. Home: 75E Narutowicza Lodz Poland Office: care Lyric Opera 20 W Wacker Dr Chicago IL 60606

KUCK, MARIE ELIZABETH BUKOVSKY, pharmacist; b. Milw., Aug. 3, 1910; d. Frank Joseph and Marie (Nozina) Bukovsky; Ph.C., U. Ill., 1933; m. John A. Kuck, Sept. 20, 1945 (div. Nov. 1954). Pharmacist and tchr. Am. Hosp., Chgo., 1936-38, St. Joseph Hosp., Chgo., 1938-40, Ill. Masonic Hosp., Chgo., 1940-45; chief pharmacist St. Vincent Hosp., Los Angeles, 1946-48, St. Joseph Hosp., Santa Fe, 1949-51; dir. pharm. services St. Luke's Hosp., San Francisco, 1951—; pharmacist Mission Neighborhood Health Center, San Francisco, 1968-72. Mem. peer rev. com. Drug Utilization Com., Blue Shield Cal. and Pharm. Soc. San Francisco. Recipient Bowl of Hygeia award Cal. Pharm. Assn., 1966. Mem. No., Cal. (legislative chmn. aux. 1967-69, chmn. fund raising luncheon 1953-71, pres. San Francisco aux. 1974), Nat. Am., No. Cal. (pres. 1955-56, pres. San Francisco aux. 1965-66, editor ofcl. publ. 1967-70) pharm. socs., Am. Pharm. Assn. (pres. No. Cal. br. 1956-57, nat. sec. women's aux. 1970-72), Cal. Council Hosp. Pharmacists (organizer 1962, sec.-treas. 1962-66), Am. Soc. Hosp. Pharmacists, Assn. Western Hosps. (gen. chmn. hosp. pharmacy sect. conv. San Francisco 1958), Internat. Pharmacy Congress (U.S. del. Brussels, Belgium 1958, Copenhagen, Denmark 1960), Fedn. Internationale Pharmaceutique, Lambda Kappa Sigma. Home: 2261 33d Av San Francisco CA 94116 Office: 3555 Army St San Francisco CA 94110

KUDIESY, NORMA MARTHA, librarian; b. Burlington, Vt., Nov. 21, 1931; d. Jacob J. and Margaret M. (Alafat) Kudiesy; B.S., U. Vt., 1954; M.L.S., Tex. Woman's U., 1969. Br. librarian Spl. Services Libraries, Ft. Bliss, Tex., 1967-69, reference librarian, 1969—. Mem. Altar Soc., Cath. Daus. Am. (financial soc. 1973-75), Am., Tex. (dist. sec.-treas. 1973-74), Border Regional (exec. bd. 1970-71, rec. sec. 1973-74) library assns., Am. Legion Aux. (sec. 1953-55), Northeast Bus. and Profl. Assn., Ninety Nines (treas. 1971-73). Roman Catholic. Home: 5401 Raymond Telles El Paso TX 79924 Office: Spl Services Libraries Fort Bliss TX 79916

KUECK, ETHEL COLLINS (MRS. WILLIAM WALTER KUECK), library dir.; b. Bevier, Mo., July 23, 1899; d. Shelby Miller and Emma Isabella (Sherman) Collins; A.B. (Nat. Methodist scholar), Neb. Wesleyan U., 1950; M.A., Northwestern U., 1952; m. William Walter Kueck, Sept. 24, 1919; children—Hazel Viola (Mrs. Aldor Peterson), Ellen Ethel (Mrs. Robert E. Cook). Tchr. rural schs. Neb., 1915, 17-18; sec. U. Neb., Lincoln, 1946-47, Neb. Wesleyan U., Lincoln, 1947-50, Northwestern U. Garrett Theol. Sem., Evanston, Ill., 1950-52; prof. Nat. Coll. for Christian Workers, Kansas City, Mo., 1952-54; dir. adult work Neb. Methodist Conf., Lincoln, 1954-65; dir. Christian edn. First Meth. Ch., North Platte, Neb., 1965-67; curator, librarian, dir. Neb. United Meth. Conf. Hist. Library, Lincoln, 1967—. Mem. Nat. Meth. Commn. on Adult Work; mem. joint com. on missionary edn. Meth. Ch. and Nat. Council; cons. on adult work Nat. Council and Meth. Ch.; alternate del. World Meth. Conf., London, Eng., 1966; del. World Meth. Conf., Denver, 1971. Mem. World Meth. Hist. Soc. (del. 1971, Am. sect. del. 1974), Phi Kappa Phi, Pi Gamma Mu, Psi Chi. Contbr. articles to mags. Home: Lincoln NE 68503 Office: United Methodist Historical Library Lucas Bldg Nebraska Wesleyan Universtiy 50th and St Paul Sts Lincoln NE 68504

KUEHN, EILEEN WILHELM, newspaper editor; b. New England, N.D., May 7, 1939; d. George M. and Viola (Beisser) Wilhelm; B.S., Dickinson State Coll., 1961; M.A., U. Minn., 1966, postgrad., 1968—; m. Lloyd D. Kuehn (div. Dec. 1966); children—Deborah Jean, Colin George. Mng. editor suburban Mpls. weekly Sun Newspapers, Edina, Minn., 1970—, redesigned format of all papers from broadsheet to tabloid, also design, edit. new publs.; freelance writer. Bd. dirs. Southwest Mpls. Parent-Tchr. Student Orgn. Recipient Suburban Press Found. Achievement award, 1970. Wall St. Jour. Newspaper Fund fellow, 1963; Coe Found. fellow, 1962. Mem. Minn. Press Women, Minn. Press Club. Home: 4412 Thomas Av S Minneapolis MN 55410 Office: 6601 W 78th St Edina MN 55435

KUEHN, LUCILLE MAISEL, educator, city ofcl.; b. N.Y.C., May 26, 1924; d. David Henry and Hildegard (Margulies) Maisel; B.A. magna cum laude, U. Minn., 1948; M.A., U. Cal. at Irvine, 1969; m. Rudolph L. Kuehn, Dec. 25, 1946 (div. Aug. 1971); children—Susan (Mrs. Ramani Ayake), Robert, David. Teaching asst. polit. sci. U. Minn., Mpls., 1943-45; mem. nat. program staff in human relations Anti-Defamation League, N.Y.C., 1946-49; program coordinator, instr. U. Cal. at Irvine, 1966, program coordinator dept. urban affairs, 1964-70, lectr. social ecology, 1970—, lectr. comparative culture, 1971—, asst. to vice chancellor student affairs, 1970-72, dir. program devel., 1970—. Cons. Santa Ana (Cal.) Unified Sch. Dist., 1969-70, U.S. Office Edn., 1971-72, Cal. State U., Los Angeles, 1971-72. Chmn. mental health com. Pasadena (Cal.) Planning Council, 1956-59; mem. Orange County Juvenile Justice Commn., 1965-66, Orange County Criminal Justice Council, 1969; mem. Orange County Mental Health Adv. Bd., 1970. Councilman, Newport Beach, Cal., 1974—. Mem. adv. bd. Claremont Colls. Center for Continuing Edn., 1968—, vice chmn., 1968—; bd. dirs. South Coast Child Guidance Clinic, 1965-67, 1st v.p. personnel relations, 1966-67; trustee Orange County Mosquito Abatement Dist., Harbor Day Sch. U.S. Office Edn. fellow, 1969; Ford Found. grantee, 1968-69. Mem. League Women Voters (state dir. 1959-60). Copy editor Symposium, Computers and Education, 1966. Home: 1831 Seadrift Dr Corona del Mar CA 92625 Office: City Hall 3300 Newport Blvd Newport Beach CA 92660

KUEKES, ROBERTA JEAN EDMONDS (MRS. EDWARD GRAYSON KUEKES), civic worker; b. Canton, O., Apr. 20, 1928; d. Ross Koester and Mary Elizabeth (Hoefer) Edmonds; student Ohio U., 1946-49; B.J., U. Tex., 1955; m. Edward Grayson Kuekes, June 3, 1950; children—Sherrill Jane, Edward David. Tech. editor Southwest Research Inst., San Antonio, 1955-57; copy editor Applied Mechanics Reviews, San Antonio, 1965-69. Bd. dirs., chmn. pub. relations Red Lands council Girl Scouts U.S.A., 1970—. Mem. Nat. Press Women, Tex. Press Women, Women in Communications (treas. San Antonio 1958-68), Zeta Tau Alpha. Democrat. Presbyn. Editor Greek and Byzantine Jour., 1960-61. Home: 6300 Commodore Lane Oklahoma City OK 73132 Office: 121 NE 50th St Oklahoma City OK 73105

KUH, JOYCE DATTEL (MRS. RICHARD HENRY KUH), editor; b. Greenville, Miss., Mar. 10, 1937; d. Milton Joseph and Hannah (Marks) Dattel; B.A., Newcomb Coll., 1959; m. Richard Henry Kuh, July 31, 1966; children—Michael Joseph, Jody Ellen. Asst. to treas. Dynatech Corp., Cambridge, Mass., 1959-63; editorial asst. McCall's mag., N.Y.C., 1963-64; articles editor Ladies' Home Jour., N.Y.C., 1964—. Democrat. Jewish religion. Home: 14 Washington Pl New York City NY 10003 Office: 641 Lexington Av New York City NY 10022

KUH, KATHARINE, editor; b. St. Louis, July 15, 1904; d. Morris and Olga (Weiner) Woolf; A.B., Vassar Coll., 1925; A.M., U. Chgo., 1928; postgrad. N.Y. U., 1929; m. George E. Kuh, Jan. 23, 1930 (div. 1936). Lectr., tchr. history of art for adult classes, 1930-39; owner, dir. Katharine Kuh Gallery, Chgo., 1935-42; dir. employment bur. sch. Chgo. Art Inst., 1937-42, pub. relations counsel, 1942-45, curator gallery of art interpretation, 1943-59, assoc. curator modern painting and sculpture, 1947-53, curator modern painting and sculpture, 1957-59, editor Bull. of Art Inst. Chgo., 1945-53; vis. prof. art U. Sch. Fine Arts, San Miguel, Guanajuato, Mexico, summers 1938-40; art editor Saturday Rev., 1959-71, World Mag., 1972-73, Saturday Review World, 1973—. Cons. San Francisco Museum of Art; art cons. So. Ill. U., 1963-68, First Nat. Bank, Chgo., 1968—. Author: Art Has Many Faces, 1951; Leger, 1953; The Artist's Voice, 1962; Break-Up: The Core of Modern Art, 1965; The Open Eye: in Pursuit of Art, 1971. Prepared adv. report on Indian carvings in Alaska for Office Indian Affairs, 1946; developed series of adult discussion groups in modern art for Fund for Adult Edn. of Ford Found., 1955. Home: 140 E 83d St New York City NY 10028 Office: care Saturday Review World Mag 488 Madison Av New York City NY 10022

KUHL, MARGARET HELEN CLAYTON (MRS. ALEXIUS M. KUHL), banker; b. Louisville, Aug. 22, 1908; d. Joseph Leonard and Maude (Mitzler) Clayton; student Loyola U. Home Study Div., Chgo., 1955—, Buena Vista Coll., Storm Lake, Ia., summer 1964-65, 66; m. Alexius M. Kuhl, Apr. 21, 1936; children—Carol Lynn (Mrs. Richard Benton Ford), James Michael (adopted). Sales lady, buyer Silverberg, Akron, Ia., 1924-34; owner dress shop, Fonda, Ia., 1934-40; librarian Fonda, 1940-43; bookkeeper, teller First Nat. Bank, Fonda, 1943-44; tchr. speech and drama, librarian asst. Our Lady Good Counsel Sch., Fonda, 1963-69; dir. Pomeroy State Bank. Recipient Adult Leadership award Cath. Youth Orgn., 1967, Pro Deo Juventute award, 1969. Mem. Cath. Daus. Am. (dist. dep. 1964-70, state chmn. ecumenism 1970-72, state treas. 1970-72), Diocesan Council Cath. Women (chmn. orgn. and devel. 1964-65), Nat. Council Cath. Women (diocesan pres. 1968-70, diocesan sec. 1966-67; chmn. Women in Community Service Sioux City Diocesan Bd. 1972-73), Internat. Platform Assn., Women in Community Service (pres. Ia. bd. 1971-72), Legion of Mary (pres. curia 1964-66, 67-70), Bus. and Profl. Women's Clubs, Marquis Library Assn., Intercontinental Biog. Assn. Club: Fonda Country. Home: Fifth and Queen Sts Fonda IA 50540

KUHLMANN, HELEN JUANITA, polit. party ofcl.; b. Vicksburg, Miss., July 22, 1926; d. Clarence Barron and Marye Ann (Cunningham) Huff; student La. State U., 1941-42; grad. Baton Rouge Bus. Coll., 1942; grad. Wilton Sch. Cake Decorating, 1959; m. Arthur Henry Kuhlmann, Nov. 11, 1945 (div.); children—Jeffrey David, Lynn Carol, Jack D'Owen, Richard Casey, Susan Anne, Barbee, Kris. Bus. machine operator, La., 1942-45; profl. cake decorator, instr., 1959-63; precinct committeewoman Wichita County, 1964-71; vice chmn. Wichita County Republican Central Com., 1966-70; chmn. Wichita County Central Com., 1971-72; 1st dist. dir. Kan. Fedn. Republican Women, 1966, state sec., 1967, 2d v.p., 1968-69, 1st vp., 1970-71, state pres., 1972-73; mem. exec. bd. Kan. Rep. State Com., 1972-73. Owner The H.K. Farm, Wichita County, Kan. Bd. dirs. Nat. Fedn. Rep. Women. Mem. Kan. Federated Women's Clubs (dist. officer 1968-69). Lutheran (tchr. coll.-age bible class 1961-66). Home: HK Farm Wichita County KS 67602

KUHN, ANNE NAOMI WICKER (MRS. HAROLD B. KUHN), educator; b. Lynchburg, Va.; d. George Barney and Annie (Hicks) Wicker; diploma Malone Coll., 1933, Trinity Coll. Music, London, 1937; A.B., John Fletcher Coll., 1939; M.A., Boston U., 1942; postgrad. (fellow) Harvard, 1942-44, 66-68, Boston U.; m. Harold B. Kuhn, June 11, 1934. Instr., Emmanuel Bible Coll., Birkenhead, Eng., 1936-37; asst. in history John Fletcher Coll., University Park, Ia., 1938-39; librarian Harvard U., 1939-44; tchr. adult edn. program U.S. Armed Forces, Fuerstenfeldbruck Air Base, Germany, 1951-52; prof. Union Bibl. Sem., Yeotmal, India, 1957-58; lectr. Armenian Bible Inst., Beirut, Lebanon, 1958; prof. German, Asbury Coll., Wilmore, Ky., 1962—. Del. Youth for Christ World Conf., 1948, 50, London Yearly Meeting of Friends, Edinburgh, Scotland, 1948, World Council Chs., Amsterdam, 1948, World Friends Conf., Oxford, Eng., 1952, World Methodist Conf., Oslo, Norway, 1961, Deutscher Kirchentag, Dortmund, Germany, 1963; participant Internat. Congress World Evangelization, Lausanne, Switzerland, 1974. Recipient German Consular award, Boston, 1965, Thomas Mann award Boston U., 1967. Fellow Goethe-Institut fur Germanisten, Munich, 1966-68; 70-71. Mem. Am. Assn. U. Women, Am. Assn. Tchrs. German, N.E.A., Ky. Ednl. Assn., Lincoln Lit. Soc., Delta Phi Alpha (award 1963, 65). Mem. Soc. of Friends. Author: (pamphlet) The Impact of the Transition to Modern Education Upon Religious Education, 1950; The Influence of Paul Gerhardt upon Wesleyan Hymnody, 1960. Home: 406 Kenyon Av Wilmore KY 40390

KUHN, BEATRICE HART, dermatologist and syphilologist; b. Cin., Feb. 12, 1919; d. Hornell Norris and Ella (Brockhausen) Hart; student U. Edinburgh, 1936-67, U. Heidelberg, 1937; A.B., Swarthmore Coll., 1939; m. Harold Hunter Kuhn, Mar. 3, 1943; children—Beatrice Brockhausen, Susan Lee, Virginia Laura. Intern Duke Hosp., 1943; research fellow medicine N.Y. U., 1944; research fellow 3d N.Y. U. med. div. Goldwater Meml. Hosp., N.Y., 1944; instr. dermatology and syphilology Duke U., 1944-46; pvt. practice medicine, specializing in dermatology, Charleston, W.Va., 1947—; chief subsect. dermatology Charleston Area Med. Center. Diplomate Am. Bd. Dermatology, Nat. Bd. Med. Examiners. Fellow Am. Acad. Dermatology; mem. A.M.A., W.Va., Monroe County, Fla., Kanawha County med. socs. Address: 3412 Staunton Av SE Charleston WV 25304

KUHN, BRENDA, estate mgr.; b. N.Y.C., June 13, 1911; d. Walt and Vera (Spier) Kuhn; student Friends Sem., N.Y.C., 1918-29. Co-mgr. Kuhn Estate, 1949-56, mgr., 1956-66; mgr. Estate of Brenda Kuhn, 1967—; pres. Kuhn Meml. Corp., 1969—; founder Cape Neddick Park, 1965, Kuhnhouse, Cape Neddick Park, 1967. Mem. State of Me. Art Commn., 1967-71. Trustee Nordica Meml. Assn. Mem. Am. Fedn. Arts, Archives Am. Art, Nat. Audubon Soc., numerous museums and art galleries, Smithsonian Assos., Nat. Trust for Historic Preservation, Friends of Art at Colby, Old York Improvement Soc., League Women Voters, Women's League York, Copley Soc. Boston, Guild Carilloneurs N. Am. Club: York Women's (pres. 1970-72), Yorksters. Home: Kuhnhouse Cape Neddick Park Cape Neddick ME 03902

KUHN, LUCILLE ROSS, naval officer; b. Washington, July 19, 1927; d. Lilburn Joseph and Flora Lee (Perry) Kuhn; A.A. with distinction, George Washington U., 1959, B.A., 1960. Ins. clk. Southwestern Life Ins. Co., Richmond, Va., 1945-48; joined U.S. Navy, 1949, advanced through grades to comdr., 1970; woman officer rep. 2d Navy Recruiting Area, Washington, 1963-65; U.S. Naval Security Sta., Washington, 1965-68; dir. mil. personnel 12th Naval Dist., San Francisco, 1968-70; mem. staff office asst. sec. def. for legislative affairs, Washington, 1971-74; dep. dir. Edn. and Tng. Center, Newport, 1974—. Aide de camp to Va. govs., 1960—. Decorated Nat. Def. Service medal with bronze star. Mem. Internat. Platform Assn., Smithsonian Assos., Psi Chi. Home: 2302 Kenmore Rd Richmond VA 23228 Office: Naval Edn and Tng Center Newport RI 02840

KUHNEN, S. MARIE, educator; b. Haledon, N.J., Sept. 12, 1917; d. Charles William and Sybil (Daniels) Kuhnen; B.A., Montclair State Tchrs. Coll., 1941; M.A., Columbia, 1946; Ph.D., N.Y.U., 1960. Tchr., Eastside High Sch., Paterson, N.J., 1941-44; teaching asst. botany Columbia, 1944-46; mem. faculty Montclair State Coll., 1946—, prof. biology, 1963—, chmn. dept., 1968—. Chmn. Valhalla Glen Purchase Com., 1963-67; sec.-treas. council Assn. N.J. State Coll. Faculties, 1962-67. Recipient Conservation award Summit Nature Soc., 1968. Fellow A.A.A.S.; mem. Bot Soc. Am., Nat. Sci. Tchrs. Assn. (life), Nature Conservancy, Nat. Audubon Soc., Wilderness Soc., Nat. Parks Assn., Kappa Delta Pi, Sigma Delta Epsilon. Home: 5 Charles Ct Clifton NJ 07013 Office: Biology Dept Montclair State Coll Upper Montclair NJ 07043

KUHNS, ANNE MCEWEN (MRS. L. JOHN KUHNS), realtor; b. Ault, Colo., Mar. 18, 1910; d. William Wilson and Emma Victoria (Heisel) McEwen; student Denver Bus. Coll., 1929; m. L. John Kuhns, June 19, 1929; children—Richard James, John Robert. Saleswoman, Rose Palmrose Realtor, Wofford Heights, Cal., 1957-63, Wofford Heights Realty, 1963-68; sales mgr. Frontier Realty Wofford Heights, 1968-69; Anne M. Kuhns realtor, Wofford Heights, 1969—. Owner, mgr. Double Dee Restaurant, Wofford Heights, 1956—. Mem. Nat. Assn. Real Estate Bds., Cal. Real Estate Assn., Cal. Real Estate Bd., Bus. and Profl. Women (chmn. 1958), C. of C. Baptist. Republican. Home: Box 57 Woodland Dr Wofford Heights CA 93285 Office: 7014 Wofford Blvd Wofford Heights CA 93285

KUJOTH, JEAN SPEALMAN (MRS. RICHARD K. KUJOTH), author; b. Champaign, Ill., Apr. 20, 1935; d. Max Lang and Dorothy Ruth (Flickinger) Spealman; B.A., U. Cal. at Berkeley, 1957; postgrad. U. Mich., 1957-59; M.A. in L.S., U. Wis., 1966; m. Richard K. Kujoth, Feb. 22, 1964. Mem. Phi Beta Kappa. Author: Readings in Nonbook Librarianship, 1968; Subject Guide to Periodical Indexes and Review Indexes, 1969; Libraries, Readers and Book Selection, 1969; Reading Interests of Children and Young Adults, 1970; The Teacher and School Discipline, 1970; Book Publishing: Inside Views, 1971; The Recreation Program Guide, 1972; Best Selling Children's Books, 1973. Home: 802 E State St Milwaukee WI 53208

KULAWIZ, JO ANNE KIELY (MRS. RUSSELL KULAWIZ), lawyer, judge; b. Derby, Conn., Jan. 24, 1935; d. Joseph Jerome and Anne Marie (Hart) Kiely; B.A. cum laude, Albertus Magnus Coll., 1956; J.D. (with honors), George Washington U., 1959; m. Russell Kulawiz, June 22, 1968. Admitted to Conn. bar, 1959, Fed. Ct. bar, 1961, U.S. Supreme Ct. bar, 1965; asso. firm Yudkin and Yudkin, Derby, 1959-63; partner firm Buckley, Kulawiz & Flynn and predecessors, Ansonia, Conn., 1963-72; corp. counsel City of Derby, 1967-72; judge Conn. Circuit Ct., 1972—. Counsel Valley Council Govts., 1971-72. Sec., dir. West Halifax Properties, Inc., 1967-72. Mem. adv. bd. Catholic Family Services, Valley chpt. A.R.C., Julia Day Nursery; sec., chmn. Ansonia Municipal Planning Commn., 1963-68; mem. Valley Regional Planning Agy., 1966-68. Vice chmn. Ansonia Republican Town Com., 1962-68; pres. Ansonia Rep. Women's Club, 1964; vice chmn. GOP-5, 1966-68. Mem. Am. Conn., Valley bar assns., Am. Arbitration Assn., Conn. Assn. Municipal Attys., Bus. and Profl. Womens Club, Phi Alpha Delta. Republican. Roman Catholic. Home and office: 984 Garden Rd Orange CT 06477

KULDAU, JANICE ELAINE MOYER (MRS. VON DEAN KULDAU), educator; b. Lima, O., Apr. 7, 1938; d. Carl Adrian and Beulah Grace (Roberts) Moyer; B.S., Manchester Coll., 1959; M.S., Ball State U., 1965, Ed.D., 1970; m. Von Dean Kuldau, July 24, 1960. Tchr., Wabash (Ind.) Pub. Schs., 1961-62, Speedway (Ind.) Pub. Schs., 1962-63, Muncie (Ind.) Pub. Schs., 1963-67; lectr. U. Minn., Duluth, 1968-69; asso. prof. psychology U. Wis., Superior, 1969—. Mem. Douglas County (Wis.) Mental Health Assn. Bd., 1970—; chmn. Superior-Univ. Com. on Chem. Dependency, 1972—. Mem. Nat. Assn. Sch. Psychologists, Am. Psychol. Assn. Home: 1 White Birch Trail Superior WI 54880

KULIK, BERNIECE HOPKINS (MRS. GEORGE KULIK), phychologist; b. Linn Creek, Mo., Oct. 14, 1924; d. Edward Everett and Hattie (Bangert) Hopkins; B.A., Okla. Coll. for Women, 1953; M.A., U. Denver, 1954, postgrad., 1961-62; postgrad. U. Wyo., 1960, Mont. State Coll., 1961-63; m. Ernest Clark Hollingsworth, June 8,

1946; m. 2d, George Kulik, July 5, 1973. Prin., tchr. Salem (Neb.) Pub. Schs., 1955-56, Nebraska City (Neb.) Pub. Schs., 1956; dir. guidance, tchr. Sunflower Consol. Sch. and Scottsbluff (Neb.) Coll., 1959-60; psychologist Scottsbluff Pub. Sch., 1961; testing supr., grad. asst. U. Denver, 1961; researcher in psychology Mont. State Coll., 1962; tchr., guidance counselor Genoa (Neb.) Pub. Schs., 1965-66; psychologist, dir. spl. edn. service unit #2, Fremont, Neb., 1967-78; office mgr. Univair Aircraft Corp., Denver, 1972—. Mem. Am. Psychol. Assn. (asso.) Home: 13606 E Bates Ave #305 Denver CO 80232

KULP, AIMEE KATHERINE, librarian; b. Mercersburg, Pa., Oct. 28, 1924; d. Benjamin Frank and Aimee (Fry) Kulp; A.B., Wilson Coll., 1946; B.S. in L.S., Drexel U., 1948. Clerical asst. Sterling Meml. Library, Yale, New Haven, 1946-47; serials librarian H. Firestone Meml. Library, Princeton, 1948-49; head librarian Mercersburg (Pa.) Acad., 1949—, instr. driver tng., 1972—. Mem. Chambersburg (Pa.) Hosp. Jr. Aux., 1973—. Recipient Best-of-Show award, also 1st prize Cumberland Valley Photog. Exhibit, 1960. Mem. Cumberland Valley Library Assn. (v.p. 1971-72). Mem. Order Eastern Star. Clubs: Avon Literary (sec. 1953-54, 60-61); Faculty Women's (pres. 1954). Home: 304 Johnston's Lane Mercersburg PA 17236 Office: Mercersburg Acad Mercersburg PA 17236

KULP, VIRGINIA KRAMER, educator; b. Tuttle, Okla., Aug. 6, 1910; d. Dexter Morris and Bertha Virginia (Hartin) Kramer; B.A., U. Okla., 1931; M.A., U. Tulsa, 1954, J.D., 1970; m. Albert G. Kulp, July 12, 1934; children—Victor K., Jon Albert. Owner Virginia Kramer Sch. Speech & Dance, Oklahoma City, 1929-40; counselor Tulsa Juvenile Ct., 1953-55; prof. sociology Tulsa Jr. Coll., 1970—; pvt. practice marriage, family problems counseling, Tulsa, 1971—; pres. Kulp Properties. Pres. Assistance League of Tulsa, 1972; pres. Pro America Womens Assn., 1958. Bd. dirs. Tulsa Planned Parenthood Assn., Tulsa Ballet Assn. Mem. Met. Opera Council, D.A.R. (mem. com. on Americanism 1962—, pres. 1974), Women in Communications, Phi Beta Kappa, Mortar Board, Alpha Kappa Delta, Kappa Kappa Gamma (pres. 1951-52), Tulsa Panhellenic (pres. 1961-62). Home: 1722 S Carson St Tulsa OK 74119 Office: University Club Towers Suite 2800 Tulsa OK 74119

KULPA, LORRAINE A., librarian; b. Buffalo, June 4, 1939; d. Stephen J. and Jane (Lewan) Kulpa; B.A., U. Buffalo, 1961; LL.B., State U. N.Y. at Buffalo, 1964; M.L.S., Syracuse U., 1965. Asst. reference librarian Los Angeles County Law Library, 1965-67; asst. law librarian Cornell Law Library, Ithaca, N.Y., 1967-71; legal staff librarian Gen. Motors Corp., Detroit, 1971—. Am. Assn. Law Libraries (chmn. directories com. 1970-72, editor newsletter 1974—), Am. Library Assn., Spl. Libraries, Internat. Assn. Law Libraries, Am. Soc. Information Specialists, League Women Voters, Nat. Orgn. for Women, Kappa Beta Pi. Editor: Biographical Directory of Law Librarians in the U.S. and Canada, 1971; The Kappa Beta Pi Quarterly, 1968—; editorial staff Law Library Jour. Home: 23560 Coach Light Dr Southfield MI 48075 Office: 3044 W Grand Blvd Detroit MI 48202

KULSRUD, HELENE ENID STEINMAN (MRS. RUSSELL MARION KULSRUD), computer scientist; b. N.Y.C., July 6, 1933; d. Edward and Mollie (Greenberg) Steinman; B.A. magna cum laude, Smith Coll., 1953; M.S., U. Chgo., 1954; m. Russell Marion Kulsrud, Nov. 6, 1955; children—Peter, Pamela, Suzanne. Programmer IBM, N.Y.C., 1954-55; head programmer Ednl. Testing Service, Princeton, N.J., 1956-57; mem. tech. staff RCA Labs., Princeton, 1957-66; research asso. Yale U., New Haven, 1966-67; sr. staff Aero. Research Assos. Princeton, Inc. 1967-68; mem. research staff Inst. Def. Analyses, Princeton, 1968—. Chmn. auction Smith Coll., 1970. Mem. Twp. Democratic Com., 1960-62. Mem. Assn. for Computing Machinery, Archeol. Soc. Am., Phi Beta Kappa, Sigma Xi. Hadassah. Club: Smith College (Princeton). Home: 16 Balsam Lane Princeton NJ 08540 Office: Inst Def Analyses 100 Prospect St Princeton NJ 08540

KUMAR, MARY LOUISE MORRISON (MRS. UNNI P. KUMAR), pediatrician; b. Chgo., Jan. 23, 1941; d. Donald Martin and Esther (Acton) Morrison; B.A., U. Colo., 1962; M.D., Case-Western Res. U., 1967; m. Unni P. Kumar, June 15, 1968; children—Krishna, Shanta. Intern pediatrics Cleve. Met. Gen. Hosp., 1967-68, resident, 1968-70, chief resident, 1970-71; teaching fellow, 1970-71, mem. staff, asst. pediatrician, 1971—; instr. pediatrics Case-Western Reserve U., 1971—. Mem. Am. Med. Women's Assn. Contbr. articles to profl. jours. Home: 2150 Harris Rd Broadview Heights OH 44147 Office: 3395 Scranton Rd Cleveland OH 44109

KUMIN, MAXINE WINOKUR (MRS. VICTOR MONTWID KUMIN), writer; b. Phila., June 6, 1925; d. Peter and Doll (Simon) Winokur; A.B., Radcliffe Coll., 1946, M.A., 1948; m. Victor Montwid Kumin, June 29, 1946; children—Jane Simon, Judith Montwid, Daniel David. Instr. English, Tufts U., 1958-61, lectr. English, 1965-68; lectr. English, Newton Coll. Sacred Heart, 1971—, U. Mass., Amherst, 1972; scholar Radcliffe Inst. Ind. Study, 1961-63; free-lance writer, 1953—. Nat. Council on Arts and Humanities grantee, 1967-68. Mem. Poetry Soc. Am. Author: Sebastian and the Dragon, 1960; (poems) Halfway, 1961; Spring Things, 1961; A Summer Story, 1961; Follow the Fall, 1961; A Winter Friend, 1961; Mittens in May, 1962; No One Writes A Letter to the Snail, 1962; (with Anne Sexton) Eggs of Things, 1963; More Eggs of Things, 1964; Archibald the Traveling Poodle, 1963; Speedy Digs Downside Up, 1964; The Beach Before Breakfast, 1964; Paul Bunyan, 1966; (poems) The Privilege, 1965; (novel) Through Dooms of Love, 1965; The Passions of 1971; Uxport, 1968; (juvenile) Faraway Farm, 1967, The Wonderful Babies of 1809, 1968; When Grandmother Was Young, 1969; When Mother Was Young, 1970; When Great Grandmother Was Young, 1971; (poems) The Nightmare Factory, 1970; (novel) The Abduction, 1971; (with Anne Sexton) Joey and the Birthday Present, 1971; (poems) Up Country, 1972 (Pulitzer prize for poetry 1973); The Designated Heir, 1974. Contbr. poems nat. mags. Address: care Curtis Brown Ltd 60 E 56 St New York City NY 10022

KUMMERFELD, CAROL ANN BONOSARO, govt. ofcl.; b. New Brunswick, N.J., Feb. 16, 1940; d. Rudolph W. and Elizabeth (Betsko) Bonosaro; B.A., Cornell U., 1961; postgrad, George Washington U., 1961-62; m. Donald D. Kummerfeld, Sept. 8, 1962 (div. Jan. 1970). Analytical statistician Bur. of Budget, Exec. Office of Pres., Washington, 1961-66; with U.S. Commn. on Civil Rights, Washington, 1966—, dir. tech. assistance div., 1969-72, spl. asst. to staff dir., 1972, dir. Women's Rights program, 1973—. Mem. membership budget com. Health and Welfare Council Nat. Capitol Area; adv. bd. Center for Resources on Instnl. Oppression. Democrat. Home: 2501 Calvert St NW Washington DC 20008 Office: 1121 Vermont Av NW Washington DC 20425

KUNDERT, ALICE E., state ofcl.; b. Java, S.D., July 23, 1920; d. Otto J. and Maria (Rieger) Kundert; elementary tchr.'s certificate No. State Coll., state tchr. certificate. Tchr. elementary grades, 1939-43, 48-54; clk., mgr., buyer Gates Dept. Store, Beverly Hills, Cal., Clifton Dress Shop, Hollywood, Cal., 1943-48; dep. supt. schs. Campbell County, S.D., 1954; county cts. clk., 1955-60; register deeds, 1955-69; town treas. Mound City, 1965-69; auditor State of S.D., Pierre, 1969—. Leader, 4-H Club, 1949-53, county project leader in citizenship, 1963-64; sec. Greater Campbell County Assn., 1955-57; organizer, leader Mound City Craft and Recreation Club, 1955-60; chmn. Heart Fund, March Dimes, Red Cross, Mental Health drives; mem. Gov.'s Study Commn., 1968—; mem. State and local adv. com. region VIII Office Econ. Opportunity; bd. mem., chmn. Black Hills Recreation Lab., 1956-61; exec. sec. Internat. Leaders Lab. Ireland, 1963. Polit. co. vice chmn. Republican Com., 1964-69, sec.-treas. finance chmn., 1968; mem. State Rep. Adv. Com., 1966-68; state and nat. counselor Teen Age Rep. Club Campbell County, 1964—. Home: 407 N Van Buren St Pierre SD 57501 Office: State Capitol Bldg Auditor Office Pierre SD 57501

KUNDSIN, RUTH BLUMFELD (MRS. EDWIN STANLEY KUNDSIN), microbiologist; b. N.Y.C., July 30, 1916; d. John David and Emily Anna (Krumin) Blumfeld; B.A., Hunter Coll., 1936; M.A., Boston U., 1948; D.Sc., Harvard, 1958; m. Edwin Stanley Kundsin, June 17, 1935; children—Andrea (Mrs. Thomas H. Dupree), Dennis. Microbiologist, Peter Bent Brigham Hosp., Boston, 1951—; with Harvard Med. Sch., 1962—, prin. asso. in microbiology and molecular genetics, 1968—. Diplomate Am. Bd. Microbiology. Fellow Am. Acad. Microbiology; mem. Am. Soc. Microbiology, A.A.A.S., N.Y. Acad. Sci., Phi Beta Kappa. Editor: Women & Success: The Anatomy of Achievement, 1974. Home: 71 Pratt Rd Squantum MA 02171 Office: 721 Huntington Av Boston MA 02115

KUNKLE, ETHEL WRIGHT, educator; b. Chgo., July 4, 1908; d. James Tweed and Bertha (John) Wright; B.S., Columbia, 1933; M.S. Northwestern U., 1938, Ed.D., 1955 1 dau., Karyl. Dir. pre-primary staff Winnetka (Ill.) Pub. Schs., 1939-42; prof. child devel. U. Wash., Sattle, 1942-44; child devel. specialist, dir. preschool activities Mayo Clinic, Rochester, Minn., 1944-46; prof. ednl. psychology, curriculum and devel. U. Wis., Milw., 1954—. Dir. Child Study Center, Am. Coll. Girls, Istanbul, Turkey, 1963-66; ednl. cons., Tehran, Iran, 1958-59. Dir. leadership devel. program Head Start, U. Wis., 1966-72. Recipient Best Pre-School Book award Am. Friends Lit., 1936. Mem. Assn. Childhood Edn. Internat., Am. Psychol. Assn., Winnetka Nursery Sch. Bd. (hon. life), Aldrich Meml. Nursery Sch. Bd. (Mayo Clinic; hon life), Delta Kappa Gamma, Pi Lambda Theta. Author: Saturday Walk, 1936; Saturday Ride, 1938; Saturday Flight, 1940; A Second Language Experience in Preschool, 1967; The Infant, 1969; The Four Year Old Experience, 2d edit., 1970. Home: 8307 N Greenvale Rd Milwaukee WI 53217

KUNSTADT, DOROTHY RUBINSTEIN (MRS. HERBERT KUNSTADT), physician; b. Stoczek, Poland, Mar. 16, 1936; d. Samuel and Hana (Graicer) Rubinstein; M.B., B.S., U. Melbourne (Australia), 1959, M.D., 1965; m. Herbert Kunstadt, Oct. 20, 1967. Came to U.S., 1966. Intern, Royal Melbourne (Australia) Hosp., 1960-61; resident, 1962-63; instr. medicine Harvard Med. Sch., Boston, 1966-68; jr. asso. in medicine Peter Bent Brigham Hosp., Boston, 1966-68; practice medicine, specializing in internal medicine, N.Y.C., 1968—; mem. staffs Lenox Hill Hosp., N.Y.C., Flower Fifth Fifth Avenue Hosp., N.Y.C.; asst. prof. medicine N.Y. Med. Coll., N.Y.C., 1968—. Diplomate Am. Bd. Internal Medicine. Fellow Royal Australian Coll. Physicians; mem. A.M.A., Am. Med. Woman's Assn., N.Y. State Med. Soc. Home: 500 E 77th St New York City NY 10021 Office: 107 E 85th St New York City NY 10028

KUNTZ, MARION LUCILE LEATHERS (MRS. PAUL G. KUNTZ), educator; b. Atlanta, Sept. 6, 1924; d. Otto Asa and Lucile (Parks) Leathers; B.A., Agnes Scott Coll., 1945; M.A., Emory U., 1964, Ph.D. (Am. Classical League scholar), 1969; children—Charles, Otto Alan (Daniels); m. 2d, Paul G. Kuntz, Nov. 26, 1970. Lectr. Latin, Lovett Sch., Atlanta, 1963-66; faculty Ga. State U., Atlanta, 1966—, asso. prof., 1969-73, prof. Latin and Greek, 1973—, acting chmn. fgn. lang. dept., 1974—. Am. Council Learned Socs. grantee, 1970. Named Latin Tchr. of Year, State Ga., 1965. Mem. Am. Philol. Assn., Renaissance Soc. Am., Archaeol. Inst. Am., Classical Assn. Midwest and South (Semple award 1965), Am. Assn. U. Profs., Am. Acad. Rome (sec., treas. 1970—), Italian Cultural Soc., Phi Beta Kappa. Roman Catholic. Club: Hellenic Study (pres. Atlanta 1974). Author: Colloquium of the Seven About Secrets of the Sublime of Jean Bodin 1974. Home: 1655 Ponce de leon Atlanta GA 30307

KUO, JANE CHEN-HSING LIAO (MRS. HENRY HSIN-SHENG KUO), librarian; b. Taiwan, July 1, 1936; d. Yu-fen and Chow (Yang) Liao; B.A. in Law, Nat. Taiwan U., 1959; M.L.S., Tex. Woman's U., 1964; m. Henry Hsin-sheng Kuo, Feb. 2, 1973. Came to U.S., 1962, naturalized, 1971. Tchr., Chin-ling Girls Middle Sch., Taiwan, 1959-61; catalog librarian Simpson Coll. Library, Indianola, Ia., 1964—. Mem. Internat. Platform Assn., A.L.A., Am. Hort. Soc., Am. Assn. U. Profs., Am. Assn. U. Women Club: Simpson Guild. Home: 501 E First Av Indianola IA 50125 Office: Simpson Coll Library Indianola IA 50125

KUPST, MARY JO, research psychologist; b. Chgo., Oct. 4, 1945; d. George Eugene and Winifred Mary (Hughes) Kupst; B.A., Loyola U., Chgo., 1967, M.A., 1969, Ph.D., 1972. Lectr. Loyola U., 1970-71; postdoctoral fellow community psychology U. Ill. Med. Center, Chgo., 1971-72; project dir. med. communication, div. child psychiatry Children's Meml. Hosp., Chgo., 1972—; instr. psychiatry/pediatrics Northwestern U. Med. Sch., 1973. Mem. Am. Psychol. Assn., Assn. Women in Psychology, Assn. Humanistic Psychology, Kappa Beta Gamma. Co-author article. Home: 902 W Wrightwood Av Chicago IL 60614 Office: 2300 Children's Plaza Chicago IL 60614

KURK, ANNA JEAN, govt. ofcl.; b. Anadarko, Okla., Apr. 7, 1927; d. Frederick Morris and Pearl (Thomas) Kurk; grad. high sch. Clk., Stanley H. Peavy Ins. & Real Estate, Graham, Tex., 1947-50, Pat Bryan Ins. Agy., Graham, 1950; clk. water tax depts. City of Graham, 1951-56, sec. to city mgr., 1956-58, 62-67, purchasing agt., 1967—; clk. Retail Mchts. Assn., Graham, 1958-62. Methodist. Club: Graham Credit Women's. Home: 804 Virginia St Graham TX 76046 Office: 429 4th St Graham TX 76046

KURKJIAN, ANN LEWKOWICZ DESANTIS (MRS. STEPHEN A. KURKJIAN), journalist; b. Schenectady, Aug. 27, 1946; d. Thaddeus B. and Jill (Young) Lewkowicz; B.A., St. Lawrence U., 1968; m. Stephen A. Kurkjian, Sept. 25, 1971; 1 dau., Erica Young. Reporter, Schenectady Gazette, 1968-70; reporter, Spotlight team researcher Boston Globe, 1970-71; publicity dir. Cahners Books, Boston, 1971-73. Recipient Pulitzer prize for spl. local reporting, 1972, Sigma Delta Chi award for pub. service journalism, 1972, New Eng. award for pub. service U.P.I., 1972. Mem. Schenectady Jr. League. Democrat. Home: 7 Highfield Rd Quincy MA 02169

KURLANDER, HONEY W. WACHTEL (MRS. NEALE KURLANDER), artist; b. Bklyn., Oct. 17, 1927; d. Charles B. and Sara (Alexander) Wachtel; certificate Pratt Inst., 1948; m. Neale Kurlander, June 25, 1949; children—Harold Michael, Susan Laurie. One man shows Gallerie Marcel Bernheim, Paris, Gallery, Hempstead, N.Y., Martey Gallery, North Bellmore, N.Y., Kaigado, Tokyo, Verzyl, Northport, N.Y., Country Art Gallery, Westbury, N.Y., Garden City Galleries Ltd., Union Am. Hebrew Congregations, N.Y.C., Adelphi. U., Garden City, N.Y., L.I. U.; exhibited in group shows Nat. Acad. Galleries (N.Y.), Smithsonian Instn., Heckscher Mus., Contemporary Arts Gallery, N.Y.C., others; represented in permanent collections C.W. Post Coll. Art Center, Greenvale, N.Y., Nassau Community Coll., Garden City, N.Y., Grumbacher, N.Y.C., L.I. U., Gregory Mus., Hicksville, N.Y. Tchr. painting East Meadow, N.Y., East Meadow High Sch., 1959—. Chmn., coordinator United Cerebral Palsy Art Show. Recipient 1st prize awards Country Art Gallery, 1961, others. Mem. Nassau County Art League, Nat. League Am. Pen Women (1st prizes 1961, 65, 67, 68, 69, 70, 71, 72, 73). Profl. Artists Guild, Artists Equity. Home: 303 Spruce Lane East Meadow NY 11554

KURLANDER, MICHELE STAGMAN (MRS. CLYDE KURLANDER), lawyer; b. St. Louis, July 20, 1944; d. Isadore J. and Bernice (Stein) Stagman; B.A., U. Mich., 1966; J.D., Northwestern U., 1969; m. Clyde Kurlander, June 15, 1968; 1 son, Eric Andrew. Admitted to Ill. bar, 1969; practiced in Chgo., 1969—; title examiner Chgo. Title & Trust Co., 1969-70; asso. firm Walsh, Case & Coale, 1970—. Dir. Michnan Corp. Vol. campaign for Ill. Constl. Conv., 1969-70; mem. Lawyer's Com. to End War in Vietnam. Mem. Am., Ill. bar assns. Office: 104 S Michigan Chicago IL 60603

KURSHAN, MYRA, psychoanalyst; b. Port Angles, Wash., Mar. 26, 1912; d. Charles and Bertha (Siegel) Shallit; B.A., U. Wash., 1935; diploma social work N.Y. Sch. Social Work, 1939; certificate Inst. Psychoanalytic Tng. and Research, 1969; m. Daniel L. Kurshan, Feb. 24, 1940; 1 son, Robert. Social worker, asst. to county supr. Wash. State Dept. Social Welfare, 1934-36; successively guidance worker, supr., borough supr. Jewish Bd. Guardians, N.Y.C., 1939-49; mem. faculty N.Y. Sch. Social Work, 1947-48; guidance cons. and therapist for dir. tchrs., children, parents, Jewish Community Nursery Sch., Gt. Neck Nursery Sch., 1948-49, 53-57; asso. Dr. P. Glauber, N.Y.C., 1953-64; pvt. practice psychotherapy, N.Y.C., 1964—; mem. faculty Inst. Psychoanalytic Tng. and Research, 1972—, chmn. faculty dept., 1973—, mem. bd., 1973—. Fellow Am. Orthopsychiat. Assn., Inst. Psychoanalytic Tng. and Research; mem. Nat. Assn. Social Workers, Council Psychoanalytic Psychotherapists. Home: Tibbits Lane Sands Point NY 11050 Office: 59 E 79th St New York City NY 10021

KURTIS, ARLENE VIVIAN (MRS. ALAN A. KURTIS), editor; b. N.Y.C., May 29, 1927; d. Arthur Hilton and Estelle Bernice (Applebaum) Harris; student U. Wis., 1945-47; B.A., N.Y. U., 1948; m. Alan A. Kurtis, Apr. 8, 1951;children—Fran Abby, Jonathan Baylor. Editor, Hillman Periodicals, N.Y.C., 1949-51; free lance writer, 1952-71; editor Wisdoms Child West Side Neighborhood Guide, N.Y.C., 1971-73; mem. editorial staff The City Record, N.Y.C., 1973—. Substitute tchr. social studies jr. high schs., Manhattan, 1965-66. Committeewoman N.Y. County Democratic Party, 1958-66. Jewish religion. Author: Puerto Ricans from Island to Mainland, 1969; The Jews Helped Build America, 1970. Home: 12 W 96th St New York City NY 10025 Office: 2223 Municipal Bldg New York City NY 10025

KURTZ, FREDA GRACE WITHEROW (MRS. CARROL T. KURTZ), operations research analyst; b. Kirksville, Mo., Nov. 23, 1919; d. Fred and Maude (Goldsberry) Witherow; B.S. in Bus., N.E. Mo. State U., 1942; M.A. in Econs. (Haggin fellow), U. Ky., 1946; postgrad. U. Mich., summer 1965, 69, 71, Ohio State U., summer 1964, U. Colo., 1972; m. Carrol T. Kurtz, May 29, 1948, children—Nancy Eleanor, Russell Carrol. Analytical statistician Hdqrs. Air Force Materiel Command, Wright-Patterson AFB, Dayton, O., 1948-54; mgmt. operations analyst Hdqrs. Air Force Logistics Command, Wright-Patterson AFB, 1954-61; mgmt. analyst Hdqrs. Air Force Systems Command, Andrews AFB, Washington, 1961; operations research analyst and financial specialist Aero. Systems div. Wright-Patterson AFB, 1961-73, operations research analyst Air Force Avionics Lab., 1973—. Instr., Braymer (Mo.) High Sch., 1943-44; instr. mgmt. Sinclair Community Coll., Dayton, 1973—; U. Colo. 1973. Mem. P.T.A., 1958—; Cub Scout den mother Miami Valley council Boy Scouts Am., 1965-67; mem. Incentive Awards Evaluation Panel, 1972—. Co-recipient Unit Presdl. citation, 1965, Outstanding Unit award Air Force, 1966; recipient Sustained Superior Performance rating and cash award Aero. Systems div. Wright-Patterson AFB, 1966-67, 69-70, various other Air Force letters commendation. Mem. Am. Statis. Assn. (pres. Dayton chpt. 1962-63), Operations Research Soc. Am., Am. Soc. Pub. Adminstrn., Federally Employed Women (treas. Miami Valley chpt. 1972-73, auditor 1973—, mem. exec. bd.), Alpha Phi Sigma, Pi Omega Pi, Kappa Delta Pi. Baptist (pres. Sunday sch. class 1967-68, gen. sec. Sunday sch. 1968-70, Sunday sch. tchr. 1973-74). Contbr. articles to profl. jours. Home: 2654 N Gettysburg Av Dayton OH 45406 Office: US Air Force Avionics Laboratory Wright-Patterson AFB OH 45433

KURTZ, HELEN GRAHAM, univ. library adminstr.; b. New Castle, Pa., 1913; d. Edward Frampton and Gertrude Diman (Graham) Kurtz; B.A., U. No. Ia., 1935; M.A., U. Denver, 1948. Documents librarian Brown U., Providence, 1947-68; chief library extension services R.I. Dept. State Library Services, Providence, 1968-71; chief tech. services Brown U. Library, Providence, 1971—. Vice pres. Fox Point Community Orgn., 1973—, pres., 1974. Mem. Am., R.I. library assns., New Eng. Tech. Services Librarians, Providence Preservation Soc., R.I. Hist. Soc. Club: Camera (R.I.). Home: 181 Williams St Providence RI 02906 Office: Brown Univ Library Providence RI

KUSHNER, SANDRA REITER (MRS. LOUIS B. KUSHNER), lawyer; b. Wheeling, W.Va., Oct. 11, 1942; d. S. Robert and Sarah Rebecca (Edelman) Reiter; student Am. U., 1963; B.A. cum laude, Case Western Res. U., 1964; J.D., U. Pitts., 1967; m. Louis B. Kushner, June 29, 1969; children—Jason Harley, Ashley Shoop. Admitted to Pa. bar, 1967, W.Va. bar, 1967; law clk. to Judge Ruggero Aldisert, 3d Circuit Ct. Appeals, Pitts., 1967-68; practiced in Pitts., 1968—; asso. mem. firm Thomson, Rhodes & Grigsby, 1968-70; staff atty. Neighborhood Legal Services Assn., 1970—. Chmn. Study on Juvenile Justice System Allegheny County (Pa.), 1973; mem. welfare and juvenile task force for Pitts. Model Cities Program, 1971-72; mem. United Mental Health and Retardation Task Force study on proposed uses for juvenile detention home, 1973-74. Bd. dirs. St. Peter's Child Devel. Center. Mem. Nat. Assn. Women Lawyers (juvenile law and procedure com. 1971-72), Allegheny County Bar Assn. (chmn. exec. com. Young Lawyers sect. 1973-74), Am. Judicature Soc., Nat. Council Jewish Women (nat. affairs com. 1973, Pa. legislative chmn. 1973), Case-Western Res. U. Alumni Assn. (Pitts. area coordinator 1972-74). Home: 13 Dunmoyle Pl Pittsburgh PA 15217 Office: 3603 Bates St Pittsburgh PA 15213

KUYKENDALL, PENELOPE LATTIMER (MRS. EDWARD T. KUYKENDALL, JR.), sch. adminstr.; b. Long Branch, N.J., Feb. 26, 1947; d. James C. and Mariagnes M. (Minor) Lattimer; B.A., Montclair State Coll., 1968, M.A., 1970; postgrad. Union Grad. Sch., Yellow Springs, O., 1973-74; m. Edward T. Kuykendall, Jr., Nov. 27, 1971. Counselor, Georgian Court Coll., Lakewood, N.J., 1968-69; dir. urban grad. program Montclair State Coll., Upper Montclair, N.J., 1969-70; asso. dean student Bloomfield (N.J.) Coll., 1970-71; dir. Gibbons Sch., New Brunswick, 1972—. Soloist with N.Y.C. Ballet Co., 1959-64. Budget chmn. N.J. State Commn. on Women, 1973—. Mem. Am. Assn. U. Women, Nat. Assn. Student Personnel Adminstrs., N.J. State Adminstrs. Guild, N.J. Secondary Sch. Tchrs. Assn. (trustee 1973—), East Brunswick Women's Caucus, Alumni

Assn. Monmouth Council of Girl Scouts (pres. 1969-71). Home: 2 Civic Center East Brunswick NJ 08816 Office: Gibbons School Cabin at Douglass College New Brunswick NJ 08816

KUYLER, PAULINE (MRS. BENJAMIN H. KUYLER), physician; b. Bklyn., Jan. 1, 1937; d. Samuel and Florence (Loeb) Lorvan; A.B., Goucher Coll., 1957; postgrad. U. Chgo., 1958-59; M.D. U. Ill. at Chgo., 1966; m. Benjamin H. Kuyler, June 25, 1972; 1 son, Raphael Philip. Biostatistician N.Y. State Dept. Health, Albany, N.Y., 1957-58; statistician U.S. R.R. Retirement Bd., Chgo., 1959-60; biochemist, technician Chgo. Med. Sch., 1963-64; intern Johns Hopkins Hosp., Balt., 1966-67; resident psychiatry Presbyn. St. Luke's Hosp., Chgo., 1967-69; practice gen. medicine Martin Luther King Neighborhood Health Center, Chgo., 1969-71; resident child psychiatry Children's Meml. Hosp., Chgo., 1971-72; resident psychiatry Meyer-Manhattan Psychiat. Hosp., N.Y.C., 1972—. Research asst. genetics Dept. Preventive Medicine, U. Ill., 1969-71. Bd. dirs. West Side Health Planning Orgn., Chgo., 1970-71. Mem. Am. Med. Women's Assn. Home: 65-02 Utopia Parkway Flushing NY 11365

KUZAWA, SISTER MARY GRACE, educator; b. Springfield, Mass., Feb. 11, 1918; d. John and Stella (Ciborowska) Kuzawa; B.A., St. John's U., 1953; M.A., Fordham U., 1957; Ph.D., N.Y. U., 1966. Chmn. math. dept. Holy Family Coll., Phila., 1957-70, prof. math., 1970—. NSF grantee, 1968, 69, 70, 71, 72. Mem. Math. Assn. Am., Nat. Council Tchrs. Math., Kappa Mu Epsilon. Author: Modern Mathematics: The Genesis of A School In Poland, 1968. Home: Grant and Frankford Aves Philadelphia PA 19114

KVINGEDAL, PAULINE ELVA LORENSEN (MRS. EARL JOHN KVINGEDAL), coop. exec.; b. Cambridge, Mass., June 19, 1931; d. Joseph Nectar and Helga Pontoria (Helstrom) Lorensen; student Academie Moderne, 1957, Harvard U., 1965, Emerson Coll., 1967; m. Earl John Kvingedal, Oct. 14, 1950; children—Donna Lee, DeAnne Leslie. With Promotions, Inc., Boston, 1955-66; display dir., designer William Filenes, Boston, 1963-65; buyer jr. and women's dept. Harvard Coop. Soc., Cambridge, 1966—. Pub. speaker to various schs., chs., clubs, bus. and social orgns. Vol. tchr., worker Salvation Army, 1950-68. Mem. Evangelical Free Ch. (pres. ladies guild 1954-58, v.p. women's club 1969-71). Home: 41 Shade St Lexington MA 02173 Office: 1400 Massachusetts Av Cambridge MA 02138

KWITNY, MARTHA KAPLAN (MRS. JONATHAN KWITNY), lawyer; b. Perth Amboy, N.J., Oct. 5, 1944; d. Isadore and Diana (Jaffe) Kaplan; B.A. (Nat. Merit scholar), Radcliffe Coll., 1966; J.D., Harvard, 1969; m. Jonathan Kwitny, June 2, 1968; children—Carolyn Ann, Susanna Lynn. Admitted to N.J. bar, 1969; asst. dep. pub. defender, Newark, 1971-72; staff atty., central appellate staff N.J. Ct. System, Trenton, 1973-74; asst. prosecutor Union County (N.J.), Elizabeth, 1974—. Recipient study grant Nat. Student Assn., 1965. Mem. Phi Beta Kappa. Home: 110 Cranford Av Cranford NJ 07016 Office: Prosecutor's Office Union County Courthouse Elizabeth NJ

KYBAL, ELBA GOMEZ DEL REY DE, economist; b. Santa Fe, Argentina, Apr. 1, 1915; d. Jose Ignacio and Concepcion (del. Rey) Gomez; came to U.S., 1942; A.B., Universidad del Litoral, Argentina, 1942; A.M., Radcliffe Coll., 1945, Ph.D. in Econs., 1946; m. Milic Kybal, July 16, 1950; children—Cynthia, Alexander. Economist, Fed. Res. Bank, N.Y., 1946-47; economist UN, N.Y., 1947-56; econ. integration adviser OAS Secretariat, Washington, 1956—. Mem. UN Tech. Assistance Mission to Haiti, 1948; liaison UN to Latin Am. fiscal authorities, 1948; secretariat mem. UN Gen. Assembly, Paris, 1951; secretariat mem. econ. conf. of orgn. of Am. States, Buenos Aires, 1957; secretariat mem. Com. of 21 of Operation Pan Am., 1958-60, Inter-Am. Econ. and Social Council, Lima, Peru, 1965, Buenos Aires, 1966, Vina del Mar, 1967, Port of Spain, 1968; mem. spl. com. Latin Am. Coordination Comml. Policies, Alta Gracia, Argentina, 1964, others; mem. Internat. Coffee Orgn. Missions, El Salvador, Trinidad and Tobago, Dominican Republic, 1965, Nicaraguq, Guatemala, 1965; secretariat mem. XI Meeting Consultation Fgn. Ministers, Washington, Buenos Aires, Punta del Este, 1967; Meeting Chiefs of States, Punta del Este, 1967; dir. Econ. Integration Seminars, Tegucigalpa 1969, Lima, 1970, Santiago de Chile, 1970, 71, Montevideo, Lima, Buenos Aires, 1972, Santo Domingo, 73; adviser 1A Commn. Women. lectr. writer. Elizabeth Cary Agassiz fellowship, 1942-43, fellowships at Radcliffe Coll., 1943-45. Mem. Am. Econ. Assn., Potomac Bus. and Profl. Women's Club, Phi Beta Kappa. Contbr. to vars. UN and OAS publs. Home: 10806 Alloway Dr Potomac MD 20854 Office: OAS 1725 I St NW Washington DC 20006

KYES, HELEN (MRS. ROGER M. KYES), civic leader; b. Marion, O., Dec. 28, 1904; d. Benjamin and Bess (Gilmore) Jacoby; B.A. Oberlin Coll., 1926; m. Roger M. Kyes, June 5, 1931; children—Carolyn, Frances, Katharine, Anne. Mem. bd. Woman's Nat. Farm and Garden, 1943-56, sec., 1943-45, 54-55; bd. dirs. Children's Aid and Home for the Friendless, 1949-69; bd. dirs. Brookside Sch., Cranbrook, 1953-58, sec., 1957-58; charter mem. bd. trustees Mich. State U. Oakland Found., 1957-70; v.p. exec. bd. Oakland U. Found., 1958—; trustee U. Oakland; mem. Woman's Assn. Detroit Symphony; com. 100 Detroit Met. Opera; capt. spl. gifts Detroit United Fund, 1959-61; mem. Detroit Mus. Art Founders Soc., mem. com. Detroit Foster Home Edn. and Recruitment Program, 1960—. Mem. D.A.R., Am. Assn. U. Women. Presbyn. (vice moderator deacons). Club: Village Woman's. Home: 945 Cranbrook Rd Bloomfield Hills MI 48013 also 6861 N Ocean Blvd Delray Beach FL 33444

KYKER, MARY MAE, librarian; b. Telford, Tenn., Mar. 7, 1925; d. Alva Burney and Ada Mae (Garvin) Kyker; B.A., Tusculum Coll., Tenn. 1948; M.A., East Tenn. State U., 1972. Tchr. librarian Baileyton High Sch., Greeneville, Tenn., 1948-57; librarian Washington Coll. (Tenn.) Acad., 1957-71; head librarian David Crockett High Sch., Jonesboro, Tenn., 1971—. Librarian Vernon Brethren Ch., Telford, Tenn. Recipient citation Washington Coll. Acad., 1971. Mem. Nat., Tenn., East Tenn., Washington County edn. assns., Southeastern, Tenn., Washington County library assns., Boone Tree Library Club. Home: Rural Route 1 Box 478 Telford TN 37690 Office: Rural Route 6 Jonesboro TN 37659

KYLE, JANET ELIZABETH (MRS. DAVID MCVICKER KYLE), charm sch. exec.; b. Portland, Ore., Aug. 14, 1918; d. Walter Berkeley and Minnie Elizabeth (Naylor) Hinkle; B. Secretarial Sci. (Union Pacific scholar), Ore. State U., 1939; m. David McVicker Kyle, May 4, 1940; children—Michaele (Mrs. Warren W. Leitch), Kris (Mrs. William L. Ross Jr.), David Magnus. Sec. Bonneville Power Adminstrn., Portland, Ore., 1939-40; columnist Mil. Press, Honolulu, 1963-65; owner, directress Turnabout Modeling Sch. and Agy., Stuart, Fla., 1971—. Active numerous civic orgns. Mem. Nat. League Am. Pen Women, Women in Communications, Modeling Assn. Am., Stuart C. of C., Phi Chi Theta, Mortar Bd., Alpha Chi Omega. Republican. Home: 428 Cocoanut Point Rd Stuart FL 33494 Office: 276 Flagler Av Stuart FL 33494

LAANO, MARIA ELEAZAR (MRS. ARCEO M. LAANO), physician, allergist; b. Lucban, Quezon, Philippines, May 25, 1939; d. Mariano V. and Belen (Pandeno) Eleazar; A.A., U. Santo Tomas (Philippines), 1957, M.D., cum laude, 1962; m. Arceo M. Laano, May 2, 1964; 1 dau., Sylvia Marie. Came to U.S., 1963. Adj. resident in pediatrics U. Santo Tomas Hosp., Manila, Philippines, 1962-63; rotating intern Hosp. of St. Raphael, New Haven, 1963-64; jr., sr. resident pediatrics Grasslands hosp., Valhalla, N.Y., 1965-67; fellow pediatric allergy L.I. Coll. Hosp., Bklyn., 1967-69; asso. fellow pediatric allergy Kings County Med. Center, Bklyn., 1967-69; attending allergist/pediatrician Nassau County Med. Center, East Meadow, N.Y., 1969—; dir. Allergy Testing Center, Hempstead, N.Y. Diplomate Am. Bd. Pediatrics. Mem. Am. Med. Women's Assn., Pan Am. Med. Assn., N.Y. Allergy Soc., Nassau County Med. Soc., Nassau Acad. Medicine, Med. Soc. N.Y., Yale-New Haven Philippine Assn., Philippine Med. Assn., Grasslands Alumni Assn., Am. Acad. Allergy. Home: 80 Stratford Av Garden City NY 11530 Office: 54 Main St Allergy Testing Center Hempstead NY 11550

LAATZ, MARY JANE, med. librarian; b. Indpls., Dec. 27, 1916; d. Jacob Philip and Nell (Carey) Laatz; A.B., Butler U., 1938; B.S. in L.S., Western Res. U., 1939. Librarian, Ind. U. Extension Div., Indpls., 1939-41; cataloger Ind. U. Sch. Medicine Library, 1941-51, reference librarian, 1951, 53-57, acting librarian, 1951-53, med. librarian, 1957—, asst. prof. med. lit., 1957-72, asso. prof. med. lit., 1973—. Chmn. Council of Midwest Regional Health Scis. Library and Coop. Information Services, 1968-70; participant Conf. on Interlibrary Communication Network, A.L.A, and U.S. Office Edn., 1970; Ind. U. rep. ednl. communications network study EDUCOM, 1966. Mem. Spl. Libraries Assn. (chpt. pres. 1960-61), Med. Library Assn. (mem. scholarship com. 1972-74, chmn. 1973-74), John Shaw Billings History Medicine Soc. (sec.-treas. 1965-67), Indpls. Symphony Soc., Delta Gamma. Presbyn. Contbr. articles to profl. jours. Home: 6824 Willow Rd Indianapolis IN 46220 Office: 1100 W Michigan St Indianapolis IN 46202

LABECKI, GERALDINE, univ. dean; b. Bklyn.; d. M. Gerard and Seraphina (Juskowska) Labecki; R.N., Hartford (Conn.) Hosp. Sch. Nursing, 1939; B.S. (Hartford Hosp. Alumnae scholar), Columbia, 1944, M.A. (Isabel Hampton Robb scholar), 1948; Ed.D., George Peabody Coll. Tchrs., 1967. Gen. staff nurse, asst. head nurse Hartford Municipal Hosp., 1939-42; asst. dir. sch. nursing, nursing service Mary Fletcher Hosp., Burlington, Vt., 1944-48, dir. sch. nursing, nursing service, 1948-56; asso. prof. Vanderbilt U., Nashville, 1956-68, asst. dean sch. nursing, 1965-68; dean, prof. nursing Clemson (S.C.) U., 1968—. Campaign worker Nashville Community Concerts Assn.; mem. exec. com. S.C. Bd. Health, 1970—, vice chmn., 1973; chmn. Pickens County Health Council, 1974—; mem. exec. com. Appalachian Health Council, 1974—; mem. S.C. Statewide Master Planning Com. for Nursing. Campaign worker Davidson County Democratic Com. Recipient medal D.A.R., 1935. USPHS fellow, 1963-64; Vanderbilt U. Sch. Nursing Alumnae scholar, 1965. Mem. Am., S.C. (council on practice 1972—) nurses assns., League Women Voters, Vt. League Nursing Edn. (pres. 1948-52), Nat., Vt. (pres. 1952-56), Tenn. (pres. 1958-62, dir. 1962-64, S.C. leagues for nursing, Am. Assn. U. Women, Am. Assn. U. Profs., So. Hist. Soc., Am. Pub. Health Assn., S.C. Council on Human Relations, Sigma Theta Tau, Kappa Delta Pi, Gamma Phi Beta, Delta Kappa Gamma. Home: 227 Lark Circle Clemson SC 29631

LABER, MARIAN ROBERTA OPPENHEIM (MRS. LAWRENCE E. LABER), real estate broker; b. Hanford, Cal., Jan. 18, 1918; d. Leon and Isabelle (Estrada) Oppenheim; student San Francisco City Coll., 1966, Golden Gate Coll., 1969; m. Lawrence E. Laber, Feb. 22, 1941; children—Lawrence E., Pamela, Deborah (Mrs. Thomas McDermott), James Harrison. Telephone operator Pacific Tel. & Tel. Co., 1936-39, instr., 1940-42; mgr. office Press Wireless, Washington, 1942-43; owner Marian Lawrence, children's shop, San Francisco, 1945-48; owner, mgr. San Bruno 5-10, San Francisco, 1947-50; girl Friday Lampley Realty, San Francisco, 1968-72, owner, real estate broker, 1972—. Active Boy Scouts Am., Girl Scouts U.S.A., Camp fire Girls; pres. local P.T.A., 1954-55. Trustee Drew Coll. Prep. Sch. Mem. A.R.C., Am. Cancer Soc., San Francisco Real Estate Bd., Cal. Real Estate Assn., Roman Catholic (pres. ch. group 1950-51). Home: 1367-35th Av San Francisco CA 94122 Office: 2101 Pine St San Francisco CA 94115

LABERGE-COLAS, REJANE (MRS. EMILE JULES COLAS), superior ct. judge; b. Montreal, Que., Can.; d. Louis Xiste and Isabelle (Lefebvre) Laberge; B.A. cum laude, Marguerite-Bourgeoys, 1943; Licence in law, U. Montreal, 1951; D.C.L. honoris causa, Bishop U., 1971; m. Emile Jules Colas, Oct. 25, 1958; children—Bernard, Hubert, Francois. Admitted to Que. bar, 1952; legal dept. Aluminum Secretariat, Ltd., Montreal, 1952-57; practiced in Montreal, 1957-69; mem. firm Geoffrion & Prud'homme, 1957-69; apptd. judge Superior Ct., Montreal, 1969—. Mem. revision com. Civil Code of Province of Que., 1964-70; mem. Pub. Security Commn. City of Montreal, 1962-68. Bd. govs. U. Montreal, 1970—. Mem. Canadian Bar Assn. (sect. chmn. 1967-68), Que. Fedn. Women (pres. 1966-67). Roman Catholic. Clubs: Women Canadian, University Womens. Home: 18 Ainslie Av Outremont PQ Canada Office: Superior Court House 1 E Notre Dame St Montreal PQ Canada

LABIN, SUZANNE ANDREE DEVOYON (MRS. EDOUARD LABIN), author; b. Paris, France, May 6, 1913; d. Louis and Eugenie (Leplatre) Devoyon; M.S., U. Paris, 1935, Degree Advanced Social and Internat. Studies, 1936; m. Edouard Labin, April 4, 1935. Journalist, lectr. in French, English, Spanish; author; chmn. League of Freedom, 1962—. Internat. Conf. on Polit. Warfare, 1960—. Mem. for France, World Anti-Communist League, 1963—. Author numerous books including: Stalin's Russia, 1950; The Ant Hill, The Human Condition in Communist China, 1958; The Technique of the Soviet Propaganda (U.S. Senate best seller); Counter-Attack, 1963; Embassies of Subversion, 1964; Le Colonialisme Chinois En Afrique, 1965; Red Foxes in the Chicken Coop, 1966; Sellout in Vietnam?, 1966; Chinese Threat in Asia, 1967; Fifty Years—The USSR vs. The U.S.A., 1968; Promise and Reality, 1968; The Red Book of Mao-Guerilla pays, 1969; Hippies, Drugs and Promiscuity, 1972. Address: 3 rue Thiers Paris 16 France

LABINE, PATRICIA ANNE, educator; b. Springfield, Mass., June 25, 1939; d. Roland A. and Marguerite A. (Faille) Labine; B.A., Mt. Holyoke Coll., 1961; Ph.D., Stanford, 1966. Postdoctoral fellow biomed. data processing U. Mich., 1966-68; asst. prof. dept. biology Williams Coll., Williamstown, Mass., 1968-72; mem. teaching staff William James Coll., Grand Valley State Colls., Allendale, Mich., 1972—. Mem. Ecol. Soc. Am., A.A.A.S. Home: 13704 Lincoln St Grand Haven MI 49417 Office: William James Coll Allendale MI 49401

LABORDE, SANDRA CATHERINE, psychometrist; b. Alexandria, La., Dec. 4, 1943; d. Philip and Eola Marie (Moreau) Laborde; student U. Rennes, St. Malo, France, 1964; B.A. in Sociology U. St. Thomas, 1965; M.S. in Psychology, U. Southwestern La., 1974. Researcher, Rice U. Fund Raising Campaign, Houston, 1965-66; research asst. S.W. Research Inst., Houston, 1966-68; bond underwriter Hartford Ins. Co., Hartford, Conn., 1968-70; psychologist psychology dept. Pinecrest State Sch. for Retarded, Pineville, La., 1970-72. Mem. Nat. Honor Soc. in Psychology, Council for Devel. for French in La., Am. Assn. Mental Deficiency, Psi Chi. Democrat. Roman Catholic. Home: 3915 Pecan Dr Alexandria LA 71301

LABRAKE, ORLYN BARRON (MRS. RICHARD F. LABRAKE), librarian; b. Bridgeport, Conn., Sept. 2, 1930; d. Robert Eglington and Minerva Crowell (Rogers) Barron; B.A. in Psychology, Skidmore Coll., 1955; summer student, U. Wis., 1951; M.S. in L.S., State U. N.Y. at Albany, 1967; m. Richard F. LaBrake, June 30, 1950; children—Bruce, Brian, Marcia. Grad. asst. charge library reading dept. Sch. Edn., State U. N.Y. at Albany, 1966-67; cataloging librarian Rensselaer Poly. Inst., 1967-68, head cataloging dept., 1968-71, chmn. library com., librarian in charge, 1970-71, asst. to dir., 1972-73, asst. dir. libraries, 1973—. Chmn. circulation com. Capital Dist. Library Council, 1973—, trustee, 1974—. Mem. expansion council 4-H Club, 1970-72, leader, 1969-70, 72-73. Mem. N.Y. State, Hudson-Mohawk library assns. Home: 13 Hidley Extension Troy NY 12180

LABRIE, ROSE CUSHING (MRS. ALFRED A. LABRIE), artist, writer; b. Boston, Aug. 31, 1916; d. James and Christine (Campbell) Cushing; grad. Margaret's Sch. Beauty Culture, 1934; student U. N.H., 1944-45, creative writing U. N.H., 1954, 55-56, U. Wis., 1958-59; m. Alfred A. Labrie, Nov. 29, 1934; children—James, Raymond, Christy Anne. Beautician, Margaret's Sch. of Beauty, Concord, N.H., 1934-35; owner Rose Ramona's Beauty Shoppe, Concord, 1936-37; free-lance writing, 1947—; press photographer Religious News Service in N.Y.C., 1954—; corr. World Press Assn., London, Eng., 1957-58. Primitive artist, 1965—; one-man shows Pease AFB, Portsmouth, N.H., 1966, 67, York, Me., 1965-67, Strawbery Banke, 1965, 66, Hampton, N.H., 1966, N.Y.C., 1971; paintings in pvt. collections. Dir. art exhibits for Strawbery Banke, Inc., Portsmouth, N.H., 1966—. Recipient first prize in Portsmouth Art Exhbn., 1965; Herald Tribune Fresh Air Contest (photo category), 1954-55. Mem. Armed Forces Writer's League, York Writer's, Piscataqua Pens Writers (dir.), Portsmouth Art Assn., Copley Soc. of Boston. Club: Piscataqua History. Author: History of Cape Neddick Light Station, Nubble Light, 1958; The Story of Pemaquid Light, 1961; Dancer's Image, 1969. Address: 127 Middle Rd Portsmouth NH 03801

LABRIOLA, MARY CARYL CONDRAN (MRS. JOSEPH CHARLES LABRIOLA), journalist; b. Nevada City, Cal., Apr. 7, 1944; d. Jeremiah James and Cathryn Adele (Riseborough) Condran; B.A., St. Mary's Coll., 1967; M.A., U. Notre Dame, 1968; m. Joseph Charles LaBriola, Aug. 5, 1967. Tchr., St. Joseph Elementary Sch., South Bend, Ind., 1967, Immaculate Conception Elementary Sch., Dayton, O., 1968-69; asso. editor Discover mag., Dayton, 1969-70; religion writer Jour. Herald, Dayton, 1970—; also corr. Religious News Service. Mem. Religion Newswriters Assn., Dayton Women's Liberation. Home: 1305 Harvard Blvd Dayton OH 45406 Office: Journal Herald 4th and Ludlow Sts Dayton OH 45401

LACASSE, MARIE LOUISE, home economist; b. Abbeville, La., Feb. 21, 1911; d. Albert Joseph and Marie Louise (LeGuenec) LaCasse; B.S., U. Southwestern La., 1940; M.S., La. State U. 1964. Home mgmt. supr. Farm Security Adminstrn., 1936-38, 40-46; home demonstration agt. La. Coop. Extension Service, 1946—. Mem. Commn. on Aging, Home Health Care, Terrebonne Civil Def., Terrebonne Cancer Assn., Terrebonne chpt. A.R.C. Recipient Distinguished Service award La. Assn. Extension Home Economists, 1965, Nat. Assn. Extension Home Economists, 1965; named Outstanding Woman of Yr., Terrebonne Parish, 1973; recipient Ferber award as outstanding bus. or profl. women of year, 1973. Mem. Houma Bus. and Profl. Woman's Club (pres. 1960), Altrusa Internat. Terrebonne Fine Arts Guild, La. State U. 25 Year Club, Terrobonne City Pan Hellenic League (pres. 1964), Epsilon Sigma Phi, Alpha Omicron Pi, Delta Kappa Gamma. Home: 518 Wilson Av Houma LA 70360 Office: 500 School St Houma LA 70360

LACEY, ALICE LOYOLA CUNNINGHAM (MRS. MAURICE J. LACEY), lawyer; b. Boston, Feb. 23, 1897; d. William G. and Margaret T. Cunningham; B.A. cum laude, Radcliffe Coll., 1918; M.A., Boston U., 1926; LL.B. cum laude, Portia Law Sch., 1933; m. Maurice J. Lacey, June 19, 1926 (dec.). Tchr. Girls Latin Sch., Boston, 1921-26; admitted to Mass. bar, 1935, Bar Interstate Commerce Commn., 1937, Fed. Bar, 1950; practice in Boston, other Mass. cities, 1935—, ICC, 1935—. Dir. Jamaica Plain Neighborhood House, Boston, 1927—, v.p., 1955—; dir. Jamaica Plain Neighborhood Council, 1937-48, v.p., 1948-60, pres., 1960-62; dist. chmn. Boston Council Girl Scouts Am., 1935-40, dep. commr., 1940-46, legal advisor, 1946-52; vice chmn. A.R.C., 1945-52. Mem. Radcliffe Coll. Alumnae Assn., Jamaica Plain Neighborhood House Assn., Mass. Assn. Women Lawyers, Sumner Hill Assn. Address: 73 Elm St Jamaica Plain MA 02130

LACEY, BEATRICE CATES (MRS. JOHN I. LACEY), psychophysiologist, educator; b. N.Y.C., July 22, 1919; d. Louis H. and Mollie S. (Libowitz) Cates; student Columbia, 1935-38; A.B. with distinction, Cornell U., 1940; M.A., Antioch Coll., 1958; m. John I. Lacey, Apr. 16, 1938; children—Robert A., Carolyn E. Mem. staff Fels Research Inst., Yellow Springs, O., 1953—, sr. investigator, 1966-72, sr. scientist, 1972—; instr. Antioch Coll., Yellow Springs, 1956-73, asst. prof., 1963-68, asso. prof., 1968-73, prof., 1973—. Mem. Soc. for Psychophysiol. Research (dir. 1972—), Soc. for Neurosci., Phi Kappa Phi. Research and publs. in psychophysiology of the autonomic nervous system. Home: 1425 Meadow Lane Yellow Springs OH 45387 Office: Fels Research Institute 800 Livermore St Yellow Springs OH 45387

LACEY, RUTH WILLIFORD (MRS. MOULTRIE B. LACEY), librarian; b. Memphis, Nov. 3, 1908; d. Henry Lee and Anna (Chumbley) Williford; B.A., U. Ala., 1933; med. technologist certificate Path. Inst., U. Tenn., 1934; M.L.S., U. Miss., 1966; m. Moultrie Brailsford Lacey, Nov. 16, 1946; 1 son, William Henry. Med. technician to Dr. Henry B. Gotten, Memphis, 1934-38, Frazier-Ellis Hosp., Dothan, Ala., 1938-39, E.I. duPont de Nemours & Co., 1939-45; prof. library sci. U. Miss., 1966-67; librarian State Tech. Inst. at Memphis, 1967—. Mem. Am. Vocational Assn., Tenn., Southeastern, West Tenn. library assns., Tenn. Tech. Edn. Council, Tenn. Tech. Edn. Assn., Kappa Alpha Theta. Episcopalian. Home: 304 Walthall St Holly Springs MS 38635 Office: 5983 Macon Cove St Memphis TN 38128

LACEY, SUSAN WILSON, mgmt. cons.; b. Ponca City, Okla., Apr. 25, 1939; d. Robert Kingston and Nina (Robertson) Wilson; A.A., Stephens Coll., 1959; B.S., Butler U., 1962; M.A., So. Methodist U., 1969; 1 son, Franklin Wilson. Tchr. Bd. Edn., Dallas, 1966; sec. Tex. Instruments Co., Dallas, 1966-67; employment mgr. Tex. Bank, Dallas, 1969-71; mgmt. cons. Lifson, Wilson, Ferguson & Winick, Inc., Dallas, 1972—. Tchr. Tulsa pub. schs., 1962-63; instr. Belhaven Coll., Jackson, Miss., 1965; sec. Nat. Surveys, Inc., 1974—. Vol. work for Dallas Symphony Orch., 1974. Mem. Am. (asso.), Tex., Dallas psychol. assns. Clubs: Centre Tennis, Chimeras. Home: 3516 Milton Dallas TX 75205 Office: 7616 LBJ Freeway Suite 505 Dallas TX 75240

LACH, ALMA ELIZABETH (MRS DONALD F. LACH), home econs. writer; b. Petersburg, Ill.; d. John H. and Clara E. (Boeker) Satorius; Diplome de Condon Bleu (Paris, France), 1956; m. Donald F. Lach, Mar. 18, 1939; 1 dau., Sandra Judith. Feature writer Children's Activities mag., 1954-55; creator, performer TV show Let's Cook, children's cooking show, 1955; food editor Chgo. Daily Sun-Times, 1957-65; pres. Alma Lach Kitchens Inc., Chgo., 1966—; lectr. U. Chgo. Downtown Coll., Gourmet Inst., U. Md., 1963; food cons. Food Bus. Mag., 1964-66; columnist Modern Packaging, 1967-68, Travel & Camera, 1969, Venture, 1970. Recipient Pillsbury award, 1958; Grocery Mfrs. Am. Trophy award, 1959, Certificate of Honor, 1961; Chevalier du Tastevin, 1962; Commanderie de l'Ordre des Anysetiers du Roy, 1963; Confrerie de la Chaine des Rotisseurs, 1964. Mem. U. Chgo. Settlement League, Am. Assn. Food Editors (chmn. 1959), Internat. Platform Assn. Clubs: Tavern, Quadrangle (Chgo.). Author: A Child's First Cookbook, 1950; The Campbell Kids Have a Party, 1953; The Campbell Kids at Home, 1953; Let's Cook, 1956; Candlelight Cookbook, 1959; Weekly TV food show CBS, 1962-66; Cooking a la Cordon Bleu, 1970; Alma's Almanac, 1972; Hows and Whys of French Cooking, 1974. Contbr. to World Book Yearbook, Grolier Soc. Yearbook, 1962. Address: 5750 Kenwood Av Chicago IL 60637

LACHANCE, ANN, librarian; b. Lakeport, Ont., Can., June 6, 1906; d. Arthur John and Evelyn (Harvey) Cracknell; R.N., Micholl's Hosp., 1929; certificate Childrens Hosp., Toronto, 1933; m. Mortimer Benedict Lachance, Apr. 24, 1948; 1 son, Michael Anthony Joseph. Registered nurse various instns., 1933-39; organizer, head First Aid Depts. Noordyn Aviation and Brit. Rubber Plants, Montreal and Lachine, Que., Can., 1942-45; women's counsellor Noordyn Aviation, Ltd., Montreal, 1940-44; founder Dorval Civic Library, Dorval, Que., Can., 1958, chief librarian, 1958-74, cons., 1974—. Bd. dirs. Regional Library Service, Pointe Claire, Que., Can., 1965. Mem. Canadian, Que. library assns., Profl. Librarians of the Province of Que., Que. Assn. for Children with Learning Disabilities. Home: 282 Martin Av Dorval PQ Canada Office: 1401 Lakeshore Dr Dorval PQ H9S Canada

LA CHARITÉ, VIRGINIA ANDING (MRS. RAYMOND CAMILLE LA CHARITÉ), educator; b. Phila., Jan. 18, 1937; d. Claude Ellis and Virginia Wilkinson (Nelson) Anding; B.A., Coll. of William and Mary, 1957; M.A., U. Pa., 1965, Ph.D., 1966; m. Raymond Camille La Charité, May 9, 1964; children—Claude Anding, Désirée DeRochebrune. Instr. French, Coll. of William and Mary, Williamsburg, Va., 1959-62; lectr. French, U. N.C., Chapel Hill, 1966-69; asso. prof. U. Ky., Lexington, 1969-74, prof., 1974—, chmn. comparative lit., 1970—. Fulbright grantee to France, 1957-58. Mem. Modern Lang. Assn., S. Atlantic Modern Lang. Assn., Am. Assn. Tchrs. French, Assn. for Study of Dada and Surrealism, Phi Beta Kappa, Kappa Delta Pi, Pi Delta Phi, Kappa Kappa Gamma. Author: The Poetics and the Poetry of René Char, 1968; Bonaventure Des Périer's Novel Pastimes and Merry Tales, 1972. Contbr. articles to profl. jours. Home: 1830 Cantrill Dr Lexington KY 40505

LACHER, FRANCES RUTLAND (MRS. SAMUEL LACHER), advt. writer, educator; b. Bklyn., June 1, 1921; d. Morris and Dora (Diamond) Rosen; B.B.A., Coll. City N.Y., 1942; m. Samuel Lacher, Feb. 23, 1947; children—Dorothy Alison, Irene Melanie. Group head Compton Advt., Inc., N.Y.C., 1953-59; v.p., creative supr. Dancer-Fitzgerald-Sample, 1959-63; group head Foote, Cone & Belding, 1964-65; creative dir. Hirsch, Tigler, Fried, 1967-68; copy supr. Schwab, Beatty & Porter, 1968-70; instr. advt., communications Fashion Inst. Tech., State U. N.Y., 1972—. Cons. in field. Recipient 3d pl. award Printers Ink, 1961, Best Grocery campaign, 1961, 3d pl. This Week, 10 Best Campaigns, 1961. Mem. Authors League Am., Advt. Women N.Y., Am. Advt. Fedn., Am. Assn. Univ. Profs., Authors Guild. Jewish religion. Author: The Brides Book, 1949. Editor: Ad Libber. Contbr. articles on travel, art to New York Times. Home: 650 Ocean Av Brooklyn NY 11226 Office: 227 W 27th St New York City NY 10001

LACHER, LINDA LUCILLE, food co. exec.; b. Pitts., Aug. 9, 1947; d. Charles Thomas and Veronica Dolores (Serilla) Lacher; B.A., Duquesne U., 1969. Tech. writer Ketchum, MacLeod & Grove, Inc., Pitts., 1969-70; with H.J. Heinz Co., Pitts., 1971—, supr. consumer communications, 1973-. Mem. Women in Communications, Am. Cause. Republican. Roman Catholic. Home: 440 Chatham Park Dr Pittsburgh PA 15220 Office: PO Box 57 Pittsburgh PA 15230

LACHERT, HANNA KATARZYNA, violinist; b. Warsaw, Poland, Nov. 25, 1944; d. Zygmunt Adam and Hanna Katarzyna (Chrzanowska) Lachert; diploma with honors Lyceum Music Warsaw, 1963; M.A., Acad. Music Warsaw; 1967, U. Conn., 1971; postgrad. Hochschule fur Musik, Hannover, Germany, 1967-68; Premier prix Conservatoire Royal de la Musique, Brussels, 1968-69. Came to U.S., 1969, naturalized, 1971. Soloist with European, Am. and Mexican orchs.; radio and TV appearances, recitals; violinist N.Y. Philharmonic, 1972—. Home: 155 W 68th St New York City NY 10023 Office: Broadway at 65th St New York City NY 10023

LACHMAN, MARLENE FAY, lawyer; b. Phila., June 27, 1946; d. Sidney S. and Bertha T. (Thalheimer) Lachman; B.A., Temple U., 1968; J.D., U. Pa., 1970. Admitted to Pa. bar, 1970; mem. firm Bernstein, Bernstein & Harrison, Phila., 1970—. Mem. Bi-Partisan Com. to Elect Qualified Judges, 1973; mem. Phila. Crime Commn., 1973, Personal Aid Bur. Bd. Jewish Family Service, Phila., 1973. Adviser to law explorers post Boy Scouts Am., 1973-74; mem. disciplinary bd. hearing panelist Pa. Supreme Ct., 1973-77. Mem. Pa. (bd. young lawyers sect. 1974), Phila. (vice chmn. young lawyers sect. 1973-74) bar assns., Nat. Assn. Women Lawyers, Am. Trial Lawyers Assn., Lawyers Club Phila., U. Pa. Law Alumni Soc. (bd. mgrs. 1972-75), Assn. Alumnae U. Pa. (dir. 1972-75). Home: 5427 N 11th St Philadelphia PA 19141 Office: 1521 Locust St Philadelphia PA 19102

LACINA, DORIS BEATRICE MILLER (MRS. JOSEPH LACINA), city ofcl.; b. Flint, Mich., Sept. 8, 1921; d. Clarence and Beatrice Amy (Bowen) Miller; grad. high sch.; m. Joseph Lacina, Oct 4, 1941; children—Judith Kaye (Mrs. Donald W. Blakely), Dorrie Jo. Sec., bookkeeper Chevrolet local 659, Flint, 1944-48, CIO Council, Flint, 1948-49; city clk. City of Grand Blanc (Mich.), 1963—. Mem. Municipal Clks. Assn. Mich., Am. Legion Aux. (local pres. 1968-69). Conglist. Home: 12408 Hillcrest Dr Grand Blanc MI 48439 Office: 203 E Grand Blanc Rd Grand Blanc MI 48439

LACKEY, ELIZABETH MCCARTHY (MRS. JAMES ALEXANDER LACKEY), counselor specialist; b. Milw., Nov. 15, 1927; d. John James and Elizabeth (Palbar) McCarthy; student U. Mexico, 1947; B.A., Lake Forest Coll., 1949; postgrad. Utah State U., 1951-53; m. James Alexander Lackey, Aug. 29, 1964; 1 step son, James Emmet. Tchr. and counselor San Mateo County (Cal.) Juvenile Hall, 1956-64; social worker social services dept., Racine, Wis., 1965-66; tchr. and counselor The Acad., Racine, 1966-71; counselor specialist United Migrant Opportunity Services, Kenosha, Wis., 1973—. Mem. U.S. Trotting Assn., Phi Sigma Iota. Home: 329 Newman Rd Racine WI 53406 Office: 6603 26th Av Kenosha WI 53140

LACKMAN, VIRGINIA MARGARET, psychiatrist; b.St. Thomas, Mo., June 15, 1939; d. Stephen Anton and Clara Johanna (Luebbering) Lackman; B.S. in Sci., St. Louis U., 1964, M.D., 1968. Intern medicine St. Louis U. Hosp., 1968-69; resident psychiatry U. Pitts. Hosp., 1969-72; pvt. practice medicine specializing in psychiatry, Pitts., 1972—; clin. asst. prof. psychiatry U. Pitts., 1972—. Mem. Sisters of St. Mary, St. Louis, 1953-71. Mem. Am., Pa. psychiat. socs., Resident's Orgn. (pres. 1971), Catholic Alumni Club (v.p. 1971), Pa., Allegheny County med. socs. Editor Psychiat. Communications, 1970-72. Home: 3301 Beechwood Blvd Pittsburgh PA 15217 Office: 3700 Fifth Av Pittsburgh PA 15213

LACKMOND, CATHERIENE MUNSELL (MRS. RICHARD WILLIAM LACKMOND), museum ofcl.; b. Houston, Apr. 8, 1910; d. Aureal Angelo and Kate (Latham) Munsell; A.B., Howard Coll., 1933; m. Richard William Lackmond, Apr. 16, 1934; children—Sallie (Mrs. James W. Dewberry), Richard William. Tchr. pub. schs., Birmingham, Ala., 1933-34, scorer, test and measurement dept. Birmingham Pub. Schs., 1934-37; agt. Mass. Mut. Ins. Co., 1961; dir. vol. services Children's Hosp., Birmingham, 1962-64; hostess Vestavia County Club, Birmingham, 1965; curator, mgr. Arlington Antebellum Home and Gardens, Birmingham, 1966—. Chmn. character edn. Birmingham Council Parents and Tchrs., 1951; chmn. Mother's March of Dimes, Birmingham, 1954-55; sec. Birmingham chpt. Nat. Found. Infantile Paralysis, 1955; pres. Jefferson County Radio and TV Council, 1955-61; chmn. Christmas caroling program Ala. Found. Speech and Hearing, 1957-58; pres. Women's Civic Club, Birmingham, 1956-57. Bd. dirs. Jimmy Morgan Zoo, Birmingham, 1954; pres. bd. dirs. Ala. Found. Speech and Hearing, 1959-61. Named Woman of Yr., Soroptomists, Birmingham, 1955, Chesty award Birmingham Community Chest, 1957, Meritorious award City of Birmingham, 1958. Mem. Ala. Fedn. Women's Clubs (dist. dir. 1952-54), Am. Contract Bridge League, Arlington Hist. Soc., Phi Mu. Baptist (supt. 3d yr. primary dept. 1934-70). Clubs: Kenilworth Literary (pres. 1950), Soroptimist (Birmingham). Home: 1619 Ridge Rd Birmingham AL 35209 Office: 331 Cotton Av SW Birmingham AL 35211

LACKNER, HENRIETTE (MRS. CECIL ABRAHAM), hematologist; b. Vienna, Austria, Feb. 27, 1922; d. Julius Franz and Caecelie (Dressler) Lackner; M.B., Ch.B., U. Leeds, 1945, M.D., 1948; m. Cecil Abraham, Apr. 28, 1949; children—Michael Jack, Susan Gail, Stephen Julian. Came to U.S., naturalized, 1968. Intern, Leeds Gen. Infirmary, 1945-46, Post Grad. Med. Sch., Hammersmith Hosp., London, 1948, Canadian, Red Cross Meml. Hosp., Taplow Bucks, Eng., 1948-49; resident Post Grad. Med. Sch. Hammersmith Hosp., London, 1952-54; practice medicine specializing in hematology Cape Town, S. Africa, 1955-62, N.Y.C., 1962—; mem. staffs Groote Schuur Hosp., Cape Town, N.Y. U. and Bellevue Med. Centers, N.Y.C.; asst. vis. physician Bellevue Hosp., N.Y.C., 1966—; asst. dept. medicine U. Hosp., N.Y.C., 1966—; instr. medicine N.Y.U., 1965-67, asst. prof. clin. medicine 1967-69, asst. prof. medicine, 1969—. Dir. Clin. Coagulation Lab., U. and Bellevue Med. Centers, 1968. Mem. council on thrombosis Am. Heart Assn., 1971. Mem. Royal Coll. of Physicians, London, England, N.Y. Soc. for the Study of Blood, Am. Soc. Hematology. Contbr. articles in field to profl. jours. Home: 648 Timpson St Pelham Manor NY 10803 Office: New York University Medical Center 550 First Av New York City NY 10016

LACLAUSTRA, VERA BERNEICIA DERRICK (MRS. SERAPHIN LACLAUSTRA), poet; b. Baker, Ore., Apr. 11, 1903; d. Edmon Treseia and Nellie Ann (Vessey) Derrick; grad. Oakland Cosmetology Coll., 1934; m. Gunnar Benson, Oct. 15, 1921 (dec.); 1 son, William Hugh; m. 2d, Seraphin LaClaustra, Apr. 15, 1933; 1 stepdau., Eleanor (Mrs. David J. Baird). Author: (poetry) By The Cool Waters, 1953, The Purple Wheel, 1954, Gongs of Light, 1971. Poems and books on display Brown U. Library, Huntington Library, Cal. Hist. Soc., U. Ky. Library. Recipient Cash prizes for poems Scientific Approach, 1961, Perseverance, 1966, Abisko Birches, 1973; certificates of merit Acad. Leonard Da Vinci, Rome, Italy, 1962-68, 70—, Internat. Mark Twain Soc., 1953. Mem. Avalon World Arts Acad., Cal. Fedn. Chaparral Poets, Am. Poetry League, Centro Studi E. Scambi Internat., World Poetry Soc. India, Internat. Mark Twain Soc., Ladies Aux. V.F.W. Contbr. poems to numerous periodicals, anthologies and newspapers. Home: 400 Perkins St Apt 209 Oakland CA 94610

LACY, ANN MATTHEWS, scientist, educator; b. Boston, May 29, 1932; d. Clive Woodbury and Mona (Matthews) Lacy; B.A., Wellesley Coll., 1953; M.S., Yale, 1956, Ph.D., 1959. Research asst. microbial genetics Carnegie Inst. Wash. Cold Spring Harbor, N.Y., 1953-54; NSF predoctoral fellow Yale, 1954-56; pub. health service pre-doctoral fellow Yale, 1956-59; instr. dept. biol. scis. Goucher Coll., Towson, Balt., 1959-61, asst. prof., 1961-67, asso. prof., 1967-73, prof., 1973—, chmn. dept., 1969-72; sr. investigator Nat. Sci. Found. Research Grants, biochem. genetics in fungi, 1960-70. Mem. Genetics Soc. Am., Bot. Soc. Am., Am. Inst. Biol. Scis., A.A.A.S., Am. Assn. U. Profs., Sigma Xi. Contbr. articles to profl. jours. Office: Dept Biol Scis Goucher Coll Towson MD 21204

LACY, LUCY GOODE GARNETT (MRS. OSBORNE WILSON LACY), psychiatrist; b. College Station, Tex., Jan. 6, 1924; d. William Edward and Lucy Goode (Puryear) Garnett; B.A., Westhampton Coll., U. Richmond, 1944; M.D., U. Va., 1948; m. Osborne Wilson Lacy, July 29, 1950; children—Sallie Wilson, Lucinda Puryear, Cabell Lyle. Intern, U. Ia., 1948-49, U. Va., 1949-50; resident Norristown (Pa.) State Hosp., 1951-53, Pa. State U. Sch. Medicine, Hershey, 1972-73; attending physician Woman's Hosp., Phila., 1950-51; physician Phila. Sch. Dist., 1950-51; pvt. practice medicine specializing in psychiatry Prince Edward County, Va., 1953-54; psychiatrist Child Guidance Clinic, Hartford, Conn., 1958-65; attending physician Seizure Control Clinic U. Va. Hosp., summers 1955-57; psychiatrist Lancaster (Pa.) Guidance Clinic, 1965—. Lectr. psychology Franklin and Marshall Coll., 1966-67, 73—, Nursing Sch. Lancaster Gen. Hosp., 1973—. Fellow Am. Orthopsychiat. Assn.; mem. Am. Psychiat. Assn. Democrat. Contbr. articles to profl. jours. Home: 452 Race Av Lancaster PA 17603 Office: 530 Janet Av Lancaster PA 17604

LADAS, ALICE KAHM (MRS. HAROLD SAMUEL LADAS), psychologist; b. N.Y.C.; d. Myron Daniel and Rosalie Heil (Blum) Kahm; B.A. with honors (William Alanson Neilson fellow), Smith Coll., 1943, M.Social Sci., 1947; Ed.D., Tchrs. Coll., Columbia, 1970; m. Harold Samuel Ladas, Jan. 30, 1962; children—Robin Lee, Pamela. Field examiner Fair Employment Practices Commn., Washington, 1944-47; social worker Payne Whitney Clinic, New York Hosp., N.Y.C., 1946; practice phychotherapy, N.Y.C., 1947—. Dir. child guidence Caldwell (N.J.) Pub. Schs., 1952-58; staff Maternal Care Adoption Service, Lakeville, Conn., 1957-60; staff Ballard Sch., YWCA, N.Y.C., 1967—. Bd. dirs. Hamilton Sch., Sheffield, Mass.; trustee Rosalie H. Blum Found. Fellow Nat. Inst. Pub. Affairs; mem. Am. Assn. Marriage Counselors, Acad. Certified Social Workers, Soc. for Sci. Study of Sex, Friends N.Y. Inst. Clin. Oral Pathology (chmn. N.Y. 1963—), Inst. Bio-Energetic Analysis, Phi Beta Kappa. Author: Breastfeeding: The Less Available Option and How to Help Mothers Breastfeed. Contbr. articles to profl. jours. Home: 42 Whippoorwill Rd Armonk NY 10504 Office: 241 Central Park W New York City NY 10024

LADD, FRANCES ROBERTA, librarian; b. Rochester, N.Y., Apr. 28, 1917; d. Frank Robert and Helen M. (Quinlivan) Ladd; B.A., U. Rochester, 1939; B.L.S., Columbia, 1941. Sr. asst. Rochester Pub. Library, 1941-44; cataloger U. Rochester (N.Y.) Library, 1944-52, asst. head, 1953-62, head, 1962—. Mem. Am. (nominating com. cataloging and classification sect. 1971-72), N.Y. (dir.-at large 1969-71, 2d v.p. 1971-72 resources and tech. services sect., tech. services com. 1974—) library assns., Am. Soc. Information Sci., Faculty Club, Delta Kappa Gamma. Republican. Baptist (clk. ch. 1971-73). Contbr. to library periodicals. Home: 163 Greystone Lane Apt 11 Rochester NY 14618 Office: University Rochester Library Rochester NY 14627

LADD, JEANNE WHEELUS (MRS. JOHN M. LADD), banker; b. Winnsboro, La., Apr. 20, 1925; d. Luther Joel and Winnie Rosalie (Cupples) Wheelus; grad. Draughns Bus. Coll., 1941; m. John McCaslin Ladd, June 23, 1945; 1 son, Charles McCaslin. Bookkeeper Winnsboro State Bank, 1940, M.W. Kellog Co., Oak Ridge, 1941-45; asst. cashier Ipava (Ill.) State Bank, 1951-60; gen. books and line teller Buckner State Bank, Dallas, 1964-65; br. mgr. Central Bank, Monroe, La., 1965—. Twp. clk., Ipava, 1960-61. Mem. Nat. Assn. Bank Women. Democrat. Presbyn. Club: Pilot. Home: 161 Bartholomew Dr Sterlington LA 71280 Office: 8019 DeSiard St Monroe LA 71201

LADD, LAURA DELPHINE, obstetrician and gynecologist; b. McColloms, N.Y., Sept. 3, 1907; d. Richard Clinton and Gertrude Augusta (Dunning) Ladd; B.A., Syracuse U., 1931; postgrad. (fellow anatomy) U. Ia., 1933-34; M.D., U. Tenn., 1937. Lab asst. Trudeau Research Found., Saranac Lake, N.Y., 1932; student instr., lab. technician U. Ia., 1934-37; instr. anatomy U. Miss., 1937-42; intern Emanuel Hosp., Portland, Ore., 1942-43, mem. staff, 1943—; preceptor with obstetrician, gynecologist, 1943-48; pvt. practice medicine specializing in obstetrics, gynecology, Portland, 1948—; mem. staff St. Vincent Hosp., Portland, 1944-68. Mem. Ore. Soc. Obstetricians and Gynecologists (asso.), Alpha Omega Alpha, Alpine Club Can. Home: 4921 NE 77th Av Portland OR 97218 Office: 1020 SW Taylor St Portland OR 97205

LADD, ROSALIND EKMAN (MRS. JOHN LADD), educator; b. Manchester, N.H., Oct. 13, 1933; d. Nathan and Sonia B. (Litvin) Ekman; B.A., Wheaton Coll., 1955; M.A., Brown U., 1956, Ph.D., 1962; m. John Ladd, July 8, 1963; children—Sarah, Deborah. Asst. prof. philosophy Smith Coll., Northampton, Mass., 1957-67; asso. prof. philosophy Wheaton Coll., Norton, Mass., 1967-74, prof., 1974—, chmn. dept., 1971—. Mem. Am. Philos. Assn., Mind Assn., Phi Beta Kappa. Editor: Readings in the Problems of Ethics, 1965. Home: 72 Taber Av Providence RI 02906 Office: Dept Philosophy Wheaton Coll Norton MA 02766

LADD, SUE CAROL, company exec.; b. Chgo., Oct. 30, 1915; d. S.M. and Carolyn (Schmidt) Lederer; student Hemper Hall, Kenosha, Wis., 1924, Nat. Park Sem., Forest Gleb, Md., 1927; m. Alan Ladd, Mar. 15, 1942 (dec. 1964); children—Carol Lee Veitch, Alana Ladd Jackson, Alan, David Alan. Actress in films, 1927-37; dir. Agy. for Acting and Writing, 1939-42; owner Alan Ladd Hardware and Gift Shop, Palm Springs, Cal., 1955—; pres. Ladd Enterprises, film prodn. and real estate, Beverly Hills, Cal., 1954—; propr. Sue Carol Interiors, 1950—. Address: 9250 Wilshire Blvd Beverly Hills CA 90212

LADECK, FLORENCE MARCELIA JOHNSTON (MRS. CARL MARTIN LADECK), city ofcl.; b. Laverne, Okla., Mar. 11, 1929; d. Sidney and Margaret Marcelia (Thompson) Johnston; grad. high sch.; m. Carl Martin Ladeck, Feb. 14, 1958; children—Susan Elaine Sprague Larkins, Lynette Kay Sprague Merrill, Stephen Richard. Typist clk. Assessor's Office, Placer County, Auburn, Cal., 1947-52, steno Sec. to Assessor, 1956-58, Assessor's Office, 1959; typist clk. City of Auburn Mgrs. Office, 1961-64, city clk. City Clks. Office, 1964—, dep. city treas., 1965. Treas., Little League, 1969-71. Mem. City Clks. Assn. Cal. Club: Soroptimist (dir. Auburn 1973-74, pres. 1972-73). Home: 145 Orrin Dr Auburn CA 95603 Office: 1103 High St Auburn CA 95603

LADER, JOAN SUMMERS (MRS. LAWRENCE LADER), opera singer; b. Kirkintilloch, Scotland, Apr. 12, 1938; d. John and Susan (Williamson) Summers; diploma Royal Scottish Acad. Music, Glasgow, Scotland, 1958; m. Lawrence Lader, Sept. 27, 1961; 1 dau., Wendy Summers. Came to U.S., 1961. Mem. Met. Opera Studio, 1962-66; opera singer N.Y.C. Opera Co., 1963—, Susanna in Figaro, 1967, 68, Lauretta in Gianni Schicchi, 1967, soprano leads in Marriage of Figaro, Don Giovanni, other roles; mem. Washington Opera Soc., Washington, 1966, Am. Opera Theater, Bklyn., 1966, Ft. Worth Opera Co., 1968, Scottish Opera Co., 1968, Portland Opera Assn., 1972—, Dallas Civic Opera, 1972, Eastern Opera Theatre, N.Y.C., 1973; Waverly consort 1970-73. Address: 51 Fifth Av New York City NY 10003

LADNER, MILDRED MAE DIEFENDERFER (MRS. JOHN LADNER), journalist; b. Allentown, Pa., June 24, 1918; d. Orlando and Mary Susan (Fahler) Diefenderfer; B.A., Moravian Coll., 1939; M.A., U. Wis., 1941; m. John Ladner, Aug. 19, 1950; children—Mary Patricia (Mrs. Michael Dunn Robertson), Edward David, Helen Louise. With Allentown Call-Chronicle Newspapers, 1939-43, A.P., Phila. Bur., 1943-45, Wall Street Jour., Washington Bur., 1945-70; corr. Nat. Observer, Tulsa, 1971—; weekly columnist Tulsa World, 1972—. Bd. dirs. Gilcrease Inst. Assn., Tulsa, 1964-74, pub. relations chmn., 1966-74; bd. trustees Moravian Coll., 1966-71. Recipient Comenius award, Moravian Coll., 1962. Mem. Women in Communications, Washington Press Club (treas. 1949), Tulsa Press Club. Home: 2116 S Detroit Av Tulsa OK 74114

LAFAYETTE, ESTHER MAE, librarian; b. Detroit, Apr. 24, 1904; d. Grove Hezekiah and Irene Jenny (DeShetler) Secor; student Toledo Pub. Library Sch., 1923-24, 27-28; m. William Carl LaFayette, Aug. 3, 1929 (dec. Oct. 1962); 1 son, William Secor. Jr. asst. Webster Sch. br. Toledo Pub. Library, 1924-28, children's librarian Navarre Sch. br., 1928-30, Nathan Hale br., 1930-31; librarian St. Francis de Sales High Sch., Toledo, 1958—. Social chmn. Notre Dame Ednl. League, 1953-57; vol. St. Vincent Hosp. Guild. Mem. Cath. (No. Ohio unit), Ohio library assns., Ohio Assn. Sch. Librarians. Home: 4156 Arnelle Rd Toledo OH 43606 Office: 2323 W Bancroft St Toledo OH 43607

LAFER, CHARLOTTE ZISKIND (MRS. DENNIS JOSEPH LAFER), physician; b. Boston, Nov. 11, 1931; d. Edward and Elizabeth (Kaminsky) Ziskind; B.A. summa cum laude, U. Rochester, 1953; M.D., Columbia, 1957; m. Dennis Joseph Lafer, Mar. 4, 1955; children—Edmund Lawrence, Leslie Rochelle, Bradley Mitchell. Intern, Kings County Hosp., 1957-58; gen. practice medicine, Bklyn., 1958-60, Bellerose, N.Y., 1960-63; jr. resident pediatrics Montreal Childrens Hosp., 1963-64; sr. resident pediatrics Jewish Hosp., Bklyn., 1964-65; practice medicine, specializing in pediatrics, Bklyn., 1965—; physician charge premature nursery, full term nurseries, div. neonatology Jewish Hosp. and Med. Center; dir. children's health services Suffolk County Dept. Health, 1970-73; attending physician

Nassau County Med. Center, 1970-73; attending physician div. human genetics dept. pediatrics L.I. Jewish-Hillside Med. Center, 1973-74, North Shore Hosp. Cornell U., 1974—; cons. neonatology St. Charles Hosp.; clin. instr. pediatrics State U. N.Y. Downstate Med. Center. Diplomate Am. Bd. Pediatrics. Fellow Am. Acad. Pediatrics; mem. A.M.A., N.Y. State, Suffolk County (com. chmn.) med. socs., Am. Soc. Human Genetics, Phi Beta Kappa, Alpha Omega Alpha. Home: 8 Woodhull Rd East Setauket NY 11733 Office: 635 Belle Terre Rd Port Jefferson NY 11777

LAFER, ESTELLE ROSENBAUM (MRS. LEON LAFER), motor co. exec.; b. Bklyn., Sept. 15, 1906; d. Louis and Doris (Cohen) Rosenbaum; grad. high sch.; m. Leon Lafer, Mar. 5, 1926; children—Linda Burger (Mrs. Lawrence Burger), Bernard, Dennis. With Century Motor & Compressor Co., Inc., Newark, 1935—, now pres.; v.p. B.H. Hull, antique jewelry, East Orange, N.J., 1952—. Mem. Order Eastern Star. Home: 1890 S Ocean Dr Hallandale FL 33009 Office: 195 Mulberry St Newark NJ 07102

LAFFERTY, BEVERLY LOU BROOKOVER, physician; b. Newark, O., Aug. 15, 1938; d. Lawrence William and Rosie (Rey) Brookover; B.S., Ohio State U., 1959, M.D., 1963; m. William Wesley Lafferty, Dec. 17, 1960 (div. Apr. 1971); children—Marla Michele, William Brookover, Wesley Voris, Latour Rey; m. 2d, W.R. Stephens, May 1972. Intern Grant Hosp., Columbus, O., 1963-64; gen. practice medicine, West Union, O., 1964—; mem. staff Adams County Hosp., v.p., 1971-72, chief of staff, 1973—. Mem. A.M.A., Ohio, Adams County (v.p. 1965-67, pres. 1972) med. assns., Am. Acad. Family Physicians, Am. Med. Women's Assn., Alpha Lambda Delta, Alpha Epsilon Iota, Alpha Epsilon Delta (sec. 1958-59). Mem. Order Eastern Star. Home: Route 3 Box 39 S West Union OH 45693 Office: 107 Wilson Dr West Union OH 45693

LAFFOON, IRENE MABEL (MRS. KENNETH H. LAFFOON), county ofcl.; b. Houghton, Ia., June 26, 1911; d. Sabert Roger and Mertie Dell (Berry) Hampton; grad. high sch.; m. Kenneth H. Laffoon, Aug. 24, 1931; children—Mary Kathryn (Mrs. Jerry Sims), Don Roger. Clk., Lessenden's Ready to Wear, Downs, Kan., 1929-33, J.C. Penney, Osborne, Kan., 1934-39; dep. clk. Osborne (Kan.) County, 1959-60, clk. dist. ct., Osborne, 1960—. Pres. Osborne P.T.A., 1949; chmn. Girl Scouts, 1949-53; county chmn. March of Dimes, 1945-56; mem. Fidelia Civic Club, 1953—, pres., 1964-65, pub. affairs chmn. 6th dist. bd., 1958, 59, rep. Internat. Conf., Athens, 1965; pres. Am. Field Service, Osborne, 1968-69; charter mem. Osborne Meml. Hosp. Aux., 1959—, pres., 1968-69; sec. Osborne County Celebrations, Inc., 1970—. Mem. Osborne High Sch. Bd., 1955-65; county chmn. women's div. Republican party, 1966. Recipient Silver pin for service March of Dimes, 1955, 10 yr. Service Pin Elected Pub. Ofcls., 1970, Service pin, life membership Osborne P.T.A., 1968. Mem. Kan. Dist. Clks. Assn. (state pres., 1967), Osborne C. of C. Methodist. Club: Quest. Home: 337 N 2d St Osborne KS 67473 Office: West Main St Osborne KS 67473

LAFONTANT, JEWEL STRADFORD (MRS. H. ERNEST LAFONTANT), lawyer; b. Chgo., Apr 28, 1922; d. Cornelius Francis and Aida (Carter) Stradford; B.A., Oberlin Coll., 1943; J.D., U. Chgo., 1946; m. H. Ernest LaFontant, Nov. 23, 1961; one son by previous marriage, John Rogers III. Trial atty. Legal Air Bur., 1947-54; mem. firm Stradford, LaFontant, Fisher & Malkin; asst. U.S. dist. atty., Chgo., 1955-58; U.S. del. to UN, 1972; dep. solicitor gen. U.S., 1973—. Dir. Trans World Airlines, Jewel Co. Inc. Mem. Ill. adv. com. to Fed. Civil Right Commn., 1958—. Commr., Family Study Commn., Ill., mem. U.S. Commn. Internat. Ednl. Cultural Affairs. Bd. dirs. Am. Civil Liberties Union, 1948-55, Parkway Community House, 1948-54, Maxwell St. YWCA, 1947-54. Recipient certificate of commendation Cook County Bar Assn., 1956; named Woman of Yr., Iota Phi Lambda, 1952, Ill. Assn. Colored Women, 1954, Antioch Baptist Ch., 1955. Trustee Lake Forest Coll. Mem. N.A.A.C.P. (sec. 1947-53), Nat. (sec. 1954-61), Fed. (exec. counsel 1956—), Chgo. (chmn. Am. citizenship com. 1957-59), Cook County (treas. 1953-57) bar assns., Bus. and Profl. Women's Club (past pres.). Methodist (trustee). Home: 4959 S Greenwood Av Chicago IL 60615 Office: 69 W Washington St Chicago IL 60602

LAGE, LOUISE CATHERINE, librarian; b. Davenport, Ia.; d. Otto A. and Louise (Harting) Lage; B.A., Augustana Coll.; B.S. in L.S., U. Mich., 1943. Asst. extension dept. Davenport Pub. Library, 1940-42, head extension dept., 1942-45; asst. librarian Lilly Research Labs., Indpls., 1945-51, asst. chief librarian, 1951-56, chief librarian, 1956—. Dir. Starlight Musicals, 1955—; mem. governing bd. Midwest Regional Med. Library, 1969-73. Recipient Recognition award Indpls. C. of C., 1970. Mem. Spl. Libraries Assn. (chmn. pharm. sect., sci.-tech. div. 1959-60, pres. Ind. chpt. 1967-68), Am. Soc. Information Sci., Am., Ind., Med. (chmn. recruitment com. 1951-52, sec. 1952-53, chmn. curriculum com. 1955-56, chmn. pharmacy group 1957-58, mem. bd. 1952-53, mem. exec. com. midwest regional group 1963-68) library assns., Drug Information Assn., Alumni Assn. Augustana Coll. (dir. 1971—), Indpls. Mus. Art, Indpls. Zool. Soc., Children's Mus., P.E.O. Presbyn. (elder 1974—). Home: 5307 Primrose Av Indianapolis IN 46220 Office: 307 E McCarty St Indianapolis IN 46206

LAGING, BARBARA STANTON MILLS (MRS. DUARD WALTER LAGING), artist, educator; b. Fargo, N.D., Oct. 16, 1914; d. Benjamin and Mary (McLaughlin) Mills; B.S., U. Minn., 1938; M.A., Kan. State U., 1963; m. Duard Walter Laging, Dec. 19, 1936; children—Marcia (Mrs. David W. Cummings), Thomas Stanton. Instr. art Mich. State Coll., East Lansing, 1947, U. Neb. art extension, Lincoln, 1949; art dir., color cons. Lincoln State Hosp., 1953-60; instr. design and interior design U. Neb., 1960-61, 62-64, asst. prof., 1964-72; design cons. environments for elderly and disabled, 1972—; sculpture exhibited in numerous shows in midwest, 1949—, including Lincoln Artists Guild, Midwest Six State Show, Mid-Am. Annual, Nelson Gallery Kansas City, Delta Phi Delta Exhbn., Afternoon Gallery, Waterloo Municipal Gallery, Ball State Coll., Springfield Mus., Neb. Centennial Invitational; represented in permanent collections Waterloo Municipal Gallery, Kansas State Friends of Art. Recipient numerous prizes and awards. Mem. Lincoln Artists Guild (past pres.), Neb. Art Assn., Am. Inst. Interior Design (ednl. asso.), Nat. Soc. Interior Designers (profl. affiliate), Kan. Fedn. Art, Neb. Wesleyan U. Elder Gallery Arts Council (bd. advisers, exec. com.), Interior Design Educators Council, Gerontology Soc. Author: Furniture Design for the Elderly, 1966; (monograph) How to Design a Non-Person—A Critical Look at an Environment for the Elderly, 1971. Home: 1140 S 20th St Lincoln NE 68502

LAGIOS, LAURA CALVERT, city ofcl.; b. South Bend, Ind., Feb. 3, 1921; d. Cory Wagner and Agnes (Lobaugh) Calvert; student Roosevelt Coll., 1949-50, U. Houston, 1946-47; m. John Lagios, Nov. 8, 1947; children—Christine (Mrs. Ray Neil Saye), Debi Jo. Dep. city clk. City of Newport Beach (Cal.), 1965-66, acting city clk., 1966-67, city clk., 1967—. Mem. citizens adv. com. Orange Coast Coll. Dist., 1969; charter mem. Newport Community Theater; mem. Newport Beach Friends of Library. Served with WAVES, 1944-46. Mem. So. Cal. Clks. Assn., Internat. Inst. Municipal Clks. (mem. constitution com. 1971-74, mem. internat. nomination com. 1972), Am. Records Mgmt. Assn., Red Barons of Orange County, Newport Harbor C. of C. (bd. dirs. women's div. 1967-72). Club: Zonta (pres. elect 1973-74) (Newport Harbor, Cal.). Home: 115 36th St Newport Beach CA 92660 Office: 3300 Newport Blvd Newport Beach CA 92660

LAGORIO, IRENE ROSE, artist; b. Oakland, Cal., May 2, 1921; d. Marcello N. and Argentina (Sarmoria) Lagorio; A.B., U. Cal., 1942, M.A., 1943. One-man shows at San Francisco Mus. Art, 1950, Gump's, San Francisco, 1958, Richmond (Cal.) Art Center, 1958, Laky Gallery, Carmel, Cal., 1961, Valley Art Center, Walnut Creek, Cal., 1962, 70, Ross-Talalay Gallery, New Haven, 1962, San Jose (Cal.) Art Center, 1962, 70, 72, Student Union Gallery U. Cal., Berkeley, 1963, Kramer Gallery, Los Angeles, 1963, Carmel Art Assn., 1971, 73, U. Ore. Art Mus., Eugene, 1972, Agnes Scott Coll. Art Mus., Atlanta, 1973, Nut Tree Gallery, Sacramento, 1973, Garden Cafe Gallery, Burlingame, Cal., 1964, Associazione Italo-Americana di Trieste, Italy, 1967, Galleria Pro-Padova, Padua, Italy, 1967, Teknik Universite Gallery, Trabazon, Turkey, 1967, Pacific Grove (Cal.) Mus. Natural History, 1970, Newman Hall Gallery, Berkeley, 1970, Modesto Jr. Coll. Art Gallery, 1970, de Saisset Art Mus., U. Santa Clara, 1971, Kennedy Gallery, Oakland, Cal., 1971, Monterey (Cal.) Peninsula Mus. Art, 1971; exhibited in USIA Traveling Exhbn., Europe, 1971-72; represented in permanent collections at San Francisco Mus. Art, Va. Mus. Fine Art, La. State Art Commn., San Francisco Women Artists Collection, Cal. State Library Collection, Germanisches Nat. Mus., Nuremberg, Germany, also pvt. collections; executed mural S.S. President Roosevelt, Am. President Lines, 1963, Soc. Nat. Bank, Cleve., 1968; participant 3d Internat. Biennial, Sao Paulo, Brazil. Bd. dirs. Ars Assn. Found., Carmel. Recipient Anne Bremer Meml. prize U. Cal., 1943, prize San Francisco Women Artists Exhbn., 1949, 51, 55, prize Cal. Watercolor Soc., 1953, San Francisco Art Assn., 1953; Best of Show award Monterey Mus. Art Ann. Competition, 1971; grant Chapelbrook Found. of Boston, 1968. Fellow Internat. Inst. Arts and Letters; mem. Am. Color Print Soc., Carmel Art Assn. (dir., pres. 1972). Illustrator: This Open Zoo—A Bestiary, 1972. Art critic Monterey Peninsula Herald, 1973—. Home and studio: 1st and Mission Sts Carmel CA 93921

LAGOWSKI, JEANNE WECKER MUND (MRS. JOSEPH JOHN LAGOWSKI), univ. adminstr.; b. St. Louis, Nov. 17, 1929; d. Ira Joseph and Josephine Emma (Weeker) Mund; B.S. (univ. scholar), Bradley U., 1951, M.S., 1952; Ph.D., U. Mich., 1957; m. Joseph John Lagowski, Feb. 13, 1954; Instr. in chemistry Bradley U., Peoria, Ill., 1951, 52; teaching asst. U. Mich., Ann Arbor, 1952-54; research chemist agrl. chemistry dept. Mich. State U., East Lansing, 1956-57; postdoctoral fellow Cambridge (Eng.) U., 1957-59; research scientist zoology dept. U. Tex., Austin, 1959-73, asst. dean in gen. and comparative studies, 1972—, lectr. zoology, 1973—. Recipient, Research Career Devel. award, NIH, 1964. Mem. Am. Chem. Soc., Internat. Soc. Heterocyclic Chemists, Mortar Bd., Sigma Xi, Phi Kappa Phi, Sigma Delta Epsilon, Iota Sigma Pi. Author: (with A.R. Katritzky) The Principles of Heterocyclic Chemistry, 1967, Heterocyclic Chemistry 1960, Chemistry of the Heterocyclic N-Oxides, 1971. Asso. editor Advances in Heterocyclic Chemistry, 1963-65. Contbr. articles to profl. jours. Home: 2105 Meadowbrook Dr Austin TX 78703

LAGRONE, DARLENE ELIZABETH LEE CAIN (MRS. KENNETH WAYNE LAGRONE), city employee; b. Langford, Kan., Jan. 14, 1936; d. William Bennett and Martha Doris (Callahan) Cain; student U. Ark., 1973-74; m. Kenneth Wayne Lagrone, Nov. 8, 1952; children—Kenneth Wayne, Carolyn Darlene, James William, Dianne Elizabeth. Requisition aircraft clk. SAC, Salina, Kan., 1952-53; co-pub., editor The Trumann (Ark.) Dem., 1959-71; sec. to mayor, city clk., treas., city insp., city commns. Trumann, 1971—; ofcl. sec. to Planning and Zoning Commn., Trumann, 1972—. Corr. Memphis Press-Scimitar and Ark. Gazette, 1964-72. Mem. Citizens Adv. Com., Trumann, 1966—; mem. Poinsett County (Ark.) Planning and Devel. Assn., 1969—. Recipient awards in state contest for editorial writing and news articles Ark. Press Women, 1967-68. Mem. Ark. Press Women, Nat. Geog. Assn., Am. Legion Aux. Baptist (mem. ch. budget com. 1969-70). Club: Twentieth Century (Trumann). Home: 548 Smith Av Trumann AR 72472 Office: Melton Av City Hall Trumann AR 72472

LAGROW, PATRICIA ANN FLEMING (MRS. LIONEL EDWIN LAGROW, JR.), irrigation co. exec.; b. Cleve., Apr. 28, 1929; d. Henry Charles and Alice (Blake) Fleming; student pub. schs.; m. Lionel Edwin LaGrow, Jr., Aug. 28, 1948; children—Lenice (Mrs. Jeffrey W. Dean), Kenneth, William, Linda, Keith. With LaGrow Irrigation, Inc., Lake Placid, Fla., 1961—, v.p., 1970—. Bd. dirs. Highlands County Youth Care, 1962—, treas., 1969-70. Mem. Fla. Irrigation Soc., Sprinkler Irrigation Assn., Sebring, Lake Placid chambers commerce. Home: 225 Park St Lake Placid FL 33852 Office: SR 621 1 Mile E Lake Placid FL 33852

LAGUAITE, JEANETTE KATHERINE, educator; b. New Orleans, June 20, 1912; d. John B. and Alma B. (Berkele) Laguaite; B.A., Tulane U., 1937, M.A., 1940; Ph.D., La. State U., 1952. Kindergarten tchr. New Orleans pub. schs., 1930-47, speech correctionist, 1947-52; prof. sect. speech pathology and audiology Tulane U. Sch. Medicine, New Orleans, 1952—, head speech pathology and audiology, 1952—. Cons. La. Evaluation Center, 1956-57, cons. La. Bd. Health Cleft Palate Team, 1959-64, VA Hosp., New Orleans, 1967—. Pres. Coalition Allied Health Professions, 1971—. Bd. dirs. Cottage Sch. for Deaf, New Orleans Area Health Planning Council. Recipient Univ. Coll. Alumni award Tulane U., 1957, John E. Robinson award La. Speech and Hearing Assn., 1970. Fellow Am. Speech and Hearing Assn.; mem. A.A.A.S., Nat. Rehab. Assn., Am. Assn. U. Profs., Am. Congress Rehab. Medicine, La. Speech and Hearing Assn. (pres. 1952-54), Am. Cleft Palate Assn., Am. Soc. Clin. Hypothesis, Am. Soc. Clin. and Exptl. Hypnosis, Internat. Assn. Logopedics and Phoniatrics. Office: 1430 Tulane Av New Orleans LA 70112

LAGUE, LOUISE ELIZABETH, journalist; b. Providence, Jan. 17, 1948; d. Maurice Euclid and Elizabeth Copeland (Laurence) Lague; degree superieur, U. Dijon, France, 1968; B.S. in French, Georgetown U., 1969. Columnist, Providence Jour. and Evening Bull., 1968-69; reporter Washington Daily News, 1969-72; reporter, mag. staff writer, performing arts and restaurant critic Washington Star-News, 1972—. Mem. alumni bd. advisers Georgetown Today, alumni mag.; panelist, cons. Georgetown U. Writers Conf. Eugene O'Neill Nat. Critics Inst. fellow, 1972. Mem. Washington Press Club, Burleith Citizens Assn., Am. Film Inst., Smithsonian Assos., Gamma Pi Epsilon. Author (with Calvin Frederick) pamphlet, Dealing with Crisis of Suicide, 1972; contbr. to Canada Today, Emblem Mag. Home: 3602 T St NW Washington DC 20007 Office: 225 Virginia Av SE Washington DC 20003

LAHEY, MARY CAROLINE, lawyer; b. Chgo., May 28, 1920; d. Harry L. and Marquetta Eugenie (Chittenden) Bemis; B.A., Mundelein Coll., 1941; M.A. in History, San Diego State U., 1966; J.D., U. San Diego, 1971; m. George Joseph Lahey, Apr. 9, 1949 (dec. Mar. 1963); children—George, Mary, Katherine. Club dir. A.R.C., France, 1945-46, Germany, 1946, Japan, 1947-48; admitted to Cal. bar, 1972; practiced in San Diego, 1972-73; legal counsel State Cal. Office Adminstrv. Hearings, Los Angeles, 1973—. Lectr. history San Diego State U., 1966-68. Mem. Cal. State Bar, Phi Alpha Delta. Home: 2658 Petaluma Long Beach CA 90815 Office: 314 W 1st St Los Angeles CA 90012

LAHR, DOROTHY ALICE FINCKE (MRS. WILLIAM JAMES LAHR), educator; b. Kansas City, Kan., Apr. 17, 1925; d. John and Alice (Bowman) Fincke; B.A., U. Wash., 1946; m. William James Lahr, May 7, 1946. Interior designer, adult edn. tchr. YWCA, 1947-52; with Seattle Art Mus., 1947—, traveling mus. curator USIS, Japan, 1957, acting head edn. dept., 1961-66, dir. edn., 1966—. Appeared in ednl. programs on Sta. KING-TV, 1954-72, Sta. KCTS-TV, 1955-72; lectr. various Guilds of Mus., P.T.A.; mem. jury selection for art works Jr. League's N.W. Art Project; mem. cultural arts adv. council Seattle Park Dept.; mem. jury selection Gov.'s Invitational Exhbn. Washington Artists, 1968; mem. jury Scholastic Art Awards, 1968; mem. Washington State Cultural Enrichment Adv. Com., 1969—; mem. Jr. League Arts for Youth Council, 1969—; mem. arts and culture program planning com. Youth div., City of Seattle; instr. humanities div. Seattle Central Community Coll., 1970—; mem. adv. com. King County Arts Commn., 1971—. Mem. Mountaineers, Arboretum Found., Lambda Rho. Home: 5224 Forest Av SE Mercer Island WA 98040 Office: Volunteer Park Seattle WA 98112

LAHR, JANICE PEARL HEDEMAN (MRS. HERBERT EDWARD LAHR), lawyer; b. Boston, Jan. 10, 1923; d. Alexander and Madeline Eloise (Levinson) Hedeman; student U. Wis., 1940-43, Hofstra Coll., 1941, N.Y. U., 1943-44; B.S., U. Ariz., 1959, J.D., 1969; m. Lawrence Sakin, Dec. 5, 1943; children—Vicki Lynne (Mrs. Michael Allen Schwager), Patricia Ann; m. 2d, Herbert Edward Lahr, Mar. 10, 1968. Sec. Hedeman Products, Inc., N.Y.C., 1943; owner, partner Towne & Sports, Inc., Tucson, 1945-49; v.p., sec. Larry Sakin, Inc., Tucson, 1948-55; admitted to Ariz. bar, 1969; asst. city atty., Tucson, 1969—. Chmn. various local drives for religious and sch. orgns., 1951-61; leader Girl Scouts Am., Tucson, 1959-61; area chmn. Cancer Drive, Tucson, 1965; mem. bd. P.T.A. Alice Vail Jr. High Sch., Tucson, 1962-63. Bd. dirs. U. Wis. Alumni, Tucson, 1972-73. Mem. Am., Ariz. bar assns., Am. Trial Lawyers, Kappa Beta Pi, Delta Zeta. Home: 4017 E Elmwood St Tucson AZ 85711 Office: 180 N Meyers St Tucson AZ 85701

LAI, SOLIDAD SALLY EUGENIO (MRS. MILTON NUUHIWA LAI), educator; b. Paauilo, Hawaii, Oct. 9, 1939; d. Pedro Mangrobang and Rosalia (Kapela) Eugenio; A.A., Maunaolu Coll., 1959; B.A., Fresno State Coll., 1962; postgrad. U. Hawaii, 1962-63; m. Milton Nuuhiwa Lai, July 18, 1964; 1 son, Leon Nawaiehaomaui. Tchr. elementary grades Hawaii Dept. Edn., 1962—. Active Pacific council Girl Scouts Am., 1963-66; chmn. Maui County Cristmas Seals, Hawaii, 1970; Maui County Parks and Recreation aide, 1972-74; mem. Hawaiian Cultural and Arts Soc.; sec. Maui Filipino Community Council, 1974. Mem. Adv. Bd. Maui Community Coll.; bd. dirs. Small World Puppetry Theatre, Waihee, Maui, trustee Eugenio Estate. Named Outstanding Young Educator State of Hawaii, 1970-71. NSF grantee, 1968, Nat. Def. Edn. Act grantee, 1966, 67. Mem. Hawaiian Canoe Club, Maui Cancer Soc., Maui Philharmonic Soc., Kappa Delta Pi. Clubs: Waihee University Extension (pres. 1970), Maui Toastmistress (pres. 1971). Home: Rural Route 1 Box 88 Wailuku HI 96793 Office: Route 1 Box 122 Wailuku HI 96793

LAI, VIOLET LAU (MRS. KUM PUI LAI), librarian; b. Honolulu, July 29, 1916; d. Say Kan and Alma Mew Ha (Wong) Lau; Ed.B., U. Hawaii, 1940, M.L.S., 1966; teaching certificate U. So. Cal., 1963; m. Kum Pui Lai, Sept. 3, 1938; children—Alma (Mrs. Bong Rin Ro), Morris Kwong You, Barbara (Mrs. John Adams Bennett). Partner, bus. mgr. Snowhite Diaper Service, Honolulu, 1944-46; instr. English, Honolulu Vocational Sch., 1949-55; instr. English, dir. publicity and publs. Honolulu Technical Sch., 1955-65; head librarian Honolulu Community Coll., 1966-74. Sec. William Paul Jarrett Intermediate ShcSch. P.T.A., Honolulu, 1958-59; mem. adv. com. Grad. Sch. Library Studies, U. Hawaii, 1971-74. Mem. Hawaii Assn. for Sch. Librarians, Hawaii Tech. Tchrs. Assn., Hawaii Library Assn. (sec. coll. and univ. sect. 1971-72), Librarians Council (sec. U. Hawaii sect. 1966-67). Author: Yearbook Planning and Production, 1959. Home: 3450 Keanu Honolulu HI 96816

LAIB, JANET, pub. relations co. exec.; b. Detroit, July 12, 1926; d. Walter and Jeanne M. (Lewenthal) Laib; student U. Mich., 1943-46; B.A. in Pub. Relations, New Sch. Social Research, 1954; m. Milton Amgott, Jan. 31, 1957; 1 dau., Margo. Beauty editor Seventeen Mag., N.Y.C., 1956; pub. relations dir. Hathaway Shirts, Inc., N.Y.C., 1956; editor McCalls Children's Wear Merchandiser, N.Y.C., 1956; pres. Janet Laib Co., N.Y.C., 1957—. Asso. Kirkland Coll., Clinton, N.Y. Mem. Pub. Relations Soc. Am., Fashion Group, Overseas Press Club Am. Home: 21 E 90th St New York City NY 10028 Office: 21 E 90th St New York City NY 10028

LAIBLIN, KATHERINE HOLT HUNDLEY, librarian; b. Salem, Va., June 5, 1910; d. Edward Roccoford and Mary Pearl (O'Neale) Holt; student U. N.C., summers 1931, 32, U. Va., eves. 1950; m. Charles Mason Hundley, Oct. 19, 1939 (dec. 1952); 1 son, Charles Marcus III; m. 2d, E. L. Nolte, Mar. 21, 1953 (div. 1956); m. 3d, George F. Laiblin, June 19, 1957 (div.). Children's librarian Olivia Raney Library, Raleigh, N.C., 1932-36; children's librarian Danville (Va.) Pub. Library, 1936-42; elementary sch. librarian, Danville, 1945-49; head librarian Ketchikan (Alaska) Pub. Library, 1949-61, Petersburg (Va.) Pub. Library, 1961-64, Astoria (Ore.) Pub. Library, 1964-65, Auburn (Wash.) Pub. Library, 1965-68; cons. instns. and physically handicapped Alaska State Library, Juneau, 1968-72, regional library coordinator S. Central region, Anchorage, 1972—; condr. children's radio program sta. KTKN, Ketchikan, 1950-58. Charter mem. Soroptimist Club, Ketchikan, 1951-61; sec. Ketchikan Bus. and Profl. Women's Club, 1958-60, Petersburg Quota Club, 1963, Midnastol Lodge Sons of Norway, 1961. Mem. Alaska, Pacific N.W. library assns., Pioneers of Alaska. Home: 2526 W 27th St Apt 4 Anchorage AK 99503 Office: 3211 Providence Dr Room 253 Anchorage AK 99504

LAIDLAW, ELIZABETH J., educator, coll. dean; b. Greenwich, Conn., June 8, 1934; d. A. Marvin and Esther C. (Carrott) Laidlaw; A.A., Colby Jr. Coll., 1954; B.S., Mich. State U., 1956, M.A., 1963; student U. Denver, summer 1965. Recreation program dir. YWCA, Greenwich, Conn., 1956-59; instr. phys. edn., resident adv. Colby Jr. Coll., New London, N.H., 1959-62; resident adv., ednl. counselor Interlochen (Mich.) Arts Acad., 1963-64; dir. womens residence hall, counselor Franklin Coll., Ind., 1964-66; dean of women Western Md. Coll., Westminster, 1966—. Mem. faculty Nat. Aquatic Sch., A.R.C., 1961-71; mem. Nat. Ski Patrol. Mem. Am., Md. personnel and guidance assns., Nat., Regional assn. women deans and counselors, Jr. League. Address: College Hill Westminster MD 21157

LAIER, JEAN BARBARA FURBUSH (MRS. CARL ROGERS LAIER), artist, poet; b. Lynn, Mass., May 26, 1926; d. Kenneth Carlyle and Elizabeth Esdale (Mac Kiel) Furbush; student Sch. Practical Arts, Boston, 1946, Decordava Mus., Northeastern U., 1972, Leslie Jr. Coll., 1973, Quinsigamond Community Coll., 1973; m. Carl Rogers Laier, Jan. 31, 1947; children—Carl Peter, Eric

Conrad, Frieda Elizabeth, Jane Ellen. Exhibited art in shows at Salem State Coll., Prestige Gallery, Peabody, Mass., Rockport, Mass., Am. Mut. Co., Wakefield, Mass.; with Forbes Lithograph Co., Chelsea, Mass., 1945-47; with Photo-Reflex Studio, Filene's, North Shore, Peabody, 1973; owner Whistling Swan Studio, comml. and residental murals, Lynnfield, Mass., 1972—. Set designer, plays Playboy Club, Boston, 1972; coordinator Saugus (Mass.) Rotary Arts Festival, 1972; chmn. Children's Poetry Contest, Lynnfield, 1970-71, Lynnfield Poetry Festival, 1972; moderator Nat. Poetry Day Festival, Lynn, 1971; numerous poetry readings, Mass., N.H., Me., N.Y., Wis., 1968—. Recipient 2d prize, nat. poetry contest Jacksonville br. Nat. League Am. Pen Women, 1971. Mem. Nat. League Am. Pen Women, New Eng. Poetry Club, Mass. Poetry Soc., Poetry Soc. N.H., Poet's Forum (Lynn, Mass.), Com. of Small Mag. Editors and Pubs., Lynnfield Art Guild, Spiritual Frontiers Fellowship, Am. Soc. Dowsers. Club: North Shore Manuscript (Lynn, Mass.). Author: Understanding the Circle, 1974. Contbr. poetry to publs., including Quill, Zahir, Ghost Dance, Softball, Brown Sweater, Legend, Premiere, Pyramid. Address: 725 Salem St Lynnfield MA 01940

LAINE, CLEO (CLEMENTINA DINAH) (MRS. JOHN PHILIP WILLIAM DANKWORTH), vocalist; b. Middlesex, Eng., Oct. 28, 1927; d. Alexander and Minnie Blanche Campbell; m. John Philip William Dankworth, 1960; children—Stuart, Alexander, Jacqueline. With Dankworth Orch., 1953—; played lead Seven Deadly Sins Edinburgh Festival also Sadlers Wells, 1961; acting roles Edinburgh (Scotland) Festival, 1966, 67; many appearances with symphony orchs., TV shows. Named Melody Maker and New Musical Express Top Girl Singer, 1956, Top Female Singer Brit. Singer, 1974; recipient Moscow Arts Theater award for acting Flesh to a Tiger, 1958, Woman of Year Golden Feather awards, 1973, Edison award (Netherlands), 1974. Home: The Old Rectory Wavendon Milton Keynes MK17 8LT England Office: Internat Artists Representation Irving House 5 Irving St London WC2H 7AT England

LAING, MELISSE, TV sta. exec.; b. Seattle, Feb. 17, 1939; d. Milo Fay and Gertrude Marie (Janson) Wilcox; B.A., Wash. State U., 1960; M.Ed., U. Wash., 1973; m. Richard L. Laing, May 4, 1973. With radio sta. KWSC Pullman, Wash., 1957-60, King Broadcasting Co., Seattle, 1959; programming asst. King Radio, Seattle, 1960-61; continuity supr. KPIX-TV, San Francisco, 1961-62; traffic mgr. KIRO-TV, Seattle, 1963-70; pub. relations dir. KCTS/9, Seattle, 1970-73, asst. program dir., 1973—. Mem. Anti-Tb. League, Seattle, 1963-71. Mem. Am. Women Radio and TV (chpt. pres. 1969-70), Women in Communications, Acad. TV Arts and Scis., Delta Delta Delta. Home: 4031 94th Av NE Bellevue WA 98004 Office: KCTS/9 University of Washington BH-10 Seattle WA 98195

LAIR, LILA MARIE GIYER, librarian; b. North Miami, Okla., Apr. 16, 1911; d. George Lesley and Bessie Jane (Ragsdale) Giyer; student Northwestern State Tchrs. Coll., Alva, Okla., 1929; A.A., Northeastern Okla. A. and M. Coll., 1931; student U. Kan., 1957; B.S., Kan. State Coll., 1961; M.L.S., U. Okla., 1964; postgrad. Appalachian State U., 1970; m. Thomas Wayne Lair, Nov. 14, 1935; (div. Sept. 1965); 1 dau., Cynthia Marie. Young people's librarian Miami (Okla.) Pub. Library, 1954-59; asst. dir. learning resources center Northeastern Okla. A. and M. Coll., Miami, 1961—. Cons. Miami (Okla.) Pub. Library, 1964, Miami (Okla.) High Sch. Library, Vinita (Okla.) Pub. Library, 1972-73, Miami Bapt. Hosp. Library, 1972. Mem. Southwestern, Okla. library assns., Higher Ednl. Alumni Council Okla., Okla. Edn. Assn. (chmn. nominating com. 1964, sec. N.E. library sect. 1965), Am. Assn. U. Profs., Internat. Platform Assn., Phi Theta Kappa, Kappa Delta Pi, Beta Phi Mu. Clubs: La Belle Maison, Reviewers (Miami, Okla.). Home: 909 J St NW Miami OK 74354

LAIRD, BETTY ANN OLSON (MRS. ROY DEAN LAIRD), ind. research analyst, actress; b. Grand Island, Neb., Dec. 19, 1925; d. Myron Ellery and Anna L. (Youtsey) Olson; B.A. cum laude, Hastings Coll., 1948; postgrad. U. Neb., 1947-48, U. Glasgow, 1952-53, U. Wash., 1956-57, U. Kan., 1960, 65-66; m. Roy Dean Laird, Sept. 3, 1946; children—Claude Myron, David Alan, Heather Lea. Tchr. English, Walnut Jr. High Sch., Grand Island, 1949-50; curriculum adviser U. Wash., Seattle, 1955-56; asst. instr. dept. English, U. Kan., Lawrence, 1958-63; research asst. (with husband), Munich, Germany, Belgrade, Yugoslavia, and U. Kan., 1963-66; project research asso. NSF, 1966-68; research analyst Jasny Project, 1969—; program adminstr. for Polish exchange, Slavic Area studies, U. Kan., Lawrence, 1972-73; ind. researcher U. Kan., Lawrence, 1973—. Historian, Bloomington-Clinton Hist. Com., 1972—. Mem. Rocky Mountain Social Sci. Assn., Friends in Council (pres. 1969-71, historian, 1971-73). Democrat. Unitarian (sec. 1962-63). Mem. Order Eastern Star. Club: University Women's (Lawrence). Author: (with Roy Dean Laird), Soviet Communism and Agrarian Revolution, 1970. Contbr. to publs. in field. Actress ednl. and comml. films Centron Corp., Lawrence, Kan., 1958—. Home: 1641 Mississippi St Lawrence KS 66044

LAIRD, CLEO FLORENCE SIEN (MRS. RUSSELL I. LAIRD), civic worker; b. Edgar, Neb., Apr. 4, 1910; d. William Foy and Lucia Swyaze (Walters) Sien; student Colo. Agrl. Coll., 1930-31; m. Russell Irving Laird, May 20, 1934; children—Julia (Mrs. Donald R. Wortham), David, Eugene, Loren, Penelope (Mrs. John L. Carroll). Co-operator Laird Farms, Worland, Wyo., 1934-58, co-owner, 1958-66, owner, 1966—. Pres., Worland Woman's Club, 1943; v.p. Wyo. P.T.A., 1946, pres., Worland; chairwoman Assn. Women's Farm Bur., 1945; chmn. Washakie County A.R.C., 1947; mem. County Welfare Bd., 1956-64; leader 4-H, 1958-62; mem. Wyo. Bd. Health, 1965-71; judge Sch. Election Bd., 1954-65; clk. Election Bd., 1962-64; pres. Democratic Women, 1938; mem. Wyo. People-to-People Travel Program, 1971—. Bd. dirs. Easter Seal Soc., Wyo. Crippled Children's Soc., 1968-72. Mem. Worland Artists Assn., Wyo. Art Assn. Democrat. Presbyn. Mem. Order Eastern Star, Daus. Nile. Clubs: Current Events (Worland); East Side. Home: 1004 Culbertson Worland WY 82401

LAIRD, ELEANOR CHILDS, author; b. Lebanon, Conn., Apr. 15, 1908; d. Harry Childs and Jane Patten (Carver) Leonard; A.B., Brown U., 1928, U. N.C. in Library Sci., 1932; L.H.D., U. Dubuque, 1971; m. Donald Anderson Laird, Apr. 18, 1940. Asst. to reference librarian Brown U. Library, Providence, 1928-35; with extension R.I. State Library, Providence, 1935-36; county librarian, Arlington, Va., 1937-39; adj. research librarian U. Dubuque (Ia.), 1965—. Bd. dirs. League Women Voters Greater Lafayette (Ind.), 1958-65. Mem. Am. Library Assn. Republican. Author (with Donald A. Laird) Psychology of Supervising the Working Woman, 1942; Technique of Handling People, 1943; Technique of Building Personal Leadership, 1944; Technique of Personal Analysis, 1945; Technique of Getting Things Done, 1947; Sizing Up People, 1951; Practical Business Psychology, 1951; Practical Sales Psychology, 1952; Human Relations in Banking, 1952; The New Psychology for Leadership, 1956; Techniques of Delegating, 1957; Sound Ways to Sound Sleep, 1959; Techniques for Efficient Remembering, 1960; Tired Feelings and How To Master Them, 1961; Dynamics of Personal Efficiency, 1961; Be Active and Feel Better, 1962; How to Get Along with Automation, 1963; Psychology; Human Relations and Motivation, 1967. Home: 912 N Grant St West Lafayette IN 47906

LAIRD, EVALYN WALSH (MRS. CHARLES HAMILTON LAIRD), lawyer; b. Chgo., Feb. 6, 1902; d. Edward J. and Mae (Tarr) Walsh; J.D., De Paul Law Sch., 1926; Ph.D. (hon.), Hamilton U., 1974; m. Charles Hamilton Laird, Aug. 8, 1925; children—Lois (Mrs. Walter P. Hillmann), Betty Ann (Mrs. Donald H. Hillmann), Charles Jr., Edward J., Jane Alice (Mrs. Daniel R. Glynn). Admitted to Ill. bar, 1926; practiced in Chgo., 1926—; mng. dir. Edward J. Walsh, ct. reporting, 1950—, owner, 1960—. Active Cub Scouts; pub. relations chmn. Rogers Park area council Girl Scouts U.S.A., Chgo., del. council, mem. personnel com.; pres. 7th dist. vicarate II, Chgo. Council Catholic Women; mem. Mayor Daley's Com. Women Lawyers; past co-chmn. Ill. Epilepsy League, Inc.; past pres. Glenola Club of Loyola Center. Former co-chmn., Women's Campaign Com. for Esther Saperstein for Senator. Mem. Women's (speakers bur.), Chgo. (past house com.; real property com., contracts and titles divs.) bar assns., Chgo. and Cook County Fedn. Women's Clubs (past mem. bd.), U.S. Figure Skating Assn., Big Sisters. Clubs: Chicago Figure Skating, Skokie Valley Figure Skating; Grand Beach (Mich.) Golf and Social. Office: 1322 Arthur Av Chicago IL 60626

LAIRD, JEAN ELOUISE RYDESKI (MRS. JACK E. LAIRD), author, educator; b. Wakefield, Mich., Jan. 18, 1930; d. Chester A. and Agnes A. (Petranek) Rydeski; Bus. Edn. degree, Duluth (Minn.) Bus. U., 1948; postgrad. U. Minn., 1949-50; m. Jack E. Laird, June 9, 1951; children—John E., Jane E., JoanAnn P., Jerilyn S., Jacquelyn T. Tchr., Oak Lawn (Ill.) High Sch. Adult Evening Sch., 1964-72, St. Xavier Coll., Chgo., 1974—. Writer newspaper column Around The House With Jean, A Woman's Work, 1965—, Chicagtown News column The World As I See It, 1969, hobby column Modern Maturity mag., travel column Travel/Leisure mag., beauty column Ladycom mag., Time and Money Savers column Lady's Circle Mag. Mem. Canterbury Writers Club Chgo. (past. pres.), Oak Lawn Bus. and Profl. Women's Club, St. Linus Guild, Mt. Assisi Acad. Parents Club. Roman Catholic. Author: Lost in the Department Store, 1964; Around The House Like Magic, 1968; Around The Kitchen Like Magic, 1969; How To Get the Most From Your Appliances, 1967; Hundreds of Hints for Harrassed Homemakers, 1971; The Alphabet Zoo, 1972; The Plump Ballerina, 1971; The Porcupine Story Book, 1974; also 95 paperback booklets. Contbr. over 500 articles to mags. Home: 10540 S Lockwood Av Oak Lawn IL 60453 also Whitewood Av Grand Beach MI 49118

LAISE, CAROLINE CLENDENING (MRS. ELLSWORTH BUNKER), govt. ofcl.; b. Winchester, Va., Nov. 14, 1917; d. James Frederic and Elizabeth Frances (Stevens) Laise; A.B., Am. U., 1938; m. Ellsworth Bunker, Jan. 3, 1967. With U.S. Civil Service Commn., 1940-45; asst. dir. personnel UNRRA, 1946-48; internat. relations officer State Dept., 1948-56; adviser U.S. delegation to UN, 1949-56, to UNESCO, 1949-56, to WHO, 1953-54; 1st sec. polit. embassy, New Delhi, India, 1956-61; dep. dir. div. South Asian affairs State Dept., 1962-65, dir. 1965-66; ambassador to Nepal, Kathmandu, 1966-73; asst. sec. state for pub. affairs, Washington, 1973—. Mem. Am. Polit. Sci. Assn., Am. Fgn. Service Assn., Asia Soc. Home: 3117 35th St NW Washington DC 20016 Office: Dept State Washington DC 20510

LAKE, ALICE DANNENBERG (MRS. LEONARD MICHAEL LAKE), mag. writer; b. N.Y.C., Nov. 29, 1916; d. Joseph and Elsie (Darmstadter) Dannenberg; B.A., Vassar Coll., 1936; m. Leonard Michael Lake, May 5, 1942; 1 dau., Ellen. Publicist, C.B.S., N.Y.C., 1937-40; propaganda analyst OWI, N.Y.C., 1940-43; sewing machine operator Big Smith Overall Factory, Carthage, Mo., 1943; housing aide USO, Rolla, Mo., 1943; reporter St. Paul Dispatch, 1943-44; free lance writer, mags. including McCalls, Good Housekeeping, Redbook, Woman's Day, Reader's Digest, Seventeen, Glamour, 1948—; pub. relations rep. Am. Soc. Plastic and Reconstructive Surgery, Am. Assn. Plastic Surgeons, 1952-60. Mem. Nat. Assn. Sci. Writers, Am. Soc. Mag. Writers, Phi Beta Kappa. Home: Glendale Rd Harrison NY 10528

LAKE, DEBBY SEGAR, publishing co. exec.; b. Walton, N.Y., Dec. 13, 1948; d. Evan B. and Ella M. (Tweedie) Segar; B.A. in Speech and Sociology (Scripps Howard Journalism scholar), Kent (O.) State U., 1971; m. Donald R. Lake, Dec. 13, 1971. Reporter, columnist Walton Reporter, 1964-67; weather girl sta. WKSU-TV, Kent, 1971; asso. editor Business Aviation, Washington, 1971-72; research asst., exec. sec., adminstrv. asst. to pres. Realty Research Corp., Atlanta, 1973; exec. sec., mem. staff Nat. Aeros. Assn., Washington, 1973-74; asst. to pub. Profl. Pilot Mag., 1974—; also treas., registered agt. Queensmith Communications. Mem. Nat. Aero. Assn., Kent State U. Alumni Assn., Ohio Speech Assn. Author articles. Office: West Bldg Washington Nat Airport Washington DC 20001

LAKE, DORIS ELIZABETH, physician; b. Sanford, Fla., July 13, 1920; d. Benjamin E. and Elizabeth Frances (Kelly) Lake; R.N., St. Vincent's Hosp. Sch. Nursing, 1941; B.S. in Nursing, Fla. State U., 1948; M.D., U. Miami, 1958. Intern, Duval Med. Center, Jacksonville, Fla., 1958-59, resident surgery, 1959-60; practice medicine specializing in family practice, West Palm Beach, Fla., 1960—; active staff Good Samaritan, St. Mary's hosps., West Palm Beach. Mem. Am., Fla. med. assns., Palm Beach County Med. Soc., Am. Cancer Soc., Alumni Assn. Fla. State U., Alumni Assn. U. Miami. Home: 319 29th St West Palm Beach FL 33407 Office: 1525 N Flagler Dr West Palm Beach FL 33407

LAKE, EDNA HELEN (MRS. EDWARD FRANK LAKE), psychologist; b. Carmel, N.Y., June 18, 1925; d. Fred Rowland and Edith Christina (Hellen) Smith; B.A., Cornell U., 1945; M.A., U. Pa., 1948; Ed.D., Columbia, 1974; m. Edward Frank Lake, May 26, 1956; children—Carolyn Jerrie, Patricia Helen. Psychol. examiner Waterbury (Conn.) pub. schs., 1952-55; sch. psychologist White Plains (N.Y.) pub. schs., 1955-56, N.Y.C. pub. schs., 1963—. Mem. Am., N.Y. State psychol. assns. Presbyn. (elder 1971-74). Home: 102-38 63rd Rd Forest Hills NY 11375 Office: 101-23 124th St Richmond Hill NY 11419

LAKE, ELLEN, lawyer; b. N.Y.C., Nov. 11, 1944; d. Leonard Michael and Alice (Dannenberg) Lake; B.A., Radcliffe Coll., 1966; J.D., Case Western Res. U., 1970; m. Peter Cummings, June 4, 1967 (div. 1972). Admitted to State Bar of Cal., 1971, Fed. Dist. Court for No. and Eastern Dists. of Cal., 1971, Ninth Circuit Court of Appeals, 1971; research atty. Cal. Supreme Court, San Francisco, 1970-71; staff atty. Legal Aid Soc. of Alameda County, Oakland, Cal., 1971-73, United Farm Workers of Am., Keene, Cal., 1973—. Reporter Louisville Times, 1966-67. Home: 2320 Prince St Berkeley CA 94705

LAKE, JEANETTE MARION, librarian; b. Oakfield, N.Y., May 27, 1913; d. August Howard and Edna Blanche (Crocker) Stein; B.A., Mt. Holyoke Coll., 1934; student Harvard Grad. Sch. Edn., 1934-35; M.S. in Library Sci., U. So. Cal., 1964; m. Ernest George Lake, Dec. 22, 1935; children—John, Margaret (Mrs. Peter D. Bulens). Grad. asst. research Harvard Grad. Sch. Edn., 1934-35; charge vocational aptitude testing Burdett Coll., Boston, 1934-35; mem. staff Cal. State Coll., Fullerton, 1964—, dir. curriculum and textbook center, 1970—. Mem. Am., Cal., Orange County library assns., Orange County Sch. Librarians, So. Cal. Tech. Processes Group, Am. Assn. U. Women. Home: 631 Cliff Dr Laguna Beach CA 92651

LAKE, VIRGINIA (MRS. KENNETH A. LAKE), cons. archivist; b. N.Y.C.; d. George Ely and Mary Frances (Brady) Pearson; B.A., Columbia, 1932; archives diploma Am. U., 1956; adminstrn. diploma (Ford Found. grant) U. Chgo., 1961; bus. law certificate U. Ill. at Springfield, 1963; m. Kenneth A. Lake, Apr. 5, 1928 (div. Dec. 1949); 1 son, Richard Alexander. Clk.-typist USAF Finance Center, Denver, 1951-54; archivist, mus. curator, custodian rare books and manuscripts U.S. Air Force Acad., 1954-58; records analyst Records Mgmt. Div., Sec. of State, Springfield, Ill., 1958-60; methods and procedures adviser Ill. Mental Health (formerly Dept. Pub. Welfare), Springfield, 1960-73; cons. on archives, records mgmt., 1973—. Cons. Bur. Records Mgmt., Manila, P.I., 1962—. Mem. Am. Records Mgmt. Assn., Adminstrv. Mgmt. Soc. (chpt. pres. 1970-71, area 9 program coordinator 1971-72; recipient award 1969, 72), Soc. Am. Archivits, Am. Acad. Polit. and Social Sci., Am. Assn. U. Women, Am. Bus. Women's Assn., Am. Soc. Pub. Adminstrn., Am. Judicature Soc. Contbr. articles to profl. jours. Profl. lectr. Home: 1208 1/2 S 7th St Springfield IL 62703

LAKELA, OLGA, botanist; b. Kesila, Finland, Mar. 11, 1890; d. Joseph Korhonen and Martha Charlotte (Kaikkonen) Lakela; diploma Valparaiso U., 1911, Normal Sch., Duluth, Minn., 1918; B.S., U. Minn., 1921, M.S., 1924, Ph.D., 1932; D.Sc., U.S. Fla., 1974. Came to U.S., 1906, naturalized, 1924. Tchr. rural sch., Kulm, N.D., 1911-12, St. Louis, County, Minn., 1914-17; tchr. biology Fairmont High Sch., 1921-25; head biology dept. State Tchrs. Coll., Minot, N.D., 1925-30; herbarium asst. U. Minn. at Mpls., 1930-35; tchr. biology dept. U. Minn. at Duluth, 1945-49, prof. botany, 1947-58, prof. emeritus, 1958—, curator, 1935-60; prof. biology State U. N.D., Grand Forks, 1959, research asst. Flora Fla. Herbarium U. South Fla., Tampa, 1960—, Hon. curator. Recipient Athena award Gulf Coast Women in Communications, 1973. Republican. Lutheran. Author: (with R.W. Long) A Flora of Tropical Florida, 1971; The Ferns of Florida, 1971—. Home: 1037 E Glenrosa Phoenix AZ 85014 Office: 170 University of South Florida Tampa FL 33620

LAKKE, DELORIS JEANETTE SHELDON (MRS. GORDON WILLARD LAKKE), civic worker; b. Lansing, Mich., May 14, 1928; d. Clifford Robert and Laura Bell (Loomis) Sheldon; student Kellogg Community Coll., 1966-68; m. Gordon Willard Lakke, Nov. 15, 1952; children—Cynthia Ann, Brenda Lynn. Pres., Woman's Aux. Calhoun County Med. Soc., 1968-69, 71-72; Mich. chmn. Edn. and Research Found., A.M.A., 1972—. Mem. Ikebana Internat., Civic Art League. Presbyn. Home: 246 Dogwood Trail Battle Creek MI 49017

LALLI, CELE GOLDSMITH (MRS. MICHAEL A. LALLI), editor; b. Scranton, Pa., Apr. 8, 1933; d. Arthur Langfeld and Viola (Wolfort) Goldsmith; B.A., Vassar Coll., 1955; m. Michael A. Lalli, Apr. 4, 1964; children—Francesca Ann, Erica Catherine. Editorial trainee, fiction dept. Ziff-Davis Pub. Co., N.Y.C., 1955-57, asst. editor, 1957-58; mng. editor Amazing Stories, 1958-60, editor-in-chief, 1960-65, mng. editor Modern Bride's Guide to Decorating Your First Home, 1965-70, exec. editor Modern Bride, 1969—. Mem. Mag. Pub. Assn., Vassar Alumni Assn. Clubs: Vassar (N.Y.C.); Vassar (Stamford). Home: 87 Hardesty Rd Stamford CT 06903 Office: 1 Park Av New York City NY 10016

LALLY, ANN MARIE, sch. adminstr.; b. Chgo., Sept. 23, 1914; d. Martin J. and Della (McDonnell) Lally; A.B., Mundelein Coll., 1935; A.M., Northwestern U., 1939, Ph.D., 1950; postgrad. Chgo. Tchrs. Coll., Chgo. Art Inst., 1935-36. Tchr. Amundsen High Sch., Chgo., 1935, Lindblom and Von Steuben, 1936-38; chmn. art dept. Schurz High Sch., 1938-40; supr. art Chgo. Pub. Elementary Schs., 1940-48; dir. art Chgo. Pub. Schs., Chgo., 1948-57; prin. John Marshall High Sch., 1957-63; supt. Dist. 16 Chgo. Pub. Schs., 1963-64, Dist. 5, 1964—; instr. creative drawing Chgo. Acad. Fine Art, 1941; instr. interior design Internat. Harvester Co., 1946-48; lectr. Wright Jr. Coll., 1948; lectr. edn. De Paul U., 1952—; lectr. edn. and art U. Chgo., 1956-59; lectr. edn. Chgo. Tchrs. Coll., 1960-62. Charter mem. woman's bd. Art Inst., Chgo.; past mem. bd. St. Joseph's Hosp. Sch. Nursing, Chgo. Trustee Pub. Sch. Tchrs.' Pension and Retirement Fund Chgo., 1957-71, sec.-treas., 1960-65, pres., 1965-70. Charter mem. woman's bd. Loyola U. Mem. Am. Assn. U. Women (Chgo. chmn. elementary and secondary edn., dir.-at-large 1962-66), Am., Ill. assns. sch. adminstrs., N.E.A. (life), Ill. Edn. Assn., Dist. Supts. Assn. (pres. 1973), Nat. Council Adminstrv. Women Edn. (profl. relations chmn. 1958-62), Assn. Supervision and Curriculum Devel., Nat., Ill. (pres. 1955) art edn. assns., Western Arts Assn. (pres. 1956-58), Chgo. Art Educators Assn. (a founder; past pres., sec. and treas.), Chgo. Pub. Sch. Art. Soc. (past dir.), Chgo. Area Reading Assn. (dir. 1963-69), Nat., Ill., assns. secondary sch. prins., Chgo. Council Fgn. Relations, Mundelein Coll. Alumnae Assn. (past pres., chmn. bd.; Mundelein Magnificant medal 1964), Pi Lambda Theta, Delta Kappa Gamma. Clubs: Ella Flagg Young, Woman's City (dir. 1963-68). Editor: Art Education in Secondary Schools, 1961. Contbr. articles to profl. jours. Home: 5701 N Sheridan Rd Chicago IL 60660 Office: 3601 N Milwaukee Av Chicago IL 60641

LALLY, KATHLEEN JEAN, journalist; b. Cleve., Dec. 13, 1946; d. Martin Charles and Jean Elizabeth (Kirk) Lally; B.S. in Journalism, Ohio U., 1967. Soc editor Painesville (O.) Telegraph, 1967-68; city hall reporter Huntington (W.Va.) Herald Dispatch, 1968-69; suburban reporter Beacon Jour., Akron, O., 1969-71, med. writer, 1971-72, chief city desk rewrite person, 1972-73; free lance journalist, 1973—. Mem. Cleve. Council Human Relations, 1964. Recipient Pulitzer prize, 1971; certificate of Merit Parents Welfare League, 1972. Mem. Nat. Orgn. for Women, Women in Communication, Zeta Tau Alpha. Home: 1929 Plymouth Rd Apt 2010 Ann Arbor MI 48105

LAM, CHARLOTTE NELL DAWSON, educator; b. Mexia, Tex.; d. Arden Earl and Maude (Merrifield) Dawson; B.S., U. Okla., 1956; Ph.D. 1967; M. Teaching, Southeastern State Coll., 1960; m. Marvin Bradford Lam, Jan. 12, 1951 (div. June 1960); children—Vicki Nell (Mrs. Norman E. Farley), Mary Lynn (Mrs. Richard M. Lenz), Bradford Earl. Tchr. pub. schs., Springer, Okla., 1950-51, Noble, Okla., 1955-56, Ione, Wash., 1956-59, Mead, Okla., 1959-61, Lawton, Okla., 1961-62; instr. English and speech Cameron State Coll., Lawton, 1962-64; grad. asst., asst. dir. reading lab. U. Okla., Norman, 1964-66; editor remedial reading program Economy Co., Oklahoma City, 1966, 67; prof. edn. and psychology Southwestern State Coll., Weatherford, Okla., 1967—. Cons. Midwest City (Okla.) Elementary Schs., 1965-66; reading and social studies Concho (Okla.) Indian Schs., 1968-69; southwestern rep. to Pres.'s Council on World Affairs, Albuquerque, 1968. Weatherford membership chmn. Lyric Theater, Oklahoma City, 1969-71. Mem. Nat., Okla. edn. assns., Internat. Reading Assn., Okla. Council Reading Tchrs., Southwestern Okla. Reading Council, Council on Higher Edn., Am. Assn. U. Women, Am. Contract Bridge League, Am. Assn. U. Profs., Kappa Delta Pi, Kappa Kappa Iota, Phi Mu. Republican. Methodist. Home: 1104 N Bryan Weatherford OK 73096

LAM, ERNA, health service adminstr.; b. Soerabaja, Indonesia, Sept. 11, 1935; d. Johan and Esther Ancy (Wolff) Kleiboer; B.S. in Occupational Therapy, Loma Linda U., 1964; 1 dau., Luzetta Carina. Came to U.S., 1961, resident, 1966. Tchr. stichting Huishoudelijke Voorlichting ten Plattelande, Netherlands, 1958-61; occupational therapy aid Loma Linda (Cal.) Sanitarium, 1962-64; staff therapist St.

John's Hosp., Springfield, Ill., 1965-66; chief therapist Lincoln (Ill.) Meml. Hosp., 1966; dir. occupational therapy Good Samaritan Hosp., Mt. Vernon, Ill., 1966-71; dept. chmn. occupational therapy assisting N.D. State Sch. Sci., Wahpeton, 1971—. Mem. adv. com. on occupational therapy curriculum U. N.D., Grand Forks, 1972—; chmn. adv. com. Minndak Vocational Career Center, Wahpeton, 1973—. Mem. Am., Dakota (v.p. Wells Fargo dist. 1972-73, pres. 1974—), Minn. occupational therapy assns., Nat. Rehab. Assn., World Fedn. Occupational Therapists. Home: 809 S 2d St Wahpeton ND 58075 Office: ND State Sch Sci Wahpeton ND 58075

LAMAR, GEORGIA RUTH CRISWELL (MRS. GRESTER H. LAMAR), librarian; b. Salem, Ind., Jan. 12, 1908; d. Arthur Preston and Maude Edith (Hunter) Criswell; A.B., U. Okla., 1933; postgrad. U. Colo., 1936-37, Okla. State U., 1965; m. Grester H. LaMar, July 22, 1941; 1 son, Robert Hal. Librarian, Panhandle State Coll., Goodwell, 1930-31, Guymon (Okla.) High Sch., 1965—; chmn. Okla. Dept. Libraries Bd., Oklahoma City, 1970—. Sec., bd. dirs. E.E. Dale Library Found., Guymon, Okla.; v.p., bd. dirs. Dunaway Library Found. Home: 418 W 4th St Guymon OK 73942

LAMB, ANTONIA, author; b. N.Y.C., Oct. 3, 1943; d. Robert Gustave and Marion (Heller) Blick; student Columbia, 1962-63; children—James Christopher, Joanna Catherine. Author: (novels) Greystones, 1966; The Greenhouse, 1967; Lady in Shadow, 1968; Remember the Summer, 1973; composer songs Morning and an Oldsmobile, 1971; Joanna, 1972; astrologer, occult cons., 1964—; ordained to ministry Universal Life Ch., 1969. Mem. Broadcast Music, Inc., 1971—. Mem. P.T.A. Mendocino, 1971—; chairperson protem Mendocino Coast Welfare Rights Orgn., 1973. Recipient St. Gaudens medal Met. Mus. Art, 1961. Mem. Nat. Soc. Lit. and Arts. Home: PO Box 395 Mendocino CA 95460 Office: care of Seligmann and Collier 280 Madison Av New York City NY 10016

LAMB, ELIZABETH SEARLE (MRS. F. BRUCE LAMB) (PSEUDONYM K.L. MITCHELL), writer; b. Topeka, Kan., Jan. 22, 1917; d. Howard Sanford and Helen Baker (Shaver) Searle; A.B., U. Kan., 1939, Mus.B., 1940; m. F. Bruce Lamb, Dec. 11, 1941; 1 dau., Carolyn (Mrs. Michael Kaye). Profl. harpist, 1939-42; writer prose and poetry in various music, inspirational, and juvenile mags., 1940—; reporter Pueblo (Colo.) Chieftain, 1957-59; dir. Am. Assn. U. Women poetry workshops N.J. Writers Seminar, 1971, 73. Mem. Canon City (Colo.) Library Bd., 1958-59. Recipient Anna Hempstead Branch Silver medal Bklyn. Poetry Circle, 1965; 2d prize Ruben Dario Internat. Meml. Poetry Contest, OAS, 1967; Haiku Orchid award Haiku Mag., 1972, 1st Haiku prize Deep South Writers and Artists Conf., 1973. Mem. Nat. League Am. Pen Women (Lady Beatrice Graham award N.Y.C. br., 1965; Ruth Mason Rice 1st prize 1966, 67, 72; biennial award 1964, 68). Haiku Soc. Am. (pres. 1971), N.Y. Women Poets, Colorado Springs Poetry Fellowship, Phi Beta Kappa, Pi Kappa Lambda, Mu Phi Epsilon, Delta Gamma. Episcopalian. Author: (with Jean Bailey, Patricia Markun) The Pelican Tree and Other Panama Adventures, 1953; Today and Every Day, 1970; Inside Me, Outside Me, 1974. Home: 4 Washington Square Village New York City NY 10012

LAMB, HELEN KEITHLEY (MRS. DONALD QUINCY LAMB), author; b. Des Moines, Sept. 7, 1908; d. Fred French and Imogene (Balliet) Keithley; B.A., Drake U., 1929; m. Donald Quincy Lamb, Mar. 24, 1934; children—Imogene (Mrs. Nathan J. Bolls, Jr.), Donald Quincy, Frederick Keithley. Actuarial student Bankers Life Ins. Co., Des Moines, 1929-34; partner Lambs' Ins. Service, Manhattan, Kan., 1937-72. Asst. chmn. Kan. Nat. Poetry Day, 1969. Recipient Magna Cum Laude World Poet award, 1970; certificate of Appreciation and Thanks, Am. Mosaic Collection, 1970; 1st prize poetry contests Kan. Authors Club, 1961, 62, 69, 71, 73. Mem. World Poetry Soc. Intercontinental, Internat. Platform Assn., Center for Study Democratic Instns., League Women Voters, Common Cause, Kan., Manhattan authors clubs, D.A.R., P.E.O., Manhattan Cultural Arts Council, Phi Beta Kappa. Democrat. Methodist. Club: Domestic Science (Manhattan). Contbr. poetry to profl. jours., mags. Home: 819 Humboldt St Manhattan KS 66502

LAMB, ISABELLE SMITH (MRS. GEORGE E. LAMB), mfg. co. exec.; b. Charteris, Que., Can., Dec. 14, 1922; d. Gordon Robert and Beatrice Leona (Dale) Smith; secretarial degree, Gowling Bus. Coll., Ottawa, Ont., Can., 1939; student Carleton U., Ottawa, Ont., 1940-42; m. George Emerson Lamb, Oct. 2, 1948; 1 son, David Emerson. Came to U.S., 1948. Sec., Gatineau Power Co., Ottawa, Ont., Can., 1942; sec. to city treas. City Ottawa, 1943; sec., Canadian Internat. Paper Co., Gatineau, Que., 1943-48; sec., dir. Ovalstrapping, Inc., Hoquiam, Wash., 1964—; corporate sec., dir. Lamb Machinery, Inc., Memphis, Meridian Machine Works (Miss.); corporate sec. Enterprises Internat., Inc., Hoquiam; dir. Gerrard Co. Ltd., Hamilton, Ont. Mem. Wash./Alaska Regional Med. Programs Adv. Com., 1966—; mem. Wash. State Comprehensive Health Planning Adv. Council, 1967—, exec. com., 1967—. Trustee St. Joseph Hosp., Aberdeen, Wash., 1970—, v.p., 1973—. Club: Zonta (sec., dir. 1973—) (Grays Harbor). Home: Cleveland St at Sunset Dr Hoquiam WA 98550 Office: Blaine and Firman Sts Hoquiam WA 98550

LAMB, JANET ARLENE (MRS. JAMES ORVILLE LAMB), race horse breeder; b. Dayton, O., Nov. 10, 1937; d. Herbert and Ethel Clara (Wright) Rothwell; grad. pub. high sch.; m. James Orville Lamb, Mar. 30, 1956; 1 son, Mark Craig. Artist, Blanchester, O., and Waynesville, O., 1948-73; teletype operator Armco Steel, Middletown, O., 1957; finish carpenter, Waynesville, 1961—; co-owner, operator farm, Blanchester, 1966—; race horse breeder, Blanchester, O., 1971—; model, 1973—. Mem. U.S. Trotting Assn., Ohio Racing Commn. Home: Route 2 1085 James Rd Blanchester OH 45107

LAMB, JULIA FLITNER (MRS. ALBERT RICHARD LAMB, JR.), conservationist, civic worker; b. Englewood, N.J., Aug. 28, 1918; d. Stanwood Edwards and Gertrude (Wellington) Flitner; B.A., Vassar Coll., 1940; m. Albert Richard Lamb, Jr., Jan. 17, 1942; children—Albert Richard III, George Stanwood, Thomas Appleton, Peter Flitner Henshaw. Asst. physician's office, Englewood, 1941-42; with reservations dept. Am. Airlines, N.Y.C., 1940-41; field sec. pub. relations, instr. math. Dwight Sch., Englewood, 1942-45. Mem. adv. bd. Scenic Hudson Preservation Conf., 1964—; mem. steering com. Save Hackensack Meadowlands Coalition, 1971—; sec. Englewood council U.S. Mail Users Council, 1968-73; environment chmn. Ch. Women United of N.J., 1971—; mem. N.J. Conservation Commn., N.J. Fedn. Shade Tree Commns., chmn. adv. com. Englewood, 1957-68; mem. social action task force on environment N.J. Council of Chs., 1972. Trustee, Dwight Sch., sec. exec. com., 1946-52; bd. govs. Englewood Sch. for Boys, 1952-71. Recipient Conservation award Am. Motors Corp., 1973, Human Relations award Negro Women's Council, 1974. Mem. Internat. Union Conservation Nature and Natural Resources, UN Assn., Am. Nature Study Soc., Palisades Nature Assn. (life; trustee 1970-73, pres. 1973—), Greenlands for Englewood Assn. (v.p. 1966-73, pres. 1973—) Sierra Club (exec. com. North Jersey group 1970-73), League of Women Voters (environmental quality Commn., Land Use Commn. Englewood), N.J. Citizens for Clean Air, Better Air for Bergen, Hudson Planning Council, Ch. Women United, Taskforce on Environment N.J., Nat. Audubon Soc., N.Y. Zool. Soc., Hudson River Fisherman's Assn. Clubs: Garden of America; Garden of Englewood (v.p. 1961-63, conservation com.), Federated Garden of N.J. Episcopalian (exec. bd. women's orgn.). Contbr. articles on conservation to periodicals. Home: 301 Lydecker St Englewood NJ 07631 also Mountainville NY 10953

LAMB, MARGARET WELDON, lawyer; b. Arlington, Mass., June 26, 1935; d. Hubert Weldon and Lydia (Cazneau) Lamb; student Wellesley Coll., 1953-56; B.A., U. Denver, 1959, law student, 1959-62; LL.B., Boston Coll., 1964. Admitted to Mass. bar, 1964, N.M. bar, 1969; atty. Hill & Barlow, Boston, 1964-65; asst. atty. gen. State of Mass., 1965-67; hearing officer Commonwealth of Mass., 1967-68; asst. atty. gen. State of N.M., 1969-71; chief pilot, counsel Air Health Kare, Denver and Taos, N.M., 1971—; practice aviation and criminal law, Taos, 1972—; co-owner, chief pilot Sangre de Cristo Aviation, Inc., Taos, 1972—; pub. defender 8th Jud. Dist., 1973—. Mem. Lawyer-Pilots Bar Assn., Mass. Bar Assn., State Bar N.M. Author: Colorado High County, 1964; also articles. Home: 918 Stagecoach Rd Santa Fe NM 87501 Office: PO Box 1134 Taos NM 87571

LAMB, MARTHA HARDY, educator; b. Charleston, W.Va., Nov. 4, 1942; d. Harold Leon and Margaret May (Hardy) Lamb; A.B., Queens Coll., 1964; M.Ed., Boston U., 1967, postgrad. (Nat. Def. Edn. Act fellow), 1967—. Tchr. social studies Atlanta secondary schs., 1965-66; grad. asst. Boston U., 1966-67; psychometrist Title I Project, Middletown, R.I., 1969; coll. counselor Gram Jr. Coll., Boston, 1969-70; psychol. counselor Framingham (Mass.) State Coll., 1970—. Mem. Nat., Mass. assns. women deans, adminstrs. and counselors, Pi Lambda Theta. Home: 38 Beverly Rd Natick MA 01760 Office: Counseling Center Framingham State Coll Framingham MA 01701

LAMB, MINA MARIE WOLF, educator; b. Sagerton, Tex., Aug. 14, 1910; d. Karl and Louise (Boeer) Wolf; B.A., Tex. Tech. Coll., 1932, M.S., 1937; Ph.D., Columbia, 1940; m. Arch G. Lamb, June 3, 1941; 1 son, Arch Karl. Tchr. pub. schs., Rule, Tex., 1933-35; with Tex. Tech, 1940—, instr., asst. prof., asso. prof., 1940-55, prof., head dept. food and nutrition, 1955-69, Margaret W. Weeks prof., 1969—. Mem. Am. Assn. U. Women, Am., Tex. (past pres.) dietetic assns., Am., Tex. home econs. assns., Am. Inst. Nutrition, Sigma Xi, Phi Upsilon Omicron, Phi Kappa Phi. Democrat. Methodist. Home: PO Box 4096 Tech Sta Lubbock TX 79409

LAMB, RUTH STANTON (MRS. RAYMOND G. LAMB), educator; B.A., Pomona Coll., 1936; M.A., Claremont Grad. Sch., 1937; Ph.D., U. So. Cal., 1943; m. Raymond G. Lamb, 1943; children—Stephan, Stanton, Robbin. Instr., Northwestern U., Evanston, Ill., 1942-44; prof., chmn. dept. Spanish and Hispanic-Am. lits., Scripps Coll., Claremont, Cal., also Claremont Grad. Sch., 1944—; mem. Instituto de la Lengua Espanola, Mexico City, Mexico, 1947; research asso. Instituto de Cultura Hispanica, Madrid, Spain, 1956; Fulbright lectr., research scholar U. Sao Paulo, Brazil, 1963, Universidad Nacional de Cuyo, Mendoza, Argentina, 1967, Rumania, 1973; lectr. Bi-Nat. Lang. Centers, Argentina, Chile, Mexico, 1966-67. Del Amo fellow, Spain, 1956. Mem. Instituto Internacional de Literatura Iberoamericana, Am. Assn. Tchrs. Spanish and Portuguese, Modern Lang. Assn. So. Cal., Western Hist. Assn., Modern Lang. Assn., Pacific Coast Council Latin Am. Studies, Internat. Assn. Hispanists, mem. Phi Beta Kappa, Phi Sigma Iota, Pi Lambda Theta, Sigma Delta Pi. Author: Breve Historia del Teatro Mexicano, 1958; Antologia del Cuento Guatemalteco, 1959; Bibliografia del Teatro Mexicano del Siglo XX, 1962; Latin America: Sights and Insights, 1963; Cuentos Misteriosos, 1964; Mexican Americans: Sons of the Southwest, 1970; Three Contemporary Latin American Plays, 1971. Home: 4442 E Live Oak Dr Claremont CA 91711

LAMBERT, B. GERALDINE, educator; b. Booneville, Ark.; d. Arthur and Bertha (Nichols) Lambert; B.A., Okla. Coll. Liberal Arts, 1946; M.Ed., U. Okla., 1958, Ph.D., 1966. Psychiat. aide Inst. of Living, Hartford, Conn., 1947; tchr., counselor Hobbs (N.M.) Municipal Schs., 1948-61; chmn. social studies dept. Classen High Sch., Oklahoma City, 1961-64; counselor Star-Spencer High Sch., Oklahoma City, 1964-66; asso. prof. psychology U. Southwestern La., Lafayette, 1966-69, prof., 1969—, chmn. dept. psychology, 1970—. Cons. Bur. Hearing and Affairs, Social Security Adminstrn., 1967-71, St. Martin Bilingual Program, 1969—, Iberia Parish Schs., 1970-73, Lafayette Mental Health Center, 1972—. Bd. dirs. Lafayette Juvenile and Adult Program, 1967—. John Hay fellow Williams Coll., Williamstown, Mass., 1964. Mem. Am., Southwestern, La. psychol. assns., Am. Personnel and Guidance Assn., N.E.A., Am. Assn. U. Women, La. Acad. Scis., Sigma Xi, Pi Gamma Mu, Delta Kappa Gamma, Phi Kappa Phi, Psi Chi, Kappa Delta Pi. Author: (with others) Adolescence: Transition for Childhood to Maturity, 1972. Home: PO Box 1571 U Southwestern La Lafayette LA 70501

LAMBERT, MARJORIE FERGUSON (MRS. E. V. LAMBERT), archaeologist, educator; b. Colorado Springs, Colo., June 13, 1910; d. John and Elizabeth (Wattson) Ferguson; B.A., Colo., Coll. 1930; M.A., U. N.M., 1931; m. E. V. Lambert, Oct. 7, 1950. Resident and teaching fellow U. N.M., 1931, instr., 1932-36, Highlands U., 1932; research asso. Sch. Am. Research, 1932; field supr. Mus. N.M. and U. N.M., 1934-37; preparator, research asso. Mus. N.M. and Sch. Am. Research, 1937-38, curator archaeology, 1938—, Palace of Govs., 1955—, also curator of anthropology exhibits, curator anthropology div. research, 1965-69; research asso. prof. Eastern N.M. U., Portales, 1969—; research asso. Sch. Am. Research, 1969—, bd. dirs., 1972—; curator anthropology exhibits Hall of Ethnology, 1969; chmn. adv. com. Picunis Pueblo Mus. Trustee Ind. Arts Fund, 1948—, chmn., 1949-50, sec., 1948-49. Mem. Am. Anthrop. Assn., Soc. Am. Archaeology, Archaeol. Soc. N.M. (sec. 1943-57, v.p. 1959—), S.W. Assn. Indian Affairs (bd. mem. 1939-59), Spanish Coll. Arts Soc. (trustee 1951—), Old Santa Fe Assn. (mem. bd.), Alpha Delta Pi. Judge Ann. Indian Market, Santa Fe, 1940—. Home: 679 E Garcia St PO Box 578 Santa Fe NM 87501

LAMBERT, MARTHA QUANDT (MRS. ROY R. LAMBERT), coll. adminstr.; b. Balt., Apr. 21, 1926; d. Roland Webster and Mary Amelia (Roland) Quandt; A.A., Johns Hopkins, 1973; m. Roy R. Lambert, Sept. 14, 1946; children—Ralph Andrew, Kathleen Joan. Office employee Davison Chem. Corp., Balt., 1946-47; supr. publs. Catonsville Community Coll., Balt., 1964—. Local sec. P.T.A., 1954-58, county sec., 1966; den mother, pack sec. Cub Scouts, 1956-59; mem. troop com. Girl Scouts U.S.A., 1960. Recipient recognition of merit Tchrs. Assn. Baltimore County, 1968. Mem. Nat. (hon.), Md. (hon.) congresses parents and tchrs., Md. Assn. Community/Jr. Colls. (sec. pub. relations affiliate 1968-72), In-Plant Printing Mgmt. Assn. (Balt. pres. 1972—), League Women Voters (county gov. 1964-66). Home: 4208 Manorview Rd Glenarm MD 21057 Office: 800 S Rolling Rd Baltimore MD 21228

LAMBERT, MARY PULLIAM (MRS. JOSEPH BUCKLEY LAMBERT), biochemist; b. Birmingham, Ala., Apr. 27, 1944; d. Arch and Laura Mae (Cannon) Pulliam; B.S., Birmingham-So. Coll., 1966; Ph.D., Northwestern U., 1971; m. Joseph Buckley Lambert, June 27, 1967; children—Laura Kirwan, Alice Pulliam. Instr. biochemistry div. Northwestern U., Evanston, Ill., 1971, 72. USPHS fellow, 1966-70. Mem. Am. Soc. Microbiology, Phi Beta Kappa, Sigma Xi. Home: 1956 Linneman St Glenview IL 60025 Office: Dept Chemistry Northwestern U Evanston IL 60201

LAMBERT, NADINE MURPHY (MRS. ROBERT E. LAMBERT), educator; b. Ephraim, Utah, Oct. 21, 1926; d. Rulon E. and Maude (Nielsen) Murphy; A.B., U. Cal. at Los Angeles, 1948; M.A., Los Angeles State Coll., 1955; Ph.D., U. So. Cal., 1965; m. David M. Allan, Dec. 28, 1950 (div. Aug. 1955); 1 dau., Laura R.; m. 2d, Robert E. Lambert, Dec. 29, 1956; 1 son, Jeffrey Ross. Psychologist, Los Nietos Sch. Dist., 1952-53, Bellflower Unified Sch. Dist., 1953-58; research cons. Cal. State Dept. Edn., 1958-64; prof. dept. edn. U. Cal., Berkeley, 1964—. Mem. edn. com., Joint Commn. on Mental Health of Children, USPHS, 1967-68; dir. sch. psychology tng. program U. Cal. at Berkeley, Behavioral Sci. Tng. Br., Nat. Inst. Mental Health Tng. Grant, 1966-70, 70-75. Fellow Am. Orthopsychiat. Assn., Am. Psychol. Assn.; mem. Nat. Council on Measurement Used in Edn., Am. Ednl. Research Assn., Am. Psychol. Assn., Cal. Assn. Sch. Psychologists and Psychometrists (pres. 1962-63). Contbr. articles to profl. jours. Asso. editor Am. Jour. Orthopsychiatry. Home: 994 Grizzly Peak Blvd Berkeley CA 94708

LAMBERT, PATTIE ANN, librarian; b. Brodnax, Va., Apr. 11, 1930; d. William Andrew and Mary Evelyn (Jones) Lambert; B.A., Coll. William and Mary, 1950; B.L.S., U. N.C., 1951. Cataloger, asst. librarian Thomas Hackney Braswell Meml. Library, Rocky Mount, N.C., 1951—. Cons. N.C. Dept. Juvenile Correction, 1971-73; writer Sunday book column, book reviewer Rocky Mount Telegram, 1961—, free-lance feature writer, 1964—; free-lance feature writer Dixie Cycle News, Nashville (N.C.) Graphic, 1965—. Co-founder Downtown Deskworkers Therapeutic Swimming League, 1959, pres., 1962-68; publicity chmn. Rocky Mount chpt. N.C. Symphony Soc., 1963-73. Mem. Am. Motorcycle Assn., N.C. Library Assn., N.C. Wild Flower Preservation Soc., Rocky Mount C. of C. (mem. arts council 1973), St. Cecelia's Guild. Democrat. Methodist. Clubs: Rocky Mount Motorcycle (hon.), Rocky Mount Rifle and Pistol (treas. 1960-63). Home: 108 Arlington Terrace Rocky Mount NC 27801 Office: Falls Rd Rocky Mount NC 27801

LAMBETH, IDA MIMS, editor; b. Houston, July 4, 1930; d. Phillip Robert and Hattie Lou (Barlow) Mims; student Lynchburg Coll., 1948-49; B.A., Longwood Coll., 1952; m. Larry Lynn Lambeth, Aug. 1, 1952 (div. July 1959); children—Lydia Lynne, Donald Lee. Caseworker, Prince William County Dept. Pub. Welfare, Manasas, Va., 1952; social sci. research asso. U. Tex. Bur. Bus. Research, Austin, 1959—, statis. researcher, 1965, editor Directory Tex. Mfrs., 1965—. Del. Travis County Rep. Conv., 1962. Episcopalian. Home: 1900 W St John's St Austin TX 78757 Office: Bur Bus Research U Tex Austin TX 78712

LAMBETH, KATHARINE COVINGTON (MRS. JAMES E. LAMBETH, JR.), mfg. co. exec.; b. Sanford, N.C., Jan. 23, 1917; d. Richard DePew and Corrinna (Chisholm) Covington; A.B. in Music, Meredith Coll., 1938; postgrad. N.C. State U., 1956-57, Parsons Sch. Design, 1958-59; m. James Erwin Lambeth, Jr., Aug. 27, 1938; children—James Erwin, III, Richard Covington, Mary Katharine (Mrs. Grady R. Cullens), Wm. Roderick. Pres. Erwin-Lambeth, Inc., Thomasville, N.C., 1947—, Interiors, Ltd., Thomasville, 1971—. Bd. mem. Resources Council Am., 1962-63. Named Outstanding Woman of Yr. in Industry N.C. Fedn. Women's Clubs, 1963. Mem. Nat. Home Fashions League (1st pres. Carolinas chpt. 1969-71, past nat. dir.), Furniture Designers Assn. (hon. life), Nat. Soc. Interior Designers, Internat. Platform Assn., Am. Assn. U. Women. Methodist. Democrat. Club: Thomasville Woman's (dir. 1960-61). Home: 214 E Lake Dr Thomasville NC 27360 Office: 201 E Holly Hill Rd Thomasville NC 27360

LAMONT, BARBARA GIBSON, librarian; b. Huntington, Ind., Nov. 8, 1925; A.B. in Classics, William and Mary Coll., 1947; M.A. in Classical Philology, Radcliffe Coll., 1952; M.S. in L.S., Simmons Coll., 1954. Tchr., Mary C. Wheeler Sch., Providence, 1949-51; clk. Lamont Library, Harvard, 1951-53; cataloguer Widener Library, Harvard, 1953-56, chief of gifts and exchange, 1956-61, adminstrv. asst. resources and acquisitions, 1961-64; librarian Douglass Coll., New Brunswick, N.J., 1964-67, Vassar Coll., Poughkeepsie, N.Y., 1967—. Cons. Keuka Coll., Keuka Park, N.Y., 1968, St. Thomas Aquinas Coll., Sparkill, N.Y., 1969. Mem. A.L.A. Office: Vassar Coll Poughkeepsie NY 12601

LAMONT, FRANCES STILES (MRS. WILLIAM LAMONT), civic leader; b. Rapid City, S.D., June 10, 1914; d. Frederick Bailey and Frances (Kenney) Stiles; B.A. in Journalism, U. Wis., 1935, M.A., 1936; m. William Mather Lamont, Oct. 6, 1937 (dec. Aug. 1973); children—William Stiles, Nancy Brereton Frances Margaret, Frederick Mather. Lectr. polit. sci. Presentation Coll., 1967-68, bd. trustees, 1969—. Active A.R.C., 1942-45; mem. S.D. Com. Edn., Gov.'s Com. White House Conf. Aging; organizer, sec. Brown County Mental Health Assn.; bd. dirs. S.D. Mental Health Assn.; state del.-at-large, bd. dirs. Nat. Assn. Mental Health, 1955-57; organizer Northeastern S.D. Mental Health Center, pres., 1958-60; mem. S.D. Women's TV Council, 1955-58; mem. Nat. Women's Adv. Council Civil Def., 1958, organizer, pres. Dacotah Prairie Mus., Inc., 1964-72, mem. Mayor's Study Com. on Low-Rent Housing, 1965—; pres. Brown County Council on Aging, 1961-68; mem. bd. Aberdeen Sr. Center Bd., 1968—; chmn. Gov.'s Com. on Aging, 1962—; gov.'s rep. Nat. Conf. State Execs. on Aging, Washington, 1963, 64, 65; vice chmn. Gov.'s Commn. on Status of Women; mem. Gov.'s Adv. Commn. on Aging, 1968—; chmn. S.D. delegation, subsect. chmn. White House Conf. on Aging, 1971; mem. S.D. Sr. Citizens Planning Council, 1971-72; mem. Foster Grandparents Council; mem. bd. Girl Scouts U.S.A., chmn. com. of regional bd., 1967-68. Named First Lady of Aberdeen for civic achievement, 1954, S.D. Mother of Yr., 1974; recipient Service to mankind award Sertoma Club, 1972, S.D. Ambassador award, 1969. Mem. Am. Assn. U. Women (state bd. 1947-71, state pres. 1958-60, state historian 1961-69, trustee Nat. Edn. Found. 1971—), D.A.R., P.E.O., P.T.A. (pres. 1948-49), Brown County Mus. and Hist. Soc. (pres. 1972), Interstate Assn. State Commns. on Status of Women (nat. dir. 1970-72), Nat. Soc. for Historic Preservation (dir.-at-large 1972), Phi Kappa Phi, Theta Sigma Phi, Kappa Alpha Theta, Mortar Bd. Republican (precinct committeewoman 1960—). Episcopalian (vestryman). Home: Meadowlark RFD Aberdeen SD 57401

LAMORA, JUDY LYNNE GRISTY (MRS. DONALD ELLSWORTH LAMORA), polit. worker; b. San Antonio, Mar. 23, 1939; d. Timothy Endemond and Clovis Ruth (Mooring) Gristy; student Tex. Technol. U., 1956-60; m. Donald Ellworth LaMora, Nov. 10, 1960; children—Grant Donald, Leigh Suzanne, Eric Jon. Proofreader, Lubbock (Tex.) Avalanche Jour., 1960; reporter Colorado Springs (Colo.) Gazette-Telegraph, 1960-61. Mem. Colo. Commn. on Status of Women, 1969-73, state vice chmn. women in govt. com., 1970-72; 2d v.p. Wagon Wheel council Girl Scouts U.S.A., 1970-72. Mem. Colo. Republican State Central Com., 1969-71, mem. exec. com.; bd. dirs., mem. exec. com. Colo. Fedn. Rep. Women, pres., 1974—; vice chmn. pub. relations Nat. Fedn. Rep. Women, 1974—. Mem. Colorado Springs Press Assn., Kappa Alpha Theta. Mem.

Christian Ch. Club: Law Wives (El Paso County). Editor: (with others) See How She Runs, A Guide for the Woman Candidate, 1972. Home: 8 Menary Way Colorado Springs CO 80906

LAMOREAUX, DELORES EVANGELINE TOM LOULA (MRS. LEE V. LAMOREAUX), coop. exec.; b. Phillips, Wis., Dec. 27, 1937; d. Joseph John and Susie (Dill) Tom; grad. high sch.; m. Franklin H. Loula, Sept. 3, 1960 (div. Mar. 1965); m. 2d, Lee V. Lamoreaux, June 7, 1969; 1 dau., Suzette Marie. With Price Electric Coop., Inc., Phillips, 1956—, sec., 1961-66, bookkeeper, 1966, mgmt. asst., 1966—, also officer Price Credit Union; owner, operator Snack Shop, Phillips, 1966-67; owner Phillips Youth Center, 1967-69. Mem. Civil Air Patrol, 1959. Mem. Wis. Assn. Rural Elec. Coops. Office Mgrs. (sec.-treas.). Methodist (lay speaker Ch. Women's Soc. 1965-70). Mem. Women of Moose (sr. regent 1957-58). Home: Luger Route Phillips WI 54555

LAMOTHE, HEATHER FIELDS, univ. dean; b. Atlanta, Nov. 23, 1947; d. James Weldon and Betty Carson (Kennedy) Fields; A.B., Ga. State U., 1970, M.A., 1972; m. Richard Surguies Lamothe, Mar. 15, 1969. Asst. dean of women Ga. State U., Atlanta, 1971-72, asst. dean for fgn. students, 1972-73, asst. dean of students, fgn. students adviser, 1973—. Dir. Atlanta Area High Sch. Model UN, 1973; mem. Gov.'s Com. for UN Day Observance, 1973, Mayor's Com. for UN Day Observance, 1973, 74. Mem. Nat., Ga. (treas. 1973-75) assns. women deans, adminstrs. and counselors, Nat. Assn. Fgn. Student Affairs, Ga. Coll. Personnel Assn., St. Andrews Soc. Christian Scientist. Club: Ga. State University Woman's. Home: 2880 Jerome Rd College Park GA 30349 Office: Fgn Student Office Ga State U 33 Gilmer St Atlanta GA 30303

LAMPE, JANE KATHLEEN, coll. dean; b. Lansing, Mich., Mar. 22, 1938; d. Waldo O. and Margaret (Flavin) Lampe; A.B., Rosary Coll., 1960; M.A. (Thomas Clarkson Trueblood Scholar), U. Mich., 1961; M.Ed., U. Va., 1967. Asst. dean women, asst. prof. speech Rosary Coll., River Forest, Ill., 1961-67; asst. dean women, dean freshmen women, dir. women's residence Salem (Mass.) State Coll., 1967-69; dean women Wilkes Coll., Wilkes Barre, Pa., 1969—. Mem. Zeta Phi Eta. Home: 63 Pringle St Kingston PA 18704 Office: Wilkes Coll Wilkes Barre PA 18703

LAMPEL, ANITA KAY, psychologist; b. Los Angeles, May 25, 1946; d. Jack Murray and Rose (Spivak) Lampel; B.A. cum laude (NSF grantee), U. Cal. at Los Angeles, 1966; Ph.D. (Nat. Def. Edn. Act grantee), Stanford, 1969. Psychologist div. child psychiatry Children's Meml. Hosp., Chgo., 1969-73; coordinator children and adolescent services San Bernardino County Mental Health, 1973—. Lectr., DePaul U., Cal. State U., San Bernardino. Area rep. Community Health Orgn., Chgo., 1971. Mem. Am., Cal. (chairperson membership com. San Bernardino-Riverside chpt. 1974) psychol. assns., Soc. for Research in Child Devel., Nat. Orgn. Women (chairperson counseling needs local chpt. 1973—), Phi Beta Kappa. Contbr. articles to profl. jours. Home: 963 W 24th St San Bernardino CA 92404 Office: 780 E Gilbert St San Bernardino CA 92404

LAMPEN, SISTER MARY JOEL, coll. pres.; b. Carlyle, Ill.; d. Joseph Conrad and Mary Johanna (Hitpas) Lampen; student Ancilla Coll., 1939-41, DePaul U., 1948; Ph.B., Loyola U., Chgo., 1949, Ed.D., 1964; M.A., St. Mary's Coll., 1956. Tchr. elementary schs., 1941-47; tchr. Angel Guardian High Sch., 1948-52, St. Augustine's High Sch., 1952-60; tchr., dir. guidance Ancilla Domini High Sch., Donaldson, Ind., 1960-64; pres. Ancilla Coll., Donaldson, 1964—. Mem. adv. council Ancilla Domini Sisters, 1966—. Mem. planning com. Marshall County (Ind.) Community Leaders Seminar, 1970—; mem. Constnl. Rev. Commn., Ind., 1972—; sec. Marshall County Devel. Study Com., 1972—. Vice pres. bd. dirs. St. Catherine's Hosp., East Chicago, Ind., 1967-72, pres. bd. dirs., 1972—. Mem. Am. Assn. Higher Edn., Nat. Catholic Ednl. Assn., Coll. Theology Soc., Ind. Acad. Religion. Office: Ancilla Coll Donaldson IN 46513

LAMPHERE, PHYLLIS (MRS. ARTHUR V. LAMPHERE), city ofcl.; B.A. in Math., Barnard Coll.; m. Arthur V. Lamphere; 3 daus. Mem. Seattle City Council, 1967—, chmn. intergovtl. relations com., mem. parks, human resources and planning coms. Chmn. health, edn. and welfare com. Puget Sound Govt. Conf.; chmn. spl. projects tech. adv. com. State Law and Justice Com.; mem. exec. com. Puget Sound Health Planning Council; mem. exec. com. Pacific Sci. Center Found. Named Woman of Achievement, Quota Club, 1968, Matrix Table Woman of Achievement, 1969. Address: Municipal Bldg Seattle WA 98104

LAMPKIN-ASAM, JULIA MCCAIN (MRS. JOSEPH ASAM), research adminstr.; b. Tuscaloosa, Ala., Feb. 27, 1931; d. Charles Barnett and Julia White (McCain) Lampkin; B.S., U. Ala., 1952; M.S., George Washington U., 1954, Ph.D., 1958; m. Joseph Asam, Apr. 7, 1971. Founder, sci. dir. Lampkin-Asam Cancer Inst., Miami, Fla., 1966-74, Tuscaloosa, 1974—. Dir. biol. scis., extension div. U. Tampa, Homestead AFB, 1970-74. Corr. sec. Women's Democratic Club, Perrine, Fla., 1968. NSF fellow, 1956-58; Am. Cancer Soc. grantee, 1963-66. Mem. Am. Assn. for Cancer Research, Sigma Xi. Author: Lymphomas: Regression, Carcinogenesis and Prevention, 1966; Malignant Intrigue, 1973. Address: PO Box 2115 Tuscaloosa AL 35401

LAMPMAN, EVELYN SIBLEY, author; b. Dallas, Ore., Apr. 18, 1907; d. Joseph E. and Harriett (Bronson) Sibley; B.S., Ore. State Coll., 1929; m. Herbert S. Lampman, May 12, 1934 (dec. June 1943); children—Linda Sibley, Anne Hathaway. Mem. Delta Delta Delta. Episcopalian. Author: Crazy Creek, 1948; Treasure Mountain, 1949; The Bounces of Cynthiann, 1950; Elder Brother, 1951; Captain Apple's Ghost, 1952; Tree Wagon, 1953; Witch Doctor's Son, 1954; Shy Stegosaurus of Cricket Creek, 1955; Navaho Sister, 1956; Rusty's Space Ship, 1957; Rock Hounds, 1958; Special Year, 1959; The City Under the Back steps, 1960 (Dorothy Canfield Fisher award 1962); Princess of Fort Vancouver, 1962; Shy Stegosaurus at Indian Springs, 1962; (under pseudonym Lynn Brandson) Timberland Adventure, 1950, Coyote Kid, 1951, Rogue's Valley, 1952, Runaway, 1953, Darcy's Harvest, 1956, Popular Girl, 1957; Mrs. Updaisy, 1963; Temple in the Sun, 1964; Wheels West, 1965; The Tilted Sombero, 1966, Half Breed, 1967 (Spur award Western Writers Am. 1968); The Bandit of Mok Hill, 1969; Cayuse Courage, 1970; Once Upon The Little Big Horn, 1971; The Year of Small Shadow, 1971; Go Up the Road, 1972; Rattlesnake Cave, 1974. Address: 3300 W Rosemont West Linn OR 97068

LAMPMAN, LOUISE CATHERINE FLETCHER (MRS. WILLIAM MORGAN LAMPMAN), univ. librarian; b. Albany, Ore., Apr. 23, 1913; d. Francis Joseph and Ida May (Beebe) Fletcher); B.A., Willamette U., 1934; postgrad. U. Wash., 1937-40; M.S., U. Ore., 1962; m. Arthur Martin Mason, Dec. 25, 1938 (dec. Dec. 1951); children—Martin Connell, Catherine Louise (Mrs. Daniel Henry Zaklan); m. 2d, William Morgan Lampman, Aug. 14, 1959. Tchr. high sch., Mill City, Ore., 1936-39, Elmira, Ore., 1940-42; tchr. jr. high sch., Eugene, Ore., 1952-67; asst. prof. librarianship, librarian Campus Lab. Sch., Central Wash. State Coll., Ellensburg, 1967-69, univ. curriculum lab. librarian, asso. prof. librarianship, 1969—. Mem. N.E.A., Am. Assn. Sch. Librarians, A.L.A., Assn. for Ednl. Communications and Tech., Assn. Coll. Research Libraries, Am. Assn. U. Profs., Am. Assn. U. Women, Delta Kappa Gamma. Contbr. articles to profl. jours. Home: 1711 College Pl Ellensburg WA 98926

LAMPSHIRE, MAXINE VIVIAN (MRS. HARVEY R. LAMPSHIRE), feature writer; b. Orchard, Colo., May 31, 1911; d. Albert Mithias and Lillian May (Miller) Firestack; student U. Colo., 1929-30, Colo. State Coll. Edn., 1933; m. Harvey R. Lampshire, Aug. 16, 1935; children—Bradford G., Geoffrey Lynn. Tchr., pub. schs. Masters, Colo., 1930-31, Snyder, Colo., 1931-32, Hillrose, Colo., 1933-36; editor Village Free Press, Harvardevens, Mass., 1948-50; women's editor Ft. Morgan (Colo.) Times, 1951-52; proof reader and contbr. Yokosuka (Japan) Sea Hawk, 1952-53; dir. pub. relations Davis Meml. Goodwill Industries, Washington, 1969-70; instr. creative writing, Alexandria (Va.) YWCA, 1971-74; writer Journal Newspapers, Alexandria, 1973—. Cons. pub. relations Arlington, Va., chpt. Am. Red Cross, 1973—. Publicist, Federated GOP Women's Clubs Va., 1962. Mem. Nat. League Am. Pen Women (v.p. 1972-74), N.E. Library Assn. (sec. 1960-61), Friends of Kennedy Center, Fairfax Cultural Assn. Republican. Author: One Giant Step for the Handicapped, 1970. Editor: Handy Caps 'n Coment, 1969-70; Wilson Blvd. Christian Ch. newsletter, 1966-67; Arlington (Va.) P.T.A. newsletter, 1954-55; Arlington GOP Women's Club newsletter, 1963-65. Home: 2145 N Quebec St Arlington VA 22207 Office: 331 N Fairfax St Alexandria VA 22314

LAMSON, AMY FLORENCE (MRS. ROGER C. LAMSON), clin. psychologist; b. Bklyn., Apr. 28, 1941; d. Lewis and Jeannette (Rothchild) Abramson; B.S. magna cum laude, Bklyn. Coll., 1961; postgrad. U. Mich., 1961-62; M.A., Boston U., 1965, Ph.D. (Nat. Inst. Mental Health fellow), 1970; m. Roger C. Lamson, Aug. 26, 1962; children—Laurie, Mark. Community psychiat. dir. Charles Drew Family Life Center, Boston; cons. Trinity Mental Health Center, Framingham, Mass.; co-therapist New Eng. Inst. Human Sexuality, Framingham. Pvt. practice psychotherapy. Mem. Am., Mass. psychol. assns., Phi Beta Kappa, Sigma Xi, Psi Chi. Home: 36 Fairlee Rd Waban MA 02168 Office: 1 Granite St Framingham MA 01701

LANAHAN, SISTER WILLIAM MARY, religious order adminstr.; b. Balt., Dec. 2, 1931; d. Leo Jerome and Myrtle Regina (Potter) Lanahan; R.N., St. Joseph Hosp. Sch. Nursing, 1952; B.S., Cath. U. Am., 1959, M.S. (USPHS grantee), 1963. Nursing supr. St. Mary Hosp., Phila., 1955-58; instr. St. Joseph Hosp. Sch. Nursing, Reading, Pa., 1959-65, dir., 1965-68; asst. adminstr. St. Francis Hosp., Wilmington, Del., 1969-73; provincial superior Sisters of St. Francis of Phila., 1973—. Mem. bd., exec. com. Health Planning Council of Del., 1971-73; vice chmn. Del. Regional Med. Program, 1972-73. Chmn. bd. trustees St. Francis Hosp., Wilmington, 1973—; trustee St. Joseph Hosp., Balt., 1973—. Mem. Leadership Conf. Women Religious, Assn. Del. Hosps. (mem. exec. com. 1969-73, pres. 1971), Sigma Theta Tau. Contbr. articles to profl. jours. Address: 7620 York Rd Towson MD 21204

LANCASTER, ALICE CUNNINGHAM (MRS. OWEN EDWIN LANCASTER, JR.), psychiat. social worker; b. Glaveston, Tex.; d. Henry Eugene and Leona (Murray) Cunningham; B.A., Southeastern La. Coll., 1949; M.S.W., Our Lady of Lake Coll., 1960; m. Owen Edwin Lancaster Jr., June 3, 1955; stepchildren—Owen Edwin III, Blake. Tchr., Ponchatoula (La.) High Sch., 1932-45, Marion High Sch., Lake Charles, La., 1952-55; recreation worker, program dir. A.R.C., Washington, Manila, Kyoto, Japan, 1945-47, social worker, Houston, 1947-48, Maxwell AFB, Ala., Camp Polk, La., Ft. Bragg, N.C., 1950-52; social worker Tex. Cradle Soc., San Antonio, 1955-60; med. social worker Bexar County Hosp. Dist. Robert B. Green Hosp., San Antonio, 1960-61; psychiat. social worker San Antonio State Hosp., 1961—, acting dir. social service dept., 1964-65, asst. dir., 1965-68, chief social worker, 1968—, adminstrv. coordinator social service dept., 1971—. Lectr. in field; mem. Nat. Council on Alcoholism, Bexar County. Vol., A.R.C., San Antonio, 1961. Mem. Nat. Assn. Social Workers, Acad. Certified Social Workers, Mental Health Assn., Worden Sch. Social Service Alumni Assn. (pres. 1967), Smithsonian Assos. (charter). Episcopalian. Contbr. articles to profl. jours. Home: 425 S Vandiver Rd San Antonio TX 78209 Office: PO Box 23310 San Antonio TX 78223

LANCASTER, JEAN FREEMAN, home economist; b. Hendersonville, N.C., Apr. 12, 1940; d. Walter Lee and Ida Ann (Barnwell) Freeman; B.S. in Home Econs., U. N.C., 1962; postgrad. Western Carolina U., 1966; m. William Eugene Lancaster, June 25, 1961; children—Mark Eugene, Angela Dawn. Tchr. Henderson County Schs., 1963-65, Hendersonville City Schs., 1965-68; extension home economist Henderson County, Hendersonville, 1968—. Mem. region B steering com. White House Conf. on Aging, 1971; mem. region B task force Council on Aging, 1973. Sec. Edneyville P.T.A., 1971-72. Mem. Agr. Workers Council (sec. 1972), Am., N.C. home econs. assns., Nat., N.C., Western Dist. (treas. 1970-71) extension home economists assns. Episcopalian. Home: Route 5 Box 352 Hendersonville NC 28739 Office: 140 4th Ave Hendersonville NC 28739

LANCASTER, WINIFRED HOEY, univ. trustee; b. County Down, Ireland, Sept. 23, 1910; d. Robert James and Mary Ann (Rea) Hoey; came to U.S., 1911, naturalized, 1941; B.S., U. Pa., 1930; M.A., U. So. Cal., 1947; m. Louis G. Lancaster, Jan. 26, 1948. High sch. tchr., Chester County, Pa., 1930-33; reporter Santa Barbara (Cal.) Morning Press, 1935; publicist, speech therapist, acting dir. counseling Santa Barbara city schs., 1936-50; successively tchr.-counselor, vice prin., dean students, dean instrn. Santa Barbara City Coll., 1950-62; lectr. U. Cal. at Santa Barbara, 1948; supr. acad. instrn. Ventura (Cal.) Sch. Girls, 1949; cons. in field, 1955-56; trustee Cal. State Univ. and Coll., 1971—; bd. govs. Cal. Community Colls., 1968-71; trustee Santa Barbara City Coll., 1965-68. Founder, pres. Channel City Women's Forum, 1966—; pres. Santa Barbara Citizens Council Crime, 1970—; arbitrator Better Bus. Bur. Tri-Counties/S. Coast; mem. Santa Barbara Citizens Continuing Edn. Adv. Com.; mem. hearing panel Western Assn. Schs. and Colls. Bd. dirs. Community TV Santa Barbara, 1971—; trustee Santa Barbara Pub. Library, 1958-63; hon. bd. dirs. Friends of Santa Barbara Pub. Library. Served to lt. WAVES, 1942-46. named Woman of Year, Santa Barbara Advt. and Merchandising Club, 1967. Wilton Park fellow, 1972. Mem. Am. Psychol. Assn., A.A.A.S., Zonta Internat. (hon. Santa Barbara), Am. Assn. U. Women, League Women Voters, Psi Chi, Phi Kappa Phi. Address: PO Drawer JJ Santa Barbara CA 93102

LANCE, MARILYN SARA, lawyer; b. Perth Amboy, N.J., Apr. 11, 1941; d. Maynard Gerard and Clara Ellen (Phillips) Lance; A.B., Douglass Coll., 1966; J.D., Seton Hall U., 1971. Asst. statistics Mental Health Amboy Clinic, Perth Amboy, 1960-63; tchr. emotionally disturbed Woodbridge Twp. (N.J.) Bd. Edn., 1966; admitted to N.J. bar, 1971; law clk. Sills, Garretson, Levine & Goceljack, Perth Amboy, 1970, Robert M. Vogel, Woodbridge, N.J., 1971; mem. firm Lance & Zacharias, Woodbridge, 1973—. Atty. Planning Bd., Perth Amboy, 1972-75. Mem. League Women Voters (atty. 1972-73), Mensa, Seton Hall U. Alumni Assn. (mem. exec. bd. 1972-75), Phi Alpha Delta, Beta Sigma. Home: 619 New Brunswick Av Perth Amboy NJ 08861 Office: 284 Amboy Av Woodbridge NJ 07095

LAND, CATHERINE ZANTHOS, advt. exec.; b. Birmingham, Ala., Jan. 10, 1922; d. Demetrius and Aglaia (Nicholas) Zanthos; B.S. in Commerce and Bus. Adminstrn., U. Ala., 1942; m. George T. Lock Land IV, June 24, 1967; children—Robert E., Thomas G., Patrick A. Financial writer United Press, N.Y.C., 1943-45; TV producer William Esty Co., N.Y.C., 1945-56; v.p., exec. TV producer Grey Advt., Inc., N.Y.C., 1957—; lectr. in field. Recipient 8 Clios Am. TV Comml. Festival, 1961—, Gold medal Cannes Film Festival, 1961, Internat. Film and TV Festival awards, 1969, Hollywood radio and TV awards, 1971, award for TV Advt. Age mag., 1973, ANNY award, 1973. Mem. Am. Acad. TV Arts and Sci., Advt. Women N.Y., Broadcast Advt. Producers Soc. Am. (pres. 1972—). Club: Hollywood Yacht. Contbr. articles to profl. jours. Home: 405 E 54th St New York City NY 10022 Office: 777 3d Av New York City NY 10017

LAND, MARY ELIZABETH, author; b. Benton, La., Sept., 1908; d. Thomas Taylor and Elizabeth (Langford) Land; student Gulf Park (Miss.) Coll., 1924-25; grad. Cheyney-Trent Sch. Poetry, Cal., 1937. Children—Patricia (Mrs. Phineas Stevens), George Thomas Lock-Land. Staff writer La. Conservation Rev. div. edn. La. Dept. Conservation, 1940-41; editor weekly syndicated column Outdoors South, 1947-48; staff writer So. Outdoors Mag., 1959-61, West Bank Guide, New Orleans, 1962-63; commentator for own conservation, outdoor program Miss. Soundings, WGCM, Gulfport, Miss. Chmn., New Orleans Spring Fiesta, 1947, 49; chmn. spring fiesta La. Poetry Soc., 1950. Recipient certificate of merit Nash Motors, 1953. Mem. D.A.R. (past program chmn. Metairie Ridge chpt.), Nat. League Am. Pen Women (Blue Ribbon award So. Region Gulf Coast br. 1948, pres. Miss.), Nat. Fedn. Am. Press Women (1st pl. award 1960), Colonial Dames, Nat. Soc. Arts and Letters (co-founder New Orleans chpt., exec. bd.), Outdoor Writers Assn. Am., La. Outdoor Writers Assn. (past dir.), Internat. Womens Fishing Assn., Fedn. Musicians Jackson, Miss. Author: (poetry) Shadows of the Swamp, 1940; Mary Land's Louisiana Cookery (co-winner So. Books of Year in ann. So. Books Competition), 1955; New Orleans Cuisine, 1969; (poetry) Abode, 1972. Home: 1314 Williams Av Natchitoches LA 71457

LAND, NELLE KEATING JOHNSTON (MRS. HARLOW H. LAND), occupational therapist; b. Princeton, W.Va., Dec. 27, 1945; d. W. Broughton and N. Louise (White) Johnston; B.S., U. Fla., 1967, M. Rehab., Counseling, 1968; m. Harlow H. Land, Aug. 21, 1968. Behavioral specialist, geriatric unit coordinator Sunland Hosp. for Mentally Retarded, Tallahassee, 1969; vocational counselor, manpower program Fla. A. and M. U., Tallahassee, 1969-70; asso. dir. Student Concern, Tallahassee, 1970-71; social services asst., counseling coordinator U.S. Army Drug Program, Dept. Def., Neu Ulm, Germany, 1973—. Mem. Am. Occupational Therapy Assn., Savant, Chi Omega. Democrat. Club: Officers Wives (New Ulm). Home: PO Box 18 Mayo FL 32066 also 7911 Ay Maderholzweg 18 Federal Republic of Germany Office: Dept of Army Office of Ulm Neu Ulm Comdr Attn: CDAAC APO New York City NY 09035

LANDAU, MURIEL ANN, coll. adminstr.; b. Schenectady, Jan. 11, 1920; d. Carl H. and Harriet B. (Hewett) Landau; student Bentley Coll., 1949-51; B.S., Suffolk U., 1960. With Gen. Electric Co., Schenectady, 1942-49; with Lasell Jr. Coll., Auburndale, Mass., 1951-55; office mgr. A.D. Jones Optical Works, Cambridge, Mass., 1955-59; faculty Bradford (Mass.) Coll., 1959—, adminstr. for non-acad. activities of coll., 1959—. Mem. Am. Accounting Assn., Nat. Assn. Accountants, Am. Soc. Women Accountants (pres. Boston chpt. 1965-66). Home: 206 River Rd Andover MA 01810 Office: Bradford College Bradford MA 01830

LANDERS, ANN (MRS. JULES LEDERER), columnist; b. Sioux City, Ia., July 4, 1918; d. Abraham B. and Rebecca (Rushall) Friedman; student Morningside Coll., 1936-39, L.H.D., 1964; L.H.D., Wilberforce U., 1972; m. Jules W. Lederer, July 2, 1939; 1 dau., Margo. Syndicated columnist Field Enterprises, Inc. Pub.-Hall Syndicate, 1955—. Chmn. Eau Claire (Wis.) Gray-Lady Corps. A.R.C., 1947-53; chmn. Minn.-Wis. council chmn. Anti-Defamation League, 1945-49; asst. Wis. chmn. Nat. Found for Infantile Paralysis, 1951-53; hon. chmn. Christmas Seal Campaign, Nat. Tb Assn., 1963; nat. bd. Am. Cancer Soc., 1972—. County chmn. Dem. Party of Eau Claire; mem. def. adv. com. Women Armed Services, 1962-63; adv. com. A.M.A., 1967—; com. for devel. and resources Harvard Med. Sch., 1967—; bd. dirs. Rehab. Inst. Chgo. Trustee Menninger Found., Nat. Dermatology Found. Recipient Nat. Family Service Assn. award, 1965, Adolph Meyer award Assn. Mental Health, 1965, Golden Stethoscope award Ill. Med. Soc., 1967, Pres. citation Nat. Council Alcoholism, 1966, Humanitarianism award Internat. Assn. Lions Club, 1967, Nat. Plaque Honor Friends Hebrew U., 1968; Nat. Service award Am. Cancer Soc., 1971; Robert T. Morse award Am. Psychiat. Assn., 1972; named one of ten most influential women in U.S., U.P.I. Poll, 1968, one of 20 most admired women in world Gallup Poll, 1968, 69, one of 10 most important women in U.S., U.P.I. Poll, 1967. Mem. League Women Voters, Brandeis U. Women (life). Author: Since You Ask Me, 1962; Ann Landers Talks to Teen-Agers About Sex, 1964; Truth is Stranger, 1968. Office: Chicago Sun Times Plaza Chicago IL 60611

LANDERS, VERNETTE TROSPER (MRS. NEWLIN LANDERS), post office clk.; b. Lawton, Okla., May 3, 1912; d. Fred Gilbert and LaVerne Hamilton (Stevens) Trosper; A.B. with honors, U. Cal. at Los Angeles, 1933, M.A., 1935, Ed.D., 1953; m. Paul Albert Lum, Aug. 29, 1952 (dec. May 1955); 1 son, William Tappan; m. 2d, Newlin Landers, May 2, 1959; children—Lawrence, Marlin. Tchr. secondary schs., Montebello, Cal., 1935-45, 48-50, 51-59; prof. Long Beach City Coll., 1946-47; asst. prof. Los Angeles State Coll., 1950; dean girls 29 Palms (Cal.) High Sch., 1960-65; dist. counselor Morongo (Cal.) Unified Sch. Dist., 1965-72, coordinator adult edn., 1965-67, guidance project dir., 1967; clk.-in-charge Landers (Cal.) Post Office, 1962—. Vice-pres., sec. Landers Assn., 1965—; sec. Landers Vol. Fire Dept., 1972—; life mem. Hi-Desert Playhouse Guild, Hi-Desert Meml. Hosp. Guild. Bd. dirs., sec. Desert Emergency Radio Service. Recipient internat. diploma of honor for community service award, 1973; Creativity award Internat. Personnel Research Assn., 1972; named Soroptimist of Year, 29 Palms Soroptimist Club, 1969. Mem. Internat. Platform Assn., Intercontinental Biog. Assn., Nat. Ret. Tchrs. Assn., Montebello Bus. and Profl. Women's Club, Postal Commemorative Soc. Clubs: Soroptimist (sec. 29 Palms 1962); Whittier (Cal.) Toastmistress (pres. 1957); Homestead Valley Women's (Landers). Contbr. articles to profl. jours. Home: 905 Landers Lane Landers CA 92284 Office: 890 Landers Lane Landers CA 92284

LANDES, GERALDINE STEINBERG (MRS. BERNARD A. LANDES), psychologist; b. Twin Falls, Ida., Mar. 5, 1933; d. Otto and Lillie (Goldman) Steinberg; student Stephens Coll., 1950-51; B.S., Northwestern U., 1954; M.A. (Office Vocational Rehab. grant), Tex. Tech. U., 1960; postgrad. U. Mich., 1954, 57, Cal. State U. at Long Beach, 1965; m. Bernard A. Landes, Jan. 30, 1954; children—Sharon Esther, Jo Denise. Child welfare caseworker Child Welfare, Lubbock, Tex., 1960-61; counselor Jewish Family Service, Long Beach, Cal., 1962; sch. psychologist Bellflower (Cal.) Unified Sch. Dist., 1966—. Mem. Nat., Cal. assns. sch. psychologists, Internat. Transactional Analysis Assn., N.E.A., Cal. Tchrs. Assn. Home: 3320 Julian St Long Beach CA 90808 Office: 16703 S Clark St Bellflower CA 90706

LANDES, RUTH SCHLOSSBERG, anthropologist; b. N.Y.C., Oct. 8, 1908; d. Joseph and Anna (Grossman) Schlossberg; B.S., N.Y.U., 1928; M.A., N.Y. Sch. Social Work, 1930; Ph.D., Columbia, 1935. Social worker, N.Y.C., 1929-31; research fellow Columbia, 1933-40; instr. anthropology Fisk U., 1937-38; instr. anthropology Bklyn. Coll., 1937; research Gunnar Myrdal's Study Am. Negro, Carnegie Corp., N.Y.C., 1939; research dir. Coordinator Inter-Am. Affairs, Washington, 1941; rep. Pres. Com. Fair Employment Practices Negro and Mexican-Am. affairs, 1941-45; dir. Fair Employment Practices Council, N.Y.C., 1945; researcher Los Angeles Met. Welfare Council, 1946-47; study dir. Am. Jewish Com., N.Y.C., 1948-51; lectr. W.A. White Psychiat. Inst., N.Y.C., 1953-55; dir. geriatrics program Los Angeles City Health Dept., 1958-59; lectr., cons. U. Cal. at Los Angeles and Berkeley, 1962, Los Angeles State Coll., 1963; prof. anthropology U. Kan., 1964; prof. McMaster U., 1965—; vis. prof. Claremont Grad. Sch., 1959-62, Columbia, 1963, Tulane U., 1964; cons. Cal. Social Work Dept. and affiliated agys. Cal. Dept. Edn., San Francisco Police, 1957—. Fulbright sr. research scholar Edinburgh U. (Scotland), 1951-52. Author: Ojibwa Sociology, 1937; The Ojibwa Woman, 1938; The City of Women, 1947; Culture in American Education, 1965; Latin-Americans of the Southwest, 1965; Ojibwa Religion and The Midewiwin, 1968; The Mystic Lake Sioux, 1969; The Prairie Potawatomi, 1970. Contbr. articles to profl. jours., also chpts. in books. Office: McMaster U Hamilton ON Canada

LANDFIELD, RUTH D'VERA GOLDBERG (MRS. SEYMOUR LANDFIELD), civic worker; b. Fargo, N.D., Feb. 2, 1918; d. Max and Anne Libby (Paletz) Goldberg; A.B., Radcliffe Coll., 1940; m. Seymour Landfield, Aug. 23, 1941; children—Mary Anne (Mrs. Hugh R. Winig), Joan, James, Frank. Research asst. psychol. research unit Santa Ana (Cal.) Army AFB, 1941-45. Bd. dirs. KFME/Channel 13 ETV, Fargo, 1963—, v.p., 1972-73; bd. dirs. F-M Civic Opera Co. Co-chmn. Met. Opera Regional Com., 1957—; mem. home and community com. N.D. Commn. on Status of Women, 1964-67; pres. Lake Agassiz Arts Council, 1970-74; vol. worker Red River Art Center, F-M Community Theater, various social service agys. Mem. Women's Assn. Fargo-Moorhead Symphony Orch. (v.p. 1954-56). Jewish religion (pres. Sisterhood 1952-54). Hadassah (pres. 1961-64, treas. 1964—). Club: Fine Arts (pres. 1967-69, chmn. drama sect. 1971-73, bd. dirs. 1964-73). Home: 1700 S 9th St Fargo ND 58102

LANDGRAF, CONSTANCE LEE (MRS. THEODORE LANDGRAF), banker; b. Honolulu; d. Lee Chew and Lee Lum Shee; grad. Roosevelt High Sch., Honolulu, 1942; m. Theodore C. Landgraf, Mar. 15, 1947; 1 son, John W. Stenographer First Hawaiian Bank, Hickam br., 1942-43, teller, 1943-45, gen. ledger clk., 1945-47, collections clk., Honolulu, 1947-54, accounting clk., 1954-56, loan rep., 1956-59, operations supr., 1959-60, dept. supr., 1960-63, asst. cashier, 1963-67, asst. br. mgr., 1967-69, credit card officer, 1969—. Mem. Honolulu Credit Women Internat. (pres. 1967-68), Waikiki Bus. and Profl. Women's Club (v.p. 1969-70), Nat. Assn. Bank Women (chmn. Hawaii group 1969-70), Zonta (Honolulu treas. 1968-70, pres. 1970-72). Home: 2120 Kalawahine Pl Honolulu HI 96822 Office: 161 S King St Honolulu HI 96813

LANDGRAF, MARY ELIZABETH NORTON (MRS. DAVID L. LANDGRAF), librarian; b. San Francisco, Aug. 7, 1937; d. Thomas Bernard and Marjorie (Milota) Norton; student San Francisco Coll. Women, 1955-58; A.B., San Francisco State Coll., 1960; M.L.S., U. Cal. at Berkeley, 1962, postgrad., 1962-63; m. David L. Landgraf, June 10, 1963; children—Robert Thomas, Lisa Marjorie. Librarian, San Francisco Pub. Library, 1958-59, 60-63; research asst. U. Cal. Grad. Sch. Librarianship, Berkeley, 1962, reviser, 1963-64; librarian San Francisco Pub. Library, 1969—. Mem. Am., Cal. library assns., No. Cal. Tech. Processes Group (sec.-treas. 1963-64), Alumni Assn. U. Cal. Library Schs., Alumnae of Sacred Heart, Beta Phi Mu. Democrat. Clubs: U. Cal. Women's Faculty (Berkeley); Viking Ski; Sausalito Cruising. Home: 119 La Verne Av Mill Valley CA 94941

LANDIS, LUELLA DANIELS (MRS. GEORGE EDWARD LANDIS), psychologist; b. Middletown, Conn., June 8, 1943; d. Orrin Elmer and Florence Jennette (Morgan) Daniels; B.S., U. Hartford, 1966, M.Ed., 1970; m. George Edward Landis, June 20, 1964. Case worker, pub. health program asst. Conn. Dept. Health, Hartford, 1966-70; psychol. examiner New Britain (Conn.) Bd. Edn., 1970-71, 73—. Mem. Nat. (Me. del. 1972-73), Conn. assns. sch. psychologists, Assn. Women in Psychology Am. (asso.), New Eng., Me. psychol. assns., Gamma Chi Rho. Episcopalian. Club: Nutmeg Doll (Conn.). Home: 16 Prospect Hill Rd Cromwell CT 06416 Office: 27 Hillside Pl New Britain CT 06051

LANDIS, SARA MARGARET SHEPPARD LESHMAN (MRS. WILLARD GRIFFITH LANDIS), editorial and promotion cons.; b. Badin, N.C., May 20, 1923; d. Thomas Coates and Ouida (Watson) Sheppard; student Flora Mac Donald Coll. for Women, 1937-38, Rice Bus. Coll., 1939; A.B. in Journalism, U. N.C., 1942; m. Willard Griffith Landis, Dec. 7, 1946; children—Susan Sheppard, Timothy Joseph, Margaret Carol. Editorial asst. Redbook Mag., N.Y.C., 1942-43; with Doubleday & Co., N.Y.C., 1944-46; Eagle Pencil Co., N.Y.C., 1953-54; personnel mgr. Workman Service, N.Y.C., 1955-56; Clay Adams Co., N.Y.C., 1957-58; job analyst Bigelow Carpet Co., N.Y.C., 1959-60; asst. to guidance dir. Childrens Village, Dobbs Ferry, N.Y., 1960-61; dir. promotion and advt. Oceana Publs., Dobbs Ferry, 1961-66; promotion mgr. Reinhold Pub. Co., N.Y.C., 1967-68, Watson Guptill Pub. Co., N.Y.C., 1968, Chilton Book Co., Phila., 1968-69; editorial and promotion cons. Editorial and Promotion Co., N.Y.C., 1969—. Home: 271 Av C New York City NY 10009

LANDMAN, RUTH HALLO (MRS. OTTO E. LANDMAN), educator, anthropologist; b. Kassel, Germany, Sept. 8, 1926; d. Rudolf and Gertrude (Rubensohn) Hallo; A.B., Vassar Coll., 1947; M.A., Yale, 1950, Ph.D., 1954; m. Otto E. Landman, Sept. 5, 1948; children—Wendy, Jessica, Jonathan. Researcher, U. Ill., Champaign-Urbana, 1954-56; lectr. Howard U., 1964-65; asst. prof. anthropology Am. U., Washington, 1965-69, asso. prof., 1969-74, prof., 1974—, chmn. dept., 1970-72. Fellow Am. Anthrop. Assn.; mem. Anthrop. Soc. Washington, Am. Ethnol. Soc., A.A.A.S. Home: 8408 Peck Pl Bethesda MD 20034 Office: Dept Anthropology Am U Washington DC 20016

LANDMANN, REBECCA JONES (MRS. WENDELL A. LANDMANN), librarian; b. Lexington, Ill., Aug. 4, 1919; d. Richard Gomer and Harriett Catharine (Gard) Jones; A.B. with highest honors, U. Ill., 1940, M.S. with honors, 1941; m. Wendell A. Landmann, Apr. 9, 1944; children—David G., Richard F. Librarian high sch., Clinton, Ill., 1941-43, Leyden High Sch., Franklin Park, Ill., 1943-44; circulation and microfilm librarian Naval Research Lab., Washington, 1944-45; librarian, children's room Anacostia Br. Library, Washington, 1945-46; library supr. River Forest (Ill.) Pub. Schs., 1956-64, Bryan (Tex.) Ind. Sch. Dist., 1964—; lectr. children's lit. Tex. A. and M. U., College Station. Pres. Stage Center, Inc., Bryan, 1973-74. Mem. Am., Ill. library assns., Tex. Assn. Sch. Librarians, Phi Beta Kappa, Phi Delta Phi, Alpha Lambda Delta. Contbr. articles to profl. jours. Home: 1602 Dominik St College Station TX 77840 Office: 2200 Villa Maria Bryan TX 77801

LANDOLFI, MARIA, educator; b. Utica, N.Y., Nov. 4, 1917; d. Thomas and Frances (Turchetti) Landolfi; B.A., Keuka Coll., 1940; M.A., Syracuse U., 1950; postgrad. Mohawk Valley Community Coll., Utica Coll.; m. Vernon Reyman, June 23, 1951 (div. May 1972). With N.Y. State Tax and Finance Dept., 1940-43; tchr. Westmoreland (N.Y.) High Sch., 1943-44, Lyons Falls (N.Y.) High Sch., 1944-46, Proctor High Sch., Utica, 1946-47; tchr. English, Utica Free Acad., 1947—. Tchr. Italian, adult evening classes Hamilton Coll., 1966; co-dir. sch. for gifted, Londonderry, Vt., summers 1956-58. Del. White House Conf. Edn., 1955. Bd. dirs. United Way Agy., Utica. Recipient Bronze medal for studies in Italian, Columbia, 1935; Keuka Coll. awards music, 1940, Alumnae award for profl. achievement, 1971. Mem. N.E.A., Am. Assn. U. Women, Utica Tchrs. Assn. (sec. 1972-73), Utica Free Acad. Tchrs. Assn. (pres. 1952, sec. 1970-72), UN Assn. U.S.A., Am. Security Council (mem. nat. adv. bd. 1972—), Dante Lit. Soc. of Harvard, Robert Browning Soc. Boston, Internat. Platform Assn. Keuka Alumnae Club. Mem. Order of Eastern Star, White Shrine of Jerusalem. Club: New Century (3d v.p.). Exhibitor, lectr. rare books, rare fabrics; pioneer teamteaching. Home: 4 Hughes Lane New Hartford NY 13413 Office: Utica Free Acad Kemble St Utica NY 13501

LANDRAM, CHRISTINA LOUELLA, librarian; b. Paragould, Ark., Dec. 10, 1922; d. James Ralph and Bertie Louella (Jordan) Oliver; A.B., Tex. Woman's U., 1945, B.S. in Library Sci., 1946, M.L.S., 1951; m. Robert E. Landram, Aug. 7, 1948; 1 son, Mark O. Cataloger, Library of Congress, 1946-48, U.S. Information Libraries, Tokyo, Japan, 1948-50, Tex. Tech. Coll., 1950-51, U.S. Dept. Agr. Library, 1953-54; librarian Yokota (Japan) Air Force Base, 1954-55; med. librarian St. Mary's Hosp., W. Palm Beach, Fla., 1957-59; librarian Jacksonville (Ark.) High Sch., 1959-61; coordinator Shelby County Libraries, Memphis, 1961-63; head catalog dept. Ga. State U., Atlanta, 1963—. Mem. Am., Southeastern, Ga. (chmn. resources and tech. services sect. 1969-71, chmn. govtl. relations com. 1973—), Metro-Atlanta (pres. 1967-68) library assns. Presbyn. Home: 1802 Alderbrook Rd NE Atlanta GA 30345 Office: 104 Decatur St SE Atlanta GA 30303

LANDRUM, ANNETTE VAUGHN, physician; b. Jasper, Ala., Mar. 9, 1932; d. Ralph Waldo and Sara Louise (Griffin) Vaughn; student Southwestern at Memphis, 1950-52, Memphis State U., 1952-53; M.D., U. Tenn., 1956; m. Samuel Edward Landrum, July 5, 1955; children—Leslie, John, Janet, Emily. Intern Druid City Hosp., Tuscaloosa, Ala., 1957-58; resident Providence Hosp., Detroit, 1958-62, St. John's Hosp., Tulsa, 1962-63; pvt. practice pathology Fort Smith, Ark., 1963—; cons. pathologist Scott County Hosp., Waldron, Ark., DeQueen (Ark.) Gen. Hosp., Booneville City Hosp., Turner Meml. Hosp., Ozark, Ark.; dir. Fort Smith Med. Lab., 1967—. Pres. League of Women Voters, 1971-72; chmn. task force on health facilities for Western Ark., 1971-72; chmn. task force on health care delivery Ark. Gov.'s Commn. on Status of Women, 1974—. Bd. dirs. Girls' Shelter of Fort Smith, 1971-72, Girls' Club, Ft. Smith, 1974—. Diplomate Am. Bd. Pathology. Fellow Coll. Am. Pathologists, Am. Soc. Clin. Pathologists; mem. Sebastian County, Ark. med. socs. Home: 15 Riverlyn Dr Fort Smith AR 72901 Office: 500 Lexington St Fort Smith AR 72901

LANDRUM, BERTHA ANN, coll. adminstr.; b. Farmington, Minn., June 11, 1938; d. Bernard H. and Norma L. (Troseth) Breyen; B.A. cum laude, U. Minn., 1960; M.A., Ariz. State U., 1965. Instr., counselor Phoenix Coll., 1965-66; counselor Mesa (Ariz.) Community Coll., 1966-72, dir. research and devel., 1972—. Mem. Ariz. Personnel and Guidance Assn. (treas. 1970-72), Ariz. Employment Counselors Assn. (treas. 1972-73). Home: 950 S Valencia St Mesa AZ 85202 Office: 1833 W Southern Av Mesa AZ 85202

LANDRUM, OPAL VIRGINIA, govt. ofcl.; b. Quinton, Ala., Nov. 17, 1918; d. Claude Wirt and Kathryn Ophelia (Skelton) Landrum; A.B., Ala. Coll. Women, 1935; M.A., Am. U., 1955, Ph.D., 1965. Tchr. pub. schs., Ala., 1935-42; operations officer Ordnance Dept., War Dept., Navajo Ordnance Dept., Flagstaff, Ariz., 1942-44, Anniston (Ala.) Ordnance Depot, 1944-46; planning officer research and devel. Q.M. Gen., Dept. Army, Washington, 1947-56, heraldic program adminstr., 1956-60, heraldic program mgr. Inst. of Heraldry, Alexandria, Va., 1960—. Cons. ofcl. symbolism and heraldry to various govt. ofcls. and agys.; lectr. to various civic and ednl. groups. Recipient Meritorious Civilian Service award Dept. Army, 1969. Mem. A.A.A.S., Confederate Meml. Lit. Soc., Am. Polit. Sci. Assn., Co. Mil. Historians, Pi Sigma Alpha. Home: 1600 S Eads St Arlington VA 22202 Office: Inst of Heraldry US Army 5010 Duke St Alexandria VA 22314

LANDRY, FRANCES LEGGIO (MRS. JULES FRANCIS LANDRY), lawyer; b. Baton Rouge, Aug. 11, 1908; d. George and Josephine (Loicano) Leggio; B.A., La. State U., 1926, LL.B., 1934, J.D., 1968; m. Jules Francis Landry, Aug. 9, 1934; 1 dau., Frances Harriet (Mrs. George Franklin Borghardt, Jr.). Admitted to La. bar, 1934; partner Landry & Landry, Baton Rouge, 1934—. Vice pres., dir. Bank Commerce & Trust Co.; dir. St. Francisville, La. Lectr. La. State U. Law Sch., 1942-43; atty. for parish tax collector, 1940-46; owner, exec. dir. Lafayette Gallery, Baton Rouge, 1969—; sec.-treas. Wooddale Comml. Properties, Inc. Mem. Beautification Commn., City of Baton Rouge, 1963-66; pres. East Baton Rouge Parish Library Bd., 1967—. Trustee Magnolia Mound for Found. for Hist. La., Inc. Mem. Internat., Inter-Am., Am. (past membership chmn. La.), La., Baton Rouge bar assns., A.L.A., La. Library Assn., Order of Coif, Phi Kappa Phi, Mu Sigma Rho. Clubs: Womans (bd. mgrs.), Quota International (pres. 1942-44). Home: 2036 Lake Hills Pkwy Baton Rouge LA 70808 Office: 348 Lafayette St Baton Rouge LA 70801

LANDRY, LENORE LOUISE, home economist; b. Gilmanton, Wis., May 8, 1923; d. Wallace J. and Cleo M. (Krampeter) Landry; B.S., Stout Inst., 1945; M.S., U. Wis., 1954. Tchr. home econs. Racine County Agrl. High Sch., Rochester, Wis., 1945-47; home economist Racine County Extension, 1947-51, Douglas County Extension, Superior, Wis., 1951-53; asst. leader State 4-H Club, Madison, Wis., 1954-55; extension textile and clothing specialist U. Wis., Madison, 1955—. Cons., author and photographer Borg Textile Group, Milw., 1968; mem. research and devel. com. Singer Sewing Machine Co., N.Y.C., 1972. Recipient Distinguished Service award Stout Alumni Assn., 1972. Mem. Wis. Home Econs. Assn. (mem. council-chmn. textile, clothing sect., 1969-71), Wis. Home Agts. Assn. (pres., 1953), Wis. Extension Worker's Assn. (dir. 1963-64, sec. 1964), Am. Home Econs. Assn. (legislative com. 1972-73), Phi Upsilon Omicron, Epsilon Sigma Phi. Home: 910 High St Madison WI 53715

LANDY, AGATHA HORRIGAN (MRS. THOMAS M. LANDY), real estate broker; b. Cleve.; d. Lawrence and Catherine (Day) Horrigan; student Cleve. Coll., 1931, John Carroll U., 1932-33; m. Thomas M. Landy, Jan. 23, 1943 (dec.); children—Thomas M., John C., Philip F., Robert J., Kevin P. Owner, pres. Agatha Horrigan Landy & Sons, Inc., realtors, Cleveland Heights, O., 1972—. Mem. Internat. Platform Assn., Chrest Child Soc., Nat. Cleve. Bds. Realtors. Clubs: Skating (Cleve.). Home: 2647 Berkshire Cleveland Heights OH 44106 Office: 30650 Pinetree St Pepper Pike OH 44124 also 2647 Berkshire Rd Cleveland Heights OH 44106

LANDY, ROSE KOTZIN (MRS. SAMUEL H. LANDY), lawyer; b. Phila., Dec. 22, 1909; d. Aaron Hayim and Goldie (Atkin) Kotzin; B.S. in Edn., U. Pa., 1929, LL.B., 1932; B.H.L., Gratz Coll., 1971; m. Samuel H. Landy, July 9, 1933; children—Arthur H., David A. Admitted to Pa. bar, 1933, practice in Phila., 1933-48; asso. Freedman, Landy & Lorry, Phila., 1948-62, Cohen, Shapiro, Polisher, Sheikman & Cohen, Phila., 1965-73. Arbitration work with Ct. of Common Pleas, Phila. Bd. dirs., chmn. library com. Gratz Coll.; chmn. legislative com. Hias and Council Migration Service, 1970—; mem. women's div. Am. Friends Hebrew U., 1965—, Dropsie U., 1972—; chmn. wills and bequests com. Phila. chpt. Hadassah, 1965—. Recipient Gratz Coll. Alumni award, 1953, Woman of Valor award Bonds of Israel Govt., 1961, Phila. Bar Assn. medallion, 1972. Mem. Pa., Phila. (chmn. citizenship com. 1972-73) bar assns., Jewish Family Service Phila., Fedn. Jewish Agys. Greater Phila., Am. Civil Liberties Union, Allied Jewish Appeal (center city vice chmn. for fund raising 1968-71), Phila. Art Mus., Acad. Fine Arts, Mus. Modern Art New York, Gratz Coll. Alumni Assn. Jewish religion. Club: Lawyers. Home: 1919 Chestnut St Philadelphia PA 19103 Office: 12 S 12th St Philadelphia PA 19107

LANE, CAROLYN BLOCKER (MRS. M. DONALD LANE, JR.), author; b. Providence, June 4, 1926; d. Harry Theodore and Margaret (Breitenfeld) Blocker; B.A., Conn. Coll., New London, 1948; m. M. Donald Lane, Jr., Apr. 28, 1951; 1 son, Jay Donald. Author: Uncle Max and the Sea Lion, 1970; Turnabout Night at the Zoo, 1971; The Voices of Greenwillow Pond, 1972; (plays) Turnabout Night at the Zoo (12th Ann. Merit award Community Childrens Theatre, Kansas City, Mo.), 1967; The Wayward Clocks (Merit award Pioneer Drama Service), 1969; The Last Grad (1st prize Theatre Guild Webster Groves, Mo.), 1970; Child of Air, 1972; The Winnemah Spirit, 1975. Mem. Authors Guild. Home: Ward Rd Salt Point NY 12578

LANE, ELAINE O'BERRY, writer, communications exec.; b. St. Petersburg, Fla., Feb. 3, 1930; d. Warren Holman and Breunita Elsie (Turner) O'Berry; A.A., St. Petersburg Jr. Coll., 1949; student New Sch. for Social Research, N.Y.C., N.Y. U.; m. Charles Zick Lane, Jan. 26, 1952 (div. 1973). With St. Petersburg Times, 1951-54, N.Y. Post, 1954-61; v.p. Milne-O'Berry Packing Co., Inc., St. Petersburg, 1961—; editor Fla. Living sect. Tampa Tribune-Times, 1968-72, with Punta Gorda Isles, 1972-73; co-owner Stephens/Lane & Assos., 1973—. Recipient excellence award Tampa Bd. Realtors, 1970. Mem. Nat. Assn. Real Estate Editors, Women in Communications, Episcopal Churchwoman. Democrat. Episcopalian. Home: PO Box 178 Punta Gorda FL 33950

LANE, EVELYN RAE CLOWERS (MRS. JOHN THOMAS LANE), educator; b. Itmann, W.Va., June 10, 1930; d. Clarence Robert and Ethel Rae (Christian) Clowers; B.S., Concord Coll., 1952; m. John Thomas Lane, Apr. 11, 1952; children—Pamela Fawn, Tammy Rae, Thomas Patrick. Phys. edn. tchr. Kensington Park Elementary Sch., Miami, Fla., 1953-54, South Miami Jr. High Sch., 1955-57; instr. phys. edn. Fla. So. Coll., Lakeland, 1963—. Vice pres. 4-H Club, 1961, leader, 1973; vol. water safety instr. trainer, first aid instr. trainer A.R.C., 1965—. Bd. dirs. Camp Fire Girls, 1965-73, leader, 1963. Mem. Fla., Dade County, Polk County assns. health, phys. edn. and recreation. Club: Faculty Women's (v.p. Lakeland 1964). Home: 14 Dos Rios Greeley CO 80631

LANE, FRONA BELL, author; b. Austin, Tex., Nov. 29, 1903; d. Henry Perry and Lula Annie (Wade) Lane; student Los Angeles State Coll., 1950-55, U. Cal. at Los Angeles, 1952-53, D.Litt. Leadership (hon.), Internat. Acad. Leadership, 1967; m. Victor Smith Amussen, Feb. 20, 1961 (dec. Nov. 1964); children by previous marriage—Arthur Perry, Marylyn Julia (Mrs. Richard D. Brugh). Script writer KMED, Medford, Ore., 1930-32; sec. PWA, Los Angeles and San Francisco, 1935-40; drama coach Gold Bond Studios, Medford, Ore., 1940-42; drama coach, pvt. studio, Ore., 1942-45, Los Angeles, 1945-51; tchr. Los Angeles City Schs., 1951-69. Tchr. accent elimination Golden State U., Los Angeles, 1955-56; script writer KYA, San Francisco, 1945-46. Active worker Democratic Central Com., Los Angeles, 1934-35. Recipient awards for poetry, prose. Mem. Nat. League Am. Pen Women (poetry workshop chmn. San Diego 1972-74, pres. 1974), Cal. Fedn. Chaparral Poets (pres. 1957). Mem. Order Eastern Star. Clubs: Women's (Escondido, Cal.); Teachers (Los Angeles, Escondido); Writers (Berkeley, Cal.); Little Theatre (Los Angeles); Music, Drama (Medford, Los Angeles). Author: Apples of Gold, 1945; The Third Eyelid, 1951; Mommy, Dear, 1954; Worm, Feed Gently, 1955; Make Believe, 1955; The Contemporary Scene, 1954; Hold the Candle, 1955; One Prayer Not Wasted, 1972; Eve Made Wise, 1974. Address: 1400 El Norte Pkwy Apt 18 San Marcos CA 92069

LANE, HELEN S. MURCHISON (MRS. EDWARD W. LANE, JR.), civic worker; b. Boston, June 1, 1924; d. Charles H. and Helen (Spratt) Murchison; A.B., Sweet Briar Coll., 1946; m. Edward W. Lane, Jr., Oct. 16, 1948; children—Edward W. III, Helen Palmer, Anna Taliaferro, Charles Murchison. Bd. dirs. Jr. League, Jacksonville, Fla., 1954-60, pres., 1959-60; chmn. Symphony Ball, Jacksonville, 1960; restorer 1893 Victorian home; regional dir. exec. com. Alumni Council Sweet Briar Coll., 1968-70; mem. Jacksonville Hist. and Cultural Commn., 1971-74; mem. fine arts com. Jacksonville C. of C., 1972-73; trustee Bartram Sch., 1972—; bd. dirs. Jacksonville Symphony, 1973; chmn. Action Plan for Arts, 1972-73; bd. dirs. Arts Assembly; mem. Adams Environmental Awards Bd., 1972-73. Mem. Acacia Garden Circle (past pres.), Colonial Dames Club: Jacksonville Garden (life). Pub.: The Best of Lucifer, 1969; The Queen Victoria Cooks, 1971. Home: 3790 Ortega Blvd Jacksonville FL 32210

LANE, LAURA GORDON, editor; b. Vernon, Tex., Nov. 15, 1913; d. William Allen and Martha (Conner) Lane; B.S. in Journalism, Tex. Women's U., 1933; postgrad. Columbia, 1944. Reporter Vernon (Tex.) Daily Record, 1936-39; asso. editor Extension service Tex. A. & M. U., College Station, 1939-42, editor, 1942-47; asso. editor Country Gentleman, Phila., 1947-55; asso. editor Farm Jour., Phila., 1955-69, women's editor, 1969-70. Recipient Nat. Headliner award Women in Communications, Inc., 1950. Mem. Asso. Country Women of World, Women in Communications. Club: Washington Press. Editor: The United States, Its People and Its Homes, 1947-53; A Country Woman's Day, 1948; Idea Book of Business Forms, 1972. Address: 2018 Spruce St Philadelphia PA 19103

LANE, MARGARET BEYNON TAYLOR (MRS. HORACE C. LANE), librarian; b. St. Louis, Feb. 6, 1919; d. Archer and Alice (Jones) Taylor; B.A., La. State U., 1939, J.D., 1942; B.A. in L.S., Columbia, 1941; m. Horace C. Lane, Jan. 6, 1945; children—Margaret Elizabeth, Thomas Archer. Reference and circulation asst. Columbia Law Library, N.Y.C., 1942-44; law librarian, asst. prof. U. Conn. Sch. Law, Hartford, 1944-46; law librarian La. State U. Law Sch., Baton Rouge, 1946-48; recorder documents La. Sec. of State's Office, Baton Rouge, 1949—. Mem. adv. council on depository libraries U.S. Pub. Printer, 1972—. Treas. Delta Iota House Bd. of Kappa Kappa Gamma, 1965-68. Mem. Am. (mem. interdivisional com. on pub. documents 1967-74, chmn. 1967-70), La. library assns., La., Baton Rouge bar assns., Phi Delta Delta, Kappa Kappa Gamma. Club: Baton Rouge Library. Home: 7545 Richards Dr Baton Rouge LA 70809 Office: PO Box 15777 Baton Rouge LA 70815

LANE, MARGARET RITCH (MRS. ISMAT HASSAN SOLIMAN), physician; b. Detroit, Jan. 18, 1926; d. Emory Wilson and Margaret Sedgwick (Norton) Lane; B.A., Carleton Coll., 1946; M.D., U. Ia., 1949; M.P.H., Harvard, 1954; m. Ismat Hassan Soliman, Feb. 13, 1968. Intern C.T. Miller Hosp., St. Paul, 1949-50; resident U. Colo. Med. Center, Denver, 1950-52; practice medicine specializing in pediatrics; physician Mansfield State Tng. Sch., 1952-53; crippled children physician Conn. State Health Dept., 1954-55; med. missionary, West Pakistan, 1955-65; crippled children physician Hawaii Health Dept., Honolulu, 1965-71; postgrad. fellow U. Colo. Med. Center, Denver, 1971-72; pediatrician Crippled Children's Service Utah Div. Health, Salt Lake City, 1972—. Bd. dirs. Pastoral Counselling Service, Honolulu, 1968-71. Diplomate Am. Bd. Pediatrics. Mem. Am. Acad. Pediatrics, Am. Pub. Health Assn., Am. Assn. for Mental Deficiency. Episcopalian. Office: 44 Medical Dr Salt Lake City UT 84113

LANE, MARION IOLA THORNBERRY (MRS. JON A. COLE), newspaper editor; b. Boulder, Colo., May 23, 1932; d. Lawrence Andrew and Amy Viola (Smith) Thornberry; grad. Am. Schs., Chgo., Ashland (Ore.) High Sch., 1954, Newspaper Inst. Am., N.Y.C., 1960; m. Lawrence Elvin Lane, Feb. 14, 1949 (div. 1967); children—Lawrence Lee, Dale Elvin; m. 2d, Jon A. Cole, Dec. 18, 1973. Reporter, feature writer, news editor weekly newspapers, 1965-68; reporter Lodi-(Cal.) News-Sentinel, 1968, farm editor, police and ct. reporter, women's page editor, 1968-70, woman's page editor, 1971—; stringer Sacramento Bee, 1970-71; author poetry and short stories. Mem. Lodi Bus. and Profl. Women's Club. Playwright: Is There Life on Other Planets?, 1966. Home: 6803 Capital Circle Sacramento CA 95828

LANE, MARION JEAN (MRS. SIDNEY LANE), artist; b. Bklyn., July 8, 1928; d. Herman and Anita (Gordon) Arrons; student Bklyn. Mus. Art Sch., 1947-59, Pratt Inst., 1948-50, Art Students League N.Y., 1953, 60, 68; B.A., William Paterson Coll., 1974; m. Sidney Lane, Dec. 25, 1953; children—Spencer, George. Exhibited in group shows at Bklyn. Mus., 1958, 59, Montclair (N.J.) Mus., 1960-64, Newark Mus., 1961, Trenton (N.J.) State Mus., 1968, 70, Jersey City Mus., 1965, Riverside Mus., N.Y.C., 1963, Everhart (Pa.) Mus., 1965, Silvermine Guild, Conn., 1965, N.Y. Worlds Fair, 1965, Lever House, N.Y.C., 1968, Lincoln Center, 1969, Philharmonic Hall, N.Y.C., 1968, Kraushaar Gallery, N.Y.C., 1974; represented in numerous pvt. collections. Chmn. art selections com. Bergen Community Mus., 1972-74; pres. Modern Artists Guild N.J., 1969-71; tchr. Edward Williams Coll., N.J., 1971-72, River Dell Adult Edn., 1961-71. Recipient awards Bklyn. Mus., 1958, Montclair Mus., 1960, 64, Jersey City Mus., 1965, Monmouth Coll., 1964. Mem. Nat. Assn. Women Artists, Silvermine Guild Artists, Art Students League N.Y. (life), Modern Artists Guild Bergen County. Home: 441 Hawthorne Pl Ridgewood NJ 07450

LANE, MARY ETHEL (MRS. JAMES WADDELL COBB), physician; b. Institute, W. Va., Dec. 4, 1929; d. David Alphonso and Juanita Jewell (Bobson) Lane; A.B., Ind. U., 1950; M.D., Woman's Med. Coll. Pa., 1954; m. James Waddell Cobb, June 21, 1959; children—Lane Leslie, Keith Hamilton, Pamela Griffin. Intern Grasslands Hosp., Eastview, N.Y., 1954-55, resident, 1955-57; practice gen. medicine, Tarrytown, N.Y., 1957-64; physician Mobile Unit Demonstration Project for Bklyn., Bronx, Queens, N.Y. Planned Parenthood World Population, 1964-66; clin. dir. contraception service Margaret Sanger Research Bur., N.Y.C., 1966-73. Cons. Naomi Gray Assos., N.Y.C., 1971—; mem. nat. med. com. Planned Parenthood/World Population. Mem. Nat. Med. Assn., Am. Assn. Planned Parenthood Physicians, Am. Assn. Sex Educators and Counselors. Home: 70 S Broadway Tarrytown NY 10591

LANE, MARY FRANCES KERNELL, educator; b. Haileyville, Okla.; d. Homer Seiber and Myrtle L. (Jones) Kernell; B.F.A., Okla. State U., M.S., 1962. Sustainer, Piano Program, KGFF Radio, Shawnee, Okla.; fed. shorthand reporter USN, Norman, Okla.; recreation dir. Vance AFB, Enid, Okla., 1956-58; head counselor Okla. State U.; instr. psychology and music Cooke County Jr. Coll., Gainesville, Tex.; sr. psychometrist research project U. Cal. at Riverside; counselor in drug control, probation officer Los Angeles County; prof. psychology East Los Angeles Coll., Los Angeles Community Coll. Dist., 1969—. Maj., Civil Air Patrol. Mem. hon. adv. bd. Addictive Drugs Edn. Found. Fellow Intercontinental Biog. Assn. (life); mem. Am., Western psychol. assns., Cal. Tchrs. Assn., Am. Fedn. Tchrs. (pres. Golden Bear chpt.), Am. Inst. Parliamentarians, Internat. Platform Assn. (sec. Western region 1968), Nat., World wildlife assns., Am. Assn. U. Women, Sigma Alpha Iota. Democrat. Presbyn. Club: Sierra (Los Angeles). Home: 1301 S Atlantic Blvd Apt 539-C Monterey Park CA 91754 Office: 5357 Brooklyn St Los Angeles CA 90022

LANE, REBEKAH JO, journalist; b. Indpls., July 5, 1948; d. Ellis Guy and Rachel Rebekah (Rice) Lane; B.S., Ball State U. (Scripps Howard grantee), 1970, M.A., 1971. Reporter, Muncie (Ind.) Star, 1968-70; reporter Anderson (Ind.) Daily Bulletin, 1971-72, wire editor, 1972-73, copy editor, 1973; copy reader Jour.-Gazette, Ft. Wayne, Ind., 1973—. Mem. Women in Communications, Nat. Orgn. Women, Kappa Tau Alpha. Republican. Methodist. Home: 1014 1/2 Van Buren St Fort Wayne IN 46804 Office: 600 W Main St Fort Wayne IN 46802

LANE, SYLVIA, lawyer; b. N.Y.C., Apr. 10, 1912; d. Benjamin and Eva (Shore) Steinberg; student St. John's U., 1931; LL.B., Bklyn. Law Sch., 1934; m. Nat Lane, June 1935; children—Stanley R., Madeline (Mrs. Harvey Howard). Admitted to N.Y. bar, 1935, since practiced in N.Y.C.; with firm Swetlow & Sugarman, N.Y.C., 1935-41; Legal cons. Central Bklyn. chpt. Hadassah 1964—. Participant N.Y. U. Conf. series on law enforcement, 1955. Legal asst. vol. Commn. Core Corrections Anna Moskowitz Kross, 1955-57; active Legal Aid Soc., Girl Scouts Am. Mem. Hadassah (editor Central Bklyn. chpt. Jour. 1955-65), B'nai B'rith. Jewish religion (editor temple bull. 1960-67). Home: 40 Clarkson Av Brooklyn NY 11226 Office: 64 Third Av New York City NY 10003

LANE, SYLVIA (MRS. BENJAMIN LANE), economist; b. N.Y.C.; A.B., U. Cal. at Berkeley, 1934, M.A., 1936; postgrad. Columbia, 1937; Ph.D., U. So. Cal., 1957; m. Benjamin Lane, Sept. 2, 1939; children—Leonard, Reece, Nancy. Lectr., asst. prof. U. So. Cal., Los Angeles, 1947-60; asso. prof. econs. San Diego State Coll., 1961-65; asso. prof. finance, asso. dir. Center Econ. Edn., Cal. State Coll., Fullerton, 1965-69; chmn. dept. finance, 1967-69; prof. agrl. econs. U. Cal. at Davis, 1969—. Econ. cons. Pres. Com. Consumer Interests, 1966—, Adv. Commn. Tax Reform, State Cal., 1968—. Project economist Los Angeles County Welfare Planning Council, 1956-59; chmn. commn. aging Community Welfare Council, San Diego, 1963-65; mem. Com. Econ. Opportunity, San Diego, 1964-65. Mem. Am., Western econ. assns., Am. Agrl. Econs. Assn., Am. Council Consumer Information, Omicron Delta Epsilon (regional dir. 1966-69, v.p. 1970, pres. 1973). Author: (with E. Bryant Phillips) Personal Finance, 1963. Home: 3028 N El Macero Dr Davis CA 95618

LANES, SELMA GORDON, critic, author, editor; b. Boston, Mar. 13, 1929; d. Jacob and Lily (Whiteman) Gordon; B.A., Smith Coll., 1950; M.S. in Journalism, Columbia, 1954; m. Jerrold B. Lanes, Nov. 21, 1959 (div. Mar. 1970); children—Andrew Oliver, Matthew Gordon. Asst. to publicity dir. Little Brown & Co., Boston, 1950-51; asso. editor Focus Mag., N.Y.C., 1951-53; travel page editor Boston Globe, 1953; spl. editorial asst., researcher Look Mag., 1956-60; children's entertainment editor Show Mag., 1961-63; critic children's books for Book World (N.Y. Herald-Tribune, later World Jour. Tribune, Wash. Post and Chgo. Tribune), 1965-71, N.Y. Times Book Rev., 1966—; articles editor Parents Mag., 1971-74; editor-in-chief Parents Mag. Press, 1974—; cons. to Penguin Books, 1967. Judge, Children's Spring Book Festival, 1970, dir., 1972; judge N.Y. Times Ten Best Illus. Children's Books, 1973. Trustee Fund for Art Investment, N.Y.C. Mem. Phi Beta Kappa. Author (juvenile) Amy Loves Good-byes, 1966; The Curiosity Book, 1968; Down the Rabbit Hole, A critical work for adults on children's literature, 1971. Office: 52 Vanderbilt Av New York City NY 10017

LANG, CHARLOTTE LOUISA, county ofcl.; b. Dunseith, N.D., July 5, 1920; d. John J. and Margaret M. (Randall) Hiatt; B.S., N.D. and Minot State Coll., 1967; m. Adam Lang, Nov. 8, 1938; children—DuWayne Lang, Dwight. Tchr. rural schs., Bottineau and Rolette Counties, N.D., 1946-59, pub. schs., Dunseith, N.D., 1960-68; county supt. schs. Bottineau and Rolette Counties, N.D., 1969—. Adviser Supplementary Ednl. Bd. Bottineau County, 1969—. County co-chmn. March Dimes, 1956—. Mem. Am. Legion Aux. (dist. pres. 1967-68, 68-69, pres. local unit 1962-67, fgn. relations chmn. for State dept. 1969-70, poppy chmn. N.D. dept. 1972-73). Methodist (active ch. bd. and ladies group). Mem. Order Eastern Star (worthy matron 1969-70, 72-73). Home: Box 156 Dunseith ND 58329

LANG, ELLEN HOPE, park superintendent; b. Sitka, Alaska, Dec. 29, 1927; d. Andrew Percy and Tillie (Howard) Hope; student Sheldon Jackson Coll., 1960, 61, 62; 1 dau., Karen (Mrs. David A. Coleman). Instructional aid Child Guidance, Bur. Indian Affairs Boarding, Mt. Edgecumbe, Alaska, 1954-62, supr. instructional aid child guidance, 1963-66; postal clk., Sitka, Alaska, 1966-67; clk.-typist Nat. Park Service, Sitka (Alaska) Nat. Monument, 1967-69, part technician, 1969-71, park ranger, 1971-74, supt., 1974—. Chmn. Sitka (Alaska) Community Action Group, 1969-73; mem. Future Alaska seminar sessions, 1969; sec. Sitka (Alaska) Village Planning Council, 1970-73; v.p. Nat. Endowment Humanities-Alaska Humanities Forum, 1972—; mem. citizens adv. com. Sitka (Alaska) Community Coll., 1970-73. Bd. dirs. S.E. Alaska Community Action Program, Rural Alaska Community Action Program; trustee Sheldon Jackson Coll., 1960-72. Recipient Spl. Service award Nat. Park Service, 1968, Spl. Achievement award, 1972, Roy E. Appleman award in history, 1971. Mem. Alaska Native Brotherhood (v.p. 1973), S.E. Alaska Indian Cultural Center (chmn. bd. 1968—). Tlingit and Haida Indian Alaska (pres. Sitka chpt. 1971—), Sitka C. of C. Presbyn. Home: PO Box 909 Sitka AK 99835 Office: PO Box 738 Sitka AK 99835

LANG, SISTER FRANZ, librarian; b. Highland Park, Mich., Sept. 7, 1921; d. Andrew and Elizabeth (Winczner) Lang; B.A., Siena Heights Coll., 1959; A.M. in Library Sci., U. Mich., 1964; postgrad. Detroit Bus. Inst., U. Chgo., U. Ill. Exec. sec., office employee, 1939-51; tchr. St. Joseph Sch., Port Huron, Mich., also Bishop Quarter Mil. Acad., Chgo., 1952-62; asst. librarian Siena Heights Coll., Adrian, Mich., 1962-63; head librarian St. Dominic Coll., St. Charles, Ill., 1963-70, Barry Coll., Miami, Fla., 1970—; library cons., 1964—. Mem. Community Relations Bd., Lake Charles, Ill., 1963-70. Served with U.S. Army Air Force, 1942-45. Mem. Am., Fla., Dade County, Cath. (chmn. Fla. unit 1973—) library assns., Southeastern Library Assn., Assn. Coll. and Research Libraries (mem. nominating com. 1973). Contbr. to publs. in field. Home: 11300 NE 2d Av Miami FL 33161

LANG, JOYCE BURNETT (MRS. IRVIN W. LANG), journalist; b. Cummings, N.D., Oct. 20, 1918; d. Mack and Bertha (Carver) Burnett; student No. State Tchrs. Coll., Marquette, Mich., 1936-37; B.A. (Sigma Delta Chi scholar), U. N.D., 1940; m. Irvin W. Lang, Aug. 22, 1942; children—Michael George, Patricia Kay. Reporter, night city, state editor, columnist Fargo (N.D.) Forum, 1940-42, 43-46; with Detroit (Mich.) Times, also San Francisco (Cal.) Call Bull., 1942; co-pub., editor Enderlin (N.D.) Ind., 1947-50; free-lance legislative reporter N.D. weeklies, 1951, 55-56; columnist, editorial writer Williston (N.D.) Herald, 1952; editor Hillsboro (N.D.) Banner, 1952-55; co-pub., editor Hebron (N.D.) Herald, 1957-65; free-lance journalist, Eugene, Ore., 1965—; founder Write-It-Right, Eugene, 1966—; publ. asst. Pacific Sociol. Review, 1967-69; information and publs. coordinator E.C. Brown Found. and Center for Family Studies, Eugene, 1969—, editor Focus on the Family, 1973—. Charter pres. Enderlin Bus. and Profl. Women's Club, 1949; state sec. N.D. Fedn. Bus. and Profl. Women's Club, 1949, editor, 1950-51; adviser Girl Scouts U.S.A., Hebron, 1959; sec. Community Hosp. Bd., Hebron, 1962-65; dir. Theodore Roosevelt Nat. Meml. Park and Badlands Assn., 1959-63; mem. P.T.A., Hebron, 1957-65. Recipient N.D. Press Woman of Achievement award, 1965; numerous awards N.D., also Nat. Fedn. Press Women, 1954-64. Mem. N.D. Press Women (charter pres. 1950-51, editor 1950-51), Nat. Fedn. Press Women, Mortar Bd., Nat. Writers Club, Am. Legion Aux., Ore. Press Women (v.p. 1973-75), Theta Sigma Phi (pres. Eugene profl. club 1971-72). Home: 4679 Barger Dr Eugene OR 97402 Office: 1802 Moss St Eugene OR 97403

LANG, MARGO TERZIAN, artist; b. Fresno, Cal., July 29, 1920; d. Nishan and Araxie (Karzarosian) Terzian; student Fresno State U., 1939-42, Stanford, 1948-50, Prado Museum, Madrid, Spain, 1957-59, Ariz. State U., 1960-61; pvt. study with Dong Kingman, Ed Whitney, Rex Brandt, others; m., Nov. 29, 1942; children—Sandra J. (Mrs. Ronald L. Carr), Roger Mark, Timothy Scott. Major exhbns. include Guadalajara, Mexico, N.Y.C., San Francisco, Chgo., Washington, Phoenix, others; paintings in various Am. embassies throughout world; represented in permanent collection Nat. Collection of Fine Arts Museum, Smithsonian Instn. Lectr., juror art shows; condr. workshops. Bd. dirs. Phoenix Symphony Assn., 1965-69, Phoenix Musical Theater, 1965-69. Recipient award for spl. achievements Symphony Assn., 1966, 67, 68, 72, spl. award State of Ariz., silver medal of excellence Internat. Platform Assn., 1971. Mem. Internat. Platform Assn., Ariz. Watercolor Assn., Nat. Soc. Arts and Letters (mem. nat. bd. 1971-72), Phoenix Art Mus., Friends of Mexican Art, Am. Artists Profl. League, English-Speaking Union, Musical Theater Guild. Home: 6127 Calle del Paisano Scottsdale AZ 85251

LANG, MARY LOUISE, camp adminstr.; b. Kalamazoo, May 6, 1922; d. Jules Herman and Florence Louise (Sergeant) Lang; B.S., Western Mich. U., 1943, M.A., 1953. Tchr. phys. edn. Battle Creek (Mich.) Jr. High Sch., 1943-45, 51-54, Albion Coll., 1945-51; resident camp dir. YWCA, Grand Rapids, Mich., summers 1951-54, program dir. resident camp and health, phys. edn. and recreation, 1954—; counselor Pretty Lake Vacation Camp, Kalamazoo, summers 1940-41, YWCA Camp Newaygo, 1939, 43-45; program dir. Kalamazoo Recreation Dept. Playground, summer 1942. Water safety instr. A.R.C., 1940—, water safety instr. trainer, 1963—; mem. Kent County Safe Boating Council, 1965-68, Gov.'s Boating Safety Council, 1964-67. Mem. Am. Camping Assn. (Mich. sect.), A.A.H.P.E.R. Home: 959 Breton Rd SE Grand Rapids MI 49506 Office: 25 Sheldon Av SE Grand Rapids MI 45902

LANG, MAUD ORA, home economist; b. Richland, Ind., Dec. 10, 1911; d. Curren Robert and Lue Tallie (Lewright) Lang; A.B., Ind. U., 1933; postgrad. Ind. State U., summers 1934, 36, 38, 40; B.S., Ball State Tchrs. Coll., 1936; postgrad U. Wis., summer 1956. Tchr. Luce Twp. High Sch., Richland, 1933-41; area extension agt. home econs. Warrick County, Ind., 1941-74, ret., 1974. Mem. Ind. Extension Workers Assn., Nat. Home Extension Agts. Assn., Ind. Acad. Sci., Am., Ind. home econs. assns., Bus. and Profl. Women Booneville. Kappa Delta Phi, Epsilon Sigma Phi (sec.-treas. 1967—). Home: RD 1 Richland IN 47634 Office: Court House Box 284 Boonville IN 47601

LANG, NATALIE SANDRA, mgmt. firm exec.; b. Chgo., Feb. 28, 1937; d. Ralph and Lillian (Unell) Lang. Vice pres. Halbrecht Assos., Inc., Chgo., 1960-64; pres. Computer Personnel Cons., Inc., Chgo., 1965-66; with Booz, Allen & Hamilton, 1966—, personnel recruiting div., 1966-70, asso. exec. personnel div., 1970-71, dir. nat. urban affairs program, Chgo., then N.Y.C., 1971-74, v.p. social responsibility and urban affairs, 1974—. Mem. Pres. Nixon's Adv. Council Minority Bus. Enterprise; mem. Black exec. exchange program adv. com. Nat. Urban League; mem. corporate urban affairs adv. com. Nat. Urban Coalition, Washington; mem. exec. com. Nat. Alliance Businessmen's Cluster; mem. corporate urban affairs div. Pub. Affairs council, Washington. Bd. dirs. Nat. Minority Purchasing Council. Recipient Woman of Year award Cosmopolitan C. of C., Chgo., 1973. Office: Booz Allen & Hamilton 245 Park Av New York City NY 10017

LANG, PEARL (MRS. JOSEPH WISEMAN), dancer, choreographer; b. Chgo., May 29, 1922; d. Jacob and Frieda Lack; m. Joseph Wiseman. Soloist, Martha Graham Dance Co., 1941-51 (1st to assume Miss Graham's own roles including El Penitente, Appalachian Spring and Letter to the World); now dancer, tchr., choreographer, presented own co. and works at Am. Dance Festival, Alvin Theater, 1952-54; founder (with Alvin Ailey) Am. Dance Center; choreographer, founder Pearl Lang Dance Found.; choreographer 35 works for concerts and TV in U.S., Israel and Europe; co-dir. Murder in the Cathedral at Shakespeare Festival, Stratford, Conn., 1965; mem. faculty Juilliard Sch. Music, Yale U., 13 years. Guggenheim fellow, 1960-61, 69-70. Address: 382 Central Park W New York City NY 10025

LANGBORT, POLLY, advt. agy. exec.; b. N.Y.C.; d. Julius and Nettie (Berman) Langbort; B.A., Adelphi U., 1954. With Young & Rubicam Internat., Inc., N.Y.C., 1956—, sr. buyer, 1962-64, media supr., 1964-68, media planning group supr., 1968-74, v.p., 1970—, dir. communications planning, 1974—. Mem. trust fund com. Marketing Planning Bd. Home: 340 E 64th St New York City NY 10021 Office: 285 Madison Av New York City NY 10017

LANGDON, BETTY (MRS. BEN LANGDON), reporter; B.S. in Journalism, U. Okla.; m. Ben Langdon; children—Ben, Nance Langdon (Mrs. Diamond). Reporter Mangum (Okla.) Star-News. Mem. Short Grass Art League (charter), U. Okla. Alumni Assn. Home: Box 340 Mangum OK 73554

LANGDON, HELEN JEAN ULIVARRI (MRS. LAWRENCE LESTER LANGDON), occupational therapist, health service adminstr.; b. Albuquerque, Feb. 3, 1933; d. John Francis and Anita Josephine (Torres) Ulivarri; student U. N.M., 1951-53; B.S. in Occupational Therapy, Colo. State U., 1955; m. Lawrence Lester Langdon, Sept. 2, 1961; children—Stephen Lawrence, Bryan John. Occupational therapist United Cerebral Palsy Assn., San Antonio, 1956-58; chief occupational therapist Rehab. Center, Albuquerque, 1958-63, workshop supr. Work Adjustment Center, 1962-63; cons. occupational therapy dept. State N.M. Maternal Health and Child Welfare, Albuquerque, 1965-67; cons. occupational therapy Riverside (Cal.) Convalescent Hosp., 1967-68, Fontana (Cal.) Convalescent Hosp., 1967-68, Alta Vista Convalescent Hosp., Riverside, 1968-69, Park Lido Convalescent Center, Flagship, Cal., 1969; dir. occupational therapy Rehab. Center, Albuquerque, 1970—. Mem. Am., N.M. occupational therapy assns. Roman Catholic. Club: Sanado Womans.

LANGE, JEAN RUTHVEN WILSHIRE, writer; b. Eastbourne, Sussex, Eng., Jan. 28, 1902; d. Ruthven Matcham and Millicent Ida (Thomson) Wilshire; student Northfield Pvt. Coll., Watford, Eng., 1919-20; m. Hans Albrecht F. Lange, Apr. 4, 1931 (dec. Aug. 1965); children—Anneliese Johanna, Jack H., (stepdau.) Ingeborg Edith. Appeared in Brit. theatre prodns. Rose Marie, 1925-27, The Barretts of Wimpole Street, 1932, Payment Deferred, 1931; appeared in Spanish theatres, Madrid, Barcelona, Valencia, 1924; appeared with Dame May Whitty's Repertory Co., London, 1928-29; news corr. Radio Free Europe, Frankfurt am Main, Germany, 1952-55; dir. pub. relations Montclair (N.J.) Art Mus., 1956-61; writer, producer Sta. KLRN-TV, ednl. TV San Antonio/Austin, 1962—. Mem. U.S. Com. for Refugees, 1960—. Recipient citation for services to refugee cause U.S. Com. for Refugees, 1961. Mem. Am. Women in Radio and Television, Women in Communications, Rho Tau Sigma. Contbg. editor San Antonio Mag., 1967-68. Contbr. articles to mags. Home: 8035 Fredericksburg Rd Apt 15 San Antonio TX 78229 Office: KLRN-TV Pavillion Texan Cultures San Antonio TX 78291

LANGE, LINDA LAURINE, educator; b. Milw., Mar. 2, 1947; d. Arnold Edwin and Laurine Marie (Johnston) Lange; B.S., Ind. U., 1969, M.S., 1971. Grad. asst. in counseling Ind. U., 1969-71; children's worker State of Ohio Bur. Services for Blind, Columbus and Cin., 1971-72; research asst., abstractor, adminstr. Systems Research Co., Cin., 1972-73; dir. counseling center Coll. Mt. St. Joseph, Cin., 1973—. Mem. Nat., Ohio assns. for women deans, adminstrs. and counselors, Am. Personnel and Guidance Assn., Ind. U. Alumni Assn., Zeta Tau Alpha, Pi Lambda Theta. Lutheran. Office: Counseling Center Coll Mt St Joseph Mount St Joseph OH 45051

LANGEN, REXINE ALLAN, ednl. cons.; b. Chgo., Feb. 27, 1920; d. Reginald Griffith and Mary (O'Leary) Allan; B.S., Wis. State U.-Platteville, 1960; M.S., U. Wis.-Milw., 1963; Ph.D., U. Wis.-Madison, 1974; m. Vincent William Souter, Aug. 23, 1942 (dec.); children—Suzanne J., Mary Anne, Pamela J.; m. 2d, Victor O. Langen, Dec. 6, 1958; 1 dau., Victoria L. Tchr., Fennimore, Reedsburg, Appleton and Whitefish Bay, Wis., 1942-58, Lab. Sch. U. Wis.-Milw., 1960-65, Lab. Sch. Wis. State U.-Stevens Point, 1968—; ednl. cons. under Dept. Health, Edn. and Welfare funding Wis. State Dept. Pub. Instrn., Madison, 1968—. Mem. Am., Wis. ednl. research assns., Am. Assn. U. Profs., Pi Lambda Theta. Christian Scientist. Home: 1523 Simpson St Madison WI 53713 Office: 126 Langdon St Madison WI 53702

LANGENFELD, ELIZABETH ANNE (MRS. FRANCIS JOSEPH LANGENFELD), pub. co. exec.; b. Rosenheim, Germany, Oct. 16, 1928; d. Ignaz and Leokadia (Steiner) Groeppner; B.A., Loretto Coll., Rosenheim, 1949; postgrad. U. Munich (Germany), 1957-58; m. Francis Joseph Langenfeld, Oct. 16, 1954; 1 dau., Mary Elizabeth. Came to U.S., 1958, naturalized, 1961; investigator, translator Dept. State, Munich, Germany, 1954-58; promotion rep. TV Guide, Triangle Publs., Moline, Ill., 1958—; lectr. inter-disciplinary workshop Western Ill. U., Macomb, 1971; guest lectr. various colls., Ia., Ill. Bd. dirs. Catholic Interracial Council, Davenport, Ia. Mem. Ia.-Ill. Pub. Relations Council, Am. Women in Radio and TV (officer Hawkeye chpt. 1968—). Club: Mississippi Valley Press (Davenport, Ia.). Home: RD 1 Alpha IL 61413 Office: PO Box 250 Moline IL 61265

LANGER, IRENE BROOKS (MRS. JERRY TANZER), mortgage banker; b. Bklyn., Oct. 13, 1925; d. Isidor and Freda (Moskowitz) Brooks; student Coll. City N.Y., 1943-46; m. Leonard H. Langer, Mar. 31, 1946 (dec. Dec. 1969); children—Diane, Barbara, Paul Andrew; m. 2d, Jerry Tanzer, Dec. 3, 1971. Office mgr. Am. Freight Bur., N.Y.C., 1941-46; sec. to chief engr. Airquipment Co., Burbank, Cal., 1946-47; sec., bookeeper Certified Chrome Mfg. Co., Los Angeles, 1947-48; pres., mgr. Insured Escrow Co., Bellflower, Cal., 1950-51; office mgr. Aldon Constrn. Co., Bellflower, 1948-50; exec. v.p. Instl. Mortgage Co., Bellflower, 1951-63; cons. Mortgage Banking, Downey, Cal., 1963-65; sr. v.p. Fidelity Bank, Beverly Hills, Cal., 1965—, mem. exec. com., finance com., 1966-69; pres., dir. Fidelity Computer Co., Beverly Hills, 1969-71; exec. v.p. Zenith Mortgage Co., Beverly Hills, 1970—, mem. exec. com., 1973—; sr. v.p. Fidelity Mgmt. Co., Beverly Hills, 1969-71. Republican. Home: 14332 Dickens St Sherman Oaks CA 91403 Office: 9665 Wilshire Blvd Beverly Hills CA 90212

LANGERMAN, BEATRICE GERTRUDE (MRS. HERBERT LANGERMAN), psycho-therapist, editor; b. N.Y.C., Jan. 9, 1937; d. Louis Samuel and Anne Carolina (Kizelstein) Shapiro; B.S. cum laude, Mich. State U., 1958; postgrad. New Sch. for Social Research, 1961, N.Y. Law Sch., 1964-66, N.Y. U., 1963-64, Rutgers U., 1963—; m. Herbert Langerman, Dec. 18, 1960. Asst. photography Ann., 1960, Ziff-Davis Pub. Co., N.Y.C., 1958-60, asst. picture editor Popular Photography mag., 1958-60; asst. dir. spl. projects Ziff-Davis Pub. Co., N.Y.C., 1960-61; free-lance non-fiction writer, N.Y.C., 1961-68; ednl. cons. Inst. for Emotional Edn., N.Y.C., 1968—, editor-in-chief Jour. Emotional Edn., 1968—. Mem. Phi Gamma Mu, Alpha Epsilon Phi. Contbr. to various publs. Home: 201 E 28th St New York City NY 10016

LANGFORD, ANNA RIGGS, lawyer, alderwoman; b. Springfield, O., Oct. 27, 1917; d. Arthur J. and Alice (Reed) Riggs; student Roosevelt U., 1946-48; J.D. with honors, John Marshall Law Sch., 1956; m. Lawrence W. Langford, Aug. 21, 1948 (div.); 1 son, Lawrence W. Clerk-typist Sec. State Ill., 1939-51; admitted to Ill. bar, 1956, since practiced in Chgo.; mem. Robinson, Farmer & Langford and predecessor firm, 1959-69; alderwoman 16th Ward, Chgo., 1972—. Pres., William H. Moore Wrecking Co. Mem. legal def. com. N.A.A.C.P., Chgo. Urban League; mem. League Women Voters, 1969—; mem. West Englewood Improvement Assn., 1969—; mem. Gov.'s Com. on Sr. Citizens, 1971-72; mem. Com. on Ill. Govt., 1971-72; del. World Congress of Peace Forces, Moscow, 1973; mem. commn. inquiry into conditions in Chili after Sept. 11 mil. coup, 1974; del. internat. prep. com. Internat. Commn. Inquiry into Crimes of Mil. Junta in Chili, Helsinki, Finland, 1974. Bd. dirs. Am. Civil Liberties Union, 1970-71, Operation Breadbasket, 1971-72, Impact, Inc., Drug Abuse Program; nat. exec. bd., mem. Operation PUSH, 1972—. Del. nat. Dem. Conv., 1972, co-chmn. Ill. del. Recipient Citation for service in cause interracial justice and brotherhood Cath. Interracial Council, 1970; Civil Rights award Cook County Bar Assn., 1968, Spl. Achievement award, 1971; Mahatma Ghandi Centennial Com. award Greater Chgo., 1969; IOTA Bus. Week award Alpha chpt. Iota Phi Lambda, 1969; James B. Anderson award for outstanding achievement in field politics Montford Point Marine Assn., 1971; Achievement award 7th Ward Ind. Orgn., 1971; award for outstanding service in govt. for human outstanding and equal justice in performance duties as alderwoman SCLC's Operation Breadbasket, 1971; Certificate award Internat. Travellers Assn., 1971; named Woman of Distinction Etta Moten Civic and Ednl. Club, 1970; numerous others. Mem. Nat., Cook County (dir. 1968-70, 74—) bar assns., Def. Attys. Chgo., Internat. Platform Assn. Home: 6036 S Bishop St Chicago IL 60636 Office: 1249-51 W 63d St Chicago IL 60636

LANGFORD, JANE E. DELANEY (MRS. JACK DWIGHT LANGFORD), banker; b. Havana, Cuba, Aug. 20, 1924 (parents Am. citizens); d. John Ralph and Edenia (Curry) Delaney; student pub. schs., Tampa, Fla.; grad. Am. Bankers Assn. Nat. Mortgage Sch., Ohio State U., 1971; m. Jack Dwight Langford, June 23, 1956. Bookkeeper, Exchange Nat. Bank, Tampa, Fla., 1942-44, exchange teller, 1944-48, various depts., 1948-59, in charge mortgage warehousing dept., 1959-61, mgr. mortgage warehousing dept., 1961, asst. cashier, 1962-69, asst. v.p., 1969—. Mem. Am. Inst. Banking (chpt. pres. 1963-64, asso. councilman dist. 1965-70), Nat. Assn. Bank Women, Beta Sigma Phi (chpt. past pres., past pres. city council). Episcopalian. Home: 3601 Waverly Circle Tampa FL 33609 Office: 601 Franklin St Tampa FL 33601

LANGHAM, NORMA, educator; b. California, Pa.; d. Alfred Scrivener and Edith (Carter) Langham; B.S., Ohio State U., 1942; B. Theatre Arts, Pasadena Playhouse Coll. Theatre Arts, 1944; M.A., Stanford, 1956, postgrad. Summer Radio-TV Inst., 1960; student Pasadena Inst. Radio, 1944-45. Tchr. sci. California High Sch., 1942-43; asst. office pub. information Denison U., Granville, O., 1955; instr. speech dept. Westminster Coll., New Wilmington, Pa., 1957-58; instr. speech and drama dept. California State Coll., 1959, asst. prof., 1960-62, asso. prof., 1962—, co-founder, sponsor, dir. Children's Theatre, 1962—. Mem. Am. Ednl. Theatre Assn., Assn. Pa. Colls. and Univ. Faculties, Internat. Assn. Theatre for Children and Young People, Children's Theatre Found., California Assn. Women Faculty (founder, pres. 1972-73), Am. Assn. U. Women (co-founder California br., 1st v.p. 1971-72, pres. 1972-73), Am. Assn. U. Profs., Theatre Assn. Pa., Alpha Psi Omega, Omicron Nu. Presbyn. Author: (play) Magic in the Sky, 1963; (text) Public Speaking; (play) John Dough (Freedoms Found. award 1968). Home: 204 Ellsworth St California PA 15419

LANGLAND, LOIS ELIZABETH, educator; b. Spring Grove, Minn., Dec. 23, 1918; d. Charley M. and Clara Elizabeth (Hille) Langland; B.S. in Edn., N.W. Mo. State Coll., 1941; M.A. in English Lit., Smith Coll., 1946; postgrad. U. Ia., 1947-51; M.A. in Psychology, U. Cal. at Los Angeles, 1958, Ph.D. in Psychology, 1962. Tchr. English, high sch., Corning, Ia., 1941-45; instr. English, Western Coll., Oxford, O., 1946-47, State U. Ia., Iowa City, 1947-51; asst. to acad. dean, dormitory counselor Cottey Coll., Nevada, Mo., 1951-53; counselor to counseling psychologist, asso. mgr. Student Counseling Center, U. Cal. at Los Angeles, 1957-65; dir. career counseling, prof. psychology Scripps Coll. and Pitzer Coll., 1965-67; prof. psychology Claremont Grad. Sch., 1967—; cons. psychologist Voorman Clinic, Upland, Cal., 1968—. Mem. com. profl. women Los Angeles Philharmonic. Mem. Am. Psychol. Assn., A.A.A.S., Am. Assn. U. Profs., Am. Assn. U. Women, Nat. Soc. Study Edn., Am. Civil Liberties Union, Am. Humanist Assn., P.E.O., Sigma Xi. Contbr. articles to profl. jours. Home: 4021 Olive Hill Dr Claremont CA 91711

LANGLEY, ELIZABETH MARIE HICKOK, educator; b. Roanoke, Va., Jan. 29, 1923; d. Ernest Stanley and Anna (Grezesiakowski) Hickok; A.A., Herzl Jr. Coll., 1943; B.A. in Sociology, Whittier Coll., 1952; M.A. in Edn., Loyola U., Chgo., 1963, Ph.D., 1968; m. Paul Bates Langley, July 1, 1944 (dec. Apr. 1960); children—Michael Paul, Robert Thomas, Joanne Margaret. Tchr. Santa Ana (Cal.) City Schs., 1952-60; lectr. edn. Loyola U., Chgo., 1964-67; prof. dept. counselor edn. Northeastern Ill. U., Chgo., 1966—, chmn., 1970—. Lectr. in field. Finance chmn. Girl Scouts U.S.A., 1967-68, active local troop activities, 1963-68. Mem. Ill. Assn. Higher Edn. (pres. chpt. 1969-70), Am., Ill., personnel and guidance assns., Am., Ill. sch. counselors assns., Am., Ill. coll. personnel assns., Ill. Assn. Counselor Edn. and Supervision, Nat., Ill. vocational guidance assns., Am. Assn. U. Profs., (v.p. chpt. 1970-71), Am. Assn. U. Women (implementation chmn. 1967-69). Contbr. articles profl. jours. Home: 3831 N Nora Av Chicago IL 60634

LANGLEY, KATHLEEN MARY (MRS. STANLEY JAMES LANGLEY), educator; b. Audley, Eng., Jan. 24, 1928; d. Reginald Charles and Hilda (Pickering) Longmore; B.Com., Birmingham (Eng.) U., 1948, M.Com., 1950; m. Stanley James Langley, July 31, 1950. Came to U.S., 1956. Sr. lectr. U. Baghdad (Iraq), 1953-56; research fellow Harvard, Cambridge, Mass., 1956-59; asst. prof. econs. Boston U., 1962-66, asso. prof., 1966—; vis. faculty mem. U. Ibadan (Nigeria), 1967-69, U. Philippines, 1970-71. Mem. Am. Econ. Assn. Author: The Industrialization of Iraq. 1961. Home: 987 Memorial Dr Cambridge MA 02138 Office: Economics Dept Boston University 226 Bay State Rd Boston MA 02215

LANGLOIS, ETHEL GALAGAN, pub. co. exec.; b. Milw., Sept. 22, 1919; d. James Edward and Emma Mary (Schroeder) Galagan; B.S., U. Wis. at Milw., 1941; m. Joseph Edward Langlois, Oct. 15, 1954; children—Edward, James, Michael, John. Tchr. Latin, Random Lake (Wis.) High Sch., 1941-42; local advt. sales Milw. Jour., 1942-43; mem. planning and prodn. staff U.S. Govt. Printing Office, Washington, 1944-46; publs. officer UN, N.Y.C., 1946-59; dir. prodn. books and sci. jours. Am. Elsevier Pub. Co., N.Y.C., 1969—. Mem. Typophiles, Am. Inst. Graphic Arts. Democrat. Roman Catholic. Home: 472 Freeman Av Oceanside NY 11572 Office: 52 Vanderbilt Av New York City NY 10017

LANGMAN, MARJORIE H. GREENE (MRS. PAUL LANGMAN), physician; b. Nazareth, Pa., Dec. 2, 1921; d. George F. and Henrietta (Knight) Greene; B.A., Syracuse U., 1944, M.D., 1946; m. Paul M. Langman, Nov. 21, 1951; children—Nancy Ann, Bette Jean. Intern Jersey City Med. Center, 1946-47, resident, 1947-48; resident Meadowbrook Hosp., Hempstead, N.Y., 1949-50, dir. dept. electrocardiography; fellow in cardiology St. Francis Hosp., Roslyn, N.Y., 1951-52; practice medicine, specializing in internal medicine, cardiology, Hicksville, 1951-72, Riverton, Wyo., 1972—; mem. cardiopulmonary team Nassau Hosp., 1955-70; tchr. fundamental advanced courses electrocardiography Nassau Acad. Medicine, 1955-72. Mem. adv. council Nassau County div. Am. Heart Assn., also chmn. sub-com. closed chest resuscitation; council mem. Nassau County br. Am. Cancer Soc.; chmn. Nassau County Coordinated Stroke Program; adv. com. Regional Med. Program Nassau Suffolk County; mem. N.Y. State Coordinating Stroke Com. Founding incorporator, pres., med. dir. Nassau Community Health Services Found.; mem. adv. Council Music Research Found. Mem. Nassau Thoracic Soc. (founder, trustee) Am., N.Y. (chmn. com. on heart disease, del.), Wyo., Nassau County (sec.), Fremont County (sec.-treas.) med. assns., Am. Soc. Internal Medicine (sec.-treas. Wyo. chpt.), Nassau County Acad. Medicine (founder, trustee), World Med. Assn., World Fedn. for Mental Health, N.Y. State Women's Med. Soc., N.Y. State Pub. Health Assn., Syracuse U. Med. Alumni Assn., Jersey City Med. Center Alumni Assn., Parents Council Friends Acad., Alpha Epsilon Iota. Club: Soroptimist. Home: Paradise Valley Route Riverton WY 82501 Office: 904 E Lincoln Riverton WY 82501

LANGNER, MILDRED CROWE (MRS. JULIAN LANGNER), med. librarian; b. Chattanooga; d. Patrick Joseph and Anna (Costello) Crowe; B.A., U. Chattanooga, 1933; B.S. in L.S., Peabody Coll. Tchrs., 1945; m. Julian Langner, Aug. 11, 1956 (dec.). Library asst. Chattanooga Pub. Library, 1933-35, div. head city and county brs. 1935-39, med. librarian, 1940-44; asst. and intern Vanderbilt U. Sch. Medicine Library, 1944-45; chief librarian, asst. prof. U. Ala. Med. Center Library, 1945-55; head librarian, asso. prof. U. Miami (Fla.) Sch. Medicine, 1955-61, 63-68, prof., also dir. med. library, 1968—; chief reference services div. Nat. Library of Medicine, Bethesda, Md., 1961-63. Mem. Fla., Med. (sec., chmn. com. on standards, chmn. refresher courses, chmn. com. publs., pres. 1966-67) library assns., Spl. Libraries Assn. (v.p. Ala. chpt.), Am. Med. Writers Assn., Am. Assn. History Medicine, Med. Faculty Wives group U. Women's Club, Phi Mu. Roman Catholic. Editor: Bull. Med. Library Assn., 1957-61; co-editor Bull. Jefferson Hillman Hosp., 1949-53. Contbr. articles to profl. jours. Home: 1408 SE Bayshore Dr Miami FL 33131 Office: U Miami Med Library PO Box 520875 Biscayne Annex Miami FL 33152

LANGNER, NOLA SPIERO (MRS. THOMAS S. LANGNER), author, illustrator; b. N.Y.C., Sept. 24, 1930; d. Gerald B. and Elsie (Feigenbaum) Spiero; student Vassar Coll., 1948-50; B.A., Bennington Coll., 1952; m. Thomas Langner, Feb. 21, 1953; children—Lisa, Josh, Eli, Gretchen and Belinda (twins). Paste-ups for movie mags. Ideal Pub. Co., N.Y.C., 1953; illustrator, constrns. for television TV Art Studio, N.Y.C., 1953-54; illustrator books Who Has a Secret, 1964; Henry the Uncatchable Mouse, 1964; Little Wolf, 1965; Hi Diddle Diddle, 1966, Three Blind Mice, 1965, Stone Soup, 1968, The Lonesome Egg, 1968; others. Author and illustrator: Miss Lucy, 1969; Go and Shut the Door, 1971; Joseph and the Wonderful Tree, 1972. Home: 271 Central Park W New York City NY 10024

LANGSETH, EDNA MARY, educator; b. Worthington, Minn., Mar. 16, 1914; d. Clarence C. and Minnie (Haggard) Langseth; B.S., Stout State U., 1933; M.S., U. Ill., 1957; postgrad. U. Cal. at Berkeley, Colo. State U. Homemaking tchr., Osceola, Wis., 1933-36; home demonstration agt. U. Wis., 1936-45; home adviser U. Cal., Kelseyville, 1946—. Women's coordinator Civil Def., San Benito County, 1955-65; mem. Cal. state 4-H adv. com., 1966-71. Mem. Am., Cal. home econs. assns., Hollister Bus. and Profl. Women's Club (Woman of Year 1965, past pres.), Phi Upsilon Omicron, Epsilon Sigma Phi. Rebekah. Contbr. articles to profl. jours. Home: Live Oak Ct PO Box 267 Lakeport CA 95453 Office: U Cal AES Office Kelseyville CA 95451

LANGSETH, FLOY LORETTA (MRS. DEVANE M. LANGSETH), bank exec.; b. Minot, N.D., Apr. 28, 1931; d. Floyd T. and Laura Oletta (Meland) Strain; student Minot State Coll., 1949, Am. Inst. Banking, 1956, 59, 71, 72; m. Devane M. Langseth, June 29, 1949; children—Melody (Mrs. Tommy Rose), Laurel Rose, Darwin Floyd. With S.S. Kresge Co., 1949, Fairmont Foods, 1949-50, Quality Lignite & Stearns Motors, 1950-51, S.S. Kresge Co., 1951, Oppen's 83, 1953-55; with 1st Nat. Bank Minot, 1955—, Supr. Comml. dept., 1956-70, asst. cashier operations, 1970—. Vice pres. Cancer Crusade Minot, 1970-71. Mem. N.D. Bank Women, Am. Inst. Banking (treas. 1970-71, sec. 1971-72, v.p. 1972-73, pres. 1973-74), Bank Adminstrn. Inst., First Nat. Bank Employees Contbn. Orgn., C. of C., Beta Sigma Phi (v.p. Xi Kappa chpt.). Lutheran. Club: Zonta (v.p. Minot chpt.). Home: 704 2d Av NE Minot ND 58701 Office: Drawer 1488 Minot ND 58701

LANGSLEY, PAULINE ROYAL, psychiatrist; b. Lincoln, Neb., July 2, 1927; d. Paul Ambrose and Dorothy Kendall (Sibley) Royal; A.B., Mills Coll., 1949; M.D., U. Neb., 1953; m. Donald G. Langsley, Sept. 9, 1955; children—Karen Jean, Dorothy Ruth, Susan Louise. Intern, Mt. Zion Hosp., San Francisco, 1953-54; resident psychiatry U. Cal. at San Francisco, 1954-57; asst. to dir., dept. psychol. medicine Cowell Meml. Hosp., Berkeley, Cal., 1957-61; psychiat. cons. pub. schs. Denver, 1962-68; staff psychiatrist U. Colo., Boulder, 1964-68; clin. instr. psychiatry med. schs. U. Cal. at San Francisco, 1957-61, U. Colo. at Denver, 1962-68; staff psychiatrist Health Service U. Cal. at Davis, 1968—, also asst. clin. prof. psychiatry. Psychiat. cons. Temple Buell Coll., Denver, 1962-68. Trustee, Mills Coll., 1974—. Fellow Am. Psychiat. Assn.; mem. Central Cal. Psychiat. Assn., Am. Orthopsychiat. Assn., Mills Alumnae Assn. (bd. govs. 1969—, nat. v.p. 1972—). Home: 524 Antioch Dr Davis CA 95616

LANIER, SISTER AGNES MARY MARGUERITE, coll. adminstr.; b. St. Albans, Vt., Apr. 18, 1914; d. Edmund and Delia (Remillard) Lanier; B.S., Rivier Coll., 1945; Ed.M., Boston U., 1950. Joined Congregation of Sisters of Holy Cross, 1932; tchr. elementary sch., Nashua, N.H., 1934-40; head bus. dept. St. Louis de Gonzague High Sch., Nashua, 1940-45, St. Anthony High Sch., Manchester, N.H., 1945-50; registrar, faculty Notre Dame Coll., Manchester, 1950—, chmn. bus. dept., 1950-67, dir. admissions, 1950-72. Rec. sec. bd. trustees Sisters Holy Cross and Notre Dame Coll., 1968—, sec. corp., 1970—; del. provincial chpt. Sisters Holy Cross, 1971-73, sec. 2d careers commn., 1972—. Mem. New Eng. Assn. Coll. Registrars and Admissions Officers. Address: 2321 Elm St Manchester NH 03104

LANIER, FRANCES BROCKMAN, ret. sch. adminstr.; b. Nez Perce, Ida., Sept. 29, 1914; d. Albert Edgar and Edna (Ellis) Brockman; Mus.B., U. Ore., 1935; Mus.M., New Eng. Conservatory, 1938; m. Sterling Lanier, July 29, 1939; children—Elizabeth Ellis, Margaret (Mrs. Robert Hargrave Brown). Concert violinist in Ore., New Eng., Balt. and Washington; soloist Portland (Ore.) Symphony, Boston Pops Symphony and other orchs.; mem. violin faculty Longy Sch. Music, Cambridge; mem. faculty, dir. prep. div. and adult study program New Eng. Conservatory Music, Boston, 1950-75, ret., 1975. Frank Huntington Beebe scholar for study and travel abroad, 1938-39. Mem. Phi Beta, Mu Phi Epsilon, Pi Kappa Lambda. Home: 6 Rutland St Cambridge MA 02138

LANKFORD, REBECCA GARNER (MRS. THOMAS BARRETT LANKFORD), assn. exec.; b. Knoxville, Tenn., May 30, 1942; d. George James and Ida Pemberton (Spahr) Garner; B.S., U. Tenn., 1964; m. Thomas Barrett Lankford, Oct. 14, 1971; children—James Sander, Robert Hood. Tech. data analyst Raytheon, Huntsville, Ala., 1971-72; mgr. research and ednl. divs. Greensboro (N.C.) C. of C., 1973—. Mem. Am. C. of C. Execs., Am. C. of C. Researchers Assn., Alpha Delta Pi. Home: 204 W Greenway S Greensboro NC 27403 Office: PO Box 3246 Greensboro NC 27402

LANPHIER, RUTH MARY, ednl. adminstr.; b. Denver, July 3, 1915; d. Joseph H. and Clara (Cleave) Lanphier; A.B., U. Denver, 1937, A.M., 1958. Civilian instr. AAF, Lowry Field, Denver, 1942-45; tchr. Denver Pub. Schs., 1945-60, coordinator instrn., 1960-61, asst. prin., dean, 1965—. Judge spelling contest Colo.-Wyo. Rocky Mountain News, 1965-74. Active vol. Colo. Gen. Hosp., St. Joseph Hosp. Recipient Tchr. Year award Denver Sertoma Club, 1965. Mem. Colo.-Wyo. Assn. Women Adminstrs. and Counselors (pres. 1973-74), Denver Deans (sec. 1967-68), Kappa Delta Pi, Pi Beta Phi, Phi Delta Kappa, Delta Kappa Gamma. Home: 1165 Columbine St Apt 12 Denver CO 80206 Office: Morey Jr High 840 E 14th Av Denver CO 80209

LANSBURGH, THERESE WEIL (MRS. RICHARD M. LANSBURGH), social worker; b. New Orleans, Oct. 29, 1919; d. Harold S. and Rosetta (Hirsch) Weil; B.A., Smith Coll., 1940; M.S.W., Tulane Sch. Social Work, 1943; m. Frankel Wolff, May 22, 1943 (dec.); children—Randolph, Deborah; m. 2d, Richard Lansburgh, Jan. 10, 1959. Founder, pres. Rebelles, AWVS U.S.O., New Orleans, 1941-43; case worker A.R.C., Boston, 1943-45; vis. tchr. Columbus, Miss., 1947-49; social worker Children's Guild, 1959-61; Pres., P.T.A. Franklin Sch., Columbus, 1953-55; bd. mem. Nat. Assn. Jr. Auxs., 1956-58, Miss. State P.T.A., 1955-57; pres. Md. Com. for Day Care Children, 1965-68, 72—, hon. pres., 1968-72; bd. mem. Nat. Com. for Day Care for Children, 1963-68, pres., 1967-68; pres. Day Care and Child Devel. Council Am., 1968-71, hon. pres., 1971-73; mem. Md. Com. on White House Conf., 1968-71; vice chmn. Developmental Child Care Forum, White House Conf. on Children, 1970. Bd. mem. Children's Lobby Md. Assn. Mental Health, Richmond Fellowship of Md. Mem. Nat. Assn. Social Workers, Nat. Conf. Social Work, Nat. Assn. for Edn. Young Children, Soc. for Research in Child Devel., Am. Orthopsychiat. Assn., Delta Kappa Gamma (hon.). Established 1st classroom for retarded children in Miss., 1951. Home: 3503 Midfield Rd Baltimore MD 21208

LANSDALE, ARLYNE, lawyer; b. Denver, July 14, 1905; d. Thomas William and Sadie Marie (Shearer) Armstrong; student Wilson's Coll., Seattle, 1922; LL.B., Southwestern U., Los Angeles, 1931; m. Dyke Lansdale, 1922 (dec. 1962); children—W.M., Dyke. Admitted to Cal. bar, 1934; pub. utility atty. Dyke Water Co., Garden Grove, 1950—. Mem. Am., Cal. bar assns., Nat. Assn. Women Lawyers, Lawyers Club of Los Angeles, Iota Tau Tau. Home: 8331 Westminster Av Westminster CA 92683 Office: PO Box 68 Garden Grove CA 92642

LANSING, ELIZABETH HUBBARD (MRS. A. TEN EYCK LANSING), author; b. Providence, May 14, 1911; d. William Brewster and Martha (Hale) Hubbard; B.S., Simmons Coll., 1933; m. A. Ten Eyck Lansing, June 18, 1937; children—Elisabeth Ten Eyck, Lydia Brewster, Robert Ten Eyck, Mary Hubbard. Editor Dodd Mead & Co., 1934-37; editorial work Cue Mag., 1936-37, Seiznick Internat., 1936-37; instr. Famous Writers Sch., Westport, Conn., 1964—; instr., cons. Inst. Children's Lit., Redding, Conn., 1973—. Author: Seeing New York, 1938; Sky Service, 1939; Cecily Drake, Movie Editor, 1940; Leonardo Da Vinci, 1941; Ann Bartlett, Navy Nurse, 1941; Nancy Naylor, Air Pilot, 1941; Kate Russell, Wartime Nurse, 1942; Ann Bartlett at Bataan, 1943; Sally Wins Her Wings, 1943; Nancy Naylor Flies South, 1944; Ann Bartlett in the South Pacific, 1944; Sandra Mitchell Stands By, 1944; Nancy Naylor, Flight Nurse, 1945; Kay Allen on Overseas Mission, 1945; Ann Bartlett Returns to the Philippines, 1946; Ann Bartlett on Stateside Duty, 1946; Nancy Naylor, Captain of Flight Nurses, 1946; Nancy Naylor, Visiting Nurse, 1947; The Disappearing Dolls, 1947; Cathy Carlisle, 1947; The Old Flag's Secret, 1948; Rider on the Mountains, 1949; The Pony That Ran Away, 1951; Shoot for a Mule, 1951; The Pony That Kept A Secret, 1952; A Pony Worth His Salt, 1952; Deer Mountain Hideaway, 1953; Jubilant For Sure, 1953; Lulu's Window, 1954; Deer River Raft, 1954; Lulu Herself, 1955; Sure Thing for Shep, 1955; The Small Circus, 1957; A House for Henrietta, 1958; Liza of the Hundredfold, 1960; Secret of Dark Entry, 1961; The Sumarians, 1971.

Contbr. articles and short stories to various mags. Democrat. Episcopalian. Home: 17 Hitchcock Rd Westport CT 06880

LANSNER, FAY, artist; b. Phila., June 21, 1921; ed. Wanamaker Inst., 1939-41, Stella Elkins Tyler Sch. Fine Arts at Temple U., 1945-47, Columbia, 1947-48, Art Students League, 1947-58, Hofmann Sch., 1948, Atelier Fernand Leger, Paris, France, 1950, Academie Andre Lhote, Paris, 1950. One-man shows at Galerie Huit, Paris, 1951, Le Gerrec, Paris, 1952, Hansa Gallery, N.Y.C., 1955, 56, 58, Hood Coll., 1961, David Herbert Gallery, N.Y.C., 1961, Zabriskie Gallery, 1963, Kornblee Gallery, 1963, 65, Benson Gallery, 1970, 72, N.Y.C. Cultural Center, 1973, U. N.D., 1973, Cite des Arts, Paris, 1973; exhibited in group shows at Southampton (N.Y.) Mus., 1960, Lyman Allen Mus., New London, Conn., 1963, Contemporary Art Mus., Houston, 1963, Am. Fedn. Arts Traveling Show, 1965, Washington Gallery Contemporary Art, 1967, Corcoran Gallery, 1967, Albright Knox Mus., Buffalo, 1967, Mus. Modern Art, N.Y.C., 1968, Bklyn. Mus., 1970, La Demeure, Paris, 1971; represented in permanent collections of N.Y.U., Weatherspoon Art Mus., Greensboro, N.C., Newsweek, N.Y.C., Rutgers Mus. Art Gallery, Kenton Corp., Jacques Kaplan Collection, N.Y.C., Ciba-Geigy Corp., Ardsley, N.Y., Cite des Arts, Paris. Address: 317 W 80th St New York City NY 10024

LANSON, LUCIENNE THERESE, physician; b. San Francisco, Mar. 18, 1930; d. Georges Emile and Anna Marie (Idiart) Lanson; B.A., U. Cal. at Berkeley, 1951; M.D., magna cum laude, Med. Coll. Pa., 1960. Intern, St. Joseph Hosp., Denver, 1960-61; resident surgery Med. Coll. Pa., 1961-62, resident obstetrics and gynecology, 1962-65; individual practice medicine specializing in obstetrics and gynecology, San Francisco, 1965-67, 69—; service S.S. Hope, Ceylon, 1968; obstetrician-gynecologist, Addis Ababa, Ethiopia, 1969; instr. Med. Coll. Pa., 1967-69. Served with Women's Med. Specialist Corps, AUS, 1952-54. Diplomate Am. Bd. Obstetrics and Gynecology. Fellow Am. Coll. Obstetricians and Gynecologists; mem. San Francisco County Med. Soc., Cal., Am. med. assns., Alpha Omega Alpha. Author: Woman to Woman-A Gynecologist Answers Questions About You and Your Body, 1975. Home: 418 Lansdale Av San Francisco CA 94127 Office: 2533 Ocean Av San Francisco CA 94132

LANTIS, MARGARET LYDIA, anthropologist, educator; b. Dayton, Ohio, Sept. 1, 1906; d. Lee Ora and Betsy (Ames) Lantis; B.A., U. Minn., 1930; Ph.D., U. Cal. at Berkeley, 1939; Social Sci. Research Council postgrad fellow, U. Chgo., 1942-43; Wenner-Gren Found. fellow, 1947. Research asso. also instr. anthropology, U. Cal., Berkeley, 1940-41; vis. prof., 1950, 1964-65; instr. U. Minn., Mpls., 1942, visiting prof., 1958; asst. prof. sociology, anthropology Reed Coll., Portland Ore., 1943-44; analyst, anthropologist with various branches U.S. govt., 1944-48, 54-63; social anthropologist, Harvard, Cambridge, Mass., 1948-52; vis. prof. Boston U., 1950; Carnegie Found. fellow McGill U., Montreal, Que., Can., 1952, vis. prof., 1963-64; vis. prof. U. Alaska, 1955, George Washington U., Washington, 1961, U. Wash., Seattle, 1962; prof. anthropology, U. Ky., Lexington, 1965—. Cons. Arctic Health Research Center, U.S. Public Health Service, 1966, Alaska Psychiat. Inst., 1967. Fellow Am. Anthropological Assn., Arctic Inst. N. Am. (research com. 1959-62, cons. 1963-64), Soc. for Applied Anthropology (eastern regional v.p. 1957, pres. 1973-74), A.A.A.S.; mem. Anthrop. Soc. Washington (exec. council 1945, 1960-61), Am. Ethnological Soc. (pres. 1964-65), Canadian Sociology and Anthropology Assn., Am. Assn. Univ. Profs., Phi Beta Kappa, Sigma Xi. Author: Alaskan Eskimo Ceremonialism, 1947; Folk Medicine and Hygiene: Lower Kuskokwim and Nunivak-Nelson Island Areas, 1959; Eskimo Childhood and Interpersonal Relationships: Nunivak Biographies and Genealogies. Editor: Ethnohistory in Southwestern Alaska and the Southern Yukon: Method and Content, 1970. Contbr. articles in field to numerous jours. and anthologies. Address: Anthropology Dept U Ky Lexington KY 40506

LANTZ, JO PULLEN (MRS. CLARENCE T. LANTZ), interior decorator; b. Chgo.; d. Ray W. and Mary Lois (Pardee) Pullen; B.A. in Psychology, U. Mo., 1948; postgrad. U. Florence, 1950-52, Chgo. Acad. Fine Arts, 1952-54; m. Clarence T. Lantz, May 19, 1956; 1 dau., Linda. Asst. designer Stoffkopf Interiors, Chgo., 1954-56; designer contract div. Mendel Bros., Chgo., 1956-58; designer Interior Guild Decorating, Chgo., 1958-60; co-owner Lantz Co., Chgo., 1961—. Corr. sec. Cradle Soc., 1967-68; mem. publicity and entertainment com. Women's Bd. of LaRabida, 1966-68. Mem. Am. Inst. Interior Designers (mem. publicity com. 1961), Nat. Home Fashion League, Ill. Opera Guild, Kappa Kappa Gamma. Home: 924 Forest Glen Dr W Winnetka IL 60093 Office: 1410 S Michigan Av Chicago IL 60605

LANTZ, JOANNE ETHEL BALDWIN (MRS. WAYNE E. LANTZ), educator; b. Defiance, O., Jan. 26, 1932; d. Hiram J. and Ethel (Smith) Baldwin; B.S., Ind. Central Coll., 1953; M.S., Ind. U., 1957; Ph.D., Mich. State U., 1969; m. Wayne E. Lantz, Oct. 22, 1955. Tchr., Arcola (Ind.) High Sch., 1953-57; guidance dir. New Haven (Ind.) High Sch., 1957-65; asso. prof. psychology, asst. dean student services Purdue U., Ft. Wayne, Ind., 1965—. Mem. Nat. Vocational Guidance Assn., Am., Ind. (sec. 1963) personnel and guidance assns., Am. Sch. Counselors Assn., Am. Coll. Personnel Assn., Delta Kappa Gamma. Home: 3118 Eastbrook Dr Fort Wayne IN 46805

LANYON, ELLEN (MRS. ROLAND GINZEL), artist; b. Chgo., Dec. 21, 1926; d. Howard Wesley and Ellen (Aspinwall) Lanyon; B.F.A., Art Inst. Chgo., 1948; M.F.A., State U. Ia., 1950; postgrad. (Fulbright fellow) Courtland Inst., U. London, 1950-51; m. Roland Ginzel, Sept. 4, 1948; children—Andrew, Lisa. One man shows Superior Street Gallery, Chgo., 1960, Stewart Rickard Gallery, San Antonio, 1962, 65, Fairweather Hardin Gallery, Chgo., 1962, Zabriskie Gallery, N.Y.C., 1962, 64, 68, 72, B.C. Holland Gallery, Chgo., 1965, 69, Richard Gray Gallery, Chgo., 1970, 73, Madison (Wis.) Art Center, 1972, Wabash Transit Gallery, Art Inst. Chgo., 1972, Smithsonian Instn., 1972, Stephens Coll., 1973, Kohler Center Arts, 1974, Odyssia Gallery, Rome, Italy, 1974; exhibited group shows, 1946—, including traveling exhbns. Am. Fedn. Arts, 1946-48, 50, 53, 57, 68-69, Art Inst. Chgo., 1946-47, 51-53, 55, 57-58, 60-62, 64, 66-71, Corcoran Gallery Art, 1961, Denver Art Mus., 1950, 52, Exhbn. Momentum, Chgo., 1948, 50, 52, 54, 56, Library of Congress, 1950, 52, Met. Mus. Art, 1952, Mus. Modern Art, 1953, 62, Phila. Mus. Art, 1946, 47, 50, 54, San Francisco Mus. Art, 1946, 50, U. Ill., 1953, 54, 57, Drawing Soc. Nat. Traveling Exhbn., 1965-66, The Painter and the Photograph traveling exhbn., 1964-65, Nostalgia traveling exhbn., 1968-69, Violence, Mus. Contemporary Art, Chgo., 1968; Birds and Beasts, Graham Gallery, N.Y.C., 1969-70; Each in His Own Way traveling exhbn., 1971, Mus. Contemporary Art, Chgo., 1972, N.Y. Cultural Center, 1972, Una Tendenza Americana, Arezzo, Italy, 1973; represented in permanent collections Art Inst. Chgo., Denver Art Mus., Library of Congress, Inst. Internat. Edn., London, Eng., Finch Coll., N.Y., Krannert Mus., U. Mass., Ill. Bell, Ill. Wesleyan U., U. Ill., U. Mass., 1st Nat. Bank, Chgo., Ill. State Mus., N.J. State Mus., A.T.&T. Corp., Galleria de Comonale de Contemporanea, Arezzo, also numerous pvt. collections. Tchr., jr. sch. Art Inst. Chgo., 1952-54, tchr. day sch., 1965, vis. instr., 1973; tchr. Rockford Coll., summer 1953, Summer Sch. Painting, Saugatuck, Mich., 1961-72; a founder, sec., treas. Chgo. Graphic Workshop, 1952-55; tchr. U. Wis. Extension, 1971—; artist-in-residence U. Ill. Chgo. Circle Campus, 1972; vis. fellow Inst. Arts and Humanistic Studies, Pa. State U.; lectr. in field. Organizer W.E.B. Women's Art Registry, Chgo., 1972. Recipient Armstrong prize, 1946, 55, Town and Country purchase prize, 1947, Blair prize, 1958, 67, Palmer prize, 1962, 64, Cahn prize, 1961 (all Art Inst. Chgo.), purchase prize Denver Art Mus., 1950, Library of Congress, 1950, Cassandra Found. award, 1970, Yaddo award, 1973, Nat. Endowment Arts, 1974. Mem. Alumni Assn. Art Inst. Chgo. Author: Wonder Production, Vol. I, 1971. Illustrator: Jakata Tales, 1975. Home and studio: 412 N Clark St Chicago IL 60610

LAO, ROSINA CHIA, educator, psychologist; b. Hong Kong, Feb. 24, 1939; d. Cheng-Chein and Ching-Chao (Soong) Chia; B.S. in Psychology, Nat. Taiwan U., 1962; M.A. in Psychology, U. Mich., 1963, Ph.D. in Social Psychology, 1969; m. Yan-Jeong Lao, June 26, 1965; children—Eugene Y., Renee Y. Instr. dept. psychology U. Mich., 1968-69; asst. prof. psychology E. Carolina U., Greenville, 1969—. Mem. Am. Psychol. Assn., Soc. for Psychol. Study Social Issues. Contbr. articles to profl. jours. Home: 201 Greenbriar Dr Greenville NC 27834

LAPCHESKA, AMY CATHERINE (MRS. RICHARD J. LAPCHESKA), banker; b. Hayes Center, Neb., May 29, 1907; d. Frank and Katherine (Kalina) Babka; student Kearney State Tchrs. Coll., 1923-24; m. Paul M. Reiss, Feb. 19, 1927; children—Mary Beth, Walter E.; m. 2d, Richard J. Lapcheska, Mar. 13, 1970. With Bruning (Neb.) State Bank, 1942—, v.p. 1965—, dir., 1953—. Mem. State Bd. Small Bus. Adminstrn., 1968-70. Bd. dirs. Rural Housing for Bruning. Mem. Bus. and Profl. Women's Club, Federated Womans Club. Lutheran. Mem. Order of Eastern Star. Clubs: County Extension. Home: Bruning NE 68322 Office: Bruning State Bank Box 222 Bruning NE 68322

LAPIN, MARY E. GAMSON, counseling supr.; b. Phila., July, 2, 1931; d. Edward and Blanche (Weintraub) Gamson; B.A., Antioch Coll., 1954; M.Ed., Boston U., 1963; m. 1960 (div. 1962). Interviewer, counselor, supr. Mass. Div. Employment Security, Boston, 1963—. Sec., Lynn Mental Health Planning Com., 1967-69. Mem. Am., Boston personnel and guidance assns., Assn. for Humanistic Psychology. Home: 2 Hawthorne Pl Boston MA 02114 Office: Charles F Hurley Govt Center Bldg Boston MA 02114

LAPOINTE, MARIELLE RITA (MRS. RAYMOND J.A. LAPOINTE), physician; b. Ottawa, Ont., Can., July 19, 1936; d. Omer Joseph and MarieAnge Irma (Roy) Pharand; M.D., U. Ottawa, 1961; m. Raymond J.A. Lapointe, Aug. 27, 1960; children—Sylvie, Lyne, Dominique, Manon, Sebastien. Intern, Ottawa Civic Hosp., 1961-62; practice medicine specializing in pub. health and Tb prevention, Ottawa, 1964-71; physician, student health services Ottawa U., 1970-71. Co-pres. Serena (nat. orgn. involved in natural family planning), Ottawa, 1970-72. Mem. Action-life and Alliance for Life, Collège des Médecins de Langue Française du Can. Home: 292 Donald St Ottawa ON K1K 1M7 Canada Office: Serena 55 Parkdale Ottawa ON K1Y 1E5 Canada also Ste Anne's Clinic 317 Murray Ottawa ON Canada

LAPORT, ALYCE HAZEL (MRS. JACOB JOHN LAPORT), chem. co. exec.; b. Chgo., Dec. 11, 1924; d. Harry and Grace (Manzer) Davis; grad. high sch.; m. Jacob John LaPort, May 27, 1961; children—Michaeleen (Mrs. Richard Fisk), Patrick Stickney. Adminstr. classified dept. Union-Sun & Jour., Lockport, N.Y., 1941; factory employee, U.A.W. officer Norton Labs., Inc., Lockport, 1942-67, personnel adminstr., 1967-68, personnel and indsl. relations adminstr., 1968—, safety coordinator, 1972—. Mem. Am. Soc. Personnel Adminstrs., Indsl. Relations Assn. Western N.Y., Indsl. Mgmt. Assn. Lockport. Home: 8 Howard Av Lockport NY 14094 Office: 520 Mill St Lockport NY 14094

LAPRAIRIE, ALLEGRA MASSEY (MRS. CLOVIS ELBERT LAPRAIRIE), social worker; b. Cypress, La., Jan. 18, 1908; d. Alfred and Mary Odalie (Scroggins) Massey; B.A., Tulane U., 1934, M.S.W., 1946; m. Clovis Elbert LaPrairie, May 29, 1930; 1 son, Clovis Elbert. Tchr. pub. schs., Natchitoches Parish, La., 1927-30, New Orleans Acad., 1930-31; social worker Fed. Emergency Relief Adminstrn., New Orleans, 1934-36, Children's Bur., New Orleans, 1937-48, Baptist Home Mission Bd., New Orleans, 1948-51; dir. Sellers Baptist Home and Adoption Center, New Orleans, 1951—. Mem. Council Social Agys., Am. Assn. Social Workers, Am. Assn. U. Women (pres. Metaire-Gretna br. 1968—, v.p. La. div. 1973—), Phi Lambda Pi. Baptist. Contbr. articles to profl. jours. Home: 1722 General Taylor St New Orleans LA 70115 Office: 2010 Peniston St New Orleans LA 70115

LAPUMA, BEVERLY ANNE (MRS. VINCENT JOSEPH LAPUMA), educator; b. Troy, N.Y., Nov. 2, 1942; d. Louis Paul and Anne Elizabeth (Smith) Draxler; B.S. (Elk scholar 1959-60), State U. N.Y. at Plattsburgh, 1963, R.N., 1963, M.S., 1966; Ph.D., N.Y. U., 1972; m. Vincent Joseph LaPuma, July 1, 1967; 1 son, Edward Vincent. Instr., health dir. Champlain Valley Sch. Nursing, Plattsburgh, 1963-65; asst. dean, residence dir. Sullivan County Community Coll., South Fallsburgh, N.Y., 1965-66; admissions counselor State U. N.Y. at Farmingdale, 1966-68; faculty N.Y.C. Community Coll., Bklyn., 1968—, asso. prof. higher edn. 1974—, also coordinator continuing edn. Mem. Am. Assn. for Higher Edn., Profl. Women's Caucus, Pi Lambda Theta, Kappa Delta Pi. Home: 44 Wynwood Rd Chatham NJ 07928 Office: 300 Jay St Brooklyn NY 11201

LARABEE, LOTTIE B(ERTHA), coll. cons., lectr.; b. Sprague, Neb.; d. Arthur Henry and Anna (Bartels) Larabee; Mus.B., U. Sch. Music, Lincoln, Neb.; Mus.M., Am. Conservatory Music; M.A., Ph. D., N.Y. U., 1955. Prin. elementary sch., Beatrice, Neb.; music instr. Albion State Normal Sch.; music instr., dir. extension U. South Dakota, Springfield; music instr., acting head music dept. Lock Haven State Coll.; dir. Own Sch., Chgo.; research coll. and univ. adminstrn., also coll. cons., 1957-67; prof. higher edn. Ft. Lauderdale (Fla.) U., 1967-69, from asst. to the pres. to v.p. for acad. affairs, 1967-69; coll. cons., 1969—; exec. dir. Am. Assn. Pres.'s Ind. Colls. and Univs., 1967-68. Recipient Distinguished Service award Am. Assn. Pres.'s Ind. Colls. and Univs. Pres., 1968. Mem. Am. Assn. Higher Edn., A.A.A.S., New Eng. Historic Geneal. Soc., Internat. Platform Assn., Kappa Delta Pi, Sigma Alpha Iota (past nat. editor). Author: Adminstrators Who Subvert Learning, Their Residence and Education, 1957; A Parent's Guide to Colleges and Universities, 1963. Home: 1201 SE 2d St Fort Lauderdale FL 33301

LARA-BRAUD, CAROLYN JEANNETTE WEATHERSBEE, biochemist; b. Waco, Tex., Jan. 4, 1940; d. Claude Harrison and Nelda Modena (Richardson) Weathersbee; A.A., Del Mar Coll., 1959; B.A., U. Tex., 1962, Ph.D. (NIH fellow, Rosalie B. Hite fellow), 1969; m. Jorge Lara-Braud, Sept. 12, 1970 (div. Aug., 1973). Research asst. dept. biochemistry Ia. State U., Ames, 1969-70; lectr. dept. home econs. U. Tex., Austin, 1971-73, research asso. Clayton Fedn. Biochem. Inst., 1970-73; asst. research scientist dept. biochemistry U. Ia., Iowa City, 1973—. Mem. Am. Chem. Soc., A.A.A.S., Phi Kappa Phi, Iota Sigma Pi, Phi Theta Kappa. Home: 3622 Parrott Av Waco TX 76707 Office: Univ of Iowa Dept of Biochemistry Iowa City IA 52240

LAREDO, RAQUEL CAMPBELL (MRS. OCTAVIO LAREDO), mfg. co. exec.; b. San Juan, P.R., Mar. 17, 1916; d. Carlos and Benigna (Fernandez-Garcia) de Choudens; grad. Mount St. Joseph Coll., 1934; postgrad. in journalism, Madrid U., 1935, 36; m. Octavio Laredo, Feb. 18, 1968. Vice pres. Impression Cutting Corp., N.Y.C., 1956-68; chmn. Standard Products Corp., New Rochelle, N.Y., 1968—. Mem. N.Y.C. Youth Bd., 1949-55, N.Y. Mayor's Com. P.R. Affairs, Mayor's Adv. Com. Aid to Dependent Children, 1949-55; chmn. subcom. Foster Homes, Dept. of Welfare, N.Y.C., 1950-52; treas. N.Y. Puerto Rican Scholarship Fund, 1952-55. Mem. Puerto Rican Journalists and Writers Assn. Home: 1026 Coral Way Coral Gables FL 33134 Office: 856 Main St New Rochelle NY 10801

LARERY, DOROTHY ALICE, educator; b. Parsons, Kan., Aug. 11, 1926; d. Frank Irving and Elsie (Bandy) Larery; A.A., Parsons Jr. Coll., 1946; B.S. in Edn., Pittsburg (Kan.) State Coll., 1948; M.S. in Household Econs., Kan. State U., 1954; Ph.D., Purdue U., 1962. Home service rep. Gas Service Co., Kansas City, Mo., 1948-51; tchr. vocational homemaking, Nevada, Mo., 1951-52; instr. home mgmt. Kan. State U., 1953-54; instr. home mgmt. U. Neb., 1954-56, asst. prof. home mgmt., family econs., 1956-61, asso. prof., 1961-65, prof., 1965-70, chmn. dept., 1964-68; head dept. home econs. Kearney (Neb.) State Coll., 1970-71; prof., head dept. home econs. U. Ark., Fayetteville, 1971—. Mem. Am., Ark. home econs. assns., Am. Council Consumer Information, Developmental Child Care Assn., Fayetteville Bus. and Profl. Women's Club, Kappa Delta Pi, Phi Upsilon Omicron, Phi Kappa Phi, Omicron Nu. Presbyn. Home: 932 Bel Air Fayetteville AR 72701

LA RIVERS, MARIAN BYRD BALLINGER (MRS. IRA LA RIVERS II), assn. exec.; b. Spencer, Ind., Aug. 16, 1915; d. Arthur Love and Caroline Louise (Graves) Ballinger; B.A., Butler U., 1936; postgrad. Ind. U., 1936, U. Tenn., 1937, Duke, 1938; M.A., U. Nev., 1969; m. Ira La Rivers II, Dec. 21, 1951; 1 son, Ira Jack III. Substitute tchr., Tenn., N.C., 1932-38; tchr., Reno, 1950-51, 61-71; exec. sec. Campus YWCA, U. Nev. at Reno, 1948-50, 51-54; trustee, sec. Biol. Soc. Nev., Verdi, 1963—; owner, adminstr. pvt. pre-sch. Cons. outdoor edn. Reno Schs., 1965-71. Mem. Gov.'s Council Econ. Devel. Mem. Am. Assn. U. Women (treas. 1951-52), N.E.A., Nev. State Edn. Assn., Nev. Library Assn., Washoe County Tchrs. Assn., Am. Women Vol. Service, Am. Friends Service Com., Tau Kappa Alpha, Kappa Alpha Theta. Home: 420 Hill Lane Verdi NV 89439 Office: Box 167 Verdi NV 89439

LARKIN, FRANCES ANN, educator; b. Damascus, O., Jan. 16, 1930; d. Willard Denny and Eleanor (Haydock) Larkin; student Earlham Coll., 1948-50; B.S., Ohio State U., 1952; M.S., U. Minn., 1958; Ph.D., Cornell U., 1968. Dietetic intern Duke U. Hosp., 1952-53; nutrition fellow Mayo Clinic, 1956-57; clinic dietician St. Luke's Hosp., Cleve., 1953-57; asso. prof. Cal. State Coll., Long Beach, 1958-61; adviser Coll. Home Econs., Dacca, Bangladesh, 1961-64; asso. prof. dept. nutrition Sch. Pub. Health, U. Mich., Ann Arbor, 1967—. Cons. Am. Home Econs. Assn. Family Planning Project, Nepal, 1973. Mem. Am. Home Econs. Assn., Am. Dietetic Assn., Am., Mich. (chmn. nutrition div. 1972—) pub. health assns. Club: Ann Arbor Women's City. Author: (with J.R.K. Robson) Malnutrition, Its Causation and Control, 1973. Home: 1945 Woodbury Av Ann Arbor MI 48104

LARKIN, HAZEL MARGARET, city ofcl.; b. Maysville, Ky., Mar. 21, 1909; d. James and Catherine (McAuliffe) Larkin; grad. high sch. Stenographer, filing clk. Wald Mfg. Co., Maysville, 1929-33; city clk. City of Maysville, 1933—, acting city mgr., 1954-60. Roman Catholic (sec. Altar Soc. 1960, sec. Council Cath. Women 1962). Home: 136 E 4th St Maysville KY 41056 Office: City Bldg Maysville KY 41056

LARKIN, JANE RITA, stock exchange exec.; b. N.Y.C.; d. Edward F. and Catherine (Keenan) Larkin; B.S., St. Johns U., 1938; postgrad. Columbia U., 1938-39. With Merrill Lynch, Pierce, Fenner, Smith, N.Y.C., 1942-59, operations mgr., 1953-59; exec. asst. to mng. partner Hirsch & Co., N.Y.C., 1959-65, gen. partner, 1966-72; v.p. du Pont, Glore and Forgan, Inc., N.Y.C., 1972—. Mem. N.Y. Stock Exchange, 1970—. Mem. Wall Street Tng. Dirs. (sec.-treas. 1965—), Women Investment Brokers (dir. 1965—). Home: 2113 Ryder St Brooklyn NY 11234 Office: 77 Water St New York City NY 10004

LARKIN, JEWELL NATION SHELL (MRS. FRANK CARLOS LARKIN), assn. exec.; b. Athens, Tenn., Nov. 26, 1919; d. David Hurley and Ann Catherine (Burns) Shell; B.A., Tenn. Wesleyan Coll., 1940; m. Frank Carlos Larkin, Nov. 26, 1943; children—Larry Frank, Lynn Edwin. Reporter, Daily Post-Athenian, Athens, 1940-41; state editor Knoxville (Tenn.) Jour., 1941-43, women's feature writer, copy reader, 1963-67; author Assn. Activities, Jour. Am. Dietetic Assn., Chgo., editor Courier, 1969-72, coordinator Ho. of Dels., 1972—. Pres., Bearden (Tenn.) Parent-Tchr. Student Orgn., 1960-61. Mem. Tenn. Jaycettes (2d. v.p. 1950-51), Tenn. Pen Women, Knoxville Jaycettes (pres. 1949-50), Women in Communication. Methodist (memb. bd. 1959-61). Home: 230 E Ontario St Chicago IL 60611 Office: 620 N Michigan Av Chicago IL 60611

LARKIN, MARITA THERESE OPPENHEIM (MRS. F. EDWARD LARKIN), civic worker; b. Coldwater, O., Jan. 31, 1921; d. Theodore Henry and Anna Elizabeth (Mathias) Oppenheim; B.A., St. Mary's Coll., 1943; M.F.A., Art Inst. Chgo., 1949; m. F. Edward Larkin, Nov. 26, 1949; children—Susie, Lynn, Michael. Tchr. English, dramatics Aurora (Ill.) East High Sch., 1946-47, Villa Carondelet, Tucson, 1947-49. Leader, Girl Scouts U.S.A., Tucson, 1958-63; librarian asst. St. Mary Hosp., 1955-56, St. Joseph Hosp., 1972-73; librarian St. Mary's and St. Joseph Aux., Tucson; docent Tucson Art Center, 1969—; pres. sustaining bd. Newman Center, Tucson, 1966-67; mem. nat. alumnae bd. St. Mary's Coll. Notre Dame, 1967-70; Rec. sec. Pima County Bar Aux., 1952-53, corr. sec., 1972-73; library vol. Sts. Peter and Paul Ch., Tucson, 1960—; courtesy chmn. Symphony Cotillion, 1968. Mem. St. Mary's Alumnae (local pres. 1963-73). Home: 160 Sierra Vista Dr Tucson AZ 85719

LARKIN, SHARON, broadcasting exec.; b. Fargo, N.D., Aug. 11, 1943; d. Aron David and Virginia Mae (Westley) Ruff; grad. high sch.; m. Patrick Matthew Larkin, Jan. 15, 1966. Traffic mgr. KXJB-TV, Fargo, 1961—. Home: 1718 14th St S Fargo ND 58102 Office: 4000 W Main St Fargo ND 58102

LAROCK, MARGUERITE FROST (MRS. LIONEL T. LAROCK), lawyer, sec.; b. Union Mills, N.B., Can., Apr. 26, 1912 (parents Am. citizens); d. Albert Raymond and Evis Hazle (Bridge) Frost; m. Lionel T. Larock, Apr. 26, 1939 (dec. Mar. 1961); children—Marcia (Mrs. Marcia Snyder), Dennis R., Norman S., Cynthia M. Apprentice, Judge Edward R. Parent, Lewiston, Me., 1931-37, legal sec., 1931-41; admitted to Me. bar, 1937, since practiced in Lewiston. Instr. to legal secretarial students Bliss Coll., Lewiston, Me., 1967-70; sec. to pres. Bates Coll., Lewiston, Me., 1970—. Mem. budget com. United Fund, Lewiston, Me., 1970-72; sec. Child and Family Mental Health Services, 1969-72; asst. v.p.

Tri-County Mental Health Services, 1972—; mem. exec. bd. Lewiston/Auburn Child and Family Service Assos., 1966-67, v.p., 1967-68. Named Woman of Year for City of Lewiston, Bus. and Profl. Woman's Club, 1972. Mem. Androscroggin County Bar Assn. (sec. 1970—). Baptist (deaconess 1971—). Mem. Order Eastern Star. Home: 461 College St Lewiston ME 04240 Office: 461 College St Lewiston ME 04240

LAROCQUE, GERALDINE ELIZABETH, educator; b. Duluth, Minn., Feb. 28, 1926; d. Weldon and June (Hill) LaRocque; B.S., U. Minn., 1947, M.A., 1952; Ph.D. (Switzer scholar, Mayr scholar), Stanford, 1965. Tchr. high sch. English, Fergus Falls, Minn., 1947-49, U. Minn. High Sch., Mpls., 1949-50, Lake Forest (Ill.) High Sch., 1950-51, U. Ill. High Sch., Urbana, 1951-53; advt and promotion dir. WTCN-Radio and TV, Mpls., 1953-55; tchr. English, Evanston Twp. (Ill.) High Sch., 1955-62; instr. Stanford, 1962-65; asst. prof. English, Tchrs. Coll., Columbia, N.Y.C., 1965-68, asso. prof., 1968-72; prof. English, U. No. Ia., Cedar Falls, 1973—. Instr. English edn. Smith Coll., Northampton, Mass., summers 1960, 61; vis. prof. English, U. Mo., Columbia, summers 1968-71; ednl. cons. to various bds. of edn., univs. and tchr. tng. insts.; mem. Nat. Council for Accreditation of Tchr. Edn. Teams, U. Mass., Amherst, 1972, U. Pitts., 1974. John Hay fellow, 1960-61. Mem. Nat. Council Tchrs. of English (ex-officio dir. 1965-72), Conf. on English Edn. (mem. exec. com. 1968-72, v.p. 1970-72), N.Y. State Com. on English Edn. (mem. exec. com. 1967-71), Ia. Council Tchrs. English (v.p. 1974-75), Phi Beta Kappa, Pi Lambda Theta, Phi Delta Kappa, Phi Alpha Theta, Kappa Kappa Gamma. Editorial bd. Teenage Book Club, Scholastic Mags., N.Y.C., 1968—, Reading Improvement, Milw., 1973—. Home: 725 Maplewood Dr Cedar Falls IA 50613

LAROCQUE, MARILYN ROSS ONDERDONK (MRS. RODNEY CLARENCE LAROCQUE), pub. relations cons.; b. Weehawken, N.J., Oct. 14, 1934; d. Chester Douglas and Marion (Ross) Onderdonk; B.A. cum laude, Mt. Holyoke Coll., 1956; postgrad. N.Y. U., 1956-57; M.Journalism, U. Cal. at Berkeley, 1965; m. Bernard Dean Benz, Oct. 5, 1957 (div. Sept. 1971); children—Mark Douglas, Dean Griffith; m. 2d, Rodney Clarence LaRocque, Feb. 10, 1973. Jr. exec. Bonwit Teller, N.Y.C., 1956; personnel asst. Warner-Lambert Pharm. Co., Morris Plains, N.J., 1957; editorial asst. Silver Burdett Co., Morristown, 1958; pub. relations cons., Piedmont, Cal., 1963—; pub. relations dir. Shaklee Corp., Hayward, Cal., 1972-73, Lung Assns. Alameda, Contra Costa and Solano Counties, 1974—. Mem. exec. bd., rep-at-large Oakland (Cal.) Symphony Guild, 1968-69; cabinet mem. Lincoln Child Center, Oakland, 1967-71, cabinet pres., 1970-71, 2d v.p. bd. dirs., 1970-71; pub. relations chmn. Food Services Council, 1974—. Mem. Cal. Republican Central Com., 1964-66. Bd. dirs. Cal. Spring Garden and Home Show, 1970—, First Agrl. Dist. Cal., 1970—. Mem. D.A.R. (chpt. regent 1960-61, 66-68), U. Cal. Alumni Assn., Museum Soc. San Francisco, Oakland Mus. Assn., Cal. Acad. Scis. Theta Sigma Phi. Clubs: Mount Holyoke Coll. Alumnae, Orinda Country. Author: Maestro Baton and His Musical Friends, 1968; Happiness is Breathing Better, 1974. Address: 70 St James Pl Piedmont CA 94611

LAROSE, WINIFRED MILLICENT STRANAHAN (MRS. HOWARD A. LAROSE), constrn. co. exec., civic worker; b. Lake George, N.Y.; d. Frederick and Jessie C. (Barber) Stranahan; grad. high sch.; m. Howard Arthur LaRose, Nov. 26, 1938; children—Howard Arthur, Cheryl Anne (Mrs. Wayne M. Young). Sec., real estate saleswoman Deininger-Leavitt, Inc., Lake George, N.Y., 1934-39; sec.-treas. Howard A. LaRose Constrn. Co., Inc., Glens Falls, N.Y., 1938—; owner Mocking Bird Hill resort, Lake George, 1954—; dir. First Nat. Bank Lake George, 1964-66. Chmn. Warren County Heart Fund, 1965-72, treas., 1967-72, Warren County rep. for Eastern N.Y., 1967—; fund raising sec. Adirondack Hudson River Assn., 1966—; mem. N.Y. State Legislative Forum, 1964—, co-chmn., 1973, mem. conservation com., 1970—; fund raising chmn. Warren County Vol. Com. on Children and Community Services, 1956—; mem. Gov.'s Adv. Council Study Commn. for Future Adirondacks, 1968-70; Warren County rep. N.Y. State Citizen's Information Service, 1970-72; membership sec. Adirondack Conservancy Com., 1971—; mem. Women's Task Force, Empire State Coll., 1971—; Adirondack regional vice-chmn. N.Y. State Environmental Planning Lobby, 1972—; mem. N.Y. Adv. Council Dept. Environmental Conservation, 1974—; mem. N.Y. Environmental Bd., 1974—. Bd. dirs. Warren County Health Assn., 1954-58; bd. govs. State U. N.Y. at Albany Found. Recipient plaque for Heart Assn. work, 1969, 72; citation for conservation work in Adirondack Park Assn., 1969; award N.Y. State Conservation Council, 1969; Community award 1968. Mem. Lake George Bus. and Profl. Women's Club (v.p. 1964-65, civic participation chmn. 1969-70, legislative chmn. 1970-72), N.Y. Forest Owners Assn. (dir. 1966-71), Adirondack Park Assn. (v.p. 1964-71, dir. 1964—, historic sites chmn. 1968-73), Lake George (corr. sec. 1964-69, pres. 1969-72, trustee 1964—, mus. chmn. 1970—), Rogers Island (trustee 1965-67) hist. assns., Wilderness Soc., Assn. for Protection Adirondacks, Lake George Assn., Soc. Archtl. Historians, Nat. Trust for Historic Preservation, Lake George Motor Ct. Assn., Lake George C. of C., Friends of the Earth, Sierra Club, Adirondack Mt. Club, Adirondack Conservancy Com. (trustee 1971—, membership sec. 1971—). Episcopalian. Mem. Order Eastern Star. Home: Mocking Bird Hill Box 112 Lake George NY 12845

LARRICK, NANCY, editor, writer, educator; b. Winchester, Va., Dec. 28, 1910; d. Herbert Scaggs and Nancy (Nulton) Larrick; A.B., Goucher Coll., 1930; A.M., Columbia, 1937; Ed.D., N.Y. U., 1955; m. Alexander L. Crosby. Tchr. pub. schs., Winchester, Va., 1930-42; publs. dir. edn. sect. War Savs. div. U.S. Treasury, 1942-44, edn. dir. War Savs. div., 1944-45; editor Young America Readers (3 weekly mags.), 1946-51; edn. dir. children's books Random House, Inc., 1951-59; free-lance writer, 1959—; lectr. N.Y.U. Grad. Sch. Edn., 1949-50; dir. workshop Ind. U. Grad. Sch. Edn., summer 1956, 61, Butler U., summer 1962; lectr. Bank Street Coll. Edn., 1955-57; adj. prof. Lehigh U., 1963—. Trustee Goucher Coll. Recipient Founders Day Certificate of Achievement, N.Y.U., 1956. Mem. Nat. Conf. Research in English, Internat. Reading Assn. (pres. 1956-57), Nat. Council Tchrs. English (mem. literature commn., distinguished lectr.), Authors Guild. Author: Printing and Promotion Handbook, 1949, 66; See for Yourself, 1952; A Parent's Guide to Children's Reading, 1958 (Edison Found. award 1959), rev. edit. 1964, 69; A Teacher's Guide to Children's Books, 1960; Junior Science Book of Rain, Hail, Sleet and Snow, 1961; A Parent's Guide to Children's Education, 1963; Somebody Turned On a Tap in these Kids, 1971. Editor: Better Readers for Our Times, 1956; Reading in Action, 1957; Piper, Pipe that Song Again, 1965; Poetry for Holidays, 1966; Piping Down the Valleys Wild, 1968; Green Is Like a Meadow of Grass, 1968; On City Streets, 1968; I Heard a Scream in the Street, 1970; The Wheels of the Bus Go Round and Round, 1972; More Poetry for Holidays, 1973; (with Eve Merriam) Male and Female under 18, 1973; Room for Me and a Mountain Lion: Poems of Open Space, 1974. Editor The Reading Teacher quar. mag., 1950-54. Contbr. articles to ednl. mags., other nat. mags. Home: Rural Route 4 Quakertown PA 18951

LARSEN, DOROTHY HUNTINGTON HILL (MRS. HAROLD THEODORE LARSEN), gerontol. cons.; b. Nora Springs, Ia., Apr. 12, 1896; d. Charles and Emily (Huntington) Hill; A.B., U. Ill., 1922, M.A., 1925; M.A., Columbia, 1956, Ed.D., 1958; m. Harold Theodore Larsen, Jan. 26, 1924; 1 son, David Page. Tchr., Scornoway, Sask., Can., 1916-18; spl. lectr. Man. Ministery Agr., Winnipeg, 1920; instr. dept. English, U. Ill., Urbana, Ill., 1922-27; counselor and gerontol. cons. Assn. Home for Women, N.Y.C., also Osborne Home, Harrison, N.Y., 1958-61; dir. Tower Leavue, Riverside Ch., N.Y.C., 1960-63; cons. gerontology Presbyn. Homes of N.J., 1965—, Sisters of St. Dominic, Caldwell, N.J., 1971. Chmn. com. on exceptional child N.Y. State P.T.A., 1948-50; chmn. Rockland County (N.Y.) Mental Health Assn., 1952-53; mem. Rockland County Mental Health Bd., 1956-58; mem. N.J. steering com. White House Conf. on Aging, 1960-61; mem. Mercer County (N.J.) Council on Aging, 1969-71, Monmouth Presbytery Task Force on Aging, 1973—, East Windsor (N.J.) Bd. Health, 1973. Bd. dirs. N.Y.C. Bd. of Sr. Centers, 1965-74. Fellow Nat. Gerontol. Soc.; mem. Women in Communications, Am. Assn. U. Women, Nat. Council Family Relations, Assn. for Community Edn. N.J., N.J. Gerontol. Soc., Kappa Delta Phi. Author: Dialogues on Aging, 1966. Home: 23-12 Meadow Lakes Hightstown NJ 08520

LARSEN, DOROTHY MURPHY (MRS. ARTHUR LARSEN), food merchandising cons.; b. Jersey City, Aug. 10, 1915; d. Joseph and Emma (Becker) Murphy; m. Arthur Larsen, Oct. 20, 1935; 1 son, Bernard. Cons. engr. Atlantic & Pacific Tea Co., hdqrs. N.Y.C., 1943-49; bakery specialist Gen. Baking Co., hdqrs. N.Y.C., 1949-56; dir. consumer service Hot Shoppes, Inc., Washington, 1957-60; creative food merchandising cons. N.J. Sch. Food Services Assn., Haledon, 1961—. Mem. Food Services Execs.' Assn., Am., N.J. (pres. 1964-67) Sch. Food Services Assns., Am. Women in Radio and TV. Contbr. articles to profl. jours. Home: Box 464 42 Merrie Trail Denville NJ 07834 Office: 70 Church St Haledon NJ 07508

LARSEN, MIRIAM CARLENE, quality control exec.; b. Chgo., May 29, 1928; d. Carl and Pansy Irene (Adams) Larsen; B.A., Harding Coll., Searcy, Ark., 1950. Mgr. composing dept. Collins Radio Co., Richardson, Tex., 1959-71; owner Van Alstyne Leader, Whitewright Sun, Weeklies, Tex., 1971-73; mgr. quality control dept. Data Communications, Dallas, 1973—. Home: 210 Ross St Denison TX 75020 Office: 11333 N Central Expressway Dallas TX 75231

LARSEN, VIRGINIA LAWRENCE (MRS. WENDELL O. LARSEN), physician, researcher; b. Chungking, China; d. Benjamin Franklin and Jennie (Borg) Lawrence; B.S., U. Wash., 1935; M.D., Woman's Med. Coll. Pa., 1939; m. Wendell O. Larsen, Aug. 6, 1943 (dec. Oct. 1948); children—Larry Wendell (dec.), Gary Lee. Intern, resident Franklin Hosp., San Francisco, 1939-43; gen. practice medicine, Richmond, Cal., 1943-46, Lynwood, Wash., 1955-57; family life educator Seattle Pub. Schs., 1950-55; chief, med. services Mental Health Research Inst., Ft. Steilacoom, Wash., 1955-70; clin. med. dir. Yakima Valley Sch., Selah, Wash., 1970, Interlake Sch., Medical Lake, Wash., 1971-72; med. dir. St. Louis Chronic Hosp. and Nursing Home, 1972—. Named Mother's Mother of Year, Seattle, 1951; Woman of Achievement, Tacoma, 1962. Fellow Am. Pub. Health Assn.; mem. St. Louis Med. Soc., Am., Mo. med. assns., Nat. Council of Family Relations, Am. Assn. U. Women, Delta Kappa Gamma. Club: Business and Professional Women's. Contbr. articles to profl. jours. Home: 5825 Southwest St St Louis MO 63139

LARSEN, VIVIAN BERTHA, mental health orgn. exec.; b. Waverly, N.Y., Aug. 11, 1933; d. Charles Oiestein and Annie Katherine (Vatnes) Larsen; student Valparaiso U., 1951-52; B.S., Ohio State U., 1958; postgrad. Case Western Res. U., 1959-60; M.S.W., Loyola U., Chgo., 1963; postgrad. (Nat. Program for Ednl. Leadership fellow) Northwestern U., 1972-74; m. Aug. 15, 1955 (div. June 1957). Tchr. high sch., Parma, O., 1958-59; tchr. elementary grade, Cleve., 1959-60; chief psychiat. social worker Katharine Wright Mental Health Center, Chgo., 1964-67; exec. dir. Proviso Twp. Mental Health Commn., Westchester, Ill., 1967-69; regional dir. mental health div. Chgo. Bd. Health, 1969-71; instr. med. sch. clinics Northwestern U., Chgo., 1963-64; asso. dir. Mental Health Task Force, Comprehensive Health Planning, Inc., Chgo., 1974. asst. prof. social work edn. div. George Williams Coll., Downers Grove, Ill., 1967—; asst. in psychiatry, dept. psychiatry Stritch Sch. Medicine, Loyola U., Maywood, Ill., 1965—. Tng. grantee Nat. Inst. Mental Health, 1960-63. Mem. Acad. Certified Social Workers. Home: 1 S 264 Windsor Lane Villa Park IL 60181 Office: Suite 226 Professional Bldg Oak Brook IL 60521

LARSON, ANN ROBERTA, editor; b. Dallas, Nov. 5, 1948; d. Lennart Vernon and Allie Belle (Moore) Larson; B.A. in Zoology, U. Tex., 1970, M.A. in Sci. Communication Journalism, 1972. Tech. publs. editor Lockheed Electronics Co., Houston, 1974—. Mem. Women in Communications, Inc., Soc. for Tech. Communication, Kappa Tau Alpha, U. Tex. Ex-Students' Assn. Home: 7608 Southwestern Blvd Dallas TX 75225 Office: Aerospace Systems Div Lockheed Electronics Co 16811 El Camino Real Houston TX 77058

LARSON, ARLENE MAE MILLER (MRS. WILLIAM PAUL LARSON), librarian; b. Milford, Neb., Apr. 9, 1928; d. Silas J. and Christine Viola (Anderson) Miller; B.S., U. Neb., 1953; M.A. (P.E.O. grant), U. Denver, 1954; postgrad. U. Colo., 1970, U. No. Colo., 1970; m. William Paul Larson, June 30, 1956; children—James William, Joann Marie. Librarian Omaha Pub. Library, 1954-56, El Paso (Tex.) Pub. Library, 1956-57, Jefferson County (Colo.) Pub. Libraries, 1963-67, Ore. Coll. Edn., Monmouth, 1967-68; librarian Jefferson County (Colo.) Pub. Schs., Denver, 1957-60, 68—. Mem. Nat., Colo., Jefferson County edn. assns., Colo. Assn. Sch. Librarians, Colo. Audio-Visual Assn., Delta Kappa Gamma. Home: 1374 S Drexel Way Denver CO 80226 Office: 200 S Harlan St Denver CO 80226

LARSON, EMILIE G., educator; b. Northfield, Minn., Apr. 28, 1919; d. Melvin Cornelius and Frieda (Christiansen) Larson; A.B., St. Olaf Coll., 1940; M.A., Radcliffe Coll., 1946; student U. Chgo., 1951-52. Tchr. Hanska (Minn.) High Sch., 1940-42, Two Harbors (Minn.) High Sch., 1942-43; tchr. J. W. Weeks Jr. High Sch., Newton, Mass., 1946-56, guidance counselor, 1956—. Mem. Boston Personnel and Guidance Assn., Am. Assn. U. Women (exec. bd. 1962-64, mem. bd. Boston 1966-68, 70—, area rep. edn. Mass. div. 1971—), Mass., Newton tchrs. assns.; N.E.A., Pi Lambda Theta. Lutheran. Clubs: Women's City (Boston); Appalachian Mountain. Contbr. articles profl. jours. Home: 75 Wyman St Waban MA 02168 Office: 7 Hereward Rd Newton MA 02159

LARSON, ESTHER ELISABETH, educator; b. Williamsport, Pa.; d. Gustaf Severin and Selma (Christiansen) Larson; B.S., West Chester (Pa.) State Coll., 1931; M.A., Columbia, 1945; Ph.D., N.Y. U., 1959. Tchr. English, Jamestown (N.Y.) High Sch., 1934-44; lectr. English Columbia, 1952-54; instr. English N.Y. U., 1957, Bennett Coll., 1954-56; asso. prof. English East Stroudsburg (Pa.) State Coll., 1959-60, prof., 1960-74, head dept., 1960-69, ret., 1974. Recipient King Gustaf V fellowship Am. Scandinavian Found., 1949-50, Founders' Day award N.Y. U., 1959. Mem. Am. Assn. U. Women, Am. Scandinavian Found., Swedish Pioneer Hist. Soc., English Grad. Union, Modern Lang. Assn., Intercontinental Biog. Assn., Nat. Council Tchrs. English (regional judge achievement awards program 1963—), Am. Studies Assn., East Stroudsburg State Coll. Faculty Assn. (treas. 1970-71), Kappa Delta Pi, Pi Lambda Theta. Clubs: Women's Graduate of Columbia University (v.p. 1950-52); Soroptimist (pres. club, 1973-74). Author: Swedish Commentators on America 1638-1865, 1963. Contbr. articles to mags. Home: 584 E Broad St East Stroudsburg PA 18360

LARSON, EVELYN MARGARET PLATT, newspaper editor; b. Racine, Wis., Sept. 3, 1923; d. Robert A. and Amanda (Block) Platt; B.S., U. Wis., 1945; postgrad. St. Mary's Coll., 1959-60, Am. Press Inst. of Columbia, 1971; m. Jack R. Larson, Feb. 14, 1948; children—Christine, Eric. Food economist Better Foods mag., N.Y.C., 1946, Practical Home Econs. mag., N.Y.C., 1947-48; home economist Ind. and Mich. Elec. Co., South Bend, 1948-50; reporter South Bend Tribune, 1967-70, women's editor, 1970—. Recipient 2d prize for feature article, AP, Ind., 1968, 71; 1st prize for feature article Hoosier State Press Assn., 1973. Mem. Am. Assn. Univ. Women, Nat. Fedn. Press Women, Women's Press Club Ind. Presbyn. Club: South Bend Press. Home: 63543 State Rd 23 North Liberty IN 46554 Office: 223 W Colfax Av South Bend IN 46626

LARSON, FRANCINE STOGIS, physician; b. Chgo., Jan. 25, 1926; d. Paul and Frances (Kwadras) Stogis; Ph.B., U. Chgo., 1945, B.S., 1946; M.B., Chgo. Med. Sch., 1950, M.D., 1951; m. Charles J. Larson, Dec. 25, 1951 (div. Apr. 1961); children—Leif John, Ingrid Ann, Anita Marie. Intern Fordham Hosp., Bronx, N.Y., 1950-51; reisdent internal medicine Detroit Meml. Hosp., 1951-52; practice medicine, Southgate, Mich., 1953-58; resident psychiatry Northville (Mich.) State Hosp., 1961-64, staff psychiatrist, 1964-67; psychiatrist, dir. Mental Hygiene Clinic of Helena (Mont.), 1967—; cons. Ft. Harrison VA Hosp. Mem. Lewis and Clark County Med. Soc., A.M.A., Mont. Med. Assn., Am., Intermountain psychiat. assns., Altrusa Internat. Home: 606 N Warren St Helena MT 59601 Office: 1415-17 Helena Av Helena MT 59601

LARSON, HELEN KAY BRANDER (MRS. MAYNARD LEON LARSON), editor; b. Avon, Mont.; d. George and Fannie E. (Markle) Brander; certificate Newspaper Inst. Am., 1950; m. Maynard Leon Larson, Mar. 25, 1949 (dec. July 1955). Various secretarial positions, 1941-58; editor, co-pub. Security Advertiser and Fountain Valley News, 1958-74; sec.-treas. Shopper Press, Inc., 1958-72, pres., 1972-74. Chmn., Fountain precinct Republican Party, 1962. Mem. Internat. Graphoanalysis Soc., Fountain Valley C. of C. (sec.-treas., mgr. 1960-65, dir. 1972-74), Colo. Presswomen, Nat. Fedn. Presswomen, Colo. Press Assn. Author: Valley of the Fountain, 1969. Home: PO Box 252 Fountain CO 80817 Office: 120 E Ohio St Fountain CO 80817

LARSON, JEAN RUSSELL (MRS. HAROLD PARKS), author; b. Marshalltown, Ia., July 25, 1930; d. Charles Reed and Myrtle Viola (Koester) Russell; student Winthrop Coll., 1948-49; m. Harold F. Parks, June 3, 1971; children—Kathleen, Richard, David, Rosemarie, William, Michael, Harold. Active Am. Arab relations. Republican. Roman Catholic. Author: Palace in Bagdad, 1965; The Silkspinners, 1966; Jack Tar, 1969 (Lewis Carroll Shelf award 1973); The Glass Mountain, 1972. Contbr. nonfiction poetry to Mass. Rev., Lit. Rev., Mich. Quar., Early Am. Life, others. Home: Box 98 Garwin IA 50632

LARSON, JESSIE, artist, educator; b. Preston, Ida.; d. Willard and Annabel (Cowley) Larson; B.S., Utah State U., 1933; M.F.A., U. Wash., 1948; student Art Student's League N.Y., 1939-40; pvt. study U.S., Europe, Mexico. Faculty Utah State U., Logan, 1941—, asso. prof., 1949-63, prof. art, 1963—; exhibited group shows Henry Gallery, Seattle, 1948, U. State, 1946, 48, 58, Bertha Eccles Galleries, 1958, 69, Art Center Galleries, 1961, 66, Springville (Utah) Annual, 1958, 68, U. Gallery, Logan, 1965, 66, 67, 2d ann. Brigham Young U. Festival Mormon Art, Provo, 1970, 4-Univ. Faculty Exhibit, 1970; represented in permanent collections Utah State U., Utah Capitol Bldg., Daughters Of Utah Pioneer, Salt Lake City, others; judge numerous exhbns. Recipient Utah State U. Research grants, 1960, 66-70, several awards Utah State Inst. Fine Arts, Utah and Ida. state fairs; 1st and 3d pl. awards Alliance for Visual Arts Spring Gala and Exhibit, 1971; 1st pl. award in fiber art crafts Utah State Fair, 1971, 3d pl. profl. award, 1973; others. Mem. Utah State U. Faculty Assn. (v.p. 1969-70), Utah Designer Craftsmen (Purchase award 1971, Phi Kappa Phi. Home: 461 N 700 E Logan UT 84321

LARSON, JO ANNA MILLER (MRS. TED C. LARSON), antique furniture cons.; b. Chgo., Aug. 16, 1924; d. John P. and Anna E. (Linden) Miller; grad. high sch.; m. Ted C. Larson, Jan. 25, 1947. Owner, The Courtyard, antiques, Antioch, 1966-74; antique furniture cons. Antique Furniture & Interior Decorating Gallery, Marshall Field & Co., Chgo., 1972—. Mem. Lake County Health, Edn. and Welfare Com., 1974—; vol. Meml. Hosp. Aux., 1962-67. Recipient 10th Dist Poetry award Lake County Fedn. Woman's Clubs, 1964. Mem. Nat. Assn. Dealers Antiques, Assn. Wives Ill. Lawyers, Ill. Fedn. Womans Clubs. Republican. Roman Catholic. Club: Antioch Womans (pres. 1963-65). Home: 100 Hawthore Lane PO Box 0 Antioch IL 60002 Office: Marshall Field & Co Antique Furniture Gallery 111 N State St Chicago IL 60690 also 384 1/2 Lake St Antioch IL 60002

LARSON, LAURA (MRS. DAVID EMMANUEL LARSON), nursing dir.; b. Herndon, Kan., Nov. 14, 1908; d. Paul and Susanna (Leitner) Goltl; diploma Research Hosp. Sch. Nursing, 1930; student Boise State Coll., 1953-54; B.S., U. Ore., 1956; M.A., Columbia, 1961; m. David Emmanuel Larson, June 2, 1934. Pub. health nurse City and County of Boise (Ida.) Health Dept., 1945-57; nursing cons. Ida. Dept. Health, 1957-65, chief medicare certification, 1965-67, coordinator nursing and allied health, 1967—; nursing cons. Ariz. Dept. Health, 1962. Commr. Boise City Housing Authority, 1967-70; mem. Nat. Ins. Benefits Adv. Council, 1972—. Bd. dirs. Boise Council on Aging. Recipient Ann. Profl. award Ida. Pub. Health Assn., 1964; named Boise's Outstanding Citizen, 1967. Mem. Am. Nurses Assn. (sec. pub. health sect. 1960-64; mem. geriatric div. exec. com. 1966-68). Contbr. articles to profl. jours. Home: 426 S Phillipi St Boise ID 83705

LARSON, MARCIA LOUISE, ednl. adminstr.; b. Knoxville, Ill., Apr. 30, 1919; d. Herman Frederick and Lillian Gertrude (Eitelgeorge) Larson; B.A., Knox Coll., 1941; postgrad. Juilliard Sch. Mus., 1947-48, Columbia, 1957; M.Ed., U. Va., 1956. Tchr., Canton (Ill.) Pub. Schs., 1941-43, Roanoke County Schs., Salem, Va., 1943-48; tchr. Roanoke (Va.) City Schs., 1948-57, prin., 1957—. Radio and T.V. performer, concert artist; soloist Temple Emanuel, 1950-60, Raleigh Ct. United Methodist Ch., 1946—. Bd. dirs. Va. Assn. Women Hwy. Safety, Sister City Com.; mem. adv. bd. Marquis Biog. Library Soc. Recipient Educators medal Freedoms Found., 1970, Good Samaritan award Civitan Club, 1971; named Most Outstanding Working Woman of Roanoke Valley, 1971. Mem. Am. Assn. U. Women, Nat. Council Adminstrv. Women in Edn., N.E.A., Va., Roanoke edn. assns., Nat., Va., Dist. dgpts. elementary sch. prins., P.T.A. (life), Roanoke Area Council for Retarded Children, Internat. Platform Assn., Wesleyan Service Guild (past pres.), P.E.O. (pres. Va. 1964), Kappa Delta Pi, Delta Kappa Gamma, Delta Zeta, Sigma Alpha Iota. Republican. Club: Pilot International. Home: 3162 Tomaranne Dr SW Roanoke VA 24018 Office: 724 Dale Av SE Roanoke VA 24013

LARSON, NETTA BELL GIRARD, lawyer; b. Riverton, Wyo.; d. George and Arranetta (Bell) Girard; student Ida. State U., 1957-58; B.S., U. Wyo., 1959, LL.B., 1961; m. Admitted to Wyo. bar, 1961, U.S. Supreme Ct. bar, 1969; practiced in Riverton, 1963-69, 73—; atty.-adviser on gen. counsel's staff Dept. Housing and Urban Devel., Washington, 1969, sect. chief, Interstate Land Sales, 1970-73; partner firm Larson & Larson, Riverton, 1973—. Chmn. sub-com. on polit., legal rights and responsibilities Gov.'s Commn. on Status Women, 1965-69, rep. Nat. Conf. Govs. Commn., Washington, 1966; local chmn. Law Day, 1966, 67; mem. state bd. Wyo. Girl Scouts U.S.A.; state vol. adviser Nat. Found., March of Dimes, 1966-69. Recipient Spl. Achievement award for Operation Breakthrough, Dept. Housing and Urban Devel., 1972; Outstanding Leadership award Girl Scouts U.S.A., 1973. Mem. Am., Wyo., Fremont County, D.C., Fed. bar assns., Women's Bar Assn. for D.C., Internat. Fedn. Women Lawyers, Am. Judicature Soc., Am. Trial Lawyers Assn. Nat. Assn. Women Lawyers (del. Wyo., nat. sec. 1969-70, v.p. 1970-71, pres. 1972-73, outstanding service award 1973), Am. Assn. U. Women (br. pres.), Wyo. Fedn. Womens Clubs (state editor, pres. elect. 1968-69), Kappa Delta. Club: Riverton Chautauqua (pres. 1965-67). Editor: Wyoming Clubwoman, 1966-68; bd. editors Wyo. Law Jour., 1959-61. Writer Obiter Dictum column Women Lawyers Jour. Contbr. articles to profl. jours. Home: 224 W Sunset St PO Box 687 Riverton WY 82501 Office: Larson & Larson 513 E Main St PO Box 687 Riverton WY 82501

LARSON, RACHEL HARRIS (MRS. JOHN WATSON HENRY), research chemist; b. Wake Forest, N.C., Aug. 1, 1913; d. Thomas Alfred and Iola (Bowling) Harris; student Campbell Coll., Buies Creek, N.C., 1930-33; B.S., Appalachian State Tchrs. Coll., 1940; M.S., Georgetown U., 1949, Ph.D., 1958; m. James Philip Larson, Aug. 27, 1956 (dec. Feb. 1967); m. 2d, John Watson Henry, Oct. 23, 1971; stepchildren—Richard Cordell Henry, David Whitcomb Henry, Margaret Elaine Henry. Tchr. high sch., Duluth, Ga., 1940, Henderson, N.C., 1941-42; indsl. hygiene research lab. tech. and sci. aid to chemist NIH, Bethesda, 1942-47; chemist to research chemist Nat. Inst. Dental Research, 1947—, chief preventive methods devel. sect. Nat Caries Program, 1972—; vis. scientist Royal Dental Coll., Denmark, 1970-71. Fellow Am. Coll. Dentists, A.A.A.S.; mem. Internat. Assn. for Dental Research, Am. Chem. Soc., Am. Inst. Nutrition, Sigma Delta Epsilon. Baptist. Contbr. articles to profl. jours. Home: 9301 Fernwood Rd Bethesda MD 20034 Office: NIH Bethesda MD 20014

LARSON, RUBY MIRIAM (MRS. CARL EDWARD LARSON), editor; b. Cleburne, Kan., Dec. 17, 1905; d. Anton N. and Ella Olivia (Berggren) Johnson; teaching certificate Kan. State Tchrs. Coll. Emporia, 1937; B.A., Augustana Coll., 1946; m. Carl Edward Larson, Dec. 25, 1963. Rural sch. tchr., Kan., 1923-32; elementary tchr. Scandia, Kan., 1936-43; parish worker Christ Ch. Am. Lutheran Missions, Willow Run, Mich., 1946-47, Augustana Ch., Omaha, 1948-51; elementary tchr., Manhattan, Kan., 1951-57; jr. high sch. English tchr., Clay Center, Kan., 1957-67; co-owner, editor Scandia (Kan.) Jour., 1965-70, owner, 1970—. Home: Scandia KS 66966 Office: Box 98 Scandia KS 66966

LARSON, VERA M., sch. adminstr.; b. Lake Benton, Minn., Nov. 4, 1914; d. John Harold and Grace (Miller) Larson; student George Fox Coll., 1939-40, Ore. Coll. Edn., 1940-42; B.S., U. Ore., 1946, M.Ed., 1955. Tchr. vocal music, Newberg, Ore., 1942-43; tchr. vocal music Portland (Ore.) Pub. Schs., 1943-51, elementary cons., 1951-53, asst. supr. personnel, 1953-57; teaching prin. Sacajawea Sch., 1957-62; supervising prin. Maplewood Sch., 1962-65; supervising prin. Grout Sch., 1965-66, supr. staff devel., 1966-70, personnel specialist, 1970—. Tchr. workshop in elementary social studies So. Ore. Coll., Ashland, summers 1958, 60, courses in curriculum constrn., elementary social studies U. Portland, summer 1958. Mem. Nat., Ore. (sec. 1954-55) edn. assns., Nat., Ore., Portland (sec. 1958-59) elementary prins. assns., Nat., Ore. assns. supervision and curriculum devel., Nat., Ore. (pres. 1956-57, 70—) assns. tchr. edn., Am. Assn. Sch. Personnel Adminstrs., Northwest Assn. Sch. Personnel Adminstrs., Nat. Soc. Study Edn., Delta Kappa Gamma (chpt. pres. 1960-62, state exec. sec. 1961-63), Pi Lambda Theta. Home: 13601 Fremont St NE Portland OR 97230 Office: 631 NE Clackamas St Portland OR 97208

LARSON, VONA ANN, educator; b. Des Moines, Sept. 27, 1930; d. Kenneth Alden and Lillian Berlin (Kampley) Larson; B.A., St. Olaf Coll., Northfield, Minn., 1952; M.S. in Edn., Drake U., Des Moines, 1962. Tchr. English, Buffalo Center (Ia.) High Sch., 1952-56; tchr., counselor Lincoln High Sch., Des Moines, 1956-61; asst. to prin. A.W. Merrill Jr. High Sch., Des Moines, 1961—. Evang. Lutheran Ch. scholar, 1952. Mem. A.A.U.W. (dir. Des Moines 1971-72), Nat. (life), Ia., Des Moines edn. assns., Nat., Ia. (pres. 1967-68) assns. women deans and counselors, Am., Ia., Des Moines personnel and guidance assns., Nat., Ia. assns. secondary sch. prins., Des Moines Adminstrs. Assn., Phi Theta Kappa, Phi Rho Pi, Delta Kappa Gamma. Lutheran (v.p. 1974-75). Home: 3929 Oakshire Rd Des Moines IA 50310 Office: 5301 Grand Av Des Moines IA 50312

LA RUE, ARLENE CATHERINE, editor; b. Syracuse, N.Y.; d. John Coughlin and Barbara (Reichert) La Rue; B.S., Syracuse U., 1934. Soc. reporter Syracuse (N.Y.) Herald, 1934; reporter Geddes News, 1934-35; reporter, city editor Rome (N.Y.) Sentinel, 1935-47; women's editor Herald Jour. and Herald Am., Syracuse, N.Y., 1947—. Tchr. journalism Syracuse U. Extension Sch., 1955, adult edn., North Syracuse, 1956, Syracuse U. Journalism Sch., 1969-71. Mem. adv. bd. Catholic Charities Assn., 1969-73. Recipient 1st prize in playwriting contest N.Y. State Fair, 1954; Hadassah award, 1953; Women Yr., Geddes Bus. and Profl. Women's Club, 1963. Mem. Theta Sigma Phi (eastern regional dir. 1955-58), Phi Kappa Phi. Roman Catholic. Club: Zonta. Home: 32 Queen's Way Camillus NY 13031 Office: Clinton Sq Syracuse NY 13201

LARUE, MARIANNA MCALLISTER (MRS. ROGER PIERRE), psychiatrist; b. N.Y.C., May 2, 1933; d. John and Virginia Archer (Exley) Buyer; B.A., Vanderbilt U., 1954; M.D., U. Tenn., 1957; m. Roger Pierre, May 12, 1960; children—Patrick McAllister, Rachel Josephine, Marguerite Virginia. Intern Jackson Meml. Hosp., Miami, Fla., 1958, resident, 1959-62; psychiatrist, Winter Park, Fla., 1962—. Mem. women's com. Fla. Symphony Soc., 1963—, Guild John Young Museum, 1968—; mem. Jr. Service League Winter Park, Inc., 1966—; mem. Drug Abuse Council Orange County, 1971-72; mem. Opera Gala Guild, 1972—. Bd. dirs. Mental Health Assn. Orange County, 1967-70, Crippled Childrens Soc. Orange County, 1963-66, Central Fla. Guidance Center, Orlando, Fla., 1964-66, Jr. Service League Winter Park, 1969-70, 72-73. Mem. Orange County Med. Soc. (asso.), Fla. Med. Soc. (asso.), Fla. Psychiat. Soc., Am. Psychiat. Assn., Alpha Omicron Pi. Presbyn. Home: 1665 Cheyenne Trail Maitland FL 32751 Office: 220 New England Bldg Winter Park FL 32789

LARUE, MAUREEN LORAINE RILEY, occupational therapist; b. Detroit, Aug. 24, 1942; d. Frank Cain and Marion Catherine (Bittinger) Riley; B.S., Wayne State U., 1966; m. Terrill James LaRue, Dec. 19, 1970; 1 dau., Michelle Marie. Staff occupational therapist Detroit Orthopaedic Clinic, 1967-70; chief occupational therapy Detroit Meml. Hosp., 1970-71; occupational therapist cons. Oakland Schs. Title VI Program, Berkley, Mich., 1971-72. Tchr. Nature for the Presch. Child, Daytona Beach Community Coll., 1973-74. Vocational Rehab. Act grantee, 1966-67, Therapy scholar. Nat. Farm and Garden Horticulture, 1965. Recipient award Meritorious Service, Oakland County Dental Soc., 1969. Mem. Am., Mich., Fla., Detroit (v.p. 1968) occupational therapy assns., Law Wives Halifax Area (treas. 1974-75), Pi Theta Epsilon. Home: 1317 Laurel Dr Daytona Beach FL 32017

LARUE, RUBY MAY DILLMAN, artist; b. nr. Silver Lake, Ind.; d. Alvah Leroy and Laura (Perry) Dillman; student Ind. U., 1952, South Bend Art Center, 1952-56; portrait painting under Harold Zisla, 1953-56, water color under Joseph Robel. Exhibited in group shows Seaway Festival Art Show, Muskegon, Mich., Town and Country Art Show, South Bend, Potpourri Art Show, South Bend, Pletcher Village Art Festival, Nappanee, Ind., Regency Sq. Art Show, Jacksonville, Fla.; portrait commns. include Dr. Robert Parks. Mem. No. Ind. Artists, Jacksonville, Fla. Art League, St. Joseph Water Color Soc. Home and Studio: Route 1 Silver Lake IN 46982

LASALA, CLARA ROSE NICOLAS, pediatrician; b. Kansas City, Mo., June 14, 1936; d. Albert Costanzo and Rose (Vaccaro) LaSala; B.S.N., Avila Coll., 1958; M.D., Creighton U., 1964; m. Jean Gerard Nicolas, Aug. 30, 1968; children—Carla Denise, Paula Anne. Intern San Francisco Gen. Hosp., 1964-65; resident U. Cal. at San Francisco, 1965-67, chief resident, 1967-68; staff pediatrician Monterey County Hosp., Salinas, Cal., 1968-70, Kaiser Permanente Hosp., Santa Clara, 1970—. Mem. Alpha Omega Alpha, Alpha Epsilon Iota. Roman Catholic. Home: 1685 Miller Av Los Altos CA 94022 Office: 900 Kiely Blvd Santa Clara CA 95051

LASBURY, LEAH B. (MRS. CLYDE P. LASBURY), realtor, artist; b. Boca Grande, Fla., Apr. 11, 1915; d. James E. and Nellie (Allen) Bartlett; B.A., Rollins Coll., 1936; B.S., Simmons Coll., 1937; m. Clyde P. Lasbury, Sept. 16, 1939; children—Cherick Pitchford, Dana Cleveland, Leah Jean. Jr. exec. trainee G. Fox & Co., Hartford, Conn., 1937-39; real estate broker, Englewood, Fla., 1951—; v.p. J.E. Bartlett & Sons, Inc., Englewood; charter mem. adv. bd. Englewood Bank. One-man shows Englewood Bank, 1960, Community Gallery, Venice, Fla., 1960, Corridor Gallery, Asheville, N.C., 1961, Italian Villa, Venice, 1963, Am. Bank, Sarasota, Fla., 1966; exhibited in group shows, 1955—, including the Nat. Assn. Women Artists, N.Y.C., 1959, N.Y.C. Pen and Brush Club, 1959, Ringling Mus., Sarasota, 1961, South Coast Galleries, Tampa Fair, 1960-61, Lowe Gallery, Miami, 1963, 68, Fla. Artist Group Shows, 1st Rollins Coll. Alumni Show, 1966, 67, 68, New Coll. Artists Group, Sarasota, Fla., 1966, St. Petersburg Arts Center, 1973, numerous others; represented in pvt. collections. Organizer Englewood Teen Club, 1952; mem. adv. bd. Sarasota County Libraries, 1966—; v.p. Ringling Mus. Mems. Guild, 1960-62; organizer 1st road commn., Englewood, 1956, 1st water commn., 1956; organizer Elsie Quirk Pub. Library, 1962, bd. dirs., 1962—, pres., 1973-74; mem. Sarasota County Community Goals Council, 1965—; charter dir. Asolo Theatre Festival Assn., 1963—. Mem. Venice Art Assn. (dir.), Englewood Realtors Assn. (organizer, charter pres.), Englewood (past pres.), Sarasota County (publicity com. 1963) chambers commerce, Englewood Women Taxpayers League (organizer, charter pres.), Sarasota Art Assn., Fla. Artist Group (pres. 1971-74), D.A.R. (charter Myakka chpt. Venice), Sarasota County Hist. Soc. (exec. com.), Internat. Platform Assn., Fine Arts Soc. Sarasota (charter mem.), Pi Gamma Mu., Phi Mu, Alpha Omega. Republican. Methodist. Clubs: Venice Yacht (charter mem.), Venice College. Home: Lee Circle Englewood FL 33533 Office: 312 Indiana Av Englewood FL 33533

LASCHE, EUNICE MARIE, physician; b. Mpls.; d. Bruno and Vittoria (Hauber) Lasche; B.S., Fla. State U., 1940; M.D., Temple U., 1948, M.S., 1953. Fellow endocrinology Phila. Gen. Hosp., 1949-51; resident internal medicine Temple U. Hosp., 1951-53, research fellow cardiology, 1953-54; practice medicine, specializing in endocrinology, Tampa, Fla., 1957—; staff physician S.W. Fla. Tb Hosp., 1955-57; clin. asst. prof. medicine U.S. Fla. Coll. Medicine; dir. Tb control Hillsborough County Health Dept., 1962-66, cons. Tb control, 1966-69; attending physician Diabetic and Metabolic Clinics, Tampa Gen. Hosp. Cons. CARE-MEDICO in Malaysia, 1965. Diplomate Am. Bd. Internal Medicine. Fellow A.C.P.; mem. A.M.A., Fla., Hillsborough County med. assns., Am., Fla. (dir.) diabetes assns., Endocrine Soc., Cath. Daus. Am. Club: Zonta (dir., pres. 1968-69) (Tampa, Fla.). Home: 7308 Ola Av Tampa FL 33604 Office: 1 Davis Blvd Tampa FL 33606

LASHER, ESTHER LU (MRS. DONALD T. LASHER), librarian; b. Denver, June 1, 1923; d. Lindley Aubrey and Irma Jane (Rust) Pim; A.A. in Fine Arts, Temple Buell Coll., 1943; B.A., Denver U., 1945, M.A., 1967; M.R.E., Eastern Bapt. Sem., 1948; m. Donald T. Lasher, Apr. 8, 1950; children—Patricia Sue, Donald Aubrey, Keith Alan, Jennifer Luanne. Tchr. pub. schs., Denver, 1945-46; dir. Christian edn. First Bapt. Ch., Evansville, Ind., 1948-50; asst. circulation librarian Evansville (Ind.) Pub. Library, 1950-51; tchr. music Dubois (Ind.) County Schs., 1951-52; br. librarian Jefferson County (Colo.) Pub. Library, 1962-64; acting head, reference librarian Colorado Springs Pub. Library, 1964-67; high sch. librarian Colorado Springs Dist. 2, 1967-68; head music library Butler U., Indpls., 1968-72; cataloger gen. collection Ind. State Library, 1972—. Leader Hoosier Indpls. council Girl Scouts U.S.A., 1972-73; leader 4-H, Perry County, Ind., 1951-53, Denver, 1956-60; block chmn. Neighborhood Improvement Orgn., 1971-72; mem. Neighborhood Republican Com., 1970-72. Mem. Music Library Assn., Internat. Music Library Assn., Christian Library Assn., Internat. Platform Assn., Indpls. Mus. Art, Sigma Alpha Iota (adviser 1969-72). Baptist (tchr. Sunday sch. 1968-72; mem. Christian edn. bd. 1969-72). Mem. Order Eastern Star. Home: 4646 Carvel Av Indianapolis IN 46205 Office: Ind State Library 140 N Senate St Indianapolis IN 46202

LASHLEY, MIRIAM, lawyer; b. Tulsa, Oct. 20, 1921; d. Edmund and Eleanor Gertrude (Starr) Lashley; student U. Tulsa, 1937-38; A.B., Wellesley Coll., 1942; LL.B., Yale, 1944; M.L.S., Okla. U., 1966. Admitted to Okla. bar, 1944; atty. appellate div. tax sect. Dept. Justice, Washington, 1944-45; instr. dept. polit. sci. U. Tulsa, 1947-48; atty. Sinclair Oil & Gas Co., Tulsa, 1950-60; librarian Tulsa City-County Library, 1962-73, Bus. and Tech. Dept., 1964-73; dir. legal services Allegheny Power Service Corp., Greensburg, Pa., 1973—. Mem. Am. Bar Assn., Okla. Bar Assn. Democrat. Presbyn. Clubs: Greensburg College; Wellesley (Pitts.). Home: Apt 1 3011 Williamsburg Dr Latrobe PA 15650 Office: 800 Cabin Hill Dr Greensburg PA 15601

LASHOF, JOYCE R. COHEN (MRS. RICHARD KENNETH LASHOF), physician; b. Phila., Mar. 27, 1926; d. Harry and Rose (Brodsky) Cohen; A.B. Duke; M.D., Womans Med. Coll. Pa.; m. Richard Kenneth Lashof, June 11, 1950; children—Judith, Carol, Danny. Intern, Bronx Hosp., N.Y.C., 1950-51, resident, 1951-52; resident Montefiore Hosp., N.Y.C., 1952-53; fellow Yale, 1953-54; USPHS fellow U. Oxford, Eng., 1964-65; practice medicine, specializing in preventive medicine, Chgo.; dir. sect. community medicine Presbyn.-St. Lukes Hosp., Chgo., 1967-71, chmn. dept. preventive medicine, 1971-73; project dir. Mile Sq. Health Center, Chgo., 1967-71; instr. medicine U. Chgo., 1956-58, asst. prof., 1958-60; clin. asst. prof. preventive medicine U. Ill., 1960-61, asst. prof., 1961-64, asso. prof., 1964-68, prof. preventive medicine and community health, 1968-71; prof. preventive medicine Rush Med. Coll., Chgo., 1971—; dir. dept. pub. health State of Ill., 1973—; research dir. Chgo. Bd. of Health, 1965. Diplomate Am. Bd. Internal Medicine. Fellow Am. Pub. Health Assn.; A.C.P.; mem. Am. Assn. Tchrs. of Preventive Medicine. Contbr. articles in field to profl. jours. Home: 4812 S Greenwood St Chicago IL 60653 Office: 1753 W Congress Pkwy Chicago IL 60612

LASKA, VERA ORAVEC (MRS. ANDREW J. LASKA), educator; b. Kosice, Czechoslovakia, July 21, 1923; M.A. in Philosophy, Charles U. (Prague), 1945, M.A. in History, 1946; Ph.D., U. Chgo., 1959; m. Andrew J. Laska, Nov. 5, 1949; children—Thomas V., Paul. Exec. sec. War Crime Commn., Prague, 1945-46; prof. U. Ill., Chgo., 1947-48, Roosevelt U., Chgo., 1948-49; fgn. student counselor U. Chgo., 1955-59, Fulbright Commn., Sao Paulo, Brazil, 1960-64; faculty U.S. history, Latin Am. civilization Regis Coll., Weston, Mass., 1966—, chmn. div. social scis., 1968—, dir. Weston history project, 1967—. Cons. Inst. Internat. Edn., N.Y.C., 1965-67. Mem. Weston Hist. Commn., 1969—, Weston Bicentennial Commn.; adv. bd. Mass. Bicentennial Commn. Internat. House fellow, 1946-48. Mem. Am. Hist. Assn., Latin Am. Studies Assn., Weston Hist. Soc., Am. Assn. U. Profs., Nat. Assn. Fgn. Student Affairs, Czechoslovak Acad. Arts and Sci. in Am. Contbr. articles to profl. jours., monthly Column Town Crier. Home: 50 Woodchester Dr Weston MA 02193

LASKER, MARY (MRS. ALBERT D. LASKER), civic leader; b. Watertown, Wis.; d. Frank Elwin and Sara (Johnson) Woodard; student U. Wis.; A.B. cum laude, Radcliffe Coll.; postgrad. Oxford U.; LL.D., U. Wis.; L.H.D. U. So. Cal., Bard Coll., Woman's Med. Coll. Pa., N.Y.U., N.Y. Med. Coll., Jefferson Med. Coll., U. Cal. at Berkeley; m. Paul Reinhardt (div.); m. 2d, Albert D. Lasker. Art dealer; asso. with Reinhardt Galleries, N.Y.C., arranging benefit loan exhbns. of outstanding old and modern French masters and selling pictures to collectors and museums; originated Hollywood Patterns, formerly subsidiary co. of Conde Nast Publs.; established with husband Albert and Mary Lasker Found., ednl. and med. research, med. journalism, 1942. Trustee N.Y.U., Kennedy Meml. Library; hon. chmn., mem. bd., exec. com. Am. Cancer Soc.; co-chmn., dir., mem. exec. com. Nat. Com. Against Mental Illness; trustee Research to Prevent Blindness Com.; chmn. Nat. Health Edn. Com.; pres. United Cerebral Palsy Research and Ednl. Found.; vice chmn. Citizens for the Treatment High Blood Pressure, Inc.; mem. Nat. Cancer Adv. Bd., Nat. Cancer Inst., N.I.H. Decorated officer French Legion of Honor; recipient Radcliffe Coll. Achievement award; Predsdl. Medal of Freedom, 1969. Home: 29 Beekman Pl New York City NY 10022 Office: 870 UN Plaza New York City NY 10017

LASKOWSKI, ROSE ANN (MRS. HENRY STANLEY LASKOWSKI), nurse; b. Detroit, July 18, 1942; d. Joseph Frank and Stella Caroline (Bartusik) Kowalski; student Bay City Jr. Coll., 1960; Asso. Sci., Henry Ford Community Coll., 1964; student Saginaw Valley Coll., 1968—; m. Henry Stanley Laskowski, July 25, 1964; 1 dau., Dawn Marie. Program dir. for mentally retarded Caro (Mich.) Regional Center, 1964—. Mem. Am. Assn. Mental Deficiency (sec.), Zeta Kappa Upsilon. Home: 5688 Lobdell St Mayville MI 48744 Office: Caro Regional Center Caro MI 48744

LASKY, ELLA, psychologist, educator; b. N.Y.C., Mar. 6, 1943; d. Morris H. Lasky and Sally (Newman) Lasky Cohen; B.A., Coll. City N.Y., 1963; Ph.D., Columbia, 1971. Lectr. Lehman Coll., City U. N.Y., 1970-72; asst. prof. psychology Manhattan Community Coll., City U. N.Y., 1973—; dir. Women's Psychotherapy Referral Service, N.Y.C., 1973—; clin. psychologist, 1973—. Mem. Am. Psychol. Assn. Assn. Women in Psychology, N.Y. Acad. Scis., Assn. Humanistic Psychology, Nat. Orgn. for Women (co-coordinator psychology com. 1971-73). Editor: Humanness: An Exploration into the Mythologies About Women and Men, 1975. Mem. editorial bd. Homosexual Counseling Jour., 1973—; editor in chief The Feminist Psychotherapy Newsletter, 1974—. Contbr. articles to profl. jours. Address: 310 W 106th St New York City NY 10025

LASSAHN, PAMELA LINNET (MRS. GORDON DENNIS LASSAHN), editor; b. Mpls., Nov. 17, 1942; d. Ralph Hayward and Thelma Evelyn (Schlick) Henry; B.S., Ia. State U., 1964, M.S., 1966; m. Gordon Dennis Lassahn, June 5, 1966; children—Nicole Elise, Jeffrey Karl. Editorial asst. Ia. Farm Service Mag., Ia. State U., Ames, 1964-66; asst. editor Ia. Agr. and Home Econs. Experiment Sta. Bulletin, 1966-69; editor of student resource papers Investigating Your Environment, Biol. Scis. Curriculum Study, Boulder, Colo., 1973—. Cons., free lance editing and indexing for various publishers, 1966—. Chmn. status of women com. YWCA, Boulder, 1971-73. Mem. Internat. Communication Assn., A.A.A.S., Women In Communications, Am. Assn. U. Women (corr. sec. 1973—). Conglist. (mem. bd. missions and social action 1973-74). Contbr. articles in field to profl. jours. Address: 783 E 17th St Idaho Falls ID 83401

LASSERS, ELISABETH STERN (MRS. WILLARD J. LASSERS), child psychiatrist; b. Offenbach, Germany; d. Robert E. and Dora (Metz) Stern; came to U.S., 1940, naturalized, 1946; M.D., U. Ill., 1949; m. Willard J. Lassers, June 30, 1946; 1 dau., Debbie. Intern, Mt. Sinai Hosp., Chgo., 1949-50; fellow Cook County Hosp., Chgo., 1950-51, pediatrics resident, 1951-52; pediatrics resident U. Ill. Research and Ednl. hosps., 1955-56, psychiatry resident U. Chgo. Hosps. and Clinics, 1963-67; med. dir. Ill. Childrens Hosp. Sch., Chgo., 1952-53; clin. instr. pediatrics U. Ill., 1954-55, 56-59; practice medicine, specializing in pediatrics, Chgo., 1956-59; mem. staff Michael Reese Hosp., 1957-63, dir. Evaluation Center for Handicapped Children, 1960-63; asso. in pediatrics Northwestern U., 1960-63; chief child psychiatry services Ill. Masonic Med. Center, Chgo., 1971—; pvt. practice child and family psychiatry; asst. prof. psychiatry and pediatrics U. Ill., 1967—; lectr. in psychiatry U. Chgo., 1972—. Psychiat. cons. Step Sch. U.S. Childrens Bur. fellow Center for Handicapped children, U. Ill., Research and Ednl. Hosps., 1959-60. Diplomate Am. Bd. Pediatrics, Am. Bd. Psychiatry and Neurology, Am. Bd. Child Psychiatry. Mem. Chgo. Council Child Psychiatry, Am. Acad. Pediatrics, Chgo. Pediatric Soc. (asso.), Am. Acad. Child Psychiatry, Am. Orthopsychiat. Assn., Am. Med. Women's Assn., Am. Psychiat. Assn., Ill. Psychiat. Soc., Soc. for Adolescent Psychiatry. Home: 1509 E 56th St Chicago IL 60637 Office: 111 N Wabash Av Chicago IL 60602

LASSETTER, MAGGIE SAMPLES (MRS. JAMES GREEN LASSETTER), realtor; b. Villa Rica, Ga.; d. Moses Monroe and Ethel (Boyd) Samples; student W. Ga. Coll., 1938-39; m. James Green Lassetter, Apr. 7, 1939; children—Margaret Annette (Mrs. Charles W. Rushing), Mary Lynn (Mrs. Earl L. Maxwell, Jr.), James William. Pvt. practice as real estate broker, DeFuniak Springs, Fla., 1954-55; partner Tallahassee Realty Co., 1958-63, v.p., 1963—. Mem. state adv. com. Fla. Dept. Edn.; v.p. Tallahassee Sister City Commn. to Pompayan, Colombia. Pres. Tallahassee Bd. Realtors, 1970—. Mem. Nat. (regional v.p. women's council), Fla. (state pres. women's council 1964, pres. Tallahassee chpt. women's council 1971, nat. dir.) assns. realtors, Nat. Inst. Real Estate Brokers, Am. Bus. Women's Assn. (pres. 1965), Bus. and Profl. Women's Club (chpt. 1st v.p. 1968, pres. 1969, dist. dir. 1971). Baptist. Mem. Order Eastern Star. Clubs: Altrusa (pres. 1968); Toastmistress. Home: 1101 Kenilworth Rd

Tallahassee FL 32303 Office: 1215 Thomasville Rd PO Box 1333 Tallahassee FL 32302

LASSILA, JEAN HANNAH DAY (MRS. KENNETH EINO LASSILA), author, lectr.; b. Rock Springs, Wyo., Oct. 23, 1934; d. Richard Charles and Helen Cecilia (Heagney) Day; B.S., U. Wyo., 1956; Ph.D. (Frederick W. Heyl fellow), Yale U., 1961; m. Kenneth Eino Lassila, Mar. 17, 1957; children—Kathrin, Ken-Erik. Spl. lectr. Case Inst. Tech., Cleve., 1961-63; research asso. Ia. State U., Ames, 1964, 67-71; lectr. U. Oulu (Finland), 1973. Mem. Am. Chem. Soc. Author: (with others) Understanding Chemistry, 1967; (with others) Programed Reviews of Chemical Principles, 1970. Contbr. articles to profl. jours. Home: 3605 Ross Rd Ames IA 50010

LASSWELL, MARCIA LEE (MRS. THOMAS LASSWELL), educator; b. Oklahoma City, July 13, 1927; d. Lee and Stella (Blackard) Eck; B.A., U. Cal. at Berkeley, 1949; M.A., U. So. Cal., 1952; postgrad. U. Cal. at Riverside, U. So. Cal., U. N.C.; m. Thomas Lasswell, May 29, 1950; children—Marcia Jane, Thomas Ely, Julia Lee. Individual practice psychotherapy, marriage and family counseling, Pomona, Cal.; asst. prof. Pepperdine Coll., Los Angeles, 1959-60; asst. prof. psychology, behavioral sci. dept. Cal. State U. at Pomona, 1960-64, asso. prof., 1965-69, prof., 1970—, chmn. dept., 1964-69; vis. asso. prof. Scripps Coll., 1968-69, U. So. Cal., 1969-70, Occidental Coll., 1971-72; lectr. various Cal. univs. Mem. staff, spl. project for alcoholics and narcotics offenders Cal. State Prison System, 1970-73; mem. Cal. Accreditation Com. for Secondary Schs., 1965—. Bd. dirs. Cal. Mental Health Authority, Planned Parenthood San Gabriel Valley, Open-Door Free Clinic. Recipient Outstanding Tchrs. award Cal. State U., 1971. Fellow Am. Assn. Marriage and Family Counselors (dir. 1970-72); mem. Am. Sociol. Assn., Pacific Sociology Assn., Nat. Council on Family Relations, A.A.A.S., Conf. of Conciliation Cts., So. Cal. Assn. Marriage and Family Counselors (pres. 1972-73), Alpha Kappa Delta, Phi Delta Gamma, Pi Gamma Mu. Author: College Teaching of General Psychology, 1967; Love, Marriage and Family, 1973. Home: 875 Hillcrest Dr Pomona CA 91766

LASSWELL, SHIRLEY ANN BASSO SLESINGER (MRS. FRED D. LASSWELL, JR.), lit. promoting co. exec.; b. Detroit, 1924; d. Michael and Clara (Leasia) Basso; grad. high sch.; m. Stephen Slesinger, Oct. 1949 (dec. 1953); 1 dau., Patricia Ann Slesinger; m. 2d, Fred D. Lasswell, Jr., June 1964. Appeared with Olsen & Johnson Show, 1941-49; pres. Stephen Slesinger, Inc., N.Y.C., Tampa, Fla., 1953—; pres. Red Ryder Enterprises, Inc., Hawley Publs., Inc., Tele-Comics, Inc.; owner U.S. and Canadian rights Winnie-the-Pooh Mdse., 1929—; owner comic strips Red Ryder, Little Beaver, King of the Royal Mounted, Ozark Ike; asso. Zane Grey, Inc. in motion picture field, promotion sales comic books based on famous Western stories. Mem. Tampa Aux. Power Squadron. Clubs: Krewe of Venus, St. Petersburg Yacht. Home: 5108 Longfellow Av Tampa FL 33609 Office: 1111 N Westshore Blvd Tampa FL 33607

LASTER, CLARA LENORA (MRS. JAMES LASTER), lit. agt., writer; b. Wainright, Ala., Feb. 14, 1914; d. James Haywood and Neila Louvenia (Martin) Thompson; student pub. schs.; D. Lit. Leadership (hon.), Internat. Acad. Leadership, P.I.,; m. James Laster, May 30, 1935; children—Shari (Mrs. William Casper), Jamie. Editor Tulsa Poetry Quar., 1968-69; lit. agt. Laster's Lit. Agy., Tulsa, 1969—. Mem. Poetry Soc. Okla. (v.p. 1965—). Mem. Ch. of Jesus Christ of Latter-day Saints. Author poetry vols.: Patter of Poems, 1948; House on Halfway Hill, 1968. Contbr. to numberous publs. including Secrets, Listen, Fate, Harvest. Address: 204 E 45th Pl Tulsa OK 74105

LATHAM, ALICE FRANCES PATTERSON (MRS. WILLIAM JOSEPH LATHAM), pub. health nurse; b. Macon, Ga., Dec. 18, 1916; d. Frank Waters and Ruby (Dews) Patterson; R.N., Charity Hosp. Sch. Nursing, New Orleans, 1937; student George Peabody Coll. Tchrs., 1938-39; B.S. in Pub. Health Nursing, U. N.C., 1954; M.P.H., Johns Hopkins, 1966; m. William Joseph Latham, July 21, 1940; children—Jo Alice (Mrs. Samuel Earl Wood), Marynette (Mrs. Myles Shannon Webb), Lauruby Cathleen. Staff pub. health nurse assigned spl. venereal disease study USPHS, Darien, Ga., 1939-40; county pub. health nurse Bacon County, Alma, Ga., 1940-41; USPHS spl. venereal disease project, Glynn County, Brunswick, 1943-47; county pub. health nurse Glynn County, 1949-51, Ware County, Waycross, 1951-52; pub. health nurse supr. Wayne-Long-Brantley-Liberty Counties, Jesup, 1954-56 dist. dir. pub. health nursing Wayne-Long-Appling-Bacon-Pierce Counties, Jesup, 1956-70; dist. nursing dir. S.E. Ga. Health Dist., 1970—, organizer mobile health services, 1973—. Exec. dir. Wayne County Home Health Agy., 1968—, Ware County Home Health Agy., 1970—. Bd. dirs. Wayne County Mental Health Assn., 1959, 60, 61, Wayne County Tb Assn., 1958-62; a non-alcoholic organizer Jesup group Alcoholics Anonymous, 1962-63; mem. adv. council Ware Meml. Hosp. Sch. Practical Nursing, Waycross, Ga., 1958. Recipient recognition Gen. Service Bd., Alcoholics Anonymous, Inc. Fellow Am. Pub. Health Assn.; mem. Am., 8th Dist. (pres. 1954-58, sec. 1958-60, dir. 1960-62, 1st v.p. 1962), Ga. (exec. bd. 1954-58) nurses assns., Ga. Pub. Health Assn. (chmn. nursing sect. 1956-57). Contbr. to state nursing manuals. Home: 115 Harper St Jesup GA 31545 Office: Wayne County Health Dept PO Drawer A Jesup GA 31545

LATHAM, EUNICE STUNKARD (MRS. JOHN R. LATHAM), ednl. adminstr.; b. N.Y.C., Sept. 4, 1923; d. Horace Wesley and Frances Grace (Klank) Stunkard; B.A., Wellesley Coll., 1945; m. John Ralph Latham, June 9, 1962. Acting dir. div. reports and analysis UNRRA, Washington, Germany and France, 1945-47; editor Unitarian Service Com., N.Y.C., 1947-49; copywriter J. Walter Thompson Co., N.Y.C., 1949-56, Lambert & Feasley, Inc., N.Y.C., 1956-62, Fuller & Smith & Ross, N.Y.C., 1962-65; v.p., creative supr. Lennen & Newell, Inc., 1965-70; headmistress Barnard Sch. for Girls, N.Y.C., 1970—. Election dist. capt. Bronx County, 1948-54; committeewoman Bronx County, 1950-62. Trustee Barnard Sch. for Girls, Antoinette Fischer Williams Fund, Barnard Sch. for Girls Money Purchase Pension Plan. Mem. Nat. Assn. Prins. Schs. for Girls, Head Mistresses of East, Guild Ind. Schs. N.Y.C., Shakespeare Soc., Soc. Mayflower Descs. Home: 1 University Pl New York City NY 10003 Office: 554 Fort Washington Av New York City NY 10033

LATHAM, MARY ELIZABETH, clergywoman; b. Cin.; d. Lawrence Lorenzo and Eugenia (Peters) Latham; B.A. cum laude, Asbury Coll., 1929. Tchr. math. and Latin, McAfee High Sch., Mercer County, Ky., 1929-32; entered ministry of evangelism Ch. of the Nazarene, 1933, ordained to ministry, 1937; traveled in work of evangelism and Christian edn., 1937-48; internat. dir. vacation Bible schs. Dept. Ch. Schs., Kansas City, Mo., 1948-67; dir. audiovisuals Ch. of the Nazarene, 1962-74. Chmn. audiovisual com. Council of Chs. Greater Kansas City, 1955-58, chmn. com. on communications edn., 1966-67; sec. Missionary Film Assos., 1969—; chmn. Latham Communications, 1975—. Mem. Assn. Ednl. Communications and Tech. Author: Vacation Bible School, Why, What, and How, 1954, 9th rev. edit., 1968; Adventures with Jesus, 1948, rev. edits., 1951, 54, 57, 60, 63; Teacher, You Are an Evangelist; also monthly articles in Adult Bible Tchr. Contbr. articles to periodicals; dir. prodn. films The Great Transition, motion picture of Nazarene Colls., 1964; Sing His Wonderful Name, 1965; Would You Believe It, 1967; The Debtors and They Do Not Wait, 1968; The Way Out and God's Word for Today's World, 1969; Moving Ahead, 1970; Just for the Love of It, 1971; To Make a Miracle, 1972; To New Worlds, 1972; The Church of the Nazarene, 1974; The Alabaster Story, 1974. Office: 10268 Cedarbrooke Lane Kansas City MO 64131

LATHAM, MILDRED BEST, book store exec.; b. Washington, N.C., June 7, 1930; d. John Milton and Ida Jane (Perry) Best; student Atlantic Christian Coll., 1961—; grad. mgmt. seminar Nat. Assn. Coll. Stores, 1971; m. Lloyd Watson Latham, Aug. 6, 1949; children—Teresa (Mrs. Lee Roy Thomas II), Angela, Watson. Bookkeeper Dr. Pepper Bottling Co., Washington, N.C., 1948-50; sec. Atlantic Christian Coll. Library, 1962-65; partner, mgr. Gen. Employment Service, Wilson, N.C., 1965-67; mgr. Atlantic Christian Coll. Bookstore, Wilson, 1967—. Recipient 2 Pick, Promote, Profit awards Coll. Store Jour. Mem. Coll. Stores Assn. N.C. (sec.-treas. 1972—, v.p. 1973, pres. 1974, dir. 1970-71). Mem. Ch. of Disciples Christ. Club: Atlantic Christian Coll. Woman's (sec. 1969-70). Home: 1412 Branch St Wilson NC 27893 Office: 600 W Gold St Wilson NC 27893

LATHOM, PATRICIA ROSS GREEN, home economist, cons.; b. San Francisco, Oct. 30, 1925; d. A.S. and Ethelyn (Ross) Green; B.A., Cal. State U., Los Angeles, 1969, postgrad., 1969-70; postgrad. U. Cal. at Los Angeles, 1971-72; m. J.W. Lathom, Sept. 15, 1945 (div. Nov. 1965); children—Jan Wesley, Christina Ross. Partner, Lathom Assos., San Marino, Cal., 1967—. Second v.p. Ynez Sch. P.T.A., 1954, membership chmn. Alhambra council, 1956-57, pres. Repetto Sch., 1955-56; Monterey Park Coordinating Council rep., 1954-56; adult adv. council rep. Monterey Park Recreation and Parks Dept., 1955; social chmn. Cal. State Coll. at Los Angeles Student Adv. Bd., 1961; founder patron Greek Theatre Assn., 1966-68; mem. County of Los Angeles Dept. Social Services, Vols. Bur., Alhambra Dist., 1969-70. Recipient Red Feather awards Community Chest, 1953, Girl of Year award Inglewood Jr. C. of C. Aux., 1952-53, Key Woman award Monterey Park Jr. C. of C., 1954. Mem. Am., Cal. home econs. assns., Nat. Council on Family Relations, Soc. for Advancement Mgmt. (exec. council, exec. sec. 1964), Am. Soc. for Tng. and Devel., Consumer Fedn. Am., Assn. Cal. Consumers, Am. Council on Consumer Interests, Consumer Panel Am., Internat. Soc. Gen. Semantics, Internat. Platform Assn., Internat. Fedn. Home Econs., Adult Edn. Assn. U.S.A., Adult Edn. Action Council, Pacific Sociol. Assn., Pasadena Mental Health Assn., Vol. Bur. Pasadena, Nat. Alliance for Family Life (founding mem.), Nat. Assn. for Female Execs., Phi Upsilon Omicron, Alpha Kappa Delta, Alpha Gamma Pi. Republican. Episcopalian. Address: 1925 Kerns Av San Marino CA 91108

LATHROP, GERTRUDE ADAMS, chemist; b. Norwich, Conn., Apr. 28, 1921; d. William Barrows and Lena (Adams) Lathrop; B.S., U. Conn., 1944; M.A., Tex. Womans U., 1953, Ph.D., 1955. Devel. chemist textiles Alexander Smith & Sons Carpet Co., Yonkers, N.Y., 1944-52; research asso. textiles Tex. Women's U., 1952-56; chief chemist Glasgo Finishing Plant div. United Mchts. & Mfrs., Inc. (Conn.), 1956-57, chief chemist Old Fort Finishing Plant div. (N.C.), 1957-63; lab. and warranty mgr. automotive div. Collins & Aikman Corp., Albemarle, N.C., 1964—. Mem. Am. Chem. Soc., Am. Assn. Textile Chemists and Colorists (sect. treas., vice chmn. 1963-64), Am. Soc. for Testing Materials (chmn. transp. fabrics on flammability com. 1973—), Bus. and Profl. Womens Club (v.p. chpt. 1973-74). Home: 301 Mountain St Black Mountain NC 28711 Office: Box 580 Albermarle NC 28001

LATHROP, JOYCE KEEN (MRS. MITCHELL LEE LATHROP), civic worker; b. Los Angeles, Nov. 25, 1939; d. William Lavern Trewin and Therese (Wenig) Keen; student Russell Sage Coll., 1957-58, Goucher Coll., 1958-59; B.A., U. So. Cal., 1961; m. Mitchell Lee Lathrop, June 29, 1959; children—Christin Lorraine, Alexander Mitchell, Timothy Trewin Mitchell. Dir. Assistance League Glendale, Pasadena (Cal.) Sr. Center, 1966-68; dir. jrs. Los Angeles Orphanage Guild, 1968-74, pres., 1974—, treas., 1972-73, v.p., 1973-74; mem. Symphonians Los Angeles Philharmonic Orch., 1969-73, Opera Assos. Music Center, 1965—, Aux. Hosp. Good Samaritan, Los Angeles; mem. nat. council Met. Opera, N.Y.C. Recipient vol. service award Huntington Meml. Hosp., Pasadena, 1967; decorated officer Mil. and Hospitaller Order St. Lazarus of Jerusalem. Mem. Founders Los Angeles Music Center. Episcopalian. Club: Goucher of Southern Cal. (treas. 1966-67, sec. 1964-66) (Los Angeles). Home: 1375 Inverness Dr Pasadena CA 91103

LATIAK, DOROTHY VIOLET SCHER (MRS. DAVID LATIAK), librarian; b. Sault Ste. Marie, Mich., July 27, 1920; d. Joseph and Rose (Saperstein) Scher; A.A., Wilson Jr. Coll., 1940; student Chgo. Pub. Library Tng. Class, 1941-42; m. David Florian Latiak, May 4, 1955. Children's librarian Chgo. Pub. Library, 1946-72, br. librarian, 1972—, editor Staff News, 1971—, councillor Staff Assn., 1971—. Cons. for Reilly and Lee on Arthur Shay's What Happens At The Library, 1971. Served with WAC, 1943-46. Mem. Children's Reading Round Table (social chmn. 1970-71, membership chmn. 1972—), Am., Ill. library assns., South Chgo. C. of C. Editor: News Letter Ridge Art Assn., 1971—. Book reviewer Sch. Library Jour., 1969-72. Home: 10658 S Michigan Av Chicago IL 60628 Office: 9055 S Houston Av Chicago IL 60617

LATIMER, HEATHER (MRS. WALTHER NEUBAUER), writer, publicist; b. Essex, Eng.; d. Robin and Jessie (Rose) Latimer; Pitman's Coll., London, Eng., 1943-45; m. Walther Neubauer, Aug. 24, 1958; Photographer's model, 1946-51; free lance writing and publicity projects, 1951-63; tv and radio publicity dir. Standard Reference Works Pub. Co., N.Y.C., 1963-65; asst. to pres. W. H. Schneider, Inc., advt., N.Y.C., 1965-67; patron relations to patrons Met. Opera, N.Y.C., 1968-70; asst. to dir. Bide-A-Wee Animal Protection Assn., N.Y.C., 1970-72; contbg. editor Dogs mag., N.Y.C., 1972—; freelance writer, 1972—. Pres., Internat. League of N.Y., 1957-67. Author: How to Make Money As A Professional Party Organizer in The Great New Leisure Time Market; Tidypet—How To Make Your Dog An Indoor Toilet and Teach Puppy or Grown Dog To Use It. Home: 155 Crary Av Mount Vernon NY 10550

LATOURETTE, ARLENE CLAIRE FERGUSON, trading stamp co. exec.; b. Elizabeth, N.J., May 21, 1930; d. Frank William and Helen Marie (Kennedy) Ferguson; student State U. N.Y., Buffalo, 1969, Newark State Coll., 1970-71; m. Leo Michael LaTourette, Sept. 9, 1950 (separated); 1 son, Richard Michael. Sr. sales mgr. Ros-Ed Products, Inc., Bronx, N.Y.. 1957-60; group savs. rep. Mchts. Green Stamps, Phila., 1960-62; group savs. dir. Sperry & Hutchinson Co., N.Y.C., 1962-70, mgr. consumer relations, 1970-73, nat. accounts mgr., 1973—. Mem. Pub. Relations Soc. Am. Home: 37-A Hussa St Linden NJ 07036 Office: 330 Madison Av New York City NY 10017

LATREILLE, LISE DIANA, hosp. ofcl.; b. Montreal, Que., Can., Nov. 30, 1945; d. Oscar Georges-Henri and Cecile Florence (Clermont) Latreille; B.A., Coll. Jesus-Marie D'Outremont, 1966; B.A. in Polit. Sci., U. Montreal, 1968, M.A. in Pub. Health Adminstrn., 1973. Asst. to dir. children's services Douglas Hosp., Verdun, Que., 1972-73; exec. asst. adult and children's services Douglas Hosp., Montreal, 1973, exec. asst. in charge paramed. and rehab. services, 1973—. Home: 6601 LaSalle Blvd Montreal PQ H4H 1R3 Canada Office: 6875 La Salle Blvd Montreal PQ H4H 1R3 Canada

LATSHAW, FRANCES ELLEN, editor; b. Kansas City, Mo., Apr. 13, 1918; d. Lawrence Wallace and Ellen (Murphy) Latshaw; grad. high sch. Civilian employee narcotics div. Med. Depot, 1942-43; with Pratt-Whitney Co., Kansas City, Mo., 1944-45; auditor, recorder deed's office County Ct. House, Kansas City, Mo. 1946-59; mng. editor Record Newspaper Co., Kansas City, Mo. 1959—. Mem. County Grand Jury, 1967. Del., Nat. Democratic Conv., 1952; sec., v.p. Kansas City Women's Dem. Club, 1955-70; county clk. nominee on Dem. ballot, 1968. Mem. Kansas City Legal Secs. Assn. (corr. sec. 1966, Day in Ct. chmn. 1967-68, parliamentarian 1969), Nat. (del. 1971), Mo. (asst. finance chmn. 1971-72) assns. legal secs. Home: 5925 Holmes St Kansas City MO 64110 Office: 3611 Troost St Kansas City MO 64109

LATSHAW, PATRICIA HERGET (MRS. GEORGE TARRANT LATSHAW), pub. relations exec., writer; b. Lakewood, O., Oct. 4, 1930; d. Walter Clyde and Helen Naomi (Jones) Herget; B.A., Principia Coll., 1951; M.A., U. Chgo., 1952; Ph.D., U. Ia., 1957; m. George Tarrant Latshaw, May 24, 1958; children—Christopher, Michael. Asst. bus. mgr. Goodman Meml. Theatre, Art Inst. Chgo., 1951-53; instr. English, U. Neb., Lincoln, 1953-55; instr. communication skills U. Ia., Iowa City, 1955-57; pub. relations writer Ill. Bell Telephone Co., Chgo., 1957-58; dir. pub. relations Cleve. YWCA, 1958-59; dir. communications and research Ursuline Coll., Cleve., 1970-73; dir. communications Univ. Services Inst., Cleve., 1973—. Ghost writer for various syndicated articles. Trainer, Episcopal Dioceses of Ohio, Mich., 1968—; mem. dept. Christian edn. Diocese of Ohio, Cleve., 1967-74. Mem. central com. Summit County Democratic party, 1970-74, precinct committeewoman, 1970-74. Mem. Nat. Assn. for Female Execs., Pub. Relations Soc. Am., Phi Beta. Episcopalian (dir. Christian edn. 1967-70). Contbr. material on children's theatre to various books. Home: 8005 Swallow Dr Macedonia OH 44056 Office: 5862 Mayfield Rd Cleveland OH 44124

LATTA, HELEN LOUISE (MRS. ROBERT ERNEST LATTA), city ofcl.; b. Marlin, Tex., Oct. 9, 1928; d. Charlie Dickie and Birtie Annie (Johnson) McKelroy; student Nat. Sch. Bus., 1946; m. Robert Ernest Latta, Feb. 27, 1948; children—Linda Elaine (Mrs. Joseph Virgil Butler), Robert Galen. Clk. City Water Works, Waco, Tex., 1946-49, clk. City Tax Office, 1952-55; city sec. City of Lacy-Lakeview, Tex., 1957-73, city tax assessor, collector, 1973—. Home: 516 Powers Waco TX 76705 Office: 501 Craven Waco TX 76705

LATTIMER, AGNES DOLORES (MRS. FRANK BETHEL, JR.), physician; b. Memphis, May 13, 1928; d. Arthur Oneal and Hortense (Lewis) Lattimer; A.B., Fisk U., 1949; M.D., Chgo. Med. Sch., 1954; m. Bernard Goss, Jan. 16, 1952 (div.); 1 son, Bernard C.; m. 2d, Frank Bethel Jr. Rotating intern Cook County Hosp., Chgo., 1954-55, resident pediatrics, 1955-56; resident pediatrics Michael Reese Hosp., Chgo., 1956-57, chief pediatric resident, 1957-58, dir. sect. ambulatory pediatrics, attending physician div. pediatrics; asso. dir. Div. Ambulatory Services, Cook County Hosp. research fellow Chgo. Heart Assn., 1958-59, Heart Disease Control Program, Chgo. Bd. Health, 1959-61; adj. physician Provident Hosp.; pediatric cons. Bethany Hosp.; mem. staff, chmn. dept. pediatrics Mary Thompson Hosp.; clin. instr. dept. preventive medicine U. Ill. Med. Sch.; asso. prof. dept. pediatrics Chgo. Med. Sch. Vice pres. bd. dirs. Greater Lawndale Conservation Commn. Diplomate Am. Bd. Pediatrics, Nat. Bd. Med. Examiners, Fellow Am. Acad. Pediatrics; mem. A.M.A. Contbr. articles to profl. publs. Home: 6815 S Paxton Av Chicago IL 60649 Office: 1825 W Harrison St Chicago IL 60612

LATTING, PATIENCE SEWELL (MRS. TRIMBLE B. LATTING), mayor, civic worker; b. Texhoma, Okla., Aug. 27, 1918; d. Frank Asa and Leila (Yates) Sewell; A.B. magna cum laude, U. Okla., 1938; M.A., Columbia, 1939; m. Trimble B. Latting, Aug. 23, 1941; children—Francelia (Mrs. Thomas A. Wilson), Nancy Sewell (Mrs. Douglas G. Spelman), James Trimble, Cynthia Longley. Asst. to research librarian Chase Nat. Bank, N.Y.C., 1938-39; dir. 1st Nat. Bank, Clinton, Okla. Mem. Oklahoma City Council, 1967-71; mayor, Oklahoma City, 1971—. Legislation chmn. Okla. Congress Parents and Tchrs., 1960-67, bd. mgrs., 1959-67, mem. exec. com., 1963-67; mem. exec. com. Oklahoma City Council P.T.A.'s, 1960-62; pres. Edgemore P.T.A., Oklahoma City, 1963-64; mem. Okla. Gov.'s Reapportionment Com., 1960, Gov.'s Adv. Com. on Edn., 1964, Mayor's Com. on Internat. Affairs, Oklahoma City, 1962-63, Oklahoma City Citizen's Emergency Finance Com., 1965; mem. bd. Okla. Inst. Justice, 1965—; mem. Okla. Commn. Tchr. Edn. and Profl. Standards, 1965-67; apptd. officer of the ct. to aid in reapportionment Okla. legislature, 1964; Named Outstanding Sr. Woman, Theta Sigma Phi, U. Okla., 1938; recipient Amy B. Onken award to outstanding undergrad. mem. Pi Beta Phi, 1938; named Woman of Yr. in Civic Work, Oklahoma City chpt. Theta Sigma Phi, 1961, Outstanding Woman award, 1968; named Outstanding Woman of Okla., Soroptimist, 1969; named hon. col. State of Okla., 1960. Mem. Am. Assn. U. Women (state mass media chmn. 1962-63), League Women Voters (mem. Oklahoma City bd. 1958-59), Oklahoma City Tennis Assn. (mem. bd. 1965—), Mortar Bd., Huguenot Soc. Founders of Manakin in the Colony Va., Phi Beta Kappa (v.p. Oklahoma City alumni 1965—), Alpha Lambda Delta, Sigma Alpha Iota, Chi Delta Phi, Pi Mu Epsilon, Pi Beta Phi (pres. Oklahoma City alumni 1947-48), Delta Kappa Gamma (hon.). Clubs: 20th Century (sec. 1961-62), Oklahoma City Golf and Country, Altrusa (hon.). Instrumental in securing passage of state law permitting local sch. bds. to prohibit high sch. fraternities and sororities, 1953; author of amicus curiae brief field on behalf of Okla. Congress Parents and Tchrs. dealing with reapportionment of state legislature, 1962. Home: 3600 Harvey Pkwy Oklahoma City OK 73118 Office: City Hall 200 N Walker St Oklahoma City OK 73102

LATZ, RUTH JEAN, polit. party ofcl.; b. Joliet, Ill., Aug. 9, 1920; d. Thomas M. and Ethel F. (Reese) Reed; student Joliet Jr. Coll., 1938-39; m. LeRoy William Latz, Oct. 14, 1938; children—Theodore T., Margaret (Mrs. Timothy Reading), David M. Jury commr. Will County Jury Commn. of 12th Dist., Joliet. Pres., Will County Republican Womens Club, 1966-70; precinct committeewoman; co-chmn. Citizens for Nixon, 14th Congl. Dist., 1968; chmn. womens div. Will County Rep. Central Com., 1970—; legis. chmn. Ill. Fedn. Rep. Women, 1971-73; co-chmn. Nixon Com., 17th Congl. Dist., 1972; mem. John Ericcson Rep. Club. Mem. exec. bd. Family Service Agy. Named Outstanding Rep. Woman of Year of Will County, 1969. Mem. Woman Power-Ill. Style. Presbyn. (deaconess, mem. Matrons Club). Home: 2220 Jasmine Dr Joliet IL 60435 Office: County Bldg 14 W Jefferson St Joliet IL 60435

LAU, JUDITH ANN (MRS. A. STEVEN WAYNE), occupational therapist; b. Detroit, Aug. 16, 1942; d. Gustave and Martha Irene (Gould) Lau; B.S., Wayne State U., 1964; m. A. Steven Wayne, Sept. 16, 1972. Staff occupational therapist, unit supr. Boston State Hosp., 1965-67; occupational therapist psychiatry unit Boston VA Hosp., 1967-73; psychiat. day hosp. unit Greater Lynn (Mass.) Community Mental Health Center, 1973—. Cons. occupational therapy Del

Manor Nursing Home, Rockland, Mass., 1969-70. Mem. Am., Mass. occupational therapy assns. Home: 24 Wheeler St Malden MA 02148 Office: Union Hosp 500 Lynnfield Rd Lynn MA 01940

LAUB, DOROTHEA BERG (MRS. RICHARD SYDNEY LAUB, JR.), leasing co. exec.; b. Chgo., June 26, 1928; d. Frank Joseph and Emily Theresa (Maier) Berg; student music U. Chgo., U. Houston, U. Tenn., Sienna Coll.; m. Richard Sydney Laub, Jr., Dec. 25, 1950; 1 son, Richard Sydney III. Concert harpist, 1959-63; owner, operator Art Leasing Co., Anaheim, Cal., 1967—, Art Rental Co., Orange, Cal., 1969—; owner Original Red Carpet Realty, Orange, 1968—. Home: 519 N Redwood Pl Anaheim CA 92806 Office: 500 S Main St NT #406 Orange CA 92668

LAUBACH, ALICE FRANCES, librarian; b. Easton, Pa., Sept. 30, 1913; d. James Howard and Edith Louise (Bercaw) Laubach; B.A., Sweet Briar Coll., 1935; M.A., U. Hawaii, 1937. Chemist, Buckeye Cotton Oil Co., Memphis, 1940-42, Casein Co. of Am., Bainbridge, N.Y., 1942-44; chemist Am. Enka Co., Enka, N.C., 1944-51, librarian, 1951—. Mem. Am. Chem. Soc., Spl. Libraries Assn., Am. Soc. Information Scientists, Bus. and Profl. Women's Club Asheville (pres. 1967-69). Home: 366 Lakeshore Dr Asheville NC 28804 Office: American Enka Co Enka NC 28728

LAUB-NOVAK, KAREN RUTH (MRS. MICHAEL NOVAK), artist; b. Cresco, Ia., Aug. 25, 1937; d. George R. and Mary (Swenson) Laub; B.A., Carleton Coll., 1959; M.F.A., State U. Ia., 1961; student Oskar Kokoschka Sch., Salzburg, Austria, 1958; m. Michael Novak, June 29, 1963; children—Richard, Tanya, Jana. Art instr. Carleton Coll., Northfield, Minn., 1961-62; instr. sr. seminar Stanford U., 1967-68, U. Cal. at Riverside, 1975; tchr. painting pvt. studios, Boston, 1962-65, Palo Alto, Cal., 1965-68, Bayville, N.Y., 1968—; lectr. Shimer Coll., 1972, U. Cal., Santa Barbara, 1972, Groton Acad., 1973, U. Hawaii, 1973, Union Theol. Sem., 1973, Boston Coll., 1973, Yale, 1974, Salzburg Seminar, 1973, Am. Acad. Religion, 1971, DePauw U., 1974, U. Tenn., 1974, U. Fla., 1974, Swarthmore Coll., 1974, numerous others; exhibited one woman shows Rochester (Minn.) Mus., Des Moines Art Center, Botolph, Boston, Union Ct., Sawyer Gallery, San Francisco, Los Robles Gallery, Rockefeller Found., Raychem. Corp., Carleton Coll., Stanford, Pacific Sch. Religion, U. Tenn., Yale, Harvard, DePauw U.; traveling shows AFA Prints, 1969-70, Am. Assn. Women Artists, 1969, 70, 71. Illustrator: A Skunk Named Zorri, 1973; (with Michael Novak) A Book of Elements, 1973. Home: 5 Snug Cove Lane Bayville NY 11709

LAUCK, MARIE THERESA, lawyer, state senator; b. Indpls.; d. Anthony P. and Marie E. (Habig) Lauck; B.A., St. Mary-of-the-Woods Coll., 1934; M.A., Butler U., 1947; J.D., Ind. U., 1955. Probation officer Municipal Ct. of Marion County, 1935-48; admitted to Ind. bar, 1955, since in pvt. practice; part-time sec. to house attys. Gen. Assembly, State Ind., 1951-57; civilian instr. The Adjutant Gen. Sch., 1950-55. Mem. Ind. Ho. of Reps., 1959-60; Dem. candidate state senator, 1960, 62, 64; mem. Ind. Senate, 1965-69, 72—. Mem. Legislative Adv. Council State of Ind., Constnl. Revision Commn. State of Ind. Mem. Ind., Indpls. bar assns., Ind. Assn. Women Lawyers (sec. 1959, pres. 1969—), Legion of Decency (chmn. Ind. chpt. 1934—), Internat. Fedn. Cath. Alumnae (past gov. Ind.), Nat. Assn. Women Lawyers (del. 1965—), Kappa Gamma Phi, Sigma Tau Delta. Democrat. Contbr. articles to profl. mags. Office: 136 E Market St Indianapolis IN 46204

LAUDA, FRANCES ELIZABETH SHAVER (MRS. FRANCIS CHARLES LAUDA), home economist; b. Evanston, Ill., May 28, 1926; d. George Jacob and Elizabeth (Siddall) Shaver; student Cornell U., 1944-45; B.S., Pratt Inst., 1948; m. Francis Charles Lauda, July 9, 1949; children—Betsy Louise, Susan Ann, Cindy Jane. Asso. homemaking editor Macfadden Publs., 1948-50; food writer, publicity dept. J. Walter Thompson Co., N.Y.C., 1950-54; free lance publicity and home econs. writer, 1954-56, 71—; food editor Seventeen mag., N.Y.C., 1956-71. Mem. Am. Home Econs. Assn., Home Economists in Bus. (chmn. pub. relations com. N.Y.C. chpt. 1952), Gamma Pi Delta. Contbr. to nat. mags. Home: Tudor Lane Sands Point NY 11050

LAUFER, BEATRICE, composer; b. N.Y.C.; d. Samuel and Fanny (Silverman) Laufer; student Juilliard Sch. Music, N.Y.C., 1944; m. Theodore Lassoff, Oct. 2, 1940 (dec. July 1955); 1 son, Samuel; m. 2d, Seymour H. Rinzler, Oct. 19, 1969 (dec. May 1970). Composer Symphony No. 1 (performed by Eastman-Rochester Symphony Orch. 1945-46, performance Germany and Japan under auspices of State Dept., 1948); Dance Festival (performed by Eastman-Rochester Symphony, 1946-47); choral compositions: Under the Pines, Spring Thunder performed Tanglewood, 1949, Song of the Fountain, Inter-racial Chorus, UN Freedom celebration, 1952; Small Concerto for Chamber Orch. performed McMillan Theatre, Columbia, 1949-50; Ile, opera, world premiere Royal Opera Co., Stockholm, Sweden, 1958; Second Symphony performed by Oklahoma City Orch., 1961; premiere concerto at Donnell Library Center, 1962; premiere performance Prelude and Fugue for Orch., Brevard (N.C.) Music Center, 1964, Cry!, orchestral prelude, Orch. of Am., Town Hall, 1966, Lyric, string trio, Bowdoin Coll. Contemporary Music Festival, 1966; Cry, performed with Eastman-Rochester Symphony, 1968; master ceremonies Young Am. Artists, radio sta. WNYC; hostess The Conductor Speaks series Sta. WNYC. Mem. A.S.C.A.P., Am. Symphony Orch. League, Am. Music Center. Home: 1045 5th Av New York City NY 10028

LAUFFER, ANNA TINKEL (MRS. OSWALD ARNO LAUFFER), librarian; b. N.Y.C., Oct. 25, 1909; d. Hyman and Matilda (Potischman) Tinkel; A.B., Hunter Coll., 1935; M.L.S., Columbia, 1940; m. Oswald Arno Lauffer, Dec. 11, 1931; children—Daniel, Elisabeth. Editorial researcher H.W. Wilson Co., N.Y.C., 1930-40, indexer Agrl. Index, 1950-63; sr. indexer Book Rev. Digest, N.Y.C., 1964—. Mem. A.L.A., Ethical Culture Soc., N.Y. Library Club, Sierra Club. Home: 150 West 96th St New York City NY 10025 Office: HW Wilson Co 950 University Av Bronx NY 10452

LAUGHLIN, ALICE MARGARET, educator; b. Malone, N.Y., Feb. 19, 1918; s. John and Roae Ellen (Murray) Laughlin; B.S., St. Joseph Coll., West Hartford, Conn., 1949; M.S., U. Vt., 1954; Ed.D., Columbia, 1965; postgrad. Fordham U., 1971—. Lab. technician S.I. Hosp., 1949-50; teaching asst. biochemistry U. Vt., 1950-52; asst. biochemist Vt. Agr. Expt. Sta., 1952-56; research chemist Nat. Biscuit Co., 1956-57; research asst. hematology and chemotherapy Columbia-Presbyn. Med. Center, N.Y.C., 1957-61; instr. sci. Sch. Nursing, St. Michael Hosp., Newark, N.J., 1961-62; asst. prof. Jersey City State Coll., 1962-67, asso. prof. chemistry, 1967-74, prof., 1974—, chmn. dept., 1969-70. Resource mem. long range planning bd. Sch. Nursing, St. Francis Hosp., Jersey City, 1963—; resource mem., cons. meeting on chem. curriculum in jr. colls. NSF, 1969. Mem. Am. Chem. Soc., N.Y., N.J. acads. scis., Am. Microchem. Soc., Am. Inst. Chemists, Chemists Club N.Y.C. Revisor Roe's Principles of Chemistry, 12th edit., 1976. Mem. editorial panel Mosby's Comprehensive Review of Nursing, 7th and 8th edits. Home: 1225 76th St North Bergen NJ 07047 Office: Chemistry Dept Jersey City State Coll Jersey City NJ 07305

LAUGHLIN, ETHELREDA ELIZABETH ROSS, educator; b. Cleve., Nov. 13, 1922; d. Edward W. and Marie C. (Solinski) Ross; A.B., Flora Stone Mather Coll., 1942; M.S., Western Res. U., 1944, Ph.D., 1962; m. James J. Laughlin III, June 14, 1951 (div. June 1956); 1 son, J. Guy. Faculty Loyola U., Chgo., 1948-49, St. John Coll., Cleve., 1949-51; tchr. various schs., 1953-61; faculty Ferris State Coll., 1962-63; prof. chemistry Cuyahoga Community Coll., Western campus, Parma, O., 1963—, dept. head scis., 1965—; vis. prof. biochemistry Case Western Res. U., 1970-71. Biochemist in charge animal research Ben Venue Labs., 1947-48, Armour Research Labs., 1948, Western Res. U. Med. Sch., 1942-47; research fellow in biochemistry Cleve. Clinic Hosp. Labs., 1953. Mem. exec. com. Two-Year Coll. Chemistry Conf. Recipient Outstanding Two Year Coll. Chem. Teaching award Mfg. Chemists Assn., 1973. Recipient grants including Nat. Sci. Tchrs. Assn. grants, 1957-58, 58-59, NSF grants, 1958, 60, 61, 63. Mem. N.E.A., A.A.A.S., Am. Chem. Soc. (chmn. two year coll. conf. 1974), Nat. Sci. Tchrs. Assn., Ohio Coll. Chemistry Tchrs. Assn., Ohio Edn. Assn., Ohio Two Year Coll. Assn., Am. Assn. U. Profs., Audubon Soc., Sierra Club, Sigma Xi. Contbr. articles to publs. Home: 6486 State Rd 12 Concord Sq Village Parma OH 44134

LAUGHLIN, MARGUERITE WARD (MRS. KYLE E. LAUGHLIN), civic worker; b. Potlatch, Ida., June 23, 1908; d. Rutherford Burchard and Mayme Aurelia (Pease) Ward; B.A., U. Ida., 1929; student U. Cal. at Berkeley, 1929-30; m. Kyle Emmett Laughlin, June 11, 1933; children—Kay (Mrs. Donald W. Driscoll), Helen (Mrs. Clarence D. Bean), John Ward. Tchr. pub. schs., Moscow, Ida., 1931-33; co.-founder Moscow Community Kindergarten, 1945; pres. Moscow P.T.A., 1946, Ida. recreation chmn., 1947; chmn. Moscow Recreation Com., 1947-49; chmn. Moscow Mayor's Recreation Commn., 1950; apptd. Ida. Library Bd., 1968—, chmn., 1970-71, 73-74. Bd. dirs. Gritman Meml. Hosp., pres. aux., 1966, 69; trustee Moscow-Latah Library System; bd. dirs. United Fund, 1966-68. Mem. Am. Library Trustees Assn. (regional dir. 1970-71), Ida. (trustee of year 1967, pres. 1973-75), Pacific N.W., Am. library assns., P.E.O. (past state pres.), Library Assos. U. Ida. (pres. 1972-74), Alpha Phi. Unitarian. Home: Box 8126 Moscow ID 83843

LAUGHLIN, NAOMI MYERS (MRS. CYRIL J. LAUGHLIN), real estate broker; b. Oliver, Ill., Mar. 11, 1913; d. Jesse and Mary Grace (Macke) Myers; A.B., George Washington U., 1934; m. Otis A. Worthington, July 24, 1936 (dec.); m. 2d, Cyril James Laughlin, Feb. 19, 1955. Asso. with husband Worthington Realty, 1942-48, owner, operator, 1948-50; operator Worthington Employment and Secretarial Service, 1948-51; exec. v.p. Montgomery County (Md.) Bd. Realtors, Inc., 1950-70; real estate broker, 1948-50, 70—; v.p. Beers Bros., Inc., realtors, Silver Spring, Md., 1970—. Lectr. real estate. Bd. govs., dir. Washington Area Realtors Council, 1954-70, recording sec. 1955, 59, 64, 68. Vice pres. Woodmoor Citizens Assn., 1949. Mem. Nat. Assn. Realtors (regional v.p. exec. officers council 1953, 59-61, sec. 1961, dir. 1967-69; bd. govs. seminar 1962-64), Md. Assn. Realtors (asst. to pres. 1954). Am. Assn. U. Women (v.p. local chpt. 1948-49), Nat. Inst. Farm and Land Brokers (dir. Md. chpt., officer 1972—), Land Execs. Assn. (sec. 1972-73), Internat. Real Estate Fedn., Am. Soc. Assn. Execs., Met. Washington Real Estate Exchangors, Omega Tau Rho, Phi Pi Epsilon. Democrat. Roman Catholic. Club: Manor Country. Author articles real estate publs. Home: 13716 New Hampshire Av Silver Spring MD 20904 Office: 818 Roeder Rd Silver Spring MD 20910

LAUH, JULIE CHANG, broker; b. Shanghai, China, June 30, 1920; d. Yih Tsai and Te-yee (Hsi) Chang; student Sch. Bus. Columbia, 1940-41; came to U.S., 1939, naturalized, 1954; m. Richard T.Y. Lee, Oct. 6, 1939 (div. 1962); children—Benson P., James P.; m. 2d, Ernest T.S. Lauh, Aug. 17, 1962. Investment broker Hayden Stone & Co., N.Y.C., 1952-54, Fahnestock & Co., N.Y.C., 1954-62; tech. analyst commodity dept. Francis I. duPont & Co., N.Y.C., 1962-69; broker Loeb Rhoades & Co., N.Y.C., 1969—. Mem. Women Investment Brokers Club. Office: 42 Wall St New York City NY 10005

LAURAIN, BEATRICE EUNICE MATTER (MRS. JEAN LAURAIN), camp dir.; b. N.Y.C., Dec. 31, 1915; d. Nathan A. and Saida (Pessin) Matter; B.A., N.Y. U., 1937, M.A., 1943; postgrad. Delcroze Sch., 1943-44, Paris Conservatoire, 1946-47; m. Peter Glushanok, Dec. 3, 1937; m. 2d, Jean Laurain, May 23, 1947; children—Jonathan, Sabina. Dir. Creston Sch. Music and Dance, N.Y.C., 1938-44; choral condr. vocal song Interpretation, group piano instr. Taft Youth and Adult Center, Bronx, 1949-54; dir. chorus Dept. Immigration and Naturalization, N.Y.C., 1949-51; piano soloist, ensemble player, 1925-55; tchr. music dept. Joan of Arc Jr. High Sch., N.Y.C., 1953-55; dir. Breezemont Camp, Armonk, N.Y., 1937-71. Vice pres., chmn. program com. P.T.A. Armonk Schs., 1960-61; chmn. Music Drama and Art Com., Armonk, 1962-63; dir. mus. prodn. North Castle Players, 1959. Mem. Am. Camping Assn. (N.Y. chmn. day camp com. 1967-69), Psi Chi. Home: PO Box 98 Canaan NY 12029

LAURENCE, ELOISE, newspaper exec.; b. Thorndale, Tex., May 7, 1907; d. Eugene Larkin and Cornelia Agnes (Sides) Laurence; B.A., Howard Payne Coll., 1931. Tchr. elementary sch., Kennedy, Tex., 1931-32; asst. dean women, faculty English, Howard Payne Coll., Brownwood, Tex., 1934-35; tchr., Thrall, Tex., 1942-47; newspaper corr. Temple (Tex.) Daily Telegram, 1946-48; advt. mgr. Thorndale (Tex.) Champion, 1953—, mng. editor, 1969—. Recipient citation of merit State Tex., 1969; Pub. Service award Tex. Alcoholic Narcotics Edn. 1971; other awards. Mem. Am. Legion, V.F.W. (historian 1963—), Thorndale C. of C. Democrat. Baptist. Mem. Order Eastern Star (life). Writer weekly column Roving Eye, 1953. Home: 200 E Michalk St PO Box 215 Thorndale TX 76577 Office: Box 247 N Main St Thorndale TX 76577

LAURENCELLE, PATRICIA, educator; b. Bklyn., June 3, 1923; d. Adrien E. and Ethel (Redmond) Laurencelle; B.A., Bklyn. Coll., 1945; certificate in occupational therapy Columbia, 1946; M.A., Tufts U., 1953; Ph.D., Boston U., 1971. Staff occupational therapist Hosp. for Spl. Surgery, N.Y.C., 1946-48; from instr. to asst. prof. occupational therapy U. Kan., Lawrence, 1948-54; instr. English lang. Inst. Am. Studies, Athens, Greece, 1954-57; dir. dept. occupational therapy Dromokaiteion Therapeuterion, Athens, 1955-57; asso. prof., chmn. dept. occupational therapy Ind. U. Sch. Medicine, Indpls., 1957-62; grad. fellow Nat. Found., Boston U., 1962-65; sociologist Walter E. Fernald State Sch. for Mentally Retarded, Waltham, Mass., 1965-66; asso. prof., acting chmn. dept. occupational therapy Coll. of Health Related Professions, asso. prof. sociology Coll. Arts and Scis., U. Fla., Gainesville, 1966-67, asso. prof. for program devel. Coll. Health and Related Professions, 1968-70; prof., coordinator health related programs No. Ill. U., DeKalb, 1970-72; dir. Central Ill. consortium for health manpower, prof. health planning Sanqamon State U., 1972-74; prof. health edn. Coll. Medicine, So. Ill. U., Springfield, 1972-74; asso. dean for allied health and nursing programs, prof. community health, Sch. Medicine, Northwestern U., Chgo., 1974—. Am. del. World Fedn. Occupational Therapists, Toronto, Ont., Can., 1965—; mem. occupational therapy adv. com., social and rehab. services Dept. Health, Edn. and Welfare; mem. allied health adv. com. Health Edn. Commn., Ill. Bd. Higher Edn., 1972—. Mem. Am. Assn. Mental Deficiency, Am., Fla. (pres.) occupational therapy assns., Am. Sociol. Assn., So. Sociol. Soc., Soc. for Applied Anthropology, Soc. for Study Social Problems, Altrusa. Democrat. Roman Catholic. Contbr. chpts. to textbooks, articles to profl. Jours. Address: 6512 N Newgard Chicago IL 60626

LAURY, JEAN RAY (MRS. STANLEY BITTERS), designer; b. Doon, Ia., Mar. 22, 1928; d. Ralph and Alice (Kloek) Ray; B.A., No. Ia. U., 1950; M.A., Stanford U., 1956; m. Frank B. Laury, Sept. 20, 1952; children—Tom, Lizabeth; m. 2d, Stanley Bitters, Oct. 3, 1971. Writer, designer numerous mag. publs. including Better Homes, House Beautiful, Womans Day, House and Garden, others; exhibited in one-man shows at Mus. Contemporary Crafts, N.Y., Stanford U. Gallery, Fresno Arts Center, Henry Gallery, U. Wash.; exhibited in group shows at Pasadena Design VIII, IX, X, Cal. Craftsmen Show; represented in permanent collections United Cal. Bank, Fresno, Savs. & Loan, Salt Lake City, Student Union, Fresno State Coll. Partner Laury-Aiken Designers, Everywoman's Studio, 1966-70. Mem. Women's Internat. League for Peace and Freedom. Author: Applique Stitchery, 1966; Quilts and Coverlets: A Contemporary Approach, 1970; Doll Making: A Creative Approach, 1970; Wood Applique, 1972; Handmade Rugs, 1972; Creative Body Coverings, 1974; New Uses for Old Laces, 1974. Address: 25090 Auberry Rd Clovis CA 93612

LAUTZENHEISER, BARBARA JEAN IDA, ins. co. exec., actuary; b. LaFeria, Tex., Nov. 15, 1938; d. Fred E. and Verna V. (Springer) Lautzenheiser; B.A. magna cum laude, Neb. Wesleyan U., 1960. With Bankers Life Neb., Lincoln, 1960—, actuarial trainee, 1960-65, asst. actuary, 1965-69, asso. actuary, 1969-70, 2d v.p., actuary, 1970-72, v.p., actuary, 1972—; lectr. Mem. agy. relations com. Lincoln Community Services. Recipient Young Alumni Service award Neb. Wesleyan U., 1971, lifetime membership grant for highest 4 yr average for women Women's Wesleyan Edn. Council, 1960. Fellow Soc. Actuaries (pub. relations com.); mem. Am. Acad. Actuaries, Neb. Actuaries Club (sec.-treas. 1971-72, pres. 1972-73, chmn. bd. 1973-74), Am. Life Ins. Assn. (com. on sex equality), Life Office Mgmt. Assn. (corp. financial planning com.), Phi Kappa Phi (Gold Key 1960), Pi Gamma Mu. Christian Scientist (local trustee). Contbr. articles to profl. jours. Home: 4835 Ginny Av Lincoln NE 68516 Office: Bankers Life Ins Co Cotner and O Sts Lincoln NE 68501

LAUX, DOROTHY CLAIRE, coll. adminstr.; b. Nashville, June 14, 1918; d. Henry and Barbara (Gabriel) Laux; diploma St. Mary's Hosp., 1939; B.S., Edgecliff Coll., 1956; M.A., George Peabody Coll., 1965. Staff nurse Vanderbilt Hosp., Nashville, 1939-40; pvt. duty nurse Nashville Hosps., 1940-41; occupational nurse Curtiss Wright, St. Louis, and Vultee Corp., Nashville, 1941-46; relief supr., head nurse VA Hosp., Nashville, 1946-60; asst. dir., instr. St. Thomas Sch. Nursing, Nashville, 1956-67; faculty U. Tenn., Nashville, 1967—, dir. div. nursing, 1967—; lectr. in field. Chmn. program com. Council of Asso. Degree Nursing Program in Tenn., 19—. Mem. Am., Tenn. (mem. standing com. on econ. and gen. welfare 1967-69) nurses assns., Nat., North Central Tenn. (chmn. nominating com.) leagues for nursing, Tenn. Edn. Assn., Am., Tenn. heart assns., Tenn. Student Nurses Assn. (panel mem. dist. 3), Council Deans and Chmn. Collegiate Programs Tenn. Home: 810 Summerly Dr Nashville TN 37209 Office: 323 McLemore St Nashville TN 37203

LAVALLARD, MARIE LOUISE (MRS. JOHN ALBERT LAVALLARD), editor, educator; b. Bklyn., July 13, 1912; d. Egmont William and Louise Christina (Koch) Froehlich; B.S., Cornell U., 1932, M.S., 1933; m. John Albert Lavallard, May 1, 1936. Sec.-technician Cornell U. Med. Center, N.Y.C., 1933-36; sec., asst. information specialist U. Vt. and State Agrl. Coll., 1936-46; asst. editor U. Ark. Agrl. Expt. Sta., Fayetteville, 1946-51, asso. editor, 1951-61, editor, research asso., 1961—, tchr. grad. course sci. writing, 1969—. Mem. U. Ark. Found. for Internat. Exchange Students, 1951—, pres., 1960-62, v.p., 1966-67, rec. sec., 1967—. Mem. Council Biology Editors, Am. Assn. Agrl. Coll. Editors, Pi Beta Phi, Gamma Sigma Delta. Club: Fayetteville Evening Lady Lions. Home: 940 Peel St Fayetteville AR 72701

LAVENDER, BEVERLY PAULINE SCHWARTZ (MRS. JOSEPH LAVENDER), psychologist; b. N.Y.C., Aug. 5, 1923; d. Louis and Miriam (Leventhal) Schwartz; student Hunter Coll., 1940-56; B.S. cum laude, U. Hartford, 1960, M.S., 1965; sch. psychologist certificate So. Conn. State Coll., 1970; m. Joseph Lavender, Aug. 16, 1942; children—Judith, Joan. Tchr. elementary sch., West Hartford, Conn., 1960-65; psychol. examiner New Britain (Conn.) Sch. Dept., 1965-69, coordinator psychol. services, 1970; therapeutic teen-age group leader Grove Hill Clinic, New Britain, 1970-71; psychol. cons., West Hartford (Conn.) Sch. Dept., 1971—. Mem. Nat., Conn. assns. sch. psychologists, Nat., Conn., West Hartford edn. assns., Assn. for Humanistic Psychology. Democrat. Home: 39 Parsons Dr West Hartford CT 06117 Office: 7 Whiting Lane West Hartford CT 06107

LAVENDER, PATZY HAUSMANN (MRS. WENDELL EUGENE LAVENDER), psychologist; b. New Orleans, Mar. 5, 1930; d. Henry and Margaret Stepbacher (Adler) Hausmann; student Tulane U., 1947-49, U. Conn., 1963-66; B.A., U. Bridgeport, 1968; M.S., So. Conn. State Coll., 1971, postgrad., 1971—; m. Wendell Eugene Lavender, Mar. 31, 1973; children—Margaret (Mrs. Peter Higle), Kathryn Ann (Mrs. Eugene Lyon). Clk., F.A.O. Schwarz Co., N.Y.C., 1949-50; water safety instr. YWCA, Stamford, Conn., 1957-63, Stamford Jewish Center, 1959-66; head waterfront dept. So. Westchester council Girl Scouts U.S.A., 1958-60; psychologist Mid-Fairfield Child Guidance Clinic, 1969-70, New Canaan Pub. Schs., 1969-70, Stamford Pub. Schs., 1970—. Dog show judge Am. Kennel Club, 1968—. Mem. Am. Psychol. Assn., Putnam (past pres.), Ox Ridge, Greenwich kennel clubs, Psi Chi. Presbyn. (deacon). Home: 90 Lawrence Hill Rd Stamford CT 06903 Office: Turn of River School Vine Rd Stamford CT 06903

LAVERY, BEATRICE CANTERBURY (MRS. EMMET G. LAVERY JR.), city ofcl.; b. Los Angeles, Jan. 20, 1926; d. Charles Milton and Bernice Mae (Peacock) Canterbury; A.B., U. So. Cal., 1948; m. Emmet G. Lavery, Sept. 27, 1963; children—Geoffrey, Tracy. Editor Whittier (Cal.) Reporter, 1944; reporter Wave Publs., Los Angeles, 1944-45; with Publicity Pfd., Los Angeles, 1946-48; press rep. NBC, Hollywood, 1949-52; fashion dir. Bullocks Dept. Store, Los Angeles, 1960-63; advt. dir. Rose Marie Reid Swimsuits, Los Angeles, 1963-65; merchandising dir. Compton Advt., Los Angeles, 1966-67; freelance advt. and pub. relations cons., 1967-70; adminstrv. coordinator to mayor of Los Angeles, 1973—. Publicity Mannequins of the Assistance League of So. Cal., 1954-56; worker pub. rleations UN Assn., Los Angeles, 1953-54, Encino Property Owners Assn., 1968-72; campaign worker Janice Bernstein candidate for Sch. Bd., Los Angeles, 1970; mem. Speakers Bur. Alan Cranston for senator campaign, 1968; pub. relations worker Tom Bradley for mayor campaign, 1969, 73. Mem. bd. gov's. U. So. Cal., 1973—. Recipient award Media Women Founder's 1970, award Los Angeles City Human Relations Bur., 1970. Mem. Women in Communications (pres. 1949-51), Los Angeles Advt. Women (Lulu award 1965), Fashion Group (dir. 1958-63), Hollywood Women's Press Club, U. So. Cal. Journalism Alumni Assn. (pres. 1972-73). Home: 5120

Encino Av Encino CA 91316 Office: 200 N Spring St Los Angeles CA 90012

LAVIETES, BEVERLY BLATT (MRS. MARC HARRY LAVIETES), biologist, educator; b. Pitts., Mar. 17, 1944; d. Simon and Sadie (Skigen) Blatt; A.B. magna cum laude, Vassar Coll., 1965; Ph.D. (NSF fellow), Case-Western Res. U., 1969; m. Marc Harry Lavietes, Aug. 13, 1966; 1 son, Bryan Ross. Am. Cancer Soc. fellow N.Y. U. Sch. Medicine, N.Y.C., 1969-70, NIH fellow, 1970-71, asst. prof. dept. pathology, 1971—. NIH research grantee, 1971—. Mem. Soc. for Developmental Biology, N.Y. Acad. Scis., Fedn. Am. Scientists, Am. Soc. Zoologists, A.A.A.S. Contbr. articles to profl. jours. Home: 35 Mercer St New York City NY 10013

LAVIN, ALICE MARIE (MRS. JAMES JOSEPH LAVIN), editor; b. Boston, Sept. 21, 1920; d. John Patrick and Alice Marie (Kaveney) Murphy; B.S., Simmons Coll., 1942; postgrad. Boston U., 1969-73; m. James Joseph Lavin, Dec. 27, 1960. Editor Topics mag., New Eng. Tel. & Tel., Boston, 1949—. Asso. in indsl. editing Simmons Coll. Dept. Publ., Boston, 1972-74. Mem. Am., Internat. assns. bus. communicators, Pub. Club Boston, Proparvulis Club. Home: 55 Hunting Rd Needham MA 02194 Office: New England Telephone and Telegraph Co 99 High St Boston MA 02110

LAVINE, BESS BLAFKIN (MRS. IRVIN A. LAVINE), judge; b. Phila., Nov. 29, 1927; d. Jacob and Bessie (Hetkin) Blafkin; B.A., George Washington U., 1949; LL.B., U. Balt., 1959; m. Irvin A. Lavine, Mar. 21, 1948; children—Sherrie, Hilary Rae, Matt. Dir. student activities Hillel Found., George Washington U., 1949; admitted to Md. bar, 1959; chief judge Orphans Ct. Prince Georges County, 1954-62; practice law, Hyattsville, 1962-69; master Juvenile Ct. Prince Georges County, 1969—. Chmn. Washington Foster Parent Program, 1964. Md. Presdl. elector, 1960; pres. Women's Democratic Club, 1963-65. Pres. Prince Georges Boys Home, 1971; v.p. Md. Commn. Fair Representation, 1962-64; bd. dirs. League Women Voters, 1952-54. Mem. Md., Prince Georges bar assns. Mem. B'nai B'rith (dir. Anti-Defamation League 1967—). Home: 10803 Pleasant Acres Dr Adelphi MD 20783 Office: Courthouse Upper Marlboro MD

LAVINE, EILEEN MARTINSON (MRS. RICHARD BENNETT LAVINE), editor, writer; b. N.Y.C., Dec. 28, 1924; d. Herman and Sylvia (Eichler) Martinson; B.A., U. Wis., 1945; M.S. in Journalism, Columbia, 1946; postgrad. U. Paris, 1950-51; m. Richard Bennett Lavine, Jan. 13, 1957; children—Michael Herman, Amy Barbara. Reporter, asst. Sunday editor New Bedford (Mass.) Standard-Times, 1946-47; asst. to moderator N.Y. Times Youth Forums, 1948-50; publicity writer Joint Def. Appeal, N.Y.C., 1952-55; editor Better Times, 1955-59, Civil Liberties in N.Y., 1955-61; writer, editor, social welfare, health, civic affairs, 1959-61; writer, editor PR Assos., Washington, 1962-68; writer, editor, bd. dirs. Information Services, Inc., Bethesda, Md., 1968—. Recipient Wis. Alumni Assn. Award, 1945. Mem. Am. Civil Liberties Union, League Women Voters, Nat. Assn. Sci. Writers. Democrat. Author: Learning to Work with the Aged; also articles. Home: 8102 Hampden Lane Bethesda MD 20014 Office: 9650 Rockville Pike Bethesda MD 20014

LAVINE, FRANCES HOFFMAN (MRS. MAX H. LAVINE), newspaper exec.; b. Chgo., Jan. 7, 1906; d. Louis and Sophie (Tauber) Hoffman; student Northwestern U., 1924, Gloucester (Mass.) Theater, 1923, Goodman Theater Sch., Chgo., 1926; m. Max H. Lavine, Dec. 26, 1935; 1 son, John Morgan. Dramatic dir. House Top Studio Theater Arts, Duluth, Minn., 1926-39; founder, dir. Children's Theater, Duluth, 1928-37; one woman show for various colls. and clubs, 1933—; narrator Nutcracker Ballet, Duluth Symphony, 1957, 59, Peter and the Wolf Symphony, 1961; drama artist in residence on number of coll. campuses, 1965—; pres. Daily Register, newspaper, Portage, Wis., 1964—; pres. Herald Telegram Pub. Co., Chippewa Falls, Wis.; adv. bd. KDAL Radio-TV Corp., Pilot tchr. Mom Program, 1965; resident volunteer tchr. Job Corps, 1968. Exec. bd. Duluth Superior Ednl. TV Corp., bd. dirs. U. Wis. Found., Superior; trustee St. Joseph's Hosp., 1965, Coll. of St. Scholastica, Duluth, Minn. Mem. Nat. Friends of Pub. Broadcasting. Home: 1 Billings Dr Superior WI 54880

LAVINE, THELMA Z. (MRS. JEROME SACHS), educator; b. Boston, Feb. 12, 1915; d. Samuel Alexander and Gussie (Pearlman) Lavine; A.B. magna cum laude, Radcliffe Coll., 1936; M.A., Harvard, 1937, Ph.D., 1939; m. Jerome Sachs, Mar. 31, 1944; 1 dau., Margaret Vera. Asst. instr. Smith Coll., 1937-38; instr. Wells Coll., 1941-43, asst. prof., 1945-46; asst. prof. Bklyn. Coll., 1946-54; asst. prof. U. Md., 1955-57, asso. prof., 1957-62, prof., 1962-65; Elton prof. philosophy George Washington U., Washington, 1965—, chmn. dept. philosophy, 1969—, mem. com. M.A. in women's studies, 1973—. Named Outstanding Faculty Mem., Md. U., 1965, Outstanding Prof. award George Washington U., 1968. Mem. Am. Philos. Assn., Washington Philosophy Club (exec. bd. 1966-67, pres. 1967-68), Am. Assn. U. Profs., Phi Beta Kappa (mem. Ralph Waldo Emerson award com. 1973—). Clubs: George Washington University; Radcliffe. Contbr. articles to profl. jours., books. Home: 1625 35th St NW Washington DC 20007

LAVOIE, LISE MARIE, med social worker; b. Lauzon, Que., Can., Dec. 8, 1936; d. Joseph and Rose (Latulippe) Lavoie; B.A., College Angele Merici Ursulines de Que., 1958; Maitrise en Service Social, U. Laval, 1961. Social worker Hotel Dieu, Quebec, 1961-62; with Hotel Dieu de Levis (Que.), 1962—, head med. social service, 1962—. Home: 335 St Joseph Lauzon PQ Canada Office: 143 Wolfe St Levis PQ Canada

LAVRICH, KATHRYN MARY DEFLER (MRS. JAMES H. LAVRICH), physician; b. Longmont, Colo., Apr. 19, 1924; d. Joseph A. and Margaret (Foidl) Defler; B.A., U. Colo., 1945; M.D., Washington U., 1951; m. James H. Lavrich, Oct. 2, 1955; children—Carol, Richard, Philip, Judith, Kenneth. Intern, Cin. Gen. Hosp., 1951-52; resident Childrens Hosp., Cin., 1952-54; pvt. practice medicine, specializing in pediatrics, Euclid, O., 1956—; asst. pediatrician Western Res. U. Mem. Adv. Bd. on Ecology, Richmond Heights, O., 1972—. Mem. No. Ohio Pediatric Soc. Home: 4908 Karen Isle Dr Richmond Heights OH 44143 Office: 25100 Euclid Av Euclid OH 44117

LAW, AMY STAUBER (MRS. WILLIAM R. LAW), biochemist; b. Phila., June 26, 1938; d. Leslie Alfred and Mabel G. (Fisher) Stauber; B.A., Mt. Holyoke Coll., 1959; M.S., U. Del., 1963, Ph.D., 1969; m. William R. Law, Oct. 29, 1965. Chemist, New Brunswick (N.J.) lab. U.S. AEC, 1957-59; research fellow U. Del., 1959-61, 65-68; research chemist AviSun Corp., Marcus Hook, Pa., 1961-65; chief lab. sect. meat inspection div. State Bd. Agr., Dover, Del., 1968-69; biochemist Wilmington (Del.) Med. Center, 1969—. Mem. A.A.A.S., Am. Assn. Clin. Chemists, Am. Women in Sci., Am. Chem. Soc. (pres. Del. biochem. sect. 1974), Sigma Xi. Club: Wilmington Trail (pres. 1970). Home: 720 Brook Dr Newark DE 19711 Office: Wilmington Med Center PO Box 1951 Wilmington DE 19899

LAW, GENEVIEVE V. PIERCE (MRS. LINWOOD BRACKETT LAW), artist; b. Newark, N.Y.; d. Frederick Russell and Anna Mary (Corey) Pierce; student Albright Art Sch., 1933-34, U. Buffalo, 1960-61; m. Linwood Brackett Law, Mar. 9, 1935; 1 son, Linwood Pierce. Exhibited one man shows Crane Library, Top of the Town, Erie County Savs. Bank, Statler Hilton Hotel; exhibited in group shows Kenan Gallery, Lockport, N.Y., Lakeview Gallery, Georgetown Gallery, Buffalo, Erie County Community Coll., Charles Birchfield Center, State U. N.Y. at Buffalo, Central Park Gallery, Buffalo, Albright-Knox Art Gallery, Buffalo, Chautauqua Inst., Carleton House, Canisius Coll., Roswell Park Gallery, Nat. League Am. Pen Women, Jr. League Art Gallery, Asso. Art Orgn. Gallery, Buffalo White House, State U. N.Y. Buffalo, Upton Hall, Wilcox Galleries, others; represented in permanent collections Cornell U., Ithaca, N.Y., Statler Hotel, N.Y.C., Am. embassies Cairo, Egypt and Istanbul, Turkey, pvt. and corp. collections. Recipient numerous awards Allentown Art Festival, Erie County Fair Fine Arts, Guild Allied Arts, Kenmore Ministers Assn. Religious Art Festival, Kenmore Art Soc., Williamstown Art Soc., Greater Buffalo Area C. of C. show, others. Mem. Nat. League Am. Pen Women, Buffalo Soc. Artists (pres. 1967-68), Kenmore, Williamsville art socs., Asso. Art Orgn. Western N.Y., Buffalo and Erie County, Morristown hist. socs. Home: 529 Norwood Av Buffalo NY 14222

LAWING, JUDITH COTTINGHAM (MRS. FORNEY FENIMORE LAWING, JR.), coll. dean; b. Georgetown, S.D., July 23, 1943; d. John DeWitte and Eleanor Gertrude (Mims) Cottingham; B.S. cum laude, Coker Coll., 1965; postgrad. Clemson U., 1969; m. Forney Fenimore Lawing, Jr., May 29, 1966; 1 dau., Wanda Stacelane. Tchr., Olanta (S.C.) High Sch., 1965-66, Landrum (S.C.) High Sch., 1966-68; instr. Horry-Georgetown Tech. Edn. Center, Conway, S.C., 1968-70, field rep., 1970-73, dean of students, 1973—. Mem. Am., S.C. (S.C. membership chmn. 1973-74) coll. personnel assns., Am., S.C. personnel and guidance assns., Am. Sch. Counselors Assn., Carolinas Assn. Collegiate Registrars and Admissions Officers, Nat. Assn. Student Personnel Adminstrs., S.C. Edn. Assn. Home: 605 Jasmine Av Myrtle Beach SC 29577 Office: Box 710 Conway SC 29526

LAWLER, LUCILLE DUFFY (MRS. JAMES T. LAWLER), educator, author; b. Ridgway, Ill., Oct. 3, 1908; d. John and Hannah (Doherty) Duffy; student So. Ill. U.; m. James T. Lawler, Dec. 27, 1932; children—Joseph, Ellen (Mrs. Gary Walsh), Patrick, Raymond, William, Lucy. Tchr., Shawneetown (Ill.) Schs., 1957-72, Ridgway (Ill.) Schs., 1972—. Leader, Gallatin County 4-H Clubs, 1949-73. First pres. Gallatin County Hist. Soc., Ill. Hist. Congress; v.p. Ill. Hist. Soc. Mem. Gallatin County Homemakers, Nat. League Am. Pen Women (pres. Ill.), Daus. of Isabella (regent). Author: Gallatin County-Gateway to Illinois, 1968; Ridgway, Our Town, 1971. Home: Rural Route 1 Ridgway IL 62979

LAWLER, RUTH CURRY, judge; b. New Orleans, Feb. 13, 1900; d. Henry Thomas and Carrie Mary (Aycock) Lawler; B.Music, H. Sophie Newcomb Coll., 1921; B.A., Our Lady of the Lake Coll., 1931. Tchr. English and dramatics, Castroville (Tex.) High Sch., 1951-61; owner, operator Landmark Inn, Castroville, 1942—; judge municipal ct., Castroville, 1965—. Councilwoman City of Castroville, Tex., 1964-72; mayor pro tem, Castroville, Tex., 1969-72. Mem. bd. trustees Medina County Hosp., 1961-63, Castroville Pub. Library, 1962-72, Castroville (Tex.) Pub. Sch., 1949-52. Recipient Woman of the Year award C. of C., 1971. Mem. San Antonio Conservation Soc. Democrat. Roman Catholic. Club: Castroville Garden. Author: The Story of Castroville: Its People, Founder and Traditions, 1968. Home: PO Box 340 Castroville TX 78009 Office: Landmark Inn PO Box 340 Castroville TX 78009

LAWLER, VIRGINIA TEMPLE, univ. adminstr.; b. Chapaign, Ill., Aug. 16, 1938; d. Arthur Rice and Leta Olga (Schissler) Temple; B.S., U. Ill., 1960; postgrad. U. N.C., 1960-62; m. Michael Henry Lawler, Apr. 27, 1962 (div. July 1972); children—Robin Lee, Brian Arthur. Columnist, Chapel Hill (N.C.) Weekly, 1960-62; sec. U. N.C. Inst. Govt., Chapel Hill, 1962-63, asst. librarian, 1963-64, acting librarian, 1964-65; adminstrv. asst. to pub. information dir. N.C. Fund Ford Found. project, Durham, 1965-67; editor U. Ill., Urbana, 1968-73, asst. dean campus programs and services, 1973-74, asso. dean campus programs and services, 1974—. Mem. nat. career merchandising bd. Mademoiselle mag., N.Y.C., 1968. Program and pub. coordinator region VIII Am. Coll. Theatre Festival, Urbana, 1971, 72. Mem. Nat. League Am. Pen Women (local v.p. 1970), Women in Communications (local v.p. 1973), D.A.R., Internat. Platform Assn., Alpha Chi Omega. Home: Route 1 Box 156 Tolono IL 61880 Office: Student Services Bldg U Ill Champaign IL 61820

LAWLESS, BETTY JO, phys. therapy cons.; b. Denver, Jan. 5, 1924; d. William W. and Ruth R. (Pomeroy) Lawless; B.S., Western Ill. U., 1945; certificate in Phys. Therapy (Nat. Found. grant), U. Minn., 1946-47; M.E. in Occupational Therapy, Colo. State U., 1954-55. Gen. therapist Quincy (Ill.) Clinic, 1947-50; chief phys. and occupational therapist Alaska Crippled Children, Anchorage, 1955-59; supervising therapist San Bernardino County (Cal.) Health, 1964-69; cons. crippled children's services Cal. Dept. Health, San Francisco, 1969—. Served with USAF, 1951-55, 59-63. Mem. Am. Phys. Therapy Assn., Am. Occupational Therapy Assn., Cal. State Employees Assn., Alpha Sigma Alpha. Mem. Order Eastern Star. Home: 10487 Westacres Dr Cupertino CA 95014 Office: 30 Van Ness Room 2006 San Francisco CA 94102

LAWLOR, CATHLEEN FRANCES MOYNAHAN (MRS. JOHN J. LAWLOR), former state ofcl.; b. N.Y.C., Aug. 20, 1912; d. Patrick A. and Catherine R. (Carroll) Moynahan; B.S., St. Johns U., 1937; diploma, Fordham U. Sch. Social Work, 1941; m. John J. Lawlor, Sept. 1, 1951 (dec. Mar. 1965). Acting dir. St. Mary's Hosp., Bklyn., 1941-42; sr. med. social worker WPA, Chronic and Acute Housekeeping Service, N.Y.C., 1942-43, Social Service Dept., Mount Sinai Hosp., N.Y.C., 1943-47; area med. social worker Bur. Med. Care, N.Y. State Dept. Social Welfare, Albany, 1948-51, sr. med. social worker, 1955-56, supr. cons. on eye health Commn. for Blind, N.Y.C., 1957-68; sr. welfare cons. (med.) Bur. Med. Care, N.Y. State Dept. Social Services, 1968-74, ret. Mem. N.Y. State Fedn. Workers for Blind (dir. 1965-66), Nat. Assn. Social Workers, Am. Acad. Social Workers, N.Y. State Welfare Conf., Civil Service Employees Assn., Sigma Chi Epsilon. Home: 3332 N Garden Roswell NM 88201

LAWN, ELISABETH REEVES CALVERLEY, educator, occupational therapist; b. York, Pa., Nov. 10, 1914; d. Edwin Elliott and Eleanor (Taylor) Calverley; B.A., Mt. Holyoke Coll., 1937; M.A., Columbia, 1941; occupational therapy certificate U. Pa., 1955; M.S. (research grantee), State U. N.Y. at Buffalo, 1971; m. Evan Lawn, May 1944 (div. July 1953); 1 son, Roger Colby. Tchr., asst. prin. Am. Sch. for Girls, Baghdad, Iraq, 1937-40; tchr. Moravian Sem. and Coll., Bethlehem, Pa., 1941-43; asst. engr. Pratt & Whitney, Hartford, Conn., 1943-44; ednl. therapist Chestnut Lodge Sanitarium, Rockville, Md., 1944-46; ednl., occupational therapy aide VA Hosp., Coatesville, Pa., 1952-53; acting dir. occupational therpy dept. Tb Sanitarium, Phila., 1955-56, Embreeville (Pa.) Neuropsychiat. Hosp., 1956-65; faculty State U. N.Y. at Buffalo, 1965—, asst. prof. occupational therapy, 1971—. Activities cons. Western N.Y. nursing homes. Mem. Am. Assn. U. Profs., Am. Assn. U. Women, Am., N.Y. State occupational therapy assns., World Fedn. Occupational Therapists, Internat. Platform Assn., Am., N.Y. civil liberties unions. Republican. Contbr. articles to publs. Home: Bldg 40 Williamstowne Ct Cheektowaga NY 14227 Office: Diefendorf Hall State U NY Buffalo NY 14215

LAWNER, ETHEL GERALDINE, physician; b. Bklyn.; d. Nicholas and Sadie (Tartikoff) Lawner; student Hood Coll., 1938-40; A.B., U. N.C., 1942; M.D., N.Y. Med. Coll., 1945; m. Irving Marshall, June 8, 1947; children—Sydne Barbara, Nina Beth, Madeline Elissa (dec.). Intern, Jersey City Med. Center, 1945-46, asst. resident, 1946-48, chief endocrine service and endocrine clinic, 1966-70, cons. staff endocrine dept., 1970—, also mem. exec. bd., 1968; asst. resident Flower Fifth Av., Hosp., N.Y.C., 1948-49; pvt. practice internal medicine and endocrinology, 1950—; med. dir. Job Corps, Jersey City, 1970-71; attending physician Fairmount Hosp., Jersey City; courtesy staff Christ Hosp. (Jersey City); attending staff The Jewish Hosp. and Rehab. Center of Jersey City; bd. mgrs. Jersey City Med. Center, 1972—. A founder, 1st pres. Citizens' Com. of Hudson County, 1965-67; chmn. Citizen's Com. to Save J.F.K. Blvd. Mem. Bus. and Profl. Women Assn. Jersey City, League of Women Voters, Nat. Council Jewish Women, Planned Parenthood Assn. Jersey City (mem. exec. bd.), Hudson County Med. Soc., Am. Med. Women's Assn., N.J. Diabetes Assn. Home: 1905 Kennedy Blvd Jersey City NJ 07305

LAWRENCE, ARLINE BERYL (MRS. WHITNEY ELMORE LAWRENCE), ednl. adminstr.; b. Berkeley, Cal., Sept. 9, 1923; d. Cecil Ray and Elaine Helen (Burwell) Roby; student McKinley Bus. Sch., 1941; m. Whitney Elmore Lawrence, June 11, 1944; children—Cynthia (Mrs. John Phillips), Kerry (Mrs. Garrett Watty), Mark, Julia. Adminstrv. sec. Mech. Trade Bld, Oakland, Cal., 1968, First Presbyn. Ch., Oakland, 1969, Albany (Cal.) Adult Sch., 1971—. Mem. Cal. Writers. Presbyn. Contbr. poetry to newspapers. Home: 645 27th St Richmond CA 94804 Office: 904 Talbot St Albany CA 94706

LAWRENCE, CHARLOTTE GRACE, educator; b. Bklyn., May 30, 1938; d. Elmer Gilbert and Eleanor Day (Foster) Lawrence; B.S., Emerson Coll., 1960; M.A., Syracuse U., 1964. Speech therapist Bd. Coop. Instrn., Onondaga County, N.Y., 1960-63; tchr. English, Fabius (N.Y.) Central Sch., 1964-66; tchr. English, speech Seminole Jr. Coll., Sanford, Fla., 1966-74, adminstr., 1974—. Mem. Nat. Assn. Parliamentarians, Nat. Council Tchrs. English, Speech Communication Assn. Am. Home: PO Box 534 Lake Mary FL 32746 Office: Seminole Jr Coll Sanford FL 32771

LAWRENCE, DEAN GRAYSON, lawyer; b. Oakland, Cal.; d. Henry C. and Myrtle (Grayson) Schmidt; A.B., U. Cal. at Berkeley, 1934, J.D., 1939. Admitted to Cal. bar, 1943, Supreme Count of U.S. bar, 1967; asso. with Pillsbury, Madison & Sutro, San Francisco, 1944-45; gen. practice, Oakland, 1946-50, San Jose, 1952-60, Grass Valley, 1960-63, 66—; county counsel Nevada County, 1964-65; bd. suprs. 2d dist., 1969—, chmn., 1971; sec. Nev. County Humane Animal Shelter Bd., 1966—, Nev. County Humane Soc., 1966—. Mem. Am. Assn. U. Women, State Bar Cal., Bus. and Profl. Women's Club, Phi Beta Kappa, Sigma Xi, Kappa Beta Pi, Pi Mu Epsilon, Pi Lambda Theta. Episcopalian. Office: Alta Vista Dr Grass Valley CA 95945

LAWRENCE, EILEEN BARNETT (MRS. EDWARD LAWRENCE), librarian; b. Centralia, Ill.; d. George Levi and Essie (Sherrod) Barnett; student Wilson Jr. Coll., 1937-40; Ph.B., Loyola U., Chgo., 1950; postgrad. Chgo. Tchrs. Coll., 1964-65; m. Edward Lawrence, Apr. 29, 1949; children—Trumagne (Mrs. Vernell Fleming), Stephanie (Mrs. Charles Pearson). Library asst. Englewood High Sch., Chgo., 1945-46, DuSable High Sch., Chgo., 1946-47; 1st asst. Oakland Br. Library, Chgo., 1958-64; br. librarian Frederick Douglass Br. Library, Chgo., 1964-69, dir. neighborhood center library, 1969—. Mem. Model Cities Edn. Task Force, 1968-69; community rep. Outreach, 1973—. Bd. dirs. Lawndale Homemakers, 1974-75; mem. Ill. Scholarship Commn., 1974—. Mem. Internat. Platform Assn. Office: 3353 W 13th St Chicago IL 60623

LAWRENCE, JOAN SMITH, lawyer; b. Seattle, Feb. 8, 1932; d. Irving D. and Dorothy C. (Cox) Smith; B.A., U. Wash., 1953, J.D. (Mortar Bd. scholar), 1969; m. Joseph C. Lawrence, 1954 (div. 1972); children—Joseph C. III, Gregory Bruce, Josanne Denise. Admitted to Wash. bar, 1969; mem. firm Skeel, McKelvy, Henke, Evenson & Betts, Seattle, 1969-73, Sullivan & Assos., Seattle, 1973—. Coordinator, Wash. Supreme Court com. on jury instructions, Seattle, 1972. Mem. Wash. (mem. rules com. 1972), Seattle-King County (chmn. judiciary and courts com. 1972-73) bar assns., Order of Coif, Mortar Bd., Law Rev., Phi Beta Kappa, Phi Alpha Delta. Home: 2127 170th St NE Bellevue WA 98008 Office: Hoge Bldg Seattle WA 98104

LAWRENCE, JOSEPHINE, author; b. Newark; d. Elijah Wiley and Mary Elizabeth (Barker) Lawrence; ed. pub. schs. and spl. courses N.Y.U.; m. Artur Platz, Oct. 19, 1940. Author books, 1921—, including: Double Wedding Ring, 1946; The Pleasant Morning Light, 1948; My Heart Shall Not Fear, 1949; The Way Things Are, 1950; The Picture Window, 1951; Song in the Night, 1952; The Web of Time, 1953; The Gates of Living, 1955; The Empty Nest, 1956; The Prodigal, 1957; The Ring of Truth, 1958; All Our Tomorrows, 1959; Hearts Do Not Break, 1960; The Amiable Meddlers, 1961; Remember When We Had a Doorman?, 1971; All the Years of Her Life, 1972; Retreat With Honor, 1973. Office: care Brandt and Brandt 101 Park Av New York City NY 10017

LAWRENCE, LOUISE (MRS. ALTUS LEON SIMPSON), educator; b. Massillon, O., Apr. 28, 1927; d. Carl Wynn and Ruth Wynetta (Moser) Lawrence; A.A., Santa Monica City Coll., 1947-49; B.A., Cal. State U., 1966, M.A., 1968; postgrad. U. So. Cal., 1972; m. Altus Leon Simpson, Dec. 20, 1970; 1 dau., Candace Warren. Tchr., lectr. John Powers Studio, Beverly Hills, Cal., 1958-62; tng. cons. Western Air Lines, Los Angeles, 1961-67, Host Internat., Inc., Los Angeles, 1961—, Rose Loos Med., Los Angeles, 1964-65, Santiago Bank, Tustin, Cal., 1972—; coordinator stewardess-hostess program Cypress (Cal.) Coll., 1966—. Pres. P.T.A., Terrance, Cal., 1957-58; chmn. Heart Fund, Terrance, 1958-59. Mem. Cal. Aerospace Edn. Assn., Cal. Tchr. Assn., Cypress Coll. Faculty Assn. Contbr. articles to profl. jours. Patentee in field. Office: Cypress College 9200 Valley View Cypress CA 90630

LAWRENCE, MARGERY H(ULINGS) (MRS. CLAY LAWRENCE), utilities exec.; b. Harmarville, Pa., June 17, 1934; d. Richard Nuttall and Alva (Burns) Hulings; student Bethany Coll., 1951-52; B.S. in Home Econs., Carnegie-Mellon U., 1955; m. 2d, Clay Lawrence, Dec. 10, 1971. Asst. mdse. buyer Joseph Horne Co., Pitts., 1955-57; home econs. editor Pitts. Group Cos. Columbia Gas System, Pitts., 1957-64, dir. home econs., 1968-72; home economist Columbia Gas Pa., Jeannette, 1964-68, dist. marketing mgr., 1972-73, mgr. dist. gas utilization, 1973—. Pub. relations chmn. Pitts. Home Economists in Bus., 1970-71, chmn. ways and means, 1972—. Mem. Am. Gas Assn. (Home Service Achievement award 1964), Am., Pa. home econs. assns., Pa. Gas Assn. (residential com.). Episcopalian.

Republican. Office: Columbia Gas Pa Inc 1405 McFarland Rd Pittsburgh PA 15216

LAWRENCE, SISTER MARY, educator; b. Toledo, June 6, 1907; d. Frank Dean and Margaret Agnes (Casey) Wilson; B.S. in Edn., Toledo Tchrs. Coll., 1936; M.A., Fordham U., 1944, Ph.D., 1948. Dean, Mary Manse Coll., Toledo, 1948-64, pres., 1964-68, dir. alumnae relations, prof. edn., 1968—, elementary sch. supr. diocese Toledo, 1972-73, curriculum coordinator, 1973—. Trustee, Med. Coll. Ohio, Toledo, 1964—. Mem. Assn. Higher Edn., Nat. Soc. Study of Edn., N.E.A., Am. Assn. U. Profs. Club: Zonta Internat. Home: 2436 Parkwood Ave Toledo OH 43620 Office: 2413 Collingwood Blvd Toledo OH 43620

LAWRENCE, MARY WELLS BERG, advt. exec.; b. Youngstown, O., May 25, 1928; d. Waldemar and Violet (Meltz) Berg; ed. Carnegie Inst. Tech., 1949; LL.D., Babson Coll., 1970; m. Harding Lawrence, Nov. 25, 1967; children—James, State, Deborah, Kathryn, Pamela. Copywriter McKelvey's Dept. Store, Youngstown, 1951-52, fashion advt. mgr. Macy's, N.Y.C., 1952-53; copy group head McCann-Erickson, N.Y.C., 1953-56; v.p., asso. copy chief Doyle, Dane, Bernbach, N.Y.C., 1957-64; sr. partner, creative dir. Jack Tinker & Partners, N.Y.C., 1964-66; pres. Wells, Rich, Greene, Inc., N.Y.C., 1966-71, chmn. bd., chief exec. officer, 1971—; Named to Copywriters Hall of Fame, Copy Club, 1969; named Marketing Saleswoman of Year, Sales Exec. Club N.Y., 1970, Advt. Woman of Year, Am. Advt. Fedn., 1971. Mem. Dallas Advt. Club. Office: 767 Fifth Av New York City NY 10022

LAWRENCE, MELODY ANN, journalist; b. Culver City, Cal., June 29, 1950; d. Glenn W. and Anna M. (Reid) Lawrence; B.S. summa cum laude, Ohio U., 1972, postgrad., 1972. Gen. assignment reporter Courier-Crescent, Orrville, O., summers 1968-70; gen. assignments Daily Record, Wooster, O., summer 1971, entertainment editor, 1972, asst. city editor, 1972—. Mem. Women in Communications (Akron chpt.), Ohio Newspaper Women's Assn., Ohio Press Women, Nat. Fedn. Press Women, Sigma Delta Chi, Kappa Tau Alpha. Methodist. Office: 212 E Liberty St Wooster OH 44691

LAWRENCE, MILDRED (MRS. CLARENCE ANTHONY LAWRENCE), author; b. Charleston, Ill., Nov. 10, 1907; d. DeWitt and Gertrude (Jefferson) Elwood; A.A., Flint Jr. Coll., 1926; B.A., Lawrence Coll., 1928; M.A., Yale, 1931; m. Clarence Anthony Lawrence, July 11, 1936; 1 dau., Mrs. James T. Schermerhorn. Society editor Flint Jour., 1928-29, reporter, feature writer, book and music critic, 1931-37; author books, stories, verses for children and young people, 1942—. Mem. Am. Assn. U. Women, Authors League Am., Phi Beta Kappa, Theta Sigma Phi, Alpha Delta Pi, Delta Kappa Gamma. Author: Susan's Bears, 1945; Peachtree Island, 1948; Sand in Her Shoes, 1949; The Homemade Year, 1950; Tallie, 1951; Crissy at the Wheel, 1952; One Hundred White Horses, 1953; Dreamboats for Trudy, 1954; Island Secret, 1955; Indigo Magic, 1956; Good Morning, My Heart, 1957; Along Comes Spring, 1958; The Questing Heart, 1959; The Shining Moment, 1960; Forever and Always, 1961; Starry Answer, 1962; Girl on Witches' Hill, 1963; Drums in My Heart, 1964; No Slipper for Cinderella, 1965; The Treasure and The Song, 1966; Reach for the Dream, 1967; Inside the Gate, 1968; Once at the Weary Why, 1969; Gateway to the Sun, 1970; Walk a Rocky Road, 1971; also short stories adult mags. Home: 1044 Terrace Blvd Orlando FL 32803

LAWRENCE, STELLA HERTCHIKOFF, educator; b. Montreal, Que., Can., Feb. 2, 1918; d. M. and Fannie (Broide) Hertchikoff; came to U.S., 1924, naturalized, 1931; B.A. magna cum laude, N.Y. U., 1938, M.S., 1941; B.E.E., Poly. Inst. Bklyn., 1949, M.E.E., 1952. Devel. engr. Control Instrument Co., 1943-47; lectr. physics City Coll. N.Y., 1958-70; mem. switching systems devel. dept. Bell Telephone Labs., 1947-60; asst. prof. Bronx Community Coll., 1960-65, asso. prof. elec. engring. tech., 1966—. Mem. Community Planning Bd. 7, Bronx, N.Y.C., 1970—. Fellow Bklyn. Engrs. Club; mem. I.E.E.E. (sr., exec. com. N.Y. sect. 1956—), Soc. Women Engrs. (sr., charter), Am. Soc. for Engring. Edn., Sigma Xi, Phi Beta Kappa, Pi Mu Epsilon, Sigma Pi Sigma. Home: 3288 Reservoir Oval E Bronx NY 10467 Office: 181st and University Av Bronx NY 10453

LAWRENCE, TELETÉ ZORAYDA (MRS. ERNEST LAWRENCE), speech and voice pathologist, educator; b. Worcester, Mass., Aug. 5, 1910; d. James Newton and Cora Valeria (Hester) Lester; A.B. cum laude, U. Cal. at Berkeley, 1932; M.A., Tex. Christian U., 1963; pvt. study voice with Edgar Schofield, N.Y.C., 1936-41, drama with Enrica Clay Dillon, N.Y.C., 1937-40; m. Ernest Lawrence, Oct. 9, 1939; children—James Lester, Valerie Alma. Mem. Am. Lyric Opera Co., 1939—; instr. speech Sch. Fine Arts, Tex. Christian U., Fort Worth, 1959-66, asst. prof., 1966-71, asso. prof., 1971—, speech pathologist specializing voice disorders Speech and Hearing Clinic, 1959—, faculty research leave, Gt. Britain, Western Europe, Hungary, 1968; pvt. practice speech and voice pathology, 1960—. Mem. bd. Sunshine Haven, home for retarded children, 1957-59; gen. chmn. Ft. Worth and Tarrant County, Nat. Retarded Children's Week, 1954; mem. family and child welfare div. Community Council Ft. Worth and Tarrant County, 1955-57, mem. health and hosp. div., 1959-60; mem. women's com. Ft. Worth chpt. Nat. Conf. Christians and Jews, Inc., 1956-59; exec. v.p. Fine Arts Found. Guild of Tex. Christian U., 1955-56, past exec. sec., past financial sec. Recipient Faculty Research grant Tex. Christian U., 1961. Mem. Nat. Council Chs. (bd. Divs. joint com. missionary edn. Pacific Coast area, 1952-55), United Ch. Women of Ft. Worth (chmn. Christian world missions dept. 1955-57, pres. 1957-59). Ft. Worth Area Council Chs. (v.p. 1955-57, exec. com. 1957-59, bd. dirs. 1959-60), U. Cal. Alumni Assn., Am. (certificate clin. competence in speech pathology), Tex. speech and hearing assns., Ft. Worth Council for Retarded Children, Speech Communication Am. (sec. speech and hearing disorders interest group 1962-63, mem. com. 1961-64), Am. Dialect Soc., Internat. Assn. Logopodics and Phoniatrics, Internat. Soc. Phonetic Scis., Am. Assn. U. Profs., Tex. Speech Assn., Lambda Ma'ams of Lambda Chi Alpha (pres. Ft. Worth 1962-63), Phi Beta Kappa Assn., Ft. Worth, Phi Beta Kappa (charter mem., v.p. Delta of Tex. chpt. 1971-73, pres. 1973-74), Delta Zeta, Psi Chi, Sigma Alpha Eta. Republican. Mem. Christian Ch. Clubs: Woman's of Fort Worth, Women of Rotary. Participant, 13th Congress of Internat. Assn. Logopedics and Phoniatrics, Vienna, 1965, 14th Congress, Paris, 1968, 15th Congress, Buenos Aires, 1971; participant 10th Internat. Congress of Linguists, Bucharest, 1967; participant 6th Internat. Congress of Phonetic Scis., Prague, 1967, 7th Internat. Congress, Montreal, 1971; participant 1st Congress Internat. Assn. Sci. Study Mental Deficiency, Montpellier, France, 1967, Semmelweis Ann. Week, Budapest Acad. Scis., 1968. Author: Handbook for Instructors of Voice and Diction, 1968. Contbr. articles to profl. jours. Home: 3860 South Hills Circle Fort Worth TX 76109

LAWRENCE, YVONNE, lawyer; b. N.Y.C.; b. Thomas F. and Raye Clark (Gilardi) Lawrence; B.S., U. Va., 1953, LL.B., 1956. Admitted to N.Y. bar, 1957; practiced in N.Y.C., 1957—; asso. Thomas F. Mullaney, Jr. and Louis L. Frank. Dir. WRVR-FM radio sta., N.Y.C., 1971—. Mem. nat. panel Am. Arbitration Assn., N.Y.C., 1965—. Bd. dirs. Am. Baptist Chs. U.S.A., 1973, Bd. Nat. Ministries, 1971—. Mem. N.Y. County Lawyers Assn., Riverside Bus. and Profl. Women's Club (pres. 1966-68). Baptist (trustee 1971). Office: 11 Broadway New York City NY 10004

LAWS, RUTH MITCHELL (MRS. WILLIAM J. LAWS), coll. adminstr.; b. Gatesville, N.C., July 25, 1912; d. Charles S. and Claire (Delk) Mitchell; B.S., Hampton Inst., 1933; M.S., Cornell U., 1943; Ed.D., N.Y. U., 1956; postgrad. U. Cal. at Berkeley, 1948; m. William J. Laws, Aug. 14, 1935; 1 dau., Cherritta. Tchr. Peabody Acad., Troy, N.C., 1933-34; rural social case worker Gates County Social Services, Gatesville, N.C., 1934-36; supr. adult edn. programs Bd. Edn., Wilmington, Del., 1936-38; tchr. Smyrna (Del.) High Sch., 1938-42; dir. tchr. educator home econs. Del. State Coll., Dover, 1942-47; supr. home econs. Del. Dept. Pub. Instrn., Dover, 1947-65, supr. planning and research in vocational edn., 1965-68. state dir. adult edn., 1968-71; asst. to pres. Del. Tech. and Community Coll., Dover, 1971—. Cons. to various ednl. instns. and agys. Mem. Del. Commn. on Children and Youth, 1951-70, chmn., 1965-70; mem. Del. Commn. on Aging, 1960-70, Gov.'s Com. on Goals for Del., 1966-69, Gov.'s Com. on Justice, 1971—; mem. Del. Manpower Council, 1971—, Nat. Council on State Coms. on Children and Youth, 1966-70; pres. Dover Area U.S.O., 1965-68. Bd. dirs. Dover YMCA. Recipient Distinguished Alumni award N.Y. U., 1957, Nat. Hampton Alumni Assn., 1957, Distinguished Vocational Educator award Del. Dept. Pub. Instrn., 1972. Mem. N.E.A. (life), Am. Home Econs. Assn., Assn. for Supervision and Curriculum Devel., Adult Edn. Assn. U.S.A., Nat. Assn. Pub. Adult and Continuing Edn., Del. Edn. Assn., Assn. for Continuing Edn. of Adults in Del. (state pres. 1973-75), Ch. Women United Del. (state pres. 1969-73), Am. Assn. U. Women (state v.p. 1966-69), Del. Assn. Sch. Adminstrs., Nat. Council Family Relations, Internat. Platform Assn., Delta Sigma Theta, Kappa Delta Pi, Pi Lambda Theta, Omicron Nu. Methodist (mem. exec. com. Peninsula Conf. 1973-74, mem. exec. com. Delmarva Ecumenical Agy. 1970-75). Home: 844 Forest St Dover DE 19901 Office: PO Box 897 Dover DE 19901

LAWSON, ELIZABETH HARRIS (MRS. CLYDE LAWSON), educator; b. Springfield, Mo., Sept. 21, 1918; d. Earl Alexander and Viola (Martin) Harris; student U. Chgo., 1938-39; B.S., Ill. Inst. Tech., 1937; M.S., Chgo. State U., 1961; m. Clyde Lawson, Sept. 18, 1943; children—Clyde Harris and Carol Harris (twins), Leonard James. Tchr. high sch. Chgo. pub. schs., 1941-61, high sch. counselor, 1961-65; adult edn. tchr., 1963-66; counselor Chgo. State U., 1965-68, asst. prof. edn., 1965—, dir. intensive edn. program, 1968-71, asst. dir. admissions, 1974—. Cons. U. S.C. Desegregation Center, 1969, 70, North Central Accrediting Assn. Secondary Schs., 1970. Mem. Art Inst. Chgo., Am. Assn. U. Profs., Am. Personnel and Guidance Assn., Ill. Guidance and Personnel Assn., Ill. Women Deans and Counselors, Delta Kappa Gamma. Episcopalian. Office: Chicago State U 95th and King Dr Chicago IL 60628

LAWSON, ELIZABETH MOULTON (MRS. DONALD WILFRED LAWSON), psychiat. social worker; b. Detroit, Sept. 19, 1924; d. Arthur A. and Bessie (Farnsworth) Moulton; B.A., St. Lawrence U., 1945; M.S.W., U. N.C., 1964; postgrad. Howard U., 1967-68, Washington Sch. Psychiatry, 1967-70; m. Donald Wilfred Lawson, Dec. 6, 1944; children—Richard Arthur, Scott Howie. Asst. dir. social service Caswell Center, N.C., 1958-62, acting dir. diagnostic clinic, 1964-66; supr. child welfare services Montgomery County Dept. Social Services, Md., 1966-70; dir. social services Great Oaks Center, Silver Spring, Md., 1970—. Mental health cons. N.C. counties, 1964-66; mem. State Planning Com. for Summer Careers in Social Work, 1970-72; field supr. U. Md. Grad. Sch. Social Work and Community Planning, 1971-74. Mem. foster care planning com. for mentally retarded, 1972-73; bd. dirs. Cerebral Palsy Day Care Center Montgomery County, 1968-70, Montgomery County Assn. Retarded Citizens, 1969-73. Recipient certificate Acad. Certified Social Workers, 1966. Mem. Am. Assn. Mental Deficiency (v.p. social work region 9 1973—), Nat. Assn. Retarded Citizens. Unitarian. Home: 610 Marcia Lane Rockville MD 20851 Office: Great Oaks Center 12001 Cherry Hill Rd Silver Spring MD 20904

LAWSON, ESTHER CHANEY (MRS. ALBERT THEODORE LAWSON), sch. adminstr.; b. Chgo., July 29, 1930; d. Thomas Roosevelt and Olie Lillie (Ford) Nelson; B.S., U. Ill., 1952; M.A., U. Chgo., 1962; m. Albert Theodore Lawson, May 2, 1954; 1 dau., Laurie Lynne. Primary tchr. Chgo. Bd. Edn., 1952-65, tchr.-counselor, 1965-69; prin. Garrett A. Morgan Elementary Sch., Chgo., 1969—. Cons. resource Wis. Research and Devel. Center, 1973-74. Registrar, 29th dist. S.E. Community Orgn., 1965. Bd. dirs. Marynook Homeowners, 1963—, Potential Sch. for Exceptional Children, 1969-74. Recipient fellowship for outstanding tchrs. Chgo. Bd. Edn., 1964. Mem. Nat. Council Adminstrv. Women, U. Chgo. Alumni, Chgo. Prins. Assn., Samuel Stratton Soc., Individually Guided Edn. Assn., Ella Flagg Young Assn., Delta Kappa Gamma, Delta Sigma Theta. Mem. Ch. of Christ. Home: 1333 E 83d St Chicago IL 60619 Office: 8407 S Kerfoot St Chicago IL 60620

LAWSON, MARGARET MOTT (MRS. RALPH E. LAWSON), home economist; b. Blairstown, N.J.; d. Lewis Aaron and Leola May (Bird) Mott; B.S. in Home Econs., Cedar Crest Coll., 1946; M.Ed. in Adult Edn., Rutgers U., 1968; m. Ralph Elmer Lawson, Sept. 3, 1960. Asst. to dir. Needlework Design Studio, McCall Corp., N.Y.C., 1946-51; home economist Bell Sewing Machine Corp., N.Y.C., 1951-54; extension home economist Mercer County Extension Service, Trenton, N.J., 1954—; needlework design cons. Flax Processing & Linen Co., N.Y.C., 1948-50. Mem. Mercer County Council on Aging, 1970—. Recipient Distinguished Service award Nat. Assn. Home Economists, 1966, Florence Hall award, 1970. Mem. Nat. (alt. regional dir. 1965-67), N.J. (pres. 1965-67) assns. extension home economists, Am. Home Econs. Assn., Adult Edn. Assn., Zonta Internat. (1st v.p. Trenton Club 1962-64). Club: Hopewell (N.J.) Valley Golf. Home: 143 W Farrell Av Trenton NJ 08618 Office: 930 Spruce St Trenton NJ 08618

LAWSON, MARION EVA (MRS. PHILIP C. LAWSON), author; b. Elkhorn, Wis., Aug. 8, 1896; d. Henry Henderson and Helen Marion (Andrus) Tubbs; B.A., Carroll Coll., 1919; m. Philip C. Lawson, Dec. 6, 1927. With various printing and advt. agencies, 1919-27. Mem. Am. Assn. U. Women (editor N.Y.C. br. Bull. 1951-54, co-editor 1957-59). Author: Solomon Juneau, Voyageur, 1960; Proud Warrior: The Story of Black Hawk (award of merit Wis. State Hist. Soc. 1969), 1968; Maggie Flying Bird, 1974. Home: 160 Cabrini Blvd New York City NY 10033

LAWSON, MARJORIE M., lawyer. Municipal judge, Washington, until 1965; pvt. practice law, Washington, 1965—. Home: 4500 Linnean Av NW Washington DC 20008 Office: 1140 Connecticut Av NW Washington DC 20036

LAWSON, MARY LOIS VEDDER (MRS. MELVIN FRANCIS LAWSON), city ofcl.; b. Gibbs, Ida., July 30, 1924; d. Edd S. and Freidaline (Herbst) Vedder; grad. high sch.; m. Melvin Francis Lawson, June 21, 1946; children—Pamela Eddean (Mrs. Marvin Vanderhoff), Frank S. Sheet metal worker Gen. Metalware, Portland, Ore., 1942-43; spray painter, painter Doernbechers Furniture, Portland, 1944-45; with shipping and receiving dept. Montgomery Ward & Co., Portland, 1945; dental asst., Coeur d'Alene, Ida., 1955-62, Seattle, 1962; cashier City of Coeru d'Alene, 1963-69, dep. treas., 1969—, city treas., 1968—, city clk., 1973—. Bd. dirs. Pub. Employees Credit Union, 1972—. Mem. Assn. Ida. Cities, Clks. and Fiscal Officers, Internat. Inst. Municipal Clks. Home: 613 Lunceford Lane Coeur d'Alene ID 83814 Office: City Hall 5th and Sherman Coeur d'Alene ID 83814

LAWSON, RUTH CATHARINE, educator; b. Batavia, N.Y., Apr. 18, 1911; d. Frank E. and Mary (Burlingham) Lawson; A.B. magna cum laude, Mt. Holyoke Coll., 1933; M.A., Bryn Mawr Coll., 1934, Ph.D., 1947; summer study Zimmern Sch., Geneva, 1932, Acad. Internat. Law, The Hague, 1939. Instr. polit. sci. and econs. Tulane U., 1936-42; successively instr., asst. prof., asso. prof. Mt. Holyoke Coll., 1942-55, prof., 1955-60, prof. polit. sci. on alumnae found., 1960—, chmn. dept. polit. sci., 1957-63, 64-65, 67-68, 72-73; asso. prof. govt., dir. Geneva Jr. year internat. studies Smith Coll., 1949-50; prof. grad. faculty U. Mass., 1971—. Vis. prof. U. Mass. Bologna Program, summer 1966; vis. fellow Center for Contemporary European Studies and Inst. Study Internat. Orgn., U. Sussex (Eng.), 1970-71. Bd. dirs. Atlantic Council U.S., 1963-71. Guggenheim fellow, 1956-57; NATO Advanced Research fellow, 1959-60; Am. Soc. Internat. Law fellow, 1962-63; U.S. Specialist grant award Dept. State, 1968; recipient Medal of Honor, Mt. Holyoke Alumnae Assn., 1972. Mem. Am. Polit. Sci. Assn. (sec. 1962-63), Am. Soc. Internat. Law (exec. council 1953-56, 68-71), Internat. Studies Assn. (sec. New Eng. sect. 1967-68, v.p. New Eng. sect. 1968-69, pres. New Eng. sect. 1969-70, mem. council internat. orgn. sect. 1973—), Internat. Inst. Strategic Studies. Am. Assn. U. Women, Phi Beta Kappa. Editor: International Regional Organizations: Constitutional Foundations, 1962. Contbr. articles and book revs. to Am. Jour. Internat. Law, Current History, Am. Polit. Sci. Rev., Internat. Orgn., Colliers Year Book, Annals of Am. Acad. Polit. and Social Sci., Politics. Home: 2 Jewett Lane South Hadley MA 01075

LAWTON, HELENA STEILBERG (MRS. EDWARD B. LAWTON, JR.), pub. relations exec.; b. Berkeley, Cal., Mar. 18, 1917; d. Walter Theodore and Rowena (Symmonds) Steilberg; B.A., U. Cal. at Berkeley, 1937; M.A., Radcliffe Coll., 1939; m. Edward B. Lawton, Jr., June 24, 1939 (dec.); children—David, Randal, Nicholas, Roger. Radio writer Consumer div. O.P.A., San Francisco, 1941-45; instr., writer U. Cal. Extension, Berkeley, 1950-62; pub. relations dir. radio sta. KPFA/FM, Berkeley, 1958-60; pub. relations dir. Planned Parenthood League Alameda County, Oakland, Cal., 1960-62; pub. relations dir. Consumers Coop. Berkeley, Inc., 1961-67; advt., pub. relations cons. Twin Pines Fed. Savs. and Loan Assn., Berkeley, 1962—. Free Lance critic, Bay Area, 1960—; cons. pub. relations occasionally for Democratic Campaigns, Assn. Cal. Consumers, Berkeley Art Co-op., Mut. Service Ins. Cos., Bay Area Funeral Soc., Gauguin Mus. Cons. pub. relations Art League East Bay, 1950-55, Berkeley Jr. Bach Festival, 1959-61, Berkeley Archtl. Heritage Com., 1970-73. Bd. dirs. Berkeley Vis. Nurse Assn., 1943-45. Anne Louise Barrett fellow in music Wellesley Coll., 1939-41. Mem. Women in Communications, Inc., Cal. Writers Club, East Bay Women's Press Club, (pres. 1965-66), Prytaneans, Phi Beta Kappa, Alpha Mu. Democrat. Author: Introduction to Musical Literature, 2 vols., 1958; Fifty Folk Songs, 1959. Editor, designer Heritage Houses, 1972, 73. Contbr. to Harvard Dictionary of Music, 1944. Address: 83 Eucalyptus Rd Berkeley CA 94705

LAWTON, MARY CECILIA, lawyer, govt. ofcl.; b. Washington, June 2, 1935; d. Frederick Joseph and Cecilia Alice (Walsh) Lawton; A.B., Seton Hill Coll., 1957, LL.D., 1972; LL.B., Georgetown U., 1960. Admitted to Washington bar, 1960, U.S. Supreme Court bar, 1964; practiced in Washington, 1960; atty. adviser U.S. Dept. Justice, 1960-72, dep. asst. atty. gen., 1972—. Trustee Seton Hill Coll., 1970—. Mem. Fed., Am. bar assns. Editor: (with Joseph Fontana) These Inalienable Rights; A Handbook of the Bill of Rights, 1965. Home: 9905 E Bexhill Dr Kensington MD 20795 Office: US Dept Justice Washington DC 20530

LAWYER, VIVIAN MOORE (MRS. CYRUS JEFFERSON LAWYER III), univ. adminstr.; b. Cleve., Jan. 6, 1946; d. Walter Frank and Everine (Stanton) Moore; B.S., Bowling Green State U., 1967, M.Ed., 1968; m. Cyrus Jefferson Lawyer III, June 8, 1968; children—Lenaye Lynne, Sonya Alyse. Asst. dean students Bowling Green (O.) State U., 1968-72, dir. office equal opportunity, 1972-73, coordinator human resources, 1973—. Mem. Lucas County health service com. Health Planning Assn. of N.W. Ohio, 1972-73, Toledo Neighborhood Health Assn., 1972-73. Trustee Toledo YWCA. Recipient distinguished service to univ. award Bowling Green State U., 1967, Midwest region adviser's award Delta Sigma Theta, 1972. Mem. Nat. Council Negro Women, Nat. Assn. Women Deans and Counselors, Ohio Assn. Women Deans, Adminstrs. and Counselors, Ohio Affirmative Action Officers. Home: 3805 Ben Lomond Ct Toledo OH 43607 Office: 231 Administration Bowling Green State U Bowling Green OH 43403

LAX, RUTH FRANCESKA (MRS. LEON A. FALIK), psychoanalyst; b. Vienna, Austria, May 26, 1921; d. Bernard and Helen (Bergman) Lax; B.A., N.Y. U., 1947, M.A., 1952, Ph.D., 1961; m. L.A. Falik, Sept. 30, 1967; 1 son by previous marriage—William B. Lax Salton. Pvt. practice psychoanalysis and therapy with adults and adolescents, N.Y.C., 1958—; faculty Inst. Psychoanalytic Tng. and Research, N.Y.C., 1964—, also mem.; asst. clin. prof. psychiatry Albert Einstein Coll. Medicine, N.Y.C., 1971—. Cons. day care div. Union Settlement, N.Y.C., 1971—. Mem. N.Y. Soc. Clin. Psychologists, Council Psychoanalytic Psychotherapists (dir.), N.Y. Soc. Freudian Psychologists (dir. 1974-76). Contbr. articles to profl. jours. Address: 164 E 81st St New York City NY 10028

LAYBOLD, LILLIAN M. VOLKERS (MRS. ELZA WALTER LAYBOLD), librarian; b. Terre Haute, Ind., May 15, 1910; d. Ivan Hayes and Emma Susan (Reed) Volkers; B.S., Ind. State Tchrs. Coll., 1932, library certificate, 1963; m. Elza Walter Laybold, July 27, 1932 (dec. 1964); children—Kay (Mrs. Larry K. Brankle), Judith (Mrs. Theodore R. Lucas). Substitute librarian McLean Jr. High Sch., Terre Haute, 1959-60; bookmobile librarian Emeline Fairbanks Meml. Library, Terre Haute, 1961-63; br. librarian Meadows br. Vigo County Pub. Library, Terre Haute, 1963—. Mem. Am., Ind. library assns., Vigo County Pub. Library Staff Assn. (pres. 1966-67, chmn. 10th ann. staff inst. 1968), Ind. State U. Alumni Assn., YWCA, Omega Sigma Chi (sec. Ind. State Tchrs. Coll. chpt. 1930, treas. 1932, v.p. alumnae group 1973), Alpha Beta Alpha. Presbyn. Clubs: Delta Gamma Mothers (charter mem., treas. 1958, v.p. 1959, pres. 1960) (Ind. State U.); Altrusa (dir. 1971-72, chmn. information 1971-72) (Terre Haute). Home: 2130 College Av Terre Haute IN 47803 Office: Meadows Br Library Meadows Shopping Center Terre Haute IN 47803

LAYCOCK, MARGERY CAROLE, educator; b. Findlay, O., Apr. 18, 1939; d. Wendell Carter and Ruth Ellen (Marshall) Laycock; student U. Colo., 1957-58, summer 1962; B.S., Ind. U., 1961, M.A., 1963, postgrad., 1965-66; postgrad. Ball. State U., 1964, Butler U., 1972, 73. Tchr. lang. arts North Central High Sch., Indpls., 1962-65, counselor, 1965—. Guest lectr. Purdue U., Indpls., 1964-65. Mem. Nat. (exec. bd. 1974—), Ind. (pres. 1972-73) assns. women deans, adminstrs. and counselors, Ind. Personnel and Guidance Assn., Delta

Kappa Gamma, Alpha Omicron Pi. Home: 949 Lake Nora N Ct Indianapolis IN 46240 Office: 1801 E 86th St Indianapolis IN 46240

LAYER, ADELAIDE BARBANES (MRS. JOSEPH C. LAYER, JR.), city ofcl.; b. Bernardsville, N.J., Nov. 21, 1905; d. Charles and Elizabeth M. (Knickel) Barbanes; student Columbia, 1930-31; m. Joseph C. Layer, Jr., Dec. 29, 1934; 1 dau., Penelope (Mrs. C. Bernie Littlejohn, Jr.). Legal sec., N.Y.C., 1929-42; supr. controller materials Aircraft Radio Corp., Boonton, N.J., 1942-47; sec. planning bd., Borough of Morris Plains, N.J., 1956-66, borough clk., office of city clk., 1959-73. Treas. Women's Aux. Fire Dept., 1948-50; treas. Morris Plains Coop. Play Sch., 1951-52; chmn. troop com., co-leader troop Girl Scouts U.S.A., 1955-59. Mem. Internat., N.J. (county rep. adv. bd. 1971-73) Morris County clks. assns. Presbyn. Club: Food, Fun and Fellowship (Morris Plains). Home: 18 Jaqui Av Morris Plains NJ 07950 Office: 531 Speedwell Av Morris Plains NJ 07950

LAYMAN, ALICE BEDELL CONNOLLY (MRS. LESTER C. LAYMAN), journalist; b. New Haven; d. Edwin Greeley and Elizabeth (Degnan) Bedell; B.S. cum laude, N.Y. U., 1931; m. Roger A. Connolly, Oct. 8, 1934 (dec. July 1953); m. 2d, Lester C. Layman, Oct. 31, 1959. Adminstrn. secondary schs., New Haven, 1931-54; asst. to dir. publicity A.R.C., New Haven, 1941-45; dir. pub. relations Quinnipiac council Boy Scouts Am., New Haven, 1953-54, New Haven Heart Assn., 1954-58, Nat. Found. for Infantile Paralysis, New Haven, 1953-57, Hosp. of St. Raphael, New Haven, 1954-58, Hosp. of Good Samaritan Med. Center, Los Angeles, 1959-69; mem. publicity com. New Haven Cancer Soc., 1957-58, Conn. Assn. for Blind, 1956-58; fashion and beauty editor Bridgeport (Conn.) Post, 1948—. Bd. dirs. Neighborhood Music Sch., New Haven, 1949-58. Mem. Am. Hosp. Assn., Am. Soc. for Hosp. Pub. Relations (dir. 1965-67), Assn. Western Hosps., Hosp. Council So. Cal. (chmn. 1964-69), Charity League New Haven (life), New Haven Advt. Club (hon.), Fashion Group, Women in Communication, Kappa Delta Pi, Clubs: El Niguel Country, Cave des Roys. Address: 34693 Camino Capistrano Capistrano Beach CA 92624

LAYMAN, EMMA MCCLOY (MRS. JAMES W. LAYMAN), psychologist; b. Danville, Va., Feb. 25, 1910; d. Charles Harold and Anna (Fisher) McCloy; A.B., Oberlin Coll., 1930; M.A., N.Y.U., 1931; Ph.D., U. Ia., 1937; m. James Walter Layman, Dec. 12, 1936. Psychol. examiner Ia. Psychopathic Hosp., Iowa City, 1934-35, 37; clin. psychologist Mich. Children's Inst., Ann Arbor, 1935-36; supr. psychol. services Ia. Bd. Social Welfare, Des Moines, 1937-41; asso. prof. psychology Woman's Coll., U. N.C., 1947-52; supervisory clin. psychologist Brooke Army Hosp., Ft. Sam Houston, 1952-54; chief psychologist Children's Hosp., Washington, 1954-60; head dept. psychology Ia. Wesleyan Coll., Mt. Pleasant, 1960—, asso. prof., 1960-61, prof., 1961—, chmn. social sci. div., 1969—, dir. East Asian Inst., 1963—, also dir. internat. studies; pvt. practice clin. psychology, 1941—; lectr. U. Chattanooga, 1946-47; vis. prof. edn. Duke, summers 1948-50; adj. prof. Am. U., 1954-60; lectr. Howard U., 1956-60; cons. Walter Reed Army Hosp. 1956-60. Served from lt. (j.g.) to lt. USN, 1943-46. Diplomate Am. Bd. Examiners in Profl. Psychology. Fellow Am. Psychol. Assn., Internat. Council Psychologists (editor newsletter 1956-58, past pres., dir.); mem. Interam. Psychol. Soc., Ia. Psychol. Assn., Am. Psychopath. Assn., Assn. Asian Studies, Phi Beta Kappa, Sigma Xi. Episcopalian. Author: Mental Health Through Physical Education and Recreation, 1955; also articles. Contbg. author publs. in field. Home: 403 S Walnut St Mount Pleasant IA 52641

LAYNE, MARIE PANNULLO, writer; b. Passaic, N.J.; d. Vincent and Jennie (Anzovino) Pannullo; grad. high sch.; pvt. study voice, writing. Debut as vocalist Carnegie Hall, 1950; writer various types articles pub. in Narcotics Education, Red Cross Youth Publications, Health, Christian Board of Education, North American Voice of Fatima, Marian Helpers Bulletin, Liguorian Publications, Our Sunday Visitor, Commissariat of the Holy Land, My Daily Visitor, Minn. Motorist, David C. Cook Pub. Co., Christian Home, Union Gospel Press, Christian Sci. Monitor, Christian Bd. Edn., Family Digest, Venture, Oratory, others; landscape artist. Home: Clifton NJ 07013

LAYNE, MILDRED ELOISE, found. exec.; b. Cardwell, Va., Mar. 1, 1911; d. Rennie Dow and Minnie Moore (Alvis) Layne; student Coll. William and Mary, 1928-31. Sec. to Am. Counsul Gen., Hong Kong, 1931-34; sec. to engineer, Washington, 1934-37; with The Colonial Williamsburg Found., Williamsburg, Va., 1937—, exec. asst. to pres., 1966—, sec. found., 1968—, v.p., 1972—. Asst. Sec., asst. treas. Jackson Hole Preserve, Inc., conservation orgn., 1952-66, v.p., 1964-66; corporate officer Grand Teton Lodge Co., Jackson Hole, Wyo., Caneel Bay Plantation, St. John, V.I., 1955-66; Mem. Am. Conservation Assn. (asst. sec., asst. treas. 1958-66). Home: Palmer House Duke of Gloucester St Williamsburg VA 23185 Office: Goodwin Bldg Williamsburg VA 23185

LAZARUS, MARJORIE ISABEL, educator; b. Egypt, Pa., Dec. 16, 1921; d. Raymond Marcus and Marguerite Ruth (Bachman) Lazarus; B.A., Pa. State U., 1942-44; spl. courses Muhlenberg Coll., 1943-44, U. Minn., 1965, 67, Syracuse U., 1968. Tchr. chemistry Whitehall (Pa.) High Sch., 1942-52, dir. publs., earth sci. tchr., 1953—. Pres. Lehigh Valley Sci. Fair, 1966-68, dir., 1969-71. Recipient Gold Key award Columbia Scholastic Press Assn., 1964, Medal of Merit, Journalism Edn. Assn., 1972, Josten's Yearbook scholarship, 1965, Wall Street Jour. Newspaper Fund fellowship, 1967, Call-Chronicle Newspaper in Classroom scholarhsip, 1968. Mem. Women in Communications, Journalism Edn. Assn. (regional dir. 1965-67, mem. bookshelf commn. 1968-71), Columbia Scholastic Press Advisers Assn. (sec.-treas. 1968-70), Columbia Scholastic Press Assn. (mem. bd. yearbook judges 1960—), Lehigh County Hist. Soc. (hon. life mem., dir. 1970—). Club: Soroptimist (1st v.p. 1973-74, dir. 1972-74) (Allentown, Pa.). Contbr. articles to various profl. publs. Home: 3570 Catherine Dr Allentown PA 18103 Office: 3800 Mechanicsville Rd Whitehall PA 18052

LAZCANO, ESTHER C. ARECHAVALETA (MRS. ANTONIO M. LAZCANO), educator; b. Havana, Cuba, Nov. 25, 1929; d. Liborio and Fannie (Brown) Arechavaleta; B.A., Matanzas Inst., 1947; Lic. in Diplomatic Law, Havana U., 1952, Lic. in Adminstrv. Law, 1953, Dr. Social Sci., 1954, LL.D., 1960; m. Antonio M. Lazcano, Apr. 2, 1955; children—Antonio M., Ana Maria, Lourdes Maria, Rosemarie. Came to U.S., 1961. Consul, Cuban Fgn. Service, Rio de Janeiro, Brazil, N.Y.C., Miami, Fla., Veracruz, Mex., Office of UN, Havana, 1952-60; mem. faculty Spanish, Wis. State U., Eau Claire, 1964—, now asso. prof. Spanish. Del., Assn. Ex-Mems. of Cuban Fgn. Service in U.S., 1964—. Mem. Modern Lang. Assn., Am. Assn. U. Profs., Am. Assn. Tchrs. Spanish and Portuguese, Circulo de Cultura Panamericano, Sigma Delta Pi. Roman Catholic. Home: 336 McKinley Av Eau Claire WI 54701

LAZDA, VELTA ABULS (MRS. JANIS O. LAZDA), immunologist; b. Riga, Latvia, Dec. 16, 1939; d. Mikelis and Emma (Viceps) Abuls; B.S., Purdue U., 1962; Ph.D., Northwestern U., 1967; m. Janis O. Lazda, Dec. 22, 1962. Postdoctoral fellow Northwestern U., Evanston, Ill., 1967-69; research asso. immunology div. Am. Dental Assn. Research Inst., Chgo., 1969—. Postdoctoral research fellow Am. Cancer Soc., 1967-69; Career Devel. award USPHS, 1972—. Mem. A.A.A.S., Am. Soc. Microbiology, Chgo. Assn. Immunologists. Home: 624 W Oakton St Evanston IL 60202 Office: Dept Immunology and Microbiology Am Dental Assn Research Inst 211 E Chicago Av Chicago IL 60611

LAZZERI, CAROL MARIE YOUNG (MRS. JOSEPH S. LAZZERI), camp adminstr.; b. Orange, N.J., Nov. 6, 1930; d. Cecil George and Caroline Grace (Varley) Young; R.N., Fitzgerald Mercy Hosp. Sch. Nursing, 1951; postgrad. Marywood Coll., part-time 1969-70; m. Brenton Salt, 1952; children—Brenton, Michael; m. 2d, Joseph S. Lazzeri, July 9, 1960; children—Jo Ann, Angela. Psychiat. nurse Mercywood Sanitarium, Ann Arbor, Mich., 1953-54; staff nurse VA Hosp., Ann Arbor, 1954-56; head nurse orthopedics U. Pa., Phila., 1956-57; asst. adminstr. cancer research U. Pa., 1957-61; head nurse med. floor St. Clare's Hosp., Denville, N.J., 1961-62; owner, operator Huckleberry Haven, Phoenix, 1962-66; adminstr. retarded children's facility Keystone Camp, Gouldsboro, Pa., 1967—. Chmn. troop Cub Scouts Am., Girl Scouts U.S.A., 1972—. Mem. Am. Assn. Mental Deficiency, Council Exceptional Children, Pa. Assn. for Retarded Children, Women's Internat. Bowling Congress. Address: RD 1 Gouldsboro PA 18424

LEA, LOLA STENDIG, lawyer; b. N.Y.C., Sept. 20, 1934; d. Hershel and Sophie (Golub) Stendig; B.A. cum laude N.Y. U., 1954; LL.B., Yale, 1957; m. Robert M. Lea, Sept. 12, 1953; 1 dau., Jennie. Admitted to N.Y. bar, 1958; law clk. to U.S. Dist. Judge, so. dist. N.Y., 1957-59; asst. U.S. atty., so. dist. N.Y., 1959-61, asso. C.C. Davis, N.Y.C., 1961-67; mem. firm Davis & Cox, N.Y.C., 1967-71, Lea, Goldberg, Goldsmith & Spellun, P.C., N.Y.C., 1971—. Spl. counsel to N.Y. 1st dept. joint interprofl. com. Drs. and Lawyers, 1972—; lectr. Practicing Law Inst., N.Y.C., 1969-70, 74; spl. mediator Med. Malpractice Mediation part Supreme Ct. N.Y., 1971—. Mem. N.Y. Bar Assn. (del. 1972—), Assn. of Bar City N.Y. (chmn. medicine and law com. 1969-71, new members com. 1973, mem. judiciary com. 1971—, grievance com. 1974—) bar assns. Home: 24 Garden Pl Brooklyn NY 11201 Office: 120 Broadway St New York NY 10005

LEACH, CAROLYN SUE (MRS. HARRISON HIBBERT HUNTOON), endocrinologist; b. Leesville, La., Aug. 25, 1940; d. Anthony Claude and Lucille (Goodwin) Leach; B.S., Northwestern La. State U., 1962; M.S., Baylor U., 1966, Ph.D., 1968; m. Harrison Hibbert Huntoon, Aug. 16, 1969; 1 dau., Sally Ann. Med. technologist U. Tex. M.D. Anderson Hosp. and Tumor Inst., 1962-66; head endocrine lab., Lyndon B. Johnson Center, NASA, Houston, 1968—, NRC research asso., 1968-70; instr. dept. physiology Baylor Coll. Medicine, Houston, 1968-70, asst. prof., 1970—. Cons. Project Sea Lab., U.S. Navy, 1968-69; cons. Project Tektite I, U.S. Navy, NASA and Gen. Electric, Dept. Interior, 1969, Project Tektite II, NASA, Dept. of Interior, 1970; asst. investigator Inst. Environmental Medicine Sch. of Medicine, U. Pa., 1970. Recipient NIH Career Devel. award, 1964-68. Mem. Endocrine Soc., Am. Physiol. Soc., N.Y. Acad. Sci., Aerospace Med. Assn., Am. Soc. Clin. Pathologists, Sigma Xi. Home: 16201 El Camino Real 1 Houston TX 77058 Office: DB62 NASA Johnson Space Center Houston TX 77058

LEACH, SALLY ANN, librarian; b. Owatonna, Minn., Dec. 23, 1923; d. Helon Edwin and Mabelle Gertrude (King) Leach; student MacMurray Coll., 1943-44; B.A., Carleton Coll., 1947; B.S. in L.S., U. So. Cal., 1948. With East Orange (N.J.) Pub. Library, 1948—, head tech. services, 1970—. Mem. East Orange Pub. Library Staff Assn. (pres. 1953-55). Methodist (v.p. in charge programs 1962-63, mem. adminstrv. bd. 1973-75). Home: 251 S Harrison St East Orange NJ 07018 Office: 21 S Arlington Av East Orange NJ 07018

LEADBEATER, ALMA DORIS ASH (MRS. HOWARD W. LEADBEATER), ednl. adminstr.; b. Jenkintown, Pa., Apr. 27, 1926; d. Leroy and Louisa Frieda (Leusch) Ash; B.S., West Chester State Coll., 1948; Ed.M., Temple U., 1951; postgrad. Northwestern U., 1955, U. Md., 1957, Pa. State U., 1966; m. Howard W. Leadbeater, July 11, 1959; stepchildren—Corey Dennis, Holly (Mrs. Clyde Jacobs, Jr.). Tchr. Highland Elementary Sch., Abington, Pa., 1948-53; helping tchr. Abington sch. dist., 1953-54, coordinator reading, 1954—; instr. reading Temple U., Phila., 1954, 62, 68. Mem. staff Ann. Temple U. Reading Inst., Phila., 1951-69; speaker Mid-Atlantic Christian Schs. Assn. Conv., Bryn Athyn and Buck Hill Falls, Pa., 1966, 70. Sec. Custis Woods Civic Assn., Glenside, Pa., 1968-70; mem. Friends of Briar Bush, Abington, 1970—. Mem. Del. Valley Reading Assn. (mem. adv. bd. 1971—; mem. exec. bd. 1973), Internat. Reading Assn., Montgomery County Reading Council. Mem. Order Eastern Star. Home: 624 Bridle Rd Glenside PA 19038 Office: 1841 Susquehanna St Abington PA 19001

LEADER, DONNA MARIA, advt. co. adminstr.; b. Evansville, Ind., Aug. 19, 1943; d. Charles Griffith and Mary Beverly (Metcalfe) Vowels; student U. Evansville, 1961-64, Ind. State U., 1972—; div.; 1 dau., Caron J. Sec., Mead Johnson & Co., Evansville, 1961-62, librarian, 1963-64; media dir. Bozell & Jacobs, Indpls., 1964-68; media dir. Ball Advt. Inc., Evansville, 1968-69, corp. sec., 1969—, asst. to pres., 1970—, also dir. Mem. Evansville Advt. Club (dir. 1971, 72), So. Ind. Arts and Edn. Council. Home: 1543 Savannah Dr Evansville IN 47715 Office: 1101 N Fulton Av Evansville IN 47710

LEAF, ANN, organist; b. Omaha, June 28, 1903; d. Charles and Augusta Hannah (Fichman) Leaf; student Juilliard Inst., 1916-18; m. Elias Kleinert, May 7, 1928 (dec. Sept. 1963); 1 son, Peter; m. 2d, Russell C. Butler, Nov. 16, 1965. Debut with Omaha Symphony, 1914; organist silent pictures, 1922-28; organist Columbia Broadcasting Co. concerts, 1929-39, organist radio serials, 1934-48, 53-60; organist Fred Allen Show, 1933-34, many other radio programs; concerts on reconditioned theatre organs throughout country, 1961—; organist revivals silent movies; appeared Filmex presentations, Los Angeles County Art Mus., Bing Theatre. Mem. A.S.C.A.P., Am. Theatre Organ Soc., Juilliard Alumni. Composer Rio Coco, Hummingbird, Aristocrat In The Automat, Mirage On the Desert, Happy Island, Waltz On a Cloud, Here Comes the Bride On a Pinto Pony, others; albums on King, Westminster, Warner Bros. Request, Concert Recs. Home: 6155 Rockcliff Dr Los Angeles CA 90068

LEAF, JEANETTE ANN BENJAMIN, educator; b. Baghdad, Iraq, Aug. 21, 1944; d. Paul Y. and Nellie (George) Benjamin; B.A., Ind. U., 1966; M.A., Northwestern U., 1967, Ph.D., 1969; m. Robert J. Leaf, June 17, 1973. Came to U.S., naturalized, 1960. Asst. prof., coordinator testing, research and evaluation for dean students office Herbert Lehman Coll., City U. N.Y., 1969—. Chmn., United Fund com. Herbert Lehman Coll., 1972-73, chmn. community affairs com., 1973-74. Mem. Nat. Assn. Women Deans, Adminstrs. and Counselors, Am. Assn. U. Profs., Nat. Orgn. Women, Am. Personnel and Guidance Assn., Am. Assn. U. Women, Nat. Assn. Student Personnel Adminstrs., Zeta Tau Alpha (Found. scholar 1966). Home: 140 E 83d St New York City NY 10028 Office: Bedford Park Blvd Bronx NY 10468

LEAF, RUTH, artist; b. N.Y.C.; d. Max and Ida (Rothman) Leaf; student Bklyn. Coll., 1939-40, Art Students League, 1942-45, Atelier 17 (Stanley William Hayter), 1945-47, New Sch. for Social Research, 1952-54; m. Hershey Lerner, June 18, 1941 (div. June 1966); children—Karen, Anita. One man shows Clark Coll., 1964, Asheville Art Mus., 1964, Western Ill. U., 1965, Brandeis U., 1965; exhibited in group shows Library of Congress, 1946, U. Pitts., 1947, Carnegie Inst., 1947, Bklyn. Mus., 1952, Seattle Art Mus., 1958, USIS, 1961, Pa. Acad., 1966, Boston Mus., 1967, Phila. Print Club, 1968; represented in permanent collections N.Y.U., Emily Lowe at U. Miami, USIA, Adelphi Coll., Art in Embassies program in Greece and Lebanon. Recipient purchase awards Library of Congress, 1946, Hofstra Coll., 1962, Olivet Coll., 1964, Hunterdon County Art Center, 1966, Nassau Community Coll., 1970; 1st prizes Village Art Center, 1959, Long Beach Art Center, 1959, North Shore Community Art Center, 1961. Mem. Phila. Print Club, Soc. Am. Graphic Artists, Boston Printmakers, Silvermine Guild, Am. Color Print Soc. (Florence Touner award 1969), Nat. Assn. Women Artists, Hunterdon County Art Center. Home: 42-30 235th St Douglaston NY 11363

LEAHY, JOAN GOMEZ-FRANCO, TV sales exec.; b. N.Y.C., Aug. 5, 1934; d. Harry M. and Ada V. (Allen) Gomez-Franco; B.S., Fordham U., 1956. Group mgr. broadcast research A.C. Nielsen Co., N.Y.C., 1957-60; supr. media analysis B.B.D.O., N.Y.C., 1960-64; v.p. network relations S.S.C. & B., 1964-72; network sales exec., NBC, N.Y.C., 1972—. Mem. Internat. Radio and TV Soc., Nat. Acad. TV Arts and Scis. Home: 350 E 54th St New York City NY 10022 Office: 30 Rockerfeller Plaza New York City NY 10020

LEAHY, SISTER MARY GERALD, educator, scientist; b. San Francisco, Oct. 11, 1917; d. Austin James and Josephine Cecilia (Coonan) Leahy; B.A., U. So. Cal., 1945; M.S., Cath. U. Am., 1947; Ph.D., U. Notre Dame, 1962; postgrad. Harvard, 1966. Joined Order Sisters St. Joseph Carondelet, 1936; prof. biology Mt. St. Mary's Coll., Los Angeles, 1966—; vis. scientist Harvard Sch. Pub. Health, 1967, U. Sheffield (Eng.), 1970; WHO grantee Israel Inst., for Biol. Scis., Ness Ziona Hebrew U., Jerusalem, 1968-70; cons. Internat. Centre for Insect Physiology and Ecology, Nairobi, Kenya, 1973, sr. research scientist collaborative project with East African Vet. Research Orgn., 1973-74. NSF research grantee for reproductive physiology mosquitoes, 1962-71; Entomol. Soc. Am. travel grantee, Canberra, Australia, SEATO Labs., Bangkok, Thailand, U.S. Naval Med. Research Unit, Taipei, Taiwan, Bishop Mus., Honolulu, 1972. Mem. Entmol. Soc. Am., A.A.A.S., Am. Inst. Biol. Scis., Am. Mosquito Control Assn., Sigma Xi, Phi Sigma. Roman Catholic. Contbr. articles to Evolution, Biol. Bull., Jour. Insect Physiology, Life Sci., Parasitology, Colloques Internationaux, Entomology London. Home: 12001 Chalon Rd Los Angeles CA 90049

LEAHY, MIRIAM KRAMER (MRS. WILLIAM E. LEAHY), assn. exec.; b. Maryland Line, Md., Nov. 6; d. Thomas Best and Luanna (Crook) Kramer; student George Washington U., 1912-13; m. William E. Leahy, Nov. 26, 1913 (dec. June 1956). Asst. vol. tchr. A.R.C., Washington, 1917-20, 39-41, chmn. Motor Corps, 1942-45, Grey Lady, Walter Reed Hosp., 1945-56, chmn. blood donor service, 1956-59, chmn. nursing services, 1959-69. Pres. Ladies Bd. Georgetown U. Hosp., 1950-52. Episcopalian. Clubs: Twentieth Century, Columbia Country (ltd. mem.), Cosmos (asso.), The Washington (v.p. 1958-59) (Washington); American Newspaper Women's. Home: 3325 Garfield St Washington DC 20008

LEAKE, JANE ACOMB (MRS. LOWELL LEAKE, JR.), educator; b. Cin., Aug. 12, 1928; d. Laurence Everett and Ruth Irene (Landwehr) Acomb; A.B. with high honors U. Cin., 1950, M.A., 1952, B.Ed., 1952; Ph.D. (fellow 1956-57, research fellow 1958-59), U. Wis., 1963; m. Lowell Leake, Jr., Sept. 5, 1959; children—Katherine Jane, Lowell G. Tchr. French and English, Walnut Hills High Sch., Cin., 1952-55; teaching asst. history and integrated liberal studies U. Wis., Madison, 1957-58, 59-60; instr. lit. U. Cin., 1961-64, asst. prof. history, 1965-69, asso. prof. history, 1969-73, prof. history, 1973—, chmn. dept. history Raymond Walters Coll., 1970—. Organizer, mem. Nat. Orgn. Women, 1968—, treas., 1968-69; mem. Am. Civil Liberties Union, 1961—. Named Outstanding Educator Am., 1971. Mem. Am. Hist. Assn., Common Cause, Mediaeval Acad. Am., Midwest Medieval Assn., Am. Assn. U. Women, Am. Assn. U. Profs. (state chmn. com. W 1973-74), Phi Beta Kappa (2d v.p. Delta Ohio 1971—, pres. elect 1973), Phi Alpha Theta. Author: The Geats of Beowulf: A Study in the Geographical Mythology of the Middle Ages, 1967. Home: 334 Whithorne Dr Cincinnati OH 45215

LEAR, BERNARDINE PINTO PADRONAGGIO (MRS. WILLIAM ROIL LEAR), educator; b. Gary, Ind., Nov. 29, 1920; d. Peter and Pauline (Pinto) Padronaggio; B.Edn., Chgo. Tchrs. Coll., 1943; M.A., Ariz. State U., 1960; m. William Roil Lear, June 30, 1946; children—Elizabeth Ann, William Roil, Robert Guy, Bruce Paul, Barbara Elaine. Tchr. pub. schs., Chgo., 1943-46, Memphis, 1947, Ariz., 1948-54; tchr., inaugurated spl. edn. program Laveen (Ariz.) Sch. Dist., 1960-69; tchr. educable mentally handicapped children Gray Sch., Phoenix, 1969-71; tchr. trainable mentally handicapped children Faith I. North Sch., Phoenix, 1971—. Mem. Nat. Assn. for Retarded Children (chpt. dir. 1959), Nat., Ariz. edn. assns., Phoenix Classroom Tchrs. Assn., Council for Exceptional Children, Am. Assn. Mental Deficiency. Roman Catholic. Home: 4522 N 53d Lane Phoenix AZ 85031 Office: 910 E Washington St Phoenix AZ 85034

LEASE, JANE ETTA, librarian; b. Kansas City, Kan., Apr. 10, 1924; d. Joy Alva and Emma (Jaggard) Omer; B.S. in Home Econs., U. Ariz., 1957; M.S. in Edn., Ind. U., 1962; M.S. in L.S., U. Denver, 1967; m. Richard J. Lease, Jan. 16, 1960; children—Janet (Mrs. Jacky B. Radifera), Joyce (Mrs. Robert J. Carson), Julia (Mrs. Earle D. Marvin), Cathy (Mrs. Edward F. Warren); stepchildren—Richard Jay II, William Harley. Newspaper reporter Ariz. Daily Star, Tucson, 1937-39; asst. home agt. Dept. Agr., 1957; homemaking tchr., Ft. Huachuca, Ariz., 1957-60; head tchr. Stonebelt Council Retarded Children, Bloomington, Ind., 1960-61; reference clk. Ariz. State U. Library, 1964-66; edn. and psychology librarian N.M. State U., 1969-71; Amway distbr., 1973—; cons. solid wastes, distressed land problems reference remedies, 1967; ecology lit. research and cons., 1966—. Ind. observer 1st World Conf. Human Environment, 1972. Mem. A.L.A., Nat., N.M. edn. assns., Am. Assn. U. Profs., Regional Environmental Edn. Research Information Orgn., Nat. Assn. Female Execs., P.E.O., D.A.R., Internat. Platform Assn., N.M. Rifle and Pistol Assn., Las Cruces Antique Car Club, Las Cruces Story League, N.M. Library Assn. Methodist (lay leader). Address: 2145 Boise Dr Las Cruces NM 88001

LEAVERTON, JEANNE WHITE, educator; b. nr. Athens, Ala., Feb. 12, 1933; d. John Baugh and Georgia (Bittick) White; B.A., Ala. Coll., 1956; M.A., U. Ala., 1968; postgrad. George Peabody Coll., 1968-69; Ph.D., Ariz. State U., 1972, Col. State Coll., 1973; m. P.A. Leaverton, 1955 (div. Oct. 1963); 1 dau., Lizabeth Courtney. Tchr. pvt. sch., Dallas, 1959-60; instr. English, So. Meth. U., Dallas, 1960-62; tchr. high sch., Morgan County, Ala., 1962-66; counselor Priceville High Sch., Decatur, Ala., 1966-68; dir., spl. edn. co-ordinator Assn. Retarded Children, Morgan, Lawrence, Limestone counties, Ala., Decatur, 1969—. Cons. mental retardation, 1969—. Instr.-grad. spl. edn. A. and M. U., Normal, Ala., 1970-71. Project dir. RESCUE for the Retarded, 1970—. Mem. Parents Without Partners (chpt. pres. 1969), Am. Assn. U. Women (br. dir. 1969-73), Decatur Ballet Assn. (treas.), League Women Voters (dir.), Huntsville Ballet

Co. (br. dir.), Decatur Womens C. of C., Am. Assn. Mental Deficiency, Council for Exceptional Children, Nat. Assn. Retarded Children, Am., Ala. personnel and guidance assns., Am. Assn. U. Women Deans and Counselors, Delta Kappa Gamma, Pi Kappa Delta, Rho Alpha Tau, Zeta Phi Eta. Home: 812 Johnston St SE Decatur AL 35601

LEAVIN, MARGO HARRIET, art gallery exec.; b. N.Y.C., Apr. 18, 1936; d. Victor David and Lillian (Green) Leavin; student U. Cal. at Berkeley, 1954-56, U. Mexico, summer 1956; B.S., U. Cal. at Los Angeles, 1958. Pvt. art dealer, 1965-70; founder, owner Margo Leavin Gallery, Inc., Los Angeles, 1970—. Mem. contemporary art council Los Angeles County Mus. Art. Bd. dirs. Otis Art Inst. Mem. Art Dealers Assn. So. Cal. Home: 1445 Miller Way Los Angeles CA 90069 Office: 812 N Robertson Blvd Los Angeles CA 90069

LEAVITT, JOAN KAZANJIAN (MRS. DONALD KEITH LEAVITT), physician; b. Boston, Jan. 14, 1926; d. Varaztad Hovannes and Marion Victorine (Hanford) Kazanjian; B.A., Radcliffe Coll., 1947; M.A., Smith Coll., 1949; M.D., Boston U., 1953; m. Donald Keith Leavitt, June 22, 1964; children—Lynda Donn, Mark Sterling. Intern, resident pediatrics Boston City Hosp., 1953-55; resident pediatrics Mass. Gen. Hosp., 1955-56; practice medicine specializing in pediatrics, Altus, Okla., 1959-64, Ponca City, Okla., 1967—; med. dir. Jackson County Health Dept., Altus, 1960-67, Ponca City-Kay County Health Dept., 1967—. Mem. Okla. State Health Planning Council. Mem. A.M.A., Okla. Med. Assn., Kay-Noble Med. Soc. (past pres.), Okla. Pub. Health Assn. (past pres.). Home: 717 Red Oak St Ponca City OK 74601 Office: Box 1959 1201 E Hartford St Ponca City OK 74601

LEAVITT, MARY JANICE DEIMEL (MRS. ROBERT WALKER LEAVITT), educator; b. Washington, Aug. 21, 1924; d. Henry L. and Ruth (Grady) Deimel; B.A., Am. U., Washington, 1946; postgrad. U. Md., 1963-65, U. Va., 1965-67, 72-73, George Washington U., 1966-67; m. Robert Walker Leavitt, Mar. 30, 1945; children—Michael Deimel, Robert Walker, Caroline Ann. Tchr., Rothery Sch., Arlington, Va., 1947; dir. Sunnyside, Children's House, Washington, 1949; asst. dir. Coop. Sch. for Handicapped Children, Arlington, 1962, dir., Arlington, Springfield, Va., 1963-66; tchr. mentally retarded children Fairfax (Va.) County Pub. Schs., 1966-68; asst. dir. Burgundy Farm Country Day Sch., Alexandria, Va., 1968-69; tchr., substitute tchr. specific learning problem children Accotink Acad., Springfield, Va., 1970—; sub-tchr. learning disabilities Children's Achievement Center, McLean, Va., 1973—. Mem. edn. subcom. Va. Commn. Children and Youth, 1973—. Den mother Nat. Capital Area Cub Scouts, Boy Scouts Am., 1962; troop fund raising chmn. Nat. Capitol council Girl Scouts U.S.A., 1968-69; capt. amblyopia team No. Va. chpt. Delta Gamma Alumnae, 1969. Mem. Am. Assn. U. Women (co-chmn. met. area mass media com. D.C. chpt. 1973-75), Council Exceptional Children, Audubon Naturalist Soc. Central Atlantic States, Delta Gamma (treas. No. Va. chpt. 1973-75). Roman Catholic. Club: Arlington Hall Officer's Wives. Home: 4902 Larno Dr Alexandria VA 22310 Office: 8519 Tuttle Rd West Springfield VA 22152

LEAVY, ELIZABETH GRAY, lawyer; b. Syracuse, N.Y., Dec. 17, 1941; d. Stanley Arnold and Margaret Huntington (Russell) Leavy; A.B. cum laude, Vassar Coll., 1963; J.D., Stanford, 1971. Admitted to Cal. bar, 1972; asso. firm O'Donnell, Waiss, Wall & Meschke, San Francisco, 1971-73; trial atty. San Francisco Litigation Center, Equal Employment Opportunity Commn., 1973—. Mem. State Bar Cal., San Francisco Bar Assn. (com. on sex discrimination). Club: Vassar (chmn. prospective students San Francisco 1972—). Home: 4229 26th St San Francisco CA 94131 Office: 1390 Market St San Francisco CA 94102

LEBAR, LOIS EMOGENE, educator; b. Olean, N.Y., Oct. 28, 1907; d. Roscoe Garfield and Alta Isabel (Hathaway) LeBar; student Geneseo (N.Y.) State Normal Sch., 1925-28, Moody Bible Inst., Chgo., 1933-35; B.A., Central YMCA Coll., Chgo., 1943; M.A., Wheaton (Ill.) Coll., 1945; Ph.D., N.Y. U., 1951. Tchr. elementary sch., Perry, N.Y., 1928-33; tchr. Moody Bible Inst., 1934-41; faculty Wheaton Coll., 1949—, chmn. grad. Christian edn., 1953—. Writer Sunday Sch. and Vacation Sch. lessons for primaries for Scripture Press, 1936-69. Named (with sister) Alumni of Year, Moody Bible Inst., 1959. Author: Children in the Bible School, 1952; Education That is Christian, 1958; Focus on People in Church Education, 1968; Family Devotions with School Age Children, 1973. Contbr. chpt. to An Introduction to Evangelical Christian Education, 1964. Home: 703 Howard St Wheaton IL 60187

LEBE, DORYANN MARIE (MRS. MELVIN STANTON LEBE), psychiatrist; b. Pasadena, Cal., Dec. 9, 1940; d. Arthur Edward and Doris Marie (Stattergren) Lamel; B.A., Stanford U., 1962; M.D., U. Cal. at Los Angeles, 1965; m. Melvin Stanton Lebe, Aug. 29, 1964; children—Anthony, Jennifer. Intern Sinai Hosp., Los Angeles, 1965-66; resident Neuropsychiat. Inst. U. Cal. at Los Angeles, 1966-69; pvt. practice psychiatry, Beverly Hills, 1970—; asso. clin. prof. U. Cal. at Los Angeles, 1970—; clin. asso. So. Cal. Psychoanalytic Inst., Los Angeles, 1970—; mem. staff Cedars-Sinai Hosp. Cons. Las Palmas Sch. for Girls, Los Angeles, 1969-71. Home: 3808 Surfwood Rd Malibu CA 90265 Office: 450 N Bedford Dr Beverly Hills CA 90210

LEBKICHER, ANNE ROSS (MRS. AUSTIN WALLACE LEBKICHER), artist; b. N.Y.C.; d. David and Anne Leslie (Lucas) Ross; student U. Wash., U. Mont., Columbia, Chouinard Art Sch., U. Wis., U. So. Cal., Oits Art Inst., Marymount Coll.; also pvt. art lessons; m. Austin Wallace Lebkicher, Sept. 15, 1926; 1 dau., Leslie Anne. Exhibited in group shows Palos Verdes (Cal.) Community Arts Assn., 1950-67, South Bay (Cal.), 1955-60, Mont. Inst. Arts, Kalispell, 1969, Flathead County Art Assn. Internat. Art Festival, 1970. Asso. weight engr. Douglas Aircraft Co. and McDonnell Douglas Missiles & Space Div., 1941-67. Mem. Flathead County Art Assn. (chmn. exhbns. 1969-72, dir. 1970—, v.p. 1973-75), Nat. League Am. Pen Women, Mont. League Profl. Women Artists, Palos Verdes Community Arts Assn. (chmn. exhbns. 1945-65, pres. 1955-56), Mont. Inst. Arts, Northwest Artists' Gallery. Contbr. articles to profl. jours. Home: Flathead Lake Rd Rollins MT 59931 Office: NW Artists' Gallery 7 1st E Kalispell MT 59901

LEBLANC, VERA ADORE, sch. ofcl.; b. Sacramento, Apr. 17, 1929; d. Clyde Floyd and Vera Aletta (Williams) Langworthy; A.A., Lamar Jr. Coll., 1950; R.N., St. Mary's Sch. Nursing, Port Arthur, Tex., 1950; postgrad. Lamar U., Beaumont, Tex., 1956, 71-72; B.S. in Nursing, U. Tex., 1973; m. Carl Nelson LeBlanc, July 1, 1951; children—Vicki Anne, Danny Michael, Greg Alan, Matthew Wayne, Terry Joseph. Instr. student nurses St. Mary's Sch. Nursing, 1952-53, pediatric supr., 1954-57, surgery supt., 1958-60; sch. nurse Nederland Ind. (Tex.) Sch. Dist., 1961-74, health occupations coop. tng., tchr., coordinator, 1974—. Pres., Little League Aux., 1961-62; sec.-treas. Jr. Football League, 1969-71, Little League, 1971-72. Bd. dirs. YMCA. Mem. Alumnae Assn. St. Mary's Sch. Nursing (pres. 1952-53), Tex. Tchrs. Assn. (pres. state sch. health sect. 1969, state legislative chmn. 1970), N.E.A. (bd. dirs. Tex., exec. com. dept. sch. nurses 1970—, legislative council dept. sch. nurses 1973-75), Internat. Platform Assn., Phi Sigma Alpha. Democrat. Roman Catholic. Home: 1517 Franklin Av Nederland TX 77627 Office: 200 S 6th St Nederland TX 77627

LEBOVITZ, CARLA SUSAN COHN (MRS. HERBERT CHARLES LEBOVITZ), interior designer, pub. relations exec.; b. York, Pa., June 19, 1932; d. Abraham D. and Sophie (Kramer) Cohn; grad. Walnut Hill Sch., 1949; B.A., Wellesley Coll., 1953; M.A., Lehigh U., 1964; postgrad. N.Y. U., 1967-68, Parsons Sch. Design, 1971-72; m. Herbert C. Lebovitz, June 21, 1953; children—Peter M., James A. Ward clk. Allentown (Pa.) Hosp., 1953-54; owner Pomeroy Leasing Co., Inc., York, Pa., 1955-60; sec. Modern Transfer Co., Inc., Allentown, 1967—; pres. The Acorn, Allentown, 1971—. Lectr. Allentown Art Mus., 1965—, docent chmn., 1965-68, adviser to dir., 1969—; tutor to handicapped Jr. High Sch. children in pub. schs., 1966-70; alumni interviewer Wellesley Coll., Lehigh Valley, 1968—, del. to alumni council, 1968, del. to Washington Conf., 1970. Mem. Community Council Fact Finding Com., 1969-71; mem. Lehigh Valley Guidance Clinic council br., 1967—, Weld United Fund, 1967—; spl. gifts chmn. United Jewish Appeal, 1967; spl. gifts co-chmn. Bonds for Israel, 1972. Bd. dirs. Arthritis Found., 1972; mem. Soc. Arts Allentown Mus. Bd., 1966—; aux. life mem. Jewish Community Center. Mem. Wellesley Club, Wellesley Club Friends Art, Nat. Trust for Historic Preservation, Smithsonian Assos., Assos. UN. Hadassah (life). Clubs: Berkleigh Country (Kutztown); Lehigh Valley Indoor Tennis (Allentown); Woman's. Home: 427 N 29th St Allentown PA 18104

LEBOWITZ, RHODA ELEANOR KOVACS (MRS. WALTER B. LEBOWITZ), civic worker; b. Bklyn.; d. William Gabriel and Shirley (Stone) Kovacs; student Manhattan Dental Sch., 1951-52, U. Miami, 1967, U. Fla., 1968; m. Walter B. Lebowitz, Feb. 14, 1954; children—Terry Lynn, Toby Jane, Jeffrey Howard. Asso., Joseph Dube Real Estate Co., Miami Beach, Fla., 1964-67, Paul Wimbish Real Estate Co., Miami Beach, 1967—; pres. Travel'n Tours, Inc.; dir. Household Burglar Alarm Co. Mem. Miami Beach Bd. Realtors. Regional chmn. Miami-Dade County March of Dimes, 1962; pres. Renanah Hadassah, 1966-67; mem. dinner dance com. Night in Italy. Mem. Democratic Exec. Com., Miami Beach, 1959-63; pres. Miami Beach Young Dem. Club, 1960. Bd. dirs. North Beach Elementary P.T.A. Recipient Woman of Year award B'nai B'rith, 1963. Mem. Miami Ballet Soc. (charter mem., bd. dirs. 1970—, corr. sec. 1971-72), O.R.T., Props. Jewish religion (v.p. temple). Mem. Rebecca Lodge. Home: 4550 N Bay Rd Miami Beach FL 33140 Office: 456 Arthur Godfrey Rd Miami Beach FL 33140

LEBOWITZ, RUTH, retail fashion chain exec.; b. St. Paul, Aug. 19, 1920; d. Isadore and Minnie (Dolinsky) Kieffer; A.A., U. Minn., 1941; m. Morris Lebowitz, Nov. 9, 1946 (dec. Dec. 1968); children—Sandra Joy, Gary Philip. Pres., owner Lieb's Corp., Mpls., 1968—; adv. bd. 1st Nat. Bank Mpls.; tchr. piano and choral music. Active P.T.A.'s, North Side Businessmen's Assn., Mpls. Fedn. Jewish Service, Com. for Israel Bonds, Mt. Sinai Hosp. Aux., Hillel House, Variety Club Heart Hosp. Recipient Nat. Leadership award Jewish Theol. Sem. of Am., 1974. Jewish religion (trustee, v.p. synagogue). Home: 4725 Minnetonka Blvd Minneapolis MN 55416 Office: 5707 W Broadway Minneapolis MN 55428

LEBRUN, VIVIAN LUCILLE DAVIS (MRS. DONALD EDWARD LEBRUN), co-owner theatre; b. Ayersville, O., Nov. 29, 1909; d. John Edgar and Nettie Ann (Eis) Davis; student pub. schs.; m. Donald Edward LeBrun, July 5, 1932; children—Suzanne (Mrs. Thomas Clark Cook), Donald Davis. Staff writer South Whitley (Ind.) Tribune, 1947-58, accounts exec., advt. dept., 1958; photographer, columnist Warsaw-Times-Union, Warsaw, Ind., 1947-72; co-owner, co-mgr. Kent Theatre, South Whitley, Ind., 1957—. Recipient award for oil painting Whitley County Art Guild Show, Columbia City, 1973. Mem. Gen. Fedn. Women's Clubs (county pres. 1941-42, dist. pres. 1956-58), Internat. Platform Assn., Nat. League Am. Pen Women, Nat. Writers Club, Ft. Wayne Hist. Soc., D.A.R. (chpt. regent 1972-74), Ladies Aux. V.F.W. (post pres. 1945), Whitley County Artist Guild, Ind. Museum Soc. (dist. dir. 1973-75). Methodist. Mem. Order Eastern Star (worthy matron 1944-45), White Shriner Jerusalem. Address: 106 N Maple St Box 495 South Whitley IN 46787

LECARIE, LORRAINE MARY, psychologist; b. N.Y.C., Oct. 20, 1926; d. David Aloysius and Marion Agnes (Halls) Lecarie; B.A., St. Joseph Coll., 1950; M.S., St. John U., 1961; M.Ed., Boston U., 1969. Joined Daus. of Wisdom, 1946, del. to provincial chpt., 1968-70; tchr. Bishop McDonnell High Sch., Bklyn., 1950-59; prin. Gate of Heaven Elementary Sch., Ozone Park, 1959-62, Christ the King High Sch., Middle Village, 1962-68, Our Lady of Wisdom Acad., Ozone Park, 1969-70; sch. psychologist Monroe County Bd. Edn., Union, W.Va., also Mercer County Bd. Edn., Princeton, W.Va., 1970—. Mem. adv. council on spl. edn. in Mercer County, 1970—; mem. adv. council for vol. services Dept. Welfare, Mercer County, 1971; vol. counselor various local social agys. Mem. Am. Psychol. Assn. (asso.), Nat. Assn. Sch. Psychologists, W.Va. Sch. Psychologists Assn. (chmn. ethics com. 1971—). Home: 601 Harrison St Princeton WV 24740 Office: Monroe County Bd Edn Union WV 24983 also Mercer County Bd Edn Princeton WV 24740

LECHNER, SISTER JOAN MARIE, coll. pres.; b. Nebraska City, Neb., July 25, 1913; d. John G. and Mary (Tongish) Lechner; A.B., Loras Coll., 1950; Ph.D., St. Louis U., 1960. Joined Soc. of Ursulines, 1934; instr. English, Latin and commerce St. Joseph's High Sch., Owensboro, Ky., 1936-48, St. Catherine's High Sch., New Haven, Ky., 1948-50; instr. English, Latin and bus., also prin. St. Francis's High Sch., Loretta, Ky., 1950-53; instr. English and bus., also treas. Brescia Coll., Owensboro, 1953-56, pres., 1959—. Recipient St. Louis U. Alumni Merit award, 1968; Liberty Bell award Daviess County Bar Assn., 1970; named Citizen of Yr., Civitan Club, 1969; Woman of Achievement of Year award Bus. and Profl. Women's Club, Owensboro br., 1974. Author: Renaissance Concepts of the Commonplaces, 1962. Address: Brescia Coll Owensboro KY 42301

LECKIE, NESSA, nursing adminstr.; b. Winnipeg, Man., Can., Apr. 21, 1911; d. Sany and Esther (Kanter) Leckie; R.N., St. Paul's Hosp., Saskatoon, Sask., Can., 1932; postgrad. in psychiat. nursing Provincial Hosp.; B. Nursing, McGill U., (Can.), 1961. Psychiat. nurse Provincial Hosp., Ponoka, Alta., 1937-47, Psychiat. Hosp., Winnipeg, Man., Can., 1947-49, Provincial Hosp., Ponoka and Edmonton, Alta., 1949-58; dir. nursing edn. Douglas Hosp., Montreal, Que., Can., 1958-69, dir. nursing, 1969—. Cons. in mental health field of nursing edn., Canadian Internat. Devel. Agy., Dept. External Affairs of Can., Trinidad, 1966; surveyor Canadian Council Hosp. Accreditation. Club: Zonta (Montreal). Home: 6875 Lasalle Blvd Montreal PQ H4H 1R3 Canada Office: Douglas Hosp 6875 Lasalle Blvd Montreal PQ Canada

LECLAIR, MARGARET FOSTER, dean; b. Elmora, Pa., Sept. 7, 1911; d. Robert Burch and Grace (Hartmann) Foster; B.A., Ohio Wesleyan U., 1933; M.A., Ohio State U., 1934, Ph.D., 1940; m. Charles George LeClair, May 30, 1945. Librarian dept. English, Ohio State U., 1934-41, instr. English, 1941-44; asst. prof. English, N.Y. State Coll. Tchrs., Buffalo, 1944-46; instr. Carnegie-Mellon U., 1946-47, asst. prof., 1947-53, asso. prof. English, 1953-60, head dept. gen. studies Margaret Morrison Carnegie Coll., 1955-56, dean, 1956-60, acting head dept. bus. studies 1957-60; dean coll. Beaver Coll., Glenside, Pa., 1960-73, dean grad. studies, 1973—, prof. English, 1960—. Fellow Fund for Advancement Edn., 1952-53. Mem. Modern Lang. Assn., Coll. English Assn., Nat. Council Tchrs. of English, Am. Assn. U. Profs., Mortar Bd., Phi Beta Kappa, Phi Kappa Phi, Kappa Delta Pi. Contbg. author: Lectures on Some Modern Poets, 1955. Home: 7614 Lafayette Av Melrose Park Philadelphia PA 19126 Office: Beaver Coll Glenside PA 19038

LE COCQ, RHODA PRISCILLA, govt. ofcl., author; b. Lynden, Wash., Jan. 31, 1921; d. Ralph B. and Nellie O. (Straks) Le Cocq; B.A., Wash. State U., 1942; M.A. in Creative Writing, Stanford, 1950; M.A. in Philosophy, U. Cal. at Santa Barbara, 1967; Ph.D., Cal. Inst. Asian Studies, 1970. Radio writer and actress sta. KHQ, Spokane, Wash., sta. KOIN, Portland, Ore., sta. KIRO, Seattle, 1939-42; owner LeCocq-Luray, N.Y.C., 1946-47; free lance writer, 1946-48; lit. scout Farrar, Straus & Cudahy, N.Y.C., 1948-53; pub. relations dir. Honolulu Acad. Arts, 1957-58; owner, propr. pub. relations counseling firm, Honolulu, 1958-61; information officer City and County of Honolulu, 1961-63, Sacramento County (Cal.) Dept. Social Welfare, 1969—; instr., lectr. U. Hawaii, 1960-61; instr. philosophy U. Cal. at Davis, 1970-71; vis. prof. Cal. Inst. Asian Studies, 1972-73; lectr. Bombay, India, 1973. Served to lt. USNR, 1942-46, ret. Res., 1970. Recipient certificate for contbn. to East-West Understanding, Cultural Integration Fellowship, 1969. Mem. Pub. Relations Soc. Am., Sacramento Pub. Relations Round Table, Cultural Integration Fellowship San Francisco, Acad. Parapsychology and Medicine Palo Alto, Internat. Platform Assn., Center for Democratic Instns., Smithsonian Inst. (asso.), USNR Assn., Mensa, Armed Forces Writers League, Kappa Alpha Theta, Theta Sigma Phi. Clubs: Sacramento Press; Marines Meml. (life) (San Francisco). Author: The Radical Thinkers: Heidegger and Sri Aurobindo, 1972; Vision of Superhumanity, 1973; short story Behold A Pale Horse included in several anthologies, dramatized TV, 1957. Home: 1500 7th St Capitol Towers Sacramento CA 95814 Office: 1725 28th St Sacramento CA 95814

LECOUNT, ADNA MARION, psychologist; b. Basin, Mont., Sept. 20, 1916; d. Charles Leroy and Adna Marion (Dunlap) LeCount; B.S., U. Cal. at Berkeley, 1940; M.A., Columbia (Sarah Sturtevant fellow 1949), 1950, Ed.D., 1950. Dean women No. Ariz. U., 1950-52; dean girls Phoenix South Mountain High Sch., 1952-57; coordinator counseling Burlingame High Sch., 1957-62; sch. psychologist Fresno (Cal.) County Dept. Edn., 1963-68; dist. psychologist Clovis (Cal.) Unified Sch. Dist., 1968—. Tchr., No. Ariz. U., 1950-52, Coll. San Mateo, 1951-52, Fresno State U., 1963-67; pvt. practice as clin. psychologist, Fresno, 1963—. Chmn. Fresno County Mental Health Adv. Bd., 1970-71; mem. Area Bd. on Mental Retardation, 1970-71. Served with USNR, 1943-46. Mem. Am. Guidance Personnel Assn., Cal. Assn. Sch. Psychologists and Psychiatrists, Kappa Delta Pi. Home: 405 E Lansing Way Fresno CA 93704 Office: 914 4th St Clovis CA 93612

LECOUNT, VIRGINIA G., communications exec.; b. Long Island City, N.Y., Nov. 22, 1917; d. Clifford R. and Luella (Meier) LeCount; B.A., Barnard Coll., 1937; M.A., Columbia, 1940. Tchr. pub. schs., P.R., 1937-38; supr. HOLC, N.Y.C., 1938-40; translator Guildhall Publs., 1940-41; office mgr. Sperry Gyroscope Co., Garden City, Lake Success, Bklyn. (all N.Y.), 1941-45; billing mgr. McCann Erickson, Inc., N.Y.C., 1945-56; v.p., bus. mgr., bd. dirs. Infoplan Internat, Inc., 1956-69; v.p., bus. mgr. Communications Affiliates Ltd., Communications Affiliates (Bahamas) Ltd., 1968-71; bus. mgr. Jack Tinker & Partners, Inc., 1969-70; mgr. office services Interpub. Group of Cos., Inc., N.Y.C., 1970-72, corporate records mgr., 1972—. Mem. Alumnae Barnard Coll. (dir.). Mem. Marble Collegiate Ch. Home: 136 E 55th St New York City NY 10022 Office: 1271 Av of Americas New York City NY 10020

L'ECUYER, ELEANOR CREED, Coast Guard officer; b. Boston, June 13, 1922; d. Eugene Wilfred and Eleanor Cary (Creed) L'Ecuyer; A.B., Suffolk U., 1944, LL.B., 1950, J.D., 1973. Enlisted to seaman recruit, USCGR, 1944, advanced through grades to capt., 1972—; mil. judge, 1971-74; chief Res. div. 12th dist., 1974—; admitted to Mass. bar, 1951, U.S. Supreme Court Bar, 1966. Sec. Utility Workers Union AFL local 387, 1952-56; mem. Mass. Wage Bd., 1954. Trustee, bd. dirs. Vinson Hall, McLean, Va., 1970-72. Mem. Am. Bar Assn., Res. Officers Am. Assn., Mass. Soc. Washington DC, Mass. Assn. Women Lawyers, Internat. Assn. Fed. Women Lawyers, Am. Legion. Democrat. Roman Catholic. Home: 405 Davis Ct San Francisco CA 94111 also 119 Andover St Apt E Sun City Center FL 33570 Office: Chief Res Div 12th USCG Dist 630 Sansome St San Francisco CA 94126

LEDBETTER, BARBARA ALLEN (MRS. HORACE RICHARD LEDBETTER), author, educator; b. Newcastle, Tex., Nov. 24, 1925; d. Cicero and Eva Pearl (Rowe) Neal; B.S., N. Tex. State U., 1947; M.E., W. Tex. State U., 1954; postgrad. Sul Ross State U., 1962; m. Horace Richard Ledbetter, May 30, 1948; children—Scarlett Eva Elena, Patricia Florence Lee. Tchr., Seymour, Tex., 1947-50, Lefors, Tex., 1950-51, White Deer, Tex., 1951-60, Bryson, Tex., 1965—. Feature writer Newcastle (Tex.) Register, 1957-68, Wichita Falls (Tex.) Record News, 1959-74, Olney (Tex.) Enterprise, 1959-66, This is West Texas Mag., 1965-70, Graham (Tex.) News, 1959-74, Young County Mag., Graham, 1972—; asst. archivist Ft. Belknap Archives, Inc., Tex., 1961-74. Del. Tex. Democrat Conv., 1960-72. Mem. Tex. Indsl. Arts Assn., Young County Hist. Commn. (treas. 1961-74), Tex. State, Jack County tchrs. assns., Ft. Belknap Soc., W. Tex. Hist. Assn. (yearbook feature writer 1964-70). Club: Graham Women's. Author: The Diary of a Frontiersman, 1858-1859, 1961; Scrapbook of Young County, Texas, 1962; Fort Belknap of Yesterday and Today, 1851-1963, 1963; The Cattlemen's Association, 1877, 1964; Civil War Days in Young County, Texas, 1861-1865, 1965; A Guide to Fort Belknap, 1965; Who Was Saint-to-Hoodle Goombi, 1966; Dr. Pope, Fort Belknap Doctor, 1860's, 1967; (brochure) An Historical Cameo of Early Twentieth Century, Texas Newcastle, Texas, 1968; Oil City, Young County, Texas, 1968; Zachariah Ellis Coombes, the Samuel Pepys of the Texas Frontier, 1969; Newcastle, Texas, the Coal Mining Town, 1907-1970, 1970; Centennial Grahamana, 1872-1972, 1972; A History of Fort Belknap, 1973; Young County Reorganized, 1874-1974, 1974. Editor: Ft. Belknap Geneal. Assn. Bull. Home and office: Murray Route Graham TX 76046

LEDBETTER, ELAINE WALKER (MRS. WILLIAM MICHAEL LEDBETTER), educator; b. Tonkawa, Okla., May 28, 1917; d. Roswell Cornell and Alta (Clark) Walker; student No. Okla. Jr. Coll., 1934-37; B.S., Okla., 1939; M.Ed., N. Tex. State U., 1954; m. William Michael Ledbetter, June 26, 1942. Tchr. biology and chemistry Blackwell (Okla.) High Sch., 1941-42; tchr. biology, chemistry, physics Shidler-Webb City (Okla.) Ind. Sch., 1942-51; tchr. chemistry, head sci. dept. Pampa (Tex.) Ind. Schs., 1951—. Profl. photographer, 1952—. Mem. scholarship com. Gray County Heart Assn., 1960-63; mem. Tex. Textbook Com., 1961-62; adv. council Nat. Sci. Fair-Internat., 1961-70; dir. Pampa Sci. Fair, 1958-68; staff coll. cooperative secondary schs. program W. Tex. State U., 1969-70; mem. com. examiners Coll. Entrance Exam. Bd., 1969-74. Named

Adult Leader of Yr., Pampa Key Club, 1961; Tex. Tchr. of Yr., 1966; Outstanding Chemistry Tchr. in Tex., 1965; Look mag. Tchr. Honor Roll, 1966, James Bryant Conant award 5th Dist., 1967. Mem. Nat. Sci. Tchrs. Assn. (sec. 1962-64, chmn. nat. conv. 1967, pres. 1972-73), Tex. Sci. Tchrs. Assn. (past pres.), N.E.A., Pampa Classroom Tchrs. Assn. (past pres.), A.A.A.S., Am. Chem. Soc., Poetry Soc. Tex. (councillor 1967-69), Internat. Platform Assn., P.E.O., Beta Sigma Phi (Woman of Yr., Pampa 1969). Democrat. Methodist. Mem. Order Eastern Star (past matron). Club: Altrusa (named Woman of Yr., Pampa 1961). Author: Triumphant Moment, 1961; Candles at Noon, 1966; Enfold the Splendor, 1973; (with John H. Marean) Introductory Physical Science: A Laboratory Approach, 1968; (with Jay A. Young) Keys to Chemistry. Home: 1611 Grape St Pampa TX 79065 Office: 111 Harvester St Pampa TX 79065

LEDERER, ANNE TRACY (MRS. H. AUSTIN LEDERER), educator; b. Chgo., Nov. 4, 1917; d. Howard Van Sinderen and Ruth Alexander Tracy; received A.B. with honors, Swarthmore Coll., 1938; A.M., Radcliffe Coll., 1940; m. William Rossmoore, June 24, 1938 (div.); 1 dau., Susan Tracy; m. 2d, H. Austin Lederer, Feb. 21, 1959; stepchildren—Meredith, Louise. Substitute tchr., Essex County, N.J., 1958—. Organizer, first chmn. N.J. chpt. Parents Without Partners, Inc., 1958—; Swarthmore Coll. rep. to Barnard Forum, 1955-57; pres. North Jersey Swarthmore Coll. Alumni Assn., 1957, 69; sec. class of 1938 at Swarthmore, 1958—. Mem. League Women Voters (mem. bd. Verona league 1971-74), Alliance Française. Clubs: Swarthmore; Radcliffe (mem. N.J. bd. 1966-69) (N.J. and N.Y.). Contbr. articles to mags. Home: 32 Otsego Rd Verona NJ 07044

LEDERER, CORINNE EDWARDS (MRS. WILLIAM J. LEDERER), coll. dean; b. Lynbrook, N.Y., Apr. 21, 1926; d. Wilbur Nelson and Ruth Pearl (MacKenzie) Edwards; B.A., Hood Coll., 1948; M.Ed., U. Vt., 1972; m. William J. Lederer, July 24, 1965; children—Paul, Kim, Kevin, Kyle. Owner, pub. Pearl Harbor Pennysaver mag., 1953-58; founder Honolulu Beacon mag., 1959, pub., advt. dir., 1959-65; chmn. bd. dirs. Kokohala Pub. corp., Honolulu, 1959-65; founder Cork Enterprises, Honolulu, 1963; with Champlain Coll., Burlington, Vt., 1971—, dir. counseling, 1971—. Co-chmn. state legislature polit. campaign, Hawaii, 1960; mem. Rep. Dist. Com., Hawaii, 1963. Named Media Woman of Yr., Advt. Agy. Assn. Hawaii, 1963. Mem. New Eng., Vt. personnel and guidance assns. Home: Peacham VT 05862 Office: Champlain Coll Burlington VT 05401

LEDESMA, JOCYLINE J. (MRS. AMANDO R. MEDINA), physician; b. Iloilo City, Phillipines, Oct. 17, 1937; d. Marcelino J. and Hermogena S. (Jaena) Ledesma; M.D., U. Philippines, 1962; m. Amando R. Medina, July 10, 1971. Intern, Philippine Gen. Hosp., Manila, 1961-62, resident pediatrics, 1962-63; rotating intern Worcester (Mass.) City Hosp., 1963-64; resident pediatrics Columbus Children's Hosp., 1964-66; fellow pediatrics Montefiore-Morrisania Hosp., N.Y.C., 1966-67; practice diagnostic and pediatric radiology, Pitts., 1967—; mem. staff P.H's. Children's Hosp. Diplomate Am. Bd. Pediatrics, Am. Bd. Diagnostic Radiology. Mem. A.M.A., Am. Coll. Radiology, Pa. Radiol. Soc., Pitts. Roentgen Soc., John Caffey Soc., Filipino Assn. Pitts. (officer 1968-69), Mu Sigma Phi. Roman Catholic. Home: 5625 Dunmoyle St Pittsburgh PA 15217 Office: 125 De Soto St Pittsburgh PA 15213

LEDFORD, EILEEN ANNE KOVALY (MRS. MARSHALL M. LEDFORD), theater owner, notary pub.; b. McKeesport, Pa.; d. Andrew E. and Mary (Skakan) Kovaly; student Douglas Bus. Coll., 1923-25; m. Marshall M. Ledford, Jan. 25, 1926 (dec. Aug. 1956); 1 son, Marshall M. Owner, mgr. Rialto Theater, Madison, W.Va., 1948—; owner A & M Corp., Logan, W.Va., 1960-70; with W.Va. Racing Commn., Charleston, 1961—, chief clk., 1963-71, exec. sec., 1971—; notary pub., Charleston, 1963—. Mem. Boone County Co-Op. Scholarship Fund, Inc., Madison, 1964—. Mem. Nat. Assn. Theater Owners Am. (bd. dirs., pres. state unit 1971—), W.Va. Allied Theaters (sec. 1963, 67—), Madison Garden Club Council (pres. 1941-43), Morris Harvey Coll. Alumni Assn. (hon.), Democrat. Methodist. Club: Womans (pres. bd. trustees 1958-62) (Madison). Home: 333 Main St Madison WV 25130

LEDLIE, MARY ELIZABETH, librarian; b. Carlisle, Ia., Feb. 23, 1918; d. Thomas Lindsay and Mabel (Sells) Ledlie; B.A., Monmouth Coll., 1939; B.L.S., Carnegie Inst. Tech., 1940. Asst. librarian Ia. State Traveling Library, Des Moines, 1940-43; 1st asst. childrens dept. Des Moines Pub. Library, 1943-44, br. librarian, 1944-46, head childrens dept., 1946-56; supr. work with children Pub. Library, Toledo, 1956-62; coordinator youth services Milw. Pub. Library, 1962—. Mem. A.L.A. (div. pres. 1970-71), P.E.O., Delta Kappa Gamma, Kappa Delta. Republican. Presbyn. Clubs: Soroptimist (pres. 1955) (Des Moines); Zonta (pres. 1969) (Milw.). Contbr. articles to library and ednl. publs. Home: 2773 N Maryland Av Milwaukee WI 53211 Office: 814 W Wisconsin Av Milwaukee WI 53233

LEDUC, HENRIETTA MARIE, chemist; b. Detroit, Oct. 26, 1918; d. Edmund Joseph and Estelle Clara (Feirer) LeDuc; B.S. (McGregor scholar) Wayne State U., 1947; Ph.D. (Harper Hosp. Kresge fellow), Mich. State U., 1956. Research chemist Harper Hosp., Detroit, 1947-50; research fellow Mich. State U., East Lansing, 1950-56; research chemist Ethyl Corp., Ferndale, Mich., 1956-65; research asso. Univ. Hosp., Ann Arbor, Mich., 1965-73, sr. research asso., 1973—. Mem. A.A.A.S., Am. Chem. Soc., Med. Electronics and Data Soc., Sigma Xi, Sigma Pi Sigma. Home: 43537 Cottisford Rd Northville MI 48167 Office: 1405 E Ann St Ann Arbor MI 48104

LEDWIDGE, MARY MARGARET, banker; b. Kansas City, Mo., June 26, 1923; d. John Patrick and Grace Mary (Dailey) Ledwidge; ed. pub. schs., Am. Inst. Banking. With Pleasant Hill Bank (Mo.), 1941—, beginning as bookkeeper, successively asst. cashier, cashier, v.p., 1941-64, exec. v.p., 1964—, dir., 1952—. Chmn. bus. dist. campaign Pleasant Hill Community United Fund, 1968-73; treas. Pleasant Hill Indsl. Found., 1961-72; sec. Pleasant Hill Planning Commn., 1968—. Recipient certificate of recognition Pleasant Hill chpt. Future Farmers Am., 1970. Mem. Nat. Assn. Bank Women, Cass County Bankers Assn. (pres. 1950), Pleasant Hill Bus. and Profl. Women's Club (pres. 1949-50). Democrat. Roman Catholic. Club: Plesant Hill Golf and Country. Home: Route 4 Pleasant Hill MO 64080 Office: PO Box 43 Pleasant Hill MO 64080

LEE, ALDORA GRAF (MRS. RONNAL L. LEE), psychologist; b. Schenectady, June 18, 1936; d. Alois W. and M. Dorothy (Swigert) Graf; A.B. with high honors and honors in Psychology (Andrew Found. scholars), Ind. U., 1958; M.A., (Ford Found. fellow), Stanford, 1960; Ph.D. (Nat. Inst. Mental Health fellow), U. Colo., 1965; m. Ronnal L. Lee, June 9, 1964. Asst. prof. U. Colo., 1965-67, research asso., 1967-68; asst. prof. Met. State Coll., Denver, 1968-70; vis. asst. prof., research asso. Ohio State U., 1971-73; vis. asst. prof. U. Ida., 1973; asst. prof. Wash. State U., Pullman, 1973—. NSF fellow U. Mich., summer 1971. Mem. A.A.A.S., Am. Psychol. Assn., Am. Sociol. Assn., Soc. Psychol. Study Social Issues, Phi Beta Kappa, Sigma Xi, Psi Chi. Contbr. articles to profl. jours. Home: 1120 N Virginia Av Moscow ID 83843 Office: Dept Psychology Wash State U Pullman WA 99163

LEE, ALEXANDRA SAIMOVICI (MRS. JACK LEE), civil engr.; b. Negresti-Vaslui, Rumania, Nov. 6, 1932; d. Leonidas and Etlea (Sraibman) Saimovici; C.E., U. Bucharest (Rumania), 1956; postgrad. U. S.C., 1973—; m. Jack Lee, July 14, 1972. Came to U.S., 1969, naturalized, 1974. Civil engr. Energo-Constructia, Bucharest, 1956-61, Elcora Construcciones Metalicas, Buenos Aires, Argentina, 1961-69; structural designer Walter Kidde, N.Y.C., 1969-70, John Kassner, cons. engrs., N.Y.C., 1971; civil engr., City of Columbia Engring. Dept. (S.C.), 1972—. Registered profl. engr., S.C. Mem. Nat. Soc. Profl. Engrs., Am. Concrete Inst. Home: 1608 Two Notch Rd Columbia SC 29204 Office: 1747 Main St Columbia SC 29201

LEE, AMY FREEMAN (MRS. FREEMAN LEE), artist, educator; b. San Antonio, Oct. 3, 1914; d. Joe and Julia (Freeman) Freeman; grad. St. Mary's Hall, 1931; student U. Tex., 1931-34; student Incarnate Word Coll., 1934-42, Litt.D. (hon.), 1965; m. Ernest R. Lee, Oct. 17, 1937 (div. Jan., 1941). Art critic San Antonio Express, 1939-41; staff art critic radio sta. KONO, 1947-51; lectr. on art humanities dept. Trinity U., San Antonio, 1954-56, San Antonio Art Inst., 1955-56; lectr. art Our Lady of Lake Coll., San Antonio, 1969-71, one man shows, 1947—, including Mus. Fine Arts, Houston, 1949, Betty Parsons Galleries, N.Y., 1950, Wellons Galleries, N.Y., 1952, Dalzell Hatfield Galleries, Los Angeles, 1952, Witte Meml. Mus., San Antonio, 1953, Tex. Fine Arts Assn., Austin, 1954, Okla. Art Center, Oklahoma City, 1954, Neptune Galleries, Marblehead, Mass., 1955, Stewart Rickard Gallery, San Antonio, Texas, 1960, 61, Haydon Calhoun Gallery, Dallas, 1961, Kendall Art Gallery, San Angelo, Tex., Amarillo Art Gallery, LaVillita Art Gallery, San Antonio, Arte A.C., Monterrey, Mexico, Chandler Gallery, Dallas, 1964, Incarnate Word Coll., 1965, 74, Beaumont Art Mus., 1966, 70, Randolph Gallery, Houston, 1966, Random Gallery, Dallas, 1966, Mexican-Am. Cultural Exchange Inst., Monterrey, Mexico, 1967, San Antonio Pub. Library, 1968, McLennan Community Coll., 1969, U. Tex., 1970, 73, Tex. Tech. U., 1970, Del Mar Coll., Corpus Christi, Tex., 1970, Southwestern U., Georgetown, Tex., 1971, L. & L. Gallery, Longview, Tex., 1971, Pioneer Meml. Library, Fredricksburg, Tex., 1971, U. Tex. Student Union, 1972, Ojo del Sol Gallery, El Paso, 1972, Shook-Carrington Gallery, San Antonio, 1972, others, Tex., Cal.; exhibited works in numerous group shows U.S., Europe, including Nat. Soc. Painters in Casein, N.Y.C., 1969, 71, 72, 73; 25th Anniversary Tex. Watercolor Soc. Exhibit, San Antonio, 1974; Nat. Tour Am. Drawings, Smithsonian Inst., 1965-66, ann. exhbns. nat. art socs., galleries, confs.; represented permanent collections. Recipient Herweck award, 1960, Elizabeth Arden Purchase prize 1961; Ann. Civic and Craftsmanship award San Antonio chpt. A.I.A., 1960; Charles Rosen award, 1950; Goode award Tex. Fine Arts Assn., 1950; purchase prize Burch-Wademan Gallery, Houston, 1963; purchase prize, juried exhbn, Hertzberg Gallery, San Antonio, 1963; Jurors' Choice, Tex. Fine Arts Assn. Exhbn., 1965; 1st prize, Jr. League purchase prize Beaumont Art Mus., 1969; others; named Woman of Distinction, Baylor U., 1967; Camellia award Joskes Tex., 1971; honorable mention 5-State Biennial Exhbn., Port Arthur, Tex., 1971; 1st prize Contemporary Artists Exhbn., San Antonio, 1973; Trevira-Hoescht Purchase Prize, 1974. Amy Freeman Lee Am. Assn. Univ. Women Ednl. Found. Fellowship named, 1973. Work reproduced in Our Expanding Vision, 1959, La Revue Moderne, 1957, 59, 63, 65, C.S. Monitor, 1959, 63, Art and the Creative Tchr., 1971, Tex. Quarterly, 1973, Tex. Trends, 1973, Character Edn. Jour., 1973. Mem. adv. com. San Antonio Blind Assn.; jury mem. children's poetry contest San Antonio Pub. Library; cons. Mexican-Am. Cultural Exchange. Inst., San Antonio; mem. adv. council Friends Sequin and Guadalupe County Pub. Libraries. Chmn. bd. dirs. Incarnate Word Coll., San Antonio; bd. dirs., nat. sec., mem. adv. bd. Gulf States br. Humane Soc. U.S.; bd. dirs. Incarnate Word Coll., Madonna Neighborhood Centers of San Antonio, Humane Soc. Bexar County, San Antonio chpt. Am. Civil Liberties Union, Arts Council San Antonio, Pub. Information Corp., Austin, Tex., First Repertory Theater, Cultural Arts San Antonio; fine arts adv. council U. Tex.; chmn. adv. com. cultural div. HemisFair '68, San Antonio; pres. Friends San Antonio Pub. Library, 1969-70; bd. mem. corp. The Cambridge Sch., Weston, Mass.; mem. exec. bd., chmn. finance Quakers Am. Friends Service com. of S.W. Region, Austin, 1947—; trustee S.W. chpt. Nat. Found. for Myasthenia Gravis; bd. mgrs. Cultural Arts San Antonio; mem. cons. bd. Kenwood Community Council; mem. adv. com. occupational edn. and tech. dept. Alamo Heights High Sch. Mem. Am. Fedn. Arts, Art Assn. New Orleans, Artists Equity Assn., Boston Soc. Ind. Artists (Smith Coll. purchase prize 1950), Mus. Modern Art, Nat. Soc. Arts and Letters, San Antonio Chamber Music Soc., Philos. Soc. Tex., Defenders of Wildlife, Am. Anti-Vivisect. Soc. (life), Tex. Art Educators, Coll. Art Assn. Am., Woman's Aux. Santa Rosa Med. Center, St. Mary's Hall Alumni Assn., San Antonio Conservation Soc., Poetry Soc. Am., Poetry Soc. San Antonio (dir.), Am. Soc. Aesthetics, Assn. Internationale des Critiques d'Art, Paris, Contemporary Artists Group San Antonio (dir.), Nat., Southwestern (purchase prize 1967, Harwood K. Smith award 1969), Tex. (purchase prize 1963, 64, 69, 74, dir.), Cal. (Figure painting award 1967) watercolor socs., San Antonio Art League (2d v.p.), Nat. Art Edn. Assn., Laguna Beach Art Assn. (hon.), Expts. in Art and Tech., Assn. Governing Bds. Univs. and Colls., Internat. Platform Assn., Bus. and Profl. Women's Assn. (hon.), Am. Assn. U. Profs., Internat. Soc. Edn. Through Art, Kappa Pi (hon.), Delta Delta Delta, numerous other groups. Author: Hobby Horses, 1940; A Critic's Notebook, 1943; Remember Pearl Harbor, 1945. Address: 127 Canterbury Hill San Antonio TX 78209

LEE, ANNABEL, educator; b. Sylvia, Kan., Mar. 24, 1915; d. Robert E. and Sarah L. (Groves) Lee; B.S. in Elementary Edn., Kansas City Tchrs. Coll., 1935; M.A. in Elementary Edn., Northwestern U., 1941; Ed.D. (Teaching fellow 1952-53), U. Wash., 1966. Tchr. schs., Heise, Ida., 1935-36, Kansas City, Mo., 1936-42; dir. Elementary Campus Sch., Harding Coll., Searcy, Ark., 1942-52; mem. faculty U. Puget Sound, Tacoma, 1953—, prof. edn., 1969—. Prin. elementary div. Am. Community Sch., Beirut, Lebanon, 1965-67. Recipient scholarship Pi Lambda Theta, 1962. Mem. Am. Assn. U. Profs., Assn. for Student Teaching (state pres. 1964-65), N.W. Philosophy Edn. Soc. (program chmn. 1971-72), Pi Lambda Theta, Alpha Delta Kappa. Club: Soroptimist (Tacoma). Office: Univ Puget Sound Tacoma WA 98416

LEE, ANNE NATALIE, nurse; b. Bklyn.; d. Taras Pavlovich and Maria (Jukovskaya) Dubovick; B.A., Hunter Coll., 1940; M.A., N.Y.U., 1948; R.N., McLean Hosp. Sch. Nursing, Waverly, Mass., 1946; M.S., Boston U., 1958; m. Henry Lee, Feb. 20, 1945; adopted children—Alice, Jennifer, Philip. Pvt. duty nurse, N.Y.C., 1946-48; staff nurse Vis. Nurse Service, 1947-48; staff nurse health dept. Schoharie Co., N.Y., 1948-51; supervising nurse N.Y. Dept. Health, Syracuse, 1951-53, cons. hosp. nursing, Albany, 1958-63, cons. nurse in service edn., 1963—; dir., coordinator nursing service instr. program co-sponsored N.Y. State Dept. Health, N.Y. State Hosp. Assn., N.Y. State League Nursing, N.Y. State Nurses Assn., 1954-57; sometimes lectr. Mem. Am. Nurses Assn., Nat. League Nursing, Am. Hosp. Assn., Am. Pub. Health Assn., Am. Soc. Tng. and Devel., Sigma Theta Tau. Contbr. articles to profl. jours. Home: 38 Grandview Dr Cobleskill NY 12043 Office: 84 Holland Av Albany NY 12208

LEE, BARBARA JILL CUMMINS (MRS. WAYNE EUGENE LEE), physician; b. Anderson, Ind., Feb. 4, 1938; d. Marion Hardin and Ruthanna (Petry) Cummins; A.B., Ind. U., 1960, M.D., 1963; m. Wayne Eugene Lee, June 29, 1963; children—Lawerance, Daniel. Intern St. Ritas Hosp., Lima, O., 1963-64; practice medicine, specializing in family practice, Wapakoneta, O., 1964—; mem. staff Lima Meml., St. Ritas hosps. Diplomate Am. Bd. Family Practice. Mem. Am. Assn. Family Practice, A.M.A., Am. Med. Women's Assn., Auglaize County Med. Soc. (v.p. 1971, pres. 1974). Home: Rural Route 3 Wapakoneta OH 45895 Office: 310 Perry St Wapakoneta OH 45895

LEE, DOROTHEA, educator; b. Yonkers, N.Y., Dec. 13, 1930; d. Charles William and Lucy (Perry) Lee; B.S., Seton Hall U., 1956, M.A., 1964, postgrad., 1967-68. Staff nurse Newark City Hosp., 1951-53; asst. supr. nurses, 1953-55, surg. clin. instr., 1955-57; instr. nurses N.J. State Hosp., Marlboro, 1957-60; sch. nurse Newark Bd. Edn., 1960-61; gen. duty nurse USAF, Chaumont, France, 1961-62; staff nurse St. Barnabas Hosp., Newark, part-time 1962-64; vocational rehab. counselor N.J. Rehab. Commn., 1964; project specialist N.J. State Hosp., Marlboro, 1964-69, asst. dir. nurses edn., 1969-70; urban health coordinator N.J. Regional Med. Program, East Orange, 1970-72; field dir. Planned Parenthood World Population, 1972—. Served to maj. USAFR, 1957-69. Mem. Am. Personnel and Guidance Assn., Nat. Rehab. Assn., United Community Corp., Am., N.J. State (unit chmn. 1970—) nurses assns., Nat. League Nursing, Am. Pub. Health Assn., N.A.A.C.P., Women's Polit. Caucus Essex County, Am. Mgmt. Assn., Newark City Hosp. Nat. Assn. Negro Bus. and Profl. Women's Club, Sch. Nursing Alumni Assn. Club: Cicuso (pres. 1965-69). Home: 42 Lehigh Av Newark NJ 07112 Office: 810 7th Av New York City NY 10019

LEE, ELEANOR PARKER, educator; b. Waycross, Ga., Sept. 17, 1917; d. Thomas Augustus and Alice (Chapman) Parker; B.S., Ga. So. Coll., 1954; postgrad. Columbia, 1958; M.A., U. Ga., 1961, 6th year degree, 1964; m. Jacob Henry Lee, Aug. 28, 1937; children—Thomas Monroe, Sandra Faye (Mrs. Jeffrey F. Gupton), Rebecca Diane (Mrs. Robert Fredrich Poland), Jacob Henry. Tchr. elementary and jr. high schs., Ware County, Ga., 1936-43, 52-59, prin., 1945-47, curriculum dir., 1959—; tchr. jr. and high schs., Coffee County, Ga., 1950-52. Instr., U. Ga., summer 1963 vice chmn. Ga. Dept. Edn. Salary Commn., 1968; pres. Ga. Dept. Instructional Supervision, 1968-69; mem. Ga. Accrediting Commn., 1965—; mem. guidance, counseling, testing adv. bd. Ga. Math. Edn. TV Com., 1963-65. Active P.T.A., 1936-69; sec. Community Action Con., Ware County, 1966-67; mem. Ware County Mental Health Com., 1967-68; participant Nat. Schs. Com. Econ. Edn., 1965, Internat. Workshop Rural Edn. Columbia, 1958. Runner-up Woman of the Year, Waycross, 1969; recipient Civic Edn. Award, 1969, award excellence Kappa Delta Pi, 1973. Mem. Am. Assn. U. Women. Nat., Ga. (dist. legislative chmn. 1969-70) edn. assns., Ga. Assn. Educators (state legislative chmn. 1969-71, mem. PACE com. 1974—), Assn. Supervision and Curriculum Devel., Kappa Delta Pi, Delta Kappa Gamma (Psi state v.p. 1966-67). Baptist. Home: 805 Cleveland St Waycross GA 31501 Office: 215 Oak St Waycross GA 31501

LEE, EVELYN GENEVA (MRS. WARREN M. LEE), educator; b. Vermillion, S.D., Apr. 19, 1920; d. Joseph Charles and Mabel Geneva (Armstrong) Dawson; B.A., U. S.D., 1942; m. Warren M. Lee, Aug. 28, 1966; stepchildren—Byron George, Milton Charles. Tchr. Rapid City (S.D.) Pub. Schs., 1948-66; Vermillion (S.D.) Pub. Schs., 1967—. Active Black Hills Playhouse, Custer, S.D., 1946—, trustee, 1966—. Am. Assn. U. Women grantee, 1967. Named Rapid City (S.D.) Tchr. of the Year, 1964. Mem. Am. Assn. U. Women, Delta Kappa Gamma, Zeta Phi Eta. Mem. Order Eastern Star. Home: 500 S University St Vermillion SD 57069 Office: 1001 E Main St Vermillion SD 57069

LEE, FERN ELLINGSON (MRS. NORMAN LEE), state legislator; b. Towner, N.D., June 6, 1909; d. John and Bessie (Hanson) Ellington; grad. high sch.; m. Norman Lee, Jan. 23, 1928; children—Dale, Jack, Russell. Editor, mgr. weekly newspaper Towner, 1943-65; editorial asst. various weekly papers, 1966—; mem. N.D. Ho. of Reps., 1967—. Mem. Nat. Fedn. Republican Women, 1965, mem. state exec. bd., 1967—. Recipient Community Betterment Leadership award, 1966; named Press Woman of Year for N.D., 1956. Mem. N.D. Press Women (past pres.), Am. Legion Aux., Nat. Fedn. Press Women (treas.), Nat. Order Women Legislators, Sigma Delta Chi. Lutheran. Mem. Order Eastern Star. Address: Towner ND 58788

LEE, FLORENCE HENRY, educator; b. New Brunswick, N.J., May 21, 1910; d. William and Frances Louise (May) Henry; A.B., Douglass Coll., 1929; M.A., Rutgers U., 1932, Ed.D., 1943; M.A., profl. diploma in psychol. counseling Columbia, 1940; m. George W. Lee, Jr., July 17, 1943 (div. 1969); children—Alfred William, Dorothy Henry. Clk., Rutgers U. Library, New Brunswick, 1929-30; parish sec., dir. religious edn. Christ Episcopal Ch., New Brunswick, 1930-35; tchr. Highland Park (N.J.) pub. schs., 1935-42; sch. psychologist Maplewood-South Orange Pub. Schs., 1942-43; lectr. edn. Douglass Coll., New Brunswick, 1949-57, coordinator tchr. edn., 1966-69, prof. edn., 1969-74, chmn. edn. dept., 1969-74, asso. prof. Grad. Sch. Edn., Rutgers U., 1957-66. Recipient Distinguished Service award for service to edn. Rutgers Grad. Sch. Edn., 1973. Mem. Phi Beta Kappa, Kappa Delta Pi, Pi Lambda Theta. Club: Douglass College Associate Alumnae (New Brunswick). Editor: Principles and Practices of Teaching in Secondary Schools - a Book of Readings, 1965. Home: 23 Delevan St New Brunswick NJ 08902

LEE, FRANCES HELEN, editor; b. N.Y.C., Jan. 6, 1936; d. Murray and Rose (Rothman) Lee; B.A., Queens Coll., 1957; M.A., N.Y.U., 1962. Editorial asst. Christian Herald Family Bookshelf, N.Y.C., 1957-62; with Gordon and Breach Sci. Pubs., Inc., N.Y.C., 1964-66, Am. Electric Power Service Corp. AEP Operating Ideas, N.Y.C., 1966-69, Indsl. Water Engring. Mag., N.Y.C., 1969-71; directory editor Photographic div. United Bus. Publs., N.Y.C., 1971—. Supr. Bronx div. N.Y. State Civil Def., 1953-59. Mem. Citizens Union Com. on N.Y.C. Charter Revision, 1974. Mem. Women's Equity Action League (chmn. research com.). Home: 170 2d Av New York City NY 10003

LEE, GEORGIA MASON (MRS. J. ROBERT LEE), psychiatrist; b. Portland, Ore., Apr. 22, 1923; d. David Townsend and Georgia Evelyn (Polleys) Mason; student Wellesley Coll., 1940-41; B.A., U. Wash., 1943; M.D., U. Ore., 1947; m. J. Robert Lee, June 21, 1947; children—Jeffrey David, Catherine Evelyn, Jonathan Townsend. Intern Providence Hosp., Portland, Ore., 1947-48; NIH fellow in radiology Columbia-Presbyn. Med. Center, 1949-51; resident in psychiatry U. Ore. Med. Sch. Hosps., 1969-71, fellow in child psychiatry, 1971-74; candidate Seattle Psychoanalytic Inst., 1973—; child devel. cons. Indian-Migrant Head Start Program, 1974—. Mem. Health Planning Council Portland Met. Area, 1969. Bd. dirs. Tri-County Community Council, 1966-70, chmn. health div., 1968-69; trustee Ore. Mus. Sci. and Industry, 1968-72, chmn. women's com., 1968-69. Mem. Multnomah County Med. Soc., Ore. Med. Assn., Ore., Multnomah County (pres. 1962-63, dir. 1963-65) med. auxs., Am. Psychiat. Assn., Am. Acad. Child Psychiatry, Nat.

Soc. Colonial Dames Am., Kappa Kappa Gamma. Home: 395 NW Brynwood Lane Portland OR 97229

LEE, GLENDA ELLA HENASY (MRS. JAMES F. LEE), coll. dean; b. Marshall, Mich., Aug. 27, 1919; d. Frank G. and Cora B. (Bucklin) Henasy; B.S., Western Mich. U., 1956, M.A., 1959; Ed.S. (Kellogg Found. fellow), U. Mich., 1968, Ed.D. (Delta Kappa Gamma scholar), 1970; m. James F. Lee, Jan. 4, 1936; children—James F., Cheryl (Mrs. Charles Bagi), Brenda (Mrs. Terry Eddy). Registrar, Kellogg Community Coll., Battle Creek, Mich., 1958-65, Oakland Community Coll., Bloomfield Hills, Mich., 1965-68; dean Middlesex Community Coll., Bedford, Mass., 1971—. Dir. Statewide Studies in Mich., 1967-68, Statewide Studies in Mass., 1968-69. Chmn., New Eng. Inter-Instl. Research Council, 1971-73; vice-chmn. Mass. Transfer Rev. Council, 1973-74; mem. council on entrance services Coll. Entrance Exam. Bd., 1973-74. Mem. N.E.A. (life), Am. Assn. Instl. Research, Delta Kappa Gamma. Mem. Ch. of Christ. Home: 241 Lexington St Woburn MA 01801 Office: Springs Rd Bedford MA 01730

LEE, JANIE CURRY, art gallery exec.; b. Shreveport, La., Apr. 22, 1937; d. Burch and Joanna (Glassell) Lee; B.A., Sarah Lawrence Coll., 1959. Ind. theatrical producer, N.Y.C., 1960-66; founder, owner Janie C. Lee Gallery, Dallas, 1968-73, Houston, 1973—. Mem. Art Dealers Assn. Am. Office: 2304 Bissonnet St Houston TX 77005

LEE, JEANIE (MRS. ROBERT E. LEE), composer, realtor; b. Chgo., Nov. 20, 1924; d. John Joseph and Hazel Marie (McNabb) Stein; B.A., Northwestern U., 1944; m. Robert E. Lee, Oct. 13, 1944; children—Randall, Scott. Realtor, owner Kensington Realty, San Diego, 1969—; television performer Assignment San Diego, 1965-70, Passport to Adventure, 1970-71, travelogues, 1958-74. Mem. San Diego Bd. Realtors. Mem. Nat. Assn. Real Estate, Internat. Fedn. Real Estate, Globe Guilders, Starlight Opera Assn. (publicity chmn. 1974), San Diego Symphony Assn. Composer music, lyrics mus. play Nostalgia, 1973; composer other songs. Office: 4104 Adams Av San Diego CA 92116

LEE, JENNIE ELIZABETH ANDREWS (MRS. HERBERT GRANT LEE), educator; b. Manchester, Ia., Mar. 23, 1906; d. Freeman Bartlett and Laura Ellen (Lindsey) Andrews; B.A., Marion Coll., 1927, B.S., 1927; M.A., U. Ia., 1941; m. Herbert Grant Lee, June 2, 1970. Pub. sch. tchr. Archer-Manly, Ia., 1928-31, prin., Ionia and Reinbeck, Ia., 1933-35, 38-45; prof. edn. Bob Jones U., Greenville, S.C., 1946-47, Kletzing Coll., University Park, Ia., 1949-51; faculty Taylor U., Upland, Ind. 1951—, dir. student teaching program, 1962—; asst. supt. Floyd County, Ia., 1936-38; dir. ednl. workshop Central Am. Mission, Siquatepeque, Honduras, 1969. Named Prof. of Yr., Taylor U., 1968. Mem. N.E.A., Assn. Tchr. Educators, Ind., Am. Assn. U. Women, Pi Lambda Theta, Delta Kappa Gamma. Home: Taylor University Upland IN 46989

LEE, JESSIE ELIZABETH (MRS. ELBERT L. LEE), assn. ofcl., former pub. co. exec.; b. Little Rock, Mar. 8, 1909; d. James Brook and Jessie Laura (Yeilding) Lankford; grad. Draughns Bus. Coll., 1930, Bish Mathis Inst., 1938; m. Elbert L. Lee, Sept. 17, 1943. Sec. treas. Longview (Tex.) News Co., Inc., bus. mgr. Longview Daily News, Longview Morning Jour., 1939-72; dir. Elderville Water Supply Corp.; sec. treas. Longview Property Co., 1971; sec. Lens Pub. Co., Inc. Mem. Longview Mus. and Arts Center, Woman's Forum, Longview Community Theatre. Bd. dirs. Longview Symphony League. Mem. Women in Communications, Longview Fedn. Women's Clubs (v.p. 1972—), Zonta (pres. Longview chpt. 1971-72). Clubs: East Tex. Knife and Fork, Longview Lion's Aux. (pres. 1973-74). Address: Route 6 Box NG 15 Longview TX 75601

LEE, JULIA MARJORIE, pub. relations exec.; b. Birmingham, Ala., May 18, 1914; d. William Austin and Mary (Vinson) McEachin; student Mercer U., 1932-34; A.B., Oglethorpe U., 1942; M.A., George Washington U., 1945; m. Thomas Evans, Sept. 6, 1933 (dec. 1934). Cryptanalyst FBI, Washington, 1937-45, 45-48; pub. relations dir. Ala. State Coll., 1948; mgr. pub. relations firm Woodward & Lothrop, Washington, 1949-62, asst. v.p., 1962-73, corporate v.p., 1973—; dir. Washington Fashion Group. Mem. Pub. Relations Soc. Am., Nat. Retail Mchts. Assn., Pub. Relations Commn., Am. Women in Radio and TV. Clubs: Advertising, Women's Advertising (Named Advt. Woman of Year 1962, 67). Home: RFD Box 536 Edgewater MD 21037 Office: Woodward and Lothrop 11th and F Sts NW Washington DC 20013

LEE, LOUISE HARPER (MRS. ERNEST M. LEE), civic worker; b. Bainbridge, Ga., Apr. 3, 1910; d. Louis Robert and Viola Carrie (Fiveash) Harper; B.S., Albany State Coll., 1948; M.Ed., Fla. and M. U., 1962; m. Ernest M. Lee, Dec. 23, 1939; children—Miriam (Mrs. Willie James Stevens), Terry Brown. Tchr., Decatur County (Ga.) Bd. Edn., 1928-52; librarian S.W. Ga. Regional Library, also Hutto High Sch., Bainbridge High Sch. (all Bainbridge), 1952-70; librarian Jones Wheat Elementary Sch., Bainbridge, 1970-71. Vol. social staff worker Decatur County Dept. Family and Children Services, Bainbridge. Bd. dirs. Am. Cancer Soc., Bainbridge, 1968—, Mental Health Assn., 1972—. Mem. Am., Ga. library assns., Nat. Edn. Assn., Ga. Assn. Educators, Ga. Assn. Ret. Tchrs., Am. Legion Aux., Decatur County Women's Council, Am. Woodmen. Democrat. Baptist (dir. youth dept. 1960—). Mem. Order Eastern Star. Clubs: Cornucopia Civic and Social, Cherokee Rose Garden. Home: 920 Albany Rd Bainbridge GA 31717

LEE, MARGARET, newspaper exec.; b. Northfield, Minn., Jan. 5, 1921; d. Edward S. and Ferne Josephine (Thompson) Lee. With accounting dept. John W. Thomas Co., Mpls., 1943-44; reporter, bookkeeper Northfield (Minn.) News, 1944-54, news editor, 1954-56, asso. editor, 1956-62, editor, 1962-67, editor, 1967—. Sec. Northfield (Minn.) Improvement Assn.; mem. Northfield Hosp. Aux., Northfield Arts Guild, Minn. Hist. Soc. Bd. dirs. Rice County Hist. Soc., 1971-73, 2d v.p., 1973-74, 1st v.p., 1974—. Mem. Nat. Fedn. Press Women (regional dir. 1955-56), Minn. Press Women (pres. 1957-58), Minn. Newspaper Assn. (com. chmn.), Bus. and Profl. Women's Club (pres. 1952-54, dist. chmn. 1954-55), Friends United to Undertake Restoration Efforts (FUTURE) (sec.), Housewives Alert to Pollution in Northfield (HATPIN). Club: Minn. Press (dir.). Editor: Gopher Tidings, 1959—. Home: 1012 Union St Northfield MN 55057 Office: Box 58 Northfield MN 55057

LEE, MARY ANN, mathematician, educator; b. Prescott, Ark., July 28, 1909; d. John Lindell and Fanny (Cordell) Lee; A.B., Randolph-Macon Woman's Coll., 1930; M.A., U. Wis., 1940; Ph.D., Cornell U., 1948. Tchr. pub. schs., El Dorado, Ark., 1930-41, St. Mary's Sch., Burlington, N.J., 1941-42; instr. Randolph-Macon Woman's Coll., 1942-43; grad. asst. Cornell U., Ithaca, N.Y., 1943-46, 47-48; asst. prof. math. Sweet Briar (Va.) Coll., 1946-49, chmn. math. dept., 1946-66, asso. prof., 1949-55, prof., 1955—. Mathematician, Rand Corp., Santa Monica, Cal., 1953-54, cons., 1955. Mem. Math. Assn. Am., Am. Math. Soc., Nat. Council Tchrs. Math., Va. Acad. Scis., Phi Beta Kappa, Sigma Xi, Sigma Delta Epsilon. Home: 3 Woodland Rd Sweet Briar VA 24595

LEE, MARY ANN, journalist; b. Memphis, July 30, 1939; d. Robert Martin and Mattye Veva (Nash) Lee; B.A., Southwestern at Memphis, 1958. Copywriter, John Cleghorn Agy., 1958; continuity dir. WMC-TV, 1959-64; TV columnist Memphis Press-Scimitar, 1964-67, TV-radio editor, 1967—; Memphis corr. Variety, 1968—. Charter mem. Critics Consensus, 1967; TV cons. Women in Cable Communications and Women in Cable, Inc., 1973. Mem. Memphis-Shelby County Democratic Women's Club. Mem. Am. Newspaper Guild, Nat. Acad. Rec. Arts and Scis., Memphis Music Inc., Women in Communications. Episcopalian. Home: 3771 Waynoka Av Memphis TN 38111 Office: 495 Union Av Memphis TN 38101

LEE, MARY ANN RAMSAY (MRS. JAMES ROBERT LEE), journalist; b. Colorado Springs, Colo., Dec. 5, 1934; d. Ruseell Lee and Lola (Searcy) Ramsay; B.J., U. Mo., 1950; m. James Robert Lee, June 16, 1957. Reporter, Free Press, Colorado Springs, 1956, soc. editor, 1962-67; continuity dir. sta. KAKE-TV, Wichita, Kan., 1957, KKTV, Colorado Springs, 1958-59; continuity-news dir. radio sta. KYSN, 1959-60; feature writer South Bay Daily Breeze, Torrance, Cal., 1967-70; staff writer Los Angeles Times, 1970—, free-lance writer non-fiction publs., 1949—. Recipient nat. award Nat. Fedn. Press Women, 1965, 1st place award, women's pages, 1967; Congl. medal merit, 1973; several awards Pacific Coast Press Club. Mem. Greater Los Angeles Press Club, Sigma Delta Chi. Home: 1615 Herrin St Redondo Beach CA 90278 Office: 3940 Compton Blvd Lawndale CA 90260

LEE, MARYAT (MARY ATTAWAY LEE), playwright; b. Covington, Ky., May 26, 1926; d. DeWitt Collins and Grace Barbee (Dyer) Lee; student Northwestern U., 1940-41; B.A., Wellesley Coll., 1945; student Middlebury Coll., summer 1944; postgrad. Union Theol. Sem., 1949-50, Columbia, 1949-51, M.A., 1955; m. David Phillips Foulkes Taylor, July 4, 1958 (dec. Sept. 1966). Engaged in film editing, 1946-48; instr. Wesleyan Coll., Macon, Ga., 1948-49; asst. to Margaret Mead, 1952-53; writer, dir. DOPE!, a street play, 1951; partner Fran Belin, Bklyn., 1966—; producer, founder, playwright Soul and Latin Theater, 1968-70, trustee, pres., 1969-70; lit. rep. Jay Hoffman Presentations, N.Y.C. Mem. faculty New Sch. for Social Research, 1965-70. Co-dir. drama workshop Fed. Reformatory for Women, 1972-73; mem. adv. panel Expansion Arts program Nat. Endowment Arts. Grantee N.Y. State Council on Arts, 1971. Mem. Dramatists Guild, Council on So. Mountains, Amateur Chamber Music Soc., Women's Farm Assos. Author (plays): Kairos, 1954; Clytemnestra, 1957; Love In 57th Street Gallery, 1960; Four Men & A Monster, 1967; The Tightrope Walker, 1963-67; Meat Hansom, 1962; FUSE, 1971, 74; (street plays) DOPE!, Day to Day, After the Fashion Show, The Classroom, Luba. Participating playwright Office for Advanced Drama Research, 1967—. Developed 1st modern street theater. Home: Route 1 Box 189 Hinton WV 25951

LEE, PATRICIA BROWNELL (MRS. GILBERT PRENTISS LEE), holly farm exec.; b. Portland, Ore., June 27, 1923; d. Ambrose Clayton and Helen Alison (Phillips) Brownell; B.A., Reed Coll., 1943; m. Gilbert Prentiss Lee, July 9, 1949; children—Gilbert Brownell, Gary Laurence, Granville Robert. Tchr. girl's health and phys. edn. Jefferson High Sch., Portland, Ore., 1943-44; recreation dir. Portland Park Bur., 1941-44; dir. women's phys. edn. Reed Coll., Portland, 1946-49; mgr. Brownell Holly Farms of Ore., Milwaukie, 1969—. Chmn. Mother's March, March of Dimes Fund Drive, 1956; camp chmn., bldg. fund drive chmn. YWCA, 1956-57; mem. budget and agy. rev. com. United Good Neighbors, 1956-58; mem. devel. com. Reed Coll., 1956-66; chmn. women's com. Multnomah County chpt. Nat. Found., 1956-58; mem. women's com. Ore. Muse. Sci. and Industry, 1959-62; pres. Jackson High Sch. P.T.A., 1966-68. Pres. Portland Met. Republican Club, 1966. Bd. dirs. Portland Br. YWCA, 1956-58, Multomah County chpt. Am. Cancer Soc., 1957-59; v.p. Reed Coll. Alumni Assn., 1962-63. Served with WAVES, 1944-46. Named Portland's Woman of Accomplishment Ore. Jour., 1971. Mem. Woman's Aux. A.M.A. (pres. 1971-72), Holly Soc. Am., Ore. Holly Growers Assn., Woman's Aux. Ore. Med. Assn. (hon.), Multnomah County Med. Soc. (hon.), Women's Soc. Christian Service (pres. 1955-56), P.E.O. Club: Stanford University Mothers'. Home: 5805 SW Brugger St Portland OR 97219 Office: PO Box 22025 Milwaukie OR 97222

LEE, PATSIE SINKEY (MRS. EARL E. LEE), motion picture producer; b. Bemidji, Minn.; d. William M. and Eva (Bradley) Vail; grad. Superior State Tchrs. Coll., 1925; postgrad. U. Minn., 1925-26, U. Wash., 1931; m. Chalmer D. Sinkey, May 14, 1932 (dec. May 1947); 1 son, Robert David; m. 2d, Hugh Richard Norrick, July 2, 1952 (dec. June 1957); m. 3d, Earl E. Lee, Oct. 28, 1960. Feature writer, rotogravure type releases Seattle Times, 1931; mag., rotogravure, non fiction releases through A.P., U.P.I., Acme, Pictorial Press of London, Seattle Times, Seattle Post Intelligence, Seattle Star, 1932-46; producer films Wash. State Game Dept., Seattle, 1946—, supr. pub. relations dept., 1949. Recipient Matrix Table award, 1946. Mem. Nat. League Am. Pen Women (award 1948). Home: Route 2 Box 1060 Pinehurst Rd Bend OR 97701

LEE, PEGGY (BORN NORMA EGSTROM), singer, actress; b. Jamestown, N.D., 1920; m. Dave Barbour (div.); m. 2d, Bradford Dexter, Jan. 4, 1955; m. 3d, Dewey Martin, Apr. 25, 1956. Singer in night clubs and on radio, Fargo, N.D., later with bands of Will Osborne, Benny Goodman; vocalist on TV; recording artist; screen debut in Mr. Music; singer Bing Crosby program, CBS; collaborator with Dave Barbour on songs Manana, It's a Good Day, What More Can a Woman Do; role in movie, Pete Kelly's Blues, 1955; collaborator songs Lady and the Tramp, 1955. Address: care CBS 485 Madison Av New York City NY 10021

LEE, POLLY JAE STEAD, librarian, author; b. Toledo, Nov. 26, 1929; d. Jonathan Everett Wheeler and Ona Katherine (Grunder) Stead; student U. Hawaii, 1945-47; m. Richard H.W. Lee, Apr. 7, 1945 (separated 1971); children—Lanie (Mrs. Reginald Lee), Karin (Mrs. Benton Robinson), Ona, Laurie, Robin (Mrs. James Scott Wallace). Film cataloger and processor U.S. Army Air Force, 1945-46; with U.S. Weatern Bur. Film Library, New Orleans, 1948-50, FBI, Wright-Patterson AFB, Dayton, O., 1952, Ohio Wholesale Winedealers, Columbus, O., 1956-58; with Coll. Engring., Ohio State U., Columbus, 1959; tech. manual writer Annie Whittenmyer Home, Davenport, Ia., 1960; with Grand Rapids (Mich.) Pub. Library, 1961-62; dir. Waterford (Mich.) Twp. Libraries, 1962-64; acquisition librarian Pontiac (Mich.) Pub. Libraries, 1965-71, dir. East Side br., 1971-73; now free-lance writer. Chmn. Oakland County br. Multiple Sclerosis Soc., 1972-73, co-chmn. Pontiac com. of Mich. area bd., 1972-73. Bd. dirs. Detroit Multiple Sclerosis Soc., 1971; mem. Mich. Area bd. Am. Friends Service Com., 1961-69, Recipient Mother of Yr. award Quad City Bus. men, Davenport, Ia. and Moline, Ill., 1960. Mem. Internat. Platform Assn. Author: Mary Dyer: Child of Light, 1973; Giant: Pictorial History of the Human Colossus, 1973. Contbr. articles to various publs. Home: PO Box 1679 San Francisco CA 94101

LEE, SALLY COCHRAN BOARDMAN (MRS. RICHARD DALLAM LEE), tchr. dramatics; b. Surbiton, Eng., Feb. 22, 1938 (parents Am. citizens); d. Thomas Volney and Dorothy Moore (Cochran) Boardman; student Prep. Acad. Royal Acad. Dramatic Art, London, Eng., 1956-57; grad. Webber-Douglas Acad. Singing and Dramatic Art, London, 1958; m. Richard Dallam Lee, Sept. 7, 1966; children—Dorothy, Katherine. Actress, state mgr., co. mgr., asst. producer Derwent Players, profl. children's theatre co., 1959-60; prodn. asst. Presentation Control Room, Rediffusion TV Co., London, 1960-61, 62-66; dir. plays, tchr. creative dramatics Rye (N.Y.) Art Centre, 1971—; tchr. acting workshops to adults and children, 1969—. Tchr. Sackerpath council Girl Scouts U.S.A. Mem. Am. Theatre Assn. Episcopalian. Address: 37 Mead Pl Rye NY 10580

LEE, SIMI, ednl. adminstr.; b. San Francisco, May 3, 1947; d. Edward S. and Winnie (Loy) Lee; B.A., U. Cal. at Berkeley, 1969, also postgrad.; postgrad. Hastings Sch. Law. Editor, reporter Peninsula Bull., San Mateo, Cal., 1970-71; human relations specialist San Mateo (Cal.) Union High Sch. Dist., 1971-73. Editor Inst. on Race and Community Relations, U. Cal. at Berkeley, 1970-71; instr. Coll. San Mateo (Cal.), 1971. Mem. San Mateo (Cal.) Conf. on Religion, Race and Social Concern, 1970—. Bd. dirs. Operation Crossroads. Mem. Assn. of Cal. Intergroup Relations Educators, Women In Communications, Chinese for Affirmative Action, Japanese Am. Citizens League, Prytanean, Delta Zeta. Editor: Multicultural Curriculums, 1972. Home: 210 S Idaho St San Mateo CA 94401

LEE, VIRGINIA YEW, author; b. San Francisco, May 5, 1926; d. S.N. and Shee (Jone) Yew; B.A., San Francisco State Coll., 1967; M.A., Lone Mountain Coll., 1969; m. Howard F. Lee (dec. Aug. 1973); children—Roberta Lee, Deirdre Moy. Author: The House That Tai Ming Built (Commonwealth Club Cal. Gold Medal award for Best Fiction by Cal. Author 1963), 1963. Home: 1232 5th Av San Francisco CA 94122

LEE, VIVIAN VASHTIA, educator, ins. co. exec.; b. Gadsden, Ala., June 24, 1917; d. John Dorsey and Annie (Waddell) Lee; B.S., U. So. Miss., 1937, M.A., 1948, profl. certificate, 1964, specialist degree, 1968; postgrad. summers Tulane U., 1939, U. Ala., 1942; Ed.D., U. Eastern Fla., 1972, Fla. State Christian Coll., 1972. Instr. social sci. Independence High Sch., Batesville, Miss., 1937-38, Carmichael (Miss.) High Sch., 1938-39; interviewer WPA, Hattiesburg, Miss., 1939-40; instr. math., girls basketball coach Sanford (Miss.) High Sch., 1940-41; instr. math., gen. sci. Hattiesburg High Sch., 1941-45; dean women Pearl River Jr. Coll., Poplarville, Miss., 1945-46; instr. sr. math., pep squad Bogalusa (La.) High Sch., 1946—, sponsor Keyette Club, 1948-53, Torch Club, 1946-60; instr. U. So. Miss., summer 1967; owner Lee's Tax Ins. and Service Bur.; parish dir. Nat. Investors Life Ins. Co., Baton Rouge, 1958—, Asso. Investors Life Ins. Co., Baton Rouge, 1958—, Investors Equity Life Ins. Co., 1965—, Am. Family Life Ins. Co., Columbus, Ga., 1967. Prin., White Non Vet. Adult Edn., 1955-63; del. La. Tchrs. Conv., 1957, 58; mem. adv. bd. Bogalusa Tchrs. Credit Union, 1958-61; judge Sci. Fair Southeastern La. Coll., 1962. Recipient plaque for outstanding service Nat. Investors Life Ins., 1960. Mem. La. Tchrs. Assn. (past pres. Bogalusa chpt.) U. So. Miss. Alumni Assn. (past pres. Bogalusa chpt.), N.E.A., Classroom Tchrs. Assn., Math. Tchrs. Assn., Internat. Platform Assn., Internat. Graphoanalysis Soc., Kappa Delta Pi, Alphega. Democrat. Baptist. Mem. Order Eastern Star. Author: The Teaching of Mathematics An Art or a Science?; The Dynamics of Success, 1971. Home: 321 Carolina Av Bogalusa LA 70427

LEECH, BESSIE BOURLAND, librarian; b. Amory, Miss., Nov. 7, 1907; d. Neal Alexander and Petra (Cheek) Bourland; B.A., U. Miss., 1929, M.A., 1942; m. Wayne C. Leech, Apr. 5, 1931; children—Bettye Neal, Judy Claire (Mrs. Carter Dobbs, Jr.). Tchr. English, Smithville (Miss.) Consol. Sch., 1931-36, Hatley High Sch., Amory, Miss., 1936-42; librarian Aberdeen (Miss.) High Sch., 1942-55, Pontotoc (Miss.) High Sch., 1955-65; tchr. Miss. State U., summer 1942, extension div. U. Miss., 1942-45; research librarian Bur. Govtl. Research U. Miss., 1965-72. Mem. finance com. Y-Teen Dist. Bd., 1957-67. Mem. N.E.A., Miss. Edn. Assn., Am. Assn. U. Women, Miss. Library Assn., Chi Delta Phi, Delta Kappa Gamma, Delta Gamma. Democrat. Methodist. Mem. Order Eastern Star. Clubs: Delphian Literary (Amory); Woman's (Aberdeen); Twentieth Century, Music Study (Pontotoc). Contbr. articles to profl. jours. Home: 406 Longest Rd Oxford MS 38655 Office: Deupree Hall Bur Govtl Research Library University MS 38677

LEEDS, ISABELLE RUSSEK, govt. ofcl.; b. N.Y.C., Dec. 6, 1926; d. Louis and Rose (Bauman) Russek; A.B., Wellesley Coll., 1947; m. Marshall Leeds, Oct. 19, 1947 (div. Apr. 1970). Spl. asst. to U.S. Senator Claiborn Pell, Providence, R.I., 1961-72; spl. asst. to lt. gov. J. Joseph Garrahy, Providence, 1968-72. Democratic nat. committeewoman, 1968-72; mem. R.I. Dem. State Com., 1968-70; del. Dem. Nat. Conv., 1964, 68; mem. R.I. adv. com. U.S. Civil Rights Commn., 1962-72. Trustee R.I. Found. for Repertory Theater; mem. corp. Miriam Hosp. Jewish religion. Clubs: Legemont, R.I. Wellesley. Home: 485 Park Av New York City NY 10022

LEEDY, EMILY L. FOSTER (MRS. WILLIAM N. LEEDY), govt. ofcl.; b. Jackson, O., Sept. 24, 1921; d. Raymond S. and Grace (Garrett) Foster; B.S., Rio Grande Coll., 1949; M.Ed., Ohio U., 1957; postgrad. Ohio State U., 1956, Mich. State U., 1958-59, Case Western Res. U., 1963-65; m. William N. Leedy, Jan. 1, 1943; 1 son. Dwight A. Tchr. Frankfort (O.) pub. schs., 1941-46, Ross County Schs., Chillicothe, O., 1948-53; elementary and supervising tchr. Chillicothe City Schs., 1953-56; dean of girls, secondary tchr. Berea City Schs., 1956-57; vis. tchr. Parma City Schs., 1957-59; counselor Homewood-Flossmoor High Sch., Flossmoor, Ill., 1959-60; teaching fellow Ohio U., 1960-62; asst. prof. edn., 1962-64; asso. prof., counselor Cuyahoga Community Coll., 1964-66; dean of women Cleve. State U., 1966-67, asso. dean student affairs, 1967-69; guidance dir. Cathedral Latin Sch., 1969-71; dir. women's service div. Ohio Bur. Employment Services, 1971—; cons. in edn. Mem. adv. com. S.W. Community Information Service, 1959-60; youth com. S.W. YWCA, 1963-70, chmn., 1964-70, bd. mgmt., 1964-70; group services council Cleve. Welfare Fedn., 1964-66; chmn. Met. YWCA Youth Program study com., 1966, bd. dirs., 1966-72, v.p., 1967-68. Mem. Am. Assn. U. Women, Am., Northeastern Ohio (sec. 1958-59, exec. com. 1963-64, pub. relations chmn. 1962-64, newsletter chmn., editor 1963-64, del. nat. assembly 1959-63) personnel and guidance assns., Nat. Vocational Guidance Assn., Am., Ohio sch. counselors assns., Am. Rehab. Counseling Assn., Nat. (publs. com. 1967-69), Ohio (program chmn. 1967, editor Newsletter 1968-71) assns. women deans and counselors, Cleve. Counselors Assn. (pres. 1966), N.E.A., Assn. Higher Edn., Am. Assn. U. Profs., Ohio Edn. Assn., Ohio Assn. Gifted Children, Nat. Assn. Student Personnel Adminstrs., Am. Coll. Personnel Assn., Am. Assn. Student Teaching, League Women Voters, Cleve. Mental Health Assn., Northeastern Ohio Tchrs. Assn., Women's Equity Action League, Zonta Internat. (exec. bd. 1968-70, treas. 1970-72), Bus. and Profl. Women's Club, Delta Kappa Gamma, Phi Delta Gamma. Club: Women's City (Cleve.). Home: 580 Lindberg Blvd Berea OH 44017 Office: 145 S Front St Columbus OH 43216

LEEDY, TAKOOHY TOPAKIAN (MRS. ROBERT EVERETT LEEDY), health services adminstr.; b. Boston, Oct. 2, 1914; d. Abraham and Loosapar (Yacobian) Topakian; certificate Phila. Sch. Occupational Therapy, 1937; postgrad. Orlando Jr. Coll., 1961-62, Fla. Tech. U., 1971-72; m. Robert Everett Leedy, June 2, 1940.

Occupational therapist N.J. State Hosp., Trenton, 1937-39; dir. occupational therapy State Tb Sanitarium, Orlando, Fla., 1937-41; occupational therapist Lawson Gen. Army Hosp., Atlanta, 1943-44; dir. occupational therapy Forrest Park Sch. for Exceptional Children, Orlando, 1957-58; dir. occupational therapy N. Brevard Rehab. Center, Titusville, Fla., 1963-70; clinic coordinator United Cerebal Palsy Clinic, Orlando, 1970—. Active Girl Scouts Am., 1927-74. Recipient Golden Eagle award Girl Scouts Am., 1927. Mem. Fla. Occupational Therapy Assn. (pres. 1967-69). Home: 2016 Crescent Rd Orlando FL 32807 Office: 506 E Colonial Dr Orlando FL 32803

LEE LOY, MARION MCGREGOR, secondary sch. tchr.; b. Honolulu, Nov. 28, 1911; d. Daniel Pamawaho and Louise Aoe (Wong) McGregor; B.A., U. Hawaii, 1933; student Ball State Tchrs. Coll., Muncie, Ind., 1963; m. Samuel Kanuuhiwalani Lee Loy, Dec. 19, 1936; children—Wilmer Kawika, Marylyn Aoe, Pilialoha Elizabeth, Samuel Kalamaku. Tchr. schs., islands Maui and Hawaii, 1935-51, Oahu, 1951—; tchr. English, social studies Farrington High Sch., Honolulu, 1960—; mem. faculty Farrington Community Sch., 1957-60. Mem. Gov. Hawaii's Commn. Status Women, 1964-66, Kamehameha Day Celebration Commn., 1952-67; pres. Hilo Civic Club Women, 1950, treas. Hawaiian Civic Club, 1951; sec. Alewa Community Assn., 1961-74. Mem. Hawaii (dir. 1963-65, 68-71, trustee 1971-74), Oahu (pres. 1964-66) edn. assns., Hawaii (pres. 1961-63), Oahu (pres. 1959-60) classroom tchrs. assns., Honolulu Bus. and Profl. Women's Club (pres. 1973-74), Fed. Bus. and Profl. Women (pres. Honolulu 1964-65), Kamehameha Alumnae Assn. (pres. 1952-55), Delta Kappa Gamma (parliamentarian Hawaii 1971-75), Kappa Kappa Iota (chpt. pres. 1968-70, pres. conclave 1971-73). Home: 1322 Kapalama Av Honolulu HI 96817 Office: 1564 N King St Honolulu HI 96817

LEEN, AGNES THEOPHILA, lawyer, state ofcl.; b. Bklyn., Sept. 7, 1912; d. Edward Aloysius and Agnes Veronica (O'Keeffe) Leen; A.B., Coll. Mt. St. Vincent, 1934; J.D., St. John's U., 1938. Admitted to N.Y. bar, 1938; asso. firm Reid & Priest, N.Y.C., 1942-48; sales mgr. Countess Mara Inc. N.Y.C., 1948-52; staff atty. Sperry Rand Inc., N.Y.C., 1952-53; trial atty. U.S. Dept. Justice Anti Trust Div., 1953-60; asst. atty. gen. Consumer Fraud Bur. N.Y. Dept. Law, N.Y.C., 1961—. Mem. Am., Bklyn. bar assns., Am. Judicature Soc., Bus. and Profl. Women Fedn. Republican. Roman Catholic. Home: 11 E 87th St New York City NY 10028 Office: #2 World Trade Center New York City NY 10047

LEEPER, VIRGINIA ANN WARD (MRS. DWIGHT M. LEEPER), banker; b. Owaneco, Ill., Jan. 18, 1914; d. Myron Orville and Tessie E. (Weist) Ward; student Brown's Bus. Coll., 1932-33; m. Dwight M. Leeper, Oct. 12, 1935 (dec. Nov. 1963); 1 dau., Marilyn Jean (dec.). Tchr. cost account and banking Brown's Bus. Coll., Decatur, Ill., 1933; clk. finance dept. A. E. Staley Mfg. Co., Decatur, 1933-35; bookkeeper Farmers State Bank, Heyworth, Ill., 1938, chmn. bd., 1939-40, v.p., 1940-43, v.p., asst. cashier, 1943-46, v.p., 1946-51, v.p., cashier, 1951-63, v.p., 1963-65, pres., 1965-70, v.p., chmn. bd., 1970—. Treas. Heyworth Community Recreation Assn., 1948-50. Mem. Am. Bus. Women's Assn. Democrat. Presbyn. Club: Federated Women's (pres. 1948-49). Home: 308 W Clarke St Heyworth IL 61745 Office: 117 E Main St Heyworth IL 61745

LEES, MARILYN ALICE, pub. relations specialist; b. Chgo., July 21, 1933; d. Glenn John and Alice Olive (Swanson) Patterson; B.S., U. Ore., 1954; postgrad. U. Ill. Extension, 1954-56, U. Cal. Extension, 1966-72, now U. Cal. at Irvine; 1 dau., Cynthia Charlotte. Writer CBS Supermarketing Services, Chgo., 1954-56; copywriter-account exec. Joseph Pedott Advt., Chgo., 1956-60, Botsford, Constantine & Gardner, Portland, Ore., 1960-64, Pub. Relations Counselors, San Francisco, 1964-66, Smoking Research, San Diego, 1966-70; program promotion mgr. U. Cal. Extension, La Jolla, after 1971; dir. advt. and pub. relations Weight Watchers, Santa Ana, Cal. Mem. Chinatown br. Youth Council YWCA, San Francisco, 1964-66; program chmn. San Diego chpt. World Future Soc., 1971. Recipient Nat. Press Women award for TV documentary program script, 1959; awards for direct mail concepts Art Dirs. Club San Francisco, 1965, San Diego, 1968. Mem. Pub. Relations Soc. Am. (nat. sec. govt. sect. 1970-71), Women in Communications (program chmn. 1969, co-chmn. nat. meeting 1970), Phi Beta. Home: 1698 Marguerite Av Corona del Mar CA 92625

LEES, MARJORIE BERMAN (MRS. SIDNEY LEES), biochemist; b. N.Y.C., Mar. 17, 1923; d. Isadore I. and Ruth (Rogal) Berman; B.A., Hunter Coll., 1943; M.S., U. Chgo., 1945; Ph.D., Harvard, 1951; m. Sidney Lees, Sept. 17, 1946; children—David, Andrew, Eliot. Sr. research asso. in pharmacology Dartmouth Med. Sch., Hanover, N.H., 1962-66; prin. research asso. biol. chemistry, mem. faculty Harvard Med. Sch., Boston 1966—. Asso. biochemist McLean Hosp., Belmont, Mass., 1966—. Nat. Inst. Neurol. Diseases and Blindness grantee, 1962—. Mem. Am. Soc. Biol. Chemist, Internat., Am. (mem. council 1971—) socs. for neurochemistry, Soc. for Neurosci., Am. Soc. for Neuropathologists, Phi Beta Kappa, Phi Sigma. Contbr. articles to profl. jours. Home: 50 Eliot Memorial Rd Newton MA 02158 Office: McLean Hospital 115 Mill St Belmont MA 02178

LEFCOURT, CAROL HOFFMAN, lawyer; b. N.Y.C., Dec. 11, 1943; d. Joshua and Marjorie (Jaffe) Hoffman; B.A., Pa. State U., 1964; LL.B., Bklyn. Law Sch., 1967; m. Robert Lefcourt, July 4, 1965; 1 dau., Janny. Admitted to N.Y. bar, 1967; mem. firm Lefcourt, Garfinkle, Crain, Cohn, Sandler, Lefcourt, Kraft & Stolar, N.Y.C., 1968-71, Lefcourt, Kraft & Libow, N.Y.C., 1973—. Cons. Richmond Coll., 1972. Mem. task force for justice N.Y. Presbytery, 1972. Mem. Nat. Lawyers Guild. Home: 260 West End Av New York City NY 10023 Office: 640 Broadway New York City NY 10012

LEFEVRE, MARGARET CLARK, educator; b. Paw Paw, Mich., Nov. 14, 1911; d. George Cathcart and Mary Allene (Lake) Clark; A.B., Western Mich. U., 1932; M.A., U. Minn., 1946; Ph.D., Western Res. U., 1957; m. Dec. 26, 1937; children—Anne, Kent, Mary (Mrs. Roland R. Paolucci). Tchr., Greenville (Mich.) High Sch., 1936-38; speech therapist Kabat-Kaiser Insts., Washington and Vallejo, Cal., 1946-50; speech therapist Sch. for Handicapped Children, Savannah, Ga., 1950-52; faculty speech pathology Western Res. U., Cleve., 1952-59, U. Akron, O., 1959-62, U. Vt., Burlington, 1962-64, Bloomsburg (Pa.) State Coll., 1964—. Cons. speech, hearing; instr. in work shops and spl. courses. Fellow Am. Speech and Hearing Assn.; mem. Am. Assn. U. Profs. (v.p. Pa. div. 1974), Pa. Speech and Hearing Assn., Internat., Pa. councils for exceptional children. Office: Bloomsburg State Coll Bloomsburg PA 17815

LEFF, RITA ZION (MRS. SYDNEY LEFF), artist; b. N.Y.C.; d. Max and Elizabeth (Rudder) Zion; student Art Students League, 1925-27, Bklyn. Mus., 1945-47; pupil Louis Shamker, 1949, Abraham Rattner, 1952; m. Sydney Leff, June 6, 1928; children—Joan (Mrs. Alfred Miller), Gail (Mrs. Martin Raab). Pvt. tchr. painting, 1965; exhibited art in one-man shows at Silvermine Guild Conn., Loring Gallery, N.Y.C., Bodley Gallery, N.Y.C., U. Me. Esterhazy Gallery, Palm Beach, Fla., Gallery Cassell, Palm Beach, Light House Gallery, Tequesta, Fla.; exhibited art in group shows at Met. Mus. Art, Bklyn. Mus., N.Y. Pub. Library, Phila. Mus., Pa. Acad., Honolulu Mus., Norfolk Mus., Riverside Mus., Tokyo Art Center, Dallas Mus., Lafayette Art Center, Butler Inst., Gallery Bosc, Paris, Maison des Arts, Brussels, Nat. Acad. Art, Oakland (Cal.) Mus., represented in permanent collections at Columbia, Pa. State U., numerous museums including Met. Mus., Bklyn. Mus., N.Y. Pub. Library, U. Me., Library Congress, Smithsonian Instn. Recipient numerous awards including Grand Prix Internat. Salon Internat. de la Femme, 1964, Grand Prize Fla. State Fair, 1969-70, prize Art Mus. Palm Beach, 1971-72. Mem. Nat. Assn. Women Artists, Audubon Artists, Soc. Am. Graphic Artists, Boston, Wash. printmakers, Nat. Soc. Painters in Casein. Address: 1707 Consulate Way West Palm Beach FL 33401

LEFFINGWELL, LOIS MENDLE (MRS. THOMAS P. LEFFINGWELL, JR.), virologist; b. Galveston, Tex., July 9, 1931; d. Frank Conrad and Ruth Lee (Crim) Mendle; B.A., U. Tex., 1953, M.A., 1955, Ph.D. (McLaughlin fellow), 1958; m. Thomas P. Leffingwell, Jr., Feb. 28, 1960; 1 son, Thomas Frank. Virologist III, Tex. Dept. Health, Austin, 1958-70, supr. virus div., 1970—. Mem. Am. Soc. Microbiologists (Tex. br.), Sigma Xi, Iota Sigma Pi. Home: 8102 Hillrise St Austin TX 78759 Office: 1100 W 49th St Austin TX 78756

LEFFLAND, ELLA, writer; b. Martinez, Cal., Nov. 25, 1931; d. Sven William and Emma (Jensen) Leffland; B.A., San Jose State Coll., 1953. Author: (novel) Mrs. Munck, 1970; short stories pub. in Best Short Stories of 1970, New Yorker, Cosmopolitan, Epoch, Quar. Rev. of Lit. Address: 1360 Vallejo St San Francisco CA 94109

LEFKOWITZ, ANNETTE SARA, educator; b. Shenandoah, Pa., Oct. 3, 1922; d. Martin A. and Libbie (Horowitz) Lefkowitz; R.N., Cornell Med. Center, 1941; B.A., Pa. State U., 1949; M.A., N.Ed. Adminstrn., Guidance, Columbia U., 1954, Ed.D., 1958. With Lock Haven (Pa.) Hosp., 1949-53, instr. nursing, 1949-50, dir. nursing service and edn., 1950-53; chmn. dept. nursing Ida. State Coll., 1954-57; prof. nursing edn., dir. sch. nursing No. Ill. U., DeKalb, 1958—. Former chmn. com. nurse examiners Dept. Reg. and Edn. State of Ill.; cons. Dist. 3 Ill. Heart Assn.; cons. DeKalb County Assn. for Retarded Children; health tng. coordinator Malayan, Thailand Peace Corps Groups. Mem. adv. com. Nat. Commn. Study Nursing and Nursing Edn. Served with Nurse Corps, AUS, 1942-46. Mem. Ida. League Nursing (past pres.), Am. Nurses Assn., Nat. League for Nursing, Am. Assn. Colls. of Nursing, Am. Assn. U. Women, Pi Lambda Theta, Kappa Delta Pi. Co-editor: Problems of the Aged, 1964. Home: 711 S Main St Sycamore IL 60178 Office: No Ill U Sch Nursing DeKalb IL 60115

LEFKOWITZ, RUTH SAMSON, mathematician, educator; b. Cin., Oct. 7, 1910; d. Bernard and Sarah Bluma (Zisling) Samson; B.A., Hunter Coll., 1930; M.A., Columbia, 1960, Ed.D., 1966; m. Charles S. Lefkowitz, Nov. 21, 1940; children—Judith R. (Mrs. Ivan G. Marcus), Jeremy Samson. Tchr. math. secondary schs., N.Y.C., 1938-59; asst. prof. math. Bronx Community Coll., City U. N.Y., Bronx, 1960-66, asso. prof. math., 1967; asso. prof. math. John Jay Coll. of Criminal Justice City U. N.Y., N.Y.C., 1967-71, prof., 1971—, chmn. dept. math., 1972—. Mem. Bd. Overseers Jewish Theol. Sem. Am. Mem. Math. Assn. Am., A.A.A.S., N.Y. State Assn. Tchrs. Math., Nat. Council Tchrs. Math., Pi Mu Epsilon, Kappa Delta Pi, Pi Lambda Theta. Home: 900 W 190 St New York City NY 10040 Office: 445 W 59th St New York City NY 10019

LEFLEY, HARRIET PHILLIPS, psychologist, educator; b. Boston, Mar. 21, 1924; d. Frederick and Bella (Shapera) Phillips; student Northeastern U., 1943-45, U. Chgo., 1945-46; B.A., Roosevelt U., 1964, M.A., 1967; Ph.D., U. Miami, 1973; m. John A. Lefley, Mar. 16, 1958; children—Keith F., Carla A. Med. librarian U. Ill., Chgo., 1947-51; ins. mgr. South Side Bank & Trust Co., Chgo., 1952-59; free-lance writer, 1959-64; psychometrician U. Chgo., 1965-66; research fellow, asst. Roosevelt U., Chgo., 1964-65; psychol. assessment officer U.S. Peace Corps, Sierra Leone, 1965-66; dir. social research Govt. Bahamas, Nassau, 1967-69; asst. prof. psychiatry U. Miami, 1973—; dir. community mental health services Dade County, Jackson Meml. Hosp., Miami, 1974—. Cons. to govt. Bahamas, 1970-72; evaluator Miccosukee bilingual edn. program, Tamiami Trail, Fla., 1973-74, NIH Indian Health Service, 1974. Ford Found. Ethnic Studies grantee, 1972-73. Mem. Am. Psychol. Assn., Interam. Congress of Psychology, Caribbean Psychiat. Assn., Am. Assn. for Social Psychiatry, Soc. for Cross-Cultural Research, Internat. Assn. of Cross-Cultural Psychology, Phi Kappa Phi. Research in cross-cultural psychology. Contbr. articles to profl. jours. Home: 5910 SW 59th St Miami FL 33143 Office: University of Miami School of Medicine Dept of Psychiatry PO Box 520875 Biscayne Annex Miami FL 33152

LEGARDEUR, MARGARET BASHFORD (MRS. GEORGE J. LEGARDEUR), physician; b. Yonkers, N.Y., June 7, 1916; d. Edward Van Sice and Jeanette (Gauthier) Bashford; A.B., Vassar Coll., 1937; M.D., Cornell U., 1941; m. George J. LeGardeur, Jan, 3, 1963. Intern N.Y. Hosp., N.Y.C., 1941-43; resident Children's Hosp., Boston, 1943-44; practice medicine specializing in pediatrics, New Orleans, 1963—; cons. several hosps. Diplomate Am. Bd. Pediatrics. Fellow Am. Acad. Pediatrics. Office: 5450 S Tonti St New Orleans LA 70125

LEGER, SISTER ANGELINE MARIE ANNE, religious orgn. adminstr.; b. Memramcook, N.B., Can., July 28, 1926; d. Sifroid and Ida (Cormier) Leger; diploma hosp. orgn. and mgmt. Can. Hosp. Assn., 1964; certificate hosp. accounting and mgmt. Ind. U., 1972. Adminstr. Hospital Stella Maris, Bouctouche, N.B., 1959-62; researcher hosp. constrn., 1962-64; adminstr. Hospital Stella Maris, Ste. Anne de Kent, N.B., 1964-74; councilor, bursar Les Religieuses N.-D. S.-C., 1974—. Mem. exec. com. Diocesan Religious Council, Moncton, N.B., 1972. Governing bd. Hosp. Stella Maris de Kent Ste. Anne de Kent, 1974. Mem. Canadian Coll. Health Service Execs., Assn. N.B. Hosp. Adminstrs. Address: 125 King St Moncton NB Canada

LEGGAT, LOIS BURNETT (MRS. JOHN A.A. LEGGAT), polit. party ofcl.; b. Warren, Pa., Aug. 23, 1917; d. John Clyde and Hazel (Filer) Burnett; grad. high sch.; m. John A.A. Leggat, Aug. 14, 1937; 1 dau., Nancy Lou. Personal shopper Halle Bros. Co., 1935-37. County chmn. Republican party, 1969-73; sec., 1st v.p. Ohio Fedn. Rep. Women, 1968-72, pres., 1972—; mem. bd. Nat. Fedn. Rep. Women, 1972—, asst. campaign chmn., 1974—. Bd. dirs. Heather Hill Home. Mem. D.A.R. Baptist. Club: Lake County (O.) Garden. Home: 4945 Waldamere Av Willoughby OH 44094 Office: 50 W Broad St Suite 3450 Columbus OH 43215

LEGGITT, DOROTHY, educator; b. Oblong, Ill., Feb. 19, 1903; d. Clarence C. and Louise Frances (Muchmore) Leggitt; diploma Eastern Ill. State U., 1923; Ph.B., U. Chgo., 1930, M.A., 1933, postgrad., intermittently, 1937-62. Tchr. rural schs., Jasper & Crawford Counties, ill., 1920-22; tchr. high sch., Glen Ellyn, Ill., 1923-35; lectr., prof. No. Ill. State U., DeKalb, 1936-37; tchr. social studies, counselor Clayton (Mo.) pub. schs., 1937-52; tchr. Decatur (Ill.) pub. schs., 1952-54, Park Ridge (Ill.) pub. schs., 1954-61; reading specialist Joliet (Ill.) Jr. Coll., 1961-62, Niles West High Sch., Skokie, Ill., 1962-63; reading cons. Kenosha High Schs., Kenosha, Wis., 1963-65; head study skills dept. Palm Beach (Fla.) Jr. Coll., 1965-73, prof. emeritus, 1973—; summer lectr. various colls. and univs. Recipient Walgreen Found. award in social, econ. and polit. instns., 1948, scholarship award Pi Lambda Theta, 1948, Distinguished Alumni award Eastern Ill. U., 1974. Mem. D.A.R. Author: Basic Study Skills and Workbook, 1942. Contbr. articles to profl. jours. Home: 401 S LaSalle St Chicago IL 60605 Office: PO Box 1432 Chicago IL 60690

LEHISTE, ILSE, educator; b. Tallinn, Estonia, Jan. 31, 1922; d. Aleksander and Julie M. (Sikka) Lehiste; Dr.Phil., U. Hamburg (Germany), 1948; Ph.D., U. Mich., 1959. Came to U.S., 1949, naturalized, 1956. Lectr., U. Hamburg. 1948-49, asso. prof. modern langs. Kan. Wesleyan U., 1950-51. Detroit Inst. Tech., 1951-56; research asso. U. Mich., 1957-63; faculty Ohio State U., Columbus, 1963—, prof. linguistics, 1965—, chmn. dept., 1965-71, dir. Linguistic Inst., 1970. Vis. prof. U. Cologne (Germany), 1965, U. Cal. at Los Angeles, 1966. Guggenheim fellow, 1969; grantee Am. Council Learned Socs., 1971, U. Vienna, 1974. Mem. Linguistic Soc. Am. (exec. com. 1971-73), Acoustical Soc. Am., Modern Lang. Assn., Internat. Soc. Phonetic Scis., A.A.A.S., Societas Linguistica Europaea. Author 6 books, latest being: Suprasegmentals, 1970; also articles, book revs. Home: 985 Kennington Av Columbus OH 43220

LEHL, MABEL BOWMAN (MRS. GEORGE PETER LEHL), educator; b. Bethany, Okla., Aug. 6, 1917; d. Ben Franklin and Dycie Ellen (Hixson) Bowman; A.A., Southwestern Ore. Community Coll., 1965; B.S., U. Ore., 1968, M.Ed., 1970, M.S., 1971; m. George Peter Lehl, June 9, 1951; children—Phyllis Golbek (Mrs. Glenn Brostrom), Harvey Golbek, Leslie Golbek, Dorothy Myers, Louise Lehl (Mrs. Kenneth Robb). Tchr. Madison Jr. High Sch., Eugene Ore., 1969-70; tchr.-therapist emotionally and socially maladjusted secondary students Springfield (Ore.) Sch. Dist., 1971—. Mem. Nat. Assn. Sch. Psychologists, Nat. Assn. Bus. and Profl. Women, Ore. Sch. Psychology Assn. Home: 346 N Cammann St Coos Bay OR 97420 also 1591 Larkspur Av Eugene OR 97401 Office: 525 Mill St Springfield OR 97477

LEHMAN, CLARA MAY HILEMAN, physician; b. Sharon, Pa., Oct. 30, 1901; d. Mayberry and Clara May (Keasey) Hileman; B.S., Pa. State U., 1924; postgrad. Columbia, 1927-28, Marine Biol. Lab., 1930-31; M.D., Woman's Med. Coll., Pa., 1935; m. Robert N. Lehman, Apr. 24, 1938; 1 dau., Mary Dorcas. Intern Lancaster (Pa.) Hosp., 1935-36, resident, 1936-37; practice gen. medicine, Pa., 1936-47; practice staff geriatrics U.S. Army Hosp., Ft. Meyer, Va., 1948-51, VA Hosp., Aspinwall, Pa., 1955-57, Woodville State Hosp., Carnegie, Pa., 1957-68; now mem. staff VA Hosp., Pitts. Mem. A.M.A., Pa., Allegheny County med. socs., Am. Geriatric Soc., Women's Med. Soc. Pitts., Royal Soc. Health, Alpha Omega Alpha, Alpha Epsilon Iota. Address: VA Hosp Pittsburgh PA 15240

LEHMAN, EVELYN JEANNE (MRS. WALTER SCOTT LONG, JR.), lawyer; b. Ann Arbor, Mich., June 13, 1930; d. Arthur Conrad and Mildred Georgianna (Pearce) Lehman; B.A., Mt. Holyoke Coll., 1951; LL.B., U. Mich., 1954; m. Walter Scott Long, Jr., Apr. 4, 1959; 1 son, Arthur Scott. Admitted to Mich. bar, 1954, N.Y. bar, 1956; practiced in Ann Arbor, 1954-55, N.Y.C., 1957—; asst. to trust officer Chase Manhattan Bank, N.Y.C., 1955-57; asso. lawyer, partner Gifford, Woody, Carter and Hays, N.Y.C., 1957—. Mem. Washington Sq. Outdoor Art Exhibit Inc., 1962—. Bd. dirs. Greenwich Village Montessori Sch., Inc., treas., 1971—. Mem. Am. Bar Assn., State Bar Mich. Club: Mt. Holyoke N.Y. (v.p. 1973—). Home: 260 W 11th St New York City NY 10014 Office: 14 Wall St New York City NY 10005

LEHMAN, LOIS JOAN, librarian; b. Danville, Pa., Apr. 25, 1932; d. Harold and Leona (Shuey) Lehman; B.A., Pa. State U., 1954; M.S., Columbia, 1959. Tchr. social studies Sunbury (Pa.) Jr. High Sch., 1955-58; librarian Lankenau Hosp., Phila., 1959-66; reference librarian U. Pa. Sch. of Medicine Library, Phila., 1966-68; asst. librarian, head pub. services Pa. State U. Coll. Medicine, Milton S. Hershey Med. Center Library, Hershey, 1968-71, acting librarian, 1972, librarian, 1972—. Mem. Med. Library Assn. (chmn. Phila. regional group 1964-65), Delta Sigma Rho. Home: 949 E Maple St Palmyra PA 17078 Office: George T Harrell Library Hershey Med Center Hershey PA 17033

LEHMAN, MARY DORCAS, physician; b. Phila., May 27, 1939; d. Robert Nathan and Clara May (Hileman) Lehman; B.S. cum laude, Pa. State U., 1960; M.D., Med. Coll. Pa., 1963. Intern Shadyside Hosp., Pitts., 1963-64; resident VA Hosp., Pitts., 1964-67; fellow Armed Forces Inst. Pathology, Washington, 1967-68; med. adviser Bd. Vets. Appeals, Washington, 1970-73; ophthalmologist Fort Myer, U.S. Army, Arlington, Va., 1972-73; asso. dir. ophthalmology Alcon Labs., Ft. Worth, 1973—. Recipient Teaching fellowship U. Pitts., 1963-67. Mem. A.M.A., Pa., Allegheny County med. socs., Am. Acad. Ophthalmology and Otolaryngology, Assn. for Research in Vision and Ophthalmology, Alumni Armed Forces Inst. Pathology. Home: 801 Washington Av Tyrone PA 16686

LEHMANN, A(LMA) REBECCA CLARK (MRS. BRYAN J. LEHMANN, JR.), bd. trade exec.; b. New Orleans; d. Robert Reese and Ada (Anderson) Clark; grad. Spencer Bus. Coll., 1941; m. Bryan J. Lehmann, Jr., Jan. 15, 1961; children—Clark James Dyson, Bryan J. III, Anne. Exec. prodn. sec. Wesco Waterpaints, Inc., Good Hope, La., Boston, Berkeley, Cal., 1941-52; legal sec., 1954-61; exec. v.p., dir., sec. bd. Destrehan Bd. Trade, Norco, La., 1961—, also dir.; partner B & B Devel. Mem. La. Conf. on Mental Health, 1962-64, La. Civil War Centennial Com., 1961-64; sec. La. Legislative Com. on Appropriations, 1960-64, La. Lesiglative Budget Study Com., 1962-64. Bd. dirs. Greater New Orleans Tourist and Conv. Commn., 1971—. Mem. Am. Mgmt. Assn., Nat. Assn. Real Estate Brokers. Democrat. Baptist. Mem. Order Eastern Star. Home: 845 Marino Dr Norco LA 70079 Office: PO Box 459 Norco LA 70079

LEHMANN, PHYLLIS LOURENE WILLIAMS (MRS. KARL LEHMANN), archaeologist, educator; b. Bklyn., Nov. 30, 1912; d. James Barnes and Lourene (Richmond) Williams; B.A., Wellesley Coll., 1934; Ph.D., N.Y.U., 1943; Litt. D., Mt. Holyoke Coll., 1971; D.F.A., Coll. of The Holy Cross, 1973; m. Karl Lehmann, Sept. 14, 1944 (dec. Dec. 1960). Asst. in charge classical collection Bklyn. Mus., 1934-36; instr. art history Bennett Jr. Coll., 1936-39; asst. prof. history of art Smith Coll., Northampton, Mass., 1946-49, asso. prof., 1949-55, prof., 1955-67, Jessie Wells Post prof. art, 1967-72, William R. Kenan, Jr. prof. art, 1972—, dean of coll., 1965-70. Asst. field dir. Excavations Archaeol. Research Fund, N.Y.U., Samothrace, 1948-60, acting dir., 1960-65, adv. dir., 1965—; research prof. Inst. Fine Arts, 1962-65, adj. prof., 1966—; mem. mng. com. Am. Sch. Classical Studies, Athens, Greece, 1958—. Fulbright research grantee, 1952-53; Guggenheim fellow, 1952-53; Bollingen fellow, 1960; named hon. citizen Samothrace, Greece, 1968. Mem. Archeol. Inst. Am. (trustee 1970-73), Coll. Art Assn., Am. Numis. Soc., Soc. Archtl. Historians, Renaissance Soc. Am., Am. Assn. U. Women (fellowship awards com.), Phi Beta Kappa (hon. Eta chpt.). Club: Cosmopolitan. Author: Statues on Coins of Southern Italy and Sicily in the Classical Period, 1946; Roman Wall Paintings from Boscoreale in the Metropolitan Museum of Art, 1953; The Pedimental Sculptures of the Hieron in Samothrace, 1962; Samothrace, vol. 3 (Alice Davis

Hitchcock Book award), 1969; (with Karl Lehmann) Samothracian Reflections, 1973; Skopas in Samothrace, 1973. Editor: Bollingen Series LX; Samothrace. Contbr. articles to profl. jours. Home: Main St Haydenville MA 01039 Office: Hillyer Hall Smith Coll Northampton MA 01060

LEHR, ANNA MAE, home economist; b. Zion Grove, Pa., Dec. 1, 1923; d. Hector and Helen Mae (Everett) Dennison; B.S. in Home Econs., Ind. State U., 1946; postgrad. U. Md., 1962, George Washington U., 1962; m. Ray O.E. Lehr, May 7, 1949; 1 son, Gregory E. Home economist extension div. Pa. State U., 1946—, mem. state health com. for Pa. State U., 1970—. Recipient Distinguished Service Ruby award for outstanding home economist Pa., 1962; Service honor Pa. State U., 1972. Mem. Bloomsburg (Pa.) Hosp. Aux. (past pres.), Bloomsburg Bus. and Profl. Women's Club, Bloomsburg Fair Assn., Epsilon Sigma Phi, Delta Sigma Epsilon. Clubs: Soroptimist, Columbia Country (pres. elect 1973-74), Inem Temple Country. Home: RD 3 Bloomsburg PA 17815

LEHRBAUMMER, MARY JANE, hosp. adminstr.; b. Milw., Nov. 30, 1946; d. Andrew Leopold and Viola Albertina (Kleinschmidt) Lehrbaummer; student Valparaiso U., 1965-68; B.A. in Journalism, U. Wis., 1969. Copywriter, Brady Co., Milw., 1968; pub. relations intern Wis. Power & Light Co., Madison, 1969; asst. pub. relations mgr. John Oster Mfg. Co., Milw., 1969-71, Med. Soc. Milw. County, Milw., 1971-73; dir. pub. relations Holiday Hosp., Orlando, Fla., 1973—. Cons., Planned Parenthood Wis. Mem. United Fund Communications Com., 1970, group chmn. 1971. Mem. Pub. Relations Soc. Am. (co-chmn. hospitality com. 1972-73), Wis. Assn. Bus. Communicators (chmn. evaluations and award program 1971-72), Pub. Relations Student Soc. Am. (chpt. pres.), Kappa Psi Omega, Theta Sigma Phi (publicity chmn. 1968-69, v.p. Milw. profl. chpt. 1971-72). Club: Milw. Players. Editor Milw. Med. Soc. Times, 1971-73, Pulse, 1971-73, Osterview, Osterechoes, Osterclips, 1970-71, Vital Signs, also Holiday Heartbeat, Precis, 1973—. Office: 92 W Miller St Orlando FL 32806

LEHTMETS-SUSI, MARLIESE LY, physician; b. Estonia, Aug. 18, 1928; d. Richard and Marliese (Renneberg) Lehtmets; student Baltic U., Hamburg, Germany, 1948-49; B.A., U. Wis., 1951, M.D., 1955; m. Heino Susi, June 18, 1955; children—Aita-Kai, Andres-Matti, Margus Rein. Came to U.S., 1949, naturalized, 1955. Intern Mercy Hosp., Buffalo, 1956-57; resident obstetrics and gynecology Phila. Gen. Hosp., 1959; practice medicine specializing in obstetrics and gynecology, 1959—; instr. Woman's Med. Coll. Pa., 1959-60; instr. Chester-Riddle Meml. Hosp., also sec. dept. obstetrics and gynecology, Media. Diplomate Am. Bd. Obstetrics and Gynecology. Fellow Am. Coll. Obstetricians and Gynecologists; mem. A.M.A., U. Wis. Alumni Assn., Internat. Sauna Assn., Internat. Fertility Assn., Pan Am. Med. Assn., Phi Kappa Phi, Alpha Epsilon Iota. Club: Soroptimist. Contbr. article to med. jour. Home and office: 1233 Hunt Club Lane Media PA 19063

LEIBENSPERGER, AMBER ALICE BALDWIN (MRS. BRUCE LEIBENSPERGER), psychologist; b. Scranton, Pa., Nov. 20, 1911; d. Darius Erastus and Catharine Lucy (Stonier) Baldwin; B.A. in Biology, Goucher Coll., 1933; M.Ed., Pa. State U., 1959; postgrad. Bucknell U., Bloomsburg State Coll.; m. Bruce Leibensperger, Nov. 30, 1934; 1 dau., Dale (Mrs. Robert Halleran). Relief visitor Dept. Welfare, Scranton, Pa., 1935; pvt. practice as elocution tchr., Summit Hill, Pa., 1935-40; tchr. high sch. Port Carbon (Pa.) Sch. Dist., 1943-45; tchr. spl. edn. West Hazleton (Pa.) Elementary and High Sch., 1956-63; county sch. psychologist Schuylkill County (Pa.) Schs., 1963-64; dist. psychologist Hazleton (Pa.) Joint Sch. System, 1964-67; coordinator spl. edn., dist. psychologist Hazleton Area Sch. Dist., 1967—. Vol. tutor Children's Home, West Hazleton, 1948-52; active Kis-Lyn, reform sch. for boys, 1954-56. Mem. Am. (asso.), Nat., Northeastern Pa. psychol. assns., Council for Exceptional Children, Hazleton Area Adminstrs. Assn., D.A.R., Delta Kappa Gamma. Contbr. articles to profl. jours. Home: 791 McKinley St Hazleton PA 18201 Office: Hazleton Sch Hdqrs Green and Laurel Sts Hazleton PA 18201

LEIBOWITZ, SARAH FRYER (MRS. MARTIN LEWIS LEIBOWITZ), educator; b. White Plains, N.Y., May 23, 1941; d. Douglas Henry and Katharine (Homer) Fryer; B.A., N.Y. U., 1964, Ph.D., 1968; m. Martin Lewis Leibowitz, June 25, 1966; children—Kimara Joy, Rebecca Tiana. Instr., N.Y. U., 1964-68; guest investigator, USPHS fellow Rockefeller U., N.Y.C., 1968-70, asst. prof. physiol. psychology, 1970—. Mem. Am. Psychol. Assn., Am. Soc. Pharmacology and Exptl. Therapeutics, Soc. Neurosci., N.Y. Acad. Scis., N.Y. State Psychol. Assn., Phi Beta Kappa, Sigma Xi, Psi Chi. Home: 60 E 8th St New York City NY 10003

LEICHTMAN, DOROTHY MOORE, librarian; b. Berlin, N.H., Feb. 28, 1915; d. Hugh Kelsea and Mary Esther (Tebbetts) Moore; B.S., Simmons Coll., 1936; M.A., Cornell U., 1939; postgrad. Harvard, 1940, Cath. U., 1953, 54, 55, 56, U. Va., 1961, 66, 71, Am. U., 1963, 64, 65; m. Edwin Sylvester Leichtman, June 27, 1943 (div. Mar. 1958); children—Hugh, Frances (Mrs. Thomas Kiska), Harry. Librarian Timber Lane Elementary Sch., Falls Church, Va., 1957-58, Annandale (Va.) Elementary Sch., 1958-60, Pine Spring Elementary Sch., Falls Church, 1957-60, Longfellow Intermediate Sch., Falls Church, 1960—. Del. to Va. Edn. Assn., 1966, 72. Mem. Asso. Sch. Librarians Fairfax County (pres. 1972-73), Fairfax, Va. edn. assns., N.E.A., Parents Without Partners, Metro Mixers Washington. Home: 1707 N Randolph St Arlington VA 22207 Office: 2000 Westmoreland St Falls Church VA 22203

LEICHTY, MARY MASON (MRS. V. ERLE LEICHTY), educator; b. Xenia, O., July 12, 1910; d. William H. and Bessie (Grant) Mason; A.B., Mich. State U., 1947, M.A., 1952, Ph.D., 1958; m. V. Erle Leichty, Dec. 23, 1929; children—Barbra (Mrs. Donovan Juliar), Erle V. Engaged in ind. research, Vietnam, 1958-59; lectr. counseling center Mich. State U., East Lansing, 1960-63, asst. prof. counseling center and dept. psychology, 1963-66, asso. prof. dept. psychology, 1966-69, prof., 1970—. Fellow Am. Orthopsychiat. Assn.; mem. Am., Midwestern, Mich. psychol. assns., Am. Orthopsychiat. Assn., Nat. Assn. for Fgn. Student Affairs, Am. Assn. U. Profs. Home: 1864 Walnut Heights Dr East Lansing MI 48823

LEIFERMAN, SILVIA WEINER (MRS. IRWIN H. LEIFERMAN), artist, civic worker; b. Chgo.; d. Morris and Annah (Caplan) Weiner; student U. Chgo., 1960-61; m. Irwin H. Leiferman, Apr. 20, 1947. Exhibited group shows Riccardo Restaurant Gallery, Chgo., 1961-62, Bryn Mawr Country Club, Chgo., 1961, 62, Covenant Club of Ill., Chgo., 1963, D'Arey Galleries, N.Y.C., 1965, Miami Mus. Modern Art, 1967, Baccardi Gallery, 1967, Hollywood Mus. Art, 1968, Gallery 99, Miami, 1968, Barry Coll., Artist's Equity at Crystal House Gallery, Miami Beach, 1968, Lowe Art Mus., 1968, Miami Museum of Modern Art, in 1970; exhibited one-man show D'Arcy Galleries, N.Y.C., 1944, Contemporary Gallery, Palm Beach, Fla., 1966, Miami Mus. Modern Art, 1966, Schram Galleries, Ft. Lauderdale, Fla., 1966, Miami Museum of Modern Art, 1970; president Active Accessories by Silvia, Chgo., 1964—. Organizer women's div. Edgewater Hosp., 1954; chairwoman for spl. sales and spl. events Greater Chgo. Com. for State of Israel, also originator Ambassador's Ball, 1956; mem. bd. Jewish Children's Bur., 1958, Mt. Sinai Hosp., 1960; chmn. women's com. Salute to Med. Research, City of Hope, 1959; chairwoman Dior-Israel Fashion Preview for State of Israel, 1962; originator, chairwoman Presentation Ball, State of Israel, 1963-64; mem. nat. bd. govs., Greater Chgo. bd. govs. Bonds for Israel; mem. bd. Brandeis U. (life); organizer, charter mem. bd. women's div. Hebrew U., 1947; mem. Miami Beach Opera Guild Commn. Bd. dirs. Nathan Goldblatt Soc. for Cancer Research, Orgn. for Rehab. and Tng. of Fox River Sanatorium; co-founder, v.p. Silvia and Irwin Leiferman Found. Recipient citations for def. bond sales U.S. Govt.; named Woman of Valor by State of Israel, 1963. Mem. Internat. Platform Assn., Am. Fedn. Arts, Artist Equity Assn., Internat. Council Museums, Nat. Council Jewish Women (mem. bd.), Art Inst. Chgo. (life). Clubs: Standard, Bryn Mawr Country (Chgo.); Westview Country (Miami, Fla.). Studio and Home: Standard Club 320 S Plymouth Ct Chicago IL 60611 also 5255 Collins Av Miami Beach FL 33140

LEIFESTE, OSIE BLACKWELL WILSON (MRS. ERWIN CHARLES LEIFESTE), writer; b. Tulia, Tex., Mar. 13, 1906; d. Arthur D. and Nancy Lee (Monroe) Blackwell; B.A., Tex. Christian U., 1933; B.J., U. Tex., 1965; m. Cliff Cicero Wilson, Sept. 30, 1933; m. 2d, Erwin Charles Leifeste, Nov. 17, 1970. Saleswoman, bookkeeper Nathan Lynch Stores, Inc., Wichita Falls, Tex., 1925-33; tchr. Samnorwood (Tex.) High Sch., 1941-42, Higgins (Tex.) High Sch., 1943, Glenpool (Okla.) High Sch., 1953, Bula (Tex.) High Sch., 1955-56; writer non-fiction Amarillo (Tex.) Daily News, Daily Oklahoman, Oklahoma City, Caller Times, Corpus Christi, Tex., Austin (Tex.) Am. & Statesman, others. Recipient various awards. Mem. Tex. Press Women (certificates merit, Golden scroll 1958, treas. 1954-58), Nat. Fedn. Press Women (life, treas. 1964-68), Am. Assn. Ret. Persons (chpt. publicity dir. 1972-74), Sigma Tau Delta, Theta Sigma Phi. Mem. Christian Ch. (chpt. publicity dir. 1956-58). Author: (with Cleo T. Terry) The Rawhide Tree, 1956. Address: 2607 Parkview St Austin TX 78757

LEIGH, ANGELA NISTAL (MRS. JAMES T. LEIGH), business exec.; b. Tampa, Fla., Feb. 6, 1926; d. Miguel Alvarez and Rita (Bustamante) Nistal; student U. Tampa, 1947, Am. U., 1958; m. James T. Leigh, May 15, 1948; children—C. Michael, J. Joseph, P. Martine, Rita Denise, Ramona Diane. With Exchange Nat. Bank, Tampa, 1945-48; tchr. St. M. Goretti Acad., Hatfield, Pa., 1962-63; pres., dir. Golden Eagle Antiques, Inc., Tampa, 1964—; v.p., dir. Hartstone Concrete Supply, Inc., Tampa, 1966-69, Waverly Arms, Inc., Tampa, 1969—; pres., dir. Heirloom Antiques Ltd., Inc., Tampa, 1972—. Mem. Nat. Assn. Dealers in Antiques, Suncoast Antique Dealers Assn., El Prado Antique Center, Hydrangea Garden Club (dir. 1969-72, pres. 1971), Catholic Women's Club. Home: 4506 San Rafael St Tampa FL 33609 Office: 4328 El Prado Blvd Tampa FL 33609

LEIGH, RUTH R. SOKOLSKI (MRS. MURRAY STUART LEIGH), realtor; b. N.Y.C., Feb. 19; d. A. Lawrence and Anne (Frieder) Sokolski; student Hunter Coll., 1934-36, U. Pa. Wharton Sch., 1942; m. Murray Stuart Leigh, June 13, 1943; 1 dau., Leslie Susan. Sales dept. mgr., buyer Saks 34th St., N.Y.C., 1935-37; radio commls. WMCA, N.Y.C., 1936-39; interior decorator Roxberg, Inc., N.Y.C., 1937-40; broker Harold N. Sloane Co., ins. brokers, N.Y.C., 1940-43; br. mgr. Manpower Inc., N.Y.C., 1952-53; interior designer Storr & Co., N.Y.C., 1949—; builder-broker Ruth S. Leigh, N.Y.C., 1965—. Dist. dir. Girl Scouts U.S.A., 1952-54; fund raiser N.Y. Heart Assn., 1955—, Salvation Army, 1960—; bd. dirs. Interfaith Neighbors, 1964-66; dist. liaison officer Black & White Assos. supporting Oddyssey House Drug Addicts, 1969-70; trustee Bloomingdale Ho. of Music, N.Y.C., 1970-71. Recipient civic awards. Mem. Unitarian-Universalist Womens Fedn. (dist. pres. 1966—), Am. Unitarian Assn. (asst. non-govtl. orgn. rep. UN, nat. chmn. UN seminars 1958-62). Republican. Unitarian (v.p. bd. 1972, deacon 1974). Home: 1010 Fifth Av New York City NY 10028 Office: 1220 Lexington Av New York City NY 10028

LEIGH, SHERREN (MRS. NORMAN J. HICKEY, JR.), advt. agy. exec.; b. Cleve., Dec. 22, 1942; d. Walter Carl and Treva (Everstine) Maurushat; B.S. in Journalism, Ohio U., 1965; m. Norman J. Hickey, Jr., Aug. 23, 1969. Pub. relations dir. Metal Lath Assn., Cleve., 1965-68; pres. Your Write Arm, Chgo., 1969-71; v.p., creative dir. Robert L. Cohn, Inc., Chgo., 1971—. Mem. Am. Women in Communications, Nat. Orgn. Women, Zeta Tau Alpha. Home: 571 Blackstone Pl Highland Park IL 60035 Office: 111 E Wacker Dr Chicago IL 60601

LEIGHNINGER, MARGARET JANE MALONY, artist; b. Dayton, O., Sept. 14, 1918; d. William A. and Pearl (Leihgeber) Malony; student Kent State U., 1936; student Western Res. U., 1948, Case Western Res. U., 1964-68, Cleve. Art Inst., 1968; B.A., Mundelein Coll. Art, 1973; m. David S. Leighninger, May 24, 1942; children—David Allan, Jenny. Social worker, Youngstown, O., 1937-42; nursery sch. tchr., 1947-48, 49-52; record room librarian U. Hosps. Cleve., 1942-46, 52-56; exhibited in one-man shows at Fine Arts Assn., Willoughby, O., Fenn Coll., Mundelein Coll.; exhibited in group shows at Malvina Freedson Galleries, Shaker Art Show, Mundelein Coll., Birmingham (Ala.) Mus. Art, Larew's Galleries, Evanston, Ill., Brewery Works Fine Arts Salon, Cedarburg, Wis. Represented in permanent collections Willoughby Fine Arts Assn., Am. Contemporary Arts and Crafts Slide Library. Mem. Cleve. Acad. Medicine, Heart Assn. Northeastern Ohio, Women's Art League Cleve., Art Inst. Chgo., North Shore Art League, Friends of Art Northwestern U., Contemporary Mus. Art, Willoughby Fine Arts Assn. Home: 2025 Sherman Av #503 Evanston IL 60201

LEIGHTON, GERTRUDE CATHERINE KERR, lawyer, educator; b. Belfast, No. Ireland, Dec. 9, 1914; d. Archibald O. and Gertrude (Hamilton) Leighton; brought to U.S., 1915, naturalized, 1918; A.B., Bryn Mawr Coll., 1938; LL.B., Yale, 1945, postgrad. in law (fellow), 1947-49. Lectr., Barnard Coll., N.Y.C., 1940-42; admitted to N.Y. bar, 1947; with firm Carter, Ledyard & Milburn, N.Y.C., 1945-47; vis. lectr. law Yale, 1949-50; asst. prof. polit. sci. Bryn Mawr (Pa.) Coll., 1950-55, asso. prof., 1955-64, prof., 1964—, chmn. dept. 1963-65, 68-71. Fund for Advancement Edn. fellow, 1953-54, Rockefeller Found. fellow, 1957-58; lectr. law U. Pa. Law Sch., Phila., 1959-61, vis. asso. research prof. law and psychiatry, 1961-65. Mem. Am. Bar Assn., Am. Polit. Sci. Assn., Am. Soc. Internat. Law, Am. Assn. U. Profs., Bryn Mawr Coll. Alumnae Assn. Episcopalian. Contbr. articles to legal jours. Research in law and psychiatry. Home: Hollow Rd Radnor PA 19087 Office: Bryn Mawr Coll Bryn Mawr PA 19010

LEIGHTON, LUCILE ADELMAN (MRS. ROBERT LEIGHTON), painter, lectr., educator; b. Chgo.; d. Charles S. and Rose (Schoen) Adelman; student Chgo. Acad. Fine Arts, 1930-31, student Evanston Acad. Fine Arts, 1932-33; spl. courses Art Inst. Chgo., 1940-50, U. Miami, Fla., 1934-35; m. Robert Leighton, Sept. 2, 1934. Painter, tchr., lectr. on art and travel, Chgo., 1950—; exhibited 16 one-man shows; exhibited maj. museums and galleries in Chgo. area, also Springfield (Mass.) Mus., Pa. Acad. Fine Arts, Rochester (N.Y.) Mus. Fine Arts, Collectors Gallery, Portland, Ore., Deauville Galleries, Atlantic City, Galerie Nouvelle, Detroit, Corinthian Gallery, Phila., Butler Mus., Youngstown, O., others; represented Chgo. Art Inst. Rental and Sales Gallery, also pvt. collections throughout U.S. Bd. dirs. Chgo. Soc. Artists. Nominated as New Talent in U.S.A., Art in Am. mag., 1956. Mem. Chgo. Council Fgn. Relations (speakers bur.), Adult Edn. Council (speakers bur.). Home and studio: 2150 N Cleveland Av Chicago IL 60614

LEIGHTON, MARGARET, actress; b. Worcestershire, Eng., Feb. 26, 1922; d. A. George and Doris Isabel (Evans) Leighton; ed. Ch. of Eng. Coll., Birmingham; m. Max Reinhardt, Aug. 1947 (dissolved 1954) m. 2d, Laurence Harvey, Aug. 8, 1957 (dissolved 1961); m. 3d, Michael Wilding, 1964. Mem. Birmingham Repertory Theatre, 1938, Old Vic Co., 1944-47; plays in London include a Sleeping Clergyman, 1947, Philadelphia Story, 1949, The Cocktail Party, 1950, The Three Sisters, 1950, Confidential Clerk, 1953, The Applecart, 1953, Separate Tables, 1954, Variation on a Theme, 1958, The Wrong Side of the Park, 1960, The Lady From the Sea, 1961; plays in N.Y.C. include Old Vic performances, 1946, Separate Tables, 1956, Much Ado About Nothing, 1959, The Night of the Iguana, 1961, Tchin Tchin, 1962, Chinese Prime Minister, 1964, Little Foxes, 1968; appeared Meml. Theatre, Stratford-on-Avon, Eng., 1952, Cactus Flower, Globe Theatre, 1967, Anthony and Cleopatra, Chichester Festival Theatre, Sussex, Eng. 1969, Girlfriend, Appollo Theatre, 1970, (film) Madwoman of Chaillot, 1969. Address: Weisberger & Frosch 120 E 56th St New York City NY 10022

LEIGHTY, EDITH GARDNER, biochemist; b. Zanesville, O., Nov. 4, 1928; d. Milton Ostius and Mildred Evelyn (Maxwell) Gardner; B.S., Marshall U., 1962; M.S., Ohio State U., 1965, Ph.D. (NIH fellow), 1967; m. David Leighty, Jan. 4, 1948 (div. Jan. 1957); 1 son, David Alan. Research chemist Standard Ultramarine Co., Huntington, W.Va., 1962-63; biochemist Battelle Columbus Labs. (O.), 1967—. Mem. Am. Chem. Soc., Sigma Xi, Sigma Delta Epsilon. Home: 2332 Hardesty Ct Columbus OH 43204 Office: 505 King Av Columbus OH 43201

LEIMAS, CAROL CHAULS (MRS. IRWIN LEIMAS), assn. exec.; b. N.Y.C., Sept. 12, 1931; d. Reuben and Lillian (Segall) Chauls; B.A., Syracuse U., 1952; Certificat d'Etudes Politiques, U. Paris, France, 1953; m. Irwin Leimas, Oct. 18, 1963; 1 dau., Stacie. Research asst. Anti-Defamation League, B'nai B'rith, N.Y.C., 1953-56; research asst. conf. group U.S. Nat. Orgn. on UN, N.Y.C., 1956-57; inquiry specialist World Affairs Center U.S., N.Y.C., 1957-60; dir. information-reference dept. Fgn. Policy Assn., N.Y.C., 1960-67; UN rep. Am. Assn. U. Women, 1969—. Mem. exec. com. Conf. UN Reps. UN Assn. Bd. dirs. N.Y. Young Democratic Club, 1959-63, 63-65, v.p., 1961-63, sec., 1962-63. French Govt. fellow, U.S. Govt. Fulbright travel fellow, 1952-53. Mem. League Women Voters N.Y.C. (dir. 1970-72), Phi Beta Kappa. Home: 60 East End Av New York City NY 10028 Office: Am Assn U Women 2401 Virginia Av NW Washington DC 20037

LEINEN, DARLENE EMILY FORSETH (MRS. JAMES THEODORE LEINEN), orgn. exec.; b. Williston, N.D., Sept. 11, 1934; d. Sigvald Arne and Lillie Virginia (Mattson) Forseth; student U. Mont., 1953-54, U. N.D., 1961-62, 73; m. James Theodore Leinen, Nov. 6, 1954; children—Jami, Mark, Christopher, Kathryn, Mary Faith, Michala. Sec., Farmers Union Ins., Williston, 1952-53, 55-57; sec., loan teller Am. State Bank, Williston, 1954-55; teller Williston Coop Credit Union, Williston, 1957-59; sec. C. of C., Williston, 1961-62; exec. sec. United Way, Williston, 1965—. Sec. Mercy Hosp. Aux., 1962-64, Community Service League, 1965-67; mem. Royal Winnipeg Ballet Com., 1967; treas., finance chmn. Williston Swim Team, 1968-72; sec. Citizen's Com. for Better Edn., 1970; pres. Jr. High Sch. Parent Tchrs. Orgn., 1972; pres. St. Joseph's Parochial Sch. Bd., 1973-74; sec. Social Service Bd. N.D., 1973—. Mem. Dem. precinct com., Williston, 1967—; del. N.D. Dem. Conv., 1968, 72. Named Outstanding Young Woman of N.D., 1970; recipient certificate of merit Williston C. of C., 1971. Mem. League Women Voters (sec. 1957-58), Beta Sigma Phi. Home: 16 W 8th St PO Box 1465 Williston ND 58801 Office: PO Box 176 Williston ND 58801

LEININGER, MADELEINE M., educator, anthropologist, univ. adminstr., nurse; b. Sutton, Neb., July 13, 1925; d. George M. and Helen Irene (Sheedy) Leininger; B.S., Mt. St. Scholastica Coll., 1950; M.S. in Nursing, Cath. U. Am., 1954; Ph.D., U. Wash., 1965. Staff nurse St. Anthony's Hosp., Denver, 1945-48; staff nurse, supr., educator Creighton Meml. St. Joseph's Hosp., Omaha, 1950-53; asso. prof. nursing U. Cin., 1954-59; prof. nursing and anthropology U. Colo., Denver and Boulder, 1965-69; dean, prof. nursing, lectr. anthropology U. Wash., Seattle, 1969-74; dean, prof. nursing and anthropology Coll. Nursing U. Utah, 1974—. Field worker, New Guinea. Bd. dirs. Lee House, Seattle. Mem. Nat. League for Nursing, Am. Assn. Coll. Nursing (pres. 1969-72), Am. Nurses Assn., Am. Anthropology Assn., N.Y. Acad. Sci., World Fedn. for Mental Health, Am. Mus. Natural History, Western Commn. for Higher Edn. in Nursing, Applied Anthropology Assn., Rocky Mountain Social Sci. Assn., Soc. for Internat. Transcultural Nursing Field Devel. Author: (with Charles Hofling) Basic Psychiatric Concepts in Nursing, 1960; Two Worlds to Blend: Anthropology and Nursing, 1970; Contemporary Issues in Mental Health Nursing, 1973. Editor Health Care Dimensions, 1973—. Contbr. articles in field to profl. jours. Home: 2789 Thunderbird Dr Salt Lake City UT 84109 Office: U Utah Coll Nursing Salt Lake City UT 84112

LEINONEN, ELLEN ANNA, educator; b. Houghton, Mich., Oct. 15, 1912; d. Matt and Maria (Gustava) Leinonen; certificate in Dental Hygiene, U. Mich., 1949, B.S. with distinction, 1956, M.S. in Anatomy, 1962; Ph.D. (Dr. A.L. Largo research scholar, Teaching fellow), Ohio State U., 1967. Instr. dentistry U. Mich. at Ann Arbor, 1949-62, asst. prof. dentistry, 1965—, asst. prof. anatomy Med. Sch., 1971—; dental hygienist, Ypsilanti, Mich., 1949-50, Canton Center, Mich., summer 1950, Wayne, Mich., 1950-52, Ann Arbor, 1953-55. Fellow Simpson Meml. Inst. U. Mich. Mem. N.Y. Acad. Scis., Am. Assn. Anatomists, Am. Inst. Chemists, A.A.A.S., Dental Hygienists Assn., Am. Assn. U. Profs., Sigma Xi, Sigma Delta Epsilon, Pi Lambda Theta, Sigma Phi Alpha (pres. 1970-71). Republican. Lutheran. Clubs: Zonta International (mem. exec. bd. 1970-73), Business and Professional Womans (Ypsilanti, Mich.). Home: 3093 Lexington Dr Ann Arbor MI 48105

LEIPZIG, LIBBY (MRS. FRED LEIPZIG), state ofcl., automotive products co. exec.; b. Easton, Pa.; d. Benjamin and Mary (Bizar) Black; student Paterson Normal Sch., N.J., 1928, Rutgers U., 1943-44, Fairleigh Dickinson U., 1962; m. Fred Leipzig, Apr. 12, 1940; 1 dau., Marta Beth. With N.J. State Employment Service, Passaic, 1941—, supr. profl. comml. dept., Paterson, N.J., 1962-69, supr. indsl. services dept., Passaic, 1969-72; v.p. Major Automotive Products Co., Inc., Clifton, N.J. 1945-69, sec.-treas., 1969—. Home: 540 Passaic Av Clifton NJ 07014

LEIS, SISTER MARY DE CHANTAL, ednl. adminstr.; b. Pitts.; d. Anthony John and Clare Elizabeth (Buettner) Leis; B.A., Seton Hill Coll., 1923; M.A., U. Pitts., 1929; Ph.D., Columbia, 1950. Joined Sisters of Charity, 1929; prof. classics Seton Hill Coll., Greensburg, Pa., 1929-41, dean of women, 1939-64, dir. of alumnae relations, 1964—. Recipient Elizabeth Seton award, 1970. Mem. Am. Assn.

Univ. Women, Pitts. Assn. of Alumnae Dirs. of Women's Colls. Address: Seton Hill College Greensburg PA 15601

LEIS, WINOGENE B. (MRS. HENRY PATRICK LEIS, JR.), nurse assn. exec.; b. Clay, W.Va., Feb. 27, 1919; d. Gruder L. and Daisy M. (Young) Barnette; R.N. cum laude, Kanawha Valley Hosp., 1939; m. Henry Patrick Leis, Jr., Jan. 8, 1944; children—Henry Patrick III, Thomas Federick. Nurse, Kanawha Valley Hosp., 1939-43. Mem. Woman's Aux. Internat. Coll. Surgeons (corr. sec. N.Y. State surg. div. 1955-57, v.p. 1961-63, pres. 1963-67; pres. U.S. sect. 1970, dir. 1970-74), Flower Fifth Av. Hosp. Woman's Aux. (dir. 1956-59, 69—), Woman's Aux. N.Y. Acad. Scis., Woman's Aux. N.Y. State Med. Soc., Woman's Aux. Internat. Coll. Surgeons (corr. sec. 1972-74). Republican. Roman Catholic. Club: Cresthaven (Whitestone, N.Y.). Home: 147-03 5th Av Whitestone NY 11357

LEISTER, LOIS ANDERSON (MRS. JOHN WARD LEISTER, JR.), poet; b. New Kensington, Pa., Oct. 14, 1928; d. Edmund Louis and Ruth P. (Bowser) Anderson; student Indiana (Pa.) U., 1945-46; m. John Ward Leister, Jr., Oct. 11, 1947; children—Kathy (Mrs. John Mallonee), David, John Ward III, Joseph, Nancy. Poetry pub. in Better Camping, Am. Poet, Cyclo-flame, Kaiku Highlights, Jean's Jour., Modern Images, Prairie Poet, United Poets, Leader mag.; pub. in anthologies, including Best in Poetry, 1969, Am. Poets Fellowship Soc. Anthology, 1969. Troop leader Girl Scouts U.S.A., 1960-69; dist. roundtable commr. Boy Scouts Am., 1969-74. Chmn. bd. dirs. St. Matthews Projects, Inc., Seat Pleasant, Md., 1967-69. Recipient 1st prize Spenserian Sonnet Contest, 1969, 1st prize Quatrain Contest, 1970, 1st prize Ballad Contest, 1970, Silver Fawn award Boy Scouts Am., 1974. Mem. Avalon World Arts Acad., Md. State Poetry Soc., Am. Poets Fellowship Soc., Internat. Culture, Poetry and Efficiency Soc. (county chmn. 1972-74). Home: 4112 Ryon Rd Upper Marlboro MD 20870

LEISTLER, MARY MARTHA GRILEY (MRS. KENNETH S. LEISTLER), ch. worker; b. Cin., Nov. 27, 1938; d. Frank Alfred and Martha (Burbank) Griley; student Denison U., 1957-58; B.A. in Polit. Sci., U. Cin., 1961; m. Kenneth S. Leistler, Nov. 4, 1961; children—John David, Elizabeth Lyn. Active YMCA, leader Tri Gra-Y group, 1960-61; state pres. Ohio Bapt. Youth Fellowship, 1958-59; dir. children's work in local ch. and missions; editor nat. mag. Crossroads, 1957-58; Ohio chmn. Girls Missionary Guild Work, 1960-64; area dir. Am. Bapt. Young People, 1963-66; area dir. leadership devel. Am. Bapt. Women, mem. Ministry to Girls through Ch. Women United. Recipient award Am. Bapt. Newspapers, 1970. Mem. W.C.T.U., Phi Beta Kappa, Chi Omega. Republican. Interpreter for Am. Indians, Latin Am. countries. Home: 2460 Montana Av Cincinnati OH 45211

LEITER, BEULAH G. (MRS. ROBERT PAUL LEITER), lawyer; b. Chgo.; d. Jehiel D. and Rose (Rossman) Liebling; J.D., John Marshall U., 1945, LL.M., 1946; student U. Chgo., U. Ga., Emory U.; m. Robert Paul Leiter, May 10, 1936; children—Darryl J., Paula S. Admitted to Ga. bar, 1945, since practiced in Atlanta; mem. firm Leiter & Leiter, 1946—; dep. sheriff, 1958—. Mem. Iota Tau Tau, 1951—, So. chancellor, 1955-57, Internat. supreme chancellor, 1955-59, mem. supreme council, 1955-63, supreme asso. dean, 1959-61, internat. supreme dean, 1961-63. Mem. nat. women's com. Brandeis U., 1961—. Mem. Internat. Fedn. Women Lawyers (legal edn. com. 1958, penal law, outer space law, UN com. coms. 1959-60), Nat. Assn. Women Lawyers (mental health com.), Am. Trial Lawyers Assn., Internat. Platform Assn., Am. Judicature Soc., Com. Women in Pub. Service, Ga. Assn. Women Lawyers (past v.p., rec. sec.; exec. com.), U. Ga. Alumni Soc., Nat. Sheriffs Assn., Ga. Bar Assn., Fulton County Lawyers Assn. (charter, trustee 1952, rec. sec. 1956—), Nat. Assn. Claimant Attys., Am. Bus. Women's Assn., P.T.A., Atlanta Art Assn., Phi Kappa Delta. Clubs: Equity (publicity com. 1959-60, 62—), Old War Horse Lawyers, Nat. Travel, Smithsonian Assos., Assos. Am. Mus. Natural History. Home: 1219 Poplar Grove Dr NE Atlanta GA 30306 Office: 520 Equitable Bldg 100 Peachtree St NW Atlanta GA 30303

LEITH, LUCIA JOHNSON (MRS. D. MALCOLM LEITH), journalist; b. South Euclid, O.; d. Delos Edward and Adelaide Caroline (Carroll) Johnson; B.A. with highest honors, Principia Coll., 1966; m. D. Malcolm Leith, Oct. 4, 1969. Copykid, clk. Christian Sci. Monitor, Boston, 1966, staff writer, Boston, 1967, staff corr., Washington, 1967-69, staff corr., Chgo., 1969; free lance journalist, 1969—. Cons. Morgan Community Ednl. Center, Inc., Washington, 1969—. Recipient Pittman Prose award Principia Coll., 1965, 66. Mem. Common Cause. Home and office: 4626 Western Av Washington DC 20016

LEMAIRE, MINNIE ETHEL, educator; b. Taunton, Mass., July 15, 1908; d. Willard W. and Maude (Poole) Lemaire; B.A., Wheaton Coll., 1930; M.A., Clark U., 1932, Ph.D., 1935. Geography instr. State Tchrs. Coll., La Crosse, Wis., 1935-43; chmn. dept. geography State Tchrs. Coll., East Stroudsburg, Pa., 1943-47; chmn. dept. geology and geography Mt. Holyoke Coll., 1947-73. Fellow Nat. Council Geog. Edn. (mem. bd. 1965-67), Am. Geog. Soc.; mem. Assn. Am. Geographers (chmn. credentials com. 1957-58), Am. Assn. U. Women (pres. Conn. Valley br. 1956-58, higher edn. com. 1961-63, standards in higher edn. com. 1963-69, mem. ednl. found. 1969-73), Am. Assn. U. Profs. (com. accrediting of colls. and univs. 1961-64; pres. Mt. Holyoke Coll. chpt. 1956-58), N.E.-St. Lawrence Valley Geog. Soc. (past pres., sec.-treas. 1951-56), Soc. Women Geographers, Phi Beta Kappa. Home: 190 Brattle St Holden MA 01520 Office: Grad Sch Geography Clark U Worcester MA 01610

LEMAY, GERALDINE, librarian; b. Sheffield, Ala.; d. Edwin Forrest and Alma (Bell) LeMay; A.B., Agnes Scott Coll., Emory U.; M.A., U. Chgo. Extension service librarian Richland County, S.C.; community librarian TVA, Norris, Tenn.; librarian U.S. Army, Camp Stewart, Ga.; library sch. librarian Emory U.; asst. dir. State Dept. Information Library, Wellington, New Zealand, dir., Melbourne, Australia; dir. Savannah (Ga.) and Chatham-Effingham-Liberty Regional Library, Savannah, 1952—. Bd. dirs. Chatham County Mental Health Assn., Savannah. Mem. Am., Southeastern, Ga. library assns., Historic Savannah, Inc., Savannah Hist. Research Assn., Telfair Acad. Arts and Scis., League Women Voters, Nat. Mental Health Assn., Altrusa, Phi Beta Kappa. Author: Story of a Dam, 1940. Home: 104 W Gaston St Savannah GA 31401 Office: 2002 Bull St Savannah GA 31401

LEMAY, MARJORIE, radiologist; b. Medical Lake, Wash., May 6, 1917; d. Samuel and Grace (Lobinger) LeMay; B.A., U. Kan., 1939, M.D., 1942; m. 1948 (div. 1964); children—Tamsin Ann, Walter Eugene. Intern Albany (N.Y.) Hosp., 1942-43; resident Presbyn. Hosp., N.Y.C., 1943-46; asst. radiologist, 1948-49, 51-52; vis. scientist Cambridge (Eng.) U., 1949-51; radiologist Boston VA Hosp., 1953-63, Harvard U. Health Services, Cambridge, Mass., 1966—; vis. prof. radiology Am. U., Beirut, Lebanon, 1961-62; asso. radiologist Peter Bent Brigham Hosp., Boston, 1964-66, Beth Israel Hosp., Boston, 1969-71, Mass. Gen. Hosp., Boston, 1972—; asso. prof. radiology Harvard, 1972—. Mem. Am. Coll. Radiology, Am. Roentgen Soc., Radiol. Soc. N.Am., New Eng. Roentgen Ray Soc., Am. Soc. Neuroroentgenology. Contbr. articles to profl. jours. Home: 64 Dudley St Brookline MA 02146 Office: 75 Mt Auburn St Cambridge MA 02138

LEMAY, PAULETTE MARIE, lawyer; b. Paterson, N.J., Sept. 17, 1940; d. Albert Thomas and Yvonne Marie (Bergeron) Lemay; A.B., Vassar Coll., 1962; LL.B., U. Pa., 1965. Admitted to N.J. bar, 1965; practiced in Paterson, 1966—; law clk. to Leon Gerofsky, judge Superior Ct., New Brunswick, N.J., 1965-66; asso. firm Cole, Berman and Belsky, attys., 1966-69; individual practice law, Paterson, 1969; sr. editor Prentice-Hall, Inc., Englewood Cliffs, N.J., 1969-73; asso. gen. counsel Unishops, Inc., Jersey City, 1973—. Mem. mayor's Charter Study Commn., Paterson, 1969, sec., 1969. Fellow The Hague, Netherlands, 1964. Mem. Am., N.J. bar assns., Amateur Horsemen's Assn. (sec. dir. 1973), Am. Horse Shows Assn. Club: Zonta. Home: 360 Park Av Paterson NJ 07504 Office: 21 Caven Point Av Jersey City NJ 07305

LEMBKE, RUTH CRAINE (MRS. EMIL S. LEMBKE), educator; b. Milw., May 13, 1910; d. George and Olive Belle (Caine) Craine; B.Edn., Milw. State Tchrs. Coll., 1932; M. Philosophy, U. Wis., 1939; m. Emil S. Lembke, June 7, 1946. Elementary tchr. Bd. Edn., Lodi, Wis., 1932-34; classroom tchr. Bd. Edn., Wauwatosa, Wis., 1934-57, sch. librarian, 1957-60, sch. psychologist, 1960-73. Cons. psychologist Upward Bound program U. Wis.-Milw., summer 1966. First aid instr. A.R.C., Milw., 1935-47; leader Girl Scouts, Wauwatosa, 1936-41; staff sgt. Civil Air Patrol, 1940-44. Mem. Nat., Wis., Wauwatosa (pres. 1953) edn. assns., Nat. Assn. Sch. Psychologists, Wis. Sch. Psychologists Assn., 99's (Wis. pres. 1944-45), Delta Kappa Gamma, Pi Lambda Theta. Mem. Order Eastern Star. Asso. editor, contbr. mags. of poetry for children, 1960-69. Home: W250 N5467 Pewaukee Rd Sussex WI 53089

LEMMON, HELEN ELIZABETH, librarian; b. Latrobe, Pa., Sept. 11, 1935; d. Nathan Paul and Carolyn Mary (Foltz) Lemmon; B.A., Westminster Coll., 1959; M.Ed., Pa. State U., 1964; M.L.S., U. Pitts., 1969. Tchr. social studies, sci. Norwin Sch. Dist., Irwin, Pa., 1959-65; asst. librarian Thiel Coll., Greenville, Pa., 1969-71; librarian Johnson Bible Coll., Kimberlin Heights Station, Tenn., 1971—. Mem. Bus. and Profl. Women Greenville (Pa.), Phi Alpha Theta. Mem. Ch. of Christ. Address: Johnson Bible Coll Kimberlin Heights Station TN 37920

LEMMON, JEAN MARIE HOLMSTRAND (MRS. RICHARD LUVERNE LEMMON), editor; b. Duluth, Minn., Nov. 11, 1932; d. Lawrence Howard and Marie (Gunderson) Holmstrand; B.A. in Art, U. Minn., 1954; m. Richard LuVerne LemMon, Apr. 17, 1965; 1 dau., Rebecca Jean. Scenic designer KDAL-TV, Duluth, 1954, 56; continuity dir. radio sta. WDSM, Duluth, 1956-61; asso. editor Home Furnishings, Better Homes and Gardens Mag., Des Moines, Ia., 1961-63; home furnishings and equipment editor Successful Farming Mag., Des Moines, 1963-67; contbg. editor Better Homes and Gardens Apt. Ideas. Free lance writer, designer, interior decorator, 1967—; pres. Jean LemMon & Assos., Inc. Mem. A.S.C.A.P., Am. Inst. Interior Designers, Mensa. Address: 646 44th St Des Moines IA 50312 Office: 1716 Locust St Des Moines IA 50303

LEMON, ALICE JOY BENIOFF, theatre producer, dir.; b. Los Angeles, Nov. 24, 1933; d. Herman and Celia (Shluker) Benioff; B.S., U. Cal. at Los Angeles, 1957; M.A. in Drama and Theatre, U. Hawaii, 1973; div.; children—Kurt Robert, Lisa Kay. Founder, Peppermint Players, Honolulu, 1971, dir., 1971-74, producer, 1971—; instr. drama Honolulu Community Theatre, 1969—. Mem. Children's Media Com., Honolulu, 1973. Mem. Am. Theatre Assn., Children's Theatre Assn. Home: 3260 Monsarrat Av Honolulu HI 96815

LEMORANDE, AGNES PELEGRIN (MRS. RALPH JOHN LEMORANDE), librarian; b. Green Bay, Wis., Jan. 20, 1923; d. Marcus Hanna and Sadie Mary (DenRuyter) Pelegrin; student U. Wis., 1941-43, library certificate, 1973; B.S. in Occupational Therapy, Western Mich. U., 1947; m. Ralph John Lemorande, June 7, 1952; children—Anne Marie, Ralph J.H., Margaret Hanna, Ruth Elaine, Lisa. Staff therapist Kalamazoo (Mich.) State Hosp., 1946; asst. chief therapist VA Hosp., Richmond, Va.. 1947-51; chief occupational therapist VA Hosp., Madison, Wis., 1951-52; librarian Washington Sch. Library, Oconto Falls, Wis., 1968—. Activity cons. Falls Nursing Home, 1971—. Pres. hosp. aux., Oconto Falls, 1952; cons. installation program Girl Scouts, 1966—. Mem. Am. Occupational Therapy Assn., Nat., Wis. edn. assns., Wis. Library Assn., Alpha Gamma Delta. Home: 323 Wisconsin St Oconto Falls WI 54154 Office: Washington School Library Oconto Falls WI 54154

L'ENGLE, MADELEINE (MRS. HUGH FRANKLIN), author; b. N.Y.C., Nov. 29, 1918; d. Charles Wadsworth and Madeleine (Barnett) Camp; A.B. with honors, Smith Coll., 1941; postgrad. Columbia, 1960—; m. Hugh Franklin, Jan. 26, 1946; children—Josephine Morrison, Maria Richmond, Bion Barnett. Appeared in Broadway plays Uncle Harry, 1944, The Cherry Orchard, 1945, The Joyous Season, 1946; appeared in summer stock, radio, TV, 1941—; tchr. St. Hilda's and St. Hugh's Sch., N.Y.C., 1960—; writer in residence Ohio State U., 1970; lectr. U. Minn., U. Mich., Ind. U., U. Rochester, Wheaton Coll., U. So. Mo.; writer-in-residence Cathedral St. John the Divine; author: The Small Rain, 1945; Ilse, 1946; And Both Were Young, 1949; Camilla Dickinson, 1951; A Winter's Love, 1957; Meet the Austins, 1960; A Wrinkle in Time, 1962 (Newbery medal 1963; Sequoyah award 1965); The Moon by Night, 1963 (Austrian State Lit. award 1970); The Twenty-Four Days Before Christmas, 1964; The Arm of the Starfish, 1965; Camilla, 1965; The Love Letters, 1966; The Journey with Jonah, 1967; The Young Unicorns, 1968; Dance in The Desert, 1969; Lines Scribbled on an Envelope, 1970; The Other Side of the Sun, 1971; A Circle of Quiet, 1972; A Wind in the Door, 1973; The Summer of The Great-Grandmother, 1975. Author stories, poems, plays. Pres. Crosswicks Found.; bd. dirs. Author's League. Recipient Lewis Carroll Shelf award, 1965; Hans Christian Anderson Internat. Runner-up award; Sequoiah award; Austrian State prize for lit., 1969. Mem. Authors League (children's book com., membership com., mem. council), Authors Guild, Colonial Dames (library com.), P.E.N., Internat. Platform Assn., Writers Guild Am. Mem. Anglican Ch. (choir dir. 1953-59). Home: 924 West End Av New York City NY 10025 also Crosswicks West St Goshen CT 06756

LENHART, MRS. JOHN JACOBS (KATHARINE BRADLEY LENHART), civic worker; b. Nyack, N.Y., Apr. 25, 1903; d. Stephen Rowe and Katharine (Scott) Bradley; B.A., Vassar Coll., 1925; certificate Miss Conklin's Secretarial Sch., 1931; student Art Students' League, 1925-26, 33-34, N.Y.U., Bank St. Coll. Edn., 1942-43; Ph.D. (hon.), U. Ariz. m. John Jacobs Lenhart, USN, Nov. 28, 1927 (killed in action Mar. 1928). Asso. decorator with Adeline de Voo, 1928-29; exec. sec. Spence Sch., N.Y.C., 1931-33; vice chmn. staff asst. service N.Y. chpt. A.R.C., 1939-42; dir. Masters Nursery, 1944-54, pres. bd. 1950-52; exec. sec. pediatric service Bellevue Hosp., 1944-45; chmn. day care com. Welfare and Health Council N.Y.C., 1950-53; mem. bd. Play Schs. Assn., v.p. bd., 1960-68, chmn. com. on Parent Conducted Activities on Coop. Housing, 1954-68; dir. Goddard-Riverside Community Centers, 1961-64, Goddard-Riverside Housing Corp. bd.; vice chmn. regional planning bd. Community Council Greater N.Y., 1965-66; bd. dirs. Fedn. Protestant Welfare Agys., 1966—, mem. exec. com., 1968—, chmn. self study com. div. youth and community services, 1967-68, mem. com. on legislation 1967-68, mem. nominating com., 1968-70, chmn. sub-com. of program planning for emerging social services, 1969; bd. dirs. Assn. Neighborhood Councils, 1964-67; bd. dirs., mem. steering com. Center for Housing Partnerships, N.Y.C., 1971—; trustee Pequot Chapel; founding dir. West Farms Land Trust, Waterford, Conn. Mem. League Women Voters New London, Tappan Zee Hist. Soc., Hudson River Conservation Soc. Episcopalian. Clubs: Garden of Am.; Skating (N.Y.); Cosmopolitan (N.Y.C.); Republican (Waterford); Pequot Point Beach; Old Lyme Country; New London Garden. Home: 2 Jordon Cove Circle Waterford CT 06385 Office: 1075 Park Av New York City NY 10028

LENHER, IRENE K. (MRS. SAMUEL LENHER), artist; b. Rye, N.Y., Oct. 4, 1907; d. John Wilkinson and Elena (Hellmann) Kirkland; student Slade Sch. Art, U. Coll. (London), 1925-26, Grande Chaumiere, Paris, 1927-28; M.A. (hon.), U. Del., 1968; m. Samuel Lenher, Dec. 14, 1929; children—John K., Ann B., George V. Exhibited one-man show Warehouse Gallery Arden, Decoy Gallery, Kennett Square, Pa., Hunter Gallery, 1965, Books, Inc., Wilmington, 1966; exhibited two and three man shows, also in group shows Wilmington (Del.) Soc. Fine Arts, Rehoboth (Del.) Art League, Cottage Tour Art, West Chester, Pa.; work represented in collections Wilmington Trust Co., Hotel Du Pont, Del. Hosp. Sustaining mem. Wilmington Jr. League, Everyman's Gallery; represented permanent collections Wilmington Soc. Fine Arts, Copeland Purchase Fund, U. Del. Asso. mem. bd. Del. Hosp. Recipient 2d prize, best of show awards Nat. League Am. Pen Women shows; award of merit Nat. League Am. Penwomen, 1962. Mem. Nat. League Am. Pen Women (state pres.), Colonial Dames Am., Am. Watercolor Soc. (asso.), Soc. Mayflower Descs. (dep. gov.), Wilmington Studio Group, Phila. Art Alliance. Episcopalian. Club: Wilmington Country. Home: 1900 Woodlawn Av Wilmington DE 19806 Office: 1616 Rodney St Wilmington DE 19806

LENKEY, SUSAN V., librarian, educator; b. Budapest, Hungary, 1910; Ph.D., Pazmany Peter U., Budapest, 1946; m. Andrew Lenkey, 1937 (dec. 1967); 1 dau., Maryll Telegdy. Came to U.S., 1957, naturalized, 1963. Asst. prof. U. Budapest, 1946-50; research asso. Municipal Mus., Budapest, 1950-56; library asst. Yale, 1960; rare book librarian, lectr. humanities Stanford, 1960—. Vis. prof. Chapman Coll. World Campus Afloat, 1969, 71, 74; lectr. U. Cal. Extension, 1962—. Mem. Archeol. Inst. Am. (hon. v.p. Stanford chpt.). Author: An Unknown Leonardo Self Portrait, 1963; Portraits, 1972; Papers, 1973. Contbr. articles on art history, museology, bibliography to profl. jours. Home: 274 San Luis Dr Menlo Park CA 94025 Office: Spl Collections Stanford U Stanford CA 94305

LENKIEWICZ, JENNIE BOLUCK (MRS. THOMAS LENKIEWICZ), city ofcl.; b. Norwich, Conn., Mar. 11, 1933; d. Samuel and Julia (Matejik) Boluck; L.P.N., Backus Hosp. Sch. Nursing, 1973; m. Thomas Lenkiewicz, Aug. 15, 1953; children—Lori, Thomas II, David. Head bookkeeper S & S Leather & Arts & Crafts Co., 1951-56; sec., receptionist, office nurse Dr. Irwin Israel, Colchester, Conn., 1956-68; borough clk., Colchester, 1965-74; clk. Borough Zoning Bd., 1965-74; exec. dir., sec. Colchester (Conn.) Housing Authority, 1973—; pediatric nurse William W. Backus Hosp., 1973—. Sec.-hostess Belmont Funeral Home, Colchester, Conn., 1965—. Mem. V.F.W. Aux. (post trustee 1972-75), Colchester Grange. Roman Catholic. Home: Old Hebron Rd Colchester CT 06415

LENNEY, ANNIE, artist, educator; b. Potsdam, N.Y.; d. Edward and Annie (Kennedy) Lenney; B.A., Coll. St. Elizabeth, Convent, N.J., 1932; postgrad. St. Lawrence U., N.Y. U., Syracuse U., Fordham U., Art Students League; pvt. study art; m. William Shannon, Oct. 6, 1935; children—Ann, Dennis, Gerald. Supr. art Main St. Sch., Tuckahoe, N.Y., 1932-35, Brookside and Montclair Acad., Montclair, N.J., 1951-53, St. Vincents Acad., Newark, 1953-55; instr. art Upsala Coll., East Orange, N.J., 1954-55; head tchr. Saturday Jr. Art Sch., Newark, 1953-55; art tchr. South Maplewood (N.J.) Adult Sch., 1952-62, Montclair Mus. Art Sch., 1955-56, Newton (N.J.) pub. sch. system, 1963-71, also Sch. Fine and Indsl. Arts, Newark, 1946-63. Exhibited Newark Mus., Montclair Mus., Trenton (N.J.) Mus., Oakland Art Gallery, Lehigh Art Gallery, Mus. N.M., Nat. Acad. Galleries, Argent Galleries, Eggleston Galleries N.Y.C., Montclair Mus., 1966, Everhart Mus., 1966, World's Fair, 1965, many others; also exhibited in Paris, Lisbon, Naples, Athens, Tokyo, Japan; numerous one man shows including Allentown Coll. St. Frances de Sales, George Washington Carver Mus., Tuskegee Inst. Ala., St. Scholastica Edn. Center, Ft. Worth, Ark., Ga. Coll., Albany (Ga.) Mus., Central Mo. State Coll., Wyo. and Colo. Coll., Seton Hall U., 1966, Borzansky Galleries, N.Y.C., 1968, Centenary Coll., Hachettstown, Hardin County Mus., Kenton, O., Wassenburg Art Center, Van Wert, O., Upper Ia. Coll., Fayette, Mayville (N.D.) State Coll., Potsdam (N.Y.) Mus., LaSalle Coll., Phila., Hayt Inst. Art, New Castle, Pa., Marathon Mus., Wausau, Wis., Spring Arbor (Mich.) Coll., Georgian Court Coll., others; represented permanent collections at Brooks Meml. Art Gallery, Everhart Mus., Norfolk Mus., Munson William Proctor Mus., Massilon Mus., Farnsworth Mus., Oklahoma City Art Center, Buie Mus., Oxford, Miss., Montclair (N.J.) Mus., Newark Mus., Paterson (N.J.) Mus., S.I. Inst. Arts and Sci., Butler Inst. Am. Art, Youngstown, O., Andrew Dickson White Mus. of Cornell U., Fairleigh Dickinson U., Seton Hall U., Notre Dame U., Minn. Inst. Art, Morris Mus., Morristown, others, also pvt. collections. Recipient Eugenie Marron award, oil, 10th Ann. Spring Lake Exhbn., 1948; 1st award water color, 15th Ann. Art Exhbn., Irvington, N.J., 1948, 12th Spring Lake Exhbn., 1948; Beth Creevy Ham award Nat. Assn. Women Artists, 1948; Samuel Karasick Meml.; 1st award, oil, 34th Ann. State Exhbn., Montclair (N.J.) Mus.; prize 62d Ann. Exhbn., Nat. Assn. Women Artists, 1954; and numerous honorable mentions. Mem. Painters and Sculptors Soc. N.J., Nat. Assn. Women Artists, N.J. Water Color Club, Asso. Artists of N.J., Audubon Artists Soc., Allied Artists, Inc. Contbr. articles to profl. jours. Address: Gaisler Rd RD 2 Blairstown NJ 07825

LENNON, DELORES RAE FRANCISCO, tchr. aide, wig and make-up artist; b. Mpls., July 11, 1940; d. Clarence Frank and Ruth Evelyn (Hayden) Francisco; student Macalester Coll., 1958, Minn. Sch. Bus., Ritter's Beauty Sch., 1960, Rasmussen Sch. Bus. (Bus. and Profl. Women's Found. grant), 1969; B.S. in Elementary Edn. (fed. grants), U. Minn., 1974, postgrad., 1974—; m. John Wermuth Lennon, Oct. 28, 1961 (div.); children—Gretchen Anne, John Edward. Telephone operator Northwestern Bell Co., 1956-57; instr. Sillouette Figure Form Internat., 1958; swimmer Water Ballet Corps Al Sheehan's Aqua Follies, summers 1957-59; sec., receptionist Mpls. Woman's Club, 1958; Hotel Pick-Nicollet, Mpls., 1958, Hotel Leamington, Mpls., 1959; pvt. sec. Home of the Good Shepherd, St. Paul, 1960; hairdresser Ritter's Beauty Shop, St. Paul, 1961; asst. wig maker Tyrone Guthrie Theatre, Mpls., 1968-69; sec., receptionist St. Paul Pub. Schs., also tchr. aide; free-lance wig and make-up artist. Vol. United Fund, 1965; model Goodwill Aux.; leader Camp Fire Girls; co-chmn. Tyrone Guthrie Theatre Teen Bd., 1964-65. Mem. Gallanteers Minn. Mus. Art, Puppeteers Am., Internat. Juggler's Assn., Mpls. Soc. Fine Arts, Walker Art Center, Am. Orff-Schulwerk Assn., Minn. Assn. Edn. Young Children, Nat. Orgn. Women, Minn. Edn. Assn., Nat. Council Tchrs. English, League Women Voters (del.

Met. council 1963-66), Minn. Woman's Polit. Caucus, Minn. Sci. Fiction Soc., Internat. Platform Assn., Minn. Civil Liberties Union, Nat. Consortium Options Pub. Edn., Phi Beta (grantee), Phi Delta Kappa. Unitarian. Home: 1867 Princeton Av St Paul MN 55105

LENNOX, MARJORIE ELIZABETH, govt. ofcl.; b. Omaha, Sept. 10, 1938; d. George Banks and Viola Marjorie (Richards) Lennox; B.S. in Edn., U. Neb., Lincoln, 1962, M.A., 1970. Tchr. Omaha elementary pub. schs., 1962-71; real estate salesman Grice and Co., Omaha, 1968-71; equal opportunity specialist Omaha area office Dept. Housing and Urban Devel., 1972—. Treas. Omaha chpt. Links, Inc., 1969-75, chairperson constrn. com. Central Links, Inc., 1973-74, Central area rep. research com. nat. orgn., 1969-70. Dist. rep. Neb. Democratic Conv., 1967; mem. Omaha Charter Revision Conv., 1973. Bd. dirs. Danner Meml. Children's Center, 1971-72, Girls Club Omaha, 1973—. Fellow Tri-Univ. Project Elementary Edn./English; recipient certificate of award Central Area Links, 1972. Mem. Am. Acad. Polit. and Social Scis., Am. Soc. Pub. Adminstrn., Conf. Minority Pub. Adminstrs., Internat. Platform Assn., Nat. Assn. Human Rights Workers, Nat. Assn. Real Estate Brokers, Nat. Assn. Women Deans, Adminstrs. and Counselors, Am. Civil Liberties Union, Nat. Urban League, N.A.A.C.P., Nat. Fedn. Settlements and Neighborhood Centers. Episcopalian (deacon). Author: Education for the '70's, 1970. Home: 722 JE George Blvd Omaha NE 68132 Office: 7100 W Center Rd Omaha NE 68106

LENOX, ANNE STOUFFER, educator; b. Hagerstown, Md., June 4, 1930; d. Brewer L. and Sara (Macias) Stouffer; B.A., William Smith Coll., Geneva, N.Y., 1952; M.A., U. Pa., 1958, postgrad., 1958—; m. Donald Porter Lenox, Sept. 7, 1957 (div. Mar. 1961). Asst. dir. admissions William Smith Coll., 1952-55; asst. instr. English, U. Pa., 1956-59, personnel officer (vice dean) Coll. For Women, 1958-61; headmistress Agnes Irwin Sch., Rosemont, Pa., 1962—. Mem. chmn.'s adv. council Childrens Hosp. Phila. Trustee Miss Hall's Sch., Pittsfield, Mass. Mem. Nat. Assn. Prins. of Schs. for Girls, Headmistress Assn. East. Home: 306 S Valley Rd Paoli PA 19301 Office: Ithan Av and Conestoga Rd Rosemont PA 19010

LENT, WANDA JUNE THOMPSON, musician, educator; b. Medina, O., Nov. 1, 1937; d. Wendell Emerson and Neva (Weimer) Thompson; certificate Sherwood Music Sch., Chgo., 1956, B.A. in Music Edn., 1959, postgrad., 1959; m. Herbert George Lent, June 12, 1965; 1 dau., Denise Yvonne. Soloist, Moody Meml. Ch. Choir, Chgo., 1955-59, Chgo. Bus. Men's Chorus and Orch., 1956-59, Sherwood Opera Prodns., 1956-59, Chgo. 11th St. Theatre Opera Prodns., 1956-59, Zion (Ill.) Symphony Orch., 1969; tchr. vocal music Ill. Children's Hosp.-Sch., 1957-59; supr. vocal music LaSalle (Ill.) Pub. Schs., 1959—. Soloist various mus. prodns., ch. choirs. Bd. dirs. Ill. Valley Community Concert Assn. Pres., Future Tchrs. Am., 1952-54; music chmn. LaSalle P.T.A., 1959-75. Mem. LaSalle Bus. and Profl. Women's Club (music chmn. 1963-75), Ill., Nat. music tchrs. assns., LaSalle Elementary Sch. Edn. Assn. (pres. 1969-71), Nat., Ill. edn. socs., Organ-Piano Tchrs. Assn. Internat., Musicians Protective Union. Republican. Conglist. (organist, choir dir.). Club: LaSalle Zonta (pres. 1967-70). Home: 618 Clark St Oglesby IL 61348 Office: 1165 St Vincents Av LaSalle IL 61301

LENZ, DOROTHY VAL, home economist; b. Bellevue, Pa., Feb. 18, 1940; d. Carl H. and Mabel Florence (Steen) Lenz; B.S., Pa. State U., 1961. Home service rep. Peoples Natural Gas Co., Pitts., 1961-63, program and tng. asst., 1963-67, supr. residential appliance promotion, 1967—. Mem. Pa. Home Econs. Assn. (chmn. Western dist. Western area 1965-66), Pitts. Home Economists in Bus. (chmn. 1970-71), Phi Upsilon Omicron. Home: 2022 Texdale St Pittsburgh PA 15216 Office: 2 Gateway Center Pittsburgh PA 15222

LEON, FLORENCE MAY PRATT (MRS. JAMES LEON), genealogist; b. Boston, Sept. 7, 1921; d. Charles Henry and Laura Mildred (Lepene) Pratt; student Hunter Coll., 1943, East Carolina Tchrs. Coll., 1951-52; m. James Leon, Feb. 16, 1944; children—Florence May (Mrs. Leon Joseph Davis), Paul James, John Charles, David George. Def. worker, Mass., 1939-43; area sec., troop leader, chmn. water safety Girl Scouts U.S.A., 1954-57, counselor, exec. bd. sec., 1954-60; den mother Cub Scouts, 1957-60; co-chmn. A.R.C., Comanche County, Okla., 1958-59; day camp dir. YMCA, West Roxbury, Mass., 1961, aquatic staff, 1961-62; staff genealogist Nat. Soc. D.A.R., Washington, 1966-67; Served with USMCR, 1943-45. Recipient certificate A.R.C. Far East Command, 1971, citation Gen. J.H. Michaelis Comdr.-in-chief UN Command, Korea, 1971, medal S.A.R., 1973. Mem. Mass. Soc. Mayflower Descs. New Eng. Historic and Geneal. Soc., Nat. Va. geneal. socs., Columbia Hist. Soc., Nantucket Hist. Assn., Nat. Soc. Daus. of Founders and Patriots Am., Nat. Soc. Children of Am. Revolution (1st v.p. D.C. 1967-69, sr. D.C. pres. 1972-74), D.A.R. (chpt. regent 1964-66, 72—, state chmn. 1966—, mem. bd. mgmt. 1964—), Nat. Soc. Women Descs. Ancient and Honorable Arty. Co. (nat. chmn. bicentennial U.S. com.), Conn. Soc. Genealogists, Soc. Genealogists London, Am. Assn. State and Local History. Club: Marine Officers Wives (Washington). Home: 3803 Maryland St Alexandria VA 22309

LEONARD, CHRISTIANA MORISON, neuropsychologist, educator; b. Boston, Jan. 22, 1938; d. Robert Swain and Beningna Ivanovna (Rempel) Morison; B.A. cum laude, Radcliffe Coll., 1959; Ph.D., Mass. Inst. Tech., 1967; m. John Leonard, June 13, 1959; children—Andrew Warren, Amy Elmore. Postdoctoral fellow Rockefeller U., N.Y.C., 1967-69, research asso., 1970-71, asst. prof. neuropsychology, 1971—. Mem. vis. com. dept. psychology Mass. Inst. Psychology, Cambridge, 1972—. Mem. Soc. for Neurosci., Eastern Psychol. Assn., Sigma Xi. Contbr. articles to sci. jours. Office: Rockefeller Univ 66th St and York Av New York City NY 10021

LEONARD, DORIS FRANCES CORCORAN (MRS. RICHARD MANNING LEONARD), conservationist; b. Denver; d. Daniel John and Luella (Shannon) Corcoran; student San Mateo Jr. Coll., 1926-28; m. Richard Manning Leonard, July 14, 1934; children—Frances (Mrs. Richard Gray Best), Elizabeth. Legal sec. pvt. law firm, San Francisco, 1929-33. Regional Agrl. Credit Corp., San Francisco, 1933-35; partner photog. studio Bridge & Leonard, Berkeley, 1935-45; sec.-treas., partner Conservation Assos., San Francisco, 1960—, treas. Sempervirens Fund, 1968-72, adviser 1972—; dir. Pacific Gas & Electric Co. Mem. Alta Bates Hosp. Vol. Assn., 1957—; sec. Dag Hammarskjold Redwood Meml. Grove Com., 1963—; gen. sec. Cal. Coastal Redwood Scenic Rd. and Trail System, 1965-66; mem. Cal. Adv. Com. on Pub. Land Law Rev., 1966-68; del. White House Conf. on Natural Beauty, 1965. Founder, v.p. Point Reyes Nat. Seashore Found., 1958-70; pres. Leonard Found., 1961—; nat. bd. govs. Nature Conservancy, 1962-68, mem. nat. council, 1968—; mem. adv. com. U. Cal. Land and Water Natural Areas System. Recipient Merit award Cal. Conservation Council, 1957; Conservation award Am. Motors, 1970; Spl. Achievement award Sierra Club, 1970. Mem. Nat. Parks Assn. (dep. sec. gen. 1st World Conf. on nat. parks 1959-62, del. 2d World Conf. on Nat. Parks 1972), Trustees for Conservation (treas. 1970-71), Alaska Conservation Soc., Wilderness Soc., Bombay Natural History Soc., Cal. Acad. Scis., Fedn. Western Outdoor Clubs, East African Wildlife Assn., Nat. Audubon Soc., Arctic Internat. Wildlife Range Soc. (founder, charter mem.), Alta Bates Vol. Assn., Assn. for Conservation Wildlife, Bangkok, Thailand, Internat. Union for Conservation Nature and Natural Resources (del. 8th gen. assembly Nairobi, Kenya, Africa 1963, 11th gen. assembly Banff, Can. 1972), Point Reyes Bird Observatory (bd. dirs. 1968—), others. Club: Berkeley (Cal.) City; Sierra (life, gen. sec. biennial confs. 1955, 57, 59). Home: 980 Keeler Av Berkeley CA 94708

LEONARD, ELIZABETH ANN ADNEY (MRS. ALAN J. LEONARD), social worker; b. Lebanon, Ind., Apr. 27, 1917; d. Frank B. and Fern (Coons) Adney; student MacMurray Coll. for Women, 1935-36; A.B., Ind. U., 1939, M.A., 1947; postgrad. Columbia, 1948; m. Alan J. Leonard, Aug. 4, 1949; children—Arthur Alan, Jean Elizabeth. Social worker A.R.C., 1944-46, Louisville Mental Hygiene Clinic, 1948-49, New Orleans Guidance Center, 1949-52; social worker Long Beach (Cal.) Psychiat. Clinic for Children, 1958—, supervisory social worker, 1965—, chief social worker, 1974—. Lectr., Cal. State U., Long Beach, 1966-68. Mem. Nat. Assn. Social Workers, Acad. Certified Social Workers, Am. Orthopsychiat. Assn., Women's Aux. Los Angeles County Med. Assn., Zeta Tau Alpha, Kappa Kappa Kappa. Home: 6851 Lees Way Long Beach CA 90815 Office: Meml Hosp Med Center 2801 Atlantic Av Long Beach CA 90801

LEONARD, EUNICE HARPER (MRS. PAUL HOLLAND LEONARD), assn. exec.; b. Harpers, S.C.; d. Edwin and Sarah (Davidson) Harper; A.B., Winthrop Coll., 1910; postgrad. U. S.C., 1935; m. Paul Holland Leonard, Dec. 27, 1917; children—Edwin Madison (killed in action), Sarah Holland (Mrs. Martin Jernigan), Robert Beverly, Davidson Harper. Exec. dir. Crippled Children's Soc., S.C., 1944-45; state dir. crippled children's div. S.C. State Bd. Health, 1945-46; exec. dir. S.C. Div. Am. Cancer Soc., 1945-65. State pres. Congress Parents and Tchrs., 1937-41, nat. v.p., 1941-44, nat. chmn. sch. lunch program, 1947-50; state pres. S.C. Council Common Good, 1939-42, pres. S.C. Coordinating Edn. Council, 1945. Trustee Columbia Twp. Auditorium Bd. Recipient citation Gov. S.C., 1944; medal and citation Am. Cancer Soc., 1958; plaque Woodmen of World, 1966; Mary Mildred Sullivan award, 1973; named Outstanding Woman of Yr., S.C. Status Women Conf., 1969. Mem. S.C. Fedn. Women's Clubs (state chmn. pub. affairs, Americanization citizenship, legislation, health), Bus. and Profl. Women's Club (pres. 1948-50), S.C., Spartanburg County, Richland County hist. assns., Historic Columbia Found. D.A.R. (chpt. regent 1961-63, state pub. relations chmn. 1961-66), Daus. Am. Colonists (state regent 1964-67, state treas., nat. chaplain, nat. chmn. historic landmarks and memls.), Daus. 1812 (pres. and registrar local chpt.), Order Knights of Royal Garter, U.S. Caroliniana Soc., Am. Assn. U. Women (pres. Columbia br. 1963-65), Colonial Dames XVII Century, Magna Carta Dames Am., U.D.C. (dist. dir., pres. Wade Hampton chpt., S.C. div. pres.), Am. Legion Aux. (state pub. relations chmn.), Palmetto Outdoor Hist. Drama Soc. (past adv. bd.), Williamsburg County Hist. Soc., S.C. Hugenot Soc., Order Crown Charlemagne in U.S.A. Methodist (pres. Women's Soc. Christian Service). Clubs: Navy Mother's, Woman's of Columbia (pres. 1933-35). Home: 900 Laurens St Columbia SC 29201

LEONARD, LOUISE (MRS. ROBERT P. LEONARD), state senator; b. Washington, Oct. 7, 1919; d. Roy Leslie and Florence Alberta (Bellows) McVey; student Sch. Govt., George Washington U.; m. Robert P. Leonard, Jan. 23, 1948. Formerly with U.S. Engrs. Dept., OSS, Dept. State, Washington, Can., Alaska, India; mem. W. Va. Senate, 1970—. Mem. W. Va. Eastern Panhandle Land and River Protective Assn., Task Force on Regional and Local Planning, 1969—. Adv. Bd. Fed. Reformatory for Women, Alderson, W. Va., 1969—, Mental Health Assn. Chmn. Republican Exec. Com. of Jefferson County; 2d v.p. W. Va. Fedn. Rep. Women; past pres. Jefferson County Fedn.; mem. bd. Nat. Fedn. Rep. Women; candidate U.S. Senate, 1972; del. Rep. nat. conv., 1972, mem. platform com. Mem. Womens Club of Harpers Ferry Dist., Hist. Assn., D.A.R., League of Women Voters, C. of C., W. Va. Garden Club, Inc. (life), Nat. Soc. State Legislators, Nat. Order Women Legislators, Alpha Delta Pi, Phi Pi Epsilon. Republican. Episcopalian. Address: Box 5 Harpers Ferry WV 25425

LEONARD, VIVITA KRIEVS (MRS. PAUL F. LEONARD), physician; b. Riga, Latvia, Apr. 16, 1932; d. Rudolfs H. and Zenta M. (Cers) Krievs; came to U.S., 1949, naturalized, 1953; B.A., U. Neb., 1953, M.D., 1956; m. Paul F. Leonard, July 18, 1957; children—Paul Arthur, Silva Kristine. Intern, Charles T. Miller Hosp., St. Paul, Minn., 1956-57, anesthesiologist, 1960; resident in anesthesiology U. Neb. Hosp., Omaha, 1957-59; fellow in anesthesiology Mayo Grad. Sch., 1960; asst. to staff Mayo Clinic, 1961; sr. staff physician Rochester (Minn.) State Hosp., 1963-69. Diplomate Am. Bd. Anesthesiology. Mem. Phi Beta Kappa, Alpha Omega Alpha, Alpha Phi. Home: 719 5th St SW Rochester MN 55901

LEONE, IDA ALBA, plant physiologist; b. Elizabeth, N.J., Apr. 28, 1922; d. Joseph and Josephine (Aprigliano) Leone; B.S., N.J. Coll. Women, 1944; M.S., Rutgers U., 1946. Research asst. Rutgers Coll. Agr., New Brunswick, N.J., 1946-50, research asso., 1950-58, asst. research specialist, 1958—, asso. research prof., 1970—. Mem. Elizabeth Mayor's Ad Hoc Com. on Air Pollution.; rep. Rahway (N.J.), treas. Central Jersey Regional Air Pollution Control Agy. Chmn. bd. dirs. Delaware Valley Citizens' Council for Clean Air; bd. dirs. Union County Tb League, 1963—. Recipient Amita award for Women of achievement, 1966—. Mem. Am. Soc. Plant Physiologists, Air Pollution Control Assn. (sec. Mid-Atlantic states sect. 1956-63), N.J. Acad. Sci., Am. Soc. Phytopathologists, Sigma Xi. Contbr. articles to profl. jours. Home: 876 Rayhon Terrace Rahway NJ 07065 Office: Dept Plant Biology Rutgers Cook Coll New Brunswick NJ 08903

LEONG, APRIL KAM YEE, social worker; b. Honolulu; d. Philip Sun and Ngo (Tom) Leong; B.A., U. Hawaii, 1955; M.S.W., Washington U., St. Louis, 1957. Program dir. Berkeley (Cal.) Community YWCA, 1957-60; east area dir. Oahu YWCA, Honolulu, 1960-64; instr. hosp.-in-service tng. program Waimano Tng. Sch. and Hosp., Honolulu, 1964-65; socialization program coordinator Hosp. Improvement Project Hawaii State Hosp., 1965-68, adminstr., 1968-71; program coordinator Crippled Children br. Hawaii Dept. Health, Honolulu, 1971—; instr. field work U. Hawaii, 1961-70. Mem. Nat. Assn. Social Workers, Acad. Certified Social Workers. Home: 3022 Kalakaua Av Honolulu HI 96815 Office: Hawaii Dept Health PO Box 3378 Honolulu HI 96801

LEPEHNE, RENATE, educator; b. Koenigsberg, Germany, Apr. 3, 1931 (came to U.S. 1939, naturalized 1945); d. George M. and Caecilie (Friedstein) Lepehne; student Western Res. U. (now Case Western Res. U.), 1947-49, Boston U., 1949-51; B.S., Northeastern U., 1970; M.Ed., Boston Coll. Supr. follow-up clinic Mt. Sinai Hosp., N.Y.C., 1952-53; market research asst. Fairchild Publs., Inc., N.Y.C., 1953-54; advt. copy writer, tech. editor Tracerlab, Inc., Waltham, Mass., 1955-56; adminstrv. sec. to asso. dean Harvard Sch. Law, Cambridge, Mass., 1956-58; instr. German, Northeastern U., 1965, German Saturday Sch., Boston, 1962; instructional programmer, tng. systems dept. Bolt Beranek & Newman Inc., Cambridge, 1961-64; officer instrn. Forsyth Dental Center Sch. for Dental Hygienists, Boston, 1966-71; acting dir. div. programmed learning Northeastern U., Office Ednl. Resources, Boston, 1969-70, instructional designer, div. instructional systems prodn., mem. faculty Northeastern U., 1964-72; dir. Office Instructional Design, The Open Coll., Bunker Hill Community Coll., Charlestown, Mass., 1972—. Bd. dirs. Internat. Inst., Internat. Student Assn., 1966-67. Mem. Soc. Instructional Tech. (treas. 1966-68), Mass., New Eng. psychol. assns., Am. Ednl. Research Assn., League Women Voters, Am. Assn. U. Women (dir. Boston chpt.), Nat. Soc. Programmed Instrn., Assn. Ednl. Communications and Tech., N.E.A., Phi Delta Pi. Pub. 20 textbooks and papers. Home: 650 Huntington Av Boston MA 02115 Office: Rutherford Av Charlestown MA 02129

LEPENDORF, BARBARA JOAN ROGERS (MRS. STANLEY LEPENDORF), lawyer; b. Buffalo, July 11, 1937; d. Maurice and Gladys (Lazerson) Rogers; B.A., U. Buffalo, 1959, J.D., 1961; m. Stanley Lependorf, Mar. 24, 1962; children—Esther Ann, Gabriel, Molly. Admitted to N.Y. bar, 1961, N.J. bar, 1972; pvt. practice law, 1961-64; asst. dist. atty. Erie County, Buffalo, 1968-70; pvt. practice law, Princeton, N.J. 1972—; pre-law adviser Princeton, 1972—; pool atty. State N.J. Pub. Defender's Office, Mercer County, 1972—. Cooperating atty. N.J. Civil Liberties Union, 1972. Mem. Princeton Cable TV Commn., 1973-74, Princeton Twp. Bd. Health, 1974—, Intergovtl. Drug Commn., Princeton, 1974—. Mem. N.J. State Bar Assn., Princeton Univ. League. Home: 640 Prospect Av Princeton NJ 08540 Office: 195 Nassau St Princeton NJ 08540

LEPESCHKIN, JULIE ANNE WILSON (MRS. EUGENE LEPESCHKIN), educator; b. Ann Arbor, Mich., Sept. 2, 1915; d. Frank Norman and Juel A. (Mahoney) Wilson; B.A., U. Mich., 1936; M.A., U. Wis., 1941; m. Eugene Lepeschkin, May 30, 1949; children—Tamara Julianne, Ludmilla Francesca Eugenia, Nina Olga Grace. Grad. asst. U. Pitts., 1941, U. Mich., 1942-43; tchr. U. Mich. Lab. Elementary Sch., 1943-47; instr. Newcomb Coll. Sch. Art, also Tulane U., New Orleans, 1947-49; resource tchr. dance and dramatics Metairie Park Country Day Sch., New Orleans, 1947-49; supt. Lower Ch. Sch. Unitarian, 1958-62; asst. prof. dept. home econs. U. Vt., Burlington, 1962—. Tchr. creative movement classes for children Fleming Mus., U. Vt., 1950-60; chmn. Community Puppeteers, 1958-60; cons. Burlington Day Care Center, 1966—; mem. U.S. Nat. Com. on Early Childhood Edn., 1967—; state presch. chmn. P.T.A. Bd., 1963-67; chmn. subcom. on day care Gov.'s Com. on Children and Youth, 1963-66, chmn. subcom. early childhood services 1967-69; mem. State Community Coordinated Child Care, 1969-72; chmn. adv. com. on day care Vt. Dept. Welfare, 1966—; regional cons. Head Start, 1967-69; mem. Gov.'s Com. Children and Youth, 1968-71, White House Conf. on Children, 1970. Recipient Distinguished Service award State of Vt., 1972. Mem. N.E.A., Nat. Assn. Edn. Young Children, World Ednl. Fellowship, Nat. Com. on Day Care, Child Study Assn., Soc. Research Child Devel., Internat. Playground Assn., Assn. Childhood Edn. Internat. (chmn. study study conf. 1971), Pi Lambda Theta. Unitarian. Author: My Daddy is in Prison. Editor: (with Gerold Greenmore) Procs. Vt. Internat. Conf. and Follow-up Conf. Home: 75 Bilodeau St Burlington VT 05401

LEPOW, MARTHA LIPSON, pediatrician; b. Cleve., Mar. 28, 1927; d. Harry A. and Anna (Miller) Lipson; B.A., Oberlin Coll., 1948; M.D., Western Res. U., 1952; m. Irwin Howard Lepow, Feb. 7, 1958; children—Lauren, David, Daniel. Intern, Univ. Hosp., Cleve., 1952-53; resident Cleve. City Hosp., 1953-56; postdoctoral fellow infectious diseases Nat. Found. Infantile Paralysis, Cleve., 1956-58; sr. instr. Cleve. Met. Gen. Hosp., 1958-61, asst. prof. pediatrics, 1961-67; cons. pediatrician hosps. U.S.; asst. prof. Western Res. U., Cleve., 1961-67; asso. prof. Sch. Medicine. U. Conn. at Hartford, 1967-72, prof. pediatrics, 1972—. Lectr. Yale U. Sch. Medicine, New Haven, 1967—. Head health sub.-com. Gov.'s Task Force on Lead, 1970. Trustee Nat. Found. Sudden Infant Death, 1969—; bd. dirs. Urban League, Hartford, 1971-72. USPHS spl. fellow, Oxford, Eng., 1961-62. Mem. Am. Soc. Pediatric Research, Am. Pediatric Soc., Am. Acad. Pediatrics, Infectious Diseases Soc. Am., New Eng. Pediatrics Soc. (councillor 1969-72), Alpha Omega Alpha. Contbr. articles to profl. jours. Home: 4 Hillsboro Dr West Hartford CT 06107 Office: Univ Conn Health Center Farmington CT 06032

LEQUIN, DORIS STEELE, chemist; b. Phila., Mar. 23, 1929; d. William Blair and Alice (Gehris) Steele; B.A., Mary Washington Coll. of U. Va., 1952; m. Paul I. Lequin, Aug. 20, 1966 (div. Apr. 1970). Chemist metall. div. U.S. Bur. Mines, College Park, Md., 1952-54; chemist chem. and corrosion sect. U.S. Naval Ordnance Lab., Silver Spring, Md., 1954-57, asso. scientist nonmetallic material div., 1957-72, sr. scientist, 1972—. Recipient Meritorious Civilian Service award, 1964. Mem. Am. Chem. Soc., Am. Sci. Affiliation, Soc. Plastics Engrs., Am. Soc. Testing and Materials. Presbyn. Contbr. articles to profl. jours. Home: 429 Branch Dr Silver Spring MD 20901 Office: US Naval Ordnance Lab White Oak Silver Spring MD 20910

LERAGER, SALLY JOHNSON, nurse, educator; b. Rockford, Ill., Apr. 24, 1923; d. Herbert A. and Aileen (Peyton) J.; R.N., Good Samaritan Hosp., 1942-45; student U. Ill., 1948-49; Ph.D. (hon.), Hamilton State U.; children—Ann Elizabeth, Stacey Aileen. John Robert Powers model, 1946, Cornet model, Miami, 1947; nurse obstetrics delivery Women's Hosp., N.Y.C., 1947-49, St. Francis Hosp., Evanston, Ill., 1953; charge, head nurse Broward Gen. Hosp., Ft. Lauderdale, Fla., 1968; night supr. Ashbrook Convalescent and Nursing Hosp., Scotch Plains, N.J., 1968—. Council chmn. Betty Merit Tchrs. Scholarship, 1962; area nat. organizer Girl Scouts U.S.A., 1962-65; Westfield (N.J.) Round-Up and Health chmn., 1962-63; pres. Tamaques Sch., 1965, adviser Parent Tchr. Orgn., 1966, fgn. relationship chmn., 1967-68; exec. bd. chmn. Westfield High Sch. P.T.A. Newsletter, 1968-70; chmn. Nat. Space Edn., Westfield, 1964; Westfield chmn. fgn. nurses Overlook Hosp., Summit, N.J., 1964-69. Mem. Am., Nat. Dist. nurses assns., Nat. Orgn. for Women (N.J. convenor 1967-72), Am. Contract Bridge League (certified instr.), Bridge Tchrs. Assn. Republican. Presbyn. Club: Mindowaskin (Westfield). Inventor Holder for Marking Device. Home: 823 Nancy Way Westfield NJ 07090 also 1212 Cordova Rd Fort Lauderdale FL 33316 Office: 823 Nancy Way Westfield NJ 07090

LERGIER, CLARA SALEVA (MRS. JULIO E. LERGIER), librarian; b. Lares, P.R., Nov. 29, 1919; d. Marcos A. and Maria L. (Torres) Saleva; B.A., Poly. Inst., San German, P.R., 1940; postgrad. U. P.R., 1941, tchr.-librarian license, 1967; m. Julio E. Lergier, Apr. 26, 1942; 1 dau., Clara Marlene (Mrs. Fernando H. Cruz Tollinche). Tchr. sci. and math., San Juan, P.R., 1941-43; coordinator, archives clk. and translator for coordination Interam. Affairs, Washington, 1943; tchr., San Juan, Mayagüez, P.R., 1944-46; librarian Bus. and Comml. Census-Statistics Bur., San Juan, 1966—; librarian St. Johns Episcopal Sch., San Juan, 1968—; exec. sec. Ateneo Puertorriqueño, San Juan, 1968-70, head librarian Ateneo Puertorriqueño Library, 1970—. Co-chmn. Red Cross House Campaign, San Juan, 1962; co-chmn. Children's Hosp. Campaign, 1962-63; first lady, chmn. Ladies Aux. Lions Internat. dist. 51-A, P.R., 1973—. Pub. relations dir. Children's Hosp., 1973—. Mem. Asoc. Esposas de Medicos, Club Civico de Damas, Union Am. Women, Assn. of Librarians, Women's Coll. Club, Lions Ladies Aux. Author: Con los ojos del Alma-Poetry, 1969. Home: 526 Carbonel Hato Rey PR 00919 Office: Box 1180 San Juan PR 00902

LERMAN, BEATRICE PRAZAK (MRS. IRVING LERMAN), physician; b. Elizabeth, N.J., May 8, 1915; d. Emil and Magdalena (Dechert) Prazak; B.A., Cornell U., Ithaca, N.Y., 1937; M.D., Temple U., 1942; m. Irving Lerman, Oct. 19, 1946; stepchildren—Samuel (dec.), Fred. Jr. intern Jersey City Med. Center, 1941; sr. intern Elizabeth (N.J.) Gen. Hosp., 1942-43; resident pediatrics Bellevue Hosp., N.Y.C., 1943-44; practice medicine specializing in pediatrics, Elizabeth, 1944-52, urology, 1952-65; physician in charge accident and emergency room Monmouth Med. Center, Long Branch, N.J., 1966-71; courtesy staff Alexian Bros. Hosp., Elizabeth, 1960-65; instr. pediatrics N.Y. U., Sch. Medicine, 1943-44; dir. medicine Janet Meml. Home, 1944-48; instr. pediatrics Elizabeth Gen. Hosp. Sch. Nursing, 1944-48, attending pediatrician, 1944-52; asst. pediatrician St. Elizabeth Hosp., Elizabeth, 1948-52; med. examiner pub. schs., Elizabeth, 1948-52; physician Monmouth County Blood Bank, 1972—. Recipient award of merit A.M.A., 1969, 70, 71. Mem. Union County Pediatric Soc. (sec. 1948-52), Am. Acad. Pediatrics, Am. Acad. Gen. Practice, Am. Acad. Family Physicians, Aesculapius (pres. 1936-37). Home: 806 Maple St West Deal Ocean NJ 07712

LERNER, CAROLE JEAN SUTYAK (MRS. PAUL LERNER), occupational therapist; b. Detroit, Aug. 28, 1938; d. Andrew B. and Maxine Curtis (Scudder) Sutyak; B.S., Eastern Mich. U., 1960; m. Paul Lerner, May 6, 1967; 1 son, Brett. Dir. occupational therapy Lenawee County Spl. Edn., Adrian, Mich., 1960-64; dir. psychiat. occupational therapy Sinai Hosp., Detroit, 1964-68, Mt. Sinai Hosp., Toronto, Ont., Can., 1973—. Mem. women's com. Art Gallery Waterloo (Ont.), 1970-72. Home: 32 Kimbark Blvd Toronto ON M5N 2X7 Canada Office: Mt Sinai Hosp 600 University Av Toronto ON Canada

LERNER, DEANA DUSKIN (MRS. LEO A. LERNER), publishing co. exec.; b. London, Eng., Aug. 6, 1906; d. Abraham and Annie (Roze) Duskin; came to U.S., 1907, naturalized, 1926; student Crane Coll.; m. Leo Lerner, July 12, 1929; children—Louis A., Robert Morris, Rosanne (Mrs. Tom Branch). Ballet dancer; pres. Lerner Home Newspaper, Chgo., 1965—; with Myers Pub. Co.; dir. Lincoln Sq. Savs. & Loan Assn. Mem. Gov.'s Commn. on Conflict of Interest, 1966—. Active Art Inst. Chgo., Shakespeare Festival (Stratford Ont., Can.), Am. Civil Liberties Union, Ams. for Dem. Action, League Women Voters, Jewish Fedn., Contemporary Art Mus. Bd. dirs. Hull House, Uptown Center, Leo A. Lerner Theater. Home: 4300 N Marine Dr Chicago IL 60613 Office: 7519 N Ashland Av Chicago IL 60626

LERNER, ERNESTINE SYLVIA STERN (MRS. SAMUEL LERNER), psychotherapist; b. Cleve., Aug. 20, 1917; d. Joseph M. and Martha (Nusbaum) Stern; B.A., Western Res. U., 1939, postgrad., 1943-46; M.Social Sci., Smith Coll., 1941; m. Samuel Lerner, Nov. 25, 1948; 1 son, Joshua Bruce. Caseworker, supr. children's dept. Jewish Social Service Bur. and Jewish Children's Bur., Detroit, 1942-46; supr. VA Mental Hygiene Clinic, Detroit, 1946-47; supr. adoption dept. Free Synagogue Child Adoption Com., N.Y.C., 1948-49; chief psychiat. social worker St. Barnabas Child Guidance Clinic, Mpls., 1951-52; casework supr., group therapist Battle Creek (Mich.) Child Guidance Clinic, 1955-60; psychotherapist, group therapist, therapeutic nursery sch. project Merrill-Palmer Inst., Detroit, 1967-68; pvt. practice as marriage counselor and psychiat. social worker, Detroit and Battle Creek, 1955—. Bd. dirs. Minges Brook Sch. P.T.A., Battle Creek, 1956-58, program chmn., 1957-58; bd. dirs. Pasteur Sch. P.T.A., Detroit, 1961-62, program chmn., 1961-62. Mem. Nat. Assn. Social Workers, Mich. Assn. Marriage Counselors (sec. 1972-74), Mich. Soc. Civilian Social Work (edn. and profl. devel. chmn.), Am. Civil Liberties Union. Home: 1686 Balmoral Detroit MI 48203

LERNER, GERDA, educator, author; b. Vienna, Austria; d. Robert and Ilona (Neumann) Kronstein; came to U.S., 1939, naturalized, 1943; B.A., New Sch. Social Research, 1963; M.A., Columbia, 1965, Ph.D., 1966; m. Carl Lerner, Oct. 6, 1941; children—Stephanie Jean, Daniel Andrew. Lectr. New Sch. Social Research, 1963-65; asst. prof. Am. history L.I. U., 1965-66, asso. prof., 1966-68; mem. faculty Sarah Lawrence Coll., 1968—; lectr. in field; asso. Columbia Seminar on Am. Civilization, 1968—. Mem. Am. Assn. U. Profs., Am. Hist. Assn., Orgn. Am. Historians, Am. Studies Assn., Authors Guild. Author: No Farewell, 1955; screenplay Black Like Me, 1964, The Grimke Sisters from South Carolina: Rebels Against Slavery, 1967; The Woman in American History, 1971; Black Women in White America: A Documentary History, 1972. Contbr. articles to profl. jours., book reviews to mags. Home: 33-60 21st St Astoria NY 11106

LERNER, MARGUERITE RUSH (MRS. AARON B. LERNER), physician; b. Mpls., May 17, 1924; d. Harry H. and Sophia B. (Goldstein) Rush; B.A. summa cum laude, U. Minn., 1945; postgrad. Barnard Coll., 1945-46, Johns Hopkins, 1946-48; M.D., Western Res. U., 1950; m. Aaron B. Lerner, June 21, 1945; children—Peter, Michael, Ethan, Seth. Intern U. Mich. Hosp., Ann Arbor, 1950-51, resident, 1951-52; resident U. Ore. Hosp., Portland, 1952-54; practice medicine specializing in dermatology, New Haven, 1955—; attending dermatology West Haven VA Hosp., 1955-57; instr. dermatology Yale, New Haven, Conn., 1957-60, asst. clin. prof., 1960-66, asso. clin. prof., 1966-73, prof., 1973—; physician U. Health Service, New Haven, 1971—; mem. staff Yale-New Haven Hosp., New Haven. Author: Color and People, 1971; Where Do You Come From?, 1967; Who Do You Think You Are?, 1963; Red Man, White Man, African Chief, 1960. Office: 333 Cedar St New Haven CT 06510

LERNER, MILDRED SHERWOOD, clin. psychologist; b. N.Y.C., Mar. 29, 1929; d. Samuel Jerome and Rose (Malina) Sherwood; B.A. with honors, Coll. City N.Y., 1951, M.A., 1952; Ph.D., N.Y. U., 1957; m. William Lerner, Aug. 26, 1950 (div. 1970); children—Andrew Roy, Julie Sue. Pvt. practice, N.Y.C., 1962—; supr. N.Y. Clinic Mental Health, N.Y.C.; instr. adult edn., Coll. City N.Y., 1952-54; chief psychologist High Point Hosp., Port Chester, N.Y., 1954-61; dean student tng. Nat. Psychol. Assn. for Psychoanalysis, N.Y.C., 1968-73, pres., 1972-74; cons. Children's Aid Soc., N.Y.C., 1961-65. Alvin Johnson scholar, 1951; Psychology fellow Coll. City N.Y., 1952-54. Fellow Am. Psychol. Assn.; mem. N.Y. State Psychol. Assn., N.Y. Soc. Clin. Psychologists, Am. Assn. Psychotherapy, Psychotherapists in Pvt. Practice, Am. Humanistic Psychol. Assn., Am. Group Psychol. Assn., Psi Chi. Club: Westport (Conn.) Country. Contbr. to profl. jours. Address: 23 Old Mill Rd Westport CT

LERNER, RUTH SPERO (MRS. JULIUS LERNER), educator; b. N.Y.C., Apr. 22, 1903; d. Phineas and Ann (Lublin) Spero; B.A., Hunter Coll., 1924; postgrad. Columbia, 1926, N.Y. U., 1932; m. Julius Lerner, Aug. 11, 1926; 1 son, Richard E. Mem. faculty Hunter Coll., N.Y.C., 1924—, prof. edn., 1959—. Cons. Coll. and Career Consultants, Inc., 1960—; pvt. practice counseling. Diplomate Am. Bd. Examiners in Profl. Psychology. Mem. Am. Psychol. Assn., Am. Assn. U. Profs., N.E.A., Phi Beta Kappa Alumnae, Phi Beta Kappa, Kappa Delta Pi. Home: 35 Sutton Pl New York City NY 10022

LERNER, SHARON RUTH GOLDMAN (MRS. HARRY JONAS LERNER), illustrator; b. Chgo., Nov. 9, 1938; d. Julius Nathan and Ethel (Kremen) Goldman; B.S., U. Minn., 1960; m. Harry Jonas Lerner, June 25, 1961; children—Adam, Mia, Daniel. Tchr. art U. Minn. Univ. High Sch., Mpls., 1960-61, White Bear (Minn.) pub. schs., 1961-62; art dir. Lerner Publs. Co., Mpls., 1962—; pres. Carolrhoda Books, Mpls., 1969—. Author, illustrator: I Found A Leaf, 1964; I Picked A Flower, 1967; I Like Vegetables, 1967; Who Will Wake Up Spring?, 1967; Square is A Shape, 1970; Straight is A Line, 1970; Orange is A Color, 1970; Butterflies are Beautiful, 1974; author: Places of Musical Fame, 1962, Self Portrait in Art, 1965; illustrator I Like Fruit, 1969. Home: 2215 N Willow Lane Minneapolis MN 55416

LESACK, LINDA LEBOWITZ (MRS. BURT LESACK), educator; b. Phila., Sept. 4, 1943; d. William Bernard and Eva (Seligson) Lebowitz; Normal certificate, Gratz Coll., 1962; B.A., Temple U., 1964, M.A., 1966; postgrad. Villanova U., 1965; Ph.D., U. Mo.-Columbia, 1973; m. Burt Lesack, June 19, 1969. Tchr., Temple Zion Religious Sch., Phila., 1961-65; grad. asst. Temple U., 1964-65; grad. asst., teaching fellow U. Mo.-Columbia, 1965-69; prin. B'nai B'rith Hillel Sunday Sch., Columbia, 1965-69; tchr. Frankford High Sch., Phila., 1973—; tchr. Hebrew adult edn., coordinator events Congregation Beth Torah, Willingboro, N.J. Recipient B'nai B'rith Hillel Found., Columbia, Gold Key award, 1969. Mem. Modern Lang. Assn. Am., Am. Assn. Tchrs. Spanish and Portuguese, Am. Assn. U. Women, Sigma Delta Pi, Pi Delta Phi. Mem. B'nai B'rith Women. Home: 86 Toledo Lane Willingboro NJ 08046 Office: Frankford High Sch Oxford and Wakeling Sts Philadelphia PA

LESER, JANET GRAHAM, physician; b. Jacksonville, Fla., Dec. 28, 1907; d. Frederick and Janet Wallace (Graham) Leser; A.B., Wilson Coll., 1931; M.D., N.Y. U., 1936; m. John Davis Graham, June 3, 1946; 1 son, John. Intern, Grasslands Hosp., Valhalla, N.Y., 1937; asst. resident medicine U. Chgo. Clinics, 1938; practice internal medicine, N.Y.C., 1939-40, Jacksonville, Fla., 1941-56; cons. div. family services State of Fla., 1955—; asso. physician Duval Med. Center, 1945-70, St. Luke's Hosp., 1942-56. Diplomate Am. Bd. Internal Medicine. Home: 408 East St Waynesville NC 28786

LESH-LAURIE, GEORGIA ELIZABETH (MRS. WILLIAM F. LAURIE), biologist, coll. dean.; b. Cleve., July 28, 1938; d. Howard Frees and Josephine Elizabeth (Taylor) Lesh; B.S. magna cum laude, Marietta Coll., 1960; M.S. (Wis. Alumni Research Found. fellow), U. Wis., 1961; Ph.D. (NIH fellow, NSF fellow), Case Western Res. U., 1965; m. William F. Laurie, Aug. 16, 1969. Tchr. Cleve. pub. schs., 1961-62; asst. prof. State U. N.Y., Albany, 1966-69; asst. prof. biology Case Western Res. U., Cleve., 1969-73, asso. prof., 1974—, asst. dean, 1973—. Cons. developmental biology to pub. cos., 1968—. NSF grantee, 1973, Research Corp. grantee, 1971, Am. Cancer Soc. institutional grantee, 1969, 70, 73. Mem. A.A.A.S., N.Y. Acad. Scis., Am. Soc. Zoologists, Soc. for Developmental Biology. Contbr. articles to sci. jours. Home: 15787 Forest Hills Blvd E Cleveland OH 44112

LESIEUR, HELEN ELAINE, pub. relations exec.; b. Coffeyville, Kan., Feb. 16, 1920; d. Frank R. and Grace (Koon) LeSieur; B.S. in Edn., Southeast Mo. State Coll., 1943; student art Washington U., St. Louis, 1943-44; student bus. adminstrn. Northwestern U., 1945-46. Dir. Municipal Concert Bur., Houston, 1950-52; free lance theatrical publicist, Chgo., 1952-54; pub. relations account exec. Aaron D. Cushman & Assos., Chgo., 1954-60; pub. relations dir. Arthritis Found., Ill. chpt., 1960-61, So. Cal. chpt., 1961—. Mem. Pub. Relations Soc. Am. (sec. Los Angeles area chpt. 1971-73), Soc. Fund Raisers, Publicity Club (pres. 1966-67), Women's Ad Club. Home: 5709 Fallsgrove St Los Angeles CA 90016 Office: 4311 Wilshire Blvd Los Angeles CA 90010

LESKI, CAROL JEAN HOWARD, editor; b. Chgo., July 31, 1926; d. Richard James and Mary Eleanor (Neilsen) Howard; student U. Ill., 1943-45, Thornton Jr. Coll., 1965-66; children from previous marriage—Janice Rhea, Bruce Edward. Sec. to J. Branch, Childcraft, 1944-46; sec. to F. Fenner, editor Popular Photography mag., 1946-50; reporter Pointer Publs., Riverdale, Ill., 1964-66, editor, 1966—. Mem. Dolton Civic Assn., 1966—; pub. relations chmn. Mid-Am. chpt. A.R.C., 1967-70; judge V.F.W. Voice Democracy Contest, 1970-74. Mem. Thornton Community Council Journalism Adv. Com., 1970-74. Recipient various citations and certificates of merit Dolton-Riverdale Jaycees, Rotary Club, Dolton Civic Assn., Am. Vets. Press, Isaak Walton League, Met. San. Dist. Greater Chgo., Genoa council K.C., numerous others. Mem. Ill. Press Assn., Nat. Editorial Assn. Roman Catholic. Clubs: Business and Professional Womans (Riverdale and Dolton). Home: 229 E 143d St Dolton IL 60419 Office: 13814 Indiana Av Riverdale IL 60627

LESLEIN, BETTY JEAN SWAYNE (MRS. WALTER IRWIN LESLEIN), educator; b. Leesburg, O., Mar. 18, 1932; d. John Franklin and Myrtle Jane (Eubanks) Swayne; B.S., Ohio State U., 1964, M.A., 1970; postgrad. Emory U., 1968-69, U. Ga., 1973; m. Walter Irwin Leslein, Aug. 22, 1954; children—Mark Edward, Peter, Kathy. Tchr., Ohio Youth Commn., Powell, 1964-66; tchr., work-study coordinator Hilliard (O.) High Sch., 1966-68; grad. asst. Emory U., Atlanta, 1968-69; tchr. DeKalb County Sch. System, Decatur, Ga., 1969—, tchr. Ga. history and Am. history Henderson High Sch., Chamblee, 1973—. Mem. Ga. Drug Abuse Adv. Commn., 1973—. Pres. Democratic Women of DeKalb, 1972-73, mem. adv. bd., 1969—; mem. Ga. Dem. Exec. Com., 1970—; DeKalb County Dem. Exec. Com., 1970—; alternate del. Dem. Nat. Conv., 1972. Recipient Outstanding Sustained Superior Service award FAA, 1961. Mem. N.E.A., Ga. Assn. Educators and Classroom Tchrs. (del. 1973 gen. assembly), DeKalb Assn. Educators, League Women Voters, Ga. Conservancy. Pythian Sisters. Home: 4033 Barr Circle Tucker GA 30084 Office: Henderson High Sch 2830 Henderson Mill Rd Chamblee GA 30041

LESLEY, EUGENIA LUKAS, clin. psychologist; b. Detroit, Oct. 2, 1920; d. John Michael and Alexandra Barbara (Snarski) Lukaszewicz; B.S., Marygrove Coll., 1940; M.S. in Biology, U. Detroit, 1941, M.A. in Psychology, 1957; postgrad. Wayne State U., 1950-52, 57-58; Ph.D., U. Denver, 1960; m. Walter Lesley, Dec. 15, 1951 (dec. 1968); 1 dau., Alexandra Dobson (Mrs. Patrick Michael Ward). Clin. psychologist Wayne County Gen. Hosp., Eloise, Mich., 1960-66, So. Fla. State Hosp., Hollywood, 1969-70, VA Hosp., Tuscaloosa, Ala., 1970—. Mem. Am., Southeastern, Ala. psychol. assns., Mensa, Psi Chi. Home: 607 Williamsburg East Tuscaloosa AL 35401 Office: VA Hosp Loop Rd Tuscaloosa AL 35401

LESLIE, BETTY JEAN CHAMBERLAIN (MRS. JOHN S. LESLIE), museum ofcl.; b. Ellicottville, N.Y., Oct. 31, 1924; d. Glenn Earl and Bertha A. (Umphrey) Chamberlain; m. John S. Leslie, Feb. 23, 1958. With Mich. State Extension Service, 1945-55; now reporter, sec., co-adminstr., mem. bd. Sanilac County (Mich.) Hist. Mus. Mem. Sanilac County Hist. Soc., Ontario Geneol. Soc., Chamberlain Family Assn., Sanilac County Hist. Soc., Smithsonian Instn., Chautauqua Inst., United Womens Soc. Christian Service. Mem. Christian Ch. Free lance writer throughout U.S. Home: 5109 6 B St E Bradenton FL 33505

LESLIE, HELEN KRAUSS (MRS. WENDELL W. LESLIE), bus. exec.; b. Newark, Apr. 7, 1921; d. Otto Edmund and Hattie (Windmuller) Krauss; B.S., Ala. Poly. Inst. (now Auburn U.), 1943; m. Wendell W. Leslie, Aug. 4, 1964. With Krauss Air Conditioning, Inc., 1943-73, successively stenographer, bookkeeper, air conditioning and refrigeration design and layout, draftsman, office mgr., 1943-53, sec., treas., dir., co-owner, 1953-73; with K & W Supply House, Inc., 1943—, sec., treas., dir., 1943-69, exec. v.p., dir., 1969-73, owner, pres., 1973; co-owner Krause Roofing Co., Inc., 1953—, sec., treas., dir. 1953—; with Conair Distbrs., Inc., 1956-63, sec., treas., dir., 1956—; co-owner, sec.-treas. Stone & Clay Products Corp.; dir. Home Fed. Savings and Loan Assn. Mem. Citizens Adv. Com. on hwy. safety, Fla., 1958-62; mem. adv. council St. Petersburg Civil Def., 1958—; pres. Nat. Fedn. Bus. and Profl. Women's Clubs, Inc., Washington, 1965, Conf. Bus. and Profl. Women Americas, El Salvador, 1972. Pres. Police Athletic League, 1969-70; nat. chmn. Know Your Am. Week of All Am. Conf. Combat Communism; chmn. Fla. Gov.'s Commn. Status Women, 1967-68; vice chmn. Fla. State Elections Commn., 1974, 75; mem. Small Bus. Adminstrn. Nat. Adv. Council, Nat. chmn. Know Your America Week of Nat. Fedn. Bus. and Profl. Women's Clubs, 1957, nat. chmn. health and safety, 1958-60, co-chmn. hemispheric friendship com., 1958-60, treas. nat. fedn. 1960-61, world affairs chmn. 1961-62, pres., 1965-66, chmn. hemispheric friendship com. for 1975 conf., Mexico City, mem. women's conf. Nat. Safety Council, mem. exec. com., 1966-69. Trustee Bus. and Profl. Women's Found. Washington; bd. visitors Air U., Maxwell AFB, 1974—; mem. president's round table Eckerd Coll. Mem. Delta Zeta. Republican. Presbyn. Home: Box 13221 St Petersburg FL 33733 Office: 1000 30 St S St Petersburg FL 33733

LESLY, RUTH (MRS. JOE LESLY), librarian; b. Stephentown, N.Y., Sept. 22, 1928; d. Mark and Pauline Clara (Waldhorn) Lilienfeld; B.A., State U. N.Y. at Albany, 1947; M.S., Columbia, 1952; m. Joe Lesly, Dec. 19, 1954; children—Meredith Ann, Mark Jonathan. Asst. children's librarian N.Y. Pub. Library, 1948-49; librarian Anti-Defamation League, B'nai B'rith, N.Y.C., 1949-51; asst. librarian Geyer Advt., Inc., N.Y.C., 1951-55; librarian Hastings-on-Hudson (N.Y.) Pub. Library, 1962-68, dir., 1968—. Mem. Am., N.Y., Westchester library assns., Pub. Library Dirs. Assn. Westchester County (mem. exec. bd. 1971-72, pres. 1972). Democrat. Jewish religion. Home: 20 Villard Av Hastings-on-Hudson NY 10706 Office: Pub Library Hastings on Hudson NY 10706

LESSE, ETTA GORDON (MRS. S. MICHAEL LESSE), psychiat. social worker; b. Trenton, N.J.; d. H. Charles and Rose (Miers) Gordon; B.A., Beaver Coll., 1936; M.Social Sci., Smith Coll., 1942; postgrad. Bryn Mawr Coll. Sch. Social Economy, 1942, 48, U. Pa. Sch. Social Work, 1947, 61; m. S. Michael Lesse, Sept. 12, 1937; children—Toni Gordon and Cathy Ross (twins). Exec. sec. Clinic for Child Psychiatry, Temple U. Med. Sch., Phila., 1941-42; psychiat. social worker Bur. Family Service, Orange, N.J., 1942-44, Family Welfare Soc., Newport, R.I., 1944-45; intake worker Bur. Family Service, Orange, N.J., 1946; case supr., asst. to chief social worker VA, Phila., 1946-51; consultant for social agys. and ct., 1969, 70. Social and health counsellor to Draft Bd., Orange, N.J., 1942-44; organizer steering com. for establishment case work sect. Council Social Agys., Newport, R.I., 1944; chmn. Workshop for Profl. Social Workers Lehigh Valley, 1953; group chmn. regional conf. pub. edn. Gov.'s Commn. Pub. Edn., 1957, Pa. Gov.'s Commn. on Aging, 1960; cons. foster home devel. Northampton County Children's Aid Soc., 1961-63; profl. participant in religion and psychiatry seminars, Easton, Pa., 1963-64; interviewer Easton-Phillipsburg (Pa.) Commn. Human Relations, 1964; mem. adv. bd. Northeastern region Pa. Dept. Pub. Welfare. Lectr. to child study group P.T.A., Easton, Pa., 1962. Bd. dirs. Lehigh Valley Center Performing Arts Assn., 1973—, v.p., 1973—. Mem. Nat. Assn. Social Workers, Acad. Certified Social Workers, Am. Assn. U. Women (br. pres. 1967-68, dir. Eastern br. 1969—), Lehigh Valley Mental Health Assn. (dir. 1969-71, chmn. com. on personnel and nominating 1970-71), Allentown Art Mus., Women's Com. Phila. Assn. Psychoanalysis, Women's Aux. Northampton County Med. Soc., (dir. 1970—, v.p. 1970-71, pres. 1972-73), Smith Coll. Alumni Assn. Home: 2768 Stephens St Easton PA 18042

LESSEN, GRACE LEOLA (MRS. W.G. LESSEN), librarian; b. Pleasant Plains, Ill.; d. William Alexander and Becky Ann (Haynes) Plunkett; A.A., Lincoln Coll., 1932; B.S., U. Ill., 1942, M.S., 1947, M.S. in L.S., 1962; postgrad. U. Ill., U. Chgo.; m. W.G. Lessen, Apr. 15, 1934; children—Larry, Sue (Mrs. Glenn Kanaby). Tchr., Logan County (Ill.) Rural Schs., 1930-39; tchr. English dept. Lincoln (Ill.) High Sch., 1953-54, Beason (Ill.) High Sch., 1955-66; asst. prof. English, Lincoln (Ill.) Coll., 1966-69, asst. librarian, 1969-70; instr. use of library facilities, asst. dir. learning center Spoon River Coll., Canton, Ill., 1970-72. Mem. Nat., Ill. edn. assns., Ill. Library Assn., Modern Lang. Assn., Assn. Coll. and Research Libraries, Ill. Assn. Sch. Librarians, Am. Assn. Univ. Women (mem. state bd. on edn. 1949-55), Kappa Delta Pi. Methodist. Home: 707 N Union St Lincoln IL 62656

LESSER, GILDA, microbiologist, biol. chemist; b. N.Y.C., June 5, 1912; d. George and Pauline (Lifshey) Lesser; B.S., N.Y. U., 1932, M.S., 1945. Research asst. dept. exptl. endocrinology and herpetology Am. Mus. Natural History, N.Y.C., 1932-33; asst. blood chemistry Bklyn. Jewish Hosp., 1933-34; asst. bacteriologist Brookdale Hosp., Bklyn., 1934-35, research in hematology, 1935-36; microbiologist, head lab. Bklyn. Cancer Inst., 1936-41; microbiologist Fordham Hosp., N.Y.C., 1941-42; chief mycologist Maclean Labs., Bklyn., 1942-44; research asso. Squibb & Sons, New Brunswick, N.J., 1944-45; microbiologist, biochemist Allied Food Industrie, Perth Amboy, N.J., 1945-51; microbiologist C.F. Kirk Co., N.Y.C., 1951-52; dir. Bio-Indsl. Research Labs., Bklyn., 1952-74, Ft. Lauderdale, Fla., 1974—. Lectr. bacteriology, histology L.I. U. Sch. Podiatry, N.Y.C., 1942-43. Mem. A.A.A.S., Mu Chi Sigma. Home: 780 NE 46 Ct Fort Lauderdale FL 33334 Office: 4560 N Dixie Hwy Fort Lauderdale FL 33334

LESSER, RUTH MANACHER, psychologist; b. N.Y.C., Dec. 4, 1923; d. Morris and Eva (Weinstein) Manacher; B.A., U. Wis., 1945; M.A., New Sch. Social Research, 1954; Ph.D., N.Y. U., 1961, certificate in psychotherapy and psychoanalysis, 1966; m. Gerson T. Lesser, Aug. 14, 1947; children—Kathy, Judith, Amy. Individual practice psychotherapy and psychoanalysis, N.Y.C., 1961—; asso. prof., dir. clin. tng. Yeshiva U., 1961-74; adj. asso. prof. N.Y. U., 1971—, dir. Postdoctoral Clinic, 1974—; mem. faculty William Alanson White Inst. Cons., VA; mem. nat. council Vis. Psychologist Program, Am. Psychol. Assn.; also mem. bd. profl. affairs, mem. accreditation teams clin. tng. programs, psychology memberships; mem. N.Y. State Bd. Psychology, N.Y. State Dept. Edn. Recipient Founders Day award N.Y. U. Mem. Am., N.Y. State (exec. council clin. div.) psychol. assns., Psi Chi. Home: 45 E 82d St New York City NY 10028 Office: 55 Fifth Av New York City NY 10003

LESSING, ELISE ELKINS, research psychologist; b. Mpls., Dec. 25, 1927; d. Alfred John and Myrtle Dona (Hull) Elkins; A.B., Oberlin Coll., Ph.D., U. Chgo., 1955; m. John Curtiss Lessing, Dec. 20, 1958 (div. 1964); children—Joel Owen, Marie-Elise. Sr. research asso. Inst. for Juvenile Research, Chgo., 1955—; asst. prof. psychology U. Ill., 1970—. Nat. Inst. Mental Health Tng. grantee, 1953-54. Mem. Am., Midwestern, Ill. psychol. assns., N.A.A.C.P., Phi Beta Kappa, Sigma Xi. Unitarian-Universalist. Contbr. numerous articles to profl. jours.

Home: 1103 S Lyman St Oak Park IL 60304 Office: 1140 S Paulina St Chicago IL 60612

LESTER, OLIVE PECKHAM, educator; b. Lancaster, N.Y., Dec. 19, 1903; d. Levant Delos and Martha Louise (Zurbrich) Lester; B.A., U. Buffalo, 1924, M.A., 1926; Ph.D., U. Chgo., 1931. Instr., U. Buffalo (now State U. N.Y., Buffalo), 1925-31, asst. prof., 1931-39, asso. prof., 1939-46, prof., 1946—, acting chmn. dept. psychology, 1952-54, chmn., 1954-64. Mem. adv. council for nursing N.Y. State Edn. Dept., 1960-66. Mem. adv. com. Council World Affairs, 1970—; mem. nominating com. Mental Hygiene Soc. Erie County, 1970—; pres. Lancaster Library Bd., 1960—. Recipient various awards State U. N.Y. at Buffalo. Fellow Am. Psychol. Assn., Soc. Psychol. Study Social Issues; mem. Phi Beta Kappa, Pi Lambda Theta. Contbr. articles to profl. lit. Home: 5454 Broadway Lancaster NY 14086 Office: Dept Psychology State U NY at Buffalo 4230 Ridge Lea Rd Amherst NY 14226

LESZCZYNSKA, SISTER M. EUNICE, instnl. adminstr.; b. Phila., Aug. 11, 1928; d. Alexander and Josephine (Sczpinski) Leszczynska; B.A. in Sociology, Marywood Coll., 1956; M.S.W., Catholic U. Am., 1958, postgrad., 1972—. Tchr. elementary sch., summer counselor Little Flower House of Providence, Wading River, N.Y., 1948-56, summer caseworker, 1956-58; tchr., summer counselor St. Peter Claver Sch., Bklyn., 1953-55; instnl. caseworker, dir. child care St. Christopher's Home, Sea Cliff, N.Y., 1958-61; dir. candidates for Religious Sisters of Holy Family of Nazareth, 1965-68; dir. St. Mary's Home for Children, Ambler, Pa., 1968—. Sec., Adminstrs. of Archdiocese of Phila., 1968-69, pres., 1969-70. Mem. Nat. Assn. Social Workers, Nat. Cath. Edn. Assn., Am. Orthopsychiat. Assn., Nat. Conf. Cath. Charities. Author manual, articles on child care. Address: St Mary's Home for Children Bethlehem Pike Ambler PA 19002

LETCHMAN, SHIRLEY SANDERS, anesthesiologist; b. Hamilton, Ala., Apr. 21, 1937; d. William Arlie and Mattie (Finch) Sanders; student Howard Coll., 1955-57; B.S., U. Ala., 1959; M.D., Med. Coll. Ala., 1963; m. Charles H. Letchman, May 14, 1965; children—Cindy, Chuck. Intern Grady Hosp., Atlanta, 1963-64; resident Lloyd Noland Hosp., Fairfield, Ala., 1968; anesthesiologist Anesthesia Services Birmingham (Ala.), 1968—; mem. staff St. Vincent's Hosp., South Highland Infirmary, Eye Found. Hosp. Mem. Am., Jefferson County, Ala. socs. anesthesiologists. Home: 1028 Jeffery Dr Birmingham AL 35235 Office: 2701 10th Av S Birmingham AL 35205

LEUCHTER, MAGDA SARA, newspaper exec.; b. Wildwood, N.J., Nov. 20, 1928; d. Irving and Olga (Fein) Shenberg; B.A., U. Wis., 1949; m. Ben Zion Leuchter, Aug. 13, 1950; children—Janet, Lisa, Sara, Miriam. Service mgr. Gimbels, Phila., 1949; asst. dir. Hillel Found., U. Pa., 1949; promotion mgr. Vineland (N.J.) Times Jour., 1956—. Pres. Vineland (N.J.) chpt. Hadassah, 1966-68, area v.p. So. N.J. region, 1969-72; chmn. women's div. United Jewish Appeal, 1950, 60; trustee Vineland Free Pub. Library, 1962—, chmn., 1971—; mem. aux. Newcomb Hosp., Vineland; del. council Vineland Sch. Democratic candidate Cumberland County Bd. Freeholders; v.p. Vineland Dem. Club. Trustee Stockton State Coll., Pomona, N.J. Mem. League Women Voters, Beth Israel Sisterhood, Hebrew Women's Benevolent Soc., Deborah. Club: Buena Vista (N.J.) Country. Home: 28 S State St Vineland NJ 08360 Office: 7 S 7th St Vineland NJ 08360

LEUSCHNER, LUCILE MARY, librarian; b. Beloit, Wis., Sept. 25, 1911; d. Charles Herbert and Rose Anna (Connell) Kline; student Beloit Coll., 1929-31; student U. Wis. at Madison, 1933-34, certificate in L.S., 1940; m. Robert Earl Leuschner, Nov. 1, 1947; children—Robert Charles, William Richard, Anne (Mrs. Leonard Edward Collins). Library asst., then reference librarian Beloit Pub. Library, 1934-44; librarian Norfolk Naval Hosp., Portsmouth, Va., 1944-46, VA Hosp., Tomah, Wis., 1947-48; head librarian Tomah Pub. Library, 1953-57; mem. staff Agnews State Hosp. library, San Jose, Cal., 1958—, sr. librarian charge med. library, 1965—. Bd. dirs. Coop. Information Network, 1972-74. Mem. Cal. Library Assn. (pres. hosp. and instns. library div. 1969-70), Med. Library Assn., No. Cal. Med. Library Group. Author chpt. in book. Home: 1970 Minna Way San Jose CA 95124 Office: Agnews State Hosp Library San Jose CA 95114

LEUTGOEB, ROSALIA ALOISIA (MRS. JOHN LEUTGOEB), educator; b. Vienna, Austria, Apr. 2, 1901; d. Ferdinand and Hermine (Dopler) Schmid; B.S., Marquette U., 1935; M.S., 1936, Ph.D., 1938; m. John Leutgoeb, Aug. 10, 1920; 1 son, John. Instr. St. Ambrose Coll., 1940-42; research chemist Red Star Yeast Co., Milw., 1942-44; research chemist U.S. Govt. Labs., Akron, O., 1944-45; asso. prof. Mundelein Coll., 1945-49; research chemist Froedtert Grain & Malting Co., Milw., 1950-52; prof. chemistry, chmn. chemistry dept. Northland Coll., Ashland, Wis., 1953-70, prof. chemistry emeritus, 1970—. Recipient Edward A. Uhrig award for teaching. Mem. Am. Chem. Soc., A.A.A.S., Internat. Platform Assn., Sigma Gamma Chi. Contbr. articles to profl. jours. Home: Route 1 Box 164 Maple Lane Ashland WI 54806

LEVALLEY, NORMA TEMPLETON GARDINER (MRS. JOHN LEVALLEY), writer; b. Lyndhurst, N.J., Oct. 21, 1930; d. Herbert Walker and Sarah Orr (McLean) Gardiner; student U. Buffalo, 1948-50; B.A. with high honors, U. Cal. at Los Angeles, 1969; m. John LeValley, June 30, 1951; children—Lisa Beth, Nancy Lynn. Performer, writer puppet shows. Named Outstanding Grad. Journalism, U. Cal. Los Angeles, 1969. Mem. Women in Communication. Contbr. articles to various mags. Address: 1459 Indiana Av South Pasadena CA 91030

LEVALLY, HAZEL WINNIE HOWARD, lawyer; b. Claypool, Okla., May 4, 1920; d. Wilton Elveston and Jessie Joe (Brown) Howard; B.A., U. Okla., 1942, LL.B., 1948; m. Earl Eugene LeVally, Feb. 2, 1945. Tchr. secondary schs. in Okla., 1942-45; admitted to Okla. bar, 1948; partner firm LeVally and LeVally, Healdron, 1948-74; pvt. practice, 1974—. Partner Howard Ranches, Ringling, Okla., 1948-64; ranch owner, Ringling, 1964—. Mem. Okla., Carter County bar assns., Healdton C. of C., Healdton Bus. and Profl. Women's Club, Kappa Beta Pi. Methodist. Home: 509 W Shell St PO Box 844 Healdton OK 73438 Office: 509 Shell St PO Box 844 Healdton OK 73438

LEVEE, LUELLA NASH, pub. relations and advt. exec.; b. Covington, Ky., Aug. 13, 1924; d. William A. and Bertha A. (Fisher) Nash; student U. Cin., 1942-45; divorced; 1 son, William N. Reporter, Ky. Post, Covington, 1945; publicist Elliot & Nelson, N.Y.C., 1945-46; asst. supr. insts. U. Mich., 1946-47; asst. news dir. U. Buffalo, 1947-51; editorial promotion dir. Buffalo Courier-Express, 1952-65; staff editor Cin. Bell, 1965-72; partner Tree House Assos., pub. relations and advt., Fort Mitchell, Ky., 1974—. Bd. dirs. Western N.Y. Safety Conf., 1953-64, pub. relations cons., 1953—. Mem. Ky. Heritage Commn., 1971-73; a founder, past pres. No. Ky. Heritage League. Recipient Carol Lane award Nat. Safety Council, 1965; named Ky. col., 1969, Ky. adm., 1969. Mem. Nat. League Am. Pen Women (pres. Cin. br. 1974—), Cin. Editors Assn. (past dir.), Women in Communications, Cin. Art Mus., Ky. Hist. Soc. (life). Contbr. articles to publs. Art work rep. pub. bldgs., pvt. collections. Address: 321 Iris Rd Fort Mitchell KY 41011

LEVEN, ANN RUTH, art adminstr.; b. Canton, O., Nov. 1, 1940; d. Joseph J. and Bessie (Scharff) Leven; A.B., Pembroke Coll., 1962; certificate with distinction Harvard-Radcliffe Program in Bus. Adminstrn., 1963; M.B.A., Harvard, 1964. Asst. product mgr. household products div. Colgate-Palmolive, N.Y.C., 1964-66; asst. account exec. Grey Advt., N.Y.C., 1966-67; financial asst. Met. Mus. Art, N.Y.C., 1967-69, asst. treas., 1970-72, treas., 1972—. Artist, awarded prizes for painting and graphic arts. Mem. exec. bd. new leadership div. Fedn. Jewish Philanthropies, 1968-70; bd. dirs. Camp Rainbow, 1970—. Recipient Young Leadership award Council Jewish Fedns. and Welfare Funds, 1968. Mem. Am. Assn. Mus., Women's Financial Assn. Clubs: Women's City (mem. finance com.), Harvard Bus. Sch. (dir.), Radcliffe, Pembroke Coll. (dir., chmn. scholarship com.). Home: 1160 3d Av New York City NY 10021 Office: Fifth Av and 82d St New York City NY 10028

LEVENE, CAROL, TV and film writer; b. Oakland, Cal., Dec. 13, 1911; d. Albert I. and Florence (Colman) Levene; A.B., U. Cal. at Berkeley, 1941; M.A., San Francisco State Coll., 1958. Pub. relations, social caseworker, social group worker, summer camp dir., 1934-42; profl. group work services overseas A.R.C., 1942-44; free-lance writer, producer radio, TV, film, 1944—; instr. TV and radio Golden Gate Coll., 1955-56; instr. TV prodn. Stanford Grad. Sch., 1956; writer U. Cal. Motion Picture Unit, 1958-60; statewide film and TV dir. U. Cal., 1961—; instr. TV and film writing U. Cal. Extension, 1960-61; Fulbright lectr. communications, adviser to faculty Sch. Journalism, Ankara (Turkey) U., 1970-71; Fulbright lectr. Cinema Inst., Rome, Italy, 1971; asst. prof. film dept. Cal. State U. at San Francisco, 1973—. Recipient Chris award Greater Columbus Film Festival, 1959, 60, 62, 64, 70; award, radio series Ohio State Inst. for Ednl. Radio and TV, 1950; award Headliners Club for live TV series, Sigma Delta Chi, 1957; selection for screening EFLA, 1960, 69; certificate of participation Brussels Internat. Film Festival, 1960, Cindy award, 1969; Top award motion pictures Los Angeles Advt. Women's Club, 1968, 70, 74, CINE Golden Eagle, 1970. Mem. Writers Guild Am. Home: 104 Corbett Av San Francisco CA 94114 Office: Univ Hall Berkeley CA 94720

LEVENSON, ROSALINE, educator; b. Phila., Sept. 10, 1915; d. Louis and Rebecca (Fishman) Levenson; B.A., U. Cal. at Santa Barbara, 1952; M.A., U. Cal. at Berkeley, 1953; M.S., U. Conn., 1962; Ph.D., 1971. Newspaper editor West Los Angeles Ind., Los Angeles, 1938-42; researcher Dept. Army, Tokyo, Japan, 1946-48; writer U.S. R.R. Retirement Bd., Chgo., 1958; tchr.-researcher Inst. Pub. Service, U. Conn., Storrs, 1958-72; asso. prof. Cal. State U., Chico, 1972—, Cal. corr. Nat. Civic Rev., 1967—. Served with AUS, 1942-45; now mem. USAF Res. Mem. Am. Polit. Sci. Assn., Am. Soc. Pub. Adminstrn., Nat. Municipal League. Author: County Government in Connecticut-Its History and Demise, 1966; also article Government in American Society—A Reader. Editor: Connecticut Government, 1958-72. Contbr. to Nat. Civic Review, Pub. Personnel Rev., Personnel Adminstrn., Am. City, Nation's Cities. Home: PO Box 3635 Chico CA 95926 Office: Dept Polit Sci Cal State U Chico CA 95926

LEVENTHAL, A. LINDA, lawyer; b. Albany, N.Y., June 10, 1943; d. David H. and Shirley R. (Asofsky) Leventhal; B.A., State U. N.Y. at Buffalo, 1965; J.D., Union Coll., 1968. Admitted to N.Y. bar, 1968; law clk. Sanford Rosenblum, atty., Albany, 1966-68; partner Rosenblum & Leventhal, Albany, 1969—. Pres. bd. mgrs., bd. dirs. The Commons of East Greenbush (N.Y.) Condominium. Mem. Am., N.Y. State bar assns., N.Y. State Trial Lawyers Assn., Nat. Assn. Women Lawyers. Home: 26 Donna Lynn Dr East Greenbush NY 12061 Office: 732 Madison Av Albany NY 12208

LEVENTHAL, RUTH LEE (MRS. BERNARD SENNET), sculptor; b. N.Y.C., Oct. 5, 1923; d. Isador H. and Ethel (Karp) Lee; student N.Y. U., Nat. Acad., Art Students League; m. Bernard Sennet, Feb. 19, 1972; children by previous marriage—Ricki (Mrs. Ivan Delbyck), Peter Leventhal. Exhibited sculpture in one-man shows at Lynn Kottler Galleries, N.Y.C., Chapman Sculpture Galleries, N.Y.C., Modern Mus. Art, Israel; exhibited in group shows at Nat. Acad. Galleries, N.Y.C., Nat. Arts Club, N.Y.C., Parke Bernet Galleries, N.Y.C.; represented in permanent collections at Musuem Modern Art, Israel, Tel Aviv (Israel) U., Riverside Meml. Chapel, Goldsmith's Hall, London, Eng. Recipient Nat. 3M award, 1969, gold medal for sculpture Catherine Lorrilord Wolff Arts Club, 1970, Gold medal Nat. Arts Club, 1973. Fellow Royal Soc.; mem. Nat. Soc. for Arts and Letters (dir.) Allied Artists Am., A.S.C.A.P., Am. Guild Authors and Composers, Catherine Lorrillard Wolfe (dir.). Club: Salamagundi (N.Y.C.). Patentee hosp. and home care equipment. Home: 440 E 57th St New York City NY 10022

LEVER, KATHERINE, educator; b. St. Louis; d. John H. and Cora (Medbury) Lever; A.B., Swarthmore Coll., 1936; M.A., Bryn Mawr Coll., 1937, Ph.D., 1943. Instr. English, U. Rochester, 1939-41; prof. English, Wellesley (Mass.) Coll., 1942—, chmn. English dept., 1959-62. Mem. Modern Lang. Assn., Am. Phiol. Assn., Milton Soc., Phi Beta Kappa. Author: The Art of Greek Comedy, 1956; The Novel and the Reader, 1961; The Perfect Teacher, 1964. Home: 14 Belair Rd Wellesley MA 02181

LEVERETTE, SARAH ELIZABETH, state ofcl.; b. Iva, S.C., Dec. 28, 1919; d. Stephen Ernest and Allie E. (McGee) Leverette; A.A., Anderson Coll., 1938; A.B., U. S.C., 1940, LL.B., 1943; postgrad. Columbia, summer 1947. Admitted to S.C. bar, 1943; legal research S.C. Labor Dept., Columbia, 1945-47; with Law Sch. U. S.C., Columbia, 1947-72, law librarian, 1947-72; commr. S.C. Indsl. Commn., 1972—. Mem. Com. to Study Constn. S.C. Mem. Am. Assn. Law Librarians (Carolinas pres. 1948-50, chmn. scholarship com. 1959-71, coms. on membership, exchange and duplicates 1963-64, pres. Southeastern chpt. 1968-70; life), S.C. Bar Assn., Am. Judicature Soc., S.C. State Employees Assn. (dir. 1958-60), League Women Voters (pres. Columbia 1958-61, past 2d v.p. S.C.), Columbia Library Assn. (pres. 1951-52), Phi Beta Kappa, Zeta Tau Alpha. Episcopalian. Club: Pilot (past pres.) (Columbia). Co-compiler Checklist of S.C. Session Laws, 1963. Home: 1718 Madison Rd Apt 102 Columbia SC 29204 Office: 1026 Sumter St Columbia SC 29201

LEVERY, MARY MAGDALENE, antiques dealer; b. Dunlap, Ill., July 13, 1923; d. Joseph Christy and Nancy Emaline (Kincaid) King; student Ellis Bus. Coll., 1944-46; m. Harold Eli Levery, July 13, 1946; children—Chris Lynn, Larry Alan. Pres., March Rachel Antique Shop, Inc., Morton, Ill., 1960-71, Washington, Ill., 1971—. Mem. Nat. Assn. Dealers in Antiques, Central Ill. Antique Dealers Assn., Appraisers Assn. Am. Home: 702 S Elm St Washington IL 61571 Office: 501 Walnut St Washington IL 61571

LEVESQUE, PENNEY JEAN, race horse driver, trainer; b. Lewiston, Me., Aug. 15, 1953; d. Fernand Louis and Dorothy Gwendolyn (Philbrick) Levesque; grad. high sch. Driver, trainer standard bred race horses, 1969—; at age 16 received F license to drive in sulky races, at age 18 received P license, received A license, 1973. First woman to race at Scarborough Downs in Me., 1971. Mem. U.S. Trotting Assn. Home: 7 Ralph Av Lewiston ME 04240

LEVI, JANICE LAWAN WEEKS (MRS. THOMAS JACK LEVI), educator; b. Refugio, Tex., July 4, 1946; d. Guy Nolen and Lillian Lorene (Whitten) Weeks; B.S., Tex. Agrl. and Indsl. U., 1968; postgrad. La. State U., 1968-70, U. Houston, 1971; m. Thomas Jack Levi, Jan. 18, 1968; children—Kimberly, Marcel. Tchr. journalism Sinton (Tex.) High Sch., 1968-70; tchr. drama Sam Rayburn High Sch., Pasadena, Tex., 1970—. Teaching asst. La. State U., 1968. Mem. Tex. Tchrs. Assn., Tex. Classroom Tchrs. Assn., Nat. Speleological Soc. Editor El Rancho yearbook Tex. Agrl. and Indsl. U., 1967, 68. Home: 9127 Barton St Houston TX 77034

LEVIEUX, ELEANOR ANNE (MRS. MICHEL LEVIEUX), linguist, author; b. Rochester, N.Y., Oct. 26, 1937; d. Jacob S. and Florence (Miller) Ross; student Middlebury Coll., 1956; B.A., with honors in Comparative Lit., Cornell U., 1959; certificate d'Etudes Francaises (Fulbright scholar), Faculte de Bordeaux, France, 1960; m. Michel Levieux, Oct. 31, 1961; children—Patricia, Valerie. English adviser Julliard Pub., Paris, 1960-64; Fulbright teaching fellow, Faculté de Strasbourg, France, 1960-61; English tchr. NATO Def. Coll., Paris, 1964-65; French translator, Internat. C. of C., Paris, 1966—. Mem. Phi Beta Kappa, Phi Kappa Phi. Author: (with Michel Levieux), Beyond the Dictionary in French, 1968. Transl. of Le Corbusier, Soustelle, Memmi, Bruckberger, Segalen, others, also numerous articles. Home: 148 rue de Lourmel 75015 Paris France Office: ICC 38 Cours Albert Ier 75008 Paris France

LEVIN, ALEXANDRA LEE (MRS. M. JASTROW LEVIN), writer; b. Washington, Apr. 16, 1912; d. Lawrence Rust and Alexandra (McDannold) Lee; student Bryn Mawr Coll., 1929-32; m. M. Jastrow Levin, Aug. 24, 1934; children—Betsy, Lawrence Lee, Sarah C., Alexandra (Mrs. Barry Cohen). Tchr. Balt. emergency Relief Com., 1933-35; free-lance writer, specializing in biography for various mags., newspaper and hist. jours., including Am. Heritage, Balt. Sun, Md. mag. Active fund-raising drives A.R.C. and March of Dimes. Recipient Book of Yr. award Phila. Hadassah, 1961, Distinguished Author award Md. Jewish Hist. Soc., 1973. Mem. Md. Hist. Soc. (mem. publ. com. 1972-75), Soc. of Lees of Va., Common Cause. Club: Bryn Mawr College (Balt.). Author: The Szolds of Lombard St., 1960; Vision, 1964; Dare to Be Different, 1972. Home: 3712 Chesholm Rd Baltimore MD 21216

LEVIN, DEBORAH YVETTE SILVER (MRS. HERBERT S. LEVIN), writer, civic worker; b. Phila., May 8, 1925; d. Irvin and Marcella (Artzt) S.; student U. Pa., 1942-44, Stenotype Inst., 1942, Music Conservatory Phila., Phila. Sch. Ballet and Drama, 1940-44, U. Miami, 1950-52; m. Herbert S. Levin, Feb. 19, 1944; children—Michele, Phillip. Reporter, Phila. Inquirer, 1942-43; mem. staff Village Post, Coconut Grove, Fla., 1965—; ct. reporter Civil Service, Phila., 1942-44; legal sec. U.S. Dist. Atty's, Office, Phila., 1941-42; fashion and photographer's model, Phila., Miami, 1944-69. Tchr. music, yoga, classic dance; sculptors' and artists' portrait model, editorial work, 1950-69. Bd. dirs. U. Miami Symphony, 1958-63; founder, bd. dirs. Greater Miami Philharmonic Soc., Theatre Arts League, Miami Ballet Soc., Women's Guild of Philharmonic, Women's Assn. Big Bros., 1964-72; bd. dirs. Miami Music Club, 1960-62; trustee U. Miami Symphony, 1962. Vice pres. Greater Miami Philharmonic Guild, 1964—; Vizcayan chmn. remembrance fund Big Bros., 1970, sec., 1971; chmn. Project Hope for Theatre Arts League, 1966, 68. Mem. Alliance Francaise Miami and Phila., Miami Dental Aux., Great Books Group Orgn., Council Internat. Visitors (membership chmn. 1971-73, dir., v.p. 1972—), Am. Symphony Orch. League. Home: 5305 SW 64th Ct Miami FL 33155

LEVIN, ELLEN KODISH (MRS. LEE M. MANNA), educator, psychiatrist; b. Chgo., Oct. 19, 1927; d. Solomon and Edith (Meyers) Kodish; B.S., U. Ill., 1949, M.D., 1953; m. Lee M. Manna, Nov. 6, 1971; children by previous marriages—Susan Cohen, Karen Cohen, Richard Levin. Intern, Meth. Hosp., Gary, Ind., 1953-54; resident Mayo Clinic, Rochester, Minn., 1958-60, Michael Reese Hosp., Chgo., 1961-64; pvt. practice medicine specializing in gen. medicine, Hebron, Ind., 1954-58; asso. dept. psychiatry Northwestern U., Evanston, Ill., 1965—. Mem. A.M.A., Lake County Med. Soc., Soc. for Adolescent Psychiatry. Address: 315 Lincolnwood St Highland Park IL 60035

LEVIN, FELICE MICHAELS (MRS. HARRY C. LEVIN), pub. affairs cons.; b. Chgo., Mar. 21, 1928; d. Harry and Fannie (Litz) Michaels; B.A. in Journalism, U. Wis., 1949, M.A. in Mass Communications and Polit. Sociology, 1967; m. Harry C. Levin, Feb. 25, 1968. Continuity writer sta. WISC, Madison, Wis., 1950-51; asst. for pub. contacts State Hist. Soc. Wis., Madison, 1951-53; dir. publs. U. Wis. Extension Div., Madison, 1953-57; staff writer Wis. State Jour., Madison, 1957-65; cons. Ford Found., N.Y.C., 1968—, WNET, 1970, Vera Inst. Justice and Community Action for Legal Services, N.Y.C. Pres., Wis. Women's Legislative Council, 1960-64, Temple Beth El, Madison, 1963-64. Mem. N.Y.C. Women in Communications, Madison Art Assn. Madison League Women Voters, Phi Kappa Phi, Theta Sigma Phi, Sigma Epsilon Sigma. Jewish religion. Club: Overseas Press. Address: 360 E 72d St New York City NY 10021

LEVIN, HELEN PEARLMAN (MRS. EZRA LEVIN), civic worker; b. Chgo., Jan. 21, 1913; d. Isadore W. and Sonya (Garber) Pearlman; ed. Los Angeles City Coll; m. Ezra Levin, Sept. 14, 1940; children—Judy, Susan, Emily. Vice pres. Cable Communications, Inc., 1972—. Vice pres. Community Found. Champaign County; mem. citizens com. Ill. Bd. Higher Edn., 1972—, U. Ill., 1972—; bd. dirs. CCDC Found., Nat. Acad. Arts, Sinai Temple. Mem. League Women Voters (nat. treas. 1968-70, pres. Ill. chpt. 1963-67). Home: 1109 W University Av Champaign IL 61820

LEVIN, KATHRYN JOANN (MRS. DAVID LEVIN), physicist; b. Lawrence, Kan., Feb. 25, 1944; d. Leonard N. and Shirley A. (Miller) Liebermann; B.A., U. Cal. at Berkeley, 1966; Ph.D., Harvard, 1970; m. David Levin, Aug. 31, 1969. NSF trainee, 1966-69; research asso. U. Rochester (N.Y.), 1970-72; asst. research physicist U. Cal. at Irvine, 1972—. Recipient NSF travel grant, 1973. Mem. Am. Phys. Soc. Home: 106 Nieto Av Long Beach CA 90803 Office: Physics Dept U Cal Irvine CA 92664

LEVIN, MURIEL IMOGENE (MRS. SHELDON LEVIN), educator; b. Chgo., Apr. 8, 1922; d. Joseph E. Kramer and Anne (Kleinberg) Heller; B.S., Northwestern U., 1963, M.A., 1971; m. Sheldon Levin, Nov. 29, 1944; children—Carol, Diane (Mrs. John Woodley), Larry. Tchr. voice tng. Columbia Coll., Chgo., 1964-66; tchr. acting voice Goodman Theatre Sch., Chgo., 1965-68; tchr. drama Evanston (Ill.) Twp. High Sch., 1970-71; tchr. drama and English, Chgo. Pub. Schs., 1972—; now chmn. performing arts dept. New Orr High Sch.; theatre coach Northwestern U., summer 1973. Television script writer; actress Country Club Theatre; dir. Hull House, Goodman Theatre, Drama Club, Evanston. Mem. Ill. Theatre Assn. (v.p.). Home: 940 Sheridan Rd Wilmette IL 60091 Office: Orr High Sch Pulaski and Chicago Av Chicago IL 60624

LEVIN, NORA, historian, educator; b. Phila., Sept. 20, 1916; d. Joseph and Bertha (Landberg) Levin; B.S. in Edn., Temple U., 1938; B.S. in Library Sci., Drexel Inst., 1941. Visitor, Pa. dept. Pub. Assistance, Phila., 1938-40; reference librarian dept. pub. documents Free Library Phila., 1941-43, Time Mag., N.Y.C., 1943-44; head editorial library Holiday Mag., Phila., 1945-47; exec. dir. Phila. Council of Pioneer Women, 1949-53; instr. history Phila. pub. high schs., 1953-71, Gratz Coll., 1971—. Mem. Am. Civil Liberties Union, 1950—, Pub. Citizen, Inc., 1972—. Bd. dirs. Jewish Community Relations Council Phila., Com. of 1000 for Soviet Jewry. Bernard de Voto fellow Breadloaf Writers' Conf., 1969. Mem. Am. Fedn. Tchrs., Ams. for Democratic Action, Authors' Guild. Democrat. Author: The Holocaust: The Destruction of European Jewry, 1933-45 (Jewish Book Council award 1969, Book-of-Month Club alternate), 1968; also articles. Home: 1220 Chelten Av Philadelphia PA 19126

LEVINE, ANNE NACHAMA (MRS. SEYMOUR LEVINE), educator; b. Augsbourg, Germany, June 17, 1922; d. Sussman and Rachel (Lewin) Zimmer; Baccalaureat, Coll. de Cannes, France, 1940-42; B.A., Georgian Ct. Coll., Lakewood, N.J., 1963; M.A., Rutgers U., 1968; m. Seymour Levine, Aug. 31, 1947; children—Joel, Denise (Mrs. Ian Sumner). Came to U.S., 1947, naturalized, 1949. Tchr. French, Lakewood High Sch., 1963-64; lectr. French, Monmouth Coll., Long Branch, N.J., 1965-66; instr., asst. prof. French, Georgian Ct. Coll., Lakewood, 1966—. Vol. A.R.C., 1957-60. Mem. French Resistance, 1943, 44. Mem. Am. Assn. Tchrs. French, Am. Assn. U. Profs., Alliance Francaise, Phi Sigma Iota, Pi Delta Phi. Home: 115 Iris Rd Lakewood NJ 08701

LEVINE, HELEN SAXON (MRS. NORMAN D. LEVINE), med. technologist; b. San Francisco; d. Ernest M. Saxon and Ann S. Dippel; A.B., U. Ill., 1939; m. Norman D. Levine, Mar. 2, 1935. Supr. lab. San Francisco Dept. Pub. Health Tb Sanatorium, 1944-46, U. Ill. Health Services, Urbana, 1952-65; research asso. in immunobiology, zoology dept. U. Ill., 1965—. Mem. Am. Assn. U. Profs., A.A.A.S., Am. Heart Assn., Ill. Acad. Sci., Ill. Pub. Health Assn., Am. Soc. Med. Technologists, Am. Soc. Clin. Pathologists, Sigma Delta Epsilon. Home: 702 LaSell Dr Champaign IL 61822 Office: Morrill Hall U Ill Urbana IL 61801

LEVINE, JOYCE CLAIRE KOENIGSBERG (MRS. HOWARD I. LEVINE), artist; b. Jersey City, Mar. 8, 1938; d. Sam W. and Rose Ann (Ressler) Koenigsberg; student Ridgeood Sch. Art, 1964; m. Howard I. Levine, Mar. 2, 1957; children—Marc, Brad, Jaime. One-man shows at FairLawn Art Center, Lord & Taylor, Jersey City Mus.; exhibited in group shows at Jersey City Mus., Newark Mus., Hudson Valley (N.Y.) Artists, Nat. Arts Gallery, N.Y.C.; represented in permanent collections at Temple Beth Or, N.J. Bd. Edn., Westwood, N.J., numerous others; tchr. art on cruise ships, 1972-74; tchr. oil painting, portraits and still life in pvt. studio, 1969—. Recipient gold ribbon Bergen Mall, 1971, Permanent Pigment prize Jersey City Mus., 1972, Meml. award Jersey City Mus., 1973. Mem. Am. Artists Profl. League, Fair Lawn, Ringwood, Pascack art assns., Bergen County Artists Guild. Home: 612 Kenneth St Westwood NJ 07675

LEVINE, JUNE (MRS. PAUL MARSHALL LEVINE), educator; b. Chgo., June 1, 1927; d. Hyman and Celia (Freedman) Rubin; A.A., Nassau Community Coll., 1968; B.S. summa cum laude, L.I. U., 1972; M.S., C.W. Post Coll., 1974; m. Paul Marshall Levine, Dec. 19, 1948; children—Deborah Sue, Karen Ann. Vol. tchr. aide Nassau County chpt. Assn. for Help of Retarded Children, 1965-66, tchr., 1966—. Mem. Wenwood Oaks Civic Assn., 1970. Recipient certificate of achievement for in-service tng. course, 1971, N.Y. State Incentive award, 1972. Mem. Am. Assn. Mental Deficiency, Council for Exceptional Children, N.Y. State Assn. Tchrs. Mentally Handicapped. Home: 746 Wenwood Dr East Meadows NY 11554 Office: 189 Wheatley Rd Brookville NY 11545

LEVINE, LENORE SARAH (MRS. ALVIN WESELEY), pediatrician; b. Ellenville, N.Y., Mar. 10, 1933; d. Herman Joseph and Pearl (Trotsky) Levine; B.A., Vassar Coll., 1954; M.D., N.Y. U., 1958; m. Alvin C. Weseley, Feb. 27, 1959; children—Phoebe, Jonathan, Matthew. Intern Bellevue Hosp., N.Y.C., 1958-59, resident, 1959-60; fellow in pediatrics N.Y. Hosp., N.Y.C., 1960-61; practice medicine specializing in pediatrics, N.Y.C., 1961—; asst. attending pediatrician N.Y. Hosp., 1968—; clin. instr. pediatrics Cornell U. Med. Coll., 1967-68, clin. asst. prof. pediatrics, 1968-71, asst. prof. pediatrics, 1971—, dir. Adolescent Clinic, 1971-73. Mem. Am. Acad. Pediatrics, Soc. for Adolescent Medicine, Endocrine Soc., Pediatric Endocrine Soc. Home: 130 E 75th St New York City NY 10021 Office: 525 E 68th St New York City NY 10021

LEVINE, MAITA FAYE, educator; b. Cin., Oct. 17, 1930; d. Aaron and Jessie (Byer) Levine; B.A., U. Cin., 1952, B.Ed., 1953, M.A. for Tchrs., 1966; Ph.D., Ohio State U., 1970. Tchr., Woodward High Sch., Cin., 1953-63; instr. math. U. Cin., 1963-70, asst. prof. math., 1970—. Writer, Nat. Longitudinal Study Math. Abilities, Sch. Math. Study Group, Stanford, Cal., 1963, Am. Coll. Testing Program, Iowa City, 1973—; lectr. NSF Insts., Kenyon Coll., 1960-61, U. Cin., 1962—. Faculty fellow NSF, 1968-69. Mem. Am. Assn. U. Women, Math. Assn. Am., Nat. Council Tchrs. Math., Am. Assn. U. Profs., Assn. Women in Maths., Commn. on History Math., Sigma Xi, Phi Beta Kappa, Delta Kappa Gamma. Democrat. Jewish religion. Home: 1106 Lois Dr Cincinnati OH 45237

LEVINE, MAUREEN JULIANNE (MRS. SAMUEL LEVINE), educator; b. N.Y.C., Nov. 30, 1930; d. Patrick and Mary (Walsh) Hanafin; R.N., Flower and Fifth Av. Sch. Nursing, 1952; B.S., Central Mich. U., 1967, M.A. (Bd. Trustees fellow), 1968; Ph.D., Mich. State U., 1974; m. Samuel Levine, Oct. 17, 1953; children—Robert Yale, Donna Marie, David Emmett. Pub. health nurse Vis. Nurse Service, N.Y.C., 1952-54; faculty mem. dept. psychology Central Mich. U., Mt. Pleasant, 1969—. Profl. adviser Mt. Pleasant Assn. for Prepared Childbirth. Mem. Am., Midwest psychol. assns., Am. Assn. U. Women, Mich. Sch. Psychologists Assn., Central Mich. U. Alumni Assn. Clubs: Triselion, Saginaw Valley College Womens (pres. 1974-75) (University Center, Mich.). Contbr. articles to profl. jours. Home: 5002 Foxcroft St Midland MI 48640 Office: Sloan Hall 226 Central Mich U Mount Pleasant MI 48858

LEVINE, RUTH LEA (MRS. MAX I. LEVINE), editor; b. Russia, Oct. 14, 1910; d. Israel and Rebecca (Raigorodetsky) Kofshelofsky; B.A., Hunter Coll., 1933; m. Max I. Levine, May 23, 1929; children—Don Eric, Tomar. Yiddish writer serial novels Jewish Day, 1937-57; editor weekly womens page, daily columns, 1937-57; writer scripts and interviews sta. WEVD, 1953-58; editor Pioneer Woman, N.Y.C., 1967—. Mem. as tapestry weaver Artists Craftsmen of N.Y., 1962. Ghost writer: And We Are Not Saved for David Wdowinski, 1963. Home: 341 W 24th St New York City NY 10011 Office: 315 Fifth Av New York City NY 10016

LEVINE, RUTH ROTHENBERG (MRS. MARTIN J. LEVINE), educator; b. N.Y.C.; d. Jacob and Jeannette (Bandel) Rothenberg; B.A. magna cum laude, Hunter Coll., 1938; M.A., Columbia, 1939; Ph.D., Tufts U., 1955; m. Martin J. Levine, June 21, 1953. Asst. prof. Tufts U. Sch. Medicine, 1955-58; asst. prof. dept. pharmacology Sch. Medicine, Boston U., 1958-61, asso. prof., 1961-65, prof. 1965—, chmn. div. med. scis. Grad. Sch., 1964—, Univ. prof., 1972—. Mem. Am. Soc. for Pharmacology and Exptl. Therapeutics, Biophys. Soc., A.A.A.S., Am. Chem. Soc., Am. Pharm. Assn., Acad. Scis., Phi Beta Kappa, Sigma Xi. Home: 212 Crafts Rd Chestnut Hill MA 02167 Office: 80 E Concord St Boston MA 02118

LEVINE, SUZANNE BRAUN (MRS. ROBERT F. LEVINE), mag. editor; b. N.Y.C., June 21, 1941; d. Imre and Esther (Bernson) Braun; B.A. cum laude, Radcliffe Coll., 1963; m. Robert F. Levine, Apr. 2, 1967. Editor Seattle mag., 1963-65; feature editor Time/Life Books, 1966-67, feature editor Mademoiselle mag., 1967-68; editorial staff McCall's mag., 1968-70; mng. editor Sexual Behavior mag., N.Y.C., 1970-71; mng. editor Ms. mag., N.Y.C., 1971—. Free-lance writer various publs., including Today's Health, Cosmopolitan, Ladies Home Jour.; free-lance book editor Macmillan & Co. Mem. Am. Soc. Mag. Editors. Club: Harvard (N.Y.C.). Home: 22 E 36th St New York City NY 10016 Office: 370 Lexington Av New York City NY 10017

LEVINE-SHNEIDMAN, CONALEE (MRS. J. LEE SHNEIDMAN), psychologist; b. N.Y.C., Feb. 22, 1930; d. Robert and Lillian (Kurlander) Levine; Ph.D., N.Y. U., 1959; m. J. Lee Shneidman, Sept. 3, 1961; children—Philip, Jack. Asst. prof. psychology Rutgers U., 1958-59; sr. psychologist Lincoln Inst. for Psychotherapy, 1959-61; asst. prof. psychology Fairleigh Dickinson U., 1959—; practice psychoanalysis and psychotherapy, N.Y.C., 1960-69; asso. prof. edn. N.Y. U., 1963—; supr. therapy grad. psychology program Yeshiva U., 1971—. Group cons. Albert Einstein Coll. Medicine, N.Y.C., 1965-66; psychol. cons. A Better Change program, Wis., 1969—. USPHS research fellow, 1958. Mem. Am. Psychol. Assn., Am., N.Y. (pres. 1968-69, trustee 1969-70) personnel and guidance assns., N.Y. Soc. Clin. Psychologists, Psychoanalytic Soc. N.Y. U. Home: 161 W 86th St New York City NY 10024 Office: 27 W 86th St New York City NY 10024

LEVINSON, ELIZABETH JOHNSON (MRS. RONALD B. LEVINSON), clin. psychologist; b. Charleston, S.C., Oct. 29, 1903; d. Clarence Edward and Madeleine (Coates) Johnson; A.B., U. Chgo., 1924; M.A. in Psychology, U. Me., 1958, Ph.D., 1963; m. Ronald B. Levinson, Jan. 10, 1924; children—Madeleine Edmondson, Oliver (dec.), Ellen (Mrs. Motoaki Sato), Edward. Psychologist Bangor (Me.) State Hosp., 1958-60; intern clin. psychology Children's Hosp. Med. Center, Boston, 1963-64; psychologist Eastern Me. Guidance Center, Bangor, 1961, 64-68; psychologist Counseling Center, Bangor, 1968—, dir. research and evaluation, 1969-74; pvt. practice, 1974—; vis. instr. U. Me., summer 1966. Mem. Me. Com. Problems Mentally Retarded, 1956—; pres. Eastern Me. Friends Retarded Children, 1955-57, Me. Assn. Retarded Children, 1956-58. Recipient Deborah Morton award Westbrook Jr. Coll., Me., 1966; Roselle Huddilston award Me. Tb and Health Assn., 1972; instn. for mentally retarded Elizabeth Levinson Developmental Center, Bangor, Me., named in her honor, 1971. Diplomate Am. Bd. Clin. Psychology. Mem. Am. Psychol. Assn., Am. Assn. Mental Deficiency, Am. Orthopsychiat. Assn., Am. Assn. Group Psychotherapy, Am. Assn. U. Women (recipient Me. achievement award 1959), Council Exceptional Children, Phi Beta Kappa, Sigma Xi. Author: Retarded Children in Maine: A Survey and Analysis, 1962. Home: 78 N Main St Orono ME 04473

LEVINSON, MEREDITH R. MOSS (MRS. JAMES ROSS LEVINSON), TV exec.; b. Youngstown, O., Nov. 8, 1942; d. Jack and Shirley (Aaron) Moss; B.S. in Speech, Northwestern U., 1964; M.A. in Communications (Moderator mag. scholar 1965, Annenberg Tuition scholar 1966), U. Pa., 1966; m. James Ross Levinson, Sept. 5, 1965; 1 son, Stephen Jay. Asso. editor Moderator mag., Phila., 1965-66; pub. affairs dir. WTVN-TV, Columbus, O., 1967-68; publicity and pub. service dir. sta. WCPO-TV, Cin., 1969-71; publicity mgr. Avco Broadcasting, Cin., 1972; dir. promotion and publicity Phil Donahue Show, Dayton, O., 1973—. Actress Northwestern U. Drama Featival, 1961, Ivanhoe Children's Theatre, Chgo., 1964; tchr. Anglican Sch., Jerusalem, Israel, 1966-67; producer, writer Let's Face It, WTVN-TV, Columbus, O., 1968. Founder, dir. Peanut Playhouse, Dayton, 1960; tutor underprivileged youth, Chgo., 1963-64; ednl. programming chmn. United Jewish Appeal, women's div., Dayton, O., 1973-74. Women's bd. Jewish Community Council, Dayton, 1973-74. Mem. Am. Women Radio and TV, Women in Communications (chpt. v.p. 1972-73), League Women Voters, Hadassah (chpt. v.p. 1972-73), Jr. League. Feature writer Nat. Jewish Monthly, 1973, author syndicated columns Newspapers Enterprise Assn. Asso. editor Scope Mag., Ford Found., 1966. Home: 1821 Burroughs Dr Dayton OH 45406 Office: WLWD-TV Avco Dr Dayton OH 45401

LEVINSON, SUSAN SHULMAN (MRS. STEPHEN M. LEVINSON), coll. adminstr.; b. Norwalk, Conn., May 30, 1946; d. Joseph I. and Doris (Levine) Shulman; B.A., U. Conn., 1968; m. Stephen M. Levinson, Dec. 29, 1968. Adminstrv. asst. to dir. financial aid Emerson Coll., Boston, 1968-70, dir. financial aid, 1970—. Staff Inst. Financial Aid Adminstrn. Coll. Entrance Exam. Bd. Mem. Nat., Eastern, Mass. (treas. 1974—) assns. student financial aid adminstrs. Home: 4615 Stearns Hill Rd Waltham MA 02154 Office: 148 Beacon St Boston MA 02116

LEVIT, LEONORE A(UGUSTE) FRANK (MRS. FRED LEVIT), psychologist; b. Frankfurt, Germany, June 20, 1926; d. William Gustave and Alma Regina (Stern) Frank; brought to U.S., 1938, naturalized, 1944; B.A., N.Y. U., 1947, M.A., 1948; Ph.D., U. Chgo., 1963; m. Fred Levit, Mar. 15, 1947; children—Creon, Theodore. Psychologist, dir. tng. Mental Health Center, Chgo., 1950-58, part-time, 1958-68; dir. crisis intervention unit Clark-Locust Community Mental Health Center, Chgo., 1968-70; conciliator Divorce Conciliation Service, Circuit Ct. Cook County, Chgo., 1970—; pvt. practice psychotherapy, Chgo., 1970—; vis. asst. prof. Inst. Family Studies St. Xavier Coll., Chgo., 1973. Vis. lectr. marriage and divorce problems to various ednl. and instns., Chgo., 1970—. Fellow Am. Orthopsychiat. Assn.; mem. Internat., Am., Ill. psychol. assns., Am. Assn. Marriage and Family Counselors, Conf. Conciliation Cts. Home: 250 Maple Av Wilmette IL 60091 Office: care Divorce Conciliation Service Civic Center Chicago IL 60602

LEVITT, JOANN NOREEN GORTON (MRS. ROBERT J. LEVITT), anesthesiologist; b. Plymouth, Mich., Sept. 25, 1925; s. Forest Warren and Frances Ermina (Ford) Gorton; R.N., Edward W. Sparrow Sch. Nursing, 1949; B.S., Mich. State Coll., 1952; M.D., U. Mich., 1956; m. Robert J. Levitt, Apr. 17, 1947; children—Robert, Patricia, William, Richard. Intern, Edward W. Sparrow Hosp., Lansing, Mich., 1956-57; contract surgeon Ireland Army Hosp., Fort Knox, Ky., 1957-59; pvt. practice medicine, Ft. Leavenworth, Kan., 1962-63; resident anesthesiology Charity Hosp., New Orleans, 1963-65; pvt. practice medicince specializing in anesthesiology, Alexandria, Va., 1965-73, Roswell, N.M., 1973—; mem. staffs St. Mary's Hosp., Eastern N.M. Med. Center. Med. missionary, Taiwan, 1969; cons. virology dept. U. Montevideo, Uraguay, 1969. Mem. Alpha Epsilon Iota. Home: 1303 N Pennsylvania Av Roswell NM 88201 Office: 200 E 1st St Roswell NM 88201

LEVITTAN, SHIRLEY RUTH, judge; b. N.Y.C.; d. Nathan William and Winifred (Silverstein) Levittan; A.B., Barnard Coll., 1939; M.A., Syracuse U., 1940; postgrad. Sorbonne U., 1947; J.D., N.Y. Law Sch., 1956. Admitted to N.Y. bar, 1956; practiced in N.Y.C.; mem. firm Wallman Kramer & Paley, 1967-70; judge civil ct. City of N.Y., 1970, criminal court, 1971—. Mem. Women's Bar Assn. (v.p. 1969-70, dir. 1969—). Home: 49 E 86th St New York City NY 10028 Office: 100 Centre St New York City NY 10013

LEVREAULT, ROSEMARY BOWERS (MRS. LIONEL P. LEVREAULT), educator; b. Beaucoup, Ill., Aug. 21, 1927; d. Raymond E. and Mary Bertha (Schwind) Bowers; B.S., So. Ill. U., 1949; M.A., Ohio U., 1953; m. Lionel P. Levreault, June 22, 1957. Residence counselor U. Ill. at Champaign, 1953-57; psychiat. social worker Chapin Hosp., Providence, 1957-61; sch. counselor Cumberland Valley High Sch., Mechanicsburg, Pa., 1962-65, Cedar Cliff High Sch., Camp Hill, Pa., 1965—. Mem. Nat. Assn. Women Deans and Counselors, Am. Personnel and Guidance Assn., Am. Assn. U. Women, Pa. Sch. Counselors Assn., Delta Kappa Gamma. Home: 103 Harrison St New Cumberland PA 17070 Office: Cedar Cliff High Sch Camp Hill PA 17011

LEVY, BARBARA MINA WEXNER (MRS. HERBERT E. LEVY, JR.), fashion writer, editor; b. Hot Springs, Ark., Jan. 30, 1927; d. Henry David and Helen Ruth (Loeb) Wexner; A.A., Lindenwood Coll., 1945; postgrad. U. Houston, 1958-59; m. Herbert E. Levy, Jr., July 25, 1945; children—Barbara (Mrs. Mark Chain), Richard, Lauren (Mrs. Vance Hughes). Feature writer Houston Town, 1957-58; regional editor Boot & Shoe Recorder, 1958-65; contbr. to Modern Retailer, Houston and Miami, Customer Service, Scholastic mags., Englewood Cliffs, N.J., 1966-67; fashion shoe editor Window Shopping the World, N.Y.C., 1967-68; women's fashion editor Boot and Shoe Recorder, N.Y.C., 1968-74; pub. Barbara's Report, Shoes and, 1974—. Mem. alumnae bd. Lindenwood Coll., 1967-68, v.p., 1969. Mem. Shoe Women Execs. (pres. 1973, chmn. bd. 1974), Fashion Group, Women in Communications. Contbr. articles to various publs. including Shoe & Leather Jour., Can., Shoe News, London, Shoes & Views, South Africa, 1970—. Address: 3 Horizon Rd Fort Lee NJ 07024

LEVY, BEATRICE KACHUCK, educator; b. Bklyn., Jan. 3, 1926; d. Joseph and Lydia (Greenberg) Kachuck; B.A., Bklyn. Coll., 1948; M.A., N.Y. U., 1955, Ph.D., 1972; m. Harold Levy, June 15, 1946; children—Paul, Dan. Tchr., Nassau County Pub. Schs., 1961-64; reading cons. Lawrence Pub. Schs., 1964-68; asst. prof. Bklyn. Coll., 1968—. Mem. Am. Psychol. Assn., Internat. Reading Assn., Nat. Council Tchrs. English, Nat. Council Research English, Am. Assn. U. Profs. Contbr. to Black Dialects and Reading, 1974. Contbr. articles to profl. jours. Home: 134 N Long Beach Av Freeport NY 11520 Office: Sch Edn Brooklyn Coll Brooklyn NY 11210

LEVY, BERTHA MARION, pediatrician; b. Oklahoma City, Dec. 21, 1914; d. Victor and Coralie (Kaufman) Levy; student La. State U., 1932-34; M.D., Tulane U., 1938. Intern Woman's Hosp., Phila., 1938-39; resident Bradford Meml. Hosp. and Children's Med. Center, Dallas, 1940-41, Children's Hosp., Cin., 1950-51; practice medicine specializing in pediatrics, Oklahoma City, 1941—; adminstrv. asst. supr. med. Units Okla. Dept. Instns., Social and Rehab. Services, 1965—; clin. prof. pediatrics Okla. U. Sch. Medicine, 1967—. Served with M.C., USNR 1945-46. Diplomate Am. Bd. Pediatrics. Mem. Am. Acad. Pediatrics (life), Women in Communications (named Woman of Yr. 1971). Home: 204 NW 54th Dr Oklahoma City OK 73118 Office: 1220 N Walker St Oklahoma City OK 73103

LEVY, BETHOE GESSNER (MRS. GUS DANIEL LEVY), graphic arts co. exec.; b. Centralia, Ill., June 14, 1926; d. George Bagur and Ruby Lee (Wilson) Gessner; student Sophie Newcomb Coll., 1943-44; B.A., La. State U., 1947; m. Gus Daniel Levy, Nov. 25, 1948; children—Joel Gessner, Robert George, Gwynneth Alice. Advt. mgr. Home Gardening mag., New Orleans, 1948; script writer WDSU-TV, New Orleans, 1953-55; editor house organ Joseph Katz Co., New Orleans, 1957-58; account exec. Hal Ross Assos., advt. agy., 1958-61; v.p., comptroller, dir. Creative Services, Inc., New Orleans, 1961—; columnist Clarion Herald, New Orleans, 1963-70. Leader S.E. La. council Girl Scouts Am., 1955-57; various offices P.T.A., New Orleans, 1959-69. Mem. adv. bd. Repertory Theatre of New Orleans, 1971-72. Mem. Women in Communications, Alpha Delta Pi. Episcopalian. Home: 3429 Metairie Ct Metairie LA 70002 Office: 535 Gravier St New Orleans LA 70130

LEVY, LILLIAN RAE BERLINER (MRS. AARON LEVY), author; b. Chgo., Mar. 16, 1918; d. Morris Abraham Berliner and Clara (Youkelson Berliner LaValle; student Birmingham So. Coll., 1936-37, U. Chgo., 1937-38, U. Chgo. Law Sch., 1938-39; m. Aaron Levy, Dec. 31, 1939; children—Esther Tekla (Mrs. Daniel Michael Eichenbaum), Steven Abraham. Asst. dir. personnel Franklin Simon on Fifth Av., N.Y.C., 1940-41; editor Am. Womens Voluntary Services Bull., N.Y.C., 1941-43; pub. relations asst. Kopeland Assos., Silver Spring, Md., 1956-57; Washington bur. chief Jewish Post & Opinion, Indpls., 1957-65; sci. reporter Sci. Service, Inc., Washington, 1960-62; asst. producer Coll. News Conf., 1963; cons. NASA, 1963-65, sr. sci. writer, Washington, 1965-70, dep. chief communications br., 1970-71, chief pub. activities support br., 1971-73, asst. dir. pub. services div., 1973—, also counselor equal employment opportunity; lectr. U.S. Grad. Sch., U.S. Dept. Agr., Washington, 1968—; mng. editor Sci. News Yearbook, Washington, 1969-70. Recipient NASA sustained superior performance award, 1970. Mem. Philos. Soc., A.A.A.S., Federally Employed Women, Am. Newspaper Womens Club, Hadassah, Sisterhood of Adas Israel. Club: Washington Press, National Press. Author: (editor-contbr.) Space: Its Impact on Man and Society, 1965, reissued, 1973; The Search for Cold, 1975; editor Washington Press Club Newsletter; articles in various jours. Contbr. to Harper Ency. Sci., Japanese Ency. Sci., History, Culture, 1972; also numerous articles. Author weekly column distributed to newspapers by NASA 'Down to Earth, A Woman's View of Space,' 1972—. Home: 4609 Norwood Dr Chevy Chase MD 20015 Office: 400 Maryland Av SW Washington DC 20546

LEVY, PAULA SARA, lawyer, state ofcl.; b. Newark, Mar. 5, 1942; d. Irving and Rose (Scharer) Levy; B.A., Brandeis U., 1963; J.D., Rutgers U., 1968. Admitted to N.Y. bar, 1969, N.J. bar, 1971; mem. firm Ravin & Ravin, Newark, 1969-72, Okin & Okin, Newark, 1972-74; asst. dep. pub. adv. State N.J., 1974—; counsel for indigents Newark Municipal Ct. Mem. legislation and social policy com. Mental Health Assn. Essex County, 1973-74. Mem. Am., N.J., Essex County bar assns., Am. Civil Liberties Union, Am. Acad. Polit. and Social Scis. Home: 5 Crestwood Dr West Orange NJ 07052 Office: Dept Pub Adv 1100 Raymond Blvd Newark NJ 07102

LEVY, TIBBIE (MRS. ELI BENNETT LEVY), lawyer, painter; b. N.Y.C., Oct. 29, 1908; d. David and Minnie (Hoffman) Goldstein; A.B., Cornell U., 1929, postgrad., 1929-30; J.D., N.Y. U., 1931; studied with Arshile Gorky, Art Students League, Andre L'Hote, Academic de la Grande Chaumiere, Cornell U., also Vincenzo; m. Eli Bennett Levy, Nov. 19, 1931; children—Lynn (Mrs. Leland S. Zaubler), John Hoffman (dec.). Admitted to N.Y. bar, 1932; pvt.

practice of law, N.Y.C., 1932—. Profl. painter under name of Lysan and Tibbie Levy; exhibited one-man shows in N.Y.C., Pa., Paris, Madrid, London, Tokyo; represented numerous permanent museum collections, Phoenix Mus. Art, Witte Mus., San Antonio, Jewish Mus. Hebrew Union Coll., Cin., Evansville (Ind.) Mus. Art and Sci., Boston U., Brandeis U., Cornell U., Ga. Mus., Jewish Mus., Cin., Mus. Modern Art, Miami, Witte Meml. Mus., Tex., George Peabody Mus., Tenn., Princeton, Palm Springs Mus., Barnard Coll., Fairleigh Dickinson U., N.J., Syracuse U., Colgate U., Rutgers U.; also pvt. and indsl. collections. Pres. patrons council Barnard Sch. for Boys; mem. Speakers Bur., Anti-Defamation League; pres. Freedom chpt., mem. Speakers Bur., B'nai B'rith; pres. Parents Assn. Calhoun Sch. Dir., Hebrew Kindergarten and Infants Home. Home: 2 Sutton Pl S New York City NY 10022

LEWALLEN, ORVEDA MAY, state ofcl.; b. Princeton, N.J., Aug. 31, 1940; d. Orville R. and Edith (Berrien) Austin; A.A., Ind. Community Coll., 1960; B.A., Washburn U., 1962; m. Lawrence Jay Lewallen, Dec. 28, 1965. Social worker Nemaha County Dept. Social Welfare, Seneca, Kan., 1966-70, dir., 1970-73; dir. Marysville Dist. Kan. State Dept. Social and Rehab. Services. Sec., Nemaha County Planning Commn., 1966-72. Recipient Leadership citation Central Bapt. Theol. Sem., Kansas City, Kan., 1972. Mem. N.E. Kan. County Ofcls. Assn. (sec. 1970-71, v.p. 1971-72, pres. 1972-73), Kan. Conf. Social Welfare (financial sec. 1972—, chmn. pub. relations com. 1974—), Kansas County Social Workers Assn., N.E. Kan. Social Welfare Assn. (dir.). Methodist. Home: 511 1/2 Main St Seneca KS 66538 Office: 1114 Broadway Marysville KS 66508

LEWICKI, ANN MARIA, med. educator; b. Kowel, Poland, Aug. 25, 1932; d. Marjan and Anna Grete (Meyer) Lewicki; came to U.S., 1952, naturalized, 1958; A.B. cum laude, Albion Coll., 1956; M.D., Wayne State U., 1959. Intern D.C. Gen. Hosp., 1959-60; resident radiology Wayne State Affiliated Hosps., Detroit, 1960-63; staff radiologist William Beaumont Hosp., Royal Oak, Mich., 1963-64; instr. radiology Stanford U. Sch. Medicine, 1964-67, asst. prof. radiology, 1967; asso. radiology Harvard Med. Sch., 1967-70, asst. prof. radiology, 1970-74, asso. prof., 1974—. Diplomate Am. Bd. Radiology. Mem. Mass. Med. Soc., New Eng. Roentgen Ray Soc., Mass. Radiol. Soc., Soc. Gastrointestinal Radiologists, Am. Coll. Radiology, Radiol. Soc. N.Am., Am. Med. Women's Assn. Home: 75 Grove St #231 Wellesley MA 02181 Office: 721 Huntington Av Boston MA 02115

LEWIN, SUSAN JANE WINIG GRANT (MRS. HAROLD LEWIN), editor; b. Phila., Feb. 25, 1939; d. Benjamin Gerald and May (Lipsky) Winig; B.A., U. Pa., 1960; m. H. Chester Grant, Aug. 1960 (div. 1966); m. 2d, Harold Lewin, June 4, 1967. Editor publs. I.R.E. (now I.E.E.E.), N.Y.C., 1960-61; reporter Fairchild Publs., N.Y.C., 1962-70; columnist Viewpoint, Home Furnishings Daily, N.Y.C., 1963-70, design editor, 1965-70; design editor House Beautiful Mag., Hearst Publs., 1970—. Recipient Distinguished Editorial award Nat. Soc. Interior Designers, 1967. Mem. Nat. Home Fashions League, Nat. Soc. Interior Designers (asso.), Am. Inst. Interior Designers (asso.), Archtl. League. Home: 118 Riverside Dr New York City NY 10024 Office: 717 Fifth Av New York City NY 10022

LEWIS, ADELAIDE LINDEMANN (MRS. RICHARD C. LEWIS), pub. co. exec.; b. Bklyn., June 28, 1938; d. Frederick Richard and Mary (Mills) Lindemann; B.A., N.Y. U., 1961; m. Richard Curtiss Lewis, Jan. 11, 1963. Prodn. mgr. Pitman Pub. Corp., N.Y.C., 1963—. Mem. exec. com. South Bklyn. Devel. Council, 1970-71; sec. Boerum Hill Assn., 1970-71. Office: 6 E 43d St New York City NY 10017

LEWIS, AUDREY ANN, anesthesiologist; b. Petrolia, Ont., Can., Jan. 5, 1936; d. Gordon Alan and Dorothy Isobel (Abbott) Lewis; M.D., U. Western Ont., 1958; came to U.S., 1962, naturalized, 1973. Intern Victoria Hosp., London, Ont., 1958-59, resident, 1959-62; resident Boston Children's Hosp. Med. Center, 1962-63; staff anesthesiologist Lemuer Shattuck Hosp., Boston, 1963-68, acting chief anesthesiologist, 1968-69; staff anesthesiologist Boston Hosp. for Women, 1970-71; sr. staff anesthesiologist Mass. Eye & Ear Infirmary, Boston, 1971—; clin. instr. anesthesia Harvard Med. Sch., Cambridge, Mass., 1970—. Diplomate Royal Coll. Surgeons (Can.), Am. Bd. Anesthesiology. Mem. Am. Soc. Anesthesiologists, Canadian Anesthetists Soc., Mass. Soc. Anesthesiologists, Alpha Omega Alpha, Kappa Alpha Theta. Home: 77 Pond Av Brookline MA 02146 Office: 243 Charles St Boston MA 02142

LEWIS, AUDREY EUBANKS (MRS. EDWARD C. LEWIS), educator; b. Chgo.; d. Horace E. and Marjorie (Leonard) Eubanks; B.S., U. Ill., 1944; M.S., U. Ill., 1949; postgrad. Middlebury Coll., summer 1958; Ed.D., George Peabody Coll. Tchrs., 1965; m. Edward C. Lewis, Dec. 22, 1948; children—Geri Marlene, Lynn Cheryl, Yvette Laraine. Tchr. phys. edn. Chgo. pub. schs., 1944-46; mem. phys. edn. faculty W.Va. State Coll., Institute, 1946-48, 50-51; dir. health edn. YWCA, Madison, Wis., 1951-53; prof. phys. edn. Tenn. State U., Nashville, 1955-67, chmn. upper div., 1968—; head dept. health and phys. edn. Ala. State Coll., Montgomery, 1967-68. Mem. Nat., So. assns. for phys. edn. coll. women, Am., Tenn. assns. health, phys. edn. and recreation, Nat. Congress Parents and Tchrs., Jack and Jill Club, Kappa Delta Pi, Alpha Kappa Alpha. Home: 3728 Westport Dr Nashville TN 37218

LEWIS, BESSIE MAE, coll. dean; b. Elizabeth City, N.C., Aug. 20, 1947; d. Isaac Kennon and Bessie (Pool) Lewis; B.S., Elizabeth City State U., 1969. Dean of women Del. State Coll., Dover, 1969—, chmn. of staff, 1970-72. Mem. Nat. Assn. Women Deans and Counselors, Am., Del. coll. personnel assns., Del. Personnel and Guidance Assn., Nat. Council Negro Women, N.A.A.C.P., Delta Sigma Theta. Address: Box 241 Delaware State College Dover DE 19901

LEWIS, BETTY AINES (MRS. CHARLES E. LEWIS, JR.), orgn. exec.; b. Kansas City, Mo., Sept. 25, 1916; d. Lewis Hopkins and Edna (Mays) Aines; A.A., Kansas City Jr. Coll., 1935; B.A., U. Kan., 1937; m. Charles Emmit Lewis, Jr., July 6, 1940; children—Bettina Anne, Laurie Jane (Mrs. William Crawford). Mem. staff The Ind., Kansas City jour. of soc., 1953-62; creative asst. Happy Home, woman's program KMBC-TV, 1955-61; pub. relations dir. Kansas City Area council Girl Scouts U.S.A., 1961, tng. cons. in pub. relations at Nat. Tng. Center Excelsior Springs, Mo.; now pub. relations dir. Mid-Continent council Girl Scouts U.S.A. Chmn. bd. govs. Kansas City Young Matrons, 1959-61; mem. People to People Council; del. radio-TV Council of Kansas City, 1958, 59, 60, bd. mem., 1961-73, chmn. good listening and viewing com., 1961-62, chmn. membership com., 1962-63, pres., 1963-65; free lance radio commns., 1963—; mem. Mayor's Environmental Seasonal Safety Cleanup Com.; bd. dirs. Save the Environment Please. Mem. Pub. Relations Soc. Am. (dir. Kansas City chpt. 1970—), Am. Assn. U. Women, Am. Women in Radio and TV (local chpt. pres. 1961-62, dir., nat. adv. council 1961-62). A.F.T.R.A., Mo. Press Women, Jackson County Hist. Soc., Assn. Girl Scout Profl. Workers (nat. bd. 1966-73, editor Bull. 1966-73), D.A.R., Heart of Am. Geneal. Soc., Alpha Chi Omega (chpt. corporate bd. 1961-63). Presbyn. Clubs: Women's City, Woodside Racket, Ball (bd. govs. 1973—). Home: 4306 Homestead Dr Shawnee Mission KS 66208 Office: 2233 Grand Av Kansas City MO 64108

LEWIS, BETTY CARROLL (MRS. THOMAS A. LEWIS), clubwoman; b. St. Paul, Apr. 27, 1920; d. Charles Parnell and Lydarene (Bryan) Carroll; student Coll. St. Catherine, 1938-40; m. Thomas A. Lewis, Sept. 21, 1940; children—Thomas Andrew, Carol Ann (Mrs. Richard A. Anderson), Mary Beth. Mem. exec. com. Stritch Ann. Award Dinner, 1957—; exec. com. presentation ball Order of Lafayette, 1960—; fellow St. Joseph Coll., 1962—; treas. women's bd. Mercy Hosp., Chgo., 1969-71; mem. women's bd. Loyola U., Chgo., 1963—, DePaul U., Chgo., 1968-71. Mem. Ill. Club for Cath. Women (v.p. 1968-73). Clubs: Fideliras Women's (v.p. 1970-72), South Shore Country, Union League (Chgo.); White Lake Yacht, White Lake Golf (Whitehall, Mich.). Home: 21 Spinning Wheel Rd Hinsdale IL 60520

LEWIS, BRENDA, singer, actress; b. Harrisburg, Pa., Mar. 2, 1921; student Pa. State U.; m. Simon Asen, Nov. 27, 1943 (div. 1959); children—Leo, Michael; m. 2d, Benjamin Cooper, 1959; 1 dau., Edith Maureen. Debut Phila. Opera Co., 1941; appeared on Broadway in Merry Widow, 1944, Lucretia, 1948, Regina, 1952, also as singing birdie Blitzstein's opera based on Little Foxes; debut N.Y.C. Center Opera Co. in Salome, 1946; appeared in Salome, San Francisco Opera, 1951, 52; debut Met. Opera Co. in La Boheme, 1953, other roles include Rosalinda in Fledermaus, Carmen, Donna Elvira in Don Giovanni, Venus in Tannheuser, Vanessa and Marie in Wozzeck; radio, TV appearances; summer stock appearances include Call Me Madam, Song of Norway, Carousel, Chocolate Soldier; leading comedy role Girl in Pink Tights, 1954; stared Vienna 4 months as Kate in Kiss Me Kate and Carmen at Volksoper, 1956; Annie Get Your Gun, Volksoper, Vienna, 1957. Recordings Allegro-Royale. Address: care NYC Opera Co Lincoln Center New York City NY 10020

LEWIS, CATHERINE HENIFORD, librarian; b. Richmond, Va., Feb. 24, 1924; d. Davis Oscar and Katherine Wright (Hammack) Heniford; B.A., Coker Coll., 1943; M.A., U. N.C., 1945, B.L.S., 1948; m. Myron Francis Lewis, 1949 (div. 1958); children—Alan, Kevin, Paul. Reference asst. U. N.C. at Chapel Hill, 1944-48; documents librarian Northwestern State Coll., La., 1948-49; asst. librarian Sch. Advanced Internat. Studies, Washington, 1950-51; reviewer, bibliographer USIA, 1951-55; librarian Coastal Carolina Jr. Coll., Conway, S.C., 1958-60; head librarian Horry County Meml. Library, Conway, 1960—. 1st v.p. S.C. Council on Human Rights, 1972, 74. Chmn. bd. dirs. Horry-Georgetown Econ. Opportunity Council, 1969-73, bd. dirs., 1973—. Named Field and Herald Woman of Year, 1973. Mem. Am., S.C., Southeastern library assns. Home: 1409 8th Av Conway SC 29526 Office: 1008 5th St Conway SC 29526

LEWIS, DOLORES JOAN, univ. dean; b. Farmville, Va., Aug. 28, 1939; d. William Joseph and Lou Edna (Carrington) Lewis; B.B.A., City U. N.Y., 1964, M.S., 1968; postgrad. Pace U., N.Y. U., New Sch. for Social Research. Personnel mgr., asst. controller Pyramid Publs., N.Y.C., 1953-70; personnel dir., bus. mgr. Hostos Community Coll., City U. N.Y., 1970-71; personnel dir. Medgar Evers Coll., Bklyn., 1971-73; dean of adminstrv. affairs Lincoln U., Jefferson City, Mo., 1973—. Mem. Am. Personnel and Guidance Assn., Am. Mgmt. Assn., Nat. Assn. Coll. and Univ. Bus. Officers, Coll. and Univ. Personnel Assn., Am. Assn. Univ. Women. Home: 5 Hiddenwood St Jefferson City MO 65101

LEWIS, DOLORES LILLIAN (MRS. MILTON TALMAGE LEWIS), ednl. adminstr.; b. Balt., June 10, 1929; d. Andrew Anthony and Catherine (Truszkowski) Golembiewski; B.S., Moore Coll. Art, 1969; M.A. in Art Edn., Glassboro State Coll., 1973; m. Milton Talmage Lewis, Dec. 21, 1945; children—Kathleen (Mrs. Larry Myers), Delores (Mrs. Arthur Milne), Mark, David. Instr. art Pine Hill (N.J.) Elementary Sch., 1969-70; asst. registrar, dir. continuing edn., Moore Coll. Art, Phila., 1970-72, registrar, dir. continuing edn., 1972—. Exhibited in group shows at Columbus (Ga.) Mus., 1950, Pa. State U., 1969, Phila. Art Alliance, 1970, N.J. State Mus., 1973. Mem. Am. Assn. Collegiate Registrars and Admissions Officers, N.J. Designer Craftsmen, Phila. Art Tchrs. Assn., Phila. Art Alliance, Artist Equity. Office: 20th and Race St Philadelphia PA 19103

LEWIS, DORIS EILEEN PRINGLE (MRS. MARSHALL E. LEWIS), librarian; b. Toronto, Ont., Can., July 20, 1911; d. Charles and Ethel (Monckton) Pringle; B.A., U. Toronto, 1933, diploma Sch. Library Science, 1934, B.L.S., 1963; LL.D., Trent U., 1969; m. Marshall E. Lewis, Oct. 17, 1936; 1 son, Peter. Gen. librarian U. Toronto, 1934-36; head librarian Waterloo (Ont.) Coll., 1951-58; chief librarian U. Waterloo, 1958-69, collections devel. librarian, 1969—. Cons. in field. Mem. Canadian Library Assn., Inst. Profl. Librarians of Ont. Home: Rural Route 4 Bright ON Canada Office: U Waterloo Waterloo ON N2L 3G1 Canada

LEWIS, ELEANOR SMITH (MRS. KENT STEWART LEWIS), lawyer; b. Salt Lake City, May 14, 1944; d. Wayne David and Jean (Hathaway) Smith; J.D., U. Utah, 1967; m. Kent Stewart Lewis, Sept. 11, 1967; 1 son, Adam Wayne. Veterans claims examiner VA, Salt Lake City, 1968-71; admitted to Utah bar, 1968; atty. Office of the Solicitor, U.S. Dept. Interior, Salt Lake City, 1971—. Mem. Utah State Bar, Am., Salt Lake County Fed. bar assns. Home: 1133 South 1400 E Salt Lake City UT 84105 Office: 125 South State Salt Lake City UT 84138

LEWIS, ELIZABETH ALLARA (MRS. F. WOODWARD LEWIS), physician; b. New Haven, Oct. 12, 1912; d. Emmanuel and Dima (Massarini) Allara; A.B., Albertus Magnus Coll., 1933; M.D., Tufts U., 1937; m. F. Woodward Lewis, Sept. 1, 1935; children—F. Woodward, Elizabeth (Mrs. James Nash), Nancy (Mrs. George Parker III), David Snow, Sarah Lewis. Intern, New Eng. Hosp. for Women and Children, Boston, 1937, Charles V. Chapin Hosp., Providence, 1939; practice gen. medicine, Groton, Mass., 1940—; mem. staff Ayer Community Meml. Hosp., 1940—, sec. staff, 1942-43, 60, v.p. staff, 1946-47, pres. staff 1948-49; mem. staff Groton Community Hosp., 1955—, sec. staff, 1959-61; active mem. staff Nashoba Community Hosp. Mem. Groton Bd. Health, 1955-60. Mem. med. alumni exec. Tufts U., 1964—, v.p. alumni exec. council, 1967-69. Diplomate Nat. Bd. Med. Examiners, Am. Bd. Family Practice (charter). Fellow Am. Acad. Family Physicians; mem. Am. Acad. Family Physicians, N.E. Obstet. and Gynecol. Soc., Mass., North Worcester med. socs., A.M.A. (recipient Physician's Recognition award). Club: Groton Woman's. Home: Main St Groton MA 01450

LEWIS, ELIZABETH HUGER MATTHEW, librarian; b. Charleston, S.C., Dec. 3, 1916; d. Charles Frederic and Margaret Eloise (Tyler) Matthew; student Richmond Profl. Inst., 1939, Ind. U., 1951, Ball State U., 1953, Cornwall Tech. Coll. (Eng.), 1964, U. London (Eng.), 1964; B.A., Purdue U., 1965; M.L.S., Pratt Inst., 1967; Ed.D., Columbia, 1974; m. Frank Christopher Sweetman, Apr. 15, 1940; m. 2d, John Chase Lewis, Feb. 24, 1950; 1 son, Christopher Tyler Sweetman. Tchr. Miami (Fla.) Art Sch., 1949-51; cartographic and statis. draftsman Pan Am. Airways, Miami, 1948-51; instr. Ind. U., Kokomo, 1952-57; v.p. Lewis Workshop Studios, Ind. and Mich., 1951-63; curator slides, dept. art Coll. City N.Y., 1971; sr. lectr. fine arts, art librarian U.S. Mil. Acad., West Point, N.Y., 1968-71, 72—. Exhibited in one-man art shows at Lafayette Art Center, Miami Mus. Modern Art, The Gallery, Ft. Lauderdale; represented in permanent collections at Miami Mus. Modern Art, Ball Mus., Muncie, Ind., Loeb Theater, Purdue U., Lafayette, Ind. Mem. chorus Metropoli Grand Opera Co., Norfolk, Va., 1973; mem. jury Am. Film Festival, 1969—; program chmn. Kokomo Art Assn., 1952-54; stage designer Little Theater, Kokomo, 1953-55. Served with U.S. Mcht. Marine, 1943-45. Mem. Spl. Libraries Assn. (mem. chpt. membership com. 1973), Nat. Art Edn. Assn., Am. Soc. Information Sci. Health Edn. Media Assn., N.Y. Library Assn., Assn. for Supervision and Curriculum Devel., Am. Assn. U. Profs., So. Assn. Sculptors, Nat. Microfilm Assn., Information Film Producers Assn., Internat. Soc. Edn. through Art, Nat. Art Workers Community, Kappa Delta Pi, Kappa Kappa Kappa, Delta Rho Kappa. Home: 9 Dale Av Apt 3 Highland Falls NY 10928 Office: US Mil Academy Library West Point NY 10996

LEWIS, ELMA INA, cultural complex adminstr.; b. Boston, Sept. 15, 1921; d. Clairmont Richard McDonald and Edwardine (Jordan) Corbin Lewis; B.Lit. Interpretation, Emerson Coll., 1943, LL.D., 1968; M.Ed., Boston U., 1944; H.H.D. (hon.), Boston Coll., 1971; H.H.D., Anna Maria Coll., 1971; Dr. Arts (hon.), Harvard, 1972, Merrimac Coll., 1973, Clark U., 1973, Regis Coll., 1973; D.F.A. (hon.), Colby Coll., 1972; L.H.D., Salem State Coll., 1973. Tchr., Boston Pub. Schs., 1945; speech therapist Mass. Mental Health Habit Clinic, Boston, 1945-47; social worker Harriet Tubman House, Boston, 1947-49; founder, dir. Elma Lewis Sch. Fine Arts, Dorchester, Mass., 1950—; founder Nat. Center Afro-Am. Artists, Boston, 1968. Played role of Julie in Liliom, Copley Theater, Boston, 1945; dir. plays, operas. Cons. office program devel. Boston Sch. Com., 1966-67; mem. Title III adv. council Mass. Bd. Edn., 1968; mem. bd. Met. Council for EPDNL. Opportunity, 1966—, Roxbury Multi-Service Center, 1965—, Com. for Community Edn. Devel., 1967—, City Missionary Soc., 1968—; mem. Spl. Mass. Commn. for Franklin Park Zoo. Bd. dirs. New African Theatre, New Eng. Theatre Conf., Theatre Communications Group. Recipient awards Lambda Kappa Mu, 1964, Omega Psi Phi, 1967, New Eng. Theatre Conf., 1967, Boston Negro Bus. and Profl. Women, 1968, citation merit Grahm Jr. Coll., 1969; Mayor's Citation, City of Boston, 1970; Outstanding Women award Campfire Girls Am., 1970; Henry C. Tanneraward Black Arts Council Cal., 1971; Regional Dir.'s Certificate for Outstanding Community Service, Dept. Health Edn. and Welfare, Boston, 1971; Meritorious Pub. Service citation Fed. Bus. and Profl. Womens Clubs, 1970; Certificate of Honor, Nat. Council Tchrs. English, 1971. Fellow Black Acad. Arts and Letters; mem. N.A.A.C.P. (award 1966), Urban League Boston (award 1968), Internat. Platform Assn., Internat. Platform Artists, Met. Cultural Alliance. Contbr. articles to mags. Home: 15 Homestead St Dorchester MA 02121 Office: 122 Elm Hill Av Dorchester MA 02121

LEWIS, ERNIE JACQULIN (MRS. GEORGE NEIL LEWIS, JR.), health service adminstr.; b. Summerfield, La., Sept. 11, 1922; d. Jack Robert and Myrtle Annie (Brown) Kimbell; grad. Homer High Sch., 1939; R.N., Highland Sanitarium Sch. Nursing, 1943; m. George Neil Lewis, Jr., Nov. 30, 1947; children—Judy Lynn, Barbara Sue. Nurse pvt. duty, Shreveport, La., 1943; office nurse, Minden, La., 1945-47; vis. nurse Pub. Health Service Claiborne Parish, Homer, La., 1947-48; office nurse, Minden, 1948-51; prin. E.J. Lewis pvt. duty nurse, Ringgold, La., 1952-66; owner, mgr. Ho-Made Soft Cream, Ringgold, 1952-66; supr. nurses Jonesboro (La.) Charity Hosp., 1966-70; supt. Minden Sanitarium, Inc., 1970, hosp. adminstr., 1971—. Served with Nurse Corps, AUS, 1943-45; ETO. Mem. La. State Nurses Assn., N.W. Dist. Adminstrs. Assn., Am. Legion Aux., 1946—. Democrat. Baptist (asst. Sunday sch. tchr. since 19—). Home: Box 325 Ringgold LA 71068 Office: 113 N Monroe Minden LA 71055

LEWIS, FAYE CASHATT, physician, writer; b. nr. Dedham, Ia., Jan. 30, 1896; d. Osa Tillman and Salome Lusetta (Corwin) Cashatt; B.A., U. S.D., 1919; M.D., Washington U., St. Louis, 1921; m. William Benjamin Lewis, July 15, 1923; children—Malcolm Richard, Mary Virginia, Elizabeth Ann (Mrs. William Matthew). Intern Halstead (Kan.) Hosp., 1921-22; gen. practice medicine, 1943-69; ret., 1969. Mem. Alpha Omega Alpha. Republican. Methodist. Mem. P.E.O. Author: Doc's Wife, 1940; Patients, Doctors and Families, 1968; A Doctor Looks at Heart Trouble, 1970; Nothing to Make a Shadow, 1972; All Out Against Arthritis, 1973. Home: 1500 Willson Av Webster City IA 50595

LEWIS, FLORA, journalist; b. Los Angeles; d. Benjamin and Pauline (Kallin) Lewis; B.A., U. Cal. at Los Angeles, 1941; M.S., Columbia, 1942; m. Sydney Gruson, Aug. 17, 1945 (div. 1973); children—Kerry, Sheila, Lindsey. Reporter, Los Angeles Times, 1941, A.P., N.Y., Washington, London, 1942-46; free-lance or contract for Observer, Economist, Financial Times, France-soir, Time Mag., N.Y. Times Mag., London, Warsaw, Berlin, Hague, Mexico City, Tel Aviv, 1946-54, Prague, Warsaw, 1956-58; editor McGraw-Hill, N.Y.C., 1955; bur. chief Washington Post, Bonn, London, N.Y.C., 1958-66; syndicated columnist Newsday, Paris, N.Y.C., 1967-72; bur. chief N.Y. Times, Paris, 1972—. Recipient awards for best interpretation fgn. affairs, 1956, best reporting fgn. affairs 1960 Overseas Press Club, Columbia Journalism Sch. 50th Anniversary Honor award, 1963. Mem. Phi Beta Kappa. Author: Case History of Hope, 1958, Red Pawn, 1964, One of Our H-Bombs Is Missing, 1967; contbr. to anthologies, books, mags. Office: NY Times 3 Rue Scribe Paris 9e France

LEWIS, FRANCES HARMAN, coll. ofcl.; b. Montclair, N.J.; d. Walter H. and Esther (Harman) Lewis; B.A., Beaver Coll., 1939. Staff mem. Times Chronicle, Jenkintown, Pa., 1944-48; asst. dir. pub. relations Beaver Coll., Glenside, 1949-51, dir. pub. relations, 1951—. Vol. chpt. fund drs. Salvation Army, United Fund, YMCA, Jenkintown; mem. Meadowbrook Aux. Abington Meml. Hosp. Bd. dirs., pres. Old York Rd. Community Council, 1964-73, pres., 1968-69; bd. dirs. Community Action Coll., 1971—; mem. devel. com. Abington Friends Sch. Art Alliance Mem. Am. Coll. Pub. Relations Assn., Pub. Relations Soc. Am., Am. Acad. Polit. and Social Scis., Am. Assn. U. Women, Beaver Coll. Alumnae Assn. (chmn. publicity com., student selection com., 1950-52, 2d v.p. 1961-65), Suburban Pub. Relations Club (pres. 1960-61). Episcopalian. Clubs: The Chesapeake; Old York Road Country; Soroptimist (local chmn. scholarship com. 1968); Beaver College Faculty (pres. 1958-59) (Glenside). Home: 721 Fairfield Rd Glenside PA 19038 Office: Beaver Coll Glenside PA 19038

LEWIS, GWENDOLYN ADELL JOHNSON (MRS. DONALD EDWIN LEWIS), psychologist; b. Litchfield, Minn., Nov. 4, 1936; d. Delphin and Iva Mae (Watkins) Johnson; student Olivet Coll., 1954-55, Pasadena Coll., 1955-57; B.A., Cal. State U. at Los Angeles, 1959, M.A., 1962; m. Donald Edwin Lewis, Aug. 28, 1961; children—Dean Joseph, Darryl Edwin. Tchr., Temple City (Cal.) schs., 1959-62; psychologist Baldwin Park (Cal.) Unified Sch. Dist., 1962-63, Charter Oak Unified Sch. Dist., Covina, 1963-66, Arcadia Unified Sch. Dist., Arcadia, Cal., 1967, Edmonds (Wash.) Sch. Dist., 1968-73, Regional Center for Deaf, Portland, Ore., 1974—. Mem.

Internat. Reading Assn., Council for Exceptional Children, Wash. State Psychol. Assn., Nat. Assn. Sch. Psychologists (Wash. state del. 1969-73), Am. Assn. U. Women, Pi Lambda Theta. Editorial adv. bd. Sch. Psychology Digest, 1969—. Home: 9 Falstaff St Lake Oswego OR 97034

LEWIS, HONEY AARON, lawyer; b. Los Angeles, July 10, 1942; d. Joseph and Esther (Lebensohn) Lewis; B.A., U. Cal. at Los Angeles, 1964; J.D., U. San Fernando, 1968; M.A. in Polit. Sci., Cal. State U. at Los Angeles, 1972. Admitted to Cal. bar, 1969, practiced in Los Angeles, 1969-70; mem. firm Joseph Lewis and Frank Waters; dep. city atty. Los Angeles, 1970—. Mem. Los Angeles Dem. Central Com., 1968-72. Mem. Am., Los Angeles County bar assns., Am. Judicature Soc., U. Cal. at Los Angeles Alumni Assn. Office: 205 S Broadway St Los Angeles CA 90012

LEWIS, JANE HAMBLIN (MRS. RICHARD CRAIG LEWIS), architect; b. Albany, N.Y., Mar. 6, 1919; d. Leon Nathan and Minnie Rauscher (Fox) Hamblin; B.Arch., Syracuse U., 1941; m. Richard Craig Lewis, May 31, 1942; children—David Wayne, James Alan, Edward Scott. Draftsman, U.S. C.E., Arlington, Va., 1942; self employed architect, Albany, 1946-50; with W. Parker Dodge Assos., Rensselaer, N.Y., 1950-51, 53-59; jr. architect N.Y. State Dept. Pub. Works, Div. Architecture, Albany, 1959-61; asst. architect N.Y. State Dept. Health, div. Hosp. Rev. and Planning, Albany, 1961-66, sr. architect, 1966-67; asst. dir., architect cons. Regional Hosp. Rev. and Planning Council of Northeastern N.Y., Inc., Albany, 1967—. Mem. A.I.A. (chpt. health and hosp. com. 1968), Sigma Upsilon Alpha. Conglist. (sec. 1968—). Home: 27 Oak Rd Delmar NY 12054 Office: 1196 Western Av Albany NY 12203

LEWIS, JOY ARVIDA SCHALEBEN (MRS. ROBERT EDWIN LEWIS), freelance writer; b. Milw., Sept. 28, 1938; d. Arville Orman and Ida Arnella (Androvandi) Schaleben; B.S. in Med. Tech., U. Wis., 1960, M.S. in Journalism, 1967; m. Robert Edwin Lewis, May 4, 1968; 1 son, Mark Joslin. Sci. writer U. Wis., Madison, 1965-67; reporter Boston Globe, 1968-69; asst. dir. publs. Tufts U., Medford, Mass., 1969; dir. pub. relations Ohio State U. Sch. Communication, Athens, 1971; freelance writer, Milw., 1972—. U.S. rep. Internat. Center Advanced Studies in Communications in Latin Am. (OAS and UNESCO), Quito, Ecuador, 1966. Mem. Women in Communications. Author: Getting the Story of Nazi Germany-Louis P. Lochner, 1969. Address: 3035 N Downer Av Milwaukee WI 53211

LEWIS, KAREN GAIL, psychiat. social worker; b. Norfolk, Va., May 29, 1944; d. Albert Samuel and Blanche Mae (Abelove) Lewis; student Cedar Crest Coll., 1964, Sorbonne, U. Paris, France, summer, 1964; B.A., Boston U., 1966, M.S. in Social Work, 1971. Social welfare worker Boston Dept. Pub. Welfare, 1966-68; social worker Children's unit Met. State Hosp., Waltham, Mass., 1968-69; psychiat. social worker Newton (Mass.) Mental Health Clinic, 1969-70, Worcester (Mass.) Youth Guidance Center, 1971—. Mem. Nat. Assn. Social Workers, Am. Assn. Psychiat. Services to Children, Am. Orthopsychiat. Assn. Office: 275 Belmont St Worcester MA 01604

LEWIS, LINDA DONELLE, neurologist; b. Columbus, O., Nov. 27, 1939; d. Donald Peter and Ann Elizabeth (Karn) Lewis; B.S., Bethany Coll., 1961; M.D., W.Va. U., 1965. Intern U. Wis. hosps., 1965-66; asst. resident St. Luke's Hosp. Center, N.Y.C., 1966-67, resident, 1967-68; asst. resident neurology Case Western Res. U., Cleve., 1968-69; resident Columbia Presbyn. Med. Center, 1969-70, chief resident, 1970-71, chief neurolgoy clinics, 1971—; practice medicine specializing in neurology, N.Y.C., 1971—; mem. staffs. Presbyn. Hosp. and St. Luke's Hosp., N.Y.C. asst. neurology Columbia, 1969-71, instr., 1971-74, asst. prof., 1974—; Mem. A.A.A.S., A.M.A., N.Y. Acad. Sci., Am. Acad. Neurology, Assn. for Research in Nervous and Mental Disease, N.Y. State, N.Y. County Med. Socs. Home: 260 W 21st St New York City NY 10011 Office: 710 W 168th St New York City NY 10032

LEWIS, MARGUERITE GARBER (MRS. WILLIAM LEROY LEWIS), civic worker; b. nr. Bellville, O., July 23, 1911; d. Horatio Seymour and Sylvia (Swank) Garber; B.A., Coll. of Wooster, 1933; M.A., U. Mich., 1936; postgrad. Northwestern U., 1937; m. William Leroy Lewis, June 16, 1937; children—Sylvia Jane, Thomas Leroy, David Garber, Catherine Carol, Linda Evelyn. Tchr., 1933-39. Troop leader Girl Scouts U.S.A., 1960-61, chmn. Am. Field Service, 1962-63; bd. mgrs. N.Y. State Congress Parents and Tchrs., 1962-65, Tex. Congress, 1973; mem. Larchmont-Mamaroneck Motion Picture Council, 1944—, pres., 1957-59; mem. Fedn. Motion Picture Councils, 1960-67, nat. conf. chmn., 1961, nat. pres., 1965-67; radio and TV chmn. Ft. Worth City Council P.T.A.'s, 1967-70; moderator weekly TV program Parents in Action, KTVT, 1967-73; co-ordinator community services courses, div. spl. courses Tex. Christian U., 1969-73. Recipient Distinguished Alumni award Coll. Wooster, 1971. Mem. Am. Assn. U. Women, Nat. Congress Parents and Tchrs. (hon. life), Delta Sigma Rho, Pi Kappa Delta. Clubs: Wooster, Womans. Presbyn. Editor: Newsreel, 1965-67. Home: 6254 Cabaret St San Diego CA 92120

LEWIS, MARIANNA OLMSTEAD (MRS. GEORGE SHERMAN LEWIS), editor; b. New Britian, Conn., July 18, 1923; d. Bertice Henry and Anna Davenport (Bodley) Olmstead; A.B., Stanford, 1949; m. George Sherman Lewis, Aug. 8, 1959. Sec. to dean of mil. programs Hamilton Coll., Clinton, N.Y., 1943-44; asst. to curator Chinese and South Asian collections Hoover Inst. and Library, Stanford, 1949-57; with Found. Center (formerly Found. Library Center), N.Y.C., 1957—, sr. research asso., 1972—, editor The Found. Directory, 1961-71. Democrat. Home: 31 E 12th St New York City NY 10003 Office: Foundation Center 888 7th Av New York City NY 10019

LEWIS, MARY GENEVIEVE, librarian; b. Vincennes, Ind., Aug. 28, 1911; d. Claudius Ervin and Isa (Hollister) Lewis; B.A., Northwestern U., 1933, M.A., 1935; B.A., Columbia, 1938. Reference asst., reference librarian Oak Park (Ill.) Pub. Library, 1935-37, 38-43, head reference dept., 1938-43, 45-50; instr. English, head dept. Warren Wilson Coll., Swannanoa, N.C., 1950-61; reference librarian Stetson U., DeLand, Fla., 1961-73. Bd. dirs. West Volusia County chpt. A.R.C. Served to capt. WAC, 1943-45; ETO. Mem. Am., Fla. library assns. Democrat. Presbyn. Home: 135 W Minnesota Av DeLand FL 32720

LEWIS, MARY LOU (MRS. CHARLES W. LEWIS), physician; b. Madison, W.Va., Nov. 5, 1931; d. Lawrence Bruce and Myrtle May (Carpenter) Lyon; A.B., Duke, 1954; M.D. cum laude, Emory U., 1965; m. Charles W. Lewis, Nov. 9, 1968; children—Tony, Dina, Lesli. Intern The New York Hosp., N.Y.C., 1965-66; research fellow physiology Cornell U. Med. Coll., 1966-68; resident Cal. Med. Center at San Francisco, 1968-71, clin. nephrology resident 1970-71; dir. medicine Charleston (W.Va.) Area Med. Center, Inc., 1971—; asso. prof. medicine W.Va. U. Med. Center, Charleston. Pres. med. adv. com. W.Va. chpt. Nat. Kidney Found., 1971—. Diplomate Bd. Internal Medicine. Mem. Am. Soc. Medicine, A.M.A., Am. Soc. Nephrology, Alpha Omega Alpha, Alpha Chi Omega. Home: 1510 Knob Rd Charleston WV 25314 Office: 3200 Mac Corkle Av SE Charleston WV 25304

LEWIS, NANCI JEANNE GETSCHINE (MRS. NORMAN H. LEWIS), occupational therapist, civic worker; b. Pasadena, Cal., Dec. 24, 1935; d. Constant Alexander and Lois Helene (Davis) Getschine; A.A., U. Cal. at Berkeley, 1955; B.S., U. So. Cal., 1957; m. Norman H. Lewis, Nov. 30, 1957; children—Janis K., Joanne K., Jon K., Joy K. Staff occupation therapist Norfolk (Va.) Cerebral Palsy Tng. Center, 1961-63; tchr. therapist Homebound Program, Norfolk Sch. System, 1963-64; head occupational therapy United Cerebral Palsy, Jacksonville, Fla., 1965-67; occupational therapy cons. Kauai Instl. Care Home, Waimea, Hawaii, 1974—. Gray Lady, A.R.C., 1967-69, water safety instr., 1955-73; v.p. P.T.A., Kekaha Elementary Sch., 1973-74. Bd. dirs. Council of Pacific, Girl Scouts U.S.A., 1973-74, assn. chmn. Island of Kauai, 1973-74. Named Kauai Mil. Wife Year, 1973. Mem. Am. Occupational Therapy Assn., Chapel Women Yokohama (Japan) (pres. 1968-70), Sierra Club, Alpha Chi Omega. Mem. United Ch. of Christ (youth adviser). Mokihana (hospitality chmn. 1973-74) (Kauai). Home: 5526 Bittern Av Ewa Beach HI 96706

LEWIS, NATALIE PUTNAM, developmental psychology researcher; b. Boston; d. Arthur Barnard and Carrie (Webber) B.; B.A., then M.A., 1969, Ph.D., 1971; m. George W. Lewis (dec. June 1965); children—G. Webber, Lochlain Putnam. Editorial asst. Harvard, Cambridge, Mass., 1952-60; developmental psychology research U.S. Govt., Boston, 1969-74; cons., mem. consumer adv. bd., 1971—. Chmn., Portsmouth (N.H.) Naval Hosp. Council, 1957-59; mem. Parents of Exeter (N.H.) Day Sch., 1965-68. Mem. Ret. Officers Assn., Navy Officers Wives Club, Guilde of Strawbery Banke (v.p. 1974), Mass. Soc. Mayflower Descs., N.H. Fedn. Garden Clubs (exec. bd. 1958-60, 65-67), Mensa. Author: Firelite Farm, 1963; To My Sons, 1966; Poems for My Husband, 1955. Home: Firelite Farm Stratham NH 03885

LEWIS, PHEBE HELEN, educator; b. Freeport, Mich., Nov. 29, 1930; s. Minard and Ruby Marion (Adams) Lewis; B.A., Houghton (N.Y.) Coll., 1951; M.A., Western Mich. U., 1964; Ph.D. (Nat. Def. Edn. Act fellow), Ohio State U., 1972. Asst. dir. child evangelism Mich. Conf. Wesleyan Ch. Am., 1951-55; elementary classroom tchr. Northview Pub. Schs., Grand Rapids, Mich., 1955-64; asso. prof. edn. Houghton Coll., 1964-68; teaching asso. Ohio State U., 1969-71; asst. prof. edn. Ind. U. at South Bend, 1971—. Cons. EPDA Internship Program, Penn-Harris-Madison Sch. Corp., Mishawaka, Ind.; book reviewer Christian Scholar's Rev. Cons. mem. editorial com. Aldersgate Graded Curriculum, 1973—. Mem. Nat. Council Tchrs. English (citation for promising research 1973), Am. Tchrs. Edn., N.E.A., Internat. Reading Assn., Nat. Soc. Study Edn. Home: 1002 S 20th St South Bend IN 46615 Office: 1825 Northside Blvd South Bend IN 46615

LEWIS, RUTH ANN NEWMAN, librarian; b. Huntington, W.Va., Nov. 1, 1938; d. James Waymer and Virginia Ruth (Booten) Newman; A.B., Marshall U., 1960; postgrad. Fla. State U., Fla. Tech. U., Stetson U.; m. Wayne Ernest Lewis, June 26, 1965; 1 son, Mark Wayne. Librarian Parkway Jr. High Sch., Titusville, Fla., 1960-65, Ceredo Kenova High Sch., Kenova, W.Va., 1965-66, Oak Park Elementary Sch., Titusville, 1966-68, Titusville High Sch., 1968—. Mem. A.L.A., Fla. Library Assn., Brevard County Librarians (chmn.), Am. Assn. Univ. Women, N.E.A., Fla. Edn. Assn., Classroom Tchr. Assn., Alpha Delta Kappa, Delta Kappa Gamma. Home: 3648 Frazier Ct Titusville FL 32780 Office: US Route 1 S Titusville FL 32780

LEWIS, SALLY BUTZEL (MRS. LEONARD THEODORE LEWIS), civic worker; b. Detroit, June 29, 1912; d. Leo Martin and Caroline (Heavenrich) Butzel; B.A., Vassar Coll., 1934; m. Leonard Theodore Lewis, Apr. 4, 1935; 1 son, Leonard Theodore. Mem. Women's City Club of Detroit, 1932-67, dir., 1935-38; dir., chmn. community services com. Village Woman's Club of Birmingham-Bloomfield dir. Franklin-Wright Settlement, Inc., Detroit, 1939-74, pres. 1959-60; trustee Oakland County Children's Aid Soc., 1950-64, Oakland U. Found., 1973-74; mem. exec. com. Detroit Fedn. Settlements, 1961; mem. steering com., women's orgn. United Fund, 1960-61; mem. Oakland planning div. United Community Services, Met. Detroit, 1959-70; membership chmn. Bloomfield Art Assn., Birmingham, Mich.; mem. scholarship com. Meadow Brook Sch. Music, Meadow Brook Festival, Rochester, Mich.; treas. Cranbrook Music Guild, Inc., 1959, dir., 1958-63, sec., 1960-61; mem. women's com. Cranbrook Galleries Art, Bloomfield Hills; exec. com. Meadow Brook Festival, Rochester, Md., 1969-72. Mem. Nat. Council Jewish Women, Am. Jewish Com., Women's Assn. Detroit Symphony, Friends Detroit Symphony. Mem. Women's Nat. Farm and Garden. Clubs: Village, Ibex. Home: 1421 Lochridge Rd Bloomfield Hills MI 48013

LEWIS, SAMELLA SANDERS (MRS. PAUL G. LEWIS), educator, artist; b. New Orleans; d. Samuel and Rachel (Taylor) Sanders; student Dillard U., 1941-43; B.S., Hampton Inst., 1945; M.A., Ohio State U., 1948, Ph.D., 1951; postdoctorate U. So. Cal., 1964-66; m. Paul G. Lewis, Dec. 22, 1948; children—Alan Stephen, Claude Anthony. Exhibited in group shows at U.S. Soviet Exchange Exhibit.; represented in permanent collections at Balt. Mus. Fine Arts, Va. Mus. Fine Arts, High Mus. of Atlanta, Ohio Union Gallery, Viktor Lowenfeld Meml. Gallery, Atlanta U. Gallery, Palm Springs Mus., Oakland Mus. Art, many others; prof. art U. State of N.Y. at Plattsburgh, 1958-68; asso. prof. art Cal. State Coll., Dominquez Hills, 1968—, Scripps Coll., Claremont, Cal., 1970-71; co-ordinator edn. Los Angeles County Mus. Art. Fulbright travel grantee, 1962; Ford Found. grantee, 1965; Nat. Def. Edn. Act postdoctoral grantee, 1964-66. Mem. Am. Soc. for Aesthetics, Coll. Art Assn. Am., Am. Assn. U. Profs., Assn. for Asian Studies. Co-editor: Black Artists on Art; Art: African American. Home: 1237 Masselin Av Los Angeles CA 90019

LEWIS, SANDRA CUTLER (MRS. PAUL LEWIS), occupational therapist; b. Phila., Sept. 29, 1936; d. Jacob W. and Ethyl (Riseman) Cutler; student U. Mich., 1954-55; B.S., U. Pa., 1958; M.F.A., 1960, occupational therapy certificate, 1965; m. Paul Lewis, Oct. 14, 1961; children—Ethan, Judith, Sharon. Jr. high sch. art tchr., Camden County, N.J., 1960, Central Bucks County Schs., Doylestown, Pa., 1962; occupational therapist Moss Rehab. Hosp., Phila., 1966; therapist Inst. Pa. Hosp., Phila., 1968-72; occupational therapist geriatric unit Norristown (Pa.) State Hosp., 1972—. Mem. Commr. Lawrence Curry's Citizens Adv. Study Group on Mental Health and Mental Retardation, Montgomery County, Pa., 1973-74. Occupational Therapy Tng. grantee, U. Pa., 1958-60. Mem. Gerontological Soc., League Women Voters, Am., Eastern Pa. occupational therapy assns. Home: 8305 Mac Arthur Rd Wyndmoor PA 19118 Office: Norristown State Hosp Norristown PA 19401

LEWIS, SHIRLEY BOOTH, educator; b. Englewood, Colo., Nov. 27, 1917; d. John J. and Ethel (Calloley) Booth; R.N., Colo. Tng. Sch. for Nurses, 1943; B.S., U. Denver, 1955; M.S., U. Colo., 1958; m. Ronald W. Lewis, June 16, 1967. Staff nurse Denver Pub. Health, 1943-45; instr., supr. Denver Gen. Hosp., 1946-49; asso. dir. nurses Gen. Rose Meml. Hosp., 1949-58; asst. prof. nursing U. Colo. Sch. Nursing, Denver, 1958-67; dir. inservice edn. Rice Meml. Hosp., Wilmar, Minn., 1972-73; nurse cons. Minn. Dept. Pub. Health Div. Crippled Children, 1973—. Cons. nurse Gideons Internat. Conv., summer 1963, Colo. Welfare Dept. for Revision of Standards for Infant and Child Day Care Nurseries. Mem. Am. Assn. U. Profs., Nat., Colo. (2d v.p. 1961-67; chmn. maternal and child nursing council 1965-66) leagues for nursing, Am., Minn., Dist. 8 Minn. (mem. com. careers and continuing edn., v.p. 1972-73, pres. 1974—) nurses assns., Colo. Mental Health Assn., U. Colo. Sch. Nursing Alumni (v.p.), N.E.A., Federated Womens Clubs, Sigma Theta Tau (hon. archivist 1966-67). Republican. Mem. United Ch. of Christ (ednl. com. local ch.). Mem. Order of Eastern Star (grand warder Minn. Grand chpt.). Home: 701 10th St S Benson MN 56215

LEWIS, VIRGINIA GRIFFIN, coll. adminstr.; b. Shreveport, La., Aug. 17, 1944; d. John Wesley and Virginia Griffin (McCuen) Lewis; B.A., Converse Coll., 1966; M.Ed., U. N.C., 1972. Tchr. English, Charlotte Mecklenburg Schs., Charlotte, N.C., 1966-67, Prince William County Schs., Manassas, Va., 1967-69, Bertie County, Windsor, N.C., 1969-70; coordinator residence halls, asst. to dean of students Queens Coll., Charlotte, 1972—. Mem. Charlotte Mayor's Com. Employment of the Handicapped, 1974-75. Mem. Nat., N.C. assns. women deans, adminstrs. and counselors. Presbyn. Home: 1900 Selwyn Av Charlotte NC 28274

LEWIS, VIVIAN FLOYD (MRS. GASTON F. LEWIS), ret. educator, civic worker; b. Memphis, Apr. 30, 1919; d. James Ernest and Lilia (Harris) Floyd; student Schauffler Coll. for Women, B.S., Wilberforce U., 1942; postgrad. Case Sch. Applied Scis., 1943; M.S., Western Res. U., 1946; Ph.D., Ohio State U., 1953; m. Gaston F. Lewis, Dec. 26, 1950; 1 stepson, Frederick G. Tchr. health and phys. edn. Central Jr. High Sch., Cleve., 1942-46; chmn. dept. health, phys. edn. and recreation Central State U., Wilberforce, O., 1946-74; cons. recreation, elementary phys. edn., sr. citizens, Columbus Sch. for Blind, Dayton Model City Youth Programs. Past v.p. Green County Steering Com. Federal Poverty Programs; mem. Pres. Nixon's Adv. Council on Edn. Disadvantaged Children, 1970; mem. phys. edn. com. Greene County YMCA; acting chmn. Greene County Head Start Project; mem. exec. com. Greene County Council Community Services; pres. Greene County Occupational Industrialization Center; v.p. Greene County Recreation Bd.; chmn. Montgomery, Warren and Greene County summer programs for disadvantaged; mem. Greene County Golden Age Sr. Citizens Center Com., SCOPE; mem. tech. adv. com. White House Conf. on Aging, White House Conf. for Children; sec. Greene Meml. Hosp. Bd. Mem. Am. Assn. U. Profs., Am. Assn. U. Women, A.A.H.P.E.R., Am. Recreation Soc., Ohio Coll. Assn., Ohio Assn. Health, Phys. Edn. and Recreation, Nat., Midwest assns. phys. edn. coll. women, N.E.A., Ohio Edn. Assn., Am. Health Assn., Greene County Mental Health Assn., Nat. Recreation and Parks Assn., Nat. Community Sch. Edn. Assn., Am. Assn. Phys. and Mental Rehab., Alpha Kappa Alpha. Home: Box 338 Wilberforce OH 45384

LEWISOHN, MARJORIE G(RETA), physician; b. N.Y.C., Nov. 28, 1918; d. Samuel A. and Margaret (Seligman) Lewisohn; A.B., U. Mich., 1940; M.D., Johns Hopkins, 1944. Rotating intern Hosp. for Women of Md., Balt., 1944; resident pathology Presbyn. Hosp., Pitts., 1944-45; asst. resident physician chest service Bellevue Hosp., N.Y.C., 1945, asst. clin. vis. physician chest service, 1951-55; research fellow, asst. resident chest diseases N.Y. Hosp., 1947; fellow Coll. Phys. and Surg., asst. in medicine Columbia, 1949-50, asst. resident physician 1st Med. Div., 1950-51, asst. clin. vis. physician, 1951-55; practice medicine specializing in internal medicine and chest diseases, N.Y.C., 1952—; asso. physician med. service Lenox Hill. Hosp., N.Y.C., 1962—; courtesy staff Drs. Hosp., N.Y.C., 1952—; clin. instr. medicine Cornell U. Med. Sch., 1955-66, clin. asst. prof. medicine, 1966—; lectr. in field. Mem. governing bd. United Negro Coll. Fund, 1960-65. Trustee Pub. Edn. Assn., N.Y.C., 1954-65, Austen Riggs Center, Inc. and Hosp., 1962—, Johns Hopkins, 1971—. Mem. N.Y. County (mem. com hosps. and dispensaries 1955-61), N.Y. State med. socs., A.M.A., A.C.P., Royal Soc. Health, N.Y., Am. Trudeau socs., N.Y. Tb and Health Assn., Harvey Soc., N.Y. Acad. Medicine, Soc. Clin. Investigation, Am. Assn. Physicians, Asia Soc. Club: Cosmopolitan (N.Y.C.). Home: 15 E 91st St New York City NY 10028 Office: 45 East End Av New York City NY 10028

LEWISON, FLORENCE (MRS. MAURICE GLICKMAN), art gallery dir., writer; b. Jersey City; d. Samuel and Fannie (Sinaberg) Lewison; student music, Italy, 1934-35; student Sch. for Art Studies, N.Y.C., 1945-50; m. Maurice Glickman, Dec. 20, 1931. Art news editor, art critic, feature writer Design mag., 1949-51; art history research, Europe, 1956-61; founder, dir. Florence Lewison Gallery, N.Y.C., 1961—. Organizer Maurice Glickman 30 year retrospective exhibit Albany (N.Y.) Inst. History and Art, 1963, organizer Theodore Robinson exhibit, 1963. Author: Theodore Robinson-America's First Impressionist, 1974, also numerous forewords to exhbn. catalogues. Contbr. articles to profl. publs. Home: 165 E 66th St New York City NY 10021 Office: 30 E 60th St New York City NY 10022

LEY, DOROTHY CORINNE HOBBS, physician, med. assn. ofcl.; b. Toronto, Ont., Can., Apr. 4, 1924; d. Charles Thomas Hobbs and Inez Corinne (Dunlop) Ley; M.D. cum laude, U. Toronto, 1948; B.Sc. (Med.) in Pathol. Chemistry, 1951. Intern Toronto Gen. Hosp., 1948-49; NRC fellow dept. pathol. chemistry U. Toronto, 1949-50; fellow in pathology Women's Coll. Hosp., Toronto, 1950-51, Banting Inst., U. Toronto, 1950-51; sr. in medicine Wellesley div. Toronto Gen. Hosp., 1951-53; asst. resident in medicine Barnes Hosp., Washington U., St. Louis, 1953-54; practice medicine specializing in hematology and lab. medicine, Toronto, 1954-72; NRC fellow Toronto Western Hosp., 1954-56; clin. research asso. Ont. Cancer Treatment and Research Found. Toronto Western Hosp., 1956-68, also attending physician, 1956-72; asst. prof. medicine U. Toronto, 1967-72; cons. to clin. labs. Oakville-Trafalgar Meml. Hosp., Oakville, Ont., 1962—. Pres. Toronto Med. Labs. Ltd., 1960-68; med. dir. Med. Data Scis., Ltd., 1968-69; dir. lab. certification and proficiency testing program, sect. on lab. medicine, Ont. Med. Assn., 1972—. Vice pres. Conservative Women's Forum, 1966, pres., 1967-68; pres. Thorah Twp. Cottagers Assn., 1973—. Fellow A.C.P., Royal Coll. Physicians Can., Internat. Soc. Hematology; mem. Acad. Medicine Toronto (pres. elect), Am. Soc. Clin. Pathologists, Am., European socs. hematology, Canadian and Ont. Med. Assn., A.A.A.S., Canadian, Ont. assns. of pathologists, Canadian, Internat. socs. of chemotherapy, Clin. Research Soc. Toronto, Canadian Soc. Immunology, Canadian Soc. for Clin. Investigation, Canadian Soc. Clin. Chemists, Fedn. Med. Women of Can., Internat. Soc. Blood Transfusion, N.Y. Acad. Scis., Royal Soc. Medicine, Soc. Nuclear Medicine, Ont. Antibody Club, Internat. Council of Women, Alpha Omega Alpha. Clubs: Granite, Lambton Golf and Country, Cedarhurst Golf, Boca Raton (Fla.) Golf and Country. Contbr. articles on hematology and pathological chemistry and lab. proficiency testing to med. jours. Home: 92 Valecrest Dr Islington M9A 4P6 ON Canada Office: 240 St George St Toronto M5R 2P4 ON Canada

LEY, KATHERINE LOUISE, educator; b. Prairie du Sac, Wis., Dec. 6, 1919; d. Ivan Herman and G. Louise (Conger) Ley; B.S., U. Wis., 1941; M.S., U. Cal. at Los Angeles, 1947; Ph.D., U. Ia., 1960. Tchr. pub. schs., Platteville, Wis., 1941-43; instr. Ia. State Coll., Ames, 1943-45; instr., asst. prof., asso. prof. U. Colo., Boulder, 1946-61; asso. prof. U. Mich., Ann Arbor, 1961-66, U. N.C., Greensboro, 1972, Tex.

Womens U., 1973; vis. prof. U. So. Cal., Los Angeles, summer 1959, U. Wash., Seattle, summer 1961; prof., chmn. womens phys. edn. dept. State U. N.Y., Coll. at Cortland, N.Y., 1966—; distinguished prof. U. Bridgeport, 1974. Cons., Ednl. Testing Service, Princeton, N.J., 1968—; chmn. Nat. Com. on Standards for Girls and Womens Sports, 1954-56; mem. governing council U.S. Track and Field Fedn., 1962-65, U.S. Gymnastics Fedn., 1962; 1st chmn. Commn. on Intercollegiate Athletics for Women, 1966-69; bd. cons. U.S. Olympic Com., 1969—. Recipient Merit award Eastern Assn. Phys. Edn. for Coll. Women, 1973. Mem. A.A.H.P.E.R. (life, v.p. 1961, mem. exec. council phys. edn. div. 1972, pres. 1974-75), Nat. Assn. Phys. Edn. Coll. Women, Am. Acad. Phys. Edn., Nat. Found. for Health, Phys. Edn. and Recreation, Am. Alliance for Health, Phys. Edn. and Recreation, Phi Kappa Phi, Delta Kappa Gamma. Mem. Order Eastern Star. Co-author: Team and Individual Sports for Women, 1955. Editor, cons. Addison Wesley Pub. Co., Reading, Mass. Contbr. articles in field to profl. jours. Home: 23 Circle Dr Cortland NY 13045

LEYDA, JEAN CRAVENS (MRS. VIRGIL WILLIAM LEYDA), author, editor, club woman; b. Granby, Mo., Jan. 15, 1903; d. William A. and Lois (Harmon) Cravens; A.A., Stephens Coll., 1920; B.A., Mt. Holyoke Coll., 1923; M.A. in English Lit., U. Wis., 1930; m. Virgil William Leyda, Aug. 10, 1945; 1 foster son, Leonard Breckler. Tchr. English, Freeport (Ill.) High Sch., 1923-26, head English dept., 1926-27; head English dept. Mishawaka (Ind.) High Sch., 1929-45, dir. English, Mishawaka Jr. and Sr. High Schs., 1938-45; co-author lit. anthologies Scott, Foresman Co., Chgo., 1940-50, editorial staff, after 1945; now ret. Pres., Chandler (Ariz.) Woman's Club, 1954-55, chmn. community service com., 1961-63; edn. chmn. Ariz. Fedn. Women's Clubs, 1955-57. Mem. founding adv. bd. Chandler Pub. Library. Recipient alumnae achievement award Stephens Coll., 1956. Former mem., past pres. Ind. Council Tchrs. English. Mem. Ind. Ret. Tchrs. Assn., D.A.R., Colonial Dames 17th Century, P.E.O., Phi Theta Kappa. Democrat. Presbyn. (trustee 1951-53, life elder). Mem. Order Eastern Star, Daus. of Nile. Club: Desert (past pres.). Author: (with others) Enjoying Life through Literature, 1951; Exploring Life through Literature, 1951. Address: 400 N Hartford St Chandler AZ 85224

LEYLAND, MARILYN JEANNE (MRS. JOHN THOMAS LEYLAND), writer, editor, pub. relations cons.; b. Peoria, Ill., Sept. 6, 1945; d. Eugene Joseph and Evelyn Mae (Strassburger) Voss; B.S. cum laude (Peoria Acad. Sci. Meml. scholar), Bradley U., 1967; M.S. in Journalism, Northwestern U., 1968; m. John Thomas Leyland, May 16, 1970; 1 son, John Thomas II. Pub. information asst., dir. Ill. Regional Med. Program, Chgo., 1968-71; free lance writer, editor, pub. relations cons., Chgo., Peoria, Charleston, S.C., 1971—. Mem. publicity com. A.A.A.S. Ann. Meeting, Chgo., 1970. Vol., Ill. Constl. Conv., 1969-70; hostess Historic Charleston Found., 1973; bd. mem., hospitality chmn., publicity co-chmn. Bazaar, Naval Officers Wives Club of Charleston, 1973; mem. bd., hospitality chmn. Destroyer Officers Wives Club of Charleston, 1973; mem. League Women Voters. Mem. Women in Communications, Inc., Am., Ill. pub. health assns., Delta Zeta, Phi Kappa Phi. Roman Catholic. Mem. editorial staff The New Home Med. Ency., 1973. Address: 3011 N Delaware St Peoria IL 61603

LEYSATH, MURDALE ANN CAMERON (MRS. ELWIN FREDERICK LEYSATH), clergywoman; b. Greenville, S.C., May 24, 1924; d. Murdo Alexander and Bertha (Love) Cameron; B.A. with distinction, Winthrop Coll., 1945; study course Vt. Conf. United Ch. Christ, 1962-65; m. Elwin Frederick Leysath, June 12, 1947; children—Albert William II, Dorothy Murdale. Pub. Social case worker Florence County (S.C.) Dept. Pub. Welfare, 1945-47, Aiken County (S.C.) Dept. Pub. Welfare, 1948; lay minister Sherburne United Ch. of Christ, Killington, Vt., 1955-65; kindergarten tchr. Rutland (Vt.) pub. schs., 1962; minister Tri-Valley Parish, 1962-71, Cornwall-Weybridge Parish, 1971—; ordained to ministry United Ch. Christ, 1965. Den mother Cub Scouts Am., 1959-60; mem. nat. council for lay life and work United Ch. Christ, 1961-67; bd. dirs. Vt. Conf. United Ch. Christ, 1966-70, chmn. jr. high com. 1966-67, chmn. Christian edn. dept., 1967-70, mem. ch. standing and extension com., 1971—; bd. dirs., an originator research leisure ministry Killington-Pico Area Ecumenical Project, 1967-70; trustee, incorporator mem. Vt. Religious Edn. Found., 1969—; pres. Rutland County Ministerial Assn., 1965-66; mem. exec. com. Nat. Conf. Christians and Jews, 1962-71, mem. clergy com., 1963-67. Bd. dirs. Family Life Found., 1962. Recipient Brotherhood award Nat. Conf. Christians and Jews, 1965. Mem. Internat. Platform Assn., Am. Assn. U. Women, Addison County Ministerial Assn. (pres. 1973—), D.A.R., Pi Gamma Mu, Alpha Psi Omega, Beta Sigma Phi (local pres. 1946-47, 48-49). Contbr. to Rev. of Books and Religion. Address: RD 2 Cornwall Middlebury VT 05753

LIANG, PEILING (MRS. KEE-BEW CHUN), artist, educator; b. Tientsin, China, Feb. 14, 1910; d. Yen-Hing and Yu-Cheng (Wang) Liang; grad. with honors St. Joseph's Sch., Tientsin, 1924; student Sofia U., Tokyo, Japan, 1951; pvt. studies, 1932-55; m. Kee-Bew Chun, Apr. 7, 1929; children—Hung Kit, Paochia (Mrs. Paul W.M. Ing). Came to U.S., 1956; naturalized, 1961. Exhibited in one man show in Barbizon Hotel, N.Y.C., 1960; exhibited in group shows in China House Group, N.Y.C., 1956, Am. Watercolor Soc., Ann. Exhbn., N.Y.C., 1957, 58, Hands Across the Sea, Internat. Art Exhbn., N.Y.C., 1957, Allied Artists Am. Ann. Exhbn., N.Y.C., 1957, Nat. Assn. Women Artists Ann. Exhibit, N.Y.C., 1958, Comerford Gallery, N.Y.C., 1959. Tchr., Chinese painting YWCA Central Bd., N.Y.C., 1959—, Long Island Adult Edn. program, Long Island, N.Y., 1959, Westchester Edgemont Adult Edn. program, N.Y.C. Bd. Edn., 1960. Recipient Grumbacher award for Watercolors, Allied Artists Am., 1957; Katherine M. Howe Meml. prize Nat. Assn. Women Artists, 1958. Mem. Am. Watercolor Soc., Nat. Assn. Women Artists, China Inst. N.Y.C. Home: 246 E 46th St New York City NY 10017

LIBAW, FRIEDA BORNSTON, psychologist, educator; b. Erie, Pa., Nov. 22, 1919; d. Abram and Jennie (Goldstein) Bornston; B.A. in Bacteriology, U. Cal. at Los Angeles, 1942; M.A. in Psychology, U. So. Cal., 1950, Ph.D. in Psychology, 1961 (div. 1946); 1 dau., Marva Lynn; m. 2d, William H. Libaw, Apr. 29, 1956 (div. Sept. 1972). Instr. Los Angeles City Coll., 1949-57; supervising tchr. U. Cal. at Los Angeles, 1951-53, research asso., 1951-53; research dir. Cal. State Coll. at Los Angeles, 1958-61, asst. prof., 1961-66; research dir. Found. for Jr. Blind, Los Angeles, 1961-62; treas. J.P. Guilford Award Fund; exec. dir. Galton Inst., Beverly Hills, Cal., 1961—; pres. Cognitive Systems, Inc., to 1970; pres. Mentrex Enterprises, Los Angeles, 1971—; dir. product devel. and evaluation Comprenetics, Inc., Beverly Hills, Cal., 1973-74. Mem. Am., Western psychol. assns., Assn. Research Growth Relationships, Am. Assn. U. Women, Nat. Assn. Gifted Children, Am. Documentation Inst., Soc. Psychophysiol. Research, A.A.A.S., Soc. for Research in Child Devel., Sigma Xi. Editor: Perceptual-Cognitive Development 1965-70. Author: (with J.C. Coleman) Successful Study, 1960; (with J.C. Coleman and W.D. Martinson) Success in College, 1960, 66; (with J. Kirschenbaum) Mentorex Student Study Skills Manual for Introductory Psychology, 1969; (with others) Computer-Assisted Test Construction, 1974. Contbr. articles to profl. jours. Home: 10514 Rountree Rd Los Angeles CA 90064 Office: PO Box 5284 Beverly Hills CA 90210

LIBBEY, DEE, composer; b. Deland, Fla., Nov. 1, 1919; d. Clifford K. and Anastasia (Schumate) R.; B. Mus., Stetson U., 1941; pupil composition Leo Sowerly, Nadia Boulanger; m. Edwin B. Libbey, June 7, 1941; 1 son, Michael R. Composer popular songs including Mangos, Silver Bird, Essence and Directions, Wee Little Boy, Tolling Bells; choral works, instrumental pieces, lit. works including The Lost Forest, under name Q'Adrianne Rohde; commd. to compose Give Honor to God, Freedom Found. for Bicentennial. Mem. A.S.C.A.P. (award 1961, 62), Phi Beta. Methodist. Address: Box 52 Goodwell OK 73939

LIBBEY, FLORENCE ELIZABETH, librarian; b. Augusta, Me., June 8, 1906; d. Benjamin F. and Anne (Young) Libbey; A.B., Colby Coll., 1929; B.S., Columbia, 1930, M.S., 1966; postgrad. Alliance Francaise, Paris, France, 1968. Dir. Bur. of Library Extension State Library, Augusta, Me., 1930-42; librarian Farmington State Tchrs. Coll., Me., 1942-45; reference librarian Colby Coll., Waterville, Me., 1945-47, instr. bibliography, 1947-49, acting librarian, 1951-54, asst. librarian, 1947-56, asst. prof., 1949-56, asso. librarian, 1956-71, emeritus, 1971—, asso. prof., 1956-71, emeritus, 1971—; curator Colbiana Collection, 1968-71; instr. library sci. workshop, summers 1961-65; asst. dir., sch. librarians workshop U. Me., summer 1950. Library cons., vol. librarian Kennebec Valley Mental Health Center, 1973—. Recipient Brick award Colby Alumni, 1970. Mem. Am., Me. (pres. 1933-35), New Eng. (sec. 1958-59) library assns., Me. Sch. Library Assn., New Eng. Coll. Librarians, Colby Library Assos. (sec. 1951-54), Am. Assn. U. Women, Columbia Sch. of Library Service Alumni Assn., Colby Coll. Alumni Assn., Alpha Delta Pi, Delta Kappa Gamma. Editor: Bureau of Library Extension, in Bull. Me. State Library, 1930-42, Bull. Me. Library Assn., 1950-53. Contbr. articles to profl. jours. Methodist. Home: 45 Winter St Waterville ME 04901

LIBERLES, LUCILLE, physician; b. Balt., Aug. 24, 1894; d. Ned and Rosa (Rosenfeld) Liberles; A.B., Goucher Coll., 1915; M.D., John Hopkins, 1919. Intern Bellevue Hosp., N.Y.C., 1919-20; practice medicine specializing in pediatrics, Balt., 1920—; mem. staff Johns Hopkins Hosp., 1920—, Sinai Hosp., 1920—; hon. pediatrician U. Md. Med. Sch., 1970—. Diplomate Am. Bd. Pediatrics. Club: Johns Hopkins. Home: 3507 N Charles St Baltimore MD 21218 Office: 1724 Eutaw Pl Baltimore MD 21217

LIBERMAN, BARBARA LEE (MRS. E. DANIEL LIBERMAN), pianist; b. St. Louis, Aug. 9, 1936; d. Edward Leonard and Annette (Miller) Rudman; student Northwestern U., 1954-55, Roosevelt U., 1955-56; B.S., Juilliard Sch., 1959; M.Music, Washington U., St. Louis, 1961; m. (Earl) Daniel Liberman, Apr. 15, 1962; children—Claude Alexander, Gabriel Abraham. Tchr., St. Louis, 1959-65, Webster Coll., Webster Grove, Mo., 1965-67; leader, dir. Bel Canto Ensemble mini-operas, 1968—; pianist St. Louis Symphony, 1971; free lance accompanist, 1959—; mem. faculty Conservatory St. Louis Inst. Music, 1974—. Mem. Ladies Friday Mus. Club St. Louis (pres. 1969—). Through more than 400 performances of Bel Canto Ensemble for children, opera and culture have been encouraged in less rigid and more meaningful presentations. Home: #7 Warson Terrace St Louis MO 63124 Office: Powell Symphony Hall 718 N Grand Blvd St Louis MO 63103

LICHTENBERG, BETTY PLUNKETT (MRS. DONOVAN ROYCE LICHTENBERG), educator; b. Lexington, Ky., Oct. 16, 1938; d. Hugh Russell and Grace Beatrice (Littleton) Kiser; B.A., U. Ky., 1960, M.A., 1963; Ph.D., U. Ill., 1967; m. Donovan Royce Lichtenberg, Mar. 18, 1972; 1 dau., Julie Plunkett. Math. tchr. Lexington, Ky., 1960-64; instr. U. Ill., Urbana, 1966-67; asst. prof. math. edn. U. Fla., Gainesville, 1967-71; asso. prof. math. edn. U. South Fla., Tampa, 1971—; also cons. math. edn. Mem. Nat., Fla. councils tchrs. maths., Am. Soc. Curriculum, Kappa Delta Pi, Pi Mu Epsilon. Contbr. articles math. edn. Asso. editor Mathematics Student Jour., 1972—. Home: 521 Rolling View Dr Temple Terrace FL 33617

LICHTENSTADTER, ILSE, educator; b. Hamburg, Germany; d. Jacob and Flora (Levi) Lichtenstadter; Ph.D., U. Frankfurt am Main (Germany), 1931; D.Phil., U. Oxford (Eng.), 1937. Came to U.S., 1938, naturalized, 1944. Librarian, Queen's Coll., Cambridge, Eng., 1933-35; specialist in Oriental langs. Oxford U. Press. 1935-38; cataloguer library Jewish Theol. Sem., N.Y.C., 1938-45; asst. prof. Arabic and Islamic culture The Asia Inst., N.Y.C., 1942, prof., 1946-52; lectr. Islamic culture N.Y. U., 1952-60, Rutgers U., 1959-60; lectr. on Arabic, Harvard, 1960-74, emeritus, 1974. Cons. Arabic, The Bollingen Found., 1954—. Notgemeinschaft der Deutschen Wissenschaft fellow, 1932-33; Social Sci. Research Council fellow, 1950, 55; Fulbright Travel grantee, 1963. Mem. Am. Oriental Soc. Clubs: N.Y. Oriental; Harvard Faculty (life mem.). Author: Women in the Aiyam al-'Arab, 1935; Islam and the Modern Age, 1958; Introduction to Classical Arabic Literature, 1974. Gen. editor: Library of Classical Arabic Literature: Vol. 1 Ibn Tufayl's Hayy Ibn Yaqzan, 1972. Contbr. articles to profl. jours. Home: 14 Concord Av Cambridge MA 02138

LICHTENSTEIN, GRACE ROSENTHAL, journalist; b. Bklyn., Dec. 25, 1941; d. Alvin and Rose (Smith) Rosenthal; A.B., Bklyn. Coll., 1962. Advt. copywriter Cambridge U. Press, N.Y.C., 1962-64, R.R. Bowker Co., N.Y.C., 1964-66; advt. copywriter N.Y. Times, N.Y.C., 1966-67, radio news scriptwriter, 1967-69, reporter, 1970—. Author: A Long Way, Baby, 1974. Contbr. articles to various mags., including N.Y. Times mag., Esquire, Seventeen, N.Y. mag., Cosmopolitan, Sat. Rev. Home: 16 W 74th St New York City NY 10023 Office: NY Times 229 W 43d St New York City NY 10036

LIDA, DENAH LEVY (MRS. RAIMUNDO LIDA), educator; b. N.Y.C., Sept. 9, 1923; d. Haim David and Ephthimia (Semos) Levy; B.A., Hunter Coll., 1943; M.A., Columbia, 1944; Ph.D., U. Nacional Autonoma de Mexico, 1952; m. Raimundo Lida, Dec. 23, 1955. Asst. prof. Spanish Smith Coll., Northampton, Mass., 1945-53, Sweet Briar (Va.) Coll., 1954-55; prof. Spanish, Brandeis U., Waltham, Mass., 1955—. Mem. Modern Lang. Assn. Am., Renaissance Soc. Am., Internat. Assn. Hispanists. Contbr. articles to various jours. Home: 19 Chauncy St Cambridge MA 02138 Office: Brandeis U Waltham MA 02154

LIDDLE, NANCY HYATT (MRS. CHARLES M. LIDDLE, 3D), art gallery ofcl.; b. Martinsville, Ind., Aug. 27, 1931; d. Ralph Romeo and Gladys (Cain) Hyatt; A.B., Ind. U., 1953; m. Charles M. Liddle, 3d, Sept. 17, 1955; children—Christopher, Matthew, Sara. Dir. 327 Gallery, Albany, N.Y., 1959-64; critic and art feature writer Knickerbocker News, Albany, 1965-67; asst. dir. Univ. Art Gallery, State U. N.Y. at Albany, 1967—. Bd. dirs. Jr. League of Albany, 1958-60, Planned Parenthood Assn. Albany, 1963-66, Albany Inst. History and Art, 1970—. Mem. Gallery Assn. N.Y. State (dir. 1969-71). Home: 34 Willet St Albany NY 12210 Office: Art Gallery State U NY at Albany 1400 Washington Av Albany NY 12222

LIDE, NEOMA JEWELL LAWHON (MRS. MARTIN JAMES LIDE, JR.), poet; b. Levelland, Tex., Apr. 1, 1926; d. Charles Samuel and Juel (Yeager) Lawhon; Secretarial certificate Draughon's Bus. Coll., 1943; student U. Tex., 1944-46; R.N., Jefferson-Hillman Sch. Nursing, 1950; m. Martin James Lide, Jr., Nov. 12, 1950; children—Martin James, III, Brooks Nathaniel, Gardner Lawhon. Writer column Baldwin Times, Bay Minette, Ala., 1964-68, Shades Valley Sun newspapers, Birmingham, Ala., 1974—; nurse Univ. Hosp., 1970, Bapt. Med. Center, 1970; charge nurse coronary intensive care unit South Highland Infirmary, 1970-72; asst. archtl. firm Martin J. Lide, Birmingham, 1972—. Mem. def. adv. com. Women in Services, for Ala., 1961-63; coordinator women's activities Nat. Vets. Day, Birmingham, 1961-70; mem. exec. com., 1968-70; poetry chmn. Women's Com. of 100 for Birmingham, 1974-75. Mem. Gorgas bd. U. Ala., Tuscaloosa, 1959. Recipient citation Merit, Muscular Dystrophy Assn. Am., 1961. Club: The Club (Birmingham). Author: Instead of Sunset, 1973. Home: 3536 Brookwood Rd Birmingham AL 35223 Office: 14 Office Park Circle Birmingham AL 35223

LIDIA, KATHLEEN VARUE (MRS. ARCH DEAN LIDIA), chem. co. exec.; b. Gordon, Tex., Jan. 4, 1899; d. Joe King and Sallie Elizabeth (Carlock) Orndorff; diploma, certificate North Tex. State Normal Coll., 1922; postgrad. U. Tex., 1923-24; m. Arch Dean Lidia, June 15, 1927 (dec. July 1951); 1 dau., Billie Jo (Mrs. William Gene Spoonts. Tchr., prin. Brazos-Gordon High Sch., Brazos and Gordon, Tex., 1918-20, 25-27; sec.-treas. State Chem. Co. hdqrs. Amarillo, Tex., 1951—, v.p., 1973—, also co-owner, dir., 1943—. Bd. dirs. A.R.C., 3 years. Named Boss of the Year Am. Bus. Women's Assn., 1969. Mem. Am. Assn. U. Women, Amarillo Study Club (pres. 1938-39), Athenaeum Study Club, Daus. of the Nile (charter), Friends of the Library (life). Clubs: Amarillo Country, Amarillo, Knife and Fork, Amarillo Garden (life), L'Aiguille. Methodist. Home: 2201 Travis St Amarillo TX 79109 Office: 100 Houston St Amarillo TX

LIDZ, RUTH WILMANNS, psychiatrist; b. Heidelberg, Germany, June 18, 1910; d. Carlos and Elisabeth (Meyer) Wilmanns; student U. Heidelberg, 1929, 31, U. Munich (Germany), 1929-30; M.D., U. Basel (Switzerland), 1935; m. Theodore Lidz, Nov. 23, 1939; children—Victor Meyer, Charles Wilmanns, Jerome Shedlin. Came to U.S., 1937, naturalized, 1940. Intern Guraba Hosp., Istanbul, Turkey, 1935-36; research asst., resident psychiatry Phipps Clinic, Johns Hopkins Hosp., 1937-39; physician Springfield State Hosp., Sykesville, Md., 1939-40; practice medicine specializing in psychiatry and psychoanalysis, Balt., 1945-51, New Haven, 1951-65; asst. psychiatrist Johns Hopkins Hosp., 1940-43, chief EEG lab., 1943-45, psychiatrist, 1950-51; instr. Johns Hopkins Med. Sch., 1940-45, asst. prof., 1945-51; psychiatrist Eastern Health Dist. Well Baby Clinic, Balt., 1942-45; mem. faculty Balt.-Wash. Psychoanalytic Inst., 1949-51; asso. clin. prof. psychiatry Yale, 1966-72, clin. prof., 1972—. Vis. prof. U. Oslo, 1970, Baylor U., 1970. Active Planned Parenthood Assn. Md., Balt., 1949-51. Fellow Am. Psychiat. Assn. (life); mem. Am. Psychoanalytic Assn., Group Advancement Psychiatry, Western New Eng. Psychoanalytic Assn. (founding mem.), Conn. Med. Soc. Contbr. articles to profl. jours. Home: 60 Orchard Rd Woodbridge CT 06525 Office: 333 Cedar St New Haven CT 06510

LIEB, BARBARA ANN, journalist; b. N.Y.C., Feb. 26, 1951; d. Robert Pelham and Ina Lee (Eichner) Lieb; B.A. (Theta Sigma Phi scholar), Cal. State U., Northridge, 1972. News asst. KGIL Radio, San Fernando, Cal., 1971-73; editorial asst. Carte Blanche mag., Los Angeles, 1973—. Named Outstanding News Editor, KEDC Radio, 1972. Mem. Women in Communications, Sigma Delta Chi. Home: 4428 Wortser Av North Hollywood CA 91604 Office: 3460 Wilshire Blvd Los Angeles CA 90010

LIEBELT, ANNABEL GLOCKLER (MRS. ROBERT ARTHUR LIEBELT), biologist, educator; b. Washington, June 27, 1926; d. Otto Gottlieb and Henley Florentina (Hallberg) Glockler; B.A., Western Md. Coll., Westminster, 1948; M.S., U. Ill., Chgo., 1955; Ph.D., Baylor U., 1960; m. Robert Arthur Liebelt, June 26, 1954; children—Ralph Arthur, Laurie Ann, Erica Lynn, Nancy Louise. Biologist pathology sect. Nat. Cancer Inst., Bethesda, Md., 1949-52; research and teaching asst. dept. anatomy U. Ill. Coll. Medicine, Chgo., 1952-54; research and teaching asst. dept. anatomy Baylor Coll. Medicine, 1954-58, instr. anatomy, 1958-62, asst. prof., 1962-67, asso. prof., 1967-71; asso. prof. cell and molecular biology Med. Coll. Ga., Augusta, 1971-74; prof. anatomy Northwestern Ohio U. Coll. Medicine, 1974—. Exec. dir. Kirschbaum Meml. Lab. Inbred Mice, 1958—. Bd. dirs. Augusta Radiation Center. Invited speaker 20th Ann. Symposium in Fundamental Cancer Research, M.D. Anderson Hosp. and Tumor Inst., 1966. Mem. Assn. Women in Sci., Am., Pan Am., So. assns. anatomists, So. Anatomists, Am. Assn. for Cancer Research, Am. Assn. Lab. Animal Care (S.E. sect.), Ga. Acad. Sci., S.E., S.W. cancer research assns., Sigma Xi. Episcopalian. Home: 1972 Pineview Dr Kent OH 44240

LIEBELT, LINDA ELIZABETH GEORGE (MRS. WOLFGANG LIEBELT), mus. ofcl.; b. San Francisco, Mar. 23, 1947; d. George Rodney and Eleanor Evangeline (Peppin) George; B.A. in Art History, U. Cal. at Berkeley, 1969; M.A. in Art History, U. Cal. at Santa Barbara, 1971; m. Wolfgang Liebelt, July 28, 1973. Health claims adjustor Met. Life Ins. Co., San Francisco, 1969; dir. Triton Mus. Art, Santa Clara, Cal., 1971—. Bd. dirs. Council Arts, San Jose, 1972-73. Mem. Am. Assn. U. Women, Am. Assn. Museums, Coll. Art Assn. Am., Steinhart Aquaium Soc., Cal. Alumnae Assn. Office: 1505 Warburton Av Santa Clara CA 95050

LIEBERMAN, CANDACE FRIEDMAN (MRS. MARK E. LIEBERMAN), editor; b. Bklyn., Mar. 18, 1950; d. Theodore and Sydell Elaine (Sackstein) Friedman; B.S., Boston U., 1970; m. Mark E. Lieberman, June 25, 1970. Copywriter, Denhard & Steward, Inc., advt., N.Y.C., 1970; press sec. State Senator Donald M. Halperin, N.Y.C., 1970-71; copywriter Auerbach Advt., Inc., N.Y.C., 1971-73; editor N.Am. Precis Syndicate, pub. relations, N.Y.C., 1973—. Mem. Kensington-Ditmas Community Council, 1973—. Founder Bklyn. Democratic Coalition, 1968. Asso. mem. Pub. Relations Soc. Am. Home: 684 E 19th St Brooklyn NY 11230 Office: 220 W 42d St New York City NY 10036

LIEBERMAN, INGA ROSENBERG (MRS. ROBERT WILLIAM LIEBERMAN), speech therapist; b. Czechoslovakia, Apr. 4, 1947; d. Albert and Elizabeth (Schicktanz) Rosenberg; B.A., U. Toronto, 1968, Diploma Speech Pathology and Audiology, 1970; m. Robert William Lieberman, Aug. 31, 1972. Speech therapist Toronto (Ont., Can.) Rehab. Centre, 1970-71, Our Lady of Mercy Hosp., Toronto, 1971-72, St. Joseph's Hosp., Toronto, 1971—. Mem. Ont. Speech and Hearing Assn. Home: 111 Raglan Av Apt 106 Toronto 10 ON Canada Office: 30 The Queensway Toronto 3 ON Canada

LIEBERMAN, JANET ELAINE RUBENSOHN (MRS. JERROLD LIEBERMAN), coll. dean; b. N.Y.C., Oct. 2, 1921; d. Samuel and Ida A. (Schubert) Rubensohn; B.A., Barnard Coll., 1943; M.A., Coll. City N.Y., 1956; Ph.D., N.Y. U., 1965; m. Jerrold Lieberman, June 30, 1957; children—Gary Andrew Chase, Randolph Hugh Chase. Psychologist, Mt. Sinai Hosp., N.Y.C., 1953-56; psychologist N.Y.C. Bd. Edn., 1957-61; lectr., tchr. Dalton Sch., Coll. City N.Y., N.Y. U., 1961-65; asst. prof. Hunter Coll., 1965-70; asso. prof., asst. dean faculty La Guardia Coll., Long Island City, N.Y., 1971—. Mem. Pi Lambda Theta, Kappa Delta Phi. Contbr. articles to profl. jours. Home: 190 E 72d St New York City NY 10021 Office: 31-10 Thomson Av Long Island City NY 11101

LIEBERMAN, JULIA, educator; b. Wilkes-Barre, Pa., Nov. 2, 1908; d. Max and Matilda (Williams) Lieberman; B.S., East Stroudsburg State Coll., 1930. Tchr. health, phys. edn. Hanover Twp. Sch. Dist., 1930-66; program coordinator, staff supr., camp adminstr. Jewish Community Center, Wilkes-Barre, 1932—. First aid instr. A.R.C., 1942-66. Mem. Nat. Jewish Welfare Bd. Mem. Assn. Jewish Center Workers (regional sec., 25 Year Spl. plaque 1963), Nat. Ret. Tchrs. Assn. (life), Nat. Council Jewish Women, Hadassah. Mem. B'nai B'rith Women. Club: Womens Service (Jewish Community Center). Home: 34 S Main St Wilkes-Barre PA 18701 Office: 60 S River St Wilkes-Barre PA 18701

LIEBERMAN, ROSE, immunologist; b. N.Y.C.; d. Jacob and Sarah (Baum) Lieberman; B.S., Columbia, 1935, M.A., 1937. Med. bacteriologist Christ Hosp., Jersey City, 1937-42; Southbury Tng. Sch. and Yale Sch. Medicine, New Haven, 1942-49; med. microbiologist VA, Dayton, O., 1949-51, Ft. Detrick, Frederick, Md., 1951-52; with NIH, Bethesda, Md., 1952—, research immunologist, 1960—. Recipient Yale Fluid Research award, 1947, Meritorious award NIH, 1953. Mem. Am. Assn. Immunologists, Research Soc. Am., Am. Microbiology Soc. Contbr. articles to profl. jours. Home: 3630 Gleneagles Dr Silver Spring MD 20966 Office: NIH Bethesda MD 20014

LIEBHABER, HENIA FISCHER (MRS. MARC LIEBHABER), physician; b. Swir, Poland, Feb. 20, 1923; d. Irving and Basia (Benes) Fischer; M.D. cum laude, Ludwig Maximilians U., Munich, Germany, 1950; m. Marc Liebhaber, July 8, 1945; children—Paul, Sharon, Howard. Came to U.S., 1950, naturalized, 1957. Intern Swedish Hosp., Mpls., 1954-55; resident internal medicine Asbury Meth. Hosp., Mpls., 1956-57; sr. staff physician Anoka State Hosp., 1957—. Recipient Outstanding Citizens award Mpls. Council of Americanization, 1959. Mem. Hennepin County Med. Soc., Minn. State Med. Assn. Jewish religion (mem. women's league 1965—). Home: 4340 Cedarwood Rd Minneapolis MN 55416 Office: Anoka State Hospital Anoka MN 55303

LIEBHAUSER, ROSELLA ANN, librarian; b. Menasha, Wis., Feb. 5, 1913; d. Joseph Anton and Anne Marie (Heidger) Liebhauser; grad. Holy Ghost Acad.; student Inst. on Hosp. Librarianship, 1960-62. Office clk. St. Mary's Hosp., Watertown, Wis., 1935-38; office clk., dental asst. to Dr. Stasney, Menasha, Wis., 1938-42; office clk., bookkeeper Central Paper Co., Menasha, 1942-45; office clk. Mercy Med. Center, Oshkosh, Wis., 1945; librarian Sch. Nursing Library, Mercy Med. Center, Oshkosh, 1945—. Instr. religion to retarded children Catholic schs. Oshkosh area, 1960—. Mem. Winnebago County Assn. Retarded Children (religion chmn. 1965-70, bronze plaque award 1970), Mercy Mission Club (founder 1945, pres. 1945—). Office: School of Nursing Library 660 Oak St Oshkosh WI 54901

LIEBOLD, MARY JANE, real estate and ins. agy. exec.; b. Chgo., June 5, 1925; d. Oscar Paul and Mary Albina (Hancock) Larson; student St. Agnes Acad., 1938-42; m. William E. Liebold, Feb. 11, 1955 (dec.). Sec.-treas. McClain-Matthews Agy., Inc., Indpls., 1957—. Mem. Ind. Real Estate Commn., 1973—, mem. Ind. Real Estate Edn. Adv. Council. Past pres. Indpls. chpt. Womens Council Indpls. Bd. Realtors; past corporate sec. Indpls. Bd. Realtors. Mem. Ind. Real Estate Assn. (dir.), Nat. Assn. Realtors (chmn. com. Indpls. chpt. Womens Council, pres. 1974), Womens Council Realtors. Club: Altrusa (corr. sec., pres. 1973-74). Home: 1751 B Pemberton Lane Indianapolis IN 46220 Office: 1901 Broad Ripple Av Indianapolis IN 46220

LIEBOWITZ, JANET GOLDMUNTZ (MRS. ROBERT LIEBOWITZ), artist; b. N.Y.C., June 23, 1920; d. Joseph and Sadye (Rosenbloom) Goldmuntz; student Elmira Coll., 1937-40, Art Students League, 1960-65; m. Robert Liebowitz, June 23, 1940; 1 son, Edward. One man shows as Westerly Gallery (N.Y.C.), Elmira Coll. (N.Y.), Flair Gallery (Cin.), Silvermine Guild of Artists, Conn.; exhibited in group shows at Hartford Atheneum, Silvermine Guild of Artists, City of N.J. Mus., Nat. Acad., N.Y.C., Mus. Arts and Scis., Bridgeport, Conn., and others; represented in permanent collections at Elmira Coll., Publix Corp., Bocour Collection, Munson-Williams-Proctor Inst., Butler Inst. Am. Art, Albrecht Gallery, Griffiths Art Center of St. Lawrence U., State U. N.Y. at Pottsdam, also pvt. collections; mem. Phoenix Gallery, N.Y.C. Mem. Nat. Assn. Women Artists, Silvermine Guild of Artists, Artists Equity Assn. N.Y. Home: 91 Central Park W New York City NY 10023 Office: 27 E 22d St New York City NY 10010

LIEF, NINA LINCOLN RAYEVSKY (MRS. VICTOR F. LIEF), physician; b. Liberty, N.Y., Feb. 12, 1907; d. Charles and Lucy (Kalina) Rayevsky; B.A., Barnard Coll., 1927; M.D., Bellevue and Univ. Med. Sch., 1931; m. Victor F. Lief, May 31, 1932; 1 dau., Carlotta (Mrs. David I. Schuster). Intern Bellevue Hosp., N.Y.C., 1931-32, resident pediatrics, 1932-33; resident psychiatry Tulane U., New Orleans, 1957-60; practice medicine specializing in pediatrics, 1933-57, in child psychiatry, 1957—; mem. staff Bellevue Hosp., 1933-57, St Joseph's Hosp., Far Rockaway, N.Y., 1935-57, Charity Hosp., New Orleans, 1957-63; dir. Childrens House at S.E. La. State Hosp., 1960-63; psychiatrist Child Devel. Center, 1963-72; asst. prof. psychiatry Tulane U., 1960-63; dir. child psychiatry N.Y. Sch. Psychiatry, 1963-67; asso. prof. child and community psychiatry N.Y. Med. Coll., 1967—; asso. attending Met. Hosp., N.Y.C., 1967—, Flower Fifth Av. Hosp., N.Y.C., 1967—; dir. Early Childhood Devel. Center, 1974—. Mem. Council Child Psychiatry, N.Y.C. Fellow Am. Acad. Pediatrics, Am. Psychiat. Assn., Am. Acad. Child Psychiatry; mem. A.M.A., Am. Acad. Psychoanalysis, Am. Assn. Orthopsychiatry. Asso. editor: (with H.I. and V.F. Lief) Psychological Basis of Medical Practice, 1963. Asso. editor Internat. Jour. Drug Addiction, 1965—. Home: 111 Old Kingdom Rd Wilton CT 06897 Office: 5 E 102d St New York City NY 10028

LIEGL, SISTER ANNE, coll. adminstr.; b. Bay Shore, Mich., Feb. 3, 1913; d. John B. and Anna (Fuchs) Liegl; B.A., Holy Family Coll., 1959; M.B.A., Notre Dame U., 1966. Joined Franciscan Sisters of Christian Charity, 1929; tchr. elementary sch., Wis., Ohio, Mich., 1932-58; bus. office employee Good Samaritan Hosp., Zanesville, O., 1961-67; admissions office Holy Family Coll., Manitowoc, Wis., 1968-70; bus. officer, treas. Silver Lake Coll., Manitowoc, 1970—. Mem. corp. Silver Lake Coll., Inc., 1973. Address: Silver Lake College Manitowoc WI 54220

LIETMAN, MARGARET CAROLINE, librarian; b. Wilkinsburg, Pa., Oct. 5, 1916; d. Edward Nicholas and Anna Bertha (Orr) Lietman; B.A., Monmouth Coll., 1938; B.S. in L.S., Carnegie Inst. Tech., 1939; postgrad. U. Pitts., 1970. Substitute librarian Mercy Hosp., also Pitts. Acad. Medicine Library, Pitts., 1939; asst. librarian Med. and Dental Library, U. Pitts., 1940-42, cataloger Sch. Social Work, 1942-44, asst. to acquisitions librarian Univ. Library, 1953-54; librarian Mercy Hosp., Pitts., 1944-48; asst. cataloguer, librarian East Carolina Coll., Greenville, N.C., 1950-52; librarian Sch. Nursing Columbia div. Forbes Hosp. System, Pitts., 1955—. Mem. Am., Med. (past treas. Pitts. region), Pa. library assns., Nat. League for Nursing, Tri-State Assn. Coll. and Research Libraries. Republican. Presbyn. Home: 717 Wallace Av Pittsburgh PA 15221 Office: Penn Av and West St Pittsburgh PA 15221

LIETWILER, HELENA CATHERINE KEEHNE (MRS. JOHN MARION LIETWILER), educator; b. Pomeroy, O., Oct. 8; d. Charles Henry and Blanche (Enzenauer) Keehne; A.B., Western Coll. for Women, 1928; M.A., George Washington U., 1956, advanced profl. certificate, 1965, Ed.D., 1967; m. John Marion Lietwiler, June 3, 1932; children—Charles John, Christian Willard. Tchr. elementary, secondary sch., Pomeroy, 1928-32; tchr. elementary sch., prin., Guam, Mariannas Islands, 1948-50; tchr. elementary sch., Alexandria, Va., 1954-56, tchr. remedial reading, 1956-58; secondary sch. reading specialist, spl. reading tchr., resource tchr. in reading Montgomery County (Md.) Pub. Schs., 1958-74, now ret. Lectr. edn. George Washington U., 1958-59, asst. professorial lectr. in edn., 1966—. Mem. Internat. Reading Assn., N.E.A., Coll. Reading Assn., Nat. Soc. for Study Edn., Md. State Tchrs. Assn., Am. Assn. U. Women, Montgomery County Edn. Assn., Greater Washington Intermediate Reading Council, Pi Lambda Theta. Home: 5907 Aberdeen Rd Bethesda MD 20034

LIFQUIST, ROSALIND CARIBELLE, food economist, ret. govt. ofcl.; b. Henning, Minn., June 5, 1903; d. John D. and Frances Myrtle (Wilcox) Lifquist; B.S. with high distinction (Caleb Dorr scholar 1935), U. Minn., 1935, M.S., 1937; m. Milton H. Simon, May 25, 1927 (dec.). Tchr. home econs. pub. schs., Algoma, Gillette, and Shawano, Wis., 1921-26; dietetics intern U. Minn. Hosp., 1926, U. Wash., 1941; dietitian City Hosp., Lock Haven, Pa., 1926-33; instr. foods U. Minn., St. Paul, 1935-37; asst. prof. foods and nutrition Ia. State Coll., Ames, 1937-41; food economist Bur. Human Nutrition and Home Econs., U.S. Dept. Agr., Washington, 1946-55, Agrl. Marketing Service, also Econ. Research Service, 1955-73. Served from lt. (j.g.) to lt. comdr. WAVES, 1942-46. Recipient certificate of merit U.S. Dept. Agr., 1961; Distinguished Service award U. Wis., 1973. Mem. Am. Home Econs. Assn. (nat. chmn. public relations com. 1958-61), Omicron Nu, Pi Lambda Theta, Phi Upsilon Omicron. Author several govt. publs. on food, consumer research, also numerous articles. Home: 1727 Massachusetts Av NW Washington DC 20036

LIFSON, BETTY ANN GLASSER, social worker; b. Cambridge, Mass., Oct. 29, 1920; d. Myer and Rose (Cohen) Sugarman; B.A., U. Pa., 1941; M.S., Simmons Coll., 1947; children—Rona-Lee, Joyce Enid. Research psychiat. social worker demonstration and research projects Mass. Mental Health Center, Nat. Inst. Mental Health, Boston, 1958-60, 60-64; research social worker in charge orgn. of adolescent unit Boston State Hosp., 1963-66, chmn. exec. com. for VISTAS, 1968; supr., case aide coll. student vols. Phillips Brooks House, mental hosps. com. Harvard, 1963-64; supr. coll. student group work Tufts and Boston Coll., 1965-66; dir. social service Dept. Mental Health, Mass., 1968-69; now coordinator aftercare services, region VI Dept. Mental Health Mass., Boston; dir. Social Rehab. Center Rockland County Mental Health Center, 1971-73; instr. dept. psychiatry Tufts U. Sch. Medicine, 1968. Vice pres. Orgn. for Rehab. Through Tng., 1950; pres. suburban region Am. Jewish Congress, 1963. Served with WAVES, 1942-45. Recipient Maida H. Solomon award Simmons Coll. Sch. Social Work Alumni, 1965, 1st Ogilby award Simmons Coll., 1971. Mem. Nat. Assn. Social Workers, Simmons Coll. Alumnae Assn. (co-chmn. awards com. 1966), Nat. Alumnae Assn. U. Pa. (bd. dirs. 1965-66). Author: (with others) The Prevention of Hospitalization, 1963, Adolescents in a Mental Hospital, 1968. Contbr. articles to profl. jours. Home: 18 Nancy Rd Chestnut Hill MA 02167

LIGGETT, FRANCES JEAN, retirement community exec.; b. Mishawaka, Ind., Oct. 9, 1946; d. Cloyd Eugene and Lois Roberta (Hardy) Liggett; B.A. with honors, Mich. State U., 1968. Traffic mgr. WYYY Radio, Kalamazoo, 1968-69; reporter Three Rivers (Mich.) Comml. Newspaper, 1969-70; service rep. Mountain Bell Telephone, Phoenix, 1970-71; editor Sun City (Ariz.) Citizen, 1971-73; community newspaper editor Rossmoor Leisure World, Mesa, Ariz., 1973—. Mem. Ariz. Press Women, Women in Communications, Theta Sigma Phi. Home: 615 S Hardy Tempe AZ 85281 Office: 908 S Power Rd Mesa AZ 85206

LIGHT, LOUISE ELIZABETH (MRS. MAX SILVER), physician; b. N.Y.C., Oct. 8, 1908; d. Noum and Annie (Pomerantz) Light; D.O., Coll. Osteo. Physicians and Surgeons, 1938; M.D., Cal. Coll. Medicine, 1962; m. Max Silver, Oct. 14, 1942; 1 son, Gerald Goldstein. Intern Los Angeles County Gen. Hosp., 1938-39; practice medicine, Los Angeles, 1939—; mem. staff Midway Hosp., Los Angeles, So. Cal. Meml. Hosp., Culver City; asso. prof. clin. pediatrics Coll. Osteo. Physicians and Surgeons, Los Angeles, 1942-62, Cal. Coll. Medicine, Los Angeles, 1962-63; tng. psychiatry U. Cal. at Los Angeles, 1955-61; tchr., mem. staff Los Angeles Suicide Prevention Center, 1963-66; staff pediatric clinics Los Angeles Bd. Edn., 1939-51; staff Benjamin Rush Psychiat. Clinic, Los Angeles, 1966-67, West Central Mental Health Center, Los Angeles, 1970—. Capt. City Coll. unit Women's Ambulance Def. Corps, 1941-45. Mem. World, Am. psychiat. assns., Am., Cal., Los Angeles County med. assns., Internat. Assn. for Prevention of Suicide, So. Cal. Psychiat. Soc., Assn. for Social and Community Psychiatry (sec. 1968-70). Home: 983 Lindenwood Lane Los Angeles CA 90049 Office: 1026 S Robertson Blvd Los Angeles CA 90035

LIGHT, PRISCILLA MILLER (MRS. WARREN CHARLES LIGHT), coll. adminstr.; b. Malden, Mass., Jan. 13, 1921; d. Willard A. and Madeleine F. (Jordan) Miller; A.B. cum laude, Tufts U., 1949; M.Ed., U. Va., 1963; m. Warren Charles Light, Aug. 24, 1946; children—Donna J., Nancy L. (Mrs. William T. Snypes, Jr.), Barbara J. Tchr., Lynchburg (Va.) Pub. Schs., 1963-65; dir. financial aid and career planning Randolph-Macon Woman's Coll., Lynchburg, 1965—. Pres., Lynchburg chpt. Am. Field Service, 1969-70; mem. adv. council Va. Coll. Work Study Program, 1970—; mem. ad hoc gov.'s com. Coll. Scholarship Service, 1971-73. Bd. dirs. Va. Edn. Loan Authority. Served with WAVES, 1943-45. Recipient Z Soc. award U. Va., 1963. Mem. League Women Voters, Am. Personnel and Guidance Assn., Nat., So. (pres. 1974-75), Va. (life, pres. 1970-72) assns. student financial aid adminstrs., Am. Assn. U. Women, So. Coll. Placement Assn., Nat. Vocational Guidance Assn., Kappa Delta Pi, Delta Kappa Gamma (Outstanding Educator Am. 1972). Presbyn. (youth adviser 1966-71). Home: 1418 Robin Hood Pl Lynchburg VA 24503

LIGHTFOOT, EVELYN LAMPREY LYONS (MRS. ROBERT MITCHELL LIGHTFOOT, JR.), librarian; b. Haverhill, Mass., May 25, 1910; d. Bartlett Leslie and Marjorie Marietta (Lamprey) Lyons; B.A., W.Va. Wesleyan Coll., 1931; postgrad. U. Va., 1931-32, Emmanuel Coll., 1933-34, Marywood Coll., 1938-39; B.S. in L.S., Syracuse U., 1944; m. Robert Mitchell Lightfoot, Jr., Dec. 23, 1935; children—Robert Mitchell III, James Ellison. Asst. librarian Montgomery County (Ala.) Library, 1952-55; reference librarian Bradley U., Peoria, Ill., 1955—, head reference dept., 1970—. Mem. Ala., Ill., Ill. Valley library assns., Chi Omega. Home: 1109 N Maplewood Av Peoria IL 61606 Office: Cullom-Davis Library Bradley U Peoria IL 61606

LIKINS, MARJORIE DOROTHEA HARJES, clergywoman; b. Grinnell, Ia., Apr. 18, 1924; d. Herman Wendt and Emma Christine (Bohstedt) Harjes; B.A., Cornell Coll., 1945; B.D., Union Theol. Sem., 1949; Ph.D., Columbia, 1963; m. Robert C. Likins, July 7, 1944 (div. May 1954). Counsellor to Protestant students Hunter Coll., N.Y.C., 1949-51; instr. Masters Sch., Dobbs Ferry, N.Y., 1951-53; ordained to ministry United Ch. Christ, 1957; dir. youth ministry Riverside Ch., N.Y.C., 1949-55; minister edn. Ch. of the Chimes, Van Nuys, Cal., 1955-60; asso. conf. minister So. Cal. Conf. United Ch., Pasadena, 1960-72. Vis. prof. edn. Rochester Center for Theol. Studies, 1972-73; asso. prof. ch. and ministry Pitts. Theol. Sem., 1973—. Mem. corporate bd. Homeland Ministries United Ch., 1971, mem. nat. task force on status of women in ch. and society, 1971-75; mem. exec. com. United Ministries in Higher Edn. So. Cal., 1960-72; mem. corporate bd. U. Religious Conf., U. Cal. at Los Angeles, 1960-72. Mem. Council Ch. Edn. Personnel, Ch. Educators Assn. West Coast. Home: 616 N Highland Av Pittsburgh PA 15206

LILJESTRAND, BETTY HORNOR (MRS. PAUL HOWARD LILJESTRAND), biologist, assn. exec.; b. Sioux Rapids, Ia., Jan. 13, 1912; d. Guy Lee and Grace Ovitt (Moore) Hornor; B.A. in pre-med. sci., Grinnell Coll., 1934; M.A. in Cytology, Columbia, 1937; m. Paul Howard Liljestrand, Nov. 28, 1937; children—Robert, Lana (Mrs. David Michael Craigo), Eric, Wendla. Biol. researcher Mass. Marine Biol. Lab., Woods Hole, 1935, 36, 37; instr. biology Barnard Coll., Columbia, 1935-37; pathologist, roentgenologist, asst. for reports Queens Hosp., Honolulu, 1938-41; adminstrv. asst. Leeward Hosp. and Clinic, Aiea, Hawaii, 1959-72; pres. Woman's Auxs., A.M.A., hdqrs. Chgo., 1974-75. Mem. finance com. Pacific Council Girl Scouts U.S., 1968-71; pres. Punahou P.T.A., 1957-59. Bd. dirs. Hawaii Heart Assn., 1959-64, sec., 1964-65. Mem. Hawaii Geog. Soc. (adv. bd. 1963-69, dir. 1970-73), Phi Beta Kappa. Conglist. (chmn. Youth and Young Adult com. 1963-65). Club: Uluniu Women's Swim (pres. 1961-64). Home: 3300 Tantalus Dr Honolulu HI 96822 Office: 981010 Haukapila St Aiea HI 96701

LILLIE, BEATRICE (LADY PEEL), actress; b. Toronto, Ont., Can., May 29, 1894; d. John and Lucie (Shaw) Lillie; ed. St. Agnes Coll., Belleville, Ont.; m. Sir Robert Peel (dec.); 1 son, Robert, 6th Baronet (dec. 1942). Made first profl. stage appearance in 5064 Gerrard, London, Eng., 1915; first N.Y. appearance Times Sq. Theatre in Andre Charlot's Revue, 1924; appeared in many plays, musicals in London, 1914-23, and N.Y.C.; other appearances in N.Y. include several variety performances Palace Theatre, also shows Oh, Please, She's My Baby, This Year of Grace, The Third Little Show, Too True To Be Good (by George Bernard Shaw), Walk a Little Faster, At Home Abroad, The Show Is On, Set to Music, Seven Lively Arts, Inside U.S.A., An Evening with Beatrice Lillie, Beasops Fables, Auntie Mame; motion pictures include Exit Smiling, 1927, The Show of Shows, 1928, Are You There?, 1930, Doctor Rhythm, 1938, On Approval, 1944, Around the World in 80 Days, 1956, Thoroughly Modern Millie, 1967; numerous radio and TV appearances including the original Bob Hope Show, Toast of the Town, An Evening with Beatrice Lillie, others; appeared in Golden Jubilee edit. Ziegfeld Follies, Winter Garden Theatre, N.Y.C., 1957; appeared in High Spirits, Alvin Theater, 1964-65. Entertained Allied troops in Scapa Flo, Eng., Europe, Middle East and North Africa, 1939-45. Decorated by Gen. Charles de Gaulle; recipient African Star, Donaldson award, 1944-45; citation Nat. Conf. Christians and Jews, 1948; cited as Greatest Comedienne of All Time, Am. Fedn. Women's Philanthropies, 1953; Antoinette Perry award, 1952; named U.S.A. Father's Favorite Female, 1953; recipient Sara Siddons award, Chgo., 1953. Author: (autobiography) Every Other Inch a Lady, 1972. Address: 25 East End Av New York City NY 10028

LILLIE, ELLA LAUSMAN (MRS. EVERETT JAMES LILLIE), educator; b. Benton Harbor, Mich., June 25, 1911; d. Gust and Olga A. (Steinke) Lausman; B.A., Western Mich. U., 1933; M.A., U. Mich., 1936, postgrad. (scholar 1938-39), 1938-41, Cal. State Coll., 1957-58, 72; m. Everett James Lillie, Dec. 18, 1949. Tchr., Howell (Mich.) High Sch., 1936-38, Lincoln High Sch., Ferndale, Mich., 1941-43; asst. prof. Western Mich. U., Kalamazoo, 1943-45; prof. math. Glendale (Cal.) Coll., 1946—. Mem. Assn. Classroom Tchrs. (pres.), Cal. (past pres., dir.), Glendale tchrs. assns., Math. Assn. Am., N.E.A. (life), U. Mich. (life), Western Mich. U. alumni assns., Omega Alpha Delta (pres. 1964-66), Alpha Delta Kappa (chpt. pres. 1972-76). Club: U. Mich. Alumnae (past pres.) (Los Angeles). Home: 1142 Paloma Dr Arcadia CA 91006 Office: Glendale Coll Glendale CA 91208

LILLIE, MARGARET ELIZABETH, judge; b. Bennington, Vt., Jan. 2, 1924; d. Daniel Frederic and Winifred Margaret (Flannery) Lillie; B.A., U. Vt., 1944; J.D., Boston Coll. Law, 1953. Admitted to Vt. bar, 1953; practiced in Bennington, 1953—; pros. atty. Bennington County, Vt., 1955-61; judge of probate Dist. Bennington, 1961-74. Trustee St. Joseph Coll., 1972—. Served with Women's Res., U.S. Navy, 1945-47. Mem. Am. (mem. jud. adminstrn. sect. 1965—), Vt., Bennington County bar assns., Vt. Probate Judges Assn. Home: 276 South Stream Rd Bennington VT 05201 Office: PO Box 108 Bennington VT 05201

LILLIE, MILDRED L., justice; b. Ida Grove, Ia., Jan. 25, 1915; d. Ottmar A. and Florence (Martin) Kluckhohn; A.B., U. Cal. at Berkeley, 1935, J.D., 1938; LL.D., Western State U. Coll. Law. m. Cameron L. Lillie, Mar. 18, 1947 (dec. Apr. 1959); m. 2d, A. V. Falcone, Aug. 27, 1966. Admitted to Cal. bar, 1938, pvt. practice law, 1938-42, 46-47; asst. U.S. atty., Los Angeles, 1942-46; judge Municipal Ct., City Los Angeles, 1947-49, Superior Ct. County of Los Angeles, 1949-58; justice Ct. of Appeal, 2d Div., Los Angeles, 1958—; asso. justice pro tem Cal. Supreme Ct., 1960. Mem. Los Angeles Orphanage Guild. Named Time's Woman of Year, 1952. Mem. Am., Fed., Los Angeles bar assns., Conf. Cal. Judges, Am. Judicature Soc., Los Angeles C. of C., Bus. and Profl. Women's Clubs, St. Anne's Guild. Clubs: Women Lawyers, Lawyers Wives, Ebell (Los Angeles); Soroptimist. Home: 2222 Av of Stars Los Angeles CA 90067

LILLY, DORIS, author; b. Los Angeles, Dec. 26, 1926; d. Otto William and Edith Marie (Humphries) Lilly; ed. pub. schs. Columnist N.Y. Post, 1958—; performer numerous TV panel shows, N.Y., Cal., other states. Author: How to Marry a Millionaire, 1951; How to Make Love in Five Languages, 1964; Those Fabulous Greeks: Onassis, Niarchos and Livanos, 1970. Address: 301 E 62nd St New York City NY 10021

LILLY, ELIZABETH ANN (MRS. JOHN RICHARD LILLY), physician; b. Gettysburg, Pa., Mar. 25, 1936; d. Donald Washington and Mary Ruth (Haverstick) Brown; A.B., Gettysburg Coll., 1958; M.D., Temple U., 1962; m. John Richard Lilly, June 15, 1958; children—John Richard, Donald Wellington. Intern Nazareth Hosp., Phila., 1962-63; practice medicine, Indian Head, Md., 1964-66; resident child psychiatry Univ. Hosp. Psychiat. Inst., Balt., 1966-70; practice medicine specializing in child psychiatry, Grofton, Md., 1970-72, Hyattsville, Md., 1972—; staff physician Levindale Nursing Home, Balt.; phychiatrist on staff D.C. Children's Center, 1968-70. Recipient Biology award Beta Beta Beta, 1957-58; Physician's Recognition award, 1970, 73. Mem. Prince George Med. Soc. Address: 6902 Chansory Lane Hyattsville MD 20782

LILLY, LUELLA JEAN, educator; b. Newberg, Ore., Aug. 23, 1937; d. David Hardy and Edith (Coleman) Lilly; B.S., Lewis and Clark Coll., 1959; M.S., U. Ore., 1961; Ph.D., Tex. Woman's U., 1971; postgrad. Portland State Coll., Ore. State U., U. Ore., U. Utah, Sacramento State Coll., Cal. State Coll. at Long Beach, State U. Coll. at Cortland (N.Y.). Tchr., Central Linn Jr.-Sr. High Sch., Halsey, Ore., 1959-60, Lake Oswego (Ore.) High Sch., 1960-63, Ore. State U., 1963-64, Am. River Coll., 1964-69; dir. women's phys. edn. U. Nev., Reno, 1969-73, dir. women's athletics, 1973—. Pres. No. Cal. Intercollegiate Athletic Conf., 1973—. Camp dir.; instr. A.R.C., 1951-59. Mem. Western Soc. Phys. Edn. for Women, Cal. Assn. Health, Phys. Edn. and Recreation (chmn. jr. coll. sect.), Nev. Bd. Women Ofcls. (chmn. bd. 1969-74), Div. Girls and Women's Sports, Western Assn. Intercollegiate Athletics for Women (exec. bd. 1973-75), Nev. Assn. Health, Phys. Edn. and Recreation. Women's Internat. Bowling Congress, Internat. Platform Assn., Theta Kappa, Phi Kappa Phi. Author: An Overview of Body Mechanics, rev. edit., 1969. Contbr. articles to profl. jours. Home: 605 Imperial Blvd Reno NV 89503

LIM, ESTHER PEI-CHENG (MRS. FRANK H. LEE), physician; b. Fukien, China, Oct. 21, 1921; d. Tiong-Kong and Chua-Szi (Huang) Lim; M.D., Nat. Central U., 1946; postgrad. N.Y. U.-Bellevue Med. Center, 1958-59; m. Frank H. Lee, Sept. 24, 1955; children—Grace E., Sylvia B. Came to U.S., 1951, naturalized, 1962. Intern Univ. Hosp., 1945-46; resident obstetrics and gynecology Lutheran Hosp. Md., 1951-53; resident anesthesiology Fordham Hosp., 1953-55, St. Luke's Hosp., 1955-58; attending anesthesiologist French Hosp., 1959-62; asso. attending physician St. Barnabas Hosp.; co-chief Manhasset Med. Center Hosp., Great Neck, N.Y., 1962—. Diplomate Am. Bd. Anesthesiologists. Fellow Am. Coll. Anesthesiologists; mem. A.M.A., Am., N.Y. socs. anesthesiologists, N.Y. County Med. Soc., N.Y. State Med. Soc. Address: 2 Jeffrey Lane Great Neck NY 11020

LIM, NODI EDITH, banker; b. Honolulu, June 26, 1925; d. Soo Chun Kim and Bong Yuen Kim (Shon) Kim; B.S., U. Wis., 1947; postgrad. U. Hawaii, 1964; m. Chester C.S. Lim, July 3, 1948; children—Richard C., Jann Patricia. X-ray technician Radiology Assos., Honolulu, 1948-62; asst. v.p. Bank of Hawaii, 1962-72, 73—; asst. v.p. Valley Nat. Bank, Phoenix, Ariz., 1973. Panel Judge Honolulu-Pacific Fed. Exec. Bd., 1972. Bd. dirs. Hawaii State Council of Churches. Named Citizen of the Day Radio Sta. KGU, 1973. Mem. Nat. Assn. Bank Women (regional v.p. 1972-73), Aloha Bus. and Profl. Club (pres. 1972, dir. 1972—). Home: 535 Kiholo St Honolulu HI 96821 Office: Bank of Hawaii PO Box 2900 Honolulu HI 96802

LIM, REBECCA ANG, anesthesiologist, educator; b. Manila, Philippines, July 10, 1942; d. Luis C.Y. and Mary (Ang) Lim; A.A., U. Santo Thomas, Manila, 1962, M.D., 1967. Came to U.S., 1968, naturalized, 1974. Intern Edgewater Hosp., Chgo., 1969; resident anesthesia Michael Reese Hosp., Chgo., 1970-71, Northwestern U., Chgo., 1971-72; practice medicine specializing in anesthesiology, Maywood, Ill., 1973—; instr. anesthesiology Loyola U., Maywood, 1973-74, asst. prof., 1974—. Diplomate Am. Bd. Anesthesiology. Fellow Am. Coll. Anesthesiologists; mem. A.M.A., Am., Ill., Chgo., socs. anesthesiologists. Home: 900 N Lake Shore Dr Apt 2304 Chicago IL 60611 Office: 2160 S 1st Av Maywood IL 60153

LIMBACH, JOANNE ELIZABETH, occupational therapist; b. Milw., Sept. 30, 1933; d. Joseph William and Margaret (Wiedmeyer) Limbach; B.S., Mt. Mary Coll., 1956. Occupational therapist VA Center, Wood, Wis., 1957-58, 60-70, supr. clin. edn. in occupational therapy, 1970—; dir. occupational therapy St. Michael Hosp., Milw., 1958-59. Mem. alumnae bd. Mt. Mary Coll., 1969-71. Mem. Am., Wis. (treas. 1964-65) occupational therapy assns., Am. Assn. U. Women, Wis. Council on Edn. Home: 3333 N Knoll Blvd Wauwatosa WI 53222 Office: VA Center Wood WI 53193

LIN, IRENE C., physician; b. Kwangtung, China, Dec. 20, 1939; d. Gene and Sue (Leong) Chin; came to U.S., 1945, naturalized, 1956; A.B., Barnard Coll., 1962; M.D., Columbia, 1966. Intern St. Luke's Hosp., N.Y.C., 1966-67; resident Presbyn. Hosp., N.Y.C., 1967-69; research fellow Columbia, N.Y.C., 1969-70; med. attending Parkway Hosp., N.Y.C., 1970-71; attending anesthesiologist North Shore Hosp., Manhasset, N.Y., 1971—. Diplomate Am. Bd. Anesthesiology. Mem. Am., N.Y. State socs. anesthesiology, Med. Soc. State N.Y. Office: 300 Community Dr Manhasset NY 11030

LIN, SAN-SU CHEN (MRS. PAUL LIN), educator; b. Hong Kong, China, June 3, 1916; d. L.O. and Nellie (Wong) Chan; B.A., Nat. Peking U., Peiping, China, 1939; M.A., Tchrs. Coll. Columbia, 1950, Ed.D., 1953; m. Paul J.S. Lin, Oct. 8, 1939; children—Betty, Jeannie. Came to U.S., 1949, naturalized, 1966. Instr. English, Provincial Tchrs. Coll., Taipei, Taiwan, China, 1948-49; prof. English, Claflin Coll., Orangeburg, S.C., 1955-64, head dept. English, 1957-64; prof. English, So. U., Baton Rouge, 1964—, dir. freshman English, 1969—. Cons. U.S. Office Edn. for evaluation project proposals. U.S. Office Edn. research grantee, 1961-64. Mem. Nat. Council Tchrs. English (spl. task force to study English programs for disadvantaged students 1965), Conf. on Coll. Composition and Communication, Commn. on Humanities, Assn. Supervision and Curriculum Devel. Author: Pattern Practice in the Teaching of Standard English to Students with a Nonstandard Dialect, 1965. Contbr. articles to English Jour., Coll. English, CLA Jour., others. Home: 8107 Branchwood Dr Baton Rouge LA 70811

LINARES, GRACIELA HEBE, physician, city ofcl.; b. Zarate, Argentina, May 21, 1936; d. Julio Argentino and Maria Elvira (Sanchez) Linares; came to U.S., 1966, naturalized, 1973; B.S., U. Buenos Aires, Argentina, 1953, M.D., 1962. Intern St. Vincent's Med. Center, S.I., N.Y., 1966-67; resident in internal medicine Ramos Mejiá Hosp., Buenos Aires, 1963-66; resident in pathology S.I. Hosp., 1967-68; resident St. Mary's Hosp., Hoboken, N.Y., 1968-69, Roosevelt Hosp., N.Y.C., 1969-70, Bklyn. VA Hosp., 1970-71; practice medicine specializing in forensic medicine, N.Y.C., 1971—; jr. med. examiner Office of Chief Med. Examiner, N.Y.C., 1971-73, asso. med. examiner, 1973—. Recipient Physician's Recognition award A.M.A., 1969, 71.

LINCOLN, SISTER ELEANOR HAMBLIN, educator; b. Mpls., May 13, 1924; d. James Shoals and Florence Townsend (Hamblin) Lincoln; B.S., Coll. St. Catherine, 1946, B.A., 1950; M.A., U. Minn., 1955; Ph.D., U. Minn., 1958. Faculty, Coll. St. Catherine, St. Paul, 1951—, prof. English, 1972—; vis. lectr. Coll. St. Rose, Albany, N.Y., 1962, Rosary Coll. Grad. Library Sch., River Forest, Ill., 1968, 71. Mem. Phi Beta Kappa, Kappa Gamma Pi, Delta Phi Lambda, Pi Gamma Mu. Author: Cultural Significance of the Origins and Development of the Minneapolis Public Library: A Study in the American Public Library Movement, 1959. Address: Coll St Catherine St Paul MN 55105

LINCOLN, ELIZABETH KITCHEL (MRS. ALEXANDER LINCOLN, JR.), social worker; b. Englewood, N.J.; d. Cornelius Porter and Edith (Ray) Kitchel; B.A., Vassar Coll., 1933; M.A., Radcliffe Coll., 1938; M.S.W., U. Pitts., 1964; m. Alexander Lincoln, Jr., May 17, 1937; children—Eleanor (Mrs. William H. Buchanan, Jr.), Alexander III, Robert Kitchel, Margaret Kitchel. Coordinator mental health planning study Vt. Dept. Mental Health, Montpelier, 1964-65, field cons., 1965-68; field cons. N.H. Com. for Older Ams. Act, Concord, N.H., 1968-69; dir. services for aging N.H. State Council on Aging, Concord, 1969-73; research asso. dept. psychiatry U. Vt. Med. Sch., 1966-69, mem. faculty, 1973—; cons. White Pines Coll., Chester, N.H., 1970—. Mem. N.H. State Commn. on Alcoholism, 1958-62; sec. Gov.'s Mental Health Survey Com., 1957-59, Gov.'s Task Force on Mental Health Reorgn., 1960-61; chmn. mental health com. N.H. Social Welfare Council, 1957, dir., 1957-62, 64—; mem. N.H. Commn. on Status of Women, 1971—; mem. adv. com. on older Ams., U.S. Dept. Health, Edn. and Welfare, 1970-73; mem. White House Conf. on Aging nat. planning bd., 1971—. Trustee Meredith (N.H.) Pub. Library, 1946-62, Spaulding Youth Center, Tilton, N.H., 1971—; bd. dirs. White Mountain Community Services, Littleton, N.H., 1964-73, Lakes Region Mental Health Assn., Laconia, N.H., 1968-72, N.H. Swiftwater Girl Scout Council, Women's Information Service Edn., N.H. Assn. Elderly; incorporator Lakes Region Gen. Hosp., Laconia, 1960—, N.H. Charitable Fund, 1971—; trustee Washingtonian Hosp., Jamaica Plain, Mass., 1955—. Mem. Nat. Assn. Social Workers, Acad. Certified Social Workers, Am. Sociol. Assn., Am. Pub. Health Assn., Boston Soc. for Gerontolgic Psychiatry, Am. Assn. Ret. Persons, Nat. Soc. Colonial Dames, Jr. League Boston, Am. Assn. U. Women (state dir. 1955-61, 67—). Club: Womens City (Boston). Home: Meredith Bay Farm Meredith NH 03253

LINCOLN, EMMA ETHEL, real estate exec., automotive service co. exec.; b. East Lyme, Conn., Jan. 20, 1914; d. Daniel and Mary Emma (Holmes) Higgins; grad. Williams Meml. Inst., 1934. Owner Lincoln Auto Service, New London, Conn., 1940—; pres. Lincoln Center, Inc., New London, 1963—. Republican Statc Central Committewoman 20th dist., Conn., 1972—; Rep. town chmn. New London Rep. Com., 1966-72. Bd. dirs., pres. YMCA, New London. Mem. Bus. and Profl Womens Club (pres.). Home: 16 Glenwood Place New London CT 06320 Office: 174 State Pier Rd New London CT 06320

LINCOLN, HELEN MARIE GARBER, librarian; b. Dayton, Va., Oct. 18, 1912; d. Edward Harrison and Ressie Sheldon (Buyer) Garber; student Shenandoah Coll., 1929-34, U. Pa., 1956, Harrisonburg Bus. Coll., 1956, Eastern Ky. U., 1965-66, Ball State U., 1966-67; A.A., Elgin Community Coll., 1968; B.S., Findlay Coll., 1969; D. Chiropractic, Bebout Chiropractic Coll., 1968; m. Ernest Erdine Lincoln II, June 20, 1937; 1 son, Ernest Erdine III. House parent Bel Air Indsl. Sch., Richmond, Va., 1950-51; tchr. Sch. Specialized Edn., Bridgewater, Va., 1960; houseparent St. Ann Sch., Albemarle County, Va., 1961; tchr. Sch. for Blind, Staunton, Va., 1963, Morgan County (W.Va.) Pub. Schs., 1964-65; tchr. spl. edn. Rockingham County (Va.) Pub. Schs., 1963-64; librarian, Bliss Coll., Columbus, O., 1969—. Instr. first aid A.R.C., 1952; guide, Massanutten Caverns, Rockingham County, Va., 1966. Home: RFD 1 Dayton VA 22821 Office: 3770 N High St Columbus OH 43214

LINCOLN, J(EANNETTE) VIRGINIA, physicist; b. Ames, Ia., Sept. 7, 1915; d. Rush B. and Jeannette (Bartholomew) Lincoln; B.A. in Physics, Wellesley Coll., 1936; M.S. in Household Equipment, Ia. State U., 1938. Research fellow Ia. State U., Ames, 1936-37, grad. asst., 1937-38, instr. household equipment, 1938-42; physicist Nat. Bur. Standards, Washington, 1942-54, Boulder, Colo., 1954-65, sect. chief Radio Warning Services, 1959-65; chief Aeronomy and Space Data Center, ESSA Research Labs., Environmental Sci. Services Adminstrn., 1966-70; chief World Data Center A for Solar-Terrestial Physics, Environmental Data Service, Nat. Oceanic and Atmospheric Adminstrn., Boulder, 1970—. Sec. for World Days, Internat. Ursigram and World Days Service, 1961—; reporter Internat. Assn. Geo-magnetism and Aeronomy, 1963-66; sec. Ionospheric Network adv. group Internat. Union Radio Sci., 1969-72, vice chmn., 1972—; mem. Internat. Astron. U. Commn. Solar Activity, 1973. Recipient Gold medal distinguished service Dept. Commerce, 1973. Fellow A.A.A.S.; mem. Research Soc. Am. (sec. Boulder br. 1971), Am. Geophys. Union, Am. Astronom. Soc., Soc. Women Engrs. (chmn. Denver Sect. 1972-73, sect. rep. 1973—), Am. Assn. U. Women, Internat. Union Radio-Sci. (U.S. commn., sec. solar terrestrial physics com. Ionosphere network adv. group 1969-72, vice chmn. 1972—), P.E.O. (chpt. pres. 1957-58). Republican. Episcopalian. Club: Soroptimist (pres. Boulder 1960-61). Co-author sunspot number prediction method; editor, compiler solar-terrestrial physics data. Home: 2005 Alpine Dr Boulder CO 80302 Office: Nat Oceanic and Atmospheric Adminstrn Boulder CO 80302

LINCOLN, JOANNE, librarian; b. Dallas, Oct. 17, 1938; d. Frank Jackson and Ruth Louise (Boedeker) Lincoln; B.A., Wheaton Coll., 1960; M.LN., Emory U., 1969. Librarian, sci. and industry dept. Dallas Pub. Library, 1960-66; librarian Atlanta Pub. Schs., 1966—. Mem. A.L.A., Metro Atlanta, Southeastern, Ga. library assns., Delta Kappa Gamma. Home: 988 Cardova Dr NE Atlanta GA 30324 Office: 2930 Forrest Hill Dr SW Atlanta GA 30315

LINCOLN, KRISTINA GRINDEE, clin. psychologist; b. Portland, Ore., June 12, 1943; d. Joel S. and Elizabeth (Thomas) Grindee; B.A., Reed Coll., Portland, Ore., 1965; Ph.D. with honors, N.Y. U., 1971, postdoctoral fellow, 1970—; m. Peter G. Lincoln, Oct. 8, 1966; 2 children. Researcher, Research Center Mental Health, N.Y.C., 1965-66, 67-68, 69-70; psychology intern Postgrad. Center Mental Health, 1968-69; staff psychologist Kings County Hosp., Bklyn., 1970-71; psychologist Neurol. Inst., N.Y.C., 1971—; pvt. clin. practice, N.Y.C., 1972—, Norwood, N.J., 1974—. Mem. Norwood Community Adv. Group, 1973—; alumni admissions counselor No. N.J. area for Reed Coll., 1973—. Recipient Founder's Day award N.Y. U., 1971. Nat. Inst. Mental Health fellow, 1965-68, 69-70. Mem. Am., N.Y. State, N.J. psychol. assns., Pascack Valley Hosp. Assn., Reed Coll., N.Y U. alumnae assns. Democrat. Office: 333 W 57th St New York City NY 10019

LINCOLN, MARJORIE HELEN (MRS. SEAMON ANDREW LINCOLN), librarian; b. Des Moines; d. Floyd and Anna (Carr) Falls; B.A., State U. Ia., 1937; B.S. in L.S., U. Chgo., 1948; m. Seamon Andrew Lincoln, July 6, 1936; children—Marjorie (Mrs. R. J. Weiner), Lynn (Mrs. Jerry Powell), Seamon Andrew. Student asst. library State U. of Ia., 1933-37; asst. circulation and catalog dept. Des Moines Pub. Library, 1939-41; with catalog dept. library U. Chgo., 1948-50; head librarian Wheaton (Ill.). Pub. Library, 1950-68, library dir., 1968—. Mem. Am., Ill. (mem. budget, profile coms. 1962-63, chmn. pub. library sect. 1969-70) library assns., West Suburban Library Club (pres. 1960-61), Library Adminstrs. Conf. No. Ill. (sec.-treas. 1961-62, pres. 1971-72), Am. Assn. U. Women, Phi Beta Kappa. Clubs: Wheaton Drama; Graduate Library School (U. Chgo.). Contbr. weekly column to Wheaton Daily Jour. Home: 850 Lorraine Av Wheaton IL 60187 Office: 225 N Cross Wheaton IL 60187

LIND, AMY INEZ, occupational therapist, educator; b. Melville, Sask., Can.; d. Charles and Agnes (Naseth) Lind; tchrs. certificate Regina (Sask.) Normal Sch., 1936; diploma in occupational therapy U. Toronto, 1947; student McMaster U., 1952; Ph.D., U. Wyo., 1965. Came to U.S., 1957, naturalized, 1962. Tchr., Sask. schs., 1936-41; instr. aircraft recognition RCAF, 1941-45; dir. occupational therapy dept. Mountain Sanatorium, Hamilton, 1947-55; occupational therapist Liverpool (Eng.) Sch. Occupational Therapy, 1952-53; occupational therapy cons. psychiat. services Dept. Health, Regina, Sask., Can., 1955-57; chmn. occupational therapy dept. U. N.D., Grand Forks, 1957—, asst. prof. occupational therapy, 1957-62, asso. prof., 1962-73, prof., 1973—. Mem. com. health care facilities N.D. Health Dept., 1970—, regional adv. com. on rehab., 1970—; chmn. ad hoc com. on A Sheltered Workshop for Grand Forks, 1972; pres. Valley Assn. Retarded Children, 1974—; chmn. com. on recruitment and tng. rehab. personnel N.D. Statewide Planning for Comprehensive Rehab., 1967—; sec. N.D. Council on Health Careers, 1971—. Mem. World Fedn. Occupational Therapy, Am., N.D. (mem. com. continuing edn. 1972—) occupational therapy assns., Nat., N.D. (mem. exec. bd., pres. 1970-71) rehab. assns., Am. Assn. U. Profs., Red River Dist. Occupational Therapy (sec.-treas.), Am. Assn. U. Women (campus rep.), N.D. Bus. and Profl. Womens Club (past dist. dir.). Presbyn. (chmn. Bus. Women's Guild 1962-63). Club: Quota (past pres. Grand Forks). Home: 1527 Chestnut Pl Grand Forks ND 58201

LIND, ARLENE FINKEL (MRS. IRVING LIND), art gallery exec.; b. Bklyn., Dec. 27, 1928; d. Samuel and Ann (Gallop) Finkel; B.A., N.Y. U., 1949; student Cranbrook Acad. Art, 1956; m. Irving Lind, Feb. 1, 1951; children—Robert, Leslie, Amy, Victoria. With Leah Salisbury, lit. agt., N.Y.C., 1949-51, Benton & Bowles Co., N.Y.C., 1952-53; founder, owner Arlene Lind Gallery, San Francisco, 1967—. Founder Art for Industry Lease Program, San Francisco, 1967; founding mem. Image Works Film Prodn. Co., San Francisco; mem. staff pub. affairs and publs. dept. Asia Found., 1973—. Area chmn. Marin Alternative, 1972—. Mem. Delancy Street Found., San Francisco. Mem. San Francisco Home Furnishing League, Terra Linda Art Assn., San Francisco Mus. Art, DeYoung Mus., Occupational Rehab. through Tng., Palace of Legion of Honor, Marin Symphony Assn. Office: 435 Jackson St San Francisco CA 94111

LIND, SYLVIA KASS (MRS. ARTHUR K. LIND), educator; b. N.Y.C., Feb. 24, 1915; d. David Siegel and Anna (Berlin) Mahr; B.S. in Edn. magna cum laude, William Paterson Coll. N.J., 1959, M.S. in Guidance, 1971; m. Irving Kass, June 1938 (dec. Sept. 1964); children—Roger Alan, David Miles; m. 2d, Arthur K. Lind, Apr. 23, 1970. Tchr. 3d, 4th grades Milnes Sch., Fair Lawn, N.J., 1959—. Pres., Cherry Hill P.T.A., 1951-53; chmn. Voter Service, Bergen County League of Women Voters, 1954-55; treas. League Women Voters, River Edge, N.J., 1955-57; chmn. Fair Lawn Lang. Arts Com., 1962; mem. student-faculty com. student personnel services William Paterson Coll., 1971-72. Bd. dirs. River Dell Adult Edn. Com., 1951-71, pres., 1961-62. Mem. Assn. Childhood Edn. N.J. (treas. 1970-72), Kappa Delta Pi. Home: 390 Oak Av River Edge NJ 07661 Office: Philip St Fair Lawn NJ 07410

LIND, VIIU SARAL (MRS. HARRY LIND), veterinarian; b. Tallinn, Estonia, Apr. 10, 1910; d. Karl and Ebba-Marie (Vimberg) Saral; D.V.M., U. Tartu (Estonia), 1936; m. Harry Lind, Aug. 22, 1936; children—Thomas Carl, Mary. Came to U.S., 1949, naturalized, 1954. Professorial asst. Small Animal Clinic, U. Tartu, 1936-42; pvt. practice vet. medicine, Marion, N.C., 1949—. Troop leader, neighborhood chmn. Girl Scouts U.S.A., Marion, 1949-68. Mem. N.C., Western N.C. (past sec.), Pietmont (past pres.) vet. medicine assns. Address: 346 State St Marion NC 28752

LINDAUER, LOIS LYONS, dietary orgn. adminstr.; b. N.Y.C., Feb. 6, 1933; d. Ken and Rose (Schneidman) Lyons; A.B., Brandeis U., 1953; m. William Seltz, Nov. 12, 1972; children by previous marriage—Karen Lyons, Amy Hope. Copywriter, Herbert Frank Advt. Agy., Boston, 1956-57; pres. Paisley workshop, handmade plaques and wall decor, N.Y.C., 1962-65; nat. dir. Diet Workshop, Inc., East Meadow, N.Y., 1965—. Diet cons. Alba Non-Fat Skim Milk. Pub. relations dir. Internat. Franchise Assn. Author: It's In to Be Thin, 1971; The Diet Workshop Restaurant Manual, 1972; The Fast and Easy Teenage Diet, 1973. Home: 749 Park Lane East Meadow NY 11554 Office: 1975 Hempstead Turnpike East Meadow NY 11554

LINDBECK, VERA LEEGER (MRS. DAVID O. LINDBECK), social worker; b. N.Y.C., Jan. 4, 1920; d. Leon L. and Anna (Helman) Leeger; B.A., Woman's Coll. U. N.C., 1939; M.S., U. Buffalo, 1958; m. David O. Lindbeck, July 7, 1961; 1 dau., Norma Jean. Caseworker, Family Service, Jamestown, N.Y., 1958, Alcoholic Rehab. Clinic, Sacramento, 1958-59; supr. Gowanda State Hosp., Helmuth, N.Y., 1959-61; dir. girls' probation services Hamilton County (O.) Juvenile Ct., 1961-64; dir. research, acting dir. group therapy Family Service, Cin., 1964-70, asst. casework dir., 1970—; field instr. U. Buffalo, 1961, Kent Sch. Social Work U. Louisville, 1963. Mem. N.Am. Assn. Alcholism Programs, Nat. Assn. Social Workers, Acad. Certified Social Workers, Am., Tri-State group psychotherapy assns., Am. Schizophrenia Found. Home: 1026 Thunderbird Dr Cincinnati OH 45231 Office: 2343 Auburn Av Cincinnati OH 45219

LINDBERG, LOIS HELEN, educator; b. Scott AFB, Ill., Sept. 1, 1932; d. Arthur John and Helen Edith (Swanson) Lindberg; B.A., San Jose State U., 1952; M.P.H., U. Cal. at Berkeley, 1958; Ph.D., Stanford, 1966. Microbiologist State Dept. Pub. Health, Berkeley, Cal., 1952-55; asso. pub. health microbiology U. Cal. at Berkeley, 1955-58; mem. faculty San Jose (Cal.) State U., 1958—, prof. biology and microbiology, 1958—. Dir. Cal. Climate Corp., Burbank, 1969—. NIH fellow, 1962-63, NSF fellow, 1963-66. Mem. A.A.A.S., Am. Soc. Microbiology, Am. Assn. Immunology, Sigma Xi. Club: Sierra (Palo Alto, Cal.). Home: 211 Santa Margarita Av Menlo Park CA 94025 Office: Duncan Hall San Jose State U San Jose CA 95152

LINDBERG, WILMA JEAN, educator; b. Canton, O., Dec. 8, 1924; d. Carl Estley and Bertha Cecilia (Franklin) Lindberg; A.B., Hanover Coll., 1946; certificate in occupational therapy Wayne State U., 1951, M.Ed., 1963; certificate U. Ala., 1974. Commd. 2d lt. U.S. Air Force, 1952, advanced through grades to capt., 1957, ret., 1961; asst. prof. occupational therapy U. Fla., Gainesville, 1961-67; asso. prof. occupational therapy U. Ala., Birmingham, 1967—, chmn. dept. occupational therapy, 1967-73, ednl. specialist Center for Research and Devel., 1974—. Cons. Bur. Nursing Home Licensure, State of Ala., 1971-73. Mem. med.-profl. adv. bd. United Cerebral Palsy of Ala., 1969-74. Mem. Am. (mem. council on edn. 1967-73), Ala.-Miss. (treas. 1971-73) occupational therapy assns., Am. Assn. U. Profs., Ret. Officers Assn., Ala. Ornithol. Soc. (sec. 1970-71), Nat. Audubon Soc. Clubs: Altrusa (rec. sec. 1970-72) Sierra (Birmingham). Mem. Eta Rho Pi, Alpha Rho Gamma, Kappa Delta Pi. Home: 2712 Millbrook Rd Birmingham AL 35243 Office: University Station Birmingham AL 35294

LINDBERGH, ANNE SPENCER MORROW (MRS. CHARLES AUGUSTUS LINDBERGH), author; b. 1906; d. Dwight Whitney and Elizabeth Reeve (Cutter) Morrow; grad. Miss Chapin's Sch., N.Y.C.; grad. Smith Coll., Northampton, Mass., 1928, M.A. (hon.), 1935; m. Charles Augustus Lindbergh, May 27, 1929; children—Charles Augustus (dec.), Jon Morrow, Land Morrow, Anne Spencer, Reeve, Scott. Recipient two prizes for lit. work Smith Coll.; cross of honor for part in survey of trans-Atlantic air route U.S. Flag Assn., 1933; Hubbard gold medal for work as co-pilot and radio operator in flight of 40,000 miles over five continents Nat. Geog. Soc.,

1934. Author: North to the Orient, 1935; Listen, the Wind, 1938; The Wave of the Future, 1940; The Steep Ascent, 1944; Gift from the Sea, 1955; Unicorn and Other Poems; Dearly Beloved, 1962; Bring Me a Unicron, 1972. Home: Scotts Cove Darien CT 06820

LINDBLOM, RITA MAE FORMAN (MRS. CHESTER W. LINDBLOM), polit. worker; b. Wahpeton, N.D., May 17, 1929; d. Arthur Max and Hazel (Miller) Forman; student N.D. State Sch. Sci., 1947-48; m. Chester W. Lindblom, May 29, 1949; children—Karen (Mrs. Lynn Angvick), Bradley. With Plentywood (Mont.) Herald, 1948-55, 62-68; sec. Fed. Crop Ins. Office, Plentywood, 1957-61; co-owner Lindblom Ranch, Outlook, Mont., 1961—; mgr. State Mont. Liquor Store, Plentywood, 1969—. County sec., treas. Mont. Constl. Revision Com., 1970. Sec., Sheridan County Central Com. Democratic party, 1958-61, vice chmn., 1964-68, county precinct committeewoman, 1966—, state committeewoman, 1967-73; mem. Mont. State Central Com. Exec. Bd., 1969—; treas. Mont. Dem. Women's Club, 1967-73, 1st v.p., 1973—; del. Dem. Nat. Conv., 1968; bills clk. Mont. State Senate, 1969, 71. Mem. Nat. Farm Orgn., Nat. Farmers Union, League Women Voters, V.F.W. Aux. (Outstanding State Pres. 1964, nat. council mem. 1972-74). Lutheran. Home: Rural Route Outlook MT 59252 Office: 101 N Jefferson St Plentywood MT 59254

LINDE, MAXINE HELEN (MRS. RONALD K. LINDE), lawyer; b. Chgo., Sept. 2, 1939; d. Jack and Lottie (Kroll) Stern; B.A. summa cum laude, U. Cal. at Los Angeles, 1961; J.D., Stanford, 1967; m. Ronald Keith Linde, June 12, 1960. Applied mathematician, research engr. Jet Propulsion Lab., Pasadena, Cal., 1961-64; admitted to Cal. bar, 1968; law clk. Stanley A. Weigel Dist. Judge U.S. Dist. Ct. No. Cal., 1967-68; mem. firm Long & Levit, San Francisco, 1968-69, Swerdlow, Glikbarg & Shimer, Beverly Hills, 1969-72; asst. to chmn., gen. counsel Envirodyne, Inc., Los Angeles, 1972—. Mem. Cal. State Bar, Beverly Hills Bar Assn., Order Coif, Phi Beta Kappa, Pi Mu Epsilon, Alpha Lambda Delta. Home: 255 S Reeves Dr #301 Beverly Hills CA 90212 Office: 1180 S Beverly Dr Los Angeles CA 90035

LINDELL, MARION DENNARD (MRS. ELWOOD TERENCE LINDELL), pub. relations counselor; b. Corsicana, Tex., Aug. 20, 1926; d. William Aubrey and Texanna (Cole) Dennard; B.A., Rice U., 1945; m. Elwood Terence Lindell, Apr. 9, 1954; 1 dau., Martha Diane. Asso. editor AGC Constrn. News, Houston, 1945-48; asst. mng. editor Gulf Pub. Co., Houston, 1948-52; editorial dir. Rittenhouse & Co., advt. agy., Houston, 1953-55; v.p. Cain Orgn., Inc., pub. relations counselor, Dallas, 1955-60; owner Marion Lindell/Pub. Relations, Dallas, 1960-69; partner Lindell-Keys Co., Dallas, 1969—; dir. pub. information Dallas Acad., 1968—. Information dir. A Beautiful, Clean Dallas, 1969—. Recipient Matrix award Dallas chpt. Women in Communications, 1973. Mem. Pub. Relations Soc. Am. (sec., dir., accreditation chmn. North Tex. chpt.). Home: 6466 Orchid Lane Dallas TX 75230 Office: 4300 N Central Expressway Dallas TX 75206

LINDEMAN, CONSTANCE JOAN TROMPETER (MRS. NEIL CARL LINDEMAN), occupational therapist; b. Winfield, Kan., Mar. 3, 1935; d. Roy Henderson and Effie Viola (Kiefer) Trompeter; B.S., Colo. State U., 1957; m. Neil Carl Lindeman, June 9, 1957; children—Mark Milton, Lisa Michele. Mem. vis. occupational therapy service East Orange Orthopedic Hosp., 1963; sec.-treas., dir. Shrewsbury (N.J.) Conf. (med. marketing consultants), 1968—. Chmn. steering com. Juvenile Justice Confs., 1973—; pres. Rumson (N.J.) P.T.A., 1969-71; mem. Bd. Edn. Rumson-Fairhaven, 1973—. Bd. dirs., pres. Jr. League Monmouth County, N.J. Mem. Am. Occupational Therapy Assn., Kappa Alpha Theta. Methodist. Home: 15 Oyster Bay Dr Rumson NJ 07760

LINDEMAN, KATHERINE JANE, librarian; b. Chgo., Dec. 3, 1921; d. John Henry and Margaret Louise (Thomas) Lindeman; A.B., MacMurray Coll., 1940-44; B.S. in L.S., U. Ill., 1944-45. Library asst. Sweet Briar (Va.) Coll. Library, 1945-46; asst. reference librarian Ill. State Library, Springfield, 1946-49; asst. order librarian Fla. State U. Library, Tallahassee, 1949-50; librarian Glenview (Ill.) Pub. Library, 1952—, head adult services, 1972—. Mem. steering com., reference sect. North Suburban Library System, 19—. Mem. Am., Ill. library assns. Club: Zonta Internat. (pres. chpt. 1973-74). Home: 850 Eldorado St Winnetka IL 60093 Office: 1930 Glenview Rd Glenview IL 60025

LINDEMANN, NORMA LEE (MRS. ROBERT ALFRED LINDEMANN), systems analyst; b. Vincennes, Ind., Oct. 19, 1922; d. Virgil Evans and Tressie Lee (Hurt) Ashby; diploma, Brevard (N.C.) Jr. Coll., 1942; student Oakland City (Ind.) Coll., summer 1942; A.B., Ind. U., 1946, M.A., 1949, postgrad., 1954-55, U. Notre Dame, 1952-54, U. Fla., 1968-69; m. Robert Alfred Lindemann, Apr. 29, 1944. Prodn. and quality control clk. Tenn. Eastman Corp., Oak Ridge, 1944-46; research asst. math. U. Notre Dame, 1949-54; statistician U.S. Naval Inspection of Ordnance, Mishawaka, Ind., 1955-57; operations analyst USAF, Patrick AFB, Fla., 1957-59, engr. RCA-MTP, 1959-61, 62—; mem. tech. staff Aerospace Corp., Patrick AFB, 1961-62; teaching asst. Ind. U., 1946-49, 54-55, lectr., 1950-51; lectr. math. operations research Fla. Inst. Tech., 1959—. Mem. Am. Math. Soc., Math. Assn. Am., Soc. Indsl. and Applied Math., Operations Research Soc. Am., I.E.E.E. Home: 149 Exeter St Satellite Beach FL 32937 Office: RCA-MTP Box 4308 Mail Unit 645 Bldg 989 Patrick AFB FL 32935

LINDEN, KATHRYN, communications cons.; b. N.Y.C., Jan. 24, 1905; d. Robert Berthold and Anna (Jaehns) Linden; B.S. with honors, Columbia, 1953, M.A., 1956; Ph.D., N.Y. U., 1972. Asst. dept. edn. Met. Mus. Art, N.Y.C., 1937-44; dir. audiovisual edn. East and West Assn., 1944-45, chmn. film com., 1945-48; cons. audiovisual program Am. Nurses Assn., 1948-53, dir. Am. Nurses Assn.-Nat. League Nursing Film Service (now Am. Jour. Nursing Co.), N.Y.C., 1953-70. Tech. cons. White House Conf. Children and Youth, 1960; chmn. Audio-Visual Conf. Med. and Allied Scis., Chgo., 1960-62, program chmn., 1963-67, vice chmn., 1959; corr. sec. N.Y. Film Council, 1959-67; chmn. film forum sessions, jury screenings in health film category Am. Film Assemblies, 1957-69, juror, active workshops, 1954-56; mem. conv. film com. Nat. Social Welfare Assemblies, 1953-58. Trustee, dir. Taraknath Das Found., N.Y.C., 1959—. Mem. Alumni Assn. Sch. Gen. Studies Columbia (sec. 1960-63, corr. sec. 1969-70, sec. 1971-74), Am. Acad. Polit. and Social Scis., Ednl. Film Library Assn., Council on Med. TV, N.Y. U. Alumni Assn. Presbyn. Contbr. articles to profl. jours. Co-producer, prodn. coordinator filmstrips, films in field. Home: 504 W 110th St New York City NY 10025

LINDEN, MARY ANN, editor; b. Kansas City, Mo., Jan. 17, 1948; d. Francis August and Ann Georgia (Prell) Linden; B.J., U. Mo. at Columbia, 1970. Feature writer The Voice Pub. Co., Miami, Fla., 1970-72; dir. TV show sta. WCKT, Miami, 1972; editor Miami Herald, 1973—. Adviser Jr. Achievement, Miami, 1973—. Mem. Women in Communications, Internat. Assn. Bus. Communicators, Sigma Delta Chi. Home: 7505 SW 82d St Miami FL 33143 Office: 1 Herald Plaza Miami FL 33101

LINDER, BARBARA ANNE, univ. dean; b. Rockford, Ill., Feb. 3, 1942; d. Marshall Leroy and Henrietta Amanda (Lerch) Linder; B.A., Millikin U., 1964; M.A., U. Denver, 1965, postgrad., 1969-72. Asst. dean of women U. Denver, 1966-69, residence hall dir., 1969-72; dean of women Ida. State U., Pocatello, 1972—. Mem. Nat. Assn. Women Deans and Counselors (mem. far west regional coordinating com. 1973—), Nat. Assn. Student Personnel Adminstrs., Am. Assn. U. Women, Pocatello Women's Polit. Caucus, Alpha Chi Omega. Lutheran. Home: 139 Appaloosa St Pocatello ID 83201

LINDER, DIANE BALL (MRS. AUBRY L. LINDER), nutritionist; b. Magnolia, Miss., Mar. 10, 1944; d. John Wesley and Loraine (Moak) Ball; student S.W. Miss. Jr. Coll., 1962-63; B.S., Miss. State Coll. Women, 1966; M.S., U. Tenn., 1968; m. Aubry L. Linder, Mar. 7, 1970. Patient food service coordinator Morrison's Food Service Consol., Mobile, Ala., 1967-68; tchr. Fruitdale (Ala.) High Sch., 1968; asst. nutrition specialist La. State U. Coop. Extension Service, Baton Rouge, after 1969, now asso. specialist. Mem. Am., La. (chmn. nutrition sect. 1970-72, editor newsletter 1973-75) home econs. assns., Miss. State Coll. Women Alumnae Assn., Am. Dietetic Assn., Gamma Sigma Delta. Home: Route 1 Box 192 Denham Springs LA 70726 Office: Knapp Hall La State U Baton Rouge LA 70803

LINDER, EMMA VANDEGRIFT (MRS. CARROLL YEATMAN LINDER), hist. soc. ofcl.; b. Russellville, Ala., July 26, 1913; d. Edgar Newton and Aurelia Mae (Alverson) Vandegrift; A.B., Brenau Coll., 1933; m. Carroll Yeatman Linder, Sept. 30, 1945; 1 son, Walton Vandegrift. Instr. biology Brenau Coll., Gainesville, Ga., 1933-36; tchr. biology Blount County (Ala.) High Sch., 1936-41, Murphy High Sch., Mobile, Ala., 1942-45. Owner Cherry Hill Farm, Oneonta, Ala., 1967-74. Mem. Blount County Farm Bur. Women's Com. Recipient Gov.'s Conservation award, 1962; named Woman of the Year Gadsden, Ala., 1955; recipient Leadership award Blount County, 1972. Mem. Ala. Hist. Assn., Blount County Hist. Soc. (pres. 1972-74), Ala. Wildflower Soc., Beta Beta Beta, Pi Gamma Mu. Methodist. Clubs: Amaryllis Garden, Tait's Gap Homemakers, Worthwhile Study, Garden (dir. 1956-74), Blount County Conservation. Contbr. to Heritage of Blount County, 1973. Contbr. articles to local newspapers. Address: Route 4 Box 156 Oneonta AL 35121 Office: Blount County Memorial Museum 308 5th Av Oneonta AL 35121

LINDER, JUDY ANNETTE, hosp. exec.; b. Spartanburg, S.C., Dec. 14, 1947; d. James Roland and Guyula Geneva (Burnett) Linder; student Lander Coll., 1965-67, Wofford Coll., 1967, U. S.C., 1969-71. Pub. information officer Spartanburg Gen. Hosp., 1968-69; placement counsellor Snelling & Snelling, Inc., 1969-70; dir. personnel Mary Black Meml. Hosp., 1970-73; dir. personnel Doctors Meml. Hosp., Spartanburg, 1973—. Mem. Am. Soc. Hosp. Personnel Adminstrs., Am. Soc. Hosp. Pub. Relations Dirs., Am. Hosp. Assn. (Am. Soc. Vol. Service Dirs. div.). Home: Route 1 Box 228 Spartanburg SC 29302 Office: 389 Serpentine Dr Spartanburg SC 29303

LINDGREN, ASTRID, author; b. Vimmerby, Sweden, Nov. 14, 1907; d. Samuel August and Hanna (Jonsson) Ericsson; ed., Stockholm, Sweden; m. Sture Lindgren, Apr. 4, 1931 (dec. 1952); children—Lars, Karin (Mrs. Carl Olof Nyman). Writer children's books, 1944—; children's book editor Raben & Sjogren Pubs., Stockholm, 1946-70. Recipient Nils Holgersson medal for children's book, 1950; Swedish state award for authors' high lit. standard, 1957; Hans Christian Anderson medal, internat. children's book award, 1958; Spring Festival award N.Y. Herald Tribune, 1959; Gold medal Swedish Acad., 1971. Mem. Union Swedish Authors. Club: Swedish Pen. Author: Pippi Longstocking, 1950; Sia Lives on Kilimanjaro, 1959; Mio My Son, 1956; Rasmus and the Vagabond, 1960; Bill Bergson Master Detective, 1952; Mischievous Meg, 1962; The Children of Noisy Village, 1962; Happy Times in Noisy Village, 1963; Lotta on Troublemaker Street, 1963; The Children on Troublemaker Street, 1964; Seacrow Island, 1969; Emil in the Soup Tureen, 1970; Emil's Pranks, 1971; Karlsson-on-the Roof, 1971; Emil and Piggy Beast, 1973. Home: Dalagatan 46 Stockholm Sweden

LINDHEIM, ROSLYN ITTELSON, architect; b. N.Y.C., 1921; grad. Lincoln Sch. Tchrs. Coll., 1938; postgrad. Radcliffe Coll., 1938-40; B.Arch. (Mckim fellow), Columbia, 1944; m. Richard Lindheim, Sept. 13, 1942; children—Daniel, Susan. Asst. dean Coll. Environmental Design, U. Cal. at Berkeley, 1967-70, asso. prof. architecture, 1968-71, prof., 1971—. USPHS grantee to develop methods of analysis for making design decision in hosps.; Nat. Inst. Mental Health grantee to explore relationship between phys. design and health. Mem. A.I.A., Inst. Medicine, Nat. Acad. Scis. Contbr. articles to profl. jours. Home: 103 El Camino Real Berkeley CA 94705

LINDLEY, HELEN CATHERINE SHAW (MRS. SAMUEL GIBBS LINDLEY), editor; b. Cicero, Ill., June 12, 1913; d. George Thomas and Marie Theresa (Lauterbach) Shaw; student St. Louis U., 1956-57, La. State U., 1958-59; m. Samuel Gibbs Lindley, Dec. 9, 1949; 1 son, Samuel Gordon. Free-lance writer, 1962—; organizer Izard County Hist. Soc., Dolph, Ark., 1969, sec., treas., 1971—; editor, pub. Izard County Historian, 1969—. Dir. activities Optimist Youth Camp, Baton Rouge, 1958-62; disaster worker A.R.C., 1956-62; telegrapher-communications Boy Scouts Am., Cub Scouts Am., Baton Rouge, 1958-62. Address: Rural Route Dolph AR 72528

LINDNER, HANNAH ELISABETH RIECKEN, dairy products co. exec.; b. Hamburg, Germany (parents Am. citizens); d. Robert and Alma (Wange) Riecken; student engring. Purdue U., 1941; Ph.D. (hon.), Hamilton State U., Tucson; m. David R. Lindner, Nov. 24, 1920 (dec. Feb. 1940); children—David R. II, Marian (Mrs. Milan C. Olbina), Wilbur H. Dir., sec.-treas. Lindner Bros., Inc., Indpls., 1929-40, pres., 1940-62, chmn. bd., 1962—; pres., dir. Herl Enterprises, Indpls., 1959—; dir., v.p. Linbro, Inc., Indpls., 1959—; pres. dir. Irving Realty, Indpls., 1959—; treas., dir. East End Dairies, Indpls., 1940-57. Mem. Nat. Assn. Retail Ice Cream Mfg. (dir. 1954-57), Ind. Dairy Assn., Indpls. Bus. and Profl. Club (pres. 1974—), Gen. Fedn. Women's Clubs, Mut. Service Orgn. (life), Indpls. C. of C. (named Outstanding Bus. Woman Indpls. 1958, dir. council women, 1963-65), Women's Dept. Club (mem. bd. 1964-68), Ind. Fedn. Clubs. (treas. 1967-69), Salvation Army Aux. Methodist (bd. stewards). Mem. Order Eastern Star. Clubs: Indpls. Propyleum; Women's Investment, Indpls. Athletic, Altrusa (dir. 1963-65) (Indpls.). Home: 11050 Presbyterian Dr Indianapolis IN 46201 Office: 6101 E Washington St Indianapolis IN 46219

LINDSAY, CATHERINE BROWN (MRS. H.S. CHOATE), writer; b. St. Paul, Mar. 24, 1926; d. Earnest C. and Marguerite (Countryman) Brown; B.A., U. Minn., 1946, M.A., 1947; m. Kenneth C. Lindsay, Feb. 7, 1943 (div. Oct. 1947); m. 2d, H.S. Choate, Nov. 16, 1970. Tchr. creative writing, Am. and world lit. U. Colo., Boulder, 1949-51, Vassar Coll., Poughkeepsie, N.Y., 1951-53, N.Y.U., 1953-57, San Francisco State U., 1959-60; fiction editor Scholastic Mags., N.Y.C., 1960-62; writer Ency. Brit., Chgo., 1964; asst. prof. English, Rock Valley Coll., Rockford, Ill., 1967-70. MacDowell Colony grantee, 1953, 71, Huntington Hartford Found. grantee, 1956. Author: The Country of the Young, 1946; How to Teach Your Students to Write, 1967. Contbr. short stories and travel articles to Am. Girl, Co-Ed. and Practical English mags. Home: Quail Ridge East Morrill Way Indian Hills Tucson AZ 85705

LINDSAY, FREDA THERESA SCHIMPF (MRS. GORDON JAMES LINDSAY), religious exec.; b. Burstall, Sask., Can., Apr. 18, 1914; d. Gottfred and Kaity (Saklofsky) Schimpf; student Life Bible Coll., Portland, Ore., 1933-35, B.A., Los Angeles, 1938; m. Gordon James Lindsay, Nov. 14, 1937; children—Carole Ann, Gilbert Livingston, Dennis Gordon. Came to U.S., 1919, naturalized, 1940. With Christ for the Nations, Dallas, 1948—, sec., 1960—, pres., 1973—; pres. Christ for the Nations Inst., Dallas. Editor Gordon Lindsays books including: Prayer That Moves Mountains, 1959; One Year to Live, 1972; One in Every Other Family, 1973; How to Be Enriched by Giving, 1974. Pub., editor Christ for Nation mag. Home: 441 Fawn Ridge Dr Dallas TX 75224 Office: Box 24910 Dallas TX 75224

LINDSAY, GRACE VICTORIA BARROWS (MRS. HAROLD MILTON LINDSAY), physician; b. Phila., June 2, 1927; d. Victor Ira and Marie (Holeton) Barrows; A.B., Columbia Union Coll., 1950; postgrad. U. Va., 1952, Coll. William and Mary, 1957, 58, 59; M.D., Howard U., 1964; m. Harold Milton Lindsay, July 8, 1948; children—John Gregory, James Harold, Joan Victoria, Julia Suzanne. Tchr. jr. high sch., Hampton, Va., 1956-60; intern Washington Sanitarium and Hosp., Takoma Park, Md., 1964-65; resident dermatology Med. Coll. Va., Richmond, 1965-68; practice medicine specializing in dermatology, Silver Spring, Md. 1969—; cons. dermatology St. Elizabeth Hosp., Washington, 1969-72, Leland Meml. Hosp., Riverdale, Md., 1972—. Mem. Seventh-day Adventist Ch. Home: 8016 Barron St Takoma Park MD 20012 Office: 831 University Blvd E Silver Spring MD 20903

LINDSAY, JUNE CAMPBELL MCKEE (MRS. POWELL LINDSAY), communications exec.; b. Detroit, Nov. 14, 1920; d. Maitland Everett and Josephine Belle (Campbell) McKee; B.A. with honors in Speech (McGregor Fund Mich. grantee), U. Mich., 1943; Electronics Engring. certificate Signal Corps Ground Signal Service, 1943; postgrad. (Inst. Gen. Semantics grantee), U. Chgo., 1944-45, N.Y. U. (Armour grantee), 1945-46, Columbia, 1946-47, Wayne State U., 1960-64, U. Mich., 1964-70; m. Powell Lindsay, Nov. 25, 1967; 1 son, Kristi Costa McKee. Coordinator, activator McKee Prodns., Detroit, 1943-56; Being Unltd., 1957—; dir. Suitcase Theatre, Inc., Ann Arbor, Mich. Cons. Cornelian Corner Detroit, Inc., 1957-63, Islamic Center Found. Soc., Detroit, 1959-62, City Ann Arbor Human Relations Commn., 1966-68, Urban Adult Edn. Inst., Detroit, 1968-69, Mich. Bell Telephone Co., Detroit, 1969, African Art Gallery Founders, Detroit Inst. Arts, 1964, WKAR-TV, Mich. State U., 1971—. Bd. dirs. Mus. Youth Internat., Saline, Mich. Chaplain's asst. Univ. Hosp., Ann Arbor, 1971-72; program dir. People-to-People, Ann Arbor, 1971-72; Suitcase Theatre tour coordinator Brit. Empire's Leprosy Relief Assn., 1972—. Recipient Award for Excellence Mich. Ednl. Assn., 1971, Mich. Assn. Classroom Tchrs., 1972. Mem. Soc. for Individual Responsibility, Am. Women in Radio and TV Broadcast Pioneers, Am. Fedn. Advt., Internat. Platform Assn., Baha'i Faith (assembly cons. 1960—). Home: 2339 S Circle Dr Ann Arbor MI 48103

LINDSAY, VAUGHNIE JEAN GARRETTE (MRS. JOSEPH D. LINDSAY III), univ. dean; b. Prague, Okla., Mar. 31, 1921; d. Irvin Frank and Cora (Kennedy) Garrette; B.S., Central State U., 1940; M. Bus. Edn. with spl. distinction, U. Okla., 1959; Ed.D. with spl. distinction, Ind. U., 1966; m. Joseph D. Lindsay III, July 25, 1947; children—Deborah Ann (Mrs. Larry D. Rogers), Sandra Jo (Mrs. Lawrence Doreson). Bus. tchr. Mooreland (Okla.) High Sch., 1940-42, Guthrie (Okla.) High Sch., 1942-43; personnel mgr. Phillips Petroleum Co., Oklahoma City, 1943-47; exec. sec. Esperanza Oils, Inc., Oklahoma City, 1956-58; asst. prof. bus. edn. Southwestern State Coll., Weatherford, Okla., 1959-62; asst. prof. bus. edn. U. Okla., Norman, 1965-66, asso. prof., 1966-70; prof. bus. edn., adj. prof. secondary edn. So. Ill. U. at Edwardsville, 1970-73, grad. dean, 1973—. Mem. Nat. Com. on Guidelines for Bus. Tchr. Edn., 1969-70; cons., lectr., writer Consortium on Okla. Guidelines for Collegiate Shorthand, 1969; curriculum cons. Job Corps Center, Guthrie, Okla., 1967. Danforth Study grantee, 1962-63, 63-64. Mem. Nat. Assn. for Bus. Tchr. Edn. (mem. exec. bd. 1970-72; mem. task force 1970-72; co-editor Rev., fall 1972), N.E.A., Nat., North Central bus. edn. assns., Am., Ill. vocational assns., Nat. Council Univ. Research Adminstrs., Ill. Bus. Edn. Assn. (mem. exec. bd. 1972-75), Ill. Bus. Educators Council, Delta Pi Epsilon (nat. research com.), Pi Lambda Theta. Asso. editor Nat. Bus. Edn. Quarterly, 1970, editor, 1971; editor sect. Forum, 1971. Co-author: Guidelines for Business Teacher Education, 1972. Contbr. articles to profl. jours. Home: 12773 Partridge Run Dr Florissant MO 63033 Office: Grad Sch So Ill U Edwardsville IL 62025

LINDSEY, ANNE LYLE BUTTON, editor; b. Newark, Feb. 23, 1923; d. John Conyers and Olive Lyle (Demarest) Button; student Washington Sch. for Secs., 1939-40, Wilson Coll., 1940-42, N.Y. U., 1942-43; m. Charles Grattan Lindsey, Jr., Aug. 15, 1970; children by previous marriage—George, Donald and Deborah Hart. Exec. sec. Lionel Edie, N.Y.C., 1945-46; with Antelope Valley Jr. Coll., Cal., 1957-58; advt. dir. Stanley Rowland Real Estate Sales, Falls Church, Va., 1959-68; newspaper columnist, feature writer Studio Creative Crafts, Arlington, Va., 1968-69; editor Enterprise Prodns., Middleburg, Va., 1970—. Mem. Va. Real Estate Bd., Huguenot Soc., Retarded Childrens Assn., Nat. League Am. Pen Women (pres. Falls Church and Arlington br. 1970), Nat. Soaring Soc. Am., Soroptimist Internat. Republican. Methodist. Club: Middleburg Garden. Author: China Painting Step by Step, 1962; Creative Ceramics for Beginners, 1968; Ceramic Painting Step by Step, 1971; Loudoun County, 1973. Address: Brookcliff Middleburg VA 22117

LINDSEY, D. RUTH, educator, corrective therapist; b. Kingfisher, Okla., Oct. 26, 1926; d. Lewis H. and Kenyon (King) Lindsey; B.S., Okla. State U., 1948; M.S., U. Wis., 1954; P.E.D., Ind. U., 1965. Faculty health phys. edn. and recreation Okla. State U., Stillwater, 1948-50, 56—, Monticello Coll., Godfrey, Ill., 1951-54, DePauw U., 1954-56. Counselor, Camp Waldemar, Hunt, Tex., 1948-56; cons. Payne County Child Welfare Dept. and County Health Dept.; fencing cons. Olympic Devel. Com., 2d Nat. Inst. Girls and Women's Sports, 1965; Okla. liaison Nat. Task Force on Perceptual Motor Devel., 1969-72; mem. governing bd. spl. Olympics, 1971—; mem. Gov's Phys. Fitness Council, 1966, 69. Bd. dirs. Payne County Sheltered Workshop, 1971-74. Recipient award Danforth Found., 1944. Mem. Am. Corrective Therapy Assn., Amateur Fencers League Am., Nat. Fencing Coaches Assn., Okla. Assn. Health, Phys. Edn. and Recreation (past v.p.; Honor award 1965), Nat., So. assns. phys. edn. for coll. Women, Okla. Bd. Women's Ofcls. (past chmn.). Republican. Baptist. Author: (with Jones, Whitley) Body Mechanics, 1968; (with others) Concepts in Physical Education, 1970. Contbr. articles to mags., profl. jours. Research on reducing racket. Home: 824 Ranch Dr Stillwater OK 74074 Office: Okla State U Stillwater OK 74074

LINDSEY, NORMA JACK, educator, microbiologist; b. Van Zandt County, nr. Canton, Tex., June 16, 1929; d. Oscar Lee and Nora Velma (Flovin) Lindsey; B.A., B.S., Tex. Woman's U., B.S., 1951; M.P.H., U. Cal. at Berkeley, 1964; Ph.D., Colo. State U., 1969.

Bacteriologist, Dallas Health Dept. Labs., 1951-54; microbiologist, chief Br. Lab., Ariz. State Health Labs., Tucson, 1956-65; chief microbiology, asst. dir. N.M. Health Labs., Albuquerque, 1969-70; research microbiologist U.S. Dept. Health, Edn. and Welfare, Kansas City, Kan., 1970-73; asst. prof. pathology U. Kan. Med. Center, Kansas City, 1973—. Served with USNR, 1954-56. Tng. grantee USPHS, 1963-64. Mem. Am. Soc. Microbiology, A.A.A.S., N.Y. Acad. Sci., Tissue Culture Assn., Research Soc. Am., Am. Pub. Health Assn., Sigma Xi. Contbr. articles to profl. jours. Home: 6317 W 58th St Shawnee Mission KS 66202 Office: 39th and Bainbow St Kansas City KS 66103

LINDSEY, RUTH, librarian; b. Dixon, S.D., Sept. 21, 1914; d. Albert Samuel and Ferne (Sours) Lindsey; A.B., Washington U., St. Louis, 1940, J.D., 1940. Admitted to Mo. bar, 1940; sec., atty. firm Armstrong & Hamilton, St. Louis, 1941-45, Sievers & Regan, 1945-49; asso. with M. Jules King, accountant, gen. practice, 1949-58; librarian Ark. Supreme Ct., Little Rock, 1960—. Mem. Ark. Assn. Women Lawyers (pres. 1966), Pulaski County (Ark.), Am., Ark. bar assns., Washington U. Law Alumni Assn., Zeta Tau Alpha, Delta Sigma Rho, Kappa Beta Pi. Presbyn. Club: Altrusa (dir., treas. Little Rock 1971-73, Altrusan of Year award 1973). Home: 6111 Ridgecrest Dr Little Rock AR 72205 Office: Justice Bldg Little Rock AR 72201

LINDSEY, SANDRA CHARLOTTE ROSE BARTON (MRS. ROBERT LINDSEY, JR.), adminstr.; b. Buffalo, July 31, 1936; d. Daniel Cornelius and Sylvia Adaline (Brandford) Barton; B.S., Tufts U., 1960; M. Pub. Adminstrn., U. So. Cal., 1970; m. Robert Lindsey, Jr., June 4, 1966. Occupational therapist City of Hope, Duarte, Cal., 1962-67; rehab. cons. therapeutics So. Cal., 1967-69; dir. Pacific Coast region Project 75, Nat. Med. Assn., Los Angeles, 1970-73; now engaged in bus. devel. Founders Savs. & Loan Assn. Bd. dirs. Los Angeles Met. YWCA, 1970—, chmn. awards com., 1971-73; bd. dirs. Clark Residence, Los Angeles, 1970—. Traineeship grantee USPHS, 1968. Mem. Am. Occupational Therapy Assn., Am. Pub. Health Assn., Am. Soc. Pub. Adminstrn., Am. Acad. Polit. and Social Sci., Alpha Kappa Alpha. Home: 3911 Olympiad Dr Los Angeles CA 90043 Office: 3910 W Santa Barbara Av Los Angeles CA 90008

LINDSLEY, INA ELIZABETH, author; b. Lyons, Minn.; d. Frank Roscoe and Mary E. (Williams) Lindsley; B.A., Macalester Coll., 1911. News reporter, 1914-20; exec. sec. Lyon County (Minn.) A.R.C., 1920-29; free lance writer, 1921—. Election bd. judge, 1930-54. Trustee Marshall-Lyon County (Minn.) Pub. Library, 1933-54. Mem. Nat. Presbyn. Bd. Christian Edn. Mem. League Minn. Poets, Am. Assn. U. Women, P.E.O. Author childrens books including The Silver Star, 1962, The Little Pine Tree (made into filmstrip for Soc. Visual Edn., Inc.), 1955; Holliday in Doll-Land, 1968; Hi, Tuffy, 1969; The Puffy Policeman of Perryville, 1971. Contbr. numerous stories and rhymes to juvenile publs. Address: 200 S 4th St Marshall MN 56258

LINEHAN, ELEANOR BARBARA, sch. adminstr.; b. Cambridge, Mass., Jan. 28, 1914; d. Edward Alfred and Amy Eleanor (Van Horn) Linehan; B.S. in Edn., Boston U., then M.S., Ed.D. Reading instr. Cobb Sch., Kingston, Mass., 1936-37; tchr. Winn Brook Sch., Belmont, Mass., 1937-42; asst. supt. elementary schs., Waltham, Mass., 1956—. Tchr. Newton (Mass.) Coll. of Sacred Heart, 1953-70. Bd. dirs. A.R.C., Beaver Brook Mental Health Center, Belmont, Monomoy Community services, Chatham, Mass. Served with USNR, 1942-45. Recipient Outstanding award A.R.C., 1970, Top Hat award Bus.-Profl. Women, 1967. Mem. Waltham C. of C. Coffee Cuppers, Alpha Gamma, Delta Gamma, Pi Lambda Theta (pres. chpt. 1954). Home: Hillcrest Rd N Chatham MA 02650

LINEHAN, MARSHA MARIE, psychologist; b. Tulsa, May 5, 1943; d. John Marston and Ella Marie (Bourg) Linehan; B.S. cum laude, Loyola U. Chgo., 1968, M.A., 1970, Ph.D., 1971. Lectr. psychology Loyola U., 1969-71; research clinician Suicide Prevention and Crisis Service, Buffalo, 1971-72; adj. prof. State U. Coll., Buffalo, 1972; postdoctoral fellow in behavior modification State U. N.Y., Stony Brook, 1972-73; asst. prof. psychology Cath. U. Am., Washington, 1973—; pvt. practice psychology, Washington, 1974—; adj. prof. Inst. Pastoral Studies, Loyola U., Chgo., 1970-73. Mem. Am., D.C. psychol. assns., Assn. for Advancement Behavior Therapy (membership chmn. 1974—), Am. Assn. Suicidology, Psi Chi. Research in sex differences in suicidal behavior, behavior modification. Home: 1301 20th St NW Washington DC 20036

LINEY, MURIEL ELISE, pub. relations exec.; b. Phila., Nov. 29, 1941; d. John Joseph and Rosa Elizabeth (Acquesta) Liney; B.A., Pa. State U., 1962. Field service A.J. Wood Research, Phila., 1962-64; pub. relations asst. Phila. Nat. Bank, 1964-70; pub. relations dir. Holy Redeemer Hosp., Meadowbrook, Pa., 1970—. Mem. Pub. Relations Assn., Delaware Valley Hosp. Council, Hosp. Assn. Pa. Office: 1648 Huntingdon Pike Meadowbrook PA 19046

LIN-FU, JANE SYCIP (MRS. CHING MARK FU), pediatrician; b. Singapore, Nov. 21, 1928 (came to U.S. 1955, naturalized 1963); d. Yu Y. and Unchong Y. (Sycip) Lin; M.D. cum laude, U. Santo Tomas, Manila, Philippines, 1955; m. Ching Mark Fu, May 30, 1958; children—Emanuel, Jeanette, Stephenie. Intern Bklyn. Jewish Hosp. and Med. Center, 1955-56; resident, 1956-58, fellow pediatric neurology, 1958-60; cons. children's bur. Dept. Health, Edn. and Welfare, 1963-69, maternal and child health service USPHS, 1969-73, White House Conf. on Children, 1970, Clin. Services Health Services, Dept. Health Edn. and Welfare, 1973—. Recipient award to work in lead poisoning Nat. Decorating Products Assn., 1972, Superior Service award Dept. Health, Edn. and Welfare, 1973. Diplomate Am. Bd. Pediatrics. Fellow Am. Acad. Pediatrics; mem. Washington Med. Soc. (asso.). Research and publs. on lead poisoning in children. Home: 6420 Hollins Dr Bethesda MD Office: 5600 Fishers Lane Rockville MD 20852

LING, CARMEL ARLENE, educator; b. Wichita, Kan., Apr. 11, 1912; d. Harry Benjamin and Ella (Wells) Ling; B.A., Whittier Coll., 1933; M.S., U. So. Cal., 1948. Musician, soprano, appearing professionally, 1928-48; harpist with Schertizinger Quintet, 1936-48; tool designer Douglas Aircraft, 1942-44; tchr. math. Excelsior Union High Sch. Dist. (now Norwalk-La Mirada Unified School Dist.), 1944-57, dist. psychologist and tchr. advanced math., 1957—. Mem. Nat. Council Tchrs. Math., Math. Assn. Am., Cal. Math. Council (regional rep. 1953—), Cal. Tchrs. Assn., N.E.A., Cal. Assn. Sch. Psychologists and Psychometrists, Whittier Bus. and Profl. Women's Club (pres. 1972-74). Home: 5401 N Mesagrove Av Whittier CA 90601 Office: Pioneer and Alondra Norwalk CA 90651

LINHARDT, ELIZABETH AGNES WEISHAAR (MRS. GEORGE ELMER LINHARDT), orgn. exec.; b. Balt., Sept. 20, 1915; d. Charles Joseph and Elizabeth Florence (Ziemer) Weishaar; ed. Balt. schs.; m. George Elmer Linhardt, July 31, 1938; children—Angela Elizabeth, George Elmer. Asst. to pharmacist St. Agnes Hosp., Balt., 1931-34, X-ray technician, 1934-38; med. sec., Annapolis, Md., 1938—. Organizer health room St. Mary's High and Grammar Schs., Annapolis, Md., 1959; state chmn. A.M.A. Edn. and Research Found., 1968-75, chmn. members-at-large, 1966-68, treas., 1970-71. Mem. Woman's Aux. A.M.A., Woman's Aux. Med. and Chirurgical Faculty Md., Woman's Aux. Am. Soc. Abdominal Surgeons, Woman's Aux. Internat. Coll. Surgeons. Club: Faculty Wives (U. Md.). Home: 3 Chesapeake Av Annapolis MD 21403

LINK, CAROLYN EARHEART, govt. ofcl.; b. Dover, Tenn., Feb. 15, 1941; d. Joseph Elijah and Eva (Durrwachter) Earheart; student Austin Peay State U., 1971; m. Ronnie Wade Link, June 12, 1963; children—Chase Riley, Amber Elaine. Bookkeeper, Dover Stone Co., 1959-61; clk.-typist, receptionist Ft. Donelson Nat. Mil. Park, Dover, 1961-65, clk.-typist, 1968-72, adminstrv. clk., 1972—; teller Farmers & Mchts. Bank, Bumpus Mills, Tenn., 1965-68. Mem. Dover Bus. and Profl. Women's Club (charter pres. 1962, corr. sec. 1973—), Stewart County Jaycettes (charter mem., pres. 1968, sec. 1966—, state dir. 1967). Mem. Christian Ch. Home: Route 2 Box 312 Dover TN 37058 Office: PO Box F Dover TN 37058

LINK, SISTER M. JEAN, hosp. adminstr.; b. Carthagena, O., Apr. 21, 1929; d. Charles J. and Anna S. (Wuebker) Link; B.S., U. Dayton, 1953; M.B.A. in Hosp. Adminstrn., Xavier U., 1964. Lab. supr. Our Lady of Bellefonte Hosp., Ashland, Ky., 1954-59; lab. supr. St. Mary Hosp., Quincy, Ill., 1960-62; adminstrv. resident St. Joseph Hosp., South Bend, Ind., 1963-64; asst. adminstr. St. Francis Hosp., Cin., 1964-66, adminstr., 1966—. Bd. trustees St. Anthony Hosp., Columbus, O., 1972—; bd. dirs. St. Francis-St. George Hosp.; asso. Franciscan Health Services, Cin., 1971—; mem. adv. bd. Hosp. Adv. Com. Mem. Am. Soc. Med. Technologists, Am. Mgmt. Assn., Am. Coll. Hosp. Adminstrs., Am. Hosp. Assn., Am. Health Assn., Soc. Personnel Adminstrs., Council Religious Cin. Home: 2144 Selim St Cincinnati OH 45214 Office: 1860 Queen City Cincinnati OH 45214

LINK, MAE MILLS (MRS. S. GORDDEN LINK), space medicine research cons.; b. Corbin, Ky., May 14, 1915; d. William Speed and Florence (Estes) Mills; B.S., George Peabody Coll. for Tchrs., 1936; M.A., Vanderbilt U., 1937; Ph.D., Am. U., 1951; grad. Air War Coll., 1965; m. S. Gordden Link, Jan. 11, 1936. Instr. social sci. Oglethorpe U., 1938-39; instr. English, Drury Coll., 1940-41; asso. dir. edn. Ga. Warm Springs Found., 1941-42; mil. historian Hdqrs. Army Air Forces, 1943-45, Office Mil. History, Dept. of Army, 1945-51; spl. asst. to surgeon gen. and sr. med. historian U.S. Air Force, Washington, 1951-62; cons. in documentation and space medicine historian NASA, Washington, 1962-64, coordinator documentation and life scis. historian, 1964-70; research asso. Ohio State U. Found., 1970-72; trustee, dir. history fellows Koontz Meml. Center Advanced Study, 1972. Mem. exec. com. D.C. area Orgn. for Advancement Coll. Teaching. Trustee, Univ. Press Fund, Amos R. Koontz Meml. Found. Recipient Meritorious Service award U.S. Air Force, 1955, Outstanding Performance award, 1956, 62; Friday Nighters cup, 1960. Fellow Am. Med. Writers Assn. (dir. Middle Atlantic region); mem. Aerospace Med. Assn. (standing com. on sci. communication in bioastronautics and space medicine), Am. Inst. Aeros. and Astronautics (hist. adv. com.), Air Force Hist. Found. (charter), Am. Assn. Med. History, Internat. Congress History Medicine, Soc. for History Tech., Am. Hist. Assn., Societe International d'Histoire de la Medecine, Am. Assn. U. Women. Republican. Episcopalian. Clubs: Garden Va. Author: (with others) Medical Support of the Army Air Forces in World War II, 1955; Annual Reports of the U.S. Air Force Medical Service, 1949-62; Space Medicine in Project Mercury, 1965. Editor: U.S. Air Force Med. Service Digest, 1957-62. Contbr. to Ency. Brit., Collier's Ency., Funk & Wagnall's New Ency., USA/USSR Joint Publ. profl. jours. Home: Dellbrook Riverton VA 22651 Office: Center for Advanced Study Riverton VA 22651

LINK, MARILYN CALMES, found. exec.; b. Glendale, Cal., Feb. 20, 1924; d. Edwin Albert and Marie (Calmes) Link; student Syracuse U., 1942-44, Stephens Coll., 1945; B.S., N.Y. U., 1946; M.S., U. Ill., 1949; postgrad. Columbia, 1952-53. Staff asst. edn. div. Link Aviation, Binghamton, N.Y., 1946-48; tchr. elementary sch., Millburn, N.J., 1949-51; exec. pilot Wood-Mosaic Co., Louisville, 1952-53; instr. air age edn. div. U. Neb. at Lincoln, 1951-53; exec. sec. Link Found., Binghamton, N.Y., 1954—; adminstrv. asst. Gen. Precision Equipment, N.Y.C., 1958-61; spl. asst., pub. relations Mohawk Airlines, N.Y.C., 1961-72; mgr. sales devel. Hughes Airwest Airlines, Eastern region, N.Y.C., 1972. Adviser Dept. Def., 1973; collaborator Nat. Air and Space Mus., Smithsonian Instn., 1954-59. Trustee Link Found., 1970—, Atlantic Found., 1973—, Harbor Branch Found., 1973—; bd. curators Stephens Coll., 1971-74. Recipient U. Aviation Assn. award 1962, Frank B. Brewer Trophy, Nat. Aero. Assns., 1963, Lady Hay Drummond-Hay Trophy, Women's Internat. Aero. Assn., 1965. Mem. Nat. Pilots Assn., Nat. Aerospace Edn. Council Aviation-Space Writers Assn., Ninety-Nines. Home: 3 Vista Palm Lane Vero Beach FL 32960 Office: 250 Park Av Suite 624 New York City NY 10017

LINK, MARION CLAYTON (MRS. EDWIN A. LINK), author; b. Ilion, N.Y., Nov. 15, 1907; d. Floyd Ashton and Elma (Gray) Clayton; B.S. in Journalism, Syracuse U., 1929; m. Edwin A. Link, June 6, 1931; children—William Martin, Edwin Clayton. Reporter, feature writer Syracuse Jour.-Am., 1925-28, Utica (N.Y.) Observer-Dispatch, 1928, Binghamton (N.Y.) Press, 1929-31; pub. relations sec. Link Aviation Inc., Binghamton, 1931-37; research, author undersea projects with husband, 1949—. Bd. dirs. State U. N.Y. at Binghamton, Syracuse U., YWCA, Binghamton. Recipient Arents Pioneer medal Syracuse U., 1963. Mem. Soc. Woman Geographers, Woman's Nat. Book Assn., Phi Kappa Phi, Pi Beta Phi, Delta Kappa Gamma, Eta Pi Upsilon. Club: Zonta Internat. Author: Sea Diver, a Quest for History Under the Sea, 1959; (with Edwin A. Link) A New Theory on Columbus' Voyage Through the Bahamas, 1958; Windows in the Sea, 1973. Contbr. articles to profl. jours., mags. Address: 10 Avon Rd Binghamton NY 13905

LINKE, FRANCES BAUR (MRS. RAYMOND J. LINKE), librarian; b. Buenos Aires, Argentina, May 3, 1924 (parents Am. citizens); d. George and Caroline (Cunioli) Baur; A.A., Los Angeles City Coll., 1962; B.S., Cal. State U., 1967; M.S. in L.S., U. So. Cal., 1972; m. Raymond J. Linke, Mar. 20, 1964. Librarian, Minn. Mining & Mfg. Co., Los Angeles, 1960-64, Blue Cross of So. Cal., Los Angeles, 1964—. Co-owner Nin-Ra Siamese Cattery, La Canada, Cal., 1967—. Mem. Cal. Library Assn., Spl. Libraries Assn. (mem. subject heading com., ins. div. 1968-74), Med. Library Group So. Cal., Am. Cat Assn., Cat Fanciers Assn., Am. Cat Fanciers Assn., Screen Actors Guild, A.F.T.R.A. Author: Gone to the Cats, bibliography of cat books, 1973. Office: 4777 Sunset Blvd Los Angeles CA 90027

LINN, MARGARET WISHON (MRS. BERNARD S. LINN), social worker; b. Yadkinville, N.C., Jan. 29, 1930; d. Luther Mark and Helen (Hendricks) Wishon; B.A., Bob Jones U., 1951; M.S.W., Coll. William and Mary, 1956; Ph.D., Union Grad. Sch., Yellow Springs, O., 1974; m. Bernard S. Linn, Oct. 2, 1955. With N.Y. State Mental Hygiene Clinic, Binghamton, N.Y., 1956-58; psychiat. social worker VA Hosp., Perry Point, Md., 1958-63; social sci. research VA Hosp., also U. Miami (Fla.) Sch. Medicine, 1963—, asso. prof. family medicine, U. Miami, 1970—. Adj. asso. prof. social work Barry Coll. Sch. Social Work, Miami, 1969—. Mem. research com. Nat. Inst. Mental Health, 1973—. Nat. Inst. Mental Health grantee, 1969-70, 70-71; Nat. Inst. Child Health Human Devel. grantee, 1972-74, United Health Fund grantee, 1971. Mem. Nat. Assn. Social Work, Am. Sociol. Assn., Am. Psychology Assn., Gerontology Soc., A.A.A.S. Contbr. articles to profl. jours. Home: 1224 Country Club Prado Coral Gables FL 33134 Office: VA Hosp 1201 NW 16th St Miami FL 33125

LINN, (MARION) JOANNE LOVELL (MRS. ROBERT JOSEPH LINN), anesthesiologist, educator; b. Centerville, Tenn., Mar. 24, 1926; d. Joe William and Annie Louise (Stephenson) Lovell; A.B., Tusculum Coll., 1946; M.D., Vanderbilt U., 1950; m. Robert Joseph Linn, Aug. 30, 1949; children—Mary Louise (Mrs. Scott Peyton Fitzhugh), Joseph Lovell, Margaret Ruth, David Robert. Intern, Balt. City Hosps., 1950-51; resident anesthesiology Vanderbilt U. Hosps., Nashville, 1951-53, George Washington U. Hosp., Washington, 1953; instr. anesthesiology Vanderbilt U., 1955-58, asst. prof., 1958-72, asso. prof., 1972—; cons. anesthesiologist VA Hosp., 1955-63, 73—, St. Thomas Hosp., 1968— (both Nashville). Mem. Am., So., Tenn. med. assns., Internat. Anesthesiology Research Soc., Am. Soc. Anesthesiology, Tenn. Soc. Anesthesiologists (sec.-treas. 1971—), So., Nashville (pres. 1956, 66, 70-71) anesthesiology socs., Am., Tenn., Middle Tenn. (exec. bd. 1970, chmn. pub. edn. com. 1973-75) heart assns., Am. Med. Womens Assn. (charter, co-founder, 1st pres. Middle Tenn. br. 1967, nat. chmn. internat. relations com. 1973—, sec. 1974), Davidson County and Nashville Acad. Medicine, N.Y. Acad. Scis., Am. Inst. Hypnosis, Am. Assn. U. Profs., Am. Assn. U. Women, Am. Profl. Practice Assn., Nashville Area C. of C., Internat. Platform Assn., Nat. Aero. Assn., Nat. Audubon Soc., Nat. Council on Alcoholism and Drug Abuse, Am. Mus. Natural History, numerous other orgns., Delta Kappa Gamma, Alpha Epsilon Delta. Presbyn. Clubs: University, Vanderbilt Woman's (Nashville), Davidson County Business and Professional Womens. Home: 6532 Jocelyn Hollow Rd Nashville TN 37205 Office: Vanderbilt U Med Center Nashville TN 37232

LINN, PHYLLIS ISAACS (MRS. D. HAROLD LINN), sculptor, educator; b. N.Y.C., Dec. 23, 1930; d. A. Joseph and Lillian (Lehrer) Isaacs; A.F.A., Ohio U., 1950; B.A., Hofstra U., 1972, M.A., 1974; m. D. Harold Linn, Dec. 25, 1952; children—Sharon, Jeffrey, Steven, Richard. Exhibited one-woman shows at Hewlett-Woodmere Library Galleries, 1973; exhibited in group shows Audubon Artists, N.Y.C., 1971, Nat. Acad. Galleries, N.Y.C., 1971-73, Lehigh (Pa.) U., 1972, Lever House, N.Y.C., 1972-73, Bergen Community Mus., Englewood, N.J., 1974. Grad. teaching fellow Hofstra U., Hempstead, N.Y., 1972, instr. art history dept., 1972—. Recipient univ. R. Fanning award, 1970, C. Lambasa award 1971. Mem. Nat. Assn. Women Artists, Artist Craftsmen N.Y., League Present Day Artists, Artist Equity Assn.

LINNETTE, VALLETA HARPER MARY, coll. dean; b. Cin., Sept. 25, 1922; d. James Edward and Mary Lavina (Baptiste) Harper; B.S., Columbia, 1942, M.A., 1944; student English lit., U. London (Eng.), 1950; m. Harry Maurice Linnette, Dec. 5, 1953 (dec. 1968). Dean women Va. State Coll., Petersburg, 1947-57, asso. prof. English, 1952-57; tchr. English San Diego High Sch., 1957-64; tchr. English, San Diego City Coll., 1964-72, dean student activities, 1973—. Dir., chmn. personnel com. Pacific Coast Bank, San Diego, 1972—. Mem. San Diego Status of Women Adv. Bd., 1973—. Pres. bd. dirs. San Diego County Citizens Scholarship Found., 1971-73; regional bd. dirs., local exec. bd. dirs. Nat. Conf. Christians and Jews; adv. bd. Project YES (Youth Edn. Service). Recipient Truth award Nat. Sojourners, 1972; named Woman of Valor in Edn., Beth Israel Sisterhood, 1970. Mem. Nat. Assn. Women Deans, Adminstrs. and Counselors, Cal. Assn. Women Adminstrs. and Counselors (chpt. dir. 1972-75), Am. Personnel and Guidance Assn., Am. Assn. U. Women (pres. San Diego 1973—), Nat. Assn. Negro Bus. and Profl. Women, Delta Kappa Gamma, Alpha Kappa Alpha (pres. 1969-72). Author: Guide to Teaching Afro-American Literature, 1969; also articles. Home: 429 Las Flores Terrace San Diego CA 92114

LINQUIST, EVELYN DUNLAVY (MRS. PETER LINQUIST), banker; b. Cheyenne, Wyo., Aug. 26, 1912; d. Dayton Atwell and Stella (Stites) Dunlavy; student York Coll., 1931, Lincoln Sch. Commerce, 1942; m. Peter Linquist, May 16, 1947; 1 dau., Constance (Mrs. John O. Dahlstet). Sec. firm Anderson, Storms and Strasbarger, Holdrege, Neb., 1948-51; mgr., sec. Holdrege Savs. & Loan, 1951—, also dir. Mem. Holdrege C. of C. Home: 1002 Morton St Holdrege NE 68949 Office: 423 Garfield St Holdrege NE 68949

LINSLEY, PRISCILLA MARY (MRS. PAUL E. LINSLEY), librarian; b. Girard, Pa., Mar. 20, 1934; d. John Carl and Charlotte (Read) Katzman; B.A., U. N.H., 1956; M.A., No. Ill. U., 1964; m. Michael A. Kahn, June 19, 1954; children—Karen, Lisa, Amy; m. 2d, Paul E. Linsley, Feb. 22, 1969. Cataloger No. Ill. U., 1964-66; asst. librarian Ednl. Testing Service, Princeton, N.J., 1966-68, librarian, 1968—; mem. adv. bd. Mercer County Community Coll. Mem. A.L.A., Spl. Libraries Assn. (pres. elect chpt. 1973-74, chairperson elect edn. sect. 1973-74), Am. Soc. Information Sci. Home: Cleveland Rd RD 2 Princeton NJ 08540 Office: Educational Testing Service Princeton NJ 08540

LINTON, MARGARET REYNOLDS, publisher; b. Camden, S.C.; d. Andrew and Louise (Gaskin) Reynolds; student Youngstown State U.; m. Amos Leo Linton, May 15, 1950 (dec.); 1 son, Gary Leo. Operator Linton Funeral Home; newspaper editor, columnist Buckeye Rev., Youngstown, O.; sec.-treas. Black Broadcasting Coalition; publisher, editor Critique Publ. Asso., Youngstown; producer, host weekly TV show One Woman's World, 1963, 70—; pres., editor bi-monthly news mag. Critique, 1966-72; sec.-treas. Youngstown Community Cablevision, Inc. Founder Broadway Theatre League; chmn. Fashion Fair; mem. N.A.A.C.P., Hostess Johnson-Humphrey Inaugural; sec. Citizens for Kennedy; mem. Youngstown Human Relations Commn.; mem. panel Dem. Nat. Com.; exec. female com. govt. Youngstown Black Polit. Assembly. Bd. dirs. McGuffey Manor, convalescent home, Housing Opportunities, low cost housing, Urban League, Cancer Soc., Children's Service, Council Blind, Black Broadcasting Coalition. Named B'nai B'rith Woman of Year, 1961. Mem. Am. Assn. Workers for Blind, Am. Assn. Instrs. for Blind, Ohio Negro Bus. and Profl. Women (1st gov.), Buckeye Funeral Dirs., Nat. Assn. Fashion and Accessory Designers, Am. Women in Radio-TV. Elk. Club: Bridge. Home: 632 Belmont Av Youngstown OH 44511 Office: 601 Arlington St Youngstown OH 44502

LINTON, MARIGOLD LORELAI, psychologist, educator; b. Banning, Cal., Sept. 30, 1936; d. Walter Alexander and Wistaria (Hartmann) Linton; B.A., U. Cal. at Riverside, 1958; postgrad. U. Ia., 1958-60; Ph.D., U. Cal. at Los Angeles, 1964. Research asso., dept. child psychiatry U. So. Cal., Los Angeles, 1963-64; lectr. San Diego State U., 1964-65, asst. prof., 1965-68, asso. prof., 1968-71; prof. psychology, 1971-74; prof. U. Utah, Salt Lake City, 1974—; vis. prof. U. Cal. at San Diego, 1971-72. Bd. dirs. Malki Mus., Banning, Cal., 1971-74; mem. talent search bd., U. Cal. at San Diego, 1970-71. Mem. Nat. Indian Edn. Assn. (founding bd. dirs., 1970-71), A.A.A.S., Am., Western psychol. assns. Author: A Simplified Style Manual, 1972; The Practical Statistician, 1975. Home: 1437 Brookes Av San Diego CA 92103 Office: Dept Psychology U Utah Salt Lake City UT 84112

LINTON, MARY ANN (MRS. GEORGE DAVID LINTON), sorority exec.; b. Pitts., Nov. 21, 1941; d. James William and Stella Grace (Huey) Sidehamer; B.A., Pa. State U., 1963; postgrad. Duquesne U., 1964; M.A., U. Pitts., 1966; m. George David Linton, Sept. 8, 1962; children—Brian David, Natasha Ann. Tchr., Falk Lab. Sch., Pitts., 1966, Edgewood Elementary Sch., 1967-69; chmn. Alpha Sigma Alpha, Springfield, Mo., 1967-70, nat. pres., 1970—. Active P.T.A., 1970—. Mem. Nat. Assn. Women Deans and Councilors (asso.), Nat. Panhellenic Conf. (area adviser). Republican. Presbyn. Club: Alpha Sigma Alpha Alumni (Pitts.). Home: 204 Gallup Rd Princeton NJ 08540 Office: 1201 E Walnut St Springfield MO 65802

LINTON, THELMA ELVIRA CARLTON (MRS. HERBERT JAMES LINTON), city ofcl.; b. Newbury, O., Feb. 28, 1904; d. Hiram Edmund and Nellie Elvira (Loveland) Carlton; A.B. cum laude, Baldwin Wallace Coll., 1924; m. Herbert James Linton, Aug. 13, 1927; children—Eltha (Mrs. Harry E. Bartels), Ralph E., H. Bruce, David A. Tchr. math. and sci. Solon (O.) High Sch., 1924-28; village clk. Village of Solon, 1949-56; dir. finance City of Solon, 1956—. Mem. Municipal Finance Officer Assn. U.S. and Can., Ohio Finance Officers, N.E. Ohio Finance Officers Assn. (charter), D.A.R. Home: 35599 Aurora Rd Solon OH 44139 Office: 6315 SOM Center Rd Solon OH 44139

LINZER, ESTELLE MURIEL, assn. cons.; b. N.Y.C., June 28, 1918; d. Martin M. and Lottie (Peist) Linzer; B.S. in Marketing and Journalism, N.Y. U., 1939. Field asst. League of Nations Assn., N.Y.C., 1942-45; field asst. Am. Assn. for UN, N.Y.C., 1945-47, field dir., 1947-53, asso. dir. for program, 1953-65, asst. to chmn. bd. dirs., 1953-62; program cons. to non-govtl. orgns., 1966—; cons. Johnson Found. Wis., 1966—. Adminstr. Dartmouth Talks in Kiev, USSR, 1971, World Assembly for Human Rights, Montreal, Que., 1968. Vice chmn. human rights com. Non-Govtl. Orgns. Affiliated with UN, 1973. Mem. Internat. Assn. for Exchange of Students for Tech. Experience (dir. 1971—), UN Assn. N.Y. (vice chmn. 1971—). Home: 333 E 79th St New York City NY 10021 Office: 866 United Nations Plaza New York City NY 10017

LIONBERGER, ERLE TALBOT LUND (MRS. JOHN S. LIONBERGER, JR.), republican committeewomen; b. St. Louis, Apr. 29, 1933; d. Joel Y. and Erle (Harsh) Lund; student Mary Inst., 1951; A.B., Vassar Coll., 1955; m. John S. Lionberger, Jr., June 23, 1956; children—Erle Talbot, Louise Shepley. Republican committeewoman Hadley Twp., St. Louis County, 1965—; mem. St. Louis County Rep. Central Com., 1965—; alternate del. Rep. Nat. Conv., 1968; mem. Rep. State Com., 1968—, del. Rep. Nat. Conv., 1972. Regional chmn. United Fund, 1964; area chmn. Arts Council Drive, 1965. Bd. dirs. Landmarks Assn. St. Louis, Inc., 1973—, coordinator Historic Preservation Pilgrimage, 1974. Mem. Jr. League St. Louis, Nat. Soc. Colonial Dames Am. Address: 21 Dartford St St Louis MO 63105

LIPE, LINDA BON, accountant; b. Clarksdale, Miss., Jan. 10, 1948; d. William Ray and Gwendolyn (Strickland) Lipe; B.B.A., U. Miss., 1970, J.D., 1971. Admitted to Miss. bar, 1971; with Arthur Young & Co., San Jose, Cal., 1971-74, sr. tax accountant, 1973-74; sr. operations analyst Kaiser Aetna, Oakland, Cal., 1974—. Mem. Am. Bar Assn., Miss. State Bar, Alpha Lambda Delta, Beta Alpha Psi, Beta Gamma Sigma, Eta Sigma Phi, Phi Gamma Nu, Kappa Beta Pi, Pi Beta Phi. Episcopalian. Home: 5104 Westmont Av Apt 13 San Jose CA 95130 Office: Ordway Bldg Kaiser Center Oakland CA 94612

LIPKIN, MARY CASTLEMAN DAVIS (MRS. ARTHUR BENNETT LIPKIN), former psychiat. social worker; b. Germantown, Pa., Mar. 4, 1907; d. Henry L. and Willie (Webb) Davis; student grad. sch. social work U. Wash., 1946-48; m. William F. Cavenaugh, Nov. 8, 1930 (div.); children—Molly C. (Mrs. Gary Oberbillig), William A.; m. 2d, Arthur Bennett Lipkin, Sept. 15, 1961 (dec. June 1974). Nursery sch. tchr. Miquon (Pa.) Sch., 1940-45; caseworker Family Soc. Seattle, 1948-49, Jewish Family and Child Service, Seattle, 1951-56; psychiat. social worker Stockton (Cal.) State Hosp., 1957-58; supr. social service Mental Health Research Inst., Fort Steilacoom, Wash., 1958-59; engaged in pvt. practice, Bellevue, Wash., 1959-61. Diplomate Conf. Advancement of Pvt. Practice in Social Work. Mem. Nat. Assn. Social Workers, Internat. Conf. Social Work, World Fedn. Mental Health, Acad. Certified Social Workers, Jr. League, Seattle Art Mus., Mus. Modern Art (N.Y.C.), Am. Symphony Orch. League, Phila. Art Alliance, Pa. Acad. Fine Arts. Clubs: Cosmopolitan (Phila.); Women's University (Seattle). Home: 1801 John F Kennedy Blvd Philadelphia PA 19103

LIPPARD, LUCY ROWLAND, author; b. N.Y.C., Apr. 14, 1937; d. Vernon William and Margaret Isham (Cross) Lippard; B.A., Smith Coll., 1958; M.A., N.Y. U., 1962; hon. degree Moore Coll. Art, 1972; m. Robert Ryman, Aug. 19, 1961 (div. May 1968); 1 son, Ethan Isham. Library asst. Mus. Modern Art, N.Y.C., 1958-60; staff writer, 1967; N.Y. editor Art Internat. mag., 1965-67; lectr. N.Y. State Council of the Arts, 1970—, Sch. Visual Arts, N.Y.C., 1969-72. Active Art Workers' Coalition, Ad Hoc Women Artists' Com., West-East Bag, N.Y. Peace Action Coalition. John Simon Guggenheim fellow, 1968; Nat. Endowment Arts critics grantee, 1973. Author: The Graphic Work of Philip Evergood, 1966; Pop Art, 1966; Surrealists on Art, 1970; Dadas on Art, 1971; Changing-Essays in Art Criticism, 1971; Tony Smith, 1972; Six Years: The Dematerialization of the Art Object, 1972. Contbg. author anthologies and mus. exhibition catalogues. Home: 138 Prince St New York City NY 10012

LIPPERT, FELICE SALLY MARK (MRS. ALBERT LIPPERT), weight reduction co. exec.; b. N.Y.C., Feb. 9, 1930; d. Charles William and Mollie (Weissblum) Mark; B.A., Hunter Coll., 1951; m. Albert Lippert, June 21, 1953; children—Keith Lawrence, Randy Seth. Tchr. elementary sch., Tuckahoe, N.Y., 1951-56; with Weight Watchers, Internat., Inc., Great Neck, N.Y., 1963—, treas., 1963-68, sec., dir., 1968-71, corp. sec., 1971—, dir. food research, 1963—. Asso. food editor W.W. Twentyfirst Corp., N.Y.C., 1968—. Chmn. fund raising Mr. & Mrs. League, City of Hope, N.Y.C., 1968—; mem. Am. Parkinson's Disease Assn., 1962—. Mem. Hadassah (life), Chi Omicron. Jewish religion. Home: Sousa Dr Sands Point NY 11050 Office: 175 E Shore Rd Great Neck NY 11023

LIPPINCOTT, SARAH LEE, educator, astronomer; b. Phila., Oct. 26, 1920; d. George E. and Sarah (Evans) Lippincott; student Swarthmore Coll., 1938-39, M.A., 1950; B.A., U. Pa., 1942; D.Sc., Villanova U., 1973. Research asst. Sproul Obs., Swarthmore (Pa.) Coll., 1941-50, research asso., 1951-72, dir., lectr., 1972—. Mem. Savoy Opera Co., Phila., 1947—. Bd. mgrs. Societe de Bienfaisance de Philadelphie, 1966-69. Recipient achievement award Kappa Kappa Gamma, 1966; Jane Bell Meml. scholar, 1937-38; Jessie Kovalenko scholar, 1950; Fulbright fellow, Paris, France, 1953-54. Mem. Rittenhouse, Am. (lectr. 1961—) astronom. socs., Internat. Astronom. Union (v.p. Commn. 26 1970, pres. 1973—), Sigma Xi (nat. lectr. 1971—). Author: (with Joseph M. Joseph) Point to the Stars, 1963, rev., 1967, 2d edit., 1972; (with Laurence Lafore) Philadelphia, the Unexpected City, 1965. Contbr. articles to profl. jours. Office: Sproul Observatory Swarthmore Coll Swarthmore PA 19081

LIPPITT, ELIZABETH CHARLOTTE, writer; b. San Francisco; d. Sidney Grant and Stella Lippitt; student Mills Coll., U. Cal. at Berkeley, 1933-34. Writer, performer own satirical monologues; contbr. articles to various newspapers including Chgo. Am., Orlando Sentinel, Phoenix Republic, Ark. Democrat, Conn. Sunday Herald. Recipient Congress of Freedom award, 1959, 71-73. Mem. Nat. Assn. R.R. Passengers, Nat. Trust for Historic Preservation, Am. Security Council, Internat. Platform Assn., Wilderness Soc., Ladies Aux. League Men Voters, 52 Vets. Assn. Pop singer, recorder song album Songs From the Heart. Home: 2414 Pacific Av San Francisco CA 94115

LIPPSETT, SHIRLEY MINERVA (MRS. HERBERT L. LIPPSETT), physician; b. Bayonne, N.J., Apr. 13, 1922; d. Barnet and Pauline (Levine) Cohen; B.A., N.Y. U., 1941, M.D., 1944; m. Herbert L. Lippsett, Mar. 28, 1946; children—Paula Barbara, Stuart Alan, Laurence Scott. Intern Newark Beth Israel Hosp., 1944-45; resident Univ. Mich. Hosp., Ann Arbor, 1944-46, Lincoln Hosp., Bronx, 1946, Emory Hosp., Atlanta, 1947; practice medicine specializing in pediatrics, Bklyn., 1948—; mem. staff Brookdale Hosp. Med. Center, Bklyn., asso. clin. prof. pediatrics State U. N.Y., Downstate Med. Center, Bklyn. Diplomate Am. Bd. Pediatrics. Fellow Am. Acad Pediatrics; mem. A.M.A., Kings County Med. Soc. (sec. pediatric sect.). Office: 1250 Ocean Av Brooklyn NY 11230

LIPSCHITZ, BEVERLY, educator; b. Bklyn., July 17, 1934; d. Jacob Irving and Sylvia (Gorchikoff) Lipschitz; B.A., Bklyn. Coll., 1955; M.S., 1956; Ed.D., N.Y. U., 1964; student Inst. Pupil Personnel Adminstrs. Harvard, summer 1967. Tchr. N.Y.C. Bd. Edn., 1955-61, guidance coordinator office dist. supt. Bklyn., 1963-65; guidance counselor Pub. Sch. 260, Bklyn., 1961-63; instr. dept. guidance and personnel N.Y. U., N.Y.C., 1965, asst. prof., 1965-66; supr. guidance N.Y.C. Bd. Edn., Bklyn., 1966—, dept. supt. Dist. 19, 1974. Instr., Yeshiva U., N.Y.C., 1969; instr. Kingsborough Community Coll., 1971-72; adj. asst. prof. L.I. U., 1972—; adj. prof. Bar Ilan U., Israel, summer 1973-74; mem. exec. bd. com. Mental Health Projects East N.Y., 1966—; mem. council of agys. Assn. for Children with Retarded Mental Devel., 1969-70; pres. Bushwick Mental Health Clinic, 1972. Mem. adv. bd. Interboro Psychiat. Center. Mem. N.Y.C. Personnel and Guidance Assn. (pres.-elect 1969), Council Suprs. Assn. (chpt. sec. 1968—), Am. Personnel and Guidance Assn., Assn. Sch. Counselors, Assn. Counselor Educators, Joint Assn. Suprs., Jewish Tchrs. Assn. (mem. exec. bd. 1971-72, treas. 1973), Internat. Platform Assn., Mensa, Phi Beta Kappa, Kappa Delta Pi, Pi Lambda Theta, Alpha Epsilon Phi. Address: 760 E 10th St Brooklyn NY 11230

LIPSCOMB, EDRA EVADEAN, educator; b. Marion, Ill., Aug. 3, 1919; d. Edgar and Anna Josephine (Wiesbrodt) Turnage; B.S., So. Ill. U., 1955; M.A., U. Mich., 1955; Ed.D., Ind. U., 1962; postgrad. U. Minn.; m. July 5, 1939 (div. Sept. 1950); 1 son, H. Alan. Tchr., Benton (Ill.) Elementary Schs., 1939-54, DeKalb (Ill.) Consol. Schs., 1955-56; faculty No. Ill. U., DeKalb, Ill., 1956—, prof. elementary edn., 1967—. Ednl. cons. to various schs. in No. Ill.; mem. vis. accreditation com. Nat. Council for Accreditation Tchr. Edn., Kent State U., 1974. Research grantee No. Ill. U., 1965, 73, State of Ill., 1972-73. Mem. Internat. Reading Assn., Internat. Assn. for Supervision and Curriculum Devel., Nat., Ill. edn. assns., Assn. for Higher Edn., Am. Edn. Research Assn., Pi Lambda Theta. Democrat. Roman Catholic. Author: Lipscomb Teacher Attitude Scale. Contbr. articles to profl. jours. Home: 212 Laurel Lane DeKalb IL 60115

LIPSCOMB, LINDA ANN WAGNER (MRS. JOHN F. LIPSCOMB), librarian; b. Cleve., Feb. 10, 1943; d. Gordon N. and Ann Linda (Musgrave) Wagner; A.B., Marietta Coll., 1965; M.S., Case Western Res. U., 1966; m. John F. Lipscomb, Apr. 13, 1968. Information specialist TRW Systems Group, Redondo Beach, Cal., 1966-68, configuration and data mgmt. specialist, 1968-72, configuration and data mgmt. adminstr., 1972—. Mem. Spl. Libraries Assn., Chi Omega, Pi Delta Epsilon. Home: 356 Hillcrest St El Segundo CA 90245 Office: R2/1076 One Space Park Redondo Beach CA 90278

LIPSCOMB, TATIANA BALKOFF DROWNE (MRS. CHARLES J. LIPSCOMB), translator, ins. broker; b. St. Petersburg, Russia, Nov. 10, 1913; d. Peter and Zenaida S. (Bosniatskaia) Balkoff; came to U.S., 1917, naturalized, 1931; student Claremont Grad. Sch.; m. Charles Lipscomb, Dec. 16, 1973; 1 dau. by previous marriage, Tatiana Gillette; stepchildren—H. Russell Drowne III, Bradley C. Drowne; C. Christopher Lipscomb, Lorraine L. Roberts. Ins. broker H. Russell Drowne, Inc., N.Y.C., 1961; pvt. practice ins. broker, N.Y.C., 1961—. Bd. dirs. Nat. Bd. Rev. Motion Pictures. Dep. chmn. Goldovsky Opera Inst., 1964—. Recipient Herald Tab Book award, 1947; Boys Club 1st prize, 1949. Club: Colony (N.Y.C.). Author: Little Magic Horse, 1941; But Charlie Wasn't Listening, 1949; I Am From Siam, 1950; Take Wing, 1951. Translator libretto's for Met. opera: Golden Cockeral, 1942, Khovanchina, 1943, Fidelio, 1946, New Eng. Conservatory Music: Eugene Onegin, Treasure Trove of the Sun, Across the Green Past, 1947, Parralax, 1965. Address: 825 5th Av New York City NY 10021

LIPSITZ, ELEANOR JEAN, lawyer; b. Balt., Jan. 7, 1943; d. Benjamin and Eleanor Irene (Plugge) Lipsitz; B.S., U. Md., 1964, J.D., 1967. Admitted to Md. bar, 1967; atty. Lipsitz & Lipsitz, Balt., 1968—. Bill drafter Gen. Assembly of Md., 1968-70. Mem. Am., Md., Balt. bar assns. Home: 217 W Lanvale St Baltimore MD 21217 Office: 10 Light St Baltimore MD 21202

LIPSKY, JOAN MILLER (MRS. ABBOTT BENNETT LIPSKY), state legislator; b. Cedar Rapids, Ia., Apr. 9, 1919; d. John F. and Ruth S. Miller; B.S., Northwestern U., 1940; postgrad. U. Ia., 1940-41; m. Abbott Bennett Lipsky, 1941; children—Ann, John, Abbott. Psychologist, U. Chgo. Hosps., 1941-42; mem. Ia. Ho. of Reps., 1967—. Mem. Mayor's Commn. Housing; chmn. Mayor's Commn. Alcoholism; chmn. com. human resources Midwest Conf. State Govts.; mem. intergovtl. relations com. Nat. Legislative Conf. Mem. Am. Assn. U. Women, League of Women Voters, Cedar Rapids Art Assn., Hadassah, Sisterhood of Temple Judah, Linn County Mental Health Assn. Republican. Jewish religion. Club: Cedar Rapids Women's. Home: 655 Cottage Grove Av SE Cedar Rapids IA 52403 Office: State Capital E Tenth & Grand Avs Des Moines IA 50319*

LIPSON, GOLDIE, artist, lectr., author; b. N.Y.C., Nov. 18, 1905; d. Herman and Tillie (Schroff) Goldman; studied with Carl Nelson; studied fresco mural painting, Mexico, 1951; m. Moe Lipson, July 24, 1924; children—Adylin (Mrs. Murray Rosenblatt), Stanley. One-man shows Uptown Gallery, N.Y.C., 1942, Charles Barzansky Gallery, N.Y.C., 1946, 47, 49, 53, 58, 64, 67; retrospective exhbn. County Center, White Plains, N.Y., 1953, Barzansky Gallery, 1967 Winter Haven (Fla.) Cultural Art Center, 1970; demonstrations Nat. Acad. Art, 1945, 46, 47, 48, 62; dir., tchr. Goldie Lipson Studio Workshop, 1947-64; instr. Arnold Coll., Milford, Conn., 1951, 52; dir. art YM-YWHA, Mt. Vernon, 1951-55; dir. art classes YMCA, Bronx, N.Y., 1940-41; exhibits in traveling shows through U.S. and Can.; exhibited Aquarelles Gallery, Paris, 1949, nat. juried shows of Am. Water Color Soc., Audubon Soc., Allied Artists Am., Nat. Acad. Art, Cosmopolitan Artists at Riverside Mus., 1951, 52, 54, N.Y. Coliseum Art, 1959, Artists Equity, 1959, Clarksville Art Center, Barzansky Gallery, N.Y.C., Mamaroneck Beach and Y Club, 1966-68; executed fresco murals, San Maguel Alanda, Mexico, 1951; mural in oil executed for Samuel Carson Collection, Purchase, N.Y., 1960, murals in tile, cement and oil, Winter Haven and Lake of the Hills, Fla., 1972-73; permanent outdoor sculpture exhbn. Orchard Springs Gardens, Winter Haven, 1970—; represented in pvt. collections. Writer weekly column Our Guru Says, Daily Highlander, Lake Wales, 1971-72; tchr., lectr. Yoga. Recipient 1st prize oil Mt. Vernon Art Assn., 1947, 49, 54, 1st prize water color, 1948, 51; 1st prize New Rochelle Art Assn., 1948-50; top prize in oil Westchester County Center, 1949, prize for colored print, 1957. Mem. Nat. Assn. Women Artists (mem. jury 1959), Fla. Fedn. Art (publicity chmn. 1970-72), Fla. League Arts Artists Equity (dir. 1956-61), Mamaroneck Artist Guild, Mt. Vernon, New Rochelle art assns., Westchester Art Assn. Author: Moods and Nudes, 1960. Author and illustrator; Rejuvenation, 1963; We, 1965; Beyond Yoga, 1970; author: Rejuvenation through Yoga, 1965; illustrator Yoga, Youth and Reincarnations, 1965. Home: Lake of the Hills Lake Wales FL 33853

LIPTAK, IRENE FRANCES, bus. exec.; b. Clifton, N.J., Feb. 22, 1926; d. George J. and Anna J. (Strelec) Liptak; student U. Newark, 1944-45; B.S., Rutgers U. 1950, M.B.A., 1955, Ed.M., 1964; postgrad. Montclair State Coll., 1960-61, Fairleigh Dickinson U., 1963-64. Exec. sec., adminstrv. asst. to pres., chmn. bd. Botany Mills, Inc., Passaic, N.J., 1942-53; treas., sec. Rowland-Johnson Co., Inc., Clifton, 1953—; tchr. Seton Hall U., Newark, 1963-65. Mem. conf. planning com. N.J. Commn. on Women, 1972. Sec., trustee Charles, Jr. and Dorothy Johnson Found. Mem. Grad. Sch. Edn. Alumni Assn. Rutgers, Friends Library of Rutherford, Rutgers U. Coll. Honor Soc., Am. Assn. U. Women (corr. sec. Nutley br. 1972-74, treas. 1974—), Rutgers U. Coll. Alumni Assn. (mem.-at-large central council 1971-74), Am. Soc. Notaries, Phi Chi Theta (chmn. nat. conv. 1972). Republican. Slovak Nat. Catholic. Club: Rutgers University College Womens (Newark). Editor: Ch. News, 1958-68. Home: 106 Ridge Rd Rutherford NJ 07070 Office: 1051 Bloomfield Av Clifton NJ 07012

LISI, EDITH CALABRISI (MRS. JOHN LISI), city ofcl.; b. Casale diCarinola, Prov Caserta, Italy, Aug. 26, 1909; d. Arcangelo and Teresa (Abronzino) Calabrisi; came to U.S., 1912, naturalized, 1921; student Ridley Sch. Bus., 1964-66; m. John Lisi, Sept. 11, 1937 (dec. June 1954). Agt., Chittenden Pvt. Investigating, Binghamton, N.Y. 1957-60; claims clk. N.Y. State Dept. Labor, Binghamton, 1961-63; clk. Broome County Clerk's Office, Binghamton, N.Y., 1964-65; dep. city clk. City of Binghamton (N.Y.), 1966-72, city clk., 1972—. Mem. Broome County Rep. Finance Com., 1966—. Mem. Binghamton Bus. and Profl. Women, Am. Civic Assn., Aux. Sons of Italy. Roman Catholic. Club: Monday Afternoon (Binghamton). Home: 24 Rutherford St Binghamton NY 13901 Office: Governmental Plaza Hawley St Binghamton NY 13901

LISTON, JANET LOUISE RENAUD (MRS. DENNIS DARYL LISTON), psychologist; b. Marshalltown, Ia., Oct. 26, 1944; d. Donald Johnson and Alice Ione (Piper) Renaud; B.A., U. Ia., 1966; M.A., Ohio State U., 1969; m. Dennis Daryl Liston, Apr. 4, 1966; 1 dau., Emily Louise. Elementary tchr. Boydstun Sch., Big Spring, Tex., 1966-67; intern as sch. psychologist Franklin County Schs., Columbus, O., 1969-70; sch. psychologist Southwestern City Schs., Grove City, O., 1970-73; psychologist Career Devel. Center, Columbus, O., 1973—. NSF grantee, 1965-66. Mem. Nat., Ohio sch. psychologists assns., Sch. Psychologists Central Ohio (pres. 1974), League Women Voters (action chmn. 1971-73, unit chmn. 1974), Phi Beta Kappa, Delta Kappa Gamma. Presbyn. Home: 2185 Harwich Rd Columbus OH 43221 Office: 3100 Sullivant Av Columbus OH 43204

LITMAN, ROSLYN MARGOLIS, lawyer; b. N.Y.C., Sept. 30, 1928; d. Harry and Dorothy (Perlow) Margolis; B.A., U. Pitts., 1949, J.D., 1952; m. S. David Litman, Nov. 22, 1950; children—Jessica, Hannah, Harry. Admitted to Pa. bar, 1952, since practiced in Pitts.; partner firm Litman, Litman, Harris & Specter, 1952—. Adj. prof. U. Pitts. Sch. Law, 1958—; permanent del. to Conf. U.S. Circuit Ct. Appeals for 3d Circuit. Chmn. Pitts. Pub. Parking Authority, 1970—. Mem. Allegheny County Bar Assn. (pres. elect 1974), Allegheny County Acad. Trial Lawyers (charter). Home: 1047 S Negley Av Pittsburgh PA 15217 Office: 1320 Grant Bldg Pittsburgh PA 15219

LITTIKEN, BARBARA L., ins. exec.; b. Columbus, Ind., Apr. 28, 1938; d. Robert Lee and Marybelle (Bryan) Littiken; B.A., DePauw U., 1960. Sales promotion asst. Ill. Mid-Continent Ins. Co., Chgo., 1960-63, agy. sec., 1963; editorial asst. Mut. Trust Life Ins. Co., Chgo., 1963, editor, 1963-67, supr. sales promotion div., 1967-72; dir. communications Scheer Financial Corp., Chgo., 1972-73; creative dir. Montgomery Ward Life Ins. Co., Chgo., 1973—. Mem. Landmarks Preservation Council. Mem. Mail Advt. Club Chgo. (dir. 1967-70), Indsl. Editors Assn. Chgo., Life Ins. Advertisers Assn. (v.p. Chgo. chpt. 1971-72, pres. 1973-74), Alpha Phi. Club: Columbia Yacht. Address: 1045 W Belden Av Chicago IL 60614 Office: 140 S State St Chicago IL 60603

LITTLE, ADELE DEE KEATLEY (MRS. GEORGE ROCKAFELLOW LITTLE), mus. adminstr.; b. Plattsburg, N.Y., Dec. 18, 1928; d. Edwin Emerson and Adele Louise (Crandall) Keatley; B.A. in English, Stanford, 1950; m. George Rockafellow Little, Dec. 15, 1956. Advt. copywriter Marguerite Tuttle, Inc., N.Y.C., 1951-56; women's editor Potsdam (N.Y.) Courier-Freeman, 1957-63; dir. curator Potsdam Pub. Mus., 1964—. Dir. No. N.Y. Pub. Co. Vice chmn. Arts and Humanities Council St. Lawrence Valley, N.Y.; active Girl Scouts U.S.A. Bd. dirs. Regional Conf. Hist. Agys. Mem. Am. Assn. Museums, Assn. for State and Local History, D.A.R., Mayflower Soc. N.Y., Victorian Soc. N.Y., N.Y. State Hist. Assn., Am. Assn. U. Women. Author: (with H. Keller) Potsdam and the Civil War, 1961. Contbr. articles to profl. publs. Home: 6 Ridgewood Lane Route 3 Potsdam NY 13676 Office: Potsdam Pub Mus Civic Center Potsdam NY 13676

LITTLE, ANGELA CAPOBIANCO (MRS. GEORGE GORDON LITTLE), educator; b. San Francisco, Jan. 12, 1920; d. Alfredo Agosto and Elizabeth (Kruse) Capobianco; B.A., U. Cal. at Berkeley, 1940, M.S., 1954, Ph.D., 1969; m. George Gordon Little, Nov. 8, 1947; 1 dau., Judith Kristine. Jr. specialist Agrl. Expt. Sta., U. Cal. at Berkeley, 1956-61, asso. specialist, 1961-69, asst. food scientist, 1969-72, asso. food scientist, 1972—, lectr. nutritional scis. dept. nutritional scis., 1969—. Bd. dir. Consumers Co-op. of Berkeley, 1970-71; mem. adv. bd. grad. minority recruitment program U. Cal. at Berkeley, 1971—. U.S. Dept. Interior grantee, 1965-70, U.S. Dept. Commerce, 1972-73, State of Cal. Wine Adv. Bd., 1968-71, Assn. of Ofcl. Analytical Chemists, 1972-74. Mem. A.A.A.S., Am. Soc. for Testing and Materials (mem. coms. E-12 and E-18, 1969—), Optical Soc. Am., Inter-Soc. Color Council, Inst. Food Technologists (counselor 1971—), N.Y. Acad. Sci., Sigma Xi, Iota Sigma Pi, Phi Tau Sigma. Author: (with G. MacKinney) Color of Foods, 1962. Contbr. articles in field to profl. jours. Home: 85 Cleary Court San Francisco CA 94109 Office: Dept Nutritional Sciences University of California Berkeley CA 94720

LITTLE, CHRISTINE E. (MRS. REX J. LITTLE), librarian; b. Paterson, N.J., June 3, 1937; d. Leo Rudolph and Helen Hinman (Martin) Etzkorn; B.A., U. Syracuse, 1958; M.S. in Library Sci., U. Mich., 1959; postgrad. Ariz. State U., 1964-66, No. Ariz. U., 1966; m. N. John Larsen, Apr. 6, 1961 (div. Nov. 1970); 1 son, Christopher John; m. 2d, Rex J. Little, Sept. 1, 1973. Librarian, researcher Western history dept. Denver Pub. Library, 1959-61; librarian supr. Bur. Indian Affairs, Dept. of Interior, Brigham City, Utah, 1963-68; asso. librarian Salk Inst. Biol. Studies, La Jolla, Cal., 1970-71; reference librarian, computer research analyst Biomed. Library U. Cal. at San Diego, 1971-72; med. librarian VA Hosp., San Diego, 1972—. Mem. Am., Med. library assns., Med. Library Group So. Cal., Am. Assn. U. Women. Home: 304 Trailview Rd Encinitas CA 92024 Office: VA Hosp 3350 La Jolla Village Dr San Diego CA 92161

LITTLE, DIANA, obstetrician; b. Detroit, Aug. 10, 1938; d. John and Charlotte (Stanard) Little; B.A., Central Mich. U., 1960; M.D., Wayne State U., 1964. Intern Oakwood Hosp., Dearborn, Mich., 1964-65, resident, 1965-68; pvt. practice obstetrics and gynecology, Ann Arbor, 1968—; mem. staff St. Joseph, Saline Community hosps. Mem. Nat. Orgn. Women, 1971-72. Mem. A.M.A., Mich., Washtenaw County med. socs. Home: 725 Skynob Ann Arbor MI 48105 Office: 2200 Fuller St # 308B Ann Arbor MI 48105

LITTLE, DOROTHY VICTRY (MRS. GEORGE W. LITTLE), educator, city ofcl.; b. Belleville, Ill., Nov. 27, 1914; d. William Muriel and Safronia Novella (Griffith) Victry; B.S., Tenn. Technol. U., 1957; postgrad. U. Tenn., 1966-67; m. George W. Little, Apr. 2, 1938; children—Franklin N., Thomas W., Bruce A. Tchr. Augusta, Ga., 1936-37, Neverfail, 1941-43, Tabor, 1943-44, Pleasant Hill, 1947-57, 59-62, 67-70, Homestead, 1962-66, Tavares (Fla.), 1957-59, Cumberland County High Sch., 1970—. Mem. City Council, City of Pleasant Hill, Tenn., 1971—. Mem. Nat., Tenn. edn. assns., Council Exceptional Children (membership chmn. 1972-73), Bus. and Profl. Women Crossville, Delta Kappa Gamma. Mem. United Ch. Christ. Mem. Order Eastern Star (asso. matron 1956-57). Home: 26 Main St Pleasant Hill TN 38578 Office: Stanley St Crossville TN 38555

LITTLE, GRETCHEN D(OHM), librarian; b. High Bridge, N.J., Nov. 7, 1913; d. James L. and Gretchen B. (Dohm) Little; A.B., Duke, 1936; B.S. in L.S., Drexel Inst. Tech., 1949. Asst. librarian devel. dept. Uni-Royal, 1936-37; tech. librarian Mead Corp., 1937-43, ICI United States Inc. (formerly Atlas Chem. Industries, Inc.), 1943—. Mem. A.A.A.S., Am. Chem. Soc., Spl. Libraries Assn. (pres. 1954-55, chmn. sci.-tech. div.; chmn. 50th ann. conv.), Am. Soc. Information Scientists, Am. Water Works Assn., T.A.P.P.I., Nat. Microfilm Assn., Med. Library Assn. Office: ICI United States Inc Wilmington DE 19899

LITTLE, IMOGENE SYLVESTER, psychiat. technician; b. Chandler, Ariz., Apr. 29, 1924; d. Delbert Hayden and Edna Melvina (Parson) Sylvester; A.A., Porterville Community Coll., 1971; m. Leonard Stewart Little, Apr. 25, 1940; children—James, Linda Wilson, Joel, Jeremy. Psychiat. technician trainee Porterville (Cal.) State Hosp., 1955-56, psychiat. technician, 1956-62, supervising psychiat. technician, 1962—. Mem. Porterville Community Concert Assn., 1970—; pres. Home-Sch. Orgn., Strathmore (Cal.) Union Elementary Sch., 1973—. Mem. Am. Assn. on Mental Deficiency, Cal. State Employees Assn., Cal. Assn. Human Services Technologists. Democrat. Baptist. Office: PO Box 2000 Porterville CA 93257

LITTLE, JEWELL SHIRLEY (MRS. VAN B. LITTLE), banker; b. Attalla, Ala.; d. Walter B. and Mattie (Gammon) Shirley; student U. Ala., 1956; postgrad. Sch. Bank Marketing, U. Colo.; m. Van B. Little, Dec. 10, 1949 (dec. Dec. 1964). Chief shipper Lawrence Products, Attalla, Ala., 1938-49; with Exchange Bank, Attalla, 1955—, v.p., cashier, 1962-73, sr. v.p., 1973—. Treas. Attalla (Ala.) City Schs., 1964—. Mem. Gadsden C. of C., Nat. Assn. Bank Women (group chmn. North Central Ala. group 1969-70), Etowah County Banks Advt. Clearinghouse Assn. Methodist (ch. sec. 1969—). Club: Attalla Country. Home: 305 Greene St SE Attalla AL 35954 Office: 923 Attalla Blvd Attalla AL 35954

LITTLE, LILLIE BRADSHAW (MRS. BLANTON PRICE LITTLE), home economist, educator; b. Walters, Va.; d. Thomas Gavin and Julia Southall (Reynolds) Bradshaw; B.S. in Home Econs., U. N.C., 1933, M.S., in Home Econs., 1965; m. Blanton Price Little, Jan. 3, 1940; 1 son, Blanton Price. Tchr. home econs. bd. edn. Cabarrus County, N.C., 1933-35, Wilson County, N.C., 1935-37; home econs. agt. N.C. Extension Service Stanly County, Albemarle, 1937-40; tchr. home econs. Bd. Edn. New Hanover County, N.C., 1943-44; dir. cafeterias Bd. Edn., Durham County, N.C., 1951-53; home econs. agt. N.C. Extension Service Pitt County, Greenville, 1953-58; specialist housing and home furnishings N.C. State U., Raleigh, 1958-70, dist. home econs. agt., 1970—. Cons. So. Furniture Mfg. Assn., High Point, N.C., 1967-70, Sears, Roebuck & Co., Chgo., 1970-71; instr. seminar for tng. personnel Belk's Stores, Charlotte, N.C., 1968—; instr. seminar for tng. personnel Norman's of Salisbury (N.C.), 1968-69; Coordinator Consumerama I and II, Winston-Salem, 1970-72. Mem. N.C. (pres. coll. 1933—, sec. dist. 1955—, treas. 1956—, chmn. housing sect. 1959-65, mem. exec. council 1959-63), Nat. (chmn. nominating com. 1963) home econs. assns., Nat. Soc. Interior Designers, Nat. Home Fashings League, Am. Home Econs Assn., Delta Kappa Gamma, Epsilon Sigma Phi. Contbr. research articles on home furnishings to profl. publs. Home: 4500 Connell Dr Raleigh NC 27609 Office: 309 Ricks Hall North Carolina State University Raleigh NC 27607

LITTLE, ROSEMARY VON STORCH ALLEN, librarian; b. Newark, June 14, 1938; d. Wilkie Chapman and Ruth (von Storch) Allen; A.B., Rutgers U., 1960, M.L.S., 1961; m. John Edwin Little, Oct. 8, 1966. Student page Rutherford (N.J.) Pub. Library, 1955-56; asst. Fairleigh Dickinson U. Library, summers 1957-60; grad. asst. Douglass Coll. Library, Rutgers U., 1960-61; asst. reference librarian Princeton Library, 1961-64, librarian, pub. adminstrn. collection, 1964—. Sec. Young Republican Club, Princeton, N.J., 1964—; alternate del. Mercer County to Young Republicans of N.J., 1964-65, del. 1965—. Librarian U.S. Pavilion, N.Y. World's Fair, 1964. Mem. Am., N.J. (sec.-treas. coll. and univ. sect. 1970-71) library assns., Spl. Libraries Assn. (sec.-treas. Princeton-Trenton chpt. 1968-69), N.Y. Library Club, Friends Princeton U. Library, Met. Mus. Art. Republican. Conglist. Home: 1 Grandview Av Lawrenceville NJ 08648 Office: Princeton U Library Princeton NJ 08540

LITTLE, RUTH ALICE OGILVIE (MRS. GORDAN LITTLE), librarian; b. Lynn, Mass., Nov. 22, 1919; d. James Robert and Joanna (Watt) Ogilvie; A.B., Radcliffe Coll., 1939; B.S. in L.S., Simmons Coll., 1940; M.A., U. Cal. at Santa Barbara, 1963; m. Gordan Little, Oct. 20, 1951; children—Alan Craig, James Robert. Cataloger, Baker Library, Harvard, Cambridge, Mass., 1940-42; historian Boston Ordnance Dist., 1942-45; records adminstr. War Assets Adminstrn., San Francisco, 1945-49; librarian Hamilton AFB, Cal., 1949-53; research asst. Library of Congress Legislative Reference Service, Washington, 1957; project dir. Fed. Library Services project Santa Barbara Pub. Library, 1958-59; head librarian Santa Barbara City Coll., 1959—. Bd. dirs. Internat. Social Sci. Inst. Mem. Cal. Library Assn., Cal. Tchrs. Assn., Jr. Coll. Faculty Assn. Home: 2521 Calle Galicia Santa Barbara CA 93109

LITTLE, SARA PAMELA, educator; b. Charlotte, N.C., Mar. 9, 1919; d. John H. and Beulah (Campbell) Little; A.B., Queens Coll., 1939, D. Humanities (hon.), 1972; M. Religious Edn., Gen. Assembly's Tng. Sch., 1944; Ph.D., Yale, 1958; postgrad. Harvard, 1965. Tchr. high sch., N.C., 1939-42; asst. regional Christian edn. dir. Synod N.C., Charlotte, 1944-50; faculty Presbyn. Sch. of Christian Edn., Richmond, Va., 1951—, prof. Christian Edn., 1951—; adj. prof. Christian edn. Union Theol. Sem., Richmond, 1966-73, prof., 1973—. Cons. Youth Research Center, Mpls., 1971—, Citizens for Excellent Pub. Schs., 1971-72, Human Relations Council, 1967—, Common Cause, 1972—. Recipient Margaret Bowen award St. Andrews Coll., 1973. Mem. Nat. Soc. Edn., Nat. Council on Religion and Pub. Edn., Religious Edn. Assn. (dir. 1972—), Assn. Profs. and Researchers in Religious Edn. (pres. 1966), Assn. for Profl. Edn. for Ministry, Delta Kappa Gamma. Presbyn. Author: Learning Together in the Christian Fellowship, 1956; The Role of the Bible in Contemporary Christian Education, 1958; Language of the Christian Community, 1965; Youth, World and Church, 1968. Contbr. articles in field to profl. jours. Editorial bds. Religious Edn., 1961—, Theology Today, 1973—. Address: 1205 Palmyra Av Richmond VA 23227

LITTLEDALE, FREYA LOTA BROWN (MRS. HAROLD AYLMER LITTLEDALE), writer, editor; b. N.Y.C.; d. David Milton and Dorothy (Passoff) Brown; B.S., Ithaca Coll., 1951; postgrad. N.Y. U., 1952;; m. Harold Aylmer Littledale; 1 son, Glenn David. Tchr. English pub. schs., Willsboro, N.Y., 1952-53; editor South Shore Record, L.I., N.Y., 1953-55; asso. editor Maco Mag. Corp., N.Y.C., 1960-61, Rutledge Books and Ridge Press, N.Y.C., 1961-62; juvenile book editor Parents' Mag. Press, N.Y.C., 1962-65; free-lance writer-editor, 1965—; writer Silver Burdett div. Time-Life Corp., 1965; editor, anthologist Arrow Book Club div. Scholastic Book Services. Author: The Magic Fish, 1967; (with Harold Littledale) Timothy's Forest, 1969; King Fox and Other Old Tales, 1971; The Magic Tablecloth, the Magic Goat, and the Hitting Stick, 1973. Editor: A Treasure Chest of Poetry, 1964; Fairy Tales by Hans Christian Andersen, 1964; Aesop's Fables, 1964; Grimm's Fairy Tales, 1964; 13 Ghostly Tales, 1966; Ghosts and Spirits of Many Lands, 1970; Stories of Ghosts, Witches and Demons, 1971. Home: 305 E 86th St New York City NY 10028

LITTLEFIELD, ELIZABETH NELSON (MRS. VERNE D. LITTLEFIELD), orgn. exec.; b. Chgo., May 5, 1912; d. William Ely and Mabelle (Moore) Nelson; B.A., Pomona Coll., 1933; postgrad. U. Cal. at Los Angeles, 1933-34; m. Verne D. Littlefield, Jan. 12, 1935; 1 son, William Nelson. Bd. mgrs. Ariz. Congress Parents and Tchrs., Phoenix, 1954-57, 62—, v.p. Central region, 1957-58, v.p., 1958-60, pres., 1960-62. Mem. adv. com. Rocky Mountain Project; sec. Ariz. Council Edn., 1961-62, pres., 1962-64; state rep. Nat. Com. Support Pub. Schs., 1964; v.p. Ariz. Citizens for Strengthening Pub. Sch. Edn., 1964, pres., 1965; participant White House Conf. on Edn., 1965; mem. ednl. TV com. State Supr. Pub. Instrn., 1965; exec. bd. Gov.'s Com. on Alcoholism, 1965; mem. tech. adv. com. State Health Dept. Alcohol and Drug Abuse Program, 1968—. Bd. dirs. Maricopa Citizens Com. Alcoholism; bd. mgrs. Nat. Congress Parents and Tchrs., 1960-62. Recipient plaque for outstanding service to pub. edn., Ariz. Edn. Assn., 1962. Mem. Am. Assn. U. Women (area rep. edn. Phoenix br. 1968-69, pres. 1969-72, gen. chmn. South Pacific regional conf. 1972-73, chmn. Survival English project Ariz. div. 1972—, pres. Ariz. div. 1974), Coordinating Council for Continuing Edn. and Counseling. Republican. Episcopalian. Club: Glendale Women's. Home: 530 W Palmaire St Phoenix AZ 85021

LITTLEFIELD, SHIRLEY DAVIS, physician; b. Clarkshill, Ind., Dec. 19, 1924; d. Haven Stanley and Martha Ada (Yount) Davis; student Butler U., 1943-44; B.S., Purdue U., 1946; M.D., Ind. U., 1949; m. Paul A. Littlefield, Sept. 13, 1947 (div. Dec. 1972); children—Anne (Mrs. James Peters), Jeffrey, Daniel and Michael (twins), Robert. Intern, St. Vincent's Hosp., Indpls., 1949-50; resident anesthesiology Ind. Univ. Med. Center Hosps., Indpls., 1954-56; gen. practice medicine, Boise, Idaho, 1950-53, specializing in anesthesiology, Indpls., 1956—; mem. staff Methodist Hosp.; cons. anesthesiologist Johnson County Hosp., Franklin, Ind., Hendricks County Hosp., Danville, Ind. Diplomate Am. Bd. Anesthesiology. Mem. A.M.A., Ind. Med. Assn., Marion County Med. Soc., Am., Ind., Indpls. socs. anesthesiologists, Marion County Assn. Retarded Children. Club: Ulen Country. Home: 4040 Crooked Creek Overlook Indianapolis IN 46208 Office: 1815 N Capital St Indianapolis IN 46212

LITTLEJOHN, MARY BOBBITT, educator; b. Ada, Okla., July 17, 1917; d. Bailey Mathewson and Rebecca Anne (Tolbert) Bobbitt; A.B., Trinity U., San Antonio, Tex., 1937; M.Ed., U. N.C., 1938, Ph.D., 1966; m. Samuel McGowan Littlejohn, Aug. 17, 1940 (div.); children—Samuel, Robert Grayson, Anne Rebecca, Jeanette Tolbert. Editor, sec. to dir. U. N.C. Press, Chapel Hill, 1938-41, 42-43; priorities supr. Mill-Power Supply Co., Charlotte, N.C., 1941-42; high sch. tchr., jr. high sch. counsellor pub. schs., Charlotte, 1961-64; prof. edn. Winthrop Coll., Rock Hill, S.C., 1965—; vis. instr. U. N.C., 1966; cons. in field. Mem. State Central and State Exec. Coms. Republican Party, Minn., 1952-56; chairwoman rural Hennepin County Rep. Com., Richfield, Minn., 1953-56. Recipient Phi Kappa Phi Award for Excellence in Teaching Winthrop Coll., 1969, 70, 71, 73; named Winthrop Coll. Distinguished Prof., 1972; named Career Woman of the Year Rock Hill Bus. and Profl. Women's Club, 1973. Mem. Am. Assn. U. Women, Am. Ednl. Research Assn., Nat. Council for Measurement in Edn., Am. Assn. for Higher Edn. Presbyn. Contbr. articles to profl. jours. Home: Rt 2 Box 422 A Fort Mill SC 29715 Office: School of Education Winthrop College Rock Hill SC 29730

LITTLES, ALTAMESE BRYANT (MRS. PERRY L. LITTLES), librarian; b. Fernandina Beach, Fla., Aug. 3, 1913; d. Melville and Maud (Bryant) (Threadcraft) Bryant; B.A., Fla. A. and M. Coll., 1944; M.A. in English, Hampton Inst., 1950; M.S. in L.S., N.C. Central Coll., 1958; postgrad. Columbia, 1947-48; m. Perry L. Littles, May 27, 1954; 1 son, Amos J. Tchr. Nichols (Fla.) Elementary Sch., 1933-41, prin., 1941-43; tchr. Roosevelt High Sch., Lake Wales, Fla., 1943-54, librarian, 1955—, also coordinator adult edn., 1966-70, Sec., Girl State chmn. Am. Legion Aux., 1960—; pres. exec. bd. Civic Club, Lake Wales, 1965—. Recipient trophy for work with students Roosevelt High Sch. Student Council, 1965. Mem. A.L.A., Fla. Edn. Assn., Polk County Sch. Assn. (regional sec. 1970-72), Sigma Gamma Rho (pres. chpt. 1967-72, plaque distinguished service 1972). Dau. of Elk. Club: Entre Nous (Bartow, Fla.). Home: 203 North St Lake Wales FL 33853 Office: 115 E St Lake Wales FL 33853

LITTLEWOOD, BARBARA SHAFFER (MRS. ROLAND KAY LITTLEWOOD), biochem. geneticist; b. Buffalo, Oct. 8, 1941; d. Charles Howard and Marcia (Brown) Shaffer; B.A., U. Rochester, 1963; Ph.D., U. Pa., 1968; m. Roland Kay Littlewood, Sept. 2, 1970; 1 son, David John. Postdoctoral fellow dept. genetics Cornell U., 1968-70; research asso. biochemistry U. Wis., Madison, 1970-73, project asso. physiol. chemistry, 1973—. Mem. Am. Soc. Microbiology, Genetics Soc. Am. Contbr. articles to profl. jours. Home: 5102 Manor Cross Madison WI 53711

LITTMAN, BERNICE FINGERHUT (MRS. ROBERT JACOB LITTMAN), lawyer; b. Manchester, Eng., Aug. 20, 1944; d. Isaac and Letty (Kay) Fingerhut; B.A., Somerville Coll., Oxford (Eng.) U., 1965, M.A., 1973; J.D., Columbia U., 1969; m. Robert Jacob Littman, Aug. 29, 1966; 1 son, Adam. Admitted to English bar, 1966, Mass. bar, 1969, Hawaii bar, 1972; asso. Nathanson & Rudofsky, attys., Boston, 1969-71; asso. Cades, Schutte, Fleming & Wright, attys., Honolulu, Hawaii, 1971—. Mem. Am., Hawaii bar assns., Honourable Soc. Inner Temple. Jewish religion (dir. congregation). Home: 1541 Kalaniwai Pl Honolulu HI 96821 Office: 165 S King St Honolulu HI 96813

LITTMAN, ELAINE HARRIET (MRS. RICHARD LITTMAN), advt. agy. co. exec.; b. Bklyn., May 13, 1934; d. Louis and Ann (Lifschitz) Borden; B.A., Coll. City N.Y., 1955; m. Richard Littman, Oct. 18, 1952; children—Nancy, Glenn; foster child Cao-Thi-Ngay. Account exec. Nationwide Advt. Co., Inc., N.Y.C., 1966—, head dept., 1973—. Pres., E & R Assos., Wayne, N.J., 1968. Active United Jewish Appeal. Democrat. Jewish religion. Mem. B'nai B'rith. Club: Advertising. Home: 9 Boonstra Dr Wayne NJ 07470 Office: 60 E 42d St New York NY 10017

LITZENBERGER, NANCY JAYNE (MRS. SAM W. LITZENBERGER, JR.), lawyer; b. Terre Haute, Ind., May 28, 1942; d. James Franklin and Betty Jayne (McCash) Lehman; A.B., Ind. U., 1964, J.D. (Krannert fellow), 1966; m. Sam W. Litzenberger, Jr., Apr. 8, 1967. Research asst. dept. sociology Ind. U., Bloomington, 1961-63, legal researcher police adminstrn. dept., 1965-66; admitted to Ind. bar, 1966; legal research Dillauou, Overaker & Schwartz, Paris, Ill., 1966-67, Lou Pearlman, Jr., Lafayette, Ind., 1967-68; asso. atty. Litzenberger & Litzenberger, Williamsport, Ind., 1968—. Mem. Ind., Warren County bar assns., Kappa Kappa Kappa, Alpha Lambda Delta, Delta Delta Delta. Home: Rural Route 2 Williamsport IN 47993 Office: 115 N Monroe St Williamsport IN 47993

LIU, CHARLOTTE TSUI (MRS. OSCAR C. LIU), pathologist; b. Wuchong, China, May 25, 1919; d. Oscar S.R. and Hsue Shoo (Chao) Ts'ui; M.D., Cheeloo U., China, 1944; M.Med. Sci. in Immunology, U. Pa., 1957; m. Oscar C. Liu, Nov. 23, 1947; children—Phyllis Anne, Robert Reber, Christopher Jay. Came to U.S., 1947, naturalized, 1953. Intern U. Hosp., Chengtu, China, 1943-44; resident in internal medicine Chungking (China) Central Hosp., 1944-47; pediatrician Childrens Seashore House, Atlantic City, N.J., 1947-51; resident in oncology Jeanes Hosp. Fox Chase, Pa., 1951-52; attending physician Childrens Hosp. of Phila., 1953-58; instr. Grad. Sch. Medicine U. Pa., Phila., 1956-59; research asso. Norristown (Pa.) State Hosp., 1961-62, Temple U., Phila., 1962-63; resident in pathology Woman's Med. Coll. Hosp., Phila., 1963-65; trainee clin. pathology dept. Phila. Gen. Hosp., 1965-67, staff pathologist, 1967-71; cons. clin. pathology dept., Grand View Hosp., Sellersville, Pa., 1967-69; instr. anatomic pathology U. Pa. Med. Sch., 1969-71; asso. pathologist Women and Infants Hosp. R.I., 1971—. Diplomate Am. Bd. Pathology. Fellow Coll. Am. Pathologists, Am. Soc. Clin. Pathologists; mem. Am. (Recognition award in continuing edn. 1969, 73, R.I. med. assns., Kent County Med. Soc., Am. Soc. Cytology, Am. Med. Women's Assn., Internat. Acad. Pathology, Sigma Delta Epsilon. Contbr. articles on immunology, pathology and cytology to profl. jours. Home: 166 Love Lane Warwick RI 02886 Office: Women and Infants' Hosp RI 50 Maude St Providence RI 02908

LIU, JOANNA KUNG HSIEN (MRS. KAI-HSIEN LIU), librarian; b. Mintsing, Fukien, China, Feb. 23, 1910; d. Cho Ching and Lien Chiu (Cheng) Liu; B.A., Hwa Nan Coll., China, 1932; M.A., Drew U. Theol. Sem., 1939; M.A., Columbia, 1949; B.S. in L.S., U. Ill., 1952; m. Kai-Hsien Liu, Dec. 29, 1951. Came to U.S., 1937, naturalized, 1961. Serials librarian Northeastern U. Library, Boston, 1952-58; cataloger Harvard U. Grad. Sch. Bus. Adminstrn. Library, 1958-60, Brandeis U. Library, 1960-63, Mass. Inst. Tech. Library, 1963-65; med. librarian VA Hosp. Library, Bedford, Mass., 1965-66, Franklin Inst. of Boston, 1966—. Mem. A.L.A., Assn. New Eng. Jr. Coll. Librarian, Nat. Assn. Govt. Employees. Methodist. Home: 203 Lake View Av Cambridge MA 02138 Office: 41 Berkeley St Boston MA 02116

LIVINGSTON, MARY JANE, social worker; b. Pitts., Mar. 25, 1930; d. Harry Edward and Charlotte (Sutter) Kroll; B.S., U. Pitts., 1951; M.S. in Social Work, U. Louisville, 1965; m. Robert LaMar Livingston, Oct. 27, 1951 (div. May 1973); children—Carol Lee and Sheryl Ann (twins). Typist, statistician Westinghouse Electric Co., Pitts., 1951-54; social worker So. Ind. Mental Health Center, Jeffersonville, 1965-67, chief social worker, 1967-69, coordinator children's services, 1972—; chief outpatient services West Central Louisville Mental Health Center, Area A region 6, 1969-72; Ky. Comprehensive Care Plan, 1970-72; field instr. U. Louisville, 1966-71; field instr. Catherine Spalding Coll., 1969-70; pvt. practice Carlton Riddick and Assos., 1972—; cons. Methodist Pastoral Counseling Service, 1966-68, Ind. Mental Health Center, Jeffersonville, 1969—. Vol. Bridgehaven, Louisville, 1961-63, asso. mem., 1961—. Mem. Nat. Assn. Social Workers, Acad. Certified Social Workers, Ky. Soc. Clin. Social Workers (exec. bd.), Am. Group Psychotherapy Assn. Home: 10105 Grand Av Louisville KY 40299 Office: 203 13th St Jeffersonville IN 47130 also Carlton Riddick and Assos St Mathews KY 40207

LIVINGSTON, MYRA COHN (MRS. RICHARD ROLAND LIVINGSTON), author, educator; b. Omaha, Aug. 17, 1926; d. Mayer Louis Bud and Gertrude (Marks) Cohn; B.A., Sarah Lawrence Coll., 1948; m. Richard Roland Livingston, Apr. 14, 1952; children—Joshua, Jonas Cohn, Jennie Marks. Profl. French horn player, 1941-48; pub. relations work for Hollywood personalities, 1950-52; book reviewer Los Angeles Daily News, also Los Angeles Mirror, Los Angeles Times, N.Y. Times, 1948—; lectr. U. Cal. on 5 campuses, 1958—, now U. Cal. at Los Angeles Extension; poet in residence Beverly Hills Unified Sch. Dist.; tchr. Los Angeles City Schs., Claremont Colls.; lectr. U. Utah, U. Neb., U. Kan., Lehigh U., Cal. State Coll., Towson, others. Exec. v.p. Friends of Beverly Hills Pub. Library; active Beverly Hills P.T.A. Recipient awards N.Y. Herald Tribune Children's Book Festival, 1958, Comprehensive Contbn. awards, 1958, Tex. Inst. Letters, 1961, award for notable book So. Cal. Council on Lit. for Children and Young People, 1972. Mem. Tex. Inst. Letters, Authors Guild, A.L.A., P.E.N. Author: Whispers and Other Poems, 1958; Wide Awake and Other Poems, 1959; I'm Hiding, 1961; See What I Found, 1962; I Talk to Elephants, 1962; I'm Not Me, 1963; Happy Birthday, 1964; The Moon and A Star and Other Poems, 1965; I'm Waiting, 1966; Old Mrs. Twindlytart and Other Rhymes, 1967; A Tune Beyond Us, 1968; A Crazy Flight and Other Poems, 1969; Speak Roughly To Your Little Boy, 1971; The Malibu and Other Poems, 1972; Listen, Children, Listen, 1972; What a Wonderful Bird the Frog Are, 1973; Poems of Lewis Carroll, 1973; When You Are Alone/It Keeps You Capone, 1973; Come Away, 1974; The Way Things Are and Other Poems, 1974. Address: 9308 Readcrest Dr Beverly Hills CA 90210

LIVINGSTON, SIDNEE, artist; b. N.Y.C.; d. Louis and Ray (Shaff) Lehr; student N.A.D.; m. Louis Livingston (dec. Aug. 1959); 1 son, Frederick Brown. Exhibited one man shows Salpeter Gallery, N.Y.C., 1947, Asso. Am. Artists Gallery, Chgo., 1949-50, Wellons Gallery ,

N.Y.C., 1951, U. Miss., 1953, Nelson Gallery, Chgo., 1953, Everhart Mus. (Pa.), 1957, U. Miami (Fla.), 1960, Condon Riley Gallery, N.Y.C., 1960, Nantucket, Mass., 1967, Columbus (Ga.) Mus., 1972; exhibited group shows Phila. Acad. Fine Arts, 1953, Art Inst. Chgo., 1949, 50, Kansas City Art Inst., Butler Art Inst., 1950, Va. Mus., Denver Mus., St. Louis Mus., 1956, U. Neb., 1953, 54, Library Congress, 1957, also travel exhibits in Eng., Scotland, France, Greece, Belgium, Japan; Nat. Assn. Women Artists travel exhibits U.S. and Europe, 1965-70; represented in permanent collections Eng., France, Switzerland, Sweden, Italy, U.S.A. Recipient First prize for watercolor Painters and Sculptors Soc. N.J., 1965; Mildred Tommy Atkins award, 1971. Fellow MacDowell Colony, 1960, 63. Address: 14 Minetta St New York City NY 10012

LIVINGSTONE, BETTY JACKSON (MRS. JOHN STANLEY LIVINGSTONE), plastics processing co. exec.; b. Chgo., July 21, 1923; d. Vestus Twiggs and Josephine Louise (Stenhouse) Jackson; B.S. in Chemistry, Fla. State U., 1944; m. John Stanley Livingstone, May 2, 1943. Research asst. Manhattan Project, Mass. Inst. Tech., 1944-45, research asso., 1947-51; research asst. Harvard, 1945-47; research and devel. chemist Stein Hall, Charlotte, N.C., 1956-63; pres. Livingstone Coating Corp., Charlotte, 1963—. Mem. Am. Chem. Soc. (sect. chmn. 1960, regional chmn. 1963), Nat. Assn. Corrosion Engrs., Soc. Plastics Industry (policy bd. fluorocarom div.), Phi Beta Kappa, Sigma Xi, Phi Kappa Phi, Gamma Sigma Epsilon. Republican. Episcopalian. Home: 2032 Princeton Av Charlotte NC 28207 Office: PO Box 8282 Charlotte NC 28208

LIVO, NORMA JOAN (MRS. GEORGE O. LIVO), educator; b. Tarentum, Pa., July 31, 1929; d. David John and Mae (Kline) Jackson; B.S., U. Pitts., 1962, M.Ed., 1963, Ed.D., 1969; m. George O. Livo, Jan. 26, 1951; children—Lauren, K. Eric, Kim, Robert. Geophys. asst. Gulf Research Lab., Harmerville, Pa., 1950-52; demonstration tchr. Falk Lab. Sch., U. Pitts., 1962-68; prof. lang. arts U. Colo., Denver, 1968—. Mem. Nat. Council of Tchrs. English, Internat. Reading Assn., Pi Lambda Theta, Phi Delta Kappa. Home: 11960 W 22d Place Lakewood CO 80215 Office: Univ of Colorado 1100-14th St Denver CO 80202

LLAMAS, ADRIENNE BOYER (MRS. NESTOR LLAMAS), retail chain exec.; b. Nanticoke, Pa., Mar. 5, 1937; d. Chester and Anna (Rogoznician) Boyer; grad. high sch.; m. Nestor Llamas, Oct. 15, 1966. Secretarial position Rose's Stores, Inc., N.Y.C., 1958-63, asst. buyer fashionwear and sportswear, 1964-73, asst. mgr. N.Y. office, 1965-73, mgr. N.Y. office, 1974—. Home: 454 W 20th St New York City NY 10011 Office: 200 Fifth Av New York City NY 10010

LLORENS, ANA MARIA RODRIGUEZ (MRS. LUIS LLORENS), librarian; b. Guayanilla, P.R., Apr. 26, 1919; d. Rapael Robustiano and Clotilde (Rodriguez-Sosa) Rodriguez; normal diploma U. P.R., 1939; B.A., La. State U., 1957, M.S., 1958; M.A. in Spanish, Fla. State U., 1970; m. Luis Llorens, Dec. 23, 1939 (div. March 1950); children—Luis, Anabel. Tchr. Liceo Puertorriqueño, San Juan, P.R., 1941-44; cataloguer Miami (Fla.) Pub. Library, 1958-59; head catalog librarian Mobile (Ala.) Pub. Library, 1959-60; sr. high sch. librarian, Mobile, 1960-62; reference librarian Fla. State U., Tallahassee, 1962-65; librarian Fgn. Langs. Grad. Library Ohio State U., Columbus, 1965—. Cons. secondary sch. library Colombia, 1971. Mem. Latin Am. Area Studies Com., Ohio State U., 1969—; chmn. ad hoc com. on Faculty Status for Ohio State U. librarians, 1970; mem. Seminar on Acquisition Latin Am. Library Materials, 1969—. Author: Periodicals in the Romance Languages and Literatures at Ohio State University, 1969; French Language Dictionaries in the Ohio State University Libraries, 1970. Home: 2100 Harwitch Rd Columbus OH 43221 Office: 1858 Neil Av Columbus OH 43210

LLOYD, DOROTHY DAVIS, assn. editor; b. Enfield, N.C., Oct. 11, 1918; d. Donald M. and Anna Elizabeth (Davis) Burgess; B.A., Duke U., 1937; m. Thomas Jones Price Murray, Nov. 19, 1937 (div. Nov. 1961); 1 son, James Thomas; m. 2d, Robert Crawford Lloyd, Jan. 20, 1962. Mem. advt. dept. Raleigh (N.C.) Times, 1939-42; copywriter Wise Advt. Agy., Balt., 1950-52; adminstrv. sec. Tchrs. Assn. Baltimore County, Balt., 1952-56; asso. editor Md. State Tchrs. Assn., 1956-62, mng. editor, 1962-68, dir. publs., 1968—. Cons. sch. law revision publ. Md. Dept. Edn., 1967, Md. Council Edn. publs., 1967. Mem. Women's Advt. Club Balt. (pres. 1961-63; dir. 1963-64), Mid-Atlantic Assn. Indsl. Editors (dir. 1956-58), Nat. Assn. State Edn. Editors, Nat. Sch. Pub. Relations Assn., Edpress Assn., N.E.A. (life), Adminstrv. Women in Edn., Phi Beta Kappa, Kappa Kappa Gamma, Delta Kappa Gamma. Republican. Methodist. Home: 3000 W Strathmore Av Baltimore MD 21209 Office: 344 N Charles St Baltimore MD 21201

LLOYD, RUTH SMITH (MRS. STERLING MORRISON LLOYD), anatomist, educator; b. Jan. 25, 1917; d. Bradley Donald and Mary Elizabeth (Morris) Smith; A.B. magna cum laude, Mount Holyoke Coll., 1937; M.S. in Zoology (Univ. fellow), Howard U., 1938; Ph.D. (Rosenwald fellow), Case Western Res., 1941; m. Sterling Morrison Lloyd, Dec. 30, 1939; children—Marilyn (Mrs. Hugh Bernard Price), Sterling Morrison, David Smith. Instr. biology Hampton (Va.) Inst., 1941-42; technician dept. physiology Howard U. Coll. Medicine, Washington, 1942-43, faculty, 1943—, asso. prof. anatomy, 1955—, dir. acad. reinforcement Coll. Medicine, 1970—. Mem. Am. Assn. Med. Colls., Sigma Xi, Delta Sigma Theta. Unitarian (trustee 1967-70). Democrat. Club: Washington chpt. of Girl Friends. Home: 2510 Irving St NE Washington DC 20018 Office: 520 W St NW Washington DC 20001

LLOYD-CAMPBELL, CRYSTAL COUSINS (MRS. EDWIN D. CAMPBELL), educator; b. Bklyn., Nov. 29, 1937; d. Jesse and Sarah Louise (Fink) Cousins; student U. Chgo., 1953-56; B.A., Northeastern U., 1963; LL.B., Boston Coll., 1966; postgrad. Harvard, 1971—; m. Edwin D. Campbell, June 7, 1973; children—Sean Lloyd, Jennifer Lloyd. Admitted to Mass. bar, 1966; atty. Peabody & Arnold, Boston, 1966-71; instr. law Northeastern U., 1971-72; instr. sociology Boston U., also chief counsel Devel. Disabilities Project, Exec. Office Human Services, 1972-73; prof. law Suffolk U., Boston, 1973—. Mem. Am., Mass., Boston bar assns., Am. Civil Liberties Union, N.A.A.C.P., Order of Coif. Author: (with Harold G. Wren) Corporate Reorganizations, 1966. Home: 100 Valentine St West Newton MA 02165 Office: Suffolk U Boston MA 02109

LOACH, JEAN CALANTHE, bus. cons.; b. Chgo.; d. George Winwood and Mary (Sipes) Loach; Mus.B., Mundelein Coll. Hostess Jean Loach TV Show, also women's editor WXYZ-TV, Detroit, 1950-60; pres. Jean Loach & Assos., Miami Beach, Fla., and N.Y.C., 1960-70, 72—; pres. Future Record Co., 1962—; dir. advt. and pub. relations Sheraton Park hotel, Sheraton Carlton hotel, Washington, 1971-72; chmn. bd. Jean Loach Assos. Corp., Washington, 1972—; asst. to pres. Wolf Internat. Enterprises, Los Angeles, 1972; dir. House of Peacock Corp., Washington. Adv. bd. Salvation Army, Miami, Fla., 1973; bd. dirs. Univ. Concert Series Seminars, 1970. Mem. A.F.T.R.A., A.S.C.A.P., Screen Actors Guild, Am. Fedn. Musicians, Am. Women in Radio and TV. Mem. Order Eastern Star, Daus. of Nile, Order of White Shrine. Club: Women's City (Detroit). Composer: Paree Still Seems the Same to Me, 1958; Where There's A Will There's A Way, 1966; Lucky, Lucky Me, 1973; A Mom Like Mine, 1973. Home: 4925 Collins Av Miami Beach FL 33140 Office: 801 S Bayshore Dr Miami Beach FL 33131

LOAR, BARBARA JEAN TYNER (MRS. NELSON ARTHUR LOAR, III), occupational therapy cons.; b. Fargo, N.D., Oct. 22, 1936; d. Edward Henry and Helen (Creamer) Tyner; B.S., U. Ill., 1959; m. Nelson Arthur Loar, III, Nov. 15, 1957; children—Steven, James, Alison. Staff occupational therapist Inst. Phys. Medicine and Rehab., Peoria, Ill., 1959-60; cons. occupational therapy Americana Nursing Centers, Inc., Monticello, Ill., 1965—; dir. occupational therapy Peoria (Ill.) pub. schs., 1970-72; cons. occupational therapy Belwood County Nursing Home, Peoria, 1972—, Apostolic Nursing Home, Peoria, 1973—, Restmor, Inc., Morton, 1972—, Americana Nursing Center, Peoria and Pekin, 1973—. Mem. profl. edn. com. Mental Health Bd., 1965-68; mem. placement and community resource com. Jr. League Peoria, 1968—; v.p. Kickapoo council Girl Scouts U.S.A., 1968-74, dir. program services for handicapped. Mem. Am. (mem. planning com. chronic ill and aging 1971-73), Ill. (pres. 1974—) occupational therapy assns., U. Ill. Alumnae Assn. (dir. 1973—), Peoria Jaycee-Ettes (hon. life mem., pres. 1962). Home: 3823 N Grandview Dr Peoria IL 61614

LOAR, PEGGY ANN (MRS. KENTON J. LOAR), museum ofcl.; b. Cin., May 14, 1948; d. Jerome Vincent and Elizabeth Ann (Ranz) Wahl; B.A., U. Cin., 1970, M.A., 1971; m. Kenton J. Loar, Sept. 5, 1970. Teaching asst. U. Cin., 1970-71; asst. curator in charge edn., acting curator Indpls. Museum of Art, 1971-72, asso. curator in charge edn., acting curator, 1972-73, curator edn. Indpls. Museum Art, 1973—, organizer exhibit Ind. Stoneware, 1974. Lectr. art appreciation Ind. U.-Purdue U., Indpls., 1972—; mem. Ad Hoc Council for Arts and Humanities in Edn., 1970—. Bd. dirs. Ind. Com. for Humanities, 1970—, Hosp. Audiences, 1973—. Mem. Coll. Art Assn., Am. Assn. Museums, Ind. Film Council, Nat. Art Edn. Assn., Am. Film Inst. Home: 3612 Watson Rd Indianapolis IN 46205 Office: 1200 W 38th St Indianapolis IN 46208

LOBER, MAUREEN MACY, lawyer; b. Streator, Ill., May 28, 1928; d. Maurice Thomas and Ila Glee (Bowman) Macy; student U. Cal. at Los Angeles, 1944-45; A.B. cum laude, Fla. State U., 1947; LL.B., Lincoln Coll. Law, 1952; postgrad. U. Ill. Law Sch., 1950, U. Havana, Cuba, 1948; m. Arlyn R. Lober, June 18, 1950; children—Rebecca, Rosemarie, Christine. Tchr. high sch., Litchfield, Ill., 1947-51; admitted to Ill. bar, 1952; mem. firm Macy & Lober, Litchfield, Springfield and Raymond, Ill., 1952—. Active YWCA, Urban League Guild, Springfield. Mem. Springfield Met. Expn. and Auditorium Authority, 1969—. Chairwoman, Sangamon County Republican party, 1971—. Mem. Ill., Sangamon, Montgomery County bar assns., Am. Assn. U. Women, Zonta Internat., Phi Beta Kappa. Lutheran. Home: 1916 N 8th St Springfield IL 62702 Office: 521 N 5th Springfield IL 62702 also News Herald Bldg Litchfield IL 62056

LOBSENZ, AMELIA BABETTE FREITAG (MRS. HARRY ABRAHAMS), pub. relations exec.; b. Greensboro, N.C.; d. Leo and Florence (Scheer) Freitag; B.A., Agnes Scott Coll., 1944; m. Harry Abrahams; children—Michael, George, Kay. Writer mag. articles and books, 1947-52; dir. mag. dept. Edward Gottlieb & Assos., N.Y.C., 1952-56; pres. Lobsenz Pub. Relations Co., Inc., N.Y.C., 1956—; lectr. in field. Mem. citizens council Hofstra U., 1960—. Recipient Mag. Writers award Soc. Mag. Writers, 1960. Mem. Pub. Relations Soc. Am. (chpt. workshops chmn. 1971—, mem. bd. pub. relations 1974), Soc. Mag. Writers, Am. Med. Writers Assn., Am. Women in Radio and TV, L.I. Pub. Relations Soc. Club: Publicity (N.Y.C.). Author: Kay Everett Call CQ, 1951; Kay Everett Works DX, 1952. Office: 745 Fifth Av New York City NY 10022

LOCKARD, BETTY PINE (MRS. LAWRENCE A. LOCKARD), educator, lawyer; b. Kansas City, Mo., May 12, 1933; d. Gayles R. and Meda (Burns) Pine; B.S. in Edn., Central Mo. State U., 1955, M.S. in Edn., 1956; J.D., U. Mo. at Kansas City, 1961; m. Lawrence A. Lockard, June 25, 1952. Tchr. elementary sch., Warrensburg, Mo., 1956-58, Topeka, 1955-56; admitted to Mo. bar, 1961; mem. firm Pine, Welling, Jones & Lockard, Warrensburg, 1961-62, Pine & Lockard, Warrensburg, 1967-71; probate and magistrate judge Johnson County, Mo., 1963-66; asst. prof. criminal justice Central Mo. State U., Warrensburg, 1971—. Vol. Cancer Fund, Heart Fund, United Fund. Bd. dirs. Wesley Found., 1970-72. Mem. Mo., Johnson County (sec., 1967-68) bar assns., Am. Judicature Soc., Mo. Tchrs. Assn., Community Tchrs. Assn., Mo. Police Chiefs Assn., Nat. Assn. Women Hwy. Safety Leaders (exec. sec.), Nat. Safety Council, Kappa Delta Pi, Alpha Phi Delta, Sigma Sigma Sigma. Republican. Methodist. Home: Route 5 Warrensburg MO 64093

LOCKARD, LEE (MRS. JACK W. LOCKARD), city ofcl.; b. Forest, La., Aug. 9, 1923; d. Benjamin Clyde and Myrtle (Standifer) Wild; student Draughon's Sch. Bus., Little Rock, 1941; City Sec. certificate, North Tex. State U., 1972; m. Jack W. Lockard, Mar. 13, 1944; children—Jackie (Mrs. R.W. Smith), Jean (Mrs. Michael Goins). City sec., West University Place, Tex., 1964—. Mem. Tex. (sec.-treas.), Harris County Area (pres.) assns. city clks. and secs. Home: 4521 Birch St Bellaire TX 77401 Office: 3800 University St Houston TX 77005

LOCKE, EDITH RAYMOND (MRS. A. RALPH LOCKE, JR.), editor; b. Vienna, Austria; d. Herman and Dora (Hockberg) Laub; naturalized, 1944; student Bklyn. Coll., Coll. City N.Y., N.Y. U.; m. A. Ralph Locke, Jr., May 29, 1963; 1 dau., Katherine. Asst. editor Harper's Bazaar, also Jr. Bazaar, N.Y.C., 1945-47; fashion dir. Abbott Kimball Advt. Agy., N.Y.C., 1947-49; asso. fashion editor Mademoiselle mag., N.Y.C., 1949-59, fashion editor, 1959-68, exec. editor, 1968-71, editor-in-chief, 1971—. Mem. The Fashion Group (pres. 1972-73), Am. Soc. Mag. Editors, Am. Fashion Critics (mem. Coty award jury). Author: (children's book) The Red Door, 1964. Office: 350 Madison Av New York City NY 10017

LOCKE, IRENE VIVIAN FISHER (MRS. JOHN LOOR LOCKE), civic worker; b. Birch Tree, Mo.; d. Oliver David and Nellie Evelyn (Hughes) Fisher; grad. pvt. schs.; m. John Loor Locke, Sept. 21, 1920; children—Peggy (Mrs. Newman), John Loor, Evelyn (Mrs. Dreitzler). Treas., dir., asst. sec. O.D. Fisher Investment Co., Seattle, 1974—. King County chmn. women's div. savs. bonds div. U.S. Treasury Dept., 1941-51, state chmn., 1948-51; bd. mem. Nat. Citizen's Com. Mental Health, summer 1963, mem. founding com.; mem. Pres.'s Nat. Emergency Com., Nat. Council on Crime and Delinquency; co-chmn. nat. conf. Jr. League Am., 1940; v.p. Jr. League Seattle, 1941; past bd. mem. Seattle council Girl Scouts U.S.A.; active United Good Neighbors, Seattle; co-chmn. O.D. Fisher Charitable Found., Seattle, 1967-74, asst. sec., trustee, asst. treas., 1974—. Trustee Intercollegiate Studies Inst. Recipient citations U.S. Treasury Dept., 1945, 51, Wash. State Treasury, 1948-51. Mem. Internat. Platform Assn. Home: 2148 Broadmoor Dr E Seattle WA 98112 Office: 3311 Seattle First Nat Bank Bldg Seattle WA 98154

LOCKETT, SISTER MARY CLODOVIA, ednl. adminstr.; b. Austin, Tex., Jan. 23, 1913; d. Edgar Stephen and Monica (Mangan) Lockett; B.S., St. Louis U., 1937, Ph.D., 1952; M.S., DePaul U., 1947. Joined Order Sisters of Notre Dame, 1935; instr. biology LeClerc Coll., Belleville, Ill., 1947-49; prof. biology Notre Dame Coll., St. Louis, 1949-65, chmn. dept., 1965; prof. biology U. Dallas, 1965-68, chmn. dept., 1968—. Bd. dirs. Inter-racial Council, Dallas, 1968, Am. Cancer Soc., Dallas, 1968. Minnie Stevens Piper prof., 1969; grantee NSF, AEC. Author: Research Problems in Biology, 1971. Contbr. articles to profl. jours. Home: Route 2 Box 4 Irving TX 75062 Office: Dept Biology U Dallas Irving TX 76060

LOCKHART, ADELAIDE B., librarian; b. Boston, July 1, 1916; A.B. in Polit. Sci., Boston U., 1950; M.S. in L.S., Simmons Coll., 1951. Library asst. Brockton (Mass.) Pub. Library, 1941-43; library asst. young people's room Boston Pub. Library, 1946-50, reference asst., 1950-52; research asst. to asso. librarian Yale Library, 1952-60; asst. coll. librarian Dartmouth Coll. Library, 1960-73, dir. library services, 1973—. Served to staff sgt. USAAF, 1943-46. Mem. New Eng. Library Assn. (pres. 1971-72). Office: Dartmouth Coll Hanover NH 03755

LOCKHART, AILEENE SIMPSON, univ. dean; b. Atlanta, Mar. 18, 1911; d. Thomas Ellis and Aileene Reeves (Simpson) Lockhart; B.S., Tex. Woman's U., 1932; M.S., U. Wis., 1937, Ph.D., 1942; D.Sc. (hon.), U. Neb., 1967. Chmn. dept. phys. edn. Mary Hardin-Baylor Coll., Belton, Tex., 1937-42; asso. prof. U. Neb. at Lincoln, 1942-49; prof. U. So. Cal., Los Angeles, 1949-73; dean, prof. Coll. Health, Phys. Edn. and Recreation, Tex. Woman's U., Denton, 1973—. Prof. Smith Coll., Northampton, Mass., 1965, 68; spl. lectr. Wellesley (Mass.) Coll., 1969-71; cons. editor William C. Brown Co., pubs., 1953—. Amy Morris Homan's fellow Wellesley Coll., 1961-62. Fellow Am. Acad. Phys. Edn., Am. Coll. Sports Medicine; mem. Nat. Assn. Phys. Edn. Coll. Women, Am. Assn. U. Women, A.A.H.P.E.R. Author books, including Anthology of Contemporary Readings in Physical Education, 1970; Chronicle of American Physical Education, 1972; Modern Dance-Building and Teaching Lessons, 1973. Contbr. to publs. in field. Asso. editor Research Quar., 1969—. Home: 1314 Windsor Dr Denton TX 76201

LOCKHART, BESS BEEBE LEMMON (MRS. FRED LOCKHART), ret. educator; b. Stewart, O., Mar. 10, 1907; d. Vernner Ashby and Mildred (Beebe) Lemmon; kindergarten-primary diploma Ohio U., 1928; student Syracuse U., 1952; B.S., Md. U., 1954, M.Ed., 1955; m. Fred Lockhart, June 29, 1963. Tchr., Green Valley Sch., Stewart, O., 1928-29, Columbia Center Sch., Newark, O., 1929-30, Stewart, O., 1930-31, Capitol Heights (Md.) Sch., 1931-38, Ft. Washington (Md.), 1938-39, Cheverly (Md.) Elementary Sch., 1939-52, Berwyn Elementary Sch., College Park, Md., 1952-64; tchr. spl. edn. Berwyn Heights Elementary Sch., College Park, 1964-71. Supervising tchr., spl. edn. classes U. Md., 1955-71. Acting pres. Berwyn Sch. P.T.A., 1964; asst. treas. Crofton (Md.) Leisure Group, 1973. Bd. dirs. Mental Health Assn. Prince George County, 1952-53. Mem. Nat., Med. (county treas. 1940-44) edn. assns., Md. Tchrs. Assn., Md. Congress Parents and Tchrs. (hon. life), Assn. for Retarded Children Prince George County, Ret. Tchrs. Assn. Prince George County, Am. Assn. Mental Deficiency, Council for Exceptional Children (county pres. 1957, v p. 1958), Md. Fedn. Women's Clubs (So. dist. credential chmn. 1972-74). Mem. Order Eastern Star. Clubs: Federated Woman's, Crofton Woman's, Crofton Village Garden, Crofton Newcomers, Christian Women's (book chmn. 1971-74) (Crofton, Md.). Home: 1764 Crofton Pkwy Crofton MD 21113

LOCKHART, JUNE, actress; d.; Gene and Kathleen Lockhart. Motion picutres include All This and Heaven, Too., Sergeant York, Miss Annie Rooney, Meet Me in St. Louis, Son of Lassie, White Cliffs of Dover, Keep Your Powder Dry, Bury Me Dead, T-Men, It's a Joke, Son, Time Limit; also TV appearances including series Lassie, Lost in Space, Petticoat Junction; theatre appearances 40 Carats, Butterflies are Free, Best of Friends, No Sex Please, We're British. Recipient Tony award for Love or Money; named Woman of Year in Drama A.P. Address: care Leonard Grant & Assos 9000 Sunset Blvd Hollywood CA 90069

LOCKHART, LORA MARGARET (MRS. LAWRENCE LEONARD LOCKHART), assn. exec.; b. Maysville, Mo., June 15, 1903; d. Worthy Hewitt and Julia Ann (Hancock) Redman; student Mo. Jr. Coll., 1926, Central Mo. State U., 1927; B.S., Northwest Mo. State U., 1955; m. Lawrence Leonard Lockhart, June 2, 1928. Tchr. rural schs. DeKalb County, Mo., 1922-68, Consol. Dist. #2, Raytown, Mo., 1956-68; staff writer, researcher DeKalb County Heritage Quar. Mag., Maysville, Mo., 1970—. Promoter, organizer, pres. DeKalb County Hist. Soc., Maysville, Mo., 1969—; promoter of Centennials, DeKalb County, 1969-70; mgr. DeKalb County Cemetery Census, 1972; organizer County Mus. and Resource Library, Maysville, 1971—. 4-H Leadership award, 1945. Mem. Ret. Tchrs. Assn., Mo. Tchrs. Assn., Womens Soc. Christian Service. Methodist. Clubs: Hedge Farm Home (cultural arts chmn. 1969-71); Farm Home Extension. Layout editor Fairport Centennial Book, 1969, Adams Twp. Book, 1970. Home and office: Route 3 Box 100 Maysville MO 64469

LOCKLAIR, ETHEL MARIE (MRS. JAMES M. LOCKLAIR), banker; b. Rutherford, N.J., Jan. 22, 1915; d. Frank Herbert and Catherine Marie (Kane) Snyder; grad. high sch.; m. James M. Locklair, Sept. 5, 1959. Sec., Ellwood S. with real estate and ins. bus., Rutherford, N.J., 1932-42; sec. engring. dept. Bendix Aviation Corp., Teterboro, N.J., 1942-46; office mgr. Ross Advt. Agy., Hackensack, N.J., 1946-58; exec. sec. to base mgr. Burroughs Corp., Eglin AFB, Fla., 1958-60; v.p., sec. Midland Bank, Paramus, N.J., 1960—. Mem. Bergen County Bankers Assn., Am. Inst. Banking, Nat. Assn. Bank Women. Roman Catholic. Home: 14 Beverridge Rd Mahwah NJ 07430 Office: 80 E Ridgewood Av Paramus NJ 07652

LOCKLEY, JEANETTE ELAINE (MRS. ARNOLD H. LOCKLEY), educator; b. Dallas, Feb. 13, 1933; d. Robert Lee and Morita Foresta (Williams) Prince; B.S., Wiley Coll., 1953; M.S., Tex. So. U., 1954; M.S. in Statistics, Stanford, 1968, Ph.D. in Edn., 1970; m. Arnold Herbert Lockley, Aug. 5, 1952 (dec. Dec. 1973); 1 son, Geoffrey Lynn. Instr. math. Tex. So. U., Houston, 1954-57; prof. math. Merritt Coll., Oakland, Cal., 1958—; asst. prof. math. and edn., research asso. Macalester Coll., St. Paul, 1969-70; also cons., ednl. statistician. John Hay Whitney fellow, 1958; NSF fellow, 1962. Mem. Am. Ednl. Research Assn., Am. Statis. Assn., Am. Math. Soc., Alpha Kappa Alpha (local pres. 1966-67), Pi Lambda Theta, Pi Mu Epsilon, Beta Kappa Chi. Club: San Francisco Links. Home: 6126 Plymouth Av Richmond CA 94805 Office: 12500 Campus Dr Oakland CA 94619

LOCKMAN, EVELYN ELIZABETH, educator, dancer; b. Bolivar, Tenn.; d. William and Mansell (Brooks) Lockman; diploma Ward-Belmont Coll., 1929; B.A., Vanderbilt U., 1931; M.A., George Peabody Coll., 1933; postgrad. summers U. Wis., 1936, 37, N.Y.U., 1939-40, 47, 56, 57; spl. dance tng. N.Y.C., 1933-45, Europe, summers 1965-67, also in the Orient, summers 1969, 70, 71, 72. Head women's phys. edn. dept. Vanderbilt U., Nashville, 1934-36; pvt. dance studio, Bowling Green, Ky., 1936-39; vis. instr. Western Ky. State Tchrs. Coll., Bowling Green, 1938; asst. prof. phys. edn. U. Southwestern La., Lafayette, 1939-40, asso. prof. fine arts, head dance dept., 1942-47; instr. Scarborough-on-the-Hudson, N.Y., 1941-42;

asso. prof. phys. edn. Bowling Green (O.) State U., 1947-48; faculty, chmn. dance Cal. State U., San Diego, 1948—, asso. prof. of phys. edn., 1956-69; prof. dance, 1969—. Dean women, dance instr. YMCA Grad. Sch., Blue Ridge, N.C., 1934-36; vis. instr. dance N.Y. state Tchrs. Coll., Cortland summers 1945-46; lectr. dance N.Y.U. Grad. Sch., N.Y.C., summers 1956-57; solo concert dancer, 1931-33, occasionally 1933-55; guest tchr. Coll. Chinese Culture at Taipei, Hong Kong, Edn. Dept. Coll. Phys. Edn. at Bangkok, Women's U. Seoul; lecture tour Am. Cultural Centers in Korea, USIS, 1971, Taiwan, 1972, Hong Kong, 1972, Bombay, India, 1972, 73, Calcutta, India, Singapore, 1973, Indonesia, 1973. Donor Dance Scholarship U. Southwestern La., 1963. Dance Research grantee San Diego State U. Found., 1964, 71. Mem. Am. Assn. U. Profs., Am. Dance Guild, N.E.A., Assn. Cal. State U. Profs. (sec.), Internat. Council Health, Phys. Edn., Recreation, Finlandia Assn., A.A.H.P.E.R., (chmn. aesthetics sect., chmn. heritage com. dance div., mem. exec. bd., v.p.), Am. Dance Guild (exec. bd.), Nat. Dance Assn. (pres.), Cal. Assn. Phys. Edn., Health and Recreation (unit v.p. dance), Iran-Am. Soc., Internat. Assn. Phys. Edn. and Sports for Girls and Women, Friends Library Cal. State U. at San Diego. Democrat. Baptist. Presented in concert, workshops, various Am. and fgn. dance artists. Author: Modern Dance Manual; Pre-Classic Music and Dance Forms; (with Eija U. Celli) Finland's Folk Dances. Editor: Guide Lines for Dance Artists-in-Residence and Host Institutions. Home: 4375 46th St San Diego CA 92115

LOCKNEY, AMELIA MARY HANSEN (MRS. MARTIN JOHN LOCKNEY), civic worker; b. New Plymouth, Ida., Sept. 8, 1914; d. Peter Knudsen and Rosa (Seigel) Hansen; student Coll. Ida., 1931-33; m. Martin John Lockney, Feb. 24, 1940; 1 son, Martin John. Pres. Benjamin Franklin P.T.A., San Diego, 1950-52; chmn. United Fund, San Diego, 1952; rec. sec. San Diego County Girl Scout Bd., 1952; chmn. consultative tumor bd. Hoag Hosp., Newport Beach, Cal., 1956-59, pres. hosp. aux., 1961-64; pres. Orange Council Council Hosp. Auxiliaries, 1964; vol. buyer Gift Box, Hoag Hosp., Newport Beach, 1966—, chmn. Gift Box, 1966-68; treas. Children's Dental Health Center, Newport Beach, 1968-70; pres. Assistance League Newport Beach (Cal.), 1973; mem. budget com. Orange County Philharmonic Soc., 1973; chmn. consumer com. of five-year long range planning com. Hoag Hosp., 1973. Home: 801 Via Lido Sound Newport Beach CA 92660

LOCKRIDGE, KATHRYN DELANA, editor; b. Indpls., Feb. 13, 1939; d. Shockley and Mary Kay (Geake) Lockridge; B.A., Miami U., Ohio, 1961; M.A., Syracuse U., 1963; postgrad., U. Hawaii, 1960. Mgr., N.Y. State Soc. Newspaper Editors, Syracuse, 1961-63; editor, reporter A.P., Buffalo and Albany, N.Y., 1963-67; mgr. legislative corr. Cuyler News Service, Albany, 1967-69; instr. journalism Mich. State U., East Lansing, 1969-73; press cons., N.Y.C., 1973—. Cons. Model Cities Newspaper, Lansing, 1972-73; v.p. Model Cities Policy Bd., Lansing, Mich., 1973. Recipient Distinguished Service award Women's Press Club, 1969. Mem. Women's Press Club N.Y. State, Aircraft Owners and Pilots Assn., Assn. for Edn. in Journalism, Legislative Corrs. Assn., Nat. Press Club of Washington, Nat. Pilots Assn., Soc. for Profl. Journalists, Women in Communications (Advisor award 1971), Kappa Tau Alpha, Alpha Omicron Pi. Contbr. articles to profl. jours. Home: 47 W 12th St New York City NY 10011

LOCKROW, DOROTHY SEARLE (MRS. CHARLES RUSSEL LOCKROW), librarian; b. Athol, Mass., Sept. 23, 1915; d. Frederic Leonard and Ruth Alice (Randall) Searle; B.S. in L.S., Simmons Coll., 1937; M.A. in Edn., So. Conn. State Coll., 1955; m. Charles Russell Lockrow, Aug. 16, 1941. Cataloger, Yale Law Library, 1938-42; asst. librarian, Southern Conn. State College, New Haven, 1946-57; cataloger, Bridgeport (Conn.) pub. Library, 1957-58; cataloger New Haven Free Pub. Library, 1958-61, head cataloging dept., 1961-63; asst. librarian U. New Haven, West Haven, Conn., 1964—. Mem. Am., Conn. (chmn. tech. services sect. 1950, 72) library assns. Home: 370 Drummond Rd Orange CT 06477 Office: 300 Orange Av West Haven CT 06516

LOCKSHIN, FLORENCE LEVIN (MRS. SAMUEL D. LOCKSHIN), composer, pianist; b. Columbus, O., Mar. 24, 1910; d. Samuel M. and Jennie (Klein) Levin; B.S., Ohio State U., 1931; M.A., Smith Coll., 1953; m. Samuel D. Lockshin, June 4, 1933; children—Richard A., Michael D. Pianist concerts and radio programs, 1920-53. Represented State of Ohio as composer-performer 1951 Biennial Nat. Fedn. Music Clubs. Mem. Am. Fedn. Musicians (hon., life). Composer works for full orch., solo piano, 4 pianos, chamber music, ballet with orch., men's chorus, women's chorus. Home: Baker Hill Northampton MA 01060

LOCKWOOD, JANE LOWRY BIGGERS, polit. worker; b. Toledo, Aug. 12, 1920; d. John David and Mary (Kelsey) Biggers; ed. Garland Jr. Coll., King-Smith Studio Sch.; m. Corwin Rees Lockwood, Jr., July 6, 1942; 1 son, Corwin Rees III. Area chmn. Mothers March of Dimes, 1956; dir. K Wives of Washington, 1955; area chmn. Am. Heart Assn., 1954. Mem. Republican Nat. Women's Finance Com., 1948-59; dir. D.C. League Rep. Women's Club, 1948-62; mem. Eisenhower-Nixon campaign com., 1952, 56; mem. Eisenhower-Nixon Inaugural Coms., 1953, 57; mem. Montgomery County Rep. Central Com., 1963—, vice chmn. women's activities, 1964-70, 72-73; del. Rep. Nat. Conv., 1968; vice chmn. hospitality com. Nixon-Agnew Inaugural, 1968-69, com. chmn. reception V.P. and Mrs. Agnew; mem. Rock Creek Women's Rep. Club, 1954—, 1st v.p., dir., 1962; co-chmn. finance com. James P. Gleason for County Exec.; pres. Rockville Rep. Women's Club, 1971-72; vols. involvement coordinator Montgomery County Re-elect the Pres. com.; Rep. elector Md. Methodist. Club: Westmoreland Hills Garden (Md.). Home: 10500 Rockville Pike Rockville MD 20852

LOCKWOOD, JEAN ELAINE (MRS. PAUL RICHARD LOCKWOOD), newspaper editor; b. Oak Harbor, O., Oct. 21, 1917; d. Otto Emery and Laura Augusta (Wilhelmsen) Reider; student Tiffin Bus. U., 1935-36, Bliss Bus. Coll., 1939; m. Paul Richard Lockwood, Oct. 17, 1942; children—Priscilla J., Paul Robert. Clk., typist Home Owners Loan Corp., Toledo, Columbus, O., 1937-41; clk. Ottawa County Welfare Dept., Port Clinton, O., 1941; clk., stenographer Erie Army Depot, LaCarne, O., 1941-42, 50; office mgr. Ottawa County News, Daily News, Port Clinton, O., Radio Sta. WRWR-FM, Port Clinton, 1950-68; editor Ottawa County Exponent, Oak Harbor, O., 1971—. Adminstrv. specialist Ottawa County Riverview Nursing Home, Oak Harbor, 1968—; v.p. R.W.R., Inc., Port Clinton, O., 1962. Mem. Oak Harbor Hist. Com., 1968-69. Treas., Ottawa County Democrat Womens Club; active in various polit. campaigns, 1937-68. Mem. Oak Harbor Businessmens Assn., Am. Legion Aux. (pres. 1947-48, Ohio dist. Americanism chmn. 1949-50), Nat. Assn. for Female Execs., Oak Harbor C. of C. Lutheran. Clubs: Press (Toledo); Catawba Island (Port Clinton); Erie Army Depot Womens (LaCarne). Home: 172 Oak Ridge Dr Oak Harbor OH 43449 Office: 106-110 N Locust St Oak Harbor OH 43449

LOCKWOOD, LINDA GAIL, biologist, educator; b. N.Y.C., May 25, 1936; d. Richard Carl and Martha Miriam (Bradford) Lockwood; B.S., Columbia, 1960, M.A., 1961, M.A., 1965, Ph.D., 1969. Lab. asst. botany Columbia, 1961-67, sci. honors instr. 1962-69, asst. prof. sci. edn., 1969-73; asso. prof. environmental sci. U. Mass. at Amherst, 1973—. NSF fellow, 1970; Jesse Smith Noyes Found. grantee, 1971-73. Mem. A.A.A.S., Am. Inst. Biol. Sci., Nat. Audubon Soc., Nat. Assn. Biol. Tchrs., Bot. Soc. Am., Wilderness Soc., Sigma Xi. Home: 50 Meadow St Amherst MA 01002 Office: Marshall Hall U Mass Amherst MA 01002

LOCKWOOD, LORNA ELIZABETH, state justice; b. Douglas, Ariz., Mar. 24, 1903; d. Alfred Collins and Daisy Maude (Lincoln) L.; A.B., U. Ariz., 1923, J.D., 1925. Admitted to Ariz. bar, 1925; mem. firm Lockwood & Savage, Phoenix, 1939-41, Cox, Lockwood & Lockwood, Phoenix, 1944-48; price atty. Ariz. OPA, 1942-44; asst. atty. gen. Ariz., 1948-50; judge Superior Ct. Maricopa County, 1951-61; justice Ariz. Supreme Ct., 1961—, vice chief justice, 1964, 69, chief justice, 1965-66, 70-71. Active promotion legislation improved mental health code, neighborhood council delinquency prevention and control, sr. citizens legislation. Mem. Ariz. Ho. of Reps., 1939-40, 41-42, 47-48. Bd. dirs. Ariz. Girls Ranch. Recipient Medallion of Merit, U. Ariz., 1960, Alumnus Achievement award, 1961; Award of Merit, Ariz. Conf. Crime and Delinquency Prevention and Control, 1955; named State Profl. Woman of Year, State Fedn. Bus. and Profl. Women's Clubs, 1961; Women of Achievement award Ariz. br. Am. Assn. U. Women, 1966; Humanitarian award Hadassah, 1965; Woman of Year, Ariz. Fedn. Women's Clubs, 1965; Woman of Year, Kansas City Advt. and Sales Execs. Clubs, 1965; award of merit Am. Trial Lawyers Assn., 1970; Builder of a Greater Ariz. Law and Govt. award, 1971; Brotherhood award Nat. Conf. Christians and Jews, 1972; Distinguished Citizens award U. Ariz. Alumni Assn., 1972. Mem. Am., Maricopa County (hon.) bar assns., Am. Law Inst., Nat. Fedn. Bus. and Profl. Women's Clubs (pres. Ariz. 1956-57, Western regional dir. 1957-58; nat. bd. chmn. pub. affairs 1959-60), Ariz. Judges Assn. (past pres.), Nat. Assn. Women Lawyers, Phoenix Bus. and Profl. Women's Club, Epsilon Sigma Alpha (hon.), Kappa Beta Pi, Delta Kappa Gamma (hon.), Chi Omega. Conglist. (trustee). Mem. Order Eastern Star (past matron). Club: Phoenix Soroptimist (past pres.). Home: Apt 37 1320 E Bethany Home Rd Phoenix AZ 85014 Office: Capitol Bldg Ariz Supreme Ct Phoenix AZ 85007

LODER, MARTHA KATHERINE, ret. educator; b. Bridgeton, N.J., July 12, 1914; d., LeRoy Ward and Maude (Woodruff) Loder; A.B., Dickinson Coll., 1934; A.M., U. Pa., 1937, Ph.D., 1943. Tchr., Bridgeton High Sch., 1935-38, 39-41, head dept. English, fgn. langs., 1943-57; tchr. Springfield Twp. High Sch., Chestnut Hill, Pa., 1941-43; supr. secondary instrn. Bridgeton Pub. Schs., 1957-71; ret., 1971. Bd. dirs. Bridgeton chpt. Nat. Conf. Christians and Jews; trustee Bridgeton Free Pub. Library. Recipient Am. Legion award for meritorious community service, 1950. Mem. D.A.R., Am. Assn. U. Women, Nat. Ret. Tchrs. Assn., Alliance Francaise, Phi Beta Kappa, Delta Kappa Gamma. Author: The Life and Novels of Leon Gozlan, 1943. Home: 8 South Dr Bridgeton NJ 08302

LODGE, ANN, psychologist; b. Cleve., July 22, 1931; d. George Townsend and Edith Pardee (Bennett) Lodge; A.B., Wilkes Coll., 1955; Ph.D. (USPHS fellow), Duke, 1960. Intern med. psychology Duke Med. Center, 1957-58; USPHS fellow Nat. Inst. Mental Health, 1960-63; staff psychologist Durham (N.C.) Child Guidance Center, 1959-60; research asso. Walter Reed Army Inst. Research, also Washington Sch. Psychiatry, Washington, 1963-65; research asso. neurology and psychiatry Children's Hosp. Research Found., Washington, 1965-72; research prof. pediatrics George Washington U. Sch. Medicine, 1968-72; asso. prof. psychology, dept. behavioral sci. George Mason U., Fairfax, Va., 1970-72; child devel. specialist, dir. infant devel. research lab. Children's Hosp. San Francisco, 1972—. Mem. faculty San Francisco State U., 1973—, Cal. Sch. Profl. Psychology, 1974—; research cons. Family Developmental Center, San Francisco, 1972—, Center for Spl. Problems, Community Mental Health Services, San Francisco Dept. Pub. Health, 1974—. Mem. Am. Psychol. Assn., A.A.A.S., Internat. Neuropsychology Soc., N.Y. Acad. Scis., Soc. Research in Child Devel., Soc. Neurosci., Sigma Xi. Contbr. to Serotonin in Down's Syndrome, 1973, also articles to profl. jours. Home: 45 Molino Av Mill Valley CA 94941 Office: Pediatrics Dept Children's Hosp 3801 Sacramento St San Francisco CA 94118

LODGE, EDITH BENNETT (MRS. GEORGE TOWNSEND LODGE), poet; b. N.Y.C., Nov. 17, 1908; d. William Mason and Mary Evans (Umstead) Bennett; B.A., Oberlin Coll., 1929; M.A., Old Dominion U., 1970; m. George Townsend Lodge, June 18, 1929; children—Ann, David Townsend. Asst., Tchr.'s Coll. Library, Columbia U., N.Y.C., 1944-45; asst. Duke U. Library, Durham, N.C., 1955-58; lectr. English, Old Dominon U., Norfolk, Va., 1970-72; poems and prose segments pub. in Saturday Rev., N.Y. Times, Kaleidograph, Lantern, Arrows in the Air, Christian Century, Presbyn. Survey, Pulpit, Oregonian Verse, The Lyric, Imprints Quar., other mags. and newspapers; poems included in Golden Year, 1960, Diamond Anthologies of Poetry Soc. Am., 1971, Golden Anthology of Poetry Soc. Va., 1974, Sandwich Isles, U.S.A., Anthology of Hawaii Writers Club, 1973. Recipient 1st prize for sonnet Irene Leache Meml. Contest, 1964, 1st prize for lyric, 1965. Mem. Poetry Soc. Am., Acad. Am. Poets, Poetry Soc. Va., Am. Assn. U. Women. Presbyn. Author: Song of the Hill, Selected Poems of Edith Lodge, 1964; Journey Through Noon (poems), 1974. Home: 1329 Oak Park Av Norfolk VA 23503

LODGE, RHEA EWALD, state ofcl.; b. Detroit, May 30; d. William R. and Rhea Elizabeth (Allen) Ewald; student Wellesley Coll., 1937-39, U. Mo. Sch. Journalism, 1940-42; m. L. Harvey Lodge, Oct. 16, 1971; children by previous marriage—Robert Brigham Ellery, Jr. (dec.), Carl Frederick Vietor III. Telegraph editor Pontiac (Mich.) Daily Press, 1945-47, women's editor, 1957-60; editor Lakeland Tribune, weekly, Waterford, Mich., 1960-63; pub. relations exec. A.R. Gloster, Detroit, 1963-66; pub. relations dir. continuing edn. div. Oakland U., Rochester, Mich., 1965-68; with News-Tribune Publs., Waterford, 1968-71; pres. Vietor-Lodge Assos., Troy, Mich., 1970-72; pub. relations, exec. asst. to dir. Mich. Dept. Labor, Lansing, 1973—. Author, narrator weekly radio program Voice of Meadowbrook for Meadowbrook Music Festival, 1967-68; chmn. Mich. Labor Dept. div. United Way Lansing, 1973-74; mem. minority bus. opportunity com., publicity com. Mich. Rehab. Assn., 1974, legislative adv. com., 1973—; treas. House and Senate Club, 1972-75. Mem. Women's Econ. Club Detroit, Detroit Press Club, Women in Communications (dir. 1942, 68-69), League Women Voters (dir.), Am. Assn. U. Women (asso.), Mich. Women's Press Club (1st place award photo. and news coverage 1970), Nat. Fedn. Press Women, Mich. Employees Assn., Founders Soc. Detroit Inst. Art, Pontiac Creative Arts Center, Alpha Phi. Clubs: Wellesley; Viernese. Home: 2572 Somerset Blvd Troy MI 48084 Office: Mich Dept Labor 300 E Michigan Av Lansing MI 48926

LODICO, CECELIA ANN, pub. relations exec.; b. Canton, O., Nov. 21, 1948; d. Louis and Theresa Catherine (Zeller) Lodico; A.A., Palomar Coll., 1968; B.A. in Pub. Relations, San Jose State U., 1971. Dir. pub. relations Santa Clara County Girl Scout Council, San Jose, Cal., 1971-74; pub. information officer Clovis (Cal.) Unified Sch. Dist., 1974—. Mem. Pub. Relations Soc. Am., Women in Communications. Roman Catholic. Home: 2205 Peach Av Apt 14 Clovis CA 93612 Office: 914 4th St Clovis CA 93612

LOEB, ELINOR EISENDRATH (MRS. LOUIS C. LOEB), pub. health ofcl.; b. Denver; d. Edwin N. and Lillian (Ettenson) Eisendrath; student Simmons Coll., 1935-38; B.S., U. Denver, 1956; m. Louis C. Loeb, Feb. 17, 1941 (dec. Dec. 1965); children—Michael E., Patricia. Dir. personnel Neusteter's, Denver, 1939-41, 44-46; instr. consumer edn. and retail selling U. Denver, 1947-48; dir. vol. services Tri County Dist. Health Dept., Englewood, Colo., 1966—. Chmn. March of Dimes Fashion Show, 1956, CARE Fashion Show, 1957-58, Denver Symphony Orch. Benefit, 1959; co-chmn. patron com. Denver Debutante Ball, 1960-61; reservations chmn. French Ball, Colo. Centennial, 1962; active Am. Field Service. Bd. dirs. Nat. Found. for Infantile Paralysis, Planned Parenthood, Cranmer Park-Hilltop Improvement Assn. Mem. Am. Assn. Vol. Services Coordinators. Clubs: Green Gables Country, Town (Denver). Home: 480 S Marion St Pkwy Apt 506 Denver CO 80209 Office: 3265 W Girard St Englewood CO 80110

LOEB, FRANCES LEHMAN (MRS. JOHN L. LOEB), city ofcl.; b. N.Y.C., Sept. 25, 1906; d. Arthur and Adele (Lewisohn) Lehman; student Vassar Coll., 1924-26; m. John L. Loeb, Nov. 18, 1926; children—Judith (Mrs. Judy Chiara), John L., Ann (Mrs. Bronfman), Arthur Lehman, Deborah (Mrs. David J. Davies). N.Y.C. commr. for UN and Consular Corps, 1966—. Exec. group Population Crisis Com., Washington; mem. Am. Friends of Can. com.; bd. mgrs. Bellevue Schs. Nursing; bd. dirs. Recreation Service for Children of Bellevue; mem. exec. com. Fedn. for Jewish Philanthropies; mem. UN Devel. Corp., 1972—; life trustee Collegiate Sch. for Boys, N.Y.C.; trustee Briarcliff Coll., Briarcliff Manor, N.Y. Home: 730 Park Av New York City NY 10021 also Anderson Hill Rd Purchase NY 10577

LOEBL, SUZANNE BAMBERGER (MRS. ERNEST M. LOEBL), author; b. Hannover, Germany; d. Hugo and Margaret (Schwarzhaupt) Bamberger; student Lycee de Forest, Brussels, 1938-42, Institut Meurice Chimie, Brussels, 1944-46, Columbia, 1946-48; m. Ernest M. Loebl, Mar. 15, 1950; children—Judith Hannah, David Albert. Came to U.S., 1946, naturalized, 1951. Research asst. Sloane-Kettering Inst. for Cancer Research, 1948-52; research asst. N.Y.U., 1952-54; free lance tech. writer, translator, 1958—; sci. editor N.Y. Heart Assn., 1969-71; sci. editor Arthritis Found., 1971—. Advanced Sci. Writing fellow Columbia U., 1968-69; recipient Matrix award N.Y. Women in Communications, 1974. Mem. Am. Med. Writers Assn., Nat. Assn. Sci. Writers., Soc. Mag. Writers. Author: Fighting the Unseen: The Story of Viruses, 1967; Exploring the Mind: Man's Search for Mental Health, 1968; Conception, Contraception, A New Look, 1974. Home: 788 Riverside Dr New York City NY 10032 Office: 1212 Av of Americas New York City NY 10036

LOEBLICH, HELEN NINA TAPPAN, paleontologist; b. Norman, Okla., Oct. 12, 1917; d. Frank Girard and Mary (Jenks) Tappan; B.S., U. Okla., 1937, M.S., 1939; Ph.D., U. Chgo., 1942; m. Alfred Richard Loeblich Jr., June 18, 1939; children—Alfred Richard III, Karen Elizabeth Lipps, Judith Anne (Mrs. David Covey), Daryl Louise (Mrs. Robert Ford). Instr. geology Tulane U., 1942-43; geologist U.S. Geol. Survey, Washington, 1943-45, 1947-57, Fullerton, Cal., 1957—; lectr. geology U. Cal. at Los Angeles, 1958-65, asso. research geologist, 1961-64, sr. lectr. geology, 1965-66, prof. geology, 1966—, vice-chmn. dept., 1973—; research asso. Smithsonian Instn., Washington, 1954-57. John Simon Guggenheim Found. fellow, 1953-54. Fellow Geol. Soc. Am.; mem. Paleontol. Soc., Soc. Protozoologists, Phycological Soc. Am., Nat. Assn. Geology Tchrs., Internat. Paleontol. Union, Palaeontographical soc., Internat. Phycol. Soc., Phycol. Soc. Gt. Britain, Cushman Found. for aminiferal Research, Marine Biol. Assn. U.K., Soc. Econ. Paleontologists and Mineralogists, Am. Assn. U. Profs., Phi Beta Kappa, Sigma Xi, Sigma Delta Epsilon. Author: (with A. R. Loeblich Jr.) Treatise on Invertebrate Paleontology, part C, Protista 2, Foraminiferida, 2 vols., 1964. Research, publs. on morphology, systematics, nomenclature of foraminifers, thecamoebians, silicoflagellates, ebridians, tintinnids, coccolithophorids, radiolarians, organic-walled phyto plankton, chitinozoa, Cretaceous-Tertiary boundary, Cretaceous of Gulf Coast, Mesozoic of N. Alaska; Jurassic of S.D.; reclassification of foraminifera, fossil phytoplankton and effect on ecosystems and atmosphere of changes in phytoplankton abundance through geologic time. Home: 11427 Albata St Los Angeles CA 90049 Office: Dept Geology U Cal Los Angeles CA 90024

LOENING, MRS. ALBERT PALMER (SARAH LARKIN), author; b. Nutley, N.J., Dec. 9, 1896; d. Adrian H. and Katherine (Satterthwaite) Larkin; student Miss Chapin's Sch., Madame Marty's Sch., Paris, 1913; m. Albert P. Loening, Nov. 28, 1922; 1 son, Albert Palmer. Author: Three Rivers, 1934; The Trevals, a Tale of Quebec, 1936; Radisson, 1938; Dimo, 1940; Joan of Arc, 1951; Zulli, 1954; The Old Master, 1958; The Old Master and Other Tails, 1967; Mountain in the Field, 1972. Chmn. arts and skill corp. A.R.C., Camp Upton, 1944, chmn. Hampton chpt., 1946; pres. Cathedral Guild St. John the Divine, 1963-66, 68-70. Mem. Pen and Brush, Nat. Soc. Colonial Dames, Gardeners of St. John's (past chmn.), Huguenot Soc. Am., Order St. John Jerusalem (asso. officer). Clubs: Colony, Cosmopolitan, Hroswithia, Southampton Garden (past pres). Home: 1 E 66th St New York City NY 10021 also Lallinden Southampton NY 11968

LOERKE, JEAN PENN, mus. curator; b. Madison, Wis., Dec. 31, 1934; d. Francis O. and Julia Mae (Stefik) Penn; B.S., U. Wis., 1957; grad. Chgo. Sch. Interior Decoration, 1959; postgrad. U. Wis.-Milw., 1972—; 1 son, Pieter Richard. Pub. relations sec. Graphic Arts Assn. Wis., Milw., 1958-60; pub. relations dir. Milw. Hosp., 1963-64; owner The Cobblestone Antique Shop, Eagle, Wis., 1964-67; county historian, curator mus. Waukesha County Hist. Mus., Waukesha, Wis., 1972—. Instr. antiques evaluation Waukesha County Tech. Inst., 1973. Mem. Mayor's Task Force on Downtown Devel., Waukesha, Wis., 1973—; mem. adv. com. Milw. Hosp. Sch. Nursing, 1964. Mem. Soc. Archtl. Historians. Bd. Friends and Alumni U. Wis. (sec. 1972—), Gamma Alpha Chi, Theta Sigma Phi. Author: Early Waukesha: A Walking Tour of Archtl. and Historic Sites, 1973. Editor: The Bottle Stopper, 1964-66. Home: Route 1 Box 52 Eagle WI 53119 Office: 101 W Main St Waukesha WI 53186

LOESCH, KATHARINE TAYLOR (MRS. JOHN GEORGE LOESCH), educator; b. Berkeley, Cal., Apr. 13, 1922; d. Paul Schuster and Katharine (Whiteside) Taylor; student Swarthmore Coll., 1939-41, U. Wash., 1942; B.A., Columbia, 1944, M.A., 1949; postgrad. Ind. U., 1953; Ph.D., Northwestern U., 1961; m. John George Loesch, Aug. 28, 1948; 1 son, William Ross. Instr. speech Wellesley (Mass.) Coll., 1949-52, Loyola U., Chgo., 1956; asst. prof. speech Roosevelt U., Chgo., 1957, 62-65; faculty U. Ill. at Chgo. Circle, 1968—, asso. prof. speech, 1970—. Recipient Golden Anniversary Prize award Speech Assn. Am., 1969. Am. Philos. Soc. grantee, 1970. Mem. Am. Soc. for Aesthetics, Linguistics Soc. Am., Speech Communication Assn., Modern Lang. Assn. Home: 2129 N Sedgwick St Chicago IL 60614

LOEW, GLORIA (MRS. CLEMENS ALEXANDER LOEW), psychotherapist; b. Jersey City, June 23, 1941; d. Felix James and Anne (Tieger) Heiman; B.A., U. Denver, 1960; M.A., Purdue U., 1962, Ph.D., 1967; m. Clemens Alexander Loew, June 9, 1968;

children—Jennifer, Shannon. Cons. Psychologist Bur. Child Welfare, N.Y.C., 1967-69; psychotherapist, N.Y.C., 1968—, Englewood, N.J., 1973—. Lectr. Ind. U., Kokomo, 1965. Postdoctoral fellow, 1967-69. Mem. Am. Psychol. Assn. Editor: Three Psychotherapists: A Clinical Comparison (Loew, Grayson & Loew), 1975. Address: 90 Booth Av Englewood NJ 07631

LOEWENSTEIN, ARLINE PERRY (MRS. JACK MAYER LOEWENSTEIN), psychologist; b. Cleve., June 4, 1932; d. Aaron and Gertrude (Sachs) Perry; A.B., U. Miami, 1954, M.Ed., 1964, Ph.D. (Nat. Def. Edn. Act fellow), 1971; m. Jack Mayer Loewenstein, Sept. 7, 1957; children—David Andrew, Linda Mayer. Copywriter, WQAM-Radio, Miami, Fla., 1954-56; pub. service WTVJ-TV, 1956-59; tchr. Dade County Bd. Pub. Instrn., Miami, 1964-66, psychologist, 1971—; faculty U. Miami, 1970, 74. Mem. Am. Psychol. Assn., Assn. for Advancement Behavior Therapy, Fla., Dade County assns. sch. psychologists, Women in Communications, Mortar Bd., Phi Kappa Phi, Alpha Epsilon Phi, Kappa Delta Pi. Home: 19631 Whispering Pines Rd Miami FL 33157 Office: 2201 SW 4th St Miami FL 33135

LOEWENSTEIN, RUTH, import exec.; b. Munich, Germany, May 29, 1929; d. Willy and Anny (Cahen) Loewenstein; came to U.S., 1940, naturalized, 1945; B.A., Hunter Coll., 1951; postgrad. New Sch. Social Research. With Willy Loewenstein Corp., 1945-63; with David E. Schwab & Co., N.Y.C., 1963—, v.p., 1972—. Active Nat. Council Jewish Women, other community orgns. Mem. Alpha Chi Alpha. Home: 63-60 98th St Rego Park NY 11374 Office: 417 Fifth Av New York City NY 10016

LOEWUS, HELEN GALLAND (MRS. FREDERICK LOEWUS), retail co. exec.; b. N.Y.C., June 1, 1925; d. Joe and Ida (Freund) Galland; B.A., Hunter Coll., 1945; m. Frederick Loewus, June 27, 1967; children (by a previous marriage)—David, Susan and Judy Frishberg; stepchildren—Barbara (Mrs. Harvey Melnick), Richard Loewus. Exec. trainee program Lord & Taylor, N.Y.C., 1945-46, asst. buyer, 1947-50; buyer Bonwit Teller, N.Y.C., 1950-63, div. mdse. mgr., 1963-69, v.p., asso. gen. mdse. mgr., 1969-71, v.p., gen. mdse. mgr., 1971-73, sr. v.p., gen. mdse. mgr., 1973—, also dir. Bd. govs. Fashion Group; trustee City Hope; adv. bd. Hunter Coll. Recipient Genesco Superior Achievement award, 1963, 70. Home: 40 W 86th St New York City NY 10024 Office: Bonwit Teller 721 Fifth Av New York City NY 10021

LOEWUS, MARY WALZ (MRS. FRANK A. LOEWUS), biochemist; b. Duluth, Minn., Feb. 15, 1923; d. Ivan George and Mary Ellen (McLennan) Walz; student Coll. of St. Scholastica, 1940-43; B.A. magna cum laude, U. Minn., 1945, M.S., 1950, Ph.D., 1953; m. Frank Abel Loewus, Dec. 26, 1947; children—Rebecca (Mrs. Howard L. Deitch), David, Daniel. Research asso. U. Cal. at Berkeley, 1956-64; research asso. State U. N.Y. at Buffalo, 1965—. NSF grantee, 1965-67. Contbr. articles to profl. jours. Home: 35 Woodhaven Rd Amherst NY 14226 Office: Dept Biology State U NY Buffalo NY 14214

LOFGREN, RUTH, biologist, educator; b. Huntsville, Utah, Nov. 25, 1916; d. Benjamin Franklin and Alice Loise (Elder) Lofgren; B.A., U. Utah, 1939, M.A., 1940; Ph.D., U. Mich., 1944. Instr. microbiology U. Mich. at Ann Arbor, 1945-48, asst. prof., 1948-53; research asso. Found. Integrated Edn., N.Y.C., 1953-56; asst. prof. biology Bklyn. Coll., 1956-63, asso. prof. sci. edn., 1963—. Instr. human physiology Adelphi U., Garden City, N.Y., 1954-56; tchr. sci. Bklyn. Ethical Culture Sch., 1958. Sec., treas. Friends Schs. Com., 1970-74; judge sch. sci. fairs. Postdoctoral fellow U. Pa., 1946, U. Cal., 1949; Faculty Research grantee, 1971-72. Mem. Am. Inst. Biol. Scis., Nat. Sci. Tchrs. Assn., Nat. Assn. Biology Tchrs., A.A.A.S., N.Y. Biology Tchrs. Assn. (faculty cons. 1973-74), Sigma Delta Epsilon, Pi Lambda Theta. Club: Women's Press (chmn. constn. and by-laws 1972-74) (N.Y.C.). Home: 3310 Av H Brooklyn NY 11210 Office: 1109 Plaza Brooklyn College Brooklyn NY 11210

LOFTS, NORAH, author; b. Shipdham, Norfolk, Eng., Aug. 27, 1904; d. Isaac and Ethel (Garner) Robinson; student Bury St. Edmund's, Eng.; m. Geoffrey Lofts, Dec. 29, 1933; 1 son, Geoffrey St. Edmund Clive. Author: I Met a Gypsy, 1935; Here Was a Man, 1936; White Hell of Pity, 1934; Requiem for Idols, 1938; Colin Lowrie, 1938; Blossom Like the Rose, 1939; Hester Room, 1940; The Brittle Glass, 1942; The Golden Fleece, 1943; Jassy, 1945; To See a Fine Lady, 1946; Road to Revelation (pub. in Eng. only), 1941; Silver Nutmeg, 1947; A Calf for Venus, 1949; Women of the Old Testament, 1949; Esther, 1950; The Luteplayer, 1951; Bless This House, 1954; Winter Harvest, 1955; Afternoon of An Autocrat, 1956; Scent of Cloves, 1957; The Town House, 1959; Heaven in Your Hand; The House At Old Vine; The House at Sunset, 1962; The Concubine, 1963; How Far To Bethlehem 1965; (with Margery Weiner) Eternal France, 1968; The Lost Queen, 1969; Lovers All Untrue, 1970; The King's Pleasure, 1970; A Rose for Virtue, 1971; Out of the Dark, 1972; Nethergate, 1973; Crown of Aloes, 1974; Knight's Acre, 1975. Home: Northgate House Bury St Edmunds Suffolk England

LOGAN, BARBARA JACQUELINE (MRS. GEORGE GRAYSON TYLER), physician; b. Lynn, Mass., Sept. 9, 1914; d. Joseph B. and Jeanne B. (Backman) Logan; B.S., Boston U., 1931-34; M.D., George Washington U., 1938; m. George Grayson Tyler, Feb. 20, 1959. Intern Jersey City Med. Center, Margaret Hague, Jersey City, 1939-41; resident Woman's Hosp., St. Luke's Hosp., N.Y.C., 1941-44; practice medicine specializing in surgery and gynecology and obstetrics, N.Y.C., 1944—; sr. cons. Gynecology and Infertility Clinics, 1945—; attending obstetrician and gynecologist Roosevelt Hosp., 1945—; asso. prof. obstetrics and gynecology Columbia U. Med. Sch., 1971—. Bd. dirs. N.Y. State Charities Aid, Child Adoption and Foster Home, Children's Aid Soc. Diplomate Nat. Bd. Med. Examiners. Fellow A.C.S., Am. Coll. Obstetrics and Gynecology, Acad. Medicine of N.Y.; mem. N.Y. Gynecology Soc., N.Y. Acad. Sci., Am. Fertility Soc., Am. Women's Med. Soc. Club: Cosmopolitan. Home: 1080 Fifth Av New York City NY 10028 Office: 930 Park Av New York City NY 10028

LOGAN, ELIZABETH MOORE (MRS. JOHN SUBLETT LOGAN), civic worker; b. Kansas City, Mo.; d. Walton Norwood and Elizabeth (Brown) Moore; student Vassar Coll., U. Cal. at Berkeley; m. John Sublett Logan, May 24, 1935; children—Walton Moore, Bailey (Mrs. George Christian Meyer III). Bd. dirs. San Francisco Opera Guild, de Young Mus. Soc., Golden Gate chpt. A.R.C. Home: 2855 Ralston Av Hillsborough CA 94010

LOGAN, GRACE ELEANOR MILLER (MRS. HENRY WHITTINGTON LOGAN), educator; b. Valencia, Pa., June 22, 1908; d. Alvah John and Lillian (Gibson) Miller; B.S., Temple U., 1930, M.S., 1931; postgrad., 1955-56; m. Henry Whittington Logan, Mar. 16, 1940; 1 son, Henry Whittington III. English instr. Temple U., 1930-33; asst. prof. to dept. head Moravian Coll., Bethlehem, Pa., 1933-42; asso. prof. edn. and philosophy Widener Coll. (formerly PMC Colls.), Chester, Pa., 1956-67, asso. prof. English and philosophy, 1969-70, prof. English, 1970—, dir. Coll. Reading Services, 1958—; dir. Fed. Office of Edn. Equal Opportunities Tng. Br. Insts., 1965—; cons., lectr.; only woman on faculty any mil. coll. U.S. for 8 yrs. Evaluator, ESEA Title I project Chester Sch. Dist., 1968-69. Mem. Am. Assn. U. Profs., Nat. Council Tchrs. English, Coll. English Assn., Internat. Platform Assn., Am. Assn. for Higher Edn., N.E.A., Coll. Reading Assn., Internat. Reading Assn., Pa. Council Tchrs., Am. Acad. Religion, Kappa Delta Epsilon, Pi Delta Epsilon. Presbyn. Home: 201 Sykes Lane Wallingford PA 19086 Office: Widener Coll Chester PA 19013

LOGAN, JEANNETTE, nursing adminstr.; b. Maywood, Ill., Mar. 1, 1933; d. Samuel and Luvena (Simmons) Logan; diploma Cook County Sch. Nursing, 1955; student U. Ill., 1968-71, Roosevelt U., 1973—. Staff nurse pediatrics Cook County Hosp., Chgo., 1955-57, head nurse, medicine, 1957-59, supr. medicine, 1959-63, 64-65, adminstrv. supr. nursing service, 1964-68, asst. dir. med. nursing, 1969-71, dir. med. nursing, 1971-72, dir. nursing services, 1972—; head nurse obstetrics Mt. Sinai Hosp., Chgo., 1963-64. Vol. chmn. health div. Operation Push, 1972—; mem. com. united health information Council for Community Services, 1972-73. Mem. Ill. Nurses Assn. (council nursing practice 1969-70, mem. council 1973—), Am. Heart Assn., Cook County Sch. Nursing Alumni Assn. (pres. 1968-70), League of Black Women. Home: 7957 S Luella St Chicago IL 60617 Office: 1835 W Harrison St Chicago IL 60612

LOGAN, NORMA ADDISON SCHLENZ (MRS. JOHN ALEXANDER LOGAN), civic worker, writer; b. Covington, La., Feb. 9, 1919; d. David Ira and Blanche (Belmont) Addison; student Newcomb Coll., La. State U., 1937-39; m. Harry E. Schlenz, Aug. 4, 1942 (dec. Dec. 1969); children—Susan (Mrs. Robert L. Moran), Dianne (Mrs. Kenton W. Gangwer), Deborah Ann (Mrs. Richard Ciancio), H. Addison; m. 2d, John Alexander Logan. Pres. womens bd. Sherman Hosp., Elgin, Ill., 1961-62, aux. bd. v.p.; v.p. Florence Crittenton Anchorage, 1943-45, Infant Welfare Soc. Chgo., 1943-44; free lance writer for newspapers, charity publs., panhellenic groups. Pres., Elgin Acad., 1961-63. Recipient Order of Lion, Art Inst. Chgo., 1960. Presbyn. Author: Contented Is a Freshman, If—, 1960. Home: 335 Robinwood Dr Terre Haute IN 47803

LOGAN, REBECCA DE LOATCH POLLARD (MRS. JOHN A. LOGAN), civic worker, philanthropist; b. Port Norfolk, Va.; d. William Andrew and Daisy (De Loatch) Pollard; student Grand Central Art Sch., 1926, Boston Sch. Mus. Fine Arts, 1931; m. William B. Van Lennep II, Sept. 6, 1926 (div. 1937); 1 son, Richard; m. 2d, M. Robert Guggenheim, Jan. 6, 1938 (dec. Nov. 1959); m. 3d, John A. Logan, Apr. 16, 1962. Exhibited art work Nat. Mus., Washington, 1948, Boston, 1931. Mem. women's bd. Washington Heart Assn., 1968—; mem. women's com. Corcoran Gallery Art, Washington, 1955—, now trustee; founder Art Barn, (name changed to Art Barn Assos. 1973), pres. Assos. of Artists Equity of Washington, 1971-73, pres. emeritus, 1973—; mem. Nat. Trust for Historic Preservation, Washington, 1966—; mem. nat. bd. Women's Med. Coll. Pa., 1957—. Bd. dirs. Children's Hosp. Washington, 1945—, asso. mem., 1964—. Trustee Nat. Ballet Soc., Washington; bd. dirs. Washington Opera Soc. Guild, Washington Performing Arts; trustee Children's Speech and Hearing Center, Washington, 1969—. Mem. Am. Newspaper Women's Assn. (asso.), Nat. Soc. Arts and Letters (pres. 1958-60), Colonial Dames Am., D.A.R. Episcopalian. Clubs: Washington, Sulgrave, 1925 F Street, City Tavern (Washington). Home: 4400 Broad Branch Rd Washington DC 20008 also Estate Bellevue Christiansted St Croix VI 00820

LOGGIE, JENNIFER MARY HILDRETH, physician, pharmacologist, educator; b. Lusaka, Zambia, Feb. 4, 1936; d. John and Jenny (Beattie) Loggie; M.B., B.Ch., U. Witwatersrand, Johannesburg, South Africa, 1959. Intern Harare Hosp., Salisbury, Rhodesia, 1960-61; gen. practice Lusaka, 1961-62; pediatric sr. houseofficer Derby Children's Hosp., St. John's Hosp., Chelmsford, Eng., 1962-64; resident in pediatrics Children's Hosp., Louisville, 1964, Cin., 1964-65; clin. pharmacology fellow Cin. Coll. Medicine, 1965-67; asst. prof. pediatrics and pharmacology U. Cin., 1967-69, asso. prof. pediatrics, 1970—, also asso. prof. pharmacology, 1972—. Am. Heart Assn. grantee, 1970-71, 71-72. Mem. Midwest Soc. for Pediatric Research. Episcopalian. Contbr. articles on pediatrics to med. jours., Am. Jour. Diseases Childhood, Jour. Pediatrics. Home: 1133 Herschel St Cincinnati OH 45208 Office: Childrens Hosp Research Foundation Elland and Bethesda St Cincinnati OH 45229

LOGSDON, GLORIA NEWTON (MRS. JOHN LAWRENCE LOGSDON), ednl. adminstr.; b. St. Louis, Aug. 12, 1941; d. David John and Frances Elizabeth (Johnson) Newton; B.A., U. Mo., 1963; M.S., Hofstra U., 1969; m. John Lawrence Logsdon, Nov. 18, 1965; children—Elizabeth Jennifer, Robert Burns II. Tchr., Suffolk State Sch., Melville, N.Y., 1966-69, edn. supr., 1969-72, mental hygiene treatment team leader, 1972-73; ednl. dir. Sagamore Children's Center, Melville, 1973—. Mem. Am. Assn. Mental Deficiency, Council for Exceptional Children, N.Y. State Assn. for Tchrs. of Mentally Handicapped, L.I. Assn. Spl. Edn. Adminstrs., Mental Hygiene Educators Assn., N.A.A.C.P. (pres. Kansas City youth council 1959-61, pres. Mo. conf. of youth councils and coll. chpts. 1960-62, chmn. region 4 youth and coll. sect. 1960-62, mem. nat. youth works com. 1961-62). Home: 7 Leigh St Huntington NY 11743 Office: Sagamore Children's Center Melville NY 11743

LOGSDON, LAURA LOUISE, psychologist; b. Carey, O., Dec. 26, 1927; d. Lloyd Cletus and Anna Rose (Kummerer) Logdson; student Loyola U., Chgo., 1945-48, M.A., 1961, postgrad., 1964-69; A.B., Mary Manse Coll., 1957. Clin. inter Cath. Charities Guidance Center, Chgo., 1957-58; Nat. Inst. Mental Health project grad. asst. Loyola U., Chgo., 1959-61; sch. psychologist intern Ill. Dept. Pub. Instrn., Springfield, 1962-63; clin. psychologist Sandusky Valley Guidance Center, Tiffin, O., 1963-64; chief psychologist S.W. Cook County Coop. for Spl. Edn., Tinley Park, Ill., 1964-65; clin. psychologist Cath. Charities Reading Clinic, Chgo., 1966-69; sch. psychologist McHenry County (Ill.) Spl. Edn., Woodstock, 1969-70, Toledo Diocesan Sch. Office, 1970-72; sch. psychologist, diagnostic reading clinic Toledo Bd. Edn., 1972—. Mem. Am. (asso.), Midwestern, Ill. (charter) psychol. assns., Maumee Valley Sch. Psychologists Assn., Nat. Assn. Sch. Psychologists, Pi Gamma Mu, Psi Chi. Home: 2526 Parkview St Toledo OH 43606 Office: 415 N St Clair St Toledo OH 43604

LOHMAN, BERNEICE THOMAS KNAGGS (MRS. BEN E. LOHMAN), orgn. ofcl.; b. Ovid, Mich., Nov. 22, 1905; d. Frederick Arthur and Evalena (Vosburgh) Thomas; grad. Baker Bus. Coll., 1925; student Central Mich. U., 1923; LL.B., Blackstone Inst. Law, Chgo., 1942; m. Daniel A. Knaggs, Mar. 11, 1944 (dec. Aug. 1957); m. 2d, Ben E. Lohman, Dec. 27, 1958. Legal sec. firm Smith, Hunter & Spaulding, St. Johns, Mich., 1925-26, Person, Marshall & Palm, Lansing, Mich., 1927-29, Office Atty. Gen. Mich., 1933-35, Miller, Canfield, Paddock & Stone, Detroit, 1937-39; com. clk. Mich. Ho. of Reps., Lansing, 1927, sec. to speaker of house, 1929-33, statistician ways and means com., 1939, 41-61; sec. to chmn. Mich. Liquor Commn., 1935-37, Mich. Dept. Labor and Industry, 1939-41; vice chmn. State Employees Retirement System Mich., 1970-73, chmn., 1973—. Nurses aide A.R.C., Mich., 1942—; sec. Monroe County Hist. Soc., 1948-50, v.p., 1950-52, pres., 1954-56; bd. dirs. Southeastern Mich. Tourists Assn., 1956-58; trustee Mich. Hist. Soc., 1946-48; sec. Sesquicentennial Com. Battle River Basin; chmn. impact Civil War on farming in Mich., Civil War Centennial Observance Commn., 1960-66, mem. adv. com., 1964. Vice pres. Mich. Fedn. Republican Women's Clubs, 1943-44; mem. election bd., Monroe, Mich., 1952-56; sec. Monroe County Rep. Com., 1952-53; pres. Monroe Rep. Women's Club, 1973—; state chmn. older Am. div. of Mich. Com. for Re-election of Pres. Nixon, 1972. Recipient citation of appreciation V.F.W., 1945, citation Mich. Ho. of Reps., 1961, citation for achievement and meritorious services D.A.V., A.R.C., 1964. Mem. D.A.R., Daus. Am. Colonists (state regent 1970—; regent Monroe chpt. 1973—). Episcopalian (v.p. ECW Woman 1954-55). Mem. Order Eastern Star. Home: 610 E Elm Av Monroe MI 48161 also 2618 Lake Shore Dr Route 2 Fennville MI 49408

LOHR DE IRIZARRY, MILDRED TUCKER (MRS. RAUL A. IRIZARRY CALDER), educator; b. Brandy, Va.; d. Robert Lee and Victoria James (Swan) Lohr; B.A., Farmville State Tchrs. Coll. (now Longwood Coll.), 1927; M.A., Columbia, 1933, postgrad., 1943-44, 64; postgrad. U. London Sch. Econs., 1954; S.S., McGill U., 1965, U. Ohio, 1966, U. Del., 1970; m. Raul Armando Irizarry Calder, June 18, 1940; children—Raul Armando II, Robert Tucker. Tchr. grade sch., Madison County, Va. and Orange, Va., 1924-25; tchr. war dept., Washington, 1928-38; chmn. dept. history and polit. sci. Poly Inst., San German, P.R., 1938-58; prof., chmn. dept. geography InterAm. U., San German, 1964—, also dean of faculty, v.p. univ. on sabbatical leave study USSR; supr. dept. edn., San Juan, P.R., 1970—. Mem. Hermandad, 1929—, v.p., 1968—; active hosp. pub. fund raising, Mayaguez and San German, 1964-65; vol. com. work and hosp. work Internat. Red Cross. Mem. Internat. Platform Assn., Marquis Biog. Library Soc. Democrat. Episcopalian. Club: Altrusa. Home: InterAm U San German PR 00753

LOHRER, MARGUERITE, social worker; b. Unionville, Mich.; d. William and Elizabeth (Wills) Lohrer; B.S., Northwestern U., 1940; A.M., U. Chgo. Sch. Social Service Adminstrn., 1954. Med. social worker Am. Nat. Red Cross, Mil. and Naval Welfare-Gardiner Gen. Hosp., Chgo., 1943-46, VA Regional Office, Chgo., 1946, VA Center, Los Angeles, 1946-53, VA Research Hosp., Chgo., 1954-56, Chgo. chpt. Muscular Dystrophy Assn., 1956-58; social service dir. Muscular Dystrophy Assns. Am., N.Y.C., 1958-62; social work cons. N.Y.C. Dept. Health, 1962-64; dir. social service Manhattan Eye, Ear and Throat Hosp., N.Y.C., 1964—. Mem. Nat. Assn. Social Workers, Acad. Certified Social Workers, Rehab. Internat., Soc. for Hosp. Social Work Dirs., Nat. Conf. Social Welfare, English-Speaking Union, Am. Assn. U. Women. Episcopalian. Home: 11 Fifth Av New York City NY 10003 Office: 210 E 64th St New York City NY 10021

LOLLOBRIGIDA, GINA, actress; b. Subiaco, Italy, July 4, 1932; d. Giovanni and Giuseppina Mercuri; diploma Arts Sch. for Painting, Sculpture, Rome, Italy, 1946; m. Milko Skofic, Jan. 15, 1949; 1 son, Milko. Motion picture actress, 1947—; films include Mad About Opera, Pagliacci, 1948, The Bridge Cannot Wait, 1948, Miss Italy, 1949, Bridge for One Night, 1951, Crossed Swords, 1952, Beat the Devil, 1952, Bread, Love and Dreams, 1953, Beautiful but Dangerous, 1955, Trapeze, 1955, Solomon and Sheba, 1958, Come September, 1960, Go Naked in the World, 1960, Hyppolita's Beauty, 1961, Imperial Venus, 1962, Woman of Straw, 1963, Strange Bed-fellows, 1964, Hotel Paradiso, 1965, Cervantes, 1966, Buonasera Mrs. Campbell, 1968, A Very Beautiful November, 1968, others. Recipient Gran Premio St. Vincent, 1952, Silver Ribbon, 1953, golden David de Donatello. Internat. Cinema Club, 1955 (Italy); La Victoire, French Oscar, 1952, 55, 58. Vichy Referendum, 1954, 56 (France); Cine Revelation, 1954, Cine Revue reward, 1955, 57, 58, 59 (Belgium); Bambi, 1956, 57, 58, 59 (Germany); Cinematographic prize, 1954 (Argentina); Photoplay mag. award, 1959 (U.S.), others. Hon. mem. jury French prize La Victorie. Address: Via Appia Antica 223 Rome Italy

LOMAN, MARY LAVERNE (MRS. COY EMIAL LOMAN), educator; b. Stratford, Okla., June 10, 1928; d. Thomas DeWitte and Mary Ellen (Goodwin) Glass; B.S., U. Okla., 1956, M.A., 1957, Ph.D., 1961; m. Coy Emial Loman, Dec. 23, 1944; 1 dau., Sandra (Mrs. Wayne Easton). Grad. asst. math. dept. Okla. U., 1956-57, instr., 1957-61; asst. prof. math. Central State U., Edmond, Okla., 1961-62, asso. prof., 1962-66, prof., 1966—. Named Central State U. Tchr. of Year, 1968-69. NSF Faculty fellow, 1965-67. Mem. Math. Assn. Am., Nat. Council Tchrs. Math., Okla. Council Tchrs. Math. (dir. 1972-76, v.p. 1974-76), Okla. Edn. Assn. (pres. local unit 1967-68), Delta Kappa Gamma (pres. chpt. 1964-66). Home: 2201 Tall Oaks Trail Edmond OK 73034

LOMANITZ, RACHEL, microbiologist; b. Mexico City, Mexico, May 23, 1915 (parents Am. citizens); d. Sebastian B. and Miriam (Feld) Lomanitz; B.S. in chemistry, U. Okla., 1935, M.S. (scholar), 1936, life certificate secondary schs., 1939, Ph.D., 1964; postgrad. Coll. Jewish Studies, 1939-41. Tchr. high sch., Okla., 1936-38; research asst. clin. chemistry Research Hosp., Ill., 1939-40; chem. technician Boiler Water Lab., Chgo., 1940-41; departmental librarian plant genetics Weizmann Inst. Sci., Rehovoth, Israel, 1954-56; chem. technician Okla. Med. Research Found., 1957; research asst. med. mycology U. Okla. Med. Center, 1960-61, co-prin. investigator med. microbiology, 1960-62; asst. microbiologist Bronx-Lebanon Hosp. Center, 1965; mem. research staff med. mycology N.Y. State Dept. Health, 1966; head microbiology dept. Smith, Miller & Patch, Inc., New Brunswick, N.J., 1966-69; microbiologist John F. Kennedy Med. Center, Edison, N.J., 1969—. Adj. faculty Middlesex County Coll. Fellow U. Okla. Med. Center, 1962-63. Mem. Am. Soc. Microbiology, Med. Mycol. Soc. Americas, Med. Mycology Soc. N.Y., Sigma Xi. Home: 101 Lincoln Av Highland Park NJ 08904 Office: James St Edison NJ 08817

LONDA, JEWELDEAN JONES (MRS. DANIEL LONDA), social worker; b. nr. Lawrenceville, Ga.; d. Vanus and Loraine (Teague) Jones; B.A., LaGrange Coll., 1947; postgrad. U. N.C., 1949-50; m. Daniel Londa, Mar. 17, 1968. Dir. teenage program, dir. camping YWCA, Birmingham, Ala., Utica, N.Y., Atlanta, N.Y.C., 1947-59; dir. health and welfare Nat. Urban League, N.Y.C., 1959—. Bd. dirs. N.Y.C. Pub. Health Assn., 1966-70; mem. Joint Commn. Mental Health for Children, 1967-69; mem. Nat. Adv. Council Med. Edn., 1966-70. Mem. Nat. Assn. Social Workers, Nat. Assn. Intergroup Relations Ofcls. Home: 145 W 93d St New York City NY 10025 Office: 55 E 52d St New York City NY 10022

LONDOW, MATTIE LEE, ednl. adminstr.; b. El Campo, Tex., Apr. 19, 1927; d. Dennis and Ona Catherine (Miller) Scott; B.S., Prairie View (Tex.) A. and M. Coll., 1948, M.S., 1953; Ph.D., Tex. Woman's U., 1969; m. Robert Londow, Apr. 20, 1957; 1 son, Kenneth. Tchr. phys. edn., Port Arthur, Tex., 1949-69; asst. prof. phys. edn. So. U., Baton Rouge, 1967-68; grad. asst. Tex. Woman's U., Denton, 1968-69; prof., coordinator women's phys. edn. Prairie View A. and M. Coll., 1969-70, 71-73; asso. prof. phys. edn. Lamar State Coll., Beaumont, Tex., 1970-71; prof., head combined phys. edn. dept. Prairie View U., 1973—. Bd. dirs. Port Arthur chpt. A.R.C., 1965-67. Mem. Nat. Assn. Phys. Edn. Coll. Women (pub. relations chmn. 1971-73), Phi Delta Kappa, Alpha Kappa Alpha (chmn. social action com. 1970-71). Lutheran. Address: PO Box 2454 Prairie View TX 77445

LONG, AMELIA REYNOLDS, mus. ofcl.; b. Columbia, Pa., Nov. 25, 1904; d. John Henry and Florence Rosalia (Hardy) Long; B.Sc., U. Pa., 1931, M.A., 1932. Writer mystery stories Phoenix Pub. Co., Ziff-Davis Pub. Co., N.Y.C., 1933-51; editor Stackpole Pub. Co., Harrisburg, Pa., 1951-58; curator William Penn Meml. Mus., Harrisburg, 1960—. Author: (poetry) Shreds and Patches, 1974; also 31 mystery novels. Editor: A Goodly Heritage: Poems of Pennsylvania, 1968. Home: 725 S 25th St Harrisburg PA 17111 Office: William Penn Memorial Museum 3d and North Sts Harrisburg PA 17102

LONG, ANNE TENNEY (MRS. RICHARD DURBIN LONG), banker; b. N.Y.C., June 2, 1923; d. Frederick William and Rose Elizabeth (Haworth) Tenney; B.A., Antioch Coll., 1945; postgrad. Pace Coll., 1947; M.S., Columbia, 1955; postgrad. N.Y. U., 1957-59, Rutgers U., 1966; m. Richard Durbin Long, Nov. 1, 1943; children—Mary (Mrs. William Fitch), Richard. Staff accountant Barrow, Wade, Guthrie & Co., C.P.A.'s, N.Y.C., 1945-47; instr. Davis Bus. Coll., Toledo, 1951-53; security analyst N.J. Bank & Trust Co., Paterson, 1955-62, asst. treas., 1962-63, asst. v.p., 1963-69; asst. investment officer Bank N.Y., N.Y.C., 1969-71, investment officer, 1971—. Thesis examiner Rutgers U. Stonier Grad. Sch. Banking, 1968-72; organizing dir. Inter-County Community Bank, South Plainfield, N.J. C.P.A., N.J. Mem. Am. Womans Soc. C.P.A.'s (past dir.), Nat. Assn. Bank Women (past dir.), Am. Inst. C.P.A.'s, N.J. Soc. C.P.A.'s, Am. Soc. Women Accountants (past pres. Toledo chpt.), N.Y. Soc. Security Analysts, Inst. Chartered Financial Analysts, N.Y. U. Grad. Sch. Bus. Adminstrn. Alumni Assn. (dir. 1972—). Republican. Unitarian. Clubs: Ridgewood College (N.J.); Arcola Country (Paramus, N.J.); New York University. Author weekly column Women's Financial World, Passaic Herald News, 1960-72. Home: 484 Ackerman Av Glen Rock NJ 07452 Office: 530 Fifth Av New York City NY 10036

LONG, BEVERLY GLENN (MRS. J. EMERY LONG), lawyer; b. Omaha, Mar. 1, 1923; d. Max Edgar and Allise Katherine Dorothy (Nielsen) Glenn; A.B., U. Chgo., 1944; J.D., Columbia, 1947; m. J. Emery Long, May 6, 1950. Admitted to N.Y. bar, 1948, R.I. bar, 1951; asso. firm Edwards & Angell, Providence, 1950—. Mem. adv. com. Child Welfare Services, R.I. Dept. Social Welfare, 1959-66; mem. personnel com. Big Bros. of R.I., Inc., 1964-67; mem. R.I. Gov.'s Commn. on Status of Women, 1965; chmn. Childrens Code Commn., 1967—. Bd. dirs. Childrens Friend and Service, Inc., Providence chpt. A.R.C., St. Marys Home for Children, R.I. Conf. on Social Work, R.I. Council Community Services, United Fund. Recipient citation for pub. service U. Chgo., 1959. Mem. Am., R.I., New Eng. bar assns. Republican. Conglist. Home: 200 Elmgrove Av Providence RI 02906 Office: 2700 Hospital Trust Tower Providence RI 02903

LONG, CALVERTA ELNORA DAVIS (MRS. WILLIE HAMPTON LONG), librarian; b. Johnsonville, S.C., Sept. 15, 1932; d. Ernest and Venus (Bartelle) Davis; B.S., S.C. State Coll., 1953; M.S., Atlanta U., 1958; m. Willie Hampton Long, Nov. 17, 1957; children—Sharon, Alicia Jeanne. Instr. English, Carver High Sch., Lake City, S.C., 1953-54, librarian, 1953-58; librarian Barber Scotia Coll., Concord, N.C., 1958-60; circulation asst. S.C. State Coll., Orangeburg, S.C., 1960-62, reference and documents librarian, 1962—. Vol. worker United Fund, Heart Fund. Mem. Am., Southeastern, S.C. library assns., Nat. Assn. Coll. Women, Assn. Coll. and Research Libraries, Alpha Beta Alpha, Delta Sigma Theta, Alpha Kappa Mu, Beta Phi Mu. Home: Box 1572 SC State College Orangeburg SC 29115 Office: Miller F Whittaker Library SC State College Orangeburg SC 29115

LONG, CLAUDIA BETH, educator; b. Freeport, N.Y., Feb. 10, 1948; d. Hartley Akin and Marguerite Andrae (Clark) Long; A.A., Nassau Community Coll., 1968; B.A., Morris Harvey Coll., 1970. Instr. phys. edn. Phila. Coll. of Bible, 1971—, dir. women's athletics, 1973—. Counselor, waterfront dir. Pioneer Girls, Camp Cherith, 1969-72, activity coordinator, 1973, div. dir., 1972-73. Mem. A.A.H.P.E.R., U.S. Field Hockey Assn. Home: 1800 Arch St Philadelphia PA 19103

LONG, DELCIE OLIVE (MRS. JAMES COMMODORE LONG), mcht.; b. Gilboa, W.Va., Aug. 24, 1916; d. Newman Wilson and Vergie Norman (Williams) Jones; grad. high sch.; m. James Commodore Long, July 26, 1936; 1 dau., Judith Anne. Floor mgr. Fields 5 cents - $1.00 Store, South Charleston, W.Va., 1941-45; owner Dixie 5 cents - $1.00 Store, Gassaway, W.Va., 1945—. Methodist (mem. ofcl. bd. 1966-74, chmn. social concerns 1966-71, chmn. edn. 1974). Mem. Order Eastern Star; Rebekah (dist. treas. 1952-54). Home: 113 State St Gassaway WV 26624 Office: 624 Elk St Gassaway WV 26624

LONG, DOROTHY CATHERINE (MRS. JOHN C. LONG, JR.), physician; b. N.Y.C., Dec. 12, 1915; d. Frank Charles and Helen Sarah (Swanson) Krause; B.A. cum laude, Hunter Coll., 1937; M.D., N.Y.U., 1941; m. John C. Long, Jr., Feb. 1, 1942; children—John C. III, Cornelia, Barbara, Patricia. Intern, Queen's (N.Y.) Gen. Hosp., 1941-42; resident pediatrics, fellow pediatrics Met. Hosp., N.Y. Med. Coll., 1942-47; practice medicine specializing in pediatrics, Bayside, N.Y., 1945-50, Plainview, Tex., 1950—; mem. staffs Central Plains Hosp., Plainview; cons. Head Start program, 1969—; asso. prof. pediatrics Tex. Tech Med. Sch., 1973—; asso. clin. prof. Tex. Tech U. Sch. Medicine, 1973—. Bd. dirs. Plainview Community Nursery. Named Woman of the Year Plainview C. of C., 1968. Diplomate Am. Bd. Pediatrics. Mem. Am. Acad. Pediatrics, Phi Beta Kappa. Home: 1300 Borger St Plainview TX 79072 Office: 2404 Yonkers St Plainview TX 79072

LONG, EDITH CATHERINE BURKEY (MRS. JOHN BOUDER LONG), librarian; b. Lebanon, Pa., Apr. 24, 1916; d. George Henry and May Elizabeth (Speece) Burkey; B.S., Millersville State Coll., 1940, M.L.S., 1969; M.Ed., Temple U., 1963; m. John Bouder Long, May 10, 1941. Tchr., Vera Cruz Sch., nr. Denver, Pa., 1940; tchr. elementary sch. Palmyra (Pa.) Area Schs., 1940-62; elementary librarian Milton Hershey Sch., Hershey, Pa., 1962-70, librarian Sr. Hall Library, 1970—. Asst. librarian Lebanon Valley Coll., Annville, Pa., 1970-71. Sec., Palmyra Pub. Library Bd., 1962—. Mem. Pa. Library Assn. Mem. United Ch. of Christ (deacon 1971—). Home: 109 W Orchard Dr Palmyra PA 17078 Office: Senior Hall Library Hershey PA 17033

LONG, ERNESTINE MARTHA JOULLIAN, educator; b. St. Louis, Nov. 14, 1906; d. Ernest Cameron and Alice (Joullian) Long; A.B., U. Wis., 1927; M.S., U. Chgo., 1932; postgrad. (NSF fellow), So. Ill. U., 1969-70. Tchr. scis. in pub. schs. Normandy dist., St. Louis, 1927-67, Red Bud, Ill., 1967-71, St. Louis, 1971—. Chmn. Neighborhood Taxpayers Assn., 1950-63. Mem. A.A.A.S., Am. Inst. Physics, Am. Personnel and Guidance Assn. (treas. St. Louis br. 1954), Am. Chem. Soc., Central Assn. Sch. Sci. Math. Tchrs., Mo., Ill. tchrs. assns., League Women Voters, St. Louis Symphony Soc., Am. Ednl. Leadership, Nat. Aerospace Council, Am. Guild Organists, N.E.A., Acad. Sci. St. Louis. Methodist (organist). Home: 245 N Price Rd Ladue MO 63124 Office: Roosevelt High Sch St Louis MO 63101

LONG, FERN, librarian; b. Cleve., Nov. 23, 1908; d. Francis Joseph and Louise (Sakryd) Long; B.A. magna cum laude, Radcliffe Coll., 1926; Ph.D., Charles U., Prague, Czechoslovakia, 1930; B.S. in Library Sci., Western Res. U., 1940. Supr. adult edn. dept. Cleve. Pub. Library, 1944-70, dep. dir., 1970-74, interim dir., 1974—. Dir. Reading Centers Project for Functionally Illiterate Adults, 1965-66; cons. Case-Western Res. U. Sch. Library Sci. Mem. Cleve. Bicentennial Commn., 1973—. Bd. dirs. Anti-Tb League of Cuyahoga County; mem. com. older persons Cleve. Welfare Edn.; del. UNESCO Sem., Malmo, Sweden, 1950; bd. dirs. Cleve. Center on Alcoholism, Cleve. Nationalities Services Center del. White House Conf. on Aging, 1961. Recipient Radcliffe Alumnae award, 1960; named Cleve. Woman of Achievement, 1961. Mem. A.L.A. (pres. adult services div. 1963-64), Phi Beta Kappa (Cleve. pres. 1962-63), Delta Kappa Gamma. Author: All about Meetings: A Practical Guide, 1966. Translator: Late Harvest; If The Mirror Break; The Hideout; Seven Times the Leading Man. Book reviewer Cleve. Press, 1971—. Home: 2364 Queenston Rd Cleveland Heights OH 44118 Office: Pub Library Cleveland OH 44114

LONG, HELEN HALTER, author, publishing co. exec., educator; b. St. Louis, Nov. 19, 1906; d. Charles C. and Ida (May) Halter; A.B., Washington U., St. Louis, 1927, A.M. (grad. fellow 1927-28), 1928; Ph.D., N.Y. U., 1937; M. Forrest E. Long, June 22, 1944. Tchr. social studies, Venice, Ill., 1928-30; asst. prof. social sci. N.Y. State Coll. for Tchrs., Albany, 1930-38; head dept. social studies The Milne Sch., Albany, 1930-38; tchr. pub. schs., Mamaroneck, N.Y., 1938-42, prin. elementary and jr. high schs., 1942-54, asst. supt. schs., 1954-61; dir. curriculum studies Inst. Instructional Improvement, N.Y.C., 1962—; pres. Books of the World, Sweet Springs, Mo., 1963—; dir. Roxbury Press. Teaching fellow Sch. Edn., N.Y.U., 1936-37, div. gen. edn., 1938-39, instr. Sch. Edn., 1939-43; asso. editor The Clearing House, 1935-55; mem. N.Y. State Regents Social Studies Curriculum Com., 1935-38. Mem. Phi Beta Kappa, Pi Gamma Mu, Kappa Delta Pi, Alpha Xi Delta (Diamond Jubilee honor 1968). Author: Society in Action, 1936; National Safety Council Lesson Units, 1944-52; (with Forrest E. Long) Social Studies Skills, rev. edit., 1972. Home: 107 Medallion Dr Sweet Springs MO 65351 Office: Roxbury Bldg Sweet Springs MO 65351

LONG, ISABEL MARGARET, med. mycologist; b. Bklyn., Nov. 11, 1932; d. Edwin J. and Margaret (Ripp) Long; B.A. in Biology, Notre Dame Coll., S.I., N.Y., 1953. Staff antibiotic chemotherapy lab. Mt. Sinai Hosp., N.Y.C., 1953-62, med. mycology lab. N.Y.C. Dept. Health, 1962-65; trainee in virology research U. Chgo., 1965-66; head diagnostic med. mycology lab. Presbyn.-St. Luke's Hosp., Chgo., 1966—, tchr. basic lab. procedures in med. mycology, 1966—. Mem. Med. Mycology Soc. Am., Med. Mycology Soc. of Ams., Am. Soc. Microbiology. Contbr. to Mycopathologia et Mycologia Applicate, vol. 40, 1970. Home: Apt 1120 4960 N Marine Dr Chicago IL 60640 Office: 1753 W Congress Pkwy Chicago IL 60612

LONG, JEWEL BERNICE, coll. adminstr.; b. Portsmouth, Va., Dec. 1, 1947; d. Richard Wellington and Leslie Carcelia (Crocker) Long; B.S., Hampton Inst., 1969, M.A., 1971. Grad. asst. Hampton (Va.) Inst., 1969-71, resident hall dir., 1971—, asst. dir. student affairs, 1971—. Youth pres. Bapt. Gen. Conv. Va., 1966-71, life mem., 1971—. Named Outstanding Young Woman of Am., Bapt. Gen. Conv. Va., 1973. Mem. Nat. Assn. Women Deans, Adminstrs. and Counselors, Nat. Assn. Personnel Workers, Am. Personnel and Guidance Assn., Am. Coll. Personnel Assn., Alpha Kappa Alpha. Home: 1138 Chisholm Circle Portsmouth VA 23704 Office: PO Box 6557 Hampton Institute Hampton VA 23668

LONG, JUANITA AMANDA OUTLAW, coll. dean; b. Phila., Nov. 9, 1918; d. Guy Darrell and Lillie Louberria (Lyell) Outlaw; diploma nursing Boston City Hosp.; B.S. in Nursing, Washington U., St. Louis, 1956, M.S. in Nursing, 1958; certificate advanced grad. study Northeastern U., 1974; m. Thomas Marshall Long, Aug. 25, 1950 (div.); 1 son, Thomas Marshall. Head nurse Boston City Hosp., 1945-47; dir. nursing Norfolk (Va.) Community Hosp., 1947-48; served with U.S. Army Nurse Corps, 1948-52; faculty Homer G. Phillips Hosp. Sch. Nursing, St. Louis, 1958-61, asso. dir., 1961-65; asso. dir. Beth Israel Hosp. Sch. Nursing, Boston, 1965-67; asst. prof. nursing Northeastern U., Boston, 1965-68, acting dean Coll. Nursing, 1968-69, dean, 1969—. Cons., Catherine Laboure Sch. Nursing, 1971—. Mem. Mass. Drug Formulary Commn., 1971—, Sch. Nursing, Peter Bent Brigham Hosp., Boston, 1968—, New Eng. Council of Higher Edn. in Nursing, 1969—; mem. corp. Lawrence Meml. Hosp., Medford, Mass., 1972—. Bd. dirs. nat. council Northeastern U. Recipient Achievement award Boston City Hosp., 1970. Mem. Am. Nurses Assn., Nat. League for Nursing, Mass. Nursing Assn. (dist. V dir.), Phi Sigma, Phi Kappa Phi. Club: Zonta (local dir.). Home: 48 Cabot St Winchester MA 01890 Office: Northeastern U 360 Huntington Av Boston MA 02115

LONG, MARY JEAN (MRS. FREDERICK CECIL LONG), educator; b. Duluth, Minn., Mar. 24, 1914; d. Joseph Parnell and Lora Sanford (Kinsman) O'Brien; B.S., Mich. State U., 1935, M.S. (Warner-Lambert scholar 1959, Dow Chem. Co. fellow 1960), 1961, Ph.D., 1968; m. Frederick Cecil Long, May 25, 1936; children—Lora (Mrs. Eric Rikans), Christopher E. Lab. technician Parke Davis & Co., Detroit, 1935-36; med. technologist Blodgett Meml. Hosp., Grand Rapids, Mich., 1951-62; instr. Mich. State U., East Lansing, 1962-68; asst. prof. dept. pathology U. Neb. Med. Center, Omaha, 1969—. Mem. Nat. Registry of Clin. Chemists, Am. Soc. for Med. Tech. (Hilkowitz award 1961), Am. Assn. Clin. Chemists, Sigma Xi, Alpha Phi, Beta Beta, Alpha Delta Theta, Sigma Delta Epsilon. Club: Zonta. Home: 1854 N 81st St Omaha NE 68114 Office: 42nd and Dewey Av Omaha NE 68105

LONG, NANCY KINDERMAN (MRS. DAVID L. LONG), advt. agy. exec.; b. Phila., Mar. 2, 1946; d. Robert H. and Loraine E. (Loewe) Kinderman; B.A., U. Colo., 1968; m. David L. Long, Apr. 24, 1971. Media dir. Norman W. Buck, Inc., Northfield, Ill., 1968—, with Wetherbee Group, Northfield, 1968—, agy. v.p., 1972—. Mem. bd. Chgo. Hearing Soc. Office: 550 Frontage Rd Northfield IL 60093

LONG, RUTH EDWARDS (MRS. FREMONT C. LONG), ednl. adminstr.; b. Bklyn., July 18, 1915; d. Caleb Morris and Irene Newey (Rice) Edwards; student N.Y. State Tchrs. Coll., Oneonta, 1935-38; B.S., U. Ala., 1941; M.S. in Library Sci., U. Miss., 1966; M.S. in Supervision and Adminstrn., Rollins Coll., 1973; m. Fremont C. Long, Oct. 2, 1948; children—Linda (Mrs. David L. Smith), Patsy Jane (Mrs. Dennis Bierschbach). Librarian high sch., Collinsville, Ala., 1941-42; insp. naval air craft Grumman Air Craft Co., Bethpage, N.Y., 1942-44; librarian St. Lawrence U., Canton, N.Y., 1944-45, Rollins Coll., Winter Park, Fla., 1946-48, Pinecrest Sch. Sanford, Fla., 1956-62; county coordinator sch. libraries Seminole County Bd. Pub. Instrn., Sanford, 1962—. Reviewer children's books Random House, 1968. Mem. Fla. Assn. Media in Edn., Fla. Assn. Supervision and Curriculum Devel., Alpha Delta Kappa (pres. Gamma Gamma chpt. 1967-68). Mem. Order Eastern Star. Home: Box 92 Main St Enterprise FL 32763 Office: 911 Palmetto Av Sanford FL 32771

LONGANETTA, EVA BEATRICE MARTIN (MRS. ERNEST WILLIS LONGANETTA), mfg. co. exec.; b. Clarksburg, W.Va., Feb. 16, 1928; d. Willis Everson and Hazel Beatrice (Freeman) Martin; student Grace Bible Inst., Coatesville, Pa., 1962-65; m. Ernest Willis Longanetta, Nov. 3, 1946. With processing dept. Pepperridge Farm, Downingtown, Pa., 1960-62; with backplate dept. Pershing div., Burroughs Corp., Downingtown, Pa., 1966-67; with Faddis Bros., Inc., Downingtown, Pa., 1968—, office mgr., 1971—, corp. sec., 1972—. Mem. Alumni Assn. Grace Bible Inst., Oriental Missionary Soc. Intecessors. Mem. Nazarene Ch. Home: PO Box 13 Uwchland PA 19480 Office: 3621 Kings Hwy Downingtown PA 19335

LONGBRAKE, MARY, trust co. exec.; b. Marysville, O.; d. Mark F. and Buretta (Shields) Longbrake; B.A., Lake Forest Coll., 1935, LL.D. (hon.), 1970. Bookstore mgr. Lake Forest (Ill.) Coll., 1935-37; file supr. Home Ins. Co., Chgo., 1937-38; sec. Griffin, Ingram & Pfaff, Chgo., 1939-41; sec. to exec. v.p. No. Trust Co., Chgo., 1941-42, 46-58, adminstrv. asst., 1958-59, asst. cashier, 1959-67, 2d v.p., 1967-73, v.p., 1973—. Bd. dirs. Kobe Coll. Corp., Chgo., Eleanor Assn., Chgo.; trustee Lake Forest Coll. Served from ensign to lt. comdr. WAVES, USNR, 1942-46. Mem. Nat. Assn. Bank Women, Lyric Opera Guild, Lake Forest Coll. Alumni Assn. (exec. bd. 1948—, pres. 1961-63), Alpha Xi Delta. Republican. Presbyn. Soroptimist. Club: Executives. Home: 2348 W Touhy Av Chicago IL 60645 Office: 50 S LaSalle St Chicago IL 60690

LONGET, CLAUDINE GEORGETTE, actress, singer; b. Paris, France, Jan. 29, 1942; d. Robert and Rolande (Dumont) Longet; ed. Ecole du Spectacle, also Coll. Hatmer, Paris; m. Andy Williams, Dec. 15, 1961; children—Noelle, Christian. Came to U.S., 1960. Theatrical appearances include Turn of the Screw, Paris, 1955, Infernal Machine, 1958, Lysistrata, Rome, Italy, 1960, also in U.S.; TV roles in U.S. include Kraft Theatre, Mr. Novak, 12 o'Clock High, Run for Your Life, Combat, Dr. Kildare, Andy Williams Show, Rat Patrol; film appearances include McHale's Navy, 1966, The Party, 1967; rec. artist, 1966—. Home: 157 Delvern Dr Los Angeles CA 90069 Office: 816 N Cienaga St Beverly Hills CA 90069

LONGHENRY, RUTH ANNE, librarian; b. Bklyn., Jan. 19, 1920; d. Ernest and Rose Catherine (Martina) Longhenry; student State U. N.Y. at New Paltz, 1937-40; B.S., State U. N.Y. at Geneseo, 1941; postgrad. Columbia, 1947-49; M.S., State Tchrs. Coll. at Shippensburg, Pa., 1972. Librarian U.S. Army 2d Service Command, Governors Island, N.Y., 1941-48, Staff Coll., Norfolk, Va., 1948-51, Army War Coll., Carlisle Barracks, Pa., 1951—. Mem. A.L.A., Spl. Libraries Assn., Am. Soc. Information Specialists, Am. Assn. U. Women, Assn. U.S. Army, Sigma Pi Sigma. Club: Allenberry. Home: 146 W High St Carlisle PA 17013 Office: Library US Army War College Carlisle Barracks PA 17013

LONGINO, NAN SMITH (MRS. JAMES FRANKLIN LONGINO), librarian; b. Fouke, Ark., July 23, 1915; d. Oscar David and Nannie Elizabeth (Dyer) Smith; B.A., Ouachita Bapt. U., 1936; M.S., E. Tex. State U., 1954; m. James Franklin Longino, Dec. 2, 1939; children—Patsy (Mrs. Lawrence L. Limpus), Kay (Mrs. John N. Williamson). Tchr. pub. schs., Emerson, Ark., 1936, Roe, Ark., 1937, Fouke, 1938-53; librarian New Boston High Sch., New Boston, Tex., 1954—. Sec. pub. library bd., New Boston, 1964-70. Del. Ark. Dem. Conv., 1954. Wall St. fellow in journalism, 1962. Mem. Am. Assn. U. Women, Tex. Tchrs. Assn. (county pres. 1971), New Boston Classroom Tchrs. (pres. 1970), Bus. and Profl. Women. Clubs: Business Women's Garden (pres. 1955-71) (New Boston). Home: 110 E Sunset St New Boston TX 75570

LONGLEY, BERNIQUE (MRS. JAMES ALEXANDER ORR), artist, muralist; b. Moline, Ill., Sept. 27, 1923; d. Eli James and Effie Marie (Coen) Wilderson; grad. Art Inst. Chgo.; m. James Alexander Orr, Apr. 15, 1968; 1 dau. by previous marriage, Bernique (Mrs. Timothy W. Glidden). Exhibited in one-man shows at Mus. N.M., 1947, Little Shop, Santa Fe, 1952-58, Maurice Appleman Gallery, Denver, 1953-54, Van Dieman Lilienfield, N.Y.C., 1953, Rotunda-City Paris, San Francisco, 1955-56, Sanger-Harris Gallery, Dallas, 1968, Lars L'Aine, Palm Springs, Cal., 1963-69, Gallery A, Taos, N.M., 1966-69; exhibited in group shows at Art Inst. Chgo., 1945-48, Denver Art Mus., 1948-49, Mus. N.M., 1947-72, also Summer Gallery, Santa Fe, De Colores Gallery, Denver, others; represented in permanent collections of Red Skelton, Greer Garson, Mark Harris, others; executed murals La Fonda del Sol, N.Y.C., home Alexander Girard, Santa Fe, 1960; represented in permanent collections First Nat. Bank Denver, Santa Fe Hilton Hotel, Dome Oil Exploration Co., San Francisco, Goodman's Santa Fe, others. Bryan Lathrop fgn. traveling fellow, 1945. Mem. Art Inst. Chgo. Alumni Assn. Home: 427 Camino Del Monte Sol Santa Fe NM 87501

LONGMEYER, JUDITH ANN (MRS. JOSEPH F. LONGMEYER), pub. relations exec.; b. Chgo., Aug. 30, 1943; d. John A. and Ann E. (Jakaitis) Shulmistras; A.A., Chgo. City Jr. Coll., 1962; B.A. in English, Roosevelt U., 1970; m. Joseph F. Longmeyer, Apr. 28, 1962. Editorial asst. Skil Corp., Chgo., 1964-65, editor, 1965, mgr. employee communications and community relations, 1969, mgr. communications and pub. relations, 1970-72; pres. The Advocates, pub. relations agy., McHenry, Ill., 1973—; asst. dir. advt. and pub. relations McGraw Edison Co., Elgin, Ill., 1973-74; free lance writer, since 19—. Mem. Nat. Orgn. for Women (convenor, pres. McHenry County chpt. 1973), Publicity Club of Chgo., Iota Sigma Epsilon (pres. 1970-71). Home: 705 W Peter St McHenry IL 60050 Office: 705 W Peter St McHenry IL 60050

LONGMIRE, MARTHA HOLMES, educator, soprano; b. Wichita Falls, Tex., June 18, 1927; d. Wayne James and Martha (Roper) Holmes; Mus.B., So. Meth. U., 1948; student Lamont Sch. Music, Denver U., 1950, Music Acad. West Santa Barbara (Cal.), 1951; m. William Chapman Longmire, Apr. 29, 1953; children—William Chapman, Martha Louise, Robert, James. Debut, Dallas Symphony, 1949, Denver Symphony, 1950, Red Rocks Concert, Denver, 1950, Oklahoma City Symphony, 1950, Lotte Lehman-Town Hall, 1952, Lincoln Symphony, 1957; concert artist radio sta. WFAA, Dallas, 1947, WFAA-TV, 1949, Denver Grand Opera, season 1950-51; program chmn. Young Women's Philharmonic Kansas City, 1957, sec., 1958; asso. prof. voice Conservatory of Music, U. Kansas City, 1960—; prof. voice U. Mo. at Kansas City; soloist Kansas City Philharmonic Orch., 1961, 63, 66, St. Joseph Symphony Orch., 1962, So. Ill. U. Orch. and Choir, 1964, Kansas City Civic Orch., 1964, 68, 69, 72, concertizing throughout Midwest, Kansas City Philharmonic Chamber series, 1972, Sedalia Symphony, 1972; for extension div. U. Mo., 1966—; with Kansas City Aria group specializing in Bach, 1966-67. Recipient Pi Phi award, 1947, others. Mem. Philharmonic League, D.A.R., Kappa Alpha Theta, Mu Phi Epsilon, Pi Kappa Lambda (hon., sec. 1971-72). Methodist (soprano soloist). Home: 10520 Mohawk Lane Leawood KS 66206 Office: 4420 Warwick St Kansas City MO 64111

LONGO, JOY PAULINE, bank librarian; b. Albany, N.Y., Aug. 6, 1931; d. Paul Basil and Angelina (Vigliante) Longo; B.A., State U. N.Y. at Albany, 1954, M.L.S., 1969. Social worker Catholic Charities, Troy, N.Y., 1954-59; ins. rater Traveler's Ins. Co., Albany, 1959-63; librarian Nat. Comml. Bank and Trust Co., Albany, 1963—. Asst. in developing library Boys Club, Rensselaer, N.Y., 1964-67; sponsor Save the Children Fedn.; mem. Friends of Albany Library; vol. United Fund Drive, 1963-71; vol. Northeastern N.Y. Arthritis Found., 1973—. Mem. Spl. Libraries Assn., Co. of Mil. Historians, Alumni Council State U. N.Y. at Albany (vice-chmn. 1973—), Nat. Hist. Soc., Am. Inst. Banking, Nat. Wildlife Fedn., Inc., N.Y. State Hist. Assn., N.Y. State Library Assn., Psi Gamma. Roman Catholic. Home: 1217 Central Av Albany NY 12205 Office: 60 State St Albany NY 12207

LONGO, MARGARET, physician; b. Alexandria, La., July 4, 1936; d. Joseph Phillip and Mary (Cangelosi) Longo; B.A. in Biology, Our Lady of the Lake Coll., 1958; M.D., La. State U., 1962. Intern Confed. Meml. Med. Center, Shreveport, La., 1962-63; resident Mayo Grad. Sch. Medicine, Rochester, Minn., 1963-67, surg. cons., 1966-67; practice medicine specializing in gen. surgery, Lafayette, La., 1968—; mem. staff Lafayette Gen. Hosp., chief surg. staff, 1971; mem. staff Our Lady of Lourdes, Charity hosps. Co-ordinator med. div. United Givers Fund, Lafayette, La., 1970. Recipient Merit award for best original research paper Tex. Acad. Sci., 1956; Minn. Surg. Essay award, 1966; Surg. Travel award Mayo Clinic, 1967. Diplomate Am. Bd. Surgery. Fellow A.C.S.; mem. A.A.A.S., Mayo Clinic Alumni Assn., Am. Med. Women's Assn., A.C.S., La., Minn. Med. socs., La. Surg. Soc., Southeastern Surg. Congress. Contbr. profl. jours. Home: 605 Claymore Dr Lafayette LA 70501 Office: 1432 S College Rd Lafayette LA 70501

LONGSTRETH, MARIAN JONES, civic worker; b. Vicksburg, Miss., Aug. 9, 1906; d. Jesse Fuller and Nina (Voeinkle) Jones; student All Saints Coll., 1922-23, grad. Gunston Hall, Washington, 1925; student Curtis Inst. Music, 1925-26; m. Edward Longstreth, July 3, 1926 (div.); 1 son, Edward. Pres., founder Theatre and Arts Found. of San Diego County, La Jolla, Cal., 1954-66, dir., 1954—; mem. Gov.'s Com. for Music of Merit, Cal., 1961-64; mem. San Diego-Yokohama (Japan) Friendship Commn., 1958-70; vice chmn., 1967-70; past mem. council Friends of Library, U. Cal., dir., 1964; pres. La Jolla Playhouse Woman's Com., 1950-64; sec. Mus. Arts Soc. La Jolla, 1955-66. Mem. World Affairs Council San Diego (exec. com. 1968-70), San Diego Opera Guild, Nat. Soc. Colonial Dames XVII Century, Hist. Found. Vicksburg, League Women Voters. Clubs: Wednesday (San Diego); Beach and Tennis (La Jolla, Cal.). Author: Directory of California Composers. Home: Oak Boughs 2432 Cherry St Vicksburg MS 39180

LONGWELL, ARLENE CROSBY (MRS. HORACE M. MAZZONE), biol. scientist; b. Buffalo, 1930; d. Vaness Joseph and Rita (McMann) Crosby; A.B., S.W. Mo. State Coll., 1953; Ph.D., U. Mo., 1957; m. John H. Longwell, Jr., 1957 (dec.); m. 2d, Horace M. Mazzone, Aug. 7, 1963; 1 dau., Anne Alicia Frances. Teaching asst. U. Mo., 1953-55, research asst., 1955-57; research asso. Argonne Nat. Lab., 1957-59; guest researcher Genetics Inst. Lund (Sweden) U., 1959-60; research asso. Childrens Cancer Research Found., Childrens Hosp., Harvard Med. Sch., 1960-65; research geneticist Milford Marine Biol. Lab., Nat. Marine Fisheries Service, U.S. Dept. Commerce, 1966—. AEC postdoctoral fellow, 1957-59, Am. Cancer Soc. fellow, 1959-63. Mem. Am. Inst. Biol. Sci., N.Y. Acad. Sci., Am., Canadian genetics socs., Radiol. Research Soc., Inter-Oceano Graphic Found. Contbr. articles to profl. jours. Home: 300 Center Rd Easton CT 06425 Office: Milford Biol Lab Nat Marine Fisheries Service Nat Oceanic and Atmospheric Adminstrn US Dept Commerce Milford CT 06460

LONGWITH, JEAN MARGUERITE, radio sta. mgr.; b. San Antonio, Mar. 15, 1918; d. Harold Eugene and Anna Frances (Marshall) Longwith; B.A. cum laude, U. Tex., 1937, M.Ed. cum laude, 1945; M.F.A. cum laude (fellow), U. Ia., 1950; Tchr. sr. high sch., San Antonio, 1938-45; dir. Community Players, San Antonio, 1942-46; dir. San Antonio Little Theatre, 1947-49; instr., communications TV Hour, U. Ia., Iowa City, 1949-50; dir. WOC-TV, Davenport, Ia., 1949-51; chmn. drama dept. Jefferson High Sch., San Antonio, 1952-64; gen. mgr. radio sta. KSYM-FM, San Antonio, 1966—; prof. radio, TV, film San Antonio Coll., 1964—. Dir. Summer Dance Festival, San Antonio Recreation Dept., 1952-69; lectr. Our Lady of Lake Coll., San Antonio, 1956-59. Recipient Service citation as entertainment dir. U.S.O., 1945. Mem. Am. Assn. U. Women (v.p., 1964-66), Women in Communications, Zeta Phi Eta, Pi Lambda Theta, Phi Theta Kappa, Delta Kappa Gamma (pres. chpt. 1966-68; pres. coordinating council 1968-70), Zonta. Episcopalian. Author: Adaptation of Three Short Stories for Television, 1950; The Community That Cares (play), 1960; Poetry for Interpretation, 1955; Ten Syllabi for Courses in Broadcasting, 1969. Home: 210 Quentin Dr San Antonio TX 78201 Office: 1300 San Pedro Av San Antonio TX 78284

LONGYEAR, MARIE MARCIA BERNSTEIN (MRS. PETER RUDSTON LONGYEAR), pub. co. exec.; b. N.Y.C., Apr. 26, 1928; d. Benno Alexander and Marcia Barbara (Trzecka) B.; B.A. cum laude, Radcliffe Coll., 1949; m. Peter Rudston Longyear, July 2, 1949 (dec. 1959); 1 son, John R. Supr. editorial tng. McGraw-Hill Book Co., N.Y.C., 1960-66, mgr. editing services, 1966-74, dir. editing services, 1974—, editor bi-monthly bull. for editors, 1968—. Lectr. pub. course Harvard, summers, also vol. career counselor. Mem. Women's Nat. Book Assn., Linnaan Soc. (conservation com. 1974). Republican. Christian Scientist. Club: Radcliffe (area chmn. N.Y.C. 1973-74). Home: 300 Riverside Dr New York City NY 10025 Office: 1221 Av of Americas New York City NY 10020

LONNI, YVONNE GWENDOLYN WINGET (MRS. LOUIS J. LONNI), physician; b. Lethbridge, Alta., Can., Mar. 16, 1935; d. Thomas Tillway and Lottie Irene (Wixom) Winget; Came to U.S., 1959, naturalized, 1966; R.N., U. Alta., 1956; B.S., U. Utah, 1967, M.D., 1967; m. Louis J. Lonni, June 16, 1962; children—Virginia, Thomas. Nurse, Edmonton (Alta., Can.) Gen. Hosp., 1957-59, El Centro (Cal.) Hosp., 1959-61, Latter Day Saints Hosp., Salt Lake City, 1962-64; intern, resident pathology U. Cal. at Los Angeles, 1967-68, 71-72; resident pathology Kern County Hosp., 1969-70; chief of pathology Kaiser Permanente Hosp., Bellflower, Cal., 1973—. Med. adviser Pakistan Research Council, Dacca, East Pakistan, Bangladesh, 1970-71. Diplomate anatomic pathology and clin. pathology Am. Bd. Pathology, 1973. Mem. A.M.A., Am. Med. Women's Assn., Am., Cal. socs. clin. pathology, Internat. Soc. Pathology, Cal. Med. Assn. Editor Am. Woman's Club Jour., Dacca, 1970-71. Home: 3914 E Country Club Dr Lakewood CA 90712

LONNQUIST, JUDITH ALICE, lawyer, educator; b. Evanston, Ill., Nov. 3, 1940; d. William J. and Dorothy (Gittere) Lonnquist; A.B. in Polit. Sci., Mt. Holyoke Coll., 1962; J.D., U. Chgo., 1965. Admitted to Ill. bar, 1966; practiced in Chgo., 1966—; asso. firm Jacobs, Gore, Burns and Sugarman, 1966—. Instr. labor law U. Ill., Chgo., 1970-74. Candidate for Ill. Gen. Assembly, 1972. Mem. Ill. Bar Assn., Nat. Assn. Women Lawyers, Nat. Orgn. for Women (nat. legal v.p. 1973-74), Am. Civil Liberties Union (dir. Ill. div. 1971-74). Home: 2069 N Larrabee Chicago IL 60614 Office: 201 N Wells Chicago IL 60606

LOOMER, ZELLA GRACE, mus. ofcl.; b. Whitewater, Wis., Dec. 26, 1897; d. Harley Henry and Emma Drusilla (Gilbert) Loomer; B.A., U. Wis., 1920, M.A., 1937. Tchr. high sch., Kewaunee, Wis., 1920-21, Darlington, Wis., 1921-22, Delavan, Wis., 1922-24, West Bend, Wis., 1924-37, Wausaukee, Wis., 1937-38; tchr. U. Wis.-Stevens Point, 1938-41, Mayville Coll., 1941-43; tchr. high sch., Waukesha, Wis., 1943-63; dir. preserving, displaying and conducting tours Washington County Hist. Mus., West Bend, 1963—. Leader Camp Fire Girls, Girl Scouts Am., Kewaunee, 1920-21, Mayville, 1941-43. Mem. Wis. (pres. 1968-70), Washington County hist. socs., Wis., Washington County Rep. Orgn., Nat. Assn. Womens Clubs, Am. Assn. U. Women (pres. 1938), Delta Kappa Gamma. Baptist. Club: Garden (pres. 1971-73) (West Bend, Wis.). Home: 815 S 7th Av West Bend WI 53095

LOOMIS, CAROL JUNGE (MRS. JOHN R. LOOMIS), journalist; b. Marshfield, Mo., June 25, 1929; d. Claus Harold and Mildred Sarah (Case) Junge; student Drury Coll., 1947-49; B.Journalism, U. Mo., 1951; m. John R. Loomis, Mar. 19, 1960; children—Barbara, Mark. Publs. editor Maytag Co., Newton, Ia., 1951-54; research asso. Fortune Mag., N.Y.C., 1954-58, asso. editor, 1958-68, bd. editors, 1968—. Club: Winged Foot Golf (Mamaroneck, N.Y.). Office: Fortune Mag Time and Life Bldg New York City NY 10020

LOOMIS, SUSAN JANE, broadcasting exec.; b. Milw., Feb. 13, 1948; d. Henry Albert and Effie Augusta (Winkler) Loomis; student Mt. Mary Coll., 1966-68; B.A., U. Wis.-Milw., 1970. Pub. relations dir. radio sta. WUWM, Milw., 1969-70; continuity dir. radion stas. WEMP/WNUW-FM, Milw., 1970-71; adminstrv. asst. nat. edn. radio Nat. Assn. Ednl. Broadcasters, Washington, 1971-73; dir. pub. affairs and publicity WGMS-AM-FM, Washington, 1973—. Bd. dirs. Arthritis Assn. Met. Washington. Mem. Am. Women in Radio and TV, Alpha Omicron Pi. Home: 6154 Edsall Rd Alexandria VA 22304 Office: 5100 Wisconsin Av NW Washington DC 20016

LOPER, MARY JANE EURE, psychologist; b. Vicksburg, Miss., Feb. 6, 1927; d. Otis Perry and Vera (Bryant) Eure; student Bellhaven Coll., 1943-44, La. State U., 1944-46; B.A., U. Okla., 1947; M.S., U. So. Miss., 1959; postgrad. U. Ia., 1959-61; children—Raymond (dec.), Gai Louise, Wesley Eure. Legal sec., Hattiesburg, Miss., 1955; dir. social activities Inst. Latin Am. Studies, U. So. Miss., 1956-57; sec. Internat Paper Co., Hattiesburg, 1957-59; spl. research asst. U. Ia., 1959-61; dir. testing and guidance, asst. prof. psychology Tex. Woman's U., Denton, 1961-63; asst. dir. testing and research Counseling and Testing Center, also asst. prof. psychology So. Ill. U., Edwardsville, 1963-68; psychologist, dir. Narcotic Addict Rehab. Family Counseling Service Clark County, 1968-71; exec. dir. So. Nev. Drug Abuse Council, 1971—. Co-producer TV series Contact, KVVU-TV, 1971-72; host radio series Drug Abuse, 1972—. Recipient Woman of Valor award Hadassah, 1972. Mem. Am. Psychol. Assn., Am. Personnel and Guidance Assn., Am. Women in Radio and TV, Nat. Vocational Guidance Assn., Am. Coll. Personnel Assn., Student Personnel Assn. Tchr. Edn., Am. Assn. U. Profs., Western Psychol. Assn., Nev. Personnel and Guidance Assn., Kappa Delta Pi, Alpha Xi Delta, Pi Lambda Theta. Democrat. Presbyn. Club: Altrusa. Home: 3784 Centennial St Las Vegas NV 89121 Office: 314 Las Vegas Blvd N Las Vegas NV 89101

LOPEZ, BARBARA EVA, coll. adminstr.; b. Vienna, Austria, Mar. 9, 1944; d. Edmund Reissmann and Margaret M. (Kinzl) R.; came to U.S., 1954, naturalized by adoption, 1955; student Whittier Coll., 1961-63, San Diego State U., 1972—; m. Robert R. Lopez, Aug. 21, 1972 (div.). With Cal. Dept. Human Resources Devel., Whittier, West Covina and East Los Angeles, 1964-70, placement supr., 1968-70; dir. financial aid and placement Mesa Coll., San Diego, 1970—; cons. in field. Rep. Nat. Adv. Council Am. Coll. Testing Program, 1972-73. Mem. Cal. State Atty. Gen.'s Citizens Adv. Council, 1972—. Mem. Chicano Democratic Assn. Mem. Western Assn. Student Financial Aid Adminstrs., Cal. Community Coll. Student Aid Officers Assn. (sec. treas. 1972-73). Home: 1410 Aries Ct Chula Vista CA 92011 Office: 7250 Mesa Coll Dr San Diego CA 92111

LORCH, IRMGARD JOAN (MRS. PETER STAPLE), biologist, educator; b. Offenbach, Germany, June 13, 1923; d. Sali and Selma (Feitler) Lorch; B.S., Birmingham (Eng.) U., 1945; Ph.D., Middleset Hosp. Med. Sch. U. London (Eng.), 1948; m. Peter Staple, Mar. 6, 1952; children—Gregory C., Alan H. Came to U.S., 1959; naturalized, 1973. Nuffield postdoctoral fellow King's Coll., London, 1949-52; research asso. Center for Theoretical Biology, State U. N.Y., Buffalo, 1964-68, asst. prof., 1968-72; asst. prof. Canisius Coll., Buffalo, 1972—. Mem. Am. Soc. Cell Biology, A.A.A.S., Am. Civil Liberties Union, Fedn. Am. Scientists, Nat. Orgn. Women, Sigma Xi. Unitarian-Universalist. Contbr. articles to profl. jours. Office: Canisius Coll Buffalo NY 14226

LORCH, MARISTELLA (MRS. EDGAR R. LORCH), educator; b. Bolzano, Italy, Dec. 8, 1919; d. Gino and Giuseppina (Cristoforetti) de Panizza; Maturita Classica, Liceo Classico, Merano, Italy, 1937; Dottore in Lettere, Universita di Roma, 1941; m. Claude Bové, Feb. 10, 1945 (div. July 1955); 1 dau., Claudia; m. 2d, Edgar R. Lorch, Mar. 25, 1956; children—Lavinia, Donatella. Prof. Latin and Greek, Liceo Virgilio, Rome, 1942-45; asso. prof. Italian and German, St. Elizabeth Coll., Convent Station, N.J., 1948-51; asst. prof. Italian Barnard Coll., N.Y.C., 1951-55, asso. prof., 1955-65, prof. Italian, 1965—. Vis. asso. prof. U. Cal. at Berkeley, 1963. Mem. adminstrv. bd. Casa Italiana, chmn., 1971—; asso. coordinator 8th Internat. Congress Lit., N.Y.C., 1973. Recipient Woman of Year Italian Lit. award, 1973. Mem. Middle Ages Seminar, Medieval Acad., Modern Lang. Assn. (sec. Medieval and Renaissance sect. 1972, chmn. 1973), Renaissance Soc. Am., Renaissance Seminar Columbia U., Am. Assn. Tchrs. Italian, Dante Soc., Pirandello Soc. (pres. 1973—). Author: Lorenzo Valla, De Vero Bono; (with W. Ludwig) Z. Ziglioli, Michaelida Editorial bd. Romanic Rev. Contbr. articles on Renaissance lit., Dante and Italian theater to profl. pubs. Home: 445 Riverside Dr New York City NY 10027

LORD, FONCHEN USHER (MRS. WILLIAM WALCOTT LORD), artist; b. St. Louis; d. Roland Greene and Florence (Richardson) Usher; A.B., Radcliffe Coll., 1933, Harvard, 1933; M.A., Washington U., St. Louis, 1935; m. William Walcott Lord, June 12, 1935; children—Fonya (Mrs. James DeLong), William Pepperell, Carter Usher, Elizabeth Usher. One man shows Artists Gallery; Orlando, Fla., 1967, Paradigm Gallery, Lakeland, 1966, Ridge Art Assn., Winter Haven, 1967, W.Va. Wesleyan Coll., 1970, Avanti Galleries N.Y., 1970, Miami Mus. Modern Art, 1970, Stetson U., Deland, Fla., 1969, St. Petersburg Pub. Library, 1971, Broward Community Coll., 1971, Polk Pub. Mus., 1972, Trend House Gallery, 1972, Fla. So. Coll., 1974; exhibited in group shows at Columbia Mus. Art, Columbus Mus. Arts and Crafts, Birmingham Mus. Art, Atlanta High Mus., Norton Gallery, Dulin Gallery of Art, Ringling Mus. Art, many others; represented in permanent collections at New Coll., Sarasota, Fla., Lowe Mus., Miami, W. Va. Wesleyan Coll., Miami Mus. Modern Art, various pvt. collections. Pres., Palm Island Corp., Barton, Fla., 1954-64, Braden River Ranchettes, Barton, 1964—; asst. treas. Paris Tanning Co., South Paris, Me., 1944-48. Gen. chmn. Lakeland Assembly, 1959-64, Lakeland Cotillion, 1964-66. Bd. dirs. Polk County chpt. Leukemia Soc. Am. Recipient Merit award Fla. State Fair, 1964; Clearwater Art Seminar award, 1961, 63; 1st prize Sunshine Art Festival, 1962; Polk County Ann., 1963, 65-67, 70, 73; award Chautaugua Nat., 1969; Cape Coral Nat., 1973, Sarasota Art Assn., 1971, 73, 74. Fellow Royal Soc. Arts, London; mem. Fla. Artists Group, Nat. Assn. Am. Pen Women, Zeta Tau Alpha. Episcopalian. Home: 4305 Oakglen Rd Lakeland FL 33803

LORD, GIGI, poet, social worker; B.S., M.A., N.Y. U.; postgrad. Columbia Sch. Social Work. Supr. teaching and tng. students and social workers in individual and group casework; rehab. positions with displaced persons, Europe; research worker with children. Recipient 1st place award for poetry Nat. Fedn. State Poetry Socs., 1968, Premium award Poetry Soc. Eng., 1968, Henry Rago award N.Y. Poetry Forum, 1973. Mem. Poetry socs. Am., Eng., Pa., Acad. Am. Poets. Author: Toppling After Itself. Contbr. poetry to numerous periodicals including Beloit Poetry Jour., Carleton Miscellany, Fiddlehead, Boston Phoenix, Wis. Rev. Address: 55 E 21st St Brooklyn NY 11226

LORD, PRISCILLA SAWYER (MRS. PHILIP HOSMER LORD), author; b. Woburn, Mass.; d. Frank Hayward and Emelyn (Strang) Sawyer; A.B., Boston U., 1933; m. Philip Hosmer Lord, Feb. 10, 1938; children—Beverly, Roberta (Mrs. William H. Moore, Jr.). Readers' adviser Woburn Pub. Library, 1933-38; story teller Book Reviewer, 1933—. Bd. dirs. Mass. Soc. U. Edn., for Women, 1965—; active Girl Scouts U.S.A.; vol. chmn. scholarship com., past v.p. Marblehead Hosp. Aid Assn. Mem. Herb Soc. Am. (nat. bd., chmn. New Eng. Unit), Mass. Descs. of Mayflower, Nat. Soc. Colonial Dames Am., Alpha Gamma Delta. Clubs: Marblehead Garden (past pres.), Winter Garden (past pres.). Author: (with Daniel J. Foley) Easter Garland, 1963, The Folk Arts and Crafts of New England, 1965, The Eagle, 1968, Easter The World Over, 1970; (with Virginia Clegg Gamage) Marblehead: The Spirit of '76 Lives Here, 1971, The Lure of Marblehead, 1973. Contbr. articles to periodicals. Home: Dennett Rd Marblehead Neck MA 01945

LORE, DEBORAH ANN, educator; b. Charleston, W.Va., July 26, 1949; d. Elmer and Suzanne (Hartman) Lore; A.A., Mt. Vernon Nazarene Coll., 1970; B.S., Trevecca Nazarene Coll., 1972; M.Ed., Middle Tenn. State U., 1974. Instr. phys. edn., dir. women's intramural and extramural sports Trevecca Nazarene Coll., Nashville, Tenn., 1972—. Vol. worker March of Dimes, Heart Fund. Mem. Am., Tenn. assn. health, phys. edn. and recreation. Mem. Nazarene Ch. Home: 1100 Thompson Place Apt A-11 Nashville TN 37217

LOREN, SOPHIA, actress; b. Rome, Italy, Sept. 20, 1934; d. Riccardo Scicolone and Romilda Villani; student Scuole Magistrali Superiori; m. Carlo Ponti, Sept. 17, 1957; 1 son, Carlo. First appearance in Aida, 1951; leading roles Italian motion pictures, including The Gold of Naples, 1954, Woman of the River, 1954, Too Bad She Is Bad, Luck of Being a Woman, 1955; actress U.S. motion pictures, 1955—, including Pride and Passion, Boy on a Dolphin, Legend of Lost, Desire Under the Elms, Houseboat, Black Orchid, The Key, That Kind of Woman, Heller with a Gun, Olympia, 1959, Bay of Naples, 1959, It Started in Naples, 1960, Heller in Tights, 1960, The Millionairess, 1961, Two Women, 1961, Bocaccio 70, 1962, Five Miles to Midnight, 1962; Madame, 1963, Marriage, Italian Style, Judith, Arabesque, The Countess from Hong Kong, Happily Ever After. Recipient award for best film performance, Japan, 1958; best fgn. actress Com. of Film Francais, and the Golden Donatello in Italy, 1958; Acad. award as best actress for Two Women, 1961. Home: Chalet Daniel Burgenstock Luzern Switzerland Office: care William Morris Agy 1350 Av of Americas New York City NY*

LORENTZEN, SANDRA LESLIE (MRS. RONALD LORENTZEN), pub. relations exec.; b. Seattle, May 12, 1946; d. Paul Porter and Vivian Lota (Gray) Henry; B.A., U. Wash., 1968; m. Ronald Lorentzen, Sept. 27, 1968. Press rep. Seattle Opera Assn., 1968-72; pub. relations dir. Portland (Ore.) Opera Assn., 1972-74; pub. relations coordinator Bumbershoot Arts Festival, Seattle, 1974—. Mem. Women in Communications. Home: 1821 Federal Av E Seattle WA 98102 Office: Seattle Center House Seattle WA 98109

LORENZ, ANDREA HELEN, psychologist; b. Clinton, Ia., Mar. 9, 1947; d. Kenneth Bowen and Helen Emily (Wetzel) Lorenz; B.A., U. No. Colo., 1968, M.A., 1970, Ed.S., 1972; postgrad. Drake U., 1968-69. Tchr. English, psychology Morrison (Ill.) Community High Schs., 1968-69; sch. psychologist Clarke/Decatur County Schs., Osceola, Ia., 1970—; instr. psychology Southwestern Community Coll., Creston, Ia., 1973. Psychol. cons. Matura Community Action Corp., Headstart Program in Ringgold County, Ia., 1972-74. Mem. Area XIV Drug Abuse Com., 1972—; Clarke County chmn. Developmental Disabilities Assn., 1973. Pub. Law grantee for grad. work in spl. edn., 1969. Mem. Am. (asso.), Ia. psychol. assns., Council for Exceptional Children, Nat. Assn. for Sch. Psychologists, N.E.A. (life). Office: Clarke County Courthouse Osceola IA 50213

LORENZ, ELAINE PATRICE (MRS. RICHARD SHORE), artist; b. N.Y.C., Dec. 8, 1945; d. Ben and Muriel (Gingras) Lorenz; B.A., Marietta Coll., 1967; m. Richard Shore, July 9, 1967. Sculptor; free-lance comml. artist; tchr. wood sculpture, ceramics, jewelry, 1972—; commd. artist-in-residence Tenafly (N.J.) sch. system; exhibited in group shows at Bergen Community Mus., 1973, Madison Sq. Garden Mus. Art, 1974, Kornbluth Gallery, Fairlawn, N.J., 1974. Recipient award 84th ann. exhbn. Nat. Assn. Women Artists, N.Y.C., 1973. Mem. Nat. Assn. Women Artists, Art Center No. N.J. Home: 130 Glenbrook Pkwy Apt 6C Englewood NJ 07631

LORENZEN, EVELYN JUNE (MRS. RALPH EDWARD TUSCANY), physician; b. El Reno, Okla., June 2, 1921; d. Jens W. and Dorothy (Montgomery) Lorenzen; student Okla. Coll. Women, 1938-40; B.S. in Home Econ., U. Okla., 1942; Ph.D. in Nutrition, Biochemistry, Cornell U., 1946; B.S. in Medicine, U. Ill. at Chgo., 1948, M.D., 1951; m. Ralph Edward Tuscany, Feb. 18, 1971. Intern, Charity Hosp., New Orleans, 1951-52, resident in pediatrics, 1952-54; practice medicine, specializing in pediatrics, Houston, 1954—; mem. staff Tex. Children's, St. Luke's Episcopal, Meth., Hermann, St. Joseph, Meml. Bapt., Rosewood hosps.; lectr. U. Houston, 1963-68. Bd. dirs. Found. for Children, Houston, Research fellow medicine Harvard, 1946-47. Diplomate Am. Bd. Pediatrics, Am. Bd. Nutrition. Fellow Am. Acad. Pediatrics; mem. A.M.A. Harris County Med. Soc., Tex. Med. Assn., Tex., Houston pediatrics socs., A.A.A.S., Phi Beta Kappa, Sigma Xi. Presbyn. Mem. Order Eastern Star. Home: 2303 Bellefontaine St Houston TX 77025 Office: 6615 Travis St Houston TX 77025

LORING, KATHRYN DOUGLASS, journalist; b. Mesquite, Tex., May 2, 1907; d. Walter Blakesley and Winifred (Dodd) Douglass; student So. Methodist U., 1924-25, U. Okla., 1925-26; m. William Riley Loring, Feb. 4, 1928 (dec. July 1959); children—William Douglass, Patricia (Mrs. William King Biggs). Soc. reporter Oklahoma City Times, 1926-27; staff Chgo. Tribune, 1942—, asst. soc. editor, feature writer, 1948-56, restaurant critic and columnist, 1956—. Mem. Chgo. Council Fgn. Relations, Connoisseurs Internat., Confrerie de la Chaine des Rotisseurs, Theta Sigma Phi. Clubs: Press, Arts (Chgo.). Home: 905 Austin Av Evanston IL 60202 Office: 435 N Michigan Av Chicago IL 60611

LORIO, MARY LEE LOVE (MRS. WILFRED ANTHONY LORIO), educator; b. Hattiesburg, Miss., Feb. 28, 1922; d. Henry Jasper and Adaline Lee (Watts) Love; Tchrs. certificate Music, Va. Intermont Coll., 1942; B.A., McNeese State U., 1969; M.A., La. State U., 1972; m. Wilfred Anthony Lorio, Apr. 6, 1947. Cashier, Johns-Manville Dist. Office, St. Louis, 1943-44; receptionist Columbia Concerts, Inc., N.Y.C., 1944-45; pvt. music tchr., Hattiesburg, Miss., West Baton Rouge, Pointe Coupee Parishes, La., 1945-58; tchr. Fordoche (La.) Elementary Sch., 1958-59; spl. edn. tchr. Rougon (La.) High Sch., 1959—. Supplementary ednl. cons. for spl. edn. Pointe Coupee Parish, La., 1973. Pointe Coupee chmn. La. Commn. on Cultural Resources, 1961-63; Pointe Coupee rep. Capital Regional Planning Commn., 1971-73; mem. Pointe Coupee Bi-Centennial Com., 1973—. Mem. La. Geneal. and Hist. Soc. (pres. 1959-60), D.A.R. (organizing regent Pointe Coupee chpt. 1961, state registrar 1965-68, state chmn. geneal. records 1968-71), La. Tchrs. Assn., La. Art Edn. Assn., La. Art and Artists Guild, So. Dames Am., Huguenot Soc. Founders Manakin, Nat. Soc. Magna Carta Dames, Colonial Order of Crown, Soc. Descs. of Knights of Most Noble Order of Garter, Daus. Am. Colonists, Phi Beta, Delta Kappa Gamma. Home: Ingleside Plantation Lakeland LA 70752 Office: Rougon High Sch Rougon LA 70773

LORY, SARAH DRURY (MRS. HILLIS LORY), psychologist; b. Early, Ia., Apr. 2, 1904; d. William and Mae (Dell) Drury; A.B. with honors, Morningside Coll., 1924; postgrad. Union Theol. Sem., 1930-31, Columbia, 1937; Coll. William and Mary, 1966; M.A., George Washington U., 1957; m. Hillis Lory, June 20, 1924; children—Priscilla (Mrs. Jonathan Bickings Kulp), Nancy Jane. Tchr., Hokkusei Jo Gakko, Sapporo, Japan, 1927-28, Profl. Children's Sch., N.Y.C., 1930-31; dir. guidance Annandale (Va.) High Sch., 1954-69. Mem. Fairfax County (Va.) Sch. Bd., 1952-54; mem. bd. nursing edn. Alexandria (Va.) Hosp., 1959—. Bd. dirs. Fairfax County Child Guidance Clinic, 1955-57. Mem. Am. Psychol. Assn., Am., No. Va. personnel and guidance assns., Nat. Vocational Guidance Assn., Am. Sch. Counselors Assn., Va. Ednl. Assn., Nat. League Am. Pen Women, P.E.O., Desert Bot. Soc. Ariz., Questers, Ikebana Internat., Internat., Ariz. State poetry socs., Psi Chi. Episcopalian. Club: Pohick Garden (Lorton, Va.). Contbr. articles to profl. jours. Address: 9109 Long Hills Dr Sun City AZ 85351

LOSCALZO, ANNE GRACE (MRS. JULIAN R. RACHELE), chemist, educator; b. N.Y.C., Sept. 2, 1917; d. Charles and Lucy (Calabrese) Loscalzo; B.A., N.Y. U., 1937, M.S., 1941, Ph.D., 1943; m. Julian R. Rachele, Apr. 20, 1940; 1 dau., Linda. Teaching fellow Washington Square Coll., N.Y. U., N.Y.C., 1937-41, asst. instr., 1941-43, instr., 1943-46; instr. Coll. City N.Y., 1953-55, lectr., 1955-59; asst. prof. chemistry L.I. U., Bklyn., 1959-65, asso. prof., 1965-71, prof., 1971—. NSF fellow, 1963. Mem. N.Y.C. Chemistry Tchrs. Club, Am. Chem. Soc. (mem. com. 1941-46), N.Y. U. Chemistry Alumni (pres. 1967-69, mem. exec. com. 1948, 65-70), Sigma Xi. Research in microchemistry, 1937-45. Home: c/o Rachele 3078 38 Long Island City NY 11103 Office: Dept Chemistry Conolly College Long Island University Brooklyn NY 11201

LOSCH, JEAN CORA (MRS. KENNETH LOSCH), aquatic dir.; b. Irvington, N.J., Oct. 23, 1927; d. Walter Logan and Genevieve (Perkins) Shaw; B.S. in Chemistry, U. Ill., 1948; postgrad. Northwestern U., 1948-49; m. Kenneth Losch, Aug. 19, 1950; children—Scott, Crystal, Barbara. Med. researcher U. Ill., Chgo., 1948-51; instr. and coach swimming North Canton (O.) YMCA, 1962-70, instr., aquatic dir., 1970—. Field agt. for aquatics in N.E. Ohio area, 1972—. Active Girl Scouts Am., 1961-72; treas. North Canton P.T.A., 1965-68. Recipient Bronze medal A.R.C., 1968, Thanks badge, Girl Scouts Am. Great Trail Council, 1970. Mem. Assn. Profl. dirs. Y.M.C.A. Methodist (youth dir. 1961-67, steward 1967-70). Home: 241 Applegrove St NE North Canton OH 44720 Office: 200 S Main St North Canton OH 44720

LOSE, LINNEA ELLEN, ednl. adminstr.; b. Richmond, Ind., June 30, 1946; d. Edward F. and Virginia D. (Dolch) Lose; B.A. in English, Ohio U., 1968; M.A., U. Minn., 1972. Tchr. English and journalism pub. high schs., Dayton, O., 1968-70; asst. dir. Minn. High Sch. Press Assn., Mpls., 1970-72; editor Minn. Dept. Edn., St. Paul, 1972-73; supr. sch. community relations for Norwood (O.) pub. schs., Cin., 1973—. Free lance writer mag. articles and advt. copy, 1970—. Mem. Audience Devel. Com. for regional dance group, Mpls., 1971-73. Mem. Women in Communications (Twin Cities corr. and recording sec. 1972-73, treas., editor Cin. chpt. 1974-75), Dayton Classroom Tchrs. Assn. (pub. relations com. 1968-70), Nat. Sch. Pub. Relations Assn. (v.p. Tri-State chpt. 1974-75), Kappa Tau Alpha. Author: filmstrip on creative graphics and copy in high sch. yearbooks, 1972. Home: 2807 Observatory Av Cincinnati OH 45208 Office: Administration Bldg 2132 Williams Av Cincinnati OH 45208

LOSE, MARGARET PHYLLIS, veterinarian; b. Phila.; d. Lloyd Levi and Margaret (Adams) Lose; grad. Immaculata Coll., 1951; V.M.D., U. Pa., 1957. Various positions involved with racing and showing horses, 1933-60; bookkeeper Lose Bros., 1939-42; asst. to Dr. Henry, D.V.M., 1943-45; trainer thoroughbred horses, 1946-57; pvt. practice as veterinarian specializing in equine medicine and surgery, Berwyn, Pa., 1957—; founder, owner equine hosp. and clinic, 1973—. Ofcl. veterinarian Devon Horse Show, 1960-74. Civil service examiner mounted police, Phila., 1962-74, ofcl. veterinarian Phila. Police Dept. mounted police div., 1962-74; preceptor students U. Pa. Sch. Vet. Medicine, 1958-67; mem. faculty Harcum Coll. Student Practicum, 1973-74. Mem. Valley Forge (Pa.) Women's Republican Com., 1948-74. Recipient State High Score Open Jumping Championship awards, 1954. Mem. Am., Pa., Women's vet. medicine assns., Am. Assn. Equine Practitioners, Am. Horse Show Assn., U.S. Animal Health Assn., Pa. Horse Breeders Assn., U. Pa. Alumnae Club. Episcopalian. Contbr. articles to profl. jours. Home: 2045 Grubbs Mill Rd Berwyn PA 19312

LOSHAEK, JOYCE RAPOPORT (MRS. SAMUEL LOSHAEK), sch. psychologist; b. Chgo., June 10, 1926; d. Louis and Jeanne (Michael) Rapoport; B.A., U. Wis., 1947; M.A., Fairfield U., 1969, postgrad., 1969-72; m. Samuel Loshaek, July 25, 1948; children—Laurie, Barbara, Paula (Mrs. Stanley Listzwan), Sally. Psychometrist, U. Wis. Vets. Guidance Center, 1948-49; psychol. examiner Stamford (Conn.) Pub. Schs., 1968-72; sch. psychologist Winnetka (Ill.) Pub. Schs., 1973—. Mem. Am., Ill. psychol. assns., Nat. Assn. Sch. Psychologists, League Women Voters, Common Cause, Psi Chi, Phi Kappa Phi. Home: 400 Greenbriar Lane Deerfield IL 60015 Office: 1155 Oak St Winnetka IL 60093

LOTHROP, KATE HAYS, clin. psychologist; b. N.Y.C., July 6, 1943; d. Jean H. Lenauer and Lora (Hays) Spindell; B.A., U. N.H., 1965; A.M., Boston U., 1966, Ph.D., 1971; m. William W. Lothrop, May 28, 1967. Jr. mental health coordinator Lynn (Mass.) Child Guidance Clinic, 1969-71; sr. psychologist Concord (N.H.) Mental Health Center, 1971—; dir. mental health services Twin Rivers Commn. Health Services, Franklin, N.H., 1972—. Mem. Am., N.H. psychol. assns. Home: Box 186 Gilmanton NH 03237 Office: Concord Mental Health Center 40 S Main St Concord NH 03301

LOTTER, ANNETTE MARIE (MRS. GEORGE W. ALLEN), physician; b. Pretoria, S. Africa, Jan. 30, 1942; d. Johannes Cornelis and Anna (Steenkamp) Lotter; N.D., Pretoria U., 1965; 1 dau., Yvette Francisca; m. George W. Allen, Feb. 14, 1974. Came to U.S., 1965. Intern Passavant Meml. Hosp., Chgo., 1966; resident otolaryngology Northwestern U., Chgo., 1967-71; practice medicine specializing in otolaryngology and maxillofacial surgery, facial plastic surgery, Chgo., 1972—; mem. staff VA Research Hosp.; instr. Northwestern U. Sch. Medicine, Chgo., 1972—. Recipient Zeiss prize radiotherapy, 1961; Norval Pierce prize otolaryngologic research, 1969. Mem. Am. Council Otolarynogology, A.C.S., Am. Acad. Facial, Plastic and Reconstructive surgery, Chgo., Ill. med. socs., A.M.A., Am. Acad. Ophthalmology and Otolaryngology. Contbr. articles to profl. jours. Home: 839 W Hutchinson Chicago IL 60613 Office: Suite 903 150 E Huron St Chicago IL 60611 also Suite 119 3223 N Ashland Av Chicago IL 60657

LOTZ, JANET HOWELL (MRS. HERBERT KARL LOTZ), psychologist; b. Springfield, O., June 4, 1923; d. Folger Branson and Catherine Sladden (Tordt) Howell; student Earlham Coll., 1941-43; B.A., U. Ia., 1945, M.A., 1948; m. Herbert Karl Lotz, May 29, 1948; children—Kathryn A., Steven K., Richard P., William H. Jr. psychologist Div. Child Welfare, State of Ia., 1947-49; psychologist Knox-Warren Spl. Edn. Dist., Galesburg, Ill., 1964—, intern supr., 1968-70; psychologist Warren Achievement Sch., Monmouth, Ill., 1972-73; individual practice, Galesburg, 1962—. Mem. Am. (asso.), Ill. psychol. assns. Democrat. Mem. Soc. Friends. Home: 220 N Chambers St Galesburg IL 61401 Office: 531 Oak St Galesburg IL 61401

LOTZ, LYNNE LARISCY (MRS. GEORGE BLAINE LOTZ II), govt. ofcl., caseworker; b. Miller, Ga., Oct. 5, 1945; d. Oswell Lester and Hilda Mavis (Stegins) Lariscy; A.B., U. Ga., 1967; m. George Blaine Lotz II, Dec. 21, 1972. Caseworker, Office of Senator Richard B. Russell, Washington, 1967-68, 70-71; media buyer, asst. to pres. McElwee & Co., Augusta, Ga., 1968-69; media buyer Liller, Neal, Battle & Lindsey, Inc., Atlanta, 1969-70; staff asst. Senator David Gambwell, Washington, 1971-73; caseworker, staff asst. to Congressman Bo Ginn, Washington, 1973—. Mem. U. Ga. Alumni Assn., Women in Communications, D.A.R., Kappa Delta. Home: 5565 Columbia Pike #206 Arlington VA 22204 Office: 508 Cannon House Office Bldg Washington DC 20515

LOU, SISTER MARY ANN, surgeon; b. Shangai, China, July 14, 1938; d. Joen Tche and Chin Shuan (Huang) Lou; B.A., U. Toronto, 1959; M.D., St. Louis U., 1964. Came to U.S., 1959. Mem. Soc. Sacred Heart, 1959—; intern Queen of Angels Hosp., Los Angeles, 1964-65, resident, 1965-69; fellow thoracic surgery Brewer Found., Los Angeles, 1969-70; mission doctor, Taiwan, 1970-71; asst. prof. surgery Charles Drew Postgrad. Med. Sch., Los Angeles, 1971—, U. Cal. Sch. Medicine, Los Angeles, 1972—; asst. chief gen. surgery Martin Luther King Jr. Gen. Hosp., Los Angeles, 1971—. Diplomate Am. Bd. Surgery. Fellow A.C.S. Roman Catholic. Home: 869 S Rimpau Blvd Los Angeles CA 90005 Office: 12021 S Wilmington Av Los Angeles CA 90059

LOUBERT, MILDRED RUTT (MRS. J. DANIEL LOUBERT), psychologist; b. West Hartford, Conn., Mar. 4, 1921; d. Simon and Dora (Cohen) Rutt; B.S., Western Conn. State Coll., 1944; M.A., Boston U., 1946; postgrad. Harvard, 1947, George Washington U., 1960-61, U. Md., 1968—; m. J. Daniel Loubert, Aug. 23, 1945; children—Byron R., Cherie Anne. Psychometrist, Children's Hosp., Boston, 1945-46; population sample, analyst, interviewer U. Mich. Survey Research Center, Ann Arbor, 1946-49; psychologist New Eng. Med. Center, Boston, 1947-48, Jewish Vocational Service, Boston, 1948-50, Greater Boston Community Service, 1950-52; sch. psychologist Bd. Edn., Washington, 1959-61; research psychologist Gallaudet Coll. for Deaf, Washington, 1961-63; psychol. cons. S.S. Hope, Republic of Guinea, 1964-65, Am. Embassy Sch., Republic of Guinea, 1964-65; sch. psychologist Prince George's County Pub. Schs., Upper Marlboro, Md., 1966—. Pres. Corporate Communities of Am., 1972; chmn. bd. Transcultural Research Co., 1973—. Bd. dirs. Future Families of World. Mem. Am., Eastern, Md. psychol. assns., Am. Personnel and Guidance Assn., N.E.A., A.A.A.S., Am. Assn. U. Profs., Am. Conv. Instructors for Deaf, Nat., Md. assns. sch. psychologists. Home: 7501 Sebago Rd Bethesda MD 20034 Office: Dept Psychol Services Prince George's Public Schs Upper Marlboro MD 20870

LOUDERMILK, LOIS ADELINE WOOD (MRS. HAYDEN C. LOUDERMILK), civic worker; b. Bigelow, Ark., Aug. 25, 1911; d. William Edgar and Mary (May) Wood; B.S., State Coll. Ark., 1948; M.L.S., Peabody Coll., 1965; m. Hayden C. Loudermilk, June 25, 1932; children—Billy Hayden, James Edwin. Tchr., librarian Perryville (Ark.) High Sch., 1942-62; librarian Joe T. Robinson High Sch., Little Rock, 1962-71. Feature writer Ark. Gazette, 1945-46, Ark. Democrat, 1946-47. Historian, Perryville Extension Homemakers, 1973-75. Mem. United Meth. Women, Alpha Delta Kappa. Mem. Order Eastern Star. Club: Garden (charter mem.) (Fayetteville), Golden Age (Perryville). Home: 301 Cedar St PO Box 38 Perryville AR 72126

LOUGHEED, JEVA ULDINE ROGERS (MRS. CRAIG SAMUEL LOUGHEED), anesthesiologist; b. Bruce Mines, Ont., Can., Apr. 22, 1922; d. Richard Merritt and Mary Jane (McCrea) Rogers; M.D., U. Toronto, 1945; m. Craig Samuel Lougheed, July 6, 1945; children—Mary-Lynne (Mrs. John T. Axler), Brandon, Alice-Anne (Mrs. Ken Morlock), Stephenson, Lawrence, Kevin, Neal, Heather. Practice medicine, specializing in anesthesiology, Toronto; mem. anesthesia staff Women's Coll. Hosp., Toronto, 1959—, mem. hypnotherapy staff, 1973—. Faculty, Toronto Bible Coll. Fellow Royal Coll. Physicians and Surgeons Can.; mem. Am. Soc. Anesthesiologists, Internat. Anesthesia Research Soc., Canadian Anesthetists Soc., Canadian, Ont. med. socs., Royal Coll. Medicine (London, Eng.), Acad. Medicine Toronto, Clin. Research Soc. Toronto. Home: 561 Broadview Av Toronto ON M4K 2N8 Canada Office: Bloor St Toronto ON Canada

LOUGHLIN, WINIFRED CATHERINE, physician; b. N.Y.C., Aug. 24, 1911; d. Patrick Dominic and Mary (Nolan) Loughlin; B.A., Bklyn. Coll., 1934; M.D., Tufts U., 1938. Intern Jersey City Med. Center, 1938-39; resident N.Y. U. div. neurolog. service Goldwater Hosp., 1940-41; practice gen. medicine, N.Y.C., 1942—; mem. staff Univ. Hosp., Bellevue Hosp., N.Y. Infirmary, chief diabetes clinic; asso. prof. medicine Sch. Medicine, N.Y. U. Mem. N.Y., New York County med. socs., A.M.A., Am. Fedn. Clin. Research, N.Y. Diabetes Assn. (past pres., dir. chmn. vocational and counselling service 1965), Alpha Omega Alpha. Contbr. profl. jours. Home: 12 E 34th St New York City NY 10016 Office: 35 E 35th St New York City NY 10016

LOUGHMAN, ALEDA JOSEPHINE POOLE, mfg. corp. exec.; b. Embreeville, Pa., Nov. 1, 1932; d. Aubrey Johnson and Maggie Lee (Wilson) Poole; grad. high sch.; 1 dau., Valerie Jean Foulk; m. Robert E. Loughman, June 25, 1967 (div. 1970); 1 dau., Janet Lee. Sec., Lukens Steel Co., Coatesville, Pa., 1950-51, Army Chem. Center, Edgewood, Md., 1952-53; with Somat Corp., Pomery, Pa., 1957—, corporate sec., 1958—. Capt. indsl. div. Coatesville (Pa.) dist. United Charities drive, 1969—. Home: 1 Lepore Dr Cedar Acres E Lancaster PA 17602 Office: Somat Corp Pomeroy PA 19367

LOUGHMAN, BARBARA ELLEN EVERS (MRS. TERRY BEAVER LOUGHMAN), scientist; b. Frankfort, Ind., Oct. 26, 1940; d. Jimmie J. and Ruth (Hoyer) Evers; B.S., U. Ill., 1962; Ph.D., U. Notre Dame, 1972; m. Terry Beaver Loughman, June 28, 1962; children—Lance Evers, Chad Elliott. Asst. research microbiologist Ames Research Lab., Miles Labs., Inc., Elkhart, Ind., 1962-67, asso. research microbiologist, 1967-71, research scientist, 1971-72; staff fellow NIH-NICHD, Balt., 1972-74; sr. immunology research asso. HDR, The Upjohn Co., 1974—. Mem. Am. Soc. Microbiology, A.A.A.S., Alpha Lambda Delta, Delta Zeta. Presbyn. Home: 10243 Foxhollow Portage MI 49081 Office: Hypersensitive Disease Research Unit The Upjohn Co Kalamazoo MI 49001

LOUI, BEATRICE L.Q., ednl. cons.; b. Honolulu; d. Heong Poo and Siu (Shee) Loui; B.A., U. Hawaii, 1930; M.A., Columbia, 1947; postgrad. U. Cal. at Berkeley, 1956. Tchr. secondary schs., Honolulu, 1930-48, counselor, 1948-56; counselor U. Cal. at Berkeley, 1956-57; counselor Hawaii Employment Service, Honolulu, 1958; dir. tests and measurements Hawaii Dept. Edn., Honolulu, 1960-72; cons. assessment and evaluation ednl. projects, 1973—. Mem. Nat. Council on Measurement in Edn., Am. Ednl. Research Assn., Am., Hawaii personnel and guidance assns., Assn. for Measurement and Evaluation in Guidance, N.E.A. (life), Hawaii Edn. Assn., Hawaii Ednl. Officers Assn., Hawaii Counselors Assn. (pres. 1954), Am. Sch. Counselors Assn., Asso. Chinese U. Women (pres. 1940), Pi Lambda Theta, Delta Kappa Gamma, Pi Gamma Mu. Mem. Community Ch. Club: Altrusa (sec. 1968). Contbr. articles to profl. jours. Home: 1562 Kanalui St Honolulu HI 96816

LOUIS, LOUISE AMELIA (MRS. GEORGE J. WHITBREAD), poet, lectr.; b. N.Y.C.; d. Charles A. and Frida (Von Volquarts) Louis; A.B., Hunter Coll., 1929; m. George J. Whitbread, Feb. 14, 1942; 1 dau., Joan Louise (Mrs. Edward Oleksiak). Instr. English, speech, creative writing Hunter Coll. and Model Sch., N.Y.C., 1929-36, 40-41; lectr. Herald Tribune Club Service, N.Y.C., 1945-48; solo programs Inst. Arts and Scis., Bklyn., 1953; lectr. Federated Womens Clubs, 1962-65. Columnist, The News, Westwood, N.J., 1957-60. Judge high sch. poetry contests, N.Y.C., N.J., 1959-61, N.Y. Poetry Forum, 1970-72; drama lectr. Girl Scouts U.S.A., N.J., 1970-71; lectr. federated clubs, 1970-71. Recipient 27 nat. awards, Bus. and Profl. Women N.J. award 1968. Mem. Poetry Soc. Am. (Speyer award 1960, critic 1970-71, nominating com.), Nat. League Am. Pen Women. Author: This is For You, 1947; Path to Peak, 1956; Helpful Hints for the Teacher, 1957; The Dervish Dance, 1958; Poetry, Personality and Power, 1961; The Wonderful Becoming, 1963; Under the Lamplight, 1963; I See a Picture, 1967; Dutchy The Rag-Tag, 1970; Finding the Way, 1970; The Scarlet Net, 1972; The Miraculous Affair, 1973. Editor: Pen-Art Publs., 1967-72. Home: 402 Fairview Av Westwood NJ 07675

LOUSIN, ANN MARIE, lawyer, parliamentarian; b. Chgo., Feb. 21, 1943; d. Max Bedros and Opal Marie (Anderson) Lousin; B.A., Grinnell Coll., 1964; postgrad. U. Heidelberg, Germany, 1964-65; J.D., U. Chgo., 1968. Admitted to Ill. bar, 1970; mem. staff Legal Aid Bur., Chgo., 1968-69; research asst. Sixth Ill. Constnl. Conv., Springfield, 1970; staff asst. Speaker of Ill. Ho. of Reps., Springfield, 1971—, parliamentarian, 1973—. Instr. legal writing John Marshall Law Sch., 1971. Mem. Ill., Chgo. bar assns., Women's Bar Assn. Ill., Chgo. Council Lawyers, Am. Civil Liberties Union. Conglist. Home: Apt 414S 1400 E 55th Pl Chicago IL 60637 Office: 630 Statehouse Springfield IL 62706

LOVE, BARBARA JOAN, editor, writer; b. Glen Ridge, N.J., Feb. 27, 1937; d. Egon and Lois Ashley (Crane) Love; student Purdue U., 1955-57; B.A., Syracuse U., 1959. Tchr. English, math. Am. Sch., Florence, Italy, 1959-61; free lance writer, 1960-61; asso. editor N.Y. Lumber Trade Jour., 1961-62; sr. editor Sponsor mag., 1962-67; program editor-writer CBS-TV Network, N.Y.C., 1967-69; pres. Foremost Americans Pub. Corp., 1969-72; asso. editor Supermarketing Mag., 1972-73, mng. editor, 1973—. Bd. dirs. Nat. Gay Task Force; adv. bd. N.Y. chpt. Nat. Orgn. for Women. Author (with Sidney Abbott) Sappho Was a Right-on Woman, 1972; Gay Liberation and Women's Liberation. Home: 43 Fifth Av New York City NY 10003 Office: 1501 Broadway New York City NY 10036

LOVE, DORIS BENTA MARIA (MRS. ASKELL LOVE), botanist; b. Kristianstad, Sweden, Jan. 2, 1918; d. Gustaf and Augusta Maria Christina (Bus) Wahlén; B.A., Kristianstad Coll., 1937; B.Sc., U. Lund, 1941, Ph.D., 1943, D.Sc., 1944; m. Askell Love, Apr. 30, 1940; children—Gunnlaug, Gay (Mrs. Theodore D. Swanson), Loa (Mrs. Loa Kaersvang). Came to U.S., 1964. Research asso. genetics Lund U., Sweden, 1941-45; research asso., bot. and plant breeding, Reykjavik, 1945-51; herbarium curator Man., Can., 1951-56; asso. research prof. U. Montreal, Que., Can., 1956-63; mus. asso., research asso. Inst. Arctic and Alpine Research, U. Colo., Boulder, 1964—. Research grantee and fellow Swedish Acad. Scis., Icelandic Cultural Fund, NRC Can., NSF, Smithsonian Instn. Mem. Internat. Assn. Plant Taxonomy, Internat. Orgn. Plant Biosystematies, Internat. Orgn. Paleobotanists, Mendelian Soc. Lund, Lund Bot. Soc., Swedish Bot. Soc., Scandinavian Soc. Geneticists, Genetics Soc. Am., Genetics Soc. Can., Soc. Study of Evolution, Am. Soc. Plant Taxonomists, Bot. Soc. Am., others. Author: Cytogenetic Studies on Dioecious Melandrium, 1944; (with Askell Love) Cytotaxonomical Conspectus of the Icelandic Flora, 1956, Chromosome Numbers of Central and Northwest European Plant Species, 1961, North Atlantic Biota and Their History, 1963; Cytotaxonomical Atlas of the Slovenian Flora, 1974; Chromosome, Cytology and Cytotechnology, 1974. Contbr. numerous articles in field to profl. jours. Home: 473 Harvard Lane Boulder CO 80303

LOVE, IRIS CORNELIA, educator, archeologist; b. N.Y.C., Aug. 1, 1933; d. Cornelius Ruxton and Audrey Barbara (Josephthal) Love; B.A., Smith Coll., 1955; student Universita di Firenze (Italy), 1953-54; postgrad. Inst. Fine Arts N.Y. U., 1955—; LL.D. (hon.), Dowling Coll., 1971. Instr. Greek and Roman art Cooper Union, N.Y.C., spring 1963, Smith Coll., Northampton, Mass., 1964-65; asst. prof. art history and archeology C.W. Post Long Island U., N.Y., 1966-67, research asst. prof., 1967—. Lectr., coordinator lecture series Inst. Community Edn. Hofstra U., N.Y.C., spring 1969, fall 1970; lectr. Sch. Continuing Edn., coordinator lecture series N.Y. U., 1968-70; Distinguished Froman prof. Russell Sage Coll., Troy, N.Y., 1972; Robert Sterling Clark lectr. art history Williams Coll., Williamstown, Mass., 1973, 74; John Hamilton Fulton lectr. in art Middlebury (Vt.) Coll., 1974; dir. archeol. expdns. to Knidos, L.I. U., 1967—; staff mem. archeol. expdn. Samothrace, Inst. Fine Arts N.Y. U., summers 1955-65. Mem. Archeol. Inst. Am., Am. Assn. U. Profs., Soc. Women Geographers, Am. Turkish Soc., Nat. Orgn. Women, Alpha Soc. Republican. Episcopalian. Contbr. articles profl. jours. Home: RFD 1 Box 301 Bristol VT 05443

LOVE, MARSHA LYNN, univ. adminstr.; b. West Palm Beach, Fla., Nov. 14, 1944; d. James Luther and Blanche Louise (Morrison) Love; B.A., Fla. State U., 1966; M.A., U. N.C., 1970. Tchr. English and journalism Forest Hill High Sch., West Palm Beach, 1967-68;

counselor, office of dean of women Fla. Atlantic U., Boca Raton, 1971; asst. to dean of student affairs, 1971—. Publicity chmn. Delray Affair, sidewalk art show, 1969; mem. cast Delray Beach Playhouse, 1967-68. Grad. counselor scholar Kappa Kappa Gamma, 1966-67. Mem. Nat. Assn. Women Deans, Adminstrs. and Counselors, Nat. Council Tchrs. English, Am. Assn. U. Women, Fla. State U. Alumni Assn., Mortar Bd., Kappa Kappa Gamma. Methodist (mem. adminstrv. bd. 1970-73). Home: 805 N Swinton Av Delray Beach FL 33444 Office: Timucua Hall Fla Atlantic U Boca Raton FL 33432

LOVE, MARY EMELINE, govt. ofcl.; b. McAdams, Miss., May 6, 1911; d. James Robert and Martha (Sanders) Love; B.A., Miss. State Coll. Women, 1932; postgrad. U. So. Cal., 1953; B.S. in Library Sci., La. State U., 1949. Tchr., librarian pub. schs. Miss., 1932-45, librarian Cleveland (Miss.) High Sch., 1945-47, field librarian pub. elementary schs., Jackson, Miss., 1947-59; asso. dir. Miss. Library Commn., Jackson, 1959-67, dir., 1968—. Mem. Title III adv. council U.S. Dept. Edn., 1968—, adv. council statewide planning vocational rehab., 1968—; mem. task force State White House Conf. on Aging, 1971—. Mem. Am., Miss. (pres. 1955-57), Southeastern library assns., Miss. Assn. Sch. Librarians (past pres.), Am. Library Trustee Assn. (v.p. 1972-73), Delta Kappa Gamma. Home: 567 Warrior Trail Jackson MS 39216 Office: 405 State Office Bldg Jackson MS 39201

LOVE, NANCY LOWE, pub. relations exec.; b. San Francisco; d. Joseph and Sophie Lowe; B.A., U. Cal. at Los Angeles, 1953; postgrad. in journalism N.Y. U., 1966; Woman's program dir. KGIL, KPAL Radio, Los Angeles, 1953; co-producer, writer KLAC-TV, Los Angeles, 1954; co-producer, writer, interviewer KVOA-TV, KGUN-TV, Tucson, 1957-60; promotional and circulation dir. Theatre Arts mag., N.Y.C., 1960-62; free-lance writer, N.Y.C., 1963-66; promotion writer Hearst Mags., N.Y.C., 1966-67; v.p. Mike Merrick Pub. Relations Co., N.Y.C., 1967-71; dir. N.Y. oeprations, pres. Nancy Love Assos., Inc., N.Y.C., 1971—. Mem. Nat. Acad. TV Arts and Scis., Assn. Theatrical Press Agts. and Mgrs. Club: Tucson Press. Author screenplay: The Auctioneer, 1962. Office: 229 E 79th St New York City NY 10021

LOVE, NEUREE M. COLLIER (MRS. JOHN J. LOVE), social worker; b. Dickson County, Tenn.; d. William Baxter and Alice S. (Barksdale) Collier; B.A. in Sociology, Fisk U., 1940; M.A., U. Chgo. Sch. Social Services Adminstrn., 1950; m. John J. Love, Dec. 23, 1949. Exec. sec.'s asst. Pub. House A.M.E. Ch. Lit., Nashville, 1940-41; social worker Tenn. Dept. Pub. Welfare, Davidson County, 1941-44, child welfare services div., 1945-52, child welfare supr., 1953-60, child welfare cons., 1960-64, supr. staff devel. and tng., Nashville Center, 1965-67, supr. interstate and intercountry services, 1967—. Mem. Blue Triangle com. on adminstrn. YWCA, Nashville, 1968—, bd. dirs. ad hoc study coms. 1963-66, 67-68, chmn. bldg. and maintenance com. program planning for br. and personnel, 1964-67, chmn. personnel practices bd. dirs., 1970-72, chmn. finance com., 1972; mem. allocations and admissions com. United Givers Fund, 1967-69. Sec. bd. dirs. Housing and Counseling Services, Nashville, 1972—. Mem. Nat. Assn. Social Workers (sec. 1952-54, mem. bylaws and constn. com. 1954-55, nominating com. chmn. 1961-62, 66-67). Methodist (chmn. women's day activities 1960-63, chmn. emeritus, trustee spl. services 1969—, chmn. bldg. fund dr.). Home: 2425 Gardner Lane Nashville TN 37207 Office: Tenn Dept Public Welfare State Office Bldg Nashville TN 37219

LOVE, ROSALIE STOCKS (MRS. FRED EMERY LOVE), educator; b. Norphlet, Ark., Oct. 31, 1913; d. Carl Lee and Ora May (Hayes) Stocks; student Magnolia A. and M. Coll., El Dorado Jr. Coll., 1931-32; Henderson State Tchrs. Coll., 1932-33; B.S., So. State Coll., 1959; m. Fred Emery Love, June 29, 1934; children—David Edward (dec.), Gerry Beth (Mrs. Lloyd V. Morris), Joe Fred. Piano tchr., Norphlet, Ark., 1930-52; state worker Ark. Baptist Tng. Union Dept., Little Rock, 1952-57; kindergarten tchr. First Baptist Ch., El Dorado, Ark., 1953-59; tchr. Union Sch., El Dorado, 1959-67, Norphlet Pub. Schs., 1967—. Mem. Internat. Reading Assn., Internat. Platform Assn., Nat. League of Am. Pen Women, Nat., Ark., Union County (pres. 1970-71), Norphlet (pres. 1972—) tchrs. assns., Delta Kappa Gamma. Contbg. author: Kindergarten Resource Book, 1965. Contbr. articles in field to profl. jours. Home: PO Box 373 Norphlet AR 71759

LOVE, VIRGINIA LEE (MRS. JOHN WARREN LOVE), educator; b. Summerfield, Tex., July 12, 1912; d. Oliver Lee and Cordelia (Parrott) Hufstedler; B.A., Tex. Tech. U., 1931, M.A., 1932; postgrad. U. Mo., 1936-37, U. Chico, 1943-45; Ed.D., U. Tex., 1948; m. John Warren Love, Mar. 28, 1955. Faculty, Abilene (Tex.) Christian Coll., 1933-34; tchr. Arkansas Pass (Tex.) Pub. Schs., 1936-40; dir. child devel. Corpus Christi (Tex.) Pub. Schs., 1940-48; asst. prof. Inst. for Child Study, U. Md., College Park, 1948-50; dir. spl. edn. and student personnel services Tex. Edn. Agy., Austin, 1950-55; asso. prof. psychology Tex. So. U., Houston, 1958-60; faculty Austin Coll., Sherman, Tex., 1960—, prof. psychology and edn., 1961—. Pres., Tex. Assn. for Mental Health, Austin, 1956-57. Mem. Am. Psychol. Assn., Am., Tex. (pres. 1960-62) personnel and guidance assns. Home: 1515 W Washington Sherman TX 75090 Office: Box E Austin College Sherman TX 75090

LOVEJOY, MARGOT R. MACDONALD, artist; b. Campbellton, N.B., Can., Oct. 21, 1930; d.John Wesley and Mary Hazel (Mowat) Macdonald; student Mt. Allison U., 1947-49, L'Academie Julian, Paris, France, 1949-50; certificate design and illustration St. Martin's Sch. Art, London, 1951; student Am. U., Cairo, Egypt, 1964, Pratt Graphics Centre, N.Y.C., 1966-71; m. Derek Roxbee Lovejoy, Aug. 1, 1953; children—Shaun, Kristin, Megan. Free-lance art work for various book pubs., also Nat. Film Bd. Can., 1954-55; docent, edn. officer Nat. Gallery Can., Ottawa, 1955-65; dir. children's art classes Nat. Mus. Can., Ottawa, 1960-62; dir. art program Ottawa Dept. Parks and Recreation, 1962-64; instr. etching Pratt Graphics Centre, N.Y.C., 1972-74, Herbert H. Lehman Coll., City U. N.Y., 1974; instr. serigraphy N.Y.-Phoenix Sch. of Design, N.Y.C., North Shore Community Center, Great Neck, N.Y., 1972-74, Nassau County Office Cultural Devel., 1973-74; exhibited in one-man shows at New Brunswick Mus., St. John, Atelier du Caire, Cairo, Prestige Gallery, Boston; exhibited in many group shows including Silvermine, AAA Galleries, Hudson River Mus., Women's Interart Centre, Contemporary Canadian Prints-A Survey, 1972, Toronto Gallery Art touring show, Nat. Assn. Women Artists touring graphics show; others; represented in permanent collections N.B. Mus., Hudson River Mus. Mem. Nat. Assn. Women Artists, Profl. Artists Guild, Canadian Soc. Graphic Art, Coll. Art Assn., Artists Equity, Women in Arts, Yonkers Art Assn. Address: 166-04 81st Av Jamaica NY 11432

LOVEKIN, LOUISE JEANNE GOUX, opthalmologist; b. Detroit, June 19, 1915; d. Louis James and Charlotte Barton (Warren) Goux; B.A., Wayne U., 1941, M.D., 1943; m. Osgood Stevens Lovekin, Oct. 25, 1947; children—Osgood Stevens, James Warren, Charles Barton. Itern The Grace Hosp., Detroit, 1942-43; resident Columbia-Presbyn. Med. Center Inst. Ophthalmology, N.Y.C.; pvt. practice opthalmology, Detroit, 1946-47, San Diego, Cal., 1947-50, Fairfield, Conn., 1951—, Norwalk, Conn., 1972—; mem. staff Park City Hosp., Bridgeport, Norwalk Hosp. Cons. opthalmologist Vis. Nurse and Pub. Health Nursing Service, 1952—. Mem. Conn., Fairfield County med. socs., A.M.A., Am. Acad. Opthalmology and Otolaryngology, Pan Am. Assn. Opthalmology, Am. Assn. Opthalmology, Assn. Research in Vision and Opthalmology. Home: 290 Beach Rd Fairfield CT 06430 Office: 10 Mott Av Norwalk CT 06850

LOVELACE, LORNA SEALE, telephone co. exec.; b. Little Rock, Sept. 11, 1944; d. Denver and June (Jennings) Seale; student Tex. Christian U., 1962-63; B.A., So. Meth. U., 1966; m. Jerry Leon Lovelace, Apr. 2, 1966 (div. May 1970); 1 dau., Laura June. Pub. relations projects, editor Southwestern Bell Telephone, North Tex. Area, Dallas, 1972-73, employee information supr., gen. hdqrs., St. Louis, 1973-74, advt. supr., 1974—. Recipient Award of Merit, Internat. Assn. Bus. Communicators, 1973; Matrix award Women In Communications, 1973. Mem. Internat. Assn. Bus. Communicators, Women In Communications (hospitality chmn. 1973, Matrix award 1973), Ad Club Two (bd. dirs. 1974—), League of Women Voters, Kappa Tau Alpha, Alpha Lambda Delta, Chi Omega. Democrat. Episcopalian. Home: 7639 Carswold Dr Clayton MO 63105 Office: 1010 Pine St Room 1222 St Louis MO 63101

LOVELACE, MARGO, puppeteer; b. Pitts., Dec. 1, 1923; d. Guy Marcus and Anna Mabel (Watts) Lovelace; student McDowell Sch. of Costume Design, 1940-41, Carnegie Inst., 1954-56, U. Pitts., 1967-68; pvt. study puppetry with Cedric Head, Erhardt Reis, Sergei Obratsov; .m. Jan Harold Visser, Oct. 1940 (div. July 1964); children—Jan Douglas, Gwen, David. Founder Lovelace Marionettes, Pitts., 1947—; builder Lovelace Marionette Theatre, Pitts., 1963—; established Marionette Theatre Arts Council, Inc., Pitts., 1968—. Cons. Carnegie-Mellon U., 1968-74, Chatham Coll., 1969-71, U. Pitts., 1963-68, Model Cities, 1970-72, Office Econ. Opportunity Headstart, 1961-63, WQED-TV, 1955-74, Pitts. Pub. Sch. Bd. of Edn., 1969-74. Recipient Bronze medal for creative puppetry Union Internat. Marionettists, 1972. Mem. Theatre Assn. Pa., Puppeteers of Am. Home: 5886 Ellsworth Av Pittsburgh PA 15232 Office: 5888 1/2 Ellsworth Av Pittsburgh PA 15232

LOVELADY, CAROL KING (MRS. JAMES EDWARD LOVELADY), educator; b. Lawley, Ala.; d. Charles Lafayette and Lillian Lovella (Crowe) King; A.B. cum laude, Tusculum Coll., 1943; M.A., U. Ala., 1963, Ed.S., 1972; m. James Edward Lovelady, July 12, 1944 (dec. July 1968); children—Charlotte Wynn, Sharon Lynn. Tchr. spl. edn. Bibb County (Ala.) Schs., 1960-68; cons. Ala. Dept. Edn., Montgomery, 1968-70; asst. prof. edn. Troy (Ala.) State U., 1970—, mem. all U. council, 1972—, student teaching council, 1970—. Mem. scholarship com. Ala. Dept. Edn., 1968-70; sponsor Council for Exceptional Children, regional state dir., 1972—. Mem. Internat., Ala. Fedn. councils for exceptional children, Am. Assn. Mental Deficiency, Ala., Youth (sponsor 1972—), Pike County (rec. sec. 1972—) assns. for retarded children, Ala. Soc. for Crippled Children and Adults, Nat. Rehab. Assn., Pike County Mental Health Assn., Ala. Assn. Tchr. Edn., Nat., Ala. (mem. legislative com. 1967), Troy State (pres. 1972-73) edn. assns., Kappa Delta Pi, Alpha Delta Kappa, Delta Kappa Gamma (chpt. v.p. 1972-73). Club: Alpha Gamma Delta Alumnae. Home: 116 Woodland Circle Troy AL 36081

LOVELESS, KATHLEEN WOOD (MRS. SCOTT WARNER LOVELESS), editor; b. Salt Lake City, Apr. 7, 1949; d. Joseph F. and Helen Cottam (Hatch) Wood; B.A., U. Utah, 1971; M.S., Am. U., 1974; m. Scott Warner Loveless, Aug. 31, 1971. Intern Pres. Utah State Senate, 1970; cultural adminstr. Internat. Exchange Sch., Salt Lake City, 1970-71; editor Reclamation Era, Bur. Reclamation, Dept. Interior, Washington, 1971—. Area rep. Internat. Exchange Sch., 1971—; dir. On Stage Europe, 1973; intern Hinckley Inst. Politics, 1969, Utah State Legislature, 1971. Recipient Meritorious Service award U.S. Dept. Interior, 1971, Outstanding Area Rep. award Internat. Exchange Sch., 1972; named Miss Utah, 1968-69. Mem. Mortar Board, Phi Beta Kappa, Phi Sigma Alpha, Delta Sigma Rho, Tau Kappa Alpha. Club: Toastmasters (area gov. 1974) (Washington). Home: 1655 N 21st St No 9 Arlington VA 22209 Office: Bur Reclamation Dept Interior Washington DC 20240

LOVELL, EMILY KALLED (MRS. ROBERT EDMUND LOVELL), journalist; b. Grand Rapids, Mich., Feb. 25, 1920; d. Abdo Rham and Louise (Claussen) Kalled; student Grand Rapids Jr. Coll., 1937-39; B.A., Mich. State U., 1944; M.A., U. Ariz., 1971; m. Robert Edmund Lovell, July 4, 1947. Copywriter, asst. traffic mgr. Sta. WOOD, Grand Rapids, 1944-46; traffic mgr. KOPO, Tucson, 1946-47; reporter, city editor Alamogordo (N.M.) News, 1948-51; Alamogordo corr., feature writer Internat. News Service, Denver, 1950-54. El Paso Herald-Post, 1954-65; Alamogordo news dir., feature writer Tularosa (N.M.) Basin Times, 1957-59; co-founder, editor, pub. Otero County Star, Alamorgordo, 1961-65; newscaster KALG, Alamogordo, 1964-65; free lance feature writer Denver Post, N.M. Mag., 1949-69; corr. Electronics News, N.Y.C., 1959-63, 65-69; Sierra Vista (Ariz.) corr. Ariz. Republic, 1966; free lance editor N.M. Pioneer Interviews, 1967-69; sec., dir. Star Pub. Co., Inc., 1961-64, pres., 1964-65; free-lance writer, 1969—. Fellow Center for Arabic Studies Abroad, Am. U. Cairo, summer 1970. Third v.p., publicity chmn. Otero County Community Concert Assn., 1950-65; mem. Alamogordo Zoning Commn., 1955-57; mem. founding com. Alamogordo Central Youth Activities Com., 1957; vice chmn. Otero County chpt. Nat. Found. Infantile Paralysis, 1958-61; charter mem. N.M. Citizens Council for Traffic Safety, 1959-61; pres. Sierra Vista Hosp. Aux., 1966; pub. relations chmn. Ft. Huachuca chpt. A.R.C., 1966; mem. Am. Mothers Com. for selection Ariz. Mother of Year, 1969. Nat. bd. dirs. Hospitalized Vets. Writing Project, 1972—. Recipient 1st Pl. awards N.M. Press Assn., 1961, 62, Pub. Interest award Nat. Safety Council, 1962, 1st Pl. award Nat. Fedn. Press Women, 1960, 62; named Woman of Year Alamogordo, 1960, Editor of Week Pubs. Aux., 1962, adm. N.M. Navy, 1962, col. a.d.c. Staff Gov. N.M., 1963. Mem. N.M. (past sec.), Ariz. (pres. 1969-70, Woman of Yr. award 1972-73) press women, N.M. Fedn. Bus. and Profl. Womens Clubs (pres. 1959-60), N.M. Fedn. Women's Club (dist. pub. relations chmn. 1957-60), N.M. Hist. Soc. (life), Tularosa Basin Hist. Soc., Am. Assn. U. Women, Pan Am. Round Table Alamogordo, Theta Sigma Phi (coordinator N.M. 1954-65, Ariz. 1965-69, nat. v.p. for mems.-at-large 1968-72). Author: A Personalized History of Otero County, New Mexico, 1963; Weekend Away, 1964; Lebanese Cooking Streamlined, 1972. Home: PO Box 26013 Tempe AZ 85282

LOVETT, IRENE EASTER (MRS. FRANK MOREHEAD LOVETT), clergywoman; b. W.Va., Oct. 18, 1910; d. Lewis Hensley and Luemmer (Young) Easter; B.A., Marietta Coll., 1949; B.D., Crozer Theol. Sem., 1950; M.Ed., Temple U., 1956; LL.D., Alderson-Broaddus Coll., 1968; m. Frank Morehead Lovett, Aug. 22, 1935. Elementary sch. tchr., Putnam County, W.Va., 1931-36; tng. sec. Bapt. Young People's Union Am., Chgo., 1935-41; asso. pastor Broadway Bapt. Ch., Parkersburg, W.Va., 1943-47, pastor, 1947-52; pastor Mt. Zion Bapt. Ch., Parkersburg, 1943-47; dir. pub. relations, prof. psychology Bapt. Inst., Bryn Mawr, Pa., 1952-58, dean, 1958-65; dean Ellen Cushing Jr. Coll., Bryn Mawr, 1965-70; dir., career counselor Am. Bapt. Center for Ministry, Wellesley Hills, Mass., 1970—. Part-time psychologist Woman's Med. Coll. Hosp., Phila., 1957-60, Sleighton Farm Sch. for Girls, Darling, Pa., 1960-65. Recipient Thornburg award for Acad. Excellence Morris Harvey Coll., 1930, award Temple U., 1956. Mem. Am. Bapt. Ministers Council, Am., Pa., Mass. psychol. assns. Home: 288 Grove St Newton MA 02166 Office: Center for Ministry 40 Washington St Wellesley Hills MA 02181

LOVETTE, JOANNE PATRICIA, educator; b. Hastings, Pa., Sept. 12, 1927; d. Daniel Robert and Anna (Flynn) Lovette; B.S., Indiana U. of Pa., 1949; M.Ed., Pa. State U., 1957. Art supr. Aspinwall (Pa.) Pub. Schs., 1949-58; producer, performer tv ednl. sta. WQED, 1955-58; head dept. Greensburg (Pa.) Pub. Schs., 1958-60; tchr. Westmoreland County Mus., Greensburg, 1959-62; supr. student tchrs. Indiana U. of Pa., 1954-62, supr. curriculum, 1960—. Works exhibited in art shows, Pa.; cons., research ednl. research art edn. Mem. Pa. Art Edn. Curriculum Guidelines Com., 1969—. Mem. Pa., Nat. art edn. assns., Eastern Arts Assn., Nat. Art Assn., N.E.A., Pa. Edn. Assn., Assn. Supervision and Curriculum Devel., Assn. for Student Teaching, Nat. Soc. for Study Edn., Assn. for Higher Edn., Assn. U. Women, Mus. Modern Art, Pitts. Soc. Artists, Allied Artists, Pi Lambda Theta, Delta Phi Delta, Alpha Delta Kappa. Democrat. Roman Catholic. Home: Box 32 Brush Valley PA 15720

LOW, EDITH MCLEAN, editor; b. Wilmington, N.C., May 23, 1928; d. Cameron Moses and Sally Rhodes (Mason) McLean; student Bob Jones Coll., 1947-48, Palmer Sch. Writing, 1956-58, U. N.D., 1965-66; m. James Edgar Low, Aug. 2, 1953 (div.); children—Cameron Lewis, Heidi Lynn, Jennifer McLean. Asst. buyer fabrics Maas Goros., Tampa, Fla., 1950-54; staff writer Cross Winds Mag., Travis AFB, Cal., 1958-62; staff writer, East Grand Forks (Minn.) Record, 1962-65; women's editor Wilmington (N.C.) Star News, 1966-68; copy editor Charlotte (N.C.) News, 1968—, homemaking editor, 1968—. Treas., Cardiac Rehab. Program, Charlotte, 1973—; active Daus. Penelope mental health clinic project, 1971-73. Recipient Food Writing award, Golden Carnation award, 1971, 73, Burlington House award, 1974. Mem. N.C. Press Women (sec. 1971-72, 1st v.p. 1973—, pres. 1974; awards 1973), Nat. Soc. Interior Designers, Women in Communications. Author: No Rank to Speak Of, 1965. Home: 3501 Donovan Pl Charlotte NC 28215 Office: 600 S Tryon St Charlotte NC 28201

LOWE, BETTY ANN, physician; b. Grapevine, Tex., Mar. 23, 1934; d. J. John Willis and Wimnie (Mercer) Lowe; B.S., U. Ark., 1953, M.D., 1956. Intern U. Ark. Med. Center, Little Rock, 1956-57, chief resident, instr., 1960-61; resident pediatrics Children's Med. Center, Boston, 1957-59; practice medicine specializing in pediatrics So. Clinic, Texarkana, Ark., 1962—; mem. staff Wadley, St. Michael's hosps.; asso. clin. prof. pediatrics U. Ark. Sch. Medicine, 1964—. Pres. Bi-State Health Planning Bd., Texarkana, 1971—; mem. adv. bd. Vocational Nursing Sch., Texarkana Jr. Coll., 1969—, area rep. Ark. Regional Med. Program, mem. cancer program. Valedictorian U. Ark. Sch. Medicine, U. Ark. Class 1956, recipient Roberts award outstanding student, 1956. Mem. Miller County Med. Soc. (past pres.), Ark. Med. Soc., Alpha Epsilon Delta, Alpha Omega Alpha. Methodist. Club: Junior League. Home: 2001 Beech St Texarkana AR 75501 Office: Southern Clinic Texarkana TX 75501

LOWE, DARLINE B. MASONHOLDER (MRS. GEORGE RALPH LOWE), oil co. exec.; b. Columbus Junction, Ia., Aug. 11, 1917; d. Guy and Elizabeth (Ross) Masonholder; grad. high sch.; m. George Ralph Lowe, Jr., Aug. 19, 1935; children—George Ralph III, Gregory Paul, David Jon. Sec. Lowe Oil Co., Clinton, Mo., 1956—; also dir.; dir. Champion Oil Co., Clinton. Democrat. Presbyn. Clubs: Jefferson Women's, Clinton Country, Lowe Country. Home: 510 Price Lane Clinton MO 64735 Office: Lowe Oil Bldg Clinton MO 64735

LOWE, ERIS LYNETTE CHAPIN (MRS. HAROLD WARD LOWE), artists rep.; b. Willow Springs, Mo., Feb. 26, 1924; d. John Fenton and Mariwill (Campbell) Chapin; student S.W. Mo. State U., 1942-43, R.I. State U., 1946-47; B.A. in Edn. cum laude, Wichita State U., 1949; postgrad. (Teaching fellow), E. Tex. State U., 1970; m. Harold Ward Lowe, Apr. 22, 1946; 1 son, Harold Chapin. Tchr. English, Arlington (Tex.) Sr. High Sch., 1955-56; tchr. govt. Greenville (Tex.) Sr. High Sch., 1968-69, 71-72; instr. polit. sci. E. Tex. State U., 1968-72; rep. community concerts Columbia Artists Mgmt., Inc., N.Y.C., 1972—. Sec., Greenville (Tex.) YMCA, 1971-72, youth sponsor, 1968-72. Pres., Arlington Republican Women, 1958, Garland Rep. Women, 1960-62, Hunt County Rep. Women, 1965-66; mem. City Council Greenville, 1970-73, mayor pro tem, 1972-73. Greenville City Council rep. N. Central Tex. Council Govts., 1971-73. Dir. Arlington Community Concerts, 1954-58, Garland Community Concerts, 1958-62, Greenville Community Concerts, 1965-73. Served with WAVES, 1945-46. Mem. Am. Assn. U. Women, Kappa Delta Pi, Pi Sigma Alpha. Episcopalian (treas. 1966-68). Clubs: Story Leagues (Arlington, Garland); Grand Prairie (Tex.) Study. Home: 7730 Meadow Park Dr Dallas TX 75230 Office: 165 W 57th St New York City NY 10019

LOWE, ETHEL BLACK, artist; b. Kiowa County, Okla., Jan. 30, 1904; d. Benjamin Alonzo and Harriet Ann (Heaton) Black; B.A., Central State U., Okla., 1926; M.A., U. Tulsa, 1937; postgrad. U. Okla., U. Colo., Columbia, U. Hawaii; m. William Glenn Lowe, June 5, 1939 (dec. 1942). Tchr. pub. schs., Okla., 1922-39, N.Y., 1942-49, 50-68, ret.; teaching prin. Dragon Sch., Sasebo, Kyushu, Japan, 1949-50; works exhibited 1945—; exhbns. include Nat. Assn. Women Artists, 1953, 55, 71 Terry Nat. Art Exhibit, 1952, Provincetown Art Assn., 1952-53, Nassau Community Coll., 1971. Reproductions of works in newspapers, mags. Mem. N.Y. State Ret. Tchrs. Assn., Nat. Assn. Women Artists, Am. Watercolor Soc., Nat. Ret. Tchrs. Assn., Delta Kappa Gamma. Home: 48-50 44th St Woodside NY 11377

LOWE, FLORENCE SEGAL, public relations exec.; b. N.Y.C.; d. Samuel I. and Rose (Cantor) Segal; B.S. in Edn., U. Pa., 1932, postgrad., 1933-34; grad. Phila. Sch. Social Service, 1935; m. Herman A. Lowe, June 27, 1935 (dec. 1961); children—Lesley (Mrs. Fred Israel), Roger. Guidance counselor Phila. pub. schs., 1931-41; Washington corr. Variety mag. and Daily Variety, 1942-58, Phila. Daily News, 1955-58, Manchester (N.H.) Union Leader, 1952-58, TV Guide, 1955-57; pub. relations dir. radio sta. WIP, Phila., 1958-60, Worldwide Broadcasting Co., 1960-61; dir. spl. projects Metromedia, Inc., 1961-70; spl. asst. to chmn. Nat. Endowment for Arts, Washington, 1970—. Mem. pub. relations adv. com. Nat. Symphony, 1948-52; mem. Sec. State Commn. Travel, 1970-71. Recipient citations for war work, 1946, Army entertainment work, 1958. Mem. Am. Women in Radio and TV (pres. Washington 1954-56), Washington Press Club (v.p. 1958), Am. Newspaper Women's Club (v.p. 1963), Am. Acad. TV Arts and Scis. (v.p. D.C. 1969), Govt. Information Officers Assn. Home: 2727 29th St NW Washington DC 20008 Office: Nat Endowment for Arts Washington DC 20506

LOWE, JUDITH MARY RULE (MRS. RICHARD K. LOWE), assn. exec., interior decorator; b. Columbus, O., Jan. 11, 1938; d. Elmer Allen and Juanita Margaret (Hoff) Rule; B.A., Ohio State U., 1960; m. Richard K. Lowe, Apr. 9, 1960; children—Anita Lynne, Amy Lois, Alison Lizabeth. Exec. office mgr. Beechwold Med. Center, Columbus, 1960-68; freelance interior decorator, 1968—; exec. sec. Central Ohio Acad. Family Physicians, 1964—. Cons. trade and indsl. edn. com. on med. assisting Ohio State U., 1973-74. Cons.

Ohio council Girl Scouts, 1973-74; v.p. Worthington Resource Center, 1973-74; docent Orange Johnson House, Worthington, 1970-73, Columbus Gallery Fine Arts, 1973. Area mgr. city council Republican candidate, Worthington, 1973. Trustee Central Ohio Diabetic Assn. Mem. Am. Assn. Med. Assts. (Ohio pres. 1972-73), Am. Assn. Med. Soc. Execs., Am. Heritage Soc., Ohio, Worthington (pres. 1971-73) hist. socs., Women's Aux. Central Ohio Diabetic Assn. (sec. 1973). Club: Little Turtle Country (Columbus). Cons. editor Quick Drug Reference, for para-med. personnel, 1968-70. Address: 285 Medick Way Worthington OH 43085

LOWE, MARGARET ANNE POWELL (MRS. JERE WHITSON LOWE), assn. exec.; b. Nashville, May 24, 1923; d. Ferdinand and Margaret (Hayes) Powell; A.B., Bernard Coll., 1946; m. Jere Whitson Lowe, Sept. 17, 1954; children—Jere Whitson, John Powell. Chmn. Putnam County Library Bd., Cookeville, Tenn., 1961—. Mem. Woman's Aux. Tenn. Med. Assn. (pres. 1973—), Library Trustees of Tenn. (chmn. 1969), Nat. Soc. Colonial Dames Am., Ladies Hermitage Assn.

LOWE, MILDRED, educator, librarian; b. N.Y.C., Apr. 4, 1927; d. Kalman and Frieda (Fuchs) Rabinowitz; B.A., Bklyn. Coll., 1960; M.L.S., Pratt Inst., 1965; D.L.S., Columbia, 1972; m. Rubin Lowe, June 16, 1946; children—Carl, Stefanie, Allen. Mus. dir. Community Theatre, Massapequa, N.Y., 1950-65; govt. documents and serials librarian State U. N.Y. at Farmingdale, 1965-68; mem. faculty St. John's U., Jamaica, N.Y., 1969—, asst. prof. library sci., 1973—. Democratic committeewoman Nassau County, N.Y., 1969—. Fellow Higher Edn. Act Title IIB, 1968-71. Mem. Am., N.Y. State (chmn. legislative com., library educators sect. 1972—), Nassau County library assns., N.Y. Library Club (exec. council 1970-71), Beta Phi Mu. Home: 120 Glengariff Rd Massapequa Park NY 11762 Office: Dept Library Sci St John's Univ Jamaica NY 11439

LOWE, PHYLLIS KINNISON (MRS. RUPERT PAUL LOWE), educator; b. Higbee, Mo., Apr. 26, 1919; d. Elerd and Grace Ethel (Houtz) Baker; B.S., U. Mo., 1941, M.S., 1950; Ph.D., U. Ill., 1960; m. Roy William Kinnison, Oct. 26, 1941 (dec.); children—Patricia Ann (Mrs. James Robert Fletcher), Shirley Kay (Mrs. Robert Dean Hunt II); m. 2d, Rupert Paul Lowe, Jan. 24, 1958. Tchr. vocational home econs. Winona (Mo.) High Sch., 1941, Birch Tree (Mo.) High Sch., 1941-42, Keytesville (Mo.) High Sch., 1946; supervising tchr. vocational home econs. Salisbury High Sch. and U. Mo., 1946-48, Higginsville High Sch. and U. Mo., 1948-50, King City High Sch. and N.W. Mo. U., 1952-53; dir. research home econs. edn. Colo. State U., 1960; vis. prof. home econs. edn. Wichita State U., 1965, U. Alaska, 1966, Wis. State U., Stevens Point, 1966; prof., researcher Purdue U., West Lafayette, Ind., 1953—; chief cost accountant for U.S. Army; test item writer Ednl. Testing Service, Princeton, N.J.; cons. div. vocational and tech. edn., field reader Bur. Research, U.S. Office Edn. Mem. Am. Ednl. Research Assn., Am. (past v.p. operations, com. chmn., award for outstanding service), Ind. (past pres., com. chmn., councilor) home econs. assns., Am. Vocational Assn. (chmn. home econs. edn. grad. fellowship 1961-65, chmn. home econs. edn. grad. awards 1966-70), Am. Vocational Edn. Research Assn., Assn. for Student Teaching, Assn. for Tchr. Educators, Assn. for Supervision and Curriculum Devel., Nat. Assn. Home Econs. Tchr. Educators, Ind. Assn. for Supervision and Curriculum Devel., Ind. Vocational Home Econs. Tchrs. Assn. (past com. chmn., mem. exec. bd.), Ind. Unit Assn. for Student Teaching, Ind. Vocational and Practical Arts Assn. (mem. exec. bd.), Nat. Council Family Relations, Delta Kappa Gamma, Omicron Nu, Kappa Delta Pi. Contbr. articles profl. jours. Home: 1937 Indian Trail Dr West Lafayette IN 47906

LOWENSTEIN, LEAH MIRIAM HILLER (MRS. JOHN LOWENSTEIN), physician, educator; b. Milw., June 17, 1930; d. Abraham and Sarah (Lucoff) Hiller; B.S., U. Wis., 1950, M.D., 1954; D.Phil., Oxford (Eng.) U., 1958, postgrad. anatomy, 1955-58; m. John M. Lowenstein, Oct. 20, 1926; children—Charles, Andrew, Mark. Intern, U. Wis. Hosps., 1954-55; research asso. dept. anatomy Oxford U., 1955-58; instr. medicine Tufts U. Sch. Medicine, 1961-64; research asso. Harvard Med. Sch., 1964-65, asst. in medicine, 1965-68, asso. medicine, 1969-70, med. dir. alcohol research unit dept. psychiatry, 1967-70; asst. prof. medicine Boston U. Sch. Medicine, 1968-71, asso. prof., 1971—, asso. prof. biochemistry, 1971—, acting dean women Sch. Med., 1973; vis. renal cons. VA Hosp., Boston, 1964—. Mem. rev. com. artificial kidney-chronic uremia program NIH. USPHS grantee, 1963—; NIH Spl. fellow, 1966-67; Mass. Heart Assn. grantee, 1968-69. Mem. Soc. for Exptl. Biology (Eng.), Royal Soc. Medicine (Eng.), Am. Fedn. for Clin. Research, Am. Assn. for Study Liver Disease, A.C.P., Tissue Culture Assn., Mass. Med. Soc., Am. Soc. Nephrology, Nat. Kidney Found., Am. Physiol. Soc., Council in Kidney in Cardiovascular Disease, Am. Heart Assn., A.A.A.S. (com. on med. sci.), Am. Med. Women's Assn. (pres. New Eng. br.), Am. Med. Soc. on Alcoholism, Salt and Water Club, Internat. Soc. Nephrology. Contbr. articles to tech. jours. Home: 170 Cliff Rd Wellesley Hills MA 02181 Office: Boston U Sch Medicine 80 E Concord St Boston MA 02118

LOWENTHAL, RUTH MARIE HUEFTLE (MRS. ALFRED LOWENTHAL, JR.), coll. librarian; b. Wichita, Kan., Apr. 17, 1923; d. Albert Frederick and B. Magdalene (Ebel) Hueftle; B.A., Fort Hays Kan. State Coll., 1945; B.S. in L.S., U. Ill., 1946; postgrad. U. Kan., 1969; m. Alfred Lowenthal, Jr., Aug. 1, 1946; children—Deborah (Mrs. Ronald Russell Teeter), Richard Mark, David Alfred, Jeffrey Dean. Asst. librarian Fort Hays State Coll., Hays, Kan., 1946-49, cons., cataloger Oakley (Kan.) Pub. Library, 1951-53; dir. library services Colby (Kan.) Community Coll., 1966—. Editor, pub. dir. Western Plains Heritage Publs., Colby, 1970—. Neighborhood chmn. Girl Scouts U.S.A., Oakley, 1960-64, dir. Day Camp, 1962-63. Mem. Fedn. Women's Clubs, Kan. Fedn. Women's Clubs, Am., Kan., Mountain Plains, Thomas County libraries assns., Kan. Assn. Pub. Community Jr. Colls., Am. Assn. U. Women. Methodist. Clubs: Shakespeare (Colby); Cameo (Oakley). Home: Route 1 Box 10K Colby KS 67701 Office: 1255 S Range St Colby KS 67701

LOWER, DOROTHY MARGARET, librarian; b. Monroeville, Ind., Feb. 5, 1914; d. Allen Virgil and Cleo (Edwards) Lower; A.B., Western Coll. Women, 1936; M.A., Ind. U., 1960. Mem. staff Fort Wayne (Ind.) Pub. Library, 1957—, head genealogy dept., 1961—. Tchr. genealogy adult edn. dept. extension Purdue U., 1968-69, Fort Wayne pub. schs., 1970-71; lectr. in field. Mem. Ind. Library Assn., D.A.R., Colonial Dames XVII Century, Soc. Indiana Pioneers, Beta Phi Mu. Republican. Presbyn. Home: 802 Three Rivers E Fort Wayne IN 46802 Office: 900 Webster St Fort Wayne IN 46802

LOWERY, PEARL VIRGINIA, ret. educator, author, civic worker; b. Parkersburg, W.Va., Dec. 9, 1897; d. Artley Elmer and Ella V. (Howard) Caskey; grad. Savage Sch. Phys. Edn., 1918; B.S., Tchrs. Coll., Columbia U., 1943, M.A., 1947; postgrad. (fellow) N.Y.U.; m. Thomas J. Lowery, June 22, 1921. Tchr., Mt. Vernon (N.Y.) High Sch., 1918-68; editor N.Y. State Bus. and Profl. Woman. Mem. Layman's Nat. Traffic Com., 1959-74; disaster chmn. local chpt. A.R.C. 1938-41, first aid chmn. 1941-52, chmn. Mt. Vernon, 1969-70; mem. N.Y. State Women's Council, Dept. Commerce, 1960-64; active Girl Scouts U.S.A.; mem. Community Narcotic Study Commn., 1968-72. Recipient Nat. Pub. Affairs award Bus. and Profl. Women's Clubs, 1950; named Distinguished Bus. Woman of Yr., C. of C., 1969; named Community Leader, 1969. Mem. Am. Assn. U. Women, Am. Acad. Polit. and Social Sci., N.E.A., Nat. Women's Party, League Women Voters, Fedn. Women's Clubs, Republican Clubs, Fedn. Bus. and Profl. Women's Clubs (N.Y. pres. 1958-60, mem. nat. bd. 1958-60), Internat. Council Women, Internat. Platform Assn., Ret. Tchrs. Club (pres. area 1970-74), Falls Village Hist. Soc. Home: 300 Hayward Av Mount Vernon NY 10552 also 34 and 58 Pine Grove Falls Village CT 06031

LOWMAN, LUELLA HEAD (MRS. EUGENE SLIPHER LOWMAN), civic worker; b. Sheridan, Wyo.; d. Clinton Milo and Beulah (Bateman) Head; B.A. cum laude, U. Mont., 1937; M.S., Purdue U., 1961; m. Eugene Slipher Lowman, Sept. 19, 1940; children—Clark Eugene, Carol (Mrs. Charles Russell Grimes). Office worker U.S. Forest Service, Missoula, Mont., 1937-40, Cummins Engine Co., Columbus, Ind., 1941, U.S. Dept. Agr., Washington, 1942; tech. editor research reports Purdue U. Sch. Elec. Engring., Lafayette, Ind., 1964-66; part-time tchr. Tippecanoe County Sch. Corp., Lafayette, 1970-71. Cons. report writing Midwest Applied Sci. Co., Purdue Research Park, Lafayette, 1968. Mem. Mortar Bd., Kappa Delta Pi, Alpha Chi Omega, Kappa Kappa Kappa. Republican. Presbyn. Clubs: Lafayette Country, Edwood Glen Country. Home: 3518 Woodcliff Dr Lafayette IN 47905

LOWMAN, MARY BETHENA HEMPHILL (MRS. ZELVIN D. LOWMAN), educator, civic worker; b. Lewis, Kan., Feb. 10, 1922; d. Frederick William and Gladys (Follin) Hemphill; A.B., Western State Coll., Colo., 1945; m. Zelvin D. Lowman, Oct. 24, 1943; children—Freda Ruth (Mrs. Douglas Farr), James Fredrick, William Martin, Elizabeth June (Mrs. Joseph Herbst). Tchr., Stout Creek Sch., Colo., 1942-43, San Diego City Sch. Dist., 1944-45, Los Angeles City Sch. Dist., 1948-50; pvt. sch. tchr. So. Inst. Music, 1956-57. Troop leader Frontier council Girl Scouts U.S.A., 1957-70, mem. exec. bd., 1961-73, 2d v.p., 1962-63, pres., 1968-71, recipient Thanks Badge, 1964, chmn. established camp com., 1963-67, dir. Camp Foxtail, 1965, 67, mem. Girl Scouts U.S.A. Region VI Com., 1973—. Mem. Am. Field Service Exchange Student Bd. So. Nev., 1961. Parliamentarian, West Chartleston P.T.A., 1957-59, Nev. Congress, 1960-61; chmn. Christian Edn. Commn., 1964-65; chmn. Commn. on Mission of Church, 1966; chmn. exec. com. Clark County Bicentennial Commn., 1974—. Family chosen as Nev. All-Am. Family, 1960. Mem. Gen. Fedn. Women's Club (dir. 1958-60, 62-64, 72—, treas. Western States Conf. 1968-70, sec. 1970-72, pres. 1972—), Nev. (past pres.), Md. (past jr. dir.), fedns. Women's clubs, Clark County Pan-Hellenic Assn., So. Nev. Alumni Club (pres. 1961-62), Internat. Platform Assn. Presbyn. (elder). Club: Las Vegas Mesquite (past pres.); Jr. Women's (past pres.) (College Park, Md.); Newcomers (past pres.), Nat. Presbyterian Mariners; (past pres.), Nevada-Sierra District Mariners; Las Vegas Nautilus Mariners. Home: 1246 Cashman Dr Las Vegas NV 89102

LOWREY, SARA NELLE (MRS. DONALD J. MACKIE), journalist; b. Gatesville, Tex., Oct. 6, 1949; d. Oliver Wendell and Nelle (Goodall) Lowrey; student Spanish, U. of Americas, 1969; B.J. with honors, U. Tex. (Marjorie Derelik scholar 1971), 1971; postgrad. So. Meth. U., 1973—. English editor Novedades de Acapulco, 1971; nat. desk gen. reporter, copy editor Mexico City (Mexico) News, 1971; anchorwoman, reporter sta. KDFW-TV, Dallas, 1972-74, KPRC-TV, Houston, 1974—. Mem. press staff George Bush for Senate Campaign, 1970. Recipient award for edn. coverage Tex. Tchrs. Assn. Mem. Women In Communications, Common Cause, Mortar Bd., Kappa Tau Alpha, Alpha Lambda Delta, Sigma Delta Chi, Chi Omega. Presbyn. Home: 167 Litchfield Lane Houston TX 77024 Office: PO Box 2222 Houston TX 76127

LOWREY, SUSAN MARY, occupational therapist; b. Oak Park, Ill., Feb. 12, 1944; d. Joseph Ralph and Florence Marie (Byrne) Lowrey; B.S., Mt. Mary Coll., Milw., 1966. Staff therapist Rehab. Inst., Chgo., 1967-70; cons. rehab. in occupational therapy Royal Ryde Homes, Sydney, Australia, 1971; supr. rehab., asst. dir. occupational therapy Mercy Hosp. and Med. Center, Chgo., 1972—. Mem. Am., Ill. (recruitment chmn. 1968-70) occupational therapy assns., Allied Health Profession of Arthritis Found., Pi Theta Epsilon, Beta Beta Beta. Home: 2052 N Lincoln Park West Chicago IL 60614 Office: Mercy Hosp and Med Center care Occupational Therapy Dept Stevenson Expressway at King Dr Chicago IL 60616

LOWRIE, REBECCA LAWRENCE, civic worker; b. Galesburg, Ill., Dec. 14, 1891; d. George Appleton and Ella (Park) L; A.B., Vassar Coll., 1913; A.M., Radcliffe Coll., 1915; m. John Marshall Lowrie, Dec. 19, 1916. Advt. copy writer Macmillan Co., 1917, later editorial reader; editorial reader Harper and Brothers, 1918-31; caption writer Yale Picture Chronicles of America; book reviewer New Yorker mag., 1928-29; reader for Book of Month Club, 1931-43. Editor, Vassar Alumnae Quar., 2 yrs. Mem. Chgo. Orchestral Assn. Clubs: Cosmopolitan (N.Y.C.); Arts (Chgo.) Friday Casino. Author: Cambric Tea, 1928. Editor: Children's Vol., Harper's History of the World War, 1919. Contbr. revs. to Saturday Rev. Lit. Home: 1255 N State Pkwy Chicago IL 60610

LOWRY, BARBARA SAWYER (MRS. JOHN BLANCHARD LOWRY, JR.), pathologist; b. Phila., Mar. 31, 1924; d. Warren Everett and Mabel Helen (Petersen) Sawyer; A.B. cum laude, Bryn Mawr Coll., 1946; M.D., Temple U., 1954; m. John Blanchard Lowry, Jr., Sept. 15, 1956; children—Arthur Samuel, John Blanchard III, Peter Alfred, Charles Warren. Rotating intern Bryn Mawr (Pa.) Hosp., 1954-55, resident in pathology, 1955-58; chief resident pathology Rochester (N.Y.) Gen. Hosp., 1958-59, asst. attending pathologist, 1959-61, part-time pathologist, 1961, lectr. pathology, 1962-64; cons. pathologist Park Av. Hosp., Rochester, 1959-61; asst. pathologist St. Mary's Hosp., Rochester, 1961; pathologist Monroe County (N.Y.) Med. Examiner's Office, 1961-62, dep. med. examiner, 1962-63; dir. Monroe County (N.Y.) Health Dept. Labs., 1962-63; temporary part-time asso. pathologist The Genesee Hosp., Rochester, 1963-64; asso. pathologist Coatesville (Pa.) Hosp., 1964-70, sec. staff, mem. exec. com., 1969-70; asso. path. Community Meml. Hosp., Jennersville, Pa., 1964-71; pathologist Embreeville (Pa.) State Hosp., 1970-73; dir. labs. VA Hosp., Coatesville, 1973—. Vis. asst. prof. pathology Med. Coll. Pa., 1968—; instr. Jefferson Med. Coll., 1974—. Den mother Cub Scouts Am., Valley Forge, Pa., 1968—, den leader, coach, 1971—. Bd. dirs. Chester County unit Am. Cancer Soc., 1970—. Diplomate Am. Bd. Pathology. Fellow Am. Soc. Clin. Pathologists, Coll. Am. Pathologists; mem. Internat. Acad. Pathology, Assn. Clin. Scientists, Am. Med. Women's Assn., Valley Forge Hist. Soc., Am. Assn. U. Women, N.Y. Acad. Scis., Temple U. Med. Alumni Assn. (dir. 1970—). Mem. Soc. of Friends. Home: Jug Hollow Rd Valley Forge PA 19481 Office: VA Hospital Coatesville PA 19320

LOWRY, BERNICE GERTRUDE, occupational therapist; b. nr. Philadelphia, Miss., Apr. 3, 1922; d. Riley Wilburn and Junie (Rucker) Lowry; B.S. in Elementary Edn., Miss. State U., 1952; postgrad. Hunter Coll., 1952; M.A. in Spl. Edn. (Jackson Central Lions Club scholar), George Peabody Coll., 1960; certificate occupational therapy Washington U., St. Louis, 1962. Tchr., Miss. Pub. Schs., 1943-51, Miss. Sch. for Blind, Jackson, 1951-53, Jackson Pub. Schs., 1953-58; instr. McNeese State Coll., Lake Charles, La., 1958-60; dir. occupational therapy Univ. Med. Center, Jackson, 1962—. Mem. Nat., Miss. (del. to conv. 1953, pres. spl. edn. sect. 1957-58), edn. assns., Capital Bus. and Profl. Women (v.p. Jackson chpt. 1966-67), Am., Ala.-Miss. (del. to nat. conv. 1965-71, v.p. 1971—) occupational therapy assns., Am. Assn. U. Women, Council for Exceptional Children. Baptist. Home: 217 Wacaster St Jackson MS 39209 Office: 2500 N State St Jackson MS 39216

LOWRY, BETTY (MRS. RITCHIE P. LOWRY), writer; b. Hollywood, Cal., July 24, 1927; d. Hans and Emily Paula (Doerges) Trishman; A.B., U. Cal. at Berkeley, 1948; m. Ritchie P. Lowry, Sept. 5, 1948; children—Peter Ritchie, Robin Emily. Copy chiefs account exec. Abbott Kimball Co., San Francisco, 1948-50; dir. young homemaker div. Jackson's Furniture Co., Oakland, Cal., 1950-52; columnist Family Travel, N.Y.C., 1968-73; free lance writer, 1946—. Pres. Family Service League, Chico, Cal., 1963; mem. Cal. Home Soc., Chico, 1957-64; mem. steering com. Hospitality and Information Service, Washington, 1964-66; chmn. Joint Ednl. Policies Com., Wayland, Mass., 1970-71. Bd. dir. Jr. Mus., 1962-64. Recipient award Chico C. of C., 1961; 1st pl. nat. poetry award Am. Assn. U. Women, 1964. Mem. Nat. League Am. Pen Women (chpt. pres. 1970-72), New Eng. Poetry Club, Women In Communications, Inc. Democrat. Home: 79 Moore Rd Wayland MA 01778

LOWRY, MRS. EDWARD G. (RUTH DRIVER LOWRY), civic and social worker; b. Phila., Sept. 17, 1905; d. William R. and Mary (Swift) Driver; A.B., Vassar Coll., 1926; postgrad. Oxford U., 1927-28; m. Edward C. Lowry, Jr., Aug. 23, 1928; children—Ruth (Mrs. Anthony Arnold), Edward G. III. Pres. women's bd. Kernan Hosp. for Crippled Children, Balt., 1940-41; pres. Jr. League of Balt., 1942-43; exec. com. Pleasant Hill Red Cross Aux., 1941-43; bd. mem. Travelers Aid Soc. Balt., 1938-43, bd. Women's Hosp., 1943. Bd. dirs. Bellevue and Mills Schs. of Nursing, 1945-69, 2d v.p., mgrs., 1953-61; bd. dirs. Recreation Service for Children of Bellevue, N.Y.C., 1949-61, adv. com., 1961—; mem. bd. Judson Health Center and Social Service Aux. Bellevue, 1944-50; mem. nursing adv. council Dept. Hosps., N.Y.C., 1960-61; mem. Bellevue Nursing Com., Inc., 1969-75; corp. mem. MacDowell Colony. Mem. Phi Beta Kappa. Episcopalian. Clubs: Colony; Chilton (Boston). Home: Brookwood Sand Hill Rd Peterborough NH 03458

LOWRY, (ELIZABETH) JEAN, geologist, educator; b. Indpls., Feb. 7, 1921; d. Ellsworth and Ethel (Stryker) Lowry; B.S. in Geology, Pa. State U., 1942; Ph.D. in Structural Geology, Yale, 1951. Jr. economist OPA, Washington, 1942-43; cons. Bd. Econ. Welfare, Washington, 1943; jr. geologist groundwater div. U.S. Geol. Survey, New Haven, Conn., 1943-45, asst. geologist, 1945-49; field geologist Tenn. Div. Geology, Erwin, 1947, 48; dist. geologist for S.W., Va. Geol. Survey, Wytheville, 1949-57; asst. prof. East Carolina U., Greenville, N.C., 1958-65, prof., 1965—; vis. prof. Universidad de Concepcion, Concepcion, Chile, 1962-63. Mem. Pitt County (N.C.) Biracial Com., 1961. Mem. Geol. Soc. Am., Nat. Assn. Geology Tchrs., Carolina Geol. Soc., N.C. Acad. Sci., War Resisters League, League of Women Voters, Am. Civil Liberties Union (chmn. chpt. 1973—), Sigma Xi. Democrat. Unitarian-Universalist. Contbr. articles to profl. jours. Home: 211 S Eastern St Greenville NC 27834

LOWRY, LAURA MAY (MRS. DAVID WILLIAM LOWRY), educator; b. Lewiston, Ida., May 8, 1928; d. Fred Donald and Lillian Pearl (McGee) Coon; B.A., U. Ida., 1950, M.S., 1969; m. David William Lowry, Jan. 30, 1948; children—William David, Mark Steven. Tchr. English Rogue River (Ore.) High Sch., 1951-52; substitute tchr. jr. and sr. high sch., Ketchikan, Alaska, 1955-56; tchr. English, history Lapwai (Ida.) High Sch., 1964-66; remedial reading tchr. Lapwai pub. schs., 1966-69; dir. Early Edn. Project for Handicapped Children North Central Ida., 1970-71. Mem. Citizen's Adv. com. Upward Bound, U. Ida., 1965-72; chmn. Lewis County com. Fund for the Performing Arts Center, U. Ida., 1967-69. Trustee Lewis County Library, 1961-72, chmn., 1961-64, 66-68, 71-72. Mem. Council for Exceptional Children (sec. br. 1972-74). Home: Route 2 Box 13 Craigmont ID 83523

LOWRY, LORETTA ANN (MRS. GLEN CLINTON LOWRY), realtor; b. Beloit, Kan., Oct. 24, 1913; d. Charles Edward and Frances (Spannan) Rasher; grad. Am. Inst. Banking, 1941; student San Bernardino Valley Coll., 1965; m. Glen Clinton Lowry, Feb. 20, 1946 (dec. Feb. 1973); children—Nancy Ann (Mrs. Ronald Thomas Newcome), Elizabeth Jane (Mrs. Thomas King Krupka). Asst. cashier First Nat. Bank, Beloit, 1943-46; co-owner, partner Lowry Real Estate & Ins., Beloit, 1946-62; co-owner, Lowry Real Estate, Calimesa, Cal., 1962—. Riverside County registrar voters, 1965-70; mem. Citizens Com. for New Gen. Plan for Riverside County, Residential and Comml., 1970-73; troop leader Girl Scouts U.S.A., Beloit, 1951-60. Mem. Nat. Assn. Real Estate Bds., Am. Assn. Ret. Persons, Am. Field Service Assn., V.F.W. Aux., Cath. Daus. Am., Bus. and Profl. Women's Club, Cal. Real Estate Assn., Sons and Daus. Soddies, Yucapia Valley Bd. Realtors (treas. 1966), Calimesa C. of C. (dir. 1965-71), Cal. Assn. Ind. Businessmen, Redlands Yucaipa Hort. Soc. Republican. Clubs: Soroptimist (charter), Yucaipa Women's. Home: 208 Summit View Dr Calimesa CA 92320 Office: 543 W County Line Rd Calimesa CA 92320

LOWTHER, BARBARA ALLEN PHILLIPS DOTY (MRS. HARRY A. LOWTHER), coll. pres., psychologist; b. Pittsfield, Mass., Dec. 23, 1933; d. Webb R. and Mrytle (Garcelon) Phillips; student U. Ark., 1951-54, Kent State U., 1957-58; B.A., Case-Western Res. U., 1956, Ph.D., 1963; m. Larry A. Doty, Feb. 10, 1960; children—Raymond, Mark; m. 2d, Harry A. Lowther, Jan. 21, 1972. Tchr., Council for Retarded Child, Cleve., 1956-57; social worker Cuyahoga County Dept. Pub. Assistance, Cleve., 1957-58; clin. intern Cuyahoga State Mental Hosp., Cuyahoga Falls, O., 1958-59; instr., asst. prof. psychology North Central Coll., Naperville, Ill., 1961-66, asso. prof., 1967-73; pres. Lincoln State U., Lombard, Ill., 1973—. Cons. Geriatric Research Unit, Chgo. Med. Sch., 1967-72. Exec. dir. Career Inst., North Central Coll., 1971-73; pres. Phillips Research Found., 1972-73. Trustee Inst. Ednl. Devel. USPHS predoctoral fellow, 1959-62; NSF grantee, 1963-70, U.S. Office Edn. Research grantee, 1968-69, 71—, U.S. Office Edn. postdoctoral fellow, 1969-70. Mem. A.A.A.S., Internat. Gerontological Soc., Midwestern Psychol. Assn., Am. Ednl. Research Assn. Contbr. articles to profl. jours. Home: Route 1 Sheridan IL 60551 Office: Lincoln State Univ Lombard IL 60540

LOYD, CORINNE ELIZABETH, art center exec.; b. Leominster, Mass., Oct. 27, 1924; d. Oliver Lamont and Ethel Angela (Stratton) Hiltz; student Cleve. Inst. Art, 1962-63, Ashtabula Arts Center, 1960-70; m. Hobart Claude Loyd, Oct. 20, 1945; children—Jacqueline (Mrs. Robert Lehto), Nancy (Mrs. Patric Huffman), Joanne (Mrs. Harry Knapp), Cynthia (Mrs. Michael Luc), Douglas. Operator, Leominster Telephone Co., 1942; clk. Dupont de Nemours, Leominster, 1943, City Leominster, 1944-47; clk., sec. Ashtabula (O.) Arts Center, 1956-59, acting dir., 1960-62, asso. dir., 1963-68, dir., 1969—, instr. ceramics, 1964-68. Nurse's aid A.R.C., Leominster, 1943-45; room mother, hospitality com. P.T.A., 1952, membership com., 1953; leader Girl Scouts U.S.A., 1954-57; den mother Boy Scouts Am., 1965-66; mem. League Women Voters. Mem. Am. Fedn. Mus., Women's Service League Ashtabula County.

Lutheran (pres. ch. women's assn. 1961-62). Home: 4114 Fargo Dr Ashtabula OH 44004 Office: 2928 W 13th St Ashtabula OH 44004

LOYD, MARY LOUISE (MRS. EMORY W. LOYD), library ofcl.; b. Hereford, Tex., June 27, 1916; d. Roland and Bessie May (Berry) Loyd; B.A., McMurry Coll., 1939; student W. Tex. State Coll., 1933-34; m. Emory William Loyd, Sept. 17, 1945; children—Roger Leroy, Douglas Emory, Robert Clark, Richard Dean. Tchr. pub. schs. Deaf Smith County, Tex., 1934-35, 36-38, Vega, Tex., 39-43, Haskell, Tex., 1945; ednl. dir. Wesley Meth. Ch., Borger, Tex., 1958-64; sec. Pleasant Valley Meth. Ch., Amarillo, 1964-66; reference asst. Amarillo Pub. Library, 1966-67, dir. group services, 1967—. Mem. A.L.A., Tex. Library Assn. Methodist. Home: 7110 Bluebonnet St Amarillo TX 79108 Office: 1000 S Polk St Amarillo TX 79101

LUBBERS, SHIRLEY A., social worker; b. Allegan County, Mich., Feb. 16, 1931; d. Edward G. and Mary (DeKleine) Lubbers; B.A. in Edn., Calvin Coll., 1955; M.S.W., U. Mich., 1958. Child welfare case aide Bethany Christian Home, Grand Rapids, Mich., 1955-56; chief probation officer juvenile div. Allegan County Probate Ct., Allegan, Mich., 1958-61, county juvenile officer, dir., juvenile div., 1961—. Mem. Allegan County Interagy. Com. on Mental Retardation, 1967—; mem. exec. com. Mental Health Com. for Allegan County, 1968-70; mem. program com. 4th and 5th Ann. Youth-Detention Home Seminars, 1967, 68; mem. organizational com. Allegan County Resource Devel. Com., 1965, Allegan County Planned Parenthood, 1969; mem. Community Mental Health Services Bd. Allegan County, 1970—, sec., 1974—; exec. com. sec.-treas. Allegan County Resource Devel. Com., 1968—; mem. S.W. Regional Mental Health Com., 1971. Bd. dirs. Family Planning Allegan County, 1968-71, Children's Charter Cts. Mich., 1968-71. Mem. Nat. Assn. Social Workers, Nat. Council on Crime and Delinquency, Mich. Assn. County Juvenile Officers (rep. to Mich. Council on Children and Youth 1971—), Mich. Assn. Children's Agys., Mich. Juvenile Ct. Officers Assn. (treas. 1964-65, corr. sec. 1965-66, v.p., conv. chmn. 1966-67, pres. 1967-68), Allegan Bus. and Profl. Women's Club (rec. sec. 1965-67, 2d v.p. 1967-68, pres. 1968-70), Internat. Platform Assn. Mem. Christian Ref. Ch. (mem. Evangelism com. 1973—). Home: Route 3 Holland MI 49423 Office: County Bldg Allegan MI 49010

LUBETSKI, EDITH ESTHER SLOMOWITZ, librarian; b. Bklyn., July 16, 1940; d. David and Leah (Aronson) Slomowitz; B.A., Bklyn. Coll., 1962; M.S., Columbia, 1965; M.A., Yeshiva U., 1968; m. Meir Lubetski, Dec. 23, 1968; children—Shaul, Uriel. Librarian, Stern Coll. for Women Library, N.Y.C., 1965—. Cons. Lawrence White Meml. Library, Bklyn., 1970-72, Social Responsibilities Round Table of A.L.A., 1972-73; chmn. Core Com. on Jewish-Am. Materials, 1972-73. Mem. A.L.A., Assn. Jewish Libraries (sec. 1967-68). Author: Writings on Jewish History: An Annotated Bibliography, 1971. Home: 1219 E 27th St Brooklyn NY 11210 Office: 245 Lexington Av New York City NY 10016

LUBIN, YOLAN JULIA SCHWARTZ (MRS. ARTHUR LUBIN), artist; b. N.Y.C.; d. Leopold and Luiza (Ungar) Schwartz; student Beaux Arts Inst., 1938-40, Nat. Acad., 1941-49, Art Students League, 1949-51; m. Arthur Lubin, Dec. 8, 1929 (dec. Mar. 1948). One-man show at Doyn Kottler Galley, 1957; exhibited in group shows, 1958—, including Kottler Gallery, Artists Equity, Riverside Mus., Jewish Club; represented in pvt. collections. Cons. and therapist Bronx VA Hosp.; dir. sculpturing sch. Kittay House. Organizer, pres. Cosmopolitan chpt. Am. Jewish Congress, 1954-58, chmn. div. Jewish affairs and edn., 1959-63. Recipient sculpture medal N.A.D., 1949. Mem. Artists Equity Assn., Hunterdon County Art Center, Hadassah. Mem. B'nai B'rith. Home: 2550 Webb Av Bronx NY 10468 Office: 893 Irvine St Bronx NY 10474

LUBKIN, GLORIA BECKER, physicist, editor; b. Phila., May 16, 1933; d. Samuel Albert and Anne (Gorrin) Becker; A.B. in Physics (univ. scholar), Temple U., 1953; M.A. in Physics, Boston U., 1957; m. Yale Jay Lubkin, June 14, 1953 (div. Apr. 1968); children—David Craig, Sharon Rebecca. Grad. teaching fellow Boston U., 1953-54; mathematician Fairchild Stratos Corp., Hagerstown, Md., 1954, Letterkenny Ordnance Depot, Chambersburg, Pa., 1955-56; physicist Control Data Corp., Syosset, N.Y., 1956-58; acting chmn. physics dept. Sarah Lawrence Coll., Bronxville, N.Y., 1961-62; v.p. Lubkin Assos., Port Washington, N.Y., 1962-68; asso. editor Physics Today, N.Y.C., 1963-69, sr. editor, 1970—. Cons. Center for History and Philosophy of Physics, Am. Inst. Physics, 1966-67. Fellow Am. Phys. Soc.; mem. N.Y. Acad. Scis., Sigma Pi Sigma. Jewish religion. Mem. B'nai B'rith (chpt. v.p. 1961-62). Author: Smithsonian, 1971; (with others) Reactor Handbook, Vol. 3 Part B, 1962. Contbr. articles to profl. jours. Home: 160 S Middle Neck Rd Great Neck NY 11021 Office: 335 E 45th St New York NY 10017

LUBKIN, VIRGINIA LEILA, physician; b. N.Y.C., Oct. 26, 1914; d. Joseph and Anna (Stern) Lubkin; B.S. summa cum laude, N.Y. U., 1933; M.D., Columbia, 1937; m. Martin Bernstein, Aug. 28, 1949; children—Ellen (Mrs. Bernard Schanzer), James, Roger, John. Intern Harlem Hosp., N.Y.C., 1938-40; asst. resident neurology, Montefiore Hosp., N.Y.C., 1940, in gen. pathology, 1940-41, research fellow ophthalmology, 1941-42; resident ophthalmology King's County Hosp., N.Y.C., 1942-43, Mt. Sinai Hosp., N.Y.C., 1943-44; practice medicine specializing in ophthalmic plastic surgery and psychosomatic ophthalmology, N.Y.C., 1945—; attending ophthalmic surgeon N.Y. Eye and Ear Infirmary, N.Y.C., 1967—, asso. plastic surgeon, 1967—; asst. clin. prof. dept. ophthalmology Sch. Medicine, Mt. Sinai Hosp., 1968—; asso. attending surgeon Beth Israel Hosp., N.Y.C., 1972-74. Vis. prof. U. de San Marcos, Lima, Peru, 1967; mem. O'Dwyer Narcotics Com., 1970-74, Am. Civil Liberties union, Citizens for Clean Air, Common Cause; med. missionary Presbyn. Mission to French Cameroon, 1951. Ophthalmology research fellow Montefiore Hosp., 1941-42. Diplomate Am. Bd. Ophthalmology. Fellow A.C.S.; mem. N.Y. Soc. Clin. Ophthalmology (pres. 1970-71), Am. Acad. Ophthalmology and Otolaryngology (recipient merit award 1966), N.Y. Acad. Medicine, N.Y. Acad. Scis., A.A.A.S., Am. Acad. Facial and Plastic Reconstructive Surgery, Am. Soc. Ophthalmic Plastic Surgeons (charter mem.), Phi Beta Kappa, Alpha Omega Alpha. Jewish religion. First woman resident King's County Hosp.; 1st woman ophthalmology resident Mt. Sinai Hosp. Home: 1 Blackstone Pl Riverdale Bronx NY 10471 Office: 41 Park Av New York City NY 10016

LUBLIN, JOANN SANDRA, journalist; b. Dayton, O., Apr. 8, 1949; d. Irving and Betty Thelma (Friedman) Lublin; B.S., Northwestern U., 1970; M.A., Stanford, 1971; m. Michael A. Pollock, June 4, 1972. Reporter, Wall St. Jour., San Francisco, 1971-73, Chgo., 1973—. Newspaper Fund Reporting Intern scholar, 1969; Nat. Fedn. Press Women scholar, 1970-71. Mem. Nat. Fedn. Press Women, Women In Communications, Sigma Delta Chi, Kappa Tau Alpha. Office: 200 W Monroe St Chicago IL 60606

LUC, NADINE ELEANOR COCHRANE (MRS. JOHN THEODORE LUC), editor; b. Sault Ste. Marie, Mich., July 26, 1922; d. William Samuel and Rose (Plaskett) Cochrane; student pub. schs.; Ph.D. honoris causa, Hamilton State U., 1973; m. Elmer Leo Tobias (div. Dec. 1943); m. 2d, William Edward Villerot, Dec. 29, 1945 (div. May 1964); 1 dau., Sheryl Rose; m. 3d, John Theodore Luc, June 8, 1964 (dec. Mar. 1974); 1 stepson, David Ronald. Coordinator, Family Services, Altus, Okla., 1956-58; soc. editor Altus Times-Democrat, 1958-61; fgn. corr. U.P.I., Halifax Bur., Montreal Bur., Goose AFB, Labrador, 1961-64; writer Goose AFB paper GAB, 1961-64; editor Ebb Tide Newspaper, Tiburon, Cal., 1966—, owner, 1967—, editor-owner Corte Madera-Larkspur Courier, 1967-70, Mill Valley Sentinel, 1968-70, Sausalito Star, 1969-70; editor Cal. Flying mag., 1972-74; owner Marin Addressing Service, Tiburon. Mem. adv. bd. Family Service Agy. Marin County. Mem. Nat. Notary Assn. Club: Sausalito Woman's. Home: 2201 Jefferson Way Antioch CA 94509 Office: 1610 Tiburon Blvd Tiburon CA 94920

LUCA, MILDRED OETJEN, physician; b. N.Y.C., Aug. 7, 1910; d. Gustav Adolf and Rosina (Marcordes) Oetjen; B.A., Hunter Coll., 1930; M.D., N.Y. U., 1934; m. Frank Luca, Apr. 3, 1937; children—Linda (Mrs. Vincent Peluso), Brenda (Mrs. Donald Stine). Intern Beekman St. Hosp., N.Y.C., 1934-35; resident N.Y. Infirmary for Women and Children, 1942-43, Monmouth Med. Center, Long Branch, N.J., 1943-44; practice medicine specializing in obstetrics and gynecology, Glenhead, N.Y., 1938-42, Long Branch, N.J., 1944-69; now mem. staff Broward County Bd. Health, Palm Beach Health Dept. Broward County Med. Soc. Home: 3050 Palm Air Dr Pompano Beach FL 33060

LUCAS, BARBARA JEANNE, pub. co. editor; b. Bedford, Va., Dec. 12, 1928; d. Leftwich Sherrill and Margaret (Rider) Lucas; student Va. Intermont Coll., 1944-46. Actress, 1949-59, founder, dir. Anglo Theatre, Stockholm, Sweden; staff fgn. news desk Time mag., N.Y.C., 1959-65; asst. to v.p., pub. juvenile dept. Harper Row, N.Y.C., 1965-68, editor in chief juvenile books G.P. Putnam's Sons, N.Y.C., 1968-73; editor-in-chief juvenile books Harcourt Brace Jovanovich, N.Y.C., 1973—. Mem. Women's Nat. Book Assn., Phi Beta. Home: 7 John Marshall Lane Madison NJ 07940 Office: Harcourt Brace Jovanovich 757 3d Av New York City NY 10017

LUCAS, CAROL, gerontologist; b. Hewlett, L.I., N.Y., July 11, 1929; d. Irving William and Julia (Cutler) Lucas; B.S., Coll. William and Mary, 1949; M.A., Columbia, 1951, Ed.D., 1953. Field dir. Greater N.Y. council Girl Scouts U.S.A., N.Y.C., 1949-51; recreation dir. Neponsit (N.Y.) Beach Hosp., 1951-53; cons. Nat. Council Jewish Women, N.Y.C., 1954-55; area coordinator Los Angeles County Heart Assn., Los Angeles, 1955-56; rehab. cons. City of Hope, Duarte, Cal., 1955-56, Los Angeles Tb and Health Assn., 1957-58; recreation cons. Fedn. Protestant Welfare Agys., N.Y.C., 1958-60; instr. Columbia, 1959—; dir. spl. pilot study in gerontology, N.Y.C., 1958-64; exec. dir. Five Towns Sr. Center; supr. adminstrn. on aging project Sr. Center of Nassau County, Uniondale, N.Y.; dir. services for aging Town of Hempstead (N.Y.), 1968—. Mem. Am. Recreation Soc., Nat. Assn. Social Workers, Nat. Recreation Assn., Acad. Certified Social Workers, Royal Soc. Health (London), Kappa Delta Pi, Delta Psi Omega. Author: (with Josephine Rathbone) Recreation in Total Rehabilitation, 1958; Recreation Activity Development in Nursing Home, Homes for the Aging and Hospitals, 1962; Recreation in Gerontology, 1963. Contbr. articles to profl. jours. Home: 141 Wyckoff Pl Woodmere NY 11598 Office: Town Hall Hempstead NY 11550

LUCAS, FLORENCE VICTORIA (MRS. DAVID REX EDWARDS), lawyer, state ofcl.; b. N.Y.C., Oct. 10, 1915; d. Charles and Maybelle (Hunter) Lucas; B.A., Hunter Coll., 1936; J.D., Bklyn. Law Sch., 1939; m. David Rex Edwards. Admitted to N.Y. State bar; enforcement atty. OPA, N.Y.C., 1942-46; practiced in Jamaica, N.Y., 1946-66; asst. commr., spl. counsel to commr. N.Y. State Div. Human Rights, N.Y.C., 1966-72, dep. commn., 1972—. Vol. atty. Youth Cts., N.Y.C. Sec., Samuel Huntington Community Center, 1955-56, v.p., 1956-57; mem. Merrick Community Center. Republican candidate N.Y.C. Council, 1957. Trustee, Marymount Manhattan Coll. Recipient certificate merit Nat. Council Negro Women; Bronze plaque N.A.A.C.P. Nat. Office. Mem. Nat. Assn. Negro Bus. and Profl. Women's Clubs (Sojourner Truth award), Nat. Conf. Christians and Jews (sec.), Nat. Council Women U.S. (chmn. human rights com.). Methodist (mem. jud. council 1972—). Home: 144-07 228th St Rosedale NY 11413 Office: 270 Broadway New York City NY 10007

LUCAS, MARGARET, ocean and elec., aquanaut; b. Kemmerer, Wyo., May 29, 1947; d. William Joseph and Mary (Motoh) Lucas; B.E.E., Villanova U., 1969; postgrad. U. Del., 1969—. Research asst. civil engring. dept. U. Del., 1969-71; aquanaut Tektite II Project, U.S. Dept. Interior, 1970; adv. specialist Sea Grant Office, U. Hawaii, Honolulu, 1971—; research engr. Oceanic Inst., Waimanalo, Hawaii, 1971-72. Recipient Conservation award U.S. Dept. Interior, 1970; Young Alumnus award Villanova U., 1971; named Hon. Citizen Chgo., mayor, 1970. U.S. Dept. Commerce grantee, Interocean, 1970, Germany, 1970. Mem. Hawaii Fedn. Bus. and Profl. Women (Young Career Woman of Hawaii 1972), Eta Kappa Nu, Sigma Tau Delta. Home: 1811 Bingham St Honolulu HI 96814

LUCAS, ROSEMARY DEAN, broadcasting exec.; b. Los Angeles; d. Roy and Juarita (Damer) Dean; grad. Ind. U., 1957; married; children—Kim, Jim. Hostess, Mid-Day, also weather girl Sta. WAPI-TV, Birmingham, Ala., 1962—. Club: Birmingham Press. Office: WAPI-TV Box 1310 Birmingham AL 35201

LUCAS, RUTH MADSON, librarian; b. Billings, Mont., May 15, 1936; d. George Albert and Frances (Coyne) Madson; B.A., Seattle U., 1958; M.L.S., U. Wash. (Seattle), 1960; m. Emmett L. Lucas, June 10, 1961 (div. Oct. 1973); children—Kevin, Christopher, Therese. With New Orleans Pub. Library, 1962—, head East New Orleans regional br., 1968-70, system book selection coordinator, 1971-72, head central library pub. services, 1972—. Mem. La. Library Assn., New Orleans Library Club. Roman Catholic. Home: 1142 Michael St New Orleans LA 70114 Office: 219 Loyola St New Orleans LA 70140

LUCCHESI, (PEGGY) MARGARET ANN CUNNINGHAM (MRS. DINO V. LUCCHESI), musician; b. Oakland, Cal., June 12, 1928; d. George M. and Helen (Hambly) Cunningham; B.A. with honors, U. Cal. at Berkeley, 1949, postgrad., 1949-51; licentiate Royal Acad. Music (London), 1952, postgrad., 1952-54; M.A. in Music Edn., San Francisco State Coll., 1957; m. Dino V. Lucchesi, Aug. 5, 1961; children—Teresa Ann, Dino Alan, Rocco G. Mem. percussion sect. San Francisco Symphony Orch., 1955—, San Francisco Opera Orch., 1961—, San Francisco Percussion Ensemble for Young Audiences, 1960-71; performer concerts throughout San Francisco Bay area, 1955—; instr. U. Cal. at Berkeley, 1967—; instr. violin, viola, percussion San Francisco Conservatory Music, 1955-62, 72—; pvt. percussion tchr., 1962—. Recipient numerous awards Royal Acad. Music, 1952-54. Alfred Hertz Meml. scholar, 1951-52. Mem. Royal Acad. Music Club (London), San Francisco Women Musicians Club, Phi Beta Kappa, Pi Lambda Theta. Republican. Catholic. Address: 31 Yorkshire Dr Oakland CA 94618

LUCE, CLARE BOOTHE, playwright, former congresswoman, former ambassador; b. N.Y.C.; d. William F. and Ann (Snyder) Boothe; ed. St. Mary's, Garden City, N.Y., 1915-17, The Castle, Tarrytown, N.Y., 1917-19; Litt.D., Colby Coll., Fordham U., Mundelein Coll.; LL.D., Temple U., Creighton U., Georgetown U., Seton Hall Coll.; A.F.D., St. John's U.; m. George Tuttle Brokaw, Aug. 10, 1923 (div. 1929); m. 2d, Henry R. Luce, Nov. 23, 1935 (dec.). Asso. editor Vogue, 1930, Vanity Fair, 1931-32, mng. editor, 1933-34; newspaper columnist, 1934; playwright, 1935—; mem. 78th-79th congresses from 4th Conn. dist.; U.S. ambassador to Italy, 1953-57; cons., mem. bd. editors Ency. Brit. First vice chmn. Nat. Rev. Bd., East-West Center; mem. President's Fgn. Intelligence adv. bd.; mem. Commn. on Critical Choices for Ams. Trustee World Wildlife Fund, Alfred E. Smith Meml. Found., Am. Mus. Immigration, Honolulu Acad. Arts. Mem. Acad. Polit. Sci., Nat. Fedn. Press Women, Internat. Platform Assn. Am. Inst. Fgn. Trade, U.S. Strategic Inst. (dir.), Aspen Inst. for Humanistic Studies. Republican. Roman Catholic. Club: Oversees Press. Author: Stuffed Shirts, 1933; Europe in the Spring, 1940; (plays) Abide with Me; The Women, 1937; Kiss the Boys Goodbye, 1938; Margin for Error, 1939; Child of the Morning, 1951; Slam the Door Softly, 1970. Contbr. articles and fiction to mags. Collector, editor Saints for Now, 1952. Home: 4559 Kahala Av Honolulu HI 96816

LUCE, DIANE RITCHEY (MRS. ROBERT JAMES LUCE), educator; b. Cambridge, Mass., Nov. 2, 1942; d. John Arthur and Frances Ann (Curtis) Ritchey; B.A., Ind. U., 1964, M.A., 1965; M.S., Drexel U., 1968; postgrad. in rehab. counseling U. Pitts., 1973—; m. Robert James Luce, July 24, 1970. Tchr. history high sch., Pitman, N.J., 1965-66; jr. cataloger Drexel U. Library, 1966-67; young adult librarian Free Library, Phila., 1968-69, young adult specialist, 1969-72; grad. teaching asst. dept. polit. sci. U. Pitts., 1972-73, research fellow Hillman Library, summer 1973, career div. intern Counseling Center, 1973—; research asst. Cross Nat. Social Surveys, Pitts., 1973—. Mem. Social Responsibilities Round Table Phila. Area Librarians, Phi Beta Kappa, Beta Phi Mu. Home: 5865 Alderson St No 13 Pittsburgh PA 15217

LUCE, HELEN, library program officer; b. South Pasadena, Cal., Oct. 17, 1912; d. Samuel Tinkham and Iva (Cary) Luce; A.B., U. Cal. at Los Angeles, 1934; B.L.S., Pratt Inst., 1936. Page and library asst. Ventura County (Cal.) Library, 1934-35; first asst. Plumas and Sierra County Library, Quincy, Cal., 1936-38; first asst. Solano County Library, Fairfield, 1938-42, acting librarian, 1942-45; librarian San Bernardino County (Cal.) Library, 1945-57; library extension specialist U.S. Office Edn., Washington, 1957-67, library program officer Region 9, 1967—. Bd. dirs. Am. Cancer Soc., 1954-57; sec. A.R.C., capt. Red Cross Motor Corps. Mem. Am. (treas. library extension sect. 1952-55), Cal. (dist. pres. 1943-44, 54), library assns., Cal. County Librarians Assn. (sec.-treas. 1946-52), San Bernardino County Hist. Soc. (dir. 1948-49), San Bernardino County Mus. Assn. (sec.-treas. 1952, sec. 1953), Pub. Libraries Execs. Assn. So. Cal. (pres. 1955), Delta Zeta, Kappa Phi Zeta. Contbr. to library publs., Building America; The Right to Find Out. Home: 1845 Green St San Francisco CA 94123 Office: Library Programs US Office Edn 50 Fulton St San Francisco CA 94102

LUCHANSKY, ELEANOR SLIPSKI (MRS. PAUL LUCHANSKY), ins. co. exec.; b. Youngstown, O., July 1, 1927; d. William J. and Anastasia (Kotowski) Slipski; student bus. adminstrn., advt., Youngstown State U., 1966; m. Paul Luchansky, Aug. 3, 1947. Coordinator student testing Bd. Edn., Youngstown, O., 1944-45; sec. Roosevelt Sch., Youngstown, 1945-47; adminstrv. mgr. Sales Hamburg Bros. Wholesalers, Pitts., 1949-70; purchasing agt. Fed. Wholesalers, Hubbard, O., 1969-70; adminstrv. mgr. Gene Boyers Ins., Inc., Youngstown, 1971—. Adviser Florence Crittendon Home, Youngstown, 1966—, Canfield (O.) Fair, since 1966—; active steel Valley Home for B Boys, Greater Youngstown Safety Council, Juvenile Research Center, speakers' bur. Y-Teens, Jr. Achievement; sponsor Woman of Year award, Youngstown Vindicator, 1966; chmn. Nat. Bus. Women's Week, 1971; sponsor Korean war orphan for Bus. and Profl. Women; adviser Ohio Fedn. 50th Anniversary, 1970; chmn. Beautiful Ams. Fashion Show, 1973. Mem. Bus. Profl. Women (pres. 1970-71, dir. 1971-72, del. nat. conv. 1971), Altrusa Internat. Home: 405 Yvonne Dr Youngstown OH 44505 Office: 113 S Canfield Niles Rd Youngstown OH 44515

LUCHINS, EDITH HIRSCH, educator; b. Breziny, Poland, Dec. 21, 1921; d. Max and Leah (Kravetsky) Hirsch; came to U.S., 1928, naturalized, 1934; B.A. cum laude, Bklyn. Coll., 1942; M.S., N.Y. U., 1944, postgrad., 1944-46; Ph.D., U. Ore., 1957; m. Abraham Samuel Luchins, Oct. 10, 1942; children—David, Daniel, Jeremy, Anne, Joseph. Inst. math. dept. Bklyn. Coll., 1944-46, 48; research asst. applied math. N.Y. U., 1946; mem. faculty U. Miami, Coral Gables, Fla., 1959-62, asso. prof., 1960-62; asso. prof. Rensselaer Poly. Inst., Troy, N.Y., 1962-70, prof., 1970—. Research asso. U. Ore., Eugene, 1957-58; research found. State U. N.Y., Albany, summers 1965—. Pres. Interfaith Orgn., Eugene, 1955-57; sec. Capital dist. Bnos Israel, 1969-71, pres., 1971—. Am. Assn. U. Women fellow, 1957-58. Mem. Am. Math. Soc., Math. Assn. Am., Soc. Indsl. and Applied Math., Propylae (now Phi Beta Kappa), Pi Mu Epsilon, Sigma Xi. Author: (with Abraham S. Luchins) Rigidity of Behavior, 1959; Logical Foundations of Mathematics for Behavioral Scientists, 1965. Home: 53 Fordham Ct Albany NY 12209 Office: Dept Math Rensselaer Poly Inst Troy NY 12181

LUCHSINGER, LAURA LOUISE (MRS. VINCENT P. LUCHSINGER), educator; b. Indpls., Dec. 20, 1926; d. Harry M. and Laura Lenore (Bigley) Bourgeois; B.S. in Bus. Adminstrn., U. Ark., 1949; M.B.A., Tex. Tech U., 1955, Dr. Bus. Adminstrn., 1972; m. Vincent P. Luchsinger, May 28, 1957; children—Gregory, Mark, Laura Lea, Vincent P., Lise Louise, Julie Kathleen. Retail buyer Foley's Dept. Store, Houston, 1949-52; prof. marketing Tex. Tech U., Lubbock, 1956—, chmn. dept., 1971—; vis. prof. U. Utah in Germany, 1970. Partner, Hub City Movers, Lubbock, 1960-64; prin. Assistance to Mgmt., Lubbock, 1970—. Pres., Family Services Assn., Lubbock, 1970-72. Bd. dirs. Mental Health and Mental Retardation Assn., 1972—. Named Outstanding Educator, Outstanding Educators Am., 1971. Mem. Am. Marketing Assn., Soc. Advancement of Mgmt., Acad. Marketing Sci., Lubbock Apt. Assn., Beta Gamma Sigma, Sigma Epsilon Iota, Zeta Tau Alpha. Roman Catholic. Home: 4407 13th St Lubbock TX 79416

LUCIER, VIRGINIA MARY ROSSI, editor; b. Framingham, Mass.; d. Casimirro and Margaret D. (Scansaroli) Rossi; grad. South Middlesex Secretarial Sch., Framingham; student Boston U.; 1 dau., Deborah Jane. Former reporter, women's editor South Middlesex News (formerly Framingham News), Framingham, now soc. editor, movie and theater critic. Speaker various clubs, schs.; writer, Boston Record Am., U.P.I., Boston Globe, Amusement Business. Chmn. publicity various civic groups. Trustee Framingham Choral Soc.; bd. dirs. Am. Cancer Soc., Framingham. Named Woman of Year, Framingham Bus. and Profl. Women's Club, 1962. Hon. mem. Beta Sigma Phi. Home: 586 Hollis St Framingham MA 01701 Office: 375 Cochitaute Rd Framingham MA 01701

LUCIOLI, CLARA ELIZABETH, librarian; b. London, Eng., June 25, 1910; d. John Marcello and Agnes (Wilkin) Lucioli; came to U.S., 1919, naturalized, 1919; Certificate, Pratt Inst., 1931; student N.Y. U., 1934-38; B.A., Case Western Res. U., 1941; B.L.S., State U. N.Y. at Albany, 1942; postgrad. Miami U., 1969-71. Children's librarian Scarsdale (N.Y.) Pub. Library, 1931-34, asst. librarian, 1935-39; asst.

Mather Coll. Library, 1941—, div. head Judd Fund Service to Homebound, 1941-46, dept. head hosps. and instns. dept., 1955-70, acting dep. personnel, 1970-71, dir. profl. services, 1971—, interim dep. dir., 1974—. Lectr. sch. library sci. Case Western Res. U., Cleve., 1946-70; lectr. several univs. throughout U.S.; chmn. adv. council Title IVA grant program State Library Ohio, 1967-70; mem. Pres.'s Com. Employment Handicapped, 1960—. Mem. Am. (mem. council 1964-68), Ohio (chmn. instn. libraries com. 1955-65, named librarian of year 1970), library assns., Assn. Hosp. and Instn. Libraries (pres. 1959-60, recipient exceptional service citation 1961), Pratt Inst. Alumni Assn. (v.p. Midwest chpt.). Club: Women's City. Co-dir., author film The Winged Bequest, 1955. Contbr. profl. jours. Home: 1225 Hathaway Av Lakewood OH 44107 Office: 325 Superior Av Cleveland OH 44114

LUCIUS, MARIAN ELIZABETH, mfg. co. exec.; b. Rochester, N.Y., May 27, 1911; d. William Irvin and Helen (Muehlmatt) Lucius; B.A., U. Rochester, 1932, M.A., 1934. Librarian Fiduciary Trust Co. of N.Y., 1938-44, Research Inst. of Am., N.Y.C., 1944-45, Price Waterhouse & Co., N.Y.C., 1946-53; exec. sec. Spl. Libraries Assn., N.Y.C., 1953-59; registrar The Rockefeller U., N.Y.C., 1960-72; treas. Simplex Ceiling Corp., Union City, N.J., 1949—. Home: 1332 Midland Av Bronxville NY 10708

LUCKETT, LAYLE STEWART (MRS. JACKSON R. LUCKETT), mgmt. cons.; b. Madisonville, Ky., June 2, 1939; d. William Lyall and Carrie (Lacy) Stewart; M.B.A., Harvard, 1965; A.B., Randolph-Macon Womens Coll., 1961; postgrad. U. Cal. at Los Angeles, 1973—; m. Jackson R. Luckett, June 23, 1967; children—Jackson R., Lee, Gregory Lawrence, Steven Brent. Saleslady, Vogue, Madisonville, 1955-60; summer trainee Woodward & Lothrop, Washington, 1960, Societe Generale, Paris, France, 1962; asst. mgr. Red Garter, Boston, 1962-63; br. dept. mgr. William Filenes, Boston, 1963-64; World's Fair cons., supr. Clairol, Inc., N.Y.C., 1964; sportswear sales mgr. L.S. Ayres, Indpls., 1965-66; cons. Arthur D. Little, Washington, 1966; research asso. Planning Research Corp., Washington, 1966-67; mgmt. cons. Harbridge House Inc., Washington, 1968-71; asso. prof. bus. enterprise U. Md., 1971; pres. Gemini Assos., Cardiff-by-the-Sea, Cal. Lectr. marketing strategy U.S. Internat. U., San Diego, 1972—; asst. profl. lectr. marketing, gen. mgmt. George Washington U., Washington, 1969-70. Mem. Assn. Internat. des Etudiants Scientific et Commerciale Alumni, Ky. Soc. Washington, Randolph-Macon Alumni Assn., Radcliffe Alumni Club Los Angeles, Am. Marketing Assn., Alpha Delta Pi. Clubs: Harvard Business School (sec. 1972-73 Washington, San Diego); Harvard (San Diego). Contbr. articles to profl. jours. Home: Apt 26 10429 Wilshire Blvd Los Angeles CA 90024

LUCKHARDT, MILDRED MADELEINE CORELL (MRS. GUSTAV GEORGE LUCKHARDT), author; b. N.Y.C., Nov. 20, 1898; d. Philip George and Mildred (McCaffrey) Corell; student Columbia; m. Gustav George Luckhardt, Sept. 20, 1921; children—Jean Corell (Mrs. Lewis Morrell Robbins), Mildred Mary (Mrs. David Emerson Kenney), Philip George. Columnist, N.Y. Sun, Woman Who Sees, 1919-28; ednl. cons. and family counselor for several chs., 1927—; mem. staff children's room Rye (N.Y.) Library, 1956-65, now trustee; librarian Wainwright House, Rye, 1959—; book panelist, lectr., children's book reviewer, hymn writer; chmn. Storytellers Guild Westchester County author 25 books including The Story of Saint Nicholas, 1960; Christmas Comes Once More, 1962; Good King Wenceslas, 1964; Thanksgiving Feast and Festival, 1966; Spooky Tales about Witches, Ghosts, Goblins, Demons and Such, 1972; The Church at Work and Worship, 1968; Spring World, Awake, 1970; Funny Stories to Read or Tell, 1974; Brave Journey, 1974. Active A.R.C., Girl Scouts U.S.A., Children's Village, Dobbs Ferry, N.Y., Carver Center, Port Chester, N.Y., YWCA. Mem. Authors Guild Am., Nat. League Am. Pen Women, Hymn Soc. Am., Westchester County Library Assn., A.L.A., Assn. U.P. Christian Educators, Delta Kappa Gamma. Presbyn. Home: 121 Argonne St Fairfield CT 06604 also Cousins Island Yarmouth ME Office: Rye Library Rye NY 10580

LUCORE, PATRICIA MILLER (MRS. RAYMOND ROBERT LUCORE), research psychologist; b. Denver, Sept. 15, 1930; d. Elwood Hoop and Bertha Ann (Huested) Miller; A.A., Colo. Women's Coll., 1950; B.A., U. Wyo., 1952, M.A., 1953; Ph.D., U. Colo., 1971; m. Raymond Robert Lucore, Dec. 27, 1950; children—Ann (Mrs. Gary A. Peterson), Robert, Paul. Research asst. U. Colo., Boulder, 1968-69; staff psychologist Arapahoe Mental Health Center, Englewood, Colo., 1969-71; research psychologist, U. Ala., Tuscaloosa, 1973—. Mem. Am. Psychol. Assn., Am. Assn. Correctional Psychologists, Phi Beta Kappa, Sigma Xi, Phi Kappa Phi. Home: Apt D6 608 River Rd East Tuscaloosa AL 35401 Office: Box 2968 University of Ala Tuscaloosa AL 35486

LUDDEN, BARBARA ANN HARRISON (MRS. JAMES GREGORY LUDDEN), govt. ofcl.; b. Washington, Nov. 6, 1932; d. William Henry and Lois (Magee) Harrison; grad. cum laude Immaculate Conception Acad., 1950; student U.S. Dept. Agr. Grad. Sch., 1950-51, Am. U., 1951-52; m. James Gregory Ludden, Dec. 28, 1957. With reactor devel. div. AEC, 1950-54; personal and polit. sec. to congresswoman, Evanston, Ill., Washington, 1954-56, 57-63; rep. Citizens Com. for Fair Labor Standards, Washington, 1957; mem. U.S. delegation to UN, 1961; adminstrv. asst. to Ill. congressman, Washington, 1963-69, 70-71; spl. asst. to dir. Office Econ. Opportunity, 1969-70; congl. liaison officer Gen. Services Adminstrn., Washington, 1971-72; dir. congl. affairs Pay Bd., Exec. Office Pres., Washington, 1972-73; asso. dir. Cost of Living Council, Washington, 1973; dir. congl. relations U.S. Consumer Product Safety Commn., Washington, 1973—. Mem. Congl. Secs. Club, Immaculate Conception Acad. Alumnae of D.C. Republican. Roman Catholic. Club: Capitol Hill. Home: 8512 Stable Dr Alexandria VA 22308 Office: US Consumer Product Safety Commn 1750 K St NW Washington DC 20508

LUDEMAN, RUTH EVELYN GROVES (MRS. IVAN DALE LUDEMAN), educator; b. Windom, Minn., Jan. 25, 1927; d. Samuel Clayton and Minnie Mae (Smith) Groves; student Bethel Coll., St. Paul, 1945-46, 48-49; diploma in elementary edn. Mankato State Coll., 1950; A.B., Colo. State Coll., 1959; M.A., U. Minn., 1961, Ph.D., 1972; m. Ivan Dale Ludeman, July 25, 1947; children—Hope, Joann, Naomi. Tchr. elementary schs., Minn., 1950-59; instr., asst. prof. edn., chmn. dept. edn. Northwestern Coll., Mpls., 1961-66; supr. student teaching U. Minn., 1966-67; asst. prof. edn. Augsburg Coll., 1967-70, dir. elementary edn., 1968-70; prof. edn. Bethel Coll., 1970—. Mem. Nat. Soc. for Study Edn., Nat. Educators Fellowship, Pi Lambda Theta. Republican. Baptist. Home: 6338 11th Av S Richfield MN 55423 Office: 3900 Bethel Dr St Paul MN 55112

LUDLAM, LILLIAN, business exec.; b. N.Y.C.; B.S., Rider Coll., 1938; m. Richard Price Ludlam, June 22, 1946. With McGraw-Hill Pub. Co., Inc., N.Y.C., 1938-44; adminstrv. asst. to gen. mgr. Lord & Taylor, N.Y.C., 1944-46; advt. mgr., asst. to v.p. Monitor Equipment Corp., N.Y.C., 1946-49; owner advt. agy., 1949-55; merchandising account mgr. B.R. Martin Assos., Skokie, Ill., 1955—; v.p., sec. Village Lumber & Oil, Inc., New Hartford, Conn., 1960—; pub. Foothills Trader, New Hartford, 1960—, also pub. Conn. West. Pres., New Hartford Community Club, 1962-64; chmn. Conn. Gov.'s Consumer Adv. Council; mem. adv. com. Small Bus. Adminstrn. Pres., Litchfield County Women's Republican Club, 1956-60; mem. Conn. Rep. Central Com., 1960—, sec., 1968—. Conglist. Home: Town Hill New Hartford CT 06057

LUDLAM, YVONNE FORTUNEE DE JOURNO (MRS. JOHN LOUIS LUDLAM), editor; b. Allentown, Pa.; d. Ernest and Stella (Labe) de Journo; student N.Y. U., 1935-38; certificate Bankers Inst. Pub. Relations, Syracuse U., 1959, Bankers Inst. Exec. Devel., West Point, 1963; m. John Louis Ludlam, June 1938; children—John Louis, Barbara (Mrs. Tad Danz). Writer/ghost writer N.Y. State Bankers Assn., N.Y.C., 1955—, sec. bd. dirs., 1958-70, editor N.Y. State Banker, 1966—. Mem. Nat. Assn. Am. Pen Women (past editor Queens br. publ.), N.Y. Assn. Indsl. Communicators (past editor publ.), N.Y. Bus. Press Editors. Presbyn. Home: 39 Tuckahoe Rd Southampton NY 11968 Office: 485 Lexington Av New York City NY 10017

LUDLOFF, MARGARET ELEANOR, coll. librarian; b. N.Y.C., Oct. 13, 1945; d. Johann Friedrich and Susan (Friedel) Ludloff; B.A. in English Lit. and Speech, U. Cal. at Los Angeles, 1967, M.L.S., 1968, Teaching certificate, 1969. Librarian, Santa Monica (Cal.) High Sch., 1968-69, Roslyn (N.Y.) High Sch., 1969-70, Chamberlayne Jr. Coll., Boston, 1970-72, Newbury Jr. Coll. and Bay State Jr. Coll., Boston, 1972—. Organizer library Katherine Gibbs Sch., Boston, 1970. Co-leader Girl Scouts U.S.A., N.Y.C., 1961-62, coordinator camp program Greater N.Y. council, Briarcliff Manor, 1967. Mem. U. Cal. Alumni Club, Am. Library Assn., Assn. Librarians Smaller Colls. Greater Boston. Home: 181 Commonwealth Av Boston MA 02116

LUDLUM, MARY ELLEN SHONTING (MRS. THOMAS LUDLUM), civic worker; b. Columbus, O., Aug. 9, 1924; d. Daniel M. and Marvene (Mills) Shonting; A.B., Capital U., 1946; M.A., Ohio State U., 1950; m. Thomas Spencer Ludlum, Dec. 27, 1946; children—John Thomas, Daniel Spencer, James Robert. Tchr., Canal Winchester High Sch., 1946-48; teaching asst. Ohio State U., 1948-50, Ohio U., 1954-56; instr. Capital U., 1959-60, 65-68. Pres., League Women Voters, Athens, 1955-56, Columbus, 1962-64, mem. Ohio bd., 1966, 69, pres., 1969-73; mem. Ohio Gov.'s Task Force on Tax Reform, 1970-71; panel Am. Arbitration Assn., 1972-74; mem. Ohio Bd. Regents, 1972—; mem. steering com. Ohio Commn. Nursing and Nursing Edn., 1973—. Trustee, Ohio Inst. Pub. Finance, 1973—. Mem. Delta Sigma Rho, Tau Kappa Alpha, Phi Beta. Home: 822 Pleasant Ridge Columbus OH 43209 Office: 88 E Broad St Columbus OH 43215

LUDVIGSON, VERNA MAE (MRS. BRUCE M. LUDVIGSON), home economist; b. Duluth, Minn., Jan. 7, 1944; d. Sydney O. and Ailie A. (Mark) Christenson; B.S. (Andresen-Ryan Home Econs. scholar), U. Minn., 1966; m. Bruce M. Ludvigson, Oct. 23, 1970. Modern living cons. Mpls. Gas Co., 1966-69; 1st home economist, consumer products Litton Microwave Cooking, Mpls., 1969-72, home econs. mgr., 1972-74, dir. consumer affairs, 1974—. Mem. Am., Minn. home econs. assns., Twin Cities Home Economists in Bus., Assn. of Home Appliance Mfrs., Elec. Women of the Round Table (chmn. microwave subcom. 1971-74). Author: An Exciting New World of Microwave Cooking, 1971. Home: 12620 W Creek Rd Minnetonka MN 55343 Office: 400 Shelard Plaza S Minneapolis MN 55426

LUDWIG, ALICE JEANNE (MRS. LOUIS I. LUDWIG), educator; b. Bklyn., Jan. 18, 1920; d. James L. and Alice E. (McKinley) Hanlin; B.A., Bklyn. Coll., 1942, M.S., 1961; Ed.D. (fellow), Columbia U., 1970; m. Louis I. Ludwig, May 11, 1942; children—Peter Joseph, David Mark. Therapeutic educator, div. pediatric psychiatry Bklyn. Jewish Hosp., 1954-60; music therapist Music Therapy Center, N.Y.C., 1960-72; asst. prof. dept. spl. edn. Fordham U., Bronx, N.Y., 1967-72; asso. prof. dept. spl. edn. Jersey City State Coll. (N.J.), 1972—. Cons. Turtle Bay Arts in Tng. Therapy Program, 1969-73, Met. Music Sch., 1969-71, Nat. Assn. for Retarded Children, 1969-70. Bd. dirs. Met. Music Sch., 1966-73, Music Therapy Center, 1973—. Mem. Am. Assn. U. Profs., Am. Assn. for Mental Deficiency, Nat. Assn. Music Therapists, Council for Exceptional Children, Mensa, Kappa Delta Pi. Democrat. Jewish religion. Office: Jersey City State College Jersey City NJ 07305

LUDWIG, AUDREY ANN, publishing co. exec.; b. Prairie du Rocher, Ill., Dec. 5, 1939; d. Albert Vernon and Aurelia Marie (Ruez) Ludwig; grad. high sch. Biller typist, stenographer A.S. Aloe Co., St. Louis, 1957-64; sec. to pres., office mgr. Milliken Pub. Co., St. Louis, 1964—. Home: 5953 Nagel St St Louis MO 63109 Office: 1100 Research Blvd St Louis MO 63132

LUDWIG, CHRISTA, mezzo-soprano; b. Berlin, Germany, Mar. 16; d. Anton and Eugenie (Besalla) Ludwig; grad. high sch.; m. Paul-Emile Deiber. 1 son, Wolfgang. Appeared with Staedtische Buehnen, Frankfurt, Germany, 1946-52, Landestheater, Darmstadt, Germany 1952-54, Landestheater, Hannover, Germany, 1954-55; appearances Vienna State Opera, also Lyric Opera, Chgo., 1955—, Met. Opera N.Y.C., Carnegie Hall, Hunter Coll., Met. Mus., Philharmonic Hall (all N.Y.C.); mem. Vienna State Opera; appeared festivals Lucerne, Salzburg, Bayreuth, Athens, Saratago, also Nissei Theatre, Tokyo, Teatro Colon, Buenos Aires, Covent Garden, London, La Scala, Milan, Italy, others. Recipient title Kammersaengerin, Austrian Govt. Home: 14 Rigistrasse 6045 Meggen Switzerland

LUDWIG, LUCKII MYLENE, pub. relations exec.; b. Albany, Ore., May 5, 1943; d. Myles Gordon and Roberta Isabelle (Dawson) Ludwig; B.A., U. Mont., 1965; M.A., Marshall U., 1969. Farm-sch. reporter Lewiston (Ida.) Morning Tribune, 1965-66; sports editor Renton (Wash.) Record Chronicle, 1966-67; grad. asst. Marshall U., Huntington, W.Va., 1967-69; reporter, photographer Antioch (Cal.) Daily Ledger, 1969-71; investigative reporter Contra Costa (Cal.) Times, 1971-72; pub. and labor relations asso. Western Electric Co., Dublin, Cal., 1972—. Recipient Sports Writing award Sigma Delta Chi, 1967; Feature Writing award Contra Costa Press Club, 1971. Mem. Internat. Platform Assn., Women In Communications, Nat., Wash. press women, Quill and Scroll, Kappa Kappa Gamma. Clubs: East Bay Press, Contra Costa Press. Home: 16219 Via Arriba San Lorenzo CA 94580 Office: 6400 Sierra Court Dublin CA 94566

LUEBBE, CAROL MARIE (MRS. LAWRENCE A. LUEBBE), investment banker; b. Omaha, Dec. 25, 1928; d. John Chris and Calla Viola (Davis) Glesmann; A.A., St. John's Jr. Coll., 1947; B.S. in Elementary Edn., U. Neb., Lincoln, 1951; m. Lawrence Arthur Luebbe, Aug. 20, 1950; children—Sandra Kay, Mark Allen, Douglas Neal, David Brian. Registered rep. Mut. Fund Assos., Inc., San Francisco, 1961-66; sec.-treas., dir. Mut. Fund Accounts, Inc., Inglewood, Cal., 1967—. Mem. Nat. Assn. Securities Dealers. Republican. Lutheran. Home: 5535 W 63d St Los Angeles CA 90056 Office: 401 E Manchester Blvd Inglewood CA 90301

LUEBKE, MARY ELLEN, librarian; b. South Bend, Ind., May 6, 1928; d. Clyde Newton and Etta (Darling) Carr; student Valparaiso U., 1955-56, Ind. U. at South Bend, 1956-57; B.S. in Edn., Bethel Coll., 1961; postgrad. Ind. U. at Bloomington, 1965-67; M.A. in Library Sci., Ball State U., 1970; 1 dau., Ruth (Mrs. Oscar Carlisle). Tchr. pub. schs. South Bend, Ind., 1961-65, media specialist, 1965—. Mem. St. Joseph County Urban League edn. com., 1967-68; mem. Ind. Adv. Com. Title III Grants, 1967-69; sec. nat. com. Educators for Human Rights, 1966—. Bd. dirs. St. Joseph County council Camp Fire Girls. Dir. research state legis. campaign Republican party, 1968, St. Joseph County campaign, 1970, St. Joseph County Commrs. campaign, 1974. Mem. Ind. Sch. Librarians Assn., Nat., Ind., South Bend Community (pres. 1965-67) edn. assns., Assn. Childhood Edn. (pres. 1968), Delta Kappa Gamma. Mem. Order Eastern Star. Editor quar. Hoosier School Libraries, 1971—. Home: 650 Turtle Creek Ct South Bend IN 46637 Office: John F Kennedy Sch 609 N Olive St South Bend IN 46628

LUECHAUER, HELYN CATHERINE ANDERSON (MRS. JARVIS H. LUECHAUER), dentist; b. Oakland, Cal., Aug. 13, 1921; d. Virgil Vinson and Lillian (Hickox) Anderson; student Pacific Union Coll., 1939-43, Fresno State Coll., 1960-62; D.D.S., U. Cal., San Francisco, 1966; m. Jarvis H. Luechauer, Feb. 26, 1944. Practice dentistry (with husband), Hollywood, Cal., 1966—. Asst. clin. prof. U. Cal. Sch. Dentistry, Los Angeles, 1967—. Mem. Am., So. Cal. dental assns., Am. Dental Soc. Anesthesiology, Am. Soc. Dentistry for Children, Assn. Am. Women Dentists (sec.-treas. 1974—), United European Am. Club, Nat. Orgn. Women, Acad. Gen. Dentistry, Upsilon Alpha (grand v.p.). Republican. Conglist. Clubs: Soroptomist, Los Angeles Athletic. Home: 3347 Charleston Way Hollywood CA 90028 Office: 6565 Sunset Blvd Hollywood CA 90028

LUELOFF, JORIE ANNE PAYNE (MRS. RICHARD FRIEDMAN), journalist; b. Milw.; d. R. T. and Marjorie (Kaltenbach) Lueloff; student U. Geneva and Inst. des Hautes Etudes Internationales (Switzerland), 1961; B.A., Mills Coll., 1962; postgrad Georgetown U. Sch. Fgn. Service, 1963; m. Richard Friedman, May 1, 1971. With CIA, Washington, 1962-63; newsfeature writer A.P., N.Y.C., 1964-65; news reporter, newscaster NBC News, Sta. WMAQ-TV, Chgo., 1965—. Mem. Chgo. Press Club (gov.), Nat. Acad. Television Arts and Scis. (gov.). Office: NBC News Merchandise Mart Chicago IL 60654

LUHN, LAUDINE STILWELL (MRS. NOLAN H. LUHN), bank exec.; b. Havana, Kan., Feb. 5, 1929; d. Roy David and Lenora Pearl (Wade) Stilwell; A.Bus. Edn., Coffeyville Jr. Coll., 1948; m. Nolan H. Luhn, Aug. 6, 1966; children—David, Christina. Sec., loan teller Coffeyville Brokerage Co. (Kan.), 1947-48; sec. Multiscope, Inc., Coffeyville, 1948-50; sec. to pres. and chmn. bd. 1st Nat. Bank Coffeyville, 1950—, asst. trust officer, 1963-73, asst. v.p., trust officer, 1973—. Mem. secretarial adv. council Coffeyville Community Jr. Coll., 1960. Mem. Nat. Assn. Bank Women (chmn. Ozarks 1965), Clubs: Feminciers, Repaso Moderno Book Review. Methodist. Home: Rural Route 1 Box 18 Coffeyville KS 67337 Office: 1st Nat Bank 102 W 8th St Coffeyville KS 67337

LUHR, ADELHEID WILHELMINE, constrn. co. exec.; b. Fountain, Ill., Apr. 8, 1917; d. Lorenz George and Emma Sophia (Rusteberg) Schanz; student pub. schs.; m. Eugene Luhr, Sept. 6, 1936 (dec. Dec. 1958). Sec., treas., dir. Luhr Bros., Inc., Columbia, Ill., 1948—, Eugene Luhr & Co., 1952—. Trustee Luhr Employees Profit Sharing Trust, 1961—; bd. dirs. Meml. Hosp., Belleville, Ill., 1965—. Mem. United Ch. of Christ. Home: 1034 N Main St Columbia IL 62236 Office: 1020 N Main St Columbia IL 62236

LUHRS, KATHLEEN, editor; b. White Plains, N.Y., Oct. 8, 1941; d. Frederick and Mary (Diviney) Luhrs; B.S., Columbia, 1965. Editorial asst., researcher NBC, N.Y.C., 1965; asst. pub. service coordinator sta. WNBC-TV, N.Y.C. 1965-66; asst. editor N.Y. Hist. Soc., N.Y.C., 1966, asso. editor, 1967-68, editor, 1968—. Office: 170 Central Park W New York City NY 10024

LUISI, MARIE BARBATO (MRS. MICHAEL LUISI), advt. agy. exec.; b. N.Y.C., Aug. 31, 1936; d. Raymond and Grace (Villa) Barbato; student N.Y. U., 1956-60; m. Michael Luisi, Aug. 9, 1960; 1 son, Michael John. Local broadcasting buyer and planner J. Walter Thompson Co., N.Y.C., 1955-61, v.p., 1963—; broadcasting buying specialist Doyle Dane Bernbach, N.Y.C., 1961-63. Home: 415 E 52nd St New York City NY 10022 Office: 420 Lexington Av New York City NY 10028

LUKAS, BETTY ANN LARSEN (MRS. HENRY V. LUKAS), editor; b. Toledo, Mar. 5, 1925; d. Neil S. and Lunetta Marie (Behnke) Larsen; B.A., U. Mich., 1947; M.A., U. So. Cal., 1972; m. Henry V. Lukas, Apr. 10, 1948; children—Brian Neil, Herbert George, Maria Elizabeth. Gen. reporter Toledo Blade and Times, 1945-46; asst. editor Plaskon Mag., Toledo, 1948-49; editor Washtenaw Post-Tribune, Ann Arbor, Mich., 1949-50; staff writer, feature editor Palos Verdes (Cal.) Peninsula News, 1967-73; copy editor Los Angeles Times, 1973—. Instr. journalism El Camino Coll., 1972, Cal. State Coll., 1973-74. Bd. dirs. Alcoholism Council South Bay, Cal., 1973. Recipient numerous awards Cal. Press Women, Cal. Newspaper Pubs. Assn., Suburban Press Found., including 1st pl. and editorial citation for best series weekly newspaper, 1973. Mem. League Women Voters (pres. 1956-58), S.W. Press Assn., Theta Sigma Phi. Presbyn. (deacon 1972—). Home: 2229 Chelsea Rd Palos Verdes Estates CA 90274 Office: 1375 Sunflower St Costa Mesa CA 92626

LUKE, KATHLEEN MCCORMICK, hotel exec.; b. Topeka, Dec. 25, 1932; d. Raymond Chesley and Kathleen (Schoffner) McCormick; B.A. with distinction, U. Colo., 1971; m. Aug. 1956 (div. Nov. 1968); 1 dau., Kathleen Serena. With Tri-State Hotel Co., Wichita, Kan., 1955—, v.p., 1960-74. Mem. Phi Beta Kappa. Club: Denver Country. Home: 27 Crestmoor Dr Denver CO 80220

LUKE, MARY MUNGER, author; b. Pittsfield, Mass., Mar. 24, 1919; d. John F. and Hazel (Fish) Munger; student Berkshire Bus. Coll., Pittsfield, Mass., 1939, writing courses N.Y. U., Columbia; m. David L. Luke, May 8, 1948 (div. Jan. 1965); 1 dau., Melinda Carey. Tudor historian, writer film documentaries, travelogues, articles. Mem. Nat. Women's Republican Club, 1950—. Mem. English-Speaking Union. Club: Silver Spring Country (Ridgefield, Conn.). Author: Catherine, The Queen, 1967; A Crown for Elizabeth, 1970; Gloriana: The Years of Elizabeth, 1973. Home: 19 Peaceable St Ridgefield CT 06877

LUKES, RITA ELIZABETH, lawyer; b. Staples, Minn., Aug. 3, 1937; d. Joseph Frank and Sarah Josephine (Collins) Lukes; B.A., Coll. of St. Benedict, St. Joseph, Minn., 1959; J.D., William Mitchell Coll. of Law, 1968. Computer programmer Univac, St. Paul, 1959-68; admitted to Minn. bar, 1968; programmer analyst Control Data Corp., Mpls., 1968-71; practice in Mpls., 1968-71; atty. firm Rider, Bennett, Egan, Johnson & Arundel, Mpls., 1971—. Mem. Am., Minn., Hennepin County bar assns., Nat. Assn. Women Lawyers, Phi Delta Delta (internat. sec. 1970-72). Home: 400 Groveland Av Minneapolis MN 55403 Office: 6750 France Av S Minneapolis MN 55435

LUKSIS, LILLIAN ANNE, roentgenologist; b. Worcester, Mass., Oct. 2, 1923; d. Adam and Rose Marie (Babbitt) Luksis; student U. Mass., 1941-42; A.B., Clark U., 1944; M.D., Boston U., 1949. Intern Meml. Hosp., Worcester, Mass., 1949-50, resident, 1951-52; resident

St. Elizabeth's Hosp., Brighton, Mass., Newton, Mass., 1952-53; roentgenologist Doctor's Hosp., Worcester, 1955—, Clinton (Mass.) Hosp., 1956—; asst. roentgenologist City Hosp., Worcester, Hubbard Regional Hosp., Webster, Fairlawn Hosp., Worcester, Holden Hosp., 1956—. Mem. Am. Coll. Radiology, New Eng. Roentgen Ray Assn., Mass. Radiology Soc., A.M.A., Mass. Med. Assn., Worcester Dist. Med. Soc. Home: 135 Sewall St Boylston MA 01505 Office: 390 Main St Worcester MA 01608

LULL, DIANA JEAN SENN (MRS. FRANK CLIFFORD LULL III), advt. agy. owner; b. Seattle, Dec. 28, 1942; d. Arthur Leland and Anna Elizabeth (Mathews) Senn; B.A., U. Wash., 1965; m. Frank Clifford Lull III, Mar. 24, 1966; 1 son, Kirby Clifford. Prodn. mgr. advt. dept. Weisfields, Inc., 1965-66; freelance advt. Rons Aquarium, Windward Mark, 1969-70; advt. mgr. Ichthyotics, Inc., Seattle and Bellevue, Wash., 1971—; owner, Aqua Ad Service, Seattle, 1972—. Docent tour guide Seattle Zool. Soc., 1970—; writer Pacific Search Mag., Pacific Sci. Center, 1970-71; coordinator math. lab. Laurelhurst Grade Sch., 1973-74. Mem. Women in Communications (chmn. coll. career conf. 1970), Seattle Advt. Fedn., Alpha Omicron Pi. Editor Tracks and Trails Seattle Zool. Soc., 1970-72. Home: 4123 42d St NE Seattle WA 98105

LUM, MARY DANG ONG (MRS. GWON H. LUM), govt. ofcl; b. Oakland, Cal., Nov. 30, 1923; d. Young Tung and Grace (Gee) Ong; A.B., U. Cal. at Berkeley, 1945, M.A. in Statistics, 1946; m. Gwon H. Lum, June 19, 1949; children—James, Donald, Penny, Carol, Robert, Gary. Teaching asst. in math. U. Cal. at Berkeley, 1945-46, Mich. State Coll., East Lansing, 1947-48; teaching and research fellow U. Mich., Ann Arbor, 1948-49, research asst. Aero. Research Center, Willow Run, 1949-50; math. statistician Aero. Research Lab., Wright-Patterson AFB, Dayton, O., 1951-68, sr. operations research analyst Hdqrs. Air Force Logistics Command, 1968-73, math. statistician Aero. Research Lab., 1973—. Cons. in statistics. Mem. Am. Statis. Assn., Inst. Math. Statistics, Internat. Assn. for Statistics in Phys. Scis., Phi Beta Kappa, Sigma Xi, Pi Mu Epsilon. Club: Circle Eight Square Dance (Dayton). Research on error analysis and reliability components guided missiles, hierarchal models in design of expts., character errors in error-correcting codes for ternary reception, math. evaluation grain counts in enlaged photographs, comparison of some forecast methods. Home: Rural Route 1 Box 19 Fairborn OH 45324 Office: Wright-Patterson AFB OH 45433

LUMABAN, JULITA ARROBIO (MRS. FELICIANO VALDEZ LUMABAN), virologist; b. Manila, P.I., Jan. 31, 1933; d. Marcelo Reboldela and Candida Quero (Ordona) Arrobio; M.D., U. Santo Tomas, Manila, 1958; m. Feliciano Valdez Lumaban, Feb. 5, 1963; children—Felicitas, Marcel. Came to the U.S., 1959. Intern, Washington (D.C.) Hosp. Center, 1959-60; resident pediatrics Children's Hosp. of D.C., 1960-62, fellow in virology, 1963-64, asso. in virology Research Found., 1965—. Home: 5426 Sargent Rd W Hyattsville MD 20782 Office: 2125 13th St NW Washington DC 20009

LUMAQUE, ROSIE MACAPINLAC (MRS. ELEUTERIO R. LUMAQUE, JR.), pediatrician; b. Manila, Philippines, Nov. 2, 1938; d. Eleuterio Galang and Marina (Pineda) Macapinlac; M.D., U. Philippines, 1963; m. Eleuterio R. Lumaque, Jr., June 1, 1964; children—Eleuterio Roel, Earl Ronald, Rosele Marina. Intern McLaren Gen. Hosp., Flint, Mich., 1964-65; resident pediatrics Hurley Hosp., Flint, 1966-68, active staff, 1971—; pediatrician Mott Children's Health Center, Flint, 1969-71; practice pediatrics, Flint, 1971—. Diplomate Am. Bd. Pediatrics. Mem. A.M.A., Mich., Genesee County med. socs. Home: 6474 Kings Pointe Rd Grand Blanc MI 48439 Office: 2740 Flushing Rd Flint MI 48504

LUMB, ETHEL SUE, educator; b. Huntsville, Mo., Dec. 21, 1916; d. George Edmund and Opal Cynthia (Hamilton) Lumb; A.A., Jr. Coll., Moberly, Mo., 1937; B.A., U. Mo., 1939, M.A., 1941, B.S. in Edn., 1941; Ph.D., Washington U., St. Louis, 1949. Tchr. Stephens Coll., Columbia, Mo., 1942-46; asst. prof. U. Rochester (N.Y.), 1949-53; prof. biology Vassar Coll., Poughkeepsie, N.Y., 1953—. Predoctoral fellow USPHS, 1949, postdoctorate research fellow NIH, 1967. Mem. Am. Soc. Zoologists, Am. Soc. Cell Biology, Soc. Devel. Biology, Am. Inst. Biol. Scis., A.A.A.S., Am. Assn. U. Profs., N.Y. Acad. Scis., Sigma Xi. Home: 13 Sheldon Dr Poughkeepsie NY 19603

LUMB, JUDITH RAE (MRS. ALAN MARK LUMB), educator; b. Bridgeport, Conn., Mar. 19, 1943; d. Thomas Herbert and Blanche Alice (Smith) Morrell; B.A., U. Kan., 1965, M.A., 1966; Ph.D., Stanford, 1969; m. Alan Mark Lumb, Sept. 5, 1964; children—Timothy Alan, Jeffrey Thomas. Asst. prof. biology Atlanta (Ga.) U., 1969—. Mem. nat. governing bd. Ripon Soc., 1972—. Grantee Research Corp., 1970-71, NIH, 1972-76, NSF, 1972-73, Am. Cancer Soc., 1973-74. Mem. Am. Soc. for Microbiology, A.A.A.S., Reticuloendothelial Soc. Home: 350 Eureka Dr NE Atlanta GA 30305 Office: Atlanta University Dept Biology Atlanta GA 30314

LUMBARD, VERNA HARRIS, journalist; b. Gary, Ind., Dec. 27, 1914; d. Arthur Bertrum and Cecelia Rosalind (Heilstedt) Harris; grad. high sch.; m. Sidney Corlis Lumbard, Oct. 9, 1937. Reporter, women's editor Gary Post-Tribune, 1931-37, 40-44; gen. writer Evanston (Ill.) News Index, 1937-40; editor Sierra Madre (Cal.) News, 1952-56; women's editor Fullerton (Cal.) News Tribune, 1957-59, 68—; spl. sects. editor, 1959-67. Mem. Nat. Assistance League, 1961—. News Tribune Recipient 1st place award for best women's interest coverage in class Cal. Newspaper Publ. Assn., 1958. Mem. Orange County Press Club, Sigma Delta Chi. Republican. Home: 1309 Cameo Lane Fullerton CA 92631 Office: 655 W Valencia Dr Fullerton CA 92632

LUMPKIN, ANNE CRAIG, radio sta. exec.; b. DeValls Bluff, Ark., Apr. 3, 1919; d. Claude Cleo and Lou (Craig) Lumpkin; grad. high sch. Adminstrv. asst. to pres., gen. mgr. Radio Stas. KVLC, Little Rock, 1948-52, KGKO, Dallas, 1952-54, KTLN, Denver, 1954-58, KLRA, Little Rock, 1958—. Mem. Am. Women Radio and TV (chpt. 1st v.p. 1973, pres. 1974-75). Home: 2909 Fair Park Blvd Little Rock AR 72204 Office: 1755 Union Nat Plaza Little Rock AR 72201

LUMPKIN, THELMA LYDIA SANTORO (MRS. GEORGE THOMAS LUMPKIN), writer; b. Waterbury, Conn., Dec. 3, 1925; d. Quirino Camillo and Flora (DiNapoli) Santoro; B.S. in English, Simmons Coll., 1947; certificate Harvard Grad. Sch. Bus. Adminstrn., 1965, Yale, 1959; m. George Thomas Lumpkin, Nov. 10, 1966. Owner Korant Advt., Waterbury, Conn., 1949-55; dir. pub. relations St. Mary's Hosp., Waterbury, 1955-60; mgr. advt. Waterbury Nat. Bank, 1960-67; free lance advt. cons., writer, graphic designer, Bethany, Conn., 1967—. Cons. advt. Vernon (Conn.) Nat. Bank, 1971—. Chmn. advt. and pub. relations United Council and Fund, Waterbury, Conn., 1955-56, 62; treas. The Bethany (Conn.) Horsemen, 1962-70, pres., 1970—. Bd. dirs. Waterbury Area Mental Health Assn., 1957-58, Family Service Assn., Waterbury, 1960-63. Recipient Financial World Ann. Report Survey awards, 1960, 63; Stockholder Communications award Nat. Security Traders Assn., 1966. Address: Sperry Rd Bethany CT 06525

LUNA, MARJORIE LEE (MRS. WELBORNE S. LUNA), dist. judge; b. South Bend, Ind., Apr. 23, 1904; d. Hardy E. and Anna V. (Wright) Lee; student Western Mich. U., 1932-34; LL.B., Blackstone Coll. Law, 1938; m. Welborne S. Luna, Nov. 30, 1922; 1 dau., Margie Lee (Mrs. J.D. Armstrong, Jr.). Admitted to Mich. bar, 1938; asst. pros. atty., Allegan County, Mich., 1938; friend of the ct., Allegan, Mich., 1939-41, circuit ct. commr., 1942-46; dist. judge Kalamazoo, Mich., 1970—; pvt. practice law in Mich. Named Woman of Year, Quota Club, 1970. Mem. Am., Kalamazoo County bar assns., State Bar of Mich., Am. Trial Lawyers Assn., N. Am., Am., Mich. Dist. Judges assns. Home: PO Box 9 Kalamazoo MI 49005 Office: 416 S Rose St Kalamazoo MI 49006

LUNA, SARAH MARIE, univ. dean; b. Rochester, N.Y., Nov. 19, 1935; d. Joseph and Mary Ann (Laiuppa) Luna; B.S., Cortland State Tchrs. Coll., 1957; M.S., St. Bonaventure U., 1970. Tchr. phys. edn. Nazareth Acad., Rochester, N.Y., 1957-59, Holy Family Sch., Watertown, N.Y., 1959-60; tchr. phys. edn., adviser Batavia (N.Y.) Sr. High Sch., 1960-62; tchr. phys. edn., adviser Cardinal Mooney High Sch., Rochester, 1962-66; tchr. phys. edn. Walsh High Sch., Olean, N.Y., 1966-67; women's athletic dir. St. Bonaventure U., St. Bonaventure, N.Y., 1967-71, dean of women, 1971-74, dean students, 1974—. Choreographer N.Y. State Jr. Miss Pageant, 1964-66; N.Y. State rep. chmn., chaperone Nat. Jr. Miss Pageant, 1966; hostess for Miss Cattaraugus County, N.Y. State Pageant, 1972. Mem. Nat. Assn. Women Deans and Counselors, Western N.Y. Personnel and Guidance Assn., Nat. Assn. Student Personnel Adminstrs., A.A.H.P.E.R., N.Y. State Health, Phys. Edn. and Recreation, Assn. Women's Phys. Edn. N.Y. State (treas. exec. bd. 1962-65, rep. to state bd. 1957-59). Home: 334 Hamilton Av Olean NY 14760 Office: Box V St Bonaventure NY 14778

LUNCEFORD, TENNIE MAE (MRS. C. DEAN DUKES), physician; b. Lanett, Ala.; d. Cornelius Edgar and Tennie C. (Jones) Lunceford; B.S., U. Ala., 1942; M.D., Washington U., St. Louis, 1946; m. C. Dean Dukes, Aug. 30, 1969; children—Maureen Anne, Karen Mercedes Dukes. Intern, Luth. Deaconess Hosp., Chgo., 1946-47; resident Municipal Contagious Disease Hosp., Chgo., 1947-48, Bobs Roberts Hosp., Chgo., 1948-49; practice medicine specializing in pediatrics, Lubbock, Tex., 1949-66, specializing in pediatric allergy, 1956-66, specializing in gen. allergy, 1966—; med. dir. Corrective Learning Center, Lubbock, 1960-66. Mem. Am., Tex. med. assns., Lubbock County Med. Soc., Pan Am. Allergy Soc., S.W. Allergy Forum, Am. Coll. Allergy, Am. Assn. for Clin. Immunology and Allergy, Internat. Congress Allergology. Home: 5235 17th St Lubbock TX 79416 Office: 3610 34th St Lubbock TX 79410

LUND, SISTER CANDIDA, coll. pres.; b. Chgo.; d. Fred S. and Katharine (Murray) Lund Heck; B.A., Rosary Coll., 1942; M.A., Cath. U. Am., 1954; Ph.D., U. Chgo., 1963; LL.D., Lincoln (Ill.) Coll., 1968. Asst. dean Rosary Coll., River Forest, Ill., 1955-58, chmn. polit. sci. dept., 1961-64, pres., 1964—. Mem. exec. com. Fedn. Ind. Ill. Colls. and Univs. Trustee Carnegie Found. for Advancement Teaching. Fellow Royal Soc. Arts; mem. Assn. Am. Colls., (dir.), Art Inst. Chgo. Contbr. to Third Branch of Government (Pritchett, Westin), 1963. Address: Rosary Coll 7900 Division St River Forest IL 60305

LUND, CATHERINE TERESA (MRS. LESTER J. SCHNELL), physician; b. Bklyn., May 5, 1924; d. Thomas Francis and Anna (Donohoe) Lund; B.S., St. Johns U., 1945; M.D., L.I. Coll. Medicine, 1949; m. Lester J. Schnell, June 2, 1951; children—Lisa, Richard, Nan. Intern, Bklyn. Hosp., 1949-50, asst. resident internal medicine, 1950-51, asst. resident, chief resident pediatrics, 1953-55; practice medicine, specializing in pediatrics, Garden City, N.Y., 1964—; physician Nassau County Dept. Health-Child Health Clinics, 1964—; sch. physician Westbury Sch. Dist., 1970—; health coordinator Garden City Sch. Dist., 1972—. Home: c/o Schnell 202 Wellington Rd Garden City NY 11530

LUND, FLORENCE ADA, editor; b. Lynd, Minn., May 12, 1921; d. Roy and Vinnie Etta (Austin) Nicholson; B.A., Hamline U., 1948; postgrad. Scarritt Coll., 1958; M.A., George Peabody Coll. for Tchrs., 1969; m. Gordon L. Lund, Aug. 21, 1948 (dec. Nov. 1954); children—William, Steven, Timothy. Dir. christian edn. First Meth. Ch., St. Cloud, Minn., 1958-62; editor children's dept. Meth. Bd. Edn., Nashville, Tenn., 1962-72; exec. editor dept. gen. publs. United Meth. Bd. Edn., 1972—. Mem. Am. Assn. Mental Deficiency, Council for Exceptional Children, Nat. Assn. Retarded Children, Christian Educators Fellowship. Methodist. Home: 4810 Old Hickory Blvd Hermitage TN 37076 Office: 201 8th Av S Nashville TN 37202

LUND, LOIS ANN, home economist; b. Thief River Falls, Minn., Aug. 9, 1927; d. Robert J. and E. Luella (Tosdal) Lund; B.S., U. Minn., 1949, M.S., 1954, Ph.D., 1966. Instr. foods dept. home econs. State U. Ia., 1951-55; instr. foods Sch. Home Econs. U. Minn., 1955-63, research fellow, 1963-66, asso. prof., dir. core studies program, 1966-68, asst. dir., 1966-68; asso. dean, dir., Sch. Home Econs. Ohio State U., 1969-73, chmn. dept. home econs. extension Ohio Coop. Extension Service, 1970-73, chmn. dept. home econs. research Ohio Agrl. Research and Devel. Center, 1969-73; dean Coll. Human Ecology Mich. State U., East Lansing, 1973—. Mem. adv. council Coll. Human Ecology Cornell U., N.Y., 1971—. Recipient Betty award for excellence in teaching U. Minn., 1958, 63, 68; named Boss of Yr. Am. Bus. Womens Assn., Columbus, 1970. Mem. Am., Mich. home econs. assns., Nat. Council on Family Relations, Am. Assn. U. Profs., Phi Lambda Theta, Phi Upsilon Omicron, Omicron Nu, Sigma Delta Epsilon. Contbr. articles in field to profl. jours. Office: Coll Human Ecology Michigan State U East Lansing MI 48824

LUNDBERG, LOIS ANN MCQUAY (MRS. TED W. LUNDBERG), polit. worker; b. Tulsa, Sept. 21, 1928; d. John T. and Anna M. (Patterson) McQuay; student Long Beach City Coll., 1945-46; m. Ted W. Lundberg, Sept. 30, 1954; children—Linda, Sharon. With Pacific Telephone, Anaheim, Cal., 1956-65, supr. bus. office 1960-65. Exec. dir. U.S. Senator George Murphy Campaign, 1970; dir. Com. to Re-Elect the Pres., Orange County, 1972; vice chmn. Rep. Central Com. Orange County, 1972-74; mem. Rep. State Central Com., 1966—; del. Rep. Nat. Conv., 1972. Trustee Nixon Law Office Preservation, Inc., 1971—. Named Woman of Yr., La Habra Rep. Women, 1972. Mem. Rep. Federated Women La Habra, Rep. Assos. Orange County (bd. govs.). Lutheran. Home: 1341 Carmela Lane La Habra CA 90631

LUNDBOM, DOROTHY BUNCE (MRS. ERNEST LUNDBOM), home economist; b. Tecumseh, Kan., Aug. 7, 1909; d. George Kress and Estella Mae (Mehaffey) Bunce; B.S., Ore. State U., 1966; m. Justin H. Zornman, June 4, 1938; m. 2d, Ernest T. Lundbom, Aug. 23, 1959; children—Dorothy Joan Zornman, Nancy Lou (Mrs. Stephen A. Day). Sec. Ore. State U. Extension Service, Multnomah County, Baker, Ore., 1952-62, home economist, Baker County, Baker, 1966—. Mem. Am. Assn. U. Women (pres. 1969-70), Am. Home Econs. Assn., Ore. Extension Home Economists Assn. (sec. 1970-71), Am. Assn. Ret. Persons, Grange. Clubs: Knife and Fork (Baker, Ore.); Soroptimists (corr. sec. 1968-70, pres. 1973-74), Baker Garden (treas. 1973-74) (Baker, Ore.). Home: 2261 4th St Baker OR 97814 Office: PO Box 747 Baker OR 97814

LUNDGREN, KATHLYN IOLA KING, librarian; b. Clark, S.D., Oct. 24, 1919; d. Charles Eugene and Jennie (Patterson) King; B.S., Mankato State Coll., 1941; M.A. in Librarianship, U. Denver, 1968, also postgrad.; postgrad. U. Colo.; m. George Andrew Lundgren, June 4, 1942; children—Thomas George, Genevieve Kathleen. Tchr. elementary sch., Danube, Minn., 1941-42; adult and children's librarian McCook Pub. Library, 1960-62; librarian Hannibal (Mo.) High Sch., 1962-64; elementary librarian, Scottsbluff, Neb., 1964-67; dir. Library Services Center, Scottsbluff, 1966-70, elementary library coordinator, 1966-70; librarian, instr. audiovisual and children's lit. Neb. Western Coll., summer 1969, 70—. Library cons. to ednl. instns., also H. W. Wilson Children's Catalog. Mem. A.L.A., Neb. (mem. sch. library devel. com. 1966—, sec. state sch. library sect. 1967-68, v.p. 1969-70, pres. 1970-71), Mountain Plains (rec. sec. 1970, sec. children's sect. 1972, v.p. 1972-73, pres. 1973-74) library assns., N.E.A., Neb. (dist. pres. library sect. 1967-68), Scottsbluff (sec. 1965-68) edn. assns., Am. Assn. U. Women (local pres. 1972-74), P.E.O. (local pres. 1970), Beta Phi Mu. Episcopalian (guild pres. 1967—). Mem. Order Eastern Star. Mem. cons. editorial bd. advisers Denison Co., 1967—, book reviewer, 1966—. Reviewer Sch. Library Jour. Home: 421 Lincoln Ct Box 1086 Scottsbluff NE 69361

LUNDQUIST, MYRTLE VERNICE, educator, author; b. Chgo.; d. Martin Luther and Anna Emily (Lorenz) Lundquist; B.A., U. Chgo., 1951, M.A., 1963. Editor, The Commentator, Fed. Res. Bank Chgo., 1942-60; tchr., Wheeling, Ill., 1960-65, Schaumburg, Ill., 1965—. Mem. Women in Communications, Internat. Assn. Bus. Communications, N.E.A., Indsl. Editors Assn. Chgo., Thimble Guild, Thimble Collectors. Author: The Book of a Thousand Thimbles, 1970. Contbr. articles to mags. Home: 630 Prairie Av Wilmette IL 60091

LUNDREGAN, JANE ELIZABETH TOBIN (MRS. WILLIAM JOSEPH LUNDREGAN III), lawyer; b. Endicott, N.Y., Mar. 6, 1942; d. Henry Loughlin and Mary Margaret (Keenan) Tobin; B.A., Manhattanville Coll., 1964; LL.B., Boston Coll., 1967; m. William Joseph Lundregan III, July 15, 1967; children—Catherine, William J., Anne. Admitted to Mass. bar, 1967; practiced in Marblehead, Mass., 1967-68, Salem, Mass., 1968—; mem. firm Crooks and O'Keefe, Marblehead, 1967-68, William B. Welch, Salem, 1968—. Clk. planning bd., City of Salem, 1970—. Bd. dirs. North Shore Cath. Charity League. Mem. Mass. Assn. Woman Lawyers, Mass., Essex County bar assns. Roman Catholic. Address: 51 Bay View Av Salem MA 01970

LUNDSTROM, HELEN, univ. dean; b. Logan, Utah, Aug. 21, 1921; d. Anders Gustav and Lucile (Olson) Lundstrom; B.A., Utah State U., 1942; M.B.A., U. Denver, 1957; postgrad. U. Utah, 1953, Inst. Ednl. Mgmt., Harvard, 1973. Tchr., Preston High Sch., 1942-44, Logan High Sch., 1944-47; sec. Lundstrom Furniture & Carpet Co., Logan 1947-50, pres., 1959—; missionary Ch. Jesus Christ of Latter-day Saints, 1950-52; asst. prof. Utah State U., Logan, 1953-66, dean of women, 1966—, asso. prof., 1973—, dir. Women's Resource Center, 1974—. Pres. stake Young Women's Mut. Improvement Assn., 1959-64; mem. stake Mut. Improvement Assn. Bd., 1964-72. Mem. Def. Adv. Com. on Women in Service, 1970-72; mem. nat. security forum Air Force War Coll., 1972; mem. No. Utah Law Enforcement Adv. Council, 1972—; mem. adv. com. Hill AFB Equal Employment Opportunity, 1973—. Bd. dirs. Logan Latter-day Saints Hosp., 1973—. Mem. Nat. Assn. Women Deans and Counselors, Nat. (state membership chmn. 1956-59, regional membership chmn. 1957-59), Western (sec. 1959, 64, treas. 1965), Utah (dir. 1960-62) bus. edn. assns., Am. Assn. U. Women, Bus. and Profl. Women, Faculty Women's League, Mortar Bd, (hon.), Spurs (hon.), Phi Kappa Phi (sec. 1957-61, 69-71, pres. 1973-74), Delta Pi Epsilon (chpt. pres. 1957), Alpha Lambda Delta, Alpha Chi Omega (chmn. bldg. corp. 1946-50). Mem. Ch. of Jesus Christ of Latter-day Saints (Sunday sch. stake bd. 1973—). Club: University Women's. Home: 125 E 2d North Logan UT 84321

LUNDY, KATHRYN RENFRO (MRS. FRANK A. LUNDY), librarian; b. Horse Cave, Ky., Aug. 15, 1918; d. Edmund Lovell and Rose (Strader) Renfro; student Colo. Coll., 1935-38; A.B. in L.S., U. Denver, 1939; m. Frank A. Lundy, Nov. 12, 1971. Catalog reviser U. Denver, summer 1939; asst. cataloger Stephens Coll., 1939-42; head catalog dept. Utah State Agrl. Coll., 1942-43; cataloger Ia. State Coll., 1943-46; with U. Neb., Lincoln, 1946—, successively sr. asst. librarian catalog dept., catalog librarian, tech. service librarian, 1946-53, asst. dir. libraries for tech. service with rank of asso. prof., 1953-64, asso. dir. libraries tech. service with rank prof., 1964-68, asso. dir. libraries for gen. services with rank prof., 1968—, acting dir. univ. libraries, summer 1973. Cons. Neb. Pub. Library Commn. on Centralized Processing, 1967-70, Eastern Ia. Community Coll. Libraries, 1970. Mem. A.L.A. (council 1957-61, 65-69, (dir. resources and tech. service div. 1957-61, exec. com. cataloging and classification sect. 1959-61), Mountain-Plains (chmn. regional cataloging group 1950-51, chmn. coll. and univ. sect. 1954-55), Neb. (pres. 1963-64) library assns., Assn. Coll. and Research Libraries (sec. univ. library sect. 1954-55, chmn. com. on coms. 1955), Am. Assn. U. Women (rec. sec. Lincoln br. 1952-54). Am. Assn. U. Profs. (sec. Neb. chpt. 1962), Kappa Kappa Gamma, Beta Phi Mu. Baptist. Club: University of Nebraska Faculty Women's (1st v.p. 1958-59). Home: 1913 Monterey Dr Lincoln NE 68506 Office: Love Meml Library U Neb Lincoln NE 68508

LUNGERSHAUSEN, ALICE MANDERBACH, musician; b. Ann Arbor, Mich., July 9, 1907; d. Henry A. and Jenny (Perry) Manderbach; A.B., U. Mich., 1926, Mus.M., 1931, B.L.S., 1933; student Franz Schmidit, Vienna, Rudolph Dolmetsch Haslemere, Eng.; m. Arnold W. Lungershausen, Mar. 22, 1941; children—Gail Christine, Jenny Ann, Arnold W. Concert harpsichordist; solo, chamber music recitals, also played with Phila., Toledo, Detroit, Saginaw (Mich.), Grosse Pointe (Mich.) symphony orchs., U. Mich. Little Symphony, Detroit Women's Symphony; mem. faculty Grosse Pointe Conservatory of Music, 1962—, Detroit Community Music Sch.; ofcl. harpsichordist Detroit Symphony Orch. Founder, mem. Detroit Baroque Ensemble. Bd. dirs. Detroit Community Music Sch., Friends of Grosse Pointe Library. Mem. Tuesday Musicale Detroit, Chamber Music Soc. Detroit, Pro Musica, Mich. Fedn. Music Clubs, Women's Assn. Detroit Symphony Orch., Grosse Pointe Symphony Soc. (bd. dirs.), Founders Soc. Detroit Art Inst., Phi Beta Kappa, Mu Phi Epsilon. Home: 849 Berkshire Rd Grosse Pointe MI 48230

LUNIN, LOIS FRUMKIN (MRS. MARTIN LUNIN), information scientist; b. Schenectady; d. Hyman and Sophie J. (Tauber) Frumkin; A.B., Radcliffe Coll., 1945; M.S., Drexel Inst. Tech., 1966; m. Martin Lunin, June 22, 1947. Research adminstr. med. research dept. Wm. D. McAdams, Inc., N.Y.C., 1956-58; research asso. dept. pathology U. Tex. M.D. Anderson Hosp. and Tumor Inst., Houston, 1959-64; co-dir. and program dir. Information Center for Hearing, Speech, and Disorders of Human Communication, Johns Hopkins U. Sch. Medicine, Balt., 1965—, instr. laryngology and otology, 1966—, instr. Sch. Hygiene and Pub. Health, 1971—. Cons. NRC Task Force on Med. Subject Headings, 1967—, div. nuclear medicine N.Y. Hosp., 1967—, dept. pathology U. Md. (Balt.) Sch. Dentistry, 1964—, Pan Am. Health Orgn., 1974—; mem. Am. Nat. Standards Inst. Com., 1970—. Fellow Inst. Information Scientists; mem. Am. Soc. for Information Sci. (sec. 1971,

72, chmn. liaison com. 1971, 72, chmn. spl. interest group for information analysis centers 1970, chmn. Chesapeake Bay chpt. 1968), A.A.A.S., Assn. for Computing Machinery, Council of Biology Editors, Drug Information Assn., Med. Library Assn., Phi Kappa Phi, Beta Phi Mu. Author: Index-Handbook of Ototoxic Agents, 1966-71, 1973. Contbr. articles to profl. jours. Exec. editor: Current Citations on Communication Disorders-Hearing and Balance, 1972—; Current Citations on Communication Disorders-Language, Speech, and Voice, 1972—; editor-in-chief bull. Am. Soc. for Information Sci., 1974—. Mem. editorial bd. Johns Hopkins Med. Jour., 1970-72. Home: 28 Olmsted Green Baltimore MD 21210 Office: B-2 Wood Basic Science Bldg Johns Hopkins Med Instns Baltimore MD 21205

LUNN, JANET LOUISE (MRS. WILLIAM RICHARD LUNN), editor, author; b. Dallas, Tex., Dec. 28, 1928; came to Can., 1946, naturalized, 1962; d. Herman Alfred and Margaret Maria (Alexander) Swoboda; student Queen's U., Kingston, Ont., Can., 1941-50; m. William Richard Lunn, Mar. 2, 1950; children—Eric, Jeffrey, Alexander, Katherine, John. Editor Clarke, Irwin & Co., Toronto, Ont., 1972—. Cons. for sch. readers; free lance reviewer, critic of children's books, 1954—. Can. Council grantee, 1967. Author: Twin Spell, 1967; (with William Richard Lunn) The County, 1967. Home: RR 2 Hillier ON KOK2JO Canada Office: 791 St Clair Av W Toronto ON Canada

LUNNON, BETTY SHEEHAN (MRS. JAMES LUNNON), librarian; b. Montgomery, Ala., May 29, 1908; d. Merrill Ashurst and Martha (Guice) Sheehan; student U. Ala., 1928, 30, 32-34; A.B., George Washington U., 1938; M.A., Appalachian State Tchrs. Coll., 1959; m. David White, Nov. 27, 1927 (div. 1936); m. 2d, James Lunnon, May 13, 1939 (dec. Nov. 1954); 1 dau., Penelope Anne (Mrs. Darrell F. Fleeger). Tchr., librarian Hayneville (Ala.) Pub. Sch., 1927-29, Seale (Ala.) Pub. Sch., 1929-31, Dadeville (Ala.) Pub. Sch., 1931-32; caseworker Ala. Dept. Pub. Welfare, Fed. Emergency Relief Adminstrn., 1933-35; statis. cataloger U.S. Govt., 1937-38; librarian Miami Edison Sr. High Sch., 1938-42, Fairlawn Elementary Sch., 1952-54, Cushman Pvt. Sch., Miami, 1973—; supr. Dade County Sch. Libraries, Miami, 1954-68; supr. libraries Dept. Edn., Pago Pago, Am. Samoa, 1968-73; now library cons.; asst. prof. U. Miami summer 1960, evening sch., 1961, 63-66; prof. summer workshop Drexel Inst., 1965; library com. cons. Field Enterprises Ednl. Corp. Gray Lady, A.R.C., 1949-52; dir. Fla. Hearing and Speech Center, 1962-63. Mem. Am. Assn. U. Women (br. v.p. 1950-51), D.A.R., Nat. Fla. edn. assns., Am., Fla. (pres. 1961-62) library assns., Dade County Sch. Library Assn. (pres. 1953), Am. (dir. southeastern states 1962-64, chmn. suprs. sect. 1966-67), Fla. (pres. 1956) assns. sch. librarians, Kappa Delta Pi, Delta Kappa Gamma. Club: Quota (lt. gov. 27th dist.). Author: Jacarezinho Vadico, 1946; Two Shoes, 1951. Home: 1002 Granada Blvd Coral Gables FL 33134 Office: 592 NE 60th St Miami FL 33137

LUNSFORD, ELIZABETH ANN, planetarium exec.; b. Haleyville, Ala., July 20, 1948; d. James Taylor and Angeline Eloise (Brooks) Lunsford; B.A. in Art, U. Montevallo, 1970. Claims clk. dept. indsl. relations State Ala., Montgomery, 1971; dir. sch. relations W.A. Gayle Planetarium, Montgomery, Ala., 1971—. Mem. council Boy Scouts Am., Montgomery, 1972—. Mem. Southeastern Planetarium Assn., Internat. Soc. Planetarium Educators. Methodist. Home: 4724 B Narrow Lane Rd Montgomery AL 36111 Office: 1010 Forest Av Montgomery AL 36106

LUONG, CORINA MONGCAL (MRS. THÊ MÂN LUONG), psychologist; b. Sagay, Negros Occidental, P.I., Aug. 13, 1935; d. Emiiiano Soto and Jacoba Zalameda (Katalbas) Mongcal; B.A. cum laude, U. Philippines, 1955; M.A. (M. Farley scholar) (Fulbright-Hays grantee), Bryn Mawr Coll., 1965, Ph.D., 1968; m. Thê Mân Luong, July 5, 1968. Came to Can., 1969. Psychologist, instr. psychology Philippine Army Tng. Command, 1955-58; guidance psychologist Nat. Mental Hosp., P.I., 1958-63; staff psychologist Children's Hosp. Phila., 1965-67; clin. child psychologist, sch. psychologist Mt. Royal Health Dept., Que., Can., 1969-74; sr. psychologist Sainte-Croix Sch. Bd., Montreal, 1974—. Am. Assn. U. Women fellow, 1967-68. Mem. Am., Canadian psychol. assns., Internat. Council Psychologists, Com. Instl. Psychiatry, Que. Assn. Children with Learning Disabilities. Author: (with Dr. T.M. Luong) The Great Image Sellers, 1972. Home: 390 Cote Vertu Montreal PQ H4N 1E3 Canada Office: 1100 Cote Vertu Montreal PQ H4L 4V1 Canada

LUPEAR, LINDA MARIE, TV reporter; b. Indpls., Sept. 14, 1940; d. John S. and Ida Marie (Qualiza) Lupear; B.S. cum laude, Butler U., 1964. PUb. relations account exec. Ruben Advt., Indpls., 1962-65; reporter WISH-TV, Indpls., 1965-72, WRTV, Indpls., 1973—; pub. information asst. to supt. Indpls. pub. schs., 1972-73. Recipient various awards including Caspar award Indpls. Community Service Council, Indpls. Press Club awards. Mem. Women's Polit. Caucus, Women in Communications, Sigma Delta Chi, Phi Kappa Phi. Roman Catholic. Home: 1048 N Holmes Av Indianapolis IN 46222 Office: 1330 N Meridian St Indianapolis IN 46222

LUPIA, CAROL CHERNEY (MRS. ARCHY LOUIS LUPIA), educator; b. Flandreau, S.D., Jan. 24, 1923; d. Frank Joseph and Mary Grace (Sellman) Cherney; B.A., U. S.D., 1944; postgrad. George Washington U., 1966; certificate U. Va., 1966, San Diego State U., 1970; m. Archy Louis Lupia, June 14, 1947; children—Christie (Mrs. Bruce Albert Gescheider), David, Jonathan, Carol. Tchr. high sch., Onawa, Ia., 1944-45; personnel trainer O'Connor, Moffatt Co., San Francisco, 1946-47; tchr. Norfolk (Va.) Pub. Schs., 1961-63, Sasebo, Japan, 1968-69; tchr. for mentally retarded San Diego Unified Sch. System, 1969-70, Fairfax County, Va., 1970—. Active Girl Scouts U.S.A., 1955-58, 64-66; Navy relief interviewer Norfolk, 1961-63, San Diego, 1968-69. Mem. Am. Assn. for Mental Deficiency, Council for Exceptional Children, Nat. Assn. for Retarded Children, No. Va. Assn. for Retarded Citizens (steering com. for group homes). Clubs: Hyde Park Garden (sec. 1950-54), African Violet (pres. 1952-53). Home: 1906 Hackamore Lane Alexandria VA 22308 Office: 7630 Telegraph Rd Alexandria VA 22310

LUPO, MARY ADELINE (MRS. NICHOLAS ARTHUR LUPO), banking exec.; b. Arlington, Mass.; d. Joseph A. and Teresa (Tangusso) Raia; J.D., Northeastern U., 1938; student grad. Am. Inst. Banking, 1941, 67-70; m. Nicholas Arthur Lupo, July 31, 1945; children—Robert N. and Joan C. (Mrs. Paul Amandio Batista) (twins). Admitted to Mass. bar, 1940; tax clk. State St. Bank & Trust Co., Boston, 1941-45; tax mgr. Seattle Second Nat. Bank, 1945-46; tax atty., asso. atty. Nicholas A. Lupo, Newton, Mass., 1957-67; instr. Chamberlayne Jr. Coll., Boston, 1966-67; asst. supr. Nat. Shawmut Bank of Boston, 1967-68, tax specialist, 1968—. Active Cancer and Heart fund drives, Waltham and Weston, Mass. Mem. Am. Inst. Banking, Mass. Bar Assn., Mass. Assn. Women Lawyers, Delta Phi Epsilon. Home: 29 Myles Standish Rd Weston MA 02193 Office: Nat Shawmut Bank Boston 40 Water St Boston MA 02109

LUPOLI, GERALDINE ALICE, lawyer; b. New Haven, Oct. 17, 1941; d. Gennaro and Alice (Mongillo) Lupoli; B.A. cum laude, Albertus Magnus Coll., 1963; J.D., U. Conn., 1966. Admitted to Conn. bar, 1966, bars U.S. Dist. Ct. Dist. Conn., 1967, U.S. Ct. Appeals 2d Circuit, 1968, U.S. Supreme Ct., 1971; asst. ct. clk., Superior Ct., New Haven, 1966-68; asso., David E. Fitzgerald, Jr., New Haven, 1968-71; chief legal clk., Probate Ct., New Haven, 1971—; practiced in New Haven, 1971—. Mem. Am., Conn., New Haven County, New Haven Jr. bar assns., Kappa Gamma Pi. Home: 1768 Boulevard St New Haven CT 06511 Office: Probate Court 161 Church St New Haven CT 06510

LUPTON, MARY HOSMER (MRS. THOMAS GEORGE LUPTON), owner rare book search service; b. Olympia, Wash., Jan. 2, 1914; d. Kenneth Winthrop and Mary Louise (Wheeler) Hosmer; student Gunston Hall Jr. Coll., 1932-33; B.S. in Edn., U. Va., 1940; m. Keith Brahe Wiley, Oct. 12, 1940 (dec. Apr. 1955); children—Sarah Hosmer (Mrs. Owen Schriver Guise), Victoria (Mrs. Russell Joseph McCurdy); m. 2d, Thomas George Lupton, Nov. 27, 1965; 1 stepson, Andrew Henshaw. Partner Wakefield Press, Earlysville, Va., 1940-55; owner, operator Wakefield Forest Bookshop, Earlysville, 1955-65, Forest Bookshop, Charlottesville, 1965—, Wakefield Forest Tree Farm, 1955—. Corr. sec. Charlottesville-Albemarle Civic League, 1963-64; sec. Instructive Vis. Nurses Assn., Charlottesville, 1961-62; chmn. pub. informations Charlottesville chpt. Va. Mus. Fine Arts, 1970-74; mem. writers' adv. panel Va. Center for Creative Arts, 1973—; mem. Ablemarle County Forestry Com., 1961-62. Mem. Am. Assn. U. Women, D.A.R., New Eng. Hist. Geneal. Soc., Va., Albemarle County hist. socs., League Women Voters, Am. Forest Assn. Chi Omega. Mem. Soc. of Friends. Address: Route 1 Box 50-B Charlottesville VA 22901

LURIA, GLORIA, art gallery owner; b. N.Y.C., Oct. 5, 1925; d. Henry S. and Frances A. (Saul) Biren; student Pratt Inst., 1938-40, Art Students League, 1941-42; B.S., Skidmore Coll., 1947; m. Leonard Luria, Nov. 13, 1949; children—Peter, Henry, Nancy. Sec. L. Luria & Son, Inc., Miami, Fla., 1961—; owner Gloria Luria Gallery, Miami, 1966—. Chmn. Am. Affairs sect. Hadassah, Miami, 1964-65; pres. women's group YM and YWHA, Miami, 1965, Jewish Fedn. Greater Miami, 1971-74. Home: 13600 SW 70th Av Miami FL 33156 Office: 14700 Biscayne Blvd Miami FL 33161

LURIA, ZELLA (MRS. SALVADOR E. LURIA), educator; b. N.Y.C., Feb. 18, 1924; d. Hyman and Dora (Garbarsky) Hurwitz; B.A., Bklyn. Coll., 1944; M.A., Ind. U., 1947; Ph.D., 1951; m. Salvador E. Luria, Aprl 18, 1945; 1 son, Daniel David. Post-doctoral fellow U. Ill. at Urbana, 1951-53, asst. prof., 1956-58, research asso. Russell Sage Found., 1953-56; asst. prof. Tufts U., 1958-62, asso. prof., 1962-70, prof., 1970—; spl. fellow Pub. Health Service Laboratoire de Psychobiologie de L'Enfant, Paris, France, 1963-64. Mem. Am. Psychol. Assn., New Eng. Psychol. Assn. (pres. 1972—), Soc. Research Child Devel. Office: Tufts U Medford MA 02155

LURIE, DIANA MARGARET, writer; b. Johannesburg, South Africa, Oct. 19, 1941; d. Harold and Rose Cecile (Brasch) Lurie; student (fellow Ford Found. 1970-71) Columbia; B.F.A. with honors, Ohio State U. Reporter Life Mag., 1961-66; asso. editor Ladies Home Jour., spl. projects Time, Inc., 1971; free lance writer, N.Y.C., 1970—. Address: care Foley Agy 34 E 38th St New York City NY 10016

LURIE, NANCY OESTREICH, anthropologist; b. Milw., Jan. 29, 1924; d. Carl Ralph and Rayline (Danielson) Oestreich; B.A., U. Wis., 1945; M.A., U. Chgo., 1947; Ph.D., Northwestern U., 1952; m. Edward Lurie, 1951 (div. 1963). Faculty, U. Wis., Milw., 1947-49, 51-53, asst. prof., 1961-63, prof., 1963-72, chmn. anthropology dept., 1967-70; curator anthropology Milw. Pub. Mus., 1972—. Lectr., U. Mich., 1956-61, cons., expert witness for attys. representing tribal clients before U.S. Indian Claims Commn., 1957-64; Fulbright-Hays Lectr., Aarhus, Denmark, 1965-66. Recipient (with co-editor) Anisfield-Wolf award for best scholarly book in intergroup relations The American Indian Today, 1968. Fellow A.A.A.S., Am. Anthrop. Assn.; mem. Am. Ethnol. Soc., Soc. Applied Anthropology, Central States Anthropol. Soc. (pres. 1967), Sigma Xi. Editor, translator Mountain Wolf Woman, The Autobiography of A Winnebago Woman, 1961. Home: 3342 N Gordon Pl Milwaukee WI 53212

LURIE, OLGA RUBINOW (MRS. WALTER A. LURIE), child psychologist; b. Long Branch, N.J., Aug. 3, 1906; d. Isaac Max and Sophie (Himwich) Rubinow; student Swarthmore Coll., 1924-26; B.A. with honors, U. Wis., 1928; postgrad. U. Berlin, 1931-32; Ph.D., U. Vienna, 1934; m. Walter A. Lurie, May 14, 1938; children—Michael Rubinow, Ruth (Mrs. Neal Kozodoy). Research asst. Psychol. Inst. U. Vienna (Austria), 1934-35; psychiat. cons. Jewish Social Service Bur., Chgo., 1936-44; parent edn. leader Assn. for Family Living, Chgo., 1944-46; lectr. Pestalozzi-Froebel Tchrs. Coll., Chgo., 1945; pvt. practice as child psychologist, Mamaroneck, N.Y., 1949—. Psychol. cons. Colonial Nursery Sch., Larchmont, N.Y., 1949-59; project dir. childhood emotional health study in Westchester County, Mental Health Assn., White Plains, N.Y., 1966-70. Chmn., Citizens Com. on Pre-Sch. Edn. in Rye Neck, N.Y., 1949-50; mem. adv. com. Guidance Center, New Rochelle, 1949—; mem. N.Y. State Com. on Children, 1970—. Nat. Inst. Mental Health grantee, 1966-69. Diplomate Am. Bd. Examiners in Profl. Psychology. Fellow Am. Orthopsychiat. Assn.; mem. Am., Eastern, N.Y. State, Westchester County psychol. assns., N.Y. Soc. Clin. Psychologists. Contbr. articles to profl. jours. Address: 742 Halstead Av Mamaroneck NY 10543

LURO, FRANCES WEINMAN (MRS. HORATIO A. LURO), mining and mfg. co. exec.; b. Nicholasville, Ky., Dec. 16, 1918; d. William J. and Caroline Frances (Wysor) Weinman; grad. pvt. schs.; m. Horatio A. Luro, Sept. 2, 1951; 1 dau., Cary Latimer (Mrs. Joseph Anthony Reagan). With Thompson-Weinman & Co., Cartersville, Ga., 1951—, chmn. bd., 1966—; co-owner, dir. Evans Clay Co., McIntyre, Ga., White Pigment Co., Rutland Vt., 1966—; owner Old Mill Farm, thoroughbred horse breeding and tng. farm, Cartersville, 1951—. Bd. dirs. Am. Cancer Soc. Clubs: Piedmont Driving (Atlanta); Surf (Surfside, Fla.); Cartersville Country. Home: 4760 North Bay Rd Miami Beach FL 33140 Office: Thompson-Weinman & Co Cartersville GA 30120

LURVEY, AMELIA COOK (MRS. LEONARD LURVEY), civic worker; b. Detroit, Mar. 8, 1917; d. Max B. and Miriam (Barrett) Gellman; A.B., Ind. U., 1939; m. David M. Cook, Aug. 20, 1940 (dec. Dec. 1967); children—Frank, Sally, Mary, Daniel; m. 2d, Leonard Lurvey, Apr. 14, 1973. Speech and hearing therapist Indpls. pub. schs., 1939-40; pvt. therapist, Indpls., 1940-45; pres. Jewish Social Services, 1953-56, life bd. dirs.; pres. women's div. Jewish Welfare Fedn., 1959-60, fund raising chmn., 1959; pres. Indpls. sect. Nat. Council of Jewish Women, 1960-61, Indpls. P.T.A. council, 1961-63; first pres. Indpls. pre-sch. centers, 1965-66, chmn. planning com., 1964-65; mem. mayor's commn. on human rights, 1960-68, chmn. edn. and welfare com., 1961-68; sec. Ind. Reorgn. Commn., 1965-69; registered lobbyist Ind. Congress Parents and tchrs., 1965-74, chmn. exceptional child com., 1963-67, dir. for central Ind., 1967-68, coordinator legislative lobby com. 1968-69, state legislative chmn., 1969-73, v.p. for Central Ind. region 1973-74; mem. bd. Concord Center, 1963-68, v.p., 1967-68, chmn. Ind. Pub. Sch. Finance Coalition, 1970-73; mem. planning staff Community Service Council Met. Indpls., coordinator demonstration, early childhood intervention program, 1971-73, chmn. childhood intervention com., 1972-74; mem. adv. council spl. edn. div. Ind. Dept. Pub. Instrn., 1971-74, mem. tchr. edn. adv. council, 1971-74. Bd. dirs. Indpls. Community Action Against Poverty, Indpls. Community Service Council, Catholic Sem. Found. Indpls., Indpls. Hebrew Congregation, Indpls. Jewish Welfare Fedn., Indpls. Jewish Community Relations Adv. Council. Named Women of Year, B'nai B'rith, 1963; recipient Brotherhood award Nat. Conf. Christians and Jews, 1970. Mem. Nat., Ind. coms. for support of pub. schs., N.E.A. (commn. on profl. rights and responsibilities, study investigation com. for Ft. Wayne 1966-67), Com. to Study Problems of Multiple Handicapped (mem. legislative adv. com. 1967-68). Home: 6877 N Pennsylvania St Indianapolis IN 46220

LUSE, RUTH PETERSON (MRS. ROBERT RAY LUSE), newspaper editor; b. Phila., May 16, 1938; d. John Victor and Jean (Williams) Peterson; B.A. in English, Westminster Coll., 1960; m Robert Ray Luse, June 18, 1960; 1 son, Jon Robert. Tchr. French, Charles Boehm Jr. High Sch., Yardley, Pa., 1960-61; editor Hopewell Valley (N.J.) News, 1966—. Adminstrv. asst. N.J. Dept. Edn.; cons. Needs Assessment, Trenton, N.J., 1970-71. Mem. Sch. Bd. Community Relations Com. 1971-72. Mem. N.J. Press Assn. (3rd place editorial 1972, 2d place pub. service award 1972), Hopewell Valley Jaycee-ettes (v.p. 1968-69), Chi Omega, Omicron Gamma (chpt. v.p. 1957—). Presbyn. Club: Hopewell Valley Garden. Home: 116 Darrow Dr Pennington NJ 08534 Office: 5 Railroad Pl Hopewell NJ 08525

LUSH, EDITH JEAN HILTON (MRS. ARTHUR LYALL LUSH), social worker; b. Murray Bridge, South Australia; d. Arthur Robert and Edith (Comley) Hilton; B.A. in Sociology, U. Wash., 1959, M.S.W., 1962; m. Arthur Lyall Lush, Mar. 20, 1937; children—Robin Margaret, David Murray Hilton, Heather Ruth (Mrs. Stewart Thorndike). Came to U.S., 1952, naturalized, 1954. Broadcaster, Over the Coffee Cup program KGDN, Seattle, 1954-65; mem. staff Seattle Family Counselling Service, 1962—, family therapist, 1962—. Speaker womens retreats and convs., 1952—. Mem. Nat. Assn. Social Worker, Nat. Council Family Relations, Acad. Certified Social Workers, Am. Assn. Marriage and Family Counsellors (clin. mem.). Columnist, Lets Talk It Over, 1969—. Home: Box 201 Granite Falls WA 98252 Office: Seattle Family Counselling Service 1600 NE 150th St Seattle WA 98155

LUSK, GLENNA RAE KNIGHT (MRS. EDWIN BRUCE LUSK), librarian; b. Franklinton, La., Aug. 16, 1935; d. Otis Harvey and Lou Zelle (Bahm) Knight; B.S., La. State U., 1956, M.S., 1963; m. John Earle Uhler, Jr., May 26, 1956; children—Anne Knight, Camille Allana; m. 2d, Edwin Bruce Lusk, Nov. 28, 1970. Asst. librarian Iberville Parish Library, Plaquemine, La., 1956-57, 1962-68; tchr. Iberville Parish Pub. Schs., Plaquemine, 1957-59, Plaquemines Parish Pub. Schs., Buras, La., 1959-61; dir. Iberville Parish Library, Carriage House Mus., Plaquemine, 1969—. Mem. Iberville Parish Econ. Devel. Council, Plaquemine, 1970-71; sec. Iberville Parish Bicentennial Commn., 1973—; mem. La. Bicentennial Commn., 1974. Named Outstanding Young Woman Plaquemine, La. Jr. C. of C., 1970. Mem. La. (sect. chmn. 1967-68), Riverland (sec. 1973-74) libraries assns., Capital Area Libraries (chmn. com. 1972-74). Democrat. Episcopalian. Author: (with John E. Uhler, Jr.) Cajun Country Cookin', 1966; Rochester Clarke Bibliography of Louisiana Cookery, 1966; Royal Recipes from the Cajun Country, 1969; Iberville Parish, 1970. Home: 206 Pecan Tree Lane Plaquemine LA 70764 Office: 712 Eden St Plaquemine LA 70764

LUSKY, LOIS FREESE, account exec.; b. Wahpeton, N.D., Sept. 28, 1931; d. James J. and Edna (Eckes) Freese; A.A., N.D. State Sch. Sci., 1952; student U. Denver, 1953-55; m. Sam Lusky, July 14, 1966; 1 stepson, Mark. Staff asst. pub. relations Denver U.S. Nat. Bank, 1953-58, asst. pub. relations dir., 1959-61, pub. relations dir., 1961-63; with Sam Lusky Assos. Inc., 1963—, exec. v.p., dir., 1965—. Mem., chmn. publicity com. Colo. Commn. on Status of Women, 1968-70; mem. pub. relations com. Mile High United Fund, 1961—; vol. publicity chmn. Boys' Clubs, Denver, 1965-68. Bd. dirs. Auraria Community Center, 1960-63. Mem. Colo. Soc. Indsl. Editors, Pub. Relations Soc. Republican. Roman Catholic. Home: 3106 S Newport St Denver CO 80222 Office: First Nat Bank Bldg Denver CO 80202

LUSTER, ARLENE DOONG CHOW LEONG (MRS. GILBERT NORMAN LUSTER), librarian; b. Honolulu, Jan. 11, 1936; d. Henry Hung Yun and Sadie Mee Yee (Chun) Leong; student Ottumwa Heights Coll., 1953-54, U. Hawaii, 1954-55, Our Lady of Lake, 1955-56, U. So. Cal., 1956, Immaculate Heart Coll., 1956; B.A., Tex. Woman's U., 1957; M.S., Western Res. U., 1958; postgrad. Sophia U., Tokyo, Japan, 1959-60; m. Gilbert Norman Luster, Mar. 25, 1960; children—Eugene Kam Hoi, Deanna Mee Yee. Hosp./med. librarian Torrance (Cal.) Gen. Hosp., 1958-59; base librarian Fuchu Air Sta., Japan, 1959-61; asst. acquisitions librarian Gregg M. Sinclair Library, U. Hawaii, 1961-63; asst. base librarian Hickam AFB (Hawaii) Library, 1963-65, base librarian, 1965-68; base librarian Wheeler Base Library, Hawaii, 1968-73; naval regional librarian Navy Ednl. and Tng. Support Detachment, Pearl Harbor, 1973—; lectr. library tech. dept. Leeward Community Coll., 1974-75. Ex-officio mem. library adv. bd. Grad. Sch. Library Studies, U. Hawaii, 1973-75; corr. Wahiawa Sun Press, 1970-73; mem. Hawaii Chinese History Center, 1973—. Dep. Equal Employment Opportunity officer, 1973—. Recipient John Cotton Dana award H.W. Wilson Co. and A.L.A., 1971-72, George Washington honor medal Freedoms Found., 1971, 72. Mem. Spl. Libraries Assn., Am., Hawaii (pres. 1973-74, editor jour. 1974—) library assns., Pub. Library Relations Council. Co-editor The Pub, 1969-71. Compiler: China, Taiwan and Hong Kong PACAF Basic Bibliographies, 1961-72; Community Recreation PACAF Basic Bibliographies, 1969-71; Directory of Libraries and Informations Sources in Hawaii and the Pacific Islands, 1970, 73. Home: 3501 Kepuhi St Honolulu HI 96815 Office: Fleet Exchange Collection Navy Education and Training Support Detachment Pearl Harbor Box 526 FPO San Francisco CA 96610

LUSTIG, DOROTHY ANN, investment cons.; b. Bklyn., July 24, 1949; d. Albert M. and Jessie (Grossberg) Lustig; grad. high sch. Exec. sec. Franklin Distbrs., N.Y.C., 1966-68; statistician, researcher investments Arthur Lipser Corp., N.Y.C., 1968-70; dealer securities Seabord Funds Distbrs., Beverly Hills, Cal., 1971-73; now cons. new mut. funds. Mem. Nat. Assn. Securities Dealers. Home: 209 Montana Av Apt 202 Santa Monica CA 90403

LUSTIG, FELICIA MITZ (MRS. OSCAR G. LUSTIG), educator, psychotherapist; b. Sofia, Bulgaria, Jan. 21, 1921; d. Jacob and Rosa (Adler) Mitz; Diploma, Sofia U. (Bulgaria), 1944; postgrad. Max Eitingon Inst. for Psychoanalysis, 1944-47; M.S., Hunter Coll., 1959; Ph.D., N.Y. U., 1970; m. Oscar G. Lustig, June 10, 1946; children—Michael, Ilana, Karen. Came to U.S., 1950, naturalized, 1955. Psychologist, Hadassah Vocational and Ednl. Guidance Center, Jerusalem, 1944-47; pvt. practice as psychotherapist, Jerusalem, 1944-47, N.Y.C., 1969—; rehab. counselor intern N.Y. State Edn. Dept., N.Y.C., 1958-59; sr. clin. rehab. counselor N.Y. U.-Bellevue Med. Center, N.Y.C., 1960—; instr. rehab. medicine N.Y. U. Med. Sch., N.Y.C., 1971-73, asst. prof., 1973—. Mem. Am., N.J. psychol. assns., Am. Assn. Marriage and Family Counselors, Am. Personnel and Guidance Assn., Nat. Rehab. Assn. Home: 803 W 180th St New York City NY 10033 Office: 27th St and 1st Av New York City NY 10016 also 332 Briar Cliff Lane Paramus NJ

LUSTIG, SUSAN GARDNER HOWELL HANSON (MRS. KARL A. LUSTIG), occupational therapist; b. Beloit, Wis., Apr. 27, 1942; d. James Idris and Sally Esson (Gardner) Howell; student U. Wis., 1959-60; B.S. with distinction, U. Minn., 1965; m. Karl A. Lustig, Aug. 16, 1969; children—Kurt, Daniel. Acting occupational therapist Oak Ridge Nursing Home, Mpls., 1961; occupational therapist, hosp. improvement program Hastings (Minn.) State Hosp., 1965-66; occupational therapy cons. Div. Vocational Rehab., Honolulu, 1966-67; occupational therapist Hawaii State Hosp., Kaneohe, 1967-68; gen. medicine and surg. occupational therapist Mpls. VA Hosp., 1968, organizer occupational therapy prevocational work evaluation unit, 1968-69, supr., 1968-70. Vol. worker Ill. Dept. Children and Family Services, 1971-73. Bd. dirs. Harrison County (W.Va.) Sheltered Workshop, 1971-73. Mem. Am., Ill. occupational therapy assns., World Fedn. Occupational Therapists. Lutheran. Home: Route 4 Deer Park Rd Ottawa IL 61350

LUSTMAN, CLAIRE ROSE, social worker, govt. ofcl.; b. Pitts.; d. David and Laura (Lvensohn) Lustman; B.A., U. Pitts., 1933, M.S., 1941. Supr., Pa. Dept. Pub. Assistance, 1935-43; asst. hosp. supr. Am. Nat. Red Cross, 1943-45; chief social worker VA Hosp., Aspinwall, Pa., 1945-50; social service field rep. Central Office Social Work Service, VA, Washington, 1950-54, chief staff devel. and edn. div., 1964-73, edn. specialist Office Acad. Affairs, 1973—; chief social worker VA Hosp., Pitts., 1955-64. Asso. prof. Howard U. Sch. Social Work, Washington, 1955—; adj. asso. prof. U. Pitts. Sch. Social Work, 1963-65. Mem. adv. council, health com. Urban League Pitts., 1961-65; casework and groupwork adv. com. U. Pitts., 1953-65; adv. profl. com. Council-House Pitts., 1964-66. Bd. dirs. Nat. Rehab. Tng. Inst. Recipient award A.R.C., 1944; Outstanding Performance commendation VA, 1965. Mem. Nat. Assn. Social Workers (Service Award So. region 1967, regional inst. program com. 1950-62), Council on Social Work Edn. (faculty and teaching com. 1968-72, practice and edn. com. 1973—), Am. Assn. Med. Social Workers (area chmn. 1951-53), U. Pitts. Alumni Assn. Grad. Sch. Social Work, (pres. 1957-61), Women's Overseas Service League, Am. Hosp. Assn., Nat. Council on Aging, Nat. Conf. Social Work, Internat. Council on Social Welfare. Contbr. articles to profl. jours. Home: 2001 N Adams St Arlington VA 22201 Office: VA Central Office 810 Vermont Av NW Washington DC 20420

LUTE, HARRIET, librarian; b. Paxton, Neb.; d. Harry D. and Lulu (Woods) Lute; A.B. cum laude, Neb. State Tchrs. Coll., 1939; M.A., U. Denver, 1954. Tchr. English, Sr. High Sch., North Platte, Neb., 1939-49; library supr. North Platte Pub. Schs., 1950-60; supervisory cons. Neb. Pub. Library Commn., 1960-69; dir. libraries Englewood (Colo.) Pub. Library, 1969—. Mem. of Gov.'s Conf. on Youth, 1957. Mem. Am., Mountain Plains, Colo., Neb. (pres. 1960-61) library assns., Nat. Neb., North Platte, Keith County (pres. 1948-49) edn. assns., Am. Assn. U. Women (br. pres. 1959-61), P.T.A. (state chmn. reading and library service, state bd.), Delta Kappa Gamma, Alpha Gamma Delta. Club: Altrusa (local pres. 1955-66, dist. editor 1966—). Editor: Newsletter, 1962—. Contbr. articles profl. jours. Home: 9655 E Center St Denver CO 80231 Office: 3400 S Elati Englewood CO 80110

LUTER, YVONNE MARIE-LOUISE SPIEGELBERG, editor; b. Hamburg, Germany, Feb. 26, 1928; d. Ernest and Marie Louise (Mankiewicz) Spiegelberg; B.A., Bryn Mawr Coll., 1949; M.A., Columbia, 1958; div. Came to U.S., 1941, naturalized, 1948. Am. editor Stern mag., Hamburg, 1951—, Mortensens Forlag, Oslo, Norway, 1960—, Sondags-B.T., Copenhagen, Denmark, 1965—. Mem. Fgn. Press Assn. Democrat. Club: York (N.Y.C.). Home: 1185 Park Av New York City NY 10028 Office: 60 E 56th St New York City NY 10022

LUTHER, FLORENCE JOAN (MRS. CHARLES W. LUTHER), lawyer; b. N.Y.C. June 28, 1927; d. John Phillip and Catherine Elizabeth (Duffy) Thomas ; J.D. magna cum laude, U. Pacific, 1963; m. William J. Regan (dec.); children—Kevin P., Brian T.; m. 2d, Charles W. Luther, June 11, 1961. Admitted to Cal. bar; mem. firm Luther, Luther, O'Connor & Johnson, Sacramento, 1964—. Mem. faculty McGeorge Sch. Law, U. Pacific, Sacramento, 1966—, prof., 1968—. Judge Bank Am. Achievement awards, 1969-71. Bd. dirs. Sacramento Suicide Prevention League, 1969-70. Mem. Am., Cal., Sacramento County bar assns., Am. Assn. U. Profs., Womens Legal Groups, Am. Judicature Soc., Iota Tau Tau. Home: 8455 Winding Way Fair Oaks CA 95628 Office: 3282 5th Av Sacramento CA 95817

LUTTERBECK, ANN GOGGIN (MRS. EUGENE F. LUTTERBECK), lawyer; b. Evanston, Ill., June 18, 1923; d. Dennis F. and Bridget Jessie (Moran) Goggin; A.B., DePaul U., 1946, J.D., 1949; LL.M., U. Ill., 1957; m. Eugene F. Lutterbeck, Sept. 6, 1952; children—Karen Maura, Steven Eugene, Deborah Ann. Admitted to Ill. bar, 1949; atty. Lumbermens Mut. Casualty Co., Chgo., 1950-52; mem. firm Stradford, LaFontant, Gibson, Fisher & Cousins, Chgo., 1967-70; asso. mem. firm Kriebel & Jorgenson, Chgo., 1970-71; asst. counsel, editor life ins. law digest Am. Life Conv., Chgo., 1971-73; counsel Am. Life Ins. Assn., Chgo., 1973; dir. div. case coordination Ill. Fair Employment Practices Commn., 1973—. Volunteer atty. Legal Aid Bur. Chgo., 1952-53, Juvenile Ct. Cook County, 1964-67. Lower sch. chmn. Parents Assn. Lab. Schs. U. Chgo., 1964-65. Bd. govs. Parents Assn. Lab. Schs. U. Chgo., 1964-70; bd. dirs. Hyde Park Kenwood Community Conf., 1966-68. Mem. Am. Chgo. bar assns., Women's Bar Assn. (bd. dirs. 1953-55). Club: Germania. Home: 4950 Chicago Beach Dr Chicago IL 60615 Office: 179 W Washington St Chicago IL 60602

LUTTINGER, LENORE MADELEINE (MRS. LIONEL LUTTINGER), physician; b. Hackensack, N.J., Apr. 9, 1929; d. Joseph and Margaret (Becker) Kremer; B.S. magna cum laude, Coll. City N.Y., 1953; M.D., N.Y. U., 1957; m. Lionel Luttinger, Sept. 30, 1955; children—Amy, Karl, Nina, Tanya. Intern Stamford (Conn.) Hosp., 1957-58; pvt. practice gen. medicine, Stamford, 1958-71, Erwinna, Pa., 1971—. Home and office: River Rd Erwinna PA 18920

LUTTRELL, MARY GRACE LEAVERTON (MRS. CURTIS LOREN LUTTRELL), club woman; b. Springfield, Ill., June 16, 1918; d. William John and Agnes (Jones) Leaverton; A.A., Springfield Jr. Coll., 1937; student James Millikin U., 1938-39; m. Curtis Loren Luttrell, July 21, 1947; children—Allen William, Grace Louise. Owner, mgr. Leaverton Apts., Springfield, 1961—. Mem. D.A.R. (chpt. regent 1963-65, dist. sec. 1965-67, 69-70, state chmn. 1966-69), Children of Am. Revolution (sr. state pres. 1967-69, sr. state chaplain 1965-67, sr. state organizing sec. 1969-71), Colonial Daus. of 17th Century (pres. 1970-73), Colonial Dames of Am. (v.p. 1969-72, pres. 1973—), Nat. Soc. Magna Charta Dames (v.p. 1971-74), Daus. Am. Colonists, Sovereign Colonial Soc. Ams. of Royal Descent, Soc. Mayflower Descs., Colonial Dames XVII Century (v.p. 1970-72, state treas. 1972-75), Nat. Soc. Dames Ct. of Honor (v.p. 1971-75), Soc. Descs. Knights Noble Order of Garter. Sigma Iota Chi. Republican. Methodist. Home: 443 W Cook St Springfield IL 62704 Office: 724 S 4th St Springfield IL 62703

LUTTRULL, JUNE WISE (MRS. STEPHEN JOHN LUTTRULL), pub. co. exec.; b. Nashville, Jan. 21, 1924; d. Harry Howard and Oma Beatrice (Jones) Wise; student Falls Bus. Coll., Nashville, 1942; m. Stephen John Luttrull, Sept. 15, 1945; 1 son, Lawrence Howard. With the Meth. Pub. House, Nashville, 1942—, supr., 1960—. Home: 1343 Kenwood Dr Nashville TN 37216 Office: 201 8th Av S Nashville TN 37203

LUTUS, EMMA JEAN (MRS. JOHN F. LUTUS), ednl. adminstr.; b. Cain, Pa., July 15, 1920; d. Ezra M. and Bessie May (Strine) Funk; student Huntington Coll., 1938-39; certificate, Shippensburg State Tchrs. Coll., 1941; B.S. in Gen. Studies U. Rochester, 1958, Ed.M., 1966; m. John F. Lutus, Mar. 19, 1945; 1 dau., Jeanne (Mrs. Joshua Benin). Tchr. Miller's Elementary Sch., York Springs, Pa., 1941-44, Thorncreek Consol. Sch., Columbia City, Ind., 1944-46; tchr. Rochester City Sch., Rochester, N.Y., 1958-62, helping tchr., 1962-65, asst. dir., 1965-73. Cons. Operation Follow-Through. Mem. family life edn. com. Family Service Center, Rochester, 1971—. Trustee Roberts Wesleyan Coll., North Chili, N.Y. Mem. Assn. for Childhood Edn., Internat. Reading Assn., N.Y. Assn. for Childhood Edn. (pres. 1969-71), N.Y. State Council for Children (pres. 1971-72), N.E.A., N.Y. State Tchrs. Assn., Rochester Tchrs. Assn., Delta Kappa Gamma (pres. Alpha Xi local chpt. 1972—), Conglist. (tchr. Sunday sch. 1960—). Home: 224 Seymour Rd Rochester NY 14609 Office: 410 Alexander St Rochester NY 14607

LUTZ, BETTY JEAN (MRS. GEORGE R. LUTZ), city ofcl.; b. Provolt, Ore., July 10, 1925; d. Jack and Dorothy M. (Stidham) Steward; student Ore. State U., 1944-46; m. George R. Lutz, July 6, 1946; 1 dau., Linda S. (Mrs. Matthias E. Lukens II). Confidential sec. Nat.-Standard Co., Clifton, N.J., 1946-64; city clk. City of Clifton, N.J., 1964—. Trustee Girls' Club of Clifton; mem. Adv. Com., 1970-72. Mem. Internat. Inst. Municipal Clks., Passaic County (sec. 1970, 71, v.p. 1972-73, pres. 1974—), N.J. municipal clks. assns., Zonta Internat., Nat. Secretaries Assn., Internat. Service Club Council. Home: 34 Phyllis Place Clifton NJ 07012 Office: City Hall Main Av Clifton NJ 07015

LUTZ, EMILY EILEEN, physician; b. Circlesville, O., July 23, 1928; d. Lorin Earl and Marion Elizabeth (Rowe) Lutz; B.A., Ohio State U., 1950, M.A., 1952, M.D., 1959. Tchr. phys. edn. U. Ill., Urbana, 1952-54, Ohio State U., Columbus, 1954-55; intern San Francisco Gen. Hosp., 1959-60; resident obstetrics and gynecology U. Cal. at San Francisco, 1960-64; practice medicine specializing in obstetrics and gynecology, San Francisco, 1964-68, Circleville, O., 1968—; attending gynecologist Orient (O.) State Hosp., 1968-71; mem. staff Berger Hosp., Circleville, Ohio State Univ. Hosp.; asst. clin. prof. U. Cal. Med. Sch., San Francisco, 1966-68, Ohio State U. Coll. Medicine, 1968—. Mem. Circleville Bd. Health, 1969—. Diplomate Am. Bd. Obstetrics and Gynecology. Fellow Am. Coll. Obstetrics and Gynecology, A.C.S.; mem. Am. Med. Women's Assn., Columbus Obstetrics and Gynecology Soc. Home: 815 Dartmouth Dr Circleville OH 43113 Office: 610 Northridge Rd Circleville OH 43113

LUTZ, HELEN IRENE DRAKE (MRS. WILFORD RAY LUTZ), city ofcl.; b. Dayton, O., Sept. 4, 1918; d. Charles Francis and Hattie May (Smith) Drake; grad. Miami-Jacobs Jr. Coll., 1937; student U. Dayton, 1938-40; m. Wilford Ray Lutz, June 26, 1948; children—Gary Ray, Lynnette Irene. Exec. sec. to advt. and sales promotion mgr. Frigidaire div. Gen. Motors Sales Corp., Dayton, 1937-40; adminstr. asst. statis. services div. USAAF Hdqrs. Air Force Logistics Command, Wright-Patterson AFB, 1940-53; with City of Kettering, O., 1956—, clk. city council, 1973—. Vice pres. Orville Wright Elementary Sch., P.T.A., Dayton, 1963-64. Mem. Ohio Municipal Clks. Assn., Kettering Hist. Soc., Aurean Lit. Soc. (pres. 1935-36), D.A.R., Children Am. Revolution (local pres. 1935-36, nat. registrar 1937-38, Ohio pres. 1936-38). Lutheran (pres. fellowship class 1973-74). Mem. Order Eastern Star. Home: 840 E David Rd Kettering OH 45429 Office: Kettering Govt Center 3600 Shroyer Rd Kettering OH 45429

LUTZ, JEANNE MENDENHALL (MRS. WILLIAM EUGENE LUTZ), educator; b. Steelton, Pa., Sept. 14, 1926; d. Francis Everett and Ruth Naomi (Brinton) Mendenhall; B.A. in Speech and Theater, Brenau Coll., Gainesville, Ga., 1948; M.A. in Speech, Pa. State U., 1967; m. William Eugene Lutz, July 8, 1950. Tchr. speech pub. schs., Harrisburg, Pa., 1949-57; tchr. speech Cedar Cliff High Sch., Camp Hill, Pa., 1960-66; instr. speech Pa. State U., University Park, 1967—, dir. forensics, 1972—. Adviser speech edn. Pa. Dept. Edn., 1967-70; dir. Pa. High Sch. Speech League, 1967—, editor newsletter, 1967—. Mem. Nat. U. Extension Assn. (adv. com. discussion and debate), Nat., Pa. (exec. sec. 1969—), Eastern speech communication assns., Delta Sigma Rho, Tau Kappa Alpha, Alpha Chi Omega. Contbr. articles to profl. jours. Home: 1881 Park Forest Av State College PA 16801 Office: 205 Sparks Bldg Pa State Univ University Park PA 16802

LUTZ, MERNA MAE (MRS. ALVIN J. LUTZ), judge; b. Stella, Neb., Aug. 19, 1929; d. Leo and Beulah I. (Prall) Duggan; grad. Nampa Bus. Coll., 1948; m. Alvin J. Lutz, Nov. 4, 1950; children—Roy, Randy, James, Katrina. Sec., Northwestern Mut. Life Ins. Co., Twin Falls, Ida., 1948-50, George Ins. Agy. (Wash.), 1964-66; justice peace, 1966-72; police judge, George, 1966—; office mgr., water records clk. Watermaster's sect. Quincy Columbia Basin irrigation dist., 1972—. Lutheran (tchr. Sunday sch. 1958—, Christian growth chmn. Luth. Women's Missionary League Wash.-Alaska dist. 1965-67). Editor: George Crier, 1965—. Home: 133 Deacon St George WA 98824 Office: PO Box 5233 George WA 98824

LUX, GWEN (MRS. THOMAS H. CREIGHTON), sculptor; b. Chgo.; d. Arend and Johanna (Van Bremen) Wickerts; student Md. Inst. Arts, 1927-28, Boston Mus. Fine Arts Sch., 1929-30; pvt. study with Ivan Mestrovic, Yugoslavia; m. Thomas H. Creighton, Dec. 26, 1959. One person shows at Delphic Studios, N.Y.C., 1932, Assn. Am. Artists, N.Y.C., 1946, Pomeroy Gallery, San Francisco, 1966, Contemporary Arts Center, Honolulu, 1970; exhibited in group shows at Phila. Mus. Arts, 1933, N.A.D., 1933, Salon d'Automne, Paris, 1934, Salon des Tuileries, Paris, 1934, Weyhe, Gallery, N.Y.C., 1935, Whitney Museum Am. Art, N.Y.C., 1947, World House Gallery, N.Y.C., 1962, San Francisco Art Inst., 1964, San Francisco Mus. Art, 1965, Hoover Gallery, San Francisco, 1969; represented in permanent collection at Detroit Inst. Arts, also in pvt. collections; major commd. works include interior free-standing works in Radio City, N.Y.C., KRON-TV Bldg., San Francisco, exterior free-standing works at Northland Shopping Center, Detroit, Gen. Wingate Sch., Bklyn., State Office Bldg., Lihue, Hawaii, exterior wall pieces at McGraw Hill Bldg., Chgo., Bristol (Tenn.) Hosp., Gen. Motors Research Center, Detroit, Aviation Trades High Sch., Queens, N.Y.C., interior wall pieces in U. Ark., Victoria Theater, N.Y.C., S.S. United States, Country Day Sch., Lake Placid, N.Y., Tex. Petroleum Club, Dallas, Socony Bldg., N.Y.C., Pub. Sch. 79, N.Y.C., Laguna Towers, San Francisco; tchr. sculpture Arts and Crafts Soc. Detroit, 1945-48. Guggenheim fellow, 1933; recipient award Detroit Inst. Arts, 1945, Nat. Lithography Assn., 1947, Nat. Assn. Women Artists, 1947, Audubon Soc., 1954, Archtl. League, N.Y.C., 1958, Municipal Arts Soc., N.Y.C., 1959, Nat. Indsl. Arts Council, 1961, San Francisco Women Artists Assn., 1965. Address: 4340 Pahoa Av Honolulu HI 96816

LUYANDA, ALMA NORELIA, educator; b. Rio Piedras, P.R., Apr. 8, 1939; d. Ignacio and Dolores (Jaramillo) Luyanda; B.S. in Phys. Therapy and Occupational Therapy, U. P.R., 1961; M.A. in Spanish, N.Y. U., 1965. Phys. therapist Middlesex Rehab. and Polio Hosp., North Brunswick, N.J., 1961-62; occupational therapist Met. Hosp., N.Y.C., 1962-63; faculty Rockland Community Coll., Suffern, N.Y., 1965—, asso. prof. Spanish, 1973—, faculty senator, 1969-71, 73-75. Vol., Good Samaritan Hosp., Suffern, 1972. Cornell U. grantee, 1969. Mem. Am. Occupational Therapy Assn., Hist. Soc. Rockland County. Club: Catholic Alumni (N.Y.C.). Home: PO Box 594 Suffern NY 10901

LYBARGER, ADRIENNE REYNOLDS (MRS. LEE FRANCIS LYBARGER, JR.), coll. adminstr.; b. Boston, Mar. 8, 1926; d. Joseph Anthony and Albertine Mouton (Drevet) Reynolds; B.A., Mills Coll., 1947; certificate Katharine Gibbs Sch., 1948; m. Lee Francis Lybarger, Jr., Sept. 15, 1955; children—Linda, Lauretta, James (dec.), Lisa, Lesie, Jeffrey (dec.), Lucia, Lana. Asst. to dir. Mid-Century convocations Mass. Inst. Tech., Cambridge, 1948, asst. to dir. West Coast regional office Mid-Century devel. program, 1949-50, asst. dir. So. regional office, 1950-51; asst. to dir. convocation program Ithaca (N.Y.) Coll., 1951; asst. to dir., devel. program U. Buffalo (N.Y.), 1951-52; asst. dir. Diamond Jubilee program Case Inst. Tech., Cleve., 1952-54; asst. to dir., expansion and improvement program John D. Archbold Hosp., Thomasville, Ga., 1954-55; partner Lybarger Prodns., comml. films, N.Y.C., 1955-61; asst. dir., then dir. regional campaigns, Ohio, Boston, Mass., N.Y.C., also supr. all other nat. regional campaigns Mt. Holyoke Coll. Fund for Future, South Hadley, Mass., 1961-63; fund-raising cons. to capital programs, Vocation Service Center and Bronx-Westchester YMCA, YMCA Greater N.Y., 1963-65; dir. devel. and pub. relations Bank Street College of Edn., N.Y.C., 1965—. Mem. Am. Coll. Pub. Relations Assn., Am. Alumni Council. Author: (with L.F. Lybarger) Proven Guides to Effective Soliciting (slide film), 1950, rev., 1960. Home: King Manor Pittstown NJ 08867 Office: 610 W 112th St New York City NY 10025

LYCAKI, HELENE, clin. psychologist; b. Tripolis, Greece, Sept. 23, 1939; d. Dimitrios and Adamandia (Okonomopoulou) Lycaki; degree philology and philosophy, U. Athens, 1963; M.A. in Clin. Psychology (Profl. scholar 1969-71), Wayne State U., 1970, Ph.D., 1971. Came to U.S., 1965, naturalized, 1971. Psychiat. social worker Dromokaition Mental Hosp., Athens, 1960-65, chief psychologist adult inpatient service Lafayette Clinic, Detroit, 1973—, asst. chief psychol. div., 1974—; adj. asst. prof. psychology Wayne State U., 1973—; pvt. practice, 1973—. Nat. Inst. Mental Health fellow, 1971-73. Mem. Am. Psychol. Assn., Greek Soc. Humanistic Studies, Psi Chi. Contbr. to profl. jours. Home: 704 Lafayette Towers E Detroit MI 48207 Office: 951 E Lafayette St Detroit MI 48207

LYKINS, DOROTHY REED (MRS. WILLIAM HENDRICKS LYKINS), library trustee; b. West Lafayette, Ind., Oct. 4, 1894; d. Worth and Della Harriet (Shoup) Reed; student De Pauw U., 1913-14, Hamilton Coll. for Women, 1914-15; A.B. cum laude, Transylvania U., 1917; m. William Hendricks Lykins, Oct. 27, 1917. Federated club columnist Indpls. Sunday Star, 1950—. Trustee Covington (Ind.) Pub. Library. Mem. Ind. Fedn. Clubs (pres. 1944-47), Ind. Library Trustee Assn. (pres. 1956-58), D.A.R., Chi Omega, Kappa Kappa Kappa. Republican. Presbyn. (deacon). Clubs: Woman's, Booklovers (Covington, Ind.). Editor: Bd. Borings publ. Ind. Library Trustee Assn., 1960-69. Home: 620 Liberty St Covington IN 47932

LYLE, GLORIA GILBERT (MRS. ROBERT EDWARD LYLE, JR.), educator; b. Atlanta, Aug. 7, 1923; d. Albert Van Buren and Edith Katherine (London) Gilbert; B.A., Vanderbilt U., 1944; M.S., Emory U., 1946; Ph.D., U. N.H., 1958; m. Robert Edward Lyle, Aug. 28, 1947. Instr. chemistry Hollins (Va.) Coll., 1946-47; research asso. U. Wis. McArdle Lab., 1947-49; instr. U. N.H., Durham, 1951-60, asst. prof., 1960-64, asso. prof. chemistry, 1964-74, prof., 1974—. Mem. Steering Com. N.H. Govs. Conf. Edn., 1964. USPHS fellow, 1958-59. Mem. Am. Assn. U. Women, Chem. Soc. (London), Am. Chem. Soc., N.Y. Acad. Scis., Sigma Xi, Gamma Phi Beta. Patentee in field. Home: 7 Hoitt Dr Durham NH 03824

LYLE, JEROLYN ROSS (MRS. FRANK ALLEN LYLE), educator; b. Meridian, Miss., Sept. 12, 1937; d. Fred A. and Everette B. (Bynum) Ross; B.A. (Univ. scholar), So. Meth. U., 1958; M.A., (Univ. fellow), U. Md., 1966, Ph.D., 1970; m. Frank Allen Lyle, June 21, 1958; children—Kathryn Everette, James Jeffrey. Tchr. Dallas pub. schs., 1958-59; tchr., curriculum specialist Houston Pub. Schs., 1959-61; tchr. Arlington County schs., Arlington, Va., 1961-62, 63-64; staff economist Office of Commr., U.S. Office Edn., Dept. Health, Edn. and Welfare, 1966-68; office mgr. No. Va. Fair Housing Assn., 1965-67; sr. economist U.S. Equal Employment Opportunity Commn., 1968-70; lectr. econ. theory Smith Coll., Northampton, Mass., 1971; econ. cons. U.S. Equal Employment Opportunity Commn., summer 1971, Urban Inst., Washington, summer 1971; asst. prof. econs. Am. U., Washington, 1971—. Econs cons. U.S. Office of Mgmt. and Budget, Exec. Office of Pres., Washington, 1971; prin. investigator for research grant U.S. Equal Employment Opportunity Commn. to Am. U., Washington, 1971-72; econs. cons. Inter Am. Devel. Bank, 1974. Precinct co-chmn. Harris County Democratic Com., Houston, 1960-61. Presdl. fellow systematic analysis U.S. Office of Mgmt. and Budget and U.S. Dept. Health, Edn. and Welfare, 1967-68. Mem. Am. Econs. Assn., Indsl. Relations Research Assn., Am. Soc. for Pub. Adminstrn. Sr. author: Women in Industry: Employment Patterns of Women in Corporate America, 1973; contbg. author (with Dennis Young and Richard) Public Policy for Day Care of Young Children, 1973; Affirmative Action Programs for Women: A Survey of Innovative Programs, 1973; Patterns of Racial Discrimination, Vol. II, Employment and Income, 1974. Contbr. articles to profl. publs. Home: 5512 Center St Chevy Chase MD 20015

LYLE, KATHERINE CH'IU (MRS. EDGAR ROCHFORD LYLE, II), librarian; b. China, July 12, 1939; d. Jui Fu and Lan Ying (Chao) Ch'iu; B.A., Tunghai U., 1960; M.S. (Internat. Peace scholar P.E.O. 1962), Syracuse U., 1962; m. Edgar Rochford Lyle, II, Feb. 1, 1964; children—May, Lorin. Came to U.S., 1960, naturalized, 1968. Cataloger East Asian collection Yale, New Haven, 1962-64; cataloger Cornell Med. Coll. Library, N.Y.C., 1964-65; bibliographer Nat. Com. on Maternal Health, N.Y.C., 1966-67; chief med. librarian, bibliographer Population Council, Rockefeller U., N.Y.C., 1967—. Tchr. Chinese lang. Columbia, N.Y.C., 1967; cons. Nat. Inst. Child Health and Human Devel., 1968. Mem. Med. Library Assn., Assn. Tchrs. Chinese Lang. and Culture, Assn. Population Library and Information Center. Mem. Soc. of Friends. Author: Chinese Fables, 1967. Home: 100 LaSalle St New York City NY 10027 Office: Tower Bldg Rockefeller U York Av and 64th St New York City NY 10021

LYLES, LOUTIE ROBERTS, banker; b. Oxford, Miss., May 21, 1909; d. William Isaac and Letitia (Wilson) Roberts; student U. Miss., 1926; m. Samuel T. Lyles, Sept. 2, 1933. With 1st Nat. Bank Oxford, 1934—, asst. to pres., 1959-64, v.p., 1964—. Treas. Lafayette County Cancer Soc., 1952-56, Lafayette County Tb Assns., 1955—. Named Women of Year Oxford and Lafayette County, Bus. and Profl. Club, 1956. Mem. V.F.W. Aux. (pres. 1951-52), Nat. Assn. Bank Women, No. Miss. Bank Auditors and Controllers (treas. 1962), Am. Legion Aux. Democrat. Baptist. Mem. Order Eastern Star. Club: Pilot. Home:

208 Bramlett St Oxford MS 38655 Office: 1203 Jackson Av Oxford MS 38655

LYMAN, HELEN LUCILLE HUGUENOR, educator, librarian, researcher; b. Hornell, N.Y., Mar. 16, 1910; d. Leon C. and Lora M. (Hamilton) Huguenor; B.A., U. Buffalo, 1932, B.S. in L.S., 1940; postgrad. U. Chgo., 1955-56; m. Vreelandt B. Lyman, Jr., Apr. 29, 1939 (dec. Feb. 1946); m. 2d, Samray Smith, June 17, 1953 (div. Feb. 1959). Circulation asst. Buffalo Pub. Library, 1932-35, co-head readers bur., 1935-42, adminstrv. asst., 1943-44, head, adult edn. dept., 1944-52; dir. adult edn. survey A.L.A., Chgo., 1952-53; adult services librarian Hild regional br. Chgo. Pub. Library, 1957-59; pub. library cons., specialist in adult services Wis. Free Library Commn., Madison, 1959-63; dir. reference dept. Lockwood Meml. Library, State U. N.Y., Buffalo, 1964-65; pub. library specialist for adult services library services br. Office Edn., Dept. Health, Edn. and Welfare, Washington, 1965-67; asst. prof. Library Sch., also dir. library materials research project U. Wis., Madison, 1968-73, asso. prof., 1973—, dir. Inst. for Tng. in Librarianship Film and Library, summer 1969, dir. workshop Adult New Reader and his Reading, 1973. Cons. evaluator adult edn. project Pub. Library, Terre Haute, Ind., 1965—; mem. adv. study panel Barss, Reitzel & Assos., Cambridge, Mass., 1970-71; cons., adviser Inst. Service to Urban Disadvantaged, dept. library sci. Wayne State U., 1972; cons., adviser Morehead State U. and Appalachian Adult Edn. Center, 1972. Trustee, University Book Store, Madison. Mem. A.L.A. (pres.-elect/v.p. adult services div. 1968-69, pres. 1969-70), Am. Assn. U. Profs., Wis. Library Assn., Adult Edn. Assn. Wis., Adult Edn. Assn. U.S., Nat. Reading Conf., Am. Assn. Library Schs. Club: Altrusa. Author: Adult Education Activities in Public Libraries, 1954; Library Materials in Service to the Adult New Reader: Phase I: The Planning Year-Final Report, 1969, 1973; also contbr. to jours. Editor library programs and services to disadvantaged issue Library Trends, 1971. Home: 3209 Stevens St Madison WI 53705 also S 4528 Freeman Rd Orchard Park NY 14127 Office: U Wis Library Sch 600 N Park St Madison WI 53706

LYMAN, SUSAN FRANCES CROWLEY (MRS. ROYAL JAMES LYMAN), historian, mus. ofcl.; b. Lawrenceville, N.Y., Sept. 17, 1913; d. George and Carrie (LaFlesh) Crowley; student Am. Inst. Banking, 1958-60, State U. Coll., Potsdam, N.Y., 1960-61; m. Royal James Lyman, May 11, 1931; children—William H., Carol A. (Mrs. Howard B. Moshier). Head bookkeeping dept. State Bank Norwood (merger St. Lawrence County Bank 1958), Norwood, N.Y., 1951-62; chmn. Norwood Hist. Assn., 1961—; asst. librarian Norwood Library, 1962; spl. feature writer Potsdam Courier-Freeman and Massena Observer, N.Y., 1964—; historian Town Potsdam, 1963—, Village Norwood, 1965—; curator Norwood Mus., 1969—. Chmn., Norwood Centennial Com., 1971-72; active Salvation Army. Recipient Champion Corr. award N.Y. Press Assn., 1968; Distinguished Service citation Norwood Hist. Assn., 1972. Mem. Norwood C. of C. (sec., treas. 1968—), N.Y., St. Lawrence County hist. assns., Nat. Assn. Ret. Persons, Assn. St. Lawrence County, Norwood Library Assn., U.S. Capitol Hist. Soc., Nat. Council Sr. Citizens. Club: Golden Agers (Norwood). Author: The Story of Norwood (N.Y.)-A Century of Progress, 1872-1972, 1972. Home: 38 Prospect St Norwood NY 13668 Office: Norwood Hist Assn and Mus 39 N Main St Norwood NY 13668

LYMAN, SUSAN STOREY (MRS. RONALD T. LYMAN, JR.), ednl. adminstr.; b. Brookline, Mass., May 17, 1919; d. Charles Moorfield and Susan Jameson (Sweetser) Storey; A.B., Radcliffe Coll., 1949; Harvard-Radcliffe Mgmt.-Tng. Program, 1950; Ed.M., Harvard, 1963; m. Samuel P. Shaw, Jr., July 21, 1939 (div. 1949); children—Jane S., Samuel P., III, Charles S. (dec.); m. 2d, Ronald T. Lyman, Jr., Dec. 30, 1950; stepchildren—Elizabeth, Jennifer (Mrs. Allard K. Lowenstein), Mabel Lowell; 1 son, Ronald T., III. Marshal Radcliffe Coll., Cambridge, Mass., 1955-58, trustee, 1958—, dir. fund office, 1970-72, chmn. bd. trustees, 1972-73, acting dean Radcliffe Inst., 1972—. Pres. Mass. Soc. for Prevention Cruelty to Children, 1972-73. Bd. dirs. Douglas A. Thom Clinic for Children, Dorchester Federated Neighborhood Houses, Inc., Radcliffe and Harvard Yard Day Care Units; corp. mem. Pregnancy Counseling Services, Florence Crittenton League, others. Home: 60 Beacon St Boston MA 02108 Office: 10 Garden St Cambridge MA 02138

LYMBERIS, MARIA TRIANTAPHYLLOU (MRS. PEDRO FRANCIS DE CORDOBA), physician; b. Athens, Greece, Aug. 7, 1938; d. Triantaphyllos K. and Stella (Orologa) Lymberis; came to U.S., 1956, naturalized, 1968; B.A. in Philosophy, Rutgers U., 1960; M.D., U. So. Cal., 1964; m. Pedro Francis De Cordoba, Sept. 14, 1963; children—Jason, Anthony. Intern, Mt. Siani Hosp., Los Angeles, 1964-65; resident neurology Mt. Sinai Hosp., N.Y.C., 1965-66; resident psychiatry Albert Einstein Bronx Municipal Hosp., N.Y.C., 1966-68; fellow child psychiatry, neuropsychiatry U. Cal. at Los Angeles, 1968-70; clin. asso. Los Angeles Psychoanalytic Inst., 1968—; pvt. practice medicine specializing in adult and child psychiatry and psychoanalysis, 1968—; med. dir. Marianne Frostig Center Ednl. Therapy; asst. clin. prof. psychiatry U. Cal. at Los Angeles; mem. staff Westwood Hosp. Soroptimist Club scholar 1961-63; USPHS fellow dept. neurology U. S.C., summers 1962-63. Nominated Outstanding Young Woman Am., 1971. Diplomate Am. Bd. Psychiatry and Neurology. Mem. A.A.A.S., Am. Psychiat. Assn., Hellenic Med. Soc. N.Y., So. Cal. Psychiat. Soc. (treas. 1974—). Home: 928 Las Pulgas Rd Pacific Palisades CA 90272 Office: 270 26th St Santa Monica CA 90402

LYNCH, ALMA MARTHA HIRSCH (MRS. WILLIAM WRIGHT LYNCH), civic worker; b. Wheeling, W.Va.; d. Conrad and Alma (Hanszen) Hirsch; B.A., U. Tex.; grad. Sullins Coll.; m. William Wright Lynch, Oct. 18, 1930; children—William Wright, Harry Hanszen. Dir., Ins. Bldg. Corp. Chmn. exec. com. Dallas Council on World Affairs, 1963-66, chmn. West Dallas Scholarship Com., 1962-66; bd. dirs. Soc. for Animal Protection, 1964-66, West Dallas Community Centers, 1962-66; mem. Women's Council Dallas County, 1969-71; mem. exec. com. So. Meth. U. Dean's Club, 1964-66; mem.-at-large, mem. steering com. Nat. Com. for Children and Youth 1966-73; chmn. women's bd. Dallas Civic Opera, 1967-68. Bd. dirs. Planned Parenthood, Dallas, 1962-68; trustee Lynch Found., Ednl. Opportunities, Dallas, Dallas Heritage Soc., Dallas Theater Center, Dallas Symphony Orch.; bd. dirs. Dallas Civic Ballet, G.B. Dealey Awards for Young Artists, MacArthur Acad. Freedom, Brownwood, Tex.; mem. devel. bd. Bishop Coll. Recipient Zonta Service award, 1967; Honor award Nat. Jewish Hosp., 1963; Service award Tex. Youth Conf., 1966. Mem. Chi Omega, Sigma Alpha Iota. Episcopalian. Clubs: Brock Hollow Golf, Dallas Women's. Office: 1710 Jackson St Dallas TX 75201

LYNCH, ALVERDA MOORE (MRS. ROBERT HUGH LYNCH), home economist; b. Arkansas City, Kan., Aug. 28, 1929; d. Herman Burtholt and Lena Mae (Shephard) Magnus; B.S., Kan. State U., 1951, M.S., 1965; m. Robert Hugh Lynch, Aug. 8, 1970; 1 son from a previous marriage, Michael James Moore. Home service rep. Gas Service Co., Mission, Kan., 1951-53; home econs. agt. Kan. Extension Service, Riley County, 1955-65; family econs. spl. S.D. Extension Service, Brookings, 1965—, bd. dirs. Fed. Credit Union, 1974—. Mem. S.D. Consumers League (sec.-treas. 1971—), Am., S.D. (legislative chmn. 1971-74, co-chmn. metric project com. 1973-74) home econs. assns., Am. Assn. U. Women, Faculty Women Club, Epsilon Sigma Phi (auditing com. 1970-73). Home: 614 12th Av Brookings SD 57006

LYNCH, BEVERLY PFEIFER (MRS. JOHN ALLAN LYNCH), assn. exec.; b. Fargo, N.D., Dec. 27, 1936; d. Joseph B. and Nellie (Bailey) Pfeifer; B.S., N.D. State U., 1957; M.S., U. Ill., 1959; Ph.D., U. Wis., 1972; m. John Allan Lynch, Aug. 24, 1968. Librarian, Plymouth (Eng.) Pub. Library, 1961-62, Marquette U., Milw., 1959-60, 62-63; head serials div. Yale Library, New Haven, 1963-68; exec. sec. Assn. Coll. and Research Libraries, Chgo., 1972—. Vis. lectr. U. Wis. Library Sch., Madison, 1971-72. Home: 1859 N 68th St Milwaukee WI 53213 Office: 50 E Huron St Chicago IL 60611

LYNCH, SISTER M. WILMA, librarian; b. New Haven, Aug. 3, 1922; d. William Francis and Alice Reginald (Gordon) Lynch; B.A., Albertus Magnus Coll., 1943; postgrad. Columbia, 1951-53, also So. Conn. State Coll.; M.A. in L.S., Rosary Coll., 1958. Librarian New Haven Pub. Library, 1943-44; tchr. St. Aloysius Sch., Wilmerding, Pa., 1946-48, St. William's Sch., East Pittsburgh, Pa., 1948-49, Holy Name Sch., Steubenville, O., 1949-50, St. Andrew's Sch., Flushing, N.Y., 1950-54, St. Mary's Sch., Marietta, O., 1954-56; tchr., librarian Newark (O.) Cath. High Sch., 1956-57, St. Vincent Ferrer High Sch., N.Y.C., 1958-61, Mary Immaculate Sch., Ossining, N.Y., 1967-68; head librarian Albertus Magnus Coll., New Haven, 1968—. Mem. Am., Conn., New Eng., Cath. library assns., Albertus Magnus Coll. Alumnae. Home: 790 Prospect St New Haven CT 06511

LYNCH, MARGARET ALBERTI, assn. exec.; b. N.Y.C., Dec. 12, 1930; d. John and Rose (Donovan) Alberti; B.A., Coll. of New Rochelle, 1952; m. Charles E. Lynch, July 4, 1953; children—Marylouise, Megan. Dir. League of Women Voters of Cohasset, Mass., 1961-65, pres. 1965-67; dir. League of Women Voters of Mass., 1967-71, pres., 1971—. Mem. Gov.'s Commn. on the Status of Women, 1972—, Mass. Council on Crime and Corrections, 1968—; spl. asst. Mass. Office Ednl. and Cultural Affairs, 1973, also mem. Cohasset adv. bd. Mem. Cohasset Com. on Structure of Town Govt., 1967-69; sec. Cohasset Housing Authority, 1969-72; mem. Governor's Joint Correctional Planning Commn., 1970-72; mem. MACE Com. on Sch. Governance, 1971; mem. Nat. Endowment for Humanities. Home: 36 Sohier St Cohasset MA 02025 Office: 18 Tremont St Boston MA 02108

LYNCH, MARGIE RUTH, librarian; b. Long Beach, Cal., June 8, 1925; d. John Lafayette and Ida Pearl (Thompson) Lynch; B.A., La. State U., 1948; B.S. in Library Sci., La. State U., 1949. Br. librarian Ouachita Parish Pub. Library, Monroe, La., 1949-50; asst. librarian Avoyelles Parish Library, Marksville, La., 1950-51; asst. librarian in charge circulation Lake Charles (La.) Pub. Library, 1951-54; parish librarian Vermilion Parish Library, Abbeville, La., 1955-56; demonstration librarian Vernon Parish Library for La. State Library, 1956-57; parish librarian Vernon Parish Library, Leesville, La., 1957-60, Calcasieu Parish Library, Lake Charles, La., 1961-74; dir. Hattiesburg (Miss.) Pub. Library System, 1974—. Exec. sec. Library Devel. Com. La., 1965-67; chmn. com. on orgn. and structure of pub. libraries La. Standards Conv., 1962-63. Mem. Am., La. (sec. 1958-59, mem. pub. relations com. 1968—), Southwestern (chmn. pub. library sect. 1971—), Calcasieu library assns., Am. Library Trustee Assn. (mem. publs. com. 1964—), Bus. and Profl. Women's Club Lake Charles (pres. 1967-68), Delta Kappa Gamma. Democrat. Baptist. Clubs: Altrusa, Pilot (Leesville, La.). Home: 620 S 28th Av Apt 222 Hattiesburg MS 39401 Office: 723 Main St Hattiesburg MS 39401

LYNCH, MARY B. HILL (MRS. JAMES WALTON LYNCH), artist; b. Pruden, Ky., Sept. 30, 1933; d. Frederick Clarence and Mary Virginia (Strange) Hill; B.A., U. Chattanooga, 1956; postgrad. U. Tenn., 1962-63; student Chattanooga Art Inst., 1967-68, Provincetown (Mass.) Art Assn., 1969; m. James Walton Lynch, Oct. 6, 1956; 1 dau., Holly Kristen. One-man shows at Anchorage Hist. and Fine Arts Mus., Miss. State Coll. Women, Next Door Gallery, Chattanooga, Belmont Coll., Nashville, Tenn. Wesleyan Coll., Athens, others; exhibited in group shows at N.A.D., 1973, 74, U.S.A. Traveling Works on Paper, 1974-75; represented in permanent collections at Little Rock Art Center, Tenn. Arts Commn. State Mus., Anchorage Hist. Fine Arts Mus.; librarian Cin. Pub. Library, 1957—; book reviewer Chattanooga Times, 1965-70, Reinhold Pub. Co., N.Y.C., 1967-69; instr. Hunter Gallery of Art, Chattanooga, 1966—. Mem. alumni council U. Tenn., 1968—; div. chmn. Bookfair Chattanooga Symphony Guild, 1973; mem. adv. panel Tenn. Arts Commn., 1973-74. Chmn. Howard Baker Campaign Hdqrs., Hamilton County, 1967-68, Sen. Bill Brock - Howard Baker Campaign Hdqrs., Chattanooga, 1968; pres. Hamilton County Rep. Women's Club, 1968. Bd. dirs. Multiple Sclerosis Soc., 1969. Recipient Medal of Honor, Nat. Assn. Women Artists, 1973, also numerous purchase awards. Mem. Tenn. Watercolor Soc. (founder, pres. 1973). Club: Lookout Mountain Laurel Wood Garden. Home: 1505 Woodnymph Trail Lookout Mountain TN 37350

LYNCH, MARY TERESA, naval officer; b. Cambridge, Mass., Aug. 30, 1925; d. Charles Leo and Teresa (Buckley) Lynch; B.A., Mt. Holyoke Coll., 1946; M.D., Tufts U., 1950; Rotating intern, Balt. City Hosps., 1950-51; intern internal medicine Johns Hopkins Hosp., Balt., 1951-52; clin. immunology fellow Mass. Meml. Hosp., Boston, 1952-54; commd. lt. U.S. Navy, 1954, advanced through grades to capt., 1968; ward med. officer, officer-in-charge allergy clinic Naval Hosp., Portsmouth, Va., 1954-56; ward med. officer contagion unit Naval Hosp., Newport, R.I., 1956-62; head active duty and disposition br. phys. qualifications and med. records div. Bur. Medicine and Surgery, Navy Dept., Washington, 1962-64; head legal medicine br., 1967-69; head, profl. pubs. div., editor U.S. Navy Medicine, Arlington, Va. 1969—. Recipient Meritorious Service medal Pres. of the U.S., 1973. Diplomate Nat. Bd. Medicine Examiners. Mem. Mass. Med. Soc., A.M.A., Mil. Surgeons U.S., Fed. Editors Assn., A.C.P., Am. Med. Writers Assn. Home: #C901 1600 S Joyce St Arlington VA 22202 Office: Navy Dept Bur Medicine and Surgery Washington DC 20372

LYNCH, PATRICIA KATHLEEN, broadcasting co. producer, author; b. N.Y.C., Mar. 5, 1938; d. Harold J. and Violet B. (Carman) Lynch; A.B., Coll. of New Rochelle, 1959; M.A., Boston Coll., 1960. Asso. producer CBS News, 1966-73; producer NBC News Betty Furness' Action 4, N.Y.C., 1973; free lance writer. Mem. Writers Guild, Nat. Acad. of TV Arts and Scis. (bd. govs. 1974). Author: The National Environment Test; What's It All About Charlie Brown. Address: 416 East 85th St New York City NY 10028

LYNCH, PEG (MARGARET FRANCES LYNCH), writer, actress; b. Lincoln, Neb.; d. Hugh Franklin and Frances (Renning) Lynch; B.A., U. Minn., 1937; m. Odd Knut Ronning, Aug. 12, 1948; 1 dau., Elise Astrid Ronning. Owner, writer, actress prin. role, radio and TV show Ethel and Albert, on ABC Radio, 1944-49, as feature Kate Smith TV show, NBC, 1950-52, regular show NBC, 1952-54, CBS, 1955, ABC, 1955-56; owner, writer actress Couple Next Door, CBS radio, 1958—, Ethel and Albert, NBC, 1962-64. Mem. Screen Actors Guild, mem. A.F.T.R.A., Gamma Phi Beta. Author: Ethel and Albert (monologues, plays), 1956. Home: High St Becket MA 01223

LYND, PRISCILLA ANN, pediatrician; b. Ironton, O., Feb. 4, 1942; d. Jacob Edward and Margaret (Richards) Lynd; A.B., U. Ky., 1964, M.D., 1968. Intern pediatrics U. Ky. Med. Center, Lexington, 1968-69, resident pediatrics, 1970-71, fellow neonatology, 1971-73, asst. prof. pediatrics, 1973—; resident pediatrics U. Va. Hosp., Charlottesville, 1969-70. Sec. U. Ky. Young Republicans, 1960-63, v.p., 1963-64; pres. Fayette County Young Reps., 1973-74; mem. Young Rep. Nat. Com., 1974. Diplomate Am. Bd. Pediatrics. Fellow Am. Acad. Pediatrics; mem. Alpha Epsilon Delta. Republican. Methodist. Home: 697 Berry Lane Lexington KY 40502 Office: Dept Pediatrics U Ky Med Center Lexington KY 40504

LYNDE, DOROTHY JEAN STRAND (MRS. LLEWELLYN DAWE LYNDE), hosp. adminstr.; b. Ellendale, N.D., Mar. 18, 1925; d. Henry John and Chlora Delpha (Payne) Strand; student S.D. State Coll., 1943-44; diploma Presentation Sch. Nursing, Aberdeen, S.D., 1947; m. Llewellyn Dawe Lynde, June 3, 1948; children—John Jay, Jon J., Vikki, Connie. Supr., St. Lukes Hosp., Aberdeen, 1947-48; head nurse St. Johns Hosp., Fargo, N.D., 1948-50; coll. student health nurse State Normal and Indsl. Sch., Ellendale, 1951-52; asst. adminstr. Dickey County Meml. Hosp., Ellendale, 1952-56, adminstr., 1956—. Sec., treas. Ellendale Clinic Pharmacy, Inc., 1958—. Mem. N.D. Hosp. Assn. (profl. relations com. 1968-70), N.D. Angus Breeders Assn. Presbyn. (sec. bd. trustees 1954-55). Home: RD Ellendale ND 58436 Office: 241 Main St Ellendale ND 58436

LYNDS, BEVERLY TURNER (MRS. CLARENCE ROGER LYNDS), astronomer; b. Shreveport, La., Aug. 19, 1929; d. Homer Emory and Nettie Lee (Robertson) Turner; B.S. magna cum laude, Centenary Coll., 1949; postgrad. Tulane U., 1949-50; Ph.D., U. Cal. at Berkeley, 1955; m. Clarence Roger Lynds, June 19, 1954; 1 dau., Susan Elizabeth. Research asso. U. Cal. at Berkeley, 1956-58; research asso. Nat. Radio Astronomy Obs., Green Bank, W.Va., 1959-61; asst. prof. U. Ariz., Tucson, 1962-65, asso. prof., 1965-71; asst. to dir. Kitt Peak Nat. Obs., Tucson, 1971—, asso. astronomer, 1972-74, astronomer, 1974—. Bd. dirs. Gilbert and Sullivan Theater, Tucson, 1968-74. Mem. Am. Astron. Soc. (mem. steering com. working group in the states for women in astronomy 1973—, counselor 1974—), Internat. Astron. Union. Author: Elementary Astronomy, 1959. Editor: Dark Nebulae, 1971. Contbr. articles to profl. jours. Home: 6725 E Opatas St Tucson AZ 85715 Office: 950 N Cherry St Tucson AZ 85717

LYNESS, VIRGINIA LEE (MRS. HARRY FISHER LYNESS), educator, lawyer; b. Spokane, Wash., Sept. 18, 1926; d. A. Robert and Rosemary (Rice) Bergman; student Whitman Coll., 1944-46; B.A. cum laude, U. Washington, 1950, J.D., 1962; m. Harry Fisher Lyness, Sept. 15, 1948. Admitted to Wash. bar, 1962, practiced in Seattle, 1962-64; asso. firm C.M. McCune, Seattle, 1962-63; instr. U. Wash. Law Sch., Seattle, 1963-66, asst. prof. law, 1966-74, asso. prof., 1975—. Instr. C.L.E.O. Inst., summer 1973; cons. trust div. Pacific Coast Banking Sch., 1968—. Mem. Citizen's Adv. Bd. Edmonds Community Coll., Mem. Wash. State, Seattle-King County bar assns., Phi Delta Delta, Delta Gamma. Editor Proceedings Pacific Coast Labor Law Conf., 1974. Home: 1856 East Shelby St Seattle WA 98112 Office: 432 Condon Hall U of Washington Seattle WA 98195

LYNN, CAROLYN LOUISE DYER (MRS. LARRY DEAN LYNN), occupational therapist, civic worker; b. Ft. Knox, Ky., Dec. 22, 1942; d. David Harold and Mary Ried (Stotts) Dyer; B.A., Cottey Jr. Coll., 1962; B.S., Kan. U., 1965; m. Larry Dean Lynn, Aug. 28, 1965; children—Larry David, Lewis Edward. Psychiat. staff therapist Dorthea Dix Hosp., Raleigh, N.C., 1965-66, supr. rehab. dept., 1966; staff therapist Alaska Native Med. Center, Anchorage, 1971-72, supr., 1972. Vol., Army Community Service, Ft. Benning, Ga., 1969-70; vol. A.R.C., Ft. Bragg, N.C., 1974—; pres. Alaska Occupational Therapy Assn., 1973. Mem. Am. Occupational Therapy Assn., P.E.O. Home: 218 N Elm St Charleston MO 63834

LYNN, DONNA MARIE JOOST (MRS. WILLIAM HENDREN LYNN), writer; b. San Francisco, Nov. 15, 1935; d. H. John and Edna Mae (Ellis) Joost; B.A., San Jose State Coll., 1957; postgrad. U. Md., 1962-63, Coll. San Mateo, 1968—; m. William Hendren Lynn, Apr. 14, 1957; children—Kelly A., Kirsten J., J. Conrad. Office sec., San Jose, Cal., 1955-57; sec. E.R. Buchser High Sch., Santa Clara, 1957-58; tchr. Lakenheath (Eng.) Elementary Sch., 1962-63; tchr. creative activities Valley U.P., Portola Valley, 1972-73; free-lance writer articles for various publs., including Family Circle, Western Collector. Co-founder Bible study and prayer group, Portola Valley. Mem. Cal. Writers, Camps Farthest Out, Alpha Phi. Writer: Seascape (children's ballet), 1970, Jump for Joy (film). Nat. editor Protestant Women of Chapel Newsletter (Eng.), 1963-64. Exhibited in one man art show Lewis and Clark Coll., 1965. Home: 203 Wyndham Dr Portola Valley CA 94025

LYNN, DOROTHY REED CORNELIA (MRS. JOHN FINTON SPELLER), dermatologist; b. Rockville Centre, N.Y., Oct. 12, 1915; d. Joseph and Nellie (Irving) Lynn; A.B., Hunter Coll., 1936; M.D., Howard U., 1940; postgrad. U. Pa., 1948-49, N.Y. U., 1949-51; m. John Finton Speller, June 20, 1940; children—Sandra, Marsha, Jeffrey. Intern Freedmen's Hosp., Washington, 1940-41, 1941-42; gen. practice medicine, Phila., 1942-48; practice medicine specializing in dermatology and syphilology, Phila., 1948—; chief dermatology Mercy Douglas Hosp., Phila., 1942—; asst. prof. dermatology Hahnemann Hosp., Phila., 1970—; med. specialist Phila. Health Dept., 1952—. Trustee Temple U. Comprehensive Group Health Services Center, Planned Parenthood Southeastern Pa. Mem. A.M.A., Pa., Philadelphia County med. socs., Pa., Phila. dermatological socs., Delta Sigma Theta. Club: Links (Philadelphia). Home: 2401 Pennsylvania Av Philadelphia PA 19130 Office: 245 N Broad St Philadelphia PA 19107

LYNN, ENID (ENID LYNN ROSENTHAL), dance co. dir.; b. Hartford, Conn., Oct. 30, 1947; d. Morton Sidney and Harriet (Schloss) Rosenthal; A.A., Hartford Coll. Women; student Hartford Ballet Co., 1960—, Martha Graham Sch., N.Y.C., 1966-67, Sigurd Leeder Sch. Dance, Switzerland, 1970. Mem. faculty, performer Hartford Ballet Co., 1964—, chmn. modern dance dept., 1969, dir. Modern Dance Theatre, 1970, exec. dir. co., 1971—; mem. dance faculty Hartt Coll. Music, U. Hartford, 1967—. Mem. Creative Arts Com., 1969—; mem. dance com. Greater Hartford Civic and Arts Festival, 1970-71. Choreographer numerous works including Dover Beach, 1970, Grandstand, 1972, also works commd. Inst. Contemporary Am. Music, Hartford Symphony. Address: Hartford Ballet Co 308 Farmington Av Hartford CT 06067

LYNN, JANET, figure skater; b. Chgo., Apr. 6, 1953; d. Florian Walter and Ethelyne (Gehrke) Nowicki; student Rockford Coll., 1972. Figure skater Ice Follies, hdqrs. Mpls., 1973—. Held ice show to benefit Shriners' Hosps. Crippled Children, 1973. U.S. Nat. Ladies Figure Skating champion, 1969-73; Bronze medalist Olympic Games, 1972, World Games, 1972; Silver medalist World Figure Skating championship, 1973. Mem. Fellowship Christian Athletes (speaker). Home: 4215 Marsh Av Rockford IL 61111 Office: Ice Follies 1600 Main Tower Minneapolis MN 55402

LYNN, MELDA GUY (MRS. RALPH COWGILL LYNN), feature writer; b. Newport, Ky., Nov. 12, 1917; d. Allen Conroy and Lanola (Taylor) Guy; student Bowling Green State U., 1965-74, Sorbonne U. of Paris, 1966, Temple U., 1966, Toledo Mus. Art, 1965-73; m. Ralph Cowgill Lynn, July 31, 1937; children—James Conroy, Lawrence Blaine. Broadcaster radio sta. WPLH, Huntington, W.Va., 1945-51; broadcaster radio sta. WGRO, Bay City, Mich., 1951-52, news editor, writer, 1952-54; broadcaster, writer radio sta. WBCM, Bay City, 1954-55; women's editor Mich. Times, Bay City, 1955-58; weekly sect. editor, reporter Daily Freeman, Waukesha, Wis., 1958-60; news editor Paddock Pubs., Arlington Heights, Ill., 1960-63; staff and feature writer Toledo (O.) Blade, 1963—, beauty editor, 1964—. Vol. Red Cross Nurse's Aide, Louiseville, 1943; active hosp. auxs., Arlington Heights, 1960-63, Magruder Hosp., Port Clinton, O., 1963—; active Little Theater, Bay City, 1951-58; mem. N.W. Ohio Regional Health Planning Commn., 1972—. Mem. Women's Equity Action League, League of Women Voters (pres. Huntington W.VA., 1948), Ohio Newspaper Women's Assn. (first place award for feature story 1974), Women in Communications, Gen. Fedn. Women's Clubs (first place award for writing radio drama 1952). Clubs: Port Clinton Yacht, Catawba Island. Author: Candlecraft Recipies, 1946. Home: 633 Orchard Dr Port Clinton OH 43452 Office: 541 Superior St Toledo OH 43604

LYNN, PAULINE JUDITH WARDLOW (MRS. ARTHUR D. LYNN, JR.), lawyer; b. Columbus, O., Nov. 14, 1920; d. Charles and Helen P. (Christman) Wardlow; student Wellesley Coll., 1938-40; B.A., Ohio State U., 1942, J.D., 1948; m. Arthur D. Lynn, Jr., Dec. 29, 1943; children—Pamela Wardlow, Constance Karen, Deborah Joanne, Patricia Diane. Admitted to Ohio bar, 1948; practiced in Columbus, 1948-49. Troop leader Girl Scouts U.S.A., 1969-71. Mem. Phi Beta Kappa, Kappa Kappa Gamma, Pi Sigma Alpha. Republican. Episcopalian. Home: 2679 Wexford Rd Columbus OH 43221

LYNN, RITA LA BILLE, sociologist, social worker, educator; b. Rocky Mount, N.C., Mar. 26, 1919; d. William D. and Anne (Quigley) Lynn; A.B. cum laude, Trinity Coll., 1943; M.S. in Social Work, Cath. U. Am., 1945, Ph.D., 1949. Lectr. in social group work Cath. U. Am., 1947-48, asst. prof. social work research, 1948-57; vis. lectr. sociology and social work Cath. U. P.R., 1953; research asso. Nat. Cath. Welfare Conf., 1950, Cath. Relief Services, spl. research internat. welfare, 1956-62; prof., chmn. dept. sociology and social work Our Lady of Cincinnati Coll., Cin., 1963-65; asso. prof. sociology, Cath. U. Am., Washington, 1965-67; prof., acting chmn. dept. sociology West Liberty (W.Va.) State Coll., 1968-70; prof. social work, dir. research Barry Coll. Sch. Social Work, Miami Shores, Fla., 1970—. Cons. com. children in need D.C. Dept. Pub. Welfare, 1954-56. Fulbright grantee, Taiwan, 1966. Mem. Am. Sociol. Assn., Nat. Conf. Social Welfare, Internat. Conf. Social Work, Urban Coalition (co-chmn. research cons. com. Miami 1970-71), Soc. Internat. Devel., Council Social Work Edn., Assn. for Sociology Religion, A.A.A.S., Am. Assn. U. Profs., UN Assn. U.S.A., Kappa Gamma Pi, Pi Gamma Mu. Author: National Catholic Community Service in World War II, 1952. Contbr. articles to profl. jours. Home: 2430 NE 135 St North Miami FL 33161 Office: Barry Coll Sch Social Work Miami Shores FL 33161

LYNN, RUTH OZELLA WHITE (MRS. CHARLES BENJAMIN LYNN), assn. exec.; b. Smith Station, Ala., Aug. 24, 1922; d. Warren Candler and Elsie Ruth (Whitten) White; student Andrew Coll., 1968-69; m. Charles Benjamin Lynn, Feb. 3, 1940 (dec. July 1971); children—Charles Benjamin, George Dewey, Elsie Jayne (Mrs. Joe E. Shepard). Office receptionist, Cuthbert, Ga., 1962-66; exec. dir. Randolph Devel. Corp., Cuthbert, 1967—, Cuthbert C. of C., 1967—. Mem. Cuthbert Edn. and Recreation Com., 1962-66; chmn. Heart Drive, Randolph County, 1965—; a founder Randolph Little Theatre, 1968, treas., 1968, dir. theatre prodn., 1969; chmn. 8 County area Health and Edn. Com., Cuthbert, 1970; chmn. continuing edn. com. Andrew Coll., 1968-69; pres. elect Patterson Hosp. Aux., 1970. Chmn. Cuthbert Planning Commn., 1970; supt. Municipal Election, City of Cuthbert, 1971. Mem. Ga. C. of C., Ga. C. of C. Execs. Assn., S.W. Ga. Chamber Council. Baptist (dir. adult dept. Sunday sch. 1970-71). Club: Pilot (chmn. finance com. 1965) (Cuthbert). Home: 401 N Highland Av St Cuthbert GA 31740 Office: On the Square Cuthbert GA 31740

LYNOTT, MARJORIE ANN, physician; b. Salt Lake City, June 16, 1942; d. Tom Tinsely and Cynthia May (Tuttle) Lynott; B.S., U. Utah, 1964; M.D., Tulane U., 1968. Intern Grady Meml. Hosp., Atlanta, 1968-69; gen. practice Emory U., 1969—. Mem. Com to Help Legalize Abortions in state Ga., 1969—. Home: 6640 Akers Mill Rd Atlanta GA 30339 Office: 277 Fairground St Marietta GA 30062

LYON, ELIZABETH ROBERTS, psychotherapist, social worker; b. Cin., Sept. 28, 1912; d. Mortimer and Hannah (Roberts) Lyon; B.A., U. Cin., 1935; M.S., Columbia, 1946; postgrad. Inst. Psychotherapy, 1948-51. Med. social worker Bronx Hosp., N.Y.C., 1938-40, Harlem Hosp., 1940-42; asst. field dir. A.R.C., 1942-45, 47-48; A.R.C. scholar Columbia, Jamaica Hosp. Neurol. Inst., 1945-46; assigned Army Hepatitis Research Center, 1948; spl. cardiac research project, psychiat. social worker Com. for Care Jewish Tb, 1948-49; psychiat. social worker Bellevue Psychiat. Hosp., N.Y.C., 1949-50, Vanderbilt Psychiat. Clinic, Columbia Med. Center, N.Y.C., 1953-55; program dir. spl. services U.S. Army, Austria, 1951-53; dir. social services Am. Found. Religion and Psychiatry, 1955-64; pvt. practice counseling and psychotherapy, 1950—; founder, exec. dir. Found. for Day Hosps. and Pilot Projects, 1959—; founder, dir. Bierer House N.Y.C., 1962—; founder Marion Tanner House, 1972—. Prof. clin. edn. Westchester Inst. Tng., Counselling and Psychotherapy, 1970—. Mem. Internat. Assn. Social Psychiatry (internat. council), Nat. Assn. Social Workers. Home: 401 W 21st St New York City NY 10011

LYON, MARGARET FERN (MRS. LUTHER LAWRENCE LYON), writer; b. Lake City, Kan., Dec. 12, 1915; d. Jesse Edward and Winning Laura (Wilson) Meuschke; B.S., Kan. U., 1941; m. Luther Lawrence Lyon, Apr. 17, 1942; children—Kay Louise (Mrs. Warren Shaffer), David Ray. Elementary tchr., Kan., 1936-39; faculty Wichita U., 1946-54; writer articles on N.M. History for various mags., 1970—. Mem. N.M. Gov's. Com. on Clean Air and Water, 1967—; mem. steering com. Resources, Conservation and Devel. Council of No. N.M., 1967-69. Bd. dirs. N.M. Water Resources Research Inst., 1966-69. Mem. League of Women Voters (dir. 1949-55, 61-64, 70—, N.M. state pres. 1965-69). Address: 3007 Woodland Los Alamos NM 87544

LYON, MARION BRADLEY (MRS. FRANK LYON), wholesale co. exec.; b. Little Rock, June 8, 1910; d. Lawrence Hodsdon and Carrie Frances (Smade) Bradley; student Brenau Coll., 1928-29, U. Ark., 1929-30; m. Frank Lyon, Dec. 26, 1931; 1 son, Frank Lyon. With securities dept. Chase Nat. Bank, N.Y.C., 1930-31; v.p. Frank Lyon Co., Little Rock, 1942—; co-owner Coca-Cola Bottling Ark., Little Rock, 1968—, Twin City Bank, North Little Rock, 1966—; dir. Interstate Hwy. Sign, Little Rock, 1957—. Bd. dirs. Lyon Found., Youth Home Inc., World Missions Presbyn. Ch. U.S., 1965-73. Presbyn. Home: 9 Sunset Dr Little Rock AR 72207 Office: 65th and Scott Hamilton Little Rock AR 72205

LYON, PATRICIA JEAN, anthropologist; b. Seattle, Jan. 9, 1931; d. William Ranft and Lorena (Ferguson) Lyon; B.A., U. Cal. at Berkeley, 1952, Ph.D., 1967; postgrad. Columbia, 1957; m. David C. Kleinecke, June 25, 1950 (div. Oct. 1958); m. 2d, John H. Rowe, Apr. 24, 1970. Mem. expdn. Am. Mus. Natural History, Peru, 1960; lectr. sociology Universidad de Huamanga, Ayacucho, Peru, 1961, Universidad del Cuzco (Peru), 1963; acting instr. anthropology U. Cal. at Berkeley, 1966-67, acting asst. prof., 1967-68, vis. asst. research anthropologist, 1969, asst. research anthropologist, 1970, lectr., 1974; asst. prof. anthropology Washington U., St. Louis, 1968-70; mus. Research fellow Wenner-Gren Found. Anthrop. Research, 1970-71; research asso. Inst. Andean Studies, 1971—; archaeol. research Peru and Bolivia, 1969, Peru, 1970, 71, 72, 73. Ethnographic investigation Wachipaeri Indians, Peru, 1954, 60, 62, 64, 65, 68. Fellow Inst. Andean Studies, 1960; Johnson Fund Am. Philos. Soc. grantee, 1968. Mem. Inst. Andean Studies, Soc. Am. Archaeology, Kroeber Anthrop Soc., Am. Folklore Soc., A.A.A.S., Latin Am. Studies Assn. Am. Ethnol. Soc., Am. Anthrop. Assn., Sigma Xi. Editor: Native South Americans: Ethnology of the Least Known Continent, 1974. Asst. editor Nawpa Pacha. Contbr. articles to profl. jours. Home: 1029 Cragmont Av Berkeley CA 94708

LYON, RUTH ALTA, editor; b. Moline, Ill.; d. Eugene Cassius and Hazel Ramona (Rouch) Lyon; B.A., Central Bible Coll., Springfield, Mo., 1958. Sec., asst. bookkeeper First Nat. Bank, McCook, Neb., 1930-36; missionary to Indians, Fond du Lac Reservation, Cloquet, Minn., 1939; supr. bus. office Southcentral Bible Inst., Fort Worth, 1940-41; posting clk. storage and issue div. Signal Corps Civil Service, Washington, 1942; price clk. Rationing Bd., McCook, Neb., 1943, chief clk., 1945; asst. to evangelist, 1947-50; with nat. Sunday sch. dept. Assemblies of God, Springfield, Mo., 1950-57, promotions editor home missions div.; 1958—. Mem. Mo. Writers Guild (sec.-treas. 1966). Editor: Superintendent's Asst., 1956-58, Christ for All, 1973—, Reach Out, 1973—. Home: 1617 Benton Av Springfield MO 65803 Office: 1445 Bonnville Av Springfield MO 65802

LYON, VIRGINIA GOLDSBORO, social worker; b. Bedford, Ind., Oct. 18, 1912; d. William Henry Goldsboro and Mattie (Kimbrel) Goldsboro; student Butler U., 1931-32, Ind. U., 1932-33; B.A., DePauw U., 1935; M.Ed., Wayne U., 1956; M.S.W., Wayne State U., 1961; postgrad. U. Mich., 1942, 67, U. Detroit, 1964-66; m. Rector F. Lyon, Nov. 10, 1935; children—Nancy (Mrs. K.A. Milburn), Rebecca Lyon. Mem. Gov.'s Commn. Unemployment Relief Ind., 1935; social worker Dept. Pub. Welfare, Detroit, 1939; sch. social worker Detroit Pub. Schs., 1953—, supr., 1963—. Social work cons. Highland Parks Model Cities Program. Trainer for leadership courses Girl Scouts U.S., 1946-56. Mem. Nat. Assn. Social Workers, Delta Kappa Gamma (pres. Zeta chpt. 1968-70), Alpha Gamma Delta (pres. Detroit alumni group 1940-44, 58-62). Conglist. Home: 137 Rhode Island Highland Park MI 48203 Office: 14111 Puritan Av Detroit MI 48227

LYONS, AUGUSTA WALLACE (MRS. EDWARD LYONS), author; b. Prospect, Ky.; d. Tom and Augusta (French) Wallace; student Sweet Briar Coll., 1929-30, Vassar, Coll., 1930-31, Sorbonne, 1931-32, Barnard Coll., 1933; m. Leo Handel, Jan. 27, 1942 (div. May 1948); children—Tom, Albert; 1 adopted dau., Leslie; m. 2d, Edward Lyons, July 14, 1954. Asso. editor Louisville Times, 1945-50; author, 1944—. Mem. N.A.A.C.P., Adoptive Parents Com., Soc. for a Sane Nuclear Policy, Mystery Writers Am. Unitarian-Universalist. Author: Season of Desire, 1961; All The Lovely Possibilities, 1968; Three Women, 1969. Contbr. short stories to various publs. including New Renaissance, Montrealer, Parents Mag., France Soir, Fifty Best American Short Stories, 1915-65, The Writer, Defenders of Wildlife News. others. Home: River Bluff Rd Prospect KY 40059 Office: care Mary Yost Assos 141 E 55th St New York City NY 10022

LYONS, BARBARA ELDORA LANTZ (MRS. WILLIAM ROBERT LYONS), physician; b. Lorain, O., July 7, 1936; d. William Blake Nelson and Ella Margaret (Merrick) Lantz; B.A., Kent State U., 1958; M.D., Woman's Med. Coll. Pa., 1962; m. William Robert Lyons, July 13, 1963; children—Nancy ElDora, Kathleen Ann. Intern Grad. Hosp. U. Pa., Phila., 1962-63; instr. pharmacology Woman's Med. Coll. Pa., Phila., 1963-65; resident in gen. practice Ventura (Cal.) County Gen. Hosp., 1965-66, in obstetrics and gynecology Abington (Pa.) Meml. Hosp., 1966-67; physician No. Mich. U. Health Center, Marquette, 1967—, dir. health center, 1969-74; practice medicine, Marquette, 1967—; mem. med. staff Marquette Gen. North, Marquette Gen. South hosps. Mem. Marquette Drug Awareness Council, 1970—; mem. Zone III planning com. Mich. Tb Assn. Mem. Am., Mich. (pres. 1972—) coll. health assns., Am. Acad. Family Physicians, A.M.A. Home: 736 W Magnetic St Marquette MI 49855 Office: 1414 W Fair Av Marquette MI 49855

LYONS, BEULAH M. WALLAR (MRS. LAWRENCE RUPERT LYONS), Christian Sci. practitioner; b. Canton, O., Jan. 27, 1912; d. Lee E. and Viola (Clinger) Wallar; student pub. sch.; m. William Charles Copley, Aug. 16, 1930; children—Wilma (dec.), Jack Victor (dec.); m. 2d, Lawrence Rupert Lyons, Feb. 19, 1937 (dec. Mar. 1972). Joined Christian Sci. Ch. Toledo, 1943, C.S. Mother Ch., Boston, 1944; 1st reader C.S. Sch., Waterloo, Ia., 1951-53, 2d reader, Enterprise, Ala., 1959; now C.S. practitioner. Dir., bylaw com. chs. at Waterloo, Cedar Rapids, Ia., Enterprise, Ala., Ottumwa, Ia. Adviser, Christian Sci. Coll. Orgn., Coe Coll., 1962-64. Mem. Christian Sci. Assn. Leslie Leland Toledo (chmn. bd. 1963-64), Internat. Platform Assn., Marine Corps League Aux. (life, past pres.), Daus. Am. (hon. life). Home: 2875 Mt Vernon Rd SE Cedar Rapids IA 52403

LYONS, CLEVA JACKIE, city ofcl.; b. South Bend, Tex., Oct. 29, 1924; d. Hubert Marvin and Myrtle Lee (Cleaves) Montgomery; grad. Brantley-Draughn Bus. Sch., 1942; m. Orville Clifford Lyons, Aug. 18, 1944 (div. June 1972); children—James Clifford, Jan (Mrs. Charles Michael Myatt), Paul Marvin. With The Fair Co., Ft. Worth, 1941-44; with Air Tech. Statis. Control, Army Air Force, Ft. Worth, 1944-45; clk. Lone Star Gas Co., Marlin, Tex., 1948-54; with Lyons the Florist, Marlin, Tex., 1954-59; asst. tax assessor, collector City of Marlin, Tex., 1959—. Absentee clk. Marlin (Tex.) Ind. Sch. Dist. Elections, 1959-74. Mem. Tex. State Tax Assessors for Schs., Assn. of Assessing Officers, W.O. Wright Soc. (pres. 1954, 60, 65, 71). Baptist. Mem. Order Eastern Star (matron 1963-64). Clubs: Past Matrons, Good Earth Garden (Marlin). Home: 910 Clark St Marlin TX 76661 Office: 100 Fortune St Box 340 Marlin TX 76661

LYONS, ELAINE TURNER (MRS. JOHN EDWARD LYONS), state legislator; b. Boston, Sept. 27, 1928; d. Maurice Steele and Edna (Grace) Turner; B.S., Sargent Coll., Boston U., 1949, postgrad., 1950-51; m. John Edward Lyons, June 14, 1952; children—Judith Ann, Stephen Turner. Supr. phys. edn. Manchester (N.H.) Sch. Dept. 1949-57; swimming instr. Manchester YWCA, 1966, 67, 70; substitute tchr. Merrimack (N.H.) Sch. Dept., 1966-70; mem. N.H. Legislature, 1971—, mem. legislative edn. com. Charter mem. Merrimack Federated Republican Woman's Club, v.p., 1970-71; co-chmn. Peterson for Gov. campaign, Merrimack, 1968, 70. Bd. dirs. Merrimack Med. Center. Mem. Am. Assn. Health, Phys. Edn. and Recreation (N.H. membership chmn. 1955-57), Manchester Coll. Women's Club. Episcopalian. Author: (with others) Curriculum Guide to Physical Education in New Hampshire, 1954. Home: Shore Dr Merrimack NH 03054 Office: State House Concord NH 03301

LYONS, LOUISE BOOTH (MRS. DWIGHT K. LYONS), educator; b. Johnson City, Tenn., Mar. 17, 1932; d. Alvin Robert and Pearl (Deakins) Booth; B.S., E. Tenn. State U., 1952; M.A., 1955; specialist in edn. degree, U. Ky., 1966, Ed.D., 1973; m. Dwight K. Lyons, Aug. 15, 1959. Tchr. elementary schs. Washington County, Tenn., 1952-54, Kingsport, Tenn., 1954-57, Brevard County, Fla., 1957-58; elementary supervising tchr. demonstration sch. Appalachian State Tchr. Coll., Boone, N.C., 1958-59; elementary tchr., librarian Jefferson County, Ky., 1959-61; coordinator instructional media, asst. prof. library sci. Eastern Ky. U., Richmond, 1961-69; instructional media specialist, asst. prof. edn. U. Louisville, 1969—. Pres., Richmond Bus. and Profl. Women's Club, 1963-64; chmn. Am. home dept. Richmond Woman's Club, 1963-64; mem. Woman's Club Central Ky., Lexington, 1965-69; sec. Saturday Matinee Mus. Richmond, 1965-67, Spindletop Hall, Lexington, 1967-69. Mem. Ky. Audio-Visual Assn. (treas., dir.), Ky. Edn. Assn., N.E.A., Ky. Library Assn., A.L.A., Ky. Assn. Sch. Librarians, Nat. Assn. Ednl. Broadcasters, Am. Assn. Sch. Librarians, Assn. for Ednl. Communications and Tech., Assn. Higher Edn., J.B. Speed Mus., Pi Tau Chi, Kappa Delta Pi. Mem. Order Eastern Star. Baptist. Club: Arts. Home: The 800 800 S 4th St Louisville KY 40203

LYONS, MARGARETA FRANZEN (MRS. WILLIAM M. LYONS, JR.), art exec.; b. Jonkoping, Sweden; d. David E. L. and Alma (Engdahl) Franzen; came to U.S., 1924, naturalized, 1928; B.S., Boston U., 1937; m. William M. Lyons, Jr., July 24, 1941 (div. Apr. 1950); 1 son, William M. (killed in Vietnam 1969). Art tchr. Jr. High, Needham, Mass., 1937-41; draftsman Stone & Webster Engring. Corp., Boston, 1942-43; textbook designer D. C. Heath & Co., Boston, 1943-46; children's book designer, prodn. mgr. Houghton Mifflin Co., Boston, 1949-52; children's book designer, prodn. mgr. Pellegrini & Cudahy, N.Y.C., 1952-53; asst. art dir. Charles Scribner's Sons, N.Y.C., 1953-65, art dir., 1966—. Mem. Am. Inst. Graphic Arts. Club: Boston University (N.Y.C.). Author: The Great Ship Vasa, 1971. Home: 132 Downing St Lakewood NJ 08701 Office: 597 Fifth Av New York City NY 10017

LYONS, PATRICIA LOUISE (MRS. MICHAEL ANTHONY DOELLMAN), librarian; b. Washington, Oct. 11, 1942; d. William Michael and Rita (Weisgerber) L.; B.A., Rosemont Coll., 1964; postgrad. Am. U., 1964-65; M.S., Villanova U., 1967; m. Michael Anthony Doellman, Oct. 6, 1973. Statistician NIH, Bethesda, Md., 1964-65; library asst. Rosemont (Pa.) Coll., 1965-67; Nat. Library of Medicine trainee in computer librarianship Washington U. Sch. Medicine Library, St. Louis, 1967-68; asst. librarian, instr. library sci. Quincy (Ill.) Coll., 1968-71; head librarian Walsh Coll., Canton, O., 1971—. Trustee Ohio Coll. Library Center, 1973—, mem. peer council, 1973—, mem. ad hoc com. on user needs, 1973—. Mem. Am., Ohio (sec. div. 7, 1973-74), Cath. (chmn. No. Ohio unit 1973—) library assns., Assn. Coll. and Research Libraries, Tri-State Assn. Coll. and Research Libraries. Home: 3496 Ivanhoe Dr Brimfield OH 44240 Office: 2020 Easton St NW Canton OH 44720

LYONS, RUTH, TV and radio broadcaster; b. Cin.; d. Samuel Spencer and Margaret (Henry) Reeves; ed. U. Cin.; m. Herman A. Newman, Oct. 4, 1942; 1 dau., Candace Laird. Pianist, organist, commentator WKRC-Radio, until 1942; with Sta. WLW-Radio-TV, Cin., 1942—, emcee 50-50 Club, 90 minute show, 5 days per week. Head dir. Ruth Lyons Xmas Fund for children's hosps. in Ohio, Ind., Ky., 1941—. Recipient Golden Mike award McCall's mag., numerous other awards from groups including Midwest Hosp. Assn., Variety Club. Mem. Broadcast Pioneers, Delta Delta Delta. Writer songs. Home: 5205 Colerain Av Cincinnati OH 45223 Office: 9th and Elm Cincinnati OH 45202

LYONS, SARAH PEARL, librarian; b. Saltsburg, Pa., Aug. 31, 1938; d. Samuel Henry and Anna Deborah (Shirley) Lyons; B.S., Ind. U. of Pa., 1960; M.R.E., Conservative Bapt. Theol. Sem., 1965; M.A., U. Denver, 1966. Tchr. New Brighton (Pa.) High Sch., 1960-62; library asst. Conservative Bapt. Theol. Sem., Denver, 1962-66, librarian, 1966—. Mem. Am. Theol. Library Assn., Christian Librarians Fellowship. Baptist. Home: 2756 S Madison St Denver CO 80210 Office: Box 10000 University Park Station Denver CO 80210

LYONS, SHEILA POWERS (MRS. GARY F. LYONS), communications dir.; b. La Crosse, Wis., May 7, 1945; d. James Francis and Leone H. (Gavin) Powers; B.A. in English, Viterbo Coll., 1967; m. Gary F. Lyons, July 9, 1967. Tchr., English, Mpls., pub. schs., 1967-70; dir. communications Greater Mpls. C. of C., 1969—. Vol. tchr. Minn. Correctional Inst. for Women, 1971-72. Bd. dirs. Minn. Opera Assn., 1971-74. Home: 2741 Ewing Av S Minneapolis MN 55416 Office: 15 S 5 St Minneapolis MN 55402

LYSTAD, MARY HANEMANN (MRS. ROBERT LYSTAD), sociologist, author; b. New Orleans, Apr. 11, 1928; d. James and Mary (Douglass) Hanemann; A.B. cum laude, Newcomb Coll., 1949; M.A., Columbia, 1951; Ph.D., Tulane U., 1955; m. Robert Lystad, June 20, 1953; children—Lisa Douglass, Anne Hanemann, Mary Lunde, Robert Douglass, James Hanemann. Postdoctoral fellow social psychology S.E. La. Hosp., Mandeville, 1955-57; field research social psychology, Ghana, 1957-58, South Africa and Swaziland, 1968; chief sociologist Collaborative Child Devel. Project, Charity Hosp. La., New Orleans, 1958-61; cons. spl. operations research office Am. U., Washington, 1962; feature writer African div. Voice Am., Washington, 1964-73; sociologist Nat. Inst. Mental Health, Washington, 1968-72, spl. asst. to dir. div. spl. mental health programs, 1973—. Cons. on youth Nat. Goals Research Staff, White House, Washington, 1969-70. Fellow Am. Sociol. Soc. Contbr. articles to profl. jours. Author: Millicent the Monster, 1968; Social Aspects of Alienation, 1969; Jennifer Takes Over P.S. 94, 1972; James the Jaguar, 1972; As They See It: Changing Values of College Youth, 1973; The Halloween Parade, 1973; That New Boy, 1973; Violence at Home, 1974; A child's World as seen in his Stories and Drawings, 1974. Home: 4900 Scarsdale Rd Washington DC 20016 Office: 5600 Fishers Lane Rockville MD 20852

MA, PEARL PIK CHUN, microbiologist; b. Hong Kong; d. Chiu Ki and Yee Mui (Lum) Ma; B.A., Rosemont Coll., Pa., 1950; M.A., U. Pa., 1954; Ph.D., Jefferson Med. Coll., Phila., 1962. Chief in microbiology Woman's Hosp. Phila., 1954, Jefferson Med. Coll. and Hosp., 1954; asso. medicine sects. pub. health, infectious disease, dermatology Hahnemann Med. Coll., Phila., 1961-63; research asso. dept. pathology Med. Coll. Va., Richmond, 1965; chief in microbiology Akron City Hosp., 1965-70, chief microbiology St. Vincent's Hosp. and Med. Center N.Y., 1970—; asst. prof. clin. pathology N.Y.U. Coll. Medicine, 1970—; cons. in microbiology, 1961—. Examiner, Nat. Registry Microbiologists. Guest speaker Critic Club, Haffkine Inst., Bombay, India, Hong Kong St. Stephen's Girl's Coll. Social chmn. Internat. House, Phila., 1953. Recipient research grant award $54,000, Nat. Inst. Allergy and Infectious Diseases, Bethesda, Md., 1965-68. Mem. Am. Soc. Clin. Sci., Nat. Am. Soc. for Microbiology, Am. Soc. for Microbiology, A.A.A.S., Mideast Soc. Electron Microscopists, Am. Soc. Clin. Pathologists, N.Y. Acad. Scis., Woman Am. Med. Assn. Club: Art, Glee, Science.

Contbr. articles to profl. jours. Office: St Vincent's Hosp and Med Center NY 153 W 11th St New York City NY 10011

MAAS, ANNE ANTONIA, physician; b. Djember, Java, Indonesia, Apr. 11, 1931; d. Geerlof Dirk and Antonia Catherine (Willinge) Maas came to U.S., 1954, naturalized, 1971; Arts diploma, U. Leyden, Leiden, The Netherlands, 1957; m. Flavio E. Cifferi, 1954 (div. 1956); 1son Robert William Ciferri. Intern Jacksonville (Fla.) Bapt. Meml. Hosp., 1958-59; resident physical medicine and rehab. Columbia, 1959-62; resident internal medicine and rheumatology Rotterdam, The Netherlands, 1962-63; staff U. Amsterdam, Wilhelmina Gasthuis, 1969-71, N.Y.U., 1969—; practice medicine specializing gen. practice and diet therapy for multiple sclerosis, Bedford, N.Y., 1970—. Mem. Netherlands-Am. Acad. Club: Home: Rural Route 2 Box 202 East Middle Patent Rd Bedford NY 10506

MAAS, SALLY ANN (MRS. ROBERT ALEXANDER MARSHALL), feature writer; b. Portage, Wis., Apr. 10, 1947; d. Franklin Arthur and Mabel Gladys (Engen) Maas; B.S. in Journalism, U. Wis., 1969; m. Robert Alexander Marshall, Aug. 3, 1973. Reporter, The Paper, Oshkosh, Wis., 1969-70; feature writer The Press, Binghamton, N.Y., 1970-71; feature writer The Press-Enterprise, Riverside, Cal., 1971—. Mem. Women in Communications, League Women Voters. Club: Twin Counties Press (dir.). Home: 22673-D Palm Av Colton CA 92324 Office: Press-Enterprise PO Box 792 Riverside CA 92502

MABERRY, ANNELLE TUCKER (MRS. ROBERT E. MABERRY), ednl. adminstr.; b. Kansas City, Mo., Dec. 22, 1928; d. James Earl and Creta Gladys (Neville) Tucker; student Art Center Sch., 1959; B.A. Humane Letters, Pitzer Coll., 1972; m. Robert E. Maberry, Jan. 5, 1953; children—Sue, Lawrence, Sharon Ann. Asst. to registrar Claremont (Cal.) Men's Coll., 1959-64; registrar Pitzer Coll., Claremont, Cal., 1964—. Mem. Am., Pacific Coast assns. collegiate registrars and admissions officers. Home: 712 Via Los Santos San Dimas CA 91773 Office: 1150 Mills Av Claremont CA 91711

MABON, EDITH MUMMERY (MRS. ROBERT GIRARD MABON), ednl. adminstr.; b. Vernon Center, N.Y., Jan. 29, 1923; d. James Arthur and Ruth Miranda (Beck) Mummery; B.S., N.Y. State Coll., 1945; M.S., Syracuse U., 1952; postgrad. Cornell U., 1956, 58, 64-65; m. Robert Girard Mabon, Aug. 21, 1954. Tchr. home econs. Webster (N.Y.) Central Sch., 1945-49, Cobleskill (N.Y.) Central Sch., 1949-51, West High, Auburn, N.Y., 1951-52; prof. N.Y. State Agrl. and Tech. Coll., Delhi, 1952-67; prof., div. chmn. N.Y. State Agrl. and Tech. Coll., Morrisville, 1967—. Cons. Dietary Technician Program So. W.Va. Community Coll., Logan; mem. exec. bd. N.Y. State Nutrition Council. Active heart, cancer and hosp. fund drives. Mem. Am. Dietetic Assn., Am. Home Econs. Assn., Am. Sch. Food Service Assn., Council on Hotel, Restaurant and Instl. Edn., Bus. and Profl. Women's Club, Delta Kappa Gamma. Presbyn. Mem. Order Eastern Star. Editor Councilor, 1971-73. Home: 14 Cambridge Av Morrisville NY 13408 Office: New York State Agricultural and Tech College Morrisville NY 13408

MABROUK, BARBARA ELAINE FORD (MRS. AHMED FAHMY MABROUK), phys. therapist; b. Cambridge, O., Dec. 2, 1927; d. Everett Lawrence and Dorotha Mathea (Alderman) Ford; A.A., Ventura (Cal.) Jr. Coll., 1948; B.S. in Zoology, Ohio U., Athens, 1949, B.A. in Sociology, 1950; M.A., Ohio State U., 1955; m. Ahmed Fahmy Mabrouk, Oct. 31, 1954; children—Patricia Ann, Sarah Lou, Suzanne Theresa. Phys. therapist Ohio State U., 1953-56, Ill. Central Hosp., Chgo., 1958, VA Hosp., Chgo., 1959. Served to 1st lt. Womens Med. Specialist Corps, U.S. Army, 1950-53. Home: 9 Wildewood Terrace Framingham MA 01701

MABRY, NELLOISE JOHNSON, educator; b. Valdosta, Ga., Sept. 8, 1921; d. Hansford Duncan and Maudelle (Williams) Johnson; student Bethel Woman's Coll., 1938-39, Wesleyan Conservatory, 1941; A.B., Mercer U., 1943, M.Ed., 1949; m. William Herbert Mabry, Mar. 5, 1942 (div. Nov. 1947); 1 son, William Herbert. Tchr., Cynthia H. Weir Elementary Sch., Macon, Ga., 1950—. Mem. Nat., Ga., Bibb County edn. assns., Ga. Assn. for Childhood Edn. (pres. 1964-66), Am. Assn. U. Women, Delta Kappa Gamma (scrapbook chmn. Delta chpt. 1966-68), Alpha Delta Pi, Alpha Psi Omega. Democrat. Baptist. Home: 1575 Adams St Macon GA 31204

MACARTHUR, DIANA TAYLOR, pub. affairs cons.; b. Santa Fe, July 7, 1933; d. Antonio J. and Elizabeth (Steele) Taylor; student U. Geneva, 1953-54, B.A., Vassar Coll., 1955; children—Elizabeth, Alexander Tschursin; m. 2d, Donald Malcolm MacArthur, Mar. 31, 1962. Cons. economist Checchi & Co., Washington, 1957-61; v.p., dir. Washington office Thomas J. Deegan Co., 1961-62; dep. chief W. Africa, Peace Corps, 1963, regional program officer N.Africa, Near E., S. Asia, 1964, dir. div. pvt. and internat. orgns., 1965-66; coordinator Nat. Youth Conf. on Natural Beauty and Conservation, 1966-68; self-employed cons. pub. affairs to corps., assns., Washington, 1968—. Mem. citizens adv. bd. Pres.'s Council on Youth Opportunity, 1968-69. Trustee Menninger Found., Topeka; Bd. dirs. Washington Area Council Alcoholism and Drug Abuse, chmn. bd., 1974. Mem. Phi Beta Kappa. Home: 5313 Albemarle St NW Washington DC 20016

MACARTHUR, GLORIA, poet; b. Washington, May 14, 1924; d. Emmet Carlyle and Genevieve (Walsh) Gudger; student Vassar Coll., 1942-43; B.A. cum laude, U. Minn., 1946; m. Colin MacArthur, Mar. 17, 1949; 1 son, Glen Cameron. Columnist Mpls. Daily Times, 1946-48; reporter, page editor Palm Springs (Cal.) News, 1948-49; poetry pub. in Poetry Soc. Am. Anthologies The Golden Year, 1960, The Diamond Year, 1971, Epos Anthology, 1958, Poets of Am. Anthology, 1957, Avalon Anthologies, 1957, 58, Poetry Soc. Tex. Book of Year 1965, Epos, PS, Antioch Rev., S.W. Rev., Voices, Epoch, The Fiddlehead. Recipient Harry Covner Meml. Peace award Poetry Soc. Tex., 1964. Mem. Poetry Soc. Am. (William Marion Reedy Meml. award 1966), Poetry Soc. Ga. (Conrad Aiken award 1963, Lucy B. McIntire Meml. award 1968), Delta Phi Lambda. Address: 9901 SW 67th Av Miami FL 33156

MACAULAY, ALICE ITTNER, physician; b. Bklyn.; d. William and Anna (Holzman) Ittner; B.A., Barnard Coll., postgrad. 1944-46; M.D., N.Y. Med. Coll., 1950; postgrad. N.Y. U., 1952-53; m. David Harvard Macaulay, July 10, 1936 (dec. 1971). Tchr. N.Y.C. high schs., until 1946; actress Columbia Lab. Players Summer Stock, Roxbury, Conn., 1933-34, Old Vic, London, Eng., 1934-35; intern and resident Grasslands Hosp., Valhalla, N.Y., 1951-56, hosp. practice medicine specializing in internal medicine Grasslands Hosp., 1956—, dir. outpatient services, 1956—, asso. attending internal medicine, 1958—, chmn. pharmacy and therapeutics com., 1967—, mem. adminstrv. team, 1961—; liaison hosp. officer, for devel. of Neighborhood Health Centers; chmn. med. adv. bd. Westchester County Pub. Health Nursing; med. cons., dir. med. affairs Westchester Community Coll.; cons. Div. Vocational Rehab. and State Med. Programs; cons. hypertension, 1956—; med. adv. bd. Westchester Heart Assn., chmn. com. on hypertension, 1973—. Prof. medicine Pace U. Grad. Sch. Nursing. Mem. Westchester Acad. Med., N.Y. State Med. Soc., Westchester, Am. heart assns., A.A.A.S. Cor et Manus, Contin, N.Y. Trudeau Soc., Alpha Epsilon Iota. Club: Soroptimists Internat. Address: Hudson House Ardsley-on-Hudson NY 10503

MACCAFFREY, ISABEL GAMBLE (MRS. WALLACE T. MACCAFFREY), educator; b. Balt., Aug. 2, 1924; d. Thomas Owen and Isabel (Davidson) Gamble; B.A., Swarthmore Coll., 1946; M.A., Radcliffe Coll., 1947, Ph.D., 1954; m. Wallace T. MacCaffrey, June 16, 1956. Faculty dept. English, Bryn Mawr (Pa.) Coll., 1949-50, 52-69, prof. English, 1966-69; prof. English, Tufts U., Medford, Mass., 1969-71; William R. Kenan, Jr. prof. history and lit. Harvard U., Cambridge, Mass., 1971—. Mem. Modern Lang. Assn., Renaissance Soc. Am., English Inst. Author: Paradise Lost as Myth, 1959. Editor: Samson Agonistes and Minor Poems of Milton, 1966. Contbr. articles to profl. jours. Home: 106 Pope Rd Acton MA 01720 Office: 952 Holyoke Center Cambridge MA 02138

MACCALLUM, JANET MEADE (MRS. ALEXANDER DUNCAN MACCALLUM), veterinarian; b. N.Y.C., Jan. 7, 1925; d. George G. and Alva (Broberg) Meade; student Cornell U., 1942-43; D.V.M., N.Y. State Vet. Coll., 1946; m. Alexander Duncan MacCallum, Aug. 25, 1946; children—Duncan James, Jill Sandys, Craig Angus, Malcolm John, Megan Heather. Asst. to veterinarian Wood Vet. Hosp., Trenton, N.J., 1947-48; co-owner Utica Animal Hosp., New Hartford, N.Y., 1948—. Bd. dirs. Utica YWCA. Mem. Empire State Horsemen's Assn. (regional v.p.), Am. Horse Shows Assn., Am. Vet. Med. Assn., Womens Vet. Med. Assn., Phi Zeta. Office: RD 2 Seneca Turnpike New Hartford NY 13413

MACCANN, DONNARAE THOMPSON (MRS. RICHARD DYER MACCANN), educator; b. Culver City, Cal., Oct. 24, 1931; d. John Olsen and Charlotte Mabel (Purkey) Thompson; student Santa Monica City Coll., 1949-51; B.A., U. Cal. at Los Angeles, 1954; M.L.S., U. Cal. at Berkeley, 1955; m. Richard Dyer MacCann, Oct. 12, 1957. Children's librarian Los Angeles Pub. Library, 1955-57; head librarian Univ. Elementary Sch., U. Cal. at Los Angeles, 1957-65; instr. arts and humanities U. Cal. at Los Angeles Extension, 1959-64; lectr. English dept. U. Cal. at Los Angeles, 1963, U. Kan., Lawrence, 1968-70. Cons. U. Cal. at Los Angeles Writers' Consultation Service, 1964—, Addison-Wesley Pub. Co., 1967-68, Scott, Foresman Pub. Co., 1971. Bd. dirs. Children's Hour Nursery Sch. and Head Start, 1966-70, v.p., 1969-70. Recipient Dutton-Macrae award A.L.A. 1963. Mem. A.L.A. (Newbery-Caldecott award com. 1968), Am. Civil Liberties Union, Women's Polit. Caucus. Democrat. Christian Scientist. Author: (with Gloria Woodard) The Black American in Books for Children, 1972; (with Olga Richard) The Child's First Books: A Critical Study of Pictures and Texts, 1973. Home: 717 Normandy Dr Iowa City IA 52240

MACCARIO, MICHELINE, neurologist; b. Lubumbashi, Zaire, Sept. 16, 1931; d. Giaccomo Antonio and Louise Leontine (Watrin) Maccario; M.B., U. London, 1952; grad. summa cum laude U. Louvain (Belgium), 1958; m. Alfred Sutherland Kissack, Jr., Dec. 5, 1959; children—Bruno, Lyle, Alec, Terence. Came to U.S., 1958, naturalized, 1969. Rotating intern Kings County Hosp., Bklyn., 1958-59; resident in neurology N.Y. U.— Bellevue Hosp., N.Y.C., 1960-63; practice medicine specializing in neurology, Bklyn., 1963-71, Socorro, N.M., 1971—; staff St. Joseph's Hosp., Albuquerque, Socorro Gen. Hosp.; instr. neurology State U. N.Y. Downstate Med. Center, Bklyn., 1963-65, clin. instr., 1965-68; asso. research scientist dept. psychiatry and neurology N.Y. U. Med. Center, 1968-69, asst. clin. prof. neurology, 1969-71; asst. prof. neurology (adj.) U. N.M. Sch. Medicine, Albuquerque, 1971-74. Diplomate Am. Bd. Psychiatry and Neurology, Am. Bd. Electroencephalography. Mem. A.M.A., Am. Acad. Neurology, Am. Electroencephalography Assn., Am. Med. Womens Assn., Mid Rio Grande Med. Soc., Med. Soc. County of Kings, Bklyn. Neurol. Soc. Contbr. articles to profl. jours. Address: PO Box 664 Socorro NM 87801

MACCART, VIRGINIA RAHM, club woman; b. Pitts., May 18, 1887; d. Edward and Maude (MacDonald) Rahm; student pvt. schs.; m. Raymond D. MacCart, Oct. 1, 1919. Hon. life regent D.A.R., 1950—; nat. rec. sec. gen. Nat. Soc. New Eng. Women, 1942-45; hon. pres. gen. Nat. Soc. Daus. Union, 1861-1865, 1951-54; hon. 1st v.p. gen. Colonial Dames of 17th Century, 1953; pres. Nat. Soc. Congress of States Soc., Inc., N.Y., 1949-73. Recipient medal for war work Nat. Soc. New Eng. Women, 1945; Mary Mildred Sullivan award Lincoln Meml. U., 1953. Mem. Daus. Am. Colonists, Colonial Dames Vt. Soc., Pa. Huguenot Soc., Pa., N.Y. hist. socs., Gen. Fedn. Women's Clubs, Dist. Rep. Women, Wash. Philatelic Soc., Nat. Soc. Patriotic Women (nat. chaplain), N.Y. Bible Soc., Salvation Army Aux., Nat., Am. philatelic socs., Bur. Specialist Stamp Assn., First Day Cover Soc. Internat. Platform Assn., Smithsonian Assos. Republican. Lutheran. Clubs: The Washington, Capitol Hill (Washington); Past Regents (N.Y.); Navy Wives; Stamp Collector's (Boston). Home: 4450 Park Av S Chevy Chase MD 20015 also 201 N Riverside Dr Pompano Beach FL 33062

MACCAULEY, SISTER ROSE AGNES, educator; b. N.Y.C., Apr. 8, 1911; d. John Henry and Helen Agnes (Mernin) MacCauley; B.A., Coll. Mt. St. Vincent, 1947; M.A. in English, Fordham U., 1956; M.A. in Theology, Manhattan Coll., 1969. Joined Sisters of Charity of N.Y., 1930; tchr. English, religious studies St. Barnabas High Sch., Bronx, N.Y.C., 1947-60, Cathedral High Sch., N.Y.C., 1960-69, Elizabeth Seton Coll., 1969—. Mem. Am. Acad. Religion, Coll. Theology Soc., Soc. Bibl. Lit. Author: Vision 20/20 (20 Psalms for the 20th Century), 1971. Address: 110 Milton Rd Rye NY 10580

MACCIA, ELIZABETH STEINER (MRS. GEORGE S. MACCIA), educator; b. St. Louis, Jan. 30, 1925; d. Anton and Walburga (Rustige) Steiner; B.S., St. Louis U., 1946; M.Ed., U. Mo., 1949; M.A., U. Man. (Can.), 1954; Ph.D., U. So. Cal., 1957; m. George S. Maccia, Feb. 10, 1947. Chemist, Atlas Powder Co., Weldon Springs, Mo., 1943, Scullin Steel Co., St. Louis, 1944-45; teaching asst. gen. chemistry and gen. zoology St. Louis U., 1945-46; instr. zoology U. Kan., Lawrence, 1947; research microbiologist Wood Treating Chems. Co., St. Louis, 1947-48; tchr. phys. and biol. sciences Kanawha (Ia.) High Sch., 1949-50; prof. anatomy Los Angeles City Coll., 1950-52; tchr. phys. and biol. scis. Los Angeles Sr. High Sch., 1951-52; instr. philosophy U. Man., 1953-54; lectr. philosophy U. So. Cal. Los Angeles, 1956-57; asst. prof. philosophy Marietta (O.) Coll., 1957-60; vis. prof. grad. studies in edn. Ohio State U. Columbus, summer 1959, research coordinator Inst. Child Devel. and Family Life, 1960-61, research asso. philosophy of edn. Bur. of Ednl. Research and Service, 1960-61, asst. prof., philosopher, 1961-62, asso. prof., philosopher, 1962-64, co-dir. Ednl. Theory Center, 1962-66, co-dir. Social Studies Curriculum Center, 1963-66, prof., philosopher Bur. Ednl. Research and Service, 1964-65, prof. edn. Div. for Study of Edn., 1965-66; vis. prof. U. B.C., summer 1960; vis. prof. U. Cal. at Los Angeles, summer 1963; vis. prof. Ind. U., Bloomington, summers 1964, 67, prof. philosophy of edn., 1967—, dir. program in ednl. inquiry, 1973—; prof. philosophy U. Southwestern La. Lafayette, 1966-67. Mem. Am. Assn. U. Profs., Am. Ednl. Research Assn., Am. Philos. Assn., Assn. for Symbolic Logic, Ohio Valley Philosophy of Edn. Soc. (pres. 1966, exec. bd. 1967), Philosophy of Edn. Soc. (exec. bd. 1967, 68, chmn. spl. interest group on edn. and women's liberation 1971, chmn. com. on status of women in philosophy of edn. 1971), Philosophy of Sci. Assn., Soc. for Gen. Systems Research (publ. com., 1968, com. on social systems 1968). Contbr. articles to profl. jours. Home: Route 12 Box 160 Bloomington IN 47401

MACCLUER, JEAN WALTERS, geneticist, educator; b. Columbus, O., March 30, 1937; d. Robert Edward and Lucy G. (Busch) Walters; B.S. cum laude, Ohio State U., 1959; M.S., U. Mich., 1963, Ph.D., 1968. Research asso. dept. human genetics U. Mich., Ann Arbor, 1968-71; research asso., dept. anthropology Pa. State U., University Park, 1971-72, asst. prof. dept. biology, 1972-74, asso. prof. dept. biology, 1974—. Co-dir. Conf. on Uses of Computer Simulation in Human Population Studies, University Park, 1972. Mem. Am. Assn. Phys. Anthropologists, Am. Soc. Human Genetics, Nat. Heart and Lung Inst. (mem. adv. com. Arteriosclerosis Research Centers 1972—), Am. Soc. Naturalists, Population Assn. Am., Soc. for Study Human Biology, Soc. for Study Social Biology. Contbr. articles to profl. jours. Office: Dept Biology 208 Life Sciences I Pa State U University Park PA 16802

MACCOBY, ELEANOR EMMONS, educator; b. Tacoma, May 15, 1917; d. H. Eugene and Viva (Johnson) Emmons; student Reed Coll., 1934-35, 36-37; B.A., U. Wash., 1939; M.A., U. Mich., 1949, Ph.D., 1950; m. Nathan Maccoby, Sept. 16, 1938; children—Janice B. (Mrs. Douglass Carmichael), Sarah, Mark. Study dir., div. program surveys Dept. Agr., 1942-46, Survey Research Center, U. Mich., 1946-48, lectr. social relations Harvard, 1950-58; faculty Stanford, 1958—, prof. psychology, 1958—, chmn. dept., 1973—. Fellow Center for Advanced Study in Behavioral Sci., 1969-70. Fellow Am. Psychol. Assn. (div. pres. 1971-72), Am. Acad. Arts and Scis.; mem. Soc. Research Child Devel. (gov. council 1963-68), Western Psychol. Assn. (pres. 1974—). Author: (with R.R. Sears, H. Levin) Patterns of Child Rearing, 1957; (with M. Zellner) Experiments in Primary Education-Same Aspects of Project Follow-Through, 1970; (with C.N. Jacklin) The Psychology of Sex Differences, 1974. Editor: Readings in Social Psychology, 1957; Development of Sex Differences, 1966. Contbr. articles to profl. jours. Home: 729 Mayfield Av Stanford CA 94305

MACDONALD, ANNE MITCHELL (MRS. JAMES STUART MACDONALD), lawyer, b. Louisville, July 31, 1915; d. Dayton Thomas and Charlotte (Keene) Mitchell; LL.B., U. Louisville, 1936; postgrad. Jefferson Sch. Law, 1936—; m. James Stuart MacDonald, Oct. 11, 1935; children—Anne (Mrs. Charles P. Porter), Elizabeth (Mrs. Barry Edmonston), Thomas C., James Stuart. Admitted to Ky. bar, 1936, Ore. bar, 1964; practiced in Louisville, 1936-64, Prineville, Ore., 1964—. Municipal judge Prineville, 1960-70, mem. Crook County (Ore.) Sch. Bd., 1957-61. Mem. Am., Ore. State, Central Ore. bar assns., Nat. Assn. Women's Lawyers. Club: Prineville Golf and Country (pres. women's assn. 1951-52). Home: 305 W 1st St Prineville OR 97754 Office: Robinson-Clifton Bldg Prineville OR 97754

MACDONALD, CLARICE IRENE, computer programming supr.; b. Jamestown, N.Y., Mar. 17, 1923; d. Gerald John and Gladys Florelle (Herrick) MacDonald; A.B., Seattle Pacific Coll., 1945; M.A., U. Wash., 1952, M.S., 1973. Instr. Roberts Jr. Coll., North Chili, N.Y., 1945-49; instr. Seattle Pacific Coll., 1951-53; engr. Boeing Co., Seattle, 1953-70; programming supr. Boeing Computer Services, Seattle, 1970—; cons. library automation. Mem. Am. Math. Soc., Assn. Computing Machinery, Am. Soc. Information Sci., Sigma Xi, Pi Mu Epsilon. Republican. Home: 5900 119th St SE Bellevue WA 98006 Office: PO Box 24346 Seattle WA 98124

MACDONALD, DONA MARIE, ednl. adminstr.; b. Langley Field, Va., Mar. 28, 1944; d. Raymond Bourke and Alice Marie (Parker) MacDonald; B.S.E., Loyola U. of South, 1966; M.Ed., Boston Coll., 1968. Research asso. Judge Baker Guidance Center, Boston, 1967-68; asst. dean women Seattle U., 1968-72, dean for women, 1972—. Bd. dirs. U. Washington YWCA, 1971—, pres., 1974-75. Mem. Northwest Coll. Personnel Assn., Am. Assn. U. Women, Washington Women Deans and Counselors, Washington Campus Child Care Coalition, Nat. Assn. Women Deans, Adminstrs. and Counselors, Nat. Assn. Edn. Young Children, Kappa Delta Pi. Home: 2029 E Howe St Seattle WA 98102 Office: Seattle U Seattle WA 98122

MACDONALD, DUNCAN, communications cons.; b. Beaumont, Tex.; d. William W. and Martha (Hammond) MacDonald; m. Jean-Pierre Biver, June 1961 (div.). Supr. women's and religious programs Du Mont TV Network, N.Y.C., 1950-53; off-camera editor NBC-TV Home show, 1954; broadcaster Yankee Network, Boston, 1955-59, radio sta. WQXR, N.Y.C., 1962-67; editor home-food-fashion Yankee mag., 1956-63; partner Women's Broadcasting Syndicate, 1959-62; columnist House Beautiful mag., 1966-67, exec. asst. to editor and communications liaison, 1967-70; exec. dir., trustee Nat. Friends Pub. Broadcasting, Inc., N.Y.C., 1970-73; pres. The Media Group, Inc., 1972—. Communications adviser Nat. Council Women U.S., 1965—, Inst. on Man and Sci., 1965—, Friends Channel 13. Founder, pres. Com. for Ams., 1963; mem. Com. Safe Bicycling; mem. nat. bd. Am. Youth Hostels, 1968-73; mem. communications panel White Ho. Conf. on Nutrition, 1969. Nat. bd. dirs. Am.-Scottish Found., 1970—. Recipient UN Children's Fund award, 1957; Aid to Physically Handicapped citation Pres.'s Com., 1957. Mem. Am. Women in Radio and Television (N.Y. pres.), Am. Inst. Decorators, Nat. Home Fashions League (Boston v.p.), Fashion Group. Club: Overseas Press. Author: (with Robb Sagendorph) Rain, Hail and Baked Beans, 1958. Contbr. to Old Farmer's Almanac. Office: 2303 Willow Way Yorktown Heights NY 10598

MACDONALD, ELEANOR JOSEPHINE, epidemiologist; b. West Somerville, Mass., Mar. 4, 1909; d. Angus A. and Catherine (Boland) Macdonald; A.B., Radcliffe Coll., 1928. Statistician, Mass. Dept. Pub. Health, Boston, 1930-35, epidemiologist, 1935-40; lectr. research methods Tufts Dental Sch., Boston, 1933-43; lectr. social scis. Regis Coll., Weston, Mass., 1936-38; lectr. Emanual Coll., Boston, 1938-41; research statistician Div. Cancer Research, Conn. Dept. Health, 1941-48; asst. clin. prof. Yale Sch. Medicine, 1948-60; prof. biostatistics U. Tex. Postgrad. Sch. Medicine, 1948-63, Grad. Sch. Biomed. Scis., 1963-65; epidemiologist, head dept. U. Tex. M.D. Anderson Hosp. and Tumor Inst., 1948—, mem. dir.'s adv. council, 1948-59, 63-65, chmn. edn. com., 1963-65. Cons. statistician Tex. Cancer Coordinating Council, 1949-63; biostatistician S.W. Cancer Chemotherapy Study Group, 1957-60; statis. cons. dept. pediatrics Baylor U. Coll. Medicine, 1958-62; cons. Meml. Hosp., N.Y.C., 1947-57; cons. epidemiologist Tex. Dept. Health, 1949-63. Chmn. definitions com. End Results Evaluation Sect. Cancer Chemotherapy, Nat. Service Center, 1958-59; mem. task force joint com. staging cancer and end results A.C.S., 1961-65; cons. Nat. Cancer Adv. Council, 1944-46. Mem. research com. social statistics div. Houston C. of C., 1949-60. Recipient Myron Gordon award VIII Internat. Pigment Cell Growth Conf., 1972, Am. Cancer Soc. award for outstanding service, 1973, Radcliffe Coll. Alumnae Recognition award, 1973. Mem. Am. Radium Soc., Am. Statis. Assn., Math. Assn. Am., Am. Math. Soc., Biometric Soc., Internat. Union Against

Cancer, N.Y. Acad. Scis., Boston Med. History Club, Am., Southwestern assns. cancer research, Am. Pub. Health Assn., Pub. Health Cancer Assn. Am. (sec., treas. 1951-57, pres. 1958), Inst. Math. Statistics, A.A.A.S., Phi Beta Kappa. Contbr. numerous articles to sci. jours. Established 1st statewide cancer record registry in Conn., 1941, 1st dept. epidemiology in a cancer hosp. U. Tex.-M.D. Anderson Hosp. and Tumor Inst., 1948. Home: 2107 University Blvd Houston TX 77025 Office: 6723 Bertner Dr Houston TX 77025

MACDONALD, EVA WADDELL MADER (MRS. CHARLES NAPIER MACDONALD), physician; b. Halifax, N.S., Can., Oct. 7, 1902; d. Anthony Ivan and Eva Anderson (Waddell) Mader; M.D.C.M., Dalhousie U., 1927; D.P.H. (Connaught Lab. fellow), U. Toronto, Ont., Can., 1929; m. Charles Napier Macdonald, Aug. 25, 1931; children—Donald Fraser, James Robert. Intern, Children's Hosp., Halifax, 1925-27; resident, N.S. Sanatorium, Kentsville, 1927-28; teaching asst. Sch. Hygiene, research asst. Connaught Lab., U. Toronto, 1929-33, univ. chancellor, 1974—; physician Toronto Children's Aid Soc., 1930-38; physician out patient dept. Women's Coll. Hosp., Toronto, 1929-66, bacteriologist, 1939-42, dir. labs., 1943-53, mem. hon. staff, 1966—; gen. practice medicine, Toronto, 1953-63; dir. Pub. Hosp. Health, 1930-66. Active YWCA, Canadian Red Cross. Banting fellow, 1935-36. Mem. Fedn. Med. Women Can., English Speaking Union, Canadian, Ont. med. assns. Club: University Women's of Toronto. Home: 58 Glen Gowan Rd Toronto ON M4N1G4 Canada

MACDONALD, EVE LAPEYROUSE, biologist, educator; b. Baton Rouge, La., Jan. 2, 1929; d. Maury and Eve (Cox) Lapeyrouse; A.B. (Wellesley Coll. scholar) Wellesley Coll., 1950; M.A., Bryn Mawr Coll., 1965, Ph.D. (Bryn Mawr Coll. grad. scholar), 1967; postgrad. in Electron Microscopy, Northeastern U., 1973; divorced; 1 dau., Amy. Teaching asst. Bryn Mawr (Pa.) Coll., 1964-66; asst. prof. biology Wilson Coll., Chambersburg, Pa., 1967—. Recipient Christian R. and Mary F. Lindback award for Distinguished Teaching, Wilson Coll., 1971; fellow NSF, 1966. Mem. Wash. Soc. Electronmicroscopy, Am. Inst. Biol. Scis., Soc. for Devel. Biology, Am. Soc. Zoologists, Electron Microscope Soc. Am., A.A.A.S., Nat. Wildlife Fedn., Sigma Xi. Home: 174 Harvest Lane Chambersburg PA 17201

MACDONALD, JUDY KATHLEEN (MRS. GARY F.W. MACDONALD), mus. ofcl.; b. Charlottetown, P.E.I., Can., Apr. 28, 1945; d. Norman Rendle and Kathleen Josephine (McGlinchey) Larter; student Prince of Wales Coll., 1961-63, U. P.E.I., 1973-74; m. Gary F.W. MacDonald, Mar. 12, 1966; children—Denise Frances, Andrea Heather. Stenographer, Civil Service Commn., P.E.I. Govt., 1963-65; sec. to dir. pub. and publicity relations Confedn. Centre of Arts, Charlottetown, P.E.I., Can., 1965-68, sec. to dir. art gallery, 1968-69, registrar, librarian Confedn. Art Gallery and Mus., Charlottetown, Can., 1969—. Dir. P.E.I. Women's Inst., 1973—, convenor home econs., 1973—. Mem. P.E.I. Action Com. on Status of Women, 1973-74. Mem. Canadian Museums Assn. (instr. 1972-73). Roman Catholic. Home: South Milton PE Canada Office: PO Box 848 Charlottetown PE Canada

MACDONALD, JULIE, sculptor; b. Los Angeles, Feb. 14, 1926; d. Alexander and Aileen (McCarthy) Macdonald; student Stanford 1943-44, Art Center Sch., Los Angeles, 1945, Chouinard Art Inst., Los Angeles, 1953, Jepson Art Inst., Los Angeles, 1948-50; m. William Harrison Hood, May 1, 1970; children—Judith Macdonald Bluechel, Alexander Macdonald II. One-man shows Esther Robles Gallery, Los Angeles; exhibited in group shows Denver Mus. Art, San Francisco Mus. Art, N.A.D., N.Y.C., Sculpture Center, N.Y.C., represented in permanent collections Joseph Hirshorn, Washington, Mrs. Reese Taylor, San Marino, Cal., Jerry Lewis, Beverly Hills, Morgan Adams, Los Angeles, Ed Janss, Westwood, Cal., Jerry Orbach, N.Y.C., Rutgers U.; commns. include: Randhurst Shopping Center, Chgo., Lincoln Sq., Urbana, Ill., K St., City Mall, Sacramento, Adams Plaza, Los Angeles. Recipient awards Sacramento State Fair, San Francisco Mus. Art, Nat. Acad. Design, N.Y.C. Author; Almost Human, 1965. Home: 485 Maylin St Pasadena CA 91105

MACDONALD, MARIE GENEVA (MRS. KING RUFUS MACDONALD), journalist; b. Ozark, Ark., June 1, 1910; d. Matthew J. and Edna Mae (Barclift) Self; occasional student Wichita State U.; m. King Rufus MacDonald, Aug. 2, 1931; (dec. Oct. 7, 1966); 1 son, Ronald (dec.); step-daus. Marion Lam, Dorothy Cardell, Molly Baca. Reporter soc. dept. Wichita Eagle, 1942-47; women's editor Wichita Beacon, 1947-49; dir. women's activities, broadcaster Radio Sta. KFBI, 1949-56, KARD-TV, 1956-58; asst. program dir. Radio Sta. KFH, 1958-61; publicity dir. YWCA, 1961-63; feature writer Wichita Eagle & Beacon, 1965—. Columnist, Person to Person, Party-Line Farm Jour., 1973—. Mem. pub. information com. A.R.C., 1952-60, regional pub. information coordinator, 1963-66, dir., chmn. pub. information com., 1970-74; mem. pub. information com. Kan. div. Am. Cancer Soc., 1972—. Recipient 1st Pl. award Nat. Fedn. Press Women, 1955, 69, Kan. Optometric Soc. Writing award, 1970. Mem. Internat. Platform Assn., Am. Women Radio and Television (pres. Wichita chpt. 1975), Women in Communications (pres. Wichita profl. chpt. 1971), Wichita (pres. 1950), Kan. (Sweepstakes award 1970, pres. 1952) press women. Home: 836 Coolidge St Wichita KS 67203 Office: 825 Douglas St Wichita KS 67201

MACDONALD, MARIE PETERSON (MRS. ALEXANDER C. MACDONALD), librian; b. Gt. Falls, Mont., Feb. 24, 1913; d. Peter Gust and Hannah Christina (Swenson) Peterson; student U. Mont., 1930; B.S. magna cum laude, U. Minn., 1936; m. Alexander Colin MacDonald, Feb. 22, 1941; children—Mariellen (Mrs. G.W. Neudeck), Alice (Mrs. A.J. MacDonald), Alexander E., Peter D., Sheila (Mrs. H.J. Stearns), Margaret. Tchr., Mee Sch., Chouteau County, Mont., 1931-33, Carter County High Sch., Mont., 1936-39; librarian Glendive (Mont.) Pub. Library, 1964—. Alderman, City of Glendive, 1957-59; Democratic congl. committeewoman Eastern Mont. Congl. Dist., 1954-60. Mem. Mont. Hist. Soc. (trustee), Am. Assn. U. Women (local pres. 1949-51), Mont. Library Assn. (chmn. local history com. 1964—), Phi Beta Kappa, Pi Lambda Theta, Delta Delta Delta. Author: After Barbed Wire, 1964; Glendive: History of a Montana Town, 1968; also various mag. articles. Editor book column Mont. Arts quar. Home: 1500 River Av Glendive MT 59330 Office: Box 1329 Glendive MT 59330

MACDONALD, RUTH LANE (MRS. ERNEST R. MACDONALD), librarian; b. Buffalo; d. Fred W. and Elizabeth G. (Thynge) Lane; B.A., State U. N.Y. at Buffalo, 1934, B.L.S., 1937, M.Ed., 1957; postgrad. Temple U., 1959, U. Del., 1960, Syracuse U., 1963, 64; m. 2d, Ernest R. MacDonald, Nov. 23, 1957; 1 dau. by previous marriage, Nancy J. Librarian Gowanda (N.Y.) High Sch., 1934-37; supr. libraries Vestal (N.Y.) Central Sch. System, 1937-42; librarian Buffalo and Erie County Pub. Library, 1942-44; head librarian Amherst Central High Sch., Snyder, N.Y., 1945-47; head coll. librarian Erie Community Coll., Buffalo, 1947—; lectr. Library Sch., State U. N.Y. at Buffalo, 1971, instr. adult reading courses Div. Continuing Edn., 1963—. Active A.R.C.; mem. Com. Woman, Buffalo, 1959-62. Exec. bd. Niagara Frontier Reading Council. Mem. Spl. Libraries Assn. (nat. chmn. metals div. 1968, pres. Upstate N.Y. chpt. 1960), Coll. Reading Assn., N.Y. Library Assn. (coll. and univ. sect. sec. 1967-71, exec. bd. 1972-73), Bus. and Profl. Women's Assn., Sch. Information and Library Sci. Alumni Assn., Internat. Reading Assn., U. Buffalo Alumni Assn., Sigma Kappa, Pi Lambda Theta (treas. 1973—). Contbr. articles to profl. jours. Home: 85 Yorktown Rd Snyder NY 14226 Office: Erie Community Coll Main and Youngs Rd Buffalo NY 14221

MACDONALD, SISTER STELLA, hosp. adminstr.; b. Little Pond, P.E.I., Can., May 22, 1915; d. Angus David and Mary Cecelia (MacKenzie) MacDonald; student Prince of Wales Coll., 1932-33. Registered nurse Charlottetown (P.E.I.) Hosp., 1941, staff nurse, 1941-46, supr. obstetrical dept., 1946-52, dir. nursing, 1952-62, adminstr., 1962—. Bd. dirs. Home Care Nursing, Basilica Recreational Centre. Fellow Atlantic Cath. Hosp. Assn.; mem. Canadian Coll. Health Execs., P.E.I. Hosp. Assn. Home: Mount St Mary's Charlottetown PE Canada Office: 17 Haviland St Charlottetown PE Canada

MACDONALD, ZILLAH KATHERINE, author; b. Halifax, N.S., Can., Jan. 15, 1885; d. Charles John and Annie Christie (MacLearn) MacDonald; student Dalhousie U., 1902, Harvard, 1906, Columbia, 1949; m. Colin MacDonald, June 8, 1960. Came to U.S., 1913. Faculty, Columbia, N.Y.C., 1919-49. Mem. Canadian Authors, Women's Nat. Book Assn., Pen and Brush. Author of numerous books including, Marcia, Private Secretary, 1949; A Cap for Corrine, 1952; (with Josie Johnston) Rosemary Wins Her Cap, 1955; Fireman for A Day, 1958; Flower of the Fortress, 1966; also Courage to Command, The Mystery of the Piper's Ghost, Tab and Berkley, Tugboat Toots for Terry, Roxanne, Industrial Nurse, Nurse Todd's Strange Summer; author of various plays including The Royal Romance, Our John, The Long Box, Markheim; author of short stories for various mags. Home: The Manor Wolfville NS B0P 1X0 Canada

MACDOUGALL, MARY KATHERINE SLATE (MRS. HAROLD ALEXANDER MACDOUGALL), author; b. Mt. Auburn, Ill.; d. Fay Dudley and Kittie May (Alexander) Slate; student Alma Coll.; B.A., U. Mich., postgrad.; postgrad. U. Tex.; m. Wayne Fox McMeans (dec.); children—David, Nancy (Mrs. Charles Richey); m. 2d, Harold Alexander MacDougall (dec.); children—Alexander, Kent, Alan Ross. Former secondary tchr., Sandusky, Mich., Austin, Tex.; former women's editor Abilene (Tex.) Reporter-News, Austin Am. Statesman, gen. reporter, editor Port Huron (Mich.) Times-Herald; instr. sch. journalism and sch. communications U. Tex., Austin. Spiritual counselor, tchr. Unity Sch. Christianity; tchr., leader Unity in Temple, Unity in Waco. Author: Black Jupiter; What Treasure Mapping Can Do For You; Prosperity Now; Healing Now; Happiness Now; Making Love Happen. Contbr. articles to profl. jours., mags. Home: 2511 Hartford Rd Austin TX 78703

MACDOUGALL, RUTH DOAN (MRS. DONALD KEITH MACDOUGALL), author; b. Laconia, N.H., Mar. 19, 1939; d. Daniel and Ernestine Elizabeth (Crone) Doan; student Bennington Coll., 1957-59; Ed.B., Keene State Coll., 1961; m. Donald Keith MacDougall, Oct. 9, 1957. Author: The Lilting House, 1965; The Cost of Living, 1971; One Minus One, 1971; The Cheerleader, 1973. Mem. Authors Guild, Authors League Am. Address: RFD 2 Box 567A Rochester NH 03867

MACELWANE, GERALDINE FRANCES, judge; b. Detroit, July 9, 1909; d. Jeremiah Joseph and Mary Elizabeth (Hannett) Connell; LL.B., U. Toledo, 1938, J.D., 1968; A.B., DeSales Coll., 1942; m. John Patrick Macelwane, July 23, 1938; children—Mary Frances (Mrs. Stephen Pero), Kathleen Anne (Mrs. Anthony Wernert). Admitted to Ohio bar, 1932; pvt. practice, Toledo, 1932-37; asst. prosecutor, Lucas County, 1937-52; judge municipal Ct., Toledo, 1952-56, Lucas County Common Pleas Ct., 1956—. Cons. Women's Traffic Council; del. White Ho. Conf. on Traffic Safety, Pres.'s Mid-West Conf. on Traffic Safety; dir. Toledo Council Social Agys., Maumee Valley council Girl Scouts U.S.A.; mem. exec. com., dir. Toledo-Lucas County Safety Council; chmn. jud. adminstrn. com. Ohio Jud. Conf., 1966; nat. chmn. safety on sts. com. women's conf. Nat. Safety Council. Recipient awards for jud. service Ohio Supreme Ct., 1972-73, for outstanding service Toledo Area Assn. Correctional Workers, 1973; Chi Omega recognition medal, 1973. Fellow Ohio Bar. Found.; mem. Am., Ohio, Lucas County, Toledo bar assns., Nat. Safety Council (program chmn. 1965, v.p., exec. com. Women's Conf.), League Women Voters, Ohio Assn. Common Pleas Judges (v.p. exec. com., chmn. rules of superintendency com.), Nat. Conf. State Trial Judges, Nat. Assn. Women Lawyers, Toledo Bus. and Profl. Women's Club, Kappa Beta Pi, Phi Kappa Phi (hon. mem. U. Toledo chpt.), Delta Kappa Gamma (state hon. mem.). Democrat. Home: 2817 Collingwood Blvd Toledo OH 43610 Office: Court House Toledo OH 43610

MACELWEE, MRS. IRVIN R., civic worker, club woman, business exec.; b. Stevens Point, Wis.; d. Joseph Victor and Jeannette M. (Gasche) Collins; B.E., U. Wis., Stevens Point; postgrad. Carroll Coll.; B.Lit. Sci., U. Wis.; m. Irvin Reed MacElwee, Dec. 29, 1927; children—Marilyn Jean (Mrs. Bruce Hamilton Throckmorton), Donald Beall. Dir. Fibremold, Inc., Woburn, Mass. Apptd. to 1960 Assay Commn. Mem. bd. Phila. Cancer Dr., 1954-64; hon. pres. St. Christopher's Hosp. Auxiliary, 1957-61. Mem. adv. com. Phila. Com. on Alcoholism. Pres. Pa. Council Republican Women, 1960-62; pres. Rep. Women Pa., 1954-60; mem. bd. Nat. Fedn. Rep. Women, 1960-64, mem. exec. bd., 1962-64; alternate del. Rep. Nat. Conv., 1972. Mem. bd. Soc. Retarded Children, March of Dimes, Phila., Women's Soc. Prevention Cruelty to Animals. Recipient Plaque for citizenship work in Swarthmore, Lions Club, 1966; Alumni Achievement award, Wis. State U., 1969. Mem. D.A.R. (Phila. chpt. regent 1956-59, state program chmn. 1957-67), Am. Acad. Polit. and Social Scis., Phila. Acad. Art, Daus. 17th Century, Colonial Dames Am., Needlework Guild Am. (dir. Swarthmore br. 1935—), Woman's Med. Coll. Aux., Sons and Daus. Pilgrims, Soc. Preservation Old Landmarks, Nat. Geog. Soc., U. Wis. Phila. Alumni Assn. (v.p. 1958-61, 64—), Emergency Aid Am., Strawberry Mansion and Com. of 1926, Delta Zeta (dir. eastern region 1926-34). Presbyn. Clubs: Swarthmore Woman's, Swarthmore Music, Players of Swarthmore; Union League; Springhaven Golf (Wallingford, Pa.); Capitol Hill (Washington). Home: 909 Mt Holyoke Pl Swarthmore PA 19081

MACEY, BARBARA ANITRA, lawyer; b. Brookline, Mass.; d. Louis Albert and Evelyn K. Macey; student fine arts Boston U., J.D., New Eng. Law Sch., 1962. Admitted to Mass. bar, 1968; practiced in Mass., 1968—; spl. asst. dist. atty. Norfolk County (Mass.), Dedham, 1968—; land ct. examiner, Boston, 1972—. Mem. Mass. Assn. Women Lawyers (pres. 1974-75), Mass. Dist. Attys. Assn., Norfolk County, Mass. (del.) bar assns., Norfolk County Prosecutors Assn. Home: 12 Thorndike Brookline MA 02146 Office: One State Boston MA 02109

MACFARLANE, MARGARET LAMOREAUX, lawyer; b. Beaver Dam, Wis., June 24, 1916; d. Harland S. and Leona (Miller) Lamoreaux; student George Washington U., 1935-38; LL.B., Nat. U., 1941; m. Archie H. MacFarlane, July 30, 1947. Jr. archivist Nat. Archives, 1935-41; admitted to D.C. bar, 1941, Wis. bar, 1971; cons. Fgn. Econ. Adminstrn., 1942-45; atty. Gen. Accounting Office, 1945-71, chief legislative unit. 1949-54, chief index-digest sect. Office Gen. Counsel, 1954-60, chief legal reference service, 1960-71; adminstrv. asst. trust dept. 1st Nat. Bank & Trust Co. Beaver Dam, 1971-72; legislative analyst Wis. Hosp. Assn., 1972—. Recipient Outstanding Service awards Gen. Accounting Office, 1950, 56, 63, 66; Career Devel. award, 1967, Comptroller Gen.'s award, 1971. Mem. Fed., D.C. Women's bar assns. Home: 328 Park Av Beaver Dam WI 53916

MACGILLIVRAY, MARGARET HILDA STOUTE (MRS. A. DEAN MACGILLIVRAY), educator, endocrinologist; b. San Fernando, Trinidad, B.W.I., Aug. 30, 1930; d. Gordon Harold and Hilda (Andrews) Stoute; M.D., U. Toronto, 1956; m. A. Dean MacGillivray, Feb. 1, 1957; children—Janet, John, Matthew. Came to U.S., 1956. Intern, then resident, and chief resident Cedars of Lebanon, 1956-60; biology fellow Cal. Inst. Tech., 1960-61; fellow Mass. Gen. Hosp.-Harvard Med. Sch., 1961-64; practice medicine specializing in pediatric endocrinology, Buffalo, 1964—; attending pediatrician Buffalo Children's Hosp., 1969; asst. prof. dept. pediatrics Sch. Medicine, State U. N.Y. at Buffalo, 1965-68, asso. prof., 1968—. Asso. mem. Center Immunology, 1970. Active Planned Parenthood Assn. Recipient award Human Growth Found. Niagara Frontier chpt., 1971. Home: 16 Soldiers Pl Buffalo NY 14222 Office: 219 Bryant St Buffalo NY 14222

MACGILLIVRAY, VERA (MRS. JAMES J. MACGILLIVRAY), ednl. adminstr.; b. Bklyn., May 19, 1919; d. Vincent and Pauline (Martina) Boshia; student Fine Arts Center, 1961-71; m. James J. MacGillivray, Apr. 19, 1941; 1 son, David. Sec., Gough & King, Inc., N.Y.C., 1938-41; David R. Blossom, atty., Bklyn., 1939-41; dir. Fine Arts Center, Clinton, Ill., 1968-73; sec., editorial asst. alumni newspaper services Ill. State U., Normal, 1973—. Den mother Boy Scouts Am., Rome, N.Y., 1950-54; sec. Mothers Club St. Peters, Rome, 1954-56; pub. relations chmn. A.R.C., DeWitt County, Ill., 1965-67; patron Y Players Theatre; mem. DeWitt County Mus. Assn. Mem. St. John's Altar Rosary Soc. (sec. 1959-61). Home: Rural Route 1 Sunset Dr Clinton IL 61727 Office: Alumni Services Ill State U Normal IL 61761

MACGREGOR, FRANCES COOKE, social scientist; b. Portland; d. Charles Francis and Margaret Cassell (Spencer) Cooke; A.B., U. Cal. at Berkeley, 1927; M.A., U. Mo., 1947. Commd. asst. in tech. research tech. coop, Bur. Indian Affairs, Soil Conservation Dept., 1937; research asso. in sociology dept. psychiatry N.Y.U. Coll. Medicine, 1949-53; co-ordinator research project Psychosocial Aspects of Facial Deformities and Plastic Surgery, Nat. Inst. Mental Health grant at N.Y.U., 1949-51; cons. to Columbia U. Research Project in Contemporary Cultures, 1947-49; Milbank fellow N.Y.U. Coll. Medicine, 1951-54; vis. asst. prof. social sci. Cornell U., N.Y. Hosp. Sch. Nursing, 1954-57, vis. asso. prof., 1957-60, asso. prof., 1960-63, prof., 1963-69; research scientist Inst. Reconstructive Plastic Surgery, N.Y.U. Med. Center, 1968—, clin. asso. prof. surgery (in sociology), 1970—. Fellow Am. Sociol. Assn., Am. Anthrop. Assn., Soc. for Applied Anthropology; mem. A.A.A.S., Eastern Sociol. Soc., Soc. for Rehab. Facially Disfigured (founding mem.), Torch and Shield, Pi Beta Phi. Author: Twentieth Century Indians, 1941; Social Science in Nursing: Applications for the Improvement of Patient Care, 1960; Transformation and Identity: The Face and Plastic Surgery, 1974. Collaborator (with Dr. Margaret Mead) Growth and Culture: A Photographic Study of Balinese Childhood, 1951; joint collaborator: Facial Deformities and Plastic Surgery: A Psychosocial Study, 1953. Collaborated Mrs. Eleanor Roosevelt, This Is America, 1942. Contbr. articles to profl. and med. jours. Home: 120 E 90th St New York City NY 10028 Office: Inst Reconstructive Plastic Surgery NYU Med Center 560 1st Av New York City NY 10016

MACHT, CAROL MALISOFF (MRS. MARTIN B. MACHT), mus. curator; b. N.Y.C., Jan. 28; d. Samuel S. and Bertha (Jacobus) Malisoff; B.A., Goucher Coll., 1940; M.A., Johns Hopkins, 1942 Ph.D. (univ. scholar), 1945; m. Martin B. Macht, Dec. 5, 1939; 1 dau., Ann E. Librarian, Enoch Pratt Free Library, Balt., 1942-45; librarian Cin. Pub. Library, 1945-46; curator decorative arts Cin. Art Mus., 1958-63, sr. curator, 1963—. Tchr., Cin. Art Acad., 1958-72, Jr. League Docent Program, Cin. 1962—. Author: Classical Sources of Wedgwood Design, 1957, also articles. Home: 2702 Johnstone Pl Cincinnati OH 45206 Office: Cin Art Museum Eden Park Cincinnati OH 45202

MACINNES, MARGO, univ. adminstr.; b. Troy, N.Y., Sept. 25, 1930; d. Harold Boyce and Julia (Storr) MacInnes; student Hiram Coll., 1949-50; B.A., U. Mich., 1971; m. Richard Henry Shackson, June 16, 1951 (div. 1970); children—Carol Ann, Russell Mark. Dir. pub. relations Hudson (O.) Sch. Dist., 1964-66; asso. producer U. Mich. TV Center, Ann Arbor, 1970-71; audio-visual cons. Parkview Med. Center, Ann Arbor, 1970-72; asst. to dean coll. lit., sci. and arts U. Mich., Ann Arbor, 1972—, guest lectr. journalism dept., 1972—. Mem. Am. Women in Radio and TV, Women in Communications. Author: Girls and Women: Images and Realities, TV series, 1971; also articles. Office: LSA Bldg State St U Mich Ann Arbor MI 48104

MACINNIS, FLORENCE ELIZABETH, physician; b. Bowdle, S.D.; d. Austin Edward and Ella (Juntilla) MacInnis; student St. Mary's Coll., Notre Dame, Ind., 1920-22; B.S., Marquette U., 1927, M.D., 1928; m. Francis C. Quilty, Sept. 8, 1951. Intern St. Anthony's Hosp., Terre Haute, Ind., 1927-28; resident Wis. Anti-TB Assn., Milw., 1928-41; dir. TB, Milw. Health Dept., 1941-44; practice medicine specializing in pulmonary diseases, Kansas City, Mo., 1944—; med. dir. TB div., TB out-patient, Gen. Hosp. Kansas City, Mo., 1944—; mem. staff St. Mary's Hosp., Research Hosp. and Med. Center, Bapt. Hosp. (all Kansas City, Mo.). Asso. clin. prof. medicine Mo. U., Kansas City, 1964—. Recipient Dearholt medal Miss. Valley TB Conf., 1965. Mem. Women's C. of C. Soroptimist. Club: Women's City. Home: 609 Romany Rd Kansas City MO 64113 Office: 4620 J C Nichols Pkwy Kansas City MO 64112

MAC INTYRE, CLARA BISHOP (MRS. MALCOLM AMES MAC INTYRE), polit. worker; b. N.Y.C., May 24, 1911; d. Irving and Clare F. (Reilly) Bishop; student pub., pvt. schs.; m. Malcolm Ames Mac Intyre, Dec. 1, 1933; children—Bruce Bishop, Clare Alden, Pamela Ames (Mrs. W. Keith Pattison). Dir. Washington Housing Bd., 1947-48, Barney Neighborhood House, 1946-48; rec. sec., dir. Scarsdale Women's Exchange, N.Y., 1951-55; Washington chmn. United Thank Offering, 1958-59; mem. N.Y. State Legislative Adv. Com. on Motor Vehicles, Traffic and Hwy. Safety, Gov. Rockefeller's Com. on Ofcl. Internat. Visitors, chmn. Distinguished Visitors Com., Westchester County; mem. N.Y. state adv. bd. Drs.-Rehab. Pilot Project. Pres., Scarsdale Women's Republican Club, 1955-57; dir. sec. Westchester County Rep. Women's Club, 1955-57, mem. Scarsdale nonpartisan nominating com., 1956-57; chmn. Westchester Women's Rally reelection Gov. Rockefeller, 1962; co-chmn. Scarsdale Rep. Citizens Com., 1969. Chmn., Westchester County UN Day program, 1967-73; sponsor N.Y. Citizens Information Service. Dir. woman;s bd. Washington Opera Soc., chmn. opera lectures; bd. women's com. Union Theol. Sem., Operations Bookshelf, Youth Consultation Service Westchester-Conn. Aux., vice-chmn. nat. Liaison com. Fedn. Women's Rep. Clubs, 1959-60; dir. Women's Nat. Rep. Club, also bd. govs.; chmn. N.Y. State Women's All Am. Com.; founder, 1st pres. Westchester County Driver Improvement Sch., founder, 1st pres. Eastern Air Lines Wives Scholarship Fund; co-chmn. Westchester

County, Keep N.Y. State Clean; Bicentennial co-chmn., Scarsdale; mem. heritage com. Westchester County Bicentennial Com.; mem. Ethical Standards Com. N.Y. State Atty. Gen. Bd. dirs. Westchester County Council on Arts, Westchester Symphony Orch. Mem. Jr. League of Washington and Scarsdale. Club: Presidents (chmn. Scarsdale). Author: Introducing Washington, D.C., 1948; Welcome to Old and New Westchester, 1973. Contbr. articles to mags. Home: The Haven 60 Mamaroneck Rd Scarsdale NY 10583

MACIVER, LOREN, artist; b. N.Y.C., Feb. 2, 1909; d. Charles Augustus Paul and Julia (MacIver) Newman; student Art Students League, 1919; m. Lloyd Frankenberg. Exhibited one-man shows East River Gallery, N.Y.C., 1938, Pierre Matisse Gallery, N.Y., 1940-44, 49, 56, 61, 66, 70, Venice Biennale, 1961, Mus. Modern Art Traveling Exhbn., 1941, Vassar Art Gallery, 1950, Wellesley Coll., 1951, Whitney Mus., 1953; Dallas Mus. Fine Arts, 1953, Musee des Beaux Arts, Lyon, Musee d'Art Modern de la Ville de Paris, Musee des Ponchettes, Nice, France, 1968, others. Works exhibited at Mus. Modern Art: exhbn. Fed. Art, 1937, Fantastic Art, Dada, Surrealism, 1938, Art In Our Time, 1939; selections from Mus. Modern Art collection, various years, Fourteen Americans, 1946; exhbn. Am. art, Jeu de Paume, Paris, 1938, St. Louis Mus. Whitney Mus., Bklyn. Mus., Corcoran Art Gallery, State Dept. exhbn. sent to Europe, 1946. Represented in permanent collections: Mus. Modern Art, Met. Mus., Detroit Inst., Los Angeles, San Francisco, Newark, Whitney museums, Addison Gallery, Wadsworth Atheneum, Boston, others. Recipient 1st prize Corcoran Art Gallery, 1957, 1st prize Art Inst. Chgo., 1962; 1st prize U. Ill., 1963; Mark Rothko Meml. award, 1972. Ford Found. grantee, 1960. Mem. Nat. Inst. Arts and Letters. Home: 61 Perry St New York City NY 10014 Office: Pierre Matisse Gallery 51 E 57th St New York City NY 10022

MACIVER, PEGGE FARMER (MRS. DONALD GORDON MACIVER), monodramatist, educator; b. Colon, C.Z.; d. Alfred Gibson and Minnie (Cuckler) Farmer; B.A., Ohio U., 1935; B.L.L., Cin. Conservatory Music, 1938; M.A., George Washington U., 1964; m. Donald Gordon MacIver, June 7, 1957; 1 stepson, Neil. Monodramatist, lectr., writer touring U.S., Can. writing, performing own plays for one woman theatre presentations, 1938-59; speech therapist D.C. Pub. Schs., 1959-67, tchr. in-service tng. programs, program coordinator Ednl. Resources Center, 1967-70, asst. dir. dept. spl. edn., 1970-72, supervising dir. for staff devel. dept. spl. edn., 1972—; tchr. in-service tng. programs D.C. Tchrs. Coll. TV moderator, panelist Its Your World and World Headliner programs; mem. speakers burs. Dayton (O.) Council World Affairs, League Women Voters, 1950-57. Mem. Nat. League Am. Pen Women, Am. (certificate of clin. competence in speech pathology), D.C. speech and hearing assns., Assn. for Supervision and Curriculum Devel., Internat. Platform Assn., Phi Beta Kappa, Pi Beta Phi, Alpha Delta Kappa, Delta Kappa Gamma. Contbr. articles to profl. publs. Home: 8500 New Hampshire Av Silver Spring MD 20903 Office: DC Pub Schs Washington DC 20004

MACK, BLANCHE HUMPHREY (MRS. THOMAS JOHN MACK), orgn. exec.; b. Scranton, Pa., Mar. 13, 1927; d. Williard Clay and Margaret Ann (Brace) Humphrey; student Broome Community Coll. Evening Div., 1958-61; student Inst. for Certifying Secs., 1960; m. Thomas John Mack, May 30, 1952. Sec. to v.p. So. Tier Elec. Supply, 1945-47; sec. to mgr. marketing research dept. Ansco div. Gen. Aniline & Film Co., 1947-50; office mgr. Broome County C. of C., 1950-68; exec. dir. Broome County Heart Chpt., Inc., 1968— (all Binghamton, N.Y.). Mem. vol. service, tchr. office practice classes Binghamton State Hosp.; coordinator continuing edn. Broome Community Coll., 1971—; mem. Broome Community Health Center Aux., Chenango Forks Civic Assn.; active Broome County chpt. A.R.C.; mem. Woman's adv. council Broome Community Coll.; warden Broome County Civil Def.; pres. Chenango Valley Kiwaniqueens, 1961-62; chmn. Central N.Y. Regional Med. Program So. Subregional Com., 1972-73; sec.-treas. Broome County Inter-Agy. Council on Smoking; pub. health com. Broome County Social Planning Council; bd. dirs. N.Y.-Penn Health Planning Council, 1971-74. Recipient certificate of merit U.S. C. of C., 1952; named Sec. of Year, Binghamton Secs. Assn., 1962. Mem. Nat. Secs. Assn. Internat. (v.p. Binghamton 1961-62, pres. 1962-63, chmn. edn. and CPS service com. N.Y. state div.), Adminstrv. Mgmt. Soc. (chmn. awards com. 1968, dir. 1973-74), Sales and Marketing Execs. (dir. 1972-74), Am. Heart Assn., N.Y. State Heart Assembly, Soc. Heart Assn. Profl. Staff, Broome County Mental Health Assn. Episcopalian (sec.-treas. altar guild 1953-57). Club: Zonta (pres. 1963-64, dir. 1972—, dist. treas. 1972-74, dist. chmn. pub. relations com., chmn. service com., mem. internat. pub. relations com.), IBM Country, IBM Travel (Binghamton). Home: Oak Hill Rd RD 4 Binghamton NY 13901 Office: 8 Riverside Dr Binghamton NY 13905

MACK, CAROLYN HOURIGAN (MRS. THOMAS J. MACK), pub. co. exec.; b. Wilkes-Barre, Pa., Feb. 2, 1907; d. John Aloysius and Caroline G. (Henderson) Hourigan; B.A., Manhattanville Coll., 1928; m. Thomas J. Mack, Sept. 20, 1956. Vice pres. Wilkes-Barre Pub. Co., 1945—; treas., dir. Bertels Metal Ware Co., Inc., Kingston, Pa., 1951—; sec., dir. Mack Supply Co., Wilkes-Barre, 1956—. Mem. Wilkes-Barre City Planning Commn., 1971—. Bd. dirs., v.p. Legal Aid Soc., Wilkes-Barre, 1955-60; bd. dirs. Wyoming Valley Heart Assn.; bd. dirs., chmn. Cath. Youth Center, Wilkes-Barre; vol. bd. dirs. Channel 44 WVIA-TV, Wilkes-Barre-Scranton; trustee Misericordia Coll., Dallas, Pa. Republican. Roman Catholic. Club: Westmoreland (Wilkes-Barre). Home: 182 S Franklin St Wilkes-Barre PA 18701 Office: 15 N Main St Wilkes-Barre PA 18711

MACK, PHYLLIS FRIEDMAN (MRS. DAVID MACK), interior designer, civic worker; b. N.Y.C., Apr. 15, 1941; d. Maurice and Anne (Price) Friedman; grad. Brearley Sch., 1958; student Vassar, 1958-60, Sorbonne, 1960; B.S., Columbia, 1963; grad. N.Y. Sch. Interior Design; m. David Mack, Oct. 8, 1961; children—Alexander H., Nicholas R. Interior designer domestic interiors, N.Y.C., 1963—. Dir. Stanley Isaacs Community Center, 1965-67; dance chmn. George Jr. Republic, also mem. jr. bd., 1966-69; mem. fund-raising com. Yorkville Youth Council; mem. pub. relations com. Asso. YM-YWHA, N.Y.C. Mem. Allied Bd. Trade, Brearley Alumnae Assn. Club: Fairview Country (Greenwich, Conn.). Home: 950 Park Av New York City NY 10028 also 100 Bedford Rd Greenwich CT

MACK, SARA ROHRBACH (MRS. GEORGE MACK), educator, librarian; b. Topton, Pa., Nov. 20, 1921; d. Jonathan H. and Alda (Heffner) Rohrbach; B.S., Kutztown State Tchrs. Coll., 1943; M.S., Columbia, 1955; postgrad. U. Pa., 1959—; m. George Mack, June 26, 1943 (dec. Jan. 1949); 1 dau., Carol Ann (Mrs. Thomas F. Foy). Tchr., Chalfont (Pa.) Elementary Sch., 1943-45; librarian Mt. Penn-Lower Alsace Joint High Sch., Reading, Pa., 1949-58; asst. prof. library edn., asst. librarian Kutztown (Pa.) State Coll., 1958-70, asso. prof., 1971—, acting dir. div. library sci., 1973-74; adj. prof. Drexel Inst. Tech., 1968. Founder, Ann. Pa. Student Assts. Workshop, 1967—; mem. Pa. Nat. Library Week Com., 1962. Mem. Am., Pa. (Merit award 1969, chmn. recruiting 1966-68, awards com. 1970-71) library assns., Nat., Pa. edn. assns., Am. Assn. Sch. Librarians (student assts. com., com. on improvement sch. libraries 1969-72, com. selection materials for minorities 1973-75) Assn. for Ednl. Communication and Tech., Assn. Supervision and Curriculum Devel., Pa. Sch. Librarians (pres. 1964-66), Pa. Learning Resources Assn., Pa. Student Library Assts. Assn. (founder, sponsor 1962-64), Pa. German Soc., Am. Assn. U. Women, Alpha Beta Alpha (sponsor 1963-71), Kappa Delta Pi (Pa. adv. book selection com. 1966-67), Delta Kappa Gamma. Club: Woman's (Topton, Pa.). Compiler: Inspirational Reading for Elementary Grades. Contbr. articles to profl. jours. Home: 44 A S Elm St Kutztown PA 19530 Office: Rohrbach Library Kutztown State Coll Kutztown PA 19530

MACK, WILMETTA MAE (MRS. HAROLD L. MACK), librarian; b. Burchard, Neb., Dec. 24, 1919; d. William Albert and Mary Elizabeth (Leitschuck) Stake; B.A., U. Wyo., 1962; M.S. in L.S., Catholic U., 1970; m. Harold L. Mack, Oct. 16, 1942; children—Harold L., Mary Elizabeth (Mrs. James McLallen), William Albert, Frederick George, John Wayne. Bookkeeper, Continental Nat. Bank, Lincoln, Neb., 1940-42; stenographer War Dept., Washington, 1942-44; receptionist Dr. John J. McGuire, Pensacola, Fla., 1944-45; stenographer Agr. Dept., Lincoln, 1946-49; librarian U. Wyo., Laramie, 1960-62; librarian Florissant (Mo.) Jr. High Sch., 1962-64; librarian Barcroft Elementary Sch., Arlington, Va., 1964—. Mem. N.E.A., A.L.A., Va. Librarians Assn., Arlington Elementary Librarians (chmn.), D.A.R., United Methodist Women (v.p. coop.), Kappa Delta Pi. Mem. Order Eastern Star. Home: 5412 N 26th St Arlington VA 22207 Office: 625 S Wakefield St Arlington VA 22204

MACKAY, JOY ROSSLYN (MRS. BRUCE MACKAY), physician; b. Winnipeg, Man., Can., Aug. 8, 1942; d. John Ross and Marjorie Lucile (Bailey) Blanchard; M.D., U. B.C., 1966; m. Bruce Mackay, June 3, '1966. Intern Vancouver Gen. Hosp., 1966-67; resident Shaughnessy Hosp., Vancouver, 1967-68, U. Wash. Affiliated Hosps., Seattle, 1968-69, Herman Hosp., Houston, 1969-70; practice medicine specializing internal medicine, Houston, 1970—; internist Kelsey-Seybold Clinic, Houston, Tex., 1970—; clin instr. dept. medicine Baylor U. Coll. Medicine, 1970—. Diplomate Am. Bd. Internal Medicine. Mem. A.M.A., Am. Med. Women's Assn. (sec.-treas. Houston 1973-74), Houston Soc. Internal Medicine. Presbyn. Home: 3159 Bonney Briar Dr Missouri City TX 77459 Office: 6624 Fannin St Houston TX 77025

MACKAY, PATRICIA JOANNE, editor; b. Niagara Falls, N.Y., Nov. 13, 1945; d. Thomas Parker and Lois Grier (Nicholson) MacKay; A.B., Smith Coll., 1966. Publicity asst. Marsteller, Inc., N.Y.C., 1967-68; copywriter Diners Club Creative Group, N.Y.C., 1968-69; asso. editor Theatre Crafts Mag., N.Y.C., 1969-73, mng. editor, 1973-74, editor, 1974—. Critic, children's theatre for N.Y. State Arts Council project, 1971-72. Bd. dir. U.S. Inst. for Theatre Tech., 1972-74, vice chmn. architecture, 1972-74. Mem. Am. Theatre Assn. Author: (with others) The Shakespeare Complex, 1975. Office: Suite 815 250 W 57th St New York City NY 10019

MACKELLAR, LILLIAN JEAN, sch. nursing adminstr.; b. Los Angeles; d. Donald and Elizabeth (Forsyth) MacKellar; R.N., Queen of Angels Sch. Nursing, 1944; B.S., Immaculate Heart Coll., 1949, M.S., 1956; postgrad. U. Cal. at Los Angeles, Immaculate Heart Coll., U. So. Cal., 1952-69. Staff nurse operating room St. Joseph Hosp., Burbank, Cal., 1945-49; nursing instr. Queen of Angels Sch. Nursing, Los Angeles, 1949-51; sch. nurse Los Angeles City Bd. Edn., 1951-57, supr. sch. nursing, 1957—; asst. prof. San Fernando Valley State Coll., Northridge, Cal., 1959-60. Rep. for sch. nurses Cal. Dept. Edn. Adv. Com. for Health in Pub. Schs., 1961-63; cons. Cal. Dept. Edn. and Dept. Pub. Health for Cal. Sch. Health Services Study, 1969—; lectr. nursing Mt. St. Mary's Coll., Los Angeles, 1972-74. Hon. life mem. P.T.A. Fellow Am. Sch. Health Assn.; mem. Am. (past chmn. Sch. Nurses Forum), Cal. (past chmn. sch. nurse sect.) nurses assns., A.A.H.P.E.R. (chmn. nat. council sch. nurses, Schering-A.A.P.H.E.R Nat. Sch. Nurse Adminstr. award 1972), Los Angeles Area C. of C. (past mem. adv. com. health and hosps.), Delta Kappa Gamma (chpt. pres. 1972-74). Home: 214 N Lima St Burbank CA 91505 Office: 6621 Balboa Blvd Van Nuys CA 91406

MACKENZIE, AMANDA FISK (MRS. JOHN P. MACKENZIE), civic worker; b. Buffalo, Jan. 18, 1936; d. Bradley and Erma (Johnson) Fisk; B.A., Smith Coll., 1957; m. John Pettibone MacKenzie, Oct. 24, 1959; children—Bradley John, Alice Fisk, Douglas Bain. Editorial asst. N.E.A., Washington, 1957-58; research asst. to prof. polit. sci., Africa, 1958; sec. to pres. Charles Scribner's Sons, N.Y.C., 1959; writer, producer Washington Ednl. TV, 1961-64. Vol. co-ordinator Adams-Morgan Community Council, Washington, 1966-68, benefit chmn., 1968; coordinator performances for children Opera Soc. Washington, 1969; chmn. Friends of Playhouse, Eagles Mere, Pa., 1969-70; mem. Mayor's Inter-Agy. Com. on Beautification. Bd. dirs. Jr. League, Washington, 1969-70, Hillcrest Children's Center, 1972—, Eagles Mere Assn., 1972—, Woodley House, 1973—, Inter/Met, 1973—; trustee Washington Theater Club, 1969-72; trustee Opera House Washington, 1969—, exec. v.p., 1973—; trustee Soc. for More Beautiful Nat. Capital, 1971—, v.p., 1972—. Democrat. Episcopalian. Clubs: Women's Nat. Democratic, International, Smith College (pres. 1972-74) (Washington); Eagles Mere Yacht (sec.-treas. 1968-72). Home: 3501 Macomb St NW Washington DC 20016

MACKEY, ANITA JOHNSON (MRS. HARVEY ALEXANDER MACKEY), social worker; b. Riverside, Cal., Jan. 1, 1914; d. Frank Hannibal and Anna (Ewing) Johnson; A.B., U. Redlands, 1937; M.A., U. Chgo., 1941; L.H.D., Andrews U., 1974; m. Harvey Alexander Mackey, June 13, 1937. Sr. med. social worker Provident Hosp., Chgo., 1940-43; case supr. Home Service, Chgo. chpt. A.R.C., 1943-46; social worker, case supr. VA, Chgo., 1946-53; clin. social worker, supervisory clin. social worker VA Out-Patient Clinic, Los Angeles, 1953-64; field social worker VA Office, Santa Barbara, Cal., 1964—; black studies instr. Santa Barbara City Coll., 1969-70. Social work cons. Seventh-day Adventist Parochial Sch., 1954-55; mem. sch. bd. Seventh-day Adventist Ch. Sch., Santa Barbara, 1964-65; mem. Human Relations com. Pacific Union Conf. Seventh-day Adventists, 1969-71; mem. South Central Welfare Planning Council, Los Angeles, 1956-64, dir., 1960-64; mem. bd. Comprehensive Health Planning Assn. Santa Barbara County, 1970—, Channel Counties Comprehensive Health Planning Assn., Citizens Planning Assn. Santa Barbara, Council on Social Services, Tb and Health Assn. Santa Barbara; bd. adminstrs. Santa Barbara; dist. A.R.C.; mem. Citizen's Adv. Com. on Elementary Instrn., 1965—, Citizens Commn. on Civil Disorders, Santa Barbara, 1970, mem. Santa Barbara Commn. on Aging, 1972—. Trustee Loma Linda (Cal.) U. Mem. Nat. Assn. Social Workers, N.A.A.C.P., Santa Barbara Mental Health Assn. Clubs: Zonta, Travelers. Home: 2 El Vedado Lane Apt 6 Santa Barbara CA 93105 Office: 1216 State St Santa Barbara CA 93101

MACKEY, HELEN THERESA (MRS. EDWARD G. HART), educator; b. Boston, Oct. 6, 1918; d. Mark John and Mary Elizabeth (McLaughlin) Mackey; B.S., Boston U., 1940, M.Ed., 1948, Ed.D., 1954; m. Edward G. Hart. Elementary tchr. phys. edn. Andover, Mass., 1940-41; health and phys. edn. tchr. Athol (Mass.) Jr. High Sch. also Athol High Sch., 1941-43, supr. phys. edn., 1943-45; tchr. health and phys. edn. W. Jr. High Sch., Watertown, Mass., 1945-50; tchr. phys. edn. Watertown High Sch.; edn. Salem (Mass.) State Coll., 1952—, head health and phys edn. dept. for women, 1961-71, asst. dean women, 1959-66. Coordinator TV series WGBH, Boston, 1958; cons. New Eng. Dairy and Food Council, 1962; mem. Mass. Outdoor Edn. Com., 1959; mem. Mass. White House Conf., 1961, Regional White House Conf., N.Y.C., 1961. Fellow Am. Sch. Health Assn., A.A.H.P.E.R. (life fellow, nat. dir. for student services 1959-62, rep. to rep. assembly 1962-63, chmn. team sports sect. 1963—); mem. Mass. Assn. Health, Phys. Edn. and Recreation (v.p. health sect. 1958, Honor award 1966), Eastern Dist. Assn. for Health, Phys. Edn. and Recreation (treas. 1962-63, mem. nominating com. 1963), U.S. (umpiring chmn. 1962-63), N.E. (selection chmn. 1961), Boston (past pres.) field hockey assns., Nat., Eastern (mem. planning com. 1962-63 assns. phys. edn. for coll. women, Mass. State Coll. Assn., Mass. Assn. for Deans and Counselors, Internat. Conf. for Phy. Edn. Coll. Women (mem. embassy com. 1961—), New Eng. Health Edn. Assn., Pi Lambda Theta, Clubs: Boston University Women's Faculty (life), Boston Sargent. Author: Field Hockey: an Internation Team Sport, 1963: (with Mackey) Women's Team Sports Officiating, 1964; also articles. Home: 764 Lynnfield St Lynn MA 01904

MACKEY, MARIAN FRANCES HOUSH (MRS. WILBUR MACKEY), pub. co. exec.; b. Galesburg, Ill., Oct. 25, 1911; d. Robert Oliver and Mary Ella (Muir) Housh; A.B., Knox Coll., 1933; B.S., U. Ill. Library Sch., 1934; m. Wilbur Mackey, Sept. 11, 1938 (dec. 1966); children—Robert, Charles. Librarian Soldiers & Sailors Childrens Sch., Normal, Ill., 1934-38; co-pub. Fallbrook (Cal.) Enterprise, 1955-66, pub. 1966—. Dir. May Co., Galesburg, Moline and Princeton, Ill., 1964—. Mem. exec. com. Fallbrook (Cal.) Citizens Planning Group Inc., 1973—. Mem. Phi Mu, Delta Sigma Rho. Club: Woman's (Fallbrook, Cal.). Home: 2914 Olive Hill Rd Fallbrook CA 92028 Office: 232 S Main St Fallbrook CA 92028

MACKEY, MARJORIE MARIE (MRS. GEORGE MACKEY), banker; b. Trenton, N.J., June 4, 1926; d. Robert and Louise A. (Burns) Morley; grad. high sch.; m. George Mackey, Oct. 21, 1953; children—George Edward, Ellen, Barbara. Sec., Met. Life Ins. Co., N.Y.C., 1944-54; br. mgr. West Orange Savs. & Loan Assn. (N.J.), 1962-65; sec. to pres. Essex County State Bank, West Orange, 1965-68, asst. sec., 1968—, treas., 1971-73, v.p., 1973—. Home: 5 Maple Terrace Verona NJ 07044 Office: 445 Eagle Rock Av West Orange NJ 07052

MACKEY, RITA F., banker. Pres. Marine Midland Bank No. N.Y., Watertown. Office: 120 Washington St Watertown NY 13601*

MACKHARDT, LUCILLE ALMA HILL (MRS. FRED R. MACKHARDT), real estate broker; b. Marion, La., May 7; d. Robert Lee and Cornelia Ann (Haile) Hill; student pub. schs.; m. Fred R. Mackhardt, July 19, 1937 (dec.). Real estate broker Lucille Mackhardt, realtor, Dallas, 1953—, Richardson, Tex., 1965—. Vice pres. City Council of Women, Hot Springs, Ark., 1946-47; mgr. Community Chest, A.R.C. drives, Hot Springs, Ark., 1945-46; with War Price Adminstrn. Bd., Garland County, Ark., 1945-46; sec. Ark. State Symphony, 1946-47. Mem. Bus. and Profl. Womens Club (ways and means chmn., personal service chmn.), Nat., Tex., Dallas real estate bds., Nat. Inst. Real Estate Brokers Farms Brokers and Traders Club, Dallas Council on World Affairs Womens Group (sec. 1954-55), Ladies Elks Aux., Phi Sigma Alpha (corr. sec. Delta Eta chpt. 1968-69, 70, extension chmn. 1970-71, v.p. 1972-73, pres. 1973-74; pres. Ft. Worth-Dallas area assembly 1974-75). Home: 4719 Cole Av PO Box 8291 Dallas TX 75205

MACKIE, SHIRLEY MARIE, educator; b. Rockdale, Tex., Oct. 25, 1929; d. John Ransom and Marie (McLean) Mackie; Mus.B., La. State U., 1949, Mus.M., 1950; postgrad. Aspen Inst., 1953, Conservatoire de Musique, Fontainebleau, France, 1959, 68. Profl. clarinetist, 1950—; pvt. tchr. clarinet, piano, 1950—; band dir. Forney (Tex.) High Sch., 1953-54; asst. prof. music Mary Hardin-Baylor Coll., Belton, Tex., 1954-57; coordinator of music McLennan County Schs., Waco, Tex., 1959-70; band dir. Axtell & Riesel High Schs., McLennan County, Tex., 1970—. Fellow Intercontinental Biog. Assn.; mem. Nat. Guild of Piano Tchrs., Tex. Composers Guild, Music Tchrs. Nat. Assn., Tex. Music Tchrs. Assn., Music Educators Nat. Conf., Tex., Waco music tchrs. assn., Tex. Tchrs. Assn., Sigma Alpha Iota, Phi Kappa Phi. Mem. Order Eastern Star. Composer in media of orch., chorus, opera, ballet, band, vocal and instrumental sols, chamber music. Home: 1815 Colonial Av Waco TX 76707

MACKIEWICZ, SISTER MARY REGINETTA, coll. adminstr.; b. Chgo., Dec. 5, 1916; d. Bruno and Sophie (Ryzy) Mackiewicz; B.S. in Edn., Loyola U., 1958; postgrad. De Paul Coll. Commerce, 1961-68, Northwestern U., 1963. Joined Congregation Sisters St. Felix, 1935; tchr. St. Joseph High Sch., Chgo., 1960-62; supr. bus. office St. Francis Hosp., Milw., 1957-59; registrar Felician Coll., Chgo., 1963—, bus. mgr., 1967-69, dir. admissions, 1971—, dir. student sorority, 1968—, student financial aid officer, 1968—. Mem. N.E.A., Am. Assn. Collegiate Registrars and Admissions Officers, Ill. Assn. Collegiate Registrars, Nat. Cath. Edn. Assn., Am. Higher Edn., Nat. Council Ind. Jr. Colls. Home: 3800 Peterson Av Chicago IL 60659 Office: Registrar Office Felician College Chicago IL 60659

MACKLER, MAXINE KURTZ (MRS. RICHARD LEOPOLD CHESNEY), lawyer; b. San Francisco, Oct. 29, 1942; d. Henry Louis and Byrdie Lee (Kauffman) Kurtz; B.A., U. Cal., 1964, J.D., 1967; m. Richard Leopold Chesney, Jan. 31, 1970. Admitted to Cal. bar, 1968; prin. trial atty. San Francisco Office of Dist. Atty., 1968—, head spl. task force. Mem. State Bar, Cal., Bar Assn. San Francisco, Bay Area Prosecutor's Assn., Queen's Bench; Am. Judicature Soc. Office: 880 Bryant San Francisco CA 94103

MACKLER, TINA, artist; b. London, Eng., May 24, 1919; d. Leon and Ethel (Tischler) Mackler; student Indsl. Sch. Design, N.Y.C., Art Students League, N.Y.C., New Sch.; 1 dau., Leonore Bloom. Came to U.S., 1926, naturalized, 1943. Formerly tchr. art Nat. Acad. Ballet, N.Y.C., 1966-69; now tchr. drawing and painting West Side YMCA, N.Y.C.; several one-woman and group shows; works of art in dance and mime represented in Museum Performing Art at Lincoln Center, U. Wis. Mus., La Jolla (Cal.) Mus., Israel Mus., Farleigh Dickinson U., Circus Hall of Fame Mus.; also pvt. collections. Mem. Graphic Artists Guild. Illustrator: The Language of Ballet, 1966. Home: 25 Central Park West New York City NY 10023

MACKWORTH, JANE FELICITY (MRS. NORMAN H. MACKWORTH), psychologist; b. Melbourne, Australia, Sept. 15, 1917; d. Walter H.C.S. and Dorothy (Wooldridge) Thring; B.A., Cambridge U., 1940, M.A., 1942, Ph.D., 1945, M.B., B.Ch., 1954; m. Norman H. Mackworth, June 12, 1941; children—Jean (Mrs. David Surry), Alan K., Hugh F. Came to U.S., 1965. Research biochemist Cambridge (Eng.) U., 1940-42; with Med. Research Council, Cambridge, Eng., 1954-58; sci. officer Def. Research Med. Labs., Toronto, Ont., Can., 1960-65; fellow Radcliffe Inst., Cambridge, Mass., 1966; cons. Right To Read Lit. Search, 1970-71, Stanford (Cal.) U., 1971-73. Author: Vigilance and Habituation, 1969; Vigilance and Attention, 1970. Home: 16232 Camellia Terrace Los Gatos CA 95030

MACLAREN, MARGARET LOUISE, coll. adminstr.; b. New Orleans; d. John A. and Merle (Van Horn) MacLaren; B.A., Swarthmore Coll., 1949; certificate occupational therapy U. Pa., 1957.

Field dir. Tarrant County council Girl Scouts U.S.A., Ft. Worth, 1949-52, Camden County council, N.J., 1953-55; asst. dir. curative workshop U. Pa., 1957-59; therapist Jefferson Hosp., Phila., 1959-60; asst. dean admissions Swarthmore Coll., 1960-62, asso. dean admissions, 1962-65, dir. financial aid, 1964-68, asso. dean students, 1965-68; dean students Wheaton Coll., Norton, Mass., 1968-73; dir. financial aid Upsala Coll., East Orange, N.J., 1974—. Chmn. membership Coll. Scholarship Service of Coll. Bd., 1968-70; financial aid cons. N.E. region Coll. Entrance Exam. Bd., 1968. Gov., Southeastern Pa. Arthritis Found., 1965-68. Bd. dirs. Daggett-Crandall-Newcomb Home, 1969-73. Mem. Eastern Assn. Financial Aid Officers, Eastern Assn. Deans and Advisers to Students (dir. 1972—). Home: 152 E 94th St New York City NY 10028 Office: Upsala Coll East Orange NJ 07019

MACLEAN, BARBARA BARONDESS, interior designer; b. N.Y.C., July 4; d. Benjamin Gregor and Stella (Sirkis) Barondess; student N.Y.U., 1925-26, U. Cal. at Los Angeles, 1937-38, Los Angeles Art Center Sch. of Design, 1939-40, Art. Sch., Paris, 1952-53; m. Douglas MacLean, June, 1936 (dec.); m. 2d, Leonard J. Knaster, Aug. 22, 1955 (div. Aug. 1974). Featured in stage plays including Crime, Riddle Me This, A Thousand Summers, Topaze, 1929-31; featured in motion pictures including Rasputin, Hold your Man, Merry Widow, Tale of Two Cities, Faithfully Yours, Pursuit of Happiness, Queen Christina, others; columnist Morning Telegraph, 1929-31; interior and textile designer, Beverly Hills, Cal., 1938—; pres. Barbara Barondess MacLean Ltd., Inc., 1947—, N.Y.C., 1952—, Discovery Unltd., Palm Beach, Fla., 1973—; columnist Morning Telegraph, 1920-31; created column Little Bo-Beep on Broadway; contbr. to Hollywood (Cal.) Reporter, N.Y. Jour., Herald-Tribune, 1962-63, Woman's Day, 1963; painting exhibited in galleries, Beverly Hills, Cal., N.Y.C., 1949—. Tchr. 1st aid A.R.C., 1941-46. Mem. A.F.T.R.A., Actors Equity, Am. Inst. Design. Home: 160 Kings Rd Palm Beach FL 33480 Office: 161 Chilian Av Palm Beach FL 33480

MACLEAN, JEAN, nurse educator; b. Stamford, Conn., Sept. 7, 1909; d. Donald Robert and Louise (Westfall) MacLean; B.S., Boston U., 1930; B. Nursing, Yale, 1933, M.A. (hon.), 1953; M.S., U. Chgo., 1948. Staff nurse Inst. Human Relations, Yale, 1933-34, instr. Yale Sch. Nursing, 1936-38, asst. prof. med. nursing Yale, 1941-45, asso. prof., 1948-53, prof., 1953-58; head nurse New Haven Hosp., 1934-36; ednl. dir. Neuro-Psychology Inst., Hartford, Conn., 1938-41; dir. nursing Inst. Living, Hartford, 1945-47; prof. nursing U. Me., Orono, 1958—, dir. Sch. Nursing, 1958-69. Mem. Nat., Me. (past pres.) leagues nursing Am. Me. nurses assns., Am. Pub. Health Assn., Am. Assn. U. Profs., Alpha Delta Pi. Conglist. Home: Stillwater ME 04489 Office: U Me Orono ME 04473

MACLEAN, NAOMI FRANCES NAZOR (MRS. HAROLD ORLANDO MACLEAN), civic worker; b. Pine Bluff, Ark.; d. Francis LeRoy and Lora (Fugette) Nazor; B.A., U. Chgo., 1923; student Chgo. Mus. Coll., 1923-27; M.A., Northwestern U. Music Sch., 1928; m. Harold Orlando MacLean, June 27, 1932 (dec. Nov. 1967); children—Dorothy Mina, Harold Orlando. Dramatic soprano Chgo. Civic Opera, 1932-40; tchr. voice Chgo. Mus. Coll., 1927-31. Mem. City Beautiful Planning Commn., Santa Barbara, Cal.; mem. exec. bd. Music Acad. of West, Santa Barbara, 1966-70; chmn. ways and means com. Alpha Sch. for Retarded, Santa Barbara, 1966—. Mem. Nat. Soc. Arts and Letters (pres. 1966-70), Community Art Music Assn. (pres. 1964-66), Encore So. Cal., Affiliates of U. Cal., Channel City Women's Forum, Mu Phi Epsilon. Republican. Episcopalian. Clubs: Cal. Women's Press, Girls (Santa Barbara, v.p. 1967-69), Coral Casino, Little Town, Valley Country (Montecito), Burnam Wood Golf. Author (book of poems): Quiet at Evening, 1959. Home: 150 Middle Rd Santa Barbara CA 93103

MACLELLAN, AUDREY MAY, librarian; b. Des Moines, May 7, 1928; d. Clinton Albert and Cora (Mantz) Terrill; B.A., Central Coll., Pella, Ia., 1949; M.L.S., Simmons Coll., 1952; m. George O. MacLellan, June 5, 1953; children—Alberta Anne, Catherine Jean. Librarian Des Moines Pub. Library, 1949-51, Detroit Pub. Library, 1953-54, Toronto (Ont., Can.) Pub. Library, 1954-56, Toronto Twp. Pub. Library, 1960-62, Weston Sch. Bd., 1962-67; chief librarian Humber Coll., Rexdale, Ont., 1967—. Mem. Colls. Applied Arts and Tech. Ont. (vice chmn. com. librarians 1970-72, chmn. com. librarians 1972-74), Inst. Profl. Librarians Ont., Spl. Libraries Assn. Home: 10 St George Blvd Weston ON M9R 1W9 Canada Office: PO Box 1900 Rexdale ON M9W 5L7 Canada

MACLELLAN, DELPHINE CAROLINE, educator, marine biologist; b. St. Andrews, N.B., Can., Aug. 1, 1914; d. Charles Marmont and Astrid Mjelde (Johannsen) Wallace; B.S., Dalhousie U., 1936; M.S., McGill U., 1964; m. Robert Maclellan, May 25, 1936 (dec. 1941); children—Janet (Mrs. J. Barry Toole), Judith (Mrs. R. John Gibson). With Fisheries Research Bd. Can., St. Andrews, 1956-60; research asst. McGill U., Montreal, Que., 1963-67, mem. faculty, 1967—, asst. prof. marine biology, 1973—, also curator marines scis., 1970—, adviser marine biology undergrads. dept. biology, 1971-74. Mem. Canadian Soc. Zoologists, Sci. Research Soc. Am. (sec.-treas. McGill U. chpt. 1972-74), Sigma Xi (nat. com. on nominations 1972—). Contbr. to profl. jours. Home: 3453 Peel St Montreal PQ Canada

MACLEOD, JENNIFER ANN SELFRIDGE, research psychologist; b. London, Eng., Nov. 26, 1929; d. Harry Gordon and Charlotte (Dennis) Selfridge (parents Am. citizens); B.A., Radcliffe Coll., 1949; M.A., Columbia, 1952, Ph.D., 1958; children—Pamela J., Scott G. Research asst. Richardson, Bellows &Henry, N.Y.C., 1950-51; research account mgr. McCann Erickson, N.Y.C., 1953-55; project dir. Ogilvy, Benson & Mather, N.Y.C., 1955-57; dir. exptl. research Package Research Inst., N.Y.C., 1957-58; research dir. Opinion Research Corp., Princeton, N.J., 1958-69, chief psychologist, 1969-71; dir. Eagleton Center for Am. Women and Politics, Rutgers U., New Brunswick, N.J., 1971; owner Jennifer Macleod Assos., 1972—. Chmn. bd. Univ. N.O.W. Day Nursery. Mem. Am. Psychol. Assn., Nat. Orgn. for Women (chpt. pres. 1969-70), Assn. for Women in Psychology, Am. Civil Liberties Union (trustee N.J. 1973—), Assn. Feminist Cons. (coordinator 1972-74), Women's Equity Action League, Nat. Women's Polit. Caucus (convenor). Home and office: 4 Canoe Brook Dr Princeton Junction NJ 08550

MACMILLAN, DALPHINE, lawyer; b. St. Anthony, Ida., Jan. 2, 1918; d. John Kerr and Martha Elizabeth (Wood) MacMillan; B.A., Cornell U., 1939; J.D., George Wash. U., 1960. Enlisted U.S. Navy, 1942, advanced through grades to comdr., 1962, ret. 1964; admitted to D.C. bar, 1961; practiced with Bd. for Correction Naval Records, Arlington, Va., 1964-71; head Income Tax br. Navy Dept., Arlington 1960-64, 71—. Mem. exec. bd. Young Republicans, Lycoming County, Pa., 1940-42. Bd. dirs. A.R.C., Jersey Shore, Pa., 1940-42. Mem. Am., Fed., D.C. bar assns., Phi Alpha Delta (internat. supreme asst. treas. 1972-74), Phi Delta Delta (internat. treas. 1968-72), Order Eastern Star. Home: 1600 S Eads St Arlington VA 22202 Office: JAG Navy Dept Income Tax Branch Washington DC 20370

MACMILLAN, DOROTHY LOU, educator; b. Portland, Ore., Nov. 11, 1910; d. William David and Sadie (LeCompte) MacMillan; B.S., U. Ore., 1932, Ed.D. (Delta Kappa Gamma scholar), 1957; M.S., U. Washington, Seattle, 1938; postgrad. U. Wyo., 1961-62. Staff YWCA, various locations, 1932-42; head phys. edn. dept. Bowie High Sch., El Paso, 1942-43; with Bur. Parks and Pub. Recreation, Portland, Ore., 1943-44, 45-48; asst. program dir. U.S.O., Aberdeen, N.C., 1944-45; supr. student tchrs. phys. edn., health U. Wyo, Laramie, 1948-62, sch. camp dir., 1949-62; dean of students, prof. edn. Sheridan Coll., 1962-64; head women's phys. edn. dept. Sul Ross State Coll., Alpine, Tex., 1964-67; prof. phys. edn., edn. Keene (N.H.) State Coll., 1967—, chmn. phys. edn. dept., 1969-70, dir. major program, 1970—. Active Girl Scouts U.S.A. Recipient Thanks badge Girl Scouts U.S.A., 1955. Fellow A.A.H.P.E.R.; mem. N.E.A., N.H., Keene State Coll. (v.p. 1965) edn. assns., Am. Assn. U. Profs., Assn. Tchr. Educators (state rep.), Tchr. Edn. and Profl. Services, N.H. Assn. Health, Phys. Edn. and Recreation, Nat. Recreation and Parks Assn., Am. Camping Assn., Nat., Eastern States assns. phys. edn. coll. women, Soroptomist, Delta Kappa Gamma (pres. 1957-59), Kappa Delta Pi (v.p. 1954-55). Author: School Camping and Outdoor Education, 1956. Home: Colonial Village Bldg 5 Keene NH 03431

MACMILLAN, KATHRYN T. (MRS. M. D. MACMILLAN), ret. educator, civic worker; b. Joplin, Mo., Jan. 25, 1907; d. Jefferson Brown and May (McClung) Thomas; B.E., U. Cal. at Los Angeles, 1928; m. Marion Duval MacMillan, June 19, 1937 (dec. Sept. 1969); 1 son, Thomas Craig. Instr. women's phys. edn. and hygiene dept. Sacramento Jr. Coll., 1929-37; dir. Sacramento council Girl Scout Camp, 1944; instr. U. Redlands, summers, 1955-57; asst. clk. engrossing and enrolling dept. Cal. Senate, 1959-60; instr. phys. edn. Jr. High Sch., Sacramento, 1961-62; chmn. phys. edn. dept. Sam Brannan Jr. High Sch., Sacramento, 1962-69. Apptd. by Sacramento City Council to Redevel. Agy. now vice chmn. Participant numerous gov.'s confs.; participant White House Conf. on Edn., 1955; layman participant Nat. Resources Conf., 1955; pres. 3d dist. Cal. Congress Parents and Tchrs., 1950-52, mem. statewide coms.; pres. Crocker P.T.A., 1948; named hon. life mem.; mem. Sacramento City Unified Sch. Bd., 1954-60, pres., 1958-59; exec. com. Sacramento County Sch. Bds. Assn., 1956-60, pres., 1959-60; chmn. Mayor's Comic Book Com., 1954; organizer, 1st pres. Sacramento Council Girl Scout U.S.A., 1938, mem. tng. com. Sacramento area, pub. relations chmn. regional conf., chmn. staff, camp coms.; mem. Sacramento Citizens Com. Mental Health, community welfare com. youth problems Child Welfare Survey, 1955-57; residential chmn. United Way, 1973-74; sec.-treas. Sacramento United Vol. Services Swing Club for Blind, 1973—. Mem. Cal. Republican Central Com., Sacramento County Rep. Central Com., 1960-62; mem. Nat. Fedn. Rep. Women. Bd. dirs. Sacramento United Crusade, also chmn. residential area, 1956-57, mem. family welfare panel, 1957-58, chmn. allocations and admissions com., 1959-60, sec., 1962-63, finance com.; bd. dirs. A.R.C., 1944-46, mem. ambulance detachment civilian disaster unit, 1941-45, comdr. officer Ambulance Corps, 1941-45; pres. bd. dirs. YWCA, 1962-64; bd. dirs. Fairy Tale Town, 1956-57. Named Sacramento Woman of Yr., 1959; recipient spl. award for service A.R.C., World War II; Cal. Senate resolution of commendation, Distinguished Service award Sacramento City Council, awards Sacramento City Prins. Assn., Sacramento City-County C. of C.; United Community Service award, 1962; The Spirit of Sacramento award, 1963. Mem. Am. Assn. U. Women, Nat. Congress Parents and Tchrs. (hon. life), Nat., Cal. ret. tchrs. assns., Nat. Assn. Housing and Redevel. Ofcls., Delta Kappa Gamma. Clubs: Tuesday, Del Paso Country. Home: 1500 7th St Apt 10J Sacramento CA 95814

MACNAUGHTON, MATILDA MARIA CARLSON (MRS. LAURENCE MACNAUGHTON, JR.), educator; b. Hoboken, N.J., Sept. 27, 1919; d. Karl Werner and Maria (Mattsson) Carlson; A.B. magna cum laude, Adelphi Coll., 1940; M.S., U. Pa., 1960; postgrad., U. Pitts., West Chester State Coll.; m. Laurence MacNaughton, Jr., Dec. 6, 1941; children—Laurence III, Bruce. With actuarial dept. Met. Life Ins. Co., N.Y.C., 1941-45; tchr. math. Pitts. area, 1958-59, Conestoga Sr. High Sch., Berwyn, Pa., 1959-67, chmn. dept., 1963-67; math. curriculum coordinator Tredyffrin-Easttown Sch. System, Berwyn, 1967—. Mem. Math. Assn. Am., Dept. Supervision and Curriculum Devel., N.E.A., Pa. Edn. Assn., Nat. Council Tchrs. Math., Delta Tau Alpha. Republican. Presbyn. Mem. Order Eastern Star. Home: 2 Bacton Hill Rd Malvern PA 19355 Office: 95 Howellville Rd Berwyn PA 19312

MACNEES, VALERIE CATHERINE KOOPS (MRS. JAMES BARRY MACNEES), journalist; b. LaCrosse, Wis., Sept. 11, 1912; d. Edward Charles and Minnie (Morley) Koops; B.A., Wis. State U., 1933; postgrad. U. Wis., 1936-37; m. James Barry MacNees, June 5, 1940; children—Valerie Ann (Mrs. Robert Van Meter), James Michael. Tchr. pub. schs., Wis., 1933-40; clk. U.S. Census Bur., Washington, 1940-42; classification clk. WPB, Washington, 1942-43; editor Fgn. Broadcast Intelligence, Washington, 1944-45; editorial staff N.C.W.C. News Service, Washington, 1946-51; womens editor Catholic Standard, Washington, 1951-63, feature editor, 1963—. Weekly columnist Prince Georges Post, Hyattsville, Md., 1969—. Author: Catholic Churches in Montgomery County, 1966. Home: 2007 Brighton Rd Washington DC 20018 Office: 1711 N St NW Washington 20006

MACNEIL, GRACE M. S. MCKITTRICK (MRS. DOUGLAS H. MACNEIL), civic worker; b. Natchez, Miss., Nov. 25, 1907; d. David Lawrence and Charlotte Linton (Surget) McKittrick; B.A., H. Sophie Newcomb Coll., Tulane U., 1929; m. Douglas H. MacNeil, Sept. 25, 1933 (dec. May 1963); children—Elizabeth C. (Mrs. William Franklin Boggess), Anne W. S. Plantation owner, operator, Miss., La., 1946—; owner Elms Ct., Natchez. Nat. staff mem. Girl Scouts U.S.A., 1930-39, dir., 1955—, chmn. nat. exec. com., 1960-69, v.p., 1960-69, pres., 1969-72, mem. world com. Girl Guides, 1972—; mem. N.J. Welfare Council, 1933-36; chmn. dental health com. Council Social Agys., Somerset County, Somerville, N.J., 1951-53; mem. Council Community Services, Princeton Day Schs., 1960-62; v.p. Council Nat. Orgns. for Children and Youth, 1960-63, mem. Nat. Com. on Children and Youth, 1960-63, mem. nat. adv. com., 1965—. Dir. Family Service Agy., Princeton, N.J., 1948-52; trustee Miss Fines Sch., 1953-55, chmn. planning com., 1956-62; trustee Princeton Day Schs., 1960-64. Mem. English-Speaking Union (br. dir. 1960-65), UN Assn. Am. (dir. 1964-67), Pi Beta Phi. Clubs: Present Day (pres. Princeton 1951-53); Tulane University Alumni (dir. N.Y.C., 1959-63); Natchez Garden (bd. mem. 1967-69, pres. 1974—). Home: Elms Ct Box 284 Natchez MS 39120

MACNEIL, JANETT SHEPARD (MRS. C. RICHARD MACNEIL), broker; b. Des Moines, Dec. 8, 1917; d. Carl Chester and Dorothy Shepard (Smith) McComb; grad. sem.; m. C. Richard MacNeil, Apr. 28, 1935; children—Peter, Heather (Mrs. Louis J. Prime), Robert. Saleslady real estate, 1961; sec., treas. Pima Land & Investment Co., Tucson, 1962—; sec., treas. Home Land and Trust Co., Tucson, 1962—, asso. broker, 1965-70, broker, 1970—; also dir. both cos. Area dir. Heart Fund, 1954-60, Community Fund, 1954-60; aux. bd. Tucson Med. Center, 1959-61. Mem. Tucson Bd. Realtors, Ariz. Assn. Realtors, Nat. Assn. Real Estate Bds. Episcopalian. Home: 814 W Chula Vista Rd Tucson AZ 85704 Office: 7123 N Oracle Rd Tucson AZ 85704

MACNEILL, ANNABEL DAISY, educator; b. Calgary, Alta., Can., Feb. 7, 1916; d. Francis Wayland and Mary Emma (Robbins) MacNeill; B.A., U. B.C., 1935; M.A., Columbia, 1949; B.D., McGill U., 1960. Tchr. elementary and secondary schs., B.C., 1937-48; field sec. Council of Christian Edn., Quebec, 1949-56; prof. edn. McGill U., Montreal, Que., 1960—. Home: 5175 Prince of Wales Av Montreal PQ H4V 2N2 Canada Office: McGill University 3700 McTavish St Montreal PQ H3C 3G1 Canada

MACNOW, RITA (MRS. DAVID GRIPPE), physician; b. N.Y.C., Mar. 1, 1939; d. Jules and Mollie (Lee) Macnow; B.S. magna cum laude, L.I.U., 1955; M.D., N.Y. Med. Coll., 1959; m. David Grippe, Jan. 12, 1968; 1 son, Jeffrey LeGrand. Intern Glen Cove (N.Y.) Community Hosp., 1959-60; resident N.Y. U. Med. Center, N.Y.C., 1960-63; practice medicine specializing in dermatology, Cedarhurst, N.Y., 1963—; cons. dermatology Bklyn.-Cumberland Med. Center, 1963—; teaching staff N.Y. State Coll. Medicine, 1964—. Mem. Woman's Med. Assn., U.S. Figure Skating Assn., L.I. Dermatology Soc., Rye Figure Skating Club, Inc., Phi Beta Kappa. Home: 544 Broadway Cedarhurst NY 11516 Office: 544 Broadway Cedarhurst NY 11516

MACOMBER, MARY FRANCES (MRS. DONALD KEITH MACOMBER), lawyer; b. New Bedford, Mass., June 4, 1943; d. John Paul and Mary Frances (Murphy) Goucher; B.A. in Math., U. Me., 1964; J.D., Suffolk U., 1970; m. Donald Keith Macomber, June 7, 1969; children—Donald Keith, Mary Frances. Computer analyst Am. Tel. & Tel., Long Lines, N.Y., 1964-66, White Plains, 1966; computer analyst then supr. Honeywell, Inc., Waltham, Mass., 1966-70; admitted to Me. bar, 1970, since practiced in Kittery. Mem. Am., Me. Bar assns. Home and office: 11 Pinkham Rd Kittery ME 03904

MACPHAIL, ELIZABETH CURTIS (MRS. ALFRED H. MACPHAIL), lawyer; b. San Diego, Aug. 21, 1912; d. Carl Otto and Delia Henrietta (Curtis) Reinbold; LL.B., Balboa Law Coll., 1944; m. Alfred H. MacPhail, June 24, 1950; 1 dau., Mary Elizabeth. Admitted to Cal. bar, 1944, since practiced in San Diego, 1944—. Mem. San Diego Hist. Sites Bd., 1972—. Pres. Central Rep. Women, San Diego, 1950—. Mem. State Bar Cal., Nat. Assn. Women Lawyers, San Diego County Bar Assn., D.A.R. Author: Story of New San Diego and Its Founder, Alonzo E. Horton, 1969. Contbr. articles on San Diego History to various hist. jours. Home and office: 3401 Granada Av San Diego CA 92104

MACPHERSON, JANET TAYLOR WOLFENDEN, civic worker; b. Phila.; d. Edward Musker and Annette (Robertson) Wolfenden; B.S., M.A., U. Pa.; m. Herbert Grenfell MacPherson; children—Janet Lynne, Robert Duncan. Pres., Franklin Sch. P.T.A., Lakewood, O., 1954-56; bd. dirs. Oak Ridge chpt. Am. Assn. U. Women, 1957-59; editor This Is Oak Ridge, 1961; pres. League Women Voters of Oak Ridge, 1961-63; bd. dirs., Oak Ridge Civic Music Assn., 1963-66; pres. Oak Ridge Civic Music Assn. Womens Guild, 1963-64, Friends of Oak Ridge Pub. Library, 1966-67, League Women Voters of Tenn., 1967-69; mem. Nat. Com. for Support Pub. Schs., 1967-70; mem. Com. of 100, Found. Better Govt. for Tenn., 1968-70; mem. Tenn. com. White House Conf. on Children and Youth, 1969-70; mem. salary structure study com. Bd. Edn. of Oak Ridge, 1969-71; chmn. Youth Com. of Oak Ridge, 1969-70; mem. state planning com. Air Quality Projects for Tenn., 1970-71; bd. dirs. Awareness House of Oak Ridge, Inc., 1970-73; mem. Oak Ridge City Charter Commn., 1972-74; counselor Contact, telephone counseling service, 1973—. Mem. United Ch. Home: 102 Orchard Circle Oak Ridge TN 37830

MACRAKIS, A. LILY CHRYSSANTHACOPOULOU (MRS. MICHAEL S. MACRAKIS), educator; b. Athens, Greece; d. Chryssanthos Michael and Irene (Carabini) Chryssanthacopoulos; B.A., Athens U., 1951; Professorat de Francais, French Inst. (Athens), 1945; postgrad. Oxford U. (Eng.), 1948-49; M.A., Radcliffe Coll., 1955; m. Michael S. Macrakis, Oct. 1, 1953; children—Stavros Michael, Michele Angelica, Kristi Irene. Asst. to Dr. Robinson, Agora excavations Am. Sch. Classical Studies, Athens, 1952; asst. to dir. Acropolis Mus., Athens, 1953; bibliographer Widener Library, Harvard, 1956-58; fellow Radcliffe Inst., 1961-63, Harvard, 1967—; lectr. Regis Coll., Weston, Mass., 1962-64, asst. prof. history, 1964—, chmn. dept. history, 1968—, co-dir. European studies program, 1969—, dir. Greek studies program, 1972—, cons. Regis Hist. Conf., 1964-66. Mem. adv. bd. Study in Greece. Bd. govs. Hellcon, 1969-73, pres., 1971-72; trustee Aegean Inst., co-dir., summer 1973. Harvard scholar for research in Crete, Greece, summer 1963. Mem. Soc. Radcliffe Inst. Fellows, Soc. for Promotion Hellenic Studies, Archaeol. Inst. Am., Am. Hist. Assn., Berkshire Hist. Conf. Women, Modern Greek Studies Assn. (exec. com. 1970—, treas. 1970-73, v.p. 1974—), Am. Assn. U. Profs. (pres. Regis 1971-73), New Eng. History Tchrs. Assn. (exec. com. 1974—), Pi Gamma Mu (hon.). Bibliographer Choice, 1972—, Clio, 1974—. Home: 24 Fieldmont Rd Belmont MA 02178 Office: 235 Wellesley St Weston MA 02193

MACVEY, JOANNE MARY STAPLES (MRS. LARRY LEE MACVEY), banker; b. Stillwater, Minn., May 2, 1945; d. Mark and Vesta Lydia (Moltz) Staples; grad. high sch.; m. Larry Lee MacVey, Aug. 31, 1963; children—Kim Larie, Terry Dale. Teller, Home Fed. Savs. & Loan Assn., Austin, Minn., 1963; sec. Sterling State Bank, Austin, Minn., 1963-65; with First Am. State Bank, Brownsdale, Minn., 1968—, asst. cashier, 1970-73, asst. to pres., 1973—. Treas. Brownsdale P.T.A., 1973-74. Bd. dirs. Mower County March of Dimes, 1971—. NSF grantee, So. Ill. U., 1962. Mem. Credit Women Internat. (v.p. Austin chpt. 1970), Am. Inst. Banking, Am. Bankers Assn. Baptist. Clubs: Christian Women's (ticket co-chmn. 1971) (Austin); Hoofbeats Saddle (Brownsdale). Home: Box 49 Brownsdale MN 55918 Office: Box 167 Brownsdale MN 55918

MACVICAR, MARGARET LOVE AGNES, physicist, educator; b. Hamilton, Ont., Can., Nov. 20, 1943; d. George Francis and Elizabeth Margaret (Thompson) MacVicar; came to U.S., 1946; naturalized, 1953; S.B. in Physics, Mass. Inst. Tech., 1964, Sc.D. in Metallurgy, 1967. Postdoctoral fellow Cavendish Lab., Cambridge, Eng., 1967-69; instr. physics Mass. Inst. Tech., Cambridge, 1969-70, asst. prof., 1970-74, asso. prof., 1974—. Cons., Detroit Inst. Tech., 1971, Edn. Devel. Center, 1971, IBM, 1973, 74, Danforth Found., 1974, Lilly Endowment, 1974; mem. tech. adv. com. Sprague Electric Co. Trustee Carnegie Found. for Advancement of Teaching; bd. dirs. Oral Edn. Center, Shared Experiences, Inc. NATO fellow, 1967-68, Marie Curie Am. Assn. Univ. Women fellow, 1968-69; Danforth Found. asso., 1972—; recipient Mass. Inst. Tech. class 1922 Career Devel. award, 1973—. Mem. Am. Vacuum Soc. (chpt. treas. 1973), Am. Soc. Metals, Am. Inst. Metall. Engrs., Am. Phys. Soc., A.A.A.S. (mem. nat. com. on sci. in promotion of human welfare 1970—). Editorial bd. Rev. Sci. Instruments, 1971—. Patentee in field. Home: PO Box 304 Mass Inst Tech Branch Cambridge MA 02139

MACY, DOROTHY, JR., physician; b. N.Y.C., Feb. 21, 1917; d. Alfred and Dorothy (Hayden) Macy; B.A. with high honors, Swarthmore Coll., 1940; M.D., Woman's Med. Coll. Pa., 1944; M.S. in Medicine (Mayo Found. fellow), U. Minn., 1948. Intern, Phila. Gen. Hosp., 1944-45, asst. vis. physician, 1949-58; asso. in physiology, instr. medicine Woman's Med. Coll. Pa., 1948-49, asso. in medicine, 1949-55, asst. prof., 1955-56; pvt. practice, Phila.,

1949-56; staff Sindoni Clinic 1959-68; dir. med. edn. Sindoni Found., 1959-68; chmn. dept. extended care Maricopa County Gen. Hosp., Phoenix, 1969-71; dir. clin. investigation unit Boswell Meml. Hosp., Sun City, 1972—. Diplomate Am. Bd. Internal Medicine, Nat. Bd. Med. Examiners. Fellow A.C.P., Coll. Physicians Phila.; mem. Blockley Med. Soc., Am. Med. Women's Assn. (asso. editor Jour. 1963—), World Med. Assn., Am. Diabetes Assn., Physiol. Soc. Phila., A.A.A.S., N.Y. Acad. Scis., Am. Geriatric Soc., Am. Heart Assn., Endocrine Soc., Alumnae Assn. Nightingale-Bamford Sch., Alumnae Assn. Woman's Med. Coll. Pa., Alumnae Assn. Mayo Found. U. Minn., Phi Beta Kappa, Sigma Xi, Zeta Phi. Republican. Episcopalian. Home: 5616 N 45th St Phoenix AZ 85018

MACY, (SARAH) ELEANOR WRIGHT (MRS. SAMUEL CECIL MACY), social service exec.; b. Birmingham, Ala., July 1, 1915; d. Ellis William and Sadie (Rushing) Wright; B.A., U. Chgo., 1938, M.A., 1958; m. George Vincent Kempf, Dec. 23, 1939 (div. Oct. 1954); children—Claudia Gaynor, George Rushing; m. 2d, Samuel Cecil Macy, May 3, 1968. Child welfare caseworker Ariz. Dept. Pub. Welfare, Phoenix, 1954-56, Chgo. Child Care Soc., 1957-60; med. social work supr. Lying-In-Hosp., U. Chgo. Hosps. and Clinics, 1960-61; psychiat. social worker Virginia Frank Child Devel. Center, Jewish Family and Community Service, Chgo., 1961-64; exec. dir. Chgo. Area council Camp Fire Girls, Inc., 1964-68, Citizens Com. on Juvenile Ct. Cook County, Chgo., 1969-72; dir. adult community day program Fox Valley Mental Health Center, Elgin, Ill., 1973—. Mem. Ill. Juvenile Ct. Com., 1969-72. Mem. Nat. Assn. Social Workers, Acad. Certified Social Workers, D.A.R. Home: 749 Algona Elgin IL 60120

MADDEN, BETTY CARROLL, artist, mus. curator, lectr.; b. Chgo., Nov. 12, 1915; d. Jerome C. and Florence (Hoover) Isenbarger; student Chgo. Art Inst., 1931-32, Northwestern U., 1933-35, Am. Acad. Art, Chgo., summers 1933-37; B.F.A., U. Ill., 1938; attended Inst. Design, Chgo., evenings 1945; m. Clifford L. Carroll, Mar. 19, 1938 (div. Apr. 1960); children—Don Allan, Dennis Bruce; m. 2d, Wilbur F. Madden, Aug. 31, 1963 (dec. Feb. 1965). Free-lance artist, 1938-40; with art dept. Consol. Book Pubs., Chgo., 1944-45; comml. artist Evans, Work & Costa Advt., Inc., Springfield, Ill., 1955-58; advt. dir., fashion illustrator S. A. Barker Co., Springfield, 1958-60; tech. asst. art dept. Ill. State Mus., Springfield, 1961-63, curator art, 1963—; exhibited in group shows Ill. State Mus., 1957, 59, Ill. State Fair Profl. Art Exhibit, 1958, Premiere Art Gallery, Springfield, 1963. Lectr. on history of arts, crafts and architecture of Ill. Mem. Am. Assn. Museums, Ill. (dir. 1973—), Sangamon County hist. socs., Springfield Art Assn., Clayville Folk Arts Guild (dir. 1972—), Kappa Delta. Author: Arts, Crafts, and Architecture in Early Illinois, 1974. Research of Ill. arts, crafts and architecture. Contbr. articles in field. Home: 1145 S 1st St Springfield IL 62704 Office: Ill State Mus Springfield IL 62706

MADDEN, CHARLOTTE SLONE (MRS. EDD MADDEN), librarian, educator; b. Pippa Passes, Ky., Sept. 19, 1928; d. John Commodore and Jeannette Elizabeth (Hammond) Slone; A.B., U. Ky., 1948, M.A., 1955; m. Edd Madden, June 1, 1949; children—Jeannette Marie, Darrell Edward. Tchr. English, sci. pub. schs. Knott County, Ky., 1947-51; head edn. dept. Alice Lloyd Coll., Pippa Passes, 1951-53, tchr. English, 1953—, librarian, 1957—. County Dem. chmn. Mem. A.L.A., Southeastern Ky. Librarians Coop. (v.p. 1973-74). Baptist (ch. clk. 1961—, treas. 1961—). Mem. Order Eastern Star. Home: Pippa Passes KY 41844 Office: Alice Lloyd College Pippa Passes KY 41844

MADDEN, SISTER FRANCES BRETT, educator; b. Banff, Alta., Can., June 25, 1918; d. George and Elizabeth Madd (Bentley) Madden; B.S. in Edn., Marylhurst Coll., 1949; M.Ed., Marquette U., 1954; Ph.D., St. Louis U., 1962. Joined Sisters of the Holy Names (Ore. Province), 1935; tchr. elementary schs., Ore. and Wash., 1937-55; prof. philosophy Marylhurst (Ore.) Coll., 1955-58, 62-74, pres., 1963-70; prof. philosophy Mt. Angel Sem., St. Benedict, Ore., 1974—; grad. asst. St. Louis U., 1959-60. Mem. edn. coordinating council Ore. Ednl. TV-Radio Com., 1966-70; mem. commn. on religion in higher edn. Am. Assn. Colls., 1967-70. Bd. dirs. Ore. Colls. Found., 1963-70, sec., 1965-66; bd. dirs. Ore. Ind. Colls. Assn., 1963-70, sec., 1967-68. Mem. Am. Assn. U. Women, Am. Cath. Philos. Assn., Northwest Philos. Assn. Address: Mt Angel Sem St Benedict OR 97373

MADDEN, JANICE CECILE LEBLANC (MRS. WARREN JAMES MADDEN), univ. adminstr.; b. Worcester, Mass., Mar. 17, 1944; d. Joseph Edgar and Marie Yvonne (Voutour) LeBlanc; ed. Salter's Secretarial Sch., 1963-64; m. Warren James Madden, Feb. 14, 1971. With New Eng. Conservatory of Music, Boston, 1964—, registrar's asst., 1969-71, registrar, 1971—. Home: 5 Emmons St East Boston MA 02138 Office: 290 Huntington Av Boston MA 02115

MADDEN, MARY LOUISE, state govt. ofcl.; b. Helena, Mont., June 9, 1942; s. Edwin Rutherford and Anne Catherine (Pissot) Van Sickle; B.A. in Math. and English, St. Mary Coll., Xavier, Kan., 1964; postgrad. Sophia U., Tokyo, Japan, 1965-66; teaching certificate with honors, Centro Internat. Studi Montessoriano, Bergamo, Italy, 1969; m. Jerry Lee Madden, Dec. 29, 1967; 1 son, Mario James. Missionary, English tchr. Koen Girls Sch., Tokyo, 1964-66; center dir. Head Start Presch. Program, Helena, 1967; supr. handicapped edn. program Mont. Dept. Edn., 1969-71; research specialist Office Commnr. Edn., Alaska Dept. Edn., 1972—. Cons. fed. program grant writing. Mem. Gov. Alaska's Task Force on Trans-Alaska Pipeline Impact; mem. com. evaluation and information systems Council Chief State Sch. Officers. Bd. dirs. Juneau 4 C's Child Care. Mem. Am. Soc. Information Sci., Internat. Montessori Assn. Roman Catholic. Editor Mont. Schs., 1969-71. Home: Box 616 Douglas AK 99824 Office: Pouch F Alaska Office Bldg Juneau AK 99801

MADDEX, EILEEN CALLAGHAN (MRS. ROBERT L. MADDEX), assn. exec.; b. Columbus, O., Apr. 18, 1921; d. Cornelius James and Martha Rebecca (Durrett) Callaghan; B.S. in Home Econs., Ohio State U., 1944; m. Robert Leo Maddex, Jan. 26, 1946; children—Douglas Edwin, Gregory Robert, Jeffrey Thomas, Norman Eugene, Paul Michael. Counselor guidance office Sch. Home Econs., Ohio State U., Columbus, 1941-45; tchr. home econs. St. Mary of Springs Acad., Columbus, 1945-46; exec. dir. Omicron Nu, Mich. State U., East Lansing, 1966—. Pres. Haslett High Sch. P.T.A., 1958; pres. Haslett Women's Club, 1965-67. Mem. Am. Home Econs. Assn., Assn. Coll. Honor Socs. (v.p.), Phi Upsilon Omicron. Roman Catholic (pres. St. Jerome Guild 1954, Haslett area rep. to parish council 1970-72). Home: 5587 Woodville Haslett MI 48840 Office: Human Ecology Bldg Mich State University East Lansing MI 48824

MADDISON, CAROL HOPKINS (MRS. ANGUS MADDISON), coll. dean; b.Ottawa, Ont., Can., Dec. 20, 1923; d. Warren Garnet and Evelyn Marion (Bunnell) Hopkins; B.A., Queen's U. (Can.), 1946; M.A. (Univ. scholar), Johns Hopkins, 1952, Ph.D. (Am. Council Learned Socs. Advanced scholar), in English, 1957; m. Angus Maddison, Apr. 2, 1953; children—Charles Henry, George Michael Alexander. Asst. prof. classics U. N.B. (Can.), 1946-49; prof. English, Am. Coll. in Paris, France, 1963—, dean, 1966—. Recipient medals in Latin and Greek, Queen's U., 1946; Canadian Fedn. U. Women Travelling scholar, 1949-50; Can. Council Post-doctoral fellow, 1961-62; Humanities Research Council Can. grantee, 1959, 63. Mem. Phi Beta Kappa. Author: Apollo and The Nine: A History of the Ode, 1960; Marc Antonio Flaminio, Poet, Humanist and Philosopher, 1964. Home: 20 Rue De Longchamp 75116 Paris France Office: 31 Av Bosquet 75007 Paris France

MADDOCK, MARY PURNELL (MRS. PAUL RANDALL MADDOCK), anesthesiologist, educator; b. Washington, July 18, 1943; d. David Hawes and Ardella Clara (Smallwood) Purnell; B.A., U. Tex., 1964, M.D., 1968; m. Paul Randall Maddock, July 10, 1965; 1 son, Paul David. Intern, Hermann Hosp., Houston, 1968-69, resident, 1969-71; practice medicine, specializing in anesthesiology, Houston, 1970—; mem. staff St. Joseph Hosp., Houston, 1971; clin. asso. prof. U. Tex. Med. Sch., Houston, 1972—. Mem. Am. Soc. Anesthesiologists, Internat. Anesthesia Research Soc., Tex. Med. Assn., Harris County Med. Soc. Clubs: American Medical Tennis Assn., Lakeway World of Tennis, Net Set Racquet. Home: 11115 Tupperlake St Houston TX 77042 Office: St Joseph Prof Bldg Houston TX 77006

MADDOX, GRACE BERYL, economist, former govt. ofcl.; b. Hayward, Wis.; d. McPherson C. and Grace (Bailey) Maddox; student U. So. Cal., 1926-27, U. Cal. at Los Angeles, 1927-28; A.B., Am. U., 1954, M.A. in Econs., 1958. With various U.S. govt. agys., 1937-67; staff of U.S. mem. Internat. Mil. Tribunal, Nuremberg, Germany, 1945-46; Near East polit. analyst CIA, Washington, 1947-51, East European economist, Washington, 1952-56; economist FTC, Washington, 1956-67; researcher in field industry and finance. Recipient Superior Service award FTC, 1961, 67. Mem. Am. Econ. Assn., D.A.R., Phi Delta Gamma. Contbr. articles to govt. publs. Home: 5796 Encina Rd Apt 5 Goleta CA 93017

MADDOX, HELEN JEAN BRANT (MRS. CRAIG MILLER MADDOX), educator; b. Sumter, S.C., May 5, 1934; d. Perry Martin and Sophia Sarah (Perritt) Brant; B.S. (Phi Kappa Zeta scholar), Gallaudet Coll., 1964; M.S., Cath. U. Am., 1969; m. Craig Miller Maddox, Jan. 14, 1956; 1 son, Sonny Timothy. Sewing machine operator Eastwill Sportswear Co., Inc., Greenwood, S.C., 1956-58, Orangeburg Mfg. Co. (S.C.), 1958-60; library asst. Gallaudet Coll., Washington, 1964-66; supervising librarian hist. br. U.S. Marine Corps, Washington, 1966-69; tchr. S.C. Sch. for Deaf, Spartanburg, 1970—. Pres. S.C. Assn. of Deaf, 1971-73, sec., 1973—. Bd. dirs. Nat. Assn. of Deaf, 1972—. Recipient Cultural Program award Nat. Assn. of Deaf, 1970. Mem. A.L.A., Spl. Libraries Assn., Phi Kappa Zeta. Baptist. Clubs: Potomac Silents (Arlington, Va.); Greenville (S.C.) Silents; Palmetto Club of Deaf (Spartanburg). Editor-in-chief S.C. News, 1960-61, 69-71. Home: PO Box 486 Taylors SC 29687 Office: SC School for Deaf Spartanburg SC 29302

MADDOX, LUCY JANE, librarian, educator; b. Port, Okla., Apr. 6, 1922; d. Robert T. and Tollie (Pierce) Maddox; A.A., Central Coll., 1942; A.B., Seattle Pacific Coll., 1944; M.A., Colo. State Coll., 1948; M.L.S., U. Mich., 1956, Ph.D., 1958. Instr. speech and English, Eaton (Colo.) Pub. High Sch., 1945-48; dean women, asst. prof. speech and English, Spring Arbor (Mich.) Coll., 1948-51, 52-53, library curriculum coordinator, 1962-63, dir. library, prof. English, 1963—; asso. prof. speech and English, Seattle Pacific Coll., 1951-52; librarian, prof. English, Owosso (Mich.) Coll., 1953-55, chmn. div. lit., langs. and fine arts, 1958-59; asst. dept. library sci. U. Mich., Ann Arbor, 1957-58, lectr., part-time 1958-65; dir., instr. library technician program Ferris State Coll., Big Rapids, Mich., 1959-62. Vis. instr. library sci. Colo. State Coll., Greeley, summers 1958-61, 65, 66. Mem. Mich. Library Assn. (dist. vice chmn. 1961-62, dist. chmn. elect 1966-67, chmn. dist. II 1967-68), Conf. Christianity and Lit., Mich. Acad., Beta Phi Mu. Free Methodist. Home: 174 E Harmony Rd Spring Arbor MI 49283

MADDOX, MARYLOU MATTINGLY (MRS. KENNETH W. MADDOX), state ofcl.; b. Louisville, July 23, 1928; d. Wilbur Orville and Amelia Alliene (Richardson) Mattingly; student pub. schs., Louisville; m. Kenneth W. Maddox, Mar. 29, 1946; children—Larry Richard, Ramona Lynn, Jennifer Sue. Asso. editor Anaconda Aluminum Co., 1963-69; dir. pub. relations Ky. div. A.R.C., 1969-72; regional dir. Ky. Hist. Events Celebration Commn., Louisville, 1972—. Mem. Internat. Assn. Bus. Communicators (v.p.), Ky. Hist. Soc., Am. Bus. Women's Assn., Pub. Relations Soc. Am. (dir.). Club: Filson (Louisville). Home; 8500 Claudia St Louisville KY 40219

MADDOX, PATILLA COLLEEN MASON, univ. ofcl.; b. Durham, N.C., May 1, 1950; d. Abner S. and Maxine (Hall) Mason; B.A. in English, Lincoln U., 1972; M.A. in Coll. Student Personnel, Bowling Green (O.) U., 1973; m. Winston H. Maddox, Aug. 17, 1974. Hall dir. Bowling Green U., 1972-73; urban program coordinator Pa. State U., Harrisburg, 1973—. Mem. Nat. Assn. Women Deans, Counselors and Adminstrs., Am. Personnel and Guidance Assn., Nat. Assn. Student Personnel Adminstrs., Nat. Assn. Extension Home Economists, Urban Black Cultural Com. Home: 5019 Wynnewood Rd Harrisburg PA 17109

MADDOX, VIVIAN, librarian; b. Harrisburg, Ark., May 14, 1916; d. Herman Peay and Ruth (Halk) Maddox; A.B., Ark. State Coll., 1939; B.S. in L.S., La. State U., 1946; M.L.S., Rutgers U., 1959. Librarian, Poinsett County Library, Harrisburg, Ark., 1944-45, Natchitoches (La.) Parish Library, 1946-47, S.E. Ark. Regional Library, Monticello, 1947-48, Garland County Library, Hot Springs, 1949-52, Springfield (Mo.) Pub. Library, 1952-57; pub. library cons. Mo. State Library, 1958; research asst. Rutgers U., 1958-59; asst. city librarian Milw. Pub. Library, 1959-72; self-employed, 1972-74; librarian Colombia library sci. project Peace Corps, Bogota, 1974—. Recipient Outstanding Achievement award Milw. Municipal Women's Club, 1963. Mem. League Women Voters, Am., Wis. (chmn. library devel. and legislation com. 1972-73, library devel. and legislation com.) library assns., Am. Assn. U. Women, Milw. Area Soc. Pub. Adminstrn., (pres. 1970-71), Delta Kappa Gamma (chpt. pres. 1970-71), Beta Phi Mu. Contbr. articles to library periodicals. Home: PO Box 566 Harrisburg AR 72432

MADDOX, YVONNE T., corp. exec.; b. Paducah, Tex., July 19, 1936; d. James W. and LaVonne (Tarlton) Maddox; student Okla. State U., 1954-57, San Antonio Coll., 1957-58. Asst. to dir. personnel U. Okla., Oklahoma City, 1959-61; asst. to asso. dean U. Colo., Denver, 1962-64; sr. sec. to dean Baylor U., Houston, 1964-65; asst. to dir. advt. Syntex Labs., Palo Alto, Cal., 1965-67; mgr. profl. services Comtact Corp., N.Y.C., 1967-70; pres. World Health Information Services, Inc., N.Y.C., 1970—. Mem. Urban Am., Washington, 1968—, Urban Coalition, N.Y.C., 1968—. Mem. Am. Women Radio and Television (treas. N.Y. chpt.), Pharm. Advt. Club N.Y., Internat. Platform Assn. Home: 340 E 51st St New York City NY 10022 Office: 145 E 49th St New York City NY 10017

MADER, MARGUERITE HELOISE CROWNOVER, educator; b. Winchester, Tenn., Feb. 7, 1914; d. Arthur and Emma (Sims) Crownover; student Ward Belmont Coll., 1934; B.S., George Peabody Coll., 1937, M.A., 1949; postgrad. Oxford U., 1955, U. Tenn., 1959, 67, Middle Tenn. State U., 1962, 63, 71, Abilene Christian Coll., 1964, Samford U., 1966, Tenn. State U., 1973-74; m. Perry Wesley Mader, Oct. 23, 1939 (div. July 1943); children—Heloise Crownover, Arthur Crownover. Tchr., John Early Sch., Nashville, 1949-59; tchr. Berry Sch., Nashville, 1959-74, prin., 1974—. Fulbright exchange tchr. St. Paul's Ch. of Eng. Sch., Bolton, Eng., 1954-55. Pres. Murphy Sch. P.T.A., Nashville, 1948-49. Vice pres. Democratic Women's Club of Davidson County, 1969, mem. bd., 1970; mem. Dems. for Gore, 1971. Freedoms Found. at Valley Forge grantee, 1966; Mem. N.E.A. (life), Tenn. (chmn. upper elementary sect. 1964-65, 66-67), Middle Tenn. (sec.-treas. upper elementary sect. 1962-63), Met. Nashville (v.p. upper elementary assn. 1958-59, dir. 1973—, mem. profl. cooperation council 1968-74, profl. negotiations commn. 1974—, honor award 1969, 71) edn. assns., Nat., Tenn. aerospace edn. assns., Am. Assn. U. Women (v.p. 1958-59, Tenn. legislative chmn. 1971-73, pres. 1974—, life mem.), Am. Legion Aux. (post pres. 1953), Internat. Platform Assn., English-Speaking Union, Tenn. Hist. Soc., Tenn. Bot. Gardens and Fine Arts Soc., Tenn Fedn. Dem. Women, Belmont Hist. Assn. Episcopalian. Club: Query (Nashville). Home: 912 Tower Pl Nashville TN 37204 Office: 2200 Winford Av Nashville TN 37211

MADFIS, MIRIAM GOSIAN (MRS. BERNARD MURRAY MADFIS), publs. co. exec.; b. Brockton, Mass., June 12, 1920; d. Maurice and Dorothy June (Aronson) Gosian; B.S., Simmons Coll., 1940; m. Bernard Murray Madfis, Oct. 22, 1944; children—Elaine (Mrs. Henry Baar), Meredith Joan. Editorial asst. Tech. Rev. mag. Mass. Inst. Tech., 1940-44; advt. asst., advt. and promotion dir. Writer mag., also Plays mag., Writer, Inc., Plays, Inc., Boston, 1944—. Writer columns Tech. Rev., Plays mag. Officer, Class of 1940 Simmons Coll., 1940—, pres., 1955-65, sec., 1965—, chmn. Alumni Fund, 1949-50, chmn. coll. reunions, 1955, chmn. alumni service awards, 1971; pres. Temple Sinai P.T.A., 1967. Mem. exec. bd. Sisterhood Temple Sinai, Brookline. Recipient Alumni Service award Simmons Coll., 1970. Mem. Simmons Coll. Alumni Assn. (exec. bd.). Club: Simmons College of Boston (exec. bd. 1960—, treas. 1965-72, sec. 1973—). Home: 21 Farmington Rd West Roxbury MA 02132 Office: 8 Arlington St Boston MA 02116

MADGETT, NAOMI LONG (MRS. LEONARD P. ANDREWS), educator; b. Norfolk, Va., July 5, 1923; d. Clarence Marcellus and Maude Selena (Hilton) Long; B.A., Va. State Coll., 1945; M.Ed., Wayne State U., 1956, postgrad., 1967-68; postgrad. U. Detroit, 1961-62; m. Julian F. Witherspoon, Mar. 31, 1946 (div. Apr. 1949); 1 dau., Jill Annette (Mrs. Edward Jay Boyer); m. 2d, William H. Madgett, July 29, 1954 (div. Dec. 1960); m. 3d, Leonard P. Andrews, Mar. 31, 1972. Reporter, copyreader Mich. Chronicle, Detroit, 1945-46; service rep. Mich. Bell Telephone Co., Detroit, 1948-54; tchr. high sch. English, Detroit Pub. Schs., 1955-65, 66-68; research asso. Oakland U., Rochester, Mich., 1965-66, mem. staff Ann. Writers Conf., 1968—; lectr. English, U. Mich., 1970-71; asso. prof. English, Eastern Mich. U., Ypsilanti, 1968-73, prof., 1973—. Poet-in-residence Humanities Center, Richmond, Va., 1973. Publicity, Nicholas Hood for Council Com., 1966—. Recipient Esther R. Beer Poetry award Nat. Writers Club, 1957, Distinguished English Tchr. of Year award, 1967. Mott fellow in English, 1965. Mem. Mich. Acad. Arts and Scis., Modern Lang. Assn., Coll. Lang. Assn., Detroit Women Writers, Nat. Council Tchrs. English, N.A.A.C.P., Delta Kappa Gamma, Alpha Kappa Alpha. Mem. United Ch. of Christ. Author: (poems) (under name Naomi Cornelia Long) Songs to a Phantom Nightingale, 1941; One and the Many, 1956; Star by Star, 1965, 70; Pink Ladies in the Afternoon, 1972; (with Ethel Tincher and Henry B. Maloney) Success in Language and Literature B, 1967. Home: 16886 Inverness Av Detroit MI 48221 Office: English Dept Eastern Mich U Ypsilanti MI 48197

MADIGAN, MARGARET MICHELE, editor; b. N.Y.C., July 24, 1944; d. Martin J. and Kathleen M. (Hassett) Madigan; student Hunter Coll., 1963, Fordham U., 1964; B.F.A., Moore Coll., 1966; postgrad. Syracuse U., 1967. With Amphoto Pub. Co., 1967-68; copy editor Cosmopolitan mag., 1968-69; supervising copy editor George Braziller Pub. Co., 1969-70; copy editor Jr. Books, Harper & Row Pubs., N.Y.C., 1970-72, prodn. editor trade dept., 1972-74; copy editing supr. Charles Scribner's Sons, N.Y.C., 1974—. N.Y. State Coll. Regents scholar, 1962. Roman Catholic. Office: 597 Fifth Av New York City NY 10017

MADIGAN, MARY JEAN SMITH, hist. mus. curator; b. Nanticoke, Pa., Feb. 26, 1941; d. Melvin and Irene (Bellegia) Smith; student Drew U., 1958-60; A.B., Cornell U., 1962; M.A., Am. U., 1968; m. Richard Allen Madigan, June 11, 1960; children—Richard Allen, Dana Smith, Reese Jennings. Asst. in history Ft. Worth Childrens Mus., 1967; curator Am. History and Decorative Art Hudson River Mus., Yonkers, N.Y., 1970—. Mem. Yonkers Hist. Soc., Victorian Soc. in Am., Am. Assn. Museums, Phi Beta Kappa. Author: The Photography of Rudolf Eickemeyer, 1971; Eastlake Influenced Am. Furniture, 1973. Home: 17 Wilson Place Hastings-on-Hudson NY 10706 Office: 511 Warburton Av Yonkers NY 10701

MADISON, AUDRE EDITH GATES (MRS. F.L. MADISON), educator; b. nr. Earlsboro, Okla., May 13, 1912; d. Perdanand Cossno and Elizabeth (Sitton) Gates; A.B., Oklahoma City U., 1931; M.A., Sam Houston State Coll., 1951; postgrad. Fla. State U., 1957-60, Ga. So. Coll., 1967-70; m. F.L. Madison, May 8, 1958 (dec. Aug. 1973). Office mgr., bookkeeper, sec. for labor orgns., 1942-47; restaurant operator, Tex., Ariz., 1947-48; real estate salesman, Cal., 1935; interviewer Okla. State Employment Service, 1935-42; tchr. bus. edn., pub. schs., Fla., Tex., Okla., Kan., Wash., 1948-57; tchr. mentally retarded children Nassau County Schs., Hilliard, Fla., 1959-61, Savannah-Chatham Schs., Savannah, Ga., 1961-67; counselor Coffee County Sch. System, Douglas, Ga., 1967-70, Pike County Sch. System, Zebulon, Ga., 1970-73; resource tchr. for mentally retarded children Meriwether County, Ga., 1973—. Mem. Am. Personnel and Guidance Assn., Am. Assn. Sch. Counselors, Internat., Am. assns. mental deficiency, Am. Assn. U. Women, Ga. Edn. Assn., Bus. and Profl. Women's Orgn. (pres. 1950-51). Home: PO Box 55 Zebulon GA 30295

MADISON, CAROLINE RABB (MRS. RICHARD KEITH MADISON), educator; b. Charleston, S.C., Mar. 25, 1921; d. Roy Givens and Minnie Belle (Doar) Rabb; B.S., U. Ga., 1942; M.S., Ohio State U., 1948, Ph.D., 1952; m. Richard Keith, Apr. 1, 1944; 1 dau., Kathi Cameron. Research asst. Am. Cyanamid Co., Stamford, Conn., 1942-46; asst. prof. Kean Coll. N.J., 1962-66, asso. prof., 1966-69, prof. biology, 1969—. AEC Predoctoral fellow, 1949-51. Mem. Genetics Soc. Am., Am. Soc. Zoologist, Am. Inst. Biol. Scis., A.A.A.S. Home: 50 Chestnut Hill Dr Murray Hill NJ 07974 Office: Kean Coll NJ Union NJ 07083

MADSEN, JOAN CAROLE, clin. psychologist; b. Santa Monica, Cal., May 16, 1939; d. David Michael and Sara Rose (Schurr) Seitz; B.A., U. Cal. at Berkeley, 1961; M.A., U. Ore., 1964, Ph.D., 1966; m. Millard Madsen, Nov. 2, 1962 (div. 1970); 1 son, Gregory Todd; m. 2d, Kenneth Roy Stonebraker, July 16, 1971; 1 son, Ryan Marc. Staff clin. psychologist Kennedy Center, St. John's Community Mental Health Center, Santa Monica, 1966-73, chief clin. psychologist, 1973—; pvt. practice clin. psychology, Santa Monica, 1967—. Mem. Am., Cal., Los Angeles County psychol. assns. Home: 720 18th St

Manhattan Beach CA 90266 Office: 1339 20th St Santa Monica CA 90404

MADSEN, NORMA LEE, musician; b. Tremonton, Utah, Dec. 2, 1927; d. Doyle Franklin and Cleo (Crawforth) Madsen; student Brigham Young U. summer 1947, San Francisco Conservatory Music, summer 1949, Music Acad. West, Santa Barbara, Cal., 1962; B.S., U. Utah, 1951; postgrad. Aspen Inst. Music, 1953. Violinist mem. Utah Symphony, 1944—, mem. Utah Opera Theatre Orch., 1951-54, Utah Ballet Theatre Orchestra, 1953—; mem. Melody Maids, 4 violins and piano, 1943-49; active chamber music circles, 1946—; concert mistress U. Utah Symphony, 1947-58, prin. violist, 1958-62; concert mistress Salt Lake Oratorio Soc. Symphony, 1972—; soloist Utah Artist Series, 1964; mem. Treasure Mountain String Quartet, Park City, Utah, 1964-66; sec.-treas., dir., mem. faculty Treasure Mountain Festival of Arts, 1965, 66; lectr. U. Utah, 1951-65, instr., 1965, adj. asst. prof. music, 1969-73, adj. asso. prof., 1973—; appeared as violin soloist U. Symphony and Ballet Theatre Orch., 1954, 56, 57; 2d violinist Utah String Quartet (affiliated with Young Audiences, Inc.), ASTA Conf. Festival Quartet, 1970—, quartet-in-residence U. Utah, Bach Festival Orch., Carmel, Cal., 1963, 69; quartet-in-residence Ida. State U., summer 1967; concertizing throughout Western states, Europe, S.Am. Adjudicator regional festivals contest, 1964; guest lectr. Mem. Music Educators Nat. Conf., Am. (state membership chmn., dir. U. Utah String Conf. 1970—), Utah (chmn. Salt Lake area, state membership chmn.) string tchrs. assns., Nat. Fedn. Music Clubs, Internat. Platform Assn., Music Tchrs. Nat. Assn. (Tchr. Recognition award 1971, 72, 73), Utah Music Tchrs. Assn. (certification bd.), Mortar Bd., Mu Phi Epsilon (nat. v.p., music adviser, province gov. 1954-58, adv. council concert series 1968—), Alpha Lambda Delta, Phi Kappa Phi, Alpha Xi Delta, Lambda Delta Sigma. Mem. Ch. of Jesus Christ of Latter-day Saints. Club: University of Utah Faculty Women's (historian). Compiler, editor: Listing of Solo Works for Strings. Contbr. numerous articles to mags. Home: 2809 Connor St Salt Lake City UT 84109 Office: 55 W 1st South St Salt Lake City UT 84101

MADSEN, PATRICIA ANNE DOLAN (MRS. PETER C. MADSEN), educator; b. Los Angeles, Dec. 5, 1930; d. Edward Francis and Perle (Williams) Dolan; B.A., Scripps Coll., 1952; M.A., U. Cal. at Los Angeles, 1955, Ph.D., 1967; m. Peter C. Madsen, May 12, 1956 (div.); 1 son, Peter Christian. Instr. Pepperdine Coll., 1955-57; asso. prof., chmn. theatre arts dept. Immaculate Heart Coll., Los Angeles, 1957-72; asso. prof. drama San Jose (Cal.) State U., 1973—; choreographer, dir. for community theatre, 1953—. Chmn. Am. Coll. Theatre Festival, region 2. Mem. Rosemary 500 Guild, Pasadena. Mem. Assistance League Pasadena. Mem. Am. Ednl. Theatre Assn., (pres. So. Cal. div., nat. chmn. Playwrights Project) Cap and Bells, Cal. Ednl. Theatre Assn. (exec. bd.). Playwright: And Someday I'll Die, 1963; Scairdy-Cat! 1964; Citizen One from Series G, 1965 (also televised on NBC, 1965); The Gospel Maker, 1965; Thistle's Kiss, 1967. Home: 120 Oak Rim Way Los Gatos CA 95030 Office: Dept Drama San Jose State U San Jose CA 95192

MADSEN, RENATE ELISABETH KRZIKALLA (MRS. PAUL O. MADSEN), physician; b. Ludwigshafen, Germany, Dec. 15, 1930; d. Johannes Alexander and Editha (Ruhl) Krzikalla; M.D., U. Heidelberg, 1955; m. Paul O. Madsen, June 7, 1955; children—Thomas, Karin, Annette. Came to U.S., 1955, naturalized, 1963. Intern, Deaconess Hosp., Buffalo, 1956-57; resident Buffalo Gen. Hosp., 1959-61; practice medicine, specializing in anesthesiology, Madison, Wis., 1962—; mem. staff Univ. Hosp., Madison; instr., dept. anesthesia U. Wis., 1962-65, asst. prof., 1965—. Diplomate Am. Bd. Anesthesiology. Home: 24 Fuller Ct Madison WI 53704 Office: 1300 University Av Madison WI 53706

MADSON, LORETTA (HARTWIG), librarian; b. Denmark, Wis., Sept. 21, 1912; B.A., U. Wis., 1930-36; postgrad. Radcliffe Coll., 1944; m. Robert Cornelius Madison. With accounting dept. Mirro Aluminum Co., Manitowoc, Wis., 1936-38; market research A.C. Nielsen Co., Chgo., 1938-41; with accounts payable dept. Manitowoc Shipbldg. Co., 1941-46; cataloger Manitowoc Pub. Library, 1947-48, asst. reference librarian, 1954-62, head reference dept., 1962—, adult services librarian, 1968—, asst. librarian, 1974—. Served with WAVES, 1943-46. Mem. Am. Assn. U. Women, Wis. Library Assn., Manitowoc County Hist. Soc., U. Wis. Alumni Assn. Lutheran. Address: 712 N 11th St Manitowoc WI 54220

MAENGWYN-DAVIES, GERTRUDE DIANE ZERNER (MRS. JOHN H. I. SCHULZ), educator; b. Paris, France, Dec. 28, 1910; d. Ernst and Irene (Porges) Zerner; came to U.S., 1940, naturalized, 1946; Pharm.M., Vienna U., 1937; Ph.D. (NIH fellow), Johns Hopkins U., 1952; m. David E. Maengwyn-Davies, Oct. 8, 1939 (div. 1946); m. 2d, John H. I.Schulz, Mar. 14, 1946; 1 dau., Evelyn Mary (Mrs. Derrill Smith). Research chemist Warwick Chem. Co. (now Sun Chem. Corp), Long Island City, N.Y., 1942-43; head analyst, organic chemist Overly Biochem. Research Found., N.Y.C., 1943-44; research asst. N.Y.U., N.Y.C., 1944-45; research chemist Quaker Oats Co. Research Labs., Chgo., 1946; Markle Found. fellow dept. pharmacology U. Md., Med. Sch., Balt., 1948; faculty Johns Hopkins U. Sch. Medicine, 1948-55, fellow ophthalmology Wilmer Inst., 1949-50, instr., 1952, asst. prof., 1953-55; asso. research prof. pharmacology George Washington U. Med. Sch., Washington, 1955-56; asso. prof. pharmacology Georgetown U. Schs. Medicine and Dentistry, Washington, 1956-63, prof. pharmacology, 1963—; cons. pharmacologist, N.Y.C., 1962-63; visitor Carlsberg Labs., Copenhagen, Denmark, 1953; vis. prof. dept. pharmacology London U., 1962; vis. scientist Lab. Clin Sci., Nat. Inst. Mental Health, NIH, 1970—. NIH grantee, 1957-67; grantee A.M.A., 1968-74. Fellow A.A.A.S., Chem. Soc. (London), Washington Acad. Scis.; mem. Am. Assn. U. Profs., Am. Soc. Biol. Chemists, Am. Soc. for Pharmacology and Exptl. Therapeutics, N.Y. Acad. Scis. (life), Internat. Soc. Biochem. Pharmacology, Soc. Exptl. Biology and Medicine, Sigma Xi. Clubs: Am. Newspaper Women's, Capital Speakers. Contbg. author: Mechanism of Enzyme Action, 1954, Topics in Medicinal Chemistry, Vol. 2, 1968. Editorial bd. Unlisted Drugs, 1968—, Neuroscis., 1970—, Biol. Handbooks, Fedn. Am. Socs. Exptl. Biology, 1974—. Contbr. articles to tech. jours. Home: 2909 34th St NW Washington DC 20008

MAGAFAN, ETHEL, artist; b. Chgo., Oct. 10, 1916; d. Peter J. and Julia (Bronick) Magafan; student Colorado Springs Fine Arts Center; m. Bruce Currie, June 30, 1946; 1 dau., Jenne Magafan. Painter seven murals including Social Security Bldg., Washington, Recorder of Deeds Bldg., Senate Chamber, South Denver Post Office; one-man shows Colorado Springs Fine Arts Center, 1968, U. Hartford, 1968, Schenectady Mus., 1970, Lehigh U., 1971; paintings exhibited Carnegie Inst. Corcoran Gallery, Pa. Acad. Fine Arts, Nat. Acad. Design, Met. Mus., Denver Art Mus., San Francisco Mus., N.Y. Exhbn., 1950-51, 53, 55, 56, 59, 61, 63, 66-69, 70-71, Nat. Gallery, Washington, 1972; works represented collections Met. Mus. Art, Denver Art Mus., Del. Soc. Fine Arts, Des Moines Art Center, Norfolk, Columbia Mus., Howard U., U. Notre Dame, U. So. Ill., Butler Inst. Am. Art, Newark Mus., Portland (Me.) Mus., Springfield (Mo.) Art Mus., State U. N.Y. at Albany, Ball State U. Art Gallery, Mus. of Tex. Technol. U., Ulster County Community Coll., Dulin Gallery of Art, Farnsworth Mus., Me., Schenectady Mus. Art, Munson-Williams Proctor Inst., Evansville (Ind.) Mus., N.A.D., Provincetown Art Assn., U.S. Dept. Interior, Canton Art Inst., also pvt. collections. John Stacey scholar, 1947; Tiffany fellow, 1949; Fulbright grantee, 1951; recipient Collectors Am. Art award, 1947, 48, Adele Hyde Morrison prize San Francisco Mus., 1950, hon. mention Am. Painting Today exhbn., Met. Mus. Art, 1950; 1st Hallgarten prize Nat. Acad. Design, 1951, Ida Wells Stroud award, Am. Watercolor Soc., 1955, purchase prize Nat. Exhbn. Comtemporary Arts, 1956, Altman prize for landscape, N.A.D., 1956, Hallmark Art award, 1952; Purchase award Ball State U. Art Gallery, 1958, Columbia Mus., 1959, Portland (Me.) Mus., 1959; Childe Hassam purchases, 1958, 1961; Medal of Honor, Audubon Artists, 1962; award Am. Watercolor Soc., 1962, Grumbacher award, 1964; Best in Show award Albany Inst. Art, 1962; Benjamin Altman award Nat. Acad., 1964; Henry Ward Ranger Fund Purchase, 1964; John Marin award Springfield Mus., 1965; award Conn. Acad. Fine Arts, 1965; purchase award Watercolor U.S.A., 1966; Frank Kirk award N.A.D., 1967; award Berkshire Art Assn., 1967; purchase award Dulin Gallery, 1968; Berkshire Art Assn. award, 1968; Hassam Fund purchase award Am. Acad. Arts and Letters, 1969; Juror's Choice award Albany Inst. Art, 1969; Stanley Grumbacher Meml. award Audubon Artists, 1970; Altman prixe N.A.D., 1973; Arches award Am. Watercolor Soc., 1973; Zimmerman award Phila. Watercolor Soc., 1973; Pres.'s award Audubon Artists, 1974. N.A. Home: RFD Box 284 Woodstock NY 12498 Office: Midtown Galleries 11 E 57th St New York City NY 10022

MAGALIFF, MARILYN (MRS. HOWARD JERRY WEISS), artist; b. Bklyn., Sept. 4, 1932; d. Max and Anna (Haber) Ackerman; B.S. magna cum laude, N.Y. U., 1953; m. Howard Jerry Weiss, Nov. 24, 1972; children—Jodi Kim Magaliff and Barry Todd Magaliff (twins). Exhibited one-woman shows Century Fed. Savings Bank, Hewlett and Cedarhurst, N.Y., 1971, Hewlett-Woodmere (N.Y.) Library, 1972, Adelphi U., Garden City, N.Y., 1974, Port Washington (N.Y.) Library, 1974; exhibited in group shows Steinhart Gallery, Westbury, N.Y., 1968, North Bellmore (N.Y.) Library, 1969, Nat. Acad. Galleries N.Y.C., 1970-72, N.Y. Bank for Savs., N.Y.C., 1970, 71, Firehouse Gallery Nassau Community Coll., Garden City, 1971, Pallazzio Vechio, Florence, Italy, 1972, Palazzio Nat., Naples, Italy, 1972, Westbury Meml. Library, 1972, C.W. Post Coll., Brookville, N.Y., 1972, Franklin Nat. Bank, N.Y.C., 1973, Port Washington Library, 1972, Bergen (N.J.) Community Mus., 1974. Recipient first prize Suburban Art League Ann. Show, 1968, 71. Mem. Nat. Assn. Women Artists, Beta Gamma Sigma. Address: 77 Muriel Av Lawrence NY 11559

MAGARET, HELENE, educator, lectr., writer; b. Omaha, May 18, 1906; d. Ernst Friedrich and Celia (Wolcott) Magaret; A.B., Barnard Coll., Columbia, 1932; A.M., State U. Ia., 1938, Ph.D. (Am. Assn. U. Women fellow), 1940. Research asst. State U. Ia., 1937-38, 1939-40; instr. English, Rockford (Ill.) Coll., 1940-41; prof. Coll. St. Teresa, Winona, Minn., 1941-44; prof. English, Marymount Coll., Tarrytown, N.Y., 1944-73, prof. emeritus, 1973—, chmn. dept. English, 1962-67. Recipient Mariana Griswold Van Rensselaer poetry prize, 1932. Mem. Am. Assn. U. Women, Phi Beta Kappa. Roman Catholic. Author: The Trumpeting Crane (narrative poem), 1934; The Great Horse (narrative poem), 1937; Father DeSmet (biography), 1940; Change of Season, 1941; Who Walk in Pride (novel), 1945; Gailhac of Beziers, 1946; Giant in the Wilderness, 1952; The Head on London Bridge, 1956; A Kingdom and a Cross, 1958; Felipe, 1962. Contbr. to mags. and poetry anthologies. Home: 2922 N 54th St Omaha NE 68104

MAGDELEINE, SISTER MARY, educator; b. Milw., May 30, 1917; d. Joseph Donald and Marie (Saib) Mueller; B.A. magna cum laude, Marquette U., 1938; M.A., Catholic U. Am., 1940, Ph.D., 1942. Instr. classical langs. Cardinal Stritch Coll., 1942-47, asst. prof., asso. prof., 1947-49, prof. classical langs., 1949—, registrar, dir. admissions, 1949-67, registrar, 1967-70, chmn. dept. research and spl. programs, 1970-71; asso. dir. Sisters St. Francis of Assisi, 1971—. Mem. Leadership Conf. Women Religious, Delta Epsilon Sigma. Author: The Vocabulary of Pope St. Leo the Great, 1942; The Sermons of St. Caesarius of Arles, Vol. I, 1956, Vol. II, 1964, Vol. III, 1973. Home: 3221 S Lake Dr Milwaukee WI 53207

MAGEE, LOIS LORENE COWGILL (MRS. JOHN PAUL MAGEE), librarian; b. De Smet, S.D., Feb. 14, 1912; d. Charles Hall and Julia (Tenney) Cowgill; student U. Wash., 1929-30; B.A., U. Cal. at Los Angeles, 1934; M.S., U. So. Cal., 1956; m. John Paul Magee, May 2, 1935 (dec. Jan. 1954); children—Marie (Mrs. Ross A. Stone), Paul Terry. Reference librarian Kern County Library, Bakersfield, Cal., 1956-57, adult extension supervising librarian, 1959-63, extension coordinator, 1963-67, county librarian, 1967—; asst. state extension librarian State of Ariz., Phoenix, 1957-58. Mem. Am., Cal. library assns., Pub. Library Execs. So. Cal., Am. Soc. Pub. Adminstrn. (Doubenmeir award 1972), Libraria Sodalitas, Kern County Hist. Soc., Planned Parenthood Assn., Am. Assn. U. Women, Bakersfield C. of C., Beta Phi Mu, Psi Chi, Delta Delta Delta. Office: 1315 Truxtun Av Bakersfield CA 93301

MAGENER, INA WINROOS, realtor, ins. broker; b. San Francisco; d. John Oscar and Elizabeth (Lacalla) Winroos; student pub. and pvt. schs., San Francisco. Ins. account analyst Marsh & McLennan, San Francisco, 1941; marketing mgmt. and ins. account exec. Withoft & Co., Oakland, Cal., 1941-50; engaged in real estate devel. and mgmt., 1950—; self-employed realtor, ins. broker, 1957—. Past pres. Pacific Beach Republican Women's Club. Mem. San Diego Bd. Realtors, Cal. Real Estate Assn. (mem. indsl., comml. and exchange div.), Nat. Assn. Realtors, Pro Am. of La Jolla, Nat. League for Woman's Service Cal., Met. Opera Guild, San Diego Zool. Soc., San Diego Cactus and Succulent Soc. Episcopalian. Club: Women's City of San Francisco. Home: 4555 (K) Bond St San Diego CA 92109 Office: Suite C 950 Hotel Circle N San Diego CA 92108

MAGGIN, JANE CORREA, univ. adminstr.; b. N.Y.C., Feb. 22, 1944; d. Rodolfo A. and Alice (Kennedy) Correa; B.A. with honors, Manhattanville Coll., 1965; postgrad., N.Y. U., 1968; m. Donald L. Maggin, Aug. 1967 (div. Jan. 1970); 1 dau., Alice Winter. Founder, exec. dir. Addie Mae Collins Community Service, N.Y.C., 1965-67, dir. 1965—; dir. for tech. assistance Human Resources Adminstrn., City of N.Y., 1967-68; dir. for community relations N.Y. U., 1968-70, dir. student affairs, 1970-74, asst. chancellor, 1974—. Cons. on poverty programs and urban affairs to various govt. agencies and pvt. industries. Home: 37 Washington Sq W New York City NY 10011 Office: New York University Washington Sq New York City NY 10003

MAGGS, MARGUERITE ANNE HIMEBAUGH (MRS. ROBERT LEONARD MAGGS), horse breeder; b. N.Y.C., Feb. 18, 1936; d. Lester C. and Margaret J. (Barry) Himebaugh; B.S. in Bus., Coll. White Plains, 1957; m. Robert Leonard Maggs, Apr. 25, 1959; children—Marguerite, Robert, Barbara, James, John, Marianne. Social worker N.Y. Foundling Hosp., N.Y.C., 1957-60; owner, mgr. stable, Farmingdale, N.J., 1968—; sec. Maker Corp., Freehold, N.J., 1969—. Pres. Deal (N.J.) P.T.A., 1969. Mem. Standard Breeders and Owners Assn. N.J., Monmouth County Med. Soc. Women's Aux. (v.p. 1973-74), Smithsonian Instn. (asso.). Home: 51 Jerome St Deal NJ 07723 Office: 303 W Main St Freehold NJ 07728

MAGIERA, MARY ANNE, journalist, state ofcl.; b. Webster, Mass., Feb. 1, 1942; d. Charles Francis and Marion (Kralik) Magiera; B.S. in Journalism, Boston U., 1963. Womens page editor Webster (Mass.) Times, 1963-66; city hall reporter Norwich (Conn.) Bull., 1966-67; edn. writer Worcester (Mass.) Telegram, 1967-71; budget analyst, ednl. adviser Mass. Senate Ways and Means Com., Boston, 1971—. Mem. Republican Town Com., Webster, 1964-70. New Eng. Newspaper Editors fellow, 1969-71. Mem. Boston U. Women Grads. Club, Alpha Sigma Alpha. Home: Lawrence Rd Dudley MA 01570 Office: Massachusetts Senate Ways and Means Committee State House Boston MA 02133

MAGINNIS, IVA ANNE APPLEYARD, tax cons.; b. Sebec, Me.; d. William and Addie (Sampson) Appleyard; A.B., Vassar, 1914; postgrad. Boston U., Pace and Pace, Berlitz Sch.; m. John J. Maginnis, Sept. 28, 1923. Accountant to mgr. tax dept. Charles H. Tenney & Co., Boston, 1917-36; owner I.A. Appleyard, Tax Cons., Boston, 1936—; 1st woman to practice before Internal Revenue Service. Mem. Worcester Art Mus., Worcester Sci. Mus., Worcester Found. Exptl. Biology. Decorated Chevalier Confrerie du Taste-Vin (France). Mem. New Eng. State Tax Ofcls. Assn., Assn. Mass. Assessors, Bradford Family Compact, Wine and Food Soc., Mass. Soc. Mayflower Descs., D.A.R., Les Dames d'Escoffier. Republican. Unitarian. Clubs: College, Vassar (Boston); Worcester County Vassar (pres. 1943-45); Seigniory (Can.); Bald Peak Colony (N.H.). Home: 53 Elm St Worcester MA 01609

MAGNENAT, GEORGIANN FORT (MRS. DAVID MAGNENAT), occupational therapist; b. Shreveport, La., Apr. 9, 1948; d. George Edward and Mary Anne (Reeves) Fort; B.S. with honors, Tex. Woman's U., 1970, postgrad. 1972—; m. Alfred David Magnenat, Apr. 6, 1969. Staff occupational therapist Tex. Inst. for Rehab. & Research, Houston, 1970-71; asst. chief occupational therapist Dallas Home for Jewish Aged, 1971-72; chief occupational therapist Dallas Rehab. Inst., 1972—. Clin. faculty mem. Tex. Woman's U., Denton, 1972, U. Tex. Med. Br., Galveston, 1972. Mem. Am., Tex. (chmn. council membership services) North Tex. (continuing edn. chmn. 1973-74, sec. 1974) occupational therapy assns., Tex. Rehab. Assn. Home: 3326 O Henry Dr Garland TX 75040 Office: 7850 Brookhollow Rd Dallas TX 75040

MAGNIFICO, JOSEPHINE HUTCHESON, educator; b. Edinburg, Va., Feb. 10, 1911; d. Joseph Clarence and Minerva Elizabeth (Miller) Hutcheson; A.B., Mary Baldwin Coll., 1932; M.Ed., U. Va., 1957; m. Leonard X. Magnifico, Dec. 28, 1941 (div. May 1952). Tchr. Edinburg High Sch., 1932-43, Warren County (Va.) High Sch., 1943-45, 47-48; tchr., personnel dir. Blackstone (Va.) Coll., 1945-47; tchr. Scottsville (Va.) High Sch., 1952-54, Albemarle (Va.) High Sch., 1954-57; prof. math. Longwood Coll., Farmville, Va., 1958—. Mem. Math. Assn. Am., Va. Edn. Assn., Nat. Council Tchrs. Math., Delta Kappa Gamma (treas. chpt. 1960), Lychnos (U. Va.), Phi Mu. Episcopalian. (chmn. group II women ch. 1966—, vestry 1973—). Club: Wedgewood Country (Farmville). Home: 509 Beech St Farmville VA 23901

MAGNUSON, DORIS JANE, county agt.; b. East Orange, N.J., Feb. 28, 1930; d. Drury Scott and Florence (Watlington) Smith; A.A., Centenary Jr. Coll., 1950; B.J., U. Mo., 1952; m. Henry A. Magnuson, Jan. 1, 1951 (div. June 1970); children—Elaine Scott, Henry A. III. Editor, Portland (Me.) Evening Express, 1958-71; pub. relations dir. Westbrook Coll., 1971-72; extension agt. Coop. Extension Service, U. Me., Portland, 1972—. Mem. Am. Assn. U. Women. Home: 1832 Congress St Portland ME 04102 Office: 96 Falmouth St Portland ME 04101

MAGNUSSON, LUCILLE INGRID, educator; b. Chgo., May 25, 1926; d. Jonas Walfrid and Charlotte (Anderson) Magnusson; B.S., U. Ill., 1947. M.A., State U. Ia., 1951, Ph.D., 1957; postgrad. U. Minn., summer 1953, U. Mich., summer 1948, U. Ind., summer 1956. Instr. Beloit Coll., Beloit, Wis., 1947-50; instr. State U. Ia., Ia. City, 1950-54, research asst., 1956-57, asst. prof., 1957-60; tchr. Austin Minn. pub. schs., 1954-56; asso. prof. phys. edn. Pa. State U., University Park, 1960-72; prof., 1972—. Mem. Nat. Eastern (past v.p.) assns. for Phys. Edn. Coll. Women, A.A.H.P.E.R. (former v.p., chmn. girls and women's sports div.), chmn. commn. on intercollegiate athletics for women Phi Kappa Phi, Pi Lambda Theta. Home: 622 E McCormick Av State College PA 16801 Office: 105 White Bldg University Park PA 16802

MAGRUDER, HELEN ELAINE HAKALA (MRS. EUGENE ROSS MAGRUDER), govt. ofcl.; b. Republic, Mich., Dec. 31, 1918; d. Jacob and Mary Louise (Lahenpera) Hakala; student Badger-Green Bay Bus. Coll., 1937-38, U. Dayton, 1956-59, U. Md., 1960-62; m. Harold Eugene Canada, May 14, 1948 (dec. Dec. 31, 1951); m. 2d, Eugene Ross Magruder, July 15, 1955; stepchildren—Lee Ann (Mrs. Richard Lee Naragon), Lawrence Ross, Kevin Michael. Claims adjuster Internal Revenue Service, Milw., 1943-49; adminstrv. asst. to sr. officer Displaced Persons Commn., Camp Grohn, Germany, 1949-50; chief custodial services br. Dept. Army, Nurnberg, Germany, 1950-51, chief real estate br., 1951; sec. psychol. warfare Hdqrs. U.S. Army, Washington, 1951-55; position classification specialist Air Force Logistics Command, USAF, Wright-Patterson AFB, Dayton, O., 1955-59; sec. counterintelligence div. Office Spl. Investigations USAF, Misawa Air Base, Japan, 1959-60, chief classification and wage adminstrn. br., 39th air div., 1960-62; position classification specialist aerospace med. div. USAF, Brooks AFB, San Antonio, 1962-64, chief classification and wage adminstrn. br., 1964-65; personnel mgmt. specialist Hdqrs. USAF, Washington, 1965-67, program devel. officer, 1967-71; chief operations br. div. personnel Office Mgmt. Services, Dept. Agr., Washington, 1971-72; dir. exec. assignment program Hdqrs. USAF, 1972—. Grad. instr. advanced flower arranging Ikenobo Sch. Japanese Flower Arrangements, Tokyo, Japan, 1962. Hostess U.S.O., 1943-45; sr. troop leader Girl Scouts U.S.A., 1947-48; Wis. state rep. Army Emergency Relief Soc., 1948-49; mem. Gray Ladies A.R.C., 1952-54. Recipient Scholastic Achievement medallion U. Md., 1961, Superior Performance awards USAF, Misawa, 1960, 62, Brooks AFB, 1965, Achievement awards Hdqrs. USAF, Washington, 1966, 68. Mem. Soc. Personnel Adminstrn. (program coordinator Dayton chpt. 1957-59), Classification and Compensation Soc. Mem. Order Eastern Star. Clubs: Faculty Women's, George Washington U. Home: 700 New Hampshire Av NW Washington DC 20037 Office: Dept of Air Force Washington DC 20330

MAGUIRE, CECILIA GERTRUDE, pub. relations exec.; b. Phila., Oct. 3; d. Francis Thomas and Mary Loretta (Farrell) Maguire; B.A., Coll. Mt. St. Vincent, 1938; postgrad. N.Y. U., 1952-54. Tchr. English high schs., Yonkers, N.Y., 1938-40; reporter, feature writer Yonkers Herald Statesman, 1940-41; dir. pub. relations Cath. Youth Orgn., N.Y.C., 1941-43; editor Office War Information, N.Y.C., 1943-45; writer, editor information services Fed. Govt., Washington, 1945-47; pub. relations specialist Nat. Tb Assn., N.Y.C., 1947-52, N.Y. U., N.Y.C., 1952-57; mgr. pub. relations Town Hall, N.Y.C., 1957-58; pub. relations specialist, writer Fordham U., Bronx, N.Y.C., 1967-68;

pub. relations specialist Lincoln Center for Performing Arts, N.Y.C., 1968-69; account exec. pub. relations Doremus & Co., N.Y.C., 1969—. Vol. worker homes for aged, 1955, reading disability Vols. of the Shelter, 1960-62. Recipient Vol. Service award Cath. Youth Orgn., 1961. Mem. English-speaking Union, Theta Sigma Phi. Republican. Roman Catholic. Home: Sunnyside Manor 2 Sunnyside Dr Yonkers NY 10705 Office: 120 Broadway New York City NY 10004

MAGUIRE, CLYDE LOUISE MERRILL (MRS. JOHN H. MAGUIRE), religious orgn. exec., author; b. Heflin, Ala., Mar. 19, 1910; d. Walter Benjamin and Lilla (Jones) Merrill; A.B., Ala. Coll. (now Montevallo U.), 1929; M.R.E., Southwestern Bapt. Theol. Sem., 1931; m. John H. Maguire, Sept. 3, 1931; children—John David, Merrill (Mrs. Calvin Skaggs), Martha (Mrs. Martha Worsley). Mem. exec. com. Fla. Bapt. Women's Missionary Union Conv., 1945-68; state dir. relief offering, 1947-48; state mission study dir., 1950-55; state jubilee dir., 1961-63, state stewardship dir., 1963-66; pres. Conf. Ministers' Wives of So. Bapt. Conv., 1966-67, mem. exec. bd. Woman's Missionary Union, 1969-73. Recipient Distinguished Service award Stetson U., 1958; named Alumna of Year, Ala. Coll., 1957, Fla. Merit Mother, 1958. Mem. Nat. League Am. Pen Women (v.p. Jacksonville br. 1966-68, sec. 1969-73), P.E.O. (pres. 1962-63), Altrusa Internat., Kappa Delta Pi, Pi Kappa Delta. Author: The Cokesbury Dinner and Banquet Book, 1953; Abingdon Party and Banquet Book, 1956; Magnify Your Office, 1956; Won by One, 1958; J.M. Price—Portrait of a Pioneer, 1960; co-author: Tell Well Stories, 1958; More Tell Well Stories, 1961; Stories With a Message, 1966; Best of All Stories, 1967; Here's A Story To Tell, 1970; also hist. pageants, devotional material, program plans. Contbr. to ch. publs. Address: 4374 Landover Dr Jacksonville FL 32207

MAGURN, RUTH SAUNDERS, art mus. curator; b. Boston, Feb. 17, 1908; d. George Henry and Grace Eliza (Dingwell) Magurn; A.B., Barnard Coll., 1929; M.A., Radcliffe Coll., 1932. Cataloguer Fogg Art Mus. Harvard, Cambridge, Mass., 1929-39, asso. curator of prints, 1940-65, curator of prints, 1965-74. Vis. lectr. U. Cal., Santa Barbara, 1970, 73. Belgian-Am. Ednl. Found. grantee, 1950, 55. Mem. Print Council Am. (dir. 1968—). Translator, editor: The Letters of Peter Paul Rubens, 1955. Home: 1572 Massachusetts Av Cambridge MA 02138

MAH, ALLA DORA, research chemist; b. Stockton, Cal., Dec. 31, 1919; B.S., U. Cal. at Berkeley, 1942; m. Wai Mah, Sept. 17, 1945; 1 dau., Vei. Analytical chemist Gen. Services Adminstrn., San Francisco, 1950-53; phys. chemist Berkeley Thermodynamics Lab., 1953-67; research chemist Albany (Ore.) Metallurgy Research Center, 1967—. Mem. Phi Beta Kappa. Baptist. Author: Thermodynamic Properties of Copper and Its Inorganic Compounds, 1973; also papers on thermodynamic properties of oxides, carbides and nitrides and compilations of thermochem. data. Home: PO Box 894 Albany OR 97321 Office: PO Box 70 Albany OR 97321

MAHAFFEY, KATHRYN ROSE, toxicologist; b. Johnstown, Pa., Dec. 24, 1943; d. William Trostle and Harriet Lucindea (Curry) Mahaffey; B.S. cum laude (State Senatorial scholar), Pa. State U., 1964; M.S., Rutgers, 1966, Ph.D. (NIH research fellow), 1968. Lectr., U. N.C., Chapel Hill, 1969, asst. prof. pathology, 1970-72; program coordinator toxicology-pathology project Fedn. Am. Soc. Exptl. Biology, Bethesda, Md., 1971-72; program mgr. lead toxicity research and toxicologist FDA, Washington, 1972—. Asst. prof. community medicine Georgetown U. Sch. Medicine, Washington, 1973—. NIH Postdoctoral research fellow U. N.C., 1968. Mem. Am. Assn. U. Women, Civic Choral Soc., Am. Inst. Nutrition, Am. Soc. Exptl. Pathology, Sigma Xi, Omicron Nu. Unitarian. Author: Pathology and Toxicology: Modern Concepts and Techniques, 1972. Contbr. articles to profl. jours. Home: 6101 Massachusetts Av Bethesda MD 20016 Office: 200 C St SW Washington DC 20204

MAHAFFEY, MARYANN, city councilwoman, social work educator; b. Burlington, Ia., Jan. 18, 1925; d. Kent and Nelle (Widener) Mahaffey; B.A., Cornell Coll., Mt. Vernon, Ia., 1946; M.S.W., U. So. Cal., 1951; m. Herman Dooha, June 8, 1950; 1 dau., Susan Margaret. Recreation dir. Japanese Relocation Center, Poston, Ariz., 1945; with Seattle YWCA, 1946-49, Girl Scouts Met. Detroit and Indpls., 1951-54, Merrill-Palmer Inst., 1954-56, 59, United Cerebral Palsy Assn. Chgo., 1956-57, Brightomoor Community Center, 1959-63; program coordinator, social service dir. Detroit Foster Homes project Merrill-Palmer Inst., 1963-65; prof. Sch. Social Work, Wayne State U., Detroit, 1965—. Commr., Detroit Commn. on Children and Youth, 1968-71; mem. exec. com. Urban Alliance, 1968-70; legislative rep., chmn. Mich. Social Work Council, 1965-68; conf. chmn. Nat. Confs. on Foster Care for Emotionally Disturbed Children, 1964-66; v.p. Detroit Fedn. Settlements, 1961-63; chmn. recreation and social services com. Youth Opportunity Council, Detroit, 1967; cons. Fedn. for Aid to Dependent Children, 1961-67; chmn. Detroit Mayor's Common Council Task Force on Hunger and Malnutrition, 1970—; mem. Gov.'s Task Force on Hunger, 1973—. Mem. exec. bd. 17th Dist. Democratic party, 1969—; mem. Mich. Dem. Central Com.; spokeswoman Mich. Dem. Women's Caucus. Bd. dirs., personnel com. Met. Detroit YWCA, 1971-74. Fellow Am. Orthopsychiat. Assn.; mem. Nat. Assn. Social Workers (mem. nat. bd., nat. exec. com., chmn. nat. pub. relations com. 1972—), Nat. Conf. on Social Welfare, Mich. Assn. for Emotionally Disturbed Children, Acad. Certified Social Workers (charter), Nat. Women's Polit. Caucus (mem. bd. founding conv.), Mich. Women's Polit. Caucus, Am. Fedn. Tchrs., N.A.A.C.P., Am. Civil Liberties Union, A.A.A.S., Am. Assn. U. Profs., Nat. Orgn. Women. Home: 19468 Avon St Detroit MI 48219

MAHAFFEY, SHIRLEY CLEARY SCOTT (MRS. E.R. MAHAFFEY), radio broadcasting exec.; b. Sylvania, Ga., May 10, 1937; d. Howard C. and Reba (Humphries) Cleary; student U. Ga., 1955-56, Ga. So. Coll., 1956-58; m. E.R. Mahaffey, Mar. 15, 1972; children—Angel, Cleary. Sec.-receptionist Sylvania Broadcasting System, Inc. (Ga.), 1956, news dir., 1956-59, program dir., 1959-63, sta. mgr., 1963-66, gen. mgr., 1966-72, owner, gen. mgr., 1972—. Mem. adv. bd. State Crime Prevention, 1973. Bd. dirs. Screven County Day Care and Tng. Center, Ga. Lung Assn. Recipient A.P. and U.P.I. broadcasting awards. Mem. Ga. Assn. Broadcasters (dir. 1974-76), Screven County C. of C. (dir. 1974—, exec. sec. 1974-75), Beta Sigma Phi. Democrat. Clubs: General Women's, Junior Woman's (sec.) (Sylvania). Home: PO Box 83 Sylvania GA 30467 Office: PO Box 519 Sylvania GA 30467

MAHAN, GENEVIEVE ELLIS, sociologist; b. Canton, O., Aug. 1, 1909; d. William and Lillian (Ellis) Mahan; A.B., Western Res. U., 1931, A.M., 1941; postgrad. (Ford Found. fellow) Yale, 1952, Akademie fur Politische Bildung, Tutzing, Germany, 1963. Tchr. high schs., Canton, 1937-52; research asst. dept. sociology Yale, New Haven, 1953-55; lectr. dept. sociology Walsh Coll., Canton, 1970—. Del., Instns. Atlantic and European Cooperation, Coimbra, Portugal, 1970. Trustee, Stark County Psychiat. Found., 1961-68. Fellow Am. Sociol. Assn.; mem. Eastern Sociol. Soc., Am. Acad. Polit. and Social Sci., Nat., Ohio (exec. bd. 1962-69, pres. 1965-66) councils for social studies, Internat. Sociol. Assn., Ohio Acad. Sci., Ohio Soc. N.Y., Am. Assn. U. Women, A.A.A.S. Clubs: Canton College; Canton Woman's. Research in polit. caricature, 1955—. Address: 804 5th St NW Canton OH 44703

MAHAR, MARY HELEN, govt. ofcl.; b. Schenectady, Feb. 12, 1913; d. John A. and Mary (Callahan) Mahar; A.B., State Coll. for Tchrs., 1935, B.S. in L.S., 1944; M.S. in L.S., Columbia, 1950. Librarian, English tchr. Pierson High Sch., Sag Harbor, N.Y., 1935-40; asst. librarian Meml. High Sch., Pelham, N.Y., 1940-42; librarian Scotia (N.Y.) Jr. and Sr. High Sch., 1942-44, Garden City (N.Y.) High Sch., 1944-54; exec. sec. Am. Assn. Sch. Librarians, A.L.A., 1954-56; vis. instr. St. John's U., 1948, Columbia, 1952-53; vis. instr. State Tchrs. Coll., Geneseo, N.Y., 1949-50, prof., 1956-57; specialist sch. and children's libraries Office Edn., U.S. Dept. Health, Edn. and Welfare, Washington, 1957-64, coordinator sch. library services div. library services Bur. Ednl. Research and Devel., 1963-65, specialist sch. library supervision and services, 1965—, chief sch. libraries sect. Bur. Elementary and Secondary Edn., 1966-67, chief instrnl. resources br. 1967, chief Western program operations br., 1968-72, program mgr. sch. med. resources, div. library programs, 1972—. Fulbright fellow, 1951-52. Mem. Am. Assn. Sch. Librarians, Catholic, Am. library assns., N.E.A. Roman Catholic. Author: Certification of School Librarians, 1958; State Department of Education Responsibilities for School Libraries, 1960, also articles in profl. jours. Home: 301 G St SW Washington DC 20024 Office: US Office of Edn Washington DC 20202

MAHER, SISTER MARIA LAURENCE, educator; b. nr. Scranton, Pa., July 16, 1897; d. Joseph Patrick and Margaret (Kerner) Maher; student Bloomsburg State Tchrs. Coll., 1915-17; B.S., Marywood Coll., 1926; M.A., Villanova U., 1939; Ph.D., Fordham U., 1946. Tchr. rural sch., 1917; tchr. New Milford Acad., Darby, Pa., 1918-23; tchr. high sch., Syracuse, N.Y., 1926-32, Susquehanna, Pa., 1932-38; instr. sci. dept. Marywood Coll., Scranton, Pa., 1938-45, asst. prof., 1945-50, asso. prof., 1950-56, prof. biol. sci., 1956—, dept. head, 1960-71. Mem. Lackawanna Luzerne Citizens Council for Clean Air. 1970—. Mem. Bot. Soc. Am., Am. Nature Study Assn., Albertus Magnus Guild, African Violet Soc., A.A.A.S., Nat. Assn. Biology Tchrs., Pa. Sci. Tchrs. Assn., Lackawanna Audubon Soc. Contbr. articles to profl. jours. Address: Div Natural Scis and Math Marywood Coll Scranton PA 18509

MAHFUZ, GISELE ARLETTE, antique dealer; b. Melun, France, Oct. 10, 1927; d. Victor Joseph and Marie Antoinette (Turgis) Kerihuel; Bachelor degree Sorbonne, Paris, 1944; m. Arthur L. Mahfuz, Dec. 26, 1955. Came to U.S., naturalized, 1960. Owner, operator Gisele's Antiques, Alhambra, Cal., 1957-60, Temple City, Cal., 1960—. Appraisal cons. French antiques, Am., French, English furniture and porcelains. Mem. Nat. Antique Dealers Am. Office: 5652 N Rosemead Blvd Temple City CA 91780

MAHL, MARY ROBERTA, educator; b. Paterson, N.J., Dec. 6, 1914; d. Howard Wallace and Henriette (Breen) Mahl; A.B. summa cum laude, Wheaton Coll., 1950; A.M., N.Y. U., 1955, Ph.D. (Andiron award), 1961. Statistician U.S. Rubber Co., N.Y.C., 1942-47; regional mgr. Daniel Starch and Staff, N.Y.C., 1947-48; missionary, fund designator Sudan Interior Mission Aden, Arabia and N.Y.C., 1948-55; office mgr. Keally and Patterson, N.Y.C., 1955-57; Conde Nast Engravers, N.Y.C., 1957-59; lectr. English, U. So. Cal., 1960-61, instr., 1961-62, asst. prof., 1962-66, asso. prof., 1966—. Bd. dirs. English-Speaking Union, Los Angeles, 1969—, Conf. on Christianity and Lit., Los Angeles, 1967-69. Recipient Founders Day award N.Y. U., 1962. Mem. Modern Lang. Assn., Am. Assn. U. Profs., Milton Soc., U. Women's Club London, Nat. Council Tchrs. English, Scholastic Honor Soc., Phi Delta Gamma (faculty sponsor 1967—), Phi Kappa Phi. Republican. Presbyn. Editor: Seventeenth Century English Prose, 1968; Sir Philip Sidney's Apology for Poetry: Sixteenth Century Manuscript, 1969. Contbr. articles to profl. jours. Home: 7121 Alvern St Apt A Los Angeles CA 90045

MAHLER, JEANNE HULL, librarian; b. Kingston, N.Y., Jan. 9, 1916; d. Leon William and Frances Hitchborn (Spear) Hull; B.S. in Edn., U. Pa., 1937, M.S. in Edn., 1938; B.S. in L.S., Drexel Inst. Tech., 1940; m. William Arthur Mahler, Jan. 25, 1957. Asst. circulation dept. Free Library Phila., 1940-45, sr. asst. pub. documents dept., 1945-48, acting head, 1948, head govt. publs. dept., 1949—. Mem. Am., Spl., Pa.library assns., Library Pub. Relations Assn. Greater Phila., Pi Lambda Theta, Pi Gamma Mu. Author articles in field. Home: 1246 Johnston St Philadelphia PA 19148 Office: Free Library Phila Philadelphia PA 19103

MAHONEY, BARBARA SMITH (MRS. DENNIS C. MAHONEY), museum theater ofcl.; b. Washington, Dec. 17, 1925; d. James Leo and June Elizabeth (Roesch) Smith; student U. Cal., 1945-46; B.A., Bennington Coll., 1949; m. Dennis C. Mahoney, May 12, 1951 (dec. 1970); children—Dennis, Curtis, Nicholas, Seamus. Account exec. fashion publicity Rosemary Sheehan, Fashion and Publicity, N.Y.C., 1951-56; writer product publicity Infoplan, N.Y.C., 1963-68; asst. dir. museum theatre publicity, asst. dir. Guild Hall, East Hampton, N.Y., 1968—. Club: Maidstone (East Hampton, N.Y.). Author: A Sensitive, Passionate Man, 1974. Home: Lily Pond Lane East Hampton NY 11937 Office: Guild Hall 158 Main St East Hampton NY 11937

MAHONEY, CAROL ELIZABETH FOERTSCH (MRS. WILLIAM H. MAHONEY, JR.), editor; b. Mpls., Mar. 15, 1940; d. Richard George and Katherine Isobel (Gorman) Foertsch; student U. Minn. Grad. Sch., 1961-62; B.A., U. Minn., 1962; m. William Henry Mahoney, Jr., May 13, 1967; children—Meredith Jean, Megan Marie. Food editor St. Paul (Minn.) Pioneer Press-Dispatch, 1962-67; copy editor Ginn and Co., Waltham, Mass., 1967-69; asst. editor publs. Boston Mus. Fine Arts, 1969; asst. dir. publs. Tufts U., Medford, Mass., 1970-71; free lance writer Arlington Advocate-Winchester (Mass.) Star, 1971—; cons. editor Cambridge (Mass.) Jr. Coll., 1971—; editor, field corr. Woburn (Mass.) Daily Times, 1972—. Mem. League Women Voters, Women in Communications (chpt. v.p. 1963-64; Boston editor membership, 1968-72), Kappa Delta (pres. Boston alumnae 1972), Phi Kappa Tau. Asso. editor: Tufts Alumni Review, 1970-71. Home: 125 Newport St Arlington MA 02174 Office: Montvale Av Woburn MA 01801

MAHONEY, SISTER COLETTE, coll. pres., biologist; b. Jamaica, N.Y., July 19, 1926; d. Timothy and Lillian (Boylan) Mahoney; B.A., Marymount Coll., 1949, LL.D., 1973; M.A., Fordham U., 1952, Ph.D., 1961; H.H.D., St. Francis de Sales, 1974. Joined Religious of Sacred Heart of Mary, 1945; tchr. biology Acad. Sacred Heart of Mary, N.Y.C., 1947-57, prin., 1965-67; instr. biology Marymount Coll., Arlington, Va., 1957-61, also chmn. sci. dept.; asso. prof. biology Marymount Coll., Tarrytown, N.Y., 1961-65; pres., trustee Marymount Manhattan Coll., N.Y.C., 1967—. Dir. Manhattan Life Ins. Co. Vice pres. Council of Higher Ednl. Instns. of N.Y.C.; mem. Pres.'s Adv. Com. on Econ. Role of Women. Fellow Am. Assn. U. Women; mem. Nat. Catholic Edn. Assn. (mem. governance com. 1971—). Contbr. articles on biology to sci. publs. Address: 221 E 71st St New York City NY 10021

MAHONEY, JANE ELIZABETH WILLIAMS (MRS. EDWARD A. MAHONEY, JR.), business exec., educator; b. Massillon, O., Oct. 5, 1922; d. Edward and Dorothy (Best) Williams; student Va. Intermont Jr. Coll., 1940-41; A.B., Coll. of William and Mary (scholar), 1943; postgrad. Columbia, 1946; m. Edward A. Mahoney, Jr., Dec. 18, 1948; 1 son, Edward A. III. Cartographer, U.S. Coast and Geodetic Survey, Washington, 1943-46, Army Map Service, Washington, 1947-48; v.p., treas., dir. Mahoney Sash & Door Co., Canton, O., 1969—. Lectr., instr. astronomy, math., space sci., 1960—. Vice chmn. vols. for records A.R.C., 1950-63, bd. dirs., 1949-69; bd. mem. Canton Garden Center, 1959-61; founding dir. Hoover-Price Planetarium, Canton, 1963, bd. dirs., lectr., 1963—, dir. planetarium, 1973—; dir. astronomy Stark County Hist. Center, 1973—; active Red Feather and community orgns. drives. Recipient local, nat. awards A.R.C. Mem. Internat. Soc. Planetarium Educators, Gt. Lakes Planetarium Assn., Jr. League Canton (treas. 1956-59), Stark County Hist. Soc. (chmn. planetarium com., mem. steering com.), Stark County Astron. Soc., Mortar Bd., Phi Beta Kappa, Phi Theta Kappa. Republican. Methodist. Clubs: Garden (pres. 1959-61), Congress Lake Garden, Congress Lake, Canton, College. Home: 3421 Parkridge Circle NW Canton OH 44718 Office: Box 483 Canton OH 44701

MAHONEY, JANET MARY (MRS. WILLIAM ARTHUR MAHONEY), health service adminstr.; b. Lansing, Mich., June 17, 1935; d. Glenn Park and Nellie Louise (Potter) Manz; B.S., Mich. State U., 1957; certificate in occupational therapy Western Mich. U., 1963; M.S., Boston U., 1973; m. William Arthur Mahoney, Feb. 3, 1965. Tchr. math. Harbor Springs (Mich.) Pub. Sch., 1957-58, West Bloomfield Sch., Orchardlake, Mich., 1958-60; dir. occupational therapy Lake County Soc. for Crippled Children, Gary, Ind., 1963-64; mem. staff occupational therapists N.H. Hosp., Concord, 1964-66, 69-72, coordinator occupational therapy edn., 1973—; mem. staff occupational therapists Tex. Rehab. Hosp., Gonzales, Tex., 1966-68; dir. occupational therapy St. Jude's Hosp., Austin, Tex., 1968-69. Mem. Am., No. New Eng. (del. 1972—) occupational therapy assns. Home: PO Box 842 Concord NH 03301 Office: 105 Pleasant St Concord NH 03301

MAHONEY, JEWEL ROSE BRAUN HOLAHAN (MRS. THOMAS PATRICK MAHONEY), bus. exec.; b. Hamilton, O., Jan. 13, 1920; d. Walter Carl and Ruth (Sheley) Braun; B.A., Pa. State U., 1940; m. David Fulton Holahan, Oct. 14, 1939, (div. Apr. 1949); children—Charmian Ellen (Mrs. Carl Keith Goudy), Janice Ruth (Mrs. Charles Albert Arthur Thieme); m. 2d, Thomas Patrick Mahoney, July 6, 1973. Proofreader Penton Press, Cleve., 1941; proofreader Ency. Britannica, Chgo., 1942-43; prodn. editor, 1946-52; editor, engr. Goodyear Aircraft Corp., Akron, O., 1952-54, asst. dept. mgr., 1954-60; dir. editorial services Follett Pub. Co., Chgo., 1960-62, mng. editor, 1962-64, mng. editor ednl. div., 1964-67, exec. mng. editor, 1973; exec. editor lang. arts Follett Ednl. Corp., Chgo., 1967-73; dir. Chgo. Book Clinic, 1966-69. Participant, Internat. Conf. Teaching and Learning English, York, Eng., 1971. Mem. Am. Mgmt. Assn., Nat. Council Tchrs. English, Internat. Reading Assn., N.E.A., Assn. for Supervision and Curriculum Devel., D.A.R., Gamma Phi Beta. Republican. Mem. Christ Ch. Contbr. articles to profl. jours., chpts. to textbooks. Address: 1412 National Av Rockford IL 61103

MAHONEY, MARGARET ANNETTE, lawyer; b. Cleve., July 12, 1900; d. Timothy and Catherine (Malloy) Mahoney; LL.B., Marshall Law Sch., 1929. Admitted to Ohio bar, 1929; practiced in Cleve., 1936—; chief div. securities State of Ohio, 1951-53; dir. Ohio Dept. Indsl. Relations, 1953-56, 59-63. Mem. Ohio Def. Council, 1941-46, Cleve. Civil Service Commn., 1957-59. Mem. Ohio Ho. of Reps., 1938-42; mem. Ohio Senate, 1943-50, pres. pro tem, 1949-50; del. Democratic Nat. Conv., 1956, 60, 64; presdl. elector Dem. Party, 1948—. Recipient Woman of Achievement award Inter-Club Council of Cleve., 1957; Top Women in Govt. award Ohio Bus. and Profl. Womens Clubs, 1960. Mem. Cuyahoga County Bar Assn., Bus. and Profl. Women's Club, Kappa Beta Pi. Address: 2623 Kingston Rd Cleveland Heights OH 44118

MAHONEY, MARGARET GERLACH (MRS. J. FRANCIS MAHONEY), physician; b. Phila., Mar. 21, 1917; d. Harry and Anne R. (McGinnis) Gerlach; A.B., Temple U., 1938, M.D., 1942; M.S., U. Pa., 1945; m. J. Francis Mahoney, Dec. 30, 1944; children—J. Francis IV, James Widmann, M. Jane, Harry G., Peter T. Intern Woman's Hosp. Phila., 1942-43; resident U. Pa. Hosp., Phila., 1943-46; practice medicine specializing in dermatology, Wynnewood, Pa., 1956—; dermatologist Lankernan Hosp., Phila., 1946—; asso. prof. dermatology Jefferson Med. Coll., Phila., 1966—. Mem. Am. Med. Women's Assn. (pres. Phila. br., 1971-72). Home and Office: 324 Ingeborg Rd Wynnewood PA 19151

MAHONEY, MARGARET PROCTOR (MRS. JOHN SHEPHERD MAHONEY), lawyer; b. Pittsburg, Kan., Feb. 3, 1940; d. Alvin Horace and Mary Faye (Cooper) Proctor; student Bryn Mawr Coll., 1960-61; B.A., Wellesley Coll., 1961; LL.B., U. Md., 1968; m. John Shepherd Mahoney, Aug. 14, 1960; children—John Proctor, Matthew Shepherd. Admitted to Md. bar, 1968; researcher firm Royston, Mueller, Thomas and McLean, Towson, Md., 1970-71, asso., 1972—. Mem. Md. Bar Assn., Order of Coif, Presbyn. Casenote editor Md. Law Rev., 1967-68. Home: Seven Village Ct Bel Air MD 21014 Office: 102 W Pennsylvania Av Towson MD 21204

MAHONEY, MARY ELIZABETH GOSSETT (MRS. PATRICK B. MAHONEY), hosp. exec.; b. Hot Springs, Ark., June 1, 1925; d. Marshall Alfred and Maude (Pierce) Gossett; student MacMurray Coll. for Women, 1944-45; B.J., U. Mo., 1948; m. William J. Barry, July 21, 1950; children—Kathleen Melissa (Mrs. Daniel Hatcher), Timothy Edwin, Matthew Marshall, Elizabeth Jane; m. 2d, Patrick B. Mahoney, May 17, 1973. Reporter, soc. editor So. Newspapers, Inc., Hot Springs, Ark., summers 1943-48; editor Osceola (Ark.) Times, 1949; clk., receptionist Ozark Bath House, Hot Springs, 1949-51; dir. pub. relations St. Joseph's Hosp., Hot Springs, 1969-73; dir. pub. relations Leo N. Levi Nat. Arthritis Hosp., Hot Springs, 1973—. Mem. exec. bd. Am. Cancer Soc., Garland County, 1969-72, Hot Springs Band Parents Assn., 1971-72; mem. Emergency Health Services Com., Hot Springs, 1969-70; sec. Garland County Health Adv. Com. Mem. Am. Assn. U. Women (chmn. pub. information, 1972-73), Am. Soc. Hosp. Pub. Relations, Am. Cath. Communications Soc. Pub. Relations Soc. Am. Roman Catholic. Home: 616 Vermelle St Hot Springs AR 71901 Office: 300 Prospect Av Hot Springs AR 71901

MAIENSCHEIN, ELSIE ANNA (MRS. WILLIAM MAIENSCHEIN), realtor; b. Evanston, Ill., Oct. 4, 1923; d. Julius and Anna (Deutsch) Jonescu; student Northwestern U., 1941-42; m. William Maienschein, Apr. 24, 1948; children—Juliana (Mrs. Ronald Daverin), Caroline (Mrs. John Aurich). Exec. sec. to comptroller Montgomery Ward & Co., Chgo., 1941-51; financial exec. Robert L. Nelson Real Estate, Inc., Arlington Heights, Ill., 1966—. Lutheran. Club: St. Peter Mother's (pres. 1963-64). Home: 3 Windemere on Duxbury Rolling Meadows IL 60008 Office: 300 E Northwest Hwy Arlington Heights IL 60004

MAIER, SISTER MARY LOUISE, chemist, educator; b. Elizabeth, N.J., July 21, 1926; d. Harry and Martha Theresa (Hake); B.S. summa cum laude, St. John's U., 1959; M.S., U. Detroit, 1966; Ph.D. (U. Mich. teaching fellow, Dupont research fellow), U. Mich., 1970. Joined Sisters of St. Joseph, 1947; lab. asst. Merck & Co., Rahway, N.J., 1944-47; tchr. elementary sch. Catholic Schs., Bklyn., 1949-59; tchr. Cath. High Schs., Bklyn., 1959-66; instr. chemistry St. Joseph's Coll., Bklyn., 1970-72; asst. prof. Medgar Evers Coll., Bklyn., 1972—. Chmn. Com. of Responsibility, Ann Arbor, Mich., 1968-70; mem. Steering Com. Interfaith Council for Peace, 1968-69; mem. campus ministry, Diocese of Bklyn., 1973—. Mem. exec. bd. Pratt Area Community Council, 1972—. NSF fellow, 1961-65; Rensselaer Poly. Inst. fellow, 1971. Mem. Am. Chem. Soc. (teaching fellow award 1969), Am. Assn. U. Profs., Phi Lambda Upsilon. Clubs: Catholic Peace Fellowship, Fellowship of Reconciliation. Research in edn. and inorganic chemistry. Home: 288 Vanderbilt Av Brooklyn NY 11205 Office: 85 S Oxford St Brooklyn NY 11217

MAILMAN, VIRGINIA SHEVLIN ADDISON (MRS. NORTON W. MAILMAN), pub. relations exec.; b. Bronxville, N.Y., Apr. 27, 1929; d. Matthew Joseph and Virginia Boyd (MacMillan) Shevlin; student U. Colo., 1947-49; B.A., Stanford, 1951; m. Norton W. Mailman, June 17, 1965; children—Bruce Addison, Matthew Addison, Christopher. Recruiter with industry A.R.C. Blood Program, Los Angeles, 1951-52; reporter Life mag., N.Y.C., 1952-61; asso. editor, asst. New York Bur. chief Show Bus. Illustrated, 1961-62; formed pub. relations firm Addison, Goldstein & Walsh, Inc., N.Y.C., 1962, v.p., 1962—; formed Syndicated Airtime, producer 5 minute radio series, 1970; producer James Beard Cook-Along cassette series, 1973. Bd. dirs. Downtown Med. Center, N.Y.C. Winner Internat. Needlepoint Show, N.Y., 1973. Club: Piping Rock (Locust Valley, N.Y.). Home: 109 E 69th St New York City NY 10021 Office: 635 Madison Av New York City NY 10022

MAINA, JILL DIANE, pub. relations exec.; b. Chgo., Apr. 6, 1942; d. Paul Alexander and Edna Mae (Burke) Maina; student Lake Forest (Ill.) Coll., 1959-61; B.Theatre Arts, Pasadena Playhouse Coll. of Theatre Arts, 1963, M.Theatre Arts, 1965. Actress, 1965-70; talk show hostess Roy Elwell Show, Girl Power—Jill Maina Show, KLAC-AM, radio announcer KMET-FM, Los Angeles, 1965-69; free lance writer Confidential and Whisper mags., Newsline Publs., Los Angeles, 1967-70; editor Confidential mag., 1970-71; free lance photographer, 1968—; free lance writer, 1968—; designer, painter Tarot figures for On a Clear Day movie party at Beverly Hilton, 1968; maj. publicity campaign for Paul Winchell and his artificial heart invention Rogers, Cowan & Brenner, Inc., Beverly Hills, Cal., 1972-73, also Euell Gibbons/Grape Nuts campaign, 1972-74. Founder mem. Cal. Citizens Action Group, 1973—; mem. Animal Protection Inst., 1973—. Mem. Intercontinental Biog. Assn., Alpha Xi Delta, Alpha Psi Omega. Democrat. Presbyn. Home and office: 11639 La Maida North Hollywood CA 91601

MAINE, VIRGINIA LOUISE MOTTORN (MRS. JOHN G. MAINE), psychiat. social worker; b. Punxsutawney, Pa., Mar. 24, 1937; d. Jacob P. and Agnes (Armstrong) Mottorn; B.A., Pa. State U., 1959; M.S.W., U. Pitts., 1963; postgrad. Ind. U., 1963-64. Smith Coll., 1966; m. John G. Maine, Oct. 21, 1967. Caseworker, Mifflin County Child Welfare Services, Lewistown, Pa., 1959-60, Cambria County Child Welfare Services, Ebensburg, Pa., 1961-62; social work supr. Larue Carter Out-Patient Clinic, Indpls., 1963-67; social service dir. Clearfield (Pa.) Hosp., 1967-70; adminstr. Clearfield-Jefferson Mental Health-Mental Retardation Program, 1969. Instr. continuing edn., sociology Pa. State U., 1959-60, 67-68; field instr. grad. student supr. Ind. U., Indpls., 1966-67; cons. Presbyn. Homes, 1968-70. Bd. dirs., mem. cancer com. Western Pa. Regional Med. Program, also mem. adv. bd.; bd. dirs. Clearfield-Jefferson Mental Health Assn. (v.p. 1967-68), Clearfield County unit Am. Cancer Soc.; mem. profl. adv. bd. United Cerebral Palsy, 1972—. Fellow Am. Orthopsychiat. Assn.; mem. Am. Group Psychotherapy Assn., Am. Hosp. Assn., Assn. Hosp. Social Work Dirs., Nat. Assn. Social Workers, Acad. Certified Social Workers, Am. Assn. U. Women, Bus. and Profl. Women's Club (chmn. civic affairs 1968-69), Newcomers of Greater Houston, Pi Gamma Mu, Alpha Kappa Delta, Alpha Lambda Delta, Zeta Tau Alpha. Clubs: College Womens, Spring Shadows Womens (1st v.p. 1973-74), Civic Assn. Home: 2730 Stetson Lane Houston TX 77043 Office: 809 Turnpike Av Clearfield PA 16830

MAINES, HAZEL ESTELLA SPANN (MRS. HARMON ROSS MAINES), city ofcl.; b. Gilmer, Tex., Nov. 12, 1909; d. Joe Morgan and Lillian (Martin) Spann; student Baylor Coll., 1926-28, Tyler Comml. Coll., 1928-29, S.W. State Tchrs. Coll., San Marcos, 1930; B.A., Sam Houston Tchrs. Coll., 1933; postgrad. S.W. State Tchrs. Coll. (Okla.), 1936; m. Harmon Ross Maines, Feb. 23, 1934; children—Dickie Joe, Don Allan. Sec., Hollands Mag., Dallas, 1929; county clk. Upshur County, summer 1934; asst. county sch. supt., Gilmer, Tex., 1942-46, 47-55; city sec., Gilmer, 1955—. Tchr., Lone Mountain Sch., Gilmer, 1930-31, E. Mountain Sch., 1931-41, Indian Rock Sch., 1941, Glenwood Sch., 1946. Officer, Upshur County Election Precinct 2, 1955-73. Mem. City Sec. Assn. E. Tex., Am. Legion Aux. (sec. 1955—). Methodist (past sec. Sunday Sch. class). Home: Route 6 Box 14B Gilmer TX 75644 Office: City Hall PO Box 760 Gilmer TX 75644

MAINETTI, BARBARA ELIZABETH MANSFIELD (MRS. G. ALFRED MAINETTI), educator; b. Poughkeepsie, N.Y., Aug. 28, 1935; d. G. Stuart and Elizabeth M. (Matteson) Mansfield; B.S., Skidmore Coll., 1957; M.S., State U. N.Y., 1960; postgrad. N.Y. U., 1967—; m. G. Alfred Mainetti, June 28, 1958; children—Maria G., Peter M. Tchr., Ungraded Sch., Elmira Heights, N.Y., 1957-58, Spackenkill Sch. System, Poughkeepsie, 1958-60; sr. kindergarten tchr., head tchr. Zion unit St. George's Sch., Poughkeepsie, 1963, 70-71, pvt. tutor, 1967-68, tchr., dir. testing, 1971—. Tchr. creative dramatics, Rock City Falls, N.Y., 1955; tchr. creative dramatics Community Children's Theatre, Poughkeepsie, 1958-68, bd. dirs., 1958-60. Bd. dirs. County Players, Poughkeepsie, 1967-70, bus. mgr., 1969, pres., 1970; bd. dirs. Community Children's Theatre, 1974—. Mem. Am. Assn. U. Women, Am. Ednl. Theatre Assn., Internat. Assn. Theatre for Children and Young People, N.Y. Theatre Festival Assn. (sec.-treas. 1969-70), Beta Delta Cast. Home: 5 Calvin Blvd New Paltz NY 12561 Office: St George's School 20 Carroll St Poughkeepsie NY 12601

MAINWARING, MARION J., author; b. Boston; d. Herbert James and Marion (Imrie) Mainwaring; B.S., Simmons Coll., 1943; A.M., Radcliffe Coll., 1944, Ph.D., 1949. Teaching fellow dept. English, Harvard, 1947-48; instr. dept. English, Mount Holyoke Coll., 1948-52; newspaper corr., Eng., France, Balkans, 1968—; fgn. editor Adams Papers, 1964-65; European corr. Boston Herald Traveler, 1968. Cons. Mass. Council on Arts and Humanities, 1967-68, 72-73; translator UNESCO, 1972—. Mem. Phi Beta Kappa. Author: Murder at Midyears, 1953; Murder in Pastiche, 1954; John Quincy Adams and Russia, 1965. Editor: Turgenev The Portrait Game, 1973. Translator: Youth and Age: Three Stories by Turgenev, 1968. Address: 103 Rue de Javel Paris XV France

MAINWARING, MARY LOUISE HUNTER, educator; b. Chgo., Apr. 18, 1911; d. Thomas Alexander and Virginia Catherine (O'Neill) Hunter; student Milw.-Downer Coll., 1928-29, Northwestern U., 1929-31; B.A. summa cum laude, U. Cal. at Los Angeles, 1950, M.A. (Sol Lesser fellow), 1951; Ed.D., Ind. U., 1954; m. Angus Macdonald Gordon, Oct. 28, 1931 (div. July 1935); m. 2d, Theodore David Mainwaring, July 28, 1937 (div. June 1946). Asst. prodn. mgr. Jam Handy Orgn., film prodn., Detroit, 1942-43; prodn. mgr. Transfilm-Caravel, film prodn., N.Y.C., 1943-45; lectr. Ind. U., 1952-54; research asso. Ency. Brit. Films, Wilmette, Ill., 1954-55; writer Scott, Foresman Co., Chgo., 1955-56; faculty, audio-visual dir. Kennedy-King Coll., Chgo. City Colls., 1956—, prof., 1969—, v.p. faculty council, 1971-73; faculty council Chgo. City Colls., 1971—, pres., 1973—. Taussig traveling fellow, 1951; Mid-career fellow Syracuse U., 1967. Mem. Am. Assn. U. Profs., Assn. Ednl. Communications and Tech., Soc. Cinema Studies, Chgo. Film Council. Republican. Presbyn. Home: 1401 E 55th St Chicago IL 60615

MAIZNER, JANET PATRICIA (MRS. NEIL L. MAIZNER), pub. relations agy. exec.; b. N.Y.C., Oct. 24, 1944; d. Salvatore and Nancy (Gulisano) La Rocco; B.A. in Sociology and Journalism, Syracuse U., 1966; m. Neil Leonard Maizner, Sept. 7, 1968. Asst. pub. relations mgr. Charles Pfizer & Co., N.Y.C., 1966-69; account exec. Dunwoodie Assos., N.Y.C., 1969-70; v.p. Ruder & Finn, Inc., N.Y.C., 1970—. Cons. pub. relations Open Channel, Inc., Samaritan Halfway Soc., Inc., Conn. Developmental Disabilities Program; chmn. N.Y.C. Conf. for Coll. Coeds, 1969, 70; founder, supr. Creative Action Force, N.Y.C., 1970—. Recipient Paul B. Zucker award Ruder & Finn, 1973. Mem. Internat. Motor Press Assn. (dir.), Publicity Club, Women in Communications (v.p. programs 1971-72), Delta Gamma. Home: 3036 Day Av Coconut Grove FL 33131 Office: Ruder & Finn 110 E 59th St New York NY 10022

MAJERCAK, JEANNE (MRS. JOHN VINCENT MAJERCAK), hosp. adminstr.; b. Boston, Apr. 18, 1931; d. Edward Allan and Madge Alma (Greer) Robinson; A.B. cum laude, Notre Dame Coll., 1952; m. John Vincent Majercak, Aug. 28, 1954; children—Robert, Catherine, Susan, John, Jeanne. Dir. pub. relations Marymount Hosp., Cleve., 1954-55, Notre Dame Coll., Cleve., 1971—. Bd. dirs., mem. exec. com. of bd. St. Julie Billiart Center for Catechetics, Cleve. Mem. Am. Alumni Council, Kappa Gamma Pi (editor nat. newspaper 1962-64). Office: 4545 College Rd Cleveland OH 44121

MAJOR, MARGUERITE LOUISE, ednl. adminstr.; b. Kansas City, Mo., Jan. 26, 1929; d. Ray Clark and Celia Marguerite (Fowler) Major; A.B., San Jose State Coll., 1950. Exec. dir. San Jose State Coll. Alumni Assn., 1953-57; publs. dir. U. Santa Clara (Cal.), 1957-60, news dir., 1960-72, dir. news and editorial services, 1972—. Mem. Pub. Relations Soc. Am., Am. Colls. Pub. Relations Assn., San Jose State Alumni Assn. (dir. 1970-71). Episcopalian. Home: 120 Carlton Av Los Gatos CA 95030 Office: University of Santa Clara Santa Clara CA 95053

MAKAR, NADIA EISSA, educator; b. Cairo, Egypt, Oct. 7, 1938; d. Michel Issa and Yvonne Bitar; student Cairo U., 1958-59, 64-65; certificate Moscow U., 1964; B.A., St. Peter's Coll., 1969; Hon. Dr. Liberal Arts, Gt. China Arts Coll., 1973; m. Boshra Halim Makar, Jan. 1, 1960; children—Ralph, Roger. Tchr. chemistry Hudson Cath. High Sch., Jersey City, 1970-72, chmn. sci. dept., 1972—. Chmn. jr. poets Ann. Internat. Poetry Festival, 1973—. Bd. dirs. World Poets Resource Center, N.Y.C. Recipient Spl. award Poetry Soc. London, 1972; named outstanding secondary educator Am., 1973. Mem. A.A.A.S., Nat. Sci. Tchrs. Assn., Nat. Sci. Supr. Assn., Poetry Soc. London (life), Assn. for Edn. Tchrs. in Sci., Am. Chem. Soc., Centro Studi e Scambi Internaziolali (mem. internat. com. on sci. 1973—), N.Y., N.J. acads. sci., Internat. Platform Assn. Home: 110 Glenwood Av Apt 402 Jersey City NJ 07306 Office: 790 Bergen Av Jersey City NJ 07306

MAKAROVA, NATALIA, ballerina; b. Leningrad, USSR, Nov. 21, 1940; ed. Vaganova Ballet Sch.; grad. Leningrad Choreographic Sch., 1959. Joined Kirov Ballet; performed as Maria in Fountains of Bakhchisarai, as Nina in Masquerade, as 1 of 3 soloists in Les Sylphides, as one of stepsisters in Cinderella; made debut as Giselle in London, 1961; danced 1st Odette-Odile in Swan Lake at Kirov Theatre, Leningrad, 1964; performed in Internat. Festival Ballet, London, 1964; appeared with Kirov in Vienna, Italy and London; guest appearance in Giselle with Netherlands Nat. Ballet, Amsterdam, 1966; danced in Vienna, 1969; joined Am. Ballet Theatre, N.Y.C., 1970; made Am. debut in Giselle at N.Y.C. Center, 1970; danced in Coppelia, Lilac Garden; appeared in duet in The River; appeared as the siren in The Miraculous Mandarin, as Juliet in Romeo and Juliet; also danced in La Sylphide, Les Sylphides, Swan Lake. Recipient Gold medal at internat. ballet competition, Varna, Bulgaria; named Honored Artist of Russian Fedn., 1969. Address: care Am Ballet Theatre 888 7th Av New York City NY 10019

MAKI, ANTONIA MARIA CIANCARELLI (MRS. THOMAS NESTOR MAKI), physician; b. Milford, Mass., Dec. 30, 1940; d. Primalto and Elisa Maria (Mucciarone) Ciancarelli; B.S. cum laude, Jackson Coll., 1962; M.D., Tufts U., 1966; m. Thomas Nestor Maki, Aug. 8, 1970. Med. intern R.I. Hosp., Providence, 1966-67, resident, 1967-70, fellow in hematology, 1970-71; staff supervising physician in internal medicine R.I. Med. Center, Howard, 1971-74; personnel health physician R.I. Hosp., Providence, 1969—. Diplomate Am. Bd. Internal Medicine. Mem. A.C.P., R.I. Employed Physicians Assn. (sec. 1971-72), Phi Beta Kappa. Home: 511 Union St Franklin MA 02038 Office: RI Med Center Box 1 Howard RI 02834

MAKIELSKI, SALLY KIMBALL (MRS. STANISLAW JOHN MAKIELSKI), health planner; b. Ft. Defiance, Ariz., Nov. 23, 1938; d. Solon Toothaker and Hannah Jackson (Price) Kimball; B.A., Barnard Coll., 1960; M.A., Columbia, 1961, Ph.D., 1965; M. Planning and Urban Design, U. Va., 1968; m. Stanislaw John Makielski, June 14, 1963. Asst. prof. dept. biol. scis. Loyola U., New Orleans, 1970-72; health planner New Orleans Area Health Planning Council, 1972—. Faculty Research grantee, Loyola U., 1971-72; Pub. Health predoctoral fellow in genetics, 1961-64. Mem. Lepidopterists Soc., Am. Soc. Cell Biology, A.A.A.S., Sigma Xi. Home: 5025 Dryades St New Orleans LA 70115 Office: 333 St Charles Av New Orleans LA 70115

MAKK, EVA HOLUSA (MRS. AMERICO MAKK), painter; b. Ethiopia, Africa, Dec. 1, 1933; d. Bert Alan and Julie Elizabeth (Ribenyi) Holusa; Agrl. Engr., Acad. Fine Arts, Paris, France, 1946-50; m. Americo Makk, Oct. 18, 1950; 1 son, Americo B. Came to U.S., 1962, naturalized, 1967. Prof. painting Acad. Fine Arts, Sao Paulo, Brazil, 1950-62; ofcl. hist. painter for Brazilian Govt., 1956-62; chmn. Internat. Carnegie Exhibit, N.Y.C., 1966-67. Exhibited in internat. one-man shows at Rome, Italy, 1949, Sao Paulo, 1950, 56, 59, Rio de Janeiro, Brazil, 1956, 59, Monte Carlo, Monaco, 1968, Paris, France, 1969, N.Y.C., 1963-67, Miami, Fla., 1968-73, Munich, Germany, 1972, Lisbon, Spain, 1973; executed numerous murals in govt. palace, Pernanbuco, Manaus, Brazil, various chs., basilicas; represented in permanent collections at Sao Paulo, Rio de Janeiro, Rome, Budapest, Monaco, others. Mem. UNICEF, Art for Heart, Honolulu, co-chmn., 1971—. Recipient numerous awards, prizes. Mem. Fifty Am. Artists Assn., Am.-Hungarian Art Assn. (dir.), World Fedn. Hungarian Artists, Am. Profl. Art League Assn. Paulista De Imprensa Brazil. Address: 1515 Laukahi St Honolulu HI 96821

MAKLE, VIVIAN BROWN, educator; b. East Orange, N.J., Mar. 25, 1915; d. Walter Richard and Emily Adele (Brown) Brown; B.S., N.Y. U., 1940; M.A., Seton Hall U., 1973; m. Lawrence Cartha Makle, June 30, 1938 (div. Mar. 1966); children—Judith (Mrs. Sidney A. Banks, Jr.), Adelbert W. Owner, dir. Busy Bee Nursery Sch., East Orange, 1946-55; kindergarten tchr. Coe's Pl. and Quitman St. Schs., Newark, 1955-58; title I project coordinator Newark Sch. Dist., 1958—. Mem. citizens adv. com. Bloomfield (N.J.) Coll., 1971—; mem. East Orange Model Cities Council, 1969-72. Mem. East Orange Bd. Edn., 1970—. Bd. dirs. Extension Br. YMCA Oranges and Maplewood, N.J.; bd. dirs. TLC Day Care Center, 1971—, pres., 1972; bd. dirs., chmn. Ill Service, 1969—. Recipient Outstanding Citizen award Civic Action League, 1968, Citizens Com. East Orange, 1969, East Orange C. of C., 1969, 5th Ward Civic Club, 1969, East Orange Tchrs. Assn., 1970, Boys Club Newark, 1972, N.J. Fed. Colored Women's Clubs, 1970, Outstanding and Dedicated Service award N.J. Fedn. Colored Women's Clubs, 1971. Outstanding Contbns. award Quitman St. Sch. Parents, 1971; named Woman of Year, Worrall Publs., East Orange, 1974. Mem. Nat., N.J. assns. sch. bd. mems., Nat., N.J., Newark tchrs. assns., N.J. Fedn. Colored Women's Clubs (community improvement chmn. 1970—), Le Cercle Civique. Presbyn. (elder 1971—). Home: 32 Park End Pl East Orange NJ 07018 Office: 21 Quitman St Newark NJ 07013

MAKOFSKY, LOUISE RAINER (MRS. ABRAHAM MAKOFSKY), social worker; b. Union Springs, Ala., Sept. 20, 1922; d. Joel H. and Louise (Wright) Rainer; A.B., Ala. Coll., 1944; M.S., Columbia, 1950; m. Abraham Makofsky, June 7, 1969. Cons. in adoption Ala. Dept. Pensions and Security, 1950-56; field supr. Md. Dept. Pub. Welfare, 1956-63; cons. Head Start Program, U.S. Govt., 1964; dir. Baltimore County Dept. Social Services, Towson, Md., 1972—. Jane Abbot Meml. fellow, 1949-50. Mem. Md. Council Local Adminstrs. Social Services (pres. 1974), League Women Voters, Nat. Assn. Social Workers (chmn. Task Force on Racism), Civil Liberties Union, Common Cause. Contbr. articles profl. jours. Home: 6602 Copper Ridge Dr Baltimore MD 21209 Office: 620 York Rd Towson MD 21204

MALACH, SHIRLEY (MRS. HARRY ROBERT BOCKOFF), lawyer; b. Alpena, Mich., July 29, 1925; d. Isaac and Getta (Weisman) Malach; LL.B., 1948, Wayne State U., 1948; m. Harry Robert Bockoff, Feb. 2, 1962. Admitted to Mich. bar, 1948; mem. firm Bockoff & Bockoff, 1962—. Mem. State Bar Mich. Republican. Jewish religion. Home: 17245 West Hampton Rd Southfield MI 48075 Office: City National Bank Bldg Detroit MI 48226

MALAMUD, PHYLLIS CAROLE, journalist; b. Bklyn., Sept. 15, 1938; d. Louis and Hannah (Unterman) Malamud; B.A., Coll. City N.Y., 1960; postgrad. (Russell Sage Found. fellow), Washington U., 1968-69. Publicity asst. Newsweek Mag., N.Y.C., 1960-62, bus. and feature researcher, 1962-65, feature reporter, 1965—, asso. editor, 1973—. Recipient Gavel award Am. Bar Assn., 1968. Home: 7 Lexington Av New York City NY 10010 Office: 444 Madison Av New York City NY 10022

MALAS, CORNELIA, bus. exec.; b. Cin.; d. John C. and Katherine (Farres) Malas; student U. Cin., 1940-42; bus. certificate Littleford Nelson Bus. Coll., 1943; student Schuster Martin Sch. Drama, 1943; certificate Patricia Stevens Modeling Sch., 1944; student Campbell Bus. Coll., 1956. Head central filing dept. Gruen Watch Co., Cin., 1945-50; expediter purchasing dept. MacGregor Sport Products, Cin., 1950-57; personnel asst. Eagle-Picher Industries, Inc., Cin., 1957—. Chmn., Rosie Reds Night at Crosley Field, Rooters Organized to Stimulate Interest and Enthusiasm in Cin. Reds Baseball Team, 1967, v.p., 1972, trustee, 1974—; mem. women's com. Nat. Gov.'s. Conf., 1968; mem. ticket com. Cin. Symphony Orch., 1968; publicity chmn. May Festival, 1969, mem. women's com., 1972-73; mem. Women's com. United Fine Arts, 1973; judge Jr., Achievement, 1965, 67. Mem. Nat. Secs. Assn. (pres. Ohio div. 1969-70), Internat. Women's Personnel Assn., Women's Personnel Assn. Cin. (dir.), Am. Mgmt. Assn., Internat. Platform Assn., Alpha Delta Pi. Clubs: Hyde Park Golf and Country, Cincinnati, Internat. Toastmistress, Williams (pres. 1966-67). Home: 3138 Parkview Av Cincinnati OH 45213 Office: 580 Walnut St Cincinnati OH 45202

MALASCHAK, DOLORES BOYER (MRS. ANTHONY MICHAEL MALASCHAK), author, educator; b. Illmo, Mo., Mar. 19, 1923; d. John Stanley and Ida Jane (Garrison) Boyer; B.S. in Edn. and English, So. Ill. U., 1972; m. Anthony Michael Malaschak, May 17, 1941; children—Gary, Susan Mondy, Michael, David, Anne. Seamstress, Angelica Jacket Co., St. Louis, 1941, St. Louis Ordinance Plant, 1942-45; nurse aide Faith Hosp., St. Louis, 1956-60; instr. creative writing Belleville (Ill.) Area Coll., 1972-73; tchr. high sch. dist. 187, Cahokia, Ill., 1972-73. Mem. Cahokia Jarrot Mansion Hist. Soc. Com., 1970-73; adivser to Creative Com. Cahokia Jr. Women, 1965—. Trustee Cahokia Library Bd. Mem. Fedn. Am. Tchrs., Avalon World Arts Acad., Friend St. Clair Hist. Soc., St. Louis Poetry Center, Nat. League Am. Pen Women, McKendree Writer's Assn., Cahokia Bus. and Profl. Women. Methodist. Author: Run in the Morning, 1968; Greenwood Days, 1974. Contbr. articles to newspaper columns. Home: 16 St Lambert Dr Cahokia IL 62206

MALDONADO, AIDA QUINONES (MRS. TEODORO MALDONADO), agrl. extension agt.; b. Cagnas, P.R., Nov. 11, 1934; d. Marcos and Dolores (Alejandro) Quinones; B.S., U. P.R., 1957, M.S. in Extension Edn., 1969; Ph.D. in Home Econs. Edn. (J.C. Penney nat. fellow 1970), Pa. State U., 1972; m. Teodoro Maldonado, Nov. 19, 1960; children—Teodoro. Orlando, Aidita. Agt. home econs. Agrl. Extension Service, U. P.R., Las Piedras, 1957—. Local pres. P.R. Cancer League Prevention, 1966; counselor Las Piedras Civic Club, 1961-63. Recipient Distinguished Service award Nat. Assn. Extension Home Economists, 1969. Mem. P.R. Farmers Assn., Am. (state v.p. 1974), P.R. home econ. assns., Nat., P.R. (treas. 1968-69, 69-70, pres. elect 1973-74) extension agts. in home econs. assns., Nat. Soc. for Nutrition Edn., Nat. Fedn. Bus. and Profl. Women's Clubs, Omicron Nu, Pi Lambda Theta, Alpha Epsilon Phi. Roman Catholic. Club: Exchange (Las Piedras, P.R.) (v.p. 1969). Home: 6 Lastorres Las Piedras PR 00661 Office: JC Barbosa Lastiedras PO Box 286 Las Piedras PR 00671

MALDONADO DE ADAIME, ADA LUZ, govt. ofcl.; b. Ponce, P.R., Feb. 23, 1927; d. Rito and Justina (Sierra) Maldonado; B. Comml. Edn., U. P.R., 1949; m. Jose Juan Adaime, Mar. 3, 1950; children—Yasmin (Mrs. Antonio Ruiz Ruiz), Jose Juan, Hamed. Employer relations rep. P.R. Dept. Labor, Ponce, 1954—, dir. employment sub-office Catholic U., 1964—. Mem. Internat. Assn. Personnel Employment Securtiy. Roman Catholic. Home: 148 Atocha St Ponce PR 00731

MALE, MARY EILEEN, editor; b. Schenectady, Sept. 22, 1949; d. William John and Dorothy Frances (Hubbard) Male; student Utica Coll., 1967-69; B.A. in Journalism and English, Syracuse U., 1971.

Copy editor columnist Design News, Cahners Pub. Co., Boston, 1971—. Mem. Women in Communications, Inc. (sec. chpt. 1973-74), Am. Soc. Bus. Press Editors. Mem. Reformed Ch. Home: 68 Daniels St Franklin MA 02038 Office: 221 Columbus Av Boston MA 02116

MALEBRANCHE, JEANNETTE FONG YOUNG (MRS. REGINALD MALEBRANCHE), occupational therapist; b. San Rafael, Cal., Dec. 25, 1935; d. Tom Chew and Joan Chai (Chew) Fong; student, U. Cal. at Berkeley, 1953-55; B.A., San Jose State U., 1957; m. Reginald Malebranche, Sept. 8, 1965; children—Brian Young, Philippe, Michelle. Supr. occupational therapy Ross (Cal.) Gen. Hosp., 1960, VA Day Treatment Center, Ft. Miley, San Francisco, 1960-66; elementary tchr. St. Peter's Sch., San Antonio, 1967-68; occupational therapist, cons. Beverly Manor Convalescent Home, Carmel, Cal., 1972-73. Active P.T.A., Palma High Sch., Salinas, Cal., Santa Catalina Sch., Monterey, Cal. Mem. Am., No. Cal. (dist. III election chmn. 1973) occupational therapy assns. Club: Ft. Ord (Cal.) Officers Wives, MEDDAC Officers Wives (Ft. Ord). Home: 265 Ardennes Circle Fort Ord CA 93941

MALEK, ZENA BELLA (MRS. LEONARD MALEK), psychologist; b. Chgo., Nov. 12, 1928; d. Jacob and Tillie (Tarakoff) Chaitman; A.A., Wright Jr. Coll., 1948; B.A., Roosevelt U., 1950; postgrad. Loyola U., 1950-52; Ph.D., U. So. Cal., 1961; m. Leonard Malek, July 9, 1949; children—Shana Elaine, Aviva Beth. Psychiat. social worker Mental Health Center, Chgo., 1950-52; teaching asst. U. So. Cal., 1955-56; intern Reiss Davis Clinic for Child Guidance, Los Angeles, 1956-57, Los Angeles Psychiat. Services, 1957-58; psychologist Rancho Los Amigos Hosp., Downey, Cal., 1958-64; pvt. practice psychology, Los Angeles, 1964—. Cons., Zahm Sch., Los Angeles, 1959-65, Marriage Guidance Inst., 1960—; instr., lectr. U. So. Cal., 1962-63. Recipient Hattie Callner award, 1949. Nat. Inst. Mental Health fellow, 1959-60. Mem. Am., Western, Cal. psychol. assns., Sigma Xi, Psi Chi. Address: 3650 S Bentley Av Los Angeles CA 90034

MALETTA, ROSE HELEN (MRS. VINCENT S. CONTI), physician; b. N.Y.C., Apr. 25, 1916; d. Frank and Carmel (Ponterio) Maletta; student Hunter Coll., 1933-36; M.D., U. Naples, 1941; m. Vincent S. Conti, Mar. 4, 1943; children—Vincent R., Gloria (Mrs. Stephen C. Foster). Intern, Met. Hosp. Center, N.Y.C., 1941-42; resident Met. Hosp., Flower-Fifth Av. Hosp., N.Y.C., 1942-44; practice medicine, specializing in anesthesiology, N.Y.C., 1944-71; Ft. Lauderdale, Fla., 1971—; dir. anesthesia St. John's Hosp., Queens, N.Y.C., 1945-50; dir. anesthesia Lutheran Hosp., Bklyn., 1950-56, cons. anesthesiology, 1956-71; asst. prof. anesthesiology N.Y. Med. Coll., 1967-71; asst. attending anesthesiology Met. Hosp. Center, N.Y.C., 1967-71; anesthesiologist Broward Gen. Med. Center, Ft. Lauderdale, 1971—, Holy Cross Hosp., Imperial Point Hosps. Mem. A.M.A., Fla., Broward County med. socs., Am., Fla. socs. anesthesiologists. Clubs: Lago Mar Country, Coral Ridge Country. Home: 3550 Galt Ocean Dr Fort Lauderdale FL 33308 Office: 4001 N Ocean Dr Fort Lauderdale FL 33308

MALIN, JOYCE ELAINE, med. librarian; b. Campbell, Mo., Apr. 8, 1936; d. John Arthur and Vergie Marie (Polsgrove) Malin; A.B., Eastern Mich. U., 1958; A.M. L.S., U. Mich., 1963. Faculty-tchr. Birmingham (Mich.) Bd. Edn., 1958-64; faculty-asst. to librarian Macomb County (Mich.) Community Coll., 1964-65; librarian Detroit Osteo. Hosp. Corp., 1965-67; dir. med. library Henry Ford Hosp., Detroit, 1967—. Mem. alumni bd. Eastern Mich. U., 1963-66. Mem. Med. Library Assn., U. Mich. (life), Eastern Mich. U. (life) alumni assns., Pi Kappa Delta. Home: 1022 E 6th St Royal Oak MI 48067 Office: Med Library Henry Ford Hosp 2799 W Grand Blvd Detroit MI 48202

MALIS, LOUISE (MRS. LOUIS A. MALIS), pub. relations ofcl.; b. Atlanta, Apr. 6, 1921; d. Benjamin and Helen (Aarons) Clein; student Wright Jr. Coll., Chgo., 1937-39, Northwestern U., 1939-40; m. Louis Albert Malis, Feb. 20, 1943; children—Susan Linda, Amy Beth. Mem. P.T.A., 1949—, various local council positions 1949-54, sch. edn. chmn. Chgo. region Ill. Congress Parents and Tchrs., 1954-58, v.p. Chgo. region, 1958-60, pres., 1960-62; pub. relations, financial devel. exec. Inst. Internat. Edn., Chgo., 1962-71; dir. pub. relations Rehab. Inst. Chgo., 1973—. Cons., Frank H. Cassell & Assos., 1973. Mem. curriculum council Chgo. Bd. Edn., 1954-58, 60-62; sec. Mayor's Commn. on Sch. Bd. Nominations, 1960, 61; nominated by Mayor's Commn. on Sch. Bd. Nominations for vacancies on Chgo. Bd. Edn., 1962, 63, 64, 69; mem. Chgo. Bd. Edn., 1964—; mem. exec. com. Council of Great City Schs.; mem. steering com. Midwest Program on Airborne TV Instn., Chgo., 1960-62; Chgo. del. to Conf. on Out-of-Sch., Unemployed Youth, Washington, 1961; chmn. Chgo. Ednl. Leadership Program, 1973-74; mem. Chgo. com. Ill. Sesquicentennial. Bd. dirs. Jewish Children's Bur., Chgo., 1970-72; bd. govs. Aspira, Inc., 1973—. Mem. Nat. (hon. life), Ill. (hon. life) congresses parents and tchrs. Democrat. Jewish religion. Contbr. articles to ednl. publs. Home: 5757 N Sheridan Rd Chicago IL 60660

MALITSON, HARRIET HUTZLER, astronomer; b. Richmond, Va., June 30, 1926; d. Maurice Leon and Clare Martha (Levy) Hutzler; A.B., Goucher Coll., 1947; M.S., U. Mich., 1951; postgrad. U. Md., 1962-65; m. Irving Herschel Malitson, June 17, 1951; children—Paul Henry, Helen Gail. Physicist, Nat. Bur. Standards, Washington, 1947-49, 51-52, Naval Research Lab., Washington, 1952-57; aerospace technologist, solar radio astronomer NASA, Goddard Space Flight Center, Greenbelt, Md., 1960—. Recipient Aerospace Edn. award, 1970, Radio Astronomy Explorer group award, 1968, both Goddard Space Flight Center. Fellow Royal Astron. Soc. (Eng.); mem. Internat. Astron. Union, Internat. Union Radio Sci., Am. Astron. Soc., Goucher Alumnae Club Washington (corr. sec. 1970-72, treas. 1972-73, v.p. 1973-74). Contbr. articles profl. jours. Home: 13315 Magellan Av Rockville MD 20853 Office: Code 693 Goddard Space Flight Center Greenbelt MD 20771

MALLAN, JEAN MARGARET, educator; b. Mt. Vernon, N.Y., Aug. 10, 1930; d. Bernard Kane and Emma M. (Feld) Mallan; B.A., U. Tex., 1951; M.A., So. Ill. U., 1960; Ph.D., Purdue U., 1964. Chemist, U.S. Dept. Agr., Peoria, Ill., 1954-58; research chemist Firestone Tire & Rubber Co., Akron, O., 1964-69; asst. prof. chemistry Kent State U., Stark-Canton, O., 1969-73, U. Ala., Birmingham, 1973—. Mem. Am. Chem. Soc. Home: 2201 Rushmore Birmingham AL 35226

MALLARD, MARY ELIZABETH KEITH (MRS. STEVE HODGES MALLARD), librarian; b. Selma, N.C., Sept. 17, 1915; d. William Herbert and Mary Kate (Cameron) Keith; A.B., East Carolina Tchrs. Coll., 1936; library certificate East Carolina U., 1965; m. Steve Hodges Mallard, Dec. 26, 1937; children—Merle (Mrs. Benjamin Monroe Morris), Patsy (Mrs. Howard McCoy Braxton). Tchr., Wallace (N.C.) Elementary Sch., 1936-38, Long Creek Grady Sch., Burgaw, N.C., 1939, Rose Hill (N.C.) Elementary Sch., 1946-57, Beulaville (N.C.) Elementary Sch., 1958-59; librarian Wallace-Rose Hill High Sch., Teachey, N.C., 1960-66, James Sprunt Inst., Kenansville, N.C., 1967, Charity High Sch., Rose Hill, 1968-69, Charity Jr. High Sch., Rose Hill, 1970—. Bd. govs. Emma Anderson Meml. Chapel, Topsail Beach, N.C. Mem. Nat. (life), N.C. (dir. 1966-69, county pres. 1971) edn. assns., N.C. Assn. Educators (life, dist. pres. 1971, dist. chmn. Mary Morrow scholarship 1968-69, Distinguished Service award), Eastern Dist. (pres. 1964), N.C. (exec. com. 1964-66) classroom tchrs. assns., Nat. Assn. Classroom Tchrs. (del. 1965-71), Southeastern, N.C. High Sch. (exec. bd. 1961-66) library assns., N.C. Assn. Sch. Librarians, Women of Ch. (pres. 1952). Presbyn. Mem. Order Eastern Star (past matron). Clubs: Wallace Woman's, Green Thumb Garden (Wallace, N.C.). Home: 227 College St Wallace NC 28466 Office: Charity Jr High Sch Rose Hill NC 28458

MALLARY, GERTRUDE ROBINSON (MRS. R. DEWITT MALLARY), civic worker; b. Springfield, Mass., Aug. 19, 1902; d. George Edward and Jennie (Slater) Robinson; student Bennett Coll., 1921-22, U. Conn., 1941-42; m. R. DeWitt Mallary, Sept. 15, 1923; children—R. DeWitt, Richard Walker. Co-owner, partner Mallary Farm, Bradford, Vt., 1936—; mem. Vt. Ho. of Reps., 1953-56, sec. agr. com., 1953, mem. appropriations com., 1955; mem. Vt. Senate, 1957-58, mem. appropriations com., clk. pub. health com., vice chmn. edn. com., mem. interim legislative com. for study nursing, 1958-59. Pres., Jr. League, Springfield, 1931-33; chmn. Springfield Council Social Agys., 1938-40; mem. Vt. Bd. Recreation, 1959-65; trustee Fairlee (Vt.) Pub. Library, 1953—, Asa Bloomer Found., 1963-71, Orange County 4-H Found., 1969-71; trustee Justin Smith Morrill Found., 1964-71, pres. 1968-71; pres. Vt. Holstein Club., 1951-53; mem. Vt. Gov.'s Commn. for Library Services, 1966; regional v.p. Nat. Beef Council, 1960-64; mem. adv. com. Swift Water council Girl Scouts U.S.A., 1971—; Vt. chmn. Nat. Library Week, 1973. Mem. Vt. Library Trustees Assn. (pres. 1965-67), Vt., Bradford (pres. 1965-69) hist. socs. Editor: New Eng. Holstein Bull., 1947-50. Address: Mallary Farm Bradford VT 05033

MALLERY, MARY SILCOX (MRS. RICHARD CARRUTH MALLERY), librarian; b. Utica, N.Y., Nov. 9, 1936; d. William H. and Maybelle (Jones) Silcox; B.S. in L.S., Simmons Coll., 1958; M.S. in L.S., Drexel Inst. Tech., 1967; m. Richard Carruth Mallery, July 16, 1960. Br. librarian U.S. Army, Ft. Chaffee, Ark., 1958-59; bookmobile librarian U.S. Army, Valley Forge Gen. Hosp., Phila. Air Defense Command, 1959-60; head librarian Lansdale (Pa.) Pub. Library, 1960-67; extension librarian Montgomery County Norristown (Pa.) Pub. Library, 1967-69; area librarian Western Md. Pub. Libraries, 1970—. Mem. Am., Md. library assns., Beta Phi Mu. Home: 533 Brown Av Hagerstown MD 21740 Office: 100 S Potomac St Hagerstown MD 21740

MALLERY, SYLVIA E., educator; b. Albany, N.Y., Mar. 10, 1934; d. Roger Henry and Margaret (Provost) Mallery; B.A., Syracuse U., 1955; Ed.M., Harvard, 1957; profl. diploma Tchrs. Coll. Columbia, 1967. Prof. social sci. State U. N.Y., Cobleskill, 1958—. Instr., Tchrs. Coll. Columbia, summer 1966. Mem. U.S. Nat. Com. for Early Childhood Edn., 1969—. Mem. Kappa Delta Pi, Pi Lambda Theta. Home: 12 Washington Av Cobleskill NY 12043

MALLET, DOROTHY BERTHA MARGOLIS (MRS. LOUIS DAVID MALLET), food co. exec.; b. Pitts., Sept. 20, 1913; d. Robert and Minnie (Price) Margolis; B.S., Carnegie Mellon U., 1935; M.S., U. Pitts., 1964; m. Louis David Mallet, June 6, 1937 (dec. 1967); children—Anne (Mrs. Stanley Gordon), Eleanor (Mrs. David Bergholz), Rita (Mrs. Gary Reiswig), Robert. With Mothers Assistance Fund, Pitts., 1935-38, Allegheny County Bd. Assistance, Pitts., 1938-41; mem. Upward Bound project Carnegie Mellon U., Pitts., 1965-67; pres. Mallet & Co., Carnegie, Pa., 1967—. Mem. Nat. Assn. Social Workers, Am. Bakers Assn., Am. Soc. Bakery Engrs., Met. Pres.'s Orgn. Home: 1444 Beechwood Blvd Pittsburgh PA 15217 Office: Box 474 Carnegie PA 15106

MALLEY, KATHLEEN JUNE MCRORIE (MRS. TERENCE MALLEY), editor; b. Leavenworth, Kan., Jan. 9, 1937; d. Henry Albert and Laura Beatrice (Lonie) McRorie; B.A. magna cum laude, Whitman Coll., 1959; M.A. in Comparative Lit., U. Wash., 1961; m. Terence Malley, Mar. 17, 1960. Editorial sec. dept. English, U. Wash., 1962-64; with Warner Paperback Library, N.Y.C., 1965—, editor, 1967-73, mng. editor, 1973—. Committeewoman Kings County Democratic Party, 1970-72. Mem. Phi Beta Kappa. Home: 191 Willoughby St Brooklyn NY 11201 Office: 75 Rockefeller Plaza New York City NY 10019

MALLICOAT, LOIS EVELYN, advt. co. exec.; b. Oak Park, Ill., Dec. 12, 1926; d. Metford Edwin and Lorene Lillian (Davis) Mallicoat; B.S. in Journalism, U. Ill., 1950. Prodn. mgr. Tempo, Inc., Chgo., 1954-57; asst. prodn. mgr. McCann-Erickson, Inc., Los Angeles, 1961-66; print prodn. mgr. Parker Advt. Inc., Palos Verdes Peninsula, Cal., 1966—. Mem. Los Angeles Prodn. Mgrs. Club. Home: 3553 Emerald Torrance CA 90503 Office: 609 Deep Valley Dr Palos Verdes Peninsula CA 90274

MALLINCKRODT, MARTHA GRAVES (MRS. CHARLES O. MALLINCKRODT), club woman; b. Louisville, Dec. 2, 1905; d. Allison and Ellen (Monks) Graves; student N.Y. Sch. Applied Design for Women, 1924, U. Louisville, 1924; m. Charles Olcott Mallinckrodt, Oct. 3, 1934; children—Charles Olcott, Ellen Louise. Active Jr. Service League, Summit, N.J., 1941-51, Girl Scouts U.S.A. and Boy Scouts Am., 1945-46, 49-55; dir. Hobby Show Palos Verdes Woman's Club, 1953-54, asst. dir., 1954-55; dir. Sr. Assembly of Palos Verdes Estates, 1953-54; dir. Palos Verdes Community Arts Assn., 1957-59; founding mem. Palos Verdes Surf-Writers, 1957, treas., 1957, asst. v.p., program adviser, 1958, 59; hospitality chmn. Palos Verdes Peninsula chpt. Am. Assn. for UN, 1958-59; vol. staff Children's Hosp., Los Angeles, 1958—; mem. Los Angeles Mayor's Citizens Com., 1964. Mem. Jr. League Los Angeles, Woodland Hills Republican Women Federated, Aux. I.E.E.E., Friends Leonis Abode. Clubs: Laurel Garden; Old Treasures (chmn. treasure mart 1965). Home: 3193-A Buena Vista Laguna Hills CA 92653

MALLORY, PHYLLIS JANE NUSZ (MRS. EDWARD SCOTT MALLORY), educator; b. Lodi, Cal., Dec. 16, 1941; d. Fred Henry and Esther Emma (Enzminger/Job) Nusz; B.A., U. Pacific, 1963, M.A., 1965; m. Edward Scott Mallory, Mar. 14, 1970. Asst. dir. student affairs Bakersfield (Cal.) Coll., 1965-68, campus center coordinator, 1965-68, prof. speech, 1968—, chmn. dept. speech, 1968—. Adviser, Cal. Community Coll. Student Govt. Assn., 1966-67. Mem. Council Communication Studies vol. San Joaquin Community Hosp. Aux. Mem. Cal. Tchrs. Assn., Am. Assn. U. Profs., Western Speech Communication Assn., Speech Communication Assn., U. Pacific Alumni Assn. (area coordinator Kern County 1969-70), Bakersfield Coll. Faculty Assn. (pres. 1972-73), Bakersfield Masterwork, Chamber Singers, Delta Kappa Gamma, Alpha Chi Omega. Lutheran. Office: 1801 Panorama Dr Bakersfield CA 93305

MALLOY, AUDREY FRANCES (MRS. THADDEUS ANTHONY MALLOY), educator; b. Pitts., Mar. 22, 1937; d. Francis John and Stella Thresea (Cygrymus) Eiben; diploma in nursing St. Francis Gen. Hosp., 1958; postgrad. U. Pitts., 1966-68; B.S., Cal. State Coll., California, Pa., 1969, Ed.M., 1972; m. Thaddeus Anthony Malloy, June 6, 1959; children—Marc Francis, Mary Eileen, Christine Marie. Emergency room nurse St. Francis Hosp., Pitts., 1958-60; gen. duty nurse S. Side Hosp., Pitts., 1961-65, St. Clair Hosp., Pitts., 1967-68; psychiat. nursing instr. Mayview State Hosp., Bridgeville, Pa., 1969—. Owner, Malloy Stable, Eighty-Four, Pa., 1969—. Brownie troop leader Washington County, Pa., 1971; Mem. Am., Pa. nurses assns., U.S. Trotting Assn., Cal. State Coll. Alumni Assn. Republican. Roman Catholic. Club: Old Crows Womens (California, Pa.). Home: Box 648 Eighty-Four PA 15330 Office: Mayview State Hospital Bridgeville PA 15017

MALLOY, IRMA THOMAS (MRS. JAMES E. MALLOY), counselor; b. Stockton, Ala., Aug. 30, 1936; d. Tom and Alberta (Askew) Thomas; B.A., Tenn. State U., 1957, M.S., 1967; postgrad. Temple U., 1965, U. Houston, 1972-73; m. James E. Malloy, July 15, 1958; children—Darryl Lynn, Christopher Thomas. Social caseworker Ala. Indsl. Sch., Mt. Meigs, Ala., 1957-58, Womens Christian Alliance, Phila., 1960-63; counselor Daniel Boone Pub. Sch., Phila., 1964-65; asst. dir. Harris Home for Children, Huntsville, Ala. 1965-66; dean of women Dillard U., New Orleans, 1966-68; counselor Tex. So. U., Houston, 1969-71, dir. Counseling Center, 1971—, asso. dir. counseling and testing, 1972-73. Dir. Lady Bronze Cosmetic Salon, Houston. Troop leader Girl Scouts U.S.A., 1959-60; chmn. curriculum and guidance com. James H. Law Elementary Sch. P.T.A. Bd. dirs. Tex. So. U. Model Cities Cuney Homes Tutoring Program. Mem. Am. Personnel and Guidance Assn., Nat. Vocational Guidance Assn., Am. Sch. Counselor Assn., Coll. Student Personnel Assn., Delta Sigma Theta (chmn. mental health com.), N.A.A.C.P., Tenn. State U. Alumni Assn., United Meth. Women (treas.). Home: 4019 Redwin Circle Houston TX 77047 Office: 3201 Wheeler Av Houston TX 77004

MALLOY, MARTHA REUSS, ednl. adminstr.; b. Cin., Oct. 2, 1942; d. Carl William and Ruth (Oexman) Reuss; A.B., Denison U., 1964; M.A., Ohio State U., 1968; 1 dau., Melissa Lynn. Tchr. Latin and English, Springfield (O.) pub. schs., 1964-65; tchr. Latin, Upper Arlington High Sch., Columbus, O., 1965-68; dir. placement N. Ky. State Coll., Highland Heights, 1970—, also instr. psychology, counselor. Mem. Cin. Personnel Assn., So. Coll. Placement Assn., Ky. Placement Officers, Eta Sigma Phi, Kappa Delta Pi, Psi Chi, Phi Beta Kappa. Home: 241 S Ashbrook St Fort Mitchell KY 41017 Office: Northern Kentucky State College Highland Heights KY 41076

MALLOY, MARY ANN MALONE (MRS. JOHN R. MALLOY), internist; b. Oak Park, Ill., Feb. 10, 1942; d. James Fabian and Bernadine Catherine (Melnanow) Malone; B.A., Vassar Coll., 1963; M.D., Northwestern U., 1967; m. John R. Malloy, Oct. 21, 1967. Intern, Chgo. Wesley Meml. Hosp., 1967-68; chief resident Passavant Meml. Hosp., Chgo., 1970-71; fellow in cardiology VA Research Hosp., Chgo., 1971—; attending staff Meml. Hosp. Dupage County, 1972—; clin. asst. in medicine Northwestern U. Med. Sch., Chgo., 1970—; clin. asso. in medicine Loyola Stritch Sch. Medicine. Bd. dirs. Dupage County chpt. Am. Heart Assn. Home: 21 Cambridge Dr Oak Brook IL 60521 Office: 135 S Kenilworth St Elmhurst IL 60126

MALMBORG, ELEANOR DONALD, educator; b. N.Y.C., July 9, 1930; d. William John Alexander and Edith (King) Donald; B.A., Wells Coll., Aurora, N.Y., 1952; M.A., Columbia, 1957, Ed.D., 1962; m. Knute Eugene Malmberg, Jr., June 29, 1963. Sec. to asso. editor Sch. Exec., Buttenheim Pub. Corp., N.Y.C., 1953-54; exec. sec. research Am. Sch. Pub. Corp., N.Y.C., 1954-59; project asso. Tchrs. Coll., Columbia, 1959-60; research asst. research div., N.E.A., Washington, 1960-64; staff asso. edn. Am. Assn. U. Women, Washington, 1964-71; program coordinator activities Nat. Ret. Tchrs. Assn., Washington, 1971-74, coordinator nat. activities, 1974—. Mem. Wells Coll. Alumnae Assn. (2d v.p. 1966-72, pres. 1974—), Nat. Council Adminstrn. Women in Edn., N.E.A., Am. Assn. Sch. Adminstrs., League Women Voters, Am. Ednl. Research Assn., D.C. Citizens for Better Pub. Edn., Nat. Com. for Support Pub. Schs. Episcopalian. Club: Wells College of Washington (pres. 1962-64). Contbr. articles to profl. publs. Home: 1900 Upshur St NW Washington DC 20011 Office: 1909 K St NW Washington DC 20006

MALONE, AUDREY JANE (MRS. WILLIAM JAMES MALONE), mag. editor; b. Mpls., Apr, 22, 1924; d. Raymond and Lillian Marie (Hanson) Snure; grad. high sch.; m. William James Malone, Jan. 12, 1947; children—James, Paul, Terry, Nancy, Joanne, David, Carl. Sec. Northwestern Nat. Life Ins. Co., Mpls., 1942-50; editor, pub. Harbor Lights, 1962—. Author: The Best of Harbor Lights, 1966; An Early Harvest (poems), 1967. Home and office: 1710 Oakwood Dr St Paul MN 55112

MALONE, JAMES DEOTHA, city ofcl.; b. Gallatin, Tenn., May 27, 1927; d. Harvey V. and Sadie L. (Fitts) Malone; B.A., Fisk U., 1949, M.A. (scholar), 1955; M.A., Tenn. State U., 1973, certificate library service, 1964; postgrad. Tech. Bus. Coll., 1955-56, Middle Tenn. State U., 1968-69, Trevecca Coll., 1971, Ala. State U., 1973-74, Tenn. Tech. U., 1973, U. Tenn., 1972; H.H.D., North Little Rock Coll., 1973. Tchr. Union High Sch., Gallatin, 1950-51, Union Elementary Sch., Gallatin, 1951-68, Union and Guild Schs., Gallatin, 1968-69; librarian Union Elementary Sch., 1964-68; instructional supr. intermediate grades Homebound Program, Sch. Unwed Mothers and Adult Basic Edn., Gallatin, 1970—; dir. Adult Basic Edn., Sumner County, Tenn., 1970—; vice-mayor City of Gallatin, 1969—; notary pub., 1958—; aux. sheriff Sumner County 1974. Cons. adult edn. Ala., Tenn., 1970-73; dir. Sumner County Headstart Program, 1966-70. Mem. adv. com. Vol. State Community Coll., 1973—; mem. adv. bd. Tenn. Assn. Licensed Practical Nurses, 1971-72; chmn. Sumner County Voter Registration Program, 1970—. Vice pres. Sumner County Democratic Women's Club, 1972-73. Bd. dirs. Gallatin (Tenn.) Day Care Center. Pepsi Cola Co. scholar, 1949. Recipient Human Relations award Citizens Humboldt, Tenn., 1971; Outstanding Woman of Year award Masons, 1972; Hon. Citizen awards Fayette, Miss., 1973, Indpls., 1974; Meritorious and Outstanding Contbns. in Adult Edn. award, 1974. Mem. Nat., Tenn. (dir.), Middle Tenn., Sumner County (chmn. human relations com. 1973) edn. assns., Tenn. Assn. Pub. Sch. Adult Edn. (pres. Middle Tenn. 1973-74), Tenn. Assn. Adult Educators, Austin Peay Area Suprs. Council (mem. nominating com. 1973-74), Phi Delta Kappa. Baptist (sr. choir 1954—, Sunday sch. tchr. 1968—, pres. Willing Workers Service Club 1968—). Home: 229 S Pardue Av Gallatin TN 37066 Office: 117 E Winchester St Gallatin TN 37066

MALONE, JEAN, educator; b. East Rochester, N.Y., July 2, 1918; d. Daniel Connor and Helen (Grant) Malone; B.A., Nazareth Coll. of Rochester N.Y., 1939; M.A. in Speech and Drama, Cornell U., 1943; Ph.D. in Speech Sci. and Pathology, U. Mich., 1954; m. James H. Loughery, May 24, 1974. From instr. to prof. Nazareth Coll., Rochester, 1943-60, pres. coll., 1960-73; asso. prof. speech pathology State U. N.Y. Coll. at Genesco, 1973—; vis. lectr. dept. speech Cath. U. Am., 1958, 59. Mem. adv. bd. on tchr. edn., certification and practice N.Y. Edn. Dept., U. State N.Y., 1963-66; mem. curriculum study com. for N.Y. State Colls. offering speech correction as major. Board of directors of Empire State Found. of Ind. Liberal Arts Colls. Recipient Nat. Cath. Theatre award National Catholic Theatre Conf., 1963. Mem. Am., N.Y. State speech and hearing assns., N.Y. State Speech Assn., Delta Kappa Gamma. Research and publs. in speech correction field. Home: 28 Court St Genesco NY 14454

MALONE, JEWELL WORKMAN (MRS. BEN F. MALONE), educator; b. Wichita Falls, Tex.; d. John E. and Caroline (Harty) Workman; B.S., N. Tex. U., 1941; M.Ed., W. Tex. U., 1951, postgrad.,

1951; postgrad. N.M. State U., U. Colo., San Jose State U., George Peabody Tchrs. Coll., Cal. State U.; m. Ben F. Malone, June 23, 1942; 1 dau., Patsy Caroline. Elementary tchr. New Liberty, Clay County, Tex., 1939-42, Argyle, Denton County, Tex., 1942-43, Letot, Dallas County, Tex., 1943-44, Deep Elm, N.C., 1944, Grand Prarie, Tex., 1945, Mountain Creek, Dallas County, 1945-46, Portales, N.M., 1946-49, Hereford, Tex., 1949-51, Bunavista Elementary, Borger, Tex., 1951-52; elementary tchr., prin. Huber Elementary, Borger, 1952-58; supr. primary grades, Borger, 1958-69, co-ordinator elementary curriculum, 1969—; summer dir., tchr. Headstart Program, Borger, 1966. Pres. city council P.T.A., Borger, 1965-67. Mem. Nat. (life), Tex. (life, pres. dist. 19 1971-73) congresses parents and tchrs., Tex. State Tchrs. Assn., Tex. P.T.A. (exceptional child service chmn.), Borger Educators Assn., N.E.A., Tex., Nat. assns. supervision and curriculum devel., Tex. Elementary Prins. and Suprs., Panhandle Sch. Leaders Assn., Internat. Reading Assn., Delta Kappa Gamma. Club: North Plains Knife and Fork (Borger). Home: 410 Santa Fe St Borger TX 79007 Office: 9th and Weatherly Sts Borger TX 79007

MALONE, RUTH MOORE (MRS. CHARLES EDMUND MALONE), author; b. Clarendon, Ark.; d. John Burton and Bessie (Branch) Moore; grad. Ward Belmont Coll., Nashville; student U. Ark.; m. Charles Edmund Malone; children—Margaret Branch (Mrs. Hubert de Marcy), Mary Bess (Mrs. Dick Lankford). Free lance writer Am. Home, Good Housekeeping, Parents, Sunday mags., Memphis Comml. Appeal, Shreveport (La.) Times, Ark. Democrat, Ark. Gazette, 1944-65; weekly syndicated feature Palmer Media Group, S. Ark. newspapers, 1959-65; asso. editor State Mag., 1961-62; food editor Holiday Inn mag., 1962—. Mem. Ark. Fedn. Womens Clubs (dist. pres. 1960-62), Nat. League Am. Pen Women (br. pres. 1966-68), Ark. Press Women, Nat. Fedn. Press Women, Pi Beta Phi (alumni pres. 1964-65). Author-editor: Where to Eat in the Ozarks—How its Cooked, 1961, 62, 64; Swiss Holiday Recipes, 1966, 69—; Holiday Inn Cookbook and Travel Guide, 1962-69; Holiday Inn International Cook and Travel Book, 1970—; Dogpatch Cook Book, 1970-72. Home: 1 River Ridge Rd Little Rock AR 72207 Office: PO Box 18216 3756 Lamar Av Holiday City Memphis TN 38118

MALONEY, SISTER ELIZABETH ANN, coll. pres.; b. Baldwin, N.Y., Dec. 12, 1925; d. Francis Xavier and Julia (Mueller) Maloney; A.B., Coll. of St. Elizabeth, 1947; M.A., Fordham U., 1951; postgrad. U. Notre Dame, summers 1957-61, full time 1960-61, Yeshiva U., 1962-65. Joined Sisters of Charity, 1947; tchr. math. St. John's High Sch., Paterson, N.J., 1949-58, St. Cecilia High Sch., Englewood, N.J., 1958-60; faculty Coll. of St. Elizabeth, Convent Station, N.J., 1961—, chmn. math. dept., 1963-69, asst. to pres., 1967-70, dean of studies, 1970-71, pres., 1971—. Bd. dirs. Assn. Ind. Colls. and Univs. N.J.; mem. council So. Province Sisters of Charity of St. Elizabeth; trustee N.J. Coll. Fund Assn. Mem. Am. Math. Assn. Address: Coll of St Elizabeth Convent Station NJ 07961

MALONEY, ELIZABETH MARY, educator; b. Eaton, N.Y., Sept. 5, 1922; d. Edward Farrell and Gena Louisa (Bagley) Maloney; B.S., Columbia U., 1951, M.A., 1952, Ed.D., 1966. Head nurse, Greystone Park, N.J., 1946-48, adminstr., 1952-54, supr., 1948-50, asst. dir., 1954-57; instr. Tchrs. Coll., Columbia U., 1957-66, asst. prof. nursing edn., 1966-71, asso. prof. nursing edn., 1971—, chmn. dept., 1971—. Cons. nursing Morristown Meml. Hosp. (N.J.), 1968—. Mem. N.Y.C. Prison Health Adv. Bd.; mem. quality of care mental health servies N.Y. Prison System. Served to lt. Nurse Corps, AUS, 1944-46. Mem. Am. Assn. Deans Univ. Schs. Nursing, Am. Assn. U. Profs., N.Y. Council on Nursing Edn. (chmn.), Am. Nurses Assn., Nat. League for Nursing, Pi Lambda Theta, Kappa Delta Pi. Editor: Interpersonal Relations in Nursing, 1969; clin. editor, Perspectives in Psychiatric Care, 1969. Contbr. articles to profl. jours. Home: 106 Morningside Dr New York City NY 10027 Office: 525 W 120th St New York City NY 10027

MALONEY, PAULETTE VERONICA (MRS. FRANK J. MALONEY), ednl. adminstr.; b. Jersey City, Apr. 29, 1941; d. John Joseph and Pauline Agnes (Kasyan) Wojciechowicz; A.B., Georgian Court Coll., 1962; postgrad. Rutgers U., 1963-64, Boudoin Coll., 1967; m. Frank J. Maloney. Tchr. math. Mommouth Regional High Sch., Shrewsbury, N.J., 1962-69; dir. placement, financial aid Georgian Court Coll., Lakewood, N.J., 1972—. Mem. Middle Atlantic Placement Assn., Met. N.Y. Coll. Placement Officers Assn., N.J. Assn. Financial Aid Officers, Nat. Assn. Student Financial Aid Officers, Georgian Court Alumni Assn. Club: Monmouth County (treas. 1973—). Home: 51 Silverside Av Little Silver NJ Office: Georgian Court College Lakewood NJ 08701

MALONZO, AIDA AVELINO (MRS. ROLANDO T. ABANGAN), physician; b. Philippines, Oct., 1939; d. Cipriano C. Malonzo and Basilia (Avelino) Malonzo; M.D., Univ. East, Philippines, 1964; m. Rolando T. Abangan, Oct. 26, 1965; 2 daus. Came to U.S., 1964. Intern, Highland Hosp., Strong Meml. Hosp., Rochester, N.Y., 1964-65; resident obstetrics and gynecology Vanderbilt U. Hosp., Nashville, 1965-66; resident obstetrics and gynecology U. Miss. Med. Center, Jackson, 1966-68, now asst. prof.; practice medicine specializing in obstetrics and gynecology, Jackson, Miss., 1968—; attending obstetrician-gynecologist U. Hosp., Jackson, Miss. Diplomate Am. Bd. Obstetrics and Gynecology. Fellow Am. Coll. Obstetricians and Gynecologists; mem. Miss. Obstet. and Gynecol. Soc., Am. Assn. U. Profs. Home: 5327 13th Pl Meridian MS 39301 Office: St Joseph Med Plaza Hwy 39 N Meridian MS 39301

MALOTT, ADELE RENEE LINDGREN (MRS. GENE E. MALOTT), editor; b. St. Paul, July 19, 1935; d. Clarence R. and Julia A. (Christenson) Lindgren; B.S., Northwestern U., 1957; m. Gene E. Malott, Oct. 25, 1957. News editor Modern Beauty Shop mag., Chgo., 1957; news coordinator KGB Radio, San Diego, 1958-60; editor, asst. dir. pub. relations St. Paul C. of C., 1960-64; night editor Daily Local News, West Chester, Pa., 1965-67; editor Hillsborough Boutique, Burlingame, Cal., 1967—, Burlingame Villager, 1971—. Del. Minn. Republican Conv., 1963; sec. Del. Citizens for Romney, 1967. Mem. Nat. Press Women, Am. Legion Aux., Cal. Press Women, Pa. Press Women, Northwestern Indsl. Editors, Burlingame C. of C. (dir.), Pub. Relations Soc. Am., Am. Assn. U. Women. Clubs: Soroptimists (sec. Burlingame-San Mateo); Peninsula Press (steering com.). Home: 407 Turner Terrace San Mateo CA 94401 Office: 1001 California Dr Burlingame CA 94010

MALOY, CHARLOTTE ANN (MRS. WILLIAM HOWARD MALOY), health service adminstr.; b. Wewoka, Okla., Apr. 26, 1930; d. Ralph Henry and Opal Jo (Sloan) Saling; student Okla. State U., 1947-50; B.S., Oklahoma U., 1951; certificate in Occupational Therapy Med. Field Service Sch., 1955; m. William Howard Maloy, Feb. 5, 1955; children—Jody Ann, William Thomas, Matthew Sean. Asst. dir. occupational therapy Houston State Psychology Inst., 1961-66; dir. occupational therapy Ben Taub Hosp., Houston, 1966-67, St. Joseph Mercy Hosp., Mason City, Ia., 1967-71, Space Center Meml. Hosp., Houston, 1973—. Vice pres. Welcome Wagon, Baytown, Tex., 1973-74. Served to 1st lt. Women's Med. Specialists Corps, U.S. Army, 1953-55. Mem. Am. Occupational Therapy Assn. Home: 800 Felton St Baytown TX 77520 Office: 2050 Space Park Houston TX 77058

MALSCH, ELLEN LISA JENSEN (MRS. JOHN MALSCH), artist; b. Denmark, Aug. 4, 1913; d. Charles J. and Ellen (Rassmusen) Jensen; came to U.S., 1919, naturalized, 1935; student Art Inst. Chgo., 1932-36; m. John I. Malsch, Aug. 1948; children—Rondi (Mrs. Ron Cox), Derry L., Tom A. Dress designer, Chgo., 1936-46; tchr. design and clothing Blackhawk Tech. Vocational Sch., Beloit, Wis., 1954-74; pvt. tchr. painting, Beloit, 1970—; one-man show U. Wis.-Janesville; exhibited in group shows Wright Art Center, Beloit Coll., West Bend (Wis.) Art Mus.; represented in permanent collections Luther Coll., Decorah, Ia., U. Wis.-Janesville, U. Wis.-La Crosse. Mem. Art League Beloit, Art League Madison, Art League Rockford (Ill.), Wis. Painters and Sculptors. Home and studio: Route 1 Walker Rd Beloit WI 53511

MALSCH, EVAMARIE KATHARINA, anesthesiologist, educator; b. Cologne, Germany, Oct. 13, 1937; d. Peter Paul and Senta (Reussner) Malsch; student U. Cologne, 1958-60; M.D., U. Freiburg (Germany), 1964. Came to U.S., 1966. Intern Lawrence (Mass.) Gen. Hosp., 1966-67; resident in anesthesiology U. Pa., 1968-70; instr. anesthesiology Temple U., Phila., 1971-73, asst. prof., 1973—. Diplomate Am. Bd. Anesthesiology. Mem. Am. Soc. Anesthesiology, A.M.A. Office: 3401 Broad St Philadelphia PA 19140

MALTBY, JANE MERRIAM (MRS. CHARLES DE WITT MALTBY), psychologist; b. Meriden, Conn.; d. Charles Andrew and Matilda (Schuirer) Merriam; B.S., N.Y. U., 1930, Ph.D., 1945; M.A., Yale, 1933; m. Charles De Witt Maltby (dec. Oct. 1947); 1 dau., Janice (Mrs. Anselm Thelen). Prin. Church St. Sch., Hamden, Conn., 1932-35; counsellor, tchr. English, Hamden High Sch., 1935-48; psychologist Hamden Schs., 1948-58; researcher children's anxieties Yale U., 1958-67; pvt. practice psychology, Hamden, 1967—. Fellow Am. Psychol. Assn., Internat. Council Psychologists; mem. N.E.A., Conn. Psychol. Assn., D.A.R., Descs. of Colonial Clergy, Hamden Civic Assn., Women Descs. of Ancient and Hon. Arty. Co., Nat. Soc. New Eng. Women, Magna Charta Dames, Delta Kappa Gamma (pres. 1954-58). Republican. Clubs: Mount Carmel Book, Reliance (v.p. 1969-72). Address: 221 N 8th Av Waite Park MN 56387

MALTZMAN, SYLVIA, journalist; b. Spring Lake, N.J., May 6, 1923; d. Israel and Libbie (Samet) Maltzman; B.A., U. Americas, 1950; B.A., Woodbury Coll., 1949. Writer, News-Jour., Daytona Beach, Fla., 1953-54, Daily Report, Ontario, Cal., 1955-56, El Centro Post-Press, Cal., 1950-53, 56-60, Ft. Lauderdale (Fla.) News, 1960-74; with South Fla. Regional Planning Council, Miami, Fla., 1974—. Journalism instr. U. Americas, Mexico, 1949-50. Served with USMC, 1943-46. Mem. Women in Communications, Inc. Home: 520 SW 27th Rd Miami FL 33129 Office: 1515 NW 167th St Miami FL 33169

MALUGEN, LOUISE DE CARL (MRS. JOHN C. MALUGEN), lawyer; b. Chgo., May 15, 1945; d. Frank Anthony and Geraldine Marie (Campo) De Carl; B.A. in Polit. Sci. and Econs., Chatham Coll., 1966; J.D., Loyola U., 1970; m. John C. Malugen, June 29, 1969. Admitted to Ill. bar, 1970, Cal. bar, 1972; staff atty. Chgo. Title & Trust Co., 1970-71; practice law, mem. firm Dunn and Malugen, San Diego, 1972—. Dir. Equal Rights Advisors, Inc. Bd. dirs. United Way San Diego. Mem. San Diego County Bar Assn., Ill., Cal. state bars, Fedn. Women's Orgns. (pres. 1972-74), Lawyers Club San Diego (dir.). Home: 3750 Bayside Walk No 14 San Diego CA 92109 Office: 303 A St San Diego CA 92101

MAMALAKIS, MARIE JOHN, educator; b. Shreveport, La.; d. John E. and Demetra (Passadakis) Mamalakis; student U. Southwestern La., 1930-33; B.A., La. State U., 1937-41; B.S. in L.S., U. Chgo., 1948; postgrad. Tulane U., 1953. Tchr. St. Landry Parish (La.) Schs., 1933-41; mem. faculty U. Southwestern La., Lafayette, 1941—, librarian, 1941-65, dir. publs., 1965—, prof., 1942—; editor Lafayette Progress, 1951-61; free lance writer, 1942—. Mayors rep. Community Action Program, Lafayette, 1973—, mem. Lafayette Municipal Civil Service Bd. Bd. dirs. S.W. La. Mardi Gras Assn., 1945—, Lafayette (La.) Community Concerts Assn., 1945—. Mem. Order Eastern Star. Home: 1018 Auburn Av Lafayette LA 70501 Office: Drawer 1009 U Southwestern La Lafayette LA 70501

MAMARCHEV, HELEN LORRAINE, univ. dean; b. Houston, Oct. 28, 1949; d. James Dimitri and Marion Helen (Prewett) Mamarchev; B.A. in Sociology and Social Sci., So. Methodist U., 1971; M.S. in Edn., Ind. U., 1973. Resident asst. So. Meth. U., 1968-71; resident asst., then asst. coordinator Ind. U., 1971-73; asst. dean women, residence hall dir., asst. dir. North Coll., U. Kan., Lawrence, 1973—. Recipient M award So. Meth. U. Mem. Am. Coll. Personnel Assn., Am. Assn. U. Women (area rep., exec. bd. Lawrence), Am. Personnel and Guidance Assn., Nat., Kan. (editor bull. 1973-74) assns. women deans, adminstrs. and counselors, Kan. Assn. Student Personnel Adminstrs., Ind. U., So. Meth. U. alumni assns., Mortar Bd., Alpha Kappa Delta, Delta Zeta (v.p. 1968-69). Home: 1115 Worthshire St Houston TX 77008 Office: 500 W 11th St Lawrence KS 66045

MAMIN, ESTHA LEE GINSBERG, real estate broker; b. Dallas; d. Jacob B. and Hinda (Bernstein) Ginsberg; B.A., U. Tex., 1945, M.Tech., 1940; student Lumbleau Sch. Real Estate, 1955-56; m. Harry Mamin, Dec. 28, 1941; children—Cynthia Anne, Victoria Lynn, H. Jonathon, Marshall Timothy. Research asst. Cancer Lab., U. Tex. Med. Coll., Galveston, 1940-41; biochemist, pathology lab. James Walker Meml. Hosp., Wilmington, N.C., 1942-44, Tex. Children's Hosp., Dallas, 1946-47; research asst., pathology dept. Harvard Med. Coll., 1947-48; med. technologist, bus. mgr. Harry Mamin, M.D., Pasadena, Cal., 1948-56; real estate salesman H. H. Armistead Co., Pasadena, 1956-64, broker Mamin Co., Pasadena, 1964—. Mem. Pasadena Bd. Realtors (edn. com. 1966, mem. com. 1967, sec. womens council, 1967), Cal. Real Estate Assn., Nat. Assn. Real Estate Bds., Los Angeles County Med. Aux. (com. chmn. 1962), League Women Voters, Am. Assn. U. Women. Clubs: Officers Wives, Curtain Raiser. Home: 1551 Pasqualito Dr San Marino CA 91108 Office: 1245 E Walnut St Pasadena CA 91106

MANAHAN, HELEN MARIE, former educator; b. Piqua, O., Nov. 14, 1906; d. George W. and Mary Caroline (Dunker) Manahan; B.S. in Edn., Ohio State U., 1929, M.S. in Physiology, 1930; M.S., Columbia, N.Y. Sch. Social work, 1947; postgrad. U. Mich., 1939-41, Smith Coll., 1954, Tulane Sch. Social Work, 1957-58. Instr. health, phys. edn. Ia. State Tchrs. Coll., Cedar Falls, 1930-32; caseworker Montgomery County, Hamilton County Welfare Depts., O., 1933-37; psychiat. social worker Newberry (Mich.) State Hosp., 1939-40, Pontiac (Mich.) State Hosp., 1940-42, St. Elizabeth's Hosp., Washington, 1942-45; psychiat. casework cons. N.Y. chpt. A.R.C., 1946-48; asst. prof. Tulane Sch. Social Work, New Orleans, 1949-59; asst. prof. dept. social work Fla. State U. Sch. Social Welfare, Tallahassee, 1959-69, ret.; free lance writer; lab. technician Capitol Circle Vet. Hosp., Tallahassee, 1972—. Mem. senate, Tulane U., 1954-56, Fla. State U., 1963-65; participant 6th Ann. Fla. Nursing Home Short Course, Gainesville, Fla., 1964; del. Internat. Congress on Mental Health, London, Eng., 1948; condr. seminars Little Rock, 1959, Jacksonville, Fla., 1960, St. Petersburg, Fla., 1960, Montgomery, Ala., 1963, Tampa, Fla., 1964, Clearwater, Fla., 1966. Mem. Nat. Ret. Tchrs. Assn., Am. Assn. U. Profs. (emeritus), LeMoyne Art Found. Home: 1922 Sunset Lane Tallahassee FL 32303

MANALEY, SHIRLEY LOGAN KEYES, librarian; b. Nashville, Oct. 18, 1931; d. Thomas Logan and Edna (Nunnally) Keyes; B.S., Middle Tenn. State U., 1954; M.L.S., George Peabody Coll. for Tchrs., 1958; m. Roy Nigel Manaley, Oct. 30, 1965. Tchr., Davidson County Sch. System, Nashville, 1954-55, Muscogee County Sch. System, Columbus, Ga., 1955-56; librarian Cajon Valley Union Sch. Dist., El Cajon, Cal., 1957-64; librarian IBM Corp., Huntsville, Ala., 1965—. Mem. Spl. Libraries Assn., Southeastern, Ala. library assns., Am. Soc. Indsl. Security. Methodist. Home: 210 Skyline Rd Madison AL 35758 Office: IBM Corp 150 Sparkman Dr Huntsville AL 35805

MANAREY, THELMA ALBERTA PREVEAU, artist; b. Edmonton, Alta., Can., May 2, 1913; d. Freeman Arthur and Ella (Desmond) Preveau; student Edmonton Normal, 1931-32, U. Alta. (Can.) Extension Art, 1947-57, Banff (Can.) Sch. Fine Arts, 1955-57; m. Richard Dymond, 1937 (div. 1940); 1 son, Richard Barrie; m. 2d, Clifford Herdman Manarey, June 1, 1944. Exhibited one-man shows including Calgary, 1961, Edmonton Art Gallery, 1962, 70, 71, 72, Focus, 1962, 63, Jacox, 1964, 68, Allied Arts Calgary, 1964, Stratford Festival Canadian Landscape Painters, 1964, Burnaby Print Show, 1969, Canadian Graphics, 1970; represented in permanent collections Edmonton Pub. Sch., Edmonton Art Gallery, Meml. U. Art Gallery Nfld., U. Ore. Bd. Tchr. adult classes Edmonton Art Gallery, 1954-64; specializing in portraiture; exhbn. miniature etchings, 1970. Rep. artists Allied Arts Council, 1954-55; mem. council Edmonton Art Gallery, 1967—. Recipient Purchase award Red River (Winnipeg, Can.) Exhbn., 1965, Winnipeg Show, 1966, award Centennial Show, 1967, Visual Arts award City of Edmonton, 1973. Mem. Alta. Soc. Artists (provincial vice chmn. 1966-67), Soc. Canadian Painter-Etchers and Engravers. Address: 12026 93d St Edmonton AB T5G 1E8 Canada

MANCHEE, KATHERYN HAIT (MRS. ARTHUR LEAVENS MANCHEE), historian, lectr.; b. Bklyn., Sept. 21, 1904; d. James Merritt and Belle (Silvey) Hait; ed. Parsons Sch. Art, 1923, Newark Sch. Art, 1924; student Western Res. U., 1941-43; m. William F. Dorflinger, Apr. 1927 (dec. 1944), 1 dau., June (Mrs. John Alexander Hardy, Jr.); m. 2d, Arthur Leavens Manchee, Sept. 21, 1957; step-children—Mrs. R.W. Bachelder, Mrs. James McD. Clark, Mrs. Harry Wortman. Instr., lectr. Cleve. Mus. Art, 1941-44; lectr., historian Steuben Glass, N.Y.C., 1946-48; dir. advt. and publicity Midhurst Importing Corp., N.Y.C., 1952-54; dir. pub. relations and product promotion Fostoria Glass Co., N.Y.C., 1954-58. Mem. Jr. League Morristown, N.J., 1930-39, 45-54, Cleve., 1939-44; vice chmn. jr. council Cleve. Mus. Art, 1943-44; vol. Cleve. Orch. Woman's Com., 1942-44, A.R.C. drives, Cleve., 1939-44; leader Girl Scouts U.S.A., Cleve., 1934-35. Mem. Am. Pottery and Glass Assn., Nat. Home Fashions League, Am. Women in Radio and TV. Presbyn. Clubs: Princeton, National Arts (N.Y.C.); Garden of Oranges; Nassau (Princeton). Contbr. articles to profl. publs. Home: 430 E 57th St New York City NY 10022

MANCINI, GLORIA S., educator; b. Ansonia, Conn.; d. Andrew J. and Anne (Hosko) Sobin; B.A., Mary Washington Coll., U. Va., 1947; M.A., Yale, 1953; profl. certificate U. Conn., 1961. Tchr. elementary sch., Prospect, Conn., 1947-49, Southbury, Conn., 1949-52; reading tchr. Derby (Conn.) Pub. Schs., 1952-57, reading cons., 1957-69, coordinator spl. edn. services, 1969—. Instr., U. Bridgeport, 1967—; cons. Random House, 1960—. Mem.-at-large bd. dirs. Conn. Trails Girl Scouts of Am., 1968—. Town chmn. Griffin Hosp. Devel. Fund. Mem. League Women Voters (dir. 1969—), N.E.A., Conn. Edn. Assn., Derby Tchrs. League (sec. 1955-61), Internat. Reading Assn. (v.p. New Haven County Council 1959-61), Conn. Assn. Reading Research, Nat. Soc. Study Edn., Delta Kappa Gamma. Club: Womans College. Home: 37 E 9th St Derby CT 06418

MANDEL, DOROTHY (MRS. SIEGFRIED MANDEL), artist; b. Boston, Mar. 30, 1920; d. Saul and Anna (Cohen) Isaacs; student Mass. Sch. Art, 1937-41, Harry Sternberg at Country Art Sch., 1955-58; m. Siegfried Mandel, Feb. 3, 1946; children—Elise Judith, Theodore Scott. Art dir. Bruce Humphries, Pubs., Boston, 1945; editorial artist Book of Knowledge, N.Y.C., 1946-49; free-lance mag., newspaper illustrator Newsday, Garden City, N.Y., 1954; exhibited woodcut prints in group shows Denver Art Mus., 1964-70, Laguna Gloria Art Mus., Austin, Tex., 1967, The Gallery, Denver, 1964, Hofstra U., 1958, Phila. Free Library, 1960, Art League L.I., 1959, Mercyhurst Coll., 1963, Gilpin County (Colo.) Art League, 1965-68, 72-73, Okla. Printmakers Soc., 1965; one-man shows U. Colo., 1964, The Octagon, Ames, Ia., 1967, Southtown Gallery, Ft. Collins, Colo., 1967, Beloit (Wis.) Coll. 1970, Whitaker Gallery, Boulder, Colo., 1970, Oberlin (O.) Coll., 1972, Mustard Seed Gallery, Boulder, 1972, Unicorn Gallery, Bloomington, Ind., 1972, Jefferson Unitarian Gallery, Golden, Colo., 1973, Internat. House, Denver, 1974; in traveling shows Nat. Assn. Women Artists, 1967-69, 73—, Boulder Artists Guild, 1963-64, Old Bergen (N.J.) Art Guild, 1973—; represented in permanent collections Mus. Art. Ein Harod, Israel, Heard Mus., McKinney, Tex., Unitarian-Universalist Religious Arts Guild, Boston, also pvt. collections U.S., Eng., Israel, Europe. Tchr. woodcut printmaking Jaladas Gallery, Boulder, 1967, Woodcut Workshop, Oberlin Coll., 1972, Boulder Fine Arts Center, 1972-73. Mem. Boulder Assembly on Arts and Humanities; sec. Community Gallery Council of Boulder, 1971-72. Recipient Ferne prize in graphics Nat. Assn. Women Artists Ann., 1970. Mem. Nat. Assn. Women Artists, Artists Equity Assn., Boulder Artists Guild (sec. 1965-67). Home: 355 Balsam Lane Pine Brook Hills Boulder CO 80302

MANDEL, MRS. LEON (CAROLA PANERAI MANDEL), found. trustee; b. Havana, Cuba.; d. Camilo and Elvira (Bertini) Panerai; educated pvt. schs., Havana and Europe; m. Leon Mandel, Apr. 9, 1938. Mem. women's bd. Northwestern Meml. Hosp., Chgo. Trustee Carola and Leon Mandel Fund Loyola U., Chgo. Frequently named among Ten Best Dressed Women in U.S.; chevalier Confrerie des Chevaliers du Tastevin. Capt. All-Am. Women's Skeet Team, 1952, 53, 54, 55, 56; only woman to win a men's nat. championship, 20 gauge, 1954, also high average in world over men, 1956, in 12 gauge with 99.4 per cent; European women's live bird shooting championship, Venice, Italy, 1957, Porto, Portugal, 1961; European woman's target championship, Torino, Italy, 1958; woman's world champion live-bird shooting, Sevilla, Spain, 1959. Named to Nat. Skeet Shooting Assn. Hall of Fame, 1970. Home: 801 South County Rd Palm Beach FL 33480

MANDEL, MARJORIE SYBLE PERLMAN (MRS. SEYMOUR MANDEL), state ofcl.; b. St. Paul, Aug. 13, 1921; d. Charles and Sarah (Mark) Perlman; student U. Minn., 1939-41, Pepin Acad. Design, 1941-43; m. Seymour Mandel, May 20, 1944; children—Leslie Ann, Avis (Mrs. Alex Price Warner), Tracy Jo. Designer, Steven-Arnold Co., Mpls., 1941-43; mem. Minn. Bd. Edn., 1970—. Mem. Mpls. Com. on Urban Environment, 1968—; mem. Nat. council Girl Scouts U.S.A., 1969—, v.p. Greater Mpls. council, 1968-70, pres., 1973—; v.p. Anti-Defamation League, 1971; Vice chmn. 13th Ward Republican Com., 1968-69; adviser Rep. Nat. Com., 1970. Bd. dirs. Goodwill Industries, Mpls. Recipient I Care award as one of Minn.'s 100 most outstanding citizens Minn. Rep. Com., 1965; Good Neighbor award Sta. WTCN, 1965; Outstanding Community Service award Sta. WCCO, 1962, 63, 65. Jewish religion (temple trustee 1966—, pres. Sisterhood 1970-72). Home: 2 Red Cedar Lane Minneapolis MN 55410

MANDELBAUM, RUTH WEISS, educator; b. N.Y.C., Feb. 12, 1918; d. Samuel and Eva (Weiss) Weiss; A.B., Vassar Coll., 1938; M.A., Columbia, 1939; m. David G. Mandelbaum, May 23, 1943; children—Michael, Susan, Jonathan. Editorial asso. Publs. Weekly, N.Y.C., 1941-43; editor OSS, Washington, 1943-46; supr. grad. internship program in tchr. edn. U. Cal. at Berkeley, 1964-69, acting dir., 1969-71; sr. devel. specialist Far West Lab. for Ednl. Research and Devel., Berkeley, 1972-73, Project Spl. Elementary Edn. for Disadvantaged, Berkeley, 1973—. Jewish religion (dir. temple 1953-56). Home: 911 Mendocino Av Berkeley CA 94707

MANDELIN, DOROTHY JANE BEARCROFT (MRS. ALLAN R. MANDELIN), yarn and needlecraft shop owner; b. Burbank, Cal., Aug. 11, 1931; d. Robert Oliver and Ella Jane (Carter) Bearcroft; B.S., U. Cal. at Los Angeles, 1955; M.S., U. Chgo., 1958, Ph.D., 1964; m. Allan R. Mandelin, Mar. 22, 1967. Chemist, Eastman Kodak, Hollywood, Cal., 1955-57; asst. prof. Kalamazoo Coll., 1960-63, Chatham Coll., Pitts., 1964-67; chemist Garrett Research & Devel., LaVerne, Cal., 1968-70; owner, mgr. Needle Art Shop, Houston, 1971—. Mem. Am. Chem. Soc., Am. Inst. Chemists, Am. Phys. Soc., Sigma Xi. Home: 1418 San Sebastian Lane Houston TX 77058 Office: 16540 El Camino Real Houston TX 77058

MANDELL, RUTH E., coll. dean; b. Rochester, N.Y., June 30, 1925; d. Sylvester T. and Antoinette (Gaudio) Mandell; diploma St. Mary's Hosp. Sch. Nursing, 1946; B.S., U. Rochester, 1958, Ed.M., 1967. Registered nurse St. Mary's Hosp., 1946-50, A.R.C. Blood Program, 1950-53; nursing educator St. Mary's Hosp. Sch. Nursing, 1953-56, 60-65, Highland Hosp. Sch. Nursing, 1957-60, 74—; counselor Monroe Community Coll., Rochester, 1966-67, acting dir. health services, adminstrv. asst. student affairs, 1967-69, asso. dean students, 1970—, acting v.p. student affairs, 1972-74. Cons. curriculum revision hosps. schs. nursing, 1959-65. Mem. health careers com., mental health com. Health Council Monroe County, 1968-72. Bd. dirs. Monroe Community Hosp. Aux., 1971-73. Mem. Nat. League Nursing (dir. 1956-57), N.Y. State Jr. and Community Coll. Assn., Am. Personnel and Guidance Assn., N.Y. State Tchrs. Assn., St. Mary's Hosp. Nurses (pres. 1953-57), U. Rochester alumni assns. Home: 229 Ellington Dr Rochester NY 14616

MANDELS, MARY HICKOX (MRS. GABRIEL MANDELS), microbiologist, govt. ofcl.; b. Rutland, Vt., Sept. 12, 1917; d. Sherman Gray and Mary Elizabeth (Bolger) Hickox; B.S., Cornell U., 1939, Ph.D., 1945; m. Gabriel Mandels, Mar. 14, 1942; children—Joan (Mrs. John Roche), Peter. Instr. plant physiology Cornell U., Ithaca, N.Y., 1944-45; research microbiologist U.S. Army Natick (Mass.) Labs., 1954—. Named Civil Servant of Year in Northeast, 1963, 73. Mem. Bot. Soc. Am., Am. Soc. for Microbiology, Sigma Xi. Contbr. articles to sci. jours. Home: 106 Everett St Natick MA 01760 Office: US Army Natick Lab Natick MA 01760

MANDEVILLE, MILDRED SCHWAGERMANN (MRS. GILBERT HARRISON MANDEVILLE), editor; b. Bronxville, N.Y.; d. William and Anna Catherine (Huehn) Schwagermann; student Columbia, N.Y. U., Syracuse U., Providence Coll., Brown U., U. Wash.; m. Gilbert Harrison Mandeville, June 20, 1936; 1 dau., Terry Melinda. Editor, pub. Tuckahoe (N.Y.) Guide, 1932-39; owner, mgr. Seattle Bookfinders, 1948-62; pub., owner Price Guide Pubs., Kenmore, Wash., 1962—; editor Used Book Price Guide, Kenmore, Wash., 1962—. Cons. to book appraisers, used book dealers, and book fairs, 1962—. Mem. Music and Art Found. Cornish Sch., Seattle, Friends of Kenmore Library. Bd. dirs. Friends of Seattle Pub. Library 1st pl. winner Ann. N.W. Air Regatta Race, 1949, co-pilot 99's Trans-Continental Air Race, 1950. Mem. U. Puget Sound Women's League, 99's (chpt. chmn. 1949-51). Presbyn. Clubs: Washington Athletic; Skiers Inc. (dir. 1968—). Home: 13041 42d Av NE Seattle WA 98125 Office: 525 Kenmore Station Kenmore WA 98028

MANDLER, JEAN MATTER, psychologist, educator; b. Oak Park, Ill., Nov. 6, 1929; d. Joseph Allen and May Roberts (Finch) Matter; student Carleton Coll., 1947-49; B.A. with highest honors, Swarthmore Coll., 1951; Ph.D., Harvard, 1956; m. George Mandler, Jan. 19, 1957; children—Peter Clark, Michael Allen. Research asso. Lab. of Social Relations, Harvard, 1957-60; research asso. dept. psychology U. Toronto (Can.), 1961-65; asso. research psychologist, lectr. U. Cal. at San Diego, 1965-73, asso. prof., 1973—. Vice pres. Cal. Parents for Gifted, 1970-71; founder, pres. San Diego Assn. for Gifted Children, 1968-71. Mem. Am. Assn. U. Women, Am. Psychol. Assn., Psychonomic Soc., Soc. for Research in Child Devel., Phi Beta Kappa. Author: (with G. Mandler) Thinking: From Association to Gestalt, 1964. Asso. editor Psychol. Rev., 1970—. Contbr. articles to profl. jours. Home: 1406 La Jolla Knoll La Jolla CA 92037 Office: Dept of Psychology Univ California La Jolla CA 92037

MANES, BELLE (MRS. MYRON MANES), painter; b. N.Y.C., Mar. 22, 1930; d. Raphael and Hilda (Kurtz) Marder; student Cooper Union Art Sch., 1947-50; m. Myron Manes, Sept. 10, 1949; children—Orianne, Alan. Tchr. painting, Linden, N.J., 1951, Jewish Community Center, Plainfield, N.J., 1956-58, Gedney Art Studio, White Plains, N.Y., 1961-64; exhibited in one-man shows at Barrett Gallery, Plainfield, 1957, Nat. Bank Westchester, White Plains, 1964, Book Gallery, White Plains, 1964, Greenwich (Conn.) Art Barn, 1972; exhibited in group shows at Bklyn. Mus., Laurel Gallery, Nat. Acad., White Plains Pub. Library, Albright Knox, Phila. Mus., Barrett Gallery, Greenwich Art Barn, Feiner Gallery, Pen and Brush Club, Buffalo Jewish Center; Recipient Canaday award Nat. Acad., 1972. Mem. Nat. Assn. Women Artists. Home: 1097 North St White Plains NY 10605

MANES, NELLA CELLINI, advt. agy. exec.; b. Steubenville, O., July 25, 1920; d. Benvenuto Marcello and Liberata (DeMarco) Cellini; grad. Steubenville High Sch., 1938; student Steubenville Bus. Coll., 1939-41; m. Robert Vincent Manes, Jan. 8, 1946 (div. 1948); 1 dau., Michele Cellini (Mrs. James W. Broadfoot III). Procurement specialist U.S. Army Q.M., Washington, 1942-46; asst. time buyer Kal, Ehrlich & Merrick Advt., Washington, 1949-50, time buyer, 1950-52, media dir., 1953-58, v.p. media, 1958-68; v.p. media Ehrlich Linkins & Assos., Washington, 1969-71; exec. v.p. Ehrlich, Harris, Manes & Assos., 1971—. Mem. Nat. Acad. TV Arts and Scis., Advt. Club Washington (named Advt. Woman of Year 1963), Media Research Council, Am. Women in Radio and TV, Fashion Group. Republican. Roman Catholic. Club: Bethesda Country. Home: 4620 N Park Av Chevy Chase MD 20015 Office: 4901 Fairmont Av Bethesda MD 20014

MANFREDI, ELEANOR A. MORONO (MRS. WILLIAM F. MANFREDI), motel, restaurant exec.; b. East Rochester, N.Y., June 10, 1928; d. Antonio and Amata (Delia) Morono; student Rochester Bus. Inst., 1950, Arlington Heights Sch. Interior Decorating, 1968; m. William F. Manfredi, Sept. 30, 1950; children—Lynn Anne (Mrs. Mark Moehling), Ellen T. (Mrs. Patrick Monson), Alan N., Craig W., Julie R. Aide, Eastman Kodak Co., Rochester, N.Y., 1946-49; key punch operator Rochester Gas & Electric Co., 1949-50; corr. Air Force Finance Corp., Denver, 1950-52; owner, operator Allenwood Motel and Restaurant, Louisville, Ga., 1970—. Hospitality chmn. Woman's Club, Rochester, 1963; nursery chmn. St. Mary's Women's Club, Aiken, S.C., 1954, chmn. publicity, 1956; chmn. arts and crafts Newcomers, Arlington, Ill., 1969. Recipient Safety award Ga. Hotel and Motel Assn., 1973. Mem. Am. Motel and Hotel Assn., Bus. and Profl. Women's Club. Home: PO Box 524 Louisville GA 30434 Office: Allenwood Motel Louisville GA 30434

MANGAN, MARGARET MARY J., state supreme ct. judge; b. N.Y.C.; d. William and Hannah (Sullivan) Mangan; ed. N.Y.U. Coll. City N.Y.; LL.B., Bklyn. Law Sch., 1930. Admitted to N.Y. State bar, 1932, U.S. Supreme Ct. bar, 1955, also dist. cts., U.S. Treasury Dept., practice law, N.Y.C., 1930-45; gen. law asst. N.Y. Supreme Ct., 1945-56; judge N.Y.C. Municipal Ct., 1956-58, City Ct., 1958-63; justice Supreme Ct. State N.Y., 1963—. Founder, incorporator Interfaith Movement, Inc.; mem. Sch. Bd. No. 14, N.Y.C., 1953-58; mem. N.Y. women's activities com. Nat. Conf. Christians and Jews, 1955-58. Recipient Ann. award Emerald Soc. N.Y., 1956; award interfaith Movement, Inc., 1965, Alumni Soc. award Baruch Sch., Coll. City N.Y., 1968, Distinguished Service citation Temple Beth Sholom, 1957; named Outstanding Profl. Woman of Year, Bus. Profl. Women's Clubs N.Y., 1969. Mem. Assn. Women Lawyers, Bar Assn. City N.Y., N.Y. County Lawyers Assn. (dir. 1949-55), Fed. Bar Assn. (exec. com. N.Y., N.J. and Conn. 1941-51, recipient certificate of merit 1956), N.Y. Guild Catholic Lawyers (gov. 1942-47), Columbiettes (hon. state pres., nat. pres. 1960-63), Ancient Order Hibernians (pres. N.Y. County 1938-44), N.Y. League Bus. and Profl. Women, Phi Delta Delta. Office: 60 Centre St New York City NY 10007

MANGAROO, JEWELLEAN SMITH, educator, univ. dean; b. Jackson, Miss.; d. Aaron and Ollie (Webb) Smith; B.S., Meharry Med. Coll., 1958; M.S., Washington U., 1961; Ph.D., Ohio State U., 1968; m. Arthur Solomon Mangaroo, Aug. 31, 1967; children—William Andrew, Terees-Yvette. Dir. health services Providence Hosp. Sch. Nursing, Chgo., 1959-60; adminstrv. supr. Homer G. Phillips City Hosp., St. Louis, 1960-61; asst. prof. N.C. A. and T. State U., 1961-62; teaching asso. Ohio State U., 1962-64, nursing fellow, 1966-68; dean, prof. nursing N.C. A. and T. State U., 1968-69, Prairie View (Tex.) A. and M. Coll., 1969—. Active Houston Area Model City Program, Head Start. Trustee Prairie View A. and M. Coll. Research Found. Mem. Nat., Tex. leagues nurses, Am., Tex. nurses assns., Assn. Higher Edn., N.E.A., Assn. Allied Health Professions, Ohio State U. Alumnae Assn. (life), Pi Lambda Theta, Delta Sigma Theta. Democrat. Contbr. articles to profl. jours. Home: 10819 Cypresswood Dr Houston TX 77070

MANGEL, MARGARET WILSON, ednl. adminstr; b. Tell City, Ind., May 13, 1912; d. Emil Henry and Lena (Wilson) Mangel; A.B., Ind. U. 1932, dietetic certificate, 1934; M.S., U. Chgo., 1940, Ph.D., 1951. Tchr. home econs., English, phys. edn. Union City (Ind.) pub. schs., 1934-39; instr. home econs. U. Mo., Columbia, 1940-43, asst. prof., 1943-47, asso. prof., 1947-50, prof., 1950—, chmn. home econs. dept., 1955-60, dir. Sch. Home Econs., 1960-73, dean Coll. Home Econs., 1973—. Fellow A.A.A.S., Am. Inst. Chemists; mem. Am. Home Econs. Assn. (chmn.-elect council for profl. devel. 1974—), Am. Dietetics Assn., Assn. Higher Edn., Mo. Assn. Social Welfare, Mo. Tchrs. Assn., Mo. Assn. Consumers, Assn. Adminstrs. Home Econs. in State Univs. and Land Grant Colls. (chmn.-elect. 1972, chmn. 1972-73, past chmn. 1973-74), N.Y. Acad. Scis., Am. Assn. U. Profs., Am. Chem. Soc., Am. Pub. Health Assn., Inst. Food Technologists, N.E.A., Am. Biometric Soc., Nat. Council Adminstrs. Home Econs. (chmn. research com. 1972), Columbia C. of C., Phi Beta Kappa, Sigma Xi, Sigma Delta Epsilon, Phi Upsilon Omicron, Omicron Nu, Pi Lambda Theta, Delta Kappa Gamma, Gamma Sigma Delta, Altrusa. Presbyn. Contbr. articles to profl. jours. Home: 705 Morningside Dr Columbia MO 65201

MANGELS, JUANITA JANET, realtor; b. New Philadelphia, O., July 18, 1932; d. William E. and Hazel Gertrude (Blackson) Lovejoy; certificate Grad. Realtors Inst.; certificate in real estate Grossmont Coll.; m. Glenn A. Mangels, Oct. 27, 1950 (div. Aug. 1971); children—Glenn A., Eugene W., Linda Lea, Jeanette Mathilda; m. 2d, Melvin L. Claus, Dec. 1, 1973. Saleswoman, Vanice Realty Centre, Spring Valley, Cal., 1955-69, owner, 1969—. Active local Cub Scouts, 1967-69; 3d v.p. Casa de Oro Elementary Sch. P.T.A., 1969-70; active Concern for Missing in Action, San Diego. Mem. La Mesa Bd. Realtors (dir.), Multiple Listing Service, Casa de Oro Bus. Assn. (pres. 1972), San Diego Bd. Realtors, Spring Valley C. of C. (dir.), Nat. Inst. Real Estate Brokers. Methodist. Home: 3841 El Canto Dr Spring Valley CA 92077 Office: 9960 Campo Rd Spring Valley CA 92077

MANGIN, SHIRLEY VOLK (MRS. MARION RICHARD MANGIN), educator; b. Chgo., Apr. 30, 1922; d. David Lorne and Edith (Edelstein) Wolk; A.B., Immaculate Heart Coll., 1954; M.S., 1957; M.A., San Francisco State Coll., 1956; div.; 1 dau., Morlee Joy; m. 2d, Marion Richard Mangin, July 30, 1972. Tchr. mental retardation Area Los Angeles City Schs., 1953-57, tchr. orthopedically handicapped, 1957-58, cons. tchr. 7 schs. handicapped, 1958-60; tng. tchr. Los Angeles city schs., Los Angeles State Coll., 1960-61; vice prin. Wash. and Pacific Blvds. Sch., Los Angeles, 1961-66; adminstr. James J. McBride School for the Physically Handicapped, Los Angeles, 1966-73, West Valley Sch., Los Angeles, 1973—; asso. prof. extension div. Cal. State Coll., lectr. psychology dept. Immaculate Heart Coll., 1960—. Research asso. John Tracy Clinic, 1958-60. Rec. sec. Tchrs. Tng. Com., Los Angeles, 1963-64; mem. curriculum study com. for retarded Los Angeles City Bd. of Edn., 1963-64; membership chmn. Wash. Blvd. Parent Guild, Los Angeles, 1963-64; hon. adv. bd. 10th Dist., 1971. Bd. dirs. A.R.C. Recipient Elk scholarships, 1954, 55, 56; Dental Health scholarship U. So. Cal., 1960; commendation Los Angeles Assembly, 1972. Fellow Am. Assn. Mental Deficiency; mem. Council Exceptional Children (sec. 1957, v.p.), Exceptional Children's Found. (group adviser adult retardates 1955-62), Cal. Congress Parents and Tchrs. (hon. life, National Cat Protection Soc. (hon. life mem.). Contbr. articles in field to profl. publs. Home: 11025 Weddington St North Hollywood CA 91601 Office: West Valley School 6649 Balboa Blvd Van Nuys CA 91406

MANGIONE, LILLIAN CORNELIO (MRS. COSMO MANGIONE), investment co. exec.; b. Waterbury, Conn.; d. Carmine E. And Alphonsina (Lovetere) Cornelio; student Brown U. Extension, 1957-60; certificate N.Y. Inst. Finance, 1964; m. Cosmo Mangione, Nov. 24, 1932; 1 son, Francis. Accountant various small businesses, Winsted, Conn., 1928-32; propr. Mangione's Boutique, Providence, 1948-57; registered rep. Diamond-Doorley, Inc., Providence, 1958-65, E.R. Davenport Investments, 1965-68, Estabrook & Co., 1968-70; asso. Barrett & Co., 1970—, portofolio mgr., 1968—; tchr. investment and stock market courses, YWCA, various women's clubs, 1962-65; lectr. Stock Market-Television, 1962-63; guest on radio talk back shows discussing stock market, 1970-71. Active League Women Voters, Warwick, R.I., 1958-62. Mem. Providence Financial Analysts Soc., Mus. Art R.I. Sch. Design. Club: Turks Head. Home: Regency East 1 Jackson Hwy Providence RI 02903 Office: 930 Hospital Trust Bldg Providence RI 02903

MANGIONE, PATRICIA ANTHONY (MRS. JERRE MANGIONE), artist; b. Seattle; d. Mark Livingstone and Ida (Bittle) Anthony; student Fleisher Art Meml., 1939-46, Barnes Found., 1952-53; m. W. Robert Evans, Mar. 9, 1939 (div. 1957); 1 son, David Alan; m. 2d, Jerre Mangione, Feb. 18, 1957. One-man shows Phila. Art Alliance, 1953, 54, 57, Carlen Gallery, 1958, U. Pa., 1964, Sesslers, 1965 (all Phila.), Wellons Gallery, 1954, Frank Rehn Gallery, 1960, 63, 65 (all N.Y.C.), Fontana Gallery, 1961 (Narberth, Pa.), U.S. Information Service Gallery, Palermo, Italy, 1965, Frank Rehn Gallery, N.Y.C., 1968, 74; exhibited in numerous group shows in U.S.; represented in permanent collections Fleisher Art Meml., Moore Coll., Phila., Inst. Contemporary Art, Dallas, West Chester (PA.) State Mus.; executed mural for Continental Bank & Trust Co., Phila. Instr. painting Fleisher Art Meml., 1949-63, Bryn Mawr (Pa.) Art Center, 1959-63. Recipient medal Fleisher Art Meml., 1948; Gold medal Plastic Club, Phila., 1953, Silver medal, 1954; Clarence Wolf Meml. prize Da Vinci Art Alliance, Phila., 1960; oil prize Saratoga Springs (N.Y.) Ann. Art Show, 1966. Resident fellow MacDowell Colony, Peterborough, N.H., 1957, 58, 59, 64, 67, 71, Yaddo, Saratoga Springs, 1962, 63, 66, 68, 72. Mem. Artists Equity Assn. Phila. (v.p., 1961-63, 70-71, dir., 1963-64), Phila. Art Tchrs. Assn. (awards), Phila. Art Alliance, Inst. Contemporary Art. Home and studio: 1901 Walnut St Philadelphia PA 19103

MANGLE, LORINE EMMA, publishing co. exec.; b. Lake City, Fla., May 26, 1926; d. Wherry Raymond and Mary Belle (Conner) Harrington; student Lakeland (Fla.) Bus. Inst., 1946-48; m. Thomas Edward Mangle, Mar. 6, 1950; children—Michael Anthony, Yvonne Elaine. Office mgr. Whitman Pub. Co., Atlanta, 1957-59; bus. mgr., asst. editor Abernethy Pub. Co., Atlanta, 1960—. Home: 2270 Pinehurst Rd Snellville GA 30278 Office: 75 3d St NW Atlanta GA 30308

MANGUM, CHARLOTTE PRESTON, educator; b. Richmond, Va., May 19, 1938; d. Ernest and Elizabeth (Wall) Mangum; A.B., Vassar Coll., 1959; M.S., Yale, 1961, Ph.D., 1963. Lab. asst. Yale U., 1959-61, asst. in research, 1963, asso. in research, 1963; asst. prof. biology, asso. in marine sci. Coll. of William and Mary, Williamsburg, Va., 1964-65, 66-68, asso. prof. biology, 1968-73, prof., 1974—. Vis. investigator, systematics-ecology program Marine Biol. Lab., Woods Hole, Mass., 1966, instr. in exptl. invertebrate zoology, 1969—; lectr. in zoo physiology U. Aarhus (Denmark), 1974. NSF predoctoral fellow, 1961-62, 65, NIH postdoctoral fellow, 1963-64. Mem. Am. Soc. Zoologists (sec. div. comparative physiology and biochemistry 1972-74, mem.-at-large exec. com. 1973—), A.A.A.S., Marine Biol. Assn. U.K., Sigma Xi. Asso. editor Jour. Exptl. Zoology, 1970—; editorial bd. Am. Zoologist, 1971—. Contbr. articles to profl. jours. Home: Route 4 Box 268C Sycamore Landing Williamsburg VA 23185

MANGUM, IVA KATHLEEN (MRS. HERBERT ELI MANGUM), mus. ofcl.; b. Three Rivers, Tex., June 1, 1919; d. Jason Obed and Elsie B. (O'Neal) Blackwell; grad. high sch.; m. Herbert Eli Mangum, May 1, 1948; children—K. June (Mrs. Lynn Bennack), E. Joan (Mrs. John Perry), James M. Hague, P. Jane (Mrs. Leroy Grote), Joyce L. (Mrs. John Sorenson). With Rockport (Tex.) Pilot, 1936-40, 46-48; with Mil. Service News and Clemons Printing Co., San Antonio, 1942-46; with Bigfoot Wallace Mus., Bigfoot, Tex., 1965—, pres., 1972—. Pres. Fenwick P.T.A., San Antonio, 1957-59. Home: 2709 W Craig Place San Antonio TX 78228 Office: Bigfoot Wallace Museum Bigfoot TX 78005

MANGUM, JOYCE ORMS (MRS. RICHARD K. MANGUM), lawyer; b. Wister, Okla., Aug. 31, 1938; d. Norris Douglas and Zoel Madelon (Thompson) Orms; B.S., U. Ariz., 1959, J.D., 1961; m. Richard K. Mangum, Aug. 22, 1959; children—Karen, Mark, Rampna. Admitted to Ariz. bar, 1961; escrow officer Ariz. Title & Trust Co., Flagstaff, 1965-66; mem. firm Mangum, Wall & Stoops, Flagstaff, 1966—. Mem. adv. bds. Flagstaff (Ariz.) Coop. Nursery, 1967—, Coconino County Family Planning Council, Flagstaff, 1972-73; chmn. citizen's adv. com. Council for Community Planning, City of Flagstaff, 1973—. Bd. dirs. Big Sisters; chmn. bd. dirs. No. Ariz. Health Devel. Council, 1973—. Named Outstanding Young Woman of Ariz., 1973. Mem. State Bar Ariz. (mem. prisons and rehabilitation spl. com. 1972-73, mem. family law com. 1973—), Coconino County Bar Assn. (sec., treas. 1967-70), League Women Voters (bull. editor, sec. 1963-68), C. of C. (v.p. for community devel., mem. edn. com. 1973—), Gamma Phi Beta. Club: Soroptimist (pres. Flagstaff 1969-70). Home: 2145 N Crescent Flagstaff AZ 86001 Office: 222 E Birch St Flagstaff AZ 86001

MANIACI, MARIE, hosp. adminstr.; b. Bklyn., Apr. 14, 1924; d. Peter and Matilda (Guadagna) Imperiale; B.S. in Edn., Hunter Coll., 1953; M.B.A. in Hosp. Adminstrn., Wagner Coll., Staten Island, 1971; m. Salvatore Maniaci, Sept. 13, 1964 (dec. 1966). Various supervisory positions Adelphi and St. John's L.I. City hosps., N.Y.C., 1945-49; tchr., supr. Methodist Hosp., Bklyn., 1949-54; asst. dir. nursing Maimonides Hosp., Bklyn., 1954-61; dir. nurses Mid Island Hosp., Bethpage, N.Y., 1961-67, adminstr., bd. govs., 1967—; tchr. in field. Bd. dirs. Am. Cancer Soc.; mem. adv. bd. vocational ednl. extension bd. State U. N.Y.; asso. mem. C.W. Post Coll. Fellow Am. Acad. Med. Adminstrs.; mem. Am. Coll. Hosp. Adminstrs., Am. Nurses Assn., Am. Pub. Health Assn., Hosp. Financial Mgmt. Assn., Royal Soc. Health. Contbr. articles to profl. jours. Office: Mid Island Hospital 4295 Hempstead Turnpike Bethpage NY 11714

MANJOS, THELMA DEXTER (MRS. PETER MANJOS), educator; b. Belfast, Me., May 1, 1910; d. Collin and Ida R. (Miller) Dexter; B.A., U. Cal. at Los Angeles, 1930; M.A., San Francisco State Coll., 1956; Ph.D., N.Y. U., 1965; m. Hartley Dean Moddox II, July 12, 1931 (dec. 1955); children—Faith (Mrs. Whitney), Hartley Dean III; m. 2d, Peter Manjos, June 27, 1959. Head autograph and manuscript dept. Dawson's Rare Book Shop, Los Angeles, 1930-32; placement officer, staff trainer Cal. Dept. Employment, San Francisco, 1942-44; asst. dir. Liltle House, Menlo Park, Cal., 1956-57; vocational rehab. counselor Aid to Retarded Children, San Francisco, 1957-59; supr. vocational dept. United Cerebral Palsey, N.Y.C., 1959-66; prof. dept. counselor edn., rehab. counseling program San Diego State U., 1966—. Planning cons. Community Welfare Council, San Diego, 1967-70; cons. Social Security Disability Program, 1962—. Bd. dirs. United Cerebral Palsy Found., San Diego, Sheltered Workshops San Diego County, Nat. Rehab. Assn., San Diego, St. James Episcopal Ch. Meml. Fund, La Jolla, Cal., 1970—. Mem. Am. Personnel and Guidance Assn., Council Rehab. Counselor Edn., Nat. Rehab. Assn., Nat. Accreditation Council for Agys. Serving Blind and Visually Handicapped, Womens Aux. U. Hosp. San Diego, San Diego County Med. Soc. Home: 7258 Romero Dr La Jolla CA 92037 Office: San Diego State Univ San Diego CA 92115

MANLAPAZ, CAROLINA PAREDES, anesthesiologist; b. Manila, Philippines, Apr. 16, 1935; d. José Carlos and Guadalupe (Paredes) Manlapaz; A.A., Santo Tomás U., 1955, M.D., 1960. Intern, Santo Tomás U., Manila, 1959-60, Doctor's Hosp., Washington, 1960-61; intern Prince George's Gen. Hosp., Cheverly, Md., 1962, resident internal medicine, 1963-64, co-chief resident, 1965, resident anatomy and clin. pathology, 1965, chief resident internal medicine, 1966; resident clin. pathology (hematology) Univ. Hosp., Balt., 1965, resident anesthesiology, 1966-67; resident anesthesiology

Georgetown U. Hosp., Washington, 1967-68; anesthesiologist Prince George's Gen. Hosp., Cheverly, Md., 1968-70; anesthesiologist Fairfax Hosp., Falls Church, Va., 1970-73, Potomac Hosp., Woodbridge, 1973—. Mem. A.M.A., Am., D.C.-Md., No. Va. socs. anesthesiologists, Prince Georges County, Fairfax County med. socs. Home: 3014 Cunningham Dr Alexandria VA 22309 Office: Potomac Hosp 2300 Opitz Blvd Woodbridge VA 22191

MANLEY, DOLORES CARLENE, financial co. exec.; b. Lufkin, Tex., Dec. 7, 1933; d. Jim White and Ruby (Aldredge) Manley; grad. Draughon's Bus. Coll., 1951; student So. Meth. U., 1952-53. With Republic Financial Services, Inc., Republic Ins. Co. Group, Dallas, 1951—, sec. cos. and subsidiaries, 1961-69, asst. v.p., 1969-72; v.p., 1972—. Home: 4118-C Bowser St Dallas TX 75219 Office: 2727 Turtle Creek Blvd Dallas TX 75219

MANLEY, JOAN A. DANIELS, publisher; b. San Luis Obispo, Cal., Sept. 23, 1932; d. Carl and Della (Weinmann) Daniels; B.A., U. Cal. at Berkeley, 1954; D.Bus. Adminstrn. (hon.), U. New Haven, 1974; m. Jeremy C. Lanning, Mar. 17, 1956 (div. Sept. 1963); m. 2d, Donald H. Manley, Sept. 12, 1964. Sec., Doubleday & Co., Inc., N.Y.C., 1954-60; sales exec. Time Inc., 1960-66, v.p., 1971—; circulation dir. Time-Life Books, 1966-68, dir. sales, 1968-70, pub., 1970—; dir. Haverhill's, Inc. Chmn. govt. adv. com. Internat. Book and Library Programs. Mem. Direct Mail Advt. Assn. (dir.), Asso. 3d Class Mail Users (dir.), Assn. Am. Pubs. (past dir.). Clubs: Hemisphere, Publishers Lunch. Home: 888 8th Av New York City NY 10019 also Shaftsbury VT 05262 Office: Time and Life Bldg Rockefeller Center New York City NY 10020

MANLEY, LILLIAN CARDWELL (MRS. RICHARD SHANNON MANLEY), educator; b. Birmingham, Ala., Oct. 22, 1932; d. William Whitt and Grace (Cameron) M.; B.S., U. Ala., 1953, M.S., 1958, Ph.D., 1961; m. Richard Shannon Manley, Aug. 23, 1953; children—Richard Shannon, Alyce Hughes. Research asst. So. Research Inst., 1953-54; teaching fellow U. Ala., 1957-58; instr. Demopolis High Sch., 1958-59; asso. prof. biology Livingston U., 1959-63; chmn. div. sci., prof. biology Judson Coll., 1963-70; exec. dir. Ala. Consortium for Devel. of Higher Edn., 1970—; lectr. vis. scientists program, 1966-68. Sec. Ala. Spl. Edn. Study Commn., 1968-69; vice chmn. Ala. Commn. on Higher Edn., 1970-72; Mem. Gov.'s Commn. on Status Women, 1962-66. Trustee, Troy State U., 1968-70. Named Distinguished Young Woman, Demopolis Jayceettes, 1968. Mem. Am. Assn. U. Women (pres. Ala. div. 1964-66, mem. Internat. fellowships awards com. 1962-68, ednl. found. devel. com. 1968—), Ala. Acad. Scis. (counselor W. Ala. region 1964-70, com. on pub. relations 1966-68, v.p. 1968-69, mem. exec. com. 1966-70), U. Ala. Nat. Alumni Assn. (v.p., chmn. women's div. 1970-71; Distinguished alumna 1971), Assn. Southeastern Biologists, A.A.A.S., Mortar Bd., Phi Beta Kappa, Sigma Xi, Alpha Epsilon Delta, Alpha Lambda Delta, Alpha Chi Omega, Lambda Tau (charter; adviser Sigma chpt.). Club: Women of Demopolis Country. Methodist (mem. adminstrv. bd.). Home: Country Club Dr PO Box 338 Demopolis AL 36732 Office: 305 N Main St Demopolis AL 36732

MANN, ALMEDA LAVONA EMERY (MRS. BYRON L. BROWN), educator; b. Lincoln, Neb., July 11, 1910; d. Guy Gilbert and Clara (DeForest) Emery; student Pacific U., 1930-31; B.A., Intermountain Union Coll., 1934; postgrad. Mont. State U., summer 1937, U. Mont., summers 1965-67, M.A., 1970; m. Lewis C. Mann, Nov. 25, 1942 (dec. Jan. 1961); m. 2d, Byron L. Brown, Dec. 20, 1969. Tchr., Dixon (Mont.) High Sch., 1934-37, Columbus (Mont.) High Sch., 1937-44, 53-65; asst. prof. English, Western Mont. Coll., Dillon, 1965—; statis. typist Todd and Hatch C.P.A.'s, Portland, Ore., 1944-50. Pres. Columbus Jr. Homemakers. Recipient Gold Key as outstanding journalism tchr. Mont. State U., 1961. Newspaper Fund fellow, 1963. Mem. Nat. Council Tchrs. English, Mont. Assn. Tchrs. English (pres. 1960-61, dir. 1960-64), N.E.A., Mont. Edn. Assn. (pres. Columbus unit 1957, 64, sec. Western Mont. faculty unit 1967-70), Nat. Assn. Journalism Dirs., Am. Classical League, Am. Assn. U. Profs., Am. Assn. U. Women (pres. Dillon br. 1971—), Mont. Press Women, Delta Kappa Gamma (chpt. corr. sec. 1968-70). Republican. Conglist. (supt. Sunday Sch. 1952-55, mem. bd. religious edn. 1955-61, deaconess). Clubs: Western Montana College Faculty Women's, Dillon Shakespeare. Home: 1006 S Pacific St Dillon MT 59725

MANN, FRANCES ANN, clin. psychologist; b. Washington, June 20, 1946; d. Ernest Daniel and Thelma Gertrude (Gheen) Mann; B.A., Westhampton Coll., U. Richmond, 1968; M.A., U. Tenn., 1971, Ph.D., 1973. Staff psychologist children and youth services, referral liaison coordinator Helen Ross McNabb Center, Knoxville, Tenn., 1973—. Mem. Am., Southeastern, Tenn. psychol. assns., Council for Advancement Psychol. Professions and Scis., Common Cause, Psi Chi. Research on friendship in kindergarten children. Office: 1520 Cherokee Trail Knoxville TN 37920

MANN, GENEVIEVE ELLEN JENKINS (MRS. THEODORE W. MANN), banker; b. St. Louis; d. James L. and Ethel M. (Holt) Jenkins; student So. Ill. U., 1936-37; m. Theodore W. Mann, Sept. 7, 1937. With Colo. Nat. Bank of Denver, 1943—, asst. cashier, 1957-66, asst. v.p. personnel dept., 1966-73, v.p., 1973—. Mem. adv. council Colo. Dept. Employment, 1972—. Mem. Nat. Assn. Bank Women Inc. (chmn. exec. com. 1968-69, chmn. nat. conv. 1967), Internat. Assn. Personnel Women (conf. finance chmn. 1972), Colo. Personnel Women (pres. 1968-69), Downtown Bus. and Profl. Women's Club (treas. 1969-70), Am. Inst. Banking, Am., Colo. socs. personnel adminstrn. Club: Altrusa (rec. sec. Denver 1969-70, 2d v.p. 1971-72, pres. 1972-73). Home: 3008 S Gilpin St Denver CO 80210 Office: Colo Nat Bank Box 5168 TA Denver CO 80217

MANN, HELENE DAVIS POWNER (MRS. CECIL W. MANN), psychologist; b. Greensburg, Ind., June 30, 1899; d. Charles Tracy and Olive (Davis) Powner; student U. Ariz., 1917-19; A.B., U. Cal. at Berkeley, 1922; M.A., U. So. Cal., 1927; postgrad. U. So. Cal., Sorbonne, Paris, U. Madrid, 1927; pvt. study, France, U.S.A.; m. Cecil William Mann, Oct. 16, 1937; 1 stepdau., Jennifer O. Psychologist, tchr. gifted children Pasadena (Cal.) city schs., 1926-29; chief psychol. examiner Los Angeles County Juvenile Hall Clinic, 1929-39; spl. lectr. U. Denver, 1939-41; psychologist Bur. Testing and Guidance, also Specialized Tng. and Reassignment Unit, U.S. Army, La. State U., 1943-45; dir. Tulane U. reading improvement program, 1953-57; author, editor Charles T. Powner Corp., Regan Pub. Co., Chgo., 1922-60; pvt. practice psychology, New Orleans, 1945-61; pvt. practice, research, Jackson County, N.C., 1961—; psychol. cons. Western N.C. U. Mental Health Center, 1969-70, Dept. Interior Bur. Indian Affairs, Cherokee, N.C., 1962-70. Mem. Am. Assn. U. Women, League Women Voters, Am., Southeastern, N.C. psychol. assns., Pi Beta Phi. Club: Book. Contbr. articles to profl. jours.; also children's stories. Address: 600 Lake Wood Rd G 11 Hendersonville NC 28739

MANN, ISABEL ROOME, educator, civic worker; b. Troy, N.Y.; d. Herbert Roome and V. Adelaide (Spicer) M.; A.B., Vassar, 1918; M.A., Columbia, 1948. Tchr. English, French, Shippen Sch., Lancaster, Pa., English, history, Kent Place Sch., Summit, N.J., 1919-21; asst. in English, Troy High Sch., 1925-60. Speaker, local leader N.Y. State English Council, 1950-53; asst. sec.-treas. N.Y. State Legislative Forum, 1967-69, registrar, 1969-73. Sec., Vassar Class of 1918, 1973—. Louise Van Loon fellow, Vassar, 1947. Mem. Am. Assn. U. Women (pres. Troy 1955-59, 1963-65, del. nat. conv. 1955, 57, 61, 63, 65, 69, 71, 73), Am. Friends of Bodleian Library at Oxford, Mod. Lang. Assn., Nat. Council Tchrs. English, N.Y. State, Rensselaer County hist. socs., Women of St. Paul's (pres. 1971-73). Republican. Episcopalian. Clubs: Alliance Francaise de Troy (pres. 1944-46), Vassar (pres. 1942-44), Thursday Morning, Ilium, Troy. Address: 1518 Sage Av Troy NY 12180

MANN, SISTER JACINTA, educator; b. Pinckneyville, Ill., May 13, 1925; d. Bernard Albert and Magdalen Rose (Ruppert) Mann; B.S., So. Ill. U., 1946; M.S., U. Wis., 1947, Ph.D., 1958. Statistician, U. Wis., 1948-50; joined order Sisters of Charity, 1950; tchr. math. secondary sch., 1952-56; asst. prof. edn. Seton Hill Coll., Greensburg, Pa., 1958—, asst. dir. admissions, 1959-60, dir. admissions, 1960-67, acad. dean, 1968-71, asso. prof.-at-large, 1971-72, prof.-at-large, 1972—. Mem. faculty Harvard Summer Admissions Inst., 1967-71. Mem. Assn. Coll. Admissions Counselors (adv. bd. Coll. Admissions Center), Catholic Coll. Coordinating Council (v.p. 1965-67), Am. Psychol. Assn., Am. Statis. Assn., Nat. Council on Measurements in Edn., Assn. Coll. Admissions Counselors. Contbr. articles to profl. jours. Address: Seton Hill Coll Greensburg PA 15601

MANN, JUDITH MARGARET (MRS. VINCENT S. VILLARD, JR.), lawyer; b. Ann Arbor, Mich., Aug. 13, 1940; d. Lawrence Gerald and Margaret Regina (Karshens) Mann; B.A., Vassar Coll., 1962; J.D., U. Cal., 1967; m. Vincent S. Villard, Jr. Admitted to Cal. bar, 1967; atty. Silver, Rosen & Johnson, San Francisco, 1967-68, Coudert Bros., N.Y.C., 1969—. Mem. Am., Cal., N.Y. State bar assns., Profl. Women's Caucus, Order of Coif. Republican. Clubs: Vassar, Metropolitan Republican (N.Y.C.). Home: 233 E 69th St New York City NY 10021 Office: 200 Park Av New York City NY 10017

MANN, MARGARET BLACKWELL (MRS. JAMES HAROLD MANN), civic worker; b. Orange, Va., Sept. 28, 1919; d. Price Barron and Mary (Gardner) Blackwell; student Averett Coll., 1936-37, George Washington U., 1943-44; m. James Harold Mann, Aug. 31, 1940; children—Margaret Blackwell, Judith Walker. Adminstrv. asst. Hecht Co., Washington, 1937-40. Active various community drives; exec. reservist Office Emergency Planning, 1967—. Pres., Woman's Suburban Democratic Club, Montgomery County, Md., 1959-61; pres. Woman's Nat. Dem. Club, Washington, 1961-63, bd. govs., 1963—, chmn. ways and means com., 1973—; mem. Dem. Central Com. Md., 1964—; mem. inaugural com. Kennedy-Johnson, 1961; chmn. Woman's Speakers Bur. for Southwestern States, Johnson-Humphrey campaign, 1964, Humphrey-Muskie campaign, 1968; chmn. invitations and tickets com. Inaugural Balls Com., 1965; chmn. Nat. Dem. Women's Conf., Washington, 1966; chmn. Washington Area Friends of McGovern, 1971—; mem. spl. adv. com. women's activities Dem. Nat. Com., 1973—. Trustee Washington Ednl. TV Assn.; bd. advisers Averett Coll., Danville, Va., 1969-72, bd. govs., 1972—; bd. visitors Frostburg (Md.) State Coll. Named Ky. col., 1969. Home: 14525 Montevideo Rd Poolesville MD 20837

MANN, MARTY (MRS.), founder Nat. Council Alcoholism; b. Chgo., Oct. 15, 1904; d. William Henry and Lillian (Christy) Mann; student Chgo. Latin Sch., Santa Barbara (Cal.) Girl's Sch., 1921-22, Montemare, Adirondacks and Fla., 1922-24, Miss Nixon's Sch., Florence, Italy, 1924-25; divorced. Asst. editor Internat. Studio, 1928-30; contbr. Town and Country Mag., 1929-34; partner photography bus., London, Eng., 1930-36; publicity jubilee season Covent Garden Opera, 1935; fashion publicity dir. R. H. Macy & Co., N.Y.C., 1940-42; research dir., radio script writer A.S.C.A.P., 1942-44; founder, exec. dir. Nat. Council Alcoholism, 1944-68, now founder-cons.; lectr. on alcoholism, profl. and lay orgns.; spl. cons. to dir. Nat. Inst. on Alcohol Abuse and Alcoholism; cons. on alcoholism, social agencies, ednl. indsl., med., church groups; ofcl. del. Internat. Congress on Alcoholism, Luzerne, Switzerland, 1948; guest of Govt. Union South Africa, to advise on govt. action on alcoholism, and to address First Nat. Conf. on Alcoholism, 1951; addressed joint sessions of state legislatures of S.C., 1946, Mich., 1952, Tenn., 1965; lectr. sch. alcohol studies, Yale, U. Wash., U. Utah, U. Tex., U. Colo., U. Ga., Millsaps Coll., Menninger Found., Columbia Tchrs. Coll.; participant Third Conf. Internat. Union for Health Edn. of Pub., Rome, Italy, 1956; guest nat. alcoholism orgns., Australia and New Zealand, 1961, London, Eng., Belfast, No. Ireland, Dublin, 1964, 67. Recipient Elizabeth Blackwell award Hobart and William Smith Coll., 1963. Fellow Am. Pub. Health Assn., Soc. Pub. Health Educators, Royal Soc. of Health London, Am. Psychiat. Assn. (hon.); mem. Soc. Study Addiction to Alcohol and other Drugs London (hon. sci. mem.). Author: Primer on Alcoholism, 1950 (pub. Eng. 1952); Primer on Alcoholism: Afrikaans Translation (pub. S. Africa), 1954; Marty Mann's New Primer on Alcoholism, 1958, Finnish translation, 1962, Spanish translation, 1969; Marty Mann Answers Your Questions About Drinking and Alcoholism, 1970. Contbr. articles popular, profl. jours. Office: 2 Park Av New York City NY 10016

MANN, OPAL HURLEY (MRS. ARNOLD CURTIS MANN), govt. ofcl.; b. Yocum, Ky., Feb. 28, 1922; d. James Allen and Lourainey (Engle) Hurley; B.S., U. Ky., 1945, M.S. (Extension supervisory fellow, Ky. Extension Home Econs. fellow, Coop Extension scholar), 1965; Ph.D., Ohio State U, 1971; m. Arnold Curtis Mann, Apr. 23, 1945; children—Patricia Kay (Mrs. Steve Ganter), Vernon Gene. Tchr. home econs. Joppa (Ill.) High Sch., 1944-45; asst. home demonstration agt. U. Ky., Breathitt County, Jackson, 1945, home demonstration agt., Pike County, Pikeville, Ky., 1945-47, 55-61, dist. leader home demonstration extension agts., Lexington, Ky., 1961-65; tchr. home econs. Virgie High Sch., Pike County, 1950-55; state program specialist Home Econs. Coop. Extension Service, U. Ky., Lexington, 1965-71; dep. asst. adminstr. extension service, home econs. U.S. Dept. Agr., Washington, 1971-73, asst. adminstr., 1973—. 1st aid instr. A.R.C., 1958-63, mem. exec. bd., 1958-61; mem. Pres.'s Com. Consumer Affairs. Recipient certificate of recognition Gov. of Ky., 1971. Mem. Adult Edn. Assn. U.S.A., Am., Ky. (state conv. chmn. 1968-69), D.C. home econs. assns., Asso. Country Women of World, Am. Assn. U. Women, Ky. Assn. Continuing Edn. (state sec. 1968-70), State Extension Specialists Assn., State Program Specialists Orgn., Orgn. Profl. Employees of U.S. Dept. Agr., Agrl. Employees Consumer Assn., Epsilon Sigma Phi (Meritorious Service award 1968). Mem. Christian Ch. (v.p. bd. dirs.). Home: 9200 Dewberry Lane College Park MD 20740 Office: Extension Service Home Econs US Dept Agr Washington DC 20250

MANN, PAULINE ZLOWE (MRS. CHARLES MANN), advt. co. exec.; b. Russia (parents Am. citizens); d. Rubin and Fredda (Pufovitz) Zlowe; certificate State Tchrs. Coll., New Britain, Conn., 1930; B.S., Columbia, 1937; M.A., Trinity Coll., 1941; m. Charles Mann, Sept. 18, 1942. Tchr. Jones Jr. High Sch., Hartford, Conn., 1930-44, head English dept., 1937-44; with Zlowe Co., Inc., N.Y.C., 1944-68, v.p., 1962-68, treas., 1952-68; v.p. Marsteller, Inc., N.Y.C., 1968—. Mem. Am. Assn. Advt. Agys. (radio-TV com. 1950—), Nat. Acad. TV Arts and Scis., Museum Modern Art. Home: 117 E 77th St New York City NY 10021 Office: 866 Third Av New York City NY 10022

MANN, RUTH KIRKPATRICK (MRS. GORDON LEE MANN), club woman; b. Commerce, Tex.; d. Silvanus B. and Roxanna (Hamilton) Kirkpatrick; ed. pvt. schs.; m. Gordon Lee Mann, Dec. 10, 1912 (dec. Feb. 1949); children—Helen Ruth (dec.), Gordon Lee. Regent, Los Angeles chpt. D.A.R., 1960-62, parliamentarian, 1962-66, historian Past and Present Regents Assn. of Cal., 1964-65, dir. press relations, 1957-67; mem. state bd. Cal. Soc. Children Am. Revolution, 1966-70, state chaplain, 1968-70; recorder crosses Cal. div. U.D.C., 1964-66, dir. patriotic activities, 1966-68; pres. Ft. Moore chpt. U.S. Daus. 1812, 1960-62; mem. Nat. Soc. Magna Charta Dames, Nat. Soc. Ams. of Royal Descent. Co-capt. fund-raising, woman's com. So. Cal. Symphony-Hollywood Bowl Assn., 1960-64. Life mem. Soc. Descs. Knights of Garter, Plantagenet Society, Colonial Order of Crown of Charlemagne. Republican. Episcopalian. Contbr. articles to nat. patriotic mags. Home: 435 S Curson Av Los Angeles CA 90036

MANNERS, NANCY THERESA, city ofcl.; b. Catania, Sicily; brought to U.S., 1922, naturalized, 1927; d. Gioacchino Jack and Maria Providenza (Virzi) Marasa; degree in pub. adminstrn. U. So. Cal., 1973; m. George Manners, Dec. 20, 1941; children—Gene David, Nancy Ellen (Mrs. Frank O. Sieh), Joan Alice. With City of Covina (Cal.), 1959—, adminstrv. sec., 1960-63, asst. to city adminstr. and personnel dir., 1963-73, asst. city mgr., 1973—. Regional chmn. San Gabriel Valley TB and Respiratory Disease Assn., 1971-73; pres. Covina Coordinating Council, 1969-70; del. East San Gabriel Valley Area Coordinating Council, 1969-70; rep. Camp Glenn Rocky Probation Camp Com., 1969-70; chmn. pub. employees United Crusade, intermittently; chmn. ways and means Covian High Sch. Drill Team Boosters Club, 1970-71; mem. Covina High Sch. Band and Orchestra Boosters Club, 1964-67, 69-72; mem. Inter-Jurisdictional Com. of Nine to develop brochures regarding drug abuse, nationwide circulation, 1967-68. Mem. Covina-Valley Unified Sch. Dist. Bd. Edn., 1973—. Bd. dirs. Fedn. Community Coordinating Councils Los Angeles County, 1969-70, San Gabriel Valley Hot Line Assn., 1970—, Covina Sister City Assn., 1964-72, Covina Safety Council, 1964-70. Mem. C. of C. (bd. dirs. women's div. 1961-63), Municipal Mgmt. Assts. So. Cal. (sec.-treas. 1972-73), Internat. City Mgmt. Assn., Am. Soc. Pub. Adminstrns., So. Cal. Civil Def. and Disaster Assn., Area D Assn. Civil Def. (bd. dirs. 1965—), So. Cal. Pub. Personnel Assn., Cal. Sch. Bds. Assn. Presbyn. Club: Altrusa (pres. 1971-72). Home: 734 N Eileen Av West Covina CA 91791 Office: 125 E College St Covina CA 91723

MANNES, MARYA, author; b. N.Y.C.; d. David and Clara (Damrosch) Mannes; student pvt. sch., N.Y.C.; L.H.D., Hood Coll., 1961, Williams Coll., 1971, Southampton Coll., 1972; m. Jo Mielziner, 1926 (div. 1931); m. 2d, Richard Blow, 1937 (div. 1943); 1 son, David Jeremy; m. 3d, Christopher Clarkson, Apr. 2, 1948 (div. 1966). Feature editor, staff writer Vogue Mag., 1933-36; intelligence analyst OSS, 1943-45; feature editor Glamour mag., 1946-47; free-lance writer, 1947-52, 63—; staff mem. Reporter mag., 1952-63; writer monthly column McCall's, 1965-67, movie critic, 1968; writer monthly column N.Y. Times, 1967; TV commentator Channel 13, N.Y.C., 1967-70; columnist United Features Syndicate, 1971-73; Chubb fellow Timothy Dwight Coll., Yale, 1973. Trustee Mannes Coll. Music, N.Y.C. Recipient George Polk Meml. award for mag. reporting, 1958; award of honor Phila. chpt. Theta Sigma Phi, 1962. Democrat. Author: Message From a Stranger, 1948; More in Anger, 1958; Subverse, 1959; The New York I Know, 1961; But Will It Sell?, 1964; They, 1968; Out of My Time (autobiography), 1971; Uncoupling, 1972; Last Rights, 1974. Office: care Harold Ober Assos 40 E 49th St New York City NY 10017

MANNEY, BLANCHE IRENE ROGERS (MRS. ENOS EDWIN MANNEY), pub. co. exec.; b. Council Bluffs, Ia., Dec. 8, 1897; d. James Chauncey and Taphena Jane (Rogers) Rogers; student U. Kan., 1913-14; m. Enos Edwin Manney, June 8, 1916; children—Dorothy (Mrs. W.E. Kirschke), Enos Edwin. Owner Ford (Kan.) Promoter, 1916-17, Panhandle (Tex.) Herald, 1920-23; co-owner Monitor, Morse, Tex., 1930-31, Sanford (Tex.) News, 1930-31, Sunray (Tex.) News, 1930-31, Handly (Tex.) News, 1936-37; owner, gen. mgr. Manney Co., Ft. Worth, 1935—. Bible tchr. KFJZ, Ft. Worth, 1936-37. Author: Bits and Pieces, 1970. Home: 1041 Isbell Rd Fort Worth TX 76114

MANNING, ALMA SQUIRES (MRS. T. WESLEY MANNING), nursing adminstr.; b. New Middleton, Tenn., Sept. 9, 1912; d. James T. and Florence (Hays) Squires; diploma St. Thomas Sch. Nursing, Nashville, 1941; certificate Middle Tenn. Tchrs. Coll., Murfreesboro, 1931; B.S. in Nursing Edn., Cath. U. Am., 1955; m. T. Wesley Manning, Aug. 26, 1947. Substitute tchr. Smith County Schs., Carthage, Tenn., 1931-38; instr. nursing St. Thomas Sch. Nursing, Nashville, 1941-44, St. Mary's Sch. Nursing, Knoxville, Tenn., 1944-48; dir. nursing Nashville Met. Gen. Hosp., 1948—. Mem. bd. examiners Tenn. Com. on Nursing Edn. and Nursing Practice, 1945-50; mem. Tenn. Bd. Nursing, 1952-54; mem. nursing council Tenn. Hosp. Assn.; mem. Nat. adv. com. SSS, 1959-71. Named One of 5 Outstanding Execs. of Yr., Davidson County Bus. and Profl. Women's Club, 1963. Methodist. Club: Zonta (charter). Home: 2514 Joya Dr Nashville TN 37214 Office: Nashville Met Gen Hosp Nashville TN 37210

MANNING, ANITA, museum ofcl.; b. Indpls., Nov. 26, 1946; d. Howard Emsley and Frances Louise (Nihma) Manning; A.A., Palomar Jr. Coll., 1967; B.A. in Anthropology, San Diego State Coll., 1969; postgrad. U. Hawaii, 1971-72. Curatorial asst. Mus. of Man, San Diego, 1968-69; Nat. Endowment for Humanities mus. intern Bernice Pauahi Bishop Mus., Honolulu, 1969-70, edn. specialist, asst. registrar, 1970-71, registrar, 1971—. Lectr. to high sch. groups on Am. Indian cultures; tng. sessions with East West Center, U. Hawaii. Grantee Williamsburg Seminar for Hist. Adminstrs., 1973. Mem. Am. Assn. Museums, Am. Assn. for State and Local History, Am. Indian Hist. Soc., Hawaii Museums Assn. (v.p. 1971), Hawaiian Hist. Soc. Club: Sierra. Home: 3075 Kalihi St Honolulu HI 96819 Office: PO Box 6037 Honolulu HI 96818

MANNING, BERTINA MARIA SUIDA (MRS. ROBERT LEE MANNING), art historian; b. Vienna, Austria, Dec. 5, 1922; d. William Emil and Eugenie (Satory) Suida; came to U.S., 1939, naturalized, 1945; B.A., Queens Coll., 1945; M.A., N.Y.U., 1958, postgrad. Inst. Fine Arts, 1945-48; m. Robert Lee Manning, Dec. 19, 1948; 1 dau., Alessandra Eugenia B. Curator collection of Walter P. Chrysler, Jr., N.Y.C., 1954-57; free lance cons. art hist. research, 1958—; collaborated selection and catalogue-compilation of first exhbn. of Genoese painters of the Renaissance and Baroque, Dayton (O.) Art Inst., other Am. museums; contbr. to catalogue Italy 1600-1700, 1965; cons. Chrysler Art Mus., Norfolk, Va., 1958—. Decorated Knight Order of Merit, Italy. Mem. Beta Sigma Omicron. Author: (with William E. Suida) Luca Cambiaso, LaVita, Le Opere, 1958. Contbr. Ency. Italiana, also articles to publs. Address: 82-54 Grenfell St Kew Gardens NY 11415

MANNING, DOROTHY CORNELL (MRS. DONALD L. MANNING), librarian; b. Dansville, N.Y., Apr. 26, 1926; d. James Edwin and Dorothea Irene (Losey) Sanford; B.A., Keuka Coll., 1966; M.L.S., State U. N.Y. at Geneseo, 1969; m. Edwin G. Cornell, 1944;

children—Peter, Michael, Lynne (Mrs. Raymond A. Bennett), Robert; m. 2d, Donald L. Manning, July 4, 1964. Elementary librarian Hammondsport (N.Y.) Central Sch., 1966-69; tech. services librarian Keuka Coll. Library, Keuka Park, N.Y., 1969-71; head librarian Lightner Library, 1971—. Mem. Am. Assn. U. Profs., Am., N.Y. library assns. Home: 531 West Lake Rd Hammondsport NY 14840 Office: Lightner Library Keuka College Keuka Park NY 14478

MANNING, ELIZABETH M(ACDONALD), publisher, editor; b. Moncton, N.B., Can., Dec. 23, 1919; d. John Henry and Lucy (Allen) McDonald; B.S. in Journalism, Boston U.; postgrad. Harvard Bus. Sch., 1957-67; widow; children—Meredith, Brian, Victoria. Account exec. Hirshon-Garfield Advt. Agy., 1944-46; v.p. Newsome Pub. Relations Agy., 1946-51; pres. Manning Pub. Relations, N.Y.C., 1951-69, Finance Pub. Corp., N.Y.C., 1965—; pres., editor-in-chief Finance Mag., 1970—. Coordinator Coatesville Conf. Econ. Freedoms. Bd. dirs., nat. council Invest-in-Am. Mem. Pub. Relations Soc. Am., Am. Mgmt. Assn., Met. Pres. Orgn. (1st v.p.), Soc. Am. Bus. Writers. Club: Nat. Press (Washington). Contbr. articles to Ency. Brit. Home: 5 E 75th St New York City NY 10021 also Daniels Island South Mashpee Cape Cod MA

MANNING, MARGUERITE, univ. dean, clergywoman; b. Phoenix; d. Walter Jerald and Elizabeth (Smith) Manning; A.B., Scarritt Coll., 1942; M.A., Boston, 1943; M.Div., Union Theol. Sem., 1957; M.A., Columbia Tchrs. Coll., 1966, Ed.D., 1972. Ordained to ministry Congl. Ch.; dir. student activities U. Tenn., 1943-46; ednl. asst. Riverside Ch., N.Y.C., 1947-55; parish worker East Harlem Protestant Parish, 1955-57; minister East Corinth Congl. Ch. and Waits River Meth. Ch., Vt., 1958-61; tchr. English and phys. edn. Baghdad (Iraq) High Sch., 1961-62; adminstrv. asst. dept. guidance and student personnel adminstrn. Columbia Tchrs. Coll., 1962-66; research asso. Bank St. Coll. Edn., N.Y.C., 1966-68; with Bur. Research, N.Y.C. Bd. Edn., 1968-69; sec. personnel United Bd. Christian Higher Edn. in Asia, 1969-71; dean student affairs Rutgers U., Newark, 1971—. Active Red Feather drive; social worker A.R.C., Camp Shanks, N.Y., World War II; moderator Grafton-Orange Assn. Congl. Chs.; mem. minister's assn. Vt. Congl. Conf., 1958; pres. Women of Grace Ch., Newark. Bd. dirs. YWCA. Mem. Nat. Assn. Women Deans and Counselors, Am. Assn. Ednl. Research, Am. Personnel and Guidance Assn., N.E.A., Am. Assn. Higher Edn., Am. Assn. U. Adminstrs., Bus. and Profl. Women's Club, Pi Lambda Theta (pres. Alpha Epsilon chpt. 1966-68, treas., 1969-72, chmn. nat. nominating com. 1966-67), Kappa Delta Pi. Home: 351 Broad St Apt 1009 Newark NJ 07104

MANNING, MARY CATHERINE, polit. scientist; b. Grand Rapids, Mich., June 18, 1925; d. William Thomas and Mary F. (Dalton) Manning; A.B. summa cum laude (Bishop Albers scholar 1943), Nazareth (Mich.) Coll., 1947; M.A. (State Coll. scholar), U. Mich., 1949; postgrad. Mich. State U., 1951-54. Instr. history and polit. sci. Nazareth Coll., 1949-51; instr. Mich. State U., 1951-54; employee Mich. Employment Security Commn., 1954-63; social sci. adviser Women's Bur., U.S. Dept. Labor, 1963-65, Midwest regional dir. Women's Bur., 1965—. Trustee Nazareth Coll. Mem. Polit. Sci. Assn., Internat. Assn. Personnel in Employment Security, Nazareth Coll. Alumnae Assn. (pres. 1950-54), Kappa Gamma Pi, Pi Lambda Theta, Pi Sigma Alpha, Phi Kappa Phi. Home: 6040 N Sheridan Rd Chicago IL 60660 Office: 219 S Dearborn St Chicago IL 60604

MANNING, MILDRED PAULINE, educator; b. Bethel, N.C., Oct. 29, 1914; d. William John O. and Minnie (Manning) Manning; A.B., E. Carolina U., 1936, M.A., 1949; postgrad. Duke, summer 1964. Tchr. pub. schs., Mayodan, N.C., 1934-37, Bunn, N.C., 1937-40, Aurora, N.C., 1940-42, Oak City, N.C., 1942-45, Rocky Mount, N.C., 1945-48, Tarboro, N.C., 1948-53; elementary supr. Martin County, Williamston, N.C., 1953-71. Treas., bd. dirs. N.C. Classroom Tchrs. Survivors Fund. Mem. (life) N.E.A., (life) N.C. Edn. Assn. (dist. sec., past dist. pres., dir.), Delta Kappa Gamma. Died Oct. 10, 1971. Home: Box 685 Bethel NC 27812 Office: Box 334 Williamston NC 27862

MANNING, SUSAN KARP, educator; b. N.Y.C.; d. Walter and Estelle Rosalind (Grossman) Karp; student Mt. Holyoke Coll., 1956-58; B.A., U. Mich., 1960, M.A., 1961; Ph.D., U. Cal. at Riverside, 1971; m. Robert E. Manning, June 22, 1963. Research asst. U. Mich., 1960-61, Harvard Med. Sch., 1964, State of Cal., 1965-66; tech. specialist Mitre Corp., Bedford, Mass., 1962-64; teaching asst. U. Cal. at Riverside, 1966-67; part-time lectr. psychology Coll. City N.Y., 1967-68, lectr., 1970-71; lectr. Hunter Coll., City U. N.Y., 1968-70, instr., 1970-72, asst. prof., 1972—. Mem. N.Y. County Democratic Com., 1969—; mem. exec. com. Murray Hill Dem. Club, 1970, 72. Mem. Am., Eastern psychol. assns., A.A.A.S. Contbr. articles to profl. jours.

MANOIL, MOYCA CHRISTY (MRS. LOU MANOIL), newspaper pub.; b. Phoenix, July 31, 1919; d. Charles Bennett and Ethel Dione (Baker) Christy; B.A., Mills Coll., 1941; m. Lou Manoil, Aug. 17, 1955; children—Colin and Geoffrey (twins), Mark Lou. Woman's editor Ariz. Republic, daily newspaper, Phoenix, 1945, 54-55; feature editor U.S. Dept. State, Washington, 1945-49; writer London Daily Express, Tokyo, Japan, 1950-51; pub. Point West mag., Phoenix, 1959-62; pub. Ariz. Living, Phoenix, 1963—. Organizer, 1st pres. Planned Parenthood Aux. Phoenix, 1958. Recipient 1st place award for gen. interest mag. regularly edited by woman Nat. Fedn. Press Women, 1962. Mem. Women in Communications, Ariz. Acad. Home: 5655 N 4th St Phoenix AZ 85012 Office: 5120 N Central St Phoenix AZ 85012

MANSER, ELLEN IRENE PIERSON (MRS. GORDON MANSER), social worker; b. Bridgeton, N.J., Aug. 17, 1917; d. Howard Wilson and Irene (McAllister) Pierson; A.B., Middlebury Coll., 1938; M.A., Bryn Mawr Coll., 1940; m. Gordon Manser, Nov. 1, 1947; children—Norris James Gordon, Clark McAllister. Caseworker, Childrens Home Soc. N.J., Trenton, 1940-41, United Family and Childrens Soc., Plainfield, N.J., 1941-45, Childrens Bur., Dallas, 1945-46, Los Angeles, 1947-49; caseworker, supr., dir. adoption dept. Family and Childrens Soc., Balt., 1951-62; cons. pub. issues, coordinator joint project on parent edn., group leadership Family Service Assn. Am., N.Y.C., 1964-65, dir. project ENABLE, 1965-67, specialist family devel., 1967-71, advocacy team dir., 1971—. Mem. Nat. Assn. Social Workers, Nat. Assembly Social Policy and Devel., Nat. Conf. Social Welfare. Presbyn. Home: 5800 Arlington Av Riverdale NY 10471 Office: 44 E 23d St New York NY 10010

MANSFIELD, LOIS EDNA, educator, mathematician; b. Portland, Me., Jan. 2, 1941; d. Robert Carleton and Mary Josephine (Bowdish) Mansfield; B.S., U. Mich., 1962; M.S., U. Utah, 1966, Ph.D., 1969. Tchr. Rowland Hall-St. Marks Sch., Salt Lake City, 1962-65; vis. asst. prof. Purdue U., 1969-70; asst. prof. computer sci. U. Kan., 1970-74, asso. prof., 1974—; vis. asst. prof. math. U. Utah, 1973-74. NASA trainee, 1967-69. Mem. Am. Math. Soc., Soc. Indsl. and Applied Math. Contbr. articles to profl. jours. Home: DD 211 Bristol Terrace Lawrence KS 66044

MANSFIELD, LOUISE WASSON (MRS. GLEN E. MANSFIELD), nurse, educator; b. Blountsville, Ind., Feb. 19, 1916; d. Frank Helm and Susie (Kilmer) Wasson; B.S. cum laude, Ohio State U., 1947; M.A., Columbia, 1951; postgrad. U. Wash.; m. Glen E. Mansfield, Aug. 29, 1955; stepchildren—Colleen (Mrs. Gordon Cook, Glenna (Mrs. Eugene Bennett), Marjorie (Mrs. Edward Wallace), Pauline, Daniel Lee. Staff nurse, head nurse Harborview Hosp., Seattle, 1938-42; instr. surg. nursing dept. nursing edn. U. Ore. Med. Sch., Portland, 1947-50; instr. U. Wash. Sch. Nursing, Seattle, 1951-52, asst. prof., 1952-65, asso. prof., 1965-69, prof., 1969—. Mem. adv. bd. Univ. br. YWCA, Seattle, 1962-67. Served with Nurse Corps, AUS, 1942-46. Mem. Am. Nurses Assn., Nat. League Nursing, Am. Assn. U. Profs., Am. Assn. Advancement Med. Instrumentation, Wash. State Heart Assn., Pi Lambda Theta, Kappa Delta Pi, Sigma Theta Tau. USPHS prin. investigator cardiac nursing, 1966-68. Contbr. articles to profl. books and jours. Home: 547 NE 130th St Seattle WA 98125

MANSFIELD, RACHELL KATHRYN COPP (MRS. JAMES PATRICK MANSFIELD, JR.), civic leader; b. Great Falls, Mont.; d. Frank and Apolonia (Zdybickie) Copp; B.S. in Edn. magna cum laude, Coll. Great Falls, 1939; postgrad. U. Mont., 1968, 72—; m. James Patrick Mansfield, Jr., June 18, 1946; children—Mary Jo (Mrs. John Wayne Gass), James Patrick III, Michael G., Colleen M. Tchr., Square Butte Pub. Sch., 1939-41, Rudyard Pub. Sch., 1941-42, Hingham Pub. Sch., 1942-43. Mem. Mont. Congress Parents and Tchrs., 1958—, mag., publs. chmn., 1958-61, sec., 1961, 3d v.p., 1961-64, 1st v.p., 1964-66, pres., 1966-68, cons. on nat. booklet com., 1967-68, chmn. pub. relations 1970-72, state, nat. life mem., 1966—; mem. Mont. Health Adv. Com. on Drugs; dir. Peabody research on schs. Judith Basin County, Mont., 1961-62; mem. com. sch. consolidations, 1961-64; mem. tchr.'s supply com., 1968, mem. com. on teenagers, 1968; ednl. dist. dir. Rural Devel., 1966—; v.p. County Council Homemakers, 1970-72; mem. state legislative com. Mont. Library Assn., 1968—, dist. dir. Mental Retardation, 1965-66; del. Mont. Constnl. Conv., 1971-72; mem. Bicentennial Com., 1973—; state legislative chmn. P.T.A., 1973—. Served with WAVES, 1943-45. Mem. Am. Legion. Home: Geyser MT 59447

MANSOUR, SISTER AGNES MARY, coll. pres.; b. Detroit, Apr. 10, 1931; d. Said Thomas and Marie (Mabarak) Mansour; B.S., Mercy Coll. Detroit, 1953; M.S., Cath. U. Am., 1958; Ph.D., Georgetown U., 1964. Joined Sisters of Mercy, 1953; mem. faculty Mercy Coll. of Detroit, 1958—, chmn. med. assos. div., 1959-61, prof. chemistry, 1964-70, chmn. dept. chemistry-physics, 1964-70, pres. coll., 1971—. Clin. lab. supr., coordinator med. tech. Mt. Carmel Mercy Hosp., Detroit, 1958-61; cons. div. allied health manpower Dept. Health, Edn. and Welfare, 1972—. Am. Council on Edn. fellow, 1970-71. Mem. Am. Chem. Soc., A.A.A.S., Nat. Sci. Tchrs. Assn., Am. Soc. Med. Technologists, Assn. Schs. of Allied Health Professions, Delta Epsilon Sigma, Kappa Gamma Pi. Address: 8200 W Outer Dr Detroit MI 48219

MANTIUS, MARJORIE ELLIS, realty co. exec.; b. Roanoke, Va., Sept. 20, 1922; s. Clarence M. and Ana (Sanderson) Ellis; student Randolph Macon Woman's Coll., 1940-42, U. N.C., 1943; m. Edward P. Lebens, Nov. 14, 1943 (div. Oct. 1957); children—Edward S., David E., Bruce P.; m. 2d, Philip K. Mantius, Oct. 26, 1957. Adv. and pub. relations dir. Peugeot Inc., Forest Hills, N.Y., 1963-69; v.p., dir. pub. relations Gift Pax, Inc., Hempstead, N.Y., 1969; pub. relations and community relations dir. Levitt Residential Co., Centereach, N.Y., 1971—. Adj. faculty mem. State U. N.Y. at Stonybrook. Chmn. com. to train women speakers for Republican party N.Y. State, 1967-68. Bd. govs. friends Sunwood Sch., Stony Brook. Recipient Gold key award Pub. Relations News, 1970; award City New Orleans, 1963. Mem. Internat. Motor Press. Clubs: St. Georges, Three Village (Setauket, N.Y.); Old Field (Stony Brook). Author: L'Histoire de Peugeot, 1968. Home: Box 581 East Setauket NY 11733 Office: 1919 Middle County Rd Centereach NY 11720

MANUELIDIS, LAURA (MRS. ELIAS E. MANUELIDIS), physician; b. N.Y.C., Sept. 8, 1942; d. Milton F. and Rose (Epstein) Kirchman; B.A., Sarah Lawrence Coll., 1963; M.D., Yale, 1967; m. Elias E. Manuelidis, Nov. 19, 1966; children—Emmanuel E., Laertes Alexis. Intern, Yale Sch. Medicine, 1967-68, resident pathology, 1968-70, NIH postdoctoral fellow, 1968-72; instr. dept. pathology, 1970-72, asst. prof. pathology, 1972—. Contbr. research articles on devel. and differentiation in nervous system to med. jours. Home: 585 Ellsworth Av New Haven CT 06511

MANZIE, MARY LOU CATHERINE, indsl. real estate exec.; b. Indpls., Jan. 17, 1948; d. Michael William and Patricia Louise (Pickard) Manzie; student (David A. Curry and Ind. Classical Conf. scholar) Ind. U., 1966-69; B.A. cum laude, Boston U. 1970. Asst. in guest relations ITT Sheraton Corp. Am., Boston, 1970-71; sales adminstrv. asst. Decatur Hopkins Bigelow Dowse Co., Needham, Mass., 1971; adminstrv. asst. to pres. and chmn. bd. High Mark Corp., Boston, 1971-72; exec. asst. indsl. real estate C.W. Whittier & Bro. Real Estate, Boston, 1972-74, broker, 1973. Mem. Am., Sr., Jr. classical leagues, Big Sister Assn. Greater Boston, Nat. Orgn. Women. Home: 16 Harvard Terrace Allston MA 02134

MAPLE, BERNICE BARBARA KARPIN (MRS. ROBERT JAMES MAPLE), educator; b. Chgo., May 15, 1922; d. Felix and Anna (Pettak) Karpin; F.A.A. in Fine and Applied Arts, U. Ill., 1944; m. Robert James Maple, Sept. 7, 1945; children—James Craig, Robin Lynne. Pvt. tchr. piano Chgo. Mus. Coll., 1937-42; pvt. tchr. piano, Chgo., 1942-65; tchr. art Wilson Jr. High Sch., Decatur, Ill., 1944; intern occupational therapy Kennedy Gen. Hosp., Memphis, 1944-45; registered occupational therapist Thayer Gen. Hosp., Nashville, 1944-45; spl. edn. tchr. Genoa-Kingston Sch. Dist., Kingston, Ill., 1966—. Reading cons. various sch. dists., 1969—. Counselor, Girl Scouts U.S.A., St. Louis, 1942, leader, Decatur, Ill., 1944-45; den mother Cub Scouts Am., Sycamore, Ill., 1955-59; leader 4-H, Sycamore, 1959-64; dental chmn. Sycamore Women's Club, 1960. Recipient U.S. Govt. Fed. grantee 1944. Mem. Am. Occupational Therapy Assn. (dist. chmn. 1973), Ill. Edn. Assn., N.E.A., Assn. Tchr. Edn., Genoa-Kingston Ednl. Assn. Home: 353 Crescent Dr Sycamore IL 60178 Office: Kingston Grade Sch Kingston IL 60145

MAPLES, EVELYN LUCILLE (MRS. WILLIAM EUGENE MAPLES), editor, author; b. Ponce de Leon, Mo., Feb. 7, 1919; d. Thomas Sherman and Bertie Josephine (Dalby) Palmer; m. William Eugene Maples, Dec. 23, 1938; children—Norman Francis, Billi Jo, Matthew McBride. Tchr. pub. sch. Rogersville, Mo., 1937-38; proofreader Herald Pub. House, Independence, Mo., 1953-63, editor, 1963—. Tchr. writing various workshops. Mem. Community Assn. for the Arts, Mo. Writers Guild. Mem. Reorganized Ch. Jesus Christ of Latter Day Saints (congregation publicity dir. 1964-68, ch. sch. tchr. 1960-70, campus ministry cons. 1964-71). Republican. Author: What Saith the Scriptures, 1961, Norman Learns About the Sacraments, 1961, Jomo the Missionary Monkey, 1966, That Ye Love, 1971, The Brass Plates Adventure, 1972; Lehi, Man of God, 1972, Norman Learns About the Scriptures, 1972, The Many Selves of Ann-Elizabeth, 1973. Home: 16216 E Sea St Independence MO 64050 Office: Drawer HH 3225 S Noland Independence MO 64055

MAPLES, MARY ANGELA FINN (MRS. NEWSOM BATTLE MAPLES), educator; b. Lynn, Mass., Apr. 2, 1934; d. John Joseph and Catherine (Ahern) Finn; B.S., Mass. State Coll., 1955, M.Ed., 1961; postgrad. U. R.I., 1962, Boston U., 1964, Ore. State U., 1970, U. Ore., 1973—; m. Newsom Battle Maples, Aug. 31, 1957; children—Michael Christopher, John Neal, Stephen Christopher. Tchr. elementary schs., Mass., Alaska, Ore., 1955-60; guidance counselor, adminstr. Regional Sch. Dist. High Sch., Bridgewater, Mass., 1960-65; counselor, instr. Maryhurst (Ore.) Coll., 1965-68, dean students, 1968-69; county dir. guidance and testing Linn-Benton Intermediate Edn. Dist., Albany, Ore., 1969-72; asst. prof. U. Ore., 1972—. Mem. N.E.A., Ore. Edn. Assn., Assn. Counselor Educators and Suprs., Nat. Assn. Student Personnel Adminstrs., Am. (chmn., treas. Western region 1973—, dir. 1972—, chmn. task force br. leadership 1974, br. council 1972-73), Ore. (pres. 1972-73) personnel and guidance assns., Nat. Vocational Guidance Assn. (state coordinator), Western Assn. Counselor Educators and Suprs. (pres. elect 1975-76), Am. Sch. Counselor Assn. (mem. editorial bd. 1973—). Roman Catholic. Home: 3331 NW Crest Loop Albany OR 97321

MAR, BEATRIZ CASTRO (MRS. FRANCIS MAR), real estate broker; b. Limon, Costa Rica, C.A.M., Feb. 23, 1917; d. Guillermo and Sara (Lee) Castro; came to U.S., 1942, naturalized, 1955; B.S. in Pharmacy, U. Costa Rica, 1941; M.S. in Nutrition, Ia. State U., 1944; m. Francis Mar, July 22, 1944; children—Dennis Ronald, Faye Lee (Mrs. Willie K. Dong). Food lab. technician Schuckl & Co., Sunnyvale, Cal., 1951-56; quality control supr. Paul Mariani Co. & Mariani Frozen Foods, Cupertino, Cal., 1957-62; real estate salesman Ken Hill Realty, Sunnyvale, Cal., 1964-66; broker asso. Referral Realty, Sunnyvale, 1966-72; broker-owner Beatriz C. Mar, Realtor, Sunnyvale, 1972—. Pan Am. scholar Inst. Internat. Edn. N.Y., 1942-44. Mem. Cal. Real Estate Assn., Nat. Assn. Realtors, Nat. Inst. Real Estate Bds., Asso. Investment and Exchange Counselors, Peninsula Exchangors, Sunnyvale and San Jose Real Estate Bds. Club: Chi-Am. Women's of Santa Clara County. Home: 575 E Olive Av Sunnyvale CA 94086 Office: 355 W Olive Av Sunnyvale CA 94086

MAR, PATRICIA S., lawyer; b. Los Angeles, Oct. 9, 1942; d. Erwin W. and May G. (Jing) Mar; B.A., U. Cal. at Berkeley, 1964; J.D., U. of the Pacific, 1969. Reporter San Francisco Examiner 1964-65; staff asst. Joint Com. on Higher Edn., Cal. Legislature, Sacramento, 1965-66; adminstrv. asst. to dir. Compensatory Edn., Cal. State Dept. Edn., Sacramento, 1966-69; admitted to Cal. bar, 1970, since practiced in San Francisco; law clk. and research atty. Cal. Ct. of Appeals, San Francisco, 1969-71; asso. firm Feldman, Waldman and Kline, San Francisco, 1971—. Dir. Chinese Am. Democratic Club, San Francisco. Bd. dirs. Bay Area Comprehensive Health Care Council, Pub. Advocates, Inc. Mem. State Bar of Cal., San Francisco Bar Assn., San Francisco Barristers Club, San Francisco Queen's Bench. Home: 733 Chestnut St San Francisco CA 94133 Office: 235 Montgomery San Francisco CA 94104

MARA, JACQUELINE FRANCES, coll. dean; b. Manchester, N.H., Oct. 23, 1927; d. Francis J. and Isabelle M. (Oliver) Mara; B.S., Mt. St. Mary Coll., 1949; Ed.M., Boston U., 1953, certificate advanced grad. study, 1957, Ed.D., 1963. Instr. bus. Mt. St. Mary Coll., Hooksett, N.H., 1950-54, dir. admissions, registrar, dir. financial aid, 1954-72, acad. dean, 1972—. Mem. N.H. Personnel and Guidance Assn. (exec. bd. 1971-72, outstanding achievement award 1972), Eastern Assn. Financial Aid Officers, N.H. Financial Aid Assn. (sec. 1972—), Delta Pi Epsilon. Home: 475 Mammoth Rd Manchester NH 03104 Office: Mount St Mary College Hooksett NH 03106

MARBOE, EVELYN CHOSTNER (MRS. ROBERT FENTON MARBOE), educator; b. Detroit; d. Grover Cleveland and Mabelle M. (Siefers) Chostner; B.S., Wayne State U., 1941; M.S., Pa. State U., 1943; m. Robert Fenton Marboe, Apr. 19, 1944; children—Charles Chostner, Carol Ann, Richard Chostner. Research asst. physiol. chemistry Parke, Davis & Co., Detroit, 1941; grad. asst. chem. Pa. State U., 1942; instr. 1943-44, research asso. glass sci. research found., 1944-47, asst. prof. glass tech. research, 1947-56, asso. prof. mineral scis., 1957—. Bd. dirs., pres. Centre County chpt. Pa. Assn. Retarded Citizens; trustee Centre Community Hosp.; chmn., mem. Centre County Mental Health and Mental Retardation Bd.; founder, pres. Family Planning Council of Central Pa., Inc. Mem. Am. Assn. U. Women (past pres. State College br.), League Women Voters, Sigma Xi, Iota Sigma Pi, Sigma Delta Epsilon. Democrat. Presbyn. Author: (with W. A. Weyl) The Constitution of Glasses: A. Dynamic Interpretation, Vol. 1, 1962, Vol. 2, 1964, Vol. 3, 1966. Home: 705 W Hamilton Av State College PA 16801 Office: Pa State U University Park PA 16802

MARCELLUS, DELIA REED (MRS. LAWRENCE WAYNE MARCELLUS), newspaper exec.; b. Lawrence, Kan., Apr. 6, 1929; d. Addison Robert and Bertha Mae (Christie) Reed; B.A. in Zoology, U. Kan., 1949; m. Lawrence Wayne Marcellus, Apr. 29, 1949; children—Laura (Mrs. Nicholas Penland), Marie (Mrs. Don Burgett, Jr.), DeWayne. Asso. editor Riley Countian, weekly, Leonardville, Kan., 1951-64, McPherson County (Kan.) News, weekly, McPherson, 1964-65; account exec. advt. sales Manhattan (Kan.) Mercury, daily, 1969—. Leader 4-H Clubs, 1958-66. Bd. dirs. Riley County Mental Health, 1953-54, Riley County Extension Council, 1957-59. Recipient award for column writing, also editing Kan. Press Assn., 1964, for advt. series, 1971. Mem. Nat. Fedn. Press Women, Kan. Press Women (v.p. 1954-55), Women in Communication (pres. Manhattan 1973). Clubs: Toastmistress, Pilot (Manhattan). Home: 801 Haid Court Manhattan KS 66502 Office: Manhattan Mercury Osage at N 5th St Manhattan KS 66502

MARCERE, NORMA SNIPES (MRS. PERCY ALLUREN MARCERE), educator; b. Canton, O.; d. Norman S. and Ida (Evans) Snipes; M.A., Kent State U., 1957; m. Percy Alluren Marcere, July 29, 1930 (dec. May 1971); children—Norma Jean Snow, Alluren Leonard. Social caseworker Stark County Welfare Dept., Canton, 1938-42; health educator Stark County Tb and Health Assn., Canton, 1944-56; tchr., counselor E.A. Jones Jr. High Sch., Massillon, O., 1957-66; guidance counselor Garfield High Sch., Akron, O., 1966-71; sch. psychologist Kent (O.) City Schs., 1971-72; psychologist Hilltop House, Akron, 1972—. Vocational counselor Human Engring. Inst., 1962-66; dir. Stoydale-Brunnerdale Summer Project, 1972-73. Sec., Canton City Charter Commn., 1961-62; mem. Stark County Bd. Mental Retardation, 1967-69, 69—, sec., 1970—; mem. Youngstown Diocesan Sch. Bd., 1969—. Bd. dirs. Urban League, 1964-66, Kent State Campus Ministries, 1974—; mem. adv. bd. Walsh Coll., 1974—. Named Woman of Year Jr. League, 1973. Mem. Ohio Edn. Assn., Ohio Sch. Counselors Assn., Ohio Sch. Psychologists, Nat. Council Catholic Women, Nat. Assn. Colored Womens Clubs, Panel of Am. Women. Contbr. articles to profl. jours. and mags. Home: 6030 Frazer Av NW North Canton OH 44720

MARCHESANO, CAROLE VIRGINIA, advt. co. exec.; b. Des Moines, Ia., July 30, 1939; d. Samuel Thomas and Geneva Carol (Horner) Mazza; B.A., Catholic U., 1970; m. Martin R. Marchesano, Aug. 7, 1956 (div. July 1963); children—Michele, Richard. Office mgr. Kieffer Assos., Des Moines, 1963-65; comptroller W.A. Lemer

Advt., Inc., Washington, 1966-69; owner Goldberg, Marchesano & Assos., Inc., Washington, 1970—. Cons. for advt. office systems. Media dir. Mayor Washington's campaign, 1974, also Congressman McClosky Presidential Nomination Orgn., Joseph Yeldell Congl. campaign. Mem. Met. Washington Bd. Trade, Advt. Club Met. Washington, Nat. Acad. TV Arts and Scis. Home: 6108 Roseland Lane Rockville MD 20852 Office: 1308 19th St NW Washington DC 20036

MARCHIONE, SISTER MARGHERITA FRANCES, educator; b. Little Ferry, N.J., Feb. 19, 1922; d. Crescenzo Louis and Felicia Rose (Schettino) Marchione; A.B., Georgian Ct. Coll., 1943; A.M., Columbia, 1949, Ph.D. (Garibaldi scholar), 1960. Instr., Villa Walsh Coll., Morristown, N.J., 1949-63; lectr. Seton Hall U., South Orange, N.J., 1963-65; asso. prof. Fairleigh Dickinson U., Madison, N.J., 1965—; pres. Walsh Coll., 1966-70. Cons., Gallery Modern Art, 1968-69. Mem. Morris Twp. Jitney Study Com., 1974—. Sec.-treas., trustee Religious Tchrs. Filippini; trustee UN Assn. Recipient Nat. Def. Edn. Act grant in French, U. Ky., 1962, AMITA, Am-Italian award in edn., 1971. Fulbright scholar U. Rome, 1964. Mem. Modern Lang. Assn., N.J. Fgn. Lang. Tchrs. Assn., Amici di Clemente Rebora, Edizioni de Storia e Letteratura. Author: L'Imagine Tesa, Edizioni di Storia e Letteratura, 1960; Carteggio di Giovanni Boine Vol. I to V, 1971-74; Twentieth Century Italian Poetry, 1974. Home: Villa Walsh Morristown NJ 07960 Office: Fairleigh Dickinson U Madison NJ 07940

MARCIANO, E. GIOIA CIPRIANO (MRS. SAMUEL LEWIS MARCIANO), lawyer; b. Bklyn., Sept. 19, 1928; d. Gaetano P. and Anna Madeline (Angelillo) Cipriano; student Upsala Coll., 1946-48; J.D., Rutgers U., 1952; m. Samuel Lewis Marciano, Apr. 15, 1956; children—Frank Peter, Gioia Anne, Lucie Allesandra. Admitted to N.J. bar, 1952; since practiced in Orange, also West Orange. Mem. Rutgers Law Sch. Alumni Assn., Rolling Green Hills Assn. Address: 6 Gregory Av West Orange NJ 07052

MARCIN, MARY JULIA (MRS. RAYMOND B. MARCIN), pediatrician; b. Wellsville, N.Y., Feb. 18, 1941; d. Thomas Francis and Gertrude (Dowling) Regan; B.S. (N.Y. regents scholar), Marymount Coll., 1962; M.D., Georgetown U., 1966; m. Raymond B. Marcin, Aug. 21, 1965; children—Shelah Eileen, Sarah Elaine, Susan Elise, Peter Regan. Intern St. Francis Hosp., Hartford, Conn., 1966-67; resident, 1967-69; practice medicine specializing in pediatrics, Hartford, 1971—; staff physician Dept. Ambulatory Services, St. Francis Hosp., Hartford, 1971, Howard County Health Dept., 1972—. Mem. Hartford County, Conn. med. socs. Home: 5018 Round Tower Pl Columbia MD 21044

MARCINKOSKI, ANNETTE MARIE, educator; b. Akron, O., Aug. 2, 1933; d. Frank J. and Barbara (Popielarczyk) Marcinkoski; B.S., U. Akron, 1955; M.A., U. Mich., 1959. Tchr. Flint (Mich.) Pub. Schs., 1955-63, tng. tchr. Coop. Tchr. Edn. Program, 1963-69, elementary tchr., 1969—. Active Big Sister program; sponsor Jr. Red Cross, 1959-63; tchr. Confraternity of Christian Doctrine. Mem. United Tchrs. of Flint, Mich. Edn. Assn., N.E.A. (regional dir. 1973—), Elementary, Kindergarten and Nursery Educators, Mich. (treas. 1970-72, pres. 1973—), Flint (sec. 1959-62) assns. childhood edn., Assn. Childhood Edn. Internat., Am. Assn. Univ. Women (v.p. 1967-69, area rep. in edn. 1969-72), Theta Phi Alpha (adviser Gen. Motors Inst. chpt. 1973—), Delta Kappa Gamma, Cath. Bus. Women (sec. 1970-72), Flint Area Reading Council, Mich. Reading Assn. Home: 1911 Laurel Oak Dr Flint MI 48507 Office: 1402 W Dayton St Flint MI 48504

MARCO, RUTH ANN OVERMANN (MRS. ROBERT J. MARCO), engring. psychologist; b. St. Louis, Feb. 13, 1944; d. John Louis and Ruth (Dudley) Overmann; B.A., Webster Coll., 1966; M.A., U. Louisville, 1969; m. Robert J. Marco, Dec. 26, 1970. Research asst. in psychology U. Louisville, 1966-68; clin. psychologist Vt. State Hosp., Waterbury, 1968-69; program dir. life scis. tng. Jewish Found. for Retarded Children, St. Louis, 1969-72; engring. psychologist McDonnell Douglas Astronautics Co., St. Louis, 1972—. Cons. Vt. State Rehab. Dept. Montpelier, 1968-69. Del. Ky. Democratic State Conv., 1968. Recipient Dean's Honor award, U. Louisville, 1967. Mem. Am. Ednl. Research Assn., Am. Psychol. Assn. Contbr. articles in field to profl. jours. Home: 7516 Marillac St Louis MO 63133 Office: Dept E422 McDonnell Douglas Astronautics Co PO Box 516 St Louis MO 63166

MARCOVITZ, MARILYN HELENE COHEN (MRS. RICHARD M. MARCOVITZ), occupational therapist; b. Phila., Aug. 7, 1943; d. Samuel Herman and Pearl Rosa (Phillips) Cohen; B.S., West Chester State Coll., 1965; certificate occupational therapy U. Pa., 1967; m. Richard M. Marcovitz, Sept. 3, 1967; children—Orah Toni, Avraham Eliezer, Uriel Baruch, Yohanan Shalom. Occupational therpist Widener Meml. Sch. for Crippled Children, Phila., 1967; dir. occupational therapy United Cerebral Palsy, Pottsville, Pa., 1967-68; dir. occupational therapy Heritage Manor, Youngstown, O., 1968-69; psychiat. asst. dir. Woodside Receiving Hosp., Youngstown, 1970. Vice pres. Pioneer Women, Youngstown, 1970-71; pres. Hillel, West Chester State Coll., 1964-65. Mem. Nat. Council Jewish Women (service chmn. 1972-73), Am. Occupational Therapy Assn. Mem. Hadassah. Home: 24 Warwick Av Toronto ON 10 Canada

MARCUS, ADABELLE GROSS (MRS. ISADORE MARCUS), composer, pianist; b. Chgo., July 8, 1929; d. Isadore Theodore and Beatrice Newman (Brelowitz) Gross; student (scholar) De Paul U. Music Sch., 1939-44, Am. Conservatory Music, 1954, Roosevelt U.-Chgo. Coll. Music, 1959, De Paul U. Music Sch., 1961; m. Isadore Marcus, Oct. 22, 1949; children—Beverly, Laura. Made debut as pianist, Chgo., 1937; concertized throughout Midwest, 1947—; piano concerts presented at North Park Coll., 1968; concert of own compositions for flute, piano, voice, Chgo., 1969; performed own works with Chgo. Artists Assn., 1970-71; vocal coach, 1942-49; piano tchr., 1959—. Mem. Internat. Soc. for Contemporary Music (dir. 1963-66), Chgo. Artists Assn., Internat. Platform Assn., Ams. for Music Library in Israel. Club: Women's Musicians (Chgo.). Composer: A Day in New York City, suite for piano, 1951; A Child's Day Suite, piano, 1957; Nocturne for Flute and Piano, 1955; Song Cycle (Robert Frost text), 1959; God, Whom Shall I Compare to Thee! (Halevy text), 1960; Theme and Variations, piano, 1961; A Setting to Seasons (Robert Frost text), 1962; Etude Erotique, piano, 1963; Piano Concertino, 4 movements, 1963; Sonata, violin and piano, 1964; Violin Concerto, string chamber orch. and harp, 1965; Snow, chamber opera (Robert Frost text), 1966; Christmas Bells (Longfellow text), 1967; Four Preludes on Playthings to the Wind, voice with piano (Carl Sandburg text), 1968; Youth in Orbit, piano suite, 1969; Jazz Prelude for sch. orch., 1969; Piano Sonata, 1970; A Song for Flute, for flute with piano, 1970; Song Cycle (Dylan Thomas text), 1971; Blue Flute (flute solo and piano), 1972; Symphony of the Spheres (orch.), 1972; Monologue (piano), 1973; The House by the Side of the Road, 1973. Address: 9374 Landings Lane Des Plaines IL 60016

MARCUS, EILEEN, pub. relations co. exec.; b. Naples, Italy, June 11, 1946; d. Isaac and Minna (Cyploskicz) Einik; came to U.S., 1947, naturalized, 1955; B.S., U. Fla., 1967; m. Zvi Marcus, May 26, 1974. Publicity asst. KTTV, Los Angeles, 1968-69; asst. to dir. pub. relations and advt. Roberts Realty of Bahamas, Ltd., Miami, Fla., 1969; dir. communications Greater Miami (Fla.) C. of C., 1969-72; account exec. Everett Clay & Assos., Coral Gables, Fla., 1972-74; dir. pub. relations Hume-Smith Mickleberry, Miami, 1974—. Mem. Greater Miami Advt. Fedn. (publicity mgr. 1972), Fla. Pub. Relations Assn., Pub. Relations Soc. Am. (asso.), Theta Sigma Phi. Home: 7825 NE Bayshore Ct Miami FL 33138 Office: 1000 Brickell Av Miami FL 33131

MARCUS, ESTHER SENITZKY (MRS. R. MARCUS), social worker, psychologist, educator; b. Vilna, Poland, June 16, 1922; d. Sender and Henia (Bloch) Senitzky; came to U.S., 1933, naturalized, 1939; B.A., Hunter Coll., 1942; M.S., Columbia U. Sch. Social Work, 1944; certificate for social workers William Alanson White Inst. Psychiatry, Psychoanalysis and Psychology, 1952; Ph.D., N.Y. U., 1970; m. Robert L. Marcus; children—David Jeffrey, Donna Helene. Research fellow Inst. for Jewish Research, N.Y.C., 1941-43; fellow, caseworker Community Service Soc., N.Y.C., 1943-45; caseworker Jewish Family Service Assn., Cleve., 1945-47; admissions interviewer Columbia U. Sch. Social Work, 1953-59; supr. counseling service of clin. services William Alanson White Inst. Psychiatry, Psychoanalysis and Psychology, N.Y.C., 1953-66, faculty, 1956—; counselor, supr. Jewish Family Service, N.Y.C., 1947-70; asst. dir. Lincoln Inst. for Psychotherapy, N.Y.C., 1960-71, cons., 1971-72; pvt. practice family counseling, psychotherapy, 1954—; asso. prof. Sch. Social Welfare, 1970-72, prof., 1972—; prof. dept. psychiatry Sch. Medicine, State U. N.Y. at Stony Brook, 1972—. Cons., Temple Emanu-El Nursery Sch., N.Y.C., 1954-58, Ednl. Alliance, N.Y.C., 1955-56, Social Work Service, VA Hosp., Lyons, N.J., 1957-58, VA Regional Office, Newark, 1961-72, VA Hosp., East Orange, N.J., 1970-72, L.I. Jewish-Hillside Med. Center, Queens Hosp. Center, 1971—. Certified psychologist, N.Y., N.J. Mem. Acad. Certified Social Workers, Nat. Assn. Social Workers, Am. Acad. Psychotherapists, Council Psychoanalytic Psychotherapists, Am. Assn. Marriage Counselors, Am. Group Psychotherapy Assn., N.Y. Soc. Clin. Psychologists, N.Y. State Psychol. Assn., Am. Psychol. Assn., Phi Beta Kappa, Pi Mu Epsilon, Psi Chi, Alpha Chi Alpha. Contbr. articles to profl. publs. Home: 430 Wolf Hill Rd Dix Hills NY 11746

MARCUS, HELEN, broadcasting exec.; b. N.Y.C.; d. Joseph M. and Augusta (Hittleman) Marcus; B.A., Smith Coll., 1947. TV casting, CBS, N.Y.C., 1951; in charge subsidiary rights, play dept. MCA Mgmt., N.Y.C., 1952-54; program coordinator Names the Same TV show, N.Y.C., 1955, Two for the Money, 1955-57; asso. producer Beat the Clock, N.Y.C., 1958-61, Number Please, N.Y.C., 1961; casting dir. To Tell The Truth, Goodson-Todman Prodns., N.Y.C., 1962-68, What's My Line, 1968—. Free lance photographer, 1966—. Pres., Council of Phoenix Theatre, 1969-72; mem. adv. bd. Smith Coll. Theatre Dept., 1965—. Mem. Nat. Acad. TV Arts and Scis., Soc. Photographers in Communications, Am. Soc. Motion Pictures. Club: Town Tennis (N.Y.C.). Home: 66 E 83d St New York City NY 10028 Office: Goodson Todman 375 Park Av New York City NY 10022

MARCUS, MARCIA, painter; b. N.Y.C., Jan 11, 1928; student N.Y. U., Art Students League; 2 children. Exhibited at Whitney Mus. Am. Art, 1960, 64, Carnegie Inst., 1964-65, Corcoran Gallery Art, 1965, Am. Acad. Arts and Letters, 1965, 71, 72, ACA Gallery, 1974; exhibited in group shows in various galleries, 1951—; represented in collections Whitney Mus. Am. Art. Newark Mus. Art, R.I. Sch. Design Mus., Woodward Found., Phoenix Mus.; faculty Vassar, 1973-74. Recipient Ingram Merrill award, 1964; Rosenthal Fund award Am. Acad. Arts and Letters, 1964. Fulbright fellow, France, 1962-63. Home: 703 E 6th St New York City NY 10009

MARCUS, MARIA LENHOFF (MRS. NORMAN MARCUS), lawyer; b. Vienna, Austria, June 23, 1933; d. Arthur and Clara (Gruber) Lenhoff; came to U.S., 1939, naturalized, 1944. B.A., Oberlin Coll., 1954; LL.B., Yale, 1957; m. Norman Marcus, Dec. 23, 1956; children—Valerie Rae, Nicole Emily, Eric Arthur. Admitted to N.Y. bar, 1961; asso. counsel N.A.A.C.P., N.Y.C., 1961-67; asst. atty. gen. N.Y. State, N.Y.C., 1967—. Mem. Assn. Bar City N.Y. (chmn. com. 1972-75). Office: 2 World Trade Center New York City NY 10047

MARCUS, MARIE SARTALAMACHIA, educator; b. New Orleans; d. John and Theresa (Ranatza) Sartalamachia; B.A., Tulane U., 1955, M.A., 1959; Ed.D., George Peabody Coll., 1964; m. William M. Marcus, Aug. 9, 1941 (div. Nov. 1952); 1 son, John William. Tchr. elementary schs., New Orleans, 1953-62; instr. George Peabody Coll. for Tchrs., Nashville, 1963-64; asst. prof. La. State U., New Orleans, 1964-66, asso. prof., 1966-70, prof., 1970—, dir. Lang. Arts Center, 1966—. Lang. arts cons. St. Bernard, Lafayette, Washington parishes schs. Mem. Internat. Reading Assn. (state chmn. 1966—), Nat. Council Tchrs. English, Assn. Supervision and Curriculum Improvement. Mem. editorial bd. Reading Improvement; mem. adv. bd. Elementary English. Home: 821 Angela Av Arabi LA 70032 Office: Lakefront New Orleans LA 70122

MARCUS, MILDRED RENDL (MRS. EDWARD MARCUS), economist, educator; b. N.Y.C., May 30, 1928; d. Julius and Agnes (Hokr) Rendl; B.S., N.Y.U., 1948, M.B.A., 1950; Ph.D. (Dean Bernice Brown Cronkhite fellow 1950-51), Radcliffe Coll., 1954; m. Edward Marcus, Aug. 10, 1956. Economist Gen. Electric Co., 1953-56, Bigelow-Sanford Carpet Co., Inc., 1956-58; lectr. econs. City Coll. N.Y., evening sessions, 1953-58; research investment problems in tropical Africa, 1958-59; instr. econs. Hunter Coll., 1959-60; lectr. econs. Columbia U., 1960-61; research econ. devel. Nigeria, Africa, 1961-63; sr. economist Internat. Div. Nat. Indsl. Conf. Bd., 1963-66; asst prof. Grad. School Bus. Adminstrn., Pace Coll., 1964-66; asso. prof. Borough of Manhattan Community Coll., City U. N.Y., 1966-71, prof., 1972—. Cons. UN Conf. on trade and devel., 1966—. Bd. dirs. N.Y.C. Council on Econ. Edn., 1970—. Fellow Gerontological Assn.; mem. Indsl. Relations Research Assn., Am. Assn. U. Women, Met. (sec. 1954-56), Am. (vice chmn. conv. com. 1973) econ. assns., N.Y. U. Grad. Sch. Bus. Adminstrn. Alumni (sec. 1956-58). Club: Radcliffe. Author: (with husband) Investment & Development of Tropical Africa, 1959, International Trade and Finance, 1965, Monetary and Banking Theory, 1965, Economic Development and the Less Developed Economies, 1971; also monographs and articles in field. Econ. and internat. research in industrialization less developed areas, also east Europe planning. Home: PO Box 814 New Canaan CT 06840 Office: Manhattan Community College 1633 Broadway New York City NY 10019

MARDER, DORIE, painter; b. Nisko, Poland; d. Leisor and Esther (Jacobi) Marder; came to U.S., 1940, naturalized, 1945; student Sorbonne, Paris, France, 1936-40. One-woman shows Village Art Center, N.Y.C., 1961, 63, Studio Art Gallery, N.Y.C., 1965—, Fed. Savs. Bank, N.Y.C., 1966, High Point Gallery, Lennox, Mass., 1970, 71; exhibited in group shows Riverside Mus., N.Y.C., 1960, Nat. Serigraph Soc., N.Y.C., 1958, Am. Color Print Soc., Phila., 1951, San Francisco Mus., 1957, Sweat Meml. Mus., Memphis, 1952, Printmakers So. Cal., 1952, Milw. Art Inst., 1955, Seattle Art Mus., 1950, Am. Contemporary Art Gallery, 1957, Audubon Artists, N.Y.C., 1970, Mus. N.J., 1966, Nassau Community Coll., 1971, Boston Printmakers, 1954, Portland (Ore.) Mus., 1952, Nat. Arts Club, N.Y.C., 1963, Knickerbocker Artists, N.Y.C., 1956, N.Y. U., 1967, N.Y. Pub. Library, 1961, New Sch. for Social Research, 1954, Nat. Acad. Design, 1970, Boston Mus. Fine Arts, 1954, Print Club of Phila., 1951, Ohio U., 1955, Art Gallery of Toronto, 1956, Stamford Mus., 1960, Tift Coll., 1961, Harding Coll., 1961, U. S.C., 1963, Mich. State U., 1962, Lehigh U., 1972; exhibited abroad at Pollazzo Vechio, Florence, Italy, 1972, Pompeian Pavilion, Naples, Italy, 1972, Arts Gallery Manila, Philippines, 1960. Recipient first prize Village Art Center, 1959, 61, Clendenen prize for graphics Nat. Assn. Women Artists, 1961. Mem. Artists Equity, Am. Color Print Soc., League Present Day Artists (dir. 1971—), Art Students League, Nat. Assn. Women Artists (Montag prize 1965). Home: 223 W 21 St New York City NY 10011

MARDFIN, JEAN TSUTAE KADOOKA (MRS. DOUGLAS WARD MARDFIN), librarian; b. Hilo, Hawaii, Mar. 16, 1944; d. Tsutomu and Masako (Mayeda) Kadooka; B.A., Western Res. U., 1966, M.S. in L.S., 1967; M.A., U. Hawaii, 1973; m. Douglas Ward Mardfin, Aug. 24, 1969. Cataloger NIH Library, Bethesda, Md., 1967-68, Municipal Reference Library, Honolulu, 1968-69; municipal librarian Honolulu, 1969-72; dir. Municipal Reference and Records Center, Honolulu, 1972—. Mem. Spl. Libraries Assn., Hawaii Library Assn., Council Planning Librarians, Am. Soc. Pub. Adminstrn. (chpt. sec. 1972-73, v.p. Honolulu 1973-74), Cactus and Succulent Soc. Hawaii, Psi Chi, Beta Phi Mu. Home: 728 C Palani Av Honolulu HI 96816 Office: Municipal Reference and Records Center City Hall Honolulu HI 96813

MAREINISS, ROSE MAURER (MRS. MAX MAREINISS), artist; b. Phila., Feb. 20, 1909; d. Ashcer and Eva (Krupert) Maurer; student Nat. Acad. N.Y.; m. Max Jerome Mareiniss, Sept. 15, 1928; children—Joel, Edgar and Martin (twins). Exhibited oils, sculpture, prints in one-woman shows Israel Mus., Jerusalem, 1965, Artz Art Gallery, N.Y.C., 1958, Mon Telan Mus., 1963, Newark Mus., 1966, Rio de Janeiro, 1967, Syracuse, N.Y., Miami, Fla.; represented in permanent collections Art Gallery Jerusalem, pvt. collections; Tchr. figure painting Newark Art Coll., Vocational Sch., Newark, pvt. instrn.; playwright, 1949—. Bd. dirs. Silo Gallery of Morriston, N.J. Mem. Nat. Women's Art Assn., Artists Equity N.Y. Address: 37 Oakland Rd Maplewood NJ 07040

MAREK, BENITA LOUISE, author; b. Brenham, Tex., Aug. 31, 1915; d. Jaroslav Joseph and Benita Louise (Schuerenberg) Marek; A.A., Washington County (Tex.) Jr. Coll., 1938; B.S. cum laude, Tex. Woman's U., 1944; m. E.L. Lawrence, July 8, 1933 (div. Feb. 1946); 1 dau., Kathleen Amalia (Mrs. R. R. Obenhaus). Tchr., Kuy Kendall Sch., Washington County, 1938-40, Pulaski Union Grove Sch., Washington County, 1940-45, tchr. Brenham (Tex.) High Sch., 1947; tchr., head sci. dept. Alamo Sch., Brenham, 1947-50; tchr. Yukan Pvt. Sch., Brenham, 1953-59. Tutor Tex. U., Austin, 1945, 49, also pvt. students, Brenham. Del. to Washington county and Tex. state Democratic convs., 1960, 66; lobbyist for Gilmer-Aiken Program, 1947-49; candidate for Gov., state of Tex., 1950. Mem. Poetry Soc. of Tex., Am. Acad. of Poets. Democrat. Episcopalian. Author: The History of the Brenham Free Public Schools, 1932; Masterpieces of the World, 1938; also poems. Address: 506 W Alamo Av Brenham TX 77833

MAREK, LOIS KAY (MRS. JAMES J. MAREK), occupational therapist; b. Watseka, Ill., Mar. 22, 1941; d. Wayne Eugene and Frieda LaFern (Brooks) Bowton; B.S., Ind. U., 1966; m. James J. Marek, Mar. 18, 1967; children—Scotty, Steven. Staff therapist Riley Children's Hosp., Ind. U. Med. Center, Indpls., 1966-67; chief occupational therapist St. Margaret Hosp., Hammond, Ind., 1967-70; occupational therapist on stroke team St. Catherine Hosp., East Chicago, Ind., 1971—. Mem. adv. bd. Certified Occupational Therapy Assts. program Thornton Jr. Coll., South Holland, Ill., 1972—. Mem. Ind., Ill. occupational therapy assns. Address: 335 Maple Dr Glenwood IL 60425

MAREK, RUTH MARIE, hosp. adminstr. Sec. bd. Mercy Med. Center, Oshkosh, Wis., 1962-66; chmn. longe range planning com. St. Elizabeth Hosp., Wabasha, Minn., 1967-68; dir., sec. Immanuel-St. Joseph Hosp., Mankato, Minn., 1968-73; now asso. adminstr. Met. Med. Center, Mpls.; lectr., cons. in field. Chmn. Wabasha Housing and Redevel. Authority, 1967-68; chmn. unit United Way campaign, Mpls., 1974, coordinator hosps. campaign, 1975. Bd. dirs. Iowa Lakes Area Health Planning Council, 1971—, Lakes Area Confedn. Hosps., 1971—, Heart-Lung By-pass Assos., 1974—; mem. Found. Health Care Evaluation Minn. Hosps., 1974—. Mem. Am. Hosp. Assn. (mem. assembly nursing care and related instrn. 1973—), Am. Cath. Hosp. Assn., Am. Med. Record Assn., U. Minn. Alumni Assn., Nat. League Nursing. Address: Met Med Center 900 S 8th St Minneapolis MN 54404

MARESCA, VIRGINIA KELLER, clin. psychologist; b. Dobbs Ferry, N.Y., Nov. 7, 1923; d. Vann D. and Louetta P. (Getsinger) Keller; R.N., Diploma Sch. Nursing, 1944; B.S., Ariz. State U., 1948, M.A., 1960, Ph.D., 1963; 1 dau., Karen K. Instr., dir. Student Health Service Meml. Hosp., Phoenix, 1947-48, also instr. Union U., Albany, N.Y., 1947-48; dir. nursing New Eng. Hosp. Women and Children, Boston, 1949-50; individual practice psychology Phoenix, 1965—. Chmn. Ariz. State Bd. Psychol. Examiners, 1973-74. Mem. Am., Western, Ariz. State psychol. assns. Home: 6318 E Lafayette Blvd Scottsdale AZ 85251 Office: 3417 N 32nd St Phoenix AZ 85018

MARGALITH, HELEN MARGARET FLEISCHER (MRS. AARON M. MARGALITH), librarian; b. N.Y.C., Nov. 19, 1914; d. Louis and Caroline (Stern) Fleischer; A.B., Hunter Coll., 1936, M.A., 1944; M.L.S., Columbia, 1958; m. Aaron M. Margalith, Jan. 26, 1947; children—Carol (Mrs. Joel Jay Levy), Joan. Supr. and editorial corr. Book of Month Club, N.Y.C., 1936-48; with N.Y.C. Bd. Edn., 1955—, sr. librarian Jr. High Sch. 143M, 1957-71, George Washington High Sch., 1971—, instr. vol. after sch. profl. devel. program, 1966—. Cons. Am. Found. Religion and Psychiatry, 1964-67; staff researcher Mt. Sinai Hosp., N.Y.C., 1970. Vice pres. Rita H. Hope Inst., St. Wise Free Synagogue. Mem. Am. Found. Religion and Psychiatry, Royal Soc. Medicine, Assn. Applied Psychoanalysis, N.Y.C. Sch. Librarians Assn. (parlimentarian 1970-71), Doctoral Assn. N.Y. Educators (dir. 1970), Ch. and Synagogue Library Assn., Fellowship of Chs. and Synagogues. Editor: Judaism in Sigmund Freud's World (Earl A. Grollman). Home: 17 W 67th St New York City NY 10023 Office: George Washington High School Audubon Av 192d St New York City NY 10040

MARGENAU, MARIE ELAINE, psychotherapist; b. Yonkers, N.Y., July 11, 1943; d. Morris Angelo and Fanny (Farano) Piemontese; student Coll. St. Elizabeth, 1960-62; B.S., Fordham U., 1965; M.A. (univ. scholar), N.Y. U., 1969. Counselor, N.Y. U., 1968-69; psychology intern St. Vincent's Hosp., N.Y.C., 1969-70; sch. psychologist N.Y. U. Med. Center, Millhauser Labs., N.Y.C., 1970-72; psychotherapist Fifth Av. Center for Counseling and Psychotherapy, N.Y.C., 1970—; individual practice psychotherapy, N.Y.C., 1972—. Mem. Am. Com. Italian Migration, 1964-69, Enrico Fermi Scholarship Fund, 1968-69; mem. central com. Feminist Therapy Referral Collective, 1973—. Mem. Am. Psychol. Assn. Home: 157-10 Riverside Dr W New York City NY 10032 Office: 150 W 13th St New York City NY 10011

MARGETTS, JOSEPHINE SHARON (MRS. WALTER T. MARGETTS, JR.), nursery owner, civic worker; b. Newport, Pa., Oct. 8, 1905; d. Samuel Adams and May Meredith (Jones) Sharon; student Ambler Sch. Horticulture, 1924-25, Columbia, 1938-39, Rutgers U., 1952-53, Drew U., 1958; m. Walter T. Margetts, Jr., July 18, 1935; children—Sharon (Mrs. Richard Doremus), Cynthia (Mrs. Charles Robinson), W. Thomas, Susan (Mrs. Charles A. Connell, Jr.). Operator comml. apple and peach orchard, Pa. 1935—; operator Holly Hill Farms, New Vernon, N.J., 1954—; mem. N.J. Gen. Assembly, 1968-73. Mem. N.J. Commn. on Higher Edn., Pres.'s Commn. on Air Quality, Adv. Council on Future N.J., N.J. Election Law Enforcement Commn. Mem. Republican State Finance Com., 1953-63, chmn. women's div., 1956, 57; mem. editorial bd. N.J. Rep. News, 1961—; state Rep. com. woman from Morris County, 1961—; v.p. Morris County Women's Rep. Club, 1959—; pres. N.J. Fedn. Rep. Women, 1963-67; mem. exec. com. Nat. Fedn. Republican Women. Trustee Morristown Meml. Hosp., Frost Valley Assn., YMCA, N.J. Camp for Blind Children, Marcella, N.J., Fairleigh Dickinson U., N.J. Symphony, N.J. Hist. Soc., N.J. Agrl. Soc., Salvation Army, Morristown, Newark Acad., Morris Area Arts Council. Episcopalian (mem. altar guild). Clubs: Passaic Valley Garden (pres. 1947-51); Garden Club of N.J. (conservation chmn. 1951-53); Morristown Garden. Home: Holly Hill Farms New Vernon NJ 07960

MARGOLIS, CLORINDA GOLTRA (MRS. JOSEPH MARGOLIS), psychologist; b. Cin., June 2, 1930; d. Sidney Ellison and Ann (Hinckley) Goltra; B.A., U. Cin., 1963, M.A. cum laude, 1966, Ph.D., 1968; m. Joseph Margolis, Aug. 26, 1968; children from previous marriage—Ann Lovegrove Hunter, Jennifer Aline Hunter. Acting dir., chief psychologist Mental Health Clinic, Lawrenceburg, Ind., 1969; chief of consultation and edn. Jefferson Community Mental Health Center 1970—, asso. dir. preventive services, 1974—, also asst. prof. psychiatry and human behavior Thomas Jefferson U., Phila., 1970—. Ossabaw Found. grantee, 1973, 74. Mem. Am. psychol. assns., Phila. Soc. Clin. Psychologists, Sigma Xi. Contbr. articles to profl. jours. Home: 422 Catharine Philadelphia PA 19147 Office: 1228 Locust Philadelphia PA 19107

MARGOLIS, DORIS MAY ROSENBERG, writer, editor, public relations specialist; b. Washington, May 10, 1936; d. Samuel J. and Eva (Mendelsohn) Rosenberg; B.A. in Psychology, George Washington U., 1958; m. Lawrence Stanley Margolis, Jan. 30, 1960; children—Mary Aleta, Paul Oliver. Editorial asst. Today's Edn., N.E.A., Washington, 1958-59; tech. editor-writer John I. Thompson Co., Washington, 1959-60; editor Jour. of Rehab. and other publs., dir. pub. relations Nat. Rehab. Assn., Washington, 1960-67; asso. editor Concrete Facts mag., 1966-67; editor publs., dir. pub. relations Nat. Assn. Sheltered Workshops, Washington, 1963-68; contbg. editor Diagnosis News, Pediatric News, Obstet.-Gynecol. News, 1968-70; columnist Jewish Week newspaper, 1968-73; founder, v.p. Editorial Assos., Silver Spring, Md., 1964—. Cons., Dept. Health, Edn. and Welfare, 1971-72, Nat. Vocational Rehab. Policy and Platform Conf. for White House Conf. on Aging, 1971; dancer various musical shows; Judge nat. essay contest for high sch. students sponsored by Pres.'s Com. on Employment Handicapped, 1962, Nat. Worker of Yr. contest of Goodwill Industries Am., 1965; editor Proc. Internat. Rehab. Seminar, 1962, Proc. Regional Inst. for Sheltered Workshop Mgrs. and Rehab. Personnel, 1963; mem. dance com. Jewish Community Center Greater Washington. Bd. dirs. Jewish Social Service Agy. Mem. Am. Med. Writers Assn., Am. Psychol. Assn., Nat. Assn. Sci. Writers, Advt. Club Met. Washington, Mortar Bd., Pi Delta Epsilon, Psi Chi, Alpha Epsilon Phi. Clubs: D.C. Lawyers Wives, American Newspaper Women's, Hexagon (Washington). Address: 107 Carlisle Dr Silver Spring MD 20904

MARGOLIS, GWEN LIEDMAN (MRS. ALLAN B. MARGOLIS), real estate broker; b. Phila., Oct. 4, 1934; d. Joseph and Rose (Weiss) Liedman; student Temple U., 1951-54; spl. course U. Tampa; m. Allan Block Margolis, Sept. 12, 1953; children—Edward, Ira, Karen, Robin. Owner, broker Gwen Margolis Real Estate, North Miami Beach, Fla., 1965—; partner 16990 Corp. Mem. human relations bd., vice chmn. bd. adjustments City of North Miami Beach. Bd. dirs. Keystone Point Homeowners Assn.; adv. bd. Big Sisters Dade County. Mem. Miami Bd. Realtors, Nat. Assn. Real Estate Bds., North Miami Beach C. of C., Fla. Women's Polit. Caucus, League Women Voters, Anti-Defamation League (dir.). Home: 13105 Biscayne Bay Dr North Miami FL 33161 Office: 1725 NE 164th St North Miami Beach FL 33162

MARGOSIAN, LUCILLE K. MANOUGIAN (MRS. ERVIN M. MARGOSIAN), artist, educator; b. Highland Park, Mich., Mar. 18, 1935; d. George Krikor and Vera Varsenig (Jernukian) Manougian; B.F.A., Wayne State U., 1957, M.A., 1958; postgrad. Cal. State U., Fresno, 1959-60, U. Cal. at Berkeley, 1960-61; m. Ervin M. Margosian, Oct. 28, 1960; children—Rebecca L., Rachel L. One-man show at Jackson's Gallery, Berkeley, Cal., 1961; exhibited in group shows at Detroit Art Inst., 1958, Oakland (Cal.) Art Museum, 1961, Wayne State U. Community Arts Center, Detroit, 1965, San Francisco Ann. Art Festivals, 1967, 68, 69, Jack London Square Arts Festival, Oakland, 1969, 70, Judah L. Magnes Meml. Mus., Berkeley, 1970, Kaiser Center Gallery, Oakland, 1970, Oakland Mus. Changing Gallery, 1969, Olive Hyde Art Center, Fremont, 1971, 73, Richmond (Cal.) Art Center, 1972, others; faculty Peralta Community Colls., Laney campus, Oakland, 1967—, prof. art, 1970—. Charter mem. univ. art mus. council U. Cal. at Berkeley, 1965—. Recipient Certificate of Distinguished Achievement, Am. Legion, 1950, Best of Show 1st prize 5th Ann. Textile Exhbn., Fremont, Cal., 1973, Merit award City of Fremont, 1973. Mem. Cal. Art Edn. Assn., Oakland Museum Assn., Richmond Art Center, Women of Wayne, Wayne State U. Alumni Assn., East Bay Watercolor Soc., Internat. Platform Assn., Am. Fedn. Tchrs., Peralta Fedn. Tchrs. Home: 747 Grizzly Peak Blvd Berkeley CA 94708 Office: Laney Coll Art Dept 900 Fallon St Oakland CA 94607

MARGOT, NORMA (MRS. ALAN TAYLOR MARGOT), country club exec.; b. Eagle Pass, Tex., Sept. 22, 1927; d. Albert Prouty and Marie (Lujan) Wilson; studied with Xavier de Leon, Mexico City, Mex.; student U. Americas, 1948-49; m. Alan Taylor Margot, July 25, 1948; children—Alan Taylor, Jeannette Marie, Norma Lea, Scott Wilson. Office mgr. Communications Engrng. Co., Porterville, Cal., 1950-70; co-owner Linda Vista Swim & Racket Club, Porterville, 1970—; owner, tennis dir. Oak Tree Tennis Club, Visalia, Cal. Pres. Barn Theatre Guild, Porterville, 1959-60, 64-66; mem. bd. Tulare County Symphony League, pres., 1974—. Mem. St. Anne's Altar Soc., Porterville Garden Club, Am. Radio Relay League, Beta Sigma Phi. Home: 1185 Linda Vista Av Porterville CA 93257 Office: 1163 Linda Vista Av Porterville CA 93257

MARGRABE, MARY VIRGINIA (MRS. CARL WILLIAM HENRY MARGRABE), librarian; b. Brunswick, Md., May 21, 1923; d. John Anthony and Lula Brunswick (Darr) McMurry; A.B., Hood Coll., 1943; M.S. in Library Sci., Catholic U., 1967; m. Carl William Henry Margrabe, Dec. 10, 1943; 1 son, Carl William Henry. Tchr. English and French, Brunswick High Sch., 1943-64; librarian Linganore High Sch., Central, Md., 1964-69, Waverly Elementary Sch., Frederick, Md., 1969—. Charter mem. Brunswick Recreation Commn., 1954-71; tchr. adult non-reader Lauback Literacy Council, 1972—; mem. Potomac River Basin Com. Frederick County, 1968-69; chmn. P.T.A. coms., 1953-69. Founder, bd. dirs. Brunswick Pub. Library; bd. dirs. Frederick County Landmarks Found., Planned Parenthood Frederick County, Brunswick Potomac River Found. Nat. Def. Edn. Act fellow in French, 1959. Mem. N.E.A., Md., Frederick County (pres. 1960-61) tchrs. assns., Ednl. Media Assn. Md., Am. Assn. Sch. Librarians, Ednl. Media Assn. Frederick County (pres. 1968-69), Brunswick High Alumni Assn. (pres. 1948), League Am. Wheelmen. Episcopalian. Author: The Now Library, 1973. Contbr. articles to mags. and newspapers. Home: Frederick MD 21701 Office: Waverley Sch Route 8 Frederick MD 21701

MARICQ, HILDEGARD RAND (MRS. JOHN G. MARICQ), physician; b. Rakvere, Estonia; d. August and Elvine (Vunderlich) Rand; M.D., Free U. Brussels (Belgium), 1953; m. John G. Maricq, Oct. 9, 1948; children—Matti, Villu, Toivo. Came to U.S., 1954, naturalized, 1959. Intern, Jersey City Med. Center, 1955-56; resident psychiatry Essex County Overbrook Hosp., Cedar Grove, N.J., 1957-61; practice medicine specializing in psychiatry, Lyons, N.J., 1961—; research asso. psychiatry VA Hosp., Lyons, 1962, clin. investigator, 1963-65, sr. psychiatrist, 1967-73, dir. schizophrenia research sect., 1969-73; fellow Postdoctoral Research Tng. Program in Biol. Scis. in Relation to Mental Health dept. psychiatry Coll. Phys. and Surg., Columbia, 1965-67, research asso. dept. medicine, 1973—; research asst. prof. dept. psychiatry Rutgers U. Coll. Medicine and Dentistry, 1971-73, clin. asso. prof. psychiatry, 1973-74. Mem. A.M.A., Am. Psychiat. Assn., Microcirculatory Soc., A.A.A.S., N.J. Acad. Sci., European Soc. for Microcirculation, Estonian Learned Soc. in Am., Soc. for Psychophysiol. Research. Office: Dept Medicine Columbia U Coll Physicians and Surgeons 630 W 168th St New York City NY 10032

MARIE-VICTOIRE, OLLIE BLEVINS, judge; b. Denver, Oct. 30, 1923; d. Charles Monroe and Ollie (Duhon) Blevins; B.A., U. Denver, 1946; LL.B., Hastings Coll. U. Cal., 1956; m. Georges Marie-Victoire, June 18, 1946; 1 dau., Jeanine. Admitted to Cal. bar, 1956; research atty. Cal. Supreme Ct., 1956-61; practice in San Francisco, 1961-74; judge municipal ct., San Francisco, 1974—. Vice pres. San Francisco chpt. Nat. Orgn. Women, 1972—. Mem. Republican State Central Com., 1972—, San Francisco County Central Com., 1972—. Mem. Bar Assn. San Francisco (dir.), Queen's Bench (pres. 1974), Cal. Trial Lawyers, Lawyers Club San Francisco, Bus. and Profl. Women, Nat. Assn. Women Lawyers, Order Coif. Home: 2737 Steiner St San Francisco CA 94123 Office: City Hall San Francisco CA 94102

MARINACCI, BARBARA ELEANOR (MRS. RUDY L. MARINACCI), author; b. San Jose, Cal., Sept. 19, 1933; d. Karl Walter and Eleanor Golden (Williams) Kamb; student Reed Coll., 1950-52, Stanford, 1952, U. Cal. at Berkeley, 1952-53; m. Rudy L. Marinacci, Aug. 30, 1958; children—Michael, Christopher, Ellen. Editor adult fiction and nonfiction Dodd Mead & Co., N.Y.C., 1955-60. Unitarian. Author (biographies) Leading Ladies, 1961; They Came From Italy, 1967; O Wondrous Singer, 1970. Home: 234 12th St Santa Monica CA 90402

MARINE, SHIRLEY JULIA, publicist, editor; b. Milw., June 25, 1930; d. Richard A. and Helen (Cyganek) Marine; B.A. cum laude, Milw.-Downer Coll., 1952. With Milw. Pub. Library, 1953-65, asst. publs., exhibits, radio and TV, 1953-65, editor Milw. reader, 1953-65; author column Happy Birthday for Milw. Jour., 1953-55, Remember When, 1963-65, A-Muse-Ums, 1968—; information officer Milw. Pub. Mus., 1965-70, pub. affairs officer, 1970—. Mem. publicity com. Comm. on Aging. United Community Services, Milw., 1961-63; publicist World Affairs Council, Milw., 1958. Mem. Mayor's Beautification Com., 1965-69, 71—, All Am. City Award Com., Summerfest '70, '74 Cultural Events Com. Mem. Am. Assn. Museums, Wis. Humane Soc., Council for Wis. Writers, Milwaukee County Hist. Soc. Democrat. Author: (juvenile) Miss Miranda, 1970. Contbr. articles to newspapers, mags., profl. jours. Home: 1014 N Astor St Milwaukee WI 53202 Office: 800 W Wells St Milwaukee WI 53233

MARINELLI, ANNE VERA, librarian; b. Hibbing, Minn.; d. John and Concetta (Varriano) Martinelli; diploma Hibbing Jr. Coll., 1927; B.A., U. Wis., 1929; B.S. in L.S., Columbia, 1931, postgrad., 1934-35, 37, 40; postgrad. U. Chgo., 1947; M.A. in Italian and Library Sci., U. Ill., 1948; postgrad. U.S. Dept. Agr. Grad. Sch., 1951, U. Stranieri, Perugia, Italy, 1951, U. Mich., 1952-59. Instr., Hibbing pub. schs., 1929-30; jr. asst. librarian N.Y. Pub. Library, N.Y.C., 1930-32, sr. asst. librarian, 1933-35, asst. br. librarian, 1935-37; head librarian, instr. library methods Coll. St. Teresa, Winona, Minn., 1937-38; head catalog dept. Carleton Coll. Library, Northfield, Minn., 1938-44; head libraries Chisholm (Minn.) pub. schs., 1944-45; bibliographer U. Ill. at Urbana Library, 1945-52; asst. prof. Fla. State U. Sch. Library Sci., 1953-55; asso. prof. Tex. Woman's U. Sch. Library Sci., 1956-60; head librarian Hibbing Jr. Coll., 1960-73, ret., 1973; Spl. assignment Pan Am. Union Library, Washington, 1949; spl. asst. to librarian Library of Congress, 1950; Fulbright lectr. cons. Italian libraries, 1951-52; chairperson seminars on libaries and librarianship, Rome, also Florence, Naples, Italy, 1952; adminstrv. asst. to Am. chmn. Internat. Fedn. Library Assns. Congress, Washington, 1950; del. Nat. Commn. UNESCO Conf., 1959. Mem. for edn. com. Nat. Bi-Centennial Celebration, Hibbing. Recipient Amita award merit, 1967, Golden Anniversary award merit Hibbing State Jr. Coll. Alumni Assn., 1967, F. Bellamy citation as outstanding alumna, Portsmouth, Va., 1968, Internat. Rotary-Hibbing Service award, 1974. Mem. Assn. Coll. and Research Libraries, Round Table on Library Service Abroad (charter), A.L.A., N.E.A., Minn. Edn. Assn., Hibbing Community Coll Alumni Assn. (exec. bd. 1973—, permanent chairperson awards com), Assn. Am. Library Schs., Amita (hon. chairperson), Am. Assn. Ret. Persons, Minn. Tchrs. Retirement Assn., Columbia U. Alumni Fedn., Iota Kappa Gamma, Alpha Beta Alpha, Pi Lambda Theta. Contbr. articles to profl. jours. Home: 909 Minnesota St Hibbing MN 55746

MARINO, ANN LOUISE, nursing adminstr.; b. Manchester, Conn., May 12, 1944; d. Dominic Anthony and Amelia Theresa (Valente) Marino; R.N., Joseph Lawrence Sch. Nursing, 1965; B.S., Central Conn. State Coll., 1974. Staff nurse Lawrence Meml. Hosp., New London, Conn., 1965-66, Kula (Hawaii) Sanitorium, 1966-67; head nurse Hartford Regional Center for Mentally Retarded, Newington, 1967-71, nursing supr., 1971-74, asst. dir. residential programs, 1974—. Mem. Am. Assn. Mental Deficiency. Home: 1310 Berlin Turnpike Wethersfield CT 06109 Office: 71 Mountain Rd Newington CT 06111

MARINOFF, MARJORIE GREENFIELD (MRS. MICHAEL P. MARINOFF), lawyer; b. Phila., Sept. 23, 1942; d. Daniel K. and Frances Lucille (Rapoport) Greenfield; B.A., Barnard Coll., 1964; LL.B. cum laude, U. Pa., 1969; m. Michael P. Marinoff, Nov. 23, 1967; 1 son, Nathan Daniel. Admitted to Pa. bar, 1969; atty. Pepper, Hamilton & Scheetz, Phila., 1969—. Counsel to Child Abuse Prevention Effort (CAPE), Phila., 1973-74; cons. child abuse Commonwealth Pa., 1973-74. Bd. dirs. Am. Civil Liberties Union Greater Phila., 1969—, Pa., 1970—, Am. Civil Liberties Found. Pa., 1970—. Mem. Am. (mem. subcom. 1972—), Pa., Phila. (mem. exec. com. sect. 1971-74; chmn. com. 1971—; vice chmn. sect. 1972-73) bar assns. Club: Germantown Cricket (Phila.). Office: 2001 Fidelity Bldg Philadelphia PA 19109

MARION, LORETTA HUNT, mag. editor; b. Glen Rock, Pa., Mar. 1, 1939; d. Nevin Elias and Ruth (Adams) Hunt; B.A., Wilson Coll., 1961; M.Ed., Rutgers U., 1965; postgrad. N.Y.U., 1961-62; m. John Addison Marion, June 29, 1968; 1 dau., Cynthia Anne. Elementary tchr., New Providence, N.J., 1961-63; writer Scholastic News Trails, 1963-64; asst. editor Scholastic Newstime, 1964-65; asst. editor Scholastic Tchr. of Scholastic Mags., Inc., N.Y.C., 1965-66, asso. editor, 1966-67, mng. editor, 1967-68, editor, 1968—. Mem. N.Y. Choral Soc., 1964-65. Named Outstanding Young Woman of Am., 1966; recipient award for feature articles Ed Press Assn. Am., 1968. Mem. Assn. Childhood Edn. Internat., Ed Press Assn. Am., Assn. Supervision and Curriculum Devel., Edn. Writers Assn., World Council Curriculum and Instrn., Nat. Sch. Pub. Relations Assn. Lutheran. Club: Wilson College (N.Y.C.). Author: Map Skills Project Book III, 1965; columnist Scholastic Tchr. Office: 50 W 44th St New York City NY 10036

MARJOLLET, JANINE ELIZABETH, advt. exec.; b. Boston, Oct. 15, 1932; d. Leon and Leona (Leglize) Marjollet; B.S., Simmons Coll., 1952. Producer Campbell Ewald Advt., N.Y.C., 1955-65; with Carl Ally Advt., Inc., N.Y.C., 1965—, v.p., 1968—. Mem. Am. Women in Radio and TV. Home: 141 E 56th St New York City NY 10022 Office: 437 Madison Av New York City NY 10022

MARJORIBANKS, SHEILA DAISY, occupational therapist; b. Toronto, Ont., Can., June 2, 1930; d. William Wilson and Jean Cameron (Wylie) Marjoribanks; diploma in Occupational Therapy, U. Toronto, 1952. Staff therapist Vets.'s Hosp., Ste. Anne de Bellevue, Que., Can., 1953-59; supr. occupational therapy L'Hopital Ste. Justine, Montreal, Que., 1959-62; asst. supr. Rehab. Inst. Montreal, 1962-65; asst. supr. Toronto Rehab. Center, 1965-72, supr., 1972-74; instr. occupational therapy Sch. Rehab., Kinki Nat. Central Hosp., Osaka, Japan, 1974—. Mem. Canadian Assn, Occupational Therapists (dir. 1966—), World Fedn. Occupational Therapists, Art Gallery Ont., Royal Ont. Mus. Editor: Canadian Jour. Occupational Therapy, 1971-74. Office: 4 New St Toronto ON Canada

MARK, ESTELLE, interior designer; b. Bklyn.; d. Harry and Eva (Goldman) Mark; student N.Y. Sch. Interior Design. Interior designer Miss Estelle Mark, Bklyn., 1926—; asso. D. Arthur Mark, appraiser, Bklyn., 1957—; partner Harry Mark Antiquary and Art Gallery, Bklyn., 1963—; Pvt. tchr. interior designing, 1926—, art, 1957-58; lectr. palmistry to faculty Stevens Inst. Tech., Hoboken, N.J., 1967. Mem. Allied Bd. Trade, N.Y.C., 1973—. Mem. 52 Assn. N.Y. Mem. B'nai B'rith. Contbr. articles on antiques to Bklyn. Eagle, 1936. Home: 96 S Portland Av Brooklyn NY 11217 Office: 751-3 Fulton St Brooklyn NY 11217

MARKEY, LUCILLE PARKER, thoroughbred horse breeder and owner; b. Maysville, Ky., Dec. 14, 1896; d. John W. and Sarah B. (Owens) Parker; ed. Weston Sch.; m. Warren Wright, Mar. 26, 1919 (dec. Dec. 1950); 1 son, Warren; m. 2d, Gene Markey, Sept. 27, 1952. Owner, propr. Calumet Farm, breeding establishment and racing stable, Lexington, Ky., 1950—; 8 winners Ky. Derby, 2 winners Triple Crown. Address: Calumet Farm PO Box 1810 Lexington KY 40501

MARKHAM, GERALDINE KATHRYN, educator, naturalist; b. Columbus, O., July 14, 1923; d. Raymond Paul and Loretta Barbara (O'Neal) Murphy; student Ohio State U., 1959-67; m. Milford Charles Markham, July 8, 1946; 1 dau., Bambi (Mrs. Phillip Hugo). Nature cons. day and established camps Girl Scout and Camp Fire Girls, 1959-67; summer camp nature adviser Seal of Ohio Girl Scout council, 1962-67; naturalist-educator Dawes Arboretum, Newark, O., 1967—; broadcaster WGSF Ednl. TV, 1967—. Participant Smithsonian Astrophys. Obs. Moonwatch Project, 1957-58; mem. bd. Ohio Environmental Council, 1972-74. Served with USNR, 1944-46. Recipient Recognition in conservation edn. award Ohio Forestry Assn. Fellow Ohio Acad. Sci.; mem. Nat. Audubon Soc., Ohio Conservation and Outdoor Edn. Assn., Ohio, Licking County hist. socs., Am. Nature Study Soc., Nature Conservancy. Contbr. articles to profl. jours. Home: 777 Pierce Av Columbus OH 43213 Office: Route 5 Dawes Arboretum Newark OH 43055

MARKHAM, LOUISE PURNELL, physician; b. Russellville, Ky., Mar. 15, 1925; d. Hugh Purnell and Mary Lee (Johnson) Markham; B.S., Western Ky. State U., 1946; M.D., Tulane U., 1950; m. J. Giamalva, June 25, 1952; children—John, David H., Bruce A., Benjamin C., Michael W., Amy. Intern Southern Baptist Hosp., New Orleans, 1950-51; resident Charity Hosp., Independence, La., 1951-52; practice medicine specializing in gen. practice, Hammond, La., 1952-58; physician Student Health Service, La. State U., Baton Rouge, 1958—; physician U.S. embassy, Somalia, 1965-67. Active Baton Rouge, Youth, Inc. Mem. East Baton Rouge Parish Med. Soc., Alpha Epsilon Iota. Club: Baton Rouge Altrusa. Home: 2067 Glendale Av Baton Rouge LA 70808 Office: Student Hosp La State U Baton Rouge LA 70803

MARKHAM, MARY ELIZABETH THORNTON (MRS. REGINALD A. MARKHAM), state ofcl.; b. Haverhill, Mass.; d. John W. and Mary E. (Murphy) Thornton; B.A., Regis Coll., 1937; M.Ed., Salem State Coll., 1968; m. Reginald A. Markham, Feb. 26, 1954. With Mass. Div. Employment Security, 1937—, prin. counselor N.E. area Mass., Lawrence, 1965-70, mgr. concentrated employment program, Lowell, 1970-71, supervising mgr., 1971-73, supervisory mgr., Lowell, 1973—. Bd. dirs. Merrimack River council Girl Scouts Am., 1965-73, chmn. personnel com., 1965-73, v.p., 1972—; sec. Medford Ancillary Manpower Planning Bd., 1972-73; mem. steering com. project vol. power Malden Mayor's Com. for Employment of Handicapped, 1972-73; bd. dirs., personnel com. Community Teamwork, Inc., Lowell, 1973—, Lowell Ancillary Manpower Planning Bd., 1973—; mem. Greater Lowell Adv. Com. for Industry, 1973—; chmn. selections com., mem. planning com. Greater Lowell Com. for Employment Handicapped, 1973—. Mem. Mass. Assn. to Advance Human Services, Am., Mass., Greater Boston personnel and guidance assns., Internat. Assn. Personnel in Employment Security, Nat. Vocational Guidance Assn., Nat. Employment Counselors Assn., Lowell C. of C. (mem. jobs and human resources adv. group). Home: 83 Kenoza Av Haverhill MA 01830 Office: 291 Summer St Lowell MA 01853

MARKLE, KATHLEEN MARY MCEVENEY (MRS. JAMES A. MARKLE), club woman; b. Sault Ste. Marie, Mich.; d. William Henry and Elizabeth (McGovern) McEveney; R.N., St. Mary's Hosp. Tng. Sch. Nurses, 1926; m. James A. Markle, Apr. 10, 1928. Sustaining mem. women's div. Project Hope, 1969—. Mem. Grand Opera Assn., Womens Assn. Detroit Symphony Orch. (life), Poetry Soc. Mich., Lawyers Wives Mich. Clubs: Womens City (vice chmn. social affairs 1964-65), Catholic Study (v.p. 1957-59), Theatre Arts. Home: 475 Fiske Dr Detroit MI 48214

MARKLE, SUSAN MEYER (MRS. PHILIP W. TIEMANN), ednl. technologist; b. Buffalo, Nov. 11, 1928; d. Alden and Ruth (Alden) Rogers; student Smith Coll., 1946-49; B.A., U. Buffalo, 1951, M.A., 1954, Ph.D., 1960; m. Philip W. Tiemann, Sept. 27, 1966; 1 son,

Alden Merrill Meyer. Research asso., fellow Harvard, 1956-60; dir. programmed instrn. Center for Programmed Instrn., N.Y.C., 1960-62; asst. prof. edn. U. Cal. at Los Angeles, 1962-65; head programmed instrn. U. Ill., Chgo., 1965—, asso. prof. psychology, 1965-69, prof. psychology, 1969—. Cons. U.S. AID, India, 1966, 70, USAF Tng. Command, 1963—, Office of Edn., 1965—, Nat. Insts. Edn., 1973—, others. Mem. Nat. Soc. for Programmed Instrn. (pres. 1966, chmn. editorial bd. jour. 1965-66, 68-71), Am. Psychol. Assn., A.A.A.S., Am. Ednl. Research Assn., N.E.A., Sigma Xi. Home: 505 N Lake Shore Dr Chicago IL 60611 Office: Office Instructional Resources U Ill Box 4348 Chicago IL 60680

MARKLEY, MARY ELIZABETH OVERHULSER (MRS. RAYMOND MARKLEY), YMCA exec.; b. Warren, O., Apr. 6, 1928; d. William Orland and Ruth Carr (Sackett) Overhulser; student Bonnie Prudden Phys. Fitness Insts., 1969, 71, 73, Aquautic Instr. Certificate, 1972; m. Raymond Markley, Nov. 28, 1947; children—Thomas Ray, Nancy, Gary Devon. Clk. accounts payable C.G. Conn Ltd., Elkhart, Ind., 1946-49; with YMCA, Elkhart, 1960—, organizer pre-sch. swim classes, 1961—, instr. swimming, 1961—, trained masseuse, 1967—, dir. Ladies Health Club, 1967—, organizer first pre-sch. gym program, 1970—, organizer first Yoga and dance-exercise classes, 1969. Den mother Cub Scouts Am., 1962-63. Home: 117 S West Blvd Elkhart IN 46514 Office: 200 E Jackson Blvd Elkhart IN 46514

MARKLEY, SALLIE ANN PRICE (MRS. HOWARD WESLEY MARKLEY), educator; b. Magazine, Ark., Dec. 26, 1903; d. William Henry and Willie Ann (Cobb) Price; student Ark. Polytech. Coll., summers 1930-38, Neb. State Tchrs. Coll., 1941-42; B.S., Ark. State Tchrs. Coll., 1946, M.S., 1957; postgrad. U. Ark., 1954; m. Howard Wesley Markley, Nov. 23, 1940; 1 stepson, J. Howard; 1dau., Laura Ann. Tchr. pub. schs., Logan County, Ark., 1923-28, Paris, Ark., 1929-41; supr. English dept., tchr. Booneville (Ark.) Jr. and Sr. High Schs., 1946—; librarian Booneville High Sch., 1951-53. Vol. worker Child Devel. Center, Booneville; vol. adminstrv. asst. to project mgr. Fed. Right to Read Program in Ark. 1st v.p. local P.T.A., 1946-50; mem. Ark. Library Bd., 1964—. Trustee Logan County Library, 1950—, Ark. River Valley Regional Library, 1959—. Mem. N.E.A., Ark. Edn. Assn., Nat., Ark. councils tchrs. English, A.L.A., Ark., N.W. Regional library assns., Rotary Anns (pres. 1968). Methodist (adminstrv. bd., past Sunday sch. tchr., pres. Wesleyan Service Guild 1970). Home: 214 W 4th St Booneville AR 72927

MARKO, KATHLEEN MARGARET BARRETT (MRS. JULIAN LEWIS MARKO), educator; b. London, Eng.; d. Tom Boevey and Mabel (Grant) Barrett; B.F.A., Columbia, 1954, M.A., 1955, profl. diploma, 1963; m. Julian Lewis Marko, Feb. 15, 1949 (dec.). Tchr. Spl. elementary classes, Tenafly, N.J., 1955-57, spl. jr. high sch. classes, Englewood, N.J., 1957-58; supr. Trenton Div. of Spl. Edn. N.J. Dept. Edn., 1961-64; mem. faculty field services Newark State Coll., 1965-66; research coordinator Lang. Devel. Lab., Wrentham (Mass.) State Sch., 1966-68; dir. Title VI Project, Foxboro, Mass., 1968-70; ednl. cons.; dir. Title IV Project, New Bedford (Mass.) Pub. Schs., 1970-72; curriculum coordinator div. mental retardation Dept. Mental Health, Boston; now N.Y. State coordinator NAPRFMR. Fellow Am. Assn. on Mental Deficiency; mem. Council Exceptional Children (bd. dirs.), Am. Ednl. Research Assn., Am. Assn. U. Women, Nat. Council Women, Nat. Assn. for Retarded Children (past chmn. nat. audio-visual com.), Kappa Delta Pi, Pi Lambda Theta. Contbr. articles to profl. jours. Home: PO Box 2750 Grand Central Station New York City NY 10017 Office: 270 Madison Av New York City NY 10016

MARKS, BARBARA S., librarian; b. N.Y.C., Feb. 7, 1918; d. Joseph Mansfield and Rhoda (Schellenberg) Schaap; B.A. magna cum laude, Radcliffe, 1938; M.S., Columbia Sch. Social Work, 1941; M.S., Columbia Sch. Library Service, 1960; m. Bennett J. Marks, Sept. 19, 1941; children—Thomas, Emily (Mrs. Arthur Agin); m. Jack McKenna, Apr. 21, 1973. Librarian Jr. High Sch., New Rochelle, N.Y., 1960-61, Valhalla, 1961-64; edn. library head N.Y.U., Washington Square, 1964-72, chief reference librarian, 1972—. Mem. research team Library Services for the Disadvantaged in Buffalo, Syracuse, and Rochester, N.Y., 1969. Sch. bd. mem. Scarsdale Dist. 2, N.Y., 1957-63. Mem. A.L.A. (chmn. edn. and behavioral sci. subsection 1968-69), Spl. Libraries Assn. (social scis. div. chmn. 1972-73), Am. Soc. Information Sci. (chpt. chmn. 1973-74), Assn. Coll. and Research Libraries (chmn. nominating com. subject specialists section 1971-72), N.Y. Tech. Services Librarians (program chmn. 1969-70). Editor: N.Y. University List of Books in Education, 1968. Home: 400 Mamaroneck Av Harrison NY 10528 Office: New York University Bobst Library 70 Washington Sq S New York City NY 10012

MARKS, DOROTHY LOUISE AMES (MRS. LEONARD H. MARKS), journalist; b. Washington, Sept. 18, 1919; d. Frank Diman and Mary (Gannett) Ames; A.B., George Washington U., 1940; postgrad. U. N.C., 1941; m. Leonard H. Marks, June 3, 1948; children—Stephen Ames, Robert Evan. Asst. dir. pub. information FCC, Washington, 1941-45; Washington corr. Variety, San Diego Jour., Sioux Falls (S.D.) Argus Leader, 1945-50; contbg. editor Democratic Nat. Com., Washington, 1952-60; corr. N.Am. Newspaper Alliance and Women's News Service, Washington, 1969—. Mem. exec. com. Fgn. Student Service Council, 1968-69. Pres., Woman's Nat. Democratic Club, 1965-67. Bd. governance George Washington U., 1970-71. Clubs: Washington Press, Am. Newspaper Women's (1st v.p. 1973-74), International, 1925 F Street. Home: 2833 Mc Gill Terrace NW Washington DC 20008

MARKS, EDITH SWARTZ BOBROFF (MRS. JASON MARKS), ednl. adminstr.; b. Maynard, Mass., June 20, 1924; d. Samuel and Rebecca (Weber) Swartz; B.A., Bklyn. Coll., 1967; M.A., Columbia U., 1969; m. Jason Marks, Aug. 4, 1963. Co-dir. Career Blazers Agy., N.Y.C., 1957-69; tchr.-in-charge P.S. 224Q, sch. for emotionally disturbed, Bklyn., 1969 project asso. Spl. Ednl. Instructional Materials Center, 1974—. Mem. Schizophrenia Found. N.Y., Assn. N.Y. Educators of the Emotionally Disturbed (exec. bd.), Council for Exceptional Children, Sigma Alpha Phi. Author: (with Adele Lewis) From College to Career, 1962, (with Adele Lewis) From Kitchen to Career, 1963; Basic Concepts, 1973. Editor: Anyseed Newsletter. Home: 35 W 90th St New York City NY 10024 Office: 75 S 4th St Brooklyn NY 11211

MARKS, LILLIAN, physician; b. Columbus, O., Jan. 6, 1917; d. Samuel and Luba (Plotkin) Marks; B.A. summa cum laude, Ohio State U., 1938, M.Sc., 1939, M.D. with honors, 1943; m. Jack Bloom, July 16, 1954; 1 son, Theodore Samuel. Intern Michael Reese Hosp., Chgo., 1943-44; resident Municipal Contagious Disease Hosp., Chgo., 1944-45; pediatric resident Cook County Hosp., Chgo., 1945-46; juvenile court physician, Chgo., 1946; practice medicine specializing in pediatrics, Columbus, O., 1946—; asso. clin. prof. pediatrics Ohio State U., 1972—. Med. dir. Ohio Services for Crippled Children, 1949-53. Diplomate Am. Bd. Pediatrics. Fellow Am. Acad. Pediatrics; mem. Central Ohio Pediatric Soc., Columbus Acad. Medicine, Sigma Xi (asso.), Phi Beta Kappa, Alpha Omega Alpha. Home: 107 S Chesterfield Rd Columbus OH 43209 Office: 4207 E Broad St Columbus OH 43213

MARKS, LILLIAN SHAPIRO (MRS. JOSEPH MARKS), ret. educator, editor; b. Bklyn., Mar. 16, 1907; d. Hayman and Celia (Merowitz) Shapiro; B.S., N.Y.U., 1928; m. Joseph Marks, Feb. 21, 1932; children—Daniel, Sheila (Mrs. Vernon Pratt), Jonathan Michael. High sch. tchr., N.Y.C., 1929-30; tchr. Evalina de Rothschild Sch., Jerusalem, Palestine, 1930-31; social worker United Jewish Aid, Bklyn., 1931-32; tchr. high sch. Richmond Hill High Sch., 1932-40, Andrew Jackson High Sch., Cambria Heights, N.Y., 1940-71; staff Vassar Summer Inst., 1946. Mem. Am. Fedn. Tchrs., English-Speaking Union, Comml. Edn. Assn., Nat. Conf. Christians and Jews (women's div. com.). Democrat. Jewish religion. Am. editor: Teeline, A System of Fast Writing, 1970. Home: 117-16 Park Lane S Kew Gardens NY 11418 Office: 52 Vanderbilt Av New York City NY 10017

MARKS, MARCIA BLISS, journalist; b. Cleve., Mar. 7, 1927; d. Lloyd Bliss and Blanche Genevieve (Beal) Marks; B.A. (Sch. of Nations scholar), Principia Coll., 1948; student U. Geneva (Switzerland), 1946-47, Middlebury Coll., 1948, Harvard, 1952-53. Editorial trainee Christian Sci. Monitor, Boston, 1948-50; publs. supr. USIS, Singapore, 1951; asst. to dir. dance sch., Singapore, 1952; copy editor Little, Brown & Co., Boston, 1954-58; mgr. children's books Doubleday Bookshop, N.Y.C., 1959-60; asso. editor Grolier, Inc., N.Y.C., 1960-66; writer-editor Woman's Day, N.Y.C., 1966—. Critic, Dance mag., 1961-71; critic Critiques of Theatre Prodns. for Children, 1970-72; cons. N.Y. State Council on Arts, 1969-71. Vol., English in Action. Mem. Soc. for Asian Music, Woodland Trail Walkers, Wilderness Soc., Audubon Soc. Democrat. Club: Appalachian Mountain. Author: Swing Me, Swing Tree, 1958. Home: 116 W 75th St New York City NY 10023 Office: 1515 Broadway New York City NY 10036

MARKS, MOLLY TERESA BENNETT (MRS. ALVIN MELVILLE MARKS), civic exec.; b. Los Angeles, July 25, 1944; d. Mervin Dreux and Valre Grace (Seidl) Bennett; student Nev. So. U., 1964; postgrad. N.Y. U., 1967-68; m. Alvin Melville Marks, Aug. 25, 1965; children—Bridget Grace, Sean Christopher, Frederick Peter; stepchildren—Sarah Ellen, Douglas Melville. Moderator, interviewer, hostess TV show KLAS-TV, Las Vegas, Nev., 1961-63; adminstrv. asst. to pres. Marks Polarized Corp., Whitestone, N.Y., 1963—. Exec. v.p. North Shore Cerebral Palsy Aux., 1972-73, pres., 1973; publicity chmn. 1973 Auction 21, TV sta. WLIW, 1972—; mgr. 1st ann. horse show Assn. for Help Retarded Children, C.W. Post Coll., 1973. Mem. Civil Liberties Union, Am. Horse Shows Assn., Nassau Suffolk Horsemens Assn. (dir. 1972—), Screen Actors Guild, Catholic Daus. Am. Contbg. editor North Shore Club Life mag. Contbr. articles equestrian mags. Home: 100 Blair Rd E Oyster Bay Cove NY 11771 Office: 153-16 10th Av Whitestone NY 11757

MARKS, RACHEL BRYANT, educator; b. Lawrenceville, Va., Oct. 22, 1911; d. Richard Harrison and Sallie Everette (Watt) Marks; A.B., Emory and Henry Coll., 1932, LL.D., 1970; M.A., Scarritt Coll., 1939; M.A., U. Chgo., 1944, Ph.D., 1950. Tchr. Va. pub. schs., 1932-37, Colegio Americano, Porto Alegre, Brazil, 1939-40; case worker Social Service Bur., Petersburg, Va., 1940-41; sec. YWCA Ward-Belmont, Nashville, 1941-42, Kan. State Coll., Manhattan, Kan., 1942-43; instr. Ind. U., 1945-46; asst. to dir. casework Ill. Children's Home and Aid Soc., Chgo., 1946-48; asst. prof. U. Ill., 1948-50, asso. prof., 1950-52; asst. prof. U. Chgo., 1952-56, asso. prof., 1956-60, prof., 1960-67, Samuel Deutsch prof., 1967—, asst. editor Social Service Rev., 1952-56, editor, 1956-73. Mem. Nat. Assn. Social Workers, League Women Voters. Home: 205 Bookerdale Rd Waynesboro VA 22980

MARKSBERRY, MARY LEE, educator; b. Blairstown, Mo.; d. James Alfred and Mary (McDonald) Marksberry; B.S., Central Mo. State U., 1935; M.A., U. Mo., 1939; Ph.D., U. Chgo., 1951. Tchr. pub. schs., Mo., 1935-40; demonstration tchr., supr. Gen. Beadle State Tchr. Coll., Madison, S.D., 1940-41; tchr. pub. sch. Hinsdale, Ill., 1941-42; demonstration tchr., supr. Bemidji (Minn.) State Coll., 1942-46; tchr. Schofield Barracks Children's Sch., Oahu, Hawaii, 1946-49; research asst. U. Ill., Urbana, 1950-51; asst. prof. edn. Wayne State U., Detroit, 1951-53; faculty U. Mo., Kansas City, 1953—, asso. prof. edn., 1956-62, prof., 1962—, chmn. div. elementary edn., 1964—. Named Outstanding prof. Sch. Edn. Faculty, 1965. Mem. Assn. Supervision and Curriculum Devel., Nat. Council Tchrs. English, Nat. Council for Social Studies, Nat. Soc. for Study Edn., Am. Assn. U. Profs., Kappa Delta Pi, Phi Lambda Theta, Kappa Omicron Phi. Author: Foundation of Creativity, 1963. Contbr. articles to profl. jours. Office: 5100 Rockhill Rd Kansas City MO 64110

MARKUSEN, JOYCE LISENBY (MRS. JACK WILLIAM MARKUSEN), coll. adminstr.; b. Chesterfield, S.C., June 20, 1944; d. Niven Bryan and Dora Corinne (McLain) Lisenby; B.A. in Psychology, Furman U., 1965; M.Ed., U. S.C., 1970; m. Jack William Markusen, July 17, 1971. Social worker Charleston (S.C.) County Hosp., 1965; tchr. James Island Elementary Sch., Charleston, 1965-68, Marietta (Ga.) Pub. Schs., 1968-69; grad. asst. U. S.C. Counseling Bur., Columbia, 1969-70; asst. dean students, dir. women's programs, dir. program for handicapped, dir. orientation Baptist Coll., Charleston, 1970-73, asso. dean students, 1973—, asst. v.p. for student affairs, dir. counseling, 1974—. Mem. Trident Forum for Handicapped, Charleston, 1971—, 4-C Steering Com. for Childcare Centers, 1971-72. Mem. Nat. Assn. Student Personnel Adminstrn., S.C. Coll. Personnel Assn., Nat. Assn. Women Deans and Counselors (state editor review). Lutheran. Club: Dental Dames. Home: 28 1/2 Pitt St Apt B Charleston SC 29401

MARLAND, EMILY JANE STAHLEM (MRS. JACKSON THORNE MARLAND), educator, author; b. Valley City, N.D., Feb. 14, 1926; d. Arthur David and Evelyn (McInnes) Stahlem; student N.D. State U., 1943-45; B.A. (Cal. P.T.A. scholar), U. Cal. at Los Angeles, 1947; M.A., Columbia, 1948; m. Jackson Thorne Marland, June 30, 1949 (dec. July 1960); children—Albert MacInnes, Jackson Thorne. Tchr., Mary E. Bennett Sch. for Deaf, Los Angeles, 1948-49; pvt. tutor deaf and aphasic children, Washington, 1950-60; faculty Hearing and Speech Center, Gallaudet Coll., Kendall Green, Washington, 1962-67, asst. prof., 1968—. Appeared in various TV shows; hearing testor pre-sch. children Washington Hearing Soc., 1949-50. Mem. Alexander Graham Bell Assn. for Deaf, A.A.A.S., Am. Assn. U. Profs., Conv. Am. Instrs. of Deaf, Council Exceptional Children, Hearing and Speech Assn. D.C., Washington Assembly, Internat. Platform Assn., Kappa Kappa Gamma. Republican. Episcopalian. Club: Garden (Westmoreland Hills). Author: Idioms -How To Teach Them to the Deaf, 1969; A Handbook for Teachers, 1969; A Workbook for Students, 1969. Home: 5404 Albemarle St Washington DC 20016

MARLATT, ABBY LINDSEY, educator; b. Manhattan, Kan., Dec. 5, 1916; d. Frederick A. and Annie (Lindsey) Marlatt; B.S. in Home Econs., Kan. State U., 1938; certificate in hosp. dietetics U. Cal. at Berkeley, 1940, Ph.D., 1947. Teaching asst. home econs. U. Cal. at Berkeley, 1940-45; asso. prof., prof. foods and nutrition Kan. State U., Manhattan, 1945-56; vis. prof. home econs. Beirut (Lebanon) Coll. for Women, 1953-54, Ky. State Coll., 1968-71; prof., dir. Sch. Home Econs., U. Ky., Lexington, 1956-63, prof. home econs., 1963-68, prof. nutrition and food sci., 1968—. Bd. dirs. Community Action Lexington-Fayette County, 1967-71, 72—; treas. Lexington com. Open Housing, 1968—. Fellow A.A.A.S.; mem. Am. Dietetic Assn. (pres. Kan. 1951-52, pres. Ky. 1958-59), Am. Assn. Land Grant Colls. and State Univs. (chmn. home econs. sect. 1958-59), Am., Ky. (program chmn. 1958) home econs. assns., Soc. for Nutrition Edn. Ky. Nutrition Council (sec. 1973—), Am. Civil Liberties Union (dir., treas. Central Ky. chpt. 1966-71), Am. Assn. U. Profs., Mortar Bd., Sigma Xi, Phi Kappa Phi, Omicron Nu, Phi Upsilon Omicron (pres. Iota alumni chpt. 1971-72), Iota Sigma Pi, Delta Omega. Unitarian (chmn. ch. bd. trustees 1968, pres. Ohio Valley Council 1972—). Contbr. articles to profl. jours. Research in human nutrition, nutritional status children, food habits, vitamin metabolism. Home: 256 Tahoma Rd Lexington KY 40503

MARLEY, MARIE ISABELLE, librarian; b. Pemberton, Minn., Nov. 21, 1916; d. Harvey George and Maude Isabelle (Kanouse) Gregerson; B.S. in Edn., No. State Tchrs. Coll., Aberdeen, S.D., 1938; B.S. in L.S., George Peabody Coll. Tchrs., 1942; m. Henry James Boerum, June 30, 1944 (div. 1957); m. 2d, Lawrence L. Marley, Feb. 19, 1972. Librarian Gallatin County High Sch., Bozeman, Mont., 1942-43, U.S. Army Pocatello (Ida.) Air Field, 1943-44, Newark Pub. Library, 1944-52, 55-57, Fresno County (Cal.) Free Library, 1952-55, 57—. Mem. Fresno County Citizens Com. on Alcoholism, 1965-66. Recipient citation Small Bus. Adminstrn., 1969. Mem. Cal. Library Assn. (pres. reference div. 1968), League Women Voters. Methodist (chmn. social concerns commn. 1969-70). Author monograph. Home: 4822 E Cambridge St Fresno CA 93703 Office: 2420 Mariposa St Fresno CA 93721

MARLIN, ALICE TEPPER (MRS. JOHN TEPPER MARLIN), research co. exec.; b. Rumson, N.J., Aug. 10, 1944; d. Walter L. and Grace A. (Comins) Tepper; B.A., Wellesley Coll., 1966; m. John Tepper Marlin, Sept. 25, 1971. Editor Tax Bull., Internat. Bur. Fiscal Documentation, Amsterdam, Netherlands, 1966; securities analyst, labor economist Burnham & Co., N.Y.C., 1967-68; mem. staff Senator McCarthy's Presdl. Campaign, 1968; financial analyst Thomas O'Connell Mgmt. & Research Co., Boston, 1968-69; founder, exec. dir. Council on Econ. Priorities, N.Y.C., 1969—; v.p. Martin Rubber Co., Long Branch, N.J., 1968—. Instr., Grad. Sch. Bus. Adminstrn., Rutgers U., 1973-74. Point Found. grantee, 1972-73; Woodrow Wilson Found. sr. fellow, 1974—. Home: 360 W 22d St New York City NY 10011 Office: 84 Fifth Av New York City NY 10011

MARLOW, DOROTHY RUTH, nursing educator, univ. dean; b. Phila.; d. Willaim and Lillian (Shisler) Marlow; diploma Children's Hosp., Phila., 1942; B.S., U. Pa., 1948, M.S., 1956; Ed.D., Columbia, 1958. Various nursing edn. and nursing service positions Children's Hosp., Phila., 1943-45; supr. pediatric dept., instr. pediatric nursing Hosp. of U. Pa., 1945-53; instr. pediatric nursing Sch. Nursing, U. Pa., 1953-56, asst. prof., 1958-61, asso. prof., 1961-65, chmn. grad. program, 1962-64; prof. pediatric nursing, asst. dean Coll. Nursing, Villanova (Pa.) U., 1965-68, dean Coll. Nursing, 1968—. Cons. curriculum in nursing to various schs. of nursing. Mem. Nat. League for Nursing, Am. Nurses Assn., Am. Assn. U. Profs., Kappa Delta Pi, Sigma Theta Tau, Pi Lambda Theta. Author: Textbook of Pediatric Nursing (best book in coll. textbook group Phila. Book Show, 1962), 1961; Textbook of Pediatric Nursing, 2d edit., 1965 (certificate of award, coll. textbook group Phila. Book Show 1966), 3d edit., 1969, 4th edit., 1973. Home: 106 E Sylvan Av Rutledge PA 19070 Office: Coll Nursing Villanova U Villanova PA 19085

MARMER, ELLEN LUCILLE (MRS. HAROLD O. SHAPIRO), pediatric cardiologist; b. Bronx, N.Y., June 29, 1939; d. Benjamin and Diane (Goldstein) Marmer; student Adelphi U., 1956-57; B.S., U. Ala., 1960, M.D., 1964; M. Harold O. Shapiro, June 5, 1960; children—Cheri, Brenda. Pediatric intern Upstate Med. Center, Syracuse, N.Y., 1964-65, pediatric resident, 1965-66; asso. dept. pediatrics Columbia Presbyn. Med. Center, N.Y.C., 1967, fellow pediatric cardiology, 1967-69; practice medicine specializing in pediatric cardiology, Rockville, Conn., 1969—; dir. pediatric cardiology St. Francis Hosp., Hartford, Conn., 1971—; cons. pediatric cardiology Manchester Meml. Hosp., 1970—; mem. active staffs Rockville Gen. Hosp., Newington Children's Hosp.; mem. courtesy staff Mt. Sinai Hosp., Hartford Hosp., mem. U. Conn. Cardiovascular Com., 1970—. Bd. dirs. Heart Assn. Greater Hartford, Manchester Child Guidance Clinic. Fellow Am. Acad. Acad. Pediatrics; mem. Am. Med. Women's Assn., A.M.A., Royal Soc. Health of London, Am. (council rheumatic fever and congenital heart disease), Conn. heart assns., Conn. Med. Assn. (perinatal morbidity and mortality com. 1970), Vernon League of Women Voters (dir. 1971-73), Tolland County Med. Soc. (sec.-treas. 1971-72). Jewish religion (chmn. temple youth commn. 1970-71). Contbr. articles to profl. publs. Home: 276 Merline Dr Vernon CT 06066 Office: 57 Union St Rockville CT 06066 also St Francis Hosp Woodlawn St Hartford CT 06105

MARMO, NIKKI ANNETTE, educator, occupational therapist; b. West Palm, Fla., Nov. 27, 1942; d. Domenick and Lola Mae (Drake) Marmo; B.S. in Occupational Therapy, U. Fla., 1964; M.A. in Psychology, Cal. State U. at Los Angeles, 1973. Staff occupational therapist Crossroads Rehab. Center, Indpls., 1965-66; staff occupational therapist Rancho Los Amigos, Downey, Cal., 1967-68, sr. occupational therapist, 1968-70; head occupational therapy Long Beach (Cal.) Community Hosp., 1971-72; staff occupational therapist Childrens Health Center, San Diego, 1972-73; asst. prof. occupational therapy U. Fla., Gainesville, 1973—. Cons. to Downey Phys. Therapy, So. Cal. Rehab. and Therapeutics, Inc., Montebello, Cal., 1971, Theramedics Home Health Agy., 1971. Mem. Am., Ind., So. Cal. (chmn. ways and means com. 1972), Fla. occupational therapy assns., So. Cal. Schs. Council (vice chmn. 1970-71), League Women Voters, Sierra Club. Club: Beach Cities Ski. Home: 404 NW 26th St Gainesville FL 32607 Office: Dept of Occupational Therapy Box 212 J Hillis Miller Health Center Gainesville FL 32601

MARMUR, MILDRED LEE ROSENBERG, publishing co. exec.; b. Bklyn.; d. Louis and Esther (Hoffman) Rosenberg; B.A., Bklyn Coll., 1950; M.A., U. Minn., 1952; m. Julius Marmur, May 8, 1958; children—Alexander George, Nathaniel Zachary. With Simon & Schuster, Inc., N.Y.C., 1953—, mgr. subsidiary rights, 1959-68, dir. subsidiary rights, 1968-74, v.p., 1972-74; v.p. adult div., dir. subsidiary rights Random House, N.Y.C., 1974—. Mem. sub-com. on fgn. rights and co-prodn. Assn. Am. Pubs. Mem. Mensa, Pi Delta Phi. Translator: Madame Bovary (Flaubert), 1964; The Imaginary Invalid (Moliere), 1963; Japanese Fairy Tales, 1962; Tender and Violent Elizabeth (Henri Troyat), 1960; Diary of a Woman in White (Soubiran), 1969. Home: 420 West End Av New York City NY 10024 Office: 201 E 50th St New York City NY 10022

MARNELL, SISTER PHYLLIS, educator; b. Girard, Kan., Jan 13, 1922; d. Philip John and Rose Ann (Brophy) Marnell; student Sacred Heart Coll., Wichita, Kan., 1940-41, summers 1940-45, 58-59, 66, Alverno Coll., summers 1946-47, 49, Fordham U., summer 1948, Kan. State Tchrs. Coll., 1951-52, Kan. State U., 1952-53; B.S., St. Mary Coll., Xavier, Kan., 1954; postgrad. Duchesne Coll., summer 1955, Creighton U., summer 1958, Notre Dame U., summer 1962, Mt. St. Scholastica Coll., summer 1967, U. Wyo., summer 1968;

Media Specialist, U. No. Colo., 1973. Various teaching assignments jr. and sr. high schs.; dir. ednl. media Andale, Kan., 1966—. Bd. dirs. Sacred Heart Coll., 1967-71. Mem. Renwick Tchrs. Assn., Kan., Nat. edn. assns., Kan. Soc. Ednl. Communications and Tech., Assn. Ednl. Communications and Tech., Am., Kan., Mountain Plains library assns., Kan. Assn. Sch. Librarians, Am. Assn. U. Women, Alpha Omicron, Pi Lambda Theta. Home: PO Box 107 Andale KS 67001 Office: PO Box 68 Andale KS 67001

MAROCK, LOUISE, security specialist; b. N.Y.C.; d. Frederic Thyssen and Katherine Sinclair (Dempster) Marock; student N.Y. U. Began as sec., became spl. partner, W.C. Langley & Co., N.Y.C., investment bankers, 1920-35; ind. security specialist, N.Y.C., 1935—. Pres. Silver Cross Philanthropic Soc., N.Y.C. Mem. Women's Nat. Republican Club, N.Y.C. Clubs: Beach, Everglades (Palm Beach, Fla.); Westchester Country (Rye, N.Y.); Regency, Metropolitan (N.Y.C.); Lake Placid. Home: South Ocean Blvd Palm Beach FL 33480 also 114 E 72d St New York City NY 10021 Office: 115 Broadway New York City NY 10006

MARPLE, DOROTHY JANE, orgn. adminstr.; b. Abington, Pa., Nov. 24, 1926; d. John Stanley and Jennie (Stetler) Marple; A.B., Ursinus Coll., 1948; M.A., Syracuse U., 1950; Ed.D., Columbia Tchrs. Coll., 1969; L.H.D., Thiel Coll., 1965. Counselor, asst. office dean undergrad. women Women's Coll., Duke, 1950-53; dean women, fgn. student adviser Thiel Coll., 1953-61; asst. social dir. Whittier Hall, Columbia Tchrs. Coll., 1961-62; exec. sec. Luth. Ch. Women, Luth. Ch. Am., Phila., 1962—, coordinator commn. on function and structure Luth. Ch. in Am., 1970-72. Bd. dirs. Ministers Life and Casualty Union, 1974—. Mem. Nat. Assn. Women Deans and Counselors, Pi Lambda Theta. Home: 8018 Anderson St Philadelphia PA 19118 Office: 2900 Queen Lane Philadelphia PA 19129

MARQUARDT, DOROTHY ANN, librarian; b. Edina, Mo., Aug. 26, 1921; d. John A. and Beatrice M. (Franz) Marquardt; student Washington U., St. Louis, 1959, Quincy Coll., 1967-68; 1 son, Nicholas L. Davis. Topographer, Army Map Service, Quincy, Ill., 1943-45; with U.S. Navy Dept., Quincy, Ill.; credit mgr. Montgomery Ward Co., Quincy, Ill., 1945-47; librarian Quincy (Ill.) Free Public Library, 1947—. Author: (with Martha Eads Ward) Authors of Books for Young People, 1964, rev. edits., 1967, 71; Illustrators of Books for Young People, 1970. Home: 3421 Lawrence Rd Quincy IL 62301 Office: Quincy Free Pub Library 526 Jersey St Quincy IL 62301

MARQUARDT, LOIS ELAINE (MRS. LESTER A. MARQUARDT), newspaper editor; b. Marion, Wis., Aug. 8, 1914; d. Harvey George and Theresa Maria Edith (Zaug) Meyer; grad. high sch.; m. Lester Arthur Marquardt, Nov. 26, 1938; children—Otto Lester, Virginia Mae (Mrs. Daniel D. Berger), Bernard, Rosemary Annette (dec.), Michael John, Mary Alice (Mrs. James D. Power), Thomas Patrick, Eileen Marie (Mrs. James Smit). Sports corr. Chgo. Tribune, 1932-36; with Marion Advertiser, 1934-36; mng. editor Tigertown (Wis.) Chronicle, 1957—; regional corr. Appleton (Wis.) Post Crescent, Milw. Sentinel. Counselor, Camp Fire Girls, 1934; pres. Tigerton Graded Sch. Mothers' Club, 1961-62; pres. Split Rock Homemakers, 1960-68, sec., 1968—; sec. Tigerton Band Boosters, 1961-71; state del. Am. Cancer Soc., 1954-65; mem. Tigerton Mothers Club, 15 years; leader 4-H, 24 years; town chmn. Heart Fund, A.R.C. and Cerebral Palsy drives; organized Tigerton Art Club, 1961, also French Club; mem., past sec. St. Anthony's Council Catholic Women, also del. to diocesan meetings. Named Wis. State Mother, 1971. Home: Route 2 Tigerton WI 54486 Office: Tigerton Chronicle 1st Nat Bank Bldg Main St Tigerton WI 54486

MARQUIS, GERALDINE MAE HILDRETH (MRS. FORREST W. MARQUIS), educator; b. Ankeny, Ia., Aug. 8; d. Vernon Otto and Alma Leona (Woods) Hildreth; student U. No. Ia.; M.A., Drake U., 1972; m. Forrest William Marquis; 1 son, Robert William. Elementary tchr., Ankeny and Ft. Dodge, Ia., 1944-49, 56—; organizer Ft. Dodge Coop. Nursery Sch. Mem. N.E.A., Ia. Ft. Dodge edn. assns., Assn. Childhood Edn. Internat. (Ia. pres. 1974—), Nat. Assn. Edn. Young Children, Civic Music Assn., TTT Nat. Soc., Delta Kappa Gamma (local pres. 1974—), Phi Sigma Alpha. Republican. Methodist. Home: 814 N 16th St Fort Dodge IA 50501 Office: 615 N 16th St Fort Dodge IA 50501

MARQUIS, PEGGY COOK, educator; b. Point Pleasant, W.Va., July 22, 1931; d. Euclid Kirby and Helen Mae (Rose) Pullem; B.A., U. N.C., 1953; M.A., Columbia, 1956, Ph.D., 1964; m. Donald G. Marquis, Jan. 7, 1959 (dec. Feb. 1973). Social psychologist schs. and mental health research project Bank St. Coll. Edn., 1958; lectr. Northeastern U., 1961, cons. Stearns study of coll. student values, 1962; lectr. Boston U., 1960; asst. prof. sociology U. Mass., Boston, 1968-73, asso. prof., 1973—, faculty chmn. univ. assembly, 1973-74, chmn. dept. sociology, 1972. Am., New Eng. (mem. steering com.) psychol. assns., Am. Sociol. Assn., Soc. for Psychol. Study Social Issues, Alpha Kappa Delta, Pi Sigma Alpha. Contbr. articles to profl. jours. Home: 101 Revere St Boston MA 02114

MARQUISS, JEANNE ELLEN (MRS. STANLEY SCHWARTZBERG), physician; b. N.Y.C., Feb. 17, 1923; d. Ralph E. and Katherine (Lockwood) Marquiss; M.D., U. Mich., 1949; m. Stanley Schwartzberg, Feb. 15, 1961; children—Martin, Laury, David, Sarah. Intern Womens Hosp., Phila., 1949-50; resident Meadowbrook Hosp., Hempstead, N.Y., 1950-51, Queens Gen. Hosp., Jamaica, N.Y., 1951-54; dir. blood bank Rochester Gen. Hosp., N.Y., 1961—, asso. pathologist, 1961—. Home: 1732 Highland Av Rochester NY 14618 Office: Rochester Gen Hosp Portland Av Rochester NY 14618

MARR, CARMEL CARRINGTON (MRS. WARREN MARR II), state ofcl.; b. Bklyn.; d. William Preston and Gertrude Clementine (Lewis) Carrington; B.A., Hunter Coll., 1945; J.D., Columbia, 1948; m. Warren Marr II, Apr. 11, 1948; children—Charles Carrington, Warren Quincy. Admitted to N.Y. State bar, 1948; law asst. firm Dyer & Stevens Esqs., N.Y.C., 1948-49; practice law, N.Y.C., 1949-53; adviser legal affairs U.S. mission to UN, N.Y.C., 1953-67. sr. legal officer Office Legal Affairs, UN Secretariat, 1967-68; mem. N.Y. State Human Rights Appeal Bd., 1968-71; commr. N.Y. State Pub. Service Commn., 1971—; lectr. N.Y. Police Acad., 1963-67. Mem. N.Y. Gov.'s Com. Edn. and Employment of Women, 1963-64; mem. Nat. Gen. Services Pub. Adv. Council, 1969-71; mem. UN Devel. Corp., 1969-72. Bd. dirs. Amistad Research Center, New Orleans, Community Service Soc., N.Y.C., Bklyn. Soc. Prevention Cruelty to Children; bd. visitors N.Y. State Sch. Girls, Hudson, 1964-71; mem. exec. bd. Plays for Living, N.Y.C.; bd. govs. Billie Holiday Theatre. Mem. Bklyn. Bar Assn., Bklyn. Women's Bar Assn., Nat. Assn. Women Lawyers, Internat. Fedn. Women Lawyers, Nat. Assn. Regulatory Utility Commrs., UN Assn. (gov.), Phi Beta Kappa, Alpha Chi Alpha. Republican. Contbr. articles to profl. jours. Home: 333 New York Av Brooklyn NY 11213 Office: Public Service Commn Two World Trade Center New York City NY 10047

MARR, EILEEN (MRS. MARSHALL D. MARR), librarian; b. Sharon, Pa.; d. Eugene and Marie E. (Meier) McKenna; B.A., U. Cal. at Los Angeles, 1941; M.A., Immaculate Heart Coll., 1956; m. div. 1955; m. 2d, Marshall D. Marr, Mar. 1966. Librarian Orange County Free Library, Santa Ana, Cal, 1946-56; order librarian Fullerton (Cal.) Pub. Library, 1956-61, supr. tech. services div., 1961—. Mem. A.L.A., Cal., Orange County library assns., Am. Assn. U. Women. Episcopalian. Club: Zonta (past pres. Fullerton). Home: 221-C N Acacia Av Fullerton CA 92631 Office: 353 W Commonwealth Av Fullerton CA 92632

MARRA, CAROLYN C., accountant; b. Niles, O.; d. Joseph and Mary (Rounds) Marra; grad. Youngstown Coll., 1935; postgrad. Youngstown U., 1949-52. Mem. staff Wean-United Inc., Warren, Youngstown, O., 1935—, receptionist, 1935-36, sec. to chief draftsman and asst. engr., 1936-39, supr. controlled materials plan, 1941-45, supr. accounts payable audit, 1945—, now sr. statistician. Mem. women's com. Trumbull New Theatre, Niles. Sec.-treas., bd. dirs. Friends of McKinley Meml. Library and Mus., Niles; bd. dirs. Tru-Mah-Col chpt. Nat. Multiple Sclerosis Soc. Mem. Am. Accounting Assn., Am. Soc. Women Accountants (charter pres. Youngstown 1960, bull. chmn.), Warren Music Civic Assn., Warren Symphony, Zonta (pres. Warren-Niles 1971-73), Chi Epsilon (past pres. Youngstown), Beta Sigma Phi (chpt. sponsor). Home: 132 Fulton Av Niles OH 44446 Office: 347 N Park Av Warren OH 44481

MARRA, DOROTHEA C. (MRS. MICHAEL D. MARRA), research chemist; b. Bklyn.; d. Salvatore and Mary (Faugiana) Polizzi; B.A., Bklyn. Coll., 1943; m. Michael D. Marra, Jan. 11, 1947; 1 child, Jacques Marra. Research chemist Foster D. Snell, Inc., N.Y.C., 1944-69; v.p. Omar Research, Inc., N.Y.C., 1969—; chem. cons. to cosmetic, toiletry and pharm. cos. in U.S. and fgn. countries. Fellow Am. Inst Chemists; mem. Sci. Research Soc. Am., Soc. Cosmetic Chemists, Sigma Xi. Patentee in field. Home: 107 Fernwood Rd Summit NJ 07901 Office: 31 Union Sq W New York NY 10003 also 29 West 15th St NYC 10011

MARRALLE, TONIA MARIE, physician; b. Cleve., Dec. 12, 1941; d. Anthony James and Maria Jane (Mummolo) Marralle; student U. Cal. at Los Angeles, 1960-63; M.D., U. Cal. at Irvine, 1967. Intern St. Mary's Hosp., Long Beach, Cal., 1967-68; resident obstetrics and gynecology U. Cal. at Irvine, 1969-71; practice medicine specializing in obstetrics and gynecology, Costa Mesa, Cal., 1971—; vol. teaching staff dept. obstetrics and gynecology U. Cal. at Irvine, 1971—. Mem. Orange County Med. Assn. Office: 175 Rochester St Costa Mesa CA 92627

MARRIOTT, MRS. JOHN WILLARD, restaurant chain exec.; b. Salt Lake City, Oct. 19, 1907; d. Edwin Spencer and Alice (Taylor) Sheets; A.B., U. Utah, 1927; m. John Willard Marriott, June 9, 1927; children—John Willard, Richard Edwin. Partner, Hot Shoppes, Inc. (co. name changed to Marriott Corp.) restaurant chain, 1927—, v.p. dir., 1929—. Dir. Arthritis and Rheumatism Found. of Met. Washington; chmn. Pres.'s Adv. Com. on Arts for John F. Kennedy Center for Performing Arts, 1970—, trustee, 1972—, mem. exec. com., 1972—. Treas. League of Republican Women of D.C., 1955-57, v.p., 1957-59, campaign chmn, 2d v.p., 1959—; Rep. Nat. com. woman for D.C., mem. State Com., 1959—; treas. Rep. Nat. Conv., 1964, 68, 72, mem. arrangements com., 1960, 64, 68, 72; vice chmn. Rep. Nat. Com., 1965—, mem. exec. com., 1965—; mem. Rep. Coordinating Com., 1965-69, 73—; mem. Women's Nat. Rep. Club; vice chmn. inaugural com., 1969, hon. vice chmn., 1973. Mem. Nat. Adv. Com. for Children and Youth. Mem. Nat. Symphony Orch. Assn., Washington Nat. Ballet Guild (trustee), Internat. Neighbors Club, Welcome to Washington Club (treas.), Goodwill Guild (dir.), Chi Omega, Phi Kappa Phi. Mem. Ch. of Jesus Christ of Latter-day Saints. Clubs: Capital Speakers (chmn. membership), Washington, Capitol Hill, 1925 F Street, Am. Newspaper Women's (asso.). Home: 4500 Garfield St Washington DC 20007 Office: 5161 River Rd Washington DC 20016

MARROIG-DE-ALCALDE, GEORGINA (MRS. JESUS ALCALDE PEREZ), physician; b. Adjuntas, P.R., Oct. 17, 1928; d. Antonio and Heroilda (Rios) Marroig; B.S., U. P.R., 1951; M.D., U. Salamanca and Universidad Central, Madrid, Spain, 1957; m. Jesus Alcalde Perez, Jan. 8, 1965; children—Gisela, Marisabel. Intern San Juan City Hosp., P.R., 1957-58, resident pediatrics, 1958-60; chief resident Fajardo Dist. Hosp., P.R., 1960-61; resident pediatric cardiology Cook County Hosp., Chgo., 1961-64; chief pediatric service Fajardo Dist. Hosp., P.R., 1964-66; attending pediatric cardiology Med. Center, U. Hosp., Rio Piedras, P.R., 1966-73. Mem. P.R. Med. Assn. Address: 110 Gautier Benitez Floral Park Hato Rey PR 00917

MARRS, AIMEE W(HITMAN), clin. psychologist, ret. naval officer; b. Catoosa, Okla., Dec. 15, 1911; d. William W. and Lillian (Querry) Whitman; A.B in Math., Northeastern State Coll., Tahlequah, Okla., 1931; M.A. in Clin. Psychology, U. Tulsa, 1948; m. Manton Lee Marrs, May 9, 1948 (dec.). Accountant, Sears, Roebuck & Co., 1936-38, Phillips Petroleum Co., 1938-41, Stanolind Oil & Gas Co., 1941-43; served from ensign to lt. (j.g.), USNR, 1943-46; accounting positions Stanolind Oil & Gas Co., 1946-48; lectr. psychology U. Tulsa, also clin. psychologist Tulsa Child Guidance Clinic, 1948-51; lt. to comdr., clin. psychologist USNR, 1951-69, comdr. M.S.C., 1958-69. certified, Cal. Mem. Am., Div. 12, 16 and 31, Cal., Va., Md. psychol. assns., Psi Chi. Home: 6843 S Toledo St Apt 349 Tulsa OK 74136

MARSDEN, ELIZABETH HARLOW, educator; b. Nashville, Mar. 17, 1923; d. Frank Ernest and Harriet Ellsworth (Rees) Harlow; B.Mus., U. Miami, 1944; M.A., Columbia, 1945; m. Edward Derwood Marsden, Dec. 23, 1946 (div. Jan. 1971); children—Elizabeth Rhys, Margaret Lee, Cathering Harlow, Harriet Ann. Tchr., Southeastern LA. Coll., 1945-47; asst. prof. music U. Miami (Fla.), 1947-52; supr. music Penn Hills Sch., Pitts., 1954-59; tchr. piano, voice, Pitts., 1959-61; judge Music Educators Nat. Conf., Miami, 1953, Tampa, Fla., 1953; tchr. Dade County Schs., 1964-65, Brevard County Schs., Cape Kennedy, Fla., 1966-72; lectr. U. Ga., Atlanta, 1972-73. Music cons. Marietta city schs., 1972—; lectr. Rollins Coll., U. South Fla.; tchr. voice, piano, Coral Gables; organist, dir. music First Presbyn. Ch., Titusville, Fla., 1967-72; organist Apostles Lutheran Ch., Atlanta, 1973—. Mem. Ga. Assn. Curriculum and Instrnl. Suprs., Am. Assn. U. Profs., Am. Assn. U. Women, Music Educators Nat. Conf., Am. Guild Organists, Nat. Tchrs. Assn., Fla. Music Educators Assn., Brevard Music Edn. Assn. (v.p.), Chi Omega, Sigma Alpha Iota, Delta Kappa Gamma. Presbyn. (v.p. women's guild). Clubs: Coral Cables (Fla.) Garden; College, Tuesday Music, Mt. Lebanon Women's (Pitts.); Flamingo Dinner. Home: 1500 Bellemeade Dr Marietta GA 30060 also 931 Obispo Av Coral Gables FL Office: Bd. Pub Instrn Marietta GA 30060

MARSH, ANNE STEELE (MRS. JAMES R. MARSH), artist; b. Nutley, N.J., Sept. 7, 1901; d. Frederic Dorr and Mary (Thyng) Steele; student YWCA Art Sch., 1917-19, Cooper Union Art Sch., 1919-20; m. James R. Marsh, Jan. 17, 1925; children—Reginald S., Janet (Mrs. William M. Hunt), Peter R. Tchr. occupational therapy Bloomingdale Hosp., White Plains, N.Y., also pvt. patients, 1921-25; tchr. pvt. art classes, 1935-45; instr. of art Newark Sch. Fine and Indsl. Art, 1945-48; co-founder Hunterdon Art Center, Clinton, N.J., 1953, tchr., 1955-57; founder, v.p. Clinton Hist. Mus., 1963; exhibited one-man shows at Contemporary Arts Gallery, N.Y.C., 1935, Rollins Coll., 1936, Morton Gallery, N.Y.C., 1937, Coop. Gallery, Newark, 1938, various galleries, N.J., 1940-60, Stove Mill Gallery, Erwima, Pa., 1964, Old Bergen Art Guild, 1962—; work in collections Met. Mus., Phila. Mus., Library Congress. Trustee Hunterdon Art Center; bd. dirs. Friends of N.J. State Mus. Mem. Nat. Assn. Women Artists, N.Y. Soc. Women Artists (treas. 1970—), Del. Valley Artists (treas. 1966—), Artists Equity Assn. N.J. (dir.), Audubon Artists (dir.), Soc. Am. Graphic Artists (council 1973—), Museums Council N.J., Pen and Brush. Home: Rural Route 1 Pittstown NJ 08867

MARSH, BETTIE JEAN MCJUNKIN (MRS. WILLIAM DALE MARSH), lawyer; b. El Campo, Tex., Sept. 27, 1941; d. Loranzo and Imogene (Neaves) McJunkin; student Lindenwood Coll. for Women, 1959-60, Okla. State U., 1960-62; B.S., U. Wis., J.D., Wis. Law Sch.; m. William Dale Marsh, Apr. 3, 1970; children—Bradley Trent, Stacey Leigh. Admitted to Wis. bar, 1967, Fed. Dist. Ct. for Eastern Dist. Wis. bar, 1967, Utah State bar, 1971; law reform coordinator Milw. Legal Services Program, Milw., 1967-69; asst. research dir. Nat. Legal Aid and Def. Assn., Am. Bar Center, Chgo., 1969-70; practice firm Marsh & Marsh, Ogden, Utah, 1970-74; asst. atty. gen. Utah, 1974—. Bd. dirs. Weber Basin Mental Health Assn., 1972-73, Utah State Mental Health Assn., 1972-73, Weber County Legal Aid Services, 1972-73. Recipient Russell Sage fellow, 1966-67. Mem. Weber County Bar Assn. (dir. 1972-73), Alpha Chi Omega, Phi Alpha Delta. Presbyn. Home: 1540 Country Hills Dr Ogden UT 84403 Office: 1018 First Security Bank Bldg Ogden UT 84401

MARSH, CAROLYN O'NEAL, mgmt. cons.; b. Florence, S.C., Dec. 28, 1926; d. Charles O'Neal and Effie (Buzhardt) Marsh; B.A. in Psychology, U. Richmond, 1947, M.A., 1948. Grad. asst. psychology U. Richmond, 1947-48, psychometrist, vocational counselor, 1948-51; with Miller & Rhoads Dept. Stores, Richmond, 1951-71, personnel mgr., 1961-71; pres., treas. Carolyn Marsh Personnel Mgmt., Inc., Richmond, 1971—. Dir. Richmond area Bank Va., 1974—. Bd. dirs., chmn. personnel and rehab. com. Richmond Goodwill Industries, 1972—, v.p., 1973-75, pres. 1975—; trustee U. Richmond, 1972—. Mem. Am. Psychol. Assn., Richmond Personnel Execs. Assn., Westhampton Coll. Alumnae Assn. (dir., exec. com. 1972—, alumnae fund chmn. 1969-71). Baptist (bd. adminstrn. 1970). Club: Willow Oaks Country (charter) (Richmond). Home: 300 W Franklin St Richmond VA 23220 Office: Mutual Bldg Richmond VA 23219

MARSH, CARYL AMSTERDAM (MRS. MICHAEL MARSH), social psychologist; b. N.Y.C., Mar. 9, 1923; d. Louis and Kitty (Weitz) Amsterdam; B.A., Bklyn. Coll., 1942; postgrad. (fellow) Coll. City N.Y., 1945-46; M.A., Columbia, 1946; postgrad. George Washington U.; m. Michael Marsh, Sept. 3, 1942; children—Susan, Anna. Psychol. cons. D.C. Recreation Dept., 1957-69; cons. Meyer Found., 1964-66, D.C. City Council, 1967-72; started Anacostia Neighborhood Mus., 1967; created Exptl. Touch exhibit Nat. Mus. Natural History, 1973; project dir. Discovery Room, spl. asst., cons. Smithsonian Instn., Washington, 1967-73. Mem., sec. D.C. Arts Commn., 1968-72; cons. beautification program White House, 1965-68; pres. Pre-Sch. Parents Council, 1956-57. NSF research and devel. grantee, 1972-73. Mem. Am., D.C. psychol. assns., Am. Assn. Museums, League Women Voters, Women's Nat. Democratic Club, Psi Chi. Home: 3701 Grant Rd NW Washington DC 20016

MARSH, CLARE ANN, psychologist; b. Manitowoc, Wis., July 7, 1934; d. Clarence Emil and Dorothy Loretta (Napiezinski) Teitgen; student Lawrence Coll., 1952-54, U. Wis.-Madison, 1954-55; B.S., U. Wis.-Milw., 1966, M.S., 1968; m. Robert Marsh, Jan. 30, 1955 (div.); children—David, Wendy, Julie, Laurie. Sch. psychologist West Allis-West Milw. Sch. System, 1968—; counselor Counseling Services, Milw., 1968-72, psychotherapist Veit Clinic, 1968—; mem. paramed. staff psychiatry St. Luke's Hosp., Milw., 1970-72. Nat. Def. Edn. Act fellow, 1966-68. Mem. Am., Wis. psychol. assns., Sch. Suburban Psychologists Assn. (co-pres. 1973—), Alpha Chi Omega, Phi Kappa Phi, Sigma Tau Delta, Kappa Delta Pi. Methodist. Home: 3214 S 23d St Milwaukee WI 53215 Office: 9333 W Lincoln St Milwaukee WI 53219

MARSH, DOROTHY JANE, physician, surgeon; b. Monrovia, Cal., Oct. 16, 1915; d. Clark Herbert and Florence (Best) Marsh; A.A., Pasadena City Coll., 1934; D.O., Coll. Osteopathic Physicians and Surgeons, 1938; M.D., Cal. Coll. Medicine, 1962. Intern Los Angeles County Hosp., 1938-39; resident Los Angeles County, 1939-42; pvt. practice specializing in obstetrics and gynecology, Glendale, Cal., 1942—; chmn. dept. obstetrics and gynecology Glendale Community Hosp., 1943—, v.p. attending staff, 1967-68; former clin. prof. obstetrics and gynecology Cal. Coll. Medicine; former attending staff dept. obstetrics Los Angeles County Hosp. Mem. Cal. Osteo. Assn. (pres. 1960-61), Alumni Assn. Cal. Coll. Medicine (trustee 1961-69, sec.-treas. 1966-70), Cal. (mortality rev. com. so. sect., chmn. infant mortality com.) Los Angeles County (ins. rev. com.) med. assns., Alumni Assn. Coll. Osteo. Physicians and Surgeons (pres. 1951-53). Republican. Mem. Christian Ch. Club: Soroptimist. Home: 3017 Scotland St Los Angeles CA 90039 Office: 1385 E Colorado St Glendale CA 91205

MARSH, ELEANOR MILLER HACK (MRS. GARNETT S. MARSH), former social worker; b. Indpls., Mar. 23, 1913; d. Oren Stephen and Elizabeth (Miller) Hack; B.S., Butler U., 1934, M.S. in Edn., 1939; M.A. in Social Service, Ind. U., 1947; m. Garnett S. Marsh, Feb. 27, 1972. Elementary sch. tchr., Boggstown, Ind., 1935-39; probation officer Marion County Juvenile Ct., 1939-40, div. spl. services, 1940-42; case worker Children's Bur., Indpls., 1943; supr. med. care and eye treatment pub. assistance div. Ind. Dept. Pub. Welfare, 1944-52; dir. admissions and asst. to med. dir. Ind. U. Med. Center, Indpls., 1953-66; supr. field service sect., div. pub. assistance Ind. Dept. Pub. Welfare, 1966-72. Pres. Ind. Conf. Social Work, 1955, dir. 1952-55, 57-63; chmn. Com. Registration Social Workers, 1950-53; sec. women's aux. Henderson County YMCA, 1974. Mem. Am. Pub. Welfare Assn. (Ind. membership chmn. 1952-55), Indpls. Social Workers Club (pres. 1951-53, chmn. legislative com. 1953-55 James L. Fieser award for distinguished service 1968), Kappa Alpha Theta, Phi Kappa Phi, Kappa Delta Pi. Presbyn. Editor: Health and Welfare Legislative Information Service, 1949-52. Address: 924 N Main St Henderson KY 42420

MARSH, FLORENCE GERTRUDE, educator; b. Rochester, N.Y., Sept. 15, 1916; d. Charles D. and Ruth (Galloway) Marsh; A.B., Mt. Holyoke Coll., 1937; M.A., U. Tenn., 1943; Ph.D., Yale, 1951. Tchr., Cayuga Lake Acad., Aurora, N.Y., 1939-41; teaching fellow U. Tenn., 1941-43; instr. English, Western Coll. For Women, Oxford, O., 1943-45; instr. English, Mt. Holyoke Coll., 1948-49; instr. English, Case Western Res. U., Cleve., 1950-51, asst. prof., 1951-60, asso. prof., now prof., chmn., 1972-74. Ford Found. grantee for improvement teaching, 1954-55. Mem. Am. Assn. U. Profs., Modern Lang. Assn., Nat. Council Tchrs. English. Author: Wordsworth's Imagery: A Study in Poetic Vision, 1952. Contbr. articles to profl. jours. Home: 4883 Countryside Rd Lyndhurst OH 44124

MARSH, GWENDOLEN, musician; b. Chetopa, Kan., Mar. 17, 1908; d. Charles Williard and Myrtle (Wolven) Marsh; student Kansas City Conservatory Music, 1921-27; advanced study in piano, voice and opera scores, N.Y.C., 1927-33. Singer, pianist, tchr., N.Y.C., 1928-33; recital performances, tchr. master classes, 1934—; adjudicator Nat. Guild Piano Tchrs., 1957—; Kansas City corr., critic Musical Leader, 1965-67. Mem. Kansas City Mus. Assn., Federated Music Tchrs. Kansas City, Mo. Fedn. Music Clubs (award outstanding composer 1974). Mem. Christian Ch. Club: Musical, Clef Music (Kansas City, Mo.). Composer trios for womens voices, elementary piano pieces. Address: 1120 E 44th St Kansas City MO 64110

MARSH, MARTHA FRANCES, coll. adminstr.; b. Lexington, Ky., Apr. 21, 1948; d. Cecil Edward and Rosetta (Sexton) Marsh; B.A., Georgetown (Ky.) Coll., 1970, M.A., 1972; student Coll. Bus. Mgmt. Inst. U. Ky., 1972, 73, 74. Sec. Winchester (Ky.)-Clark County C. of C., 1968; instr. bus. Southeastern Christian Coll., Winchester, 1970-72, bus. mgr., 1972—; notary pub., 1973—. Active United Heart Fund drive, 1972—. Mem. So. Assn. Coll. and Univ. Bus. Officers, Ky. Assn. Student Financial Aid Adminstrs., Clark County Bus. and Profl. Women's Club (2d v.p. 73-75; Young Career Woman's award 1972). Baptist (choir). Home: 417 Boone Av Winchester KY 40391

MARSH, MARY VAL, educator; b. Uniontown Pa., Apr. 28, 1925; d. Roy William and Mary (Hickman) Marsh; A.B., U. Cal. at Los Angeles, 1946; M.A., Claremont Grad. Sch., 1953; m. Dwight Ellsworth Twist, Aug. 4, 1962. Tchr. Mission Elementary Sch., Redlands, Cal., 1946-48; curriculum cons. San Bernardino County Schs., San Bernardino, Cal., 1948-52, coordinator music edn., 1952-59; supr. music edn. Beverly Hills (Cal.) Unified Sch. Dist., 1959-62; lectr. music edn. San Diego State U., 1963-73; mem. Contemporary Music Project, Ford Found.-Music Educators Nat. Conf., 1963-65; supr. opera edn. project San Diego Opera Guild, Nat. Endowment for Arts, 1971—; dir. numerous music edn. workshops, 1954—. Mem. Music Educators Nat. Conf. (life, clinician biennial, div., state meetings), Sigma Alpha Iota (patroness), Delta Kappa Gamma, Pi Lambda Theta. Presbyn. (ch. soloist). Author: Choruses and Carols, 1964; Here a Song, There aSong, 1969; Explore and Discover Music, 1970; co-author The Spectrum of Music, textbook series, 1974. Home: 879 Rosecrans St San Diego CA 92106

MARSH, NGAIO DAME, writer; b. Christchurch, New Zealand, Apr. 23, 1899; d. Henry Edmund and Rose Elizabeth (Seager) Marsh; student St. Margarets Coll., New Zealand, 1910-14, Canterbury U. Coll. Sch. Art, 1915-20, Litt.D., 1963. Actress, 1920-23; theatrical producer, 1923-27; interior decorator, London, Eng., 1928-32; producer, dir. Shakespeare plays in New Zealand; writer detective novels, 1933—; dir. 1st all-New Zealand Shakespearian Co. student players, 1946. Served as head sect. leader, Red Cross, Transport, New Zealand, 1939. Decorated Dame of Brit. Empire. Fellow Royal Soc. Arts; mem. Brit. Authors, Playwrights and Composers Soc., P.E.N. Mem. Church of Eng. Club: University Canterbury. Author: Death in a White Tie, 1938; Death of a Peer, 1941; Colour Scheme, 1944; Died in the Wool, 1945; Final Curtain, 1945; A Wreath for Rivera, 1948; Opening Night, 1951; Spinsters in Jeopardy, 1953; Scales of Justice; Death of a Fool; Singing in the Shrouds, 1957; False Scent, 1959; Off With His Head, 1960; Three-Act Special, 1960; Night at the Vulcan, 1960; Hand in Glove, 1962; Dead Water, 1963; Black Beech and Honeydew (autobiography), 1965; Killer Dolphin, 1966; A Cluth of Constables, 1969; When in Rome, 1970; Tied Up In Tinsel, 1972; Black Ashe's Painted, 1974. Home: 37 Valley Rd Christchurch S 2 New Zealand Office: Messers Harold Ober Assoc 40 E 49th St New York City NY 10017

MARSH, PAMELA OLIVE, editor; b. Warwickshire, Eng.; d. James Frederick and Alice Irene (Ashmore) Marsh; ed. Sutton Coldfield High Sch., Warwickshire, Birmingham (Eng.) Secretarial Tng. Coll. Book rev. editor Christian Sci. Monitor, Boston. Home: 249 111 Perkins St Boston MA 02130 Office: 1 Norway St Boston MA 02115

MARSH, PHRONSIE IRENE (MRS. HERBERT CECIL FITZ ROY SITWELL), poet, feature writer, educator; b. nr. Lynchburg, Va., Apr. 1, 1907; d. Peter Addison and Constance (Fisher) Marsh; student Lynchburg Coll., 1924-26; B.S., Mary Washington Coll., 1927; M.A., Columbia, 1932; summer study U. Va., 1925, Inst. on World Affairs, Geneva, Switzerland, 1935, N.Y.U., U. Pa.; postgrad. Va. Poly. Inst., 1966-67, U. Va., 1970-71; m. Erik Solling Monberg, Apr. 25, 1943 (div. 1947); 1 son, Edmund Marsh; m. 2d, Herbert Cecil Fitz Roy Sitwell, May 14, 1961 (dec. Aug. 1965). Tchr. Salem (Va.) High Sch., 1927-28, E. C. Glass High Sch., Lynchburg, Va., 1928-30, Oyster Bay, N.Y., 1930-34, Washington, 1935-44; adminstrv. asst. TVA, 1933; gen. supr. edn. Wythe County Schs., Wytheville, Va., 1945-46; with Phillips Coll., Lynchburg, 1946-47; ednl. adviser Sullins Coll., Bristol, Va., 1947-49; social studies chmn. Capitol Page Sch., 1949-50; tchr. Washington pub schs., 1950-62; instr. History and English, Central Va. Coll., Lynchburg, 1967-68; owner, dir. historic properties, Bedford, Lynchburg, Va., 1949—. Ofcl. visitor 3d Internat. Congress on Comparative Law, The Hague, 1937. Del. Va. Democratic Conv., 1970-72; mem. Bedford County Dem. Com. Recipient fellowship to Nat. Music Camp, Interlochen, Mich., to write scripts for NBC broadcast, 1940, fellowship to N.Y.U., 1941, U. Pa., summer 1957. Recipient Nat. Poetry prize U.D.C., 1930, Va. Poetry prize Lynchburg Poetry Festival, 1962, 72. Mem. Am., Phila., N.Y.C. acads. polit. sci., Soc. Archtl. Historians, Poetry Soc. Va., Nat. Trust Historic Preservation, League Am. Pen Women (v.p. charge creative activities D.C. br. 1939-41), Modern Lang. Assn., N.Y., Internat. Platform Assn., Assn. Preservation Va. Antiquities, Lynchburg, Bedford hist. socs., Am. Assn. U. Women, Writers Club Va., Bedford Poetry Soc. (pres. 1962-63, 69-70), Arts Club Washington, English Speaking Union, U.D.C., Va. State Mus., Pi Gamma Mu. Episcopalian. Clubs: Specs, Woman's (pres. Oyster Bay, N.Y. 1932-34). Author numerous poems and articles in field. Home: Three Otters Estate RFD 2 Bedford VA 24523 also Townhouse 1106 Federal St Lynchburg VA 24504

MARSHALL, BARBARA HELEN (MRS. CHARLES LEWIS MARSHALL), assn. exec.; b. Collbran, Colo., July 14, 1943; d. Charles Nathaniel and Eleanor Barbara (Reed) Nichols; student, Western State Coll., 1961-63; m. Charles Lewis Marshall, June 6, 1963; children—Diana Lynn, Darren Charles. Various office positions City of Gunnison, Colo., 1963-65, 66-67; sec., bookkeeper, receptionist Cross & Rigg, C.P.A.'s, Glendive, Mont., 1968-70; exec. dir. Lake County Civic Center Assn., Leadville, Colo., 1971—. Home: 603 W 8th St Leadville CO 80461 Office: 102 E 9th St Leadville CO 80461

MARSHALL, BETTY JEAN (MRS. HOWARD MELSON MARSHALL), librarian; b. Scircleville, Ind., Mar. 20, 1926; d. Charles Cleveland and Blanche (McKinney) Jones; B.S., Ind. U., 1947; M.S., Purdue U., 1966; m. Howard Melson Marshall, July 19, 1947; children—Charles, James, Michael. Tchr. Tippecanoe Sch. Corp., Elston Rd., Ind., 1947-50, Lafayette (Ind.) Sch. Corp., 1961-66; librarian West Lafayette (Ind.) Community Schs., 1966—. Mem. steering com. Wabash Valley Media Center, West Lafayette, 1970-71. Mem. Nat., West Lafayette (exec. bd. 1970-72, v.p. 1972-74) edn. assns., Ind. Tchrs. Assn., North Central Assn. Colls. and Secondary Schs. (mem. North Central evaluation team 1974), Ind. Sch. Librarians Assn., Ind. Library Assn. (area publicity chmn.), Pi Lambda Theta, Kappa Delta Pi, Alpha Delta Kappa (sec. 1972), Tri Kappa. Mem. Christian Reformed Ch. Home: 1264 Meadowbrook Dr Lafayette IN 47905 Office: 1200 N Salisbury St West Lafayette IN 47906

MARSHALL, BETTY VOIGT (MRS. RICHARD DOUGLAS SPAULDING MARSHALL), pub. relations exec.; b. Los Angeles; d. Don Harvey and Helen (Pang) Lyou; B.A., U. Cal. at Berkeley, 1943; m. Richard Douglas Spaulding Marshall, Jan. 2, 1960. Asst. bur. chief Los Angeles bur. Newsweek mag., 1953-60; nat. mgr. mag. sect. NBC-TV Press Dept., N.Y.C., 1962-68; nat. dir. mags. McFadden, Strauss, Eddy and Irwin Co., N.Y.C., 1968-70; v.p. The James Eddy Co., N.Y.C., 1970-71; nat. dir. mags., corporate, entertainment and TV divs. Rogers, Cowan & Brenner, Inc., N.Y.C., 1971-72; pub. relations counsel The Marshall Plan, N.Y.C., 1972—. Mem. Pub. Relations Soc. Am., Nat. Press Club, Cal. Press Women Assn. (Nat. Flame award 1959—), Greater Los Angeles, Hollywood Women's press clubs. Home: 186 Riverside Dr New York City NY 10024 Office: 65 E 55th St New York City NY 10022

MARSHALL, CAROL ANN (MRS. JOSEPH KENDALL MARSHALL), newspaper exec.; b. Oakland, Cal., Aug. 21, 1940; d. Robert Wilson and Irene Evelyn (Kelman) Will; A.A., Stephens Coll., 1960; postgrad. U. Ariz., 1960; B.J., U. Mo., 1963, postgrad., 1964-65; postgrad. So. Colo. State Coll., 1967-68; m. Joseph Kendall Marshall, May 9, 1964; children—Jennifer, Michelle, Camille. Reporter, Beaumont (Tex.) Jour., 1963-64; publicist Golden Gate Coll. San Francisco, 1965; instr. So. Colo. State Coll., Pueblo, 1969; editor, pub., sec., dir. Rev.-Miner, Inc., Lovelock, Nev., 1971—. Mem. Nev. State Press Assn., Theta Sigma Phi. Club: Soroptimist (Lovelock). Home: 475 15th St Lovelock NV 89419 Office: 1055 Dartmouth Lovelock NV 89419

MARSHALL, CAROL FRANCES, educator; b. Lawrence, Kan., Oct. 14, 1933; d. Cameron Field and Frances (Allen) Marshall; B.A., U. Kan., 1955; M.A., U. Mo., 1959; Ed.D., Fla. State U., 1962. Tchr. elementary sch., Shawnee Misson, Kansas City, Kan., 1955-58, Tallahassee, 1958-59, Kansas City, Mo., 1962; grad. asst. dept. adminstrn. and supervision Fla. State U. Sch. Edn., Tallahassee, 1960-62; faculty Kan. State Tchrs. Coll., Emporia, 1962—, asso. prof., 1964-71, prof., 1971—, dir. early childhood edn., 1969—. Cons. Head Start, Emporia; coordinator early childhood program Menninger Found., Topeka, 1969—; mem. exec. com. White House Conf., 1970; mem. Kan. Adv. Council Edn., 1965-71, Kan. Tchr. Edn. Profl. Standards State Bd., 1965-71; instl. rep. Head Start Regional Tng. Office, 1973—. Bd. dirs. Emporia Community Day Care Center. Kan. State Tchrs. Coll. research grantee, 1964-66. Mem. Kan. Tchrs. Assn., N.E.A., Nat., Kan. (dir.) assns. edn. young children, Assn. Supervision and Curriculum Devel. Methodist. Home: 1107 Topeka St Emporia KS 66801

MARSHALL, DORIS BINKLEY (MRS. FRED TAYLOR MARSHALL), information scientist; b. Troy, O., June 27, 1918; d. Charles Gordon and Onda Marie (Quinn) Binkley; B.A. in Chemistry, Ohio State U., 1940; postgrad. U. Chgo., 1940-41, U. Mo., 1973—; m. Fred Taylor Marshall, Mar. 28, 1942; children—Karen Louise (Mrs. Stephen Paul Booth), Carol Ann (Mrs. Paul Edward Derrickson), Fred Gordon. Asst. tech. librarian Universal Oil Products Co., Chgo., 1940-41; tech. librarian Monsanto Co., Dayton O., 1941-44; librarian Am. Zinc, Lead & Smelting Co., Kirkwood, Mo., 1956-60; owner pvt. bus., Kirkwood, 1960-64; librarian mgmt. information center Ralston Purina Co., St. Louis, 1966-72, information scientist, 1972—. Mem. Spl. Libraries Assn. (pres. St. Louis chpt. 1972-73, mem. internat. adv. council, 1971-73, editor chpt. bull., 1968-70; mem. nominating com. food librarians div. 1973, chmn. 1974; mem. internat. nominating com. 1974-75), Internat. Assn. Agrl. Librarians and Documentalists, Am. Soc. for Information Sci., Am. Chem. Soc., Nat. Geneal. Soc. Am., Soc. Mayflower Descs., Ch. Women United (chmn. nominating com. St. Louis area 1964, auditor 1965-68), Lutheran Ch. Women (del. nat. conv. 1970). Lutheran. Contbr. articles to profl. jours. Home: 477 Burns Av Kirkwood MO 63122 Office: Ralston Purina Co Checkerboard Sq St Louis MO 63188

MARSHALL, DOROTHEA SWIGERT (MRS. ALFRED LEWIS MARSHALL), mus. ofcl.; b. Newcomerstown, O., Aug. 14, 1905; d. Elisha Dent and Stella (Stephon) Swigert; student, Ithaca Coll., 1926-27; A.B., Wittenberg U., 1930; postgrad. Capital U., 1952-53; m. Alfred Lewis Marshall, June 3, 1938; Tchr. Newcomerstown, O., 1930-38, Reynoldsburg, O., 1953-66; pres. Newcomerstown (O.) Hist. Soc., 1974—. Mem. Bus. and Profl. Womens Club (pres. 1969-71), Theta Alpha Phi, Alpha Delta Pi. Mem. Order Eastern Star. Home: 414 Cross St Newcomerstown OH 43832 Office: Museum 215 W Canal St Newcomerstown OH 43832

MARSHALL, ELEANOR CLAIRE DOUR, assn. exec.; b. Bklyn., Dec. 20, 1927; d. Louis Frederick and Claire (Eydeler) Dour; B.A., Queens Coll., 1943; postgrad. St. John's U., 1971-72; m. Edward V. Marshall, Dec. 7, 1947 (div. 1967); 1 dau., Sandra (Mrs. Mark Greenspan). Dir. dept. research and statistics Am. Nurses Assn., N.Y.C., 1961-72; asst. dir. health unit dept. pub. affairs, health unit Community Service Soc., N.Y.C., 1972—. Mem. Am., N.Y. pub. health assns., Am. Acad. Polit. Sci. Author, editor: Health Legislation in New York State, 1973, 74; Facts About Nursing: An Annual Statistical Summary, 1959-71. Home: 84-50 169 St Jamaica NY 11432 Office: 105 E 22 St New York City NY 10010

MARSHALL, HELEN LOWRIE (MRS. JOHN S. MARSHALL), writer; b. Atlanta, Neb., Aug. 21, 1904; d. Charles Stuart and Louella Evelyn (Barr) Coffey; student Kearney State Tchrs. Coll., summers 1921, 22, Colo. U. Extension, 1925, 26; grad. Parks Bus. Coll., 1926; m. Patrick Houston Lowrie, Dec. 9, 1929; children—Patrick Houston, Harold Watkins III; m. 2d, John S. Marshall, July 23, 1950. Tchr. country sch., Axtell, Neb., 1922-25; sec. Lowrie & Co. brokers, Denver, 1926-28, Senator Charles Thomas, Denver, 1929, Chevrolet Motor Div., Denver, 1939-50. Recipient Nat. award for work as universal poet Nat. League Am. Pen Women, 1966. Mem. Colo. Authors League, Nat. League Am. Pen Women (state pres. 1968-69), Poetry Soc. Colo., Colo. Press Women, Nat. Fedn. Press Women, P.E.O., Delta Kappa Gamma (hon.). Methodist. Clubs: Executives; Women's Press. Author: Bright Horizons, 1954; Close to the Heart, 1958; Dare to be Happy, 1962; Aim for a Star, 1964; Hold to Your Dream, 1965; The Gift of Wonder, 1967; Moments of Awareness, 1968; A Gift So Rare, 1969; Walk the World Proudly, 1969; Quiet Power, 1970; Starlight and Candleglow, 1971; A World That Sings, 1971; Aren't You Glad!, 1973. Home: 3241 S Holly Pl Denver CO 80222

MARSHALL, INEZ MILDRED JOYNES (MRS. JAMES FRANKLIN MARSHALL, JR.), writer; b. New Orleans; d. Solon Frank and Bertha Caroline (Westholz) Joynes; grad. high sch.; m. James Franklin Marshall, Jr., July 15, 1927; 1 dau., Arline Faye. Sec., stenographer Swift & Co., New Orleans, 1911-19; sec. to mgr. Sinclair Agy. Travelers Ins. Co., 1919-29; U.S. Govt. stenographer, clk. Kelly Field, San Antonio, 1942-44; trust dept. Frost Nat. Bank, San Antonio, 1950-59, ret., 1959; temporary positions with law firm, Meth. Mission Bd., 1959-61. Writer poetry, programs Stallings Co., San Antonio, 1959—. Mem. Am. Poetry League. Mem. Daus. Nile, Order Eastern Star. Author: Dream Patterns, 1949. Home: 6442 Av A New Orleans LA 70124

MARSHALL, JEAN MCELROY, educator; b. Chambersburg, Pa., Dec. 31, 1922; d. Frank Lester and Florence (McElroy) Marshall; A.B., Wilson Coll., 1944; M.A., Mt. Holyoke Coll., 1946; Ph.D., U. Rochester, 1951. Instr., Johns Hopkins Med. Sch., Balt., 1951-56, asst. prof., 1956-60; research postdoctoral fellow Oxford (Eng.) U., 1954-55; asst. prof. Harvard Med. Sch., Boston, 1960-66; asso. prof. physiology Brown U., Providence, 1966-69, prof., 1969—. Mem. physiology study sect. NIH, 1967-71, mem. tng. com. engring. in biology and medicine, 1971—; physiol. test com. Nat. Bd. Med. Examiners. Mem. Am. Physiol. Soc., Am. Pharmacol. Soc., N.Y. Acad. Sci., Soc. for Reproductive Biology, Soc. Gen. Physiologists, Phi Beta Kappa, Sigma Xi. Editor: The Initiation of Labor, 1964; mem. editorial bd. Jour. Pharmacology and Exptl. Therapeutics, 1965-69, Am. Jour. Physiology, 1969—, Circulation Research, 1973—. Contbr. articles to profl. jours. Home: 14 Aberdeen Rd Weston MA 02193 Office: Div Med Scis Brown U Providence RI 01912

MARSHALL, LOIS, soprano; b. Toronto, Ont., Can., 1924; d. David and Florence Marshall; grad. Royal Conservatory, Toronto (Eaton award). First recital at age 15, then sang with leading Canadian orchestras; debut at Town Hall, 1952; soloist with Arturo Toscanini in Missa Solemnis, also with Sir Thomas Beecham in works of Handel and Mozart; opera debut in La Boheme, Boston Opera Co., 1959; other appearances include Royal Festival Hall, London, Amsterdam Concergebouw, Edinburgh Festival; also in Hamburg, Dublin and USSR. Recipient Naumburg award 1952.

MARSHALL, LOIS EMILI, ednl. adminstr.; b. N.Y.C., May 11, 1932; d. Leonard and Glafys (Driver) Leaver; B.A., William Paterson State Coll., 1963; M.A., Montclair State Coll., 1967; postgrad. Columbia, 1973—; 1 dau., Sherry Joanne. Tchr. high sch. English, speech Ridgefield Park (N.J.) Bd. Edn., 1963-67, dir. adult edn., 1966-67; dir. adult edn. Plainfield (N.J.) Bd. Edn., 1967-69; dean community services Bergen Community Coll., Paramus, N.J., 1969—; lectr. Columbia, Rutgers U., Montclair State Coll. Mem. White House Conf. Children, 1970; mem. N.J. Gov.'s Pub. Services Inst. Bd., 1973; mem. Nat. adv. Council Adult Edn., 1973; mem. N.J. State Commn. Humanities. Mem. Bergen County (N.J.) Bd. Freeholders Narcotics Adv. Council, Cultural and Heritage Commn. Trustee YWCA; bd. dirs. Bergen County Urban League. Recipient Distinguished Service award Assn. Adult Edn. N.J., 1973. Mem. Nat. Assn. Pub. Continuing and Adult Edn. (dir. 1970), N.J. Cultural Council (v.p. 1971-73), League Women Voters, Am. Assn. U. Women. Contbr. articles to profl. jours. Home: 31 Barnes Dr Ridgefield Park NJ 07660 Office: Bergen Community Coll 400 Paramus Rd Paramus NJ 07654

MARSHALL, MADELEINE (MRS. ROBERT A. SIMON), educator; b. Syracuse, N.Y., Oct. 26, 1899; d. Benjamin and Ida (Strauss) Marshall; Mus.B., Syracuse U., 1919; m. Robert A. Simon, Mar. 27, 1924; children—John G., Peggy. Pianist, concert accompanist, chamber music pianist throughout U.S., 1919—; coach, diction tchr. for opera, concert and oratario singers, 1920—; faculty Juilliard Sch. Music, N.Y.C., 1935—, Sch. Sacred Music Union Theol. Sem., 1951-73. Author: The Singer's Manual of English Diction, 1953, 2d edit., 1974. Address: 151 W 86th St New York City NY 10024

MARSHALL, MARA BLUMBERG (MRS. SYLVAN MITCHELL MARSHALL), artist; b. Nice, France, July 21, 1926 (parents Am. citizens); d. Joseph and Leah (Kristeller) Blumberg; grad. Scudder-Culver Jr. Coll., 1945, N.Y. Sch. Interior Decoration, 1946; student Art Students' League, N.Y.C., 1945-46; m. Sylvan Mitchell Marshall, Feb. 11, 1951; children—Douglas Wayne, Bradley Ross. One-man shows 1st Fed. Gallery, 1971, 1st Fed. Savs. and Loan Assn. Chgo., 1971, Nat. League Am. Pen Women, 1972, Am. Art League 34th ann. exhbn., 1972, 39th ann. exhbn. Miniature Painters Sculptors and Gravers Soc. Washington, 1972; exhibited in group shows Cosmos Club, Washington, Am. Art League Exhibit, Washington, Exhibit for Kennedy Center for Performing Arts, Washington, Julius Garfinckel & Co., Am. Art League Gallery, Washington, Washington Gallery Art, Nat. League Am. Penwomen, Pres. Park Exhibit, Washington; represented in permanent collections. Mem. bd. Salvation Army Aux., 1954-56; mem. Pan Am. Liaison Com. of Women's Orgns., 1954—; mem. White House Spanish-Portuguese Study Group, 1953—, mem. bd., corr. sec., 1956-57. Mem. Nat. League Am. Pen Women (Ann. award Biennial Contest in Art., D.C. br., 1967, 69, Ann. award, 1st prize oils nat. biennial contest 1969, 1st prize in still life 1972, exec. bd. D.C. br. 1968-70, corr. sec., 1968-70, pres. 1970-72, 74—, nat. hospitality chmn. nat. exec. bd. 1972-74, co-chmn. biennial conv.), Rehobeth Art League, Artists Equity Assn., Am. Art League. Club: Internat. Home: 2929 Ellicott St NW Washington DC 20008

MARSHALL, MARGARET ANNE GUEST (MRS. PHILIP GREGORY MARSHALL), ednl. adminstr.; b. New Lyme, O., Nov. 26, 1922; d. Benjamin Thomas and Dorothy Leila (Stevens) Guest; diploma New Castle Hosp. Sch. Nursing, 1943; B.S., Rutgers U., 1956, M.S., 1957; m. Philip Gregory Marshall, Sept. 29, 1945; 1 dau., Phyllis Anne. Head nurse, supr. maternity Barnert Meml. Hosp., Paterson, N.J., 1950-55; clin. specialist psychiat. nursing Essex County Overbrook Hosp., Cedar Grove, N.J., 1957-58; instr. Rutgers U., New Brunswick, N.J., 1958-63; cons., coordinator psychiat. nursing St. Joseph's Hosp., Paterson, N.J., 1964-67; adminstr. sch. nursing and allied health William Paterson Coll., Wayne, N.J., 1967—. Mem. Health Professions Master Plan, State N.J., 1971-73, Health Professions Edn. Adv. Council, 1971-73. Served to lt., Nurse Corps, USNR, 1944-46. Nat. Inst. Mental Health Career Tchr. fellow, 1958-59. Mem. Nat. League Nursing, Am. Assn. State Colls. and Univs., Am. Cancer Soc. (mem. curriculum com. N.J. chpt. 1970—), Sigma Theta Tau. Editor: (with Shirley F. Burd) Some Clinical Approaches to Psychiatric Nursing, 1963. Home: 43 White Rock Blvd Oak Ridge NJ 07438 Office: 300 Pompton Rd Wayne NJ 07470

MARSHALL, MARY LOU, physician; b. Quincy, Mich., Aug. 8, 1935; d. Clinton Wayne and Agnes Catherine (Failing) Marshall; student U. Mich. Sch. Literature, Sci., Arts, 1953-56; M.D., U. Mich., 1960. Intern Barnes Hosp., St. Louis, 1960-61; resident U. Mich. at Ann Arbor, 1961-68; asst. pathologist Emma L. Bixby Hosp., Adrian, Mich., 1968-69; asso. pathologist Miami Valley Hosp., Dayton, O., 1969—. Diplomate Am. Bd. Pathology. Fellow Am. Soc. Clin. Pathologists, Coll. Am. Pathologists; mem. Internat. Acad. Pathologists, A.M.A. Home: 221 Lonsdale Av Dayton OH 45419 Office: 1 Wyoming St Dayton OH 45409

MARSHALL, MARY PATRICIA, psychologist; b. Kansas City, Mo., Aug. 14, 1945; d. Joseph Quentin and Mary Elizabeth (Donahue) Marshall; B.A., U. Mo. at Kansas City, 1967, M.A. in Psychology, 1969. Social worker Jackson County (Mo.) Welfare Orgn., 1967-69; clin. psychologist Western Mo. Mental Health Assn., Kansas City, 1969—, Ozanam Boys Home, Kansas City, Mo., 1970-71; instr. psychology Avila Coll., Kansas City, Mo., 1972-73, U. Mo. at Kansas City. Mem. Am. Psychol. Assn., Am. Assn. Family and Marriage Counselors. Home: 8756 W 79th Circle Overland Park KS 66214 Office: 600 E 22d St Kansas City MO 64108

MARSHALL, MILDRED DELEVETT, ret. educator; b. Balt., Aug. 15, 1904; d. William Amoss and Lutie (Kemp) Delevett; grad. Balt. Tchrs. Tng. Sch., 1922; student Johns Hopkins, 1923-24, N.Y.U., 1927; m. William Harvey Marshall, Aug. 15, 1931. Tchr. pub. schs., Balt., 1922-71; demonstration tchr.; mem. curriculum com. Balt. pub. schs.; mem. supt. com. ednl. tests and measurements. Supporting com. Walter's Art Gallery, Balt. Mus. Art; mem. women's com. Balt. Symphony Orch. Mem. Pub. Sch. Tchrs. Assn., Md. Tchrs. Assn., N.E.A., Alumnae Assn. Samuel Ready Sch., Daus. Colonial Wars, Hartford County Assn. (sec. 1950-52), Bishop's Guild, Md. Hist. Soc., Hist. Annapolis Inc., Nat. Trust Historic Preservation, English Speaking Union, Balt. Civic Opera Guild, Soc. Preservation Md. Antiquities, Colonial Dames XVII Century, Descs. Colonial Govs., D.A.R. Democrat. Episcopalian. Address: 3701 Edgewood Rd Baltimore MD 21215

MARSHALL, NAOMI VERNON DAMONTE (MRS. HAROLD K. MARSHALL), ret. photog. products co. exec., civic worker; b. New Orleans, Aug. 2, 1913; d. Joseph Roger and Laura (Nelson) Damonte; student Soule Bus. Coll., 1929-30; m. Harold K. Marshall, Feb. 4, 1938; children—Keith Cooper, Donald Kaye. Owner art materials bus. and art gallery, 1935-38; So. regional mgr., Latin Am. export mgr. Chemco Photoproducts Co., 1938-68, br. mgr. Dallas, Atlanta, Houston, Ft. Lauderdale, Fla., New Orleans, 1968-71. Sec., Mississippi Valley World Trade Conf., 1950-55; bd. dirs. New Orleans Bd. Trade, 1953-56. Founder, Downtown Art Gallery, 1956, Marshall Art Found., 1961; chmn. nat. conv. Amateur Athletic Union U.S., New Orleans, 1968; mem. Pres.'s Adv. Com. on Arts, J.F.K. Center for Performing Arts, 1969; pres. Community Vol. Services, New Orleans Art Assn.; mem. La. Art, Cultural and Hist. Preservation Com., 1973—. Co-chmn. Nixon-Lodge presdl. campaign, New Orleans, 1960; pres. Women's Republican Club New Orleans, 1973—. Pres., bd. dirs. Womens Guild, New Orleans Opera House Assn.; sec. Nat. Multiple Sclerosis Soc. New Orleans; bd. dirs. Repertory Theatre, New Orleans. Recipient award of merit City of New Orleans, 1964, Germaine Monteil Beautiful Activist award for contribution to civic and cultural affairs fo the community, 1971. Mem. Advt. Club New Orleans (past pres), Art Dirs. and Designers Club, La. Watercolor Soc., Am. Museums Assn., La. Hist. Soc., La. Landmarks Assn., New Orleans Art Assn. (past pres.), U.D.C., New Orleans Ballet Found., Spring Fiesta Assn. Methodist. Club: Altrusa. Contbr. articles to profl. jours. Home: 21 Maryland Dr New Orleans LA 70124 Office: 532 Chartres St New Orleans LA 70130

MARSHALL, NATALIE JUNEMANN (MRS. HOWARD D. MARSHALL), educator; b. Milw., June 13, 1929; d. Harold E. and Myrtle (Findlay) Junemann; A.B., Vassar Coll., 1951; M.A., Columbia, 1952, Ph.D., 1963; m. Howard D. Marshall, Aug. 7, 1954 (dec. Aug. 1972); children—Frederick S., Alison B. Instr., Vassar Coll., Poughkeepsie, N.Y., 1952-54, 59-60; teaching fellow Wesleyan U., Middletown, Conn., 1955-56; from asst. prof. to asso. prof. State U. Coll., New Paltz, N.Y., 1964-69, prof., 1969-73; prof. econs., dean studies Vassar Coll., 1973—. Bd. mgrs. Childrens Home, Poughkeepsie, 1968-71. Mem. Am. Assn. U. Women (br. pres. 1961-63, div. 3d v.p. 1964-66). Club: Vassar (pres. 1965-67) (Poughkeepsie). Co-author: Collective Bargaining, 1971. Editor: Keynes: Updated or Outdated, 1970. Home: 114 Boardman Rd Poughkeepsie NY 12603 Office: Vassar Coll Poughkeepsie NY 12601

MARSHALL, NORMA ELIZABETH (MRS. CLAUDE J. MARSHALL), ednl. adminstr.; b. Shepherd, Mich., Jan. 20, 1926; d. William Ernest and Ila Lucille (Stimer) Kirkconnell; diploma Edward W. Sparrow Hosp. Sch. Nursing, 1947; student Mich. State U., 1948-51; B.S., Case Western Res. U., 1952, M.S., 1953; m. Claude J. Marshall, Apr. 25, 1959; 1 dau., Anne Marie. Instr., E.W. Sparrow Hosp. Sch. Nursing, Lansing, Mich., 1947-51; asst. prof. U. Mich. Sch. Nursing, Ann Arbor, 1953-56, asst. to dean, asst. prof., 1956-60, asst. to dean, asso. prof., 1960-66, asst. dean, asso. prof., 1971-72, acting dean, asso. prof., 1972-73, asst. dean, prof. nursing, 1973—, chmn. acad. affairs bd., 1973-74. Mem. Mich. Bd. Nursing, 1973—. Treas., mem. exec. bd. King Elementary Sch. Parent Tchr. Orgn., Ann Arbor, 1972-74. Mem. Mich. Nursing Assn. (chmn. conv. program 1973—), Washtenaw Dist. Nurses Assn. (pres. elect 1973-74), Mich. League for Nursing, U. Mich. Alumni Soc., Case Western Res. U. Alumni Assn., Women in Adminstrn., Sigma Theta Tau, Phi Delta Gamma. Presbyn. Home: 121 N Dixboro Rd Ann Arbor MI 48105

MARSHALL, ROSEMARIE, bacteriologist, educator; b. Medford, Ore., Jan. 28, 1944; d. Emanual Cara and Lee (Eckert) Marshall; B.S., U. Wash., 1964; M.S., Ia. State U., 1966, Ph.D., 1968. Head dept. microbiology Grays Harbor Hosp., Aberdeen, Wash. 1970-71; asst. prof. biology Ga. So. Coll., Statesboro, 1971—. NIH postdoctoral fellow, 1968-70; Faculty Research grantee, 1972, 74. Mem. A.A.A.S., Am. Soc. for Microbiology, Am. Assn. U. Profs. (treas. local chpt. 1971—, pres. elect 1974), Am. Assn. Southeastern Biologists, Sigma Xi (research grantee 1971), Phi Kappa Phi. Contbr. research articles to sci. jours. Office: Ga So Coll Statesboro GA 30458

MARSHALL, SHARON KAY SEIFFERT (MRS. FRANK JOHN MARSHALL), occupational therapist; b. Minot, N.D., Apr. 12, 1939; d. Garnet Sanford and Loraine Grace (Burns) Seiffert; B.S. in Occupational Therapy, U. N.D., 1961; m. Frank John Marshall, Sept. 6, 1959; children—John, Kathryn, Garnet. Staff occupational therapist Med. Center Rehab. Hosp., Grand Forks, N.D., 1961-64; asst. prof., supr. clin. affiliations U. N.D., Grand Forks, 1964-67. County supr. N.D. Council Health Careers, Grand Forks, 1972—. Co-capt. picture lady program Kelly Sch., Grand Forks, 1973-74; mem. Citizens Com. for Grand Forks Symphony Orch., 1974—. Sec., Grand Forks County Fedn. Republican Women, 1973—. Named N.D. Outstanding Young Woman, Outstanding Young Women of Am. Program, 1973. Mem. Am., Dakota (pres. 1965-66, legislative chmn. 1971) occupational therapy assns., Red River Dist. Occupational Therapy (v.p. 1964), United Hosp. Aux., Grand Forks County Hist. Soc., P.E.O., Delta Gamma. Presbyn. Home: 3112 W Elmwood Dr Grand Forks ND 58201

MARSHALL, SHEILA HERMES (MRS. JAMES JOSIAH MARSHALL), lawyer; b. N.Y.C., Jan. 17, 1934; d. Paul Milton and Julia Angela (Meagher) Hermes; B.A., St. John's U., 1959; LL.B., N.Y. U., 1963; m. James Josiah Marshall, Sept. 30, 1967; 1 son, James J.H. Admitted to N.Y. bar, 1964, since practiced in N.Y.C.; asso. firm LeBoeuf, Lamb, Leiby and Mac Rae, N.Y.C., 1963-72, mem. firm, 1973—. Mem. Am., N.Y. bar assns. Home: 252 E 19th St Brooklyn NY 11226 Office: 1 Chase Manhattan Plaza New York City NY 10005

MARSHALL, SIMONE PAULETTE VERNIERE (MRS. ROBERT J. MARSHALL), psychologist, psychoanalyst; b. Paris, France; d. Urbain and Gabrielle (Cadiergues) Verniere; Licence de Psychologie, Sorbonne, 1949; certificate in Statistics and Neuro-Physiology Institut de Psychologie, 1949; M.A. (Fulbright scholar), Columbia, 1952, Ph.D., 1959; grad. W. A. White Inst., 1970; m. Robert J. Marshall, Sept. 13, 1953; children—Gabrielle S., Annette M. Came to U.S., 1951, naturalized, 1958. Researcher sch. psychology Nat. Bd. Edn., Paris, France, 1948-51; clin. psychologist Children's Hosp., Buffalo, 1953-54, N.J. State Colony, New Lisbon, 1956-58; instr., clinician Rutgers U. Clinic, New Brunswick, N.J., 1958-59; psychotherapist Rockland County Mental Health Center, Monsey, N.Y., 1961-64; cons. Ossining (N.Y.) Bd. Edn., 1960-64; individual practice psychology, psychoanalysis, N.Y.C., 1965—. Edn. chmn. bd. dirs. Croton Community Nursery Sch., 1963-65; mem. div. related professions White Inst., 1969-72. Mem. Am., Eastern psychol. assns., White Soc., Soc. Psychol. Study Social Issues. Office: 103 E 86th St New York City NY 10028

MARSHALL, VIRGINIA LEE BOGAR (MRS. WILLIAM A. MARSHALL), advt. exec.; b. Deary, Ida., Nov. 10, 1921; d. Chester Arthur and Sarah Lavinia (Drury) Bogar; student Ft. Wright Coll. Holy Names, 1939-42; m. Fayne Malbrook Bayes, Sept. 20, 1942 (div. Apr. 1952); 1 son, Gregory Xavier; m. 2d, William A. Marshall, May 23, 1953; 1 son, Jaye Bogar. Display and advt. trainee Sears Roebuck & Co., Spokane, Wash., 1942-43; fashion coordinator Palace Dept. Store, Spokane, 1946-47; mgr. interior displays Crescent Dept. Store, Spokane, 1947-48; head fashion copywriter Bon Marche Dept. Store, Spokane, 1948-49; creative dir. Tomowske Advt. Agy. (name changed to Miller, Ogle & Myers), Spokane, 1949-52; jr. partner William A. Marshall & Assos., advt. agy., Spokane, 1953—. Active Sacred Heart Hosp. Service League, 1963—, Pine Tree Players, 1964—, Pacific N.W. Unltd., 1963-66; radio, TV news chmn. Champagne Ball, 1962, 1963. Bd. dirs. Holy Family Hosp. Women's Aux., pub. relations and news chmn. 1960-62. Mem. Nat. Trust for Historic Preservation, E. Wash. State Hist. Soc., Philomathea Club of Gonzaga U. (dir. 1959—, news and pub. relations chmn. 1963—), Spokane C. of C. (Indsl. devel. com. 1961-64), Am. Advt. Fedn., Am. Acad. Advt., Coeur d'Alene (Ida.) Athletic Round Table. Clubs: Toastmistress (Avant pres. 1967-68, v.p. 1970-71; sec. council 1, Snake River region 1968-69, treas. 1969-70), Early Birds. Home: E 324 Montgomery Av Spokane WA 99207 Office: W 1515 3d Av Spokane WA 99204

MARSHALL, VIVIAN ASHLEY (MRS. MILBERT L. MARSHALL), bus. exec.; b. Orleans, Ind., Aug. 30, 1908; d. Omar O. and Minnie (Mead) Ashley; student New Albany Bus. Coll., 1926-27; m. George Russell Howe, 1934 (dec. 1939); m. 2d, Milbert L. Marshall, May 11, 1946; 1 step-dau., Rebecca (Mrs. Robert Bernhard). Bookkeeper, Monyhan Furniture Co., Paoli, Ind., 1927; office mgr. Orleans Chair Co. (Ind.), 1928-31; sec.-treas., office and credit mgr. Paoli Chair Co. (Ind.) 1931—. Mem. Womens Soc. Christian Service (charter), Kappa Kappa Kappa (past pres., state pub. relations dir.). Methodist (chmn. commn. on missions). Home: 310 Adams St Orleans IN 47452 Office: Box 30 Paoli IN 47454

MARTELL, ARLENE JORDAN (MRS. LEONARD J. MARTELL), state legislator; b. Milton, Vt., July 19, 1926; d. Edward W. and Eva (Messier) Jordan; grad. high sch., 1944; m. Leonard J. Martell, Aug. 28, 1945; children—Donna Ann (Mrs. Peacock), John, Steven, Gregory, Anthony. Mem. Vt. Ho. of Reps., 1969—. Bd. dirs. No. Grand Isle Mental Health Service, Inc., Champlain Valley Mental Health Assn. Mem. Farm Bur., Vt. Assn. for Children with Learning Disabilities, Kerbs Hosp. Aux. Democrat. Roman Catholic. Club: Ga. Sch. Address: RFD 3 Fairfax VT 05454*

MARTENS, SISTER MARY HARRIET, educator; b. Allegan, Mich., Jan. 20, 1925; d. Charles Frederick and Mary Harriet (Meyers) Martens; A.A., Grand Rapids Jr. Coll., 1944; B.A., Aquinas Coll., 1950; M.S., U. Notre Dame, 1960; Ph.D., U. Wis., 1967; postdoctoral fellow Mich. State U., 1971-72. Instr. Cath. Central High Sch., Grand Rapids, 1952-53; adminstr. Pioneers Meml. Hosp., Brawley, Cal., 1953-54; instr. Cath. Central High Sch., Alpena, Mich., 1954-55; chmn. dept. mathematics SS Peter and Paul High Sch., Saginaw, Mich., 1955-59; asso. prof. math. Aquinas Coll., Grand Rapids, 1960—, chmn. acad. assembly, 1972—; research com. Dominican Sisters of Marywood; in-service edn. tchrs. Dominican Edn. Assn. Kellogg fellow, 1971-72; NSF sci. faculty fellow, 1964-65. Mem. Am. Assn. Higher Edn., Am. Assn. Univ. Profs., Math. Assn. Am., Nat. Council Tchrs. of Math.; Assn. Ind. Colls. and Univs. Mich. (coordinator faculty devel. program 1972—), Pi Lambda Theta. Home: 1607 Robinson Rd SE Grand Rapids MI 49506

MARTENSEN, MARILYN RUTH, librarian; b. Rochfort Bridge, Alta., Can., Sept. 28, 1939; d. Edward H. and Emma (Schmidt) Neben; Came to U.S., 1945, naturalized, 1967. B.S., Chadron State Coll., 1960; M.L.S., Denver U., 1963; postgrad. Ariz. State U., 1969-73; m. Arvin Gerhard, Dec. 25, 1961 (div. July 1969); children—David, Joan. Catalog and acquisitions librarian Colo. State U., Ft. Collins, 1964-67; instr. edn. media U. No. Colo., Greeley, 1967-69; dir. library services Mesa (Ariz.) Community Coll., 1969-73; dir. library tech. services Maricopa County Community College Dist., Phoenix, 1973—. Mem. Ariz. State Library Assn. Home: 1517 E Broadmor Dr Tempe AZ 85282 Office: 106 E Washington St Phoenix AZ 85004

MARTH-SNADER, ELLA CAROLYN MARTH, educator; b. Alton, Ill.; d. Louis George and Elizabeth (Krauskopf) Marth; A.B., Harris Tchrs. Coll., 1930; M.S., St. Louis U., 1935, Ph.D., 1944; m. Daniel W. Snader, July 28, 1956 (div. Aug. 1972). Tchr. pub. schs., St. Louis, 1930-44; asst. prof. math. Harris Tchrs. Coll., St. Louis, 1945-47, dean of women, asso. prof., 1947-52; prof., chmn. div. math. and bus. edn. D.C. Tchrs. Coll., 1952-56, prof., 1960—; asso. prof. div. math. Chgo. Tchrs. Coll., 1956-59; specialist elementary math. U.S. Office of Edn., Washington, 1959. Cons. elementary math. Mem. St. Louis Assn. for Human Relations, 1950. Mem. Am. Math. Soc., Nat. Council Tchrs. Math., Central Assn. Sci. and Math. Tchrs. (dir. 1949, 51-53), N.E.A., Am. Personnel and Guidance Assn., Sigma Xi, Pi Mu Epsilon, Delta Kappa Gamma. Unitarian. Contbr. articles to profl. jours. Home: 3701 Connecticut Av NW Washington DC 20008

MARTIKAINEN, A(UNE) HELEN, health edn. specialist; b. Harrison, Me., May 11, 1916; d. Sylvester and Emma (Heikkinen) Martikainen; A.B., Bates Coll., 1939, D.Sc. (hon.), 1957; M.P.H., Yale, 1941; D.Sc., Harvard U., 1964, Smith Coll., 1969. Health edn. sec. Hartford Tb and Pub. Health Assn., 1941-42; cons. USPHS, 1942-49; chief health edn. WHO, Geneva, Switzerland, 1949—. Trustee Bridgton Acad., North Bridgton, Me. Recipient Delta Omega award Yale; Nat. Adminstrv. award Am. Acad. Phys. Edn.; Bates Key award; Internat. Service award, France, 1953; Prentiss medal, 1956; spl. medal, certificate for internat. health edn. service Nat. Acad. Medicine for France, 1959; profl. award Soc. Pub. Health Educators, 1963. Fellow Am. Pub. Health Assn. (chmn. health edn. sect.); mem. U.S. Soc. Pub. Health Educators, Internat. Union Health Edn., Royal Soc. Health, Acad. Phys. Edn. (asso.), Phi Beta Kappa. Lutheran. Home: 26 Morningside Dr Laconia NH 03246 Office: WHO Av Appia Geneva Switzerland

MARTIN, AGNES HUDSON MACQUEEN (MRS. WILLIAM CLAYTON MARTIN), librarian; b. Hummelstown, Pa., Jan. 3, 1900; d. James Michael and Emma Rachel (Martin) Macqueen; certificate Carnegie Library Sch., 1930; student U. Pitts., 1934-36; m. William Clayton Martin, Aug. 1, 1937; 1 stepdau., Mary (Mrs. Jay Crawford Painter). Asst., Sewickley (Pa.) Pub. Library, 1918-29; catalog asst. Carnegie Library of Pitts., 1929-38; librarian D.T. Watson Home for Crippled Children, Leetsdale, Pa., 1942-44; asst. Roselle (N.J.) Pub. Library, 1959-60; children's librarian Orange (N.J.) Pub. Library, 1960—. Mem. Am., N.J. library assns. Republican. Episcopalian. Home: 1280 Shetland Dr Union NJ 07083 Office: 348 Main St Orange NJ 07050

MARTIN, ALICE J. WILLIAMS (MRS. PERRY MARTIN), town ofcl.; b. Ferriday, La., Jan. 15, 1909; d. Arther B. and Mary A. (Powell) Williams; B.A., Miss. Indsl. Coll., 1950; m. Perry Martin, Dec. 13, 1925 (dec. 1961); 1 son, Arthur L. Formerly tchr. elementary and jr. high sch.; recorder Norvell (Ark.) Town Council, 1972—. Pres. Earle Neighborhood Action Council, 1970-74. Mem. state bd. Ark. Council Farm Workers, 1973, mem. regional bd. 1973-74. Mem. N.A.A.C.P. Baptist (ch. clk. 1932-74, dist. dir. young people 1939-74). Mem. Order Eastern Star. Home: 1800 Cartwright St Norvell AR 72331

MARTIN, ALLIE BETH (MRS. RALPH F. MARTIN), librarian; b. Annieville, Ark., June 28, 1914; d. Carlton G. and Ethel (McCaleb) Dent; A.B., Ark. Coll., 1935; B.S. in L.S., George Peabody Coll., 1939; M.S., Columbia, 1948; m. Ralph F. Martin, Oct. 6, 1937; 1 dau., Elizabeth Erhard. Librarian, Batesville Pub. Library, 1935-36, Little Rock Jr. Coll., 1936-37; asst. to exec. sec. Ark. Library Commn., 1937-38, 42-47; librarian Miss. County Library, 1941-42; head children's and extension depts. Tulsa Pub. Library, 1950-62; dir. Tulsa City-County Library, 1963—. Asso. prof. Sch. Library Sci., U. Okla., 1957—; library cons. Library Design Assos., 1965—. Mem. Okla. Humanities Com., 1972; chmn. Tulsa Humanities Commn. Mem. A.L.A. (council, project coordinator pub. library goals study, exec. bd., pres. elect), Ark. (pres.), Okla. (pres.), Southwestern (pres.; project dir. continuing edn. library staffs) library assns., Delta Kappa Gamma. Methodist. Editor: Ark. Libraries, 1945-47, Okla. Librarian, 1953-55. Author: A Strategy for Public Library Change. Contbr. to profl. publs. Home: 120 E 26th St Tulsa OK 74114 Office: Tulsa City County Library Tulsa OK 74103

MARTIN, ANITA LOUISE, educator; b. Wellington, Kan.; d. William Morgan and Edith (Myers) Martin; A.B., U. Kan., 1927; M.A., U. Wis., 1936, Ph.D., 1951. Instr., Spanish, Coll. Wooster (O.), 1945-47; grad. asst. dept. art history U. Wis., 1948-50; prof. Spanish, chmn. dept. modern langs. Western Coll. for Women, Oxford, O., 1954-58; prof., chmn. dept. Spanish, Wilson Coll., Chambersburg, Pa., 1958-61; residence dir. Cook County Sch. Nursing, Chgo., 1961-62; prof. Spanish, art history Grove City (Pa.) Coll., 1962-67; prof. fine arts U. Pitts. at Johnstown, 1967—. Tchr. art to young people Glosser Meml. Library, 1972. Served with WAC, 1943-45. Am. Assn. U. Women fellow, Spain, 1952-53; U. Pitts. grantee, Florence, Italy, 1969, Amsterdam, Holland, 1970, 71, also European travel grantee, 1972, 73. Mem. Modern Lang. Assn. Am., Johnston Area Arts Council, Vets. in Pitts., Coll. Art Assn., Women's Assn. U. Pitts. at Johnstown, Phi Sigma Iota, Delta Kappa Gamma. Contbg. author: Catholic Ency. Am. Office: Dept Fine Arts Biddle Hall U Pitts at Johnstown Johnstown PA 15904

MARTIN, ANN LAVINIA, physician; b. N.Y.C., Aug. 26, 1913; d. Arthur H. and Alice Armenia (Fish) Martin; A.B., Cornell U., 1935, M.D., 1938; m. Archibald N. Beare, Nov. 7, 1945; 1 son, Arthur. Intern Jersey City Med. Center, 1939-40, U. Minn. hosps., Mpls., 1940-41; resident Denver Children's Hosp., 1942-43; practice medicine specializing in pediatrics, Colorado Springs, Colo., 1943-45, Flagstaff, Ariz., 1952-55; pediatrician United Mine Workers Am., Cumberland, Ky., 1956, Trinidad, Colo., 1956-61; pediatrician Colo. Dept. Health and Hosps., Denver, 1961—. Clin. instr. pediatrics U. Colo. Med. Sch., 1967—. Diplomate Am. Bd. Pediatrics. Mem. Am. Acad. Pediatrics, Rocky Mountain Pediatric Soc., D.A.R., Colonial Dames. Unitarian. Home: 1270 S Fairfax St Denver CO 80222 Office: Denver Gen Hosp W 6th Av and Cherokee St Denver CO 80204

MARTIN, CAROL ANNE, nat. park service adminstr.; b. Los Angeles, Nov. 7, 1935; d. Larry C. and Florrie Amelia (Schofield) Larsen, A.B. magna cum laude, Occidental Coll., 1957; postgrad. (Fulbright scholar), U. Innsbruck, Austria, 1957-58; m. Philip DePons Martin, June 11, 1960 (dec. 1965); children—Richard Douglas, Ronald Philip. Records clk. Consol. Electrodynamics Co., Pasadena, Cal., 1959-61; clk. typist Tuzigoot Nat. Monument, Clarkdale, Ariz., 1965-67, supt. park service, 1971—; adminstrv. officer Custer Battlefield Nat. Monument, Mont., 1967-71. Mem. Ariz. Parks and Recreation Assn., Phi Beta Kappa, Beta Sigma Phi, Epsilon Sigma Alpha. Author: (with William E. Brown and Erni Escalante) People of the Stone Villages, 1973. Home: Tuzigoot National Monument Clarkdale AZ 86324 Office: Box 68 Clarkdale AZ 86324

MARTIN, CECILIA ANN, educator; b. Broken Bow, Okla., Nov. 10, 1934; d. Cecil C. and Faye (Burks) Martin; B.S., Baylor U., 1955; M.Ed., North Tex. State U., 1962. Instr. phys. edn. Stripling Jr. High Sch., Ft. Worth, 1955-65; cons. in phys. edn. Ft. Worth Ind. Sch. Dist., 1965—. Mem. N.E.A., Tex. Tchrs. Assn., Ft. Worth Council Adminstrv. Women, Am., Tex. (asso. conv. mgr. 1970-71) assns. health, phys. edn. and recreation, Tex. Assn. for Supervision and Curriculum Devel., Assn. for Childhood Edn., Ft. Worth Elementary Prins. and Suprs. Assn., Tex. Driver Edn. Assn., Ft. Worth Driver and Traffic Safety Edn. Assn., Ft. Worth Adminstrv. Womens Assn., Kappa Delta Pi, Delta Psi Kappa. Home: 3421 Hamilton Fort Worth TX 76107 Office: 3210 W Lancaster St Fort Worth TX 76107

MARTIN, CORA ARLETA, govt. ofcl.; b. Dean, Tenn., Sept. 30, 1923; d. Thomas Crawford and Florice (Gardner) Martin; certificate Bowling Green Bus. U., 1943. Clk. typist War Dept. Tullahoma, Tenn., 1943-46; payroll clk. VA AND U.S. Dept. Agr., Atlanta, 1946-51; personnel rep. U.S. Army Corps Engrs., Tullahoma, Tenn., 1951-60; personnel staffing specialist, equal opportunity specialist and coordinator fed. women's program Army Rocket and Guided Missile Agy., U.S. Army Missile Support Command and U.S. Army Missile Command, 1960—. Mem. Tenn. Gov.'s Com. for Employment of Handicapped, Mayor's Com. for Employment of Handicapped; chmn. Bedford County Heart Unit. Recipient citation Am. Heart Assn., 1967. Mem. Internat. Personnel Mgmt. Adminstrs., Shelbyville Bus. and Profl. Women's Club, Tenn. Fedn. Bus. and Profl. Women's Clubs, Inc. (pres. 1963, parliamentarian 1965-66, 71-72), Federally Employed Women (v.p. North Ala. chpt. 1970, pres. 1971-72), Bedford County African Violet Soc. Home: 502 Riverview Dr Shelbyville TN 37160 Office: US Army Missile Command Equal Opportunity Office Redstone Arsenal AL 35809

MARTIN, DEANNA RENEE DUDA (MRS. RANDALL BLAINE MARTIN), psychologist; b. Chgo., July 1, 1944; d. Walter S. and Lilyan M. (Dywan) Duda; B.A., No. Ill. U., 1965, M.A. in Clin. Psychology, 1972; m. Randall Blaine Martin, Sept. 6, 1968. Staff psychologist Elgin (Ill.) State Hosp., 1966-68; exec. dir. mental health fund adv. commn. Ill. State Legislature, 1968-69; asst. research coordinator, early childhood counselor No. Ill. U. Lab. Sch., DeKalb, Ill., 1969-72; clin. psychologist Gordon Community Mental Health Center, DeKalb, 1972-74; psychologist in mgmt. devel. United Airlines, 1974—. Instr. drug edn. No. Ill. U. Coll. Edn., 1972. Pres., Democratic Women of DeKalb County, 1971-73; Dem. precinct committeewoman DeKalb County, 1972; dep. registrar DeKalb County, 1970-74. Bd. dirs., co-founder DeKalb County Drug Council, 1970-72, DeKalb County Crisis Line, 1969-70; bd. dirs. DeKalb County Villages, 1974—. Mem. Am. Psychol. Assn.

MARTIN, DOLORES MOYANO (MRS. WILLIAM CLYDE MARTIN, JR.), Latin Am. affairs editor; b. Cordoba, Argentina; d. Horacio Moyano-Navarro and Catherine (Cocke) Moyano; B.A., Vassar Coll., 1956; postgrad. in Latin Am. Area Studies Am. U.; m. William Clyde Martin, Jr., June 6, 1959; children—Eric Barraud, Christian Bryan. Research and writer on Latin Am., Affairs, Argentine embassy, Washington, 1956-63; research cons. Inter-Am. Devel. Bank, Washington, 1965-66, 70; program adminstr. S.Am. telecommunication study Page Communications Engrs., Inc., Washington, 1966; research asso. Cultural Information Analysis Center, Am. U., Washington, 1966-69; asst. editor Handbook of Latin American Studies, Latin Am. div. Library of Congress, Washington, 1970—. Mem. Latin Am. Studies Assn., Vassar Coll. Alumnae Assn. Home: 5116 Duvall Dr Washington DC 20016

MARTIN, DOROTHY RANDOLPH, psychologist, educator; b. Denver, Apr. 19, 1912; d. Frank Bedard and Evelyn (Knapp) Martin; B.A., U. Colo., 1934, M.A., 1936, Ph.D., 1947. Instr. psychology U. Colo., Boulder, 1938-48, asst. prof., 1948-57, asso. prof., 1957-72, prof., 1972—; dir. rehab. counseling program, 1955-67, chmn. faculty council, 1973—. Vis. asso. prof. U. Kan., 1948-49; cons. U.S. Bur. Hearings and Appeals, 1960—. Recipient Robert L. Stearns award for extraordinary service U. Colo., 1962. Fellow Am. Psychol. Assn., Sigma Xi; mem. Colo. Psychol. Assn., Mortar Bd., Kappa Kappa Gamma. Home: 834 13th St Boulder CO 80302

MARTIN, EDITH KINGDON GOULD (MRS. GUY MARTIN), pianist, civic worker; b. N.Y.C., Aug. 20, 1920; d. Kingdon and Annunziata (Lucci) Gould; student Barnard Coll., N.Y.C., 1939-40; pvt. study piano; m. Guy Martin, Oct. 12, 1946; children—Isaiah Guyman III, Jason Gould, Christopher Kingdon, Edith Maria Theodosia Burr. Actress, Barter Theater, 1941, Summer Stock, Nyack, 1942, A Young American, 1946, Louis Bromfield's West of the Moon, 1946, Agatha Christie's Hidden Horizons, 1946; guest pianist Werner Lywen Quartet, 1965—. Bd. dirs. Nat. Symphony Orch., Washington; trustee Nat. Ballet; trustee, pres. Opera Soc. of Washington. Served with USNR, 1942-46. Decorated Navy Expert Pistol medal. Mem. Jr. League N.Y.C. Club: City Tavern (Washington). Author: Poems, 1934. Composer: Song Cycle on Poems of Lenau and Schiller, 1968. Home: 3300 O St NW Washington DC 20007

MARTIN, FLORENCE GIFFIN, cons.; b. Newark, Apr. 4, 1899; d. Clarence Shepard and Elizabeth Burnside (MacDonald) Giffin; B.A., St. Lawrence U., 1919, L.H.D., 1973; postgrad. N.Y. U. Sch. Commerce, 1923-24; m. Nathan Barnert Martin, Aug. 29, 1937 (dec. Nov. 1956). New bus. clk. Chase Manhattan Nat. Bank, 1919-21; sec. to editor Good Housekeeping mag., 1921; advt. asst. F. H. Bennett Biscuit Co., 1921-26; head, new bus. dept. Bank of N.Y., 1927-30; supr. prospect and donor records Emergency Unemployment Relief Com., 1931-35; office mgr. The Don Herold Co., 1935-40, sec. of corp., 1937-40; organized prospect records N.A.M., 1940; organized prospect and donor records Brit. War Relief Com., 1940-41; personnel specialist Johns-Manville Corp., N.Y.C., 1941-58; organizer women's fund raising activities Community Service Soc., 1958-61; now trustee emeritus St. Lawrence U.; adv. cons. com. bus. tech. N.Y. State Agr. and Tech. Inst., Farmingdale, 1953-60. Mem. N.Y. Personnel Mgmt. Assn. (pres. Personnel Assn. N.Y. 1952-53), Internat. Assn. Personnel Women, New Eng. Historic Geneal. Soc., St. Lawrence County Hist. Assn., Conn. Soc. Genealogists, St. Lawrence U. Alumni Assn. (v.p. 1955-57), Am. Assn. U. Women, Pan Hellenic, Delta Delta Delta. Presbyn. (chmn. local employment counseling com. 1952-55, mem. budget com., 1949-52, Women's Assn. 1949—, Lenten sch. com. 1966-68). Compiler: Simon Giffin and His Descendants, 1971. Home: 205 E 72d St New York City NY 10021

MARTIN, FRANCES FRANKLIN (MRS. WAYNE S. MARTIN), educator, club woman; b. Gary, W.Va., May 3, 1915; d. John Thomas and Mabel (Marion) Franklin; student Concord Coll., 1935; A.B., Fairmont State College, 1942; M.A., in psychology, Chapman Coll., 1963; m. Wayne S. Martin, Nov. 25, 1937; children—Carolyn Noel (Mrs. Maynard William Gurnsey, Jr.), Marilyn Curtis. Tchr. pub. schs., McDowell County, W.Va., 1935-39; exec. dir. Girl Scouts U.S.A., Fairmont, W.Va., 1954-59, Retarded Children's Council, Fairmont, 1960-61; psychol. and ednl. cons., Anaheim, Cal., 1962-63; ednl. specialist for retarded and disturbed children, Sparks, Nev., 1963—. First v.p. Fairmont Woman's Club, 1953-55; dist. dir. W.Va. Garden Club, 1959-61; pres. Fairmont Music Club, 1952-55, Marion County (W.Va.) Garden Council, 1954-56, Marion County council Girl Scouts U.S.A., 1952-54; mem. Nev. Tax Commn., 1972—. Named Woman of Year Beta Sigma Phi, 1955; recipient nat. certificate of recognition Assn. for Spl. Class Tchrs. of Handicapped, 1968, Distinguished Service award Washoe County Tchrs. Assn., 1971. Mem. Nat., W.Va. edn. assns., Nat., W.Va. assns. retarded children. Republican. Presbyn. Author: Current Trends in Elementary School Guidance Programs, 1963; Guidance Handbook for Teachers, 1964. Home: 1019 LaRue Av Reno NV 89502 Office: McKinley Park Sch Reno NV 89502

MARTIN, HELEN HICKAM, journalist; b. Pauls Valley, Okla.; d. Andrew Richard and Josephine (Sperry) Hickam; A.B., Vassar, 1929; M.A., U. Mich., 1936; m. John Butlin Martin, Sept. 5, 1934; children—Richard H., Judith (Mrs. Richard Hartig), Gillian (Mrs. Theodore C. Sorensen). Writer column Sound the Gavel, Grand Rapids (Mich.) Press, 1943-69, column Direct from Washington, 1968-71; free-lance journalist, 1971—; tchr. adult edn.; pub. speaker. Pres., Washington Planned Parenthood Assn., 1945-46, bd. dirs., 1969—; founder, pres. Kent County (Mich.) Planned Parenthood Assn., 1962-69; mem. adv. com. on population Dept. Health, Edn. and Welfare, 1970-73; hon. mem. United Community Services of Grand Rapids and Kent County, 1966; v.p., dir. Mich. Congress Parents and Tchrs., 1948-60; moderator Panel of Ams., 1962-69; residential chmn. United Community Services, 1965-68; dist. and regional chmn. Mich. Week, 1960-69; sec. Greater Mich. Found., 1960-69. Named Citizen of Year, Civitan Club of Grand Rapids, 1967; recipient award Shepard Broadcasting Corp., 1967, Republican Women's Club of Kent County, 1969. Mem. Jr. League English Speaking Union. Clubs: Am. Newspaper Women's, Capitol Speakers. Home: 7607 Glendale Rd Chevy Chase MD 20015

MARTIN, HELEN IONE STREEKS (MRS. CRAIG COLBY MARTIN), med. social worker; b. Akron, O., Mar. 3, 1919; d. Francis D. and Margaret (Cormany) Streeks; B.A., Akron U., 1942; M.S., Case-Western Res. U., 1946; m. Craig Colby Martin, May 14, 1955; children—Craig Colby II, John Francis. Caseworker, Dept. Pub. Charities, Akron, 1939-41; caseworker Div. Aid for Aged, Akron, 1942-43, asst. casework supr., 1943-45; med. social worker A.R.C., Valley Forge Gen. Hosp., Phoenixville, Pa., 1945-50, Walter Reed Army Hosp., Washington, 1950-53; asst. dir. social service dept. U. Neb. Sch. Medicine, Omaha, 1953-54; med. social worker social service dept. Akron Gen. Hosp., 1954-55, dir. out-patient dept., 1955-59, dir. social service dept., 1959-65; dir. casework service United Services for Handicapped, Akron, 1965-69, asst. exec. dir., 1969-71; project dir. comprehensive services to unwed parents Family and Childrens Service, Akron, 1971—. Mem. Summit County Home Adv. Bd., 1965-68, sec. bd., 1966-68; mem. Gov.'s Council on Vocational Rehab. Comprehensive state-wide planning com.; 1967-68; trustee Nat. Multiple Sclerosis Soc., 1973—. Mem. Nat. Assn. Social Workers (chpt. sec. 1965-69), Acad. Certified Social Workers, Nat., Ohio rehab. assns., Summit County Hist. Soc., Ohio Council Interpreters for Deaf, Delta Zeta Alumni Assn., Mu Phi Omega. Episcopalian. Home: 365 Alden Av Akron OH 44313 Office: 1082 S Main St Akron OH 44301

MARTIN, HELEN LOUISE EVERALL (MRS. GEORGE H. MARTIN), librarian, educator; b. Monona, Ia., Nov. 6, 1913; d. Bruce B. and Myrtle R. (Trumpler) Everall; B.A., State U. Ia., 1934; certificate in L.S., U. No. Ia., 1964; M.A. in L.S., U. Wis., 1969; m. George H. Martin, Aug. 9, 1934; 1 son, William B. Tchr. pub. high schs., Shell Rock, Ia., 1934-41, La Porte City, Ia., 1941-48; librarian, mem. faculty pub. sch., Monona, Ia., 1960—. Mem. Nat., (hon. life mem.), Ia. State edn. assns., Ia. Edn. Media Assn., N.E. Dist. Sch. Librarians (pres. 1971-72), Ia. High Sch. Speech Assn. (judge), Woman's Club (pres. Monona chpt. 1957-58), Delta Delta Delta. Mem. Order of Eastern Star. Home: 307 N Page St Monona IA 52159 Office: MFL Community School Monona IA 52159

MARTIN, IDA ELVIE, home economist; b. Covington, La., Mar. 17, 1915; d. Emile Victor and Katherine Earl (Jenkins) Martin; student U. Southeastern La., 1936-38; B.S., U. Southwestern La., 1940; postgrad. U. Ark., 1952, Tex. Woman's U., 1961; M.S., La. State U., 1960. Home supr. Farmer's Home Adminstrn., New Roads, La., 1940-41, Edgard, La., 1941-47; home demonstration agt. La. State U. Coop. Extension Service, Napoleonville, 1947-66, Franklinton, 1966—. Active Am. Cancer Soc., A.R.C. Recipient certificate of recognition A.R.C., 1958. Mem. Nat. Assn. Extension Home Economists (So. regional councilor 1955-57, chmn. profl. improvement com. 1971-72, Distinguished Service award 1959), La. Home Demonstration Agts. Assn. (pres. 1953-55), Catholic Daus. Am. (vice-chmn. 1945-46), Delta Kappa Gamma, Epsilon Sigma Phi. Home: Route 5 Box 250 Covington LA 70433 Office: La State U Coop Extension Service Courthouse Franklinton LA 70438

MARTIN, IRENE ANNA (MRS. WILLIAM P. MARTIN), editor; b. Venice Twp., O., July 6, 1922; d. Bernard J. and Helen Gertrude (Schreiner) Keller; grad. high sch.; m. William P. Martin, Sept. 28, 1943; children—Ardis (Mrs. Donald Medley), Robert, Marjorie (Mrs. Stephen Bogner), Gregory. Office worker Telling Belle Vernon Co., 1941-43, Heabler & Heabler Mill, 1943-45; asst. editor Attica (O.) Hub, 1965-67, editor, 1967—. Adviser 4-H, 1957-73. Mem. Bd. Edn., Attica, 1964-68, Seneca East Bd. Edn., 1974—. Mem. Nat., Ohio newspapers assns., Am. Legion Aux., Grange. Roman Catholic. Home: Route 2 Attica OH 44807 Office: Route 224 E Attica OH 44807

MARTIN, JANIS L., mezzo soprano; b. Sacramento, Aug. 19, 1939; d. Emil Wilson and Helen (Roberts) Martin; student Sacramento State Coll., U. Cal.; m. Boris Igor Rybka, Nov. 21, 1962. Selected to study Merola Tng. Program, San Francisco Opera Co., 1958-59, on contract, 1960-64; won final auditions Met. Opera, 1962, contract, 1962-64; contract Nurnburg Opera, 1965, 66; singing guest appearances in Europe; recs. Columbia Recording Co.; performed roles in Carmen, Love of Three Kings. NBC-TV, also appeared as soloist Bach Cantata, ABC-TV; oratorios performed include Verdi Requiem, Messiah, King David, Samson; roles performed with Met. Opera Co. include Otello, Cavalleria Rusticana, Faust, Tales of Hoffmann; Turn of the Screw performed with N.Y. City Opera, Hansel and Gretel with Chautauqua Summer Opera, Madame Butterfly, Chgo. Grant Park. Home: 8501 Behringersdorf uber Nurnberg Zum Bruhl 1 Germany Office: Opernhaus Lessingstrasse 1 Nurnberg Germany

MARTIN, SISTER JOAN MARIE, med. services adminstr.; b. Joplin, Missouri, Aug. 14, 1932; d. John Andrew and Josephine Marie (Mehring) Martin; B.S., Coll. St. Mary, 1957; M.H.A., St. Louis U., 1968. Joined Religious Sisters of Mercy, 1950; surg. supr. Bergan Mercy Hosp., Omaha, 1964-66; adminstrv. asst. Mercy Hosp., Council Bluffs, Ia., 1968-69; adminstr. Mercy Hosp., Roseburg, Ore., 1969-70; St. John's Med. Center, Joplin, Mo., 1970—. Bd. dirs. St. Anthony's Hosp., Pocatello, Ida., Ozark Community Mental Health Center, Joplin. Mem. Am. Coll. Hosp. Adminstrs., Joplin C. of C. (dir.), St. Louis U. Alumni Assn. Home: 2734 Picher St Joplin MO 64801 Office: 2727 McClelland Joplin MO 64801

MARTIN, JUDITH SYLVIA (MRS. ROBERT MARTIN), journalist; b. Washington, Sept. 13, 1938; d. Jacob and Helen (Aronson) Perlman; B.A., Wellesley Coll., 1959; m. Robert Martin, Jan. 30, 1960; children—Nicholas Ivor, Jacobina Helen. Reporter, Washington Post, 1960—. Recipient Newspaper Guild award for humorous writing, 1973, Am. Assn. U. Women award for feature writing, 1973. Mem. Washington Press Club, White House, State Dept. corrs. assns. Author: The Name on the White House Floor, 1972. Home: 1651 Harvard St NW Washington DC 20009 Office: 1150 15th St NW Washington DC 20005

MARTIN, JULIA MAE, biochemist, educator; b. Snow Hill, Md., Nov. 9, 1924; d. Frank and Helen Christine (McKissick) Martin; B.S. (Carver Research Found. fellow), Tuskegee Inst., 1946, M.S., 1948; Ph.D., Pa. State U., 1963. Asst. prof. chemistry Fla. A. and M. U., Tallahassee, 1949-63; asso. prof. chemistry Tuskegee (Ala.) Inst., 1963-66; prof. chemistry So. U., Baton Rouge, La., 1966—. Union Carbide Research fellow, 1968, Hoffmann La Roche fellow, 1969. Mem. Am. Chem. Soc., Am. Inst. Chemists, A.A.A.S., Am. Assn. U. Profs., Alpha Kappa Mu, Beta Kappa Chi, Iota Sigma Pi, Sigma Delta Epsilon. Home: 1564 78th Av Baton Rouge LA 70807

MARTIN, JUNE JOHNSON CALDWELL, journalist; b. Toledo, Oct. 6; d. John Franklin and Eunice Imogene (Fish) Johnson; A.A., Phoenix Jr. Coll., 1939-41; B.A., U. Ariz., 1941-43, 53-59; student Ariz. State U., 1939, 40; m. Erskine Caldwell, Dec. 21, 1942 (div. Dec. 1955); 1 son, Jay Erskine; m. 2d, Keith Martin, May 5, 1966. Free-lance writer, 1944—; columnist Ariz. Daily Star, 1956-59; editor Ariz. Alumnus mag., Tucson, 1959-70; edn. writer, columnist Ariz. Daily Star, Tucson, 1970—. Panelist, co-producer TV news show Tucson Press Club, 1954-55, pres., 1958. Mem. Tucson Civil Def. Com., 1961. Worker campaigns of Samuel Goddard, U.S. Rep. Morris Udall, U.S. ambassador Raul Castro. Recipient award Nat. Headliners Club, 1959, Ariz. Press Club award, 1957-59, Am. Alumni Council, 1966, 70. Mem. Jr. League of Tucson, Pi Beta Phi. Democrat. Methodist. Club: Tucson Press. Contbg. author: Rocky Mountain Cities, 1949. Contbr. articles and stories to mags. Home: PO Box 2631 Tucson AZ 85702 Office: PO Box 5846 Tucson AZ 85703

MARTIN, JUNE ROBERTSON, librarian; b. Charleston, W.Va., Oct. 9, 1922; d. Ernest Luster and Hazel Twila (Heeter) Martin; B.A., W.Va. U., 1943; M.A. in Modern History (Adams fellow), U. Wis., 1944, M.A. in L.S. (U. Wis. Regents scholar), 1963. Faculty, Ill. State Normal U., 1945-47; tchr. Sarah Dix Hamlin Sch., San Francisco, 1947-49; exec. sec. Kanawha County Soc. for Crippled Children, Charleston, W.Va., 1951-63; reference and interlibrary loan librarian Kanawha County Pub. Library, Charleston, 1963—. Publicity chmn. YMCA Travel Film Club, 1971-72; exec. dir. W.Va. Nat. Library Week, 1966, 67; mem. Vol. Service Bur. Bd., 1965-67. Mem. Am. Assn. U. Women (sec. 1968-70), Am. (sec.-treas. Jr. Mems. Round Table 1965-67), W.Va. (sec. 1965-66) library assns., English-Speaking Union (chpt. treas. 1967-71), League Women Voters (chpt. speaker's bur. 1974—), Kanawha County staff Assn. (v.p. 1974), Phi Beta Kappa, Kappa Delta Pi, Beta Phi Mu. Club: Quota (Charleston, W.Va.). Home: 1627 Quarrier St Charleston WV 25311 Office: 123 Capitol St Charleston WV 25301

MARTIN, SISTER KATHRYN ANN, performing arts, ednl. adminstr.; b. Rhinelander, Wis., Apr. 4, 1940; d. Harry Wright and Mildred Marie (Van Zutphen) Martin; B.A., St. Mary-of-the-Woods Coll., 1963; M.A., Ind. State U., 1971. Joined Sisters of Providence, 1965; chmn. speech and drama dept. Xavier High Sch., Appleton, Wis., 1963-65, Marywood High Sch., Evanston, Ill., 1967-68; instr. speech and drama St. Mary-of-the-Woods (Ind.) Coll., 1968-70, chmn. speech and drama dept., 1970—. Chmn. spl. projects com. Ind. Arts Commn., 1972-73, edn. com., 1973-74, theatre adv. com., 1972—; chmn. Wabash Valley Arts Council, 1971-72. Bd. dirs. Ind. Repertory Theatre, 1973-76. Named Dir. of the Best Play, Terre Haute Community Theatre, 1972-73. Mem. Am. Theatre Assn., Ind. Speech Assn. Address: St Mary of the Woods College St Mary of the Woods IN 47876

MARTIN, KATHRYN WORLEY, educator; b. Nashville; d. Winfield Hansford and Alice (Meacham) Martin; B.A., Vanderbilt U., M.A., 1943; student U. Madrid, Spain, 1956-59. Tchr., Litton High Sch., Nashville, 1943-46; instr. Coll. of Wooster, 1946-49; asst. prof. Maryville (Tenn.) Coll., 1950-56, 59—. Mem. Am. Assn. Tchrs. Spanish and Portuguese, Modern Lang. Assn. Am., Am. Assn. U. Women (v.p. Maryville br. 1952-56, pres. Maryville br. 1971-73, sec. Tenn. div. 1955-57, 2d v.p. 1973-74), Am. Assn. U. Profs. (sec.-treas. chpt. 1973—), Sigma Delta Pi (chpt. adviser), Phi Sigma Iota. Methodist. Home: 129 Stanley Av Maryville TN 37801

MARTIN, LOIS ESTELLE, educator; b. Berry, Ala., Jan. 1, 1914; d. John W. and Eliza (Moore) Baker; B.S., North Tex. State U., 1940, Ed.D., 1964; M.S., U. Ill., 1942; m. H. Gebhard Martin, Aug. 26, 1933 (dec. Jan. 1952); children—Lois Elizabeth (Mrs. James A. Ross), Kenneth Gebhard. Tchr. elementary sch., Cleburne, Tex., 1934-39, Forsan, Tex., 1939-40, Sweetwater, Tex., 1941-42; elementary and secondary tchr., counselor, Wichita Falls, Tex., 1952-64; prof. edn. Hardin-Simmons U., Abilene, Tex., 1964-67, dir. guidance edn., 1965—, head dept. spl. edn. and guidance, 1970—. Cons. jr. coll. Pres. Woman's Missionary Soc., 1950-51; dist. chmn. Guidance Assn., 1959-60; pres. P.T.A., 1937-38; coordinator Guidance Services, 1963-64; sponsor Tex. Student Edn. Assn., 1964—. Recipient Distinguished Alumni award North Tex. State U., 1964; Hometown honoree, 1969; Citizen-of-the-Day. Mem. Am. Assn. U. Women, U. Women's Club (pres. 1966-67), City Tchrs. Assn. (pres. 1962-63), Woman's Study Club (pres. 1956-57), Tex. Soc. Coll. Tchrs. Edn., N.E.A., Tex. Tchrs. Assn., Student Edn. Assn., Tex. Personnel and Guidance Assn., Delta Kappa Gamma (pres. 1965-66). Baptist (Sunday sch. tchr. 1942-46 tng. union dir. 1942-51, Sunday sch. supt. 1947-62). Mem. Order Eastern Star (past worthy matron). Contbr. to mags. and newspapers. Home: 641 Westwood Dr Abilene TX 79603

MARTIN, LUCILLE CAIAR (MRS. HAMPTON MARTIN), artist; b. Carlsbad, N.M., June 7, 1918; d. Homer E. and Angie May (Schmidt) Caiar; pvt. study art with LaVora Norman, 1953-56; diploma Merlin Enabnit Art Sch., 1969; m. Hampton Martin, May 11, 1936; children—Hal Arthur, Ned Allen, Guy Wesley. One-man shows N.M. State U., Las Cruces, 1965, Copper Gallery-Mining Club, 1971, others; exhibited in group shows at El Paso (Tex.) Mus. Art, 1964, West Tex. State U., Canyon; represented in permanent collections Carlsbad Library and Mus., Colliers Miller Gallery, St. Joseph's Mo., Western Tradition Gallery, Boulder City, Colo., Winters Gallery, Tucson; commns. include mural in Hillcrest Bapt. Ch., Carlsbad, N.M., 1962, First Bapt. Ch., McCrory, Ark., 1963, Security Savs. & Loan, Carlsbad, N.M., 1964, also N.M. state bird, roadrunner for Office of Gov., Santa Fe, 1964. Named Choice Artist, Am. Assn. U. Women, 1963; recipient 1st place award Carlsbad Area Art Assn. Exhibit, 1964, 65, 66; 2d place award Nat. Parks Art Show at Carlsbad Caverns, 1972, 1st place award, 1973. Mem. Women's Aux. Inst. Mining and Metall. Engrs. Home: 5901 E 3d St Tucson AZ 85711

MARTIN, MARGARET MARION (MRS. FLOYD AUGUST MARTIN), librarian; b. Nevada, Mo., June 6, 1912; d. Clyde Churchell and Florence Julia (Palmer) Norman; A.A., Cottey Coll., 1932; A.B., U. Mo., 1953; M.L.S., U. Ill., 1965; m. Floyd August Martin, Nov. 14, 1936; children—Emilie York (Mrs. Delmer Eugene Moore), David Norman. Asst. librarian Columbia (Mo.) Pub. Library, 1953-54, U. Mo. Med. Library, Columbia, 1954-61; spl. services librarian Army Library, Okinawa, 1961-63, Vitry-le-Francois, France, 1965-66, Nurnberg, Germany, 1966-67; head readers services U.S. Naval Acad. Library, Annapolis, Md., 1967-73; documents librarian U. Mo., Columbia, 1973-74, journalism librarian, 1974—. Mem. A.L.A., P.E.O., Phi Beta Kappa. Home: 2901 W Rollins Rd Columbia MO 65201 Office: U Mo Library Columbia MO 65201

MARTIN, MARGERY MAE, educator; b. Marshfield, Wis., Dec. 17, 1932; d. Alvin P. and Laura C. (Steinhoff) Martin; B.S., Valparaiso U., 1954; M.S., U. Wis., 1962; Ph.D., U. Utah, 1969. Tchr. phys. edn., supr. elementary sch. phys. edn. Antigo (Wis.) Pub. Schs., 1954-56; instr. Lake Forest (Ill.) Coll., 1956-62, chmn. women's dept., 1958-62; mem. faculty Cal. State Coll. at Hayward, 1962—, asst. prof., 1962-65, asso. prof. phys. edn., 1965-70, prof., 1970—. Mem. Western Soc. Phys. Edn. for Coll. Women, Nat. Assn. Phys. Edn. Coll. Women, A.A.H.P.E.R., Cal. Assn. Health, Phys. Edn., Recreation, Cal. Tchrs. Assn., Delta Kappa Gamma. Home: 21071 Ashfield Av Castro Valley CA 94546

MARTIN, MARTHA JO (MRS. JAMES ALFRED MARTIN), ednl. adminstr., journalist; b. nr. Maysville, Mo., June 16, 1941; d. Clifford H. and I. June (Gaskell) Duce; B.S. in Home Econs. Journalism, U. Mo., 1964, M.S. in Home Econs. Communications, 1969, postgrad., 1971; m. James Alfred Martin, June 21, 1959; 1 son, Gregory Lynn. Adminstrv. asst. to dean Sch. Home Econs., U. Mo., Columbia, 1964-69, coordinator ednl. resources and information specialist Sch. Veterinary Medicine, 1971—; fashion and feature writer Cal. Apparel News, Los Angeles, 1970. Mem. Am., Mo. (editor mag. 1971—) home econs. assns., Altrusa Internat., Kappa Delta Pi (treas. 1973-74), Phi Upsilon Omicron, Theta Sigma Phi (pres. prof. club 1968-69), Gamma Sigma Delta. Home: 216 Sarazen St Columbia MO 65201

MARTIN, MARTINA MOCKAITIS (MRS. JOHN H. MARTIN), physician; b. Phila., Nov. 2, 1939; d. Joseph Julius and Helen Anna (Carl) Mockaitis; R.N., Jefferson Hosp. Sch. Nursing, 1960; B.S., U. Pa., 1964; M.D., Jefferson Med. Coll., 1968; m. John H. Martin, Oct. 28, 1972. Intern, Bryn Mawr Hosp., 1968-69, resident in internal medicine, 1969-70, chief med. resident, 1970-71; fellow in rheumatology Temple U. Hosp., 1971-73; asst. coll. physician Bryn Mawr (Pa.) Coll., 1971—. Mem. A.C.P., Phila. Soc. Clin. Hypnosis, Am. Rheumatism Assn., Phila. Rheumatism Soc., Alpha Omega Alpha. Home: 829 Coopertown Rd Bryn Mawr PA 19010 Office: 933 Haverford Rd Bryn Mawr PA 19010

MARTIN, SISTER MARY, hosp. adminstr.; b. Atlanta, Ind., Mar. 22, 1935; d. Charles Joseph and Martha Margaret (Buscher) McEntee; B.A., Coll. of Mt. St. Joseph, 1966; M.H.A., St. Louis U., 1968. Sec. to auditor First Nat. Bank, Kokomo, Ind., 1952-54; joined Sisters of St. Joseph, 1954; jr. high tchr. Diocesan Schs., Lafayette, Ind., 1958-64; adminstrv. resident Spohn Hosp., Corpus Christi, Tex., 1967-68; with St. Joseph Meml. Hosp., Kokomo, 1968—, adminstr. 1968—. Dir. Mercy Hosp., Elwood, Ind., 1970-76. Mem. Blue Cross Rate Rev. Com., Indpls., 1972-75. Mem. adv. bd. Ind. U., Kokomo, 1973—; bd. dirs. Kokomo Opportunities Industrialization Center, 1973—, sec., 1973—. Named Exec. of Year, Nat. Secs. Assn., 1973. Mem. Am. Coll. of Hosp. Adminstrs., Ind. Hosp. Assn. (dir. 1972—), Sisters of St. Joseph mem. adminstrv. bd. 1970—), Kokomo C. of C. (dir. 1972—). Home: 417 Magnolia Dr Kokomo IN 46901 Office: 1907 W Sycamore Kokomo IN 46901

MARTIN, MARY CATHERINE, lawyer; b. Hillsboro, Ill., May 20, 1908; d. Robert James and Margaret (Wilkie) Martin; LL.B., Lincoln Coll. Law, 1936. Admitted to Ill. bar, 1936, D.C. bar, 1938, Supreme Ct. U.S., 1943; asst. state's atty., Springfield, Ill., 1937; pros. atty. War Crimes Trials, Manila and Tokyo, Japan, 1947-49; claims atty., legal adviser Horace Mann Ins. Co., Springfield, 1957-63; asst. atty. gen. State Ill., Springfield, 1963—. Mem. staff Inter-Parliamentary Union Conf., Washington, 1953; adminstrv. asst. U.S. Congressman Peter F. Mack, III, Washington,1954-56; asst. to dir. Commn. Govt. Security, Washington, 1956-57. Served to capt. AUS, 1942-46. Decorated Army Commendation medal. Home: 205 W Dodge St Springfield IL 62702 Office: 500 S 2d St Springfield IL 62706

MARTIN, MARY JEANETTE (MRS. JAMES W. MARTIN, JR.), occupational therapist; b. Milw., May 21, 1933; d. Ernest Ferdinand and Beatrice Fay (Orth) Krembs; B.S. cum laude, Mt. Mary Coll., Milw., 1955, postgrad., 1956; postgrad. Ga. State Coll., 1967-69; m. James W. Martin, Jr., Dec. 28, 1957; children—Michael C., Patrick K. Student intern occupational therapy Curative Workshop Milw., 1955, Norwich (Conn.) State Hosp., 1955, VA Hosp., Wood, Wis., 1955-56; mem. occupational therapy staff St. Josephs Sanitarium, Dubuque, Ia., 1956-57, Curative Workshop Milw., 1957, Aidmore Childrens Hosp., Atlanta, 1958-59; occupational therapy cons. amputee program Crippled Childrens div. Ga. Dept. Health, 1958-62; occupational therapy supr. Peachtree Hosp., Atlanta, 1962-63, Dayroom Project, Multiple Sclerosis Soc., Atlanta, 1960-66; occupational therapy cons. Mary B. Moody Nursing Home, Decatur, Ga., 1963-66; sr. occupational therapist Emory U. Rehab., Research and Tng. Center, Grady Hosp., Atlanta, 1966, dept. phys. medicine Emory U. Hosp., 1966-67; cons. occupational therapist Convocare Convalescent Center, Atlanta, 1969; staff occupational therapist Ward 7D, Grady Hosp., 1969; dir. occupational therapy dept. Ga. Retardation Center, Atlanta, 1969—. Temporary chmn., allied health professions sect. Ga. chpt. Arthritis Found., 1970. Mem. Am., Ga. (pres.) occupational therapy assns., Nat. Rehab. Assn. (program com. 1969 meeting Ga. chpt.), Am. Assn. Mental Deficiency, Eta Sigma Phi, Delta Epsilon Sigma. Home: 2800 Spring Dr Smyrna GA 30080 Office: 4770 N Peachtree Rd NE Atlanta GA 30341

MARTIN, MARY MARGARET, surgeon; b. Cleve., Oct. 31, 1925; d. William H. and Eva (Parker) Martin; B.A., Ohio State U., 1943, M.D., 1948; m. John H. Patterson, Jr., Sept. 21, 1961. Intern Ohio State Med. Center, 1948-50, resident in plastic surgery, 1953-55; asst. resident surgery Presbyn. Hosp., N.Y.C., 1950-51; surg. resident burn surgery Med. Coll. of Va., 1951-54, plastic surgery Ohio State U., 1953-55; fellow plastic surgery Cleve. Clinic, 1955; practice medicine specializing in surgery Cin., 1956—; chief sect. plastic surgery Good Samaritan Hosp.; mem. staff St. Francis, Providence, Deaconess, Children's Mercy hosps., Cin. Diplomate Am. Bd. Surgery, Am. Bd. Plastic Surgery. Fellow A.C.S. (pres. Ohio chpt. 1971-72); mem. Am. Med. Woman's Assn. (Cin. sec. 1958-60, pres. local br.), Ohio Valley Plastic Surgery Soc., Am. Soc. Surgery Trauma, Am. Cleft Palate Soc., Ohio, Cin. surg. socs. Clubs: Robert M. Zollinger (Columbus, O.); Cincinnati Cat (pres.). Home: 1111 Tahoe Terrace Cincinnati OH 45238 Office: 5948 Glenway Av Cincinnati OH 45238

MARTIN, MIRIAM, holding co. exec.; b. N.Y.C., June 30, 1919; d. Cornelius and Marie (Ruddock) Elsasser; grad. high sch. With Lubanko Tool Co., N.Y.C., 1957—, treas., 1958—; treas., dir. Technol. Devices, Inc., Long Island City, N.Y., 1968—. Mem. Women's Republican Club, 1972—. Home: 110-56 71st Av Forest Hills NY 11375 Office: 38-25 Greenpoint Av Long Island City NY 11101

MARTIN, PATRICIA JANE, pharm. co. exec.; b. Croton-on-Hudson, N.Y., June 25, 1928; d. Patrick Joseph and Laura Amanda (Tobin) Martin; B.A. summa cum laude, Coll. New Rochelle (N.Y.), 1947. Editor, W/C Pharm. Co., 1947-56; pub. relations dir. Internat. Silk Assn., 1956-57; mgr. creative services Warner-Lambert Co., Morris Plains, N.Y., 1957—; cons. Clair de Lune, Inc.; asso. dir. Bassinova Workshop. Mem. Mayor N.Y.C. Com. for Better N.Y. Mem. Advt. Women N.U. (pres. 1969-71, dir. found. 1966—; Ela award 1971, President's award 1969), Am. Advt. Fedn. (lt. gov. 2d dist.), Pharm. Advt. Club. Home: 66 Center Av Morristown NJ 07060 Office: 201 Tabor Rd Morris Plains NJ 07950

MARTIN, PATRICIA MILES (MRS. EDWARD R. MARTIN), author; b. Cherokee, Kan.; d. Thomas J. and Nell (White) Miles; spl. courses U. Wyo., 1919-20; m. Edward R. Martin, Oct. 24, 1942. Sch. tchr., Genoa, Colo., 1918, Arminto, Wyo., 1919-20, Denver, 1921; author books for children. Mem. Burlingame (Cal.) Writers, Cal. Writers. Author books for children, 1958—, including: The Pointed Brush (N.Y. Herald Tribune Honor Book), 1958; Happy Piper and the Goat, 1960; Little Two and the Peach Tree (Jr. Lit. Guild selection), 1963; The Greedy One (Jr. Lit. Guild selection), 1964; Jump Frog Jump (Jr, Lit. Guild selection), 1965; Teacher's Pet (Jr. Lit. Guild selection), 1966; Fox and the Fire, 1966; Trina's Boxcar, 1967; Pieces of Home (Jr. Lit. Guild selection), 1967; Rabbit Garden, 1967; Dolls from Cheyenne, 1967; Dolley Madison, 1967; Uncle Fonzo's Ford (Jr. Lit. Guild selection), 1968; One Special Dog (Jr. Lit. Guild selection), 1968; Nobody's Cat, 1969; Apricot ABC, 1969; That Cat 1, 2, 3, 1970; Gertrude's Pocket (Jr. Lit. Guild selection), 1970; Eddie's Bear, 1970; Hoagie's Rifle-Gun (Jr. Lit. Guild selection), 1970; Annie and the Old One (Jt. Lit. Guild selection, honor book Newbery com. A.L.A. bronze medal Christophers, silver medal Commonwealth Club Cal.), 1971; Wharf Rat (N.Y. Acad. Sci. citation 1972); Be Brave, Charlie, 1973; Two Plays About Foolish People, 1973; Somebody's Dog, 1973; Otter in the Cove, 1974. Home: 910 Bromfield Rd San Mateo CA 94402

MARTIN, RACHEL SANGSTER, librarian; b. Mt. Olive, N.C., Aug. 18, 1918; d. Leon Forrest and Bertha (Reaves) Martin; B.A., Brenau Coll., 1939; B.S. in L.S., U. N.C., 1949; M.A., State U. Ia., 1955. Tchr. pub. schs., N.C., 1939-49; asst. reference librarian Auburn (Ala.) U., 1949-51; librarian Mary Baldwin Coll., Staunton, Va., 1951-56; head humanities div. library Fla. State U., Tallahassee, 1956-57; reference and serials librarian Furman U., Greenville, S.C., 1957-72, asso. librarian, 1972—. Mem. Am. (reference and subscription books rev. Com. 1968—, Southeastern (chmn. nominating com. reference services div. 1960, vice chmn., chmn. reference services div. 1964-66), S.C. (sec. 1959, chmn. membership com. 1960-61) library assns., Am. Assn. U. Profs. (pres. Furman U. chpt. 1962-63), Delta Kappa Gamma, Beta Phi Mu, Zeta Tau Alpha. Baptist. Club: Altrusa (rec. sec. Greenville, 1959-61, archivist 1961-63, pres. 1966-68, parliamentarian 1970-71, corr. sec. 1972-73). Compiler index to articles Furman Studies 1959. Home: 220 Covington Rd Greenville SC 29609 Office: Furman U Library Greenville SC 29613

MARTIN, ROSE GODLOVE (MRS. JOSEPH E. MARTIN, JR.), assn. exec.; b. Balt., Dec. 4, 1915; d. Joseph V. and Rosa (Hayward) Godlove; R.N., South Balt. Gen. Hosp. Sch. Nursing, 1941; postgrad. Davis and Elkins Coll., 1956; m. Joseph E. Martin, Jr., Feb. 19, 1942; children—Joseph Ernest III, John Samuel. Exec. dir. Randolph Co. chpt. A.R.C., 1943-46; dir. nursing service Meml. Gen. Hosp., Elkins, W.Va., 1955-56; pres., exec. dir. Nat. Assn. for Practical Nurse Edn. and Service, Inc., N.Y.C., 1966-74; state sec. Senator Jennings Randolph, 1974—. Mem. adv. commn. to health professions N.Y.C. Bd. Edn., 1967-74. Home nursing instr. A.R.C., 1943-54. Mem. Elkins (W.Va.) City Council, 1957-61, Elkins-Randolph Co. Airport Authority, 1960-66, Randolph County Woman Jury Commr., 1965-68. Served to 2d lt. Nurse Corps, 1941-42. Recipient Woman of Achievement award Elkins Bus. and Profl. Women's Club, 1962, Nat. award for Outstanding Achievement Nat. Assn. Practical Nurse Edn. and Service, 1967. Ky. col. Mem. Nat. Council Women of U.S. (co-chmn. health com.), Assn. Schs. Allied Health Professions, Gen. Fedn. Women's Clubs, Nat. Fedn. Bus. and Profl. Women, W.Va. Assn. Mental Health (mem. exec. com. 1965-67), Nurses' Assn. (dist. pres. 1962-66), Am. Pub. Health Assn., Am. Soc. Assn. Execs., Nat. Assn. Practical Nurse Edn. and Service, Nat. Assn. Parliamentarians. Club: Woman's (Elkins, pres. 1952-54). Home: Box 450 Elkins WV 26241 Office: 315-316 Postoffice and Courthouse Bldg Elkins WV 26241

MARTIN, ROSEMARY BERNICE MARKEE (MRS. ARTHUR A. MARTIN), library adminstr.; b. Brighton, Colo., Jan. 1, 1923; d. Verne Wren and Veva (Utterback) Markee; grad. high sch.; m. Arthur Alvin Martin, Sept. 20, 1942; children—Bobbie Jo (Mrs. T. David Wise), Michael Jean (Mrs. John C. Ratliff, Jr.). Sec. Land Bank Assn., 1955-56; adminstrv. sec. Wyo. State Library, Cheyenne, 1956-63, acting state librarian, 1963, 68, 70, adminstrv. asst., 1963—. Rec. sec. State Library, Archives and Hist. Bd., 1965—. Mem. Mountain-Plains, Wyo. library assns., Cheyenne Jay Shees (charter), Wyo. Employees Assn. Methodist. Mem. Order Eastern Star, Daus. of Nile. Home: 406 Carlson St Cheyenne WY 82002 Office: Supreme Ct Bldg Cheyenne WY 82001

MARTIN, RUTH GEARIN (MRS. GORDON FRANKLIN MARTIN), reading cons.; b. Pinehurst, Ga., June 25, 1916; d. George Joseph and Annie Maude (Childers) Gearin; B.S. in Edn., Oglethrope U., 1954; M.Ed., U. Ga., 1967, Ed.D., 1969; m. Gordon Franklin Martin, June 21, 1941; children—Linda Ruth, Donna Layne. Tchr., Lamar County Bd. Edn., Milner, Ga., 1935-41; tchr. Marietta (Ga.) Bd. Edn., 1950-65, remedial reading coordinator, 1965-67, cons. reading, 1969—. Off-campus instr. U. Ga., Athens, 1969—; cons. staff devel. Houston County Bd. Edn., 1971-72. Sponsor, Girl Scouts U.S.A., 1956-60. Leader, Democratic Women Ga., 1970—. Mem. Internat. (pres. 1972-73), Southeastern Regional Internat. (speaker 1972) reading assns., Marietta Edn. Assn. (Tchr. of Year 1964, pres. 1963-64), Ga. Assn. Educators, Assn. Supervision and Curriculum Devel. (dist. dir. 1973), Ga. Assn. Instructional Suprs., Kappa Delta Epsilon, Delta Kappa Gamma, Kappa Delta Pi. Baptist. Home: 3351 Elm Creek Dr Marietta GA 30060 Office: 145 Dodd St Marietta GA 30062

MARTIN, RUTH L. DICKSON (MRS. ERIC W. MARTIN), editor, writer; b. Oyster Bay, N.Y., Oct. 15, 1915; d. John B. and Ruth (Golden) Dickson; student Pineland Coll., 1929-31, U. N.C., 1931-33, U. S.C., 1945, Bklyn. Coll., 1952; hon. Ph.D., 1973; m. Eric W. Martin, July 15, 1961; children—Edward Vaughn, Janie (Mrs. John H. Ploeger), Ann (Mrs. Nolan P. Clark), John Vaughn, Rosemary. Research in bone and vitamins Jewish Hosp., Bklyn., 1952-57; tchr., research in South Viet Nam, 1957-58; asso. editor Spectrum, Charles Pfizer Co., 1958-62; free-lance editor, writer, 1962—. Mem. N.Y. Acad. Scis., Am. Med. Writers Assn., Drug Information Assn., Asso. editor Techniques of Medication, Hazards of Medication, Martins Manuals. Home: 66 Woodland Rd Montvale NJ 07645

MARTIN, SHEILA WALSH (MRS. HOWARD BERNARD MARTIN), writer; b. N.Y.C., Sept. 15, 1924; d. Thomas Hugh and Nell Sarah (Overpeck) Walsh; B.A., U. Del., 1948; m. Howard Bernard Martin, June 19, 1948; children—Thomas, Kathleen, James, Eileen. Tchr., P.S. Dupont High Sch., Wilmington, Del., 1948-49; tutor, Hatboro, Pa., 1961-71; editor, writer Bucks County Panorama, regional mag., Doylestown, Pa., 1968-74; asso. pub. paper Am. Revolution, 1974—; columnist newspaper Today's Spirit, Hatboro; free lance writer, 1968—. Served with WAVES, 1944-46. Mem. Bucks County Writers' Guild, Phila. Writers' Conf., Phi Kappa Phi. Democrat. Episcopalian. Home: 28 Home Rd Hatboro PA 19040

MARTIN, SHIRLEY PEARL, ins. co. supr., athlete; b. Rib Lake, Wis., Dec. 1, 1922; d. Edwin Arthur and Pearl Ann (Skon) Martin; ed. Wasau Vocational Sch., Milw. Vocational Sch. Supr. Mass. Mut. Life Ins. Co., Milw., 1942—, agt., 1960—; chmn. Amateur Athletic Union Women's Basketball Rules Com., 1957-68, Wis. state chmn., 1945—; mgr., coach, player women's basketball and softball; mgr. women's basketball team on tour in Russia, 1958; chmn. joint DGWS-Am. Athletic Union Nat. Women's Basketball Com., 1973-74. Named to All-Am. basketball team, Nat. Am. Amateur Union Basketball Tourney, 1956. Home: 3862 N 75th St Milwaukee WI 53216 Office: 600 E Mason St Milwaukee WI 53202

MARTIN, SHIRLEY WITHAM (MRS. NATHAN EUGENE MARTIN), physician; b. Portland, Me., Oct. 6, 1925; d. Walter Herbert and Gertrude Mae (Johnson) Witham; A.B. cum laude, Syracuse U., 1946; M.D., U. Pa., 1950; m. Nathan Eugene Martin, June 14, 1950; children—Gerald, Dale, Alan, James. Intern Grace Hosp., Detroit, 1950-51; resident Univ. Hosps., Syracuse, N.Y., 1951-52; resident anesthesiology Los Angeles County Gen. Hosp., 1952-53; practice medicine specializing in anesthesiology, North Hollywood, Cal., 1954, Los Angeles, 1955, Pomona, Cal., 1956-65; med. dir. pulmonary therapy dept. Pomona Valley Community Hosp., Pomona, Cal., 1965—; mem. inhalation therapy com. Los Angeles Tb and Respiratory Disease Assn., 1970—. Adv. bd. Mt. San Antonio Jr. Coll. Sch. Inhalation Therapy, 1967—. Mem. Assn. Med. Dirs. Respiratory Therapy of Cal., Trudeau Soc. Conglist. Home: 762 Via Santo Tomas Claremont CA 91711 Office: 1798 N Garey Av Pomona CA 91767

MARTIN, SUSAN KATHERINE OROWAN (MRS. DAVID S. MARTIN), librarian; b. Cambridge, Eng., Nov. 14, 1942; d. Egon and Jolan (Schonfeld) Orowan; came to U.S., 1950, naturalized, 1961; A.B. cum laude, Tufts U., 1963; M.S., Simmons Coll., 1965; m. David S. Martin, June 30, 1962; specialist in data processing Harvard Library, Cambridge, Mass., 1965-68, systems librarian, 1968-73; head Library Systems Office, Gen. Library, U. Cal. at Berkeley, 1973—. Cons., Inforonics Inc., 1972, Information Design Inc., 1972-73. Council on Library Resources fellow, 1972-73. Mem. A.L.A. (instr. information sci. and automation div. 1969-71, dir. div. 1972—), Am. Soc. for Information Sci., Phi Beta Kappa. Editor: Jour. Library Automation, 1973—. Contbr. articles to profl. jours. Home: 23 Sao Augustine Way San Rafael CA 94903 Office: General Library University of Cal Berkeley CA 94720

MARTIN, THERESE FRANCIA, banker; b. Chgo., May 6, 1938; d. John Thomas and Virginia Elizabeth (Briggs) Martin; certificate U. Fla., 1965. With Am. Bankers Ins. Co., Miami, Fla., 1956-60; with accounting dept. Ships, Inc., Miami, 1960-61; sec. trust dept. First Nat. Bank, South Miami, Fla., 1961-65; with Bank of Commerce of Fla., Fort Lauderdale, 1965-73, trust officer, 1969-73; corporate trust officer Broward Nat. Bank, Ft. Lauderdale, 1973—. Mem. Nat. Assn. Bank Women, Inc. (chmn. group 1972-73), Am. Inst. Banking, Southeastern Stock Transfer Assn. Home: 4040 NW 30th Terrace #2 Fort Lauderdale FL 33309 Office: PO Box 100 Ft Lauderdale FL 33302

MARTIN, VIRGINIA LORELLE, educator; b. Mt. Olive, N.C., Nov. 29, 1939; d. Robert Reaves and Virginia Lorelle (Franck) Martin; student Greensboro Coll., 1957-59; B.S., Wake Forest Coll., 1961; M.S. (fellow), Emory U., 1963, Ph.D. (fellow), 1967. Faculty, Queens Coll., Charlotte, N.C., 1966—, asso. prof. dept. biology, 1972—. Research asst. Nat. Center for Disease Control, Atlanta, 1970-71. Mem. Am. Soc. Parasitologists, Am. Inst. Biol. Scis., A.A.A.S., Assn. Southeastern Biologists, N.C. Acad. Scis., Sigma Xi. Republican. Baptist. Club: Charlotte (N.C.) Dog Training. Home: 301 Wakefield Dr Charlotte NC 28209

MARTIN, YVONNE CONNOLLY (MRS. WILLIAM BRADY MARTIN), biochemist; b. St. Paul, Sept. 13, 1936; d. Elvert Farrell and Irene Mildred (Aitken) Connolly; B.A., Carleton Coll., 1958; Ph.D. (NSF fellow) in Chemistry, Northwestern U., 1964; m. William Brady Martin, Dec. 14, 1963; children—Margaret Anne, Catherine Irene. Lab. asst. Abbott Labs., North Chgo., Ill., 1958-60, research pharmacologist, 1964-69, asso. research fellow, 1969-74, research fellow, 1974—; instr. chemistry Northwestern U., Evanston, Ill., 1963-64. Mem. A.A.A.S., Am. Chem. Soc., Am. Pharm. Assn., Acad. Pharm. Scis., Nat. Orgn. Women, Sigma Xi, Phi Beta Kappa. Editorial bd. Jour. Medicinal Chemistry, 1971—. Contbr. articles to sci. jours. Patentee in field. Home: 2415 N Jackson St Waukegan IL 60085 Office: Dept 463 Abbott Park Abbott Labs North Chicago IL 60064

MARTINDELL, ANNE CLARK (MRS. JACKSON MARTINDELL), educator, nat. Democratic committeeman; b. N.Y.C., July 18, 1914; d. William and Marjory (Blair) Clark; student Smith Coll., 1932-33, Sir George Williams Coll., Montreal, Que., Can., 1946-47; m. Jackson Martindell, Aug. 12, 1948; children—Marjory (Mrs. K. A. Luther), George C. Scott, David C. Scott, Roger. Tchr. reading Miss Mason's Sch., Princeton, N.J., 1963—, reading supr., 1965—; trustee Marquis Biog. Library Soc., Inc., 1961—, pres., 1967—. Dir. First Nat. Bank Princeton. Treas. N.J. Neuropsychiat. Inst., 1960-63, pres., 1963-65; mem. N.J. Pub. Broadcasting Commn., 1969-73; mem. adv. council Am. Women in Politics Eagleton Center Rutgers U., 1972—. State co-chmn. finance N.J. Vols. for McCarthy, 1967-68; state finance chmn. N.J. New Democratic Coalition, 1969; sec. Commn. on Reform Dem. party in N.J., 1969; vice chmn. Dem. State Com., 1969-73; mem. Dem. Nat. Policy Council, 1971—, del. nat. Dem. conv., 1972; dep. dir. nat. conv. McGovern for Pres., 1972; mem. nat. Dem. Com., 1973—, mem. charter commn., 1973—; Bd. mgrs. N.J. State Diagnostic Center, Menlo Park, N.J., 1965-71, v.p., 1966—; trustee St. Timothy's Sch., 1954-56; trustee North County Sch., Lake Placid, N.Y., 1967-73, chmn. bd., 1970-73; trustee Mercer County Community Coll., 1970—. Mem. League Women Voters (dir. Princeton 1951-53). Democrat. Episcopalian (mem. Altar Guild 1948-59). Home: 1 Battle Rd Princeton NJ 08540

MARTINEZ, ANITA (MRS. ALFRED MARTINEZ), city ofcl.; b. Dallas, Dec. 8, 1925; d. Joe Franco and Anita Trevinio (Mongaras) Nanes; student Dallas Coll. So. Meth. U., 1945; m. Alfred Martinez, Jan. 27, 1946; children—Alfred Joseph, Steve Dan, Priscilla Ann, Rene Orlando. Mem. Dallas City Council, 1969—. Mem. Dallas Community Action Head Start Program, 1969—; fund solicitor West Dallas Youth Center, 1965—; mem. criminal justice com. North Tex. Central Council Govts.; mem. text book adv. com. Dallas Ind. Sch. Dist.; mem. designs of city com. Goals for Dallas; active fund raising Children's Med. Center; founder Mexican-Am. Block Partnership Program; mem. gen. council Dallas Young Adult Inst.; mem. Jesuit Parents Club, Children's Sch. Safety Com.; active Mobility Adjustment Retrained Workers, So. Methodist U.; initiated Weekly Council Report column in El Sol newspaper. Bd. dirs. Met. YWCA, Nat. Center for Vol. Action. Recipient Worthy Woman award Citizens Nat. Bank, 1968; named One of 10 Outstanding Women News Shapers, Dallas Times Herald, 1968, 69, 70; recipient 39th Ann. Zonta Service award, 1972; nominated Outstanding Texan Youth Leader by Nat. Leadership Methods. Mem. Ladies Aux. Dallas Restaurant Assn. (promoter Tasting Bee for charity), Women's Council Dallas County, St. Monica Spanish Lit. Guild, Tex. Municipal League. Home: 3866 Beutel Ct Dallas TX 75229 Office: City Hall Dallas TX 75201

MARTINEZ, HERMINIA, see Neufeld, Herminia Martinez

MARTINEZ, MARY STELLA PINO (MRS. PALEMON R. MARTINEZ), social worker; b. Santa Fe, Aug. 21, 1917; d. Apolonio and Manulita (Romero) Pino; B.A., U. N.M., 1944; M.A., Sch. Social Work, Columbia, 1948; m. Palemon R. Martinez, Sept. 5, 1949. Tng. supr. N.M. Dept. Pub. Welfare, 1941-57; probation officer Juvenile Ct. of Taos (N.M.), 1957—; chief probation officer 8th Jud. Dist. Ct., 1968—. Mem. N.M. Com. on Children and Youth, 1966—, chmn. corrections com., 1967-70, vice-chmn., 1972-73, chmn., 1973; forum mem. White House Conf. on Children, 1970. Bd. dirs. E.C. Cabot Meml. Boys Club of Taos Valley, N.M. Council Crime and Delinquency, 1973. Mem. N.M. Corrections Assn. (v.p. 1969-70, pres. 1970—), Nat. Assn. Social Workers, Acad. Certified Social Workers. Address: PO Box Q Taos NM 87571

MARTINEZ, SUSANNE SITTON (MRS. THOMAS MANUEL MARTINEZ), lawyer; b. San Francisco, Mar. 3, 1945; d. Floyd Weldon and Mary Katherine (Grier) Sitton; B.A. in Sociology, U. Cal. at Davis, 1967; J.D., U. Cal. at San Francisco, 1970; m. Thomas Manuel Martinez, June 12, 1965; 1 dau., Jennifer Sue. Law clk. San Francisco Neighborhood Legal Assistance Found., 1968-70; admitted to Cal. bar, 1971, since practiced in San Francisco. Staff atty. Youth Law Center, San Francisco, 1970-74; instr. poverty law Golden Gate Law Sch., San Francisco, 1970. Mem. Cal. State Bar, San Francisco Bar Assn., Order of Coif, San Francisco Lawyers Club (dir. 1973-75). Home: PO Box 21 Moss Beach CA 94038 Office: 795 Turk St San Francisco CA 94102

MARTINEZ-PICO, AMALIA, pediatric cardiologist; b. Coamo, P.R., July 10, 1929; d. Juan Martinez Morales and Catalina (Pico-Matos); B.S., Coll. A. and M. Arts, Mayaguez, P.R., 1950; M.D., U. P.R., 1955. Asst. in biology Coll. A. and M. Arts, Mayaguez, 1948-49, asst. in chemistry, 1949-50; intern San Juan (P.R.) City Hosp., 1955-56; resident Kan. U. Med. Center, Kansas City, 1956-58, fellow pediatric cardiology, 1958-59; practice medicine specializing in pediatric cardiology, San Juan, P.R.; dir. pediatric cardiology sect. P.R. Med. Center, San Juan, 1960—; dir. pediatric cardiovascular program, 1970—; courtesy staff Auxilio Mutuo Hosp., Hato Rey, Drs. Hosp., Santurce, San Jorje Hosp., Santurce; instr. pediatrics U. P.R. Sch. Medicine, 1959-60, asso. in pediatrics, 1960-62, asst. prof., 1962-69, asso. prof., 1969—; cons. emeritus pediatric cardiology U.S. Army, U.S. Navy, U.S. Coast Guard, U.S. Air Force, USPHS. Named Cardiologist of Yr., P.R. Heart Assn., 1969, Woman of Year P.R. C. of C., 1973-74. Diplomate Nat. Bd. Med. Examiners. Fellow Royal Soc. Health; mem. Am. Coll. Cardiology, Am. Acad. Pediatrics, Pan Am. Med. Assn., P.R. Heart Assn. (pres. 1972-73), Internat. Platform Assn., Alpha Omega Alpha. Home: 157 Guadalquivir Urb El Paraiso Rio Piedra PR 00926 Office: 400 Domenech Av Las Americas Hato Rey PR 00918

MARTINI, TERI, educator, author; b. Teaneck, N.J.; d. Charles and Irene (Josephy) Martini; B.S., Trenton Tchrs. Coll., 1952; M.A., Columbia, 1961. Elementary tchr. Stillman Sch., Tenafly, N.J., 1965—. Mem. Authors Guild, Women's Nat. Book Assn., N.E.A., N.J. Edn. Assn. Author children's books including, The True Book of Indians, 1954; The True Book of Cowboys, 1955; What A Frog Can Do, 1962; Mystery of the Hard Luck House, 1965; The Lucky Ghost Shirt, 1971; Patrick Henry, Patriot, 1972; The Woman in the Mirror, 1973; John Marshall, 1974. Contbr. stories, articles to mags. including Young Miss, Scholastic, Grade Teacher, Venture, Trailblazers. Home: 216 Overlook Av Leonia NJ 07605 Office: Stillman Sch Tenafly Rd Tenafly NJ 07670

MARTINSEN, ELLA BARBARA LUNG (MRS. PERRY J. MARTINSEN), writer; b. near Dawson City, Yukon Terr., Can., Jan. 6, 1901; d. Edward Burchall and Velma Deborah (Clement) Lung; student Santa Barbara State Tchrs. Coll., 1931; m. Perry J. Martinsen, Aug. 25, 1921; 1 dau., Rowena Barbara (Mrs. Charles McQueen Taylor). Concert singer appearing Tacoma, 1917, 34, 35, Santa Barbara, Cal., 1923, 30, 42-48; lectr. Alaska-Yukon gold rush history Dawson City, Whitehorse City, 1967, Santa Barbara, 1967, 72; writer for various publs. City music chmn. P.T.A., Santa Barbara, 1935-36; part-founder, treas. Cross Town Freeway Com., 1961-65. Mem. Santa Barbara Hist. Soc., Nat. League Am. Penwomen (br. pres. 1966-67, 70-71, 74-75). Clubs: Alaska (v.p. 1968-69), Strollers (pres. 1942-43, 68-69), Woman's Montecito Country (Santa Barbara). Author: Black Sand and Gold, 1956, centennial edit., 1967; Trail to North Star Gold, 1969. Contbg. author: New Voices in Am. Poetry, 1973. Contbr. articles to various mags. Home: 3033 Lomita Rd Santa Barbara CA 93105 Office: 30 E Victoria St Santa Barbara CA 93101

MARTINSON, FRANCES SIROTA (MRS. PAUL MARTINSON), lawyer; b. N.Y.C., Mar. 7, 1923; d. Herman and Augusta (Simon) Steyer; A.B., Cornell U., 1944; J.D., Columbia U., 1945; m. Nathan H. Sirota, Dec. 25, 1951 (dec. Jan. 1964); m. 2d, Paul Martinson, Aug. 21, 1969; children—John, Linda. Admitted to N.Y. bar, 1945; asso. Proskauer, Rose, Goetz & Mendelsohn, N.Y.C., 1945-47; with gen. counsel's office Dept. Labor, Washington, 1947-48, gen. counsel's office Dept. Agr., Washington, 1949; gen. counsel Port of N.Y. Authority, 1950-52; mem. firm Sirota, Bernstein & Steyer, N.Y.C., 1952—. Dir. J.S. Inskip, Inc., 1968—. Village justice, Croton-on-Hudson, N.Y., 1960-61. Mem. League Women Voters (pres. 1959-60). Home: 870 United Nations Plaza New York City NY 10017 Office: 747 3d Av New York City NY 10017

MARTINSON, JODIE HAWKINS HOUGH (MRS. DAVID WIGHT MARTINSON), newspaper editor; b. Uniontown, Pa., Nov. 22, 1936; d. H. Harrison Null and Josephine (Hawkins) Hough; B.A. in Journalism, Pa. State U., 1958; m. David Wight Martinson, Aug. 22, 1959; children—Eric, Bruce, Sarah. Asst. to editor H.J. Heinz Co. employee newspaper, Pitts., 1958-59; reporter Marlboro (Mass.) Daily Enterprise, 1967-68; editor Northborough (Mass.) Star, 1968—. Mem. Northborough Pub. Relations Com., 1966-68. Mem. Women in Communications, Northborough Hist. Soc., League Women Voters Westboro Area, D.A.R., Pi Beta Phi. Mem. Unitarian Ch. (mem. standing com. 1973—). Home: 50 Coolidge Circle Northborough MA 01532 Office: Box 199 Northborough MA 01532

MARTUFI, ROSEMARY VIVIAN, photographer; b. Huntington, W. Va., Dec. 14, 1932; d. Manuel John and Virginia Hartley (Griffith) Martufi; student Chevy Chase Jr. Coll., 1949-50. Staff photographer Washington Star-News, 1956—. Active Washington Humane Soc. Mem. White House News Photographers Assn., Senate, House press photographers' galleries, Potomac Valley Dressage Assn. Home: 4413 Chase Av Bethesda MD 20014 Office: 225 Virginia Av SE Washington DC 20061

MARTYL (Mrs. Alexander Langsdorf Jr.), artist; b. St. Louis, Mar. 16, 1918; d. Martin and Aimee (Goldstone) Schweig; A.B., Washington U., St. Louis, 1938; m. Alexander Langsdorf, Jr., Dec. 31, 1941; children—Suzanne, Alexandra. Instr. art dept. U. Chgo.; one-man shows at Cal. Palace of Legion of Honor, 1956, Chgo. Art Inst., 1949, Feingarten Galleries, N.Y.C., Beverly Hills, and Chgo., 1961, 62, 63, St. Louis, 1962, N.Y.C., 1963, Los Angeles, 1964; Kovler Gallery, Chgo., 1967, Washington U., 1967, Oriental Inst. Mus., 1969, Lake Forest Acad., 1970, Rockford, Ill., 1970, Martin Schweig Gallery, 1970, Deson-Zaks Gallery, Chgo., 1974; artist-in-residence Tamarind Inst. U. N.M., 1974; represented in permanent collections Whitney Mus. Am. Art, Davenport Mus., Met. Mus. Art, Chgo. Art Inst., Pa. Acad. Fine Arts, Ill. State Mus., Los Angeles County Mus., City Art Mus., St. Louis, Washington U., U. Ariz., Greenville County (S.C.) Mus. Recipient first prize City Art Mus., St. Louis, 1943, 44; Armstrong prize Chgo. Art Inst., 1947, William H. Bartels award, 1953, Frank Logan medal and prize, 1950; Walt Disney purchase award Los Angeles Mus.; Portrait of Am. award; purchase award Colorado Springs Fine Arts Center, 1961; honor award for mural A.I.A., 1962; named Artist of Yr., Am. Fedn. Arts, 1958. Mem. Artists Equity, Renaissance Soc. Unitarian. Club: Arts of Chicago. Address: Rural Route 1 Box 228 Meacham Rd Schaumburg IL 60172

MARTYN, MARGARET MCMILLAN, clin. psychologist; b. Ada, Okla., Apr. 12, 1919; d. Claude and Zona (Cummings) McMillan; B.A., East Central State (Okla.) Coll., 1941; M.A., U. Colo., 1960, Ph.D., 1966; m. John Morley Martyn, June 4, 1940 (div. Dec. 1965); children—Ann (Mrs. Ken Tagawa), John McMillan, Robert C.; m. 2d, Joseph G. Sheehan, June 4, 1966. Staff psychologist Camarillo (Cal.) State Hosp., 1967-69; clin. psychologist Olive View Hosp., Los Angeles, 1969—; research asst. dept. psychology U. Cal. at Los Angeles, 1964; cons. in psychology Porterville (Cal.) State Hosp., 1966-67. Active Community Theater, Denison, Tex., 1950-56, Boulder, Colo., 1957-64. Mem. Am. Psychol. Assn., A.A.A.S., Psychologists in Pub. Service, Am. Speech and Hearing Assn., Common Cause (community coordinator Santa Monica 1973—). Contbr. articles to profl. jours. Home: 371 20th St Santa Monica CA 90402 Office: Mental Health Center Olive View Hosp Los Angeles CA 91342

MARVICK, ELIZABETH WIRTH (MRS. DWAINE MARVICK), educator; b. Chgo., 1925; d. Louis and Mary (Bolton) Wirth; Ph.B., U. Chgo., 1944, M.A., 1946; Ph.D., Columbia, 1968; m. Dwaine Marvick, Dec. 31, 1948; children—Louis Wirth, Andrew Bolton. Instr., Elmira (N.Y.) Coll., 1946-47, City Coll. N.Y., 1947-51; research asso. U. Mich. at Ann Arbor, 1951-54; instr. U. Cal. Extension, Los Angeles, 1958-67, Santa Monica City Coll., 1967-68; vis. asso. prof. Cal. State Poly. Coll., Pomona, 1969; lectr. Cal. Inst. Tech., 1970-71, Claremont Grad. Sch., 1972—. Mem. Am., Internat. polit. sci. assns., Am. Sociol. Soc., Am. Assn. Pub. Opinion Research, French Hist. Studies Assn. Contbr. articles to profl. jours. Home: 10499 Wilkins Av Los Angeles CA 90024

MARVIN, ELEANOR DREYFUS (MRS. EARL MARVIN), clubwoman; b. N.Y.C., July 28, 1913; d. Emil and Hortense (Heinbach) Dreyfus; B.A., Barnard Coll., 1934; m. Ralph Heymsfeld, Feb. 20, 1936 (dec.); children—David, Jeremy, Joel, Daniel; m. 2d, Earl Marvin, June 14, 1964; stepchildren—Peter, Benjamin, Elizabeth. Former treas. Nat. Council Jewish Women, N.Y.C., v.p., chmn. nat. finance com., pres. Peninsula sect., v.p. N.Y. region, vice chmn. com. on 1968 dist. conv., now pres.; former financial sec. Woodmere P.T.A.; chmn. Pearl Larner Willen Inst., Balt., 1969; mem. President's Com. on Employment of Handicapped, Conf. of President's of Major Am. Jewish Orgns.; treas. WICS; mem. exec. com. Am. Israel Pub. Affairs Com. Bd. dirs. A.R.C.; bd. govs. Hebrew U. Recipient Hannah G. Solomon award Peninsula sect. Evenings br. Nat. Council Jewish Women, 1968. Home: 185 Alden Rd Woodmere NY 11598 Office: 1 W 47th St New York City NY 11364

MARVIN, JANE KING (MRS. J. RICHARD MARVIN), occupational therapist; b. Aberdeen, S.D., Feb. 18, 1924; d. Harmon John and Eva Idella (Kibler) King; student Grinnell Coll., 1947-48; B.S., U. Minn., 1952; postgrad. Temple U., 1973; m. J. Richard Marvin, Apr. 24, 1954; children—Richard King, Elizabeth Ann. Occupational therapist Montgomery County Cerebral Palsy Center, Silver Springs, Md., 1961-63, Home of the Merciful Savior, Phila., 1965-68; dir. occupational therapy Montgomery County Sch. for Handicapped Children, Norristown, Pa., 1968-70; occupational therapy cons. in pvt. practice, Phila., 1970—. Occupational therapy instr. U. Pa., 1967-70. Pres., Community Theater, 1953-56. Served to 1st lt. Women's Med. Service Corps, AUS, 1952-54. Mem. Am. Assn. U. Women, League Women Voters, Assn. Children with Learning Disabilities, Council Exceptional Children, Am., Eastern Pa. occupational therapy assns., Alpha Gamma Delta. Methodist. Home: 220 E Mermaid Lane #222 Philadelphia PA 19118

MARVIN, JANIS ELIZABETH, TV broadcasting co. exec.; b. Iowa City, Dec. 17, 1930; d. Kenneth Reese and Eleanor Christy (Morning) Marvin; student Ia. State U., 1949, postgrad., 1955; B.A., Grinnell Coll., 1953; Continuity writer sta. KRNT, KRNT-TV, Des Moines, 1955-56; continuity dir. sta. WOI-TV, Ames, Ia., 1956-63, also traffic mgr., traffic supr., 1963-71, programming co-ordinator, 1971—. U.S.O. rep., Ames, 1970. Mem. Women in Communications, Am. Women in Radio and TV (chpt. pres. elect 1965-66, pres. 1966-67, nat. v.p. 1968-72), Advt. Women Des Moines (v.p. 1966-67, pres. 1967-68). Home: 1822 Duff Av Ames IA 50010 Office: WOI-TV Ames IA 50010

MARVIN, JEAN MARTHA SOMMER, social work adminstr.; b. Chippewa Lake, O., June 12, 1924; d. Charles Wesley and Martha (Tanner) Sommer; B.A., Coll. of Wooster, 1945; M.S. in Social Adminstrn., Western Res. U., 1949; m. Walter J. Marvin, June 26, 1948 (div. Mar. 1961); children—Claudia, Gregory. Child welfare worker Medina and Summit counties, Akron, O., 1948-51; cons., dist. rep. Ohio Dept. Pub. Welfare, 1960-61; with Welfare Fedn. Cleve., 1961-72, asst. dir. agy. allocations 1967-72; asst. dir. agy. relations and allocations United Torch Services, 1972-74, campaign asso., 1974—. Mem. Little Hoover Commn., Berea, O., 1966-71; mem. adv. com. Div. Child Welfare, Cuyahoga County, 1966-71; mem. profl. adv. bd. S.W. chpt. (Cleve.) Parents Without Partners, 1969—. Mem. adv. com. child devel. div. Cuyahoga Community Coll., Cleve., 1965-71, mem. adv. com. child care tech., 1971-73. Trustee Donna Adkins Trust Fund, Cleve. Press. Mem. Nat. Assn. Social Workers, Acad. Certified Social Workers (Cleve. sec. 1962-64), Am. Pub. Welfare Assn., Ohio Welfare Conf. (pres. 1973), League Women Voters (pres. 1957). Club: Zonta (pres. Berea 1968-70). Home: 133 Meadow Dr Berea OH 44017 Office: 3100 Euclid Av Cleveland OH 44115

MARVIN, JEAN MURRAY, civic worker; b. Bklyn., Sept. 30, 1891; d. William and Jennie (Barre) Murray; student Colo. Coll., 1941; m. Walter Sands Marvin, May 26, 1917; children—Murray Sands, John Howland, Matthew Marvin. Exec. sec. Council Nat. Def., Washington, 1916-18; trustee Montclair (N.J.) Day Nursery, 1925-35, N.J. Symphony Orch., 1943—; founding dir. Met. Opera Guild, 1935, bd. dirs., 1938—, chmn. edn. com., 1948-56, v.p., 1940-45; bd. dirs. Children's Home and Welfare Soc., Montclair, 1935-45, pres. bd., 1940-42; bd. dirs. 3d St. Music Sch. Settlement, 1941—, pres. bd., 1957-64; bd. dirs. Montclair br. A.R.C., 1940-43, Montclair Community Chest, 1940-42. Mem. Nat. Inst. Social Sci. Republican. Clubs: Colony, Cosmopolitan (N.Y.C.). Home: 200 E 66th St New York City NY 10021 also Fair Acres Quogue NY 11959

MARVIN, PATRICIA HARMON, librarian; b. Idabel, Okla., Sept. 21, 1927; d. Alton Ernest and Louise Ann (Park) Harmon; B.A., U. Denver, 1948, M.A., 1950; m. John Robert Marvin, Aug. 14, 1948; children—Stephen Anthony, Timothy Andrew. Circulation librarian U. Neb. at Lincoln, 1950-51; reserves librarian U. Denver, 1952-53; cataloger Johns Hopkins, Balt., 1953-54; head circulation U. Notre Dame (Ind.), 1960-61; supr. circulation Newton (Mass.) Free Library, 1967—. Mem. Mass. Library Assn. Democrat. Episcopalian. Poetry reviewer Library Jour., 1968—; editor Newton Free Library Jour., 1973—. Home: 60 Anthony Circle Newtonville MA 02160 Office: 414 Centre St Newton MA 02158

MARX, ANN VIRGINIA BENNETT (MRS. ARTHUR H. MARX), clin. psychologist; b. N.Y.C., Dec. 5, 1914; d. Robert Lester and Marie Elizabeth (Page) Bennett; B.A., Hunter Coll., 1934; M.A., Columbia, 1935; postgrad. New Sch. Social Research, also N.Y. Sch. Social Work; m. Arthur H. Marx, May 3, 1941; children—Virginia Page, Leslee Marie, Roberta Ann. Research analyst Psychol. Corp., N.Y.C., 1935-37; child guidance clinic worker N.Y. State Dept. Mental Hygiene, Hudson River State Hosp., Poughkeepsie, 1937-41, sr. clin. psychologist Child Guidance Clinic, Day Care Center and Hillcrest Acad., 1946-65; psychiat. social worker Rockland State Hosp., Sloatsburg, N.Y., 1941; time study engr. Bendix Aviation Corp., N.Y.C., 1942; ct. psychologist Family Ct. State of N.Y., Dutchess County, 1965-68; psychologist Wappingers Central Schs., 1968-69; chief psychologist Day Care Center, Dutchess County Dept. Mental Hygiene; cons. psychologist Maplebrook Sch., Amenia, N.Y., Rehab. Center, St. Francis Hosp.; exec. sec. VA clinic, Poughkeepsie. Mem. Am., N.Y. State, Mid-Hudson psychl. assns., Soc. for Autistic Children, Civil Service Employees Assn., N.Y. State, Dutchess County mental hygiene assns. Clubs: Zonta, Dutchess County City and Country Woman's. Home: 34 Greenbush Dr Poughkeepsie NY 12601 Office: 230 North Rd Poughkeepsie NY 12601

MARX, DOROTHY J., orgn. exec.; b. Ansonia, Conn., Jan. 6, 1926; d. Max and Kathryn (Fields) Sachs; B.S. cum laude, N.Y. U., 1962; m. Maurice Levine, June 21, 1944 (div. Feb. 1972); children—Tedra (Mrs. Jonathan Schneider), Michael; m. 2d, Mr. Herbert Marx, June 12, 1973. Research asst. to arbitrator, N.Y.C., 1962-64; asst. to grievance bd. chmn. Hotel Trades Council, N.Y.C., 1964-65; personnel mgr. Burnell & Co., Pelham Manor, N.Y., 1966-69; mgr. adminstrv. services Nytronics, Inc., Pelham Manor, 1969-72, corp. personnel dir., 1972-73; office and personnel adminstr. Nat. Hadassah, N.Y.C., 1973—. Mem. Indsl. Relations Research Assn., Beta Gamma Sigma, Alpha Kappa Delta. Home: 20 Waterside Plaza New York City NY 10034 Office: 65 E 52d St New York City NY 10022

MARX, GERTIE FLORENTINE (MRS. ERIC P. REISS), physician; b. Frankfurt am Main, Germany, Feb. 13, 1912; d. Joseph and Elsa (Scheuer) Marx; student U. Frankfurt (Germany), 1931-36; M.D., U. Bern (Switzerland), 1937; m. Eric P. Reiss, Sept. 26, 1940 (dec. 1968). Came to U.S., 1937, naturalized, 1943. Intern, resident anesthesiology Beth Israel Hosp., N.Y.C., 1939-43, adj. anesthesiologist, 1943-50, asso. anesthesiologist, 1950-55; attending anesthesiologist Bronx Municipal Hosp. Center, 1955—; attending anesthesiologist Bronx VA Hosp., 1966-72, cons. anesthesiologist, 1972—; asst. prof. anesthesiology Albert Einstein Coll. Medicine, 1955-60, asso. prof., 1960-70, prof., 1970—. Diplomate Nat. Bd. Medical Examiners, Am. Bd. Anesthesiology. Fellow Am. Coll. Anesthesiology, N.Y. Acad. Medicine; mem. Am. (com. obstetric anesthesia 1972-74), N.Y. State (chmn. anesthesia study com. 1967-69) socs. anesthesiologists, A.M.A., Bronx County Med. Soc., N.Y. Acad. Scis. Author: (with Orkin) Physiology of Obstetric Anesthesia, 1969. Asso. editor Survey Anesthesiology, 1957—; editor Parturition and Perinatology, 1973. Contbr. articles to profl. jours. Home: 155 Crary Av Mount Vernon NY 10550

MARX, JEAN CAROLE LANDGRAF, journalist; b. Cin., Mar. 2, 1939; d. August W. and May Marie (Reis) Landgraf; B.A., Mt. St. Joseph Coll., 1961; M.S., Purdue U., 1964, Ph.D., 1967. Asst. prof. Fontbonne Coll., St. Louis, 1967-71, asso. prof., 1971-72; journalist Science mag., Washington, 1972—. NSF Summer fellow, 1970. Mem. A.A.A.S., Am. Chem. Soc., Iota Sigma Pi. Office: 1515 Massachusetts Av NW Washington DC 20005

MARZELL, LILLIAN RUTH KOENIGSBERG (MRS. ROBERT PAUL MARZELL), artist; b. Irvington, N.J.; d. Solomon and Augusta (Ring) Koenigsberg; student Bklyn. Mus. Art Sch., 1952-56; studied privately with Victor Candell, Leo Manso and Morris Davidson; m. Robert Paul Marzell, Dec. 17, 1939; children—Madeline (Mrs. John Loder), Jane (Mrs. Richard Wyckoff). Exhibited in group shows at Riverside Mus., Argent Gallery, N.A.D., Argonaut Gallery, Montclair Mus., Bklyn. Mus., Newark Mus., Kennedy Galleries, U. N.M., Edward Williams Coll., others; 14 one-man shows, also retrospective at Fairleigh Dickinson U.; represented in permanent exhibits at David L. Yunich Collection, L. Bamberger & Co., Newark, Paramus Pub. Library, John F. Kennedy Meml. Library, Art Center No. N.J., N.J. Cultural Council, Bergen Community Mus., Bank Paterson (N.J.), Radio Sta. WBAI, Am. Civil Liberties Union, Newark; dir. Paramus Art Workshop; art instr. Englewood Cliffs Upper Sch., Art Center of No. N.J.; painting in U.S.A. traveling show for Nat. Assn. Women Artists. Recipient purchase prize Bamberger's 6th Ann. Exhbn., 1962; award Monmouth Coll., 1962-63; William W. Skinner award for abstract oils Montclair Mus., 1962, Rhea Montag award Nat. Assn. Women Artists, first prize Internat. Art Exhbn., Cannes, France, many others. Mem. Bklyn. Mus. Alumni, Nat. Assn. Women Artists, Modern Artists Guild, Silvermine Guild Artists. Home: 189 Mayfair Rd Paramus NJ 07652

MARZITELLI, MARCELLA DIANE (MRS. MICHAEL JOSEPH MARZITELLI), pub. relations exec.; b. St. Paul, July 6, 1937; d. William Welford and Elnora (Jackson) Sayles; student Macalester Coll., St. Paul, 1955-58; B.A., Roosevelt U., 1963; m. Michael Joseph Marzitelli, Sept. 2, 1960; children—Frank Dominic, Patric Alexander. Instr. evening sch. Central YMCA High Sch., Chgo., 1963-66; spl. instr. Chgo. Bd. Edn., 1966-67; instr. English Central YMCA High Sch., Chgo., 1967-68, founder and chmn. Afro-Am. Studies Dept., 1968-69; curriculum coordinator, 1969-71; fund raising exec. Step, Inc., Chgo., 1973—. Reviewer of text and trade books The Curriculum Adv. Service, Chgo., 1972—. Mem. Am. Inst. for Fgn. Study (chaperon 1971—). Home: 4734 S Kimbark Av Chicago IL 60615 Office: 6740 South Shore Chicago IL 60649

MARZOLF, MARION TUTTLE, educator; b. Greenville, Mich., July 6, 1930; s. Stuart K. and Signe M. (Johnson) Tuttle; B.A. in Journalism, Mich. State U., 1952; M.A. in Journalism, U. Mich., 1963, Ph.D. in Am. Culture, 1972; m. Kingsbury Marzolf, May 7, 1953. Copywriter, Wallace-Lindeman, advt., Grand Rapids, Mich., 1952-53; reporter Biloxi (Miss.) Bull., 1953-54; reporter, asst. Washington Post, 1955-57; editorial layout asst. Nat. Geog. mag., 1957-63; lectr. Eastern Mich. U., Ypsilanti, 1964-68; mem. faculty U. Mich., Ann Arbor, 1967—, asst. prof. journalism, 1973—; city desk copy editor Ann Arbor News, 1973. Faculty adviser Women in Communications. Mem. Am. Studies Assn., Assn. Edn. in Journalism, Immigration History Soc. Author: (bibliography) Women in American Journalism, 1972. Home: 1420 Granger St Ann Arbor MI 48104

MASER, JULIA CHANDLER SCOTT (MRS. MORTON R. MASER), architect; b. N.Y.C., Apr. 8, 1934; d. Irvin Leslie and Dorothy Chandler (French) Scott; B.Arch., Cornell U., 1956; m. Morton R. Maser, May 16, 1959; children—Scott David, Benjamin Mark, Michael Henry. Designer Perkins & Will, architects, White Plains, N.Y., 1957-58, Architects Collaborative, Cambridge, Mass., 1958-59, Klaus Gehrmann, Wiesbaden, Germany, 1959-60; sr. designer Moore &Hutchins, architects, N.Y.C., 1961-63; design cons. Perkins & Will, White Plains, 1963-66; architect Albert A. Hoover & Assos., Palo Alto, Cal., 1967-69, 71—. Recipient Edward Langley prize A.I.A., 1955. Fulbright scholar, 1956-57. Mem. Gargoyle Soc., Kappa Alpha Theta, Tau Beta Pi, Alpha Alpha Gamma. Home: 761 DeSoto Dr Palo Alto CA 94303

MASEY, MARY LOUISE (MRS. JACK MASEY), author; b. Phila., Apr. 8, 1932; d. William James and Ruth Virginia (Busse) Leach; student Middlebury French Summer Sch., 1951; B.A., Ohio State U., 1954; postgrad. (Fulbright scholar), Brussels U., 1954-55, Columbia, 1956-59, George Washington U., 1962; m. Jack Masey, Dec. 27, 1959. Guide U.S. Nat. Exhbn., Moscow, USSR, 1959; guide for graphic arts exhbn. to USSR, 1963-64; research asst. Dumbarton Oaks, trustees for Harvard, Center for Byzantine Studies, Washington, 1971—. Author: Branislav the Dragon, A New Tale of Old Russia, 1967; Stories of the Steppes, Kazakh Folktales Retold, 1968; The Picture Story of the Soviet Union, 1971. Home: 2716 N St NW Washington DC 20007 Office: Dumbarton Oaks 1703 32nd St NW Washington DC 20007

MASGAI, BEVERLY ELAINE BISCH (MRS. ROGER L. MASGAI), ednl. ofcl.; b. Worthington, Minn., July 26, 1939; d. Henry J. and Flora Fanny (Doeden) Bisch; student Worthington State Jr. Coll., 1957-58; B.S. in Edn., Mankato State Coll., 1965; m. Roger L. Masgai, July 29, 1972; 1 son, Roger L. Tchr., Luverne (Minn.) Sr. High Sch., 1965-67, Berthoud (Colo.) High Sch., 1967-68; parish worker St. Matthews Luth. Ch., Worthington, 1968-69; recorder Worthington Community Coll., 1969—. Mem. Assn. Coll. Registrars and Admissions Officers (com. for nat. conv. 1972—), Upper Midwest

Assn. Coll. Registrars and Admissions Officers. Lutheran. Home: 1201 8th Av Worthington MN 56187 Office: Box 107 Worthington MN 56187

MASHBURN, HELEN LEE LIGON (MRS. C.E. MASHBURN), bank exec.; b. Little Rock, Sept. 4, 1921; d. Cyrus McDonald and Alice French (Potter) Ligon; student Draughan's Sch. Bus., 1956-57; m. Clovis Ely Mashburn, Aug. 1, 1941; 1 dau., Christie Lee. Posting clk. credit office Pfeifer's Dept. Store, Little Rock, 1939-42; bookkeeper, savs. teller Union Bank, Little Rock, 1944-56; exchange teller Republic Nat. Bank, Dallas, 1956-58; bookeeping supr. Union Nat. Bank, Little Rock, 1958-68, asst. cashier customer service dept., 1968—. Mem. Nat. Assn. Bank Women Inc. (publicity chmn. Ark. chpt. 1973-74), Am. Instn. Banking, Am. Bus. Women Assn. (pres. 1970-71, membership chmn. 1971-72, chpt. Woman of Year 1972-73), Ark. Bankers Assn. (bd. edn. 1971-72). Home: 209 Hiawatha Dr Little Rock AR 72205 Office: No 1 Union Nat Plaza Little Rock AR 72203

MASHBURN, MARIAN GRIFFIN, realtor, civic worker; b. Tallapoosa, Ga., June 13, 1919; d. Charter W. and Emma (MacDonald) Griffin; grad. U. Ala., 1942; m. John Blaine Mashburn, Oct. 24, 1942; 1 dau., Marsha Anita. Sales rep. W. C. and A. N. Miller Devel. Co., Washington, 1955-60; asso. realtor Belle Harris Realtor, Jacksonville, Fla., 1961-64, Stockton, Whatley, Davin & Co., 1964-69; owner firm Marian G. Mashburn, Realtor, 1970—. Publicity dir. Girl Scouts Am., Wilmington, N.C., 1953; bus. mgr. Jr. League Children's Theatre, Wilmington, 1954; docent Smithsonian Inst. Washington, 1955; mem. advt. staff Antique Show, Washington, 1959; mem. Jr. League Am., 1949. Recipient White House Youth Conf. award, 1959. Mem. Realtors Assn., Jacksonville Bd. Realtors. Home: 4613 Waverly Lane Jacksonville FL 32210 Office: 2000 Corporate Square Blvd Jacksonville FL 32216

MASON, AIMEE HUNNICUTT ROMBERGER (MRS. SAMUEL VENABLE MASON), educator; b. Atlanta, Nov. 3, 1918; d. Edwin William and Aimee Greenleaf (Hunnicutt) Romberger; B.A., Conn. Coll., 1940; postgrad. Emory U., 1946-48; M.A., Stetson U., 1968; m. Samuel Venable Mason, Aug. 16, 1941; children—Olivia Elizabeth (Mrs. James Butcher), Christopher Leeds. Jr. exec., merchandising G. Fox & Co., Hartford, Conn., 1940-41; air traffic controller CAA, Atlanta, 1942; partner Coronado Concrete Products, New Smyrna Beach, Fla., 1953—; adj. faculty Valencia Jr. Coll., Orlando, Fla., 1969; instr. philosophy and humanities Seminole Jr. Coll., Sanford, 1969—. Area cons. A.R.C., 1947-50; del. Nat. Red Cross, Washington, 1949; founding mem. St. Joseph Hosp. Aux., Atlanta, 1942-43; v.p., treas. P.T.A., New Smyrna Beach, 1955-60. Bd. dirs. Atlanta Symphony Orch., Fla. Symphony Orch., 1954-59. Served to lt. USCGR, 1943-46. Recipient award in graphics Nat. Assn. Women Artists, 1939, 41, Golden Hatter award Stetson U., 1973. Mem. Am. Assn. U. Profs., Am. Assn. U. Women (founding mem. New Smyrna Beach), Fla. Assn. Community Colls. Home: 2103 Ocean Dr New Smyrna Beach FL 32069 Office: Seminole Junior College Sanford FL 32771

MASON, ANNA KATHLEEN GALBREATH (MRS. CLARENCE E. MASON JR.), banker; b. Tulsa, Sept. 16, 1923; d. George Francis and Nelle Charleen (Hogan) Galbreath; grad. high sch.; m. Clarence E. Mason, Jr., Aug. 15, 1949; 1 dau., Frances Patricia (Mrs. Anthony Dando). With 1st City Nat. Bank, Houston, 1952-55; with Highland Village State Bank, Houston, 1957—, v.p. 1968—. Committeeman Houston Livestock Show and Rodeo, 1962—; pres. Houston women's div. Nat. Jewish Hosp. and Research Center, Denver, 1971-73; co-chmn. Rosewood Hosp. Fund, 1971-72; active fund raising projects Alley Theatre, 1972—. Mem. Nat. Assn. Bank Women, Spain and Tex. Soc. (trustee 1969—). Club: National A (Houston). Home: Rural Route 1 Box 340AK Pearland TX 77581 Office: PO Box 22205 Houston TX 77027

MASON, ARETHA HAMMOND (MRS. JAMES FREDERICK MASON), occupational therapist; b. Alma, Mich., July 24, 1925; d. Ernest Sylvester and Pearl Hammond (Van Core) Hammond; student Alma Coll., 1943-45; B.S., Western Mich. U., 1948; m. James Frederick Mason, Dec. 21, 1950; children—Constance Lynn, Donald James. Staff, VA Hosp., Bath, N.Y., 1948-50; chief occupational therapy Cerebral Palsy Assn., Miami, Fla., 1951-52; dir. Crippled Children Soc., Miami, 1952-53; staff therapist VA Hosp., Coral Gables, 1953-54; spl. edn. tech. Lincoln Elementary Sch., Owosso, Mich., 1958-59; therapist, substitute tchr. Sarasota (Fla.) Pub. Schs., Happiness House Rehab. Clinic, Sarasota, 1959-65; pvt. practice occupational therapy in area neurol. disfunction, Sarasota, 1965-67; occupational therapy cons. Hillhaven Nursing Homes, Sarasota and Venice, Fla., 1968—. State rep. occupational therapy Dept. Health Edn. and Welfare and Am. Nursing Home Assn. for program improvement and guidelines activity programs in nursing home facilities. Mem. Am. (chmn. publicity and recruitment 1970-71), Fla. (chmn. publicity and recruitment 1970-71, mem. nominating bd. 1971-72) occupational therapy assns., Am. Assn. U. Women (chmn. scholarship fund raising 1972-73, co-chmn. state conv. 1972-73), Sigma Philo. Conglist. (mem. ch. bd.). Address: 3172 Espanola Dr Sarasota FL 33580

MASON, BARBARA HUTCHINS (MRS. DANIEL JOSEPH MASON), advt. co. exec.; b. Auburn, Ga., Jan. 14, 1941; d. Albert Grady and Sammie Lillian (Parks) Hutchins; student Truett-McConnell Coll., 1959-60; m. Daniel Joseph Mason, Sept. 24, 1960; children—Steven Joseph, Janet Michelle. Sec. Nat. Lead Co., Atlanta, 1960-64; asst. account exec. Tucker Wayne & Co., Atlanta, 1964-68, account exec., 1968—. Home: Parks Mill Road Auburn GA 30203 Office: 2700 Peachtree Center Bldg Atlanta GA 30303

MASON, DRUSILA MARK (MRS. JOHN MASON), bus. cons.; b. Duluth, Minn., May 22, 1925; d. James Vincent and Mary (Mazzi) Mark; student pub. schs.; m. John R. Mason, Mar. 1, 1946; children—Mark Dale, John Roger, Pamela Ann, Sandra Jean. Office mgr. Mason Hayes & Co., Detroit Lakes, Minn., 1953—; v.p., dir. Gabor Trucking, Inc.; sec. N.W. Securities, Inc., 1960—; v.p., dir. Wheatland Grain & Trucking, Inc., 1963—; sec., dir. Jondru, Inc., 1963—; sec., dir. Profl. Properties, Inc., Detroit Lakes, 1971—. Charter mem. St Mary's Hosp. Aux.; mem. Sr. Citizens Council on Aging, Detroit Lakes, 1967-73; chmn. Home Delivered Meals, 1972—. Mem. Women's Div. C. of C. (pres. 1966-68), Cath. Daus. Am. (grand regent, charter mem.), V.F.W. Aux., Minn., Detroit Lakes (pres. 1959) women's golf assns., Minn. Soc. C.P.A's Wives Club, Internat. Platform Assn. Republican. Roman Catholic. Eagles Aux. (pres. 1971-72), Elkette (pres. 1971-73). Home: 302 Langford St Detroit Lakes MN 56501 Office: 1148 Washington Av Detroit Lakes MN 56501

MASON, EDA NANCY (MRS. WILLIAM DANIEL MASON), librarian; b. N.Y.C., Feb. 2, 1932; d. Abraham W. and Lillian S. (Saperstein) Eisen; student Goddard Coll., 1949-51; B.A., U. Denver, 1962, M.A., 1963; m. William Daniel Mason, Dec. 21, 1950; children—Ruth Lee, Lawrence William. Librarian grad. sch. internat. studies and social sci. found. U. Denver, 1963-69, adminstrv. asst. to dir. libraries, 1969-70, acting asst. dir. pub. services, 1970, asso. dir. pub. services, 1971—, asso. prof., 1970—; tchr. course Grad. Sch. Librarianship, 1965-69; cons. gerontology pub. library field, 1973. Recipient grad. asst. fellowship Communications Dept. U. Denver, 1963. Mem. A.L.A., Phi Beta Kappa (chpt. sec. 1967-69). Club: Sierra (San Francisco). Home: 429 Salem St Aurora CO 80011 Office: U Denver Penrose Library Denver CO 80210

MASON, FRANCES LILIAN, editor; b. Atlanta; d. James Clifford and Lily Jackson (Stier) Mason; B.A., U. Cal. at Berkeley, 1923. Reporter, Monterey (Cal.) Peninsula Daily Herald, 1926-27, Paris (France) Herald, 1929-30, Paris Bur.-N.Y. Herald Tribune, 1936-37; editorial asst., financial reporter Phoenix News Bur., N.Y.C., 1927-29, 30-36; editor govt. publs., Washington, 1936-37; researcher Mary Margaret McBride Radio Program, WOR, N.Y.C., 1937-40; with pub. relations dept. United China Relief, N.Y.C., 1941-43, United War Fund, N.Y.C., 1943-44; pub. relations dir., adminstrv. asst. to Gover Whalen, Civil Def. Vol. Orgn., N.Y.C., 1944-45; account exec., writer Reuel Estill & Co., N.Y.C., 1945-54; pub. relations writer Nat. Salvation Army, N.Y.C., 1945-47, Am. Mus. Natural History, N.Y.C., 1947-49, N.Y. Pub. Library, N.Y.C., 1949-50, YWCA, N.Y.C., 1950-52, Community Chest, Stamford, Conn., 1952-53; fund raiser Psychiat. Clinic for Children, Stamford, Mid-Fairfield County Youth Mus., Westport, Conn., Stamford Mus. and Nature Center, Fairfield County Council Alcoholism, Westport, Conn., 1954-64; pub. relations dir. Girls Clubs Am., Inc., N.Y.C., 1964-69, editor Newsletter, 1969-74. Home: 275 Rockrimmon Rd Stamford CT 06903

MASON, JANE ADDAMS, lawyer; b. Chgo., Dec. 28, 1938; d. Herman Charles and Beryl Imogene (Troxell) Mason; student U. Mich., 1956-57, U. Laval, 1956-57; B.A., U. Wash., 1960, LL.B., 1963. Admitted to Wash. bar, 1964, practice in Seattle, 1964-65, Olympia, 1965-70, Bellingham, 1970—; asso. firm Jonson and Jonson, attys., 1964-65; asst. atty. gen. Office of Washington State Atty. Gen., 1965-70; mem. firm Davis and Mason, 1970-71; pros. atty. Whatcom County, Bellingham, 1971—. Mem. Am., Wash. State bar assns., Nat. Dist. Attys. Assn., Wash. State Pros. Attys. Assn., YWCA. Democrat. Club: Soroptimist. Home: 521 West Indiana Av Bellingham WA 98225 Office: 311 Grand St Bellingham WA 98225

MASON, JIMILU, sculptor; b. Las Cruces, N.M., Oct. 19, 1930; d. Lowell Blake and Rose (d'Amore) Mason; A.A., Am. U., 1951; A.B., George Washington U., 1953. One woman show Potters House Gallery; 1962; exhibited group shows Smithsonian Instn., Washington, 1953, 56, Corcoran Gallery, Washington, 1952, 53, 57, 62, Pa. Acad. Fine Art, Phila., 1956, Detroit Mus. Fine Art, 1957, Arts Club Washington, 1957, Potter's House Gallery, Washington, 1957; represented in permanent collections Colo. State Capitol, Denver, U.S. Supreme Ct., Bklyn. Inst. Tech., Consumer's Coop. Assn. Bldg., Kansas City, Mo., S.C. Johnson & Son, Inc., Racine, Wis., S.C. Johnson & Son, Ltd., London, Eng., YMCA, Racine, Nat. Portrait Gallery, U.S. Capitol, Washington, also numerous pvt. collections; executed stained glass trilon meml. to Alma White, Denver, 1962; works include bronze busts of numerous prominent U.S. govt. figures; executed bust of Pres. Lyndon B. Johnson, 1964; 8 foot bronze figure of Pres. Johnson, for Johnson City, Tex.; bust Dag Hammarskjold, 1969, Constatino Brumidi, U.S. Capitol, Fred Vinson, Chief Justice Supreme Ct.; executed stainless steel circle fountain Columbia Shopping Mall, Columbia, Md. (Dept. Housing and Urban Devel. award 1972), 1971, stained glass window St. Albans Sch., Washington, 1971. Mgr., dir. Heritage Art and Framing, Inc., Alexandria, Va., 1963-73; dir. Potters House Gallery, 1960-67. Mem. Nat. Council Art, 1967-72. Mem. bd. overseers Dag Hammarskjold Coll., Washington. Recipient hon. mention for bronze of Peter Vaghi, Corcoran Art Gallery, 1962; Alumna award George Washington U., 1971. Mem. Artists Equity. Mem. Ch. of Saviour. Office: 415 Jefferson St Alexandria VA 22314

MASON, LUCILE, orgn. exec.; b. Montclair, N.J., Aug. 1, 1925; d. Mayne Seguine and Rachel (Entorf) Mason; A.B., Smith Coll., 1947; M.A., N.Y. U., 1968. Asst. script editor, promotion writer ABC, N.Y.C., 1949-50, asst. TV dir., 1950-51; asst. casting dir. prodn. supr. Compton Advt., Inc., N.Y.C., 1951-56, casting dir., music rec. dir., dept. head, 1956-65; conf. mgr. Camp Fire Girls, Inc., N.Y.C., 1965-66; exec. dir. Assn. Jr. Leagues Am., Inc., N.Y.C., 1966-68; cons. coordinator also spl. asst. to nat. exec. dir. Girl Scouts U.S.A. 1969, dir. pub. affairs div., 1969-71; dir. pub. relations YWCA of City N.Y., 1971-73; dir. community relations and devel. Girl Scout council Greater N.Y., 1973—; lectr. Am. Theatre Wing, N.Y.C., 1951-58. Mem. theatre com. Smith Coll., 1962-74, chmn. com., 1969-74, mem. bd. counselors, 1964—, mem. bd. counselors exec. com., 1969-74. Mem. Am. Women in Radio and Television (pres. N.Y.C. chpt. 1958-59, dir. 1973—, eastern membership chmn. 1959-61; co-chmn. internat. broadcasters program 1964, vice chmn. 14th ann. nat. conv. 1965), Am. Assn. U. Women, Nat. Acad TV Arts Scis., Internat. Platform Assn., Pub. Relations Soc. Am., Internat. Communication Assn., Community Agys. Pub. Relations Assn. (v.p. membership 1974-75), Assn. Fund Raising Dirs., Alpha Kappa Delta, Pi Lambda Theta, Kappa Delta Pi. Republican. Club: Smith College of N.Y. Home: 142 N Mountain Av Montclair NJ 07042 Office: 335 E 46th St New York City NY 10017

MASON, MARIE, psychologist, educator, coll. dean; b. Swan Quarter, N.C., July 29, 1916; d. Joseph Redden and Ina (Bennett) Mason; R.N., Parkview Hosp. Sch. Nursing, 1937; A.A., Campbell Coll., 1941; A.B., Meredith Coll., 1947; M.A., U. Ky., 1949, Ph.D., 1966; div. Dir. nursing edn. Good Samaritan Hosp., Lexington, Ky., 1952-54, Central Bapt. Hosp., Lexington, 1954-56; dir. nursing edn. and nursing service Ky. Bapt. Hosp., 1956-63; teaching fellow, asst. prof. counselor edn. U. Ky., Lexington, 1966-69; dean students, asso. prof. psychology Meredith Coll., Raleigh, N.C., 1969—. Cons. R.N. workshops, 1969. Served with Nurse Corps, AUS, 1943-46. Decorated Bronze Star. Mem. Am. Personnel and Guidance Assn., Am., So. coll. personnel assns., Nat. Vocational and Guidance Assn., N.C. Psychol. Assn., N.C. Assn. Women Deans, Am. Assn. U. Women, Ky. Nurses Assn. (dir.), Kappa Delta Phi, Beta Sigma Phi (pres. 1966-69). Home: 1108 Millbrook Rd Raleigh NC 27609

MASON, (MARY) THOMASINE GRAYSON (MRS. E. FLEMING MASON), lawyer; b. Summerton, S.C., Nov. 7, 1918; d. James Fulton and Anne (Gentry) Grayson; A.B., U. S.C., 1938, LL.B., 1942; m. Edgar Fleming Mason, June 30, 1939. Engaged in recruiting and personnel work U.S. Civil Service Commn., Ga., also S.C., World War II; admitted to S.C. bar, 1941, since practiced in Manning; asso. Grayson-Elliott, Inc., 1952-63, sec. bd. dirs., 1947-73; trial atty. civil div. U.S. Dept. Justice, Washington, 1968-70; adminstrv. law judge Bur. Hearings and Appeals, Social Security Adminstrn., Dept. Health, Edn. and Welfare; mem. S.C. Senate, 1966-68. Dist. vice chmn. A.R.C., 1955-56; chmn. Tb seals dr., 1965-67. Del. Democratic nat. conv., 1960. Bd. dirs. Palmetto Girls State; trustee Clarendon Meml. Hosp. Mem. Clarendon County Farm Bur., Clarendon County C. of C., D.A.R., Am. Legion Aux. (v.p. S.C. dept.), S.C. Bar Assn. (v.p. 3d jud. circuit 1965-67), S.C. State Bar, Am. Trial Lawyers Assn., Fed., Am. bar assns., Bus. and Profl. Women's Club, Alpha Delta Pi. Clubs: Booster, Garden (Summerton). Home: Summerton SC 29148 Office: Middleburg Plaza Suite 221 2712 Middleburg Dr Columbia SC 29204

MASON, RUTH E., social worker; b. Lawrence, Kan., June 25, 1919; d. Horace Mann and Grace (Connel) Mason; A.B., U. Kan., 1942; M.S.S.A., Western Res. U., 1948. Med. social worker Benjamin Rose Inst., Cleve., 1948-53, Benjamin Rose Hosp., Cleve., 1953-65; dir. social work Chronic Illness Center, Cuyahoga County, Cleve., 1965-70; dir. social work Cleve. Clinic Hosp., 1970—. Lectr. Sch. Applied Social Sci., Case Western Res. U., spring 1968, summer 1969. Mem. Cleve. Welfare Fedn. Voluntary Health Agy. Com., 1968-71; mem. Path Pub. Housing Com., 1969-71. Mem. Nat. Assn. Social Workers, Acad. Certified Social Workers, Am. Soc. Hosp. Social Work Dirs., N.E. Ohio Soc. Hosp. Social Work Dirs. (chmn. 1972-73), Phi Beta Kappa. Home: 2252 Newbury Dr Cleveland OH 44112 Office: 9500 Euclid Av Cleveland OH 44106

MASON, VIRGINIA LILLY (MRS. JAMES MASON), civic worker; b. Chgo., Feb. 25, 1908; d. Paul Foster and Ione J. (McBroom) Lilly; grad. Chgo. Tchrs. Coll., 1927; student U. Chgo.; m. James Mason, Oct. 17, 1931; children—Eleanor (Mrs. Carl C. Hanke, Jr.), Frances Virginia (Mrs. Joel P. Smith), John Paul. Ednl. cons. Carson Pirie Scott & Co., Chgo., 1963-73; asst. to dir. DuPage County Nutrition Program, 1974—. Mem. staff George Williams Coll. Camp. Pres., Citizen's Sch. Com. Chgo., 1953-57; chmn. edn. com. Chgo. Commn. Human Relations, 1952-70; mem. Nat. Citizen's Council Better Schs., 1956-60; vice chmn. Ill. Citizens Edn. Com., 1959-64; chmn. adv. bd. to urban youth program Chgo. Pub. Schs., 1964-70, chmn. distributive edn. adv. com., 1969—, pres. distributive edn. adv. council, 1970—. Chmn. sch. and child com. Mayor's Commn. on Youth Welfare, 1956-60. Mem. bd. mgrs. Met. Chgo., YMCA, 1955-71, mem. bd. Ill. area, 1955-60, mem. nat. council, 1958-64; world service chmn. S.W. Suburban YMCA, Chgo., 1964; mem. Nat. Citizens Com. for Support Pub. Schs.; mem. bd. Girl Scouts Chgo., 1958-60; bd. dirs. Ill. Distributive Edn. Found.; trustee Garrett Theol. Sem., 1970-74. Recipient award Chgo. Commn. Human Relations, 1950; award Citizens Schs. Com., 1957, Met. Chgo. YMCA, 1967. Home: 442 S Monroe St Hinsdale IL 60521

MASOUREDIS, MARION MYKYTEW (MRS. S. P. MASOUREDIS), physician, educator; b. Detroit, Jan. 16, 1924; d. John and Anna (Hedio) Mykytew; B.S., Wayne U., Detroit, 1945; M.D., U. Mich., 1946; M.P.H. (Thomas Parron fellow), U. Pitts., 1957; m. S. P. Masouredis, Oct. 2, 1943; children—Claudia, Linus. Clinician, Oakland (Cal.) Health Dept., 1950-53; chief Bur. Family Services, Oakland Health Dept., 1953-55; adminstrv. asst. to chief med. services Allegheny County Health Dept., 1957-59, chief disease control, 1959; dist. health officer San Francisco Health Dept., 1961-65; lectr. dept. preventive medicine U. Cal. Med. Sch., San Francisco, 1959-67; asst. dean, asso. coordinator regional med. program Marquette U. Sch. Medicine, Milw., 1967-69, asst. prof. preventive medicine, 1967-69; asso. coordinator continuing med. edn., regional med. program U. Cal. at San Diego, La Jolla, 1969—. Mem. quality med. care com. Comprehensive Health Planning Assn. San Diego, 1972—. Active A.R.C., United Community Fund; chmn. personnel com., bd. dirs. San Francisco Planned Parenthood Assn., 1963-65. Diplomate Am. Bd. Preventive Medicine. Fellow Am. Coll. Preventive Medicine; mem. Am. Pub. Health Assn., A.A.A.S. Home: 2745 Inverness Ct La Jolla CA 92037

MASSENBURG, KATHERINE BLACK, govt. ofcl.; b. Balt., July 1, 1921; d. Walter Evan and Margaret Lee (Rice) Black; B.A., Randolph-Macon Woman's Coll., 1943; postgrad. Johns Hopkins, 1943-44; m. George Y. Massenburg, Jr., Nov. 25, 1944 (div. May 1956); children—George Yellott III, Walter Black. Tchr. pub. schs., 1944-45; law clk., librarian firm Marshall, All, Carey & Doub, 1945-47; vol. polit. and community worker, 1947-60; tech. officer 7th Congl. Dist., Md. 1960 Census; adminstrv. asst. to mayor, 1965-67; confidential asst. to mem. Renegotiation Bd., Washington, 1969—. Co-chmn. RMWC Phila. Devel. Fund drive, 1956; pres. Woman's Soc. Ardmore Bapt. Ch., 1955-57; mem. govtl. affairs com. Md. Assn. Retarded Children, 1963-72, chmn., 1963-64; mem. legislative com., bd. dirs. Md. Assn. for Mental Health, 1963-72; active P.T.A. exec. com. and Civic Assn.; den mother Cub Scouts, 1954-58; mem. United Christian Citizens, 1960-67, Citizens Planning and Housing Assn., 1960—, League Women Voters, 1954—, Balt. City Community Relations Commn., 1963-65; chmn. Md. Commn. on Status of Women, 1968-70; mem. Presdl. Task Force on Women's Rights and Responsibilities, 1969; mem. Census Adv. Com. on Privacy and Confidentiality Dept. Commerce, 1972—. Republican precinct worker, 1950-70; sec. Md. Fedn. Young Reps., 1950-53, vice chmn., 1957-58; co-chmn. campaign com. Ind. Reps., Haverford Twp. Pa., 1956-57; chmn. Baltimore City Neighbor-to-Neighbor drive, 1958; 2d v.p. Md. Fedn. Rep. Women, 1959-63, pres., 1963-64; mem. Rep. State Central Com., 1962-66; chmn. 3d legis. dist. com., 1962-66; del. Rep. Nat. Conv., San Francisco, 1964, also mem. platform com.; mem. Rep. Nat. Com. from Md., 1964-72; del. Rep. Nat. Conv., Miami, 1968, also mem. platform com.; precinct chmn. 72d precinct 27th ward Balt., 1957-70. Mem. N.A.A.C.P., Urban League, Phi Beta Kappa, Tau Kappa Alpha, Pi Beta Phi. Baptist (mem. Christian edn. com. 1957-64, area leader for ch. 1957-69; tchr. Sunday sch. 1947-65). Home: 5608 Purlington Way Baltimore MD 21212 Office: 2000 M St NW Washington DC 20446

MASSETT, ELIZABETH VOLLMER, extension home economist; b. Syracuse, N.Y., July 26, 1921; d. Harry Herman and Mildred Amelia (Schuyler) Collmer; B.S., Syracuse U., 1944, postgrad., 1969—; m. Robert Phillip Massett, June 30, 1951; 1 dau., Jean Lynette. With Coop. Extension Assn. Onandaga County, various locations, 1944—, extension specialist food and nutrition, Cornell U., Ithaca, N.Y., 1947-52, extension home economist, Syracuse, 1958—. Supt. demonstration kitchen N.Y. State Fair, 1957-58. Program chmn. P.T.A., Cicero, 1959-60, pres., 1961, 62. Recipient life membership award P.T.A., 1963. Mem. Nat. Assn. Extension Home Economists (Distinguished Service award, 1964), N.Y. State Assn. Extension Home Economists (pres. 1966, 67), N.Y. State, Am. home econs. assns. Home: Box 127 Cicero NY 13039 Office: 1050 W Genesee St Syracuse NY 13202

MASSETTO, SANDRA LYNNE, lawyer; b. Phoenix, Sept. 4, 1945; d. John and Ruby Opal (Sanders) Massetto; B.A. in History and Oriental Studies, U. Ariz., 1967, M.A. in Oriental Studies, 1968; J.D., Ariz. State U., 1971. Admitted to Ariz. bar, 1971; asso. Freederick E. Kallof, Phoenix, 1971—. Vol. KAET, Tempe, 19—. Vice pres. State Ariz. Young Dems., 1971-72; nat. com. woman Dem. Party, 1972-73; vice chmn. Maricopa Dem. Party, 1970-72. Research Asst. grantee Coll. Law, 1970-71. Mem. Ariz. Women's Polit. Caucus, Ariz., Maricopa Bar assns., Ariz. State U. Alumni Assn. (dir. 1974-75), Alpha Delta Pi. Home: 5721 N 19th Dr Phoenix AZ 85015 Office: 100 W Clarendon St Phoenix AZ 85013

MASSEY, DOROTHY BUTLER (MRS. GUY M. MASSEY), accountant; b. LaFayette, Ga.; d. R. Maihue and Cora (Sisemore) Butler; student U. Chattanooga, 1949; L.B., Atlanta Law Sch., 1957, LL.M., 1958; B.B.A., Ga. State Coll., 1966; m. Guy M. Massey, Feb. 21, 1953. Accountant Gulf Oil Corp., Chattanooga, 1944-53, Crawford and Porter, Atlanta, 1953-54; accountant Baker Audio Assos., 1955-70, sec.-treas., 1955-70, also dir.; accountant Glenkaron Assos., Inc., 1955-68, sec.-treas., 1957-68; pres. Massey Co., 1971—; dir.; real estate agt. Shotz Assos. Mem. Am. Soc. Women Accountants (dir.), Women in Constrn., Notaries Pub. Assn., Bus. Profl. Women, Internat. Platform Assn., Kappa Delta. Home: 1544 Peachtree Battle Av NW Atlanta GA 30327

MASSEY, LOUISE HASH (MRS. KENNETH CARVER MASSEY), educator; b. Jacksboro, Tex., Aug. 18, 1912; d. John and Lydia (Gifford) Hash; B.A., Baylor U., 1936; M.R.E., Southwestern Bapt. Theol. Sem., 1940; postgrad. Northwestern U., 1944, Columbia, 1953; m. Kenneth Carver Massey, Nov. 25, 1948. Tchr. elementary sch., Salt Gap, Tex., 1932-35, Mildred, Tex., 1936-37; Christian ednl. dir. N. Shore Bapt. Ch., Chgo., 1939-42; faculty Baylor U., Waco, Tex., 1943-48; tchr. English, speech and drama Lambertville (N.J.) High Sch. (now South Hunterdon Regional High Sch.), 1950—, chmn. English dept., 1950-73. Dir. workshops in religious drama Am. Bapt. Assembly, Green Lake, Wis., 1948-58; dir. drama workshops Nat. Mission Conf., Silver Bay, N.Y., 1959-61; chmn. drama com. N.J. Bapts., 1956-65; dir. Nat. Bapt. Women's Pageant, Phila., 1957; mem. drama com. Nat. Drama Commn., Nat. Council Chs. Am., 1958-68. Mem. Nat., N.J., Hunterdon County, South Hunterdon Regional High Sch. edn. assns., Nat. Council Tchrs. English, Internat. Platform Assn., Hist. Soc. Lambertville, Delta Kappa Gamma. Mem. Order eastern Star. Club: Women's Federated (pres. Lambertville 1968-70). Home: 42 York St Lambertville NJ 08530

MASSEY, MARY OLIVE, home economist; b. Chester, Ga., Oct. 24, 1922; d. Wilbon Franklin and Mary Augusta (Burch) Massey; B.S., Ga. Coll., 1943; postgrad. U. Ga., 1967-68. Dist. home economist Ga. Power Co., Dublin, 1943-46, Jonesboro, Ga., 1946-51, home improvement specialist, Atlanta, 1951-52, home equipment specialist, 1952-59, home service supr., Athens, Ga., 1959—. Bd. dirs. Hope Haven Sch. for Retarded Children, sec., 1971-73; bd. dirs. Community Chest, 1971-72. Mem. Ga. Home Econs. Assn. (pres. 1966-68), Home Economists in Bus. (chmn. elect 1958-59), Residence Lighting Forum (program chmn. 1958-59), Pres. Council Athens (treas. 1964-65), Ga. Power Womans Club Athens (parliamentarian 1971-73), Entre Nous Club of YWCA (pres. 1969-70), Pilot Club Internat. (pres. Athens 1962-63, dist. community service chmn. 1972-73). Baptist. Home: 510 Riverhill Dr at Beechwood Dr Athens GA 30601 Office: 1001 Prince Av Athens GA 30601

MASSEY, NEVELLA HARRIS (MRS. JAMES WILLARD MASSEY), dietitian; b. Kentwood, La., Mar. 18, 1919; d. James Franklin and Stella Ernestine (Tycer) Harris, Sr.; B.S., Miss. State Coll. for Women, 1941; m. James Daniel Snyder, Sr., Sept. 24, 1950; children—Maude June, James Daniel, Ann Lynn; m. 2d, James Willard Massey, Mar. 10, 1962. Dietitic intern Montefiore Hosp., N.Y.C., 1941-42; with Civil Service, 1942-43; therapeutic, clin. and teaching dietitian, Med. Center, Columbus, Ga., 1956-64; dietitian hosps. Meridian, Miss., 1964-72; dietary cons. for east Miss., 1964-72; dietitian F.G. Riley Meml. Hosp., Meridian, 1968—; cons. for nursing homes and small hosps. in Meridian area. Served to capt. Dietetic Corps, AUS, 1943-52. Decorated Bronze star (2). Named Woman of the Year, Am. Bus. Women's Assn., 1972. Mem. Am. Dietitic Assn., Miss. State Coll. for Women Alumni Assn., Southeastern Hosp. Conf. for Dietitians, Am. Bus. Women's Assn., Phi Upsilon Omicron, Gamma Sigma Epsilon. Baptist. Club: Altrusa (Meridian). Home: 2328 33d Av Meridian MS 39301 Office: 1102 21st Av Meridian MS 39301

MASSEY, SUE ELLEN, physician; b. Smithfield, N.C., Sept. 25, 1939; d. Charlie Wilbert and Elsie Mae (Stallings) Massey; A.B. in Chemistry, Duke, 1961; M.D., U. N.C., 1965; m. Edward T. Kirkpatrick, Oct. 1968; 1 son, Andrew T. Intern Upstate Med. Center, Syracuse, N.Y., 1965-66; resident in obstetrics and gynecology Stanford, 1966-69; practice medicine specializing in obstetrics and gynecology; cons. Palo Alto (Cal.) Vet.'s Hosp., 1969-72; obstetrician-gynecologist Alviso (Cal.) Family Health Center, 1969-71; with Stanford U. Hosp., 1972—. Diplomate Am. Bd. Obstetrics and Gynecology; mem. Peninsula Obstet.-Gynecol. Soc., Santa Clara County Med. Soc. Home: 346 Johnson Av Los Gatos CA 95030 Office: Cowell Student Health Stanford CA 94035

MASSIAS, JEANNETTE BERTHE, assn. exec.; b. Nice, France, June 3, 1919; d. Joseph and Elizabeth (MacLeod) Massias; grad. Nice Coll., France, 1939. Came to U.S., 1957. Exec. sec. Helicop-Air, Paris, France, 1949-57; adminstrv. asst. Nat. Bd. Med. Examiners, Phila., 1959-67, comptroller, 1967—. Served to capt. with Women Aux. Air force of Free French Army, 1940-46. Decorated Legion d'Honneur, Croix de Guerre with Palm, Medaille de la Resistance, Medaille de l'Aeronautique, Def. Medal (Eng.). Mem. Adminstrv. Mgmt. Soc. Home: 62-11 Drexelbrook Dr Drexel Hill PA 19026 Office: 3930 Chestnut St Philadelphia PA 19104

MASSIE, LYNEL COVINGTON (MRS. STANTON EDWARDS MASSIE, JR.), govt. ofcl., lawyer; b. Hazlehurst, Miss., Aug. 8, 1924; d. Walter Lynn and Nel (Robertson) Covington; grad. with honors Copiah-Lincoln Jr. Coll., 1943; student Jackson Sch. Law, 1955-58; m. Stanton Edwards Massie, Jr., July 6, 1967. Clk. Liberty Mut. Ins. Co., Jackson, Miss., 1948-51, officer supr., 1951-53, sales asst., 1953-58; admitted to Miss. bar, 1958, practiced in Jackson, 1958—; asso. firm Courtney and Echols, 1958-71; with Social Security Adminstrn., Dept. Health, Edn. and Welfare, Jackson, 1971—, adminstrv. law judge Bur. Hearings and Appeals, 1971-72, adminstrv. law judge in charge office, 1972—. Mem. Fed., Miss., Hinds County bar assns., Nat. Assn. Women's Lawyers, Quota Internat. (pres. 1962-63, dist. gov. 1966-67), Assn. Adminstrv. Law Judges, Bus. and Profl. Women's Club (dist. officer 1958-59). Home: 107 Cardinal Circle Brandon MS 39042 Office: 802N State St Executive Bldg Jackson MS 39201

MASSOTH, SISTER MARY COLETTA, hosp. adminstr.; b. Piqua, Kan.; d. William Joseph and Christine T. (Kipp) Massoth; R.N., St. John Hosp., St. Louis, 1949; B.S. in Nursing Edn., Incarnate Word Coll., San Antonia, 1950; M.S., Cath. U. Am., 1956. Joined order Religious Sisters of Mercy, 1942; supr. nursing service Mercy Hosp., Oklahoma City, 1950-51, dir. Sch. Nursing, 1951-55, hosp. adminstr., 1956-62, 66-68, exec. dir., 1968-71, pres., 1971—, pres. corp., chmn. gov. bd., 1956-62, 66-71. Speaker before numerous profl. groups. Mem. personal health services com. Oklahoma City Community Council Areawide Health Planning Orgn.; vice chmn. health facilities adv. council Okla. Bd. Health, 1970-71; mem. Gov.'s Task Force on Uterine Cancer, 1972—. Bd. dirs. St. Edward Mercy Hosp., Ft. Smith, Ark., 1972—, Archbishop Bergan Mercy Hosp., Omaha, 1972-74; adv. bd. Oklahoma City Tech. Inst. Recipient award Ark. League Nursing for Service to Nursing in Ark., 1962-66. Mem. Nat., Okla., Oklahoma City (dir.) leagues for nursing, Okla. Hosp. Assn. (trustee, recipient Appreciation award for service rendered 1956-62), Oklahoma County Heart Assn., Oklahoma City Area Hosp. Council (pres. 1961-62), Okla. Council on Alcoholism (recipient Extra Mile award 1961), Okla. Conf. Cath. Hosps. (pres. 1961-62, 73, trustee 1970), Oklahoma City C. of C., Am. Coll. Hosp. Adminstrs., A.R.C., Pi Gamma Mu, Theta Sigma Phi (named woman of the year in field of health Okla. City chpt. 1970). Address: Mercy Health Center 4300 W Memorial Rd Oklahoma City OK 73120

MASSOW, ROSALIND (MRS. NORTON LUGER), journalist; b. N.Y.C.; d. Morris and Ida (Kahn) Massow; B.A., Hunter Coll., 1945; m. Norton Luger, Jan. 31, 1959. Reporter, city desk, feature writer, ski, travel columns N.Y. Jour. Am., 1945-61; feature writer, women's editor Parade Publns., N.Y.C., 1961-71; free-lance writer. Mem. Gov.'s Com. on Minority Groups in News Media, 1968; mem. Women's Aux. Booth Meml. Hosp.; mem. Pres.'s Commn. on Status of Women, 1964. Recipient Front Page award, 1956, 60, 66; Pegasus award, 1966. Mem. Overseas Press Club (bd. govs. 1965-66, 71—), Newswomen's Club N.Y. (pres. 1965-66), Deadline Club, Travel Writers of N.Y., Am. Soc. Travel Writers, Silurians, Sigma Delta Chi. Home: 530 E 72d St New York City NY 10021 Office: 530 E 72d St New York City NY 10021

MASSY, PATRICIA GRAHAM BIBBS (MRS. RICHARD OUTRAM MASSY), social worker; b. Newbury, Eng., Mar 21, 1918; d. Oswald Graham and Dorothy (French) Bibbs; B.A., U. B.C., 1941, M.S.W., 1962; m. Richard Outram Massy, July 22, 1944; children—Patricia Lynn (Mrs. James Holmes), Julie Suzanne, Shaun Adele (Mrs. Bruce Brink). Came to U.S., 1963, naturalized, 1969. With B.C. Welfare Field Service, Vancouver, Kamloops, Abbottsford, 1942-44; social worker Brandon Welfare Dept., Man., Can., 1945; with Childrens Aid Soc., Vancouver, 1948-62; supr. Dept. Pub. Social Service, Los Angeles, 1963-70, staff devel. specialist-social work, 1970—. Mem. Am. Assn. U. Women (treas. 1970), Nat. Assn. Social Workers, Alpha Phi. Methodist. Home: 601 Acacia Lane West Covina CA 91791 Office: 3401 Rio Hondo Av El Monte CA 91731

MASTERS, BETTIE SUE SILER, educator, biochemist; b. Lexington, Va., June 13, 1937; d. Wendell Hamilton and Mildred Virginia (Cromer) Siler; B.S. in Chemistry, Roanoke Coll., 1959; Ph.D. in Biochemistry, Duke, 1963; m. Robert Sherman Masters, Aug. 6, 1960; children—Diane Elizabeth, Deborah Ann. Postdoctoral fellow Duke, 1963-66, advanced research fellow, 1966-68, asso. on faculty, 1967-68; mem. faculty U. Tex. Southwestern Med. Sch., Dallas, 1968—, asso. prof. biochemistry, 1972—. Am. Cancer Soc. fellow, 1963-65; fellow Am. Heart Assn., 1966-68, established investigator, 1968-73; NIH research grantee, 1970-78; Robert A. Welch Found. research grantee, 1971—. Mem. Am. Soc. Biol. Chemists, Am. Chem. Soc., A.A.A.S., Sigma Xi. Methodist. Author papers, abstracts. Reviewer Archives Biochemistry and Biophysics, others. Home: 4115 Deep Valley Dr Dallas TX 75234

MASTERS, LAURA LANE (MRS. EDGAR MORSMAN MASTERS), librarian; b. N.Y.C., July 23, 1941; d. Cedric Raymond and Alice (Lay) Lane; A.B., Lake Erie Coll., 1963; M.L.S., U. Cal., Berkeley, 1964; m. Edgar Morsman Masters, Apr. 28, 1973. Acquisitions librarian Harvard U., Fogg Art Mus., Fine Arts Library, 1964-67; humanities cataloger U. Minn., Wilson Library, Mpls., 1968-69; librarian Am. Heritage Pub. Co., N.Y.C., 1969—. Mem. A.L.A., Spl. Libraries Assn., Save the Redwoods League, South St. Seaport Assn., Sierra Club. Office: Am Heritage Pub Co 1221 6th Av New York City NY 10020

MASTERS, MARGARET LEE (MRS. JOSEPH H. MASTERS), pediatrician; b. Canton, China, Dec. 3, 1924; d. Shau Yan and Wah Ying (Yip) Lee; came to U.S., 1940, naturalized, 1949; A.A., William and Mary Coll., 1945; M.D., Med. Coll. Va., 1950; m. Joseph H. Masters, Aug. 27, 1947; children—Margo Dianne, David Joseph, Katherine Mildred. Intern French Hosp., San Francisco, 1950-51; resident pediatrics Children's Hosp., San Francisco, 1951-53; pediatrician 98th Gen. Hosp., U.S. Army, Germany, 1954-57; practice of medicine specializing in pediatrics, Sacremento, 1959—; mem. staff Sutter Community Hosp., Sacramento, asst. clin. prof. pediatrics U. Cal. at Davis, 1970—. Diplomate Am. Bd. Pediatrics. Fellow Am. Acad. Pediatrics; mem. Am., Cal. med. assns., Sacremento County Med. Soc., Sacramento Pediatric Soc. Address: 3937 Orangewood Dr Fair Oaks CA 95628

MASTERTON, DOROTHY GREEN (MRS. ALEXANDER ROBERT MASTERTON), constrn. co. exec.; b. Bklyn., Aug. 13, 1908; d. George William and Sarah Wright (Smith) Green; A.A., Packer Collegiate Inst., 1921-27; postgrad. Fordham U., 1928, Miss Conklins Sch., 1929; m. Alexander Robert Masterton, Aug. 14, 1931; children—Joan (Mrs. Elihu Edelson), Dona (Mrs. Paul Watkeys), Jule (Mrs. John Stengel). Vice pres. So. Contractors, Inc., Sarasota, Fla., 1963-68, pres., 1968—; v.p. Siesta Gardens, Inc., 1963-72, pres., 1972—; propr. Dorothy G. Masterton, Realtor, 1970—; owner Mchts. Exchange Service, Sarasota, 1959—. Vice chmn. Minimum Housing Appeals Bd., Sarasota County, Fla., 1970-71. Mem. Nat. Soc. Pub. Accountants, Sarasota Bd. Realtors. Episcopalian. Home: 3531 Central Av Sarasota FL 33580 Office: 5860 Midnight Pass Rd Sarasota FL 33581

MASTRI, ANGELINE ROSE, neuropathologist, educator; b. Rochester, N.Y., Aug. 9, 1933; d. Ralph and Jeanette (Finocchio) Mastri; B.A., Manhattanville Coll., 1955; M.D., State U. N.Y., 1959. Intern Upstate Med. Center, Syracuse, N.Y., 1959-60, resident, 1960-61; asso. neuropathology Columbia, N.Y., 1966-68, asst. prof. neuropathology, 1968-69; asst. prof. neurology U. Minn., Mpls., 1969-73, asso. prof., 1973—. Diplomate Am. Bd. Pathology. Mem. Am. Assn. Neuropathologists, Am. Acad. Neurology, Assn. for Research in Nervous and Mental Diseases, Alpha Omega Alpha. Contbr. articles on neuropathology to med. jours. Home: 1770 Bryant Av S Minneapolis MN 55403 Office: Box 275 Dept of Neurology Univ of Minnesota Hospitals Minneapolis MN 55455

MASTROTTO, LILLIAN V(ERA), educator; b. Birmingham, Ala.; d. Angelo B. and Stella (Corallo) Mastrotto; B.S., U. Pitts., 1936, M.Ed., 1939; postgrad. State U. Pa., U. Chgo., Cornell U., 1954-55, 56-57. Tchr. New Kensington (Pa.) Pub. Sch., 1938-45; supr. Slippery Rock (Pa.) State Tchrs. Coll., 1945-47; prof. edn. State Tchrs. Coll., Millersville, Pa., 1947-53; elementary supr., psychologist, reading coordinator Dryden and Groton Central Schs., Tompkins County, N.Y., 1953-54; asst. prof. edn. Cornell U., 1953-54, summers 1955, 56, research asso. 1955-56; Ford Found. for Advancement Edn. teaching fellow, 1954-55, 56-57; reading coordinator First Supervisory Dist., Clinton County, N.Y., 1957-63; reading specialist Byram Hills Central Schs., Armonk, N.Y., 1963—, master tchr., 1971—; reading cons. Arrow Book Club Scholastic Mags., N.Y.C., 1957-72, Wonder Books, 1961-72; dir. reading clinic for children, Millersville, Cornell U.; co-dir. Reading Alert Title I Program Westchester County, Summer 1972. Former mem. council camp dir. Girl Scouts. Mem. Am. Psychol. Assn., N.E.A., N.Y. State Tchrs. Assns., Assn. Supervision and Curriculum Devel., Assn. Student Teaching, Internat. Reading Assn., Nat. Elementary Prins. Assn., Am. Assn. U. Women, Assn. for Help of Retarded Children, Assn. Higher Edn., Bus. and Profl. Women's Club, Nat. Council Tchrs. English, Armonk Little Theater Group, Pi Lambda Theta, Delta Kappa Gamma. Author books on reading, also articles in field. Home: 2 Byram Brook Pl Armonk NY 10504

MATARAZZO, RUTH GADBOIS (MRS. JOSEPH D. MATARAZZO), educator; b. New London, Conn., Nov. 9, 1926; d. John Stuart and Elizabeth (Wood) Gadbois; A.B., Brown U., 1948; M.A., Washington U., 1952, Ph.D., 1955; m. Joseph D. Matarazzo, Mar. 26, 1949; children—Harris Starr, Elizabeth Wood, Sara Holt. Research fellow pediatrics Washington U. Sch. Medicine, 1954-55; research fellow psychology Harvard U. Sch. Medicine, 1955-57; asst. prof. med. psychology U. Ore. Med. Sch., 1957-63, asso. prof., 1963-68, prof., 1968—. Bd. dirs. Portland Opera Assn., sec., 1960-63; bd. dirs. Community Child Guidance Clinic, Mental Health Assn. Ore., Portland Met. Mental Health Assn. Diplomate Am. Bd. Examiners in Profl. Psychology. Fellow Am. Psychol. Assn.; mem. Western, Ore. (past sec.-treas.), Portland (past pres.) psychol. assns., Am. Assn. U. Profs., A.A.A.S., Ore. Soc. Mayflower Descs. (bd. assts. 1966-68, treas. 1968-70, dep. gov. 1972-74, gov. 1974—), Sigma Xi. Editorial bd. Women, An Annual, 1974—. Contbr. articles to profl. jours. Home: 1934 SW Vista Av Portland OR 97201

MATASOVIC, STELLA (MRS. JOHN L. MATASOVIC), mech. products co. exec., ranch exec.; b. Lovington, Ill., July 19, 1916; d. Charles K. and Agnes (Nickus) Butkauskas; B.E., Ill. State Normal U., 1935; m. John L. Matasovic, Feb. 26, 1938; children—Linda Swiercinsky, Marilyn. Tchr. elementary sch., Pana, Ill., 1935-37; partner OXO Welding Equipment Co., New Lenox, Ill., 1944—; partner Universal Welding Supply Co., New Lenox, Ill., 1944—; mgr. Oxo Hereford ranches, Mokena, Ill., 1952—. Mem. Nat. Welding Supply Assn., New Lenox C. of C. (sec. 1969), Am. Nat. Cattlemen's Assn., Ill., Colo. hereford assns., Am. Hereford Aux. (pres. 1969-70), Ill. Beef Aux. Home: Rural Route 1 Mokena IL 60448 Office: Cedar and Oak Sts New Lenox IL 60451

MATER, JEAN (MRS. MILTON H. MATER), engring. co. exec.; b. N.Y.C., June 18, 1916; M.A., Columbia, 1940; Ph.D., Ore. State U., 1954; m. Milton H. Mater, June 21, 1940; children—James Lee, Michael Scott. Mgr., Mater Machine Works, Corvallis, Ore., 1945—; asst. mgr. Mater Engring. Co., Corvallis, 1953—; asst. sales mgr. Mater div. Appleton Machine Co., Corvallis, 1960-66; v.p. Mater Internat., Inc., Corvallis, Ore., 1966—; marketing cons. Auto-Lift Corp., Corvallis. Pres. Willamette Valley Research Council, 1966; mem. Coordinated Community Devel. Com. Chmn. Benton County chpt. Girl Scouts Am., 1950; mem. Benton County Charter Com., 1961-62; mem. Def. Adv. Com. on Women in Services, 1972; chmn. Living Conditions Commn., 1973; mem. Portland adv. council Small Bus. Adminstrn., 1972. Alternate vice chmn. Benton County Republican Central Com., v.p. Benton County Rep. Club, 1965-66. Bd. dirs. Dr. Jean Mater Bark Utilization Research Inst., Corvallis, Ore. Recipient Man of Yr. award Willamette Valley Research Council, 1970; Golden Torch award Bus. and Profl. Women, 1970; (with husband) Gottschalk award Forest Products Research Soc., 1973. Mem. Am. Chem. Soc., T.A.P.P.I., Forest Products Research Soc. (chmn. bark utilization com. 1968—, chmn. mgmt. div. 1973-74), C. of C. (chmn. congl. com. 1968—, v.p. 1970, pres. 1972, chmn. bd. 1973), Am. Assn. U. Women (v.p. 1964). Club: Altrusa (dir. Corvallis, 1960-61). Editor: Making and Selling Bark Products, 1970; Marketing Bark Agricultural and Horticultural Products, 1971; Processing Bark for Bark Products, 1972. Home: 1415 SW Brook Lane Dr Corvallis OR 97330 Office: PO Box 0 520 SW 1st St Corvallis OR 97330

MATESEVAC, ELAINE BARBARA (MRS. WILLIAM PETER MATESEVAC, JR.), editor; b. Braddock, Pa., Jan. 18, 1949; d. Steven Stanley and Mary Helen (Radatovic) Crnkovic; B.A., Duquesne U., 1970; m. William Peter Matesevac, Jr., Feb. 27, 1971. Asst. editor Oral Hygiene Publs., Pitts., 1970-72; asso. editor Leisure Publishing, Inc., Pitts., 1972—. Mem. Women in Communications, Croatian Fraternal Union, Kappa Tau Alpha, Zeta Tau Alpha (sec. 1969-70). Democrat. Roman Catholic. Home: 11083 Azalea Dr Pittsburgh PA 15235 Office: 711 Penn Av Pittsburgh PA 15222

MATESICH, SISTER MARY ANDREW, univ. dean, chemist; b. Zanesville, O., May 5, 1939; d. Matthew Michael and Margaret (Gonda) Matesich; A.B., Ohio Dominican Coll., 1962; M.S., U. Cal. at Berkeley, 1963, Ph.D. (Woodrow Wilson fellow, NSF fellow), 1966. Joined Dominican Sisters of St. Mary of Springs, 1957; asst. prof. Ohio Dominican Coll., Columbus, 1965-70, asso. prof. chemistry, 1970—, chmn. dept. chemistry, 1965-73, chmn. natural scis., 1967-72, acting acad. dean, 1973—. Research asso. Case Western Res. U., Cleve., 1969—, Carnegie Mellon U., Pitts., 1972—. Petroleum Research Fund grantee, 1966, NSF grantee, 1969. Mem. A.A.A.S., Ohio Acad Sci., Am. Chem. Soc., Sigma Xi. Contbr. articles on phys. chemistry to sci. jours. Home and office: 1216 Sunbury Rd Columbus OH 43219

MATHER, BETTY BANG, musician, educator; b. Emporia, Kan., Aug. 7, 1927; d. Read Robinson and Shirley (Smith) Bang; B.Mus., Oberlin Conservatory, 1949; M.A., Columbia, 1951; m. Roger Mather, Aug. 3, 1973. Mem. faculty U. Ia., Iowa City, 1952—, prof. music, 1973—. Author: Interpretation of French Music from 1675-1775, 1973. Home: 308 4th Av Iowa City IA 52240

MATHER, ELIZABETH HENRY, interior designer; b. Chgo.; d. H. Harry and Sally M. (Taylor) Henry; student parochial schs., Ky.; m. Orion A. Mather, April 23, 1949. Treas. Nat. Am. Woman's Council, Miami Beach, Fla. Bd. dirs. Blowing Rock (N.C.) Hosp., 1958—; mem. com. Crippled Children Soc., Miami Beach, 1956—. Mem. debutante com. Miami Beach, 1960—. Mem. Blowing Rock Art Assn. (life), Miami Opera Guild. Clubs: Blowing Rock Country; Lenoir (N.C.) Country; Surf (Miami Beach); Jockey (Maimi, Fla.). Address: 5855 N Bay Rd Miami Beach FL 33140 (summer) Cloudswept Blowing Rock NC 28605

MATHESON, JEAN MARIE, coll. adminstr.; b. Oconomowoc, Wis., Oct. 1, 1930; d. James and Elfrieda (Hartman) Matheson; B.A., U. Wis., 1952, M.A., 1964; m. James D. Selk, Mar. 10, 1962 (div. Nov. 1967); 1 dau., Jennifer Selk. Reporter Racine (Wis.) Jour.-Times, 1955-60; news bur. chief Milw. Sentinel, 1960-62; specialist Wis. Union Theatre, Madison, 1963-68; lectr. U. Wis. Sch. Journalism, Madison, 1968-72; asst. prof. journalism, dir. pub. information St. Mary's Coll. of Md., St. Mary's City, 1972—. Mem. St. Mary's County Youth Commn., 1972—. Mem. St. Mary's County Journalists Assn. (sec. 1972—), Phi Beta Kappa. Home: 387 Town Creek Dr Lexington Park MD 20653 Office: St Mary's Coll of Md St Mary's City MD 20686

MATHEWS, GEORGIE MARGARET MILSTEAD (MRS. GRANT ELSTON MATHEWS), ednl. adminstr.; b. West Plains, Mo., Mar. 12, 1918; d. Albert and May (Henry) Milstead; student Park Coll., 1935-37; B.A., Lewis and Clark Coll., 1955; M.A., U. Ore., 1962; m. Grant Elston Mathews, Aug. 28, 1937; 1 dau., Patricia Mae (Mrs. Patricia Walhood). Elementary tchr. Caldwell (Ida.) Pub. Schs., 1951-53, Portland (Ore.) Sch. Dist. 1, 1953-65; clin. prof. Portland State U., 1965-68; elementary prin. Markham Annex Primary Sch., Portland, Ore., 1968-70; area adminstr. Portland Pub. Schs. Area III, 1970—. Group leader, supr. student tchrs. Clin. Supervision Inst., Portland State U., summer sessions, 1965-70. Mem. N.E.A., Assn. for Supervision and Curriculum Devel., Ore. Edn. Assn., Ore. Elementary Sch. Prins. Assn., Assn. Area and Central Adminstrs., Delta Kappa Gamma. Presbyn. Democrat. Home: 10307 NE Brazee St Portland OR 97220 also Road's End Lincoln City OR 97368 Office: 1221 SE Madison St Portland OR 97214

MATHEWS, JANE DEHART, educator, historian; b. Asheville, N.C., Dec. 31, 1936; d. Horace Maxwell and Ruby (Sherron) DeHart; B.A., Duke, 1958, M.A., 1962, Ph.D., 1966; m. Donald G. Mathews, Aug. 22, 1959. Instr., then asst. prof. history Douglass Coll., Rutgers U., 1964-68; lectr. Am. studies U. N.C. at Chapel Hill, 1970-71, asso. prof. history, Greensboro, 1971—; asst. in social studies, test devel. Ednl. Testing Service, 1962-64; project dir. for Rockefeller Found. and Asso. Council Arts, 1968-69. Mem. adv. com. Nat. Project Center for Film and the Humanities, 1974—. Recipient Disertation award Duke Research Council, 1967. Woodrow Wilson fellow, 1958-59; Coll. Teaching Career fellow, 1959-61; fellow Am. Assn. U. Women, 1969-70. Mem. Am., So. hist. assns., Am. Studies Assn., Orgn. Am. Historians, Berkshire Conf. Women Historians, Am. Civil Liberties Union, N.C. Women's Polit. Caucus. Author: The Federal Theatre, 1935-1939; Plays, Relief and Politics, 1967. Home: PO Box 1156 Gray Bluff Trail Chapel Hill NC 27514 Office: Dept History Univ NC Greensboro NC 27412

MATHEWS, LINDA MCVEIGH (MRS. THOMAS JAY MATHEWS), journalist; b. Redlands, Cal., Mar. 14, 1946; d. Glenard Ralph and Edith Lorene (Humphrey) McVeigh; A.B., Radcliffe Coll., 1967; J.D., Harvard, 1972; m. Thomas Jay Mathews, June 15, 1967; 1 son, Joseph McVeigh. Reporter Los Angeles Times, 1967-69, Supreme Ct. corr., Washington, 1972—, sr. writer, 1973—; editor Women's Legal Def. Fund, Washington, 1971-73. Recipient Untermeyer Poetry prize, 1964, Lincoln Univ. award, 1973. Nat. Merit scholar, 1963. Mem. White House Corrs. Assn., Harvard Law Sch. Assn. Democrat. Editor Harvard Civil Rights, Civil Liberties Law Rev., 1969-72; contbg. editor Race Relations Reporter, 1973—. Contbr. articles on law and crime to Atlantic Monthly, The Nation and other publs. Home: 4600 Connecticut Av NW Washington DC 20008 Office: 1700 Pennsylvania Av NW Washington DC 20006

MATHEWS, NADENE, editor; b. Vancouver, Wash.; d. Wendell H. and Lee Retta El Dora (Parsons) Mathews; B.A. (Sr. scholar in Journalism), Willamette U.; M.A. (teaching fellow in English), U. Wis.; postgrad. City Coll. N.Y. Asst. pub. relations dir. C.E. Hooper, Inc., N.Y.C., 1951-53; office mgr., field supr., sec. Facts Consol. Market Research Co., San Francisco and Los Angeles, 1954-61; gen. mgr., field supr. Penfield & Assos. Market Research, San Francisco, 1961-68; propr. Mathews Interviewing Service, 1968; asst. editorial services officer, pub. relations Bank of Am., San Francisco, 1968—, also editor bank publs. Mem. Women in Communications (treas. San Francisco Bay Area chpt. 1971—), Am. Assn. U. Women, Bus. and Profl. Women, YMCA, Theta Sigma Phi (sec. N.Y. profl. chpt. 1953-54, treas., historian San Francisco profl. chpt. 1959-62, 70-71), Beta Chi, Delta Tau Gamma. Democrat. Methodist. Author: Corporate Responsibility for Social Problems, 1974. Co-author, co-editor: California: People, Problems, Potential, 1970. Home: 1750 Broadway San Francisco CA 94109 Office: PO Box 37000 San Francisco CA 94137

MATHIAS, MILDRED ESTHER (MRS. GERALD L. HASSLER), botanist; b. Sappington, Mo., Sept. 19, 1906; d. John Oliver and Julia (Fawcett) Mathias; A.B., Washington U., 1926, M.S., 1927, Ph.D., 1929; m. Gerald L. Hassler, Aug. 30, 1930; children—Frances Jane, John M., Julia E., James B. (dec.). Research asst. Mo. Bot. Garden, 1929-30; research asso. N.Y. Bot. Garden, 1932-36. U. Cal. at Berkeley, 1937-42; with U. Cal. at Los Angeles, 1947—, asso. prof., 1958-62, prof. botany, 1962-74, prof. emeritus, 1974—. Dir. Bot. Garden, 1957-74. Mem. exec. com. Mus. Assn., 1955-60; chmn. hort. adv. com. Los Angeles Beautiful, 1957-66. Hon. trustee Cal. Arboretum Found.; nat. bd. govs. Nature Conservancy, 1966-72; pres. bd. trustees Orgn. for Tropical Studies, 1968-70; councilor Assn. Tropical Biology, 1968-70; trustee Inst. Ecology, 1974—. Fellow A.A.A.S.; mem. Am. Soc. Plant Taxonomist (chmn. council 1960-62, pres. 1964), So. Cal. Botanists (past pres.), Cal. Bot. Soc. (former v.p.), Santa Barbara Bot. Garden (mem. adv. council), So. Cal. Hort. Inst. (past pres.), Internat. Soc. Plant Taxonomists, Bot. Soc. Am., Am. Inst. Biol. Scis., Soc. for Study Evolution, Am., Western (pres. 1965) socs. naturalists. Author sci. papers. Home: 446 S Bentley Av Los Angeles CA 90049 Office: Dept Biology U Cal Los Angeles CA 90024

MATHIES, LORRAINE, librarian; b. Newton, Ia., Oct. 29, 1919; d. Walter Henry and Mable Una (Quick) Mathies; A.B., U. Denver, 1948; M.A., U. Cal. at Los Angeles, 1957, Ed.D., 1967. Coll. librarian Fed. Advanced Tchrs. Coll., Lagos, Nigeria, 1962-63; co-investigator Eric Clearinghouse Jr. Colls., U. Cal. at Los Angeles, 1966-69; spl. cons., 1970—; head edn. and psychology library U. Cal. at Los Angeles, 1964—, dir. Inst. Operation Edn. Information Centers, 1968; library cons. U.S. AID, Nigeria, 1962-63, Nigerian Ministry Edn., 1962-63; cons. Ombudsman Found., 1970-73, Rosemead Grad. Sch. Psychology, 1970-72. Mem. Am., Cal. library assns., Spl. Libraries Assn., Am. Soc. Information Sci., U. Cal. at Los Angeles Alumni Assn., Delta Kappa Gamma, Pi Lambda Theta (mem. nat. publs. adv. bd. 1971—). Author: (with William G. Thomas) Overseas Opportunities for Educators and Students; (with Peter G. Watson) Computer-based Reference Service; asso. author Information Sources and Services in Education; Sources of Information in the Social Services. Contbr. articles to profl. jours. Home: 1115 14th St Santa Monica CA 90403 Office: Edn and Psychology Library U Cal at Los Angeles Los Angeles CA 90024

MATHIESON, HEATHER COLEEN, puppeteer, musician; b. Hershey, Pa., Nov. 6, 1950; d. Daniel Lloyd and Arlene June (Mengel) Mathieson; student U. Wash., 1969-70; B.A. in Drama, Ariz. State U., 1971. Performer with Win' Jammers, 1966-67; appeared at San Juan Melodrama Theater, Colo., 1967; prodn. asst., puppeteer Promotional Planners, Phoenix, 1968-71; puppeteer Lovelace Marionette Theater, Pitts., 1971-73; designed, executed puppets for prodns. including Rags to Riches, Rootabaga Stories, The Unicorn, Gorgon and Manticore at Ariz. State U.; propr. Rocky Mt. Puppet Troupe, Phoenix, 1973—. Occasional dir. Scottsdale Childrens Theater. Home: 1330 W Vermont St Phoenix AZ 85013

MATHIS, BETTY, pub. relations exec.; b. Atlanta, Oct. 5, 1918; d. Walter Rylander and Evelyn Battle (Epting) Mathis; student Agnes Scott Coll., 1934-36. Sports columnist Atlanta Constitution, 1934-36, gen. news and feature writer, 1936-38, spl. asst. for spl. promotions, 1938-39, feature writer, daily columnist, 1940-42; pub. relations dir. Atlanta Housing Authority, 1940; asst. regional information exec. OPA, Atlanta, 1943-45; partner Mathis, Murphey & Bondurant, Pub. Relations, Atlanta, also Nashville, Tenn., 1945-53, Mathis & Bondurant, Pub. Relations, Ft. Lauderdale, Fla., 1953—. Mem. Am. Soc. Hosp. Pub. Relations Dirs. (charter), Fla. Hosp. Assn. Pub. Relations Council (founder), Women in Communications (pres. Broward County br., nat. del. 1967-68). Editor Sun Colony mag., 1950-53. Home: 1628 NE 15th Av Fort Lauderdale FL 33305

MATHIS, BEULAH (MRS. MEYER MATHIS), statistician, govt. ofcl.;d. Maurice and Anna (Selikoff) Nechemias; B.A., Hunter Coll., 1938; m. Meyer Mathis, Apr. 27, 1941; children—Mark, Jeremy, Maurice. Math. statistician Internal Revenue Service, Washington, 1965—. Treas. P.T.A., 1955; treas., pres. Sisterhood Congregation Har Tzeon, Silver Spring, Md., 1963. Mem. Am. Statis. Assn. Home: 4508 Falcon Court Rockville MD 20853 Office: 1111 Constitution Av Washington DC 20024

MATHIS, LUCY EDENBOROUGH (MRS. LEE ROY MATHIS, JR.), physician; b. LaHabra, Cal., Dec. 29, 1928; d. Spencer N. and Beulah (White) Edenborough; A.B., Fresno State Coll., 1950; M.D., Womens Med. Coll. Pa., 1954; m. Lee Roy Mathis, Jr., June 28, 1957; children—Lee Spencer, Ryan Eric. Intern Womans Med. Coll. Pa., Phila., 1954-55, fellow pathology and oncology, 1955-58, instr. pathology, 1958-59; pathologist, dir. labs. Meml. Hosp. Lab., Palestine, Tex., 1959—; sec. bd. dirs. Park Place Convalescent Center, Inc.; cons. pathologist East Tex. Tb Hosp., 1960-65, Grapeland Community Hosp. Bd. dirs. Anderson County unit Am. Cancer Soc., 1960—, pres., 1965; bd. dirs. N.E. Tex. Tb and Respiratory Disease Assn., 1968-69. Mem. A.M.A., Tex. Med. Assn., 11th Dist. (sec.), Anderson-Leon County (pres. 1974) med. socs. Club: Altrusa (Palestine). Home: 303 S Royall St Palestine TX 75801

MATHIS, MARY LE TELLIER, ret. librarian; b. Frederick, Okla., July 13, 1910; d. John Anderson and Kate Nevins (Buchanan) Mathis; student Okla. Coll. Women, 1928-30, Central State Coll., summer 1930; B.S., Okla. State U., 1932; postgrad. Northeastern U., part time 1932-34, U. Okla., summer 1936, U. So. Cal., summer 1941; B.S. in L.S., Okla. U., 1943. Asst. in extension N.E. State U., Tahlequah, Okla., 1932-34; tchr. Frederick (Okla.) Pub. Sch., 1934-38, El Reno (Okla.) Pub. Sch., 1939-42; 1st asst. Westport br. Kansas City (Mo.) Pub. Library, 1949-50; post librarian Ft. Polk, La., 1950, Ft. Gordon, Ga., 1950-52; chief librarian Ft. Hood, Tex., 1952-54, Ft. Sill, Okla., 1954-65; head librarian Morris Swett Tech. Library, Ft. Sill, 1965-73; ret., 1973. Recipient various performance awards, U.S. Army. Mem. Am. (life), Okla. library assns., Kappa Delta (house pres. 1932). Democrat. Presbyn. Home: 515 N 11th St Frederick OK 73542 Office: Room 16 Snow Hall Fort Sill OK 73503

MATHIS, MRS. ROBERT LEE (MARIE WILEY MATHIS), religious exec.; b. Bellevie, Tex.; d. Thomas Dan and Callie (Spradling) Wiley; student Hardin Jr. Coll., Wichita Falls, Tex., 1921, evening student So. Meth. U., 1943-44; LL.D., Hardin-Simmons U., 1955; D.Litt., Mary Hardin Baylor Coll., 1956; m. Robert Lee Mathis, July 2, 1922; 1 dau., Jane Marie (Mrs. Cleo Coffey, Jr.). Youth sec. Woman's Missionary Union, Tex., 1939-45, exec. bd., 1948-50, exec. sec.-treas., 1945-48, pres., 1948-55; pres. Women's Missionary Union Aus. to So. Bapt. Conv., 1956—, mem. fgn. missions, 1953—, mem. exec. com., pres., 1956—, treas. N-Am. Bapt. Women's Union, 1955; mem. exec. com. Bapt. World Alliance 1958—, treas. women's dept., 1960—; dir. ch. activities 1st Bapt. Ch., Dallas, 1948-51; dir. student union Baylor U., 1952—; mem. Bapt. Joint com. Pub. Affairs, 1956-58. Pres. bd. trustees Carver Sch. Missions and Social Work, 1956-57. Mem. So. Bapt. Found. Home: 105 N 29th St Waco TX 76708

MATHIS, RUBY MADELEINE, educator, librarian; b. Dover, Tenn., Aug. 15, 1929; d. Johnnie Jefferson and Ruby Ester (Hall) Mathis; B.S., Austin Peay State Coll., Clarksville, Tenn., 1958; M.A. in L.S., George Peabody Coll., 1962; student Nat. Def. Edn. Act Inst. Advanced Study Ednl. Media, U. Louisville, 1968. Tchr. elementary schs. in Tenn. and Ky., 1947-59; sales rep. F.E. Compton & Co., 1956-57; librarian Sinking Fork Sch., Hopkinsville, Ky., 1959-68; asst. librarian, asst. prof. library sci. Ky. Wesleyan Coll., Owensboro, 1968—. Treas. Bear Spring (Tenn.) P.T.A., 1948-49. Mem. Ky. Tchrs. Assn. (sec. Christian County 1957-58), Ky. Assn. Sch. Librarians (dir. 1969-71), Nat., Ky., 2d Dist. edn. assns., Southeastern, Ky. library assns., Ky. Audiovisual Assn., Kappa Delta Pi. Democrat. Mem. Ch. of Christ, Club: Wesleyan Women's. Spl. work audiovisual materials and equipment. Home: 1706 Tamarack Rd Owensboro KY 42301

MATHIS, THELMA ATWOOD, artist; b. Creal Springs, Ill.; d. Hubert L. and Mima (Hutchison) Atwood; B.S., So. Ill. U., 1955, M.F.A., 1957; student Art Students League, 1957-59; m. John A. Mathis, Sept. 1, 1928 (div. 1950); children—John Atwood, Shirley (Mrs. Frank Woosley), James Stevens. One-man shows So. Ill. U., 1957, 59, Sparta (Ill.) Pub. Library, 1960, Art Mart, Inc., St. Louis, 1961, St. Louis Artists Guild, 1962, Midwestern Coll. (Ia.), 1967; two-man show Madison Galleries, N.Y.C., 1963; juried N.Y.C. Center, 1958, 59, Madison Sq. Garden, N.Y.C., 1958, Nat. Old Testament, St. Louis, 1961, 62, Mo. Art Show, St. Louis City Art Mus., 1954, 55, Nat. Arts & Crafts, Wichita, Kan., 1953, 55; instr., asst. prof. art dept. Midwestern Coll., Denison, Ia., 1965-70. Recipient Grand prize oil and drawing DuQuoin State Fair, 1955, 56, 58, 59. Mem. St. Louis Artists Guild, Am. Assn. U. Women, Pi Lambda Theta. Baptist. Home: Box 13 Pinckneyville IL 62274

MATHISON, LAURA FRANCES JONES (MRS. LESLIE KERMIT MATHISON), univ. adminstr.; b. New Market, Ala., June 28, 1919; d. William Hereford and Mary Elizabeth (Clopton) Jones; B.S., U. Montevallo, 1941; m. Leslie Kermit Mathison, Sr., May 30, 1943; children—Leslie Kermit, Stephanie Frances. Tchr., Hanceville (Ala.) High Sch., 1941-43, Riverside High Sch., Decatur, Ala., 1943-44, Brookwood (Ala.) High Sch., 1946-47, Greensboro (Ala.) High Sch., 1947-63; legal sec., Greensboro, 1948, 51; dir. alumni affairs U. Montevallo (Ala.), 1963—, editor U. Bull. alumni edit., 1963—, dir. devel., alumni area, 1963—. Mem. Library Bd. Greensboro, 1957-60. Mem. Am. Assn. U. Women (br. pres. 1971-73), Wesleyan Service Guild (pres. 1958, 64), Nat. Alumni Assn. U. Montevallo (v.p. 1954-56, pres. 1956-58, mem. alumni council 1956—), Alpha Delta Pi. Club: Metropolitan Dinner (Birmingham, Ala.). Home: 627 Sequoia N Montevallo AL 35115

MATHYS, NEL, librarian; b. Beaver Falls, N.Y., Jan. 27, 1918; d. Andrew and Mary (Wickman) Mathys; A.A., Utica Coll., Syracuse U., 1955. Library technician Watson Labs., Red Bank, N.J., 1949-51; librarian tech. library Rome Air Devel. Center, Griffiss AFB, N.Y., 1951-53, librarian in charge, 1953-58, dir. libraries, 1958—. Mem. Spl. Libraries Assn., Griffiss AFB Exec. Club. Home: 140 Glen Rd S Rome NY 13440 Office: Rome Air Devel Center Griffiss AFB NY 13440

MATIN, DOROTHY HORWITZ (MRS. HARMON MATIN), pub. relations exec.; b. Chgo., July 29, 1920; d. Harry and Eva (Light) Horwitz; student Wright Jr. Coll., 1937-38, Northwestern U., 1938-41, U. Wash., 1946-48; m. Harmon Matin, May 30, 1942; 1 son, Lowell Reed. Pub. relations Hamrick Evergreen Theatres, Seattle, 1958-61, Nat. Gen. Theatres, Seattle, 1961-66, Sterling Recreation Orgn., Seattle, 1966-70; founder, owner Dorothy Matin Agy., Seattle, 1970—. Active vol. work Brandeis U., Seattle; membership chmn. Seattle Conv. Bur., 1966—; mem. Hadassah, City of Hope. Mem. Nat. Assn. Press Women, Press Women Wash., Nat. Acad. TV Arts and Scis. (bd. govs.), Foremost Women Communications, Nat. Council Jewish Women, Seattle Symphony Womens Assn., Nat. Platform Assn. (com.). Mem. B'nai B'rith. Home: 9711 Mercerwood Dr Mercer Island WA 98040 Office: 217 9th Av N Seattle WA 98109

MATON, MARY ELLEN, educator; b. Gridley, Cal., Sept. 12, 1921; d. Chris and Bertha (Bonk) Maton; student U. Cal., summer 1943, 44; A.B., Chico State Coll., 1944; M.A., Columbia, 1946; postgrad. summers Claremont Coll., 1951, U. Hawaii, 1960. Head phys. edn. dept. Napa Jr. Coll.-Jr. High Sch., 1943-46; group therapist Napa State Hosp., 1945-46; dean girls Redlands High Sch., 1947-48; supr.-coordinator pupil personnel services Contra Costa County Schs., 1948-65; coordinator guidance and spl. edn. John Swett Unified Sch. Dist., Crockett, Cal., 1965—. Project dir. Pilot Compensatory Edn., 1963-65, Pilot Headstart Pre-sch. Programs, 1965-66; established guidance programs Contra Costa County; established spl. edn. programs Mentally Retarded, Educationally Handicapped. Active Contra Costa Assn. Mentally Retarded, Contra Costa Assn. Mental Health, Cal. Assn. Neurologically Handicapped. Mem. Cal. Tchrs. Assn., Council Exceptional Children, Cal. Psychol. Assn., No. Cal. Guidance Assn., Cal. Assn. Sch. Adminstrs., Cal. Adminstrs. Spl. Edn., Phi Lambda Theta, Kappa Delta Phi. Home: 2 Los Amigos Orinda CA 94563 Office: PO Box 847 Crockett CA 94525

MATORY, DEBORAH LOVE, psychologist; b. Norfolk, Va., Apr. 20, 1929; d. David Curthbert and Nannie Mae (Reid) Love; B.S., Howard U., 1950, M.S., 1955; m. William E. Matory, July 26, 1949; children—William Earle, Yvedt Love, James Lorand. Instr. psychology Armed Forces Inst., Misawa, Japan, 1956; psychol. intern Willoughbrook State Sch., S.I., N.Y., 1958; clin. psychologist D.C. Pub. Schs., 1959-66; pvt. practice, Washington, 1959—; asso. prof. psychology Washington Tech. Inst., 1967-69; dir. health program Model Cities, D.C., 1971—; mgr. closed circuit TV, Nat. Med. Assn., 1967-71; cons. in field. Mem. U.S. Commn. Civil Rights, D.C., 1967—; pres. Civic League N. Portal Estates, 1973—; mem. ad hoc com. mental health D.C. Commr.'s Ad Hoc Commn. Mental Health, 1963; chmn. staff devel. Community Council D.C. Sch. Bd., 1967. Bd. dirs. D.C. Social Hygiene Soc., 1969—, D.C. Inst. Mental Hygiene, 1968—, D.C. Mental Health Assn., 1963—; bd. mgrs. D.C. P.T.A., 1961-64. Named Woman of Year, Greyhound and Afro-Am. Newspaper, 1968. Mem. Am., D.C. psychol. assns., Am. Pub. Health Assn., Women's Aux. to Medico-Churargical Soc. (pres. 1965-68; Woman of Year 1967), Psi Chi, Delta Sigma Theta, Gamma Phi Delta. Home: 1645 N Portal Dr NW Washington DC 20012 Office: 1875 Connecticut Av NW Washington DC 20009

MATOUSEK, ELIZABETH GRAW (MRS. O. RALPH MATOUSEK), lawyer; b. Homestead, Fla., Nov. 9, 1925; d. G. LaMonte and Lillian I. (Mills) Graw; student Stetson U., 1943-45; B.S., Northwestern U., 1947; J.D., U. Miami, 1968; m. O. Ralph Matousek, Dec. 28, 1946; children—Robert, Charles, Martha Lynne. Catalog copywriter Sears, Roebuck & Co., Chgo., 1947-50; admitted to Fla. bar, 1968, U.S. Supreme Ct. bar, 1971; now practice law, Homestead, Fla. Pres. Avocado Elementary P.T.A., 1964; sec. Homestead Pioneer Mus., 1972-73. Mem. Fla. Assn. Women Lawyers, Fla. Bar, Homestead Bar Assn. (pres. 1972-73), Greater Homestead C. of C. (dir. 1971-74, pres. 1972-73), Delta Delta Delta. Presbyn. (pres. women of the ch. 1951-52). Elk Women. Clubs: Woman's (pres. 1953-54), Soroptomist (pres. 1972-74) (Homestead). Home: 4 NW 22d St Homestead FL 33030 Office: 234 N Krome Av Homestead FL 33030

MATSON, MOLLY HOFFMAN, librarian; b. Cleve., Oct. 14, 1921; d. John Charles and Elsa Marie (Zuern) Hoffman; student Northwestern U., 1939-40; B.A., U. Mich., 1943; M.L.S., Rutgers U., 1967; M.A., Boston, Coll., 1973; m. Kenneth H. Matson, May 11, 1946; children—Lucy, Kate, Martha. Head bibliog. search sect. Goldfarb Library, Brandeis U., Waltham, Mass., 1967-68; reference librarian U. Mass. at Boston, 1968-72, pub. services librarian, 1972—. Mem. Beta Phi Mu. Home: 101 Monmouth St Brookline MA 02146 Office: 100 Arlington St Boston MA 02116

MATSON, VIRGINIA MAE FREEBERG (MRS. EDWARD J. MATSON), educator, author; b. Chgo., Aug. 25, 1914; d. Axel George and Mae (Dalrymple) Freeberg; B.A., U. Ky., 1934; M.A., Northwestern U., 1941; m. Edward John Matson, Oct. 18, 1941; children—Karin (Mrs. Rudolf A. Renfer, Jr.), Sara M. (Mrs. Carl Bigelow Drake III), Edward Robert, Laurence D., David O. Tchr. high schs., Chgo., 1934-42, Ridge Farm, 1944-45, Lake County Pub. Schs., 1956-59; founder, dir. Grove Sch., 1958—. Mem. woman's council Brain Research Found. U. Chgo., 1966—. Recipient Chgo. 100 I Will award, 1971. Mem. Soc., Midland Authors, Friends of Lit. (fiction award 1972). Democrat. Author: Shadow on the Lost Rock, 1958; Abba, Father, 1970; Buried Alive, 1970; A School for Peter, 1974. Home: 950 N Saint Mary's Rd Libertyville IL 60048 Office: 40 E Old Mill Rd Lake Forest IL 60045

MATSUYMAMA, JANET, educator; b. Tacoma, Sept. 3, 1923; d. Hitoshi Harry and Hatsune (Sawada) Kawashima; B.S., St. Cloud (Minn.) State Coll., 1946; M.S., U. So. Cal., 1963; m. Arthur Matsuyama, Aug. 9, 1950; 1 son, Jon Randall. Tchr., Osseo (Minn.) High Sch., 1946-56, Fullerton (Cal.) Union High Sch., 1958-61; instr. div. bus. edn. Fullerton Jr. Coll., 1961—; cons. bus. edn. cons. services Cal. Dept. Edn., 1970-72. Bd. govs. Found. Advancement Bus. Edn., 1968-71. Recipient Nat. Outstanding Service award for bus. and office edn. Am. Vocational Assn., 1969. Mem. Western Assn. Schs. and Colls. (mem. accreditation team for jr. colls. 1969-72, accrediting commn. for jr. colls. 1974—), N.W. Assn. Secondary and Higher Schs. (mem. accreditation team for jr. colls. 1972), Nat. (chmn. jr. and community coll. program 1975), Western (exec. bd. 1968-73), Cal. (exec. council 1968-73, pres. 1969-70) bus. edn. assns., Cal. Vocational Assn. (exec. bd. 1968-71), Delta Pi Epsilon (exec. bd. Psi chpt. 1967-68). Contbr. profl. jours. Mem. publ. bd. Cal. Bus. Edn. jour., 1967-71. Home: 801 N Concord Pl Fullerton CA 92631

MATTA, HENRIETTA GENEVIEVE, accountant, polit. leader; b. Boston; d. Massoud and Ameena (Osseph) Matta; student Harvard U. Extension, 1948-50, Boston Coll., 1950-51, Burdett Coll., 1952-56; postgrad. Suffolk U., 1956-57, Bentley Sch. Bus. and Finance, 1958-59. Social service clk. Dept. Pub. Welfare, Brockton, Mass., 1951-56; sr. staff accountant Federated Accounting Services, Boston, 1956-59; staff accountant, auditor Coven & Suttenberg, C.P.A.'s, Boston, 1959-60; owner, accounting service, Santa Maria, Cal., 1960-61; staff accountant, auditor Aaron & Blum, C.P.A.'s, San Francisco, 1962-65; owner, accountant, M-D Bus. Services, San Francisco, 1965—; asso., also exec. producer John Robert Prodns., San Francisco, 1969—; real estate salesman Alta Assos., San Francisco, 1974—. Membership drive vol. San Francisco Symphony Assn., 1962—; grey lady A.R.C., Brockton, Mass., 1950. County sec. San Francisco Young Republicans, 1965; mem. Cal. Rep. State Central Com., 1966—; Rep. party candidate state senator, San Francisco, 1966; dist. sec. Cal. Rep. Assembly, 1965. Chmn. bd., chmn. publicity dept. Old St. Mary's Center, San Francisco, 1962-66; judge San Francisco Film Festival, 1970. Mem. Am. Accountants Assn., Women in Film, Internat. Platform Assn., Information Film Producers Assn., Nat. Acad. TV Arts and scis. (treas. San Francisco chpt. 1971-74), Cal. (asso.), San Francisco real estate bds., Am. Coll. Accredited Tax Accountants. Club: Cal. Pacific (founder, dir., sec.-treas., 1966-67). Author poetry included in Cloverleaf Book of Verse, 1970. Asso. editor San Francisco County Young Rep. Challenger, 1963-64, Cal. Young Rep. Wire, 1964-65. Home: 755 Burnett Av San Francisco CA 94131 Office: MD Bus Services 755 Burnett Av San Francisco CA 94132 also 186 Francisco St San Francisco CA 94133

MATTERA, GLORIA, educator; b. Rochester, N.Y., Apr. 16, 1930; d. Joseph and Antonietta (Sciannamea) Mattera; B.S. in Edn., State U. N.Y. Coll. at Brockport, 1952, M.S., 1955; Ed.D., Pa. State U., 1961. Elementary tchr., Greece Central Sch., Rochester, 1952-54;

demonstration tchr. Campus Elementary Sch., State U. N.Y. Coll. at Geneseo, 1954-61, prof. edn. Coll. Art and Sci., 1961—, mem. adv. council interdepartmental com. on migrant labor, and minimum wage; dir. N.Y. State Migrant Center, 1968—. Cons. social studies several N.Y. State sch. dists.; dir. Summer Workshop for Tchrs. Migrant Children, 1966-74; dir. Summer Sch. for Migrant Children, 1967, 68, Va. State Workshop for Migrant Tchrs., 1968, 71, Ala. Migrant Tchrs., 1969, 70; dir. Taba Social Studies Teaching Strategies Workshop, summer 1968; asst. summer European tour dir., 1953, 56-64, 67; mem. adv. council N.Y. State Rural Devel.; mem. adv. bd. Clearinghouse for Rural Edn. and Small Schs., N.Y. Bur. Migrant Edn. Cons. to several states on migrant edn. Great Books discussion leader, 1953-59. Recipient Honor award N.A.A.C.P., 1971. Mem. Rural Edn. Assn., Civil Service Employees Assn., Nat. Com. Edn. Migrant Children (adv. bd.), Faculty Assn. State U. N.Y., Nat. Assn. Migrant Edn., Kappa Delta Pi. Co-author: Exemplary Programs for Migrant Children, 1974. Reviewer, New Materials column Instructor mag., 1962—; sr. writer Educating Migrant Children, spring 1968. Contbr. articles to profl. publs. Home: 41 Alford St Rochester NY 14609

MATTFELD, JACQUELYN PHILLIPS ANDERSON, coll. ofcl.; b. Balt., Oct. 5, 1925; d. David Lindsay and Dorothy (Wheless) Anderson; diploma Peabody Conservatory Music, 1947; B.A. magna cum laude, Goucher Coll., 1948; Ph.D., Yale, 1959; m. Victor Henry Mattfeld, Aug. 28, 1949 (div. Aug. 1970); children—Stefanie, Felicity. Tchr. music, 1947-55; music therapist Children's Center, Hamden, Conn., 1953-55; dir. music theory dept. New Eng. Conservatory Music, Boston, 1956-58; dir. financial aid Radcliffe Coll., 1958-60, asso. dean instrn., also dean of East House, 1960-63; asso. dean student affairs Mass. Inst. Tech., 1963-65; dean Sarah Lawrence Coll., Bronxville, N.Y., 1965-69, provost, also dean of faculty, 1969-71; prof. music, asso. provost, dean acad. affairs Brown U., Providence, 1971—; lectr. dept. music Harvard, 1960-63. Mem. Commn. Leadership Devel. Higher Edn. Am. Council Edn., 1974-75, Conf. Faculty Adminstrv. Mgmt. U. Mich. 1974—; ednl. cons. Kenyon Coll., 1965; cons., asso. Kirkland Coll., 1965-72, Princeton, 1967-68; chmn. com. edn. women Yale, 1973—. Mem. project selection bd. Nat. Endowment for the Humanities, 1970-71, 71-72. Bd. dirs. Japan Internat. Christian U. Found., Inc., 1966-68, Assn. for Mentally Ill Children Westchester, 1967-71; adv. bd. Cambridge Soc. for Early Music; bd. dirs. Exptl. Center for Visual Edn., also pres. bd. trustees. Mem. Am. Musicol. Assn., Am. Conf. Acad. Deans, Eastern Assn. Coll. Deans and Advisers of Students (exec. com. 1969—), Renaissance Soc. Am., Am. Assn. U. Women, Assn. Am. Colls. (policy bd. project change undergrad. edn.), Phi Beta Kappa. Contbr. numerous articles to profl. jours. Home: 100 Brown St Providence RI 02906

MATTHAEI, PEARL VIOLA (MRS. CARL L. STABBERT), physician; b. Swanton, Neb.; d. Peter William and Louise (Muenzenmayer) Matthaei; A.B., Central Wesleyan Coll., 1919; M.D., Kan. U., 1926; m. Carl L. Stabbert, Dec. 10, 1942 (dec.); stepchildren—Orlando C. (dec.), Walter (dec.). Intern Children's Hosp., San Francisco, 1926-27; resident San Francisco City and County Hosp., 1927-28; practice medicine, Fessenden, N.D., 1929-35; staff physician N.D. State Hosp., 1935-37; staff San Antonio (Tex.) State Hosp., 1937-42, asst. supt., 1942-43, 44-49, clin. dir., 1947-59; instr. psychiatry San Antonio Coll., 1949-59, San Antonio State Hosp., 1948-58. Mem. adv. council, adult home and family life edn. program San Antonio Ind. Sch. Dist., 1967—; bd. dirs. Mental Health Assn. Bexar County, 1951-57, San Antonio Lit. Council, 1960-69; bd. govs. Girls Council San Antonio, 1965-69. Recipient awards including Theta Sigma Phi Matrix Headliner, 1956, Woman of Achievement awards Tex. div. Am. Assn. U. Women, 1967, San Antonio Bus. and Profl. Womens Club, 1969. Fellow Am. Psychiat. Assn.; mem. A.M.A., Am. Med. Women's Assn. (br. pres. 1968, br. sec. 1969-72), Tex. Neuropsychiat. Assn., Tex. Soc. Mental Health, Mental Health Assn. Bexar County, World Med. Assn., Am. Assn. U. Women (mem. div. fellowships com. 1962-67). Am. Legion Aux., Bus. and Profl. Womens Club, Tex. Fedn. Bus. and Profl. Womens Club, Tex. Fedn. Bus. and Profl. Womens Clubs, Alpha Epsilon Iota (charter mem., 1st pres., 1924-25), Delta Kappa Gamma (hon.). Club: Zonta International (San Antonio v.p. 1961-62, hon. mem.). Home: 315 Rockhill Dr San Antonio TX 78209

MATTHAI, CLARE MURRAY EAGER (MRS. ALBERT DILWORTH MATTHAI, JR.), civic worker; b. Balt., Sept. 16, 1920; d. Auville and Clara (Murray) Eager; B.A., Sweet Briar Coll., 1943; certificate in fundamentals of engring. Johns Hopkins, 1944; m. Albert Dilworth Matthai, Jr., Oct. 22, 1949; children—Clare Murray, Christopher Dilworth. Jr. engr. Glenn L. Martin Co., Balt., 1944-47; proofreader Balt. Gas & Electric Co., 1948-49; reporter Gallup Poll, 1973—. Gallery guide Munson Williams Proctor Inst. Mus., 1960-67. Trustee Civic Music Soc., Utica, N.Y., 1960—, mem. exec. com., 1967-68, 72—; active various community drives; mem. Mid-State Com. Areawide Health Planning Inc., 1968—; mem. exec. com., bd. of women Grace Episcopal Ch., Utica, 1962-70, 72—, mem. vestry, 1970-73; trustee Utica Children's Hosp. and Rehab. Center, 1961—, exec. com., 1964—, pres., 1969-71; bd. dirs. Balt. Ch. Home and Hosp., 1944-49, Vis. Nurse Assn., Utica, 1950-55, Utica Day Nursery, 1952-56; exec. com. Jr. League of Utica, 1955-58. Mem. Munson Williams Proctor Inst. Clubs: Fort Schuyler (mem. womens bd. 1967-69, chmn. arts com. 1968-69), 100,000 (Oneida County); Sadaquada Golf, Sweet Briar College (Utica); Brookside Racquet. Home: 108 Clinton St Whitesboro NY 13492

MATTHEW, JEANNETTE MORROW, librarian; b. St. Louis; d. Harry W. and Ruth (Wilkinson) Morrow; A.B., Park Coll., 1946; m. Neil E. Matthew, Dec. 22, 1963. Librarian Denver Pub. Library, 1946-48, Columbia, 1948-50, N.Y. Pub. Library, 1950-51, The Adj. Gen. Sch. Library, Ft. Harrison, Ind., 1951-56, Regional Campus Library and Sch. Social Service (now Downtown Campus Library) Ind. U., 1956—. Exec. dir. Nat. Library Week Ind., 1963-64; co-founder Adult Edn. Council Indpls. (v.p. 1956-57, sec. 1957-59, 1st woman pres. 1960-62); mem. Ind. State Adult Edn. Council. Mem. program planning com. YWCA, 1954-56, chmn. adult program planning com., 1960-62, mem. long-range planning com., 1962-65; sec. Community Manpower Planning Com., 1961-66. Mem. Spl. Libraries Assn. (pres. Ind. chpt. 1956-57, dir.-at-large Ind. chpt. 1974—, chpt. adviser, chmn. nat. membership com. 1957-61, mem. personnel com. 1962-68), Am. Assn. U. Profs. (sec. chpt. 1973—), Ind. Library Assn., A.L.A. Home: 212 E 49th St Indianapolis IN 46205 Office: 420 Blake St Indianapolis IN 46202

MATTHEWS, BURNITA SHELTON, judge; b. Burnell, Miss., Dec. 28, 1894; d. Burnell and Lora Drew (Barlow) Shelton; LL.B., Nat. U. Law Sch., 1919, LL.M., 1920, LL.D., 1950; m. Percy Ashley Matthews, Apr. 28, 1917. Admitted to D.C., Miss. bars; practice at Washington, 1920; active in securing equal rights for women; formerly mem. faculty, Washington Coll. Law; judge U.S. Dist. Ct. D.C., 1949—. Mem. Com. Experts Women's Work ILO; formerly mem. research com. Inter-Am. Commn. Women; former mem. nat. council Nat. Woman's Party. Mem. nat. bd. Woman's Med. Coll. Pa.; nat. devel. com. Am. U. Mem. Am. Bar Assn., Nat. Assn. Women Lawyers (ex-pres.). Drafted many laws sponsored by Nat. Woman's Party. Home: 4500 Connecticut Av NW Washington DC 20008 Office: US Ct House Washington DC 20543*

MATTHEWS, DORIS BOOZER (MRS. CHARLES L. MATTHEWS), educator; b. Lexington, S.C., Aug. 18, 1932; d. Otto Raymond and Ruth (Sox) Boozer; B.S., Newberry Coll., 1952; M.Ed., U. S.C., 1955, advanced certificate, 1971, Ph.D., 1972; m. Charles L. Matthews, Aug. 20, 1952; children—Shirley Ruth, Charles Ray, Sylvia Ann. Tchr., Brennen Sch., Columbia, S.C., 1952-64; supr. counseling S.C. State Employment Service, Columbia, 1964-66; counseling supr. and basic edn. specialist S.C. Com. for Tech. Edn., Columbia, 1966-68; instr. elementary edn. U. S.C., Columbia, 1968-72; asst. prof. Coll. of S.C. State Coll., Orangeburg, 1972—. Chmn., Columbians Youth Com., 1968-72, treas., 1966-72; chmn. Cayce Neighborhood Center, 1967-70. Mem. S.C. Edn. Assn., S.C. Assn. Supervision and Curriculum Devel., Employment Counselors Assn., Am. Vocational Guidance Assn., Am., S.C. personnel and guidance assns., S.C. Dept. Audio-Visual Instrn., Am. Vocational Assn. Lutheran (pres. ch. women 1971—). Clubs: Cayce Womens (pres. 1965-67), Fashion Rose Garden (pres. 1962-64). Home: 101 Deliesseline Rd Cayce SC 29033 Office: SC State Coll Orangeburg SC 29115

MATTHEWS, DRUE ELLA, educator; b. Orono, Me., Oct. 16, 1914; d. James M. and Ina (Grahame) Matthews; A.B., Mt. Holyoke Coll., 1935, M.A., 1938. Asst. to dean The Stuart Sch., Boston, 1938-39; asst. to dean, instr. history Sweet Briar (Va.) Coll., 1939-43; personnel asst. Gen. Electric Co., Bridgeport, Conn., 1943-44, Lowell, Mass., 1944-45; asst. personnel mgr. Kendall Mills, Walpole, Mass., 1945-49; young adult exec. YWCA, Seattle, 1949-51; employee relations counselor Seattle 1st Nat. Bank, 1951-55; asso. dir. Coop. Program, Antioch Coll., Yellow Springs, O., 1955-58; dir. vocational planning and placement Mt. Holyoke Coll., South Hadley, Mass., 1958—. Pres. Coll. Placement Council, 1969-70. Mem. Am. Personnel and Guidance Assn., Am. Coll. Personnel Assn., Nat. Vocational Guidance Assn. (chmn. women's sect. 1962-63), Eastern Coll. Personnel Officers (pres. 1963-64), P.E.O., Phi Beta Kappa. Home: 16 Ashfield Lane South Hadley MA 01075

MATTHEWS, ELAINE LOUISE (MRS. ROBERT THOMAS MATTHEWS), antique dealer; b. East St. Louis, Ill., June 17, 1925; d. Joseph M. and Josephine L. (Quiros) Garcia; student So. Ill. U., 1955-57, St. Louis U., 1958-62; m. Robert Thomas Matthews, Aug. 4, 1945; 1 dau., Elaine Lila (Mrs. Robert J. Kern). Owner, Antiques by Elaine, Belleville, Ill., 1964—; antique show exhibitor, 1965—; tchr. pub. schs., Belleville, 1958-71. Bd. dirs. Belleville Girl Scouts, 1957-58, neighborhood chmn., 1958-59; bd. dirs. A.R.C., 1958-59, 1st aid instr., 1958-62. Recipient award NSF, 1963. Mem. Nat. Antique Dealers Assn. Club: Soroptimist (pres. Metro-East (Ill.) club 1972-73, dist. dir. South Central region). Home: Route 3 Box 381A Belleville IL 62221 Office: Antiques by Elaine 510 Freeburg Av Belleville IL 62221

MATTHEWS, ELIZABETH SMITH (MRS. CORNELIUS D. MATTHEWS), educator; b. nr. Georgetown, Miss., Sept. 26, 1916; d. George A. and Nina (Beasley) Smith; student Central Inst. for the Deaf, St. Louis, 1954-56, Millsaps Coll., 1956-57; B.S., Miss. Coll., 1967; m. C. D. Matthews, Feb. 21, 1941; children—Mark Dulaney, George Keith. Sec. for three drs. Miss. State Hosp., Whitfield, 1938-41; clk. for referee in bankrupcty So. Dist. Miss., Jackson Div., 1941-42; sec. Lotterhos, Travis and Dunn, attys., Jackson, Miss., 1942-43; stenographer Dept. Justice, U.S. Courts, U.S. Atty., 1943-44; dep. clk. U.S. Courts, Clerk's office, 1944-47; founder, dir., tchr. Magnolia Speech Sch. for the Deaf, Jackson, 1956—. Coordinator, Alexander Graham Bell Assn. for the Deaf, Washington, 1964—, ednl. cons., 1970—. Mem. Beta Sigma Phi. Baptist. Club: Capital Lionetts (program chmn. 1964-65). Contbr. articles and revs. to mag. Home: 2969 Angela Circle Jackson MS 39209 Office: PO Box 10373 Jackson MS 39209

MATTHEWS, ERNESTINE FAYE (MRS. DOUGLAS KAY MATTHEWS), lumber co. exec.; b. Rivervale, Ark., Oct. 7, 1932; d. Harvin Cleo and Lela Marie (Huffman) Richmond; m. Douglas Kay Matthews, Aug. 3, 1948; children—Ronald D., Linda (Mrs. Barry Gardner), Terry L., Mikel L., Kevin D., Greg A. Telephone operator Gen. Telephone Co., North Branch, Mich., 1949; with Marvin C. Richmond Lumber Corp., Dowagiac, Mich., 1949-51, 1954-56, accountant, office mgr., sec.-treas., 1962-72; accountant Donald Schlager, St. Charles, Mich., 1956-57; v.p. Continental Equipment Co., Michigan City, Ind., 1967-72; sec.-treas. Southwestern Mich. Hardwoods, Inc., Dowagiac, 1973—. Mem. Beta Sigma Phi. Antlerettes. Home: Route 7 Box 430 Dowagiac MI 49047 Office: 714 N Front St PO Box 525 Dowagiac MI 49047

MATTHEWS, ESTHER ELIZABETH, educator; b. Princeton, Mass., June 20, 1918; d. Ralph E. and Julia (Cronin) Matthews; B.S., State Coll. Worcester, Mass., 1940; Ed.M., Harvard, 1943, Ed.D., 1960. Tchr., high sch. counselor, dir. guidance Holden (Mass.) pub. schs., 1942-53; dir. guidance, sch. psychologist Wareham (Mass.) pub. schs., 1954-57; high sch. guidance counselor Newton (Mass.) High Sch., 1957-60; supr. counseling practicum Harvard-Newton Summer Guidance Inst., 1956-64; head counselor Newton South High Sch., 1960-66; lectr. on edn. Boston U. 1963; instr. Nat. Def. Edn. Act Inst. Tchrs. Coll. Columbia, summer 1965; lectr. edn. Harvard, 1963-66; asso. prof. edn. U. Ore., Eugene, 1966-70, prof., 1970—; vis. prof. U. Toronto, summer 1971. Mem. Internat. Assn. Ednl. and Vocational Guidance, Am. Psychol. Assn., Am., Ore. personnel and guidance assns., Am. Assn. U. Profs., Nat. Vocational Guidance Assn. (sec., trustee, chmn. commn. on occupational status women 1968-71, pres. 1974-75). Mem. editorial bd. Vocational Guidance Quar., 1966-68. Contbr. articles to profl. jours. Home: 832 Lariat Dr Eugene OR 97401

MATTHEWS, IRMA A. (MRS. ALAN R. MATTHEWS), lawyer; b. Belmont, Mass., Oct. 20, 1913; d. Raymond L. Robbins;; LL.B. cum laude, Portia Law Sch., 1939; m. Alan R. Matthews, 1946; children—Carol J., Russell R., Duncan W., Wendy N. Admitted to Mass. bar, 1940, N.H. bar, 1958; now N.H. state atty.; also asst. atty. gen., 1967—. Home: 30 Essex St Concord NH 03301 Office: State Capitol Bldg Office of the Atty Gen Concord NH 03301

MATTHEWS, JUDITH ANN (MRS. PHILIP LAWRENCE MATTHEWS), pub. relations exec.; b. St. Charles, Mo., Oct. 21, 1946; d. Archie Burton and Wanda Mary (Bazan) Null; B.J. (Mo. Curators scholar, LaVerne Noyes scholar), U. Mo., 1968; m. Philip Lawrence Matthews, Jan. 11, 1969. Communications and publications analyst Conductron-Mo., St. Charles, 1968-69; with Ivy Bend Devel., Inc., Sedalia, Mo., 1969—, dir. advt. and pub. relations in real estate, 1969—. Recipient Winchester Distinguished Shooters award, 1973. Mem. Women In Communications, Mo. U. Alumni Assn., Amateur Trapshooting Assn., Mo. Trapshooting Assn., Gamma Phi Beta. Republican. Roman Catholic. Clubs: Walnut Hills Country, Westmoreland Country (Sedalia), Sedalia Rod/Gun. Home: 1911 W Broadway Sedalia MO 65301 Office: Box 390 Sedalia MO 65301

MATTHEWS, MARGERY IDA HARRINGTON (MRS. THOMAS JAMES MATTHEWS), librarian; b. Foster, R.I., Sept. 8, 1923; d. Herman Battey and Mary Hannah (Griffiths) Harrington; B.S., U. R.I., 1944, M.L.S., 1968; postgrad. R.I. Coll., 1969-72; m. Thomas James Matthews, Oct. 27, 1945; children—Marcia (Mrs. James Bowden), Marilyn Ida. Home economist Bristol-Myers Co., N.Y.C., 1944-45; librarian Ponaganset High Sch., North Scituate, R.I., 1964—. Mem. bldg. com. Foster Glocester Regional Sch. Dist., 1964-72; mem. Foster Bicentennial Commn., 1973—. Mem. Foster Democratic Town Com., 1970. Mem. R.I. Sch. Library Assn. (treas. 1965-71), D.A.R. Conglist (moderator 1964-72, clk. 1972—). Home: Box A30 Cucumber Hill Foster RI 02825 Office: Ponaganset High School Rural Route 2 North Scituate RI 02857

MATTHEWS, MARY HAMMER, librarian; b. Sidney, N.Y., Feb. 12, 1944; d. Harold E. and Oliver (Ober) Hammer; B.A., U. Rochester, 1965; M.S. in L.S., Columbia, 1966. Asst. catalogue, then head catalog dept. U. Alaska, Fairbanks, 1966-72; regional coordinator Alaska Div. State Libraries, 1972—. Mem. Alaska Telecommunications Consortium, 1972—. Mem. Am. (council 1974—), Pacific N.W. (chmn. coll. div. 1973—), Alaska (pres. 1970-71) library assns. Home: PO Box 80685 College AK 99701 Office: PO Box 1267 Fairbanks AK 99707

MATTHEWS, MARY JEAN O'LEARY (MRS. JOHN LEE MATTHEWS), physician; b. Holyoke, Mass., Apr. 11, 1923; d. Martin Joseph and Agnes (Burke) O'Leary; A.A., Immaculata Jr. Coll., 1942; A.B., George Washington U., 1946, M.D., 1949; m. John Lee Matthews, June 19, 1948; children—Mary Ann, Susan Jean, John Edward, Margaret Louise, Robert Joseph. Intern, D.C. Gen. Hosp., 1949-50, asso. dir. Main Lab., 1954-62; resident pathology Georgetown U. Med. Sch., 1950-54, asst. clin. prof. pathology, 1961-72; Nat. Cancer Inst. fellow, 1950-53; practice medicine, specializing in pathology, Washington, 1954—; asst. chief VA Hosp. Lab. Service, D.C., 1962-64, chief, 1964-70; asso. clin. prof. pathology Med. Sch. Howard, 1965-68, prof., 1968-72; professorial lectr. George Washington U., 1968-72, prof. pathology, 1972—; oncology pathologist, chmn. working party for lung cancer therapy Nat. Cancer Inst.-VA, 1972-73, co-chmn., 1973—. Recipient Achievement citation Washington Womens Advt. Club, 1967. Diplomate Am. Bd. Pathologic Anatomy. Mem. A.M.A., Washington Soc. Pathologists, Internat. Acad. Pathology, D.C. Med. Soc., Am. Women's Med. Assn., A.A.A.S., Am. Soc. Cytology. Roman Catholic. Home: 6604 Virginia View Ct Washington DC 20016 Office: VA Hosp 50 Irving St Washington DC 20420

MATTHYSSE, ANN GALE, educator, microbiologist; b. Chgo., Oct. 25, 1939; d. George Washington and Ann (Van Nice) Gale; A.B. magna cum laude, Radcliffe Coll., 1961; student Rockefeller U. (fellow), 1961-63; Ph.D. (NIH fellow), Harvard, 1966; m. Steven W. Matthysse, Aug. 25, 1962; 1 son, Michael. NIH postdoctoral research fellow Cal. Inst. Tech., 1966-69; research fellow, Med. Sch., Harvard, 1969-70, lectr., biology, 1970-71; asst. prof. microbiology Ind. U. Sch. Medicine, 1971—. NIH research grantee, 1972—. Mem. Am. Soc. Microbiology, Am. Soc. Plant Physiologists, Am. Inst. Biol. Sci., A.A.A.S., Tissue Culture Assn., Phi Beta Kappa, Sigma Xi. Home: 5587 Scarlet Terrace Indianapolis IN 46224

MATTINGLY, ALETHEA ELIZABETH SMITH (MRS. CHARLES PERCY MATTINGLY), educator; b. Chgo.; d. Albert E. and Mary E. (Randall) Smith; B.A. with honors, U. Wis., 1924, M.A., 1931; Ph.D., Northwestern U., 1954; m. Charles Percy Mattingly, Oct. 8, 1935. Instr., U. Minn., 1924-28; asst. prof. Fla. State Coll. for Women, 1928-34; asst. prof. U. Ariz., Tucson, 1934-42, asso. prof., 1942-54, prof. speech, 1954-74, prof. emeritus, 1974—, dir. Nat. Def. Edn. Act Inst. for Advanced Study in English, 1966, 67. Mem. Western Speech Assn. (past v.p., interpretation counselor 1964-66), Ariz. Speech and Drama Assn. (pres. 1964-66), Speech Communication Assn. (past chmn. interpretation interest group, publs. chmn. interpretation div. 1971-74), Nat. Collegiate Players, Am. Assn. U. Profs., P.E.O., Zeta Phi Eta. Author: Interpretation: Writer, Reader, Audience, 1st edit. (with Wilma H. Grimes), 1961, author of 2d edit., 1970. Editorial bd. Quar. Jour. Speech 1966-69. Asso. editor Players mag., 1934-40. Cons. editor Western Speech, 1973—. Contbr. articles to profl. jours. Home: 1312 E Adams St Tucson AZ 85719

MATTINGLY, CAPITOLA BLACK, educator; b. Georgetown, Ky., Dec. 31, 1909; d. Lewis Edward and Cordelia (Sherritt) Mattingly; A.B., Asbury Coll., 1935; M.A., Scarritt Coll., 1938; M. Nursing, Yale, 1943; M.S. in Nursing, Cath. U. Am., 1951; postgrad. U. Chgo., 1945, U. Minn., 1957. Asst. prof. U. Ga., 1944-45; nurse pub. health agys., Ga., La., 1944-49; sch. nursing Arlington County (Va.) Schs., 1952-57; asst. prof. Cath. U. Am., 1957-62; asso. prof. Duke, 1962-65; asso. prof. nursing Mercy Coll. of Detroit, 1965-68; now nursing adminstr. The Arnold Home, Inc. Cons. VA, Washington, 1959-65, Washington Heart Assn., 1958-62, Chesapeake and Potomac Telephone Cos., 1958-65. Mem. Am., Mich. nurses assns., Nat., Mich. leagues for nursing, Sigma Theta Tau, Pi Gamma Mu. Contbr. articles to profl. jours. Mem. adv. editorial bd. Nat. Rehab. Assn. Jour., 1965-68. Home: 24224 W Seven Mile Rd Detroit MI 48219 Office: Arnold Home Detroit MI 48219

MATTINGLY, SUSAN SHOTLIFF (MRS. RICHARD E. MATTINGLY), educator; b. Kansas City, Mo., Oct. 12, 1941; d. Wilmot H. and Edna E. (Grebe) Shotliff; B.A., U. Kan., 1963; Ph.D., U. Tex., 1968; m. Richard E. Mattingly, Sept. 3, 1963. Part time lectr. philosophy Westminster Coll., Fulton, Mo., 1966-67; instr. philosophy and humanities Lincoln U., Jefferson City, Mo., 1967-69, asst. prof. philosophy, 1969-72, asso. prof., head dept., 1972—. Sec. County Health Commn., 1973-74. Woodrow Wilson fellow, 1963, dissertation fellow, 1966. Mem. Am. Assn. U. Profs., Am., Mo. philos. assns., Soc. for Women in Philosophy, League Women Voters (sec. 1971—), U. Kan. Alumni Assn., Phi Beta Kappa. Home: 905 Julian Lane Fulton MO 65251

MATTIS, NOÉMI PERELMAN, psychologist; b. Lodz, Poland, Oct. 16, 1936; d. Chaim P. and Fela (Liwer) Perelman; B.A., Université Libre de Bruxelles (Belgium), 1955, LL.D., 1958; M.A., Columbia, 1964, Ph.D., 1973; m. Daniel C. Mattis, Nov. 9, 1958; children—Michael, Olivia. Came to U.S., 1958, naturalized, 1962. Trainee VA Hosp., Montrose, N.Y., 1967-68, Bronx, N.Y., 1968-69; staff psychologist Cage Teen Center and Educage, White Plains, N.Y., 1973—. Mem. Am., N.Y. State, Westchester County psychol. assns., Psi Chi, Kappa Delta Pi, Pi Lambda Theta. Home: 26 Olmsted Rd Scarsdale NY 10583 Office: 5 New St White Plains NY 10512

MATTISON, DELIA MAY, librarian; b. Clyde, Kan., Apr. 25, 1913; d. William Norman and Mary (Fessenden) Mattison; B.S., U. Ark., 1937; M.L.S., U. So. Cal., 1948. Tchr. pub. high schs., Ark., 1937-42, 46; aircraft worker Douglas Aircraft, El Segundo, Cal., 1942-45; jr. asst. library U. Ark., 1946-47, library asst., 1948-64, asst. librarian, head catalog dept., 1964—. Mem. Ark., Southwestern library assns., Am. Assn. U. Profs., Beta Phi Mu. Home: 305 Kate Smith St Prairie Grove AR 72753 Office: University of Ark Library Fayetteville AR 72701

MATTOX, AUDREY BLANCHE (MRS. THOMAS C. MATTOX), real estate broker; b. Fayetteville, Ark., Oct. 21, 1893; d. Jesse Benton and Mary Elizabeth (Woolverton) Easter; student Northeastern State Tchrs. Coll., Tallequah, Okla., 1910-11; m. Thomas C. Mattox, Mar. 31, 1915; 1 dau., Thelma Carden (Mrs. Leonard C. Smith). Tchr. Cherokee, Adair Counties, Okla., 1910-14; tchr. accounting El Dorado (Kan.) Bus. Coll., 1919-20; real estate broker J.C. Hoyt & Co., El Dorado, 1920—; agt. Railroad Bldg., Loan & Savs. Assn., El Dorado, 1940-72. Mem. El Dorado Devel. Co., 1974—. Mem. El Dorado C. of C., Bus. and Profl. Club, El Dorado Ins. Women (founder 1949, pres. 1949-50), Soc. Real Estate Appraisers, Butler County Real Estate Bd. (founder 1947), D.A.R. (registrar), Am. Legion Aux., V.F.W. Aux., Soroptomist. Democrat. Methodist. Mem. Order Eastern Star, White Shrine. Home: 534 Post Rd El Dorado KS 67042 Office: 208 W Central St El Dorado KS 67042

MATTOX, VERNA DALGAS (MRS. TILDEN MATTOX), civic worker; b. Neb., July 14, 1916; d. Fred C.H. and Jacobina K. (Madsen) Dalgas; grad. pub. high sch., 1933; m. Tilden Mattox, Apr. 19, 1941 (dec. 1969); children—Frederick, Judy (Mrs. Gabriel Tellez). Owner, Tilden's Sport Shop, Manhattan Beach, 1941-69. Mem. Citizens for Decent Lit. Mem. Manhattan Beach Recreation Commn., 1952; pres. South Bay Republican Women, 1961-62; pres. Los Angeles County Fedn. Rep. Women, 1969-70; sec. Rep. Central Com., Los Angeles County, 1971-72; Cal. Rep. Pres. Elector, 1972; asst. treas. Rep. State Central Com., Los Angeles, 1973—, asst. sec., 1975—. Mem. adv. bd. Citizens Legal Defense Alliance. Named Mrs. Manhattan Beach, C. of C., 1955. Mem. Freedoms Found. Valley Forge, Greater Los Angeles Zoo Assn., Am. Assn. Ret. Persons, Torrance Area C. of C. Home: 22647 B Nadine Circle Torrance CA 90505 Office: 6151 W Century Blvd Suite 926 Los Angeles CA 90045

MATTSON, LAURA MAE JEWETT (MRS. ROY ALBIN MATTSON), banker; b. Dunseith, N.D., Mar. 21, 1926; d. Theodore Earl and Grace Hannah (Cain) Jewett; student Am. Banking Inst., 1958, Ketchikan Community Coll., 1956, 57, 59, 67, 68, U. Wis., 1972, 73, 74; m. Roy Albin Mattson, Oct. 1, 1949. With First Nat. Bank, Ketchikan, Alaska, 1956—, cashier, 1971—. Mem. Women of Moose (recorder 1968-70, sr. regent 1971, jr. grad. regent 1973). Clubs: Emblem Club 92, Soroptimist (Ketchikan). Home: 100 Martin St PO Box 282 Ketchikan AK 99901 Office: 331 Dock St Ketchikan AK 99901

MATTSON, SUE LAU, govt. ofcl.; b. Honolulu, Feb. 1, 1925; d. A. Chung and Yuk Moi (Wong) Lau; student U. Hawaii, 1943; m. David Mattson, Aug. 15, 1955 (div. June, 1960); 1 son, Carl Lani. Statistics clk. Bur. Sight Conservation and Work with the Blind, Honolulu, 1943-50, information specialist, 1950-60, Dept. Social Services, 1960-71; information specialist Dept. Hawaiian Home Lands, 1972—. Mem. Am. Pub. Welfare Assn., Nat. Assn. Housing and Redevel. Ofcls., Hawaii Govt. Employees Assn., Internat. Platform Assn. Home: 1717 Keeaumoku St Honolulu HI 96822

MATUNAS, MARIAN STARRETT (MRS. ANTHONY L. MATUNAS), psychoanalyst; b. Indpls., June 12, 1929; d. Wendell Holmes and Evalyn Elizabeth (Haig) Starrett; B.S., Northwestern U., 1950; M.A., N.Y. U., 1954, Ph.D., 1960; diploma in psychoanalysis Center for Mental Health, N.Y.C., 1970; m. Anthony L. Matunas, Nov. 7, 1956; 1 son, Anthony Laurence. From clin. psycologist to sr. psychologist Kings Park State Hosp., 1955-58; sch. psychologist Hicksville (N.Y.) Pub. Schs., 1958-60; staff psychologist Kings County Hosp., Bklyn., 1960-64; dir. psychol. services Jewish Meml. Hosp., N.Y.C., 1964-67; supervising clin. psychologist Postgrad. Center, 1967-69; pvt. practice psychoanalysis and psychotherapy, N.Y.C., 1965—. Adj. prof. Union Grad. Sch. at Antioch, 1969—. Mem. Am., N.Y. State psychol. assns., Soc. for Projective Techniques, Psi Chi, Pi Lambda Theta, Kappa Delta Pi. Home: 333 E 30th St Apt 3L New York City NY 10016 Office: 11 E 68th St Suite 1B New York City NY 10021

MATUSOW, LYNNE, personnel co. exec.; b. N.Y.C., Apr. 28, 1942; d. Abraham Perlin and Helen (Garman) M.; A.B., Ind. U., 1962, postgrad., 1962-63; postgrad. George Washington U., 1964. Translator Library of Congress, Washington, 1964; asst. to Rep. James H. Scheuer, N.Y.C., 1964-65; editorial sec., prodn. editor Internat. Pubs. group Reuben H. Donnelly Corp., N.Y.C., 1966-68; layout editor Thomas Pub. Co., N.Y.C., 1968-69; adminstrv. asst. to pres., placement mgr. Oxford Personnel, Inc., N.Y.C., 1969-72, placement mgr., 1973—. pres. Fun City Personnel, Inc., N.Y.C., 1972-73. Aux. police officer N.Y.C. Police Dept., 1972—. Pres. Concourse Claremont Ind. Democrats, 1966-67; treas. Bronx Com. for Democratic Voters, 1967-71; del. Dem. Jud. Conv., 1965; mem. Bronx County Dem. Com., 1966—. Mem. Ind. U. Alumni Assn. Ind. U. Alumni Club N.Y. (pres. 1969-73, v.p. 1973—), Theta Sigam Phi. Home: 201 17th St New York City NY 10003 Office: 341 Madison Av New York City NY 10017

MATZ, MARY JANE PHILLIPS (MRS. CHARLES ALBERT MATZ, JR.), musicologist; b. Lebanon, O., Jan. 30, 1926; d. William Mason and Hazel (Spencer) Phillips; B.A., Smith Coll., 1947; M.A., Columbia, 1950; student New Sch. Social Research, 1947-48, Cin. Conservatory Music, 1943-44, City U. N.Y., 1968-69; m. Charles Albert Matz, Jr., Dec. 31, 1949; children—Mary Ann, Margaret Spencer, Catherine Eleanor, Clare Ann, Charles Albert III. Editor, writer Opera News, Met. Opera Guild, Inc., N.Y.C., 1948—; asst. prof. English, St. Mary's Coll., Notre Dame, Ind., 1964-68; prof. English, U. Venice and U. Feltre (Italy), 1969-72. Gen. mgr., fund raiser Festival of Two Worlds, Spoleto, Italy, 1960-62, pub. relations, 1962—. Mem. D.A.R., Ohio Hist. Soc., Ohioana Soc., Modern Lang. Assn., Authors League, Met. Opera Guild, Nat. Council Coll. Publs. Advisers, Am. Musicol. Soc., Accademia Spoletina. Author: Opera Manual, 1956; Stars in the Sun, 1956; The Many Lives of Otto Kahn, 1964; Opera: Grand and Not So Grand, 1966; Verdi: A Critical Biography, 1974; Cesare Vigna: His Life and Work, 1974; numerous articles in profl. jours. Home: Fondamenta Soranzo 340 Venice Italy Office: Opera News Met Opera Guild Inc 1865 Broadway New York City NY 10023

MATZ, NANCY BURWELL CHESTON (MRS. WILLIAM EDMUND MATZ), occupational therapist; b. Balt., Sept. 29, 1941; d. Daniel Murray and Elizabeth Anne (Long) Cheston; A.A., Briarcliff Coll., 1959-61; B.A., U. Md., 1963; certificate occupational therapy Richmond Profl. Inst., 1965; postgrad. Ohio State U., 1967; m. William Edmund Matz, July 29, 1967; 1 son, Andrew Louis. Head psychiat. occupational therapy clinic VA Hosp., Washington, 1965; chief occupational therapy United Cerebral Palsy Center, Columbus, O., 1966-68; staff tchr. Darrell Dale's Sch. for Exceptional Children, New Orleans, 1969-70; dr.'s office receptionist, asst., Thornton, Colo., 1968-69, 70-72; chief occupational therapy Castle Garden Nursing Home, Northglenn, Colo., 1972-74. Dept. Health, Edn. and Welfare scholar, 1964. Mem. Am. Occupational Therapy Assn., Gamma Theta Upsilon. Episcopalian. Home: 6498 S Marion St Littleton CO 80121

MATZKIN, ROSE ELLIS (MRS. MAX N. MATZKIN), orgn. exec.; b. N.Y.C., Sept. 1; d. Louis and Jennie (Susman) Cohen; tchr.'s certificate New Haven State Tchrs. Coll.; m. Max N. Matzkin, Dec. 23, 1934; children—Michael, Hannah (Mrs. Barry Levine). Tchr. grammar sch. Lisbon, Conn., remedial reading and dramatics, Waterbury (Conn.) sch. system, 1931-38; v.p. Hadassah, Women's Zionist Orgn. Am. Inc., 1962-65, nat. pres., 1972—; del. World Zionist Congress, Jerusalem, 1951, 60, 64, 68, 72; vice-chmn. Conf. Pres. Maj. Am. Jewish Orgns.; Hadassah rep. Nat. Conf. Soviet Jewry; vice-chmn. World Jewish Congress-Am. sect.; mem. exec. bd. World Confedn. Gen. Zionists; mem. exec. com. Am. Israel Pub. Affairs Com.; mem. governing council World Jewish Congress, 1972—. Bd. govs. Hebrew U., Jerusalem; trustee Am. Friends Hebrew U. Mem. Waterbury Jewish Fedn. Mem. Woman's Aux. Am. Dental Assn., Waterbury Hosp., St. Mary's hosps. women's auxs., League Women Voters. Office: Hadassah 65 E 52d St New York City NY 10022

MATZNER, ALEXANDRA MARIA, physician; b. Skarszewy, Poland; d. Mieczyslaw Jerzy and Pelagia Klara (Kasicka) Markiewicz; M.D., Med. Acad. Gdansk (Poland), 1952; m. Joseph M. Matzner, Mar. 5, 1961; 1 dau., Karen. Came to U.S., 1961, naturalized, 1964. Intern Med. Acad., Gdansk, 1952-53; resident Urbanowicz and Mielecki Hosp., Chorzow, 1953-60; practice medicine specializing in internal medicine and infectious diseases, Chorzow, 1953-60, specializing in radiology, Boston, 1966-70, Saugus, Mass., 1970—; radiologist Saugus (Mass.) Gen. Hosp., 1970—; mem. staff VA Hosp., Boston, 1966-70, Mt. Pleasant Hosp., Lynn, Mass. Home: 12 Forbes Lane Andover MA 01810 Office: 136 Boston St Lynn MA 01902

MAUK, DOROTHY BRITTON (MRS. C. DALLAS MAUK), journalist; b. Newark, Oct. 25, 1927; d. William G. and Esther (Silva) Britton; A.B. cum laude, Middlebury Coll., 1949; m. William Ralph Eccles, Jr., June 9, 1951 (div. Dec. 1968); 1 son, Timothy Alden; m. 2d, C. Dallas Mauk, Apr. 28, 1970. Asst. to classified mgr. Long Branch (N.J.) Daily Record, 1945, rewrite reporter, summer 1946, feature reporter, summer 1948; coll. yearbook counselor Jahn & Ollier Engraving Co., N.Y.C., 1949-51; edit. researcher, pub. relations dept. DuPont Co., Wilmington, Del., 1951-54; gen. reporter Denver Post, 1964-66, sports reporter, 1966—, recreation sports editor, 1969—. Mem. Gov.'s Local Affairs Study Comm. of 100, 1963-66; goodwill ambassador People-to-People Sister City Program, Littleton, Colo. to Bega, NSW, Australia, 1966. Bd. dirs. Colo. Youth Tennis Found., Denver, 1970—. Mem. Denver Symphony Guild, 1970—, Littleton Friends of Library, 1961—. Recipient Bud Robineau award Colo. Tennis Assn., 1970, Service award Colo. Assn. Swimming Ofcls., 1971, Appreciation award Columbine Soccer League, 1971. Mem. Am. Assn. U. Women (pres. Denver 1964-66, sec. Colo. 1969-71), Mortar Bd. Alumnae, Phi Beta Kappa. Republican. Methodist. Home: 6673 S Grant St Littleton CO 80121 Office: PO Box 1709 Denver CO 80201

MAUK, GERTRUDE, educator; b. Greenup County, Ky.; d. James Logan and Ada (Horn) Mauk; A.B., Morehead State Coll., 1938; M.Ed., Wayne State U., 1948, D.Ed., 1952. Dir. personnel adminstrn. Children's Hosp., Detroit, 1951-57; head tchr., prin. Greenup (Ky.) Ind. High Sch., 1956-57; asso. prof. edn. Georgetown Coll., 1957-61; instr. Jr. Coll. Broward County, Ft. Lauderdale, Fla., 1961-64; counselor Wayne (Mich.) Community Schs., 1964—. Mem. Am. Assn. U. Women (pres. Ft. Lauderdale 1963-64), N.E.A., Mich. Personnel Guidance Assn., Nat. Sch. Counselors Assn., Mich. Counselors Assn., Mich., Wayne edn. assns., Coll. Edn. Alumni Assn. Wayne State U. (governing bd.), D.A.R., Beta Sigma Phi, Kappa Delta Pi. Methodist. Author (with others) Choices in Daily Living. Address: PO Box 312 Garden City MI 48135

MAULDIN, E. EUGENIA, librarian; b. Baldwyn, Miss., Nov. 4, 1916; d. Thomas Andrew and Reba (Welsh) Mauldin; B.A., Millsaps Coll., 1938; M.Ed., U. Miss., 1950; M.L.S., U. Ill., 1956. Tchr., Carmichael (Miss.) High Sch., 1938-39, Ashland (Miss.) Grade Sch., 1939-41, Glen Allan (Miss.) Grade Sch., 1941-42, Guntown (Miss.) Grade Sch., 1942-43, New Albany (Miss.) Grade Sch., 1946-47; librarian Baldwyn High Sch., 1947-51; teaching asst. U. Ill. Grad. Sch. Library Sci., 1955-56; librarian Corinth (Miss.) High Sch., 1956-57; asst. prof. dept. library service Coll. Edn., U. Tenn., Knoxville, 1957-69, asso. prof., 1969-71, asso. prof. Grad. Sch. Library and Information Sci., 1971—; instr. library service Miss. State U., summer 1966. Mem. com. on tchr. edn. So. Regional Edn. Bd., 1964-67; mem. continuing library edn. network Am. Assn. Library Schs., 1973—; acting editor Tenn. Librarian, 1958-59. Bd. dirs. U. Tenn. Wesley Found., sec. exec. bd, 1970—. Mem. E. Tenn. Edn. Assn. (chmn. audiovisual sect. 1960-61), Tenn. Library Assn. (A.L.A. councilor 1965-69, chmn. nominating com. 1971, sec. library edn. sect. 1973-74), Am. Assn. Sch. Librarians, Southeastern (chmn. librarianship as a career com. 1968-70), Miss. library assns., N.E.A., Am. Assn. U. Profs., Alpha Beta Alpha, Pi Lambda Theta (v.p. local chpt. 1967-69, faculty adviser Alpha Xi chpt. 1969-74), Delta Kappa Gamma (chmn. research com. Zeta chpt. 1971-74). Methodist (adminstrv. bd.). Home: 1631 Laurel St Knoxville TN 37916

MAULL, FLORA DAVIS (MRS. BALDWIN MAULL), sculptor, civic worker; b. Mar. 1, 1904; d. A. S. Johnston and Ella (Thomas) Davis; A.B., Vassar Coll., 1925; sculptor Art Students League, N.Y.C., 1925-26; grad. study sculpture, N.Y.C., Paris, France, 1927-33; m. Baldwin Maull, Dec. 7, 1929; children—Baldwin, Diana. One man show Milch Gallery; exhibited group shows Archtl. League; represented in pvt. collections. Benefit chmn. United Neighborhood Houses, Inc., N.Y.C., 1942-43; founder, chmn. womens com. Payne Whitney Clinic N.Y. Hosp., 1943-46; bd. dirs. Mental Health Assn. N.J., 1950-52; dir., del 5th Internat. Inst. Child Psychiatry, Toronto, Can., 1954; dir., sec., treas. bd. Grosvenor Neighborhood House, Inc., N.Y.C., 1936-54, mem. bd. assos., 1954—; dir., sec., treas. bd. Psychiat. Clinic Buffalo and Erie County, 1953-62; mem. Children's Aid Soc. Com. Foster Home Care, 1960-69; mem. White House Conf. Com., 8th Jud. Dist. Mental Health, 1959-60, bd. dirs. N.Y. State Assn. for Mental Health, 1964-66; mem. Nat. Com. on Crime and Violence, 1967-69; guest White House Conf. on Aging, 1971; docent Art Mus., Princeton, 1971—. Mem. Archaeol. Inst. Am., Albright-Knox Art Gallery (life), Nat. Soc. Colonial Dames in State N.Y. (hist. activities com., Gunston Hall com.), English Speaking Union (del. 1971-73). Clubs: Colony, Badminton (N.Y.C.); Vassar (founder, alumna rep. pres. 1947-51, 69—) (Central N.J.); Present Day (Princeton, N.J.). Author: Three Centuries of Custom Houses, 1972. Address: 25 Alexander St Princeton NJ 08540

MAULLER, PATRICIA JOAN, home economist; b. Hartford City, Ind., May 15, 1923; d. Cecil Everett and Hanna Alita (Anderson) Mauller; B.S., Ball State U., 1945; postgrad. U. Wis., 1952, Purdue U., 1970. Tchr. Miami County Schs., Peru, Ind., 1945-46; home economist Ind. Coop. Extension Service, Huntington County, 1946-55, Elkhart County, 1955-66, Marion County, Indpls., 1966—. Nutrition com. chmn. Community Service Council, 1968-70. Recipient Distinguished Service award Nat. Assn. Extension Home Economists, 1956, Horace Moses Extension fellowship, 1952, 25 Year Service award Ind. Coop. Extension Service, 1971. Mem. Adult Edn. Assn. (sec. 1970-72), Am., Nat. home econs. assns., Ind. Extension Arts. Assn. (home econs. chmn. 1956), Epsilon Sigma Phi, Phi Upsilon Omicron. Methodist. Club: Altrusa (pres. 1971-72) (Indpls.). Home: 2111 Stop 11 Rd Indianapolis IN 46227 Office: City County Bldg Indianapolis IN 46202

MAUNEY, GLORIA JUANITA MEANS, librarian; b. Whitmire, S.C., Feb. 26, 1927; d. Barney Floyd and Sallie Coleman (Hunter) Means; B.S., Allen U., Columbia, S.C., 1950; M.S. in Library Sci., Cath. U. Am., 1968; m. Percy Eugene Mauney, Dec. 26, 1953; children—Shari Corinne, Louis Alvin. Reference librarian Natural History Library, Smithsonian Instn., Washington, 1960-64, br. librarian dept. entomology, 1965-68; librarian D.C. Pub. Schs., 1968—. Mem. A.L.A., D.C. Assn. Sch. Librarians, Smithsonian Assos., Alpha Kappa Alpha. Home: 23 Jefferson St NE Washington DC 20011 Office: 4501 Kansas Av NW Washington DC 20011

MAURER, CAROL JANET NELLIS (MRS. KENNETH O. MAURER), psychiatrist; b. Franklin, Pa., May 15, 1933; d. Charles Nelson and Grace (Woods) Nellis; A.A., Colo. Women's Coll., Denver, 1953; B.A., Goucher Coll., 1956; M.D., Temple U., 1960; m. Kenneth O. Maurer, July 5, 1958; children—Timothy Charles, Kathleen Cynthia, Sabrina Lynn. Rotating intern Nazareth Hosp., Phila., 1960-61; physician Polk (Pa.) State Sch. and Hosp., 1962-65; resident psychiatry Warren (Pa.) State Hosp., 1965-68, sr. psychiatrist, 1968; practice medicine specializing in psychiatry, 1968—; staff psychiatrist Venango County Mental Health Center, Oil City, Pa., 1969-72; med. dir. Titusville Hosp. Mental Health Center, 1971-73; active staff Oil City Hosp., 1972—; cons. psychiatry Franklin (Pa.), 1969—, Titusville (Pa.) Hosp., 1971—, also Famliy Service Agy. and Clarion County Child Welfare Agy. Active Shubert Club (rec. sec. 1970-71). Mem. Oil City Area Sch. Bd., 1971—; mem. Venango County and Pa. Rep. Women. Bd. dirs. Community Concert Assn., 1969-72, Venango County Health Planning Council, 1973—; med. adviser, pres. Venango County bd. Nat. Found., 1972—; adv. bd. VenArc Sheltered Workshop, 1972-73; bd. dirs. Family Service Agy., 1973—. Recipient Alumni citation Temple Buell Coll., 1966; named One of Outstanding Young Women of Am., 1966, 67. Mem. Pa. (mem. com. medicine and religion 1974—), Venango County (sec.-treas. 1970—) med. socs., Am. Psychiat. Assn., Am. Profl. Practice Assn., Pa. Psychiat. Soc., Zonta Internat. Lutheran (social welfare com.). Contbr. articles to profl. jours. Home: 15 Stewart Rd Oil City PA 16301 Office: 222 Seneca St Rm 328 Oil City PA 16301

MAURER, EVA DELL, psychologist, counselor; b. Bloomington, Ill., Nov. 4, 1924; d. John Springer and Ione (Goodrich) Maurer; B.S., Ill. State Normal, 1959; M.A., U. Ill., 1963, Ph.D., 1973. Chemist, Alpha Cellulose Corp., Bloomington, 1951-57; sch. psychologist pub. schs., Urbana, Ill., 1965—; pvt. practice counseling psychology, Champaign, Ill., 1974—. Mem. Am. Psychol. Assn., A.A.A.S. Democrat. Presbyn. Home: 1001 1/2 E Washington St Urbana IL 61801 Office: 1201 S Vine St Urbana IL 61801 also 501 S 6th St Champaign IL 61820

MAURER, HELEN STATIA (MRS. WILLIAM E. JOHNSTONE), physician; b. Meadows, Ill., Mar. 27, 1937; d. Hugh Harry and Gaynell Frieda (Rice) Maurer; student Bob Jones U., 1956-58; B.S., U. Ill., 1960, M.D., 1964; m. William E. Johnstone, Jan. 3, 1970. Intern U. Cin. Gen. Hosp., 1964-65; resident pediatrics Cin. Children's Hosp., 1965-67; hematology fellow U. Ill. Dept. Pediatrics, 1967-70, asst. prof. pediatrics, 1970—. Mem. Am. Acad. Pediatrics, Am. Soc. Hematology, Midwest Soc. Pediatric Research. Office: 840 S Wood St Chicago IL 60612 also 3030 N Normandy St Chicago IL 60634

MAURER, LORETTA ANNA, educator; b. Bklyn., Sept. 2, 1936; d. Joseph and Anna (Mader) Maurer; diploma Bklyn. Hosp. Sch. Nursing, 1960; B.A. in Health Edn., Jersey City State Coll., 1970, M.A. in Health Adminstrn., 1973. Staff nurse Willowbrook Developmental Center, S.I., N.Y., 1963-66, head nurse, 1966-69, nurse instr., 1969—, coordinator rehab. unit, 1965. Mem. Phenylketonuria Screening Com.; del. postgrad. symposium Elwyn Inst., Media, Pa., 1973. Mem. N.Y. State Legislative Adv. Com., 1970—; mem. policy making seminars of Med. Adv. Bd. N.Y.C., 1969. Mem. Royal Soc. Health, Am. Nurses Assn., Am. Assn. on Mental Deficiency (in-service rep. regional 9 conf. Del. 1972), Columbiettes K.C. Club: South Mountain Figure Skating. Home: 481 Bard Av Staten Island NY 10310 Office: 2760 Victory Blvd Staten Island NY 10314

MAURER, MADELLA JOHNS RIGBY (MRS. ROLAND MAURER), psychologist; b. Chester Pa., Jan. 4, 1903; d. William Harlan and Madella (Cheetham) Rigby; B.S., U. Pa., 1926, M.A., 1930; m. Roland Maurer, June 24, 1933 (dec. July 1966). Tchr., Chester Jr. High Sch., 1926-27; sec. to dean of women U. Pa., Phila., 1927-28, recorder psychol. clinic, 1928-30; psychologist Chester Sch. Dist., 1930-33, Survey Poor Houses, State of Del., 1933; visitor Phila. County Relief Bd., 1934; analyst Pa. State Employment Service, Phila., 1935; psychologist Allentown (Pa.) State Hosp., 1936-38, Phila Bd. Compulsory Edn., 1939; tchr., Elmira, N.Y., 1955-56, Haddonfield (N.J.) Meml. High Sch., 1956-59; asst. dir. spl. edn., tests and measurement Upper Darby (Pa.) Sch. Dist., 1959-60; staff psychologist Stockley (Del.) Hosp. for Mentally Retarded, 1960-64, acting chief psychology, 1961-64; clin. psychologist Mental Health Clinic, Del., 1963-64, Selinsgrove (Pa.) State Sch. and Hosp., 1964—. Mem. Nat. Assn. Women Deans and Counselors, Am. Assn. U. Women, Council Exceptional Children, D.A.R. (regent Conrad Weiser chpt. 1971—, vice chmn. mag. com. 1974—), Am., Eastern, Del., Pa. psychol. assns., Pa. Assn. Retarded Children, A.A.A.S., Nat. Audubon Soc., Mortar Bd., Kappa Alpha Theta. Club: Woman's Triangle (2d v.p. 1972-74). Home: Box 264 Selinsgrove PA 17870 Office: Box 500 Selinsgrove PA 17870

MAURER, MARILYN ANN, motel co. exec.; b. E. Detroit, Mich., May 4, 1935; d. Charles Oren and Bernice Elnora (Wynn) Mumford; student Western Mich. U., 1954; divorced; children—Cheryl Lee, Max Timothy. With Howard Johnson's Motor Lodge, Brookville, Pa., 1969—, mgr., 1970—, area mgr. for Pa., also trainer mgmt. personnel and new motels for company, 1973—. Active local Girl Scouts, P.T.A. Bd. dirs. Laurel Festival, Brookville United Fund. Mem. Am., Pa. hotel-motel assns., Women's Soc. Christian Service (pres. 1968-69). Republican. Methodist (mem. ch. bd. 1966-69, policy com. 1967-69). Home: Route 4 Brookville PA 15825 Office: Howard Johnson's Motor Lodge I-80 Exit 13 Brookville PA 15825

MAURER, VICKIE SUE, orgn. exec.; b. Lansing, Mich., June 12, 1942; d. Gearld Lee and Margaret Ellen (Washer) Maurer; B.S., Eastern Mich. U., 1964; postgrad. Central Mich. U., 1968-69, Mich. State U., 1966—. Tchr. phys. edn. Dundee (Mich.) High Sch., 1964-65, Manistee (Mich.) Pub. Schs., 1965-69; camp dir. field adviser, dir. program services Girl Scouts Southwestern Mich., St. Joseph, 1969-72; camping services adminstr. Girl Scouts Singing Sands, Niles, Mich., 1972-74; program services camp adminstr. No. Oakland County Girl Scouts, Pontiac, Mich., 1974—. Instr. first aid A.R.C., St. Joseph, 1970—. Mem. Assn. Girl Scouts Profl. Workers (regional sec. 1971-73), Am. Mich. camping assns. Home: 100 S River Pontiac MI 48055 Office: 91 S Telegraph Pontiac MI 48053

MAURIELLO, EDNA ANNE, coll. dean, educator; b. Beston; d. Eugene and Angela (Caggiano) Mauriello; B.S., Salem State Coll., 1946; Ed.M., Boston Coll., 1951; Ed.D., Boston U., 1960. Lang. retng. therapist, Boston Vets. Hosp., Boston, 1950-58; asst. dir. Office Testing Services, Boston Coll., 1958-59; guidance counselor Needham High Sch., Needham, Mass., 1959-60; research asso. Mass.

Council for Pub. Schs., 1960-62; asso. prof. Salem State Coll., 1962-65, asso. dean of students, 1965—, prof. grad. div., 1962—. Exec. com. Project COPE (task force on drug abuse), 1969—. Mem. sch. bd. St. John's Sch., Swampscott, Mass., 1968-70; vice chmn. master plan com. Town Swampscott, 1969-70. Mem. Mass. Assn. Women Deans and Counselors (exec. bd. 1968-70), Am. Personnel and Guidance Assn. (profl. ethics com. 1968—), Delta Kappa Gamma (exec. bd. Mass. chpt. 1969-70), Pi Lambda Theta. Home: 2 Smith Lane Swampscott MA 01907 Office: Salem State Coll Salem MA 01970

MAURO, EILEEN FRANCES, hosp. adminstr.; b. Phila., May 18, 1944; d. Guy James and Catherine Elizabeth (Morrow) Mauro; B.A., Duquesne U., 1967. Summer intern Newsletter Office, State Dept., Washington, 1965; writer/reporter S. Hills Community Newspapers, Pitts., 1966-67; asst. dir. pub. relations Duquesne U., 1967-70, Mercy Cath. Med. Center, Darby, Pa., 1970—. Free-lance pub. relations cons., 1969, 72. Mem. planning com. Del. County (Pa.) Health Fair, 1972; mem. Darby-Colwyn (Pa.) Drug Abuse Com., 1971. Named Outstanding Woman in Journalism, Duquesne U., 1967; recipient In the Pub. Interest award radio sta. WDUQ, 1967; MacEachern award Acad. Hosp. Pub. Relations, 1971. Mem. Hosp. Assn. Pa., Del. Valley Assn. Communicators, Del. Valley Hosp. Pub. Relations Assn., Am. Soc. Hosp. Pub. Relations Dirs., Women in Communications (treas. Phila. chpt. 1972-74). Home: 1600 Garrett Rd Upper Darby PA 19082 Office: Mercy Cath Med Center Lansdowne Av and Baily Rd Darby PA 19023

MAUTZ, KATHRYN ANN, judge; b. Wallace, Ida., Jan. 27, 1930; d. Anton F. and Katherine (Barbieri) Mautz; J.D., U. Ida., 1952. Admitted Wash. bar, 1952; practiced law in Spokane, 1952-54; judge Dist. Ct. No. 4, Spokane, 1955—; juvenile traffic commr. Superior Ct., 1960-64. Adv. bd. Spokane County Mental Health Assn., 1961, v.p. exec. bd., 1962-63; mem. bd. Community Action Council, 1969-71, Spokane Alcoholism Bd., 1968-71, Spokane Legal Services Bd., 1972—; trustee Spokane County Family Counseling Service, 1964-66. Mem. Wash. (chmn. state family law com. 1967-68), Spokane County bar assns., Am., Wash. mental health assns., Spokane C. of C. (indsl. devel. bur., edn. bur., recipient trophy as toastmistress of year 1953), N.Am. Benefit Assn., Wash. Magistrates Assn. (pres. 1965-66), U. Ida. Alumni Assn., Am. Assn. U. Women (life mem., nat. by laws com. 1973-74, pres. Spokane 1967-69, treas. Wash. State div. 1974-76), Am. Judicature Soc., Am. Judges Assn. (chmn. Wash. 1964, nat. gov. 1965-67, 71-72, nat. treas. 1967-69). Club: Toastmistress (pres. 1954, area winner speaking contest 1953) (Spokane). Office: Pub Safety Bldg Spokane WA 99201

MAVES, BARBARA ANN BANER, home economist; b. Chgo., Apr. 14, 1934; d. Charles Martin and Ella (Detweiler) Baner; student Eureka Coll., 1952-53; B.S., Bradley U., 1957; student Howard County Jr. Coll., 1957-58, N.Y. State Coll. at Buffalo, summer 1961; M.A., Ball State U., 1965; m. Ronald Stanley Maves, Dec. 30, 1955 (div. 1974); children—Scott Stanley, Steven Snyder. Women's staff writer Peoria (Ill.) Jour. Star, 1954-55; tchr. Big Spring (Tex.) Ind. Sch. Dist., 1956-58; pub. relations Gen. Mills, Buffalo, 1959; home economist Ind. & Mich. Electric Co., Marion, Ind., 1963-66; with Muncie (Ind.) Community Schs., 1966-70; dir. Ind. Consumer Adv. Council, Ind. Dept. Commerce, 1970; v.p. consumer sales div. Investment Diamonds Inc., Muncie, Ind., 1971-72; dir. Indpls. Office of Consumer Affairs, Indpls., 1972; adminstr. operations div. Community Service Program, Indpls., 1973-74; exec. dir. Planned Parenthood Delaware County, Muncie, 1974—. Adv. com. Ind. Family Planning Project. Co-chmn. 5th Congl. Dist. Young Republicans, 1966-67; co-chmn. Delaware County Young Republicans, 1967-69, chmn., 1969-70; state program chmn. Ind. Young Rep. Fedn., 1967-68, state co-chmn., 1968-70; membership chmn. Young Rep. Nat. Fedn., 1969-71; mem. Ind. Rep. Central com., 1968-70; mem. Rep. nat. com. voter registration, 1968, chmn. Ind. mil. absentee voting, 1968. Mem. Am., Ind. (exec. bd. 1972—) home econs. assns., Am. Assn. U. Women, Muncie Community Welfare Council (exec. bd.), Ind. Polit. Women's Caucus, Internat. Platform Assn., Psi Iota Xi. Methodist. Home: 2100 Twickingham Dr Muncie IN 47304 Office: Johnson Bldg Muncie IN 47305

MAVROLAS, HELEN PATRICIA JOANIDES (MRS. LEON N. MAVROLAS), writer, editor, photographer; b. Cleve., Aug. 16, 1925; d. Albert and Catherine (Jacobs) Joanides; student Ohio State U., 1945; m. Leon N. Mavrolas, July 25, 1948; children—Pamela, Cathy, Steven. With Will, Inc., advt., Cleve., 1945-46, Meldrum & Fewsmith Advt., Cleve., 1946-48; with West Life, Westlake, O., 1964—, feature writer, 1964—, photographer, 1965—, copy editor, 1969—. Mem. Women in Communications. Club: Rocky River (O.) Coterie. Home: 2540 Hampton Rd Rocky River OH 44116 Office: 26915 Westwood Rd Westlake OH 44145

MAW, ETHEL WILDEY (MRS. WALLACE HENRY MAW), educator; b. Moscow, O., June 21, 1918; d. Tom and Texie Lenox (Kirk) Wildey; certificate Wilmington Coll., 1938; B.S., U. Cin., 1947; M.S., U. Pa., 1951, Ph.D., 1959; m. Wallace Henry Maw, Aug. 31, 1946. Tchr. Monroe Twp. Pub. Sch., New Richmond, O., 1938-47, Cin. Pub. Sch., 1947-50, Lower Merion Twp. Pub. Schs., Ardmore, Pa., 1951-52, Springfield (Pa.) Pub. Schs., 1952-54; Fulbright lectr. Delhi (India) U., 1954-55; tchr. reading Sch. of Edn., U. Pa., Phila., 1951; lectr. Bryn Mawr (Pa.) Coll., 1957-62, asst. prof., 1962-67, asso. prof., 1968-71, prof., chmn. dept. edn. and child devel., 1971—; vis. fellow Inst. Advanced Studies, Australian Nat. U., Canberra, 1972. Cons. psychology Sch. of Edn., U. Pa., 1948-49. Bd. dirs. New Gulph Child Care Center. Mem. Assn. for Supervision and Curriculum Devel., Am. Ednl. Research Assn., League of Women Voters, Am. Assn. U. Women (legislative chmn. 1959-60), Kappa Delta Pi, Pi Lambda Theta, Delta Kappa Gamma. Home: Rural Route 2 Kennett Square PA 19348 Office: Bryn Mawr Coll Bryn Mawr PA 19010

MAWARDI, BETTY HOSMER (MRS. OSMAN K. MAWARDI), educator; b. Elkhart, Ind., Feb. 1, 1921; d. George H. and DeLoscia (Longacher) Hosmer; A.B., Radcliffe Coll., 1943, M.T.P., 1946, Ph.D., 1959; M.A., Wellesley Coll., 1952; m. Osman K. Mawardi, Nov. 23, 1950. Counselor placement office Wellesley Coll., 1946-52, asst. dir., 1953-54; research asst. Harvard, 1955-59, research asso., 1959-60; asst. prof. med. edn. research, asst. clin. prof. psychology Case-Western Res. U., 1960-66, asso. prof., asso. clin. prof., 1966—. Mem. Am., Eastern psychol. assns., Soc. Psychol. Study Social Issues, Am. Sociol. Assn., Assn. Am. Med. Colls., A.A.A.S., Sigma Xi. Contbr. articles to profl. jours. Home: 15 Mornington Lane Cleveland Heights OH 44106 Office: 2119 Abington Rd Cleveland OH 44106

MAWER, MURIEL ALICE, lawyer; b. Vancouver, B.C., Can., Dec. 20, 1912; d. Douglas Fred and Edith Mary (Freeman) Mawer; B.A. magna cum laude, U. Wash., 1933, J.D., 1935. Admitted to Wash. bar, 1935; gen. practice, partner firm Mawer & Wigle, 1935-42; dist. price atty., dist. atty. OPA, 1942-47; regional counsel Office of Price Stblzn., 1951-53; partner firm Karr, Tuttle, Koch, Campbell, Mawer & Morrow, Seattle, 1954—. Mem. Seattle Civic Center Adv. Com., 1963-71; adv. bd. Seattle-King County Council on Aging, 1956—; citizen rep. to CARE; exec. dir. Seattle Junior Programs, Inc. Mem. finance bd. St. Joseph's Parochial Sch.; trustee Seattle-King County chpt. Nat. Found., Seattle Prep. Sch., Forest Ridge Sch.; adv. bd. Convent of the Sacred Heart, Forest Ridge; bd. regents Gonzaga U. Mem. Am., Washington State, Seattle-King County (trustee 1968-72, mem. exec. bd.) bar assns., Am. Assn. U. Women (past pres. Seattle Br. and Wash. div.). Club: Altrussa (internat. pres.). Home: 1631 Interlaken Pl E Seattle WA 98112 Office: Seattle First Bank Bldg Seattle WA 98154

MAXWELL, BARBARA ANN, educator; b. Keokuk, Ia., Aug. 11, 1931; d. Fred Wilson and Grace Eileen (Jester) Maxwell; A.S., St. Joseph Jr. Coll., 1951; B.S., U. Mo., 1953. Tchr. 2d grade Lindbergh Sch., St. Joseph, Mo., 1953—. Mem. St. Joseph Sch. Dist. Curriculum Council, 1972—. Mem. Mo. State Tchrs. Assn. (resolutions com. 1967-72, exec. com. 1972—, credentials com. for Assembly of Delegates 1970), Community Tchrs. Assn. (sec. 1969-70, pres. 1972-73), St. Joseph Dist./St. Joseph Community Tchrs. Assn. (instructional procedures com.), Mo. (corr. sec. 1969-71), St. Joseph (pres. 1965-67) assns. for childhood edn., Am. Assn. U. Women, U. Mo. Edn. Alumni Assn. (sec.-treas. 1968-72), Delta Kappa Gamma, Pi Lambda Theta, Phi Theta Kappa. Presbyn. (chmn. Ladies Circle 1967-70). Home: 1830 Lovers Lane Terrace St Joseph MO 64505 Office: Lindbergh Sch St Joseph Av at Concord St St Joseph MO 64505

MAXWELL, ELIZABETH STARBUCK (MRS. CHARLES RICHARD MAXWELL), chemist; b. Birmingham, Ala., June 6, 1918; d. Edwin Guy and Byrd Viola (Burks) Starbuck; B.S., U. Ala., 1938; Sc.D., Johns Hopkins, 1948; m. Charles Richard Maxwell, July 25, 1942; children—Richard, Sarah (Mrs. David Murray Elliot). Microbiologist, Ala. Health Dept., Montgomery, 1939-40; chemist Los Alamos labs. U. Cal. at Berkeley, 1942-46; with NIH, Bethesda, Md., 1950—, research biochemist, 1956—. Bd. dirs. Found. for Advanced Edn. in Scis., Inc., Bethesda. Mem. Am. Chem. Soc., Am. Soc. Biol. Chemists, Sigma Xi. Mem. Unitarian Ch. Contbr. articles to profl. jours. Home: 4510 Gretna St Bethesda MD 20014 Office: Molecular Biology Nat Inst Arthritis and Metabolic Diseases Nat Inst Health Bethesda MD 20014

MAXWELL, FLORENCE HINSHAW (MRS. JOHN WILLIAMSON MAXWELL), civic worker; b. Nora, Ind., July 14, 1914; d. Asa Bennet and Gertrude (Randall) Hinshaw; B.A. cum laude, Butler U., 1935; m. John Williamson Maxwell, June 5, 1936; children—Marilyn, William Douglas. Coordinator, Sight Conservation and Aid to Blind, 1962-73, nat. chmn., 1969-73, active various fund drives; chmn. jamboree, hostess coms. North Central High Sch., 1959, 64; Girl Scouts U.S.A., 1937-38, 54-56; mus. chmn. Sr. Girl Scout Regional Council, 1956-57; scorekeeper Little League, 1955-57; bd. dirs. Nora Sch. Parents' Club, 1958-59, Eastwood Jr. High Sch. Triangle Club, 1959-62; bd. dirs. women's com. Ind. State Symphony Soc., 1965-67; vision screening Indpls. innercity pub. sch. kindergartens, pre-schs., 1962—; chmn. vision screening Head Start, 1967—; asst. Glaucoma screening clinics Gen. Hosp., Glendale Shopping Center, City County Bldg., Am. Legion Nat. Hdqrs., Ind. Health Assn. Conf., 1962—; chmn. sight conservation and aid to blind Nat. Delta Gamma Found., Indpls., Columbus, O., 1969-73; mem. telethon team Butler Univ. Fund, 1964; Symphoguide hostess Internat. Conf. on Cities, 1971, Nat. League of Cities, 1972; bd. dirs. Ind. Soc. Prevention Blindness, 1962—, exec. com., sec., 1971—; mem. Women's com. Ind. State Symphony Soc. Recipient Key to City of Indpls., 1972. Mem. Ind., Nat. (Sight-Saving award 1974) socs. for prevention blindness, Delta Gamma (Cable award 1969, Outstanding Alumna award 1973). Republican. Address: 1502 E 80th St Indianapolis IN 46240

MAXWELL, HAZEL DELORIS BRAMLETTE (MRS. JOHN W. MAXWELL), civic worker; b. Chgo.; d. John Mitchell and Katherine (Heard) Bramlette; grad. Chgo. Normal Sch., 1931; A.B. in Edn., Howard U., 1935; m. Virginius D. Johnston, Feb. 26, 1926 (dec. Aug. 1955); children—Anna Katherine (Mrs. Charles C. Diggs, Jr.), Lowell Douglass; m. 2d, John W. Maxwell, Nov. 29, 1958. Tchr. pub. schs., Washington, 1944-58. Mem Wis. Trade Mission to Europe, 1964-65, Far East, 1967. Mem. community planning com. United Community Services, 1965-67; mem. adv. bd. Cedarcrest Girls' Home, 1966—; mem. adv. council on library devel., Wis., pres. St. Anthony Hosp. Aux., 1960-62; aux. parliamentarian Nat. Med. Assn., 1966-68. Bd. dirs. Milw. YWCA, 1960-66, pres., 1967—; trustee Milw. Pub. Library, pres. bd., 1967—; chmn. adv. com. Sickle Cell Center, Deaconess Hosp., 1970-72; mem. women's adv. bd. Heritage Bank of Milw., 1971—; mem. Gimbel's Fashion Forum Bd. Recipient Woman of Yr. in Community Service award Milw. chpt. Theta Sigma Phi, 1969; Headliner award Milw. Press Club, 1970; Pro Urbe award Mt. Mary Coll., 1971. Mem. Wis. Library Trustees Assn. (pres. 1970-72), Woman's Aux. Nat. Med. Assn. (pres. Women's aux. 1973-74), Am. Assn. U. Women, Am. Library Trustees Assn. (sec. 1973-74), Links, Inc. (founder, 1st pres. Milw. chpt.), Alpha Kappa Alpha. Episcopalian (vestrywoman, treas. Altar Guild, 1965—). Home: 1610 N Prospect Av Milwaukee WI 53202

MAXWELL, JESSICA MARY, journalist; b. Los Angeles, Aug. 11, 1950; d. Norman Scot and Mary Meeker (Nacol) Maxwell; student San Jose State Coll., 1968-69, U. So. Cal., 1969-70, Inst. Am. Univs., Aix, France, 1970-71; B.A., U. Ore., 1973. Free lance journalist, 1973—; guest editor Mademoiselle Mag., 1973—. Mem. Women in Communications. Contbr. articles to various mags. Address: 1800 Highland Manhattan Beach CA 90266

MAXWELL, JOANNE LOUISE DUTCHER (MRS. DONALD P. MAXWELL), editor; b. Chgo.; d. William Rodney and Phoebe (Hirshey) Dutcher; A.B., Monmouth Coll., 1953; m. Donald Philip Maxwell, Oct. 6, 1956; children—Donna Jo, Barbara Lee. Gen. reporter suburban life, LaGrange Park, Ill., 1953-54; asso. editor Glen Ellyn (Ill.) News, 1954-55; founder DuPage County News Service, Inc., 1955, pres., 1955-59; founder DuPage Assos., pub. relations, 1955, pres., 1955-65; editor Naperville Clarion, also Lisle Clarion, 1956-63, Warrenville Clarion, 1958-63; adminstrv. asst. to U.S. Rep. from Ill. 14th Congl. Dist., 1965-67; exec. asst. to U.S. Rep. John N. Erlenborn, 1967—; pres. DuPage Consultants, 1963-66; sec. Attention, Inc., 1965—, also dir.; sec., dir. Westin & Assos., Inc.; corr. to various newspapers. Tag Day chmn. Salvation Army, Naperville, 1962, 63; adv. bd. Martin Mitchell Mus., 1971—. Campaign mgr. press dir. various county and state polit. campaigns, also John N. Erlenborn for U.S. Rep. campaign, 1964, 66, 68, 70; mem. DuPage County exec. bd. Young Republicans, 1958-59, 65-68, sec., Naperville, 1957-58, editor county publ., 1965-66; press dir. ann. conv. Abraham Lincoln Nat. Rep. Club, 1955-57; Recipient numerous awards for articles, Good Neighbor award Japanese Am. Citizens League, 1959. Mem. Nat. Editorial Assn., Ill. (Editor of Year 1961), DuPage (charter, sec. 1958-60) press assns., DuPage Hist. Soc., Monmouth Coll. Alumni Assn. (sec. Chgo. chpt. 1960), Naperville Heritage Soc., Women in Communications (nat. legislative chmn. 1969-71), Sigma Tau Delta, Pi Kappa Delta, Phi Alpha Theta, Kappa Kappa Gamma. Episcopalian. Home: 30 Maple Lane Naperville IL 60540 Office: 108 N Main St Wheaton IL 60187

MAXWELL, MADALYN, lawyer; b. Nashville, Ill., Jan. 9, 1926; d. Judge Ralph L. and Beulah (House) Maxwell; student Whitworth Coll., 1943-45; B.S., U. Ill., 1947, M.A., 1949; m. Thomas H. McGary, 1968. Admitted to Ill. bar, 1951; practiced in Nashville, Ill., 1951-53; (position) with inheritance tax div. Ill. Atty. Gen. Office, Springfield, 1953-55, asst. atty. gen. in charge pub. assistance claims enforcement div., 1956—; asst. to treas. Sangamo Electric Co., Springfield, Ill., 1955-56. Mem. Am., Ill., Sangamon County bar assns., Ill., Sangamon, Washington County hist. socs., Am. Judicature Soc. Episcopalian (lay reader). Home: 1520 Bates Av Springfield IL 62704 Office: Ridgely Bldg Springfield IL 62706

MAXWELL, MARTHA ANN, librarian; b. Paragould, Ark., Mar. 16, 1938; d. Lloyd Carroll and Jessie Leone (Fairchild) Maxwell; student S.E. Mo. State Coll., 1956-57; B.S., Ark. State U., 1960; M.A., George Peabody Coll. for Tchrs., 1961. Reference and extension librarian Scenic Regional Library, Union, Mo., 1961-63, asst. librarian, 1963-64; coordinator S.E. Mo. Library System, Cape Girardeau, 1965—; adminstrv. librarian Cape Girardeau Pub. Library, 1966—. Sec. steering com. Citizen's Goals for Cape Girardeau, 1968-70; chmn. Community Enrichment Task Force, 1968-70. Mem. Mo. Libraries Film Coop. Bd., 1972—. Bd. dirs. Cape Girardeau Voluntary Action Center, 1973—; bd. dirs. Christian Arts Council. Mem. Mo. Library Assn. (pres. pub. libraries div. 1973-74, A.L.A., Mo. Adult Edn. Assn., Am. Assn. Univ. Women (v.p. 1966-68, pres. 1969-73), Bus. and Profl. Women (v.p. 1969-71, sec. 1967-69, 71-72), League of Women Voters (membership chmn. provisional league 1967, bd. dir. 1967-70), C. of C. (edn. com. chmn. 1971). Democrat. Methodist. Home: 410 Themis St Apt D Cape Girardeau MO 63701 Office: Cape Girardeau Pub Libarary Courthouse Park Cape Girardeau MO 63701

MAXWELL, MARTHA JANE ORR, educator; b. Washington, Apr. 30, 1923; d. Thomas F. and Jessie (Anderson) Orr; B.A., U. Md., 1946, M.A., 1948, Ph.D., 1960; m. George A. Maxwell, Nov. 17, 1941 (div. Oct. 1965); children—Martha Christine (Mrs. Walter A. Fendley), George A., Barbara Elizabeth. Dir. reading and study skils Lab., asso. prof. psychology U. Md., College Park, 1951-68; dir. reading services, lectr. edn. U. Cal. at Berkeley, 1968-73, dir. Student Learning Center, 1973—. Fellow Am. Psychology Assn. (div. 17); mem. N. Reading Conf. Am. (exec. bd. 1973), Nat. Council Research in English, Internat. Reading Assn. (research com. 1966-70), Phi Delta Kappa. Author: Skimming and Scanning Improvement, 1969. Contbr. articles to profl. jours. Home: Box 745 Berkeley CA 94704

MAXWELL, MARY DALE BRETT (MRS. CHARLES LEROY MAXWELL), educator, clubwoman; b. Cordell, Okla., July 5, 1910; d. Rutherford and Gertrude (Whitaker) Brett; B.F.A., U. Okla., 1938; m. Charles Leroy Maxwell, Mar. 9, 1944; children—Marilyn Dale, William Brett. Tchr. pub. sch. and music, Verden, Okla., 1931-36, Alva Pub. Schs., 1938, Ardmore Pub. Schs., 1939-43; screener Bechtel McCone Fgn. Employment Corp., Los Angeles, 1943-44; corr. U.S. Treasury, Chgo., 1944; job adviser U.S Employment Service, Chgo., 1944-45. Active A.R.C., United drive, Boy Scouts Am., March of Dimes. Pres. Alva Research Club, 1955-56. Mem. D.A.R. (regent Cherokee Outlet chpt. 1960-62, del. Continental Congress, Washington 1961), P.E.O. (pres. local chpt. 1956-58, treas. Okla. chpt. 1968-69, corr. sec. 1969-70, rec. sec. 1970-71, organizer 1971-72, 1st v.p. 1973-74), Alva Women's Golf Assn. (pres. 1968), Alpha Phi. Baptist. Home: 502 Lake Dr Alva OK 73717

MAXWELL, MILDRED L. LAYMAN (MRS. GEORGE ROBERT MAXWELL), educator; b. Bristow, Okla., Sept. 18; d. Harry Elmer and Myrtle A. (Knight) Layman; student Wichita U., 1937-38; B.S., Okla. State U., 1941; M.E., U. Ark., 1967; m. George Robert Maxwell, Dec. 30, 1939; children—Robert Richard, Jon Michael. Tchr. pub. schs., Searcy, Ark., 1960-62, Searcy Sr. High Sch., 1962-65; guidance counselor Searcy Jr. High Sch., 1965—. Exec. bd., sec.-treas., pres. White County Sheltered Workshop. Mem. Am. Assn. U Women, Am., Ark. personnel and guidance assns., Ark. Sch. Counselors Assn., Searcy Edn. Assn. (exec. bd. 1971-72), Zeta Tau Alpha, Omicron Nu, Beta Sigma Phi (pres. 1968-70), P.E.O. (pres. 1970-72). Baptist. Home: 110 Ridge Pl Searcy AR 72143

MAXWELL, MURIEL OMDAHL, phys. therapist; b. Boston, Sept. 29, 1929; d. Oscar Emanuel and Helia Maria (Mattson) Omdahl; B.S. in Edn., Tufts Coll., 1952; diploma Boston Sch. Occupational Therapy, 1952; certificate phys. therapy Columbia, 1958; m. Harry Lee Maxwell, July 2, 1966 (dec. Apr. 1967). Joined USAF, 1952, discharged, 1955, re-enlisted, 1959, advanced through ranks to lt. col., 1973; chief therapist USAF med. centers, Scott AFB, Ill., 1967-70, Andrews AFB, Md., 1970-71, USAF regional hosps., Westover AFB, Mass., 1971-73, Eglin AFB, Fla., 1973—. Mem. Am. Phys. Therapy Assn., Am. Occupational Therapy Assn. Home: 67 Dartmouth St Belmont MA 02178 Office: 32 Denton Blvd Fort Walton FL 32548

MAXWELL, VERA JORDAN (MRS. ROBERT ROSCOE MAXWELL), librarian; b. DeSota, Ga., Nov. 19, 1917; d. James Gordon and Lilla Jefferson (Kilcrease) Jordan; student Ga. Southwestern Coll., 1934-36, Asbury Coll., 1936-37; B.S., Ga. State Coll. for Women, 1940; M.S., Fla. State U., 1950; m. Robert Roscoe Maxwell, July 22, 1951; children—Vera Elaine, Pamela Ann, Lee Robert. Tchr. elementary sch., Crawford County, Ga., 1937-43; tchr.-librarian high sch., Byron, Ga., 1943-47; librarian Jordan Vocational High Sch., Columbus, Ga., 1947-51; tchr. English, Thomasville (Ga.) High Sch., 1951-53; chief librarian VA Domiciliary, Thomasville, 1960-62; librarian Birdwood Jr. Coll., Thomasville, 1966—; v.p. Maxwell Sheet Metal Works, Inc., Thomasville, 1951—. Chmn. fund drive Thomas County Heart Assn., 1953; librarian Thomasville Garden Center, 1957—; pres. Jerger Sch. P.T.A., 1962-63; mem. Thomas-Colquitt Regional Library Bd., 1972—. Adv. bd. Salvation Army, 1956-73; bd. dirs. Community Chest, 1967-70. Named Woman of Yr., 2d Dist. Federated Woman's Club, 1958. Mem. Thomasville (pres. 1952-53), Peach County (pres. 1945-46) tchrs. assns., Woman's Soc. Christian Service (pres. 1964-66), Elks Woman's Aux., Theta Omega. Methodist. Clubs: Thomasville Woman's (pres. 1971-73), Killarney Queen Garden. Home: 107 Pastime Dr Thomasville GA 31792 Office: PO Box 1308 Thomasville GA 31792

MAY, BEATRICE M., educator; b. New Brunswick, N.J.; d. Louis F. and Margaret E. (Funk) May; A.B., Douglass Coll., 1949; postgrad. Traphagen Sch. Design, summer 1949, Va. Poly. Inst., summer 1958; M.S., Drexel U., 1956, postgrad., summer 1957. Instr. textiles and clothing U. R.I., Kingston, 1956-60, asst. prof., 1960-61; instr. Simmons Coll., Boston, summer, 1960; asst. 4-H extension specialist, asst. prof. N.J. Coop. Extension Service, Rutgers U., New Brunswick, 1961-67, asso. 4-H extension specialist, asso. prof., 1967-69, prof., chmn. dept. home econs. extension, 1969—. Mem. consumer affairs coordinating com. Nat. Retail Mchts. Assn., 1972—. Mem. Am. (sec. textiles and clothing sect. 1962-64), N.J. (pres. 1966-68, state trustee and mem. exec. council 1962—) home econs. assns., Middlesex County Home Econs. Council (chmn. 1961-62), Am., N.J. assns. adult edn., N.E. Admistrs. Home Econs. (chmn. 1972-74, mem. at large exec. bd. 1974—), Home Econs. Edn. Assn., Drexel U., Douglass Coll. alumni assns., Damien Dutton Soc., Epsilon Sigma Phi. Home: 530 Allgair Av North Brunswick NJ 08902

MAY, ELAINE, entertainer; b. Phila., 1932; d. Jack Berlin; ed. high sch; studied Stanislavsky method of acting with Marie Ouspenskaya; m. Marvin May (div.); 1 dau., Jeannie. Stage and radio appearances as child actor; performed Playwright's Theatre, Chgo.; with Mike

Nichols, others, appeared with improvisational theatre group in night club The Compass, Chgo., to 1957; with Mike Nichols appeared N.Y. supper clubs Village Vanguard, Blue Angel, also nigh clubs other cities; TV debut on Jack Parr Show, also appeared Steve Allen Show, Omnibus, 1958, Dinah Shore Show, Perry Como Show, TV specials; mem. panel Laugh Line, NBC, 1959; rec. spoken comedy Improvisations to Music, Mercury Records; weekly appearance NBC radio show Nightline; appeared with Mike Nichols, N.Y. Town Hall, 1959, An Evening with Mike Nichols and Elaine May, Golden Theatre, N.Y.C., 1960-61. Author: (play) A Matter of Position. Office: care Jack Rollins 200 W 57th St New York City NY 10019*

MAY, FLORENCE ELSIE, nurse, educator; b. Brunswick, O., Oct. 22, 1917; d. Arthur William and Clara Emma (Brasse) May; R.N., M.B., Johnson Sch. Nursing, 1939; B.S., Case-Western Res. U., 1951, M.A., 1952. Pvt. duty nursing Elyria (O.) Meml. Hosp., 1939-42; staff nurse, head nurse, instr. and supr. VA Hosp., Brecksille, O., 1942-49; coordinator nursing edn., asst. prof. U. Toledo, 1952-53; asst. to dir. nursing edn. Akron (O.) City Hosp., 1953-56; dir. nursing Euclid-Glenville Hosp., Euclid, O., 1956-60, West Allis (Wis.) Meml. Hosp., 1961-66; dir. Commn. on Statewide Planning for Nursing Edn. in Wis., 1967-69; asso. chmn. dept. nursing U. Wis. Extension, 1970—; nursing coordinator Milw. Regional Med. Instrnl. TV Stas., Inc., 1971—. Mem. Am. Nurses Assn. (mem. council continuing edn.), Nat. (dir. and chmn. steering com. dept. hosp. nursing 1963-67), Wis. (2d v.p.) leagues for nursing, Adult Edn. Assn., Olmsted Grange. Methodist. Club: Zonta (pres. 1967-68) (Milw.). Contbr. articles to profl. jours. Home: 8750 W Forest Home Av Greenfield WI 53228 Office: 600 W Kilbourn Av Milwaukee WI 53203

MAY, GITA, educator; b. Brussels, Belgium, Sept. 16, 1929; d. Albert and Blima (Sieradska) Jochimek; came to U.S., 1947; naturalized, 1950; B.A. magna cum laude, Hunter Coll., 1953; M.A., Columbia, 1954, Ph.D., 1957; m. Irving May, Dec. 21, 1947. Lectr. French, Hunter Coll., N.Y.C., 1953-56; instr. French, Columbia Coll., Columbia U., 1956-58, asst. prof. French, Columbia, 1958-61, asso. prof., 1961-69, prof., 1968—, departmental rep., 1968—. Lecture tour English univs., 1965. Recipient award Columbia U. Council for Research in Humanities, 1960, 67, 69, Am. Council Learned Socs., 1961, award for outstanding achievement Hunter Coll., 1963; Fulbright research grantee, 1964-65; Guggenheim fellow, 1964-65; decorated chevalier Ordre des Palmes Academiques, 1968; Nat. Endowment for Humanities Sr. fellow, 1971-72. Mem. Am. Assn. U. Profs., Am. Assn. Tchrs. French, Modern Lang. Assn. Am., Am. Soc. 18th Century Studies, Societe Francaise d' Etude du Dix-Huitieme Siecle, Am. Soc. French Academic Palms, Phi Beta Kappa. Author: Diderot et Baudelaire, critiques d'art, 1957; De Jean-Jacques Rousseau a Madame Roland; essai sur la sensibilite preromantique et revolutionnaire, 1964; Madame Roland and the Age of Revolution, 1970 (Van Amringe Distinguished Book award). Co-editor: Diderot Studies III, 1961. Contbr. articles and reviews to profl. jours. Home: 404 W 116th St New York City NY 10027

MAY, GRACE BUCKNER (MRS. MICHAEL HUGO MAY), civic worker; b. Los Angeles; d. Manfred R. and Jean Ann (Naftalin) Buckner; student U. Cal. at Los Angeles, 1946-49; B.A., Los Angeles State Coll., 1955; m. Michael Hugo May, Dec. 23, 1948; children—Carolyn Estherlee, Michael Werner, Jonathan Gustav. Docent, Los Angeles County Mus. Natural History; mem. art council U. Cal. at Los Angeles. Bd. dirs. Helping Hand, Los Angeles. Home: 5444 Corteen Pl North Hollywood CA 91607

MAY, LOLA JUNE, educator; b. Kenosha, Wis., Oct. 29, 1923; d. Arthur F. and Eleanor (Henzler) May; B.S., U. Wis., 1945; M.A., Northwestern U., 1950, Ph.D., 1964. Tchr., Ft. Atkinson (Wis.) High Sch., 1945-48, Nat. Coll. Edn. Lab. Sch., Evanston, Ill., 1948-51, New Trier Twp. High Sch., Winnetka, Ill., 1951-60; math. cons. Winnetka Pub. Schs., 1960—. Joint prof. edn. Northwestern U., 1966—; prof. math. edn. U. Hawaii, summers 1966, 68; master tchr. math. Harvard-Newton plan Harvard Grad. Sch. Edn., 1962—; speaker regional, nat. meetings Nat. Council Tchrs. Math., 1963—; participant NBC modern math series More Modern Math, 1966. Named Tchr. of Year, Grade Tchr. Mag., 1966-67. Mem. Ill., Nat. edn. assns., Nat. Council Tchrs. Math, Pi Lambda Theta. Author: Major Concepts of Elementary Modern Math, 1962; Mathematical Background for Primary Teachers, 1966; New Math for Adults Only, 1966; Teaching Mathematics in the Elementary School, 1971. Home: 2760 Marcy Av Evanston IL 60201 Office: 1155 Oak St Winnetka IL 60093

MAY, MARELIZABETH DEPP (MRS. MARTIN LEO MAY, JR.), mathematician; b. Olean, N.Y., Nov. 13, 1943; d. Leon William and Katherine Eulalia (Kelly) Depp; B.S. with honors in Math., Villanova U., 1972, postgrad., 1974—; m. Martin Leo May, Jr., Aug. 9, 1969; 1 dau., Martha Bridget. Operations research analyst Boeing Vertol Co., Phila., 1965—; tutor in math. Mem. Operations Research Soc. Am., Am. Helicopter Soc., Pi Mu Epsilon, Alpha Sigma Lambda, Nat. Sci. Club. Home: 2 Waterview Rd Apt 0-3 West Chester PA 19380 Office: Boeing Center PO Box 16858 Philadelphia PA 19142

MAY, MARGUERITE P., educator; b. Morgan City, La.; d. Emile Louis and Virginia (Welsh) Petty; B.A., Xavier U., 1943; M.A., U. So. Cal., 1954; m. Rollo G. May, Aug. 5, 1948. Tchr. Carver Jr. High Sch., Los Angeles, 1944-45, Garden Gate High Sch., Los Angeles, 1945-52, Mark Twain Jr. High, 1952-60, 64-65; cons. secondary sch. English curriculum Los Angeles City Schs., 1960-64. cons.-writer specially funded programs, 1966-67; curriculum specialist Neglected and Delinquent Children's project, 1967; supr. ESEA, Title I Secondary Sch. Projects, 1968, dir. curriculum Jordan Ednl. Complex ESEA, Title III, 1968-71, dir. reading task force developmental reading program for black learners, 1971—. Demonstration tchr. U. Cal. at Los Angeles, 1954-60, instr. extension sch., mem. drama profl. adv. com. ARTS IMPACT Project, Glendale (Cal.) City Schs. Mem. Drama Tchrs. Assn. So. Cal. (past pres.), Nat. Council Tchrs. English, Reading Council of Los Angeles (charter mem.; sec. 1961-62), Cal. Assn. Thcrs. English (state curriculum com.), So. Cal. Council Tchrs. English, P.T.A. (hon. life), Community Relations Conf. So. Cal., Cal. Assn. Tchrs. English, Los Angeles Area Reading Assn. (bd. dirs.), Assn. Supervision and Curriculum Devel., Internat. Reading Assn., Am. Ednl. Research Assn., Council Dirs. and Suprs., Pacesetters, Town Hall, Delta Kappa Gamma (Beta Eta chpt.). Editorial cons. Rise of the American Nation, also America, Its Peoples and Values. Mem. team of authors of books for Aardvark Media Inc., 1974. Author articles in field. Adv. bd. Los Angeles Times Student Outlook Newspaper, 1968. Home: 4910 Angeles Vista Los Angeles CA 90043 Office: 450 N Grand Av Los Angeles CA 90054

MAY, NELL CLEVELAND, lawyer; b. Fulton, Miss., Sept. 11, 1923; d. Arthur Thomas and Effie Eulalia (Senter) Cleveland; B.A., Blue Mountain (Miss.) Coll., 1941-44; student Delta State Coll., Cleveland, Miss., 1948; m. Albert Edwin May, May 14, 1948; children—Michael, Mary (Mrs. Garry Summerford), Arthur William, Albert Edwin. Sec. to Arthur T. Cleveland, Fulton, 1938-41, 44-46, 51-62; tchr. Fulton Grammar Sch., 1946-47, Itawamba Agrl. High Sch., Fulton, 1946-47; sec. to county agt., Indianola, Miss., 1948-49; bookkeeper Central Buick Co., Indianola, 1949-51; admitted to Miss. bar, 1964, since practiced in Fulton. Chmn. Regional Rehab. Center, Itawamba County, 1958—; bd. dirs. Regional Rehab. Center, Tupelo, Miss. Mem. Miss. Bar Assn., Bonneville (Miss.) Bus. and Profl. Women's Club. Baptist (treas. 1961-71). Mem. Order Eastern Star. Home: 513 S Cummings St Fulton MS 38843 Office: PO Box 538 Fulton MS 38843

MAY, PEGGY ANNE (MRS. MAXEY DESTIN MAY), newspaper writer; b. Gainesville, Fla., Oct. 21, 1928; d. Harold Gray and Harriette (Ray) Clayton; student Fla. State U., 1946-47, U. Fla., 1947-49; m. Maxey Destin May, June 11, 1949; children—Lee Clayton, Mark Destin, Nancy Harriette. Women's page editor Playground Daily News, 1963—. Mem. Alpha Chi Omega. Democrat. Baptist. Club: Fla. Press (sec.). Home: 19 Pryor Rd SE Fort Walton Beach FL 32548 Office: PO Drawer 1307 Fort Walton Beach FL 32548

MAY, SHIRLEY S. (MRS. ROBERT C. MAY), civic worker, educator; b. Plainfield, N.J.; d. Morris and Anna (Barishaw) Steinberg; B.S. in Edn., N.J. State Coll., 1942; postgrad. N.Y.U.; m. Robert C. May, May 8, 1943 (dec. 1967); children—Michael L., Carol S. Sch. tchr., 1942-46, 52; founder, organizer Masterwork Music and Art Found., 1955, now cons., trustee; exec. dir. Morris-Sussex chpt. Am. Heart Assn. Established audio-visual lab. Whippany (N.J.) Pub. Schs.; v.p. Citizens Council for Pub. Schs., Whippany; bd. dirs., program chmn. Whippany P.T.A.; chmn. audio-visual aids Morris County P.T.A.; bd. dirs. Hanover Twp. Adult Sch., 1956-64; an organizer Parents' Assn., Chatham Sq. Music Sch., N.Y.C. Mem. Music Tchrs. Nat. Assn., Nat. Assn. Am. Composers and Condrs., Internat. Platform Assn., Com. for N.Y. Choruses, League for N.Y. Music, Am. Mgmt. Assn. Home: 23 Pleasant Valley Rd Whippany NJ 07981 Office: 55 Maple Av Morristown NJ 07960

MAY, STEPHANIE MIDDLETON (MRS. JOHN M. MAY), sculptor; b. N.Y.C., Apr. 16, 1928; d. Thomas Hazelhurst and Ruth (Stephens) Middleton; student Stephens Coll., 1948, Columbia, 1950, Art Students' League, 1951; m. John M. May, Oct. 21, 1949; children—Elizabeth Evans, Geoffrey Middleton. Exhibited on group shows at New Britain Mus., 1954, Wadsworth Atheneum, 1954, 55, 56; Treas., Conn. McCarthy for Pres. Campaign, 1968; finance chmn. Conn. senate Democratic campaign, 1970; treas. Conn. McGovern for Pres., 1972; del. Dem. Nat. Conv., Chgo., 1968. Bd. dirs. Nat. Com. for Sane Nuclear Policy, 1958-68. Fellow, Royal Soc. Arts; mem. Conn. Acad. Fine Arts, Greater Hartford Council Chs. (v.p. 1960-64), Jr. League Hartford. Sculptor: Eleanor Roosevelt Peace award, 1963. Home: 113 Duncaster Rd Bloomfield CT 06002

MAYBEE, CHARLOTTE ANN, educator; b. Clarkston, Mich., Feb. 22, 1927; d. James Russell and Vera (Miller) Maybee; B.A., Mich. State U., 1948, M.A., 1954; postgrad. summers U. Mich., 1964, Temple U., 1965. Tchr. kindergarten Flint (Mich.) Bd. Edn., 1948-63, elementary sch. counselor, 1963-64, instructional specialist pre-kindergarten program, 1964-68; day care center licensing center, 1968-69; supr. day care center licensing, also nursery schs. Mich. Dept. Social Services, 1969—. Dir. Flint Head Start Program, summers 1966-67; adv. bd. Cedar St. Children's Center, 1967. Ola Hiller scholar Flint inter-chpt. council Delta Kappa Gamma, 1965. Mem. Nat., Mich., Flint (bd. dirs. 1961-63) edn. assns., Assn. Childhood Edn. (pres. Flint 1963-65, state nursery sch. v.p. 1965-67, state dir. 1969-73), Mich. Council Family Relations (state dir. 1971-73), Nat. Assn. for Edn. Young Children, Am. Assn. U. Women, Delta Kappa Gamma (chpt. rec. sec. 1964-66), Alpha Lambda. Home: 1116 Poplar Lane East Lansing MI 48823 Office: Dept Social Services 300 S Capitol Lansing MI 48926

MAYDIAN, PEGGY WITHROW STOCK (MRS. THOMAS CARLYLE MAYDIAN), coll. librarian; b. Clifton Forge, Va., Feb. 17, 1929; d. Cecil Fredrick and Suella (Withrow) Stock; student Milligan Coll., 1947-49; B.S., E. Tenn. State U., 1951, postgrad., 1968; M.A. in L.S., George Peabody Coll., 1959; m. Thomas Carlyle Maydian. Tchr., Henry County (Va.) Pub. Schs., 1951-52; tchr. English, coach girls' basketball team U.S. Army Spl. Service, Indiantown Gap, Pa., 1952-53; service club asst. dir. Air Force Spl. Services, Tagu, Korea, 1953-54, service club dir., Duluth, Minn., 1955-56; tchr., librarian Truman Elementary Sch., Key West, Fla., 1957-58; librarian State Vocational Tng. Sch. for Boys, Nashville, 1958-59, U.S. Army Dept. Sch., Pirmasens, Germany, 1959-61; audiovisual librarian Dabney S. Lancaster Community Coll., Clifton Forge, Va., 1967—. Mem. base community relations bd. 343d Fighter Group, Duluth, Minn., 1955-56. Mem. Am., Va. library assns., Beta Phi Mu. Clubs: Va. Business and Professional Women; Dabney S. Lancaster Faculty Wives and Women's (treas. 1974-75). Home: Box 28 Selma VA 24474 Office: Dabney S Lancaster Community Coll Clifton Forge VA 24422

MAYER, ANNETTE PERLMUTTER (MRS. KENNETH EDMUND MAYER), univ. adminstr.; b. Bklyn., Sept. 5, 1932; d. Jack and Bertha (Schwartz) Perlmutter; A.B., U. Ky., 1954, postgrad., 1967-68; m. Kenneth Edmund Mayer, June 14, 1959; children—Michele, Michael. Publicity asst. WLW-TV, Cin., 1954-56, Community Chest and Council, Cin., 1956-59; dir. news bur. Transylvania U., Lexington, Ky., 1959—. Mem. Nat. Council Coll. Publs. Advisers. Mem. Spindletop Hall. Club: Lexington (U. Ky.). Home: 1611 Altanta Dr Lexington KY 40505 Office: 300 N Broadway Lexington KY 40508

MAYER, CHARLOTTE M. YOUNG (MRS. MERL G. MAYER), sci. editor; b.Hutsonville, Ill., Nov. 5, 1914; d. Ralph M. and Beulah (Lionberger) Young; B.S., Butler U., 1937; M.S., U. Ill., 1939; M.A., Syracuse U., 1956; student No. Ill. State U., 1968; m. Merl G. Mayer, Dec. 25, 1961; 1 son Michael; step-children—Judith Dalche, Mary Lynn Villareal, Mark, Marshall; foster-children--Penney Fowler, Debbie Fowler. Tchr. sci., pub. and pvt. schs., Ill., Ohio, N.C., 1937-63; camp dir. Charlotte Country Day Camp, Charlotte, N.C., 1957-61; counselor Dist. 21, Wheeling, Ill., 1963-68, 70-73; sci. editor Laidlaw Pub. Co., River Forest, Ill., 1968—. Dist. chmn. Sci. Fairs, N.W. suburbs, Chgo., 1966-68. Ford fellow, 1955-56. Mem. Nat. Assn. Sci. Tchrs., Ill. Guidance and Personnel Assn., N.E.A., Ill. Edn. Assn., Am. Assn. U. Women. Conglist. Home: 2268 Elmira St Des Plaines IL 60018 Office: Madison and Thatcher Sts River Forest IL 60305

MAYER, FLORENCE EMILY, physician; b. Karuizawa, Japan, Sept. 26, 1923; d. Paul S. and Frances L. (Frank) Mayer; M.D., Northwestern U., 1951. Intern Cin. Gen. Hosp., 1951; resident pediatrics Cin. Children's Hosp., 1951-53, Boston Children's Med. Center, 1953-54; fellow cardiology Boston Children's Med. Center, 1954-57, Hosp. for Sick Children, London, Eng., 1957-58; instr. N.Y.U. Sch. Medicine, 1959-60, asst. clin. prof. pediatrics, 1960-61; research fellow Royal Alexandra Hosp. for Children, Sydney, Australia, 1961-62; pediatric cons. Nat. Inst. Child Health and Human Devel., NIH, Bethesda, Md., 1963-72, sr. staff scientist Nat. Heart and Lung Inst., 1972—. Diplomate Am. Bd. Pediatrics. Fellow Am. Acad. Pediatrics; mem. A.A.A.S., Am., Washington heart assns., Alpha Omega Alpha. Home: 5822 Bradley Blvd Bethesda MD 20014 Office: NIH Bethesda MD 20014

MAYER, GRETA MIRJAM, social work cons.; b. Worms, Germany; d. Jacob J. and Rose (Loeb) Mayer; State Diploma Social Work, Soziale Frauenschule Mannheim, 1929; Certificate Psychology, U. Mainz, 1932; M.S.W., Boston U., 1950; Came to U.S., 1947, naturalized, 1952 Social worker, Germany, 1929-36; dir. children's homes, Israel, 1936-47, Children's Study Home, Boston, 1949-50; caseworker, child therapist Jewish Bd. Guardians, 1950-56; supr. Guidance Centre, New Rochelle, N.Y., 1956-58; dir. parent counseling Child Study Assn., Am., 1960-69; supr. child psychiatry Mt. Sinai Hosp., N.Y.C., 1969-73; cons. Horace Mann Sch., 1969—; pvt. practice psychotherapy, children and adults, N.Y., 1954—. Cons. to nursery schs. and day care centers. Fellow Am. Orthopsychiat. Assn.; mem. Nat. Assn. Social Workers, Am. Assn. for Psychotherapists. Home: 160 W 96th St New York City NY 10025

MAYER, JANET, ednl. adminstr.; b. N.Y.C., Feb. 13, 1931; d. Ernest de Wael and Jean (Heffernan) Mayer; A.B., Vassar Coll., 1952; M.A., Georgetown U., 1959. Tchr. history and French Holton Arms Sch., Washington, 1952-54, 56-60, Castilleja Sch., Palo Alto, Cal., 1955-56; asst. dir. admissions Vassar Coll., 1960-65; head upper sch. Kent Pl. Sch., Summit, N.J., 1965-69; headmistress The Hewitt Sch., N.Y.C., 1969—. Mem. Headmistresses Assn. East, Nat. Assn. Prins. Schs. Girls, Guild Ind. Schs. Home: 245 E 63d St New York City NY 10021 Office: 45 E 75th St New York City NY 10021

MAYER, LILLIAN ROSE ZDARSKY (MRS. EDWARD BURGARD MAYER), educator; b. Buffalo, Aug. 9, 1908; d. Joseph and Marie (Smolka) Zdarsky; teaching certificate State U. Coll. at Buffalo, 1930; student Eastman Sch. Music, 1930-36; B.S. in Music Edn. in Strings, U. Buffalo, 1957; D.Edn. in Music honoris causa, Hamilton State U., 1973; m. Edward Burgard Mayer, July 9, 1940; children—Lillian Marie (Mrs. David Becherer Newbert), Suzanne (Mrs. Donald Stephen Biskin), Rosemarie (Mrs. Barton Roen). Tchr., music dir. Wanakah Sch., Hamburg, N.Y., 1930-42; tchr. string orchs. Orchard Park (N.Y.) Central Sch., 1952—. Pvt. instr. violin, Buffalo, 1935-42, Orchard Park, 1955—; concertmistress Orchard Park Symphony Orch., 1955-65, bd. dirs., 1955—, audition chmn., 1955-65; cons. clinician music educators, 1959—; cons. string teaching. Bd. dirs. Civic Music Assn. Orchard Park. Mem. Nat., N.Y. State (reporter 1966-67), Erie County music educators assns., Am. String Tchrs. Assn. (2d v.p. chpt. 1962-68), Erie County Tchrs. Assn., Alpha Sigma Tau. Republican. Roman Catholic. Club: Zonta (past pres.). Home: Makaha Valley Towers 622 Waianae HI 96792

MAYER, MYRA LOU, banker; b. Cleve., Oct. 24, 1944; d. Louis E. and Marie (Klein) Mayer; student Bard Coll., 1961-62, Am. Coll. in Paris (France), 1962, Sorbonne, Paris, 1962; B.B.A., U. Ariz., 1965; M.B.A., Am. U., 1972. Security analyst 1st Nat. Bank Chgo., 1965-68; trust investment officer Union Trust Co. of D.C., Washington, 1969—. Mem. Nat. Assn. Bank Women, Washington Soc. Investment Analysts, Financial Analysts Fedn., Phi Delta Gamma, Phi Chi Theta. Club: National Economists. Home: 3001 Veazey Terrace NW Washington DC 20008 Office: Union Trust Co of DC 15th and H Sts NW Washington DC 20005

MAYER, PAULINE IVERSEN, cvic worker; b. Pitts., Sept. 12, 1909; d. Lorenz and Gertrude (Adlesperger) Iversen; student St. Marys Acad., 1924-26, Mt. Mercy, Pitts., 1926-27; m. Casper Peter Mayer, June 8, 1927; 1 dau., Antoinette (Mrs. John Thomas Fallon). Dir. woman's bd. Duquesne U., 1957-61; dir. Civic Light Opera Guild, Pitts., 1960-61, pres., 1964-66; v.p., dir. Civic Light Opera. Mem. Pitts. Symphony Soc. Republican. Roman Catholic. Home: 340 Fox Chapel Rd Pittsburgh PA 15238

MAYER, SHIRLEY ANNA (MRS. WILLIAM A. BARNES), physician; b. N.Y.C.; d. Frank and Elizabeth (Groh) Mayer; A.B. cum laude, Hunter Coll., 1940; M.D., U. Chgo., 1943; M.P.H., Columbia, 1964; m. William A. Barnes, July 1, 1945; children—William Christopher, Esme (Mrs. Frederick Sessler), Robin, George. Practice medicine specializing in pediatrics; asst. prof. clin. pediatrics Columbia Coll. Phys. and Surg.; dist. cons. pediatrician N.J. Dept. Health; sr. pub. health physician; Am. Acad. pediatric cons. to Head Start Programs, N.J.; coordinator Newark Maternity and Infant Care Project; dir. Bur. Child Health, N.Y.C. Dept. Health, asst. commr. Maternal and Child Health Services, also supervising physician secondary sch. health program; now regional dir. health services delivery, med. dir. maternal and child health services region II Dept. Health, Edn. and Welfare. Instr. pediatrics, fellow Cardiology Clinic, N.Y. Hosp. and Cornell Med. Center; U.S. rep. to com. on biol. and social aspects of perinatal mortality WHO. Trustee, mem. med. adv. com. Planned Parenthood Bergen County; mem. med. adv. com. N.Y. chpt. Nat. Found. March of Dimes. Diplomate Am. Bd. Pediatrics, Am. Bd. Preventive Medicine. Mem. Am., N.J. pub. health assns., Am., N.J. acads. pediatrics, Phi Beta Kappa, Alpha Omega Alpha. Club: Women's City (N.Y.C.). Home: 303 E Franklin Turnpike Ho Ho Kus NJ 07423 Office: Dept Health Edn and Welfare Region II 26 Federal Plaza New York City NY 10007

MAYER, VELIA ANN, lawyer; b. nr. Mt. Pleasant, Tex., Feb. 13, 1943; d. Velia John and Opal (Dale) Mayer; B.A. cum laude, U. Miss., 1965, J.D., 1968. Admitted to Miss. bar, 1968; practiced in Jackson, 1971—; law clk. for judge of Miss. Supreme Ct., Jackson, 1968-69; spl. asst. atty. gen. State of Miss., Jackson, 1969-71; asso. firm Watkins and Eager, attys. at law, Jackson, 1971—. Mem. Am., Miss., Hinds County bar assns., Am. Judicature Soc., Jackson Young Lawyer's Assn. Home: 220 Edgewood Terrace Dr Jackson MS 39206 Office: Box 650 Jackson MS 39205

MAYES, DOROTHY LEE (MRS. FRED MAYES), editor; b. San Angelo, Tex., May 7, 1948; d. William Lee and Evelyn Loraine (Summers) Bundrant; B.A., U. Okla., 1970; m. Fred Mayes, June 6, 1970. Editorial asst. Jour. Rehab., Nat. Rehab. Assn., Washington, 1970-72; editor U.S. Dept. Agr., Econ. Research Service, Washington, 1972—. Mem. Women in Communications, Inc. (2d v.p. Nat. Capital chpt.). Presbyn. (editor monthly mag. Gateway Beacon). Home: 6820 Walker Mill Rd District Heights MD 20027 Office: US Dept Agr Econ Research Service Div Information Washington DC 20250

MAYES, EDYTHE BEAM, novelist, poet; b. Kings Mountain, N.C., May 9, 1902; s. Charles Lemuel and Mary Florence (McGinnes) Beam; ed. Lenoir Rhyne Coll., Juilliard Sch. Music, N.Y. U.; m. LeRoy H. Mayes, Sept. 26, 1926 (dec.). Former mem. staff N.Y. Times; in charge fgn. dept. Macfadden Publs., N.Y.C., 1924; active (with husband) in fund raising for colls., univs. and founds. Author: The Gift (containing Our Debt to the Negro, Prose Poem to Chardin), 1973; Washington . . . God's Workshop, 1973; Flesh is Grass, 1974; Never Too Old, 1974; also numerous published poems, essays, short stories. Address: 358 Clark Av Staten Island NY 10306

MAYFIELD, SARA MARTIN, writer, editor; b. Tuscaloosa, Ala., Sept. 10, 1905; d. James Jefferson and Susan Fitts (Martin) Mayfield; student U. Paris (France), 1926, U. Chgo., 1927; A.B., Goucher Coll., 1928; M.A., U. Ala., 1931; postgrad. Tulane U., 1943; m. John Allen Sellers, Nov. 12, 1924 (div. Jan. 1927). Playreader, casting dir. Bela Blau, Inc., N.Y.C., 1931-32; with Rockland County Theater, 1932; spl. corr. Balt. Sunpapers, 1928-29, Paris Herald, 1929, N.Y. Herald Tribune 1931, The Birmingham (Ala.) News, 1945-46, Transradio Press, N.Y.C., 1938-45; asst. editor U. Ala. Press, University, 1967-69, contbg. editor, 1969-72. Observer, U.S. Mil. Intelligence, 1940-49. Recipient award Ala. Library, 1970. Mem. Jr. League, Phi

Beta Kappa. Democrat. Author: The Constant Circle: The Menckens and Their Friends, 1968; Exiles From Paradise, 1972; Mona Lisa: The Story of the Woman in the Portrait, 1974. Patentee in field. Office: Box 3435 U Ala University AL 35486

MAYHALL, DOROTHY ANN, museum ofcl.; b. Portland, Ore., May 31, 1925; d. Nelles H. and Myrtle Jane (Pye) Mayhall; student U. Omaha, 1944-46; B.F.A., U. Ia., 1948, M.F.A., 1950; Fulbright scholar Ecole des Beaux Arts, Paris, France, 1950-51. With Mus. Modern Art, N.Y.C., 1961-65; dir. Aldrich Mus. Contemporary Art, Ridgefield, Conn., 1965-71, Storm King Art Center, Mountainville, N.Y., 1971—. Exhibited sculpture in one-man show at A.M. Sachs, N.Y.C., 1972; exhibited in many group shows. Served to 1st lt. WAC, 1952-56. Home: Old Pleasant Hill Rd Mountainville NY 10953

MAYHALL, JANE FRANCIS (MRS. LESLIE G. KATZ), author; b. Louisville, May 10, 1921; d. Howard Wesley and Loula Eliza (Bennett) Mayhall; student Black Mountain Coll., 1937-40, Black Mountain Music Sch., 1944, Middlebury Music Sch., 1939, Longy Music Sch., 1940-41, New Sch. for Social Research, 1946-48, Claremont Coll., summer, 1948; m. Leslie George Katz, June 4, 1940. Mem. faculty New Sch. for Social Research, N.Y.C., 1948; mem. summer workshop faculty Morehead (Ky.) State Coll., 1960-62, Alice Lloyd Coll., Pippa Passes, Ky., 1968. Guest lectr. Ohio U., Athens, 1968, N.Y. U., 1950, New Sch. for Social Research, 1950. Fletcher Pratt prose fellow Breadloaf Sch. English, 1958, Yaddo fellow, Edward MacDowell fellow. Author: Cousin to Human, 1960; Ready for the Ha-Ha, 1966; Givers and Takers, 1969. Contbr. articles, poems, short stories, critical essays to various pubs. including Cross Sections, Best Am. Short Stories, Botteghe Oscure, New World Writing, N.Y. Times Book of Verse, Partisan Rev., Modern Lang. Quar., Nation, Harpers Bazaar, Aphra, Quar. Rev. of Lit., Paris Rev., others. Translator: (with Otto Guth) Die Kluge, 1968. Author: (play) Eclogue, 1954. Home: 50 Remsen St Brooklyn NY 11201

MAYHALL, MARY MILDRED PICKLE (MRS. TEMPLE B. MAYHALL), author; b. Austin, Tex., Dec. 20, 1902; d. David Jones and Birdie Mildred (Givens) Pickle; B.A., U. Tex., 1924, M.A., 1926, Ph.D., 1939; postgrad. U. Chgo., 1929, 30, 33; m. Temple B. Mayhall, Sept. 12, 1925; children—David, William. Tchr. gen. sci. Allan Jr. High Sch., Austin, 1924-25; tutor in anthropology U. Tex., Austin, 1925-27; instr., 1927-45; tchr. social studies Stephen F. Austin High Sch., Austin, 1956-64; dir. Graphic Ideas, Inc., Austin, 1973—. Lectr., cons. in history. Active P.T.A., March of Dimes, Cancer drives; mem. Summerfield G. Roberts prize com. Sons of Republic Tex., 1974—. Mem. Anthrop. Assn., Am., Austin (editor 1973—) rose socs., Heritage Soc., Tex., W. Tex. hist. assns., Okla. Hist. Soc., Collectors Inst., Friends of U. Tex. Library, Daughters of Republic Tex., D.A.R. Democrat. Methodist. Club: Kwill Klub (Austin, Tex.). Author: The Kiowas, 1962, rev. edit., 1971; Indian Wars of Texas (Writers Round Up award Theta Sigma Phi 1966), 1965; (with Robert Holz and Samuel W. Newman) Texas and Its History, 1972. Editor: Texas Wild Flowers, with biography of Eliza Griffin Johnston (Summerfield G. Roberts award 1973), 1972. Contbr. articles to profl. jours. Home: 1906 Raleigh Av Austin TX 78703

MAYNARD, BEVERLY ANN, educator; b. Dallas, Nov. 29, 1948; d. Ogle Leslie and Ernestine Beverly (Russell) Maynard; B.F.A. in Theatre and Speech Edn., So. Meth. U., 1971; M.S., N. Tex. State U., 1971-72, predoctoral student, 1973—. Tchr. Dallas Fashion Merchandising Coll., 1972; communications instr. Eastfield Coll., Dallas, 1972—; theatre cluster curriculum writer Skyline Center Theatre program, Dallas, 1973; hostess Tips for Teens, daily radio interview program, teen coordinator radio sta. KVIL, Dallas, 1967-68; an organizer Mam'selle Coll. Fashion Instr. Program, 1967-69. Mem. women's com. Dallas Theatre Center; mem. Dallas Friends of Channel 13, Am. Theatre Assn. conv., 1972, 73. Baptist. Home: 658 Harter Rd Dallas TX 75218

MAYNARD, JEAN PATRICIA, coll. adminstr.; b. Bklyn., Nov. 28, 1927; d. Charles Arthur and Gladys (Van Meter) Finley; student Barnard Coll., 1945-46; certificate Katharine Gibbs Secretarial Sch., 1946-47; m. John Walter Maynard, Nov. 6, 1948; children—John Paul, Preston Charles, Peter Brooks. Exec. sec. CBS, N.Y.C., 1947-48; sec. to John Martin, A.I.A., Middletown, Conn., 1962-65; exec. sec. Honors Coll., Wesleyan U., Middletown, 1965-68, asst. to dir., 1968—. Acting dir. Conn. Poetry Circuit, 1970-72, dir., 1972—; charter mem. Middletown chpt. Am. Field Service, 1967—, sec., 1963-65, chmn. Ams. Abroad com., 1968-69, chmn. publicity com., 1965-68, 70-71, v.p., 1971-72, 74-75; mem. Jr. Matinee Com., Middletown, 1959-65. Mem. Wesleyan Potters (charter). Home: 115 Brown St Middletown CT 06457

MAYNARD, MARIANNE, educator, occupational therapist; b. Detroit, Oct. 3, 1931; d. Henry Raymond and Hazel Louise (Shaw) Maynard; B.A., Wayne State U., 1953, M.A., 1955; postgrad. U. Wis. Cons., dir. tng. Wis. Dept. Health and Social Services, Div. Mental Health, Madison, Wis., 1964-72; specialist in activity therapy programs dept. mental health U. Wis. Extension, Madison, 1972—. Cons., mem. Nat. Inst. Mental Health Region V grant com.; rev. com., cons. W.I., U.S. aide to mental health, 1967; mem. Wis. Ednl. Congress on Aging, 1973—; cons. Am. Occupational Therapy Assn. Resource Panel, Nat. Inst. Health Project, 1972-73, Center for Allied Health Instructional Personnel, U. Fla., 1973. Mem. N.A.A.C.P. (chpt. chmn. 1970-71), Am., Wis. (chmn. edn. 1969-71) occupational therapy assns., Gerontological Soc., Wis. Adult Edn. Assn., Am. Personnel and Guidance Assn., Nat. Rehab. Assn., Pi Lambda Theta. Contbr. articles to profl. jours. Home: 2502 Brentwood Pkwy Madison WI 53704 Office: 610 Langdon St Madison WI 53706

MAYNARD, MIRIAM CLARK, journalist; b. Kinston, N.C., Jan. 8, 1922; d. Thomas Spurgeon and Ione (Lane) Maynard; student Greensboro Coll., 1938-39, Am. U., 1948. Project supr. Nat. Youth Adminstrn., 1940-41; chief auditor Navy Disbursing Dept., Cherry Point, N.C., 1941-44; office mgr. Farmers Home Adminstrn., Kinston, 1944-47; adminstrv. asst. Dr. Rachel Davis, Kinston, 1947-48; editorial asst. Public Affairs Inst., Washington, 1948-51; city editor, reporter Kinston Daily Free Press, 1951-73, mng. editor, 1973—. Charter mem. Environment Unltd., 1969—. Sec. Lenoir County Democratic Exec. Com., 1952-53; sec. Lenoir County Democratic Women's Club, 1960-64; active in various polit. campaigns. Recipient awards N.C. Press Women, 1952, 53, 73, N.C Press Assn., 1970, 72. Mem. N.C. Press Women's Assn., N.C. Press Assn. (bd. dirs.), Lenoir County Hist. Assn. (pub. relations dir. 1970—). Clubs: Kinston Collectors, Kinston Coin. Home: 310 Sherwood Pl Kinston NC 28501 Office: Free Press North St Kinston NC 28501

MAYNARD, OLIVIA BENEDICT, polit. party ofcl.; b. Cin., June 24, 1936; d. Samuel and Elizabeth Brewster (Carruthers) Benedict; student Sweet Briar Coll., 1954-57; B.A., George Washington U., 1958; M.S.W., U. Mich., 1971; children—Elizabeth, Benjamin, John. Mem. exec. com. Democratic party Genesee County, Mich., 1967-71; recording sec. Mich. Dem. Party, Detroit, 1967-71, vice chmn., 1971—; alternate del. Dem. nat. conv., 1968, 72. Mem. Flint Urban League, Flint League Women Voters, Nat. Assn. Social Workers (exec. bd. 1974—). Home: 2026 Calumet St Flint MI 48503 Office: 1535 E Lafayette St Detroit MI 48207

MAYNE, MABELLE ELAINE ADAMS (MRS. LESLIE LEWELLEN, JR.), biochemist; b. Wichita Falls, Tex., May 13, 1926; d. Bill Tom and Irene (Kitchen) Adams; B.S., Baylor U., 1946, Ph.D., 1963; M.S., Tulane U., 1952; postgrad. Univ. Coll., U. London (Eng.), 1952-54; m. Weldon Thurman Mayne, Dec. 27, 1958 (div. Apr. 1966); children—Cathleen Elizabeth, Michael Patrick, Martin Douglas; m. 2d, Leslie Lewellen, Jr., May 14, 1972. Chemist So. Regional Research Lab., USDA, New Orleans, 1946-52, Brit. Gelatine & Glue Research Assn., London, Eng., 1952-54, Samuel Roberts Noble Found., Ardmore, Okla., 1955-59; with U. Tex., M. D. Anderson Hosp. & Tumor Inst., Houston, 1959-71, Nat. Health Labs., Inc., lab. dir. 1971-72, biochemist, 1965-71, tchr. biochemistry Grad. Sch. Biomed. Sci., 1965-71; clin. chemist dept. pathology Tex. Children's Hosp., 1972—. William Osler lect. Phila. Gen. Hosp., 1967; Welch Found. fellow U. Tex., 1963-65. Mem. Am. Chem. Soc., A.A.A.S., N.Y. Acad. Sci., Am. Assn. Cancer Research, Am. Med. Writers Assn., Am. Assn. Immunologist, Am. Assn. Clin. Chemists, Soc. Acad. Achievement, Sigma Xi. Episcopalian. Contbr. articles on hormone structure and protein chemistry to profl. jours. Home: 3310 Aberdeen Way Houston TX 77025 Office: Dept Pathology Tex Children's Hosp 6621 Fannin St Houston TX 77025

MAYNE, RUTH YVONNE, microbiologist; b. New Orleans, June 10, 1915; d. Bruce and Marion (Spitzer) Mayne; student Memphis State Coll., 1932-34; B.S., U. Minn., 1936; postgrad. Ia. State Coll., 1943-44; M.S., Tulane U., 1946. Med. technologist La. State U. Med. Sch., New Orleans, 1936-40, with pvt. doctor, New Orleans, 1940-41, Ft. Bragg (N.C.) Sta. Hosp., 1941; med. technologist LaGarde Gen. Hosp., New Orleans, 1941-42, in charge plasma bank lab., 1942-43; teaching fellow Ia. State Coll., 1943-44; grad. asst. bacteriology Tulane U. Med. Sch., 1945-46, bacteriologist dept. gynecology, 1946-47; asst. microbiologist So. Regional Research Lab., U.S. Dept. Agr., New Orleans, 1947-53, asso. microbiologist, 1953-56, asso. bacteriologist, 1956-62, research microbiologist, 1962—. Recipient Best Paper award La. Soc. Med. Technologists, 1947, Superior Service Group award Dept. Agr., 1952. Mem. Inst. Food Technologists, Am. Soc. Microbiology, Mycol. Soc. Am., Soc. Indsl. Microbiology, Assn. Milk, Food and Environmental Sanitarians, A.A.A.S., Sigma Xi. Research on diphtheroids, Candida species, trichomonads, urinary tract infections, lipolytic organisms, chem. protection against deteriorative micro-organisms on cotton fiber, plasticizers, varnishes, mycotoxins, bacterial contamination of feed meals. Address: PO Box 19687 New Orleans LA 70119

MAYO, CORA LOUISE (MRS. MARION WESLEY MAYO), educator; b. Chgo., Oct. 31, 1925; d. Charles Amos and Mary (Elder) Scott; B.S., U. Ill., 1949, advanced certificate in edn., 1973; M.A., U. Chgo., 1962; m. Marion Wesley Mayo, July 21, 1948; children—Lynne Karen, Janice Kathleen, JoAnn, Thomas Bolton III. Life guard, instr. first aid, water safety and accident prevention Chgo. Park Dist., 1943-48; elementary tchr. Chgo. Bd. Edn., 1955-66, parent co-ordinator, 1966-69, human relations staff asst., 1969-72, acting human relations coordinator, 1973-74. Instr., group leader human relations classes and insts., 1966—; instr. Inst. for Community Leaders, 1967-69; cons. Volt Information Sci., 1968, Pacific Tng. and Tech. Assistance Corp., 1970-73, Social Dynamics, 1974, lectr. human services Kennedy-King Coll., 1969; founder firm From the Black Experience, Inc., Chgo., 1973. Pres. Parkway Community Service Guild, 1954, Englewood Mental Health Center, 1968; sec. Stony Island Park Civic Assn., 1969; dir. Citizens Information Service, 1969; del. Southeast Community Orgn. Schs. Com., 1971-72; P.T.A. (chmn. tutoring com. 1969-70). Recipient award Englewood Community Service, 1969, achievement award sta. WJRT, 1969, sta. WJPC, 1974. Mem. Nat. Sch. Pub. Relations Assn. (communications cons. 1969—, v.p.-at-large 1970-71), N.E.A., Chgo. Urban League, N.A.A.C.P. (edn. com. 1968-69), Nat. Assn. Media Women, Women in Communications, Delta Sigma Theta, Phi Delta Kappa. Clubs: Debonnettes Social, Parents Guild (Chgo.). Editor: Human Relations Digest, 1969-72. Home: 1618 E 85th Pl Chicago IL 60617

MAYO, GEORGIA THELMA RILEY (MRS. HARRY RELVIA MAYO), banker; b. Macon, Mo., Sept. 16, 1897; d. Andrew Edwin and Elizabeth Ann (Archer) Riley; student Mo. Wesleyan Coll., 1918-19, 19-20, Kirksville State Coll., 1921; m. Harry Relvia Mayo, Aug. 30, 1922 (dec. Sept. 1961); children—Elizabeth Ann (Mrs. Robert Sibbit), George Edwin, Harry Riley (dec.), John William. Tchr. pub. schs., Brookfield, Mo., 1920-21, Mendon, Mo., 1921-22; with Peoples State Bank, Spickard, Mo., 1961—, v.p., dir., 1962—. Sec., Mo. Ninth Congl. Republican Com., 1962-67. Pres., Mo. dept. Am. Legion Aux., 1941-42, mem. exec. com., 1973—, dir. Mo. Girls' State, 1949, 51-53; conf. sec. Christian social relations Methodist Woman's Soc. Christian Service, 1963-67. Mem. D.A.R. (past regent), Order Eastern Star (past matron). Home: 1225 E 13th Ct Trenton MO 64683 Office: PO Box 458 Trenton MO 64683

MAYS, CARRIE JONES, city ofcl.; b. Lincoln County, Ga., Aug. 30, 1928; d. Joe and Minnie (Leverett) J.; m. William H. Mays III; 1 son, William H. III. Funeral dir., Augusta, Ga., 1962—; mem. Augusta City Council, 1971—. Mem. Augusta Planning and Zoning Commn., Augusta Waterworks Com., Recorders Ct. and Stockade Com. Augusta, Augusta Recreation Com.; Augusta mayor's rep. Office Equal Opportunity bd., 1971. Co-chmn. Paine Coll. Build-it-Back drive, 1972; mem. Ga. Alcoholism Adv. Com.; mem. expansion com. Augusta YM-YWCAs; voting del. Nat. YWCA Conv., 1967. Chmn. bd. Phyllis Whealty br. YWCA; bd. dirs. Greene St. YWCA, Augusta Library. Named Woman of Year, Lincoln League, 1971. Mem. Nat., Ga. funeral service practitioners assns., N.A.A.C.P., Augusta Black Caucus, Paine Coll. Alumni Assn. Methodist. Club: Pinnacle (Augusta). Address: 1221 9th St Augusta GA 30901

MAYS, ELLA KEMP (MRS. HORACE N. MAYS), pub. relations cons.; b. Atlanta; d. James and Mattie F. (Bell) Kemp; student (scholar) Baptist Inst., Temple U.; A.B., U. So. Cal.; m. Horace N. Mays; children—Velva Ann, Ronald. Supr. placement div. Nat. Youth Adminstrn., asst. supr. USES, Washington; asst. supr. housing adminstrn. Dept. Agr., Arlington, Va.; supr. placement div. 12th U.S. Civil Service Commn., Los Angeles; dir. religious activities 2d Baptist Ch., Los Angeles; tchr. released time Ch. Fedn., Los Angeles Pub. Schs.; mgr. Western Avenue Realty & Investment Co., Los Angeles; women's dir. radio sta. KDAY; mem. dept. profl. and vocational standards Cal. Bd. Social Work Examiners; pub. relations specialist, 1963—; dir. Ella Kay Mays Agy. (pub. relations); cons. Pub. Relations Bus. Enterprise. Tchr. pub. schs., Connellsville, Uniontown, Pa. Bd. dirs. Cal. Commn. on Crowded Jails and Narcotics; social worker Family Services, Phila.; 2d v.p., sec. YWCA, Los Angeles; bd. dirs. Los Angeles Urban League; bd. dirs., v.p. 39th Street P.T.A.; mem. speakers bur., dir., charter mem. So. Central Area Welfare Planning Council; chmn. Nat. Negro History Week, 1951; mem. mothers com. Girl Scouts U.S.A., Los Angeles, Boy Scouts Am., Los Angeles; mem. region X Cal. adv. com. Dept. Health, Edn. and Welfare; mem. Cal. Dept. Health and Welfare; mem. adv. bd. Dist. Atty.'s Office, Bank of Finance; mem. Mayor's Community Relations Com.; mem. Carnegie Urban Exec. Leadership Adv. Com.; moderator Office of Minority Bus. Enterprise, Dept. Commerce. Named Woman of Year, Los Angeles Urban League, 1951; recipient award Zeta Phi Beta, citation P.T.A., 1960, certificate of merit award in Christian edn. Western Bapt. State Conv., 1962, Community Service award Wheels of Progress; Communications award Nat. Council Negro Women; Carnegie Found. fellow. Mem. Western Av. Bus. and Profl. Assn. (1st nat. v.p.), Nat. Assn. Media Women (past pres. Los Angeles chpt.), Los Angeles Advt. Women, Am. Advt. Fedn., chpt.), Nat. Assn. Market Devel. (regional dir.), Cal. Press Women (dir.), Beverly Hills C. of C., Theta Sigma Phi, Theta Kappa. Baptist. Home: 3966 Hepburn Av Los Angeles CA 90008 Office: 9350 Wilshire Blvd Beverly Hills CA 90212

MAYS, MAXINE PARKER, educator; b. Eureka, Kan., Jan. 1, 1928; d. James E. and Pearl M. (Burkhart) Parker; A.B., U. No. Colo., 1965; M.S. (Fed. Spl. Edn. fellow), State U. N.Y. at Buffalo, 1968, Ed.D., 1974; m. J.R. Mays, Mar. 14, 1948 (div. 1964); children—Teresa (Mrs. Ronald Ikner), Shelley (Mrs. James Scott). Tchr. retarded children, Casper, Wyo., 1958-67; prin. Woods Sch., Casper, 1962-67; prof. mental retardation State U. N.Y. Coll. at Buffalo, 1967—. Dir. Sheltered Workshop, Rehab. Workshop, Casper, 1962-66; cons. in field. Bd. dirs. Services for Mentally Retarded Erie County, Niagara Assn. Retarded Children. Recipient Distinguished Service award Kiwanis Internat., 1967; sch. dedicated in her honor, Casper, 1970. Mem. N.E.A., Council Exceptional Children, Am. Assn. Mental Deficiency, Assn. Supervision and Curriculum Devel. Author: Student Teaching in Special Classes, 1973; also articles. Home: 102 St James Pl Buffalo NY 14222

MAYSILLES, ELIZABETH, educator; b. Sleepy Creek, W.Va., Dec. 17, 1920; d. Evers and Rose (Scott) Maysilles; A.B., W.Va. U., 1944; M.A., Hunter Coll., 1963; postgrad. N.Y. U., 1975—. Radio announcer, news reporter sta. WAJR, Morgantown, W.Va., 1945-46; radio interviewer sta. WGHF-FM, N.Y.C., 1948-50; tchr. pvt. classes in personal improvement, N.Y.C., 1954-60; lectr. edn. N.Y. U., N.Y.C., 1964-74; lectr. edn. Montclair (N.J.) State Coll., 1974-75, faculty adviser to distinguished speakers series, 1970-71. Chmn. UN Inst., N.Y. U., 1969-71. Mem. exec. bd. Grad. Students Orgn., N.Y. U., 1969-71. Ida M. Bodman scholar, 1971. Mem. Speech Communications Assn., Internat. Platform Assn., Kappa Delta Pi, Alpha Psi Omega. Home: 155 E 77th St New York City NY 10021 Office: 829 Shimkin Hall New York Univ New York City NY 10003

MAYWHORT, HELEN MARGARET (WOOTEN), librarian; b. Chattanooga, Dec. 24, 1915; d. Walter B. and Nelle Grace (Shoupe) Wooten; B.A. cum laude, U. Tenn., 1938; B.S. in L.S., Drexel Inst. Tech., 1942; m. John Arthur Maywhort (dec. Dec. 1970), June 20, 1942; children—William Walter, Marilyn (Mrs. F.W. Keith). Librarian Tyner High Sch., Hamilton County, Tenn., 1938-41; fine arts librarian Free Library, Phila., 1942; periodicals librarian, cataloger Temple U., Phila., 1943-46; librarian Chattanooga High Sch., 1949-51, The McCallie Sch., Chattanooga, 1959—. Bibliographer So. Newspaper Publishers Assn., Chattanooga, 1950; indexer Chattanooga C. of C., 1951—; cataloger Hamilton Countywide libraries, 1952; instr. library sci. U. Tenn. extension, 1971. Den mother Cub Scouts Am., Chattanooga, 1953-55. Bd. dirs. P.T.A., Sunnyside Sch., Chattanooga, 1955-57. Mem. Chattanooga Area Library Assn. (pres. 1950, sec. 1963), Mid-South Assn. Ind. Schs. (library chmn. 1960, 65, 73), Woman's Athletic Assn., Chi Omega. Presbyn. Clubs: Grace Reading, Brainerd Garden (dir. 1958). Home: 325 Belvoir Av Chattanooga TN 37411 Office: McCallie School Kyle St Chattanooga TN 37404

MAZIN, NANCY RUTH SPITALNICK (MRS. AARON MAZIN), lawyer; b. Atlantic City, Mar. 23, 1945; d. Joseph and Alice (Rothman) Spitalnick; B.S. in Bus. Adminstrn., Boston U., 1967; postgrad. Am. U. Sch. Law, 1967-68; J.D., Temple U., 1968-70; m. Aaron Mazin, June 23, 1968; 1 dau., Robin. Admitted to Pa. bar, 1970, N.J. bar, 1971; asso. Klovsky, Kuby & Harris, Phila., 1970-73; Dept. Def. atty., Phila., 1970-73; pvt. practice law, Phila., 1970—, Atlantic City, 1971—; with firm Horn, Weinstein & Kaplan, Atlantic City, 1974—. Adj. prof. Stockton State Coll., 1974—. Named Dept. Def. Women of Year, 1973. Mem. N.J., Pa., Atlantic County bars, Fed. Bar Assn., Women's Jr. C. of C., Phi Alpha Delta. Jewish religion. Club: Soroptomist. Home: 15 S Cornwall Av Ventnor NJ 08406 Office: Guarantee Trust Bldg Atlantic City NJ 08401

MAZUR, HELEN LOUISE JONES GROUTEN (MRS. ALBIN M. MAZUR), civic worker, med. sec.; b. Wilkinsburg, Pa., Aug. 2, 1923; d. Edward and Helen (Cooper) Jones; student Burroughs Secretarial Sch., 1941; m. Walter A. Grouten, July 21, 1946 (div. June 1969); 1 son, Barry Alan; m. 2d, Albin Mazur, Sept. 25, 1971; stepchildren—Dean Anthony, Kim Michael. Chief adminstr. United Fund, Avon, Conn., 1963-72, also bd. dirs.; med. sec. Fitzsimons Gen. Hosp., Denver, 1942-46, Gilbert W. Heublein, M.D., Hartford, Conn., 1946-53, 59-67, Garner Lewis, M.D., Simsbury, Conn., 1959—. Pres., Tunxis council United Ch. Women, 1965-68, sec. Ch. Women United Conn., 1967; pres. Woman's Club, Avon, 1967; dir. pub. relations Conn. Yankee council, Girl Scouts U.S.A., 1966-67. Bd. dirs. Conn. Health League; mem. Avon Pub. Health Nursing Bd. Mem. Avon Republican Town Com., 1964-72, sec., 1966-67, 68-72; justice of peace, Avon, 1968-72. Recipient Service award United Fund, Avon, 1966, Amblyopia Clinics, Conn. Soc. Prevention Blindness, 1965-68. Mem. UN Assn. Hartford (sec. 1968—), Pub. Health Assn. Conn. (legislative chmn. 1966-67), Avon Pub. Health Nursing Assn. (dir. 1960-70), League of Women Voters. Conglist. Club: Avon Woman's (editor newspaper 1968-71). Home: 88 Spring Lane West Hartford CT 06107 Office: 720 Hopmeadow St Simsbury CT 06070

MAZUR, STELLA MARY, orgn. exec.; b. Lowell, Mass.; d. Stanley and Katherine (Cichowicz) Mazur; B.S., Mass. State Coll.; student ARC Mgmt. Tng. Sch., 1962, Nat. Tng. Lab. for Applied Behavioral Sci., 1963. U.S.O. club dir. Windsor Locks, Conn., 1942; gen. field rep. A.R.C., 1944, exec. dir., Waltham, Mass., 1944—. Spl. assignment State Dept. USIA Graphic Arts Cultural Exchange Program, Eastern Europe, Poland, 1965. Recipient Waltham Rotary Club spl. citation, 1952, Waltham Community 25 Year Service award, 1969, Recognition award Waltham chpt. A.R.C., 1971. Mem. Nat. Recreation Assn., Internat. Platform Assn., State Coll. Alumni Assn. Clubs: Vesper Country (Tyngsboro, Mass.); Longmeadow Golf, Country (Lowell). Home: 170 Andover St Lowell MA 01852 Office: ARC 22 Appleton St Waltham MA 02154

MAZUY, CORDELIA KAY KNIGHT (MRS. JON CLAUDE MAZUY), banker; b. Springfield, Mo., Nov. 22, 1938; d. William Horace and Charline (Bentley) Knight; A.B. with honors in English, U. N.C., 1960; M.S. in Statistics, N.C. State U., 1962; m. Jon Claude Mazuy, Aug. 31, 1959; children—Katharine Michelle, Christopher Knight. Statistician, Research Triangle Inst., Durham, N.C., 1960-63; statis. cons. Arthur D. Little, Inc., Cambridge, Mass., 1963-67; marketing research project mgr. Polaroid Corp., Cambridge, 1967, dir. marketing research 1968-69, mgr. marketing planning and analysis, 1969-70; dir. marketing and bus. planning Transaction Tech. Inc., Cambridge, 1970-72; pres. Mazuy Assos., Boston, 1972-73; v.p. Nat. Shawmut Bank, Boston, 1973-74; sr. v.p. Shawmut Assos., 1974—. Tchr., Amos Tuck Grad. Sch. Bus., 1964-65. Mem. Am. Statis. Assn., Am. Marketing Assn., Bank Marketing Assn., Phi Beta Kappa, Phi Kappa Phi, Kappa Alpha Theta. Home: 115 Lincoln Rd Wayland MA 01778 Office: 40 Water St Boston MA 02109

MAZZANTI, DEBORAH SZEKELY SHAINMAN (MRS. VINCENT E. MAZZANTI), health and beauty resort exec.; b. N.Y.C., May 3, 1922; d. Harry and Rebecca (Seidman) Shainman; student pub. schs., U.S.A., Tahiti, Mexico; m. Edmond Bordeaux Szekely, Dec. 26, 1939 (div. Dec. 1969); children—Livia Soledad, Alexandre Odin; m. Vincent E. Mazzanti, June 16, 1971. Co-founder Rancho La Puerta, Tecate, Baja, Cal., 1940; founder, pres., dir. Golden Door, Inc., Escondido, Cal., 1959—; pres., Golden Door Cosmetics, San Diego, 1959—. dir. Vannier Tea, Inc., N.Y.C. nat. sponsor Save the Children Fedn., 1965—; mem. women's com. Salk Inst., 1968—; mem. San Diego Opera, San Diego Symphony, Fine

Arts Soc., Planned Parenthood, Mental Health Assn.; mem. Pres.'s Conf. Phys. Fitness and Sports, 1968—; a founder Free Family Fitness and Fun Centers, San Diego. Bd. dirs. Combined Arts and Edn. Council San Diego, Theatre and Arts Found., Old Globe Theatre, Francis Parker Sch.; bd. dirs., mem. Community Assos. Sch. Medicine, U. Cal. at San Diego, also mem. Chancellor's Club, vice chmn. bd. overseers; sec., bd. govs. San Diego Stadium Authority; trustee Menninger Found. Author: The Golden Door Book of Health and Beauty, 1961. Home: 3232 Dove St San Diego CA 92103 Office: 2104 Hancock St San Diego CA 92110

MAZZARO, JANICE FOLEY (MRS. ANTHONY MAZZARO), theatrical dir.; b. N.Y.C., Nov. 14, 1928; d. Michael Joseph and Mary (De Mare) Foley; B.S., N.Y. U., 1950, postgrad., 1950; postgrad. Am. Theatre Wing, 1951-52, Herbert Berghof Studio, 1952-53, Towson State Coll., 1973; m. Anthony Mazzaro, Apr. 19, 1958; children—Deborah Monique, Lesley Diane. Mng. dir., drama dir. Creative Arts Workshop, Towson, Md., 1965-70; drama dir. Jewish Community Center, Balt., 1962-64; prodn. dir., drama instr. Community Mus. Theatre, Community Coll. Balt., 1969-72; exec. dir., prodn. dir. Dulaney Summer Theatre, Towson, 1967-74; drama cons. Balt. County Dept. Recreation and Parks, 1968-71; makeup cons. Roland Park Country Sch., 1968-73; prodn. dir., coordinator Md. Jr. Miss Pageant, 1968-69; co-founder, dir. Theatre Art Studios, Lutherville, Md., 1970-72; guest dir. Country Players, Pikesville, Md., 1969, Barnstormers, Johns Hopkins, 1969, Conservatory Players, Pikesville, 1969, Stafford Players, 1970, Kenwood Sr. High Sch., 1970-73, Theatre Hopkins, Johns Hopkins, 1971; instr. drama and speech Catonsville Community Coll., 1972-74; instr. speech Essex Community Coll., 1972; prodn. exec., dir. Stembridge Community Theatre, 1973. Cons. on mus. theater Gov.'s Conf. on Recreation and Parks, Towson, 1972. Address: 816 Ivydale Av Reistertown MD 21136

MAZZO, KAY, ballerina; b. Chgo., 1947; student of Bernadene Hayes, Sch. of Am. Ballet. Ballerina with Ballet U.S.A., 1961-62; with N.Y.C. Ballet, 1962—, soloist, 1965—. Home: 160 West End Av New York City NY 10023 Office: New York City Ballet Lincoln Center New York City NY 10023

MCADAMS, INA MAY OGLETREE (MRS. KELLY E. MCADAMS), bus. exec., club woman; b. Wetumka, Okla., May 28, 1906; d. George Royden and Londa (Pickett) Ogletree; student E. Tex. State Coll., 1922-24, Baylor U., 1926, Tex. A. and M. Coll., 1926; B.S., Sam Houston State Coll., 1930; M. Journalism, U. Tex., 1959; m. Kelly Edgar McAdams, May 30, 1928; children—Kelly Roy, Martha Lucille (Mrs. Ralph William Vertrees), Billye May (Mrs. Herbert Oscar Muecke). Tchr., 1926-28; free-lance writer, 1930—; owner, v.p. M. and O. Timber Co., Austin, Tex., 1952—. First Woman mem. Tex. Good Neighbor Commn., 1955—; mem. Am. Revolution Bicentennial Commn. of Tex.; city coordinator Ground Observer Corps, 1955-57; hon. mem. Internat. Relations Council, San Antonio, 1956—; mem. Internat. Good Neighbor Commn., Travis County Hist. Survey Com. Recipient Freedoms Found. Honor award, 1965. Mem. Tex. Fedn. Women's Clubs (chmn. status woman com. 1956-58, bd. mem. 1953-57, chmn. pub. relations 1958-60, platform chmn. 1962-64), Tex. Fine Arts Assn., Tex. Hist. Found., Austin Women's Fedn. (pres. 1953-55), D.A.R. (regent 1954-56, mem. state bd. 1952-58, state registrar 1958-60), Delphian Soc., Daus. of 1812 (Tex. pres. 1954-56, mem. state bd. 1950-58), Austin Woman's Symphony League, Huguenots of Manakintowne, Magna Charta Dames, Ams. of Royal Descent, Alpha Gamma Delta, Theta Sigma Phi, Epsilon Sigma Omicron. Baptist. Clubs: San Antonio Breakfast, Violet Crown Garden (life), Woman's (life). Editor and compiler Tex. Women Distinction, 1962, The Building of Longwood, 1972. Home: 1425 Preston Av Austin TX 78703 also McAdams K-Bar Ranch Arcata CA 95521

MCAFEE, CARRIE R. HAMPTON (MRS. JOSHUA O. MCAFEE), educator; b. Galveston, Tex., Dec. 30, 1932; d. Tom and Daisy (Charlton) Hampton; B.A., Tex. So. U., 1952, M.A., 1963; postgrad. Lincoln U., 1958, Columbia, 1960, U. Cal. at Berkeley, 1964; m. Joshua O. McAfee, July 31, 1964; children—Rhonda Maria, Roy Bernard. Tchr., Houston Ind. Sch. Dist., 1953-65, counselor, 1965-68, vice prin., 1968-74, prin., 1974—. Counselor, Neighborhood Youth Corps, 1969—; vol. nurses aid A.R.C., 1964—; active YWCA. Mem. Am. Personnel and Guidance Assn., Am. Assn. Sex Edn. and Counselors, Nat., Tex. assns. women deans, Assn. Supervision and Curriculum Devel., Tex. Tchrs. Assn., Tex., Houston assns. supervision and curriculum devel., Houston Sch. Adminstrs. Assn., Am. Bridge Assn. (dir.), Am. Contract Bridge League, Nat., Tex. assns. secondary sch. prins., Nat. Assn. Female Execs., Zeta Phi Beta. Roman Catholic. Home: 3618 S MacGregor Way Houston TX 77021

MCALISTER, ISABEL MILEY (MRS. GEORGE ALEXANDER MCALISTER), health service adminstr.; b. Chambersburg, Pa., Jan. 29, 1906; d. Harry Mellvill and Orpah A. (Schaff) Miley; student Moore Inst. Illustration 1926-28; diploma Phila. Sch. Occupational Therapy, U. Pa., 1935; m. George Alexander McAlister, June 24, 1942. Staff occupational therapist Norristown (Pa.) State Hosp., 1935-43, Spring Grove State Hosp., Catonsville, Md., 1955-57, also head occupational therapy, 1955-57; occupational therapist Washington County Soc. for Crippled Children and Adults, Washington, Pa., 1957-61; staff occupational therapist Montebello State Hosp., Balt., 1961-65; dir. occupational therapy, supr. of tng. aides South Mountain (Pa.) Restoration Center, 1965—. Mem. Am. Legion Aux., Am., Md., Pa. occupational therapy assns., D.A.R. (circle pres. 1949-51). Presbyn. (sec. missionary soc. 1945-46). Home: 79 North Main Chambersburg PA 17201

MCALISTER, MARJORIE MAXINE, librarian; b. Des Moines, Sept. 25, 1915; d. Walter Ace and Myra Phoebe (Hutt) Keith; B.A., Drake U., 1936; B.S. in Library Sci., U. Denver, 1940; m. Ned Walter McAlister, Aug. 18, 1940. Tchr., librarian Radcliffe (Ia.) High Sch., 1936-38; librarian Cowles Library, Drake U., Des Moines, 1938-43, U.S. Army Library, Ft. Des Moines, 1943-46, VA Hosp., Des Moines, 1947-48; with Des Moines Pub. Library, 1950—, coordinator adminstrv. services, 1969—. Mem. Des Moines Library Club (pres. 1959), A.L.A., Ia. Library Assn. (chmn. membership com. 1958, chmn. adult services com. 1962), Bus. and Profl. Women's Club. Mem. Order Eastern Star. Home: 1227 River Vista Dr Des Moines IA 50315 Office: 100 Lucust St Des Moines IA 50309

MCALLISTER, ANN BROOKS (MRS. BOBBY DARRELL MCALLISTER), coll. dean; b. Fairfield, Ala., Apr. 14, 1936; d. James Clarence and Annie Hala (Bullock) Brooks; B.S., Samford U., 1964; M.A., U. Ala., 1967; Ph.D., 1973; m. Bobby Darrell McAllister, Sept. 29, 1956 (dec. 1961); children—Darrell Britton, Leslie Mara. Counselor U. Ala., University, summer, 1966; counselor, tchr. history Fairfield City schs., Ala., 1964-67; asst. dean students Miss. State Coll. for Women, Columbus, 1967-68, dean of students, 1968-72; research asso. research and tng. center So. Region Sch. Bd. Assn., U. Ala., University, 1972-73; prof. edn., dean of students Miss. State Coll. for Women, Columbus, 1973—. Mem. adv. bd. Nat. Bank Commerce. Mem. Am. Personnel and Guidance Assn., Nat. Assn. Women Deans, Adminstrs. and Counselors, So. Coll. Personnel Assn. (chmn. research com. 1973-74), Miss. Chief Personnel Adminstrs. (chmn. conf. coordinator 1972), Kappa Delta Pi, Kappa Delta Epsilon, Pi Gamma Mu, Omicron Kappa Pi, Pi Tau Chi. Baptist. Contbr. articles on ednl. adminstrn. to profl. jours. Office: Mississippi State College for Women Columbus MS 39701

MCALLISTER, JOSEPHINE KELLER (MRS. HOWARD MCALLISTER), real estate co. exec.; b. Cowan, Tenn., Nov. 14, 1926; d. Joseph Sevier and Bonnie Annie Laurie (Allen) Keller; grad. high sch.; m. Howard McAllister, Nov. 11, 1949; children—Donna, Jon Howard. Sec., War Dept., Washington, 1945; legal sec. Jack Politz, Washington, 1946-53; with Huntington Realty, Pacific Palisades, Cal., 1962—, mgr. Huntington's Red Carpet Realtors, 1973—. Mem. Cal. Real Estate Assn., Los Angeles Realty Bd. (v.p., dir. 1973—, chmn. Pacific Palisades div. 1973—), Pacific Palisades Womens Club. Home: 535 Mount Holyoke Pacific Palisades CA 90272 Office: 15129 Sunset Blvd Pacific Palisades CA 90272

MCALLISTER, PATRICIA LOUISE CYONE (MRS. JAMES JACOB MCALLISTER), pallet and container co. exec.; b. Ridgway, Pa., June 28, 1944; d. John Nick and Grace Mary (Gier) Cyone; A.A., Robert Morris Coll., 1964; m. James Jacob McAllister, May 25, 1968; children—James Jacob, Stephen James, Douglas James. Sec. to controller Keystone Carbon Co., St. Marys, Pa., 1964-67, sec. to exec. sec., 1968-69; controller Elk Pallet & Splty. Co., Inc., St. Marys, 1969—, v.p. of bd. dirs., 1970—. Sec. for sec. Young Republicans Elk County, 1968-69. Mem. Elk County Civic Music Assn., Alpha Iota. Address: PO Box 579 St Marys PA 15857

MCANDREW, CATHERINE DOLCH (MRS. WALTER JOSEPHE MCANDREW), lawyer; b. Madison, Wis., Jan. 13, 1918; d. Edward William and Marguerite (Pierce) Dolch; B.S., U. Ill., 1937; M.A., U. Mich., 1940; J.D., Rutgers U., 1960; m. Walter Josephe McAndrew, Feb. 28, 1944; children—Catherine, Walter John, Lawrence Edward. Tchr. high sch., Polo, Ill., Scarsdale and Riverside, N.Y., 1937-38, 40; prof. speech and dramatics Fayette (Ia.) U., 1940-41, Montclair (N.J.) Tchrs. Coll., 1945-46, Douglas Coll., New Brunswick, N.J., 1955-57; sec. Edison Twp. Planning Bd., N.J., 1958-59; radio broadcaster, writer sta. WELL, Battle Creek, Mich., 1943-44, sta. WWL, New Orleans, 1945-46, sta. WHBF, Champaign, Ill., 1942; admitted to N.J. bar, 1960, Cal. bar, 1963, also U.S. Supreme Ct. bar; practiced in New Brunswick, 1960-63, San Francisco, 1964; asso. firm Strong and Strong, 1960-62, Price, Postel and Parma, 1963; state atty. Cal. Pub. Utilities Commn. dept. Housing and Community Devel., Motor Vehicle dept., Sacramento, 1964—. Tchr. bus. law Sacramento City Coll., 1972—. Served with WAC, 1943-44. Mem. D.C., N.J., Cal. bar assns. Home: 5943 Klamath Dr Sacramento CA 95860 Office: 2415 First Av Sacramento CA 95809

MCANULTY, MARY CATHERINE CRAMER (MRS. CHARLES GILBERT MCANULTY), ret. educator; b. Braddock, Pa., June 26, 1908; d. Albert R. and Sara (Kelly) Cramer; A.B., Fla. So. Coll., 1929; M.A., Tchrs. Coll. Columbia, 1937; postgrad. Fla. State U., 1946-50; m. Charles Gilbert McAnulty, Dec. 25, 1937. Elementary tchr. Lake Ann Sch., Lake Garfield, Fla., 1930-31, elementary prin., 1932-34; prin. South Winter Haven Elementary Sch., Winter Haven, Fla., 1935-55; adminstrv. asst. to supervising prin. Winter Haven Area Schs., 1956-60; prin. Fred Garner Elementary Sch., Winter Haven, 1961-68, Lake Alfred Elementary Sch., 1969-70. Asst. chmn. vols., asst. tng. chmn., local chpt. A.R.C., 1967-68, 2d v.p., also chmn. vols., 1969-70, bd. mem., chmn. service to mil. families, 1970-71, chmn. coll. youth, 1971-72. Mem. Am. Assn. Supervision and Curriculum Devel., Internat. Reading Assn. (Polk County chmn.), N.E.A., Fla. Edn. Assn. (dir. dept. elementary sch. prins. 1965-67), Polk County Elementary Prins. Assn. (sec.), League Women Voters (local dir. 1962), Am. Assn. U. Women (local br. chmn. status women com. 1963), D.A.R. (chpt. treas. 1967-68, historian 1969-70, regent 1970-72, state chmn. jr. Am. citizens 1972—, dir. dist. VI 1973-74), Fla. So. Coll. Alumni Assn. (sec.), Internat. Platform Assn., P.E.O. (chpt. treas. 1970-74), Pi Gamma Mu, Delta Kappa Gamma (State Achievement award 1964, Fla. pres. 1962-63, chpt. parliamentarian 1968-73). Methodist (choir mem., chmn. commn. edn. 1959-60, supt. study program 1969-70, organist 1970-74, pres. Wesley fellowship class 1972-73). Clubs: Pilot (charter, pres. 1954-55, 61-62), Poinsettia Garden (sec.), Winter Haven Woman's (edn. chmn. 1967-68). Home: 333 W Lake Howard Dr Apt 303D SE Winter Haven FL 33880

MCARDLE, CONSTANCE, librarian; b. Boston; d. Henry F. and Marie (Olney) McArdle; A.B., Chestnut Hill Coll., Phila., 1946; M.L.S., Queen's Coll., 1974. Fund raiser Plimoth Plantation, Boston, 1957-58; fashion publicity with Eleanor Lambert Co., N.Y.C., 1958-59; with Grolier Inc., pubs., N.Y.C., 1960—, editorial librarian, 1970—. Mem. Spl. Libraries Assn., N.Y. Library Club. Home: 330 E 56th St New York City NY 10022 Office: 575 Lexington Av New York City NY 10022

MCARTHUR, JANET WARD, physician; b. Bellingham, Wash., June 25, 1914; d. Hyland Donald and Alice Maria (Frost) McArthur; A.B., U. Wash., 1935, M.S., 1937; M.B., Northwestern U., 1941, M.D., 1942; Sc.D., Mt. Holyoke Coll., 1962. Intern Cin. Gen. Hosp., 1941-42, asst. resident in medicine, 1942-43; asst. resident, research fellow in medicine, H.P. Walcott fellow clin. medicine Mass. Gen. Hosp., Boston, 1943-44, asso. physician, 1959—; instr. Harvard Med. Sch., Boston, 1955-57, asst. prof., 1960-64, asso. prof., 1964-73, prof., 1973—, mem. Center for Population Studies, 1970—; mem. scientific adv. com. Med. Research Inst. Worcester, 1963—; adv. com. Harvard Center for Population Studies, 1971—; cons. physician Mass. Eye and Ear Infirmary, Boston, 1952—; asso. to children's service, Mass. Gen. Hosp., 1968—. Diplomate Am. Bd. Internal Medicine. Fellow A.C.P.; mem. A.M.A., Endocrine Soc., Am. Fertility Soc., A.A.A.S., Boston Obstetrical Soc., Phi Beta Kappa, Sigma Xi, Alpha Omega Alpha. Author: (with others) Functional Endocrinology from Birth Through Adolescence, 1952. Editor: (with Theodore Colton) Statistics in Endocrinology, 1970. Contbr. articles to profl. pubs. Home: 19 Brimmer St Boston MA 02108 Office: 32 Fruit St Boston MA 02114

MCARTHUR, JEANETTE BENNETT, artist, author, ednl. adminstr.; b. Reidsville, N.C., Jan. 22, 1919; d. Charles Robert and Maggie Norman (Waynick) Bennett; A.B., Greensboro Coll., 1939; M.A., Columbia, 1951; m. Joseph R. McArthur, Dec. 8, 1940 (div. Aug. 1950); 1 dau., Sarajean (Mrs. Demetrio Joseph Capua). Dir. art edn. Broward County Pub. Schs., Ft. Lauderdale, Fla., 1961—; exhibited group shows Madison Gallery, N.Y.C., 1968, Arkep Gallery, N.Y.C., 1969, N.C. Mus. Art, Raleigh, 1970, Mint Mus., Charlotte, N.C., 1971, Hollywood (Fla.) Art Mus., 1971, Village Gallery, Coral Gables, Fla., 1972; represented in pvt. collections; illustrator, script writer comml. filmstrips. Mem. Nat., Fla., Broward art edn. assns., Internat. Soc. for Edn. through Art, Delta Kappa Gamma. Author: Stitchery, 1970; Holiday Ideas, 1970; Jewelry Anyone Can Make, 1970; Printing Without a Press, 1970; Creative Crayon Techniques, 1970; Ends and Odds to Art, 1970; also stories in children's mags. Editor: Fla. Art Education mag., 1967. Home: 526 N Rainbow Dr Hollywood FL 33021 Office: 1320 SW 4th St Fort Lauderdale FL 33312

MCARTHUR, LESLIE ANN ZEBROWITZ, psychologist, educator; b. Detroit, Nov. 8, 1944; d. Aaron Harry and Esther (Milgrom) Zebrowitz; B.A., U. Wis., 1966; M.S. (Woodrow Wilson fellow), Yale, 1968, Ph.D. (Nat. Inst. Mental Health fellow), 1970; m. A. Verne McArthur, July 14, 1968; 1 son, Caleb Jonathan. Asst. prof. psychology Brandeis U., Waltham, Mass., 1970—, Ford Found. faculty fellow for research on role of women in soc., 1973-74, Nat. Inst. Mental Health grantee, 1973-74. Mem. Am. Psychol. Assn., Phi Beta Kappa. Editorial cons. Jour. Personality and Social Psychology, 1970—; mem. editorial rev. bd. Jour. Personality, 1972—. Research in causal attribution, effects of mass media on children's sex-role behavior. Office: Brandeis Univ Dept Psychology Waltham MA 02154

MCARTHUR, NADEAN ORR, dairy co. exec.; b. Bellefontaine, O., July 31, 1936; d. James Starl and LaVaughn Leuna (Haver) Orr; grad. high sch.; m. Charles M. McArthur, June 12, 1959 (dec. June 1973); 1 dau., La Nae. Sec., treas. Charles McArthur Dairies, Okeechobee, Fla., 1959—, pres., 1973—. Sec., treas. bd. dirs. Americable TV, 1970—. Sec. Fine Arts, Okeechobee, 1963. Clubs: Everglades (Palm Beach, Fla.); Surf, Palm Bay (Miami, Fla.); Womans (pres. Okeechobee 1960-61). Home: 309 SW 15th St Okeechobee FL 33472 Office: PO Box 1205 Okeechobee FL 33472

MCAULIFFE, ROSEMARY, lawyer; b. New Rochelle, N.Y.; d. William and Rose (Payne) McAuliffe; A.B., Regis Coll., 1949; J.D., New Eng. Sch. Law, 1954; M.Ed., Boston State Coll., 1970. Admitted to Mass. bar, 1956; practiced in Boston, 1956—; asso. firm McAuliffe & McAuliffe, 1957—. Mem. Mass. Assn. Women Lawyers. Roman Catholic (pres. ch. council, 1970—). Home: 84 Prince St Boston MA 02113

MCAVOY, RITA CLOUTIER (MRS. GEORGE EDWARD MCAVOY), bus. exec., civic worker; b. Lewiston, Me., June 9, 1917; d. Gideon Edward and Eva Mary (Lambert) Cloutier; grad. high sch.; m. George Edward McAvoy, July 5, 1948; children—Richard Dixon, Suzanne Bette (Mrs. Richard Hopgood). Owner, operator Thayers Hotel, Littleton, N.H., 1949-69; operator, part owner Crawford House, Crawford Notch, N.H., 1969-73; postmaster Crawford House P.O., 1970-73. Pres. women's aux. Littleton Hosp., 1966-67, 71; sec., organizer fund drive Dollars for Scholars program, 1963—; mem. N.H. Network Fund Raising Com., 1968-74, Littleton Bicentennial Com., 1973-75, Pres.'s Assay Commn., 1970; mem. selection com. Nat. Resources Conservation Awards, 1974—. Pres. Profile Republican Women's Club, 1957-58, 71; mem. N.H. State Rep. Com., 1967-73; women's chmn. Littleton Rep. Town Com., 1964—; pres. N.H. Fedn. Rep. Women, 1974—. Trustee Littleton Hosp. Named Rep. Woman of Yr., Profile Rep. Women's Club, 1969, Woman of Yr., Colonial Club, 1972. Mem. N.H. Hotel and Motel Assn., N.H. Audubon Soc., Littleton Hist. Soc., League Women Voters. Clubs: Littleton Garden (pres. 1961-62), Littleton Colonial (pres. 1956-57). Address: Bethlehem Rd Littleton NH 03561

MCBAIN, DIANE, actress; b. Cleve., May 18, 1941; d. Walter G. and Cleo (Ferguson) McBain; student pub. schs.; m. Rodney Leroy Burke, Feb. 6, 1972. Appeared in starring roles in movies including Ice Palace, 1959, Parrish, 1960, Claudelle Inglish, 1961, The Caretakers, 1962, Mary, Mary, 1963; Distant Trumpet, 1963, Spinout, 1966, The Sidehackers, 1969, The Delta Factor, 1970, Savage Season, 1970, The Deathhead Virgin, 1972, Wicked, Wicked, 1973; also appeared in TV series Surfside Six, 1960-61. Mem. A.F.T.R.A., Screen Actors Guild.

MCBAIN, OLIVIA LEONA SNELL (MRS. CLAIR ADRIAN MCBAIN), educator; b. Pauline, Neb., Nov. 30, 1917; d. William Jesse and Margaret (Merkel) Snell; A.B., San Francisco State U., 1958, M.A., 1961; m. Clair Adrian McBain, May 25, 1948; 1 son, Robert Lee Brown. Engaged in property mgmt., Oakland, Cal., 1947-58; intern Sonoma State Hosp. for Retarded, Glen Ellen, 1958-59; tchr. educable mentally retarded Oakland (Cal.) Sch. Dist., 1959-60; tchr., counselor for mentally retarded San Leandro High Sch., San Leandro (Cal.) Unified Sch. Dist., 1960—. Home: 2933 Georgia St Oakland CA 94602 Office: 2200 Bancroft Av San Leandro CA 94578

MCBEE, LOUISE, educator; b. Strawberry Plains, Tenn.; d. John Wallace and Nina (Umbarger) McBee; B.S., E. Tenn. State U., 1946; M.A., Columbia U., 1951; Ph.D., Ohio State U., 1961. Geography tchr. Marion (Va.) High Sch., 1946-47; instr. phys. edn. E. Tenn. State U. Johnson City, 1947-50, dir. housing, 1951-56, asst. dean women, 1957-59, dean women and prof. psychology, 1961-63; Fulbright tchr., Rotterdam, Holland, 1956-57; dean women, asso. prof. psychology U. Ga., Athens, 1963-74, dean student affairs, asso. prof. psychology, 1974—. Prof. psychology World Campus Afloat. Mem. Ga. Gov.'s Commn. on Status Women. Mem. Am., Southeastern psychol. assns., Nat., Ga. assns. women deans and counselors, So. Coll. Personnel Assn., Am. Assn. U. Women, Mortar Bd., Phi Kappa Phi, Kappa Delta Pi, Pi Lambda Theta, Delta Kappa Gamma, Psi Chi, Kappa Delta. Home: 145 Pine Valley Pl Athens GA 30601

MCBEE, SUSANNA BARNES, journalist; b. Sante Fe, Mar. 28, 1935; d. Jess Stephen and Sybil Elizabeth (Barnes) McBee; A.B., U. So. Cal., 1956; M.A., U. Chgo., 1962. Staff writer Washington Post, 1957-65, 73-74, asst. nat. editor, 1974—; Washington corr. Life mag., 1965-69; Washington editor McCall's mag., 1970-72. Recipient Penney-Missouri mag. award, 1969. Mem. Washington Press Club, Sigma Delta Chi (Pub. Service award 1969). Club: Internat. (Washington). Home: 3834 T St NW Washington DC 20007 Office: 1150 15th St NW Washington DC 20005

MCBRIDE, BEVERLEY BOOTH, psychologist; b. Richmond, Va., June 29, 1929; d. Edward Lee and Myrtle Grace (Woodlief) Booth; student Randolph-Macon Womans Coll., 1949-51; B.S., Va. Commonwealth U., 1951, postgrad., 1951-53; M.S., Va. Poly. Inst. and State U., 1964; postgrad. Ohio U., 1969; m. John William McBride; children—John David, William Stephen, Philip Anthony, James Andrew. Staff psychologist Mountain Empire Guidance Clinic, Radford, Va., 1959-67, acting dir., 1963-65; cons. psychologist Greenbrier Valley Mental Health Clinic, Lewisburg, W.Va., 1964-70, chief psychologist, 1970—; pvt. practice, Parkersburg, W.Va., 1967-69. Program cons. Headstart-Day Care Program, W. Central W.Va. Community Action Assn., Parkersburg, 1967-70, dir. counseling unit Manpower Program, 1968-70; cons. psychologist Allegheny Mental Health Clinic, Clifton Forge, Va., 1971—; faculty Radford Coll., 1962-64, W.Va. U., Parkersburg, 1968-70; cons. psychologist Div. Vocational Rehab., Richmond Area, 1953-58, Monroe County Bd. Edn., Union, W.Va., 1965-68, Greenbrier County Bd. Edn., Lewisburg, 1965-72, Monroe County Mental Health Clinic, Union, W.Va., 1970-73. Chmn. fine arts com. Radford Jr. Womans Club, 1960-61, program chmn., 1961-62, v.p., 1962-63, pres., 1963-64; mem. Gov.'s Study Commn. on Youth, 1962-63, Gov.'s Study Commn. on Mental Health, 1964-65; chmn. Multicounty Interagy. Council, Radford, 1963-64; mem. Parkersburg Fine Arts Center, 1967-70; chmn. conservation dept. Parkersburg Womans Club, 1968-69; mem. adv. bd. Radford Fine Arts Council, 1963-65, Greenbrier Tng. Center, 1973—. Mem. Nat. (del. 1971-73), W.Va. (pres. elect 1973—) assns. sch. psychologists, W.Va. Psychol. Assn. Episcopalian. Home: 409 E Washington St Lewisburg WV 24901 Office: 100 Church St Lewisburg WV 24901

MCBRIDE, DOROTHY LEE ANDERSON (MRS. HENRY JOHN MCBRIDE), motel owner, operator; b. Clint, Tex., Apr. 12, 1920; d. R.C. and Ruby Estelle (Ford) Anderson; B.A., Sul Ross State U., 1940; m. Henry John McBride, Mar. 15, 1941; children—Ann Estelle (Mrs. Billy Paul Stewart), Nina. Legal sec. Swearingen & Bledsoe, Marfa, Tex., 1940-43; co-owner, operator Western Auto Asso. Store, Alpine, Tex., 1941-60, Motel Bien Venido, Alpine, 1956—. Registered rep. Financial Programs, Inc., Denver, 1956-72, Cornerstone Financial Services, Boston, 1972—. Mem. Alpine City Council, 1966—, mayor, 1970—. Mem. planning com. Sul Ross State U., Alpine, 1970—. Mem. Alpine C. of C. (dir.), W. Tex. Council

Govts. (dir.). Baptist (past pres. women's group). Mem. Order Eastern Star. Clubs: Beauceant, Pilot (past dist. gov. Alpine). Home: 108 E Eagle Pass Alpine TX 79830 Office: 807 E Holland St Alpine TX 79830

MCBRIDE, LUCIA, ret. radiographer; b. Cleve., Oct. 20, 1907; d. Malcolm Lee and Lucia (McCurdy) McBride; student Mills Coll., 1927-29, Cleve. Coll., 1931-32, Zimmern Sch., Geneva, Switzerland, 1929-30; B.S., Western Res. U., 1936; grad. Ia. State U., 1939. Formerly tchr. pvt., pub. schs., Cleve.; head pre-sch. dept. Laurel Sch., Cleve., 1936-38; head emergency x-ray dept. Roosevelt Hosp., N.Y.C., 1948-72, head Beisler X-ray suite, 1967-72. Past mem. examining bd. exams. N.Y. State Council Roentgen Ray Technicians. Past dir. Child Health Assn., Cleve. Assn. Nursery Edn., Jr. Council Cleve. Mus. Art. Fellow Am. Geog. Soc.; mem. Am. Assn. U. Women, Nat. Hist. Soc., N.Y. Zool. Soc., Nat. Audubon Soc., Plato-Pythagorean Council (pres., treas.), Am. Mus. Nat. History, Health and Light Research Inst., English Speaking Union, Met. Mus. Art, N.Y. Cultural Center, Archeol. Inst. Am., Assos. of Lincoln Center, Nat. Trust for Historic Preservation, Oceanographic Found., Community Opera, Soc. Archtl. Historians, Menninger Found., N.Y. Bot. Gardens, Correctional Assn., Humane Soc., Smithsonian Assos., N.Y. Geneal. and Biog. Soc., Mus. Am. Indian, Bklyn. Mus., D.A.R., Nat. Assn. Am. Composers and Condrs. Contbr. articles to profl. jours. Home: 264 W 73d St New York City NY 10023

MCBRIDE, MARIAN BERNICE (MRS. RAYMOND E. MCBRIDE), editor, author; b. Wallace, Ida., Feb. 16, 1923; d. Pierce Joseph and Julia (Flynn) Dunne; B.J., Marquette U., 1943; m. Raymond E. McBride, Apr. 29, 1946; children—Joseph, Genni (Mrs. John Caspari), Michael, Patrick, Dennis, Mark, Timothy. With pub. relations dept. Bruce Pub. Co., 1943-45; with Milw. Jour., 1945-46; free lance writer, 1946-63; staff writer Milw. Sentinel, 1963-69; account exec. Barkin-Herman, Milw., 1969-70; asso. editor HER/Milw. mag., 1973—. Vice chmn. Wis. Democratic party, 1960-63. Recipient Am. Bar Assn. Gavel award, 1968; Best Feature Story of Year award Milw. Press Club, 1969; named Woman in Action, U. Wis. in Milw., 1965; Outstanding Journalist in Wis., U. Wis., 1967. Mem. Women in Communications, Milw. Press Club. Author: Discrimination in Private Clubs, 1965; (booklets) Women's Legal Rights in Wis., 1968. Home: 7631 Rogers Av Wauwatosa WI 53213

MCBROOM, FLETCHER PEARL RILEY, physician; b. Louisville, Miss.; d. Thomas and Augusta (Dooley) Riley; A.B., U. Chgo., 1946; B.S., Columbia, 1949, M.D., 1953; certificate (fellow in cardiology) U. So. Cal., 1958; m. Marcus S. W. McBroom, Jan. 21, 1956 (div. 1969); children—Lorelei Joyce, Pamela Carol. Intern internal medicine Bellevue Med. Center, N.Y.C., 1953-54; resident internal medicine, research fellow cardiovascular disease, asst. internal medicine Columbia Coll. Phys. and Surg., N.Y.C., 1954-55; resident internal medicine, house staff officer U. Cal. at Los Angeles, 1955-57; practice medicine specializing in internal medicine and cardiology, Los Angeles, 1958—; prin. investigator cardiovascular research Inst. for Med. Research, Cedars of Lebanon Hosp., Los Angeles, 1958-63, attending med. staff, 1961—; cons. internist, cardiologist Univ. Hosp., Los Angeles; attending med. staff Temple Hosp., Los Angeles. Organizer, Los Amigos, 1963-64; lectr. P.T.A.'s, high schs., sororities, chs., 1958—. Treas. Frederick Douglas Child Devel. Center. Recipient citation and certificate of honor Our Author Study Club, 1961, 62, Trailblazer award for med. research Nat. Aux. Negro Bus. and Profl. Women, 1962, Finer Womanhood award Zeta Phi Beta, 1960, awards for outstanding achievements in medicine Golden West Mag., 1962, 63, 66, citation of merit for achievements in medicine and med. research Internat. Congress Women, 1961. Mem. A.M.A., Los Angeles County, Charles Drew med. assns., Med., Dentists, Pharm. Assn., Urban League, N.A.A.C.P., Alpha Kappa Alpha. Contbr. articles to med. jours. Office: 1828 S Western Av Los Angeles CA 90006

MCBROOM, RUBY CUREINGTON (MRS. HASKELL L. MCBROOM), poet; b. Nichol, La., Dec. 21, 1918; d. Aaron Green and Mary Louisa (Smith) Cureington; student La. State Normal Coll., summer 1940; m. Haskell L. McBroom, June 18, 1949 (dec. Dec. 1967); children—Charles M., Jennifer S., Mary (Mrs. D. Dawson Wright). Asst. postmaster U.S. P.O., Zenoria, 1941-52; poetry pub. in Progressive Farmer, other mags., newspapers; poems included Fellowship Poetry Book, anthology of poetry, 1973. Recipient Gertrude B. Saucier humerous award La. State Poetry Soc. Festival, 1971. Mem. La. Poetry Soc. Baptist. Home: Route 1 Box 81 Trout LA 71371

MCBRYDE, MARY BERNICE HARWELL, ins. co. exec.; b. Texhoma, Okla., Feb. 2, 1907; d. Baker and Jessie B. (Chicken) Harwell; grad. high sch.; children—William R., Ann (Mrs. John J. McLaughlin), Truda Mae (Mrs. Gerald Hibbs), Beth (Mrs. David Kahmar), June. With Res. Nat. Ins. Co., Oklahoma City, 1958—, treas., 1963—. Mem. Hugenot Soc., D.A.R. Republican. Methodist. Mem. Order Eastern Star. Home: 2515 Dittmer Rd Oklahoma City OK 73127 Office: 418 NW 5th St Oklahoma City OK 73102

MCBURNEY, LIDIE SLOAN (MRS. ANDREW M. MCBURNEY), civic worker; b. New Orleans; d. Matthew Scott and Lottie E. (Lane) Sloan; grad. Sarah Lawrence Coll., 1936; m. Andrew M. McBurney, Feb. 26, 1938; children—A. Sloan, F. Lane. Mem. com. N.Y.C. Cancer Commn., 1949-52; mem. benefit com. N.Y. Infirmary, 1949; co-chmn. Community Chest Campaign, Lake Placid, 1951; mem. fund raising com. Boys Club of N.Y.C., 1960-63; vice chmn. women's div. Travelers Aid Soc., 1955, spl. gifts com. 1955—. Bd. dirs. Salvation Army Assn. of N.Y., 1950-64, v.p., 1955-64, chmn. women's div., 1954-56, rep. on Com. for Armed Forces, 1951-54; mem. com. U.S.O. of N.Y.C., Inc., 1954-58, mem. bd., 1969—, chmn. women's div., mem. exec. com., 1970—. mem. nat. council U.S.O., 1960—, nat. bd., 1961—, nat. bd. U.S.O. Corp., 1964—, sec., 1968—, sec. U.S.O., Inc., 1968—; bd. dirs. Placid Meml. Hosp., 1970—, chmn. ann. campaign, 1971—. Mem. Knickerbocker Greys (dir. 1952—, pres. 1956-59), N.Y. Jr. League, Lenox Hill Neighborhood Assn. (dir. 1965-72), Women's Nat. Republican Club (4th v.p. bd. 1966-68). Clubs: Colony (N.Y.C.); Lake Placid. Home: 190 E 72d St New York City NY 10021 also River Ranch Lake Placid NY 12946

MCCABE, CYNTHIA JAFFEE (MRS. LAWRENCE MCCABE), curator; b. N.Y.C., Feb. 8, 1943; d. Harry and Pauline (Titefsky) Jaffee; B.A., Cornell U., 1963; M.A., Columbia, 1967; m. Lawrence McCabe, Nov. 23, 1969. Organizer fine arts sect., catalogue, bibliography Lower East Side: Portal to American Life (1870-1924), Jewish Mus., N.Y.C., 1966; research Nakian Retrospective, Mus. Modern Art, N.Y.C., 1966; organizer fine arts sect. Erie Canal Sesquicentennial, N.Y. State Council Arts, 1967; research Venice 34, Nat. Collection of Fine Arts, Smithsonian Instn., Washington, 1968; curator painting and sculpture Hirshhorn Mus. and Sculpture Garden, Smithsonian Instn., Washington, 1967—. Mem. Internat. Council Museums, Am. Assn. Museums (curators' com.), Am. Assn. U. Women, Coll. Art Assn. Am., Soc. Archtl. Historians, Women's Caucus on Arts (nat. adv. bd.). Organizer catalogues. Home: 3106 Dogwood St Washington DC 20015 Office: Hirshhorn Mus and Sculpture Garden Smithsonian Instn Washington DC 20560

MCCABE, GENEVIEVE RUTH MATTHEWS (MRS. JAMES PATRICK MCCABE), village ofcl.; b. Lima, N.Y., Apr. 3, 1912; d. Almeron Evert and Nora (Perkins) Matthews; B.A., Houghton Coll., 1933; m. james Patrick McCabe, Dec. 27, 1941; 1 dau., Lenora Elizabeth. Sense tng. tchr. N.Y. State Dept. Mental Hygiene, Letchworth Village, Thiells, N.Y., 1937-43; village clk., registrar vital statistics Haverstraw, N.Y., 1947-74. Registrar, Local Selective Service Bd., 1956-72. Trustee, treas. Haverstraw Pub. Library, 1968—. Democratic committeewoman, Haverstraw, 1974; mem. Haverstraw Dem. Assn. Recipient Quarter Century certificate Pub. Service award N.Y. State Conf. Mayors, 1973. Mem. Library Assn. Rockland County (com. mem. 1969—), N.Y. State Assn. City and Village Clks., Rockland County Hist. Soc. Methodist. Club: 42 (Haverstraw). Home: HiTor Apts Dowd St Haverstraw NY 10927 Office: Fairmount Av Haverstraw NY 10927

MCCABE, LUBERTA MARIE HARDEN (MRS. FRANCIS THOMAS MCCABE), jour. editor; b. Wheaton, Minn., Oct. 29, 1900; d. Richard Dewey and Pauline (Schluep) Harden; B.A., Washington State Coll., 1922; M.A., Clark U., 1926, Ph.D., 1929; m. Francis Thomas McCabe, Aug. 18, 1934; children—Richard M., Thomas F., Robert J. Tchr. high schs. Valleyford and Ritzville, Wash., 1922-25; asst. editor Clark U. Press, Worcester, Mass., 1929-34; asso. editor Jour. Abnormal and Social Psychology, Washington, 1940-50; mng. editor Jour. of Pastoral Care, N.Y.C., 1952—. Bd. dirs. The Ednl. Exchange of Greater Boston. Home: 61 Lexington Av Cambridge MA 02138

MCCAFFERTY, AUDREY JANE, pub. relations exec.; b. Batavia, O.; d. Hubert Joseph and Lillian Marie (Berger) McCafferty. Sec. Cin. C. of C., 1947; with The Kroger Co., Cin., 1947—, pub. relations asst., 1955-70, mgr. press and publicity pub. affairs dept., 1970-73, mgr. pub. information, 1973—. Mem. Cin. Commn. Hunger and Malnutrition, 1971—. Mem. Consumer Conf. Greater Cin., Southwestern Ohio Consumers Assn., Am. Women in Radio and TV, Pub. Relations Soc. Am., League of Women Voters, Women in Communications. Club: Cincinnati Zonta (pres. 1964-65). Home: 2540 Ferguson Rd Cincinnati OH 45238 Office: 1014 Vine St Cincinnati OH 45201

MCCAFFREE, MARY KATHERINE, physician; b. Schell City, Mo., Feb. 24, 1933; d. William Taylor and Katherine Peterson (Grinstead) McCaffree; student Cottey Coll., 1951-52; A.B., Mo. U., 1956; M.D., U. Mo., 1963. Intern St. Luke's Hosp., St. Louis, 1963-64; resident internal medicine U. Mo. Med. Sch., Columbia, 1964-67; practice medicine specializing in internal medicine, St. Joseph, Mo., 1967-70, Jefferson City, Mo., 1971—; mem. staff St. Mary's Hosp., staff sec., 1973; mem. staff Meml. Community Hosp., Jefferson City. Active Boy Scouts Am. Mem. A.C.P., Am. Philat. Soc., Am., Mo. So., Cole County, med. assns., Am. Soc. Internal Medicine, Am. Heart Assn., U. Mo. Alumni Assn., Cole County Hist. Soc., Conservation Fedn. Mo., Am. Med. Women's Assn., Delta Delta Delta. Home: 903A Southwest Blvd Jefferson City MO 65101 Office: 1505 Southwest Blvd Jefferson City MO 65101

MCCAIN, ELIZABETH, state ofcl.; b. Memphis, Sept. 16, 1898; d. Vannoy Hugh and Maggie (Stephenson) McCain; B.S., Memphis State U., 1935; M.A., Peabody Coll., 1940; LL.B., So. Law U., 1958. Tchr. Shelby County and Memphis city schs., 1918-40; instr. reading clinics Ill. State Normal U., summers, 1942-50; dir. child guidance and testing Memphis city schs., 1941-50; judge Memphis Juvenile Ct., 1950-63; research specialist, cons. State of Tenn. Commn. on Children and Youth, 1964—. Admitted to Tenn. bar, 1958. Named Woman of Year in Memphis, Pilot Club, 1951; award Kiwanis Club, Memphis, 1959, Memphis Optimist Club, 1963; spl. award of merit Tenn. Council Juvenile Ct. Judges, 1973, Nat. Council Juvenile Ct. Judges, 1973. Mem. Nat. (treas. 1961-65), Tenn. (exec. sec. 1964—) councils juvenile ct. judges, Tenn. Edn. Assn. (pres. 1948-49), Tenn. Congress P.T.A. (bd. mgrs. 1965—). Mem. Order Eastern Star. Clubs: Kate Trader Barrow Book (pres. 1933-36), Quota (local pres., dist. gov. 1945-46). Home: 612 Metro Manor 500 5th Av N Nashville TN 37219 Office: 104 Capital Towers Nashville TN 37219

MCCAIN, ELLA BYRD (MRS. JOHN H. MCCAIN), librarian; b. Dothan, Ala., Mar. 8, 1925; d. Erskine Bell and Lydia Claudia (Woods) Byrd; B.S., Ala. A. and M. U., 1945; M.L.S., U. Mich., 1953; m. John H. McCain, June 17, 1947. Tchr. Opelika (Ala.) Bd. Edn., 1945-47, Jefferson County Bd. Edn., Birmingham, Ala., 1947-52; librarian, 1952—. Vis. instr. S.C. State Coll. Library Sch., Orangeburg, summer 1954, Atlanta U. Sch. Library Service, 1955—; cons. workshops and confs. Mem. evaluation com. Ala. and So. Assn. Accreditation of Schs., 1954-64; mem. Ala. Profl. Media Standards Com., 1970—, Ala. Com. Teaching Use Library Media, 1970; pres. Jefferson County Library Group, 1957-69; mem. State Right to Read. Com., 1969. Mem. A.L.A., Ala. (sec. Children's young people div. 1971—), Southeastern library assns., Ala. Assn. Sch. Libraries (pres. 1954-56), Ala. Instructional Media Assn., Am. Assn. Sch. Librarians (ad hoc com. 1967-69), N.E.A., Ala., Jefferson County (financial sec. 1954-58) tchrs. assns., Am., Ala., Jefferson County vocational assns., Jefferson County Edn. Assn. Home: 1 Greenspring Av SW Birmingham AL 35211 Office: PO Box 515 Gardendale AL 35071

MCCAIN, JO ANN MARKS (MRS. WILLIAM THOMAS MCCAIN), clubwoman; b. Shelby, Miss., May 18, 1934; d. William C. and Mae (Maxwell) Marks; student Memphis State U., 1953-54; m. William Thomas McCain, Dec. 1954. Fashion show chmn., parliamentarian, bd. dirs. 19th Century Club, Memphis, 1962, 1st v.p., 1966-67, gen. chmn. Germantown Charity Horse Show, 1965-66, publicity, program chmn., 1967; chmn. Christmas Ball Ladies St. Jude, 1962-63, reservations chmn., 1964, bd. dirs., 1962-64, 1st v.p., 1964-66, fashion show chmn., 1965; exec. sec. to County Commn. chmn., 1962-67; gen. chmn. Heart Sunday for Memphis and Shelby County, 1967; co-chmn. Mothers March of Dimes, 1967; sec. to chmn. bd. United Inns, Inc., 1968—; co-chmn. Hemophilia Ball, 1969. Mem. Symphony League Memphis, Dress Circle, Memphis Symphony Chorus, Memphis State Oratorio Chorus. Methodist. Clubs: Suburban Garden; Germantown Business and Professional Women's; Colonial-Countrywood Garden. Home: 1788 Poplar Estates Pkwy Germantown TN 38138

MCCALL, EDITH (MRS. HOWARD C. WORLEY), author; b. Charles City, Ia., Sept. 5, 1911; d. William John and Mary Catherine (May) Sansom; student U. Wis., 1928-30; M.A., U. Chgo., 1949; m. Merle R. McCall, June 8, 1935 (div. Jan. 1963); children—Constance (Mrs. David R. Johnston), Mary (Mrs. Tony R. Legato); m. 2d, Howard C. Worley, July 16, 1971 (dec. July 1974). Elementary sch. tchr., Elmhurst, Ill., 1930-35, Western Springs, Ill., 1943-47; reading cons. La. Grange, Ill., 1947-55; author, 1955—. Cons., lectr. to various schs. in U.S. Recipient Gold Plaque award Mo. Writers, 1960; Recognition award Central Mo. State U., 1970. Mem. Authors Guild, White River Valley (organizer, sec., editor 1961-62), others hist. socs., Mo. Writers Guild (pres. 1971-72, chpt. pres. 1970-71), Pi Lambda Theta. Author: 12 book series The Button Books, 1953-59; 19 book series Frontiers of America, 1958-70; 8 book series Butternut Bill, 1965-69; 4 social study readers, 1961; English Village in the Ozarks, 1969; co-author numerous textbooks. Address: PO Box 255 Hollister MO 65672

MCCALL, ELIZABETH REGINA, chemist; b. Columbus, O., May 16, 1922; d. Austin John and Genevieve Marie (Krause) McCall; B.S., La. State U., 1943. Asst. sci. aide analytical chemistry So. Regional Research Center Dept. Agr., New Orleans, 1943-44, chemists, 1944-61, analytical chemist, 1961-65, research chemist, 1965—. Recipient Superior Service award U.S. Dept. Agr., 1952. Mem. Am. Chem. Soc., Am. Oil Chemists Soc., Am. Assn. Textile Chemists and Colorists, Soc. for Applied Spectroscopy, Coblentz Soc., Sigma Xi. Contbr. articles to sci. jours. Office: Box 19687 New Orleans LA 70179

MCCALL, HAZEL BRADFIELD (MRS. JOHN DEAN MCCALL), club woman; b. Fiskville, Tex.; d. Thomas Bascom and Martha (Colvin) Bradfield; grad. Kenilworth Hall, Austin, Tex.; student U. Tex.; m. John Dean McCall, June 21, 1933; children—Paul Bradfield Horton, Mary Helen Horton (Mrs. Horton Brownell), John Dean, Thomas Screven. Pres. Dallas Lawyers Wives' Club, 1952-53, Dallas Soc. Meml. Assn., 1956-57; dir. Women's Council Dallas County, 1959—; mem. scholarship com., 1963-64, 72; dir. Dallas Fedn. Women's Club Girl's Found., Inc., 1962—; bd. mem. women's bd. Dallas Civic Opera, Dallas Civic Ballet, Friday Forum. Pres. Dem. Women Dallas County, 1949-50. Mem. D.A.R., U.D.C., Dallas Fedn. Women's Clubs, Dallas Women's Symphony League, Dallas Pan Am. Round Table Number 1, Shakespeare Followers (pres. 1963-64). Clubs: Dallas Woman's, Marianne Scruggs Garden (auditor 1972-73), Dallas Country. Home: 3628 Beverly Dr Dallas TX 75205

MCCALL, JANET LOUISE, actress, dir., playwright; b. Washington, June 26, 1935; d. Garland Erskine and Mildred Louise (Beard) McCall; Mus.B. in Piano, Eastman Sch. Music, 1954-57; grad. student Cath. U. Am., 1957; M.A. in Theatre, Pa. State U., 1968; student Cleve. Playhouse Summer Sch., Shakespeare at Circle in Sq. Sch., N.Y.C.; repertory with Washington Players Theatre, also pvt. voice and dance, N.Y.C. Actress and dir. numerous summer and winter regional, stock, univ., off-Broadway theatres, including Lincoln Center Library and Equity Theater; off-Broadway appearances in The Golden Apple, Jacques Brel is Alive and Well and Living in Paris, The Bacchants; Broadway appearances in Camelot; Two By Two (standby), 1776 (standby), Jacques Brelis Alive and Well and Living in Paris, Cyrano. Mem. Penn. Sch. State Players, Sigma Alpha Iota (hon.). Address: 349 W 44th St New York City NY 10036

MCCALL, MARY M., social worker; b. Eagle, N.Y.; d. James J. and Marie (Devin) McCall; B.A., U. Buffalo, 1936, M.S.W., 1950. Social case worker, supr. family dept., supr. Niagara Falls office, supr. intake, sec. mental health clinic, supr. unmarried mother dept. Cath. Charities, Buffalo, 1937-47; chief social work service VA Hosp., Batavia, N.Y., 1947—. Cons. Arnold Gregory Hosp., Albion, N.Y., Batavia Nursing Home, Elmcrest Sanatarium, Churchville, N.Y. Treas., Genesse County Citizens Comm. for Mental Health, 1963; pres. Genesee County Inter-Agy. Council, 1957-58, 63-64. Bd. dirs. Genesee County Mental Health Assn. Mem. Cath. Daus. Am., Nat. Assn. Social Workers, N.Y. State Welfare Conf., Am. Soc. Hosp. Social Work Dirs., St. Jeromes Hosp. Guild, Am. Assn. U. Women, Acad. Certified Social Workers, Nat. Council Cath. Women. Roman Catholic. Home: 6 Brooklyn Av Batavia NY 14020 Office: VA Hosp Batavia NY 14020

MCCALL, NINA (MRS. JOHN T. MCCALL), civic worker; b. Hancock, Mich., Aug. 24, 1924; d. Emery and Florence (Kroll) Tourville; student U. Mich., 1942-44, Mich. State U., 1944-46, 57-59; m. John Thompson McCall, Sept. 6, 1946; children—Bonnie Elizabeth, Maryann. Mem. League Women Voters, 1952—, bd. dirs. Mich. chpt., 1956-59, N.J., 1964-71, pres., Mountain Lakes, N.J., 1961-64, pres. N.J., 1971—; mem. Mich. Ednl. Adv. Com., 1957; mem. Mich. Ednl. Finance Study Com., 1959; active P.T.A., Girl Scouts U.S.A. Mem. N.J. Energy Crisis Study Commn., 1973—, vice chmn., 1973—. Bd. dirs. Center for Analysis Pub. Issues (N.J.), 1971-72, Eagleton Inst. Politics Rutgers U., 1971-72; mem. acad. affairs com. Bloomfield Coll., 1971-72. Mem. N.J. Audubon Soc. Episcopalian. Home: 122 Powerville Rd Mountain Lakes NJ 07046 Office: 460 Bloomfield Av Montclair NJ 07042

MCCALL, VIRGINIA NIELSEN (MRS. JOSEPH R. MCCALL), author; b. Idaho Falls, Ida., June 14, 1909; d. Jesse Hans and Florence (Kingston) Nielsen; student U. Ida., 1927-29, Utah State Agr. Coll., 1931-32; m. Robert M. Pressey (dec. 1939); m. 2d, Joseph R. McCall, Apr. 21, 1943. Mem. Authors Guild, Authors League Am., Cal. Writers Club. Author: Try to Forget Me, 1942; Cadet Widow, 1942; Bewildered Heart, 1946; The Golden One, 1947; Journey to Love, 1959; Remember Me, 1960; The Road to the Valley, 1961; Dangerous Dream, 1961; The Mystery of Fyfe House, 1962; The Whistling Winds, 1964; Keoni, My Brother, 1965; Kimo and Madame Pele, 1966; Navy Nurse, 1968; The Mystery of Secret Town, 1969; Nurse in the Navy, 1969; (with Joseph R. McCall) Your Career in Parks and Recreation, 1970; Adassa and Her Hen, 1971; Seven Tides, 1972. Address: 9028 Talisman Dr Sacramento CA 95826

MCCALLION, HAZEL MARY MURIEL JOURNEAUX (MRS. SAMUEL MCCALLION), town ofcl., editor; b. Port Daniel, Que., Can., Feb. 14, 1921; d. Herbert and Maude Amanda (Travers) Journeaux; grad. high sch.; m. Samuel McCallion, Sept. 29, 1951; children—Peter, Linda, Paul. Office mgr. Canadian Kellogg Co., Ltd., Toronto, Ont., Can., 1948-61; editor Streetsville Ont., Booster, 1962—; chmn. Streetsville Planning Bd., 1964-66; mayor Town Streetsville, 1970-73; councillor City Mississauga, 1974—. Mem. Streetsville C. of C. (pres. 1964-65), Assn. Municipalities Ont. (v.p. 1972-73), Ont. Anglican Young People's Assn. (provincial pres. 1945-46), Anglican Young People's Assn. (nat. pres. 1949-51). Home: 1560 Britannia Rd Streetsville ON Canada Office: 167 Queen St S Streetsville ON Canada

MCCALLUM, BARBARA EILAND (MRS. DONALD GEORGE MCCALLUM), lawyer; b. Fresno, Cal., Jan. 1, 1938; d. Edward Marvin and Alma Bernice (Pratt) Walker; student Santa Monica City Coll., 1955-57; J.D., U. of Pacific, 1967; m. Donald George McCallum, Apr. 28, 1970. Admitted to Cal. bar, 1967; owner, atty. Barbara Lynn (Walker) Eiland, Sacramento, 1967-70; partner Wong, McCallum & McCallum, Sacramento, 1970-73, McCallum & McCallum, Sacramento, 1973—. Cons. Crisis Clinic, Sacramento, 1969-70; vis. instr. Cal. State U., Sacramento, 1972; mem. adv. panel Law in a Free Soc. Project, 1972—. Mem. Children Center, Sacramento, 1968-73; workshop leader women's legal rights various seminars, 1972-73. Dist. 3 mem. El Dorado County Democratic Central Com., 1974—. Mem. Women Lawyers Sacramento (pres. 1971-72), Sacramento County Bar Assn. (council 1971-72), Barristers (dir. 1972-73), Am., San Francisco, El Dorado County bar assns., Judicature Soc., Internat. Fedn. Des Femmes Des Carriers Juridiques, Nat. Women Lawyers, Internat. Fedn. Women Lawyers, Cal. Trial Lawyers Assn. (chmn. women's rights com. 1974), Law Sch. Assos., Sacramento Law Plan (dir. 1972-73), Sacramento Community Commn. for Women (pres. 1972-73), Am. Assn. U. Women, Women's Equity Action League (mem. com. 1972—), Lawyers' Wives. Bus. and Profl. Women. Soroptimist (chmn. various coms. 1971—). Home: 3715 Toronto Rd Shingle Springs CA 95682 Office: 717 K St Suite 500 Sacramento CA 95814 also 3280 Royal Dr Cameron Park Shingle Springs CA 95682

MCCALLUM, FREDDIE LAIRD (MRS. WILLIAM ROGER MCCALLUM), ednl. adminstr.; b. Pelion, S.C., Aug. 25, 1912; d. Jacob Henry and Annie Frances (Cupstid) Laird; B.A., Limestone Coll., 1932; M.Ed., U. S.C., 1950; m. William Roger McCallum, Feb. 27, 1937 (dec. Sept. 1960). Tchr. elementary schs., S.C., 1932-43; prin. Fort Jackson Elementary Sch., Columbia, S.C., 1943-50, Columbia Pub. Schs., 1954-56, 63-72; adminstrv. staff, dir. alumni affairs Limestone Coll., Gaffney, S.C., 1972—. Mem. Nat., S.C., Richland County (pres. 1946-47) edn. assns., S.C., Nat. prins. assns., S.C. (pres. 1965-67), Columbia Br. (pres. 1962-64) assns. for childhood edn., Assn. Supervision and Curriculum Devel., Am. Assn. U. Women (v.p. Columbia Br. 1970-72), Future Home Makers Assn. (counselor S.C. edn. dept. 1962-63, dir. summer camp 1963-64), Delta Kappa Gamma (pres. Alpha chpt. 1950-52, rec. sec. Alpha Eta chpt. 1963-65), Kappa Kappa Iota (pres. 1969-70). Home: 3231 Lakewood Av Columbia SC 29201 Office: Limestone Coll Gaffney SC 29340

MCCALLUM, PHYLLIS MAE JORGENSEN (MRS. GEORGE ALEXANDER MCCALLUM), playwright; b. Pacific Grove, Cal., Apr. 5, 1911; d. Henry Garfield and Delia Mae (Hull) Jorgensen; B.A., Stanford, 1936; m. George Alexander McCallum, Dec. 20, 1936; children—Alexsan (Mrs. Paul L. Dillon, Jr.), Michael Douglas. Mem. adv. bd. Pioneer Drama Service, Denver, 1970—. Vice pres. Entertainment Commn., San Jose, Cal., 1955-71; pres. San Jose State Coll. Faculty Wives, 1968-69, San Jose Jr. Theatre Adv. Bd., 1968-70. Recipient 1st prize for The Pale Pink Dragon, Seattle Jr. Programs Nat. Playwriting Contest, 1958, Kangalou, Community Children's Theatre, Inc., Kansas City, 1963; 2d. Prize The Touch and the Tender Troll, 1967; Ada Tallman prize Chi Omega alumnae, 1970; 1st prize Nat. League Am. Pen Women, 1974, 3d prize Children's Theatre Richmond, 1974. Mem. Nat. League Am. Pen Women (br. pres. 1971-73), Iota Delta. Playwright The Pale Pink Dragon, 1958; The Uniform Unicorn, 1967; The Grateful Griffin, 1968; The Touch and Tender Troll, 1967; The Vanilla Viking, 1969; Hansel and Gretel and the Golden Petticoat, 1973; Crumple, Rumpelstiltskin, 1974. Home: 1187 Clark Way San Jose CA 95125 Office: Pioneer Drama Service 2172 S Colorado Blvd Denver CO 80222

MCCALLUM, THELMA BEARD, educator; b. Hardinsburg, Ky., Feb. 18, 1902; d. Charles and Mary Moorman Beard; B.Pedagogy, Ky. State Coll., 1924; B.S. in Edn., Northwestern U., 1940; M.A. in Edn., Roosevelt U., 1968; m. William H. McCallum, Nov. 26, 1934. Asst. prin., then prin., high sch., Hardinsburg, Ky., 1928-32; tchr. elementary sch., Columbus, O., 1940-50, Chgo. Pub. Schs., 1950-56, 64-72; nat. leader in charge libraries Methodist Ch., U.S.A. and 42 fgn. countries, 1960-64. Del., World Council Chs., 1954, World Meth. Council, London, Eng., 1966, Denver, 1970, World Fedn. Meth. Women, 1966, 70; mem. council on world service and finance United Meth. Ch., Evanston, Ill., 1968-72; hon. v.p. women's div., 1960-64. Trustee Clark Coll., Atlanta, Nat. Coll., Kansas City, Mo., 1960-64. Active YWCA, Urban League, N.A.A.C.P., Found. of Ewha U., Seoul, Korea. Mem. Delta Sigma Theta (life). Home: 635 E 84th St Chicago IL 60619

MCCAMAN, MARILYN RUTH WALES (MRS. RICHARD EUGENE MCCAMAN), pharmacologist; b. Oak Park, Ill., Oct. 10, 1928; d. Franklin Earl and Mildred Ruth (Albert) Wales; B.A., Grinnell Coll., 1950; Ph.D., Washington U., St. Louis, 1958; m. Richard Eugene McCaman, Feb. 8, 1953; children—Michael, David, Judith, Sandra, Christopher. Research asso. dept. pharmacology Washington U., St. Louis, 1957-58; research asso. Ind. U. Med. Sch., Indpls., 1959-61, instr., 1961-63, asst. prof., 1963-67; sr. research scientist City Hope Med. Center, Duarte, Cal., 1970—. Research grantee Muscular Dystrophy Assn. Am., 1965-67. Contbr. articles to profl. jours. Home: 2808 Warren Way Arcadia CA 91006 Office: City Hope Med Center Duarte CA 91010

MCCAMMAN, CAROL VERNE, editor; b. Oakland, Cal., Nov. 1, 1908; d. William J. and Mabel Lambert (Taylor) McCamman; A.B., U. Cal. at Berkeley, 1929, M.A., 1930; postgrad. U. Cal. at Berkeley, U. Chgo., U. Mich., U. Cal. at Los Angeles, Rutgers. Examiner phys. scis. div. U. Chgo., 1931-33; editorial work Psychol. Inst., Washington, 1933-36; tchr. high sch. math. Washington Pub. Schs., 1936-69; mng. editor The Math. Tchr., Nat. Council of Tchrs. of Math., Washington, 1969—. Part time tchr. Cath. U. Am., Am. U., George Washington U. Recipient Meyer award NSF Insts., 1957, 62. Mem. Am. Assn. U. Women, Math. Assn. of Am., Phi Beta Kappa, Delta Kappa Gamma. Home: 1901 Wyoming Av NW Washington DC 20009 Office: National Council of Teachers of Mathematics 1906 Association Dr Reston VA 22091

MCCAMMON, HELEN MARY ZABORNIAK (MRS. RICHARD BALDWIN MCCAMMON), govt. ofcl.; b. Winnipeg, Man., Can., Aug. 16, 1933; d. Joseph and Mary (Choman) Zaborniak; B.S. with honors, U. Man., 1955; M.S., U. Mich., 1956; Ph.D. (Grad. Found. fellow), Ind. U., 1959; m. Richard Baldwin, Sept. 5, 1956; children—Catherine Ann, Ian David. Came to U.S., 1956, naturalized, 1963. Research technician Man. Dept. Mines and Natural Resources, Winnipeg, 1952-59; faculty U. N.D., Grand Forks, 1961; lectr. U. Pitts., 1963, asst. prof., 1964-68, asso. prof., 1968; vis. asso. prof. U. Ill., Chgo., 1968-70; research asso., dept. invertebrates Field Mus. Natural History, Chgo., 1970-72; Tech. adviser-editor Indsl. Bio-Test Labs., Northbrook, Ill., 1972; dir. office research programs Region 1, U.S. Environmental Protection Agy., Boston, 1973—. Cons. Denoyer Ceppert Co., 1972—. OAS fellow, 1969-70. Mem. A.A.A.S., Am. Soc. Limnologists and Oceanographers, Am. Soc. Zoologists, Soc. Econ. Mineralogists and Paleontologists, Systematics Assn., Internat. Assn. Gt. Lakes Research, Marine Tech. Soc., Assn. Women in Sci., Sigma Xi. Home: 12 Inman St Cambridge MA 02139 Office: US Environmental Protection Agy Region 1 JF Kennedy Fed Bldg Boston MA 02203

MCCAMY, JEAN BOND (MRS. ROBERT JULIAN MCCAMY, JR.), journalist, author; b. Windsor, N.C., May 17, 1938; d. James Nurney and Grace Artemecia (Bazemore) Bond; student Greensboro Coll., 1956-58, Coll. of William and Mary, 1958, Campbell Coll., 1958-59; m. Robert Julian McCamy, Jr., Aug. 22, 1959; children—Bond, Cameron, Charlotte. Scriptwriter The Househunter, Raleigh, N.C., 1970; staff writer Wake Weekly, Wake Forest, N.C., 1971—; corr., Raleigh (N.C.) Times, 1972-73; free lance writer, 1965—. Writer-in-residence N.C. Dept. of Pub. Instrn. Poetry-In-The-Schs., Raleigh, 1972-74; poetry cons. N.C. Dept. of Corrections, 1973—. Pres. Wake Forest (N.C.) Coll. Birthplace Soc., Inc., 1973—; mem. Wake Forest Good Neighbor Council, 1972-74. Mem. Wake Forest Municipal Elections Bd., 1973—. Bd. dirs. Student Theatre Guild of N.C., Inc., Wake Forest Pub. Library. Recipient Writing award Baldwin County (Ala.) Writers Club, 1965, Writing award Tarheel Writers Round Table, 1966. Mem. N.C. Poetry Soc. (awards 1971-74, v.p. 1973-74), N.C. Press and Presswomen's Assn., N.C. Arts Council, Wake Forest C. of C. (sec. 1971—), N.C. Writers Conf. Episcopalian. Club: Wake Forest Newcomer's (pres. 1968) Contbr. poems, articles and short stories to lit. mags. Home: 145 West Sycamore Wake Forest NC 27587 Office: The Wake Weekly PO Box 192 Wake Forest NC 27587

MCCANCE, ELIZABETH FRANCES, educator; b. Pitts., Oct. 8, 1910; d. Frank Keller and Mary Stuart (Stevenson) McCance; student Ind. U., 1964; hon. grad. secretarial sci. Robert Morris Jr. Coll., 1967. Dean of women Robert Morris Jr. Coll., Pitts., 1942-68; dean students Bradford Sch., Pitts., 1968—. Mem. Pitts. Personnel Assn. (exec. bd.), Nat. Assn. Women Deans, Adminstrs. and Counselors, Pa. Assn. Women Deans and Counselors, Nat. Council Adminstrv. Women in Edn. (pres. elect Pitts. council), Jr. League, Zonta Internat. (pres. Pitts. 1970-72, lt. gov. dist. IV 1973-74, gov. dist. IV, dir. 1974-76). Clubs: Pittsburgh Golf. Home: Royal York Apts 3955 Bigelow Blvd Pittsburgh PA 15213 Office: Bradford Sch 355 5th Av Pittsburgh PA 19220

MCCANDLESS, ANNA LOOMIS, club woman; b. Aspinwall, Pa., July 21, 1897; d. George Wilberforce and Estella (Loomis) McCandless; B.S., Carnegie-Mellon U., 1919. Pres. Vis. Nurses Assn. of Allegheny County, 1955-57; mem. vis. com. Margaret Morrison Carnegie Coll., 1962-66; v.p. Alumni Fedn. Carnegie Inst. Tech., 1963-66. Trustee Carnegie, Mellon U., 1966—. Mem. Am. Assn. U. Women. Clubs: College, Twentieth Century (pres. 1956-58) (Pitts.); Appalachian Mountain. Home: Park Plaza Apts Craig St Pittsburgh PA 15213

MCCANDLESS, BARBARA J., state ofcl.; b. Cottonwood Falls, Kan., Oct. 25, 1931; d. Arch G. and Grace (Kittle) McCandless; B.S., Kan. State U., 1953; M.S., Cornell U., 1959; postgrad. U. Minn., 1962-66, U. Cal. at Berkeley, 1971-72; m. Allyn O. Lockner, 1969. Home demonstration agt. Kan. State U., 1953-57; teaching asst. Cornell U., 1957-58, asst. extension home economist in marketing, 1958-59; consumer marketing specialist, asst. prof. Ore. State U., 1959-62; instr. home econs. U. Minn., 1962-63, research asst. agrl. econs., 1963-66; asst. prof. U. R.I., 1966-67; asso. prof. family econs., mgmt., housing, equipment dept. head S.D. State U., 1967-73; asst. to sec. Dept. Commerce and Consumer Affairs, S.D., 1973—. Dir. Nat. Council Occupational Licensing, 1973-75. Mem. Am. Marketing Assn., Am. Agrl. Econs. Assn., Am. Home Econs. Assn., Nat. Council on Family Relations, Am. Council Consumer Interests, League Women Voters, Kan. State U. Alumni Assn., S.D. Consumers League, Pi Gamma Mu. Club: Brookings (S.D.) Country. Research on profl. and occupational licensing bds. Address: 1100 E Church Pierre SD 57501

MCCANDLESS, PAULINE WILLIAMS (MRS. GARRETT CLAIR MCCANDLESS), physician; b. nr. Franklin, Pa., Feb. 10, 1916; d. Moses Perry and Mabel Agnes (McDowell) Williams; B.S., U. Pitts., 1946, M.D., 1948; m. Garrett Clair McCandless, Apr. 10, 1948; children—David Perry, Priscilla Jan. Intern St. Margaret Meml. Hosp., Pitts.; practice gen. medicine, Franklin, Pa., 1949—; mem. staff Franklin (Pa.) Hosp.; lectr. to various women's groups and high sch. girls. Adv. bd. U. Pitts., Titusville. Recipient citizenship award Franklin C. of C., 1966, outstanding service award Clarion County unit Am. Cancer Soc., 1971. Fellow Am. Geriatrics Soc.; mem. Am. Acad. Family Physicians, Am. Med. Womens Assn., Am., Pa., Venango med. socs., Delta Kappa Gamma. Mem. Order Eastern Star. Club: Zonta. Home: Star Route Franklin PA 16323 Office: 1228 Elk St Franklin PA 16323

MCCANN, CECILE NELKEN (MRS. ALBERT HEWS MCCANN, JR.), art jour. editor, pub.; b. New Orleans, July 13, 1917; d. Abraham and Leona (Reiman) Nelken; student Vassar Coll., 1934-36, Tulane U., 1936-37; B.A., San Jose State Coll., 1963, M.A., 1964; student U. Cal. at Berkeley, 1966-67; m. Albert Hews McCann, Jr., Mar. 6, 1937; children—Dorothy (Mrs. Edward J. Collins, Jr.), Cecile Isaacs, Annette Lassen, Denise McCann, Albert Hews III. Tool designer Convair Corp., New Orleans, 1942-45; archtl. draftsman, various companies, New Orleans and Clinton, Ia.; owner, operator ceramics studio, Clinton; instr. San Jose State Coll., 1964-65, Cal. State U., Hayward, 1964-65, Chabot Coll., Hayward, 1966-69, Laney Coll., 1967-70; founder, editor, pub. Artweek mag., Oakland, Cal., 1970—; exhibited in one man shows at Davenport Mus. Art, Robert North Galleries, Chgo., Crocker Gallery, Sacramento, Barrios Gallery, Fair Oaks, Cal., Cal. Coll. Arts and Crafts, Oakland, Illi, The Gallery of Beautiful Things, San Francisco, others; exhibited in group shows at DeYoung Mus., San Francisco, Everson Mus. Art, Syracuse, N.Y., Oakland Mus., Richmond Art Center, Pasadena Mus., Los Angeles County Mus. Art, others; represented in permanent collections San Jose State Coll., Mills Coll., Coll. Holy Names, others. Adv. bd. Center Folk Art and Contemporary Crafts. Mem. Assn. San Francisco Potters, Am. Crafts Council. Home: 4974 Vannoy Av Castro Valley CA 94546 Office: 1305 Franklin St Oakland CA 94612

MCCANN, EITHNE CARMEL (MRS. B. CAIRBRE MCCANN), physician; b. Birr, Ireland, Oct. 5, 1926; d. Edward Lowry and Mary (Mooney) Madden; M.D., Nat. U., Dublin, Ireland, 1952; postgrad. N.Y. U., 1955-58; m. B. Cairbre McCann, June 2, 1953; children—Dervilla, Una, Sean, Sheila. Came to U.S., 1961, naturalized, 1967. Intern St. Johns (Nfld.) Gen. Hosp., 1953-54; resident Bellevue Hosp., 1955-56, Goldwater Meml. Hosp., 1956-58; asst. med. dir. rehab. Crotched Mountain Rehab. Centre, Greenfield, N.H., 1961-68; dir. rehab. medicine St. Joseph's Hosp., Providence, 1968—; mem. staff Zambarano Hosp., Providence. Mem. exec. com. R.I. Arthritis Found. Bd. dirs., home maker, med. and scientific com. Arthritis Found. Active PTA groups of Barrington Sch. System, R.I., 1968-72. Mem. R.I., Providence med. socs. Home: 206 Nayatt Rd Barrington RI 02806 Office: 200 High Service Av North Providence RI 02904

MCCANN, FRANCES VERONICA (MRS. ELDEN J. MURRAY), physiologist, educator; b. Manchester, Conn., Jan. 15, 1927; d. John Joseph and Grace E. (Tuttle) McCann; A.B. with distinction and honors, U. Conn., 1952, Ph.D. (Nat. Heart Inst. fellow), 1959; M.S., U. Ill., 1954; m. Elden J. Murray, Sept. 20, 1962. Investigator Marine Biol. Lab., Woods Hole, Mass., 1952-62; instr. physiology Dartmouth Med. Sch., Hanover, N.H., 1959-61, asst. prof. 1961-67, asso. prof. physiology, 1967-73, prof., 1973—, mem. admissions com., 1965—. Cons. research Mary Hitchcock Meml. Hosp.; cons. physiology study sect. NIH, 1973—; established investigator Am. Heart Assn.; chmn. Internat. Symposium on Comparative Physiology of the Heart, 1968. Nat. Heart Inst. grantee, 1960—, N.H. Heart Assn., 1964-65, Vt. Heart Assn., 1966—. Mem. Am. Physiol. Soc., Soc. Gen. Physiologists, A.A.A.S., Biophys. Soc., Am. Heart Assn. (council on basic sci. 1972—), Sigma Xi, Phi Kappa Phi. Editor: Comparative Physiology of the Heart: Current Trends, 1969. Contbr. numerous publs. Home: 5 Dunster Dr Hanover NH 03755

MCCANN, JEAN JUANITA WILSON (MRS. GEORGE FREDERIC MCCANN, JR.), editor; b. Chgo., Feb. 6, 1923; d. John Gilbert and Hazel Lillian (Anderson) Wilson; student Northwestern U., 1940-44; m. George Frederic McCann, Jr., Aug. 2, 1948. Reporter Centralia (Ill.) Sentinel, 1939, Kenosha (Wis.) Labor, newspaper, 1941; N.Y. bur. chief Chgo. Jour. Commerce, 1944-48, Cleve. Jour. Commerce, of N.Y., Chgo. Jour., 1948-49; editor house organ Lake Erie council Girl Scouts U.S.A., 1961-66, 71-72; owner Med. News Service, Cleveland Heights, Ohio, 1966-73; med. writer Sci. & Medicine Pub. Co., N.Y.C., 1968-73, Med. Post, Toronto, Ont., 1971-73; asso. editor Biomed. News, Washington, 1971—. Recipient United Torch 1st place award Fedn. Community Planning, 1972. Mem. Nat. Assn. Sci. Writers, Am. Med. Writers Assn., Internat. Platform Assn., Women in Communications (chpt. pres. 1968-69, 73-74). Address: 2980 Berkshire Rd Cleveland Heights OH 44118

MCCANN, KATHLEEN BURNETT, educator; b. Rye, N.Y., Mar. 26, 1912; d. Edward and Ethel Raymond (Mason) Burnett; A.B., Barnard Coll., 1935; M.F.A., Yale, 1939; student London Sch. Econs., 1932; m. Peter Francis McCann, June 23, 1942; children—Peter Paul, Kathleen Burnett DesMaisons. Mgr., dir. Lake Placid (N.Y.) Stock Players, 1938-40; instr. drama, speech and English, Tusculum Coll., Greenville, Tenn., 1939-41, Juanita Coll., Huntingdon, Pa., 1941-43; mgr., dir. Tucson Little Theatre, 1950-53; instr. English and speech Lasell Jr. Coll., Auburndale, Mass., 1958-59; asst. prof. drama and speech Lesley Coll., Cambridge, Mass., 1959-62; asso. prof. communication arts and scis. Curry Coll., Milton, Mass., 1962—, dean women, 1964-68; leader writing workshop, Starr Island, Me., 1970. Mem. Speech Communication Assn., New Eng. Theatre Conf., Am. Assn. U. Profs. Author: (plays) Out of Despair, 1960; Scatter the Dreams, 1963; Suffolk Resolves, 1974. Home: 64 Bradlee Rd Milton MA 02186

MCCANN, RUTH ICENOGLE, realtor; b. Atlanta, Dec. 28, 1931; d. Karl Luster and Inez (Allen) Icenogle; A.B., Huntingdon Coll., 1951; m. Robert R. McCann, June 23, 1956; children—Robert R., Alice, Carole. Salesman Walter Scott Realty Co., Decatur, Ga., 1964-70, v.p., sales mgr., 1970—. Mem. Nat. Assn. Real Estate Bds. (state 2d v.p. women's council 1972). Episcopalian. Home: 864 Stratford Rd Avondale Estates GA 30002 Office: 3326 N Druid Hills Rd Decatur GA 30033

MCCARDLE, DOROTHY BARTLETT, journalist; b. Jonesboro, Tenn., July 25, 1904; d. George Edwin and Kate (Deaderick) Bartlett; B.A., U. Pa., 1927; m. Carl W. McCradle, Sept. 15, 1934 (dec.); 1 dau., Marcia (Mrs. S. Ruffin Maddox, Jr.). Reporter Phila. N. Am., 1922-24, Phila. Inquirer, 1924-37, Washington Post, 1960—; Columnist, reporter N. Am. Newspaper Alliance, 1949-64. Mem. White House Corr. Assn. Club: Washington Press. Home: 6109 Ramshorn Pl McLean VA 22101 Office: Washington Post 1150 15th St Washington DC 20005

MCCARLEY, CAROLYN JOSEPHINE SPENCE (MRS. CLINT WELDON MCCARLEY), shoe store exec.; b. Emporium, Pa., Oct. 16, 1919; d. Charles Burnell and Marguerite (Schoenbohm) Spence; student W. Tex. State U., 1938-40; B.A., Tex. Arts and Industries, U., 1942; postgrad. U. Guadalajara, 1944; m. Clint Weldon McCarley, June 8, 1945; children—Clint Weldon, Philip Allen, Charles Aubra, Kelvyn Joe. Tchr., Kingsville, Tex., 1942-43, Falfurrias, Tex., 1943-44, Gregory, Tex., 1944-45, Clarkwood, Tex., 1948-49, Harlingen, Tex., 1952-53; co-owner Carolyn's Shoe Store, Harlingen, 1954—, McAllen, Tex., 1973—. Vice pres. Stephen F. Austin Sch. P.T.A., Harlingen, 1964-65; sec. St. Paul's Luth. Sch. P.T.A., 1966-68; chmn. Project Goodwill, 1966-68. Recipient citation State Fine Arts Commn., 1966-67. Mem. S. Tex. Dist. (pub. affairs dept. chmn. 1968-70, pres. 1970-72), Rio Grande Valley (conv. coordinator 1969-71, hospitality chmn. 1971—, Tex. (internat. hostess chmn. 1972—, sec. scholarship fund com. 1973-74) fedns. women's clubs. Presbyn. (chmn. Christian edn. com.), Lower Rio Grande Valley Hist. Mus. Assn. (pres. 1973—). Clubs: Zonta (pres. 1968-70, service chmn. 1971-72), Afflatus (sec. 1969-70, pres. 1970-72), City Federation Past Presidents (sec. 1969) (all Harlingen). Home: 102 Wildwood St Harlingen TX 78550 Office: 705 Coronado Village Harlingen TX 78550

MCCARRAN, SISTER MARGARET PATRICIA, educator; b. Reno, July 22, 1904; d. Patrick Anthony and Martha Harriet (Weeks) McCarran; Mus.B., Mount St. Mary's Coll., 1931; B.A., Coll. Holy Names, 1935; M.A., Cath. U. Am., 1946, Ph.D., 1952. Instr. music, musicology, secondary schs., So., No. Cal., 1926-46; asso. prof. history and polit. sci. Coll. of Holy Names, Oakland, Cal., 1952-63, dir. Office of Research, 1954—. Lectr. No., So. Cal., 1953-69; collecting, editing Senator Patrick A. McCarran's papers, 1952—. Mem. Bd. Rehab. Washoe County, Nev., 1969—; chmn. bd. Washoe State Rehab., Inc.; mem. Gov.'s Commn. Nev. Am. Bicentennial com.; pres. Nev. Alcoholism Assn. Mem. Hispanic Am. Soc., Brit. History Soc., Nat. League Am. Pen Women, Pi Beta Phi. Author: Fabianism in the Political Life of Britain, The Fabian Transmission, 1952. Contbr. articles, poetry pub. to various mags. Home: McCarran Ranch Hwy 40 Via Sparks NV 89431 Office: Coll of Holy Names Oakland CA 94619

MCCARRON, MARGARET MARY, physician, educator; b. Chgo., Aug. 14, 1928; d. Patrick Joseph and Rose E. (Stewart) McCarron; B.A., St. Xavier Coll., 1950; M.D., Loyola U., Chgo., 1954. Intern, Los Angeles County Hosp., 1954-55, resident internal medicine, 1955-58; fellow NIH Endocrine & Metabolic Disease, U. So. Cal., Los Angeles, 1958-59; asst. med. dir. Los Angeles/U. So. Cal. Med. Center, Los Angeles, 1964—; asso. prof. medicine, pharmacy U. So. Cal., Los Angeles, 1961—, chmn. dept. clin. edn. and services, 1970-73. Cons. various orgns., 1961—. Recipient Dart award for acad. innovation U. So. Cal., 1970. Diplomate Am. Bd. Internal Medicine. Fellow A.C.P. Home: 5071 Ambrose Av Los Angeles CA 90027 Office: 1200 N State St Los Angeles CA 90033

MCCARTHA, ALICE PAULUKAS, educator; b. Springfield, Ill., July 19, 1913; d. Michael Andrew and Martha Alleda (McDonald) Paulukas; B.Ed., Ill. State U., 1935; M.A., U. Ill., 1940; Ed.D., U. Fla., 1949; postgrad. Chgo. Art Inst., Columbia, U. S.C., George Washington U., Coll. William and Mary, Va. Commonwealth U.; m. Carl Webster McCartha, June 8, 1946. Tchr., Ill. and Ind., 1933-34, 35-42; dir. instrn., Kanapolis, N.C., 1942-43; dir. elementary edn. Guilford County, N.C., 1949-50; asso. prof. U. S.C., 1950-53; asst. prof. San Diego State Coll., 1953-55; dir. instrn. York County, Va., 1955-65; adj. prof. Coll. William and Mary, 1955-72; prof. acad. div. Va. Commonwealth U., 1969—. Cons. sch. systems; dir. tchr. workshops; mem. N.C. Ednl. Planning Commn., 1943-45. Bd. dirs. PreSchool for Retarded Children, Friends Day Care Center, Richmond, Va., 1969-70. Mem. N.E.A., Nat. Assn. Edn. Young Children, Nat. Council Social Studies, Kappa Delta Pi. Asso. editor N.C. Edn., 1943-46. Home: 151 Queens Dr W Williamsburg VA 23185 Office: 920 Park St Richmond VA 23220

MCCARTHY, AGNES BLANDFORD (MRS. HAROLD L. WISE), author; b. N.Y.C., June 20, 1933; d. Daniel Charles and Agnes Cleary (Blandford) McCarthy; A.B., Cath. U. Am., 1954; M.A., State U. N.Y., 1972; m. Harold L. Wise, Sept. 4, 1965; 1 son, Daniel Charles. Asst. editor TV Program Week, Curtis Pub. Co., Washington, 1954-55; elementary tchr., Casper, Wyo., 1956-58; coordinating editor Scholastic Mags., N.Y.C., 1960-62; editor lang. arts texts Harcourt Brace Jovanovich, N.Y.C., 1962-65; profl. material editor Am. Edn. Pubs., Middletown, Conn., 1965; research asso. Center Study Instrn., San Francisco, 1966-69. Mem. Nat. Council Tchrs. English, Am. Folklore Assn., Am. Anthrop. Assn., Nat. Assn. Humanities Edn. Author: Let's Go to a Court, 1961; Let's Go to Vote, 1962; Giant Animals of Long Ago, 1963; Creatures of the Deep, 1963; Worth Fighting For, 1965; New York State, Its Land and People, 1959; Room 10, 1966; The Impossibles, 1968; The Social Sciences,

Concepts, 1970; Expression: Black Americans, 1972; The Humanities: Self-Expression and Conduct, 1974. Home: Woodstock NY 12498 Office: Box 573 Woodstock NY 12498

MCCARTHY, CHARLOTTE ELLEN (MRS. LAWRENCE MCCARTHY), composer; b. Tangier, Ind., Sept. 12, 1918; d. Leslie Adam and Mary Lucinda (Wann) Norman; grad. Colo. Women's Coll., 1940; m. Edward Powers, Feb. 22, 1946 (div. Sept. 1955); children—Noreen (Mrs. Darrell Peck), Steve; m. 2d, Lawrence McCarthy, Sept. 19, 1956. Composer popular ballads including I Don't Want to be Hurt Anymore, 1964, Can't You See I'm Sorry, 1965. Mem. A.S.C.A.P. Home: 1207 Moraga St San Francisco CA 94122

MCCARTHY, SISTER CLARE D'ASSISI, librarian, educator; b. Boston, Feb. 19, 1900; d. Timothy J. and Ellen A. (Sullivan) McCarthy; B.A., Fordham U., 1929; B. in Library Sci., Mt. St. Vincent U., Halifax, N.S., Can., 1949. Joined Sisters of Charity, 1923; tchr. jr. high sch. and high sch., Bklyn., 1926-41, 44-48; tchr., librarian Mt. St. Agnes Acad., Hamilton, Bermuda, 1941-44; tchr., librarian St. Patrick's High Sch., Lawrence, Mass., St. Peter's High Sch., Dorchester, Mass., after 1948; now librarian John F. Kennedy Youth Library, Dorchester. Mem. New Eng., Catholic (chmn. New Eng. unit 1961-67) library assns., Women's Nat. Book Assn. Home: 307 Bowdoin St Dorchester MA 02122 Office: John F Kennedy Youth Library 294 Bowdoin St Dorchester MA 02122

MCCARTHY, JANET LEE GORRELL (MRS. JOHN MCCARTHY), educator; b. Seymour, Ind.; d. Ivan Collins and Lenore (Davis) Gorrell; B.S., Ball State U., 1952, M.A., 1958; Ed.D., Ind. U., 1968; m. John McCarthy, Aug. 10, 1963. First grade tchr., Hartford City, Ind., 1952-55, Columbus, O., 1955-56; kindergarten dir., Muncie, Ind., 1956-60; kindergarten instr. U. Chgo., 1960-62; asst. prof. edn., psychology, Ind. State U., Terre Haute, 1962—, prof., 1973—. Cons. Project Head Start, also schs. throughout Ind.; mem. Gov.'s Commn. on Child Care Services, 1969—; chmn. State Community Coordinated Child Care Com., 1970—. Bd dirs. Northside Day Care Center, Southside Day Nursery, Terre Haute. Recipient Outstanding Alumni award Ball State U., 1971; Outstanding Tchr. award Ind. State U., 1973. Mem. Ind. State Tchrs. Assn., Nat. (dir. 1973—), Ind. (pres. 1969-70), Midwest (bd. dirs., pres. 1971-72) assns. for edn. of young children, Assn. for Childhood Edn. Internat., N.E.A., U.S. Com. of Organisation Mondiale pour l'Education Prescolaire, Assn. Supervision and Curriculum Devel., Elementary-Kindergarten-Nursery Edn. Assn., Am. Assn. U. Women (chpt. v.p. 1958, 59), Pi Lambda Theta, Delta Kappa Gamma, Alpha Lambda Delta (chpt. hon. mem.), Chi Omega (alumnae chpt. v.p. 1968). Presbyn. Home: 805 S 6th St Terre Haute IN 47807

MCCARTHY, KATHRYN AGNES, physicist, ednl. adminstr.; b. Lawrence, Mass., Aug. 7, 1924; d. Joseph Augustine and Catherine (Barrett) McCarthy; A.B., Tufts U., 1945, M.S., 1946; Ph.D., Radcliffe Coll., 1957. Instr. in physics Tufts U. 1946-53, asst. prof., 1953-59, asso. prof., 1959-62, prof., 1962—, dean grad. sch. arts and scis., 1969-74, provost, sr. v.p., 1973—; research fellow in metallurgy Harvard, 1957-59; research asso. Baird Assos., 1947-49, 51, Boston U. Optical Research Lab., summer 1952; asso. research engr. U. Mich., summer 1957-58. Dir. Mass. Electric Co. Mem. exec. council Council Grad. Schs., 1972—; mem. commn. on institutional affairs Assn. Am. Colls., 1972—. Trustee Southeastern Mass. U., 1972—, Merrimack Coll., 1974—. Fellow Optical Soc. Am. (pres. New Eng. sect. 1971-72), Am. Phys. Soc.; mem. New Eng. Assn. Colls. and Univs. (commn. on higher edn. 1972—, chmn. 1973—), Phi Beta Kappa, Sigma Xi. Home: 26 High St Andover MA 01810 Office: Tufts U Medford MA 02155

MCCARTHY, MARGARET, educator; b. Hattiesburg, Miss.; d. Frederick T. and Mary (O'Connor) McCarthy; B.S., U. So. Miss., 1939, M.A., 1956, postgrad.; postgrad. Fla. State U., 1940, U. Miss., 1948; Ph.D., La. State U., 1970. Tchr. pub. schs., Ft. Walton, Fla., 1939-42; food service mgr. U.S. Army Post Exchange, Camp Shelby, Miss., 1942-46; supr. sch. lunch area Miss. Dept. Edn., Jackson, Miss., 1947-64; asst. prof. home econs. U. So. Miss., 1964-70, asso. prof., 1970-71, prof., chmn. dept. food and nutrition, 1972—. Mem. Am. (vita shows), Miss. sch. food service assns., Am., Miss. dietetic assns., Miss. Nutrition Council, Am., Miss. home econs. assns., Am. Assn. U. Women, Forrest County Home Econs. Alumni Assn., Delta Zeta, Delta Kappa Gamma. Club: Altrusa. Home: 314 S 32d Av Hattiesburg MS 39401

MCCARTHY, MARY BETH, editor; b. Worcester, Mass., June 23, 1943; d. Martin Justin and Agnes Bertha (Hanlan) McCarthy; grad. high sch. Sec., Worcester (Mass.) Telegram & Gazette Publishing Co., Inc., 1961-63, TV writer, editor, 1963—. Roman Catholic. Home: 57 Camp St Worcester MA 01603 Office: 20 Franklin St Worcester MA 01613

MCCARTHY, MARY CONSTANCE, librarian; b. Potsdam, N.Y., May 7, 1928; d. Michael Maurice and Katherine Agnes (Sullivan) McCarthy; B.E., State U. N.Y. at Potsdam, 1948; M.A., Sch. Librarianship, U. Denver, 1951; M.S., State U. N.Y. at Buffalo, 1967; Certificate of Advanced Study, Grad. Library Sch., U. Chgo., 1969. Spl. services librarian U.S. Army in Europe, 1951-53; asst. librarian Niagara U., Niagara Falls, N.Y., 1953-57, State U. N.Y. at Potsdam, 1957-62; head circulation dept., State U. N.Y. at Buffalo, 1962-68, bibliographer in polit. sci., 1965-68; asst. reference librarian U. Ill. at Chgo. Circle, 1970-72; reference librarian, acting head reference dept. Northwestern U., Evanston, Ill., 1972—. Mem. A.L.A., Beta Phi Mu. Home: 1722 Monroe St Evanston IL 60202

MCCARTHY, SISTER MARY FRANCES, educator; b. Springfield, Mass., July 25, 1916; d. Charles James and Elizabeth (Weeks) McCarthy; A.B., Trinity Coll., Washington, 1937; M.A., Cath. U. Am., 1938; Ph.D., Johns Hopkins, 1961; postgrad. Cath. U., Middlebury Coll., Mainz U., Goethe Inst., Munchen, Georgetown U. Tchr. Latin and English, Archdiocesan High Schs., Phila., 1941-56; instr. English, Trinity Coll., Washington, 1957-59; Fulbright travel award and fellowship from Deutscher Akademischer Austauschdienst. research at Johannes Gutenberg Universitat, Mainz, Germany, 1959-60; asst. prof. German and Russian, Trinity Coll., Washington, 1960-62, asso, prof., 1962-65, prof. German and Russian, 1965—, chmn. dept. German, 1960—, chmn. dept. Russian 1960-67. Trustee Trinity Coll., Washington, 1965-68. Nat. Endowment for Humanities sr. fellow, 1972-73. Mem. Mediaeval Acad. Am., Am. Assn. U. Profs., Modern Lang. Assn., Am. Tchrs. German. Contbr. articles in field to various publs., including New Cath. Ency. Translator: On Modern German Literature (P.K. Kurz), 3 vols., 1970, 71, 73. Address: Trinity Coll Washington DC 20017

MCCARTHY, SISTER MARY LORRAINE, ednl. adminstr.; b. Meriden, Minn., May 10, 1901; d. Joseph S. and Margaret (Kane) McCarthy; B.A., Coll. of St. Teresa, 1927; M.A., U. Minn., 1939. Joined Sisters St. Francis, 1920; tchr. elementary sch. St. Casimir Sch., Wells, Minn., 1921-23, St. Theodore Sch., Albert Lea, Minn., 1924-25, St. John Sch., Rochester, Minn., 1925-26; tchr. St. Mary High Sch., Portsmouth, O., 1927-28; prin. Mary McCahill High Sch., Lake City, Minn., 1938-39, St. Augustine High Sch., Austin, Minn., 1940-46, Cathedral High Sch., Winona, Minn., 1946-52; prin. Coll. of St. Teresa, Winona, Minn., summer 1940, 42, 43, 45, instr., 1947—, sec. and dir. admissions, 1952-60, dir. publicity, 1960-67, dir. pub. information, 1967—. Trustee Coll. St. Teresa, sec. 1967-70. Mem. Nat. Catholic Edn. Assn. (editor coll. newsletter 1962-65), Pi Delta Epsilon. Contbr. articles to profl. jours. Address: College of Saint Teresa Winona MN 55987

MCCARTHY, MARY PHYLLIS MASCITTI, social worker; b. Leominster, Mass., Oct. 12, 1928; d. Pelino and Anna (DiNino) Mascitti; B.A. in Psychology, U. Cal. at Los Angeles, 1954; M.S.W., Cath. U. Am., 1963; postgrad. Bryn Mawr Coll., 1972—; m. Walter Joseph McCarthy, May 21, 1955 (dec.). Joined Cath. Sisters in Social Service, 1956; psychometrist, U. Cal., Los Angeles, 1953-55; caseworker Cath. Social Services, Vallejo, Cal., 1959-61; tchr. Immaculate Heart Coll., Hollywood, Cal., 1963-65, St. Mary's Coll., Los Angeles, 1966-68; casework dir. Holy Family Adoption Service, Los Angeles, 1963-71; local dir. Sisters of Social Service, Figueroa Way, Los Angeles, 1968-71, del., 1967, chmn. edn. commn., 1968; marriage, family counselor State Cal., 1969—; student counselor Rosemont (Pa.) Coll., 1971-73. Mem. Los Angeles Welfare Planning Council Com. on Community Devel. Services in Child Welfare, 1966-71; mem. Cal. Social Welfare Bd. child welfare study task group services to unmarried parents, 1968-69; free lance lectr., 1970—. Mem. Acad. Certified Social Workers, Internat. Conf. Social Work, Nat. Assn. Social Workers (del. to nat. assembly 1967, 69), Los Angeles Nat. Assn. Social Workers (bd. dirs. 1967-71, div. chmn. div. social policy and action 1966-67). Sigma Kappa. Address: 1101 S Arlington Av Los Angeles CA 90019

MCCARTIN, ROSEMARIE ELIZABETH, psychologist; b. Colorado Springs, Colo., July 18, 1926; d. Emmet J. and Rula (Raymond) McC.; B.A., Coll. Great Falls, 1955; M.A., Immaculate Heart Coll., 1960; Ph.D., U. So. Cal., 1964; postgrad. Seattle U., 1959-60, U. Notre Dame, 1955-56, Marquette U., 1957-58, U. Cal. at Los Angeles, 1964. Tchr. various schs., Wash., Cal., 1946-56; instr. psychology, edn. Seattle U., 1960, Immaculate Heart Coll., Los Angeles, 1961-62; staff psychologist Immaculate Heart Psychol. Clinic, Los Angeles, 1962-64; child therapist Braille Inst. Am., Los Angeles, 1962-64; research asst. Center for Research in Mental Retardation, Pacific State Hosp., Pomona, Cal., 1963-65; asst. prof. psychology and edn. Seattle U., 1964-67, asso. prof. psychology, 1967-69; asso. prof. U. Wash., Seattle, 1969—, sr. research fellow Research and Evaluation in Med. Edn., 1971-72, dir. Interdisciplinary Tng. Clin. Tng. Unit Center Devel. Mentally Retarded Children, 1973—; research cons. Center for Research in Mental Retardation, Pomona, 1965-70; cons. Martin Luther King Day Home Center, Seattle, 1968—. Mem. Am., Western, Wash. State, Puget Sound psychol. assns., Am. Assn. on Mental Deficiency, Sci. Research in Child Devel., A.A.A.S., Am. Ednl. Research Assn., Wash. Edn. Assn., Assn. Advancement Behavior Therapies (br. sec. 1967-69), Am. Assn. U. Profs., Pi Lambda Theta. Contbr. articles in field to profl. jours. Home: 505 Belmont E Seattle WA 98102 Office: Miller Hall U Washington Seattle WA 98105

MCCARTNEY, DOROTHY WILSON (MRS. JOHN RICHARD MCCARTNEY), writer; b. Stroudsburg, Pa.; d. George Zabriskie and Winifred Russell (Hanna) Wilson; B.A., Pa. State U., 1934; M.A., Cornell U., 1943; postgrad. E. Stroudsburg State Tchrs. Coll., 1935-36; m. John Richard McCartney, Jan. 23, 1943; children—Elaina Maureen, Michael Scott. Tchr. Music elementary sch., Needmore, Pa., 1936-37; tchr. English jr. high sch. Falls-Overfield Consol. Sch., Mill City, Pa., 1937-40, tchr. English sr. high schs., 1940-42; music librarian Cornell U., Ithaca, N.Y., 1942-44; asst. librarian West Chester (Pa.) State Coll., 1962-65; writer poetry, juvenile and adult short stories, articles, songs pub. in numerous newspapers, mags., anthologies. Sec., treas., pianist, writer musical score Film Perspectives, non-profit film soc., Wilmington, Del., 1954-65. Recipient Sidney Lanier Sonnet award N.C. Poetry Soc., 1966, 69, 72; Traditional Poetry award Nat. Fedn. State Poetry Socs., 1972; Thomas H. McDill award N.C. Poetry Soc., 1972; James Brady Simonton Meml. award Mid-South Poetry Festival, Tenn., 1972, Haiku award, 1972; Oscar Arnold Young Meml. book award Poetry Council N.C., 1974, many others. Fellow Internat. Poetry Soc.; mem. Acad. Am. Poets (founder), N.C., Pa., Alaska, Mass., Md. poetry socs., Nat. Fedn. State Poetry Socs., Am. Assn. U. Women (pres. writers group Wilmington, Del. 1953-54), Poetry Soc. Tex. (asso.), Chester County Art Assn., Centro Studi e Scambi Internazionali. Author: Lemmus Lemmus and Other Poems, 1973. Home: Box 34 Westtown PA 19395

MCCARTNEY, LEAH BROCK (MRS. VICTOR A. MCCARTNEY), judge; b. Ellisville, Miss., Dec. 1, 1911; d. Thomas Anderson and Lillie Lee (Grangent) Brock; B.S. in Edn., Lincoln U., 1938; LL.B., Nat. U., 1954; m. Victor A. McCartney, Nov. 14, 1959. Tchr. bus. edn. St. Louis pub. schs., 1940-42; tchr. Pioneer Bus. Sch., Phila., 1942-44; admitted to Ill. bar, 1956, Mo. bar, 1971, U.S. Supreme Ct., 1968; congl. sec., 1951-54; mem. firm Brooks, Hodge & Savage, 1956-65; asst. prof. law Fla. A. and M. U., 1961-62; atty.-adviser U.S. Dept. Treasury, 1965-68; atty. estate tax Internal Revenue Service, St. Louis, 1968-73; municipal judge City of Kinloch (Mo.), 1973—. Mem. commn. on status and role of women United Meth. Ch., 1972, dean sch. of missions Mo. East Conf., 1972, 73. Cited as 1st woman municipal judge in state Mo. Senate, 1973. Mem. N.A.A.C.P. (field sec. N.Y. 1949-51). Home: 5906 Jefferson St Kinloch MO 63140 Office: 5625 Martin Luther King St Kinloch MO 63140

MCCARTNEY, SUSAN, photographer; b. Indpls., June 2, 1933; d. Stafford and Virginia (Witt) Dickens; student Hammersmith Coll. Art, London, Eng., 1948-52, Cooper Union, N.Y.C., 1953-58; div. Free lance photographer, 1964—; work has appeared in numerous nat. mags., including Life, Time, Glamour, Venture, Travel and Camera, Popular Photography, Modern Photography, Redbook, Womans Day; instr. photography Cooper Union, 1972. Mem. Am. Soc. Photographers in Communications (bd. govs.). Address: PO Box 166 Wallkill NY 12589

MCCARTY, MARIANNE BIER KEATING (MRS. CHARLES STONEHAM MCCARTY), writer; b. Ritzville, Wash., Apr. 18, 1928; d. Philip N. and Amanda (Ott) Bier; student Cornish Sch. Arts, 1944; B.A., U. Wash., 1947; m. John G. Keating, May 30, 1947 (dec. 1968); 2d, m. Charles Stoneham McCarty, Dec. 2, 1970. Actress on stage, films, radio, vaudeville and TV, including Life With Father, Kiss and Tell, Storm Operation, 1947-56; co-author non-fiction articles for various mags., 1947-56; news program commentator WOR-TV, N.Y.C., 1956; with J. Walter Thompson Advt., N.Y.C., 1956-69; grant officer, sec., asst. treas. John and Mary R. Markle Found., N.Y.C., 1970-72; information office adminstr. Population Council, N.Y.C., 1972-73; free lance writer, 1973—. Mem. Actors Equity, Am. Guild Variety Artists, A.F.T.R.A., Screen Actors Guild, Advt. Women of N.Y. Democrat. Address: 39 Fifth Av New York City NY 10003

MCCARTY, VIRGINIA DILL (MRS. MENDEL O. MCCARTY), lawyer; b. Plainfield, Ind., Dec. 15, 1924; d. E. Millard and Martha Gertrude (Paddack) Dill; A.B., Ind. U., 1946, LL.B., 1950; m. Mendel O. McCarty, Apr. 26, 1946 (dec. Mar. 1973), children—Michael Brent, Janet Martha. Admitted to Ind. bar, 1950; with Wasson's Dept. Store, Indpls., 1950; legal staff OPS, Indpls., 1950-52, final title examiner Union Title Co., Indpls., 1952-53; dep. atty. gen. Ind., 1965-66, asst. atty. gen., 1966-69; partner law firm Dillon, Kelley, McCarty, Hardamon, & Cohen, Indpls., 1969—; pres. Dill-Fields Implement Co., Inc., Greenfield, Ind., 1967—; mem. and sec.-treas. Ind. Bd. Law Examiners, 1971—. Mem. Indpls. Mayor's Task Force Women, 1972—, chairperson legal status com., 1974—. Pres. Greater Indpls. Women's Polit. Caucas, 1971—, Ind. Women's Polit. Caucus, 1972-73; precinct vice committeeman, 1966-69; chairperson orgn. com. Nat. Women's Polit. Caucus, 1973—; v.p. Hoosiers for Equal Rights Amendment, 1973-74. Bd dirs. Concord Center, Info, Inc. Mem. Ind., Indpls. (legislative chmn. 1972) bar assns., Order of Coif, Phi Beta Kappa. Club: Stansfield Circle (Indpls.). Home: 5809 Washington Blvd Indianapolis IN 46220 Office: 120 E Market St 511 Indianapolis IN 46204

MCCASH, JUNE TULLY HALL, educator; b. Newberry, S.C., June 8, 1938; d. James DeLeon and Martha Williemae (Stone) Hall; student Reid Hall, Paris, France, 1958-59; B.A., Agnes Scott Coll., 1960; M.A., Emory U., 1963, Ph.D., 1967; m. Marvin Hampton Martin, Apr. 8, 1961 (div. June 1971); children—Michael Hall, Christopher Brenden; m. 2d, William Barton McCash, June 26, 1974. Teaching asst. English, U. Fla., 1960-61; grad. teaching asst. French, Emory U., Atlanta, 1962-64, instr., 1964-66; asst. prof. French Middle Tenn. State U., Murfreesboro, 1967-70, asso. prof., 1970—, dir. honors program, 1973—. Actress, dir. Murfreesboro Little Theatre, 1969—. Mem. Rutherford County Democratic Exec. Com., 1973—. Faculty research grantee Middle Tenn. State U., 1970. Mem. Medieval Acad. Am., Societe Roncesvals, Modern Lang. Assn., South Atlantic Modern Lang. Assn., Am. Assn. Tchrs. French, Am. Assn. U. Profs. (v.p. 1971-72), Tenn. Fgn. Lang. Teaching Assn., Phi Sigma Iota, Alpha Mu Gamma. Democrat. Episcopalian. Author: Love's Fools: Aucassin, Troilus, Calisto and the Parody of the Courtly Lover, 1972. Contbr. articles to profl. jours. Home: 135 Cherry Lane Murfreesboro TN 37130

MCCASKEY, MARY MATTHEWS (MRS. GREGORY M. MCCASKEY), physician; b. Three Rivers, Tex., Apr. 21, 1927; d. William C. and Gertrude (Lewis) Matthews; A.B., Trinity U., 1946; M.D., Baylor Coll. Medicine, 1950; m. Gregory M. McCaskey, Feb. 9, 1951; children—Elizabeth, Martha, Neil, Ruth, Morgen. Intern Hermann Hosp., Houston, 1950-51; resident Meth. Hosp., Houston, 1952-54; practice medicine specializing in pediatrics, Corpus Christi, Tex., 1953-63; staff physician, children and youth project, Dept. Health Edn. and Welfare, Driscoll Found., Children's Hosp., Corpus Christi, Tex., 1970—. Mem. Am., Tex. med. assns., Nueces County Med. Soc., League Women Voters, The Theresians. Home: 250 Cape Henry St Corpus Christi TX 78412 Office: 1001 Louisiana St Corpus Christi TX 78404

MCCASLIN, NELLIE, educator; b. Cleve., Aug. 20, 1914; d. Paul G. and Nellie (Wagner) McCaslin; B.A., Western Res. U., 1936, M.A., 1937; Ph.D., N.Y.U., 1957. Mem. faculty Tudor Hall Sch., 1937-44, Nat. Coll. Edn., 1944-54, Columbia Tchrs. Coll., 1960-67, Rockford Coll., summers 1962-63; mem. faculty Mills Coll. Edn., N.Y.C., 1957-72, dir. student personnel services, 1964-72; mem. faculty N.Y. U., 1972—. Coordinator, dir. program for children radio sta. WABC, N.Y.C., weekly 1965-68; dir. two children's records ABC Paramount, 1966. Mem. Am. Edn. Theatre Assn. (program chmn. 1963, regional chmn. 1964), Children's Theatre Conf. (regional gov. 1959-62, nat. sec. 1964-65, governing bd. 1961—), Children's Theatre Assn. (pres. 1973—). Author: Legends in Action, 1945; More Legends in Action, 1950; Tall Tales and Tall Men, 1956; Pioneers in Petticoats, 1960; The Little Snow Girl, 1963, The Rabbit who Wanted Red Wings, 1963; Creative Dramatics in the Classroom, 2d edit., 1974; A History of Children's Theatre in the United States, 1971. Home: 40 E 10th St New York City NY 10003

MCCATHRIN, ZOE (MRS. JOHN ELWOOD MCCATHRIN), bank ofcl.; b. Columbus, O., Aug. 23, 1936; d. Edwin Lester and Nora Elizabeth (Horlocker) Bargdill; student Ohio U., 1954-56, Otterbein Coll., 1965—; m. John Elwood McCathrin, Apr. 12, 1968; 1 son, Lee Edwin. TV emcee WTVN, 1954; columnist Westerville (O.) Pub. Opinion; reporter, apprentice Columbus Dispatch, Columbus Citizen Jour.; free-lance writer, journalist Columbus Dispatch, Cleve. Plain Dealer, trade publs.; writer, office pub. relations Otterbein Coll., Westerville, 1965-74; dir. communications Ohio Nat. Bank, 1974—. Mem. Ohio Commn. on Status of Women. Mem. Pub. Relations Soc. Am. (dir.), Women in Communications, Westerville Hist. Soc. Home: 178 Moss Rd Westerville OH 43081

MCCAUGHEY, ANNE MARY, civic worker; b. Phila., Aug. 2, 1915; d. Harry Moses and Mary (Orr) McCaughey; A.B., Pa. State Coll., 1937. Asso. editor Woman's Day mag., N.Y.C., 1946-50; women's editor Germantown Courier, Phila., 1954-68. Vol. editor newsletter Southeastern Pa. chpt. A.R.C., 1966—; mem. women's com. Deshler-Morris House of Germantown Hist. Soc., 1971—. Red Cross worker with 50th Gen. Hosp., U.S. Army, 1943-45. Mem. Am. Overseas Assn., Alpha Chi Omega. Presbyn. Home: Sedgwick Gardens Philadelphia PA 19119

MCCAULEY, ELFRIEDA BABNEY (MRS. LEON MCCAULEY), sch. adminstr.; b. Milw., Aug. 11, 1915; d. Rudolph and Louise (Hetzel) Babney; B.Ed., U. Wis., 1948; M.S., Columbia, 1965, Dr. in L.S., 1971; m. Leon McCauley, June 10, 1938; children—Brian, Christopher, Kevin, Matthew. With Milw. Pub. Library, 1935-40; reporter Religious News Service, N.Y.C., 1941-43; free lance pub. relations, N.Y.C., 1943-46; sec., treas. McCauley Enterprises, Greenwich, Conn., 1961-65; high sch. librarian Greenwich Pub. Schs., 1965-69, coordinator sch. libraries, 1969-73, dir. media services, 1973—. Vis. lectr. Columbia Sch. Library Service, 1972-73. Mem. Internat. Reading Assn., N.E.A., Am., Conn. Sch. library assns., Conn. Audio Visual Edn. Assn., N.Y. State Ednl. Communications Assn. Author: Book of Prayers, 1955; A Treasury of Faith, 1957; Book of Family Worship, 1958; Prayers for Girls, 1956. Contbr. articles to profl. jours., anthologies. Home: 32 Longmeadow Rd Riverside CT 06878 Office: Greenwich Pub Schs Box 292 Greenwich CT 06830

MCCAULEY, HANNAH JO (MRS. ROBERT MITCHEL MCCAULEY), librarian; b. Houston, Sept. 14, 1929; d. Moye Damascas and Deborah Ellen (Jordan) Vansau; A.A., Kilgor Jr. Coll., 1947; B.S., U. Tex., 1950; postgrad. George Peabody Coll., 1952; m. Robert Mitchel McCauley, June 26, 1953; 1 dau., Deborah Ann. Tchr., librarian Judson Grove Sch., Longview, Tex., 1950-53; librarian Lancaster (O.) City Schs., 1956-68; librarian Ohio U., Lancaster, 1968—, asst. prof. library technology, 1972—. Chmn., Lancaster City Sch. Libraries, 1960-68, Ohio U. Br. Libraries, 1968—; dir. Library Tech. Assts. Program, 1971—. Recipient Martha Holden Jennings scholarship, 1967. Mem. Ohio (bd. dirs. 1969, sec. 1972, pres. 1974), Am. (2d v.p.) assns. sch. librarians, Am., Ohio library assns., Edn. Media Council Ohio, Council Library Tech., League Women Voters, Am. Assn. U. Women, Fairfield County Heritage Assn., Phi Theta Kappa. Mem. Ch. Christ (pres. Christian Womens Assn. 1958).

Home: 155 Berkley Dr Lancaster OH 43130 Office: 1570 Granville Pike Lancaster OH 43130

MCCAY, JOAN ELIZABETH, editor; b. Sioux Falls, S.D., Dec. 1, 1926; d. Charles Homer and Mary Theresa (Kenneally) McCay; B.A., U. S.D., 1947, M.A., 1948; postgrad. U. Tex., 1965, U. Mass., 1968. Tchr. high sch. English, Milbank, S.D., 1947-48; membership sec. Am. Swedish Inst. Art, Lit. and Sci., Mpls., 1948-50; radio script writer, announcer Schuneman's, Inc., St. Paul, 1950-53; sec., dept. publs. U. Tex.-M.D. Anderson Hosp. and Tumor Inst., Houston, 1954-59, asst. editor, dept. publs., 1959-66, asso. editor, 1966-69, mng. editor, supr. publs., 1969—; mng. editor Med. Arts Pub. Found., Houston, 1961—; co-investigator Nat. Cancer Inst. grant Oncological Word Bank, 1967-70; asso. prof. med. journalism U. Tex. Grad. Sch. Biomed. Scis., Houston, 1971—; lectr. U. Tex. Dental Br., Houston, 1971—. Recipient merit award for outstanding retail promotion Nat. Retail Dry Goods Assn., 1951, spl. award for outstanding radio coordination with other media, 1952, grand award, 1952. Mem. Soc. for Tech. Communication, Zeta Phi Eta, Tau Kappa Alpha. Mng. editor Cancer Bull., 1961—; co-editor Year Book of Cancer, 1955—; editor (with R.L. Clark, R.W. Cumley and M.M. Copeland) Oncology 1970, 5 vols., 1971. Editor Textbook of Radiotherapy (by G.H. Fletcher), 1973. Home: 3029 Carnegie St Houston TX 77005 Office: Publications Dept MD Anderson Hosp Houston TX 77025

MCCHESNEY, KATHRYN MARIE (MRS. THOMAS DAVID MCCHESNEY), univ. dean; b. Curwensville, Pa., Jan. 14, 1936; d. Orland William and Lillian Irene (Morrison) Spencer; B.A., U. Akron, 1962; M.L.S., Kent State U., 1965, postgrad., 1971—; m. Thomas David McChesney, June 12, 1954; 1 son, Eric Spencer. Tchr. English, Springfield Local High Sch., Akron, O., 1962-63, librarian, 1963-64, head librarian, 1965-68; asst. to dean, instr. Kent (O.) State U. Sch. Library Sci., 1968-69, asst. dean, asst. prof., 1969—. Rep., Uniontown Community Council, 1964-66. Mem. Am., Ohio (chmn. Library Edn. Roundtable 1971-72, exec. council Div. VI Library Edn. 1972—) library assns., Am. Assn. Univ. Profs., Am., Ohio assns. sch. librarians, Beta Phi Mu, Phi Sigma Alpha, Phi Alpha Theta, Sigma Phi Epsilon. Club: Uniontown Junior Womans (pres. 1965-66). Contbr. articles, book revs. to profl. periodicals. Home: 3611 Edison St NW Uniontown OH 44685 Office: Kent State U Kent OH 44242

MCCLAIN, ALICE, library adminstr.; b. Telluride, Colo., Apr. 20, 1918; d. Henry Griffiths and Rebecca Sophia (Kesner) McClain; student U. Mont., 1935-37, State U. Ia., 1938-39; A.B., U. Denver, 1940; M.A., Western State Coll., Colo., 1942. Asst. librarian Western State Coll., Gunnison, Colo., 1940-43; army librarian U.S. Armed Services, Hill Field, Utah, 1943-45, Am. Army, Germany, 1945-47; circulation asst. Seattle Pub. Library, 1948-51; reference librarian Ida. State U., Pocatello, 1952, asso. librarian, 1953-66; asso. dir. Mont. State U. Library, Bozeman, 1966-69, dir. libraries, 1970—. Great Decisions chmn., Pocatello, Ida., 1962; UN Day Coordinator for Pocatello, 1956. Grad. fellow Western State Coll., 1940-42. Mem. Am., Pacific Northwest (pres. 1966-67), Mont. (mem. council 1973—) library assns., Am. Assn. U. Women, Am. Assn. U. Profs., PEO Sisterhood, Delta Kappa Gamma. Home: 710 S 16th Av Bozeman MT 59715 Office: Montana State Univ Library Bozeman MT 59715

MCCLAIN, SISTER MARY PATRICK, coll. adminstr.; b. Pitts., Nov. 30, 1911; d. Patrick Francis and Stella Grace (Shiring) McClain; B.A., Mount Mercy Coll., 1938; M.A., Cath. U. Am., 1942; postgrad. U. Lavel, 1951; Ph.D., Fordham U., 1957. High sch. tchr. Spanish, Latin Our Lady of Mercy Acad., Pitts., 1936-42; high sch. tchr. French, English Academic Catolica, San Juan, P.R., 1942-47; asst. prof. French Carlow Coll., Pitts., 1947-57, asso. prof. French, 1957-63, prof., 1969—, acad. dean, 1963-71, acad. v.p., dean instrn., 1971-74. Mem. deans' com. Pitts. Council of Higher Edn., 1969-73. Mem. Bd. trustees Carlow Coll., 1963-73, v.p., 1971-74; exec. bd. Pitts. Council Pub. Edn., 1968-70. Mem. Am. Assn. Higher Edn., Am. Assn. Tchrs. French. Home: 5090 Warwick Terrace Pittsburgh PA 15213 Office: Carlow Coll Pittsburgh PA 15213

MCCLAIN, ROSELLA (MRS. EDWARD MCCLAIN), coll. adminstr.; b. nr. Covington, Tenn., Feb. 14, 1933; d. Malcolm Elmore and Ruby Norris (Max) Overall; B.S., Memphis State U., 1954, M.A., 1962; m. Edward McClain, Dec. 30, 1950; 1 son, Edward. Tchr., Tipton County Sch. System, 1954-55, Covington City Sch. System, 1955-69; dir. admissions and records Dyersburg (Tenn.) State Community Coll., 1969—. Bd. dirs. Tipton County Hist. Soc. Named Outstanding Educator in Higher Edn., 1973. Lion Oil scholar, 1955. Mem. Tenn. Edn. Assn., Tenn. Personnel and Guidance Assn., Tenn. Assn. Collegiate Registrars and Admissions Officers (sec.-treas.), Alpha Delta Kappa. Home: Route 1 Box 201A Covington TN 38019 Office: Lake Rd Dyersburg TN 38024

MCCLANAHAN, MABEL RUBY, bus. exec.; b. nr. Doering, Wis., Feb. 14, 1918; d. John Joseph and Myrtle Adeline (Means) Krause; student adult study classes evening schs.; m. William G. McClanahan, July 8, 1937 (div. Oct. 1938); 1 son, Garrett W. Bookkeeper, sec. radio sta. WSAU, Wausau, Wis., 1936-37; sec. Marathon Finance Corp., Wausau, 1938-41; adminstrv. asst. U.S. Govt., Wausau, 1941-46; bus. mgr. Crane Engring. Sales, Inc., Appleton, 1946—, dir., corp. sec., 1952—; dir. No. State Bank, Appleton, 1972—. Bd. dirs. Anti-Tb Assn., Appleton, 1956-57, seal sale chmn., 1956-57, 60-61; mem. Wis. Council of Safety, 1958-59, Wis. Brotherhood Com., 1957-59, Wis. Roadside Council, 1957-70, Wis. adv. council Small Bus. Adminstrn., 1965-69; mem. Appleton Bd. Edn., 1969-72, pres., 1973; mem. Gov.'s Commn. Status Women, 1964-69, Nat. Women's Adv. Council on Poverty, 1967-70; sec., dir. Appleton Taxpayers Assn., pres., 1966-67; chmn. Nat. Career Advancement Scholarship Com., 1970—; mem. adv. com. Center for Studies in Vocational and Tech. Edn., U. Wis., 1973—. Trustee Bus. and Profl. Women's Found., 1960-68, 72—. Named Post-Crescent Woman of Year, 1972-73. Mem. Wis. (rec. sec. N. Central region 1957-59, state pres. 1957-59), Nat. (nat. pres. 1967-68) fedns. bus. and profl. women's clubs, Luth. Ch. Women, Appleton Area C. of C. (dir. 1972—). Lutheran. Home: PO Box 467 Appleton WI 54911 Office: 1601 S Seminole Dr Appleton WI 54911

MCCLARY, JANE MCILVAINE STEVENSON (MRS. NELSON C. MCCLARY), author; b. Pitts., Feb. 19, 1919; d. William Cooper and Elizabeth (Walker) Stevenson; grad. high sch.; m. Nelson C. McClary, Dec. 15, 1956; children—Stevenson, Christopher. Named Woman of Achievement, Va. Press Women, 1973. Author numerous books including: Cinta's Challenge, 1954; My Antarctic Honeymoon, 1956; Cammie's Choice, 1961; Cammie's Challenge, 1962; Cammie's Cousin, 1963; To Win the Hunt, 1966; The Will to Win, 1966; A Portion for Foxes, 1972. Contbr. numerous articles to profl. jours. Home: Zulla Rd Middleburg VA 22117

MCCLATCHY, ELEANOR, pub., pres., dir. McClatchy Newspapers, pubs. Fresno Bee, Sacramento Bee, McClatchy Broadcasting Co. of Nev., McClatchy Broadcasting Co. Newspapers Pulitzer prize, 1935 (for exposing polit. corruption in Nev.). Office: Fresno Bee Van Ness and Caliveras Fresno CA 93721

MCCLEAVE, MILDRED ATWOOD (MRS. BEN F. MCCLEAVE, JR.), educator, counselor; b. Memphis, Dec. 19, 1919; d. Carl Rivers and Ellen Morning (Winston) Poston; B.A., Le Moyne Coll., 1941; M.A., Denver U., 1971; m. Ben F. McCleave, Jr.; children—Ben III, Bob, Bill, Bruce. Tchr. pub. schs., Memphis, 1941-53, acting prin.; playground dir. Recreation Dept., Memphis, 1939-48, Davenport, Ia., 1952; city director enumerator, Denver, 1957-58; tchr. pub. schs., Denver, 1958—, also counselor, 1971—. Tchr. Headstart program Children's Edn. Fund, Denver, summers, 1965, 66; co-instr. minority culture for Denver pub. schs., 1968. Counselor Memphis council Girl Scouts Am., 1942-48; mem. Memphis Cotton-Makers Jubilee com., 1949-53. Sec. East Denver Coordinating Council, 1955-58; alternate del. to Republican conv., Miami, Fla., 1972. Recipient achievement award YMCA, 1959. Mem. Nat., Colo. edn. assns., Colo. Personnel and Guidance Assn., Colo. Sch. Counselors Assn., Denver Classroom Tchrs. Assn., Colo.-Wyo. Assn. of Women Deans and Counselors, Inter-Alumni Assn., Alpha Kappa Alpha. Episcopalian (pres. churchwomen). Mem. Order Eastern Star. Home: 2236 High St Denver CO 80205 Office: Hill Junior High School 451 Clermont St Denver CO 80220

MCCLELLAN, DOROTHY WOMACK (MRS. REED H. MCCLELLAN), banker; b. Roosevelt, Utah, May 9, 1920; d. Henry Edgar and Thelma Dorothy (Prigmore) Womack; student U. Ill., 1955-56, Gonzaga U., 1964-68, Spokane Community Coll., 1970; m. Reed H. McClellan, Oct. 18, 1938; 1 dau., Gail (Mrs. Leland Mercy). Teller, bookkeeper Roosevelt State Bank, 1943-48, First Nat. Bank, Rantoul, Ill., 1948-52; head teller Old Nat. Bank, 1955-57; owner, mgr. Snelling & Snelling, Spokane, Wash., 1957; sec. Citizens Savs. & Loan Soc., Spokane, 1957; asst. sec. Wash. Mut. Savs. Bank, 1966-67, asst. mgr., 1967-68, mgr. Northtown br., 1968—. Loaned exec. United Crusade, 1969-70, mem. budget com., 1968-71. Mem. Inland Empire Group Nat. Assn. Bank Women (group chmn. 1967-68), v.p. northwestern region 1969-70), Bank Adminstrn. Inst. (dir. 1971-72, sec. 1972-73, treas. 1973-74). Methodist (ofcl. bd. 1971-72). Mem. Order Eastern Star. Club: Zonta. Home: East 1309 57th Av Spokane WA 99203 Office: East 103 Queen Av Spokane WA 99207

MCCLELLAND, ANN SAMONIAL (MRS. STEWART W. MCCLELLAND), educator, lectr.; b. Vincennes, Ind., Jan. 31, 1917; d. Charles Edward and Martha Ann (Love) Samonial; A.A., Vincennes U., 1936; B.S., Peabody Coll., 1938, M.A., 1941; postgrad. Vanderbilt U.; Litt.D. (hon.), Steed Coll., 1957; m. Stewart Winning McClelland, Aug. 2, 1947. Tchr., Bogalusa (La.) High Sch., 1938, Holmes High Sch., Covington, Ky., 1939-45; instr. Okla. Coll. Women, 1938-39; dean women Lincoln Meml. U., 1945-47; sponsor Dale Carnegie courses, Fla., Ind., 1947—; asso. with Mrs. Dale Carnegie in Dorothy Carnegie Courses Women, 1956—. Fellow Royal Soc. Arts (London); mem. Indpls. Propylaeum, Internat. Platform Assn., Herron Museum Alliance, Am. Assn. U. Women, Wedgewood Internat. Seminar, Wedgewood Soc. (London), English Speaking Union, D.A.R., Am. Ceramic Circle, Kappa Kappa Kappa, Pi Gamma Chi. Republican. Roman Catholic. Affiliated with husband in Lincoln research; authority on Coin glass and Wedgwood. Home: 730 Braeside Ct Indianapolis IN 46260

MCCLELLAND, ANNE R., ret. govt. ofcl.; b. N.Y.C., Aug. 12, 1914; d. Victor and Deborah (Farber) Rosenberg; B.S., Douglass Coll., 1933; postgrad. Columbia, 1933-34, 37-38; m. Donald Hawthorne McClelland, Jan. 16, 1952. Edn. statistician Rutgers U., 1934-35; financial statistician SEC, 1940-42; economist, bus. economist OPA, 1942-47; fgn. trade economist SCAP, Tokyo, Japan, 1947-50; with AID and predecessor agys., 1950—, asst. program officer, Korea, 1957-58, country desk officer, Washington, 1961-65, evaluation officer, Saigon, Vietnam, 1970-72, agrl. economist, 1973-74. Mem. Am. Econ. Assn., Soc. for Internat. Devel. Address: AID/ADEPP APO San Francisco CA 96243

MCCLELLAND, SUE, winery co. advt. exec.; b. Cleve., May 17, 1934; d. Walter B. and Barbara P. (Pinnell) McClelland; student Harvard Bus. Sch., 1960; B.A., Mills Coll., 1956. Price clk. purchasing div. C. & O. Ry., Cleve., 1956-57; mgr. student corr. Cleve. Inst. Electronics, 1957-59; advt. asst. Scott Paper Co., Phila., 1960-62, asst. media mgr., 1962-63, advt. media mgr., 1963-72; dir. media planning Gallo Winery, 1972—. Mem. Phila. Center for Internat. Visitors, 1961—. Republican. Conglist. Clubs: Philadelphia Club of Advertising Women (bd. dirs. 1965-67, v.p. 1967-68), Harvard Business School Club Television-Radio Advertising (bd. dirs. 1969-72). Home: 1229 Brighton Av 241 Modesto CA 95355 Office: E and J Gallo Winery Modesto CA 95353

MCCLEMENTS, N. RUTH, coll. dean; b. Ballston Springs, N.Y., Jan. 30, 1931; d. Stewart and Elizabeth (Hill) Walker; B.A., Tusculum Coll., 1959; M.A. (assistantship), Ball State U., 1971; m. Lawrence Ellery McClements, Sept. 6, 1953 (dec. 1969); children—Donna Ruth, Larry Stewart, Ronna Beth, Timothy James. Instr. psychology Ind. Vocational Tech. Coll., Muncie, 1971-72; dean of women Nyack (N.Y.) Coll., 1972—. Leader, Cub Scouts Am., Muncie, 1964-66. Named Mother of Year, Christian Missionary Alliance Ch., 1970. Mem. Christian Missionary Alliance Ch. Address: Nyack Coll Nyack NY 10960

MCCLENDON, ERNESTINE EPPS (MRS. GEORGE WILTSHIRE), theatrical agt.; b. Norfolk, Va.; d. Edward and Lillie (Warren) Epps; grad. high sch.; m. George Wiltshire, Aug. 20, 1946. Actress, Woodstock Playhouse, N.Y.C., 1958, Casino Theatre, Newport, R.I., 1959, North Jersey Playhouse, 1959, Jan Hus House, N.Y.C., 1959, Lenox Hill Playhouse, 1959-60, 60-61, toured summer theatres as Lena in A Raisin in the Sun, 1961; also appeared in numerous films including A Face in the Crowd, 1957, The Last Angry Man, 1959, The Apartment, 1960, The Rat Race, 1960, The Young Doctors, The World by Night, Warner Brothers, 1961, The Young Savages, United Artists, 1961; also TV appearances, ABC, NBC, CBS, 1950; artists rep. Ernestine McClendon Enterprises, Inc., N.Y.C. 1962—, Hollywood, Cal., 1972—. Mem. Actors Guild Assn., Screen Actors Guild, A.F.T.R.A. Composer songs AGAC, 1966. Home: 8440 Sunset Blvd Los Angeles CA 90069 Office: 56W 45th St New York City NY 10036 also 8440 Sunset Blvd Hollywood CA 90069

MCCLENDON, JOAN PARSONS (MRS. CLAUDE M. MCCLENDON), banker; b. Boston, Apr. 21, 1925; d. Jack and Victoria Muriel (Adams) Parsons; student Long Beach Jr. Coll., 1942-43, Los Angeles City Coll., 1944, U. Miss. Sch. Banking, 1973-74; m. Claude M. McClendon, Nov. 17, 1945; 1 dau., Joan Diane (Mrs. Glenn Wayne Kuykendall). Teller, bookkeeper S.W. Miss. Bank (formerly Magnolia Bank), Magnolia, Miss., 1953-59, asst. cashier, 1960-74, asst. to pres., 1974—. Pres., Pike County chpt. Am. Cancer Soc., 1971-72; maj. gift chmn. Magnolia United Givers, 1973. Del. Democratic State Conv., 1968—; sec. Pike County Democratic Exec. Com., 1966—. Mem. Am. Inst. Banking (chmn. Tri-County study group 1972—), Nat. Assn. Bank Women (state chmn. 1971-72), Banking Adminstrn. Inst. (dir. S.W. Miss. chpt. 1972—, v.p. 1974-75), Miss. Bankers Assn. (edn. com. 1974—), Magnolia Area C. of C. (dir., sec. 1973-74). Episcopalian. Home: Route 4 Magnolia MS 39652 Office: PO Box 109 Magnolia MS 39652

MCCLENNEN, SANDRA ELAINE SWISS, educator; b. Huntington, W.Va., Oct. 28, 1942; d. Sol Stuart and Doris Ruth (Weintraub) Swiss; B.S., U. Mich., 1963, M.A., 1965, M.A., 1970, Ph.D., 1973; m. Douglas McClennen, Aug. 20, 1966; children—Michael, Marjorie. Tchr. blind, retarded children Plymouth Child Devel. Center, Northville, Mich., 1963-66, dir. mental retardation program, 1966-70; univ. supr. student teaching Eastern Mich. U., Ypsilanti, 1970-71, instr. dept. spl. edn., 1971-73, asst. prof., 1973—. Bd. dirs. Community Opportunity Center. Mem. Am. Psychol. Assn., Am. Assn. Mental Deficiency, Nat. Assn. for Retarded Children and Adults, Am. Assn. Workers for Blind, Mich. Assn. Tchr. Educators, Assn. for Humanistic Psychology, League Women Voters, Plymouth Assembly for Equal Opportunity, Phi Kappa Phi. Home: 619 N Sheldon Rd Plymouth MI 48170 Office: 236 Rackham Ypsilanti MI 48197

MCCLINTOCK, BARBARA, geneticist; b. Hartford, Conn., June 16, 1902; d. Thomas Henry and Sara (Handy) McClintock; B.S. in Botany, Cornell U., 1923, A.M., 1925, Ph.D., 1927; Sc.D. (hon.), U. Rochester, 1947. Instr. botany Cornell U., 1923-31, research asst., 1934-36; fellow NRC, Guggenheim Found., 1933-34; asst. prof. botany U. Mo., 1936-41; investigator in genetics Carnegie Inst., Washington, 1941-47, research, Cold Spring Harbor, L.I., N.Y. Recipient ann. achievement award Am. Assn. U. Women, 1947, Nat. Medal Sci., 1970. Mem. Genetics Soc., A.A.A.S., Bot. Soc., Soc. Am. Naturalists, Nat. Acad. Scis., Am. Philos. Soc., Sigma Xi. Contbr. to various biol. jours. Office: Carnegie Instn 1530 P St NW Washington DC 20005*

MCCLINTOCK, BETTIE LOU (MRS. HOYT MINGUS MCCLINTOCK), physician; b. Calmer, Ark., Apr. 21, 1930; d. Joseph Lyndon and Nanie Cross (Reed) Brown; M.D., Baylor U., 1955; m. Hoyt Mingus McClintock, Sept. 16, 1955; children—Joseph Milton, Michael Ray, Roy Alan, Marsha Ann. Intern Bethany Hosp., Kansas City, Kan., 1955-56; resident pediatrics Childrens Mercy Hosp., Kansas City, Mo., 1958-60; practice medicine specializing in pediatrics, Clovis, N.M., 1961—; asso. physician McClintock Pediatric Clinic, 1961—; cons. pediatric staff Clovis Meml. Hosp.; dist health dir. N.M. Health and Social Service, 1968—. Diplomate Am. Bd. Pediatrics. Fellow Am. Acad. Pediatrics, N.M. Pediatric Soc. (sec.-treas. 1970—); mem. Am., N.M., Curry-Roosevelt County (sec. 1966-67) med. assns., Am. Assn. U. Women, Internat. Platform Assn. Baptist. (nursery com. 1965—). Club. Soroptimist (corr. sec. 1964-65). Home: 1412 Eastridge Dr Clovis NM 88101 Office: 1633 Prince St Clovis NM 88106

MCCLINTOCK, ELAINE SARAH SNELL (MRS. JOHN ROBERT MCCLINTOCK), ednl. adminstr.; b. Cloverdale, B.S., Can., Mar. 15, 1935; d. Edward James and Gertrude Clara (Parnell) Snell; B.S. in Nursing, U. B.C., 1957; M.Ed., Queens U., 1974; m. John Robert McClintock, May 30, 1959; children—James Douglas, Michael John. Staff nurse Victorian Order Nurses Can., Brockville, Ont., 1957-59; tchr. med. surg. nursing Sch. Nursing, Brockville Gen. Hosp., 1960-64, asst. dir. nursing edn., 1964-66, dir. regional sch. nursing, 1966-73; chmn. health scis. dept. St. Lawrence Coll., Brockville, 1973—. Mem. Registered Nurses Assn. Ont. (pres. local chpt. 1963-64). Home: 82 Bennett St Brockville ON Canada

MCCLINTOCK, ELIZABETH MAY, botanist; b. Los Angeles, July 7, 1912; d. Arthur Polk and Margaret Christina (Stoveken) McClintock; B.A., U. Cal. at Los Angeles, 1937, M.A., 1939; Ph.D., U. Mich., 1956. Herbarium botanist, dept. botany U. Cal. at Los Angeles, 1941-46; with Cal. Acad. Scis., San Francisco, 1948—, curator botany dept., 1969—. Mem. Internat. Assn. Plant Taxonomy, Bot. Soc. Am., Am. Assn. Bot. Gardens and Arboreta, Am. Soc. Plant Taxonomists, Nature Conservancy, Cal. Natural Areas Coordinating Council, Cal. Native Plant Soc., Cal. Bot. Soc., Sierra Club. Home: 1335 Union St San Francisco CA 94109 Office: Cal Academy of Sciences San Francisco CA 94118

MCCLINTOCK, FRANCES STEIDEL (MRS. JOHN CHAMBERLAIN MCCLINTOCK), civic worker; b. Logan, W.Va., Apr. 1, 1917; d. Joseph Heber and Lucia (Raymond) Steidel; student Stanford, 1933-36; m. John Chamberlain McClintock, May 5, 1937; children—Susan (Mrs. Robert L.M. Vas Dias), John Mills, Lucia (Mrs. Samuel Giles Payne V), Deborah (Mrs. John Rudolph Vitek, III), Robert Michael. Dir. pub. relations Boston YMCA, 1955-57; sec. Human Relations Com. City of Newton, 1956-59; v.p. The Hospitality and Information Service (THIS) for diplomatic residents and families, Washington, 1961-67, pres., 1967-69; vice-chmn., dir. Internat. Visitors Information Service, Washington, 1962-70, Nat. Council Community Services to Internat. Visitors, 1967—. Mem. adv. council Corp. Pub. Broadcasting, 1973—, adv. com. U.S. Center Internat. Women's Year, 1975. Trustee, Meridian House Internat., Washington; trustee, dir. Greater Washington Ednl. Tele-Communications Assn., Inc.; bd. dirs. Vol. Action Center, Greater Washington Health and Welfare Council. Mem. Nat. Council Women of U.S. (western hemisphere liaison chmn. 1968-70), League of Women Voters (pres. D.C. chpt. 1948-50, Newton, Mass., 1954-56), Stanford Alumni Assn., Internat. Platform Assn., Am. Acad. Polit. Sci., Nat. Orgn. Women, Delta Gamma. Democrat. Episcopalian. Home: 218 S Royal St Alexandria VA 22314 Office: 1630 Crescent Pl NW Washington DC 20009

MCCLINTON, HELEN ELIZABETH AUGE (MRS. ROBERT JOSEPH MCCLINTON), civic worker; b. Denver, Nov. 14, 1928; d. Charles Robert and Jessie Mary (Ackermann) Auge; B.F.A., U. Denver, 1950, grad. student spl. edn., 1969-70; postgrad. art edn. So. Colo. State Coll., 1967-69; m. Robert Joseph McClinton, Oct. 20, 1956; children—Michele, Michael. Artist, Alexander Film Co., Colorado Springs, 1951-52; spl. services club program dir., Camp Hale, Colo., 1954-55, Salzburg Mil. Post St. Johann, Pongau, Austria, 1952-54; spl. services arts and crafts shop dir., Ft. Carson, Colo., 1955-58; tchr. spl. edn. Pikes Peak Bd. Coop. Services, Colorado Springs, 1969-70; tchr. art Palmer High Sch., Colorado Springs, 1972. Founder Mother's Mut. Com., 1965, state chmn., 1968—; founder dir. Colorado Springs Spl. Religious Edn. Program, 1966—; v.p. El Paso County Assn. for Retarded Children, 1967-68; com. chmn. Nat. Assn. Retarded Child Conv., 1971; Colorado Springs co-chmn. Coloradans for '76 Olympics, 1972. Trustee Rocky Mountain Rehab. Center, 1968-69; bd. dirs. Colo. Assn. for Retarded Children, 1968-71, founder dir. ski program, 1968—; bd. dirs. Nat. Apostolate for Mentally Retarded, 1970—. Recipient Lt. Joseph P. Kennedy Jr. Found. scholarship, 1970, Distinguished Service to Univ. award U. Denver, 1973. Mem. Nat. Cath. Edn. Assn., Council for Exceptional Children, U. Denver Alumni Assn. (treas. nat. bd. 1973), Delta Phi Delta, Gamma Phi Beta. Roman Catholic. Clubs: University Denver Alumni (charter mem. Colorado Springs, Colo.). Author: Mothers Mutual Manual, 1967. Illustrator: The Water and the Power (by Albert N. Williams), 1951. Home: 128 N Brentwood Dr Colorado Springs CO 80909

MCCLOSKEY, EUNICE L. (EUNICE LONCOSKE), author, artist; b. Ridgway, Pa., May 25, 1904; d. Fred William and Ada Amelia (Nelson) Loncoske; student Columbia, 1930-31; m. Lewis Frank McCloskey, Jan. 9, 1932; 1 dau., Mimi Marie. Sec., Olson & Larson, Inc., 1926-38; author and illustrator books Coal Dust and

Crystals, 1938; Strange Alchemy, 1940; The Heart Knows This (prize awarded by Driftwind Press), 1944; This Is the Hour, 1949; The Golden Hill, 1952; These Rugged Hills, 1954; This is My Art, Vol. 1, 1956, Vol. 2, 1957, Vol. 3, 1958, Vol. 4, 1962; So Dear to my Heart, Vol. I (biography), 1964; Potpourri (biography), 1966; Songs and Paintings for The Heart, 1969; Symbols of My Life, 1970; O Shana, Shana, 1972; contbr. poetry, articles, essays and short stories to magazines U.S. and Can., including Ladies Home Jour., McCall's, Good Housekeeping, Household. Water colors and etchings exhibited at Carnegie Inst., Pitts., Nat. Museum, Washington, Nelson Art Gallery, (Kansas City), Creative Art Gallery, Hammer Gallery (both N.Y.C.), Edwin Forrest Gallery, Everyman's Gallery (Phila.), Pitts. Plan for Art Gallery, Upstairs Gallery, Raymond Duncan Galleries, Ligoa Duncan Gallery; paintings at Galerie Paula Insel, N.Y.C., Women's City Club, Phila., Philbrook Art Center, Tulsa; one-man show art, Chautauqua, N.Y., 1957, Theil College, 1960, Langenheim Gallery, Greenville, Pa., Indiana (Pa.) State Coll., 1960, Upstairs Gallery Asso. Artists, Pitts., 1961, 72; art show Lioga Duncan Gallery, 1967, Carnegie Gallery, Raymond Duncan Gallery, Paris, 1970, 71. other mus.; one artist show Lynn Kottler Galleries, N.Y.C., 1974. Publicity dir. Jr. Women's Club, Girl Scouts, Art Club (Ridgway, Pa.); dir. Pitts. Assn. Artists; chmn. edn. V.I.A.; chmn. ann. Clothesline Exhibit, Ridgway; poetry chmn. for Elk County. Recipient prizes for poems, articles and short stories Pa. Fedn. Women's Clubs, 1st prize for interior decoration Good Housekeeping, 1941, 1st prize for art Nat. League Am. Penwomen, Asso. Artists prize for watercolor Carnegie Mus., 1950, 53, Henry Posner prize for watercolor Carnegie Museum, 1950, Aimee Jackson Short prize for art, Phila. for watercolor chosen as best watercolor to rep. Pa. and sent to Nat. Mus., Washington; poetry prizes, Ted Malone, Am. Lit. Assn.; elected Woman of the Yr., Ridgway, 1958-59; 1st prize for watercolor Bryn Mawr State Show, 1959, honorable mention for watercolor Carnegie, 1959, Nat. 1st prize for lyric Nat. League Am. Pen Women, 1954; elected to Hall of Fame, 1966. Fellow Internat. Inst. Arts and Letters; mem. Phila. Art Alliance, Nat. League Am. Pen Women (v.p. Oil City br.; nat. poetry editor 1950-52, poetry prizes; 1st prize nat. 1953; asst. art chmn., nat. editor Sonnets 1958-60, short story editor 1972), Pa. Fedn. Women's Clubs (fine arts chmn.), Pitts. Assn. Artists, Mark Twain Soc., Am. Lit. Assn., Centro Studi, Scampi Internationale, Delta Kappa Gamma. Home: 403 Oak St Ridgeway PA 15853

MCCLOSKEY, MAXINE ELAINE MUGG (MRS. JOHN MICHAEL MCCLOSKEY), educator; b. Portland, Ore., Apr. 26, 1927; d. Leslie and Lydia (Sarajarvi) Mugg; A.A., U. Cal. at Berkeley, 1948; B.S., Portland State U., 1962; M.A., Reed Coll., 1963; m. John Michael McCloskey, June 17, 1965; children—Claire Johnson (Mrs. J. Phillip Jacob), Laura Johnson, James Johnson, Rosemary Johnson. Intern tchr. sr. social studies Grant High Sch., Portland, Ore., 1962-63; instr. sr. social studies St. Helen's Hall, Portland, Ore., 1963-64; instr. Am. history Portland State U., 1964-65; instr. Am. instns. Coll. Marin, Kentfield, Cal., 1965-66; instr. U.S. history and polit. sci. Merritt Coll., Oakland, Cal., 1968—. Mem. Ore. staff U.S. Senator Richard Neuberger, 1955-56, 59; mem. campaign staff Maurine Neuberger, candidate U.S. Senator, 1960; pres. Jane Jefferson Democratic Women's Club, 1962-64; alternate del. Dem. Nat. Conf., 1964, mem. exec. com. platform com., 1964. Bd. dirs., sec. Project Jonah. Mem. Am. Hist. Assn., Ore. Hist. Soc., Regional Parks Assn. (v.p. 1973), Fedn. Western Outdoor Clubs (editor publs. 1973), Sierra Club. Unitarian. Editor: (with James P. Gilligan) Wilderness and the Quality of Life, 1969; Wilderness, the Edge of Knowledge, 1970. Home: 93 Florada Av Piedmont CA 94610 Office: 12500 Campus Dr Oakland CA 94619

MCCLUNEY, DOROTHY JACKSON (MRS. CHARLES F. MCCLUNEY), motel exec.; b. Birmingham, Ala., Aug. 17, 1928; d. William Edward and Myrtle Mae (Jackson) Arrowood; extension student advanced accounting, U. Tenn.; m. Charles F. McCluney, Jan. 7, 1951; 1 dau., Kayron. With Goodyear Tire Co., Gadsden, Ala., 1946-54; office mgr. Namie Packing Co., wholesale meats, Mobile, 1954-57; with Pub. Accounting Office, Tullahoma, Tenn., 1957-59; owner, mgr. McCluney's Employment-Secretarial Agy., 1965-69; adminstr. Commodore Motor Inn, Tullahoma, 1969—; owner, mgr. Picadilly Pub Lounge, 1969—. Recipient Certificate of Appreciation, U.S. Navy, 1973. Mem. Tullahoma C. of C., Am., Tenn. hotel-motel assns., Am. Legion Aux., Toastmistress Club. Baptist. Home: 201 Kaywood Av Tullahoma TN 37388 Office: Box 726 Tullahoma TN 37388

MCCLUNG, GALE STUBBS (MRS. ROBERT M. MCCLUNG), editor; b. Akron, O., July 1, 1923; d. Elmer Joseph and Florence Nightingale (Harris) S.; A.B., Mt. Holyoke Coll., 1945; m. Robert M. McClung, July 23, 1949; children—William M., Thomas C. Systems and methods analyst IBM Corp., N.Y.C., 1945-55; editor Alumnae Quar. Mt. Holyoke Coll. Alumnae Assn., Mt. Holyoke Coll., South Hadley, Mass., 1962—. Corporator Amherst (Mass.) Savs. Bank. Mem. Amherst Town Meeting, 1964-73. Recipient medal of honor Mt. Holyoke Alumnae, 1967. Conglist (deacon 1971-74, chmn. deacons, 1973-74, moderator 1974—). Home: 91 Sunset Av Amherst MA 01002 Office: Mary E Woolley Hall Mount Holyoke College South Hadley MA 01075

MCCLUNG, KAREN LEE, publicity mgr.; b. Glendale, Cal., Apr. 16, 1946; d. Walter Herbert and Gloria Emily (Bloom) Harvey; B.A. in English, Stanford, 1968; M.A. in Lang. Arts, San Francisco State Coll., 1969; m. William James McClung, Sept. 6, 1970. With U. Cal. Press, Berkeley, 1969—, publicity mgr., 1970—. Mem. Pubs. Publicity Assn., U.S. Lawn Tennis Assn. Home: 240 Alvarado Rd Berkeley CA 94705 Office: 2223 Fulton St Berkeley CA 94720

MCCLURE, BARBARA JANE KIMBALL (MRS. JAMES MARVIN MCCLURE), educator, churchwoman; b. Snead, Ala., May 15, 1932; d. Willie Luther and Vera (Browning) Kimball; B.S., Jacksonville State U., 1958; M.Ed., W.Ga. Coll., 1969, Ednl. Specialist degree, 1971; m. James Marvin McClure, Mar. 3, 1948; children—Donald Earl, Annita Lynn, William Thomas. Tchr. biology, sci. Haralson County Bd. Edn., Buchanan, Ga., 1957-58; tchr. Cedartown (Ga.) Sch. System, 1958-61, 63-64, 65-66; tchr. world and Am. lit. Cedartown City System, 1966-67; counselor Polk Sch. Dist., Cedartown, 1967-71, curriculum dir., 1971—. Asst. dir. In-service on Elementary Sch. Counseling Program, Cedartown, 1969—; mem. ednl. standards com. Ga. Dept. Edn., mem. Ga. Tchr. Edn. Council, 1973—. Pres. primary assn. Ch. of Jesus Christ of Latter-day Saints, 1968—, pres. mut. improvement assn., 1957-61, counselor relief soc., 1962-64, mem. State Sunday Sch. Bd. Active Polk County Republican Com., 1964-66. Mem. Ga. Home Econs. Assn. (7th dist. pres. 1960), Future Homemakers Am. (hon. life). Home: 305 Lakeside Dr Cedartown GA 30125

MCCLURE, GILLIAN MARY, physician; b. London, Eng., Nov. 26, 1930; d. Wilson and Muriel Mary (Nutt) Smith; M.B.B.S., U. Coll., London, 1954, Diploma, Royal Coll. Obstetrics and Gynecology, 1957; m. Richard J. McClure, July 19, 1958; children—Joyce Deane, Austin Gavin. House physician Univ. Coll. Hosp., St. Pancras Hosp., London, 1955; house surgeon Central Middlesex Hosp., London, 1956-57; asst. resident Wellesley Hosp., Toronto, Ont., 1958-59; research asst. Cal. Inst. Tech., Pasadena, 1960-63; intern Huntington Meml. Hosp., Pasadena, 1968-69; practice internal medicine, Pasadena, 1969-73; staff teaching service Huntington Meml. Hosp., 1969—. Mem. Los Angeles County Med. Assn., Pasadena Med. Soc., A.M.A. Home: 1654 E Loma Alta Dr Pasadena CA 91001

MCCOLL, MARGARET CALDWELL, librarian; b. Port Deposit, Md., Apr. 1, 1924; d. Hugh and Margaret (Caldwell) McColl; B.A., U. Pa., 1944, M.A., 1946; M.S. in Library Sci., Drexel U., 1955. Proofreader Curtis Pub. Co., Phila., 1946-47; bibliog. asst. U. Pa. Library, 1949-55; cataloger Temple U. Library, Phila., 1955—. Mem. A.L.A., Assn. Coll. and Research Libraries, Beta Phi Mu, Delta Phi Alpha. Home: 229 E Front St Media PA 19063 Office: Temple Univ Library 13th and Berks St Philadelphia PA 19122

MCCOLLOUGH, JANE P., physician; b. Tarentum, Pa., Nov. 21, 1920; d. William Sherman and Kathleen (Power) McCollough; A.B., Vassar Coll., 1942; M.D., Western Res. U., 1945. Intern Babies and Children's Hosp., Cleve., 1945-46; resident Lowman Pavillion, Cleve. Met. Hosp., Cleve. 1946-48, physician outpatient dept., 1961—; sr. staff physician E. Side County Clinic, Cleve., 1948—; cons. Woman's, St. Alexis, Hawthornden State hosps.; clin. instr. medicine Western Res. U., 1970—. Trustee Woman's Gen. Hosp., 1956—, pres., 1971—. Mem. Am., Ohio med. assns., Am. Med. Women's Assn., Cleve. Acad. Medicine, Am., Ohio thoracic socs., Cleve. Chest Soc., Women's Med. Soc. Republican. Presbyn. Home: 12700 Lake Av Cleveland OH 44107 Office: 4520 Carnegie St Cleveland OH 44103

MCCOLLOUGH, LUCILLE HANNA (MRS. CLARENCE LINDSAY MCCOLLOUGH), state legislator; b. Huron County, Mich., Dec. 30, 1905; d. William and Stella (Stover) Hanna; grad., Western Mich. U., 1923; m. Clarence Lindsay McCollough, June 16, 1925; children—Clarence, Marilyn (Mrs. Edwards), Patrick. Past tchr., sec., stenographer; mem. Mich. Ho. of Reps., 1955—. Active Dearborn Fedn. Civic Assns., N. Am. Benefit Assn., Citizens Traffic Safety Council, YWCA. Mem. Aviation Property Owners Assn., McDonald Sch. Mothers' Club, Navy Mother's Club, Ladies Aux. VFW, League of Women Voters, Nat. Order Women Legislators, Hist. Soc., Nat. Fedn. Bus. and Profl. Women. Recipient Sr. Auto Worker award U.A.W. Ret. Workers, 1964, citation for service Nat. Ret. Tchrs. Assn. and Am. Assn. Ret. Persons, 1965, certificate of appreciation Vets. World War I, 1966, citation VFW Mich., U.S., citation Allied Vets. Council, Dearborn, 1966, Outstanding Health Service award Mich. Med. Soc., 1969; named Bus. Woman of the Year, Mich. Fedn. Bus. and Profl. Women, 1965, 68. Democrat. Presbyn. Mem. Women of the Moose. Home: 7517 Kentucky Av Dearborn MI 48126 Office: Mich State Capitol Ho of Reps Lansing MI 48901

MCCOLLUM, MARY BAUMGARTNER (MRS. WILLIAM BALLEW MCCOLLUM), psychiatrist; b. Wichita Falls, Tex., Mar. 3, 1943; d. Walter John and Louise Helen (Hartman) Baumgartner; A.B. magna cum laude, U. Kan., 1964; M.D., Baylor U., 1968; m. William Ballew McCollum, Aug. 23, 1964. Intern Meml. Baptist Hosp., Houston, 1968-69; resident psychiatry Baylor Coll. Medicine, 1969-71, chief resident, 1971-72; adminstr. psychiatry ward VA Hosp., Houston, Tex., 1971-73; asst. prof. Baylor Coll. Medicine; dir. Baylor Psychiat. Clinic. Nat. Inst. Mental Health grantee, 1967-68, NIH grantee, 1964-65, 65-66; named outstanding woman med. student Am. Med. Women's Assn. Mem. Phi Beta Kappa, Alpha Omega Alpha, Pi Beta Phi, Mortar Bd. Home: 1828 Dunstan Rd Houston TX 77005 Office: Baylor Coll Medicine 1200 Moursund Av Houston TX 77025

MCCOLSKEY, ANN SHEDDEN (MRS. ROBERT N. MCCOLSKEY), psychologist; b. Boston, Sept. 27, 1925; d. William M. and Ruth H. (Blodgett) Shedden; B.A., Vassar Coll., 1946; M.A., U. Fla., 1955, Ph.D., 1958; m. Robert N. McColskey, Apr. 12, 1947; children—Anne M., Wendy H., Erin S. Staff psychologist Volusia County Child Guidance Clinic, Daytona Beach, Fla., 1958-59; clin. psychologist, Daytona Beach, 1960-68; sr. clin. psychologist, dir. crisis intervention Escambia County Community Mental Health Center, Pensacola, Fla., 1968-71; asst. prof. Pensacola Jr. Coll., 1972; pvt. practice clin. psychology, Pensacola, 1972—; adj. prof. psychology U. W. Fla., 1969—. Mem. Fla. Psychol. Assn. (sec. 1967-69, treas. 1970-72, pres. 1973-74), Am. Psychol. Assn., Phi Beta Kappa, Phi Kappa Phi. Home: 5790 Avenida Robledal Pensacola FL 32504 Office: 215 N Palafox St Pensacola FL 32501

MCCOMAS, ELIZABETH MAE VEITCH, civic and polit. worker; b. N.M., June 17, 1929; d. Raymond J. and Erminda J. (Fountain) Veitch; R.N., Hotel Dieu Sch. Nursing, El Paso, 1950; student St. Louis U., 1950-52; m. Robert E. McComas, June 4, 1952; children—Robert E. III, Timothy S., Kathryn E., Annmarie M., Mark A., Rachael E., Johanna M. Pct. chairwoman Republican Party, 1961-64; pres. Rep. Fed. Woman's Orgn., 1964-67; co-chmn. N.M. Rep. Party, 1967-69, vice chmn., 1967-71; del., mem. platform com. Rep. Nat. Conv., 1968; mem. Dona Ana City Rep. Exec. Com., N.M. Rep. Central Com., N.M. Rep. Ballot Security Com.; mem. N.M. Constn. Jud. Revision Com., 1964. Mem. U.S. Assay Commn., 1972. Program chmn. N.M. Nurses Assn., 1965, dist. bd. dirs., 1970-73, mem. legislative com.; bd. dirs. Community Concert Assn.; dist. pub. edn. chmn. Am. Cancer Soc.; mem., former water safety chmn. A.R.C. Recipient local and state Rep. awards. Home: Box 436 Mesilla NM 88046

MCCOMBS, BARBARA LEHERISSEY ADOLF, psychologist; b. Galesburg, Ill., Nov. 30, 1942; d. Raymond Louis and Emily Marie (Schulz) Adolf; B.A., Fla. State U., 1967, M.S. in Ednl. Research, 1969, Ph.D. in Ednl. Psychology, 1971; m. George Murray McCombs, Aug. 19, 1972; 1 dau., Heather Rae. Research asso. Fla. State U., Tallahassee, 1969-71; sr. engring. psychologist McDonnell Douglas Corp., St. Louis, 1971—. Mem. Am. Psychol. Assn., Am. Edn. Research Assn., Human Factors Soc. Contbr. articles, papers to profl. publs. Home: 12295 E Bates Circle Denver CO 80232 Office: PO Box 30204 Lowry AFB Denver CO 80230

MCCOMBS, FREDA SILER (MRS. JAMES MCCOMBS), educator; b. Asheville, N.C., Feb. 26, 1933; d. Arthur Allen and Mary Lucille (Pattillo) Siler; B.S. cum laude, Salem Coll., 1955; M.Ed., U. N.C., 1959, Ed.D., 1963; m. James McCombs, June 7, 1962; children—Mary Amanda, Allen Siler, Thomas Philip. Tchr. sci. Woodrow Wilson High Sch., Portsmouth, Va., 1955-56, Franklin (N.C.) High Sch., 1957-58; instr. Longwood Coll., Farmville, Va., 1961-63; asst. prof. Central Va. Community Coll., Lynchburg, 1967-69, asso. prof., 1969-70; asst. prof. Longwood Coll., Farmville, Va., 1970-71, asso. prof. natural scis., 1971—. Cons. for planning 5th and 6th grade TV sci. lessons WCVE-TV, Richmond, Va., 1972—; planning cons. State Elementary Sci. Conf., 1973—. Acad. Year Inst. grantee NSF, 1958-59. Mem. Am. Assn. U. Profs. (sec. 1972-74), A.A.A.S., Am. Educators Tchrs. Sci. Democrat. Roman Catholic. Home: 600 Buffalo St Farmville VA 23901

MCCONNAUGHEY, ESTHER LOIS (MRS. THOMAS ALBERT MCCONNAUGHEY), home economist; b. Eaton, Ind., Apr. 16, 1914; d. Earl and Edna C. (Campbell) Michael; B.S., Ball State U., 1960, M.A., 1964, guidance and counseling license, 1965; m. Thomas Albert McConnaughey, Jan. 24, 1933 (dec. Feb. 1972); children—Hal David, Dana Jane (Mrs. James Bradley Banter), Edna Anne (Mrs. Robert Dennis O'Brien), John Ross. County 4-H leader, county coordinator Blackford County, Purdue U., Ind., 1952-59, home economist, area extension agt., Portland, 1969—; tchr. Muncie Community Schs., (Ind.), 1960-69. Counselor and guidance personnel Muncie Community Schs., 1967-69. Pres. Hartford City council Girl Scouts Am., 1947-50. Mem. Licking County Dem. com., 1945-47. Mem. Am., Ind. home econs. assns., Nat. Assn. Extension Home Econs. Roman Catholic. Office: Extension Office Portland IN 47371 Home: Rural Route Hartford City IN 47348

MCCONNAUGHEY, MARIANNE BELL, lawyer, govt. ofcl.; b. Mar. 22, 1914; d. Robert Cook and Mamie (Collins) Bell; B.Sc., U. Minn., 1935; LL.B., U. Va., 1937; m. Robert K. McConnaughey, Sept. 8, 1941 (dec. 1966); children—Robert S., John B., David T., Terry W. Admitted to D.C. bar, 1937, U.S. Ct. Appeals, 1942, U.S. Supreme Ct. bar, 1948; atty. NLRB, Chgo., 1937-38; atty. antitrust div. Dept. Justice, Washington, 1938-42; office solicitor Dept. Agr., Washington, 1948; staff atty. Bd. Immigration Appeals Dept. Justice, 1948-66, bd. mem., 1966—. Recipient Atty. Gen.'s Spl. Commendation, 1974. Mem. D.C. Bar Assn., Alpha Gamma Delta. Democrat. Episcopalian. Clubs: Chevy Chase (Md.). Home: 5220 Parkway Dr Chevy Chase MD 20015 Office: Dept Justice 12th between E and F Sts NW Washington DC 20015

MCCONNELL, BEVERLY JOY (MRS. JOSEPH M. BATTERSBY), lawyer; b. Chgo., Mar. 10, 1931; d. Robert N. and Beatrice M. (Benyon) McConnell; B.A., U. Ariz., 1953, J.D., 1955; m. Joseph M. Battersby, Dec. 20, 1969; 1 stepdau., Franki M. Admitted to Ariz. bar, 1955; dep. county atty. Pinal County Atty.'s Office, Florence, Ariz., 1955-58; asso. with David Wilson, atty., Phoenix, 1958-60; mem. firm Wilson, McConnell & Moroney and predecessor firm, Phoenix, 1960—. Mem. Comml. Law League Am., State Bar Ariz., Maricopa County Bar Assn. Office: 114 W Adams St Phoenix AZ 85003

MCCONNELL, CATHERINE SANDERS (MRS. CHARLES LEE MCCONNELL), author, ret. bacteriologist; b. Chilhowie, Va., Apr. 14, 1902; d. Marvin and Rachel Graham (Cox) Sanders; grad. So. Sem., 1920, So. Sch. Commerce, 1921; completed course in Med. Tech., U. Va., 1922; m. Charles Lee McConnell, July 22, 1924; children—Charles Lee, Jean Bradley (Mrs. Shankel), Harold Sanders, Kitty Marvin (Mrs. Gerald C. Henninger). Head lab. technician Johnston Meml. Hosp., 1922-25; bacteriologist Va. Dept. Health, 1941-67; chmn. publs. com. Hist. Soc. Washington County, Va., Inc., Abingdon, 1964—. Mem. Am. Legion Womens Aux., D.A.R., Bus. and Profl. Womens Club. Democrat. Presbyn. Author: High on a Windy Hill, 1968; Sanders Saga, 1972. Home: PO Box 153 Abingdon VA 24210 Office: PO Box 484 Abingdon VA 24210

MCCONNELL, DOROTHY FRAISER (MRS. FREDRICK EARL MCCONNELL), coll. dean; b. Cocoa, Fla., Sept. 4, 1924; d. Albert Bateman and Norma (Statzer) Fraiser; student U. Tampa, 1949-51, 55; B.A., Pan Am. Coll., 1956; M. Ed., Auburn U., 1960; Ed.D., Baylor U., 1967; m. Fredrick Earl McConnell, Mar. 29, 1947; children—Lester Earl, Ronald Fraiser, Oma Elizabeth. Bookkeeper, Eelbeck Milling Co., Columbus, Ga., 1942-46; elementary tchr. Harlingen (Tex.) pub. schs., 1954-59, Colquitt County sch. system, Moultrie, Ga., 1959-61, Connally ind. sch. system, Waco, Tex., 1961-65; prof. edn. Mary Hardin-Baylor Coll., Belton, Tex., 1965-69, dean of students, 1969—. Bd. dirs. REACH Center, Belton. Served with WAVES, USNR, 1946-47. Mem. Nat. Ednl. Assn., Tex. State Tchrs. Assn., Am. Assn. for Higher Edn., Nat. League for Nursing, Am., Tex. personnel and guidance assns., Tex. Sch. Counselors Assn., Tex. Soc. Coll. Tchrs. Edn., Am. Assn. U. Women, Ex-Students Assn. Baylor U., Auburn Alumni Assn., Alpha Delta Kappa. Baptist. Address: 2810 Del Norte St Temple TX 76501

MCCONNELL, EMMA JOSEPHINE, educator; b. Collinsville, Okla., Aug. 29, 1930; d. Clayton Devere and Bennie (Chitwood) McConnell; B.A., U. Tulsa, 1951, postgrad. (asst. fellow), 1951-52; M.A., Smith Coll., 1954. Grad. teaching fellow Smith Coll., 1952-54; tchr. Williamsburg (Mass.) Jr. High Sch., 1957, Northampton (Mass.) High Sch., 1957-58, Poughkeepsie Day Sch., 1958-65; dir. secondary edn. Vassar Coll., Poughkeepsie, 1965-74, dir. tchr. preparation, 1969-74, asst. prof. edn., chmn. dept. edn., 1971-74, Mary Conover Mellon House fellow, 1967-70. Lectr., cons. in edn.; evaluator Ednl. Books, 1967—. Active coll., community, summer and children's theatre, 1948-60; chmn. Poughkeepsie Model Cities Edn. Com., 1967-68, adviser, 1968-70. Recipient scholarships, fellowships including Bus. and Profl. Women's scholarship, Tulsa, 1948-51. Mem. Am. Assn. U. Profs., Nat. Soc. Study Edn., Am. Assn. U. Women, N.E.A., N.Y. State Council for Tchrs. English, Nat. Audubon Soc., Nat. Wildlife Assn., Mus. Natural History (asso.). Address: 142 A College Av Poughkeepsie NY 12603

MCCONNELL, GERALDINE ASHLEY (MRS. CONRAD N. MCCONNELL), pharmacist; b. Denver; d. Frederick D. and Mary (Owens) Ashley; B.S., U. Colo., 1950; m. Conrad N. McConnell, Oct. 7, 1950; 1 son, C. Peter. Pharmacist, Rocky Mountain Arsenal, Dept. Army Chem. Corps, 1951-55, VA Outpatient Clinic, Portland, Ore., 1957-68; pharmacy mgr. Crestview Convalescent Hosp., Portland, 1968-73. Mem. community services com. Urban League of Portland, 1964-66, bd. dirs., 1970—, sec. bd., 1972-74; mem. sch. bd. adv. com. Portland Pub. Schs., 1973—. Mem. Ore. Soc. Hosp. Pharmacists, N.A.A.C.P. (life mem.), Alpha Kappa Alpha (award 1966, pres. 1959-61, scholarship chmn. 1957, 60, 62, 64), Jack and Jill of Am. (treas. 1966-67). Club: Links (v.p. 1968, pres. 1969-72). Designed 1st aid kit for Chem. Corps. Home: 3640 N Winchell St Portland OR 97217 Office: VA Outpatient Clinic 426 SW Stark St Portland OR 97202

MCCONNELL, JUDITH DOBSON, lawyer; b. Lincoln, Neb., Feb. 10, 1944; d. Raymond Arnott and Maren Ellen (Dobson) McConnell; B.A., U. Cal. at Berkeley, 1966, J.D., 1969; m. Randall Collins, June 1970; 1 dau., Lindsay Collins. Admitted to Cal. bar, 1970; trial atty. Cal. Dept. Transp., San Diego, 1969—. Adj. prof. law U. San Diego, 1973—; lectr. U. Cal. Extension, San Diego, 1973—. Dir. San Diego County Water Authority, 1973—; mem. Senator James Mills' Adv. Panel on Equal Rights Amendment, 1972. Mem. Nat. Orgn. for Women, San Diego County Bar Assn., Lawyers Club San Diego (pres. 1972-74), Phi Beta Kappa. Home: 3619 Front St San Diego CA 92103 Office: 110 West C St San Diego CA 92101

MCCONNELL, MARY HELEN (MRS. RALPH HUGO SCHWARZKOPF), physician; b. Abingdon, Va., June 11, 1926; d. John Thomas and Helen (Harton) McConnell; A.B., George Washington U., 1947, M.D., 1950; m. Ralph Hugo Schwarzkopf, July 12, 1971; 1 dau., Helen Harton McConnell. Intern Gallinger Municipal Hosp., Washington, 1950-51; resident Children's Hosp., Washington, 1953-54, N.C. Bapt. Hosp., Winston Salem, 1954-55; pvt. practice medicine specializing in pediatrics, Asheville, N.C., 1955—; mem. staffs Meml., St. Josephs, Orthopedic hosps. Mem. A.M.A., N.C., Buncombe County med. socs. Home: Box 92 Route 3 Arden NC 28704 Office: 675 Biltmore Av Asheville NC 28803

MCCONVILLE, FRANCES BORDEN (MRS. DANIEL J. MCCONVILLE, JR.), retail trade co. exec.; b. Boston, Nov. 26, 1918; B.A. cum laude, Radcliffe Coll., 1939; m. Daniel J. McConville, Jr., June 28, 1968. Mgr. consumer products promotion Pfizer, Inc., N.Y.C., 1964-70, cons., 1973—; v.p. McConville, Inc., Ogdensburg, N.Y., 1970—, McConville, Inc. Export Sales Div. chain duty-free shops, Logan Internat. Airport, Boston, Ogdensburg, N.Y., Buffalo, other locations, 1973—. Co-owner, breeder Standardbred racing horses. Served with WAC. Mem. U.S., Canadian trotting assns., North River Power Squadron, Am. Women in Radio and TV. Home: One Dolomite Plaza Ogdensburg NY 13669 also 151 Tremont St Boston MA 02111 also 333 N Ocean Blvd Deerfield Beach FL 33441 Office: McConville Inc One Dolomite Plaza PO Box 500 Ogdensburg NY 13669

MCCORD, JOAN FISH (MRS. CARL SILVER), educator; b. N.Y.C., Aug. 4, 1930; d. Robert and Mildred (Stern) Fish; B.A., Stanford U., 1952, M.A., 1966, Ph.D., 1968; Ed.M., Harvard, 1956; m. William McCord, Mar. 27, 1951 (div. Mar. 1965); children—Geoffrey, Robert; m. 2d, Carl Silver, July 24, 1970. Research asst; Lab. Social Relations, Harvard U., 1953-55, research asst. Lab. Human Devel., 1955-56; research asso. Sociology Dept., Stanford U., co-dir. personality devel. research project, 1959-65; asso. prof. sociology Drexel U., Phila., 1968—. Research asso. Med. Research Found., Palo Alto, Cal., 1964-65; lecturer sociology Stanford U., 1962. Recipient Josiah Royce fellowship Radcliffe, 1957, Stanford Wilson fellowship Stanford U., 1962-63, fellowship NIH, 1965-68. Mem. Am. Sociological Assn. Author: (all with William McCord) Psychopathy and Delinquency, 1956; Origins of Crime, 1959; Origins of Alcoholism, 1960; The Psychopath, 1964. Contbr. articles to profl. pubs. Home: 1279 Montgomery Av Wynnewood PA 19096 Office: 32d and Chestnut Sts Philadelphia PA 19104

MCCORKLE, JEAN SOLARI (MRS. DAVID ALLEN MCCORKLE), pub. relations officer; b. Memphis, July 26, 1950; d. Anthony J. and Mavis (Selby) Solari; A.A., U. Fla., 1970; B.A., Memphis State U., 1972; m. David Allen McCorkle, June 26, 1971. Reporter Comml. Appeal, Memphis, 1971-72; staff writer Connection mag. Memphis Light, Gas and Water, 1972-73, publs. editor, 1973-74, pub. relations officer, 1974—. Mem. Internat. Assn. Bus. Communicators, Women in Communications (chpt. v.p. 1974). Democrat. Roman Catholic. Home: 5323 Scrivener Dr Memphis TN 38134 Office: PO Box 388 Memphis TN 38145

MCCORKLE, LOIS PAKE (MRS. HUGH FAGNANI MCCORKLE), physician; b. Akron, O., Feb. 8, 1927; d. Charles Edward and Gladys Ruth (Thornton) Pake; B.A., Oberlin Coll., 1947; M.D., Western Res. U., 1951; m. Hugh Fagnani McCorkle, Aug. 27, 1949; children—Daniel Charles, Martha Ruth, Georgianna Lynn. Intern Watts Hosp., Durham, N.C., 1951-52; fellow instr. biostatistics Western Res. U., Cleve., 1952-58, USPHS fellow immunohematology, 1955-59, instr., asst. prof. biostatistics, research statistician, 1962-70; biostatistician, dir. dept. University Hosps., Cleve., 1971—. Mem. Research com. Blue Cross of Northeast Ohio, 1969—. Trustee Case Western Res. U. Med. Alumni Asso. Mem. Am. Assn. Blood Banks, Am. Med. Women's Assn., Am. Pub. Health Assn, Phi Beta Kappa, Alpha Omega Alpha. Democrat. Presbyn. Home: 2245 Harcourt Dr Cleveland Heights OH 44106 Office: University Hospitals University Circle Cleveland OH 44106

MCCORMACK, BOBBIE JEANE ROLAND (MRS. PAUL JOSEPH MCCORMACK), physician; b. Houston, Dec. 12, 1934; d. Howard D. and Lois (Neel) Roland; R.N., Bapt. Meml. Hosp. Sch. Nursing, 1955; B.A., Baylor U., 1958; M.D., U. Tex., 1962; m. Paul Joseph McCormack, May 30, 1964; children—Sheila Marie, Karen Lynn, Paul Joseph, David Michael. Rotating intern St. Elizabeth's Hosp., Brighton, Mass., 1962-63; resident in obstetrics, gynecology U. Tex. Med. Br., Galveston, 1963-67, instr., 1967; practice of medicine, specializing in obstetrics and gynecology, Brockton, Mass., 1967—; mem. staff Brockton Hosp. Diplomate Am. Bd. Obstetrics and Gynecology. Fellow Am. Coll. Obstetrics and Gynecology; mem. A.M.A., Am. Med. Women's Assn., Mass., Plymouth County med. socs., Willard R. Cooke Obstet. and Gynecol. Soc., Mu Delta. Address: 5 Crestfield Dr Brockton MA 02402

MCCORMACK, ELIZABETH J., found. exec.; b. N.Y.C., Mar. 7, 1922; d. George H. and Natalie (Duffy) McCormack; B.A., Manhattanville Coll.; M.A., Providence Coll.; Ph.D., Fordham U.; LL.D., Brandeis U., Princeton. Headmistress, Convent Sacred Heart, Greenwich, Conn., 1954-58; asst. to pres. Manhattanville Coll., Purchase, N.Y., 1958-62, acad. dean, 1962-66, pres., 1966-74; found. exec. Rockefeller Bros. Fund, Inc., 1974—. Chmn. commn. on higher edn. Middle States Assn. Coll. and Secondary Schs., 1970—; mem. adv. council N.Y. State Joint Legislative Com. on Higher Edn.; IBM fellowship com. United Negro Coll. Fund. Bd. dirs. Rye (N.Y.) Country Day Sch.; trustee Hampshire Coll.; bd. visitors Coll. City N.Y., Nat. Commn. on Competency-Based Edn. Address: 30 Rockefeller Plaza New York City NY 10020

MCCORMACK, GERALDINE HEATHWOOD (MRS. WILLIAM MICHAEL MCCORMACK), physician; b. N.Y.C., May 21, 1938; d. Charles and Mary Ellen (Burns) Heathwood; B.S., Coll. Mount Saint Vincent, 1960; M.D., State U. N.Y., 1964; m. Wiliam Michael McCormack, June 15, 1963; children—William Michael, Glenn Charles, Charlotte Ann. Intern pediatrics Kings County Hosp. Center, Bklyn., 1964-65; med. adv. Am. consulate, Dacca, East Pakistan (Bangladesh), 1965-68; resident pediatrics Mass. Gen. Hosp., Boston, 1968-70; teaching fellow pediatrics Harvard Med. Sch., Boston, 1968-70; practice medicine specialzing in pediatrics, Melrose, Mass., 1971—; mem. staffs Melrose Wakefield Hosp., Mass. Gen. Hosp., Boston. Home: 56 Lorena Rd Winchester MA 01890 Office: 792 Main St Melrose MA 02176

MCCORMACK, GRACE, microbiologist, educator; b. Rochester, N.Y.; d. Walter and Maud (Brimacomb) McCormack; A.B., U. Rochester, 1941; M.S., U. Md., 1951. Technician, U. Rochester Sch. Medicine and Dentistry-AEC, Rochester, N.Y., 1942-48; bacteriologist U.S. Fish and Wildlife Service, U.S. Dept. Interior, College Park, Md., and East Boston, Mass., 1948-53; asso. bacteriologist Md. Dept. Health, Balt., 1953-55; bacteriologist-technologist VA Hosp., Canandaigua N.Y., 1955-66; faculty dept. biol. scis. Monroe Community Coll., Rochester, N.Y., 1966—, now asso. prof. Recipient Sustained Superior Service award VA Hosp., 1963. Fellow Royal Soc. Health (Eng.), Am. Inst. Chemists; mem. Soc. Microbiologists, Am. Chem. Soc., Am. Pub. Health Assn., Inst. Food Technologists, A.A.A.S., Am. Inst. Biol. Scis., N.Y. Acad. Scis. Contbr. numerous articles to profl. jours. Home: 162 Raleigh St Rochester NY 14620

MCCORMACK, MARJORIE HARRIS (MRS. F.A. MCCORMACK), osteo. physician; b. Murphysboro, Ill., Mar. 24, 1915; d. George W. and Mary S. (Piquard) Harris; B.S., Ark. State U., 1952; D.O., Kansas City Coll. Osteopathic Medicine, 1958; m. F.A. McCormack, May 10, 1936. Intern, Osteo. Hosp., Kansas City, Mo., 1963-64; pvt. practice osteopathic medicine, Bernie, Mo., 1959-64, Malden, Mo., 1964—; co-owner Country Aire Smorgasbord, Murphysboro, 1968—. Mem. Am., Mo. osteo. assns., Internat. Platform Assn., Delta Omega. Home: RFD 3 Murphysboro IL 62966 Office: 201 N Decatur St Malden MO 63863

MCCORMACK, PATRICIA SEGER (MRS. DONALD P. MCCORMACK), editor; b. Pitts.; d. Arthur J. and Anna (McCaffrey) Seger; B.A., U. Pitts., 1949; m. Donald P. McCormack, Apr. 28, 1951; 1 son, Christopher Paul. News editor Mt. Lebanon News, Pitts., 1951-53; reporter, med. editor Pitts. Sun-Telegraph, 1953-57; asst. sci. information dir. Nat. Found., N.Y.C., 1957; med. sci. editor Internat. News Service (merger with UPI 1958), 1957-60, columnist, 1960—, family news editor, 1972. Recipient George Washington Honor medal Freedoms Found., 1953; Biennial Nat. Media award Family Service Assn. Am., 1960. Mem. A.A.A.S., Nat. Assn. Sci. Writers, Mortar Bd., Pi Delta Epsilon. Club: New York Newspaperwomen's. Home: 45 Marion Rd Westport CT 06880 Office: 220 E 42d St New York City NY 10017

MCCORMACK, REGINA CLAIRE, physician, educator; b. Bayonne, N.J., Apr. 30, 1928; d. Joseph T. and Marcella E. (Earle) McCormack; B.A. in Math., Coll. New Rochelle, 1949; B.S. in Nursing, Cornell U., 1952, M.D., 1958. Intern, Cornell U.-N.Y. Hosp. Med. Center, 1958-59; resident U. Va. Hosp., Charlottesville, 1959-60; staff physician Boston VA Hosp., also asst. medicine Tufts U. Sch. Medicine, 1963-64; instr. preventive medicine and internal medicine U. Va. Sch. Medicine, Charlottesville, 1964-66, asst. prof., 1966-69, asso. prof., 1969-72, dir. USPHS apprenticeship tng. program, 1965-72, dir. med. care and community medicine program, 1965-72, clin. asso. prof. internal medicine, 1972—; pvt. practice internal medicine, Charlottesville; vis. asso. prof. community medicine Albert Einstein Coll. Medicine, 1970-71; spl. asst. Montefiore Hosp. and Med. Center, Bronx, N.Y., 1970-71. Milbank Meml. Fund faculty fellow, 1967. Fellow Am. Pub. Health Assn., Am. Coll. Preventive Medicine, A.C.P.; mem. Am. Fedn. Clin. Research, Am. Heart Assn., Assn. Am. Med. Colls., Assn. Tchrs. Preventive Medicine, Va., Albemarle County med. socs., Va. Pub. Health Assn., N.Y. Acad. Scis., Sigma Theta Tau. Contbr. articles in field to profl. jours. Home: Route 3 Box 30 Flordon Dr Charlottesville VA 22901

MCCORMACK, SARAH MILLER, ret. med. social worker; b. Stanford, Ky.; d. Augustus and Laura (Messer) McCormack; student Fugazzi Bus. Coll., 1928-29, Ky. Wesleyan Coll., 1931-32; A.B., U. Ky., 1936; M.S.W., U. Louisville, 1949. Legal sec., Lexington, Ky., 1929-30; elementary tchr., Stanford, 1933-35; tchr. Goshen (O.) High Sch., 1936-40; office sec. U. Ky., 1940-46; clk. VA Regional Office, Louisville, 1946-47; med. social worker Cook County Hosp., Chgo., 1949-50, Commn. for Handicapped Children, Lexington, 1950-73. Bd. dirs. Cardinal Hill Nursery Sch. for Handicapped Children, Lexington, also various local health orgns. Mem. Nat. Assn. Social Workers (local sec. 1950—), Acad. Certified Social Workers, Ky. Welfare Assn., Ky. Soc. for Crippled Children, Am. Angus Assn., Lexington Bus. and Profl. Women's Club (Woman of Achievement award 1974), Ky. Edn. Assn., Bluegrass Organic and Consumer Assn., Meadowthorp P.T.A. Methodist. Home: 109 Hamilton Park Lexington KY 40504

MCCORMICK, ADOREEN MARY, govt. ofcl.; b. Helena, Mont., Aug. 20, 1936; d. Walter Nelson and Cecilia Adoreen (Burke) McCormick; B.A., Seattle U., 1958; M.A., Georgetown U., 1962. Information and editorial asst. Library of Congress, Washington, 1958-59, information and editorial specialist, 1959-60, adminstrv. asst., 1960-61, spl. asst., 1961-66, legislative liaison officer, 1966—. Pres., 4000 Tunlaw Rd. Tenants Assn., 1971—. Mem. D.C. Library Assn., Kappa Gamma Pi. Contbr. articles to profl. jours. Home: 4000 Tunlaw Rd Nw Washington DC 20007 Office: Office Asst Librarian Library of Congress Washington DC 20540

MCCORMICK, DOROTHY FRANKLIN (MRS. RICHARD HARRISON MCCORMICK), editor; b. Tacoma, Dec. 9, 1906; d. Clarence James and Alma Mae (Brewer) Franklin; student U. Ore., 1926-29; m. Richard Harrison McCormick, Aug. 15, 1931; 1 dau., Jean. Reporter, Jour. Commerce, Portland, Ore., 1929-31, part-time editor, 1931-44; editor Northwest Constrn. News, constrn. news editor PBE, Pacific Builder and Engr., Seattle, 1952—. Free lance pub. relations work. Mem. Women in Constrn. (Seattle pres. 1962-63), Women in Communications. Republican. Presbyn. Club: Soroptimist (Seattle). Home: 3619 13th W Seattle WA 98119 Office: 109 W Mercer St Seattle WA 98119

MCCORMICK, DOROTHY MAY LAMKIN (MRS. JOHN SHERIDAN MCCORMICK, JR.), state legislator; b. Greenwich, Conn., May 3, 1932; d. Harold Otis and Frances (Bing) Lamkin; student Farmington Tchrs. Coll., 1951; m. John Sheridan McCormick, Jr., July 8, 1952; children—Bonny, Scott, Patricia, Kathleen, Christopher, Jeffery, Karen. Saleswoman, Consol. Real Estate & Engring. Co., 1969—; mem. Me. Ho. of reps., 1971—. Mem. Knox County Republican Com., 1968—. Trustee Knox County Gen. Hosp. Named Me. Homemaker of Year, 1972. Mem. Grange. Club: Union Woman's Community. Home: Box 422 Union ME 04862

MCCORMICK, HOPE BALDWIN (MRS. BROOKS MCCORMICK), polit. party ofcl.; b. N.Y.C., July 9, 1919; d. Alexander Taylor and Loise (Bisbee) Baldwin; student Ethel Walker Sch., Simsbury, Conn.; m. Brooks McCormick, June 26, 1940; children—Martha (Mrs. William O. Hunt, Jr.), Brooks, Mark B., Abby D. Mem. Ill. Ho. of Reps., 1965-67; Republican Nat. committeewoman for Ill., 1968—. Past mem. women's bd. Children's Meml. Hosp., Lyric Opera; founder, past pres. Ill. Epilepsy League; mem. women's bd. Rush-Presbyn.-St. Luke's Med. Center, Art Inst. of Chgo., Field Mus. Natural History. Chmn. women's div. United Republican Fund, 1957-61; past pres. Rep. Citizens Com. of 9th Congl. Dist., 1961-66; bd. govs. United Rep. Fund of Ill., Recording for the Blind; exec. com. Ill. Fedn. Rep. Women; mem. exec. com. Rep. Nat. Com., 1971-72, vice chmn., 1972—. Trustee Ill. Children's Home and Aid Soc., Mus. Sci. and Industry, MacMurray Coll. Address: 1530 N State Pkwy Chicago IL 60610

MCCORMICK, JO MARY, art critic, journalist, editor, artist, author; b. N.Y.C., Mar. 6, 1918; d. Mochichika and Bridget Anne (McCormick) Sakurai; student Columbia, 1947-55, Art Students League, Nat. Acad. Design. Feature editor N. Am. News Corp., N.Y.C., 1952-56; woman's page editor The Rural New Yorker mag., 1959-61; art critic Pictures on Exhibit mag., 1959—; exhibited in group shows Burr Gallery, Barzansky Galleries, Gallery East; columnist Of Life and Books in N. Am. News, 1952—, New York column newspaper, 1971; book reviewer N.Y. Times, 1971; editor Bus. and Commercial Aviation mag., 1969-72. Founder, pres., bd. dirs. Good Samaritan's Awards. Mem. Women's Land Army U.S. Crop Corps War Food Adminstrn., 1944. Mem. Art Students League (life), Alumni Assn. Columbia, Women's Press Club, Women's Internat. Assn. Aeros. Contbr. articles to nat. profl. mags.; lectr. in field. Home: 444 2d Av New York City NY 10010

MCCORMICK, SISTER MARY JOHN ALOYSE, educator; b. Phila., Mar. 3, 1910; d. John Aloysius and Mary Elizabeth (King) McCormick; B.A., Rosemont Coll., 1931; postgrad. U. Pa., 1931, Pierce Bus. Coll., 1931-32; M.A. in Latin, Villanova U., 1943, postgrad., 1950, 53; Ph.D., Catholic U. Am., 1964; postgrad. U. Laval (Que., Can.), 1951. Joined Congregation of Religious Sisters of Mercy, 1933; instr. Cath. high schs., 1935-48; faculty Gwynedd-Mercy Coll., Gwynedd Valley, Pa., 1948-59, prof. classics, chmn. dept., 1964-72, dir. admissions, 1964-68, registrar, 1948-59; rare book librarian Ryan Meml. Library, St. Charles Borromeo Sem., Overbrook, Pa.; asst. coordinator retirement program Sisters of Mercy. Translations of Latin, French and Greek. Address: Convent of Sisters of Mercy 515 Montgomery Av Merion Station PA 19066

MCCORVEY, BARBARA JEAN (MRS. WILLIAM H. MCCORVEY, SR.), constrn. co. exec.; b. Montgomery, Ala., Sept. 30, 1939; d. Carl G. and Thelma Jane (Thackston) Edgar; student Modern Bus. Acad., 1958; student Auburn U., Montgomery; m. William H. McCorvey, Sr., July 17, 1958; children—William H., Bradley S., Barton E. Asst. sec.-treas. Stallings & McCorvey, Inc., Montgomery, 1967—. Mem. Planning and Devel. Bd., City of Montgomery, 1973—; precinct worker Republican party, 1972-73. Bd. dirs. Cystic Fibrosis Assn., 1970-73, publicity chmn., 1973—. Mem. Ladies Aux. Asso. Gen. Contractors Am. (chpt. pres. 1973—). Club: Christian Womens (v.p. 1973—, dir. 1972—) (Montgomery, Ala.). Home: 3535 Dalraida Ct Montgomery AL 36107 Office: PO Box 7029 Montgomery AL 36107

MCCOSKEY, JEAN MENDYK (MRS. RICHARD L. MCCOSKEY), savs. and loan exec.; b. West Hammond, Ill., Sept. 26, 1917; d. Anton and Kyrstyna (Glosek) Mendyk; student Hartnett's Bus. Coll., Hammond, Ind., 1944-45, Am. Savings and Loan Inst., Chgo., 1961-66; m. Richard L. McCoskey, May 30, 1946. Sec. to Postmaster, Post Office Dept., Hammond, Ind., 1943-55; asst. sec.-treas., asst. mgr. Lake Fed. Savs. and Loan Assn., Hammond, 1957—. Mem. Order of the Amaranth, Inc.; Order Eastern Star. Mem. First Ch. of Christ (sec. ladies orgn. 1955-58). Club: American Business Women's (treas. 1972-73) Chicago Heights, Ill.). Home: 8850 Woodward Av Highland IN 46322 Office: 7048 Kennedy Av Hammond IN 46323

MCCOTTER, MARGARET ROSEMOND PALMER (MRS. BURNEY RICHARD MCCOTTER), librarian; b. Thomasville, N.C., Nov. 7, 1921; d. Jacob Alexander and Etna (Little) Palmer; A.B., Catawba Coll., 1942; B.S. in L.S., U. N.C., 1944; m. Burney Richard McCotter, June 21, 1946; children—Richard Palmer, Karen Ellen. Librarian, Southern Pines (N.C.) Sch. System, 1944-47; post librarian Fort Story (Va.), 1950-51; librarian LeRoy Martin Jr. High Sch., Raleigh, N.C., 1959-62, 65—; library cons. N.C. Dept. Pub. Instrn., Raleigh, 1963-65. Mem. N.E.A., U.D.C., N.C. Library Assn., N.C. Assn. Educators, N.C. Soc. for Preservation of Antiquities, Delta Kappa Gamma, Beta Phi Mu, Sigma Pi Alpha. Democrat. Presbyn. Club: Carolina Country (Raleigh). Joint author AV Cataloging and Processing Simplified, 1971. Editor: Reference Materials for School Libraries, 1965. Home: 332 Buncombe St Raleigh NC 27609 Office: 1701 Ridge Rd Raleigh NC 27607

MCCOURT, DELMA CHANEY, extension home economist; b. New Athens, O., July 20, 1916; d. Willis Craig and Clairbel (Sparrow) Chaney; B.Sc., Ohio State U., 1940; M.Sc., Ariz. State U., 1961; m. Eskeridge A. McCourt, June 8, 1941. Home economist Farmers Home Adminstrn., various counties, 1940-45; home econs. agt. W.Va. U., Wellsburg, 1945-54, Ohio State U., Steubenville, 1964—. Mem. Electric Women's Round Table, Ohio County Extension Agts. Assn., Am., Jefferson County, Ohio home econs. assns. Club: Goodwill Garden. Home: 132 Walker Rd Follansbee WV 26037 Office: Federal Bldg Steubenville OH 43952

MCCOWN, JEAN MACQUARRIE (MRS. CYRUS B. MCCOWN), social worker; b. Pitts.; d. David P. and Bertha (Culbertson) MacQuarrie; A.B., Muskingum Coll., 1933; M.S.W., U. Pitts., 1938; m. Cyrus B. McCown, May 30, 1937; children—Joseph Robert, Sara Jean (Mrs. Samuel K. Dogbe), Mary Hallie (Mrs. Robert M. O'Brien). Caseworker, Family Soc., Pitts., 1935-38; caseworker Travelers Aid Soc., Los Angeles, 1953-56, supr., 1956-57, dist. dir., 1957-68; psychiat. social worker Family Service of Rio Hondo Area, Whittier, Cal., 1969-72; caseworker Family Service and Children's Aid, Jackson, Mich., 1972—. Mem. Nat. Assn. Social Workers, Acad. Certified Social Workers. Democrat. Presbyn. Home: 1010 S Brown St Jackson MI 49203 Office: 729 W Michigan Av Jackson MI 49201

MCCOY, EVA LEAH ROBINSON (MRS. WILLIAM E. MCCOY), social worker; b. Marion, Ill., Feb. 2, 1930; d. James Harry and Della (McGough) Robinson; B.A., Bapt. Mission Tng. Sch., 1953; m. William E. McCoy, Dec. 16, 1953; children—Paula Christine and Patricia Kathleen (twins). Program dir. Emmanuel Christian Center, Bklyn., 1954-55; caseworker Gallia County Child Welfare, 1966-67; acting dir. social services Gallipolis State Inst., Gallipolis, O., 1967-74, admissions worker, 1974—. Pres. elementary P.T.A., Rio Grande, O., 1967-68. Mem. Nat. Assn. Social Workers, Ohio State Social Workers, Am. Assn. Mental Deficiency, Gallia Assn. Chs. (charter bd. mem. 1965). Baptist (pres. bd. Christian edn. 1961-62, 72—). Club: Writers. Home: Box 109-B Route 2 Bidwell OH 45614 Office: Gallipolis State Inst Gallipolis OH 45631

MCCOY, GLADYS SIMS (MRS. WILLIAM MCCOY), educator; b. Atlanta, Feb. 28, 1928; d. Willie Tilman and Lucille (Duke) Sims; B.A., Talladega Coll., 1949; M.S.W., Portland State U., 1967; m. William McCoy, Feb. 28, 1951; children—Krista A., William A., Paul T., Mary M., Cecilia R., Peter J., Martha L. Teen-age program dir. YWCA, Portland, Ore., 1949-51; program coordinator, sch. affiliation service Am. Friends Service Com., Portland, 1963; camp dir. Jewish Community Day Camp, Portland, 1966; dir. social services Vancouver (Wash.) Headstart, 1967-70; instr. sociology Clark Coll., Vancouver, 1970-71; asst. prof. sociology Pacific U., Forest Grove, Ore., 1971—. Mem. Portland Sch. Bd., 1970-74; del. Democratic nat. conv., 1972. Mem. Western Interstate Commn. for Higher Edn., 1973—. Recipient Charlotte Chapman Turner award Am. Friends Service Com., 1965. Mem. Nat. Assn. Social Workers, Urban League. Home: 6650 N Amherst St Portland OR 97203 Office: Pacific U Forest Grove OR 97116

MCCOY, IDELLA MARIA THERESA BROWN (MRS. GENE GUY MCCOY), bus. exec.; b. Woodriver, Ill., July 21, 1928; d. Mayo Clinton and Loretta (Weisaupt) Brown; student Shurtleff Coll., Ill., 1946-48; m. Gene Guy McCoy, Aug. 8, 1948; children—Gene Guy III, Vicki V., Randall R., S. Sherman. Prodn. mgr. Ad Craft of Ark., Inc., Little Rock, 1958, sec.-treas., 1958-65, exec. v.p., 1965—. Residential chmn. United Fund Pulaski County, 1962-63, pub. relations, 1969. Mem. Am. Advt. Fedn. (dir. S.W. dist. 1969—), Little Rock Advt. Club (pres. 1970-71), Gamma Alpha Chi (Spl. Service award 1969). Home: 12000 Rivercrest Dr Little Rock AR 72207 Office: 1122 W 3d St Little Rock AR 72201

MCCOY, KATHLEEN LYNNE, editor; b. Dayton, O., Apr. 25, 1945; d. James Lyons and Ethel Elizabeth (Curtis) McCoy; B.S. in Journalism, Northwestern U., 1967, M.S. in Mag. Journalism, 1968. Faculty, Flintridge Sacred Heart Acad., Pasadena, Cal., 1959-63; free lance writer, 1965—; feature editor 'TEEN Mag., Los Angeles, 1968—. Frequent guest various TV, radio talk shows. Recipient award for article research Readers Digest, 1966. Mem. Com. Single Taxpayers, Screen Actors Guild, Am. Guild Variety Artists, Am.

Fedn. TV and Radio Artists, Nat. Orgn. Women, Women in Communications, Sigma Delta Chi. Democrat. Roman Catholic. Home: 4420 Los Feliz Blvd Los Angeles CA 90027 Office: Teen Mag 8490 Sunset Blvd Los Angeles CA 90069

MCCOY, LEAHMAE, educator; b. Chgo., Sept 3, 1912; d. Charles Raymond and Florence (Berry) Brown; A.B., U. Kan., 1933; M.A., Tufts U., 1935; Ph.D., U. Ill., 1937; m. Charles F. McCoy (div.); children—Barry Malcolm, Jan Salter, John Raymond (dec.), Catherine. Research asst. dept. econs. Princeton, 1937-39; mem. faculty dept. econ. U. Ariz., Tucson, 1953—, asso. prof., 1964-69, prof., 1970—, dir. grad. studies Coll. Bus. Adminstrn., 1973—. Cons. elderly, physically handicapped econ. problems. Recipient Standard Oil Found. Good Teaching award, 1969. Mem. Am., Western econ. assns., Econ. History Assn., Western Regional Sci. Assn., A.A.A.S., Phi Beta Kappa, Phi Kappa Phi, Beta Gamma Sigma. Contbr. profl. jours. Home: 4037 E 4th St Tucson AZ 85711

MCCOY, MARY HILLE, home economist; b. Balt., Jan. 11, 1920; d. George Price and Mabel Hille (Jones) McCoy; B.S., Longwood Coll., 1941; M.S., U. Wis., 1956; postgrad. U. Ark., 1955-56, George Washington U., 1961. Tchr. home econs. Fairfax (Va.) High Sch., 1941-49; home demonstration agt. Loudon County, Va., 1949-54; dist. home demonstration agt at large Va. Poly. Inst., Blacksburg, 1954-58, dist. agt. east central dist., 1958-67, program leader home econs. E. central dist., Va., 1967—. Recipient farm found. fellow. U. Wis., 1955. Mem. Am., Va. home econs. assns., Va. Extension Agts. Assn., Adult Edn. Assn. Va., Pi Lambda Theta, Epsilon Sigma Phi (sec. 1966-67). Methodist. Home: Box 592 Appomattox VA 24522 Office: Dist Extension Office Appomattox VA

MCCOY, TERESA MARIE, occupational therapist; b. Phila., Mar. 25, 1909; s. Joseph Jerome and Claire Josephine (Tinaro) McCoy; B.S., N.Y. U., 1952; M.A. (Nat. Found. fellow), U. So. Cal., 1959. Cons. nursing home program Ohio Dept. Health, Columbus, asst. prof. occupational therapy Ohio State U., Columbus, 1961-65; dir. occupational therapy assts. program Mt. Aloysius Jr. Coll., Cresson, Pa., 1965-67; occupational therapist, coordinator field programs Tufts U.-Boston Sch. Occupational Therapy, 1969—. Cons. nursing homes, adult aphasia. Mem. Am. (chmn. ad hoc com. on guidelines/occupational therapy asst. programs 1969-71), Mass. (council on standards) occupational therapy assns., World Fedn. Occupational Therapists. Home: 213 Washington Lane Jenkintown PA 19046 Office: 136 Harrison Av Boston MA 02111

MCCRACKEN, BOBBIE ADKINS (MRS. WILLIAM O. MCCRACKEN), civic worker; b. Clarksville, Ark., May 15, 1920; d. Robert E. and Elzada (Storm) Adkins; student Coll. Ozarks, 1937-41, Am. Conservatory of Music, Chgo., 1944, U. Ark., 1943; postgrad. U. Ark., 1969-70; m. William O. McCracken, Apr. 13, 1945; 1 dau., Kay Lynn. Clk., Ark. State Selective Service System, 1941-46; sec., clk. FBI, 1940; tchr. Little Rock Pub. Sch. System, 1953-54; v.p. McCracken Realty Co. Pres., Little Rock Dist. Ark. Fedn. Women's Clubs, 1966—, state bd. dirs.; pres. Meml. chpt. U.D.C., 1966—, Ark. Pioneers Pulaski County Assn., 1967—; mem. President's Com. on Safety, 1959-62, Gov.'s Commn. on Status of Women; v.p. Sears Civic Center; chmn. Gov.'s Commn. Ark. Childrens Hosp.; adviser to Dept. of Def., 1973—; ofcl. County of Pulaski Magistrate's Ct., 1973—; bd. mem. Ark. Safety Commn.; mem. Gov.'s Consumer Affairs Commn., State Econs. Commn.; adv. bd. Ark. Nurses Assn., 1972—. Mem. Ark. Women in Pub. Affairs (pres. 1970—), Greater Little Rock Fedn. Women's Clubs (past pres.), Pulaski Bus. and Profl. Women's Clubs (past pres.), Nat. Jr. Fedn. Music Clubs (past pres.). Clubs: Women's City (pres. 1968-70, 1st pres. 1969-70, dir. 1972—, editor directory 1972), Women's (organizer, treas. 1973-74) (Little Rock); Ark. Aero. Home: 90 Indian Trail Little Rock AR 72207

MCCRACKEN, EVA HENNEN, clubwoman; b. New Orleans, Apr. 24, 1908; d. John Clark and Eva Harding (Buddecke) McCracken; student Soule Bus. Coll., 1926. Cashier, Columbia Theatre, Hammond, La., 1926-30; mgr. Globe Indsl. Loan Co., Hammond, 1930-34; legal sec., Hammond, 1934-64; owner, operator income tax service, Hammond, 1964—. Mem. adv. bd. to local Draft Bd., 1942-45; sec. Hammond United Givers Fund, 1960—; mem. Tangipahoa Parish Council of Aging, 1963—. Pres. Aux. B. Grace Meml. Episcopal Ch., 1951, sec. St. Elizabeth Guild, 1972—; pres. Hammond Lioness Club, 1954; organizer, 1st pres. Hammond Bus. and Profl. Women's Club, 1956-58; state rec. sec. Soc. Mayflower Descs., 1960—. Named Bus. Woman of Yr., Hammond Bus. and Profl. Womens Club, 1959. Mem. Am. Assn. Ret. Persons, Assn. Profl. Notaries, S.E. La. Hist. Assn. Home: 411 E Charles Av Hammond LA 70401 Office: Guaranty Bank Bldg 100 E Thomas St Hammond LA 70401 also PO Box 608 Hammond LA 70401

MCCRACKEN, SALLY ROSE, educator; b. Cambridge, O., Aug. 24, 1942; d. Arthur James and Lavena Faye (Orr) McCracken; B.A., Muskingum Coll., 1964; M.A., Bowling Green State U., 1965; Ph.D., Wayne State U., 1968. Instr. Wayne State U., 1967-68; asso. prof. speech communications Eastern Mich. U., Ypsilanti, 1968—, chief negotiator with Am. Assn. U. Profs., 1974; cons. in field. Chmn. bd. dirs. Theatre Co. Ann Arbor, Mich., 1972-73; Recipient Excellence in Teaching award Eastern Mich. U., 1969. Wolfram fellow, 1966-68. Mem. Speech Communication Assn., Internat. Communications Assn., A.A.A.S., Central States Speech Assn. (program developer 1973-74). Contbr. articles to profl. jours. Home: 13348 Wales St Huntington Woods MI 48070 Office: 134 Quirk Hall Eastern Mich Univ Ypsilanti MI 48197

MCCRACKEN, URSULA NAYLOR ELAND (MRS. EDWARD PHILLIP MCCRACKEN), mus. editor; b. N.Y.C., Jan. 31, 1942; d. Michael John Naylor and Ursula Ellen Mary (Brockwell) Eland; B.A. (scholar), Wellesley Coll., 1963; m. Edward Phillip McCracken, Sept. 26, 1964. Curatorial asst. Albright-Knox Art Gallery, Buffalo, 1963-64; editor publs. Walters Art Gallery, Balt., 1965—. Mem. Balt. Bibliophiles. Editor: Gatherings in Honor of Dorothy E. Miner, Baltimore, 1974. Home: 3024 N Calvert St Baltimore MD 21218 Office: Walters Art Gallery 600 N Charles St Baltimore MD 21201

MCCRANE, RUTH MAE, artist, educator; b. Corpus Christi, Tex., Jan. 18, 1929; d. Henry and Blanche (Labostrie) McCrane; B.A., Tex. So. U., 1952, M.A., 1955; student Nat. Gallery Art, Geroge Washington U.; Ed.D., Ohio St. Matthew U., 1971; Ed.D. (hon.), Mt. Sinai U. and Theol. Sem., 1971. Tchr. English to refugees, Houston, 1950-51; head art dept., instr. Spanish, Jarvis Christian Coll., Hawkins, Tex., 1952-54; became instr. art edn. Tex. So. U., 1954; tchr. art and Spanish L.C. Anderson High Sch., Austin, Tex., also dir. mural and scenery Pan Am. Dance Recitals; head art dept. Booker T. Washington Jr.-Sr. High Sch., Houston; headed Jr. Art Workshop, Houston, 1959—; instr. art G.C. Scarborough Jr.-Sr. High Sch., Houston, 1970—; illustrator lit. on audio-visual transparencies; works exhibited Tex. So. U., Jarvis Christian Coll., Bishop Coll., 5th Houston Post Easter Exhbn., Mus. Fine Arts Houston, Tex. So. U. Pharm. Auditorium; Catholic Newman Hall Center, Houston, Jerusalem Missionary Bapt. Ch., Amanda Dixon Library and Lonnie B. Smith Library, Houston; executed murals for Jarvis Christian Coll., 1952, New Hope Bapt. Ch., Hawkins, 1953, Tex. So. U., 1955, Imperial Club, Houston, St. Elizabeth's Hosp., St. Nicholas Sch., Houston, United Ministry Bldg. and Main Bldg., Tex. So. U., Morning Star Bapt. Church Houston; relief work 34th St. Meth. Ch., Our Mother of Mercy, Houston, art dir. stage prodns. 1954; dir. dance groups, 1952-54; adv. bd. Newman Hall Tex. State U. Treas. St. Elizabeth Hosp. Guild. Mem. Art in Am. Soc., Tex., Central Tex. Dist. tchrs. assns., Coll. Classroom Tchrs. Assn., Assn. Study Negro Life and History, N.E.A., Houston Classroom Tchrs.' Assn., Tex. Assn. Tchrs., Nat. Geog. Soc., Internat. Platform Assn., Austin Edn. Assn., Western Tex. art assns., Nat. Art Edn. Assn., Houston Art Tchrs. Assn., Nat. Council Negro Women, Nat. Alliance Postal Employees, Alpha Kappa Mu, Sigma Gamma Rho (del. Southwestern Regional, Dallas 1959). Roman Catholic. Illustrator: A Simplified Spanish Guide, 1972. Author audiovisual materials: Bilingual-Environment Art Education Curriculum, 1974. Home: 5622 Weaver Rd Houston TX 77016

MCCRARY, EUGENIA LESTER (MRS. DENNIS DAUGHTRY MCCRARY), civic worker; b. Annapolis, Md., Mar. 23, 1929; d. John Campbell and Eugenia (Potts) Lester; A.B. cum laude, Radcliffe Coll., 1950; M.A., Johns Hopkins, 1952; postgrad. Harvard, spring 1953, Pa. State U., 1953-54, Drew U., 1957-58; m. John Campbell Howard, July 15, 1955. (dec. Sept. 1965); m. 2d, Dennis Daughtry McCrary, June 28, 1969. Grad. asst. dept. romance langs. Pa. State U., 1953-54; tchr. dept. math. The Brearley Sch., N.Y.C., 1954-57; dir. Sch. Langs., Inc., Summit, N.J., 1958-69, trustee, 1960-69. Dist. chmn. Eastern regional auditions Nat. Council, Met. Opera Nat. Council, N.Y.C., 1960-66, dist. dir. publicity, 1966-67, nat. vice chmn. publicity, 1967-71, nat. chmn. pub. relations, 1972—. Mem. Nat. Soc. Colonial Dames, Jr. League Summit, N.J. Mem. Playhouse Assn. Summit, Inc., Met. Opera Nat. Council, Mayflower Soc., Pi Lambda Theta. Republican. Episcopalian. Clubs: Radcliffe of New Jersey (bd. dirs. 1957-69, pres. 1958-60) (Summit); Colony, Radcliffe (N.Y.C.); Harvard. Home: 24 Central Park S New York City NY 10019

MCCRARY, MARTHA ELIZABETH, cons.; b. Cleve.; d. William John and Emma Sophia (Baehr) Pohle; R.N., Met. Gen. Hosp., 1925; B.S., Ohio State U., 1937; M.S. in Nursing, Case Western Res. U., 1952; m. Harry Barkalow McCrary, Oct. 17, 1925; 1 son, Ralph W. Dir. nursing Elyria (O.) Meml. Hosp., 1940-42; chief nurse br. office VA, Phila., 1946-49, Brecksville VA Hosp., Cleve., 1949-69; program planner Northeast Ohio Regional Med. Program, Cleve., 1969—. Commr. on Ohio Gov's. Council for Nursing, Columbus, 1973-75. Bd. dirs. Council Post Retirement Inst., Case Western Res. U., 1972-74. Served to lt. col. Army Nurse Corp, 1942-45. Named Woman of Year VA, 1956. Mem. Cleve. Area League for Nursing (pres. 1973), Res. Army Officers Assn. (nat. v.p. 1961-62), Women's Overseas League, Am. Nurses Assn., Am. Legion, Ret. Officers Assn., Res. Officers Assn. (state council 1960—, dir. 1965-74), League Women Voters, Sigma Theta Tau. Club: Zonta (Cleve.). Address: 6712 Stafford Dr Mayfield Heights OH 44124

MCCRARY, MARY JANE KING (MRS. CARL MCCRARY), historian; b. Brevard, N.C.; d. Alexander Henry and Hessie (Clayton) King; student Furman U. (formerly Greenville Woman's Coll.), 1915-17; Mus. Arts, Tift Coll., 1918; m. Hugh R. Walker, Oct. 1, 1920 (dec.); children—John S., Jane (Mrs. Jon T. Freeman); m. 2d, Carl McCrary, Jan. 20, 1931; children—Thomas K., Martha (Mrs. Joseph W. McGuire, Jr.). Tchr. pub. sch. music, Brevard Schs., 1923-25; owner, mgr. Walker Ins. Agy., 1929-57; pres. Brevard Bd. of Realtors, 1964-65; mem. Nat. Real Estate Bd. County chmn. blood com. A.R.C.; mem. N.C. Am. Revolution Bicentennial Commn., N.C. Confederate Centennial Commn.; chmn. Transylvania County Hist. Commn., 1960—. Recipient blue, purple ribbons for paints, ceramic works. Mem. Cherokee Hist. Assn. (mem. exec. bd.), Nat. Soc. Am. Colonists, D.A.R., League Am. Pen Women (pres.), N.C., Western N.C. hist. assns. Episcopalian. Home: 228 Maple St Brevard NC 28712 Office: 37 W Jordan St Brevard NC 28712

MCCRAY, MARY ANNICE, librarian; b. Waterford, Pa., May 24, 1918; d. Rollo and Annice Gertrude (Ensworth) McCray; B.A., Mercyhurst Coll., 1940; B.S. in L.S., Western Res. U., 1941. Reference asst. reference dept. Toldeo Pub. Library, 1941-43; asst., reference dept. Warder Pub. Library, Springfield, O., 1943-49; librarian children's dept. Bklyn. Pub. Library, 1950-51, reference librarian Crown Heights br., 1951-53; head reference dept. Erie (Pa.) Pub. Library, 1954—. Mem. Am., Pa. (chmn. N.W. dist. 1964-65) library assns., Erie County Hist. Soc., Mental Health Assn. Erie County, Arts Council of Erie, Erie Art Center. Home: 9 E 33d St Erie PA 16504 Office: 3 S Perry Sq Erie PA 16507

MCCREA, JOAN MARIE RYAN (MRS. ALOYSIUS MCCREA), educator; b. Chgo., Jan. 24, 1922; d. Alexander Charles and Sophia (Hagan) Ryan; B.A., Ind. U., 1942; M.A., U. Cal. at Los Angeles, 1958; Ph.D., U. Cal. at Los Angeles, 1965; m. James Aloysius McCrea, Jan. 26, 1946. Instr. econs. U. Cal. at Riverside, 1958-60; asst. prof. econs. Hollins Coll., 1960-65; asso. prof. econs. U. Tex., Arlington, 1966—. Mem. Am. Assn. U. Profs., Am., Western econ. assns., Indsl. Research Assn., Rocky Mountain Social Sci. Assn., Mensa. Democrat. Roman Catholic. Contbr. articles to profl. jours., encys. Home: 3512 Hampshire Dr Arlington TX 76013

MCCREADY, PAULINE ISABEL, rehab. adminstr.; b. Bangor, Me., July 4, 1911; d. Cyrus David and Grace (Grant) McCready; B.A., U. Me., 1932; M.S. in Social Adminstrn. (Buhl Found. fellow 1945-46), U. Pitts., 1946; Ed.D., Boston U., 1963. Adminstr. health and welfare agys., 1942-67; dir. Christamore House, Indpls., 1950-55; dir. Crotched Mountain Rehabilitation Centers for Children and Adults, Greenfield, N.H., 1955-62; supt. Stevens Tng. Center, Hallowell, Me., 1963-67; engaged in pvt. practice, 1967-74; dir. Mo. Girls Town, Mountain Grove, 1974—. Mem. Pres.'s Com. Employment Handicapped, Gov.'s Com. Children and Youth. Fellow Royal Soc. Health; mem. Mem. Am. Assn. U. Women, Nat. Conference Supts. Correctional Instns. for Girls and Women, Nat. Assn. Tng. Schs., Nat. Assn. Social Workers, Nat. Rehab. Assn., Acad. Certified Social Workers, Assn. Rehab. Centers, Inc., Airedale Terrier Club of Am., Delta Delta Delta, Pi Lambda Theta. Address: Route 3 Box 83 Mountain Grove MO 65711

MCCREARY, JOYZELLE HEROD, educator, psychologist; b. Pampa, Tex., Feb. 14, 1937; d. Thomas and Florence Elizabeth (Cooley) Herod; B.S., North Tex. State U., 1959; M.S., U. Cal. at Los Angeles, 1961; Ph.D., U. Tex. at Austin, 1968; m. Richard Duerr McCreary, Mar. 21, 1970; 1 dau., Jennifer Lynn. Tchr. high sch., Odessa, Tex., 1959-60; instr. U. Cal. at Santa Barbara, 1961-64; trainee in psychology VA Hosp., Dallas and Houston, 1964-68; staff psychologist VA Hosp., Houston, 1968-69; asst. prof. psychology U. Houston, 1969—, dir. applied psychology tng. program, 1970—; pvt. practice psychology, Houston, 1969—. Cons., leadership tng., 1966-68, adviser tng., 73—, mem. nominating com., 1972-74. Mem. Am., Tex., Houston psychol. assns., Delta Gamma. Home: 4927 Valerie St Bellaire TX 77401 Office: Dept Psychology Univ Houston Houston TX 77004

MCCRORY, ELLANN, radiologist; b. Butler Springs, Ala., Mar. 22, 1936; d. William Bryant and Eva Estelle (Stabler) McCrory; B.S., U. Ala., 1956; M.D., Med. Coll. Ala., 1960. Rotating intern Univ. Hosp., Birmingham, Ala., 1960-61; resident Bapt. Meml. Hosp., Memphis, 1961-64; instr. radiology U. Fla., 1964-65; pvt. practice radiology, Andalusia, Ala., 1965-66, Langdale, Ala., 1966—; speaker. Recipient Bausch and Lomb sci. award, 1953. Mem. Am. Coll. Radiology, Radiol. Soc. N.A., A.M.A., Am. Med. Women's Assn., So. Radiol. Assn., Am. Roentgen Ray Soc., Mid-South Med. Assn., Med. Assn. Ala., Chambers County Med. Soc., So. Med. Assn., Ala. Radiol. Soc., Valley C. of C., Phi Beta Kappa, Alpha Lambda Delta. Methodist. Home: PO Box 425 Lanett AL 36863 Office: Lanier Hospital Langdale AL 36864

MCCRORY, JAN KATHLEEN (MRS. RONALD LEROY MCCRORY), marina operator; b. Beaumont, Tex., Apr. 2, 1950; d. Fred Elwyn and Lelia Caroline (O'Brien) Andrews; A.A., San Antonio Coll., 1970; B.J., U. Tex., 1972; m. Ronald Leroy McCrory, Feb. 24, 1973. Asst. dir. pub. relations Santa Rosa Med. Center, San Antonio, 1972-73; co-operator Sunrise Marina, Llano, Tex., 1973—. Mem. Women in Communications, Alamo Indsl. Editors Assn. (v.p. San Antonio 1972-73), Sigma Delta Chi. Mem. Order Eastern Star. Home and office: Click Route Llano TX 78643

MCCRORY, MARGARET ANNE, educator; b. St. Cloud, Minn., May 26, 1932; d. John Raymond and Mary Lee (Rutter) McCrory; R.N., B.S., U. Rochester, 1955, Ed.M., 1961; Ed.D., Boston U., 1966. Pub. health nurse-sch. nurse tchr. Dist. Nursing Assn. North Westchester County, Mt. Kisco, N.Y., 1955-56; coll. nurse, asst. prof. health edn. State U., N.Y., at Geneseo, 1956-65; asst. prof. Purdue U., 1966-67, U. Rochester, 1967-70; dir. counseling services, asst. program adminstr. World of Inquiry Sch., Rochester, N.Y., 1970—. Head resident, asst. head resident Boston U., 1962-63. Cons., Health Edn. Workshop for Latin Am. Educators, 1960-61; chmn. Coll. Safety Edn. Com., 1960-61. Sec., Project Unique, 1973—. Bd. dirs. Counseling Research. Active Rochester Oratorio Soc., Civic Music Assn. Trustee Project Unique. Mem. Am. Assn. U. Women (co-chmn. N.Y. State Biennial Conf. 1962), Am. Personnel and Guidance Assn., Am. Coll. Personnel Assn., N.Y. State Faculties Assn. (sec., mem. faculty cabinet 1960-61), Am. Assn. U. Profs., Assn. Counselor Educator Suprs., Am. Psychol. Assn., Pi Lambda Theta, Delta Kappa Gamma. Presbyn. Editorial bd. N.Y. State Personnel and Guidance Jour. Home: 20 Hillcrest Pkwy Brookport NY 14420

MCCRORY, MARTHA, educator, musician; b. Quincy, Ill.; d. Joseph W. and Florence (Bastert) McCrory; student Northwestern U., 1937-38; B.M., U. Mich., 1941; M.M., Eastman Sch. Music, 1944, also artists diploma; postgrad. U. London, summer 1955, Berkshire Music Center, 1941, Music Acad. of West, 1952. Cellist, All Am. Youth Orch., 1940, U. Mich. Little Symphony, 1940, Rochester Philharmonic, 1942-46; asst. prof. music Drake U., 1946-47, Trinity U., San Antonio, 1947-52; asst. prin. cello San Antonio Symphony, 1947-53, Chattanooga Symphony, 1955-62, mgr., 1958-62; asst. prof. music U. of South, Sewanee, Tenn., 1962-69, asso. prof., 1969—; dir. Sewanee Summer Music Center, 1963—; cellist Chattanooga, Nashville, Knoxville symphonies, Cumberland Trio, 1967—; staff musician Nashville rec. studios. Mem. adv. panel Tenn. Arts Commn. Mem. Nat. Sch. Orchestra Assn. (chpt. chmn., chpt. pres.), Am. Fedn. Musicians, Tenn. Fedn. Music Clubs (dir.), Am. String Tchrs. Assn. (past chpt. pres.), Pi Beta Phi, Sigma Alpha Iota, Pi Kappa Lambda. Republican. Conglist. Home: Sewanee TN 37375 Office: U of the South Sewanee TN 37375

MCCUE, BETTY FOSTER, ednl. adminstr.; b. Pitts., June 5, 1916; d. William Francis and Harriet (Foster) McCue; B.S., U. Pitts., 1943; M.S., MacMurray Coll., 1947; Ph.D., U. Ia., 1952. Chmn. dept. health edn. YWCA, Warren, O., 1943-44, Denver, 1945-47; instr. phys. edn. MacMurray Coll., Jacksonville, Ill., 1947-50; research asst. U. Ia., Iowa City, 1950-52, asso. prof. U. Neb., Lincoln, 1953-55; prof., chmn. dept. phys. edn. for women Oberlin (O.) Coll., 1955-64, Duke, 1964-68; prof., chmn. dept. phys. edn. for women U. Ore., Eugene, 1968-71, prof., asso. dean Sch. Health, Phys. Edn. and Recreation, 1972—. Mem. audio-visual com. Nat. Council Chs., Oberlin, 1962-66. Bd. dirs. Lordin County (O.) chpt. A.R.C., 1959-66. Mem. Am. Assn. U. Women (pres. 1960-63), Nat. (hon. membership chmn.), Midwest (pres. 1961-63) So. (bd. dirs. 1966-68) assns. phys. edn. coll. women, A.A.H.P.E.R. (jour. editorial bd. 1965-68, dist. treas.), Am. Acad. Phys. Edn., N.Am. Soc. Sport History (dir., jour. rev. editor), Pi Lambda Theta, Delta Kappa Gamma. Author: Physical Education Activities for Women, 1969. Chmn. bd. Quest mag., 1966-69. Home: 1728 W 34th Pl Eugene OR 97405

MCCUE, CAROLYN MOORE (MRS. HOWARD M. MCCUE), pediatric cardiologist; b. Richmond, Va., June 26, 1916; d. Thomas Justin and Caroline (Willingham) Moore; student Wellesley Coll., 1933-35; A.B., Leland Stanford U., 1937; M.D., Med. Coll. Va., 1941; m. Howard M. McCue, Jr., Apr. 5, 1941; children—Carolyn (Mrs. Robert T. Osteen), Howard McDowell III. Intern, Wis. Gen. Hosp., Madison, 1941-42; resident Children's Hosp., Phila., 1942-43, Med. Coll. Va., 1946-47; dir. pediatric cardiology Med. Coll. Va., Richmond, 1947—, prof. pediatrics, 1963—; clin. dir. pediatric cardiology clinics State of Va., 1958—. Fellow Am. Acad. Pediatrics, Am. Coll. Cardiology; mem. A.C.P., Richmond Acad. Medicine (pres. elect 1975), Richmond Area Heart Assn. (pres. 1959-60), Phi Beta Kappa, Alpha Omega Alpha. Club: Country (Richmond). Contbr. articles to profl. jours. Home: 12 Huntly Rd Richmond VA 23226 Office: Box 272 Med Coll VA Richmond VA 23298

MCCUE, LAURETTA GRACE (MRS. ELBERT MERRILL MCCUE), hosp. adminstr.; b. nr. Ulysses, Kan., Oct. 8, 1919; d. Leoran Quintillis and Bertha Belle (Anderson) Carter; grad. high sch.; m. Elbert Merrill McCue, Mar. 15, 1942; children—Wilma Jeane (Mrs. Leonard Kleeman), Merry Lynn King, Merrilyn Lee (Mrs. W.J. Mohan), Merrill Leoran. Sec. to supt. Lakin (Kan.) High Sch., 1952-57; sec. Kearny County Hosp., Lakin, 1957-70, adminstr., 1970—. Mem. Kan. Hosp. Assn. Home: 509 W Kingman Lakin KS 67860 Office: 305 Kansas Av Lakin KS 67860

MCCUE, MIRIAM EUGENIA, clin. psychologist; b. Denver, Nov. 4, 1917; d. Frank Joseph and Miriam Genevieve (Keliher) Crowley; A.B., U. Wyo., 1939; M.A., Fordham U., 1940, Ph.D., 1944; m. John Joseph Gerald McCue, Dec. 19, 1949; 1 son, Brian Gerald. Asst. prof. psychology Rosemont (Pa.) Coll., 1941-44; Smith Coll., Northampton, Mass., 1946-50; clin. psychologist Cushing VA Hosp., Framingham, Mass., 1950-52; chief psychologist Mental Hygiene Clinic, VA Hosp., Lowell, Mass., 1952-54; staff psychologist VA Hosp., Bedford, Mass., 1963—. Mem. adv. bd. Cary Meml. Library, Lexington, Mass., 1956-63. Served with WAVES, 1944-46. Mem. Am., Mass. psychol. assns., Am. Assn. Advancement Behavior Therapy, Sigma Xi, Psi Chi (nat. sec.-treas. 1949-52), Kappa Kappa Gamma. Clubs: Lexington (Mass.) Golf; Cambridge (Mass.) Boat; Middlesex (Mass.) Swim and Tennis. Home: 20 N Hancock St Lexington MA 02173 Office: VA Hosp 200 Springs Rd Bedford MA 01730

MCCULLAGH, BETTE L., bus. exec.; b. Peoria, Ill., Apr. 11, 1920; d. F. W. and Helen (Hermanson) Link; student Santa Monica Jr. Coll., U. Cal. at Los Angeles; m. William T. Pattison, May 18, 1938 (div. 1947); children—William T., Martin L.; m. 2d, John T. McCullagh, 1956 (dec.); stepchildren—Patricia, Teresa, Sandra, Debora. Partner in trucking bus., Honolulu, 1939-47; in sales work Honolulu, until

1951; gen. office mgr. Clef TV, Santa Monica, Cal., 1951-53; co-owner Ni-Plate Engring. Corp., Santa Monica, 1956-59; personnel mgr. Hoover Electric Co., Los Angeles, 1959—. Active VA Pacer Program to relocate vets. West Los Angeles Vets. Center. Mem. Am. Soc. for Personnel Adminstrn., Personnel Indsl. Relations Assn. Club: Business and Professional Womens. Office: 2100 S Stoner Av Los Angeles CA 90025

MCCULLEY, MARY CATHERINE RENSCH (MRS. VICTOR LEE MCCULLEY), educator; b. Laredo, Mo., July 7, 1916; d. Earnest Firm and Stella (Roach) Rensch; grad. Trenton Jr. Coll., 1936; B.S. in Elementary Edn., N.E. Mo. Tchrs. Coll., 1952; m. Victor Lee McCulley, June 24, 1939; 1 dau., Lyalla Lee. Tchr. rural schs., Grundy County, Mo., 1936-44, 48-53; tchr. elementary schs., Galt, Mo., 1944-47, Spickard, Mo., 1953-54, Cameron, Mo., 1954-65, Mitchell Elementary Sch., Atwater, Cal., 1955-64, Aileen Colburn Sch., Atwater, 1964—. Leader Sunset 4-H Club, 1969—; pres. Mitchell Sch. P.T.A., 1969-70. Mem. N.E.A. (life), Cal. Tchrs. Assn. (treas. 1973-74), Atwater Elementary Tchrs. Assn. (pres. 1958-59, v.p. 1972-73), Bus. and Profl. Womens Club (2d v.p. 1969-70), Cal. Dept. Classroom Tchrs. (pres. 1962-64), Merced-Mariposa Cowbells. Baptist. Home: 8100 W Sunset Dr Atwater CA 95301

MCCULLOCH, ETTA SMITH, educator, nurse; b. Carveton, Pa., Nov. 23, 1912; d. Samuel T. and Emma C. (Stackhouse) Smith; student State Tchrs. Coll., Bloomsburg, Pa., 1929-31; R.N., Mt. Sinai Hosp. Sch. Nursing, N.Y.C., 1934; B.S., Fla. State U., 1968, M.S., 1972, Ph.D., 1974; m. John McCulloch, Aug. 22, 1932 (dec. Jan. 1963). Head nurse Lenox Hill Hosp., N.Y.C., 1935; teaching supr. Met. Hosp., N.Y.C., 1936; asst. night supr. Westchester Sq. Hosp., N.Y.C., 1937; obstet. supr. Royal Hosp., N.Y.C., 1937-40; supr. Parkchester Gen. Hosp., N.Y.C., 1940-47; dir. nursing Westchester Sq. Hosp., 1948-56, Waterman Meml. Hosp., Eustis, Fla., 1956-58; gen. duty nurse Theresa Holland Hosp., Leesburg, Fla., 1958-60; nursing instr. Orange County Vocational Sch., Orlando, Fla., 1960-72. Mem. Am. (dist. pres. 1970-72), Fla. nurses assns., Nat. League for Nursing, N.E.A., Am., Fla. (sec. health occupations edn. sect.) vocational assn., Iota Lambda Sigma. Club: Orlando Altrusa (pres. 1970-72). Inventor terminal sterlization of infant formula, 1943. Home: 717 Lake Shore Dr Eustis FL 32726

MCCULLOCH, PEGGY JANE (MRS. ARTHUR RUPERT MCCULLOCH), educator; b. Billings, Mont., Sept. 5, 1926; d. John Sherman and Anna Marguerite (Timken) Campbell; B.S., Eastern Mont. Coll., 1950, M.S., 1967; postgrad. U. Wyo., 1967, 71, Central Wyo. Coll., 1969-70; m. Arthur Rupert McCulloch, Sept. 15, 1945; children—Gerrene Kay (Mrs. Willard Paul Walrath, Jr.), Arthur Lee. Tchr. 5th and 6th grades, high sch. drama coach, Joliet, Mont., 1950-51; clk., buyer Hart Albin Co., Billings, Mont., 1956-66; recreation dept. City Billings, 1953-65; tchr.'s aid., spl. edn. Sch. Dist. 2, Billings, 1966; spl. edn. tchr. Emerson Sch., Wyo. State Tng. Sch., Lander, Wyo., 1966-73, counselor Mitchell Center, 1973—. Mem. Am. Assn. on Mental Deficiency, Council for Exceptional Chidren, Wyo. Personnel and Guidance Assn., Billings Studio Theater, Daughters of the Nile, Oriental Band, Trails End Extension Club, Alpha Psi Omega. Address: Wyoming State Training School Lander WY 82520

MCCULLOUGH, FRANCES SUGG (MRS. RAYMOND R. MCCULLOUGH), librarian; b. Carlisle, Ky., Aug. 16, 1913; d. Russell Lee and Jessie D. (Scott) Sugg; B.A., Berea Coll., 1936; postgrad. U. Cin.; m. Raymond R. McCullough, Jan. 9, 1937; children—Margaret, Mary. Periodical, reference librarian U. Cin. Gen. Library, 1937-47; librarian Mercy Hosp. Sch. Nursing, Hamilton, O., 1960-70, health sci. librarian, 1960—. Mem. Am., Med., Cath. library assns., Spl. Libraries Assn., Cin. Area Health Scis. Libraries Assn. (treas. 1973—). Editor health scis. column Cath. Library World, 1966-68. Home: 1025 Oakmont Av Hamilton OH 45013 Office: 111 Buckeye St Hamilton OH 45011

MCCULLOUGH, H. A., registered nurse; b. Pratt, Kan., July 28, 1913; d. Ole Elmo and Inez Louise (Mawdsley) McCullough; diploma Baylor U. Sch. Nursing, 1941, B.S. cum laude, 1953; B.R.E., Southwestern Bapt. Theol. Sem., 1950; M.A., Columbia U., 1954, profl. diploma, 1958. With F.W. Woolworth Co., 1929-38; nurse's staff Baylor Hosp., 1941-42, Wichita Hosp., 1947; supr. Bethesda under supervision Buckner Orphans Home, San Antonio, 1950-51; pvt., gen. duty nurse, Waco, Tex., 1952-53; instr. dept. nurse edn. Ft. Hays State Coll., 1954-56; asst. prof. sch. nursing U. Okla., 1958-60; edn. dir. Susan B. Allen Meml. Hosp. Sch. Nursing, El Dorado, Kan., 1960-61; nursing coordinator psychiat. nursing VA, Wadsworth, 1962-64, clin. instr. nursing, Fort Lyon, Colo., 1964-66; asso. chief nursing service for edn., North Little Rock (Ark.) div. VA Hosp., 1966-68; staff nurse Wichita (Kan.) VA Hosp., 1969-71, relief supr., 1971-73, nurse clinician, 1973—. Active McCullough Scholarship Fund, Trust Agreement, Immanuel Bapt. Ch., Wichita. Served with Nurses Corps, AUS, 1942-47. Decorated Purple Heart. Mem. Nat. League Nursing (mem. nominations com. 1967), Am. Nurses Assn., Alpha Kappa Delta, Pi Lambda Theta. Baptist (ch. librarian 1962-64, 66-68). Mem. Order Eastern Star. Home: 2367 S Estelle Av Wichita KS 67211

MCCULLOUGH, KORLEEN WESTCOTT (MRS. B. KEITH MCCULLOUGH), banker; b. Watertown, N.Y., Nov. 12, 1916; d. Arthur Jesse and Edith (McQuinn) Westcott; m. B. Keith McCullough, Oct. 29, 1938. Asst. clerk SSS, Massena, N.Y., 1939-41; exec. sec. Massena (N.Y.) C. of C., 1942-51; sec. Massena Banking & Trust Co., 1951-63; asst. cashier Nat. Bank No. N.Y., Massena, 1963-68, loan and operations officer, 1969—. Residential chmn. United Fund, Massena, 1967, 69. Mem. Massena Bus. and Profl. Womens Club (pres. 1969-70), St. Lawrence County Bankers Assn. (dir. 1973—), N.Y. State Banking Assn. (chmn. St. Lawrence County women's com. 1962-67, 71—), Massena C. of C. (treas., dir. 1972—). Mem. Order Eastern Star (auditor 1966—). Home: 76 Grove St Massena NY 13662 Office: 41 Main St Massena NY 13662

MCCULLOUGH, MABELLE G., educator; b. Mt. Pleasant, Ia., Feb. 27, 1914; d. Thomas E. and Martha (Cone) McCullough; B.A. summa cum laude, Ia. Wesleyan Coll., 1943; M.A. in Religious Edn., Yale, 1945; postgrad. U. Minn., 1949-54; Ed.D. in Guidance and Student Personnel Adminstrn., Columbia, 1956; wards—Maryam Ali Abadi, Elaheh Ali Abadi, Hossein Ali Abadi, Bardia Kamrad. Asso. dir. Wesley Found., St. Paul campus U. Minn., 1945-49; dir. student housing bur., office dean of students U. Minn., Mpls., 1949-69, office v.p. for student affairs, 1969—, asst. prof. edn., 1956-66, asst. dean students, asso. prof. edn., 1966—; certified cons. psychologist, Minn., 1962—. Mem. Gov.'s Commn. Status of Women, 1963-67, also chmn. edn. com.; mem. Nat. Adv. Council on Health Professions Ednl. Assistance, 1970-71. Mem. Women's Adv. Council Civil Def., State Minn., 1962-61; St. Paul alumni rep. Ia. Wesleyan Coll.; adv. bd. YWCA, 1943-46, 62-65, treas., 1963-64, adv. bd. chmn., 1964-66, 70—; bd. dirs. Mpls. YWCA, 1968—, chmn. personnel com., 1969-73; bd. dirs., chmn. program com., mem. exec. com. Wesley Found., U. Minn., 1960-64. Mem. Shoreview Village Planning Commn., 1968-71, chmn., 1971—. Mem. Am. Assn. U. Women (status of women chmn. Mpls. br. 1958-60, dir. Mpls. br. 1968-69; Minn. div. status of women chmn. 1960-62, roster chmn. 1962-64, chmn. com. study financing pub. edn. 1961-63, producer 2TV programs on pub. sch. financing, mem. nat. com. on standards in higher edn. 1967-73, chmn. 1969-73, bd. dirs. Edn. Found. 1969—, internat. fellowships com. 1973—), Am. Assn. Higher Edn., Nat. Assn. Women Deans and Counselors (mem. by laws com. 1968-70), Nat. Council Adminstrv. Women in Edn., Am. Personnel and Guidance Assn., Am. Coll. Personnel Assn., Assn. Coll. and Univ. Housing Officers (institutional rep., co-chmn. 5th nat. conf., chmn. off-campus housing com., mem. internat. com.). Methodist. Club: Columbia University Alumni of Minnesota (dir., sec.). Author publs. in fields of student housing, internat. edn., and status of women. Home: 5883 Carlson St St Paul MN 55112 Office: 16 Morrill Hall U Minn Minneapolis MN 55455

MCCUNE, SHIRLEY DICKINSON (MRS. WESLEY MCCUNE), assn. exec.; b. Sterling, Colo., Dec. 1, 1934; d. Donald Dewey and Elma Irene (Smith) Dickinson; B.A., Colo. State Coll. Edn., 1957; M.S.W., U. Denver, 1960; D. Social Work, Cath. U. Am., 1966; m. Wesley McCune, Aug. 1, 1959. Sr. scientist, manpower research group George Washington U., Washington, 1962-67; asso. dir. Am. Assn. U. Women, 1967-71; mgr. tchr. rights N.E.A., Washington, 1971—. Lectr. George Washington U., Washington, 1962-72. Mem. D.C. Commn. on Status of Women, 1973. Home: 325 2d St SE Washington DC 20003 Office: 1201 16th St NW Washington DC 20036

MCCURRY, ELEANORE PAULINE ERDAHL, occupational therapist; b. Frost, Minn., May 16, 1922; d. Absalon A. and Sarah Maryann (Brekke) Erdahl; B.S., N.D. State U., 1943; registered occupational therapist U. Ill., 1946; m. Robert Max McCurry, Dec. 14, 1946 (div. Aug. 1971); children—Geraldine Ann (Mrs. Gary G. Howard), Jeanne Ellen. Staff therapist Wakeman Gen. Hosp., Camp Atterbury, Ind., 1946; staff therapist Clinton Valley Center (formerly Pontiac (Mich.) State Hosp.), 1947-48, asst. dir. occupational therapy, 1948-53, dir. occupational therapy, 1953-72, coordinator activity therapy, 1972—. Cons. occupational therapy schs. Wayne State U., Eastern Mich. U., Western Mich. U.; cons. on hort. therapy Mich. State U. Leader, Girl Scouts U.S.A., Pontiac, 1959-69. Bd. dirs. Jay Shop. Mem. Am., Mich. (sec. 1960-64, Minuteman award 1972) occupational therapy assns., Woman's Nat. Farm and Garden Club. Lutheran. Home: 2208 Garland Pontiac MI 48053 Office: 140 Elizabeth Lake Rd Pontiac MI 48053

MCCURRY, KATHRYN MAREE, educator; b. White Pond, S.C., July 17, 1929; d. William Earle and Mildred Ruth (Owens) McCurry; B.A., Converse Coll., 1950; M.A., U. S.C., 1951; postgrad. Dell Sch. Med. Tech., 1954, U. S.C., 1960-61, 63, 68. Lab. tech. Dr. W.E. McCurry's Clinic, Ridge Spring, S.C., 1952-55; instr. French and English, asst. to dean Greenbrier Coll., Lewisburg, W.Va., 1955-59; tchr. French, Columbia (S.C.) Coll., 1960; tchr. English, Brooklyn-Cayce High Sch., West Columbia, S.C., 1960; tchr. French, A.C. Flora High Sch., Columbia, 1960—. Counsellor Fgn. Lang. Study League, Orsay, France, 1967. Mem. Am. Med. Technologists, S.C. Soc. Am. Med. Technologists (sec., treas. 1961-62), S.C., Richland County edn. assns., S.C. Lang. Assn., Central States Modern Lang. Assn., City French Tchrs. (chmn. 1969-70), Am. Assn. U. Women, Colonial Dames XVII Century, French Huguenot Soc., Internat. Platform Assn. Home: 6433 Eastshore Rd Columbia SC 29206

MCCUSKER, SISTER MARY LAURETTA, educator; b. Sillery, Que., Can., Jan. 18, 1919; d. Albert James and Laura (Cleary) McCusker; brought to U.S., 1929, naturalized, 1942; B.A., Western Md. Coll., 1942; M.L.S., Columbia U., 1950, D.L.S., 1963. Librarian Annapolis (Md.) High Sch., 1942-44, McDonogh Mil. Sch., 1944-47; part time librarian N.Y.C. Pub. Library, 1947-48; asst. prof. library sci. Ia. State Tchrs. Coll., 1948-59; teaching fellow Columbia, 1952-53; asso. prof. library sci. Rosary Coll., River Forest, Ill., 1963-67, dean Grad. Sch. Library Sci., 1967—. Mem. Ill. State Library Adv. Com., 1972—. Mem. Am. (legislative com. 1970-71, nominating com. 1970-71), Chgo. (chmn. elementary sect. 1964-65) library assns. Editor: Major Problems in the Education of Librarians (R.D. Leigh, 1954). Gen. editor CLA Booklist, 1965-69, Seminar on Automation in the Library dept. Library sci. Rosary Coll., 1966, Style Manual, rev. edit., 1967. Address: 7900 W Division St River Forest IL 60305

MCCUTCHEON, NANCY SUSAN, educator; b. Columbia, S.C., July 10, 1937; d. Samuel Durant and Nancy (Milford) McCutcheon; B.A., U. S.C., 1957, M.Ed., 1966, Ph.D., 1969; diploma, tchrs. certificate in piano Sherwood Music Sch., Chgo., 1959. Tchr., Belvedere Elementary Sch., Columbia, 1957-65; grad. teaching asst. Sch. Edn., U. S.C., Columbia, 1965-68, instr., 1968-70, asst. prof., on-site coordinator career opportunities program, Williamsburg County, S.C., 1970-73, dir. career opportunities program, 1973—. Pvt. piano tchr., 1955—; cons. substitute teaching program Williamsburg County, S.C., 1969-70. Mem. N.E.A., S.C. Edn. Assn., Assn. Supervision and Curriculum Devel., Soc. Research Child Devel., Am. Ednl. Research Assn., Columbia Music Tchrs. Assn. (sec. 1964-66), So. Assn. Schs. and Colls. (vis. com.) Nat. Assn. Edn. Young Children, S.C. Fedn. Music Clubs (adjudicator piano festivals 1960—), Nat. Council Tchrs. English, Nat. Soc. Study Edn., So. Assn. Children Under Six, Phi Beta Kappa (sec.-treas. Alpha of S.C. chpt. 1971—), Delta Kappa Gamma, Kappa Delta Epsilon, Alpha Delta Kappa, Beta Sigma Phi (chpt. pres. 1961-62). Baptist. Club: Sherwood Music School Seminar (pres. 1967, 68). Contbr. to profl. publs. Home: 2911 Devine St Columbia SC 29205

MCCUTCHEON, ROSEMARY (MRS. WILMER G. MCCUTCHEON), agribusiness exec.; b. Orlando, Fla., May 10, 1927; d. William Isaac and May Belle (Patterson) Barber; student Maryville Coll., Rollins Coll. extension; m. Herbert A. Smith, Jr., Oct. 21, 1947 (dec. July 1960); children—Hannah (Mrs. Luciano P. Maldonado, Jr.), SeBelle (Mrs. Gary L. Dymme), Dosia M., Miranda R.; m. 2d, Wilmer G. McCutcheon, Dec. 26, 1968. Gen. mgr., trustee Herbert A. Smith, Jr. Trust, Kissimmee, Fla., 1960—; dir. Golden Gem Growers, Umatilla, Fla., Citizens State Bank, St. Cloud, Fla. Mem. Osceola County Planning Commn., Kissimmee, 1963-68. Life mem. Fairchild Tropical Garden, Miami, 1959—; asso. mem. Am. Mus. Natural History, N.Y.C., 1966—. Bd. dirs. Osceola County Art and Culture Center, 1963-64. Mem. Fla. Hort. Soc., Soil and Crop Sci. Soc. Fla., Am. Quarter Horse Assn., Am. Forestry Assn., Nat., Fla. Aububon socs., Fla. Citrus Prodn. Mgrs. Assn., Am. Polled Hereford Assn. Home: PO Box 488 St Cloud FL 32769 Office: 519 E Vine St Kissimmee FL 32741

MCDANIEL, AGNES M. MCLAUGHLIN (MRS. JOHN W. MCDANIEL), cattle rancher; b. nr. Clewiston, Fla., Feb. 6, 1907; d. Robert Elonzo and Susie (Brewer) McLaughlin; student Fla. State U., 1924-27; m. John W. McDaniel, June 7, 1928 (dec. Sept. 1957); 1 son, Robert E. Cattle rancher, Clewiston, Fla. Mem. So. Bapt. Annuity Bd., 1966—. Mem. Internat. Platform Assn., Phi Sigma Alpha. Baptist. Home: Westover Bldg 102 6611 Cypress Lake Dr Ft Myers FL 33901

MCDANIEL, AUDREY STANSELL (MRS. VALRIE SHIELDS MCDANIEL), author; b. Washington, Feb. 24, 1908; d. Dwight David and Jennette Marie (Nolan) Stansell; student pub. schs., pvt. tutors; m. Valrie Shields McDaniel, Sr., Feb. 1, 1941; 1 son, Val. Bd. dirs. Arlington Temple and Community Center, Rosslyn, Va., 1965—; pres. Audrey McDaniel Faith and Hope Found. Mem. A.S.C.A.P., London Poetry Soc., Nat. League Am. Pen Women (nat. chaplain 1966-68). Author: The Greatest of These is Love, 1962; Forget-Me-Nots of Love, 1964; Garden of Hope, 1966; God is There, 1969; A Christmas Rose, 1971; Abiding Love, 1973 (books have been produced on radio and TV). Composer lyrics Hymn Gems from Sacred Memory Time, 1967. Home: 5800 N 11th St Arlington VA 22205

MCDANIEL, CLAUDETTE BLACK (MRS. SYLVESTER W. MCDANIEL), broadcasting exec.; b. Richmond, Va., Dec. 12, 1939; d. Lawrence Nicklos and Leolia C. (Cheatham) Black; B.A., Va. Union U., 1964; postgrad. Va. Commonwealth U., 1965—; m. Sylvester W. McDaniel, Mar. 21, 1969; 1 dau., Claudine Renee. With radio sta. WANT, Richmond, 1950-68; pub. service dir. radio sta. WENZ, Richmond, 1968—; producer, dir. Claudette and Guest radio program. Spl. activities supr. Dept. Occupational Therapy, Health Sci. Center, Med. Coll. Va., 1960—; publicity chmn. Nat. Council of Coll. Women; sponsor creative workshop at Va. State Penitentiary; mem. pub. relations com. Richmond br. A.R.C.; mem. Va. State Bd. Corrections. Recipient Music Scholarship, Va. State Coll., 1957. Mem. Nat. Recreation and Park Assn., Va. Recreation and Park Soc. (Va. therapeutic recreation interest sect.), Peoples Polit. and Civic Assn., Zeta Phi Beta. Home: 105 E 15th St Richmond VA 23224 Office: 111 N 4th St Richmond VA 23219

MCDANIEL, ELIZABETH ALICE LOGAN (MRS. DAVID C. MCDANIEL), psychologist, educator; b. Youngstown, O.; d. Lawrence A. and Henrietta (Villnave) Logan; B.A., U. Cal. at Los Angeles; M.S., U. Ill.; Ph.D., U. Tex., 1967; m. David C. McDaniel; children—David C., Steven, Donna, William, Susan. Prof., S.W. Tex. State U., San Marcos, 1969—; sch. and clin. psychology, child behaviour cons.; research in self concept, geriatrics. Recipient Am. Assn. U. Women Coll. Faculty Program award, 1963. Nat. Inst. Mental Health scholar, 1964-67. Mem. Am. Psychol. Assn., Am. Assn. U. Women, Am. Assn. U. Profs., Assn. Childhood Edn. Internat., Tex., S.W. psychol. assns., Tex. State Tchrs. Assn., Tex. Assn. Coll. Tchrs., Delta Zeta, Psi Chi, Pi Lambda Theta. Soroptimist. Author: Inferred Self Concept Scale; also articles in field. Editor: A Manual to Assist the New Observer and Others Studying Children's Behavior. Home: 6514 Bradley Dr Austin TX 78723 Office: 512 E Riverside Dr Austin TX 78723

MCDANIEL, ELIZABETH HOLLAND, artist; b. Detroit, July 23, 1913; d. Edward Morton and Elsie (Nicols) Holland; student Grand Central Sch. Art, 1930-31, Sarah Lawrence Coll., 1932-33, Ecoles d'Arts Americaines, Fontainebleau, France, 1932-33; m. George Edgar Naylon, Jr., July 20, 1934 (div. Jan. 1939); m. 2d, Gene Winans McDaniel, Dec. 29, 1940 (div. Sept. 1968); children—Gene Ross, Lauralyn. Artist, 1929—; one-man shows Casa de Manana, La Jolla, Cal., 1941, Nev. Art Gallery, Reno, 1965, St. Mary's Art Gallery, Virginia City, Nev., 1966-68, Depot Gallery, Yountville, Cal., 1968, Torrance Gallery, San Anselmo, 1969; exhibited in group shows Oakland (Cal.) Anns., Marin Soc. Artists Shows, Soc. Western Artists Shows, Winblad Gallery, San Francisco, Town and Country Gallery, Palo Alto, Gold Hill Gallery, Round Hill Mall, Zephyr Cove, Nev.; represented in permanent collection Artists Studio, Bolinas, Cal. Tchr. landscape in oils, acrylics and color theory Marin Art and Garden Center, Ross, Cal., 1968—, Napa Valley Art Assn., Napa, 1967—. Juror Marin Soc. Artists and Soc. Western Artists. Recipient awards including Purchase award St. Mary's in Mountains, 1968. Mem. Marin Soc. Artists, Soc. Western Artists, Mendocino Art League, Napa Valley Artists Assn. Home: Horseshoe Hill Bolinas CA 94924

MCDANIEL, ELLEN GARB (MRS. JOHN PERRY MCDANIEL), psychiatrist; b. Cleve., Dec. 21, 1941; student Carnegie Inst. Tech., 1959-62; M.D., U. Mich., 1966; m. John Perry McDaniel. Intern Delaware Hosp., Wilmington, 1966-67; resident Ohio State U., Columbus, 1967-68, U. Md., Balt., 1968-69; chief resident U. Md., Balt., 1969-70, instr. Med. Sch., 1970-72, asst. prof. Med. Sch., 1972—. Diplomate Am. Bd. Psychiatry and Neurology. Mem. Am. Psychiat. Assn., Am. Psychoanalytic Assn. (affiliate), Md. Psychiat. Soc. Home: 235 Chancery Rd Baltimore MD 21218

MCDANIEL, HELEN MARIE, social worker; b. Columbus, O., Nov. 6, 1918; d. Dennis S. and Marie (Carter) McDaniel; B.S., Ohio State U., 1941, M.A. in Social Adminstrn., 1942, postgrad., 1962-63, 67, Ph.D., 1969. Girl's work dir., asst. camp dir., Franklin Settlement, Detroit, 1942-44; social work instr. Ohio State U., 1946; caseworker Cath. Welfare Bur., Columbus, 1946-49, supr., 1949-60, casework dir., 1960-70; dir. Cath. Social Services, Columbus, 1970—; clin. instr. Ohio State U., 1970—. Field work coordinator St. Mary Springs Coll., Columbus, 1958—. Pres., Cath. Interracial Com., 1954; mem. profl. adv. council United Way, Franklin County, 1971—; mem. Council on Social Work Edn.; mem. Nat. Conf. on Social Welfare. Named Woman of Year, Citizen Jour., 1960. Mem. Nat. Conf. Cath. Charities (mem. commn. on families and children 1964—, mem. bd. 1969—), Ohio State U. Sch. Social Work Alumni (pres. 1973-74). Democrat. Roman Catholic (mem. diocesan council cath. women 1946—). Author essays in field. Home: 419 Derrer Rd Columbus OH 43204 Office: 197 E Gay St Columbus OH 43215

MCDANIEL, LUCY VIRGINIA, phys. therapist; b. Pocatello, Ida., Feb. 27, 1920; d. Edward Henry and Lucy Lavon (Gibbs) McDaniel; B.S., U. Cal. at Los Angeles, 1942, Ed.D., 1961; M.Ed., U. Mo. at Columbia, 1943; certificate phys. therapy U.S. Army Phys. Therapy Sch., 1944. Staff and supervisory phys. therapist U.S. Army hosps., Modesto, Cal. and Japan, 1944-47, Orthopaedic Hosp., Los Angeles, 1947-53; asso. curriculum in phys. therapy U. Cal. at San Francisco, 1953-57; phys. therapist in doctor's office, 1957-60; instr. research methods U. So. Cal., 1964-67; research coordinator phys. therapy Los Amigos Hosp., Downey, Cal., 1961-73; cons. Allied Health Professions, Palos Verdes, Cal., 1973—. Pres. Los Angeles unit Women's Overseas Service League, 1966-68, 73-74. Grantee Dept. Health, Edn. and Welfare, 1965-71. Mem. Am. Phys. Therapy Assn. (chmn. sect. research 1964-66), Nat. Soc. Programmed Instrn., Pi Lambda Theta. Author: Brain and Nerves, Bones, Joints and Muscles, 1965; Major Systems of the Human Body, 1970; Selected Orthopaedic Disabilities and Selected Medical Disabilities, 1973; Selected Neurological Disabilities, 1974; also articles. Address: 27907 Centuria Dr Palos Verdes CA 90274

MCDANIEL, MARY LOU (MRS. JOHN LEONARD MCDANIEL), coll. adminstr.; b. Mountain Home, Ark., Feb. 21, 1939; d. Chester Clifton and Doris Jane (Hickman) Studdard; B.S., Ark. State U., 1961, M.S., 1967; m. John Leonard McDaniel, Jan. 21, 1973. Instr. bus. edn. Blytheville (Ark.) Sr. High Sch., 1961-66, chmn. dept., 1963-66; counselor for women student personnel staff Ark. State U., 1967—. Mem. Ark. Gov.'s Commn. Status Women, 1971—; sec. Jonesboro Area City Panhellenic, 1973, v.p., 1974. Recipient Distinguished Service award Ark. State U., 1961. Mem. Nat. Assn. Women Deans, Adminstrs. and Counselors, Ark. Assn. Women Deans and Counselors, S.W. Assn. Student Personnel Adminstrs., Ark. Coll. Personnel Assn. (sec.-treas. 1971-72), Delta Kappa Gamma, Pi Omega Pi (recipient award 1961), Alpha Lambda Delta, Kappa Delta Pi. Mem. Ch. of God. Club: Ark. State University Faculty Women's. Home: 3604 Medallion Circle Jonesboro AR 72401 Office: PO Box 393 State University AR 72467

MCDANIEL, MILDRED MAXINE, retail store exec.; b. Garrett, Ind., Nov. 28, 1916; d. Martin L. and Cletus Gertrude (Beber) Miller; grad. high sch.; m. Dwight Darwin McDaniel, July 14, 1945; children—Linda (Mrs. Joseph DePew), Debra Kaye. With Haffner Stores, Garrett, 1939—, sec., treas., 1939—, sec. to pres., 1962-72, now dir. Mem. Bus. and Profl. Women's Club (treas. 1973-74). Mem. Ch. of Christ. Mem. Order Eastern Star. Home: 204 Harrison St Garrett IN 46738 Office: 214 S Randolph St Garrett IN 46738

MCDANIEL, PATSYE MABRY, psychologist; b. Galax, Va., Sept. 6, 1935; d. Hugh Irvin and Cora Lee (Jones) Mabry; student Madison Coll., 1952-54; B.S. in Edn., Radford Coll., 1957; M.A., Mich. State U., 1968; m. Quannah McDaniel, Nov. 29, 1958; children—Quannah Patrick, Amanda. Tchr. elementary sch. Wythe County, Wytheville, Va., 1954-55, tchr. high sch., 1955-56; psychometrist Portsmouth (Va.) City Schs. 1957-61, 65-66; psychologist U. Cal. Med. Center, San Francisco, 1961-64; tchr. jr. high sch. Richmond County, Augusta, Ga., 1964-65; tchr. educable mentally retarded Prince William County Schs., Woodbridge, Va., 1966-67; psychologist Prince William County, Manassas, Va., 1968-70. Psychometrist, Va. Dept. Mental Health, Mt. Empire Guidance Center, Radford Coll., summer 1958; pre-sch. tchr. Wythe County Schs., Wytheville, summer 1970. Civilian co-chmn. Post Co-op. Nursery Sch., Aberdeen Proving Ground, Md., 1971-73. Mem. Am. Psychol. Assn. (asso.), Assn. Am. Coll. Women (Manila, P.I.). Home: care LTC QL McDaniel 450489256 JASMAG Philippines APO San Francisco CA 96528 Address: care E Jones Austinville VA 24312

MCDANIEL, SUSAN J. GRIFFITH (MRS. JAMES S. MCDANIEL), ednl. adminstr.; b. Kansas City, Kan., Dec. 3, 1938; d. William Edwin and Elene E. (Peters) Griffith; B.S., Kan. State Tchrs. Coll., 1959, M.S., 1962; postgrad. Kan. State U., 1961-62; Ph.D., U. Okla., 1966; m. James S. McDaniel, June 11, 1966. Asst. prof. biology East Carolina U., Greenville, N.C., 1967—, asst. provost, 1973—. Cons. various ednl. programs. NSF fellow, 1961-64, NIH trainee, 1966. Mem. Assn. Southeastern Biologists, N.C. Acad. Sci. (sec. 1973—), Am. Mus. Natural History, Nat. Orgn. Women (chpt. sec. 1973), Sigma Xi, Phi Sigma, Beta Beta Beta. Home: Route 7 Box 195 Greenville NC 27834

MCDANIEL, THELMA LOUISE (MRS. FRED RUSSELL MCDANIEL), educator; b. S.I., N.Y., Sept. 20, 1923; d. Carl Lee and Marie Elena (Frasula) Richardson; student Hunter Coll., 1941, Maryville Coll., 1942-45; B.F.A., U. Ia., 1946; M.A., Eastern Mich. U., 1964; postgrad. U. Mich., 1966-71; m. Fred Russell McDaniel, Aug. 26, 1946; children—Susan, Jamie Ruth. Mem. faculty Eastern Mich. U., 1961—, asso. prof. drama, 1973—. Dir. Little Theatre of the Young. Mem. League Women Voters (local membership chmn., dir.). Home: 210 N Wallace Ypsilanti MI 48197 Office: Quirk Bldg Eastern Mich U Ypsilanti MI 48197

MCDAVID, SARAH ANN (MRS. O.C. RANDOLPH MCDAVID), lawyer; b. Talladega, Ala., Mar. 23, 1930; d. Milton Blair and Bobbie (Pennington) Samuel; student U. Hawaii, 1948-49; B.A., U. Ala., 1952; postgrad. U. Mo., 1952-53; L.L.B., Jackson Sch. Law, 1966; m. O.C. Randolph McDavid, Jan. 11, 1959. Soc. editor Jasper (Ala.) Mountain Eagle, 1952; reporter The Birmingham (Ala.) News, 1953-57; editorial writer New Orleans (La.) Item, 1957; reporter New Orleans (La.) States-Item, 1958; admitted to Miss. bar, 1966; law clk. Miss. Supreme Court, Jackson, Miss., 1966-67; with firm Hedgepeth & Hedgepeth, Jackson, 1967-70; partner Hedgepeth & McDavid, Jackson, Miss., 1971-73; partner McDavid & Rimmer, Jackson, 1973—; legal counsel Blue Cross & Blue Shield of Miss., 1973—, Miss. Hosp. Assn., 1971—. Mem. Am., Miss., Hinds County bar assns., Soc. of Hosp. Attorneys, Nat. Assn. Women Lawyers, Delta Delta Delta, Theta Sigma Phi. Episcopalian. Home: 359 Forest Av Jackson MS 39206 Office: PO Box 1467 Jackson MS 39205

MCDERMID, ALICE MARGUERITE CONNELL (MRS. RALPH MANEWAL MCDERMID), civic worker, polit. worker; b. Sterling, Ill., May 25, 1910; d. William Hayes and Margaret (Durr) Connell; A.B., U. Ill., 1931; m. Ralph Manewal McDermid, Nov. 28, 1931; children—Ralph Manewal, Jane Dillon (Mrs. Anders Wiberg), Michael Metcalf, John Fairbanks. Bd. dirs. Scarsdale Womans Exchange, 1953-60; mem. social service bd. N.Y. Infirmary, 1960—, vice chmn., 1964—; trustees team United Hosp. Fund, 1965—; case policy bd. Spence-Chapin Adoption Service, 1960—; fund raising Vis. Nurse Assn., 1960-64, Greer Sch., 1958-73. Sec., Young Republicans Ill., 1930-31, mem. bd. Scarsdale (N.Y.) Womens Rep. Club, 1961-65, pres., 1965-67; del. Washington Conf. Nat. Fed. Rep. Women, 1965-72; mem. council Fedn. Womens Rep. Clubs N.Y. State, 1967—; Rep. dist. leader, 1967—; del. Rep. Jud. Conv., 1969-71; vice chmn. Rep. Town Com., 1969—, mem. N.Y.C. Womans Nat. Rep. Club, Rep. Presidents Club; mem. N.Y. State Rep. Com., 1970—; committee woman 90th Assembly Dist. Mem. English Speaking Union U.S. Alpha Xi Delta. Episcopalian. Clubs: Scarsdale Womens, Scarsdale Golf, Fox Meadow Tennis, Village; Capitol Hill (Washington); Ladies Harvard (N.Y.C.); Racquet (Winter Park, Fla.). Home: 10 Windsor Lane Scarsdale NY 10583 also 682 Granville Dr Winter Park FL 32789

MCDERMOTT, AGNES CHARLENE SENAPE (MRS. VINCENT MCDERMOTT), educator; b. Hazleton, Pa., Mar. 11, 1937; d. Charles Gerard and Conjetta C. (Ranieri) Senape; B.A. with honors, U. Pa., 1956; Ph.D., U. Pa., 1964; postgrad. U. Cal., Berkeley, 1960-61, U. Amsterdam, Netherlands, 1965-66, U. Wis., 1968-69; m. Vincent McDermott, Sept. 10, 1959; 1 son, Robert; adopted children—Lisle, Jamie. Grad. fellow U. Pa., 1961-62; tchr. State U. N.Y., Buffalo, 1964-65, Hampton Inst., Va., 1966-67, U. Wis., Milw., 1967-69; mem. faculty U. N.M., Albuquerque, 1970—, asso. prof. philosophy, 1970—. Samuel Fels Found. fellow, 1963, Am. Assn. U. Women fellow, 1965, Nat. Endowment Humanities fellow, 1971. Mem. Am. Oriental Soc., Tibet Soc., Soc. Eastern and Comparative Philosophy, Am. Philos. Assn., Phi Beta Kappa, Pi Mu Epsilon. Author: An Eleventh Century Buddhist Logic of Exists, 1969. Contbr. articles to profl. pubs. Home: 2804 E Linnwood St Milwaukee WI 53211 Office: Dept Philosophy U NM Albuquerque NM 87106

MCDERMOTT, FRANCES MCCLELLAN (MRS. LEON A. MCDERMOTT), educator; b. Warsaw, Ind.; d. George Edmund and Millie (Axtell) McClellan; A.B., Eastern Mich. U., 1930; M.A., U. Mich., 1933; Ed.D., Mich. State U., 1963; m. Leon A. McDermott, July 23, 1939. Tchr. Armada (Mich.) High Sch., 1930-32; sec. Washtenaw County (Mich.) Sch., 1933-36; tchr. St. Louis High Sch., 1936-39, tchr., librarian, 1949-54; tchr. Livingston County Sch., 1940-42; asst. librarian Dow Chem. Co., 1943-47; sec. to placement officer Central Mich. U., 1947-48; prin. Beal City (Mich.) High Sch., 1948-49; mem. faculty Ferris State Coll., Big Rapids, Mich., 1954—, prof. English, 1966—. Vis. prof. Coll. William and Mary, Williamsburg, Va., summers 1961-64, 67. Mem. Nat. Councils Tchrs. English, Mich. Coll. English Tchrs. Assn., Mecosta County Hist. Assn., Kappa Delta Pi, Delta Kappa Gamma, Pi Lambda Theta, Sigma Kappa. Home: 1152 Highland St Mount Pleasant MI 48858 Office: Ferris State Coll Big Rapids MI 49307

MCDERMOTT, IDARUTH MITCHELL (MRS. EDWARD BRIAN MCDERMOTT), business exec.; b. Hingham, Mass., Oct. 9, 1921; d. Henry Forrester and Rebecca (Gerrold) Mitchell; B.A., Radcliffe Coll., 1938; postgrad. N.Y. Inst. Finance, 1940, Am. Inst. Banking, 1942; m. Edward Brian McDermott, Feb. 11, 1939; children—Brian Emerson, Bruce Burnham, Diane Lee. Acting head investment dept., adminstrv. asst. to the trust officer Comml. Nat. Bank & Trust Co., N.Y.C., 1939-49; adminstrv. asst. to the dir. sales promotion SKO, Inc., N.Y.C., 1966-70, adminstrv. asst. to pres., 1970-74; corporate sec.-treas. Specialized Components, Inc.; owner McDermott's Surgi-Clip, Inc. Mem. N.Y. Soc. Security Analysts, Nat. Soc. D.A.R. Address: 23 Flower Lane Manhasset NY 11030

MCDERMOTT, IRENE WILDER (MRS. THOMAS JOHN MCDERMOTT), author; b. Veedersburg, Ind.; d. Edward and Ida (Keeling) Wilder; student Coll. Music and Arts, Indpls., 1918-19; m. Thomas John McDermott, Feb. 17, 1927; 1 son, Thomas John. Writer articles, fiction stories and poetry appearing in mags., newspapers, 1947—; author daily column Evening Outlook, Santa Monica, 1968—; judge creative writing classes Venice (Cal.) High Sch., 1950-55, Westchester (Cal.) High Sch., 1959-67, Nat. Fedn. Women's Clubs, Marina Dist., Cal., 1967—. Mem. Nat. Soc. Arts and Letters (sec., 1960-63, 66-67, v.p., 1964-65), Nat. League Am. Pen Women (pres., 1962-64; awards). Republican. Rotarian. Club: Santa Monica (Cal.). Author: Enter the Temple Called Beautiful, 1969. Address: 1051 20th St Santa Monica CA 90403

MCDERMOTT, MARIA CONCEPTA, educator; b. Dubuque, Ia., Apr. 1, 1913; d. John Charles and Mary Agnes (O'Connell) McDermott; B.A., St. Mary's Coll., 1938; M.A., Catholic U. Am., 1948; Ph.D., U. Notre Dame, 1962; Tchr., prin., supr. high schs. St. Paul's High Sch., Washington, 1948-51; supr. Holy Cross High Schs. in Midwest, 1951-57; mem. faculty St. Mary's Coll., Notre Dame, Ind., 1958—, prof. theories of learning, 1964—. Field rep. Glasser Inst. Reality Therapy, Los Angeles; mem. Ind. State Project English, Carnegie Study Cath. Schs. in Action; draft counselor; juvenile rehab. worker county cts. Recipient Spes Unica award as prof. of year, 1972. Mem. Am. Assn. U. Profs., Nat. Council Tchrs. English, N.E.A., Authors Indiana History, Am. Assn. Colls. Tchr. Edn., Am. Council Higher Edn., Center for Democratic Instns. Author: Making of a Sister-Teacher, 1962; also articles. Co-editor films in series Are You Listening? for ednl. TV. Address: St Mary's College Notre Dame IN 46556

MCDERMOTT, PATRICIA LOUISE (MRS. RICHARD H. BIEBER), lawyer, state legislator; b. Washington, Feb. 19, 1938; d. Peter A. and Emily L. (Wolfe) McDermott; student Ida. State U., 1954-55, B.A., 1958; student Creighton U., 1955-56; J.D., George Washington U., 1961; LL.M., Georgetown U., 1964; m. Richard H. Bieber, Dec. 15, 1971. Admitted to D.C. bar, 1961, Ida. bar, 1966; mem. staff U.S. Senator Frank Church, Washington, 1958-61; atty. solicitor's office U.S. Labor Dept., Washington, 1961-65; house counsel United Planning Orgn., Washington, 1965; cons. U.S. Labor Dept., Washington, 1966; partner McDermott & McDermott, Pocatello, Ida., 1966—; mem. Ida. Ho. of Reps., 1968—. Del. Ida. Democratic Conv. 1966, 70, 72; pres. Bannock County Young Dems., 1966-68; regional v.p. Ida. Young Dems., 1966-68. Mem. legislative adv. com. Ida. Alcohol Safety Action Project; mem. Pocatello Bicentennial Com., 1973—. Mem. alumni bd. Ida. State U., 1973—. Mem. Am., Ida. trial lawyers assns., Ida. State Bar, Am., Fed., 6th Dist. (sec.-treas. 1966) bar assns., Western State Conf. Legislators (law and criminal justice com.), St. Anthony Council Catholic Women, Bus. and Profl. Women's Club, Alpha Omicron Pi. Roman Catholic. Home: 218 N 10th St Pocatello ID 83201 Office: PO Box 3 Pocatello ID 83201

MCDEVITT, ELLEN, physician; b. Shubuta, Miss., Sept. 3, 1907; d. James Andrew and Alma (McManus) McDevitt; A.B., Miss. State Coll., 1930; M.D., U. Utah, 1949. Chief technician vascular clinic N.Y. Post Grad. Hosp., 1934-46; intern Meadowbrook Hosp., Hempstead, N.Y., 1949-50; asst. resident Hackensack (N.J.) Hosp., 1950-51, Bellevue Hosp., N.Y.C., 1953-54; research asso. medicine N.Y. Hosp.-Cornell U. Med. Coll., 1951-52; provisional asst. physician out patient dept. N.Y. Hosp., 1951-52; mem. staff, chief 2d med. div. vascular clinic Bellevue Hosp.; instr. medicine Cornell U., 1954-56, asst. prof., 1957-63, asso. prof., 1963-72; asso. attending N.Y. Hosp., dir. vascular sect., 1968-72; courtesy staff N.Y. Hosp. Fellow Am. Soc. Geriatics; mem. A.M.A., Miss., East Miss. med. socs., Am. (fellow council on circulation, fellow council on stroke), N.Y., Miss. heart assns., Sigma Xi. Contbr. articles to profl. jours. Home: 1520 Olive St Gulfport MS 39501

MCDEVITT, SISTER MILDRED MARY, educator; b. Pawtucket, R.I., Feb. 21, 1897; d. William Henry and Sarah (Simpson) McDevitt; student Brown U., 1914-15; B.A., Trinity Coll., 1919; M.A., Emmanuel Coll., 1926; Ph.D., Boston Coll., 1934; M.A., Russian Sch. Middlebury Coll., 1959. Joined Order of Sisters of Notre Dame de Namur, Cin., 1917; organizer French dept. Emmanuel Coll., Boston, 1919, dir., 1919-57, prof. French lang. and lit., 1919—, chmn. Spanish dept., 1934-38, chmn. Slavic dept., 1957—, chmn. modern lang. dept., 1959-62, initiator, dir. Russian Center, 1960—, dir. Research Lang. Center, 1961-63; prof. dept. modern lang. Hampton (Va.) Inst., 1969-71, vis. lectr. French, 1969-71; assoc. prof. modern lang. dept. Talladega (Ala.) Coll., 1971—; vis. fellowship to Slavic dept. Harvard, 1955, Yale, 1956-57. Bd. dirs. Va. Lower Peninsula chpt. Am. Civil Liberties Union, 1970-71, 74—, Common Cause, 1970—. Recipient Palmes d'argent, ruban violet French Govt., 1949, violet rosette, 1964. Mem. Am. Assn. Tchrs. Slavic and Eastern European Langs. (pres. Eastern Mass. chpt. 1957, 60, Mass. pres. 1964), Modern Lang. Assn. Am. (v.p. N.E. chpt. 1956-57), Am. Assn. Tchrs. French (dir. Boston chpt. 1955-57), Am. Assn. U. Profs. Author: Louis Veuillot d'apres sa correspondance, 1935; La metrique de Francis Jammes, vue dans le cadre de celle de ses contemporains et de ses predecesseurs immediats, 1958; Catherine (lyric verse French), 1964; Pocket Poems, 1968. Asso. editor Le Bayou, 1945-63. Contbr. articles to various mags. Address: Modern Language Dept Talladega College Talladega AL 35160

MCDONALD, AUBREY BARTON (MRS. JONAS BARENHOLTZ), cosmetic co. exec.; b. LayFayette, Tenn., Aug. 7, 1911; d. William Dobson and Dona May (Miller) Barton; student Murfreesboro State U., 1933-34, Watkins Sch., Nashville, 1937-38, Vanderbilt Extension Sch., 1939-40; m. Paul Roy McDonald, Dec. 23, 1933 (div. Apr. 1955); 1 dau., Judy (Mrs. Duane Barnes); m. 2d, Jonas Barenholtz, Oct. 7, 1969. Co-founder Fashion Two Twenty, Inc., cosmetics firm, Aurora, O., 1962, exec. v.p., 1962—, dir., 1962—. Home: 2563 Covington Rd Akron OH 44313 Office: Fashion Two Twenty Inc 1263 S Chillcothe Rd Aurora OH 44202

MCDONALD, BARBARA HOLLIS BUCK (MRS. FRANK J. MCDONALD), recreational exec., nurse; b. Melrose, Mass., Oct. 1, 1907; d. William F. and Lucy G. (Hollis) Buck; B.S., Simmons Coll., 1931; R.N., Mass. Gen. Hosp., 1931; postgrad. Boston U., 1932; m. F. Russell Metcalf, Sept. 23, 1932; 1 son, William S.; m. 2d, Frank J. McDonald, Feb. 1, 1952. Dist. nurse Boston Vis. Nurse Assn., 1931-38; nurse Children's Aid Soc., Boston, 1938-41; exec. dir. Winchester (Mass.) Girl Scouts, 1941-52, Laconia (N.H.) Girl Scouts, 1952-54; co-dir., nurse Camp Nokomis, Lakeport, N.H., 1952—. Mem. Am. Camping Assn., N.H. Camp Dirs. Assn., Phi Theta Psi. Editor: Girl Scout Specialty Books, 1944-46. Home: 30 Palm St Weeki Wachee Hills Brooksville FL 33512 Office: Camp Nokomis Bear Island Lakeport NH 03246

MCDONALD, BLANCHE, librarian; b. Woonsocket, R.I.; d. Cuthbert J. and Clara (Saint Germain) McDonald; student Cath. U., 1940, Columbia U., 1942-44; B.A., U. R.I., 1974. Tchr. Acad. Jesus Mary, Woonsocket; with Harris Inst. Library, Woonsocket, 1926—, social br. librarian, 1927-40, 41—. Mem. A.L.A., R.I. Library Assn. Contbr. articles to profl. publs. Home: Woonsocket RI 02895 Office: 571 Social St Woonsocket RI 02895

MCDONALD, BONNIE BELLE, educator; b. Quitman, Miss.; d. Daniel W. and Mattie B. (Irby) McDonald; B.S., Miss. State Coll. for Women, 1939; M.S., U. Tenn., 1949; Ph.D., Tex. Woman's U., 1969. Tchr. home econs. Pachuta (Miss.) High Sch., 1939-41; head homemaking dept. Sumrall (Miss.) High Sch., 1941-44, 46-48; grad. asst. nutrition U. Tenn., Knoxville, 1948-49, asst. prof. human nutrition, 1949-57; specialist in food and nutrition Agrl. Extension Service, U. Fla. and Fla. State U., Tallahassee, 1957-61; dietitian Emory U. Hosp., Atlanta, 1961-62; research asso. nutrition Med. Coll. Ga., Augusta, 1962-64; asst. prof. home econs. Wis. State U., Stevens Point, 1964-67, asso. prof., 1967-71, prof. home econs., dir. dietetic program, 1971-72, program coordinator, 1973—. Cons. Head Start Project, 1966-72; curriculum cons. Dept. Pub. Instrn., 1973-74; grad. asst. Tex. Woman's U., Denton, 1967-69. Served with WAVES, 1944-46. Fellow Royal Soc. Health; mem. Internat. Fedn. Home Econs., Am., Wis. (mem. exec. bd. 1966-68), No. Wis. (pres. 1967-68) dietetics assns., Am., Wis. (chmn. research com. 1969-70) home econs. assns., N.E.A., A.A.A.S., Am. Wis. pub. health assns., Soc. Nutrition Edn., Wis. Acad. Scis., Wis. Nutrition Council (pres. 1974), Am. Assn. U. Women, Bus. and Profl. Women's Club. Contbr. articles to pubs. Home: 1609 4th Av Stevens Point WI 54481

MCDONALD, DOROTHY VERNELL, sch. adminstr.; b. Double Springs, Ala., Aug. 25, 1934; d. Lester W. and Elsie L. (Moody) Mize; B.S., Florence State U., 1955; M.A., Ball State U., 1966; m. Charles Thomas McDonald, Dec. 22, 1955 (div. 1967); 1 dau., Deborah Kay. Sec. Delco Battery div. Gen. Motors Corp., Muncie, Ind., 1955-56; substitute tchr. Muncie Community Schs., 1960-62, tchr. bus., counselor, 1962-70; dean women Southside High Sch., Muncie, 1970—. Bd. dirs. Youth Service Bur., 1973-74. Mem. Nat. Assn. Women Deans, Adminstrs. and Counselors, Ind. Assn. Women Deans and Counselors. Home: 2116 S Grant St Muncie IN 47302

MCDONALD, SISTER GRACE, religious order adminstr.; b. Spokane, Wash., Nov. 26, 1917; d. John V. and Justine (Reimringer) McDonald; B.A., Viterbo Coll., 1946; M.A., Cath. U. Am., 1949, Ph.D., 1954. Joined Franciscan Sisters Perpetual Adoration, 1935; tchr. parochial schs., Wis., Ia., 1937-48; prin. St. Robert Sch., Halder, Wis., 1946-48; prof. history Viterbo Coll. La Crosse, Wis., 1952—, dir. residence, 1952-60, pres. coll., 1960-70; pres. Franciscan Sisters of Perpetual Adoration, 1970—. Mem. nat. bd., chmn. region IX Leadership Conf. of Women Religious. Mem. Wis. State Ethics Bd. Bd. dirs. La Crosse Citizens Planning Corp., Viterbo Coll. Mem. Am. Assn. U. Women, Am. Cath. Hist. Assn., Wis. Cath. Conf., Nat. Cath. Edn. Assn., La Crosse County Hist. Soc., Greater La Crosse C. of C. (edn. com.), Pi Gamma Mu. Author: History of the Irish in Wisconsin in the Nineteenth Century, 1954. Address: 912 Market St La Crosse WI 54601

MCDONALD, IRENE MABLE DARNEILLE (MRS. JAMES MCDONALD), writer; b. Crescent City, Cal., Mar. 23, 1891; d. Hynson Lane and Martha Angeline (Sanders) Darneille; A.B., San Jose State U., 1927; postgrad. U. Cal. at Berkeley, 1949, 50, San Francisco State Coll., 1952; m. James McDonald, Feb. 20, 1916 (dec. 1968); children—James Darneille, Herbert R. Tchr. pub. schs., Ore., 1909-10; pianist Lyceum, 1911-15; mem. singing group Darneille Sisters, 1927-29; tchr. Escuela Professional, Panama, 1929-31; checker in high explosives Benicia Arsenal, Cal., 1940-42; tchr. Mt. Diablo Unified Sch., 1942-55; writer articles for Instructor mag., 1954-60, other non-fiction articles, 1954—. Recipient award as best art chmn. in Cal., Cal. Fedn. Woman's Clubs. Mem. Nat. League Am. Pen Women (pres. Santa Clara County 1970-72, parliamentarian 1972—), San Jose Art League, Cal. Writers. Club: San Jose Music Study. Contbg. editor on art markets Pen Woman, 1968-72. Designer stationery for Internat. Center, San Jose, 1968. Home: 260 S 15th St San Jose CA 95112

MCDONALD, JANE HALL (MRS. HAROLD WOOD MCDONALD), museum ofcl.; b. Coronado, Cal., Mar. 8, 1916; d. Robert Archibald and Margaret (Powers) H.; student U. Ariz., 1933-34; m. Harold Wood McDonald, June 6, 1937; children—Judith (Mrs. Edwin John Bradley, Harold Wood. Hostess, Hammond Harwood House, museum, Annapolis, Md., 1961-72, exec. sec., 1972—. Club: Naval Academy Women's. Home: 214 King George St Annapolis MD 21401 Office: 19 Maryland Av Annapolis MD 21401

MCDONALD, JULIE JENSEN (MRS. ELLIOTT R. MCDONALD, JR.), journalist, author; b. nr. Fiscus, Ia., June 22, 1929; d. Alfred Julius and Myrtle (Faurschou) Jensen; B.A. in Journalism, U. Ia., 1951; Litt. D. (hon.), St. Ambrose Coll., 1972; m. Elliott R. McDonald, Jr., May 6, 1952; children—Beth, Elliott R. III. Women's editor Rockford (Ill.) Register-Republic and Morning Star, 1951-52; writer, arts reviewer, Davenport (Ia.) Times-Democrat, 1962—; tchr. English, Black Hawk Jr. Coll., Moline, Ill., 1964; lectr. journalism St. Ambrose Coll., Davenport, Ia., 1974. Active Scott County Assn. Mental Health; chmn. Ia. Arts Council, 1969-73, Quad City Arts Council. Sec. Scott County Republican Central Com., 1957—. Named Writer of Year, Quad City Writers Club, 1969. Mem. Questers Study Club, Octave Thanet Book Club, Nat. League Am. Pen Women, Friends of Art, P.E.O., Phi Beta Kappa. Presbyn. (deacon). Author: The Wives, 1960; Man Running, 1963; Amalie's Story, 1970. Home and Office: 2802 E Locust St Davenport IA 52803

MCDONALD, LOIS BELLE EASTER (MRS. ROY LOCKWOOD MCDONALD, SR.), civic worker; b. Clifton, Ill., Apr. 19, 1927; d. Merle George and Margaret Jane (Domville) Easter; grad. high sch.; m. Roy Lockwood McDonald, Sr., Aug. 28, 1950; children—Roy Lockwood, Jr., Linda Gail. Profl. ice skater Holiday on Ice, 1946-53. Women's aquatic dir. YMCA, Green Bay, Wis., 1962—; chmn. synchronized swimming Wis. Amateur Athletic Union, 1970—. Named Sportswoman of Yr., Elks Club, 1972. Conglist. Home: 1821 Packerland Dr Green Bay WI 54303 Office: 235 N Jefferson St PO Box 490 Green Bay WI 54305

MCDONALD, LUCILE SAUNDERS, newspaper corr., author; b. Portland, Ore., Sept. 1, 1898; d. Frank M. and Rosa (Wittenberg) Saunders; student U. Ore.; courses in writing Columbia; m. Harold D. McDonald, Dec. 25, 1922; children—Richard, Carol. Mem. staff Bend (Ore.) Bull., Salem (Ore.) Statesman and Oregonian; writer mag. articles in S.Am., staff Buenos Aires Herald; night editor U.P.I. for S. Am.; with U.P.I., N.Y.C.; with Standard News Assn., Morning World, N.Y.C.; staff World Traveler mag.; news editor Cordova (Alaska) Daily Times.; N.Y. Times corr.; Turkey; feature writer Seattle Times

Sunday Mag., 1942-66, ret., 1966. Recipient Torchbearer award Washington Press Women, 1970. Mem. Puget Sound Maritime (editorial staff Sea Chest), Wash. hist. socs., Pacific N.W. Writers Conf. (a founder), Authors League Am., Western Writers Am., Seattle Free Lances, Women in Communications (Nat. Headliner award 1959). Author: Dick and the Spice Cupboard, 1936; Jewels and Gems (Jr. Lit. Guild selection); The Giant With Four Arms, 1941; Sheker's Lucky Piece, 1942; Bering's Potlatch, 1944; The Mystery of Catesby Island (Jr. Lit. Guild selection), 1950; Stormy Year 1952; Washington's Yesterdays, 1953; Friday's Child (Jr. Lit. Guild selection), 1954; The Mystery of the Long House, 1956; Pigtail Pioneer, 1956; Wing Harbor (Jr. Lit. Guild selection), 1957; The Courting of Ann Maria, 1958; Search for the Northwest Passage, 1958; Assignment in Ankara (Jr. Lit. Guild selection), 1959; Winter's Harvest, 1961; Coast Country, 1966; The Sunken Forest, 1968; For Glory and The King, 1969; Where the Washingtonians Lived, 1969; Garden Sass: the Story of Vegetables, 1971; The Look of Old Time Washington, 1971; Swan Among the Indians, 1972. Home: 3224 109th St SE Bellevue WA 98004

MCDONALD, MADONNA LEIGH FARRIS (MRS. PAUL LEACH MCDONALD), assn. exec.; b. Nashville, May 21, 1940; d. Paul Knox and Mable Ruth (Coleman) Farris; student Middle Tenn. State Coll., 1957-58, U. Tenn., 1960; m. Paul Leach McDonald, July 20, 1957; children—Richard Knox, Russell Wade, Robert Scott. Asst. to office mgr. NDPR, Inc., pub. relations, Nashville, 1967; collections specialist Steltemeier, Westbrook & Harvey, attys., Nashville, 1968-69; asst. to dir. Am. Assn. for State and Local History, Nashville, 1969-71, dir. adminstrv. services, 1971—. Bd. dirs. Franklin Rd. Acad. Mem. Middle Tenn. Bus. Press Club. Home: 5233 Kincannon Dr Nashville TN 37220 Office: 1315 8th Av S Nashville TN 37203

MCDONALD, MARGARET LEE (PEGGY), editor; b. El Reno, Okla., Oct. 2, 1911; d. Benjamin Coleman and Katherine (Chiles) McDonald; student Okla. Coll. Women, 1928-30, U. Okla., 1931-32; B.M., Centenary Coll., 1932. Tchr. music, 1932-34; with Electrolux Corp., 1937-39, Tex. State Employment Service, 1939-40, Tex. Harvey Oil Co., 1940-44; sec. to pres. Oilwell div. U.S. Steel Corp., Dallas, 1944—, also editor Oilwell News. Pres. Downtown Republican Club. Mem. Internat. Assn. Bus. Communicators, Exec. Secs., Inc., Desk and Derrick Club Dallas. Baptist. Club: Press (Dallas). Home: 4425 Caruth Blvd Dallas TX 75225 Office: PO Box 478 Dallas TX 75221

MCDONALD, MARGARET SPAIN (MRS. WILLIAM C. MCDONALD JR.), civic worker; b. Chevy Chase, Md., Feb. 22, 1919; d. Frank Edward and Margaret Ketchum (Cameron) Spain; student Goucher Coll., 1935-37, Sophie Newcomb Coll., 1937-38; A.B., Birmingham-So. Coll., 1939; m. William Clifford McDonald, Jr., Aug. 1, 1944; children—Margaret Cameron, William Clifford III. Women's page editor Birmingham (Ala.) Age-Herald, 1939-41; club worker A.R.C., CBI, 1943-45; former pres. Family Counseling Assn.; dir. Jefferson County (Ala.) Community Chest, 1965-72; exec. dir. Greater Birmingham Found., 1966—; mem. Regional Health Planning Commn., Birmingham, 1969—, Community Action Com., Birmingham, 1969—. Bd. dirs. Birmingham Beautification Bd., Operation New Birmingham. Named woman of year Birmingham Bus. and Profl. Womens' Club, 1971. Episcopalian. Clubs: Mountain Brook, Junior League, Birmingham Country (Birmingham). Home: 2201 Crest Rd South Birmingham AL 35209

MCDONALD, MARION, editor, ednl. adminstr.; b. Detroit, Aug. 19, 1907; d. Samuel Grant and Emma Christine (Waterfall) McDonald; A.B., U. Mich., 1930. Reporter Down River Press, Wyandotte, Mich., 1936-37; free lance publicity, 1939-41; editor U. Mich. Extension Service News, Ann Arbor, 1941—, asst. Detroit office, editor and publicist, 1942-48, publs. editor, 1948-49, Ann Arbor, 1949-71, dir. publs., 1971-72, dir. information and publs., 1972—. Mem. Women in Communications (adviser U. Mich. chpt. 1951-61), Adult Edn. Assn. Am., Adult Edn. Assn. Mich., Nat. Univ. Extension Assn. (mem. editorial com. 1957-59, publs. pub. affairs com. 1967-69), Women in Communications (pres. chpt. 1936-42), Alpha Xi Delta. Mem. First Ch. of Christ Scientist. Home: 2180 Medford Rd Apt 5 Ann Arbor MI 48104 Office: 412 Maynard St Ann Arbor MI 48104

MCDONALD, MARY JANE HOWE (MRS. WALLACE MCDONALD), educator, civic worker; b. Omaha, Jan. 15, 1926; d. Donald Kenneth and Rachel (Farrington) Howe; A.B., Vassar Coll., 1946; M.Ed., Boston U., 1974; m. Wallace McDonald, Sept. 11, 1947; children—Martha, Alan, Susan, Donald Bruce. Tchr., Mary C. Wheeler Sch., Providence, 1946-47; sec. Harvard Fatigue Lab., Cambridge, Mass., 1948; lab. technician Bio-Physics Lab., Harvard Med. Sch., Cambridge, 1948-49, Mass. Gen. Hosp., Boston, 1949-50; now tchr. math. Deerfield (Mass.) Acad. Mem. exec. bd., rec. sec. McCall Jr. High Sch. Parents Assn., 1964-65; v.p. Wyman Sch. Parents Assn., 1966-67, pres., 1967-68; den mother Boy Scouts of Am., 1959-60; leader Girl Scouts of U.S., 1965-67, asst. leader, 1967-69. Bd. dirs. Neighbors for an Open Winchester, Inc., 1967-71. Mem. Nat. Council Tchrs. Math., Jr. League Holyoke. Congilist. Club: Brewster Park (treas., dir. 1967-70). Home: Box 265 Deerfield MA 01342

MCDONALD, MARY JO, librarian; b. Cooper, Tex., May 3, 1930; d. John Thomas and Florence (Combs) Boyd; B.A., East Tex. State U., 1950, M.S., 1952; postgrad. Tex. Woman's U., U. Tex.; m. Reuben B. McDonald, June 28, 1955; children—Jon, Carol, Monika, Doris. Tchr. English, Rosebud (Tex.) High Sch., 1951-52; librarian Yoe High Sch., Cameron, Tex., 1952-55, S.W. Tex. State U., 1956-66; librarian, audiovisual coordinator New Braunfels (Tex.) High Sch., 1966—. Mem. Tex. Library Assn. (dist. sec. 1974—), N.E.A., Tex. Edn. Assn., Am. Assn. U. Women. Democrat. Methodist. Home: 587 Lakeview Circle New Braunfels TX 78130

MCDONALD, PATRICIA EILEEN, librarian; b. Mitchell, S.D., May 6, 1941; d. Francis Earl and Lillian Ellen (Grady) McDonald; B.S., S.D. State U., 1963; postgrad. U. Colo., 1965-66; M.L.S., U. Denver, 1969. Tchr., Denver Pub. Schs., 1963-66, 69-70, Sacramento Pub. Schs., 1966-68; asst. librarian, cataloger Yankton (S.D.) Coll., 1970-71, dir. library, 1971—. Mem. Am., Mountain Plains, S.D., Yankton (sec.-treas. 1971-72, chmn. 1973—) library assns., Am. Assn. U. Profs. Home: 818 Linn St Yankton SD 57078 Office: 1016 Douglas St Yankton SD 57078

MCDONALD, PAULINE ELIZABETH WILLIAMS (MRS. DENNIS ANTHONY MCDONALD), owner nursery sch.; b. Remsen, N.Y., Apr. 20, 1907; d. Orson and Edith Grace (Hughes) Williams; life teaching certificate State U. Coll. Edn., Oneonta, N.Y., 1928; postgrad. Columbia, 1932, U. So. Cal., 1948-49, U. Cal. at Los Angeles, 1967-69; m. Dennis Anthony McDonald, Oct. 12, 1935; children—Patricia Ann (Mrs. James Arthur Fountain), Kay Roberta (Mrs. Richard Scott Heineman). Kindergarten tchr., Huntington, N.Y., 1928-36; tchr. Culver City (Cal.) Unified Schs., 1947-49; owner, dir. Palms Tiny Tots Nursery Sch., Los Angeles, 1949—. Mem. Mayor's Com. on Health and Welfare, 1959; mem. West Area Planning Council, 1965-69; mem. U. Cal. Extension Core Program Com., 1965; charter mem. Culver City Guidance Clinic, 1961, v.p., 1971-73. Mem. Pre Sch. Assn. (charter mem., pres. Los Angeles 1959-61), So. Cal. Pre Sch. Assn. (v.p. 1964-65), Cal. Assn. for Edn. Young Children (treas. Los Angeles 1971-72), Early Childhood Edn. (exec. state bd. com. 1969-71). Methodist (mem. ednl. com. 1965—). Club: Soroptimist (Culver City, Cal.). Author: (with Doris V. Brown) Creative Art for Home and School, 1961, rev. edit., 1974; (with D.V. Brown) Learning Begins at Home, 1969, rev. edit., 1971. Home: 5243 Shenandoah Av Los Angeles CA 90056 Office: 3614 Motor Av Los Angeles CA 90034

MCDONALD, SARAH FRANCES, lawyer; b. Jefferson, Ga., Aug. 9, 1915; d. Edward Monroe and Belle (Braselton) McDonald; A.B., Agnes Scott Coll., 1936; L.L.B., Woodrow Wilson Coll. Law, 1951. Admitted to Ga. bar, 1951; gen. practice law, Decatur, Ga., 1951—. Dir. Fulton-DeKalb County chpt. Nat. Found., 1957-58; mem. Atlanta Estate Planning Council, mem. exec. bd., 1973-74, bd. dirs. Atlanta Legal Aid Soc., 1957—, sec., 1967-68, 3d v.p., 1970-71; women's adv. com. Civil Def. Div., Ga., 1957-59. One of 3 women dirs. Margaret Mitchell Safety Council 1956-65; dir. Atlanta Traffic and Safety Council, 1957-59; mem. Gov.'s Comm. Status of Women, 1964-70; pres. Leafmore-Creek Park Civic Assn. 1972-73; chmn. Women under Law Com. Pioneered driver edn. in all DeKalb County high schs., resulting in Decatur Bus. and Profl. Women's Club winning 1st pl. in nation in Carol Lane awards Nat. Safety Council, 1956. Bd. dirs. Decatur-DeKalb YMCA, 1974—. Recipient citation Civitan Good Citizenship Award, 1955; named Atlanta's Woman of Year in Professions, 1957. Mem. Am. (sect. on real property, probate and trust 1972-73), Ga. (vice chmn. ins. program com., continuing edn. com., mem. legal ethics and grievances com.), Decatur-DeKalb (1st woman mem., mem. com. draft Handbook for Jurors 1955, chmn. com. to revise Jury Handbook, chmn. com. initiate new courthouse facility to house cts., related depts. 1956, co-chmn. program com. 1969-71, 73-74), Stone Mountain bar assns., Ga. Assn. Women Lawyers (pres. 1957-58), Ga. Fedn. Bus. and Profl. Women's Clubs, Decatur Bus. and Profl. Women's Club (charter pres. 1954-56), Ga. Congress Parents and Tchrs. (hon. life), DeKalb County C. of C. (3d v.p. 1957—, chmn. meetings and forums com. 1959—), Agnes Scott Coll. Alumnae Assn. (bd. mem. 1959—, nat. pres. 1962-64, chmn. ann. giving fund 1966—), State Bar Ga. (program coordinator estate planning Seminar 1966). Presbyn. (homes and edn. com.). Club: Druid Hills Golf (dir.). Home: 1423 Vistaleaf Dr Decatur GA 30033 Office: One West Court Sq Suite 430 Decatur GA 30030

MCDONALD, VERNA GREENLEAF PAGENSTECHER (MRS. DUANE C. MCDONALD), pub. relations exec.; b. San Antonio, Nov. 15, 1923; d. Gustav Adolph and Verna Cleves (Greenleaf) Pagenstecher; student U. Tex., 1942-43; B.A. in French Langs. and Lit., Randolph-Macon Women's Coll., 1944; M.A. in Germanic Langs. and Lit., U. Colo., 1965; Ph.D. in Coll. Student Personnel Adminstrn. U. No. Colo., 1971; m. Duane Clifford McDonald, Nov. 8, 1944; children—Kent Stuart, Lynne. Instr. French and German, Greeley (Colo.) Central High Sch., 1959-68; asst. dean women U. No. Colo., Greeley, 1969-70, instr. French and German, 1970-71; indsl. relations staff mem., dept. head employee relations Kodak Colo. div. Eastman Kodak Co., Windsor, 1971—, editor monthly KCD Scanner. Americans Abroad coordinator Greeley chpt. Am. Field Service, 1963-65; Region VIII dir. Assn. Jr. Leagues Am., Inc., 1956-57; bd. dirs. Community Center for Creative Arts. Named Tchr. of Year, Greeley Central High Sch. chpt. Future Tchrs. Am., 1967. Mem. Delta Delta Delta. Episcopalian. Home: Box 566 Windsor CO 80550 Office: Employee Relations Eastman Kodak Co Kodak Colo Div Windsor CO 80550

MCDONALD, VIRGINIA BURGEY (MRS. JAMES EDWARD MCDONALD), city ofcl.; b. Schenectady, May 30, 1913; d. William Dillon and Frances Edith (Farrell) Burgey; R.N., St. Peter's Hosp. Sch. Nursing, Albany, N.Y., 1934; m. James Edward McDonald, Jan. 15, 1937 (dec. June 1969); 1 son, James Edward III (dec.). Supervisory nurse, nursery Brady Maternity Hosp., Albany, 1934-36; mayor, City of Cohoes, N.Y., 1970—. Vol. service worker Cohoes Meml. Hosp., 1948-63; initiated, organized bd. dirs. Cohoes Community Center, v.p. bd. dirs., 1964—; mem. steering com. N.Y. State Conf. Mayors, 1971—, mem. legislative com., 1970—; mem. community devel. com. U.S. Conf. Mayors, 1971-72; mem. Capitol Dist. Transp. Study Policy Com., 1970—; mem. Albany County Sewer Dist. Com.; mem. bldg. com. Cohoes Pub. Library, 1966-67, now mem. planning com.; mem. Cohoes Civil Def., 1970—; vol. nurse A.R.C. Blood Bank Program, Cohoes, 1966-68; mem. Cohoes Hosp. Aux., 1948—; mem. Albany County Charter Commn., 1972—; co-chmn. community fund drive for Cohoes Community Center. Mem. Cohoes Citizens Party Aux., 1963—, mem. exec. com., 1970—. Bd. dirs. Renesselaer br. A.R.C. bd. govs. Cohoes Model Cities Program; adv. bd. Keveny Meml. Acad.; bd. dirs. United Community Services Hudson-Mohawk Area, 1967—. Mem. Am. Pub. Works Assn., Alumnae Assn. St. Peter's Hosp. Roman Catholic. Home: 27 Sunset Court Cohoes NY 12047 Office: Mayor's Office Mohawk St Cohoes NY 12047

MCDONELL, BETTY NEWMAN, editor; b. Miami, Fla., July 14, 1929; d. Frank Douglas and Elizabeth Louise (Schafer) Newman; B.A. cum laude, U. Miami, Coral Gables, Fla., 1951; m. Charles Oliver McDonell, Sept. 12, 1950 (div. Jan. 1972); children—Bruce Scott, Katie Wallace, Brian Douglas, Mary Charles. With copy dept. Miami Daily News, 1946-48; sec. U. Miami, 1950-51; tchr. Dade County (Fla.) Schs., 1955-56; editor Fla. Audubon Soc., Maitland, 1965—; mng. editor Fla. Ornithol. Jour., 1972—; free lance bibliographer, editor, writer. Pub. Access TV Workshop tchr., 1972—. Mem. Fla. Com. on Rare and Endangered Plants and Animals, 1973-74, Winter Park Hosp. Aux., 1961-65; dist. capt. United Fund, 1972. Mem. Fla. Mag. Assn. (dir.), Fla. Forestry Assn. (hon.), Greater Orlando Press Club, Greater Miami Alumni Assn. (pres. 1956), Kappa Kappa Gamma. Democrat. Episcopalian. Editor: Florida Naturalist, 1968—. Home: 640 Mojave Trail Maitland FL 32751 Office: PO Drawer 7 Maitland FL 32751

MCDONNELL, BARBARA MOCK (MRS. JERRY MCDONNELL), pub. relations exec.; b. Chgo., Jan. 22, 1945; d. Harry Edgar and Beulah (Holland) Mock; B.A., DePauw U., 1966; M.A., Ind. U., 1969; m. Jerry McDonnell, May 20, 1972. Tchr. English and journalism, dir. pub. information Oak Park and River Forest (Ill.) High Sch., 1967-69; advt. mgr. CNA Financial Corp., Chgo., 1969-73; pub. relations dir. Broyles, Allebaugh & Davis, Advt., Inc., Englewood, Colo., 1973—. Mem. Women in Communications (Chgo. pres. 1972-73, nat. chmn. Clarion awards 1973-74), Kappa Kappa Gamma. Home: 1095 Monaco Pkwy Denver CO 80220 Office: 2 Executive Park Englewood CO 80110

MCDONNELL, HELEN MARGARET, educator; b. Bogata, N.J., July 31, 1923; d. Maurice Martin and Helen (Vollmer) McDonnell; B.A., Monmouth Coll., 1958; M.A., Seton Hall U., 1959; postgrad. Oxford (Eng.) U., summer 1964; Ph.D., (Woodrow Wilson fellow) Rutgers U., 1970. Civil service employee, Ft. Monmouth, N.J., 1942-58; tchr. English, Asbury Park (N.J.) High Sch., 1958-59; chmn. English dept., tchr. English, Wall High Sch., Wall Twp., N.J., 1959-64; chmn. English dept., tchr. English Ocean Twp. High Sch., Oakhurst, N.J., 1965—. Lectr. English, Monmouth Coll., part-time, 1960-62. Recipient Ford Found. grant summer study, 1959. Mem. N.J., Monmouth County edn. assns., N.J. Secondary Sch. Tchrs. Assn., Assn. Secondary Sch. Dept. Heads N.J., N.J. Assn. Tchrs. English, Nat. Council Tchrs. English (mem. com. on comparative and world lit. 1966—, asso. chmn. 1970 —). Co-author: (anthology series) Man in Literature, 1970; England in Literature, 1972. Address: 2927 Bangs Av Neptune NJ 07753

MCDONNELL, KATHLEEN MARIE, retail store ofcl.; b. London, Eng., May 16, 1947; d. John Joseph and Mary Bridget (Lunney) McDonnell; A.S. in Marketing, Westchester Community Coll., 1967. With W.T. Grant Co., various locations, 1963-70, asst. buyer N.Y. Office, 1970-71, buyer, 1971—. Office: 1515 Broadway New York City NY 10036

MCDONNELL, SISTER M. GERALDINE, nursing educator; b. San Francisco, Mar. 20, 1920; d. Michael Joseph and Elizabeth Agnes (Moran) McDonnell; diploma St. Mary's Coll. Nursing, San Francisco, 1941; B.A., Russell Coll., Burlingame, Cal., 1956; B.S. in Nursing cum laude, U. San Francisco, 1960; M.S., Catholic U. Am., 1962; postgrad. Brigham Young U., Provo, Utah. Joined Sisters of Mercy, Roman Catholic Ch., 1953; operating room supr., tchr. St. Mary's Med. Center, 1941-53; nursing service dir. St. Mary's Hosp. and Med. Center, 1962-65; asso. prof. Sch. Nursing, U. San Francisco, 1966-69, dean, 1969—; cons. in field. Mem. San Francisco consortium N.L.N. Baccalaureate Higher Degree Assn. Cal.; mem. Health Professions Council San Francisco, health adv. bd. Sisters of Mercy. Bd. dirs. St. Mercy High Sch., San Francisco. Mem. Nat. League Nurses, Am. Assn. U. Profs., Am. Assn. U. Deans., Cath. Hosp. Assn., San Francisco Heart Assn., Sigma Theta Tau, Alpha Sigma Nu. Home: 2200 Hayes St San Francisco CA 94117 Office: 2130 Fulton St San Francisco CA 94117

MCDONNELL, PATRICIA MARY, govt. ofcl.; b. San Mateo, Cal., Sept. 25, 1933; d. Harold James and Frances Isabel (Safarik) McDonnell; A.B., Coll. of Notre Dame, Cal., 1955; M.S., St. Louis U., 1958; postgrad. Am. U., 1963-64. Asso. editor Chem. Abstracts Service, Columbus, O., 1958-63; patent research specialist U.S. Patent Office, Washington, 1963—. Tech. cons. World Intellectual Property Orgn., Geneva, Switzerland, 1971-72. Mem. Am. Chem. Soc. (treas. div. chem. lit. 1968-72), Am. Soc. for Information Sci. (treas. Potomac chpt. 1963-64), Patent Office Soc. (sec. 1965-66), Nat. Microfilm Assn., Assn. for Computing Machinery, A.A.A.S., Gamma Pi Epsilon. Contbr. articles to profl. publs. Home: 6214 Hollins Dr Bethesda MD 20034 Office: US Patent Office Washington DC 20231

MCDONNELL, VIRGINIA BLEECKER (MRS. JOHN HENRY MCDONNELL), author; b. Short Hills, N.J., Nov. 24, 1917; d. J. Barclay and Helen Borden (Farley) Bleecker; R.N., Samaritan Hosp. Sch. Nursing, Troy, N.Y., 1941; postgrad. Russell Sage Coll., 1942; m. John Henry McDonnell, Feb. 13, 1954; 1 son, Gordon Rutherford. Night supr. male surg. ward N.Y. Post Grad. Med. Sch. and Hosp., N.Y.C., 1942-43; co-dir. Gore Mountain Ski Sch., North Creek, N.Y., 1947-55; mem. N.Y. State Winter Sports Council, 1950-60; asst. to exec. dir. pubs. and pub. relations Grand Lodge, Free and Accepted Masons, N.Y.C., 1958; reporter, feature writer Macy Westchester Rockland Newspapers, Westchester County, N.Y., 1959-61, editor, 1961-63; free lance author, 1963—. Recipient citation Leukemia Soc., 1959, City of Hope, 1959. Mem. Authors' Guild and League, Mystery Writers of Am., Huguenot-Thomas Paine Hist. Assn., Am. Forestry Assn. Author: Your Future in Nursing, 1963; Aerospace Nurse, 1966; The Irish Helped Build America, 1969; Careers in Hotel Management, 1971; Miscalculated Risk, 1972; Silent Partner, 1972; The Deep Six, 1973; The Long Shot, 1974, others. Author numerous short stories and articles. Home: 79 Hudson Park Rd New Rochelle NY 10805

MCDONOUGH, IRMA KAARINA, librarian; b. Sault Ste. Marie, Ont., Can., Nov. 19, 1924; d. Eino Jacob and Kerttu (Heinonen) Laakso; B.A., U. Toronto, 1965, B.L.S., 1966, diploma in library scis., 1946; divorced, 1960; 1 dau., Dale Marion; m. 2d, H.N. Milnes, 1966. Librarian Sudbury Pub. Library, 1952-54, Toronto Pub. Library, 1954-64; coordinator Children's Library Service, Provincial Library Service, Toronto, 1965—. Mem. Canadian, Ont. (pres. 1970-71) library assns. Editor, Ont. Library Rev., 1965—; editor, Initiator In Rev., 1967—. Home: 98 Willcocks St Toronto ON M5S 1C8 Canada Office: 14th Floor Mowat Block Queen's Park Toronto ON M7A 1C5 Canada

MCDONOUGH, ISABELLE MARY RICKEY (MRS. DAYLE C. MCDONOUGH), clubwoman; b. Oskaloosa, Ia., Apr. 4; d. Lindsey Vinton and Heddy (Lundee) Rickey; B.A. in Govt., George Washington U., 1947, postgrad., 1947-49; m. Dayle C. McDonough, Jan. 20, 1949. Dep. tax assessor and collector Aransas Pass. Ind. Sch. Dist., 1939-41; sec. to city atty., Aransas Pass, Tex., 1939-41; information specialist U.S. State Dept., Washington, 1942-48. Treas., Mo. Fedn. Women's Clubs, 1964-66, 2d v.p., 1966-68, 1st v.p., 1968-70, pres., 1970-72, exec. com., dir., 1972—; exec. com. Missourians for Clean Water. Bd. dirs. Gen. Fedn. Women's Clubs; bd. dirs. DeKalb County Pub. Library, pres., 1966; bd. dirs. Mo. Girls Town Found. Mem. Am. Soc. in Glasgow (Scotland), DeKalb County Hist. Soc., Internat. Platform Assn., Am. Assn. U. Women, Nat. League Am. Pen Women, Epsilon Sigma Omicron, Zeta Tau Alpha, Phi Delta Delta, Phi Delta Gamma. Democrat. Episcopalian. Clubs: Tri Arts, Wimodausis, Gavel, Ledgers (pres.), Isabelle McDonough Girls Town, DeKalb County Women's Democratic (pres. 1964), Shakespeare, Mo. Democratic, Fifty Year. Editor Mo. Clubwoman Mag. Home: 608 S Water St Maysville MO 64469

MCDONOUGH, LEAH BROOKS (MRS. JOSEPH M. MCDONOUGH), psychologist, county ofcl.; b. N.Y.C., Apr. 24, 1924; d. Nicholas J. and Leah G. (Griffin) Brooks; A.B., Coll. of New Rochelle, 1944; M.A., Fordham U., 1946; Ph.D., Mich. State U., 1958; m. Joseph M. McDonough, July 3, 1949; 1 dau., Susan. Clin. psychologist VA Hosp., Lyons, N.J., 1949-50, Coral Gables, Fla., 1958-61; chief Cts. and Corrections unit, San Mateo County Mental Health Service, Redwood City, Cal., 1962—. Mem. Am. Psychol. Assn. Contbr. articles on mental health and criminal justice to profl. publs. Home: 2150 Cowper St Palo Alto CA 94301 Office: 590 Hamilton St Redwood City CA 94063

MCDOWALL, MARY RUTH WOODS (MRS. JOHN KENNEDY MCDOWALL, JR.), educator; b. Coal Valley, Ala., Oct. 18, 1914; d. James Lucius and Etha Ozella (Sherer) Woods; B.S., Livingston State Tchrs. Coll., 1942; M.Ed., Miss. Coll., 1971; m. John Kennedy McDowall, Jr., Feb. 5, 1944; children—Mary Kennedy (Mrs. Varnell), Frances Ozella. Tchr. elementary sch., Walker County, Ala., 1935-45, Jackson (Miss.) Separate Sch. Dist., 1947—, Boyd Sch., 1967—. Active March of Dimes, Heart Fund, United Giver's Fund, P.T.A. Mem. Miss., Jackson edn. assns., Women's Gideon Aux. Internat., Assn. Childhood Edn. (pres. Jackson chpt. 1969-70, Miss. v.p. 1971-74), Alpha Delta Kappa (v.p. Jackson chpt.). Presbyn. Home: 4131 Oaklawn Dr Jackson MS 39206

MCDOWELL, MARJORIE ELLEN, advt. co. exec.; b. Saginaw, Mich., Aug. 25, 1939; d. Frederick Peter and Dora Carleta (Ladd) Simon; grad. high sch. Asso. media dir. J. Walter Thompson Advt. Co., Los Angeles, 1964-68; media buyer Compton Advt. Co., Los

Angeles, 1968; v.p., media dir. Kaufman Lansky Advt. Co., San Diego, 1969—. Mem. adv. com. 78th Assembly Dist. Cal., 1974. Mem. Nat. Orgn. for Women, Nat. Acad. of TV Arts and Scis. (bd. govs. 1973-75), San Diego Advt. Club (mem. com. 1973-74), Media Club. Office: 654 India San Diego CA 92101

MCDOWELL, MARY ADDLINE PROFFIT (MRS. CINNCINATTAS MCDOWELL), bus. dir.; b. Claybonne Co., Tenn., Feb. 4, 1904; d. James Henderson and Ellan (Beeler) Proffit; student Carson Jr. Coll., 1932-33; m. Leonard Maxwell Evans, Feb. 16, 1921 (div. June 1950); 1 son, J. Conally Evans; m. 2d, Cinncinattas McDowell, Apr. 16, 1960 (dec. Sept. 1965). Supr. garment factory, Bristol, Tenn., 1932-42; supr. Hercules Powder Co., 1942-44; dir. Young Women's Aux., Nalachuckee, Tenn., 1944-46; dir. Woman's Missionary Union, 1946-54; youth dir. and dir. ch. activities Belmont Baptist Ch., 1954-64; real estate and investment bus., 1964-67; sr. dir. Mary Kay Cosmetics, Inc., Odessa, Tex., 1967—, also cons. Worked with Odessa Boy's Club, 1955-56; mem. Ector County Park Bd., 1966—; mem. Ector County Children's Service Bd., 1972—; mem. YMCA bd., 1963—, dir., 1963-65. Bd. dirs. Baptists Nursing Home, Knoxville, Tenn. Mem. C. of C., Pioneer Study Club, Contemporary Garden Club. Mem. Order Eastern Star. Address: 2208 Salinas St Odessa TX 79760

MCDOWELL, MAY ROSS (M.A. ROSS), mfg. exec., lawyer; b. Buffalo, May 11, 1898; d. Elmer A. and Susan C. (Turner) Ross; LL.B., E. Tenn. Law Sch., 1934; LL.D., Steed Coll. Tech., 1962; m. George Howard McDowell, Aug. 29, 1938 (dec. Apr. 1971); 1 son, George Ross (dec.). Admitted to Tenn. bar, 1934; corp. sec. Empire Chair Co., Johnson City, Tenn., 1921-33; practice law, Johnson City, 1935-43; gen. counsel, corp. sec. Johnson City Foundry & Machine Co., 1943-46; v.p., gen. counsel Johnson City Foundry & Machinery Works, Inc., 1946-68, pres., treas., 1968—. Chmn., Metal Fabricating and Mfg. Apprenticeship Com., Johnson City 1947-48. Mem. council, chmn. pub. relations com. Appalachian county Girl Scout council; mem. adv. council bd. Salvation Army; mem. corp. Boys Clubs of Johnson City; chmn. bd. People To People of Johnson City. First woman commr. Johnson City, 1957-65, vice-mayor, 1959-61, mayor, 1961-63; ofcl. rep. Johnson City Power Bd., 1957-59; mem. Johnson City Planning Commn., 1959. Ofcl. del. Inter-Am. Conf., Punta del Este, Uruguay, 1962. Trustee Steed Coll. Tech. Exec. com. state exec. com. Republican party, 1938-52, vice chmn. Washington County exec. com., 1934-50. Recipient certificate Meritorious Service, U.S. Dept. Labor, 1963; named 1st Distinguished Woman in Residence at U. Colo., 1965, Woman of Achievement, Tenn. Fedn. Bus. and Profl. Women's Clubs, 1966, Outstanding Woman, Civitan Internat. Appalachian Dist., 1970. Mem. C. of C., Soc. Daus. Colonial Wars, So. Dames, Daus. Am. Colonists, Sons and Daus. of Pilgrims, Tenn. Soc. Colonial Dames XVII Century (charter, recipient certificate for outstanding contbn. to def. of republic 1970), D.A.R. (chpt. regent 1968, state chmn. bicentennial com. 1971-74), Patrick-Henry Allied Families of Patrick and Henry Counties Va. (founder, historian), Am., Washington County bar assns., Bar Assn. Tenn., Nat. Assn. Women Lawyers, Bus. and Profl. Women's Club (1st pres. 1924, state pres. Tenn. fedn. 1925-27), Rocky Mount Hist. Assn. (dir.), Town Affiliation Assn. U.S. Kappa Delta (past pres. Tri-Cities area alumni assn). Baptist. Mem. Order Eastern Star. Clubs: Monday, Johnson City Country, National Lawyers. Home: 426 Highland Av Johnson City TN 37601 Office: 920 W Walnut St Johnson City TN 37601

MCDUFF, MARJORIE MCLEAN (MRS. JOSEPH REA MCDUFF), editor; b. New Orleans, July 22, 1918; d. Clarence Eugene and Leah (Briede) McLean; grad. high sch.; m. Joseph Rea McDuff, June 8, 1940; children—Rebecca Lynn (Mrs. Anthony T. Kramer), Alan Rea, Nancy Gail (Mrs. Randolph J. Ross). Office asst. Geiger Printing Co., Hattiesburg, Miss., 1936-38; office mgr., asst. treas. Julius Kayser & Co., Hattiesburg, 1938-41; office mgr., asso. editor, sec. Who's Who in Am. Edn., Inc., Hattiesburg, Nashville, 1955-68, asso. editor Presidents and Deans of Am. Colls and Univs., Leaders in Am. Sci., 1955-68; mng. editor CCM Corp. subsidiary Crowell Collier Ednl. Corp., 1968-71; accountant, treas. Univ. and Coll. Press of Miss., Hattiesburg, 1971-73. Asso. editor Who's Who in Am. Coll. and U. Adminstrn., 1970, Ofcl. Mus. Directory, 1970. Sec., Forrest County Safety Council, 1957-58. Mem. Jr. Aux. Hattiesburg. Republican. Episcopalian. Club: Hattiesburg Country. Home: 800 S 17th Av Hattiesburg MS 39401

MCELHINEY, FAYE CATHERINE (MRS. GLYNN LYLE MCELHINEY), city ofcl.; b. Lewistown, Ill., May 17, 1910; d. Edwin and Ruth Ann (Wileman) Parkinson; student Brown's Bus. Coll., Galesburg, Ill., 1928-29; m. Glynn Lyle McElhiney, Aug. 23, 1930; children—Ted, Darlene (Mrs. Leo Henry), Richard Lyle. Sec. to atty., 1928-30; saleslady Avon Products, 1945-54; bookkeeper City of Kewanee, Ill., 1955-68, city clk., 1968—. Active various civic drives. Mem. Kewanee Pub. Hosp. Aux., Ill. Municipal League, Ill. Municipal clks., Internat. Municipal clks., Grange. Methodist. Mem. Order Eastern Star. Club: Business and Professional Womens. Home: 1026 Pine St Kewanee IL 61443 Office: 200 W 3d St Kewanee IL 61443

MCELLIGOTT, PEGGY LORRAINE (MRS. PAUL D. KETCHUM), city ofcl., lawyer; b. San Francisco; d. Thomas William and Annapeg (Svendsen) McElligott; A.B., Stanford, 1948, J.D., 1950; m. Paul D. Ketchum, Nov. 29, 1964. Admitted to Cal. bar, 1950; house counsel Getz Bros. & Co., San Francisco, 1950-55; staff adviser fgn. trade, counsel Ampex Corp., Redwood City, Cal., 1955-57; with Wilson, Jones, Morton & Lynch, San Mateo, 1957—, partner, 1964—, specialist in tax exempt pub. finance. Legislative adv. municipal law, 1957-64; acting city atty. Town of Los Gatos (Cal.), 1963-64; dep. city atty. Town of Portola Valley (Cal.), 1964—. Chmn. atty's com. Cal. Assn. Sanitation Agys. Mem. Am. Bar Assn., State Bar of Cal., Am. Judicature Soc. Contbr. articles to profl. jours. Home: 1469 Dana Av Palo Alto CA 94301 Office: 630 N San Mateo Dr San Mateo CA 94401

MCELROY, CATHRYN JEAN, curator; b. Lincoln, Neb., Jan. 2, 1946; d. Robert Walter and Virginia DeEtte (Eis) McElroy; B.A. magna cum laude, U. Colo., 1968; M.A., U. Del., 1970. Curator, Henry Morrison Flagler Museum, decorative arts and history museum, Palm Beach, Fla., 1970—. Mem. prop and wardrobe com. Jr. Opera Guild, Civic Opera of Palm Beaches, 1971—. Mem. Am. Assn. Museums, Nat. Trust for Historic Preservation, Palm Beach County Hist. Soc., Phi Alpha Theta. Home: 2111 N Flagler St Apt 27 West Palm Beach FL 33407 Office: Box 969 Palm Beach FL 33480

MCELROY, ELIZABETH WARNER (MRS. ROBERT MCELROY), librarian; b. Dixon, Ill., Jan. 29, 1923; d. Robert L. and Mary (Morrison) Warner; B.A., Carleton Coll., 1944; M.A., U. Chgo., 1967; m. Robert McElroy, May 31, 1947. Research chemist Container Corp. Am., Chgo., 1944-50; reference librarian J. Walter Thompson Co., Chgo., 1967-68; chief reference librarian Atmospheric Scis. Library, Dept. Commerce, Silver Spring, Md., 1969—. Mem. A.L.A., Spl. Library Assn. (rep. to A.L.A. com. on interlibrary loan), League Women Voters. Contbr. articles to profl. jours. Home: 3016 Tilden St NW Washington DC 20008 Office: Atmospheric Sciences Library 8060 13th St Silver Spring MD 20910

MCELROY, HILDA NJOKI (MRS. CLENAN C. MCELROY), cosmetic co. exec.; b. Sherman, Tex., Feb. 12, 1925; d. J.D. and Marian Acquilla (Washington) Hampton; B.S., Xavier U., New Orleans, 1945; M.A. (Ford Found. fellow), Northwestern U., 1970, Ph.D., 1973; m. Clenan C. McElroy, Mar. 3, 1946; children—Ronald, Phillip, David, Marian, Harry and Larry (twins). Tchr., Chgo. Pub. Schs., 1948-50; tchr. emotionally disturbed children Gary (Ind.) Schs., 1950-56, North Chicago (Ill.) Schs., 1962-69; tchr. interpretation black lit. Northwestern U. and Barat Coll., 1969; v.p. customer relations Black Fox Enterprises Ltd., North Chicago, 1971—; producer, hostess TV Series Black Arts 71, Chgo., 1971. Founder, dir. Cultural Workshop of North Chicago, 1968. Mem. adv. bd. Contemporary African Festival, Field Mus. Natural History, Chgo., 1973. Dissertation Fellowship grantee Northwestern U., 1973. Mem. Internat. Black Writers Conf., Delta Sigma Theta. Author: Black Journey, Black History Pageant, 1968; co-author Bibliography of Black American Playwrights 1960-1970, 1971. Contbr. articles to profl. jours. Address: 1700 20th St North Chicago IL 60064

MCELROY, LILLIAN MAE, state legislator; b. Maynard, Ia., Apr. 28, 1917; d. Harry LaVern and Caroline Katherine (Meyer) Arthur; student Upper Ia. U., 1936; m. Paul E. McElroy, June 28, 1936 (dec. 1965); children—Sheryl (Mrs. James F. Hunter), Sharon (Mrs. Dale Hirz), Diane (Mrs. William F. Obert), Paul Rodney. Farm owner, nr. Percival, Ia., mem. Ia. Ho. of Reps., 1971—. Pres. Fremont County Republican Women's Orgn., 1960-61. Named Ia. Master Farm Homemaker, Wallace Farmer Mag., 1958. Mem. Nat. Order Women Legislators, Ladies Legislative League, Federated Women's Club, P.E.O. Methodist. Address: Percival IA 51648

MCENIRY, SISTER BLANCHE MARIE, educator; b. Sedalia, Mo.; d. Matthew H. and Anne (Hefron) McEniry; B.A., Coll. St. Elizabeth, 1927; M.A., Columbia, 1934; Ph.D., Cath. U. Am., 1937. Joined Sisters of Charity of St. Elizabeth, 1930; lectr. Seton Hall U., 1938-48; vis. prof. Al-Hikma U., Baghdad, Iraq, 1965-66; chmn., prof. history Coll. St. Elizabeth, Convent Station, N.J., 1953—. Mem. senate Western province Diocesan Council of Sisters, Paterson, N.J. Trustee Coll. St. Elizabeth; bd. dirs. Ams. for Middle East Understanding. Mem. Am., Am. Cath. hist. assns. Coll. St. Elizabeth Alumnae Assn. (dir. 1954-59, 61-66), Phi Alpha Theta. Author: Woman of Decision, 1953, American Life Series textbooks, 1948; Three Score and Ten, 1970. Contbr. to New Cath. Ency. Address: College of St Elizabeth Convent Station NJ 09761

MCENTEE, HELEN MARIE SCHROEDER, librarian; b. Bklyn., Mar. 30, 1915; d. Henry John and Mary Elizabeth (Fuchs) Schroeder; Dental Hygienist, Eastman Sch. Dental Hygiene, 1938; student Cornell U., summers 1937-39, N.Y. U., 1941; B.A., Ladycliff Coll., 1946; B.L.S. (Faculty scholar), St. John's U., 1948; postgrad. Vassar Coll., 1950; M.A., Tchrs. Coll., Columbia, 1956; m. Girard L. McEntee, May 31, 1941 (dec. Jan. 1957); stepchildren—Ducat, Girard L. III. Dental hygiene tchr. N.Y. State Oral Hygiene Commn., 1937-40, Port Chester (N.Y.) Pub. Schs., 1940-41; dental hygienist, Kingston, N.Y., summer 1940; tchr. English, librarian Maybrook (N.Y.) High Sch., spring 1948; librarian South Jr. High Sch., Newburgh, N.Y., 1948-54, Edgewood-Greenacres Elementary Schs., Scarsdale, N.Y., 1954-55, Sr. High Sch., Glen Rock, N.J., 1956-66; asst. prof. dept. library sci. Grad. Sch. St. John's U., Jamaica, N.Y., 1966-69; coordinator, media specialist, librarian Peekskill (N.Y.) City Schs., 1969-73; asst. librarian Tchrs. Coll., Columbia, N.Y.C., 1955-56. Instr. St. John's U., 1960, Paterson State Coll., 1963. Vice pres. Bds. Coop. Ednl. Services Media Council, Putnam/Westchester County; mem. Bergen Com. for Library Service Edn., Constn. Island Assn.; chmn. stated meeting Met. Sch. Study Council, 1957; mem. N.Y. State Library Com. for New Standards. Mem. A.L.A., N.J., N.Y., Canadian. Cath. library assns., N.E.A., N.J. Edn. Assn., Bergen County Sch. Librarians (exec. bd.), Am. Assn. U. Women (pres. N.W. Bergen br.), Am. Bookwoman's Assn., Ladycliff, St. John's U., Columbia Tchrs. Coll. alumni assns. Clubs: Women's, West Point Officers. Contbr. articles to profl. publs. Home: 2 Weyant Terrace Highland Falls NY 10928 Office: 1072 Elm St Peekskill NY 10566

MCENTEE, KATHRYN RAE JONES (MRS. A. RAYMOND MCENTEE), newspaperwoman; b. Atlantic City, N.J., Mar. 3, 1908; d. Samuel C. and Emma R. (Turpin) Jones; B.A. cum laude, Rosemont Coll., 1930; m. A. Raymond McEntee, Nov. 11, 1936; children—Raymond, Robert, Richard. Reporter Atlantic City Press, 1930-33, soc. editor, 1933-38; editor Vailsburg Leader, Irvington, N.J., 1950-73; soc. editor Irvington (N.J.) Herald, 1950-73. Bd. dirs. Vailsburg First Aid Ambulance Squad, 1965-68. Named Firewoman of Year, Newark Fireman Benevolent Assn., 1965, Ch. Reporter of Year, Vailsburg Lions Club, 1973. Mem. Kappa Gamma Pi. Home: 215 N Dorset Av Ventnor NJ 08406

MCEWAN, MARY CATHERINE FEE (MRS. IGNATIUS MCEWAN), psychiatrist; b. Glasgow, Scotland, May 4, 1919; d. Patrick and Bridget (McGovern) Fee; B.S., Glosgow U., 1939, M.B., Ch.B., 1942; m. Ignatius McEwan, Apr. 2, 1945; children—Patricia, Vincent, Veronica, Alex. Intern, Royal Hosp. Sick Children, Eastern Gen., Royal Maternity and Women's hosps., all Glasgow; resident Strathclyde Hosp., Lanarkshire, Scotland, Darnley Hosp., Renfrewshire, Scotland; med. officer in charge Antenatal Clinics, Renfrewshire, 1945-46; gen. practice medicine, Toronto, Ont., 1957-62; practice medicine specializing in psychiatry, Toronto, 1968—; mem. staff St. Michael Hosp., Toronto. Pres., Acad. Medicine, Toronto, 1968-69. Fellow Royal Coll. Physicians; mem. Ont. Med. Assn. (dir.). Home: 23 Vintage Lane Thornhill ON Canada Office: 202 St Clair Av W Toronto ON Canada

MCFADDEN, RUTH MARILYN, librarian; b. Paris, Tenn., May 22, 1933; d. Homer Bryant and Ruth Taylor (Jones) McFadden; B.A., Murray State U., 1955, M.A. in Edn., 1957; M.A. in L.S., George Peabody Coll., 1963; certificate of advanced studies in L.S., U. Ill., 1970. Tchr. lit. Grove Jr. High Sch., Paris, 1955-63; asst. head catalog dept. Murray (Ky.) State U., 1963-74, head catalog dept., 1974—. Student worker, catalog dept. U. Ill. Library, Urbana, summers 1967-72. Mem. Beta Phi Mu, Kappa Delta Pi. Home: 714 N Poplar St Paris TN 38242 Office: Murray State University Library 15th St Murray KY 42071

MCFADDEN, SUSAN MEADE (MRS. JOHN J. MCFADDEN, JR.), occupational therapist; b. Washington, Nov. 13, 1941; d. Seibert Dwight and Josephine Adeline (Blacklock) Meade; B.S., Va. Commonwealth U., 1963; M.Ed. (Univ. fellow), Pa. State U., 1973; m. John J. McFadden, Jr., June 19, 1971. Staff occupational therapist Richmond (Va.) Cerebral Palsy Center, 1964-65, James Ryder Randall Elementary Sch., Clinton, Md., 1965-67; resource occupational therapist, cons. Prince George's County Pub. Schs., Upper Marlboro, Md., 1967-71; ednl. cons. State College (Pa.) Presbyn. Ch., 1972-73; head dept. occupational therapy Child Devel. Center, Memphis, 1973—; asst. prof. child devel. U. Tenn., 1973—. Mem. Am., Tenn. occupational therapy assns., Am. Assn. Mental Deficiency, Council for Exceptional Children, Pi Lambda Theta. Home: 5925 Poplar Pike Extd Apt 15 Memphis TN 38138 Office: Child Devel Center 711 Jefferson Av Memphis TN 38105

MCFADDEN, WILMOT CURNOW HAMM, chief librarian; b. Lead, S.D., Oct. 3, 1919; d. William and Ingeborg (Christianson) Curnow; student S.D. State Coll., 1938-41; m. Kenneth G. Hamm, Jan. 8, 1944 (div. 1963); 1 dau., Wilmot Christine; m. 2d, John Stinson McFadden, Mar. 1965. Asst. librarian Rock Springs (Wyo.) Pub. Library, 1947-48, head librarian, 1953—. Exec. dir. Wyo., Nat. Library Week, 1969. State committeewoman Democratic party, 1952—, also state vice chmn. Mem. adv. bd. Fed. Commn. Civil Rights, 1963—; treas. Dist. 4 Sch. Bd., 1966—, clk. dist. 1, 1969—; adv. bd. Western Wyo. Community Coll. Bd. dirs. State Library Archives and Hist. Bd., 1959-64, 66-71, mem., 1967—. Recipient Grolier Nat. Library Week award 1969. Mem. Federated Woman's Club, Am. Legion Aux., Mountain Plains (Wyo. rep. 1967-68, v.p. 1972, pres. 1972-73), Am., Wyo. (chmn. conf. 1966, v.p. 1972, pres. 1972-73) library assns., Am. Library Trustees Assn. Author: Handbook Wyoming Library Trustees. Home: 28 Cedar St Rock Springs WY 82901 Office: 300 Blair St Rock Springs WY 82901

MCFALL, GENE PAULIN (MRS. JAMES C. MCFALL), social worker; b. Dallas, Nov. 19, 1907; d. Vasco Ferdinand and Elizabeth (Britain) Hallum; A.B., San Diego State Coll., 1931; M.S.W., U. So. Cal., 1948; m. James C. McFall, Feb. 14, 1928. Psychiat. social worker, div. chief Dept. Pub. Welfare, San Diego, 1936-44; home service field rep., psychiat. social worker western region A.R.C., San Francisco, 1944-46; exec. dir. San Diego County council Girl Scouts U.S.A., 1947-63; chief psychiat. social worker Douglas Young Clinic, San Diego, 1964-67; clin. social worker State of Cal., 1967-72; pvt. practice as social worker, 1972—; case work cons. First Presbyn. Ch., San Diego; guest lectr. social work San Diego State Coll. Organizer Camp Safari, 1960, adminstr., 1960-63. Chmn. San Diego City Social Work Commn., 1953-58. Bd. dirs. San Diego Community Welfare Council, Assistance League San Diego, Cal. Assn. Health and Welfare, Mental Health Assn. San Diego, Am. Field Service, San Diego-Yokohama Sister City Program, San Diego Hist. Soc.; bd. govs. United Fund San Diego. Recipient certificate of commendation as med. field agt. S.S.S., U.S. Pres., 1945; named San Diego Woman of Year, 1956, Citizen of Week, 1963. Mem. Nat. Assn. Social Workers, (past chmn. San Diego chpt.), Acad. Certified Social Workers, Chi Omega. Home: 666 Upas St San Diego CA 92103

MCFARLAND, GRACE MARY, educator; b. Los Angeles; d. Ray A. and Helen D. (Brinckmann) McFarland; A.A., Citrus Jr. Coll., 1937; student Pasadena City Coll., 1938, U. Cal. at Los Angeles; B.A., U. Cal. at Santa Barbara, 1941; M.S., U. So. Cal., 1950. Tchr. Rosemead (Cal.) schs., 1941-50, Webster Sch., Pasadena, 1950-53; asst. prin. Willard Sch., 1953-54; prin. Allendale Sch., 1954-55, Don Benito Sch., 1955-59; asst. supt. elementary schs., Pasadena, 1959-73, asso. supt. for schs. and ednl. services, 1973—. Bd. dirs. Pasadena Girls Club. Mem. Cal. Congress Parents and Tchrs. (hon. life), N.E.A., Nat. Elementary Prin. Assn., Cal. Tchrs. Assn., Cal. Elementary Sch. Adminstrs. Assn., Cal. Assn. for Childhood Edn., Pasadena Edn. Assn., Elementary Sch. Sci. Assn. So. Cal., Pasadena C. of C., Phi Lambda Theta, Delta Kappa Gamma. Clubs: Pasadena Women's, Zonta. Home: 907 Monterey Av Monrovia CA 91016 Office: 351 S Hudson Av Pasadena CA 91106

MCFARLAND, KAY ELEANOR, judge; b. Coffeyville, Kan., July 20, 1935; d. Kenneth W. and Margaret E. (Thrall) McFarland; B.A. magna cum laude, Washburn U., 1957; J.D., Washburn Sch. Law, 1964. Admitted to Kan. bar, 1964; pvt. practice law, Topeka, 1964-71; probate, juvenile judge Shawnee County, Topeka, 1971-73; dist. judge, Topeka, 1973—. Owner, operator Quilts by Kay McFarland, Topeka, 1961-64. Mem. Am., Kan., Topeka bar assns., Dist. Judges Assn., Nat. Assn. Juvenile Judges, Nat. Assn. Probate Judges. Home: 4401 W 10th St Topeka KS 66604 Office: Ct House Topeka KS 66603

MCFARLIN, ANNJENNETTE SOPHIE, educator; b. Pensacola, Fla., July 14, 1935; d. Clifford and Thecimar (Brown) McFarlin; B.A., Cal. State U., Long Beach, 1967; M.A., U. Cal. at Los Angeles, 1968; postgrad. U. Wash., 1974—; 1 adopted dau., Annjennette E. Coordinator interdisciplinary skills curriculum No. Ill. U., DeKalb, 1968-70; dir. Dept. Health, Edn. and Welfare grant San Diego State Coll., 1971-72; staff asst. dean student dean student affairs for counseling Wash. State U., Pullman, 1972—. Chmn. edn. div. Mayor San Diego Youth Council, 1971-73; mem. minority adv. bd. sta. KFMB, Radio-TV, San Diego, 1971. Danforth fellow, 1967; recipient Intercollegiate Forensics award, 1964. Mem. Nat. Assn. Negro Bus. and Profl. Women's Clubs, Speech Communication Assn. Democrat. Mem. A.M.E. Ch. (pres. Young Womens Missionary Soc. 1970-72). Author article, book reviewer. Home: 110 Orange Dr Chula Vista CA 92011 Office: 330 College Hall Pullman WA 99163

MCFEATERS, MARGARET MARSHALL (MRS. GEORGE F. MCFEATERS), educator; b. Noblestown, Pa., May 21, 1910; d. Frederick D. and Lillian (Wells) Marshall; B.S., U. Pitts., 1944, M.Ed., 1947, D.Ed., 1954; m. George F. McFeaters, Sept. 22, 1939. Elementary tchr. Penn. Twp. Schs., Allegheny County, Pa., 1930-48, teaching prin., 1936-41; core tchr., curriculum coordinator Penn Jr. High, 1948-53; prin. Freedom (Pa.) area elementary schs., 1955-61; asst. prof. edn. Geneva Coll., Beaver Falls, Pa., 1962; asso. prof. edn. Slippery Rock (Pa.) State Coll., 1963-70, prof., 1970—, supr. student tchrs., 1963—. Mem. Pa. State Edn. Assn. (pres. Pa. dept. supv. and curriculum 1964-66), Assn. Supervision and Curriculum Devel. (nat. bd.), N.E.A., U. Pitts. Doctoral Assn., Assn. Tchr. Educators, Am. Assn. U. Profs., Assn. U. Women, Adminstrv. Women in Edn., Internat. Platform Assn., Slippery Rock Speakers Bur. Author: Guide book for New Professionals in Education, 1971. Home: 608 Browns Lane Pittsburgh PA 15237 Office: Slippery Rock PA 16057

MCFEE, JUNE KING (MRS. MALCOLM MCFEE), educator; b. Seattle, June 3, 1917; d. Cleo P. and Betty (Smith) King; student Whitman Coll., 1935-37; B.A., U. Wash., 1939; M.Ed., Central Wash. Coll., 1954; Ed.D., Stanford, 1957; m. Malcolm McFee, Sept. 27, 1941; 1 son, John King. Instr. Yakima Valley Jr. Coll., 1952-54; instr., asst. prof. art edn. Stanford U., 1955-63; vis. asso. prof. Ariz. State U., 1964-65; prof. art edn. and edn. U. Ore., Eugene, 1965—, also dir. Inst. for Community Art Studies. Vis. lectr. No. Ill. U., U. Ariz., U. Alaska, Fla. State U.; vis. prof. U. Ill., Ind. U.; cons. Los Angeles County schs., Pa. State U. Seminar, Hawaii Dept. Edn., JDR III Fund Arts Program, edn. com. A.I.A. Mem. Nat. Art Edn. Assn. (Pacific regional pres. 1968-70), Kappa Delta Pi, Pi Lambda Theta. Editor: Studies in Art Education. Contbr. to books, also articles to profl. jours. Home: 2375 Bailey Hill Rd Eugene OR 97405

MCGAFFEY, EDNA SILCOCK (MRS. CLAUDE W. MCGAFFEY, JR.), historian, columnist; b. Riverton, Utah, Apr. 15, 1920; d. Wilford T. and Florence (Bills) Silcock; student U. Utah, 1937-39; B.A., St. Mary's U., San Antonio, 1955; m. Harold L. Monteer, 1939 (div. 1943); 1 son, David Harold; m. 2d, Claude W. McGaffey, Jr., Aug. 21, 1948. Civilian employee U.S. Army, USAF, 1942-73, adminstr. San Antonio Air Materiel Area USAF hist. program, Kelly AFB, Tex., 1949-73, chief SAAMA Hist. Office, 1955-73; ret., 1973; columnist San Antonio Express-News, 1973—. Recipient Superior Performance award for work as historian, 1965; Woman of Achievement award Tex. Press Women, 1973; named Outstanding Toastmistress Mortar Bd. Toastmistress Club, 1961, 63, Outstanding Clubwoman of Year, Express-News Readers, 1971.

Mem. Am. Assn. U. Women (br. publicity chmn. 1969-70, corr. sec. 1970-72, rec. sec. Tex. div. 1973-75), San Antonio Art League, Women's Aux. Goodwill Industries, San Antonio Garden Center, San Antonio Conservation Soc., Tex. Press Women (historian 1969, dist. pres. 1970, rec. sec. 1971, parliamentarian 1972, corr. sec. 1973-74), Tex. (3d v.p. Alamo Dist. 1970-71, 2d v.p. 1971-72, 1st v.p. 1972—), San Antonio (4th v.p. 1961-62, rec. sec. 1966-68) fedns. womens clubs, Nat. Assn. Parliamentarians, Am. Assn. Ret. Persons, Theta Sigma Phi (pres. local profl. chpt. 1966-68, 2d v.p. 1971-72, Headliner award 1969). Clubs: Women's of San Antonio (life, chmn. Cosmopolitan Round Table 1963-65, 69-71, 1st v.p. in charge programs 1964-65, chmn. Amaranthine Round Table 1966-67), Mortar Bd. Clubs: Zonta San Antonio (mem. bd. publicity chmn. 1969-71, bull. chmn. 1971-73, chmn. antique show and sale 1974); Toastmistress (pres. 1961-62, council treas. 1965-66). Contbr. articles to nat. mags. Home: Apt 1114 6701 Blanco Rd San Antonio TX 78216

MCGAFFEY, HAZEL LOUISE ANDERSON, pathologist; b. Opheim, Mont., Aug. 21, 1924; d. Daniel Gideon and Anna Louise (Arnold) Anderson; B.M., U. Minn., 1949, M.D., 1950; m. Byron K. McGaffey, June 12, 1949; children—Ann Louise, William Grant. Rotating intern Swedish Hosp., Seattle, 1949-50; resident internal medicine Firland Sanatorium, Seattle, 1950-51, mem. staff, 1951-53; resident internal medicine Bellevue Hosp., N.Y.C., 1954; resident pathology U. Colo. Med. Center, also Denver VA Hosp., 1955-60; asst. chief pathology, chief pathology Oklahoma City VA Hosp., 1960-63; dir. pathology and Sch. Med. Tech. of Sacred Heart Hosp., Idaho Falls, Ida., 1963-73, pvt. lab., 1973—; coroner Bonneville County, 1965-69. Bd. dirs. Ida. Am. Cancer Soc., 1969-71. Fellow Am. Soc. Clin. Pathology (Ida. state councilor), Coll. Am. Pathology, Ida. Soc. Pathologists (sec. 1972, pres. 1973); mem. A.M.A., Pacific N.W. Soc. Pathologists. Home: 2055 S Higbee St Idaho Falls ID 83401 Office: 1206 E 17th St Idaho Falls ID 83401

MCGALL, EMMA CATHERINE, lawyer; b. North Plainfield, N.J., Aug. 29, 1907; d. James T. and Mary Frances (Kreger) McGall; J.D., Rutgers U., 1936. Admitted to N.J. bar, 1936, U.S. Supreme Ct. bar, 1964; practiced in Westfield, 1936—; partner Beard & McGall, attys., 1947—. Mem. Westfield Bd. Edn., 1970-73. Trustee Westfield YWCA, sec., 1954-57, now bd. dirs.; trustee N.J. Youth Correctional Instns. Mem. Union County Bar, N.J. State Bar, Am. Bar Assn., Nat. Assn. Women Lawyers, Bus. and Profl. Women's Clubs (mem. internat. legislation commn. 1966-69, pres. N.J. Fedn. 1960-62, legislative chmn. Nat. Fedn. 1964-67). Club: Westfield (pres. 1940-42). Home: 151 N Euclid Av Westfield NJ 07090 Office: 66 Elm St Westfield NJ 07091

MCGARRY, HELEN ELIZABETH, community services exec.; b. Novinger, Mo., Sept. 26, 1918; d. John Christopher and Mary Lou (Kinney) Burns; student real estate schs.; m. James Gordon McGarry, Mar. 24, 1935; children—James Gordon, Charles Michael. Gen. mgr. D&S Devel. Corp., Phoenix, 1960; exec. dir. Colo. River Indian Tribes, Office Econ. Opportunity, Parker, Ariz., 1966-71; spl. cons. Indian programs, states Ariz. and Cal., 1972; project dir. aged programs Maricopa County Community Services, Phoenix, 1973—. Pres. Parker C. of C., 1966-67. Pres. Parker Democratic Women's Club, 1971-72; mem. exec. bd. Dem. Women's Assn. Phoenix, 1972-73. Bd. dirs. Havasu City (Ariz.) Concert Assn., 1972-74, Yuma County Fair, 1966-73, Graham Meml. Hosp., Parker, 1966-72; life mem. Parker Hosp. Aux., 1973—. Mem. Save the Jail Found., Colo. River Devel. Assn. Elk. Home: 3626 N 37th St Phoenix AZ 85018 Office: 3645 E Washington St Phoenix AZ 85034

MCGAUGHEY, FLORENCE HELEN, educator, author; b. Roachdale, Ind., Mar. 1, 1904; d. Charles E. and Sallie E. (Brumfield) McGaughey; student Western Coll. for Women, 1922-23; A.B., DePauw U., 1926, postgrad., 1930, 42, 56; A.M., Middlebury Coll., 1932; postgrad. Ind. U., 1938, Ind. State U., 1943, 51, 56. Asst. prof. English, Ind. State U., Terre Haute, 1946-57, asso. prof., 1957-61, prof., 1961-70, prof. emeritus, 1970—. Columnist, Poets Corner. Adv. mem. MBLS. Bd. dirs. Terre Haute Symphony, Women's Symphony Soc. Recipient award of honor, gold cup gold medals, Poets Corner, 1959, Talisman Key Internat., 1969; Alumni citation DePauw U., 1959; diploma Segnalazione and poet laureate award in English, Centro Studi e Scambi, 1962. Fellow Internat. Poetry Soc.; mem. Nat. League Am. Pen Women (1st prizes 1948, hon. mention 1959), Am. Poets Fellowship Soc. (publs. grantee 1967), Modern Lang. Assn., Ind. State Fedn. Poetry Clubs (Poet Laureate award 1973-74), Poetry Soc. Australia, Comitato Internazionale Centro Studi e Scambi (Rome hon. rep.), Accademia Internazionale Leonardo da Vinci (corr. Rome, diploma merit, gold medal 1968), Wedgewood Collectors Soc., World Poetry Soc. (Magna Cum Laude distinguished service citation 1970), Acad. Am. Poets, Alpha Psi Omega, Delta Delta Delta (Golden Circle award), Delta Kappa Gamma, Alpha Phi Gamma. Clubs: National Arts; Faculty Women's; University; Pen and Brush; Poets' Study of Terre Haute; Wabash Valley Press. Author: Wind Across the Night, 1938; Music in the Wind, 1941; Spring is a Blue Kite, 1946; Reaching for the Spring, 1958; Selected Poems, 1961; Shadows, 1965; Petals From a Plum Tree, 1967 (with Jon J. Polifrone) Four Songs of Sorrow, Holy Night. Ind. editor Poet 1972; editor, contbr.: History of 1st Christian Ch., Greencastle, Ind., 1972. Contbr. poems, essays, articles to various newspapers, mags., profl. jours. Home: 136 S 25th St Terre Haute IN 47803

MCGAW, JESSIE BREWER, author, educator; b. Clarksville, Tenn., Oct. 17, 1913; d. Lewis Vernon and Birdie (Basford) Brewer; A.B., Duke, 1935; M.A., Peabody Coll., 1940; postgrad. Columbia, 1948-50, (Fulbright scholar) Am. Acad. Rome, 1959; m. Howard Franklin McGaw, Dec. 28, 1939 (div. 1958); children—Miriam Katherine, Vernon Howard; m. 2d, Harold L. Geis, Aug. 1964 (div. 1972). Tchr. Latin, Ward Belmont Sch., Nashville, 1938-40; tchr. Lausanne Sch., Memphis, 1940-42; asst. prof. English and Latin, U. Houston, 1952—. Bd. dirs. YWCA, 1957-59, Day Care Assn., 1956-61, Houston Civic Music Assn., 1958-60, Houston Council Human Relations. Recipient Cokesburg Juvenile award; Theta Sigma Phi lit. award. Research grantee, 1964, 72. Mem. Tex. Folklore Soc., South Central Modern Lang. Assn., Houston Council, Tchrs. Fgn. Lang. (treas.), League Women Voters, Am. Assn. U. Women, Tex. Inst. Letters, U. Houston Women's Assn. (pres. 1967-68), Delta Kappa Gamma, Kappa Kappa Gamma. Democrat. Methodist. Club: University Houston Woman's (pres. 1954-55, 67-68). Author: How Medicine Man Cured Paleface Woman, 1956; Painted Pony Runs Away, 1958; Little Elk Hunts Buffalo, 1961. Home: 2405 Dickey Pl Houston TX 77019

MCGEE, DOROTHY HORTON, author, historian; b. West Point, N.Y., Nov. 30, 1913; d. Hugh Henry and Dorothy (Brown) McGee; ed. Sch. of St. Mary, 1920-21, Green Vale Sch., 1921-28, Brearley Sch., 1928-29, Fermata Sch., 1929-31. Asst. historian Inc. Village of Roslyn, N.Y., 1950-58; historian Inc. Vilage of Matinecock, 1966—. Author: Skipper Sandra, 1950; Sally Townsend, Patriot, 1952; The Boarding School Mystery, 1953; Famous Signers of the Declaration, 1955; Alexander Hamilton—New Yorker, 1957; Herbert Hoover: Engineer, Humanitarian, Statesman, 1959, rev. edit., 1965; The Pearl Pendant Mystery, 1960; Framers of the Constitution, 1968; author booklets, articles hist. and sailing subjects. Chmn., Oyster Bay Am. Bicentennial Revolution Commn., 1971—; mem. Nassau County Am. Revolution Bicentennial Commn. Dir., The Friends of Raynham Hall, Inc.; treas. Family Welfare Assn. Nassau County, Inc., 1956-58; dir. Family Service Assn. Nassau County, 1958-69, chmn. Oyster Bay Am. Revolution Bicentennial Commn., 1971—. Recipient Certificate of award for outstanding contbn. children's lit. N.Y. State Assn. Elementary Sch. Prins., 1959; award Nat. Soc. Children of Am. Revolution, 1960; award N.Y. Assn. Supervision and Curriculum Devel., 1961; hist. award Town of Oyster Bay, 1963. Fellow Soc. Am. Historian, Inc.; mem. Soc. Preservation L.I. Antiquities (dir.), N.Y. Geneal. and Biol. Soc. Oyster Bay Hist. Soc. (pres. 1971—), Nassau County Hist. Soc., Nat. Trust Historic Preservation, L.I. Hist. Soc., others. Republican. Address: Box 142 Locust Valley NY 11560

MCGEE, KAREN MARIE OELTJEN (MRS. RICHARD PELHAM MCGEE), mfg. co. exec.; b. Schribner, Neb., Feb. 13, 1939; d. Edwin John and Magdalene Caroline (Wulf) Oeltjen; student Midland Coll., 1956-57; m. Richard Pelham McGee, June 1, 1958; 1 dau., Kristal Dawn. Sec., George Hormel, Fremont, Neb., 1957-58, Russell Stover Candies, Lincoln, Neb., 1959-60; v.p. Bird Engring., Inc., Fremont, 1960—. Bd. dirs., capt. Fremont Community Chest. Mem. Ch. of Christ (bd. edn. 1966-70). Home: 1957 E 3d St Fremont NE 68025 Office: PO Box J Fremont NE 68025

MCGEE, MARJORIE LAMONT (MRS. JOHN MCGEE), physician; b. Canton, O., Nov. 20, 1919; d. Charles Augustus and Eva (Bowman) LaMont; A.B., Duke U., 1941; M.D., Johns Hopkins U., 1944; m. John McGee, Nov. 21, 1943; children—Nancy Jochem (Mrs. F. Stephens), John Bruce, Marilyn, Stephen Douglas. Intern Johns Hopkins Hosp., Balt., 1944-45; part time cons. San Joaquin County health dept., Stockton, Cal., 1951-53, Marin County health dept., San Rafael, Cal., 1963—. Mem. Ross Elementary Sch. bd. edn., 1962-69. Bd. dirs. Sunny Hills Residential Treatment Center, San Anselmo, Cal. Mem. Woman's Aux. Cal. Med. Soc., Kappa Delta. Republican. Presbyn. Club: Meadow Golf and Country (Fairfax, Cal.). Address: 54 Winship Av San Anselmo CA 94960

MCGEE, MARTHA, univ. dean; b. Savannah, Ga., Oct. 8, 1933; d. Robert Winston and Myrtle (Tomlin) McGee; A.B., Judson Coll., 1955; M.A., Duke, 1958; postgrad. U. Miami, Fla., 1964, 66. Tchr., Chatham County Bd. Pub. Instrn., Savannah, 1955-57; asst. head resident counselor U. Miami, 1958-59, head resident counselor, 1959-61, asst. dean of women, 1961-67; dean of women Jacksonville (Fla.) U., 1967—. Chmn. personnel services, bd. dirs. Girl Scout council Tropical Fla., 1964-67, bd. dirs. Gateway council, Jacksonville, 1967—, chmn. personnel services, 1969-72; regional interviewer Girl Scouts U.S.A. bd. dirs., chmn. residence com. Jacksonville YWCA, 1968-70, v.p., 1970-72. Mem. So. (editor Newsletter, 1961-64, 71-73, sec. 1959-60), Fla. (pres.) coll. personnel assns., Fla. Personnel and Guidance Assn., Nat. Assn. Women Deans and Counselors. Home: 2962 Charme Dr Jacksonville FL 32211

MCGEEVER, MARGARET E. COOK (MRS. JOHN F. MCGEEVER), educator; b. Girard, Pa.; d. Charles D. and Maude Ruth (Freeman) Cook; B.S., Ohio U., 1940; M.S., U. Cal. at Los Angeles, 1952; Ed.D., Columbia, 1959; m. John F. McGeever, Oct. 8, 1943 (dec. Jan. 1969); 1 dau., Kelly Ann. Tchr., Linesville (Pa.) High Sch., 1940-41; with Agr. Extension Service, Kittanning, Pa., 1941-43; home econs. supr. Fairview (Pa.) High Sch., 1945-46; tchr. high sch., Saegertown, Pa., 1946-47; tchr. pub. sch., Conneaut Lake, Pa., 1947-50, Edinboro (Pa.) High Sch., 1950-51, Conneaut Valley Joint Sch., Conneautville, Pa., 1952-55; tchr. Miami (Fla.) Jackson High Sch., 1955-60; chmn. home and family life dept. Dade County Jr. Coll., Miami, 1960-61; asst. prof., head dept. home econs. Western Carolina Coll., Callowhee, N.C., 1961-63; asso. prof. home econs. San Diego State Coll., 1963-65, 1969; prof., dean Sch. Home Econs. Indiana (Pa.) U., 1969-70; prof. Bowling Green (O.) State U., 1970-73; head dept. child devel. Cal. Poly. State U., San Luis Obispo, 1973—. Mem. Cal. Home Econs. Assn., Am. Home Econs. Assn. (life), Nat. Council Family Relations (life), A.A.A.S., Am. Assn. U. Women, Am. Assn. U. Profs., Am. Pub. Health Assn., Cal. Assn. Marriage and Family Counselors, Day Care and Child Devel. Assn., Child Study Assn., Assn. Childhood Edn. Internat., Nat., Tri-County, Cal. assns. edn. young children, Council Basic Edn. Mem. Ch. Jesus Christ of Latter-day Saints. Club: Altrusa. Home: 2830 Flora St San Luis Obispo CA 93401

MCGEHEE, NAN ELIZABETH, univ. ofcl.; b. Chgo.; d. Winston T. and Ethel S. (Davis) McGehee; A.B., U. Chgo., 1947; M.S., Northwestern U., 1959; Ph.D., 1962. Asst. prof. U. Ill., Chgo., 1962-66, asso. prof. psychology, 1966—, dir. univ. honors programs, 1967-70, asso. dean faculties, 1970-72, asso. chancellor, 1972—. Mem. Alpha Kappa Alpha. Home: 9100 S Throop St Chicago IL 60620

MCGETTIGAN, LORRAINE JEAN RODRIGUEZ (MRS. EDWARD T. MCGETTIGAN, SR.), ins. co. exec.; b. N.Y.C., Mar. 27, 1926; d. Arthur E. and JeanElizabeth (Cahill) Rodriguez; student Katharine Gibbs Bus. Sch., 1944-46, New Rochelle Coll., 1966-68; m. Edward T. McGettigan, Sr., May 6, 1950; children—James, Edward, Susan, Joan. Treas., dir. R.A.E. Herbhold & Co., N.Y.C., High Risk Excess Corp., N.Y.C.; dir. Transp. Mgmt., Inc., Dover, Del.; co-owner Going Away Stables, Wilton, Conn. Vol. worker St. Vincents Hosp., Westchester, N.Y., 1966—; pres. Sch. Holy Child Mothers Club, Rye, N.Y., 1972-73. Mem. U.S. Trotting Assn., Harness Horse Breeders N.Y. State and North East Conn., Rosary Soc. (pres. 1972-73). Club: Shorehaven Country (Norwalk, Conn.). Home: 31 W Meadow Rd Wilton CT 06897 Office: 570 7th Av New York City NY 10018

MCGEVNA, MARGARET MURREN, city ofcl.; b. Orange, N.J., Oct. 16, 1919; d. Thomas A. and Margaret M. (McIntyre) Murren; student Newark State Coll., 1971; m. (dec. Aug. 1963); children—James, Maureen (Mrs. Richard Basta), Thomas, Sharon. Owner, Marge's Bridal Shop, Kenilworth, N.J., 1958-63; borough clk., purchasing agt., personnel dir. City of Kenilworth, 1963—. Recipient citation Pioneer Boys Am., 1972. Mem. Internat. Clks. Assn., Purchasing Agts. Assn. N.J., Municipal Clks. Assn. N.J. Home: 160 Boulevard Kenilworth NJ 07033 Office: Office of Borough Clk Borough Hall Kenilworth NJ 07033

MCGIBBON, PAULINE MILLS (MRS. DONALD WALKER MCGIBBON), Canadian provincial ofcl.; b. Sarnia, Ont., Can., Oct. 20, 1910; d. Alfred William and Ethel (French) Mills; B.A., U. Toronto, 1933; LL.D., U. Alta., 1967; Dr. Univ., U. Ottawa, 1972; m. Donald Walker McGibbon, Jan. 26, 1935. Dir. IBM, Canada, 1972-74; chancellor U. Toronto, 1971-74; lt. gov. Province Ont., 1974—. Mem. U. Toronto Senate, 1952-63; pres. Dominion Drama Festival, 1957-59; mem. Can. Council, 1968-71; pres. Can. Conf. Arts, 1972-73; v.p. Massey Hall, 1973-74. Bd. dirs. du Maurier Council for Performing Arts, 1973-74, Nat. Theatre Sch. Can., 1962-74; chmn. bd. dirs. Women's Coll. Hosp., 1970-74; gov. Upper Can. Coll., 1971-74. Decorated officer Order of Can., dame comdr. Order St. Lazarus Jerusalem; recipient Can. drama award, 1957; civic award of merit City of Toronto, 1966; Centennial medal, 1967. Mem. Imperial Order Daus. Empire (pres. nat. chpt. 1963-65). Home: 20 Avoca Av Toronto ON Canada Office: Queen's Park Toronto ON Canada

MCGILL, GERTRUDE MARION, assn. exec.; b. Marblehead, Mass., Aug. 24, 1911; d. Edward Joseph and Ellen (Gavin) McGill; A.B., Radcliffe Coll., 1932; certificate program in bus. adminstrn. Harvard-Radcliffe, 1943; postgrad. Simmons Sch. Social Work, 1941-42. Wage and salary adminstr. Walsh-Kaiser Co., Providence, 1943-46, Walsh Constrn. Co., N.Y.C., 1946-47; employment mgr. Textron, Inc., Manchester, N.H., 1947-48; personnel dir. Quincy (Mass.) City Hosp., 1948-51, City of Quincy, 1951-56; personnel adviser Girl Scouts U.S.A., Boston, 1956-65, regional dir., 1965-68, personnel specialist, 1968—. Mem. Harvard Bus. Sch. Assn. Boston, Greater Boston Personnel and Guidance Assn., Marblehead Hist. Soc., Irish Georgian Soc. Clubs: North Shore Radcliffe, Women's Personnel of Boston, Friends of Peabody Mus. Home: 6 Walnut St Marblehead MA 01945 Office: 10 Charles River Plaza Boston MA 02116

MCGILL, (SHIRLEY) FRANCES, educator; b. Fordyce, Ark., Dec. 24, 1919; d. Edwin H. and Ena (Speer) McGill; B.A., Mills Coll., 1941; M.S., U. Wash., 1943; postgrad. U. Colo., 1950, Ind. U., 1952, U. Wash., 1961; Ph.D., Ohio State U., 1963. Asst. instr. U. Wash., 1941-43; program dir. overseas A.R.C., 1943-46; instr. U. N.M., Albuquerque, 1946-53, asst. prof., 1953-64, asso. prof. phys. edn., 1964—, asso. dir. Human Performance Lab., 1965—. Research asso. Lovelace Found. for Med. Research, 1964—; chmn. Nat. Commn. Intercollegiate Athletics for Women, 1969—, Nat. Gymnastics Rating Com., 1968-69. Mem. Bernalillo County Red Cross Water Safety Com., 1948—, water safety chmn., 1954-60; mem. Com. Recreation Facilities State Dept. Edn., 1954-56. Recipient Honor award N.M. Assn. Health, Phys. Edn., Recreation. Mem. U.S. Gymnastics Fedn. (mem. governing council 1967—), A.A.H.P.E.R. (nat. bd. dirs. 1965-67, chmn. prins. and technics officiating com. 1962-64), Amateur Athletic Union (nat. sports medicine com. 1964-66), Div. for Girls and Women's Sports (mem. bd. 1946-52, 60-62, 64, dist. chmn. 1954-57), Western Soc. Phys. Edn. Coll. Women (pres. 1973-74). Home: 904 Girard St NE Albuquerque NM 87106

MCGILL, SHIRLEY STEFFEN (MRS. JAMES PATRICK MCGILL), antiques dealer; b. St. Louis, Sept. 1, 1925; d. Edward Charles and Claire Marie (Miller) Steffen; student U. Ariz., 1943-45; m. James Patrick McGill, July 14, 1961; children—Dianne (Mrs. Gerald Thomas Gibbons), Claire Miller Codding. Owner, Shirley McGill Antiques, Geneva, Ill., 1962—; exhibitor, mgr. antiques shows, 1962—. Mem. Nat., No. Ill. (dir. 1971-72) assns. dealers in antiques, Chgo. Suburban Antiques Dealers Assn. (pres. 1963-65, dir. 1965-74), Chi Omega. Mem. Order Eastern Star. Home: 323 E Washington St West Chicago IL 60185 Office: 717 E State St Geneva IL 60134

MCGILL, THEODORA, librarian; b. Orlando, Fla., Oct. 30, 1921; d. Theodore and Eunice Beatrice (Thomas) McGill; B.S., Miner Tchrs. Coll., 1941; postgrad. Howard U., 1941-42; M.S., Cath. U., 1952, postgrad., 1970-71; postgrad. George Washington U., 1969-70. Staff asst. program dir. A.R.C., Europe, 1944-49; librarian Nat. Cath. Sch. Social Service, Cath. U. Am., 1952-55; supervisory librarian Spl. Services in Korea, 1955-67; reference librarian Dept. Health, Edn. and Welfare, 1967-68; librarian Export-Import Bank U.S., Washington, 1968—. Recipient Certificate of Achievement U.S. Army Spl. Services, 1960; Meritorious Civilian Service award Dept. Army, 1966. Mem. spl. Libraries Assn. (archivist D.C. chpt. 1971—, chairwoman social sci. group 1971-72), D.C. Library Assn., Law Librarians Soc. Washington, Cath. U. Alumni Assn. Office: 811 Vermont Av NW Washington DC 20571

MCGILLEY, SISTER MARY JANET, coll. pres.; b. Kansas City, Mo., Dec. 4, 1924; d. James P. and Peg (Ryan) McGilley; B.A., St. Mary Coll., 1945; M.A., Boston Coll., 1951; Ph.D., Fordham U., 1956; postgrad. U. Notre Dame, 1960, Columbia, 1964. Social worker, Kansas City, 1945-46; joined Sisters of Charity of Leavenworth, 1946; tchr. English, Hayden High Sch., Topeka, 1948-50, Billings (Mont.) Central High Sch., 1951-53; faculty dept. English, St. Mary Coll., Leavenworth, Kan., 1956-64, pres. Coll., 1964—. Mem. Leavenworth Mayor's Adv. Commn. Bd. dirs. Asso. Ind. Colls. of Kan.; bd. dirs., exec. com. Kansas City Regional Council for Higher Edn., Ind. Coll. Funds Am. bd. dirs. Kan. Found for Pvt. Colls., pres., 1972-74. Recipient Alumnae award St. Mary Coll., 1969. Mem. Nat. Council Tchrs. English, Am. Council Edn., Cath. Poetry Soc. Am., Am. Assn. Higher Edn., Leavenworth C. of C. (hon. mem. bd. dirs.), Assn. Am. Colls. (commn. on higher learning 1970-73), Delta Epsilon Sigma. Democrat. Contbr. articles, fiction, poetry to various jours. Address: St Mary Coll Leavenworth KS 66048

MCGILLIARD, KATHLEEN LYNETTE (MRS. GEORGE STANLEY MCGILLIARD), choreographer, educator; b. Tacoma, Jan. 7, 1946; d. C.W. and Shirley Maxine (Fox) Coffin; student Pacific Luth. U., Tacoma, 1964-65; B.F.A. in Dance, U. Utah, 1968; M.F.A. in Dance, U. N.C., 1972; m. George Stanley McGilliard, May 10, 1970. Soloist, Concert Ballet Group of Tacoma, 1958-65; performer Tacoma Little Theatre, 1958-60; dance tchr., Vashon Island, Wash., 1961; soloist Tacoma Civic Ballet, 1963-64; dance tchr. Tacoma Pub. Schs., 1968; tchr. Met. Park Bd. Tacoma, 1967; dance tchr., choreographer State U. N.Y., Geneseo, 1968—. Cons. Am. Revolutionary Bi-Centennial Commn., Gig Harbor, Wash., 1973; performer, dir. Theatre West, Gig Harbor, 1973; adminstr., dance tchr. Gig Harbor Sch. Performing Arts, 1973. Mem. Am. Dance Guild, Am. Theatre Assn., Orchesis (v.p. 1967-68), Alpha Psi Omega, Phi Delta Chi. Choreographer: Another Coming, 1969; A Day for Dancing, 1970; Coppelia, 1971. Home: 804 Fox Dr Fox Island WA 98333 Office: Harbor Landing Mall Gig Harbor WA 98335

MCGILLIVRAY, KATHERINE FRANCES POLLAK, hotel exec.; b. Vienna, Austria, June 4, 1922; d. Ernest and Frances (von Kollmann) Pollak; student U. Sask. (Can.), 1938-39; m. Frank Aikins McGillivray, June 27, 1942 (div. 1950); children—Frank Ernest, Stanley Gordon. Profl. child actress, Vienna, 1926-31; reporter Der Courier, Regina, Sask., 1937-41; free lance cons. pub. relations, 1945-61; sec. Registered Nurses Assn. Ont., 1945-51; exec. asst. Manton Bros. Ltd., Toronto, Ont., 1951-53; office mgr., dir. Canadian Charcoal Corp., Toronto, 1953-57; adminstrv. asst. to pres. Lake Ont. Cement Co., Ltd., Toronto, 1957-62; dir. pub. relations and advt. Allied Chem. Can., Ltd., Montreal, Que., Can., 1962-72; dir. pub. relations and advt. Queen Elizabeth Hotel and Hilton Can. Ltd., Montreal, 1973—. Lectr. McGill U., Montreal, 1969-72. Mem. Advt. and Sales Exec. Club (v.p. 1966-68), Canadian Pub. Relations Soc., Canadian Advt. and Sales Assn. (pres. 1973). Presbyn. Club: Zonta (Montreal). Home: 3555 Cote des Neiges Rd Montreal PQ Canada Office: Queen Elizabeth Hotel Montreal PQ H3B 1X8 Canada

MCGINLEY, JULIANNE IMPERATO (MRS. PATRICK W. MCGINLEY), endocrinologist; b. N.Y.C., Sept. 22, 1939; d. Thomas and Marian (Crispinelli) Imperato; B.S. cum laude in Chemistry, Coll. Mt. St. Vincent, 1961; M.D., State U. N.Y., 1965; m. Patrick W. McGinley, Aug. 27, 1966. Intern St. Vincent's Hosp. and Med. Center, N.Y.C., 1965-66, resident in medicine, 1966-68; fellow in therapeutics Lenox Hill Hosp.-N.Y. U., 1968-69; NIH research fellow in endocrinology N.Y. Hosp.-Cornell Med. Coll., 1969—; asst. physician N.Y. Hosp., 1969—, instr. medicine, 1972—; attending physician Mt. Carmel Home for Aged, N.Y.C., 1967—. Mem. Kappa Gamma Pi. Office: NY Hosp 1300 York Av New York City NY 10021

MCGINLEY, PHYLLIS (MRS. CHARLES HAYDEN), writer of verse; b. Ontario, Ore., Mar. 21, 1905; d. Daniel and Julia (Kiesel) McGinley; student U. Utah, U. Cal.; D.Litt., Wheaton Coll., 1956, St. Mary's Coll. of Notre Dame, 1958, Marquette U., 1960, Dartmouth Coll., 1961, Boston Coll., 1962, Wilson Coll., 1963, Smith Coll., 1964, St. John's U., 1965; m. Charles Hayden, June 25, 1937; children—Julia E., Phyllis L. Writer of light verse, articles and lit. criticisms for nat. mags. Recipient Christopher medal, 1955, Cath. Writers Guild award, 1955, Poetry Soc. award, 1955, St. Catherine of Sienna medal, 1956; Pulitzer prize for poetry, 1961. Mem. Nat. Inst. of Arts and Letters, Poetry Soc. Am., P.E.N., Kappa Kappa Gamma. Roman Catholic. Author: (collections of verse) On the Contrary, 1934; One More Manhattan, 1937; Pocketful of Wry, 1940; Husbands Are Difficult, 1941; Stones From a Glass House, 1946; A Short Walk from the Station, 1951; Love Letters of Phyllis McGinley, 1954; (children's book) The Horse Who Lived Upstairs, 1944; The Plain Princess, 1945; All Around the Town, 1948; The Most Wonderful Doll in the World, 1950; Blunderbus, 1951; The Horse Who Had His Picture in the Paper, 1951; Make Believe Twins, 1952; The Year Without a Santa Claus, 1957; (collections of verse) Merry Christmas, Happy New Year, 1958; (lyrics for revue) Small Wonder, 1948; (film narration) The Emperor's Nightingale, 1951; Lucy McLockett (children's book), 1959; The Province of the Heart (collection of essays), 1959; Times Three (collections verse), 1960; Sugar and Spice (children's book), 1960; Mince Pie and Mistletoe, 1961; Arent' Boys Awful, 1962; Six Pence in Her Shoe (collection essays), 1964; Wonderful Time, 1966; Wreath of Christmas Legends, 1967; Wonders and Surprises, 1968; Saint Watching, 1969; (verse) Confessions of a Reluctant Optimist, 1974. Address: 16 N Chatsworth Av Larchmont NY 10538

MCGINNIS, MARY LOUISE MALONEY (MRS. ALBERT MCGINNIS), orgn. exec.; b. Carrollton, Ill., Aug. 18, 1916; d. Edward C. and Louise C. (Baltz) Maloney; grad. high sch.; m. Albert McGinnis, June 15, 1938; children—Connie (Mrs. Gerald Eskoff), James Michael, Patrick Sean. Exec. dir. Ill. Prairie council Girl Scouts U.S.A., Jacksonville, Ill., 1967—. First v.p. Inter-Agy. Council, 1969, pres., 1972-74. Mem. Republican Women. Bd. dirs. Jacksonville Childrens Found., 1969—, sec., 1971—. Recipient Thanks badge Girl Scouts U.S.A., 1968. Mem. Cath. Daus. Am. (program chmn. 1968-70). Roman Catholic. Clubs: Toastmistress (treas. 1972), Altrusa (treas. 1972, pres. 1972-74), Woman's (Jacksonville). Home: 238 E Michigan Av Jacksonville IL 62650 Office: 535 W Lafayette Av Jacksonville IL 62650

MCGINNIS, MARY ROBERTS, med. sec.; b. Rogers, Tex., Aug. 2, 1924; d. Frank C. and Lucy (Thornton) Roberts; B.B.A., Southwestern U., Georgetown, Tex., 1945; children by previous marriage—Mark A., Cathy L., Angela S. Med. sec. Scott & White Clinic, Temple, Tex.; exec. sec. Bell County Med. Soc., Temple. Mem., past officer local chpt. and regional council Parents Without Partners. Mem. Pi Gamma Mu. Mem. Order Eastern Star. Home: 1922 S 49th St Temple TX 76501 Office: 2401 S 31st St Temple TX 76501

MCGINNISS, BARBARA MACE (MRS. CARLOS A. FRANCO), fashion publicist, writer; b. Des Moines; d. Brice M. and Gladys (Langford) Mace; student Mt. Holyoke Coll., 1942-43; A.B., George Washington U., 1944; m. Harry W. McGinniss III, June 28, 1942 (div. Feb. 1950); m. 2d, Carlos A. Franco, June 16, 1951 (dec. July 1967). Advt. mgr. Neusteter Co., Denver, 1945-47, I. Miller Shoes, N.Y.C., 1953; publicity dir., display dir., fashion coordinator Cavendish Buying Office, N.Y.C., 1948-52; publicity dir. White Stag, N.Y.C., 1954-58; dir. pub. relations Bergdorf Goodman, N.Y.C., 1959-60; publicity dir. Mister Pants, N.Y.C., 1960-62; fashion news service mgr. Montgomery Ward, N.Y.C., 1966-72; account supr. Bell & Stanton Pub. Relations, N.Y.C. 1972; account exec., writer Robert Rolnick Assos., TV films, 1972-74. Guest lectr. retail advt. U. Denver, 1946. Reader, The Lighthouse, 1950-53; remedial reading Vols. of the Shelter, 1962-67. Mem. Pub. Relations Soc. Am., Am. Women in Radio and TV, Home Fashion League, Fashion Group (publicity com. 1963-65, fashion therapy com. 1966-71), Amateur Comedy Club, Chi Omega. Home: 355 E 72d St New York City NY 10021

MCGINNISS, DOROTHY AGNES, librarian, educator; b. Schenectady, Apr. 11, 1911; d. James and Margaret (O'Neil) McGinniss; A.B., N.Y. State Coll. Tchrs., Albany, 1932, B.S. in L.S., 1939; M.S. in L.S., Columbia, 1951. Tchr., sch. librarian, N.Y. State, 1934-44; librarian, head childrens work Newark Pub. Library, 1944-52; tchr. library sci. So. Ill. U., Carbondale, 1953-58; supr. library service Balt. County Bd. Edn., 1958-62; exec. sec. Am. Assn. Sch. Librarians, Chgo., 1962-66; prof. Syracuse (N.Y.) U. Sch. Library Sci., until 1974, prof. emeritus, 1974—; librarian Chilmark Pub. Library, Martha's Vineyard, Mass., 1974—. Mem. Am., N.Y. library assn. Home: State Rd Vineyard Haven MA 02568

MCGIVNEY, MELBA CLARE MATTHEWS, educator; b. Salt Lake City, Sept. 20, 1938; d. Weldon Clarence and Melba Bernice (Goff) Matthews; B.S. in Phys. Edn. and Dance, U. Utah, 1959, M.A. in Phys. Edn. and Ednl. Adminstrn., 1966, postgrad. 1974-75; m. Donald B. McGivney, Dec. 28, 1959; children—Claren Dawn, Michael Patrick, Cauleen. Tchr. in pub. and pvt. schs., Utah, 1959-60, 63-66; recreational work with Ute Indians, 1960-63; mem. faculty Westminster Coll., Salt Lake City, 1966—, asso. prof. health, phys. edn. and recreation, 1972—, chmn. dept., 1969—. Mem. conv. planning com. Utah Bd. Edn. Trustee Westminster Coll. Mem. Am. Assn. U. Profs., Utah Conf. Higher Edn., Am., Utah assns. health, phys. edn. and recreation, Western Soc. Phys. Edn. Coll. Women. Home: 3830 S 3060 East Salt Lake City UT 84109

MCGLYNN, BETTY LOCHRIE HOAG (MRS. THOMAS ARNOLD MCGLYNN), mus. archivist; b. Deer Lodge, Mont., Apr. 28, 1914; d. Arthur James and Elizabeth Tangey (Davey) Lochrie; B.A., Stanford, 1936; M.A., U. So. Cal., 1967; m. Thomas Arnold McGlynn, July 28, 1973; children (by previous marriage)—Peter L., Jane (Mrs. Richard Fargo Brown), Robert D. So. Cal. researcher Archives Am. Art, 1964-67; research dir. Carmel (Cal.) Mus. Art, 1967-69; dir. Triton Mus. Art, Santa Clara, Cal., 1970; archivist, editor jour. San Mateo (Cal.) County Hist. Assn. Mus., 1971—. Tchr. art extension Monterey Peninsula Coll., 1970, San Jose (Cal.) City Coll., 1971. Rec. sec. Coordinating Arts Council Monterey Peninsula, 1968-70. Mem. Am. Assn. U. Women, Chinese Hist. Soc. Am. Author: World of Mary DeNeale Morgan, 1970. Home: 1708 Lexington Av San Mateo CA 94402 Office: 1700 Hillsdale Blvd San Mateo CA 94402

MCGOEY, NOELLE THERESA, librarian; b. New Orleans, Dec. 25, 1927; d. James Patrick and Edna Louise (Crane) McGoey; B.A., Newcomb Coll., 1947; M.A., Tulane U., 1950. Tchr., Orleans Parish Sch. Bd., 1947-53; librarian I, New Orleans Pub. Library, 1954-67, library acquisitions officer, 1968—. Mem. La. Library Assn. Home: 317 Seattle St New Orleans LA 70124 Office: 219 Loyola Av New Orleans LA 70140

MCGOVERN, ELEANOR STEGEBERG, wife of U.S. Senator from S.D.; b. nr. Woonsocket, S.D., Nov. 25, 1921; student bus. adminstrn. Dakota Wesleyan U.; student George Washington U.; m. George Stanley McGovern, Oct. 31, 1943; children—Ann (Mrs. Wilbur Mead), Susan (Mrs. James Rowen), Teresa, Steven, Mary. Vol. in family edn. Parent and Child Care Center, Washington. Co-chmn. dist. hdqrs. George McGovern campaign for U.S. Ho. of Reps., Mitchell, S.D., 1956; co-chmn. program com. Women's Nat. Democratic Club; treas. Dem. Congl. Wives' Forum; mem. Suburban Women's Dem. Club, Montgomery County, Md. Bd. dirs. Psychiat. Inst. Found., Odyssey House, Erickson Inst., Chgo. Mem. Am. Acad. Med. Adminstrs. (hon.). Address: Mitchell SD 57301 also Washington DC

MCGOWAN, DIANNE ALICE, assn. exec.; b. Medford, Mass., Oct. 3, 1933; d. Clifton Otis and Esther Kathleen (Morang) Dyer; B.S. in Journalism, Boston U., 1955; children—Michael Kevin, Matthew Richard. Asst. editor J. Walter Thompso.., N.Y.C., 1955-57; editorial asst. St. Regis Paper Co., N.Y.C., 1957-58; publns. editor Acacia Life Ins. Co., Washington, 1962-69; with Savs. Bonds div. Treasury Dept., 1969-74, dep. dir. nat. orgns., Pitts., 1973-74; mgr. Women's activities Hwy. Users Fedn. for Safety and Mobility, Washington, 1974—. Bd. dirs. Parents-Without-Partners, 1970; bd. dirs., v.p. Montgomery County Single Parents, 1969. Recipient award Freedoms Found., 1965. Mem. Internat. Council Indsl. Editors (pres. Washington chpt. 1969), Am. Assn. Indsl. Editors (treas., dir.), Internat. Assn. Bus. Communicators (treas.; Editor of Year award Washington chpt. 1968), Am. Soc. Assn. Execs., Washington Advt. Club, Pitts. Indsl. Communicators, Nat. Assn. Women Hwy. Safety Leaders. Author poems. Home: 8811 Montgomery Av Chevy Chase MD 20015 Office: 1776 Massachusetts Av NW Washington DC 20036

MCGOWAN, JANICE MAE MARY, physician; b. Chgo., Oct. 11, 1928; d. Dominic Joseph and Helen Margaret Mary (Croft) McGowan; B.S., Coll. St. Theresa, Winona, Minn., 1950; postgrad. U. Ill., 1955; M.D., U. Ill., 1960. Med. Technologist Am. Soc. Clinic Pathologists, St. Joseph's Hosp., Kansas City, Mo., 1950-51; med. technologist, chief No. Ill. Blood Bank, 1953, Columbus Hosp., Chgo., 1953-60; intern Cook County Hosp., Chgo., 1960-61; resident St. Luke's Hosp., San Francisco, 1961-62, U. Cal. Hosp., San Francisco, 1962; practice medicine specializing in alcoholism, San Francisco, 1962—; med. dir. Alcoholism Clinic, Presbyn. Hosp., 1964—; San Francisco State U. Health Service, 1964—, Pacific Med. Center, San Francisco, 1962—. Cons., Behavior Inst., Sausalito, Cal., 1968—. Active United Jewish Community Center, 1965-70, N.A.A.C.P. Diplomate Am. Bd. Family Practice (Charter mem.). Mem. A.M.A., San Francisco Med. Soc., Am. Med. Soc. on Alcoholism, San Francisco Acad. Hypnosis, Womens' Physician Club. Home: 575 San Bruno Av San Francisco CA 94107 Office: 2398 Sacramento St San Francisco CA 94115

MCGOWAN, MARY LYNCH (MRS. ROBERT V. MCGOWAN), ins. co. exec.; b. Providence; d. James H. and Grace (Hackett) Lynch; student Am. Inst. Banking, 1955, Ins. Library Assn. of Boston, 1957, Hickox Secretarial Sch., Boston, 1966, Am. Mut. Ins. Alliance, 1971, Ins. Inst., Northeastern U., 1974; m. Robert V. McGowan, Dec. 8, 1973. With Norfolk & Dedham Mut. Fire Ins. Co., Dedham, Mass., 1956-73, editor, pub. relations and advt. mgr., 1963-73; v.p. McGowan Ins. Agy., Inc., North Attleboro, 1974—. Mem. Nat. (sec. regional conf. 1972, chmn. printing regional conf. 1972, chmn. resolutions com. 1973, mem. nominating com. 1974, award for outstanding state chmn. mag., advt. and reporting coms. 1973, regional chmn. mag. advt. com. 1974), Mass. (editor state mag. 1969-71, state sec. 1971-72, state v.p. 1972-73, state pres. 1973-74, Ins. Woman of Year 1974) assns. ins. women, Mutual Ins. Communicators (award for editorial excellence 1967, 68), Ind. Mut. Agts. New Eng. (dir.), Greater Boston C. of C. (mem. execs. club). Home: 8 Rathbun Willard Attleboro MA 02703 Office: 188 N Washington St North Attleboro MA 02760

MCGOWAN, SHERRY ANN, hosp. exec., publisher; b. Richmond, Va., May 11, 1946; d. Benjamin Stanley and Imelda Catherine (Dawson) Smith; student U. Kan., 1966-68, Washburn U., Topeka, 1970—; m. Jay S. McGowan, Nov. 1, 1965. Library asst. U. Kan., 1966-68; sec. in Topeka, 1969; mem. staff Topeka State Hosp., 1970—, sec. spl. services sect., 1973—, mem. staff devel. advt. com. and employees council, 1970-72, mem. secretarial staff devel. com., 1970-73, mem. grievance com., 1970—; owner Feminist Press of Topeka, 1975—. Mem. founding steering com. Women Aware, Topeka, 1971, v.p., 1972, coordinator, 1973, editor newsletter, 1972; charter mem. Lawrence (Kan.) Peace Center, 1966-68. Speaker's dir. Kan. Young Democrats, 1973; mem. com. 2d dist. Kan. Dem. Central Com., 1972—, precinct committeewoman Shawnee County, 1972—; alt. del. Dem. Nat. Conv., 1972; del. Kan. Dem. Conv., 1972; mem. Young Dem. Clubs, 1969—; founder New Dem. Coalition Kan., 1969-71; active local campaigns. Author poems, editor newsletters. Home: 1526 Harrison St Topeka KS 66612 Office: Spl Services Sect Topeka State Hosp Topeka KS 66606

MCGOWAN-SASS, BRENDA KATHLEEN (MRS. ROBERT CARL SASS), neuropsychologist; b. Winchester, Mass., May 23, 1939; d. Thomas Patrick and Katharine Louise (Regan) McGowan; B.A., Northeastern U., 1962; M.S., U. Mass., 1965, Ph.D., 1967; postgrad. U. Geneva, Switzerland, 1964; m. Robert Carl Sass, Oct. 18, 1969. Research psychologist Stanley Cobb Labs., Mass. Gen. Hosp., Boston, 1964-65; research fellow in Psychiatry Harvard Med. Sch., Boston, 1966-68; research asso. div. neurobiology Barrow Neurol. Inst., Phoenix, 1968-70; research asso. dept. physiology, anatomy U. Cal. at Berkeley, 1971—, cons. to program in Med. Health Scis. Recipient Abram Aaron Levy award, 1962. Mem. Am., Western psychol. assns. Contbr. articles on neurobiology to sci. jours. Home: 375 River View Dr San Jose CA 95111 Office: Dept of Physiology Anatomy Univ of California Berkeley CA 94720

MCGOWN, PEARL KINNEAR, cons., author; b. Clinton, Mass., Feb. 27, 1892; d. Duke Marlborough and Emma (Stevens) Kinnear; student pub. schs.; m. Maurice J. McGown, Mar. 14, 1914; 1 son, Winthrop Hart. Legal sec. Dodge & Saunders, Worcester, Mass., 1907-49; pres. Pearl K. McGown, Inc., West Boylston, Mass., 1948—; cons. Sturbridge (Mass.) Corp., 1970—; pres. Nat. Guild Pearl K. McGown Rug Hookrafters, Inc., Sturbridge, 1972—. Condr., workshops Cedar Lakes Arts and Crafts, Ripley, W.Va., 1954—, Holy Cross Coll., Worcester, 1950—; exhibited art one-woman show Milton Eisenhower Library Galleries, 1973. Mem. Nat. League Am. Pen Women (past pres.), Hookrafters Guild (pres. 1944-46), Inter-Soc. Color Council, Internat. Platform Assn. Author: The Dreams Beneath Design, 1939; You Can Hook Rugs, 1951; Color in Hooked Rugs, 1954; Persian Orientals, 1958; The Lore and Lure of Hooked Rugs, 1966. Home: 135 Sterling St West Boylston MA 01583 Office: Sturbridge Corp Old Sturbridge Village Mus Sturbridge MA 01566

MCGRATH, HAZEL FERRIS, journalist; b. Sturgeon Bay, Wis., Jan. 12, 1910; d. Joseph Ferdinand and Catherine Julia (Klaubauf) Ferris; B.A. in Journalism U. Wis., 1944, postgrad., 1952; m. Malcolm F. McGrath, July 13, 1931 (div. July 1949); children—Michael Ferris, Patricia Helen (Mrs. Polo V. Niño), Terence William. Asst. editor U. Wis. News Service, Madison, 1945-49, editor, 1949-63, pub. information officer, 1963-73. Mem. Women in Communications (pres. 1959-60). Clubs: Madison Civics (dir. 1973-74), Madison Press. Home: 2516 Commonwealth Av Madison WI 53711

MCGRATH, MARIANNE SMITH (MRS. DONALD JOSEPH MCGRATH), pediatrician; b. Pitts., May 25, 1941; d. Raymond Francis and Ann Jane (Schneider) Smith; A.B., Thomas More Coll., 1963; M.D., U. Ky., 1968; m. Donald Joseph McGrath, July 5, 1969; children—Jane Patrice, Matthew Donald. Tchr. biology Seton High Sch., Cin., 1963-64; intern pediatrics St. Francis Hosp., Pitts., 1968-69; resident pediatrics Good Samaritan Hosp., Cin., 1969-70, Community pediatric fellow, 1970-71; pediatrician Family Health Clinic, Dayton, Ky., 1971-73; instr. pediatrics U. Cin., 1973—; pediatrician Cin. Adolescent Clinic, 1973—. Mem. A.M.A., Cin. Pediatric Soc., Cin. Acad. Medicine, Kenton-Campbell County Med. Soc. Home: 3137 Brookwood Dr Fort Mitchell KY 41017 Office: Cin Adolescent Clinic Children's Hosp Med Center Cincinnati OH

MCGRATH, PHYLLIS ANN KETLER, real estate broker; b. Benkelman, Neb., Mar. 15, 1937; d. C. Merle and Eva Marie (Cooley) Ketler; student Colo. State U., 1957-58; student U. No. Colo., 1958-59; m. John I. McGrath, June 1, 1958 (div. 1971); children—John Robert, Jeffrey Alan. Pvt. sec. Miner & Miner Cons. Engrs., Greeley, Colo., 1955-63; exec. sec. to city mgr. City of Greeley, 1965-67; dir. pub. relations Greeley Nat. Bank, 1967-70; pvt. cons. in pub. relations and polit. exemptions, Greeley, 1970-73; real estate saleswoman Wheeler Realty, Greeley, 1973—. Regional cons. Office Econ. Opportunity, Denver, 1973. Sec. Young Republican Nat. Fed., 1971-73, nat. co-chmn., 1973—. Bd. dirs. Greeley United Fund, v.p., 1965-69. Mem. Greeley Concert Assn., Am. Women in Radio and TV, Nat. Assn. Realtors, Greeley C. of C., Kappa Delta. Home: 1616 Montview Blvd Greeley CO 80631 Office: 1331 8th Av Greeley CO 80631

MCGRATH, RUTH EHRIG, educator; b. Buffalo, Dec. 29, 1908; d. Ernest and Clara Catherine (Eichhorn) Ehrig; B.S., State Tchrs. Coll. Buffalo, 1930; postgrad. Merrill Palmer Inst., Detroit, 1930; Ed.M., U. Buffalo, 1950, Ed.D., 1953; m. John McGrath, Aug. 13, 1932; children—Garry Wayne, Earl James. Tchr. home econs. Northside High Sch., 1930-32; head tchr. lab. preschool, lectr. edn. U. Buffalo, 1938-50; dir. lab. preschool, asso. prof. edn. State U. N.Y. at Buffalo, 1959—. Cons., Headstart, 1967-69, Jewish Center, 1955-57, Jack and Jill Nursey of YWCA, 1965-70; mem. U.S. Nat. Com. for Early Childhood, 1972. Mem. Nursery Assn. Ont. (dir. 1957-63), World Orgn. Early Childhood Devel., N.Y. State Council Children (pres. 1970-71), N.Y. Assn. Edn. of Young Children (pres. 1968-70), Early Childhood Edn. Council Western N.Y. (pres. 1958-60. 64-66), Pi Lambda Theta (faculty adviser 1965—). Editor: (with Marna Burstein) Cooking with Children, 1969. Contbr. articles profl. jours., encys. Home: 55 Marjann Terrace Kenmore NY 14223 Office: 3435 Main St Buffalo NY 14214

MCGREAL, DOROTHY WINIFRED (MRS. JAMES D. MCGREAL), editor, publisher; b. Grand Forks, N.D.; d. Albert and Doris Marguerite (Packard) Jans; student N.Y. Sch. Interior Decoration, 1938-39; m. James D. McGreal; children—Terrence J., Patrick B. Comml. artist, N.Y.C., 1942-43; bus. mgr. Stamford (Conn.) Pioneers Baseball Club, 1948; editor, pub. World of Comic Art Publs., Hawthorne, Cal., 1966—. Lectr., Los Angeles County Pub. Library groups, 1966—. Warden, Los Angeles County Disaster Relief Authority, 1955—. Recipient Pub. Service award Community Chest, 1958, Boy Scouts Am., 1959. Mem. Fine Arts Assn. Centinela Valley (pres. 1971—), Friends of Huntington Library, Comic Art Hist. Soc. (founder 1967). Home: 3839 W 139th St Hawthorne CA 90250 Office: PO Box 507 Hawthorne CA 90250

MCGREGOR, DOLORES, advt. agy. exec.; b. Minot, N.D., June 14, 1924; d. Donald A. and Margrith (Bieri) McGregor; student N.D. State U., 1942, Ia. State U., 1944; B.S., U. Wash., 1946. Home economist Seattle Times, 1946-49, Seattle Post Intelligencer, 1949-52, King Broadcasting Co., Seattle, 1952-62; home econs. dir. Pacific Nat. Advt. Agy., Seattle, 1962—; free lance food photography supervision and cons. for television tapes, newspapers. Mem. adv. council home econs. dept. Wash. State U., 1959-62, Mem. Wash. Home Economists in Bus. (chmn. edn. found.), Am., Wash. (com. chmn.) home econs. assns., Am. Women in Radio and Television (chpt. pres. 1970—). Editor: Bea Donovan's Favorites, 1962. Home: 2587 Nob Hill N Seattle WA 98109 Office: 217 6th Av N Seattle WA 98109

MCGREGOR, LOUISE KEITH HILL (MRS. ROBERT DRAKE MCGREGOR, JR.), educator; b. Gainesville, Fla., Jan. 1, 1922; d. Franklin Jeremiah and Eva Harriett (Johnson) Hill; B.S., Hampton Inst., 1943, M.S., 1951; postgrad. Temple U., summer 1953, Va. State Coll., U. Va., George Washington U.; m. Robert Drake McGregor, Jr., June 23, 1956. Tchr. home econs. Lincoln High Sch., Gainesville, 1943-56; tchr., chmn. dept. spl. edn. Arlington County Pub. Sch., Arlington, Va., 1958-73; tchr. Kenmore Jr. High Sch., Arlington, 1969—. Vol. aide gift shop Red Cross Hosp., Louisville, 1957; mem. Adv. Com. for Child Care Arlington County, 1971-73; mem. Arlington Health and Welfare Council, 1971-73. Mem. Am. Assn. on Mental Deficiency, Nat., Va., Arlington edn. assns., Council for Exceptional Children, No. Va. Assn. Assn. for Retarded Citizens, Am. Assn. Jack and Jill, Delta Sigma Theta. Conglist. Co-author, editor Cirriculum Guide for the Instruction of Educable Mentally Handicapped, 1968. Home: 5266 19th Rd N Arlington VA 22207

MCGREGOR, MARJORIE JOE, educator; b. Oklahoma City, Dec. 6, 1928; d. Roy and Violet Almeta (Reigh) Holland; B.F.A., Okla. U., 1963, M.A. in Oral Communication, 1965, Ph.D., 1971; m. Lewis Walter McGregor, June 18, 1949; children—Stanley Lewis, Jeffrey Paul. Owner, tchr. Marjorie's Sch. Dance, Oklahoma City, 1951-62; asso. prof. oral communication Central State U., Edmond, Okla., 1965—. Mem. Okla. Speech Communication Assn. (pres. 1973-74, editor newsletter 1971-72, editor jour. 1975), Central States Speech Assn. (sec. adv. com.), Speech Communication Assn. (vice-chairperson adv. council), Am. Assn. U. Women, Delta Kappa Gamma, Delta Zeta. Mem. Christian Ch. Author article. Home: 1220 Mockingbird Lane Edmond OK 73034

MCGREW, ELIZABETH A., physician; b. Faribault, Minn., Aug. 30, 1916; d. Charles Dana and Edna (Rosebrook) McG.; student Rockford Coll., 1933-35; B.A., Carleton Coll., 1938; M.D., U. Minn., 1945. Intern Milw. County Hosp., 1944-45; resident pathoiogy Research and Edn. Hosp., U. Ill., 1945-49, asst. pathologist, 1949-54, asso. pathologist, 1954-62, pathologist, 1962—; instr. Coll. Medicine, U. Ill., 1948-54, asst. prof., 1954-58, asso. prof., 1958-62, prof., 1962—; teaching cons. Cook County Hosp., W. Side and Hines VA hosps. Bd. dirs. Ill. div. Am. Cancer Soc. Fellow Am. Soc. Clin. Pathologists, Coll. Am. Pathologists, Pan Am. Med. Assn.; mem. A.M.A. (Hektoen Gold medal 1958), Med. Women's Internat., Internat. Acad. Cytology, Am. Assn. Pathologists and Bacteriologists, Am. Assn. for Cancer Research, Am. Soc. Cytology (Papanicolaou award 1958, v.p.), Ill. (v.p.), Chgo. (past pres.) path. socs., Am. Med. Women's Assn. (pres.), Chgo. Inst. Medicine Contbg. author: Atlas of Exfoliative Cytology (Papanicolaou), 1958. Research on collab isolation of tumor cells from blood. Home: 548 Judson St Evanston IL 60202 Office: 1853 W Polk St Chicago IL 60612

MCGUFFEE, ANNE ROSE GUICE (MRS. JOHN MERRIT MCGUFFEE), mus. ofcl.; d. Harper Sessions and Annie Josephine (Cooper) Guice; grad. high sch.; m. John Merrit McGuffee, Dec. 21, 1944; children—John Joseph, James Michael. Clk. typist U.S. Engrs., Vicksburg, Miss., 1942-44; receptionist Ct. House Mus., Vicksburg, 1964-65, mgr. Souvenier Shop, 1965-67, asst. to dir., 1967-68, acting dir., 1969—. Vice pres. St. Aloysius Mother's Club, Vicksburg, 1954-56; den mother Cub Scouts Am., Vicksburg, 1954-56; mem. Vicksburg Warren Beautiful, 1972—. Mem. Vicksburg and Warren County Hist. Soc. (3d v.p. 1970-71), Am. Legion, Smithsonian Assos. Roman Catholic. Ladies of Elks, K.C. Ladies Aux. (v.p. 1971). Home: PO Box 988 Vicksburg MS 39180 Office: 1008 Cherry St Vicksburg MS 39180

MCGUFFEE, FRANCES JACKSON (MRS. WALTER MCGUFFEE), educator; b. Pontotoc, Miss.; d. Francis Lee and Maude (Pickering) Jackson; B.S., Miss. State Coll. Women, 1940; M.S., U. Tenn., 1949; Ph.D., Tex. Women's U., 1966; m. Walter McGuffee, Dec. 21, 1948; 1 dau., Linda Jean. Tchr. home econs. McAdams (Miss.) High Sch., 1940-43, Lena (Miss.) High Sch., 1943-44; faculty Miss. Coll., Clinton, 1944—, asso. prof. home econs., 1954-69, prof., 1969—, head dept., 1948—. Mem. Am. Assn. U. Women (pres. br. 1966-68, treas. 1972—), Am., Miss. (treas. 1959-61, scholarship chmn. 1961-64, pres. 1971-72, counselor 1972—, coll. and univ. sect. chmn.) home econs. assns., Nat., Miss. councils on family relations, So., Miss. (1st v.p. 1967-68) assns. children under six (pres. 1974-75), Kappa Delta Pi, Delta Kappa Gamma (2d v.p. 1972—). Home: 304 W Madison St Clinton MS 39056

MCGUIGAN, DOROTHY SOPHIA GIES (MRS. BERNARD JOSEPH MCGUIGAN), writer; b. Ann Arbor, Mich., Nov. 12, 1914; d. Charles George and Jane Elizabeth (Sturman) Gies; A.B., U. Mich., 1936; postgrad. U. London (Eng.), 1937-38; M.A. (Univ. fellow), Columbia, 1939; m. Bernard Joseph McGuigan, Aug. 3, 1946 (dec.); children—Michael John, Cathleen Mary. With sales promotion dept. Macmillan Pub. Co., N.Y.C., 1939-42; staff asst. A.R.C., Eng., France and Germany, 1944-46; writer, Stars and Stripes, Germany, 1946-49; instr. bus. writing U. Mich., Ann Arbor, 1955-58, writer, editor Center for Continuing Edn. Women, 1970—. Recipient Avery Hopwood awards U. Mich., 1933, 34, 35, 36; Lucy Elliott fellow, 1937, Kappa Kappa Gamma fellow, 1937. Mem. Mortar Board, Phi Beta Kappa. Democrat. Episcopalian. Author: The Habsburgs, 1966; A Dangerous Experiment, 1970; Metternich and the Duchess, 1975. Home: 470 Rock Creek Dr Ann Arbor MI 48104 Office: 330 Thompson St Ann Arbor MI 48108

MCGUIGAN, LEE ANN, producer, film editor, writer; b. McKeesport, Pa., June 6, 1946; d. Philip and Zelma Marie (Lostetter) McGuigan; B.A. in Journalism with high honors, Pa. State U., 1968; M.A. in Journalism, U. Mo., 1974. Editor Pitts. Motion Pictures Lab., Pitts., 1968; news film editor KDKA-TV, Pitts., 1969; motion picture, still photographer, editor WQED-TV, Newsroom Program, Pitts., 1969-71; media producer U. Pitts. Instructional Prodn. Services, 1972; photographer, radio-TV publicity editor Stephens Coll., Columbia, Mo., 1972-73, guest lectr., 1973-74; news producer KOMU-TV, Columbia, 1974—. Free lance writer, photographer Pitts. Renaissance Mag., 1971-72; free lance film editor U. Mo. at Columbia, 1973—. Recipient Student Journalism award Pa. Press Women, 1968. Mem. Women in Communications, Phi Kappa Phi, Kappa Tau Alpha. Editor film When Gary Allen Runs, 1971. Producer, photographer, editor Login: The University of Pittsburgh Computer Center, 1972 (2d pl. Mo. Student Assn. Film Festival 1974). Home: 300 N 9th St Columbia MO 65201 Office: KOMU-TV Hwy 63 South Columbia MO 65201

MCGUINN, DOROTHY IRENE HEYN (MRS. JAMES JOSEPH MCGUINN), pub. relations co. exec.; b. Chgo., July 28; d. Louis Anton and Irene (Sullivan) Heyn; B.A., Northwestern U.; student Moser Bus. Coll., Chgo., Chgo. Art Inst.; m. James Joseph McGuinn, Oct. 19, 1940; children—James Joseph III, Brian Mitchell. Reporter, Chgo. Am., 1937-38, Lerner Community Papers, Chgo., 1938-40; syndicated columnist Charm Chatter, 1938-40; columnist Tarrytown (N.Y.) Daily News, 1949-51; head trade publicity Chgo. Internat. Trade Fair, 1959-60, v.p. Pub. Relations Internat., Chgo., 1960-66; columnist Rochelle (Ill.) Leader and Mt. Morris (Ill.) Index, 1966-67; market research Boylhart, Lovett & Dean, Los Angeles, 1968-69, Capital Res. Corp., 1970-71; partner Writers' Adv. Service, also sec., 1973—. Mem. Soc. Midland Authors (rec. sec. 1955-63, pres. 1963-65), Soc. Southwestern Authors (founder, sec. 1972-74, pres. 1974—), Chgo. Playreaders (founder), Chgo. Cultural Com. (sec.). Club: Publicity (Chgo.). Author: (with husband) Parents Can't Win, 1947. Contbr. articles to mags., newspapers. Address: 510 Windy Peak Pl Tucson AZ 85704

MCGUINNESS, ADELAIDE HELEN, sales exec.; b. Yonkers, N.Y., Mar. 19, 1922; d. James John and Adeline Isabelle (Kern) Kavanaugh; ed. Washington Sch. for Secs., Pa. State U.; div.; children—Kevin, Darcy. Sales coordinator Coppercraft Guild subsidiary Armor Bronze & Silver, Taunton, Mass., 1960-62; co-originator, sales mgr. Princess House, North Dighton, Mass., 1962-64, nat. v.p. sales, 1964—; dir. G.A. Rogers Inc., North Dighton. Home: 501 Fletcher Rd North Kingstown RI 02852 Office: 455 Somerset Av North Dighton MA 02764

MCGUIRE, AVA MARIA, ednl. adminstr.; b. N.Y.C., Dec. 24, 1944; d. John Philip and Gertrude Eileen (Newe) McGuire; B.S., C.W. Post Coll., 1968, M.S., 1969; diploma St. John's U., 1973. Adminstr. Edn. Council, Mineola, N.Y., 1967-69; adminstr. div. gen. services Nassau County Bd. Co-op Ednl. Services, Jericho, N.Y., 1967—. Ednl. cons. to Freeport Sch. dist., Freeport, N.Y., 1972. Bd. dirs. Internat. Grad. Sch. Edn., Denver; mem. Grad. Program Policy Bd. Grad. Edn. Dept., St. John's U., Jamaica, N.Y. Mem. L.I., N.Y. State assns. for supervision and curriculum devel., Delta Kappa Gamma, Phi Delta Kappa. Democrat. Roman Catholic. Home: 1 East Rogues Path Huntington Station NY 11746 Office: 125 Jericho Turnpike Jericho NY

MCGUIRE, CHRISTINE HARRISON (MRS. JULES H. MASSERMAN), ednl. adminstr.; b. Jenkins, Ky., Aug. 11, 1918; d. Samuel Harrison and Esther Ethel (Lykens) McGuire; B.A., Muskingum Coll., 1937; M.A., Ohio State U., 1938; postgrad. U. Chgo., 1938-41; m. Jules H. Masserman, Feb. 20, 1943. Mem. faculty U. Chgo., 1941-61; mem. faculty U. Ill. Coll. Medicine, Chgo., 1961—, prof., 1965—. Cons. WHO, med. colls. and med. splty. socs. Mem. Nat. Council Measurement in Edn. (pres. 1974-75), Assn. Am. Med. Colls. (group chmn. 1974-75). Author: (with Charvat and Parsons) Nature and Use of Examinations in Medical Education, 1968; (with Solomon) Clinical Simulations, 1971; (with Muslin, Thurnblad and Templeton Evaluative Methods in Psychiatric Education, 1974. Home: 2231 E 67th St Chicago IL 60649 Office: 835 S Wolcott St Chicago IL 60612

MCGUIRE, MARGARET MARY, librarian; b. Morton, Minn., Sept. 8, 1911; d. Charles Stewart and Myrtle Agnes (McGowan) McG.; B.A., Coll. St. Catherine, 1933; B.L.S., U. Minn., 1937. Children's librarian Mpls. Pub. Library, 1937-42, reference librarian, 1948-53, audio-visual librarian, 1953-55, head visual aids, 1955-72; pvt. audio-visual cons., 1972—; research librarian Time, Inc., N.Y.C., 1946-47. Chmn., Mpls. and Hennepin County Pub. Employees Week, 1948-50; registry clk. Mpls. and Hennepin County AFL-CIO Com. for Polit. Action, 1950-62, chairwoman state and nat. polit. campaigns, 1952-58. Sec., Democratic Farmer Labor Party, Mpls. 7th Ward, 1950-52, Minn. Fifth Legislative Dist., 1950-52, Hennepin County Council, 1954. Served to lt. comdr. USNR, 1942-46. Recipient Mayor of Mpls. Outstanding Citizen award, 1950, 51. Mem. A.L.A. (mem. library-labor com. 1953-56, 68-70, audio visual com. 1960-72, library adminstrn. pub. relations com. 1967-70), Mpls. Pub. Library Staff Assn. (pres. 1949), Mpls. Employees Retirement Assn. (pres. 1954, sec. 1966-68, 70-72), Minn. State Fedn. Labor, Retired Officers Assn., Am. Legion. Roman Catholic (sec. Archdiocese Labor Sch. 1949-51). Author (with others) Guidelines for AV Materials and Services for Public Libraries, 1970. Contbr. articles to pub. employee, union and library publs. Home: 52 Groveland Terrace Minneapolis MN 55403 Office: Public Library 300 Nicollet Mall Minneapolis MN 55401

MCGUIRK, MARGARET ANNE, pediatrician; b. N.Y.C., Apr. 29, 1942; d. Terence Joseph and Teresa (Regan) McG.; B.A., City U. N.Y., 1963; M.D., Med. Coll. Pa., 1967. Intern, Lenox Hill Hosp., N.Y.C., 1967-68; resident pediatrics, 1968-69, chief resident pediatrics, 1969-70, attending physician, 1970—; practice medicine, specializing pediatrics, N.Y.C., 1970—; attending physician Drs. Hosp., N.Y.C.; clin. instr. pediatrics N.Y.U. Diplomate Am. Bd. Pediatrics. Mem. A.M.A., County Med. Soc. N.Y., Alpha Omega Alpha. Office: 59 E 79th St New York City NY 10021

MCGURK, PATRICIA HELEN, librarian; b. Beacon, N.Y.; d. Patrick James and Helen J. (Keating) McGurk; B.S., State U. N.Y. at New Paltz, 1964; M.L.S., State U. N.Y. at Albany, 1967. With Howland Circulating Library, Beacon, 1949-59, Readers Services div. Vassar Coll., Poughkeepsie, N.Y., 1959-61; multi-media librarian Wappingers Falls (N.Y.) Central Sch. Dist., 1964-69, library supr., 1969—. Active Girl Scouts U.S. Mem. A.L.A., N.Y., Dutchess County (pres. 1973-74) library assns., N.Y. State Tchrs. Assn., Sch. Librarians Southeastern N.Y., N.E.A., Dutchess County Librarians, N.Y. State Ednl. Communication Assn. Home: 25 Weston Ave Fishkill NY 12524 Office: Wappingers Falls Central School District Wappingers Falls NY 12590

MCHARG, MARGARET JANE, lawyer; b. Fond-Du-Lac, Wis., July 13, 1946; d. George Edward and Margaret Minnie (Refer) McHarg; B.B.A., U. Ia., 1968, J.D., 1971, M.A., 1971. Admitted to Ia. bar, 1971; accountant H.G. Petershagen, C.P.A., Iowa City, 1971-72; friend of court atty. Cedar Rapids, Ia., 1972—; jud. magistrate Ia. County, Ia., 1973—. Mem. U. Ia. Alumni Assn., Phi Gamma Nu, Kappa Beta Pi. Lutheran. Home: 304 Washington St Victor IA 52347 Office: Linn County Courthouse Cedar Rapids IA 52240

MCHOLICK, MARY JOYCE RAYMOND, journalist; b. Isabel, S.D., July 22, 1927; d. Ray A. and Leona (Henry) Raymond; B.S., Ore. State U., 1952; M.S., U. Ore., 1969; m. William John McHolick, June 26, 1948; children—Sandra Joyce, Rebecca Mary, William Raymond. Feature writer, reporter Eugene (Ore.) Register-Guard, 1970—; free lance pub. relations cons., 1969-70. Bd. dirs. S.W. Ore. Mus. Sci. and Industry, 1965-66, Broadway Theater League, 1965-66, Lane County Auditorium Assn., 1968-71, Ore. Arts Council, 1970-71; mem. Mall Arts Adv. Com., Eugene, 1971; mem. Gov.'s Ore. Arts Commn. Adv. Com., 1970—. Mem. Lane County Med. Aux., Eugene Jr. League (pres. 1964-65), Mu Phi Epsilon Patrons, Kappa Tau Alpha. Presbyn. (elder). Club: Eugene Fortnightly. Home: 955 Coburg Rd Eugene OR 97401 Office: PO Box 10188 Eugene OR 97401

MCHUGH, DOROTHY BARBREE, mem. Republican Nat. Com.; b. Oakland, Cal.; d. Joseph and Nellie (Snowden) Barbree; student U. Cal. at Berkeley; m. Harry G. Miller, July 4, 1932 (dec. 1947); children—Michael B., Harry; m. 2d, Keith S. McHugh, Dec. 14, 1957. Republican County campaign mgr. for N.Y.C. Mayoral Campaign, 1961, N.Y. State Gubernatorial Campaign 1962; co-campaign dir. Rep. Gubernatorial campaign, 1966; mem. Rep. Nat. Com. for N.Y., 1963—; mem. adv. bd. N.Y.C. Rep. Women, 1963—. Pres. Assistance League, Glendale, Cal., 1940-41; dir. women's aux. Inst. Phys. Medicine and Rehab., 1959—, Assn. Homemaker Service, N.Y.C., 1961-62; mem. bd. Inwood House for Unwed Mothers, 1966. Mme. Sigma Kappa. Address: 10 Gracie Sq New York City NY 10028

MCHUGH, GEORGIA ALICE, ins.-investment co. exec.; b. Lawrence, Mass., July 25, 1924; d. Edward Joseph and Alice Gertrude (Doyle) McHugh; B.S. in Math., U. Mass., 1946; postgrad. Boston U., 1947-48, Northeastern U., 1950-51. Statistician Babson Reports, Inc., Wellesley, Mass., 1946-48; econ. and investment analysis Keystone Custodian Funds, Inc., Boston, 1948-53; financial analyst Fireman's Fund Am. Ins. Cos., San Francisco, 1953-65, asst. sec. investments, 1965-66, sec. investments, 1966-67, asst. v.p., mgr. property and casualty common stock portfolio, 1967—, v.p., mgr. property and casualty common stock portfolio, 1971—; v.p. Am. Express Investment Mgmt. Co., San Francisco, 1968-71. Bd. dirs. Bay Area council Girl Scouts U.S.A.; bd. dirs. San Francisco YWCA, v.p., chmn. finance com., 1972—; bd. dirs. Golden Gate Coll. Assos., 1970—. Mem. Inst. Chartered Financial Analysts, Security Analysts San Francisco (chmn. tng. standards 1968-70, gov. 1966-68), Financial Women's Club San Francisco (founding mem.), Soroptimist (treas. San Francisco 1971-72, v.p. 1972-73, pres. 1973-74). Club: Commonwealth Cal. (San Francisco). Home: 3130 Canyon Rd Burlingame CA 94010 Office: PO Box 3395 San Francisco CA 94119

MCHUGH, LILLIAN WEED TRIPLETT (MRS. GODFREY TURNER MCHUGH), civic worker; b. Lenoir, N.C., Apr. 12, 1935; d. Roger B. and Lilyan (Weed) Triplett; A.B., Hollins Coll., 1957; m. Boyd Edwards Fall, Sept. 7, 1957 (dec. Dec. 1963); children—Katherine, Boyd, Lillian; m. 2d, Godfrey Turner McHugh, Mar. 25, 1967; 1 dau., Allison Turner. Mem. exec. com. Nat. Symphony Ball, Washington, 1969, Washington Internat. Horse Show, 1969; patron Washington Performing Arts, 1971-72; women's com. Nat. Ballet Soc., 1972; exec. women's com. Washington Performing Arts Ball, 1972; vol. worker A.R.C., 1959—; life mem. women's com. Nat. Symphony Orch. Mem. UN Assn. (asso. chmn. 1968). Home: 5241 Partridge Lane Washington DC 20016

MCILRATH, PATRICIA ANNE, educator; b. Kansas City, Mo., Jan. 25, 1917; d. George D. and Ethel (Howard) McIlrath; A.B., Grinnell Coll., 1937; M.A., Northwestern U., 1946; Ph.D., Stanford, 1951. Instr., asst. prof. speech and drama U. Ill., 1946-54; chmn. dept. speech and drama, dir. U. Playhouse, asso. prof. speech and drama U. Mo., Kansas City, 1954-62, prof. speech and theatre, 1962—, also dir. U. theatres. Artistic dir. Mo. Repertory Theatre, Mo. Vanguard Theatre. Mem. Mo. Council on Arts, 1965-69, mem. adv. commn., 1969—, chmn. adv. com. on theatre, 1965-67; mem. adv. bd. Community Children's Theatre. Recipient Matrix Honored Women award, Theta Sigma Phi, 1967, Avila medal, 1968; award of excellence Am. Coll. Theatre Festival, 1972; Pro Merita award Rockhurst Coll. Mem. Univ. Resident Theatre Assn. (exec. bd.), Nat. Assn. Schs. Theatre (v.p.), Nat. Collegiate Players (v.p.), ANTA, Am. Theatre Assn. (dir.), Speech Assn. Am., Zeta Phi Eta, Delta Kappa Gamma, Phi Kappa Phi. Roman Catholic. Home: 1300 E 72d St Kansas City MO 64131 Office: 5100 Rockhill Rd Kansas City MO 64131

MCINNES, SISTER CATHERINE VALARIA, hosp. adminstr.; b. Westlock, Alta., Can., Jan. 9, 1927; d. David and Margaret Mary (Campbell) McInnes; diploma St. Joseph Hosp. Sch. Nursing, 1950; B.S. in Nursing, Seattle U., 1961; M.S. in Nursing, St. John's U., 1963. Asst. head nurse St. Joseph Hosp., Victoria, B.C., Can., 1950-51; supr. operating room Sacred Heart Hosp., Eugene, Ore., 1953-57; supr. operating room St. Joseph Hosp., Bellingham, Wash., 1957-59, adminstr., 1968—; adminstr. Josephinum, Seattle, 1963-68. Treas., Wash. State Cath. Hosp. and Health Care Assn., 1971-73, v.p., 1973-75; pres. N.W. Hosp. Council, 1972-73. Mem. implementation com. Whatcom County Mental Health Adminstrn. Bd., 1972-73. Mem. Am., Cath. hosp. assns., Assn. Western Hosps., Comprehensive Health Planning, Theta Sigma Tau. Club: Altrusa (Bellingham). Home: 3201 Ellis St Bellingham WA 98225 Office: St Joseph Hosp 3201 Ellis St Bellingham WA 98225

MCINNIS, IRA MAURINE, librarian; b. Sylvania, Ark., Apr. 10, 1903; d. William Ira and Mary Lou (McCallum) McInnis; B.A., Belhaven Coll., 1924; M.A. in L.S., George Peabody Coll., 1955, postgrad., 1964. Tchr., E. Side Sch., Jackson County, Miss., 1924-25, French Camp (Miss.) Acad., 1925-28, Pascagoula (Miss.) High Sch., 1928-32, Coxburg Vocational High Sch., Eden, Miss., 1933-34; tchr., dean of girls French Camp (Miss.) Acad., 1934-37; tchr. Madison-Ridgeland High Sch., Madison, Miss., 1937-39, Nettleton (Miss.) High Sch., 1939-42, Macon (Miss.,) High Sch., 1942-44; librarian Moss Point (Miss.) High Sch., 1944-46; tchr. Macon High Sch., 1946-48; librarian Benton (Miss.) High Sch., 1948-49; chmn. English dept., tchr. Moss Point High Sch., 1949-51; tchr. LaFayette (Ga.) High Sch., 1951-52, librarian, 1952-53; librarian Corinth (Miss.) High Sch., 1953-56, Miss. Delta Jr. Coll., Moorhead, 1956-71, French Camp (Miss.) Acad., 1971—. Mem. Miss. Edn. Assn., Miss. Library Assn. (sect. chmn. 1965, co-chmn. registrations 1968), Beta Phi Mu, Delta Kappa Gamma (chpt. corr. sec. 1964-66, chpt. pres. 1968-70, state chmn. profl. affairs com. 1969-71). Democrat. Presbyn. Mem. Order Eastern Star (worthy matron 1961, 62). Home: Box 100 Pickens MS 39146 Office: French Camp Academy French Camp MS 39745

MCINNIS, LYNN WILLIARD (MRS. ELLIS THAD MCINNIS), banker; b. Jamestown, N.C., Nov. 18, 1925; d. Hervie Nicola and Vivian McGee (Hayworth) Williard; student Salem Coll., 1942-45, U. N.C., 1946; A.B., High Point Coll., 1948; m. Ellis Thad McInnis, Jan. 5, 1946; children—Elizabeth Jane, Robert Hervey. With High Point (N.C.) Bank & Trust Co., 1946—, v.p., 1959—, also dir. Mem. High Point chpt. N.C. Symphony Soc. Bd., 1953-54; mem. High Point Community Concert Bd., 1955-57. Mem. Am. Inst. Banking, N.C. Fedn. Music Clubs (corr. sec. 1964, chmn. N.C. state conv. 1965), Altrusa Club (pres. 1971-72), Mus. Art Club (pres. 1955-56), Friday Morning Music Study Club, Hum-N-Hoe Garden Club. Presbyn. Mem. Order Eastern Star. Home: 909 Forrest Hill Dr High Point NC 27262 Office: PO Box 428 High Point NC 27261

MCINTOSH, CAROLYN SUE (MRS. JOE C. RUDE III), dentist; b. Dallas, Nov. 3, 1942; d. Henry and Suzie (Hazel) McIntosh; student U. Tex., 1961-62, D.D.S., 1966; M.P.H.. U. Mich., 1969. Asst. dir. dental pub. health, also clinician Dept. Pub. Health, Houston, 1966-67; staff dental cons., clinician Tex. Inst. Rehab. and Research, Tex. Med. Center, Houston, 1966-67; staff dental cons. continuing edn. br. Dental Health Center U.S. Dept. Health, Edn., Welfare Pub. Health Service, San Francisco, 1967-68; resident dental pub. health U. Mich., 1970; dental dir. Children and Youth Project No. 660 Driscoll Found. Children's Hosp., Corpus Christi, Tex., 1970-73; clin. asst. prof. pedodontics U. Tex. Dental br. Instr. Del Mar. Coll., Corpus Christi, 1970-73; asst. dir. dental program Ga. Retardation Center, Atlanta, 1973—; clin. asst. prof. pedodontics Emory U. Dental Sch., 1973—. Mem. Am., Tex. dental assns., Nueces Valley Dist. Dental Soc., Am., Tex. pub. health assns., Am. Assn. Pub. Health Dentists, Am. Soc. Preventive Dentistry. Home: 1458 Meadowcreek Ct Dunwoody GA 30338 Office: 4770 N Peachtree Rd Atlanta GA 30341

MCINTOSH, ELLEN MARIE, educator; b. Flag Pond, Tenn., Jan. 5, 1920; d. Clifford Millard and Annie (Tipton) McIntosh; B.A., Carson Newman Coll., 1948; M.R.E., Carver Sch. Missions and Social Work, 1950; M.A., Geo. Peabody Coll., 1956; student Ariz. State Coll., 1951-52. Instr. religion, head resident Grand Canyon Coll., 1950-51, instr. sociology, head resident, 1951-52, asst. prof. social studies, acting dean women, 1952-56, asso. prof. social studies, dean women, 1956-65; dean of women So. Bapt. Seminary, 1965-68; dean women Shorter Coll., Rome, Ga., 1968-71; asso. prof. sociology Mo. Baptist Coll., Manchester, 1971—. Trustee Carver Sch. Missions and Social Work, 1952-60. Mem. Women's Missionary Union Ariz. (past exec. bd.), Bus. and Profl. Women, Am. Assn. U. Women, Nat., Ga. assns. women deans and counselors, Nat. Council Family Relations, S.W. Social Sci. Assn., Ariz. Assn. Deans and Counselors, Nat., Ariz. edn. assns., Ky. Assn. Deans of Women and Counselors, Delta Kappa Gamma. Baptist. Address: 402 Enchanted Pkwy Manchester MO 63011

MCINTOSH, MARGARET MAE MOLLISON (MRS. DONALD WALDRON MCINTOSH), educator; b. Belfast, Me., Oct. 22, 1929; d. Edwin and Catherine (Hamilton) Mollison; B.A., U. Me., 1950, M.Ed., 1952; m. Donald Waldron McIntosh, July 20, 1963; 1 dau., Meredith Mary. English tchr. N.H. Fay High Sch., Dexter, Me., 1950-51, Old Town (Me.) High Sch., 1951-53; asst. exec. dir. Gen. Alumni Assn. of U. Me., Orono, 1953-63; instr. dept. speech U. Me., Portland, 1965—. Vice pres. Me. State Bd. Edn., 1968—. Mem. exec. com. Alumni council U. Me., Orono, 1965—. Recipient Black Bear, U. Me. Alumni Council, 1968. Mem. Am. Assn. U. Women (sec. Me. chpt. 1961-63), York Art Assn. (pres. 1973—). Republican. Conglist. Home: Norwood Farms Rd York Harbor ME 03911

MCINTURF, FAITH MARY, racing exec.; b. Grand Ridge, Ill., Aug. 22, 1917; d. Lynne E. and Margaret (Garver) McInturf; grad. high sch. With The J. E. Porter Corp., Chgo., 1963-65, v.p., 1951-65, sec., 1951-65, also dir.; v.p., sec. Potomac Engring. Corp., 1941—; sec.-treas., dir. Chgo. Harness Racing Inc., Balmoral Jockey Club, Inc., Balmoral Park Trot, Inc., Horse Racing Promotions, Inc., all 1967-72. Mem. Art. Inst. Chgo. Roman Catholic. Home: 1360 Lake Shore Dr Chicago IL 60610 Office: 664 N Michigan Av Chicago IL 60611

MCINTYRE, JANE O'NEILL MAHADY (MRS. CARL M. MCINTYRE), lawyer, govt. ofcl.; b. Latrobe, Pa., Feb. 18, 1922; d. James J. and Katharine (O'Neill) Mahady; B.A., Seton Hill Coll., 1942; LL.B., U. Pa., 1945; m. Carl M. McIntyre, Dec. 30, 1954; 1 son, James Joseph. Admitted to Pa. bar, 1946; law clk. Conlen, LaBrum & Beechwood, Phila., 1945-46; researcher Legislative Reference Bur., Library of Congress, Washington, 1947; partner firm Mahady and Mahady, Greensburg, Pa., Latrobe, 1947-62; chief, devel. loans br. Office Gen. Counsel, Small Bus. Adminstrn., Washington, 1961-64, chief, inter-agency br., 1964-65, atty. Office Congl. Relations, 1965-66, spl. asst. to adminstr., 1966-69; atty., adviser claims and litigation real estate div. Office C.E., Dept. Army, Washington, 1971-72, chief claims and litigation, 1973—. Pres. Latrobe Civic Club, 1950-51, Quota Club, Greensburg, 1947-54, Hui O Wahine Officers Wives Club, Honolulu, 1959-60. Pa. nat. committeewoman Young Democratic Club Am., 1949-56; mem. governing bd. Pa. Fedn. Dem. Women's Groups, 1950-56; mem. exec. and policy com. Pa. Dem. Com., 1950-56; organizer Westmoreland County Young Dem. Group, 1948, past sec., v.p.; v.p. Young Dem. Clubs Am., 1951-53; alt. del. at large Dem. nat. conv., 1952. Named one of five top women qualified for high level presdl. appointment D.C. Fedn. Bus. and Profl. Women. Mem. Am., Fed., Pa., Westmoreland, Phila. bar assns., Met. Bus. and Profl. Women's Club (dir. Latrobe), Washington Forum, Women United (sec., dir.). Mem. editorial bd. U. Pa. Law Rev., 1944-45. Home: 12906 Crisfield Rd Silver Spring MD 20906 Office: Corps Engrs Dept Army Washington DC 20314

MCINTYRE, MARY SHELLEY, musician; b. Good Pine, La.; d. Archibald Ormsby and May (Rawlings) McIntyre; student Ward-Belmont Jr. Coll., 1 year, New Orleans Conservatory, 1 year; grad., also postgrad. Juilliard Inst. Mus. Art, N.Y.C.; student Columbia, 1 summer, pvt. study with Vlado Kolitsch, N.Y.C. Solo violinist concert ensemble The Homestead, Hot Springs, Va., 8 years; solo violinist concert ensemble Lauderdale Beach Hotel, Ft. Lauderdale, Fla., 5 winters; solo violinist concert ensemble Grindstone Inn, Winter Harbor, Me., 3 summers, violinist Houston Symphony, 1943—; violist Brevard (N.C.) Festival 2 seasons. Mem. Am. Fedn. Musicians. Presbyn. Home: 2724 Nottingham Rd Houston TX 77005 Office: Houston Symphony Soc Jesse H Jones Hall for Performing Arts 615 Louisiana St Houston TX 77001

MCINTYRE, PATRICIA ANN, physician; b. Christopher, Ill., Sept. 1, 1926; d. Clyde and Irma Theora (Ahlers) McI.; A.B., Kalamazoo Coll., 1948; M.D., Johns Hopkins, 1948-52. Intern internal medicine Mass. Gen. Hosp., Boston, 1952-53; asst. resident internal medicine Johns Hopkins Hosp., Balt., 1953-55; fellow in medicine hematology div. Sch. Medicine, Johns Hopkins, Balt., 1955-57, instr. dept. medicine, 1957-58, research asso., 1964-65, instr., 1965-67, dept. radiol. sci., 1966-67, asst. prof. depts. medicine, radiology and radiol. scis., 1967-71, asso. prof., 1971—, asso. prof. environmental health div. radiation health, 1973—. Diplomate Am. Bd. Internal Medicine, Am. Bd. Nuclear Medicine. Fellow A.C.P.; mem. A.M.A., Balt. City Med. Assn., Am. Fedn. for Clin. Research, Am. Soc. Hematology, Soc. Nuclear Medicine, Reticuloendothelial Soc. (mem. panel internat. com. standardization in haematology). Contbr. articles to med. jours. Home: 5623 Gardenville Av Baltimore MD 21206 Office: 615 N Wolfe St Baltimore MD 21205

MCINTYRE, VERNA MARGUERITE, musician; b. Good Pine, La.; d. Archibald Ormsby and May (Rawlings) McIntyre; student New Orleans Conservatory 1 yr., Juilliard Inst. Mus. Art, N.Y.C., 3 yrs., Smith Coll. Summer Sch. Music, 4 yrs., Berkeley Summer Music Colony, Harrison, Me., 4 yrs., La. State U. 2 yrs.; pvt. study with Harold Berkley, N.Y.C. Mem. concert ensemble The Homestead, Hot Springs, Va., 2 yrs., New Orleans Symphony, 2 yrs., Brevard (N.C.) Festival Orch., 2 seasons; now violinist Houston Symphony; instr. string classes Houston Ind. Sch. Dist. Mem. Am. Fedn. Musicians. Presbyn. Home: 2724 Nottingham Rd Houston TX 77005 Office: Houston Symphony Soc Jesse H Jones Hall for Performing Arts 615 Louisiana St Houston TX 77001

MCIVER, SUSAN BERTHA, educator; b. Hutchinson, Kan., Nov. 6, 1940; d. Ernest Dale and Thelma Faye (McCrory) McIver; B.A., U. Cal., at Riverside, 1962; M.S., Washington State U., 1964, Ph.D., 1967. Asst. prof. dept. parasitology Sch. Hygiene, U. Toronto, 1967-71, asso. prof., 1971—. NIH fellow, 1966-67; Inter-Am. fellow in tropical medicine, 1973. Mem. Entomol. Soc. Am., Entomol. Soc. Can., Canadian Soc. Zoologists, P.E.O. Home: 68 Boswell Av Toronto ON Canada Office: Dept Parasitology Sch Hygiene U Toronto Toronto ON Canada

MCIVOR, SHIRLEY K., ednl. adminstr.; b. Lynchburg, Va.; d. Labron Eugene and Katherine (Cox) McIvor; A.B., Randolph-Macon Woman's Coll., 1949; M.Ed., U. Va., 1957, diploma advanced grad. study, 1968. Tchr. Lynchburg (Va.) Schs., 1949-60; dean of girls E.C. Glass High Sch., Lynchburg, 1960-68, asst. prin., 1968-73, asso. prin., 1973—. Mem. Am. Assn. U. Women (co-chmn. edn. com. 1967-69), Delta Kappa Gamma (parliamentarian 1968-70), Kappa Delta Pi, Gamma Phi Beta. Methodist. Club: Lynchburg Woman's. Home: 2740 Link Rd Lynchburg VA 24503

MCKAIG, DIANNE L., lawyer; b. Canton, O., Nov. 17, 1930; d. Sherman J. and Kathryn (Shaidnagle) McKaig; B.A., U. Ky., 1952, J.D., 1954; LL.M., Harvard, 1955. Admitted to Ky. bar, 1954, Mass. bar, 1956; law clk. Ky. Ct. Appeals, Frankfort, 1954; atty. Palmer, Dodge, Gardner & Bradford, Boston, 1955-56; practice law, Boston, 1956-58; atty.-adviser Office of Solicitor, U.S. Dept. Labor, Washington, 1958-62, regional dir. Women's Bur., Atlanta, 1963-66, chief div. legislation and standards, Women's Bur., Washington, 1966-68; spl. asst. to sec. (consumer interests) U.S. Dept. Health, Edn. and Welfare, Washington, 1968, dir. Office Consumer Services, 1968-69; exec. dir. Mich. Consumers Council, 1969-72; asst. v.p. consumer affairs Coca-Cola Co., Atlanta, 1972-74; v.p. Coca-Cola U.S.A., 1974—. Mem. Major Appliance Consumer Action Panel, 1970-72. Bd. dirs. Nat. Council for Family Financial Edn., 1970-72, Nat. Council Better Bus. Burs., 1971-72. Mem. Ky. Fed., Mass. bar assns., Soc. Consumer Affairs Profls. (dir. 1973—, 1st v.p. 1974—), U. Ky. Alumni Assn. (pres. Washington 1962), Bus. and Profl. Women's Clubs, Order of Coif, Mortar Bd., Alpha Delta Pi (chpt. outstanding alumna 1965), Eta Sigma Phi, Phi Beta. Asso. editor Ky. Law Jour., 1953. Home: 119 Rosaire Pl Cross Creek NW Atlanta GA 30327

MCKAIG, MAUREEN LOUISE, extension agt.; b. Logansport, Ind., Dec. 8, 1945; d. Edward Elliott and Elizabeth Jane (Martin) McKaig; B.A., Purdue U., 1967, M.S., 1969. Resident counselor Purdue U., Lafayette, Ind., 1968-69; tchr. elementary sch. Southeastern and Pioneer Sch. Corp., Logansport, 1968; area extension agt.-youth Purdue U., Peru, Ind., 1969—; state dir. Ind. Extension Service. Recipient Community Service award Peru C. of C., 1974; Rural Youth Adviser Meritorious award, 1974. Mem. Bus. and Profl. Women, Nat. Assn. Extension Agts., Miami County Young Adults, Internat. Farm Youth Exchange Alumni, Farm Bur. Methodist (council ministries 1970—, work chmn. evangelism 1970, work chmn. social concerns and ecumenical affairs 1974). Home: 457 W 11th St Peru IN 46970 Office: Court House Peru IN 46970

MCKAY, EDNA BARTLETT, fashion writer; b. Elgin, Ill., June 12, 1908; d. Edmund Frederick and Edna (Allanson) Wellinghoff; B.S., Northwestern U., 1928; m. Loring C. Bartlett, Aug. 21, 1945 (dec. Aug. 1968); m. 2d, Louis D. McKay, May 10, 1973. Women's dir. radio sta. WELM, Elmira, N.Y., 1947-73; columnist Fashion Scene Elmira Telegram, 1969—; free-lance fashion coordinator and reports; cons. in field; producer fashion shows. Mem. Friends of Steele Meml. Library, Arnot Mus. Aux. Recipient Golden Slipper award Am. Footwear Assn., 1965, Fravy award Fashion Reporting, 1967; named Advt. Woman of Year Elmira-Corning Advt. Club, 1969. Mem. Jr. League, Am. Women in Radio and TV. Home: 84 Greenridge Dr Elmira NY 14902

MCKAY, HELEN BEATRICE RONK (MRS. CHARLES NELSON MCKAY), village ofcl.; b. Highland, N.Y., Aug. 15, 1917; d. Frederick and Beatrice Emma (Rhoades) Ronk; student Orange County Community Coll., 1968, 71-72, Syracuse U., 1968; m. Charles Nelson McKay, Oct. 15, 1939; children—Nelson Craig, Brian Glenn. Office clk. Walden Coal Co., 1937-39; area enumerator Bur. Census, 1950; payroll and personnel staff Interstate Bag Co., Walden, N.Y., 1950-57; clk., registrar vital statistics, dep. treas. Village of Walden, N.Y., 1957—. Recipient Attendance award N.Y. State Fiscal Officers and Municipal Clks., N.Y. State Conf. Mayors and N.Y. State Dept. Audit and Control, 1973. Mem. N.Y. State Assn. City and Village Clks. Assn. (chmn. com. N.Y. State municipal handbook 1971-74), Internat. Inst. Municipal Clks., Kappa Sigma. Methodist. Mem. Order Eastern Star. Club: Woman's (pres. 1957-59, treas. 1972—) (Walden). Home: 32 Church St Walden NY 12586 Office: 8 Scofield St Walden NY 12586

MCKAY, JOY H., real estate exec.; b. Warrenville, N.J., June 14, 1914; d. Arthur and Helen (Milius) Hofheimer; grad. Dalton Sch., N.Y.C., 1932, Sarah Lawrence Coll., 1934; m. Joseph J. Siccardi, Sept. 5, 1934 (div. 1952); children—Helene Gay, Carol Ann (Mrs. William Williams Wyman), Arthur J., Marilyn Jill (Mrs. Thomas Iuliucci, Jr.); m. 2d, Raymond Roth, Aug. 25, 1955 (dec.); m. 3d, Samuel J. McKay, Dec. 1970. Mem. Bd. Edn. Warren Twp., N.J., 1940-47, pres. 1947; chmn. Warren Twp. A.R.C.; v.p. Mental Hygiene Soc. Union County, N.J., 1946-49, pres. 1949-51; bd. mgrs. N.J. Neuropsychiat. Inst., Princeton, N.J., 1951-55, v.p., 1953-54; pres. N.J. Assn. for Mental Health, 1951-56, mem. bd., 1951-64, exec. com. 1951-63, chmn. planning com., 1958-62; chmn. com. orgn. Nat. Assn. Mental Health, 1953-57, dir., 1951-62, mem. exec. com., 1953-62, chmn. planning com. 1959-61, mem. program com., 1961-63, chmn. direct services com., 1961-63; exec. dir. Somerset County Assn. for Mental Health, 1965-67; dir. div. services N.J. Heart Assn., 1967-70; supr. Heart Sunday Broward County (Fla.) Heart Assn., 1970-71, dir. fund raising, 1971-72; asso. J.G. Realty, Deerfield, Fla., 1972-73; asso. Gold Palm Realty, Boca Raton, Fla., 1973—. Trustee Nathan Hofheimer Found., 1945-70. Unitarian. Home: 750 NE Spanish River Blvd Boca Raton FL 33432

MCKEE, FRANCES GWENDOLYN MARTIN (MRS. DAVIS BELL MCKEE, JR.), nursing educator; b. Lawrence, Mass., Nov. 10, 1923; d. William Guy and Bertha Etta (Ferris) Martin; B.S., Merrimack Coll., 1958; M.S., Boston U., 1959, Ed.D., 1974; m. Davis Bell McKee, Jr., July 30, 1944; children—Linda Karen, Leslie Susan, Davis Bell, Guy Martin. Staff nurse Bon Secours Hosp., Methuen, Mass., 1955-69, Lawrence (Mass.) Gen. Hosp., 1970—. Prof., St. Anselm's Coll., Manchester, N.H., 1959—; instr. N.H. Coll., Manchester, 1971-72; project dir. federal grant Dept. Health, Edn. and Welfare, 1968-71. Woman's adviser Dist. 5 March of Dimes of N.H., 1972—. Trustee Manchester (N.H.) Area Family Planning Clinic, 1968-71, chmn. personnel com. 1968-71. Mem. Am. Nurses Assn., Nat. League for Nursing, V.F.W. Aux. (pres. 1953-54). Home: New Boston Rd Bedford NH 03102 Office: St Anselm's Dr Manchester NH 03102

MCKEE, HEATHER GERTRUDE (MRS. LARRY ROY MCKEE), hosp. adminstr.; b. East London, South Africa, May 18, 1940; d. Bernard Michael and Ruth Little-John (Gower) Kieser; Degree in Nursing and Midwifery, Witwatersrand Nursing Coll. (South Africa), 1961; m. Larry Roy McKee, Dec. 3, 1966; children—Laurel Vee, Michael James. Came to Can., 1965, naturalized, 1966. Staff nurse Germiston (Transvaal, South Africa) Gen. Hosp., 1961-63, head nurse, 1962-63; staff nurse Cullinan (Transvaal) Mine Hosp., 1963-64, Weyburn (Sask., Can.) Gen. Hosp., 1965-66; staff nurse Drumheller (Alta., Can.) Gen. Hosp., 1966-67, supr., 1969-74, dir. nursing, 1974—. Mem. Am. Assn. R.N.s, Dirs. of Nursing for Small Hosps. Home: PO Rowley AB Canada Office: Box 4500 Drumheller AB Canada

MCKEE, KATHRYN LORENA KELLOGG (MRS. ROBERT KYLE MCKEE), mfg. co. exec.; b. Jeffersonville, Ind., Nov. 15, 1918; d. John Boaz and Lorena Vivian (English) Kellogg; student Monte Cassino Jr. Coll., 1936-37, Tulsa Secretarial Sch., 1946-47, Willis Bus. Coll., 1957, Valley Coll., 1964-66; certificate in indsl. relations, U. Cal. at Los Angeles, 1970; m. Robert Kyle McKee, July 1, 1960; children by previous marriage—Jeffrey L. Duncan, Christopher K. Duncan. Sec., Okla. Natural Gas Co., Tulsa, 1937-38; adminstrv. sec. Ashland Oil & Refining Co., Tulsa, 1947-49; exec. sec. Schlumberger Well Surveying Corp., Tulsa, 1949-57; bus., personal, social sec. D.D. Feldman Oil & Gas Co., 1957-59; exec. sec., adminstrv. asst., editor house orgn. Avdel, Inc. (name now Avibank Mfg. Inc.) Burbank, Cal., 1966—, personnel dir., 1971—, sec., dir., 1971-73; sec. Avdisc, Inc., 1972—; sec., dir. LTL Industries, Inc., 1973—. Active United Crusade. Mem. Internat. Assn. Personnel Women (membership com. 1970), Personnel and Indsl. Relations Assn. (generalist subcom. 1971-72, mem. generalist com. 1973-74), Personnel Women Los Angeles (program com. 1970-71, rec. sec. 1972—, chmn. continuing edn. com. 1973-74), Tulsa Desk and Derrick (dir. 1952-53), U. Cal. at Los Angeles Alumnae Assn., Beta Phi Gamma, Eta Upsilon Gamma. Republican. Mem. Ch. of Religious Sci. Author: Speaking of Sceptre, 1966. Home: 3325 Adina Dr Hollywood CA 90028 Office: 210 S Victory St Burbank CA 91502

MCKEE, LOIS IRENE (MRS. GEORGE E. MCKEE), educator; b. Navarre, O., June 18, 1909; d. Malvern Sylvester and Blanche (McIntosh) Slutz; B.S. summa cum laude, Ohio U., 1937; M.Ed., Kent State U., 1955; postgrad. Akron U., 1959; m. George E. McKee, June 12, 1943. Tchr. Valley Sch., Columbiana County O., 1928-29, Salem (O.) city schs., 1929-46; prin. Elkton Sch., Lisbon, O., 1946-47; tchr. Canal Fulton (O.) Sch., 1948-51; tchr. Canton (O.) pub. schs., 1951—, tchr. academically gifted, 1959—. Jennings scholar, 1966-67; Martha Holden Jenning Master Tchr., 1967; recipient Valley Forge Tchrs. medal Freedoms Found., 1968; named Canton Tchr. of Yr., 1973. Mem. N.E.A., Ohio Edn. Assn., E. Central Ohio Tchrs. Assn. (chmn. gifted children sect. 1963), Ohio Assn. Childhood Edn., Canton Profl. Educators Assn., Nat. Congress Parents and Tchrs., Ohio Assn. for Supervision and Curriculum Devel., Assn., Childhood Edn. Internat. Canton Assn. Childhood Edn. (pres. 1958-60, adviser 1960-64), Am. Assn. U. Women (Canton pres. 1967-69, treas. Ohio div. 1972-74), Kappa Delta Pi. Club: Quota. Author chpt. of book. Home: 3219 Glen Pl NW Canton OH 44708

MCKEE, MARGARET JEAN, polit. analyst; b. New Haven, June 20, 1929; d. Waldo McCutcheon and Elizabeth (Thayer) McKee; A.B., Vassar Coll., 1951. Staff asst. United Republican Finance Com., N.Y.C., 1952; staff asst. N.Y. Rep. State Com., N.Y.C., 1953-55; staff asst. Crusade for Freedom (name later changed to Radio Free Europe Fund), N.Y.C., 1955-57; researcher Stricker & Henning Research Asso., Inc., N.Y.C., 1957-59; exec. sec. New Yorkers for Nixon (name later changed to N.Y. State Ind. Citizens for Nixon Lodge), N.Y.C., 1959-60; asst. to Raymond Moley, polit. columnist, N.Y.C., 1961; asst. campaign com. Louis J. Lefkowitz for Mayor, N.Y.C., 1961; research programmer, treas. Consensus, Inc., N.Y.C., 1962-67; spl. asst. to U.S. Senator Jacob K. Javits, N.Y., 1967-73, adminstrv. asst., 1973—. Commr. N.Y. State Bingo Control Authority, 1965-72; pres. Bklyn. Heights Slope Young Republican Club, 1955-56; co-chmn. Bklyn. Citizens for Eisenhower-Nixon, 1956; chmn. 2d Jud. Dist. Assn. N.Y. State Young Republican Clubs, Inc., 1957-58, vice-chmn., mem. bd. govs., 1958-60, v.p., 1960-62; pres., 1962-64; mem. exec. com. Fedn. Women's Rep. Clubs N.Y. State, Inc., 1960-64, mem. council, 1964—; mem. exec. com. N.Y. Rep. State Com. 1962-64; co-chmn. spl. assts. Rockefeller for Pres. Nat. Campaign com., N.Y.C., 1964; co-dir. N.Y. Rep. State Campaign Com., 1964; asst. campaign mgr. Kenneth B. Keating for Judge Ct. Appeals, N.Y., 1965; dir. scheduling Gov. Rockefeller campaign, 1966, Sen. Charles E. Goodell campaign, 1970; dir. scheduling and speakers' bur. N.Y. Com. to Re-elect the Pres., 1972. Mem. bd. govs. Women's Nat. Rep. Club, N.Y.C., 1963-66. Mem. Jr. League of Bklyn. (past dir.). Episcopalian. Club: Vassar (past dir.) (Bklyn.). Home: 3001 Veazey Terrace NW Washington DC 20008 Office: Old Senate Office Bldg Washington DC 20510

MCKEE, MARJORIE ANN BRAND (MRS. ROBERT E. MCKEE), educator; b. Detroit, Aug. 13, 1922; d. George Edward and Elsie Bertie (Jones) Brand; A.A., Stephens Coll., 1942; B.Ed., Nat. Coll. Edn., Evanston, Ill., 1944; M.S.W., U. Mich., 1951; Ed.D., Wayne State U., 1969; m. Robert Eugene McKee, May 27, 1952; 1 dau., Marjorie (Mrs. John Welborn Mitzel). Tchr. Children's Inst., Chgo., 1944-45; elementary tchr. Detroit Pub. Schs., 1950-53; tchr., prin. Firestone Staff Sch., Harbel, Liberia, 1952-60; supr., tchr. spl. edn. Detroit Pub. Schs., 1960-69; asst. prof. spl. edn. No. Mich. U., 1969-73, asso. prof., 1973—. Chmn. edn. sect. Inter Agy. Cadre on Mental Retardation. James Cozens fellow in social work, 1945-46. Mem. N.E.A., Council Exceptional Children (pres. Detroit chpt. 1967), Am. Assn. Mental Deficiency, Nat. Assn. Retarded Children, Alpha Delta Kappa (pres. Gamma Epsilon chpt.). Home: 653 Lakewood Lane Harvey MI 49855 Office: Northern Michigan University Marquette MI 49855

MCKEE, MRS. WALDO MCC. (ELIZABETH BROOKS THAYER MCKEE), club woman; b. Bklyn; d. John Van Buren and Elizabeth B. (Chatfield) Thayer; grad. Bklyn. Heights Sem., 1914; m. Waldo McCutcheon McKee, Oct. 3, 1925; children—Elizabeth Brooks (Mrs. J. Eugene Lewis), M. Jean. Hon. dir. Orphan Asylum, Bklyn.; past chmn. social service com. Cumberland Hosp., Bklyn.; past treas. Bklyn. com. Met. Opera; past mem. N.Y. Philharmonic Com.; mem. Cheshire Bicentennial Commn. Polit. edn. chmn. Woman's Republican Club, Cheshire. Mem. Bklyn. Jr. League (past pres.), Nat. Soc. Colonial Dames (past v.p. N.Y.), New Haven Colony, Cheshire (membership chmn.) hist. socs., Conn. Antiquarian and Landmarks Soc. Cheshire Historic Dist. Com. Clubs: Civitas (past v.p.), Mrs. Fields Literary (past v.p.). Home: 532 S Brooksvale Rd Cheshire CT 06410

MCKEEMAN, DOLORES EVELYN BOE (MRS. DANIEL WALLACE MCKEEMAN), realtor; b. Mpls., Mar. 17, 1914; d. Christopher Alfred and Mary Evelyn (Taylor) Boe; student Sacramento Real Estate Sch., 1957; m. Daniel Wallace McKeeman, Dec. 23, 1933; children—Michaelyn (Mrs. Hamilton Curry McKelvey), Myron Dennis, Timothy Daniel. Salesperson, Beguette Realtors, Sacramento, 1957-58; realtor Channel Real Estate, Sacramento, 1958-61, McKeeman Real Estate, Auburn, Cal., 1964-73, Channel Real Estate, Salinas, Cal., 1966-67. Active Historic Auburn restoration. Mem. Auburn, Placer County chambers commerce, Bus. and Profl. Women. Club: Soroptomist (Auburn). Address: 197 Aeolia Dr Auburn CA 95603

MCKEEMAN, GWEN MARIE MOSS (MRS. ROBERT LEWIS MCKEEMAN), clubwoman; b. Stigler, Okla., Feb. 28, 1926; d. Leonard McDonald and Marie (Gatlin) Moss; B.S. in Bus. Edn., Northeastern State Coll., Tahlequah, Okla., 1947; m. Robert Lewis McKeeman, Mar. 31, 1951; children—Robert Moss, Marianne, Scott Randall. Pres., Tulsa Alumnae chpt. Delta Zeta, 1958, Province Alumnae dir., 1960-64, nat. chmn. State Days, 1963-64, pres. Tulsa City Panhellenic, 1965, nat. v.p. Alumnae, 1964-69, Nat. Panhellenic Conf. del., 1969—, mem. exec. com., treas., 1971-73, with Office of Sec., 1973—. Sec.-treas. Magic Empire Distbg., Inc., Broomtown, Inc. Vol. March of Dimes, 1971-73. Bd. dirs. Tulsa Recreation Center for Physically Limited, 1970-71; bd. mgrs. Tulsa Cerebral Palsy Assn., 1967—, pres., 1970-71. Named Delta Zeta of Okla., 1965. Mem. Tulsa City Panhellenic, Tulsa Lion Tamers, Sports Buggies of Tulsa, Meml. High Sch. P.T.A., Nat. Assn. Women Deans, Adminstrs. and Counsellors. Presbyn. Club: Delta Upsilon Mothers (U. Okla.). Home: 5517 S 74th E Av Tulsa OK 74145

MCKEEVER, CATHERINE PATRICIA O'MALLEY (MRS. FRANCIS MICHAEL MCKEEVER), civic worker; b. Kewanee, Ill.; d. William Henry and Nellie Louise (Maegher) O'Malley; B.Ed., Ill. State Normal U., 1934; m. Francis Michael McKeever, Jan. 19, 1946; children—Sheila Ann, Francis Michael, Patricia Catherine. Tchr. Dunlap Grade Sch., 1937-38, East Peoria (Ill.) Grade Sch., 1938-41, East Peoria (Ill.) High Sch., 1941-42; recreational dir. A.R.C., Amarillo, Tex., 1942-44, Percy Jones Gen. Hosp., Battle Creek, Mich., 1944-45. Treas. St. Vincent's Hosp. Bd., 1965-67, program chmn., 1967-69; mem. Good Samaritan Hosp. Bd., 1962-66; mem. St. Anne's Hosp. Guild Bd., 1960-68; mem. Social Service Aux. Bd., 1969-70, chmn. presentation ball, 1970-71, pres., 1973-75; coordinator Jr. Mannequin Assisteens, Assistance League So. Cal., 1968-69, membership com., 1970-71. Recipient Certificate of Merit award A.R.C., 1946. Home: 139 S Plymouth Blvd Los Angeles CA 90004

MCKEITHEN, MARJORIE HOWELL FUNDERBURK (MRS. JOHN JULIAN MCKEITHEN), civic worker; b. Grayson, La., Aug. 30, 1919; d. Aaron John and Katie Lee (Howell) Funderburk; B.S., La. Poly. Inst., 1939; m. John Julian McKeithen (former Gov. La.), June 14, 1942; children—Jesse Jay, Walter Fox, Rebecca Ann, Melissa Sue, Pamela Clare, Jenneva Maude. Tchr. math. La. high schs., 1939-42. Mem. Commn. Social Welfare, 1964—, Commn. La. Assn. Retarded Children, 1964—; v.p. Band Booster's Club, 1962. Democrat. Methodist (pres. women's soc. 1961). Home: Hogan Plantation Columbia LA 71418

MCKENNA, CATHERINE A. (MRS. WILLIAM F. MCKENNA), educator; b. Berlin, Conn.; d. Daniel Francis and Margaret (Monahan) Donahue; student Pequod Bus. Coll., Meriden, Conn., 1925-27; m. William Francis McKenna, June 25, 1935; children—William Francis (dec.), Daniel. Retail asst., Meriden, 1928-29; instr. St. Rose Sch., Meriden, 1930-35; athletic instr. St. Rose Community Bldg., 1932-35; playground instr. City of Meriden playgrounds, 1933-34. Hon. hostess in Washington for Nat. Assn. Mut. Savs. Banks, 1959-63; hostess in Washington, Nat. League Insured Savs. Assns., 1963—, vice chmn. hospitality com., 1968—. Active A.R.C.; mem. aux. com. Holy Cross Hosp., Silver Spring, Md. 1969—. Campaign aide to U.S. Senator Francis T. Maloney, 1932. Adv. mem. MBLS. Mem. Conn. State Soc. Democrat. Roman Catholic. Home: 8004 Park Crest Dr Silver Spring MD 20910

MCKENNA, SISTER MARGARET MARY, educator; b. Teaneck, N.J., May 26, 1930; d. Walter Francis and Stella Marie (Schnell) McKenna; A.B., Chestnut Hill Coll., 1955; M.A. (scholar), U. Notre Dame, 1960; postgrad. U. Pa., 1971—. Joined Med. Mission Sisters, 1948; designer, co-editor Med. Missionary Mag., 1956-65; adminstr. St. Theresa's Inst. and Med. Mission Sisters, 1960-67; prof. dept.

theology LaSalle Coll., Phila., 1970—. Mem. Pa. Gov.'s Commn. on Status Women, 1965-66; mem. program com. on Cath.-Jewish Relations Phila. Cardinal's Commn. on Human Relations, 1970-72. Bd. dirs. O.P.E.N. Inc., Phila., Holy Family Hosp., Atlanta. Mem. Cath. Bib. Assn., Coll. Theology Soc., Am. Acad. Religion, Phila. Seminar on Christian Orgins. Democrat. Roman Catholic. Author: Women of the Church, 1967; If It Matters. Home: 438 E Walnut Lane Philadelphia PA 19144

MCKENNA, MARIAN CECILIA, educator; b. Scarsdale, N.Y., July 3, 1926; d. John Francis and Marguerite Veronica (Hanfling) McKenna; Tchrs. diploma, N.Y. Coll. Music, 1946; B.S., Tchrs. Coll., Columbia, 1949, M.A., 1950, Ph.D. in History, (Erb fellow 1953), 1954. Instr. history Hunter Coll., City U. N.Y., 1953-59; asst. prof. Manhattanville Coll., Purchase, N.Y., 1959-64, asso. prof., 1964-66; prof. history U. Calgary, (Alta., Can.), 1966—. Danforth fellow, 1965; grantee Can. Council, 1969, 70, 71, 72. Mem. Am., So. hist. assns., Orgn. Am. Historians, Canadian Assn. Am. Studies, Immigration History Soc. Author: Borah, 1961; Pictorial History of Catholicism, 1962. Contbr. articles to various publs. Home: 3343 Upton Pl NW Calgary AB T2N 4G9 Canada

MCKENNA, MARY LOESCH (MRS. MAURICE A. MCKENNA), bus. exec.; b. N.Y.C., Aug. 14, 1918; d. George J. and Jane A. (Black) Loesch; B.S., Columbia, 1939; m. Maurice A. McKenna, June 11, 1940. Dir. media research Benton & Bowles, N.Y.C., 1942-54; v.p. in charge research and sales devel. Metromedia, N.Y.C., 1954-68, v.p. in charge market research, 1968—. Past pres. Radio and TV Research Council; sec. Internat. Radio and TV Found., 1965—; past dir. Television Bur. Advt.; tech. chmn. All-Radio Methodology Survey. Mem. Am. Marketing Assn., Media Research Dirs. Assn., Radio and Television Research Council, Internat. Radio and Television Execs. Soc., Internat. Radio and Television Found. Republican. Roman Catholic. Home: Heritage Village Southbury CT 06877 Office: 485 Lexington Av New York City NY 10017

MCKENNEY, FLORENCE REA (MRS. W. GIBBS MCKENNEY, JR.), civic worker, club woman; b. Canton, N.C., Nov. 6, 1914; d. William and Roberta (Payne) Rea; B.S., U. Md., 1936; m. W. Gibbs McKenney, Jr., July 17, 1939. Tchr. home econs. pub. schs., Balt., 1936-40, Washington, 1940-45. Asso. dir. Delta Delta Delta, 1958-62. Chmn. orientation and tng. A.R.C., Balt., 1961-64, dir., 1961—, vice chmn. community relations, 1964-66, chmn. uniformed vols., 1966-67, vice chmn. vols. Balt. regional chpt. 1967-69, chmn. vols., 1969-72; mem. Hampton Nat. Historic Site Com., 1963—; 2d v.p. Balt. Civic Opera Guild, 1968-72; financial sec. Cylburn Wildflower Preserve and Garden Center, 1971—. Bd. dirs. Meals on Wheels; pres. bd. mgrs. J. Bennett Home, 1974—. Mem. Federated Garden Clubs Md. (dist. dir., state pres. 1967-69), Mortar Bd., Alpha Lambda Delta, Omicron Nu, Phi Kappa Phi. Methodist. Clubs: Baltimore Country, Lutherville Garden (pres. 1957-58), Woodbrook Murray Hill Garden, Woman's of Roland Park (gov. 1971-73). Home: 102 Estes Rd Baltimore MD 21212

MCKENRY, COLETTA, librarian; b. Pitts., Jan. 13, 1913; d. Ralph Marland and Marie Josephine (Harrington) McKenry; B.S., Indiana U. of Pa., 1935; postgrad. Grace Martin's Secretarial Sch., 1937; M.Ed., U. Pitts., 1943, M.L.S., 1965. Sec. to editor Jour. Applied Physics, U. Pitts., 1937-39; sec. to sales mgr. Lyon Metal Products, Inc., Pitts., 1939-41; supr. reference bur. U.S. Steel Corp., Pitts., 1941—, staff asst. indsl. relations dept., 1942-68, librarian, 1968—. Nurses aide Magee Hosp., 1941-47. Mem. Am., Pa., Spl. library assns. Clubs: Beaver Lakes Country (Aliquippa, Pa.); Womans City (Pitts.); Chesapeake (Irvington, Va.). Home: 621 Olympia Rd Pittsburgh PA 15211 Office: 600 Grant St Pittsburgh PA 15230

MCKENZIE, ANN SPENCER LLEWELLYN (MRS. CLAUDE FLEATUS MCKENZIE), lawyer; b. Oxford, N.C., Dec. 18, 1925; d. Clement Manly and Ruth Spencer (Pitchford) Llewellyn; certificate of laws U. N.C., 1955; m. Herbert B. Greene, Jr., Feb. 19, 1944; 1 son, Herbert B. III; m. 2d, Claude Fleatus McKenzie, Dec. 27, 1957. Admitted to N.C. bar, 1955, Md. bar, 1958, N.C. Supreme Ct. bar, 1955; practiced in Concord, N.C., 1955-66, Balt., 1966—; mem. firm Llewellyn & Greene, Concord, 1955-57, Llewellyn & McKenzie, Concord, 1957-61, Llewellyn, McKenzie & Llewellyn, Concord, 1961-66; individual practice, Balt., 1966—. Pioneer female defense counsel mil. ct. martial, Ft. Bragg, N.C., 1956. Home: 500 Druid Hill Av Baltimore MD 21201 Office: 646 Jasper St Baltimore MD 21201

MCKENZIE, ELIZABETH ADAMS (MRS. LEONARD JOHN MCKENZIE), ednl. adminstr.; b. Carlton, Ga., Mar. 17, 1926; d. Robert Amos and Evelyn Cleo (Colson) Adams; student Gary Jr. Coll., 1942-44; B.S., Ind. U., 1946; m. Leonard John McKenzie, June 20, 1948. Publs. coordinator U. Wis. Extension Div., Madison, 1957-58; publs. editor Nat. Assn. Ednl. Broadcasters, Urbana, Ill., 1959-66; editor Office dean of students, vice chancellor for campus affairs U. Ill. at Champaign, 1966—. Mem. corp. bd. Univ. YWCA, Champaign, 1967—, chmn. bd., 1971-72. Mem. Women in Communication (chpt. pres. 1972—), Edn. Writers Assn. Unitarian. Home: 703-A Holiday Park Dr Champaign IL 61820

MCKENZIE, MARY LOUISE, physician; b Vienna, Ill., Oct. 3, 1933; d. Ralph Herbert and Margaret Elizabeth (Gourley) McKenzie; student Blackburn Coll., 1951-53; A.B., U. Ill., 1955; M.D., Woman's Med. Coll., 1959. Intern, Presbyn. St. Lukes Hosp., Chgo., 1959-60, gen. surgery resident St. Francis Hosp., Evanston, 1960-64; resident plastic surgery Cook County Hosp., Chgo., 1964-67; practice medicine specializing in plastic surgery, St. Charles, Ill., 1968—; mem. staffs Delnor, Geneva Community, Central Dupage, Winfield, Shriners hosps. Diplomate Am. Bd. Surgery, Am. Bd. Plastic Surgery; Mem. A.C.S. Contbr. articles to profl. pubs. Home: 1805 Allen Lane St Charles IL 60174 Office: 24 Mosedale St St Charles IL 60174

MCKEON, CLEMENTINE CECELIA, physician; b. New Orleans; d. John Vincent and Mary (Maillho) McKeon; B.S., Tulane U., 1930, M.D., 1932. Rotating intern New England Hosp., Boston, 1932-33; sr. physician Met. State Hosp., Waltham, Mass., 1933-42; practice of psychiatry Boston, 1942-43; staff VA Hosp., Bedford, 1946-68, chief of staff, 1965-68, acting hosp. dir., 1968; clin. dir. Westwood (Mass.) Lodge, 1969-70; practice medicine, specializing in psychiatry, Arlington, Mass., 1971—. Mem. faculty Tufts U. Med. Sch., Boston, 1946-68. Served to surgeon USPHS, 1943-46. Recipient citation for outstanding service D.A.V., 1968. Diplomate Am. Bd. Psychiatry and Neurology. Mem. A.M.A., Pan Am., Mass. med. socs., Middlesex Central of Mass. Med. Soc., Am. Psychiat. Assn., New Eng. Soc. Psychiatry (pres. 1953-54), Am. Med. Women's Assn., N.Y. Acad. Scis., World Mental Health Orgn., Boston Bus. and Profl. Club. Home: 11 Bedford St Lexington MA 02173 Office: 3 Valley Rd Arlington MA 02174

MCKEOWN, ELSYE, mental health cons., educator; b. Orange, N.J., Feb. 26, 1917; d. Samuel C. and Anna (Spann) McKeown; B.S. in Sociology and Psychology, U. S.C., 1950; M.S. in Psychiat. Social Work, Columbia, 1952; postgrad. Harvard, 1959-60. Chief psychiat. social worker Richland County Mental Health Clinic, Columbia, S.C., 1952-54; mental health cons. S.C. Dept. Mental Health, Columbia, 1954-64, Nat. Inst. Mental Health, Dept. Health, Edn. and Welfare Region IV, Atlanta, 1964—. Asst. prof. psychology dept. U. S.C., Columbia, 1956-60; cons. Child Study Project, Sumter, S.C., 1960-64. Nat. Inst. Mental Health fellow, Harvard, 1959-60. Fellow Am. Orthopsychiat. Assn.; mem. Nat. Assn. Social Workers, Am. Pub. Health Assn. Home: 1098-H North James Town Rd Decatur GA 30033 Office: MH Serv USPHS HEW 7th St NE Atlanta GA 30323

MCKEOWN, MARY ELIZABETH, educator; b. Chgo., Nov. 26, 1921; d. Raymond Edmund and Alice (Fitzgerald) McNamara; B.S., U. Chgo., 1946; M.S., DePaul U., 1953; m. James Edward McKeown, Aug. 6, 1955. Supr. high sch. dept. Am. Sch., 1948-68, prin., 1968—. Mem. Nat. Assn. Secondary Sch. Prins., Central States Assn. Sci. and Math Tchrs. Nat. Council Tchrs. Math., Adult Edn. Assn., Women's Math Club., League Women Voters. Home: 1469 N Sheridan Rd Kenosha WI 53140

MCKERALL, MARY JEANETTE, lawyer; b. Springfield, Mo., Dec. 23, 1944; d. Josiah Danforth and Eileen Virginia (Carter) McKerall; B.A. in History, Nicholls State U., 1966; postgrad. La. State U., 1966, U. Houston Coll. Law, 1966-67; J.D., U. Tex., 1969. Admitted to Tex. bar, 1969; examiner abstract dept. Stewart Title Co., Houston, 1969; staff atty. Houston Legal Found., 1969-70; pvt. practice, 1970-74; asst. county atty. Harris County Atty.'s Office, Houston, 1974—. Mem. State Bar Tex., Houston Bar Assn., Nat. Assn. Women Lawyers, Nat. Assn. for Community TV, Nat., Harris County women's polit. caucuses, Houston Grand Opera Guild, Kappa Beta Pi (dean 1971-72). Home: 1206 Stanford Houston TX 77019 Office: Harris County Courthouse Houston TX 77002

MCKEWEN, JANE B., physician; b. Baltimore County, Md., Jan. 5, 1923; d. Edward M. and Ethel L. (Bell) McKewen; B.S., Johns Hopkins U., 1945; certificate Peabody Conservatory of Music, 1944; M.D., Johns Hopkins Med. Sch., 1951. Intern, Johns Hopkins Hosp., Balt., 1951-52; resident Johns Hopkins Hosp., 1952-54, Doctors Hosp., Washington, 1954-56; practice medicine specializing in anesthesiology, Washington, 1956-58, Republic of Haiti, 1958-60, Balt., 1960-68, Boise and Nampa, Ida., 1968—; mem. staff Mercy Hosp., Nampa, Ida. Bd. dirs. Ida. Humane Soc. Diplomate Am. Bd. Anesthesiologists. Fellow Am. Coll. Anesthesiology; mem. Am. Soc. Anesthesiologists, Assn. Am. Physicians and Surgeons, Ida. Med. Soc., Sons of Norway. Address: 3617 Hillcrest Dr Boise ID 83705

MCKIBBIN, ELSIE HOLMES, occupational therapist; b. Lansing, Mich., Apr. 5, 1917; d. Clifford Worden and Ruth (Mead) McKibbin; B.S., Mich. State U., 1939; certificate occupational therapy Colo. State U., 1958; M.A., U. Ala., 1968. Tchr. home econs. Grayling (Mich.) High Sch., 1940; home service rep. Mich. Consol. Gas Co., Muskegon, 1940-42; lab. asst. serology U. Mich. at Ann Arbor, 1942-45; hosp. worker A.R.C., San Antonio, 1945-47; dir. conf. registration continuing edn. dept. Mich. State U., 1951-56; sr. occupational therapist Ia. Meth. Hosp., Des Moines, 1959-63; chief occupational therapist U. Ala. Hosps. and Clinics, Birmingham, 1963-67; dir. occupational therapy Center Devel. and Learning Disorders U. Ala., Birmingham, 1968—, asst. prof. occupational therapy, 1968—. Bd. dirs., mem. exec. bd. United Cerebral Palsy Greater Birmingham, Ala.; sec.-treas., bd. dirs. South Highland Day Care Center, Inc. Mem. Am. Occupational Therapy Assn. (regional coordinator council on practice 1965-67), Am. Assn. U. Women, Alpha Phi. Presbyn. Home: 1711A Valley Av Birmingham AL 35209

MCKILLOP, LUCILLE MARY, coll. pres.; b. Chgo., Sept. 28, 1924; d. Daniel and Catherine (Hamill) McKillop; B.A., St. Xavier Coll., 1951; M.S., U. Notre Dame, 1959; Ph.D., U. Wis., 1965. Tchr. pub. schs. Chgo. and Ottawa, Ill., 1946-58; instr. Edgewood Coll., Madison, Wis., 1961-62; vis. prof. Ill. Inst. Tech., Chgo., 1969; mem. faculty St. Xavier Coll., Chgo., 1958-59, 63-73; pres. Salve Regina Coll., Newport, R.I., 1973—. Cons. and speaker to various religious communities. Mem. Govt. Commn. Inst. of Mercy in U.S., 1970-72, chmn., 1969-72. Bd. dirs. Mercy Action Found., Washington, 1972-73; bd. dirs. Sisters of Mercy, Province of Chgo. Mem. Am. Assn. U. Women (mem. exec. bd. 1965-68). Address: Salve Regina College Ochre Point Av Newport RI 02840

MCKIM, CHARLOTTE B., civic worker; b. Bklyn., Apr. 20, 1899; d. David Peyton and Maude (Logan) Bevans; student Art Students League, 1920-24, Harvard, summer 1934; m. William Lee McKim, Oct. 15, 1924. Sec. Soc. of Four Arts, 1951-56, dir., 1951—. Mem. Norton Gallery of Art, Mus. Modern Art N.Y.C., English-Speaking Union Palm Beach. Compiler: The Salles Letters 1825-50, 1957. Address: 322 Eden Rd Palm Beach FL 33480

MCKIM, JUDITH LOUISE, educator; b. Waterloo, Ia., Sept. 1, 1936; d. Francis Marion and Bess (Ogden) McKim; B.A. in English-Journalism, Grinnell Coll., 1958. Coll. recruiting Tex. Instruments, Inc., Dallas, 1958-63; adminstrv. asst. dept. sociology and anthropology U. Ia., Iowa City, 1964-70, project coordinator Ia. Urban Community Research Center, 1970—. Mem. Population Assn. Am., Nat. Audubon Soc., Women in Communications. Republican. Contbr. articles to profl. jours. Education and the Absorption of Inmigrant Mexican-Americans. Home: 706 George St Iowa City IA 52240 Office: Ia Urban Community Research Center U Ia Iowa City IA 52242

MCKINLEY, ALICE ELIZABETH, librarian; b. Champaign County, O., Feb. 23, 1921; d. Herman Toomire and Sarah Rebecca (Siebert) McKinley; B.A., Blackburn U., 1940; B.A., Park Coll., 1942; B.L.S., U. Denver, 1943 librarian Minot Pub. Library, N.D., 1943, Park Coll. Library, Parkville, Mo., 1943-45, Kan. City (Mo.) Pub. Library, 1946-47; spl. services librarian, U.S. Army, Europe, 1947-55; library cons. Mich. State Library, Lansing, 1956-64, U.S. Office Edn., Dept. Health, Edn. and Welfare, Washington, 1965-67; exec. dir. DuPage Library System, Wheaton, Ill., 1967—. Mem. Am., Ill. library assns. Home: PO Box 682 Wheaton IL 60187 Office: DuPage Library System PO Box 826 Wheaton IL 60187

MCKINLEY, MARGERY ANN MCDONALD (MRS. CHARLES WILLIAM MCKINLEY), pub. co. exec.; b. Lakewood, O., Mar. 18, 1926; d. Thomas Fraser and Helena (Jongewaard) McDonald; B.A., U. Ia., 1948; m. Charles William McKinley, Aug. 27, 1948; children—Karen Lane, Laura Ann, Leslie Marie, Margery Lynn, Charles William. With Brownsville Pub. Corp., Brownsville, Pa., 1955—, v.p., treas., 1970—. Mem. Centerville Borough Planning Commn., 1972-74. Mem. Adv. bd. March of Dimes, 1971-74. Home: 200 Indian Rock Dr Brownsville PA 15417 Office: 16-18 Bridge St Brownsville PA 15417

MCKINNEY, HELEN MATHEWS (MRS. JACK W. MCKINNEY), state legislator; b. Idaho Falls, Ida., Oct. 30, 1917; student U. Utah, U. Ida.; m. Jack W. McKinney; 1 son, John S. Past tchr. jr. high sch., 1940-55; mem. Ida. Ho. of Reps., 1965—, sec., Republican caucus, vice chmn. appropriations com. Mem. adv. bd. Challis Nat. Forest. Past sec., committeewoman, Ida. Rep. Centennial Com.; mem. Gov.'s Status of Women Commn. Mem. Bus. and Profl. Women's Club, Internat. Toast Mistresses, Nat. Edn. Assn., Ida. (v.p.), North Ida. C. of C. (dir., 1st woman pres. 1973), U. Ida. Alumni Assn. (exec. bd.), Alpha Chi Omega. Recipient Outstanding Citizen's award, 1965; named Woman of the Year, 1966. Republican. Episcopalian. Address: Box 457 Salmon ID 83467

MCKINNEY, LINDA LEA (MRS. PHILIP ANTHONY MCKINNEY, JR.), retail exec.; b. Indpls., Sept. 4, 1944; d. Arthur Lee and Hariet (Struve) Bess; student Ind. U., 1962-67; m. Philip Anthony McKinney, Jr., Feb. 4, 1967. Sec. Standard Life Ins. Co., Indpls., 1962-67; publicity mgr. Ind. U. Press, Bloomington, 1967-72; owner Baskin-Robbins Ice Cream Store, Nashville, Ind., 1971—; Brown County Bus. and Profl. Women's Club (v.p.), Brown County C. of C. (dir. 1972—). Mem. Ind. Fedn. Bus. and Profl. Women's Clubs, owner, cons. Bridal Elegance, Nashville, 1972—. Home and office: Box 173 Nashville IN 47448

MCKINNEY, LORELLA A., educator; b. Lafayette, O., June 7, 1925; d. Donovan Stanley and M. Lucile (Ewing) McK.; B.S. in Edn., Ohio No. U., 1947; M.A., Ohio State U., 1950; Ph.D., 1963; postgrad. Purdue U., 1954, Carnegie Inst. Tech., 1955, Case Inst. Tech., 1956. Tchr. math. Ohio No. U., Ada, 1947, Swanton (O.) High Sch., 1947-48, Ohio State U., 1949, Washington High Sch., Washington Court House, O., 1950-52, Kenton (O.) High Sch., 1952-55, Wooster (O.) High Sch., 1955-57; adminstrv. asst. North High Sch., Willoughby, 1957, asst. prin., 1958-60, 63-65; instr. dept. secondary edn. Ohio State U., 1960-62; guest instr. dept. edn. Emory U., Atlanta, summers, 1961-64, Oglethorpe Coll., Atlanta, summer 1965, asso. prof., dir. tchr. edn., 1965-67; asst. dir. edn. State U. Coll., New Palta, N.Y., 1967-68, asso. prof., asso. dir. edn., 1968-70, asso. dean edn., 1970-71; asst. dir. program devel. Comprehensive Career Edn. Model, Ohio State U., 1971-73, program dir. spl. projects, research and devel. specialist, 1973—. Westminister Found. fellow, 1948-50; Gen. Electric fellow, 1954; Westinghouse fellow, 1955; Du Pont fellow, 1956. Mem. N.E.A. (life), Ohio (life) edn. assns., Assn. Tchr. Educators, Am. Assn. U. Profs., Am. Assn. Sch. Adminstrs., Nat. Sch. Pub. Relations Assn., Comparative Edn. Soc., Nat. Soc. Profs. of Edn., N.Y. State Assn. Tchr. Educators, (exec. com., corr. sec.), Nat. Council Adminstrv. Women in Edn., Nat. Soc. Study Edn., Ednl. Research Assn., Am. Vocational Assn., Nat., Ohio assns. secondary sch. prins., Nat., N.Y. State (legislative com.), Ramapo-Catskill (rec. sec.) assns. supervision and curriculum devel., Internat. Platform Assn., Faculty Assn. State Univ. N.Y., Assn. Higher Edn., Ohio No. U., Ohio State U. alumni assns., Delta Kappa Gamma, Pi Lambda Theta. Republican. Methodist. Club: Quota. Contbr. profl. jours. Research in staff utilization practices in pub. secondary schs. of Ohio. Home: 2853 Zollinger Rd Upper Arlington OH 43221

MCKINNEY, NANCY BROWN, state agy. ofcl.; b. Brockton, Mass., May 25, 1947; d. Joseph True and Elsie Jane (Brindle) Brown; B.S. in Sociology, McPherson Coll., 1969; postgrad. Central Conn. State Coll., 1972, Lebanon Coll., 1974; m. Herbert George McKinney, July 28, 1973. Area coordinator for 4-H and Youth, U. Conn. Coop. Extension Service, Litchfield County, Conn., 1969-74; case technician div. welfare, N.H. Dept. Health and Welfare, Claremont, 1974—. Chmn. Lebanon (N.H.) United Way, 1974; sec.-treas. Community Resources Com. Northwestern Conn., 1972-73, mem., 1969-74. Mem. Coalition on Human Rights, Conn. Council on the Family, Nat. (chmn. profl. improvement com. 1973-74, nat. center devel. com. 1973-74), New Eng. (v.p. 1974), Conn. (sec.-treas. 1970-72) assns. extension 4-H agts., League Women Voters. Home: 35 Seminary Hill West Lebanon NH 03784 Office: 137 Broad St Claremont NH 03743

MCKISSICK, MABEL FRANCES RICE (MRS. WALLACE T. MCKISSICK), librarian; b. Union, S.C., June 12, 1922; d. Phillip and Charity (Morman) Rice; B.A., Knoxville Coll., 1943; M.A., Columbia, 1954, M.S. in L.S., 1966; postgrad. Allen U., 1946-48, S.C. State Coll., 1949-50; m. Wallace T. McKissick, Dec. 22, 1946; 1 son, Wallace T. Tchr., Sims High Sch., Union, 1943-48, librarian, 1948-68; librarian New London (Conn.) Jr. High Sch. 1968—. Recipient certificate of appreciation Student Library Assts. Assn. S.C., 1964, 65; certificate of merit Dictionary Internat. Biography, 1968. Mem. A.L.A. (treatment of minority groups in library books and other instructional materials com., Coretta Scott King awards com.), New Eng. Sch. Library Assn., New Eng. (student leadership com.), Conn. (1st v.p. 1971-72, pres. 1973-74) sch. library assns., N.E.A. (dept. audiovisual instrn.), Conn., New London edn. assns., New London Service League (dir.), Am. Assn. Sch. Librarians, Knoxville Coll., Columbia Sch. Library Service alumni assns., Delta Kappa Gamma, Delta Sigma Theta. Mem. Order Eastern Star. Clubs: Zonta, Gayette (pres. New London). Home: PO Box 1122 201 Hempstead St New London CT 06320 Office: New London Jr High Sch Lincoln Av PO New London CT 06320

MCKISSICK, PAMELA LOUISE, advt. co. exec.; b. Louisville, Mar. 8, 1946; d. William Harper and Louise (Faith) McKissick; student Northwestern U., 1963, Am. Acad. Dramatic Arts, 1964-66. Broadcaster, WNEW-FM, N.Y.C., 1966-67; writer RSVP-pilot series, Los Angeles, 1968; film producer Erwin Wasey Advt., Los Angeles, 1969; writer comml. music and lyrics for Eddy Arnold, 1970-72; creative dir. William Cook Advt., Jacksonville, Fla., 1971-72, dir. creative services, 1972-74, v.p., 1974—; pres. Bullet Pub. Co., Jacksonville, Fla., 1973-74. Mem. Jacksonville Mayor's Advt. Council on Arts, 1972-73. Mem. A.F.T.R.A. Republican. Baptist. Club: Pilots (Jacksonville). Home: 193 San Juan Dr Ponte Vedra Beach FL Office: Am Heritage Bldg Jacksonville FL 32202

MCKNIGHT, ALICE LORRAINE POLLAKOFF (MRS. ROBERT VICTOR MCKNIGHT), business exec.; b. El Paso, Tex.; d. Phillip Lipman and Josephine (Gardner) Pollakoff; student U. Tex. at El Paso, 1949-50; m. Robert Victor McKnight, Aug. 12, 1950. With Popular Dry Goods Co., El Paso, 1947-70, asst. buyer jr. and infants wear, 1947-55, buyer cosmetics, 1955-70; dir. sales Yves St. Laurent and Lanvin Parfums, N.Y.C., 1970-72; v.p. Leni Inc., 1972—; pres. Alice McKnight Merchandising, Ltd., N.Y.C., 1973—. Cons. distributive edn. Home: 750 Park Av New York City NY 10021 Office: 730 Fifth Av New York City NY 10019

MCKNIGHT, ELIZABETH CHAPMAN (MRS. CHARLES JACKSON MCKNIGHT), journalist; b. Balt., June 20, 1907; d. Robert William and Ida (Sternberg) Evans; B.A., Coll. of Pacific, 1928, postgrad., 1928-29; m. Robert H. Chapman, June 25, 1932; children—Betty (Mrs. Rudolph Dyck), David, Arthur; m. 2d., Charles Jackson McKnight, Sept. 23, 1964 (dec. May 1972). Tchr., McClymonds High Sch., Oakland, Cal., 1929-32; project supr. WPA Sewing Project, Bakersfield, Cal., 1938-40; reporter Stockton Daily Record, 1945-59, central Cal. news editor, 1959-66, asst. city editor, 1966—, writer weekly column, Take the Back Road, 1962—. Mem. Stockton Redevel. Agy., 1963—; adv. com. Stockton Bd. Edn., 1953-56; mem. Cal. Commn. on Status of Women, 1969-71. Named Woman of the Year, Stockton Quota Club, 1964, Am. Assn. U. Women, 1960, Stockton Bus. and Profl. Womens Club, 1970. Mem. Cal. Fedn. Bus. and Profl. Women, (pres. 1960-61), Pi Kappa Delta. Republican. Clubs: Business and Professional Women, Zonta. Home: 332 E Robinhood Dr Stockton CA 95207 Office: 530 E Market St Stockton CA 95202

MCKOWN, ANNE HOWARD (MRS. BARRETT L. MCKOWN), educator; b. Balt., Mar. 5, 1934; d. John F. and Isabel T. (Willson) Grim; B.S., Washington Coll., 1956; M.Ed., Am. U., 1972; m. Barrett L. McKown, Sept. 24, 1965. Tchr. math, sci., jr. high sch., Balt.,

1956-57; tchr. elementary sch., St. Simons Island, Ga., 1957-58; tchr. sci. jr. high sch., Guam, 1958-59; tchr. sci. sr. high sch., Hyattsville, Md., 1960-70; guidance counselor Friendly Sr. High Sch., Oxon Hill, Md., 1970-74; instructional asst. pub. schs., Upper Marlboro, Md., 1974—. Supr. student tchrs. and counselor practicum candidates U. Md., College Park, 1966-70; del. to Sci. and Humanities Symposiums. Mem. Loch Haven Civic Assn., Edgewater, Md. Recipient Tchr. Sci. Talent Search award Westinghouse Corp., 1968. NSF grantee, 1963, 65, 68. Mem. Nat., Md. assns. biology tchrs., N.E.A., Md., Prince George's County tchrs. assns., Nat., Md., Prince George's County personnel and guidance assns., Zeta Tau Alpha. Episcopalian. Home: 3580 South River Terrace Edgewater MD 21037 Office: Prince Georges County Pub Schs Instructional Services Upper Marlboro MD 20870

MCKUSICK, ANNE BISHOP, physician, educator; b. Rochester, N.Y., Sept. 7, 1922; d. Fred Margeson and Grace (Common) Bishop; student McMaster U., 1939-42; A.B., Cornell U., 1944; postgrad. U. Cal. at Berkeley, 1946; M.D., Johns Hopkins, 1950; m. Victor Almon McKusick, June 11, 1949; children—Carol Anne, Kenneth Andrew, Victor Wayne. Jr. physicist Manhattan Project, Oak Ridge, 1944-45; intern Johns Hopkins Hosp., Balt., 1950-51, asst. resident, in medicine, 1951-52, staff out-patient dept., 1952—, part time active staff, 1967—; faculty Johns Hopkins U. Sch. Medicine, 1953—, asst. prof. medicine, 1969—; practice medicine specializing in rheumatology, Balt., 1954—. Vis. physician out-patient dept. Balt. City Hosps., 1954—. Mem. Am. Rheumatism Assn., Johns Hopkins Women's Med. Alumnae Assn. (pres. 1960-61, 73-75), Md. Soc. for Rheumatic Diseases, Kappa Alpha Theta. mem. med. and sci. com. Md. chpt. Arthritis Found., 1963—. Presbyn. Club: Ice of Baltimore. Home: 221 Northway Baltimore MD 21218 Office: Johns Hopkins Hosp Baltimore MD 21205

MCKUSICK, MARJORIE JANE (MRS. BLAINE C. MCKUSICK), physician; b. Buffalo, Jan. 27, 1923; d. James F. and Hattie (Oberglock) Kirk; B.A., Bryn Mawr Coll., 1943, M.A., Radcliffe Coll., 1944; M.D., Harvard, 1949; m. Blaine C. McKusick, Oct. 18, 1952; children—Marshall Kirk, James Chase, Kathleen Blaine. Rotating intern. Phila. Gen. Hosp., 1949-51; asst. resident Babies Hosp. Columbia-Presbyn. Med. Center, 1951-53; pvt. practice pediatrics, Wilmington, 1953-74; attending chief pediatrics Wilmington Med. Center, 1958—, dir. adolescent clinic, 1968-71; courtesy staff pediatrics St. Francis Hosp., 1953-71; dir. Well Baby Clinics—Kingswood Community Center, 1954-71; mem. med. staff Children's Hosp., Phila., 1973—; asso. prof. pediatrics Jefferson Med. Coll., 1973—; dir. Student Health Services, U. Del., 1974—. Chmn. bd. Del. Adolescent Program, Inc., 1968—; mem. med. adv. bd. Del. League for Planned Parenthood; del. White House Conf. on Children, 1970; mem. Del. Gov.'s Comprehensive Health Planning Council, 1972—. Bd. dirs. Del. Guidance Services Children and Youth, 1973—. Diplomate Am. Bd. Pediatrics. Mem. A.M.A., Am. Acad. Pediatrics (Del. chmn. 1970-73, exec. com. 1973—, mem. com. long-range planning 1973—), Am. Pub. Health Assn. (mem. youth com. 1972—), Soc. Adolescent Medicine (charter, treas. 1970-73), New Castle County Med. Soc. (v.p. 1973—), Med. Soc. Del. (trustee 1970-73), Del. Acad. Medicine, Del. Valley Soc. Adolescent Health (exec. com. 1973—), Sigma Xi. Contbg. author Modern Woman's Med. Ency., 1966. Editorial bd. Del. Med. Jour., 1972—; mem. adv. council to editorial bd. Postgrad. Medicine, McGraw-Hill, 1974—). Home: 1101 N Broom St Wilmington DE 19806 Office: Laurel Hall U Del Newark DE 19711

MCLACHLAN, PATRICIA JOSEPHINE POORE (MRS. JACK CAMERON MCLACHLAN), psychologist, educator; b. Jersey City, Jan. 10, 1939; d. Joseph O. and Josephine (Kujalowicz) Poore; A.B., Cath. U. Am., 1960; M.A., Fairleigh Dickinson U., 1963, postgrad. Monclair State Coll., 1963-68; m. Jack Cameron McLachlan, Dec. 26, 1972. Personnel asst. Sterns Allied Corp., Paramus, N.J., 1960-61; elementary tchr. Mt. Carmel Sch., Ridgewood, N.J., 1961-62; biology instr., counselor Immaculate Heart Acad., Washington Twp., N.J., 1962-63, dir. guidance, 1963—; psychology instr. Fairleigh Dickinson U., Teaneck, N.J., 1964-67. Engaged in therapy with teenage narcotics addicts Msgr. Wall Social Service Center, Hackensack, N.J., 1970-71, Valley Center, Ridgewood, N.J., 1972—; mem. Middle States Evaluation Com., Summit, N.J., 1972, Union City, N.J., 1973; mem. Archdiocese Newark Guidance Council. Mem. Nat. Vocational Guidance Assn., Am., N.J. personnel and guidance assns., Assn. for Counselor Edn. and Supervision, Am. Sch. Counselors Assn., Assn. for Measurement and Evaluation in Guidance, N.J. Assn. for Measurement and Evaluation in Guidance, Am., Eastern, N.J. (mem. com. on edn. and standards 1969) psychol. assns., Am. Coll. Personnel Assn., Bergen County Cath., Bergen County (mem. exec. council 1969-70) guidance assns., Dirs. of Guidance of Bergen County, N.J. Mental Health Assn., Cath. U., Fairleigh Dickinson U. alumni assns., Psi Chi (pres. 1964), Theta Phi Alpha. Home: 735 Elm Av Teaneck NJ 07666 Office: Van Emburgh Av Box 300 Washington Twp c/o Westwood PO NJ 07675

MCLAIN, BETTY JEAN (MRS. CHARLES H. MCLAIN), coll. dean; b. Coeur d'Alene, Ida., Sept. 13, 1923; d. Grover Cleveland and Hazel Elizabeth (Marshall) Cardwell; B.S. in Bus. Edn., U. Ida., 1945; M.Ed., Whitworth Coll., 1973; m. Charles H. McLain, Aug. 21, 1948; children—Susan, Ellen, Sarah, Patrick. Instr., Coeur d'Alene High Sch., 1945-50; instr. dept. bus. edn. N. Ida. Coll., Coeur d'Alene, 1963—, dean of women, 1967—. Sec., Kootenai Meml. Hosp., 1968. Bd. dirs. U. Ida. Parents Assn. Named Mother of Year, U. Ida., 1972. Mem. Nat., Western bus. edn. assns., Gamma Phi Beta, Kappa Delta Pi, Phi Chi Theta, Delta Kappa Gamma. Presbyn. (elder 1969—). Clubs: Coeur d'Alene Mother's, Art Study, P.E.O. Home: 815 Hastings Av Coeur d'Alene ID 83814 Office: 1000 W Garden Coeur d'Alene ID 83814

MCLAIN, JANICE DARLENE, journalist; b. Ottumwa, Ia., Dec. 20, 1943; d. Arthur George and Daisy Darlene (Thompson) Sells; B.S., Ia. State U., 1967; m. Richard McLain, July 4, 1964; 1 son, Christopher. Asst. women's editor LaCrosse (Wis.) Tribune, 1967-68, women's editor Focus-Food, 1969—. Commentator local fashion shows; judge local beauty contests; speaker local orgns.; vol. nursery dir. LaCrosse County Dept. Social Services, 1969; mem. P.T.A., 1972—. Bd. dirs. LaCrosse County Republican Women, 1966-69; publicity chmn. LaCrosse County Republican Party, 1966-67, del. state conv. 1968, 70. Bd. dirs. Newcomer's Club of YWCA, 1967-68; bd. dirs. Woman of the Month award sponsored by LaCrosse Tribune and LaCrosse C. of C., 1971-73. Recipient 1st place award Internat. Reading Assn., 1971; Vesta awards Am. Meat Inst., 1972—. Mem. Am. Assn. U. Women (state bd. dirs. 1969), LaCrosse Montessori Soc. (bd. dirs. 1970-72), Nat. Fedn. Press Women, League of Women Voters, Kappa Delta, Beta Sigma Phi (hon.). Editorial adv. bd. Encounters: A Journal of Regional Interactions, 1972-73. Home: 2734 Hagen Rd LaCrosse WI 54601 Office: 401 N 3d St LaCrosse WI 54601

MCLAIN, MYRTLE SUNDBERG, physician; b. Ensign, Mich., Dec. 24, 1930; d. Ferdinand Isaac and Marie Ingeborg (Hagglad) Sundberg; B.S. in Chemistry, U. Mich., 1952, M.D., 1966; m. Ernest Linton McLain, Sept. 1, 1951; children—Alice L., Jan M., Dawn C., Carol P., Kenneth W., Ross A. Intern, St. Mary's Hosp., Grand Rapids, Mich., 1966-67, emergency physician, 1967—, also med. dir. Emergency Care Center; mem. staff Butterworth Hosp., Grand Rapids hosps.; asst. clin. prof. Coll. Human Med. Recipient Moses Gomberg prize chemistry, 1951. Mem. Am. Coll. Emergency Physicians (charter), A.M.A., Mich., Kent County med. socs., Am. Women's Med. Assn., Am. Soc. Psychol. Research, Alpha Epsilon Iota. Home: 645 Oakleigh Rd NW Grand Rapids MI 49504

MCLANE, HELEN J., exec. search cons.; b. Indpls.; d. Alvin R. and Ethel (Ranck) McLane; B.S. with distinction, Northwestern U., 1951, M.B.A., 1965. Pub. relations writer Chgo. Assn. Commerce and Industry, 1952-53; press dir. Community Fund Chgo., 1953-56; asso. Beveridge Orgn., Inc., 1956-61, v.p., 1961-66; pub. relations cons. Internat. Harvester Co., 1966-69, asst. to pub. relations dir., 1969-70; asso. Heidrick & Struggles, 1970— (all Chgo.). Mem. Women's Polit. Caucus, Common Cause, Better Govt. Assn., Nat. Orgn. Women, Nat. Assn. Investment Clubs (dir. 1957-69, trustee 1969-72, adviser 1972—). Author: (with Patrica Hutar) The Investment Club Way to Stock Market Success, 1963. Home: 124 Robsart Rd Kenilworth IL 60043 Office: 20 N Wacker Dr Chicago IL 60606

MCLANE, SUSAN NEIDLINGER, state legislator; b. Brookline, Mass., Sept. 28, 1929; d. Lloyd Kellock and Marion Ruth (Walker) Neidlinger; student Mt. Holyoke Coll., 1948; m. Malcolm McLane, Apr. 30, 1948; children—Susan B., Donald W., Deborah, Alan, Ann L. Mem. N.H. Legislature, 1968—, vice chmn. ways and means com., 1970—, chmn. exec. depts. and adminstrn. com. 1973-74. Pres. aux. N.H. Hosp., 1966. Bd. dirs. N.H. Council on World Affairs, 1958—; bd. dirs., editor N.H. League Women Voters, 1960-68; bd. dirs. Eastern conf. Council State Govts., 1973-74. Home: 5 Auburn St Concord NH 03301

MCLARTY, SALLIE GORDON, coll. adminstr.; b. Winston-Salem, N.C., Dec. 28, 1945; d. Emmett Kennedy and Margaret Gertrude (Harrell) McLarty; B.A., Greensboro Coll., 1971. Library clk. Olivia Raney Pub. Library, Raleigh, N.C., 1966-68; switchboard operator, receptionist Greensboro (N.C.) Coll., 1969-71, dir. alumni, 1971—, adviser to G.C. Sons and Daus., Alpha Kappa Omega. Mem. com. to interview prospective students for colls. in N.C. for Philpott Scholarship, 1972—. Mem. Greensboro Regional Consortium for Higher Edn. (sec. alumni div.), Am. Alumni Council. Democrat. Methodist. Editor: Greensboro Coll. Alumni Bull., 1973—. Designer ch. bulls., programs, displays for confs., Logo for Tar Heel Realty. Home: 217 N Cedar St Greensboro NC 27401 Office: 815 W Market St Greensboro NC 27420

MCLAUGHLIN, BARBARA LEADER (MRS. JAMES JOSEPH MCLAUGHLIN II), corp. exec., polit. worker; b. Hackensack, N.J., Mar. 20, 1936; d. Albert Kingsland and Evelyn M. (Sottung) Leader; B.A., Rutgers U., 1958; postgrad. U. Minn., 1964-66; m. James Joseph McLaughlin II, June 5, 1958 (div. 1974); children—James Joseph III, Albert Elliot, Kathryn Evelyn. Free-lance work in data processing application, Mpls. and St. Paul, 1968-73; tech. writer and data mgmt. Customer Engring. div. Control Data Corp., 1973-74; applications analyst Control Data Profl. Services Div., 1974—. Mem. community edn. task force City of Crystal Planning Commn., 1969-74; mem. Crystal Environmental Commn. Chairwoman Crystal Republican com., 1970-74; mem. Rep. State Central Com., 1971-74; mem. Minn. Rep. Electronic Data Processing Adv. Com., 1970-73; del. Minn. Rep. Conv., 1970-74. Mem. North Hennepin Montessori Assn., League Women Voters, Math. Assn. Am. Episcopalian. Home: 1 MacArthur Blvd Apt 311 Westmont NJ 08108

MCLAUGHLIN, DENA RAE BINGHAM (MRS. GLENN W. MCLAUGHLIN), sch. adminstr.; b. Blue Mound, Kan., July 23, 1915; d. Fred A. and Lottie A. (Rice) Bingham; A.B., Baker U., 1958; M.Ed., U. Kan., 1963; m. Glenn W. McLaughlin, Mar. 8, 1935; children—Arden B., Patti (Mrs. Fred Zaborsky). Tchr., Monticello Sch., DeSoto, Kan., 1945-64, prin., 1953-64; prin. Woodsonia-Monticello, DeSoto, 1964—. Mem. N.E.A., Johnson County Prins. Assn. (pres. 1962-63), Monticello Grange, Alpha Kappa Delta (pres. 1965-66). Methodist. Club: Monticello Homemakers (DeSoto). Home: Clear Creek Rd DeSoto KS 66018 Office: Woodsonia-Monticello W 55th St DeSoto KS 66018

MCLAUGHLIN, DOROTHY ANN JENSEN (MRS. HERBERT MCLAUGHLIN), photographer, assn. exec.; b. Manti, Utah, May 10, 1912; d. James Joseph and Mary Alice (Downard) Jensen; grad. Snow Jr. Coll., 1931; m. Marion D. Jolley, July 24, 1932 (dec. 1947); 1 son, Joseph M.; m. 2d, Herbert McLaughlin, June 3, 1950. Co-owner Jolley Turkey Co., Mt. Pleasant, Utah, 1932-50, McLaughlin & Co. Photographers, Phoenix, 1950-55; sec., treas. Ariz. Photog. Assn., Phoenix, 1955—. Pres., Inter-Club Council Phoenix, 1953-54. Recipient Best of Show award Art Dirs. Club Phoenix, 1964; Outstanding Citizen award Civic Plaza Bus. Assn. Phoenix, 1971. Mem. Nat. Press Photographers Assn., Press Club, Copperstate News Photog. Assn., Profl. Photographers Am., Am. Soc. Mag. Photographers, Beta Sigma Phi (hon.). Republican. Mem. Ch. of Jesus Christ of Latter-day Saints. Club: Soroptimist (pres. Phoenix 1952-53). Pub.: (with husband) Phoenix, 1870-1970, 1970. Illustrator: (with husband) Arizona the Beautiful (Don Dedera), 1974. Home: 1129 W Royal Palm Rd Phoenix AZ 85021 Office: 2350 W Holly St Phoenix AZ 85009

MCLAUGHLIN, GEDDES M., coll. dean; B.S., Peabody Coll.; M.P.H., U. Minn.; Ed.D., North Tex. State U. Prof., dean Sch. Nursing, Baylor U., Waco, Tex. Office: Sch Nursing Baylor U 3616 Worth St Dallas TX 75246

MCLAUGHLIN, GERALDINE MARGARET, educator; b. Corydon, Pa., June 6, 1918; d. James A. and Romaine (Griffin) McLaughlin; B.S. in Edn., State Tchrs. Coll., Buffalo, 1938; M.A., St. Bonaventure U., 1945; postgrad. St. Lawrence U. 1949-50, Syracuse U., 1954. Tchr., Allegany (N.Y.) Central Sch., 1938-48, guidance counselor, 1949-58, elementary supr., 1949—. Cons. State Edn. Dept., 1963-64; lectr. grad. dept. St. Bonaventure U. Sch. Edn., 1972. Mem. nat. council Camp Fire Girls, 1970—; pres., dir. Campfire Girls of Olean; sec., dir. Olean Community Chest; sec., dir. Cattaraugus County Mental Health Assn., Allegany Meml. Library; sec. Tb and Respiratory Disease Assn. Cattaraugus County, Cattaraugus County Health Assn.; mem. adv. council Children with Learning Disabilities. Mem. N.E.A., N.Y. State, Allegany tchrs. assns., Cattargus County Elementary Sch. Adminstrs. (pres.), Delta Kappa Gamma. Clubs: Zonta, Women's College. Home: 133 N 5th St Allegany NY 14706

MCLAUGHLIN, LINDA HODGE (MRS. HUGH T. MCLAUGHLIN), lawyer; b. Los Angeles, Feb. 13, 1942; d. Rowland Stanley and Reva Mae (Swecker) Hodge; A.B. with honors, Stanford U., 1963; LL.B., U. Cal. at Berkeley, 1966; m. Hugh Thomas McLaughlin, July 12, 1968; children—Margaret, Robert, Mark. Admitted to Cal. bar, 1967; asso. Keatinge and Sterling, Los Angeles, 1967-70; partner Bergland, Martin and McLaughlin, Newport Beach, Cal., 1970—. Mem. Am., Orange County bar assns., State Bar Cal., Women Lawyers Club Los Angeles, Nat. Assn. Women Lawyers, Cap and Gown Hon. Soc. Clubs: Lawyers, Women Lawyers' (Los Angeles). Home: 13411 Gimbert Lane Santa Ana CA 92705 Office: 369 San Miguel Dr Newport Beach CA 92660

MCLAUGHLIN, MARILYN JEAN (MRS. PHILLIP JOSEPH MCLAUGHLIN), city ofcl.; b. Dayton, O., Jan. 23, 1935; d. Robert Joseph and Catherine Josephine (Durkin) Janning; student U. Dayton, 1954-55; m. Phillip Joseph McLaughlin, June 16, 1956; 1 son, Scott Phillip. Sec. to mayor City of Centerville, O., 1964-68, clk. city council, 1968—, clk. mayor's ct., dep. clk. Kettering Municipal Ct., 1972—. Notary pub. Montgomery County, O., 1968—. Mem. Centerville Hist. Soc., Ohio Municipal Clk.'s Assn., Ohio Council Nat. Accredited Flower Show Judges. Clubs: Country Corner Garden (pres. 1963, treas. 1972), Jr. Progress (pres. 1964). Home: 7660 Rolling Oak Dr Centerville OH 45459 Office: 100 W Spring Valley Rd Centerville OH 45459

MCLAUGHLIN, (MARTHA) ANNE, retail co. exec.; b. Dallas, Oct. 27, 1936; d. Gail Edward and Claudia Marguerita (Betry) McLaughlin; student U. Kansas City, 1955-56; postgrad. Hunter Coll. Sales clk. Pecks Dept. Store, Allied Inc., Kansas City, Mo., 1955-58, asst. buyer, 1958-61; buyer Almart Stores div. Allied Stores, 1961-69, divisional mdse. mgr., 1969-72; dir. advt. Robert Hall Village, N.Y.C., 1972—. Mem. Advt. Club N.Y.C., Adventure Soc., Natural History Soc. Republican. Home: 37 E 63d St New York City NY 10021 Office: 333 W 34th St New York City NY 10001

MCLAUGHLIN, MARY C., health adminstr. Health commr. N.Y.C. Health Dept. until 1971; dep. adminstr. Health Services Adminstrn., N.Y.C., 1971-73; commr. health services Suffolk County, 1974—. Lectr. on subject. Office: H Lee Dennison Exec Office Bldg Vets Meml Hwy Hauppauge NY 11787

MCLAUGHLIN, RITA E., educator; b. Boston; d. William Joseph and Elizabeth A. (Dunn) McLaughlin; B.S., Boston Tchrs. Coll., 1938, M.Ed., 1939; postgrad. Boston U., 1951-53, City Coll. N.Y., 1956-58. Tchr., Town of Somerset, Mass., 1939-41; tchr. reading Boston Tchrs. Coll., 1942-43; time study engr. Hood Rubber Co., Watertown, Mass., 1943-44; placement dir. Miss Bridges, Boston, 1945-49, dir. spl. services Norwood, Mass., 1949-56; psychologist Westchester (N.Y.) Boces, 1956-58; ednl. cons. Houghton Mifflin Co., Boston, 1958-60; psychologist Swampscott (Mass.) Schs., 1960-63; asst. prof. reading-lang. arts, supr. student teaching Framingham State Coll., Mass., 1963—. Mem. Manhattan Reading Council (sec. 1957), Nobscot Reading Council (pres. 1967), Mass. Bay Regional Reading Council (pres. 1969), Mass. State Council (pres. 1971-72), Mass Sch. Psychologists, Nat. Soc. Study Edn., N.E.A., Nat. Council Tchrs. English, Internat. Reading Assn. (state chmn. 1972—), Am. Assn. U. Profs., Smithsonian Assos., Nat. Hist. Soc., Bus. and Profl. Womens Clubs, Boston Mus. Fine Arts. Delta Kappa Gamma. Author: The Literature Sampler. Home: 126 University Rd Brookline MA 02146

MCLEAN, ARLENE ELIZABETH ANDREWS (MRS. LEWIS FOLLETT MCLEAN), biometrician; b. nr. Coatesville, Pa., Nov. 11, 1941; d. William and Maude Elizabeth (Wheatley) Andrews; B.S. in Biology, Ursinus Coll., 1962; M.S. in Applied Statistics, Villanova U., 1967; Ph.D., Thomas Jefferson U., 1975; m. Lewis Follett McLean, Oct. 26, 1964. Research asst. Wyeth Labs., Radnor, Pa., 1962-64, adminstrv. asst., 1964-65; jr. statistician Merck, Sharp & Dohme Research Labs., West Point, Pa., 1966-67, statistician, 1967-69, sr. statistician, 1969-70, biometrician, 1970-71, head planning, coordination and analysis unit, 1971—. Lectr. Villanova U., 1968-71. Mem. Am. Statis. Assn., Biometrics Soc., Am. Soc. Clin. Pharmacology and Therapeutics, Physiol. Soc. Phila., Sigma Xi. Home: 176 Kinsey Rd Harleysville PA 19438 Office: Merck Sharp & Dohme Research Labs Sumneytown Pike West Point PA 19486

MCLEAN, ELIZABETH JACKSON (MRS. CHARLES H. MCLEAN), traffic engr.; b. Mineral Point, Wis., Apr. 26, 1931; d. Edwin and Anna (Speich) Jackson; B.S. in Civil Engring., U. Wis., 1954; m. Charles H. McLean, Oct. 6, 1956; children—Carla, Kristina. City planner City of Chgo., 1954-56, traffic engr., 1956-65, asst. commr. Dept. Pub. Works, 1965-73, 1st dep. commr., 1973—. Mem. U.S. Com. on Transp. Quality, Commn. on Urban Area Govt.; co-chmn. Chgo. Beautiful Com.; sec. Lincoln Park Renewal Corp.; mem. women's aux. Salvation Army. Registered profl. engr. Mem. Am. Soc. Pub. Adminstrs., Inst. Traffic Engrs., Nat. Assn. Housing and Redevel. Ofcl., Am. Pub. Works Assn., Am. Soc. C.E., Western Soc. Engrs., Council Fgn. Relations, Lincoln Central Assn., Am. Inst. Planners, Nat. Soc. Profl. Engrs., Art Inst., Lincoln Park Conservation Assn., Alliance Profl. and Bus. Women, Lincoln Park Zool. Soc., Chi Epsilon, Tau Beta Pi. Home: 2002 N Mohawk St Chicago IL 60614 Office: City Hall Chicago IL 60602

MCLEAN, MARGARET STONER (MRS. MALCOLM DALLAS MCLEAN), microfilm researcher; b. Victoria, Tex., June 5, 1915; d. Thomas Royal and Mame Victoria (Stoner) Stoner; A.A., Victoria Jr. Coll., 1936; B.S., U. Tex., 1939; m. Malcolm Dallas McLean, Feb. 11, 1939; 1 son, John Robertson. Receptionist, postmaster San Jacinto Mus. History, Houston, 1939-41; microfilm camera operator Library of Congress, Washington, 1942; bibliog. researcher, 1947-53; tchr. elementary sch., Fayetteville, Ark., 1954-55; elementary tchr. Am. Sch., Tegucigalpa, Honduras, 1957-58; tchr. English, U.S. Binat. Center and Am. High Sch., Guayaquil, Ecuador, 1959-61; newspaper microfilm archivist Amon Carter Mus. Western Art, Ft. Worth, 1963-73; microfilm research specialist Spanish Tex. Microfilm Center, Presidio La Bahia, Goliad, Tex., 1973—. Club: Texas Christian University Woman's (Ft. Worth). Contbr. articles to profl. jours. Address: 2555 Cockrell St Fort Worth TX 76109

MCLEAN, MARQUITA SHEILA MCLARTY (MRS. CECIL P. MCLEAN), educator; b. Richmond, Va., Aug. 5, 1933; d. William Charles and Daisey (Dabney) McLarty; B.A. with distinction, Va. State Coll., 1953; M.A., Ohio State U., 1956; postgrad. U. Cin., 1957-69; m. Cecil P. McLean, July 25, 1958. Tchr. girls' sch., Delaware, O., 1954-57, Robert A. Taft Sr. High Sch., Cin., 1957-62; counselor Sawyer Jr. High Sch., Cin., 1962-65, Withrow High Sch., Cin., 1965-67; asso. Guidance Services div. Cin. Pub. Schs., 1968-73; dir. Office Univ. Commitment to Human Resources, U. Cin., 1973—. Active Pres.'s Youth Campaign, Cin., 1968—; mem. Sch.-Community Guidance Task Force, 1970—, Mayor's Com. Youth Program, Cin., 1970—, City of Cin. Manpower Commn., 1970-71; Antioch Scholarship Selector Com., Cin., 1969, 70, Pres.'s Council Youth Opportunity, 1968—; mem. alumni adv. council Ohio State U., 1971—. Past trustee Cin. Tech. Coll. Mem. Ohio Edn. Assn., Am., Cin. (pres. 1967-68) personnel and guidance assns., Am. (nat. task force counselor negotiations 1969—, v.p. middle sch. 1970-71), Ohio (Southwestern rep. 1969) sch. counselor assns., Assn. Counselor Edn. and Supervision (co-chairperson commn. non-white concerns), Nat. Assn. Sch. Counselors (nat. dep. chmn.-v.p. 1972), Delta Sigma Theta (pres. 1963). Club: Ohio State Alumni (Greater Cin., scholarship chmn. 1969-72). Home: 5324 Kenwood Rd Cincinnati OH 45227 Office: Office Univ Commitment-Human Resources Beecher Hall Cincinnati OH 45221

MCLEAN, MILDRED MURRAY (MRS. JOHN MCLEAN), advt. exec.; b. Summit, N.J.; d. Edward Everett and Lilliam (Williams) Murray; grad. Coleman Bus. Coll., 1929; m. John McLean, Oct. 9, 1935. Office mgr., accountant William C. Siebert, Summit, N.J., 1929-39; controller Overlook Hosp., 1940-46; personnel dir., gen. supr., sec. bd. dirs. Martindale-Hubbell, Inc., 1946-55; advt. prodn.

dir. Silver Burdett Co., Morristown, N.J., 1955-72; advt. prodn. mgr. Gen. Learning Corp., 1972—. Co-chmn. Seminar on Status of Women, Fairleigh Dicksinson U., 1963; mem. N.J. State Commn. Women, 1970-72, charter chmn., 1971-72. Bd. dirs. Tri-County Children's Center, Morristown, N.J.; trustee YWCA, Summit, N.J. Recipient Industry award State of N.J., 1971. Mem. Bus. and Profl. Women's Club Summit (charter mem., pres. 1958-60, Woman of Achievement award 1972), N.J. Fedn. Bus. and Profl. Women's Clubs (career advancement chmn. 1960-62, 3d v.p. 1962-64, 2d v.p. 1964-66, 1st v.p. 1966-67, pres. elect 1967-68, pres. 1968-69, Nat. Fedn. Bus. and Profl. Women's Clubs (resolutions chmn. nat. conv. 1970), Athenaeum. Club: Zonta (charter mem., dir. 1956-59), Zonta Golden Z (adv. chmn. Fairleigh Dickinson U. 1964-66); Fortnightly (Summit). Home: 13 Ridgedale Av Summit NJ 07901 Office: care Silver Burdett Div Gen Learning Corp Morristown NJ 07960

MCLELLAN, PATRICIA ANNE (MRS. WILLIAM Z. LEAVITT), physician; b. Glen Ridge, N.J., Nov. 6, 1932; d. John Douglas and Helen Dorthy (Blanchard) McLellan; student Colby Jr. Coll., 1950-53; A.B., Boston U. Coll. Liberal Arts, 1954; M.D., Boston Sch. Medicine, 1958; m. William Z. Leavitt, July 11, 1960; children—James Alan, John David, William Robert. Intern, Newton-Wellesely Hosp., Newton, Mass., 1958-59; resident in radiology University Hosp., Boston, 1959-62; asso. radiologist U. Hosp., Boston, 1962-65; radiologist St. Elizabeth Hosp., Boston, 1965—; instr. radiology Tufts Med. Sch., 1965—. Diplomate Am. Coll. Radiology. Home: 130 Franklin St Newton MA 02158 Office: 736 Cambridge St Boston MA 02135

MCLEMORE, ETHEL WARD, research geophysicist, mathematician; b. Sylvarena, Miss., Jan. 22, 1908; d. William Robert and Frances Virginia (Douglas) Ward; B.A., Miss. Woman's Coll., 1928; M.A., U. N.C., 1929; postgrad. U. Chgo., 1931, Colo. Sch. Mines, 1941-42, So. Meth. U., 1962-64; m. Robert Henry McLemore, June 30, 1935; 1 dau., Mary Frances. Head math. dept. Miss. Jr. Coll., 1929-30; instr. chemistry, math. Miss. State Coll. for Women, 1930-32; research mathematician Humble Oil & Refining Co., Houston, 1933-36; ind. geophys. research, Tex. and Colo., 1936-42, Ft. Worth, 1946—; geophysicist United Geophys. Co., Pasadena, Cal., 1942-46; tchr. chemistry, physics, Hockaday Sch., Dallas, 1958-59, tchr. math., 1959-60; tchr. chemistry Ursuline Acad., Dallas, 1964-67, Hockaday Sch., 1968-69. Mem. Am. Math. Soc., Math. Assn. Am., Am. Geophys. Union, Seismol. Soc. Am., Soc. Exploration Geophysicists, A.A.A.S., Soc. Indsl. and Applied Math., Tex Acad. Sci., Sigma Xi. Contbr. various articles to profl. jours. Home: 11625 Wander Lane Dallas TX 75230

MCLENDON, BILLYE BURRELL, psychologist; b. Coppers Cove, Tex.; d. Norwood W. and Lena Mae (McGonagill) McLendon; A.A. first honors, Temple Jr. Coll., 1948; B.A. magna cum laude (Delta Delta Delta scholar 1949), U. Tex., 1950, M.A., 1956, Ph.D., 1965. Classroom tchr. Ind. Sch. Dist., Port Arthur, Austin, Tex., 1950-54; research and teaching asst. dept. psychology U. Tex., 1955-56, asst. psychologist, intern Testing and Counseling Center, 1957-59, teaching asst., lectr. dept. ednl. psychology, 1959-61; psychologist Austin Community Guidance Center, 1956-57; sch. psychologist St. Andrews Episcopal Sch., 1958; clin. psychologist Child Psychiatry Center, Milw. Children's Hosp., also instr. psychology depts. psychiatry and pediatrics Marquette U. Sch. Medicine, Milw., 1964-67; elementary sch. counselor, psychologist San Antonio Ind. Sch. Dist., 1969-70; psychologist Harlandale Ind. Sch. Dist., San Antonio, 1970-71; psychologist Lebe Hoch Learning and Treatment Center, Fredericksburg, Tex., 1972-73; practice counseling and clin. psychology, 1965—. Mem. Am., Southwestern, Tex. psychol. assns., UN Assn., Internat. Platform Assn., Am. Mus. Natural History, Nat. Council on Family Relations, Nat. Wildlife Fedn., Phi Beta Kappa, Pi Lambda Theta, Psi Chi. Democrat. Methodist. Contbr. articles to profl. jours. Research in origin of person, creativeness, student-centered teaching, psychotherapy, community mental health. Home: 1205 S 27th St Temple TX 76501

MCLENDON, DOROTHY JOSEPHINE, sch. psychologist; b. Crawfordsville, Ind., Feb. 20, 1918; d. Joseph Newton and Dora (Ryall) Fullenwider; A.B., Olivet Coll., Kankakee, Ill., 1942; M.A., Boston U., 1945, Ed.D., 1970; postgrad. Harvard, 1958-61, N.Y. U., 1965-66; m. Hiram James McLendon, May 23, 1942; 1 son, Hiram James. Sch. psychologist pub. schs. Alameda County (Cal.), 1948-51, Berkeley, Cal., 1951-52, Army Schs., Paris, France, 1957-58; sch. psychologist pub. schs., Brookline, Mass., 1958—. Diplomate Am. Bd. Profl. Psychology. Mem. N.E.A., Am. Psychol. Assn., League Women Voters (dir. Cambridge chpt., chmn. voters service 1955-57). Home: 100 Memorial Dr Cambridge MA 02142 Office: Town Hall Brookline MA 02146

MCLENDON, ETHEL MATTHEWS, librarian; b. St. Augustine, Fla., Oct. 7, 1916; d. Frank Buffington and Mary Heyward (Wright) Matthews; B.S., George Peabody Coll. for Tchrs., 1939; M.A., Fla. State U., 1955; m. Lewis McLendon, Aug. 25, 1940. Librarian pub. sch., Crestview and Jacksonville, Fla., 1950-59; instr. library sci. Albany State Coll., U. Okla., summers 1958-60; county librarian Duval County (Fla.) Schs., Jacksonville, 1960-64, supr. sch. libraries, 1971—; asst. prof. library sci. U. Fla., 1965-71. Hon. founder, mem. planning com. Episcopal High Sch., Jacksonville; mem. Mayor's Community Sch. Task Force, spring 1973. Mem. Am., Southeastern, Fla. library assns., Assn. for Ednl. Communications and Tech., Fla. Assn. Tchr. Edn., Fla. Assn. Curriculum Devel., Pi Gamma Chi, Beta Phi Mu. Democrat. Episcopalian (vestrywoman 1973—). Home: 5836 Oliver St Jacksonville FL 32211

MCLENNAN, MARGARET THOMAS (MRS. CHARLES E. MCLENNAN), physician; b. Chgo., Mar. 1, 1913; d. David Edward and Rose Blanche (Brewster) Thomas; A.B., U. Mo., 1932, B.S., 1934; M.D., U. Minn., 1936; m. Charles E. McLennan, June 26, 1937; children—James E., Nancy (Mrs. Douglas L. King), Jane (Mrs. Goeffrey B. Stearns), Thomas C. Intern, University of Minn. hosps., 1936-38; resident Mpls. Maternity Hosp., 1938-39, research fellow hematology U. Utah Coll. Medicine, 1944-47; med. staff Planned Parenthood Assn., San Francisco, 1947-56; research asso., dir. gynecologic cytology lab. Stanford U. Sch. Medicine, Cal., 1957-72, asst. prof. gynecology, obstetrics, 1972—. Mem. Am. Soc. Cytology. Home: 701 Tennyson Av Palo Alto CA 94303 Office: 300 Pasteur Dr Palo Alto CA 94304

MCLEOD, CHRISTIE ELLEN, physician; b. South Barre, Vt., Aug. 7, 1909; d. Lowell and Dora (Bancroft) McLeod; B.S., U. Vt., 1931, M.D., 1934. Intern New Eng. Hosp. for Women and Children, Boston, 1936-37; resident Worcester (Mass.) City Hosp., 1934-35, Belmont Hosp., Worcester, 1935-36; asst. pathologist Middlesex Meml. Hosp., Middletown, Conn., 1937-40, pathologist, 1940—, sec. med. staff, 1968—. Chmn. dirs. and teaching suprs. Conn. Schs. Med. Tech. Adv. Com. on Hosp. Licensing, 1954-69; corporator Middletown (Conn.) Savs. Bank. Mem. Conn. Council on Hosps., 1970-72. Bd. dirs. YMCA, Middletown, 1956—, pres., 1966-67; pres. Community Chest, Middletown, 1956, United Fund, Middletown, 1956; bd. dirs. Middlesex Meml. Hosp., Middlesex Heart Assn., Conn. Cancer Soc., A.R.C., Middletown Homemakers Assn.; trustee No. Middlesex YMCA. Served to lt. M.C., WAVES, 1944-46. Recipient service awards United Fund, 1958, V.F.W., 1961, Middletown C. of C., 1964, Americanism award B'nai B'rith, 1954, Woman of Achievement award New Eng. Region Soroptimists, 1971, Distinguished Alumni award U. Vt., 1972. Fellow Am. Soc. Clin. Pathologists (mem. joint commn. continuing edn. med. tech. 1963-66), Coll. Am. Pathologists; mem. Conn. Soc. Pathologists (pres. 1958-60), Am. Soc. Study Neoplastic Diseases, A.M.A., N.Y. Acad. Scis., Middlesex County Med. Assn. (pres. 1958-60), Conn. State Med. Soc. (mem. ho. of dels. 1956-58, mem. pub. health com., blood bank com., chmn. com. on hosps.). Club: Soroptomists (hon.). Home: Maple Shade Rd Middletown CT 06457 Office: 28 Crescent St Middletown CT 06457

MCLEOD, EMILIE WARREN, editor; b. Boston, Dec. 2, 1926; d. Shields and Alice (Springfield) Warren; B.A., Mt. Holyoke Coll., 1948; m. Guy Collingwood McLeod, June 23, 1950; children—Sara K., Susan W., Stuart C. Editorial asst. Ladies Home Jour., 1948-49, Presbyn. Life, 1949-50; asst. editor children's books Houghton Mifflin Co., 1950-52; children's book editor Atlantic Monthly Press, 1956—; Sec. Sea Farm Research Found. Bd. dirs. Shared Ednl. Experience. Mem. A.L.A., A.I.G.A., Mt. Holyoke Alumnae Assn., Colonial Dames Am. Conglist. Clubs: Mt. Holyoke (bd. dirs. 1962-73, pres. 1970-72) (Boston); Waquoit Bay Yacht (Falmouth, Mass.). Author: Seven Remarkable Bears, 1952; Clancy's Witch, 1958; One Snail and Me, 1962; The Bear's Bicycle, 1975. Home: 60 Carlton Rd Waban MA 02168 Office: 8 Arlington St Boston MA 02112

MCLEOD, ETHEL MCCARTHY (MRS. ROBERT DONALD MCLEOD), telephone answering service exec.; b. Albuquerque, Sept. 30, 1922; d. Walter Harry and Marie Harriett (Adams) McCarthy; student Albuquerque Bus. Coll., 1939; m. Robert Donald McLeod, Aug. 19, 1944. Sec., Harold O. Waggoner, atty., Albuquerque, 1939-44, Consol. Vultee Aircraft Co., San Diego, 1944-45, Goodyear Aircraft Co., Phoenix, 1945-46, Lawyers Title Ins. Corp., Dallas, 1946-49; ct. reporter Reese AFB, Tex., 1949-50; conveyancer Service Abstract & Title Co., Lubbock, Tex., 1950-55; co-owner Stenocall, Lubbock, 1955—; exec. sec. Lubbock-Crosby-Garza County Med. Soc., 1968—; dir. Tex. Bank, 1968—. Gen. chmn. Cancer Drive, 1969; chmn. advt./communications sect. fund raising com. for new YWCA, 1973. Pres., Better Bus. Bur.; sec. Vol. Blood Donors Com., Lubbock Symphony Orch. Recipient Silver medal award Lubbock Advt. Fedn., 1973, Answering Service award for community service, 1973, Outstanding Bus. Woman award Bus. and Profl. Women, 1973; named Boss of Year, PBX Club, 1960. Mem. Asso. Telephone Answering Exchanges (nat. chmn. conducted seminars), Lubbock C. of C. (chmn. advt./pub. relations com. 1972), Lubbock Advt. Club (exec. sec. 1958-69), Phi Mu. Episcopalian. Home: 5414 20th St Lubbock TX 79407 Office: 1212 13th St Lubbock TX 79401

MCLEOD, HEATHER ANNE, dinnerwear co. rep., theater dir., actress; b. Great Falls, Mont., Feb. 9, 1937; d. Archie Donald and Violet Victoria Mires (Palagi) McLeod; B.A. in Fine Arts, U. Mont., 1959; postgrad. Ottumwa Coll., 1960-61; M.A. in Profl. Directing and Acting, U. Wash., Seattle, 1970. Drama and English tchr. Missoula (Mont.) High Sch., 1959-60; speech and drama tchr. Ottumwa (Ia.) Coll., 1960-61; speech, English and drama tchr. Pl Polson (Mont.) High Sch., 1962-64; chmn. dept. drama Carroll Coll., Helena, Mont., 1964-69; dir. pub. relations and publicity, drama dept. U. Wash., Seattle, 1969-70; tour dir., actress Pacific Repertory Co., Xenia, O., 1971; freelance dir., actress dinner theaters and community theaters off-off Broadway, N.Y.C., 1972; marketing asst. Denby Ltd., N.Y., also N.J., Pa., 1973, saleswoman, 1974—. Pres. Whitefish (Mont.) Summer Theater, 1967. Campaigner for women candidates for pub. office in N.Y.C. area, 1972-73. Mem. A.F.T.R.A., Delta Delta Delta. Roman Catholic. Home and office: 19 Willoughby Av Apt 2 Brooklyn NY 11205

MCLEOD, JONNIE HORN (MRS. WILLIAM LESLIE MCLEOD), pediatrician; b. Lucedale, Miss., Oct. 30, 1923; d. John William and Zula (Thigpen) Horn; B.A., Sophie Newcomb Coll., 1945; M.D., Tulane U., 1949; m. William Leslie McLeod, July 15, 1951; children—Laura, Melissa, Katherine, William Leslie. Intern Charity Hosp. of La., New Orleans, 1950-51, resident, 1951-52; practice medicine, specializing in pediatrics, Charlotte, N.C., 1952—; pediatrician Charlotte Dept. Health, 1953—. Cons. health edn. Charlotte Pub Schs., 1956—; mem. U.S. Council on Communicable Disease, 1969-71; producer TV series for Charlotte elementary schs. Family Talk; mem. adv. council N.C. Drug Authority, 1972—; mem. N.C. Mental Health Commn., 1972—. Bd. dirs. Drug Edn. Center Charlotte, Mental Health Assn. N.C., Charlotte Family Life Councils. Named Woman of Year, Charlotte Downtown Assn., 1968, 1969; recipient Oak Leaf award N.C. P.T.A., 1967; Citizen of Yr. award Charlotte Civitan Club, 1972. Baptist. Club: Charlotte Country. Home: 1504 Biltmore Dr Charlotte NC 28207 Office: 1416 E Morehead Charlotte NC 28204

MCLEOD, MARIE VIRGINIA, editor; b. Montclair, N.J., Apr. 28, 1933; d. Thomas Donald and Marie Catherine (Houchens) McLeod; A.B., Caldwell Coll., 1954. With Time, Inc., N.Y.C., 1954-59, newsmarker, 1956-59; sec. E.I. DuPont de Nemours & Co., Inc., N.Y.C., 1960; editor Colonial Life Ins. Co., East Orange, N.J., 1960-65; editor Royal Globe Ins. Co., N.Y.C., 1965-68; editor Nabisco, Inc., N.Y.C., 1969—. Bd. govs. N.Y. Assn. Bus. Communicators, 1969—. Mem. Caldwell Coll. Alumnae Assn. Roman Catholic. Clubs: Gregory (Montclair, N.J.). Office: 425 Park Av New York City NY 10022

MCLEROY, NELLIE MAE, educator; b. Haskell, Tex., June 2, 1909; d. Charles Jefferson and Annie Eugenia (Keeling) McLeroy; B.S., W. Tex. State Coll., 1938; M.R.E., Southwestern Bapt. Theol. Sem., 1945, D.R.E., 1959; postgrad. Ariz. State U., 1964—, U. Ariz., No. Ariz. U. Tchr. pub. schs. Brownfield, Tex., 1930-39. Tahoka, Tex., 1939-42; ednl. dir. 1st Bapt. Chs., Levelland, 1943-44, Winters, 1945-46. Kerrville, 1946-47 (all Tex.). North Side Bapt. Ch., San Antonio, 1947-48; ednl. field worker Tex. Bapt. Tng. Union Dept., Dallas, 1948-53, 55-57; ednl. dir. Bellaire (Tex.) Bapt. Ch., 1953; chmn. div. religious edn. Western Bapt. Sem., Kansas City, Mo., 1953-55; dean of women Decatur (Tex.) Bapt. Coll., 1957-58; dean-registrar N.M. Bapt. Coll., Hobbs, 1958-60, pres. coll., 1960-62; pres. Coll. of S.W. Hobbs, 1962-64, acad. dean and adminstrv. asst., 1964-65; elementary tchr. pub. schs., Apache Junction, Ariz., 1964-65; asso. prof. edn. and psychology Grand Canyon Coll., Phoenix, 1965-66; tchr. adult edn. White Mountain Apache Tribe, Ariz., 1967-70; asso. prof. psychology Eastern Ariz. Jr. Coll., 1969-71; test instrument project Whiteriver Elementary Sch., 1970-71; elementary tchr., curriculum cons. Seven Mile Elementary Sch., Whiteriver, Ariz., 1966-71; dir. associational tng. union Southeastern Bapt. Assn. N.M., 1959-62. Ednl. rep. Manpower Devel. Adv. Com., Hobbs, 1963-64; sec.-treas. Navajo County Ednl. Council. Mem. Nat. Tex. parent-tchr. assns., Nat. Geog. Soc., Southwestern, N.M. Bapt. religious edn. assns., Tex. Assn. Deans of Women, Tex. State Tchrs. Assn., N.E.A., N.M., Ariz. edn. assns., Ariz. Coll. Assn., Nat. Council Exceptional Children, Whiteriver Educators Assn. (pres. 1967-68), Alpha Delta Kappa (chaplain Ariz. Alpha Eta chpt. 1970-71). Democrat. Editor (with Ethel Fulton), compiler Gomez Souvenir Cook Book, 1937. Home: PO Box 867 Brownfield TX 79316

MCLOUGHLIN, ELLEN V(ERONICA), ret. editor; b. Utica, N.Y.; d. James Henry and Mary Frances (Riley) McLoughlin; student Utica Free Acad.; A.B., Smith Coll., 1915; postgrad. Radcliffe Coll., 1921-22; L.H.D., Lincoln Coll., 1949. Asst. editor woman's page Country Gentleman, 1915-17; circulation promoter Crowell Pub. Co., 1922-24; asst. advt. mgr. Grolier Soc., 1924-34, advt. mgr., 1934-41, editorial dir., 1947-59, v.p., 1956-64; mng. editor Book of Knowledge, Children's Ency., 1936-42, editor Book of Knowledge Annuals, 1940-53, Book of Knowledge, 1942-60, Story of Our Time, 1947-53, L'Encyclopedie de la Jeunesse, 1948-60, Le Livre de l'Annee, 1950-60, La Science Pour Tous, 1960-64. Pres. bd. trustees Cragsmoor (N.Y.) Library, 1967-70. Roman Catholic. Club: Nat. Arts. Author: The Murder of Doctor Casenova (with Lucile Rathbun, Anetia McLoughlin), 1934. Contbr. verse to mags. Home: 181 Bay View Av Cornwall-on-Hudson NY 12520

MCMAHON, BEVERLY EDITH, geologist; b. Los Angeles, Apr. 11, 1922; d. James and Helen Virginia (Albee) McMahon; B.A., U. Colo., 1944, Ph.D. (NSF fellow), 1966. Exploration geologist Shell Oil Co., midcontinent and Rocky Mountain states, 1944-60; teaching asst. dept. geol. scis., U. Colo., Boulder, 1960-66; research asso. Mass. Inst. Tech., Cambridge, 1966-68; asst. prof. geology and geophysics Central State U., Wilberforce, O., 1968-70; asst. prof. Ohio State U., Columbus, 1970-73, research asso., 1973—. Grad. fellow U. Colo., 1960-66. Mem. North Tex. Geol. Soc. (v.p. 1951-52), Am. Assn. Petroleum Geologists, Am. Geophys. Union, Geol. Soc. Am., Rocky Mountain Assn. of Geologists, Ohio Acad. of Sci., Ohio Geol. Soc., Zonta Club of Denver (sec. 1959-60), Sigma Xi. Asso. editor: Oil and Gas Fields of Nebraska, 1956. Contbr. articles on paleomagnetism and subsurface stratigraphy to profl. publs. Home: 1499 Lafayette Dr Columbus OH 43220

MCMAHON, CHRISTINE EUPHRASIA SMITH (MRS. EUGENE FRANCIS MCMAHON), lawyer; b. Chgo., Dec. 4, 1940; d. Raymond James and Bernice Susan (Lickus) Smith; A.B. magna cum laude, Loyola U., Chgo., 1962; J.D., De Paul U., 1965; m. Eugene Francis McMahon, Aug. 5, 1967. Asst. to a supr., personnel dept. Marshall Field & Co., Chgo., 1959—; admitted to Ill. bar, 1965; atty. Tim J. Harrington, law firm, Chgo., 1965-68; asso. atty. Paulson & Ketchum, Chgo., 1968—. Recipient various scholarships. Mem. Am., Ill., Southside Chgo. bar assns., Women's Bar Assn., Chgo. Trial Lawyers Club. Roman Catholic. Home: 11935 S Ridgeway St Alsip IL 60658 Office: 120 W Madison St Chicago IL 60602

MCMAHON, DORIS MAY BOTSCH (MRS. JOHN EDWARD MCMAHON), educator; b. Hempstead, N.Y., May 13, 1928; d. Charles William and Vera Mae (Ivanhoe) Botsch; B.S., Boston U., 1950; M.A., Tchrs. Coll. Columbia, 1953; postgrad. N.Y. U., 1954-70; m. John Edward McMahon, Aug. 6, 1972; children—Michael, Sharon, Kathryn, Monica. Tchr. phys. edn., sci. health Cathedral Sch. St. Marys, Garden City, N.Y., 1950-52; tchr. phys. edn. Great Neck (N.Y.) North Sr. High Sch., 1952-58; tchr. phys. edn., chmn. girls' phys. edn. dept. South Sr. High Sch., Great Neck, 1958—. Mem. L.I. (pres. 1953-56), New Atlantic (pres. 1959-60) field hockey assns., Assn. Women Phys. Edn. N.Y. State (Service award 1973, pres. 1961), N.Y. State Assn. Health, Phys. Edn. and Recreation (pres. 1970-71), N.Y. State Pub. High Sch. Athletic Assn. (pres. women's sect. 1972-74), N.Y. State, Great Neck tchrs. assns. Home: 33 Old Pine Dr Manhasset NY 11030 Office: Great Neck South High Sch 341 Lakeville Rd Great Neck NY 11020

MCMAHON, ELIZABETH MILDRED, educator; b. Bridgeport, Conn., June 16, 1918; d. Frederick Francis and Elizabeth (Collins) McMahon; A.B., Coll. of New Rochelle, 1940; M.A., Fairfield U., 1952, Certificate Advanced Study, 1963. Tchr. English, Roger Ludlow Jr. High Sch., East Norwalk, Conn., 1942, Center Jr. High Sch., Norwalk, Conn., 1943; tchr. English, counselor Center Jr. High Sch., Norwalk, 1945-53; head guidance counselor Nathan Hale Jr. High Sch., Norwalk, 1953—. Instr. tests and measurements Danbury State Coll., 1953-54. Mem. Conn. Tchrs. Certification Adv. Bd., 1967-72, chmn., 1969, vice chmn., 1970-71. Gen. Electric fellow 1959, Dept. State Fellow, 1965, Ford Found fellow, 1966. Mem. Am., Conn. personnel and guidance assns., Am. Sch. Counselor Assn., N.E.A., Conn. Edn. Assn. (dir. 1964-68), Norwalk Tchrs. Assn. (pres. 1957-60), Am. Assn. U. Women (Norwalk 3d v.p. 1948-49), Coll. of New Rochelle Alumnae Assn. (chpt. pres. 1945). Home: 128 Gregory Blvd East Norwalk CT 06855 Office: Nathan Hale Middle Sch Strawberry Hill Av Norwalk CT 06855

MCMAHON, LUCILLE MARGARET (MRS. JOHN PATRICK MCMAHON), librarian; b. Wellesley, Mass., Apr. 7, 1910; d. James Patrick and Mary Catherine (Slamin) Keating; B.A., Wellesley Coll., 1930; B.S., Columbia, 1940; m. John Patrick McMahon, Oct. 13, 1941; children—John James, Mary (Mrs. Paul Cramer), Jane (Mrs. Robert E. Kennedy), Margaret (Mrs. John Lareau). Asst. librarian Wellesley Coll. Library, 1930-41; reference librarian Wellesley Free Library, 1963-71, staff asso., mem. exec. bd., 1970-71, reference coordinator, 1971—. Sec. Town of Wellesley Library Bldg. Planning Commn., 1953-60. Mem. Mass., New Eng. library assns., Catholic Internat. Newman Club Fedn. (v.p. 1939-41), John Henry Newman Honor Soc. Home: 98 Oak St Wellesley MA 02181 Office: Wellesley Free Library Wellesley MA 02181

MCMAHON, MARGARET JEAN, banker; b. Forest City, Ia., May 10, 1925; d. Peter J. and Katherine Louise (Sloan) McMahon; student Waldorf Coll. Accountant, Forest City (Ia.) Motor Co., 1946-54; with Forest City Bank & Trust Co., 1954—, now v.p. Finance chmn. Easter Seal Soc. Crippled Children and Adults, Inc., 1968-72; active Am. Cancer Soc., Retarded Assn.; pres. North Central Ia. Heart Assn., 1973-75; sec. Forest City Vol. Ambulance Service, 1973. sec.-treas. Carrie M. Frandsen Nursing Home, Inc. Mem. Nat. Assn. Bank Women (state sec. 1973-74). Roman Catholic (adv. council). Home and office: Forest City IA 50436

MCMAHON, MARION, psychologist, educator; b. N.Y.C., Aug. 30, 1907; d. Thomas Paul and Mary Ellen (O'Brien) McMahon; B.A., Coll. Mt. St. Vincent, 1930; M.A. cum laude, Fordham U., 1946, Ph.D. cum laude, 1955. Tchr. N.Y.C. Pub. Schs., 1930-33, Acad. Mt. St. Vincent, 1933-37; tchr. Latin and sci. Cathedral High Sch., 1937-45; tchr. chemistry Acad. Mt. St. Vincent, 1945-49, St. Gabriel High Sch., New Rochelle, N.Y., 1949-54; tchr. psychology Coll. Mt. St. Vincent, 1954-62; prof., chmn. dept. psychology Elizabeth Seton Coll., Yonkers, N.Y., 1962-70, dir. Children's Learning Center, 1970—. Chmn., N.Y. Archdiocesan Guidance Council, 1958-63; co-chmn. first theol. confs. between Roman Catholics and Mo. Synod Lutherans for scholars, 1963-70; chmn. Yonkers Christian Ecumenical Council, 1966-72; mem. N.Y. Archdiocesan Ecumenical Commn., 1969—. Mem. adv. council edn. div. Human Rights Commn., Yonkers, 1967-73. Recipient NSF grant, 1962, plaque Archdiocese of N.Y. for Guidance Council, 1963, award Mo. Synod Luth. Pastoral Confs., 1965-67. Mem. Am., Eastern, N.Y. State psychol. assns., Psychologists Interested in Religious Issues. Participant symposium Internat. Congress Psychologists, Brussels, Belgium, 1958. Address: 1061 N Broadway Yonkers NY 10701

MCMAHON, ROSEMARY, librarian; b. Kenton, O., June 12, 1931; d. Maurice A. and Martina J. (Dolan) McMahon; student Ohio No. U., 1949-50, Coll. St. Mary of the Springs, 1951-52, U. Dayton, summer 1961; B.S. in Edn., Ohio Dominican Coll., 1962; postgrad. Rosary Coll., summer 1972, 74. Receptionist, switchboard operator San Antonio Hosp., Kenton, 1953-55, Cath. Welfare Bur., Columbus, O., 1955-61; tchr. St. Augustine Sch., Columbus, 1961-62; cataloger State Library of Ohio Catalog Center, Columbus, 1962-73, Columbus Tech. Inst., 1973—. Mem. Am., Ohio, Catholic, Franklin County library assns., Ohio Assn. Sch. Librarians. Home: 1407 Doten Av Columbus OH 43212

MCMAHON, SHIRLEY ANNE, physician; b. Cambridge, Mass., Aug. 8, 1934; d. Earl Chatham and Miriam Ethelyn (Thompson) McMahon; A.B. magna cum laude, Middlebury Coll., 1956; certificate occupational therapy Columbia U., 1958; M.D., Boston U., 1965. Intern pediatrics, Stanford Med. Center, Palo Alto, Cal., 1965-66; resident pediatrics New England Med. Center, Boston, 1966-68; fellow child psychiatry Children's Hosp. of Washington, D.C., 1968-69; instr. pediatrics George Washington U., 1969-71, asst. prof. child health and devel., 1971-72; cons. Potomac Found. for Mental Health, 1971-72; asst. prof. psychiatry, asso. in psychopharmacology research Tufts U., 1972-73; instr. in pediatrics Harvard, 1972—; pediatrician coordinator Ambulatory Center, Beth Israel Hosp., Boston, 1972—. Diplomate Am. Bd. Pediatrics. Fellow Am. Acad. Pediatrics; mem. Phi Beta Kappa, Begg Soc. Home: 53 Brackett Pl Marblehead MA 01945 Office: 330 Brookline Av Boston MA 02215

MCMANUS, MARIANNE LEE, psychologist, educator; b. N.Y.C., July 30, 1932; d. James William and Mary Julia (Lee) McManus; B.A., Coll. of New Rochelle, N.Y., 1953; M.A., U. Wis., 1956, Ph.D., 1963. Learning skills specialist U. Wis. Counseling Service, 1955-56, clin. psychologist, 1958-68; psychology intern Wis. Diagnostic Center, Madison, 1956-57, clin. psychologist, 1958; clin. psychologist U. Wis. Counseling Service, 1958-68, Ia. State U. Counseling Service, Ames, 1968—, asst. prof. psychology, 1968-73, asso. prof., 1973—, chmn. Univ. Recreation Com., 1974; pvt. practice cons. psychologist, 1958—; hostess weekly radio broadcast Psychology for Today, WOI AM/FM, 1969-72. Mem. Ia. Women's Polit. Caucus, 1973—. Recipient Faculty Travel grant Internat. Congress Psychology, Tokyo, 1972. Mem. Am. Psychol. Assn., A.A.A.S., Am. Assn. U. Profs., Am. Personnel and Guidance Assn., Ia. Acad. Sci., Found. for Creative Behavior, Sierra Club (outings chmn. 1969-71, v.p. 1971-73 Ia. chpt.), Psi Chi, Phi Lambda Theta. Author: Learning How to Study, 1974. Home: 414 Briarwood Pl Ames IA 50010

MCMANUS, MAUREEN ELEANOR, publicity exec.; b. N.Y.C.; d. Terence J. and Mary Eleanor (Lynn) McManus; student pvt. schs. In charge recruitment blood donors A.R.C. Blood Bank, Bklyn., 1941-45; publicity dir. G.P. Putnam's Sons, N.Y.C., 1945-48, Henry Holt & Co., (now Holt, Rinehart & Winston, Inc.), N.Y.C., 1948-52, 54-68, Cowles Book Co., 1968-71; publicity dir. Stephen Greene Press, Brattleboro, Vt., 1971-73; free lancer, 1954—; publicity, researcher Readers Digest, Pleasantville, N.Y., 1952-54. Lectr., Radcliffe Coll., Georgetown U. Mem. Nat. Book Awards Com., 1948—. Mem. Women's Nat. Book Assn., Pubs. Publicity Assn. Home: RFD 3 Brattleboro VT 05301

MCMASTER, GLORIA MAE BUGNI, mezzo-soprano, educator; b. Montreal, Wis.; d. Anton George and Rose (Gatto) Bugni; student U. Minn.; B.S., Juilliard Sch. Music, N.Y.C.; postgrad. Columbia, U. Detroit, State U. N.Y., Brockport; Mus.M., Eastman Sch. Music, U. Rochester; m. Chester L. McMaster (dec. Dec. 8, 1972); children—Chester Anthony, Raymond Dale, Brian Monroe, Maureen Anne, Heather Lynn. Performed in concert, oratorio, opera throughout U.S., including solo appearances with Juilliard Opera Theater, Chautauqua Opera Assn., Rochester Opera Theater; appeared as soloist with Mpls. Symphony, Rochester (N.Y.) Philharmonic, Buffalo Philharmonic, Music Theater of Rochester, Eastman Rochester Symphony, Rochester, Hornell (N.Y.) Symphony; recitals at Youngstown, O., Ironwood, Mich., Hornell, Alfred and Rochester, N.Y.; concerts Nazareth Art Center, Nat. Opera Assn., New Orleans; dir. Dansville (N.Y.) Music Theater. Asst. prof. Youngstown State U., State U. Coll., Geneseo, N.Y.; now asso. prof. Houghton (N.Y.) Coll.; dir. Dansville Music Theater, 1972—. Appeared in title role Nat. Edn. Television prodn. The Medium. Mem. exec. com. Livingston County Young Republicans. Mem. Am. Assn. U. Women (past pres. Dansville area br.), Am. Assn. U. Profs. (past chpt. exec. bd.), Nat. Opera Assn., Nat. Assn. Tchrs. Singing, Juilliard Alumni Assn., Eastman Alumni Assn., N.Y. Music Tchrs. Assn. Home: 8470 Mt Morris Rd Dansville NY 14437

MCMICHAEL, SYLVIA (BETTY) HEARN, internat. investment exec.; b. Los Angeles, Aug. 16, 1933; d. Joseph Charles and Leona May (Crocker) Hearn; pvt. tutoring; m. Ernest McMichael II (div. 1962); children—Patricia May Hulbert, Pamela Frances (Mrs. Douglas Anderson), Debra Stacy, Ernest John III. Real estate salesman, broker, Cal. and Hawaii, 1955—; investment properties and syndicate packaging, 1963—, constrn. high rise residential and resort bldgs., subdivs., plantations and conversion European castles for modern living, 1968—; pres. Mt. View Investments, Ltd., Honolulu, 1965—; pres. New Ventures, Ltd., 1968-71; pres. McMichael & Nevels, Ltd., 1970—; sec., dir. Tara Plantations, Ltd. (Brit.), 1970—; sec., dir. Claiefontaine, Ltd. (Brit.), 1970—; propr. Industries Du Pacifique (French), 1971—; partner New Hebrides Real Estate Co., 1969—; dir. Jones Shore Investments Pty., Ltd., Terr. of Papua and New Guinea, 1970—; pres. Castle Holdings Ltd., 1972—. Mem. Honolulu Bd. Realtors. Hawaiian del. Republican Platform Com., 1968. Mem. Nat. Inst. Real Estate Brokers, Nat. Home Builders Assn., Fedn. Internat. Des Professions Immobilieres, Big Island Press Club, Hawaii Horse Breeders Assn. Club: Hilo Yacht. Home: 1166 Waiholo Pl Honolulu HI 96821 also Chateau de Levis Lurcy-Levis 03320 France Office: 1441 Kapiolani Blvd Suite 920 Honolulu HI 96814

MCMILLAN, CAROLINE OSGOOD, mfg. co. exec.; b. Boston, July 23, 1929; d. John Endicott and Caroline (Cutter) McMillan; student N.Y. U., 1972. Sr. writer, editor J. Walter Thompson Co., N.Y.C., 1957-61; supr. financial and stockholder relations Schering Corp., Bloomfield, N.J., 1964-69; dir. pub. affairs Athlone Industries, Inc., Parsippany, N.J., 1972—. Trustee St. Mary's-in-the-Mountains, 1953-60, White Mt. Sch., 1975—. Asso. mem. alumnae presidents council Ind. Secondary Schs., 1958—. Founding editor Investornews Mag., 1960-62. Home: 215 E 80th St New York City NY 10021 Office: 200 Webro Rd Parsippany NJ 07054

MCMILLAN, CYNTHIA ELLEN SWISHER (MRS. ROBERT GLENN MCMILLAN), pediatrician; b. Grand Junction, Colo., Nov. 25, 1943; d. Paul Wesley and Julia Vera (Smith) Swisher; A.B., U. N.C., 1965, M.D., 1969; m. Robert Glenn McMillan, Dec. 17, 1966; 1 son, Richard David. Intern, U. Tenn. Med. Research Center and Hosp., Knoxville, Tenn., 1969-70, pediatric resident physician, 1970-73; med. asso. Birth Defects Evaluation Center, Knoxville, 1973—. Methodist. Home: 316 Heritage Dr E Concord TN 37922

MCMILLAN, HELEN ELVIRA DAVIS (MRS. KENNETH K. MCMILLAN), state legislator; b. Ortonville, Minn.; d. Guy O. and Alice (Eldred) Davis; student U. Minn., 1930; m. Kenneth K. McMillan, July 10, 1937 (dec. 1971). Mem. Minn. Ho. of Reps., 1963—, 1st chairwoman crime prevention and corrections com. Sec., Gov.'s Human Rights Commn., Mower County, Minn., 1960—; mem. Gov.'s Status of Women Commn., 1963—; bd. dirs. A.R.C., Mower County, 1960-65, chmn. blood program, 1954-59; mem. Minn. Bd. Planned Parenthood; mem. adv. com. to women's affairs div. Human Rights Dept. Mem. Nat. Council Ch. Women (v.p. 1961-63), Minn. League Women Voters (pres. 1951-53). Home: 1230 2d Dr NE Austin MN 55912 Office: State Capitol St Paul MN 55101

MCMILLAN, MAE FRANCES, physician, educator; b. Austin, Tex., May 12, 1936; d. Ben Sanders and Annie Mae (Walker) McMillan; B.S., Wiley Coll., 1955; M.D., Meharry Med. Coll., 1959; postgrad. Baylor Coll. Medicine, 1960-65. Intern, Wayne County (Mich.) Gen. Hosp., Eloise, 1959-60; resident VA Hosp., Houston State Psychiat. Inst., 1960-63, Tex. Children's Hosp., child study clinic Houston State Psychiat. Inst., 1963-65, Hampstead Child Therapy Clinic, London, Eng., 1965-67; practice medicine specializing in child psychiatry, Houston, 1965—; instr. psychiatry Baylor Coll. Medicine, 1961-65, asst. prof., 1966—, mem. admissions com., 1973—; asst. prof. Faculty for Advanced Studies, U. Tex. Grad. Sch. Bio-med. Sci., 1969; asst. dir. div. child psychiatry Tex. Research Inst. Mental Scis., 1966-72, dir., 1972—; mem. staff, cons. Riverside Gen., St. Elizabeth's, St. Joseph's, Tex. Children's, Meth. hosps.; attending physician Harris County Hosp. Dist., Ben Taub Gen. Hosp.; cons. Houston Children's Mental Health Services, 1966—, Child Welfare div. Harris County, 1970—, St. Joseph's Mid-Houston Community Mental Health Center, 1966-72; cons. spl. edn. com. Houston Ind. Sch. Dist., 1970—; mem. Harris County Grand Jury Interium Com., 1967—; sec. Child Care Council Greater Houston, 1969-71; mem. Tex. Commn. Services to Children and Youth; mem. policy com. Am. Community TV, 1970-72; mem. grant rev. com. Center for Studies Met. Problems, Nat. Inst. Mental Health. Diplomate Am. Bd. Psychiatry and Neurology. Mem. Am., Nat., Tex. med. assns., Am. Psychiat. Assn. (sec.-treas. com. black psychiatrists), Nat. Council Negro Women (life mem.; chmn. health and social welfare com. 1968—), Tex. Soc. Child Psychiatry (counselor), Harris County Med. Soc., Houston Med. Forum, Houston Psychiat. Soc., Assn. Adolescent Psychiatry, Delta Sigma Theta (Founders Day award), Alpha Kappa Mu. Democrat. Methodist (chmn. work area on Christian social concern 1969—). Contbr. articles to profl. jours. Home: 4114 Cornell St Houston TX 77022 Office: 1300 Moursund Av Houston TX 77025

MCMILLAN, MARGARET LANGSTAFF, librarian; b. Eagle Grove, Ia., Sept. 23, 1902; d. Harry C. and Elizabeth Louise (Knowlen) McM.; B.S., Central Mo. State U., Warrensburg, 1921; M.A., U. Mo., 1923; postgrad. U. Neuchatel (Switzerland), 1947. Dir. library Columbia (Mo.) Coll., 1926-59; librarian Mo. State Hist. Soc. Library, Columbia, 1959-60; head reference research Mid Continent Library Service, Independence, Mo., 1961—; faculty summers Central Mo. State U. at Warrensburg, N.W. Mo. State U. at Maryville, U. Mo. at Columbia. Mem. Am. Assn. U. Women, Am., Mo. library assns., Pi Lambda Theta, Delta Kappa Gamma, Alpha Pi Zeta. Methodist. Club: Women's City (Kansas City). Author articles on Mo. history; also weekly column From the Library Book Shelve. Home: 2525 Lees Summit Rd Independence MO 64055 Office: Mid Continent Library Service Spring and W 24 Hwy Independence MO 64050

MCMILLAN, PATRICIA ANN, librarian; b. Kendallville, Ind., Jan. 1, 1940; d. James W. and Frances Lucille (Guymon) McMillan; student Butler U., 1958-60; B.S. in Elementary Edn., Ind. U., 1962; M.A. in Library Sci., U. Denver, 1965; M.S. in Edn., No. Ill. U., 1972. Social sci. reference librarian U. Notre Dame Library, 1963-66; asst. reference librarian Wis. State U. at Eau Claire, 1966-67; asst. head reader's aid St. Paul Pub. Library, 1967-68; asst. reference librarian No. Ill., U. Library, DeKalb, 1968—. Mem. A.L.A., Bus. and Profl. Women's Club DeKalb (rec. sec. 1972-73). Home: 711 S Main St Apt 204-A Sycamore IL 60178 Office: No Ill Univ Library DeKalb IL 60115

MCMILLEN, VIRGINIA NODE (MRS. JOHN THOMAS MCMILLEN JR.), mus. curator, ranch adminstr.; b. Austin, Tex., Nov. 20, 1945; d. John Golden and Sybil Dean (Fred) Farmer; student Ft. Lewis Coll., 1964-67; B.A., Ariz. State U., 1969; postgrad. Western N.M. U., 1972—; m. John Thomas McMillen Jr., July 25, 1971. Curator, Silver City (N.M.) Mus., 1969-73; partner Flying E Ranch, Grant County, N.M., 1971—. Tchr. English, St. Mary's Acad., Silver City, 1970. Mem. Grant County Art Guild, 1973—. Mem. Am. Assn. U. Women (pres. 1972-74), Hist. Soc. Southwest N.M. (pres. 1971—), Am., N.M. (program chmn. 1972) assns. museums. Author: Silver Echoes, 1971. Home: Box 962 Silver City NM 88061 Office: Box 962 Silver City NM 88061

MCMILLIN, MARGARET JUNE, mcht.; b. Butler, Mo., Feb. 2, 1921; d. L. Lloyd and Ethel Blanche (Coonrod) Gaines; student U. Kan., 1939-40; m. Eugene Stewart McMillin, Oct. 12, 1940 (dec.); children—Carol (Mrs. Hilton Wayne Nuffer), Daniel Alan. Receptionist, Dr. D.H. Sillix, O.D., 1954-58; personal receptionist Kan. Congressman Newell A. George, 1958-60; with advt. dept. Radio Sta. KLWN, Lawrence, Kan., 1961-62; mgr. Kirstens, 1962-66; mgr., buyer Alley Shop and Attic, Lawrence, 1966—. Mem. Downtown Lawrence Assn., 1970. Mem. Democratic State Com., 1966—; vice chmn. Douglas County Dem. Central Com., 1966—; del. Dem. Nat. Conv., 1968; vice chmn. 3d Dist. Kan. Democrats, 1968-70, sec., 1972—; commr. Kan. to Dem. Nat. Commn. on Del. Selection and Party Structure, 1973—; mem. state bd. Kan. Fedn. Women's Dem. Clubs; Kan. alternate Nat. Dem. Mini-Conf., 1974. Mem. Lawrence, Lawrence Women's (dir.) chambers commerce, Am. Legion Aux., Douglas County Hist. Soc. (life), Beta Sigma Phi, Alpha Delta Pi. Home: 1801 NW 5th St Route 4 Box 173 Lawrence KS 66044 Office: 843 Massachusetts St Lawrence KS 66044

MCMULLAN, DOROTHY, nurse educator; b. Bloomfield, N.J., June 19, 1911; d. Samuel H. and Anne (Gardiner) McMullan; grad. Cornell U., N.Y. Hosp. Sch. Nursing, 1935; B.S., N.Y. U., 1948, M.A., 1950, Ed.D., 1962. Pub. health nurse Henry St. Vis. Nurse Service, N.Y.C., 1935-39; pvt. duty nurse, N.Y.C., 1939-41; instr. Cornell U., N.Y. Hosp. Sch. Nursing, 1947-55; supr. N.Y. Hosp., Cornell Med. Center, 1947-50, asst. dept. head, 1950-53, adminstrv. asst. nursing service, 1953-55; dir. Sch. Nursing, prof. nursing Russell Sage Coll., 1955-61; dean, prof. nursing Ind. State U., Terre Haute, 1962-71; dir. nursing programs Nat. League for Nursing, N.Y.C., 1971—. Mem. Ind. Regional Med. Program Adv. Group; mem. bd. Community Services Found. of Wabash Valley; sec., treas. exec. com. Ind. Health Planning Council, 1968-71; mem. adv. com. on women in services Dept. Def., 1971—. Served from 2d lt. to 1st lt. Army Nurse Corps, 1942-46. Mem. Am. Assn. U. Profs., N.E.A., Assn. for Higher Edn., Am. Nurses Assn., Nat. (chmn. Gt. Lakes regional assembly 1968-71), Ind. (pres. 1966-71), N.Y. State (chmn. dept. baccalaureate and higher degree programs 1960-62)leagues for nursing, Am. Pub. Health Assn., Am. Assn. U. Women, Common Cause, UN Assn., Kappa Delta Pi. Author: (with Emanuel Hayt, Groeschel) Law of Hospital and Nurse, 1958. Home: 1 Lincoln Plaza New York City NY 10023

MCMULLAN, JEAN FRANCES GENTRY (MRS. ANDREW J. MCMULLAN, JR.), camp exec.; b. Hartford, Conn., June 7, 1926; d. Charles Burt and Kathleen (Moore) Gentry; B.A., U. Conn., 1947, Spl. certificate in Edn., 1948, M.A., 1949; m. Andrew J. McMullan, Jr., Mar. 31, 1950; children—Kathy Jean, Mark Andrew, Bruce Gentry (dec.), Keith Charles. Tchr., Coventry (Conn.) Country Day Sch., 1947-48; head counselor Camp Wyonegonic, Denmark, Me., 1948-50, co-dir., 1950-62; supr. music Riverside (Conn.) Sch., Old Greenwich (Conn.) Sch., 1950; supr. music pub. elementary schs., Willimantic, Conn., 1950-51; owner, dir. Alford Lake Camp, South Hope, Me., 1963—. Cellist, Willimantic Symphony, 1941-47, Portland (Me.) Symphony, 1955-72; helper, organizer Fund for Advancement Camping Durham Symposium, 1973. Adv. trustee Susan L. Curtis Found., Me., 1973. Mem. Me. Camp Dirs. Assn. (pres. 1962-63, dir.), Am. (v.p. 1973-74, exec. com. 1970-74), New Eng. (pres. 1970-71, dir.) camping assns., Nat. Camping Edn. Com. (mem. bd. 1972-73), Mortar Bd., Phi Beta Kappa. Republican. Conglist. Home: 17 Pilot Point Rd Cape Elizabeth ME 04107 Office: Alford Lake Camp RFD 2 Union ME 04862

MCMULLAN, JUNE BARBARA GUNTER (MRS. CHARLES E. MCMULLAN), banker; b. nr. Agricola, Miss., June 2, 1938; d. Hascal and Addie Lavern (Hathcock) Gunter; grad. high sch.; m. Charles E. McMullan, Aug. 4, 1957; children—Ricky Steven, Peggy Suzanne, Martin Douglas. With Bank Lucedale (Miss.), 1956—, teller, 1959-64, asst. cashier, 1965-69, asst. v.p., 1970-72, v.p. advt. and public relations, personnel and gen. bank operations, 1972—. Sec.-treas. bd. George County Heart Assn., (1968-72; lady col. Hon. Bill Waller Gov's. Staff, 1972-76. Mem. Nat. Assn. Bank Women (vice-chmn. Coast group Miss. 1971-72, pres. 1972-73). Selected All State Championship Basketball Team, 1955, 56. Home: PO Box 774 Lucedale MS 39452 Office: PO Box 647 Lucedale MS 39452

MCMULLIN, LORETTA DENT (MRS. CHARLES R. MCMULLIN), artist; b. Birmingham, Ala.; d. William Wirt and Regina (Weltman) Dent; student U. Ala., 1920-22, Samford U., 1957-58, Nat. Acad. Art, summers 1962, 64; pvt. study art Lem McDaniel, William Wilson, Walter Steumfig; m. Charles R. McMullin, Dec. 18, 1926 (dec. Sept. 1931); children—Charles James (dec.), David Dent. Exhibited in group shows Birmingham Mus. Art, 1957—, Pen Women State Show, Birmingham, Ala. State Fair, 1962, Montgomery Mus. Art, Mobile Mus. Art, others; represented in pvt. collections. State dir. Am. Art Week, 1966. Recipient Special Achievement award Am. Artists Profl. League; prizes Ala. Pen Women Show, 1971, 73. Mem. Nat. League Am. Pen Women (art chmn. 1966-72), English Speaking Union (bd. mem. 1954-60), Ala. Writers Conclave. Methodist. Home: 2647 Montevallo Rd Birmingham AL 35223

MCMURRAY, LADONNA LYLE, eductor; b. DuQuoin, Ill., May 20, 1935; d. Walter A. and Ruth C. (Schwinn) McMurray; B.S. in Edn., So. Ill. U. at Carbondale, 1957, M.S. in Speech, 1961; Ph.D. in Speech Communication, U. So. Cal., 1975; m. John Kennedy Geddes, Jr., Sept. 8, 1973. Tchr., Flora (Ill.) High Sch., 1957-60; grad. teaching asst. So. Ill. U., 1960-61, lectr. radio-TV, 1961-63; instr. speech Portland (Ore.) State U., 1963-67; asst. prof. speech and drama Central Wash. U., Ellensburg, 1967-68; grad. teaching asst. U. Wis.-Madison, 1968-69; mem. vis. faculty speech and drama Tex. So. U., Houston, summer 1969; adminstrv. asst., then research asst. U. So. Cal., 1969-73; instr. Los Angeles County Sheriff's Dept., spring 1973; spl. instr. S.W. Coll., Los Angeles, 1973-74; now with research unit Ky. State Dept. Justice, Frankfort. Asst. prof. speech Cal. State U. at Los Angeles, 1973-74. Mem. Western Speech Assn., Speech Communication Assn., Internat. Communication Assn., Sigma Beta Gamma, Pi Kappa Delta, Zeta Phi Eta. Home: 313 E North St DuQuoin IL 62832 Office: 209 St Clair St Frankfort KY 40601

MCNAIL, EDDIE GATHINGS (MRS. JOHN LEONARD MCNAIL), educator; b. Prairie, Miss., Nov. 28, 1905; d. James Covington and Lavinia (Prewett) Gathings; B.A., U. Miss., 1927; postgrad. U. Tex., 1945; M.A., Agrl. and Indsl. U., 1948; m. John Leonard McNail, Apr. 5, 1928; children—Mary (Mrs. Grover Cleveland Williams), Joseph Covington (dec.). Sr. English tchr. La Feria Ind. Sch. Dist., 1927-28, 41-49, elementary tchr., 1959-68; sr. English tchr. Mercedes Ind. Sch. Dist., 1949-59. Chmn. pub. safety com., La Feria, Tex., 1971-72. Named Tchr. of the Year, Rio Grande Valley Fedn. Women's Clubs, 1967; recipient plaque Tex. Pub. Schs., 1968. Mem. Am. Legion Aux. (pres. 1960-61), D.A.R. (regent Lt. Thomas Barlow chpt. 1967-68), Tex. State Tchrs. Assn., Daus. Am. Colonists (v.p. Quinton Stockwell chpt., chmn. nat. com. patriotic edn., Thatcher award), Ret. Tchrs. Assn. (1st v.p. Harlingen Mid-Valley 1970-72, pres. 1972-73), Rio Grande Valley Fedn. Women's Clubs (1st v.p. 1971-73, pres. 1973-75), Delta Kappa Gamma (pres. 1964-66). Methodist (chmn. ch. adminstrv. bd. 1973, pres. Unith Meth. Women 1973). Mem. Order Eastern Star (matron 1937-38). Club: Cultura (pres. 1934) (La Feria). Author: The Silver Cord, 1971. Home: 204 West St La Feria TX 78559

MCNAIR, BARBARA, singer, actress; b. Racine, Wis., Mar. 4; d. Horace and Claudia (Taylor) McNair; student U. So. Cal. Formerly night club singer; theatrical appearances include The Body Beautiful, 1958; The Merry World of Nat King Cole, 1961; No Strings, 1962; films include Spencer's Mountain, 1962; Stiletto, 1969; Change of Habit, 1969; Venus in Furs, 1970; They Call Me Mister Tibbs, 1970; Pajama Game, 1973; star weekly TV show Barbara McNair Show. Mem. Am. Guild Variety Artists, Stage Artists Guild, A.F.T.R.A., Actors Equity Guild. Home: 404 Torry Av Bronx NY 10472 Office: care of Berger Ross & Steinman 15 Central Park W New York City NY 10017*

MCNAIR, KATHRYN LOUISE MALLORY (MRS. JAMES DUNLAP MCNAIR), author; b. Mattoon, Ill., Aug. 4, 1911; d. Jesse Francis and Mabel (Harris) Mallory; A.B., U. Ill., 1936; m. James Dunlap McNair, May 6, 1937; children—Edward Anthony, Susan (Mrs. Sidney J. Blatt). Recipient Distinguished Writing award Ind. U., 1966. Mem. Am. League Penwomen, Delta Kappa Gamma. Republican. Methodist. Author: A Sense of Magic, 1965; A Book of Directions, 1970. Contbr. articles to profl. jours., short stories to Ladies Home Jour., Woman's Day. Home: 3400 Petty Rd Muncie IN 47304

MCNALL, PEARL GERTRUDE, anesthesiologist; b. Carnegie, Pa., Feb. 3, 1923; d. James Bell and Mabel Grace (Weston) McNall; B.S., Westminster Coll., 1943; M.D., U. Pitts., 1949. Research asso. Mellon Inst., Pitts., 1944-45; intern Mercy Hosp., Pitts., 1949-50, resident, 1950-52, now mem. staff; practice medicine specializing in anesthesiology, Pitts., 1952—; mem. staff St. Margaret Meml., St. Clair Meml. hosps., Pitts., Mem. med. adv. bd. Myasthenia Gravis Found., 1959—, also sec.; instr. anesthesiology U. Pitts., 1952—. Mem. Am., Pa., Western Pa. socs. anesthesiologists; Royal Soc. Medicine, Am., Pa. med. assns., Allegheny County Med. Soc., Am. Med. Women's Assn., Internat. Anesthesia Research Soc. Methodist. Mem. Order Eastern Star. Club: Chartiers Country (Pitts.). Home: 20 Winthrop Rd Carnegie PA 15106 Office: 1400 Locust St Pittsburgh PA 15219

MCNALLY, CRYSTAL ELAINE, ednl. adminstr.; b. Hiattville, Kan., Sept. 23, 1914; d. John and Mae Ann (Attkisson) McNally; B.S., Kan. State U., 1935; M.A., Columbia, 1954. Librarian, tchr. Bucklin (Kan.) High Sch., 1935-43; view schs., Wichita, Kan., 1943-49; dir. library media services Wichita schs., 1949—. Mem. Speaker's Bur., P.T.A., Wichita, 1949—. Goodwill ambassador for UNESCO to Orleans, France, 1949. Mem. Am., Kan. library assns., Am. Kan.

assns. of sch. librarians, P.E.O., Kan. Authors. Delta Kappa Gamma. Methodist. Mem. Order Eastern Star. Editor Sch. Media Quar., 1953. Home: 119 South Estelle Wichita KS 67211 Office: 1847 North Chautauqua Wichita KS 67214

MCNALLY, JEAN ELIZABETH, physician; b. Sioux City, Ia., May 31, 1930; d. John and Mary (Brennan) McNally; A.B., Briar Cliff Coll., Sioux City, 1953; M.D., U. Ia., 1957; m. Peter Carbonara, Apr. 28, 1960; children—Peter, Paul, John, Mary. Intern, St. Vincent's Hosp., N.Y.C., 1957-58; resident in medicine St. Vincent's Hosp., 1958-59, Englewood (N.J.) Hosp., 1964-65, 73-74; practice medicine specializing in internal medicine, Englewood, N.J., 1969—; mem. staff Englewood Hosp. Home: 276 E Linden Av Englewood NJ 07631 Office: 229 Engle St Englewood NJ 07631

MCNALLY, JOAN MARY (MRS. JOSEPH MICHAEL MCNALLY), editor; b. Chokio, Minn., July 4, 1928; d. John Herman and Clara Justine (Herman) Wensman; student pub. schs.; m. Joseph Michael McNally, July 17, 1946; children—William, Daniel, Kay. Newspaper editor Chokio Rev., 1968-71, 73—; reporter, photographer Morris (Minn.) Sun & Tribune, 1971-73. Sec., Chokio Community Center Com., 1970—, pres., 1972—; sec. Youth For Understanding Com. 1969—; past pres. Chokio United Fund; mem. Region C Crime Commn., 1974—. Roman Catholic. Club: Chokio Commercial (pres. 1970). Editor, pub. St. Mary's Bell Ringers Cook Book, 3 edits., 1968-72. Home: Chokio MN 56221 Office: Chokio Rev Chokio MN 56221

MCNALLY, MARY DOWNING, librarian; b. Fall River, Mass., July 4, 1922; d. Leo Augustine and Emma Mary (Barlow) McNally; B.S., Seton Hill Coll., 1943; M.S., Sch. Pub. Relations and Communications, Boston U., 1953; M.S., in L.S., Fla. State U., 1963. Sci. Instr. Sturdy Meml. Hosp., Attleboro, Mass., 1945-46; dietition, instr. nutrition and diet therapy, St. Anne's Hosp., Fall River, Mass., 1946-50; editor, publicist Bordon Co., N.Y.C., 1952-54; head consumer relations Waste King Corp., San Francisco, 1954-56; recreation supr. U.S. Army Spl. Services, Germany, Korea, Panama, 1957-61; adult librarian pub. services, and asst. chief pub. relations Enoch Pratt Free Library, Balt., 1963-67; area branch librarian Prince Georges County Meml. Library, Hyattsville, Md., 1967-70; dir. Dorchester County Pub. Library, Cambridge, Md., 1970—. Mem. Dorchester Arts Center, Cambridge, Md., 1970—; mem. Dorchester Gen. Hosp. Aux., 1970—; chmn. Dorchester County Council Health and Social Agys., 1974-75. Mem. Dorchester County Hist. Soc., A.L.A. (activities com. 1974-77), Md. Library Assn. (chmn. publicity com. 1964-66, nominating com. 1967-68, 1st v.p. 1972-73, pres. 1973-74, scholarship chmn. 1974-75), League of Women Voters, Tau Mu Epsilon, Theta Phi Mu. Roman Catholic. Club: Quota (rec. sec. 1971-72) (Cambridge). Home: 112 Oakley St Cambridge MD 21613 Office: 301 Gay St Cambridge MD 21613

MCNAMARA, CAROLYN LEE, inst. exec.; b. Wayne, Mich., Oct. 16, 1944; d. Manuel Maurice and Virginia Lee (Tapp) Graddy; B.S., Murray (Ky.) State U., 1966; M.A., Purdue U., 1969, Ed.D., 1971; m. Donald James McNamara, June 15, 1968. Family living editor, agrl. information dept. Purdue U., 1969-72; tech. asso. Center Vocational and Tech. Edn., Ohio State U., Columbus, 1972, residence hall dir., 1972-74; project interviewer Vera Inst. Justice, N.Y.C., 1975—. Vol. Children's Receiving Home, Tarrytown, N.Y., 1975—. Mem. Am. Personnel and Guidance Assn., Am. Coll. Personnel Assn., Nat. Assn. Women Deans, Adminstrs. and Counselors, Speech Communication Assn., Alpha Omicron Pi (dir. region II), Alphecca (hon.), Chi Delta Phi, Lambda Iota Tau. Methodist. Contbr. articles to profl. jours. Home: 410 Benedict Av Apt 1-F Tarrytown NY 10591

MCNAMARA, MARGART C. (MRS. ROBERT S. MCNAMARA), civic worker; b. Seattle, Aug. 22, 1915; d. Thomas J. and Margaret (McKinstry) Craig; B.A., U. Cal., Berkeley, 1937; m. Robert S. McNamara, Aug. 13, 1940; children—Margaret Elizabeth, Kathleen, Robert Craig. High sch. tchr. Alameda and San Rafael, Cal., 1938-40. Regional dir. White House Conf. Children and Youth, 1960; dir. Widening Horizons, City of Washington summer program for youth, 1964-65; chmn. bd. Reading is Fundamental program Smithsonian Instn., 1966—; mem. nat. adv. council Office Econ. Opportunity, 1965-68; mem. Nat. Com. U.S.-China Relations. Trustee Chatham Coll., Pitts., Eugene and Agnes E. Meyer Found., Washington; bd. dirs. Smithsonian Assos. Mem. League Women Voters. Presbyn. Home: 2412 Tracy Pl NW Washington DC 20008

MCNAMARA, MAUREEN ANN, ednl. adminstr.; b. Burlington, Vt., June 11, 1923; d. Joseph Augustine and Mary Patricia (Magner) McNamara; B.S., Regis Coll., 1945; postgrad. St. Michael's Coll., 1965, 70. Coll. recorder, asst. registrar St. Michael's Coll., Winooski, Vt., 1960-67, coordinator extension services and grad. program, 1967-69, registrar, 1969—. Mem. bd. corporators Burlington Savs. Bank, 1973—; dir. Chittenden Trust Co. Mem. Adv. Council U.S. Catholic Bishops, 1969—; mem. Vt. Diocesan Ecumenical Commn., 1971—. Mem. Burlington Democratic City Com., 1973—, Chittenden County Dem. Com., 1973—; mem. zoning bd. City of Burlington, 1968—. Trustee Vt. State Colls., 1973—. Mem. New Eng. Assn. Registrars and Adminstrv. Officers (treas. 1971—), Vt. League Women Voters (v.p. 1969—), Vt. Catholic Press Assn. (dir. 1969—), Delta Epsilon Sigma. Home: 14 Summit St Burlington VT 05401 Office: St Michaels College Winooski VT 05404

MCNAMEE, RUTH ELEANOR BRADEN (MRS. WILLIAM A. MCNAMEE), city ofcl.; b. N.Y.C.; d. Charles William and Johanna (Schnebbe) Braden; A.B., Bucknell U., 1942; postgrad. Sch. Bus. Practice and Speech, 1943; m. William A. McNamee, May 11, 1946; children—JoAnne, Jeffrey. Mem. City Planning Bd., Birmingham, Mich., 1964-65, mem. City Commn., 1965—, mayor, 1970-71; mem. Spl. Commn. on Local Govt., 1970—. Pres. Quarton Sch. P.T.A., 1961-62; mem. Commn. on Women, 1969-70; mem. Gov.'s Commn. on Pub. Employment Relations Act, 1973—. Bd. dirs. Community House, Birmingham, Mich.; trustee Cranbrook Schs., Bloomfield Hills, Mich., Mich. Municipal League. Named Ford Citizen of the Year, 1968. Mem. Am. Assn. U. Women, League Women Voters. Club: Village Womans (Bloomfield Hills). Home: 1271 Lakeside St Birmingham MI 48009

MCNANAMY, EVE LYN WEEKS (MRS. THOMAS J. MCNANAMY), clin. psychologist; B.Ed., U. Miami (Fla.), 1957, M.Ed., 1958, Ph.D., 1966; m. Thomas J. McNanamy, Dec. 6, 1963. Instr. Broward County Bd. Pub. Instruction, Ft. Lauderdale, Fla., 1954-56; children's counselor Miami Lighthouse for the Blind, 1962; psychol. counsellor U. Miami Sch. Medicine, 1963; clin. intern Jackson Meml. Hosp., Miami, 1961, clin. psychologist; 1964-66; psychologist Community Mental Health Clinic, Miami, 1966-69; pvt. practice as psychotherapist, marriage and family counselor, Miami, 1968—. Profl. adviser Mental Health Assn., Miami, Fla., 1965-66; community programs dir. Mental Health Assn. Dade County, 1966-67; cons. Ednl. Guidance Services, Miami. Bd. dirs. S. Dade Mental Health Found., Women's Alcoholic Edn. Center. Recipient Myrtle Wreath award for community service Hadassah, 1965; Presdl. Service award Nat. Employ the Handicapped Com. Mem. Am., Fla., Dade County psychol. assns., Nat., Dade County rehab. assns., Council for Exceptional Children, Am. Assn. Marriage and Family Counselors, Am. Orthopsychiat. Assn., Am. Assn. U. Women (mem. doctoral fellowship com.), South Dade C. of C. (dir., mem. speakers bur.) Jr. League Miami, Phi Kappa Phi. Clubs: Zonta; Alumni Century. Home: 4706 Granada Blvd Coral Gables FL 33146 Office: Dadeland Med Bldg 7400 N Kendall Dr Miami FL 33156

MCNATT, MURIEL COWDEN (MRS. JAMES MATTHEW MCNATT), tax assessor; b. Eunice, N.M., Dec. 27, 1914; d. Liddon and Muriel (Oliver) Cowden; grad. high sch.; m. James Matthew McNatt, June 19, 1932; 1 dau., Esther Monteine (Mrs. James William Baird). Asst. Otero County Abstract and Title Co., Alamogordo, N.M., 1954-62; co-owner Home and Bus. Service, Alamogordo, 1958-71; assessor Otero County, 1967-70, chief dep. assessor, 1962-66, 71—. Vice pres. McNatt Mfg. Corp., 1957—. Del. numerous legislative com. hearings, 1966-71; speaker, writer in field. Mem. com. for preservation hist. material Alamogordo Pub. Library. Mem. N.M. Assn. Assessors (sec. 1969-71). Home: 2400 Lawrence Blvd Alamogordo NM 88310 Office: Court House Alamogordo NM 88310

MCNEAR, BETTE HITCHCOCK, newspaperwoman; b. Norristown, Pa., May 13, 1924; d. Craig Burt and Emma Maude (Watkins) Hitchcock; student St. Lawrence U., 1942-45; m. James Joseph McNear, Nov. 25, 1944 (div. May 1967); children—Wendy (Mrs. Kevin Wright), Mary (Mrs. David Fischbach), Francis C. Feature writer Post-Standard, Syracuse, N.Y., 1958-60, Times-Union, Albany, 1960-63; asst. women's editor News-Jour., Wilmington, Del., 1963-68, women's editor, 1968-71, food editor, 1970—, travel editor, 1971—, asso. features editor, 1971-73. Adv. bd. Salvation Army. Mem. Nat. Press Women, Soc. Am. Travel Writers, Women in Communications, Delta Delta Delta, Pi Delta Epsilon. Clubs: Washington Press; Delaware Press (1st v.p. 1971, 72) (Wilmington, Del.); Soroptimist. Home: 171 Villas Dr New Castle DE 19720 Office: 831 Orange St Wilmington DE 19899

MCNEELY, PHOEBE CHAPMAN (MRS. GEORGE HANSBROUGH MCNEELY), educator; b. Sacramento, Mar. 7, 1922; d. Calvin Chadiock and Jane (Greeley) Chapman; B.S., U. Cal., 1943; M.S., Cal. State U. at Hayward, 1968; m. George Hansbrough McNeely, July 3, 1948; children—Barbara (Mrs. Michael Burton Genung), Florence, Louise, William Mills. Tchr. social scis. Livermore (Cal.) High Sch., 1960-63, 72—, dean girls, 1966-72; counselor Granada High Sch., Livermore, 1963-66. Mem. Livermore Drug Abuse Prevention Com., 1969-71. Mem. Nat. Assn. Women Deans Adminstrs. and Counselors, Cal. Assn. Women Adminstrs. and Counselors (pres. 1971-73), Delta Kappa Kappa (chpt. v.p. 1974-76, pres. elect 1976—). Episcopalian (mem. bishop's com. 1959-61). Home: 3884 Harvard Way Livermore CA 94550

MCNEELY, SHIRLEY FARRELL (MRS. JOHN C. MCNEELY, JR.), newspaperwoman; b. Salina, Kan., Apr. 15, 1949; d. John Pierce and Betty (Hinton) Farrell; B.A., Tex. Christian U., 1971; m. John C. McNeely, Jr., July 14, 1973. With Columbus (O.) Dispatch, 1971—, copy editor, 1971—, page editor, 1972—. Mem. Ohio Newspaper Women's Assn., Women in Communications, Press Club Ohio. Clubs: Gridiron (Columbus, O.); Press (sec., dir. 1972-75) (Columbus, O.). Home: 669 1/2 S Grant Av Columbus OH 43206 Office: 34 S 3d St Columbus OH 43216

MCNEER, LENORE LEE WHITMAN (MRS. RICHARD MASON MCNEER), educator; b. Logan, W.Va., May 16, 1922; d. Grover C. and Altha (Cooper) Whitman; A.B., Berea Coll., 1944; M.A., U. Chgo., 1947; postgrad. U. Vt., 1954-55, Boston U., 1956-57, Nat. Tng. Lab., Bethel, Me., 1956, 58, U. Mass., 1973—; m. Richard Mason McNeer, Sept. 1, 1946; children—Richard Mason, Craig Selden. Asst. to dir. Internat. House, U. Chgo., 1944-51, sec. dept. polit. sci., 1945-47; psychiat. social worker Vt. Dept. Mental Health, 1953-61, cons. community orgn. Office Mental Retardation, 1966-68; faculty Vt. Coll., Montpelier, 1961-72, mem. exec. com. faculty forum, 1965-72; asso. prof. Norwich U., 1972—. Cons., Nat. Inst. Mental Health, 1971-73. Cons. New Eng. Mgmt. Corp. Vice pres. State Episcopal Women, 1957-60; sec., mem. exec. com. regional conf. Child Welfare League Am., 1958-61; mem. nat. com. leadership edn. United Ch. Women, 1958-61, state pres., 1958-61; sec., mem. exec. com. N.E. State Govts. Conf. Mental Health, 1960-61; mem. area com. Am. Field Service, 1963-66; mem. Gov.'s Commn. Status Women, 1964-65; mem. Commn. Ecumenical Relations, Episcopal Diocese Vt., 1965—; mem. joint Ecumenical com. Episcopal Ch. Vt., Cath. Diocese Burlington and Vt. Ch. Council, 1965-66; mem. Faith and Order Commn., Vt. Council Chs., 1967-71; mem. selection com. Montpelier Dollars for Scholars, 1968; chmn. Gov.'s Commn. Status of Women, 1970-72; mem. Vt. Welfare Adv. Council, 1972-74; mem. task force on mental health materials So. Regional Edn. Bd., 1973—; mem. adv. council on aging Am. Assn. Community Colls., 1972—. mem. nat. com. Japan Internat. Christian U., 1962—; mem. task force So. Regional Edn. Bd.; chmn. New Eng. Regional Conf. Faculty Devel. Trustee Vt. Council Chs. Mem. Washington County Dem. Women's Com., 1965-67. Mem. Nat. Assn. Social Workers (v.p. Vt. chpt. social work edn. com. 1966-69), Common Cause. Home: 42 Mountain View Montpelier VT 05602

MCNEIL, HELEN HOWERY (MRS. RAYMOND W. MCNEIL), civic worker; b. Farmington, Md., Dec. 13, 1925; d. Ernest Preston and Ada Elizabeth (Calvert) Howery; student pub. schs., Oxford, Pa.; m. Raymond W. McNeil, July 14, 1943; children—Connie (Mrs. Welby D. Jones), William, Kimberly, Kevin, Marc. Exec. sec. Oxford Civic Assn., 1956-74; campaign co-chmn., Oxford Community Chest-A.R.C., 1969-74; sec. Oxford Human Needs Study Group, 1969-73; treas. Neighborhood Services Center, 1970-74; sec. St. Christophers Kindergarten, 1969-73; sec. bldg. fund Community Meml. Hosp. Recipient Citizens award Oxford C. of C., 1948. Methodist (sec. bldg. fund 1957). Home: RD 1 Box 14 Oxford PA 19363

MCNEIL, MARY CAROLYNN, physician; b. Memphis, Feb. 16, 1927; d. James Edward and Jamie (Burrow) McNeil; student So. Missionary Coll., 1945-47, LaSierra Coll., 1947-49; M.D., Loma Linda U., 1953. Intern Nashville Gen. Hosp., 1953-54; resident obstetrics and gynecology Vanderbilt U. Hosp., Nashville, 1954-55; resident pathology VA Hosp., Martinsburg, W.Va., 1955-56; resident obstetrics and gynecology John Gaston Hosp., Memphis, 1956-58, St. Luke's Hosp., St. Louis, 1964-65; med. missionary Giffard Meml. Hosp., Nuzvid, Andhra Pradesh, India, 1960-63; practice medicine, specializing in obstetrics and gynecology, Cumberland, Ky., 1958-60, Long Beach, Cal., 1965—; vice chief obstetrics-gynecology dept. Long Beach Community Hosp., 1972-73, chief obstetrics-gynecology dept., 1974—. Diplomate Am. Bd. Obstetrics and Gynecology. Fellow Am. Coll. Obstericians and Gynecologists; mem. Am. Med. Women's Assn. (br. pres. 1968-69), A.M.A., Cal., Los Angeles County med. assns. Republican. 7th Day Adventist. Office: Security Bldg 110 Pine St Long Beach CA 90802 also 5199 E Pacific Coast Hwy Suite 508 Long Beach CA 90804

MCNEILL, EDNA EARLE ADAMS (MRS. CARL T. MCNEILL), govt. ofcl.; b. nr. Mayfield, Ky., Nov. 26, 1934; d. William Mason and Lula Mae (Johnson) Adams; grad. high sch.; m. Carl T. McNeill, Oct. 10, 1954; children—Carl, Elizabeth, Beverly, Janice. Credit clk. Montgomery Ward, Mayfield, 1953, credit mgr., Hopkinsville, Ky., 1956, asst. cashier, Jackson, Tenn., 1956-59; ins. agt. Barnett & McNeill Ins. Agy., Parsons, Tenn., 1965-71; exec. dir. Housing Authority Parsons, 1967—. Home: Elizabeth St Parsons TN 38363 Office: 301 Rose Av Parsons TN 38363

MCNEILL, ESTHER SHAW (MRS. RODNEY JOHNSON MCNEILL), coll. dean, educator; b. Clarkton, N.C., Jan. 2, 1923; d. Macy and Lee Jetta (Andrews) Shaw; B.A. (W.J. Trent scholar), Livingston Coll., 1944; M.A., N.Y. U., 1961; postgrad. (So. Edn. Found. fellow), N.C. Central U., 1968-70; m. Rodney Johnson McNeill, Apr. 22, 1946; children—Rodney Ellsworth, Glenda Cartrelle. Tchr. B.T. Washington Sch., Clarkton, N.C., 1944-62; spl. edn. tchr. Oxford (N.C.) city schs., 1962-64; supr. Henderson (N.C.)-Vance County elementary schs., 1964-68; dir. secondary edn. Vance County Schs., Henderson, 1968-70; asso. prof. edn. St. Augustine's Coll., Raleigh, N.C., 1970—, also asso. dean students, 1972—. Lectr. N.C. Central U., Durham, 1964—; cons. edn. to Human Relations Center, St. Augustine's Coll., 1969—, Lumberton (N.C.) city schs., 1970—, Martin County (N.C.) schs., 1970—. Mem. Oxford (N.C.) Layman Council, 1965—; sec. Bladen County chpt. N.A.A.C.P. Nat. Def. Edn. Act fellow, 1965, Danforth fellow, 1973. Mem. Am. Assn. Adminstrs., Nat. Edn. Assn., N.C. Assn. Edn., N.C. Assn. Supervision and Curriculum Devel. (dir. 1970—), N.C. Assn. Women Deans, Vance County Women's Voters League (co-dir. 1968—), Nat. Assn. Coll. Women, Students Voter League (dir. 1970—), Zeta Phi Beta. Home: 1309 E Martin St Raleigh NC 27610 Office: Saint Augustine's College Raleigh NC 27611

MCNEILL, SHIRLEY JEAN MOTTERN, social worker; b. Johnson City, Tenn., Apr. 6, 1944; d. Edward and Anna Katherin (Mottern) Lane; A.A., Essex Community Coll., 1972; student Coppin State Coll., 1971—; m. Leroy McNeill, July 19, 1963 (div. Sept. 1969); 1 son, Charles Lee. Program coordinator Title III Program, Coppin State Coll., Balt., 1971—. Tech. cons. Dept. Health, Edn. and Welfare, 1970-72; nat. coordinating chmn. for Md. to Nat. Welfare Rights Orgn., 1968—; mem. Balt. Welfare Rights Orgn., 1968—; sec. client adv. com. Baltimore County Dept. Social Service, 1968-71. Bd. dirs. Columbia Law Center, Md. Dept. Employment and Social Services, Md. Conf. Social Welfare. Home: 912 Orems Rd Baltimore MD 21221 Office: 2500 W North Av Baltimore MD 21216

MCNICHOLS, LYDIA ALICE ANDREWS, coll. adminstr.; b. Kennebec, S.D., Oct. 29, 1913; d. George Harrison and Lydia Armette (Coen) Andrews; B.S., Seattle Pacific Coll., 1945; m. Donald McNichols, Sept. 1, 1940; 1 son, Melvin Donald. Elementary tchr., S.D., 1934-36; registrar, instr. Los Angeles Pacific Coll., 1945-50; asst. prof. music George Fox Coll., Newberg, Ore., 1950-55; dir. music and Christian edn. 1st Free Methodist Ch., Seattle, 1957-60; asst. registrar Seattle Pacific Coll., 1963-67, asso. registrar, 1967-70, dir. registration and records, 1970—, v.p. inter-coll. relations commn., 1973-74, pres. 1974-75. Bd. dirs. Children's Center, Seattle World's Fair, 1962. Mem. Am. Assn. Collegiate Registrars and Admissions Officers, Pacific Assn. Coll. Registrars and Admissions Officers, Am. Assn. U. Women, Puget Sound Choral Conductors Guild (pres. 1962). Methodist (co-chmn. worship). Club: Seattlean (pres. 1957). Home: 3207 10 Av W Seattle WA 98119

MCNULTY, FAITH TRUMBULL CORRIGAN (MRS. RICHARD H. MARTIN), writer; b. N.Y.C., Nov. 28, 1918; d. Joseph E. and Faith (Robinson) Corrigan; student Barnard Coll., 1936-37; m. John McNulty, Sept. 24, 1945; 1 son, John Joseph; m. 2d, Richard H. Martin, Dec. 13, 1957. Researcher Life Mag., N.Y.C., 1943-44; asst. editor Colliers, 1949-50, Cosmopolitan, 1951-53; staff writer New Yorker Mag., N.Y.C., 1953—. Recipient Dutton Animal award, 1966. Author: The Whooping Crane, 1966; Must They Die?, 1971; The Great Whales, 1974. Home: Box 370 Wakefield RI 02880 Office: The New Yorker 25 W 43d St New York City NY 10036

MCNUTT, DOLLY HITE (MRS. HOUSTON MCNUTT), mayor; b. Henderson, Ky., June 22, 1917; d. Leslie P. and Mary Gladys (Flaherty) Hite; student, Paducah Jr. Coll., 1936, Am. Acad. Dramatic Arts, 1938; m. Houston McNutt, Feb. 25, 1941. Partner Royal Crown-Nehi Bottling Co., Paducah, Ky., 1941-73; commr., mayor pro-tem City of Paducah, 1968-70; mayor City of Paducah, Ky., 1972—. Vol. A.R.C., Paducah; seal chmn. McCracken County Tb. Assn., 1969-71; chmn. civic beautification bd. City of Paducah, 1965-66; mem. Home and Neighborhood Devel. Soc. Recipient Distinguished Woman award Fraternal Order of Eagles, 1972; Citizen of Year award, Southside Kiwanis Club, 1972; Woman of Year award, Bus. and Profl. Women's Club, 1971, Meritorious Service award Greater Paducah C. of C., 1974, others. Mem. Jackson Purchase Hist. Soc., Bus. and Profl. Women's Club, Greater Paducah C. of C. (mem. all Am. city com. 1969-70), Internat. Platform Assn. Democrat. Roman Catholic. Club: Paducah (Ky.) Garden. Home: 105 Country Club Lane Paducah KY 42001 Office: PO Box 891 Paducah KY 42001

MCNUTT, MRS. DOROTHY, cons. librarian; b. Cin., Jan. 17, 1903; d. Milton G. and Emily (Thompson) Conger; A.B., Ohio Wesleyan U., 1926; m. Clyde D. McNutt, July 3, 1928 (div.). With Cin. Pub. Library, 1926-72, mem. library tng. class, 1926-27, asst. pub. documents dept., 1934-36, asst. sci. and industry dept., 1927-34, 36-52, head sci. and industry dept., 1952-72; library cons., 1972—. Mem. A.L.A., Ohio Library Assn. (exec. bd. 1955-56, editor Bull. 1955—), Spl. Libraries Assn., Alliance Francaise, D.A.R., Bus. and Profl. Women's Club, Nat. Huguenot Soc., Alpha Chi Omega. Methodist. Clubs: Monnett, Soroptimist, College. Contbr. articles to profl. jours., local newspapers. Home: 4239 Hamilton Av Cincinnati OH 45223 Office: 28 Woodlawn Av Fort Mitchell KY 41017

MCNUTT, SARA JEAN, educator; b. Memphis, Mich., Nov. 24, 1932; d. Esbon Newton and Anna (Henderson) McNutt; B.S. cum laude, Central Mich. U., 1954; M.A., Mich. State U., 1961; postgrad. U. Wyo. Ph.D. (hon.), Colo. Christian Coll., 1973. Student tchr. supr. Lakeview Sr. High Sch., Battle Creek, Mich., 1954-57; dept. head Utica (Mich.) Sr. High Sch., 1957-59; bus. tchr., adult edn. instr. Oak Park (Mich.) Sr. High Sch., 1959-62; tchr. U. High Sch., Laramie, Wyo., 1963; instr. dept. office adminstrn. and secretarial sci. U. Wyo., 1963-65; faculty Central Mich. U., Mt. Pleasant, now asst. prof. bus. data processing and bus. edn.; acting dir. N. campus Data Processing Center, 1966-71. Asst. adviser Wyo. Vocational Edn. Tchr. Conf., 1963. Mem. Nat., North-Central, Mich. bus. edn. assns., Nat., Mich. edn. assns., Mich. Assn. Higher Edn., Internat. Soc. Bus. Edn., Soc. Automation in Bus. Edn., Smithsonian Assos. Home: 1211 Glen Av Mount Pleasant MI 48858

MCPHAIL, MARY KUJAWA (MRS. HUGH DUNCAN MCPHAIL), physician; b. Luck, Poland, Dec. 28, 1920; d. Jacob and Vera Makarewich Kujawa; B.A., U. Sask. (Can.), 1942; M.D., U. Man. (Can.), 1945; m. Hugh Duncan McPhail, Oct. 24, 1949; children—Alexandra Mary, Hugh John, Tamara Myra. Intern St. Boniface Hosp., Winnipeg, Man., Can., 1944-45; resident Univ. Hosp., Saskatoon, Sask., Can., 1959; practice medicine specializing in anesthesia, St. Walburg, Sask., 1947, Wilkie, Sask., 1948-51, North Battleford, Sask., 1959—; mem. staffs Battlefords Union Hosp., North Battleford. Sec. McPhail Air Services, Ltd., Sask., 1952—, Patco Farms, Ltd., North Battleford, 1973. Trustee North Battleford Dist. Pub. Sch., 1961—, v.p., 1967-68, pres., 1969-70. Mem. provincial bd. Riverside Home, Battleford, 1973. Mem. Dist. Med. Soc. (pres. 1972), U. Alumni Assn. Club: University (pres. 1958, 72-73), Home and School (pres. 1958) (North Battleford). Office: 500 11th Av North Battleford SK S9A 2S6 Canada

MCPHERSON, ALICE RUTH, physician, educator; b. Regina, Sask., Can., June 30, 1926; d. Gordon and Viola (Hoover) McP.; B.S., U. Wis., 1948, M.D., 1951. Intern Santa Barbara Cottage Hosp., 1951-52; resident anesthesiology Hartford Hosp., 1953; resident ophthalmology Chgo. EENT Hosp., 1953, U. Wis. Hosp., 1953-55; ophthalmologist Davis & Duehr Eye Clinic, 1955-57, Scott and White Clinic, 1958-60, Houston, 1960-62; fellow retina service Mass. Eye and Ear Infirmary, 1957-58; pvt. practice medicine, specializing in ophthalmology, retinal diseases, Houston, 1962—; mem. staffs Meth. Hosp., Houston, St. Luke's Hosp., Houston, Tex. Children's Hosp., Houston; clin. instr. U. Wis., 1956-58; clin. asso. prof. ophthalmology Baylor Coll. Medicine, Houston, 1960-63, 1969—, asst. prof. ophthalmology, 1963-69, chief retina service dept. ophthalmology, 1960—. Lectr. ophthalmology U. Tex., 1958—; cons. retinal diseases VA Hosp., 1959—, Ben Taub Hosp., Houston, 1960—. Pres. Retina Research Found., Houston. Trustee Retina Found., Boston. Diplomate Am. Bd. Ophthalmology, Am. Acad. Ophthalmology and Otolaryngology, A.C.S. Mem. A.M.A., Tex. Med. Assn., Harris County Med. Soc., Houston Ophthal. Soc., Am. Med. Women's Assn., Nat. Med. Found. for Eye Care, Pan-Pacific Surg. Assn., French Ophthal. Soc., Internat. Med. Assembly Southwest Tex., Am. Assn. Ophthalmology, So. Med. Assn., Assn. Research Ophthalmology, Assn. Am. Physicians and Surgeons, Retina Soc., Soc. Eye Surgeons, Internat. Coll. Surgeons, Am. Soc. Contemporary Ophthalmology, Pan Am. Med. Soc., Jules Gonin Club. Author: New and Controversial Aspects of Retinal Detachment, 1968, Research in prevention blindness. Office: 6436 Fannin Med Center Profl Bldg Houston TX 77025

MCPHERSON, EMMA LOU, banker; b. Pottsville, Tex., July 9, 1928; d. Winsor Barton and Emma Elmira (Clabaugh) McPherson; grad. high sch. With Hamilton Nat. Bank (Tex.), 1952—, v.p., 1970—. Home: Pottsville TX 76565 Office: Box 873 Hamilton TX 76531

MCPHERSON, MARY KATHRYN DAVENPORT (MRS. WILLIAM VANN MCPHERSON, JR.), editor; b. Durham, N.C., June 26, 1948; d. Robert Benton and Margaret Elizabeth (Smith) Davenport; B.A. in Journalism (Carl Council scholar), U. N.C., 1970; m. William Vann McPherson, Jr., Jan. 15, 1972. Staff writer Durham (N.C.) Morning Herald, 1970-71, woman's editor, 1971—. Mem. Jr. League Durham, N.C., 1974—. Bd. dirs. Allied Arts Durham, N.C., 1973—, U. N.C. Alumni Assn., 1972-73. Recipient award for best interview story N.C. Press Women, 1971, best news story, best house and garden story, best layout, 1974. Mem. Women in Communications, N.C. Press Women, Delta Delta Delta. Democrat. Methodist. Club: Hope Valley Country (Durham). Home: 108 Briarcliff Rd Durham NC 27707 Office: 115 Market St Durham NC 27702

MCQUAID, GERTRUDE ANN, telephone co. exec.; b. Belfast, No. Ireland, Nov. 2, 1924; d. William and Ellen (McKegney) McQuaid; came to U.S., 1928, naturalized, 1933; B.A., Hunter Coll., 1949; M.A., N.Y. U., 1954, postgrad., 1955-65; postgrad. Columbia, 1954-55, Coll. City N.Y., 1966-68, New Sch. for Social Research, 1970-73. Research asst. Dun & Bradstreet, Inc., N.Y.C., 1949-54; statistician Econometric Inst., Inc., N.Y.C., 1955-56; research analyst Gen. Cable Corp., N.Y.C., 1956-59; statistician Englehart, Leggett & Cornell, N.Y.C., 1959; statistician, econ. analyst, statistical economist Am. Metal Climax, Inc., N.Y.C., 1959-66; economist Bank of N.Y., N.Y.C., 1967-69; asso. economist J. Carvel Lange, N.Y.C., 1969-70; staff economist Internat. Tel. & Tel. Corp., N.Y.C., 1970—. Ind. cons. as economist for various firms. Mem. Nat. Assn. Bus. Economists, Am. Statis. Assn., N.Y. Assn. Bus. Economists, Nat. Economists Club, Met. Econs. Assn. Home: 2960 Grand Concourse Bronx NY 10458 Office: 320 Park Av New York City NY 10022

MCQUATER, BETTY MARGUERITE PHELPS (MRS. OTIS DARRELL MCQUATER), citrus co. exec.; b. Trinidad, Colo., Nov. 11, 1923; d. James Cash and Helen Marguerite (Anderson) Phelps; A.A., San Bernardino Valley Coll., 1972; m. Otis Darrell McQuater, June 19, 1943; children—Judy (Mrs. Ronald Gene Dreiman), John. Stenographer II Norton Air Base, San Bernardino, Cal., 1942-43; sec. C. of C., Colton, Cal., 1956-58; exec. sec. Cal. Citrus Pulp div. Plant Industries, Inc., Colton, 1958-68, controller, 1968—. Troop Leader Girl Scouts U.S.A., Colton, 1951-58, dir. day camp, 1955-56, chmn. council, 1956-57; pres. Colton Jr. High P.T.A., 1956-58; officer Colton Council P.T.A., 1958-59. Mem. Nat. P.T.A., Colton (pres. 1969), San Orco Dist. (chmn. No. sect. 1973) bus. and profl. women's clubs. Home: 1001 N 2d St Colton CA 92324 Office: 316 W D St Colton CA 92324

MCQUEEN, DORIS JANICE, sch. exec.; b. Marshall, Tex., May 27, 1930; d. Alvy Lee and Cora (Jones) McQueen; student Kilgore Coll., 1954-55. Sec., Office of Supt. Schs., Longview (Tex.) Ind. Sch. Dist., 1948-55, financial sec. Sch. Bd., 1955-58, dir. bus. services, 1958—. Dir. E. Tex. Tchrs. Credit Union, 1953—. Mem. Am. Bus. Women's Assn., Am., Tex. assns. sch. bus. ofcls., Tex. Tchrs. Assn., N.E.A. Presbyn. Home: 2605 Fleetwood Longview TX 75601 Office: 515 N Court St Longview TX 75601

MCQUEEN, MARGARET LOUISE WARNKEN, civic worker; b. Austin, Tex., Sept. 30, 1912; d. Edwin and Louise (Walton) Warnken; B.A., U. Tex., 1933, M.A., 1934; postgrad. Tulane Sch. Social Work, 1935, La. State U., 1936, Radcliffe Coll., 1936-37; m. Bryce Ryan, Aug. 10, 1935 (div. Dec. 1953); 1 son, Bruce Barnett; m. 2d, Robert C. McQueen, Sept. 30, 1955 (div. Aug. 1967). Research editor (Ford Found. grantee) Cornell Social Sci. Research Center, 1953-54; research editor, analyst Tex. Research League, Austin, 1954-61; dir. research, information Tex. Social Welfare Assn., Austin, 1961-63; health program analyst Statewide Program Com. for Mental Health and Mental Retardation Planning, Austin, 1963-64; asso. dir. Community Council of Austin and Travis County, Austin, 1964-70; vocational counselor Tex. Rehab. Commn., Austin, 1970—; teaching cons. U. Tex. Head Start Tchrs., summer 1965; cons. Lear Sigler, Inc., 1967-68, Voit Tech. Corp., Tex., 1968—. Sec. bd. dirs. Austin Symphony Orch. Soc. Mem. Women in Communications, Delta Delta Delta. Democrat. Author: (with Robin Williams) Schools in Transition, 1954. Home: Route 9 Box 815 Austin TX 78703 Office: 105 W Riverside Dr Austin TX 78704

MCQUILLAN, ELIZABETH, ednl. adminstr.; b. Hudson, Mass., May 1, 1918; d. William A. and Julia A. (O'Neil) McQuillan; B.S., Regis Coll., 1940; M.Ed., Boston U., 1950; postgrad. Boston Coll., Framingham State Coll., Worcester State Coll. Tchr., Hudson High Sch., 1941-61, dir. guidance, 1961-68, asst. prin., 1968—, dir. Adult Evening Sch., 1968-69. Real estate broker, 1940—. Mem. Mass. Assn. Women Deans and Counselors, Am. Personnel and Guidance Assn., Middlesex County Tech. Assn. (exec. bd. 1964-67), Nat., Mass. secondary sch. prins. assns., Regis Coll. Alumnae Assn., Boston U. Alumni Assn., St. Michael's Ladies Sodality. Club: Regis (Framingham). Home: 8 Kathleen Rd Hudson MA 01749

MCQUILLAN, MARGARET MARY, pub. co. exec.; b. N.Y.C.; d. John A. and Margaret (Higgins) McQuillan; A.B., Coll. New Rochelle, 1945; M.A., Columbia, 1948. With Harcourt Brace Jovanovich, Inc. (formerly Harcourt, Brace & World), N.Y.C., 1949—, asst. sec., 1960-70, sec., 1971—. Home: 125 Crestwood Av Tuckahoe NY 10707 Office: 757 3d Av New York City NY 10017

MCQUILLEN, LINDA KAY, lawyer; b. Okmulgee, Okla., Mar. 16, 1944; d. James Dudley and Virginia (Thomas) McQuillen; B.S., U. Okla., 1966, J.D. (Law Sci. Acad. Am. fellow, Liberty Nat. Bank & Trust Co. scholar), 1969. Admitted to Okla. bar, 1969; atty. Cities Service Oil Co., Tulsa, 1969—. Jr. Achievement adviser, 1970-71, 74-75. Republican state committeewoman, 1968-70. Mem. Am. Assn. U. Women, Am. (com. 1969—), Okla. bar assns., Mid Continent Oil and Gas Assn. (mem. com. 1972—), Kappa Beta Pi, Alpha Gamma Phi Beta. Methodist (youth coordinator 1973-74, dist. shepherd 1974—). Club: Evening Pilot Tulsa (publicity com. 1973-74, editor Newspaper 1973-74, rec. sec. 1974-75, chmn. outreach div. 1974-75). Home: 3287 S Cincinnati St Tulsa OK 74105 Office: PO Box 300 Tulsa OK 74102

MCQUITTY, EDITH ANGEL (MRS. JOSEPH GUY MCQUITTY), librarian; b. St. Louis, Nov. 16, 1912; d. Frederick Francis and Amelia Edith (Maunder) Zelle; A.B., U. Mo., 1934; m. Joseph Guy McQuitty, June 8, 1935; children—Jacqueline (Mrs. Michael B. Kavanaugh), Robert. With St. Louis Pub. Library, 1955-63; asst. librarian St. Louis Police Library, 1963-65, librarian, 1965—. Mem. Spl. Libraries Assn. (sec. Greater St. Louis chpt. 1967-68, employment chmn. 1970-72). Home: 2875 Derhake Rd Florissant MO 63033 Office: 315 S 12th St St Louis MO 63102

MCQUITTY, MARTHA WARREN (MRS. JAMES THOMAS MCQUITTY), physician; b. Hartwell, Ga., May 4, 1913; d. Mark Thornton and Sarah (Herndon) Warren; B.S., U. Ga., 1934; M.S. (fellow), Emory U., 1935; M.D., Med. Coll. Ga., 1939; m. James Thomas McQuitty, Sr., Apr. 11, 1941; children—James Thomas, Joseph Warren, Martha (Mrs. John William Mister, Jr.), Sarah Jane. Intern, Touro Infirmary, New Orleans, 1939-40, courtesy staff, 1950—; resident pediatrics, Egleston Hosp., Atlanta, 1940-41; resident pediatrics Charity Hosp. of La., New Orleans, 1941-42, sr. vis. physician, 1960—; instr. pediatrics Med. Coll. Ga., Augusta, 1943-44; practice medicine, specializing in pediatrics, New Orleans, 1960—; clinician City Health Dept., New Orleans, 1946—; asso. clin. prof. pediatrics La. Sch. Med., La. State U., New Orleans, 1960—; mem. staffs Touro Infirmary, La. Charity Hosp. (both New Orleans). Pediatric cons. Child Devel. Program Total Community Action. Mem. La. Med. Soc., Orleans Parish Med. Soc., New Orleans Pediatrics Soc., Phi Beta Kappa, Phi Kappa Phi. Home: 32 Killdeer St New Orleans LA 70124 Office: 3600 Prytania St New Orleans LA 70115

MCRAE, VERA MARIE, advt. agy. exec.; b. Moline, Ill., Jan. 14, 1939; d. Melford G. and Inez Marie (Edwards) McRae; student Normal U. Exec. sec. Deere & Co., Moline, Ill., 1958-62; sec. U.S. Hdqrs. Army, Heidelberg, Germany, 1962-63; exec. sec. Champion Papers, Chgo., 1964-65; with Stern, Walters & Simmons, Inc., Chgo., 1966—, v.p. adminstrn., 1970—. Home: 301 Eugenie St Chicago IL 60614 Office: 150 E Huron St Chicago IL 60611

MCSHERRY, ENID FORD JONES, coll. ofcl.; b. New Haven, Apr. 23, 1940; d. William Ford and Elinor (MacBrayne) Jones; A.A., Briarcliff (N.Y.) Coll., 1960; student N.Y. Sch. Interior Design, 1961, Silvermine Coll. Art, 1961-62; m. John Anthony McSherry, Jan. 21, 1967. Asst. to dir. devel. Met. Mus. Art, N.Y.C., 1965-70; dir. alumnae affairs Finch Coll., N.Y.C., 1970—, also editor alumnae publns. Mem. Am. Alumni Council, Alumnae Adv. Center. Home: 130 E 94th St New York City NY 10028 Office: 52 E 78th St New York City NY 10021

MCSWEEN, SALLY FOSTER (MRS. HAROLD BARNETT MCSWEEN), civic worker; b. New Orleans, Nov. 6, 1927; d. Charles Shearer and Bessie (Long) Foster; B.A., Tulane U., 1948; postgrad. La. State U., 1949-50; m. Harold Barnett McSween, Dec. 21, 1948; children—John Charles, Robert Douglas, Elizabeth, Sally Foster. Pres., Alexandria (La.) Service League, 1964-65; v.p. Alexandria Community Concert Assn., 1965—; bd. mem. Rapids Symphony Orch., 1967—, fund raising chmn., women's com., 1969; bd. mem. YWCA, Alexandria, 1963-66; pres. bd. trustees Kent Plantation House, Inc., 1970—. Mem. Chi Omega. Methodist (chmn. kindergarten 1969—). Clubs: Matinee Musical (Alexandria), Alexandria Golf and Country; Kenwood, 86th Congress (Washington). Home: Grove Lane Alexandria LA 71301

MCSWEENEY, JOSEPHINE, reference librarian, educator; b. N.Y.C., May 5, 1931; d. Martin Patrick and Nora (Molloy) McSweeney; B.A., State U. N.Y. at Plattsburgh, 1951; M.A., Columbia, 1952; M.L.S., Pratt Inst., 1960. Tchr. Bd. Edn., Huntington Station, N.Y., 1951-54; tchr. Dependent Sch. System, Japan, 1954-55, Phillippine Islands, 1955-56, Germany, 1956-58, Italy, 1958-59; reference librarian, asso. prof. Pratt Inst. Library, Bklyn., 1960—. Mem. Pratt Inst. Alumni Soc. (exec. council, v.p. 1972-73), Pratt Inst. Faculty Council, Am. Library Assn. (life), Am. Assn. U. Profs. (chpt. sec-treas. 1965-67), Met. Coll. Inter Library Assn. (sec.-treas. 1964-66), Pratt Inst. Grad. Library Sch. Alumni Assn. (exec. bd. 1962-64, 66-68, 70-72, v.p. 1964-66, pres. 1967-69), Vols. of the Shelter, Beta Phi Mu (chpt. treas. 1970—). Clubs: Book League of N.Y.; N.Y. Library. Home: 453 E 14th St New York City NY 10009 Office: Pratt Institute Library Brooklyn NY 11205

MCTAVISH, RUTH SHIRLEY (MRS. HAROLD B. MCTAVISH), librarian; b. Central City, Ia., Dec. 5, 1902; d. Karl Godfrey and Clara Catherine (Kolb) Schmickle; B.A., U. No. Ia., 1925; postgrad. U. Ia., 1928; m. Harold B. McTavish, May 28, 1932; children—Donald G., Marian (Mrs. Ronald L. Siders), Bruce B. Instr. English, pub. schs., Cherokee, Ia., 1925-27; tchr. English, librarian, pub. schs., Northwood, Ia., 1928-29; librarian pub. schs., Cedar Rapids, 1929-32; organizer, dir. health sci. library St. Luke's Meth. Hosp., 1960-69; planner, organizer, dir. Mercy Hosp. Library, 1969—. Mem. Ia. Regional Med. Program Adv. Com. on Libraries, 1970-72. Mem. Med. Library Assn., Ia. Library Assn. Presbyn. Mem. Order Eastern Star. Home: 3015 Kenridge Terrace NE Cedar Rapids IA 52402 Office: 701 10th St SE Cedar Rapids IA 52403

MCVAY, ROSE ROMEO, lawyer; b. Italy, May 27, 1911; d. Frank and Mary (Licata) Romeo; student Ohio State U., 1932-35; LL.B., Akron Law Sch., 1939; m. Horace McVay, Jan. 8, 1938 (dec. Nov. 1968); children—Noreen Mary, Mary (Mrs. John D. Menches). Admitted to Ohio bar, 1944; individual practice law, Akron. Mem. Ohio, Akron bar assns., Cath. Daus. Am. Democrat. Roman Catholic. Clubs: Quota, St. Paul's Study (Akron). Address: 6009 Manchester Rd Akron OH 44319

MCVAY, SHIRLEY JOAN, constrn. co. exec.; b. Gassville, Ark., June 17, 1937; d. L. R. and M. Maye (Powell) Byrd; grad. high sch.; m. L. McVay (div.); children—Larry, Sherri. Owner, corporate sec. Wiseman Homes, Inc., Lexington, Ky., 1965—. Mem. Lexington Real Estate Bd.; mem. exec. com. Com. to Insure Good Govt.; mem. adv. com. Water Quality Control Com. Mem. Republican Exec. Com., Fayette, Ky., 1966-72; mem. Fayette County Rep. Adv. Com., 1967-72; alternate del. Rep. Nat. Conv., 1972. Bd. dirs., treas. Lexington Housing for Handicapped. Mem. Lexington Home Builders Assn. (dir., pres.-elect). Mem. Order Eastern Star. Office: 3080 Richmond Rd Lexington KY 40502

MCVEY, JANICE MARTENE, coll. adminstr.; b. Neelyville, Mo., Feb. 25, 1934; d. Kenneth R. and Wanda Lucille (Brandon) McVey; B.S. in Edn., Ark. State U., 1961. Tchr. schs. in Mo., 1952-54, 61-62; with Allstate Ins. Co., 1954-60; asst. club dir. Army Spl. Services, Heidelberg, Germany, 1962-64; customer service adviser Gen. Telephone Co., Bloomington, Ill., 1964-68; asso. dir. admissions Lindenwood Coll., St. Charles, Mo., 1968-71; dir. admissions Coll. of Ozarks, Clarksville, Ark., 1971—, also mem. admissions com. Learning Disabilities Center. Mem. Nat. Assn. Coll. Admissions Counselors, So. Assn. Admissions Counselors, Mo. Tchrs. Assn., Alpha Phi. Methodist. Mem. Order Eastern Star, White Shrine. Home: 503 Ash St Clarksville AR 72830

MCWHINNEY, MADELINE H. (MRS. JOHN DENNY DALE), economist; b. Denver, Mar 11, 1922; d. Leroy and Alice (Houston) McWhinney; B.A., Smith Coll., 1943; M.B.A., N.Y. U., 1947; m. John D. Dale, June 23, 1961; one son, Thomas Denny. Economist, Fed. Res. Bank N.Y., 1943-73, chief financial and trade statis. div., 1955-59, mgr. market statistics dept., 1960-65, asst. v.p., 1965-73; pres. First Women's Bank, N.Y.C., 1974—; trustee Retirement System Fed. Res. Bank, 1955-58. Trustee Carnegie Corp. N.Y. Recipient Smith Coll. medal, 1971, Alumni Achievement award N.Y. U. Grad. Sch. Bus. Adminstrn. Alumni Assn., 1971. Mem. Am. Finance Assn. (past dir.), Money Marketeers (v.p. 1960, pres. 1961-62), Nat. of Bank Women, Alumni Assn. Grad. Sch. Bus. Admin. N.Y.U. (dir. 1951-63, pres. 1957-59), Am. Econ. Assn., Soc. Meml. Center, Phi Beta Kappa. Home: PO Box 458 Red Bank NJ 07701 Office: First Women's Bank 111 E 57th St New York City NY 10022

MCWHINNIE, MARY ALICE, educator; b. Chgo., Aug. 10, 1922; d. David Anthony and Ruth M. (Brann) McWhinnie; B.S., DePaul U., 1944, M.S., 1946; Ph.D., Northwestern U., 1952. Faculty zoology DePaul U., Chgo., 1952—, prof., 1960—, acting chmn. dept. biol. scis., 1964-66, chmn. dept., 1966-68. Mem. panel on biology and medicine Nat. Acad. Scis., 1973—. Am. Soc. Physiology fellow, summer 1956; Lalor Found. fellow, summer 1957; NSF research grantee, 1958-60, 60-66, Antarctic div. grantee, 1962-63, 65, 67, 70-72, 73-74. Mem. Am. Inst. Biol. Scis., A.A.A.S., Midwest Benthological Soc., N.Y. Acad. Scis., Am. Soc. Zoologists, Soc. for Cell Biology, Biophys. Soc., Soc. for Cryobiology, Marine Tech. Soc., Arctic Inst. N.Am., Internat. Oceanographic Found., Ill. Acad. Scis., Internat. Assn. for Gt. Lakes Research, Sigma Xi. Contbr. articles to profl. jours. Home: 746 S Wesley Av Oak Park IL 60304 Office: 1036 Belden Av Chicago IL 60614

MCWHIRTER, GLENNA SOTIER, newspaper editor; b. Peoria, Ill., June 28, 1929; d. Alfred Leon and Lorene Garnet (Short) Sotier; B.A., U. Mich., 1951, postgrad., 1956-57; m. Edward Ford McWhirter, May 16, 1952 (div. Aug. 1973); children—Suzanne, Charles, James. Editorial asst. to pub. Detroit Labor Trends, 1951-53; editorial asst. Detroit news bur. McGraw-Hill. Pub. Co., 1953-55; staff writer, women's dept. Detroit Free Press, 1963-65, staff writer, city desk, 1965-69, asst. city editor, 1969—; copywriter Campbell-Ewald Advt., Detroit, 1964-65. Recipient gold medallion Detroit Press Club, 1965, award for best one-minute color film comml. N.Y. Film Critics, 1965. Mem. Women in Communications, Detroit Press Club (sec. 1973), Sigma Delta Chi. Home: 660 Whitmore Rd Detroit MI 48203 Office: 321 W Lafayette St Detroit MI 48231

MCWHITE, IRENE MCVAY, educator; b. Atlanta, Aug. 1, 1943; d. Hugh and Irene (Yeilding) McVay; A.B. in Psychology, Ga. Coll., Milledgeville, 1965; M.S. in Psychology, U. Ga. at Athens, 1966; m. James Henry McWhite, Sept. 12, 1970. Chief psychometrist, counselor Guidance Center, U. Ga. at Athens, 1966-68; instr. psychology West Ga. Coll., Carrollton, 1968-70; psychoednl. evaluator Ga. Dept. Edn., Atlanta, 1970; asst. prof. psychology Birmingham (Ala.)-So. Coll., 1971-74; coordinator consultation and edn. Eastside Mental Health Center, Birmingham, 1974—. Mem. Am., Southeastern psychol. assns., Psi Chi, Pi Gamma Mu. Baptist.

MCWHORTER, SUZANNE SCHIRRMAN (MRS. PAUL MCWHORTER), educator; b. Portsmouth, O., Jan. 16, 1931; d. George J. and Frances (Hicks) Schirrman; B.S., U. Ark., 1952, M.B.A., 1954; Ph.D., Ohio State U., 1957; m. Paul McWhorter, Dec. 20, 1949. Instr. mgmt. U. Ark., 1951-54; teaching fellow Ohio State U., 1954-57; asst. prof. bus. Tex. Technol. Coll., 1957-58; asso. prof. bus. N. Tex. State U., Denton, 1958-71, prof. marketing, communications and internat. bus., 1971—. Commr. Gov.'s Commn. on Status of Women in Tex., 1970-72. Mem. Tex. Assn. Coll. Tchrs., Am. Marketing Assn., Southwestern Social Sci. Assn., D.A.R., Dallas Symphony League, Fine Arts Soc. Tex. (dir. 1973—), Pan Hellenic Alumni Assn. (pres. 1961-63), Beta Gamma Sigma, Delta Delta Delta Alumnae Assn. (pres. 1971-73), Phi Gamma Nu. Presbyn. Home: 2825 Foxcroft Circle Denton TX 76201

MCWILLIAMS, BETTY JANE, speech pathologist, educator; b. Martins Ferry, O.; d. Harry J. and Martha (McClure) McWilliams; B.S., Ohio State U., 1949; M.S., U. Pitts., 1950, Ph.D., 1953. Instr. to asso. prof. U. Pitts., 1953-69, prof., dir. Cleft Palate Center, 1969—; cons. hosps. and crippled children's socs. Bd. dirs. United Cerebral Palsy, Am. Cleft Palate Ednl. Found. Fellow Am. Speech and Hearing Assn. (mem. joint com. speech and dentistry); mem. Am. Psychol. Assn., Am. Cleft Palate Assn. (pres. 1965). Contbr. articles to profl. jours. Asso. editor Cleft Palate Jour., 1970—. Home: 512 Bigham Rd Pittsburgh PA 15211

MCWILLIAMS, DORIS DALEY (MRS. WILLIAM GILBERT MCWILLIAMS), civic worker; b. Indpls., Oct. 1, 1924; d. Roland Bigelow and Mary Adelaide (Pitkin) Daley; B.A., Butler U., 1946; m. William Gilbert McWilliams, Sept. 25, 1946; children—Mary (Mrs. Robert Martin Fredriksen), Marjorie (Mrs. John Howard Payne), Martha Lucinda. Past sec. League Women Voters, Middletown Twp., N.J., past v.p., pres., Shreveport, La., past sec. of La., now state pres.; mem. exec. com. La. Com. for Humanities, 1972—; mem. state and local govt. com. Goals for La., 1972—; mem. La. Library Devel. Com., 1972—. Bd. dirs. Am. Cancer Soc., Middletown, N.J., Shreveport, 1965-71; bd. dirs. Shreveport chpt. Nat. Conf. Christians and Jews, 1971—. Mem. Mortar Bd., Phi Kappa Phi, Alpha Chi Omega. Presbyn. Home: 10021 Smitherman Dr Shreveport LA 71105 Office: Municipal Auditorium Shreveport LA 71101

MCWILLIAMS, JETTIE MANNING CRISP (MRS. WILEY E. MCWILLIAMS, JR.), educator; b. nr. Mt. Creek, Ala., May 5, 1928; A.B., Berea Coll., 1958; postgrad. Bluffton Coll., 1957, Ohio State U., 1964; M.A. (Haggin fellow), U. Ky., 1963, Ed.D., 1966; m. Robert Alton Crisp, Jr., May 5, 1949 (dec. Mar. 1961); children—Jane Rae, Victoria Anne, Kathryn Dianne, Yvonne Nell; m. 2d, Wiley E. McWilliams, Jr., June 4, 1967 (dec. Apr. 1972). Pub. high sch. English tchr., Wheelwright, Ky., 1950-52, Pandora, O., 1959-61; guidance counselor Bryan St. Jr. High Sch., Lexington, Ky., 1963-64; instr. U. Ky., Lexington, 1965-66; asst. prof. ednl. psychology and guidance, then asso. prof. Tenn. Tech. U., Cookeville, 1966—. Cons. ednl. systems and Project Upper Cumberland, Cookeville, 1967-70. Leader, Girl Scouts U.S.A., Beaverdam, O. 1959-61; sec. Cookeville P.T.A., 1960-61, historian, 1961-62, 2d v.p., 1967-68. Bd. dirs. Tenn. Vocational Tng. Center, Cookeville, Wesley Found. Named

Outstanding Alumnus, Bluffton Coll., 1971. Mem. Am. Assn. U. Women, Am. Personnel and Guidance Assn., Nat. Vocational Guidance Assn., Am. Coll. Personnel Assn., Am. Assn. U. Profs. (pres. Tenn. Tech. chpt. 1973-74), Tenn. Assn. Counselor Educators and Suprs., Nat., Tenn. edn. assns., Internat. Platform Assn., Kappa Delta Pi, Beta Sigma Phi. Contbr. articles to profl. jours. Home: 1131 Flatt Circle Cookeville TN 38501

MCWILLIAMS, MARGARET ANN (MRS. DONALD A. MCWILLIAMS), educator; b. Osage, Ia., May 26, 1929; d. Alvin Randall and Mildred Irene (Lane) Edgar; B.S., Ia. State U., 1951, M.S., 1953; Ph.D., Ore. State U., 1968; m. Donald A. McWilliams, Sept. 20, 1953; children—Roger, Kathleen. Asst. prof. home econs., Cal. State U., Los Angeles, 1961-66, asso. prof., 1966-68, prof., chmn. dept., 1968—. Mem. Greater Los Angeles Nutrition Council, 1967—; mem. home econs. adv. coms. East Los Angeles Coll., Harbor Coll. Recipient nat. founders fellowship Phi Upsilon Omicron, 1964, Nat. Found. fellowship, 1967; alumni centennial award Ia. State U., 1971. Mem. Am. Home Econs. Assn., Am. Dietetic Assn., Inst. Food Technologists, Am. Inst. Chemists, Am. Pub. Health Assn., Phi Kappa Phi, Phi Upsilon Omicron, Omicron Nu, Iota Sigma Pi, Sigma Alpha Iota. Author: Food Fundamentals, 2d edit., 1974; Nutrition for the Growing Years, 1967; (with L. Kotschevar) Understanding Food, 1969; Illustrated Guide to Food Preparation, 1970; (with L. Davis) Food for You, 1971; The Meatless Cookbook, 1973; (with F. Stare) Living Nutrition, 1973, Nutrition for Good Health, 1974. Tech. cons. Am. Home Econs. Assn. Jour. Home: 1916 N Gilbert St Fullerton CA 92633

MCWILLIAMS, ROSE ANNA PEJASZEK (MRS. ERWIN SHERWOOD MCWILLIAMS), hosp. adminstr.; b. Ft. Sheridan, Ill., June 18, 1930; d. Stanley Ployer and Frances Edna (Smith) Pejaszek; R.N., U. Denver-Presbyn. Sch. Nursing, 1951; m. Erwin Sherwood, June 18, 1952; children—Karen Ann, Karla Diane, Gary Lynn. Staff nurse Presbyn. Hosp., Denver, 1951-52, Malone Hogan Hosp., Big Spring, Tex., 1952; instr. Reagan County Hosp., Big Lake, Tex., 1966-67, charge nurse, 1967-69, dir. nursing, 1969-72, adminstr., 1972—. Active P.T.A., Candy Striper Orgn. Bd. dirs. Reagan Meml. Hosp., Big Lake, 1972-74, Big Country Tb Assn., San Angelo, Tex., 1970-74. Home: 1010 Main St Big Lake TX 76932 Office: 805 Main St Big Lake TX 76932

MEACHAM, CATHERINE VOSE UNDERWOOD (MRS. NOLAND FONTAINE MEACHAM), editor; b. Detroit, June 2, 1908; d. Robert Boyden and Katherine (Edgington) Underwood; A.B., Southwestern U., 1929; m. Noland Fontaine Meacham, Nov. 8, 1933; (dec. Dec. 1969); children—Catherine (Mrs. Ralph F. Colin, Jr.), Fontaine (Mrs. David F. Taylor). Mem. editorial staff Press-Scimitar, Memphis, 1941—, fashion editor, 1963-74. Mem. D.A.R., Colonial Dames, P.E.O., Alpha Omicron Pi. Clubs: Le Bonheur, Les Passees (Memphis). Home: 172 Kimbrough St Memphis TN 38104

MEAD, PEARL EDELMANN, advt. agy. exec.; b. N.Y.C., N.Y., May 3, 1914; d. Alfred M. and Rebecca (Sarzin) Edelmann; B.S., Bklyn. Coll., 1935; m. Daniel S. Mead, Oct. 22, 1954 (dec. Apr. 1971). Dietitian, Hosp. for Joint Diseases, 1935-38, Beth David Hosp., 1938-39; with L.C. Gumbinner Advt. Agy., N.Y.C., 1953-54; with William Douglas McAdams, Inc., advt. agy., N.Y.C., 1954—, media dir., 1956—. Guest lectr. Bklyn. Coll. Pharmacy, 1965, N.Y. U. Sch. Advt., 1965. Named Advt. Woman of Year, Gamma Alpha Chi, 1964; recipient Pres.'s award Pharm. Advt. Club, 1971. Mem. Advt. Fedn. Am. (dir. 1964-65, Advt. Women N.Y. (dir. 1964-67), Pharm. Advt. Club (dir. 1967, 68), Gamma Alpha Chi (hon.). Home: 185 E 85th St New York City NY 10028 Office: 110 E 59th St New York City NY 10022

MEAD, SYLVIA (ALICE) EARLE (MRS. GILES W. MEAD), biologist, aquanaut, educator; b. Gibbstown, N.J., Aug. 30, 1935; d. Lewis Reade and Alice Freas (Richie) Earle; student St. Petersburg Jr. Coll.; B.S., Fla. State U., 1955; postgrad. (NSF fellow) U. Va., summer 1955; M.A. (NSF, Gen. Foods fellows), Duke, 1956, Ph.D., 1966; postgrad. U. Fla., 1959-60, 64; m. Giles W. Mead; children—Parry W., Jane W., Elizabeth R., J. Richie, G. Whitaker, Gale Graf. Asst. in botany Fla. State U., summer 1952, herbarium asst., 1955; herbarium asst. Duke, 1956-57, U. Fla., 1959-60; fisheries biologist U.S. Fish and Wildlife Service, Beaufort, N.C., 1957; instr. botany St. Petersburg Jr. Coll., 1963-64; marine biologist, phycologist NSF Internat. Indian Ocean Expdn., 1964, Southeastern Pacific Biol. Oceanographic Program, Caribbean Sea, Panama, Ecuador, Chile, Galapagos Islands; research asso. Cape Haze Marine Lab., 1965, resident dir., 1966; research scholar Radcliffe Inst., 1967-68; research fellow Farlow Herbarium, Harvard, 1967—; mission leader Tektite II Underwater Research project, V.I., 1970; coordinator, lectr. marine ecology and aqua culture U. Cal. at Los Angeles Extension; asso. sci. Marine Sci. Inst., U. So. Fla.; research asso. in botany U. Cal. at Berkeley; asso. in botany Los Angeles County Mus. Natural History. Diver, New Eng. Aquarium and Steinhart Aquarium, Smithsonian-Link Man-in-Sea Project, Bahamas, 1968, also cons.; cons. U.S. Sea Grant Program, 1969—; cons. on study marine plants Smithsonian Tropical Research Inst., Panama, 1971; chief scientist R/V Searcher Cruise 72-1, Galapagos Islands, 1972; chief scientist, aquahaut Mission P-7 Flare Project, Fla. Keys, 1972. Recipient Conservation Service award Dept. Interior, 1970, commendation County of Los Angeles, 1970, Woman of Year award Los Angeles Times, 1970; named hon. citizen of Chgo., 1970. Mem. Bot. Soc. Am., Phycological Soc. Am., Internat., Brit. phycological socs., Internat. Assn. Plant Taxonomists, Am. Soc. Ichthyologists and Herpetologists, Ecol. Soc. Am., Internat. Assn. Profl. Diving Scientists, Steinhart Divers, Sigma Xi. Co-editor: Scientific Results of the Tektite Project, 1972. Research on systematics and ecology of marine plants in Gulf of Mexico, N.W. Indian Ocean, S.W. Pacific Ocean, interrelationship between marine animals and plants. Home: 100 S June St Los Angeles CA 90004 Napa CA Office: Los Angeles County Museum of Natural History Los Angeles CA 90007

MEADE, SISTER ELLEN PATRICIA, hosp. adminstr.; b. N.Y.C.; d. Patrick and Ellen (Sullivan) Meade; B.S. in Bus. Adminstrn., Coll. St. Elizabeth Convent, N.J., 1953, M.S., St. Louis U., 1958. With HOLC, 1937-46; adminstrv. asst., office mother gen. Sisters of Charity of St. Elizabeth, 1946-54; asst. adminstr. St. Elizabeth Hosp., Elizabeth, N.J., 1954-57, adminstr., 1957—. Vice pres. region 3 Union County Mental Health Hosp. and Health Council; pres. Elizabeth Tri-Hosp. Fund; mem. Union County Charter Commn. Fellow Am. Coll. Hosp. Adminstrs.; mem. N.J. Cath. Hosp. Conf., St. Louis U. Hosp. Adminstrn. of Alumni Assn. (exec. council, past pres.), Mental Health Assn. Union County, Union County Social Planning Council, Am. Assn. Maternal and Child Health, Hosp. Personnel Mgmt. Assn., Nat. Conf. Cath. Charities, Am. Assn. Hosp. Accountants, Am., N.J., Union County (chmn. exec. com.) hosp. assns., Eastern Union County C. of C. Address: 225 Williamson St Elizabeth NJ 07207

MEADOWS, LAURA LOU, lawyer; b. Cin., May 10, 1932; d. Alvin Louis and Laura Marie (Fox) Muckerheide; B.A., Miami U., 1952; J.D., Harvard, 1960. Admitted to Mass. bar, 1960, N.Y. bar, 1967; asso. firm Choate, Hall & Stewart, Boston, 1960-66, Lord, Day & Lord, N.Y.C., 1966-68, Shearman & Sterling, N.Y.C., 1969; tax lawyer Mobil Oil Corp., N.Y.C., 1970-74; asst. tax dir., tax counsel Merck & Co., Inc., Rahway, N.J., 1974—. Served to 1st lt. USAF, 1954-57. Mem. Am. Bar Assn. (tax sect. 1960—), Assn. Bar N.Y.C. (tax com. 1971—). Methodist. Club: Harvard of New York City. Home: 351 E 84th St New York City NY 10028 Office: 126 Lincoln Av Rahway NJ 07065

MEAHL, HELEN EIDSON BUCHANAN, educator, family sociologist; b. Springdale, Ark., Sept. 3, 1912; d. Robert A. and Ruby O'Neal) Eidson; B.S. in Home Econs., U. Ark., 1936, M.A. in Sociology, 1954; Ed.D. in Family Relationships, Pa. State U., 1961; m. Leslie W. Buchanan, June 3, 1937 (dec. 1944); m. 2d, Robert P. Meahl, Aug. 15, 1964; 1 dau., Helen Buchanan (Mrs. James O. Crust); stepdaus.—Ann B. (Mrs. Harold Lane), Sue B. (Mrs. Guy Eroh). Home demonstration agt. Nevada County, Ark., 1936-37; tchr. NYA project, 1940-41; mem. Ark. legislature from Nevada County, 1945-46; edn. sec. for ch., Prescott, Ark., 1946-48; asst. editor weekly mag. Ark. Baptist, 1948-49; dean women, publicity dir. Central Coll., Little Rock, 1949-50; Pub. schs. tchr., 1937-38, 51-54; instr., then asst. prof. Pa. State U., 1954-61; asso. prof. child devel. and family relationships U. Tenn., 1961-64; asso. prof. sociology Juniata Coll., Huntingdon, Pa., 1965-70, also supr. child services project; faculty dept. sociology Pa. State U., University Park, 1970—. Family life cons., speaker on family. NSF Postdoctoral fellow. Mem. Nat. Council Family Relations (mem.-at-large exec. com. 1961-64, sec. 1965-66, chmn. certification and standards com., mem. adv. com. 1963—), Am. Social Health Assn., Am. Home Econs. Assn. (chmn. sect. family relations and child devel. 1964-65), Am. Sociol. Assn., Soc. Research Child Devel., Am. Assn. U. Profs., Eastern Sociol. Soc., Am. Assn. U. Women. Author: (with Jessie Bernard and William M. Smith Jr.) Dating, Mating and Marriage, 1958; also articles. Home: PO Box 90 Boalsburg PA 16827 Office: 504 Liberal Arts Bldg University Park PA 16802

MEALING, ISABEL THORPE, social worker; b. Townsend, Ga., Oct. 4, 1907; d. Elisha McDonald and Maude (Davis) Thorpe; student Ga. State Tchrs. Coll., 1924-26; A.B., Randolph-Macon Woman's Coll., 1928; M.S.W., Tulane U., 1943; postgrad. U. Va., 1929; m. John Pace Mealing, Jr., Aug. 15, 1929 (div. Dec. 1939); children—Elisha Thorpe, Margaret Mae (Mrs. Wayne Frederick Orlowski). Visitor, Fulton County Dept. Pub. Welfare, Atlanta, 1937-38; dir. McIntosh County Dept. Pub. Welfare, Darien, Ga., 1938-40; child welfare cons. State of Ga., Atlanta, 1941-44; social worker A.R.C., Lawson Gen. Hosp., Atlanta, 1944-45; asst. field dir. Lawson Gen. Hosp., Atlanta and Station Hosp., Fort Benning, Ga., 1945-46; chief social work service VA Regional Office, Fort Jackson, S.C., 1947-48; pub. welfare officer Dept. Army, Japan, 1949-51; sr. social worker Valley Forge Army Hosp., 1951; chief social work Service VA Hosp., Richmond, Va., 1951-52, VA Center, Wadsworth, Kan., 1952-68, Dublin, Ga., 1968—. Mem. Social Planning Council Leavenworth, Kan., 1952-68, v.p., 1955-56, 67-68, pres. 1956-57; chmn. welfare com. Mayor's Adv. Com. Leavenworth, 1968; organizational bd. mem. Leavenworth Community Action Program, 1966; adviser social work Explorer Scouts, Dublin, 1972. Bd. dirs. Leavenworth Mental Health Assn., 1959-68, pres., 1964-66; bd. mem. A.R.C., Leavenworth, 1960-68, chmn. services to mil. families com.; mem. bd. govs. United Fund, Leavenworth, 1967-68; bd. dirs. YWCA, Leavenworth, 1962-68, pres., 1964-65; bd. dirs. Laurens County Mental Health Assn., pres., 1972—. Mem. Nat. Assn. Social Workers (exec. bd. Mo.-Kan. chpt. 1954-56, pres. Central Ga. chpt. 1970-71, del. assembly 1971), Am. Assn. Med. Social Workers (pres. Mo.-Kan. chpt. 1954-55), Nat., Internat., Ga. (mem. nominating com. 1945) confs. on social welfare, Daus. Am. Colonists, Community Resources Forum (pres. 1971-72), Nat. Soc. Colonial Dames XVII Century (surgeon gen. Matthew Fuller chpt.). Club: Pilot (Dublin). Address: VA Center Dublin GA 31021

MEANS, FLORENCE CRANNELL, author; b. Baldwinsville, N.Y., May 15, 1891; d. Phillip Wendell and Fannie Eleanor (Grout) Crannell; student Henry Read Sch. Art, 1910-11; spl. student Kansas City Bapt. Theol. Sem., 1912, U. Denver, 1923-24, McPherson (Kan.) Coll., summer 1922-29; m. Carleton Bell Means, Sept. 19, 1912; 1 dau., Eleanor Crannell (Mrs. Angus C. Hull, Jr.). Lectr., Writers Conf. Rocky Mts., U. Colo., 1947, 48. Recipient ann. nat. award Child Study Assn., 1945, Nancy Bloch award, 1957; Churchmanship citation Central Bapt. Sem., 1962. Mem. Internat. Inst. Arts and Letters (asso.), Authors League Colo., Delta Kappa Gamma, Zeta Tau Alpha. Baptist. Clubs: Denver Woman's Press, Soroptimist International (hon.). Author: (with Harriet Fullen) Rafael and Consuelo, 1929; A Candle in the Mist, 1931; (with Frances Somers Riggs) Children of the Great Spirit, 1932; Ranch and Ring, a Story of the Pioneer West, 1932; Dusky Day, 1933; A Bowlful of Stars, 1934; Rainbow Bridge, 1934; Penny for Luck, 1934; Tangled Waters, 1936; The Singing Wood, 1937; Shuttered Windows, 1938; Adella Mary in Old New Mexico, 1939; Across the Fruited Plain, 1940; At the End of Nowhere, 1940; Children of the Promise, 1941; Whispering Girl, 1941; Shadow Over Wide Ruin, 1943; Teresita of the Valley, 1943; Peter of the Mesa, 1944; The Moved Outers, 1945; Great Day in the Morning, 1946; Assorted Sisters, 1947; The House Under the Hill, 1949; (with Carl Means) The Silver Fleece, 1950; Hetty of the Grande Deluxe, 1951, Carvers' George, 1952; Alicia, 1953; The Rains Will Come, 1954; Sagebrush Surgeon, 1956; Knock At the Door, Emmy, 1956; Reach for a Star, 1957; Borrowed Brother, 1958; Emmy and the Blue Door, 1959; Sunlight on the Hopi Mesas, the Story of Abigail E. Johnson, 1960; But I Am Sara, 1961; That Girl Andy, 1962; Tolliver, 1963; It Takes All Kinds, 1964; Us Maltbys, 1966; Our Cup is Broken, 1969; Smith Valley, 1973. Contbr. fiction articles, verse to mags. Home: 595 Baseline Rd Boulder CO 80302

MEANS, JULIA JUANITA, librarian; b. Dale, Okla.; d. David Howard and Kate Lee (Cormack) Means; B.S., U. Okla., 1933; M.A., U. Denver, 1952. Tchr., Tecumseh (Okla.) Pub. Schs., 1925-31, Maud (Okla.) Pub. Schs., 1931-32, Graham (Okla.) Pub. Schs., 1933-37, Nicoma Park (Okla.) Pub. Schs., 1937-43; jr. accountant Douglas Aircraft Co., Oklahoma City, 1943-45; circulation asst. Oklahoma City Pub. Library, 1945-49, reference asst., 1949-50; faculty Oklahoma City U., 1950-73, asso. prof. library sci., reference librarian 1969-73; serials librarian Oklahoma City Southwestern Coll., 1973—. Mem. Am. Assn. U. Women, Am., Okla. (sec. 1962), Ark., Southwestern library assns., Chi Delta Phi. Democrat. Presbyn. Home: 1501 NW 31st St Oklahoma City OK 73118

MEANS, MARIANNE HANSEN, newspaper columnist; b. Sioux City, Ia., June 13, 1934; d. Ernest Maynard and Else Marie Johanne (Andersen) Hansen; B.A., U. Neb., 1956. Copy editor Lincoln (Neb.) Jour., 1955-57; woman's editor No. Va. Sun, Arlington, 1957-59; Washington bur. corr. Hearst Headline Service, 1959-61, White Ho. corr., 1961-65; King Features Syndicate columnist, 1965—. Mem. D.C. Woman's Savs. Bond Com., 1959-62. Recipient Front Page award N.Y. Newspaper Women, 1962. Mem. White House Corrs. Assn., Phi Beta Kappa, Delta Delta Delta, Theta Sigma Phi, Kappa Tay Alpha, Gamma Alpha Phi. Clubs: Federal City, Washington Press. Author: The Woman in the White House, 1963. Home: 1521 31st St NW Washington DC 20007 Office: 1701 Pennsylvania Av Washington DC 20020

MEANY, SARAH ANN, occupational therapist; b. Warren, O., Feb. 20, 1928; d. Edward Anthony and Ida May (Van Cleef) Meany; B.A., Lake Erie Coll. for Women, 1950; certificate in Occupational Therapy, Washington U., St. Louis, 1962. Recreational asst. USAF, Korea, 1952-53, recreation program dir., 1954-55, recreation dir., P.R., 1956-58, U.S., 1958-60; occupational therapist Canton (O.) Rehab. Center, 1962-64, Childrens Rehab. Center, Warren, 1964-66; dir. occupational therapy services Hillside Hosp., Warren, 1966—; owner-operator Pirate Sam Co.; clin. instr. Washington U., 1973—. Mem. Am., Ohio (pres. 1968-70) occupational therapy assns. Club: Altrusa (Warren). Book reviewer Am. Jour. of Occupational Therapy, 1964-66. Home: 957 Adelaide St SE Warren OH 44484 Office: 8747 Squires Lane NE Warren OH 44484

MEARA, NAOMI MARIE, educator; b. Columbus, O., Feb. 26, 1937; d. Joseph Raymond and Naomi (Conway) Meara; B.A., Ohio State U., 1958, B.S., 1960; M.A., Syracuse U., 1962; postgrad. U. Ill., 1964-65; Ph.D., Ohio State U., 1967. Service rep. Ohio Bell Telephone Co., Columbus, O., 1958-59; student asst. Ohio State U., 1959-60; grad. asst. Syracuse U., 1960-62; residence hall dir. U. Ill., 1962-65; psychology trainee VA, 1965-66; teaching asst. Ohio State U., 1965-67; asst. prof. Wis. State U., LaCrosse, 1967-69, asso. prof. psychology, 1969-70; sr. vis. research asso. Ohio State U., Columbus, 1970-72; asso. prof., chmn. dept. psychology Ohio Dominican Coll., Columbus, 1972—. Mem. Am. Psychol. Assn., Am. Assn. Personnel and Guidance, Am. Assn. U. Profs., Sigma Xi, Mortar Bd., Pi Lambda Theta. Home: 1526 Presidental Dr Columbus OH 43212

MEARIG, JUDITH SUZANNE, educator, child psychologist; b. Reading, Pa., May 23, 1935; d. Luther Benjamin and Erma Viola (Angstadt) Mearig; student U. St. Andrews (Scotland), 1956-57; A.B., Oberlin Coll., 1957; M.A., U. Mich., 1961, Ph.D. (Horace H. Rickham scholar, fellow), 1964. Elementary tchr. Sayville (N.Y.) Pub. Schs., 1957-59, 60-61; sch. psychologist Univ. Sch., Ann Arbor, Mich., 1961-63; coordinator grad. program in sch. psychology, asso. prof. ednl. psychology St. Lawrence U., Canton, N.Y., 1964—, coordinator counseling center, 1964-69; cons. psychologist Sunmount State Sch., Tupper Lake, N.Y., 1966-67, St. Lawrence State Hosp. Children's Unit, 1969-70; psychologist Franklin County Outpatient Diagnostic Clinic, 1967-68; pvt. practice child psychology, Potsdam, N.Y., 1967—. Chmn., County Headstart Adv. Council, 1967-68, mem., 1968-69; mem. nursery ednl. adv. council State U. Coll., Canton, 1968—. Bd. dirs. Potsdam Child Devel. Center. Diplomate Am. Bd. Profl. Psychology. Fellow Am. Orthopsychiat. Assn.; mem. Am., N.Y. psychol. assns., Phi Kappa Phi, Pi Lambda Theta. Home: 17 Bay St Potsdam NY 13676 Office: Atwood Hall St Lawrence U Canton NY 13617

MEARS, DARLENE WANDA HIND (MRS. DAVID EDMUND MEARS), lawyer; b. Oceanside, N.Y., July 19, 1946; d. Ira Flint and Wanda Mary (Terry) Hind; student El Camino Jr. Coll., 1965; B.A., Valparaiso U., 1968, J.D., 1971; m. David Edmund Mears, Jan. 25, 1969. Admitted to Ind. bar, 1971; nat. examining and closing atty. Chgo. Title & Trust Co., 1971-72; pvt. practice law, Hammond, Ind., 1971—; dep. prosecutor Lake County Ind. Juvenile Div., Hammond, 1972—. Dir. Calumet Area Humane Soc., Inc., Hammond, 1971—, atty., 1971-74. Mem. Am. Assn. U. Women, Am., Ind., Hammond bar assns., Nat. Orgn. Women, Animal Protection Assn., Fund for Animals, Wild Horse Organized Assistance, Pet Pride, Defenders of Wildlife, Nat. Cat Protection Soc., Humane Soc. U.S. Valparaiso U. Sch. Law Alumni Assn. (treas. 1973-74, dir.), Phi Alpha Delpha, Kappa Tau Zeta (sec. alumni 1972). Home: 3133 Condit St Highland IN 46322 Office: 5217 Hohman Av Hammond IN 46320

MEBANE, MARGARET ANNE, psychiat. social worker; b. Burlington, N.C.; d. Sidney Robert and Margaret (Murphy) Mebane; B.A., U. N.C., 1954, M.S.W., 1960; m. Carl Putnam Parker. Case work asst. Lee County Dept. Pub. Welfare, Sanford, N.C., 1954-56, Alamance County Dept. Pub. Welfare, Burlington, 1956-58; psychiat. social worker, social service VA Hosp., Salem, Va., 1960-64; social work unit coordinator, social service VA Hosp., Salisbury, N.C., 1964—. Field work instr. U. N.C. Sch. Social Work, 1965-70, Livingstone Coll., 1971-72, U. S.C., 1972-73. Mem. Nat. Assn. Social Workers, Acad. Certified Social Workers, D.A.R. Methodist. Home: 803 Wesley Dr Brentwood Acres Salisbury NC 28144

MECHANIC, JANET LOVE (MRS. MELVIN OLIVER ARONSON), optometrist; b. Cambridge, Mass., June 30, 1921; d. Leon and Clarice Olga (Hameson) Mechanic; Dr. Optometry, Mass. Coll. Optometry, 1942, postgrad., 1946—, U. Me., 1942-43, Frankfort Arsenal, 1943-44; m. Melvin Oliver Aronson, Oct. 25, 1953; children—Leanne Ruth, Joyce Merle. Chief optical insp. Boston Ordnance Dept., 1942-45; editor sci. optical material Mass. Inst. Tech., Cambridge, 1945-46; pvt. practice optometry, Brookline, Mass., 1947—; head optometrist New Eng. Hosp., 1949-70; cons. indsl. optometrics, 1949-70; optometrist for various rehab. instns. Mem. Mass. (contact lens com.) Boston Socs. optometrists, Am. Optometric Assn., Mass. Coll. Optometry Alumni Assn. (class agt. 1967-69), Epsilon Omicron Sigma. Contbr. articles to profl. jours. Home: 105 Gardner Rd Brookline MA 02146 Office: 1146 Beacon St Brookline MA 02146

MECOM, DOROTHY MAE (MRS. ROBERT WAYNE MECOM), banker; b. Tulsa, Oct. 25, 1933; d. Hulet Mayes and Myrtle Ione (Silkey) Waybourn; grad. high sch.; m. Robert Wayne Mecom, July 25, 1952; children—Larry Wayne, Pamala Ione, James Michael, Robby Dale. Proof operator 4th Nat. Bank, Tulsa, 1951-53; proof operator and bookkeeper Peoples State Bank, Tulsa, 1953-55; bookkeeper Admiral State Bank, Tulsa, 1956-57; head bookkeeper North Side State Bank, Tulsa, 1958—, asst. cashier, 1970—. Mem. Tulsa Jr. Girls Activities Assn. (treas. 1969—), Am. Inst. Banking, Nat. Assn. Bank Women. Clubs: Tulsa Bankers Wives, Northeast Mustangs Quarterback (dir. girls 1968-70). Home: 3544 E King Pl Tulsa OK 74115 Office: 601 E Apache St Tulsa OK 74106

MEDALIA, JUDITH HILDA KLUBOCK (MRS. AVROM I. MEDALIA), ednl. adminstr.; b. Boston, Nov. 4, 1926; d. Max Bernard and Mollie (Ruttenberg) Klubock; B.S., Wheelock Coll., 1959, M.S. in Edn., 1967; m. Avrom I. Medalia, Feb. 15, 1956; children—Jonathan, James, Deborah, Janet. Substitute tchr. Newton (Mass.) pub. schs., 1960-63; tchr. emotionally disturbed children South Shore Mental Health Center, Quincy, Mass., 1967-68; practicum supr. grad. students Wheelock Coll., Boston, 1967; supr. Community Clin. Nursery Schs. and Day Care, Dept. Mental Health, Comm. Mass., Region V, Dedham, Mass., 1968—. Adv. team mem. Mass. Office for Children Region V, Newton, 1973-74; coordinator Brookline-Newton Presch. Program, 1974—; cons. Head Start and pvt. nursery schs. Mem. Democratic Ward Com., 1960-62; mem. aux. Dem. Ward Com., 1964-70. Nat. Inst. Mental Health grantee, 1966-67. Mem. Boston Assn. Edn. Young Children, Am. Assn. Mental Deficiency. Home: 30 Dorr Rd Newton MA 02158 Office: Peabody Sch 474 Brookline St Newton MA 02159

MEDARIS, FLORENCE ISABEL, osteo. physician and surgeon; b. Kirksville, Mo.; d. Charles Edward and Nellie (Finley) Medaris; B.A., Coll. Wooster, 1932; D.O., Kirksville Coll. Osteopathy and Surgery, 1939; postgrad. U. Wis., Marquette U. Pvt. practice osteo. medicine and surgery, Milw., 1940—. Active YWCA, Milwaukee County Mental Assn., Milw. Art Center, Friends of Art; mem. med. bd. dirs. Milw. Soc. Multiple Sclerosis Soc., 1973—; mem. Mayor's Beautification Com., 1968—. Dir. Zonta Manor, 1957-67, Brace Fund Bd. of Advt. Women of Milw., 1958-64, pres. bd., 1962-63; bd. mem. Bookfellows Milw.; finance com. Coll. Womens Club Found., 1971—. Mem. Am. Osteo. Assn. (com. mental health 1964), Wis. Assn. Osteo. Physicians and Surgeons, Milw. Dist. Soc. Osteo. Physicians and Surgeons, Am. Coll. Gen. Practitioners, Applied Acad. Osteopathy, Am. Assn. U. Women, Inter-Group Council Women (pres. 1947-49, dir.), Wis. Pub. Health Assn., Council for Wis. Writers, Photog. Soc. Am., Wis. Acad. Scis., Arts and Letters, Delta Omega (nat. pres. 1952-53). Presbyn. Club: Zonta (bd. mem. Milw. 1968-69). Home: 1121 N Waverly Pl Milwaukee WI 53202 Office: 161 W Wisconsin Av Milwaukee WI 53203

MEDBERRY, LYNN (MRS. EDWARD FRANCIS FREEMAN), advt. exec.; b. Detroit, Apr. 10, 1920; d. Laurence Earl and Myrtle (Stewart) Morris; student Wayne U., 1938-41; m. Edward Francis Freeman, Nov. 17, 1956. Regional advt. mgr. J.L. Hudson, Detroit, 1940-41; asst. advt. mgr. I. Himelhoch, 1941-42; asst. advt. mgr. Bullock's Wilshire, Los Angeles, 1942; writer news bur. Ford Motor Co., Dearborn, Mich., 1942-45; mgr. radio sta. YWR, Willow Run, Ford Motor Co., Detroit, 1945; pub. dir. Mich. Nat. Found. Infantile Paralysis, Detroit, 1945-46; mng. editor Milady of Cal., Los Angeles, 1946-49; co-owner Medberry & Barth, advt. agy., 1949-51; account exec. Carson/Roberts Advt. Agy., 1951-56, v.p. women's products, 1958-66, sr. v.p., dir. creative merchandising, after 1966; prin., owner Klein Medberry Advt., Inc., Beverly Hills, Cal., 1973—; marketing dir. Cole of Cal., 1956-58; dir. Fashion Group, Los Angeles. Mem. Los Angeles County Democratic Central Com., 1947-49. Bd. dirs. Little Flower Home, 1949-53. Recipient Advt. Lulu, 1st place award for most unique method of advt., Los Angeles Advt. Women, 1952, award for best direct mail campaign, 1955, award for qualitative research, 1961-64, award for best complete campaign, 1964. Mem. Mus. Assn. (asso.). Mem. Ch. of Religious Sci. Home: 9432 Sierra Mar Pl Los Angeles CA 90069 Office: 9024 Olympic Blvd Beverly Hills CA

MEDBERY, MAXINE MITSUYE, physician; b. Los Angeles, Mar. 28, 1938; d. Robert Akira and Michi (Sagawa) Kubota; B.A., U. Mich., 1962, M.D., 1967; m. Bruce Wolters Medbery, Oct. 5, 1965 (div. May 1967). Intern, Orange County Med. Center, Orange, Cal., 1967-68; resident obstetrics and gynecology Meml. Hosp., Long Beach, 1968-69; emergency physician Daniel Freeman Hosp., Inglewood, Cal., 1969—. Mem. Am. Coll. Emergency Physicians. Home: 13360 Maxella Av Marina del Rey CA 90291 Office: 333 N Prairie St Inglewood CA 90301

MEDEIROS, ELIZABETH JONES, educator; b. Berryville, Va., Sept. 17, 1924; d. Thomas and Maria Thornton (Shugart) Jones; B.S. in Edn., Longwood Coll., 1946; postgrad. U. Hawaii, 1951-72, Pepperdine U., Los Angeles, 1967-68; m. Joseph Soares Mederios, Feb. 3, 1951; 1 dau., Rose Marie (Mrs. Dwayne L. McCorkle). Tchr. schs. in Va. and Hawaii, 1945-47; stenographer, Hawaii, 1947-51; tchr. Maui (Hawaii) Dept. Edn., 1951-52, 54, 65, 65-70; dir. Maui Econ. Opportunity, Inc., 1965-67; vice prin. Lihikai Elementary Sch., Kahului, Hawaii, 1970-74; prin. Maunaloa (Hawaii) Elementary Sch., 1974—. Tchr. tng. cons. Head Star, Guam, summers 1967, 68. Chmn., Maui Com. Status Women, 1973-74. Mem. Maui Bus. and Profl. Women's Club (pres. 1973-74), Delta Kappa Gamma. Mem. United Ch. Christ (v.p. 1973-75, chmn. bd. Christian edn. 1971). Home: Kula Maui HI 96790 Office: PO Box 128 Maunaloa HI 96770

MEDER, MARGARETE ANNA (MRS. FRANCIS MEDER), banker; b. Dortmund, Germany, Mar. 3, 1920; d. Alfred George and Regina (Lippe) Claus; grad. Comml. Coll. Dortmund, 1938; m. Francis Meder, May 10, 1945; children—Peter F., Robert V. Came to the U.S., 1951, naturalized, 1957. Clerk, Prodn. Control, Harpener Bergbau, Dortmund, W. Germany, 1938-43; supr. systems Dornier Aircraft and Zeppelin Luftschiffbau, Friedrichshafen Am Bodensee, 1943-45; with Wilmette (Ill.) State Bank, 1952—, bookkeeper, 1952-57, head bookkeeper, 1957-62, asst. cashier, 1962-69, asst. v.p., 1969-70, v.p., 1970, v.p., comptroller, 1971—. Mem. Nat. Assn. Bank Women. Republican. Roman Catholic. Club: Executives (Chgo.). Home: 1431 Forest Av Wilmette IL 60091 Office: 1200 Central Av Wilmette IL 60091

MEDER, MARYLOUISE DUNHAM, educator; b. Danbury, Conn.; d. Francis Bryan and Ruth (Dunham) Meder; B.A., U. Va., 1947; M.L.S., Carnegie Mellon U., 1949; M.A., Trinity Coll. at Hartford, 1962; Ph.D., U. Mich., 1964. Cataloger Ohio State U., Columbus, 1949-53; asst. librarian Central Conn. State Coll., New Britain, 1953-62; asst. prof. Sch. Library Sci. Rutgers State U., New Brunswick, N.J., 1964-66; prof. Tex. Woman's U. Sch. Library Sci., Denton, 1967-71; prof. librarianship Kan. State Tchrs. Coll., Emporia, 1971—. Mem. A.L.A., Kan. Library Assn., Assn. Am. Library Schs., Bibliog. Soc. Am., Mediaeval Acad., Conn. Hist. Soc., Am. Assn. U. Profs., Am. Assn. U. Women, Beta Phi Mu. Republican. Conglist. Home: 1233 Tomahawk Rd Emporia KS 66801

MEDINA, ANN HILLYER, network corr.; b. N.Y.C., May 9, 1943; d. Harold Raymond and Janet Brevoort (Williams) Medina; B.A. in Philosophy, Wellesley Coll., 1965; M.A. in Philosophy (Herschel fellow 1966), U. Chgo., 1967; postgrad. U. Ill., 1968, Cleve. State Law Sch., 1971-72. Legal researcher Am. Bar Found., Chgo., 1966; news trainee NBC News, Chgo., 1969, TV reporter, Cleve., 1970, network producer, 1972; network corr., documentary producer ABC News, N.Y.C., 1973—. Grad. asst. instr. philosophy U. Ill., Chgo., 1968; speaker to various groups, 1970-72. Organizer First Offender Juvenile Female Program, Chgo., 1966-67; mem. Lakeview Citizens Council, Chgo., 1968. Democrat. Club: Cosmopolitan (N.Y.C.). Home: 15 W 81st St New York City NY 10024 Office: 7 W 66th St New York City NY 10023

MEDITZ, ELIZABETH CAGNEY, coll. adminstr.; b. Poughkeepsie, N.Y.; d. Joseph Jefferson and Jeannette (Page) Cagney; B.S., Columbia, M.A., 1940; m. Walter J. Meditz, Jan. 9, 1944; children—Jeannette, Marybeth. Chmn. bus. edn. dept. Penn Hall Jr. Coll., Chambersburg, Pa., 1940-42; instr. commerce Mary Washington Coll., U. Va., 1942-44; tchr. social sci. and bus. Montclair (N.J.) pub. schs., 1964-68; registrar Katherine Gibbs Sch., 1968-70; asst. dir. charge acad. placement Columbia, 1970-71; dean admissions Edglewood Cliffs (N.J.) Coll., 1971-74; asst. dir. admissions Centenary Coll. for Women, Hackettstown, N.J., 1974—. Pres. Parents Guild, St. Mary's Sch., 1956-58. Mem. Am. Assn. U. Women (pres. br. 1961-63). Clubs: Columbia Faculty; Englewood Field; Buck Hill Falls Tennis. Home: 268 Chestnut St Englewood NJ 07631 Office: Centenary Coll Women Hackettstown NJ 07840

MEDLEY, PATRICIA JOAN, former govt. ofcl.; b. Pasadena, Cal., June 17, 1928; d. Howard A. and Lois (Krauter) Medley; B.A., Pepperdine Coll., 1950; M.S.W., U. Cal. at Berkeley, 1952. Psychiat. social worker A.R.C., 1952-55; chief psychiat. social worker USAF, Parks AFB, Cal., 1955-58; chief psychiat. social worker Santa Clara County Mental Health Services, San Jose, Cal., 1958-65, adminstr. mental health, 1965-72; part-time work Psychiat. Med. Group, San Jose, 1963—. Cons. Conf. Local Mental Health Dirs., State Dept. Mental Hygiene, 1968—, Parents of Handicapped Children in Santa Clara County, 1964-66, State of Cal. Dept. Edn., 1960-61, Am. Psychiat. Assn., 1968-69. Mem. Santa Clara County Social Planning Council, 1967—, Mid-Pennisula Com. on Services to Children, 1966-68. Mem. Nat. Assn. Social Workers (registrar 1964-69), Assn. Mental Health Adminstrs., Am. Acad. Social Workers., Santa Clara County Mental Health Assn., Ret. Officers Assn., Am. Assn. Ret. Persons. Home: 21491 Burr Way Hayward CA 94541

MEDVEN, DUSANKA ANNA ZUZIC, chem. engr.; b. Zagreb, Yugoslavia; d. Marko and Zora (Popovic) Zuzic; candidate engr. Inst. Tech., U. Belgrad, 1951; student Sorbonne, 1951-52; Chem.E., Cath. U. Louvain, 1955; grad. student Carnegie Inst. Tech., 1957-60; m. Anton Medven, May 14, 1967 (div. 1974); 1 dau., Ann Dana. Came to U.S., 1957, naturalized, 1963. Research chem. engr. Ateliers de Constructions d'Evere, Brussels, Belgium, 1956-57; research chemist Am. Petroleum Inst. Research Project at Carnegie Isnt. Tech., 1957-61; chem. engr. phys. properties data cons. Union Carbide Corp., 1961-72; sr. chem. engr., engring. data specialist Thermodynamic Research Center, Tex. A. and M. U., College Station, 1972—. Pres., Divine Shepherd of Souls Found., Inc. Mem. Soc. Women Engrs. (membership chmn. Pitts. sect. 1960-61), Am. Chem. Soc., Am. Inst. Chem. Engrs., Am. Assn. U. Women, Bus. and Profl. Womens Clubs. Home: 305 Fairway Dr Bryan TX 77801 Office: Thermodynamic Research Center Tex A and M U College Station TX 77843

MEE, MARY JEAN ALLEN (MRS. JOHN H. MEE), lawyer; b. San Francisco, Jan. 24, 1938; d. Homer Jay and Jean Victoria (Berquist) Allen; A.A., Sacramento City Coll., 1961; student, U. Pacific McGeorge Coll. of Law, 1967; m. John H. Mee, Jan. 31, 1956; children—Michael, Barbara. Tng. technician State Cal., 1958-71; admitted to Cal. bar, 1971; staff counsel Cal. State Dept. Employment Devel., Sacramento, 1971—. Mem. Am., Cal., Sacramento County bar assns., Barristers, League Women Voters, Sacramento Women Lawyers. Democrat. Home: 6541 Driftwood St Sacramento CA 95831 Office: 800 Capitol Mall Sacramento CA 95814

MEEHAN, KATHLEEN MARY, educator; b. Muncie, Ind., Nov. 28, 1904; d. Michael J. and Dora Ann (Conroy) Meehan; A.B., Ball State U., 1925, M.A., 1949. Soc. editor Muncie Star, 1924-25; tchr. Blaine Sch., Muncie, 1925-30; tchr. English, newswriting Wilson Jr. High Sch., Muncie, 1930-31; English tchr. Central High Sch., Muncie, 1931-71, English tchr. Adult Edn. Center, 1971-73, sponsor sch. newspaper, 1931-55, ann. Magician, 1931-35. Supr. publs. Muncie Community Schs., 1954-59. Recipient Distinguished Alumni award Ball State U. Alumni, 1963; named Woman of Year, Beta Sigma Pi, 1956; recipient awards including Muncie Bus. and Profl. Women's Club Civic award, 1964, 1st Pl. awards Women's Press Club of Ind., 1965, 66, 70, 71, 72, 73; Journalism Alumni award Ball State U., 1973. Mem. Nat. League Am. Pen Women (Ind. pres. 1962-64, Muncie pres. 1961-63, sec. 1969—), Ind. (publicity chmn. E. div. 1961—), Muncie tchrs. assns., Muncie Arts Assn. (sec. bd. 1951-54), Ind. High Sch. Press Assn. (div. pres. 1948-49), Ball State U. Alumni Assn. (exec. bd. 1960-63), Women in Communication (chpt. pres. 1958-60, historian 1969—), Delta Kappa Gamma, Alpha Chi Omega, Tri Kappa (past chpt. v.p.). Democrat. Roman Catholic. Clubs: Administrative Women's Muncie Schs. (pres. 1964-65), Women's Press, Alpha Alumnae. Columnist, feature writer Lafayette edit. Our Sunday Visitor. Contbr. stories, articles to publs. Home: 2125 W Main St Muncie IN 47303

MEEK, MARGUERITE PATTERSON, storage co. exec.; b. Texarkana, Tex., Dec. 17, 1904; d. Robert Alexander and Mona (Rountree) Patterson; student Sul Ross State Tchrs. Coll., 1922-23, Centenary Coll., 1926-28; m. Benjamin Louie Meek, Dec. 25, 1927; children—Barbara Rose, Elmo Coleman (dec.). With Kroger Co., Air Reduction Sales Co., Shreveport, La.; sec.-treas. Dixie Moving and Storage Inc., Monroe, La., 1954—, B.L. Meek Inc., Monroe, 1972—. Mem. Bus. and Profl. Women's Club (past pres.), Altrusa (pres.). Mem. Ch. Christ. Home: 703 Tarver St Monroe LA 71201 Office: 313 Walnut St Monroe LA 71201

MEEK, VURNETTA GETHORIA, ednl. adminstr.; b. Marshall, Tex., Oct. 28, 1947; d. Edward Johnson and Marjorie Faye (Yancy) Meek; student Wiley Coll., 1966-67; B.A., Xavier U. La., 1971. Dir. pub. relations, coll. photographer Wiley Coll., Marshall, 1971—. Home: 2503 Holland St Marshall TX 75670

MEEKER, BARBARA MILLER (MRS. WILLIAM MEEKER), artist, educator; b. Peru, Ind., Dec. 31, 1930; d. George Curtis and Ruth (Burton) Miller; A.B. in Art, cum laude, DePauw U., 1952; studied with various artists; m. William F. Meeker, Aug. 10, 1952; children—David George, Stephen George. Tchr. art Hammond Pub. Schs., 1952-57; asst. prof. art Purdue U., 1965—. Exhibited one man shows: Purdue U., Calumet Campus, Bibo Gallery, Peoria, Ill., Oak Park-River Forest High Sch., (Ill.), others; exhibited Art Galleries, Park Forest (Ill.) Rental and Sales, Town Gallery, Munster, Ind., Station Gallery, Crown Point, Ind., South Bend (Ind.) Art Center, John Herron Art Gallery, Indpls., Indpls. Mus. Art, Bibo Gallery, Peoria, Ill., Left Bank Art Gallery, Saugatuck, Mich.; represented pvt. collections. Judge, Juried Art Shows and Regional Sci. and Art Fairs. Mem. State House (Ind.) Art Com., 1963-65. Mem. Hammond City Panhellenic Assn. (pres. 1961), Am. Assn. U. Profs., Hoosier Salon, Indiana Artists, Gary Artists League, Artists Equity, Kappa Kappa Gamma Alumnae Assn. (pres. 1961). Home: 8314 Greenwood Av Munster IN 46321 Office: 2233 171st St Hammond IN 46319

MEEKER, SYLVIA CARSTENS (MRS. RUSLEY COLEY MEEKER), educator; b. N.Y.C., Sept. 22, 1931; d. Cedric Stephens and Louise (Moyle) Carstens; A.B. (Sophia Smith scholar), Smith Coll., 1953; certificate in Occupational Therapy, Columbia, 1956; m. Rusley Coley Meeker, Feb. 21, 1957; children—Rusley Coley, David Robert. Chief occupational therapist U.S. Naval Hosp., Corona, Cal., 1956-57; staff occupational therapist U.S. Naval Hosp., San Diego, 1957-58, San Diego Childrens Hosp., 1958-59; chief occupational therapist Palm Beach County Home, West Palm Beach, Fla., 1966-70; instr. Palm Beach Jr. Coll., Lake Worth, Fla., 1970—. Served with Med. Service Corps, USNR, 1956-58. Fellow, grantee Smith Coll. So. Mountain Workship, 1953. Mem. Am., Fla. occupational therapy assns., World Fedn. Occupational Therapists. Democrat. Presbyn. (trustee). Home: 969 SW 9th Av Boca Raton FL 33432 Office: 4200 S Congress Av Lake Worth FL 33460

MEEKS, LINDA BROWER (MRS. JACK NORWOOD MEEKS, JR.), educator; b. Toledo, June 9, 1945; d. James Calvin and Elsie Margaret (Day) Brower; B.S., U. Toledo, 1968; M.S., U. Wis., 1969; m. Jack Norwood Meeks, Jr., Dec. 19, 1970; children—Kristen Ann. Asst. prof. health edn. Ohio State U., Columbus, 1969—. Mem. A.A.H.P.E.R. (Midwest chmn. elementary health sect. 1973), Ohio Council Family Relations (dir. 1971-73), Alpha Kappa Delta. Author: (with John Burt) Education for Sexuality: Concepts and Programs for Teaching, 1970, 75, Toward A Health Sexuality, 1973. Home: 1825 Victorian Ct Columbus OH 43220

MEEMA, SILVIA VEERUS (MRS. HELDUR ERIK MEEMA), physician; b. Tallinn, Estonia, Sept. 19, 1923; d. Johannes Voldemar and Olga Louise (Wutter) Veerus; student U. Tartu, Estonia, 1942-44; Med. Lic., Karolinska Institutet, Stockholm, Sweden, 1951; m. Heldur Erik Meema, July 6, 1946; children—Ann Karin, Karl Eric, Kersti, Marion. Intern, Toronto (Ont., Can.) Gen. Hosp., 1953-54; physician Gage Inst. Chest Clinic, Toronto, 1954-56; asso. staff, research dept. radiology Toronto Western Hosp., 1962—. Licentiante Med. Council Can. Mem. Fedn. Med. Women Can., Assn. for Advancement Baltic Studies. Home: 38 Princess Margaret Blvd Islington Ontario Canada Office: 399 Bathurst St Toronto ON Canada

MEGLIN, MARY ANN KEMENT (MRS. ANTHONY J. MEGLIN), librarian; b. Suffield, Conn., Aug. 15, 1926; d. Stanley Joseph and Patronela (Mickunas) Kement; grad. high sch.; m. Anthony J. Meglin, May 31, 1947; children—Barbara M., Linda M. Sec., Conn. Bank & Trust Co., 1945-49; librarian, McKew Parr Library, Chester, Conn., 1955—. Asso. mem. Burndy Library, Norwalk, Conn. Bd. dirs. Chester Pub. Library, 1973—. Mem. Am., Conn. library assns. Home: Railroad Av Chester CT 06412 Office: Straits Rd Chester CT 06412

MEGLINO, JOSEPHINE BUGLIONE (MRS. NICHOLAS MEGLINO), mfg. co. exec.; b. Bklyn., Dec. 28, 1928; d. Donato and Olimpia (Ceretta) Buglione; B.A., Hunter Coll., 1949, M.A. (fellow), 1951; m. Nicholas Meglino, May 13, 1951; children—Patricia, James, Don. Tchr. math. N.Y.C. pub. schs., 1950-57; engring. asst. Bell Telephone Lab., 1951-52; v.p. Jodee Plastics, Inc., Bklyn., 1964-66; pres. Patrician Products Inc., Bklyn., 1966—. Home: 107 Ridgewood Av Brooklyn NY 11208 Office: Patrician Products Inc 483 E 99th St Brooklyn NY 11236

MEGOWAN, PEGGY CHARLENE, editor; b. Mexia, Tex., Dec. 9, 1931; d. Charles Louis and Naomi Catherine (Stewart) Wofford; student Los Angeles Trade Tech. Jr. Coll., 1961; children—Debra Kay (Mrs. Mathew Sweeney), Mark Edward, Patrick Michael. Cashier, Nautilus Hotel, Miami Beach, Fla., 1952; overseas and long distance telephone operator; profl. model; publicity, promotion and photography North Hollywood Figure Skating Club; freelance photojournalist for Los Angeles Examiner, Los Angeles Times, Great Falls (Mont.) Tribune, A.P., U.P.I., Long Beach News Service, Valley Times, Santa Barbara News Press, Jerry Schnitzer Prodns., Frank Werber Enterprises, to 1964; contbg. editor Sports Car Graphic mag., 1964-65; editorial asst. Teen, Rod and Custom mags., 1965; asst. to editor Super Tuning and How to Build and Race a Hot Rod, 1966; mng. editor Raceway mag., 1966; chief copy editor Legal Directories Pub. Co., 1967-68; asso. editor Nat. Dragster, 1968-69; asst. editor Argus Pub. Corp., mng. editor 1001 Custom and Rod Ideas, asst. editor Off-Road Vehicles mag., 1970; freelance editor, 1970-71; asst. mng. editor, prodn. editor Wheels Afield, 1971-73; mng. editor Par Golf mag., 1973, Photog. Equipment Buyer's Guide, 1973—all for Petersen Pub. Co. Judge, U.S. Figure Skating Assn. Served as 2d lt. Civil Air Patrol, 1956. Mem. Am. Auto Racing Writers and Broadcasters Assn. Home: 11018 Aqua Vista North Hollywood CA 91602 Office: 8490 Sunset Blvd Los Angeles CA 90069

MEHAU, MILDRED GRACE, realty exec.; b. Trinidad, Colo., Aug. 9, 1918; d. Selby and Grace (Lee) Benedict; student in bus. adminstrn. Trinidad Jr. Coll., 1936-38; student in hosp. adminstr. U. Cal. at Los Angeles Extension, 1950-51; m. Henry Kalaione Mehau, Oct. 6, 1964 (dec.). Adminstr., Edgemont Hosp., Los Angeles, 1949-64; activities dir. Mauna Kea Beach Hotel, Kamuela, Hawaii, 1965-70; gen. mgr. Kona Plantations, Kailua-Kona, Hawaii, 1970—; sales rep. Tony Leeb Realty, Kailua-Kona, 1973—. Sec., USCG Aux., Los Angeles, 1950-53. Club: Catalina Island (Cal.) Yacht. Address: Kona Plantation 48 Kuakini Hwy Kailua-Kona HI 96740

MEHEARG, LILLIEN ERL (MRS. GEORGE E. VOLZ), psychologist, educator; b. Parkdale, Ark.; d. Thomas Albert and Lillie (Massey) Mehearg; B.A., Millsaps Coll., 1957; M.A., La. State U., 1958; Ph.D., U. So. Miss., 1963; m. George E. Volz, Jan. 2, 1956 (dec. 1959). Intern psychology N.Y. State Dept. Mental Hygiene, Poughkeepsie, 1959-60; psychologist, dir. Lake Charles (La.) Mental Health Center, 1960-61; psychologist, research dir. Hammond (La.) Mental Health Center, also coordinator Region VII Mental Health Planning Council, also chief psychologist Hammond State Sch. Retarded, 1962-64; asst. prof. U. So. Miss., Hattiesburg, 1964-65, asso. prof., 1965-68, prof., 1968—, dir. Psychol. Clinic, 1964—, dir. psychol. tng., 1966—. Cons. VA and various state agys.; chmn. Miss. Bd. Psychol. Examiners. Mem. Miss. Gov.'s Council on Children and Youth. Mem. Am., Miss., Southeastern, Southwestern psychol. assns., Psi Chi, Phi Kappa Phi. Home: 3601 Morningside Dr Hattiesburg MS 39401

MEHLMAN, JULIA (MRS. F.W. GREENHUT), child psychiatrist; b. N.Y.C., Oct. 8, 1907; d. Jacob S. and Regina (Seidner) Mehlman; A.B., Cornell U., 1929; M.A., Columbia, 1932; M.D., Yale, 1937; m. F. W. Greenhut, Nov. 11, 1939; 1 son, Jeffrey. Intern, Jewish Hosp., Bklyn., 1937-38; resident pediatrics N.Y.U., 1948-49; extern pediatric pathology Beth Israel Hosp., 1949; extern pediatric psychology Bell Hosp., 1949; resident N.Y. Foundling Hosp., 1950; resident psychiatry Creedmoor State Hosp., 1959-60, Hillside Hosp., 1960-62; attending pediatrician N.Y. Infirmary, 1953-61, attending psychiatrist, 1964—; staff psychiatrist Jewish Child Care Assn., 1962-64; psychiatrist N.Y.C. Bur. Child Guidance, 1964—, Lifeline Center for Child Devel., 1966—; child psychiatrist Hillside div., Queens Gen. Hosp., Great Neck, N.Y., 1964—. Instr. dental tng. for mental retardation L. I. Jewish Med. Center. Bd. dirs. Great Neck (N.Y.) Sr. High Sch. P.T.A. Mem. Am. Med. Women's Assn., Am. Acad. Pediatrics, A.M.A., N.Y. Council on Child Psychiatry, Nassau County Med. Soc., Nassau Neuro Psychiat. Soc. (chmn. com. on mental retardation). Address: 10 Preston Rd Great Neck NY 11023

MEIER, NOELLYN PIERCE HILL (MRS. MICHAEL ARTHUR MEIER), occupational therapist; b. Wilmington, Del., Dec. 24, 1944; d. Arthur Joseph and Clerna Evelyn (Pierce) Hill; student Emory U., 1962-64; B.S., U. Fla., 1966; m. Michael Arthur Meier, Aug. 17, 1968; 1 son, Robert. Staff therapist Sinai Hosp., Balt., 1967-68; therapist Diagnostic Adjustive and Corrective Center for Learning, Portsmouth, Va., part-time 1970; therapist Bapt. Hosp., Pensacola, Fla., part-time, 1971-72. Mem. Officers Wives League (treas. 1972). Home: 15282 Calle Juanito San Diego CA 92129

MEIGHAN, SISTER CECILIA, coll. pres.; b. Wilkes-Barre, Pa., Oct. 29, 1933; d. James Gibbons and Rose Angela (Timony) Meighan; B.A., Coll. Misericordia, 1958; M.A., U. Scranton, 1964; Ed.D. (Kellogg fellow), Columbia, 1972. Tchr., Diocese of Scranton (Pa.) Schs., 1956-65; instr. English dept. Mt. Aloysius Jr. Coll., Cresson, Pa., 1965-66, asso. prof., chmn. English dept., 1966-69, asst. to pres., 1971-72, pres., 1972—. Mem. Community Coll. Arena Com., United Ministries for Higher Edn. Trustee, Coll. Misericordia, Dallas, Pa.; bd. incorporators Mercy Hosp., Johnstown, Pa. Mem. Am. Assn. for Higher Edn., Assn. Governing Bds., Nat. Catholic Ednl. Assn., Pa. Assn. Two-Year Colls. (exec. com.). Address: Mt Aloysius Jr Coll Cresson PA 16630

MEILLER, JOAN MASON (MRS. RICHARD MUDIE MEILLER), child psychiatrist; b. Mineola, N.Y., June 22, 1927; d. Henry Hoezle and Chloe (Herring) Mason; A.B., Mt. Holyoke Coll., 1948; M.D., State U. N.Y., Bklyn., 1952; m. Richard Mudie Meiller, Nov. 11, 1950; children—Elizabeth, Scott, John. Intern, Norwalk (Conn.) Hosp., 1952-53; resident Duke Med. Center, Durham, N.C., 1953-58; practice medicine specializing in child psychiatry, Durham, 1958-61, Richmond, Va., 1961—; mem. staff St. Mary's Hosp., Richmond. Home: 6632 Belmont Rd Chesterfield VA 23832 Office: 3800 Patterson Av Richmond VA 23221

MEILY, ESTHER RIDENOUR (MRS. DAVID R. MEILY), educator; b. Lima, O.; d. Joshua Mechling and Jennie (Hitchkock) Ridenour; student Wittenberg U., 1926-28, Ball State U., 1956-57, Bluffton Coll., 1932-33, U. Mich., 1950-51; B.A. in Music Edn. Lawrence U., 1963; m. David R. Meily, May 23, 1934 (dec. 1972); children—Helen Adelia (Mrs. Melvin L. Bayer), Martha Frances (Mrs. Edward C. Senechal), Sara Elizabeth. Elementary vocal music tchr., Lima, 1930-34, Morgan Sch., Appleton, Wis., 1963—; substitute tchr., Washington, 1934-36, Pontiac and Birmingham, Mich., 1945-55; high sch. music tchr., Marion, Ind., 1955-58. Asst. organist Nat. City Christian Ch., Washington, 1934-36; organist, choir dir. First Bapt. Ch., Birmingham, 1950-53, All Sts. Episcopal Ch., Appleton, 1958-64, St. Thomas Episcopal Ch., Menasha, Wis., 1964—. Vol. tchr., programmer Children's Hosp., Detroit, 1950-54; dir. Civic Music Series, Marion, 1952; music tchr. Retarded Children's Sch., Marion, 1954-55; asst. music therapist Winnebago State Hosp., Oshkosh, Wis., 1967-71. Mem. Organ Guild, Wis. Acad. Arts, Nat., Wis. music educators guilds, Am. Contract Bridge League (life master). Composer: St. Thomas Mass, other sacred works. Home: 10 Brokaw Pl Appleton WI 54911 Office: St Thomas Episcopal Ch Menasha WI

MEINDERS, HILDRED MCCANTS (MRS. WESLEY H. MEINDERS), lawyer; b. Guthrie, Okla., Jan. 27, 1908; d. James Franklin and Maude Alberta (Putman) McCants; B.S., Okla. Coll. for Women, 1932; law degree John B. Ogden Sch. Law, Ardmore, Okla., 1941; m. Wesley H. Meinders, May 22, 1937; children—Janet Ruth (Mrs. K.D. Charalampous), Don W., Anne (Mrs. John H. Heaton), Mary (Mrs. Floyd W. Johnson). Tchr. pub. schs., Carter County, Okla., 1927-31; office sec. Soil Conservation Service, Ardmore, 1933-40; admitted to Okla. bar, 1942; individual practice law, Pauls Valley, 1956-61; county atty. Garvin County, Okla., 1961-67; individual practice law, Davis, Okla., 1967—. Pres. P.T.A., Wynnewood, Okla., 1945-46, Woodland, Okla., 1949-50, Yukon, Okla., 1953-54; active fund drives A.R.C., Salvation Army, Boy Scouts, Girl Scouts. Regent Okla. Coll. Liberal Arts, 1972—; bd. dirs. State P.T.A., 1943-56. Democratic precinct chmn., Pauls Valley, 1958-60. Mem. Am. Assn. U. Women (state legislative chmn. 1963-65, state bd. dirs. 1963-65), Okla. Bar Assn., Bus. and Profl. Women. Methodist. Mem. Order Eastern Star (past matron). Address: West Route Davis OK 73030

MEINERSMANN, ROSALI VERA BRONENKANT (MRS. HERMAN THEODORE MEINERSMANN), librarian; b. Milw., Mar. 21, 1918; d. George John and Marie Sylvia (Nowakowski) Bronenkant; B.A., Milw. Downer Coll., 1940; M.A., U. Wash., 1942; m. Herman Theodore Meinersmann, Dec. 10, 1945; children—Jonna (Mrs. Stephen Johnson), Karen (Mrs. Leonard Lake), Tedd George, Richard John, Mark David. Children's librarian, Youngstown, O., 1943-45; hosp. librarian Downey VA Hosp. (Ill.), 1949-51; acting librarian, Antioch, Ill., 1946; librarian, Lake Villa, Ill., 1947-51; med. librarian Maxwell AFB Hosp., 1955-57; med. librarian Del. Bd. Health, 1962-63; librarian, Simpson Sch., Camden, Del., 1964-66, Laurel (Del.) Pub. Library, 1966-69; dept. head library tech. curriculum Del. Community and Tech. Coll., Georgetown, 1969-70; adminstr. Md. Materials Center, Md. State Div. Libraries, Salisbury, 1970—. Cons. dependent's library Kindley AFB, 1958-62. Pres. Bermuda council Girl Scouts Am., 1961-62; mem. Gov.'s. Council for Women, 1970—. Bd. dirs., sec.-treas. Sussex Mental Health Assn., 1973—; bd. dirs. Sussex County Arts Council, 1970—, v.p., 1971. Mem. Laurel (Del.) Planning Commn., 1971-73. Recipient Outstanding Librarian award Maxwell AFB Hosp., 1957, Grant N.E.A., 1965, Del. Library Grant, Drexel U., 1967. Mem. Am. Assn. U. Women (v.p. Dover chpt. 1966), Audubon Soc., Nat. Parks Assn., Appalachian Trail Conf., League Women Voters, Del. Library Assn. (pres. 1971-72), Sussex County Bus. and Profl. Women (pres. 1973—), Laurel Am. Field Service (pres. 1973—). Club: New Century (Laurel, Del.). Home: 505 S Central Av Laurel DE 19956 Office: 655 S Salisbury Blvd Salisbury MD 21801

MEINKOTH, MARIAN RICHARDS (MRS. NORMAN A. MEINKOTH), educator; b. nr. Fairfield, Ill., June 30, 1914; d. Thomas E. and Bertha (Berry) Richards; B.Ed., So. Ill. U., 1935; M.A., U. Ill., 1936, Ph.D., 1947; m. Norman A. Meinkoth, Dec. 26, 1938; 1 dau., Pantip. Grad. asst. U. Ill. at Urbana, 1942-45, instr., 1945-47; mem. faculty Temple U., Phila., 1947—, asso. prof., 1961-73, prof. econs., 1973—; Fulbright lectr. Thailand, 1957-58. Home: 431 W Woodland Av Springfield PA 19065 Office: Broad and Montgomery Avs Philadelphia PA 19122

MEIR, GOLDA (CHANGED NAME FROM GOLDA MYERSON 1956), former Israeli govt. ofcl.; b. Kiev, Russia, May 3, 1898 brought to U.S., 1906; ed. pub. schs., Milw.; m. Morris Myerson, 1917; children—Menachem, Sara. Active Zionist Labor Party, Milw.; immigrated Palestine, 1921; mem. collective farm village, 1921-24; with the Solel Boneh, 1924-26; sec. Women's Labor Council, Histadruth, 1928; mem. exec. and secretariat, Fed. Labour, 1929-34; chmn. bd. dir. Workers Sick Fund, 1936; head polit. dept., Fedn. Labour, Labour party del. Actions Com., World Zionist Orgn., 1936; mem. War Econ. Adv. Council, Palestine Govt., 1939; leading mem. Hagana struggle; head polit. dept. Jewish Agy. for Palestine, 1946-48; ambassador to USSR, 1948; minister labor and social inst., 1949-52; minister of labour, 1952-56; minister fgn. affairs, Govt. of Israel, 1956-66; mem. parliament, sec. gen. Israel Labour Party, 1966-68; prime minister of Israel, 1969-74. Address: 8 Baron Hirsh St Tel Aviv Israel

MEISER, SISTER MARY ADELE, hosp. adminstr.; b. Pitts., Aug. 15, 1903; d. Joseph J. and Mamie T. (Murphy) Meiser; B.A., Duquesne U., 1930, M.A., 1933; M.B.A., U. Chgo., 1940. With Jones Merc. Agy., 1919-20; with Warrington Auto Constrn. Co., 1920-22; with Rex-Oil Co., 1922-24; novitiate Sisters St. Francis, Mt. Alvernia, Millvale, Pa., 1924-26, mem. council, 1962-74; adminstrv. asst. St. Francis Gen. Hosp., Pitts., 1926-38, asst. adminstr., 1940-58, adminstr., 1958-66, exec. dir. 1966—, also bd. dirs. adminstr. Evanston (Ill.) Hosp., 1939-40. Past cons. Nat. Center for Health Services, Dept. Health, Edn., Welfare. Bd. dirs. Lawrenceville Econ. Action Program; past trustee Point Park Coll., Pa. Citizens Council Commn. on Aging; past bd. dirs. Pitts. Playhouse. Fellow Am. Coll. Hosp. Administrs.; mem. Am. Assn. Hosp. Accountants, Am. Assn. Maternal and Infant Health, Am. Hosp. Assn., Hosp. Assn. Pa. (past v.p., trustee), Cath. Hosp. Assn., St. Louis C. of C., Health and Welfare Assn. Allegheny County, Hosp. Council Western Pa. (past trustee), Nat. League Nursing, Nat. Rehab. Assn., Western Pa. Assn. Women Deans, Counselors and Personnel Workers, Hosp. Planning Assn. Allegheny County, Urban League, Pa. Welfare Forum, United Mental Health Services Allegheny County. Past mem. editorial bd. The Modern Hosp., 1940—. Contbr. articles profl. jours. Home: Sisters of St Francis Mt Alvernia 146 Hawthorne Rd Millvale Pittsburgh PA 15209 Office: St Francis Gen Hosp 45th St off Penn Av Pittsburgh PA 15201

MEISNER, PHYLLIS O'DELL HUGOS (MRS. JOHN FREDERICK MEISNER), sorority exec.; b. Belleville, Kan., July 24, 1926; d. Karl Adolph and Wanda Frances (Figgins) Hugos; B.S., Kan. State U., 1947; m. John Frederick Meisner, Feb. 9, 1947; children—Sharon (Mrs. Craig S. Rowlen), Kendall, Merle Beth. Pres. Sigma Gamma chpt. Kappa Delta, Manhattan, Kans., 1946-47, financial adviser, Manhattan, 1955-67, pres., Manhattan, 1956-57, province alumnae officer, 1967-69, nat. treas., 1969-71, nat. pres., 1971—; treas. Kan. State Day, 1965, pres., 1967; pres. Marlatt P.T.A., Manhattan, 1969-70. Mem. Am. Assn. U. Women. Mem. Christian Ch. (deaconess 1967-71). Address: 7206 S Xenia Circle Englewood CO 80110

MEISSINGER, RUTH ANNEMARIE, physician; b. Frankfurt am Main, Germany, July 23, 1924; d. Wilhelm and Antonie Elisabetha (Schwebel) Meissinger; Dr.med., J. W. Goethe U., Frankfurt, Germany, 1949; M.D., 1954; m. B. L. Garrison, July 11, 1959. Came to U.S., 1952. Intern, Cal. Luth. Hosp., Los Angeles, 1953-54, resident in obstetrics and gynecology, 1954-57; med. officer Internat. Refugee Orgn., Frankfurt, Germany, 1950-51; practice medicine specializing in obstetrics and gynecology Permanante Med. Group, Fontana (Cal.) Med. Center, 1957—; mem. staff, tchr. resident physicians Kaiser Found. Hosp., Fontana. Mem. Mus. Chaffey Communities Cultural Center, Upland, Cal., 1971—; sponsor West End Opera Assn., Ontario, Cal., 1971—; patron Humane Soc. Chaffey Community, Inc. Mem. Riverside-San Bernardino Obstretics and Gynecology Soc., Animal Protection Inst. Am. Home: 1790 N Euclid Av Upland CA 91786 Office: 9985 Sierra Av Fontana CA 92335

MEISTER, EMMA AGNES, ednl. adminstr.; b. West Hoboken, N.J.; d. William and Agnes (Devereaux) Meister; B.S., N.Y. U., 1950, M.A., 1954; postgrad. Columbia, Purdue U., Jersey City State Coll., Newark State Coll., Seton Hall U. Sec., prin. elementary sch. Union City (N.J.) Pub. Schs., 1934-47, dir. spl. services dept., 1961—; sch. social worker Union City Pub. Schs., 1948-61; instr. Rutgers U., 1961—. Dir. Hudson County Council Social Agys., 1955-60; mem. citizens adv. com. Union City PAL, 1959-64; sec. Union City Juvenile Conf. Com., 1953-64; dir. Hudson County Homemaker Service, 1959-64, Hudson County Mental Health, 1961-64; mem. adv. bd. N. Hudson chpt. A.R.C., 1962-64; pres. citizens adv. bd. Union City Pub. Health, 1959-64; mem. Hudson County com. White Ho. Conf. on Aged, 1960; adviser to Pres. Kennedy's Com. on Juvenile Delinquency, Youth and Crime, 1962. Coordinator for spl. services program City of Union, 1965. Served as capt. USAAF, 1943-46. Named Woman of Achievement, Hudson County, 1965. Mem. Hudson County Social Workers Orgn. (past pres.), N.J. Assn. Sch. Social Workers, Nat. Assn. Social Workers, Internat., Nat. confs. social welfare, N.J. Welfare Council, N.J., Union City edn. assns., Am. Assn. U. Women (pres. North Hudson Coll. club 1966), Internat. Council Exceptional Children, Am. Personnel and Guidance Assn., Assn. Counselor Edn. and Supervision, Acad. Certified Social Workers. Home: 140 78th St North Bergen NJ 07047 Office: Bd Edn Bldg 3912 Bergen Turnpike (32d St) Union City NJ 07087

MEITZEN, EDWINA MAY (MRS. GEORGE EDWARD MEITZEN), newspaper editor; b. Dallas, Dec. 19, 1931; d. John Edward and Dorothy May (Moore) Fitzgerald; student Jacksonville Bapt. Coll., 1949-50; m. George Edward Meitzen, Sept. 5, 1959; children from previous marriage—Charles Wilson Kratzer III, Edwin Matthew Kratzer, Colleen. Linotype operator Jacksonville (Tex.) Times, 1950-52, Manney Pub. Co., Ft. Worth, 1954-57, Aspen (Colo.) Times, 1959-60, Oregonian, Portland, Ore., 1960-64; linotype operator Dayton (Ore.) Tribune, 1964—, editor, 1964—. Mem. Dayton (Ore.) Library Bd., 1966. Sec. Lafayette (Ore.) Planning Commn., 1970; mem. Lafayette City Council, 1971-73, Yamhill County Parks Bd., 1971-73; mayor of Lafayette, 1973-74. Mem. Dayton J-C-Ettes (pres. 1966-67). Republican. Baptist. Home: 485 Weashington St Lafayette OR 97127 Office: 3d and Ferry St PO Box 68 Dayton OR 97114

MEIZNER, PAULA (MRS. ISRAEL MEIZNER), sculptor; b. Poland; d. Meyer and Sally (Stam) Warshawsky; student Westchester County Workshop, White Plains, N.Y.; m. Israel Meizner, Feb. 8, 1931; children—Clair (Mrs. Donald Wyner), Lilly (Mrs. Steven Toback). Came to U.S., 1940, naturalized, 1946. Exhibited one-man shows at Silvermine Guild Artists, New Canaan, Conn., 1966, Art Barn, Greenwich, Conn., 1972; exhibited in group shows at Pa. Acad. Fine Arts, Detroit Inst. Fine Arts, Katonah Gallery, Hudson River Mus., Lever House, others; represented in permanent collection at Larry Aldrich Mus., Ridgefield, Conn.; tchr. sculpture Westchester Ethical Culture Soc., New Rochelle, Rye (N.Y.) Art Center, also pvt. classes. Recipient prize for sculpture New Eng. Exhbns., 1959, 61, 70, 72; prize N.J. Painters and Sculptors, others. Mem. Audubon Artists, Knickerbocker Artists (medal of honor for sculpture 1961), Silvermine Guild Artists, Conn. Acad., Nat. Assn. Women Artists (Charles N. Winston Meml. award Ann. Exhbn. 1972), Yonkers Art Assn., Westchester Art Soc. (1st prize 1963). Home: 126 Seacord Rd New Rochelle NY 10804

MELAMED, BARBARA GREENSTEIN, psychologist, educator; b. Bklyn., Mar. 31, 1943; d. Alexander Isidore and Frances Anna (Elovich) Greenstein; B.A. with distinction, U. Mich., 1964; M.S., U. Wis., 1967, Ph.D., 1969; m. Lawrence Ervin Melamed, June 14, 1964; children—Jodi Lynn, Douglas Matthew. Research asso., mem. grad. faculty Kent (O.) State U., 1969-71; staff psychologist Akron Guidance Center, 1969-71; asso. prof. psychology and asst. prof. psychiatry Case Western Res. U., Cleve., 1971—. Cons. VA Hosp., Brecksville, O., Walter Reed Army Hosp., Washington, Bellefaire Residential Children's Treatment, Shaker Heights, O. NIH grantee; Cleve. Found. grantee. Mem. Am., Midwestern, Ohio psychol. assns., Assn. Advancement of Behavior Therapy, Phi Beta Kappa. Editorial bd. Psychotherapy: Theory Research and Practice. Contbr. articles to profl. jours. Exec. producer films Ethan Has An Operation, 1974, Behavioral Guidance in Pedodontics, 1973. Home: 1590 Wrenford Rd South Euclid OH 44121 Office: Dept Psychology Mather Meml Bldg Case-Western Res Univ Cleveland OH 44106

MELCHER, BETSY FLAGG (MRS. JOHN MELCHER), artist; b. N.Y.C., Apr. 8, 1900; d. Ernest and Margaret Elizabeth (Bonnell) Flagg; pvt. study with Cecilia Beaux, Elsie Dodge Pattee, Alfred Hoen, Mabel R. Welch; m. John Melcher, May 6, 1925; children—Pamela, Ursula (Mrs. Marc deF. De Logeres). Painter portraits various persons including Adm. Samuel Eliot Morrison, Mrs. Vincent Astor, Mrs. August Belmont. Home: 170 E 78th St New York City NY 10021 also Northeast Harbor ME

MELCHER, SANDRA JEAN (MRS. FRANK THEODORE MELCHER), painter, printmaker; b. Cleve., May 24, 1932; d. William Anthony and Elizabeth Charlotte (Jarabek) Vago; B.F.A., Cleve. Inst. Art, 1953; postgrad., Montclair Coll., 1965-66, Ridgewood Sch. Art, 1967-68; m. Frank Theodore Melcher, Jan. 12, 1952; 1 dau., Renee Janine. One-woman shows Galt's Gallery, Chatham, N.J., 1968, Sea Gallery, N.Y.C., 1970, 71, Gallery 64, N.Y.C., 1972, Petersen Studios, Saddle River, N.J., 1973, Simon's Rock Early Coll., Great Barrington, Mass., 1973; group shows Cleve. Mus., 1955, Newark Mus., Jersey City Mus., 1968-69, Bergen Community Mus., Paramus, N.J., 1972, Montclair (N.J.) Mus., 1972, 73; traveling exhbtns. N.J. Council on Arts, 1972, Nat. Assn. Women Artists, 1973—; represented in permanent collections at Carnegie Inst. Tech. Mus. Art, J.C. Penney corporate collection, Gould Inc. corporate collection, Bloomingdale Designer collections, Paramus, N.J. Free lance art work for IBM, Franklin Lakes, N.J., 1970—, spl. advt. agys., 1973—. Mem. Nat. Assn. Women Artists, Modern Artists Guild N.J., Hunterdon Art Assn., Art Center of No. N.J. Address: 1504 Clubside Rd Lyndhurst OH 44124

MELCHOR, OLLIE MAE JOHNSON (MRS. JOHN CALVIN MELCHOR), educator; b. Atlanta; d. Leon Matthews and Emma (Slaigh) Johnson; A.B., Rust Coll., 1944; M.A., U. Denver, 1956; m. John Calvin Melchor, June 15, 1948. Tchr. math., home econs., Ruleville, Miss., 1945; math. tchr., Hattisburg, Miss., 1947-49; asst. prin., math. tchr. Higgins Jr. Sr. High Sch., 1949-65; prin. Riverton Jr. High Sch., 1966, Clarksdale (Miss.) Jr. High Sch., 1967-70, Riverton Elementary Sch., 1970—. Trustee Daus. of Elks Lola Whitehead Temple 1139. Mem. N.E.A., Nat. Secondary and Elementary Prins. Assn., Nat. Math. Assn., Am. Legion Aux. (state pres. 1965—), V.F.W. Aux. (past local pres.), Rust Coll. Alumni Assn. (nat. v.p. 1960—). Methodist. Club: Social Les Pitetes Amis (pres.). Home: 104 5th Clarksdale MS 38614

MELCONIAN, LINDA JEAN, govt. ofcl.; b. Springfield, Mass., Mar. 28, 1948; d. George and Virginia Elaine (Noble) Melconian; B.A. magna cum laude, Mt. Holyoke Coll., 1970; M.A., George Washington U., 1974, postgrad. Law Sch., 1973—. Polit. sci. intern Rep. E.P. Boland of Mass., summer 1969; research asst. to Sen. E.S. Muskie Senatorial Campaign, 1970; legislative asst. to House Majority Whip, T.P. O'Neill, Jr., now House Majority leader, 1971—. Lectr., cons. polit. sci. faculty George Washington U., Am. U., Mt. Holyoke Coll. Active participant Mass. Democratic Party campaigns. Mem. Young Dems., League Women Voters, Springfield, Mass. Area. Clubs: Mount Holyoke (Springfield); Women's Business and Professional of Western Mass. Home: 465 Dwight Rd Springfield MA 01108 Office: Room H-148 Office of Majority Leader US Capitol Washington DC 20515

MELECHEN, PATRICIA JUSTICE HANSEN, hosp. adminstr.; b. Olympia, Wash., Mar. 15, 1934; d. James Watson and Corinne Harriet (Currier) Justice; B.S., Wash. U., 1956; m. Berner L. Hansen, July 29, 1955 (div. 1968); 1 dau., Karen Sue; m. 2d, Norman E. Melechen, Mar. 8, 1974. With Oakland County div. Pontiac (Mich.) State Hosp., 1956-61, 63-68, chief occupational therapy, 1964-68; with St. Louis U. Hosp., Wohl Mental Health Inst., 1968—, dir. activities therapy, 1969—; clin. instr. occupational therapy Washington U., St. Louis, 1973—. Mem. Mo. Occupational Therapy Assn. (chmn. council on practice 1973—). Club: St. Louis Ski. Home: 9572 Chancellorsville Dr St Louis MO 63126 Office: 1221 S Grand Blvd St Louis MO 63104

MELGAARD, RUTH LYNN ORR, owner brokerage co.; b. Jonesville, Va., Aug. 11, 1926; d. Claude David and Lena Virginia (Sprinkle) Orr; R.N., St. Mary's Meml. Hosp. Sch. Nursing, 1948; student U. Tenn., 1959; m. Erick Gilbert Melgaard, Jr., Dec. 15, 1945 (dec.); children—Erick III, David. Supr. nursing St. Marys Hosp., Knoxville, Tenn., 1955-62; dir. nursing service U. Tenn. Hosp., Knoxville, 1965-69; dir. nursing Eastern State Psychiat. Hosp., 1969-72; owner, operator Melgaard Brokerage Co., Knoxville, 1972—. Instr. Knox County chpt. A.R.C., 1971-73; chmn. West Haven Health Com., 1968-70. Judge West Haven precinct Knox County Election Com., 1968-69. Mem. Nat. Food Brokers Assn., Am. Nurses Assn., St. Mary's Meml. Hosp. Alumnae Assn. Methodist. Home: 4005 Elderwood Rd Knoxville TN 37921 Office: 6209 Baum Dr Knoxville TN 37921

MELLETTE, ELOISE AVERY HOLLADAY (MRS. ROBERT SIDNEY MELLETTE), ret. newspaperwoman; b. Winnsboro, S.C., Nov. 26, 1908; d. James Minor and Syme (Ayres) Holladay; ed. bus. sch., 1927; m. Robert Sidney Mellette, Oct. 6, 1928; children—Robert Sidney, Polly Ayres (Mrs. Loren B. Mead), William Wheeler, Laura Martinez. Soc. editor Marion (S.C.) Star, 1926-28, 45-47; corr. News and Courier, Charleston, S.C., 1929-30, Columbia (S.C.) Record, 1940-45, 45-47; sec. Seed Loan, govt. project, Orangeburg, S.C., 1942-45; comml. tchr. New Youth Adminstrn., Orangeburg, 1943-44; gen. office Clk. U.S. Agrl. Stblzn. and Conservation Service, Orangeburg, Marion, and Florence, S.C., 1950-52; owner, operator plant nursery, Florence, 1953-63; substitute tchr. Florence Pub. Schs., 1963-64, 71-73; women's writer Florence Morning News, 1964-67; communications tchr. T-Sq., Office Econ. Opportunity, Florence, 1967-68. Vol. Mental Health Assn., Orangeburg-Florence, 1969-74, Am. Cancer Soc., Florence, 1970-73; mem. bd. Florence County Council Aging; vol. worker Hotline, telephone counseling. Mem. P.T.A. (past sec., v.p.), Am. Legion Aux. Presbyn. Home: 401 Greenway Dr Florence SC 29501

MELLING, CAROL ANN (MRS. RODGER CLAYTON MELLING), editor; b. Plainfield, N.J., May 29, 1943; d. Robert Walter and Pearl Rosetta (Acker) Fitzsimmons; A.A. cum laude, Keystone Jr. Coll., 1962; B.A., Syracuse U., 1964, postgrad. 1966-68; m. Rodger Clayton Melling, June 11, 1966; 1 son, Cameron Lee. Copy editor Am. Baptist Conv., Valley Forge, Pa., 1964-65, asst. production mgr., 1965-66; editorial asst. Inter-Univ. Case Program, Syracuse, N.Y., 1966-68; staff asso. C&P Telephone, Charleston, W.Va., 1968-70; information writer W.Va. Dept. Hwys., Charleston, 1971—. Mem. Women In Communications, W.Va. Communicators (sec., treas. 1973, v.p. 1974), Phi Theta Kappa, Sigma Tau Sigma, Theta Sigma Phi. Republican. Baptist. Home: Route 1 Box 302 Elkview WV 25071 Office: Room 152 1900 Washington St Charleston WV 25305

MELLINK, MACHTELD JOHANNA, archaeologist; b. Amsterdam, Netherlands, 1917; d. Johan and Machteld (Kruyff) Mellink; B.A., U. Amsterdam, 1938, M.A., 1941; Ph.D., Utrecht U., 1943. Staff mem. Excavations at Tarsus, Turkey, 1947-49, Gordion Excavations, 1950—; field dir. excavations at Karatas-Semayuk, Lycia, Turkey, 1963—; asst. prof. dept. classical, Near Eastern archaeology Bryn Mawr (Pa.) Coll., 1949-53, asso. prof., 1953-63, prof., 1963—, also chmn. dept. Research asso. U. Mus. U. Pa. Fellow Am. Acad. Arts and Scis.; mem. Archaeol. Inst. Am.; corr. mem. Royal Netherlands Acad. Scis., German Archaeol. Inst. Contbr. articles to profl. jours. Home: 221 N Roberts Rd Bryn Mawr PA 19010

MELLISH, MARJORY SCOTT CRIST (MRS. EUGENE WILLIAM MELLISH), social worker; b. N.Y.C.; d. Henry Monell and Margaret (Scott) Crist; B.A. (Caroline Mathilde Behre scholar), Adelphi U., 1932; M.S.W., Hunter Coll., 1963; m. Eugene William Mellish, Oct. 20, 1933; 1 son, Stephen Eugene. Caseworker family service Nassau County (N.Y.) Dept. Social Services, Mineola, 1959-61, sr. caseworker adoption services, 1963-64, supr. undercare unit, childrens' services, 1964-66; supr. foster homefinding, children's services, 1966-73, asst. dir. children's services, 1973—; caseworker, family services Cath. Charities, Bklyn., 1961-62; social worker Bklyn. Home for Children, Forest Hills, N.Y., 1962-63. Mem. Nat. Assn. Social Workers, Acad. Certified Social Workers, D.A.R. (del. nat. conv. 1961, del. state conv. 1964, chmn. Children Am. Revolution com. 1964-65), Pi Gamma Mu, Delta Tau Alpha. Home: 27 Wellington Rd Garden City NY 11530 Office: Nassau County Dept Social Services County Seat Dr Mineola NY 11501

MELNICK, MATILDA BENYESH (MRS. JOSEPH LOUIS MELNICK), educator; b. Russe, Bulgaria, Feb. 7, 1926; d. Sinto and Rachel (Farchy) Benyesh; M.B., U. Sofia, Bulgaria, 1949; M.D., Hebrew U., Jerusalem, Israel, 1952; m. Joseph Louis Melnick, June 12, 1958. Came to U.S., 1955, naturalized, 1960. Research asst. Tel. Hashomer Hosp., Israel, 1953-55; research fellow Yale Sch. Medicine, New Haven, 1955-57; vis. scientist NIH, Bethesda, Md., 1957-58; asst. prof. Baylor U. Coll. Medicine, Houston, 1958-64, asso. prof., 1964-67, prof. virology and epidemiology, 1967—. Del. Soviet Am. Conf. on Poliomyelitis, Moscow, 1960. Recipient Humanitarian award Jewish Inst. Med. Research, 1964; 60th Anniversary award Hadassah, 1972. Mem. Am. Soc. Microbiology, Am. Assn. Cancer

Research, A.M.A., Am. Assn. Immunologists. Contbr. numerous articles to profl. jours., also chpts. to med. textbooks, revs. in virology and cancer research. Home: 8838 Chatsworth St Houston TX 77024 Office: 1200 Moursund Av Houston TX 77025

MELOGRANO, LILLIAN GRIMM, real estate broker; b. N.Y.C., Sept. 16, 1924; d. Joseph Nicholas and Anna Emma (Simon) Grimm; student U. Cal. at Los Angeles, 1962-65; children—Paul Francis, Lisa Maree. Exec. asst., sec. to corporate officers Republic Aviation Corp., N.Y.C., 1941-44, Gen. Aircraft Co., N.Y.C., 1944-45, IBM, N.Y.C., 1946-48; pres. Lil Melograno Assos., Inc., Beverly Hills, Cal., 1962—. Pres. Benedict Canyon Assn., 1965, 70, Hillside Fedn., 1966, 67; mem. citizens adv. com. Mulholland Scenic Pkwy., 1972—; chmn. Bel Air-Beverly Crest Dist. Plan Adv. Com., 1971; mem. Mayor's Commn. Recommendations Com., 1973—; mem. City Atty.'s Citizens Adv. Com. on Planning, 1973—; mem. adv. com. Citizens Asso. for Educating Youth, Inc., 1972—; chairwoman Los Angeles Internat. Airport Property Acquisition Bd., 1973—. Bd. dirs. Friends of Santa Monica Mountains, Parks and Seashore, 1973—, Benedict Canyon Assn., 1963—, Family Sch. Alliance at Univ. Elementary Sch. at U. Cal. at Los Angeles, 1964-69. Mem. Nat. Assn. Real Estate Bds., Cal. Real Estate Assn., Los Angeles, Beverly Hills (dir. 1974, chairwoman membership com.) realty bds. Home: 9725 Hensal Rd Beverly Hills CA 90210 Office: 9405 Brighton Way Beverly Hills CA 90210

MELONAS, ALEXANDRA KUPROWICZ (MRS. MICHAEL M. MELONAS), city ofcl.; b. Weirton, W.Va., Feb. 4, 1932; d. William and Maxine (Mostowski) Kuprowicz; student Steubenville Bus. Coll., 1950-51; m. Michael M. Melonas, July 4, 1954; children—Neo, Anthony. With Weirton Steel div. Nat. Steel Corp., 1951-54; sec., receptionist Weir High Sch., Weirton, 1968; city clk. City of Weirton, 1968—; sec. to Police Civil Service Commn., Fire Civil Service Commn., Traffic Commn., Commr. City Elections, 1968—. Den mother Cub Scouts, 1962-68; treas. P.T.A., 1961-63. Mem. Municipal City Clks. Assn., Daus. Penelope (marshall 1962-66), Greek Ladies Philoptohos Soc., Weirton Baseball Assn. Aux. Mem. Greek Orthodox Ch. Home: 326 Bennett Dr Weirton WV 26062 Office: Office of City Clk City Hall Weirton WV 26062

MELOY, LORETTA MARIE SCHRADER (MRS. HAROLD MELOY), judge; b. Shelbyville, Ind., Apr. 26, 1924; d. Conrad and Anna Elisabeth (Kranz) Schrader; B.S., Ind. U., 1946, J.D. (Wendell Willkie law scholar), 1968; m. Harold Meloy, Sept. 9, 1951. Admitted to Ind. bar, 1969; individual practice law, Shelbyville, 1969—; judge City Ct. Shelbyville, 1972—. Address: PO Box 454 Shelbyville IN 46176

MELOY, SYBIL PISKUR (MRS. PAUL W. MELOY), pharm. co. exec.; b. Chgo., Dec. 1, 1939; d. Michael M. and Laura (Stevenson) P.; B.S., U. Ill., 1961; J.D., Chgo.-Kent Coll. Law, 1965; m. Paul W. Meloy, June 29, 1963; children—William, Bradley. Admitted to Ill. bar, 1965; patent chemist G.D. Searle & Co., Skokie, Ill., 1961-65, patent atty., 1965-69, sr. patent atty., 1969-71, dir. internat. legal affairs, 1971-72; regional counsel Abbott Labs., North Chicago, Ill., 1972—. Mem. Am. Chem. Soc., Am., Chgo. bar assns., Am. Patent Law Assn., Women's Bar Assn. Ill., Licensing Execs. Soc., Phi Beta Kappa, Phi Kappa Phi, Iota Sigma Pi, Kappa Beta Pi, Sigma Kappa. Home: 212 E Kathleen Dr Park Ridge IL 60068 Office: 14th St and Sheridan Rd D-364 North Chicago IL 60064

MELROSE, ALICE G., sch. adminstr.; b. Cold Spring Harbor, N.Y., Apr. 10, 1919; d. John George and Signe Marie (Carlson) Melrose; B.A., Randolph-Macon Womens Coll., 1938; M.A., N.Y. U., 1940. Asst. tchr. jr. high sch. Manhasset, N.Y., 1938-39; tchr. St. Margaret's Sch., Mendham, N.J., 1939-41, Gardner Sch., N.Y.C., 1941-42; research and office mgr. OSRD Project, Oyster Bay, N.Y., 1942-45; corr. Doubleday & Co., Garden City, N.Y., 1945-47; office mgr. Nat. Acad. Design, N.Y.C., 1947-66, asst. to dir., 1961-67, dir., 1967—. Sec., treas. E. A. Abbey Scholarships in Mural Painting, Inc., N.Y.C., 1949. Episcopalian. Home: 21 Mayfair Dr Huntington NY 11743 Office: 1083 Fifth Av New York City NY 10028

MELROSE, MARY JANE, lawyer; b. Hazelton, Pa., Jan. 11, 1919; d. J.L. and E.M. (Campbell) Halter; B.A., Bethany Coll., 1940; M.A., U. Pitts., 1942; J.D., U. Miami, 1953. Admitted to Fla. bar, 1953, since practiced as mem. firm Helliwell, Melrose & DeWolf, Attys., Miami, and Orlando; gen. counsel, v.p., sec. Grand Bahama Port Authority Ltd. and affiliated cos., Freeport, Grand Bahama, 1968—; v.p., gen. counsel Intercontinental Diversified Corp.; dir. Bank Perrine (Fla.), Bank Cutler Ridge (Fla.), Fla. Shares, Inc. Mem. Am., Fla., Dade County, Orange County bar assns., Zeta Tau Alpha, Kappa Beta Phi. Clubs: Lucayan Country (Freeport); National Lawyers (Washington). Home: Silver Point PO Box F 904 Freeport Grand Bahama Office: Grand Bahama Port Authority Ltd PO Box F 2666 Freeport Grand Bahama

MELTON, DONNA FAYE, city ofcl.; b. Detroit, Sept. 25, 1928; d. Clifton Othello and Donna Irene (Hoyt) Melton; B.S. in Recreation Leadership, Wayne State U., 1960, M.A. in Recreation, 1970. With Dept. Parks and Recreation, Detroit, 1956—, recreation leader, 1956-60, recreation instr., 1960-65, community house supr., 1965-67, specialist girls and women's sports, 1967-71, mem. exec. com. Div. Girls and Womens Sports, 1972-74, asst. recreation supr., 1974—. Mem. women's volleyball com. U.S. Olympic Com., 1972—, women's basketball com., 1972—, sec., 1972—; mem. women's basketball com. Nat. Amateur Athletic Union Com., 1973-74. Mem. Mich. Recreation and Park Assn. (mem. athletic bd. 1967-71, mem. exec. bd. 1969-72), Mich. Amatuer Athletic Union (sec. 1970-72). Home: 17444 Marene St Detroit MI 48219 Office: 3020 Wreford St Detroit MI 48208

MELTZER, JUDITH NAOMI STETTIN (MRS. GEORGE MELTZER), advt. exec.; b. Bklyn., Oct. 2, 1929; d. Albert Boaz and Blanche (Baron) Stettin; student Hunter Coll., 1945; m. George Meltzer, Sept. 10, 1949; children—Mindy Ann, Donald Bruce. Advt. mgr. Mid Island-Levittown Times, Bethpage Newsgram, Syosset Advance, Centre Island News, Jericho News Jour., Litmor Publs., Hicksville, N.Y., 1969—. Home: 35 Lantern Rd Hicksville NY 11801 Office: 22 W Nicholai St Hicksville NY 11801

MELVILLE, MARYLOU ALLIEN, real estate broker; b. Stevenson, Wash., June 5, 1919; d. Urban and Leah Mary (Tom) Jensen; student, Benke-Walker Bus. Sch., 1938-39, Santa Barbara State Coll., 1941-42, San Bernardino Valley Coll., 1948-49; m. Robert Edward Melville, Apr. 18, 1973; 1 dau. by previous marriage, Shirley Jean (Mrs. McCollister). Instr. arts and crafts San Bernardino (Cal.) Coll., 1949-52; with Stewart Realty Co., Hermosa Beach, Cal., 1959-62; owner, real estate broker Marylou Graddy Realty, Hermosa Beach and Baywood Park, Cal., 1962-70, Palm Desert, Cal., 1970-73. Tchr. arts and crafts, Colstrip, Mont., 1973—; lectr. to various real estate groups. Recipient Omega Tau Rho award Nat. Assn. Realtors, 1971; Realtor of Year award S. Bay Bd. Realtors, 1971. Mem. Nat. Inst. of Farm and Land Brokers (Cal. state pres. 1973), Soc. Exchange Counselors (bd. govs. 1972-74). Home: PO Box 142 Colstrip MT 59323 Office: PO Box 916 Forsyth MT 59327

MELVIN, SISTER M. CONSTANCE, librarian; b. Pittston, Pa., Oct. 28, 1918; d. Francis L. and Kathryn (Hughes) Melvin; A.B., Marywood Coll., 1940; B.S. in L.S. Columbia, 1941; Ph.D., U. Chgo., 1962. Librarian pub. schs., Eastport, L.I., N.Y., 1941-43, Mt. Kisco, N.Y., 1943-46; gen. asst. librarian Pub. Library, Scranton, Pa., 1943; asst. librarian Marywood Coll., 1946-48; joined Order of Sisters, Servants of Immaculate Heart of Mary, 1948; tchr. Cath. schs. Scranton Diocese, 1950-60; lectr. Marywood Coll., 1952-60, prof. 1960—, chmn. dept. librarianship, 1960—. Mem. A.L.A., Cath., Pa. library assns., Pa. Sch. Librarians Assn., Am. Assn. U. Profs., Am. Assn. U. Women, Kappa Gamma Pi, Beta Phi Mu. Home: Marywood College 2300 Adams Av Scranton PA 18509

MELZER, FLORENCE (MRS. HENRY MELZER), newspaper pub.; b. N.Y.C., Nov. 20, 1926; d. Sam and Sophie (Hutnick) Winkler; grad. Walton High Sch., 1943; m. Henry Melzer, June 1, 1946; children—Barbara, Steven. Sec., Manhattan Mut. Ins., N.Y.C., 1943-46; advt. rep. Fairlawn (N.J.) Shopper News, 1957-63, layout artist, 1959-63, columnist, 1960-63; co-pub. Town News North, Paramus, N.J., 1963-73; started new publ. Town News South, Hackensack, N.J., 1973—; sec. treas. LCS Co., Inc., Public relations Democratic Com., Bergen County, N.J., 1972—. Mem. Paramus C. of C., Profl. Women's Orgn. (chairwoman). Mem. B'nai B'rith. Home: 39-11 Tierney Pl Fair Lawn NJ 07410 Office: Box 267 Parmus 583 Winters Av Paramus NJ 07652

MEMFORD, PATRICIA RAE (MRS. DONALD EARL MUMFORD), pub. relations exec.; b. Oklahoma City, Feb. 25, 1932; d. Raymond W. and Mildred Louise (Wisdom) Gallagher; student Okla. State U., 1949-50; m. Donald Earl Mumford, Apr. 6, 1951; children—Raymond Scott, Kenneth Earl, Robert Paul. Continuity/traffic dir. radio sta. KRMG, Tulsa, 1951-52; continuity traffic/merchandising dir. sta. KLAS-TV, Las Vegas, Nev., 1953-54; continuity/traffic dir. radio sta. KTVK, Phoenix, 1955-56, sta. KBTV, Denver, 1956-57, radio sta. KKUA, Honolulu, 1967-71; pub. relations exec. Hawaii Council of Churches, Honolulu, 1971—. Free lance writer, 1971—. Mem. Women in Communication, Ch. Women United in Windward Oahu (pres. 1965-67), Ch. Women United in Hawaii (pres. 1968-71), Church Women United (dir. 1968-71). Mem. Christian Ch. (elder 1971-73). Home: 1478 Uluhala Place Kailua HI 96734 Office: Hawaii Council of Churches 200 N Vineyard Room 403 Honolulu HI 96817

MENAKER, BONNIE DOUGLASS (MRS. J. THOMAS MENAKER), lawyer; b. Harrisburg, Pa., Sept. 26, 1939; d. William Tyler and Mary Alice (Hicks) Douglass; A.B., U. N.C., 1961, LL.B., 1964; m. J. Thomas Menaker, June 18, 1960. Admitted to Pa. bar, 1965; jud. law clk., Harrisburg, 1964-65; mem. firm Hepford, Zimmerman & Swartz, Harrisburg, 1965-72, partner, 1972—. Mem. Commn. on Status of Women, 1966—. Mem. Am., Pa. bar assns., Am. Civil Liberties Union, League Women Voters, Phi Delta Phi. Republican. Home: 4707 N Galen Rd Harrisburg PA 17110 Office: 22 S 3d St Harrisburg PA 17101

MENAKER, SHIRLEY ANN LASCH (MRS. MICHAEL MENAKER), educator; b. Jersey City, July 22, 1935; d. Frederick Carl and Mary Elisabeth (Thrall) Lasch; B.A., Swarthmore Coll., 1956; M.A., Boston U., 1961, Ph.D., 1965; m. Michael Menaker, June 4, 1955; children—Ellen Margaret, Nicholas. Adminstrv. asst. N.J. State Fedn. Dist. Bds. Edn., Trenton, 1956-59; trainee clin. psychology Mass. Mental Health Center, Boston, 1960-61; intern clin. psychology Thom Guidance Clinic for Children, Boston, 1961-62; research asso. ednl. psychology U. Tex., Austin, 1964-67, asst. prof. edn. psychology, 1967-70, asso. prof. ednl. psychology, 1970—, psychol. cons. Research and Devel. Center for Tchr. Edn., 1965-67, faculty investigator, 1967—. Nat. Inst. Mental Health Predoctoral research fellow, 1963-64. Mem. Am. Psychol. Assn., Am. Ednl. Research Assn. Home: 3302 Cherry Tree Circle Austin TX 78731

MENCHER, JOAN PHYLLIS (MRS. FRANKLIN C. SOUTHWORTH), anthropologist, educator; b. N.Y.C., Jan. 29, 1930; d. Irving W. and Mae (Bodin) Mencher; B.A. magna cum laude, Smith Coll., 1950; Ph.D., Columbia, 1958; m. Franklin C. Southworth, June 21, 1966. Instr. Hofstra Coll., Hempstead, L.I., 1960-61; Ogden Mills fellow Am. Mus. Natural History, N.Y.C., 1961-62; NSF postdoctoral fellow in India, 1962-64; vis. asst. prof. Cornell U., 1964-65; research asso. Columbia, N.Y.C., 1965-67, vis. asso. prof., 1967-68, sr. research asso. dept. anthropology, 1969-72; asso. prof. anthropology Lehman Coll., City U. N.Y., N.Y.C., 1968-73, prof., 1974—. Am. Assn. U. Women postdoctoral fellow, also Fulbright fellow in India, 1958-60; Nat. Inst. Mental Health grantee in India, 1966-67; NSF grantee for research in India, 1969-71; Guggenheim fellow, 1974. Fellow Am. Anthrop. Assn.; mem. Royal Anthrop. Assn. Gt. Britain and Ireland, Soc. Asian Studies, Soc. Applied Anthropology, Indian Sociol. Soc., Phi Beta Kappa, Sigma Xi. Home: 315 Riverside Dr New York City NY 10015 Office: Dept Anthropology Lehman College New York City NY 10468

MENDELOWITZ, MARY JANE, assn. exec.; b. Denver, Mar. 7, 1921; d. Louis Gerson and Jennie (Cohen) Keinon; student U. Denver, 1939-42; m. Monroe Richard Mendelowitz, May 5, 1943; children—Andrea Jo, David. Exec. sec. conv. dept. Lions Internat., Chgo., 1960-65; conv. coordinator A.M.A., Chgo., 1965-71; asst. exec. v.p. Am. Soc. Plastic and Reconstructive Surgeons, Chgo., 1971—. Active Chgo. Community Theater, 1956-73. Mem. Profl. Conv. Mgmt. Assn., Am. Assn. Med. Soc. Execs., Conf. Med. Soc. Execs. Greater Chgo. Democrat. Jewish religion. Home: 2411 W Jarvis St Chicago IL 60645 Office: 29 E Madison St Chicago IL 60602

MENDES, HELEN ALTHIA DAVENPORT, social worker; b. Bronx, N.Y., May 20, 1935; d. Arthur L. and Louise (Dow) Davenport; B.A., Queens Coll., 1957; M.S.W., Columbia, 1964. Caseworker Jewish Family Service, Bklyn., 1964-67; acting dir. Big Bros. Residence, N.Y.C., 1967-69; mental health cons. Albert Einstein Coll. Medicine, Bronx., N.Y., 1969; social work cons. Big Bros., Inc., N.Y., 1970-72; social work cons. Wiltwyck Sch. for Boys, N.Y.C., 1972; asso. U. Cal. at Los Angeles, 1972—; pvt. practice psychotherapy, N.Y.C., 1968-70. Mem. family service adv. com. Community Service Soc., 1969-72; mem. women's com. African-Am. Insts., 1967-72; mem. adv. bd. Bklyn. Urban League, 1967-72. Mem. Assn. Black Social Workers, Nat. Assn. Social Workers, League Women Voters, N.Y. Civil Liberties Union, Fedn. Black Histroy and Arts. Author: The African Heritage Cookbook, 1971. Home: 1047 Meadowbrook Av Los Angeles CA 90019 Office: Sch Social Welfare U Cal at Los Angeles 405 Hilgard Av Los Angeles CA 90024

MENDUKE, PHYLLIS BONOW HIRSCH (MRS. HYMAN MENDUKE), pub. relations exec.; b. Phila., May 5, 1924; d. Harry W. and Ella (Bonow) Hirsch; B.S., Temple U., 1945; m. Hyman Menduke, Apr. 14, 1946; 1 dau., Judith Ellen (Mrs. Paul Schwartz). Writer, AM, Inc., Phila., 1945-49; free-lance editorial and pub. relations cons., 1950-66; writer, publicist Fedn. Jewish Agys. Greater Phila., 1966—, copy chief, 1973—. Mem. Women in Communications, Phila. Pub. Relations Assn. (dir. 1972—), League Women Voters Phila. (dir. 1950-55), Phi Sigma Sigma. Jewish religion. Home: 7808 Haines Rd Cheltenham PA 19012 Office: 1511 Walnut St Philadelphia PA 19102

MENENDEZ, SHIRLEY ANN CORBIN (MRS. ALBERT JOHN MENENDEZ), librarian; b. Richmond, Va., Feb. 5, 1937; d. Daniel and Madeline (Euring) Corbin; B.A., Mary Baldwin Coll., 1961; M.L.S., Drexel U., 1965; m. Albert John Menendez, June 15, 1974. Library asst. Staunton (Va.) Pub. Library, 1955-61; tchr. Robert E. Lee High Sch., Staunton, 1961-62; reference librarian and cataloger Fed. Res. Bank of Phila., 1963-65; circulation supr., reader's services librarian, Hyattsville (Md.) br. Prince George's County Meml. Library, 1965-69, br. librarian College Park (Md.) br., 1969-71, adminstrv. asst. pub. services, Hyattsville, 1971—. Mem. Md., (corr. sec. 1969-70), D.C. library assns. Home: 14151 Castle Blvd Silver Spring MD 20904 Office: 6532 Adelphi Rd Hyattsville MD 20782

MENES, PAULINE HERSKOWITZ (MRS. MELVIN MENES), state legislator; b. N.Y.C., July 16, 1924; d. Arthur Benjamin and Hannah Herskowitz; B.A., Hunter Coll., 1945; m. Melvin Menes, Sept. 1, 1946; children—Sandra Jill, Robin Joy, Bambi Lynn. Economist, Q.M.C., 1945-47; geographer Army Map Service, 1949-50; substitute tchr. Prince Georges Pub. High Schs., Md., 1965-66; mem. Md. Ho. of Dels., 1967—. Sec., Prince Georges County Ind. Democrats, 1962; chief clerk Suprv. of Elections, Md., 1963; sec. Prince Georges County Dem. Steering Com., 1966. Democrat. Jewish religion. Home: 3517 Marlbrough Way College Park MD 20740

MENNEMEYER, SISTER MARY HERMIAS, educator; b. St. Louis; d. August and Ida (Keisker) Mennemeyer; B.S. in Edn., St. Louis U., 1934; M.S. in Chemistry, DePaul U., 1943; postgrad. nuclear sci. St. Louis U., 1957, 67; postgrad. (NSF or AEC scholar at following), U. Mo., summer 1957, 67, Oak Ridge Inst. Nuclear Studies, 1957, Kan. State Tchrs. Coll., 1959, U. Okla., 1960, 61, Inst. Sci. Research, Las Vegas, N.M., 1962-63. Mem. Order Sch. Sisters Notre Dame; tchr., head scis. dept. St. Paul High Sch., Highland, Ill., 1934-39, Aviston (Ill.) Community High Sch., 1939-45, 49-54, LeClerc Coll., Belleville, Ill., 1945-49, St. Francis Borgia High Sch., Washington, Mo., 1954-62, St. Francis de Sales High Sch., St. Louis, 1963-67, Notre Dame Coll., St. Louis, 1967—. Tchr. coll. sci., summers 1944-56; tchr. AEC-NSF Inst. in Radiation Biology St. Mary's Coll., Winona, Minn., summers 1965-66; participant sci. programs TV; mem. regional bd. Future Scientists Am., 1964; mem. com. for tech. day St. Louis Research Council, 1972; mem. com. for space sci. month McDonnell Planetarium. Recipient Distinguished Service citation Mo. Civil Def., 1961, Apple for Tchr. award St. Louis, 1965; Mo. Sci. Educator award, 1972. Mem. Nat. Sci. Tchrs. Assn. (life, Sci. Tchr. Achievement Recognition award 1960), A.A.A.S., N.E.A., Nat. Catholic Edn. Assn., St. Louis Archdiocesan Sci. Council (chmn. 1963), Sci. Tchrs. Mo. (bd. dirs., mem. exec. com.; St. Louis suburban rep.; chmn. Mo. Sci. Educator award), Internat. Platform Assn. Co-author: Radioactivity-Fundamentals and Experiments, 1963; How to Use Radioisotopes in High School Science Teaching, 1966. Editor: Missouri Science News, 1969—. Research and publs. in sci. field. Home and office: Notre Dame Coll 320 E Ripa Av St Louis MO 63125

MENNEN, DOROTHY RUNK (MRS. HAROLD E. MENNEN), performing arts adminstr., educator; b. Marshfield, Wis., July 17, 1915; d. Jon Cleveland and Minnie Pearle (Walker) Runk; B.S. in Edn., Kent State U., 1938; M.A., Purdue U., 1964; m. Harold E. Mennen, Jan. 5, 1943; children—Ferol, Laurel (Mrs. Bruce Miller Robb). Tchr., choral dir. Twinsburg (O.) pub. sch., 1938-41; tchr. speech, English Aurora (O.) High Sch., 1941-42; tchr. Cuyahoga Falls (O.) High Sch., 1941-42; tchr. English, Wea High Sch., Tippecanoe County, Ind., 1951-53; tchr. vocal music West Lafayette (Ind.) pub. schs., 1957-60; asst. prof. theatre Purdue U., West Lafayette, Ind., 1964—, also vocal coach, 1964—. Contralto soloist, 1946—. Bd. dirs. Lafayette Symphony, 1958-60, Civic Theatre, Lafayette, 1972-73. Mem. Am. Theatre Assn. (nat. chairperson theatre, speech and voice 1968-71, 73—), Nat. Assn. Tchrs. of Singing, Speech Communication Assn., Am. Assn. U. Profs. (chairperson com. W on Status of Women 1972-74, pres. chpt. 1974-75), Women's Equity Action League, League of Women Voters. Democrat. Methodist. Home: 1804 Ravinia Rd West Lafayette IN 47906

MENNINGER, JEANETTA LYLE (MRS. KARL MENNINGER), editor; b. St. Louis; d. Edward Gerard and Jeanetta (Patterson) Lyle; A.B., Park Coll., 1923; postgrad. Columbia, 1930; m. Karl Menninger, Sept. 9, 1941; 1 dau., Rosemary. Prin. preparatory sch. Central Coll. for Women, 1925; reporter, feature writer Utica (N.Y.) Daily Press, 1925-30; with pub. relations dept. Columbia U., 1930; editorial worker, writer Menninger Clinic, Topeka, 1931; research asst. Carnegie Found. proj., Hollywood, Cal., 1937; freelance writer, 1937-41; editor Bull. of Menninger Clinic, Topeka, Kan., 1936—; dir. publs. Menninger Found., 1946-64; cons. editor Correctional Programs News, 1971—; asso. editor Presbyn. Outlook, Richmond, Va., 1973—; bd. dirs. A.R.T., Inc., 1972—. Active in various drives as A.R.C., Am. Cancer Soc., Multiple Sclerosis, Mental Hygiene, Art Center, others. Trustee Mulvane Art Center, Washburn Municipal U., 1954—, Family Service and Guidance Center, Topeka, 1957-71, The Villages, Inc., 1969—, Park Coll., Parkville, Mo., 1970—. Fellow Am. Med. Writers Assn.; mem. Kan. Press Women, Nat. Fedn. Press Women, Nat. Assn. Sci. Writers, YWCA, Theta Sigma Phi. Democrat. Presbyn. Collaborator (with husband) in Love against Hate (book), 1942. Contbr. numerous articles to profl. jours., various mags. Home: 1819 Westwood Circle Topeka KS 66604 Office: Menninger Found Box 829 Topeka KS 66601

MENSORE, LAVAUGHN TULANE BOUCH (MRS. JOHN JOSEPH MENSORE), lawyer; b. Weston, W.Va., Feb. 2, 1940; d. Russel Edward and Lora Lavaughn (Finster) Bouch; A.B., W.Va. U., 1961; J.D., 1964; m. John Joseph Mensore, Nov. 7, 1964; children—Michelle Tulane, John Charles II, Nicole Tulane. Admitted to W.Va. bar, 1964; partner Mensore & Mensore, New Martinsville, W.Va., 1965—; sec.-treas. J.C. Mensore Distbr., Inc., New Martinsville, W.Va., 1969—. Active Ming Twig, Wetzel County Hosp. Aux., Citizen's Scholarship Found. N.M., New Martinsville (W.Va.) Woman's Civic League; charter mem. Friends of WWTU-TV, Morgantown, W.Va. Named Outstanding Sr. Woman, W.Va. U., 1961. Mem. Am., W.Va. bar assns., W.Va. State Bar, Kappa Kappa Gamma Alumni Assn. Clubs: Quota (charter), Magnolia Yacht (New Martinsville); Sistersville (W.Va.) Country. Home: 343 Clark Dr New Martinsville WV 26155 Office: Main St New Martinsville WV 26155

MENTENDIEK, MARY ANN, physician; b. Indpls., Sept. 12, 1942; d. Maurice Henry and Dorotha Beatrice (Price) Mentandiek; A.B., Ind. U., 1964, M.D., 1967. Intern, Meth. Hosp. Ind., 1967-68, resident internal medicine, 1968-71, mem. staff, 1971—; practice medicine specializing in internal medicine, Indpls., 1971—. Diplomate Am. Bd. Internal Medicine. Mem. A.M.A., Marion County Med. Soc., Delta Delta Delta. Presbyn. Home: 141 Buckingham Dr Indianapolis IN 46208 Office: 5699 E 71st St Indianapolis IN 46220

MENYUK, PAULA NICHOLS (MRS. NORMAN MENYUK), psycholinguist, educator; b. N.Y.C., Oct. 2, 1929; d. Louis and Helen (Weissman) Nichols; B.S., N.Y. U., 1951; D.Ed. (Nat. Inst. Mental Health fellow 1958-60), Boston U., 1961; m. Norman Manyuk, Mar. 5, 1950; children—Curtis R., Diane E., Eric D. Tchr. speech and

English high schs., N.Y.C., 1951-52; speech therapist Mass. Gen. Hosp., Boston, 1952-54; Nat. Inst. Mental Health postdoctoral fellow Mass. Inst. Tech., 1961-64, mem. research staff, after 1964; prof. Boston U., 1972—; cons. Children's Hosp. Med. Center, Boston, Nat. Inst. Neurol. Diseases and Stroke, 1972-76. Mem. Brookline Council Pub. Schs., v.p., 1966-68; mem. Brookline Civil Rights Com.; mem. bd. Brookline High Sch. P.T.A. Mem. Brookline Democratic com., 1966—. Fulbright fellow, 1970. Fellow Am. Speech and Hearing Assn.; mem. Soc. Research Child Devel., Linguistic Soc. Am. Author: Sentences Children Use, 1969; The Acquisition and Development of Language, 1971; Speech Development, 1972. Home: 162 Mason Terrace Brookline MA 02146 Office: 264 Bay State Rd Boston MA 02115

MENZEL, FEROL JEAN SCHRICKER (MRS. BRUCE W. MENZEL), occupational therapist; b. Cin., Mar. 12, 1946; d. Raymond and Esther (Meikle) Schricker; B.S., Ohio State U., 1968; M.S., Ia. State U., 1975; m. Bruce W. Menzel, Aug. 9, 1969. Occupational therapist Spl. Children's Center, Ithaca, N.Y., 1969-70; occupational therapist Woodward (Ia.) State Hosp. Sch., 1970-71, work evaluator, 1972-73, dir. developmental center, 1973—. Bd. dirs., pres. Story County Developmental Center. Mem. Ia. Occupational Therapy Assn. (treas. 1973—). Home: 1123 Scholl Av Ames IA 50010

MENZEL, (MARY) MARGARET YOUNG (MRS. ROBERT WINSTON MENZEL), educator; b. Kerrville, Tex., June 21, 1924; d. Walter Patterson and Mary (Hightower) Young; B.A. magna cum laude, Southwestern U., 1944; Ph.D., U. Va., 1949; m. Robert Winston Menzel, Apr. 9, 1949; children—Robert Winston, Gary Patterson, Mary Linda. Instr. agronomy Tex. A. and M. Coll., College Station, 1949-54; plant geneticist U.S. Dept. Agr., Tallahassee, 1955-62; research asso. Fla. State U., Tallahassee, 1954-63; asso. prof., 1963-68, prof. dept. biol. scis., 1968—, asso. chmn. dept., 1972-73. Recipient Research prize Assn. of Southeastern Biologists, 1950. Research grantee Sigma Xi, 1954, 55; grantee Am. Philos. Soc., 1954, 66; AEC grantee, 1964—. Mem. Nat. Orgn. for Women (pres. chpt. 1972—), Assn. of Southeastern Biologists (v.p. 1966), League of Women Voters, Sigma Xi, Alpha Delta Pi. Methodist. Contbr. articles in field to profl. jours. Editor: Assn. of Southeastern Biologists, 1971—. Office: Dept Biological Science Florida State University Tallahassee FL 32306

MENZIES, ELIZABETH GRANT CRANBROOK, author, photographer; b. Princeton, N.J., June 24, 1915; d. Alan Wilfrid Cranbrook and Mary Isabella (Dickson) Menzies; pvtly. ed. Recipient N.J. Tercentenary medal for photo of Albert Einstein, 1964; citation of commendation Am. Assn. for State and Local History, 1970, award of merit, 1968; Author award N.J. Assn. Tchrs. English, 1970. Mem. Am. Audubon Soc., N.J. Hist. Soc. Author: Before The Waters: The Upper Delaware Valley, 1966; Millstone Valley, 1969; co-author: Princeton Architecture: A Pictorial History of Town and Campus, 1967. Contbr. articles to various publs. Home: 926 Kingston Rd Princeton NJ 08540

MENZIES, JEAN STORKE (MRS. ERNEST F. MENZIES), ret. newspaperwoman; b. Santa Barbara, Cal., Dec. 30, 1904; d. Thomas More and Elsie (Smith) Storke; B.A., Vassar Coll., 1927; M.A. in Physics, Stanford, 1931; m. Ernest F. Menzies, Oct. 20, 1937; children—Jean Storke (Mrs. Dennis Wayne Vaughan), Thomas More. Teaching asst. dept. physics Stanford, 1928-29; instr. of physics Vassar Coll., 1929-30; tchr. math., chemistry, gen. sci. Sarah Dix Hamlin Sch., San Francisco, 1931-34; press reporter, spl. writer Santa Barbara News-Press, 1954-71. Rec. sec. YWCA, India, Burma and Ceylon, 1941-42; rec. sec., Calcutta, 1942-47, v.p., 1949-51; sec. Tri-County adv. council Children's Home Soc., Santa Barbara, 1952-54; founding dir., sec. corp. Santa Barbara Film Soc., Inc., 1960-66. Bd. dirs. Santa Barbara County chpt. Am. Assn. UN, 1954-59; bd. friends U. Cal. at Santa Barbara Library; sec. bd. trustees Crane Country Day Sch., 1955-57; trustee Mental Hygiene Clinic of Santa Barbara; adv. council Santa Barbara Citizens Adult Edn., 1958-62, v.p., 1960-62; bd. dirs. Internat. Social Sci. Inst., sec., 1963-68, mem. adv. bd., 1969; bd. dirs. Planned Parenthood Santa Barbara County, Inc., 1964-65, adv. council, 1966-67; trustee Santa Barbara Botanic Garden, 1967—, Santa Barbara Trust for Historic Preservation, 1967-68, 72-74; mem. affiliates bd. dirs. U. Cal. at Santa Barbara, 1960-61, 67-70, 72—; sec. Santa Barbara Mission Archive-Library, 1967—. Mem. Santa Barbara Hist. Soc. (dir. 1957-62, founding mem. women's projects bd. 1959-63, sec. 1961-62), Channel City Women's Forum (v.p. 1969-73, bd. dirs.), Phi Beta Kappa, Sigma Xi. Club: Vassar of Santa Barbara and the Tri-Counties (1st v.p., founding com. 1956-57, 2d v.p., 1959-61, chmn. publicity com. 1961—). Home: 2298 Featherhill Rd Santa Barbara CA 93108

MERCER, CAROLINE GASTON, educator; b. Mpls., Apr. 13, 1908; d. Hugh Victor and Edith (Crawford) Mercer; B.A., Vassar Coll., 1929; M.A., Radcliffe Coll., 1931; Ph.D., U. Chgo., 1948. Tchr. pvt. schs., 1929-36; faculty Vassar Coll., 1938—, successively instr., asst. prof., asso. prof., prof., asst. dean, 1938-40, chmn. English dept., 1956-58, 62-69, Mary A. Scott Found. prof., 1956-73, prof. emeritus, 1973—. Mem. Am. Assn. U. Women, Modern Lang. Assn., Phi Beta Kappa. Home: 528 Belgravia Ct Poughkeepsie NY 12603

MERCER, CAROLYN MALINA (MRS. SMITH ABNER MERCER), psychologist; b. Brenham, Tex., Oct. 1, 1915; d. Frank and Caroline (Marek) Malina; B.A., U. Tex., 1936; M.A., U. Houston, 1961, Ph.D., 1968; m. Smith Abner Mercer, June 7, 1941; children—Smith A., Thomas Frank. Reporter, Temple (Tex.) Daily Telegram, 1936-40; editor Bellaire Texan, 1953-55; tchr. Houston Sch. System, 1955-58, counselor, 1958-65; teaching fellow psychology dept. U. Houston, 1965-68, acting dir. reading clinic, 1966-68; staff psychologist Richmond State Sch., Tex. Dept. Mental Health-Mental Retardation, 1968-69, chief psychologist, 1969-71; owner, chief psychologist Psychol. Services Assos., Houston, 1968—; dir. Texan Pub. Co., Houston. Mem. Tex. Citizens Adv. Commn. on the Handicapped. Mem. Am. Psychol. Assn., Tex., Southwestern, Houston psychol. assns., Psi Chi, Theta Sigma Phi. Home: 7702 Braeburn Valley Dr Houston TX 77036 Office: 5433 Westheimer St 1106 Houston TX 77027

MERCER, JEANNE EMILY KEHOE (MRS. THOMAS H. MERCER), pediatrician; b. Joliet, Ill., June 3, 1924; d. John Joseph and Marjorie (Moss) Kehoe; B.A., U. Ill., 1944, B.S., 1945, M.D., 1947; m. Thomas H. Mercer, Feb. 12, 1949; children—Margaret, Emily, Mary Anne. Intern, Cook County Hosp., Chgo., 1947-48, resident, 1948-50; practice medicine specializing in pediatrics, Oak Park, Ill., 1950—; mem. staff Oak Park, West Suburban, Presbyn-St. Lukes, Gottlieb hosps.; asso. prof. Rush Med. Sch., 1971—; mem. teaching staff Foster McGaw Med. Sch., Loyola U., 1973—. Head Start cons. Rock Island Area. Active Community Nursing Service. Diplomate Am. Bd. Pediatrics. Home: 1015 Park Av River Forest IL 60305 Office: 715 Lake St Oak Park IL 60301 also 837 S Westmore Lombard IL 60149

MERCER, MARGARET, psychologist; b. Ridgway, Pa., Oct. 8, 1907; d. Edwin Talmadge and Mary Agnes (O'Keefe) Mercer; A.B., Pa. State U., 1929, M.S., 1934, Ph.D., 1938. Tchr. math. Renovo High Sch., Pa., 1929-35; asst. prof. counseling service Cornell U., 1937-42; intern psychologist N.Y. State Psychol. Intern. Tng. Program, 1942-43; psychologist, State Tng. Sch. for Girls, Hudson, N.Y., 1943-44, State Hosp., Torrance, Pa., 1944-46; chief psychologist VA Hosp., Coatesville, Pa., 1947-52; dir. tng., psychology br., St. Elizabeth Hosp., Washington, 1952-57, dir. research, 1958-61, dir. research in clin. psychology, behavioral studies br., 1961-70; chmn. psychology dept. Lock Haven (Pa.) State Coll., 1970-73; psychologist Rehab. Center, Williamsport (Pa.) Hosp., 1973—. Diplomate clin. psychology Am.. Bd. Examiners in Profl. Psychology. Fellow Am. Psychol. Assn., Sigma Xi. Home: 324 Rural Av Williamsport PA 17701 Office: Rehab Center Williamsport Hosp Williamsport PA 17701

MERCER, MARIAN, actress, singer; b. Akron, O., Nov. 26, 1935; d. Samuel and Nelle Mercer; B.Mus., U. Mich., 1957. Appeared in Hotel Paradiso, 1959, Greenwillow, 1960, The Tunnel of Love, 1960, Fiorello!, 1959, Little Mary Sunshine, 1959, New Faces of 62, and numerous other plays; appeared on TV shows The Dave Garroway Show, 1961, Mike Wallace Show, 1961, Andy Williams Show, 1962. Recipient Antoinette Perry award, 1968-69. Office: 1 W 72d St New York City NY 10023*

MERCER, MARILYN, editor; b. White Plains, N.Y., June 10, 1923; d. Harold and Clara Smith (Whelpley) Mercer; B.A., Smith Coll., 1945. Editor/columnist Bell-N.Am., 1949-57; feature writer, editor Sunday mag. N.Y. Herald Tribune, 1957-60, 62-63; feature editor Glamour mag., 1960-62, 63-70; women's service editor McCall's mag., N.Y.C., 1970—; cons. editor Allied Publs., 1970. Mem. Authors Guild, Am. Soc. Mag. Editors, N.Y. Newswomen's Club. Author: (with Joyce Peterson) Adultery for Adults, 1967. Contbr. articles to profl. jours. and mags. Home: 340 E 64th St New York City NY 10021 Office: 230 Park Av New York City NY 10017

MERCK, BARBARA JEAN HOLT (MRS. DANIEL E. MERCK), educator, med. adminstr.; b. Pensacola, Fla., June 17, 1924; d. Mack Haley and Geneva (James) Holt; A.B., Fla. State U., 1946; M.A., Stetson U., 1948; postgrad. U. Paris, 1953; m. Daniel E. Merck, Aug. 28, 1955; 1 son, Daniel Michael. Tchr. English, speech Pensacola High Sch., 1946-47; civilian actress technician U.S. Govt., Far East, 1948-49; pvt. elementary sch. instr., Bluefield, Nicaragua, 1949-50; instr. English, speech, drama Pensacola Jr. Coll., 1950-54; instr. English, Samford U. (formerly Howard Coll.), Birmingham, Ala., 1955-58, asst. prof., 1958-61, 63-66; med. adminstr. Baptist Med. Center, Birmingham, 1969—. Mem. Woman's Aux. Jefferson County Med. Soc. Faculty Wives Club Med. Coll. Ala., Sigma Tau Delta. Address: Profl Bldg Bapt Med Center 801 Princeton Av Suite 217 Birmingham AL 35211

MERCKENS, ROSEMARY EILEEN HEMINGER (MRS. RUSSELL NEIL MERCKENS), editor; b. Oak Harbor, O., Sept. 30, 1931; d. Oscar John Fred and Irene Esther (Bovia) Heminger; grad. high sch.; m. Russell Neil Merckens, Oct. 21, 1950; children—Rhonda (Mrs. Michael Botti), Rita (Mrs. James Mahler), Russell Neil, Ruthe (Mrs. Tom Sisson). Sec., Worthy R. Brown & Sons, Lakeside, O., 1948-51; distbr. Toledo Blade newspaper, 1960-61; reporter, sec. Peninsular News, 1963; co-owner, editor Peninsular Printing Co., Marblehead, O., 1968—. Leader, troop organizer service team Erie Shores council Girl Scouts Am., 1959-71; v.p. programming, membership P.T.A., 1960's. Mem. Tuscarawas (hon.), Ottawa County (corr. sec. 1971—) hist. socs., Nat. Fedn. Independent Bus. Republican. Lutheran. Home: 230 E 2d St Lakeside OH 43440 Office: PO Box 27 710 Cedar Av Marblehead OH 43440

MERCOURI, MELINA, Greek screen actress, b. 1929. Has appeared in Stella, 1955; He Who Must Die, 1956; Gipsy and the Gentleman; Never on Sunday, 1959; Phaedra, 1961; The Victors, 1963; Light of Day, 1963; Topkapi, 1964. Address: care Jules Dassin 25 rue du Montparnasse Paris France*

MEREDITH, FANNIE MAE HOWELL (MRS. DANIEL THOMAS MEREDITH), assn. exec.; b. Waco, Tex., Sept. 29, 1917; d. Rufus Jefferson and Cordie Lee (Ricketts) Howell; student Baylor U., 1935-36, Bus. Coll., Waco, 1936; B.A. cum laude, Grand Canyon Coll., 1960; m. Daniel Thomas Meredith, Dec. 23, 1943; children—Gloria (Mrs. Dan W. Walton), James Harris, Daniel Robert. Auditor, Sears, Roebuck & Co., Waco, Tex., 1936-41, employee auditing office, Dallas, 1941-42; employee auditing office United Gas Pipe Line, Dallas, 1942-43; alumni sec. Grand Canyon Coll. Phoenix, 1961-72, exec. sec. (alumni), 1972—. Pres. Women's Aux. Orangewood Retirement Home, Phoenix, 1967-70; local pres. Am. Bapt. Women, 1960-64, area pres., 1970-72, regional sec., 1970-72. Recipient Alumnus of yr. award Grand Canyon Coll. Alumni Assn., 1972, service award, 1965. Republican. Home: 5309 N Palo Cristi Rd Paradise Valley AZ 85253 Office: 3300 W Camelback Rd Phoenix AZ 85017 also PO Box 11097 Phoenix AZ 85061

MEREDITH, MARTHA EDIE SCHICK (MRS. C. SPENCER MEREDITH III), physician; b. Connellsville, Pa., Feb. 19, 1916; d. John Lawrence and Mary Carson (Edie) Schick; B.S., U. Pitts., 1946, M.D., 1947; m. C. Spencer Meredith III, July 23, 1949; children—Mary Edie (Mrs. Louis J. Rovelli), C. Spencer IV, John Lawrence. Intern, Phila. Gen. Hosp., 1947-49; resident pathology VA Hosp., Dallas, 1951-54; pracitce medicine specializing in pathology, Dallas, 1954-57, New Orleans, 1967-72, Biloxi, Miss., 1970—; chief lab. service VA Hosp., Dallas, 1955-57; mem. staffs VA Hosp., New Orleans, La. State U. Hosp., New Orleans, VA. Hosp., Biloxi, Miss. Home: 501 Brookside Av Biloxi MS 39531 Office: Biloxi VA Hosp Biloxi MS 39531

MERENBACH, ALICE THACKER, lawyer; b. Santurce, P.R., Feb. 21, 1936; d. William Jennings and Alice Lorena (Sherry) Thacker; A.A., Santa Monica City Coll., 1955; B.A., U. Cal. at Los Angeles, 1958; J.D., Loyola U., Los Angeles, 1966; m. Dennis G. Merenbach, Dec. 20, 1964 (div. 1974); children—Michael, Susan. Admitted to Cal. bar, 1966; dep. dist. atty., Santa Barbara, 1966-68, 1974—; practice law, Santa Barbara, 1968—; judge pro tem Santa Barbara Superior Ct., 1971; referee Juvenile Ct., Santa Barbara, 1972-74. Mem. continuing edn. adv. council Santa Barbara City Coll., 1973—; co-chmn. Community Support Com. to Establish Methadone Program in Santa Barbara, 1970-71. Pres. Eastside Republican Women's Club, 1971-72; mem. Santa Barbara County Rep. Central Com., 1972—; asso. mem. Cal. Rep. Central Com., 1972-73. Mem. State Bar Cal., Santa Barbara County Bar (dir. 1973—), Barristers, Lawyers Wives (pres. 1973), Am. Assn. U. Women (charter mem. Goleta br.), D.A.R. (corr. sec. 1970-73), Loyola Advocates, U. Cal. at Santa Barbara Affiliates, U. Cal. at Los Angeles Alumni Assn. (life), Nat. Orgn. for Women, Phi Alpha Delta. Clubs: La Cumbre Country, Channel City Women's (Santa Barbara). Home: 3913 Camellia Lane Santa Barbara CA 93110 Office: 118E Figueroa St Santa Barbara CA 93105

MERHILL, HARRIETTE DICK, educator; b. N.Y.C.; d. Jacob and Frances (Weiss) Dick; B.A., John B. Stetson U., 1956, M.A., 1960; m. Cyril E. Merhill, Feb. 25, 1943 (dec. Jan. 1958); 1 dau., Linda Kay (Mrs. George E. Mayo). Staff mem. Sterling House Community Center, Stratford, Conn., 1941-43, Volusia County council Girl Scouts U.S.A., Daytona Beach, Fla., 1951-52; elementary tchr., Orange County, 1956-60, elementary tchr., counselor, 1960-62; tchr., counselor, dir. in-service tng. Gateway Sch. for Emotionally Disturbed Children, Orange County, 1962-63; guidance counselor Union Park Jr. High Sch., Orange County, 1963-68; exec. staff Assn. for Childhood Edn. Internat., Washington, 1968-69; supr. guidance Orange County Pub. Schs., Orlando, Fla., 1969—. Mem. exec. bd. Volusia council Girl Scouts U.S.A., 1950-53; Volusia County council PTA, 1953-56; membership chmn. Fla. Com. for Children and Youth. Recipient fellowship Assn. for Childhood Edn. Internat., 1968-69. Mem. Am., Fla., Central Fla. (pres. 1967-68) personnel and guidance assns., Assn. for Childhood Edn. Internat., Fla. Assn. for Curriculum and Supervision, Fla. Council for Research, Orange County Edn. Assn. (pres. 1960-61), Orange County Guidance Assn. (pres. 1963-64), Central Fla. Council Continuing Edn. for Women (dir.), Fla. (treas. 1969-71), Orlando-Central Fla. (pres. 1967-68, 69-71) assns. childhood edn., Orange County Classroom Tchrs. Assn. (dir. 1st v.p. 1963-66), Fla. Assn. Counselor Educators and Suprs. (pres.-elect 1973), Alpha Delta Kappa, Kappa Delta Pi. Contbr. articles to profl. jours. Address: 3624 Wren Lane Orlando FL 32803 also 410 Woods Av Orlando FL 32806

MERITT, LUCY SHOE, archaeologist, educator; b. Camden, N.J., Aug. 7, 1906; d. William Bonaparte and Mary Esther (Dunning) Shoe; A.B., Bryn Mawr Coll., 1927, M.A., 1928, Ph.D., 1935; L.H.D., Brown U., 1974; m. Benjamin Dean Meritt. Fellow Am. Sch. Classical Studies, Athens, Greece, 1929-32; fellow Am. Acad. in Rome, 1936-37, research fellow, 1949-50; asst. prof. art, archaeology and Greek, Mt. Holyoke Coll., 1937-42, asso. prof., 1942-50, counselor, chief counselor of students, 1943-47; mem. Isnt. for Advanced Study, Princeton, 1948-49, 50-73; vis. prof. Washington U., St. Louis, 1958, 60; vis. lectr. Princeton, 1959; prof. U. Tex., Austin, 1973-74, vis. scholar, 1973—. Mem. excavation staff at Cosa, 1950, Morgantina, 1957. Mem. mng. com. Am. Sch. Classical Studies, 1937—, exec. com., 1948-52, chmn. publs. com., editor publs., 1950-72. Mem. Archaeol. Inst. Am. (recorder 1960-68, 71, acting gen. sec. 1962, pres. Princeton soc. 1963-67), Soc. Archtl. Historians, Alumni Assn. Am. Sch. Classical Studies (sec.-treas. 1940—), Classical Soc. Am. Acad. in Rome (pres. 1952), German Archaeol. Inst. (corr.), Internat. Assn. Classical Archaeology (corr.). Clubs: Bryn Mawr of Princeton (pres. 1956-57, 59-63; Austin Womans; Pathfinders. Author: Profiles of Greek Mouldings, 1936; Profiles of Western Greek Mouldings, 1952; Etruscan and Republican Roman Mouldings, 1965. Contbr. articles to profl. publs. Home: 712 W 16th St Austin TX 78701

MERIWETHER, BETTY ANN, physician, naval officer; b. nr. Clarksville, Tenn., Feb. 22, 1934; d. Bowman S. and Drusilla (Clendenin) Meriwether; B.A., Asbury Coll., 1956; M.D., U. Tenn., 1959. Intern, Mobile (Ala.) Gen. Hosp., 1960-61; dir. pub. health Warren and White Counties, Tenn., 1961; gen. practice medicine, McMinnville, Tenn., 1961-62; resident gen. surgery St. Thomas Hosp., Nashville, 1962-63; resident obstetrics and gynecology U. Ala., Birmingham, 1963-66; practice obstetrics and gynecology, Grand Prairie, Tex., 1969-70; chief obstetrics and gynecology dept. Gt. S.W. Gen. Hosp., Grand Prairie, 1969-70; dir. gynecol. nurse practicioner program U.S. Naval Hosp., Portsmouth, Va., mem. faculty, 1970—. Served to comdr. USN, 1966-69, 70—. Diplomate Am. Bd. Obstetrics and Gynecology. Fellow Am. Coll. Obstetrics and Gynecology; mem. A.M.A. Republican. Methodist. Address: Box 601 care Portsmouth Naval Hosp Portsmouth VA 23708

MERIWETHER, LEE, actress; b. Los Angeles, May 27, 1939; d. Gregg and Ethel (Mulligan) M.; ed. City Coll. San Francisco; m. Frank Aletter, Apr. 1958; children—Kyle, Lesley. Films include 4-D Man, Courtship of Eddie's Father, Batman, Angel in My Pocket, The Undefeated, The Bros. O'Toole; TV series Time Tunnel, Andy Griffith Show, Barnaby Jones; stage appearances include Tunnel of Love, Affairs of State, Hatful of Rain, Aesop in the Park, Spoon River Anthology. Named Miss Am., 1955. Address: care Esine Chandler Pub Relations 195 S Beverly Dr Beverly Hills CA 90212

MERJOS, ANNA, editor; b. N.Y.C.; d. Stavros and Helen (Papavasiliou) Merjos; B.A., Hunter Coll., 1944. Asst. mathematician Columbia, N.Y.C., 1944-45; econ. analyst Econometric Inst., N.Y.C., 1945-51; asst. v.p. Merrill Lynch, Pierce, Fenner & Smith, Inc., N.Y.C., 1951—. Mem. Phi Beta Kappa, Pi Mu Epsilon. Home: 205 W End Av New York City NY 10023 Office: One Liberty Plaza 165 Broadway New York City NY 10006

MERLINO, MAXINE OLLIE SEELBINDER (MRS. DANTE R. MERLINO), educator, artist; b. Portland, Ore., July, 1912; d. Ernest August and Ollie (Shuey) Seelbinder; scholar. Mus. Art Sch., Portland, 1933-36, Art Students League, N.Y.C., 1936-39; B.A., Long Beach (Cal.) State Coll., 1952, M.A., 1952; Ed.D., U. So. Cal., 1961; m. Dante R. Merlino, Nov. 23, 1936; 1 son, Dante R. Free lance artist, murals and illustrations, N.Y.C., Washington, 1939-43, Long Beach, 1945-46; sci. illustrator USAAF, 1944-45; set designer and interior murals Preston Sturges, Hollywood porducer and dir., 1946-52; prof. art, dean Sch. Fine Arts, Cal. State U., Long Beach, 1952—; exhibited in group shows Eastern U.S., 1937-43, Western U.S., 1952—. Illustrator, art cons. Teaching Tools (periodical), 1954-59. Active YWCA, Children's Theater. Mem. Art Student's League N.Y.C. (life), Am. Assn. U. Profs. Contbr. illustrations to popular mags. Home: 359 Panama Av Long Beach CA 90814

MERMAN, MARY MARGUERITE (MRS. JOHN RICHARD GIBEL), lawyer; b. Pitts., Jan. 25, 1928; d. Frank J. and Marguerite M.J. (Compston) Merman; A.B., Duquesne U., 1950; certificate in comml. art Ad-Art Coll., 1948; J.D., U. Pitts., 1953; m. John Richard Gibel, Jan. 27, 1968; children—Marsia L., Jeannine M. Admitted to Pa. bar, 1954, D.C. bar, 1954; law preceptor Seif, Schultz & Frost, Pitts., 1953-54; pvt. practice law, Pitts., 1955, 59-62; atty. Rose, Rose & Houston, Pitts., 1955-58; counsel Pitts. dist. office Small Bus. Adminstrn., Pitts., 1962—. Mem. Pa., Fed. (pres. Pitts. chpt. 1965, sec. 1962-63, first v.p. 1963-64, mem. exec. bd. 1966-67), Allegheny County bar assns., Allegheny County Lawyers Club (v.p. 1968-69, mem. exec. bd. 1961-66, sec. 1960-61). Home: 617 St James St Pittsburgh PA 15232 Office: 1401 Federal Bldg 1000 Liberty Av Pittsburgh PA 15222

MEROLA, EMMA M. VARVARO, physician; b. N.Y.C., Jan. 1, 1908; d. Ettore and Anna (Borghini) Varvaro; B.S., Douglass Coll., 1930; student Woman's Med. Coll., 1930-33; M.D., Middlesex Coll., 1936; m. Joseph F. Merola, Nov. 30, 1939; children—Frank, Joseph, Henry, Anthony, Marianne. Intern Glens Falls (N.Y.) Hosp., 1936-37; X-ray, lab. work Victory Meml. Hosp., Bklyn., 1937-39; practice, Waltham, Mass., 1939—; staff Waltham Hosp. Tchr. elementary sch., 1964-65; instr. in Teaching English as Fgn. Lang. program, 1968-69. Leader Girl Scouts and Boy Scouts. Mem. adv. bd. Salvation Army of Waltham, 1961-65; mem. Am. Med. Polit. Action Com. Mem. A.M.A., Mass. Med. Soc., Middlesex Aux. Mass. Med. Soc., Am. Med. Women's Assn. (pres. 1960), Douglass Boston Alumnae Club (pres. 1959), League Women Voters, Grapho-Analyst Study Group, Charles River Med. Soc., Charles River Aux., Internat. Platform Assn., St. Luke's Guild Mass. Cath. Physicians. Club: College. Home: 114 Church St Waltham MA 02154 Office: 117 Summer St Waltham MA 02154

MERRIAM, EVE (MRS. LEONARD C. LEWIN), poet, author; b. Phila., July 19, 1916; student pub. schs.; m. Leonard C. Lewin; children—Guy Michel, Dee Michel. Recipient Yale Younger Poets prize, 1946, Colliers Star Fiction award. Mem. Soc. Mag. Writers, Dramatists Guild. Author: The Double Bed From the Feminine Side, 1958; The Voice of Liberty, 1959; The Trouble With Love, 1961; Figleaf: The Business of Being in Fashion, 1961; Mommies at Work, 1962; Basics—An I Can Read Book for Grownups, 1962; There is No Rhyme for Silver, 1962; It Doesn't Always Have to Rhyme. After Nora Slammed the Door, 1964; Independent Voices, 1968; The Inner City Mother Goose, 1969; The Nixon Poems; Finding A Poem, 1970; Growing Up Female in America: 10 Lives, 1971; Inner City (Broadway musical), 1971-72; Out Loud, 1973. Co-editor Male and Female Under 18, 1973. Contbr. to mags. and anthologies in U.S. and fgn. countries. Address: 10 Water St Stonington CT 06378

MERRIAM, IDA CRAVEN (MRS. MYLON MERRIAM), govt. ofcl.; b. Phila., Nov. 6, 1904; d. William Ayres and Amelia (Sonntag) Craven; A.B., Wellesley Coll., 1925; student U. Chgo., 1925-26; Ph.D., Brookings Grad. Sch. Econs. and Govt., 1928; m. Mylon Merriam, Feb. 17, 1933; 1 dau., Hannah Greene. Assn. editor Ency. of Social Scis., 1928-34; asst. prof. econs. Conn. Coll. Women, 1934-36; with Social Security Adminstrn., Dept. Health, Edn. and Welfare, 1936—, successively econ. analyst, asst. dir., dir. research and statistics, 1956-65, asst. commr. for research, 1965-72, spl. asst. to commr., 1972—; expert, tech. adviser, social security ILO, Govt. of Thailand, 1955-56. Recipient Fed. Women's award, 1966; distinguished service award Nat. Conf. on Social Welfare, 1969. Fellow Am. Statis. Assn.; mem. Am. Econ. Assn., Am. Pub. Welfare Assn., Phi Beta Kappa. Author articles in field. Home: 2908 Brandywine St NW Washington DC 20008 Office: Social Security Adminstrn Washington DC 20201

MERRICK, BARBARA HALL, art gallery exec.; b. Sioux Falls, S.D., Jan. 3, 1937; d. Philip Taylor and Clara Belle (Owens) Hall; B.F.A., State U. Ia., 1959, postgrad., 1960; div. Staff mem. N.Y. U., 1961; asst. display dir., fashion coordinator Gilchrests Dept. Stores, Boston, 1961-62; fashion coordinator Alexanders Dept. Stores, N.Y.C., 1962-63, asst. fashion dir., 1964-65, exec. fashion dir., head coordinator, 1965-68; owner, dir. Gallery Modern Art, Taos, N.M., 1969—. Mem. Taos C. of C. (dir. 1971), Pi Beta Phi. Contbr. articles to profl. jours. Home: Box 1072 Taos NM 87571 Office: Gallery of Modern Art Box 1072 Taos NM 87571

MERRICK, EUNICE PEACOCK (MRS. GEORGE E. MERRICK), civic worker; b. Coconut Grove, Fla.; d. Alfred and Lillian (Frow) Peacock; student pvt. and pub. schs.; m. George Edgar Merrick, Feb. 5, 1916. Treas. George E. Merrick, Inc., real estate, 1934-42, pres., 1942-45. Active in establishing Dade County Schs., Coral Gables, 1922-25. Recipient Book of Golden Deeds, Exchange Club Coral Gables, 1957. Mem. Hist. Soc. So. Fla., Fla. Hist. Soc., Fairchild Tropical Garden, Nat. League Am. Pen Women (patroness), Sigma Alpha Iota (patroness). Christian Scientist. Clubs: Coral Gables Woman's (charter mem., dir.), Coral Gables Garden (past pres.), George E. Merrick, the original owner, founder Coral Gables, Fla. Home: 1015 Coral Way Coral Gables FL 33134

MERRILL, DINA (MRS. CLIFF ROBERTSON), actress; b. N.Y.C.; d. E.F. Hutton and Marjorie Merriweather Post; ed. Mt. Vernon Sem.; student George Washington U., Am. Acad. Dramatic Arts, Am. Mus. and Dramatic Acad.; m. Stanley M. Rumbough, Jr., Mar. 23, 1946 (div. Dec. 1966); children—Stanley, Nina; m. 2d, Cliff Robertson, Dec. 21, 1966; 1 dau., Heather. Motion picture debut in Desk Set, 1957, co-starred movies including Don't Give Up the Ship, 1958, Operation Petticoat, 1959, The Sundowners, 1960, Butterfield 8, 1961, Courtship of Eddie's Father, 1963, I'll Take Sweden, 1964; Walking Major, 1970, Throw Out the Anchor, 1972, Running Wild, 1974; Shakespeare debut with Helen Hayes Equity Group in Twelfth Night, Othello, 1960; summer theatre tours in Voice of the Turtle, 1961, Write Me a Murder, 1963, Shaw Festival Repertory, Major Barbara, Misalliance, 1965; guest star various TV shows including Playhouse 90, 1958, What Makes Sammy Run?, 1959, DuPont Show of Month, Desilu Playhouse, 1961, Dr. Kildare, Westinghouse Presents, U.S. Steel Hour, 1962, Dick Powell Show, 1962, 63, Alfred Hitchcock Hour, 1963, The Rogues, 1963, 64, Mickey, Kraft Suspense Theatre, 1964, The FBI, Bob Hope Chrysler Theatre, Daktari, 1965, Bonanza, Bob Hope Special, 1966, Run For Your Life, 1967, Batman, 1967, Seven in Darkness, 1969, Mission Impossible, 1969, The Lonely Profession, 1969. Bd. dirs. N.Y.C. Mission Soc., Joslin Diabetes Found., Am. Mus. and Dramatic Acad., Inc. Com. Olympic Ski Team, Am. Mus. and Dramatic Acad. Office: 35 W 53d St New York City NY 10019

MERRILL, DOROTHY, educator; b. Abington, Mass., Jan. 1, 1927; d. Byron Hill and Olive Thorne (Miller) Merrill; B.S., Bridgewater State Coll., 1947; A.M., U. Mich., 1959, Ph.D. (Delta Kappa Gamma scholar 1960-61, Rackham fellow 1962-63), 1964. Tchr. high sch., Hanover, Mass., 1947-57, Brockton, Mass., 1957-60; instr. zoology U. Mich. at Ann Arbor, 1963-64; asst. prof. biol. sci. Smith Coll., Northampton, Mass., 1964-70; faculty Western Coll., Oxford, Ohio, 1970-74, asso. prof. biology Biol. Coll. IV Grand Valley State Colls., Allendale, Mich., 1974—. Mem. Am. Soc. Zoologists, A.A.A.S., Animal Behavior Soc., Sigma Xi, Kappa Delta Pi. Episcopalian. Home: 4097-4 Pine Creek Rd Grandville MI 49418 Office: Coll IV Grand Valley State Colls Allendale MI 49401

MERRILL, JEAN FAIRBANKS, writer; b. Rochester, N.Y., Jan. 27, 1923; d. Earl Dwight and Elsie (Fairbanks) Merrill; B.A., Allegheny Coll., 1944; M.A., Wellesley Coll., 1945. Feature editor Scholastic Mags., 1947-50; editor Lit. Cavalcade, 1956-57, publs. div. Bank St. Coll. Edn., 1964-65. Fulbright fellow, India, 1952-53. Mem. N.Am. Mycol. Assn., Authors League, Am. Civil Liberties Union, War Resisters League, Vt. Inst. Natural Scis., Audubon Soc., Phi Beta Kappa. Author children's books: Henry, the Hand-Painted Mouse, 1951; The Woover, 1952; Boxes, 1953; The Tree House of Jimmy Domino, 1955; The Travels of Marco, 1956; A Song for Gar, 1957; The Very Nice Things, 1959; Blue's Broken Heart, 1960; Shan's Lucky Knife (Jr. Lit. Guild selection), Emily Emerson's Moon (Jr. Lit. Guild selection), 1960; The Superlative Horse (Jr. Lit. Guild selection, Lewis Carroll Shelf award 1963), 1961; Tell About the Cowbarn, Daddy, 1963; The Pushcart War (Lewis Carroll Shelf award, Boys' Club Am. Jr. Book award), 1964; High Wide and Handsome (Jr. Lit. Guild selection), 1964; The Elephant Who Liked to Smash Small Cars, 1967; Red Riding, 1968; The Black Sheep, 1969; Here I Come—Ready or Not!, 1970; Mary, Come Running, 1970; How Many Kids Are Hiding on My Block?, 1970; Please, Don't Eat My Cabin, 1971; The Toothpaste Millionaire, 1972; The Second Greatest Clown in the World, 1972; The Jackpot, 1972; The Bumper Sticker Book, 1973; The Girl Who Brightened Up the World, 1974; Maria's House, 1974. Editor: (poetry) A Few Flies and I, 1969. Address: 29 S Main St Randolph VT 05060 also Washington VT 05675

MERRILL, MARY ANN, biologist, author; b. Toledo, Dec. 10, 1930; d. George L. and Dorothy (Borton) Merrill; B.A., U. Ariz., 1953; M.A., U. Miami (Fla.), 1957; grad. De Vry Tech. Inst., 1966, Locksmithing Inst., 1969. Operator marine biol. and fresh water labs., Ray, Ind. and Coral Gables, Fla., 1953; tchr. Shenendoah Jr. High Sch., Miami, 1958-59, Exmoor Sch., Miami, 1959-60; exhibited in group shows at Lowe Art Gallery, Miami, 1955—. Fellow Internat. Oceanographic Found. (life); mem. Audubon Soc., D.A.R., Toledo Art Mus., Lowe Art Gallery, Film Soc., Am. Radio Relay League, Delta Delta Delta. Methodist. Author: Angels & Corners, 1958; Hermit, 1965; Chaoborus, 1965; Shadows, 1969; Synathidae, Vols. I, II, III, 1968-70; Melon Patch, 1969; Survey, 1969; New Mama for Christmas, 1969; Diary of a Lady Spy, 1970; Toledo to Miami by Train, 1970; Richard Basehart, Vols. I-IV, 1970; The Family Speaks for Itself, 1973, others. Home: 1210 S Alhambra Circle Coral Gables FL 33146 Office: 372 Spitzer Bldg Toledo OH 43604

MERRILL, NANCY OSBORNE, curator; b. Somerville, Mass., Nov. 26, 1920; d. Daniel C. and Carrie M. (Matheson) Merrill; B.A., Jackson Coll. Tufts U., 1942. Office mgr. surety dept. Employers Ins. Co., Boston, 1942-52; asst. mgr. Family Summer Hotel, Gifford House, Provincetown, Mass., 1952-63; curator of glass Chrysler Art Mus., Provincetown, 1963-71; curator of glass Chrysler Mus., Norfolk, Va., 1971-73; dir., curator Sandwich (Mass.) Glass Mus., 1973—. Lectr. Corning Glass Mus. Seminar, 1973, Nat. Early Am. Glass Club, 1972, 74, Chrysler Mus. at Norfolk, 1973. Mem. Am. Assn. Museums, Nat. Early Am. Glass Club (2nd v.p. 1973). Club: Cape Cod Tufts (treas. 1969). Home: 13 A School St Sandwich MA 02563 Office: 129 Main St Sandwich MA 02563

MERRILL, SHIRLEY KIMBALL (MRS. CHARLES A. MERRILL), state ofcl.; b. West Peabody, Mass., Sept. 11, 1922; d. Linwood and Carrie Maude (Sawyer) Kimball; B.S., U. N.H., 1944; m. Charles A. Merrill, Nov. 16, 1946; children—John Charles, Nancy Sawyer (Mrs. Marshall Jordan). Mem. city council, Lebanon, N.H., 1967-70; mayor, Lebanon, 1969-70; mem. N.H. Ho. of Reps., 1967-73, chmn. labor com., 1970-73; pub. utilities commr. State of N.H., 1973—. Mem. adv. com. reins. U.S. Dept. Housing and Urban Devel., 1971—; mem. N.H. Appeals Tribunal Dept. Employment Security, 1971-72. Alt. del. Republican Nat. Conv., 1968, 72; asst. chmn. N.H. Rep. Com., 1973—. Club: Woman's (Lebanon). Address: 22 Perley Av Lebanon NH 03766

MERRIMAN, MARGARITA LEONOR DIETEL (MRS. JAMES HOUSTON MERRIMAN), educator; b. Barcelona, Spain, Nov. 29, 1927; d. Victor Ernest and Mary Belle (Holder) Dietel; Mus.B., U. Tenn., 1948; Mus.M., U. Rochester, 1953, Ph.D., 1960; postgrad. U. Mich., 1949, Boston U., 1970; m. James Houston Merriman, June 10, 1956; children—Harold Lyndon, Merri Lynn. Dir. music Shenandoah Valley Acad., 1948-51; asst. prof. music Andrews U., 1951-56, So. Missionary U., 1956-58; prof. music Atlantic Union Coll., South Lancaster, Mass., 1959—. Active Am. Music Center. Mem. Mass. Music Tchrs. Assn. (corr. sec. 1967). Seventh-Day Adventist. Composer: Symphony No. 1, 1959; Psalm 24, 1964; Behold, the Tabernacle of God, 1967; To Him That Overcometh, 1970; (oratorio) The Millennium, 1973. Home: Box 704 South Lancaster MA 01561

MERRIMAN, PATRICIA ANN LLOYD (MRS. KENNETH LEE MERRIMAN), editor; b. Lynchburg, Va., Oct. 5, 1934; d. Corrie Flemming and Mary Irene (Whitten) Lloyd; grad. high sch.; m. Kenneth Lee Merriman, Sept. 5, 1958; 1 dau., Diane Paige. Editorial asst. News Leader, Richmond, Va., 1956-63, asso. editor editorial page, 1963—. Recipient First Place editorial writing Va. Press Assn., 1970, First Place Va. Press Women, 1967, 68, 70, 71. Mem. Nat. Conf. Editorial Writers (chmn. nominations com. 1974—), Va. Press Women (pres. 1972—), Va. Press Assn. (co-chmn. news com. 1973—), Am. Soc. Newspaper Editors, Sigma Delta Chi. Home: 2504 Three Willows Ct Richmond VA 23229 Office: 333 E Grace St Richmond VA 23213

MERRITT, DORIS HONIG (MRS. ARTHUR DONALD MERRITT), univ. dean; b. N.Y.C., July 16, 1923; d. Aaron and Lillian (Kunstlich) Honig; B.A., City U. N.Y., 1944; M.D., George Washington U., 1952 children—Kenneth Arthur, Christopher Ralph. Pediatric intern Duke Hosp., 1952-53; teaching and research fellow dept. pediatrics George Washington U. Sch. Medicine, 1953-54; pediatric asst. resident Duke U. Hosp., 1954-55, cardiovascular fellow dept. pediatrics, 1955-56, instr. dept. pediatrics, dir. pediatric cardiorenal clinic, 1956-57; exec. sec. cardiovascular study sect., gen. medicine study sect., div. research grants NIH, 1957-60; dir. med. research grants and contracts Ind. U. Sch. Medicine, 1961-62, asst. prof. pediatrics, 1961-68, asst. dean med. research, 1962-65, asst. dir. med. research, aerospace research application center, 1963-65, asso. dir. med. research, 1965-68, asst. dean for research, office v.p. for research and dean advanced studies, 1965-67, dir. sponsored programs, asst. to provost, 1965-68, asso. dean for research and advanced studies, office v.p. and dean for research and advanced studies, 1967—, asso. prof. pediatrics, 1968-73, prof., 1973—. Cons. USPHS, NIH, Div. Research Grants, Div. Health Research Facilities and Resources, Nat. Heart Inst., 1963—, Am. Heart Assn., 1963—, Ind. State Med. Assn. Commn. on Vol. Health Orgns., 1964-67, Bur. Health Manpower, Health Profession's Constrn. Program, 1965—, Nat. Library Medicine, Health Center Library Constrn. Program, 1966—; dir. office sponsored programs Ind. U.-Purdue U., Indpls, Office Chancellor, 1968-71, dean research and sponsored programs, 1971—; mem. Nat. Library Medicine biomed. library review com., 1970-74. Chmn. Indpls. Consortium for Urban Edn., 1971—; v.p. Greater Indpls. Progress Com., 1974; mem. Community Service Council, 1969—. Bd. dirs. Bd. for Fundamental Edn., Community Addiction Services Agy., Inc. Served to lt. (j.g.) USNR. Diplomate Nat. Bd. Med. Examiners, Am. Bd. Pediatrics. Fellow Am. Acad. Pediatrics; mem. A.A.A.S., George Washington U., Duke U. med. alumni assns., Phi Beta Kappa, Alpha Omega Alpha. Contbr. articles to profl. jours. Office: 1219 W Michigan St Indianapolis IN 46202

MERRITT, JANET BURTON SCARBOROUGH (MRS. SAMUEL MICKLEBERRY MERRITT), state legislator, musician, writer, educator; b. Americus, Ga., Jan. 4, 1909; d. Robert Henry and Janet Augusta (Burton) Scarborough; B.A., Valdosta State Coll., 1959; m. Samuel Mickleberry Merritt, June 6, 1933; children—Thomas Burton, Mary Ella, Janet. Tchr. pub. schs. Ga. Sch. System, 1928-33; real estate, ins. broker; mem. Ga. Ho. of Reps., 1964—, vice chmn. juvenile affairs com., mem. appropriations com., state instns. and property com., mem. com. state planning and community affairs, sec. long-range planning U. Ga. com. Nat. accredited flower show judge. Mem. Civil Def. Women's Com. of Ga., 1955—; mem. Red Cross Nurses Aide organizing chmn. Gray Ladies, Sumter County chpt. A.R.C., 1964; sec. long range planning U. Ga. com.; mem. Andersonville Prison Park Improvement Com., Andersonville Meml. Monument Com.; mem. Ga. Bicentennial Commn.; mem. Ga. Gov.'s Commn. Planned Growth Ga., Status of Women in Ga.; mem. adv. council State Federated Com. Humanities. Trustee Meadow Garden, Augusta, 1962-68; mem. adv. bd. Tamasee D.A.R. Sch., 1962-65; mem. adv. council Whittaker Center Children with Learning Problems, Atlanta, 1970—; bd. dirs. Americus Goodwill Industries. Mem. D.A.R. (mem. nat. bd. 1960-62, hon. life state regent Ga. Soc.; v.p. gen. Nat. Soc., 1963-66, mem. resolutions com. 1962—), Nat., Ga. music tchrs. assns., Colonial Dames Am. (town chmn. 1964-66), Nat. Order Women Legislators (rec. sec.), Federated Garden Clubs Sumter County (parliamentarian 1964), Jr. Welfare League Americus (charter), Alpha Chi Omega. Democrat. Episcopalian. Clubs: Chi Omega Mothers (U. Ga.); Daylily Garden. Home: 234 W Dodson St Americus GA 31709 Office: 300 Peachtree St Atlanta GA

MERRITT, MARY MARTHA PRESLEY (MRS. CHARLES W. MERRITT), state legislator; b. Tutwiler, Miss., Nov. 2, 1922; d. Curtis Edward and Martha E. (Johnston) Presley; B.A., U. Ky.; m. Charles W. Merritt, July 19, 1947; children—Presley McDonald (Mrs. Joel M. Wagoner), Charles Wesley, Ann Whitten. Mem. W.Va. Ho. of Dels., 1970—. Mem. So. Regional Edn. Bd. Conf., New Orleans, 1972. Named Woman of Year, Jr. Woman's Club, 1971; named Outstanding Woman Legislator, Eagleton Inst. Politics, Rutgers U., 1972. Democrat. Episcopalian. Home: 1518 Harper Rd Beckley WV 25801

MERRITT, MYRTLE AGNES, educator; b. Norway, Ia., Sept. 23, 1925; d. Clarence Edward and Caroline Marie (Zuber) Merritt; B.A., No. Ia. U., 1946; M.A., U. Ia., 1951, Ph.D., 1961. Instr., Maquoketa (Ia.) pub. schs., 1946-48, U. No. Ia., 1948-51, 51-52; prof. health, phys. edn. State U. Coll. Arts and Scis., Geneseo, N.Y., 1952—. Mem. Youth Recreation Com., Geneseo, 1971-72; rec. sec. for bd. dirs. Geneseo Interfaith Center, Inc., 1971—. Trustee Dorothea Deitz Meml. Scholarship Fund. Mem. Nat. Found. Health, Phys. Edn. and Recreation, Am. Assn. U. Profs., Am. Assn. U. Women, A.A.H.P.E.R. (sec.-treas. eastern dist. 1971—, Service award 1973), Nat., Eastern (pres.-elect 1972) assns. phys. edn. coll. women, Assn. Women Phys. Edn. N.Y. State (pres. Central Western area 1966-68, Merit award 1972), N.Y. State Assn. Health, Phys. Edn. and Recreation (sec.-treas. 1966-69, zone pres. 1972—), Pi Lambda Theta. Methodist. Editor Nat. Assn. Phys. Edn. Coll. Women Biennial Record, 1969-71. Home: 12 W View Crescent Geneseo NY 14454

MERRY, ANNABEL PAYTON (MRS. LOUIS GEORGE MERRY), civic worker; b. Clinton, Ind., May 5, 1905; d. James Augustus and Laura Jane Elizabeth (Dugger) Payton; B.A., Ind. State Tchrs. Coll., 1947, postgrad., 1953, 63; m. Louis George Merry, Sept. 24, 1933; 1 dau., Lora (Mrs. Paul E. Lehman). Tchr. rural sch., Clinton Twp., Vermillion County, Ind., 1922-24; elementary tchr., Blanford, Ind., 1924-29, Clinton, Ind., 1929-32, Hammond, Ind., 1932-33; primary tchr., New Marion, Ind., 1942-45, Rockville, Ind., 1945-70. Tchr. Bible, Correctional Center, Rockville, 1969—; restored, researched history of dolls in Parke County Mus.; lectr. on dolls to various clubs; condr. song service at nursing homes. Mem. Nat., Ind., Parke County ret. tchrs. assns., Parke County Hist. Soc. (pres. 1971-72), Sr. Citizens. Methodist (mem. ch. adminstrv. bd. 1968—, mem. welfare adv. bd. 1969-70). Home: 604 E Indiana St Rockville IN 47872

MERRY, FRANCES ROBINSON (MRS. ERNEST BRISCOE MERRY, JR.), civic worker; b. Jacksonville, Fla., May 15, 1914; d. Philip Frank and Lorene (Youngblood) Robinson; student Ward-Belmont Sch., Nashville, 1930-31, Mary Baldwin Coll., 1931-32; m. Ernest Briscoe Merry, Jr., Nov. 1, 1933; children—Frances Robinson (Mrs. George Bryan Simkins), Ernest Briscoe 111, Philip Robinson, Anne Somers. Bd. dirs. Girl Scouts U.S.A., Augusta, Ga. area, 1938-40; bd. dirs. Jr. League, 1936-41, 50-53; pres. Episcopal Day Sch. Assn., 1951-52; with Gray Ladies A.R.C., 1942-44; bd. dirs. Augusta Assembly, 1955-56; chmn. meml. petit point furnishing St. Paul's Episcopal Ch., 1957-66, dir. Jr. Dau. King, 1954-55, pres. Women's Aux., 1943-44. Pres. Augusta Symphony Orch. Guild, 1960-63; bd. dirs. Augusta Symphony and Historic Augusta, Inc.; trustee Augusta Prep. Sch., 1961-72. Clubs: Augusta Country; Town and Country Garden (pres. 1951-52, 66-67), Pinnacle. Home: 16 Indian Cove Rd Augusta GA 30904

MERSEL, MARJORIE KATHRYN PEDERSEN (MRS. JULES MERSEL), lawyer; b. Manila, Utah, June 17, 1923; d. Leo Henry and Kathryn Anna (Reed) Pedersen; A.B., U. Cal., 1948; LL.B., U. San Francisco, 1948; m. Jules Mersel, Apr. 12, 1950; 1 son, Jonathan. Admitted to D.C. bar, 1952, Cal. bar, 1955; Marjorie Kathryn Pedersen Mersel, atty., Beverly Hills, Cal., 1961-71; staff counsel Dept. Real Estate State of Cal., Los Angeles, 1971—. Mem. Beverly Hills Bar Assn., Trial Lawyers Assn., So. Cal. Women Lawyers Assn. (treas. 1962-63), Beverly Hills C. of C. Home: 13007 Hartsook St Sherman Oaks CA 91403 Office: Dept Real Estate 107 S Broadway Los Angeles CA

MERSEREAU, ANNIE RUTH CROSS (MRS. PAUL ELIJAH MERSEREAU), ednl. adminstr.; b. Chapel Hill, N.C., Nov. 3, 1921; d. Coy Robert and Martha Estelle (Lutterloh) Cross; B.A., N.C. Central Coll., 1943; M.A., N.Y. U., 1950; postgrad. Columbia, 1962; m. Paul Elijah, Oct. 12, 1957; 1 son, Robert Elliott (dec.). Tchr. pub. schs., N.Y.C., 1947-55; sch. community coordinator dist. 19 Bd. Edn., N.Y.C., 1955-58; tchr., guidance counselor pub. sch., N.Y.C., 1958-66; dir. Title I pub. schs. Central Harlem dist., N.Y.C., 1966-73; dep. supt. dist. 1 Bd. Edn., N.Y.C., 1973—. Ednl. cons. Flower and Fifth Av. Hosp., N.Y.C., 1956-57, 369th Vets. Assn., 1956-57, Local 372, Profl. Household Workers, 1973-74; mem. council suprs. N.Y.C. Bd. Edn., 1969—. Pres. Friends United for Harlem Prep., 1971—. Trustee Teaneck (N.J.) Bd. Edn., 1972—; mem. N.Y. State Democratic Com., 1961-66, N.Y. County Dem. Com., Teaneck, N.J., 1969—. Bd. dirs. YWCA, Hackensack, N.J. Recipient Tchr. of Yr. award Mayor of N.Y.C., 1955; award B'nai B'rith, 1957. Mem. Nat. Assn. Bus. and Profl. Women (Teaneck pres. 1971—), N.A.A.C.P., Delta Sigma Theta. Democrat. Home: 1181 Congress Av Teaneck NJ 07666 Office: 75 Av B New York City NY 10009

MERTENS, PATRICIA FURLONG, cons.; b. Trenton, Mo., Sept. 27, 1944; d. Stanley Francis and Rema A. (Nea) Furlong; A.A. (Sadie Yates scholar), Trenton Jr. Coll., 1964; B.S. in Edn. (Regents scholar) N.W. Mo. State Coll., 1966; M.A. . in L.S., U. Mich., 1967; m. John Fray Mertens, Aug. 17, 1969. Clk., typist Grundy County-Jewett Norris Library, Trenton, 1962-64; children's librarian Daniel Boone Regional Library, Columbia, Mo., 1967-71, regional cons. for children's service, 1971-74. Mem. children's book selection com. Mo. State Library, Jefferson City, 1967-74. Recipient John Cotton Dana Spl. award A.L.A. and H.W. Wilson Co., 1973. Mo. State Library scholar, 1966; Fed. Library Services and Constrn. Act grantee, 1971. Mem. Am. Assn. U. Women (social chmn. 1970-71), Mo. Library Assn., Phi Theta Kappa, Gamma Sigma Sigma. Home: 405 N Main Poplar Bluff MO 63901

MERTZ, EVA JULITTA, dentist; b. Wilno, Poland, Dec. 14, 1935 (parents Am. citizens); d. Witold Waclaw and Anna (Szadziewicz) Putkowski; B.A., Rutgers U., 1957; D.D.S., U. Pa., 1961; postgrad. Phila. Coll. Pharmacy and Sci., 1964; m. Roland F. Mertz, Sept. 2, 1957 (dec. Apr. 1973). Practice gen. dentistry, Drexel Hill, Pa., 1961; translator, abstractor Med. Lit., Inc., Phila., 1962-65; med. writer, editor drug regulatory affairs dept. E.R. Squibb & Sons, Inc., 1965-70; dental asso. Dental Clin. research dept. Johnson & Johnson, New Brunswick, N.J., 1970-72, asst. dir., 1972—. Mem. Am., N.J., Middlesex County dental assns., Assn. Am. Women Dentists, Internat. Assn. for Dental Research, Federation Dentaire Internationale, Am. Soc. Preventive Dentistry, Am. Assn. Dental Schs., Am. Soc. Dentistry for Children, Am. Pub. Health Assn., Pa. Women's Dental Soc., Am. Med. Writers Assn., MEDICUS. Office: Johnson & Johnson Dental Clin Research Dental Products Co 20 Lake Dr East Windsor NJ 08520

MERTZ, JOANNE ELIZABETH, pediatrician; b. Lafayette, Ind., May 12, 1926; d. J. Harold and Esther (Simons) Mertz; B.S., Purdue U., 1947; M.D., Duke, 1951. Intern, Cin. Gen. Hosp., 1951-52; resident Children's Hosp., Cin., 1952-54, asst. dir. out-patient clinic, 1954-55; instr. pediatrics U. Cin. Sch. Medicine, 1954-55; active staff Little Traverse Hosp., Petoskey, Mich.; mem. dept. pediatrics Burns Clinic, Petoskey. Mem. Petoskey Area Mental Health Clinic Bd., 1974—. Diplomate Am. Bd. Pediatrics. Fellow Am. Acad. Pediatrics (sec. Mich. chpt.); mem. Western Mich. Pediatric Soc., Am. Assn. U. Women. Home: Rural Route 1 Resort Pike Petoskey MI 49770 Office: Burns Clinic Petoskey MI 49770

MERTZ, MARY KATHRYN BECK (MRS. HAROLD L. MERTZ), govt. ofcl.; b. Milton, Pa., Jan. 31, 1933; d. Earl Starrett and Bernice (Diehl) Beck; grad. high sch.; m. Harold L. Mertz, Feb. 15, 1952; children—Vickie (Mrs. Doren Edward Berkheimer, Jr.), Dann Andrew, Keith Alan. Sec., Fox Knapp Mfg. Co., Milton, Pa., 1953-55; clk. sec. Montgomery Mills, Inc. (Pa.), 1955-60; chief clk. Borough of Milton (Pa.), 1960—. Sec. Little League Aux. Milton, 1963. Sec. Milton Planning Commn., 1972; rec. sec. Milton Zoning Hearing Bd., 1968—. Mem. Nat. Fedn. Bus. and Profl. Women's Clubs (local v.p.), Pa. Assn. Notaries. Club: Union County Sportsmen (Weikert, Pa.). Home: 14 Sycamore Lane Milton PA 17847 Office: 28 N Front St Milton PA 17847

MESCALL, SISTER ELOISE THERESE, educator; b. Los Angeles, Dec. 20, 1919; d. Thomas Francis and Ottilia Mary Louise (Durazzo) Mescall; B.A., U. Cal. at Los Angeles, 1946; M.A., 1949, Ph.D., 1959; hon. diploma U. Madrid, 1952. Joined Order, 1937; vis. prof. Dominican Coll., San Rafael, summer 1947; mem. faculty Mt. St. Mary's Coll., Los Angeles, 1948—, prof. romance langs., 1959—, chmn. modern lang. dept., 1948-61, dir. Doheny campus, 1959-64, dir. devel., 1964-67. Dir. various travel study tours; exchange prof. Fontbonne Coll., St. Louis, 1967-68; mem. audit com. bilingual programs Cal., HEW, 1969-73; evaluator proposals Title VII, U.S. Office Edn., 1969-73. Mem. Mayor's Com. for Internat. Visitors, 1966—, Cal. Com. on Fgn. Langs., 1961-62. Travel grantee Instituto de Cultura Hispanica, 1952, Mexican Govt., 1953, Nat. Assn. Fgn. Student Advisers, 1957, Austrian Govt., 1960; postdoctoral fellow Laval (Que.) U., summer 1967, U. Lauzanne (Switzerland), summer 1968, Louvain (Belgium) U., 1972-73; Richlieu Inst. scholar, Sorbonne, Paris, summer 1955. Recipient Les Palmes Academiques French Govt., 1960, honor plaque Modern and Classical Lang. Assn. So. Cal., 1969; Mem. Am. Assn. Tchrs. French (pres. 1958-59, exec. com. 1962-64, nat. com. fgn. langs. for elementary schs. 1962-64), Modern Lang. Assn. (exec. council 1956-59, 61-63, 74—, publicity chmn. 1971-72), Council Internat. Students (exec. council 1955-70), Western States Council Edn. Travel (treas., 1961-63), Nat. Cath. Edn. Assn. (exec. com., 1966-69), Alliance Francaise, Am. Assn. Tchrs. Spanish, Am. Council Teaching Fgn. Langs., Am. Mems. Palmes Academiques, Alpha Mu Gamma (nat. pres., 1956-58, 59-60), Pi Delta Phi (nat. v.p., 1962—), Sigma Delta Pi. Editor: Modernism, 1970; The Sounding Solitude (M. Drouin), 1971. Home: 12001 Chalon Rd Los Angeles CA 90049 Office: Dept Romance Langs Mt St Mary's College Los Angeles CA 90049

MESCHAN, RACHEL FARRER (MRS. ISADORE MESCHAN), physician; b. Sydney, Australia, May 21, 1915; d. John Hanbury and Gertrude (Powell) Farrer; M.B., B.S., U. Melbourne (Australia), 1940; M.D., Bowman Gray Sch. Medicine, 1957; grad. trainee marriage council U. Pa., 1966; m. Isadore Meschan, Sept. 3, 1943; children—David, Jane (Mrs. Miles Foy III), Rosalind (Mrs. James Weir), Joyce Irene. Came to U.S., 1946, naturalized, 1950. Research asso., dept. radiology Bowman Gray Sch. Medicine, Wake Forest U., Winston-Salem, N.C., 1957—, asst. clin. prof. marriage counseling, dept. obstetrics and gynecology, 1973—. Cons. Winston-Salem Forsyth County Sch. System, 1962—. Mem. Am. Assn. Marriage and Family Counselors, Nat. Council Family Relations, Am. Fertility Soc. Asst. author: (with I. Meschan) Atlas of Normal Radiographic Anatomy, 1951, rev. edit., 1959, Roentgen Signs in Clinic Diagnosis, 1956, Synopsis of Roentgen Signs, 1962, Roentgen Signs in Clinical Practice, 1966, Radiographic Positioning and Related Anatomy, 1968; Analysis of Roentgen Signs in General Radiology, 1973. Address: 2716 Bartram Rd Winston-Salem NC 27106

MESERVE, MARILYN MOSES (MRS. EDWIN A. C. MESERVE), pediatrician; b. Ticonderoga, N.Y., Oct. 2, 1926; d. Luther Horace and Marion (Card) Moses; A.A., Green Mt. Jr. Coll., 1944; A.B., Boston U., 1946, M.D., 1950; m. Edwin A. C. Meserve, Dec. 18, 1948; children—John, William, Donald, Thomas, Mary Beth, Charles. Intern, Worcester Meml. Hosp., 1950-51; resident, New Eng. Med. Center, 1951-52; practice medicine specializing in pediatrics, Southboro, Mass., 1952—; mem. staff Marlboro (Mass.), Framingham (Mass.) hosps. Vice-pres. Marlboro Westboro Area Bd., 1971-72. Bd. dirs. Teen Canteen, Inc., Southboro, Mass., Washingtonian Hosp., Jamaica Plains, Mass., Marlboro Westboro Mental Health Assn. Conglist. (trustee 1971-72). Address: 81 Middle Rd Southboro MA 01772

MESINGER, MAXINE DAVID (MRS. EMIL M. MESINGER), journalist; b. Houston, Dec. 19, 1925; d. Julian Max and Ella (Dorfman) David; student Tex. State Coll. for Women, 1942-43, Ind. U., 1943-44; m. Emil Meyer Mesinger, Mar. 21, 1944; children—Julianne (Mrs. Thomas J. Haas), Jay Monroe. Columnist Houston Press, 1959-63, Houston Chronicle, 1963—; broadcaster radio sta. KXYZ, Houston, 1959-71, TV sta. KHOU, Houston, 1971—; also free-lance writer. Named St. Jude Woman of Year, 1969. Home: 2226 S Piney Point Houston TX 77042 Office: 801 Texas Av Houston TX 77002

MESROBIAN, ARPENA SACHAKLIAN (MRS. WILLIAM JOHN MESROBIAN), editor; b. Boston; d. Aaron Harry and Eliza (Der Melkonian) Sachaklian; student Armenian Coll. Beirut, 1937-38; A.A., Syracuse U., 1959; B.A. magna cum laude, 1971; m. William John Mesrobian, June 22, 1940; children—William Stephen, Marian Elizabeth (Mrs. Bruce MacCurdy). Editor, Syracuse U. Press, 1955-58, exec. editor, 1958, asst. dir., 1961, acting dir., 1965-66, asso. dir., editor 1968—. Mem. pubs. bd. The Courier, 1970—. Pres. Syracuse (N.Y.) chpt. Armenian Relief Soc., 1972—. Mem. Internat. Platform Assn., Women in Communications, Am. Assn. U. Adminstrs., Assn. Am. U. Presses (mem. nominating com. 1973) Alumni Assn. U. Coll. Syracuse U. (mem. steering com. 1972-73), Phi Kappa Phi. Mem. Armenian Apostolic Ch. (trustee 1972—). Club: Zonta (dir. 1973) (Syracuse, N.Y.). Book review editor Armenian Review, 1967—; editor Syracuse Zonta Club Newsletter, 19—. Home: 108 Winkworth Pkwy Syracuse NY 13215

MESSER, TERESA WINTER (MRS. JOHN PHILIP MESSER), pub. relations cons.; b. Portland, Me., June 3, 1946; d. William Clarence and Emily Tommasina (Vacca) Winter; B.A., Simmons Coll., 1968; m. John Philip Messer, June 21, 1969; 1 son, Kevin Walter. Pub. relations counselor, writer Creative Assos., Portland, Me., 1968-69; police, ct. edn. and gen. reporter Peabody (Mass.) Times, 1969; copy editor Lynn (Mass.) Daily Evening Item, 1969-70; dir. pub. relations dept. Chellis, Conwell, Gale & Poole Advt. Agy., Portland, Me., 1970-72; pub. relations, media cons., writer, Scarborough, Me., 1972—. Club: Greater Portland Simmons College (pres. 1973-75). Author: Influential Novels, 1970. Home: 16 Tall Pines Rd Scarborough ME 04074

MESSERSCHMIDT, RAMONA ONEITA, psychologist; b. Naperville, Ill., June 25, 1907; d. Frank August and Emma Dorothea (Kailer) Messerschmidt; A.A., Toledo U., 1924; B.A., U. Wis., 1926; M.A., Ohio State U., 1927, Ph.D., 1937; postgrad. Columbia, 1927-29, N.Y. Sch. Social Work, 1930-31, U. Cal. at Berkeley, 1946-48, U. Wash., 1956. Chief psychologist N.Y. State Reformatory Women, Bedford Hills, 1927-29, Child Guidance Clinic, White Plains, N.Y., 1929-34; asst. psychology dept. Ohio State U., 1934-36; chief psychologist Milw. Pub. Schs., 1936-42; cons. psychologist Child Welfare Dept., Olympia, Wash., 1942-47; psychologist VA Mental Hygiene Clinic, San Francisco, 1947-51; chief psychologist VA Mental Hygiene Clinic, Spokane, Wash., 1951-71; psychologist Outpatient Clinic, VA Hosp., Chillicothe, O., 1971—. Mem. Wash. Gov.'s Planning Commn. Vocational Rehab., 1969. Fellow Am. Psychol. Assn. (dir.); mem. Am. Group Therapy Assn. (dir. 1949-55); past mem. A.A.A.S., Am. Assn. Mental Deficiency, Nat. Com. Mental Hygiene, Orthopsychiat. Assn., Delta Delta Delta, Pi Lambda Theta, Psi Chi. Contbr. articles to profl. jours. Home: 602 Commanche Rd Chillicothe OH 45601 Office: VA Hosp Chillicothe OH 45601

MESSITTE, EDITH WECHSLER (MRS. JESSE B. MESSITTE), govt. ofcl.; b. Bklyn., Nov. 10, 1917; d. Samuel and Leona (Dichter) Wechsler; student Am. U., 1958-62; m. Jesse B. Messitte, Nov. 28, 1936; children—Michael, Toni (Mrs. Alan D. Mason), Peter. Pub. information specialist Nat. Inst. Neurol. Diseases and Stroke, NIH, Bethesda, Md., 1953—. Home: 7602 Glenbrook Rd Bethesda MD 20014 Office: NIH Bldg 31 Bethesda MD 20014

MESSNER, JEAN THORSEN (MRS. KENNETH HAROLD MESSNER), anesthesiologist; b. Cleve., June 11, 1937; d. Robert Ingman and Ruth Barbara (Weigand) Thorsen; B.S., Albright Coll., 1959; M.D., Temple U., 1963; m. Kenneth Harold Messner, Aug. 29, 1959; children—Liede, Eric, Keith. Rotating intern, Reading (Pa.) Hosp., 1963-64; gen. practice medicine, Guam, 1964-66; resident in anesthesia R.I. Hosp., Providence, 1966-68; fellow in anesthesia, Tufts New Eng. Med. Center Hosp., Boston, 1968-69, instr. anesthesia, 1969-71; asst. prof. anesthesia Miami (Fla.) U. Med. Sch., 1971-72, Hershey (Pa.) Med. Center, 1972—. Diplomate Am. Bd. Anesthesiology. Fellow Am. Coll. Anesthesiologists; mem. Am., Pa. socs. anesthesiologists, A.M.A., Pa., Dauphin County med. socs., Internat. Anesthesia Research Soc. Address: Dept Anesthesiology Hershey Med Center Hershey PA 17033

MESSNER, KATHRYN HERTZOG, civic worker; b. Glendale, Cal., May 27, 1915; d. Walter Sylvester and Sadie (Dinger) Hertzog; B.A., U. Cal. at Los Angeles, 1936, M.A., 1951; m. Ernest Lincoln, Jan. 1, 1942; children—Ernest Lincoln, Martha Allison. Tchr. social studies Los Angeles schs., 1937-46; mem. Los Angeles County Grand Jury, 1961. Mem. alumni council U. Cal. at Los Angeles, 1942-46; mem. exec. bd. Los Angeles Family Service, 1959-62, adv. bd., 1965—; mem. Dist. Atty.'s Adv. Com., 1965—, chmn. San Marino chpt. Am. Cancer Soc.; bd. dirs. Pasadena Rep. Women's Club, 1960-62, San Marino dist. council Girl Scouts U.S.A., 1959-68; pres. San Marino High Sch. P.T.A., 1964-65; bd. dirs. Pasadena Vol. Placement Bur., 1962-68; mem. adv. bd. Univ. YWCA, 1956—; co-chmn. Dist. Atty's. adv. bd. Young Citizens Council, 1968—; mem. San Marino Red Cross Council, 1966—, chmn., 1969-71, vice chmn., 1972—; mem. San Marino bd. Am. Field Service, 1971—; mem. Atty. Gen.'s Vol. Adv. Council, 1972—; mem. adv. bd. Beverly Hills-West Los Angeles YWCA, 1973—; mem. San Marino Community Council, 1964-73. Recipient spl. commendation Am. Cancer Soc., 1961, 73. Mem. D.A.R., Pasadena Philharmonic, Las Floristas, Huntington Meml. Clinic Aux., Nat. Charity League, Pasadena Dispensary Aux., Gold Shield (co-founder), Pi Lambda Theta, Pi Gamma Mu, Mortar Bd., Prytanean Soc. Home: 1786 Kelton Av Los Angeles CA 91108

MESSORE, CONSTANCE LORNA JEREMIAH (MRS. MICHAEL B. MESSORE, JR.), lawyer; b. Providence, June 30, 1932; d. Jeremiah S. and Lorna G. (Long) Jeremiah; A.B., Radcliffe Coll., 1954; LL.B., Boston U., 1957; m. Michael B. Messore, Jr., Oct. 11, 1958; children—Michael III, Gregory. Admitted to R.I. bar, 1957; asst. U.S. atty. Dist. R.I., Providence, 1970—. Home: 360 Nayatt Rd Barrington RI 02806 Office: US Atty's Office Fed Bldg Providence RI 02903

MESTRE, ROSALIND RHODELL TISHFIELD (MRS. DAVID MESTRE), occupational therapist; b. N.Y.C., Mar. 19, 1948; d. Sidney and Florence (Krelenstein) Tishfield; student Hunter Coll., 1965-67; B.S., Columbia, 1970; m. David Mestre, Feb. 21, 1968; children—David, Marissa. Staff therapist Kingsbrook Jewish Med. Center, Bklyn., 1970-74; chief occupational therapist Bklyn.-Cumberland Med. Center, 1974—. Cons. to Congl. Home; home care therapist Bklyn.-Cumberland Home Med. Center, St. Mary's Hosp., Methodist Hosp. Home: 1381 Linden Blvd Brooklyn NY 11212

METCALF, JOANNA JEANNE, anesthesiologist; b. Waterbury, Vt., Feb. 22, 1921; d. Harris H. and Greta F. (Perkins) Metcalf; B.S., U. Vt., 1942, M.D., 1945. Intern, Newton-Wellesley Hosp., Newton, Mass., 1945-46, anesthesia resident, 1948-51, anesthesiologist, 1952-70, treas. staff, 1958-62; teaching fellow medicine U. Vt. Coll., 1946-48; practice medicine specializing in anesthesiology, Boston, 1948—; asst. anesthesiologist Peter Bent Brigham Hosp., Boston, also teaching fellow anesthesia Harvard, 1950-52; anesthesiologist Faulkner Hosp., Jamaica Plain, Mass., 1970—. Mem. A.M.A., Am., Mass. anesthesiology socs., New Eng., Charles River, West Roxbury med. socs., League Women Voters, Pi Beta Phi. Republican. Home: 24 Southwick Rd Waban MA 02168

METCALF, WANDA CHARLENE, real estate broker; b. Norman, Okla., May 29, 1931; d. Charlie Columbus and Martha Beulah (Armitage) Henderson; grad. high sch.; m. Raymond Harold Metcalf, Oct. 30, 1948; children—Debra Jean (Mrs. Mike Gary Olson), Ronnie Harold. Real estate salesman Irvin Bender, Galt, Cal., 1961-64; office mgr. B.O. Katzahian and Ben Shaffer, Galt, 1964-68; real estate broker Real Estate by Metcalf, Redding, Cal., 1973—. Pres. Women's Missionary Council, Redding, 1969-71. Republican. Home: 3691 Bechelli Lane Redding CA 96001 Office: PO Box Redding CA 96001

METFORD, MARTHA ELIZABETH, lawyer; b. Madison, Ind., Jan. 16, 1934; d. George Rumpler and Martha Francisco (Roberts) Metford; student Vassar Coll., 1951-53; A.B., Ind. U., 1955; J.D., Yale, 1958; postgrad. George Washington U., 1970. Admitted to Ind. bar, 1958; atty. Metford & Hensley, Madison, 1958-59, office gen. counsel U.S. Gen. Accounting Office, Washington, 1959-66, office gen. counsel Fed. Home Loan Bank Bd., Washington, 1970-71; counsel U.S. Senate Democratic Policy Com., Washington, 1971—. Exhibited in group show Studio Gallery, Washington, 1973. Mem. Am. Judicature Soc., Fed. Bar Assn., D.A.R., Women's Bar D.C., Kappa Beta Pi, Chi Omega. Home: 134 11th St SE Washington DC 20003 Office: S 318 The Capitol Washington DC 20510

METRINKO, MICHELE BETTINA, lawyer, govt. ofcl.; b. N.Y.C., Mar. 23, 1945; d. Michael J. and Elizabeth (Sedor) Metrinko; B.S. in Fgn. Service, Georgetown U., 1965, J.D., 1968, LL.M. in Taxation, 1970. Admitted to D.C. bar, 1969, Fed. bar, 1970, D.C. Ct. Appeals, 1971, U.C. Ct. Claims bar, 1971, U.S. Supreme Ct. bar, 1973; mem. legislative research staff Rep. Seymour Halpern, Washington, 1964-65; law clk. firm Keatinge & Sterling, Los Angeles, summer 1967; mem. staff legal advisers' office Dept. State, Washington, 1967; staff atty. div. corporate regulation SEC, Washington, 1968-71; trial atty. tax div. Dept. Justice, Washington, 1971-72; spl. asst. to adminstr. Environmental Protection Agy., Washington, 1972-74; asso. solicitor, div. conservation and wildlife Dept. Interior, Washington, 1974—; disc jockey, pub. affairs announcer radio sta. WGTB, Washington, 1961-65; moderator, appearances numerous TV spls. and programs. Toured with Bob Hope U.S.O. troupe, Middle East and Mediterranean area, Christmas, 1963. Recipient oratory awards Cath. Youth Orgn., 1959, B'Nai B'rith, 1960, Forensic League, 1961, Am. Legion, 1960, K.C., 1961; numerous beauty pageant titles including Miss U.S.A., 1963-64. Mem. Fed. Bar Assn., Am. Soc. Internat. Law, Nat. Symphony Com., Nat. Steeplechase and Hunt Assn. Club: Blue Ridge Hunt (Boyce, Va.). Home: London House 1001 Wilson Blvd Arlington VA 22209 Office: Dept of Interior Office of Solicitor Washington DC 20240

METTEY, KATHLEEN ELIZABETH GRIFFITH (MRS. HECTOR NORMAN METTEY), realtor; b. Andersonville, Va., Feb. 3, 1921; d. Noah Clinton and Grace Elizabeth (Martin) Griffith; certificate Anthony's Sch. Real Estate, 1969; m. Hector Norman Mettey, Sept. 29, 1948; 1 dau., Kathyrn Rhoda (Mrs. Everet Charles Surdez). Owner, Santee Realty, El Cajon, Cal., 1953—, real estate salesman, 1953-69, broker, 1969—. Mem. exec. bd. Santee Citizen Planning Com., 1968—; mem. Make Am. Better Com., 1970-74; chmn. early childhood edn. com. Santee Sch., 1973-74; sec.-treas. Santee Lakes Festival, 1962-64, Queen chmn., 1963; active P.T.A. Santee C. of C., 1971. Mem. El Cajon Valley Bd. Realtors, Santee C. of C. (Citizen of Year award 1971, sec. 1971-72). Clubs: Santee Woman's (Woman of Year plaque 1972); Suburban Toastmistress (San Diego). Home: 1371 Pepper Dr El Cajon CA 92021

METZ, BETTY ANN, coll. dean; b. Passaic, N.J., Sept. 12, 1927; d. Albert and Marion (Chrisfield) Metz; B.A., Wellesley Coll., 1949; M.F.A., Yale, 1952; M.Pub. Adminstrn., N.Y. U., 1957, Ph.D., 1966. Theatrical dir., producer, 1952-56; interviewer N.Y. State Employment Service, 1956-59; evaluator, asst. dir. div. field services Newark State Coll., 1959-66; dean continuing edn. Bristol Community Coll., Fall River, Mass., 1966—, dean in charge, 1973. Mem. bd. Citizens for Citizens, Fall River, 1967-73, pres. bd., 1970; mem. Sec. Edn.'s Task Force on Prison Edn., 1971-72; mem. Title I Com. on Higher Edn., 1971—, chmn., 1974—. Mem. Nat. Council Community Services (charter, New Eng. rep. 1973—), Mass. Adult Edn. Assn. (regional v.p. 1968—). Home: 1219 Main Rd Westport MA 02791 Office: 64 Durfee St Fall River MA 02720

METZ, DIANE BAILEY (MRS. R. ANTHONY METZ), law librarian; b. Putnam, Conn., May 27, 1946; d. Francis and Gertrude (LaRose) Bailey; B.A., Clark U., 1968; J.D., Creighton U., 1971; m. R. Anthony Metz, Aug. 7, 1971; 1 dau., Andrea Rose. Admitted to Neb. bar, 1971; reference librarian Creighton U. Sch. Law Library, Omaha, 1971-72; law librarian Kutak Rock Cohen Campbell Garfinkle & Woodward, Omaha, 1972—. Mem. Am., Neb., Omaha bar assns. Home: 6530 N 31st Av Omaha NE 68112 Office: 600 Woodmen Tower Omaha NE 68112

METZ, MARY KANOUSE, banker; b. nr. St. Paul, Ind., Sept. 8, 1908; d. James Lewis and Margaret Violet (Colee) Kanouse; grad. high sch.; m. Russell L. Metz, July 25, 1925 (dec. May 1973); 1 son, Jack R. Sec., Herbert C. Jones, Atty., 1925-33; sec. HOLC, 1933-38; 1st dep. clk. Office Shelby Circuit Ct., 1941-47; with Farmers Nat. Bank, Shelbyville, Ind., 1947-73, asst. mgr. installment loans and credit checking, now ret. Mem. Bus. and Profl. Women's Club (past pres. Shelbyville). Democrat. Home: 845 Main St Shelbyville IN 46176

METZ, PATRICIA ANNE HARRIS (MRS. FLOYD A. METZ), social worker; b. Detroit, May 10, 1936; d. Hugh and Frances (Alvord) Harris; B.A., Albion Coll., 1958; M.S.W., Wayne State U., 1960; m. Floyd A. Metz, Aug. 23, 1958; children—Marcia Anne, Kevin Harris. Caseworker, Family Service of Oakland County, Berkley, Mich., 1958-59, Clinic for Child Study, Wayne County Juvenile Ct., Detroit, 1959-65, N.W. Wayne County Child Guidance Clinic, Garden City, Mich., 1965-67; exec. sec. Met. Detroit chpt. Nat. Assn. Social Workers, 1967-70; dir. counseling Friends Sch. in Detroit, 1970-73. Dir. I.C. Harris, Inc., Detroit. Bd. dirs. Met. Detroit YWCA, 1967—, treas., 1972—; mem. comprehensive child care com. United Community Services, 1971-73; bd. dirs. Mich. Council YWCAs, 1974—. Mem. Nat. Assn. Social Workers (chpt. sec. 1966-67, finance chmn. 1970-72), Wayne State U. Sch. Social Work Alumni Assn. (treas. 1964-66), Inkster Coop. Services Com. (sec. 1966-67), Acad. Certified Social Workers. Mennonite. Home: 18951 Rosemont St Detroit MI 48219

METZGER, BARBARA ANN, govt. ofcl.; b. N.Y.C., June 10, 1948; d. Max and Veronica E. (McDermott) Metzger; B.A., San Diego State U., 1970; postgrad. Cal. State U. Grad. asst. journalism San Diego State U., 1970; writer, producer, reporter KFMB-TV, San Diego, 1970-73; cons. Cal. State Assembly, Sacramento, 1973—. Mem. Women In Communications. Democrat. Home: 615 23d St Sacramento CA 95816 Office: State Capitol Sacramento CA 95814

METZGER, ERIKA ALMA (MRS. MICHAEL M. METZGER), educator; b. Berlin, Germany, Apr. 8, 1933; d. Otto A. and Alma H. (Nitschke) Hirt; diploma U. Goettingen, 1954; staatsexamen U. Berlin, 1958; M.A., Cornell U., 1961; Ph.D., State U. N.Y. at Buffalo, 1967; m. Michael M. Metzger, Aug. 30, 1958. Came to U.S., 1958, naturalized, 1964. Teaching asst. Cornell U., 1958-61; instr. U. Ill., 1961-63; instr., asst. prof., asso. prof. State U. N.Y. at Buffalo, 1963—, also dir. undergrad. studies dept. German and Slavic. Mem. Am. Assn. Tchrs. German, Modern Lang. Assn., Internat. Vereinigung Germanistik. Author: (with Michael Metzger) Stefan George, 1972; textbooks in field. Editor: Baroque Anthologies, 1970, 73; jour. Lyrik und Prosa, 1972—. Contbr. revs., articles to profl. jours. Home: 54 Niagara Falls Blvd Buffalo NY 14214

METZGER, EVELYN RUTH BORCHARD (MRS. HERMAN A. METZGER), artist; b. N.Y.C., June 8, 1911; d. Samuel and Eva (Rose) Borchard; student Horace Mann Sch., 1925-28; A.B., Vassar Coll., 1932; studied painting with George Grosz, Raphael Soyer, others; sculpture with Sally Farnham; m. H.A. Metzger, June 28, 1934; children—James B., Edward A., Eva B. One-man shows including Galeria Muller, Buenos Aires, 1950, Selected Artists Galleries, N.Y.C., 1962, Vassar Coll. Art Gallery, Poughkeepsie, N.Y., 1963, Everhart Mus., Scranton, Pa., 1963, Gallerie Bellechasse, Paris, 1963, Norfolk (Va.) Mus. Art, 1965, Frank Partridge Gallery, N.Y., 1964, Ga. Mus. Fine Arts, Athens, 1966, Van Diemen-Lilienfeld Galleries, N.Y., 1966, Mus. Modern Art, Miami, 1967, Columbus (Ga.) Mus., 1966, Mexican-Am. Cultural Inst., Mexico City, 1967, U. Me., Orono, 1967, Albion (Mich.) Coll., 1969,

Graham Eckes Sch., Palm Beach, Fla., 1970, Bartholet Gallery, N.Y.C., 1973; exhibited in group shows including Allied Artists Am., Nat. Acad. Galleries, 1960, Artists N.Y. '72, Union Carbide Bldg., N.Y.C., Art in Embassies program U.S. State Dept.; represented in numerous permanent mus. collections. Mem. Phi Beta Kappa. Clubs: Cosmopolitan, Vassar (N.Y.C.). Home: 815 Park Av New York City NY 10021

METZLER, DOROTHY JEAN MASTERS (MRS. JERRY DON METZLER), occupational therapist; b. Lexington, Ky., Nov. 12, 1937; d. Everett Debb and Maurice Florence (Bridges) Masters; student Ariz. State Coll., 1955-57; B.S. in Occupational Therapy, San Jose State Coll., 1961; postgrad. U. Cal. at Riverside, 1968-69; m. Jerry Don Metzler, Aug. 18, 1962. Staff occupational therapist U.S. VA Hosp., Tucson, 1961-62, Samuel Gompers Meml. Rehab. Center, Phoenix, 1962-63, Sunshine Orthopedically Handicapped Sch., Fresno, Cal., 1963-67; tchr. primary sch. Parlier (Cal.) dist., 1967-68, San Jacinto sch. dist., Cal., 1968-69; occupational therapist Frances Stevens Orthopedically Handicapped Sch., Palm Springs, Cal., 1969-71, Katherine Finchy Orthopedically Handicapped Sch., Palm Springs, Cal., 1971-72, Maricopa County Gen. Hosp., Phoenix, 1972—. Mem. Phoenix Symphony Chorale, 1973—; coordinator Christian Global Concerns United Methodist Women, Aldersgate United Meth. Ch., 1973—. Mem. Am., Ariz. (mem. child devel. com. 1973—), No. Cal., So. Cal. occupational therapy assns., Wesleyan Service Guild (v.p. 1972), Ind. Order Foresters. Methodist. Home: 4414 N 25th St No 10 Phoenix AZ 85016 Office: 2601 E Roosevelt St Phoenix AZ 85008

METZLER-SMITH, SANDRA JOY, museum curator; b. Santa Barbara, Cal., July 26, 1950; d. Fred Herman and Pattie Ruth (Eaton) Metzler; A.B. in Anthropology, U. Cal. at Berkeley, 1972; m. Kenneth Ogden Smith III, Sept. 1, 1973. Instr. archaeology elementary summer sch. Mt. Diablo Sch. Dist., Concord, Cal., 1972; curator Mendocino County Mus., Willits, Cal., 1972—; cons. cultural resources for evaluation environmental impact reports. Home: 166 Wood St Willits CA 95490 Office: 400 E Commercial St Willits CA 95490

METZNER, CLARA LOUISE HEENAN (MRS. THEODORE EDWARD METZNER), ch. ofcl.; b. Louisville, June 27, 1915; d. Joseph Harper and Mary Lowe (Stanley) Heenan; student U. Louisville, 1934; m. Theodore Edward Metzner, Nov. 13, 1935; 1 dau., Mary Kaye (Mrs. Talbot W. Trammell). Advt. rep. Christian Sci. Monitor, Louisville, 1945-50; became Christian Sci. practitioner, Boston, 1953, now in Louisville; clk. 1st Ch. of Christ Scientist, Louisville, 1957-58, 2d reader, 1963-65. Bd. dirs. Brimmer and May Sch., 1952. Vol. worker Ky. Correctional Instns., 1970—. Mem. Nat. Trust for Historic Preservation. Home: 2407 Top Hill Rd Louisville KY 40206

MEUDT, EDNA KRISTIN (MRS. PETER MEUDT), author; b. Wyoming Valley, Wis., Sept. 14, 1906; d. John William and Kristin Marie (Nielsen) Kritz; student pub. sch., Sacred Heart Acad., Madison, Wis.; m. Peter Meudt, Oct. 10, 1924 (dec. May 1972); children—Richard E., Howard E. (dec.), Kathleen E. (Mrs. George Ott), Christine (Mrs. Daniel Parkinson), (ward) Christopher H. Meudt. Tchr. poetry Rhinelander Sch. Arts, U. Wis. Extension, 1962—; tchr., mem. bd. Valley Studio, Spring Green, Wis., 1971—; speaker at confs., convs., workshops; poetry pub. in Am. Forests, Nature mag., Nat. Wildlife, Chgo. Tribune mag., Christian Century, Cats mag., Sign mag., Rotarian, Univ. Rev., Wis. Trails, Wis. Acad. Rev., Poetry Australia, Poet Lore. Active in various local civic orgns.; chmn. creative writing panel Wis. Arts Bd., 1974. Recipient Gov.'s award for creativity in the arts Wis. Arts Council, 1970; award Writers Digest, 1969; Council Wis. Writers, 1973. Mem. Nat. Fedn. State Poetry Socs. (award, pres. 1961-63), Nat. League Am. Pen Women (Wis. br. v.p. 1957-59), Wis. Fellowship of Poets (pres. 1954-56, 62-64), Wis. Acad. Scis., Arts and Letters (v.p. for letters), State Hist. Soc. Wis., Wis. Regional Writers Assn. (bd. 1954-57), Theta Sigma Phi (Gold Writers cup for book of poems 1965). Roman Catholic. Author poetry: Round River Canticle (honors award 1962), 1960; In No Strange Land (1st prize 1964), 1964; No One Sings Face Down, 1970; The Ineluctable Sea, 1974; also short stories, articles, one-act plays. Editor poetry for mags., anthologies. Home: Box 95 Rural Route 3 Dodgeville WI 53533

MEULENDYKE, ANN-MARIE, economist; b. N.Y.C., Oct. 24, 1944; d. Bruce and Ruth (Chadsey) Meulendyke; A.B., Cornell U., 1966; M.A., U. Chgo., 1970. Research asst. Fed. Res. Bank Chgo., summer 1968; economist Fed. Res. Bank N.Y., N.Y.C., 1970—. Mem. Am. Econ. Assn., Omicron Delta Epsilon. Home: 13 W 13th St New York City NY 10011 Office: 33 Liberty St New York City NY 10045

MEULI, ESTHER ADELLE WEBSTER (MRS. JASPER G. MEULI), judge; b. Oakland, Cal., Jan. 9, 1918; d. John Calvin and Blanch (Hagler) Webster; student Coll. Pacific, 1937-38; LL.B., U. Cal. at Berkeley, 1946; m. Jasper G. Mueli, Oct. 4, 1954. Asst. mgr. theatres, Sonora, Anglos, San Andreas, Cal., 1943-53; clk. Justice Ct. 1st Jud. Dist., Sonora, 1953-60, clk. to judge, 1967-70, judge, 1973—. Mem. Am. Acad. Jud. Edn., Bus. and Profl. Women's Club, Assn. Peace Officers, Judges and Marshalls. Republican. Roman Catholic. Club: Soroptimist (Sonora). Home: 173 Bradford Av Sonora CA 95370 Office: 82 N Washington St Sonora CA 95370

MEWES, ISABELLE KLEBANOW, counselor, therapist; b. N.Y.C., July 5, 1922; d. Leo E. and Ella (Danowitz) Klebanow; student Alfred U., 1939-40; B.S., N.Y. U., 1945; M.S., Barry Coll., 1963; div.; children—Leo K. Vogel, Marilyn (Mrs. Steve Myers), Deborah E., Melanie M. Tchr. English, jr. high schs., Miami, Fla., 1957-65; tchr. remedial English, Parkway Jr. High Sch., Miami, 1962-65, guidance counselor, 1965-71; counselor Miami Dade Community Coll., 1972-73; counselor, therapist Center Family Learning, Miami, 1973—. Pvt. practice as counselor for adolescents and family counselor, North Miami Beach, 1965—. Mem. N.E.A., Fla. Edn. Assn., Classroom Tchrs. Assn. (mem. human relations commn. 1969-70), Nat. Council Tchrs. English, Am., So. Fla., Dade County personnel and guidance assns., League Women Voters, Mental Health Assn., Kappa Delta Pi (v.p.). Hadassah. Home: 670 NE 179th Terrace North Miami Beach FL 33162 Office: 8740 N Kendall Dr Miami FL 33156

MEYER, ALBERTA LOUISE, educator; b. St. Louis, Mar. 4, 1913; d. Otto H. and Alvina D. (Schnellbacher) Meyer; A.B., Harris Tchrs. Coll., 1933; A.M., Columbia, 1943. Tchr. pub. elementary schs., St. Louis, 1936-48, 49-50; fellow Assn. for Childhood Edn. Internat., Washington, 1948-49, exec. sec., 1959—; audio-visual cons. St. Louis Pub. Schs., 1950-59. Vice chmn. Women's Joint Congl. Com., 1960-61, chmn., 1961-62; sec. U.S. Nat. Com. on Early Childhood Edn., 1960-71; mem. exec. com. Council Nat. Orgns. for Children and Youth, 1960-72, chmn., 1968-70; mem. nat. adv. conf. on internat. tchr. exchange U.S. Office Edn., 1959—; mem. tech. assistance com. White Ho. Conf. on Children, 1970; mem. Nat. Adv. Council Prevention Speech and Lang. Handicaps, 1971-72; chmn. planning com. Citizen's Conf. Priorities and Action for Children and Youth, 1971; alternate rep. bd. dirs. Child Devel. Asso. Consortium, 1972—. Mem. Nat. Council Orgns., Assn. Childhood Edn. Internat., Adminstrv. Women in Edn. (pres. D.C. council 1962-63), Alliance of Assns. for Advancement Edn. (exec. com. 1973—), Nat. Audubon Soc., Kappa Delta Pi, Delta Kappa Gamma, Sigma Sigma Sigma. Home: 3201 Wisconsin Av NW Washington DC 20016 Office: 3615 Wisconsin Av NW Washington DC 20016

MEYER, ARLENE NAOMI HOCHMAN (MRS. JOHN H. MEYER), deisgner, advt. exec.; b. N.Y.C., Mar. 25, 1930; d. Robert and Lillian (Menken) Hochman; B.A., Conn. Coll., 1952; m. John H. Meyer, Jan. 18, 1953; children—Elise Ann, Robert Adam, Emily Ione. Advt. copywriter Abraham & Straus, Bklyn., 1951-53; tchr. Norwich Sch. System, 1953-54; designer John Meyer of Norwich (Conn.) div. W.R. Grace, 1955-63, sec. corp., head designer, advt. dir., 1963-68, dir. design and advt., 1968—. Organizer, tchr. Head Start program, Norwich, 1966; chmn. Hosp. Aux., 1961-63; mem. adv. bd. Lyman Allyn Mus., 1968. Trustee Southeastern Conn. Hearing and Speech Center; bd. dirs. Conn. Bd. Literacy Vols., 1973. Recipient Alumni of Distinction award Conn. Coll., 1973. Mem. Nat. Council Jewish Women (pres. Norwich chpt. 1956-58), Hadassah (life), Conn. Coll. Alumni Assn. Home: 66 Reynolds Rd Norwich CT 06360 Office: 1 Connecticut Av Norwich CT 06360

MEYER, BETTY ANNE (MRS. JOHN R. BASKIN), lawyer; b. Cleve.; d. William Henry and Monica (McSherry) Meyer; student Denison U., 1941-43; A.B., Flora Stone Mather Coll., Western Res. U., 1946, LL.B., 1947; m. John R. Baskin, 1967. Admitted to Ohio bar, 1947; asst. to dean Adelbert Coll., Western Res. U., 1948-49; asso. Kiefer, Hunter, Knecht & Williams, Cleve., 1965—. Mem. Alpha Phi. Home: 2679 Ashley Rd Shaker Heights OH 44122 Office: Terminal Tower Cleveland OH 44113

MEYER, BETTY JANE, librarian; b. Indpls., July 20, 1918; d. Herbert R. and Gertrude (Sanders) Meyer; B.A., Ball State Tchrs. Coll., 1940; B.S. in L.S., Western Res. U., 1945. Student asst. Muncie Pub. (Ind.) Library, 1936-40; library asst. Ohio State U. Library, Columbus, 1940-42. with Ohio State U., 1945—, successively cataloger, asst. circulation librarian, acting circulation librarian, adminstrv. asst. to dir. libraries, acting asso. reference librarian, 1945-58, cataloger in charge of serials, 1958-65, head serial div. catalog dept., 1965-68, head acquisition dept., 1968-71, instr. prof. in library adminstrn., 1958-63, asst. prof., 1963-67, asso. prof. library adminstrn., 1967—, asst. dir. libraries tech. services, 1971—; library asst. Grandview Heights Pub. Library Columbus, 1942-44; student asst. Case Inst. Tech. Cleve., 1944-45. Mem. Am., Ohio, Ohioana. Franklin County library assns., Am. Assn. U. Profs., Assn. Coll. and Research Librarians, Ohio Valley Group Tech. Service Librarians. P.E.O., Beta Phi Mu.

MEYER, EDITH PATTERSON (MRS. SHELBY RIDER MEYER), author; b. Chatham, Mass., June 2, 1895; d. John Nelson and Etta (Briant) Patterson; certificate in L.S., Pratt Inst., 1916; postgrad. Columbia, U. Chgo., Western Res. U.; m. Shelby Rider Meyer, July 2, 1921 (dec. 1943). First asst., children's librarian Pub. Library Fond du Lac, Wis., 1916-18; children's librarian Cleve. Pub. Library, 1918-21; with A.L.A., Chgo., 1921-23; asso. children's book editor Rand McNally, Chgo., 1923-43; children's book editor Abingdon Press, N.Y.C., 1944-55; free-lance writer, 1956—. Tchr. writing for children, summer confs., Ridgewood, N.C., 1956, 58. Mem. Am., Conn. library assns., Women's Nat. Book Assn., Stamford Forum for World Affairs, Am.-European Friendship Assn. Author: Go It Alone Lady, 1957; Bible Stories for Young Readers, 1958; Dynamite and Peace, the Story of Alfred Nobel, 1958; Champions of Peace (Jane Addams award), 1960; The Three Guardsmen and other stories from the Apocrypha, 1960; Pirate Queen, 1961; The Friendly Frontier, 1962; Meet the Future—Books and Ideas in Libraries of Today and Tomorrow, 1964; Champions of the Four Freedoms, 1966; That Remarkable Man—Justice Oliver Wendell Holmes, 1967; First Lady of the Renaissance-A Biography of Isabella d'Este, 1970; For Goodness Sake! Growing Up in A New England Parsonage, 1973; Not Charity But Justice, the Story of Jacob Riis, 1974. Contbr. articles to various mags. including Scholastic, Jr. Red. Cross News, Christian Home. Address: 83 Morgan St Stamford CT 06905

MEYER, ELIZABETH, lawyer; b. Detroit, Apr. 16, 1944; d. Ruben and Irene (Saliter) Meyer; B.A., Kalamazoo Coll., 1965; J.D. magna cum laude, Wayne State U., 1968. Admitted to Mich. bar, 1968, Cal. bar, 1971; atty. narcotic and dangerous drug sect., criminal div. U.S. Dept. Justice, Washington, 1968-70, atty. Southwestern unit narcotic and dangerous drug sect., 1970—. Recipient Am. Jurisprudence award for criminal law Bancroft-Whitney Co., 1966; Spl. Achievement award U.S. Dept. Justice, 1972. Mem. State Bar Mich., Bar Assn. D.C., State Bar Cal., Internat. Oceanographic Assn., Nat. Orgn. for Women. Democrat. Club: Sierra (San Diego). Office: US Courthouse 325 West F St San Diego CA 92101

MEYER, FLORENCE EVELYN (MRS. RAYMOND LOWELL MEYER), antique dealer; b. Providence, Apr. 7, 1923; d. John and Alice May (Ledger) Lindell; stepdau. Otto Benjamin Graemiger; grad. high sch.; m. Raymond Lowell Meyer, Apr. 13, 1946. Bookkeeper, R.I. Hosp. Nat. Bank, Pawtucket, 1941-46; med. record librarian, med. sec. St. John's Hickey Meml. Hosp., Anderson, Ind., 1948-52; med. record librarian Hancock County Meml. Hosp., Greenfield, Ind., 1952-54; accountant Delco-Remy div. Gen. Motors Corp., Anderson, 1954—; owner Flo's Antiques, House of Nippon, Anderson, 1968—. Mem. Nat. Assn. Dealers in Antiques. Episcopalian. Author: The Colorful World of Nippon, 1971; Pins, For Hats & Cravats, 1974. Contbr. to publs. in field. Home: Anderson IN 46011

MEYER, FRANCES ELIZABETH (MRS. HAROLD THEODORE MEYER), coll. ofcl.; b. St. Peter, Minn., Aug. 25, 1904; d. Thomas James and Regina (Krohn) Pettijohn; B.A. magna cum laude, Gustavus Adolphus Coll., St. Peter, 1926; postgrad. summers Mankato (Minn.) State Tchrs. Coll., 1927, U. Wis., 1958-59; m. Harold Theodore Meyer, June 24, 1929; children—Robert James, Richard T., Donald Jon. Librarian, tchr. Lake Crystal (Minn.) High Sch., 1926-29; substitute tchr. Superior (Wis.) High Sch., 1943-45; homemaker Family Service, Madison, Wis., 1952-53; asst. librarian Hawthorne Library, Madison, 1958; with Madison Bus. Coll., 1958—, Student Council adviser, dir. student activities, 1961-73, dean women, 1973—. Grand Observer Corps supr. Civil Def., Madison, 1955-58; den mother Cub Scouts; social chmn. P.T.A. East High Sch., 1951-52. Mem. Wis. Library Assn., Alpha Iota. Lutheran. Home: 2421 Hoard St Madison WI 53704

MEYER, HELEN CHASE, educator; b. Medford, Mass., June 22, 1927; d. Elton Fletcher and Eleanor Marden (Jones) Chase; B.A., Denison U., 1949; M.A., U. Ala., 1965, Ph.D., 1970; divorced; children—Cynthia Anne, Karl Frederick, Richard Werner, Thomas Alan, Mary Katharine. Tchr. Granville (O.) Coop. Nursery Sch., 1950-51, Granville Exempted Village Sch., 1952-56; tutor, teaching asst. Denison U., Granville, 1952-58; tutor Wake Forest U., Winston-Salem, N.C., 1958-60; tchr. Tuscaloosa (Ala.) City Schs., 1963-64; psychometrist State of Ala., 1966-68; grad. teaching fellow U. Ala., Tuscaloosa, 1966-67, research fellow, 1967, counseling lab. supr., 1967-68; asst. prof. edn. Cal. State U. at Hayward, 1968-73, asso. prof., 1973—. Cons. to sch. systems, 1967—. Bd. mgrs. Carlmont (Cal.) YMCA, 1972—, asst. chmn. bd. mgrs., 1974—; mem. com. Pacific Region YMCA High Sch. Conf., San Mateo, Cal., 1971—, chmn., 1974—. Mem. Am. Psychol. Assn., Am. Personnel and Guidance Assn., Cal. Reading Assn., Am. Edn. Research Assn., Nat. Council for Social Studies, Phi Beta Kappa, Kappa Delta Pi, Pi Lambda Theta, Pi Delta Phi, Alpha Phi. Episcopalian (Sunday Sch. tchr., chmn. Altar Guild). Contbr. articles to profl. jours. Home: 824 Canyon Drive Redwood City CA 94062 Office: Dept of Teacher Edn California State University Hayward CA 94542

MEYER, HELEN (MRS. ABRAHAM J. MEYER), publisher; b. Bklyn., Dec. 4, 1907; d. Bertolen and Esther (Greenfield) Honig; student pub. schs.; m. Abraham J. Meyer, Sept. 1, 1929; children—Adele (Mrs. Roger Harrison Brodkin), Robert L. With Popular Sci., McCall's mag., 1921-22; pres., dir. Dell Pub. Co., Inc., N.Y.C., 1923-57; pres., dir. Dell Distbg., Inc., 1957—, Dell Internat., Inc., 1957—; pres. Dial Press, Inc., Noble & Noble Pubs., Inc., Montville Warehousing Co., Inc., v.p. Dellprint, Inc., Dunellen, N.J. Mem. Assn. Am. Pubs. (dir.). Home: 231 Montrose Av South Orange NJ 07079 Office: 1 Dag Hammarskjold Plaza New York City NY 10017

MEYER, KERSTIN, mezzo soprano; b. Stockholm, Sweden, Apr. 3, 1928; tng. piano, voice; student Royal Acad. Music, 1948-50; Opera Sch., 1950-52; tng. Mozarteum, Salzburg, also studied in Italy. Debut as Azucena in Il Travatore, Royal Opera, Stockholm, 1952, later appeared in Delilah and Carmen, also as Magdalena in Rigoletto, Octavian in Rosenkavalier, Brangane in Tristan und Isolde, Fricka in Das Rheingold, Walkure, title role in Orfeo; sang Eboli, State Opera, Vienna, appeared in Verdi's Requiem, Vienna; sang Carmen, Hamburg Opera, 1958, Berlin, 1960, Covent Garden, London, 1960; recital BBC, London, 1959; performed at Venice Festival, 1960, in Mahler's Eighth Symphony, Berlin Festival, 1960; debut Met. Opera Co., 1960, returned to London, 1961, 62, Teatro Colon, Buenos Aires, Argentina, 1961, Glyndebourne Festival, 1961, 62, 64, 70, San Francisco Opera, 1962, Paris Opera, 1962, Bayreuth Festival, 1962, 63, 64, 65, Salzburg Festival, 1966, La Scala, 1968, 69, Kundry, Geneva, 1970; concert tour Australia, 1967; performing with Berlin, Hamburg and Stockholm Operas. Home: Benergatan 71 Stockholm Sweden Office: Met Opera Co New York City NY 10018

MEYER, MARGARET ELEANOR, microbiologist; b. Westwood, Cal., Feb. 8, 1923; d. Herman Henry and Eleanor (Dobson) Meyer; B.S., U. Cal. at Berkeley, 1945; Ph.D., U. Cal. at Davis, 1961. Pub. health analyst USPHS, Bethesda, Md., 1945-46; swine Brucellosis control agt. U.S. Dept. Agr., Davis, 1946-47; bacteriologist U. Cal. at Davis, 1947-61, research microbiologist Sch. Vet. Medicine, 1961—, U. Cal. Med. Sch. at Los Angeles, 1961—, supr. Brucella Identifications Lab, WHO, U. Cal. at Davis, 1964—, prof. vet. pub. health, 1973—. Cons. subcom. on Brucella, Internat. Com. on Bacterial Taxonomy, 1962—, mem., 1966—; mem. 5th Pan Am. Congress Veterinary Medicine. Venezuela, 1966, Internat. Congress Microbiology, Moscow, Russia, 1966, Mexico City, 1970; mem. adv. com. to Bergey's Manual Defermerative Bacteriology, 1967; mem. Internat. Conf. on Culture Collections, Tokoyo, 1968; cons. in residence Pan Am. Health Orgn., Zoonoses Lab., Buenos Aires, 1968. Recipient Research Career Devel. award USPHS-NIH, 1963. Fellow Am. Pub. Health Assn., Am. Acad. Microbiology; mem. Soc. Am. Microbiologists, N.Am. Conf. Animal Disease Research Workers, (chmn. com. on genus Brucella 1964—), Am. Coll. Vet. Microbiologists (hon. affiliate), Internat. Assn. Microbiol. Socs. (mem. 1st intersectional congress 1974), Am. Assn. U. Women (membership com., chmn. evening sci. sect. Sacramento br.), No. Cal. Womens Golf Assn., U. Cal. Alumni Assn., Sigma Xi (publicity dir., program dir. Davis chpt. 1971-72, pres. Davis chpt. 1973-74). Clubs: U. of Cal. Faculty (Davis); El Dorado Royal Country (Shingle Springs, Cal.); Reno Women's Golf. Author articles to profl. jours. Home: 5611 Fair Oaks Blvd Carmichael CA 95608 Office: Dept Epidemiology and Preventative Medicine Sch Vet Medicine U Cal Davis CA 95616

MEYER, MARIE BARNHART ZEISLER (MRS. DAVID A. MEYER), civic worker; b. Marion, O.; d. John Fredrick and Glen (Barnhart) Zeisler; grad. Grant Hosp. Nurses Tng. Sch., 1933; m. David A. Meyer, May 17, 1933; children—David A., Frank J., Betty (Mrs. Brooksie Legene Perkins). Charter mem., chmn. patient transp. Shelby County chpt. Muscular Dystrophy, Memphis, 1956-59; pres. 9th dist. Tenn. Fedn. Women's Clubs, 1964-66, Tenn. Fedn. Women's Clubs, 1966-68; mem. exec. bd. Gen. Fedn. Women's Clubs, 1966-70, editor Internat. News Bull., 1968-70; vice chmn. Gov.'s Commn. on Status Women, 1968-70; mem. adv. com. Atlantic Union, 1969-70; v.p. Cranbury (N.J.) Hist. and Preservation Soc., 1973—; program chmn. Cranbury Hist. Tour, 1973. Bd. dirs. Tenn. Home for Incurables, Memphis, 1962-65, Mid South Fair, 1964—. Named col. a.d.c. Gov.'s Staff State Tenn., 1966-70. Mem. Internat. Platform Assn. Presbyn. (choir mem., circle leader, Bible tchr.). Clubs: Beethoven Music Soc., 19th Century, Outlook (pres. 1968-70), Lunch Forum (pres. Memphis 1962-64), Cranbury Women's (sec. 1972—). Address: 1 Woodview Dr Cranbury NJ 08512

MEYER, MARILYN ROSE, extension agt.; b. N.Y.C., May 4, 1938; d. Claude G. and Anna M. (Krueger) Meyer; B.S., State U. N.Y., Brockport, 1954; postgrad. Hofstra U., 1959; M.A., N.Y. U., 1962. Tchr. phys. edn. East Meadow (N.Y.) schs., 1954-57; coop. extension agt. 4-H Div. Nassau County, West Hempstead, N.Y., 1957—, camp mng. dir., 1964—. Recipient Danforth Leadership award Nassau County 4-H, 1971, Nat. Distinguished Service award Nat. Assn. Extension 4-H Agts., 1970, Leadership award N.Y. State chpt. Epsilon Sigma Phi, 1968. Mem. Am. Camping Assn., A.A.H.P.E.R., Nat., N.Y. State 4-H agents assns., Pi Lambda Theta, Epsilon Sigma Phi, Kappa Delta Pi. Home: 35 Madison St Lynbrook NY 11563 Office: 300 Hempstead Turnpike West Hempstead NY 11552

MEYER, MARION RICH WATERMAN (MRS. JOHN A. MEYER), univ. adminstr.; b. Auburn, Me., June 11, 1921; d. Ira Herbert and Georgia (Rich) Waterman; student Auburn (Me.) Sch. Commerce, 1941; B.S., U. Me., 1951; M.A., Syracuse U., 1955; m. John A. Meyer, Aug. 13, 1955. Bus. tchr. Pemetic High Sch., Southwest Harbor, Me., 1941-48, Knox Sch. for Girls, Cooperstown, N.Y., 1948-49; adminstrv. asst. Briarcliff Jr. Coll., Briarcliff Manor, N.Y., 1949-50; bus. tchr. Gloucester (Mass.) High Sch., 1951-53; instr. in office adminstrn. Sch. of Mgmt., Syracuse U., 1955-57, counselor to undergrad. students, instr. bus. writing, 1957-70, dir. undergrad. studies, 1970—, asst. dean, 1972—. Mem. Acad. Affairs Adminstrs. (nat. sec. 1965-73, pres.-elect 1973—, chmn. N.E. regional council 1965-67, exec. com. 1965—), Am. Coll. Personnel Assn. (commr. 1965-67, 71—), Am. Personnel and Guidance Assn., Am. Bus. Writing Assn., Nat. Assn. Women Deans and Counselors, Grad. Students Assn. Syracuse U. (pres. 1954-55), N.Y. State Assn. Deans and Guidance Personnel, N.Y. State Fedn. Bus. and Profl. Women's Clubs (chmn. youth leadership conf. 1965-67), Bus. and Profl. Women's Club Syracuse (pres. 1962-63, chmn. Women in Mgmt. seminar 1972—), Delta Pi Epsilon, Beta Gamma Sigma. Home: 149 Vincent St Syracuse NY 13210

MEYER, PRISCILLA ANN SMITH (MRS. RONALD D. MEYER), journalist; b. Paterson, N.J., Jan. 14, 1940; d. Elmer Lambert and Mary Emma (Shaffer) Smith; B.S., U. Fla., 1962; m. Ronald D. Meyer, Aug. 15, 1959; children—Pamela Ruth, Victoria

Lynn. Asst. editor Fla. Agrl. Extension Service, U. Fla., 1962-63; editor Tobacco Reporter, Cin., 1964-70; reporter Wall St. Jour., N.Y.C., 1970—. Home: 3 Volz Pl Yonkers NY 10701 Office: 22 Cortlandt St New York City NY 10007

MEYER, RUTH ANN, educator; b. Aplington, Ia., Dec. 30, 1935; d. Henry R. and Nancy (Janssen) Meyer; B.A., U. No. Ia., 1958; M.A., Colo. State Coll., 1964. Profl. basketball player, 1955-56; tchr. Sr. High Sch., Newton, Ia., 1958-63; instr. Wartburg Coll., Waverly, 1963-65; asso. prof. phys. edn. Western Mich. U., Kalamazoo, 1965—, chmn. dept. phys. edn. for women, asst. dir. athletics, 1972—. Intercollegiate chmn. Mich. Div. for Girls and Women's Sports, 1968-70. Active Community Chest, Inc., Kalamazoo, 1969-71; program com. mem. YWCA, Newton, 1958-63. Recipient Honor award Ia. Assn. Health, Phys. Edn., and Recreation, 1965. Mem. A.A.H.P.E.R., Mich. Assn. Health, Phys. Edn. and Recreation (pres. 1971-72), Midwest (commr. 1972), Mich. (commr. 1972) assns. intercollegiate athletics for women, Delta Kappa Gamma, Pi Lambda Theta, Kappa Delta Pi. Republican. Mem. Reformed Ch. of Am. Home: 8542 Sylvan Lane Kalamazoo MI 49002

MEYER, SYLVIA FRANCES RAISSEN (MRS. MORRIS J. MEYER), physician; b. Kroonstad, South Africa, Aug. 15, 1921; d. Mendel and Yetty (Smiedt) Raissen; M.B. B. Ch., U. Witwatersrand, 1943, D.P.H., 1945; M.D., State U. N.Y., 1967; m. Morris J. Meyer, Jan. 4, 1942; 1 son, Steven Leslie. Came to U.S., 1966. Intern, Boksburg-Benoni Hosp., Boksburg, S. Africa, 1944; resident Johannesburg (South Africa) Gen. Hosp., 1947-48; physician Johannesburg Gen. Hosp., 1948-61; asst. med. officer health, London, Eng., 1961-65; prin. med. officer Redbridge, London, Eng., 1965-66; dir. home care dept. Bklyn. Cumberland Med. Center, 1966-68; med. dir. Charles Drew Health Center, Bklyn., 1968-70; dir. med. clinic Montifiore-Morrisania Med. Centre, 1970-71; dir. ambulatory care Catholic Med. Center, Bklyn., 1971-74; clin. instr. dept. community health Albert Einstein Coll. Medicine, 1970-71; dir. community medicine South Shore div. L.I. Jewish-Hillside Med. Center, 1974—. Mem. British Med. Assn., Am. Pub. Health Assn. Home: 18 Dunster Rd Great Neck NY 11021 Office: 327 Beach 19th St Far Rockaway NY 11691

MEYER, VESTA GREEN (MRS. JAMES RAYMOND MEYER), plant geneticist; b. Bay City, Mich., July 22, 1919; d. Lloyd John and Vesta Grace (Boyer)) G.; B.S., Mich. State U., 1939; M.S., Pa. State Coll., 1940; m. James Raymond Meyer, Aug. 17, 1940; children—Mary (Mrs. Phillip Hembree), Harry, Charles, Ferolyn. Instr. botany U. Tenn., Knoxville, 1947; research asso. Delta br. Miss. Agrl. Expt. Sta., Stoneville, 1954-67; asso. geneticist Delta br. Miss. Agrl. and Forestry Expt. Sta., Stoneville, 1967—. Violist, Greenville (Miss.) Symphony, 1957—. Mem. A.A.A.S., Am. Soc. Agronomy, Am. Genetic Assn., Bot. Soc. Am., Crop Sci. Soc. Am., Soc. Econ. Botany, Grad. Women in Sci., Sigma Xi, Phi Kappa Phi. Methodist. Home: 108 Redbud St Leland MS 38756 Office: Delta Br Expt Sta Stoneville MS 38776

MEYERS, ANNA BRENNER, lawyer; b. Lodz, Poland, Dec. 18, 1897; d. Joseph and Edith (Gutman) Brenner; came to U.S., 1900, naturalized, 1925; R.N., Bklyn. Jewish Hosp. Nurses Tng. Sch. 1918; student Tchrs. Coll., Columbia, 1920-22, N.Y. Sch. Social Work, 1922-23; LL.B., St. Lawrence U., 1928; LL.D., Bethune-Cookman Coll., 1964, U. Miami, 1972; m. Benjamin Meyers, May 18, 1939 (dec. 1974). Tchr. elementary sch., Stepney, Conn., 1913-14; vis. nurse Henry Street Settlement, 1919-20; dir. farm and rural program Nat. Council Jewish Women, 1922-29; social worker Crime Prevention Bur., N.Y.C. Police Dept., 1929-30; dir. social service Maimonides Hosp., Bklyn., 1930-31; dist. office adminstr. N.Y. Emergency Home Relief Bur., 1931-33; admitted to N.Y. State bar, 1934, Fla. bar, 1936, U.S. Supreme Ct. bar, 1941, ICC bar, 1942; practiced in N.Y.C., 1934-35, Miami, Fla., 1936—; social worker Fed. Emergency Relief Adminstrn., Miami, 1935; sec., dir. Miami Bottled Gas, Inc., 1936-60. Mem. budget com. Community Chest of Dade County, Fla., United Fund; pres. Jewish Family and Children's Service, Miami; nat. v.p. Am. Jewish Congress; mem. Dade County Sch. Bd., 1953-71; founder Miami-Dade Jr. Coll.; founder Miami pub. TV channel; founding mem. Miami Jewish Hosp. and Home for Aged; mem. Miami Beach Devel. Commn., 1965-67, Miami Beach Rent Control Commn., 1973; del. White House Conf. on Children, 1970, World Zionist Congress, Basle, Switzerland, 1945. Trustee, Mt. Sinai Hosp., Miami Beach, 1973—, Miami Beach Pub. Library, 1961—; past trustee Cedars of Lebanon Hosp.; chmn. bd. trustees Miami Beach Art Center; trustee, sec. bd. Greater Miami Jewish Fedn.; mem. bd. Welfare Planning Council. Recipient Outstanding Citizen of Dade County award, 1957; State of Israel medallion, Eleanor Roosevelt-Israel Humanitarian award, 1964, Tower of David award, Jerusalem Liberation award; Man of Year award U. Miami chpt. Delta Kappa, 1969, Abess Human Relations award Anti-Defamation League, 1971; Sch. Bell award Dade County Classroom Tchrs. Assn., 1971; Morrison Meml. award South Fla. Pharm. Assn.; award Greater Miami Jewish Fedn.; others. Mem. Miami C. of C. (chmn. internat. relations women's div.), Nat. Assn. Women Lawyers (past treas.), Fla. Fedn. Bus. and Profl. Women's Clubs (state legislation chmn.), Internat. (v.p., treas.), Fla. (organizer, 1st pres.) assns. women lawyer, Am. Judicature Soc., Phi Theta Kappa. Democrat. Jewish religion. Home: 5055 Collins Av Miami Beach FL 33140 Office: 420 Lincoln Rd Miami Beach FL 33139

MEYERS, EDNA OCKO, psychologist; b. N.Y.C., Oct. 8, 1909; d. Isaac and Bessie (Wofsey) Ocko; B.A., Hunter Coll., 1929; M.S., City Coll. N.Y., 1961; Ed.D., Columbia, 1966; m. Sidney Meyers, May 26, 1930 (dec. 1969); 1 son, Nicholas. Tchr. English in secondary schs., N.Y.C., 1931-34; profl. pianist, dancer, 1933-37; a founder New Dance Group, 1934; dance critic Cue, 1936-38; feature writer N.Y. Post, 1937; editor in chief Theatre Arts Com. mag., 1936-39; with pub. relations dept. Hadassah, Albert Einstein Coll. Medicine, other nat. orgns., 1940-50; teaching asso. Tchrs. Coll. Columbia, 1964; chief psychologist Northside Center, psychiat. clinic, N.Y.C., 1967—; faculty City Coll., N.Y.C., 1967—. Dept. Health, Edn. and Welfare grantee, 1970-72. Fellow Am. Orthopsychiat. Assn.; mem. A.A.A.S., Am. Psychol. Assn., N.Y. Soc. Clin. Psychologists. Home: 545 West End Av New York City NY 10024 Office: Northside Center 31 W 110th St New York City NY 10026 Office: City Coll New York City NY 10031

MEYERS, ELAINE HARRIET SCHWARZBACH (MRS. DAN MEYERS), pub. relations cons.; b. Chgo., Apr. 10, 1927; d. Michael Mitchell and Mary (Miller) Schwarzbach; B.A., U. Wis., 1948; m. Dan Meyers, June 20, 1954; children—Lawrence Jay, Neal Steven. Pub. relations cons. Athens Athletic Club, Oakland, Cal., 1966-69, Alameda County Easter Seal Soc., Oakland, Cal., 1969—. Third v.p. Oakland (Cal.) Symphony Guild, 1964-66. Mem. Women in Communications, Inc. (pres. Oakland-Berkeley chpt. 1973—), East Bay Press Club, East Bay Women's Press Club, Ad/Mark. Address: 4861 Geranium Pl Oakland CA 94619

MEYERS, INA STUART (MRS. HAROLD H. MEYERS), editor; b. Warsaw, Poland, Mar. 20, 1921; d. Michael and Niusia (Szereszewski) Szabad; came to U.S., 1934, derivative citizenship; student Hunter Coll., 1936-38; m. Harold H. Meyers, Aug. 7, 1941; children—Michael, Paul, Kim. Asst. women's editor Daily Times, Mamaroneck, N.Y., div. Westchester-Rockland Newspapers, 1961-62, gen. reporter, 1962-68, city editor, 1968-74, mng. editor, 1974—. Mem. selection com. Mamaroneck (N.Y.) Bd. Edn., 1960-62, mem. adult edn. adv. com., 1956-59. Mem. Sigma Delta Chi. Home: 304 Fenimore Rd Mamaroneck NY 10543 Office: 126 Library Lane Mamaroneck NY 10543

MEYERS, MAE ESTELLE, civil engr.; b. Cameron, Tex., Nov. 26, 1908; d. E.L. and Sallie Mae (Hodges) Meyers; B.A., Rice U., 1930; M.A., U. Tex., Austin, 1933; postgrad. Air Nav. Instr.'s Sch., USN, 1943, Art Students League, N.Y.C., 1946-49, Columbia Coll. Physicians and Surgeons, 1949-51. Art tchr. pub. schs., Dayton, Tex., 1934-39; advt. artist Mears Advt., N.Y.C., 1946-48; asst. to supr. engrng. changes Chance Vought Aircraft Co., Dallas, 1953-56; designer engrng., 1956-59; designer, engr. for paving city streets, Dallas, 1959—; occupational therapist VA Hosp., McKinney, Tex., 1951-52. Served to lt. comdr. USNR, 1943-46. Named One of Top Ten Women in Bus., Am. Bus. Women's Assn., 1970. Mem. U.S. Naval Inst. (asso.), Am. Bus. Women's Assn. (treas. Tercera chpt. 1969-70), D.A.R. (vice regent), Colonial Dames XVII Century. Roman Catholic. Painted altar pieces, 1935, 37, 39-42. Patentee nav. device. Home: 2038 Mather St Irving TX 75061 Office: 1500 W Mockingbird Lane Dallas TX 75235

MEYERS, MATTIE BURTON, educator; b. Durham, N.C., Dec. 10; d. Fred Langston and Julia Mae (Tedder) Burton; B.S., N.C. Central U., 1946; M.A., Fresno State Coll., 1966; postgrad. U. So. Cal., 1967-68; m. Earl Randolph Meyers, Nov. 16, 1946 (div. Dec. 1969); children—Earl Randolph, Eric L., Gayle K.F., Michael R., David K. Tchr., Kerman-Floyd Sch. Dist., Kerman, Cal., 1967-69; tchr. remedial reading, sci., social studies Fresno (Cal.) City Unified Sch. Dist., 1969-71, math. resource specialist, 1971-72; instr. Center for Urban Edn., Fresno State Coll., 1971; staff writer Grapevine mag., 1971-74; instr. sociology, sec. to supt. Lincoln Hosp. Sch. Nursing, Durham, N.C., 1945-47. Mem. womens adv. council Cal. Fair Employment Practices, 1966; mem. Study Com. on Patterns of Edn., Fresno, 1962-63; mem. Fresno Biracial Council, 1963-65; mem. Fresno Community Council Housing Com., 1961-62; edn. chmn. N.A.A.C.P., Fresno, 1963-68; mem. Fresno Citizens Exec. Com., 1966-67; mem. minority adv. com. KFSN TV. Candidate for Mayor of Fresno, 1965. Recipient Hon. Mayor of Fresno citation, 1962, Outstanding Pres.'s award Fresno br. N.A.A.C.P., 1962, Social Action award Gamma Xi chpt. Phi Beta Sigma Fraternity, 1962; named Woman of Year, Gamma Eta chpt. Iota Phi Lambda Sorority, 1962. Mem. Cal. Tchrs. Assn., N.E.A., A.A.A.S., Black Educators Assn. Fresno (sec.), Nat. Council tchrs. Math., Beta Kappa Chi. Home: 210 E Hawes Av Fresno CA 93706 Office: Mary McLeod Bethume Elementary Sch 1616 S Fruit Av Fresno CA 93706

MEYERS, MURIEL C., physician, educator; b. N.Y.C., Mar. 31, 1916; d. G. Roland and Helen V. (Lyons) Meyers; A.B., Hood Coll., 1937; M.D., Duke, 1941; Sc.D. (hon.), Hood Coll., 1963. Intern, Duke Hosp., 1941-42, asst. resident, 1942-43; resident U. Mich., 1944, instr. internal medicine, 1944-47, asst. prof., 1947-53, asso. prof., 1953-62, prof., 1962—; practice medicine specializing in internal medicine hematology, Ann Arbor, Mich., 1947—; research asst. Simpson Meml. Inst., U. Mich., Ann Arbor, 1944-47, research asso., 1947-59, acting dir., 1959-60, asso. dir., 1960—; cons. hematology Ann Arbor VA Hosp., 1958—. Recipient Citation in Sci. Hood Coll., 1952, Sr. Med. Residents' award U. Mich. Med. Center, 1968. Diplomate Am. Bd. Internal Medicine. Mem. A.C.P., Am. Fedn. Clin. Research, Am. Soc. Hematology, Internat. Soc. Hematology, Central Soc. Clin. Research, Alpha Omega Alpha. Contbr. articles to profl. jours. Home: 818 Lincoln Av Ann Arbor MI 48104 Office: Simpson Inst Observatory St Ann Arbor MI 48104

MEYERSON, NANCY ROBBINS, pub. relations exec.; b. Chgo., Aug. 5, 1947; d. Harry and Sonya (Roiter) Robbins; B.S., Northwestern U., 1968; m. Gerald Hirsch Meyerson, Dec. 23, 1967 (div. Feb. 1974). Dir. pub. relations Ill. Pharm. Assn., Chgo., 1968-69, Am. Inst. Baking, Chgo., 1969-71, A. Epstein Cos., Inc., Chgo., 1971—; partner Small Bus. Communications, Chgo., 1973—. Pub. relations dir. Equal Rights Amendment Central, 1973—. Mem. Women in Communications (v.p. 1971-72, archivist-historian 1973—). Co-author: A Shopping Guide to Nutrition. Office: 2011 W Pershing Rd Chicago IL 60609

MICEK, KATHERINE SCHOLES DANLEY (MRS. EDWARD WILLIAM MICEK), physician; b. Phila., Dec. 27, 1925; d. Hollis Lapp and Marian Earl (Scholes) Danley; A.B., Gettysburg Coll., 1945; M.D., Temple U., 1950; m. Edward William Micek, Sept. 3, 1950; 1 dau., Andrea Madelaine. Technician, Med. Research Labs., Sharp & Dohme, Inc., Glenolden, Pa., 1945-46; technician, Temple U. Hosp., Phila., 1947-50, intern, 1950-51, resident anesthesia, 1953-56; practice medicine specializing in anesthesia, Phila., 1956-70; anesthesia asst. Lankenau Hosp., Phila., 1960-70; chief anesthesia Shriners Hosp. for Crippled Children, Phila., 1960-63, asso., 1963-67; clin. asso. Merck Sharp & Dohme Med. Research Labs., 1963-67; cons. Internat. Information, Inc., 1967-69; gen. practice medicine, Phila., 1970—. Mem. A.M.A., N.Y. Acad. Sci., Pa. State, Philadelphia County med. socs. Clubs: Bala Golf (Phila.); Wilmington (Del.) Skating.

MICELI, MARGARET ELIZABETH, sch. exec.; b. New London, Conn.; d. Salvatore and Delia Agnes (Alger) Mugovero; ed. Williams Meml. Inst., 1938; m. John J. Miceli, Oct. 23, 1938 (dec. Jan. 1973); children—J. Dennis, Keith L., Suzanne (Mrs. Verne Anton), Jeffrey J. Day camp dir. Girl Scouts Am., 1950-56; teen age dir. YWCA, 1960-63; exec. dir. New London unit Am. Cancer Soc., 1963-70; devel. coordinator New London YMCA, 1970-73; devel. dir. Waterford Country Day Sch., 1974—; staff YWCA confs. Sarah Lawrence Coll., 1961, LaSalle Coll., 1962-63. Nat. Cancer Crusade Conf. Workshop coordinator, 1969; corporator Southeastern Conn. Speech and Hearing Center; organizer Womens World of Am. Cancer Soc., 1967, New London unit, 1967; vice chmn. New London Arts Festival, 1973. Campaign mgr. Republican City Councilor Dr. Elsie Tytla, 1963, 65, 67; campaign adviser Dr. R.C. Weller for Bd. Edn. seat, 1965; advt. cons. New London Rep. Party, 1973. Bd. dirs. Heart Assn., Girl Scouts Am.; mem. adv. council Joseph Lawrence Sch. Nursing; charter mem. Friends of Mitchell Coll., Community Health Council. Recipient plaque Conn. div. Am. Cancer Soc., 1970. Club: Zonta International (New London). Pub., editor Action Report house organ YMCA, 1971-73. Home: 100 Glenwood Av New London CT 06320 Office: 58 Hunt's Brook Rd Quaker Hill CT 06385

MICHAEL, PATRICIA GORDON (MRS. JACK L. MICHAEL), mus. ofcl.; b. S.I., N.Y., July 3, 1940; d. George E. and Mary Victoria (Klugewicz) Gordon; B.A., Notre Dame Coll. of S.I.; M.A., Pa. State U.; m. Jack L. Michael, May 19, 1967. Adminstrv. asst. N.Y. Acad. Scis. Interdisciplinary Communications Program, 1963-67; registrar Kalamazoo Pub. Mus., 1967—. Mem. Kalamazoo City Planning Commn., 1974—. Mem. Midwest, Mich. museums assns., Oakland Dr. Assn. (rec. sec. 1974—), Chamber Music Soc. Kalamazoo (bus. mgr. 1972—), Hist. Soc. Mont. Home: 1832 Brentwood Av Kalamazoo MI 49008 Office: 315 S Rose St Kalamazoo MI 49006

MICHAEL, PHYLLIS CALLENDER (MRS. ARTHUR L. MICHAEL), hymnwriter; b. nr. Berwick, Pa., Dec. 24, 1908; d. Bruce Miles and Emma (Harvey) Callender; grad. Bloomsburg Coll., 1928; B. Mus., U. Extension Conservatory, Chgo., 1953; m. Arthur L. Michael, Aug. 21, 1933; children—Robert Bruce, Keith Winton. Elementary tchr. Berwick Schs., 1928-33; substitute tchr. Shickshinny and Northwest Area, Pa., 1954-66; tchr. Northwest Area High Sch., 1966-71; gen. tchr. piano, organ, theory and voice, 1943—; hymnwriter, poet, author, composer, 1943—. Recipient first place in Nat. Favorite Hymns contest for Take Thou My Hand, 1953, Certificate of Merit for distinguished service to composition outstanding hymns, 1967, and others. Adv. mem. MBLS. Mem. N.E.A., Pa. Edn. Assn., Internat. Platform Assn., Hymn Soc. Am. Author: Poems for Mothers, 1963; Poems From My Heart, 1964; Beside Still Waters, 1970; Fun to Do Showers, 1970; Bridal Shower Ideas, 1972; contbr. songs, articles, poems to books, hymn-books, booklets, mags. Address: Oak Haven RFD 3 Shickshinny PA 18655

MICHAEL, SANDRA DALE, geneticist; b. Sacramento, Jan. 23, 1945; d. Gordon Greenwood and Ruby Frances (Johnson) Michael; B.A. cum laude, Cal. State Coll. at Sonoma, 1967; Ph.D. (NIH fellow), U. Cal. at Davis, 1970; m. Dennis Powell Murr, Aug. 12, 1967 (div.). NIH/Health Sci. Advancement Award postdoctoral fellow U. Cal. at Davis, 1970-73, research geneticist, 1973-74; asst. prof. State U. N.Y. at Binghamton, 1974—. Mem. Genetics Soc. Am., Soc. Study Reprodn. Research with electron microscopy of neurologic mutants; hormonal studies during pregnancy. Contbr. to profl. jours. Office: Dept Biol Scis State U NY Binghamton NY 13901

MICHAELS, LINDA ANN, pub. relations exec.; b. Pitts., Aug. 20, 1945; d. Stanley John and Anne Dolores (Fleisher) Michaels; B.A., Duquesne U., 1967; certificate in pub. relations Allegheny Community Coll., 1970; M.Pub. Adminstrn., U. Pitts., 1973. Editor-in-chief Signal-Item, newspaper, Carnegie, Pa., 1967-68; exec. sec., community orgn. specialist for borough Carnegie Code Enforcement Program, Carnegie, 1968-72; dir. pub. relations Century Fed. Savs. & Loan Assn. Pitts., 1972—. Com. chmn. United Fund, Pitts., 1972. Recipient certificate of commendation for community service Boys Clubs Am., 1968; Carnegie plaque for community service, 1968; commendation for excellence in journalism U.S. Army, 1968; commendation for creative reporting U.S. Dept. Forest and Waters, 1968. Mem. Savs. Instn. Marketing Assn., Pa. Assn. Notaries, Internat. Platform Assn., Women in Communications. Home: Essex House Apt 1610 Pittsburgh PA 15206 Office: 5912 Penn Mall Pittsburgh PA 15206

MICHAK, HELEN BARBARA, educator, nurse; b. Cleve., July 31, 1926; d. Andrew and Mary (Patrick) Michak; Diploma Cleve. City Hosp. Sch. Nursing, 1947; B.A., Miami U., Oxford, O., 1951; M.A., Case Western Res. U., 1960. Staff nurse Cleve. City Hosp., 1947-48; pub. health nurse Cleve. Div. Health, 1951-52; instr. Cleve. City Hosp. Sch. Nursing, 1952-56; supr. nursing Cuyahoga County Hosp., Cleve., 1956-58; pub. information dir. N.E. Ohio Am. Heart Assn., Cleve., 1960-64; dir. spl. events Higbee Co., Cleve., 1964-66; exec. dir. Cleve. Area League for Nursing, 1966-72; dir. continuing edn. nurses, adj. asso. prof. Cleve. State U., 1972—. Trustee N.E. Ohio Regional Med. Program, 1970-73; mem. adv. com. Dept. Nursing Cuyanoga Community Coll., 1967—; mem. policy bd. Center Health Data N.E. Ohio, 1972-73; mem. Rep. Assembly and Health Planning and Devel. Commn., Welfare Fedn. Cleve., 1967-72; mem. Cleve. Community Health Network, 1972-73; mem. nursing adv. com. Cleve. Maternal and Infant Care Project, 1972-73; mem. United Appeal Films and Speakers Bur., 1967-73; mem. adv. com. Ohio Fedn. Licensed Practical Nurses, 1970—; mem. tech. adv. com. TB and Respiratory Disease Assn. Cuyahoga County, 1967—; mem. Ohio Commn. on Nursing, 1971—; mem. Citizens com. nursing homes Fedn. Community Planning, 1973—; mem. com. on home health services Met. Health Planning Commn., 1973—. Mem. Nat. League Nursing (mem. com. 1970-72), Am., Greater Cleve. (joint practice com. 1973—) nurses assns., Zeta Tau Alpha. Club: Zonta (Cleveland). Home: 4686 Oakridge Dr North Royalton OH 44133 Office: Cleve State Univ 2344 Euclid Av Cleveland OH 44115

MICHAUD, SISTER FERNANDE, nursing home adminstr.; b. Bic, Que., Can., Dec. 7, 1918; d. Isidore and Alice (Garneau) Michaud; diploma hosp. adminstrn. U. Sask. (Can.), 1965. Supr. lab. and radiology dept. St. Paul's Hosp., Saskatoon, Sask., Can., 1944-50, St. Theresa Hosp., St. Paul, Alta., Can., 1950-56, 65-68, Edmonton (Alta.), Gen. Hosp., 1956-65; adminstr. Youville Home, St. Albert, Alta., 1968—. Bd. dirs. Edmonton Gen. Hosp., 1970-73. Mem. Canadian Council Health Service Execs., Canadian Soc. Med. Technologists. Address: 9 St Vital Av St Albert AB T8N 1K1 Canada

MICHAUX, MARY HELEN TATOM (MRS. WILLIAM WHITEHEAD MICHAUX), psychologist; b. Huttig, Ark., Apr. 26, 1911; d. Bascom Guinn and Helen Viola (Y'Blood) Tatom; B.A., George Washington U., 1947; M.A., Catholic U. Am., 1949, Ph.D., 1952; m. William Whitehead Michaux, Mar. 18, 1961. Tchr., Ark. Pub. Schs., 1930-44; trainee VA, Catholic U., 1947-51; staff psychologist VA Mental Hygiene Clinic, Washington, 1951-57; chief psychologist Legal Psychiat. Services D.C. Dept. Pub. Health, 1957-59; research psychologist Friends of Psychiat. Research, Spring Grove State Hosp., Balt., 1959-67, Springfield State Hosp., Sykesville, Md., 1967—. Served with Women's Res., AUS, 1944-46. Fellow Md. Psychol. Assn.; mem. Am. Psychol. Assn., Sigma Xi. Democrat. Methodist. Contbr. articles to profl. jours. Home: 501 Colleen Rd Baltimore MD 21229 Office: Springfield State Hospital Sykesville MD 21784

MICHEL, JOAN HESS (MRS. FREDERICK A. MICHEL), mag. editor; b. Bklyn., June 24, 1929; d. James and Mildred (Horak) Hess; B.A., Sweet Briar Coll., 1951; M.A., George Peabody Coll. for Tchrs., 1952; m. Frederick A. Michel, Oct. 4, 1959; children—Jennifer, Frederick, Christopher. Asst. copy editor Town & Country mag., N.Y.C., 1955-56; editorial asst. Am. Artist mag., N.Y.C., 1956, asst. editor, 1957-58, mng. editor, 1958-59, contbg. editor, 1959—; contbg. editor Fence Industry mag., N.Y.C., 1972—. Carnegie fellow, 1951-52. Mem. Pi Gamma Mu. Democrat. Home: 108 Manhasset Woods Rd Manhasset NY 11030

MICHELET, FAYE IRENE FULLERTON (MRS. CHARLES JULES MICHELET, JR.), clubwoman; b. Tuscola, Ill., Oct. 13, 1902; d. Frank Alexander and Anna (Slaughter) Fullerton; student MacMurray Coll., 1921-22, Northwestern, 1922-23; A.B., U. Ill., 1926; m. Charles Jules Michelet, Jr., June 28, 1937; 1 dau., Michele Fay (Mrs. Michael Verne Boyer). Tchr., Barstow Sch., Kansas City, Mo., 1927-30, Bancroft Sch., Worcester, Mass., 1930-31; supr. Thurston Sch., Pitts., 1931-34, Punahou Sch., Honolulu, 1934-35; tchr. Milw.-Downer Sem., 1935-37. Nat. corr. sec. Daus. Am. Colonists, 1964-67, nat. chmn. resolutions, 1967-68, nat. organizing sec., 1968-70, state regent, 1961-64, state chmn. insignia, 1967-70, chpt. chmn. ann. benefit, 1967-69, nat. pres., 1970-73, hon. life pres. 1974—; chpt. regent D.A.R., 1959-61, state chmn. membership, 1962-64; rec. sec. Ill. State Officers Club D.A.R., 1965-67; state v.p. Colonial Dames XVII Century, 1968-70, chpt. pres., 1968-70, State Parliamentarian, 1974—; sr. pres. William Dawes Soc. Children Am. Revolution, 1957-59. Mem. Nat. Soc. Sons and Daus. of Pilgrims,

Nat. Soc. Daus. Colonial Wars, Nat. Soc. Desc. Colonial Clergy, Nat. League Am. Pen Women (historian Chgo. br. 1974—), Magna Charta Dames, Ill. Hist. Soc., Am. Legion Aux., Soc. Ind. Pioneers, Nat. Soc. Ladies Grand Army of Republic, Ill. Audubon Soc., Wilmette Hist. Soc., Am. Assn. U. Women, U. Ill. Alumnae Assn., Delta Gamma Alumnae Assn. Republican. Episcopalian (mem. woman's guild). Clubs: National Officers (Daus. Am. Colonists, rec. sec. 1974—), Michigan Shores, National Gavel, D.A.R. Ex-Regents (corr. sec. 4th div. 1967-69). Home: 1028 Sheridan Rd Wilmette IL 60091

MICHELS, AGNES KIRSOPP LAKE (MRS. WALTER C. MICHELS), educator; b. Leiden, Netherlands, July 31, 1909 brought to U.S., 1914, naturalized, 1924; d. Kirsopp and Helen (Forman) Lake; student St. Paul's Girls' Sch., London, 1925-26; B.A., Bryn Mawr Coll., 1930, M.A., 1931, Ph.D., 1934; fellow Am. Acad., Rome, 1931-33; m. Walter Christian Michels, June 4, 1941; 1 stepdau., Leslyn Jane (Mrs. Charles H. Goodrich, Jr.). Instr. Bryn Mawr Coll., 1934-38, asst. prof. Latin, 1938-46, asso. prof., 1946-55, prof., 1955—, Mellon prof. humanities, 1970—; Martin lectr. Oberlin Coll., 1969. Faculty fellow Found Advancement Edn., 1953-54; Guggenheim fellow, 1960-61; recipient Goodwin Merit award, 1970. Mem. Am. Philol. Assn. (pres. 1972), Am. Inst. Archaeology, Soc. Promotion Roman Studies (Eng.), Internat. Archaeol. Assn., Alumni Soc. Am. Acad. Rome, Bryn Mawr Coll. Alumnae Assn. Mem. Soc. Friends. Author: The Calendar of The Roman Republic, 1967. Home: 532 Red Fox Lane Wayne PA 19087 Office: Bryn Mawr Coll Bryn Mawr PA 19010

MICHELSEN, PHYLLIS BUCKLEY (MRS. FREDERICK C. NACHOD), statistician; b. Fall River, Mass.; d. John Joseph and Frances Lilly (Brightman) Buckley; A.B., Barnard Coll., 1949; M.S., Columbia, 1952; D.Sc., Harvard, 1971; m. Walter J. Michelsen, Dec. 31, 1950; 1 dau., Sarah A.; m. 2d, Frederick C. Nachod, May 27, 1972. Asso. in biostatistics Columbia, 1950-65; asst. prof. Albany (N.Y.) Med. Coll., Union U., 1968-72; sr. research scientist demography, vital statistics N.Y. State Health Dept., Albany, 1972—. Mem. Am. Statis. Assn., Biometric Soc., Sigma Xi. Home: PO Box 345 Kinderhook NY 12106 Office: 84 Holland Av Albany NY 12208

MICHELSON, BETTIE ELIZABETH NELSON, educator; b. DeKalb, Ill., Sept. 7, 1920; d. Carl Emil and Lucile Evelyn (Martin) Nelson; B.E., No. Ill. U., 1942, M.S., 1966; diploma in occupational therapy U. Ill., 1948; postgrad. McGill U., 1964, U. Kan., 1965, Columbia, 1969, U. Americas, Mexico, 1967; m. G.W. Michelson, Apr. 17, 1948; children—Monica, Mark. Tchr. pub. schs., Brookfield, Ill., 1942-43, Aurora, Ill., 1943-44; therapist Shick Army Hosp., Clinton, Ia., 1945-46; dir. Madigan Neuropsychiatric Occupational Therapy facility, Ft. Lewis, Wash., 1946-48; tchr. pub. schs., DeKalb, Ill., 1948-52, 64—, Grant Sch., Washington, 1952-53, pub. schs., Geneva, Ill., 1961-62; cooperating tchr. dept. spl. edn. No. Ill. U., DeKalb, 1965—. Mem. U.S. delegation to 7th Caribbean Conf. for Mental Health, Trinidad, 1969; participant conf. art and spl. edn. Nat. Art. Edn. Assn., 1974; lectr. on spl. edn. to various civic and ch. groups; active summer recreation program for retarded children DeKalb County. Bd. dirs. Project Alert, DeKalb County, 1973-74. Fellow in occupational therapy Center for Developmental and Learning Disorders, U. Ala., 1970-71. Mem. Nat., Ill. edn. assns., Am. Occupational Therapy Assn., Council for Exceptional Children, Ill., DeKalb assns. for tchr. educators, League Women Voters, English-Speaking Union, Delta Kappa Gamma. Home: 330 Sycamore Rd DeKalb IL 60115 Office: 145 Fisk Av DeKalb IL 60115

MICHELSON, GERTRUDE G. (MRS. HORACE MICHELSON), business exec.; b. Jamestown, N.Y., June 3, 1925; d. Thomas and Celia (Cohen) Rosen; B.A., Pa. State U., 1945; LL.B., Columbia, 1947; m. Horace Michelson, Mar. 28, 1947; children—Martha Ann (dec.), Barbara Jane. With Macy's, N.Y.C., 1947—, adminstr. staff personnel, 1957-63, v.p., 1963-70, sr. v.p. for consumer and labor relations, 1970-72, sr. v.p. personnel, labor and consumer relations, 1972—; dir. Quaker Oats Co., Chubb Corp., Inc., Webster Apts., Inc. Mem. Com. for Specialized Placement Handicapped; adv. council Cornell Sch. Indsl. Relations, 1972—; trustee Markle Found.; adv. council Nat. Coalition Edn. Women; bd. dirs. Greater N.Y. Safety Council, Better Bus. Bur. N.Y., Interracial Council Bus. Opportunity. Home: 70 E 10th St New York City NY 10003 Office: 151 W 34th St New York City NY 10001

MICKA, HELEN KRANICK (MRS. THOMAS JAMES MICKA), ret. educator; b. Helena, Mont., Sept. 12, 1908; d. Charles Wesley and Mary Anne (Muscos) Kranick; B.A., Intermountain Union Coll., 1930; M.A., U. Mont., 1967; m. Thomas James Micka, June 6, 1935; 1 dau., Mary Ann. Tchr. English, Latin, Baker (Mont.) High Sch., 1930-35; tchr. English, Hinsdale (Mont.) High Sch., 1936-37; tchr. English, Latin, journalism Corvallis (Mont.) High Sch., 1943-62; tchr. English, journalism Bozeman (Mont.) High Sch., 1962-73. State youth chmn. Mont. State Grange, 1946-49; leader 4-H Club, 1955-59; dist. pres. P.T.A., 1949-51, state treas., 1951-54, state historian, 1954-61; counselor Flathead Lake Methodist Camp for Jr. High, 1951-53. Recipient newspaper fund fellowship Wall Street Jour., 1962, Gold Key award Mont. Interscholastic Editorial Assn., 1969, Valley Forge Tchrs. medal Freedoms Found., 1970. Mem. Mont., Nat. edn. assns., Am. Assn. Univ. Women, Journalism Educators Am., Modern Lang. Assn., Mont. Assn. Tchrs. English (state pres. 1965), Mont. Ret. Tchrs. Assn. (local v.p., state publicity chmn.), United Meth. Women (dist. pres. 1973—, mem. conf. exec. com.), White Shrine, Daus. of Nile, Order Eastern Star, Methodist (lay leader 1948-56). Author: History of Montana Congress of Parents and Teachers, 1915-1965, 1965. Home: Route 4 Box 114 Bozeman MT 59715 Office: Bozeman Sr High School 1211 W Main St Bozeman MT 59715

MICKA, MARY ANN, pediatrician; b. Hamilton, Mont., Sept. 24, 1940; d. Thomas James and Helen May (Kranick) Micka; B.S., Mont. State U., 1962; M.D. (Nathan Hoffheimer fellow, Alpha Gamma Delta Founders Meml. Fund grantee, Mortar Bd. fellow, Alice Crocker Lloyd fellow), Case Western Res. U., 1966; M.P.H. (Cross Cultural grantee, pub. health trainee), U. Tex., 1974. Intern Cleve. Met. Gen. Hosp., 1966-67, resident pediatrics, 1967-68; resident pediatrics Bernalillo County Med. Center, Albuquerque, 1971-72; physician Peace Corps, Cameroon, West Africa, 1968-70; emergency room physician Bataan Meml. Hosp., Albuquerque, 1972; med. cons. Child Health Services Maternal and Child Health, Tex. State Dept. Health, Austin, 1974—. Cons. Title XIX Med. Screening Program, Tex. Pub. Health Region 10, Harlingen, pediatric screening examiner, 1973-74. Mem. Christian Med. Soc., Population Assn. Am., U.S.-Mex. Border Health Assn., Mortar Bd., Alpha Gamma Delta, Alpha Lambda Delta, Phi Sigma, Phi Kappa Phi, Phi Sigma. Methodist. Home: Route 4 Box 114 Bozeman MT 59715 Office: 1100 W 49th St MCH Austin TX 78756

MICKANS, VIKTORIJA, psychiatrist, psychoanalyst; b. Nautreni, Latvia; d. Joachims and Helena (Mugins) Mickans; tchr. State Tchrs. Tng. Inst., 1936; Dr. med. dent., U. Munich, 1951, Dr. med., 1954. Came to U.S., 1951, naturalized, 1959. Tchr., Latvia, 1936-43; rotating intern Greenpoint Hosp., Bklyn., 1954-55; resident psychiatry Bellevue Hosp., N.Y.C., 1955-58; fellow psychiatry Inst. Phys. Medicine and Rehab., 1958-59; staff psychiatrist Cath. Charities Guidance Inst., N.Y.C., 1960—, Bur. Child Guidance, N.Y.C. Bd. Edn., 1967—; psychiatrist Family Ct., N.Y.C., 1960-67; psychoanalyst Am. Inst. Psychoanalysis, 1967-71, Karen Horney Clinic, N.Y.C., 1967—. Fellow Am. Geriatrics Soc., Am. Acad. Psychoanalysis; mem. A.M.A., Am. Psychiat. Assn., Assn. for Advancement Psychoanalysis, N.Y. Council Child Psychiatry, Assn. for Advancement Psychotherapy. Address: 120 E 34th St New York City NY 10016

MICKIEWICZ, ELLEN PROPPER (MRS. DENIS MICKIEWICZ), educator, author; b. Hartford, Conn., Nov. 6, 1938; d. George and Rebecca (Adler) Propper; B.A., Wellesley Coll., 1960; Ph.D., Yale, 1965; m. Denis Mickiewicz, June 2, 1963; 1 son, Cyril. Lectr. polit. sci. Yale, 1965-67; asst. prof. polit. sci. Mich. State U., East Lansing, 1967-69, asso. prof., 1969-73, prof., 1973—. Mem. exec. com. Midwest Conf. on Slavic Studies, 1969-72. Ford fellow, 1962-63; Fgn. Area Tng. fellow, 1963-65; Guggenheim fellow, 1973-74; Sigma Xi grantee, 1973-74. Mem. Am. Assn. for Advancement Slavic Studies, Am., Midwest polit. sci. assns., Phi Beta Kappa. Author: Soviet Political Schools, 1967. Author, editor: Handbook of Soviet Social Science Data, 1973; cons., guest editor Soviet Edn., 1972. Contbr. articles to profl. jours. Home: 361 Southlawn Av East Lansing MI 48823

MIDDIONE, ELIZABETH DERBY (MRS. CARLO MIDDIONE), assn. exec.; b. Jackson, N.C., Jan. 6, 1923; d. Roger Alden and Elizabeth Palmer (Harlan) Derby; student Barnard Coll., N.Y.C., 1942-44; Mus.B., Juilliard Inst. Music, N.Y.C., 1944; postgrad. Hunfer Coll., N.Y.C., 1945, U. Oslo, Norway, 1947; m. Carlo Middione, June 1, 1968. Script reader Twentieth Century Fox, 1941-43; mgr. import and distbn. Vaco Co., N.Y.C., 1947-52; mgr. nat. wholesale div. Georg Jensen, Inc., N.Y.C., 1952-57; ind. cons., San Francisco, 1957-71; exec. sec. Stern Grove Festival Assn., 1963-71; instl. cons. San Francisco Boys Chorus, 1966-71, now dir.; pub. relations cons. Blum & Middione, 1967-71; exec. dir. Contra Costa County Assn. for Mentally Retarded, Inc., Walnut Creek, Cal., 1971-74; devel. dir. Goodwill Industries Greater East Bay, Oakland, 1974—. Mem., participant Aspen Internat. Design Conf., 1952-57; mem. adv. bd. Cal. Coll. Arts and Crafts, 1957-63; mem. exhibit com. Cal. Hist. Soc., 1959-65. Bd. dirs. Young Audiences, San Francisco Chamber Music Soc.; trustee United Bay Area Crusade. Mem. exec. com. Contra Costa County Coordinating Council. Recipient awards San Francisco Bay Area Publicity Club, 1969, 70. Mem. Assn. Agy. Adminstrs. (1st v.p. Contra Costa County). Home: 131 Delmar St San Francisco CA 94117 Office: 212 9th St Oakland CA 94607

MIDDLEHURST, BARBARA MARY, astronomer, astrophysicist; b. Penarth, Wales, U.K., Sept. 10, 1915; d. George Frederick and Gladys (Sadler) Middlehurst; B.A., Girton Coll., Cambridge, Eng., 1936, M.A., 1947. Observer, St. Andrews U. Obs., Scotland, 1951-54, lectr., 1954-59; vis. astronomer Hamburg (Germany) Obs., 1951; research asso. Ind. U., 1953-54, Yerkes Obs., Williams Bay, Wis., 1959-60, U. Ariz., Tucson, 1960-68; asso. editor Ency. Brit., 1968-72; vis. scientist Luna Sci. Inst., Houston, 1973—. Fellow Am. Geophys. Union, Royal Astron. Soc. (London); mem. Am. Astron. Soc., Internat. Astron. Union (sec. commn. 17 1967). Editor: (with G.P. Kuiper) series Stars and Stellar Systems, 1959; The Solar System, vol. 3, 1961, vol. 4, 1963. Research, publs. on photog. and photoelectric stellar photometry, stellar spectroscopy, lunar and planetary studies. Address: Luna Sci Inst 3303 NASA Rd Houston TX 77058

MIDDLEMAN, ROSE RUTH, physician; b. Pitts., Apr. 14, 1911; d. Harry and Fanny Rachel (Opachevsky) Schechter; B.S., U. Pitts., 1932, M.D., 1934, M.P.H., 1961; postgrad. N.Y. Postgrad. Med. Sch., 1937; m. Leo Silverblatt, June 7, 1934; children—Norma (Mrs. Harold Caplan), Howard, Alan. Practice medicine, 1936-37, specializing in gynecology, Youngstown, O., 1937-42, Pitts., 1943-59; asst. to chief, div. maternal and child health Allegheny County Health Dept., Pitts., 1962-63, chief div., 1963-68; med. coordinator Planned Parenthood Center Pitts., 1968-72, med. dir., 1972—. Lectr. Population div. Grad. Sch. Pub. Health U. Pitts., 1968—. Unit chmn. League Women Voters, 1966-67; mem. Pa. Abortion Law Commn., 1972. Bd. dirs. Abortion Justice Assn., 1969-70, 71-73, vice chmn., 1970-71. Mem. Allegheny County, Pa. med. socs., Assn. Planned Parenthood Physicians, Am. Pub. Health Assn., Am. Civil Liberties Union, Alpha Omega Alpha. Home: 3421 Ridgewood Dr Pittsburgh PA 15235 Office: 526 Penn Av Pittsburgh PA 15222

MIDDLEMAN, RUTH J. ROSENBLOOM, educator; b. Pitts., Nov. 11, 1923; d. Alfred A. and Corinne (Lorch) Rosenbloom; B.S. with highest honors, U. Pitts., 1944, M.S., 1946; postgrad. U. Pa., 1960-61; Ed.D., Temple U., 1972; m. Donald J. Middleman, Jan. 30, 1949; children—Karl D., Philip H. Dir. Jewish Center Day Camps, Phila., 1949-53; departmental supr. Jewish Centers, Phila., 1946-51; dir. activities Neighborhood Centre, Phila., 1951-53; supr. students Carnegie Inst. Tech. and U. Pa., 1946-53, 66—, Temple U., 1950-53; faculty U. Pa. Sch. Social Work, 1950-68, Sch. Occupational Therapy, 1960-61, 66-69; prof. Temple U. Sch. Social Adminstrn., 1968—; social worker Pa. Assn. for Retarded Children, Phila., 1957-58; supr. Florence Crittenton Service, Phila., 1957-60, program dir., 1965-66; group work supr. Children's Aid Soc. Pa., Phila., 1965-68; cons. Phila. Bd. Edn., 1967—. Active N.J. Div. Corrections. Mem. Am. Orthopsychiat. Assn., Nat. Assn. Social Workers, Am. Acad. Certified Social Workers, Council on Social Work Edn., Am. Assn. U. Profs., Mortar Bd., Alpha Epsilon Phi, Alpha Kappa Delta, Pi Lambda Theta. Jewish religion. Author: The Non-Verbal Method in Working with Groups, 1968. Contbr. articles to profl. jours. Collector paper folk art. Home: Cooper River Plaza 915E Pennsauken NJ 08109 Office: Temple U Sch Social Adminstrn Philadelphia PA 19122

MIDDLETON, ANNETTA VIRGINIA, transp. co. exec.; b. Marshall, Mo., Aug. 8, 1917; d. Thomas Richard and Virginia Ellen (Hamilton) Breeden; student Missouri Valley Coll., 1936-37; m. Howard A. Middleton, Aug. 9, 1938 (div.). With Cramer Chair Co., Kansas City, Mo., 1938-42; office mgr. Hartford Knitting Mills, Unionville, Conn., 1942-43; sec. Mchts. Delivery Co., Kansas City, 1943—. Mem. Womens C. of C. Clubs: Transportation, Business Womens (Kansas City, Mo.). Home: 9419 Hayes Dr Overland Park KS 66212 Office: 1212 E 19th St Kansas City MO 64108

MIDDLETON, AVA ELIZABETH JACKSON (MRS. JOSEPH LEONARD MIDDLETON), educator; b. Raleigh, N.C.; d. Donald Rudolph and Bessie (Mull) Jackson; A.B., Meredith Coll., 1939; B.D., Crozer Theol. Sem., Chester, Pa. 1943; postgrad. Union Theol. Sem., N.Y.C., 1945, E. Carolina U., Greenville, N.C., 1964-65, N.C. State U., Raleigh, 1965, U. Hawaii, Honolulu, Summer 1967, N.C. State U., 1970; m. Joseph Leonard Middleton, Sept. 19, 1940; children—Mildred Marilyn, Jacilyn Sue. Tchr. pub. schs., Rolesville, N.C., 1939-40, Blue Ridge Sch. for Boys, Hendersonville, N.C., 1945-46; associational missionary Raleigh (N.C.) Bapt. Assn., summers 1940-41; pres. Crozer Guild, 1941-42; playground dir. YMCA, Chester, Pa., summer 1942; postal clk., Chester, 1943-44; co-dir. Roanoke Bapt. Assn., Rocky Mount, N.C., 1945-46; prof. sociology, econs., govt. and speech Lees-McRae Coll., Banner Elk, N.C., 1947-48; instr. dept. sociology and anthropology N.C. State of U. N.C. at Raleigh, 1961—. Faculty sociology and psychology Peace Coll., Raleigh, 1962, 66-70, mem. sociology seminar com., 1963-64, prof. sociology and psychology, 1966-70. Sec., N.C. Family Life Council, 1959-61, pres., 1961-64; sec. Southeastern Council on Family Relations, 1964-66; mem. teen-age com. YWCA, Raleigh, 1953-59; 3d v.p. State Coll. Woman's Club, 1958-59; chmn. parent edn. and family life Frances Lacy Sch. P.T.A., 1959-60, 63-64; pres. Needham B. Broughton High Sch. P.T.A., 1966-67; bd. mgrs. N.C. Congress Parents and Tchrs., 1967-71, chmn. high sch. service com.; organizer Child Study Group, 1949; cons. Raleigh Pre-Sch., 1955-56; counselor Girl Scout Day Camp, 1958; condr. confs., speaker to chs., colls., community groups, 1939—. Bd. dirs. YWCA, Raleigh, 1959-60. Mem. family and welfare services com. N.C. Gov.'s Commn. on Status Women; mem. adv. com. on materials and tools of instrn. Gov.'s Study Commn. on Pub. Sch. System N.C., 1967-68; chmn. Southeastern Council on family relations Family Life Edn. in Pub. Schs., 1967-70. Mem. Nat. Council on Family Relations (dir.), So. Sociol. Soc., Population Assn. Am., Am. Social Health Assn., N.C. Sociol. Assn., Council Women's Orgns. N.C. State U. (organizer, 1st pres. 1969—), N.C. Council Women's Orgns., Raleigh Chamber Music Guild, N.C. Mental Health Assn., N.C. Adult Edn. Assn., Meredith Coll. Alumnae Assn., N.C. U. Woman's Club (pres.-elect 1967-68, pres. 1968-69), Am. Assn. U. Profs., Am. Assn. U. Women, Masque and Gavel, Phi Rho Pi. Club: Past Pres.'s N.C. State U. Woman's (sec.-treas. 1972-73). Home: 903 Runnymede Rd Raleigh NC 27607

MIDDLETON, CATHERINE BROWN, physician; b. Savannah, Ga., Jan. 30, 1916; d. Charles Clayton and Jimmie Belle (Bugg) Middleton; student Shaw U., 1930-31; B.S. in Zoology, Howard U., 1934, postgrad., 1935-36, M.D. with honors, 1944; M.S. in Zoology, U. Mich., 1938; M.P.H., U. N.C., 1967. Externe pediatrics Freedmens Hosp., Washington, 1943-44; rotating intern Harlem Hosp., N.Y.C., 1944-45, resident internal medicine, 1945, attending physician internal medicine, 1945-48; resident gen. medicine St. Agnes Hosp., Raleigh, N.C., 1950; physician N.Y.C. Pub. Schs., 1946-47; attending physician internal medicine Fordham Hosp., N.Y.C., 1948-50; pediatric staff St. Agnes Hosp., Raleigh, 1951-61; charge Community Children's Clinic, Wake County Meml. Hosp., 1965-66; gen. practice staff assigned pediatrics Wake County Meml. Hosp., 1961-67; dir. maternal and child health services Del. State Bd. Health, Dover, 1968—, acting dir. div. maternal, child and crippled children's Services, 1968-70, dir., 1970—; instr. drama Shaw U., 1934-35; instr. biology Washington High Sch., Raleigh, 1936-37; instr. biology and math. E.E. Smith High Sch., Fayetteville, N.C., 1938-40; regular attendant Saturday ward rounds Duke U., 1950-52; pvt. practice gen. medicine, N.Y.C., 1945-50, specializing pediatrics, Raleigh, 1950-66. Vol. med. care Negro Indigent Children, Wake County, N.C., 1951-65; bd. mem. Wake County Mental Health Center, 1952-56; cons. speaker Presch. clins. and P.T.A., Raleigh, 1950-66; vol. Wake County Rehab. Center, 1966; mem. Del. Sch. Health Adv. Com., 1970—; adv. bd. Del. Assn. Retarded Children, 1970-71; med. adv. com. Del. League Planned Parenthood, 1971—; mem. med. clinic com. Del. Adolescent Program, 1968—; mem. ad hoc adv. health com. Greater Wilmington Devel. Council, 1968-70, day care adv. com., 1970—, ad hoc health forum com., 1971—; med. adv. com. dept. child devel. and guidance Wilmington Pub. Schs., 1968-71, coordinating com. family life edn., 1968-71; Del. designee Regional Community Coordinated Child Care Com., 1969—; chmn. task force maternal health White House Conf. Children and Youth, 1970—. Mem. L.A. Scruggs Med. Soc., Nat. Med. Assn., Am. Pub. Health Assn., Del. Acad. Medicine, Kent County Med. Soc., Assn. State Maternal and Child Health and Crippled Children Dirs., Am. Acad. Pediatrics (mem. com. handicapped Del. chpt.), Delta Sigma Theta, Kappa Pi. Home: Route 4 Box 253-B Dover DE 19901 Office: Div Pub Health Dept Health and Social Services Dover DE 19901

MIDDLETON, MARGARET JOSEPHINE REESE (MRS. WILLIAM SAMUEL MIDDLETON), lawyer; b. Lawrence, Mich., Feb. 13, 1915; d. Emerson Anthony and Josephine Olivia (LaDuke) Reese; B.S., U. Ill., 1936, J.D., 1959; postgrad. U. Ind., 1939-40; m. William Samuel Middleton, June 27, 1940; children—Julia Ann (Mrs. Richard Stanley Govan), William Richard. Tchr., Lafler Sch., Bangor, Mich., 1935-36; tchr. speech and English, Benjamin Harrison Jr. High Sch., South Bend, Ind., 1937-40; admitted to Ill. bar; partner Middleton & Middleton, attys. at law, Gibson City, Ill., 1961—; spl. asst. atty. gen. for revenue LaSalle, Grundy, Kendall, Ford, Iroquois and Livingston counties, 1970—. Ford County chmn. White House Conf. on Children and Youth, 1968-70, del. to Washington, 1970, mem. state family study com., 1969-70; mem. Ford County Case Coordinating Council; pres. Gibson City Community Migrant Council, 1968, 69, sec., 1973-75. Chairlady Ford County Republican Com., 1970—. Mem. Ill. State, Ford County bar assns., Council Cath. Women (past deanery and diocesan pres., pres. parish 1971-73), Ill. Cath. Conf. (dir., sec.-treas. 1971-75), Nat. Council Cath. Laity (dir. 1971-73), Gibson City Bus. and Profl. Women's Club, Delta Delta Delta. Home: 529 N Church St Gibson City IL 60936 Office: 110 E 9th St Gibson City IL 60936

MIDDLETON, PATRICIA JEAN, psychiatrist; b. Phila., May 7, 1937; d. William Vernon and Miriam Kathleen (Horst) Middleton; B.A., DePauw U., 1959; M.D., Temple U., 1964, M.S., 1966. Intern, York (Pa.) Hosp., 1964-65; postdoctoral research fellow Lab. Clin. Sci., Nat. Inst. Mental Health, Bethesda, Md., 1965-68; resident neurology Temple U. Hosp., 1968-69; resident in psychiatry Inst. Pa. Hosp., Phila., 1969-72. Lectr. Spiritual Frontiers Fellowship, 1970—, mem. exec. com. Phila. area chpt., 1969—; nat. exec. council, 1972—. Mem. Am. Med. Women's Assn., A.A.A.S., Am. Acad. Neurology, Babcock Surg. Soc., Phi Beta Kappa, Sigma Xi. Methodist. Home: 201 W Evergreen Av Philadelphia PA 19118 Office: 111 N 49th St Philadelphia PA 19139

MIDKIFF, MARY ELIZABETH MATZKE (MRS. PATRICK CLAYTON MIDKIFF), editor; b. Galveston, Tex., Dec. 3, 1920; d. August and Uarda Caroline (Butts) Matzke; grad. high sch.; m. Patrick Clayton Midkiff, Apr. 1, 1945. Reporter, feature writer, society editor Galveston (Tex.) News & Tribune, 1938-42; reporter, feature writer, asst. night city editor Houston Post, 1943-47; editor Action, Houston C. of C., 1947-49, editorial asst., 1964-66, asso. editor, 1966-69, exec. editor, 1969-72, editor, mgr. Houston mag., 1972-74, mgr. publs. Houston C. of C., 1974—; copy editor Houston Chronicle, 1949-53; co-owner Waller County Record, weekly newspaper, Waller, 1952-59. Cons. publs. Am. C. of C. Execs. Communications Council, 1973—. Mem. adv. panel in pub. affairs Houston-Harris County chpt. A.R.C., 1971-72; mem. pub. relations com. Houston-Galveston Regional Transp. Study, 1972-73. Recipient Headliner award Houston profl. chpt. Women in Communications, 1973. Mem. Am. C. of C. Execs., Am. C. of C. Exec. Communications Council (chmn. 1974—), Am. Assn. Commerce Publs. (dir. 1970-72), Tex. C. of C. Mgrs. Assn., Women in Communications, Press Club Houston. Democrat. Methodist. Home: 908 E Whitney Dr Houston TX 77022 Office: PO Box 53600 Houston TX 77052

MIDLARSKY, ELIZABETH STECKEL (MRS. MANUS I. MIDLARSKY), psychologist, educator; b. N.Y.C., Apr. 29, 1941; d. Abraham Allan and Frances Lucille (Wiener) Steckel; B.A. magna cum laude, Bklyn. Coll., 1961, postgrad. (grad. fellow), 1961-63; M.A., Northwestern U., 1966, Ph.D. (univ. scholar), 1968; m. Manus I. Midlarsky, June 25, 1961; children—Susan Rachel, Miriam Joyce. Intern VA Hosp., Downey, Ill., 1964-66; lectr. Northwestern U.,

Evanston, Ill., 1965-67; asst. prof. psychology U. Denver, 1968—. Am. Assn. U. Women postdoctoral research fellow, 1974-75. Mem. Am., Colo., Rocky Mountain psychology assns., Assn. for Women Working in Mental Health (steering com.), Phi Beta Kappa, Sigma Xi, Psi Chi. Contbr. articles to profl. publs. Jewish religion. Contbg. author: The Social Process of Helping and Sharing. Home: 2100 Dartmouth Av Boulder CO 80303

MIEDEMA, SYLVIA ANN SERP (MRS. JACOB A. MIEDEMA), savs. and loan assn. exec.; b. Chgo., June 19, 1904; d. Celestin and Julia (Kropacek) Serp; student pub. schs.; m. Charles L. Klima, Jr., June 28, 1924 (dec. Sept. 1951); children—Carol L. (Mrs. Thomas J. Martin), Charles L. III; m. 2d, Jacob A. Miedema, Oct. 24, 1953 (dec. Oct. 1966). Dir., asst. sec. Clyde Savs. & Loan Assn., 1927-33; co-mgr., 1933-51, dir., pres., mgr., 1951—; pres., dir. Klima Ins. Co., Inc., North Riverside, Ill.; chartering dir. Cashier Bank Savs. & Loan Assns., Chgo., 1968—, Darien Bank (Ill.), 1972—. Mem. Com. on industry devel. Ill. Savs. and Loan Comm., 1974—. Founder, past pres. Burnham P.T.A.; past pres. Cicero Edn. Council; campaign mgr. North Riverside Community Chest, 1973. Bd. dirs. Central Suburban unit Ill. div. Am. Cancer Soc.; bd. govs. Cicero Community Chest. Recipient Spike Club award Nat. Home Builders, citation U.S. Treasury Dept. Mem. U.S. (mem. com. internal operations 1973), Ill. (chmn. adv. com. to bd. dirs. 1971-73) savs. and loan leagues, Lyric Opera Guild. Clubs: Bus. and Profl. Women's Cicero, Cicero Women's (past pres.), Berwyn Women's Civic. Home: 342 Eastgrove Riverside IL 60546 Office: 7222 W Cermak Rd North Riverside IL 60546

MIEL, ALICE MARIE, educator; b. Six Lakes, Mich., Feb. 21, 1906; d. Lucas Marcus and Ane Marie (Jensen) Miel; life certificate Central Mich. U., 1924; A.B., U. Mich., 1928, M.A., 1931; Ed.D., Columbia, 1944; L.L.D., Central Mich. U., 1954. Tchr. pub. schs., Ann Arbor, Mich., 1937-39; curriculum coordinator Mt. Pleasant (Mich.) Pub. Schs., 1939-42; prof. edn. Columbia U., N.Y.C., 1945-71, emeritus prof., 1971—; specialist social studies Ministry of Edn., Kabul, Afghanistan, 1971-73. Recipient Human Rights award N.E.A., 1968. Mem. World Edn. Fellowship (sec.-treas. U.S. sect. 1964-69, v.p. 1969-72); mem. Assn. for Supervision and Curriculum Devel. (pres. 1953-54), World Council for Curriculum and Instrn. (exec. sec. 1973—). Author: (with others) Democracy in School Administration, 1943; Changing the Curriculum, 1946; Cooperative Procedures in Learning, 1952; (with Peggy Brogan) More Than Social Studies, 1957; (with Arthur J. Lewis), Supervision for Improved Instruction, 1972; author, editor: Creativity in Teaching, 1961; (with Edwin Kiester) The Shortchanged Children of Suburbia, 1967. Address: 549 W 123d St New York City NY 10027

MIELKE, THELMA JANE, librarian; b. Rochester, N.Y., Dec. 14, 1916; d. Charles Frederick and Sophia Louise (Gottschalk) Mielke; A.B., Elmhurst Coll., 1937; M.A., U. Rochester, 1939; postgrad. Union Theol. Sem., Columbia, 1941-45, N.Y.U., 1954-60; M.S., Columbia, 1961. Asst. dept. philosophy U. Rochester, 1937-39; group worker Baden St. Settlement House, 1939-41; resident Ch. of All Nations, N.Y.C., 1942-43; librarian Harlem Boys Club, 1943-45; UN corr. Revista, P.R., 1945-50; observer UN, 1945-50, OAS, Commn. of Dependent Territories, Havana, Cuba, 1949; pub. relations Hill & Knowlton, N.Y.C., 1952-54; reference asst. to sr. reference librarian, N.Y. U., 1954-63; reference librarian L.I.U., Bklyn., 1963—, asst. prof., 1963-65, asso. prof. 1965—. Exec. sec. Eastern States Hist. Clearing House, 1965—. Mem. Am. Assn. U. Prof., A.L.A., United Fedn. Coll. Tchrs. (sec., exec. bd. 1972—), Nat. Orgn. Women, Nat. Women's Polit. Caucus, Salalm. Editor: Library Leaves, 1964—. Home: 175 W 12th St New York City NY 10011 Office: 385 Flatbush Av Extension Brooklyn NY 11201

MIGALA-WIECLAW, LUCYNA (MRS. KAZIMIERZ WIECLAW), TV news producer; b. Krakow, Poland, May 22, 1944; d. Joseph and Estelle (Suwala) Migala; came to U.S., 1947, naturalized, 1955; student Loyola U., Chgo., 1962-63; student Chicago Conservatory of Music, 1963-68; B.S. in Journalism, Northwestern U., 1966; m. Kazimierz Wieclaw, Nov. 27, 1971. Radio announcer, producer sta. WOPA, Oak Park, Ill., 1963-66; writer, reporter, producer NBC news, Chgo., 1966-69, 1969-71, producer NBC local news, Washington, 1969; producer, coordinator NBC news, Cleve., 1971—. Soloist, mgr. Lira Singers, Chgo., 1965—; mem., chmn. various cultural coms. Polish Am. Congress, 1970—. Washington Journalism Center fellow, spring 1969. Home: 10301 Lake No 703 Cleveland OH 44102 Office: 1403 E 6th St Cleveland OH 44114

MIGEON, BARBARA LOU RUBEN (MRS. CLAUDE JEAN MIGEON), pediatrician; b. Rochester, N.Y., July 31, 1931; d. William Saul and Sara (Gitin) Ruben; B.A., Smith Coll., 1952; M.D., U. Buffalo, 1956; m. Claude Jean Migeon, Apr. 2, 1960; children—Jacques, Jean-Paul, Nicole. Intern, Johns Hopkins, 1956-57, resident, 1957-59; fellow in pediatric endocrinology Harvard, 1959-60; instr. pediatrics Johns Hopkins, Balt., 1962-65, asst. prof., 1965-70, asso. prof., 1970—, head pediatric-genetic counseling clinic, 1970—. Recipient Grants, Joseph Kennedy Found., 1968, Nat. Genetics Found., 1969, NIH, 1971, Citation, Med. Coll. Pa., 1971. Mem. Soc. Pediatric Research, Am. Pediatric Soc., Am. Soc. Human Genetics. Contbr. articles to profl. jours. Home: 502 Somerset Rd Baltimore MD 21210

MIHALENKO, RUTH MADELINE PETERSON (MRS. JOSEPH F. MIHALENKO), assn. exec.; b. Camden, N.J., July 9, 1938; d. LeRoy and Anna M. (Mooz) Peterson; B.A., Douglass Coll., 1960; m. Joseph F. Mihalenko, July 1, 1961; children—Alyson, Geoffrey, Sandra. Reporter, Home News Pub. Co., 1960-66; editor, Alumnae Bull., Douglass Coll., 1967-69; editor, Suburban Weekly, 1971; staff writer Sentinel Publs., East Brunswick, N.J., 1971-73; dir. pub. relations YWCA Central Jersey, New Brunswick, 1972—. Mem. N.J. Press Assn. Methodist. Club: Douglass Alumnae (treas. Class 1960, 1970—) (New Brunswick, N.J.). Address: 805 Hoover Dr North Brunswick NJ 08902

MIHARA, TOSHIKO JOYCE, ednl. adminstr.; d. Iwao and Shizuko (Nagai) Mihara; B.A., U. Neb.; M.A., U. Denver; m. Carl. W. Schlaphoff, Aug. 25, 1973. Asst. librarian Arapahoe Community Coll., Littleton, Colo., 1969-71; head librarian Investors Mgmt. Scis., Denver, 1971-72; dir. learning center, tchr. polit. sci. Colo. Mountain Coll., Leadville, 1972—. Chmn. Lake County Young Democrats, 1973—. Mem. Am., Colo. library assns. Home: PO Box 881 Leadville CO 80461 Office: Colorado Mt College East Campus Leadville CO 80461

MIJANOVICH, ALICE BURNS (MRS. MLADEN MIJANOVICH), physician; b. Oak Park, Ill., July 3, 1921; d. Thomas and Henrietta Marie (Otis) Burns; B.A., Ripon Coll., 1943; M.D., U. Ill., 1949; m. Mladen Mijanovich, June 19, 1948; children—Susan Alice, James Robert, Ann Beth. Intern, Broadlawns Polk County Hosp., Des Moines, 1949-50; gen. practice medicine, Marengo, Ill., 1951—; mem. staffs Highland, St. Joseph's hosps. (both Belvidere, Ill.); dir. well-baby clinic Chanute AFB, 1954-55. Fellow Am. Acad. Family Practice; mem. Am. Med. Women's Assn., A.M.A., Ill., McHenry County med. socs. Presbyn. (elder 1966, clk. of sessions 1969-70). Home: 614 W Grant St Marengo IL 60152 Office: 556 E Grant St Marengo IL 60152

MIKLAS, PAULINE ROBINSON (MRS. MICHAEL J. MIKLAS), clubwoman, writer; b. Balt., Nov. 15, 1913; d. Emmanuel Ellinger and Mary Alice (Dunn) Robinson; grad. Inst. de Notre Dame; m. Michael J. Miklas, Dec. 23, 1946; children—Patricia (Mrs. Rudolph Henning), Joanne P. Free-lance advt. and pub. relations, Balt., Miami Beach, Fla., Tampa, Fla.; dir. pub. relations Miami Beach Pub. Co., 1946-49, Coppertone, Inc., Coconut Grove, Fla., 1947-48. Chmn. TV and communications Mother's March of Dimes, 1955-58; pres. Women of Gallery, Tampa Art Inst., 1956-58; cons. Clearwater (Fla.) Symphony League, 1957-60; pres. Tampa Philharmonic Women's League, 1957-60, United Cerebral Palsy Assn., Tampa, 1958, Sunstate Opera Guild, Tampa, 1965-69; Eastern U.S. chmn. Am. Art Week, Am. Artists Profl. League, 1965. Bd. dirs. Tampa Gen. Hosp. Women's Aux., 1955-58, Tampa Philharmonic Assn., 1952-63, Multiple Sclerosis Assn., 1962-64, Religious Arts Theatre, Tampa, 1964-66. Named Outstanding Woman of Fla., 1960. Mem. Nat. League Am. Pen Women (pres. Davis Island br. 1960-64, Fla. pres. 1970-72, nat. biennial chmn. 1972-74), Internat. Platform Assn., U.D.C. (chpt. v.p. 1968-70), Fla. Fedn. Music Clubs (dir. 1955-62, Tampa C. of C. (chmn. edn. for Davis Island 1958), League Women Voters (dir. 1960-64), Hillsborough County Fedn. Women's Clubs (chmn. 1962-66), Friday Morning Musicale (artistic dir. 1962-66). Clubs: Tampa Women's, Davis Island Garden (Tampa). Editor Crescendo mag., 1963-65. Home: 75 Ladoga Davis Island Tampa FL 33606

MIKULSKI, BARBARA ANN, city ofcl.; b. Balt., July 20, 1936; d. William and Christina Eleanor (Kutz) Mikulski; B.A., Mt. St. Agnes Coll., 1958; postgrad. Loyola Coll. at Balt., 1961; M.S.W., U. Md., 1965; LL.D., Goucher Coll., 1973. Tchr., Mt. Saint Agnes Coll., 1969, Community Coll. Balt., 1970-71, VISTA Tng. Center, 1965-70, St. Mary's Sem., 1971; with Balt. Dept. Social Services, 1961-63, 66-70, York Family Agy., 1964, Asso. Cath. Charities, 1958-61; now city councilwoman 1st dist. Balt. Adj. prof. Loyola at Balt.; cons. orgns. including Nat. Center Urban Ethnic Affairs, HUD, U.S. Senate Com. on Aging, Md. Higher Edn. Council on Urban Affairs, Balt. Dept. Edn., Anne Arundel County Dept. Mental Hygiene, U. Md. Sch. Library Sci. and Pub. Information. Mem. Polish Women's Alliance, Polish Am. Congress, Citizen Planning and Housing Assn., S.E. Community Orgn.; chmn. commn. community devel. Archiocesan Urban Commn. Mem. Nat. Women's Polit. Caucus; mem. nat. com. Muskie for Pres., 1971-72; chairperson commn. del. selection and party structure Democratic Nat. Com. Nat. bd. dirs. Urban Coalition; bd. dirs. Valley House. Named One of Outstanding Young Women in Am.; Md. Outstanding Young Woman of Year, 1968. Mem. Am. Fedn. Tchrs., Nat. Assn. Social Workers, League Women Voters. Contbr. articles to N.Y. Times, U.S. Steelworker Jour., Red Book and others. Home: 309 Folcroft St Baltimore MD 21224 Office: City Hall Baltimore MD 21202

MIKULSKY, JOAN MARILYN, coll. dean; b. Dobbs Ferry, N.Y., Feb. 27, 1932; d. Fred and Helen (Henshaw) de Serres; B.A., Hunter Coll., 1953, M.A., 1963; m. Walter Mikulsky, Aug. 5, 1956 (div. Aug. 1967). Chmn. art dept. Hendrick Hudson High Sch., Montrose, N.Y., 1953-61; instr. art Hunter Coll., City U. of N.Y., N.Y.C., 1961-65, asst. prof., 1965-65, asst. prof., asst. dean for campus planning Grad. Div. City U. N.Y., 1966-67, asso. prof., asst. dean, 1968-70, prof., dean of adminstrn. grad. sch. and univ. center, 1973—. Design cons. City U. N.Y. Grad. Center, Computer Facility, 1967-74. Recipient various awards and certificates. Mem. Nat. Soc. Interior Designers. Home: 345 East 69th St New York City NY 10022

MILAM, BEVERLY HORN, advt. agy. exec.; b. Chgo., July 9, 1936; d. Alex F. and Amelia Ann (Hayna) Horn; ed. Drake U., Des Moines, 1954-57; m. David Carter Milam, Oct. 28, 1972; children—Ellen Thurau, Russell Thurau. Broadcast buyer, media dir. W.W. Sherrill Co., Inc., Dallas, 1971—. Mem. Assn. Broadcasting Execs. Tex., Chi Omega. Home: 9722 Broken Bow Dallas TX 75238 Office: 3200 Maple Av Dallas TX 75201

MILANOV, ZINKA, soprano; b. Zagreb, Yugoslavia; d. Rudolf and Ljubica (Smiciklas) Kunc; grad. Girl's Evangel. Sch., Zagreb; diploma Zagreb Acad. Music; pupil Maria Kostrencic, Milka Ternina, Prof. Carpi, Prof. Stueckgold, Prof. Bozidar Kunc. European operatic debut, Yugoslavia, as Leonora in Il Trovatore, Met. Opera debut, same role, 1937; leading dramatic soprano roles Met. Opera, Chgo. Civic Opera, San Francisco Opera, Cin. Summer Opera, also in Buenos Aires, Rio de Janeiro, Sao Paulo, Vienna, Salzburg Festival, La Scala, Covent Garden, Lucerne Festival, and others. Opened Met. season, four times, 1940-66; lead roles in: Aida, L'Amore dei Tre Re, Un Ballo in Maschera, Madam Butterfly, Cavalleria Rusticana, Don Giovanni, Ernanl, Faust, La Gioconda, La Juive, Fidelio, Mefistofole, Norma, Otello, Pique Dame, Der Rosenkavalier, Simon Boccanegra, Il Tabarro, Tannhauser, Tosca, Il Trovatore, Turandot, Die Walkure, William Tell, Andrea Chenier, Forza del Destino, Girl of the Golden West, Louise, Manon Lescaut. Concert tours U.S., Can., Mexico, C.A., S.A., Europe. TV and radio artist; recorded with RCA Victor. Address: Met Opera New York City NY 10023

MILAS, HELEN GOGO (MRS. ANGELO MILAS), editor; b. Salonica, Greece, July 15, 1939 (parents Am. citizens); d. Samuel and Christina (Choleva) Gogo; B.A., N.Y. U., 1961; m. Angelo Milas, Jan. 21, 1973. Met. editor TV Guide, Radnor, Pa., 1961-63; asst. to editorial dir. Ideal Pub. Co., N.Y.C., 1963-65, editorial dir., 1972—; mag. editor Movie Mirror mag. Sterling Pub. Co., N.Y.C., 1965-72. Recipient Joyce Kilmer award N.Y. U., 1961. Home: 200 E 15th St New York City NY 10003 Office: 575 Madison Av New York City NY 10022

MILAZZO, MILDRED MARYANN, statistician; b. N.Y.C., Dec. 21, 1912; d. Paul Zachary and Laura Virginia (Manzo) Milazzo; B.C.S., Columbus U., 1951, postgrad., 1951-52; postgrad. U.S. Dept. Agr. Grad. Sch., 1943-66, George Washington U., 1963-64. Statis. clk. WPB, Washington, 1943-44, econ. statistician, 1944-45; cost accounting clk. OPA, Washington, 1945-47; fiscal accounting clk. VA, Washington, 1948-51, Dept. Commerce, Bur. Pub. Rds., Washington, 1951-54, engring. aide, 1954-56, statis. asst., 1956-66; statistician in social sci. Dept. Justice, Washington, 1966-68; fiscal analyst Health, Edn. and Welfare, Vocational Rehab. Services Adminstrn., Washington, 1968—. Mem. Am. Statis. Assn., Alpha Chi Upsilon. Home: 200 Branch Rd SE Vienna VA 22180 Office: 330 C St SW Washington DC 20201

MILBRADT, RUTH ANN SCHULENBURG LEE (MRS. EARLE G. MILBRADT), auditor; b. Portland, Ore., May 30, 1931; d. Carl Fredrick William and Augusta Wilhelmina (Otto) Schulenburg; student Valparaiso U., 1948-49; B.S. (Am. Soc. Women Accountants scholar), Portland State U., 1967; m. Earle G. Milbradt, May 14, 1971; children—(by previous marriage) David Douglas Lee, Daniel Jeffrey Lee. Account clk., auditor's office City of Portland, 1950-56; supervisory auditor U.S. Gen. Accounting Office, Portland, 1967—. C.P.A., Ore. Mem. Am. Soc. Women Accountants (chpt. dir. 1970-71). Lutheran. Home: 2015 NE 50th Av Portland OR 97213 Office: 527 E Burnside St Portland OR 97214

MILBURN, NANCY STAFFORD (MRS. RICHARD HENRY MILBURN), coll. dean; b. Syracuse, N.Y., Sept. 7, 1927; d. George Edward and Margaret Jeannette (Martin) Stafford; A.B., Radcliffe Coll., 1949; M.S., Tufts U., 1950; Ph.D., Harvard, 1959; m. Richard Henry Milburn, Aug. 25, 1951; children—Sarah Stafford, Anne Douglas. Faculty dept. biology Tufts U., Medford, Mass., 1958—, prof., 1969—, asso. dean instrn., 1972—, dean Jackson Coll., 1972—. Mem. adv. com. NRC Inst. for Lab. Animal Resources, 1970—, mem. Sr. Fulbright Fellowship Rev. Com., 1973—; mem. project rev. B com., neurol. disorders program NIH, 1973—. Bd. dirs. Harvard Apparatus Found., Harvard Apparatus Corp., bd. visitors to biology dept. Harvard. Mem. Am. Zool. Soc., Biophys. Soc., Am. Physiol. Soc., Entomol. Soc. Am., New Eng. Soc. Electron Microscopy, Am. Micros. Soc., Am. Women in Sci., Women in Sci. and Engring., Am. Assn. U. Women, Sigma Xi. Editor: Physiology Tchr. Home: 1 Plymouth Rd Winchester MA 01890 Office: Jackson Dean's Office Dept Biology Tufts U Medford MA 02155

MILBY, DOROTHY MARIE (MRS. CECIL HENRY MILBY), ednl. adminstr.; b. Dayton, O., Aug. 20, 1915; d. Ray Lafee and Teresa Caroline (Hoerth) Messler; B.A., Miami U., Oxford, O., 1936, M.Ed., 1963; postgrad. U. Dayton, 1963, Wright State U., 1965; m. Cecil Henry Milby, June 19, 1937; children—Linda (Mrs. Richard T. Hoppe), Steven Ray. Tchr., Kettering (O.) Bd. Edn., 1962-66; faculty Sinclair Community Coll., Dayton, 1966—, asso. prof. govt., chmn. div. gen. studies, 1970—. Mem. faculty adv. com. Ohio Bd. Regents, Dayton, 1967-69. Pres., Dorothy Lane P.T.A., Kettering, 1953-54, Van Buren Jr. High P.T.A., Kettering, 1954-55; mem. Kettering Bd. Edn., 1956-60, pres. 1958-59; mem. Kettering Council P.T.A.'s, 1954-56, pres., 1955-56. Mem. Kettering Republican Club, 1940-62, pres. 1950-51; clk., treas. Van Buren Twp., 1952-54; exec. sec. Montgomery County Rep. Exec. Com., 1960-62. Recipient Dayton area C. of C. Service award, 1958; Dayton Area Top Ten Women award, 1971. Mem. Ohio Congress Parents and Tchrs. (hon.), Sigma Sigma Sigma. Mem. Order Eastern Star. Home: 7750 Yankee St Dayton OH 45459

MILDVAN, DONNA TEBET, physician; b. Phila., June 20, 1942; d. Carl David and Gertrude (Tebet) Mildvan; A.B. magna cum laude, Bryn Mawr, 1963; M.D., Johns Hopkins (Henry Strong Denison scholar), 1967. Intern, Mt. Sinai Hosp., N.Y.C., 1967-68, resident internal medicine, 1968-70, fellow infectious diseases, 1970-72, asst. Sch. Medicine, 1970-72, asso. Sch. Medicine, 1972—; attending physician in infectious diseases Beth Israel Med. Center, N.Y.C., 1972—. Mem. Am. Soc. for Microbiology (med. com. human rights 1971—), A.A.A.S. Office: Beth Israel Hosp 10 Nathan D Perlman Pl New York City NY 10003

MILDVAN, PATRICIA J. TARR (MRS. ALBERT SAMUEL MILDVAN), physician; b. Bklyn., June 21, 1932; d. Burton Frederick and Ruby A. (Burns) Tarr; B.A. (Meth. scholar 1950-54), Cornell Coll. of Ia., 1954; M.D., Johns Hopkins, 1959; m. Albert Samuel Mildvan, Mar. 15, 1957; children—Heather, Pamela, Margo. Intern pediatrics Balt. City Hosp., 1959-60; pediatrician Covenant House Health Services, 1973—; clin. instr. pediatrics Temple U., 1968—; asst. attending pediatrician St. Christopher's Hosp. for Children, Phila., 1968—. Mem. Phi Beta Kappa. Home: 301 Holmecrest Rd Jenkintown PA 19046 Office: 251 E Bringhurst St Philadelphia PA 19144

MILES, ESTHER EMERY (MRS. HENRY GAINES MILES), ednl. adminstr.; b. Centralia, Wash., Sept. 9, 1928; d. Lawrence Ward and Leta Caroline (Denny) Emery; B.S., U. Wash., 1949; M.Ed., U. Fla., 1959; m. Henry Gaines Miles, May 27, 1949; children—David Henry, John Andrew, William Emery. Classroom tchr., elementary grades Duval County Pub. Schs., Jacksonville, 1949-56, coordinator Title 1 Clin. Reading Program, 1966-69, supr. reading, 1969—. Cons. Croft Ednl. Services, Salem (Ore.) Sch. Dist., various Fla. sch. dists. Mem. Fla. State Textbook Com., 1969-71. Mem. Internat. Reading Assn. (state orgn. chmn. 1969-71, nat. chmn. orgn. and membership 1973—), Fla. (pres. 1968-69), Duval County (pres. 1961-63) reading councils, Phi Delta Kappa, Phi Kappa Phi. Contbg. editor Fla. Reading Quar., 1971-73; editor I.R.A. Newsletter to Council Leaders, 1973—. Home: 11945 Little Creek Lane Jacksonville FL 32217 Office: 1741 Francis St Jacksonville FL 32209

MILES, JEANNE PATTERSON, artist; b. Balt.; d. Walter and Edna (Webb) Miles; B.F.A., George Washington U.; studied art Philips Meml. Gallery Sch., Atelier Gromaire, Grand Chaumiere, Paris, France; m. Frank Curlee, Dec. 31, 1935 (dec.); m. 2d, Johannes Schiefer, Feb. 11, 1939 (div.); 1 dau., Joanna Schiefer. Exhibited in one-man show Betty Parsons Gallery, N.Y.C., 1945, 52, 56, Grand Central Moderns, N.Y., 1968, Wesbeth Galleries, N.Y.C., 1972; exhibited group shows at N.Y. Rome Found., Walker Art Gallery, Corcoran Biennial, Yale Mus., Chateau Gagnes, France, Whitney Mus., Nat. Fedn. Am. Art, Mus. Modern Art, Riverside Mus., Guggenheim Mus., Gedok Am. Woman show, Hamburg and Berlin, Germany, 1972, others; represented in permanent collections N.Y. U., Santa Barbara Mus., Munson Proctor Mus., Rutgers Coll., U. Ariz., Guggenheim, Cin. and Newark Mus., White Art Mus. Cornell U., Ecumenical Inst., Graymoor, Garrison, N.Y., Springfield (Mass.) Art Mus., Weatherspoon Art Mus., U. N.C.; pvt. collections N.Y., France. Recipient Charles C. Ladd painting scholarship, Tahiti, 1956, traveling scholarship, France, 1937-48; Am. Inst. Arts and Letters grantee, 1968, Mark Rothko Found. grantee, 1970, 73; Pelham-von Stoeffler Art Fund grantee, 1974. Mem. Abstract Artists Am. Home: Wesbeth Apt A 1103 463 West St New York City NY 10014

MILES, JULIA LOUISE BEATTY (MRS. ARTHUR PARKER MILES), social worker; b. Waverly, Ill., Feb. 20, 1912; d. Francis Argus and Ethel (Swift) Beatty; B.A., U. Ill., 1933; M.A., U. Chgo., 1939; m. Arthur Parker Miles, Feb. 23, 1935; children—Nancy Ann (Mrs. Peter Walker Townsend), Sarah Louise (Mrs. John Lewis Gerken), James Howard. Tchr., Anna-Jonesboro High Sch., Anna, Ill., 1933-34; case aide Ill. Emergency Relief Commn., Peoria, Ill., 1934; caseworker, Family Service Bur., United Charities, Chgo., 1936-37; field work supr. U. Chgo., 1937-38, Tulane U., New Orleans, 1940-42; casework supr. Childrens Bur., New Orleans, 1942-43; field work supr. U. Wis., Madison, 1946-47; casework supr. Mendota State Hosp., Madison, Wis., 1957-66; social work cons. Div. Mental Hygiene, State Dept. Health and Social Services, Madison, Wis., 1966—. Sec., Madison Welfare Council, 1966-69; founder, sec. Wis. Civil Liberties Union, 1950-56; mem. Madison Youth Commn., 1957-63; dir. Madison Neighborhood Centers, 1964-70, Child Devel., Inc., 1966-69. Univ. League, 1964-66. Mem. Nat. Assn. Social Workers, Acad. Certified Social Workers, League Women Voters (bd. dirs. 1946-54), Alpha Phi. Democrat. Unitarian. Home: 1101 Lincoln St Madison WI 53711 Office: 1 W Wilson St Madison WI 53702

MILES, LEE, editor; b. N.J., June 22, 1940; d. David Phillips and Claire Lucille (Reeser) Miles; diploma Havergal Coll., Toronto, Ont., Can., 1958; A.A., Bennett Jr. Coll., Millbrook, N.Y., 1960. Dept. mgr., asst. buyer Saks Fifth Av., N.Y.C., 1960-63; asst. editor fashion Redbook mag., N.Y.C., 1963-65, editor needlework, patterns, crafts, 1965—. Bd. mem. Friends Henry St. Settlement, 1971-72. Mem. Fashion Group. Office: 230 Park Av New York City NY 10017

MILES, SARAH WILLIE THOMAS (MRS. EDWARD O. MILES), collection agy. exec.; b. Burlington, Kan., Aug. 15, 1910; d. Thomas W. and Grace Mildred (Fowler) Jones; A.A., Napa (Cal.) Coll., 1951; postgrad., Pacific Union Coll., 1952—; m. Howard W. Thomas, July 26, 1932 (dec.); 1 dau., Jacquelyn Sue (Mrs. Roland R. Henson); m. 2d, Edward O. Miles. Bookkeeper Reece Produce, Clovis, N.M., 1930-31; pub. stenographer, Big Springs, Tex., 1932—; room clk. Cal. Hotel, Oakland, Cal., 1946-47; Conner Hotel, Napa, Cal., 1947-49; asst. mgr. Merchants Coll. Service, 1950-53; collector Retail Credit Assn., Woodland, Cal., 1954-55; office mgr. Credit Bur., Willows, Cal., 1955-57; owner, Dr. and Mchts. Credit Bur., Woodland, Cal., 1957—, Retail Merchants Credit Assn., Davis, Cal. Mem. Nat. Fellowship Meth. Musicians, Am. Collectors Assn., Cal. Assn. Collectors, Bus. and Profl. Women Club, C. of C. Republican. Methodist. Club: Soroptimist (pres. 1958-59) (Woodland, Cal.). Home: 100 W Casa Linda St Woodland CA 95695 Office: 201 4th St Woodland CA 95695

MILES, SUSIE ELIZABETH (MRS. GEORGE W. MILES), instnl. adminstr.; b. Middlesburg, N.C., Oct. 9, 1907; d. William and Betsie (Burwell) Bullock; B.A., Howard U., 1931, M.A., 1940; postgrad. Am. U., 1940-41; m. George W. Miles, Jan. 24, 1939. Ednl. placement officer John Hawkins High Sch., Warrenton, N.C., 1931-35; tchr. Dunbar High Sch., Washington, 1937-39; U.S. govt. chief office statist. analysis and cons. low rent programs, Washington, 1962-70; exec. dir. Home for the Aged, Washington, 1971—. Mem. Washington planning commn. Am. Statistics Assn., 1960-71. Trustee John F. Kennedy Coll., Wahoo, Neb. Recipient Meritorious awards Howard U., 1953, N.A.A.C.P., 1966, Afro Am. Newspaper 1957, Zeta Phi Beta 1970. Mem. Nat. Assn. of Housing and Urban Redevel. Ofcls., Nat. Housing Conf., N.A.A.C.P., Howard U. Alumni, Zeta Phi Beta. Baptist (trustee, chmn. 1972—). Clubs: Howard U. Womens Club. Home: 2619 11th St Washington DC 20001 Office: 1818 Newton St Washington DC 20001

MILES, VERA, actress; b. Boise City, Okla., Aug. 23, 1930; d. Thomas and Burnice (Wyrick) Raltson; m. Keith Larsen; children—Debra, Kelley, Michael, Eric; m. 2d, Robert Jones, Jan. 1, 1973. Film roles include Rose Bowl Story, Charge at Feather River, Wichita, The Searchers, 23 Paces to Baker St., Autumn Leaves, Wrong Man, Beau James, Web of Evidence, F.B.I. Story, Back Street, Psycho, Man Who Killed Liberty Valance, Gentle Giant, Kona Coast, Hellfighters, Mission Batangos, Wild Country, Follow Me, Boys, Cactus, Castaway Cowboy; guest star dramatic TV programs latest being Owen Marshall, Counsellor at Law, Marcus Welby, M.D., Colombo, Runaway, others; stage role 40 Carats. Address: care Esme Chandler 195 S Beverly Dr Beverly Hills CA 90212

MILGRAM, GAIL GLEASON (MRS. WILLIAM H. MILGRAM), educator; b. South Amboy, N.J., June 14, 1942; d. John Thomas and Evelyn Patricia (Lynch) Gleason; B.S., Georgian Ct. Coll., 1963; M.Ed., Rutgers U., 1965, Ed.D., Rutgers U., 1969; m. William H. Milgram, Aug. 6, 1966; children—Lynn Patricia, Anne Melissa. Tchr. pub. schs., Sayreville, N.J., 1963-69; ednl. project dir., cons. Center Alcohol Studies, Rutgers U., New Brunswick, N.J., 1971—. Cons. alcohol edn. N.J. Dept. Health, also pub. sch. systems, pvt. ednl. assn. Grantee Nat. Inst. Alcohol Abuse and Alcoholism, 1971-73. Democrat. Roman Catholic. Author: The Teenager and Alcohol, 1970; The Teenager and Smoking: Tobacco and Marijuana, 1972; Annotated Bibliography of Alcohol Education, 1974; The Teenager and Sex, 1974. Home: 15 Dodson Rd East Brunswick NJ 08816 Office: Center Alcohol Studies Rutgers U New Brunswick NJ 08903

MILGROM, BETTY (MRS. HARRY MILGROM), educator; b. N.Y.C.; d. Israel and Annie (Selverstone) Geltman; B.S. (MAJ. Namm scholar), N.Y. U., 1933, M.S., 1934; m. Harry Milgrom, June 26, 1969; 1 dau., Barbara. Instr. merchandising Baruch Sch. City U., Bklyn. Coll., 1942-56; cons., prof. Lab. Inst. Merchandising, N.Y.C., 1956—; profl. artist. One man water color show Pietrantonio Gallery, N.Y.C., 1970. Mem. Composers, Authors and Artists Am., Artists Equity Assn., Burr Artists, Eta Mu Pi. Author: (with Wingate and Gillespie) Know Your Merchandise, 1944, rev. edit., 1974. Home: 185 E 85th St New York City NY 10028 Office: Lab Inst Merchandising 12 E 53d St New York City NY 10022

MILHAM, MARY ELLA, educator; b. Waukesha, Wis., Mar. 22, 1922; d. James Curtis and Ocallia Jessie (Pardee) Milham; B.A., Carroll Coll., 1943; M.A., U. Wis.-Madison, 1944, Ph.D., 1950. Tchr. Stevens Point (Wis.) High Sch., 1944-46; instr. U. Wis.-Madison, 1950-54; mem. faculty U. N.B. (Can.), 1954—, prof. classics, 1968—. Can. Council leave fellow, 1961-62, 68-69; research grantee Can. Council, 1963, 72, 73, Am. Council Learned Socs. grantee, 1966. Mem. Am. Philol. Assn., Linguistic Soc. Am., Classical Assn. Can. (exec. council 1968-70, 73-76), Humanities Assn. Can. (sec.-treas. 1966-68), Episcopalian. Author: A Glossarial Index to De re Coquinaria of Apicius, 1952; College English I and II, 1952; Apicii Decem Libri Qui de re Coquinaria, 1969. Home: 20900 W Cleveland Av New Berlin WI 53151 Office: Univ New Brunswick Fredericton NB E3B 5A3 Canada

MILLAN, ELLEN ANN DAGON (MRS. LYLE JORDAN MILLAN IV), physician; b. Balt., Feb. 3, 1936; d. Emmett Paul and Annie (Sollers) Dagon; A.B., George Washington U., 1959; M.D., U. Md., 1964; postgrad. Johns Hopkins U., 1965-68; m. Lyle Jordan Millan IV, Dec. 21, 1963; children—Lyle Jordan V, Elizabeth Lyle, Ann Sheridan Worthington. Intern, Union Meml. Hosp., Balt., 1964-65; resident anesthesiology Johns Hopkins Hosp., Balt., 1965-68, fellow, 1965-68; practice medicine specializing in anesthesiology, Balt., 1968—; attending staff Union Meml. Hosp., Church Home and Hosp., Franklin Sq. Hosp., Children's Hosp. (all Balt.); faculty Church Home and Hosp., Balt., 1969—, affiliate cons. emergency room, 1969—, mem. med. audit and utilizations com., 1970-72, mem. emergency and ambulatory care com., 1973-74, chief emergency dept., 1973-74; cons. anesthesiologist Md. State Penitentiary, 1971. Mem. A.M.A., Am. Coll. Emergency Physicians, Met. Emergency Dept. Heads, Am., Md. socs. anaesthesiologists, Balt. City Med. and Chiurgical Soc., Internat. Congress Anaesthesiologists. Episcopalian. Address: 215 Northway St Baltimore MD 21218

MILLAR, HILARY ETHEL CLARA (MRS. EUGENE C. TEODORESCU), physician; b. Beccles, Suffolk, England, Aug. 16, 1922; d. Frederick George and Dorothy Ann (Aldred) Millar; student St. Brandon's Clergy Daughters' Sch., England, 1936-41; Scottish Conjoint Med. License, Sch. Medicine of Royal Colls., Edinburgh, Scotland, 1947; M.P.H., Johns Hopkins Sch. Pub. Health, 1958; m. Eugene C. Teodorescu, Feb. 13, 1958; 1 dau., Anna Maria Millar. Casualty officer Northampton County Hosp., Northampton, Eng., 1948; House physician internal medicine City Hosp., Northampton, 1949; house surgeon Ipswich and E. Suffolk Hosp., England, 1950; house physician Lincoln County Hosp., England, 1950; pediatric house physician Sheffield Children's Hosp., England, 1951; resident pathologist Lincoln County Hosp., 1951-52; resident pediatrics Vancouver Gen. Hosp., Vancouver, B.C., Can., 1952-53, Children's Hosp., Washington, 1953-54; resident psychiatry St. Elizabeth's Hosp., 1954-55; sr. house officer pediatrics, St. James' Hosp., Balham, London, Eng., 1955-56; instr. Sch. Pub. Health, Johns Hopkins U., 1956-58; chief infant and preschool div. Bur. Maternal and Child Health, D.C. Dept. Pub. Health, 1958-67, dir. children and youth project, 1967-70; prin. cons. maternal and child health service, Internat. Health Services and Mental Health Adminstrn., Dept. Health, Edn. and Welfare, Washington, 1970-71, specialist maternal and child health Health Services div. Maternal and Child Health Service, 1971-73, acting chief Health Services Quality Br., 1973—; attending staff Children's Hosp., Washington, 1960—; instr. George Washington U., 1960—. Mem. White House Com. Prevention Mental Retardation, 1963-65, Inter-agency Adoption Com. for Greater Washington Area, 1962-65. Fellow Am. Acad. Pediatrics, Am. Pub. Health Assn.; mem. British Med. Assn., Royal Soc. Health, D.C. Med. Soc. (child welfare com. 1960-68), Royal Faculty Community Medicine. Contbr. articles to profl. pubs. Home: 3011 Rodman St NW Washington DC 20008 Office: 5600 Fishers Lane Rockville MD 20852

MILLAR, IRENE PYLE, harpist, educator, dramatic coach; b. South Bend, Ind., Mar. 27, 1909; d. Dan and Zoula (Johnson) Pyle; student Am. U., 1927-28; St. Mary's Coll., 1934-35, Ind. U. Extension, 1933-35; grad. Alviene Sch. Theatre, N.Y.C., 1931, LeLand Powers Sch. Theatre, Boston, 1933; m. Frank Estes Millar, June 1, 1935; children—Dan Pyle, Frank Estes III. Pub. and pvt. sch. tchr., 1933-34; profl. stock and radio actress, 1927; pres. dir. South Bend Community Theatre, Fed. Theatre Project, 1935-42; organizer Home Studio, 1948; tchr. speech and drama, coach, dir., 1933—; staff mem. WETL; spl. coach in radio, stage, TV technique for models, salesmen; pub. speaker; ghost writer; dir., v.p. Presbyn. Players, little theatre; dir. Jr. Players and Exptl. Theatre weekly radio show Playshop of the Air, 1953—; dir., sec. Broadway Theatre League, South Bend. Active A.R.C., Tb League; mem. bd. YWCA; mem. women's bd. Meml. Hosp., 1957—; mem. South Bend Sch. Bd., 1957—, sec. 1958—; dir. 4-H Talent Show and Style Shows; mem. South Bend Library Bd., 1957—; chmn. Presbyn. Players Playwriting Contest, 1955; v.p. St. Joseph County chpt. UN Assn. U.S.A., 1968-71; chmn. Mayor's Com. 25th Anniversary Celebration UN. Mem. South Bend Recreation Com., 1956—. Vice pres. St. Joseph County Scholarship Fund Found., 1958-62, sec., 1962-66, pres., 1966—; trustee South Bend Art Center, 1957—, also mem. women's aux.; bd. dirs. Family and Children's Center. Named Woman of Year, 1964. Mem. Women's Div. South Bend-Mishawaka C. of C., Internat. Platform Assn., Speech and Hearing Aux., Nat., Ind. sch. bd. assns., D.A.R., (former regent Schuyler Colfax chpt., state bd., Ind. librarian 1952-55, winner Ind. lit. contest 1972), Creative Arts Assn. St. Mary's Alumnae Assn. (2d v.p. 1972-73), Children Am. Revolution (past Ind., pres.), Nat., Ind. library assns., Ind. Sch. Bd. Assn., Nat. Recreation Assn., N. Ind. Hist. Soc., Psi Iota Xi, Delta Kappa Gamma. Presbyn. (adult adviser youth group). Clubs: Mother's Study (pres.), Phi Delta Theta Mother's (pres.), Altrusa (v.p. South Bend, rec. sec. 1969-72), South Bend St. Mary's. Address: 3406 Woodmont Dr South Bend IN 46614

MILLAR, LEOLA FAUDREE (MRS. CHARLES J. MILLAR), librarian; b. Evansville, Ind., Dec. 4, 1905; d. Thomas Lee and Martha (Harris) Faudree; student Stephens Coll., 1923-25, Mo. Sch. Mines, 1926, U. Mo., summers 1951-53; m. Charles J. Millar, Dec. 25, 1925 (dec. Feb. 1955); children—Nancy Lee (Mrs. W. K. Mengel), James Bruce. Librarian Rolla (Mo.) High Sch., 1950-53, Rolla Free Pub. Library, 1954—. Mo. exec. dir. Nat. Library Week, 1960. Bd. dirs. Arthritis Found. Mo. Mem. A.L.A., Mo. Library Assn. (sec. 1961-63; chmn. legislative com. 1967-69), Mo. Adult Edn. Assn. (dir.), P.E.O. Episcopalian. Home: 1400 Pine St Rolla MO 65401 Office: Box 248 Rolla MO 65401

MILLARD, KATHLEEN MARGARET AGNETE HARLAND (MRS. BEN MILLARD), physician; b. St. Vincent, B.W.I., Sept. 6, 1916; d. Sydney Cross and Emily Wilson (Cameron) Harland; M.B. Ch. B., U. Bristol, 1941; m. Ben Millard, June 25, 1943; children—Frances (Mrs. Lescek Toparowski), Katherine (Mrs. Kenneth Nesper), Michael, Bronwyn, Peter, Julie. Intern, Southmead, Bristol, 1942; resident Bristol Maternity Hosp., 1947-48, Maine Med. Center, Portland, 1958-61, 67-69; gen. practice medicine Bristol, 1944-49, New Market, N.H., 1952-57; practice medicine specializing in pediatrics, North Windham, Me., 1957—. Mem. British Med. Assn., Am. Fedn. Astrologers. Home: Windham Center Rd South Windham ME 04082 Office: White Bridge Rd North Windham ME 04062

MILLEDGE, SARAH FRANKLIN (MRS. STANLEY MILLEDGE), civic worker; b. Melrose, Mass., July 8, 1906; d. Albert Barnes and Edith (Bradbury) Franklin; B.A, Wellesley Coll., 1927; m. Stanley Milledge, Sept. 1, 1928 (dec. Oct. 1965);children—Allan Francis, Sarah (Mrs. Harold S. Nelson), Eleanor (Mrs. Barry Decker). Dir. community service Sta. WCKT-TV, Miami, Fla., 1962—; dir. Sunbeam TV Co., Miami, 1954-70. Mem. nat. bd. Girl Scouts U.S.A., 1952-66; chmn. Fla. Com. Children and Youth, 1968-70; pres. Miami YWCA, 1969-73; pres. Council Continuing Edn. of Women, 1971-72; co-chmn. womens div. Fla. chpt. Nat. Conf. Christians and Jews, 1966-70. Mem. Am. Women in Radio-TV (v.p.), Soc. Mayflower Descs., Theta Sigma Phi. Conglist. Clubs: Wellesley. Home: 1600 S Bay Shore Lane Miami FL 33133 Office: Box 118 Miami FL 33138

MILLENA, NILDA JACOB, physician; b. Daraga, Albay, P.I., Aug. 22, 1941; d. Jesus and Natalia (Jacob) Millena; A.A. with high honors, Legaspi Coll., 1958; M.D. cum laude, U. Santo Tomas, 1964. Adj. resident medicine Albay (P.I.) Provincial Hosp., 1965-66; practice gen. medicine, Daraga, Albay, 1966-67; rotating intern medicine Kenmore Mercy Hosp., 1967-68; resident Millard Fillmore Hosp., 1968-70; chief resident internal medicine St. Joseph Infirmary, Louisville, 1970-71; practice medicine specializing in internal medicine, Daraga, 1972—. Mem. Philippine Med. Assn., Philippine Med. Women's Assn. Home: Arboleda St Daraga Albay Philippines Office: Rizal St Daraga Albay Philippines

MILLER, A. ELIZABETH, ret. educator; b. Youngstown, O.; d. Jesse LeRoy and Ada (Ritter) Miller; A.B., Thiel Coll., 1928; M.A., Columbia, 1938; postgrad. U. Chgo., Denver U., U. Mich., Kent State U., Ohio State U., 1938-52. Tchr. elementary and jr. high schs., 1928-45; speech therapist, 1945-67; speech and hearing therapist, 1947-67; speech cons. pub. schs., Youngstown, O., 1950-74, chief sect. for speech and hearing services, 1969-70, coordinator sect. speech, lang. and hearing, 1971-72, coordinator Programmed Approach to Lang. Services, 1972-74; part-time instr. Youngstown State U. Mem. Pa. Com. Speech and Hearing Therapy, White House Conf., Youngstown, 1950; mem. adv. com. Youngstown Hearing and Speech Center, 1958—. Named Outstanding Community Leader, Ohio Bus. and Profl. Women, 1963, Women of Year, Delta Kappa Gamma, 1960; recipient certificate Clin. Competence, Am. Speech and Hearing Assn., Distinguished Alumnus award Thiel Coll., 1973. Mem. Ohio Speech and Hearing Assn. (v.p. 1951-52, recipient certificate for pioneer work in a prevention program 1972), Speech Assn. Am., Am. Assn. U. Women (dir. 1944-47), N.E.A. (life), Ohio, Northeastern (chmn. speech and hearing sect. 1928—) edn. assns., Council Exceptional Children (pres. 1950-51), Bus. and Profl. Women (pres. 1965-66). Lutheran. Home: 4071 Glenwood Av Youngstown OH 44512

MILLER, AGNES CHAMBLESS (MRS. FRED MAHER MILLER), educator; b. Ruston, La., Apr. 8, 1918; d. Marion Christopher and Rhoda (Liner) Chambless; B.S., La. Poly. Inst., 1938; M.S., La. State U., 1944; Ph.D., Fla. State U., 1964; m. William L. Cofer, Aug. 17, 1949 (div. 1959); children—Rhenda Scott, Claire Frances; m. 2d, Fred Maher Miller, Aug. 7, 1965. Tchr. high sch., Belcher, La., 1938-40; asst. dining hall dir. La. State U., 1941; food service dir. Standard (Oil) Restaurant Co., Baton Rouge; tchr. high sch., Start and Rayville, La., 1942-44; supr. nutrition and lunchroom edn. A.E. Phillips Tchr. Tng. Sch., La. Tech. U., Ruston, 1944-46, instr. food and nutrition La. Tech., 1946-49, prof. home econs., 1955-59, 61-62, 64-70, dean Coll. Home Econs., 1970—; parish sch. lunch supr. Natchitoches, La., 1949-50, Lake Charles, La., 1954-55. Chmn. home econs. adminstrs. La. Coll. Conf., 1973-74. Mem. Am., La. home econs. assns., Am. Dietetic Assn., Southeastern Council Family Relations, Nat., Gulf Coast sect. assns. inst. food technologists, Am. Assn. Adminstrs. Home Econs., Soc. for Nutrition Edn., La. Acad. Sci., La. Tchrs. Assn. (v.p. Tech. chpt. 1967-68), Coll. and U. Tchrs. Food and Nutrition (sect. pres. 1968-69), Delta Zeta, Alpha Tau Delta, Phi Kappa Phi. Home: 503 S Sparta Ruston LA 71270

MILLER, ALICE PATRICIA MCCARTHY (MRS. WARREN HUDSON MILLER), author; b. Lynn, Mass.; d. William Henry and Julia (McCarthy) McCarthy; A.B., Hunter Coll., M. Social Science, New Sch. Social Research; M.A., Columbia, 1963; m. Warren Hudson Miller, Apr. 3, 1942; children—Nancy Lynn, Jacqueline. Instr. communication arts and skills N.Y.C. Community Coll., Bklyn., 1960-61; instr. psychology Pratt Inst., 1961-63; instr. psychology, sociology Juilliard Sch. Music, 1965-66; instr. sociology Helen Fuld Sch. Nursing, 1973—, free lance work Harper & Row, 1969—. U.S. del. to Internat. Psychol. Congress, Moscow, 1966. Trustee Levittown (N.Y.) Pub. Library, 1950-52; charter mem. Creative Edn. Found. Recipient awards for writing Ind. U. Found., 1958. Mem. Am. Psychol. Assn. (asso.) Authors Guild, Phi Beta Kappa. Democrat. Author: The Heart of Camp Whippoorwill, 1960; Make Way for Peggy O'Brien!, 1961; The Little Store on the Corner, 1961; In Cold Red Ink, 1968; A Kennedy Chronology, 1968; It Happened in 1918, 1968; Who Shares Your Birthday?, 1970; The 1910-1919 Decade, 1972. Contbr. stories, articles, verse to mags. and anthologies. Home: 3701 Henry Hudson Pkwy Bronx NY 10463

MILLER, ANASTASIA PIDD (MRS. ALFRED W. KOBS), physician; b. Houston, Jan. 16, 1922; d. Newton Edd and Anastasia (Johnston) Miller; B.A., Sam Houston State U., 1943; M.D., Baylor U., 1947; m. Alfred W. Kobs, Sept. 22, 1950; 1 dau., Pidd Anastasia. Intern, St. Luke's Hosp., Kansas City, Mo., 1947-48; resident Charleston (W.Va.) Gen. Hosp., 1948-50; resident Baylor Program, Hermann Hosp., Houston 1962-64, mem. staff spl. clinic pediatrics, 1965-72, dir. chromosome lab., 1967-72; med. dir. Cerebral Palsy Treatment Center, Houston, 1966-70; clin. asst. in pediatrics M.D. Anderson Hosp., Houston, 1969—. Co-founder Camp Kno Koma, camp for diabetic children, Charleston, 1950; troop leader Girl Scouts, 1960-65. Diplomate Am. Bd. Pediatrics. Mem. Am. Acad. Pediatrics, Am. Acad. Cerebral Palsy, Tex., Harris County med. socs., Houston Pediatric Soc. Home: 7619 Windswept Lane Houston TX 77042 Office: 11105 Bellaire St Houston TX 77072

MILLER, A(NNA) KATHRINE, bacteriologist; b. East Orange, N.J., June 8, 1913; d. William B. and Anna (Hartman) Miller; B.S., Moravian Coll. Women, 1934; M.S., Columbia, 1936; Ph.D., Cornell U., Ithaca, N.Y., 1942. Instr. dept. biology Moravian Coll. Women, Bethlehem, Pa., 1934-41, Wells Coll., Aurora, N.Y., 1942-43; research asso. Sharp & Dohme, Inc., 1943-56; bacteriologist, Merck Inst. for Therapeutic Research, Merck Sharp & Dohme, Rahway, N.J., 1943—, sr. research fellow, 1974—. Trustee Moravian Coll., Bethlehem, Pa., 1954—. Fellow and diplomate Am. Acad. Microbiology; fellow A.A.A.S.; mem. Am. Soc. Microbiology, N.Y. Acad. Scis., Soc. Gen. Microbiology, Soc. Indsl. Microbiology, Sigma Xi, Phi Kappa Phi, Sigma Delta Epsilon. Republican. Lutheran. Home: 104 B Duncan Hill Westfield NJ 07090 Office: Merck Inst for Therapeutic Research Rahway NJ 07065

MILLER, ANNE MARIE TIEFENBACH (MRS. LARRY FRANK MILLER), editor; b. Pennewang, Austria, Aug. 8, 1947; d. John and Elizabeth (Fichtel) Tiefenbach; student Ohio State U., 1965-68; m. Larry Frank Miller, July 12, 1969; 1 dau., Elizabeth Shahan. With Mansfield (O.) News Jour., 1966—, women's editor, 1969-73, editor Hot Line column, 1973—. Mem. Ohio State Adv. Council for Continuing Edn., 1969-70; mem. women's com. Mansfield Symphony Orch., 1966-72. Mem. Ohio Newspaper Women's Assn. (recipient Top award, 1970-71), Mansfield Fedn. Women. Roman Catholic (mem. ch. council 1968-72). Home: 649 Bennington Dr Mansfield OH 44904 Office: 70 W 4th St Mansfield OH 44901

MILLER, ARLYN HOCHBERG, psychologist; b. N.Y.C., Dec. 2, 1925; d. Nathaniel and Marie (Weinstein) Hochberg; B.S., Coll. City N.Y., 1946, M.S., 1948; Ed.D. in Psychology, Temple U., 1965; m. Arthur M. Miller, May 29, 1947 (div. June 1971); children—David, Eve. Tchr. elementary schs., N.Y.C., 1946-48, tchr. spl. edn., 1948-52; dir. spl. classes, Gloversville, N.Y., 1953-58, sch. psychologist Fulton County (N.Y.), 1953-58; instr. psychology and sociology Littauer Hosp. Sch. Nursing, Gloversville, 1955-58; sch. psychologist Cherry Hill Pub. Schs., 1958-63; staff psychologist Children's Hosp., Phila., 1963-64; sr. psychologist Community Child Guidance, Camden, N.J., 1964-69; adj. faculty Drexel U., Rutgers U., Glassboro Coll., Camden County Coll.; pvt. practice as child and adolescent psychologist; psychologist N.J. Div. Youth and Family Services. cons. N.J. Assn. for Learning Disabilities; dir. singles seminars, cons., mem. adv. bd. Robins Nest Home for Delinquent Girls. Mem. profl. adv. bd., bd. dirs. Camden County (N.J.) Mental Health Assn., Camden County Assn. for Children with Learning Disabilities; mem. profl. adv. bd. Parents Without Partners. Mem. Am., N.J., Camden County (charter) psychol. assns., Am. Acad. Psychotherapists, Am. Group Psychotherapy Assn., Psychologists in Pvt. Practice. Contbr. articles to profl. jours. Home: 311 Graisbury Av Haddonfield NJ 08033

MILLER, AURELIA TOYER (MRS. CLAUDE L. MILLER), assn. exec.; b. Balt.; d. Francis Asbury and Isa Lee (Robinson) Toyer; B.S., Bluefield State Coll., 1938; M.A., Atlanta U., 1942; Ph.D., N.Y. U., 1952; m. Claude L. Miller. Asst. prof. econs. Washington Sq. Coll., N.Y. U., N.Y.C., 1952-53; lectr. dept. econs. Queens Coll., City U. of N.Y., 1953-57; economist N.Y. State Consumer Counsel, Albany, 1957-58; dir. labor research N.Y.C. Dept. of Labor, 1964-67; consumer cons., asso. dir. bur. research, Nat. YWCA, N.Y.C., 1967-70, dir. data center, 1970—; lectr. econs. Baruch Sch., City U. N.Y., 1959—, Sch. Labor and Indsl. Relations, Cornell U., N.Y.C., 1970—. Mem. Maj. Appliance Consumer Action Panel, 1970-72; pub. mem. Nat. Advt. Rev. Bd.; mem. consumer adv. panel N.Y.C. Dept. Consumer Affairs. Vice pres. bd. dirs. Sheltering Arms Childrens Service; trustee Underwriters Labs. Mem. Am. Econ. Assn., Am. Council Consumer Interests. Author: Get Your Money's Worth, 1965. Home: 388 Clinton Av Brooklyn NY 11238 Office: 600 Lexington Av New York City NY 10022

MILLER, BARBARA ANN KAUFMAN (MRS. HAROLD I. MILLER), lyric soprano; b. Morgantown, W.Va., Aug. 2, 1932; d. Nathan and Ethel (Ritchin) Kaufman; student U. Mich., 1950-51, Pa. State U., 1951-53; A.B., U. Pitts. 1955; m. Harold I. Miller, Feb. 10, 1963; 1 son, Bruce. Lyric soprano appearing with popular mus. shows, 1958—, including Call Me Madam, 1953, Blossom Time, 1953, Gentlemen Prefer Blondes, 1953, The Mikado, 1953, Louisiana Purchase, 1953, Naughty Marietta, 1953, Three Wishes for Jamie, 1953, Music In The Air, 1953, Lady In The Dark, 1953, The Great Waltz, 1953. Performer for community and charity orgns., Altonna, Pa., 1954—, Danville, Ky., 1963—. Mem. Council Jewish Women (gen. chmn. spl. projects Lexington 1963—), Sisterhood Adath Israel Temple, Lexington, Ky., Ohio Valley Fedn. Temple Sisterhoods (mem. bd. 1968—, program chmn.), Little Garden Club of Danville, Am. Assn. U. Women, Women Guild Lexington Philharmonic, Sigma Delta Tau. Hadassah (bd. mem. 1963-64). Home: 470 Boone Trail Danville KY 40422

MILLER, BARBARA ROCHELLE STOLER (MRS. JAMES ROBERT MILLER), philologist, educator; b. N.Y.C., Aug. 8, 1940; d. Louis O. and Sara (Cracken) Stoler; student U. Mich., 1958-59; B.A. magna cum laude, Barnard Coll., 1962; M.A. (Fgn. Area fellow 1963-65), Columbia, 1964; Ph.D. (Univ. fellow 1965-66) with honors in Oriental Studies, U. Pa., 1968; m. James Robert Miller, Aug. 13, 1960; 1 dau., Gwenn Alison. Asst. prof. Oriental studies Barnard Coll., Columbia U., 1968-72, asso. prof. Oriental studies, 1972—. Am. Inst. Indian Studies fellow, 1966-67, 74-75; Am. Assn. U. Women fellow, 1966-67, Nat. Endowment for Humanities summer fellow, 1971; Guggenheim fellow, 1974-75. Mem. Am. Oriental Soc., Assn. Asian Studies, Asia Soc. (mem. adv. com. Asian lit. program 1971—). Author: Bhartrihari: Poems, 1967; Phantasies of a Love-Thief: The Caurapancasika Attributed to Bilhana, 1971; A Syllabus of Indian Civilization, 1971. Guest editor spl. Sanskrit issue Jour. South Asian Lit., formerly Mahfil: A Quarterly of South Asian Literaure, 1971. Home: 175 Riverside Dr New York City NY 10024

MILLER, BARBARA SIMMONS (MRS. THOMAS R. MILLER), librarian; b. Chattanooga, Tenn., Aug. 19, 1909; d. Andrew Warren and Katie Vivian (Truss) Simmons; B. Music, U. Mich., 1933; B.S., Spalding Coll., 1951, M.A., 1953; m. Thomas R. Miller, July 8, 1935; Tchr. music Russell Jr. High Sch., Louisville, 1933-35; children's librarian, Western br., Louisville Pub. Library, 1951-59, asst. head. children's dept., 1959, head children's dept., 1960, coordinator children's services, 1970—. Instr., Spalding Coll., 1951-72, U. Ky. Extension, Louisville, 1970-72. Bd. dirs. Norton Children's Hosp., 1973—. Recipient Caritas medal Spalding Coll., 1971; Woman of Achievement award Louisville Women's Club. Mem. Am., Ky., Southeastern library assns., N.A.A.C.P., Urban League, Links, Inc., Girl Friends, Inc., Zonta, Bellarmine Women's Council, Louisville Theatrical Assn. (bd. dirs. 1969-72, children's service div. bd. dirs. 1972—), Delta Sigma Theta. Roman Catholic. Democrat. Editor: Children's Record Critique, 1960-72. Home: 215 N 46th St Louisville KY 40212 Office: 301 York St Louisville KY 40203

MILLER, BARBARA STALLCUP (MRS. LELAND FRANK MILLER), pub. relations exec.; b. Mayten, Cal., Sept. 4, 1919; d. Joseph Nathaniel and Maybelle (Needham) Stallcup; B.A., U. Ore., 1942; m. Leland Frank Miller, May 16, 1946; children—Paula Bechtold, Susan (Mrs. Tom Thrasher), Daniel, Alison. Women's editor Eugene (Ore.) Daily News, 1941-43; law clk. J. Everett Barr, atty., Yreka, Cal., 1943-45; mgr. Yreka C. of C., 1945-46; dir. pub. relations Columbia River Girl Scout Council, Portland, Ore., 1962-67; dir. pub. relations and information U. Portland, 1967—. Pub. relations cons. Portland Jr. Civic Theatre, 1964-71, Vols. Am. Ore., Inc., 1968-71, Women for Agr., 1970-71. Bd. dirs., mem. edn. com. Portland Civic Theatre, 1964-71; bd. dirs., pub. relations chmn. Portland Columbia River council Girl Scouts Am., 1960-62, leader, 1954-72. Recipient Rose award Alpha Xi Delta, Presidential Citation, Ore. Editors and Communicators. Mem. Women in Communications (N.W. regional v.p. 1973), Ore. Assn. Editors and Communicators (edn. chmn. 1972-73), Ore. Press Women, Alpha Xi Delta. Club: Portland Zenith (sec. 1972-73). Home: 5930 SW Meadows Rd Lake Oswego OR 97034 Office: 5000 N Willamette Blvd Portland OR 97203

MILLER, BERNICE G. METZEL (MRS. RALPH B. MILLER), lawyer; b. Cleve., Apr. 1, 1917; d. Charles and Rose (Beck) Metzel; student Darvas Sch. Design, Cleveland Art Sch., Cleve. Coll., 1939, Cleve. State Coll., 1946; grad. Cleveland Marshall Law Sch., 1951, LL.M., 1963, LL.D., 1968; m. Ralph B. Miller, Apr. 14, 1946; children—Harrison Simon, Curtis Arvin. Fashion designer; self-employed as pub. accountant; owner, Ace Distbg. Co.; admitted to Ohio bar, practiced in Seven Hills, Cleve. Active P.T.A. Councilwoman, City of Seven Hills. Recipient Certificate of Appreciation, Cuyahoga County Bar Assn. Mem. Nat. Assn. Women Lawyers, Am., Ohio State (mem. council dels.), Cuyahoga County (trustee), Parma (trustee) bar assns., Cleve. Women Lawyers, Citizens League, Kappa Beta Pi. Mem. B'nai B'rith Sisterhood. Club: Women's City. Home: 2065 Ridgeview Dr Seven Hills OH 44131 Office: 7543 Broadview Rd Cleveland OH 44131

MILLER, C. KAY RICHARDSON (MRS. CRAIG A. MILLER), social worker; b. Oswego, Kan., Dec. 9, 1941; d. Luther Cordell and Janice Elfreda (Martin) Richardson; A.B. in Sociology, Ft. Hays (Kan.) State Coll., 1963; M.S.W., U. Kan., 1965; m. Craig A. Miller, Feb. 6, 1971; 1 son, Lance Allen. Social worker in surg. specialities U. Kan. Med. Center, Kansas City, 1965-67, social worker in psychiatry, 1967-71, teaching asso. in psychiatry Sch. Medicine, 1969-71, field instr. Sch. Social Welfare, 1969-71; social work supr. Larned (Kan.) State Hosp., 1971—; field instr. sociology Tabor Coll., 1971-72. Adv. council Sch. Social Welfare, U. Kan. Bd. dirs. Florence Crittenton Home, Kansas City, 1965-69, corr. sec., 1967, rec. sec., 1968, also mem., chmn. numerous coms. Mem. Nat. Assn. Social Workers, Acad. Certified Social Workers, Am. Orthopsychiat. Assn., Pawnee County Mental Health Assn., U. Kan. Social Work Alumni Assn. (treas. 1968-71), Mortar Bd., Delta Zeta (alumni chpt. pres. Johnson-Wyandotte counties 1966-67, alumni chpt. treas. 1967-69). Methodist. Home: 823 Santa Fe St Larned KS 67550

MILLER, CATHERINE BROWN (MRS. JAMES R. MILLER), coll. dean, psychologist; b. Rochester, N.Y., May 17, 1941; d. Selden S. and Olive C. (Miller) Brown; B.S., State U. Coll. at Cortland, 1963; M.A., Ohio State U., 1965; postgrad. State U. N.Y., Albany, 1970—; m. James R. Miller, May 18, 1968. Asst. dir. Morrison Tower, Ohio State U., Columbus, 1963-65; asst. dean students State U. N.Y., Albany, 1965-67, asso. dir. residences, 1967-69; asso. dean students, faculty psychology Simon's Rock Early Coll., Great Barrington, Mass., 1969-71, faculty psychology, dean students, 1971—. Vol. counselor sch. system So. Berkshire Regional Sch. System, Sheffield, Mass., 1972. Mem. Am. Psychol. Assn., Am. Assn. U. Profs., Nat. Assn. Student Personnel Adminstrs., Am. Personnel and Guidance Assn. Home: Box 7 Sheffield MA 01257 Office: Simon's Rock Early Coll Great Barrington MA 01230

MILLER, CATHERINE LANHAM (MRS. ROBERT BLAKE MILLER), author; b. Greensburg, Ind., May 9, 1917; d. William Henry and Ethel Rosa (Ewing) Lanham; B.Pub. Sch. Music, Ind. U., 1938; m. Robert Blake Miller, June 30, 1950; children—Robert Blake, Ross Lanham, Melissa Ewing. Music, drama tchr., Evansville, Ind., 1938-41; with OWI, Washington, 1941-44; advt. copywriter Crowell Collier Pub. Co., N.Y.C., 1945-49; copywriter Young & Rubicam Advt., N.Y.C., 1949-51; advt. copywriter TV Guide, Radnor, Pa., 1959-61; copy chief Gerald F. Selinger Advt., Phila., 1961-65; columnist Beating the Blahs, Phila. Inquirer, 1972-73; traveled for Listerine to promote product on television and radio, 1973; lectr. clubs, womens groups. Mem. Soc. Mag. Writers, Kappa Kappa Gamma. Club: Aronimink Golf (Newton Square, Pa.). Author: How to Say Yes to Life-A Woman's Guide to Beating the Blahs, 1971. Contbr. articles to mags. Address: RD 1 Box 191 Malvern PA 19355

MILLER, CECELIA ELEANOR LOTKO (MRS. GEORGE E. CHAMBERS), anesthesiologist; b. Chgo., Oct. 24, 1917; d. Joseph S. and Zofia H. (Baizer) Lotko; student Northwestern U., 1945-47; B.S., U. Ill., 1949, M.D., 1951; m. James R. Miller, Sept. 3, 1938 (div. 1958); 1 dau., Josephine Ann (Mrs. John E. Mitchell); m. 2d, George E. Chambers, Dec. 5, 1970; stepchildren—Ronald, Lawrence, Leon, Marilyn (Mrs. Dale Stacy). Intern, Cook County Hosp., Chgo., 1951-53; resident Hines (Ill.) VA Hosp., 1953-54; practice medicine, specializing in anesthesiology, Hammond, Ind., 1955, Chgo., 1956—; sr. staff Jackson Park Hosp., Chgo. Mem. Field Mus. Natural History, Art Inst. Chgo. Fellow Am. Coll. Anesthesiologists; mem. A.M.A., Am. Med. Women's Assn., Ill., Chgo. med. socs., Am., Ill., Chgo. socs. anesthesiologists, Hines Surg. Soc., Cook County Hosp. Interns and Residents Alumni Assn., U. Ill. Alumni Assn., Dean's Club U. Ill. Coll. Medicine (charter), Alpha Epsilon Iota, Alpha Sigma Lambda. Home: 14730 S Central Av Bldg A Oak Forest IL 60452 Office: 7531 Stony Island Av Chicago IL 60649

MILLER, CECILIA LORRAINE PARSONS (MRS. H. LIONEL MILLER), author, editor; b. Mansfield, O., July 15, 1909; d. Walbridge and Katharine Hooker (Whiteman) Parsons; A.B., Hillsdale Coll., 1932; m. H. Lionel Miller, May 13, 1934; children—Thomas Kenyon, Daniel Benjamin, Damaris Ray (Mrs. Roger E. Milo), Elizabeth Walbridge (Mrs. Thompson). Mem. exec. com., arts festival Harrisburg Arts Council, 1967-68, chmn. by laws com., 1969-70, membership chmn., 1969-70, sec., 1971-72, v.p., 1972—, pres., 1973-74. Recipient Distinguished Alumni Achievement award Hillsdale Coll., 1962; Endorsement for Merit Pa. Poetry Soc., 1962, 2d Place Book Publ. award Nat. Fedn. State Poetry Socs., 1966; Carl Sandburg award N.C., 1971; Carlisle award, 1971. Mem. Nat. Fedn. State Poetry Socs. (1st pres. 1959-60 editor, founder newsletter Strophes, 4th v.p. 1966-68, adv. bd. 1972-74), Pa. Poetry Soc. (pres. 1957-61, trustee 1965-69, editor newsletter and ann. prize poems 1957-69, librarian, historian 1959—), Am. Poetry League, South and West, Inc., Pa. Folklore Soc., Chi Omega. Presbyn. (pres. interracial fellowship 1967-69). Author: Not Less Content, 1960; Peculiar Honors, 1962; To March to Terrible Music, 1967; Stand At the Edge, 1970; Space Where Once a Husband Stood, 1972. Editor Ch. Women United News, Greater Harrisburg, Pa., 1962—; Nat. Fedn. State Poetry Socs. Prize Poems Anthology, 1968, 69. Contbr. articles to profl. jours. Home: 264 Walton St Lemoyne PA 17043

MILLER, CHRIS (DOROTHY JUNE MILLER), state legislator; b. Boston, June 15, 1926; d. Charles Dana and Dorothy Evelyn (Noyce) Chrisman; student Wheaton Coll., 1943, Mills Coll., 1944, Tex. Christian U., intermittently 1964-67; m. June 22, 1944 (div. 1965); children—Louis Chrisman, Gerald Lee. Advt. mgr. Ft. Worth C. of C., 1967-68; neighborhood services coordinator, community health coordinator Community Action Agy., Ft. Worth, 1968-69; owner Chris Pub. Relations, Ft. Worth, 1969-72; mem. Tex. Ho. of Reps., 1973—; dir. Christnight Office Services, Inc., Fort Worth. Mem. Ft. Worth Human Relations Commn., 1970-72, Mayor's Com. on Status of Women, 1972-73; adv. bd. Tex. Women's Equity Action League, Inst. for Women. Mem. Am. Women in Radio and TV, Women in Communications, Nat. Orgn. Women, Bus. and Profl. Women's Club, League Women Voters, Press Club Ft. Worth (co-recipient Female Newsmaker of Year award 1972). Club: Zonta. Home: 2524 Ridgemar Fort Worth TX 76116 Office: PO Box 9063 Forth Worth TX 76107

MILLER, DOROTHEA WELSH (MRS. FLOYD IRVING MILLER), mus. ofcl.; b. Newton, Kan., Sept. 7, 1904; d. Burt Watson and Lila (Fossey) Welsh; student, Bethel Coll., 1923-24; A.B., Southwestern Coll., 1926; B.S., George Peabody Library Sch., 1943; m. Floyd Irving Miller, Aug. 28, 1948. Tchr. Windom (Kan.) High Sch., 1926-30, Canton (Kan.) High Sch., 1931, Bison (Kan.) High Sch., 1932-33, Newton (Kan.) Jr. High Sch., 1934-43; reference librarian Wichita (Kan.) U., 1943-46, Boeing Aviation Library, Wichita, 1947; head librarian Southwestern Coll., Winfield, Kan., 1947-48; dir. Chisholm Trail Mus., Wellington, Kan., 1971—. Mem. N.E.A., A.L.A., Kan. Hist. Assn., Pi Gamma Mu. Clubs: Wellington Book, Federated Music, Garden (Wellington). Home: 520 N H St Wellington KS 67152 Office: 502 N Washington Av Wellington KS 67152

MILLER, DOROTHY INMAN (MRS. J.A. MILLER), judge; b. Lamesa, Tex., Oct. 27, 1921; d. E.B. and Freddie M. (Haley) Inman; grad. high sch.; m. J.A. Miller, Mar. 5, 1941; children—Linda (Mrs. Ronnie McMillan), Lynn (Mrs. Bill O'Brien), Robert. With police dept. City of Lamesa, 1955-58, ct. clk., 1958, municipal ct. judge, 1958—. Mem. Coprock Fed. Credit Union (v.p., dir.). Baptist. Home: 1509 N. 4th Pl Lamesa TX 79331 Office: 302 N 1st St Lamesa TX 79331

MILLER, DOROTHY LORA, sociologist; b. West Liberty, Ia., Mar. 8, 1920; d. Edward and Gertrude Ellen (McKillop) Pressler; B.A., State U. Ia., 1955, M.A., 1957; D.S.W., U. Cal., Berkeley, 1966; div.; children—Ann (Mrs. William Rosenthal), Sherry (Mrs. James Sesko). Social research Sch. Psychiatry, U. Ia., 1955-60; dir. social research lab. Cal. Dept. Mental Hygiene, 1960-67; dir. research Sci. Analysis Corp., San Francisco, 1967—; lectr. Sch. Social Work, Sch. Nursing, U. Cal., Berkeley; cons. Research West. Sponsor, Cal. Com. Prisoner Humanity and Justice. Recipient Koshland award Cal. Health and Welfare, 1967. Mem. Nat. Assn. Social Workers, Social Psychiatry Research Assn. (dir.), Am. Sociol. Assn., Phi Beta Kappa, Alpha Kappa Delta. Am. Indian traditional religion. Author: Worlds That Fail, 1965. Contbr. articles profl. jours. Home: 98 Kelloch Av San Francisco CA 94134 Office: 4339 California St San Francisco CA 94118

MILLER, DOROTHY RISLEY, state ofcl.; b. East Hartford, Conn., Apr. 1, 1920; d. John Strong and Winifred Irene (Cooley) Risley; grad. high sch.; m. Robert Arnold Miller, Nov. 23, 1950 (dec. July 27, 1968); 1 dau., Diane. Personnel dept. supr. Aetna Life and Casaulty Co., Hartford, Conn., 1938-63, 66-71; now ret. Mem. Conn. Ho Reps., 1959-63, 69—; mem. Republican State Central Com., 1960-63, 69-72; mem. Rep. Town Com., Bolton, Conn., 1954-69; mem. 2d Congl. Dist. North Rep. Women's Assn., 1968-72. Mem. Bolton Fire Aux. Mem. Nat., Conn. (pres. 1971-73) orders women legislators, 1st Congl. Dist. Rep. Women's Assn. Methodist (trustee 1972—). Home: 23 Cook Dr Bolton CT 06040

MILLER, ELAINE NOVINSKY (MRS. HERMAN P. MILLER), psychotherapist; N.Y.C., Aug. 21, 1922; d. Sam and Miriam (Greenberg) Novinsky; B.A., George Washington U., 1949; M.A., Am. U., 1962; m. Herman P. Miller, Aug. 8, 1942; children—June (Mrs. Roya Larry Lipsky), Judi (Mrs. Ken Glasser). Psychologist Md. Correctional Inst., Jessup, 1962-68; individual practice psychotherapy, Washington, 1968—. Mem. Am., Md., D.C. psychol. assns., Am. Group Psychotherapy Assn. Home: 105 Bluff Terrace Silver Spring MD 20902 Office: 5415 Connecticut Av NW L-32 Washington DC 20015

MILLER, ELIZABETH JANE BARKER (MRS. RONALD EARL MILLER), educator, clubwoman; b. Kline, S.C., Aug. 24, 1936; d. William Donleigh and Pearl (Ayer) Barker; B.S. magna cum laude, Newberry Coll., 1959; postgrad. Rollins Coll., Fla. State U., Fla. U., U. S.C., S.C. State Coll.; m. Ronald Earl Miller, June 4, 1960; 1 son, Burton Ronald. Tchr., Lexington (S.C.) Elementary Sch., 1959-60, Springfield (Ga.) Elementary Sch., 1960-61, Winter Park (Fla.) Elementary Sch., 1961-63, Allendale Fairfax (S.C.) High Sch., 1963-67, Bamberg-Ehrhardt High Sch., Bamberg, S.C., 1969-71, Andrew Jackson Acad., Ehrhardt, S.C., 1971—. Mem. D.A.R., U.S. Daus. 1812 (S.C. pres. 1970-73, nat. historian 1973—), S.C. Hist. Soc., Am. Legion Aux., Delta Kappa Gamma. Republican. Lutheran. Club: Dixie Garden (Ehrhardt, S.C.). Address: PO Box 37 Ehrhardt SC 29081

MILLER, ELIZABETH P. (MRS. JAMES RUMRILL MILLER), conservationist; b. Phila.; d. Irvin and Eliza S. (Pleasants) King; grad. Springside Sch., 1925; student Pa. Sch. Horticulture, 1927; grad. Nat. Sch. Elocution and Oratory, 1929; m. James Rumrill Miller, Jr., Oct. 17, 1931; children—Laura P. (dec.), James Rumrill III. Pres. Planters Garden Club, 1956-57; zone rep. to interchange fellowship in horticulture Garden Club Am., 1959-61; chmn. Symposium on Pa. Gardens, 1958-59; lectr. horse husbandry Ambler Campus, Temple U., 1953-55; dir. Wissahickon Valley Watershed Assn., 1958—, chmn. Penllyn Natural Area, 1964-71, Project Trend Teaching Response to Environmental Demands, 1969—; lectr. on conservation to orgns.; chmn. steering com. Montgomery County Conservation Workshop, 1967—. Chmn. of Land Use, Garden Club of Am. Conservation com., 1968-73. Co-chmn. Penllyn Hunter and Pony Show, 1946-50; mem. women's adv. bd. to Coll. Women, U. Pa. Bd. dirs. Environmental Planning and Information Center Pa., 1970-73. Recipient Zone IV Conservation certificate Garden Club Am., 1966, Margaret Douglas medal for conservation edn., 1973. Mem. Phila. Conservationists, Pa. Hort. Soc., Conservation Council Eastern Pa., Pa. Environmental Council, Alumnae Assn. Springside Sch. (pres. 1949-52). Episcopalian. Address: Grasshopper Lane Gwynedd Valley PA 19437

MILLER, ELIZABETH RUBY SHANK (MRS. JOHN BASCOM MILLER), state senator; b. Marshalltown, Ia., Aug. 24, 1905; grad., high sch., 1923; m. John Bascom Miller, Sept. 5, 1923; children—John Bascom, Edward James, Mary Louise (Mrs. Tom Speas), Elizabeth Arlene (Mrs. Russell Weeden, Jr.). Mem. Ia. Ho. of Reps., 1969-72, Ia. Senate, 1972—. Home nursing chmn. Red Cross, 1950-60; Marshall County rural chmn. Am. Cancer Soc., 1955-56; mem. Marshall County Jury Commn., 1962-68. Precinct committeewomen Marshalltown Republican Com., 1940-68; twp. clk., 1956-68; Marshall county Fedn. Rep. Women, 1965-66; Ia. Rep. campaign chmn., 1968-69. Named Marshall County Rep. Woman of the Year, 1969, Outstanding Civic Leader of Am., 1967. Mem. Gen. Fedn. Women's Clubs, Farm Bur., Bus. and Profl. Women, Internat. Platform Assn., Am. Inst. Parliamentarians. Republican. Conglist. Home: Rural Route 3 Marshalltown IA 50158

MILLER, ELLA MAY (MRS. SAMUEL EBERSOLE MILLER), radio speaker; b. Harper, Kan., May 22, 1915; d. Reuben Musser and Lucinda Ella (Neuhauser) Weaver; B.A., Th.B., Goshen Coll., 1941; postgrad. Richmond Theol. Sem., 1966; m. Samuel Ebersole Miller, June 10, 1941; children—Samuel Ernest, John David, Martin Robert, Jeanne Susan. Mission worker, Kansas City, Kan., 1935-37; missionary to Argentina, Mennonite Bd. Missions and Charities, 1941-52; free lance writer, Argentina and Harrisonburg, Va., 1954—; conf. speaker Mennonite Ch., Harrisonburg, 1958—; radio speaker Mennonite Broadcasts, Inc., Harrisonburg, 1958—; dir. Heart to Heart Fellowship groups, 1965—. Nominee Va. Mother of Year, 1967. Mem. Eastern Mennonite Coll. Profs. Wives Assn. Author: Heart to Heart Poetry Album, 1963; Ella May's Favorite Recipes, 1965; I Am a Woman, 1967; A Woman In Her Home, 1969; Ella May's Favorite Recipes for Heart and Hearth, 1971; Ella May's Hints for Homemakers, 1972; Happiness Is Homemaking, 1974. Editor bimonthly Heart to Heart Letter, 1958—. Home: 1312 College Av Harrisonburg VA 22801 Office: 1251 Edom Rd Harrisonburg VA 22801

MILLER, ELVA RUBY CONNES (MRS. JOHN R. MILLER), civic worker, entertainer; b. Joplin, Mo.; d. Edward and Ada (Martin) Connes; student Pomona Coll., part-time, 1936-56; m. John R. Miller, Jan. 17, 1934 (dec. Nov. 1968). Entertainer various night clubs, supper clubs, also Hollywood Bowl, 1967; tv appearances; rec. artist Capitol Records, 1966—, Amaret Records, 1969—; appeared in motion pictures Active Girl Scouts U.S.A., 1933-58; hon. mem. Mayor's Com. for Sr. Citizens, Los Angeles, 1966. Mem. Cal. Republican Assembly. Recipient awards including Thanks badge Girl Scouts U.S.A., 1956, Key to City, Mayor San Diego, 1967, plaque Dept. of Def. for trip to Viet Nam, 1967. Mem. So. Cal. Symphony Assn., Town Hall Cal. Republican. Home: 4411 Los Feliz Blvd Los Angeles CA 90027

MILLER, ETHEL BERYL, educator; b. Mound City, Ill., Sept. 9, 1915; d. Charles Sumner and Charlotte (Austin) Miller; student So. Ill. U., 1932-34; B.S., U. Ill., 1936; M.A., George Peabody U., 1946, Ed.D., 1965; 1 foster son, Steven Johns. Tchr. pub. schs., Mounds, Ill., 1936-46; asst. county supt. schs., Mounds Ill., 1946-49, elementary supt., 1949-53; asst. to state supt. pub. instrn., Springfield, Ill., 1953-59; asst. prof. MacMurray Coll., Jacksonville, Ill., 1959-61; research asst. Peabody Coll., Nashville, 1961-63; asst. prof. Butler U., Indpls., 1963-64; asso. prof. elementary edn. Murray (Ky.) State U., 1964-67, No. Ill. U., DeKalb., 1967—. Sponsor, Sigma Lambda Sigma service sorority, 1969—; Assn. Childhood Edn. br., 1970—. Mem. Internat. Reading Assn., Nat. Soc. Study Edn., Assn. Childhood Edn., Internat. Platform Assn., Am. Assn. U. Profs., Delta Kappa Gamma (v.p. 1970-72), Kappa Delta Pi. Methodist. Contbr. articles in field to profl. jours. Home: 337 Kishwaukee Dr Sycamore IL 60178 Office: Graham Hall DeKalb IL 60115

MILLER, EVE STONE (MRS. JOHN B. MILLER), investment co. exec., realtor; b. New Haven, Jan. 27, 1918; d. David Bernard and Katherine Margaret (Lee) Stone; grad. high sch.; m. John B. Miller, May 9, 1942; children—David A., Peter J., Mary L. Real estate broker Gold Coast Homes, Inc., Boca Raton, Fla., 1958—, pres., 1959—; mortgage broker, sec. Gold Coast Mortgage Corp., Boca Raton, 1960—; treas., asst. sec. EMS Industries, Inc., Boca Raton, 1967—; sec., dir. Custom Engring. & Test Co., Inc., St. Petersburg, Fla., 1968—. Bd. dirs. S.E. Palm Beach County Home Nursing Service, pres., 1969-72; bd. dirs. Vis. Homemaker Service Palm Beach County, Inc. Mem. Bd. Realtors Boca Raton. Club: Soroptimist (charter pres.

Boca Raton 1960-61). Home: Route 4 Box 519 Fort Myers FL 33905 Office: 110 E Palmetto Park Rd Boca Raton FL 33432

MILLER, EVELYN BAILEY (MRS. CHARLES ROBERT MILLER), assn. exec.; b. Atlanta; d. Thomas Francis and Willie (Groves) Bailey; student Spelman Coll., N.Y. U., 1943-44, Hunter Coll., 1945-46, New Sch. for Social Research, N.Y. U., Columbia U.; B.A., Southeastern U.; m. Charles Robert Miller, Aug. 28, 1955. With Harlem Br. YMCA, N.Y.C., 1949—, membership-program asst., 1955-63, membership sec., 1963-66, membership/pub. relations dir., 1966-71, membership/adult program dir., 1971—. Chmn. membership-pub. relations cabinet YMCA Greater N.Y., 1968-70. Mem. adv. council Sch. Bd. 5; mem. Met. Com. of 100. Bd. dirs. Com. on Civil Rights in N.Y., 1958-65, Childville, Inc. Recipient Pres.'s trophy YMCA, 1966, Honorable Mention plaque YMCA, 1972; Loyalty and Dedication award Met. Com. of 100, 1973. Mem. Assn. Profl. Dirs. (mem. commn. on personnel and security matters 1973—, commr. on white racism 1969-72), Assn. Black Social Workers, N.A.A.C.P., Knickerbocker Bus. and Profl. Women. Methodist. Home: 415 Central Park W New York City NY 10025 Office: 180 W 135th St New York City NY 10030

MILLER, FANNIE CAROLYN ROLL (MRS. WILLIAM PEOPLES MILLER), educator; b. Kansas City, Mo.; d. Edward Francis and Louisa Caroline (Chambers) Roll; B.A., U. Buffalo, 1927; postgrad. U. State N.Y., State Tchr. Coll., Buffalo, Canisius Coll., Buffalo, Beaver Coll., Jenkintown, Pa.; Temple U.; m. William Peoples Miller, Nov. 24, 1937 (dec. May 1961); children—Frances Roll (Mrs. Robert Alan Barnett), Janet Peoples (Mrs. Harold Robert Crooks). Tchr. Pub. Schs., Clarence, N.Y., 1927-28; tchr. English and social studies, librarian Lewiston High Sch., Lewiston, N.Y., 1928-32, Buffalo Sch. System, 1932-38; tchr., chmn. social studies St. Basil Acad., Phila., 1959-70. Mem. Assn. Am. U. Women, Nat. League Am. Pen Women, Internat. Platform Assn., Nat. Council Social Studies. Republican. Roman Catholic. Contbr. Verses and poems to childrens publications, also original radio plays for amateur childrens productions. Home: 7719 Jansen Dr Springfield VA 22152

MILLER, FANNIE (MRS. SHERMAN E. MILLER), educator; b. Winchester, Ky., May 30, 1914; d. Sam and Ethel (Schwartzman) Herman; A.B., U. Ky., 1935, M.A., 1937; postgrad. Columbia, summer 1936, U. Ky., 1937—; m. Dr. Sherman E. Miller, May 30, 1937; children—Freda Grace (Mrs. Michael H. Lerner), Joseph Herman, Samye Norene (Mrs. Norman L. Auerback), Faith Sarah. Supervising tchr. English, speech, drama U. Sch., U. Ky., Lexington, 1936-41, substitute tchr., 1944-59, supervising tchr., 1959-62, coordinator student teaching, 1962—, asst. prof. student teaching, 1966—. Cons. English tchrs., English depts., 1960—; mem. editorial adv. bd. Lit. Cavalcade, 1964-67. Pres., 7th dist. P.T.A., 1960-63; mem. state bd. mgrs. Ky. Congress Parents and Tchrs., 1960-63; pres. Lexington City Council, 1957-58, bd. dirs., 7th Dist., chmn. com. Reading and Library Service, 1966—; mem. Ky. Gov.'s Citizens Com. for Ky. Village, 1964, Gov.'s Commn. on Status Women, 1964-66; chmn. area resource com. Midwest Program Airborne TV Instrn., 1960-63; founder Lexington Children's Theater; mem. budget com. United Community Fund. Trustee, vice chmn., chmn. planning com. Lexington Pub. Library. Recipient United Jewish Appeal award, 1950; YMCA citation for Outstanding Service to Youth of Lexington and Fayette County, 1952; March of Dimes certificate Appreciation, 1954; Delta Zeta Outstanding Woman of Year award, 1968; named as Pacesetter in Kentuckian, 1968; Outstanding Woman faculty mem. Assn. Women Students U. Ky., 1970; citation for religious leadership Union Am. Hebrew Congregations, 1972. Mem. Ky. Congress Parents and Tchrs. (life), Nat., Ky., Central Ky. (pres. English sect. 1964-65) edn. assns., Assn. Tchr. Educators, Ky. Communication Arts Assn. (past v.p.), Nat., Ky. (pres. 1967-68) councils tchrs. English, Mortar Bd. (past v.p., adviser 1973—), Phi Beta Kappa, Kappa Delta Pi (past pres.), Delta Kappa Gamma, Gamma Beta Phi (U. Ky. advisor). Jewish religion (past pres. sisterhood; past supt. religious sch. tchr. religious sch. 1933—). Home: 311 Holliday Rd Lexington KY 40502

MILLER, FLORENCE DAVIS (MRS. ORVAL I. MILLER), physician; b. Los Angeles, Feb. 16, 1927; d. Ward B. and Opal Ruth (Hart) Davis; B.A., Whittier Coll., 1947; M.D., U. So. Cal., 1952; m. Orval I. Miller, June 8, 1952; children—Luana Lynne, Brian Douglas. Intern, Gen. Hosp., Riverside County, Cal.; practice medicine specializing in gen. practice, anesthesiology, Perris, Cal., 1953-58; sch. physician Corona Unified Sch. Dist., 1958-70; physician Riverside County Pub. Health Dept., 1970—. Mem. Nuview Elementary Sch. Dist., 1968—. Republican. Conglist. Home: 28960 Lakeview Nuevo CA 92367

MILLER, FRANCES ALMA, physician; b. North Benton, O., July 5, 1908; d. Delbert Joseph and Viola (Day) Miller; B.A., Ohio Wesleyan U., 1930; M.D., Western Res. Sch. Medicine, 1937. Intern, University hosps., Cleve., 1937-38; resident Youngstown (Ohio) Hosp. Assn., 1942-45; practice medicine specializing in radiology, Youngstown, 1945—; dir. dept. radiology South Unit Youngstown Hosp., (Ohio), 1961-67, radiologist, 1967—; sec. med. staff Youngstown Hosp., 1968. Diplomate Am. Bd. Radiology. Fellow Am. Coll. Radiology; mem. Radiological Soc. N.A., Am. Med. Soc., Cleve., Ohio State (exec. com. 1960) radiological socs., Ohio, Mahoning County med. socs., Phi Beta Kappa, Alpha Omega Alpha. Home: 4118 Oak Knoll Dr Youngstown OH 44512 Office: South Unit Youngstown Hospital Assn Youngstown OH 44501

MILLER, FRANCES HALL (MRS. HUGH MILLER), educator, lawyer; b. Boston, Dec. 25, 1938; d. Addison Smith and Winston (Ivey) Hall; A.B., Mt. Holyoke Coll., 1960; J.D., Boston U., 1965; postgrad. London Sch. Econs., 1965-66; m. Hugh Miller, June 3, 1961; children—Hugh, Christopher. Econ. analyst Bur. Indian Affairs, Washington, 1960-62; asst. editor Am. Trial Lawyers Assn., Cambridge, Mass., 1966-71; instr. law Boston U. Sch. Law, 1967-71, lectr. law, 1971-73, adj. asso. prof. law, 1973—; admitted to Mass. bar, 1965; asso. Powers & Hall, Boston, 1973—. Mem. Hill-Burton Adv. Council, 1973—; mem. Health Policy Devel. Group, Dept. Pub. Health, 1973—; consumer rep. CHAMP State Com., 1973—. Commr. Mass. Rate Setting Commn., 1974—. Trustee, bequests and annuities subcom. Mt. Holyoke Coll., 1972—. Mem. Mass. Bar Assn., Mass. Assn. Women Lawyers. Club: Longwood Cricket (Brookline, Mass.). Asso. editor Am. Soc. Law and Medicine Newsletter, 1973—. Home: 42 Cliff Rd Wellesley MA 02181 Office: 765 Commonwealth Av Boston MA 02127

MILLER, FRANCES LOUISE ASHTON, librarian; b. Shannon City, Ia., Feb. 25, 1918; d. James Thomas and Mary Elizabeth (Olson) Ashton; A.B., Drake U., 1941; B.S. in L.S., Columbia, 1947; postgrad. Drake U., Washington U., St. Louis, U. Minn., U. Ia., State U. N.Y., Albany; m. John Robert Miller, Oct. 22, 1948 (div. June 1970). Tchr. English, Leland (Ia.) pub. schs., 1941-42; tchr. English and social sci. Guthrie Center (Ia.) pub. schs., 1942-43; jr. librarian Pub. Library, Des Moines, 1945-46, circulation librarian, 1947; asst. librarian Drake U., Des Moines, 1947-51; librarian County Library, St. Louis, 1951; cataloger A. and M. Coll. Tex., College Station, 1951-52; tchr. English, A. and M. Consol. Schs., College Station, 1952; tchr. English, Webster Groves (Mo.) high sch., 1952-58; librarian Excelsior (Minn.) High Sch., 1958-60, Lyons Twp. High Sch., La Grange, Ill., 1960-61; research librarian, information service Field Enterprises, Chgo., 1961-62; librarian, curriculum center Community Pub. Schs., Cedar Rapids, Ia., 1962-64; catalog librarian, asst. prof. Coe Coll., Cedar Rapids, 1964-65; edn. bibliographer, asst. prof. State U. N.Y. at Albany, 1965-71; librarian, media specialist Balston Spa (N.Y.) High Sch., 1971-73; asst. law librarian N.Y. State Dept. Law, Albany, 1973-74; librarian N.Y. State Dept. Motor Vehicles, Albany, 1974—. Vol. worker Meml. Hosp., Albany, 1970-71; mem. Festival of Praise Choir, Albany, 1971—; chmn. pub. edn. com. Saratoga County unit Am. Cancer Soc., 1972-73. Served with USNR, 1943-45. Mem. Am., N.Y., Hudson Mohawk library assns., Eastern N.Y. Sch. Librarians, Coll. and Research Librarians Assn., Am. Assn. Sch. Librarians, Spl. Library Assn., Am. Fedn. Tchrs. Assns., N.E.A., N.Y. United Tchrs. Assn. Presbyn. Contbr. to profl. publs. Home: 4 Colonial Ct Rural Route 4 Ballston Lake NY 12019 Office: Research Library NY State Dept Motor Vehicles 45 Empire State Plaza S Swan Albany NY 12228

MILLER, FRAULEIN YVONNE ESSEX (MRS. SILAS S. MILLER), educator; b. New Orleans, Apr. 11, 1930; d. Alfred Bernard and Ernestine (Crump) Essex; B.A., So. U., 1950; postgrad. Chgo. Tchrs. Coll., 1957-58, De Paul U., 1958-59, U. Chgo., 1960; m. Silas S. Miller, June 29, 1948; children—Diedra Shirrube, Rodney Llewellyn. Tchr. English, Covington (La.) High Sch., 1951-52, Du Sable High Sch., Chgo., 1956; tchr. English, Englewood High Sch., Chgo., 1956—, head dept. English, 1964—. Tutor, St. Joachim Parish Sch., 1964—. Mem. Citizens Sch. Com., Chgo., 1964—. Recipient award Chgo. Commn. on Human Relations, 1964; named Tchr. of Yr., Kate Maremont Found., 1964. Mem. Chgo. Tchrs. Union. Home: 414 E 89th St Chicago IL 60619 Office: 6201 S Stewart Chicago IL 60621

MILLER, GENE WILLIAMS (MRS. RICHARD L. MILLER), civic worker; b. Winterset, Ia., Oct. 17, 1906; d. Orlo David and Edna Katherine (Bonebrake) Williams; B.A., U. So. Cal., 1928; m. Richard L. Miller, June 7, 1931; children—Richard W., Damon C. Tchr. English, Grand Junction (Colo.) Pub. Schs., 1928-30; tchr. English, Des Moines Pub. Schs., 1930-32; mem. Summit (N.J.) Welfare Bd., 1940-57, N.J. Library Commn., 1944-47, N.J. Bd. Edn., 1947-57, Duval County Sch. Bd., Jacksonville, Fla., 1969—; mem. Community Planning Council, Jacksonville, 1970—. Pres., League Women Voters, Summit, 1942-44, mem. N.J. state bd., 1944-57; del. N.J. Constl. Conv., 1947. Recipient Woman of Year awards Soroptimist Club, 1965, Council Jewish Women, 1970, Fla. Pub. Co., 1971, Jr. Womens Club, 1971. Mem. P.E.O., Am. Assn. U. Women, Beta Sigma Omicron, Pi Kappa Sigma. Republican. Unitarian. Home: 9134 Beauclerc Circle W Jacksonville FL 32217

MILLER, GERALDENE AGNES (MRS. WILLIAM JAMES MILLER), lawyer; b. Galena, Kan., Oct. 27, 1928; d. Oscar Maxel and Pearl (Berry) Yount; A.B., U. Kan., 1951; J.D., U. Mo., 1958; m. William James Miller, June 24, 1951; children—Carolyn Agnes, Barbara Anne, Elizabeth Pearl. Admitted to Kan., Ia. bars, 1958, Okla. bar, 1960; with firm Miller & Miller, Mission, Kan., 1958; Cedar Rapids, Ia., 1958-59, Ponca City, Okla., 1960—. Mem. Ponca City P.T.A., 1959-69. Mem. Kay County Women's Republican Club, 1959—, pres. 1964-68. Bd. dirs. Opportunity Center, Reconciliation Com. Mem. Am. U. Women, Kay County Bar Aux., C. of C., Phi Delta Delta. Methodist (pres. women's soc. ch. services). Home: 727 Monument Ponca City OK 74601 Office: 104 N 2nd St Ponca City OK 74601

MILLER, GLORIA LEE, state ofcl.; b. N.Y.C., Aug. 9, 1927; d. Otto and Gertrude (Goldstein) Kaplan; student U. Miami, 1945-46; div.; children—Arleen (Mrs. Bernard Milmoe), Madelyn (Mrs. George Kellert), Richard. Dir. recreation Town of Surfside, Fla., 1955-67; information specialist State of Fla., Dept. Commerce, Miami, 1967—; broadcaster Job Line, WPLG-TV, 1969—, Community Report, WCKT-TV, 1968—; writer weekly column Random Thoughts, Miami Times, 1971—. Recipient Nat. award for outstanding community service Parents Mag., 1965-66; Gold Image award Fla. Pub. Relations Assn., 1972; Commendation from Pres. Johnson for outstanding community service, 1966. Mem. Am. Women in Radio and TV (pres. 1970), Women In Communications (communications chmn. 1971), Council for Continuing Edn. Women, C. of C. (mem. human resources devel. com. 1973-74). Home: 16950 W Dixie Hwy North Miami Beach FL 33162 Office: 1350 NW 12th Av Miami FL 33136

MILLER, GRACE LAVINIA GREGORY (MRS. NOBLE L. MILLER), educator; b. Morley, Mo., Feb. 22, 1913; d. Oscar Lee and Rachael (Cavaness) Gregory; B.S. in Edn., S.E. Mo. State Coll., 1951; M.S. in Edn., So. Ill. U., 1956, specialist in edn., 1967; postgrad. U. Mo., 1959, Northwestern State Coll., Natchitoches, La., 1961; Ed.D., U. Tulsa, 1970; m. Noble L. Miller, June 16, 1935; children—Ted G., Donald T., Alora Kay (Mrs. Norman F. Johns). Tchr. pub. sch., Vanduser, Mo., 1944-45; prin. elementary pub. sch., Diehlstadt, Mo., 1951-53; tchr. jr. high sch. Shawnee Community Unit, Wolf Lake, Ill., 1953-58; counselor pub. sch., Cape Girardeau, Mo., 1958-67; counselor educator Central Mo. State Coll., 1965, S.W. Mo. State Coll., 1966, N.W. Mo. State Coll., 1969, supr. practice tchrs. U. Tulsa, 1968-69; prof. edn., counselor educator Lincoln U., Jefferson City, Mo., 1969—, dir. program for guidance and counseling, 1969—. Recipient Nat. Def. Edn. Act scholarships, 1959, 61. Mem. N.E.A., Am. Personnel and Guidance Assn., Am. Vocational Assn., Bus. and Profl. Women, Mo. Guidance Assn. (pres. 1965), Kappa Delta Pi. Mem. Order Eastern Star (past matron). Home: 1412 Bold Hill Rd Jefferson City MO 65101

MILLER, HAZEL BELLE (MRS. ESMOND A. VAN NAME), physician; b. Bklyn., Sept. 17, 1912; d. Frank W. and Florence (Brodie) Miller; B.S., N.Y. U., 1929; M.D cum laude, Woman's Med. Coll. Pa., 1934; m. Esmond A. Van Name, June 7, 1934; children—Barry Allen, Kerry Everett. Intern, Jersey Med. Center and Margaret Hague Maternity Hosp., 1934-35; gen. practice Hollis, L.I., 1935-60, Garden City, N.Y., 1960—; physician in clinics N.Y. Skin and Cancer Hosp., 1935-41; mem. obstet. staff Mary Immaculate Hosp., 1936—, obstet. clinic, 1936-63. Active Boy Scouts Am. Fellow Am. Acad. Family Physicians (charter, past chpt. pres.), Nassau Acad. Medicine; mem. Am. Geriatrics Soc., Am. Soc. Clin. Hypnosis, Women's Med. Soc. N.Y. State (pres. 1966-68), Am. Med. Womens Assn. (del. to Med. Womens Internat. Assn., rep. to UN), Soroptomists, Alpha Omicron Pi, Zeta Phi, Alpha Omega Alpha. Address: 125 Cherry Valley Av Garden City NY 11530

MILLER, HELEN MAY, librarian; b. Conway, Mo., Sept. 13, 1918; d. Lloyd Schmalhorst and Olive Frazier (Smith) Miller; A.B., Drury Coll., 1940; B.S. in L.S., U. Denver, 1941. Engring. librarian U. Ark., 1941-43; circulation librarian Springfield (Mo.) Pub. Library, 1943-45; librarian U.S. Army, Ft. George G. Meade, Md., 1945-46, Cole County Library, Jefferson City, Mo., 1947-49, Jefferson City and Cole County libraries, 1949-55; librarian USAF bases in Germany and Eng., 1955-58; pub. library cons. W.Va. Library Commn., 1959-61; state librarian Ida. State Library, 1962—. Mem. Am., Pacific Northwest, Ida. library assns. Author articles in field. Editor: The Idaho Librarian, 1962-69. Home: 2410 State St Boise ID 83702 Office: 325 W State St Boise ID 83702

MILLER, HELENA A., educator; b. Rudolph, O., Apr. 25, 1913; d. Royal James and Bertha (Hansen) Miller; B.A., Ohio State U., 1935, B.S. in Edn., 1935, M.S., 1938; Ph.D., Radcliffe Coll., Harvard, 1945. Tchr., dean of girls Montgomery Twp. High Sch., Wayne, O., 1935-37; asst. botany Ohio State U., Columbus, O., 1938-39; lectr. biology Hiram Coll., O., 1939; biology instr. Milton (Mass.) Acad., 1939-40, biology instr., head sci. in lower sch., 1940-41; teaching fellow in biology Radcliffe Coll., Cambridge, Mass., 1942-43, Harvard, 1943-44; cons. to War Dept., 1944; botany instr. Conn. Coll. Women, New London, Conn., 1944-45, Wellesley Coll., Wellesley, Mass., 1945-48; asso. prof. biology Duquesne U., Pitts., 1948-59, prof., 1959—, asst. dean Coll. of Arts and Sci., 1966—. Mem. Bot. Soc. Am. (vice chmn. teaching sect. 1966, chmn. 1967), Taxonomic Soc. Am., Internat. Assn. Plant Taxonomy, A.A.A.S., Nat. Geog. Soc., Torrey Bot. Soc., Soc. for Study Evolution, Nat. Assn. Standard Med. Vocabulary, Soc. Econ. Botany, Center Intergrative Edn., Am. Asso. U. Adminstrs., Nat. Sci. Tchrs. Assn., Internat. Assn. Plant Morphologists, Internat. Platform Assn., Soc. Exptl. Biology, Am. Inst. Biol. Scis., Soc. Developmental Biology, Am. Assn. U. Women, Nat. Assn. Biology Tchrs., Intercontinental Biog. Assn. (life), Pa. Cath. Round Table Sci. (past exec. sec.-treas.), Western Pa. Conservancy, Phi Beta Kappa, Sigma Xi, Sigma Pi Sigma, Phi Epsilon Phi, Alpha Epsilon Delta. Contbr. numerous articles to profl. jours. Home: 532 Highview Rd Pittsburgh PA 15234

MILLER, IDA MAE GOOD (MRS. JOHN CHESTER MILLER), librarian; b. Indpls., Mar. 25, 1919; d. Irby J. and Mabel Iota (Rivir) Good; A.B., Ind. Central Coll., 1939; B.L.S., Columbia U., 1948; B. Music, Butler U., 1952; m. John Chester Miller, May 6, 1950; children—Susan Marie, Julia Christina, David Alan, Carl Edward. Tchr., Indpls. Pub. Sch., 1941-43, high sch. library asst., 1946-47, sr. librarian Indpls. Pub. Library, 1948-52; historical librarian Plainfield (Ind.) Pub. Library, 1967-73; pamphlet cataloger Ind. Hist. Soc. Library, Indpls., 1973—. Served with WAC, 1943-45. Mem. A.L.A., Ind. Library Assn., Ind., Hendricks County, Guilford Twp. hist. socs., Hymn Soc. Am., Ind. Geology and Gem Soc., Sigma Alpha Iota. Republican. Mem. Soc. Friends (choir dir. 1956-65). Contbr. articles to profl. pubs. Editor music: Quaker Life, 1959-73, writer monthly column, 1959-69. Joint editor: Friends Sing, 1963, Let Friends Sing, 1967. Home: 525 E Main St Plainfield IN 46168 Office: 140 N Senate Av Indianapolis IN 46204

MILLER, IRMA GANZ, pub. co. exec.; b. Scranton, Pa., Dec. 25, 1916; d. Jacob and Dora (Weinberger) Ganz; B.A., Pa. State U., 1938; m. Milton Miller, Sept. 3, 1939 (dec. Dec., 1969); children—Jeffrey H., Lee James. Dir., Soccer Assos., New Rochelle, N.Y., 1948—; bus. mgr. Jeffrey Lee Syndicate, New Rochelle, 1953—; pres. Sport Shelf, New Rochelle, 1953—; bus. mgr. Wide World Book Center, Ltd., New Rochelle, 1966—; mng. editor Soccer News, New Rochelle, 1968—. Mem. Soccer Writers Assn. Am. (pres. 1969—), Am. Assn. Health, Phys. Edn. and Recreation, Nat. Recreation Assn., Nat. Parks and Recreation Assn., Internat. Platform Assn., Nat. Sportscasters and Sportswriters Assn., Pa. State Alumni Assn. Office: 359 North Av New Rochelle NY 10802 also PO Box 634 New Rochelle NY 10802

MILLER, ISABEL MOUNT (MRS. TOM POLK MILLER), architect; b. Justin, Tex., Mar. 27, 1916; d. Jess Wallace and Nancy Ellen (Donald) Mount; B.A. with distinction, Rice Inst., 1936, B.S. in Architecture, 1937; m. Tom Polk Miller, Aug. 10, 1947; children—Crispin Mount, Abigail Mount. With Burns Roensch Co., architects, Houston, 1938-42; with drafting div. Stran-Steel Co., Detroit, 1942-43; with Pietro Belluschi, architect, Portland, Ore., 1946, Robert Pope, architect, Santurce, P.R., 1946, Kemper Nomland, architects, Los Angeles, 1948-49, Mount-Miller Architects, Denton, Tex., 1949—. Vice chmn. Denton County Hist. Survey Com., 1973-74. Bd. dirs. Denton Arts Council, 1971-74. Recipient Mary Alice Elliott Loan fund for travel and archtl. study Rice Inst., 1940. Mem. League Women Voters (Denton pres. 1973—). Democrat. Unitarian (pres. Denton 1966-67). Prin. archtl. works include Denton County Electric Coop. Bldg., 1954, Denton Unitarian Fellowhsip Bldg., 1959; designer Dem. election hdqrs., 1956, 60, 64, 68, 72. Address: 711 W Sycamore St Denton TX 76201

MILLER, JANICE MARGARET (MRS. LYLE DEVON MILLER), veterinarian; b. McPherson, Kan., Nov. 11, 1938; d. Charles Harris and Margaret Irene (Tolle) Lilly; B.S., Kan. State U., 1960, D.V.M., 1962, M.S., 1963; Ph.D., U. Wis., 1969; m. Lyle Devon Miller, Apr. 18, 1962; children—Donald Devon, Brenda Joanne. Research asso. Mass. Inst. Tech., Cambridge, 1964-65; vet. pathologist Nat. Animal Disease Lab., Ames, Ia., 1972—. Mem. young exec. com. U.S. Dept. Agr., 1973—. Leukemia Soc. Am. fellow, 1970-72. Mem. Nat. Assn. Fed. Veterinarians, Am. Vet. Med. Assn., Am. Coll. Vet. Pathologists, Phi Kappa Phi. Republican. Methodist. Contbr. articles to profl. jours. Home: 2803 Northwood Dr Ames IA 50010 Office: Nat Animal Disease Lab Box 70 Ames IA 50010

MILLER, JEANNE-MARIE ANDERSON (MRS. NATHAN JOHN MILLER), educator; b. Washington, Feb. 18, 1937; d. William and Agnes Catherine (Johns) Anderson; B.A., Howard U., 1959, M.A., 1963; m. Nathan John Miller, Oct. 2, 1960. Instr. dept. English Howard U., Washington, 1963—, also asst. dir. Inst. for Arts and Humanities, 1973—. Cons. Am. Studies Assn., 1972—. Mem. Washington Performing Arts Soc., 1971—, Friends of WETA-TV, 1971—, Mus. African Art, 1971—, Arena Stage Assos., 1972—. Ford Found. fellow, 1970-72, So. Fellowships Fund fellow, 1972—. Mem. Nat. Council Tchrs. of English, Coll. English Assn., Am. Studies Assn., Am. Theatre Assn., Am. Assn. U. Profs., Am. Assn. U. Women, League Women Voters, Common Cause, Civil Liberties Union, Am. Acad. Polit. and Social Sci., Coll. Lang. Assn., Modern Lang. Assn., Friends Kennedy Center for Performing Arts. Democrat. Episcopalian. Contbr. articles in field to profl. jours. Home: 1101 3d St SW Washington DC 20024

MILLER, JOAN ANN (MRS. WILLIAM RICHARD MILLER), librarian; b. Albany, N.Y., Mar. 9, 1941; d. Leslie Fey and Margaret Elizabeth (Till) Glenck; B.A., State U. N.Y., 1963, M.L.S., 1964; m. William Richard Miller, Oct. 13, 1967. Research librarian, character research project Union Coll., Schenectady, N.Y., 1963-64; reference and circulation librarian Albany Med. Coll., (N.Y.), 1964; reference librarian, Hawley Library, N.Y. State U., Albany, 1964; sr. med. librarian N.Y. State Med. Library, State Edn. Dept., Albany, 1964-68; asso. instructional materials for handicapped children, N.Y. Spl. Edn. Instructional Materials Center, N.Y. State Edn. Dept., 1968—. Cons. in field to various state and local agys. Mem. Council Exceptional Children, N.Y. Ednl. Communications Assn., N.Y. Library Assn., Assn. Ednl. Communication and Tech., Upstate N.Y. Regional Med. Library Assn. Editorial staff: Reading Aids for the Physically Handicapped, A.L.A., 1970. Author: (with others) Instructional Materials Thesaurus for Special Education, 2d edit., 1964. Editor: Proceedings of the Institute on Improving Library Services for Handicapped Children, 1971. Compiler: CEC/ERIC Information Center, IMC/RMC Network Professional Film Collection, 1971. Contbr. articles to profl. jours. Home: 6 Woodridge Court RD 4 Ballston Lake NY 12019 Office: 55 Elk St Albany NY 12224

MILLER, JOYCE (LARAYNE) (MRS. R. WARBURTON), marriage, family and child counselor; b. South Bend, Ind., July 29, 1925; d. Estal Ellis and Blendena (Keltner) Maxey; A.B., U. Redlands, 1959, M.A., 1962; m. Robert Warburton Miller, Mar. 24, 1946; children—Pamela Joyce, Brent Warburton, Page Layne. Practice as marriage, family and child counselor, speech pathologist, San Bernardino, Cal., 1957—; staff cons. Citrus Care Convalescent Hosp., Fontana, Cal., 1969—. Dir., v.p. AVORA, Inc., 1973—. Mem. steering com. Mentally Gifted Minors Program, San Bernardino City Schs., 1971-72; mem. San Bernardino chpt. City of Hope, 1959—, chpt. pres., 1964-66, also trustee; active San Bernardino Civic Light Opera Assn., 1959—; v.p. Carriage Club of Civic Light Opera, 1963-64; mem. San Bernardino Area Mental Health Assn., 1959—, P.T.A., 1954—, 1st v.p., 1956-57; mem. Nat. Charity League, 1972—; mem. unit 2 planning com. Golden Valley Jr. High Sch., 1973, mem. citizen's adv. com., 1972—; exec. bd. mem. ad hoc com. Performing Arts for Students, 1973; ofcl. chaperone Nat. Miss Teenager Pageant, 1974; mem. ad hoc com., treas. Support Creative Arts Now, 1973—. Pres., San Bernardino County Young Democrats, 1955-56; Dem. state committeewoman, 1955-57. Univ. Redlands fellow, 1966—. Mem. Am. Speech and Hearing Assn., Nat. Council on Family Relations, Inland Psychol. Assn. So. Cal. (sec.-treas. 1971-72), So. Counties Psychologist's Assn., Music Edn. Support Assn. (dir.), Pi Kappa Delta, Beta Lambda Mu. Methodist. Mem. Order Eastern Star (life). Clubs: Wilsonian (San Bernardino, Cal.), San Bernardino Women's, 1955. Author: (with Robert Warburton Miller) Dealing With The Behavioral Problems In The Elementary School, 1969; A Therapy Guide for the Families of Adult Aphasics, 1972. Home: 3621 Valencia Av San Bernardino CA 92405 Office: 1308 N D St San Bernardino CA 92405

MILLER, JUDITH MIRIAM STATMAN (MRS. PAUL P. MILLER), bus. exec.; b. Dallas, June 1, 1938; d. Joseph and Lillian (Tolmich) Statman; student U. Tex., 1955-56; m. Paul P. Miller, Dec. 20, 1970; 1 stepson, Steven. With Bloom Advt., Dallas, 1957-71, head media dept., 1965-71; broadcast supr. Tracy-Locke, Inc., Dallas, 1971—. Mem. Assn. Broadcast Execs. Tex. (sec. 1963-64, 65-66, 67-67). Home: 3801 Turtle Creek Dr Dallas TX 75219 Office: 1407 Main St Dallas TX 75250

MILLER, JUNE LEE, govt. ofcl.; b. Richmond, Va., Feb. 25, 1923: d. Harry Lee and Laura (Severson) Camp; student Zeith Bus. Sch., 1942; m. Earl J. Abendshein, Sept. 27, 1944 (div. Sept. 1955); children—Harry Michael, April Lee; m. 2d, Marshall E. Miller, Nov. 19, 1960. Proof reader Hanover (Pa.) Sun, 1949-52; teletypist St. Petersburg (Fla.) Times, 1952-56; publ. planner Congl. Quar., Washington, 1957-62, dir. spl. supplements dept., 1962-66; editor Vanguard, VA, Washington, 1966-68, staff asst. Adminstr. Vets. Affairs, 1968-69, personnel staffing specialist, 1969-71, incentive awards officer, 1971—. Pa. state pres. AMVETS Aux., 1950-51, nat. Americanism chmn., 1951-52, nat. liaison officer, 1954-55, nat. legislative dir., 1956-57, nat. pres., 1957-58; editorial cons. AMVETS, 1968—. Mem. editorial bd. All Am. Conf. to Combat Communism, 1957-59; mem. awards com. Pres.'s Com. Employment Physically Handicapped, 1958—. Mem. Foremost Women in Communications. Club: Lawyers Wives (Washington). Author: Code of An American Mother, 1957; To Care for Him Who Shall Have Borne the Battle, 1966; Twenty-three Years of AMVETS Auxiliary, 1969. Home: 1616 Wainwright Dr Reston VA 22090 Office: VA Washington DC 20420

MILLER, KAY JOHNS, pub. relations cons., Shreveport, La., Nov. 13, 1921; d. Walter Neville and Lucile Katherine (Simpson) Jackson; grad. Franklin Sch. Art, N.Y.C.; student U. N.M., 1940-41; m. Josef M. Miller, Oct. 19, 1946 (dec. Apr. 1973); children—Victoria R., Laurie R. Graphics designer, Los Angeles, 1945-67; advt. copywriter Kay Miller Advt., Los Angeles, 1960-67; editor Homebuyers mag., Los Angeles, 1967-69; prin. Kay Miller, pub. relations cons., Los Angeles, 1969—. Mem. Los Angeles Beautiful. Bd. dirs. Country Joe's. Recipient commendation Los Angeles City Council, 1971. Mem. Common Cause, Publicity Club of Los Angeles. Democrat. Episcopalian. Address: 108 S Almont Dr Los Angeles CA 90048

MILLER, LAURA ANNE WIMER (MRS. ROBERT WILLIAM MILLER), state ofcl.; b. San Antonio, Oct. 4, 1919; d. Kenneth Robert and Cecile Clarita (Janin) Wimer; student U. San Antonio, 1936-39; med. tech. certificate Robert B. Green Meml. Hosp., San Antonio, 1939; m. Robert William Miller, Jan. 11, 1942; children—Richard Frank, Patsy Ann (Mrs. Joseph Lambert Marshall). Med. Technologist Austin (Tex.) State Hosp., 1939-41; mem. Colo. Ho. of Reps., 1970—. Mem. Colo. Health Facilities Adv. Council, 1970—; mem. adv. com. Colo. Commn. Higher Edn., 1973—. Precinct committeewoman Jefferson County (Colo.) Republican Com., 1961-70. Trustee Jefferson County Pub. Library. Home: 6100 W Bowles Av Littleton CO 80123

MILLER, LILLIAN VICTORIA (MRS. ELMER JOE MILLER), real estate broker; b. Castle Rock, Wash., July 23, 1925; d. Victor Morrell and Esther Loring (Anderson) Anderson; B.A., Walla Walla Coll., 1947; m. Elmer Joe Miller, July 15, 1945; children—Victor Joe, Craig Revere, Marcia Louise. Social worker San Bernardino County (Cal.), 1954-56; sec., coordinator Miller Constrn. Co., Loma Linda, Cal., 1957-64; real estate salesman University Realty, Loma Linda, 1964-67, real estate broker, 1967—. Mem. Loma Linda Elementary Sch. Bd., 1965-67; mem. Acad. High Sch. Sch. Bd., Loma Linda, 1965-67; mem. bldg. com. 1970. Named One of Top Ten Salesman, San Bernardino Bd. Realtors, 1971-72; 1st salesperson in San Bernardino Bd. Realtors to receive membership Million Dollar Club, 1973. Mem. Redlands Bd. Realtors (dir., mem. edn. com. 1972—). Seventh-day Adventist (mem. bd. deaconesses 1961-73). Home: 11554 Richmont Rd Loma Linda CA 92354 Office: 11156 Anderson St Loma Linda CA 92354

MILLER, LINDA B., educator; b. Manchester, N.H., Aug. 7, 1937; d. Louis and Helene (Chase) Miller; grad. cum laude Emma Willard Sch., 1955; A.B. cum laude, Radcliffe Coll., 1959; M.A., Columbia, 1961, Ph.D., 1965. Asst. prof. Barnard Coll., 1964-67; research asso. Princeton, 1966-67; research asso. Harvard, Cambridge, Mass., 1967-71, lectr., 1968-69; asso. prof. polit. sci. Wellesley (Mass.) Coll., 1969—, Council on Fgn. Relations Internat. Affairs fellow, 1973-74. Mem. Am. Polit. Sci. Assn., Am. Assn. U. Profs., Inst. for Stretegic Studies, Am. Soc. Internat. Law. Author: World Order and Local Disorder: The United Nations and Internal Conflicts, 1967; Dynamics of World Politics: Studies in the Resolution of Conflicts, 1968; Cyprus: The Law and Politics of Civil Strife, 1968. Contbr. articles to profl. jours. Home: 287 Harvard St Cambridge MA 02139 Office: Wellesley Coll Wellesley MA 02181

MILLER, LOIS HEPLER, newspaper editor; b. Morgantown, W.Va., Mar. 24, 1928; d. George A. and Jean C. (Long) Anderson; student Ind. State Tchrs. Coll., 1946-49; postgrad. Sch. Edn., Temple U., 1950-53; m. Lloyd F. Hepler, May 20, 1950 (dec.); children—Alan, Harold, Margaret Jean; m. 2d, Willard E. Miller, Sr., Apr. 19, 1974. Formerly with Canonsburg (Pa.) Daily Notes, Indiana (Pa.) Evening Gazette; various secretarial positions, Phila.; with Montgomery Pub. Co., Jenkintown, Pa., 1961—, gen. news reporter, 1961-73, women's editor, 1965-73, asso. news editor, 1970-73, mng. editor Times Chronicle, Jenkintown, Glenside News, Huntington Valley Globe, 1973—. First aid vol. 2d Alarmers Rescue Squad of Montgomery County. Recipient ann. state journalist conv. awards, 1965-66, 68-72. Mem. Pa. Women's Press Assn. (named News-woman of Year 1966, 71), Pa. Soc. Newspaper Editors, Women in Communications, Inc., D.A.R., Old York Rd Hist. Soc., Sigma Delta Chi. Mem. Order Eastern Star. Home: 416 Leedom St Jenkintown PA 19046 Office: Times Chronicle 413 Johnston St Jenkintown PA 19046

MILLER, LOUISE DEAN (MRS. MICKEY L. MILLER), journalist; b. Lubbock, Tex., Dec. 10, 1921; d. Arlie David and Ludie Lee (Hart) Dean; B.A., B.S., Tex. Woman's U., 1943; m. Mickey L. Miller, Aug. 30, 1946; children—Mary Linda, Myra Lee, Mickey Lynne. Gen. reporter Vernon (Tex.) Daily Record, 1943-44; feature writer Tinker AFB Paper, Oklahoma City, 1944-46; woman's page editor Albuquerque Tribune, 1946-48; publicist United Community Fund, Albuquerque, 1951; information specialist Albuquerque Pub. Schs., 1967-68; pub. information and program dir. YWCA, Albuquerque, 1970-72; researcher-writer Albuquerque Jour., 1972—. Active with Girl Scouts Am., and various other civic orgns. Mem. Am. Assn. U. Women, Women In Communications. Home: 1201 Richmond Dr NE Albuquerque NM 87106 Office: Action Line Drawer J Albuquerque Journal Albuquerque NM 87103

MILLER, LOUISE HESS (MRS. MARLIN MILLER), ret. educator; b. Etna Green, Ind.; d. William T. and Anna (Melick) Hess; A.B., Ind. U., 1928; postgrad. Vassar Coll., summer 1938; M.A., U. Notre Dame, 1952; m. Marlin Miller, Dec. 28, 1929; children—Marlin, James Hess, Terry Stuart. Reporter, feature writer South Bend (Ind.) News-Times, 1928-29; tchr. Jefferson, Muessel schs., South Bend, 1949-63, J. W. Riley High Sch., South Bend, 1963-70. Mem. Am. Assn. U. Women, Women in Communications. Presbyn. Home: 1733 Southwood Av South Bend IN 46615

MILLER, LOUISE ROSEMAN (MRS. RAY E. MILLER), occupational therapist; b. Lancaster, Pa., Oct. 25, 1946; d. Donald Kramer and Elizabeth Oswald (Colt) Roseman; A.B., Wilson Coll., 1968; certificate proficiency in occupational therapy U. Pa., 1970; m. Ray E. Miller, Aug. 2, 1969. Occupational therapist Montgomery County intermediate unit Sch. for Physically Handicapped Children, Norristown, Pa., 1970-74; occupational therapist Pennhurst State Sch. and Hosp., Spring City, Pa., 1974—. Cons. St. Edmond's Home for Crippled Children, Rosemont, 1972—; cons. spl. edn. dept. Cabrini Coll., 1973. Mem. Am., Eastern Pa. occupational therapy assns. Home: RD 1 Box 452 Bechtelsville PA 19505 Office: Pennhurst State Sch and Hosp Spring City PA 19475

MILLER, MARCIA ANN (MRS. LARRY REED MILLER), educator; b. Fremont, O., Nov. 23, 1942; d. Elery L. and Rachel E. (Bartholomew) Wolfe; student Mich. State U., 1960-62; B.S., Bowling Green State U., 1965, M.A., 1966; Ph.D., Ohio State U., 1970; m. Larry Reed Miller, Dec. 27, 1962. Instr., Bowling Green (O.) State U., 1966-68; instr. div. infectious diseases Ohio State U. Coll. Medicine, Columbus, 1970-71; asst. prof. microbiology U. Ill. Coll. Medicine, Peoria, 1971—; adj. prof. microbiology Ill. State U., Normal, 1971—. Mem. bd. govs. Nat. Found., March of Dimes, Peoria-Stark-Marshall chpts., Ill., 1972—. Ill. Lung Assn. grantee, 1971—; Chgo. and Ill. Heart Assn. grantee, 1973—; Sigma Xi grantee, 1971-72; U. Ill. grantee, 1971-72; March of Dimes grantee, 1972-73. Recipient Interstate Postgrad. Med. Assn. Research award, 1973. Mem. A.A.A.S., Am. Soc. for Microbiology, Am. Fedn. for Clin. Research, Sigma Xi, Beta Beta Beta, Phi Sigma, Phi Kappa Phi. Home: 1017 Gregory St Normal IL 61761 Office: 1400 W Main St Peoria IL 61606

MILLER, MARIAN ELIZABETH (MRS. WILLIS JAMES MILLER, JR.), data processing co. exec.; b. Gary, S.D., Sept. 26, 1929; d. Thomas and Grace (Merrill) Adams; B.S. magna cum laude, S.D. State U., 1951; m. Willis James Miller, Jr., Sept. 17, 1961; 1 dau., Michele Regina (dec.). Jr. engr. Boeing Airplane Co., Seattle, 1952-56; mathematician IBM Corp., Washington, 1957-58; programmer Philco-Ford Co., Palo Alto, Cal., 1958-61; sr. programmer Lockheed Missiles & Space Co., Palo Alto, 1962-66; sr. programmer, analyst Litton Industries, Culver City, Cal., 1966-67, Pascagoula, Miss., 1972; sr. analyst United Tech. Center, Sunnyvale, Cal., 1968-69; nat. project leader financial systems Miller-Ellis Computer Systems, Palo Alto, 1969-70; dir., sec. treas. Clough's Enterprises, Inc., Palo Alto, 1968-71; dir., exec. v.p., sec., treas. Data Plan, Inc., Los Altos, Cal., 1971—; partner W.J. Miller Asso., Los Altos, 1964—. Mem. Assn. for Computing Machinery, Phi Kappa Phi. Methodist. Home: 950 Oxford Dr Los Altos CA 94022

MILLER, MARIE ALICE OED (MRS. GEORGE W. MILLER, JR.), newspaper editor; b. N.Y.C., Feb. 21, 1925; d. Jules J. and Mary Alice (Lenehan) Oed; grad. high sch.; m. George W. Miller, Jr., Aug. 17, 1945; children—George III, Gayle, Michael, Steven, Douglas. Free-lance writer, 1947—; mng. editor L.I. Graphic & Roosevelt Press, weekly newspaper, Freeport, N.Y., 1969—. Pres. Bellmore P.T.A., 1960-61; sec. Freeport Waterfront Assn., 1965-69; pres. Dodd Jr. High Sch. P.T.A., Freeport, 1970-71. Bd. dirs. Freeport Econ. Opportunity Council, 1973—. Served with USNR, 1943-45. Mem. Nassau County Press Assn., Am. Legion. Republican. Roman Catholic. Home: 935 S Long Beach Av Freeport NY 11520 Office: 80 Church St Freeport NY 11520

MILLER, MARIE LOUISE (MRS. MILTON LLOYD MILLER), wholesale trade exec.; b. St. Louis, Aug. 29, 1924; d. Leo Sylvester and Elizabeth Mary (Ogden) La Blaine; grad. high sch.; m. Milton Lloyd Miller, Sept. 15, 1945; 1 dau., Mary Beth. IBM operator J.C. Penney Co., 1945-57; tng. personnel Internat. Shoe Co., Topeka, 1957; office mgr. Vulcan Corp., St. Louis, 1957-61; treas. World Tire Corp., St. Louis, 1961—; dir. Am. Brick Co. Served with USMCR, 1950-51. Mem. Data Processor Mgrs. Assn. Clubs: Midwest Sprots, Bellefontaine Country. Home: 10632 E Grantview Dr St Louis MO 63123 Office: 4156 Hoffmeister Rd St Louis MO 63125

MILLER, MARILYN EVELYN, educator; b. Canton, O.; d. Willard and Evelyn (Voss) Miller; B.S. cum laude, Kent State U., 1949, M.A., 1950; Ph.D., Ind. U., 1960. Mem. faculty U. Wis., Milw., 1957—, asso. prof. psychology, 1965-74, prof., 1974—, chmn. psychology dept., 1971—. Statis. cons. NIH grantee, 1965, 66; Nat. Inst. Child Health grantee, 1969. Mem. Am., Midwestern, Milwaukee County (pres. 1968-69) psychol. assns., Am. Assn. U. Profs., Sigma Xi, Psi Chi. Contbr. articles to profl. publs. Home: 1031 E Ogden Av Milwaukee WI 53202

MILLER, MARILYN JEAN (MRS. ALFRED A. HORMEL, JR.), artist; b. San Francisco, Nov. 12, 1925; d. Herbert Delmar and Helen (Reno) Miller; grad. Cal. Sch. Fine Arts, San Francisco, 1951; postgrad. Art Students League, N.Y.C., 1951-54; m. Alfred A. Hormel, Jr., Sept. 20, 1952; children—Richard Alfred, Phillip Christian, Quentin. Free-lance illustrator, working with numerous indsl. firms, advt. agys., mags. and book pubs., 1951—; exhibited lithography numerous group shows in mus. in San Francisco area, 1944-51, various galleries, N.Y.C. area, 1951—; one-woman show San Francisco Art Assn., 1959. Recipient prizes San Francisco Art Assn., 1950, Oakland (Cal.) Art Mus., 1950; represented in permanent collections Ford Motor Co., Albion Coll., Cedar Rapids (Mich.) Pub. Library, numerous pvt. collections; work featured in Am. Artist mag., 1954. Illustrator children's books, most recent being: Up from the Sea Came An Island, 1962; Mutiny in the Time Machine, 1963; Earthquake in Antioch, 1964; The Children of Long Ago Street, 1964; Hurricane Guest, 1964; Ice King, 1965; Gracie, 1965; The Fish in the Castle, 1965; The Dog That Watched the Mountain, 1967; May Day for Samoset, 1968; A Ghost Around The House, 1970; The Resident Witch, 1970; The Long Blonde Wig, 1970; The Tide, 1970; Uncle Morgan's Ghost, 1971, Naughty Little Pilgrim, 1971; Stars, 1972; The Witch Who Saved Halloween, 1972; Pilgrims to the Rescue, 1972; Pietro and Brother Francis, 1972; Wind is to Feel, 1973; The Vandals of Treason House, 1973; The Treasure of Kilvarra, 1973; The Watchcat, 1973; illustrator textbooks, and for various mags. including The Reporter, Saturday Rev., Reader's Digest, Good Housekeeping, Harpers, Esquire, Archtl. Record, Gourmet, This Week, N.Y. Times Sunday Mag. Home and studio: Curiosity Lane Weston CT 06883

MILLER, MARJORIE CAVINS LEEPER (MRS. EDWARD ERNST MILLER), educator, state legislator; b. Morgantown, W.Va., June 8, 1922; d. Lorimer V. and Neva (Adams) Cavins; student Spokane Jr. Coll., 1939-40, Morris Harvey Coll., 1940-41; B.A., U. Mich., 1944; M.A., U. Wis., 1962; m. Harry Dean Leeper, Nov. 5, 1944 (dec. 1954); children—Steven Lloyd, David Dean, Linda Jean, Kenneth Chandran; m. 2d, Edward Ernst Miller, May 12, 1963; stepchildren—Mark, Sterling, Jeffrey, Nancy, Randy. Teen-age program dir. Ann Arbor YWCA, 1944-45; married women's program dir. New Haven YWCA, 1945-46; teaching asst. U. Wis., Madison, 1957-60, asst. dean letters and sci., 1960-66, coordinator univ. religious activities, 1966—; mem. Wis. State Assembly, 1970—. Vice chmn. Dane County Democratic Com., 1967-68. Mem. adv. bd. U. Wis. YWCA. Mem. Assn. Coordinators Univ. Religious Activities, Student Personnel Club, Nat. Orgn. Women Legislators, New Dem. Coalition (nat. steering com.), Nat. Women's Polit. Caucus (nat. adv. com.). Methodist. Home: 1937 Arlington Pl Madison WI 53705

MILLER, MARJORIE MASON (MRS. HARLAND H. MILLER, SR.), pub. relations cons.; b. Birmingham, Ala., Sept. 13, 1913; d. Charles Edward and Blanche Marie (Wasson) Mason; student Tex. U. Women, 1932-33, U. Tex., 1934; B.A., U. Mo., 1935; postgrad. U. Houston, 1962; m. Harland H. Miller, Sr., Jan. 4, 1944; children—Harland Harold, Sarah Jane. News reporter Houston Chronicle, 1929-32, feature writer, 1957-60, publicity suburban press, 1961-62; pub. relations Houston YWCA, 1957-68; information officer Center Human Resources, U. Houston, 1969-70, cons. pub. relations, 1971—. Mem. Gov.'s Commn. on Status of Women in Tex., 1970-72. Mem. Women in Communications, Inc. (sec. Houston profl. chpt. 1966), Tex. Press Women, Inc. (dist. pres. 1972-74), Am. Assn. U. Women (legislative chmn. 1972-75, registered lobbyist), U. Mo. Alumni Assn. (pres. Houston br. 1957-59). Democrat. Club: Houston Press. Home: 2116 Bartlett St Houston TX 77006

MILLER, MARTINA M. CALIHAN (MRS. HAROLD CHALMERS MILLER), civic worker; b. Rochester, N.Y., May 12, 1914; d. Walter A. and Anne T. (Messer) Calihan; B.A., Vassar Coll., 1936; postgrad. Oxford U., 1936-37; m. Harold Chalmers Miller, Sept. 18, 1948; children—Anne (Mrs. Charles S. Arensberg), Elizabeth French. Bd. dirs. Jr. League Rochester, 1939-42, editor mag., 1940-42; bd. dirs. Jr. League Chgo., 1951-54, placement chmn., 1952-53, edn. chmn., 1953-54; mem. exec. com. Vol. Bur., Welfare Council Met. Chgo., 1953-55; bd. dirs. United Charities Chgo., 1953-63, chmn. nursery center counselling service, 1959-61; mem. women's aux. United Charities Chgo., 1953-71, mem. com. from agy. bd. to organize aux., 1954, bd. dirs., 1966-67; active Crusade of Mercy, 1963-68, chmn. women's spl. gifts, 1966; dir. communications Infant Welfare Soc. Chgo., 1972—. Bd. govs. St. Vincent's Orphanage, 1954-57. Served to lt. (j.g.) USNR, 1943-45. Recipient Distinguished Service award Met. Crusade of Mercy Chgo., 1965; named Woman of Day radio sta. WAIT, Chgo., 1968. Mem. Vis. Nurse Assn. Chgo. (mem. nurse's adv. com. 1968—, mem. exec. com. 1968-72, 2d. v.p. 1968-70, 1st v.p., 1970-72; chmn. coordinated home care com. 1968-69). Republican. Roman Catholic. Address: 1411 N State Parkway Chicago IL 60610

MILLER, MARY, educator; b. Lebanon, Ind., July 15, 1900; d. George T. and Lydia Ann (Etchison) Miller; student MacMurray Coll., 1918-20; A.B., U. Ill., 1923, M.A., 1924; grad. student Denver U., Mich. State U., U. Mich., Butler U. Tchr., English, head English dept. 1926-62, dir. dramatics Danville (Ill.) High Sch., 1926-61, asst. dir. Danville Jr. Coll., 1946-48, exec. dean, 1948-66, pres., 1966-72, pres. emeritus, 1972—; coordinator English, Jr. and Sr. High Schs., 1961-62. Pres., Danville Jr. Coll.-Community Symphony, 1973—. Named Danville Woman Yr., 1965; Boss of Yr., Danville br. Nat. Secs. Assn., 1970. Mem. Ill. Assn. Tchrs. English (pres. 1941), Danville Assn. Secondary Edn. (pres. 1949), Nat. Council Tchrs. English (com. mem.), Nat., Ill., Danville edns. assns., Am. Assn. U. Women, Ill. Assn. Jr. Colls. (sec.-treas. 1965-66), Vermilion County Mus. Soc., Ill. Assn. Women Deans, Danville Jr. Coll. Found. (exec. sec. 1972—), Delta Kappa Gamma, Alpha Psi Omega, Delta Delta Delta, Psi Iota Xi, Red Mask, Thespians (regional dir. 1959—). Club: Altrusa. Author plays: S'No Haven, 1954, Murder Walks Among Us, 1956, Remember the Mayne. Contbr. articles profl. jours. Home: 1618 N Vermilion Danville IL 61832

MILLER, MARY ALICE BOURNE, judge; b. Chgo., Jan. 26, 1922; d. Culvin Forde and Nila (Hunt) Bourne; student Central Coll., Fayette, Mo., 1938-40; LL.B., U. Mo., 1944; m. Orlando W. Miller, Nov. 2, 1952. Admitted to Mo. bar, 1944, Colo. bar, 1947, Alaska bar, 1956; practice law, Steamboat Springs, Colo., 1947-52, Fairbanks, Alaska, 1956-67; judge Alaska Dist. Ct., Fairbanks, 1967—. Mem. Alaska Bd. Parole, 1960-67; mem. standing com. on criminal procedure Alaska Supreme Ct. Mem. Muskox Service Area Commn., 1966-69, also sec.; mem. adv. bd. Fairbanks Rehab. Center; mem. Fairbanks Council on Alcoholism. Mem. Am., Alaska, Tanana Valley (pres. 1965-66) bar assns., Am. Judicature Soc., Nat. Council on Crime and Delinquency, Zonta Internat. Mem. P.E.O. Home: Red Fox Dr Box 5753 College AK 99701 Office: District Court 604 Barnette St Fairbanks AK 99701

MILLER, SISTER MARY AQUIN, former coll. pres.; b. Kewaskum, Wis., Feb. 12, 1904; d. Edward F. and Margaret (Mueller) Miller; B.S. magna cum laude, Marquette U., 1936; Ph.D., Cath. U. Am., 1943. Joined Order of Sisters of St. Francis of Assisi, Milw., 1929; tchr. St. Mary's Acad., Milw., 1932-39; faculty dept. biology Cardinal Stritch Coll., Milw., 1942-62, prof. biology, 1952-64, pres., 1955-74. Treas. Wis. Found. Ind. Colls., 1969-74. Recipient Gold Key scholarship award Marquette U., 1936. Mem. A.A.A.S., Delta Epsilon Sigma. Address: 6801 N Yates Rd Milwaukee WI 53217

MILLER, MARY FRANCES CECIL (MRS. SHANNON OSBORN MILLER, JR.), bus. exec.; b. Richards, Tex., June 11, 1919; d. Albert Nolan and Lynn (Wood) Cecil; student Victoria Jr. Coll., 1937; m. Shannon Osborn Miller, Jr., Apr. 7, 1944 (dec. 1960); children—Shannon Osborn III, Martha (Mrs. Joe Lane). Office mgr. Navarra Motors, Key West, Fla., 1945-49, Peebles Motor Co., South Norfolk, Va., 1949-52, Can. Dry Bot-tling Co., New London, Conn., 1952-55, Crippo Motor Co., 1955-57, Snelling Motor Co., Houston, 1957-60, Taylor Buick, Ft. Pierce, Fla., 1967-68; sec.-treas. Pores'

Inc., Ft. Pierce, 1960-67, Dave Snelling Lincoln-Mercury, Inc., Houston, 1968-71; office mgr. Leo Jarnagin Pontiac Co., Houston, 1971—. Named to 1st place in automobile accounting Ford Motor Co., Gen. Motors Corp., Chrysler Corp., Am. Motors, 1949-69. Presbyn. Club: Pelican Yacht. Home: 8354 Ruthby St Houston TX 77017 Office: 2600 Travis St Houston TX 77006

MILLER, MERRILY DALE DULMAN (MRS. EDWARD RICHARD MILLER), educator; b. Yonkers, N.Y., Mar. 3, 1943; d. Stanley and Pearl (Colin) Dulman; A.B., cum laude, Vassar Coll., 1965; M.A., Memphis State U., 1968; Ed.M., Tchrs. Coll., Columbia, 1972, Ed.D., 1974; m. Edward Richard Miller, Dec. 24, 1964. Grad. asst., dept. music Memphis State U., 1965-67; partner, Miller Mgmt., Memphis, 1965-68; tchr. spl. edn. Bd. of Edn., Yonkers, N.Y., 1968, tchr. emotionally disturbed, 1968-72; instr. Fairleigh Dickinson U. Coll. Edn., 1972-73, Tchrs. Coll., Columbia, 1973; coordinator ednl. services M.E.N.D. Center Human Devel., N.Y.C., 1973—; guest lectr. behavior modification Marymount Manhattan, 1973; participant workshops in behavioral observations for paraprofls., 1973—. Mem. Assn. N.Y. State Educators Emotionally Disturbed, Council for Exceptional Children, Fawn Ridge Civic Assn. Club: Westchester Vassar. Contbr. articles to profl. jours. Exptl. behavioral research in edn. Home: 19 Amherst Dr Yonkers NY 10710

MILLER, META HELENA, educator; b. Balt., Jan. 29, 1897; d. Charles A.A.J. and Mary (Bonnet) Miller; A.B., Goucher Coll., 1917; M.A., Johns Hopkins, 1919, Ph.D., 1922; postgrad. Columbia, Sorbonne; certificat d'etudes practiques de prononciation Institut de Phonetique, 1931. Instr. French Wells Coll., 1919-21; with U. N.C. at Greensboro, 1922—, successively asst. prof. romance langs., asso. prof., 1927-37, prof., 1937-66, prof. emeritus, 1966—, acting head dept., 1953-56, head dept., 1956-62; now tutor. Am. adviser Brit. U. summer schs., 1961—. Am. Aid to France, 1940-45. Mem. fgn. langs. com. N.C. Curriculum Study Com. Mem. Modern Lang. Assn., S. Am. Archaeol. Soc., World Federalists, Alliance French, Am. Assn. Tchrs. Spanish, N.C. Edn. Assn., Atlantic Modern Lang. Assn., Am. Assn. Tchrs. Francaise, Lutheran Acad. Scholarship, P.E.O., Kappa Kappa Gamma, Alpha Delta Pi, Tau Psi Omega. Democrat. Lutheran. Club: Johns Hopkins. Author: Chateaubriand and English Lit., 1925; (with Chinard, Gilbert, others) Les Natchez, 1932; (with Hooke, Malcolm) French Review Grammar, 1945. Home: 1908 Walker Av Greensboro NC 27403

MILLER, MILDRED, opera, concert singer; b. Cleve.; d. William and Elsa (Friedhofer) Mueller; Mus.B., Cleve. Inst. Music, 1946; artists' diploma, N.E. Conservatory Music, 1948; Mus.D. (hon.), Bowling Green U., 1960; hon. doctorate New Eng. Conservatory Music, 1966; m. Wesley W. Posvar, Apr. 30, 1950; children—Wesley William, Margot Marina, Lisa Christina. Operatic debut in Peter Grimes, Tanglewood, 1946; mem. N.E. Opera Theater, 1946-49, Stuttgart State Theater, Germany, 1949-50, Glyndebourne Opera, Edinburgh Festival, 1951, San Francisco Opera, 1960, Chgo. Lyric Opera, 1960, Cin. Zoo Opera, 1966, San Antonio Opera, 1968; debut as Cherubino in Figaro, Met. Opera, 1951, now mem. Met. Opera Assn., Vienna, Berlin, Munich, Frankfurt, Pasadena, Ft. Worth, Kansas City, Pitts., Tulsa, St. Paul opera cos.; radio debut Telephone Hour, TV debut Voice of Firestone, 1952; first film Merry Wives of Windsor, 1966; bd. dirs. Gateway To Music, Inc.; adv. bd. music dept. Bowling Green State U.; bd. dirs. Mendelssohn Choir, Pitts., Pitts. Ballet Theater. Recipient of Frank Huntington Beebe Award for study abroad, 1949, 50; Boston C. of C. award Outstanding Achievements in Field of Mus., 1959; Grand Prix du Disque for Songs of the Wayfarer, 1965; named 1 of outstanding women 1968 in Pitts., Pitts. Press and Pitts. Post-Gazette, Distinguished Dau. of Pa., 1972. Mem. Soc. Arts and Letters, Women's Assn. U. Pitts. (hon. pres.), Internat. Hugo Wolf Soc., Nat. Council Arts (music panel) Sigma Alpha Iota. Club: Tuesday Musical. Home: 718 Devonshire St Pittsburgh PA 15213 Office: Judd Concert Artist Bur 127 W 69th St New York City NY 10023

MILLER, MILDRED SAYRE, psychologist; b. Lockport, N.Y.; d. Edward Merritt and Mary Ella (Jones) Bunce; B.S., U. Wis., 1935, Ph.M., 1938; M.A., Columbia, 1949, Ed.D., 1950; m. Baxter Page Sayre (dec.); m. 2d, Harold Page Miller (dec.). Asst. to dean U. Chgo., 1938-43; dean of students Ariz. State U., 1943-52; dean of students, prof. psychology, 1952-58; psychologist, counselor trainer U. Cal. at Los Angeles, 1958—; psychologist El Camino Coll., 1960-67. Mem. Am. Psychol. Assn., Am. Personnel and Guidance Assn., Am. Acad. Polit. and Social Sci., N.E.A., Am. Assn. U. Women, A.A.A.S., Internat. Platform Assn., Kappa Kappa Delta, Alpha Delta Pi (Achievement award 1971), Kappa Delta Pi, Phi Delta Gamma, Pi Lambda Theta, Phi Upsilon Omicron. Clubs: Soroptimist, Zonta, Las Vecinas. Author articles profl. jours. Address: Riviera Village Redondo Beach CA 90277

MILLER, NAN COURTNEY, pub. relations co. exec.; b. La Crosse, Wis., Jan. 22, 1925; d. Henry Daniel and Winifred (McMahon) Miller; B.A., Northwestern U., 1957, J.D., 1961. Pres., Nan Miller Prodns. & Theatrical Agy., Denver, 1945-53; pres., chief exec. officer Nan Miller & Assos., Inc., Pub. Relations, Chgo., 1963—; Intercomco Internat., Inc., Chgo., 1971—. Recipient Service to Youth award YMCA Camp Channing, 1968. Mem. Chgo. Assn. Commerce and Industry, Pub. Relations Soc. Am., Premium Industry Club, Small Industry Council, Presidents Club, Publicity Club of Chgo., Public Safety Council (crime prevention com.), Phi Beta Kappa, Alpha Lambda Delta. Club: Executives (Chgo.). Home: 1444 W Cullom Chicago IL 60613 Office: 55 E Washington St Chicago IL 60602

MILLER, NANCY HUBER (MRS. WILLIAM CONRAD MILLER), journalist; b. Chambersburg, Pa., June 30, 1941; d. J. Lin and Blanche (Musselman) Huber; B.A., Pa. State U., 1962, M.A., 1969; m. William Conrad Miller, June 4, 1966; 1 son, Martin Huber. Teaching asst. dept. speech Pa. State U., 1962-64, radio/TV producer dept. pub. information, 1964—. Reporter, Voice of Am., 1973—. Mem. Am. Assn. U. Women, Mortar Board. Home: RD 1 Box 127 Bellefonte PA 16823 Office: 312 Old Main University Park PA 10802

MILLER, NORMA JEAN ROSS (MRS. ALDEN FRANK MILLER, JR.), civic worker; b. Butler, Pa., Oct. 3, 1920; d. William Bryson and Doris Mae (Ferguson) Ross; student spl. courses Pa. State U., 1944-46, Yale, 1954-57; m. Alden Frank Miller, Jr., Apr. 16, 1940; 1 son, Alden Frank III. Exec. mgr. Donora (Pa.) C. of C., 1950-57, Donora Community Chest, 1950-57; office mgr. Donora Golden Jubilee, 1951; staff writer Herald-Am., Donora, 1957, city editor, 1957-70; asso. editor Daily Herald, Donora, 1970-73. Mem. Mayor's Adv. Council, Donora, 1965-69, Citizens' Adv. Council, Donora, 1965-69. Mem. Donora Bd. Edn., 1954-60, pres., 1960; mem. Donora Borough Council, 1970-72. Bd. dirs. Mon Valley chpt. A.R.C., 1964—, sec. bd., 1966—; bd. dirs. Washington-Greene County Tourist Promotion Agy., 1970—, Washington County History and Landmarks Found. 1971—, Mon Valley council Camp Fire Girls, 1965—, Mon Valley Drug and Alcoholism Council, 1971—; bd. dirs. United Way Mon Valley, 1973—, chmn. pub. relations, 1973-74. Mem. Pa. Soc. Newspaper Editors, Pitts. Press Club, Donora C. of C. (pres. 1971-72), D.A.R. Mem. Order Eastern Star (worthy matron 1966-67), White Shrine of Jerusalem, Order of Amaranth (royal matron 1966, dist. dep.). Clubs: Donora Forecast (pres. 1962-63), Donora Unidon (pres. 1965-66, 56-57). Home: Overlook Terrace Donora PA 15033

MILLER, PATRICIA ALINE MIRMAN (MRS. DONALD LEE MILLER), occupational therapist; b. N.Y.C., Apr. 15, 1941; d. Cornelius Edward and Katherine (Steinfeld) Mirman; B.S., N.Y. U., 1962; m. Donald Lee Miller, Dec. 22, 1962; children—Alec, Nina Lynn. Mem. staff, supervising therapist Bronx (N.Y.) Municipal Hosp., 1962-64; pvt. practice as occupational therapist, Orleans, France, 1964-66; cons. occupational therapy Rofay Nursing Home, Bronx, 1967-69; cons. occupational therapy and activities program Park Av. Nursing Home, East Orange, N.J., 1968-69, Sarah Newman Nursing Home, Mamaroneck, N.Y., 1969-70; cons. occupational therapy and activities New Rochelle (N.Y.) Hosp. Med. Center, 1971—. Lectr., Jewish Home and Hosp. for Aged, N.Y.C., 1971-72. Mem. Am., N.Y. Met. Dist. occupational therapy assns. Home: 1 Durham Rd Larchmont NY 10538 Office: New Rochelle Hosp Med Center New Rochelle NY 10801

MILLER, RUTH LOUISE, found. exec.; b. Akron, O., July 11, 1915; d. Arthur W. and Elizabeth (Pfeiffer) Miller; B.S., U. Akron, 1939; M.A., Hartford Sem. Found., 1941. Nat. sec. girls missionary work United Brethren Ch., Dayton, O., 1942-46; coordinator non-Western dels. to World Conf. Christian Youth, Oslo, Norway, 1946-47; administrv. sec. Japan Internat. Christian U. Found., N.Y.C., 1948—, exec. dir., 1963—. Mem. Japan Soc. N.Y.C. Presbyn. Home: 180 West End Av New York City NY 10023 Office: 475 Riverside Dr New York City NY 10027

MILLER, RUTH MARY HELEN, physician, army officer, pianist; b. La Crosse, Wis.; d. Carl Frederick and Helen Adelaide (Klosheim) Miller; student Rosary Coll., 1936-38; B.A., U. Wis., 1941, M.D., 1945; postgrad. Los Angeles State Coll., 1956; certificate N.Y. Polyclinic Med. Sch. and Hosp., 1958; Ph.D., Belin U., 1959; m. William H. Ferguson, Mar. 28, 1943 (dec. Jan. 1944). Concert pianist throughout Mid-West, 1939-41; intern Goldwater Meml. Hosp., Welfare Island, N.Y.C., 1944-45, resident neurology, 1945-47; practice medicine, Avon Park, Fla., 1948-51, specializing in neurology and internal medicine, Fall River, Mass., 1959-66, Somerset, 1966—. Served to lt. col., M.C., 1951-55; now col. Army Res. ret.; hosp. comdr. 399th Evacuation Hosp., Taunton, Mass., 1970-71. Fellow Am. Coll. Angiology, Internat. Coll. Angiology, Am. Geriatrics Soc., Acad. Psychosomatic Medicine, Am. Coll. Emergency Physicians, Royal Soc. Health; mem. A.M.A., Am. Med. Womens Assn., Mass. Council Pub. Justice, Mass. Citizens Rights Assn., Assn. Mil. Surgeons, Internat. Platform Assn., Res. Officers Assn., WAC Vets Assn. (hon.), Rosary Coll. Alumnae Assn., U. Wis. Alumni Assn., Phi Sigma, Psi Chi, Alpha Epsilon Iota. Mem. Order Eastern Star, Order White Shrine. Home: 161 Johnson St Somerset MA 02726 Office: 161 Johnson St Somerset MA 02726

MILLER, SHARON ANN NINTEMAN (MRS. JOHN DENNIS MILLER), educator; b. Bakersfield, Cal., Feb. 2, 1938; d. Vincent John and Margaret Ann (McMullan) Ninteman; student Bakersfield City Coll., 1956-57; A.A., San Diego City Coll., 1958; B.A., Cal. State U., 1960; postgrad. Cal. Western U., 1961-66, Cal. State U., 1967-69, 72—; spl. edn. credential U. Cal. at Davis, 1972; m. John Dennis Miller, Nov. 26, 1969; stepchildren—Jonda, James. Asso. editor N. Shores Sentinel, San Diego, 1960-61; dist. dir. San Diego County council Camp Fire Girls, 1961-64, camp dir., 1967, coordinator devel. and information, 1964-69; partner Nugget Printing Co., Yreka, Cal., 1969—; spl. edn. tchr. Siskiyou County Schs., Yreka, Cal., 1970—. Mem. Save Our Wild Rivers, Siskiyou County, Yreka, 1971-72; mem. recreation com. Home of Guiding Hands, Santee, Cal., 1968-69; pub. relations chmn. Yreka Vols. for Handicapped People, 1970—; delegation leader Cultural Olympics of Internat. Olympics, U.S. State Dept., Mexico, 1968. Dir. news election survey for Reagan-Brown gubernatorial campaign San Diego County, 1966. Bd. dirs. Siskiyou Opportunity Center, 1971—. Mem. Am. Camping Assn. (pub. relations chmn. 1962-68), Childrens Home Soc. (mem. ways, means and publicity com. 1970—), Am. Assn. U. Women (corr. sec. 1972—), Women in Communications, Cal. Council for Exceptional Children. Home: 221 Wetzel Way Yreka CA 96097 Office: 317 W Miner St Yreka CA 96097

MILLER, SHARON KAY, educator; b. Cambridge, Md., Apr. 4, 1943; d. James Hugh Howard and Elsie Virginia (Campbell) O'Ferrall; B.S., Frostburg (Md.) State Coll., 1965; postgrad. Towson (Md.) State Coll., 1967—; m. James Goodwin Miller, Nov. 27, 1964; 1 son, William Jeffrey. Tchr., Norfolk (Va.) City Schs., 1966-67; tchr. Harford County (Md.) Schs., 1967—, Edgewood (Md.) Sr. High Sch., 1967—, coach girls' varsity field hockey, 1968—, coach, adviser high sch. gymnastics, 1969—. Chmn., Md. Dist. III Field Hockey Tournament, 1971-72; mem. Harford County Athletics Policies Legislative Com., 1973—. Mem. Harford County Edn. Assn. (bldg. rep. 1968-71, mem. pub. relations com. 1969-70, chmn. com. 1970-71, editor newsletter 1970-71), United Teaching Profession. Republican. Methodist. Home: 12 W Ring Factory Rd Bel Air MD 21014 Office: Edgewood Sr High School Edgewood MD 21040

MILLER, SHEILA REYNOLDS, lawyer; b. Hutchinson, Kan., Aug. 21, 1944; d. H. Newlin and Lois Alliene (Brickey) Reynolds; B.A. with distinction, U. Kan., 1966, J.D., 1971; postgrad. (Woodrow Wilson fellow), Harvard, 1966-67; m. Timothy Alan Miller, June 8, 1967. Admitted to Kan., Mo. bars, 1971; atty. Legal Aid Soc. of Greater Kansas City, Mo., 1971-73, Topeka, 1973—. Mem. Order of Coif. Home: Rural Route 1 Lecompton KS 66050 Office: 121 E 6th St Topeka KS 66603

MILLER, SHIRLEY UNGER (MRS. CARL B. MILLER), artist; b. N.Y.C., Jan. 3, 1918; d. William and Cecilia (Schatzman) Unger; certificate in Fine Arts Cooper Union, 1939; m. Carl B. Miller, Nov. 6, 1947. Free lance advt. artist, 1945-60; one woman shows at Aspects Gallery, N.Y.C., 1967, Peter Cooper Gallery, N.Y.C., 1968, Contemporary Arts Gallery, N.Y. U., 1970, Silvermine Guild, New Canaan, Conn., 1972, Roko Gallery, N.Y.C., 1971, 74, L.I. U., 1973; exhibited paintings and drawings in group shows at Butler Inst., Youngstown, O., 1967, Wadsworth Athenaem, Hartford, Conn., 1970-71; represented in permanent collections at Hudson River Mus., Yonkers, N.Y., Evansville Mus. of Art, Evansville, Ind., Rutgers U., New Brunswick, N.J. Recipient Newmasters award New Eng. Exhbn., 1966, Audubon Artists medal for oil, 1968, Medal of Honor, 1970. Mem. Nat. Assn. Women Artists. Address: 340 East 64th St New York City NY 10021

MILLER, SUNNE MAEDELL SENN (MRS. HYMAN PHILIP MILLER), pub. relations exec.; b. Fostoria, O., May 12, 1912; d. Jesse Frank and Della May (Myers) Senn; student Ohio State U., 1924-27; m. Hyman Philip Miller, Oct. 22, 1928; 1 son, Murray David. Mdse. control dept. F.R. Lazarus & Co., Columbus, O., 1926-29; optical asst. Gate City Optical, St. Louis, 1933-35; optical asst., reading instr. Dr. F.W. Staubach, Toledo, 1935-46; sta. mgr. WTOD, Toledo, 1946-60; editor Toledo Monitor, 1960-63, Sylvania (O.) Sentinel, 1964-67; exec. v.p. Thomas Hart Asso., Toledo, 1967—. Address: 338 N Erie St Toledo OH 43624

MILLER, VIRGINIA STAUB (MRS. HERMAN STUART MILLER), librarian; b. Hampstead, Md., May 13, 1909; d. John Henry and Ethel (Gettier) Staub; B.A., Coll. William and Mary, 1932; M.S., Columbia, 1940; m. Herman Stuart Miller, Oct. 16, 1966. Library asst. Med. Coll. Va., Richmond, 1932-43; head cataloger Coll. William and Mary, Williamsburg, Va., 1943-50; library asst. NASA, Langley Field, Va., 1950-60; head librarian U.S. Army Transp. Sch., Ft. Eustis, Va., 1960—. Recipient Civilian Meritorious award Dept. Army, 1961. Mem. Va. Library Assn., Spl. Libraries Assn. Home: 6 Shore Park Dr Newport News VA 23602 Office: US Army Transp Sch Fort Eustis VA 23604

MILLER, WILMA HILDRUTH, educator; b. Dixon, Ill., Mar. 8, 1936; d. William Alexander and Ruth Karin (Hanson) Miller; B.S., No. Ill. U., 1958, M.S., 1961; D.Ed., U. Ariz., 1967. Elementary tchr. pub. schs., Dixon, Ill., 1958-63, Tucson, Ariz., 1963-64; asst. prof. edn. Wis. State U., 1965-68; asso. prof. edn. Ill. State U., Normal, 1968-72, prof., 1972—; vis. prof. edn. Western Wash. State Coll., summer, 1970. Recipient citation of merit Internat. Reading Assn., 1968. Mem. Internat. Reading Assn., Am. Ednl. Research Assn., Nat., Ill. edn. assns., Ill. Assn. Higher Edn., Am. Assn. U. Profs. Author: The First R: Elementary Reading Today, 1972; Identifying and Correcting Reading Difficulties in Children, 1971; Elementary Reading Today, 1972; Diagnosis and Correction of Reading Difficulties in Secondary School Students, 1973. Home: 302 N Coolidge Normal IL 61761 Office: Illinois State University Normal IL 61761

MILLER, ZOYA DICKINS (MRS. HILLIARD EVE MILLER), civic worker; b. Washington, July 15, 1923; d. Randolph and Zoya Pavlovna (Klementinovski) Dickins; grad. Stuart Sch. Costume Design, Washington, 1942; student Sophie Newcomb Coll., 1944, New Eng. Conservatory Music, 1946; grad. Internat. Sch. Reading, 1969; m. Hilliard Eve Miller, Dec. 6, 1943; children—Jeffrey Arnot, Hilliard Eve III. Fashion coordinator, cons. Mademoiselle mag., 1942-43; instr. Stuart Summer Sch. Costume Design, Washington, 1942; fashion coordinator Julius Garfinckel, Washington, 1942-43; star TV show Cowbelle Kitchen, 1957-58, Flair for Living, 1958-59; model mags. and comml. films, also nat. comml. recs., 1956—; dir. program devel. Webb-Waring Lung Inst., Denver. Mem. exec. com. El Paso County Tb and Respiratory Disease Assn., 1954-63; chmn. radio and TV council Colo. Tb and Respiratory Disease Assn., 1963-68, mem. med. affairs com., 1965-72, pres., 1965-66, procurer found. funds, 1965-72; developer nat. radio ednl. prodns. for internat. use Nat. Tb and Respiratory Disease Assn., 1963-68, coordinator statewide screening programs Colo., other states, 1965-72; chmn. benefit fund raising El Paso County Cancer Soc., 1963; coordinator Colorado Springs Debutante Ball, 1967-72, Nat. Gov.'s Conf. Ball, 1969; chmn. Colo. Gov.'s Comprehensive Health Planning Council, 1967-72; chmn. Colo. Chronic Care Com., 1969-72, chmn. fund raising, 1970-72, chmn. spl. com. congl. studies on nat. health bills, 1971-72; mem. Colo.-Wyo. Regional Med. Program Adv. Council, 1969—; mem. Colo. Med. Found. Consumers Adv. Council, 1972—; mem. decorative arts com. Colorado Springs Fine Arts Center. Recipient James J. Waring award Colo. Conf. on Respiratory Disease Workers, 1963. Mem. Nat. (chmn. nat. father of year contest 1956-57), Colo., El Paso County (pres. 1954, TV chmn. 1954-59) cowbelle assns. Club: Broadmoor Garden (ways and means chmn. 1967-69, civic chmn. 1970-71, publicity chmn. 1972)(Colorado Springs, Colo.). Contbr. articles, lectures health care systems. Home: 74 Cheyenne Mountain Blvd Colorado Springs CO 80906

MILLICAN, HAVILAND HOUSTON (MRS. LAYTON WADE MILLICAN), assn. exec.; b. Fort Valley, Ga., July 11, 1931; d. Lawrence Edward and Etta Wylie (Carithers) Houston; A.B., Asbury Coll., 1952; M.C.E., Emory U., 1958; m. Layton Wade Millican, Nov. 20, 1965. Pub. sch. tchr., Thomasville, Ga., 1952-53; youth dir. Wesley Monumental Meth. Ch., Savannah, Ga., 1953-57; dir. Christian edn. Peachtree Rd. United Meth. Ch., Atlanta, 1958-63; asst. dir. student devel. Sch. Nursing, Emory U., Atlanta, 1963-65; dir. Christian Edn. Peachtree Rd. United Meth. Ch., Atlanta, 1965-71; exec. dir. YWCA, Atlanta, 1972—. Cons., Leadership Edn. and Devel., 1969-72. Bd. assos. Sch. Nursing, Emory U.; bd. dirs. Chs. Homes for Girls, Atlanta. Methodist (sec. bd. edn. N. Ga. conf. 1968-72, dir. Christian Educator's Fellowship 1968-72). Author: Teamwork Without Tears, 1968. Home: 411 Allison Dr NE Atlanta GA 30342 Office: 1027 Columbia Av NE Atlanta GA 30309

MILLIGAN, BARBARA WILLARD WORKING (MRS. RICHARD HARROLD MILLIGAN), psychologist; b. Palo Alto, Cal., June 7, 1927; d. Holbrook and Helen (Rider) Working; B.A. in Social Scis., Stanford, 1949; M.S. in Psychology, Cal. San Jose State U., 1970; m. Richard Harrold Milligan, Mar. 5, 1955; children—Brook Gunderson, Lyle Elizabeth, Cathlin Harrold. Sch. psychologist Union Sch. Dist., San Jose, Cal., 1970—. Mem. Am. Psychol. Assn., Cal. Assn. Sch. Psychologists and Psychometrists, Sierra Club, Nat. Audubon Soc. Editor Monthly Rev. Fed. Res. Bank San Francisco, 1952-56. Home: 4260 Pomona Av Palo Alto CA 94306 Office: 5175 Union Av San Jose CA 95124

MILLIGAN, IDA VICTORIA COLLINS (MRS. RANDOLPH HALL MILLIGAN), lawyer; b. N.Y.C.; d. Charles Henry and Ida Barbara (Baer) Collins; grad. Burdett Bus. Coll.; LL.B., Northeastern U., 1929; m. Randolph Hall Milligan, Dec. 31, 1942. Stenographer, bookkeeper First Ch. of Christian Scientist, Boston, 1918-48, also sec. to bd. trustees charitable instns. stenographer, State Library, Concord, N.H.; legal sec. Upton, Sanders & Upton, Concord, N.H., 1951-61; admitted to Mass. bar, 1931, N.H. bar, 1949; practiced in Newbury, N.H., to 1969. Mem. Republican State Constitutional Conv., 1964; mem. N.H. Legislature, 1965-66. Mem. Nat. Assn. Women Lawyers, OWLS (Women in Legislature), N.H. Bar Assn. Christian Scientist (trustee, pres., chmn. bd. 1959, 1st reader). Home: 618 SE 29th Terrace Ocala FL 32670

MILLIGAN, MARGARET MARY PETERS (MRS. CHESTER EDWARD MILLIGAN), bus. exec., city ofcl.; b. Chgo., Sept. 28, 1920; d. Martin John and Rose (Bloom) Peters; grad. high sch.; Certificate Bus. Adminstrn., YWCA, Chgo., 1941; Certificate Pub. Relations, Whittier (Cal.) Adult Edn., 1957; m. Irvin J. Steinert, Nov. 22, 1945 (div. Oct. 1957); children—Edward John, Donald Michael; m. 2d, Chester Edward Milligan, Oct. 10, 1958; stepchildren—Gary Lee, Gloria (Mrs. L. Dean McKee). Service rep. supr. Ill. Bell Telephone Co., Chgo., 1938-45; sec. to gen. mgr. Gen. Metals Corp., Los Angeles, 1953-55; pvt. sec. to 1st v.p. Nat. Screw & Mfg. Co., Los Angeles, 1955; office mgr. Electro Refractories and Abrasives Corp., Los Angeles, 1955-58; owner-mgr. Ka Ce Stock Farms, Tarzana, Cal., 1959—; mgr. Casa de Vida Lindley Apts., Encino, Cal., 1971—. Commr., Human Relations Comm., City of Los Angeles, 1968-71, pres., 1969-71, chmn. edn.-schs. subcom., chmn. procedures com., mem. budget com., 1968-69. Capt. Ill. Bell Telephone chpt. Women's Def. Corps Am., 1943-45; chmn. exec. bd. Mayor's Community Adv. Com., Los Angeles, 1968-69; chmn. bd. Career Training Program, Liaison League Rehab. Group, Inc., Sybil Brand Inst. for Women, Los Angeles County Sheriff's Dept., 1966-69; charter sec. Mass. Rapid Transit Devel. Found., Inc., So. Cal., 1965-68; mem. bd. United Way, Inc., 1965-66; city residential chmn. United Crusade, 1965; chmn. liaison unit subcom. Valleywide Better Govt. Com., 1964-67; mem. jr.

guild Inst. for Cancer and Blood Research, 1969-70. Mem. Republican Nat. Com., 1968-70; pub. relations chmn. Tarzana Rep. Women's Club, 1967-68. Recipient First Year Pioneer award Woodland Hills Freedom Season, 1961; Press Book and Press Clippings awards Sierra-Cahuenga dist. Cal. Fedn. Women's Clubs, 1963, 1st Place State Press Clipping award, 1963, 1st Place award for leadership and mblzn., 1964, Personal award Achievement, 1963-64, Certificate of Recognition Los Angeles Recreation Corps, 1964, Certificate of Appreciation Tarzana Kiwanis Club, 1964, Award of Merit Los Angeles County Bd. Suprs., 1965; named Woman of Year, Ven-Tar Bus. and Profl. Women's Club, 1963, Tarzana Bus. and Profl. Women's Club, 1965; recipient commendation Los Angeles City Council, 1964-65, Cal. Legislature, 1965, Mayor Sam Yorty, 1968; Mayor's City Seal award, 1968-69. Mem. Hall of Fame of the Trotter, Cal. Racing Hall of Fame (charter), Nat. Assn. Harness Drivers, Inc., U.S. Trotting Assn., Western Standardbred Assn., Cal. Horse Racing Assn., Ill. Racing Assn., Ill. Harness Horsemen's Assn., San Fernando Valley Pub. Relations Roundtable, Tarzana Bus. and Profl. Women's Club (pres. 1968-69), Asso. Chambers Commerce San Fernando Valley (2d v.p. 1965), Tarzana C. of C. (pres. 1964-65), Delphian Soc. Presbyn. Clubs: Tarzana (Cal.) Newcomers, Tarzana (Cal.) Woman's (mem. bd. 1962-65, 68). Author: The First Authentic History of Tarzana, 1963. Address: 5334 Lindley Av Apt 330 Encino CA 91316

MILLIKEN, HELEN WALLBANK (MRS. WILLIAM G. MILLIKEN), wife of gov. of Mich.; b. Denver, Dec. 4, 1922; d. Stanley Thomas and Nellie (Sillik) Wallbank; B.A., Smith Coll., 1945; m. William G. Milliken, Oct. 20, 1945; children—William G., Elaine. Wife of gov. of Mich. Chmn., Mich Artrain. Mem. Mich. Soc. Architects (hon.). Christian Scientist. Home: 6103 Peninsula St Traverse City MI 49684 Office: Governor's Residence Lansing MI

MILLIKEN, MARY ELIZABETH BATES, educator; b. Winston-Salem, N.C., Nov. 3, 1922; d. Howard Edward and Mattie Elfreda (Gammel) Bates; B.S., Duke, 1946; M.S., N.C. State U., 1966, Ed.D. (Nat. Def. Edn. Act fellow 1967-69), 1969; m. Harry Arthur Milliken, Apr. 22, 1947; children—Harry Arthur, Betty Jane (Mrs. Richard Honeycutt), Howard, Susan (Mrs. L.E. Mingledorff), Scott. Registered nurse, 1946-57; tchr., coordinator practical nurse edn. Raleigh (N.C.) Pub. Schs., also Holding Tech. Inst., 1957-64; curriculum specialist health occupations N.C. Community Coll. System, 1964-67; asso. prof. Marshall U., 1969-71; asst. prof. vocational edn. U. Ga., 1971—; cons. tchr. edn. for health profls.; project dir. numerous workshops, confs. in field. Mem. Am. Ednl. Research Assn., Am. Vocational Assn., Nat. League Nursing, Nat. Assn. Indsl. and Tech. Tchr. Educators, Am. Assn. Allied Health Professions Phi Kappa Phi, Epsilon Pi Tau. Author: Understanding Human Behavior: a Guide for Health Workers, 1969, 2d edit., 1974; Problems and Approaches in Student Evaluation, 1970. Contbr. articles to profl. jours. Home: 170 Holly Lane Athens GA 30601

MILLIKEN, MRS. PETER H. (SUSAN JOHNSTONE), govt. ofcl.; b. Woodstock, Conn.; d. Francis U. and Violet Floyd (Ward) Johnstone; A.B., Vassar Coll.; M.A., Columbia; m. Peter H. Milliken, Dec. 15, 1950; children—Peter H. III, Frances U. Johnstone. Chief statistician, research analyst E. W. Axe & Co., investment counsel, N.Y.C., 1940-42, 48-52; economist War Prodn. Bd., Washington, 1943-44; chief economist for sugar and allied products OPA, 1945-46; head sugar price control in U.S. and its possessions U.S. Dept. Agr., 1947; profl. genealogist, 1953—; tutor in statistics, math., French, econs. Columbia, 1962—; instr. math. N.Y. Bd. Edn., 1966—. Life mem. Gov. William Bradford Compact, editor bull., 1963-69. Mem. Colonial Dames Am. (docent, house com.), Soc. Daus. Holland Dames, N.Y. Geneal. and Biog. Soc. Episcopalian. Author articles in field. Home: 423 W 120th St New York City NY 10027 Office: 110 Livingston St New York City NY 11201

MILLMORE, ANNE OBREITER (MRS. ROBERT WALTER MILLMORE), investment analyst; b. Glen Ridge, N.J., Nov. 27, 1940; d. Joseph William and Gertrude Jean (Shafer) Obreiter; B.S., U. Vt., 1962; M.B.A., U. Pa., 1964; m. Robert Walter Millmore, Jan. 25, 1969. Mutual fund custodian New Eng. Mchts. Nat. Bank, Boston, 1962-63; computer programmer Prudential Ins. Co., Newark, 1965-67; investment analyst Nuveen Corp., brokerage, N.Y.C., 1967-68, Prudential Ins. Co., Newark, 1969—. Mem. N.Y. Soc. Security Analysts, N.Y. Consumer Analysts (Splinter group), Alpha Chi Omega. Club: Montclair (N.J.) Ski (treas. 1966-68, dir. 1968—). Home: 52 East Lake Blvd Morris Township NJ 07960 Office: Common Stock Dept 22 Plaza Newark NJ 07101

MILLS, AGNES (MRS. SAUL MILLS), painter, sculptor; b. Bklyn., Apr. 2, 1917; d. Herman J. and Celia (Ducoffe) Karlin; student Cooper Union Art Sch., 1934-38, N.Y. U., 1940-42; B.F.A., Pratt Inst., 1970; m. Saul Mills, July 16, 1938; children—Karen, Margret. Art tchr., art coordinator N. Shore Community Art Center, Great Neck, N.Y., 1958—; painter, sculptor, printmaker; exhibited in one-woman shows at Alfredo Valente Gallery, N.Y.C., North Truro Art Gallery, Cape Cod, Mass., Carus Gallery, N.Y.C., Harbor Gallery, Cold Spring Harbor, N.Y., Unitarian Soc., Manhasset, N.Y.; exhibited in group shows at Butler Inst. Am. Art, Bklyn. Mus., Smithsonian Instn., Pa. Acad., Audubon Soc., Pratt Graphics Art Center, Silvermine Art Guild, Seattle Art Mus., others; represented in permanent collections at Hunterdon County Art Mus., U. Me. Art Dept., C.W. Post Coll., Cal. Sch. Arts and Crafts, others; important sculptural works include Homage to Alwin Nikolais (plexiglass), Bird Form (welded steel), Icharus (bronze). Recipient Purchase prizes C.W. Post College., 1968, Wash. Soc. of Sculptors, Painters and Printmakers, 1970, U. Me., 1971, Nassau Community Coll., 1971, Hunterdon County Mus., 1970. Mem. Nat. Assn. Women Artists, Profl. Artists Guild, Experimenfs in Art and Tech., Women in Arts. Club: Print (Phila.). Address: 323 Melbourne Rd Great Neck NY 11021

MILLS, DALE DOUGLAS (MRS. WILLIAM RUSSELL MILLS), writer; b. Seattle, Oct. 4, 1930; d. Donald Emery and Antoinette (Kinleyside) Douglas; B.A., U. Wash., 1952; m. William Russell Mills, Aug. 13, 1955; children—Lida, William Russell, Peter, Jane. Reporter, Seattle Times, 1954-55, part-time 1972—; asst. librarian Harvard, 1955-56; free-lance nonfiction journalist Puget Soundings, Seattle Post Intelligencer, Seattle Times, 1967—. Mem. Citizens Com. for Sign Control, 1970-72. Research dir. Bruce Chapman City Council campaign, 1971. Bd. mgrs. King County Juvenile Ct.; trustee Allied Arts Seattle. Mem. Women in Communications, Wash. State Press Women (award for excellence in reporting 1972, 73), Kappa Kappa Gamma. Editor: Puget Soundings mag., 1968-70.

MILLS, KATHLEEN COVENTON (MRS. FRANCIS DONALD MILLS), educator; b. Port Angeles, Wash., Oct. 26, 1918; d. Harry and Edna (Burns) Coventon; B.A., U. Wash., 1960; M.A. (Teaching fellow), San Francisco State Coll., 1967; m. Francis Donald Mills, June 10, 1967; children by previous marriage—Kris Kauffman, Richard Kauffman, Kathy Kauffman. Tchr. Shoreline Sch. Dist., Seattle, 1958-73. Instr. Western Wash. State Coll., Bellingham, summers 1968-72; adult edn. tchr. and supr. family life Seattle Pub. Schs., 1955-58. Pres. Haller Lake Sch. P.T.A., Seattle, 1952-53; mem. Haller Lake Improvement Club, Seattle, 1949-73. Mem. Nat., Wash. edn. assns., Am. Assn. Mental Deficiency, Council Exceptional Children, Assn. Shoreline Spl. Edn. Tchrs. (pres. 1968-69). Home: 1746 N 128th St Seattle WA 98133 Office: Educational Service Center NE 158th and 20th Av NE Seattle WA 98155

MILLS, NELDA JO, librarian; b. Sylva, N.C., Aug. 1, 1947; d. Joseph Way and Willa Mae (Blanton) Mills; B.S. in Edn., Western Carolina U., 1969; postgrad. Appalachian State U., 1975. Asst. circulation librarian Hunter Library, Western Carolina Coll., 1969-70; asst. librarian Southwestern Tech. Inst., Sylva, 1970-71, librarian, 1971—. Mem. Am., N.C. library assns., Learning Resources Assn. N.C., Alpha Delta Kappa. Baptist. Home: Route 1 Box 346 Sylva NC 28779

MILLS, RUTH HARPER, govt. ofcl.; b. Seattle, Dec. 15, 1922; d. Robert W. and Agnes (Olsen) Harper; B.A., Mt. Holyoke Coll., 1943; postgrad. U. Louisville, 1961; m. C. Wright Mills, July 10, 1947 (div. June 1959); 1 dau. Kathryn. Tech. asst. Bell Telephone Labs., Inc., N.Y.C., 1943-45; exec. sec. N.Y. State League Women Voters, N.Y.C., 1946-47; with Bur. Census, U.S. Dept. Commerce, Washington, 1958—, survey statistician, 1958—. Huntington Hartford fellow, 1954. Recipient Silver Medal award U.S. Dept. Commerce, 1971. Mem. Am. Statis. Assn. Home: 7516 River Hill Rd Oxon Hill MD 20021 Office: Bur Census Washington DC 20233

MILLS, RUTH INA, educator; b. Pittsfield, Mass., Apr. 24, 1919; d. Emery James and Grace (Langdon) Mills; B.A., Rockford Coll., 1941; postgrad. U. Wis., 1942-43; M.Ed., Mass. State Tchrs. Coll., 1946; profl. diploma in edn. U. Conn., 1956; Ed.D., U. Md., 1959. Tchr. Central Jr. High Sch., Pittsfield, 1943-49, High Sch., Pittsfield, 1949-53; core curriculum specialist Pub. Jr. High Schs., Pittsfield, 1954-57; grad. asst. U. Md., College Park, 1958-59; asst. prof. edn. U. Wis., Milw., 1959-64; asso. prof. edn. Concord Coll., Athens, W.Va., 1964-68, prof. edn., 1968—. Instr. grad. program extension div. Marshall U., Huntington, W.Va., W.Va. U., Morgantown, 1967-73; adj. prof. W.Va. Coll. Grad. Studies, 1973—; cons., lectr. on Headstart, pre-school programs, core curriculum to profl., coll. and univ. groups, 1954—. Recipient Travel Grant Fund for the Advancement of Edn., 1953-54, fellowship Regional Council for Internat. Edn., 1963. Mem. N.E.A., Nat. Soc. for Study Edn., Nat. Conf. Core Tchrs. (dir. 1958-61), Council for Basic Edn., Internat. Platform Assn., Delta Kappa Gamma (pres. local chpt.). Author: So You Don't Want to Raise a Brat!, 1971. Contbr. articles to profl. jours. Home: 215 Vermillion St Athens WV 24712

MILLSOM, CAROL ANN, educator; b. Cleve., Feb. 10, 1935; d. Alfred Leroy and Lucy Frances (Burnham) Millsom; B.S., Carnegie Mellon U., 1957; M.S., Cornell U., 1960, Ph.D. (Nat. Inst. Mental Health fellow), 1965. Sr. lectr. Specialist Tng. Coll., Winneba, Ghana, West Africa, 1965-66; asst. prof. N.Y. U., 1966-69, asso. prof. edn., 1969-72; asso. prof. edn. U. Mich., Ann Arbor, 1972—. Cons. to C.C. Bd. Edn., also pub. cos. Contbr. articles to profl. jours. Home: 1249 Island Dr Ann Arbor MI 48105

MILLSOP, LILLIAN ARLIE, educator; b. Sharon, Pa., Aug. 6, 1932; d. Thomas Charles Fremont and Adah Viola (Schaller) Millsop; B.S., Edinboro State Tchrs. Coll., 1954; M.Ed., Pa. State U., 1957; postgrad. Ind. U., 1962—. Tchr., Sharon (Pa.) City Schs., 1954—. Tchr. Shenango Valley campus Pa. State U., 1959-71, Thiel Coll., Greenville, Pa., 1971-73. Mem. Right to Read Task Force, 1972—; sec. Sharon Tchrs. Assn., 1955-56, treas., 1956-58, pres. elect, 1958-59, pres., 1959-60; recording sec. Mercer County Coordinating Council, 1959-62. Grantee Center Applied Linguistics, 1968-69. Mem. N.E.A. (life), Nat. Soc. Study Edn., Pa. State Edn. Assn., Internat. (pres. Shenango council 1972-73), Keystone State (recording sec. 1973-74) reading assns. Republican. Mem. Christian Ch. (mem. Christian Edn. com. 1969—, deaconess 1964—). Club: College (Sharon). Home: 1324 Stanton St Sharon PA 16146 Office: Sharon Jr High Sch Case Av Sharon PA 16146

MILLSPAUGH, DORIS HAZEL RINTELMANN (MRS. ABBOTT MILLSPAUGH), editor; b. Milw., Dec. 17, 1916; d. Walter J. and Elsa (Gathmann) Rintelmann; grad. Prospect Hall Secretarial Sch., 1939; m. Abbott Millspaugh; children—Susie M. (Mrs. Richard Trudeau), Judy M., Doris A. (Mrs. Michael Connell). Tchr. piano, Milw., 1933-39; sec. to dir. Bobley Pub. Corp., Glen Cove, N.Y., 1960-67, sec. to dir., asso. editor, dir. consultation, research dept. Illus. World Ency., Woodbury, N.Y., 1966—. Asso. editor, staff writer, music book library Magnus Organ Corp., 1972—. Office: 311 Crossways Park Dr Woodbury NY 11797

MILMAN, DORIS HOPE (MRS. NATHAN KREEGER), physician; b. N.Y.C., Nov. 17, 1917; d. Barnet S. and Rose (Smoleroff) Milman; B.A., Barnard Coll., 1938; M.D., N.Y.U., 1942; m. Nathan Kreeger, June 15, 1941; 1 dau., Elizabeth Rose. Intern, resident Jewish Hosp., Bklyn., 1942-48; practice medicine, specializing in child and adolescent psychiatry, Bklyn., 1948-70; mem. staff Jewish, Jewish Chronic Disease, Maimonides, Kings County hosps.; asso. prof. pediatric psychiatry Downstate Med. Center, 1964-73, prof., 1973—, acting chmn. dept. pediatrics, 1973—; asso. Kings County Hosp., 1956-73, chief-of-service pediatrics, 1973—; chief-of-service State U. N.Y. Hosp., 1973—. Fellow Am. Acad. Pediatrics; mem. Kings County Med. Soc., Bklyn. Psychiat. Soc., N.Y. Pediatric Soc., Bklyn. Acad. Pediatrics, Am. Psychiat. Assn. Home: 126 Westminster Rd Brooklyn NY 11218 Office: 450 Clarkson Av Brooklyn NY 11203

MILNE, MARGERY (MRS. LORUS J. MILNE), lectr., author; b. N.Y.C.; d. S. Harrison and Beatrice (Gutman) Greene; A.B., Hunter Coll., 1933; M.A., Columbia, 1934; M.A., Radcliffe Coll., 1937, Ph.D., 1939; research study Woods Hole Marine Labs., Scripps Instn. Oceanography, field study N. and Central Am., Panama, Dutch Guiana and Caribbean Islands, Africa, also Europe, Near East, Southeast Asia, New Zealand and Australia.; m. Lorus J. Milne, Sept. 10, 1939. Instr. biology U. Me., 1936-37, Randolph-Macon Woman's Coll., 1938-39; asst. prof. William and Mary Coll., 1941-42, Beaver Coll., 1942-47, U. Pa., 1943-44, U. Vt., 1947-48, U. N.H., 1948-50; asso. prof. State Coll., Fitchburg, Mass., 1955-56; vis. prof. Northeastern U., 1958, Wesleyan U., 1961; cons.-writer biol. scis. curriculum study, U. Colo., 1960, leader (sci. writing), 1962, 67; cons.-writer Dept. Edn., New Zealand, 1966; lectr., 1948—; lectr. U. N.H., 1967—; vis. prof. environmental scis. Fla. Internat. U., 1974. Recipient Geo. Westinghouse Sci. Writing award, 1947, Nash Conservation award, 1954, Saxton lit. fellowship, 1954, U.S.-S. Africa Leader Exchange fellowship, 1959, research grants from Sigma Xi, Am. Philos. Soc., Am. Acad. Arts and Sci. Mem. Phi Beta Kappa, Sigma Xi, Phi Sigma. Author (with husband): A Multitude of Living Things, 1947; Famous Naturalists, 1952; The Biotic World and Man, 1952; The Mating Instinct, 1954; The World of Night, 1956; Paths Across the Earth, 1958; Animal Life, 1959; Plant Life, 1959; The Balance of Nature, 1960; The Lower Animals, 1960; The Mountains, 1962; The Senses of Animals and Men, 1962; The Valley: Meadow, Grove and Stream, 1963; Because of a Tree, 1963; Growth and Age, 1964; Water and Life, 1964; The Crab That Crawled Out of the Past, 1965; Gift From the Sky, 1967; Living Plants of the World, 1967; Patterns of Survival, 1967; The Ages of Life, 1968; The Phoenix Forest, 1968; The Nature of Animals, 1969; North American Birds, 1969; When the Tide Goes Far Out, 1970; The Nature of Life, 1970; The Cougar Doesn't Live Here Any More: Does the World Still Have Room for Wildlife?, 1971; The Nature of Plants, 1971; The Arena of Life: The Dynamics of Ecology, 1972; The How and Why of Growing, 1972; Invertebrates of North America, 1972; The Animal in Man, 1973; also articles in field. Home: 1 Garden Lane Durham NH 03824

MILNER, DOROTHY SOULE, occupational therapist; b. Syracuse, N.Y., Jan. 28, 1940; d. Benjamin Charles and Dorothy Bigelow (Soule) Milner; Asso. Applied Sci., Briarcliff Coll., 1960; B.S., Columbia, 1963. Staff occupational therapist Duke U. Med. Center, Durham, N.C., 1963-66; sr. therapist U. Fla. Med. Center, Gainesville, 1966-67; sr. therapist Inst. Rehab. Medicine, N.Y. U. Med. Center, N.Y.C., 1967—, supr. prevocational evaluation, 1967—. Club: New York Briarcliff Coll. Alumnae (pres. 1972-75). Home: 340 E 74th St New York City NY 10021 Office: Inst Rehab Medicine NY U Med Center 400 E 34th St New York City NY 10016

MILNER, MARGARET BEVERLY WIEBUSCH (MRS. JAMES WILBOURNE MILNER), civic worker; b. Waco, Tex.; d. Arthur Casper and Ada Margaret (Rogers) Wiebusch; A.B. cum laude, Baylor U., 1936, M.A. cum laude, 1938; postgrad. U. Heidelberg, 1946-47, U. Mich., 1952-54; m. James Wilbourne Milner, Apr. 5, 1941; children—Mary Margaret (Mrs. John Lawrence Richardson), James Wilbourne (dec.). High sch. tchr., Tex., 1936-41; asst. English dept. Baylor U., 1936-38. Chmn. blood bank service A.R.C., West Point, N.Y., 1949-52; council pres. Girl Scouts U.S.A., Ft. Sill, Okla., 1956-57; mem. Laubach Lit. Council, Washington, 1962—; mem. Army Distaff Aux. Com., 1961—; mem. women's council Internat. Christian Leadership, 1962—; mem. Internat. Prayer Fellowship Council, Lake Junaluska, N.C., 1969—. Trustee, Hope Valley Camp, Washington. Recipient Thanks badge Girl Scouts U.S.A. Mem. Women's Soc. Christian Service (hon. life), Young Life Bd. No. Va., D.A.R. (nat. mem.-at-large), Order of St. Luke, Ednl. Communications Assn. (coordinator cons. com.), Salvation Army Aux., Kappa Delta Pi, Beta Pi Theta, Kappa Epsilon Alpha, Alpha Chi. Methodist (mem. ofcl. bd. 1963—, mem. commn. on missions 1964—). Clubs: Army Research and Development Wives (pub. relations chmn. 1963-64). Capital Speakers, Washington. Home: 3830 N Woodrow St Arlington VA 22207

MILNER, VIRGINIA VAN NUYS VOORHIES (MRS. RICHARD PIERCE MILNER), physician; b. Rockwell City, Ia., July 16, 1912; d. Gilbert and Edna (Van Nuys) Voorhies; B.S. cum laude, Parsons Coll., 1934; M.D., U. Ia., 1937; m. Richard Pierce Milner, Sept. 12, 1941; children—Virginia (Mrs. Robert Edward Garlitz), Richard Pierce, Marilyn (Mrs. Steven Warren Kline). Intern, Passavant Hosp., Pitts., 1937-38; resident Woman's Hosp., N.Y.C., 1938-39; staff physician Bklyn. Cottage Hosp., Dixon, N.M., 1939-40, Embudo Presbyn. Hosp., Embudo, N.M., 1940-41; practice medicine specializing in gen. practice and obstetrics, Albuquerque, 1941—; mem. staffs St. Joseph's, Presbyn. hosps., Albuquerque; med. adv., camp physician Camp Fire Girl Resident Camp, Cuba, N.M., 1958-59; bd. dirs. Visiting Nurse Service, 1964-66. Mem. Am. Bd. Family Practice, Am. Acad. Gen. Practice, N.M., Albuquerque Bernalillo County med. socs., Med. Soc. U.S. and Mexico, Inter Acad. Metabology, Am. Heart Assn., N.M. Mus. Found., Assn. Indian Affairs, N.M. and Albuquerque Opera Guild, N.M. Synodical Soc., P.E.O. (pres. 1949). Presbyn. (pres. women's orgn. 1954-55). Club: Altrusa. Home: 3600 Mackland St NE Albuquerque NM 87110 Office: 106 Girard St SE Albuquerque NM 87106

MILOTTE, ELMA MOORE JOLLY (MRS. ALFRED GEORGE MILOTTE), motion picture producer; b. Seattle, July 1, 1907; d. Elmer Ellsworth and Eva E. (Moore) Jolly; B.A. in Edn., U. Wash., 1930; m. Alfred George Milotte, June 15, 1934. Tchr. high sch., Orting, Wash., 1930-32, Dryden, Wash., 1933-34; owner photographic studio, Ketchikan, Alaska, 1934-39; assisted husband in photography and lecturing with nature films, 1939-42, 66-68; asst. in filming true life adventures Walt Disney Prodns., Burbank, Cal., 1946-57; ind. producer TV commls. and children's nature films Milotte Prodns., Sumner, Wash., 1958—. Asst. curator photography U. Puget Sound Museum Bd., 1970—. Mem. Soc. Women Geographers, Phi Sigma, Delta Zeta. Christian Scientist. Author: (with Alfred Milotte) The Story of An Alaskan Grizzly Bear, 1969. Home: 9710 Angeline Rd E Sumner WA 98390

MILSTEAD, AGNES MCDOW (MRS J.B. MILSTEAD), educator, librarian; b. Covington, Tenn., July 23, 1915; d. John Bernard and Onie (Adkins) McDow; B.A., U. Wyo., 1959; M.S., La. State U., 1966; m. Henry T. Bigelow, Sept. 7, 1936 (dec. Dec. 1959); 1 son, John Henry; m. 2d, J.B. Milstead, Apr. 12, 1960 (dec. May 1969). Elementary sch. tchr. Laramie County, Wyo., 1953-59, Cheyenne, Wyo., 1959-60; librarian Ouachita Parish, Sterlington, La., 1960-66; asst. prof. library sci. U. Wyo., Laramie, 1966—. Mem. N.E.A., Assn. for Supervision Tchr. Edn., Am. Wyo., Mountain Plains (chmn. sch. and children's sect. 1972) library assns., Am., La. (pres. 1965-66), Wyo. (pres. 1969-70) assns. sch. librarians, Wyo. Edn. Assn., Kappa Delta Pi, Phi Kappa Phi. Democrat. Baptist. Mem. Order Eastern Star. Contbr. articles to profl. jours. Home: 321 S 13th St Laramie WY 82070

MILTON, DIXIE TYLER, librarian; b. Boston, Aug. 17, 1910; d. John William and Emma Ray (Tyler) Milton; B.S., Tex. State Coll. for Women, 1941, postgrad., 1952-53; postgrad. Baylor U., 1950-52. Librarian Garden City (Tex.) High Sch., 1940-41; librarian Army Air Force, Waco, Tex., 1942-46; catalog librarian Waco Pub. Library, 1947-49; cataloger area library Mo. State Library, Jefferson City, 1949-50; order librarian Baylor U., Waco, Tex., 1950-53; librarian, curator Masonic Grand Lodge Library and Museum, Waco, 1953—. Cons. librarian Lee Lockwood Scottish Rite Library and Museum, 1970—. Mem. A.L.A., Spl. Libraries Assn., Tex. Mus. Assn., Oral History Assn. Republican. Baptist. Home: 4108 Sherry Lane Waco TX 76711 Office: 715 Columbus St Waco TX 76703

MILTON, ELIZABETH NASIF, recreation dir.; b. Birmingham, Ala., Dec. 14. 1927; d. Nasif Elias and Mary (Harika) Milton; B.S., Ala. Coll., 1950; M.A., Columbia U., 1959. Tchr., Sacred Heart and Mt. Carmel High Schs., New Orleans, 1950-52; program dir. YWCA, New Orleans, 1952-62; recreation and camp dir. Kingsley House, New Orleans, 1962—. Recreation cons. to various agencies and groups. Fellow A.A.H.P.E.R.; mem. Nat., La. (mem. research com. 1972-73) recreation and park assns., Am. Camping Assn. Democrat. Club: Syrian, Lebanon, American (New Orleans). Home: 1831 Bordeaux New Orleans LA 70115 Office: 914 Richard New Orleans LA 70130

MILUSCHEWA, SIMA, mech. engr.; B.S. in Mech. Engring.; M.S. in Mech. Engring., Newark Coll. Engring., 1955. Design engr. design and devel. dept. Westinghouse Electric Co., Bloomfield, N.J., 1951-56; project engr. aero. group Research div. Curtiss-Wright Co., Clifton, N.J., 1956-58; space systems specialist advanced systems operations analysis group Astro-Electronics div. RCA, Princeton, N.J., 1958-68; sr. scientist, advanced concepts group Grumman Aerospace Corp., Bethpage, L.I., N.Y., 1968—. Recipient Salute to Women in Elec. Living award for space vehicle design work, Elec. Women's Round Table, Inc., 1963. Mem. Am. Soc. M.E., Am. Inst. Aeros. and Astronautics, Am. Geophys. Union, Soc. Women Engrs.

MIMS, HARRIET MARTHA, lawyer; b. Phila., Sept. 7, 1915; d. John Andrew and Louise (McCullough) Mims; B.S., Temple U., 1937; M.A., U. Pa., 1942, J.D., 1949. Admitted to Pa. bar, 1950, Supreme Ct. Pa. bar, 1951; individual practice law, Doylestown, Pa., 1950—. County clk. Criminal Cts., Doylestown, 1972—. Served with WAC, 1942-46. Home and office: 460 Pebble Hill Rd Doylestown PA 18901

MIMS, NANCY CROCKETT (MRS. MATTHEW HANSFORD MIMS), editor, librarian; b. Stony Point, Tenn., Nov. 6, 1909; d. Stuart Raper and Marie Langley (Ramsey) Crockett; A.B., Agnes Scott Coll., 1931; grad. study Grensboro Coll. for Women, 1932; m. Charles R. McCarty, Dec. 27, 1933 (dec. Mar. 1936); m. 2d, Matthew Hansford Mims, Feb. 21, 1940; children—Julian Landrum III, Matthew Hansford, Marie Crockett. Tchr. English dept. Waynesville (N.C.) High Sch., 1931-33, Wilkes County (Ga.) pub. schs., 1935-37, Edgefield High Sch., 1937-39, Franklin (N.C.) High Sch., 1939-40; editor Edgefield Advertiser, county weekly, 1942-45, Johnston Herald, 1942-45, Palmetto White Ribbon, W.C.T.U. publ., 1945—; corr., feature writer Augusta (Ga.) Chronicle, Augusta (Ga.) Herald, 1949—, Columbia (S.C.) Record, 1949-59; head librarian Edgefield County Aiken-Barnwell-Edgefield Regional Library, 1958—. Dir. Civic League Courtesy Center, 1967—. South Carolina exec. dir. Nat. Library Week, 1967; Edgefield County chairman of Tricennten. Chmn. bd. trustees D. A. Tompkins Meml. library, 1943—; Edgefield County chmn. White House Conf. on Children and Youth, 1960. Vice chmn. County Dem. conv., 1956. Recipient spl. grant Porter Fleming Found., 1964, Community Leader of Am. award, 1968. Mem. Edgefield County Hist. Soc. (sec. 1960—), S.C. Library Assn. (sec. pub. library sect. 1960-61), Caroliniana Soc., Clan Campbell Am., D.A.R. (chpt. regent 1964-66), Daus. Colonial Wars, Daus. Am. Colonists, Nat. Soc. So. Dames Am., U. Archives Inst., S.C. Geneal. Soc., Clan Buchanan. Contbr. Chronicle Sunday Mag., 1953-55. Home: 610 Buncombe St Edgefield SC 29824

MIMS, ROSETTA JOHNSON (MRS. ALEX LOUIS MIMS), educator; b. Birmingham, Ala., Oct. 18, 1942; d. Edward and Erma Bell (Sledge) Johnson; B.S., Ala. State U., 1964, postgrad., 1973; postgrad. U. South Ala., 1970; m. Alex Louis Mims, Dec. 30, 1968. Second grade tchr. Birmingham (Ala.) City Schs. Systems, 1965-66; kindergarten tchr. Troy (Ala.) City Schs., 1966-68; first grade tchr. Mobile (Ala.) Pub. Sch. System, 1968—. Mem. N.E.A., Ala., Mobile County edn. assns., Fedn. Women's Clubs. Roman Catholic. Club: Kosmos Social (Mobile). Home: 641 S Wasson St Whistler AL 36612 Office: Calcedeaver Sch Mt Vernon AL 35592

MINDEL, TOBY MATHILDE HEIMAN (MRS. SAM ARTHUR MINDEL), ednl. adminstr.; b. Tarrytown, N.Y.; d. Ezidor Levi and Rose (Sussman) Heiman; B.A., Wayne State U., 1954, M.Ed., 1956, Ed.D., 1964; postgrad. (W. T. Grant fellow) Merrill Palmer Inst., 1965-66; m. Sam Arthur Mindel, June 5, 1939 (dec. Nov. 1948); 1 son, Joel Phillip. Kindergarten tchr. Detroit Pub. Schs., 1950-59, guidance counselor, 1960-66, adminstr. guidance and counseling dept., 1966-71; dir. GED Testing Service, 1971—. Vis. prof. Cal. State Coll., 1962, 63. Vice-pres. exec. bd. YWCA, Detroit, 1969. Fellow Detroit Round Table Catholics and Jews; mem. Pi Lambda Theta. Home: 8801 Kingswood St Detroit MI 48221 Office: 10100 Grand River Av Detroit MI 48204

MINDELL, DORIS, lawyer; b. Bklyn., Apr. 6, 1922; d. David and Pauline (Isaacs) Friedman; student Bklyn. Coll., 1937-40; J.D., U. Ariz., 1963; m. Robert E. Mindell, Oct. 1, 1940; children—Alan, Gerald, Paula. Retail buyer Levy's Dept. Store, Tucson, 1950-54; admitted to Ariz. bar, 1963; practiced law, Tucson, 1963-65; research atty. Ct. of Appeals, Tucson, 1965—. Vice pres. Pantano Republican Women, Tucson, 1972-74; mem. Pima County Rep. Club, 1970—. Mem. adv. bd. Awareness House, 1969-70. Recipient Am. Jurisprudence Book awards, 1962-63; Estate Planning award So. Ariz. Bank, 1963; Lawyers Title Ins. award, 1963. Mem. Am., Pima County (sec., treas. 1973-74) bar assns., Kappa Beta Pi. Home: 3722 E 4th St Tucson AZ 85716 Office: 415 W Congress Tucson AZ 85701

MINER, FRANCES MESSERSMITH, ret. curator, educator; b. Plainfield, N.J., Apr. 23, 1905; d. Ralph Kinney and Charlotte (Messersmith) Miner; A.B., Smith Coll., 1927; M.A., N.Y.U., 1942. Dir. Girl Scouts U.S.A., Elmira, N.Y., 1927-30; instr. Bklyn. Bot. Garden, 1930-37, 38-45, curator instrn., 1945-73; ret., 1973; field rep. Childrens Gardens, Nat. Recreation Assn., 1937-38. Recipient Smith Coll. medal, 1964, citation Am. Hort. Soc., 1968. Mem. Am. Assn. Bot. Gardens and Arboreta (dir. 1966-69), Bus. and Profl. Womens Club (pres. 1943-45), Delta Kappa Gamma. Mem. Christian Ch. Author: Adventure Book of Growing Plants, 1959. Contbr. articles to profl. jours. Home: 88 Morningside Dr New York City NY 10027

MINER, KATHERINE DELARYE (MRS. ARTHUR D. MINER), educator; b. Houghton, Mich., July 28, 1908; d. Angus Ronald and Victoria (Priniski) MacDonald; B.S., No. Mich. U., 1940; M.A., U. Mich., 1950; m. Arthur D. Miner, Mar. 1, 1952; 1 son, David M. Delarye. Tchr., Sault Ste. Marie, Mich., 1940-47, Flint, Mich., 1947-50; audiologist Sch. for the Deaf, Flint, 1950-54; tchr. Cal. Sch. for the Deaf, Riverside, 1954-55; cons. hearing Oakland County, Mich., 1955-56; tchr. Portland (Ore.) Oral Deaf, 1956-62; asso. prof. spl. edn. Kent (O.) State U., 1962—. Mem. Council of Exceptional Children, A.G. Bell Assn. for Deaf, Am. Instrs. of Deaf, Mu Iota Sigma. Home: 3267 Sandy Lake Rd Ravenna OH 44266 Office: Kent State University Kent OH 44242

MINER, LISBETH (MRS. ALASDAIR WILLIAM SPENS-THOMSON), writer, photographer; b. Litchfield, Conn., Oct. 14, 1915; d. Ellsworth Frost and Mary Helen (Kennard) Miner; B.A., Ohio Wesleyan U., 1937; postgrad. N.Y. U., 1938, U. Conn., 1973; m. Alasdair William Spens-Thomson, Sept. 19, 1949; children—Alasdair William, Shena Elisabeth. Free lance writer and photographer, 1937—; woman's editor Soundings Mag., Wethersfield, Conn., 1964—. Part time tchr. lang. arts and communications in various secondary schs., 1966—. Established Small Craft Safety Program, Norwalk (Conn.) Youth, 1961. Recipient certificate of Appreciation, USCG, 1972; Dir.'s award certificate merit Nat. Assn. Engine and Boat Mfrs., 1973. Mem. League Women Voters (dir. 1956-57), Women in Communications, U.S. Power Squadrons, N.Am. Yacht Racing Union, Long Island Sound Yacht Racing Assn. Episcopalian. Contbg. editor: Small Boat World Mag., 1972—. Home and office: Sylvester Ct East Norwalk CT 06855

MINER, RUTH, lawyer, educator; b. Galesburg, Ill., May 29, 1920; d. A. Burns and Anna Lee (Dilworth) Miner; A.B., Knox Coll., 1941; M.A., U. Ill., 1951; J.D., U. Chgo., 1953; postgrad. London Sch. Econs., 1965, Acad. Internat. Law, The Hague, 1965. Tchr. high sch., 1946; tng. officer VA, 1947-49; admitted to Ill. bar, 1953, Fed. bar, 1955; editor Commerce Clearing House, 1953-54; with Chgo. br. Fidelity & Deposit Co. Md., 1954-57; mem. faculty U. Wis., Whitewater, 1958—, asso. prof. polit. sci., 1962-74, prof., 1974—, internat. student adviser, 1962-66. Alternate del. Dem. Nat. Conv., 1972. Served with WAVES, 1943-45. Mem. League Women Voters. Home: 327 Ann St Whitewater WI 53190

MINER, SANDRA, physician; b. Walla, Walla, Wash., Apr. 12, 1939; d. James Harvey and Helen (Grams) Miner; B.A., Whitman Coll., 1961; M.D., Med. Coll. Pa., 1965. Intern, Virginia Mason Hosp., Seattle, 1965-66; resident Fresno (Cal.) Gen. Hosp., 1966-67, Kaiser Found Hosp., San Francisco, 1967-68; fellow City of Hope Med. Center, Duarte, Cal., 1968-69; practice medicine specializing in pediatrics, San Diego, 1969—; mem. staffs Mercy, Sharp Meml., Children's, University hosps.; pediatrician Rees Stealy Med. Clinic, San Diego, 1969-72. Mem. A.M.A., Cal. Med. Assn., San Diego Med. Soc., Am. Med. Women's Assn., Am. Acad. Pediatrics, San Diego Pediatric Soc. Address: 2001 4th Av San Diego CA 92101

MINER, THELMA MAY SMITH (MRS. WARD L. MINER), educator; b. Ocean City, N.J., Jan. 15, 1915; d. Benjamin Franklin and Myrtle Estelle (Simkins) Smith; B.A., Dickinson Coll., 1935; M.A., U. Pa., 1942; Ph.D., 1945; m. Ward L. Miner, Oct. 27, 1950. Tchr. 5th grade, Ocean City, N.J., 1935-42; instr. English dept. Temple U., 1945-48; asst. prof. Dickinson Coll., 1948-51; research in France, 1951-53; instr. English dept. Vassar Coll., 1953-55, U. Kan., 1956-57; asst. prof. English dept. Youngstown (O.) State U., 1957-59, asso. prof., 1959-65, prof., 1965—. Fulbright prof. Internat. People's Coll., Elsinore, Denmark, 1960-61. Recipient Distinguished prof. award Youngstown State U., 1972; Am. Council of Learned Socs. fellow, 1951-52. Mem. Modern Lang. Assn., Am. Studies Assn., Am. Assn. U. Profs. Author: The Uncollected Poems of James Russell Lowell, 1950; (with husband) Transatlantic Migration: The Contemporary American Novel in France, 1955; also articles, book revs. in profl. jours. Home: RFD 1 North Jackson OH 44451 Office: Youngstown State U Youngstown OH 44503

MINGE, CAROL TILLMAN BLAND (MRS. JERRY LEE MINGE), civic worker; b. Hazlehurst, Ga., Aug. 4, 1938; d. Daniel Ed and Mary Alice (Thomas) Bland; student U. Ga., 1956-58; m. Jerry Lee Minge, Mar. 27, 1958; children—Mary Angela, Jennifer Bland, Anne Marguerite. Div. chmn. March of Dimes, Rome, Ga., 1969—. Am. Cancer Soc., Rome, 1968—; mem. day camp bd. YMCA, Rome, 1968-69. Mem. Ga. Gov.'s commn. Status Women. Alternate del. Democratic Nat. Conv., 1972. Mem. Nat. Accredited Flower Show Judges, N.W. Ga. Judges Council, Jr. Service League, Coosa Valley Tennis Assn., Kappa Delta. Baptist. Clubs: Green Thumb Garden (pres. 1964-65), Coosa Country (Rome). Home: 10 Saddle Rd Rome GA 30161

MINGE, JEANNE, radio and TV producer, writer; b. Louisville; d. James Elmore and Veda (Viner) Hooker; m. J. Chadwick Minge, Jr. (div. Jan. 1969); children—Lucius Hastings, James Hooker, Dorothy Pembroke, Jackson Chadwick III. Radio and TV producer, writer Tulane U., New Orleans, 1950-54, 58-60, originator, writer-producer Tulane Close-Up, syndicated TV program, 1950-60; dir. TV U. Cal. at Berkeley, 1954-55; mgr. sta. WNPS, New Orleans, 1958-64; tchr. Radio-TV Writing Am. Sch. Found., Mexico City, 1967-68; cons. prodn. Canal Trece-TV, Mexico City, Mexico, 1968-69; feature writer Auge de Mexico, 1972-73. Recipient Emmy award best pub. service program year No. Cal. Acad. TV Arts and Scis., 1955; Gold Bell award best Cath. short film of year, 1960. Mem. Alpha Phi. Office: Tulane Alumni House 6319 Willow St New Orleans LA 70118

MINGOLELLI, JENNIE LEE DEKLE (MRS. RALPH A. MINGOLELLI), b. Plant City, Fla., Feb. 24, 1944; d. George W. and Frances C. (Parker) Dekle; B.A., Stetson U., 1966; M.A., Syracuse U., 1968, postgrad. 1968—; m. Ralph A. Mingolelli, June 29, 1968; 1 son, Ralph Christopher. Admissions counselor U. Ga., Athens, summer 1967; undergrad. counselor Syracuse (N.Y.) U., 1968, residence hall dir., 1968-71; dean of women Le Moyne Coll., Syracuse, 1971-74; real estate salesman, 1974—. Mem. community affairs com. A.R.C., 1966-69; mem. Priority One Greater Syracuse, Inc., Inner City Opera Com. Republican chmn. 17th ward 10th dist. Syracuse, N.Y., 1973—. Bd. dirs. Support: Pregnancy Counseling Service Syracuse, 1974—. Mem. Am. Personnel and Guidance Assn., Nat. Assn. Women Deans, Adminstrs. and Counselors, Am. Assn. U. Women, Nat. Assn. Student Personnel and Adminstrs., N.Y. State Personnel and Guidance Assn. Home: 101 Claire Rd Syracuse NY 13214

MINICK, KARAN FRIEDA, lawyer; b. Los Angeles, July 13, 1935; d. Louis and Frieda (Karan) Minick; A.B., U. Cal. at Berkeley, 1957; postgrad., 1965; LL.B., U. So. Cal., 1960. Admitted to Cal. bar, 1960; dep. corp. commr. State of Cal., 1961; counsel, com. on adminstrn. justice State Bar Cal., 1961-64; dep. counsel San Joaquin County, 1964, 70—; prof. Humphreys Sch. Law, Stockton, 1964-65; research atty. League Cal. Cities, 1965; atty. Office of Solicitor, U.S. Dept. Labor, Washington, 1965-70. Mem. Am. (mem. com. jud. adminstrn. 1961), Los Angeles County bar assns., State Bar Cal., Am. Assn. U. Women, Legion Lex, Phi Delta Delta. Office: 222 E Weber Av Stockton CA 95202

MINK, PATSY TAKEMOTO, lawyer, congresswoman; b. Paia, Hawaii, Dec. 6, 1927; d. Suematsu and Mitama (Tateyama) Takemoto; student Wilson Coll., 1946, U. Neb., 1947; B.A., U. Hawaii, 1948; J.D., U. Chgo., 1951; m. John Francis Mink, Jan. 27, 1951; 1 dau., Gwendolyn Matsu. Admitted to Hawaii bar; pvt. practice law, Honolulu, 1953—; prof. bus. law U. Hawaii, Honolulu, 1952-56, 59-63; atty. Territorial Ho. of Reps., 1955; mem. 89th-93d Congresses, Hawaii, chmn. subcom. mines and mining Interior and Insular Affairs Com. U.S. del. to Young Polit. Leaders Conf., Paris. Charter pres. Young Dem. Club of Oahu, 1954-56; charter pres. Territory of Hawaii Young Democrats, 1956; nat. v.p. Young Dem. Clubs of Am., Ams. for Dem. Action, 1973—; mem. Territorial Ho. of Reps., 1956-58; mem. Territorial Senate, 1958-59; mem. Hawaii Senate, 1963-64. Trustee Palama Settlement, 1957-60, Dag Hammarskjold Coll., 1974—; former dir. Hawaii Assn. to Help Retarded Children. Office: Ho of Reps Washington DC 20515

MINKIN, CONSTANCE (MRS. NOAH MINKIN), editor; b. Toledo, Nov. 25, 1923; d. Henry and Pearl (Friedlander) Rappaport; B.S., Northwestern U., 1944; postgrad. U. Wis., 1947-48; m. Noah Minkin, June 19, 1948. Asst. to program dir. pub. relations Amvets, Washington, 1951-60; with Smithsonian Instn., Washington, 1960—, chief exhibits editor, 1968—, asst. chief Office Exhibits Central, 1974—. Mem. Am. Assn. Museums, Nat. Trust Historic Preservation, Women in Communications. Editor: The Men and Machines of American Journalism (Peter C. Marzio), 1973. Home: 1251 S Oakcrest Rd Arlington VA 22202 Office: 900 Jefferson Dr Washington DC 20560

MINKOFF, MARGARET MILLER (MRS. LEONARD MINKOFF), merchandising exec.; b. Gary, Ind., Oct. 24, 1928; d. George and Esther (Bassan) Miller; student Beloit Coll., 1946-47; m. Leonard Minkoff, Jan. 23, 1948; children—Gregg, Ellen Margaret. Asst. buyer, buyer O. Connor Millinery, Chgo., 1947-49; dept. head Continental Casualty Ins. Co., Chgo., 1953-54; buyer A & G Millinery, Chgo., 1964-69; buyer, merchandising exec. Charles A. Stevens & Co., Chgo., 1969—. Bd. Dirs. Uptown Chgo. Commn., 1961-63. Named Mother of Year, Chgo. Boys Clubs, 1956. Home: 152 Western Av Roselle IL 60172 Office: 25 N State St Chicago IL 60602

MINNER, SISTER JEANNE FRANCIS, educator; b. Colusa, Cal., Mar. 30, 1917; d. Oscar Lee and Minnie (Postlethwaite) Minner; student San Antonio Jr. Coll., 1935-37; B.S., Our Lady of Lake Coll., 1939; M.A., Catholic U. Am., 1949; Ph.D., U. Tex., 1965. Tchr., St. Vincent's Coll. and Acad., Shreveport, La., 1939-41; tchr. Incarnate Word Acad., Corpus Christi, Tex., 1941-46, tchr. biology, head sci. dept., 1948-63; tchr. Villa Maria High Sch., Brownsville, Tex., 1946-48; dean, head div. natural sci. and math. Christopher Coll., 1963-66, dir. Piper Meml. Lab. 1965-68, pres., 1966-68; chmn. dept. edn. Coll. Santa Fe, 1968-70; chmn. dept. St. Mary's U., San Antonio, 1970—. Fellow Tex. Acad. Sci., mem. A.A.A.S. (life), Nat. Assn. Biology Tchrs. (Tex. chmn. pvt. schs. 1963-68), Nat. Sci. Tchrs. Assn. (life), Sci. Tchrs. Assn. Tex. (v.p. 1964, adv. bd. 1963, pres. elect 1965, pres. 1966, editor 1967-68, hon. life mem.), Tex. State Tchrs. Assn. (life), Am. Inst. Biol. Scis. (life), Ex-Students Assn. U. Tex. (life), Am. Radio Relay League (life), N.E.A. (life), Corpus Christi Interracial Council, Am. Assn. U. Profs., Nat. Wildlife Fedn., Pilot Internat., Assn. Supervision and Curriculum Devel., M.B.L.S. Club: Corpus Christi Outdoor. Contbr. articles to profl. jours. Home: 2930 S Alameda St Corpus Christi TX 78404 also 1243 Babcock Rd San Antonio TX 78201 Office: Saint Mary's U San Antonio TX 78284

MINNICH, VIRGINIA, hematologist, educator; b. Zanesville, Ohio, January 24, 1910; d. Rufus Humphrey and Ollie (Burley) Minnich; B.S. in Home Econs., Ohio State U., 1937; M.S. in Nutrition, Ia. State Coll., 1938; D.Sc., William Woods Coll., 1972. Research asst. dept. medicine div. hematology Washington U. Sch. Medicine, St. Louis, 1939-54, research asso., 1954-58, research asst. prof., 1958-67, research asso. prof., 1967-74, prof., 1974—. Named St. Louis Woman of Achievement, Group Action Council, 1947; Fulbrigh-Hays research award, Turkey, 1964. Mem. Am. Fedn. for Clin. Research, Soc. for Exptl. Biology and Medicine, Internat. Soc. Hematology, Am. Soc. Hematology, Sigma Xi, Omicron Nu, Phi Upsilon Omicron. Contbr. numerous articles to profl. jours. Home: 4501 Maryland Av St Louis MO 63108

MINNICK, ELEANORE JEAN STERRETT (MRS. PAUL FLOYD MINNICK), univ. librarian; b. Mansfield, O., Apr. 7, 1920; d. William Dwight and Florence (Clemens) Sterrett; student Ball State U., 1939-40; B.S., Wittenberg U., 1963, postgrad., 1970—; m. Paul Floyd Minnick, Jan. 23, 1940; children—Mary (Mrs. Gibson D. Walker), Margaret (Mrs. Hysel Caldwell), Paul James, Gwendolyn. Tchr. elementary schs., South Solon, O., 1958-63; librarian Southeastern High Sch., South Charleston, 1963-68; acquisitions librarian Clark Tech. Coll., Springfield, O., 1968—; librarian Houston br. Warder Pub. Library, South Charleston, O., 1958-68. Home: 422 Possum Rd W Springfield OH 45506 Office: 570 E Leffels Lane Springfield OH 45505

MINNIER, JANE DEDRICK (MRS. FRANK RAYMOND MINNIER), ednl. adminstr.; b. Ticonderoga, N.Y., Sept. 7, 1927; d. G. Earl and Lois Dean Dedrick; B.A., Keuka Coll., 1949; postgrad. U. Md., 1950-54; m. Frank Raymond Minnier, Aug. 20, 1955; children—Gwen Elizabeth, Douglas Earl. Tchr. Montrose Sch., Reisterstown, Md., 1949-52; instr. and asst. to dean Keuka Coll., Keuka Park, N.Y., 1952-54; dir. guidance Ticonderoga (N.Y.) High Sch., 1954-55; tchr. Somersworth (N.H.) Sch. System, 1961-64; financial aid officer and dir. State U. N.Y., Plattsburgh, 1965—, also chmn. chancellor's Financial Aid Adv. Bd., 1973—. Cons. financial aid to several colls. Sec. Council of Community Services, 1971-72, v.p., 1972-74. Mem. N.Y. State Financial Aid Assn., Eastern Assn. Financial Aids. Democrat. Presbyn. (choir mem. 1967—). Clubs: Beartown Ski (sec. treas. 1972-74), Figure Skating. Home: 38 Morrison Av Plattsburgh NY 12901 Office: KEHOE No 211 State Univ New York Plattsburgh NY 12901

MINNIS, JEAN REYNOLDS, educator; b. Ia., Jan. 15, 1916; Harry Elmer and Josephine Erma (De Booy) Reynolds; B.A., U. No. Ia., 1937; postgrad. U. Denver, 1952-53, U. Md., 1966; M.A., U. Colo., 1970, postgrad., 1970—; m. Roy Barker Minnis, June 28, 1940; children—David Alan, Paul Edward. Tchr. high sch., Lamoille, Ia., 1937-38, Paulina, Ia., 1938-40; with Hartford Accident & Indemnity Co., San Francisco, 1943-45; tchr. high sch., Montgomery County, Md., 1964-66, Denver, 1966—. Bass violist Waterloo (Ia.) Symphony Orch., 1933-37, Aurora (Ill.) Symphony Orch., 1940-42. Mem. Disciples of Christ, mem. gen. bd., 1960—, mem. deaconess bd., 1960—, sec., 1968-70, treas., 1972-73, librarian ch., 1963-65, corr. sec. Christian Women's Fellowship, 1971-73, mem. dept. campus ministries Rocky Mountain region, 1973—. Bd. dirs. United Commn. Campus Ministries in Colo., 1973—. Mem. Modern Lang. Assn., Rocky Mountain Modern Lang. Assn., English Speaking Union, Am. Assn. U. Women, Sigma Tau Delta, Kappa Delta Pi. Contbr. poetry to mags. and newspapers. Home: 7889 E Kenyon Av Denver CO 80237

MINNIS, MHYRA SCHWAY, educator, sociologist; b. Dvinsk, Latvia; d. Hersh and Beth Ann Schway; B.A., Oberlin Coll., 1939, M.A., 1940; Ph.D., Yale, 1951; m. Dean Hugh Minnis, June, 1932 (div. Nov. 1945). Instr. sociology Bowling Green (O.) State U., 1946-48; asst. prof. sociology U. Ida., 1954-56, asso. prof., 1957-60; asst. prof. Skidmore Coll., Saratoga Springs, N.Y., 1956-57, San Fernando Valley State Coll., 1960-62; asso. prof. sociology Tex. Tech U., 1962-65, prof., 1965—. research grantee, 1970-71. Research analyst USPHS, Adminstrv. Div., Plans and Reports Br., Washington, 1951; sr. research analyst Library of Congress, 1951-54. Recreational social worker, asst. program dir., head recreation worker A.R.C., 1943-46; occupational and recreational dir. County Tb Hosp., Amherst, O., 1940-41. Trustee Lubbock City-County Child Welfare Bd., Council on Alcoholism. Recipient Merit award A.R.C., Tex. 1946; scholarships Case Western Res. U., Oberlin Coll., Yale; Tech. U. research grantee 1964-65, Hogg Found. for Mental Health grantee, 1964-65. Fellow Am. Sociol. Assn.; mem. Am. Assn. U. Profs., Tex. Assn. Coll. Tchrs., Soc. Internat. Criminology, So. Sociol. Assn., S.W. Sociol. Assn. (v.p., program chmn. 1972-73, pres. 1973-74), Tex. Acad. Sci., T.A.C.T. Sr. editor: Sociological Perspectives: Readings in Social Problems and Deviant Behavior 1968; Tornado: The Voice of the People in Disaster and After, A Study in Residential Integration, 1971. Contbr. articles to profl. jours. and books. Home: 4512A 65th St Lubbock TX 79414

MINNIS-BAILEY, GLADYS ALENE HODGES (MRS. JOHN LEE BAILEY), hosp. adminstr.; b. Daytona Beach, Fla., Oct. 13, 1923; d. Eugene Everett and Louvenia (Lavatte) Hodges; student Russell Kelly Bus. Coll., 1948-49, Carnegie Inst., 1953-55; B.S., Wayne State U., 1970; m. Thomas Minnis, Apr. 17, 1946 (dec.); children—Lillia (Mrs. Edward W. Dodson), Katie; m. 2d, John Lee Bailey, Feb. 12, 1972. Med. asst. Dexter Lab., Detroit, 1955-56; electroencephalograph technician Detroit Gen. Hosp., 1959-62; instr. electroencephalograph technologists Wayne State U. Sch. Medicine, Detroit, 1962-70; head dept. electrographics Harper Hosp., Detroit, 1968—. Co-chmn. women's rights for equal ednl. grant fellowship State of Mich., 1970. State central mem. Mich. Democratic party, 1965-70; precinct del. county Dem. convs., 1950, 70; mem. exec. bd. 1st dist. Dem. party, 1967-70. Office Econ. Opportunity Manpower Devel. and Tng. program grantee Wayne State U. Sch. Medicine, 1965. Mem. Am., Canadian socs. electroencephalographic, N.A.A.C.P., Am. Civil Liberties Union, Central (treas. 1969-70),

Great Lakes (dir. 1968-70) socs. electrographic technologists, Am. Assn. Physicians Assts. Home: 17414 St Aubin St Detroit MI 48212

MINOR, IRENE CARTER (MRS. HARRY H. MINOR, JR.), govt. ofcl.; b. Kansas City, Kan., July 22, 1932; d. Manzer and Ruth (Simmons) Carter; diploma in nursing Kan. U., 1950-53; B.S., Avila Coll., 1960; M.A., U. Mo., 1969; postgrad. Mo. U., 1971-72, Kan. State Tchrs. Coll., Emporia, 1970-71; m. Harry Harold Minor, Jr., Sept. 18, 1967; children—Bruce Condore Sims, Harriet Virginia. Charge nurse, instr. Psychiat. Receiving Center, Kansas City, Mo., 1954-56; asst. dir. nursing, faculty mem. St. Margaret's Hosp. Sch. Nursing, Kansas City, 1957-61; organizer, dir. nursing edn. program Kansas City Community Jr. Coll., 1970-72; nat. coordinator affirmative action program Am. Nurses Assn., Kansas City, 1972-74; equal opportunity specialist Office Civil Rights, U.S. Dept. Health, Edn. and Welfare, Kansas City, 1974—. Cons. health careers program Kaw Valley Med. Soc., 1971-72; planning cons. Kan. Regional Med. Program, 1972. Adv. com. nursing edn. program Johnson County Community Coll., 1971-72. Mem. Am., Kan. nurses assns., Nat. League for Nursing, Nat. Assn. Human Rights Workers, Nat. Drifters, Inc. (nat. v.p. 1959, chmn. nat. pub. relations 1970-71), Sigma Theta Tau. Contbr. articles to profl. jours. Home: 105 Johnston Dr Raymore MO 64083 Office: 12 Grand Bldg 12th and Grand Av Kansas City MO 64106

MINOT, ANNA SEDGWICK (MRS. JOSEPH WARREN), actress; b. Boston; d. Wayland Manning and Anna (Shaughnessy) Minot; grad. Buckingham Sch.; B.A., Vassar Coll.; m. Arthur S. Franz, Oct. 25, 1942 (div. 1947); 1 son, Michael Minot; m. 2d, Joseph Warren, June 7, 1953. Debut as actress in The Strings, My Lord, Are False, N.Y.C., 1942; appeared in Broadway prodns. including The Russian People, 1943, The Visitor, 1944, The Iceman Cometh, 1946, An Enemy of the People, 1951, The Love of Four Colonels, 1953, The Trip to Bountiful, 1953, The Tunnel of Love, 1957, Ivanov, 1966; TV appearances include Bachelor Party, 1953, Terry de Marco in The Edge of Night, 1958-59, Martha Wilson in As The World Turns, 1966-70, Meg Johns in A World Apart, 1970-71, Esther Geller in Somerset, 1973—; stage mgr. Broadway prodn. Ivanov, 1966; staff playreader, copywriter Play of the Month Guild, 1957-67. Reader Recording for the Blind, Inc., 1968—; performer Plays for Living, Family Service Assn. Am., 1965—. Mem. Urban League Greater N.Y., Actors' Fund, Phi Beta Kappa. Democrat. Home: 226 W 10th St New York City NY 10014 Office: care Actors Equity Assn 165 W 46th St New York City NY 10036

MINTON, YVONNE FAY (MRS. WILLIAM BARCLAY), mezzo soprano; b. Sydney, Australia, Dec. 4, 1938; d. Robert and Violet (Dean) Minton; student Sydney Conservatorium Music, 1957-60; m. William Barclay, Aug. 21, 1965; children—Malcolm Alexander, Alison Elizabeth. Prin. mezzo soprano Royal Opera House Coventgarden, London, Eng., 1965—. Guest prin. Cologne (Germany) Opera House, 1969, Chgo. Opera, 1970. Recordings include Rosenkavalier, Cosi Fan Tutte, Mahler Songs.

MINX, PRISCILLA MCCORMICK (MRS. L. PAUL MINX), interior designer; b. Logansport, Ind.; d. John Jay and Florence (Dritt) McCormick; student Purdue U., 1933-35; m. L. Paul Minx, Nov. 24, 1949; children—Paul William, Martha Sue, Kathryn Ann. interior designer Minx Co., Indpls., 1950—. Cub den mother Boy Scouts Am., Indpls., 1961-63; co-leader Girl Scouts U.S.A., 1965-66. Mem. policy com. Jordan YMCA, 1963-64. Mem. Am. Inst. Interior Designers (gov. Ind. 1970—), Indpls. Panhellenic Assn. (pres. 1957-58), Kappa Kappa Kappa (chpt. pres. 1964-65), Alpha Chi. Presbyn. (exec. bd. United Presbyn. Women 1968—). Home: 744 Sherwood Dr Indianapolis IN 46240 Office: 4214 College Av Indianapolis IN 46208

MIRMOW, ESTHER LEE, psychologist; b. Summerville, S.C., Dec. 1, 1922; d. Aaron and Raye (Wilensky) Mirmow; B.A., Smith Coll., 1943, M.A., 1945; Ph.D., Washington U., St. Louis, 1952. Instr., Smith Coll., Northampton, Mass., 1945-47; psychologist pub. schs., San Diego, 1947-49; asst. prof. psychology Mills Coll., Oakland, Cal., 1952-58, asso. prof., 1958-66, prof., 1966—, head dept. psychology, 1956—, chmn. div. natural scis., 1972—; Nat. Inst. Mental Health postdoctoral fellow Michael Reese Hosp., Chgo., 1958-59. Bd. dirs. Ann Martin Services for Children. Fulbright fellow, 1964. Mem. Am. Psychol. Assn., Phi Beta Kappa, Sigma Xi. Home: 6 Faculty Village Mills Coll Oakland CA 94613

MIRRAS, ANASTASIA VASELIKE, psychologist; b. Vancouver, B.C., Can., Mar. 6, 1946; d. John Steve and Mary (Petroulias) Mirras; B.A., Lewis and Clark Coll., 1968; M.A., Portland State U., 1971; postgrad. U. Portland, 1968-69, U. Ore., 1972, 74. Substitute tchr. math. Sch. Dist. 1, Portland, Ore., 1971-72; Sch. psychologist Vancouver Sch. Bd., 1972—; instr. Western Bus. U., Portland, Ore., 1972. Mem. Kitsilano Task Force for Resource Bd., Vancouver, 1974; mem. Vancouver Neighborhood Services Assn., 1972—. Mem. Kitsilano Citizens Com. for Mental Health, 1973-74. Mem. Kitsilano Neighborhood House Bd. of Gov.'s, 1972—. Mem. Am., Canadian, Western, B.C. psychol. assns., Ore. Council Tchrs. of Math., Nat. Council Tchrs. of Math., Nat. Assn. Sch. Psychologists, B.C. Tchrs. Fedn., Vancouver Elementary Sch. Tchrs. Assn., Daus. of Penelope. Home: 7206 North Kerby Av Portland OR 97217 also 102-2265 West 3rd Av Vancouver BC V6K 1L5 Canada Office: 1595 West 10th Av Vancouver BC Canada

MIRTI, BARBARA (MRS. MICHAEL MIRTI), physician; b. N.Y.C., Nov. 6, 1937; d. John and Albina (Gaeta) DeStefano; A.B., N.Y.U., 1958; M.D., Bologna U. Sch. Medicine, Bologna, Italy, 1963; m. Michael Mirti, Dec. 29, 1962. Intern, Orange (N.J.) Meml. Hosp., 1966-67; resident East Orange (N.J.) VA Hosp., 1967-68; resident internal medicine St. Michael Hosp., Newark, 1968-69, fellow in cardiology, 1969-70; practice medicine specializing in internal medicine and cardiology, Succasunna, N.J., 1972—; vis. physician N.J. Rehab. Commn., 1970—; mem. staffs St. Michael Med. Center, Newark, Dover (N.J.) Gen. Hosp. Mem. A.M.A., Essex County Med. Soc. Address: 57 Pleasant Hill Rd Succasunna NJ 07876

MISCHLER, IRENE BEULAH, librarian; b. Danvers, Ill., Aug. 23, 1912; d. Arnold John and Bertha (Kohler) M.; B.Ed., Ill. State U., 1938; B.L.S., U. Ill., 1939. Circulation and registration librarian Hoyt Pub. Library, Saginaw, Mich., 1939-43; head Butman Fish Library, 1943-51; asst. head circulation div. Indpls. Pub. Library, 1951-53; profl. asst. Grosse Pointe (Mich.) Pub. Library, 1953-59; reference asst. Indpls. Pub. Library, 1959-61, head social scis. div., 1961—. Mem. Am., Ind. library assns., Indpls. and Marion County Pub. Library Staff Assn., Marion County Hist. Soc., Audubon Film Series. Republican. Presbyn. Home: 1434 N Delaware St Indianapolis IN 46202 Office: 40 East St Clair St Indianapolis IN 46204

MISENHIMER, VIOLET ELIZABETH SNYDER (MRS. JOY B. MISENHIMER), artist; b. Flora, Ill.; d. Martin Thomas and Trophie Jane (Amerman) Snyder; student Sch. Art Inst. Chgo., 1941-42, Art Students League, 1950; m. Joy B. Misenhimer; children—Martin David, Joy Burrell. Tchr. painting adult edn. classes Scarsdale (N.Y.) High Sch., 1946, Sch. Art Guild, Boca Raton, Fla., 1968-72; pvt. tchr.; exhibited art in one-man shows Wellons Gallery, N.Y.C., Mamaroneck (N.Y.) Free Library, First Westchester Bank, Mamaroneck, Aeolian Corp., White Plains, N.Y.; exhibited art in group shows at Art Inst. Chgo., Art Club Washington, Am. Water Color Soc., Nat. Acad. Galleries, Hamilton Art Gallery, Ont., Soc. of Four Arts, Palm Beach, Fla., Hortt Meml., Fort Lauderdale Mus. Arts, Fla. Watercolor Soc., Art Guild Boca Raton, Arts Club Washington, Perry Art Mus., Miami, Fla., Whitney Mus. Am. Art, Internat. Art Gallery, N.Y.C.; represented in permanent collections in pvt. collections. Judge 12th Ann. Art Exhbn. Mamaroneck, Mamaroneck Womens' Club Ann. Exhbn., Boca Raton Center for the Arts. Recipient numerous awards including Scarsdale Art Assn., Westchester Arts and Crafts Guild, Art Guild Boca Raton. Fellow Internat. Inst. Arts and Letters; mem. Nat. Assn. Women Artists, Art Guild Boca Raton, (pres. 1970-71; mem. art adv. bd. 1971-72; advisor to pres. 1971-72), Fla. Watercolor Soc. Home: 850 West Royal Palm Rd Boca Raton FL 33432

MISHKIN, BARBARA FRIEDMAN (MRS. MORTIMER MISHKIN), bioethicist; b. Phila., Feb. 19, 1936; d. Maurice Harold and Gertrude Berliner (Sanders) Friedman; A.B. cum laude, Mt. Holyoke Coll., 1957; M.A., Yale, 1958; m. Mortimer Mishkin, May 27, 1971; children by previous marriage—Diane, Paul, David, Amy. Research psychologist sect. on neuropsychology Nat. Inst. Mental Health, 1968-69; spl. asst. for health scis. to chief judge U.S. Ct. Appeals for D.C., 1971; cons. Boston U. Center for Law and Health Scis., 1971-73; cons., also lectr. law and ethics Johns Hopkins Med. Sch., 1971-74; spl. asst. for bioethics to sci. dir. Nat. Inst. Child Health and Human Devel. for devel. Dept. Health, Edn. and Welfare-NIH policy for protection of human subjects in biomed. research, 1973-74; sr. asst. to exec. dir. Nat. Commn. Protection Human Subjects of Biomed. and Behavioral Research, 1974—. Bd. dirs. Howard County Pub. Health Assn., 1963-65. Mem. Am. Psychol. Assn., Phi Beta Kappa. Contbr. papers to profl. convs., jours. Home: 6404 Highland Dr Chevy Chase MD 20015 Office: Bldg 31 Room 2A50 NIH Bethesda MD 20014

MISHKIN, EVELYN CUTLER (MRS. RALPH D. MISHKIN), social worker; b. N.Y.C., Aug. 12, 1921; d. Solomon and Dora (Cohen) Cutler; student, U. Wis., 1939-41; B.A., Hunter Coll., 1944; M.S.W., Columbia U., 1946; m. Ralph D. Mishkin, Jan. 23, 1942 (dec. 1971); children—Lynn, Cathy. Psychiat. social worker Youth House, N.Y.C., 1946-49; with Bur. of Child Guidance, Queens office N.Y.C. Bd. Edn., 1949—, psychiat. sch. social worker, 1956—. Mem. Nat. Assn. Social Workers, Am. Assn. Psychiat. Social Workers, Am. Orthopsychiat. Assn. Home: 20 Lodge Rd Great Neck NY 11021 Office: Bureau of Child Guidance Queens Center 101-23 124th St Richmond Hill NY 11419

MISHNE, JUDITH MARKS, educator; b. Cleve., Feb. 21, 1932; d. Moses Issac and Lillian (Kemelman) Marks; B.S., U. Wis., 1953; M.S., Case-Western Res. U., 1955; grad. child therapy program Chgo. Inst. Psychoanalysis, 1974; 1 son, Jonathan Michael. Caseworker, Akron (O.) Child Guidance Center, 1955-56, Cleve. Child Guidance Center, 1956-58, Jewish Family Service, Cleveland Heights, N.Y., 1959-62; sch. social worker Orange Bd. Edn., Pepper Pike, N.Y., 1962-66; supr. Bellefaire of Cleve. Jewish Children's Bur., 1964-66; asst. prof. field instrn. Sch. Social Service Adminstrn., U. Chgo., 1966—. Cons., Pritzker Children's Hosp., Chgo., 1967—, Madden Hosp., Chgo., 1971-72; pvt. practice as psychotherapist. Mem. Council Social Work Edn., Nat. Assn. Social Workers, Acad. Certified Social Workers, Orthopsychiatry, Assn. Child and Adolescent Psychotherapy, Ill. Clin. Social Workers (v.p.). Editorial bd. Jour. Sch. Social Work. Home: 5705 S Blackstone St Chicago IL 60637

MITCHELL, ANNIE MARTIN (MRS. CHARLES A. MITCHELL), civic worker assn. exec.; b. Rockwood, Tenn., Apr. 8, 1921; d. Robert Amis and Ruth (Cashion) Lauderdale; B.S. magna cum laude, U. Tenn., 1942; m. Charles Austin Mitchell, Aug. 7, 1942; children—Virginia (Mrs. Rodolphe Nessim Zarka), Charles Austin, Robert. Active local, state nat. levels P.T.A., 1952—, v.p. nat. P.T.A. region III, 1972—; pres. Tenn. Congress Parents and Tchrs., 1969-72; mem. Tenn. United Orgns. for Edn., 1966-69; mem. exec. com. Highland Rim council Girl Scouts U.S.A., 1955-65, pres., 1960-62; Cumberland Valley council Girl Scouts U.S., 1965—; del. White House Conf. on Food, Nutrition and Health, 1969, on Children and Youth, 1970; mem. Five County Med. Aux., Tenn. Comprehensive Health Planning Council, 1969—, Tenn. Fulbright-Hayes Scholarship Com., 1970—, Gov.'s Adv. Council Edn. Handicapped, 1972—. Lewishon art fellow, 1941-42; Merrill Palmer child devel. scholar, 1941. Mem. Tenn., Fla., Ky., N.Y., Nat. (hon. life mem.) congresses parents and tchrs., Phi Kappa Phi, Delta Kappa Gamma, Omicron Nu. Methodist. Club: Sparta (Tenn.) Women's. Home: 108 S Highland Dr Sparta TN 38583

MITCHELL, BARBARA ANN STEPPER (MRS. TOM B. MITCHELL), state ofcl.; b. Eureka, S.D., Oct. 30, 1937; d. John and Rosalind (Helmer) Stepper; B.S., U. Ore., 1959, M.S., 1973; m. Tom B. Mitchell, Sept. 2, 1961; children—Dayna, Stuart, Derek. Reporter Yakima Herald Republic, Yakima, Wash., 1959-60; news editor Med. Sch. U. Ore. Portland, 1960-61, univ. publs. editor, sci. writer, 1961-62, dir. publs., Eugene, 1964-66, dir. local govt. communication project, 1970-72, tchr. journalistic writing, 1972-73; editor Field Emission Corp., McMinnville, Ore., 1962-63; owner, pres. Mitchell Pub. Relations Agy., Eugene, 1966-73. Legislative asst. to State Rep., 1973; communication cons. Ore. Sch. Bds. Assn., 1971-72, League of Ore. Cities, 1971-72, Assn. Ore. Counties, 1972-73. Dir. communication and govt. relations Ore. State Dept. Edn., Salem, 1973—. Mem. Women in Communications (pres. Eugene chpt. 1969, treas. 1973), Ore. Sch. Pub. Relations Assn. (v.p. 1973—), Ore. Assn. Editors and Communicators (nat. conf. pubs. chmn. 1973—, awards chmn. 1969). Author: Communication Handbook for Local Governments, 1972. Editor: Women on the Move: A Feminist Perspective, 1973. Home: 1923 Sylvan St Eugene OR 97403 Office: 942 Lancaster Dr NE Salem OR 97310

MITCHELL, CHARLOTTE STUDER (MRS. PHILIP JAMES MITCHELL), librarian; b. Milw.; d. Erwin Henry and Clara (Krahn) Studer; A.B., Milwaukee-Downer Coll.; B.S., U. So. Cal.; M.A., U. Chgo.; m. Philip James Mitchell, Aug. 10, 1957; 1 son, Mark Philip. Asst. librarian Berwyn Pub. Library, Berwyn, Ill., 1940-43; censorship clerk U.S. Office of Censorship, 1943-44; librarian Michael Reese Hosp. Sch. Nursing, Chgo., 1944-51; head librarian Miles Labs., Inc., Elkhart, Ind., 1951-72, dir. library resources and services, 1972—. Dir. Elkhart Concert Club, 1960—, sec., 1963-65, pres., 1970-71; v.p. Elkhart County Arts and Humanities Council, 1972-74; v.p. Michiana Ballet Co., 1973—. Mem. Med., Am. library assns., Spl. Libraries Assn. Club: Altrusa. Home: 2601 E Jackson Blvd Elkhart IN 46514 Office: 1127 Myrtle St Elkhart IN 46514

MITCHELL, DOROTHY DEVINNEY (MRS. WILLIAM C. MITCHELL, SR.), mfg. co. exec.; b. Blairsville, Pa., June 12, 1912; d. Wilbert L. and Lottie Mae (Crusan) Devinney; grad. Cambria Row Bus. Coll., 1932; m. William C. Mitchell, Sr., July 26, 1936; children—Pamela (Mrs. Anthony H. Geletka), Betty Lou (Mrs. Robert J. Repinski), William C. Corp. sec. Blairsville Wilbert Vault Co., Inc. Mem. Order Eastern Star. Home: 158 N Brady St Blairsville PA 15717 Office: 100 N East Lane Blairsville PA 15717

MITCHELL, GEORGIA BONE (MRS. WILLIAM A. MITCHELL), physician; b. Nashville; d. James Asbury and Ethel (Bell) Bone; B.A., Fisk U., 1947; M.A., Middlebury Coll., 1948; M.D., Meharry Med. Coll., 1958; student McGill U., Montreal, Que., 1947, U. Colo., 1966; spl. study internal medicine, Nairobi, Kenya, East Africa, Vienna, Austria, infectious diseases, Acapulco, Mexico, P.R., cardiology, Geneva, Switzerland, 1973; m. William A. Mitchell, Aug. 23, 1952; 1 dau., Anne Elizabeth. Intern, St. Mary Mercy Hosp., Gary, Ind., 1958-59; practice medicine, Gary, 1959—; mem. staff St. Mary Mercy Hosp., Meth. Hosp. Asst. leader Girl Scouts U.S.A., Gary, 1964—; mem. Holy Angels Parish Sch. Bd., 1971—. Mem. A.M.A., Ind. State, Lake County med. assns., Am. Med. Womens Assn., Jack and Jill of Am., Inc., Alpha Omega Alpha, Phi Beta Kappa, Delta Sigma Theta. Episcopalian. Home: 8733 Lake Shore Dr Gary IN 46403 Office: 1706 Broadway Gary IN 46407

MITCHELL, GRACE LOUISE (MRS. DONALD BATES MITCHELL), ednl. adminstr.; b. Natick, Mass., Jan. 10, 1909; d. Aubrey A. and Ruperta M. (Woodward) Forster; B.S., Tufts U., 1954; M.Ed., Harvard, 1962; m. Donald Bates Mitchell, Aug. 26, 1948; children from previous marriage—F. Lee Bailey, Nancy C. Bergstrom, William E. Bailey. Dir. Green Acres Day Sch., Waltham, Mass., 1933—; ednl. dir., exec. v.p. Living and Learning Centres, 1970—; prof., coordinator early childhood Ednl. program Quinsigamond Community Coll., Worcester, Mass., 1968-71. Pres. Waltham Family Service, 1953; corporate mem. Waltham Hosp., 1970—. Bd. dirs. Jr. Achievement, Boston. Mem. Assn. Childhood Edn., Waltham C. of C. (dir. 1944), Am. Camping Assn. (pres. new Eng. sect. 1966-67). Author: Fundamentals of Day Camping, 1960. Home: 439 Lexington St Waltham MA 02154 Office: 764 Main St Waltham MA 02154

MITCHELL, ILA MAE (MRS. LEWIS VERNIE MITCHELL), newspaper exec.; b. South Haven, Mich., Sept. 26, 1927; d. Clinton Lindsay and Frances Mary (Benedict) Fleming; secretarial certificate Western Mich. U., 1947; m. Lewis Vernie Mitchell, Aug. 1, 1947; children—Michele Lynn (Mrs. Barney Ray Cargile), Robert Lewis, William Clinton. Bookkeeper, Fayette County Times, Fayette, Ala., 1958-60; steel inventory clk. Portland Forge & Foundry (Ind.), 1962-66; bookkeeper, asst. to gen. mgr. Iroquois County Daily Times, Watseka, Ill., 1966-70; mus. sec. Iroquois County Hist. Soc. Mus., Watseka, 1971-72; co-owner Milford (Ill.) Herald News, 1972—. Sec., Gideons Aux., Kankakee, Ill., 1967-70. Methodist (tchr. Sunday sch. 1966-72, v.p. women's soc. Christian Service 1971-72). Club: Woman's of Watseka (pres. 1971-73, 18th dist. Ill. bicentennial chmn.). Home: 600 E Lyle St Milford IL 60953 Office: 18 S Axtel St Milford IL 60953

MITCHELL, JONI, singer, songwriter; b. Ft. MacCleod, Alta., Can., Nov. 7, 1943; d. William A. and Myrtle M. (McKee) Anderson; student Alta. Coll. Art. Albums include Song to a Seagull; Clouds. Address: care Asylum Records Geffen-Roberts Co 9120 Sunset Blvd Hollywood CA 90069

MITCHELL, JOSEPHINE GRAY (MRS. T. A. MITCHELL), musician; b. Bonham, Tex.; d. Moses Vashti and Bertie (Hoy) Gray; B.S., Tex. Women's U., 1926, M.A., 1971; m. T.A. Mitchell, Mar. 21, 1929; children—Richard Gray, Thomas Albert. Pianist profl. concerts, Tex., Okla., Colo., 1927—; tchr. music Port Arthur (Tex.) High Sch., 1928-29. Lectr. on Tex. music and composers in Southwest area. Established Southwestern Folk Music Archive in Ft. Worth Library; mem. bd. Tex. Girls Choir, Youth Orch. Greater Ft. Worth. Recipient citation Nat. Fedn. Music Clubs, 1962-70, Am. Fedn. Musicians, 1965, Sigma Alpha Iota, 1966. Nat. Fedn. Musicians, 1967; named 1st Lady Music Ft. Worth, 1967. Mem. Am. Coll. Musicians, Fort Worth League Composers (founder, pres.), Fine Arts Guild, Nat. Fedn. Music Clubs (nat. folk music archivist 1963-65, research chmn. 1958-68), Tex. Fedn. Music Clubs (pres. 4th dist. 1964-65), Tex. Composers Guild (state chmn. 1952—), Nat. Fedn. Music Clubs (nat. chmn. folk music 1971—), Tex. Women's U. Alumnae Assn. (past. pres.), Fort Worth Ballet Assn. (charter), Symphony League (charter), Ft. Worth Opera Guild (charter), Fine Arts Council, Nat. Guild Piano Tchrs. (nat. adjudicator), Sigma Alpha Iota (pres. 1961-62), Episcopalian. Clubs: Fort Worth Piano Forum, Fort Worth Women's, Euterpean Music (pres. 1952-54), E. Clyde Whitlock Music (past pres., charter mem.). Editor: Tex. Composers Handbook, 1955, 2d. edit., 1974. Home: 5120 Malinda Lane S Fort Worth TX 76112

MITCHELL, JOSEPHINE MARGARET (MRS. LOWELL SCHOENFELD), educator; b. Edmonton, Alta., Can.; d. Benjamin Foster and Kate Josephine (Russell) Mitchell; came to U.S., 1938, naturalized, 1950; B.S. with honors, U. Alta., 1934; M.A., Bryn Mawr Coll., 1941, Ph.D., 1942; m. Lowell Schoenfeld, Aug. 10, 1953. Tchr. women's colls., 1942-47; asst. prof. Okla. State U., 1947-48, U. Ill., 1948-54; mathematician Gen. Electric Co., Ithaca, N.Y., 1955-56, Westinghouse Research Lab., Pitts., 1956-57; asso. prof. U. Pitts., 1957-58; asso. prof. Pa. State U., 1958-61, prof., 1961-68; prof. math. State U. N.Y. at Buffalo, 1968—; mem. Inst. Advanced Study, Princeton, 1954-55; mem. math. research center, U. Wis., 1964-65, summer 1967; Math. Assn. lectr., 1965-72. Research grantee Am. Philos. Soc., 1948; Am. Assn. U. Women Nat. fellow, 1954-55; NSF Sr. Postdoctoral fellow, 1964-65, grantee, 1952-53, 68-71; Air Force grantee, 1960-63. Fellow A.A.A.S.; mem. Am. Math. Soc., Math. Assn. Am. Contbr. articles math. jours. Research in math., 1942—. Home: 1701 W River Rd Grand Island NY 14072 Office: 4246 Ridge Lea Rd Amherst NY 14266

MITCHELL, MARIANNE HELEN, educator; b. Toledo, Apr. 8, 1937; d. Frank H. and Helen (Metzger) Mitchell; B.A., U. Toledo, 1958, M.A., 1961, Ed.D., 1964. Tchr. secondary English, Toledo Pub. Schs., 1958-60; supr. student tchrs. U. Toledo, 1961-62, research asso., 1963-64; asst. prof. counselor edn. Central Mich. U., 1964-66; asso. prof. counselor edn. Ind. U., Bloomington, 1966—. Asso. dir. comparative edn. studies between U.S. and U.K., 1963—. Mem. Am. Personnel and Guidance Assn., Phi Kappa Phi, Pi Lambda Theta, Pi Beta Phi, Delta Kappa Gamma. Author: The High School Dropout: Can He Succeed in College; The Development and Management of School Guidance Programs; The Counselor and Sexuality. Office: Sch Edn Ind U Bloomington IN 47401

MITCHELL, MARION MIRANDA MCWILLIAMS (MRS. WILLIAM HENRY MITCHELL), social work adminstr.; b. Elgin, Ill., Nov. 14, 1914; d. Henry Edgar and Ada (Young) McWilliams; B.A., U. Chgo., 1936, M.A., 1959; m. William Henry Mitchell, Jan. 11, 1941. Caseworker, Chgo. Relief Adminstrn., 1938-41; library asst. Chgo. Pub. Library, 1941-42; caseworker Chgo. Orphan Asylum, 1943-44, caseworker spl. day care project, 1947-50; probation officer Juvenile Ct. of Cook County (Ill.), 1945-47; caseworker Chgo. (Ill.) Child Care Soc., 1950-54, supr. child placement and adoptions, 1954—. Chmn. Chgo. chpt. Nat. Council on Illegitimacy, 1966—; del. to Ill. Commn. on Children, 1970, mem. state cooperating orgns. com., 1972-73, mem. adoptions com., 1972-73, mem. adv. com. Subsidies for Black Adoptions, 1972-74. Bd. dirs. Midwest Adoption Facilitating Service, 1971—, Council on Unplanned Pregnancy, 1971-73. Mem. Ill. Welfare Assn. (mem. study course com. 1965-73, dir. 1972—), Nat. Assn. Social Workers, Nat. Conf. Social Welfare, Child Care Assn. Ill., Acad. Certified Social Workers. Home: 7552 S

Wabash Av Chicago IL 60619 Office: 5467 S University Av Chicago IL 60615

MITCHELL, MONA GENEVIEVE WOLF (MRS. BRUCE AMBROSE MITCHELL), occupational therapist; b. Ames, Ia., Aug. 13, 1940; d. Leonard Lauritzen and Elva Lucille (Kreamer) Wolf; student Grinnell Coll., 1958-59; B.S., Western Mich. U., 1963; m. Bruce Ambrose Mitchell, June 8, 1968; children—Heather Rosine, Laura Kathleen. Staff therapist Children's Psychiat. Hosp., Ann Arbor, Mich., 1963-66; staff therapist So. Ariz. Mental Health Center, Tucson, 1966-69, acting dept. head, 1968; head occupational therapy dept. Partridge Sch., Tucson, 1969-70; staff therapist Good Samaritan Hosp., Phoenix, 1970-71. Mem. Am., Ariz. (pres. 1969-71) occupational therapy assns., Mohare County Assn. Retarded Children (treas. 1972-73). Home: 2419 Lillie St Kingman AZ 86401

MITCHELL, NELLIE L., physician; b. Jersey City; d. Cullie and Eloise (Casey) Mitchell; B.A., N.Y.U., 1945; M.A., Columbia, 1949; M.D., Howard U., 1950; 1 son, Edward H. Intern Jersey City Med. Center, 1950-51; resident Freedmen's Hosp., Washington, 1951-56; practice medicine, specializing in child psychiatry Rochester, N.Y., 1965—; mem. staff Rochester Gen. Hosp.; tng. dir. child psychiatry Rochester Mental Health Center, 1971—; clin. instr. psychiatry U. Rochester, 1965—; cons. Monroe County Dept. Social Services, E. Irondequoit Central Sch., Hillside Children's Center. Diplomate Am. Bd. Psychiatry and Neurology. Fellow Am. Orthopsychiat. Assn., Am. Psychiat. Assn.; mem. Am. Med. Womens Assn., Nat. Med. Assn., Am. Acad. Child Psychiatry, Alpha Kappa Alpha. Presbyn. Home: 345 Highland Av Rochester NY 14620 Office: Rochester Mental Health Center Rochester NY 14620

MITCHELL, RUTH KAY, information scientist, librarian; b. Wauwatosa, Wis.; d. Albert and Ruth Pauline (Weber) Schulke; B.S., U. Wis., 1957, M.A., 1966; postgrad. U. Pitts., 1967—, advanced certificate information sci., 1968; 1 dau., Beth Kay. Librarian, Milw. Sch. Engring., 1960-67, dir. information services, 1967; research asst. U. Pitts., 1967-69; project lead engr. Westinghouse Information Systems Lab., 1967-70; dean of libraries services office, head research and systems Ore. System Higher Edn., Eugene, 1970—; asso. prof. U. Ore., 1970—. Mem. A.L.A., Am. Soc. Information Scis., Am. Assn. U. Profs., Engrs. and Scientists, Nat. Orgn. Women. Author: Information Science and Computer Basics, 1971. Home: 6195 Thurston Rd Springfield OR 97477 Office: U Oregon Room 112-C Library Eugene OR 97403

MITCHELL, SUSAN CATHERINE (MRS. JOHN WILLIAM MITCHELL), coll. adminstr.; b. Boston, Dec. 1, 1944; d. Robert Miller and Catherine (Penrose) Lewis; B.A., U. Colo., 1966; M.A., U. Ore., 1968, M.S., 1969; m. John William Mitchell, Aug. 27, 1966; 1 dau., Heather Catherine. Dean women Boise (Ida.) State Coll., 1972-73, dir. student residential life, 1973—. Mem. Boise Opera Guild, 1971—; co-chmn. regional Women's Conf., 1972. Mem. Nat. Assn. Women Deans, Adminstrs. and Counselors, Am. Assn. Higher Edn., N.W. Coll. Personnel Assn., Ida. Personnel and Guidance Assn. Club: Madrigal (soloist). Home: 3225 Camrose Lane Boise ID 83704

MITCHELL, VERDA RAYE (MRS. PAT MITCHELL), city ofcl.; b. Stonewall County, Tex., Feb. 20, 1929; d. Fred David and Edna Inez (Trammel) Graham; student Draughan's Bus. Coll., 1947; m. Pat Mitchell, Jr., May 31, 1950; children—Verdonna (Mrs. Bobby Durham), Monty. Bookkeeper, First Nat. Bank, Aspermont, Tex., 1952-61; sec. Aspermont Ind. Sch. Dist., 1964-65; bus. mgr. Stonewall Meml. Hosp., Aspermont, 1965-72; city sec. City of Aspermont, 1972—. Sec., 4-H Adult Leadership Club, Aspermont, 1972—, Future Farmers Am. Booster Club, Aspermont, 1973—. Baptist. Clubs: Aspermont Golf, Bridge, Things Going On (Aspermont). Home: PO Box 310 Aspermont TX 79502 Office: PO Box 277 Aspermont TX 79502

MITFORD, JESSICA (MRS. ROBERT TREUHAFT), author; b. Batsford Mansion, Eng., Sept. 11, 1917; d. Lord and Lady Redesdale; m. Esmond Romilly, 1937; m. 2d, Robert Treuhaft, June 21, 1943; children—Constancia Romilly, Benjamin Treuhaft. Came to U.S., 1939, naturalized, 1944. Sec., East Bay Civil Rights Congress, 1949-55. Author: Daughters and Rebels (autobiography), 1960; The American Way of Death, 1963; The Trial of Dr. Spock, 1969; Kind and Usual Punishment: The American Prison Business, 1973. Address: 6411 Regent St Oakland CA 94618

MITSTIFER, DOROTHY IRWIN, assn. exec.; b. Gaines, Pa., Aug. 17, 1932; d. Leonard Robert and Laura (Crane) Irwin; B.S., Mansfield State Coll., 1954; postgrad. Cornell U., 1955; M.Ed., Pa. State U., 1972; m. Robert Mitchell Mitstifer, June 17, 1956; children—Kurt Michael, Brett Robert. Tchr., Tri-County Joint Sch. Dist., Canton, Pa., 1954-56, Loyalsock Twp. Sch. Dist., Williamsport, Pa., 1956-62; nat. exec. sec., mgr. nat. office Kappa Omicron Phi home econ. honor soc., 1964—. Bd. dirs. Williamsburg Pub. Library. Mem. Am. Home Econs. Assn., Kappa Delta Pi, Kappa Omicron Phi, Omicron Nu. Club: Women's Civic (Williamsburg). Address: 1411 Lafayette Pkwy Williamsport PA 17701

MITSUDO, SUMI MARY (MRS. SAMUEL S. KOIDE), physician; b. Longview, Wash., Oct. 22, 1929; d. Sotaro and Asa (Uyeda) Mitsudo; B.A., Swarthmore Coll., 1951; M.D., Woman's Med. Coll. Pa., 1956; m. Samuel S. Koide, Nov. 26, 1960; children—Sumi Lynn, Mark Kenji, Eric Akira. Intern, Germantown Dispensary & Hosp., Phila., 1956; resident pathology Michael Reese Hosp., Chgo., 1957-59, Temple U. Med. Center, Phila., 1959-61; asst. pathologist Bellevue Hosp., N.Y.C., 1961-66; asst. prof., N.Y. U. Med. Sch., N.Y.C., 1963-66; asso. dir. labs. Morrisania Hosp. Affiliation, Bronx, 1966—; asso. pathologist Montefiore Hosp. Med. Center, Bronx, 1966—; asst. prof. pathology Albert Einstein Coll. Medicine, Bronx, N.Y., 1967—. Vice pres. Dobbs Ferry Employment Service, Inc.; chmn. Narcotic Guidance Council Dobbs Ferry. Fellow Am. Soc. Clin. Pathology; mem. N.Y. Pathol. Soc., N.Y. Pathology Club, Soc. Urban Physicians, League Women Voters. Unitarian (trustee 1970-73). Home: 134 Lefurgy Av Dobbs Ferry NY 10522 Office: 111 E 210th St Bronx NY 10452

MIURA, MURIEL REIKO KAMADA, home economist; b. Honolulu, Jan. 23, 1935; d. Minoru and Rose (Masako) Kamada; B.S., U. Hawaii, 1958; M.A., Columbia, 1959; 1 dau., Shari Akemi. Tchr. Hawaii Dept. Edn.; Honolulu, 1958-59; now home econs. dir. Gasco, Inc., Honolulu. Food cons.; demonstrator TV series Cook Japanese for sta. KHET, Hawaii, 1973. Recipient McCall's Home Service Achievement award, 1961-63, Festival of Gas award N.Y. World's Fair 1965. Mem. Am. Home Econs. Assn., Am. Sch. Lunch Service Assn., Food Service Execs. Hawaii. Author: Cook Japanese-Hawaiian Style, 1974. Address: 1050 Bishop St Honolulu HI 96813

MIZUNO, IKUKO, musician; b. Tokyo, Japan, Dec. 5, 1942; d. Hisao and Hiroko (Hibi) Mizuno; B.A., ToHoGakuen Sch. Music, Japan, 1965; diploma, Accademia Musical Chigiana, 1968, Conservatoire de Musique de Geneva, 1968; M.M., Boston U., 1969. Began playing violin at age 5; 7 debuts in Tokyo playing Bach Violin Concerto; tour with Toho-Gakuen Sch. Music String Orch., U.S.A., 1964; solo violinist with Boston Pops, 1966—, also several recitals; mem. 1st violin sect. Boston Symphony Orch., European tour, 1971; debut recital, N.Y.C., 1972; concert tours to Japan, 1969—. Recipient Music award, 1965. Mem. Phi Kappa Lambda. Appeared TV, radio, Italy, Switzerland, Japan, U.S.A. Home: 33 Pond Av Brookline MA 02146 Office: Symphony Hall Boston MA 02115

MIZUNO, NOBUKO SHIMOTORI, biochemist; b. Oakland, Cal., Apr. 20, 1916; d. Shinichiro and Kil (Niiyomura) Shimotori; A.B., U. Cal. at Berkeley, 1937, M.A., 1939; Ph.D., U. Minn., 1956; m. Walter Mizuno, Mar. 20, 1942 (dec.). Research asst. U. Cal. at Berkeley, 1937-41; instr. Macalester Coll., St. Paul, 1946-51; research asso. U. Minn., 1956-62; research biochemist VA Hosp., Mpls., 1962—. Mem. Am. Chem. Soc., A.A.A.S., N.Y. Acad. Scis., Am. Inst. Nutrition, Am. Assn. Cancer Research, Phi Beta Kappa, Sigma Xi, Iota Sigma Pi, Phi Zeta. Contbr. articles to profl. jours. Home: 1282 Hewitt Av St Paul MN 55104 Office: VA Hospital Minneapolis MN 55417

MOALLEM, ANITA LOUISE GROSS, educator, radiologist; b. N.Y.C., Dec. 30, 1939; d. Herman and Jessie (Schuman) Gross; B.S., Bklyn. Coll., 1960; M.D., Albert Einstein Coll. Medicine, 1964. Intern, resident Bronx-Lebanon Hosp. Center, N.Y.C.; practice medicine specializing in radiology, N.Y.C.; mem. staff Flower and Fifth Av Hosp., N.Y.C.; asst. prof. radiology N.Y. Med. Coll., N.Y.C., 1971—. Diplomate Am. Bd. Radiology. Mem. Am. Coll. Radiology, Am. Inst. for Ultrasound in Med., Soc. Nuclear Med., A.M.A. Office: 1249 Fifth Av New York City NY 10029

MOBBERLY, BELVA ADELLE, city ofcl.; b. Ohio County, Ky., Oct. 4, 1912; d. Eugene and Belva Lockwood (Jackson) Stroud; grad. Owensboro (Ky.) Bus. Coll., 1933; certificate Internat. City Mgr.'s Assn., 1956; m. Hubert Shelton, June 16, 1935 (dec. 1953); children—Dallas, Linda (Mrs. P.E. Egeler), Kaye (Mrs. Wayne Greenwall), Michael; m. 2d, James S. Mobberly, Mar. 10, 1973. Legal sec., 1933-42; with local SSS, 1942-43; office mgr. Suburban Plumbing & Heating Co., 1946-52; legal sec. to mayor, Owensboro, 1954-55; personnel dir. City of Owensboro, city clk., 1955—, sec. city employees bd. trustees Pension Fund. Past sec. D.A.V. Assn.; pres. Spastic Home-Sch. Inc. Parents Club, 1969, sec., 1960—; sec., dir. Owensboro Regatta, 1969—. Mem. Internat. Inst. Municipal Clks. (membership chmn. 1964), Internat. City Clks. Assn., Ky. Hist. Soc., Ky. Cols. Home: 2121 Cedar St Owensboro KY 42301 Office: PO Box 208 Owensboro KY 42301

MOBERLY, ISABEL CAROL, mem. Republican Nat. Com.; b. Alliance, Alta., Can., Sept. 12, 1909; d. Carl J. and Elizabeth Emma (Hogan) Quisberg; came to U.S., 1923, naturalized, 1931; ed. pub. schs., Mont.; m. Waldo Young Moberly, Oct. 6, 1926. Partner, v.p., treas. with husband in W. Y. Moberly, Inc., and predecessor, U.S. customhouse brokers, Sweetgrass, Mont., 1926-68. Mem. Rep. Party, 1931—; pres. Toole County Rep. Womens Club, 1958-59; v.p. Mont. Fedn. Rep. Women, 1959-60; vice chmn. Mont. Rep. Central Com., 1960-64; mem. Rep. Com. from Mont., 1964—, also mem. exec. com., 1964-68; vice chmn. Rep. Nat. Com., 1972—. Mem. Mont. Hosp. Adv. Council, 1958-62. Dir. Mont. Girls State, 1963-65. Named Woman of the Year, Mont. Fedn. Bus. and Profl. Women's Clubs, 1968. Mem. Am. Legion Aux. Home: 485 Judy Av Shelby MT 59474

MOBLEY, JEAN BELLINGRATH, educator; b. Norfolk, Va., Mar. 13, 1927; d. George Council and Margaret (Shive) Bellingrath; student Agnes Scott Coll., 1944-46; A.B., Duke U., 1948; M.A., U. N.C., 1954, Ph.D., 1970; m. Carroll Wade Mobley, Mar. 12, 1949; children—Larry Wade, Julia Elizabeth. Tchr. pub. schs., N.C., 1949-56; asso. prof., head math. dept. Flora MacDonald Coll., Red Springs, N.C., 1956-61, St. Andrew's Presbyn. Coll., Laurinburg, N.C., 1961-63; prof. Pfeiffer Coll., Misenheimer, N.C., 1963—. Cons. math. to pub. schs. NSF fellow, 1961-62, Presbyn. fellow, 1962-63. Mem. Nat. Council Tchrs. Math., N.C., Council Tchrs. Math., N.E.A., N.C. Assn. Educators (N.C. pres. math. dept. 1961-62, N.C. pres. div. higher edn. 1963-64), N.C. Acad. Sci. (pres. math. dept. 1962-63), Math. Assn. Am., Delta Kappa Gamma. Presbyn. Author: Supervision in Mathematics, 1968. Home: 227 Camelot Dr Salisbury NC 28144 Office: Pfeiffer Coll Misenheimer NC 28109

MOCHARY, MARY VERONICA (MRS. STEPHEN E. MOCHARY), lawyer; b. Budapest, Hungary, Sept. 7, 1942; d. Alexander and Elisabeth (Aranyi) Kasser; came to U.S., 1949, naturalized, 1957; B.A., Wellesley Coll., 1963; J.D., U. Chgo., 1967; m. Stephen E. Mochary, Sept. 25, 1965; children—Alexandra Veronica, Matthew Neal. Translator, trainee Bank of Am., Internat. Hdqrs., San Francisco, 1963-64; admitted to Ark. 1968, N.J. bar, 1970; pvt. practice law, Fayetteville, Ark., 1968; partner Mochary & Mochary, Montclair, N.J., 1970—. Bd. dirs. Manhatten Indsl. Home for Blind League; bd. dirs. Kasser Art Found., mgr., 1969—. Mem. Ark., N.J. bar assns., League Women Voters. Republican. Mem. Ref. Ch. Clubs: N.J. Wellesley, Essex Fells Country. Home: 60 Undercliff Rd Montclair NJ 07042 Office: 26 Park St Montclair NJ 07042

MOCK, ESTHER GILLILAND (MRS. LAVERNE FRANCIS MOCK), pub. relations exec.; b. LaJunta, Colo., Sept. 18, 1915; d. John Lawrence and Sophia Catherine (Fisher) Gilliland; student U. Colo., 1933-34; m. LaVerne Francis Mock, Dec. 13, 1934; children—Michael Stephen, Eric Vaughan, John Allan, Douglas Wayne. Columnist Winston-Salem Jour., 1956-57; dir. news bur. Salem Coll., Winston-Salem, 1961-71, dir. pub. relations, 1972-73; dir. pub. information, community action program Expt. in Self Reliance, Winston-Salem, 1968-69, asst. to pres. for pub. relations, 1973—. Bd. dirs. Halfway House, Winston-Salem. Mem. League Women Voters, Nat. Orgn. for Women, Delta Delta Delta. Home: 1105 Brookstown Av Winston-Salem NC 27101 Office: Salem Coll Winston-Salem NC 27108

MOCK, JOANNE MCKESSON, TV exec.; b. Buffalo, Aug. 7, 1930; d. Harold Jackson and Ruth Elizabeth (Straight) Mock; B.A., U. Cal. at Los Angeles. With TV prodn. ABC-TV, Fuller & Smith & Ross Advt., N.Y.C., 1954-60; producer, dir. KQED-TV, San Francisco, 1961-70, Cal. Instructional TV Consortium State Colls. and Univs., Rohnert Park, Cal., 1973—; cons. U.S. Office Edn., Washington, 1974. Recipient award for excellence Nat. Ednl. TV, 1967, Broadcast Preceptor award San Francisco State Coll., 1966. Mem. Western Ednl. Soc. Telecommunications, Common Cause (West coast TV coordinator 1971-73), Pacific Heights Assn. Home: 2400 Pacific Av San Francisco CA 94115 Office: 1801 E Cotati Av Rohnert Park CA 94928

MOCK, SANDRA LYNNE, social worker; b. Chgo.; d. Eugene W. and Myra (Freward) Mock; B.A., Franklin Coll., 1960; M.S.W., Tulane U., 1962; postgrad. John Marshall Law Sch., 1967. Psychiat. and clin. social worker VA Hosp., Seattle, 1962-64; med. social worker Evanston (Ill.) Hosp., 1964—. Field instr. U. Chgo. Sch. Social Services Adminstrn., 1967-70; instr. Northwestern U. Med. Sch., 1966-73. Northminster Ch. fellow, 1970-73, v.p., 1973—. Mem. Nat. Assn. Social Workers (med. council 1964-70), Acad. Certified Social Workers, Franklin Coll. Alumni Council, Tulane U. Alumni Assn., Evanston Mental Health Soc., Women in Communications. (Hoosier Headliner award 1958), Delta Delta Delta. Episcopalian. Club: Unicorn Ski (Chgo.). Home: 408 Barton Pl Evanston IL 60202

MODE, JUDY KEY (MRS. DAVID LUKE MODE), journalist; b. Chattanooga, July 22, 1949; d. Vernie Lee and Ruby Elizabeth (Smith) Key; student Wesleyan Coll., Macon, Ga., 1967-68; B.A. cum laude, U. Ga., 1972; m. David Luke Mode, Aug. 8, 1970. Asst. dir. pub. relations Reinhardt Coll., Waleska, Ga., 1972, dir. pub. relations, 1973; staff writer Cherokee Tribune, Canton, Ga., 1973; exec. asst., head copywriter Sullivan Agy., Columbia, S.C., 1974—. Mem. Phi Kappa Phi, Gamma Alpha Chi, Kappa Tau Alpha, Kappa Delta. Baptist. Home: Landmark Dr Columbia SC 29210

MODEL, ELISABETH DITTMAN, sculptor; b. Bayreuth, Bavaria, Germany; d. J.M. and Therese (Dittman-Fleisher) Dittman; student Coll. Art, Munich, Bavaria, Acad. Art, Amsterdam, Netherlands; pupil sculptor M. Kogan, Paris, France; m. Max Model, Sept. 5, 1922 (dec.); children—Wolfe F., Frank P. Came to U.S., 1941, naturalized, 1947. One-woman shows Europe, N.Y.C., Washington; group shows Stedelijk Mus., Amsterdam, Brit.-Am. Art Center, Mus. Fine Arts, Boston, Mus. Fine Arts, Phila., Bklyn. Mus., Riverside Mus., Mus. Natural History, Galleria L'Obelisco, Rome, The Contemporaries, N.Y.C., others; represented in collections including Corcoran Gallery, Washington, Ryks-Prenton-Kabinett, Amsterdam, Atheneum Mus., Hartford, Conn., Jewish Mus. N.Y., Norfolk (Va.) Mus., Wichita (Kan.) U., Brandeis U. Recipient numerous awards and prizes. Mem. Fedn. Modern Painters and Sculptors (corr. sec.), Bklyn. Soc. Artists. Home: 340 W 72d St Apt 1-A New York City NY 10023 also Bedford Village NY

MODJESKA, JANET ELAINE (MRS. PAUL A. MODJESKA), outdoor advt. co. exec.; b. Saugerties, N.Y., Aug. 25, 1937; d. Durwood and Margaret Elizabeth (Van Vlierden) Swart; grad. high sch.; m. Paul A. Modjeska, Nov. 24, 1957; children—Steven, Pamela, Nancy, Sharon. Exec. v.p. Modjeska Sign Studios, Inc., Kingston, N.Y., 1966—; exec. v.p. Twin Poster Corp., Kingston, 1966—, Midport Outdoor, Inc., Middletown, N.Y., 1968—, Forty Thomas Street Corp., Kingston, 1966—. Home: 21 Barclay St Saugerties NY 12477 Office: 40 Thomas St Kingston NY 12401

MOE, MILDRED MARY MINASIAN (MRS. OSBORNE KENNETH MOE), physicist; b. Phila., Nov. 18, 1929; d. Hagop and Nevart (Azhderian) Minasian; B.A. in Physics, U. Cal. at Los Angeles, 1951, M.A., 1953, Ph.D. (Univ. fellow), 1957; m. Osborne Kenneth Moe, Aug. 20, 1951; children—Robert Arthur, Karen Elizabeth Nevart. Teaching asst. U. Cal., Los Angeles, 1951-52; grad. research asst. Scripps Instn. Oceanography, 1953; mem. tech. staff TRW Systems, 1956-60; cons. E.H. Plessent Assos., 1963-64; asst. prof. physics Loyola U., Los Angeles, 1967-70, research asso., 1971-73; asst. research physicist U. Cal. at Irvine, 1973—. Mem. Am. Phys. Soc., Am. Assn. Physics Tchrs., Phi Beta Kappa, Sigma Xi, Pi Mu Epsilon. Home: 6892 Manhattan Dr Huntington Beach CA 92647

MOEHLMAN, MARGUERITE CAROLINE REICHENBOURG (MRS. ARTHUR H. MOEHLMAN), educator; b. Nice, France (parent Am. citizen); d. Frank and Madeleine (Arnauld) Reichenbourg; B.Sc., U. Nancy, 1927; B.S., U. Pa., 1927, M.S., 1929, Ph.D., 1932; diploma Inst. Phonetique, U. Paris, 1935; postgrad. Harvard, 1931; m. Arthur H. Moehlman, Dec. 23, 1933; children—Michael Scott, Stephen Mackaye, Patricia des Roses, Jacqueline Arnauld (Mrs. Frank McCreary III). Tchr. French, Sayward Sch., Phila., 1928-32; asst. prof. French, modern lang. edn., chmn. dept. Ohio State U., 1932-38; tchr. Arlington (Va.) Pub. Schs., 1943-45, Haddonfield (N.J.) High Sch., 1945-46, Austin (Tex.) Pub. Sch., 1955-67; head dept. modern langs. St. Stephen's Sch., Austin, 1966—. Mem. Modern Lang. Assn. U.S., Save the Children Fedn. Episcopalian. Author: Les Lectures de Jean-Jacques Rousseau, 1934. Joint research with husband higher edn., internat. edn., summers 1967, 70, 72, 73. Contbr. articles to profl. jours. Home: 4107 Farhills St Austin TX 78731

MOEHRLE, PHYLLIS HORTON (MRS. JAMES HOLDEN MOEHRLE), assn. exec.; b. Hamburg, N.Y., June 12, 1914; d. Roy Austin and Grace Valentine (Spencer) Horton; B.A., Hunter Coll., 1935; postgrad. U. Buffalo, N.Y. U.; m. James Holden Moehrle, Feb. 10, 1942. Staff asst. Nat. Assn. Mfrs., Washington, 1945-66, asst. to v.p. indsl. relations, dir. Indsl. Relations Inst., 1966-72, asst. v.p., N.Y.C., 1972-73, v.p., Washington, 1973—. Mem. bus. adv. council Bur. Labor Statistics, 1969-73. Bd. dirs. World Relief Commn., 1957-68. Recipient Gold Key award Pub. Relations News, 1974. Mem. Am. Soc. Assn. Execs., Indsl. Relations Research Assn. Contbr. articles to profl. and popular mags. Home: 500 23d St NW Washington DC 20037 Office: 1776 F St NW Washington DC 20006

MOELLER, AVIS GABRIELSON, educator; b. St. Croix Falls, Wis., Dec. 24, 1936; d. Theodore Russell and Elma N. (Schipper) Gabrielson; B.S., U. Minn., 1958, M.A., 1966; m. James W. Moeller, Aug. 3, 1970. Tchr. high sch., 1958-64; instr. Coll. Home Econs. U. Minn., 1965-66; asst. prof. textiles and clothing, chmn. dept. St. Olaf Coll., Northfield, Minn., 1966-70; asst. prof. Mundelein Coll., Chgo., 1970—; tchr. workshops, instr. Head Start programs. Mem. Am., Ill./Minn. home econs. assns., Coll. Tchrs. Textiles and Clothing, Phi Upsilon Omicron. Author curriculum guides. Home: 9338 Harding Av Evanston IL 60203 Office: 6363 Sheridan Rd Chicago IL 60660

MOELLER, DOROTHY WILSON (MRS. LESLIE GEORGE MOELLER), writer; b. Dawson, N.D., Nov. 14, 1902; d. Richard Miller and Lucie Emma (Mumby) Wilson; student Mason City Jr. Coll., 1921-22; B.A., certificate in journalism, U. Ia., 1925; postgrad. U. Ia., 1950-51; m. Leslie George Moeller, Mar. 24, 1926; children—Richard Kent, Margaret Lou (Mrs. Theodore Cooke Nelson). Reporter, Waverly (Ia.) Newspapers, Inc., 1928-43, mgr., 1943-45; researcher, writer Classroom Use of Daily Newspapers, nat. study, 1956-58; mem. staff Jour. Speech and Hearing Research, Am. Speech and Hearing Assn., Washington, 1958-63; editorial and research asso., archivist U. Ia., 1963-69; writer psychosocial aspects of communications, 1958—. Cons. student orientation U. Ia., 1950-65. Mem. council Cardinal council Girl Scouts, 1947-51; chmn. county blood drive A.R.C., 1951. Bd. dirs. Iowa City Community Chest, 1952-54. Recipient Headliner award U. Ia. Women in Communication, 1973. Mem. Women in Communications, Ia. Designer Craftsmen, League Women Voters (Ia. dir.), editor Iowa Voter 1952-55, P.E.O. Republican. Clubs: Nineteenth Century Study, University, International, University Athletic (Iowa City). Author: (with Wendell Johnson) Living with Change, 1972. Editor: (with Wendell Johnson) Speech Handicapped School Children, 1967. Address: 623 E College St Iowa City IA 52240

MOELLER, ESTHER LOUISE (MRS. A. DEWITT BROWN), physician; b. Utica, N.Y., Aug. 6, 1916; d. Alfred L. and Hannah A. (Steinhorst) Moeller; student Barnard Coll., 1938; M.D., Albany Med. Coll., 1942; m. A. Dewitt Brown, Dec. 29, 1941; 1 son, Jared Moeller Brown. Gen. intern Meml. Hosp., Albany, N.Y., 1942-43; pathology intern Albany Hosp., 1943-44; gen. practice medicine, New Hartford, N.Y., 1944—; mem. staff Faxton Hosp., Utica, 1944—; asso. staff St. Luke's Meml. Hosp., Utica, 1970—; mem. geriatric screening team Utica State Hosp., 1968—. Mem. Nat. Bd. Med. Examiners, Am., N.Y., County of Oneida med. assns., Central N.Y. Acad. Medicine, Munson Williams Proctor Inst., Am. Orchid Soc., N.Y. Conservation Council, Nat. Hist. Soc., Defenders of Wildlife,

Smithsonian Assos., Assn. N.Y. Mental Hygiene Physicians and Dentists. Mem. Order Eastern Star. Clubs: Bide A Wee Home, Gardening Under Lights. Home: 86 Genesee St New Hartford NY 13413 Office: 86 Genesee St New Hartford NY 13413

MOEN, OLLIE MAE ALLISON (MRS. GEORGE JENS MOEN), ednl. adminstr.; b. nr. Osage, Tex., Mar. 14, 1910; d. William Patrick and Elbie Isle (Hancock) Allison; student Tex. Luth. Coll., summers 1946-49; m. George Jens Moen, May 26, 1934; children—George James, Allison J. Clk., Woolworth Co., Waco, Tex., 1927; operator S.W. Bell Telephone Co., Waco, 1928, instr., observer central office, 1930-31, bus. office rep., 1932-38; dir. Youth Cultural Center, Waco Sch. System, 1964—. Pres. Provident Heights Sch. P.T.A., 1961-62, Waco City Council P.T.A., 1965-66; cultural arts chmn. 9th Dist. Tex. P.T.A., 1967-68. Bd. dirs. Sunset Luth. Home, Clifton, Tex., 1962-71. Mem. Tex. Museum Assn. (dir. 1969-73), Evangelical Luth. Ch. Women (nat. life mem), Tex. P.T.A. (life), Waco Garden Council (1st v.p. 1969). Clubs: Blossom Garden (pres. 1967). Home: 2025 Sugg Dr Waco TX 76710 Office: 815 Columbus Av Waco TX 76703

MOFFAT, GRACE HARRIET, educator; b. N.Y.C.; B.S., M.A., City Univ. of N.Y.; Ph.D., N.Y. U., 1966; 2 children. Teaching fellow N.Y. U., 1961-62, instr., 1962; research asst. Brookhaven Nat. Lab., Upton, N.Y., 1961-63; research asst. Strangeways Research Lab., Cambridge, Eng., 1963-65; instr. Downstate Med. Center State U. N.Y., Bklyn., 1965-71; adj. asst. prof. dept. physiology Sch. Medicine U. N.M., 1972—, adj. asst. prof. dept. of anatomy, 1973—. NSF fellow, 1959, 61, AEC fellow, 1960, Brit. Empire Cancer Campaign for Research fellow, 1963-65. Mem. Am. Assn. Anatomists, Beta Lambda Sigma. Office: Basic Medical Science Bldg N Campus Albuquerque NM 87131

MOFFAT, HELEN MOORE, librarian; b. Garland, Utah, Apr. 26, 1917; d. Harvey Lemuel and Harriet A. (Miller) Moore; B.A., U. Utah, 1942; M.A., Ariz. State U., 1955; M.A., U. Denver, 1958; m. Lloyd Brown Moffat, June 5, 1946 (div. 1947); 1 son, Riley Moore. Tchr., librarian Weber County Schs., Utah, 1942-48, Mesa dist. schs., Ariz., 1948-66; guest prof. library sci. U. Utah, Salt Lake City, 1962-63, Ariz. State U., Tempe, 1960-67; librarian Ch. Coll. of Hawaii (now Hawaii campus Brigham Young U.), Laie, 1966—. Mem. Ariz., Mesa edn. assns., Ariz. State, Hawaii library assns., Phi Kappa Phi, Beta Phi Mu, Delta Kappa Gamma. Home: 55-170 Puuahi St Laie HI 96762 Office: Brigham Young U-Hawaii Campus Laie HI 96762

MOFFETT, MARTHA LEATHERWOOD, editor; b. St. Clair, Ala., Jan. 3, 1934; d. William Elbert and Martha (Funderburk) Leatherwood; B.S. in English Edn., U. Ala., 1955; M.S. in L.S., Columbia, 1972; m. Robert Knight Moffett, Jan. 30, 1955; children—Cameron, Tyler, Kirsten. Editor Grolier Inc., N.Y.C., 1966-68; sr. copy editor Am. Heritage Dictionary, N.Y.C., 1968-70; editor Ladies' Home Journal, N.Y.C., 1973—. Mem. Forum of Writers for Young People (pres. 1973-74). Author: Whales in Fact and Fiction, 1967; The First Book of Dolphins, 1971; A Flower Pot Is Not A Hat, '72; Great Women Athletes, 1974. Home: 201 W 94th St New York City NY 10025 Office: 614 Lexington Av New York City NY 10017

MOFFETT, SANDRA GAIL ROBINSON (MRS. WILLIAM D.A. MOFFETT III), occupational therapist; b. Temple, Tex., July 29, 1949; d. Ural Sylvester and Constance Marie (Rountree) Robinson, Jr.; B.S. in Occupational Therapy, Tex. Women's U., 1971; m. William D.A. Moffett, III, Aug. 18, 1973. Staff occupational therapist VA Center, Temple, Tex., 1971—. Mem. Am., Tex. (treas. central Tex. dist. 1973-75) occupational therapy assns. Home: 1419 E Av C Temple TX 76501 Office: 1901 S 1st St Temple TX 76501

MOFFITT, MARY ELIZABETH WEIMER, educator; b. Somerset, Pa., Aug. 8, 1907; d. Chauncey W. and Sarah (Woy) Weimer; B.S., Susquehanna U., 1928, Ped.D. (hon.), 1973; M.A., Columbia, 1930, Ed.D., 1953; m. Leon G. Moffitt, Sept. 30, 1934 (dec. Jan. 1961). Tchr. pub. schs., Pa., 1930-40; tchr. Horace Mann-Lincoln Tchrs. Coll., Columbia, N.Y.C., 1940-48; tchr. pub. schs., Punta Gorda, Fla., 1948-50; mem. faculty Queens Coll., City U. N.Y., Flushing, L.I., 1950—, prof. edn., 1965—. Cons. early childhood edn. Chmn. U.S. Nat. Com. for Early Childhood, 1971-73. Mem. Nat. Assn. Childhood Edn. Internat., Nat. Assn. Edn. Young Children, Assn. Curriculum Devel., Am. Ednl. Research Assn., Nat. Sci. Tchrs. Assn., World Edn. Fellowship, others. Author: vols. 1 and 2 of Science/Life series, Macmillan Co., 1959. Contbr. profl. jours. Home: 25 Solar Lane Albertson NY 11507 Office: Queens Coll Kissena Blvd Flushing NY 11367

MOFFO, ANNA, opera singer; b. Wayne, Pa.; d. Nicolas and Regina (Cinti) Moffo; grad. with honors Curtis Inst.; hon. degrees Temple U., Ursinus Coll.; Singer, Italian radio stas.; appeared TV opera Madame Butterfly, Italy; singer opera houses, Paris, London, Salzburg, also Italy; Am. debut Lyric Opera Co., Chgo., 1957, Met. Opera Co., N.Y.C., 1959; appeared Voice of Firestone telecast, 1957; operatic roles (soprano) include LaBoheme, Mignon, Rigoletto, Falstaff, Madame Butterfly, La Traviata, Turandot, La Juive, Barber of Seville, Marriage of Figaro; recs. Angel Records, RCA Victor; collaborator with husband in writing popular songs. Decorated commendatore Order Merit Republic of Italy. Fulbright scholar, 1956. Recipient numerous profl. awards. Address: care S A Gorlinsky Ltd 35 Dover St London W 1 England

MOGGE, HARRIET MORGAN, pub. co. personnel exec.; b. Cleve., Jan. 2, 1928; d. Russell VanDyke and Grace (Wells) Morgan; B.M.E., Northwestern U., 1959; postgrad. Ill. State U., 1969; m. Robert Arthur Mogge, Aug. 17, 1948; 1 dau., Linda Jean. Instr. piano, Evanston, Ill., 1954-58; instr. elementary music pub. schs., Evanston, 1959; editorial asst., archivist Summy-Birchard Co., Evanston, 1964-66, asst. to editor-in-chief, 1966-67, cons., 1968-69, ednl. dir., 1969-74, also historian, 1973-74; asst. dir. profl. programs Music Educators Nat. Conf., Vienna, Va., 1974—. Supr. vocal music jr. high sch., Watseka, Ill., 1967-68. Active various community drives. Mem. Music Educators Nat. Conf., Am. Choral Dirs. Assn., In and About Chgo. Music Educators Assn. (dir.), Suzuki Assn. Ams. (exec. sec. 1972—), Mu Phi Epsilon, Kappa Delta (province pres. 1960-66, 72—). Republican. Presbyn. Clubs: Evanston Woman's (music chmn.); Business and Professional Women's (dir. 1968-70) (Watseka); Antique Automobile Club, Model T Ford Internat. (v.p. 1971-72, dir. 1971—). Mng. editor Am. Suzuki Jour. Home: 1554 Northgate Sq #21B Reston VA 22090 Office: 8150 Leesburg Pike Vienna VA 22180

MOHANNA, ALTA JEAN BROWN (MRS. RICHARD J. MOHANNA), newspaper editor; b. Newport, Neb., July 24, 1930; d. James Price and Lena Alberta (Bishop) Brown; grad. high sch.; m. Richard J. Mohanna, Oct. 1, 1949; children—Mitchell James, Timothy Joseph. Co-editor, pub. Cairo Record, Cairo, Neb., 1954—. Methodist. Mem. Order of Eastern Star (worthy matron 1963-64). Elk. Home: 508 W Medina St Cairo NE 68824 Office: 120 High St Cairo NE 68824

MOHLER, EUNICE CAZIER, constrn. co. exec.; b. Twin Bridges, Mont., May 30, 1918; d. Evan Willard and Francena (Cazier) Christensen; student Woodbury Business Coll., Los Angeles, 1938; m. William W. Mohler, Apr. 23, 1945 (div. Mar. 1956). Sec., Ballinger Ins. Co., Los Angeles, 1938-41; with Grafe Callahan Constrn. Co., Los Angeles, 1941—, corporate officer, 1945—, also dir. Mem. Phi Beta Kappa. Republican. Mem. Ch. Jesus Christ of Latter-Day Saints. Home: 356 S Burnside Av Los Angeles CA 90036 Office: 714 W Olympic Blvd Los Angeles CA 90015

MOHLMAN, MARGARET ANN, advt. agy. exec.; b. Lafayette, Ind., Aug. 30, 1932; d. Robert Joseph and Margaret Mary (Horan) Mohlman; B.A., Sweet Briar Coll., 1954. Copywriter Compton Advt., N.Y.C., 1957-62, Foote, Cone & Belding, advt., N.Y.C., 1962-65; copy group head Needham, Harper & Steers, Inc., N.Y.C., 1965-69, account exec., 1969-73, asst. to chmn., v.p., 1973-74; account exec. Cunningham & Walsh, Inc., N.Y.C., 1974—. Home: 333 E 49th St New York City NY 10017 Office: care Cunningham & Walsh Inc 261 Madison Av New York City NY 10016

MOHNS, GRACE UPDERGRAFF BERGEN (MRS. EDWARD A. MOHNS), composer-pianist; b. Dubuque, Ia., Nov. 20, 1907; d. John Tallmadge and E. Grace (Updegraff) Bergen; student Lake Forest Coll., 1925-29; B.A. magna cum laude, U. Minn., 1930; spl. student McPhail Sch. Music, Mpls.; m. Rev. Edward A. Mohns, June 28, 1932; children—Grace Updegraff (Mrs. Laurance Redington Hoagland, Junior), Edward Bergen. Composer, recitalist, pianist, tchr. piano, 1923—; tchr. piano and theory pub. and pvt. schs., Mpls., 1930-32; organist, choir dir. N.J., Mich., Wash., Ore. Mem. bd. Community Concerts in Mich., Ore. Awarded composition fellowship Juilliard Sch. Music, 1930, 31. Mem. Nat. Assn. U. Women, Jr. League Am., Mich. Composers, Tex. Composers Guild, D.A.R., Dallas Symphony League, Nat., Ore. music tchrs. assns., Nat. Fedn. Bus. and Profl. Women's Clubs, Internat. Piano Library, Tex. Fine Arts Soc. (charter), Marquis Biog. Library Soc., Music Tchrs. Assn. Cal., Rossmoor Music Assn., Delta Gamma, Sigma Alpha Iota. Republican. Presbyn. (Bible tchr.). Clubs: Fronian, Musical Arts, Craig Class (Dallas). Compositions include Thine Is the Power, This Is God's Gift, Nocturne, Gaelic Hornpipe, Firemist, Maid of Spring, Anchored Hearts, Music Everywhere, Christ Is Risen, Ring, Ye Bells, L'Armistice, Sea Suite, Sands of the Desert, Dawnmist, At Bethany. Old Love Is Best, Undertones of Life, He Is Saving Some Glory for Me, Fidelity to Delta Gamma, Two Sea Songs Without Words, Intermezzo, Sunset Hill, Sing, Toys, Sing!; lectr., recitals on Am. indian. Home: Highover 2889-2 Ptarmigan Dr Walnut Creek CA 94595

MOISSIDES, LYDIA ELIZABETH, chemist; b. Newton, Mass., Mar. 11, 1948; d. George Lazarus and Chryso (Andreadou) Moissides; student Lasell Jr. Coll., 1963-64; B.S., Aurora Coll., 1967; M.S., U. Ill., 1969, Ph.D., 1971. Sr. scientist Mead Johnson & Co., Evansville, Ind., 1971—. Prof. chemistry U. Evansville, 1973-74. Alto soloist Evansville Choral Soc., 1972—; first aid instr., disaster vehicle vol. A.R.C., 1972—; bd. dirs. YWCA, 1972—, treas., 1973—, folk dancing instr., 1973—; adv. bd. women's continuing edn. U. Evansville, 1972—. Bd. dirs. Young Life, 1973—, sec., 1974—, NSF fellow, 1969-71. Mem. Am. Chem. Soc., A.A.A.S., Metric Assn., Phi Kappa Phi, Phi Lambda Upsilon, Sigma Alpha Iota. Home: 2530-A W Franklin St Evansville IN 47712 Office: Research Center Mead Johnson & Co Evansville IN 47721

MOKE, EMILY HILLIER, hotel exec.; b. Chgo., Dec. 13, 1921; d. Harry Elias and Alice W. (Weed) Hillier; bus. degree, Cleary Coll., Ypsilanti, Mich., 1942; m. Blaine H. Moke, Aug. 5, 1950 (div. 1967); 1 son, Lynn Whitney. Sec., Bldg. Div. State of Mich., Lansing, 1942-45; adminstrv. asst. Employment Security Commn., Phoenix, 1945-50; campaign office mgr. Mayor's Hdqrs., Tucson, 1954-56; exec. sec. Pima County Democratic Hdqrs., Tucson, 1956-58; asst. corp. sec. Glacier Park, Inc., Tucson, East Glacier, Mont., 1962-66, conv. coordinator, 1966—, corp. sec., 1966—, gen. mgr., exec. sec., 1962—; corp. sec. Glacier Park Transport Co., 1966—, Waterton Transport Co., 1966—. Corr. sec. Conf. Nat. Park Concessioners, 1963-66, 70—. Wedding dir. 1st Congl. Ch., Phoenix, 1946-50; womens chmn. Pima County March of Dimes, 1957; del. DATO Fgn. Travel Agts. Pow-Wow, Tucson, 1973. Recipient Distinguished Service award Mont. Heart Assn., 1973. Home: 3139 N Laurel St Tucson AZ 85712 Office: PO Box 4340 Tucson AZ 85717 also Glacier Park Inc East Glacier MT 59434

MOLETTE, BARBARA JEAN (MRS. CARLTON WOODARD MOLETTE II), educator; b. Los Angeles, Jan. 31, 1940; d. Baxter Robert and Nora Lee (Johnson) Roseburr; B.A., Fla. A. and M. U., 1966; M.F.A., Fla. State U., 1969; m. Carlton Woodard Molette II, June 15, 1960; children—Carla Evelyn, Andrea Rose. Instr., Spelman Coll., Atlanta, 1969—. Mem. Dramatists Guild, Am. Theatre Assn., Nat. Assn. Dramatic and Speech Arts. Author plays: Rosalee Pritchett, 1971; Dr. B.S. Black, 1972; Booji, 1972. Home: 3174 Mangum Lane SW Atlanta GA 30311 Office: Spelman College Atlanta GA 30314

MOLHO, LAURA (MRS. JOSEPH THEODORE SARD), physician; b. Salonika, Greece, Mar. 22, 1933; d. Mordecai and Bella (Counne) Molho; M.D., U. Salonika, Greece, 1956; m. Joseph Theodore Sard, June 24, 1960; children—Mark, Bonnie. Came to U.S., 1957, naturalized, 1965. Intern, Lebanon Hosp., Bronx, N.Y.; resident L.I. Jewish Hosp., 1958-59, Montefiore Hosp., Bronx, 1959-62; asst. pathologist Long Island Jewish Hosp., New Hyde Park, N.Y., 1962-64; asso. pathologist Queens Gen. Hosp. Center, Jamaica, N.Y., 1965—; clin. asst. prof. pathology State U. N.Y., Stony Brook. Diplomate Am. Bd. Pathology. Fellow Coll. Am. Pathologists; mem. Med. Soc. County Queens, Med. Soc. N.Y., A.M.A., Am. Soc. Clin. Pathologists. Office: Queens Gen Hosp Center 82-68 164th St Jamaica NY 11432

MOLHOLM, ALICE BURNS (MRS. HANS BARSO MOLHOLM), social worker; b. Glasgow, Scotland, Aug. 21, 1911; d. John Thomas and Alice Gallagher (Corcoran) Burns; came to U.S., 1924, naturalized, 1943; B.S., St. Xavier's Coll., 1932; M.A. (Univ. scholar) Loyola U. Sch. Social Work, 1935; m. Hans Barso Molholm, Feb. 6, 1949 (dec. June 1971); stepchildren—John T., Thomas B. With Cook County Bur. Pub. Welfare, 1933-35; supr. field work, instr. advanced casework Loyola U. Sch. Social work, Chgo., 1935-42; dist. supr. home service dept. Chgo. chpt. A.R.C., 1942-44; dir. intramural service Chgo. State Hosp. Mentally Ill, 1944-45; exec. dir. Forest Park Children's Center, St. Louis, 1945-47; asst. chief social service Inst. Juvenile Research Chgo., 1947-49; with East St. Louis Child Guidance Clinic, 1949; asso. prof. social work George Warren Brown Sch. Social Work, Washington U., St. Louis, 1950-54; ednl. dir. Columbus (O.) State Hosp. for Mentally Ill, 1954-57; dir. social service dept. Mental Health Inst., Independence, Ia., 1958; asst. dir. social service dept. U. Ark. Med. Center, Little Rock, 1958-65, 66-67, asso. prof. social work, 1966-67; dir. casework services Ark. State Hosp., Little Rock, 1967-73, dir. social service dept., 1973—; asso. prof. social work U. Ark., Little Rock, 1970—. Cons. social work to various pub., pvt. instns., agys.; mem. child protection com. U. Ark Med. Center. Fellow Am. Orthopsychiat. Assn.; mem. Acad. Certified Social Workers, Nat. Assn. Social Workers, Council on Social Work Edn. Home: 7318 Ouachita Dr Little Rock AR 72205 Office: 4313 W Markham St Little Rock AR 72201

MOLINERO, MARIA ISABEL, univ. adminstr.; b. Pamplona, Spain, Feb. 5, 1933; d. Francisco and Cataline (Fernandez) Molinero; B.B.A., Cath. U. P.R., 1972; M.B.A., Intern Am. U., 1974. Dir. adminstrv. personnel Center for Univ. Studies, Madrid Central U., Pamplona Spain, 1967-71; dir. financial affairs Bayamon Central U., Bayamon, P.R., 1971—. Mem. Am. Mgmt. Assn., Internat. Accountants Soc. Home: I-36 Capt Correa Reparto Flamingo Bayamon PR 00619 Office: PO Box 1725 Bayamon PR 00619

MOLLENKOTT, VIRGINIA RAMEY, educator; b. Phila., Jan. 28, 1932; d. Robert Franklin and May (Lotz) Ramey; B.A., Bob Jones U., 1953; M.A., Temple U., 1955; Ph.D., N.Y. U., 1964; m. Friedrich H. Mollenkott, June 17, 1954 (div. July 1973); 1 son, Paul Friedrich. Chmn. English dept. Shelton Coll., 1955-63, Nyack Coll., 1963-67; prof. English, William Paterson Coll. of N.J., Wayne, 1967—, chmn. dept. English, 1972—. Asst. editor Seventeenth-Century News, 1965—; stylistic cons. New Internat. Bible Translation Com.; guest speaker various colls., civic and religious groups. Recipient Andiron award, 1964, Penfield fellowship, 1963, Founders Day award, 1964 (all from N.Y. U.). Mem. Modern Lang. Assn., Milton Soc. Am., Conf. Christianity and Lit. (chief bibliographer, dir.). Author: Adamant and Stone Chips: A Christian Humanist Approach to Knowledge, 1967; In Search of Balance, 1969; Adam Among the Television Trees, 1971. Contbr. articles profl. jours. Home: Route 1 Box 16-C Hewitt NJ 07421 Office: William Paterson Coll of NJ Wayne NJ 07470

MOLLER, ANITA JOHANNE (MRS. DAVID LAIRD), interior designer; b. Hoboken, N.J., Aug. 12, 1909; d. Edward M. and Jessie (Nilssen) Moller; student Parsons Sch. Design, N.Y.C., 1928-30; m. David Livingstone Laird; stepchildren--David Currier, Robert Livingstone. Asst. designer St. James's Galleries, Ltd., N.Y.C., 1936-38; interior design asst. to Jane Christian, N.Y.C., 1939-43; prodn. illustrator for three engring. firms, N.Y.C., 1943-46; free lance interior design, N.Y., 1946-48; dir. interior design fgn. bldgs. operations Dept. State, Washington, 1948-72; now in own design bus., Newtown Square, Pa., Key Biscayne, Fla. Mem. com. fine arts Grad. Sch. Dept. Agr., Washington, 1964—. Fellow Am. Inst. Interior Designers (Elsie de Wolfe award N.Y. chpt. 1971); hon. mem. A.I.A. Presbyn. Home: 181 E Kenilworth Av Newtown Square PA 19073 Office: 1111 Crandon Blvd Key Biscayne FL

MOLLOY, JULIA SALE (MRS. FRANCIS HENRY MOLLOY), educator; b. La Grange, Ill., Oct. 19, 1905; d. William Benson and Dagmar (McKinley) Sale; B.S., U. Cin., 1926; postgrad. Am. Acad. Art, 1927-28, U. Wis., 1935-39; certificate in phys. therapy Harvard Med. Sch., 1938; M.A. in Spl. Edn., Northwestern U., 1951, postgrad., 1951-60; m. Francis Henry Molloy, May 20, 1939; children—Francis Henry, Christopher Hugh. Tchr. health edn. and dramatics, pub. schs., Owensboro, Ky., also Webster Groves, Mo., 1926-28; writer, producer children's plays Marshall Field's Children's Theatre, Chgo., 1929-34; dir. Chuliwi Lodge for Handicapped Children, Pompano Beach, Fla., 1934-35; tchr. McKinley Orthopedic Sch., Wis. Dept. Handicapped Children, 1935-39; tchr. homebound Evanston (Ill.) Pub. Sch., 1940-47; lang. pathologist Outpatient Clinic for Retarded Children, Dr. Julian D. Levinson Research Found., Cook County Hosp., Chgo., 1951-60, 72—; dir., prin. Orchard Sch. for Spl. Edn., Skokie, Ill., 1952-69; prin. Julia S. Molloy Edn. Center, Morton Grove, Ill., 1969-72; Prof. spl. edn. U. San Diego, 1972—; vis. lectr. Northwestern U., U. Chgo., Nat. Coll. Edn., Ont. (Can.) Dept. Edn., Toronto, U. Miami (Fla.), Ohio U., 1953—; cons. to numerous states, counties, pub. schs. on spl. edn., 1954—; mem. adv. bd. Mongoloid Devel. Council, Clearbrook Center, Inter-Village Mental Health Assn., Orchard Center for Mental Health; mem. citizens adv. bd. mental health program Niles Twp. Bd. Assessors. Recipient Community Service award Skokie C. of C., Service award Am. Legion. Fellow Am. Assn. on Mental Deficiency (sub-sect. organizing com. speech and audiology); mem. Council for Exceptional Children (Ill. exec. council, sec. North Shore chpt., legislation chmn.), Am., Ill. speech and hearing assns., Mortar Bd., Kappa Delta. Author: Teaching the Retarded Child to Talk, 1960, rev. edit., 1974 (also Brit., Spanish, Hindi, German edits.); Trainable Children: Curriculum and Procedures, 1963, rev. (Edn. Today award), 1972; Mental Retardation: Readings—Resources, 1971. Mem. editorial bd. John Day Co. Contbr. articles to profl. jours., chpts. to books. Home: 9217 Ewing Av Evanston IL 60203

MOLLOY, MARILYN, ednl. adminstr.; b. Caney, Kan., Apr. 24, 1931; d. James Joseph and Marguerite Muriel (Johnston) Molloy; B.S., Our Lady of the Lake Coll., 1955; M.A., U. Tex., 1961, Ph.D., 1966. Tchr. elementary and secondary schs., Dallas, 1952-58; tchr. math., physics Our Lady of the Lake, San Antonio, 1959-72, asso. dean, 1972—. NSF grantee, 1959. Mem. Am. Math. Soc., Math. Assn. Am. Address: SW 24th St San Antonio TX 78285

MOLLOY, MAUREEN KATHERINE, physician; b. N.Y.C., Aug. 15, 1932; d. James X. and Helen C. (Reidy) Molloy; B.A., Barnard Coll., 1953; M.D., State U. N.Y., 1957; M.S. in Hygiene, Harvard, 1964. Intern, Royal Victoria Hosp., Montreal, Que., Can., 1957-58, resident, 1958-59; resident Montreal Childrens Hosp., Childrens Hosp., Mass. Gen. Hosp., Boston, 1960-63; practice medicine specializing in orthopedics, Burlington, Vt., 1966—; dir. orthopedics Handicapped Children's Service, Vt. Dept. Health, Burlington, 1966—; asst. clin. prof. orthopedic surgery U. Vt. Coll. Medicine, Burlington, 1969—; asso. attending orthopedic surgeon Med. Center Hosp. of Vt., Burlington, 1970—. Vt.; Trustee Camp Thorpe, Goshen, Vt. Diplomate Am. Bd. Orthopedic Surgery. Mem. Am. Acad. Orthopedic Surgery, Assn. Dirs. State Maternal and Child Health and Crippled Childrens Services, Am. Acad. Pediatrics, Vt. Med. Soc. Home: 348 College St Burlington VT 05401 Office: 115 Colchester Av Burlington VT 05401

MOLONY, WINIFRED DELANEY (MRS. JOHN E. MOLONY), lawyer, govt. ofcl.; b. Laramie, Wyo., Nov. 30, 1912; d. John Vincent and Winifred Veronica (Higgins) DeLaney; student Rosary Coll., 1929-31; LL.B., J.D. Loyola U., Chgo.; m. John E. Molony, Oct. 30, 1954 (dec. Sept. 1958). Admitted to Ill. bar, 1938, practiced in Chgo. and Oak Park, 1938-40; with WPB Chgo., 1940-42; mem. staff office gen. counsel U.S. Dept. Agr., Chgo., 1942—, asst. regional atty., 1970—. Trustee, mem. exec. com. bd. Loyola U., Chgo., 1971—. Named Woman of Year, Women's Share in Pub. Service, 1974. Mem. Am., Fed. (recipient Milton Grodon award 1971), Chgo. Bar assns., Women's Bar Assn. Ill. (v.p. 1946-47), Catholic Lawyers Guild, Loyola Alumnae Assn. (pres. 1960-61, pres. Gen. Alumni Assn. 1962-63), Kappa Beta Pi. Home: 3550 Lake Shore Dr Chicago IL 60657 Office: 230 S Wacker Dr Chicago IL 60606

MOLTER, RITA JEAN, editor; b. Kentland, Ind., Apr. 21, 1926; d. Samuel Edward and Margaret Genevieve (O'Neil) Molter; A.B., Ind. U., 1949. Copy editor city desk Jour. Gazette, Fort Wayne, Ind., 1949-50; book editor Meredith Pub. Co., Des Moines, 1950-54; product publicity mgr. The Pillsbury Co., Mpls., 1954-56; account exec. Gen. Pub. Relations, N.Y.C., 1956-60; food copyeditor Family Circle Inc., N.Y.C., 1960-65, food editor, 1965-70; food editor

Parents' Mag., N.Y.C., 1970—. Mem. Women in Communication. Office: 52 Vanderbilt Av New York City NY 10017

MOLVEAU, HELEN LOUISE (MRS. CLAUDE MOLVEAU), rehab. counselor; b. Billings, Mont., Nov. 23, 1913; d. Chester and Louise (Hill) Naeseth; B.S., Columbia, 1935, M.A., 1962, Profl. diploma in Rehab. Counseling, 1962; m. Claude Molveau, Oct. 15, 1938. Profl. singer concerts and on Broadway, 1945-62, including lead song of Norway, concert tours; rehab. counselor Workmen's Compensation Bur., N.Y.C., 1963; rehab. counselor Office Vocational Rehab. State N.Y., N.Y.C., 1963-72, supr., 1972—. Mem. Pub. Edn. Broadcasting Network. Office Vocational Rehab. Fed. Grant scholar. Mem. Am., N.Y. State psychol. assns., Nat. Rehab. Assn., Nat., N.Y. Met. (chmn. profl. standards com.) rehab. counselors assns., Common Cause. Home: 4 Washington Sq Village New York City NY 10012 Office: 225 Park Av S New York City NY 10003

MOMIYAMA, NANAE, artist; b. Tokyo, Japan, Sept. 2, 1924; d. Tokutaro and Kimie (Ito) Momiyama; B.A., Bunka Gakuin Coll., Tokyo, 1944; M.A., Tokyo Women's Coll., 1947; student Art Students League N.Y., 1954-56; m. Martin Momiyama, Feb. 23, 1962; children—Haniwa, Kesa, Kaoru. Came to U.S., 1954. One-man shows Bruce Mus., Greenwich, Conn., Brata Gallery, N.Y.C., Form Gallery, Tokyo, Gima Gallery, Honolulu, Takemiya Gallery, Tokyo, Seibu Gallery, Tokyo; exhibited group shows Mus. Modern Arts, Tokyo, Met. Mus. Tokyo, Salon Internat. di Pittura, Rome, Grand Prix International de Deauville, France, Nat. Acad., N.Y. Lever House, others; represented in permanent collections Gallerie Raymond Creuze, Paris, Gallerie Rene Borel, Deauville, many pvt. collections; art instr. Bunka Gakvin Coll., Tokyo, 1948-54, Midorigaoko Sch., Tokyo, 1947-54; lectr., art instr. Japan Soc., Inc., N.Y.C., 1954—; art instr. Westchester County Art Workshop, 1971—, State U. N.Y., Purchase, 1973—; lectr. Columbia, Bklyn. Coll., Coll. City N.Y., Pratt Inst., Wagner Coll., Vassar Coll., U. Rochester, Bklyn. Mus., Phila. Mus., Pittsfield Mus., others. Recipient award Salone International de Pittura at Palazzo della Esposizioni, Rome, 1972, Grand Prix International de Peinture de Deauville, France, 1972. Mem. Nat. Assn. Women Artists, Modern Arts Assn. (chpt. dir. 1967—), Japanese Artists Assn., Assn. Internationale des Artists Plastique l'UNESCO, Modern Arts Assn. Japan, Jiyu Bijitsuka, Kyokai Japan, Westchester Art Assn., Old Greenwich Art Assn. (hon.). Author: Sumi-e, An Introduction to Ink Painting, 1967. Illustrator Makaranososhi, 1967; Dairy of Lady Sarashina, 1971. Home: Woodland Dr Port Chester NY 10573 Office: PO Box 44 Glenville Sta Greenwich CT 06830

MOMJIAN, MARY KALAJIAN, candy co. exec.; b. N.Y.C., Apr. 4, 1916; s. David and Rose (Hagopian) Kalajian; student N.Y. U., 1935-37; grad. Eastman Bus. Sch., 1938; student Columbia, 1942-44, Manhattan Coll., 1944; m. James Harout Momjian, May 15, 1949; 1 son, Arthur. Stenographer, asst. bookkeeper Duro-Test Corp., North Bergen, N.J., 1939-40; sec. to regional supr. U.S. Dept. Labor Bur. Apprentice Tng., N.Y.C., 1940-49; partner Atlantic Candy Co., Atlantic City, 1949—. Financial v.p. P.T.A. Massachusetts Av. Sch., Atlantic City, 1962-64; mem. women's aux. Shore Meml. Hosp., Somers Point, N.J., 1964—; mem. parents council Columbia. Mem. Nat. Right to Work Group Washington. Home: Linwood NJ 08221 Office: Atlantic City NJ 08401

MONACK, LOUISE CHARLOTTE, educator; b. Charleroi, Pa., June 16, 1919; d. N. James and Stephanie (Clement) Monack; A.B., W. Va. U., 1942, M.S., 1944; Ph.D., Bryn Mawr Coll., 1951. Chemist, E.I. duPont de Nemours & Co., Inc., Buffalo, N.Y., 1943-45; instr. Sweet Briar (Va.) Coll., 1945-47; instr. chemistry Wilson Coll., Chambersburg, Pa., 1950-52, asst. prof., 1952-57, asso. prof., 1957-67, prof., chmn. dept., 1967—. Mem. Am. Chem. Soc., Middle Atlantic Assn. Liberal Arts Chemistry Tchrs., A.A.A.S., Phi Beta Kappa, Sigma Xi. Home: 135 Highland Rd Chambersburg PA 17201

MONAGHAN, KATHLEEN M., sociologist, educator; b. Quincy, Mass., Sept. 30, 1936; d. William Francis and Mary V. (Clinton) Whalen; B.A., Emmanuel Coll., 1958; M.A., Fordham U., 1960; postgrad. N.Y. U., 1962—; div.; children—Megan, Maura. Instr., Coll. of New Rochelle, 1960-63; asst. prof. Marymount Manhattan Coll., N.Y.C., 1964—, chmn. dept. sociology, 1967—. Mem. Catholic Interracial Council, 1961-62. Mem. Sociologists for Women in Soc. (co-pres. met. chpt. 1973), Am. Sociol. Assn., Eastern Sociol. Assn., A.A.A.S., Am. Civil Liberties Union, Am. Assn. U. Profs. Home: L Stuyvesant Oval New York City NY 10009 Office: 221 E 71st St New York City NY 10021

MONDALE, MADELYN KAHRS SNAPP (MRS. WALTER E. MONDALE), civic worker; b. N.Y.C.; d. Marvin Leslie and Irene (Bear) Snapp; student George Washington U., 1929-31, U. Minn., 1964; m. Walter Edward Mondale, Oct. 14, 1934; children—Elinor Irene (Mrs. Henry Pendleton Gersman), Jason Edward, Richard Warfield. Staff pathology dept. George Washington U. Med. Sch., 1929-34, in charge endocrine research lab., 1930-34; mem. staff Lewistown (Mont.) Carnegie Pub. Library, 1962—, librarian, 1962-69, asst. city librarian, 1969-73; dir. Central Mont. Hist. Assn. Mus., 1964-70, pres., 1970—. Chmn., Jr. Red Cross, Andover, Mass., 1952-54; pres. P.T.A., Council, Andover, 1947-49, Lewistown, Mont., 1958-60; state chmn. State Congress Parents and Tchrs., Mass., 1948-50, Mont., 1960-62; organizing mem. Priscilla Abbot chpt. D.A.R., Andover, 1948—, regent Julia Hancock chpt., Lewiston, 1962-64, state registrar, Mont., 1964-66, state vice-regent, 1966-68, state regent, 1968-70, U.S.A. bicentennial celebration chmn. for Mont. to Nat. D.A.R. Mem. Lewiston City Bicentennial Com., Lewiston Study Commn. Local Govt., 1974—. Methodist. Home: 801 5th Av South Lewistown MT 59457

MONEY, ISABEL STIRLING, physician; b. Rangoon, Burma, July 3, 1913; d. James Berry and Isabella Stirling (McCartney) Money; brought to U.S., 1914, naturalized, 1922; B.S., Boston U., 1937, M.D., 1940 Intern, New Eng. Hosp. for Women and Children, Boston, 1940-41, resident, 1941-43; practice medicine specializing in obstetrics and gynecology, Boston, 1943-63, Needham, Mass., 1963-72; former mem. staff Faulkner Hosp., Boston, Glover Meml. Hosp., Needham; former mem. courtesy staff Leonard Morse Hosp., Natick, Mass.; asso. physician Student Health Service, Smith Coll., Northampton, Mass., 1972—. Mem. A.M.A., Am. Coll. Obstetricians and Gynecologists, Mass., Hampshire Dist. med. socs., Phi Beta Kappa. Episcopalian. Address: Student Health Service Smith Coll 69 Paradise Rd Northampton MA 01060

MONGAN, LAURENE ATKINSON (MRS. EDGAR J. MONGAN, JR.), real estate broker; b. Fond du Lac, Wis., Sept. 2, 1922; d. Elisah Maynard and Laurene (Wallichs) Atkinson; student Carroll Coll., 1940-41; m. Edgar J. Mongan, Jr., Dec. 17, 1946; children—Michael James, Sean Meynard, Patrick Kevin. Pres. Cordova Realty Co., Rancho Cordova, Cal., 1958—; dir. Sacramento Multiple Listing Service, 1974—. Chmn. Cancer Crusade, 1972-73, State Police Olympics, Rancho Cordova, 1974. Mem. Nat. Assn. Real Estate Bds., Cal. Real Estate Bd., Rancho Cordova C. of C. (dir. 1967—), Sacramento Bd. Realtors, Cal. Real Estate Assn. (chmn. dist. 3, 1974). Club: Mather Officers Wives (Sacramento). Home: Point West Tennis Club Heritage Lane 3002 Sacramento CA Office: Box 96 Rancho Cordova CA 95670

MONK, JOANNE THOMPSON (MRS. JOHN COLBURN MONK, JR.), librarian; b. Carrsville, Ky., Apr. 16, 1931; d. Carlos D. and Callie B. (Sisk) Thompson; B.A., Murray State Coll., 1951; M.A., George Peabody Coll., 1951; M.L.S., U. Okla., 1968; m. John Colburn Monk, Jr., June 19, 1957; 1 son, John Colburn III. Asst. librarian Southwestern State Coll., Weatherford, Okla., 1952-54; librarian Labette County Community High Sch., Altamont, Kan., 1954-57; reference librarian George Washington U. Library, Washington, 1957-61; acquisitions librarian Oklahoma City U. Library, 1964-68; supr. acquisitions Fairfax County Pub. Library, Springfield, Va., 1968—. Mem. Am. Assn. U. Women, Va. Library Assn., Kappa Delta Pi, Beta Phi Mu. Home: 3949 Fairfax Sq Fairfax VA 22030 Office: 5502 Port Royal Rd Springfield VA 22151

MONROE, BARBARA GRANGER (MRS. DONALD MCGILL MONROE), anatomist, educator; b. N.Y.C., Aug. 23, 1913; d. Abbott Dean and Jane Sherman (Peters) Granger; B.A., Mount Holyoke Coll., 1935, M.A., 1937; Ph.D., Cornell U., 1943; m. Donald McGill Monroe, July 7, 1951; 1 son, Richard Dean. Instr. zoology U. Ariz., Tucson, 1943-45; instr. U. So. Cal., Los Angeles, 1945-48, asst. prof. anatomy, 1948-52, asso. prof., 1952-66, prof. anatomy, 1966—. USPHS grantee, 1960-71. Mem. Am. Soc. Zoologists, Am. Assn. Anatomists, Electron Microscope Soc. Am. Contbr. articles to profl. jours. Home: 4232 Don Alegse Place Los Angeles CA 90008 Office: Dept of Anatomy University of Southern California Los Angeles CA 90033

MONROE, MARGARET ELLEN, educator; b. N.Y.C., May 21, 1914; d. Ralph Brigham and Ruth Hungerford (Cleaveland) Monroe; B.A., N.Y. State Coll. Tchrs., 1936, B.L.S., 1937; M.A., Tchrs. Coll., Columbia, 1939, D. Library Sci., 1962. Librarian, N.Y. Pub. Library, N.Y.C., 1939-51; dir. Am. Heritage project A.L.A., Chgo., 1951-53; prof. library sci. Rutgers U., 1953-63; dir. U. Wis. Library Sch., Madison, 1963-70, prof., 1970—. Pres. Welfare Council S.I., 1946-47. Fund for Adult Edn. Leadership fellow, 1953-54. Recipient Beta Phi Mu award for distinguished service to edn. for librarianship, 1972. Mem. A.L.A. (pres. adult services div. 1960-61), Assn. Am. Library Schs. (pres. 1971). Author: Library Adult Education, 1963; Alcohol Education for the Layman, 1957; Reading Guidance and Bibliotherapy in Public, Hospital and Institutional Libraries, 1971. Home: 1219 Rutledge St Madison WI 53703

MONSEN, ELAINE RANKER (MRS. R. JOSEPH MONSEN), educator; b. Oakland, Cal., June 6, 1935; d. Emery R. and Irene Stewart (Thorley) Ranker; B.A., U. Utah, 1956; M.S. (Mead Johnson Grad. scholar 1959), U. Cal. at Berkeley, 1959, Ph.D. (NSF fellow), 1961; postgrad. (NSF Sci. Faculty fellow) Harvard, 1968-69; m. R. Joseph Monsen, Jan. 21, 1959; 1 dau., Maren Ranker. Asst. prof. Brigham Young U., 1960-63; asst. prof. U. Wash., 1963-71, asso. prof. nutrition, 1973—, chmn. Nutrition Studies Com., 1969—; research fellow Harvard, 1968-69; vis. scholar Stanford, 1971-72. Mem. Sci. Adv. Com. for Food Fortification, Pan-Am. Health Orgn., Sao Paulo, Brazil, 1972—. Witness to State of Wash. Legislative Com., 1972. Bd. dirs. Contemporary Theatre, 1969-72; trustee Seattle Found. Nutrition Found. grantee, 1965-68, Agrl. Research Service grantee, 1969—; Center for Research in Oral Biology grantee, 1970. Mem. Am. Inst. Nutrition, Am. Dietetic Assn. (mem. sci. resource panel 1971—), Soc. for Nutrition Edn., Wash. State Heart Assn. (mem. nutrition council 1973—), Sigma Xi, Phi Beta Kappa, Phi Kappa Phi. Contbr. articles on lipid metabolism and iron absorption to profl. jours. Office: 203 Raitt Hall U Washington DL 10 Seattle WA 98195

MONSON, CAROLYN (MRS. DALE A. MONSON), journalist; b. Salt Lake City, Aug. 16, 1936; d. Hyrum Claud and Ruth (Wilson) Bennion; student U. Utah, 1954-56; m. Dale A. Monson, Jan. 4, 1969; 1 son, D. Brady. Staff writer Salt Lake Tribune, 1956-67, fashion editor, 1967—. Mem. Sigma Delta Chi. Home: 7009 S 85 E Midvale UT 84047 Office: Box 867 Salt Lake City UT 84110

MONSON, ROBERTA ANN (MRS. THOMAS PHILLIP MONSON), physician; b. Niagara Falls, N.Y., Apr. 10, 1942; d. Stanley Allen and Elizabeth Katherine (Harding) Mills; B.S., Allegheny Coll., 1963; M.D., Harvard, 1967; m. Thomas Phillip Monson, Apr. 20, 1968; 1 dau., Kristina Karin. Intern, Cleve. Met. Gen. Hosp., 1967-68, resident internal medicine, 1969-71; chief resident internal medicine U. Wis., VA Hosp., Madison, 1971-72; Stetler Research fellow, 1971-74; chief outpatient dept. VA Hosp., 1974—. Am. Viscose Corp. scholar, 1962, Huidekoper-Harvard fellow, 1963-64, NSF grantee, 1960-62, 64-65. Diplomate Nat. Bd. Med. Examiners, Am. Bd. Internal Medicine. Mem. A.C.P., Assn. U. Faculty Women, Phi Beta Kappa. Contbr. articles to profl. pubs. Home: 1235 Wellesley Rd Madison WI 53705 Office: 2500 Overlook Terrace Madison WI 53705

MONT, HALLIE BUCHANAN, pediatrician; b. Los Angeles, May 9, 1922; d. Alfred Gordon and Edith Ellen (Hamilton) Buchanan; B.A., U. Cal. at Los Angeles, 1944; M.D., U. Buffalo, 1947; m. Charles Hansen Mont, June 26, 1944; children—Diane, Charmain. Intern, Cal. Hosp., Los Angeles, 1947-48; resident Children's Hosp., Los Angeles, 1948-50; pvt. practice pediatrics, Burbank, Cal., 1950—; mem. staff Children's, St. Joseph, Valley Presbyn. hosps.; dir. Burbank Retarded Children's Center, 1963—. Recipient Soro award for outstanding profl. woman of San Fernando Valley, 1960. Diplomate Am. Bd. Pediatrics. Mem. Am. Acad. Pediatrics, Southwestern Pediatric Soc., Am. Assn. Univ. Women. Mem. Christian Ch. Home: 637 N California St Burbank CA 91505 Office: 2813 W Alameda St Burbank CA 91505

MONTAGUE, BARBARA ANN, chemist; b. Hagerstown, Md., Aug. 29, 1929; d. Daniel Junkin and Alma Hazel (Lehman) Montague; B.A., Randolph-Macon Woman's Coll., 1951. Chemist plastics dept. research div. E.I. DuPont Co., Wilmington, Del., 1951-60, information chemist, 1960, head plastics dept., information center, 1961-64, development coordinator DuPont Central Report Index, 1964-67, supr. Central Report Index, 1967-74, mgr. adminstrv. services, photo products dept., internat. div., 1974—. Promotion mgr. DuPont sec.'s dept. United Fund Campaign, 1973. Mem. Am. Chem. Soc. (chmn. div. chem. lit. 1975), Am. Soc. Information Scis., Alpha Delta Pi. Republican. Presbyn. Contbr. articles to profl. jours. Home: RD 2 Box 26A Friends Meeting House Rd Hockessin DE 19707 Office: E I Du Pont Co Concord Plaza Wilmington DE 19898

MONTAGUE, ELEANOR MARIE DINO (MRS. MEREDITH MONTAGUE III), physician; b. Genoa, Italy, Feb. 11, 1926; d. Frank and Sylvia (DeMaestri) Dino; came to U.S., 1928, naturalized, 1928; A.B., U. Ala., 1947; M.D., Woman's Med. Coll. Pa.; 1950; m. Meredith Montague III, Nov. 12, 1953; children—Eleanor, Meredith, Leontyna, Melanie. Rotating and med. intern Kings County Hosp., Bklyn., 1950-52, resident in pathology, 1952-53; resident in radiology Columbia-Presbyn. Med. Center, N.Y.C., 1953-56; Am. Cancer Soc. fellow in radiotherapy U. Tex., M.D. Anderson Hosp. and Tumor Inst., Houston, 1959-61; practiced medicine specializing in radiotherapy; radiologist 6160th USAF Hosp., Japan, 1956; staff physician Am. Telehone and Telegraph Co., N.Y.C., 1957; asst. radiotherapist U. Tex., M.D. Anderson Hosp. and Tumor Inst., 1961-66, asso. radiotherapist, 1966-68, radiotherapist, 1968, asso. prof. radiotherapy, gen. faculty, 1965-66, asso. prof., 1966-68; radiotherapist Meth. Hosp., Houston, 1969-72; clin. asso. prof. radiotherapy Baylor Med. Coll., Houston, 1969-72; prof. radiotherapy, radiotherapist M.D. Anderson Hosp., 1973—. Mem. cancer research tng. com. Nat. Cancer Inst. Diplomate Am. Bd. Radiology. Mem. A.M.A., Am. Radium Soc., Am. Soc. Therapeutic Radiologists, Am. Coll. Radiology, Radiol. Soc. N.Am., Tex. Med. Assn., Harris County Med. Soc., Breast Cancer Task Force, Phi Beta Kappa, Alpha Omega Alpha. Contbr. articles to profl. jours. Home: 5230 Yarwell St Houston TX 77035 Office: MD Anderson Hosp Houston TX 77025

MONTAGUE, JEANNE ODELL, journalist; b. St. Louis, Oct. 9, 1944; d. Richard Thomas and Vesta M. (Spurgeon) Odell; student Vanderbilt U., 1962; B.A. (Eugene Field scholar), U. Mo., 1967, B.J., 1967, M.A., 1969; m. Richard W. Montague, Dec. 21, 1968 (div. 1973). With pub. relations work N.E.A., Washington, 1967-68; writer, editor Anchorage (Alaska) Daily News, 1968—. Bd. dirs. Alaska Heart Assn., Anchorage, Anchorage Symphony Assn. Recipient feature writing prize Theta Sigma Phi, 1967. Mem. Anchorage Symphony Women's League, Alaska Conservation Soc., Anchorage Fine Arts Mus. Assn., Phi Beta Kappa, Kappa Tau Alpha, Phi Sigma Iota. Home: 1212 W 5th Av Anchorage AK 99503 Office: 133 Post Rd Anchorage AK 99501

MONTAGUE, JOANNE, ednl. adminstr.; b. Birmingham, Ala., Nov. 10, 1931; d. Wayland Pharis and Rachel (Deanhardt) Montague; B.A., Winthrop Coll., 1954; M.A., Duke, 1964. Tchr. English and journalism Statesville (N.C.) High Sch., 1959-66; asst. prof. dept. English, Gardner-Webb Coll., Boiling Springs, N.C., 1966-68; instr. dept. English, Furman U., Greenville, S.C., 1968-71; editor Municipal South and So. Hosps., Greenville, 1971-72; mem. evaluation staff Piedmont Schs. Project, Greer, S.C., 1972—. Pres., Orgn. Democratic Women Greenville County, 1973—; mem. S.C. Dem. Party. Mem. N.E.A. Baptist. Home: 202 Robinson St Greenville SC 29609 Office: 206 Church St Greer SC 29651

MONTAGUE, KATHERINE KARASSIK (MRS. PETER GUNN MONTAGUE), research orgn. exec.; b. N.Y.C., Oct. 27, 1939; d. Igor John and Mary Eugene (Ragosin) Karassik; B.A., Oberlin Coll., 1961; student Sorbonne, Paris, France, 1959-60; postgrad. State U. Ia., 1961-62; m. Peter Gunn Montague, Oct. 18, 1970; stepchildren—Tyree, Timothy, Jessica. Trilingual translator with various firms, Paris, France and Madrid, Spain, 1963-67; adminstrv. asst. to dir. Center for Study of Responsive Law, Washington, 1970; dir., chmn. bd. dirs. S.W. Research and Information Center, Albuquerque, 1971—. Co-chmn. Albuquerque chpt. N.M. Citizens for Clear Air and Water, 1972—; mem. City of Albuquerque Com. on Environmental Concerns, 1972. Mem. Soc. Mag. Writers. Author: (with Peter Gunn Montague) Mercury, 1971. Co-contbr. articles to various mags., including Environment, Audubon, Sat. Rev. Home and office: PO Box 4524 Albuquerque NM 87106

MONTCHALIN, YVONNE CORNELL (MRS. LEON PAUL MONTCHALIN), lawyer; b. Siebert, Colo., Dec. 9, 1909; d. Hubert Clyde and Byrde (Stouffer) Cornell; J.D., Willamette U., 1930; m. Leon Paul Montchalin, June 25, 1950; children—William Clyde, Karen (Mrs. William A. Allinger). Admitted to Wash. bar, 1932; Title examiner, legal dept. Home Owners Loan Corp., Seattle, 1932-35; pvt. practice law, Camas, Wash., 1935-50; founding sec., transfer agt. Washington State Bank, Washougal, 1969—, also dir., corporate sec.; city atty., Camas and Ridgefield, 1945-50. Chmn. Civil Service Commn., Skamania County, Wash., 1959-65; mem. Wash. State White House Conf. on Children and Youth, 1960; mem. Skamania County Bd. Edn., 1960-66. Mem. Wash. Republican Central Com., 1964—, mem. state exec. bd., 1971-72, sec., 1973—. Clark County bd. dirs. Wash. Children's Home Soc., 1945-47; bd. dirs. Skamania Sch. Dist. 2, 1958-64, S.W. Wash. Intermediate Sch. Dist. 112, 1966-68. Mem. Wash. State Bar Assn. (mem. travel com.), Nat. Fedn. Bus. and Profl. Women, Am. Judicature Soc., Am. Bar Assn., Internat. Platform Assn. Methodist. Mem. Order Eastern Star, Amaranth. Clubs: Touring of France (Paris), Chichester (Eng.) Yacht. Contbr. articles mags. Home: Route 1 Box 1585 Washougal WA 98671 Office: 640 E St Washougal WA 98671

MONTGOMERY, ASHLEY HANNAH, assn. adminstr.; b. Palmyra, Va. Mar. 20, 1922; d. William Nathanial and Cora Bell (Wills) Hannah; student Longwood Coll., 1939-40; R.N., Med. Coll. of Va., 1943; B.S. in Nursing Edn., U. Va., 1950; m. Robert Paul Montgomery, Sept. 30, 1950; children—Dan Thomas, Linda, Laura, Dinah, Judy. Operating room nurse, Med. Coll. of Va. Hosp., Richmond, U. Va. Hosp., Charlottesville, 1943-49; adminstrv. asst. Arlington County (Va.) Med. Soc., 1968-69, exec. sec., 1969—. Mem. D.A.R. (regent 1961-63), Huguenot Soc. of Va. Presbyn. Home: 6635 McLean Ct McLean VA 22101 Office: 4615 Lee Highway Arlington VA 22207

MONTGOMERY, CATHERINE LEWIS, govt. ofcl., civic worker; b. Washington; d. Lloyd and Catherine (Branch) Lewis; student Howard U., 1944-46, Internat. Finish Sch., San Francisco, 1948, U. Cal. extension div., San Francisco, 1948-49; m. Alpha LeVon Montgomery, Aug. 23, 1947 (div. Aug. 1964); 1 son, Alpha LeVon. With OPA, Washington, 1941-47; sec. U.S. Naval Radiol. Def. Lab., San Francisco, 1947-49; adminstrv. asst. tech. dir. USN Electronics Lab., San Diego, 1950-62; adminstrv. asst. state field dir. Republican State Central Com., San Diego, 1966; adminstrv. asst., personnel dir. Econ. Opportunity Commn., San Diego, 1966-69; commr. Cal. Fair Employment Practices Commn., 1969—; planning commr. City San Diego, 1966-73, vice chmn., 1970. Mem. Pres.'s Council on Minority Bus. Enterprise, 1972—. Unit chmn. San Diego League Women Voters, 1963, finance chmn., 1964, bd. dirs., 1964-66; mem. county pub. information and edn. com. San Diego br. Am. Cancer Soc., 1966-67, bd. dirs. 1967-68; mem. Mental Health Services adv. bd., San Diego County, 1968—; mem. southeast San Diego devel. com., sec., 1965; mem. steering com. Southeast Women for Better Edn., 1965; charter mem. Women's Assn. for Salk Inst., 1965; charter mem. San Diego Ballet Assn., 1964; mem. youth and incentives com. San Diego Urban League, 1964, bd. dirs., 1971—; active N.A.A.C.P., 1958—. Mem. Cal. Republican Women Federated of San Diego; exec. com. Rep. State Central Com. of Cal. Pres. bd. dirs. Girls' Club San Diego, Inc., 1967-68, sec., dir., 1964, publicity, pub. relations chmn., 1964; bd. dirs. Girls Clubs Am., Inc., 1972, recipient Distinguished Community Service award, 1972. Recipient Superior Accomplishment award OPA, Washington, 1944; Outstanding Performance award USN Electronics Lab., 1955-58; Woman of Year award for civic activities Women, Inc., 1967; Nat. Sojourner Truth Meritorious Service award for community service and advancing the status of women Negro Bus. and Profl. Women's Clubs Assn., 1967; Woman of Valour award for youth activities Temple Beth Israel Sisterhood, San Diego, 1967; award of merit San Diego sect. Am. Inst. Planners, 1973; certificate of appreciation Nat. Assn. Planners, 1973; named Woman of Distinction, Bus. and Profl. Clubs San Diego, 1974. Mem. The Links, Inc. (charter mem. San Diego, pres. 1963-65, parliamentarian 1965-66), Nat. Inst. Pub. Affairs (asso. in urban affairs), Soroptimist Club San Diego. Home: 5171 Roswell St San Diego CA 92114 Office: 1350 Front St San Diego CA 92101

MONTGOMERY, ELEANOR (MRS. A. MOORE MONTGOMERY), former editor; b. Chgo.; d. Herbert Joseph and Edith (Olson) Scully; A.B., U. Chgo., 1930; m. A. Moore Montgomery, Sept. 21, 1942 (dec. Nov. 1965). Asso. fashion editor Vogue mag., N.Y.C., 1935-51; exhibited paintings Parrish Art Mus., Southampton, Galeries Raymond Duncan, Paris, France; pub. poetry abroad. Pres., Sri Aurobindo Internat. Center Found., N.Y.C., 1955—; involved in bldg. new city Auroville, South India. Active various charitable orgns. Decorated dame Order St. John Jerusalem, Knights of Malta, Ordre des Palmes d'Or (France). Mem. Mortar Board (pres. 1929-30). Clubs: Old York (N.Y.C.); Meadow (Southampton, L.I.). Home: 875 Fifth Av New York City NY 10021

MONTGOMERY, ELIZABETH FLANAGAN (MRS. STEWART MAGRUDER MONTGOMERY), ch. and civic worker; b. Cary, Miss., July 25, 1898; d. Robert Edward Lee and Annie May (Purdy) Flanagan; grad. Northwestern Sch. Speech, 1918; A.B., Miss. State Coll. for Women, 1924; summer study Peabody Coll., U. Cal., Columbia; m. Stewart Magruder Montgomery, Jan. 5, 1935. Instr. elementary grades, high sch. English and dramatics, Cary, Miss., 1924-51. Mem. King's Daus. and Sons, state pres. 1949-51, 55-56, dir. Indian work, speaker internat. conv.; state pres. Miss. Women's Cabinet, 1954-55; mem. adv. council Miss. Children's Code Commn.; edn. com. Miss. Assn. Mental Health, 1958—, dir., exec. com., nominating com., 1963-66, dir., 1966—, sec., 1973—; chmn. Miss. Mental Health Conv., 1964; county commr. Fifth Region Mental Health Center, 1967—; del. Nat. Mental Health Conv., 1963, meeting, N.Y.C.; dir. State Mental Health Bd.; sec. Miss. Mental Health Assn., 1971-73; county campaign chmn. A.R.C., 1962. Mem. pub. relations com. Miss. Women's Cabinet, 1961—, now also recreation chmn.; mem. Gov.'s Ladies Staff, Miss., 1960-64 sec. Miss. Mental Health, 1969—; mem. Sharkey County Mental Health Commn., 1967—. Trustee King's Daus. Home, Natchez, Miss., 1948-52, pres. gov.'s bd., 1956—, gov.'s bd. trustees, 1965—. Recipient Woman of Achievement award Rolling Fork Bus. and Profl. Women, 1965; named Outstanding Civic leader Am., 1967. Mem. Miss. King's Daus. and Sons (historian 1969—, parliamentarian), Internat. Platform Assn., Daus. Am. Colonists, Order of Washington, Daus. of 1812, Colonial Dames of XVII Century (chpt. pres. 1971-73, state 1st v.p. 1971-73, state pres. 1973—), Dames of Court Honor, Daus. Confederacy, Soc. Magna Charta Dames, Ams. Royal Descent, Zeta Phi Eta. Episcopalian (state pres., women's orgn., 1952-55; pres. IV province Episcopal Ch. 1957-60). Club: Highland (pres. aux. 1963-64), Delta Debutante (patron 1961—).

MONTGOMERY, ELIZABETH RIDER (MRS. ARTHUR JULESBERG), author; b. Huaras, Peru, July 12, 1902 (parents Am. citizens); d. Charles Q. and Lula (Tralle) Rider; student Western Wash. Coll. Edn., 1924-25, U. Cal. at Los Angeles, 1927-28; m. Norman A. Montgomery, Aug. 15, 1930 (div.); children—Janet E., Robin A.; m. 2d, Arthur Julesberg, May 30, 1963. Elementary tchr. Los Angeles pub. schs., 1928-36; staff writer Scott, Foresman & Co., Chgo., 1938-63. Co-author: Sally Does It, 1940; We Look and See, 1940, We Work and Play, 1940, We Come and Go, 1940, Good Times With Our Friends, 1941, Three Friends, 1944, Five in the Family, 1946, Girl Next Door, 1946, You, 1948, Happy Days With Our Friends, 1948, Just Like Me, 1957, Being Six, 1957, Seven or So, 1957, Eight to Nine, 1957, Going on Ten, 1958, About Yourself, 1949, Health for All, series, 1965. Author: Bonnie's Baby Brother, 1942; The Story Behind Great Inventions, 1944; The Story Behind Great Medical Discoveries, 1945; The Story Behind Great Books, 1946; Keys to Nature's Secrets, 1946; The Story Behind Great Stories, 1947; The Story Behind Modern Books, 1949; All Kinds of People, 1950; Three Miles An Hour, 1952; The Story Behind Musical Instruments, 1953; Half-Pint Fisherman, 1956; The Story Behind Popular Songs, 1958; Second-Fiddle-Sandra, 1958; Till Time Be Conquered, 1959; Susan and the Storm, 1960; The Mystery of Edison Brown, 1960; Alexander Graham Bell, 1963; The Klep, 1963; Tide Treasure Camper, 1963; Hernando De Soto, 1964; Chief Seattle, 1966; Lewis and Clark, 1966; Two Kinds of Courage, 1966; Toward Democracy, 1967; Old Ben Franklin's Philadelphia, 1967; Hans Christian Andersen, 1968; When A Ton of Gold Reached Seattle, 1968; William C. Handy, Father of The Blues, 1968; Chief Joseph, Guardian of His People, 1969; Henry Ford, 1969; Will Rogers, 1970; When Pioneers Pushed West to Oregon, 1970; Mahatma Gandhi, 1970; Albert Schweitzer, Great Humanitarian, 1971; Walt Disney, Master of Make-Believe, 1971; Duke Ellington, King of Jazz, 1972; Dag Hammarskjold, 1973; Three Jazz Greats, 1973; Indian Patriots, 1974; Super Showmen, 1974. Recipient playwriting awards Seattle Jr. Programs, 1948, YMHA, 1950, Henry Broderick, 1963, Wilmette Children's Theatre, 1965, Wilmington Drama League, 1964, Theatre Americana, 1965. Mem. Seattle Free Lances, Author's Guild, Wash. State Press Women, Nat. League Am. Penwomen. Conglist. Home: 10203 47th Av SW Seattle WA 98146

MONTGOMERY, GLADYS K. (MRS. VICTOR MONTGOMERY), civic worker; b. Albuquerque, N.M.; d. Frank James and Anna (Simonsen) Kreamer; B.A., U. Cal. at Berkeley, 1917; D.F.A. (hon.), Pomona Coll., 1970; m. Victor Montgomery, Mar 31, 1917; children—Victor, Jeanne (Mrs. J. Glennon Cahill, Jr.). Anne (Mrs. William H. Erwin). Mem. organizing com. Beverly Hills High Sch. P.T.A., 1936—, historian, 1936-37; mem. organizing com. Stanford Mothers Club, So. Cal., 1938; gov. Guild Opera Co. of Los Angeles, 1950, exec. com., chmn. Western region Nat. Council Met. Opera Co. 1958, mem. at large exec. com., 1967; dir. Women's Com. Los Angeles Philharmonic Orch., 1947, 1st v.p. 1955—, del. to biennial conf. of Nat. Assn. Women's Coms. for Philharmonic Orchs., Houston, 1953, Mpls., 1955, Atlanta, 1957, Chgo., 1959; mem. patroness com. Hollywood Bowl, 1958—; dir. Assistance League So. Cal., 1950, corr. sec. 1952-53; mem. adv. bd. Jr. Auxiliary of Assistance League, 1946—, hon. bd., 1967; membership com. Opera Guild of So. Cal. 1955-57; bd. dirs. Affiliates U. Cal. at Los Angeles, 1959-62; trustee Academic Rewards Coll. Scientists, Inc., 1959-66, rec. sec., 1963-64. Mem. of the Friends of Colls. at Claremont, Honnold Library Soc., art council U. Cal. at Los Angeles, Florence Crittendon Home; dir. Boys Club of Hollywood, 1957; trustee Pomona Coll., co-donor Montgomery Art Center; women's council KCET channel 28. Mem. Met. Opera Nat. Council (exec. com.), So. Cal. Sym. Assn., Los Angeles County Mus. Assn., Air Force Aid Soc. (life), Hollywood Bowl Assn., Phi Beta Kappa Assos. (v.p. 1967-72), Phi Beta Kappa. Clubs: Women's (dir. 1942-43, chmn. scholarship and welfare com.). Garden (dir. 1940-42, sec. 1941), University (Beverly Hills); Women's Campus (Pomona Coll. dir. 1940—, founding pres. 1940, chmn. organizing com. 1939-40); California; Los Angeles County. Home: 10375 Wilshire Blvd Los Angeles CA 90024

MONTGOMERY, GLADYS TAYLOR, writer; b. Natick, Mass.; d. Charles Norton and Myrtle (Cates) Taylor; B.A., Wellesley Coll.; m. Alexander John Montgomery (dec. 1955). Writer, McGraw-Hill mags. in Washington office, 1942-62, Washington editor Textile World, 1943-46, Washington corr. Electronics, 1943-44, Washington editor same, 1944-57, Washington corr. Nucleonics, 1947-52, mem. Washington staff Bus. Week, 1952-62; past sci. and tech. writer Washington News bur. McGraw-Hill; now freelance and pub. relations. Mem. Pres. Nixon's Adv. Com. on Arts, 1970—. Recipient citation Armed Forces Communications and Electronics Assn., 1970. Mem. A.A.A.S., Nat. Assn. Sci. Writers, Washington Press Club (pres. 1957-58), Am. Newspaper Women's Club, English-Speaking Union. Clubs: Sulgrave, Chevy Chase, Wellesley College (Washington). Home: 2725 29th St NW Washington DC 20008

MONTGOMERY, JAYNE NASH (MRS. HENRY H. MONTGOMERY), lawyer; b. Edmond, Okla., June 20, 1921; d. Mell A. and L. Mae (Clark) Nash; A.B., Okla. Coll. for Women, 1942; LL.B., U. Okla., 1949; m. Henry H. Montgomery, July 1, 1950; children—Nancy (Mrs. Bill Ford), Holly, Sally. Admitted to Okla. bar, 1949; practiced in Purcell, Okla., 1950—; mem. firm Montgomery & Montgomery, 1950—; lectr. law U. Okla. Coll. Law, 1951-54; city atty., Purcell, 1956-60; spl. justice Supreme Ct. Okla., 1968. Active Girl Scouts U.S.A. Pres., Sch. Bd., Purcell, 1971-72, 74-75. Mem. Okla. (chmn. com. on uniform jury instrns. 1964-68), McClain County bar assns., Okla. Assn. Women Lawyers (pres. 1955), Order of Coif. Mem. Order Eastern Star. Home: Box 87 Purcell OK 73080

MONTGOMERY, JEAN ANN, lighting designer; b. Hanover, Pa., Jan. 16, 1946; d. William Moffit and Ruth Babette (Eiseman) Montgomery; B.A., U. Del., 1967; M.F.A., U. Minn., 1971. Tech. dir. Allenberry Playhouse, Boiling Springs, Pa., 1967-68; lighting designer U. Minn., Mpls., 1968—, stage supr., 1968—, asst. prof. tech. theatre, 1973. Lighting designer Coliseum Summer Theatre, Latham, N.Y., summers 1970-74. Mem. Am. Theatre Assn., U.S. Inst. Theatre Tech., Theatre Assn. Pa. Office: Rarig Center U Minn Minneapolis MN 55455

MONTGOMERY, KATHRYN EVELYN ROVER (MRS. ROY TAYLOR MONTGOMERY), civic worker; b. Lafayette, Ind., Nov. 11, 1942; d. Edward Ernest and Marjorie Belle (Pierson) Rover; B.A., Purdue U., 1964; M.A., Ind. U., 1966; m. Roy Taylor Montgomery, June 6, 1964; children—Karyn Lynn, Robert Edward. Tchr. elementary grades East Sch., Martinsville, Ind., 1964-65; homebound tchr. Clermont County Sch. System, Cin., 1966-67; presch. and developmental tchr. United Cerebral Palsy of Cin., 1967-69; tchr. educable retarded Fond du Lac (Wis.) Sch. Dist., 1969-70. Soloist, mem. chorus Cin. Musical Theater, 1967-68; performer Fond du Lac (Wis.) Community Theater, 1970, 72, 73; adviser, vol. tchr. tng. babysitters for handicapped United Cerebral Palsy, 1971, Division St. United Meth. Ch. Sch. for Retarded, Fond du Lac, 1971-73. Exec. bd. dirs. United Cerebral Palsy-Winnebagoland, 1969—. Mem. Council for Exceptional Children, Am. Assn. U. Women, Lawyers Wives Wis., Round Table. Methodist. Club: South Hills (Fond du Lac, Wis.). Home: 2320 Thornton Ct Fond du Lac WI 54935

MONTGOMERY, LUCILE HASSELL HARRIS, civic worker; b. Williamston, N.C., June 18, 1911; d. Cushing Biggs and Mary Lee (Woodard) Hassell; B.A., Salem Coll., 1930; student U. N.C., summers 1930-33, N.Y. Sch. Social Work, 1934; m. Thomas Everett Harris, Dec. 7, 1934 (div. July 1943); children—Marvin Bryan, Ruffin Kirby; m. 2d, Kenneth Floyd Montgomery, Apr. 12, 1947 (div. 1972); children—Henrietta Lee (Mrs. Peter Northrop Heydon), Kenneth Haywood. Tchr. jr. high sch., N.C., 1931-33; dir. women's work Civil Works Adminstrn., Washington, 1933; county adminstr. N.C. Emergency Relief Adminstrn., 1934; case worker Travellers Aid Soc., Washington, 1935-36; v.p. League of Women Voters, Winnetka, Ill., 1949-54; v.p. bd. trustees Music Center of North Shore, Winnetka, 1959-64; founding co-chmn. Fine Arts Quartet Concert Com., 1959-63; founding mem., v.p. Voters for Peace, Chgo., 1962-63; dir. Workshops on Voter Edn. and Campaign Techniques for Polit. Candidates, S.C., Ga., Tenn., Miss., 1964-67; chmn. 13th congl. dist. Chgo. Com. for Ind. Polit. Action, 1965-66; dir., mem. conv. steering com. Nat. Conf. for New Politics, 1966-68; Ill. organizer Jeannette Rankin Brigade, 1968; mem. radical caucus Coalition for an Open Conv., 1968; del. Nat. Democratic Conv., 1968. Bd. dirs. Lyric Opera, Poor People's Devel. Found., Glenrock Community Sch., Highlander Research and Edn. Center, Voter Edn. Project, Unicorn; mem. adv. council Common Unity. Recipient Clarence Darrow Humanitarian award, 1964. Home: 1734 N Wells St Chicago IL 60614

MONTGOMERY, MARTHA BARBER (MRS. DE WITT HALL MONTGOMERY, JR.), educator; b. Palo Alto, Cal., June 17, 1929; d. Willard Foster and Gladys Rebecca (Dorris) Barber; A.B., Bryn Mawr Coll., 1949; A.M., U. Pa., 1970, Ph.D., 1971; m. De Witt Hall Montgomery, June 18, 1949; children—De Witt Hall, Mary Willard, Owen Canterbury, Ruth Rebecca. Asst. prof. philosophy Drexel U., Phila., 1970—. Mem. sch. com. Haverford (Pa.) Friends Sch., 1964—. Mem. corp. Haverford Coll., 1971—. Nat. Endowment for the Humanities grantee, 1974. Mem. Jean Piaget Soc. (sec. 1974—, also mem. bd. dirs.), Am. Assn. Univ. Profs., Am. Philos. Assn., Soc. for Women in Philosophy. Mem. Soc. of Friends. Contbr. revs. of books of philos. jours. Home: 335 Aubrey Rd Wynnewood PA 19096 Office: Drexel U Philadelphia PA 19104

MONTGOMERY, MARY ELLA, librarian; b. Detroit, Dec. 6, 1925; d. Burton Vaughn and Rae Montgomery; A.B., Wayne State U., 1948; M.A. in L.S., U. Mich., 1951. Bookmobile librarian Dearborn (Mich.) Pub. Library, 1951-56; reference librarian Gen. Motors Research Labs., Warren, Mich., 1956-62; librarian Burroughs Corp., Detroit, 1962-66; research librarian Eaton Corp., Southfield, Mich., 1966—. Mem. Spl. Libraries Assn. (pres. Mich. 1961-62). Home: 7902 Bingham Av Dearborn MI 48126 Office: Eaton Corp Research Center 26201 Northwestern Hwy Southfield MI 48076

MONTGOMERY, MARY HELEN, univ. adminstr.; b. Independence, Mo., Apr. 7, 1931; d. Walter William and Josephine (Buchanan) Montgomery; B.A. in Journalism, B.S. in Econs., U. Okla., 1953; postgrad. U. Minn. Asst. pub. relations dir. Baptist Conv. Okla., 1953; photographer, feature writer, Enid, Okla., 1953; advt. mgr. asst. Southwestern Dailies, Miami, Okla., 1954-56; advt. dir., Del Rio, Tex., 1956-60; advt. and bus. mgr. student publs. U. Okla., Norman, 1960—. Media adviser Pres.'s Commn. on Consumer Protection; co-chmn. City Com. to Establish Juvenile Retention Shelter, 1967-69; media print adviser Region IV, Girl Scouts Am., 1969—; mem. Mayor's Task Force to Coordination Vol. Services, Norman, 1972. Mem. Am. Assn. U. Women, Am. Advt. Fedn., Nat. Assn. Parliamentary Officers, Gamma Alpha Chi (nat. exec. dir. Ednl. Fund 1971). Club: Altrusa International. Home: 917 Cruce St Norman OK 73069 Office: 860 Van Vleet St Norman OK 73029

MONTGOMERY, MERLE, musician, ednl. cons.; b. Davidson, Okla., May 15, 1904; d. Herman and Grace Frances (Williams) Campbell; B.F.A., U. Okla., 1924; diploma Am. Conservatory, Fontainbleau, France, 1933; Mus.M., Eastman Sch. Music, Rochester, N.Y., 1938, Ph.D., 1948; m. Pleasant Parx Montgomery, June 11, 1924 (dec. 1928); 1 adopted son, Milton Carl; m. 2d, A. Walter Kramer, Nov. 16, 1957 (dec. Apr. 1969). Extension tchr. piano and theory U. Okla., 1931-33; pvt. tchr. piano and theory, Oklahoma City, 1933-34; head piano and theory Southwestern State Coll., Weatherford, Okla., 1934-38; asst. state supr. Okla. Music Project, 1938-41; state supr. Okla. W.P.A. Music Project, 1941-43; tchr. Eastman Sch. Music, Rochester, 1943-45, vis. prof. summer, 1960; lectr. Schillinger System Mus. Composition, 1945-50; nat. ednl. rep. Carl Fischer, Inc., 1947-54; coordinator Symphonic Repertory, 1967—, v.p. in charge pub. relations, 1968-71; ednl. cons. Oxford U. Press, 1956-67; composer: A Cappella chorus; song for child, Jack and Jill mag., Phila., 1939; 17 songs for children, 1936; 8 songs for children, 1939. Gov. U. Rochester, 1953-55, mem. alumni council to trustees, 1964-68, hon. life mem. trustees council, 1969—. Recipient Alumni citation U. Rochester, 1964. Mem. Music Tchrs. Nat. Assn., Nat. (chmn. biennial conv., N.Y.C. 1953, 67, dir. 1955—; nat. v.p. in charge Northeastern region 1965-67; nat. 1st v.p. 1967-71; nat. pres. 1971—), N.Y. (pres. 1958-59) fedns. music clubs, A.S.C.A.P., Music Tchrs. Nat. Assn., Mu Phi Epsilon, Kappa Kappa Iota. Author: (with Mrs. Marguerite Meeks) Correspondence Course in music theory, 1937; Music Theory Papers, I-II-III, Music Composition Papers, 1959, manual for Vol. I, 1970. Editor: Oklahoma Music News, 1940. Compiler, editor Scribner Music Library, Vol. I, 1956, Vol. IV, 1972. Contbr. to mus. mags. Home: 222 E 80th St Penthouse B New York City NY 10021

MONTGOMERY, MILDRED CARTER (MRS. JAMES B. MONTGOMERY), librarian; b. Parkin, Ark., Dec. 28, 1915; d. Don Carlos and Ida Lee (Fields) Carter; A.B., Ark. State U., 1937; M.A. in Zoology, U. Ark., 1958; M.L.S., U. Ill., 1959; m. James B. Montgomery, Sr., Aug. 24, 1939 (dec. Aug. 1955); children—James Braxtol, David Carter. Substitute tchr., various locations, 1938-54; library sci. tchr., catalog librarian Ark. State U., Jonesboro, 1959-63; catalog and map librarian Memphis State U., (Tenn.), 1963-72; head catalog librarian U. So. Miss., 1972—. Active sch., Cub Scouts Am., 1949-55. Mem. Am., Miss., Southeastern library assns., Pi Gamma Mu. Methodist (active various work). Home: Apt 14 3500 Hardy St Hattiesburg MS 39401

MONTGOMERY, NANCY SCHWINN (MRS. HOWARD H. MONTGOMERY, JR.), editor; b. Claxton, Ga., July 23, 1921; d. Karl Christian and Nancy Leigh (Elmore) Schwinn; B.A., Mt. Holyoke Coll., 1942; postgrad. U. Paris, 1960, Am. U., 1964-66; m. Howard H. Montgomery, Jr., June 6, 1942; children—Nancy (Mrs. John R.V. Dickson), Morgan O'Neille. Asst. editor Army Motion Picture Service, Washington, 1942-43; contbg. writer Seabury Press, 1952-53; dir. primary sch. Am. Cathedral, Paris, France, 1958-60; asst. to publicity dir. Washington Cathedral, 1961-63, staff writer, 1963-66, editor publs., 1967-74, acting communications dir., 1974—. Cons. INTER-MET, Washington, 1972-73. Chmn. quar. bd. Mt. Holyoke Coll. Alumnae Assn.; mem. adv. bd. continuing edn. for women George Washington U. Mem. Asso. Ch. Press (dir. 1972—), Nat. Orgn. for Women, Am. Civil Liberties Union, Nat. Press Club, Nat. Cathedral Assn., Episcopal Peace Fellowship. Democrat. Author: A Guide to Washington Cathedral, 1964; Stitches for God, 1967; The Herb Cottage Cook Book, 1965; Washington Cathedral Coloring Book, 1968. Office: Washington Cathedral Mount St Alban Washington DC 20016

MONTGOMERY, PATRICIA HOY, pub. relations exec.; b. Evanston, Ill., Sept. 27, 1923; d. Kenneth Osborn and Margaret Elizabeth (Wood) Hoy; A.A., Stephens Coll., 1943; B.J., U. Mo., 1945; m. William G. Hancock, Oct. 9, 1948 (div.); 1 dau., Diane; m. 2d, Robert C. Montgomery, Apr. 14, 1956 (div.). Mem. staff U.P. Assn., Chgo., 1945-49; feature writer Chgo. Daily News, 1951-56; asso. editor House and Garden mag., N.Y.C., 1957-59; successively women's editor, mgr. women's news, mgr. women's programs, pub. relations dept. Am. Airlines, Inc., N.Y.C., 1960-71; account supr. Bell & Stanton Pub. Relations, N.Y.C., 1972; mem. staff pub. relations dept. Gen. Motors Overseas Operations, N.Y.C., 1973—. Mem. Am. Women in Radio and Television, Soc. Am. Travel Writers, Fashion Group N.Y., Theta Sigma Phi, Delta Gamma. Contbr. articles nat. mags. Home: 415 E 52d St New York City NY 10022 Office: Gen Motors Bldg 767 Fifth Av New York City NY 10022

MONTGOMERY, RUTH SHICK (MRS. ROBERT H. MONTGOMERY), author; b. Sumner, Ill.; d. Ira Whitmer and Bertha (Judy) Shick; student Purdue U.; student Baylor U., LL.D., 1956; LL.D., Ashland Coll., 1958; m. Robert H. Montgomery. Formerly news reporter Waco (Tex.) News-Tribune; woman's editor Louisville Herald-Post; feature writer St. Louis Post-Dispatch, Indpls. Star; news reporter Detroit Times, Detroit News, Chgo. Tribune; Washington corr. N.Y. Daily News 1944-55; fgn. corr. South Am., Europe, Far and Middle East intermittently, 1946-68; spl. Washington corr. for Internat. News Service, 1956-58; syndicated columnist Hearst Headline Service and King Features, 1958-68; only woman selected to cover Pres. Roosevelt's funeral, 1945. Recipient Pall Mall Journalistic award, 1947; Front Page award Indpls. Press Club, 1957; George R. Holmes journalism award, 1957; best non-fiction award Ind. U., 1966; Most Valuable Alumna award, Baylor U., 1967. Mem. White House Corrs. Assn., State Dept. Corrs. Assn., Alpha Chi Omega, Theta Sigma Phi (woman of the year award Indpls. chpt. 1966, Cal. chpt. 1967), Kappa Kappa Kappa. Clubs: Women's Nat. Press (pres. 1950-51, bd. govs. 1951-54), Washington Press. Author: Once There Was a Nun; Mrs. LBJ, A Gift of Prophecy: The Phenomenal Jeane Dixon; A Search For The Truth; Flowers At The White House; Here and Hereafter; Hail To The Chiefs, 1970; A World Beyond, 1971; Born To Heal, 1973; Companions Along the Way, 1974. Home: Apartado 923 Cuernavaca Morelos Mexico

MONTIE, IRENE CURRAN (MRS. WALTER GEORGE MONTIE), govt. ofcl., statistician; b. Tannersville, N.Y., Dec. 12, 1921; d. Michael Edward and Catherine (Keogh) Curran; student Wayne U., 1958-59; A.A. summa cum laude, Prince Georges Coll., 1972; B.S., N.Y. U., 1974; student Georgetown U., 1971, Coll. Notre Dame, U. Cal. at Berkeley, 1973; B.A. summa cum laude, Upper Ia. U., 1973; M.A., No. Colo. U., 1974; m. Walter George Montie, Nov. 21, 1940; children—Michael, Thomas, John, Kitty, Suzanne. Hotel and restaurant mgr., Elka Park, N.Y., 1940-48; owner, mgr. Manor Nursery Sch., Royal Oak, Mich., 1949-54; supr. statis. surveys U.S. Census Bur., Detroit, 1957-65; chief sampling procedures for statis. methodology U.S. Census Bur., Washington, 1965—. Lectr. statis. procedures at various colls., govtl. groups, 1965—; speaker radio, TV, profl. groups, 1963—. Instr. first aid, med. aux., Royal Oak, 1955-56. Recipient Superior Performance awards U.S. Bur. Census, 1958, 59, 65, Superior Contbn. award, 1970, Spl. Achievement award, 1973. Mem. Am. Statis. Assn., Am. Soc. for Quality Control, Nat. Soc. for Programmed Instrn., Internat. Assn. Survey Statisticians. Contbr. articles to profl. publs. Home: 5411 Old Temple Hill Rd Washington DC 20031 Office: Statis Methods Div US Bur Census Washington DC 20233

MONTIN, ALICE EMMA BERTHA (MRS. JOHN RAGNAR THEODORE MONTIN), writer; b. Oakland, Cal., Aug. 1, 1910; d. Charles Bartholomew and Annette Mathilda (Jespersen) Klambt; A.B., U. Cal. at Berkeley, 1931, gen. teaching credential, 1932; postgrad. San Francisco Theol. Sem., San Francisco State U., San Miguel de Allende, Mexico; m. John Ragnar Theodore Montin, June 10, 1934; children—Sonya (Mrs. Douglas White), Marcia (Mrs. Norman Kennedy Grant). High sch. tchr., Alameda, Cal., 1934-40; Presbyn. missionary to Colombia, S.Am., 1946; pioneer in released time religious teaching, Contra Costa, Cal., 1946-48; co-owner Impresora Mexicana S.A. pubs., Mexico City, Mexico, 1950-58; tchr. Henrietta St. Elementary Sch., Martinez, Cal., 1953-54; travel cons. Carroll Travel service, Alameda, Cal., 1952-53, 57-58; librarian Pleasant Hill Library, Central Library, Contra Costa County, 1958-60;

sec. missions Presbyn. ch., Walnut Creek 1974—; columnist various newspapers including Contra Costa (Cal.) Times, 1969—. Free lance writer, organizer, dir. Writers' Confs., Cal., 1970-73, Guatemala, 1970; founder, chmn. Christian Writers' Confs., Mt. Hermon, Cal., 1970—. Recipient Dwight L. Moody award for excellence in Christian writing, 1964. Mem. Am. Bible Soc. (co-ordinator 1960-74), Presbyn. Republican. Club: Cal. Writers' (Berkeley). Home: 1610 3d Av Walnut Creek CA 94596 Office: PO Box 5543 1720 Oakland Blvd Walnut Creek CA 94596

MONTLICK, ROSLYN ZEE PESSIN (MRS. BEN MONTLICK), lawyer; b. Hartford, Conn., Aug. 4, 1923; d. Israel George and Gussie Elizabeth (Marcus) Pessin; student St. Joseph Coll., 1942; J.D., U. Conn., 1946; m. Ben Montlick, July 14, 1946; children—Linda, Susan. Admitted to Conn. bar, 1946, since practiced in New Haven. Mem. Conn., New Haven County bar assns. Jewish religion. Home: 100 Stevenson Rd New Haven CT 06515 Office: 384 Whalley Av New Haven CT 06511

MONTOYA, JUANITA DURAN (MRS. MAX E. MONTOYA), ednl. adminstr.; b. Rainsville, N.M., June 24, 1923; d. J. Margarito and Lucia F. (Fernandez) Duran; B.A., N.M. Highlands U., 1953, M.A., 1958; Ph.D., U. N.M., 1971; m. Max E. Montoya, Oct. 17, 1949; children—Carl Alonzo, Lloyd Anthony, Allen Michael. Tchr., prin. elementary and jr. high schs., Mora, N.M., bookkeeper, clk. supt. office Mora Sch. System, 1942-61; counselor, spl. edn. coordinator, dir. bilingual programs, remedial reading tchr. Las Vegas (N.M.) City Sch., 1961-71; asst. prof. counseling courses N.M. Highlands U., Las Vegas, 1971-73, dir. guidance, counseling and testing, 1971—. Mem. Am. Assn. Univ. Profs., N.M. Personnel and Guidance Assn., N.M. Counselors Assn., Las Vegas City Edn. Assn., Am. Personnel and Guidance Assn., N.E.A. (dist. mem. state hall of fame com.), League Women Voters, Delta Kappa Gamma. Home: 1315 8th St Las Vegas NM 87701

MONTOYA, SUZANNE DAVID (MRS. LAWRENCE CORLEY MONTOYA), newspaper editor; b. Provo, Utah, May 10, 1950; d. Kenneth Ray and Annette Bessette) David; B.A. cum laude, Cal. State U. at Northridge, 1971, postgrad., 1971—; m. Lawrence Corley Montoya, June 7, 1969. Instr. Rosamond (Cal.) High Sch., 1971-72; sports writer Daily Ledger-Gazette, Lancaster, Cal., 1971-72, newspaper entertainment editor, staff writer, 1973—; newspaper editor Enterprise newspaper, California City, 1972-73. Mem. Women in Communications, Sigma Delta Chi. Roman Catholic. Club: Antelope Valley Press (dir.). Home: 1746 W Jackman St Lancaster CA 93534 Office: 45815 Fig Av Lancaster CA 93534

MOO, SUSAN HORN (MRS. CHARLES A. MOO), lawyer; b. Newark, Dec. 15, 1939; d. Max and Mona (Lyons) Horn; B.A., Wellesley Coll., 1961; postgrad. Brandeis U., 1961-62; LL.B., Harvard, 1968; m. Charles A. Moo, June 2, 1960; children—Lauren Rachel, David Benjamin. Physicist, Apollo project Mass. Inst. Tech. Instrumentation Lab., Cambridge, 1962-64; math. textbook editor Ginn & Co., Boston, 1964-65; admitted to Mass. bar, 1968; asso. Bingham, Dana & Gould, Boston, 1968-70; gen. counsel Center for Community Econ. Devel., Cambridge, 1971—, trustee, 1972—. Bd. dirs. Parent Tchrs. Orgn., Driscoll Sch., Brookline, 1973-74; trustee KLH Day Care Center, Cambridge, 1971—. Mem. Am., Boston (mem. land use planning com. 1972—) bar assns., Mass. Assn. Women Lawyers (membership chmn. 1973—), Nat. Orgn. Women (gen. counsel Eastern Mass. 1973—), Phi Beta Kappa. Office: 5 Upland Rd Cambridge MA 02138

MOODY, BARBARA GAREY, nursing educator; b. Medford, Mass., June 23, 1931; d. DeMelle and Mildred (Holman) Garey; B.A., William Jewell Coll., Liberty, Mo., 1953; M.Ed., Northeastern U., Boston, 1964; m. Richard H. Moody, May 15, 1954; children—Meredith, Heather, Richard B., Janice. Dir. personnel P.W. Moody Co., Andover, Mass., 1954-70; guidance counselor Lawrence (Mass.) Gen. Hosp. Sch. Nursing, 1971—. Dir., sec. Gale Systems, 1972-74; dir. Coulter Fibers, Inc., 1968-74. Pres. Andover Vis. Nurse Assn., 1964-74. Mem. Andover Sch. Com., 1963-66. Bd. dirs. Andover Girl Scouts, 1956-60, Andover YMCA, 1968-73, Andover Family Services, 1973-76. Mem. Nat. Assn. Women Deans, Adminstrs. and Counselors, League Women Voters, Nat. League Nursing, Am. Personnel and Guidance Assn., Pi Kappa Delta. Mem. United Ch. Christ (bd. Christian edn.). Club: Andover Tennis. Home: 12 Suncrest Rd Andover MA 01810 Office: 1 General St Lawrence MA 01842

MOODY, MAXINE JOHANNA (MRS. JOHN HENRY ROWLAND, JR.), physician; b. Jacksonville, Fla., Sept. 25, 1941; d. Maxey Dell and Dorothy Johanna (Boyd) Moody; B.A., Fla. State U., 1963; M.D., U. Fla., 1967; m. John Henry Rowland, June 14, 1969; children—Mary Kelly, John Henry III. Intern, Cin. Gen. Hosp., 1967-68; resident anesthesiology Johns Hopkins Hosp., 1968-69; practice medicine, specializing in emergency medicine, Holy Cross Hosp., Fort Lauderdale, Fla., 1969—; local med. adviser La Leche League Internat., 1972—; health career adviser, community concern chmn. Womens Med. Wives Aux., Broward County Med. Assn., Fla. Mem. Bel Air (Fla.) Civic Assn., 1969-71, Community Concert Series Ft. Lauderdale, 1969—; v.p. Broward County Right to Life Com.; mem. Nat. Right to Life Com. Bd. dirs. Fla. Right to Life. Mem. Am. Coll. Emergency Physicians (charter), Broward County Med. Soc., Fla. Med. Assn., Am. Assn. Pub. Health, Maternal and Child Health, La Leche League Internat., The John Birch Soc. Roman Catholic. Home and office: 4904 Empire Av Jacksonville FL 32207

MOODY, MYRTLE ANNETTE, librarian; b. Rochester, Minn., May 9, 1915; d. Thomas Arthur and Blanche Pearl (Pike) Moody; B.S., U. Minn., 1937. In charge order work U. Minn. Law Library, Mpls., 1937-42; head acquisitions Harvard Law Sch. Library, Cambridge, Mass., 1943-67, asst. librarian, tech. services, 1968—. Bd. dirs. Harvard Employees Credit Union, 1947. Mem. Am. Assn. Law Libraries, Internat. Assn. Law Libraries, Law Librarians New Eng. Contbr. articles to profl. jours. Home: 17 Prince Av Winchester MA 01890 Office: Harvard Law Sch Library Cambridge MA 02138

MOODY, YVONNE KIRKLAND, nurse; b. Jacksonville, Fla., Nov. 27, 1936; d. William Thomas and Lula Mae (Durham) Kirkland; diploma Grady Meml. Hosp. Sch. Nursing, Atlanta, 1957; B.S. in Nursing, Tuskegee Inst., 1965; M. Nursing Service Adminstrn., DePaul U., 1972; divorced; 1 dau., Angela. Staff nurse VA Hosp., Tuskegee, Ala., 1958-66; head nurse, med. nursing supr., asst. chief nursing service VA Research Hosp., Chgo., 1966-73; chief nursing service VA Hosp., Allen Park, Mich., 1973—. Guest lectr. DePaul U. Sch. Nursing, U. Ill. Coll. Nursing (both Chgo.). Mem. Am. Nurses Assn., Am. Soc. Nursing Service Adminstrs., Detroit Met. Area Assn. Nursing Service Adminstrs., League of Black Women. Home: 23300 Providence Drive Apt 716 Southfield MI 48075 Office: W Southfield and Outer Drive Allen Park MI 48101

MOOK, NELLA DENNY, writer, editor; b. Tarentum, Pa., Apr. 12, 1911; d. Joseph Simeon and Nana Elizabeth (Ross) Denny; student Mather Coll. Western Res. U., 1929-30; m. Emerson Hadley Mook, June 25, 1932 (div. Apr. 1949); children—Douglas Greenwood, Delo Emerson. Copywriter, Don Kemper Advt. Agy., Dayton, O., 1950-52, Advt., Inc., Washington, 1952-60; writer, editor Aminco Lab. News Am. Instrument Co., Silver Spring, Md., 1960—. Vol. Democratic party, 19—. Recipient Erma Proetz award for TV comml. Women's Advt. Club St. Louis, 1952. Mem. Internat. Assn. Bus. Communicators, Am. Med. Writers Assn., A.A.A.S. Unitarian. Home: 124 Hilltop Rd Silver Spring MD 20910 Office: 8030 Georgia Av Silver Spring MD 20910

MOON, ANN FERGUSON, clin. psychologist; b. Lubbock, Tex., Dec. 10, 1930; d. Breit Robert and Molly Bernard (Speed) Ferguson; B.A. magna cum laude, U. Tex., 1952; M.A. in Psychology, U. Houston, 1966, Ph.D. in Clin. Psychology, 1967; m. John Beverly Moon, Nov. 25, 1954; 1 son, John Michael. Clin. intern Baylor Coll. Medicine, 1966-67; staff psychologist Hedgecroft Hosp. Community Mental Health Center, Houston, 1967, chief clin. psychologist, 1968-69; cons. clin. psychologist Harris County Mental Health Center, Houston, 1969; individual practice clin. psychology, Houston, 1968—. Cons. to Parents Alert, Houston, 1968-69; co-founder Harris County Com. on Drug Abuse, 1968. Mem. Gov.'s Commn. on Status of Women, 1970—. NIH grantee, 1964-66; USPHS grantee 1966-67. Mem. Am., Southwestern, Tex., Houston psychol. assns., U. Tex. Ex-Students Assn., U. Houston Ex-Students Assn., Phi Beta Kappa, Alpha Chi Omega. Episcopalian. Home: 14 Bayou Shadows Houston TX 77024 Office: 3931 Essex Lane Houston TX

MOON, JULIA ANDRUS (MRS. F. FRANKLIN MOON), civic worker; b. N.Y.C., Apr. 20, 1915; d. Hamlin Foster and Mary (Hotchkiss) Andrus; grad. Emma Willard Sch., 1933; B.A., Smith Coll., 1937; m. Frederick Franklin Moon, Sept. 10, 1938; children—Margaret Andrus (Mrs. Frederick S. Gilbert, Jr.), Frederick Franklin III, Carol Browning (Mrs. Patrick D. Cardon). Mem. Stryker's Lane Aux., Inc., 1944-53, treas., 1948-53; mem. Ballard Sch. com. YWCA of N.Y., 1945-48, com. of mgmt., 1948-53; chmn. Goddard Neighborhood House Benefit, 1953; exec. com. women's div. Legal Aid Soc. of N.Y., 1952-68, chmn. women's div., 1959; alumnae trustee Emma Willard Sch., 1956-61, nat. chmn. Emma Willard Day, 1961, pres. alumnae assn., 1958-60, pres. N.Y. chpt., 1948-49; dir. Smith Coll. Club of N.Y., 1946-58, chmn. house com., 1948-52, scholarship com., 1952-58; v.p. Alumnae Pres.'s Council of Ind. Secondary Schs., 1959-62; dir. Grosvenor Neighborhood House, 1960—, pres., 1961-64; dir. Internat. Center N.Y., Inc., 1972—; trustee Leopold Shepp Found., Smith Coll., 1967-72; nat. chmn. Smith Coll. Capital Campaign, 1968-70. Republican. Presbyn. Club: Cosmopolitan. Home: 17 E 89th St New York City NY 10028 also Lloyd Neck Huntington NY 11743

MOON, MARJORIE RUTH, state ofcl.; b. Pocatello, Ida., June 16, 1926; d. Clark Blakeley and Ruth (Gerhart) Moon; student Pacific U., 1944-46; A.B. in Journalism, U. Wash., 1948. Reporter, Pocatello Tribune, 1944; reporter Caldwell (Ida.) News-Tribune, 1948-50; reporter, also Boise (Ida.) bur. chief Deseret News, Salt Lake City, 1950-52; owner Ida. Pioneer Statewide, Boise, 1952-55; founder, owner Garden City (Ida.) Gazette, 1954-68; owner Sawtooth Lodge, Grandjean, 1958-60, Modern Press, Boise, 1958-61; Ida. state treas., 1963—. Mem. Ida. Commn. on Women's Programs. Mem. Nat., Ida. fedns. press women, Nat. Assn. State Auditors, Comptrollers and Treasurers, Western Regional Treasurers Assn. (chmn. 1971-72). Democrat. Conglist. Club: Soroptimist (pres. 1971-73). (Boise). Home: 2227 Heights Dr Boise ID 83702 Office: State House Boise ID 83720

MOONAN, WENDY LYON, magazine editor; b. N.Y.C., May 20, 1947; d. Reginald Lyon Francis and Joanne Moonan; B.A. with honors, Wellesley Coll., 1968; certificate Sorbonne, 1969. Reporter, Bergen Record, Hackensack, N.J., 1969; founder, editor Univ. Rev., book rev. coll. students, 1969-70; mng. editor Juris Doctor, N.Y.C., 1971, editor, 1971—; law editor Single mag., 1973. Nieman fellow Harvard, 1974-75. Club: Fifth Avenue Racquet (N.Y.C.). Contbg. author: The New Professionals. Home: 240 E 53d St New York City NY 10022 Office: Juris Doctor 555 Madison Av New York City NY 10022

MOONEY, JEAN, exec. journalist; b. Cleve.; d. John Joseph and Elsie Marie (Longabaugh) Mooney; student Western Res. U., 1940, 41, 48. Asst. to exec. v.p. Cuyahoga Abstract Title and Trust Co., Cleve., 1939-47; pub. relations dir. women's div. Am. Inst. Banking, Cleve., 1940-44, Dale Carnegie Schs. Northeastern O., 1944-47; dir. women's services Newspaper Enterprises Service, Cleve., 1947—, lectr. seminars Am. Press Inst., Columbia, 1951—. Mem. women's div. President's Council Civil Def., 1952-56; U.S. del Asian-Am. Writers' Conf., Honolulu, 1967. Recipient J.C. Penney-U. Mo. medal, 1967. Mem. Women's Advt. Club Cleve. (award 1947), Advt. Women N.Y., Women in Communications (regional dir. 1956-61; recipient Headliner award, 1955). Author monograph on women's readership, 1961. Home: 19413 Argyle Oval Rocky River OH 44116 Office: Newspaper Enterprise Assn 1200 W 3d St Cleveland OH 44113

MOONEY, JEANETTE (JEN) CECILIA, banker; b. Davenport, Ia., Aug. 30, 1921; d. James David and Maybelle (Watson) Koerner; student Drake U., 1940-42, Washington U., St. Louis, 1949-50, U. Colo., 1971; m. Jack Hamilton Mooney, May 2, 1949; children—David Coyle, Christopher. Pub. relations asst. First Nat. Bank Montgomery (Ala.), 1958-61, community affairs, pub. relations officer, 1968-71, asst. v.p., 1971—; asst., Dr. James Koerner, Lexington, Mass., 1961-62; ednl. asst. USAF, Maxwell AFB, Ala., 1966-68; hostess Money Matters, TV series, Auburn, Ala., 1969—. Tchr. money, banking classes pub. high schs., profl. and civic orgns. Pres. Montgomery Art Guild, 1969-70; chmn. Arts Council Montgomery, 1969—, Seminar of the Arts, Montgomery, 1969—. Trustee Montgomery Mus. Fine Arts, 1968-71. Named Ala. Woman of Achievement, Bus. and Profl. Women's Clubs, 1971. Mem. Nat. Assn. Bank Women, Bus. and Profl. Women's Club, mem. Zonta Internat., League Women Voters, Am. Women in Radio and TV, Nat. Orgn. Women. Author: Let's Talk about Money, 1968, rev. edit., 1973; The Wonderland of a Women's Division, 1971; Widow's Guide and Checklist, 1973. Editor, illustrator: Money-Saving Recipes, 1971; Calorie Saving Recipes, 1972. Artist. Home: 2659 Oxford St Montgomery AL 36111 Office: PO Box 511 8 Commerce St Montgomery AL 36101

MOOR, JOAN THORNTON ROTHWELL (MRS. EDGAR JACQUES MOOR), biochemist; b. Lynn, Mass., Feb. 19, 1921; d. Paul Taylor and Adeline (Magrane) Rothwell; A.B., Vassar Coll., 1942; S.M., Mass. Inst. Tech., 1945; m. Edgar Jacques Moor, Aug. 5, 1950. Instr., Vassar Coll., Poughkeepsie, N.Y., 1946; research asst. Children's Hosp., Boston, 1947-48; research asst. New Eng. Deaconess Hosp., Boston, 1949-51; staff div. sponsored research Mass. Inst. Tech., Cambridge, 1952—. Treas., dir. Multinational Bus. Assos., Inc., Cambridge, 1967—. Fellow Internat. Acad. Law and Sci.; mem. Am. Chem. Soc., A.A.A.S., Boston Council Fgn. Relations (exec. com.), Pan Am. Soc. New Eng., Inc. New Eng. Council Latin Am. Studies, Sigma Xi. Republican. Roman Catholic. Contbr. articles to profl. jours. Home: Taborknoll Lincoln MA 01773

MOORE, ALDERINE BERNICE JENNINGS (MRS. JAMES F. MOORE), club woman; b. Sacramento, Apr. 17, 1915; d. James Joseph and Elise (Thomas) Jennings; A.B., U. Wash., 1941; m. James Francis Moore, Aug. 14, 1945. Sec to div. plant supr. Pacific Tel. & Tel. Co., Sacramento, 1937-39; exec. sec. Sacramento Community Chest Fund Raising Dr., 1941; sec. USAAF, Mather Field, Sacramento, 1942; statistician Cal. Western States Life Ins. Co., 1943; treas. Women's Aux. Stranger's Hosp., Rio de Janeiro, Brazil, 1964-65. Vice pres. Douglaston (N.Y.) Women's Club, 1955; mem. Douglaston Garden Club, 1951-55; pres. Nina Opland chpt. Women's Cancer Assn. U. Miami, 1960-61; corr. sec. Coral Gables (Fla.) Garden Club, 1960-62; pres. Miami Alumnae Club of Pi Beta Phi, 1961-62; mem. Putnam Hill chpt. D.A.R., Greenwich, Conn.; mem. Woman's Club, Greenwich, Conn.; mem. Women's Panhellenic Assn., Miami, 1961-62; internat. treas. Ikebana Internat., Tokyo, Japan, 1966-67, parliamentarian Tokyo chpt., 1966-67, N.Y. chpt., 1968-69; mem. Coll. Women Assn. Japan, 1965-66; mem. Tchrs. Assn. Sogetsu Sch. Japanese Flower Arranging, 1966—. Served to lt. USNR, 1943-45. Mem. Internat. Platform Assn., Am. Assn. U. Women, Pi Beta Phi (local v.p. alumnae club 1969-71). Baptist. Club: Steamboat Investment (pres. 1972-73). Home: 630 Steamboat Rd Greenwich CT 06830

MOORE, ALICE JOSEPH, educator; b. Hampshire, Ill., Mar. 19, 1914; d. John Francis and Alice (Hogan) Moore; Ph.B., Siena Heights Coll., 1939; M.A., Catholic U. Am., 1940, Ph.D., 1956. Joined Adrian Dominicans, 1932; tchr. Visitation Sch., Detroit, 1933-40, St. Lawrence Sch., Chgo., 1940-47; prin. St. Brendan Sch., San Francisco, 1947-53; supr. elementary Dominican schs. for Mich., O., N.Y., Detroit, 1954-55; supr. Siena Heights Coll., Adrian, Mich., 1957-64; prof. psychology and edn., dir. placement services Barry Coll., Miami, 1965—. Mem. N.E.A., Catholic Edn. Assn., Assn. Supervision and Curriculum Devel., Am. Assn. Colls for Tchr. Edn. Author: Retention of College Students, 1957. Address: 11300 NE 2d Av Miami FL 33161

MOORE, ALMA CHESNUT, journalist, author; b. Washington, Sept. 18, 1901; d. Victor King and Olive (Spohr) Chesnut; A.B., Goucher Coll., 1922; m. H.S. Moore, July 3, 1931 (div.); children—Peter, Anthony, Christopher. Reporter, woman's editor Balt. Am., 1922-25; head newspaper publicity Nat. A.R.C., Washington, 1925-28; mem. editorial staff American Forests, Am. Forestry Assn., Washington, 1928-29; woman's editor Pitts. Press, 1929-30; woman's editor Transradio Press Service, N.Y.C., 1937-42; editor She mag., N.Y.C. Free lance author, free lance editor of books manuscripts, 1959—. Author: How to Clean Everything, 1952; The Friendly Forests, 1954; Betty Bissell Book of Home Cleaning, 1959; The Grasses, 1960. Home: 5 Rockledge Rd Hartsdale NY 10530

MOORE, SISTER ANNE JOACHIM, coll. pres.; b. Loretto, Minn., Nov. 9, 1916; d. Earl Emara and Grace Ann (Elsenpeter) M.; R.N., St. Mary's Hosp. Sch. Nursing, 1937; B.S., Coll. of St. Catherine, 1946; B.S.L., St. Paul Coll. Law, 1950; M.Ed., U. Minn., 1958. Indsl. nurse United Aircraft Co., East Hartford, Conn., 1941-42, 45-46, 3M Co., St. Paul, 1947-50; asso. dir. Sisters of St. Joseph Sch. Nursing of N.D., Fargo, 1953-57; dir. St. Mary's Sch. Nursing, Mpls., 1958-64; founder St. Mary's Jr. Coll., Mpls., 1964, pres., 1964—. Dir. 4th Northwestern Nat. Bank, Mpls. Chmn., adv. com. nursing edn. in Minn. for Higher Edn. Coordinating Commn. Pres. bd. dirs. Vis. Nurse Service, Mpls.; bd. dirs. Bridge for Runaway Youth, Mpls., Am. Lung Assn. Hennepin County, Univ. Community Devel. Corp., West Bank Process, Mpls., Minn. Respiratory Health Assn. Served with Nurse Corps, AUS, 1942-45. Mem. A.M.A. (adv. com. allied health edn.), Am. Assn. Community and Jr. Colls. (adv. com. study allied health edn.), Assn. Schs. Allied Health Professions, Nat. Assn. for Higher Edn. Home: 601 26th Av S Minneapolis MN 55406 Office: 2600 S 6th St Minneapolis MN 55406

MOORE, BARBARA JEAN DE SANTI, occupational therapist; b. Jackson Heights, N.Y., Apr. 18, 1943; d. Fred Louis and Jeanette Anna (Bradley) De Santi; B.S., Ohio State U., 1965; postgrad. Coll. City N.Y., 1968; m. Brian Arthur Moore, May 7, 1966 (div.); children—Arthur, Bradley. Therapist, Mt. Sinai Hosp., N.Y.C., 1967-68; tchr., Lowell, Mass., 1968-69; occupational therapist VA Hosp., Northport, N.Y., 1971-73, Orange County Regional Mental Health Team, Buena Park, Cal., 1973—. Nursing home cons. N.Y. State, 1971-73. Mem. Am. Occupational Therapy Assn. (exec. bd. L.I. chpt. 1971-73). Home: 3701 Parkview Lane 1A Irvine CA 92664 Office: 6820 Orangethorpe Buena Park CA 90620

MOORE, BARBARA JORDAN (MRS. GARY RAY MOORE), mag. editor; b. Charleston, W.Va., June 8, 1936; d. Edward Earl and Mary Frances (Fitzwater) Jordan; student Trevecca Coll., Nashville, 1953-54, Morris Harvey Coll., 1954-55, Hunter Coll., 1968; m. Gary Ray Moore, Mar. 21, 1965; 1 son, Edward Sean. News reporter Daytona Beach (Fla.) News-Jour., 1964-66; news reporter-columnist Freeport (Bahamas) News, 1967; staff writer Assn. Jr. Leagues Am., 1967-68; mgr. information services Bolt, Beranek and Newman, Inc., cons., N.Y.C., 1968-70; editor Title VII Report, Crowell, Collier and Macmillan, Inc., N.Y.C., 1970; editor Women Today, Today Publns. and News Service, 1970—; dir. publns. and pub. relations Catalyst, Inc., N.Y.C., 1972—; cons. women's rights, including affirmative action programs. Chmn. Volusia County Heart Assn., Deland, Fla., 1963-64; v.p. Jr. Women's Club, Deland, 1963-64; co-chmn. Assn. Retarded Children, Deland, 1963-64; co-founder, 1st pres. N.Y. State div. Women's Equity Action League, 1971-72. First v.p. Democratic Women's Club, Deland, 1964-65. Mem. Women in Communications, Nat. Orgn. Women, Pub. Relations Soc. Am. Home: 245 W 107th St New York City NY 10025 Office: Nat Press Bldg Washington DC 20004

MOORE, BERNICE MILBURN (MRS. HARRY E. MOORE), mental health adminstr., author; b. San Antonio, June 17, 1904; d. Ted Hatton and Carrie (Coley) Milburn; B.J., U. Tex., 1924; M.A., 1932; Ph.D., U. N.C., 1937; m. Harry Estill Moore, Nov. 27, 1924 (dec. July 1966). Reporter, Austin Am. and Statesman, 1924-26; dir. Child Welfare Survey of Tex., Tex. Relief Commn., 1933-34; asst. Inst. for Research in Social Sci., U. N.C., 1934-37; asst. dir. Austin (Tex.) Regional Office, Profl. Projects, WPA, 1938-41; cons. Hogg Found. for Mental Hygiene (name now Hogg Found. for Mental Health), U. Tex., 1941-55, asst. to dir. community and profl. edn., 1955-72, exec. asso., 1972—, asso. dir. Philanthropy in Southwest, 1964-71; cons. Home and Family Edn. div. Tex. Edn. Agy., 1941-64, chmn. state adv. com., innovation and assessment in edn.; chmn. state adv. com. med. and dental edn., mem. coordinating bd. Tex. State Coll. and U. System; spl. cons. Clin. Facilities div. Research Utilization br. Nat. Inst. Mental Health 1963-65; mem. program adv. com., cons. social devel. curriculum S.W. Ednl. Devel. Lab.; cons. Gov.'s Task Force on Child Devel.; mem. Task Force on Youth; Joint Commn. on Mental Health Children; coordinator Tex. Coop Youth Study and profl. edn., adviser seminars for chaplains in marriage and family counseling, USAF, sponsored By Hogg Found. for Mental Health, 1956-66. Recipient Nat. Headliner award, Theta Sigma Phi, 1956; Spl. Service award, Tex. Soc. for Mental Health, also Ft. Worth-Tarrant County Soc. for Mental Health; award of merit Am. Vocational Assn., 1963; Moore-Bowman award of excellence Tex. Council on Family Realtions; Bernice Milburn Moore scholarship for continuing edn. for women established by Ex-Students Assn., U. Tex. Fellow Am. Assn. Marriage and Family Counselors (hon.); mem. Am. Social. Soc., Nat. Assn. for Mental Health, Am. Home Econs. Assn., Southwestern

Social Sci. Assn., Tex. Soc. for Mental Health, Tex. Council on Mental Health (past pres.), Philos. Soc. Tex., Tex. Council Mental Health Research, Future Homemakers of Am. (nat. hon. mem.), Women in Communications, Alpha Kappa Delta, Delta Kappa Gamma, Phi Upsilon Omicron. Democrat. Mem. Disciples of Christ Ch. Author: (with Harry Estill Moore) Through Your Own Front Door, 1945; (With Dorothy M. Leahy) You and Your Family, 1948, rev. 1954; (with Robert L. Sutherland) Family, Community and Mental Health, 1950; Juvenile Delinquency, Research, Theory, Comment, 1959; (with Wayne H. Holtzman) Tomorrow's Parents, 1965; pamphlets and study guides on mental health and the family. Contbr. to ednl. yearbooks, profl. jours. Home: 1215 W 22 1/2 St Austin TX 78705 Office: Hogg Found for Mental Health U Tex Austin TX 78712

MOORE, BETTY MAE, editor; b. Lukin Twp., Ill., Feb. 24, 1924; d. Willis Bennett and Maymie Lee (Tadlock) Moore; grad. high sch. With Lawrence County News, 1944—, shop foreman, 1948-58, asst. editor, shop foreman, 1958-64, editor, 1964—. Recipient Trusty Typewriter award Coca-Cola Co., 1967, Med. Journalism award Ill. Med. Soc., 1969, Best Photography and Best Feature Story awards So. Ill. Editorial Assn., 1971. Mem. Ill. Press Assn., So. Ill. Editorial Assn., Wabash Valley Assn., Beta Sigma Phi, Xi Gamma Lambda. Mem. Christian Ch. Home: 1111 Charles St Lawrenceville IL 62439 Office: 1209 State St Lawrenceville IL 62439

MOORE, DAWN FRANCES (MRS. EDWARD W. MOORE), data processor; b. Lansing, Mich., June 19, 1931; d. James Ernest and Frances Matilda (Magley) Bishop; student Mich. State U., 1954-55; m. Edward William Moore, Nov. 12, 1960. Supr. programming, systems analyst Mich. Dept. Revenue, Lansing, 1958-66; mgr. systems design and programming Mich. Dept. Treasury, Lansing, 1966-73; mgr. systems Mich. Central System Data Center, Lansing, 1973-74; mgr. exec. systems Mich. Dept. Treasury, 1974—. Mem. Data Processor Mgmt. Assn. (sec. 1969-74), Assn. Systems Mgmt. Episcopalian. Mem. Order Eastern Star. Home: 109 Bessemaur Dr East Lansing MI 48823 Office: Treasury Bldg 4th Floor Lansing MI 48922

MOORE, DEANIE FRAZIER (MRS. DANIEL M. MOORE), broadcaster; b. Dallas, Dec. 6, 1921; d. Clifton Lamar and Marie (Montgomery) Frazier; student N.Y. U., 1940; B.A., La. State U., 1942, Ph.D., 1974; postgrad., Malone Coll., 1964-66, Kent State U., 1965-67; M.A., U. Akron, 1968; postgrad., Northeast La. U., 1969; m. Daniel M. Moore, Aug. 19, 1967; children—Peg, John Bauer, Milton Moore. News editor KWKH-KTBS, Shreveport, 1942; woman's editor WHBC, Canton, O., 1959-67; grad. asst. Akron (O.) U., 1966-67; free lance broadcaster, 1969-72; pres. N.E. La. Research Inst., Monroe, 1972-73; asst. prof. sociology Northwestern State U., Natchitoches, La., 1974—. Mem. exec. bd. United Givers, Monroe, La., 1970, mem. quota and admissions com. 1972. State v.p. Nat. Women's Polit. Caucus, Baton Rouge, 1972. Bd. dirs. La. for Ednl. TV, 1973-74, N.E. La. Health Planning Council, 1970-73. Served to lt. WAVES, 1942-46. Mem. Internat. Platform Assn., Nat. Assn. for Better Broadcasting, Am. Assn. U. Women (dir. 1972-73), Am. Women in Radio and TV, Am. Sociol. Assn., Assn. Feminist Cons., La. Council of Family Relations, Sociologists for Women In Soc., Women's Equity Action League, Nat. Orgn. Women, Mortar Bd., Jr. League, Kappa Delta. Home: 3908 Deborah Dr Monroe LA 71201 Office: Box 7155 Monroe LA 71201 also Box 440 Route 2 Natchitoches LA

MOORE, DOLORES MCCORD, costume designer; b. Jacksonville, Fla., Feb. 11, 1937; d. Hershel D. and Della Ruth (Cooper) McCord; student Pasadena (Cal.) Playhouse Coll. Theatre Arts, 1955-58; B.A. in Drama summa cum laude, U. West Fla., 1969; M.A. in Theatre, U. Ill. at Urbana, 1971. Co-founder, asst. curator Pensacola (Fla.) Hist. Mus., 1960-63; audio-visuals asst. Pensacola Pub. Library, 1963-67; grad. asst. Costume Shop, Krannert Center Performing Arts, Urbana, Ill., 1969-71; costume designer dept. speech and theatre U. Ill. at Chgo., 1971-72; costume cons., adj. prof. theatre U. West Fla., Pensacola, 1973—; publicity and pub. relations West Fla. Regional Library System, Pensacola, 1973—. Mem. Am. Theatre Assn., Fla. Pub. Relations Assn. Democrat. Roman Catholic. Home: 3331 Summit Blvd Apt 115 Pensacola FL 32503 Office: Pensacola Pub Library 200 W Gregory St Pensacola FL 32501

MOORE, DOROTHA (MRS. COLLIS P. MOORE), Republican nat. committeewoman; b. Portland, Ore., Dec. 29, 1903; d. John Clyde and Verna (Lyman) Huntley; student Ore. Normal Sch., Monmouth, 1922, U. Ore., 1923-24; m. Collis P. Moore, May 24, 1925; 1 son, David Huntley. County chmn. Rep. Com.; mem. Rep. Nat. Com., Ore., 1956—, vice chmn., 1964-72. Appointed mem. Ore. Ednl. Coordinating Council, 1968-73; mem. Ore. Capitol Planning Commn., 1972-76. Sherman County chmn. Nat. Found., vol. adviser Ore. unit. Mem. D.A.R. Presbyn. Club: Federated Women's (pres. 4th Dist. Ore. 1929). Address: Box 225 Moro OR 97039

MOORE, DOROTHY CHRISTINE SEXTON (MRS. ALBERT LYNWOOD MOORE), educator; b. Enfield, N.C., Nov. 27, 1912; d. Joseph Thomas and Annie Juanita (Cooke) Sexton; certificate Mars Hill Jr. Coll., 1936; B.S., East Carolina Coll., 1953, M.A., 1964; m. Albert Lynwood Moore, Mar. 22, 1941. Tchr. Dawson Sch., Scotland Neck, N.C., 1937-39, New Hope Sch., Roanoke Rapids, N.C., 1939-40, William R. Davie Sch., Roanoke Rapids, N.C., 1940-46, Enfield (N.C.) Grade Sch., 1947-62; supr. early childhood edn. Halifax County Schs., Halifax, N.C., 1962—. Mem. N.E.A., N.C. Edn. Assn. (pres. local unit 1953), Delta Kappa Gamma (pres. 1964-66). Baptist. Clubs: Woman's, Tuesday Afternoon Study (Enfield). Home: Route 2 Box 32 Enfield NC 27823 Office: Box 468 Halifax County Schs Halifax NC 27839

MOORE, DOROTHY O., editor, pub.; b. St. Louis, Oct. 6, 1906; d. Richard Henry and Mahala (Polk) Woltien; extension student U. Mo., 1946-50; m. Howard S. Moore, Oct. 18, 1924; 1 son, H. Denis. Free-lance feature writer St. Louis Globe-Democrat, 1946-49, St. Louis Post-Dispatch, 1949-52; free lance mag. writer, 1946-52; writer radio show weekly KMOX, St. Louis, 1949-50; lectr. 1946-52; editor, pub. St. Clair (Mo.) Chronicle, 1952—, Sullivan (Mo.) Tri-County News, 1954—; pres., treas. Moore Enterprises Inc., Happy Sac Investment Co., St. Clair, Mo.; owner office supply and equipment stores. Mem. St. Clair Devel. Assn., Planned Progress Commn. St. Clair, chmn. 1952-58. Trustee Phoebe Apperson Hearst Hist. Soc. Mem. Franklin County Hist. Soc., St. Clair C. of C. (v.p.), Mo. Press Women (dir.). Club: Booster (Sullivan, Mo.). Home: St Clair MO Office: 525 N Commercial St St Clair MO 63077 also 226 W Main St Sullivan MO

MOORE, DOROTHY UPPERMAN (MRS. ROBERT DAVID MOORE), sch. adminstr.; b. Jersey City, Jan. 31, 1923; d. Arthur James and Iola Winifred (Harris) Upperman; B.S., Jersey City State Tchrs. Coll., 1945; M.A., Queens Coll., 1958; m. Robert David Moore, May 12, 1940; 1 dau., Patricia (Mrs. Robert Lewis Anderson). Tchr. elementary sch. Pub. Sch. 23, Bronx, 1946-50; guidance counselor N.Y. City Bd. Edn., 1959-68; asst. prin. Pub. Sch. 116, N.Y.C., 1968-73; prin. Pub. Sch. 251, Springfield Gardens, N.Y., 1973—. Cons. South Queens Counseling Service, Jamaica, N.Y., 1965-67. Mem. spl. awards com. 103d Precinct Community Council, 1969—; exec. sec. South Jamaica Community Council, 1971-72; mem. adv. com. Creedmore State Hosp., N.Y.C., 1965-71. Recipient Community award B'nai Brith, 1966. Mem. Council Suprs. and Adminstrs. City N.Y. Home: 115-23 173d St St Albans NY 11434 Office: 144-51 Arthur Av Springfield Gardens NY 11413

MOORE, DOROTHY WHITSELL (MRS. JAMES C. MOORE), librarian; b. Lewisburg, Tenn., May 2, 1916; d. Virgil M. and Bonnie K. (Long) Whitsell; B.A., Vanderbilt U., 1937; B.L.S., Peabody Coll., 1940; m. James C. Moore, Nov. 26, 1941; children—James C. III, Gwendolyn. Librarian Walker County Library, Jasper, Ala., 1940-41; asst. librarian Peabody Coll. Library Sch., Nashville, 1941-42; librarian Tullahoma (Tenn.) High Sch., 1942-46, Ch. of Christ Mission Sch. Library, Frankfurt am Main, Germany, 1950-52; cataloger Harding Coll. Library, Searcy, Ark., 1956-58; librarian Pepperdine Coll. Library Los Angeles, 1958-69; univ. librarian Pepperdine U., Malibu, Cal., 1969—. Bd. dirs. Information Center for So. Cal. Libraries, 1971-73. Mem. Cal. Library Assn., Asso. Women for Pepperdine, Christian Librarians Assn. Democrat. Mem. Ch. of Christ. Home: 23922 DeVille Way Malibu CA 90265

MOORE, ELEANOR HOLLINGSWORTH (MRS. NEAL WORDEN MOORE), social services adminstr.; b. Indianola, Ia., Sept. 23, 1919; d. John Emory and Luda Eleanor (Smith) Hollingsworth; A.B. Washburn U., 1942; M.S.W., Kan. U. 1963; certificate Tulane U., 1965; m. Neal Worden Moore, Dec. 27, 1939; children—Nancy, Daphne (Mrs. Jack Allen), Cynthia. Instr. sociology and psychology Washburn U., Topeka, Kan., 1949-53; child welfare worker Greene County, Springfield, Mo., 1955-58; supr. casework services Med. Center for Fed. Prisoners, Springfield, 1958-66; dir. social services Springfield Regional Clinic for Mental Retardation, Mo. Div. Mental Health, 1967—. Recipient Sustained Superior Service award Dept. Justice, 1961. Nat. Inst. Mental Health Ednl. grantee, 1961-62. Mem. Am. Assn. for Mental Deficiency, Greene County Assn. for Retarded Children, Springfield Community Planning Council, Nat. Assn. of Social Workers (certificate leadership tng. program Greene County Guidance Clinic 1971), (past dir.), League of Women Voters (past dir.), Springfield Pub. Agy. Council. Home: 1112 S Fremont Springfield MO 65804 Office: 1515 E Pythian Springfield MO 65802

MOORE, ELLEN BRYAN (MRS. DARROW HAYWOOD MOORE), state ofcl., bus. exec.; b. Baton Rouge, Apr. 13, 1912; d. Alex Dunn and Louise (Rhodes) Bryan; B.A., La. State U., 1933, M.A., 1950; grad. student Tulane U., 1935; m. Darrow Haywood Moore, Jan. 27, 1944; children—Margaret L'Mell, Ellen Victoria. Tchr. pub. schs. Baton Rouge, 1933-40; builder, personal property mgmt., 1935—; register of state lands, La., 1952—; state ofcl. register State Land Office. Mem. State Recreation and Park Commn., 1952—, La. rep. to Nat. Park Conf., 1953—, dir., 1964-66; nat. chmn. of membership com. Nat. Conf. on State Parks, 1969—; state rep. Pub. Land Law Rev. Commn.; vice chmn. La. Office Bldg. Corp.; mem. Gov.'s adv. council La. Bur. Outdoor Recreation; chmn. State Park Com., 1960-66; state chmn. Gov.'s Commn. Status of Women; mem. adv. council La. Tourist Commn. State rep. Nat. Civilian Def. Women's Adv. Council, Washington, 1955. Bd. dirs. United Givers Fund; state chmn. Multiple Sclerosis dirve; vice chmn. La. Rental Commn.; zone chmn. March of Dimes, 1957, chmn. govtl. div., 1966—; budget com. Community Services Council; Pres. East Baton Rouge Lioness orgn., 1950-51; mem. bd. Girl Scouts Am., 1954-55, Camp Fire Girls, 1957. Dir. United Democrats La.; dir. Operation Crossroad (So. div.), Nat. Dem. Party, 1956. Served from pvt. to capt. AUS, 1941-45. Hon. mem. Pelican Girls State. Mem. Am. Legion (del. nat. conv. 1953-54), La. Edn. Assn., Am. Assn. U. Women, Am. Right of Way Assn., Am. Forestry Assn., Bus. and Profl. Women's Club, Amvets, YMCA, Delta Zeta, Phi Lambda Phi, Psi Chi, Alpha Delta Kappa. Clubs: Pilot (pres. Baton Rouge chpt. 1940-41), Merry-Go-Round (past pres.). Home: 2222 Government St Baton Rouge LA 70806 Office: State Land and Natural Resources Bldg Baton Route LA 70804

MOORE, EMMA ROSE DUPREE (MRS. DAN KIRK MOORE), educator; b. Vinita, Okla., Nov. 17, 1926; d. William Wright and Rosa May (Wright) Dupree; student Okla. Bapt. U., 1945-46; B.A., U. Okla., 1967; postgrad. Northeastern State Coll., Tahlequah, Okla., 1967; m. Dan Kirk Moore, Apr. 17, 1949; children—Mary Gail (Mrs. Raymond D. Brown), Curtis, Glen. With Vinita (Okla.) Daily Jour., 1943-45, city editor, 1944-45; editor, mgr. Craig County Democrat, Vinita, 1949-50; staff, women's dept. Oklahoman & Times, Oklahoma City, 1952-53; pub. relations asst. Bapt. Gen. Conv. Okla., Oklahoma City, 1953-54; various editorial positions Vinita Jour., 1956-62, 66; tchr. jr. and sr. high schs., Adair, Okla., 1968, Vinita High Sch., 1968—. Editorial cons. N.E. Okla. Electric Coop., Inc., 1972. Vice pres. Vinita Camp Fire Council, 1959; mem. Craig County Child Welfare Com., 1960-61; leader 4-H Club, 1961-66; mem. Eastern Trails Arts and Humanities Council, 1973; project dir. Craig County Humanities Task Force, 1973—; pres. Will Rogers P.T.A., 1965-66. Mem. Nat., Okla. councils tchrs. English, Okla. Edn. Assn. (county pub. relations chmn. 1969-70), Okla. Journalism Edn. Assn., Okla. Interscholastic Press Assn. Advisers, Am. Assn. U. Women (2d v.p. 1970-72, pub. information chmn. Vinita, 1972, pub. information chmn. Okla. 1973—; Okla. dir. 1973—), U. Okla. Assn. (life), Women in Communications. Democrat. Baptist. Home: Box 263 Vinita OK 74301 Office: Box H Vinita OK 74301

MOORE, ETHEL MAE MARSHALL, business ofcl.; b. Vaux Hall, N.J., Sept. 14, 1917; d. Martin and Laura (Monger) Marshall; student Newark Bus. Coll., 1938-40, Rutgers U., 1965-66; m. 1935; children—Chester, Leroy. Advt. mgr. N.J. Afro Am. Newspaper, 1948-55; copywriter Scheer Advt. Agy., 1957-65; merchandizing coordinator Amalgamated Pubs., newspaper advt. reps., N.Y.C., 1965—; owner, mgr. EMOORE Assos., advt. and pub. relations, 1970—; syndicated columnist Ethel's Cookery, since 1967—. Bd. dirs. N.A.A.C.P. Newark Sickle Cell Anemia Project. Mem. Nat. Assn. Media Women (charter, nat. financial sec. 1965-67), Nat. Assn. Negro Bus. and Profl. Women (v.p. 1961-65). Mem. A.M.E. Ch. Home: 540 Chestnut St Orange NJ 07050 Office: 45 W 45th St New York City NY 10036

MOORE, EUDORAH MORSE (MRS. ANSON C. MOORE), museum curator; b. Denver, June 15, 1918; d. Bradish P. and Anna R. (Reynolds) Morse; A.B., Smith Coll., 1940; postgrad. U. Cal. at Los Angeles; m. Anson C. Moore, July 2, 1940; children—William A. II, Anna R., Anson C., Reynolds. Founder, Art Alliance, Pasadena (Cal.) Art Mus., pres. bd. dirs. mus., 1957-62, curator design, 1961-74, bd. dirs., 1956-69; dir. Cal. Design, Pasadena, 1974—. Bd. dirs. Encounters Contemporary Music, Otis Art Assos., Smith Coll. alumni assn., Arboretum Found., Los Angeles State and County Arboretum. Recipient Cultural Achievement award Pasadena C. of C., 1962; Trailblazer award Nat. Home Fashions League, 1971; Smith Coll. medal, 1973. Home: 1080 Glen Oaks Blvd Pasadena CA 91105 Office: 300 E Green St Pasadena CA 91101

MOORE, FREONA CLARE, social worker; b. Coffeyville, Kan., May 21, 1910; d. Fred Earl and Addie (Beatty) Moore; B.S., Pittsburg (Kan.) State Coll., 1933; M.S.W., Washington U., St. Louis, 1959. Social worker Montgomery County (Kan.) Dept. Social Welfare, 1934-39; adminstr. Coffeyville (Kan.) Welfare Office, 1939-44; county dir. Finney County Dept. Social Welfare, Garden City, Kan., 1944-46; field rep. Kan. Dept. Social Welfare, Topeka, 1946-61, dir. div. of staff devel., 1961—. Mem. adv. com. Kansas City Regional Council for Higher Edn., 1969—; mem. profl. adv. com. on social work edn. Wichita State U., 1968—, profl. adv. com. U. Kan. Sch. Social Welfare, 1968—; dir. Licensing Kan. Social Workers, 1974—. Mem. Acad. Certified Social Workers, Nat. Assn. Social Workers, Am. Pub. Welfare Assn. (pres. Southwestern regional conf. field reps. 1950-51), Nat. (rep. region VII to nominating com. 1972—), Kan. (v.p. 1959-60, rec. sec. 1970-71) confs. social welfare, Am. Assn. U. Women, Kan. County Dirs. Assn. (pres. 1946), Kan. Family Life Assn. Assn. (v.p. 1959-60), Council Social Work Edn., Am. Soc. Pub. Adminstrn. (Kan. chpt. sec.-treas. 1965-66, chpt. pres. 1968-69), League Women Voters, Kansas Native Sons and Daus. Presbyn. (elder, mem. ministerial relations com. Presbytery No. Kan. 1973—). Mem. Order Eastern Star; Ancient Order of Toltee. Club: Topeka Star (pres. 1961-63). Home: 1162 Collins Av Topeka KS 66604 Office: State Office Bldg Topeka KS 66612

MOORE, GAYLE P., office supply co. exec.; b. McKeesport, Pa., Oct. 6, 1930; d. Richard Harold and Mildred Francis (Landis) Paul; B.S. in Phys. Edn., Davis and Elkins Coll., 1952; m. Richard W. Moore, Aug. 2, 1952; children—Machelle L., Mark D. Tchr., Cumberland County, N.C., 1954-56; tchr., Randolph County, 1957-60; kindergarten tchr. Elkins (W.Va.) YMCA, 1967-70; pres. McManus Office Supply, Inc., Elkins, 1962—. Pres. 3d ward P.T.A.; mem. Davis Meml. Hosp. Aux., Elkins Band Aux. Mem. Chi Omega. Presbyn. (ch. sch. tchr. 1968-73, mem. ch. sch. council, 1973—, deacon 1972—, sec.-treas. circle 1973—). Home: 205 Wilton Av Elkins WV 26241 Office: 322 Davis Av Elkins WV 26241

MOORE, GLENDA SUE, advt. agy. exec.; b. Roscoe, Tex., Oct. 23, 1937; d. Donald Weldon and Oda (Roberts) Moore; B.A., North Tex. State U., 1959. Reporter, Dallas Morning News, 1959-60; asst. to pub. relations mgr. Tex. Instruments, Inc., Dallas, 1960-61; account exec., v.p. Wyatt & Williams, Inc., Dallas, 1961-72; gen. mgr. Holiday Advt. Agy., Arlington, Tex., 1972—. Mem. Dallas Advt. League, Ft. Worth Advt. Club. Home: 3451 Chaparral Dr Dallas TX 75234 Office: Box 5151 Arlington TX 76011

MOORE, IVY PEARL SIMMONS (MRS. WILLIAM ROBERT MOORE), librarian; b. Quail, Tex., Jan. 13, 1932; d. William Sanford and Curtis Mollie (Cagle) Simmons; student Wayland Bapt. Coll., 1949-52; B.S., West Tex. State Coll., 1955; M.L.S., Tex. Woman's U., 1957; m. John William Reber, Mar. 21, 1952 (div. 1953); 1 son, William Lee; m. 2d, William Robert Moore, Apr. 6, 1958; children—Lucinda Yvonne, Martha Jane. Acting librarian Floyd County Pub. Library, Floydada, Tex., 1954-55; catalog librarian Hardin-Simmons U., Abilene, 1957-58; asst. catalog librarian North Tex. State U., Denton, 1958-62; catalog librarian San Diego Pub. Library, 1962-65; chief library staff FAA, Alaskan region, Anchorage, 1965—. Mem. Alaska Library Assn. (treas. 1968), Nat. Rifle Assn., Alpha Beta Alpha, Alpha Chi. Baptist. Home: 1620 E 27th St Anchorage AK 99504 Office: 632 6th Av Anchorage AK 99501

MOORE, JANE ROSS, librarian; b. Phila., Apr. 24, 1929; d. John William and Mary (McClure) Ross; A.B., Smith Coll., 1951; M.S. in L.S., Drexel U., 1952; postgrad. Columbia; M.B.A. (with distinction), N.Y. U., 1965; Ph.D., Case Western Res. U., 1974; m. Cyril Howard Moore, Jr., June 1, 1956 (div. Mar. 1967). Cataloguer Yale U. Library, 1952-54; chief tech. processes librarian Lederle Labs., Am. Cyanamid Co., Pearl River, N.Y., 1954-58; chief serials catalog librarian Bklyn. Coll. Library, 1958-65, asst. prof., chief catalog div., 1965-70, asso. prof., chief catalog div., 1971-73, asso. prof., asso. librarian adminstrv. services, 1973—; lectr. Syracuse U. Grad. Sch. Library Sci., summer 1967, 69, Queens Coll. Grad. Dept. Library Sci., 1967-69. HEW Title II & fellow Case Western Res. U. Sch. Library Sci., 1970-72. Mem. N.Y. Library Assn. (pres. resources and tech. services sect. 1966-67, councilor 1966-67, sec.-treas. coll. and univs. libraries sect. 1973—), A.L.A. (membership com. 1967-71; chmn. council of regional groups, resources and tech. services div. 1968-69, dir. div. 1968-70), N.Y. Tech. Services Librarians (pres. 1963-64), Am. Assn. U. Profs., Spl. Libraries Assn., N.Y. U. Grad. Sch. Bus. Adminstrn. Alumni Assn. (rec. sec. 1967-69, dir. 1969-70) Phi Kappa Phi. Presbyn. (elder). Clubs: New York Library (sec. 1964-66, council 1966-70, 73—); Smith College (pres. 1966-67, 67-68), Civitas (Bklyn.). Home: 35 Schermerhorn St Brooklyn NY 11201 Office: Bklyn Coll Library Brooklyn NY 11210

MOORE, JEAN-MARIE, nurse, adminstr.; b. N.Y.C., July 24, 1934; d. Patrick and Jane (Phillips) Moore; diploma Mary Immaculate Hosp. Sch., Nursing, 1955; B.S., Adelphi U., 1959; M.A., N.Y.U., 1962. Staff nurse John T. Mather Hosp., Port Jefferson, N.Y., 1955-58; clin. instr. Bellevue and Mills Schs. Nursing, N.Y.C., 1958-62; instr. Nassau Community Coll., Garden City, N.Y., 1962-63; asst. prof. Skidmore Coll., N.Y.C., 1963-68; nurse edn. adviser to Phong Dinh Province Nursing Sch., Can Tho, Vietnam Mission, AID, Dept. of State, Washington, 1968-69; asst. dir. devel. and research N.Y.U. Hosp., N.Y.C., 1970—. Mem. Nat. League Nursing, Am. Pub. Health Assn., League Women Voters. Home: 340 E 34th St New York City NY 10016 Office: 560 1st Av New York City NY 10016

MOORE, JOANNE IWEITA, pharmacologist, educator; b. Greenville, O., July 23, 1928; d. Clarence Jacob and Mary Edna (Klepinger) Moore; A.B., U. Cin., 1950; Ph.D., U. Mich., 1959. Asst. prof. pharmacology U. Okla. Coll. Medicine, Oklahoma City, 1961-66, asso. prof., 1966-71, prof., 1971—, also vice chmn. dept. pharmacology, 1966-69, acting chmn., 1969-73, chmn., 1973—. Bd. dirs. Okla. Heart Assn., chmn. research com., 1973-74. Postdoctoral fellow Emory U., 1959-61; USPHS grantee, 1963-69. Mem. Am. Soc. for Pharmacology and Exptl. Therapeutics, N.Y. Acad. Scis., Soc. for Exptl. Biology and Medicine, Am. Fedn. for Clin. Research, Soc. for Neurosci., Assn. for Med. Sch. Pharmacology, Sigma Xi. Contbr. articles on pharmacology to profl. jours. Home: 5725 Rushing Rd Oklahoma City OK 73132

MOORE, JOYCE CAMPBELL, educator; b. Lawrence County, Ala., Apr. 21, 1935; d. John Luther and Zora (Lansdell) Campbell; B.S., Florence (Ala.) State U., 1956; M.Ed., Auburn (Ala.) U., 1961; grad. student Loyola U., New Orleans, 1972; m. Gary Dale Moore, Sept. 8, 1956; children—Gregory James, Susan Janaan. Instr. phys. edn. Opelika (Ala.) Jr. High Sch., 1956-59, Auburn U., 1960-61, Danville (Ala.) High Sch., 1961-62, Gadsden (Ala.) State Jr. Coll., 1965-68; instr. gen. sci. Ozark (Ala.) city schs., 1959-60; asst. prof. phys. edn. Loyola U., New Orleans, 1972—; cons. in field, summer recreation dir. Mem. President's Com. for Athletes, 1971-72. Mem. Am., So., La. assns. health, phys. edn. and recreation, La. Tchrs. Assn., Hyman-Pl.-River Oaks Civic Assn., Kappa Delta Pi. Baptist (active children and youth coms.) Club: Plantation Athletic, Aurora Country (New Orleans). Home: 3001 Hyman Pl New Orleans LA 70114

MOORE, KAY, plastic surgeon; b. McComb, Miss., Aug. 9, 1938; d. John Kirkman and Willie J. (Beard) M.; B.S., La. State U., 1957, M.D., 1961. Intern, City of Memphis (Tenn.) Hosp., 1961-62; resident,

Charity Hosp., New Orleans, 1962-66, Jacksonville (Fla.) hosps., 1966-68; practice medicine specializing in plastic surgery, Baton Rouge, La., 1968—; mem. staff Baton Rouge Gen. Hosp., Our Lady of Lake Hosp., Baton Rouge; cons. Bogalusa Community Med. Center, 1968—. Diplomate Am. Bd. Surgery, Am. Bd. Plastic Surgery. Fellow A.C.S.; mem. Am. Soc. Plastic and Reconstructive Surgeons, Am., Southeastern socs. plastic and reconstructive surgeons, So. Med. Assn., Southeastern Surg. Soc. Home: 2659 July St Baton Rouge LA 70808 Office: 3849 North Blvd Baton Rouge LA 70806

MOORE, LOLA PEARL RAMSEY, realtor; b. Omaha, Ill., Oct. 14, 1910; d. Floyd and Fannie Ann (Dillard) Ramsey; certificate in real estate U. Cal. at Berkeley, 1967; student Long Beach Secretarial Coll., 1942, Diablo Valley Coll., 1961-63; m. J. L. Cook, Dec 30, 1929 (div. Oct. 1937); 1 son, James C.; m. 2d, Forrest R. Moore Jan. 22, 1938 (div. Jan. 1970); 1 son, Warren A. Accountant various firms, 1940-61; with various real estate firms, 1961-64; owner Moore Realty, Concord, Cal., 1964-65; pres., gen. mgr. Moore Realty Inc., Concord, 1965-72; owner Loma Realty, Camarillo, Cal., 1972—. Recipient awards Contra Costa Bd. Realtors, 1965, 66. Mem. Contra Costa Bd. Realtors (chmn. library com. 1965-66), Cal. Real Estate Assn., Nat. Assn. Realtors (mem. woman's council 1964—; pres. Contbr. chpt. 1965), Nat. Inst. Real Estate Brokers, Camarillo Bd. Realtors (sec. 1974—), Concord C. of C. (mem. com. Concord coordinated services project 1967-68, dir. 1970-72), League Women Voters. Presbyn. Mem. Order Eastern Star. Clubs: Soroptimists (pres. 1970-71) (Concord); International Traders. Home: 2269 Sherborne St PO Box 337 Camarillo CA 93010 Office: 1820 Ventura Blvd Camarillo CA 93010

MOORE, LORETTA MARIE STULTS (MRS. ROBERT PAUL MOORE), psychologist; b. Vernon, Ind., Sept. 12, 1935; d. James Henry and Ellen Marie (Snyder) Stults; student Ball State U., 1957-59; B.A., Butler U., 1962; M.A., Wayne State U., 1969, postgrad., 1969—; m. Robert Paul Moore, July 26, 1953; children—Linda Lynn, Michael Allen. Sec., Delco Battery Plant, Gen. Motors Corp., Muncie, Ind., 1955-59; indsl. relations analyst personnel and orgn. staff World Hdqrs., Ford Motor Co., Dearborn, Mich., 1967-69; instr. psychology Wayne State U., part-time 1969-73; individual practice psychol. cons., Lincoln Park, Mich., 1973—. Mem. Nat. Orgn. Women (employment chairperson, dir., state rep. to Detroit Met. chpt.), Am., Midwestern, Mich. psychol. assns., Psi Chi. Home: 1133 Mill Lincoln Park MI 48146

MOORE, LUCILLE SANDERS GRAVES (MRS. GEORGE ALFORD MOORE), garment worker, union ofcl.; b. Greensboro, N.C., Apr. 6, 1920; d. Alexander Farrmington and Bessie (Patillo) Graves; student U. Conn., 1973; m. George Alford Moore, Sept. 26, 1954 (dec. Aug. 1973); children—C. Sanders, Edward, Welton, James Sanders, Myra (Mrs. Marvin L. Robinson Jr.), Charlene Sanders, Alicia Sanders, Georgia. Presser, I. Dibner & Bros., Waterbury, Conn., 1960—. Vice pres. local 223, Internat. Ladies Garment Workers Union. Mem. Model Cities Citizen Bd., Waterbury; mem. Central Naugatuck Valley Drug Com., Waterbury, 1973—. Mem. Waterbury Republican Town Com., 1958-68; mem. Bd. Edn., Waterbury, 1969—. Bd. dirs. Research Found., St. Mary's Hosp., Waterbury. Mem. N.A.A.C.P. (mem. exec. bd. 1971—), Waterbury C. of C. Republican. Baptist. Elk; mem. Order Eastern Star. Home: 188 Cherry St Waterbury CT 06702

MOORE, SISTER M. IGNATIA ANN, educator; b. Seattle, Apr. 17, 1929; d. Philip H. and Helen Mae (Connell) Moore; student Seattle U., 1947-49; B.A., Marylhurst Coll., 1955; M.A., Cath. U. Am., 1966; postgrad. U. Reading (Eng.), 1968, Royal Acad. Dramatic Art, London, Eng., Summer 1974. Joined Community of Sisters of Holy Names, 1949; tchr. St. Francis High Sch., Eugene, Ore., 1951-53, St. Mary's Acad., Portland, Ore., 1954, Star of Sea High Sch., Astoria, Ore., 1955-58, St. Mary's Acad., Portland, 1958—. Faculty Marylhurst (Ore.) Coll., 1969—, drama dir., 1970—. Evaluation cons. Ore. Shakespeare Festival Assn., 1972—; mem. bd. Am. Theatre Co., 1970-71. Mem. Am. Theatre Assn., Nat. Cath. Theatre Conf., Secondary Schs. Theatre Assn., ANTA, Ore. Theatre Arts Assn. (pres. 1969-71), N.W. Drama Assn. Home: 1615 SW 5th St Portland OR 97201 Office: Marylhurst Coll Marylhurst OR 97036

MOORE, MARGARET ELEANOR MARCHMAN, librarian; b. Pinckard, Ala., Nov. 6, 1913; d. Robert Lee and Eleanor Rowena (Paris) Marchman; A.B., Fla. State Coll., for Women, 1936; B.S. in Library Sci., George Peabody Coll. for Tchrs., 1947, M.A. in Library Sci., 1962; m. James William Moore, Feb. 22, 1934 (div. 1940); 1 son, John Robert. Tchr. Alva (Fla.) High Sch., 1938-40, Wacissa (Fla.) Jr. High Sch., 1940-43; librarian Bartow (Fla.) Sr. High Sch., 1943-45, 48-67, Bartow Pub. Library, 1945-48; cataloger Roux Library, Fla. So. Coll., Lakeland, 1967-70, reference librarian, 1970—. Mem. N.E.A., Fla. Library Assn., Beta Phi Mu, Delta Kappa Gamma. Democrat. Baptist. Home: 175 Lake Morton Dr Apt 61-G Lakeland FL 33801 Office: Roux Library Fla So Coll Lakeland FL 33802

MOORE, MARGARET RUMBERGER (MRS. JOHN TRAVERS MOORE), librarian, author; b. DuBois, Pa.; d. George F. and Mary E. (Means) Rumberger; B.S. in L.S., Syracuse U., 1926; m. John Travers Moore, June 16, 1928. Children's librarian Dayton (O.) Pub. Library, 1926-41; freelance writer, 1942—; asst. library dir., asst. prof. Xavier U., Cin., 1947-68; cons., 1969-71. Mem. Pi Lambda Sigma, Zeta Tau Alpha. Author: They Saw Him Fly, 1966; Pretty Kitty, 1966; Guess What I Am, 1974; (with John Travers Moore): Sing Along Sary, 1951; Little Saints, 1953; Big Saints, 1954; The Three Tripps, 1959; On Cherry Tree Hill, 1960; The Little Band and the Inaugural Parade, 1968; Pepito's Speech, 1970; Certainly, Carrie, Cut the Cake, 1972. Contbr. articles, (fiction) to profl. jours., children's mags. Home: 525 Ehringhaus St Hendersonville NC 28739

MOORE, M(ARGUERITE) CAROLYN, anesthesiologist; b. Wilmington, Del., Feb. 20, 1918; d. William Walton and Marguerite Carolina (Nicolussi) Moore; B.A., U. Del., 1960; M.D., Hahnemann Med. Coll., 1964. Intern, Huntington Meml. Hosp., Pasadena, Cal., 1964-65; resident Los Angeles County Gen. Hosp., 1965-67; practice medicine, specializing in anesthesia, 1967—; mem. staff Med. Center of El Monte (Cal.), 1972—. Fellow Am. Coll. Anesthesiology; mem. A.M.A., Am., Cal. socs. anesthesiologists. Home and office: 1760 State St South Pasadena CA 91030

MOORE, MARIA JUSTICE, health planner; b. Norfolk, Va., Dec. 22, 1943; d. Benjamin Eugene and Marie Justice Dewey (Chadwick) Moore; student U. N.C., 1962-65. Staff reporter, music and theatre critic Virginian Pilot Newspaper, Norfolk, Va., 1967-71; health planner Tidewater Regional Health Planning Council, Norfolk, 1971—. Active Soc. for Aid Sickle Cell Anemia. Mem. Va. Pub. Health Assn., Common Cause (publicity coordinator Tidewater chpt. 1973-74). Home: 6305 Ardsley Sq Virginia Beach VA 23462 Office: Koger Exec Center Norfolk VA 23502

MOORE, MARTHA ANNELL, furniture co. exec.; d. James Edwin and Mattie Ardeen (Rice) Moore; student Draughn's Bus. Coll., 1935-36. With Firestone Tire & Rubber Co., Akron, O., 1940-43; bookkeeper, office mgr. Fortner Furniture Co., Inc., Memphis, 1943-64, sec., 1964-74, sec.-treas., 1974—. Methodist (chmn. Ch. Sch. edn. 1968—). Home: 4088 Walnut Grove Rd Memphis TN 38117 Office: 3400 Summer Av Memphis TN 38122

MOORE, MARTHA ELIZABETH (MRS. LOUIS A. BURNETT), artist; b. Bayonne, N.J.; d. Arthur James and Florence Veronica (Kiefer) Moore; student (scholar), Art Students League, 1958-62; m. Louis Anthony Burnett, June 24, 1936. One-woman show, Jerusalem, Israel, 1970; represented in permanent collection Harvard U., Norfolk (Va.) Mus. Art and Sci., Mcht. Marine Acad., Kings Point, L.I., Tyler (Tex.) Art Mus., Glassboro (N.J.) State Coll. Recipient Maynard Portrait award Nat. Acad. Design, 1962; Gold medal honor Nat. Assn. Women Artists, 1963, Catherine Lorillard Wolf Art Club, 1963, 66 and others. Mem. Art Students League N.Y.C. (life), Rockport Art Assn., Allied Artists Am. (treas., 1963-65), Audubon Artists (corr. sec., 1963), Nat. Assn. Women Artists, Catharine Lorillard Wolfe Art Club. Home: 4 Hoffman Rd High Bridge NJ 08829 Studio: 17 Dock Square Rockport MA 01966

MOORE, MARY ELIZABETH, physician; b. New London, Conn., Dec. 7, 1930; d. Stansell Pickens and Mary Alice (Streckfuss) Moore; A.B., Douglass Coll., 1952; M.S., Rutgers U., 1958, Ph.D., 1960; M.D., Temple U., 1967; m. Stanley A. Greenstein, Aug. 3, 1974. Research asst. sociology Rutgers U., 1952-56, research asso., 1956-59; asso. in psychology Swarthmore Coll., 1959-60; asso. psychology, psychiatry U. Pa., 1960-63; intern, Temple U. Sch. Medicine, 1967-68, resident, 1968-70, fellow, 1970-72, asst. prof. medicine, 1972—; practice medicine specializing in rheumatology, Phila., 1972—; mem. staff Temple U., Episcopal hosps., Phila. Diplomate Am. Bd. Internal Medicine. Fellow A.C.P.; mem. Am. Rheumatism Assn., Phila. Rheumatism Soc. Contbr. articles to profl. jours. Home: 500 Manning Walk Philadelphia PA 19106 Office: Temple U Hosp 3401 N Broad St Philadelphia PA 19140

MOORE, MARY HELEN LEGRAND (MRS. WADE HAMPTON MOORE), home economist; b. Carthage, N.C., Apr. 20, 1928; d. Matthew Thomas and Hannah Pine (Watkins) LeGrand; student N.C. Coll., 1944-45; B.S. in Home Econs., Agrl. and Tech. U., 1948; M. Ed., N.C. State U., 1968; m. Wade Hampton Moore, May 30, 1970. Tchr. home econs. Belhaven (N.C.) High Sch., 1949-51; extension home economist N.C. Agrl. Extension Service, Cumberland County, Fayetteville, 1951-70, Coop. Extension Service, Washington, 1970-71; home economics specialist Md. Coop. Extension Service, College Park, Md., 1971—. Mem. Policy Adv. Com., Cumberland Community Action Agy., 1968-70. Mem. Steering Com., Fayetteville, 1965. Recipient Distinguished Service award Cumberland County, 1970. Mem. Am., N.C. (chmn. textile and clothing com. 1966) home econs. assns., Nat. (Distinguished Service award 1970), N.C. (2nd. v.p. elect 1970) assns. extension home economists, Epsilon Sigma Phi, Delta Sigma Theta (pres. 1954-56, 58-60). Home: 9431 Ardmore Rd Landover MD 20785 Office: Univ Maryland College Park MD

MOORE, MAY LOU, librarian; b. Oklahoma City, Apr. 11, 1927; d. Harry Raymond and Helen (Sailors) Lasley; B.A., Tex. State Coll. for Women, 1948, B.S., 1948; m. Charles W. Moore, Dec. 17, 1948 (div. Apr. 1960). Librarian Getty Oil Co., Houston, 1956-63, Exxon Co., Houston, 1963—. Mem. Spl. Libraries Assn. (treas. Tex. chpt. 1966-67, treas. petroleum div. 1968-70, vice chmn. 1970-71, chmn. 1971-72). Home: 3119 Fairhope Houston TX 77025 Office: 800 Bell Houston TX 77002

MOORE, PAMELA LOUISE RAU (MRS. THOMAS MOORE), newspaper pub.; b. Bryan, Tex., Sept. 22, 1946; d. Frederick Adolph and Era G. (Gaulden) Rau; student Pan Am. Coll., 1964-66, Sam Houston State Coll., 1967; m. Thomas Sutton Moore, Apr. 29, 1967; children—Melissa Kay, Frederick Thomas. Co-mgr. The Almeda Texan, Houston, 1971; pub. The Cheney (Kan.) Sentinel, 1971—, The Goddard (Kan.) Sentinel, 1973—. Mem. Extension Homemakers Unit, Kappa Delta. Home: 213 Harrison St Cheney KS 67025 Office: 129 Main St Cheney KS 67025

MOORE, PATRICIA KEARNS (MRS. EDWIN CECIL MOORE), real estate broker; b. Chgo., May 27, 1924; John Clifford and Margaret (Plankey) Kearns; B.S., Beloit Coll., 1946; m. Edwin Cecil Moore, May 21, 1955; 1 son, John Geoffrey. Office sec. Asso. Gen. Contractors, Los Angeles, 1947-49; admissions counselor Beloit (Wis.) Coll., 1949-51; recreation dir. mil. hosps. A.R.C., Japan, Cal., Korea, 1951-55; asso. broker Tri-City Real Estate, Monterey, Cal., 1962—. Coordinator fund campaign Blood Bank Program, 1956; chmn. vols. A.R.C., Subic Bay, P.I., 1959-60; entertainment service chmn. Red Cross Vol. Services, Monterey, 1956. Recipient Spl. award for outstanding service to bd. Monterey Bd. Realtors, 1971. Mem. Cal. Real Estate Assn. (dist. chmn. 1971-73), Monterey Bd. Realtors (dir. 1969), Pi Beta Phi. Club: Monterey Peninsula Country, Monterey Civic. Home: 1043 Lost Barranca Pebble Beach CA 93953 Office: Tri-City Real Estate Washington and Pearl Monterey CA 93953

MOORE, PATRICIA (MRS. HERBERT JOSEPH BRUDER, JR.), pub. relations exec.; b. Phila., Dec. 29; d. Joseph Francis and Mary Patricia (Smith) Moore; student Clarke Conservatory of Music, 1934-39, Julliard Sch. Music, 1939-41; m. Herbert Joseph Bruder, Jr., Oct. 10, 1953. Pub. relations and spl. events dir. Strawbridge & Clothier Dept. Store, Phila., 1948-71; dir. women's div. Gray & Rogers, Inc., advt. agy., Phila., 1971-73; v.p. pub. relations and advt. T. Gray Assos., Inc., Phila., 1973—. Pres. Women's Aux. Am. Heart Assn., 1972-73, chmn. heart ball, 1974; pub. relations chmn. Salvation Army; active Phila. council Girl Scouts Am.; mem. Phila. Tourism Com., 1971—. Mem. Women in Communications, Phila. Pub. Relations Assn. (dir. 1964—), Fashion Group of Phila. (exec. bd.), Phila. Club Advt. Women, Am. Women in Radio and TV (pres. 1970-71). Club: Colonial Village. Home: Abbey and Country Rds Berwyn PA 19312 Office: T Gray Associates Inc 3 Parkway Philadelphia PA 19102

MOORE, PAULINE RUYLE (MRS. J. CORDELL MOORE), lawyer; ed. MacMurray Coll., George Washington U., Am. U., Washington Coll. Law; m. J. Cordell Moore, July 29, 1939. Adminstrv. sec. to Ill. Congressman James M. Barnes 1939-42; adminstrv. work Democratic Nat. Com., 1945-47; chief clk. and counsel Dem. Policy Com., U.S. Senate, 1948-70; now practice law, Washington; admitted to Tenn. bar, U.S. Supreme Ct. Mem. Phi Delta Delta. Home: 9701 Fields Rd Gaithersburg MD 20760 Office: 1001 Connecticut Av SW Washington DC 20036

MOORE, PHYLLIS SKAFF (MRS. CLARK D'ARCY MOORE), zool. gardens adminstr.; b. Charleston, W.Va., July 26, 1939; d. Phillip Samuel and Erma Louise (Patterson) Skaff; B.A., Rice U., 1961; m. Clark D'Arcy Moore, Dec. 21, 1962; children—Philip Dyer, Lorra Lee. Research asst. Baylor U. Coll. Medicine, Houston, 1961-64; curator edn. and children's zoo Houston Zool. Gardens, 1968—. Chmn. adv. bd. Houston Community High Sch., 1973—; bd. dirs. Cooperative Preschs. of Houston, 1967-69. Fellow Am. Assn. Zool. Parks and Aquariums (mem. pub. edn. com. 1972—); mem. Internat. Assn. Zoo Edn. Officers. Unitarian. Author, editor: (with Berry, Logan, Quick) Houston Zoological Gardens Docent Training Handbook, 1970. Home: 1922 Lauderdale Houston TX 77025 Office: PO Box 1562 Houston TX 77001

MOORE, RAYLYN (MRS. WARD MOORE), writer; b. Waynesville, O., Jan. 5, 1928; d. James Byrl and Ethelyn (Coverston) Crabbe; B.A., Ohio State U., 1949; M.A., Cal. State U. at San Jose, 1972; m. Ward Moore, June 28; children—Beth, Jeanne, John, Sara. Newspaper reporter, various newspapers, including Prescott (Ariz.) Evening Courier, Deseret News, Salt Lake City, 1949-60; free lance journalist, 1960-66; editor Exec. Housekeeper trade mag., N.Y.C., 1966-69; instr. writing Monterey (Cal.) Peninsula Coll., 1969—. Mem. Authors League Am., Theta Sigma Phi. Unitarian. Author: Mock Orange, 1968; Wonderful Wizard, Marvelous Land, 1973. Contbr. short stories and articles to various popular and lit. mags., anthologies. Address: 302 Park St Pacific Grove GA 93950

MOORE, RITA JEANNETTE (MRS. J. EARL MOORE), dean bus. sch.; b. Moosup, Conn., Jan. 24, 1917; d. J. Herman and Elizabeth (Burke) Dore; B.S., State Coll. at Worcester, Mass., also M.Ed.; m. J. Earl Moore, May 4, 1940; children—Ann C., John E. Tchr. Salter secretarial Sch., Worcester, 1959-65, dean of women, 1965—, v.p., 1968—; tchr. accounting, dir. New Eng. Sch. Accounting, Worcester, Mass., 1973—. Mem. Mass. Bus. Educators Assn. (v.p. 1974—), Eastern Bus. Tchrs. Assn., Nat. Assn. Accountants (dir. 1973—). Home: 20 Saybrook Rd Worcester MA 01604 Office: 45 Cedar St Worcester MA 01609

MOORE, SONIA, theatre dir., drama coach; b. Gomel, Russia; d. Evser and Sophie (Pasherstnik) Shatzov; student U. Kiev, U. Moscow, 1918-20, Drama Studio Solovzov Theatre, Kiev, 1919-20, Studio of Moscow Art Theatre, 1920-23; diploma, Alliance Francaise, Paris, 1927, Istituto Interuniversitario Italiano, Rome, 1938, Reale Conservatorio de Musica Santa Cecilia, 1939, R. Accademia Filarmonica, Rome, 1939; m. Leon Moore, May 11, 1926 (dec. Mar. 1957); 1 dau., Irene (Mrs. Jack Jaglom). Came to U.S., 1940, naturalized, 1946. Appeared at Russian Theatre in Germany, 1923-26; Off Broadway dir., co-producer The Painted Days, 1961; dir. Sharon's Grave prodn. Irish Players, 1961; dir. Sonia Moore Studio of Theatre, N.Y.C., 1961—; founder, pres. Am. Center for Stanislavski Theatre Art, Inc., 1964, artistic dir. ACSTA 1 Reperatory Co., 1970—, prodns. include The Cherry Orchard, Desire Under the Elms, The Man With the Flower in his Mouth, The Stronger, others; lectr. series on Stanislavski System, Library and Museum of the Performing Arts at Lincoln Center, 1967-68; lectr. on WNYC-FM, 1968-69, 73. Supr. Stanislavski System Workshop under auspices Recreation and Cultural Affairs Adminstrn. City N.Y., seminar Stanislavski Canadian Govt., 1969, 73; also various univs. and workshops. Author: The Stanislavski Method, 1960; The Stanislavski System, 1965; Training an Actor; The Stanislavski System in Class, 1968; Stanislavski Today, 1973. Contbr. articles to profl. jours., Ency. Brit. Address: 485 Park Av New York City NY 10022

MOORE, WOODY STURDIVANT (MRS. JOHN CALHOUN MOORE), librarian; b. Marion, Ala., Aug. 1, 1917; d. Edwin Woody and Mattie Garland (Perkins) Sturdivant; A.B., Judson Coll., 1939; certificate in sch. librarianship U. Ala., 1960, M.A., 1962; postgrad. U. Mich., summer 1961; m. John Calhoun Moore, Nov. 25, 1948. Staff artist Birmingham (Ala.) Pub. Library System, 1940-41; clk., state accounting office So. Bell Tel. and Tel. Co., Birmingham, 1941-42; asst. sec.-treas. Nat. Farm Loan Assn., Marion, 1945-51; asst. to bus. mgr. Marion (Ala.) Inst., 1958-60, librarian, 1960—. Cons. Judson Coll. Library, Marion, 1964. Mem. Marion City Commn. on Arts and Humanities, 1973—; chmn. Marion Inst. Art Show, 1973—. Mem. Am., Ala. (2d v.p. 1969) library assns., Ala. Jr. Coll. Library Assn. (pres. 1965-66), Perry County Hist. and Preservation Soc. (dir. 1973—), Women's Soc. Christian Service (life). Democrat. Methodist. Clubs: Triad Study (pres. 1958, v.p. 1973), Marion Ladies Golf Assn. (Marion). Home: 213 Polk St Marion AL 36756 Office: Marion Inst Marion AL 36756

MOOREHEAD, NITA FAYE BROWN (MRS. NORMAN LEON MOOREHEAD), psychologist; b. Hawkins, Tex., June 11, 1936; d. Jesse Frank and Mary (Berry) Brown; B.S., Tex. Coll., 1958; M.Ed., North Tex. State U., 1963; Ed.D., East Tex. State U., 1974; m. Norman Leon Moorehead, June 5, 1958; 1 dau., Audrey Faye. Tchr. high sch. Laneville (Tex.) Ind. Sch. Dist., 1959-63; prin. elementary sch. Canton Ind. Sch. Dist., 1963-64; dean of women Tex. Coll., Tyler, 1968-72, head dept. freshman studies, 1974—; teaching asst. East Tex. State U., Commerce, 1973-74. Faculty Improvement grantee Tex. Coll., Tyler, 1972-74. Mem. Am. Personnel and Guidance Assn., Am. Coll. Personnel Assn., Nat. Assn. Women Deans, Adminstrs. and Counselors, Top Ladies of Distinction, Phi Delta Kappa, Alpha Kappa Delta, Alpha Kappa Alpha. United Methodist. Mem. Pride of Hawkins. Home: 2305 N Grand St Tyler TX 75701 Office: 2404 N Grand St Tyler TX 75701

MOORHEAD, JULIANA REGESTER, editor; b. Richmond, Va., Dec. 12, 1942; d. Eldridge Veitch and Juliana (Hartsook) Regester; student Shorter Coll., Rome, Ga., 1959-61, U. Ga., 1961-63; m. N. Eugene Moorhead, Aug. 10, 1963; children—Carey Louise, Elizabeth Stacy. Staff writer Rome News-Tribune, 1962-63; asst. woman's editor Durham (N.C.) Sun, 1968-74, asst. city editor, 1974—. Mem. Women in Communications, N.C. Press Women. Democrat. Presbyn. Clubs: Durham Junior Women's (pres. 1973), Durham Newcomers (pres. 1968-69). Home: 2714 Heather Glen Durham NC 27705 Office: Box 2092 Durham NC 27702

MOORMAN, PAMELA ANN, psychologist; b. Passaic, N.J., Dec. 7, 1942; d. Wynant Clair and Jeannette Frances (Rentzsch) Moorman; B.A., Bucknell U., 1964; M.A. in Psychology, Assumption Coll., Worcester, Mass., 1970. Psychologist Westboro (Mass.) State Hosp., 1965, prin. psychologist, also asst. to supt., 1973—; research psychologist Wrentham (Mass.) State Sch., 1966, Cushing Hosp., Framingham, Mass., 1967; prin. psychologist, also asst. to supt. Grafton (Mass.) State Hosp., 1967-72; individual practice psychology pvt. community mental health clinic, 1974—. Mem. Am. (asso.), New Eng., Mass. psychol. assns., Assn. Advancement Psychology. Research, publs. on state hosp. closings. Home: 157 Hayden Rowe Hopkinton MA 01748 Office: Westboro State Hosp 211 Lyman St Westboro MA 01581

MOOSE, SANDRA OHRN (MRS. ALAN J. ZAKON), mgmt. consulting firm exec.; b. Boston, Feb. 17, 1942; d. Fritz Andrew and Esther (Bastey) Ohrn; A.B. summa cum laude, Wheaton Coll., 1963; M.A., Harvard, 1965, Ph.D., 1968; m. Alan J. Zakon. Teaching fellow, Harvard, Cambridge, Mass., 1965-66; cons. Fed. Deposit Ins. Corp., Washington, 1966-68; mgmt. cons. The Boston Cons. Group, 1968—. Trustee Geoffrey and Elizabeth May Found. Recipient 100th Anniversary award Wheaton Coll. Alumnae Assn., 1970, Catherine Filene prize, 1962. Wheaton scholar, U. Vienna (Austria), 1962; Woodrow Wilson fellow, 1963-64. Mem. Am. Econ. Assn., A.A.A.S., Radcliffe, Wheaton alumnae assns., Phi Beta Kappa. Home: 85 E India Row Boston MA 02110 Office: 1 Boston Pl Boston MA 02106

MOOTS, DORIS DEAN WHITE (MRS. OWEN L. MOOTS), hosp. adminstr.; b. nr. Bethel, Mo., Nov. 13, 1923; d. William Jacob and Mary Hazel (Turner) White; student Kirksville (Mo.) State Tchrs. Coll., 1944-45; m. Glen Edward Moots, June 19, 1945 (div. July 1971); children—Judy Cheryl (Mrs. Larry Joe Freeman), Glenda Gail; m. 2d, Owen L. Moots, Mar. 6, 1973. Sec., Shelby County Social

Security Office, Shelbyville, Mo., 1941-43, sec. Dist. Office, Kirksville, 1943-45; bus. mgr., surg. technician Moots Hosp. and Clinic, Pryor, Okla., 1947-51, adminstr., surg. technician, 1951-71, cons. adminstr., 1971-73. Mem. Am. Coll. Osteo. Hosp. Adminstrs., Northeastern Okla. (past pres. aux.), Okla. (past pres. aux.) osteo. assns., Okla. Gen. Fedn. Women's Clubs (past dist. chmn. pub. affairs), Pryor Women's Golf Assn. (past sec.-treas.), Alpha Sigma Alpha. Democrat. Mem. Christian Ch. Club: Monday Forum (past pres.). Home: 202 Park Plaza Kirksville MO 63501 Office: 202 N Franklin St Kirksville MO 63501

MORALES, GOLDIE PEARL LADEN, educator; b. Idabel, Okla., Aug. 29, 1909; d. Roland Lee and Mary Tricy (Riggs) Laden; B.A. in Philosophy, U. Cal. at Los Angeles, 1957; M.A. in English, Cal. State U. at Los Angeles, 1960; A.M. in Philosophy, U. So. Cal., 1962; m. Anthony Augustine Morales, Sept. 23, 1940. Instr. English, East Los Angeles Coll., 1964-67, asst. prof. English, 1967-69, asst. prof. philosophy, 1970-72, prof. philosophy, 1973—. Mem. Nat. Fed. State Poetry Socs., Cal. Poetry Soc., Pi Lambda Theta. Contbr. poetry to lit. mags. Home: 1340 College View Dr Monterey Park CA 91754 Office: East Los Angeles Coll 5357 E Brooklyn Av Los Angeles CA 90022

MORAN, ANN ELIZABETH, librarian; b. Franklin, Tenn.; d. James Walker and Emma Mai (Fly) Moran; B.S., Middle Tenn. State U., 1940; B.S. in L.S., George Peabody Coll. for Tchrs., 1943, M.A., 1953. Librarian various schs., Tenn., 1943-61; tchr. Franklin City Schs., 1961-65; tchr., librarian Williamson County (Tenn.) Schs., Franklin, 1940-43, library supr., 1965—, Chmn. fund drive Heart Assn., Franklin, 1969, chmn. bus., 1970, co-chmn. rural fund dr., 1972. Mem. Nat., Tenn., Middle Tenn. edn. assns., Am., Tenn. library assns., Bus. and Profl. Women's Club (sec. 1969-70), Women's Nat. Book Assn. (sec. 1971-73), Delta Kappa Gamma (treas. 1972-74). Home: Route 3 Franklin TN 37064 Office: Columbia Av Franklin TN 37064

MORAN, IRENE ELIZABETH, library ofcl.; b. Jersey City, June 25, 1927; d. Walter J. and Mary F. (Watson) Moran; student N.Y. U. Sch. Commerce, 1951. Editorial asst. Am. Banker, N.Y.C., 1944-51; with publicity dept. DuMont TV Network, N.Y.C., 1951-54; press editor Sta. WOR-AM-TV, N.Y.C., 1955-58; asst. Maurice Feldman-Pub. Relations, N.Y.C., 1958-60; pub. relations asst. Bklyn. Pub. Library, 1961-63, dir. pub. relations, 1963—. Mem. Pub. Relations Soc. Am., A.L.A., Pub. Relations Officers Soc. Home: 2770-A Kennedy Blvd Jersey City NJ 07306 Office: Bklyn Public Library Grand Army Plaza Brooklyn NY 11238

MORAN, IRENE VARNEY, city ofcl.; b. Gloucester, Mass., Apr. 10, 1924; d. Manuel F. and Irene (Fraga) Santos; B.A. in English and Psychology, U. N.H., 1945; M.A. in Pub. Adminstrn., Syracuse U., 1971; m. Walter Raymond Varney, June 29, 1945 (dec. 1956); m. 2d, John E. Moran, Mar. 1959 (div. 1968); 1 son, John Edward. City clk. City of Edmonds, Wash., 1958—. Sec. City of Edmonds Firemen's Relief and Pension Bd. Mem. Adv. Bd. Edmonds Community Coll. Mem. Internat. Inst. Municipal Clks., Wash. Municipal Clks. Assn. (sec. 1973-75), Wash., Suburban finance officers assns. Clubs: Soroptimist (finance chmn. Sno-King chpt. 1973-74, corr. sec. 1974-75), Edmonds Yacht. Home: 941 Daley Edmonds WA 98020 Office: Civic Center Edmonds WA 98020

MORAN, JULIA PORCELLI, sculptor; b. N.Y.C., Apr. 18, 1917; d. Francis Paul and Maria (Franchina) Porcelli; pvt. study art; student Art Students League; m. Philip R.L. Moran, Apr. 8, 1953; children—Terese, Angela Jean, Joseph Philip, Lauren Frances. Profl. sculptor, exhibited numerous group shows; head Cultural Arts Assembly program elementary schs. system, Westchester County, N.Y.; chmn. Arts and Culture program, Greenburgh, N.Y.; initiator monthly cultural programs; lectr. in field; judge art shows, N.Y.C. and Westchester County. Executed life-size statue St. Thomas Aquinas, Buffalo. Dir. pub. relations White Plains (N.Y.) bd. Girl Scouts U.S.; co-chmn. cultural arts dist. P.T.A. exec. bd. Chmn. Elmsford (N.Y.) Democratic party. Recipient 1st prize sculpture Art in the Park, Tarrytown, N.Y., 1970, 2d prize Village Art Center, 1973, numerous others. Mem. Art Students League (life), Westchester Art Soc., Marmaroneck Artists Guild. Roman Catholic (Mother's Guild). Address: 48 N Mortimer Av Elmsford NY 10523

MORAN, MIRIAM L., educator; b. White Plains, N.Y.; d. Martin M. and Ellen V. (Brown) Moran; B.A., Good Counsel Coll., 1943; M.A., Fordham U., 1944; Ph.D., St. Johns U., 1957. Chmn. dept. history Good Counsel Coll., White Plains, N.Y., 1947-60, acad. dean, 1960-71; v.p. coll. relations Coll. White Plains, 1971—. Mem. Am. Hist. Assn., Am. Acad. Polit. and Social Sci., Am. Catholic Hist. Assn., Westchester County Assn., White Plains C. of C. Address: 52 N Broadway White Plains NY 10603

MORANI, ALMA DEA, surgeon; b. N.Y.C., Mar. 21, 1907; d. Salvatore N. and Amalia (Gracci) Morani; B.S., N.Y.U., 1928; M.D., Woman's Med. Coll. Pa., 1931; L.H.D. (hon.), Chestnut Hill Coll., 1974. Intern St. James Hosp., Newark, 1931-32; surg. resident Woman Med. Hosp., Phila., 1932-35; fellow plastic surgery U. Wash. Med. Sch., St. Louis, Mo., 1946-47; pvt. practice plastic surgery, Phila., 1948—; asso. surgeon Roxborough Meml. Hosp., 1940—; chief plastic surgery St. Marys Hosp., 1948—; cons. VA Hosp., 1955—; prof. clin. surgery Woman's Med. Coll. Pa., 1950—; vol. vis. prof. plastic surgery Nat. Def. Med. Center, Taipei, Taiwan, 1964. Pres. Am. Women's Hosps. Service, Inc., N.Y.C., 1967—. Decorated Order Sons of Italy, 1955, Order of Merit Cavaliere Ufficiale, Republic Italy; recipient Alumnae Achievement award Woman's Med. Coll. Pa., 1964, Achievement award South Phila. Lions Club, 1965, Friendship Fete Fame award, 1968; award of distinction Soroptimist Fedn. Am., 1970; Elizabeth Blackwell award Am. Med. Women's Assn., 1972; Distinguished Dau. Pa. award, 1973. Diplomate Am. Bd. Surgery. Fellow Am., Internat. colls. surgeons; mem. Am. Soc. Plastic and Reconstructive Surgery, Robert H. Ivy Soc. Plastic Surgery, Phila. Coll. Physicians, Am. Physicians Art Assn. (past pres.), Am. Med. Women's Assn. (regional dir.), Alumnae Assn. Woman's Med. Coll. (pres. 1957-58), Med. Women's Internat. Assn. (pres. 1972-74), Phila. County Med. Soc. (treas., dir.), Chinese Med. Soc., Philippine Med. Woman's Assn., Royal Soc. Medicine (affiliate), Phila. Acad. Surgery. Contbr. articles to med. jours. Home: 704 Kenilworth Apts Philadelphia PA 19144 Office: 3665 Midvale Av Philadelphia PA 19129

MORATZ, VIRGINIA ANNE, occupational therapist; b. N.Y.C., Nov. 3, 1947; d. Frank and Barbara Elizabeth (Mugdan) Moratz; B.A. in Psychology, Susquehanna U., 1969; Certificate in Occupational Therapy, Boston U., 1971. Staff occupational therapist U. Md. Hosp., Balt., 1971—. Occupational Therapy cons. Md. Manor, Glen Burnie, 1974—. Mem. Nat. Paraplegia Found., Am. Occupational Therapy Assn. Office: 22 S Greene St Baltimore MD 21201

MORE, VIRGINIA WAKEMAN, ins. co. exec.; b. White Plains, N.Y., Aug. 7, 1919; d. Tyndall Wells and Laura Elvira (Judd) Wakeman; student Am. U., 1936-37; B.S. magna cum laude, Syracuse U., 1940; postgrad. George Washington U., 1944; m. John W. More, June 26, 1940 (div. 1967); children—Alan Clyde, Bonnie Jean, Syver Wakeman, Jan Leslie. Asst. chemist U.S. Army Ordnance dept., Syracuse, N.Y., 1942-44; lab. technician, nurse pvt. med. office, Washington, 1944-45; lectr. Am. U. Assn. Lang. Tng. Center, Bangkok, Thailand, 1957-60; tchr. Queen Mother's Palace, Bangkok, 1957-58; mem. staff personnel div. Chase Manhattan Bank, Monrovia, Liberia, 1962; mem. adminstrv. staff AID, Nairobi, Kenya, 1962-63; sec., adminstrv. staff Am. embassy, Nairobi, 1963-64; office mgr. News Express, Bowie, Md., 1965-66; legislative aid to Md. senator, Bowie, 1966-68; examiner Govt. Employees Ins. Co., Washington, 1968, subrogation examiner, Miami, Fla., 1972—. Mem. Kappa Alpha Theta (life), Phi Kappa Phi (hon.). Home: 1595 NE 135th St North Miami FL 33161 Office: 99 NW 183d St Miami FL 33169

MOREAU, JEANNE, actress; b. Paris, France, Jan. 23, 1929; d. Anatole and Kathleen (Buckley) Moreau; student pub. schs., Paris; m. Jean-Louis Richard, Sept. 27, 1949 (div. 1962); 1 son, Jerome. Star motion pictures Ascensur pour l'Echafaud, 1958, Les Amants, 1958, Les Liaisons Dangereuses, 1959, Le Dialogue des Carmelites, 1959, Moderato Cantabile, 1960, La Notte, 1959, Jules et Jim, 1961, Peau de Banane, 1963, Le Journal d'Une Femme de Chambre, 1963, Mata-Hari, 1964, The Yellow Rolls-Royce, 1964, Viva Marial, 1965, The Immortal Story, 1966, Great Catherine, 1967. Address: 9 rue du Cirque Paris 8 France

MOREHEAD, MILDRED ADA, coll. adminstr., physician; b. Norristown, Pa., May 11, 1919; d. Turner Gustavus and Sara Mildred (Bachenheim) Morehead; student Duke, 1937-40; M.D., Columbia, 1943; M.P.H., Harvard, 1948. Rotating intern Englewood (N.J.) Gen. Hosp., 1944; resident internal medicine Bellevue Hosp., N.Y.C., 1944-45; epidemiologist Inst. Inter-Am. Affairs, Brazil, 1948-52; asso. dir. quality med. care studies Health Ins. Plan Greater N.Y., 1953-57, dir., 1957-59; asso. med. dir. Union Family Med. Fund, Hotel Industry N.Y.C., 1959-63; dir. med. audit unit Teamster Center Program, 1959-69; adj. asst. prof. adminstrv. medicine Columbia Sch. Pub. Health and Adminstrv. Medicine, 1959-68; asso. prof. community health, dir. evaluation unit dept. community health Albert Einstein Coll. Medicine, N.Y.C., 1968—; cons. Office Econ. Opportunity, 1967-73, N.Y. State Med. Soc., 1968-70, Dept. Health, Edn. and Welfare, 1970—, N.Y. Hosp. Corp., 1972—. Served with USPHS, 1944-47. Mem. Am. Pub. Health Assn., Am. Acad. Preventive Medicine. Contbr. articles to profl. jours. Home: Harbor Dr Port Chester NY 10573 Office: 1300 Morris Park Av New York City NY 10461

MOREHEAD, NORMA NELLE BULLARD (MRS. EDWIN LEE MOREHEAD), social worker; b. Jasper, Fla.; d. Clifton Price and Emily (McClellan) Bullard; student U. Miami (Fla.), 1932, Appalachian State Tchrs. Coll., 1932-34; B.S., Aurora Coll., 1936; M.S. in Social Work, St. Louis U., 1944; postgrad. Washington U., St. Louis, 1941-42; m. Edwin Lee Morehead, Nov. 19, 1944; children—Marjorie Nelle (Mrs. Thomas Charles Ney), Emilee Ellen (Mrs. Rodney Allen Hawkins). Tchr., Wilcox Sch., Oswego, Ill., 1936-37; welfare worker Dist. Welfare Bd., Miami, Fla., 1937-40; recreation worker Epworth Sch. for Girls, Webster Groves, Mo., 1940-41; vocational counselor St. Louis br. A.R.C., 1941-43; med. social worker U. Kan. Med. Center, 1944, 45, 46, 48, 49; asst. to dir. adoption services Jackson County Juvenile Ct., Kansas City, Mo., 1951—, supr. adoption services, 1969-71, supr. foster home unit, 1971—; field supr. student U. Kan., 1961-62. Mem. Nat. Assn. Social Workers, Acad. Certified Social Workers, Mo. Assn. for Social Welfare; Beta Sigma Phi. Baptist. Home: 106 E 63d St Kansas City MO 64113 Office: 625 E 26th St Kansas City MO 64106

MORENO, MARGUERITE THERESA CUSACK (MRS. PETER H. MORENO), educator; b. N.Y.C., Feb. 6, 1922; d. John Francis and Elizabeth (Robinson) Cusack; A.B., Coll. Mount St. Vincent, 1943; M.A., Seton Hall U., 1958; postgrad. Paterson State Coll., 1959-60, N.Y. U., 1962-64; Ph.D. in Ednl. Psychology, Fordham U., 1971; m. Peter H. Moreno, Nov. 24, 1946; children—John H., Mary Ellen. Elementary tchr. St. Philip's Sch., Saddle Brook, N.J., 1953-56, Rochell Park (N.J.) pub. schs., 1956-60; reading specialist, learning disabilities cons. Hackensack (N.J.) pub. schs., 1960-65; teaching asst. N.Y. U., 1963-64; reading clinician, adj. instr. Reading Center St. Peters Coll., 1960-65; asst. prof. reading dept. counseling and spl. services Sch. Edn., Seton Hall U., South Orange, N.J., 1965-70, dir. reading program and coordinator ednl. services center, 1965-70; asso. prof., chmn. dept. early childhood edn. William Paterson Coll. of N.J., Wayne, 1970-72, adj. asst. prof. Grad. Sch. Edn. N.Y. U., 1972—; ednl. cons. Yavneh Acad., Project Direct Follow Through Workshop, others. Mem. N.J. Edn. Assn., N.E.A., Am., N.J. reading assns., Assn. Exceptional Children, N.J. Reading Tchrs. Assn. (dir., pres. 1973-74), Phi Lambda Theta, Kappa Delta Pi. Home: 803 Albemarle St Wyckoff NJ 07481 Office: William Paterson Coll New Jersey Wayne NJ 07079

MORENO, MARÍA EUGENIA, editor; b. Mexico City, Mexico, Feb. 16, 1939; d. Eugenio Moreno Stadelmann and Amparo Gómez Alcalde de Moreno; B. in Humanities, Motolinia (Mexico) U., 1954; postgrad. Nat. U. Mexico, 1956; m. Higinio Ureta, Feb. 14, 1959; children—Gina, Higinio. Founder, mgr. Lupita mag. for women, 1957; founder, dir. Le Mujer de Hoy mag., 1960; founder Kena mag., 1963, since mng. dir.; mng. dir. Diseño mag., 1971—. Conductor TV programs for women, 1959—. Founder Juvenile Work Center, Mexico City, 1970, v.p., 1973—; originator Women of Year celebration in Mexico, 1960—. Bd. dirs. Nat. Advt. Council Mexico, 1970. Recipient Tourism medal Mexican Fed. Govt., 1973. Mem. World's Newspaper and Writers Women Assn. (pres. 1974), Mexico Advt. Ladies Club (past pres.), Fashion Group. Home: 117 Magdalena St México DF 12 Mexico Office: 44 Saturno St México 14 DF Mexico

MORENO, RITA, actress; b. Humacao, P.R., Dec. 11, 1931. Spanish dancer since childhood, night club entertainer; motion picture debut, 1950; films include Pagan Love Song, Toast of New Orleans, Singin' in the Rain, The Ring, Cattle Town, Latin Lovers, Jivaro, Yellow Tomahawk, Garden of Evil, Untamed, Seven Cities of Gold, Lieutenant Wore Skirts, King and I, This Rebel Breed, Summer and Smoke, West Side Story. Recipient Acad. Award for best supporting actress, 1962. Address: 140 Riverside Dr New York City NY 10024

MORESCHI, PATRICIA ROE REED (MRS. ANTHONY F. MORESCHI), child psychiatrist; b. Kansas City, Mo., Dec. 22, 1927; d. Roe Bernard and Alva Cleo (Wiley) Reed; B.S., Ia. State Coll., 1949; M.D., Woman's Med. Coll., 1954; m. Anthony F. Moreschi, July 12, 1953; children—Michelle, Anthony P., Patrice, Lynn. Intern, U. Ia. Hosp., Iowa City, 1954-55; resident pediatrics Woman's Med. Coll., Phila., 1961, adult psychiatry resident, 1969-71; child psychiatry resident Einstein Hosp., Phila., 1967-69; practice medicine specializing in pediatrics Wayne, Pa., 1961-67; practice medicine specializing in child psychiatry, King of Prussia, Pa., 1971—; mem. staff Women's Med. Coll. Hosp., Phila., Bryn Mawr (Pa.) Hosp.; psychiatric cons. Montgomery County Retarded Children, 1971—, Norristown Sch. Dist., 1971—, St. Christopher Hosp., Phila., 1971—. Bd. dirs. Freedom Valley council Girl Scouts Am. Fellow Am. Acad. Pediatrics; mem. A.M.A., Am. Med. Woman's Assn., Am. Acad. Child Psychiatry, Regional Council Child Psychiatry, League Woman Voters, Woman's Internat. League for Peace and Freedom. Home: 909 Croton St Wayne PA 19087 Office: 491 Allendale St King of Prussia PA 19087

MORETON, ANN DEPRIEST (MRS. FREDERICK PERKINS MORETON), writer, photographer; b. Polkville, N.C., Apr. 3, 1910; d. William Wesley and Minnie Jane (Philbeck) DePriest; student Am. U., 1928-29; m. Frederick Perkins Moreton, June 18, 1933 (dec. 1960); children—Thomas Perkins, Judith. Asst. buyer Woodward & Lothrop's, Washington, 1930-31; feature writer various newspapers, 1950-64; numerous stories in mags., newspapers illustrated with photographs, including Progressive Farmer, Home Gardening, Holland's, Profitable Hobbies, Dixie Roto mag., Nations Bus., 1955-60, Smithsonian, 1971, Ranger Rick, 1972; photographer Gulf Coast Research Lab., Ocean Springs, Miss., 1955-61, Ferson Optical Co., Ocean Springs, 1955; exhibited at Frame House Gallery, Louisville, 1970, Lauren Rogers Mus., Laurel, Miss., 1970, Am. Mus. Natural History, 1970-71, Smithsonian Instn., 1971, Newport News (Va.) Nature Museum, 1972, Tallahassee Nature Mus., 1972. Mem. Nat. League Am. Pen Women, Internat. Platform Speakers Assn., Nat. Audubon Soc., Miss. Gulf Coast Photographers Assn., Nat. Arachnid Soc. (founder 1966). Author: Spiders of the United States, 1974. Address: Route 2 Powhatan VA 23139

MOREY, BARBARA LOUISE, librarian; b. Shrewsbury, Mass., Sept. 11, 1916; d. William Eaton and Ethel Marion (Bement) Morey; B.A., U. Pa., 1938; B.S., Simmons Coll., 1939. Children's Librarian Rochester (N.Y.) Pub. Library, 1939-44; head children's work Elmwood Library, Providence, 1944-46; children's librarian Berkshire Athenaeum, Pittsfield, Mass., 1946-48; regional bookmobile librarian Western Regional Pub. Library System, Pittsfield, 1940—. Mem. cemetery com. Richmond, Mass., 1951-52; sec. Richmond Civic Assn., 1959-61; mem. Richmond Conservation Com., 1974—. Library trustee Richmond, 1955-57. Mem. Mass., Western Mass. library assns., Berkshire Museum, Audubon Soc. Conglist. Home: Canaan Rd Richmond MA 01254 Office: 184 South St Pittsfield MA 01201

MORGAN, ALICE ANNETTE, coll. adminstr.; b. Sciotoville, O., June 26, 1918; d. William M. and Janetta (Nickel) Morgan; A.B., Ky. Christian Coll., 1941; postgrad. Butler U., 1941; M.A., Marshall U., 1955. Prof. Ky. Christian Coll., Grayson, 1941—, registrar, 1953—. Mem. Am. Judicature Soc., Am. Assn. U. Profs. Mem. Christian Ch. Home: Grayson KY 41143 Office: Ky Christian Coll Grayson KY 41143

MORGAN, ANNE CUTLER MITCHELL (MRS. VANCE NEILY MORGAN), assn. exec.; b. Albany, N.Y., Oct. 21, 1935; d. Roy Herman and Helen DeMille (Cutler) Mitchell; B.A., Wellesley Coll., 1957; m. Vance Neily Morgan, Sept. 18, 1971. Coordinator internat. div. Kenyon & Eckhardt, advt. agy., N.Y.C., 1956-69; officer mgr. Montgomery, Day & Co., N.Y.C., 1969-70; coordinator customer relations Boston Safe Deposit & Trust Co., 1970-72; exec. dir. Wellesley Coll. Alumnae Assn., Wellesley, Mass., 1972—. Mem. Am. Alumni Council. Episcopalian. Clubs: Wellesley College (Wellesley); Wellesley (Boston and Middlesex, Mass.). Home: 13 Peckham Hill Rd Sherborn MA 01770 Office: Wellesley College Wellesley MA 02181

MORGAN, ANTONIA BELL (MRS. WILLIAM J. MORGAN), psychologist; b. London, Eng., Oct. 5, 1914 (came to U.S. 1946, naturalized 1948); d. James Young and Jean (Macnair) Bell; B.A., U. Oxford, 1936, M.A., 1945; tchrs. diploma U. London, 1938; m. William James Morgan, Nov. 2, 1944; children—William James, Jean Elizabeth, Robert Macnair. Chmn. dept. classical studies St. Albans Sch., Hertfordshire, Eng., 1938-41; Walter Hines Page scholar, lectr. English Speaking Union, 1941-42; lectr. Brit. Ministry of Information, 1942-43, asst. prin., India Office, 1943-45; sec. Aptitude Assos., Inc., 1946-49, asso. dir., 1949—. Lectr. Nat. Mental Health Assn.; sec. of No. Va. Mental Health Assn., 1955-56, v.p., 1958-59; cons. to ch. Sch. of the Diocese of Va. Licensed clin. psychologist, Va. Mem. A.A.A.S., Am. Personnel and Guidance Assn., Nat. Assn. Sch. Psychologists. Episcopalian. Author psychol. tests, articles on edn. of gifted children, and psychol. testing. Address: 2816 Gallows Rd Vienna VA 22180

MORGAN, BARBARA JEANETTE, librarian; b. nr. Greenfield, O.; d. Oliver Mack and Blanche Gertrude (Hamm) Morgan; B.S., Capital U.; M.S., Western Reserve U., 1952. Analytical chemist Mead Corp., Chillicothe, O., 1942-52, asst. librarian, 1952-64, librarian, 1964—. Mem. T.A.P.P.I., Am. Assn. U. Women, Spl. Libraries Assn., Soc. Ohio Archivists. Republican. Presbyn. Home: 3 Shawnee Dr Chillicothe OH 45601 Office: Mead Corp Central Research Lab Library 8th and Hickory Sts Chillicothe OH 45601

MORGAN, DONNA LOU ARCHIBALD (BONNIE LAKE) (MRS. DEMAR A. MORGAN), journalist; b. Malad, Ida., June 21, 1928; d. Robert Donald and Afton (Timpson) Archibald; B.S., U. Utah, 1949; m. DeMar A. Morgan, Apr. 7, 1949; children—Marcia (Mrs. Kurt Higgins), Arnie, Michele, Clay, Eric. Tchr. pub. schs., Seattle, 1949-52; with Salt Lake Tribune, 1954—, food editor, 1962—. Mem. Alumni bd. U. Utah, 1967—. Mem. Delta Delta Delta. Author: The Best of Bonnie Lake, 1972; co-author The Wit and Wisdom of Brigham Young with Pioneer Recipes, 1973. Home: 4565 Willow Rd Salt Lake City UT 84117 Office: Salt Lake City Tribune 143 S Main St Salt Lake City UT 84110

MORGAN, DOROTHY HOAGLAND (MRS. CHARLES RICHARD MORGAN), horsebreeder; b. Louisville, Mar. 29, 1950; d. Frank Morris and Ethel (Graves) Hoagland; B.S. (Block and Bridle jr. scholar, Keenland scholar), U. Ky., 1971, postgrad., 1972; m. Charles Richard Morgan, May 23, 1971. Co-mgr. with Frank M. Hoagland, standardbred horses, Fern Creek, Ky., 1964-70; co-trainer Charles Morgan Stable, Troy, O., 1971—. Mem. Ohio Horseman's Assn., U.S. Trotting Assn., Gamma Sigma Delta. Address: 3293 Wright Rd Laura OH 45337

MORGAN, HELEN BOSART, sculptor; b. Springfield, O., Oct. 17, 1902; d. Harley John and Mary Ellen (Grove) Bosart; A.B., Wittenberg U., 1923; postgrad. sculpture Daylen Art Inst., 1941-42, 46, Chgo. Art Inst., 1952-53; m. Joseph Wayland Morgan, Jan. 30, 1930 (dec. June 1969). One woman show Springfield Art Center, 1972; exhibited in group shows Flair Gallery, Cin., 1964-67, Cin. Mus., 1967, Ohio State Fair, 1968, Nat. Assn. Women Artists, N.Y.C., 1969, Merton G. Boyd Gallery, Columbus, 1970, Capitol U., Columbus, 1971, Gallery 200, Columbus, 1972; represented in permanent collections Wittenberg U., Butler Inst. Am. Art, Ohio U., Warder Library, Springfield, Cin. Art Mus., Mary E. Johnson Art Center, London, O., others. Founder, 1st pres., instr. Springfield Art Assn., 1946-63. Bd. dirs Clark Meml. Home, Springfield, 1950—. Mem. Nat. Assn. Women Artists, Internat. Inst. Arts and Letters. Home: 845 E High St Springfield OH 45505

MORGAN, HELEN (JEAN) NADEN (MRS. WALTER CLIFFORD MORGAN), educator, artist; b. Oak Park, Ill., Sept. 13, 1930; d. Donald Irvine and Helen Anna (Danhoff) Naden; student Hope (Mich.) Coll., 1948-50; B.A.E., Sch. Art Inst. Chgo., 1953, M.A.E., 1964; certificate Academie Voor Beeldende Kunsten, Belgium, 1969; m. Walter Clifford Morgan, May 14, 1966. Tchr. art jr. high sch., Cicero, Ill., 1953-62; tchr. art high sch. Maine Twp. schs., Park Ridge, Ill., 1964-65; asst. prof. art S.D. State U., Brookings, 1965—. Mem. Civic Fine Arts Center, Sioux Falls, S.D., Meml. Art Center, Brookings. paintings, textile design exhibited numerous art shows. Mem. Am., World crafts councils, Nat. Art Edn. Assn.,

Midwest Weavers Conf., Delta Phi Delta. Home: 1610 1st St Brookings SD 57006

MORGAN, JANET CAUDELL, psychologist; b. Buffalo, Aug. 8, 1925; d. Richard William and Blanche Ruth (Smith) Caudell; B.A. in Psychology, Denison U., 1947; M.A. in Psychology, U. Colo., 1948; postgrad. State U. of N.Y., Buffalo, 1958-60; m. Ben F. Morgan, Jr., Sept. 8, 1949 (div. May 1963); children—Benjamin Franklin III, Gary Caudell. Psychologist VA Dept., U. N.M., Albuquerque, 1948-49; sch. psychologist Bd. of Cooperative Edn. Services, Erie County, N.Y., 1958-74, coordinator of services for handicapped children, 1961-65; sch. psychologist Williamsville (N.Y.) Central Sch., 1974—. Cons. for pre-kindergarten summer program, Williamsville, 1971-73; speaker TV programs on brain injured children, 1965—. Mem. adv. bd. Buffalo Area Council on Alcoholism in Schs., 1964. Mem. Am., Western N.Y. psychol. assns., Nat. Assn. for Children with Learning Disabilities (v.p. Western N.Y. chpt. 1970-72), Nat., Upstate N.Y. assns. of sch. psychologists, Mental Health Assn. of Erie County (mem. task force on mental health in schs. 1973), Psi Chi, Alpha Phi. Home: 260 Roycroft Blvd Amherst NY 14226 Office: 5225 Sheridan Dr Williamsville NY 14221

MORGAN, JUNE MATHEWS, banker; b. Unionville, Mo., May 3, 1931; d. Ralph Sherman and Margaret Nancy (Creek) Mathews; student St. Petersburg Jr. Coll., 1967-68; children—Mark, Jacqueline. Sec., Mo. Dept. Health and Welfare, 1949-54, Law Office, Hon. Clare Magee, U.S. Rep., Unionville, Mo., 1958-60; v.p. Caladesi Nat. Bank, Dunedin, Fla., 1960-70; asst. v.p. Sun Bank of Tampa Bay (Fla.) 1970-73; v.p., cashier Key Bank of Tampa, 1973—. Mem. devel. bd. Mease Hosp., 1970-72. Mem. Nat. Assn. Bank Women, Am. Inst. Banking, Fla. Bankers Assn. Club: Tampa Racquet. Home: 5820 N Church St Tampa FL 33614 Office: 3601 W Waters Av Tampa FL 33614

MORGAN, LAURA GREY, physician; b. Mineola, N.Y., Jan. 25, 1919; d. Joseph and Sophie (Nemotka) Grey; R.N., Mt. Sinai Hosp. Sch. Nursing, 1939; student N.Y.U., 1941-44; M.D., N.Y. Med. Coll., 1949; m. J. Robert Morgan, Oct. 11, 1941. Intern, Morrisania City Hosp., 1949-50, resident pediatrics, 1950-52; pediatric cons. N.Y.C. Health Dept., 1953—; practice medicine, specializing in pediatrics, Stamford, Conn., 1956—. Diplomate Nat. Bd. Med. Examiners. Fellow Am. Pub. Health Assn.; mem. A.M.A., Conn. (del.), Stamford med. socs., Fairfield County Med. Assn. (trustee), Am. Acad. Pediatrics. Club: Soroptimist (Stamford). Home: 269 Palmer Hill Rd Old Greenwich CT 06870 Office: 21 Bridge St Stamford CT 06905

MORGAN, MARIANNE, bus. exec.; b. Muncie, Ind., Oct. 13, 1940; d. Clarence Wilson and Mary Estle (Shafer) Morgan; student Ball State U., 1958-61; B.A., Cal. State U., 1963; M.S., U. So. Cal., 1968; postgrad. U. Cal. at Irvine, 1970-74, So. Fla. U., 1974—. Library asst. Anaheim (Cal.) Pub. Library, 1963-65, sr. library asst., 1965-68; librarian Orange Coast Coll., Costa Mesa, Cal., 1968-74, exec. asst. to pres. F.E. Brady Products, Inc., Clearwater, Fla., 1974—. Alice M. Kitselman scholar, 1958. Mem. Cal., Orange County library assns., Faculty Assn. Cal. Community Colls., Wilderness Soc., Am. Civil Liberties Union, Sierra Club, Common Cause, Gamma Theta Upsilon, Beta Phi Mu. Republican. Home: 2455 W Moore Haven Dr Woodgate at Countryside Clearwater FL 33515 Office: PO Box 5304 2151 Logan St Clearwater FL 33515

MORGAN, MARTHA NAYLOR, lawyer; b. Evanston, Ill., Mar. 30, 1938; d. Ralph Edmond and Esther Grace (Severance) Naylor; A.A., Stephens Coll., Columbia, Mo., 1958; student U. Ill., 1958-60; J.D., Loyola U., Los Angeles, 1967; m. Coleman Adalbert Swart, Aug. 11, 1973; m. Richard Jon Larsen, Nov. 24, 1960 (div. Dec. 1968); 1 son, Frederick Roy. Admitted to Cal. bar, 1967; sr. tax accountant Security Pacific Bank, Los Angeles, 1968-69; asso. atty. Delbridge, Linton & Waterhouse, Pasadena, Cal., 1969-70; individual practice law, Pasadena, 1970—. Guest lectr. med. and legal ethics Queen of Angeles Sch. Nursing, Los Angeles, 1969—. Mem. Cal., Los Angeles, Pasadena (chmn. law day 1972) bar assns., Phi Theta Kappa. Republican. Home: 2885 Sheffield Rd San Marino CA 91108 Office: 150 S Los Robles Pasadena CA 91101

MORGAN, MARY LYNN (MRS. RALPH EMERSON MCGILL), dentist; b. Texarkana, Tex., Apr. 5, 1921; d. Mac Rogers and Delana (Lynn) Morgan; student John B. Stetson U., 1938-40; D.D.S., Emory U., 1943; m. Ralph Emerson McGill, Apr. 20, 1967; 1 stepson, Ralph Emerson. Practice dentistry, specializing in pedodontics, Atlanta, 1947—; faculty Sch. Dentistry Emory U., Atlanta, 1951—. Mem. Am. Acad. Pedodontics (dir.), Am. Coll. Dentists, Am., Ga. (sec.-treas., pres.) socs. dentistry for children, Am., No. Dist., Ga. dental socs., Omicron Kappa Upsilon. Episcopalian. Home: 3399 Piedmont Rd NE Atlanta GA 30305 Office: 490 Peachtree St NE Atlanta GA 30308

MORGAN, METALEEN CLINE, educator; b. Hickory, N.C., Nov. 23, 1940; d. Neil Montell and Metaleen Elizabeth (Cline) Morgan; A.B., Greensboro Coll., 1963; M.R.E., Garrett Theol. Sem., 1965; postgrad. Appalachian State U., 1971-73. Dir. Christian edn. First United Meth. Ch., Lenoir, N.C., 1965-69; instr. religion, philosophy and sociology Caldwell Community Coll. and Tech. Inst., Lenoir, 1970—; instr. Lenoir Rhyne Coll., Hickory, N.C., 1973. Leader Girl Scout U.S.A., 1969-74; chmn. Caldwell Community Coll. Heart Fund, 1973, Mother's March, March of Dimes, 1973. Bd. dirs. Yokefellow Christian Service Center, Lenoir. Mem. Am. Assn. U. Women, N.C. Sociol. Assn., N.C. Speech and Drama Assn., Community Coll. Social Sci. Assn., Christian Educator Fellowship. Methodist. Home: 109 Valencia Pl NE Lenoir NC 28645

MORGAN, NELLE WELLS, editor; b. Kenefic, Okla., Nov. 20, 1925; d. Virgil C. and Margaret L. (Smith) Wells; student George Washington U., 1942-45; asso. degree in drama Keene Smith Sch. Contemporary Arts, 1945-47; asso. degree in theatre arts Inst. Contemporary Arts, 1949; m. Woodruff S. Morgan, June 7, 1945 (div. Mar. 1973); children—Thomas B., Woodruff S., Martha M. Free-lance actress, 1949-59; mgr. Vic Tanny Health Clubs, N.Y.C., 1959-62; asst. to personnel mgr. Macke Vending Co., Washington, 1962-65; gen. mgr. Thompson Book Co., Washington, 1965-69; mng. editor Am. Fedn. Information Processing Societies, Montvale, N.J., 1969—. Editorial cons. various tech. assns. Mem. Com. for Cherry Blossom Festival, Washington, 1945-46, Com. for Pres.'s Birthday Ball, Washington, 1945-47. Mem. Washington Personnel Assn., Profl. and Bus. Club Ridgewood, Chi Omega. Democrat. Methodist. Home: 365 Cedar Av Ridgewood NJ 07450 Office: 210 Summit Av Montvale NJ 07645

MORGAN, NORMA LUCILLE (MRS. HAROLD JOHN MORGAN), home economist; b. Ames, Ia., Nov. 26, 1925; d. Harley Sylvester and Mabel Eleanor (Cotton) Shellito; B.S., Ia. State U., 1946, postgrad., 1965-71; m. Harold John Morgan, Mar. 23, 1946; children—Robert Paul, John Daniel, Thomas Harold, Catherine Margaret. Mgr. sch. hot lunch program, Ruthven, Ia., 1947; extension home economist Extension Service, Kossuth County, Ia., 1961-64; tchr. Headstart program, Auburn, Ala., 1965; home economist Extension Service, Crawford and Ida counties, Denison, Ia., 1965—. Chmn. seven county area Family Life Conf., Ia., 1969-72. Mem. Denison Community Sch. Bd. Edn., 1970—, pres., 1971. Bd. dirs. Community Nursery Sch., Denison, Ia., 1967-69. Mem. Ia. Assn. Extension Home Economists (pres. 1971), Ia. State U. Extension Assn. (v.p. 1971, sec. 1973-74), Am. Assn. U. Women (cultural insterests chmn., 1968-69), Ia. Council Family Relations, Am. Home Econs. Assn., Ia. Home Econs. Assn., Nat. Assn. Extension Home Economists, Ia. State U. Home Econs. Alumni Assn. Home: 2405 2d Av S Denison IA 51442 Office: Box 376 Courthouse Denison IA 51442

MORGAN, PHYLLIS JANE, recreational adminstr.; b. Homestead, Pa., Aug. 29, 1927; d. Clarence V. and Nellie J. (Wilson) Morgan; grad. Moody Bible Inst., Chgo., 1950. Dir. girls' work Peniel Community Center, Chgo., 1950-53; gen. program dir. First U.P. Community House, Pitts., 1953-59; regional rep. Pioneer Girls, Wheaton, Ill., 1959—. Mem. Am. Camping Assn., Nat. Rifle Assn., Christian Camping Internat. Home: 767 Highland Parkway Buffalo NY 14223

MORGAN, RUTH LORENE PROUSE (MRS. VERNON EDWARD MORGAN), educator; b. Berkeley, Cal., Mar. 30, 1934; d. Ervin Joseph and Thelma (Prcesang) Prouse; B.A. summa cum laude, U. Tex., 1956; M.A., La. State U., 1962, Ph.D., 1966; m. Vernon Edward Morgan, June 3, 1956; children—Glenn Edward, Renee Ruth. Tchr., O. Henry Jr. High Sch., Austin, Tex., 1957; instr. Victoria Coll., Tex., 1958-60; asst. prof. polit. sci. So. Meth. U., Dallas, 1966-70, asso. prof., 1970-74, prof., 1974—, chmn. faculty senate, 1972-73. Recipient Outstanding Prof. award, 1969, 74. Mem. Am. Assn. U. Profs., Am., Western, So. polit sci. assns., Acad. Polit. Sci., Phi Beta Kappa, Pi Sigma Alpha, Theta Sigma Phi, Phi Kappa Phi. Author: The President and Civil Rights: Policy-Making by Executive Order, 1970. Home: 7736 Woodstone St Dallas TX 75240

MORGAN, SARA RUTH, educator; b. Andrews, N.C., May 11, 1915; d. Garland Temple and Willabelle (Sandlin) Posey; B.S., Asheville Coll., 1942; M.S., U. Tenn., 1944; postgrad. Woman's Coll., U. N.C., 1945, Case Inst. Tech., 1956; J.D., Samford U., 1969; m. Frank McConaughy Morgan, Apr. 6, 1946; 1 son, George William. Asst. cashier Citizens Bank & Trust Co., Murphy, N.C., 1935-41; teacher Chapel Hill (N.C.) High School, 1942-43; teaching fellow U. Tenn., 1943-44; instr. Ala. Coll., Montevallo, 1944-45, asst. prof., 1948-54, asso. prof., 1954-71, prof. U. Montevallo, 1971—; coordinator distributive edn. Asheville (N.C.) City Schs., 1945-46; admitted to Ala. bar, 1969. Program specialist distbn. and marketing U.S. Office Edn., Washington, summer 1966. Recipient certificate merit Ala. Fedn. Women's club. Mem. Am. Assn. U. Women, United Bus. Edn. Assn., Southeastern Bus. Writers Assn., Am., Shelby County bar assns., Ala. Bar, D.A.R., Sigma Alpha Sigma, Pi Omega Pi, Phi Delta Delta. Democrat. Contbr. articles to profl. jours. Home: 346 Moody St N Montevallo AL 35115

MORGAN-BAWS, VIOLET YOLANDA (MRS. ROBERT E. BAWS), real estate broker; b. Canandaigua, N.Y., Sept. 11, 1915; d. Joseph Anthony and Mary Dominica (Campese) Emmanuel; student Mt. San Antonio Coll., 1971-72; m. Robert E. Baws, Mar. 8, 1962; children—Gloria, George Peter. Owner, operator Violet Morgan Real Estate, El Monte, Cal., 1959—. Cons. real estate probate sales. Named Realtor of Year, San Gabriel Valley Bd. Realtors, 1972. Mem. San Gabriel Valley Womens' Council Realtors (charter pres. 1972), San Gabriel Valley Bd. Realtors (pres. 1974). Clubs: Soroptimist (El Monte); Toastmistress (co-founder 1972) (Covina, Cal.). Address: 10717 Garvey Av El Monte CA 91733

MORGANROTH, JANICE MARILYN COHN (MRS. FRED MORGANROTH), lawyer; b. Detroit, Mar. 14, 1940; d. Sidney Lewis and Beverly Monica (Shapero) Cohn; student U. Colo., 1958-59; B.A., Mich. State U., 1961; J.D., Wayne State U., 1964; m. Fred Morganroth, June 23, 1963; children—Greg Scot, Candi Lyn, Erik Jon. Admitted to Mich. bar, 1964; asso. Lebenbom, Morganroth & Stern, Southfield, 1963—. Corr. and rec. sec. Parent Tchrs. Orgn. Franklin Sch., 1973-74; dist. chmn. March of Dimes, 1973-74; sec. Rosemond Estates Assn.; block chmn. Muscular Distrophy, 1973; chmn. women's com. Met. Opera. Mem. State Bar Mich., World Wide Sportsman Club, Music Study Club, Chaine des Routisseurs, Alpha Epsilon Phi. Clubs: Detroit Tennis, Danish-Am., Lady Adms. Home: 30920 Woodcrest Ct Franklin MI 48025 Office: 1115 Travelers Tower Southfield MI 48075

MORGENLANDER, ELLA KRAMER, artist; b. Bronx, N.Y., Aug. 7, 1931; d. Bernard and Sarah (Walawelsky) Kramer; secretarial degree Bklyn. Coll., 1953; student N.Y. U., 1961; student (scholar) Bklyn. Mus. Art Sch., 1964-72; m. Lee Jay Morganlander, Dec. 25, 1963. One-man shows at N.A.D. Galleries, Community Arts Gallery Bklyn. Mus.; exhibited in group shows at N.A.D., Community Gallery of Bklyn. Mus., Artists Equity Gallery, N.Y.C.; tchr. creative art activities for pre-sch. children Bank St. Early Childhood Center, Operation Headstart programs, N.Y.C., 1965-67. Bd. dirs. Barnes Found., Merion, Pa., 1973-74. Recipient Adele M. Schiff prize Nat. Assn. Women Artists, 1973, painting award Bklyn. Mus., 1973, Mortimer N. Haber sculpture scholarship Roslyn (N.Y.) Sch. Painting and Sculpture, 1972-73. Mem. Artist Equity Assn., Nat. Assn. Women Artists. Home: 210 Park Place Brooklyn NY 11238

MORGENSEN, HELEN STEWART, retail stores exec.; b. Mpls., Oct. 15, 1924; d. Carroll Merle and Vena Alwilda (Hilton) Stewart; student U. Mont., 1942-46, Seattle U., 1957; m. Christian Walter Morgensen, Oct. 25, 1952 (div. July 1967); 1 dau., Judy Lee (Mrs. Richard Otis Dunn). Sec., Pacific Island Engrs., Guam, 1946-47; sec. to gov. of Mont., 1948; sec. to Mont. Liquor Control Bd., 1949-52; sec. to pres. Universal Services, Inc., Seattle, 1953-62, office mgr., 1958-62; office mgr. Bonanza Stores, Inc., Renton, 1962-65, adminstrv. asst., 1965-70, treas., 1970—. Trustee Bonanza Stores Profit Sharing Trust, 1971—. Mem. Nat. Secs. Assn. Home: 1425 Puget Dr Apt 314 Renton WA 98055 Office: 705 SW 7th St Renton WA 98055

MORGENSTERN, LUCILE CAMPBELL (MRS. MARVIN W. MORGENSTERN), partner pub. co.; b. Fairmont, Minn., Dec. 9, 1916; d. Leslie Earl and Ethel Arelia (Frakes) Campbell; student pub. schs.; m. Marvin W. Morgenstern, July 25, 1938. Society editor, bookkeeper Hector (Minn.) Mirror, 1935-42; printer Pensacola (Fla.) Daily, 1944; printer, lino operator New Bern (N.C.) Daily, 1944; proofreader Brown and Bigelow, St. Paul, 1945-62; owner, co-partner Times-Reporter Printing Co., Adams, Wis., 1962—, pub., bus. mgr., 1962—. Bd. dirs., treas. Adams County Meml. Hosp., Friendship, Wis. Mem. Wis. Press Assn., V.F.W. Auxiliary. Club: Golf (Friendship, Wis.). Home: Friendship WI 53934 Office: Adams WI 53910

MORGENSTERN, SALLI WEIDENFELD (MRS. JACK MORGENSTERN), librarian; b. Dorna, Rumania, Apr. 6, 1918; d. Simha and Etty (Klinghoffer) Weidenfeld; B.A., U. Czernoutz, 1937-39; m. Jack Morgenstern, July 3, 1947; 1 son, Nicky. Came to U.S., 1967, naturalized, 1973. Asst. librarian Acad. Socialist Republic Rumania, Bucharest, 1949-52, librarian, 1952-56; chief librarian Israel Med. Assn., Haifa, 1960-67; rare book cataloguer N.Y. Acad. Medicine, N.Y.C., 1967—. Cons. for orgn. hosp. libraries, Haifa, Hedera and Naharya, Israel, 1964-67; cons. history of medicine. Mem. Med. Library Assn. Home: 68-13 Fleet St Forest Hills NY 11375 Office: 2 E 103d St New York City NY 10029

MORGENTHAU, JOAN ELIZABETH (MRS. FRED HIRSCHHORN, JR.), physician; b. N.Y.C., Oct. 9, 1923; d. Henry and Elinor Joan (Fatman) Morgenthau; B.A., Vassar Coll., 1945; M.D., Columbia, 1949; m. Fred Hirschhorn, Jr., Oct. 6, 1957; children—Elizabeth, Joan, Elinor. Intern in internal medicine Maimonides Hosp., Bklyn., 1949-50; resident in pediatrics N.Y. Hosp., 1950-54; asst. dir. pediatrics comprehensive care and teaching program N.Y. Hosp., 1953-59, dir. adolescent clinic, 1965-67; dir. adolescent unit Mt. Sinai Med. Center, N.Y.C., 1957—; asst. prof. pediatrics Cornell U. Med. Sch., 1958-67; asso. prof. pediatrics also community medicine Mt. Sinai Sch. Medicine, City U. N.Y., 1967—. Diplomate Am. Acad. Pediatrics. Club: Cosmopolitan (N.Y.C.). Home: 55 Binney Lane Old Greenwich CT 06870 Office: Mt Sinai Hosp 5th Av and 100th St New York City NY 10029

MORIARTY, FLORENCE JARMAN (MRS. VINCENT P. MORIARTY), editor; b. Flushing, N.Y.; d. George W. L. and Sarah (Tuite) Jarman; A.B., N.Y.U., 1936; m. Robert Austin Schetty, Jan. 22, 1938 (div.); m. 2d, Vincent Paul Moriarty, June 16, 1961. Coll. textbook editor Prentice-Hall, Inc., N.Y.C., 1936-38; schoolbook editor Iroquois Pub. Co., Syracuse, N.Y., 1938-40; asso. editor Modern Romances, Dell Pub. Co., 1940-43; mng. editor Personal Romances, Ideal Pub. Corp., 1943-48, editor Intimate Romances, 1948-53; editor, originator of title True Life Stories, Pines Publs., 1953-54; editor-in-chief True Confessions, Macfadden-Bartell Corp., N.Y.C., 1954—. Mem. Theta Upsilon. Club: N.Y. University (bd. govs.). Home: 69 W 9th St New York City NY 10011 Office: 205 E 42d St New York City NY 10017

MORICONI, JANIE KATHRYN MCKELVEY (MRS. JOHN JOSEPH MORICONI), editor; b. Tyler, Tex., July 20, 1943; d. Samuel Houston and Frankie Pearl (Duke) McKelvey; student Tex. Technol. U., 1962; student Kan. State Coll. of Pittsburg, 1970-72; m. John Joseph Moriconi, Nov. 24, 1962; children—Charlotte Ann, Jana Maria. Gen. assignment reporter Roswell (N.M.) Daily Record, Record Pub. Co., 1964-66; women's editor The Morning Sun, Pittsburg Pub. Co., Pittsburg, Kan., 1966—. Mem., vol. bd. sec. Mt. Carmel Guild; bd. mem., troop leader Redbud Trail Girl Scout Council, 1970—; lit. chmn. Pittsburg City Fedn., 1970—; founding co-chmn., incorporator, chmn. bd. Pittsburg Area Arts and Crafts Assn., 1973-74; state publicity chmn. Kan. Assn. Community Arts Council, 1973-74; local publicity dir. art tour Mid-Am. Arts Alliance, 1974. Bd. dirs. Youth for Environmental Action. Roman Catholic. Club: Kansas (dist. conv. publicity 1973-74, conservation chmn. 1970—). Home: 107 N Goodhall Frontenac KS 66762 Office: 701 N Locust Pittsburg KS 66762

MORIEARTY, SUE ELLEN (MRS. RICHARD F. ROGAL), psychologist; b. Manitowoc, Wis., Feb. 24, 1944; d. Louis Michael and Elizabeth Ellen (Lentz) Moriearty; B.A., U. Wis., Oshkosh, 1966; M.A., U. Mo., Kansas City, 1969; Ph.D. (USPHS grantee), U. S.D., 1972; m. Richard F. Rogal, Dec. 23, 1972. Instr., U. Wis., Green Bay, 1969; program dir. Behavior Modification Unit, also career chief psychology Jacksonville (Ill.) State Hosp., 1972—. Cons., Three Rivers Sch. Dist., Jacksonville, 1973. Mem. exec. bd. Community Health Areawide Planning of Elm City, 1974—. Nat. Inst. Mental Health fellow, Kansas City, Mo., 1971-72. Mem. League Women Voters, Am. Assn. U. Women, Nat. Orgn. Women, Am., Midwestern, Ill. psychol. assns. Home: 30 Chateau de Fleur Jacksonville IL 62650 Office: Jacksonville State Hosp Jacksonville IL 62650

MORITZ, GAYNELLE MARGUERIETE, city ofcl.; b. Seymour, Ind., Jan. 22, 1910; d. Henry Joseph and Henrietta Ethel (Reedy) Moritz; ed. Seymour Bus. Coll., 1941. County recorder Jackson County, 1946-54; clk.-treas. City of Seymour (Ind.), 1956—. Mem. Seymour Bus. and Profl. Women's Club (pres. 1951-52), Am. Legion Aux. (post pres. 1953-54), Phi Beta Psi. Democrat. Home: 411 S Poplar St Seymour IN 47274 Office: 220 N Chestnut St Seymour IN 47274

MORIWAKI, SHARON YURIKO, educator; b. Honolulu, Dec. 29, 1945; d. Yutaka and Jean Shizuko (Muramoto) Moriwaki; B.A., U. So. Cal. at Los Angeles, 1967, M.A., 1969, Ph.D., 1971. Research asst. III Center for Tng. in Community Psychiatry, Los Angeles, 1970-71; research asso. Rancho Los Amigos Hosp., Downey, Cal., 1971-72; asst. prof. research methods, statistics, sociology of lifecycle U. So. Cal. at Los Angeles, 1972—. Cons. VA Hosp. Central Research Unit Task Force on Asian Mental Health, Task Force on Suicide Prevention. Nat. Inst. Mental Health fellow, 1967-71, Cecilia O'Neill scholar, 1971. Biomed. Research grantee, 1971. Mem. Am. Psychol. Assn., Am., Pacific sociol. assns., Asian Am. Social Workers, Gerontology Soc., Asian Am. Educators. Contbr. research articles on ethnicity, mental health and aging to profl. publs. Home: 1002 North Mariposa No 23 Los Angeles CA 90029 Office: Univ of So Cal University Park Los Angeles CA 90077

MORKOVSKY, MARY CHRISTINE, educator; b. San Antonio, Dec. 13, 1931; d. Henry John and Mary Amalia (Kucera) Morkovsky; B.A., Our Lady of the Lake Coll., 1954; M.A., St. Louis U., 1961, Ph.D., 1966. Prof. Our Lady of the Lake Coll., San Antonio, 1962—; curator exhibits San Jose Mission, San Antonio, 1971-73; researcher in Europe San Jose Mission Hist. Research Library, 1972-73. Grad. teaching asst. St. Louis U., 1966. Mem. Am. Philos. Assn., Am. Assn. U. Profs., Am. Metaphys. Soc., Southwestern Philos. Soc. Mem. Congregation of Divine Providence (del. to gen. chpt. 1967-68, 73—). Office: 411 SW 24th St San Antonio TX 78285

MORLANG, BARBARA LOUISE BLAUVELT (MRS. CHARLES MORLANG, JR.), nutrition cons.; b. Danbury, Conn., May 24, 1944; d. Starr Chester and Dorothy Olive Mae (Schofield) Blauvelt; B.S., Brigham Young U., 1960; M.S., Columbia, 1964; Ph.D., U. Mass., 1969; m. Charles Morlang, Nov. 12, 1964. Dietetic intern Yale-New Haven Hosp., 1961; therapeutic dietitian Yale-New Haven Community Hosp., 1960-62, St. Luke's Hosp., N.Y.C., 1962-64; nutrition cons. Bur. Nutrition N.Y.C., 1964-65; dir. Springfield (Mass.) Dairy Council, 1965-66; nutrition cons. Va. Dept. Health, Roanoke, 1969—. Pres. Adult Activities Council, 1972; finance officer Civil Air Patrol, 1972—. Mem. Am. Pub. Health Assn., Bot. Soc. Am., Va. (registration chmn. 1973), Roanoke (pres. 1971) dietetic assns., Va. Home Econs. Assn. (treas. 1971-73), Va. Council Health and Med. Care, Sigma Xi, Phi Sigma, Omicron Nu. Home: 6828 Ardmore Dr Hollins VA 24019 Office: 703 Townside Rd Roanoke VA 24014

MORLEY, FRANKIE LANELL PETERSON, advt. exec.; b. Turkey, Tex., Nov. 7, 1934; d. James Frank and Bessie Mae (Dennis) Peterson; student Tex. A. and M. U., 1950, S.W. Tex. State Coll., 1951; m. Robert Edward Morley, Dec. 21, 1952; children—Joel Blake, Mark Edward. Continuity dir. radio sta. KITE, 1961-64; dir. radio-TV, bus. mgr. Westberry/LeMessurier Advt. Agy., 1964-66; time buyer Pitluk Group Advt. Agy., 1967-68; propr. Morley Media Services, San Antonio, 1969—. First v.p. San Antonio Council Chs., 1959-60; sec. Larkspur P.T.A., 1963-64; pres. Christian Women's Fellowship, 1960-61. Bd. dirs. San Antonio Camp Fire Girls. Mem. Am. Women in Radio and TV (pres. San Antonio chpt. 1970), Sales and Marketing Execs. (dir.), San Antonio Advt. Fedn. (various coms.). Home: 4430 Shavano Woods San Antonio TX 78249 Office: 9720 Data Point San Antonio TX 78229

MORLEY, MAE GRIGG, medical librarian; b. Montreal, Que., Can.; d. Hugh and Emma Bertha (Keefe) Grigg; B.Arts, McGill U., 1947, M.L.S., 1971; B.L.S., U. Toronto, 1953; m. William Morley, July 3, 1953; children—Primo, Minou. Librarian Allan Meml. Inst., psychiat. hosp., Montreal, 1953-57; library asst. Health Scis. Library, Queens U., Kingston, Ont., 1964-70; librarian Kingston Psychiat. Hosp., 1972—. Home: 147 Norman Rogers Dr Kingston ON K7M 2R1 Canada Office: Box 603 Kingston ON K7L 4X3 Canada

MORLOCK, LOIS ANN, banker; b. Bowling Green, O., Apr. 30; d. William H. and Vivian Reynolds Reynolds; M.A. in Finance and Banking Ohio U., 1964; postgrad. Rutgers U., 1969, Harvard, 1970; children—Larry, Beth, Timothy, Todd. With First Nat. Bank, Bowling Green, O., 1954—, v.p., 1967-68, exec. v.p., 1968—. Guest lectr. Bowling Green U., 1970-71. Mem. City Govtl. Adv. Com., Bowling Green, 1971-72; mem. nat. edn. com. Nat. Assn. Bank Women, 1971-72, Ohio Co-op. Office Edn. Bd., 1969-72, finance com. Ohio Sch. Bd., 1972—. Mem. Bowling Green City Dist. Sch. Bd., 1971—, pres., 1974. Bd. dirs. Practical Nurses Assn., Northwestern Ohio. Named to Outstanding Young Women Am., Bus. and Profl. Women, Bowling Green, 1967-70; recipient Community Service award City of Bowling Green, 1970, 71, 72. Mem. Nat. Assn. Bank Women (v.p.), Ohio, Am. (nat. pub. speaker for edn. com. 1971-72, dir. 1972-74) banker assns., Bowling Green C. of C. (chmn. Promote Bowling Green com.), Bus. and Profl. Women's Club, Alpha Chi Omega. Club: Women's of America N.Y.C.). Home: 1047 Melrose Estates Bowling Green OH 43402 Office: 222 S Main St Bowling Green OH 43402

MORMINO, KAY TITUS (MRS. FRANK MORMINO), publisher, editor; b. San Francisco; d. Louis and Charlotte (Hill) Titus; B.A., U. Cal. at Los Angeles, 1942, M.A., U. So. Cal., 1947; m. John Allison Bell, June 24, 1927 (dec. 1950); children—Charles Gordon, Charlotte Alison (Mrs. Thomas A. Baird); m. 2d, Frank Mormino, Sept. 6, 1962 (dec. Oct. 1974). Tchr. pub. high schs., Los Angeles, 1943-67; editor haiku poetry sect. Nutmegger Mag., Danbury, Conn., 1967-68; editor, pub. Modern Haiku mag., Los Angeles, 1969—. Founder, leader Haiku Workshop, Los Angeles, 1964-70. Recipient 1st prize Virgilio Meml. Haiku Contest, 1963. Fulbright grantee, 1953-54. Mem. Cal. Fedn. Chaparral Poets, League Am. Penwomen, Japan-America Soc., Kappa Kappa Gamma. Editor: Haiku Anthology, 1967. Contbr. articles, poetry to various publs.

MORNING, JANE GRAY (MRS. LAROY MORNING), librarian; b. Oak Park, Ill., Jan. 5, 1928; d. George Foster and Lillian Ruth (Urgos) Gray; B.A., Elmhurst Coll., 1949; M.L. S., U. R.I., 1968; m. LaRoy Morning, Dec. 18, 1971; children by previous marriage—Amy Dillenbeck, Thomas Gray Dillenbeck, David Dillenbeck. Head adult services Pawtucket (R.I.) Pub. Library, 1968-69; acquisitions librarian No. Ill. U., DeKalb, 1969; head librarian Judson Coll. Library, Elgin, Ill., 1969-73, Batavia (Ill.) Pub. Library, 1973—. Trustee, Elgin Community Coll. Mem. A.L.A., Ill. Library Assn., Am. Assn. U. Women, Am. Civil Liberties Union, Nat. Orgn. Women, League Women Voters. Unitarian. Home: 1038 Center St Elgin IL 60120 Office: 11 N Batavia Av Batavia IL 60510

MORPHONIOS, ELLEN JAMES, judge; b. Ponzer, N.C., Sept. 30, 1929; d. Wesley L. and Lydia (Winfield) James; J.D., U. Miami, 1957; m. Alex G. Morphonios, 1950 (div. 1971); children—Dale, Dean; m. 2d, John Joseph Rowe, Mar. 20, 1972 (div.). Admitted to Fla. bar, 1958, also U.S. Supreme Ct. bar, Circuit Ct. Appeals bar, U.S. Dist. Ct. bar; practiced in Miami, 1958-61; asst. state's atty. State of Fla., 1961; trial atty., chief prosecutor Criminal Ct., 1961-70; judge Criminal Ct. Record in and for Dade County, Miami, 1971—. Mem. Fla. Bd. Bar Examiners, 1968; lectr. Police Acad.; mem. com. on criminal ct. relief Fla. Supreme Ct., 1971; commentator Sta. WKAT, Miami, 1968-72; guest commentator Sta. KNOX, St. Louis; speaker to civic, polit. and fraternal orgns. Mem. judges adv. com. to Standing Com. on Ethics and Profl. Responsibility; mem. jud. selection, tenure and discipline com. Conf. Fla. Circuit Judges. Recipient Gen. Douglas McArthur Meml. award League Am. Ideals, 1970, Good Citizenship award Dept. Fla. Ladies Aux., Jewish War Vets. U.S.A., 1971; named Lady of Year, Miami Beach Democratic Club, 1972, Outstanding Woman of Dade County, Voters and Taxpayers League Dade County, 1972. Mem. Am. Bar Assn., Fla. Bar, Nat. Assn. Women Lawyers, Nat. Orgn. Women, Bus. and Profl. Womens Club. Home: 8640 SW 84th Ave Miami FL 33143 Office: 1351 NW 12th St Miami FL 33125

MORPHOS, DIANE BELOGIANIS (MRS. PANOS PAUL MORPHOS), civic worker; b. Chgo.; d. Demetrios and Alice (Rousseas) Belogianis; B.S., U. Chgo., 1937, M.A., 1938; m. Panos Paul Morphos, Dec. 11, 1948; children—Evangeline, Paul. Mem. faculty U. Chgo. Orthogenic Sch., 1938-45, U. Chgo. Remedial Reading Clinics, 1945-48; vis. lectr. Tulane U., 1947. Bd. dirs. S.E. La. council Girl Scouts U.S., New Orleans, 1959-65, v.p., 1965-68, pres., 1968—; mem. bd. Am. Assn. U. Women, New Orleans, 1969, v.p., 1970—. Mem. Athenee Louisianais, France-Amerique, Maison Hospitaliere, League Women Voters. Mem. Greek Orthodox Ch. Clubs: Greek Women's University (Chgo.); Tulane University Women's (New Orleans, La.). Home: 1404 Audubon St New Orleans LA 70118

MORRILL, MILLY FREEMAN (MRS. RALPH K. MORRILL), artist; b. Cleve., Apr. 19, 1940; d. Hal E. and Mildred (Real) Freeman; A.B., Smith Coll., 1961; M.A., Yale, 1964; Ed. D. in Art, Columbia, 1972; m. Ralph K. Morrill, July 24, 1964. Grad. asst. fine arts Oberlin Coll., 1961-62; asst. in instrn. dept. art history Yale, 1963-64; reference asst. library Mus. Fine Arts, Boston, 1964-65; instr. art dept. Auburn (Ala.) U., 1965-68; cons. Birmingham (Ala.) Bd. Edn., 1966-67; v.p., art cons. Environmental Research Assos., Inc., Auburn, 1966-69; pres. Epoch Estates, Wevertown, N.Y., 1969—; co-dir., exhibitor Caligallery Art Cabinet, Chestertown, N.Y., 1970—; instr. woodcut N. Country Art Center, Warrensburg, N.Y., 1972, Lower Adirondack Regional Arts Council, Glens Falls, N.Y., 1973; cons. Hyde Collection, Glens Falls, 1973. visual designer; one-man show, 60's Retrospective, Columbia U., 1970; exhibited group shows Ala. Council on Arts, 1968, 7th Dixie Ann., 1966, 9th Dixie Ann., 1968, Nat. Print Exhbn., State U. N.Y. at Potsdam, 1967, Water Color Soc. Ala. Ann., 1967. Recipient Purchase award Tuskegee Inst. Ann., 1966; Ala. Art League Ann. award 1967, Glen Falls Area Ann. awards, 1970, 71; Winter Art Ann. award Lower Adirondack Regional Arts Council, 1973. Mem. Coll. Art Assn., Am. Soc. Aesthetics, D.A.R. Home: Antler Lake Box 106 Wevertown NY 12886

MORRIS, ALDYTH VERNON (MRS. RAYMOND LLEWELLYN MORRIS), playwright; b. Logan, Utah, Aug. 24, 1901; d. Weston and Frances (Maughan) Vernon; B.A., Utah State U., 1921; postgrad. Columbia, 1925, U. Hawaii, 1958; m. Raymond Llewellyn Morris, June 27, 1929; 1 son, Richard Vernon. Bus. mgr. War Manpower Commn., Honolulu, 1943-46; editor U. Hawaii Press, 1950-53, mng. editor, 1953-65; editor East-West Center Press, Honolulu, 1965-67. Asst. to editor Philosophy East and West jour., 1953-65; asst. to editor Japanese Mind, also Chinese Mind, Indian Mind, Status of Individual East and West, 1967. Bd. dirs. King's Daus. Home, Honolulu. Mem. Nat. Soc. Arts and Letters, Nat. League Am. Pen Women, Dramatists Guild, P.E.N. (charter mem., mem. exec. com. Honolulu). Author: (plays) Fourth Son (Carefree Tree), 1955, Secret Concubine, 1957, Damien Letter, 1963, Sword and Samurai, 1966, The Clone, 1971, Damien, 1973; also one-act plays. Home: 1028 15th Av Honolulu HI 96816

MORRIS, BETTY BRYANT (MRS. JAY W. MORRIS), lawyer; b. Mountain Grove, Mo., Oct. 9, 1940; d. James Andrew and Joyce D. Martin (Cramer) Bryant; student South Western Sch. Law, 1964-66; LL.B., Beverly Coll. Law, 1968; m. Jay W. Morris, May 29, 1971. Sec., Office of Los Angeles County Supr., 1958-60; supr. legal steno pool Dist. Atty.'s Office, Los Angeles, 1960-63; clk. Superior Ct., Los Angeles County, 1963-69; admitted to Cal. bar, 1969; asso. trust counsel Security-Pacific Nat. Bank, Los Angeles, 1969-73; asso. counsel Union Bank, Los Angeles, 1973—. Mem. adv. bd. Girls Week, Los Angeles City Sch. Dist., 1973-74. Recipient Outstanding Career Woman certificate Cal. Fedn. Bus. and Profl. Women, 1973. Mem. Internat., Nat. (mem. status of women com. 1970-74) assns. women lawyers, Women Lawyers Assn. Los Angeles (pres. 1973-74), Am. Bar Assn., State Bar Cal., Nat. Bus. and Profl. Women Los Angeles (pres. 1974-75), Los Angeles County Bar, Am. Inst. Banking, Los Angeles C. of C., Beverly Coll. Law Alumni Assn. (dir.) Phi Alpha Delta. Office: 445 S Figueroa St Los Angeles CA 90017

MORRIS, CAROLINE JANE STEWART (MRS. FRANCIS J. MORRIS), librarian; b. Ridley Park, Pa., Sept. 14, 1923; d. James Sterrett and Mildred M. (McCloskey) Stewart; B.S. in Commerce, Drexel U., 1950; M.S. in L.S., 1964; m. Francis Joseph Morris, Feb. 3, 1950; 1 son, Edward James Stewart. Adminstrv. trainee John Wanamaker, Phila., 1946-50; serials librarian Penn Morton Colls., Chester, Pa., 1964-65; dir. libraries Pa. Hosp., Phila., 1965—; instr., leader several library workshops Am. Hosp. Assn., Cath. Hosp. Assn., Med. Library Assn. Mem. Emergency Aid Pa., 1960—. Served with WAVES, 1943-45. Mem. Nat. Med. Library Assn. (sect. chmn. 1970), A.L.A., Spl. Libraries Assn., Med. (local chpt. pres. 1969-70), Prospect Park library assns., Am. Assn. U. Profs., D. of R. (pres. Pa. 1947—), Victorian Soc. Am., Delaware County Hist. Soc., Historic Delaware County, Valley Forge Hist. Soc., Geneol. Soc. Pa., Hort. Soc. Pa., Dames Loyal Legion (state pres. 1966-68), Phila. Mus. Art, Inst. Contemporary Art, Drexel U. Alumni Assn. (pres. 1969-71). Club: Art Alliance (Phila). Home: 555 13th Av Prospect Park PA 19076 Office: 8th and Spruce Sts Philadelphia PA 19107

MORRIS, CYNTHIA HERRON TAFT (MRS. DONALD RICHARD MORRIS), educator; b. Cin., Apr. 28, 1928; d. Charles Phelps and Eleanor (Chase) Taft; B.A., Vassar Coll., 1949; M.Sc., London Sch. Econs., 1951; Ph.D., Yale, 1959; m. Donald Richard Morris, Sept. 18, 1955; children—David Taft, Michele Taft. Econ. analyst information sect. Mut. Security Agy., Paris, France, 1951-52; research asst. L.G. Reynolds, econs. dept. Yale U., 1953-55; teaching fellow econs. dept. Harvard U., 1955-57; research fellow Am. Assn. U. Women, 1958-59; cons. electricity power com. Econ. Commn. of Europe, Geneva, Switzerland, 1960; mem. faculty Am. U., Washington, 1964—, prof. econs. dept., 1969—. Cons. policy planning div., office program and policy coordination AID, 1962-71. NSF grantee, 1965-68, 68-70, 70-73. Author: (with L.G. Reynolds) Evolution of Wage Structure, 1956; (with I. Adelman) Society, Politics and Economic Development: A Quantitative Approach, 1967, Economic Growth and Social Equity in Developing Countries, 1973. Home: 3030 Arizona Av NW Washington DC 20016

MORRIS, DOROTHY HELEN, occupational therapist; b. Kansas City, Mo., Sept. 16, 1932; d. William Robinson and Nellie Mae (Burns) Morris; B.S., U. Kan., 1955; postgrad. U. So. Cal., 1956. Occupational therapist Children's Hosp., Denver, 1955-57; instr. phys. medicine U. Kan., Kansas City, 1957-66; exec. dir. Crippled Children's Nursery Sch., Kansas City, Mo., 1966—. Adviser or cons. United Cerebral Palsy of Kansas City, Kansas City Assn. Retarded Children, Infant Devel. Center, Shawnee Mission, Kan., Shawnee Mission Sch. Dist., Developmental Disability Council, Co-op. Areawide Transp. Service, Children's Mercy Hosp. Mem. Am., Kan. occupational therapy assns., United Way Exec. Assn. Home: 5608 Barkley Rd Shawnee Mission KS 66202 Office: 24th at Gilham St Kansas City MO 64108

MORRIS, EFFIE LEE (MRS. LEONARD VIRGIL JONES), librarian; b. Richmond, Va.; d. William H. and Erma (Caskie) Morris; B.A., Case Western Res. U., 1945, B.L.S., 1946, M.S. in L.S., 1956; m. Leonard Virgil Jones, Aug. 25, 1971. Br. children's librarian Cleve. Pub. Library, from 1946; children's specialist Library of the Blind, N.Y. Pub. Library, 1958-63; coordinator children's library services San Francisco Pub. Library, 1963—. Chmn. Library of Congress Adv. Com. of Children's Librarians on Selection of Books for Blind, 1958-63. Guest prof. Atlanta U., 1954; lectr. Case-Western Res. U., 1953-55. Cons. reading project San Francisco chpt. Nat. Council Christian and Jews, 1967—. Mem. Newbery Caldecott award com., 1950-56, 66-67, Laura Ingalls Wilder award com., 1953-54, 58-60; mem. prodn. rev. com. Nat. Aid to Visually Handicapped; mem. library adv. bd. New Book Knowledge; cons. E.S.E.A. services Chgo. Pub. Library Study, 1968-69; mem. adv. com. E.S.E.A. State of Cal., 1965—, Library Sch., San Jose State U., 1972—; del. White House Conf. on Children, 1970. Bd. dirs. YWCA, San Francisco, 1968-73; asso. council Mills Coll., 1973—. Recipient E.P. Dutton-John Macrae award for advancement of library service to children and young people, 1958. Mem. A.L.A. (sec. children's library assn. 1955-56, dir. children's services div. 1963-66, council 1967-71, pres.-elect pub. library assn. 1970-71, pres. 1971-72), League Women Voters, Women's Nat. Book Assn. (chpt. pres. 1968-70), Nat. Council Tchrs. English Nat. Braille Club (pres. 1961-63), Am. Assn. U. Women, N.A.A.C.P., Urban League (Bay area), Cal. Library Assn. (dist. pres. 1966; pres. children's services div. 1970-72), Cal. Black Librarians Caucus (organizer), Common Cause, Cal. Writers Club (hon.), Beta Phi Mu, Alpha Kappa Alpha. Conglist. Club: Altrusa (v.p. 1968). Contbr. articles profl. jours. Home: 66 Cleary Ct Apt 1507 San Francisco CA 94109 Office: San Francisco Pub Library Civic Center San Francisco CA 94102

MORRIS, ELINOR LOUISE, ednl. adminstr.; b. N.Y.C.; d. Frank and Marie (D'Ambrose) M.; A.B., Hunter Coll.; postgrad. Columbia, New Sch. Social Research. With Fed. Res. Bank, 1951-56; student adviser, vet. adviser Parsons Sch. Design, N.Y.C., 1956-61, fgn. student adviser, counselor, dir. placement, 1962—; cons. in field. Mem. Am., N.Y. State personnel and guidance assns., Eastern Coll. Placement Dirs. Contbr. articles to profl. jours. Home: 81 Irving Pl New York City NY Office: Parsons Sch Design 66 Fifth Av New York City NY 10011

MORRIS, EVELINE ROSE (MRS. G.G. WIRT), lawyer; b. France, June 28, 1941; d. Jules and Elizabeth Morris (Guild) Stefanuccio; came to U.S., 1945, naturalized, 1946; B.A., U. Cal. at Northridge, 1964; J.D., San Fernando Valley State Coll., 1971; m. G.G. Wirt, Dec. 19, 1966; children—G.G. III, Carrie Everle. Sales asso. Gribin von Dyl Realtors, Los Angeles, 1961-64; pres. Emco Cos., real estate, Los Angeles, 1964; pres. Red Giant, Inc., Aba Red Carpet Realtors; dir. Universal Giant Cos., J-G Frontage, Inc. Admitted to Cal. bar, 1972. Mem. Nat. Assn. Real Estate Bds., Cal. Real Estate Assn., Los Angeles, San Fernando Valley bar assns. Home: 23086 Cass St Woodland Hills CA 91364 Office: 22555 Ventura Blvd Woodland Hills CA 91364

MORRIS, HEATHER SHANE, physician; b. London, Eng., Nov. 5, 1935; d. Abraham Nathaniel and Ivy Miriam (Simmonds) Morris; M.B., Ch.B., U. Edinburgh, Scotland, 1960. Came to Can., 1966, naturalized, 1971. Intern, Maidenhead Hosp., Eng., 1960-61; resident Solihull Hosp., Eng., 1961-66, Women's Coll. Hosp., Toronto, Ont., Can., 1966-67; practice medicine specializing in obstetrics and gynecology, Toronto, 1966—; mem. staffs Women's Coll. Hosp. Guest lectr. univs., radio, TV, 1971—. Bd. dirs. Alliance for Life, pres., chmn., 1971—. Fellow Can. Royal Coll. Physicians and Surgeons; mem. Royal Coll. Obstetricians and Gynecologists, Canadian Med. Assn., Soc. of Obstetrics and Gynecology Can., Acad. Medicine, Toronto. Jewish religion. Home: 1 Rosedale Rd Toronto ON M4W 2P1 Canada Office: Ste 708 99 Av Rd Toronto ON M5R 2G5 Canada

MORRIS, HELEN GLADYS, endocrinologist; b. Denver, May 3, 1932; d. Harry and Bessie (Barshop) Morris; B.A., U. Colo., 1953, M.D., 1956. Intern U. Colo. Med. Center, 1956-57, resident medicine, 1957-59, fellow endocrinology, 1959-61; Damon Runyon research fellow, 1961-63; staff physician Denver VA Hosp., 1963-68, clin. investigator, 1964-68, cons. endocrinology, 1965-68; dir. endocrinology Children's Asthma Research Inst., Denver, 1968-71; endocrinologist Nat. Jewish Hosp., Denver, 1971—; mem. faculty U. Colo. Sch. Medicine, 1959—, asst. prof. medicine, 1965—; cons. Gen. Rose Meml. Hosp., 1971. Recipient Jim Fielder cancer research award, 1953, 54, Nat. Polio Found. research award, 1955; NIH research grantee, 1966-68, 72—. Diplomate Am. Bd. Internal Medicine. Mem. Am. Fedn. Clin. Research. Author articles. Home: 130 Pearl St Denver CO 80203 Office: 3800 E Colfax Av Denver CO 80220

MORRIS, HELENE THERESA, mgmt. cons.; b. Phila., Jan. 21, 1936; d. Mark M. and Elizabeth D. (Carroll) Morris; B.S. in Bus. Adminstrn., St. Joseph's Coll., 1969; M.B.A., Drexel U., 1972; student Talus C.P.A. Sch., 1973. With personnel dept. Pacific Nat. Ins. Group, Phila., 1953-58; adminstrv. asst. accounting dept. Bull. Co., Phila., 1959-70; bus. mgr. Pa. Coll. Optometry, Phila., 1970-74; mgmt. cons. Peat, Marwick, Mitchell & Co., Phila., 1974—; also pvt. accounting practice and tax accountant for secondary tchrs. Cons. Phila. Center for Health Careers. Committeewoman, Jr. Republicans, 1956-69; mem. Young Reps. of Upper Darby, Pa., Delaware County Rep. Women's Club. Bd. govs. Alumni Assn. St. Joseph's Coll.; fiscal officer Civil Air Patrol, 1954-59. Mem. Coll. and U. Personnel Assn., Nat. Assn. Coll. and U. Bus. Officers, Eastern Assn. Coll. and U. Auditors, Bus. and Profl. Women's Club. Home: 111 Maplewood Av Upper Darby PA 19082 Office: 1500 Walnut St Philadelphia PA 19101

MORRIS, JANET PATRICIA, assn. exec.; b. N.Y.C., Feb. 8, 1917; d. Edward Francis and Anne Helena (Harvey) Morris; B.A. cum laude, St. Joseph's Coll., 1937; postgrad. Heffley Bus. Sch., 1938, Columbia, 1952-53. Sec. to assn. officer Life Ins. Assn. Am., N.Y.C., 1938-56, asst. sec., 1957-63, asst. to pres., 1964-68, sec., 1969-72; sec. Am. Life Ins. Assn., 1973—, also editor News. Mem. N.Y. League Bus. and Profl. Women (dir. 1962-70). Club: Internat. (Washington). Home: 4201 Cathedral Av NW Washington DC 20016 Office: 1730 Pennsylvania Av NW Washington DC 20006

MORRIS, JEAN AARON (MRS. JOE TERRY MORRIS), ednl. adminstr.; b. Athens, Ga., Feb. 11, 1929; d. Ralph Edward and Ruth (Llewallyn) Aaron; B.S., U. Tampa, 1959; M.A. in Spl. Edn., U. South Fla., 1969; m. Joe Terry Morris, July 2, 1946; children—Jean Karen, Laura Susan, Teresa Ruth. Music dir. radio Sta. WFLA, Tampa, Fla., 1957-59, radio and TV talent scout, sta. WFLA Radio & TV, 1960-62, account exec., 1962-65, TV producer, 1962-65; broadcasting sta. exec. radio sta. WGTO, Cypress Gardens, Fla., 1965; account exec. radio Sta. WALT, Tampa, 1965-70; broadcast exec., air personality radio sta. WINQ, 1968-70; prodn. and utilization specialist for instructional TV, WJCT Community TV, Jacksonville, 1970-72; coordinator information/mgmt. spl. programs dept. Duval County Sch. System, Jacksonville, 1972-74, dir. information services, 1974—; TV coordinator Hillsboro County Sch. System, Tampa, 1959-60; instr. speech Patricia Stevens Career Coll. Mem. Mayor's Commn. on Status Women, 1973. Bd. dirs. N.E. Fla. chpt. U.S.O., YWCA, Program Resources, Fla. West Coast chpt. Multiple Sclerosis Soc. Mem. Am. Women in Radio and TV (pres. Fla. chpt. 1962-64), Nat. Pen Women, Tampa Advt. Club (sec., dir.), Tampa U. Alumni Assn., Nat. Sch. Public Relations Assn., Green Key Honor Club, Council for Exceptional Children, Pi Delta Epsilon, Sigma Tau Delta, Phi Delta Kappa, Kappa Delta Pi. Clubs: Toastmistress (charter mem.); Forest Hill Junior Women's (v.p. 1962-63). Home: 1856 Challen Av Jacksonville FL 32205 Office: 1325 San Marco Blvd Jacksonville FL 32207

MORRIS, JOAN HELEN JURISCH (MRS. VINCENT E. MORRIS), antique dealer; b. N.Y.C., May 16, 1911; d. Alfred and Johannah (Goldsmith) Jurisch; m. Vincent E. Morris, Aug. 30, 1942; children—John Morrison, Patrica Kathleen (Mrs. Robert E. Schaberg). Editor, Assn. Nat. Advertisers, N.Y.C., 1936-39; editor books on antiques Barrows & Co., N.Y.C., 1950; co-owner The Morris House, Stamford, Conn., 1942—; lectr., writer on antiques and early cookery, 1949—; cons. to museums and hist. restorations. Curator Stamford Hist. Soc., 1960-64; Conn. chmn. House and Garden Tour to benefit Inst. of Rehab. Medicine, N.Y. U., 1970. Bd. dirs. St. Joseph's Hosp., Stamford, 1958-60, Stamford Girls' Club, 1966-69, 73—, Stratford Shakespeare Guild, 1964—. Mem. Nat. League Am. Pen Women (v.p. Conn. Pioneer br. 1966-70, pres. 1974—). Club: Indian Harbor Yacht (Greenwich, Conn.). Home: 1296 High Ridge Rd Stamford CT 06903

MORRIS, JOYCE TAYLOR (MRS. ROBERT ARTHUR MORRIS), librarian; b. Auburn, N.Y., Oct. 2, 1924; d. Nelson Edward and Gladys Azalie (Chatelle) Taylor; A.B., Allegheny Coll., 1946; M.S. in L.S., Syracuse U., 1969; m. Robert Arthur Morris, Sept. 7, 1946; children—Susan Anne (Mrs. James Smith Ewing), Gregory Evan. Asst. librarian Jamestown (N.Y.) Community Coll., 1966-70, library dir., 1970—. Mem. exec. bd. Council Head Librarians, State U. N.Y. System, 1972-73, mem. com. to revise by-laws, 1973-74. Mem. A.L.A., N.Y. State, State U. N.Y. library assns. Democrat. Home: 37 Linwood Av Jamestown NY 14701

MORRIS, LAURA CATHARINE GAETJENS (MRS. J. PERRY MORRIS), physician; b. Bklyn., Feb. 21, 1910; d. Charles Francis and Adele (Schmitt) Gaetjens; B.S. cum laude, Elmira Coll., 1931; M.D., Coll. Phys. and Surg., Columbia, 1935; m. J. Perry Morris, Feb. 19, 1939; children—Mary (Mrs. Lawrence Kameya), Nancy Catherine, Joanne (Mrs. Charles Melba Stant) (dec.). Intern Luth. Med. Center, Bklyn., 1935-36, resident, 1936-37; individual practice medicine, Pensacola, Fla., 1938-39, Norfolk, Va., 1942-44; clin. physician King's Daus. Children's Clinic, Norfolk, 1939-62, sec., treas., 1961-66; dir. sch. health services Norfolk City Schs., 1962-66; dir. supportive services, dir. sch. health program Norfolk Dept. of Health, 1966-71, acting dir. Tb program, 1967-70; dir. health and nutrition program Norfolk pub. schs., 1971-72; dir. Chesapeake (Va.)

Health Dept., 1972—. Sch. physician Norfolk City Schs., 1945-62; mem. profl. adv. com. Health Welfare Recreation Planning Council, Norfolk, 1965—, pres., 1965-67; chmn. Chesapeake Mental Health and Mental Retardation Services Bd.; bd. dirs. S.E. Va. Tb and Respiratory Disease Assn. Fellow Am. Sch. Health Assn., Chesapeake (pres. 1973), Va. State, Norfolk County med. socs., Va., Tidewater pediatric socs., Va. Thoracic Soc. (dir.), Am., Va. pub. health assns., Va. (regional v.p. 1968-70), Tidewater (pres. 1966-68, 72—) assns. mental health, Va. Council Social Welfare (mem. regional bd. 1972—), Va. Edn. Assn. (hon. sch. nurse sect.), Edn. Assn. Chesapeake, C. of C. Soroptimist (pres. 1969-71). Home: 6442 Duquesne Pl Virginia Beach VA 23462 Office: 300 Cedar Rd Chesapeake VA 23320

MORRIS, LETTYE MARIE NOBLES (MRS. MELVIN A. MORRIS), educator; b. Ayden, N.C.; d. William Lloyd and Cornelia (Nobles) Nobles; A.B., Meredith Coll., 1929; M.Ed., U. Richmond, 1963; m. Melvin A. Morris, Dec. 31, 1935; children—James L., Arnold N. Tchr. English and French, Chowan High Sch., Edenton, N.C., 1929-31, Pink Hill (N.C.) High Sch., 1931-33, Ayden High Sch., 1933-35, Robersonville (N.C.) High Sch., 1935-36; tchr. English and journalism, also counselor Manchester High Sch., Richmond, Va., 1948-63, sr. counselor, 1963-65, asst. prin., 1965-67; coordinator informational services and pupil placement Chesterfield County Sch. System, Chesterfield, Va., 1967—. Judge newspapers So. Interscholastic Press Assn., Washington and Lee U., 1956-69. Recipient Washington and Lee U. Advisers' award, 1955; Columbia Scholastic Press Assn. Gold Key, 1964; Freedom Found.'s Classroom Tchrs. medal, 1959; Richmond Area Youth Safety Council citation, 1959. Mem. Nat., Va. (communications chmn. 1970), Chesterfield edn. assns., Nat. Sch. Pub. Relations Assn (audit com. 1972), Richmond Pub. Relations Assn., Richmond Club Printing House Craftsmen (bull. editor), Kappa Delta Pi, Delta Kappa Gamma, Alpha Delta Kappa (state treas. 1968-70, state v.p. 1970-72, state pres. 1972—). Baptist. Author (with Marjorie Webb) play Evenhanded Justice—Dr. Christian Radio Series, 1954. Home: 3934 Lake Hill Rd Richmond VA 23234 Office: Chesterfield County Sch Adminstrn Bldg Chesterfield VA 23832

MORRIS, LOUISE ELIZABETH BURTON (MRS. HARRY JOSEPH MORRIS), author, editor, genealogist, lectr., club woman; b. Arleston, Tex., Dec. 6, 1905; d. Edgar Lee and Myrtie Etoile (Black) Burton; student Oklahoma City U., 1922-24, spl. courses Okla. U., Samford U., Brigham Young U.; m. Harry Joseph Morris, Nov. 3, 1945. Factory rep. for U.S. Ohio Plastic Co., Frazeyburg, O., 1941; spl. rep. for Tex., Richard Hudnut Co., N.Y.C., 1942, for 4 states, Coty, Inc., N.Y.C., 1944; factory rep. for 11 states Sharpe & Sheehan, N.Y.C., 1951; factory rep. for Cook County, Ill., H.H. Ayres div. Lever Bros., N.Y.C., 1953. Lectr. biography, genealogy, heraldry, history. Conducted geneal. and heraldic seminars; geneal. forum at ann. Gathering Scottish Clans, Salado, Tex., 1967, 69, 71, 72; mem. program com., speaker World Conf. Records and Genealogy, 1969; speaker Internat. Congress Genealogy and Heraldry, Vienna, Austria, 1970, Liege, Belgium, 1972, English Heraldry Congress, Oxford, 1973. Chmn. adminstrv. Com. Dallas County Hist. Survey Com.; apptd. Tex. chmn. Tex. state Magna Charta Com. Chmn. library, trustee Central Tex. Area Mus., Inc.; mem. bd. Academico Correspondiente Academia de Gene. and Heraldry, Guadalajara, Mexico, Academia Mexicana de Genealogia y Heraldica, Mexico City. Recipient awards for articles books and essays. Certificates of Merit, Dictionary Internat. Biography, 1967, 72, Augustan Soc., 1968; decorated Companion of merit Order St. Lazarus of Jerusalem. Fellow Tex. Geneal. Soc. (v.p., 1st state historian, gen. conv. chmn.), Heraldic and Geneal. Studies Soc. Eng. (founder), Harry S. Truman Research Inst. (hon.), Scottish Soc. Antiquaries, Tex. Hist. Research Inst. (founder), Heraldry Soc. Malta; mem. Heraldry Soc. London (Eng.), Heraldry Soc. Can., So. Soc. Genealogists, Soc. Genealogists, London, Eng., Royal Soc. St. George, Eng., Scottish Genealogy Soc., Scottish Soc. San Antonio, Smithsonian Assos., D.A.R. (Ill. and Tex. chmn. pub. relations; organizer and 1st regent Capt. Thomas Black chpt., hon. life regent), Nat. Soc. Children of Am. Revolution (life; nat. and state promoter; hon. life sr. pres. Sgt. Amos Boynton Soc.), Gen. Soc. Mayflower Descs. (dep. gov. gen. Tex.; hon. life colony gov.; Tex. rec. sec.), Nat. Soc. Women Descs. of Ancient and Honorable Arty. Co. (nat. 1st v.p., nat. corr. sec.; organizer and 1st Tex. pres., hon. life state pres.; state parliamentarian), Nat. Soc. Magna Charta Dames (1st Tex. regent, hon. life state regent; hon. life regent various colonies; state parliamentarian, dir.; chmn. Tex. 750th anniversary Magna Charta com., ofcl. rep. Tex. and Dallas ceremonies Eng., 1965), Dallas So. Meml. Assn., Augustan Soc. (life; v.p. Keystone states; permanent rep. to Internat. Geneal. and Heraldic Congresses), S.W. Council Geneal. and Hist. Soc. (v.p.), Nat. Soc. New Eng. Women (organizer and 1st Tex. pres., hon. life state pres.; state parliamentarian), Nat. Soc. Daus. Am. Colonists (hon. life state regent; hon. life regent various chpts.), Ams. Royal Descent (life), Colonial Order Crown (life), Plantagenet Soc. (life), Nat. Soc. Old Plymouth Colony Descs. (organizing state pres.; hon. life state pres.; life), Colonial Dames Am., Inc., Nat. Soc. Daus. Colonial Wars (Tex. parliamentarian; state chmn. frontier nursing service), Am., S.W. archivists assns., Orgn. Am. Historians, Capitol, Western Res., Tex. hist. socs., Washington-on-the-Brazos State Park Soc., Tex. Pioneers Assn., Tex. Hist. Found., Nat. Soc. Dames of Ct. of Honor, Nat. Soc. U.S. Daus. of 1812, U.D.C. (hon. life pres. Chgo. chpt.; Tex. chmn. radio, TV; 1st v.p. Dallas chpt. 6), Coastal Bend Area Genealogy Soc. (hon.), Crockett Genealogy Soc. (hon.), Mesquite (hon.), San Angelo (hon.), Central Tex. (Hon.), Lubbock (hon.) geneal. socs., Nat., Internat. Order San Jacinto Descs. (1st v.p.; founder-pres. Dallas chpt.), Daus. Republic Tex. (chpt. hon. pres., editor Tex. State Lineage Book), Geneal. Soc. Victoria (Australia), Am. Soc. Heraldry, Nat., Ala., Ill., Okla., St. Louis, Ark.-La.-Tex. geneal. socs., Dallas County Heritage Soc., Inc. (charter), Soc. of Friends of St. George and Descs. of Knights of Garter (life), Brit.-Am. Soc. (life). King William I, The Conqueror, And His Companions At Arms, Ltd., (life; Tex. rep.-genealogist), Sovereign Order Alfred The Great (Dame Grand Cross; grand genealogist-heraldist), Nat., Central Tex. (hon.), Ft. Worth geneal. socs., Nat. (charter mem., founder asso.), Tex. (life) hist. socs., Nat. Soc. Arts and Letters (Chgo. chpt., Dallas Patriotic Assn. (2d v.p. 1964), Dallas Local History and Geneal. Soc. (v.p., editor), Dallas Civic Opera Guild, Friends of Tex. U. and Dallas Pub. Library, Dallas Symphony Orch. League, Ladies Hermitage Assn., New Eng. Historic Geneal. Soc., Genealogy Club Am. (charter), Dallas chpt. Freedom Found. (charter), Peyton, Skipworth family assns., Nat. Trust for Historic Preservation, Am. Assn. State and Local History, Order of Washington, Phila. (life), Nat. Fedn. Press Women, Tex. Press Women, Marquis Biog. Library Soc. (adviser), Nat. Geog. Soc., Dallas Council World Affairs, Dallas Woman's Forum (gen. civic chmn.), Internat. Platform Assn., Collectors Inst. (charter). Alpha Chi Omega. Methodist. Clubs: Knife and Fork, Public Affairs Luncheon (Dallas). Author: Ladies of the White House, 1957; The Ancient and Honorable, 1963; First Ladies of Texas-Wives of Texas Governors, 1964; Primer of Genealogical Research, 1965; Lineages and Genealogical Notes, 1967; Instant Historical Programs, 1968. Compiler-editor Founders and Patriots of Republic of Texas, The Local History and Genealogical Society Handbook of Seminars in Genealogical Research. Author articles, book reviews, essays in various mags. Editor: The Local History and Genealogy Society Quar., 1963-65. Home: Hacienda Tejas 2515 Sweetbrier Dr Dallas TX 75228

MORRIS, MARGARET ANN, librarian; d. Berry and Dora Ellen (Gordy) Morris; A.A., Eastern Pilgrim Coll., 1957-59; B.S., Kutztown State Coll., 1961; M.S., Syracuse U., 1966; m. Paul Michael Apostolos, Aug. 17, 1974. Bookkeeper, Salisbury Nat. Bank (Md.), 1948-57; librarian Eastern Shore Book Processing Center, Salisbury, 1961-65; head librarian Owosso (Mich.) Coll., 1966-70; cataloger Kutztown (Pa.) State Coll. Library, 1970-71, chief cataloger, 1972—. Sec. Aux. Penn Wesleyan Coll., Allentown, Pa., 1971—. Recipient Library Edn. award Kutztown State Coll., 1961. Mem. Am., Pa. library assns., Kappa Delta Pi, Beta Phi Mu. Mem. Wesleyan Ch. Home: 41-B South Elm St Kutztown PA 19530 Office: Kutztown State Coll Library Kutztown PA 19530

MORRIS, MARGARET FRANCINE, librarian; b. Gilmer, Tex., June 26, 1938; d. Gus S. and Margaret (Aldredge) Morris; B.A., U. Tex., 1961; M.S., E. Tex. State U., 1964. Bookmobile librarian Tex. State Library, Lockhart, 1964; asst. reference librarian Arlington State Coll., 1964-67; chief reference librarian U. Tex., Arlington, 1968-72, curator spl. collections, 1972—. Mem. Am. Assn. U. Profs., Sherlock Holmes Soc. London, Am., Tex. (chmn. reference round table) library assns., Western History Assn., Tex. Assn. Coll. Tchrs. (chpt. pres. 1969-70), Fort Worth Corral, The Westerners, Tex. Hist. Assn. Editor: Essays on the Gilded Age, 1973. Co-editor: Essays on American Foreign Policy, 1974; Essays on Urban America, 1974. Contbr. articles to profl. jours. Office: Library U Tex at Arlington Arlington TX 76019

MORRIS, MARGARET JONES, judge; b. Murray, Ky., Oct. 8, 1922; d. Lyman and Emma (Stamps) Jones; B.A., Ind. U., 1945; J.D., Northwestern U., 1949; m. Robert Stanley Morris, Dec. 21, 1948; children—Stephen Robert, David Randolph. Admitted to Ill. bar. 1949, Cal. bar, 1953; staff atty. Chgo. Land Clearance Commn., Chgo., 1949-52; dep. county counsel San Bernardino County, 1955-61, chief asst. county counsel, 1961-63; judge Municipal Ct., San Bernardino County, Cal., 1963-66; judge Superior Ct., San Bernardino County, 1966—, elected presiding judge, 1969—. Bd. dirs. Legal Aid Soc. San Bernardino County, 1969, Crafton Hills Coll. Found., San Bernardino County Heart Assn. Mem. Conf. Cal. Judges, Nat. Assn. Women Lawyers, San Bernardino County Bar Assn., Delta Kappa Gamma (hon.). Club: Zonta (San Bernardino). Lutheran. Home: 1332 Arroyo Crest Redlands CA 92373 Office: 351 N Arrowhead Av San Bernardino CA 92415

MORRIS, MARY ELLEN FRANCES, anesthesiologist, educator; b. Windsor, Ont., Can., Jan. 2, 1932; d. Frank Elijah and Frances Charlotte (Cock) Morris; M.D., C.M., Queen's U., 1955; Ph.D., McGill U., 1970. Rotating intern Montreal (Que., Can.) Gen. Hosp., 1955-56; resident in anesthesia McGill U., Montreal, 1957, research trainee in neurophysiology dept. anesthesia research, 1965-70, demonstrator, lectr. anesthesiology, 1965-69, asst. prof., 1969—, research in neurophysiology and anesthesia, 1970—, lectr. dept. physiology, 1971—, faculty dentistry, 1971—, Sch. Physiotherapy, 1974—, Med. Research Council Can. scholar, 1972—; resident in anesthesiology Western Res. U. Hosp., Cleve.; research fellow Montreal Neurol. Inst., 1960-61, clin. fellow in anesthesiology, 1962-63; clin. fellow anesthesiology Montreal Childrens Hosp., 1962; staff Hotel Dieu de St. Joseph de St. Jerome, 1964; staff Lakeshore Gen. Hosp., Pointe-Claire, Que., 1965-70, cons. anesthesiologist, 1970—. Diplomate Am. Bd. Anesthesiology. Mem. Canadian Anesthesists Soc., Soc. for Neuroscis., Canadian Physiol. Soc. Contbr. articles to med. jours. Home: 3470 Stanley St Apt 420 Montreal PQ H3A 1R9 Canada Office: 3655 Drummond St Montreal PQ H3G 1Y6 Canada

MORRIS, M(ARY) ROSALIND, educator; b. Wales, Gt. Britain, May 8, 1920; d. Aneurin Edmund and Celia Charles (Evans) Morris; came to U.S., 1942, naturalized, 1954; B.S.A., Ont. Agrl. Coll., 1942; Ph.D., Cornell U., 1947; postgrad. (Johnson Faculty fellow), Cal. Inst. Tech., 1949-50. Asst. in agronomy U. Neb. at Lincoln, 1947-51, asst. prof., 1951-53, asso. prof., 1953-58, prof., 1958—. Guggenheim fellow, 1956-57. Fellow A.A.A.S.; mem. Genetics Soc. Am., Genetics Soc. Can., Crop Sci. Soc. Am., Am. Assn. U. Women, Am. Inst. Biol. Sci., Sigma Xi, Gamma Sigma Delta, Sigma Delta Epsilon. Club: Audubon Naturalists (Lincoln). Contbr. articles to profl. jours. Home: 3018 O St Lincoln NE 68510

MORRIS, PATRICIA JOSEPHINE COLLINS (MRS. JOHN F. MORRIS), educator; b. Mpls., Jan. 15, 1912; d. Patrick and Kathryn (Hennessy) Collins; B.S., U. Minn., 1933, M.A., 1941; Ed.D., Temple U., 1960; m. John F. Morris, Dec. 21, 1951. Asst. prof. phys. edn. Temple U., Phila., 1938-52; tchr. Springside Sch., Chestnut Hill, Pa., 1953-57; asso. prof. phys. edn. Trenton (N.J.) State Coll., 1961-70, prof., 1971—. Dir. Phila. Hockey Day Camps 1955-70. Recipient Certificate of Merit, 1967. Fellow Am. Coll. Sports Medicine; mem. Am. Assn. Coll. Women Tchrs. Phys. Edn., Am. (chmn. body mechanics sect. E.D.A. 1970), N.J. assns. health, phys. edn. and recreation, N.J. Edn. Assn., Am. Assn. U. Profs., Psi Chi, Delta Psi Kappa (service pin 1960), Sigma Kappa. Research on somatotypes and body structure. Home: Box 154 Croydon PA 19020 Office: Packer Hall Trenton State Coll Trenton NJ 08625

MORRIS, PORTIA MARIE (MRS. DAVID DAVIS MORRIS), educator; b. Coeur d'Alene, Idaho, Mar. 27, 1911; d. Henry Peter and Laura May (Buchanan) Glindeman; B.S., U. Wis., 1932; M.A., Columbia U., 1935; Ph.D., U. Wis., 1940; m. David Davis Morris, July 7, 1940; children—Margaret (Mrs. Stephen Ludwig Lowe), Thomas, Edward, John. Tchr., Marshfield High Sch., (Wis.), 1932-34, N.J. Sch. for Deaf, 1935-36; instr. U. Wis., 1936-38, research asso., 1938-40; asst. prof. chemistry U. Idaho, 1944-45, home econs. Whitworth Coll., Spokane, Washington, 1945-47, U. Ia., 1947-48; asso. prof. Albion Coll., 1950-63, Mich. State U., Lansing, 1963-72, prof., 1972—. Mem. Am., Mich. home econs. assns., Am., Mich. dietetics assns., Soc. Nutrition Edn., Phi Kappa Phi, Omicron Nu, Pi Lambda Theta. Author bulletins Mich. Coop. Extension Service. Home: 1046 Lilac Av East Lansing MI 48823 Office: 103 Human Ecology Bldg Michigan State University East Lansing MI 48823

MORRIS, RUBY PEARL (MRS. M.B. MORRIS), ednl. adminstr.; b. Thornton, Tex., Jan. 11, 1918; d. J. H. and Mattie (Alston) Laurence; B.A., North Tex. State U., 1949, M.Ed., 1953, Ed. D., 1964; m. M.B. Morris, Feb. 28, 1938; 1 dau., Marion Beth (Mrs. Ken Cott). Supr. counseling and guidance Denton County Coll., Denton, Tex., 1953-59; asst. dir. psychol. services Dallas Ind. Sch. Dist., 1959-68, dir. psychol. services, 1968-71, adminstr. pupil personnel services, 1971-72, dep. asst. supt. pupil personnel services, 1972—. Vis. adj. prof. So. Meth. U., 1961, Okla. State U., 1962, Ark. State Coll., Jonesboro, 1965, East Tex. State U., Commerce, 1972-74, Dallas County Jr. Coll., 1967-69, North Tex. State U., Denton, 1970-71. Bd. dirs. Girls Adventure Trails. Mem. Tex. Personnel and Guidance Assn. (pres. 1957), Tex. Psychol. Assn. (pres. 1972), Dallas County Mental Health Assn. (dir. 1974-76), Dallas Sch. Adminstrs. Assn. (v.p. 1962-63). Contbr. articles on guidance and psychology to profl. pubs. Home: 6707 Winton Dallas TX 75214 Office: 3700 Ross Dallas TX 75204

MORRIS, RUBY TURNER, educator; b. Pepperell, Mass., 1908; d. George Freeman and Martha (Sibley) Turner; A.B., Vassar Coll., 1929; M.A., Stanford, 1930, Ph.D., 1937. Instr. Vassar Coll., Poughkeepsie, N.Y., 1930-35, asst. prof., 1936-39, asso. prof., 1939-52; prof. econs. Conn. Coll., New London, 1952-72, chmn. dept., 1952-72, Lucretia L. Allyn prof. emeritus econs., 1972—. Mem. New London Democratic Town Com., 1952—; mem. New London City Council, 1971—, dep. mayor, 1972-73. Mem. League Women Voters, Phi Beta Kappa. Author: The Theory of Consumer Demand, 1937; Fundamentals of Economics, 1967; Consumers Union, 1971. Home: 8 Winchester Rd New London CT 06320

MORRIS, RUTH FALLS (MRS. VESTAL L. MORRIS), educator; b. Gastonia, N.C., Jan. 23, 1913; d. Charles Newton and Bryte (Stroupe) Falls; B.S., East Carolina Coll., 1951; M.A., Tchrs. Coll. Columbia U., 1958; m. Vestal L. Morris, Oct. 22, 1943. Tchr. Lucia Sch., Mt. Holly, N.C., 1935-40; typist U.S. Army Engr. Corps., Am. Consulate, Colon, Panama, 1943-45; tchr. Gatun Sch., Gatun, C.Z., 1946-54; tchr. primary, intermediate educable mentally handicapped children Margarita Sch., Margarita, C.Z., 1958-66; staff mem. Ft. Gulick Elementary Sch., 1967-70, tchr. acad. enhancement, 1970-72; ednl. prescriptionist, vis. tchr. spl. classes Coco Solo (C.Z.) Elementary Sch., 1973—. Named Outstanding Tchr. Panama Canal Zone Schs. Div., 1967, 73. Mem. Am. Assn. U. Women, Atlantic Tchrs. Guild (v.p. 1952, treas. 1953), Am. Assn. Mental Deficiency (asso.), Council Exceptional Children, Internat. Platform Assn., Assn. Exceptional Children, Internat. Reading Assn., Isthmian Anthropology Soc., Sierra Club, Common Cause, Federally Employed Women (Atlantic area coordinator), Beta Sigma Phi (v.p. 1956). Clubs: Cristobal Woman's, Caribbean Coll. (charter pres. 1952), Soroptimist (pres. 1960, vice gov. Costa Rica and Panama 1965-69) (Colon, Panama). Contbr. articles to profl. jours. Home: Box 144 Gatun CZ Office: Box 5008 Coco Solo CA

MORRIS, TERRY LESSER (MRS. EUGENE J. MORRIS), writer; b. N.Y.C., Feb. 19, 1914; d. Samuel and Lena (Weissmann) Lesser; B.A., Hunter Coll., 1933, M.A., 1937; m. Eugene J. Morris, Mar. 29, 1934; children—Richard, Samuel. Tchr. English, N.Y.C. High Schs., 1937-43; feature writer Battle Creek (Mich.) Enquirer and News, 1943-44; writer, producer radio series WKZO, Kalamazoo, 1944-45; writer short stories, mag., articles for publs. including Am. mag., McCall's, Good Housekeeping, Woman's Home Companion, Cosmopolitan, Family Weekly, Life, New Republic, Redbook, Saga, This Week, Family Circle, Reader's Digest, 1945—. Lectr. mag. article writing N.Y. U., 1958-59; guest lectr. mag. article writing New Sch. Social Research, N.Y.C., 1960-61; lectr. Queens Coll., Bklyn., 1966-67. Recipient Blakeslee award for mag. article Am. Heart Assn., 1964. Mem. Soc. Mag. Writers (v.p. 1961, chmn. 1968, exec. council 1968-71, membership chmn. 1973-74, pres. 1974-75). Author: No Hiding Place, 1945; Cross Section (short story anthology), 1947; Strange Desires (short story anthology), 1954. Editor, contbr.: Prose by Professionals, 1961; Dr. America: The Story of Tom Dooley, 1963; Shalom, Golda, 1971. Address: 200 Central Park S New York City NY 10019

MORRIS, VERA, real estate broker; b. Manteca, Cal., Apr. 27, 1928; d. Alex A. and Anna (Harshenien) Reibin; student Delta Jr. Coll., 1961-70, Modesto Jr. Coll., 1970; m. Jack R. Morris, Jan. 8, 1946 (dec. May 1961); children—Jeanette, Jack, Scott. Saleswoman, Yosemite Realty, Manteca, 1963-64; broker, owner Continental Realty, Manteca, 1965—; owner Continental Mobile Home Sales, Stockton, Cal., 1971-73, Mobile Sales lot, Manteca, 1972—, Atwater and San Jose, Cal., 1974—. Instr., Red Cross swimming, Manteca, 1951-62; active Girl Scouts U.S.A., 1954-58; sec. Lincoln P.T.A., Manteca, 1958. Mem. Bus. and Profl. Women's Manteca, Nat., South San Joaquin bd. realtors, No. Cal. Golfers Assn., Nat. Bowlers Assn., Sigma Chi Delta. Democrat. Clubs: Spring Creek Country, MiTee Niners, Square Wheelers Square Dance. Home: 311 S Powers Av Manteca CA 95336 Office: 1840 E Yosemite Manteca CA 95336

MORRIS, VISTA LORENE, educator; b. Patesville, Ky.; d. Lorenzo Elisha and Rena (Pulliam) Morris; student Ky. Wesleyan Coll., 1927-30; A.B., Western Ky. State Coll., 1930-31. Tchr. Lee Elementary Sch., Owensboro, Ky., 1934-41, Central Jr. High Sch., 1941-47, Jefferson Jr. High Sch., 1947-48; tchr. English, Owensboro High Sch., 1948—, also chmn. English dept.; instr. English Ky. Wesleyan Coll., summer 1963. Mem. Nat. (dir. 1957-59, mem. achievement awards com. 1957-73), Ky. (chmn. 2 dist.) councils tchrs. of English, Owensboro Tchrs. Assn. (pres. 1957-58), Tchr. Edn. and Profl. Standards (chmn. 2d dist. Ky. 1960—; mem. commn. 1960-63), N.E.A., Ky. Edn. Assn., Delta Kappa Gamma (sec. Kappa chpt. 1960—, state pres. 1969-71, mem. internat. exec. bd. 1969-71, mem. com. leadership devel. 1972-74). Democrat. Methodist. Home: 1432 E 4th St Owensboro KY 42301 Office: 1800 Frederica St Owensboro KY 42301

MORRISEY, MARLENE DALKE (MRS. JOHN A. MORRISEY), govt. exec.; b. St. Mary's, Kan.; d. D. L. and Annabelle (Garber) Dalke; A.B., Baker U., 1935; postgrad. Cath. U. Am., 1952-54; m. James Kelly Wright, July 2, 1938 (div. 1950); 1 son, Jay Kelly; m. 2d, John A. Morrisey, Feb. 12, 1954. Asst. to registrar U. Mo., 1936; asst. to v.p. Page Mill Co., Topeka, 1937-41; with Library of Congress, Washington, 1941—, exec. asst. to librarian, 1946—. Vol. worker Planned Parenthood Assn.; mem. League Women Voters Arlington, Va. Recipient Superior Service award Library of Congress. Mem. Delta Delta Delta, Alpha Delta Sigma. Unitarian (trustee). Club: Washington Arts. Contbr. articles profl. jours. Home: 5023 N Washington Blvd Arlington VA 22205 Office: Library of Congress Washington DC 20540

MORRISON, ALICE LEE (MRS. DON HARLAN MORRISON), coll. dean; b. St. Louis, Nov. 27, 1910; d. George and Florentine (Orth) Douglas; B.A., U. Ill., 1932, M.A., 1934; m. Don Harlan Morrison, Apr. 8, 1939; 1 son, David Douglas. Chmn. dept. English Cerro Gordo (Ill.) Twp. High Sch., 1935-39; instr. English Danville (Ill.) Jr. Coll., 1952—, dept. chmn., 1968-69, baccalaureate dean, 1966—. Mem. League Women Voters, 1942-52, v.p., 1950; mem. Girl Scout Council, 1945-47; mem. bd. Civic Symphony, 1970—, sec., 1973-75; mem. steering com. Lay Study City Schs., 1948-53. Mem. Am. Assn. U. Women (v.p. 1948-49), Symphony Guild, Delta Kappa Gamma (v.p. 1967-68), Pi Delta Phi. Republican. Presbyn. Author: Laymen Study Their Schools 1948-52, 1953; The Miller Years, 1973. Home: 909D Georgian Dr Danville IL 61832 Office: 2000 E Main St Danville IL 61832

MORRISON, BARBARA STILL (MRS. ROBERT WOODBURY MORRISON), advt. agy. exec.; b. Boston, Apr. 14, 1938; d. Edward M. and Elma F. (Carnes) Still; grad. Katharine Gibbs Secretarial Sch., 1958; m. Robert Woodbury Morrison, Sept. 6, 1958; children—Lynne Marie, Robert Woodbury. Exec. sec. to v.p. N.E. Mut. Life Ins. Co., Boston, 1958-60; exec. sec. to pres. O.A. Both Corp., Ashland, Mass., 1960; media buyer Wellesley Advt. Assn., Wellesley Hills, Mass., 1965-67; account exec. Arnold & Co., advt., Boston, 1967—. Tchr. Medfield (Mass.) State Hosp., 1963-64. Mem. New Eng. Broadcasters Exec. Club. Conglist. Home: High St Extension Lancaster MA 01523 Office: 1111 Park Square Bldg Boston MA 02116

MORRISON, CHLOE ANTHONY (PSEUDONYM TONI MORRISON), editor, author; b. Lorain, O., Feb. 18, 1931; d. George and Ella Ramah (Willis) Wofford; B.A., Howard U., 1953; M.A., Cornell, 1955; children—Harold Ford, Slade Kevin. Instr. English and humanities Howard U., Washington, 1958-64; editor Random House, N.Y.C., 1965—. Lectr. State U. N.Y., 1971-72. Mem. lit. panel Nat. Endowment for Arts, 1971—. Mem. Author's Guild (counsel 1972). Author: The Bluest Eye, 1970; Sula, 1973. Office: 201 E 50th St New York City NY 10022

MORRISON, EILENE M(AY), ret. librarian, educator; b. Bellingham, Wash., Nov. 19, 1912; d. John Reid and Lillian (Cramer) Morrison; B.A., Western Wash. Coll. Edn., 1935; M.A., Columbia U., 1947, postgrad., 1947-48, 61; B.A. in Librarianship, U. Wash., 1950. Tchr., Wash. pub. schs., 1935-46; instr. demonstration sch. San Francisco State Coll., 1948-49; library supr., high sch. librarian Aberdeen (Wash.) pub. schs., 1950-54; asst. prof. library sci., asst. reference librarian Mont. State Coll., Bozeman, 1954-60; dist. librarian Bremerton (Wash.) Sch. Dist., 1961-73; vis. asst. prof. library sci. U. Ore., summer 1960; asst. prof. extension sch. librarianship U. Wash., Seattle, winter 1963; vis. asst. in edn. Pacific Lutheran U., Parkland, Wash., summer 1963-64; asst. dir. Nat. Def. Edn. Act Sch. Library Inst., U. Okla., summer 1966. Mem. Am. (dir. 1965-67), Wash. (treas. 1963-65, chmn. region 2 1966-67, v.p. 1967-68, pres. 1968-69, editor Library Leads 1973-74) assns. sch. librarians, Wash. Assn. Ednl. Communications and Tech., Am., Pacific Northwest. Wash., library assns., N.E.A., Wash., Bremerton Edn. assns., Am. Assn. U. Women, Delta Kappa Gamma (treas. Alpha Sigma chpt. 1972-74), Pi Lambda Theta, Kappa Delta Pi. Club: Soroptimist. Contbr. to profl. jours. Home: 2185 Lakehurst Dr Bremerton WA 98310

MORRISON, EVALINE PEARL CUTLER, journalist; b. Starkey, N.Y., 1890; d. Walter Charles and Sarah Caroline (Gulick) Cutler; student Los Angeles State Normal Sch., 1913-15; A.B., U. Cal. at Berkeley, 1919; m. Gail L.V. Morrison, July 23, 1925 (dec. Sept. 1949). Tchr., Red Hill Sch., Yoncalla, Ore., 1915-16, Los Angeles High Sch. System, 1929-46; teaching fellow psychology U. Cal. at Berkeley, 1923-25; counselor George Washington High Sch., Robert Louis Stevenson Jr. High Sch., Los Angeles, 1937-45; reporter-photographer Riverside (Cal.) Daily Enterprise, 1954—; feature writer, columnist, photographer Riverside Press-Enterprise and Daily Enterprise, 1954—. Dir. Red Cross work U. Cal., at Berkeley, 1917-18. Home: Lake Elsinore CA 92330 Office: 3512 14th St Riverside CA 92501

MORRISON, EVELYN, psychologist, educator; b. Perth Amboy, N.J.; d. Nathan and Minnie (Greenberg) Morrison; B.A. in Psychology, Rutgers U., 1961, M.Ed., 1963, Ed.D., 1967. Sch. psychologist Woodbridge Twp. (N.J.) Pub. Schs., 1966-70; dir. spl. services Edison Twp. Pub. Schs., Edison, N.J., 1970—. Instr. Rutgers U., Trenton State Coll., 1965-71. Mem. Am., N.J. psychol. assns., N.J. Assn. Pupil Personnel Adminstrn. Office: 2825 Woodbridge Av Edison NJ 08817

MORRISON, JOY SOUTH (MRS. THOMAS LAMAR MORRISON), pub. co. editor; b. Montpelier, Ida., June 3, 1924; d. Edward Marshall and Ruth Eldora (Heath) South; student Idaho State U., 1941-43; B.A., U. Wis., 1946; postgrad. Coll. So. Utah, 1950, U. Utah, 1951; m. Thomas Lamar Morrison, Mar. 25, 1950; 1 dau., Michele Ann. Bus. mgr. Uncle Ray's mag., Madison, Wis., and Cleve., 1946-47; reporter Ida. State Jour., Pocatello, 1947-50; tchr., journalism, English, East High Sch., Salt Lake City, 1950-51; continuity writer Radio station KWIK, Pocatello, 1952-55; women's editor Ida. State Jour., 1955—. Tech. staff Pocatello Community Players. Bd. dirs. Salvation Army. Named Ida. Women's Editor of Year, 1971. Mem. Order Job's Daus. Theta Sigma Phi. Presbyn. Home: 1015 E Elm St Pocatello ID 83201 Office: 305 S Arthur St Pocatello ID 83201

MORRISON, KATHRYN JAYDENE WALKER (MRS. MICHAEL HOWE MORRISON), educator; b. Cherokee, Okla., Aug. 22, 1933; d. Jay Frank and Kathryn (Johnson) Walker; B.S., Okla. State U., 1955, M.S., 1957; student U. Colo., 1965, Central State Coll., 1969; m. Michael Howe Morrison, Aug. 12, 1955; children—Jay Edward, Michael McCullough. Tchr. pub. schs., Cushing, Okla., 1955-57, Indpls., 1958-59; tchr. Helena (Okla.) Pub. Sch., 1965-72, counselor, 1965-72; spl. edn. tchr. Helena-Goltry Sch., 1969-72; psychometrist N.W. Okla. Edn. Center, 1973—. Recipient Masonic Tchr. of Year award 1968. Mem. Okla. Counselors Assn. (pres. N.W. dist. 1970-71), Am., Okla. personnel and guidance assns., N.E.A., Okla. Edn. Assn., Woods County Tchrs. Assn. (pres. 1972-73), Nat., Okla. assns. sch. psychologists, Am. Psychol. Assn., Okla. Div. Learning Disabilities, Chi Omega (chpt. v.p. 1954), Chi Omega Alumni Assn. Mem. Disciples of Christ Ch. Home: Box 585 Helena OK 73741

MORRISON, LAURA EMILY (MRS. WILLIAM H. GOTTLIEB), pub. relations exec.; b. Kansas City, Mo.; d. Lacey Harvey and Emma (Snow) Morrison; B.A., Mo. U., 1932; B.S., Columbia Sch. Journalism, 1934; m. William H. Gottlieb, Sept. 7, 1940; 1 son, William Pearis. Asst. editor Diesel Power, N.Y.C., 1934-35; asso. editor Conover-Mast Publs., N.Y.C., 1935-38; partner Morrison-Gottlieb, Inc., pub. relations, N.Y.C., 1940-43, pres., 1947—; mng. editor Modern Plastics Mag., N.Y.C., 1943, editor, 1947. Bd. dirs. Community Chest, Port Washington, N.Y., 1973—. Pres. Council Bard Coll. (Alumni Medal 1974). Mem. Pub. Relations Soc. Am., Publicity Club N.Y., Women in Communications, Delta Delta Delta. Club: Plandome Country. Home: 7 Woodland Dr Sands Point NY 11050 Office: 555 Fifth Av New York City NY 10017

MORRISON, LUCILE PHILLIPS, psychologist, author; b. Los Angeles, Sept. 8, 1896; d. Lee A. and Catherine (Coffin) Phillips; A.B., Vassar Coll., 1918; M.A., George Pepperdine Coll., 1958; m. Wayland Augustus Morrison, Dec. 27, 1917; children—Wayland Lee, Richard Holt, Lee Allen, Keith Norman; 1 adopted dau., Patricia Lee. Dir. Lee A. Phillips, Inc., 1930-49, v.p., 1938-42, pres., 1942-49; intern Am. Inst. Family Relations, Los Angeles, 1952-53, asso. counselor 1954-55, counselor, 1955-64, also v.p. bd. dirs., until 1964. Pres. (founder mem.) of the Duarte (Cal.) Community Service Council, 1946-48, editor newsletter, 1946-48, v.p., 1948-50, health chmn., 1951-54; dir., mem. Duarte Community Center Bd., 1949-57; dir. Children's Hosp., Los Angeles, 1921-44; trustee, mem. coms. Scripps Coll., 1930-72, hon. trustee, 1972, chmn. ednl. policy com., 1965-70; bd. trustees Westminster Gardens Presbyn. Ch. U.S.A., 1953-66, hon. life trustee, 1966; constituent mem. bd. fellows Claremont (Cal.) U. Center, 1967-70, mem. grad. sch. com., 1968-70, mem. adv. bd. Inst. Antiquity and Christianity, Claremont Grad. Sch., 1968—, mem. bldg. and grounds com.; v.p., dir., mem. staff Psychol. Guidance Center, Anaheim, Cal., 1960-63; bd. dirs. Cal. Sch. Profl. Psychology, 1972—, exec. council, 1973-74, mem. acad. commr., 1974—. Dir. Psychol. Publs., Inc., Los Angeles, 1966—. Active mus., hist., archeol. socs., So. Cal. Symphony Assn., Hist. Soc. So. Cal. Licensed psychologist, also marriage, family and child counselor State of Cal. Mem. N.Y. Acad. Scis., Child Study Assn. Am., Am. Assn. U. Women, Acad. Psychologists in Martial Counseling, Am. (asso.), Cal., Western psychol. assns., D.A.R., Am., Cal. So. Cal. assns. marriage and family counselors, Cal. State Marriage Counseling Assn., Am. Assn. Humanistic Psychology, Acad. Religion and Mental Health, Inst. Achievement Human Potential, Phi Beta Kappa, Delta Kappa Gamma, Psi Chi. Club: Women's University (Los Angeles). Author: Mystery Gate, 1928; The Attic Child, 1929; Blue Bandits, 1930; The Lost Queen of Egypt, 1938; (with Robert M. Taylor) Taylor-Johnson Temperament Analysis; Research and Development of Test and Manual, 1963-67; also articles. Editor: Doll Dreams (4 vols.), 1927-32; The World of Books, 1934. Home: 1134 Rancho Rd Arcadia CA 91006 Office: 5300 Hollywood Blvd Los Angeles CA 90027

MORRISON, NANCY JANE, educator; b. Washington, Nov. 24, 1933; d. Morris J. and Esther (Ellinger) Morrison; B.A., Allegheny Coll., 1955; M.Ed., Cal. State Coll., 1972. Tchr. Greensburg-Salem (Pa.) Sch. Dist., 1955-57, New Castle (Pa.) Sch. Dist., 1957-61; tchr. Zachariah Connell Sch., Connellsville, Pa., 1961-71; reading diagnostician Connellsville area sch. dist., 1971—. Mem. Pa. State Edn. Assn., N.E.A., Pa. Assn. Study and Edn. Mentally Gifted, Western Pa. Conservancy, Delta Kappa Gamma, Alpha Xi Delta, Beta Sigma Phi. Republican. Methodist. Club: Uniontown College. Home: Box 43-B RD 1 Hopwood PA 15445 Office: 711 Ridge Blvd Dunbar Twp Elementary Sch Connellsville PA 15425

MORRISON, SELLA B., pub. relations exec.; b. Culver, Ind., Aug. 21, 1913; d. Ralph A. and B. May (Hinton) Cook; student Northwestern U., 1931-32, State U. Ia., 1932-33, 34-35; m. Gerald Charles Morrison, July 21, 1935 (div. July 1949); 1 son, J. Gerard. Pub. relations dir. Lincoln Library, Springfield, Ill., 1962—. Bd. dirs. Copper Coin Regional Ballet, Sangamon County Easter Seal Soc. Recipient Pacesetter award for community service, 1970. Mem. Ill. Library Assn., Springfield Theatre Guild (charter mem., dir. 1947-51). Editor: Ill. Library Assn. Reporter, 1969-71, Lincoln Library Bull., 1962—. Home: 1129 Fayette St Springfield IL 62704 Office: 326 S 7th St Springfield IL 62701

MORRISSEY, PATRICIA ROSE MARY, pub. relations ofcl.; b. Flint, Mich., Aug. 3, 1946; d. William Henry and Sigrid Mabel (Zachariasen) Morrissey; A.S., A.A., Flint Community Jr. Coll., 1966; B.S., U. Miami, 1968. Mng. editor Times Now, Miami, Fla., 1969-70; pub. relations with Charles Cinnamon Assos., Miami, 1970—, account exec. Mus. Sci. and Space Transit Planetarium, 1973—. TV presentation writer-collaborator, 1970—; pub. relations WPBT-TV Ednl. TV Sta. Auction, 1973; TV and radio dir. Miami hearings Fla. Commn. on Status Women, 1973; pub. relations dir. Mary Bailey's Miami Lectures, Lucis Trust, N.Y., 1972. Mem., pub. relations Central Grove Homeowners. Mem. Women in Communication (directory chmn. 1972-73, chpt. adviser U. Miami 1973—), War Resisters League, Astrological Assn. Fla. Democrat. Columnist, You Are What you Eat, 1969-70. Home: 3191 Day Av Coconut Grove FL 33133 Office: 3280 S Miami Av Miami FL 33129

MORRISSEY, SISTER ROSE ELLEN, art educator; b. Oak Park, Ill., Mar. 31, 1921; d. John Anthony and Rose Mary (McGrath) Morrissey; B.A., St. Mary's Coll., Notre Dame, Ind., 1943; B.Art Edn., Art Inst. Chgo., 1957, M.Art Edn., 1961. Joined Sisters of Holy Cross, Roman Catholic Ch., 1944; mem. faculty St. Mary's Coll., 1944—, prof. art, 1972—, chmn. dept., 1962—. Grantee Ford Found., 1965-66, Dept. Health, Edn. and Welfare, 1966; recipient awards for ceramics and enamels. Mem. Am. Assn. U. Profs., Nat. Assn. Schs. Art, No. Ind. Artists, Nat. Art Edn. Assn., Nat. Assn. Art Adminstrs., Internat. Soc. Edn. through Art. Illustrator: The Man Who Made a Cross, 1945; A Child Asks for a Star, 1965; Building the Earth, 1966. Address: St Mary's Coll Notre Dame IN 46556

MORRONI, JUNE ROSE, librarian; b. Smithmill, Pa., Jan. 8, 1938; d. Camille and Marie (Klesser) Morroni; student Lebanon Valley Coll., 1955-56; B.S., Pa. State U., 1959; A.M., U. Chgo. Grad. Library Sch., 1968. Librarian, Steele Meml. Library, Elmira, N.Y., 1961-66, Elmira City Sch. Dist., 1967-69, Corning (N.Y.) Community Coll., 1968-69; reference librarian Pa. State U., University Park, Pa., 1969—, dir. Gompers, letterbooks project, 1970—, editor Newspapers in Microform, 1970—. Friends of Steele Meml. Library research grantee, 1966. Mem. A.L.A., Pa. Library Assn., Nat. Microfilm Assn., Am. Assn. U. Profs., Mu Phi Epsilon. Democrat. Episcopalian. Home: 955 Old Boalsburg Rd State College PA 16801 Office: 6 East Pattee Library University Park PA 16802

MORSE, ELEANOR REESE (MRS. A. REYNOLDS MORSE), plastic accessory co. exec.; b. Cleve.; d. George William and Elsie Frances (Douds) Reese; Mus.B., Rollins Coll., 1935; M.A. in French, Case Western Res. U., 1970; m. A. Reynolds Morse, Mar. 21, 1942; 1 son, Bradish. Bookkeeper, sec. Injection Molders Supply Co. (name changed to IMS Co. 1969), Cleve., 1949-60, sec.-treas., 1960-65, Beachwood, O., 1965—. Vice pres. Reynolds-Morse Found., operator Salvador Dali Mus. Mem. Le Cercle des Conference Francaises (pres. 1965-67), Maison Francaise de Cleve. (pres. 1969—). Office: 24050 Commerce Park Rd Beachwood OH 44122

MORSE, EUGENIA MAUDE, architect, educator; b. Houston, Feb. 23, 1920; d. Robert Emmett and Eugenia Elizabeth (Maddox) Morse; B.A. in Architecture, Rice U., 1941, B.S. in Architecture, 1942. Practicing architect, 1949—; asso. prof. U. S.W. La., 1954-59; prof. architecture Tex. Tech. U., Lubbock, 1959—. Pres. bd. dirs. Storm Def. Club, 1970-73. Mem. West Tex. Watercolor Assn. (treas., dir. 1971-72), Nat. Geog. Soc., Museum Natural History, Smithsonian Instn. Prin. works include Seitter Photography Bldg., Corpus Christi, Tex., Miles Ramagosa Clinic, Lafayette, La., also residences. Home: 2621 33d St Lubbock TX 79410

MORSE, EVA MAE WITHAM, city ofcl.; b. South Fayston, Vt., Oct. 28, 1938; d. Lawrence George and Eloise Mae (McCullough) Witham; grad. high sch.; m. David Fred Morse, Aug. 25, 1956 (div. 1969); children—Peter John, David Lindsay, Sheila Kay. Town clk., treas., Calais, Vt., 1963—, zoning adminstr., 1971—; mem. Vt. Gen. Assembly, 1971—; spl. dep. sheriff Washington County, 1972—. Mem. Vt. Rural Devel. Adv. Council, 1973—. Trustee Washington Elec. Co-op., Inc., 1973—; bd. dirs. Coop. Health Information Center Vt., Inc., 1973—. Address: Calais VT 05648

MORSE, HAZEL ELLA FOSGATE (MRS. LEW HARLOW MORSE), museum ofcl.; b. Rindge, N.H., Sept. 26, 1892; d. Elmer Gilman and Julia Tower (Bliss) Fosgate; B.A., Mt. Holyoke Coll., 1914, M.A., 1916; postgrad. Harvard, 1925, Columbia, 1929-30; L.H.D. (hon.), Am. Internat. Coll., 1958; m. Lew Harlow Morse, Sept. 26, 1938; step-children—Lew Harlow, Douglas Conrad, Blanche Aldea (Mrs. Ernest John Dowler), Jon Caroll, Alma Louise (Mrs. Peter Lippard). Tchr. English East Me. Conf. Acad., Bucksport, 1916-18, New Britain (Conn.) High Sch., 1918-19, Leominster (Mass.) High Sch., 1919-21; faculty Am. Internat. Coll., Springfield, Mass., 1921-58, acad. dean, 1957-58; curator Ashburnham (Mass.) Hist. Soc. Inc., 1958—. Mem. Ashburnham Hist. Soc. Republican. Home: 74 Main St Ashburnham MA 01430 Office: 77 Main St Ashburnham MA 01430

MORSE, HELEN WINNIFRED, hosp. lab. exec.; b. Port Williams, N.S., Can., Nov. 12, 1926; d. Avard Ratchford and Leah Maude (Rawding) Morse; Registered Technician, Canadian Soc. Lab. Technologists, 1947. Gen. med. technologist Newton Wellesley Hosp., Newton, Mass., 1947-49; gen. med. technologist N.S. Sanatorium, Kentville, 1950-67, lab. supr., 1967—. Mem. Canadian Soc. Lab. Technologists. Baptist. Home: 29 Klondyke St Kentville NS B4N 1J1 Canada Office: Laboratory NS Sanatorium Kentville NS B4N 1C4 Canada

MORSELL, AURINE BOYDEN (MRS. WILLIAM SEWELL MORSELL, JR.), realtor; b. Balt., Sept. 25, 1907; d. Dwight Frederic and Mabel Nora (Hayward) Boyden; grad. high sch.; m. William Sewell Morsell, Jr., June 29, 1948; 1 dau., Mary (Mrs. Kenneth Cameron Miller, Jr.). Saleswoman, Roland Park Co., 1938-51; saleswoman, Roland Park Realty Co., Balt., 1951-56, pres., 1956—; dir. Security Title Co., Md. Mortgage Co. Trustee St. Mary's Coll. Md. Clubs: Elkridge, Baltimore Country, Mount Vernon (Balt.). Home: 10 Over Ridge Ct Baltimore MD 21210 Office: 4810 Roland Av Baltimore MD 21210

MORTHLAND, CONSTANCE AMELIA GRANT (MRS. ANDREW MORTHLAND), civic worker; b. Eng., Mar. 31, 1915 (came to U.S. 1919, naturalized 1940); d. Douglas Gordon and Maud (Smith) Grant; ; A.B. summa cum laude, Stanford, 1936; m. Andrew Morthland, Aug. 8, 1937; children—Joan (Mrs. Ian Elcock Bush), Patricia (Mrs. Joseph M. Hamer). Research asst. RKO Studios, 1936-39; story dept. analyst Paramount Studios, 1941-46; free lance writer, 1955-60. Exec. bd. mem. Friends of Claremont Colls., 1965—; mem. Friends of Radcliffe Coll., 1962—; chmn. finance com. Episcopal Ch. Women, 1959—; mem. exec. bd. Assistance League, 1968-69; staff mem. Laguna-Moulton Community Playhouse, 1961-69, editor Callboard, 1955—; community adviser Jr. League, 1973—. Trustee Pitzer Coll., Claremont, Cal.; bd. overseers Claremont Coll., 1965-73; bd. dirs. Lyric Opera Assn. Orange County, 1973—, Continuing Edn. at Claremont Coll., 1973—. Recipient Journalism award Sigma Delta Chi, 1936, Cal. Internat. Woman award 1971. Mem. Soc. Preservation Rural Eng. (hon.), Daus. Brit. Empire (regent 1972-73), Clubs: Stanford (Orange County sec. 1936—); Women's University (London); Newport Harbor Yacht. Home: 165 Moss Point Laguna Beach CA 92651

MORTIMER, CHARLOTTE PFAU (MRS. JOHN ATTERBURY MORTIMER), writer, cons.; b. Newton, N.J., Nov. 26, 1933; d. Karl Otto and Wilhelmina (Otterbach) Pfau; student Douglass Coll., 1952-54; B.S., R.N., Columbia U. Presbyn. Hosp., 1957, postgrad., 1957-59; postgrad., N.Y. U., 1959-60; m. John Atterbury Mortimer, Nov. 20, 1964; children—Meredith Elizabeth, Mandy Leigh. Spl. assignment nurse Columbia-Presbyn. Med. Center, N.Y.C., 1957-59; med. advt. copywriter Paul Klemtner & Co., N.Y.C., 1959-61, William Douglas McAdam Agy., N.Y.C., 1961-62; account exec. Arndt, Preston, Chapin, Lamb & Keen, N.Y.C., 1962-63; Rocky Mountain corr. Med. World News, Denver, 1963-64; owner Publicite, Denver; gen. mgr. Center Marketing Asso., Palo Alto, Cal., 1964-66; free lance writer, pub. relations cons., Palo Alto, 1966—. Mem. Palo Alto-Stanford Hosp. Aux., 1968—; pub. relations assistance Peninsula Children's Center, Menlo Park, Cal., 1968—, Triton Mus. Art, San Jose, Cal., 1966—. Bd. dirs. N.J. Jr. C. of C./UNICEF/ African Project, 1960-61. Mem. Am. Med. Writers Assn., Publicity Club N.Y., San Mateo County Horsemen's Assn. Club: Northern Cal. Morgan Horse (mem. nat. youth com.). Home: 700 Kings Mountain Rd Woodside CA 94062 Office: PO Box 4136 Woodside CA 94062

MORTIMER, RUTH, librarian; b. Syracuse, N.Y., Sept. 16, 1931; d. Donald Cameron and Lillian Ruth (Burk) Mortimer; A.B., Smith Coll., 1953; postgrad. Shakespeare Inst., U. Birmingham (Eng.), 1955; M.S., Columbia, 1957. Pre-profl. librarian Bklyn. Pub. Library, 1953-54; asst. in serials Smith Coll. Library, Northampton, Mass., 1954-56; rare book cataloger for printing and graphic arts Houghton Library, Harvard U., Cambridge, Mass., 1957—. Cons. editor English lit. renaissance; lectr. book arts. Chmn. Council of Friends of Smith Coll. Library, 1969-72. Guggenheim fellow, 1966. Mem. Renaissance Soc. Am., Bibliog. Soc. Am., Printing Hist. Soc., A.L.A., Dante Soc. Am. Club: Zonta (Boston). Author: French 16th Century Books, 1964; Italian 16th Century Books, 1974; Haiku, 1972. Contbr. articles to profl. jours. Home: 76 Grozier Rd Cambridge MA 02138 Office: Houghton Library Harvard U Cambridge MA 02138

MORTON, ELIZABETH WILLIAMS, realtor; b. Chgo.; d. Charles Albert and Alice Mae (Ellsworth) Williams; student U. Ill., 1925-26; B.S., Conn. Coll. for Women, 1929; m. Arthur M. Moody, Jr., Jan. 23, 1933 (div. Apr. 1945); 1 son, Arthur M. III; m. 2d, William B. Morton, Sept. 9, 1950 (separated May 1963). Sr. caseworker Cook County Dept. Pub. Welfare, Chgo., 1929-30; social worker Chgo. Municipal Ct. System, 1930-32; asst. supr. Queens Emergency Relief Bd., N.Y.C., 1935; home service worker, dir. A.R.C., Providence, East Greenwich, R.I., Norwalk, Greenwich and Bridgeport, Conn., N.Y.C., 1941-52; real estate saleswoman Vick Realty Co., Stamford, Conn., 1953-54; broker, partner Morton Realty Co., New Canaan, Conn., 1954-63; broker, owner E. W. Morton Realty Co. (now William Pitt, Inc.), New Canaan 1963-66, broker, mgr. br., 1966-69; self-employed as realtor, 1970—. Dir. Norwalk Community Chest, 1945, Norwalk Council, 1946, chmn. health div. 1944; adminstrv. dir. New Canaan Community Council, 1962, real estate bd. del., 1963-64; chmn. Civic Study Forum, 1970. Bd. dirs. Pub. Health Nursing Service, Southbury and Roxbury. Mem. New Canaan Bd. Realtors (dir., sec. 1960-64), Heritage Village Civic Assn. (dir. 1972), Waterbury Bd. Realtors, Conn. Assn. Real Estate Bds. (sec. 1963), Nat. Assn. Real Estate Bds. (exec. officers council 1960-64), C. of C., League Women Voters, Alpha Xi Delta (pres. 1960). Republican. Clubs: Women's of Heritage Village (dir.) (Southbury, Conn.); Connecticut College Alumna. Address: 898B Heritage Village Southbury CT 06488

MORTON, JANE ISABEL (MRS. BENJAMIN V. SIEGEL), immunologist; b. Madison, Wis., Oct. 21, 1930; d. Walter Albert and Rosalie (Amlie) Morton; B.A. in Zoology, Pomona Coll., 1952; M.A. in Zoology, U. Wis., 1954; m. Benjamin V. Siegel, June 30, 1961; children—Benjamin, Andrew. Research asst. dept. biochemistry U. Wis., Madison, 1952-54, res. asso. dept. physiol. chemistry, 1954-58; research asst. dept. biochemistry U. Cal., Berkeley, 1960-61; research asst. dept. pathology U. Ore. Med. Sch., Portland, 1964-67, research asso. div. immunology dept. medicine, 1967—. Fellow Am. Inst. Chemists, Norwegian Cancer Soc.; mem. Am. Assn. Immunologists, Am. Assn. for Cancer Research, Internat. Soc. Exptl. Hematology, Radiation Research Soc., Reticuloendothelial Soc., Sigma Xi. Contbr. numerous articles to profl. publs. Home: 3900 SW Pendleton St Portland OR 97221 Office: Dept Pathology U Ore Med Sch Portland OR 97201

MORTON, LILLIAN ELLEN, cosmetic co. exec.; b. Parsons, Kan., Jan. 8, 1918; d. Frank Porter and Lillian Felicites (McGill) Morton; A.A., Parsons Jr. Coll., 1937. With Parsons Sun, 1935-38, Manhattan (Kan.) Tribune, 1939-41, Beatrice (Neb.) Sun, 1941-42, U.S.O., Manhattan-Ft. Riley, 1942-45, Katz Drug Co., Kansas City, Mo., 1945-64; with Luzier Cosmetics, Fairway, Kan., 1965—, asst. publs. mgr., 1965—. Mem. Nat. Fedn. Press Women, Women in Communications, Mo. Press Women. Republican. Home: 1319 W 44th Terrace Kansas City MO 64111 Office: 4220 Johnson Dr Fairway KS 66205

MORTON, PRISCILLA ROSE, writer, counselor; b. Binghamton, N.Y.; d. P.D. and Alice (Brown) Morton; B.A., State U. N.Y. at Albany, 1941, M.A., 1944; diploma Tchrs. Coll., Columbia, 1960. Sch. librarian, tchr. English, Pierson High Sch., Sag Harbor, L.I., 1942-45; asst. sch. librarian, instr. library methods English, Sewanhaka High Sch., Floral Park, L.I., 1945-46; asst. sch. librarian, instr. English, Johnson City (N.Y.) High Sch., 1946-53; dean women, instr. English, Albright Coll., Reading, Pa., 1953-58; instr. English, asst. counselor Princeton (N.J.) High Sch., 1958-59; asst. dir. placement Queens Coll., Flushing, N.Y., 1959-60; asso. dean of students, asst. prof. psychology, dir. reading lab. Eastern N.M. U., Portales, 1960-61; asso. student personnel State U. N.Y. at Albany, 1961-62; dean of women, asso. prof. Mansfield (Pa.) State Coll., 1962-63; dir. student activities, asst. dean students State U. N.Y. at Farmingdale, 1963-64; dean women, asso. prof. English, Ohio No. U., Ada, 1964-66; prof. Am. lit. and composition, student adviser Centenary Coll. Women, Hackettstown, N.J., 1966-69; instr. student personnel services, counselor, reading specialist City U. N.Y. summer 1964. Mem. bishop's commn. on Black Meth. Coll. Danforth scholar Union Theol. Sem., N.Y.C. summer 1955; Bd. dirs. FISH, Floral Park-Bellerose. Mem. Nat. Assn. Women Deans, Counselors and Adminstrs. (mem. jour. 1973—), State U. N.Y. at Albany Alumni Assn., Tchrs. Coll. Alumni Assn. (Ambassador chmn. Tchr. Coll. Fund 1963-64), Am. Personnel and Guidance Assn., Am. Coll. Personnel Assn. (former mem. nat. commn. student life), Am. Assn. U. Women (founder-pres. Hackettstown N.J. br. 1967-69, pres. Sewanhaka, N.Y. br. 1971-72), Am. Guild Organists, Kappa Delta Pi, Beta Sigma Phi, Alpha Lambda Delta (hon.), Alpha Omicron Pi (hon. mem.; regional nominations chmn.). Methodist (local and conf. coordinator Christian personhood, local chmn. Christian social concerns). Author: The Role of the Student Resident Assistant in College Women's Residence Halls, 1954; Hints for Head Residents, 1954; Reminders for Receptionists in Women's Residence Halls, 1954; The College Academic Probationer: A Diagnosis and Prognosis, 1959; A Study of Some Recent Outstanding Resources in College Reading Programs, 1960; Ave Atque Vale: From Dinks to Mortar Boards: Talks With College Women; The Role of College Students in Curricular and Co-Curricular Concerns. Home: 140 Floral Pkwy Floral Park NY 11001

MOSAL, MARGARET JAMES (MRS. WILLIAM LOUIS MOSAL), assn. exec.; b. Canton, Miss., Apr. 2, 1911; d. Charles Henry and Mary (Newsom) James; A.A., Whitworth Coll., 1931; H.H.D., Pffeifer Coll., N.C., 1972; m. William Louis Mosal, Apr. 23, 1933; children—William Louis, Mary Margaret (Mrs. Lamar Fortenberry). Admissions counselor Miss. State Coll. for Women, Columbus, 1953-69; exec. dir. Phi Theta Kappa, 1934—. Pres. 20th Century Civic Club. Address: Box 230 Canton MS 39046

MOSBACKER, WANDA CHRISTINE BATH (MRS. JOHN ROGER MOSBACKER), univ. dean; b. Cin., August 28, 1911; d. Charles and Ellenore (Binne) Bath; Comml. Engr., U. Cin., 1934, M.Ed., 1957; postgrad. U. Delft (Netherlands), summer 1956, Nat. Inst. Indsl. Psychology, London, summer 1964, Albert Schweitzer Coll., Switzerland, summer 1967; m. John Roger Mosbacker, Aug. 28, 1937. Supr. women's employment Kroger Co., Cin., 1934-42; instr. coordination U. Cin., 1945-52, asst. prof., 1952-56, asso. prof., 1956-65, prof. profl. devel., 1965—, asso. dean, 1969—. Mem. Internat. Assn. Personnel Women (pres. 1965-66, mem. exec. bd. 1963-67), Women's Personnel Assn. Cin. (pres. 1950-51, mem. exec. bd. 1949-53, 70-72), Coop. Edn. Assn. (treas. 1973-74, mem. exec. bd. 1972-74), Assn. Coll. Admissions Counselors (v.p. 1954-55), Beta Gamma Sigma, Kappa Delta Pi, Pi Chi Epsilon. Home: 2106 Harrison Av Cincinnati OH 45214

MOSCRIPT, DOROTHA MARGUERITE (MRS. DONALD ELMER MOSCRIPT), librarian; b. Cheney, Kan., May 10, 1913; d. Robert Herr and Grace Ann (Jones) Yoder; student Wichita State U., 1941, Emporia State U., 1969, Northwestern U., 1970; m. Donald Elmer Moscript, Nov. 21, 1943 (dec. May 1972); children—James Tracy, William Otis. Reporter Cheney (Kan.) Sentinel, 1931-32; sec. Northcutt Oil Co., Cheney, 1939; clerk I.G.A. store, Cheney, Kan., 1940; accountant Beechcraft Co., Wichita, 1942-44, Moscript Blacksmith, Zenda, Kan., 1944-50; bookkeeper Zenda Grain, (Kan.), 1950-59; office mgr. Strong's Ins., Zenda, 1960-66; librarian Zenda (Kan.) Pub. Library, 1966—; research work in library sci. Micronesia Research Center, Guam, June 1972. Active Cub Scouts Am., 1953-59; project leader 4-H, Zenda, 1953—, book project leader, 1971-74. Mem. Am., Kan. library assns. Methodist. Mem. Order Eastern Star (worthy matron 1957). Home: Box 57 Zenda KS 67159 Office: Zenda Pub Library Box 57 Zenda KS 67159

MOSELEY, ALICE-KAREN LEWIS (MRS. PAUL W. MOSELEY III), advt. exec.; b. Mpls., Sept. 10, 1926; d. Charles Frederick King and Karen Marie (Larsen) Lewis; B.A., U. Minn., 1946; student Macalester Coll., St. Paul, 1944-45; m. Paul W. Moseley III, Aug. 31, 1946; children—Paul W. IV, Alexandra A. Asso. creative dir., v.p., mem. creative plans bd. McCann-Erickson, Inc., N.Y.C., 1949-66; asso. creative dir., v.p. Grey Advt., Inc., N.Y.C., 1966-70; pres., creative dir. Moseley Advt. Co., Westport, Conn., 1970—; cons. Bridgeport U. Advt. Marketing Course, 1973-74; tchr. advt. writing course N.Y. Ad Club, 1957-58. Chmn. United Fund, Weston, Conn., 1958; chmn. fund-raising Westport Women's Club, 1957. Recipient Clio Advt. awards, 1957, 58, 59, 60, top award, 1964, 70; Art Dir.'s Club awards, 1959, 60, 61, 66. Clubs: Aspetuck Valley Country (entertainment chmn. 1968), Weston Field (entertainment chmn. 1956-57) (Weston, Conn.). Contbr. articles to Advt. Age, Anny, Printer's Ink, 1956-71, County mag., 1974. Home: 25 Norfield Woods Rd Weston CT 06880 Office: 431 E State St Westport CT 06880

MOSELEY, MARY LYDA, dept. store exec.; b. Picayune, Miss., July 20, 1922; d. George Harry and Maye (Williams) Mitchell; grad. pub. high sch.; m. William L. Moseley, Jan. 26, 1939 (dec. Nov. 13, 1968); children—Mary (Mrs. Billy W. Miller), Linda (Mrs. Travis R. Simmons); m. 2d, Roland C. Kleinfeld, Mar. 1, 1974. Owner, prin. M L M Co., theatres, Picayune, 1965—, Lane's Dept. Store, Picayune, 1949—; founder, owner radio sta. WRJW, Picayune, 1948-51, Picayune Transp. Co., 1950-54, Picayune Air Service, 1963-66, Pine Hill Apts., Carriere, Miss., 1965—. Mem. Nat. Assn. Theatre Owners. Baptist. Home: 420 Elmwood St Picayune MS 39466 Office: PO Box 370 Picayune MS 39466

MOSELEY, PATSY JO, banker; b. Manes, Mo., Dec. 4, 1933; d. Gus and Lois (Shelby) Moseley; student S.W. Mo. State Coll., 1951-52. Bookkeeper, Security Bank, Mountain Grove, Mo., 1954-55, teller, bookkeeper, 1955-57, asst. cashier, 1958-59, asst. v.p., 1960-68, v.p., 1969—, also sec. bd. dirs. Baptist. Home: Box 13 Graff MO 65660 Office: PO Box 230 Mountain Grove MO 65711

MOSELEY, VIRGINIA DOUGLAS, educator; b. Gainesville, Tex., Jan. 31, 1917; d. Edward Hilary and Leslie (Jones) Moseley; B.A., U. Okla., 1938, M.A., 1948; Ph.D., Columbia, 1958. Instr. Gainesville (Tex.) High Sch., 1938-44, Gainesville Jr. Coll., 1938-44; asst. prof. Southeastern State Coll., Durant, Okla., 1947-55; prof. No. Ill. Univ., De Kalb, 1955-65, Tex. Women's Univ., Denton, 1965-69; prof. English U. Ottawa, Ont., Can., 1969—. Organist St. Paul's Episcopal Ch., Gainesville, Tex., 1938-44. Served to lt., WAVE, 1944-46. Delta Kappa Gamma fellow, 1954. Mem. Modern Lang. Assn., Am. Assn. U. Profs. (treas. 1963), Alpha Chi Omega. Presbyn. (elder 1963, chmn. finance 1973). Author: James Joyce and the Bible, 1969; translator: Those Americans (Mikhailov and Kossenko), 1963. Contbr. scholarly articles on literary criticism to lit. jours. Home: Apt 814 1833 Riverside Dr Ottawa ON K1G 0E8 Canada Office: University of Ottawa ON Canada

MOSER, ANNA JO NAY (MRS. ROBERT ELMER MOSER), advt. agy. exec.; b. Buckhannon, W.Va., Mar. 10, 1938; d. Robert Emerson and Merle Marie (McLaughlin) Nay; student W.Va. Wesleyan Coll., 1956-57; student George Washington U., 1957-58; m. Robert Elmer Moser, Oct. 12, 1957; 1 dau., Pamela Ann. Sec., Emmco Ins., Arlington, Va., 1958-60, Honeywell, Inc., Richmond, Va., 1960-65; with Robin Frayser Assos., Richmond, 1965—, bus. mgr., 1969—. Del., Henrico County Council P.T.A.'s, 1971—, chmn. action com., 1972-73, chmn. motorcade, 1971-72; pres. Henrico High Sch. P.T.A., 1973—. Club: Brook Run Jr. Woman's (Richmond). Home: 8204 Franconia Rd Richmond VA 23227 Office: 1906 N Hamilton St Richmond VA 23230

MOSER, DOROTHY LOUISE, univ. dean; b. Trenton, N.J., May 19, 1932; d. Roland Lambert and May (Williams) Moser; B.S., W.Va. Wesleyan Coll., 1954; M.A., Ohio U., Athens, 1956. Dir. women's programs Redbank (N.J.) YMCA, 1956-57; resident counselor, then asst. dean students Douglass Coll., Rutgers U., 1957-63; asst. dean women U. Cin., 1963-71; asst. dean student life U. Ala., 1971-74, asso. dean, 1974—. Mem. Nat. Assn. Women Deans, Adminstrs. and Counselors (resolutions com. 1974, chmn. placement com. 1975—), Ala. Assn. Women Deans and Counselors (sec. 1973-75), Ohio Women Deans and Counselors (program chmn. 1970), League Women Voters (chmn. edn. 1972), Am. Assn. U. Women (br. sec. 1972-74, br. chmn. scholarship com. 1974—, state chmn. Community service), Ala. Council Student Personnel Educators, Mortar Bd. (sect. coordinator 1969-71, 73—), Alpha Delta Pi, Delta Psi Kappa. Presbyn. (chmn. com. for faith and learning community). Clubs: Univ. Ala. Women's. Home: 24H Northwood Lakes St Northport AL 35476 Office: Box 1932 University AL 35486

MOSER, EDDA, soprano; b. Berlin; State Conservatory, Berlin. Appearances include Salzburg Festivals, 1968-72, Edinburgh, Berlin, Aix-en-Provence, Munich, Rio de Janeiro; mem. Met. Opera N.Y., 1969—, Staatsoper, Vienna, Austria, 1971—, Hamburg State Opera, 1971—. Numerous recordings.Salzburg, 1968. Address: care Metropolitan Opera Lincoln Center New York City NY 10023 also: D 5 Koln 41 Elsenborner Strasse 19 Federal Republic of Germany

MOSER, MARGARET BLACK (MRS. MANVILLE CLIFFORD MOSER), librarian; b. Wellington, Kan., Feb. 14, 1915; d. Asa Robert and Pauline (Murray) B.; student Western Coll. Women, 1933-35; B.L.S., U. Okla., 1937; m. Manville Clifford Moser, June 25, 1941; children—Robert Scott, Murray Clifford, Mark David. Librarian, Little Rock High Sch., 1937-44, Little Rock Jr. Coll., 1947-49; reference librarian Little Rock Pub. Library, 1961; librarian U. Ark., Little Rock, 1962—. Mem. Am., Ark., Southwestern (sec.-treas. resources and tech. service div. 1969-71) library assns., Am. Assn. U. Profs. (treas. 1971—), Delta Kappa Gamma, Kappa Kappa Gamma. Presbyn. Home: Route 4 22 Pine Rose Circle Little Rock AR 72206

MOSER, REBECCA GRIFFIN (MRS. WILLIAM LEX MOSER), printing equipment and supply co. exec.; b. Hamlet, N.C., May 17, 1919; d. James Raymond and Blake (Ashcraft) Griffin; diploma in sch. bus. Queens Coll., 1937; m. Joseph Alvin Morris, Nov. 27, 1942 (dec. 1958); children—Jane (Mrs. Fenton T. Erwin), Carol A., Edwin Lee, James Thomas; m. William Lex Moser, July 1, 1961. With Lindale Dairy, High Point, N.C., 1937-38; payroll clk. Hudson Hosiery Co., Charlotte, N.C., 1939-42; with Printing Equipment & Supply Co., Charlotte, 1942-60; co-owner Morris Co., Charlotte, 1960—. Leader Community 4-H Club, Charlotte, 1962-66; mem. vocational com. Mecklenburg (N.C.) County Farm Bur., 1967, projects com., 1968, publicity com., 1972. Precincts vice-chmn. Democratic party, 1966-70, county treas., 1972-73. Recipient A&P Leadership award Extension Homemakers, 1972. Mem. Charlotte Rose Soc. (treas. 1973), Extension Homemakers Assn. (treas. Mecklenburg County council 1967-72, southwestern dist. treas. 1969-70, N.C. State rec. sec. 1971, del. to nat. council, 1971, del. to workshop, 1970). Baptist (mem. mission com. 1961-65, mem. finance com. 1974). Home and office: 5217 N Tryon St Charlotte NC 28213

MOSES, LOUISE CLAY, ednl. adminstr.; b. Cin., Apr. 14, 1929; d. John Robert Parker and Velma A. Clary; student Loyola U. of South, New Orleans, 1949, Georgetown U., 1952; m. Peter John Moses, June 23, 1954 (div. Feb. 1964); children—Christine, David, Mark. X-ray technician Columbia Hosp., Washington, 1953-55; med. asst. to physician, Ann Arbor, Mich., 1967; dir. book clk., x-ray technician U. Mich. Dental Sch., Ann Arbor, 1963-67, exec. sec., 1967—. Mem. Bus. and Profl. Woman's Orgn. of Mich. Home: 332 S 7th St Ann Arbor MI 48103 Office: 708 W Huron St Ann Arbor MI 48103

MOSES, WILMA BRACKETT (MRS. LAWRENCE L. MOSES), city ofcl.; b. Belfast, Me., Nov. 17, 1928; d. William E. and Alice Louise (Gray) Brackett; student various courses U. Me.; m. Lawrence L. Moses, July 26, 1946; 1 son, Lawrence L. II. Dept. city clk. City of Belfast (Me.), 1959-66, city clk., city auditor, 1966—, acting city mgr., 1967, 71. Sec. to Belfast Planning Bd., 1968—; mem. Belfast Rep. Com., 1970; del. County and State Rep. Com., 1970, 73. Mem. New Eng., Me. (legislative com. 1970—) town and city clks. assns. Home: 35 Charles St Belfast ME 04915 Office: 71 Church St Belfast ME 04915

MOSESSON, GLORIA RUBIN, editor; b. Bklyn., Dec. 16, 1924; d. Louis and Regina B. (Greenfield) Rubin; B.A. cum laude, Bklyn. Coll., 1943; M.S., Cornell, 1945; m. Norman D. Mosesson, Aug. 16, 1955; children—Eric D., Neil A., Roger E., Carl E., Carol R. Teaching fellow chemistry Cornell U., Ithaca, N.Y., 1943-45; asst. editor Chem. Pub., N.Y.C., 1947-48; editor Chartwell House Pub., N.Y.C., 1948-55; editor Ednl. Pub. Co., N.Y.C., 1956-61; juvenile editor Bobbs-Merrill Pub. Co., N.Y.C., 1961-63; jr. books editor Meredith Press, N.Y.C., 1964-70; editor Thomas Nelson Pub. Co., N.Y.C., 1970—. Mem. Women's Nat. Book Assn., Authors League Am. Author: Breeding Laboratory Animals, 1968; The Jewish War Veterans Story, 1971; Jewelry Craft for Beginners, 1974. Contbr. articles to mags. and encys. Home: 290 West End Av New York City NY 10023 Office: 30 E 42d St New York City NY 10017

MOSHER, FRANCES ELIZABETH (MRS. JOHN WILLIAM MOSHER), composer, artist; b. Saint John, N.B., Can., Oct. 23, 1911; d. Gilbert Clark and Lillian Elizabeth (Roberts) Jordan; grad. Saint John High Sch., 1929; grad. Modern Bus. Coll., 1930; m. John William Mosher, Apr. 22, 1937; children—Joanne (Mrs. France Buoninsegni), Gretchen Elizabeth (Mrs. Churchill A. Firth). With secretarial staff Sun Life Co., Saint John, 1930-37; one woman shows at Royal Hotel, St. John, Climo Studios, St. John; exhibited in group shows at N.B. Mus., St. John, also maritime art travelling shows; composer, 1945—. Recipient award in mus. composition N.B. Music Festival, 1952. Mem. Trafalgar Old Girls Assn., St. John Art Club, Canadian Authors and Composers Assn. Mem. Anglican Ch. (Sunday sch. tchr. 1937, jr. choir dir. 1954-55). Clubs: Riverside Golf, St. Andrews Curling. Composer: A Salt and Pepper Shaker. Address: 144 Douglas Av Saint John NB EZK 1E4 Canada

MOSK, EDNA MITCHELL (MRS. JUSTICE STANLEY MOSK), polit. worker, artist; b. Winnipeg, Man., Can., Sept. 16, 1915; d. Max and Katharine (Blond) Mitchell; came to U.S., 1923, naturalized, 1924; student U. Cal. at Los Angeles, 1933-35; m. Justice Stanley Mosk, Sept. 27, 1936; 1 son, Richard Mitchell. Exhibited paintings Lawson Galleries, San Francisco, Soc. Cal. Pioneers, San Francisco; works represented in pvt. collections; dir. H&M Co., Co., Los Angeles, 1943-45; self-employed realtor Beverly Hills, Cal., 1946-58. Mem. exec. com. Econ. Opportunity Council, San Francisco, 1967-69. Campaign mgr. Mosk-for Atty. Gen. of Cal., 1958; mem. Democratic State Central Com. of Cal., 1960-62; del. Dem. Nat. Conv., 1968; mem. exec. com. Dem. Finance Com. Cal., 1968-72; mem. Chmn.'s Adv. Com. of Dem. State Central Com., 1968-73. Founder, bd. dirs. Constl. Rights Found. of No. Cal. Clubs: Burke Tennis San Francisco Lawyers Wives (San Francisco); Beverly Hills (Cal. Tennis). Home: 1200 California St San Francisco CA 94109

MOSKAL, VIRGINIA VALENTINA, polit. worker; b. Utica, N.Y., Oct. 20, 1928; d. Joseph J. and Helen (Plona) Moskal; student Utica Coll., 1951-54, Mohawk Valley Tech. Inst., 1960—. Asst. treas. Oneida County Dem. Women's Club, 1952-54, pres., 1954-55, bd. dirs., 1961—; apptd. chmn. gubernatorial campaign forum, Syracuse, N.Y., 1954, ofcl. page for Gov. Harriman at Dem. State Conv., N.Y.C., 1954; del. at large N.Y. State Conv. Young Democrats, 1957; nat. committeewoman for N.Y. State, 1957-59, first v.p., 1961—, N.Y. State rep. to women's div., chmn. Oneida County Dem. Club, 1956-60; vice chmn. Dem. State Conv., 1959; sec. N.Y. State Council of Polish Dem. Clubs, Inc., 1951-56; rep. Oneida County Civil Service Employees Assn., 1956-58, sec. 1952-53, treas., 1953-56, v.p. 1959—; sr. accountant City of Utica (N.Y.), 1960—. Treas. Gamma Chi, Inc., 1956-57; sec. Women's Aux. of Orchard Lake (Mich.) Sem., 1959-60, bd. dirs., 1961—; del. Inter-Club Council, 1961—, v.p., 1964—; bd. dirs. Central N.Y. chpt. Multiple Sclerosis, 1964—. Active civic fund-raising drives Am. Cancer Soc., Heart Fund, Easter Seal Fund, United Fund; com. chmn. Mentally Retarded Children in Utica, 1956. Mem. Am. Council Polish Cultural Clubs, Interclub Council (dir.), Christ Child Soc., Polish Am. Hist. Assn. Home: 912 State St Utica NY 13502 Office: 1 Kennedy Plaza Utica NY 13502

MOSKOWITZ, EDITH C., educator; b. Syracuse, N.Y., June 7, 1927; d. George and Ida (Rebeck) Cohen; B.A., Bklyn. Coll., 1948; M.S., Columbia Sch. Social Work, 1950; postgrad. Yeshiva U.; m. Joseph Moskowitz, Feb. 2, 1951; children—Keith, Hope. Dir. suburban services Essex County Jewish Community Center, N.J., 1956-60; psychiat. case worker Jewish Child Care Assn., N.Y.C., 1963-69; field instr. Sheild Inst., Adelphi U., Garden City, N.Y., 1969-72; instr. human service field Rockland Community Coll., Suffern, N.Y., 1972—. Cons. Assn. for Help Retarded of Retarded Children Rockland County, 1963-65; lectr. Adelphi U. Sch. Social Work, 1970—. Mem. Am. Assn. Social Workers, Am. Assn. Mental Deficiency. Home: Route 45 Pomona NY 10970

MOSS, BARBARA ANN DOWLER (MRS. JAMES DONALD MOSS), ednl. cons.; b. Midway, Pa., Sept. 23, 1939; d. Edgar W. and Isabel Ann (Massey) Dowler; B.S., N. Tex. State U., 1965, M.S., 1967, postgrad., 1969; m. James Donald Moss, Aug. 23, 1958; children—James Richard, Scott David. Group worker Dallas County Juvenile Detention Home, 1958-65; speech therapist Irving (Tex.) Ind. Sch. Dist., 1965-67; dir. speech and hearing dept. Denton (Tex.) State Sch. for Mentally Retarded, 1969-71; cons. ednl. services Dallas County Mental Health and Mental Retardation Center, Dallas, 1971—. Chmn. speech and hearing working party Tex. Gov.'s Office Comprehensive Health Planning, 1971-72; chmn. legislative com. Dallas County Child Care Council, 1971-72. Mem. Am., Tex. speech and hearing assns., Am. Assn. Mental Deficiency. Home: 423 Robin Hood St Irving TX 75061 Office: 414 S Thornton Freeway Dallas TX 75203

MOSS, ELIZA WALLER EASLEY, educator, physiologist; b. Martinsville, Va., Mar. 26, 1928; d. Owen Randolph and Cassie Louise (DuVal) Easley; B.S., Longwood Coll., Farmville, Va., 1950; M.S., U. Fla., 1957; Ph.D., N.Y. U., 1967; m. Charles George Gordon Moss, July 22, 1972. Tchr. biochemistry Va. Poly. Inst., 1953-55, 58-59; tchr., research physiology Boyce-Thompson Inst., 1960-62; tchr., researcher cytology Harvard, 1962-63; jr. adminstrv. asst. phys. chemistry Rockland State Hosp. Research Facility, Orangeburg, N.Y., 1963-64; tchr., researcher cell physiology Rockefeller U., 1967-69; asst. prof. biology St. Paul's Coll., Lawrenceville, Va., 1970—, coordinator natural sci., 1971-72. Mem. Farmville Council Human Relations. Mem. Am. Chem. Soc., Harvey Soc., Am. Inst. Chemists, Am. Civil Liberties Union, N.A.A.C.P. Home: 507 Buffalo St Farmville VA 23901 Office: Dept Natural Sci St Paul's Coll Lawrenceville VA 23868

MOSS, IRENE GREENFIELD (MRS. NAT MOSS), artist; b. Eperjes, Czechoslovakia; d. Wolf and Bella (Wolf) Greenfield; came to U.S., 1924, naturalized, 1929; student Bklyn. Mus. Sch. Art, 1948-49; m. Nat Moss; children—Robert, Ralph. One-man shows at Columbia, N.Y.C., N.Y. U., Bklyn. Coll., Suffolk Mus., State U. N.Y. at Stony Brook, others; exhibited in group shows at Rochester Meml. Art Gallery, U. N.C., Ft. Worth Art Center, Stamford Mus., others; represented in permanent collections at Finch Coll. Mus., N.Y.C., New Britain (Conn.), Mus., Norfolk (Va.) Mus., Akron (O.) Art Inst., Rose Art Mus. of Brandeis U., Waltham, Mass. Editor: Feminist Art Jour., 1972-73. Home: 214 West End Av Brooklyn NY 11235

MOSS, IRMA FAYE (MRS. ROY E. MOSS), accountant; b. Clovis, N.M., Dec. 4, 1911; d. Delbert Earl and Shadye Colbert (Haynes) Allen; student Ark. Tech., summer 1930, Northeastern State Tchrs. Coll., 1932-33, (corr.) Boulder U., Colo., 1956-57; m. John F. Elliot, Jr., July 18, 1948 (dec. 1954); 1 dau., Jean (Mrs. Edward W. Doss, Jr.); m. 2d, Roy E. Moss, Apr. 28, 1957 (dec. Nov. 1972). Accountant, Allen Canning Co., Siloam Springs, Ark., 1929—; tchr. Fairmount Sch., Gentry, Ark., 1930-33. Mem. City Planning and Zoning Commn. Siloam Springs, 1973—; pres. P.T.A., 1957, chmn. ways and means com. 1956; sec., treas. United Fund Bd., 1960-63. Named Woman of Year, Bus. and Profl. Women's Club, 1958. Mem. Christian Ch. (adult Sunday sch. tchr. 1956—, pres. ch. circle, 1954-62, chmn. decorating com. new ch. bldg. 1972-73). Pub. poems, articles, 1940-60; also poetry booklets, 1940. Home: 821 S Maxwell Siloam Springs AR 72761 Office: 305 E Main St Siloam Springs AR 72761

MOSS, JACKIE NAN, editor; b. Quonset Point, R.I., Nov. 29, 1950; d. Ira Bailey and Ardith Christine (Martindale) Moss; B.A., Pepperdine U., 1971. Editor Traveler mag., Long Beach, Cal., 1971—. Mem. Women in Communications. Mem. Ch. of Christ. Home: 7582 Rhine Dr Huntington Beach CA 92647 Office: 1207 Pine Av Long Beach CA 90814

MOSS, MARILYN, journalist; b. Spencer, Ind., July 9; d. William G. and Marie C. (Million) Moss; A.B., Ind. U., 1954. Columnist reporter Monticello Herald Jour., Monticello, Ind., 1956-58; asst. publicity mgr. TV Guide Mag., Radnor, Pa., 1958-66; columnist Lafayette (Ind.) Jour.-Courier, 1966-69, copy editor, 1966-72; now free-lance writer. Recipient Nat. Headliner award Atlantic City Press Club and City of Atlantic City, 1968, Merit award Am. Assn. Indsl. Editors, N.Y. U., 1965. Mem. Women in Communications (pres. Lafayette chpt. 1971-72), Atlantic City Press Club (judge news competition 1968), Delta Zeta, Kappa Kappa Kappa. Presbyn. (financial sec. 1967-68). Mem. Order Eastern Star. Home: 1001 Calley Dr Monticello IN 47960

MOSS, MAXINE MERTZ (MRS. RONNIE E. MOSS), editor; b. Ft. Wayne, Ind., Nov. 19, 1914; d. Edward L. and Weltha May (Coppock) Mertz; student (voice scholar) Arthur Jordan Conservatory Music, 1934-35; m. Ronnie E. Moss, June 10, 1944; 1 son, Steven Lane. Personnel counselor Ind. Bell Telephone Co., Indpls., 1940-44; with Nat. Muzzle Loading Rifle Assn., Friendship, Ind., 1960—, editor Muzzle Blasts, 1964—, office mgr., 1966—. Mem. Bi-centennial Ripley County (Ind.) com., 1970—, Historic Hoosier Hills, 1970—. Mem. Nat. Rifle Assn., Nat. Muzzle Loading Rifle Assn., N.W. Council, Mich. Sportsmen's Council, Ohio Gun Collectors, Smithsonian Assos., Mus. Fur Trade. Home: PO Box 33 Friendship IN 47021

MOSS, RACHEL SCOTT BYBEE (MRS. JAMES MERCER MOSS), civic worker; b. Charlottesville, Va., Feb. 2, 1920; d. Aubrey Walker and Wirtie (Williams) Bybee; R.N., U. Va. 1941; m. James Mercer Moss, Sept. 6, 1941; children—James Marion, Fred Aubrey (dec.), William Wallace, Robert Edward. Head nurse on medicine U. Va. Hosp., 1941-42. Dir. Security Savs. and Loan Assn., Alexandria. Mem. ladies bd. Georgetown U. Hosp., 1954—, Heart Assn. No. Va., 1963—; treas. Alexandria Crew Booster's Club, 1965-67; sec. Va. Med. Polit. Action Com., 1967-68; pres. Mansion Drive Club, 1968-69; chmn. Alexandria Tiny Tots Concert, 1965; mem. nurses com. on continuing edn. Va. Heart Assn., 1969-71; mem. ARCS Found., Inc., 1969—; mem. Va. Med. Polit. Action Com., Am. Med. Polit. Action Com.; vol., instr. A.R.C., 1973—; mem. Circle Terrace Hosp. Aux., 1973—. Mem. Alexandria (Va.) Democratic com., 1954-55; mem. Finance Com. to Re-elect Pres. Nixon, 1972. Mem. Woman's Aux. Med. Soc. Va. (pres. 1963-64, dir. 1964-67, finance chmn. 1972-73), Am. Med. Edn. and Research Found., Woman's Aux. So. Med. Assn. (v.p. 1965-66), Woman's Aux. A.M.A. (del. from Va. 1954-64), Woman's Aux. Alexandria Med. Soc. (pres. 1961-62), Alumni Assn. U. Va. Hosp. Sch. Nursing. Presbyn. Clubs: Mansion Drive Garden, Beverly Hills Women's (pres. 1973-74). Home: 319 Mansion Dr Alexandria VA 22302

MOSS, SADIE MARIE SPARKS (MRS. THEODORE L. MOSS), librarian; b. Smiths, Ala., June 17, 1918; d. Edward, Sr., and Rosa (Prince) Sparks; B.S., A. and M. Coll., Normal, Ala., 1949; M.L.S., U. So. Cal., 1959; m. Theodore L. Moss, Aug. 11, 1943; children—Larry E., Yvonne. Tchr. Lee County Tng. Sch., Auburn, Ala., 1946-49, Tuscaloosa, Ala., 1949-51; librarian Brighton High Sch., Jefferson County, Ala., 1951-52; counselor Juvenile Hall, Los Angeles, 1954-58; librarian City of Los Angeles, 1959-61, Vanguard Jr. High Sch., Compton, Cal., 1961-68, Lincoln Elementary Sch., 1968-72; dist. library cons. Pasadena United Sch. Dist., 1972—; writer short stories for children. Adviser Y-Teens; mem. library tech. adv. com. Pasadena City Coll. Bd. dirs. YWCA. Mem. Soroptimists, Iota Phi Lambda (Soror of Year 1973), Phi Lambda Theta, Delta Kappa Gamma. Democrat. Baptist. Home: 1666 E Mendocino St Altadena CA 91001 Office: 740 W Woodbury Rd Pasadena CA 91109

MOSSMAN, SALLIE LOUISE, pub. relations exec.; b. Huntington, W.Va., Dec. 7, 1948; d. Robert Lee and Jane Evelyn (Dudding) Mossman; B.S. in Journalism, Ohio U., 1970; M.A. in Journalism and Communications, U. Fla., 1971. Advt. and editorial asst. Gallipolis (O.) Daily Tribune, summers, 1967, 68; pub. relations intern Univ. Hosps., Cleve., summer, 1969; pub. relations dir. St. Johns River Jr. Coll., Palatka, Fla., 1972—. Recipient Golden Image award Fla. Pub. Relations Assn., 1973. Mem. Fla. Assn. Community Colls., Women in Communications (pres. chpt. 1974-75), Fla. Community Coll. Publs. Advisers (state sec. 1973-74), Fla. Pub. Relations Assn. (dir. 1973—), Kappa Tau Alpha, Sigma Delta Chi, Phi Kappa Phi. Home: 702 1/2 Fern St Palatka FL 32077 Office: 5001 St John Av Palatka FL 32077

MOSTELLER, BETTE VAUGHAN, librarian; b. Amelia County, Va., Feb. 1, 1937; d. Lawson Paul and Rosa Vaughan (Mottley) Mosteller; B.A., Longwood Coll., 1958; M.A. in L.S. (Va. State Library fellow), George Peabody Coll., 1959; postgrad. in history Coll. William and Mary, 1973—. Cataloger, Va. State Library, Richmond, 1959-62; readers adviser Richmond Pub. Library, summer 1962; head librarian Christopher Newport Coll., Newport News, Va., 1962—. Library adv. com. State Council Higher Edn., 1971—; mem. Eastern Va. Hist. Orgn. for the Bi-Centennial Celebration, 1970—. Mem. Va. (exec. asst. nat. library week com. 1969-71), Southeastern library assns. Home: 163 Yeardley Dr Newport News VA 23601 Office: PO Box 6070 Newport News VA 23606

MOTE, WINNIFRED KATHLEEN, pharmacist; b. Des Moines, Oct. 13, 1918; d. Frederick Garfield and Mary Rebecca (Trevillyan) Mote; B.S., Drake U., 1942. Chief pharmacist Broadlawns Polk County Hosp., Des Moines, 1942-62, instr. student nurses, 1946-58, acting dir. pharmacy service, 1962-64; instr. Drake U. at Broadlawns, 1949—. Mem. bd. YWCA, 1962-63; spl. projects chmn. S.S. Hope, 1964-66; nominating chmn. Broadlawns Guild, 1968-69. Sec. Pharmacy and Therapeutic Com., 1973-74. Recipient Good Citizenship award, 1963. Fellow Royal Soc. Health; mem. Des Moines Bus. and Profl. Women's Club, Drake U. Alumnae Assn., Am. Assn. U. Women., Am. Pharm. Assn., Am. (ho. of dels. 1973-74), Ia. (pres. 1948-49, v.p. 1966, 67, dir. 1973—) socs. hosp. pharmacists, Ia. (hosp. liaison com. 1967-68, com. on instnl. practice 1969-71), Polk County pharm. assns., Lambda Kappa Sigma (internat. resolution chmn.). Mem. Order Eastern Star (worthy matron 1963). Club: Zonta (pres. 1953-54, 66, 67; chmn. 1964-65, dir. 1968-70, 73—, service chmn. 1970-71, v.p. 1973-74, Amelia Earhart chmn. 1973-74). Home: 3512 S Union St Des Moines IA 50315 Office: 18th and Hickman Rd Des Moines IA 50314

MOTHERSHEAD, ALICE BONZI (MRS. MORRIS WARNER MOTHERSHEAD), civic worker; b. Milan, Italy, Dec. 25, 1914 (came to U.S. 1920, naturalized 1925); d. Ercole and Alice (Spalding) Bonzi; pvt. pupil music and art; student Pasadena City Coll., 1958-60; m. Morris Warner Mothershead, Sept. 15, 1935; children—Warner Bonzi, Maria (Mrs. Andrei Rogers). Partner Float Toy Co., Pasadena, Cal., 1942-44; community adviser Fgn. Student Program Pasadena City Coll., 1952—. Chmn. Am. Field Service Internat. Scholarships, Pasadena, 1953-55; mem. West Coast adv. com. Inst. Internat. Edn., San Francisco, 1957—. Vice pres. San Rafael Sch. P.T.A., Pasadena, 1945-46; active Community Chest, A.R.C., Pasadena; chmn. Greater Los Angeles Com. Internat. Student and Visitor Services, 1962; mem. Woman's Civic League Pasadena, 1972. Mem. Nat. Assn. Fgn. Student Affairs (chmn. community sect. and v.p. 1964-65, chmn. U.S. study abroad com. 1969-70), Am. Assn. UN (chpt. 2d v.p. 1964), Am. Friends Middle East, Omicron Mu Delta. Club: International (Pasadena). Author: Social Customs and Manners in the United States, 1957; co-author: 15 Years of the Foreign Student Program at Pasadena City College, 1965. Editor Students to People to Future, 1971. Home: 675 Burleigh Dr Pasadena CA 91105 Office: Pasadena City College 1570 E Colorado St Pasadena CA 91106

MOTT, DOROTHY HALE WILLIAMS (MRS. GEORGE FOX MOTT), editor; b. Mpls., Oct. 3, 1910; d. Edward Hale and Margaret (Ladd) Williams; student Ginling Coll., Nanking, China, 1932-33; A.B., U. Minn., 1937; postgrad. Columbia, 1941; m. George Fox Mott, Feb. 12, 1944; children—David Edward Way, Jonathan Loren Gould. Librarian, tchr. social studies Marine Corps Children's Sch., Quantico, Va., 1941-43; adminstrv. asst. Mott of Washington & Assos., 1950-53, tech. writer, research asst., 1953-64, supervising editor, 1964—. First v.p. Friends of D.C. Youth Orch., 1964-70, hon. sponsor, 1970—; treas. Chevy Chase Community Council, 1965—(Distinguished Service award, 1972); mem. bd. Children's Theatre Washington, 1966—. Bd. dirs. Noyes Sch. Rhythm Found. (editor Rhythm mag. 1969—, instr. summers, 1972—). Home: 3745 Kanawha St NW Washington DC 20015 Office: Dupont Circle Bldg Washington DC 20036

MOTTAZ, MABEL MANES (MRS. CLARENCE E. MOTTAZ), civic worker; b. Waynesville, Mo., Sept. 20, 1900; d. Seth McCulley and Olive Matilda (Mayfield) Manes; B.S., Mo. U., 1940; M.A., Columbia U., 1943; m. Edward Newton Henson, Feb. 20, 1920; 1 son, Drury E.; m. 2d, Sam T. Rollins, Apr. 1, 1944; m. 3d, Clarence E. Mottaz, Apr. 3, 1948. Tchr., rural schs., Pulaski, Mo., 1918-40; tchr., counselor, Waynesville, 1941-56; mem. staff Ozark Mountaineer Mag., 1956—; byline and feature writer Pulaski County Democrat, Waynesville, 1941—, Daily Guide Newspapers, 1970—. Mem. Waynesville council U.S.O., 1943—; writer by-laws Waynesville P.T.A., 1941, Pulaski County Hosp. Aux., 1946; mem. Pulaski Betterment Commn., 1970—. Organizer Pulaski County Women's Democratic Club, 1965. Mem. Am. Assn. U. Women (organizer Waynesville 1962), Pulaski County Hist. Soc. (organizer Waynesville 1969), St. Roberts-Waynesville C. of C. (dir. 1956—), Pulaski County Landowners Assn., Sho-Me-State Heritage Assn., Kappa Kappa Iota. Baptist. Mem. Order Eastern Star. Club: Harmony Home Achievement (Waynesville, Mo.). Author: Lest We Forget, 1960. Home: 306 Hwy 17 N Waynesville MO 65583

MOTTL, MARY ARNOLD (MRS. ROBERT O. MOTTL), pianist; b. Indpls., Aug. 9, 1943; d. Francis Donald and Kathryn Louise (Klingner) Arnold; Mus.B. summa cum laude, Ind. U., 1965, Mus. M., 1966 (Ford Found. fellow), postgrad., 1966—; m. Robert O. Mottl, Jan. 28, 1967; children—Richard Alan, David Brian. Tchr. U. Nev., Reno, 1966-67, Kansas State Coll. at Pittsburg, 1967-68, Webster Coll., Webster Groves, Mo., 1969-71; pianist St. Louis Symphony, 1971—; accompanist St. Louis Bach Soc., 1971—. Pvt. instrn. piano, 1966—. Recipient Young Artist award Terre Haute Symphony, 1960, Youth Appreciation award Plainfield (Ind.) Optimists, 1961, Roseanna M. Enlow award, 1965; Tri-Kappa scholar, 1961. Mem. Pi Kappa Lambda, Sigma Alpha Iota. Presbyn. Home: 522 Angenette St Kirkwood MO 63122 Office: 718 N Grand Av St Louis MO 63103

MOTTLEY, JACQUELINE VIRGINIA, educator; b. St. Cloud, Minn.; d. Joseph Bernard and Eleanore (Staunton) Weisser; B.A., Coll. of St. Catherine, 1949; postgrad. U. Wash., 1950-51, Mont. State U., 1964-67; m. Rudolph Herzog, Aug. 23, 1951 (div. Nov. 1964); children—Robert, Mark, Joseph, Thomas, Richard; m. 2d, Renwick Ferrell Mottley, June 18, 1967 (div. Sept. 1972). Tchr. art Park High Sch., Livingston, Mont., 1966-67; dir. fashion Skadron Fashion Inst., San Bernardino, Cal., 1970—; exec. asso. Carr & Assos., San Rafael, Cal. Actress in Three Penny Opera prodn. at the Loft Theater, Bozeman, 1964. Sec., Overlake div. Community Chest drive, Seattle, 1953; State of Mont. Centennial TV rep., Mont., Utah, Ida., speaker Centennial Women's Fashions, Bozeman, 1964; chmn. Project H.E.Y. (family service orgn. for USAF wives), Mather AFB, Cal., 1967; coordinator family services USAF, 1968. Recipient 1st award in black and white photography, film and TV dept. Mont. State U., 1965; 1st pl. photography 5th Ann. Art Show, 1965; hon. mention N.W. Photography Internat., 1965. Mem. Am. Assn. U. Women, Nat. Art Edn. Assn. Home: 19135 Knollwood Dr Rialto CA 92376 Office: 798 4th St San Bernardino CA 92410

MOTTO, ANNA LYDIA (MRS. JOHN R. CLARK), educator; b. N.Y.C.; d. Michael Angelo and Mollie (Gross) Motto; B.A. cum laude, Queens Coll., 1946; M.A., N.Y.U., 1948; Ph.D., U. N.C., 1953; m. John R. Clark, Nov. 7, 1959; children—Valerie Mollie, Bradford Russell. Grad. asst. U. N.C. at Chapel Hill, 1949-50, teaching fellow, 1950-51, instr. Latin, 1951-52; instr. French, Mars Hill (N.C.) Coll., summer 1953; asst. prof. langs. Washington Coll., Chestertown, Md., 1953-57; tchr. Latin and French, Northport (L.I., N.Y.) High Sch., 1957-58; asst. prof. dept. classics, chmn. Alfred (N.Y.) U., 1958-65, asso. prof.; chmn., asso. prof. classics Muhlenberg Coll., Allentown, Pa., 1965-66; asso. prof. classics St. John's U., Jamaica and Bklyn., N.Y., 1966-68; chmn., asso. prof. dept. classics Drew U., Madison, N.J., 1968-71, prof., 1971—. Fulbright grantee, Rome, Italy, summer 1956. Mem. Am. Philol. Assn., Classical Assn. Atlantic States (v.p. 1971-72), Classical Soc. of Am. Acad. in Rome, Vergilian Soc. of Cumae, N.Y. Classical Club. Author: Seneca Sourcebook: Guide to the Thought of Lucius Annacus Seneca, 1970; Satire: That Blasted Art, 1973; Seneca, 1973. Contbr. articles to profl. jours. Home: 30 Woodcliff Dr Madison NJ 07940

MOTTOROS, THERESA MARY, dept. store exec.; b. Bklyn., Oct. 5, 1932; B.A. in Econs., U. Mich., 1953; postgrad. N.Y. U., St. John's Law Sch.; m. Pierre P. Mottoros, Dec. 30, 1957. With Ford Motor Co., 1956; asst. traffic mgr. internat. div. Union Bag-Camp Paper Corp., 1957-62; sales mgr. Macy's Dept. Store, N.Y.C., 1962-64, asst. buyer, 1964-66, buyer, 1966-70, mdse. mgr., 1970-72, store mgr., 1972—, v.p., 1973—. Home: 8 Cardinal Lane Hauppauge NY 11787 Office: Macy's 34th St New York City NY

MOTZ, DIANA GRIBBON (MRS. JOHN FREDERICK MOTZ), lawyer; b. Washington, July 15, 1943; d. Daniel McNamara and Mary Jane (Retzler) Gribbon; B.A., Vassar Coll., 1965; LL.B., U. Va., 1968; m. John Frederick Motz, Sept. 20, 1968; 1 dau., Catherine Jane. Admitted to Md. bar, 1969; asso. Piper and Mawbury, Balt., 1968-71; asst. atty. gen. State of Md., Balt., 1972—. Bd. dirs. Jr. League Balt., 1973—; bd. dirs. YWCA, 1970—, sec. bd., 1972-74; bd. dirs. Union Meml. Hosp., 1971—, asst. sec., 1973-74. Home: 215 Chancery Rd Baltimore MD 21218 Office: 1100 N Eutaw St Baltimore MD 21201

MOTZKIN, EVELYN HERSZKORN (MRS. DONALD MOTZKIN), psychiatrist; b. Warsaw, Poland, Jan. 12, 1933 (came to U.S. 1937, naturalized 1943; d. Joseph and Eda (Itzkowitz) Herszkorn; B.S., Queens Coll., N.Y.C., 1953; M.D., State U. N.Y. at N.Y.C., 1958; m. Donald Motzkin, Dec. 17, 1955; children—Patricia, Linda, Neil, Nancy, Richard, Lisa. Instr. biology Queens Coll., 1953-54; intern Vassar Bros. Hosp., Poughkeepsie, N.Y., 1958-59; fellow endocrinology Coll. Medicine, Baylor U., Houston, 1960-62; resident psychiatry VA Hosp., Houston, 1962-64, VA Hosp., Sepulveda, Cal., 1965-67; practice psychiatry, Encino, Cal., 1967—; clin. asso. So. Cal. Psychoanalytic Inst., Los Angeles, 1968—; mem. staff Woodview-Calabassus Hosp., Van Nuys, Cal., Calabassas (Cal.) Psychiat. Hosp., West Valley Community Hosp., Encino, Cal., Sherman Oaks (Cal.) Community Hosp.; clin. instr. psychiatry U. Cal. at Los Angeles, 1969-71; cons. VA Hosp., Sepulveda, Jewish Home Aged, Reseda, Cal., 1968—. Mem. Am., So. Cal. psychiat. assns., Am. Psychoanalytic Assn. (affiliate). Office: 5353 Balboa Blvd Encino CA 91316

MOTZKIN, SHIRLEY MITTMAN (MRS. DON JACK MOTZKIN), educator; b. N.Y.C., Jan. 12, 1927; d. Julius and Margit Gertrude (Ullman) Mittman; B.S. cum laude, Bklyn. Coll., 1947; A.M., Columbia, 1949; Ph.D., N.Y. U., 1958; m. Don Jack Motzkin, June 22, 1952; children—Shelly, Beth, Glenn. Instr., Bklyn. Coll., 1947, then adj., to 1959; instr. N.Y. U. Coll. Dentistry, 1951-58, asso. prof. biology, 1959-66; asso. prof. biology Poly. Inst. Bklyn., 1966-73; prof. biology Poly. Inst. N.Y., N.Y.C., 1973—, chmn. life scis., 1966—. Guest lectr. Guggenheim Dental Clinic, 1960-66; research cons. N.Y. U. Coll. Dentistry, 1966-69, W.A. Benjamin & Co., N.Y.C., 1967-69. Recipient outstanding tchrs. award Coll. Dentistry, N.Y. U., 1962. NIH grantee, 1959-66, NSF grantee, 1969-71, Hartford Found. grantee, 1971-73. Mem. Internat. Assn. Dental Research, Sci. Research Soc. Am., A.A.A.S., N.Y. Acad. Scis., Teratology Soc. (charter), Internat. Assn. Cranio-Facial Biology, Cleft Palate Assn., Am. Assn. U. Profs., Sigma Xi. Home: 171 Valley Rd New Rochelle NY 10804 Office: 333 Jay St Brooklyn NY 11201

MOUAT, LUCRETIA PALMER, journalist; b. Janesville, Wis., Jan. 23, 1936; d. Malcolm Palmer and Gertrude (McPherson) Mouat; student Pomona Coll., 1954-56; B.A., U. Wis., 1958; M.A., Fletcher Sch. of Law and Diplomacy, 1961. Sec. Speakers Bur. Fgn. Policy Assn., N.Y.C., 1959; staff corr. Christian Sci. Monitor, 1961—, stationed in Washington, 1969—. Recipient Rudolphe Elie Award Boston Press Club, 1965, First place award Edn. Writers assn., 1966, award for Excellence in Bus., Econ. and Financial Reporting U. Mo., 1970, Certificate of Merit Am. Bar Assn., 1973. Mem. Am. Newspaper Women's Club (v.p. 1971-72). Club: Washington Press. Home: 4390 Lorcom Ln Arlington VA 22207 Office: 910 16th St NW Washington DC 22207

MOULD, LILIAN J., psychologist; b. Locust Valley, N.Y., June 27, 1914; d. Jesse Hays and Lillian Weir (Cook) Mould; A.B., Barnard Coll., 1935; M.A., Columbia, 1947; Ph.D., N.Y. U., 1957. Tchr. pub. schs., Hartsdale, N.Y., 1939-51; psychologist N.Y. State Child Guidance Clinic, Binghamton, 1953-57; chief psychologist Hartley-Salmon Child Guidance Clinic, Hartford, 1957-63; staff psychologist Silver Hill Found., New Canaan, Conn., 1963-70; chief psychologist Mid-Fairfield Child Guidance Center, Norwalk, Conn., 1970—; individual practice psychology, Westport, Conn., 1969—; cons. Norwalk Head Start, 1970-73, Coop. Nursery Sch., Rowayton, Conn., 1970—. Bd. dirs. Westport Nursery Sch. Mem. N.Y. State, Conn. psychol. assns., World Fedn. Mental Health, Westport-Weston Community Council, Conn. Assn. for Children with Learning Disabilities. Club: Barnard (Fairfield County). Address: 33 Cross Hwy Westport CT 06880

MOULIN, LINDA KATHRINE, audiologist; b. Canton, O., Dec. 29, 1937; d. Clinton S. and Kathrine Jane (Henning) Moulin; B.S., Kent State U., 1959, M.A., 1962; Ph.D., Case Western Res. U., 1968. Speech pathologist and audiologist Youngstown (O.) Hearing and Speech Center, 1960-64; teaching and research asst. Case Western Res. U., Cleve., 1965-68; clin. audiologist Cleve. Clin., summers 1967, 68; asst. prof. audiology and psychoacoustics State U. N.Y. at Buffalo, 1968-73, dir. Speech Communication Research Lab., 1971-73; dir. audiology dept. Environmental Tech. Corp., Cleve., 1973—. Audiological cons. Dr. Joel Bernstein, Buffalo, 1971-73, O.L. Angevine & Assos., East Aurora, N.Y., 1972-73; tchr. certification programs for audiometric technicians, 1971—; traineeship vocational rehab. adminstrn. U. Pitts., 1964-65; career-investigator traineeship NIH, Case Western Res. U., 1965-68. Recipient Easter Seal Research Found. award State U. N.Y. at Buffalo, 1972-73. Mem. Am., Ohio (editorial cons. jour. 1967) speech and hearing assns., Acoustical Soc. Am. (registration chmn. 83d conv. 1972), Psi Chi (sec. 1959-60), Sigma Alpha Eta (publs. chmn. 1958-60). Contbr. articles to profl. jours. Home: 2899 Lander Rd Pepper Pike OH 44124 Office: 3439 W Brainard Cleveland OH 44122

MOULTON, JOY WADE (MRS. EDWARD QUENTIN MOULTON), civic worker, genealogist; b. Oxnard, Cal., Nov. 30, 1928; d. Merle Elwood and Elouise (Morgan) Wade; A.B., U. Cal. at Berkeley, 1950; M.S., Wellesley Coll., 1953; m. Edward Quentin Moulton, Jan. 2, 1954; children—Jennifer Fairchild, Charles Wade, David Frederick II, Alison Joy. Instr. women's phys. edn. Ohio State U., 1954-66. Residential area chmn. United Appeals, 1959-60; dir. Columbus Symphony Orch. Women's Assn., 1961-66, rec. sec., 1965-66; dir. Lewis and Clark Symphonette, 1966-68; gen. chmn. Greater Columbus Arts Festival, 1973-74. Bd. dirs. Columbus Symphony Orch., 1969-71. Mem. Columbus Gallery Fine Arts, Mortar Bd. (nat. treas. 1964-70), Internat. Platform Assn., Gavel and Quill, Panile, Prytanean, Mu Phi Epsilon (patroness), Nu Sigma Psi, Pi Lambda Theta. Conglist. Clubs: Columbus Wellesley (v.p. 1957-59), Mortar Board Alumnae (pres. 1957-58), University Women's, Crichton (dir.). Author: The Podium, 1969-71; also works on genealogy. Address: 1303 London Dr Columbus OH 43221

MOUNCE, CAROLYN PITTS, librarian, educator; b. Ecru, Miss., Dec. 18, 1938; d. Walter Gerald and Mary Ozelle (Pitts) Mounce; B.A., Blue Mountain Coll., 1960; M.A. in L.S., George Peabody Coll. Tchrs., 1963, postgrad., 1969-70. Asst. librarian Blue Mountain (Miss.) Coll., 1960-70, head librarian, 1971—, chmn. dept. library sci., 1971—, prof. library sci., 1967—. Mem. Miss. Library Assn. (sect. sec. 1973-74), Am. Assn. U. Profs., Am. Assn. U. Women (br. pres. 1966-68, div. area rep. 1968-69), Blue Mountain Coll. Nat. Alumnae Assn. (exec. bd. 1968-71), Blue Mountain Coll. Local Alumnae Club (sec. 1966-67, pres. 1968), Blue Mountain Woman's Club (pres. 1971, sec.-treas. 1972, dist. officer 1972-74). Woodmen of the World. Baptist. Club: Blue Mountain College Faculty (treas. 1965-66). Home: Ecru MS 38841 Office: Box 113 BMC Blue Mountain MS 38610

MOUNT, WARD (PAULINE WARD), painter, sculptor; b. Batavia, N.Y.; d. Fred Kendall and Nellie L. (Dowsey) Ward; grad. Flushing High Sch.; student N.Y.U., Art Students League; pvt. study with Gertrude Gardner, Kenneth Hayes Miller, Albert P. Lucas, Joseph P. Pollia; m. Dr. Elmer M. Mount, Apr. 6, 1920; 1 son, Marshall Ward. Former head of dept. oil painting and sculpture N.J. State Tchrs. Coll.; founder, former dir. art classes Jersey City Med. Center, 1948-49; dir., instr. Ward Mount Art Classes. Represented by paintings and sculptures, Columbia U. Library, Irvington Pub. Library, Delgado Mus., New Orleans, Hudson River Mus., Montclair Art Mus., Los Angeles Mus., Trenton State Mus., Jersey City Mus., N.A.D., Marquis Biog. Library, Library of Congress, Nat. Sculpture Soc., Archtl. League (N.Y.), Verona Pub. Library, N.Y. Pub Library, Municipal Art Galleries, Allied Artists Am., Allied Arts Mus. (N.Y.), Riverside Mus., Nat. Arts Club (N.Y.C.), Grand Central Palace, Acad. Allied Arts (N.Y.C.), Am. British Art Center, N.Y. Hist. Mus., Kearney Mus., N.J. Gallery, Macy Galleries, Fine Arts Bldg. (N.Y.C.), Essex, Sussex and Warren, Monmouth hotels (Spring Lake, N.J.), Berkley Carteret (Asbury Park, N.J.), Palm Beach (Fla.) hotel, Alford Hotel (East Orange, N.J.), Brentanos, Audubon Artists, Pa. Acad., Smithsonian Instn., Carlebach Galleries (N.Y.C.), Terry Art Inst. (Fla.), Worlds Fair, N.Y., 1965, Madison Sq. Garden, F. D.

Roosevelt Mus., Archives Am. Art (Eng.), Westchester Art Galleries, Lever House, N.Y.C., Jersey City Mus., also fgn. countries. Designed bronze Medal of Honor for Painters and Sculptors Soc. N.J., 1947; designed and executed The Bell of Am., Bell Assn., 1950. Represented in many collections, including the late Pres. Franklin D. Roosevelt, Hon. Charles B. Howard of Canada, Georgia Timken Fry, Bernard U. Gimbel. Recipient 1st prize for watercolor, Jersey City Art Exhbn., 1923; 1st prize for oil painting, Jersey City Mus., 1941; 1st prize for sculpture, Painters and Sculptors Soc., 1943, 1951; Clayton E. Freeman 1st prize sculpture, ann. state exhbn., Montclair Art Mus., 1945; 1st prize sculpture, N.J. Artists (Union, N.J.), 1945; 1st prize sculpture, Asbury Park Soc. Fine Arts, 1946; purchase Jersey City Museum for permanent collection, 1946; first sculpture prize, Kearney Mus., N.J., 1947; 1st prize bronze sculpture, Art Fair, N.Y.C., 1950; Jersey Jour. Woman Achievement Gold medal, 1971; decorated Knight Mark Twain. Past mem. faculty Acad. Allied Arts (N.Y.). Fellow Internat. Inst. Arts and Letters (life), Royal Soc. of Arts (Eng.); mem. N.Y. Soc. Painters, Artists Equity, N.Y., Painters and Sculptors Soc. N.J. (founder, hon. pres.), D.A.R., Internat. Platform Assn. Designed and executed Xmas card for Am. Heart Assn., 1971. Home and studio: 74 Sherman Pl Jersey City NJ 07307

MOUNTFORD, HELEN HARVENE (MRS. DAMON W. MOUNTFORD), lawyer; b. Dallas, Mar. 13, 1942; d. Roger Parkhurst and Cornelia Harvene (Wells) Turner; student U. Kan., 1960-62, J.D., 1969; B.S., U. Ia., 1964; m. Damon William Mountford, Nov. 10, 1961; children—Hilary, Sarah. Admitted to Kan. bar, 1969; asst. to dean, coordinator legal clinics U. Kan. Law Sch., Lawrence, 1969-71; practice law, Leavenworth, Kan., 1971—. Judge, Municipal Ct., Lansing, Kan., 1973—. Mem. Am., Kan., Leavenworth County (sec. 1973, treas. 1974) bar assns., Am. Trial Lawyers Assn., Order Coif. Home: 115 Meadow Lane Lansing KS 66043 Office: 520 S 4th St Leavenworth KS 66048

MOUNTZ, LOUISE CARSON SMITH (MRS. GEORGE EDWARD MOUNTZ), librarian; b. Fond Du Lac, Wis., Oct. 20, 1911; d. Roy Carson and Charlotte Louise (Scheurs) Smith; student Western Coll., Oxford, O., 1929-31; A.B., Ohio State U., 1933; M.A., Ball State U., 1962; postgrad. Manchester Coll., 1954, Ind. U., 1960-61; m. George Edward Mountz, May 4, 1935 (dec. Oct. 1951); children—Peter Carson, Pamela Teeters (Mrs. George Edmund McDonald). Tchr., high sch., Monroeville, Ind., 1953-54, Riverdale High Sch., St. Joseph, Ind., 1954-55; tchr., librarian high sch., Avilla, Ind., 1955-58; head librarian Penn High Sch., Mishawaka, Ind., 1958-67, Northwood Jr. High Sch., Fort Wayne, 1967-69, McIntosh Jr. High Sch., Auburn, Ind., 1969-74; dir. Media Center DeKalb Jr. High Sch., Auburn, 1974—. Cons. media center planning Penn Harris Madison Sch. Corp., Mishawaka, 1966—. Bd. dirs. DeKalb County Red Cross, 1938-42, 51-53, DeKalb County Heart Assn., 1946-52, DeKalb County Community Concert Assn., 1946-58, Am. Field Service chpt., Mishawaka, 1960-67. Mem. Am. Assn. U. Women, A.L.A., World Confedn. Orgns. Teaching Professions, Nat. Council Tchrs. English, N.E.A., Ind. Sch. Librarians Assn. (dir. 1963-67), Internat. Assn. Sch. Librarianship, Ind. Assn. Ednl. Communication and Tech., Ind. Tchrs. Assn., Ind., Garrett, DeKalb County, Allen County hist. socs., Delta Kappa Gamma, Kappa Kappa Kappa (state officer 1941-45), Delta Delta Delta (house pres.). Methodist. Mem. Order Eastern Star. Club: Athena (hon. mem.) (Garrett, Ind.). Author: Biographies for Junior High Schools. Contbr. articles to profl. jours. Home: 412 E King St Garrett IN 46738

MOUTON, JANE SRYGLEY, indsl. psychologist; b. Port Arthur, Tex., Apr. 15, 1930; d. Theodore and Grace (Stumpe) Srygley; B.A. in Edn., U. Tex., 1950, Ph.D. in Psychology (Univ. fellow 1954-55), 1957; M.S. (Lewis fellow) U. Fla., 1951; m. Jackson C. Mouton, Jr., Dec. 22, 1953; children—Jane, Jacquelyne. Research asst. U. Tex., Austin, 1953-57, social sci. research asst., 1957-59, instr. in psychology, 1957-59, asst. prof. psychology, 1959-62; v.p. Scientific Methods, Inc., Austin, 1961—. Diplomate Am. Psychol. Assn. Mem. A.A.A.S., N.Y. Acad. Scis., Southwestern Psychol. Assn., Interam. Soc. of Psychology. Author: The Marriage Grid, 1971; The Grid For Sales Excellent, 1970; Corporate Excellence Through Grid Organization Development, 1968; How To Assess The Strengths And Weaknesses Of A Business Enterprise, 1972, Corporate Darwinism, 1966; Managing Intergroup Conflict, 1964; The Managerial Grid, 1964. Contbr. articles to profl. jours. Home: 2305 Hartford Rd Austin TX 78703 Office: PO Box 195 Austin TX 78767

MOW, ANNA BEAHM (MRS. BAXTER MERRILL MOW), educator; b. Daleville, Va., July 31, 1893; d. Isaac N.H. and Mary (Bucher) Beahm; B.A., Manchester Coll., 1918; B.D., Bethany Theol. Sem., 1921, M.R.E., 1941, M.Th., 1943; D.D., 1959; m. Baxter Merrill Mow, Mar. 30, 1921; children—Lois (Mrs. J. Ernest Snavely), Joseph, Merrill. Missionary to India, 1923-40; prof. Christian edn. Bethany Theol. Sem., 1942-58. Mem. gen. bd. Ch. of Brethren, 1967—. Recipient alumni award Manchester (Ind.) Coll., 1963; named Va. State Mother of Year, 1973. Author: Say 'Yes' to Life, 1961; Your Child, 1963; Going Steady with God, 1965; Your Teenager and You, 1967; Who's Afraid of Birthdays, 1969; The Secret of Married Love, 1970; Your Experience and the Bible, 1973. Address: 1318 Varnell Av NE Roanoke VA 24012

MOWER, HELEN KLARNER, coll. dean; b. Liberty, Ill., June 9, 1910; d. Otto G. and Mollie (Franks) Klarner; A.B., Knox Coll., 1962; M.A., Columbia, 1968; m. Robert F. Mower, June 24, 1939 (div. June 1952). Adminstrv. asst. Knox Coll., Galesburg, Ill., 1953-62, placement dir., 1964-68, 68—, asst. dean of students, 1968—. Mem. Am. Assn. U. Women, Midwest Coll. Placement Assn., Am. Coll. Personnel Assn., Am. Personnel and Guidance Assn., Ill. Assn. Women Deans, Counselors and Adminstrs., Nat. Assn. Women Deans, Adminstrs. and Counselors. Home: Whiting Hall Knox College Galesburg IL 61401

MOWERY, DOROTHY DUNSING (DEE DUNSING) (MRS. WILLIAM BYRON MOWERY), author; b. Hammond, Ind.; d. Julius H. and May (Bunker) Dunsing; A.B., U. Ill., 1925; M.Ed., U. Fla., 1962; m. William Byron Mowery, Aug., 1935; 1 dau., Leda Jo. Feature writer, copyreader Chgo. Sun, 1942-47, Los Angeles Times, 1947-48; woman's editor Fla. Times Union, Jacksonville, 1949-54; tchr. English Lake Shore Jr. High Sch., Jacksonville, 1955-66, St. John's River Jr. Coll., Palatka, Fla., 1966-68; supervising tchr. Jacksonville (Fla.) U., 1970-71. Mem. Nat. League Am. Pen Women, Alpha Gamma Delta. Author: Swamp Shadows, 1948; War Chant, 1954; Seminole Trail, 1956. Contbr. numerous juvenile stories to mags. and anthologies. Address: 1273 Menna St Jacksonville FL 32205

MOWLES, CYNTHIA ELIZABETH, govt. ofcl.; b. Manchester, N.H., Aug. 4, 1938; d. Henry Michael and Eleanor (Hanlan) Mowles; B.A., U. N.H., 1960, postgrad., 1962-65; Ed.M., Boston U., 1962, Ed.D., 1972. Tchr. pub. schs., Deerfield, N.H., 1960-61, Rye, N.H., 1961-63, Oyster River Coop., Lee, N.H., demonstration tchr. U. N.H., Durham, 1964-66; guidance dir. elementary schs., Bedford, N.H., 1966-68; dir. Head Start, Hillsboro County, N.H., 1967; early childhood cons. N.H. Dept. Edn., State House Annex, Concord, 1968—. Pres. Day Care and Child Devel. Council N.H., 1972-74; chmn. N.H. Early Childhood Devel. Task Force; mem. Gov.'s Day Care Adv. Com. Mem. Am. Assn. U. Women (pres. N.H. div. 1974—), Nat. Assn. Edn. Young Children, Internat. Reading Assn., Phi Mu, Pi Lambda Theta. Democrat. Roman Catholic. Home: Olde Deerfield Rd Candia NH 03034 Office: 64 N Main St Concord NH 03301

MOWRER, LILIAN T. (MRS. EDGAR ANSEL MOWRER), author; b. London, Eng.; d. Octavius Leopold and Eliza Jane (Green) Thomson; student Liverpool U., 1911-13, Sorbonne, Paris, 1907, Sapienza, Rome, 1920-21; m. Edgar Ansel Mowrer, Feb. 8, 1916; 1 dau., Diana (Mrs. Jean Beliard). Author: Journalist's Wife, 1937; Arrest and Exile, 1940; Riptide of Aggression, 1942; Concerning France, 1944; The U.S. and World Relations, 1950; John Scott of L.I., 1960; I've Seen It Happen Twice, 1969; (with Edgar A. Mowrer) UMANO and The Price of Lasting Peace, 1973. D.C. chmn. Women's Action Com. for Lasting Peace, 1943-49. Decorated for meritorious work with Red Cross (Italy). Mem. Am. Newspaper Women's Club, Pen and Brush, Inc., Women in Communications. Home: Wonalancet NH 03897

MOXLEY, ANN WEIMER, clin. psychologist; b. N.Y.C., Mar. 14, 1946; d. Rae Otis and Ruth Adrienne (Meister) Weimer; B.A. with high honors, U. Fla., 1967, M.S., 1968, Ph.D., 1970; m. James Edward Moxley, Mar. 16, 1968. Asso. psychologist Monroe Developmental Services, Rochester, N.Y., 1970-73, prin. psychologist, chief psychol. services, 1973—; clin. instr. psychiatry Sch. Medicine, U. Rochester, 1973—. Mem. Am. Psychol. Assn., Am. Assn. Mental Deficiency, Mortar Bd., Phi Beta Kappa, Phi Kappa Phi, Psi Chi, Chi Omega. Contbr. articles to profl. jours. Home: 56 Heatherhurst Dr Pittsford NY 14534 Office: 620 Westfall Rd Rochester NY 14620

MOYE, ELIZABETH GILBRETH (MRS. JOHN HOWELL MOYE), editor; b. Raleigh, N.C., May 18, 1937; d. Frank Bunker and Elizabeth (Cauthen) Gilbreth; student Smith Coll., 1955-56; m. John Howell Moye, June 9, 1966; children by previous marriage—Elizabeth Gilbreth Sams, Ellen Taylor Sams. With News and Courier, also Charleston Evening Post, Charleston, S.C., 1956—, bridal and amusements editor, 1961-69, exec. women's editor, 1969—. Mem. S.C. Press Assn., Sigma Delta Chi. Episcopalian. Club: Junior League (Charleston). Home: 853 Montgomery Rd Charleston SC 29412 Office: The News and Courier Charleston SC 29402

MOYER, GRACE SIMS, state ofcl.; b. Moweaqua, Ill., Aug. 31, 1911; d. Herman and Martha (Rarick) Sims; student Brenau Conservatory, Gainsville, Ga., 1929-30; Browns Bus. Coll., Decatur, Ill., 1931. Personnel work, bookkeeping Electric Products Co., LaGrange, Ill., 1934-43; asst. state dir. Div. Vocational Rehab. State Ill., Springfield, Ill., 1946—. Bd. dirs. Sangamon County Mental Health Assn., 1960-65, Ill. Tb Assn., 1958-72; bd. dirs. Springfield Urban League; bd. dirs. Land of Lincoln Goodwill Industries, 1960-72, pres., 1966-71, pres. emeritus, 1971—. Served from 3d officer to capt., WAC, 1943-46. Mem. Am. Legion (post comdr. 1952-53, state rehab. com. for women vets. 1956-59), Am. Legion Auxiliary, Ill. Rehab. Assn. (pres. 1957), Ill. Welfare Assn. (dir. 1956-58, 1st state chmn. functional div. rehab. dir. 1956-58), Ill. Pub. Health Assn., Ill. Conf. Respiratory Disease Workers, Ill. Hist. Soc., Nat. Hist. Soc., Nat. Geog. Soc., YWCA, Franklin Mint Coin Club, Delta Sigma Omicron. Mem. Christian Ch. Club: Altrusa. Home: PO Box 387 Hickory Ridge Lane Shelbyville IL 62562 Office: 227 S 7th St Springfield IL 62706

MOYNAHAN, ELIZABETH REILLY (MRS. JULIAN LANE MOYNAHAN), architect; b. Jamaica Plain, Mass., June 6, 1925; d. Eugene Edward and Mary Ellen (McNeese) Reilly; A.B., Radcliffe Coll., 1946; M. Arch., Harvard, 1952; m. Julian Lane Moynahan, Aug. 6, 1945; children—Catherin Maria, Brigid Elizabeth, Mary Ellen. Draftsman, Albert Goldberg Engr. Inc., Boston, 1948-52; James Harris, architect, Cambridge, Mass., 1952-55; designer, Fulmer and Bowers, Princeton, N.J. 1955-58; architect Ronald Vaughn Assos. architects, 1958-66; individual practice, Princeton, 1966—. Vis. critic Archtl. Sch., Dublin Ireland, 1966; vis. prof., U. Utah, 1974; instr. Princeton Adult Sch., 1968—. Mem. Lawrence Township (N.J.) Bldg. Commn., 1968—. Mem. A.I.A., N.J. Soc. Architects (chmn. careers com. 1973-74, mem. exec. bd. 1973—). Democrat. Prin. works include: Health, Edn. and Welfare Neighborhood Facilities Center, N.J.; Bell Telephone of N.J. Tng. Sch.; Office Bldg., Lawrence, N.J. Address: 3439 Lawrenceville Rd Princeton NJ 08540

MOZLEY, DOROTHY, librarian; b. Boston, Apr. 12, 1916; d. Fred and Mabel Dudley (Snow) Mozley; B.A., Russell Sage Coll., 1937; B.S., Simmons Coll., 1945; postgrad. Katharine Gibbs Sch., 1938. Sec., Oak Grove Sch., Vassalboro, Me., 1938-40; editor Bellman Pub. Co., Boston, 1940-41; asst. supr. index dept. Rec. and Statis. Corp., 1941-44; library asst. Enoch Pratt Free Library, Balt., 1945-47; librarian Mass. Mut. Life Ins. Co., Springfield, 1947-49; head. reference dept. Life Ins. Agy. Mgmt. Assn., Hartford, Conn., 1949-50; reference asst., genealogy and local history librarian Springfield (Mass.) City Library, 1950—. Mem. Am., Mass., New Eng. Western Mass. library assns., New Eng. Historic Geneal. Soc., Western Mass. Geneal. Soc., Am. Assn. State and Local History, Friends of The Quadrangle-Springfield Library and Mus. Assn., Friends of Oral History Center Am. Internat. Coll., Adult Edn. Assn., Russell Sage Coll., Simmons Coll. alumnae assns. Independent. Conglist. Home: 252 Union St Springfield MA 01105 Office: Springfield City Library 220 State St Springfield MA 01103

MRAZ, RUTH REED (MRS. ARTHUR J. MRAZ), ednl. adminstr.; b. Ft. Fairfield, Me., Feb. 8, 1927; d. Walter Manley and Eva Ruth (Seeley) Reed; student R.I. Sch. Design, 1945-46; A.A., Erskine Coll., 1948; student Boston U., 1946-48; m. Arthur J. Mraz, Aug. 7, 1948; children—Randall, Nancy. Feature writer, dist. corr. Gannett Pub. Co., Portland, Me., 1959-70; dir. univ. relations U. Me., Presque Isle, 1970—. Free-lance writer, 1959—; cons. pub. relations, also antiques and restorations. Mem. Me Potato Blossom Festival Com., 1960—; mem. Gov.'s Task Force for Rehab., 1968-69, Me. State Museum Commn., 1966—. Bd. dirs. N.E. Dist. YMCA, 1968-71, Me. YMCA, 1969-72; bd. dirs. Found. U. Me. at Presque Isle, 1973—, clk., 1972—. Recipient Woman of Yr. award Philomathian Club, 1968. Mem. Am. Coll. Pub. Relations Assn. (New Eng. membership chmn. 1973—, hospitality chmn. 1973-74), Beta Sigma Phi (hon.). Club: Philomathian (pres. 1952-53) (Fort Fairfield, Me.). Home: Monson Pond Fort Fairfield ME 04742 Office: U Maine at Presque Isle Presque Isle ME 04769

MRAZEK, THELMA STEVENS (MRS. JAMES E. MRAZEK), writer, editor, assn. exec.; b. Macon, Ga., Sept. 22, 1930; d. Samuel Levi and Vivian Chloe (Pierce) Stevens; B.A., Duke U., 1952; M.A., U. Pa., 1954; m. James Edward Mrazek, Nov. 28, 1970. Mem. staff Congressman Charles E. Bennett of Fla., Washington, 1952-53; adminstrv. and editorial work Fgn. Policy Assn., N.Y.C., 1954-61; chief research World Events, 1962-63, The Science Library, 1964-66, Great Ages of Man, Time Life Books, Time, Inc., N.Y.C., 1966; editor The Challenge of Crime in a Free Soc., Pres. Commn. on the Adminstrn. of Justice, Nat. Crime Commn., Washington, 1966-67; founder, editor Appalachia, dir. tech. information services, Appalachian Regional Commn., Washington, 1967-71, free lance editor and writer, 1971-74; dir. communications Mech. Contractors Assn. Am., Inc., Washington, 1974—. Interne, UN, N.Y.C., 1954. Recipient 1st prize award Fed. Editors Assns., 1968, 3d prize, 1969; commendation Appalachian Regional Commn., 1970. Democrat. Contbr. articles to profl. pubs. Address: 8811 Colesville Rd Silver Spring MD 20910

MROZINSKI, MILDRED B. FISHER (MRS. MICHAEL E. MROZINSKI), banker; b. South St. Paul, Minn., Mar. 29, 1922; d. John and Anna (Kuntz) Fisher; grad. Sch. Banking U. Wis. at Madison, 1971—; m. Michael E. Mrozinski, Sept. 28, 1946. With Drovers State Bank, South Saint Paul, Minn., 1941—, successively clk., bookkeeping dept., teller, head paying and receiving teller, in charge savs. dept., 1941-63, asst. cashier, 1964-66, asst. v.p., 1967-71, v.p., 1971—. Mem. Nat. Assn. Bank Women, Am. Inst. Banking, Bus. and Profl. Womens Group (treas. 1964-65). Club: Southview Country. Home: 604 7th St S South St Paul MN 55075 Office: 633 S Concord St South St Paul MN 55075

MUCHA, MARY ANN JANE, physician; b. Noranda, Que., Can., Oct. 25, 1944; d. Alex Sacha and Therese (Cadieux) Mucha; B.A., U. Ottawa (Ont., Can.), 1965, M.D., 1969. Intern U. Alta. (Can.) Hosp., Edmonton; resident Vancouver (B.C., Can.) Gen. Hosp., 1970-71; practice gen. medicine, Shawville, Que., 1971-72, Maniwaki, Que., 1973—; mem. staffs Riverside Hosp., Ottawa, Grace Hosp., Ottawa. Mem. Ont. Med. Assn. Office: 1516 D Merivale Rd Ottawa ON Canada

MUCHA, MARY JO, educator; b. Gary, Ind., June 5, 1949; d. Joseph John and Mary Vincent (Ippolito) Mucha; B.S. in Journalism (Demotte journalism scholar), Ball State U., 1971; M.S. in Edn., Ind. State U., 1973; postgrad. Purdue U. Tchr. English, psychology, journalism West Side High Sch., Gary, Ind., 1971—. Counselor, Rapline, Gary, 1971-73. Mem. Am. Humanist Assn., Women in Communications, Sigma Delta Chi. Clubs: Press, Headliner (Chgo.). Home: 6949 Birch Av Gary IN 46403 Office: 9th Av and Gerry St Gary IN 46405

MUCK, RUTH EVELYN SLACER (MRS. GORDON E. MUCK), educator; b. Buffalo, July 17, 1910; d. Robert A. and Hattie E. (Sheridan) Slacer; B.S., State U. Coll. at Buffalo, 1938, M.S., 1952; Ed.D., State U. N.Y. at Buffalo, 1966; m. Gordon E. Muck, Dec. 27, 1934; 1 dau., Linda Mae (Mrs. Richard Wezolowski). Tchr. pub. schs., Lockport, N.Y., 1931-42; tchr. primary level campus sch. State U. Coll., Buffalo, 1942-66, prof. edn. div. elementary edn. 1966—. Cons. tchr. edn. workshops, Minn., Fla. Mem. Assn. Tchr. Educators (state pres. 1972-73), Internat. Reading Assn. (chmn. 1969-71), Delta Kappa Gamma, Pi Lambda Theta. Methodist (dir. youth edn. 1960-69). Home: 1091 Stony Point Rd Grand Island NY 14072 Office: 1300 Elmwood Av Buffalo NY 14222

MUCKELSTON, SANDRA R., univ. dean; b. Lewistown, Mont., June 23, 1944; d. Oren F. and Alyce G. (Nation) Muckelston; B.A., Rocky Mountain Coll., 1967; J.D., U. Mont., 1971. Admitted to Mont. bar, Fed. bar, 1971; research analyst, counsel Mont. Constntl. Conv., 1971-72; asst. prof. torts, asst. dean Law Sch., U. Mont., Missoula, 1972—. Cons. local govt. research project Mont. County Commrs. Assn., 1972-73; mem. U. Mont. Faculty Senate, 1973-74. lMem. Gov.'s Commn. on Status of Women, 1972—; mem. Equal Rights Amendment Ratification Council, 1973. Mem. Nat. Orgn. Women. Contbr. articles to profl. jours. Office: U Mont Missoula MT 59801

MUDD, EMILY HARTSHORNE, counselor, educator; b. Merion, Pa., Sept. 6, 1898; d. Edward Yarnall and Clementine (Rhodes) Hartshorne; M. Social Work, U. Pa., 1936, Ph.D., 1950, D.Sc. (hon.), 1972; D.Sc. (hon.), Hobart and William Smith Colls., 1958; D.H.L., Washington and Jefferson Coll., 1973; m. Stuart Mudd, Sept. 12, 1922; children—Emily Borie (Mrs. Emily Mitchell), Stuart Harvey, Margaret Clark, John Hodgen. Vol. research asst. Harvard Med. Sch., Rockefeller Inst., N.Y.C., Henry Phipps Inst. for Tb, Phila., Sch. Medicine U. Pa., 1922-33; dir. Marriage Council of Phila., 1936-67, cons., 1967—; asst. prof., also dir. div. family study in psychiatry U. Pa., 1952-56, prof., 1956-67, prof. emeritus, 1967—, cons. behavioral sci., div. human reprodn., dept. obstetrics and gynecology Sch. Medicine, 1969—, vis. prof. family relationships, 1969—; asso. dept. psychiatry Pa. div. Phila. Gen. Hosp., 1970—; vis. prof. to upgrade skills of med., social work and outreach personnel Jessie Smith Noyes Found.; prin. investigator research marriage counseling USPHS, 1947-55, on alcoholism and marital conflict, Dept. Health Commonwealth of Pa., 1955-65; faculty marriage counseling V.A. Resident Tng. Program for Psychiatrists in Phila., 1947-64; mem. adv. com. family div. Health and Welfare Council, Phila., 1956-58. Family Life subcom. Pub. Affairs Pamphlets, New York, 1957—; asso. dir. continuing edn. Reproductive Biology Research Found., St. Louis, 1970—; cons. Ency. Mental Health, 1961-63, Family Health Program in Miss., 1969-72. Lectr. at Bryn Mawr Coll. and Swarthmore Coll., 1940-55. Mem. steering com. Social Work Research Group, 1949-52; profl. adv. com. Pa. Mental Health, Inc., 1953; chmn. exec. com. Interprofessional Commn. Marriage and Divorce Laws and Family Cts. (sponsored by Am. Bar Assn.), 1951-57; vice chmn. gov.'s adv. council on alcoholism Pa. Dept. Health, 1963-67; mem. task force on alcoholism Comprehensive Mental Health Plan, Dept. Welfare, 1964; exec. com., bd. dirs. Pathfinder Fund, Boston, 1969—; mem. bd. Sex Information Edn. Council U.S., 1964-70; co-chmn. Pa. Abortion Law Commn.; nat. adv. bd. Assn. Couples for Marriage Enrichment; adv. bd. Family Center Assos., Lexington, 1974—, Women in Transition, Phila., 1974—. Named Pa. Mother of the Year, 1961; recipient John Fleming medal Am. Inst. Geonomy and Natural Resources, 1967; recipient Medaille D'Honneur, 1966. Fellow Am. Assn. Marriage Counselors (past pres.), World Acad. Art and Sci. (exec. com. Am. div.), Am. Sociol. Soc., Am. Orthopsychiat. Assn., Coll. Physicians Phila. (hon.); mem. Soc. Sci. Study of Sex, Nat. Council on Family Relations (dir. 1963-68), Royal Soc. Promotion Health London, Am. Assn. Social Workers, Am. Group Psychotherapy Assn., Internat. Platform Assn., Gen. Alumni Soc. Grad. Sch. U. Pa. (exec. com.; rep. of Grad. Sch. Arts and Scis.), Acad. Certified Social Workers. Club: Cosmopolitan (Phila.). Author: The Practice of Marriage Counseling, 1951: co-author: Success in Family Living, 1965; also articles profl. and lay jours. Co-editor: Readings on Marriage and Family Relations, 1954; Man and Wife, a Source-book on Family Attitudes, Sexual Behavior and Marriage Counseling, 1957; Marriage Counseling: A Casebook, 1958; (with Robert C. Leslie) Professional Growth for Clergymen Through Supervised Training in Marriage Counseling And in Family Problems, 1970. Asso. editor Jour. of Marriage and the Family, 1963-67. Home: 734 Millbrook Lane Haverford PA 19041 Office: Room 1023 Courtyard Bldg Hosp U Pa 34th and Spruce St Philadelphia PA 19104

MUDGE, JOY JEAN NORTH (MRS. GLEN R. MUDGE), librarian; b. Cleve., Mar. 14, 1929; d. John Edward and Doris Eileen (McKinnon) North; A.B., Beaver Coll., 1951; postgrad. Kent State U., 1955; M.S., Wayne State U., 1962; m. Glen R. Mudge, Dec. 27, 1955. Tchr., Glenmoor Sch., East Liverpool, O., 1951-55; librarian Wayne State U., Detroit, 1955-58; librarian Oak Park, Clinton Jr. high schs., Oak Park, Mich., 1958-68; dir. sch. librarian Charlevoix (Mich.) Schs., 1968—. Named Girl Scout Career Woman of Yr., East Liverpool, 1963. Mem. A.L.A., Mich. Sch. Librarians Assn., Alpha Delta Kappa,

Pi Lambda Theta. Home: Box 96A Ellsworth MI 49729 Office: Charlevoix Pub Schs Garfield St Charlevoix MI 49720

MUDGE, RHEA AMANDINE (MRS. GROVER C. MUDGE, JR.), lawyer; b. Trenton, Feb. 9, 1909; d. Pasquale A. and Carmela (Sena) Cella; LL.B., N.J. Law Sch., 1929; postgrad. Rider Coll., 1930-32; J.D., Rutgers U., 1970; m. Grover C. Mudge, Jr., Aug. 30, 1949; 1 son, Braddock S. Social case worker, welfare dept. City of Trenton, 1929-31; admitted to N.J. bar, 1930, since practiced in Trenton. Supr. intake and certification Fed. Works Program, Trenton, 1931-35; chief clk., exec. sec. OPA, Trenton, 1942-45; vocational and ednl. counsellor, separation div. Army Dept., Fort Dix, N.J., 1946-48; chief clk. SSS, Trenton, 1949-53. Soprano soloist with Eagle Philharmonic Band. Mem. Mercer County Bar Assn. Mem. Order Eastern Star. Episcopalian (soloist 1945-60). Republican. Club: Contemporary of Trenton. Address: 25 Mountain View Rd Trenton NJ 08628

MUECK, LENORA CAROLINA, mortgage banker; b. San Diego, Tex., Oct. 26, 1935; d. William and Hortensia (Rios) Mueck; student Am. Inst. Banking, 1954-69, Tex. State Coll. Women, 1954, Stanford, 1970-71; grad. Sch. Mortgage Banking, Northwestern U., 1972. Processor land div. City of San Antonio, 1954-57; with Broadway Nat. Bank, 1957-63, loan processor Mortgage Loan Dept., 1958-61, 62-63; real estate loan processor Mfrs. Bank, Los Angeles, 1963-69, dept. supr., 1969-72, asst. sec., 1969-72, asst. v.p., 1972-73; v.p. Bradley Mortgage Co., Los Angeles, 1973—. Bd. dirs. Los Angeles Escrow Assn. Ednl. Scholarship Fund, 1968-72. Mem. Los Angeles Escrow Assn. (pres. 1974), Nat. Assn. Bank Women, Mortgage Bankers Assn., Nat. Assn. Women in Constrn., Smithsonian Assos., League Women Voters. Home: 412 S Verdugo Rd Glendale CA 91502 Office: 5655 Wilshire Blvd Los Angeles CA 90037

MUEHL, LOIS BAKER (MRS. SIEGMAR MUEHL), educator; b. Oak Park, Ill., Apr. 29, 1920; d. Arthur Franklin and Mary Ellen (Hull) Baker; B.A., Oberlin Coll., 1941; M.A., U. Ia., 1967; m. Siegmar Muehl, Apr. 15, 1944; children—Erika, Sigrid, Torsten and Brian (twins). Tchr. high sch. English, Ohio, 1941-42; with WBKB-TV, Chgo., 1942-43; ad writer, news commentator Radio Sta. WIS, Columbia, S.C., 1944; tchr. creative writing, adult edn., Iowa City, Ia., 1960-65; faculty U. Ia., Iowa City, 1965-67, 69—, asst. prof. communication, dir. reading lab., rhetoric program, 1965—; reading specialist Johnson C. Smith U., Charlotte, N.C., 1967-69. Recipient Old Gold Creative fellowship, 1970. Mem. Internat. Reading Assn., Nat. Council Tchrs. English, Ia. Hist. Soc., Phi Beta Kappa. Author: My Name Is (Jr. Lit. Guild selection), 1959; Worst Room in the School, 1961; The Hidden Year of Devlin Bates, 1967. Contbr. articles to profl. jours. Home: 430 Crestview Iowa City IA 52240

MUEHLBERG, NANCY RUTH, psychologist; b. Flint, Mich., Sept. 30, 1943; d. John Robert and Harriet Winifred (Quick) Muehlberg; B.A., State U. N.Y. at Buffalo, 1967, M.A., 1969, Ph.D., 1971. Psychologist child devel. program Children's Hosp., Buffalo, 1968-73, psychologist Speech and Hearing Clinic, 1972—, psychologist Child Psychiatry Clinic, 1973—; psychologist Buffalo Hearing and Speech Center, 1972-73, cons., 1973—. Mem. Am. Psychol. Assn. Home: 9233 Main St Clarence NY 14031 Office: 219 Bryant St Buffalo NY 14222

MUEHLECK, REBECCA BREWER (MRS. J. ROBERT MUEHLECK), librarian; b. Trenton, N.J.; d. Eben Joseph and Mary Lillian (Howard) Brewer; A.B cum laude, Mt. Holyoke Coll., 1940; B.S., Columbia, 1941; m. J. Robert Muehleck, Apr. 15, 1944; children—Robin (Mrs. Robert W. Brown), Robert Eben. With reference dept. Trenton Free Pub. Library, 1957—, head reference dept., 1960—. Mem. Trenton commn. N.J. Tercentenary, 1962-64, Trenton Bicentennial Commn., 1973—, Trenton Museum Commn., 1971—. Mem. N.J. Library Assn. (editor N.J. Bibliographer, 1962-67, pres. history and bibliography sec. 1968-69), Trenton Hist. Soc. (v.p. 1972—). Home: 322 S Main St Pennington NJ 08534 Office: 120 Academy St Trenton NJ 08608

MUEHLMEIER, RUTH EWART (MRS. PEYTON ALBERT MUEHLMEIER), artist, educator; b. Milw., Oct. 13, 1925; d. William Gladstone and Mabel (Anderson) Ewart; student Wis. State Coll., 1943-46; B.F.A., Chgo. Art Inst., 1948, postgrad. 1960; postgrad. New Sch. Social Research, 1949; m. Peyton Albert Muehlmeier, Jan. 24, 1951; children—Christine, Pamela, Peyton Scot, Daniel. One-man shows Milw. Art Inst., Coll. Women's Club, Brookfield High Sch., Milw. Jewish Center, Milw. Art Center, Rental Gallery, Cardinal Stritch Coll., Layton Sch. Art; exhibited in group shows at Wis. Salon, Walker Art Gallery, Jacques Seligman Gallery, Atelier Gallery; represented in permanent collections Milw. Art Center, Chgo. Art Inst.; murals executed at Wauwatosa Presbyn. Ch., Muridale Sanitorium, Blue Crest Motel, Brookfield Congl. Ch., others; tchr. Milw. Art Inst., 1945, 47-48, 60, Cardinal Stritch Coll., 1949-51; indsl. designer Karl Brocken Assn., Milw., 1949-50; textile designer, N.Y.C. and Nantucket, N.Y., 1948-49; lectr. Milw. Art Center, 1958-67, U. Wis. at Milw., 1963; tchr. art history Layton Sch. of Art, Milw., 1963; tchr. art history Layton Sch. of Art, Milw., 1959—; chmn. art history dept. Marquette U., 1954—. Layton art travel grantee, 1965. Mem. Wis. Painters and Sculptors (pres. 1966-67, 70-72, dir. 1968-73), Nat. League Am. Pen Women, Wis. Designer Craftsmen. Conglist. Home: Design Contract Comml Interiors Wildwood 2919 W Mill Rd Oconomowoc WI 53066

MUELLER, SISTER GERARDINE L., artist; b. Newark, Sept. 16, 1921; d. Francis Joseph and Teresa Barbara (Saalmuller) Mueller; B.A., Caldwell Coll., 1954; M.A., Notre Dame U., 1959, M.F.A., 1966; postgrad. Instituto Cultural, Guadalajara, Mexico, 1971. Art tchr. St. Dominic Acad., Jersey City, 1954-63, Fordham U., summer 1961; chmn. art dept. Caldwell (N.J.) Coll., 1963—. Chmn. art syllabus Secondary Schs. of Newark Archdiocese; seminar dir. pre-Colombian art and architecture, Mexico; mem. fine arts com. N.J. Dept. Higher Edn., 1973; lectr. in field. Mem. Caldwell Twp. Bicentenary Com. Trustee Mt. St. Dominic, Caldwell. Mem. Coll. Art Assn., Nat. Art Edn. Assn., Art Educators N.J., Am. Craftsmen's Council, Soc. for Italic Handwriting, Miniature Art Soc. N.J., Cath. Fine Arts Soc. (pres. 1969-71). Works include: walnut sculpture Last Supper, mosaic mural panels Caldwell Coll.; mosaic design Notre Dame U.; liturgical hanging Holy Cross Sem., South Bend, Ind.; stained glass windows St. Catherine's Convent, Caldwell; exhibited N.J. Artists nat. tour, 1969, 72-74; lettered, illuminated book Ceremonial, 1966. Home: Caldwell College Caldwell NJ 07006

MUELLER, IRIS WESSEL (MRS. WHEELER KAY MUELLER, JR.), coll. dean; b. St. Louis, Oct. 20, 1928; d. Cecil Henry and Dorothy Mary (Luetkenholder) Wessel; A.B., Washington U., 1948, M.A., 1949; Ph.D., U. Ill., Urbana, 1954; m. Wheeler Kay Mueller, Jr., July 15, 1950; 1 dau., Julie Kay. Mem. English faculty Finch Coll., N.Y.C., 1954—, prof., 1971—, dean, 1970—. Recipient Jessie Barr fellow, Washington U., 1948; teaching fellow U. Ill., Urbana, 1949-53. Mem. Modern Lang. Assn., Am. Assn. U. Profs., Am. Conf. Acad. Deans, Am. Assn. Higher Edn., Phi Beta Kappa, Kappa Delta Phi, Phi Kappa Phi. Author: John Stuart Mill and French Thought, 1954. Home: 340 W 28th St New York City NY 10001 Office: 52 E 78th St New York City NY 10021

MUELLER, LAURA ANN, physician; b. Grant City, Mo., Mar. 3, 1942; d. Hollis Clark and Helen Lena (Cousins) Seat; B.A., U. Mo., 1964, M.D., 1968; A.A., S.W. Baptist Coll.; m. Robert Dwight Mueller, Sept. 6, 1964; children—Amy Rae, Heidi Jo. Intern Swedish Hosp., Seattle; gen. practice, Seattle, 1969-70; med. dir. methadone maintenance program Puget Sound Social Programs, Inc., Seattle, 1970-73; physician Alcoholism Center Assos., Inc., Kirkland, Wash., 1973—. Mem. Wash., King County med. socs. Home: 636 154th Av SE Bellevue WA 98007 Office: 10322 NE 132d St Kirkland WA 98033

MUELLER, MARION LOUISE BEYER (MRS. LOTHAR W. MUELLER), sales and advt. exec.; b. Detroit, Dec. 25, 1922; d. Carl August and Anna (Werth) Beyer; B.S., Wayne State U., 1946, postgrad., 1946-47; m. Lothar W. Mueller, Aug. 21, 1948; children—Paul, Susan. Tchr. Detroit Pub. Schs., 1945-46, Highland Park (Mich.) Pub. Sch., 1946-49; bus. mgr. Harlo Printing Co., Highland Park, Mich., 1949—; in charge sales, advt. Harlo Press, Highland Park, 1964—, Wayfarer Travel Books, Highland Park, 1968—. Sec. Am. Tradion Corp., 1958-61. Pres. Oakland County Afflicted Infants Found., 1955. Mem. Art Edn. Alumni Assn. (pres. 1950-51). Club: Highland Park Women's (pres. Alpha chpt. 1963-64). Home: 424 W Oakridge St Ferndale MI 48220 Office: 16721 Hamilton St Highland Park MI 48203

MUELLER, NANCY SCHNEIDER (MRS. HELMUT C. MUELLER), educator; b. Wooster, O., Mar. 8, 1933; d. Gilbert D. and Winifred P. (Porter) Schneider; A.B., Coll. Wooster, 1955; M.S., U. Wis., 1957, Ph.D., 1962; m. Helmut C. Mueller, Jan. 29, 1959; 1 son, Karl. Hon. fellow, instr. zoology U. Wis., Madison, 1965-66; vis. asst. prof. zoology N.C. State U., Raleigh, 1968-71; vis. prof. biology N.C. Central U., Durham, 1971-72, asso. prof. biology, 1972—. Mem. Am. Soc. Cell Biology, Am. Soc. Zoologists, Assn. Women in Sci., Am. Civil Liberties Union, Sigma Xi, Beta Kappa Chi. Home: Route 5 Box 103 Chapel Hill NC 27514

MUELLER, PATRICIA ANN, psychiatrist; b. Dallas, Oct. 19, 1940; d. Nicholas John and Sarah Jane (Matthews) M.; B.A., Earlham Coll., 1962; M.D., U. Chgo., 1966; tng. Chgo. Inst. Psychoanalysis, 1972—. Intern, Michael Reese Hosp., Chgo., 1966-67, resident psychiatry, 1967-70; pvt. practice medicine specializing in psychiatry, Chgo., 1970—; asst. dir. outpatient clinic Ill. State Psychiat. Inst., 1970—, tchr. social work and med. students, 1970—; mem. faculty U. Ill. Med. Sch., 1971—. Home: 5519 S Hyde Park Blvd Chicago IL 60615 Office: 55 E Washington St Chicago IL 60602

MUELLER, SABINA GERTRUDE (MRS. ROBERT N. SULGROVE II), botanist, county ofcl.; b. Binghamton, N.Y., Apr. 29, 1940; d. F.W. Hellmut and Dorothea (Hofmann) Mueller; B.A., Swarthmore Coll., 1961; Ph.D. (NSF Summer Grad. Teaching fellow, Coker fellow), U. N.C., 1968; m. Robert N. Sulgrove II, Dec. 19, 1970; children—Rebecca Lynn, David Robert. Asst. prof. botany Shippensburg (Pa.) State Coll., 1966-68, asso. prof., 1968-70; mem. staff plant records Cox Arboretum, Dayton, O., 1972-73, botanist ednl. services, div. Dayton-Montgomery County Park Dist. 1973—. Bd. dirs. Dayton Council of Garden Clubs, horticulture chmn., 1973, 74. Mem. Internat. Assn. Plant Taxonomists, Am. Hort. Soc., Am. Assn. Bot. Gardens and Arboreta., Am. Daffodil Soc., Am. Assn. U. Women. Clubs: Hillview Garden, Welcome Wagon Garden. Home: 5512 Woodbridge Lane Dayton OH 45429 Office: Cox Arboretum 6733 Springboro Pike Dayton OH 45449

MUELLER, VIRGINIA SCHWARTZ (MRS. PAUL F. C. MUELLER), lawyer; b. Palo Alto, Cal., Apr. 27, 1924; d. William Leonard and Anstrice (Bryant) Schwartz; B.A., Stanford, 1944; LL.B., Cornell, 1946; Docteur en Droit de L'Universite de Paris, U. Paris, 1950; m. Paul Frederick Charles Mueller, Sept. 24, 1945; children—Christian William, Lisa. Admitted to Cal. bar, 1946, Wash. bar, 1952, before Supreme Ct., 1966; research atty., 1st Dist. Ct. of Appeal, Div. 1, State of Cal., 1946-49; individual practice law, 1949-53, 71—; dep. pros. atty. King County, Wash., 1953-56; dep. supr. Inheritance Tax Div., Tax Commn. of State of Wash., 1956-58; dep. dist. atty., Sacramento, 1959-66; counsel Legal Aid Soc. Sacramento County, 1966-71. Co-chmn. Stanford Conf. of Sacramento, 1961; pres. Community Welfare Council of Greater Sacramento Area, Inc., 1964-66; women's adv. council State Cal. Fair Employment Practice Commn., 1964— rep. No. Cal., U.S. com. UNICEF, 1972—. Credentials chmn. 3d Congl. Dist. Council of Democratic Clubs, 1964; pres. Dem. Women's Club, 1964; del. Dem. nat. conv., 1972. Bd. dirs. Vis. Nurse Assn., Sacramento, 1961-64; sec. adv. council Fairhaven Home and Hosp., 1961-64; mem. com. for History and Art, Stanford Law Sch., 1971—, chmn. bd. visitors spl. com. on women in law, 1973—. Mem. Nat. Dist. Attys. Assn. (pres. pros. atty.'s seminar, 1966), Am. (chmn. internat. cts. com. internat. law sect. 1974—), Fed. (v.p. Sacramento chpt. 1971-72, 73-74), Wash., Cal., Sacramento County bar assns., Queen's Bench, Thurston County Mental Health Assn. (pres. 1957-58), World Affairs Council Sacramento (pres. 1971-72), World Peace Through Law Center (rapporteur Abidjian world conf. 1973), Am. Assn. U. Women (bd. dirs. Olympia br. 1957-58, state legislative com., Cal., 1960-65, legislative advocate, 1960-65, 66-70), Causeries Francaises (pres. 1963-64), Federation Internationale des Femmes des Carrieres Juridiques (mem. bd. 1967—), Women Lawyers of Sacramento (treas. 1964, pres. 1965-66), Assn. Internat. du Droit Penal (Am. sect.), People to People, UNA-U.S.A. (pres. Sacramento chpt. 1969-71, pres. No. Cal. council 1970-71), Cornell Law Assn., Phi Delta Delta, Delta Sigma Rho. Clubs: Stanford Women's (pres. 1961-62) (Sacramento); Soroptimist (dir. Sacramento 1963-65, 72-73, v.p. 1973-74). Author article profl. jour. Home: 4310 Moss Dr Sacramento CA 95822 Office: 3401 Freeport Blvd Suite 4 Sacramento CA 95818

MUETH, JANE ELLEN, educator; b. Bellevill, Ill., Feb. 19, 1946; d. Charles John and Marjorie Jane (Hempen) Mueth; A.A., Belleville Jr. Coll., 1966; B.A., So. Ill. Univ., 1969. Tchr. oral communication, theatre Belleville Twp. High Sch. W., 1970—. Mem. Cath. Youth Orgn., sec., 1963-64. Mem. Am., Ill. Speech theatre assns., Delta Psi Omega. Home: 300 N 49th St Belleville IL 62223

MUFSON, ANN MAUSER (MRS. MARVIN R. MUFSON), lawyer; b. N.Y.C., July 3, 1935; d. Charles and Syd (Feldstein) Mauser; A.B., Goucher Coll., 1955; LL.B., Columbia, 1958; m. Marvin R. Mufson, June 2, 1956; children—Steven, Laura, Daniel. Admitted to N.Y. bar, 1958, N.J. bar, 1965; mem. firms Cravath, Swaine & Moore, N.Y.C., 1958-59; part-time asso. Jerome N. Wanshel, Larchmont, 1959-60; individual practice, Bronxville, N.Y., 1960-62; researcher Hutt & Berkow, Perth Amboy, N.J., 1963; organizer, asst. adminstr. Middlesex County Legal Services Corp., New Brunswick, 1966—. Bd. dirs. N.J. Welfare Council. Recipient community service award Am. Assn. U. Women, 1967. Mem. N.J., Middlesex County bar assns., Perth Amboy Hosp. Women's Aux., Phi Beta Kappa. Jewish religion. Mem. Hadassah, B'nai B'rith. Home: 43 Clive Hills Rd Edison NJ 08817 Office: 335 George St New Brunswick NJ 08903

MUHICH, DOLORES ROSE KLOBUCAR, ednl. psychologist; b. Muskegon Heights, Mich., Nov. 7, 1926; d. Stephen and Rose (Slobodnik) Klobucher; B.S. in Edn., So. Ill. U., 1961, M.S. in Edn., 1966, Ph.D., 1970; m. Frank William Muhich, June 16, 1946; children—Frank William, Marietta Rose, Ronald Anthony, John Stephen. Adminstrv. asst. Joliet Twp. High Sch.-W.T. Grant Co.-Assn. Commerce, Joliet, Ill., Nat. Aero. Lab., NASA, Hampton, Va., 1942-46; teaching asst., research asso. So. Ill. U., Carbondale, 1961-63, lectr., 1964, adminstrv. asso., 1966-68, asst. prof. guidance and ednl. psychology, 1970-72. Lectr., Southeastern Ill. Coll., Harrisburg, 1963; coop. office occupations coordinator Carbondale Community High Sch., 1966-67; cons. psychologist Tidewater Health Found., Norfolk, Va., 1972; cons. Ill. Commn. on Status of Women, 1972-74. Mem. Am. Psychol. Assn., Assn. for Women in Psychology (liaison chairperson 1973-74), Nat. Assn. Women Deans Adminstrs. and Counselors, Council for Advancement Psychol. Professions and Scis., Caucus for Women in Statistics, Fedn. Orgn. Profl. Women, Am. Ednl. Research Assn., Nat. Council on Measurement in Edn., Univ. and Coll. Women Ill. (acting chairperson steering com. 1972), Women's Equity Action League (convenor-pres. Ill. div. 1972-73), Nat. Orgn. Women. Contbr. articles to profl. jours. Address: 516 S University Av Carbondale IL 62901

MUILENBURG, GRACE EVELYN METCALF (MRS. VIRGIL CARL MUILENBURG), educator; b. Dexter, Kan., Sept. 19, 1913; d. Guy Emmit and Lucy Myrtie (Sinclair) Metcalf; teaching certificate Southwestern Coll., 1933; student Kan. State Tchrs. Coll. of Pittsburg, 1939-40; B.S., U. Kan., 1947; M.A., U. Mo., 1970; m. Virgil Carl Muilenburg, Dec. 28, 1936 (dec. 1939); 1 son, George Neal. Tchr. rural schs., Cowley and Chautauqua counties, Kan., 1933-37, 39-41; engring. draftsman N.Am. Aviation, Kansas City, Kan., 1943-45; drafting room supr., informational writer Kan. Geol. Survey, Lawrence, 1947-55, pub. relations dir., 1955-66; proctor Western civilization U. Kan., Lawrence, 1946-47; editor, tech. writer, research adminstrn. U. Mo., Columbia, 1966-69; asst. prof., asst. agrl. editor Kan. State U., Manhattan, 1969-74, asso. prof., asso. agrl. editor, 1974—. Pub. relations com. worker Kan. Geol. Soc., 1955, 57, 59, Midcontinent meeting Am. Assn. Petroleum Geologists, 1959, Geol. Soc. Am., 1958, 65. Mem. Geol. Soc. Am., Kan. Press Women, Nat. Fedn. Press Women, Kan. Hist. Soc., Am. Assn. Agrl. Coll. Editors, Women in Communications, Inc. Author: (with Ada Swineford) Land of the Post Rock, 1975. Home: 2075 College View Manhattan KS 66502

MUIR, HELEN, author; b. Yonkers, N.Y., Feb. 9, 1911; d. Emmet A. and Helen T. (Flaherty) Lenneham; student pub. schs.; m. William Whalley Muir, Jan. 23, 1936; children—Mary (Mrs. Frederick W. Burrell), William Torbert. With Yonkers Herald Statesman, 1929-30, 31-33, N.Y. Evening Post, 1930-31, N.Y. Evening Jour., 1933-34, Carl Byoir & Assos., N.Y.C., and Miami, Fla., 1934-35; syndicated columnist Universal Service, Miami, 1935-38; columnist Miami Herald, 1941-42; children's book editor, 1949-56; woman's editor Miami Daily News, 1943-44; free-lance mag. writer, numerous nat. mags., 1944—; drama critic Miami News, 1960-65. Trustee Coconut Grove Library Assn., Friends U. Miami Library, Friends Miami-Dade Pub. Library; bd. dirs. Miami-Dade County Pub. Library System. Recipient award Delta Kappa Gamma, 1960; Fla. Library Assn. Trustees and Friends award, 1973. Mem. Women in Communications (Community Headline award 1973). Club: Florida Women's Press (award 1963). Author: Miami, U.S.A., 1953. Home: 3855 Stewart Av Miami FL 33133

MUIRHEAD, JEAN DENMAN, lawyer, state senator; b. nr. Charleston, Miss., May 12, 1929; d. Joseph Madison and Eva (Bufkin) Denman; student Delta State Coll., 1945-47; LL.B., Jackson Sch. Law, 1967. children—Michael Denman, Walter Scott, Melissa Jean. Sec., Miss. atty. gen.'s office, 1947-50; legal sec., 1947-67; admitted to Miss. bar, 1967, since practiced in Jackson; mem. Miss. Senate, 1968-72; Miss. rep. sub-com. on hwy. beautification, 1968-72, nat. legislative transp. and hwy. safety com. Council State Govts., 1970-72; apptd. by Pres. to 1970 Assay Commn. Legislative chmn. Jackson P.T.A. Council, 1969-70; vol. counsellor Manship Youth Ct., 1969—; 1st v.p., bd. dirs. Hinds County Kidney Found. Mem. Am., Miss., Hinds County bar assns., Nat. Assn. Women Lawyers, Jackson Bus. and Profl. Womens Club, Nat. Orgn. Women (state legislative coordinator), Common Cause, Hinds County Mental Health Assn. Republican. Home: 4035 Redwing Av Jackson MS 39216 Office: Suite 203 Highland Village Jackson MS 39211

MULAC, MARGARET ELIZABETH, recreation cons.; b. Parma, O., Sept. 21, 1912; d. James Michael and Anna M. (Teska) Mulac; A.B., Western Res. U. (now Case Western Res. U.), 1930, M.A., 1953. Supr. girls and women's activities City of Cleve., 1936-43; program dir. U. Settlement, 1943-45; organizer, pres. Recreation Cons. Service, Inc., 1945-59; lectr. recreation Western Res. U. (now Case Western Res. U.), 1943—; instr. occupational therapy assisting Cuyhoga Community Coll., 1971—; diversional therapist Cleve. City Infirmary, also Highland View Hosp., 1946-53; mgr. Cleve. Golden Age Hobby Show, 1945-64; crafts and recreation dir. A. M. McGregor Home, 1960-70; tchr. Circle Work Shop, 1955-57. Planning cons. Recreation Regional Planning Assn., 1952-53; lectr. workshops for spl. services U.S. Army in Germany and France, 1957; co-chmn. Book Fair for Boys and Girls, chmn. 1966. Mem. Am. Recreation and Parks Assn., A.A.H.P.E.R., Cleve. Women's Phys. Edn. and Recreation Assn. (charter mem.), Civil Liberties Union, Council Human Relations, Consumers League. Ams. for Dem. Action. Unitarian. Author: The Playleaders Manual, 1941; The Game Book, 1946; The School Game (with Marian S. Holmes), 1950; (with Marian S. Holmes), The Party Game Book, 1951; The Fun and Games Book, 1956; Family Fun and Activities, 1958; Hobbies, the Creative Use of Leisure, 1959; The Party Fun Book, 1960; Leisure Time for Living and Retirement, 1961; Games and Stunts for Schools, Camps and Playgrounds, 1964; Educational Games for Fun, 1972. Home: 3141 Scarborough Rd Cleveland OH 44118

MULBERY, EMILY LENORE DONER (MRS. TRUMAN L. MULBERY), journalist; b. Denver, Nov. 6, 1923; d. Harold Barkley and Annie Laurie (Sanders) Doner; B.A., U. Colo., 1944, B.E., 1944; m. Truman L. Mulbery, Sept. 6, 1945; children—Ronald, Donald. Tchr. English, Spanish Amache Japanese Relocation Center, Granada, Colo., 1944-45; area corr. Pueblo (Colo.) Chieftain, 1964-67; mem. staff Lamar (Colo.) Tri-State Daily News, 1967—, corr. editor, 1967—. Episcopalian (mem. altar guild 1958—, chmn. United Thank Offering 1958—). Home: Rt 2 Box 159 Lamar CO 81052 Office: 310 S 5th St Lamar CO 81052

MULDER, LINDA ROSE MOTTL (MRS. LEE BENSON MULDER), univ. adminstr.; b. Chgo., July 4, 1945; d. Irvin Joseph and Rose Kathryn (Nyc) Mottl; B.S. with honors, U. Wis., 1967; m. Lee Benson Mulder, Sept. 16, 1967. Tchr. Madison (Wis.) Pub. Schs., 1967-68, Oshkosh (Wis.) Pub. Schs., 1968-70; spl. projects asst. to v.p. for fiscal affairs U. Health Scis. Chgo. Med. Sch., 1970-72, dir. personnel, 1972—. Mem. Coll. and Univ. Personnel Assn. Home: 1003 N Elmwood St Oak Park IL 60302 Office: 2020 W Ogden Av Chicago IL 60612

MULHAUSER, RUTH ELIZABETH, educator; b. Cleve., Nov. 20, 1913; d. Frederick Ludwig and Helen (Fletcher) Mulhauser; A.B., Oberlin Coll., 1935; M.A., Western Res. U., 1937; Ph.D., Radcliffe Coll., 1941. Instr., Coll. of Wooster, 1938-39; instr. Hiram Coll.,

1941-42; instr., asst. prof. Hollins Coll., 1942-46; asso. prof., prof. Case Western Res. U., Cleve., 1946—, chmn. romance languages, 1955-60. Decorated chevalier dans l'ordre des Palmes academiques. Mem. Modern Language Assn., Am. Assn. Tchrs. French, Renaissance Soc. Am., Am. Assn. U. Women, Phi Beta Kappa, Phi Sigma Iota. Author: (with Desberg and Saisselin) Le francais d'aujourd'hui, 1961; (with Ericksson and Forest) Foreign Languages in Elementary Schools, 1964. Editor: (with Kupersmith and Lusseyran) Albert Camus' La Chute, 1965; Sainte-Beuve Cahier de notes grecques, 1955; Sainte-Beuve and Greco-Roman Antiquity, 1969. Office: Div Modern Langs and Lit Case-Western Reserve U Cleveland OH 44106

MULHEARN, ALWINE LOUISE (MRS. LEROY SMITH), lawyer; b. Monroe, La., July 28, 1913; d. Peter Sherlock and Alwine Louise Johanna (Peters) Mulhearn; A.A., Principia Coll., 1932; J.D., Tulane, 1935; m. LeRoy Smith, 1947; children—LeRoy, Caroline (Mrs. Michael L. Thompson). Admitted to La. bar, 1935; individual practice law Tallulah, La., 1935-72; partner Mulhearn & Smith, Tallulah, 1972—; spl. asst. atty. gen. La., 1954; atty. for inheritance tax Coll. La., 1965-73; town atty., Delta, La., 1973-74; judge 16th jud. dist., La., 1974—. Former pres. Smith Abstract Co., Inc. Active Silver Waters council Girl Scouts, 1938-64, dist. dir., 1964; den mother Cub Scouts, 1956-57; pres. Band Boosters, 1964-65, P.T.A., 1965-66. Judicial bd. Delta Christian Sch., 1967—. Mem. 6th Dist. (pres. 1945), La., Am. bar assns., Am. Judicature Soc., Tallulah C. of C. (chmn. indsl. com. 1956-57). Christian Scientist. Club: Madison Parish Book. Index editor Tulane Law Rev. Bd., 1934-35. Home: 100 N Lincoln St Tallulah LA 71282 Office: 306 N Cedar St Tallulah LA 71282

MULHOLLAND, EMILIE EHMANN, pub. relations exec.; b. Phila., Apr. 4, 1934; d. Thomas Henry and Emilie (Ehmann) Mulholland; B.S., Temple U., 1955. Mem. pub. relations staff, statistician Pitts. Pirates Baseball Club, 1955-64; staff writer, office pub. information Temple U., Phila., 1964-67, asst. to dir. office pub. information, 1967-69, dir. news bur., 1969—; free-lance writer covering profl. ice hockey, 1967—. Mem. adv. com. Phila. Ret. Sr. Vol. Program. Mem. Women in Communications, Phila. Pub. Relations Assn., Phila. Club Advt. Women, Am. Assn. U. Women, Nat. Orgn. Women, Beta Gamma Sigma, Phi Alpha Theta. Club: Poor Richard (Phila.). Home: Haddon View Apts 1215E Westmont NJ 08108 Office: University News Bureau University Services Bldg Temple U Philadelphia PA 19122

MULHOLLEN, BETTY JUNE GONDER (MRS. ORANGE LYNFORD MULHOLLEN), museum curator; b. Lititz, Pa., June 11, 1923; d. Ralph William and Lillie (Mohler) Gonder; B.S., Millersville State Coll., 1950; postgrad. Pa. State U.; m. Orange Lynford Mulhollen, June 10, 1950; children—Cindy Louise (Mrs. Joseph J. Duffey), Laureen, Annalisa. Sec., Armstrong Cork Co., Lancaster, Pa., 1941-43; tchr. remedial reading Central Cambria High Sch., Ebensburg, Pa., 1967, tchr., 1967-68; curator Cambria County Hist. Soc. Museum, Ebensburg, 1969—. Served with WAVES, 1943-46. Mem. D.A.R. Mem. Order Eastern Star. Home: 604 N West St Ebensburg PA 15931 Office 521 W High St Ebensburg PA 15931

MULL, BARBARA, lawyer; b. Sacramento, Oct. 29, 1932; d. Archibald and Josephine Margaret (Richardson) Mull, Jr.; A.B., Stanford, 1954; J.D., Hastings Coll. Law, 1971. Real estate broker MacBride Real Estate, Sacramento, Cal., 1954-58; ind. real estate broker, San Francisco, 1959—. Admitted to Cal. bar, 1972; asst. court commr. Superior Ct. San Francisco, 1972—. Home: 440 Davis Ct San Francisco CA 94111 Office: City Hall San Francisco CA 94102

MULL, JANE ADDAMS, art researcher; b. Mpls., July 23, 1915; d. John Albright and Lillian (McCloud) Mull; B.A., Wellesley Coll., 1936, M.A., 1938; certificate Inst. Art and Archaeology, Paris, summer 1938. Reader, index Christian art Princeton (N.J.) U., 1938-43; researcher Am. Commn. for Protection and Salvage Artistic and Historic Monuments in War Areas, U.S. Dept. State, 1943-46; research asso., art dept. Fortune mag., N.Y.C., 1946—. Asst. editor Art Bull., 1943-44. Office: Time & Life Bldg Rockefeller Center New York City NY 10020

MULLANEY, BEATRICE HANCOCK (MRS. JOSEPH E. MULLANEY), probate judge; b. Fall River, Mass.; d. Fred and Margaret E. (O'Loughlin) Hancock; LL.B., Boston U., 1927, LL.M., 1928; LL.D., Stonehill Coll., 1956; D.Sc., Bradford Durfee Coll., 1958; m. Joseph E. Mullaney, Oct. 23, 1929 (dec. Mar. 1961); children—Vincent S., Arline (Mrs. William G. Angell), Margaret A. (Mrs. James S. Panos), Joseph E., Leonard M. Admitted to Mass. bar, 1927; practiced law Fall River, 1927-55; judge Probate Ct., Fall River, 1955—. Bd. advisers Stonehill Coll., also chmn. bd. trustees; chmn. bd. Marine Mus. Fall River. Named Lady of Equestrian Order Holy Sepulchre Jerusalem; recipient Silver Shingle award Boston U. Law Sch., 1972. Mem. Mass. Assn. Women Lawyers (bd. dirs.), Boston U. Law Sch. Alumni Assn. (mem. nat. alumni adv. bd. 1966—, v.p. 1966—), Am., Mass., Fall River bar assns., Bristol County Bar. Home: 715 High St Fall River MA 02720 Office: 441 N Main St Fall River MA 02720

MULLEN, BUELL (MRS. J. BERNARD MULLEN), artist; b. Chgo., Sept. 10; d. Charles Clinton and Modrea (Hoyne) Buell; grad. Univ. Sch. for Girls; grad. Miss Spence's Sch.; student Audubon Tyler Art Sch., Brit. Acad., Rome; studied with Petrucci and Lipinsky, Rome, Cucquier, Belgium; D.F.A., Lake Erie Coll., 1970; m. J. Bernard Mullen, Dec. 29, 1920; children—J. Bernard, Modrea Hoyne (Mrs. William H. Mitchell, Jr.), Clinton Buell. Muralist and portrait painter. After 8 years of research and experimentation has developed a method of painting on metals; this is to make the pictures permanent and to express this period of tech. devel.; works with gold, stainless steel, monel, aluminum, copper, chromium, etc. Exhibitions: Salon, Paris, Gruppo Moderno, Rome, Italy; Dayton Art Inst.; All-Ill. One-man shows: Birmingham (Ala.) Mus. of Art, also Findlay, Chgo.; Feragil, N.Y.C.; Nat. Collection of Fine Arts, Smithsonian Instn., Washington, D.C. Murals on stainless steel: Hispanic Room, Library of Congress (first mural to be painted on steel), U.S. Naval Ordnance Labs., Western Electric, Ross Hall, Great Lakes Naval Tng. Station, Searle Lab., Skokie, Ill., Ministry of War, Buenos Aires, Chase Manhattan Bank, Republic Steel Co., Case Inst. Tech., Physics Bldg., Keith Glenman Space Center; mural panels for Inland Steel, Dun & Bradstreet, I.T.&T., Gen. Motors Research, Am. Chem. Soc., North Adams Hosp., N.Y.U., Courant Inst. Math., Simon Frazer U., Vancouver, Paul Wolfe Meml. Chapel Inter-Am. U. P.R., Internat. Nickel, Internat. Minerals and Chems., other instns. Portraits on metal include: Gen. John J. Pershing, Gen. Geo. Marshall, Adm. Ben Moreell, Eugene Ormandy, Dwight D. Eisenhower, Vilhjalmur Stefansson, Jacqueline Cochran, Mme. Chiang Kai-Shek; hist. portrait Capt. James Lawrence for Battleship New Jersey; Reaching for the Ball, for Mrs. Lou Gehrig; latest portraits include: Gen. O. R. Cauldwell, Gen. Albert Wedemeyer, Cardinal Cushing, others. Rep. Internat. Assn. Arts on U.S. Nat. Commn. for UNESCO. Fellow Royal Soc. Arts; mem. Nat. Soc. Mural Painters (1st v.p.), N.Y. Fedn. Fine Arts. Clubs: Arts, Onwentsia, Architectural League, Contemporary, River, Lotos. Author: Movie Short, Painting on Metals; Art on Staines steel. Contbr. mag. articles. Studio: 222 Central Park S New York City NY 10019

MULLEN, DOROTHY JOAN, psychologist; b. Los Angeles, Aug. 29, 1929; d. Thomas James and Jean Sistine (Morigeau) Mullen; B.Mus., Immaculate Heart Coll., 1955, M.S. in Ednl. Psychology, 1959; postgrad. NSF Inst. Math., U. So. Cal., 1963-64, San Jose State NSF Inst. Math., summer 1965; M.S., Cal. State U. at Los Angeles, 1968. Tchr. parochial elementary schs., Los Angeles, 1948-58, jr. high sch., Los Angeles, 1958-62; tchr. math. Immaculate Heart High Sch., 1962-68; sch. psychologist Los Angeles County Schs. Div. Spl. Edn., Los Angeles, 1968—. Mem. Am., Western psychol. assns., Nat. Assn. Women Religious, Cal. Assn. Sch. Psychologists and Psychometrists, Foothill Assn. Sch. Psychologists. Home: 4426 Irvine Av North Hollywood CA 91602 Office: 9300 E Imperial Hwy Downey CA 90242

MULLEN, FRANCES ANDREWS (MRS. URBAN JOSEPH MULLEN), cons. edn. handicapped children; b. Chgo., Nov. 27, 1902; d. Edmund Lathrop and Ethel (Baker) Andrews; Ph.B., U. Chgo., 1923, M.A., 1927, Ph.D., 1939; m. Urban Joseph Mullen, Oct. 11, 1929; children—Urban Edmund, Ann (Mrs. Robert Cramer), William Lampe, Katherine (Mrs. Walter Dane). Tchr. high sch. math., Pocatello, Ida., 1923-25; instr. Chgo. Tchrs. Coll., 1925-26; tchr. pub. schs. Chgo., 1926-29, 31-39, 53-66, psychologist, 1939-47, prin. elementary sch., 1947-48, dir. Bur. Mentally Handicapped Children, 1949-53, asst. supt. schs. for spl. edn., 1953-66; pvt. cons. edn. handicapped children, Chgo., 1966—. Mem. psychology adv. panel Office Vocational Rehab., Dept. Health, Edn. and Welfare, 1961-63; mem. city and state bds. of youth, pvt. agys. Recipient Distinguished Service awards Chgo. Council Exceptional Children, Ill. Council Exceptional Children, 1967, N.Y. U., Ill. Epilepsy League. Diplomate Am. Bd. Examiners in Profl. Psychology. Fellow Internat. Council Psychologists (pres. 1973), Am. Psychol. Assn., Am. Orthopsychol. Assn., Am. Assn. Mental Deficience; mem. Ill. Assn. Cons. Psychologists (treas. 1944-45), Council Exceptional Children, Am. (pres., 1953-54), Ill. psychol. assns., Chgo. Psychology Club (pres., 1954-55), Council Adminstrs. Spl. Edn. in Local Sch. Systems (pres. 1961-62). Contbr. articles to profl. jours. Home and office: 2901 King Dr Chicago IL 60616

MULLEN, VIRGINIA TRUITT, zoologist; b. Wilmington, Del., Nov. 11, 1941; d. Ernest A. and Mary W. (Wilkins) Truitt; B.S., Fla. So. Coll., 1963; M.S., U. Ga., 1970; m. Michael A. Mullen, Dec. 15, 1965 (div. Apr. 1973). Tchr. biology and phys. sci. Clark County (Ga.) Schs., 1966-67; research technician R.G. Wiegert, U. Ga., 1968-70; zoologist Savannah (Ga.) Sci. Mus., 1971-73; biologist Chatham County Mosquito Control Commn., 1973—. Pres., Consumer Action Group, Athens, Ga., 1970; tchr. sailing A.R.C., Savannah, 1971. Trustee Savannah Sci. Mus., 1973—. Mem. Am., Ga. entomol. socs., Am. Mosquito Control Assn., Savannah Zool. Soc. (pres. 1973), Ecological Soc. Am., Am., Fla. anti-mosquito assns., A.A.A.S., Sigma Xi. Home: 818 Wilmington Island Rd Savannah GA 31404 Office: 1321 Eisenhower Dr Savannah GA 31405

MULLENEX, SHIRLEY LEE, mobile home mfg. co. exec.; b. Dyess, Ark., Sept. 11, 1938; d. William Robert and Lillie Lee (Stringer) Metcalf; B.S., Ark. State Coll., 1961; m. George Edward Mullenex, Dec. 19, 1964. Tchr. Cash Schs., (Ark., 1958-59, Jonesboro, 1959-60, Las Vegas, Nev., 1960-64; with Lakewood Industries, Inc., Gardena, Cal., 1965—, pres., 1970—. Bd. govs. T.C.A., 1974—. Home: 8689 Hillcrest Rd Buena Park CA 90621 Office: 18026 S Broadway St Gardena CA 90247

MULLER, ELSIE CHRISTINE, educator; b. Wakefield, Neb., Dec. 7, 1912; d. Fred George and Sophie Adele (Havekost) Muller; B.A., Wayne State Coll., 1935; M.A., U. Mich., 1944; Ph.D., Ia. State U., 1963. Tchr. math., pub. schs., Neb., S.D., Ia., Mich., 1932-47; prof. math. U. Ill., Galesburg, 1947-49, Britt (Ia.) Jr. Coll., 1949-50, LaSalle-Peru-Oglesby Jr. Coll., LaSalle, Ill., 1950-55; prof. math. Normingside Coll., Sioux City, 1955-58, 63—, chmn. math. dept., 1964—; instr. Ia. State U., Ames, 1958-63. Program chmn. Sioux City Women Democrats, 1973—. Mem. Math. Assn. Am. (state chmn. 1969-70), Nat. Council Tchrs. Math., Am. Math. Soc., A.A.A.S., Soc. Indsl. and Applied Math., Iowa Women's Polit. Caucus, Am. Assn. U. Women (treas. Sioux City 1968-70), League Women Voters (treas. Sioux City 1968-70), Sioux City Bus. and Profl. Women's Club (program chmn. 1973—), Kappa Mu Epsilon (nat. historian 1971—), Pi Mu Epsilon, Delta Kappa Gamma. Lutheran. Home: 1421 S Mulberry St Sioux City IA 51106

MULLER, EMMA FLEER, educator; b. Brillion, Wis., July 11, 1896; d. E. John and Emma (Collatz) Fleer; Mus. B., Marquette U., 1918; B.S. (Honor Entrance Scholarship 1921, Marie Mergeler scholar 1922-23, 23, 24), U. Chgo., 1923, postgrad., 1924-32, 50-53; m. Frederick H. Muller, Aug. 2, 1930 (dec. Nov. 1954); 1 son, Carl H. Instr. music Marquette U., 1915-21; organist and choir dir. Milw. and Chgo.; asst. dept. physiology U. Chgo., 1924, 25; tchr. sci. Chgo. Tchrs. Coll., 1924-28, dean, 1928-38, dir. personnel, 1938-61, ret.; dean women Woodrow Wilson Jr. Coll., 1934-37. Vol. worker Chgo. Wesley Meml. Hosp. (name changed to Northwestern Meml. Hosp. 1972), 1961—. Recipient citation from the Marquette U., 1965. Mem. Nat. (citation 1961), Ill. (citation 1953) assns. women deans and counselors, Ill. Assn. Deans Women (pres. 1940-42), Art Inst. Chgo., Lyric Opera Guild, Chgo. Symphony Soc., Am. Personnel and Guidance Assn., Ill. Guidance and Personnel Assn., Student Personnel Assn. for Tchr. Edn., Am., Ill. assns. collegiate registrars and admissions officers, Chgo. Conf. Collegiate Registrars and Admissions Officers (pres. 1953-54), Nat., Ill. edn. assns., Am. Assn. Sch. Adminstrs., Chgo. Ednl. TV Assn., Sigma Xi, Phi Beta Delta, Pi Lambda Theta, Delta Kappa Gamma, Sigma Delta Epsilon. Clubs: Woman's University, Chicago Woman's. Contbr. articles to profl. jours. Home: 1360 N Lake Shore Dr Chicago IL 60610

MULLER, JULIA KING (MRS. JON DAVID MULLER), univ. adminstr.; b. Salina, Kan., Nov. 14, 1941; d. Richard Weldon and Julia Constance (Koester) King; A.A., Stephens Coll., 1961; B.S., U. Kan., 1963; M.S., So. Ill. U., 1967; m. Jon David Muller, Jan. 27, 1963. Tchr., Stoneham (Mass.) High Sch., 1963-66; instr. elementary edn. So. Ill. U., Carbondale, 1967-68, acad. adviser, 1967-70, coordinator ednl. and cultural programming, 1970—. Mem. Nat. Assn. Women Deans, Adminstrs. and Counselors, Am. Assn. U. Women (Carbondale pres. 1973—), Phi Theta Kappa, Pi Lambda Theta. Home: 1004 Taylor Dr Carbondale IL 62901

MULLER, LYNETTE HELDMAN, educator; b. Yonkers, N.Y., Oct. 30, 1914; d. Walter A. and Henrietta Aird (Ryan) Heldman; A.B., Mt. Holyoke Coll., 1935; M.A., U. N.C., 1938; m. Donald (Medford) Muller, Sept. 28, 1940 (div. 1946); 1 dau., Jennifer. Asst. dept. drama Mt. Holyoke Coll., 1935-37; tchr. Fairfax Hall, Waynesboro, Va., 1938-39; asst. playmakers U. N.C., Chapel Hill, 1939-40; research asst. to prof. Yale U., 1941-43; tchr.-dir. drama Lower Sch., Halsted Sch., Yonkers, N.Y., 1948—, also trustee. Sec. Lincoln Republican Com., 1966-71. Bd. dirs. Jr. Workshop Westchester Dance Council. Mem. Am. Nat. Theatre Assn., Am. Ednl. Theatre Assn., Yonkers Soroptimists, Delta Kappa Gamma. Presbyn. (bd. sessions 1967). Home: 293 N Broadway Yonkers NY 10701

MULLER, MILDRED CARSON (MRS. HAROLD P. BRICK MULLER), author; b. Barstow, Tex., June 6, 1906; d. Burch and Maida Alice (Walker) Carson; B.A., U. Tex., 1925; postgrad. U. Cal. at Berkeley, 1936-37, 68; m. Harold P. Brick Muller, June 18, 1941; 1 son, Scott Carson. Elementary tchr., San Antonio, 1925-35; English tchr. Elk Grove (Cal.) High Sch., 1938-41, John Swett High Sch., Crockett, Cal., 1963-71. Pres. drs.' wives Alta Bates Hosp., Berkeley, 1960; Alta Bates vols., 1945-62. Editor, Republican Women's Bull., 1973-74. Recipient award N.E.A. Writing Contest, 1965. Mem. Am. Assn. U. Women (chmn. 1969-72), Cal. English Tchrs. Assn. (hostess 1970-71), Cal. Writers' Club, Phi Beta Kappa, Phi Mu Social (treas. 1923-25), Theta Sigma Phi. Author: seven lit. guides pub. Am. Book Co., 1970-73. Contbr. poem Nat. Poetry Anthology, 1966; also stories, articles, poems. Home: 1116 Singingwood Ct 2 Walnut Creek CA 94595

MULLER, PRISCILLA ELKOW (MRS. C. ROBERT MULLER), art historian, curator; b. Bklyn., Feb. 15, 1930; d. John and Katherine (Bulka) Elkow; A.B. cum laude, Bklyn. Coll., 1951; A.M., Inst. Fine Arts N.Y. U., 1959, Ph.D., 1963; m. C. Robert Muller, May 6, 1950. Research asst. Inst. Fine Arts N.Y. U., 1961-64; asst. curator Hispanic Soc. Am., N.Y.C., 1964-66, curator, 1966—, curator paintings, metalwork and mus., 1970—; lectr. Bklyn. Coll., 1966. Mem. Hispanic Soc. Am., Real Academia de Ciencias Bellas Letras y Nobles Artes de Cordoba (Spain) (corr.). Author: Jewels in Spain, 1500-1800, 1972. Contbr. numerous articles, exhbns. and book revs. to periodicals. Home: 41 Eastern Pkwy Brooklyn NY 11238 Office: 613 W 155th St New York City NY 10032

MULLER-EBERHARD, URSULA, med. educator; b. Goettingen, Germany, June 14, 1928; d. Ulrich and Marta (Steinhaeuser) Fleck; D.Medicine, U. Goettingen, 1953; m. Hans Muller-Eberhard, Dec. 30, 1953; children—Monika, Kristina. Came to U.S., 1954, naturalized 1966. Rotating intern Wyckoff Heights Hosp., Bklyn., 1954-55; asst. resident pediatrics Wyckoff Heights Hosp., also Kingston Av. Hosp., Bklyn., 1955-56; asst. resident pediatrics Univ. Hosp., Bellevue Med. Center, N.Y.C., 1956; fellow pediatrics Swedish Med. Research Council, U. Uppsala, 1957-59; sr. asst. resident pediatrics Bellevue Med. Center, 1959-60; fellow pediatric hematology, asst. pediatrics Cornell U. Med. Center, N.Y.C., 1960-62; instr. pediatrics, head div. pediatric hematology Bellevue Med. Center, 1962-63; asso. biochemistry Scripps Clinic and Research Found., La Jolla, Cal., 1963-69, asso. mem., 1969—; asso. adj. prof. pediatrics U. Cal. at San Diego Med. Sch., 1970—. Recipient Career Scientist award Health Research Council N.Y.C., 1962; Research Career Devel. award Nat. Inst. Arthritis and Metabolic Diseases, NIH, 1963-68, 68-71. Diplomate Am. Bd. Pediatrics. Mem. Soc. Biol. Chemists, Pediatric Research Soc., Soc. Exptl. Biology and Medicine, Am. Soc. Experimental Pathology, Am. Soc. Hematology, Am. Soc. Clin. Investigation, Am. Soc. Pharm. and Exptl. Therapy, Harvey Soc. Contbr. numerous articles profl. publs. Home: 1237 Muirlands Vista Way La Jolla CA 92037

MULLETT, ELIZABETH LOUISE MCKINNON (MRS. EDWARD J. MULLETT), educator; b. Waltham, Mass., Oct. 17, 1916; d. Warren J. and Edith F. (Tyzzer) McKinnon; B.S., Simmons Coll., 1950; Ed.M., Boston U., 1956, Ph.D., 1966; m. Edward J. Mullett, Dec. 17, 1971. Instr. Beth Israel Hosp. Sch. Nursing, Boston, 1950-58, Flint (Mich.) Community Coll., 1958-59; asso. prof. Boston U., 1965-70, U. Conn. at Storrs, 1970-72; mem. faculty Lowell (Mass.) State Coll., 1972—, asso. prof. dept. nursing, since 19—. Bd. dirs. Labourne Jr. Coll., Dorchester, Mass., 1972—. Dept. Health Edn. and Welfare Predoctoral fellow, 1960-66, Postdoctoral fellow, 1966-68. Author: (with Gerald Whipple, Mary Ann Peterson, Virginia Haines, Theodore Lerner) Acute Coronary Care, 1971. Home: 69 Hurd St Melrose MA 02176 Office: Lowell State Coll Dept Nursing Rolfe St Lowell MA 01852

MULLIGAN, BARBARA E., coll. adminstr.; b. Grand Rapids, Mich., June 25, 1927; d. Raymond Christopher and Gertrude (Moran) Mulligan; B.A., Marquette U., 1962, M.A., 1964. Instr. polit. sci., asst. dir. continuing edn. Alverno Coll., Milw., 1966-68, dir. continuing edn., 1968-71, asst. dean, 1971-72, co-dir. Research Center on Women, 1970-72; asst. dir. Div. Continuing Edn. Marquette U., 1972—. Mem. Govs. Commn. on Status of Women, 1967-71; govs. appointee Wis. Ednl. Approval Bd., 1968-71. First vice chmn. Wis. Women's Republican Club, 1964-68. Bd. dirs. Greater Milw. chpt. A.R.C., 1973-74, also personnel com., community services programs com. Mem. Adult Edn. Assn. Wis. (dir. 1969-71), Wis. Polit. Sci. Assn., (treas. 1970-72), Milw. Council Adult Learning (dir.), Adult Edn. Assn., Wis. Soc. Health and Tng., Nat. Univ. Extension Assn., Marquette U. Alumni Assn., Am. Assn. U. Women. Home: 2703 N Hackett Av Milwaukee WI 53211

MULLIN, PATRICIA EVELYN, lawyer; b. Dubuque, Ia., Aug. 13, 1926; d. Cornelius Edward and Isabelle Julia (Healey) Mullin; B.A., Clarke Coll., 1948; J.D., DePaul U., 1959. Admitted to Ia. bar, 1960, Ill. bar, 1960; with Bankers Life & Casualty Co., Chgo., 1961—, corporate and litigation atty., 1962—. Chmn. com. to select outstanding supervisory employee of yr. Chgo. Fed. Exec. Bd., 1971. Mem. Women's Bar Assn. Ill. (pres. 1970-71), Cath. Lawyers Guild Chgo. (gov. 1971). Office: 4444 W Lawrence Av Chicago IL 60630

MULLINS, JUNE BONNER, educator; b. Chgo., June 13, 1927; d. Gordon Wilson and Agnes (Russell) Bonner; B.S., U. Chgo., 1948; M.Ed., U. Pitts., 1958, Ph.D., 1968; m. William W. Mullins, June 26, 1948; children—William W., Oliver, Timothy, Garrick. Counselor emotionally disturbed children Orthogenic Sch. U. Chgo., 1946-48; tchr. disturbed and brain damaged children Western Psychiat. Inst. U. Pitts., 1958-61, asst. prof. spl. edn. and rehab., coordinator program for crippled and other health impaired, 1967-74, asso. prof., div. specialized profl. devel., Sch. of Edn., 1974—; mem. staff Home for Crippled Children, Pitts., 1960-63; tchr. Point Park Coll., Pitts., 1963-66. Mem. Am. Psychol. Assn., Council Exceptional Children, Pitts. Doctoral Assn., Pitts. Area Pre-Sch. Assn., Pitts. Assn. Arts in Edn. and Therapies, League of Women Voters (voter registration drive 1971). Contbr. articles to profl. jours. Home: 509 S Linden Av Pittsburgh PA 15208

MULQUEEN, EVELYN LOUISE (MRS. CARL F. MULQUEEN), govt. ofcl.; b. Chillicothe, O., June 1, 1912; d. John and Minnie Gertrude (Dennison) Amann; grad. high sch.; m. Carl Frederick Mulqueen, Aug. 5, 1935; children—John Joseph, James Lawrence. Clk., N.J. Div. Motor Vehicles, Pompton Lakes, 1955-59; sec. Instrument Masters, Inc., Riverdale, N.J., 1960-63; accounts receiving clk. Matzner Publs., Wayne, N.J., 1964; dep. municipal clk. Borough Pompton Lakes, 1965—. Pres., Pompton Lakes Democratic Club, 1960-61; mem. City Council, 1963. Clubs: Pompton Lakes Woman's (chmn. publicity 1972-73). Home: 36 Garden Rd Pompton Lakes NJ 07442 Office: Borough City Clerk City Hall Pompton Lakes NJ 07442

MULQUEEN, MOYA JOSEPHINE CLARKE (MRS. HERBERT J. MULQUEEN), polit. worker; b. Belfast, Ireland (came to U.S. 1922, naturalized 1928); d. Joseph Richard and Christine (O'Boyle) Clarke; B.A., Coll. New Rochelle, 1938; M.A., Fordham, 1939; m. Herbert J. Mulqueen, June 22, 1956; children—Herbert J., Jane Ann.

With Conn. Gen. Life Ins. Co., Hartford, 1942-45, Great Western Life Ins. Co., Newark, 1945-50; life ins. agt. U.S. Life, N.Y.C., 1951-56. Pres. Parents and Friends Coll., Notre Dame, Balt., 1965-67, co-chmn. inaugural com.; chmn. Millburn-Short Hills (N.J.) March of Dimes, 1961. Precinct capt. Republican Party, 1st Assembly Dist., N.Y.C., 1952-56; bd. dirs., pres. Severna Park Rep. Women's Club, 1969-70; conf. publicity chmn. Md. Fedn. Rep. Women, 1973, chmn. state fund raising, 1967-69, pub. relations chmn., 1973—; mem. nat. council Women's Nat. Rep. Club; finance com. Nat. Fedn. Rep. Women; ways and means chmn. Fedn. Rep. Women Anne Arundel County. Pres. Parents and Friends Coll. Notre Dame, 1973-74. Mem. alumnae council Coll. New Rochelle (N.Y.), 1950-54. Mem. Achievement Rewards for Coll. Scientists. Clubs: Annapolis Yacht, Sherwood Forest, Governor's (Balt.), Tail of the Fox (Timonium, Md.), Capitol Hill (Washington). Home: 121A Edgehill St Sherwood Forest MD 21405

MULRENNAN, SISTER CECILIA AGNES, educator; b. Everett, Mass., Aug. 4, 1925; d. James P. and Margaret (Grogan) Mulrennan; A.B., Regis Coll., 1946; M.S., Fordham U., 1957, Ph.D., 1959. Mem. faculty, Regis Coll., Weston, Mass., 1959—, asso. prof. biology, 1965-71, prof., 1971—, chmn. dept. biology, 1965—. Mem. Am. Genetic Assn., Sigma Xi. Address: 235 Wellesley St Weston MA 02193

MULVANEY, MARY JEAN, educator; b. Omaha, Jan. 6, 1927; d. Marion Fowler and Blanche Gibons (McKee) Mulvaney; student U. Colo., 1944-46; B.S., U. Neb., 1948; M.S., Wellesley Coll., 1951. Instr. Kan. State U., Manhattan, 1948-50; instr. U. Neb. at Lincoln, 1951-55, asst. prof., 1955-62; asst. prof. U. Kan., Lawrence, 1962-66; asso. prof., chmn. women's phys. edn. U. Chgo., 1966—, also dir. women's athletics. Mem. spl. com. women's athletics Nat. Collegiate Athletic Assn. Mem. Am., Midwest, Ill. assns. for health, phys. edn. and recreation, Nat., Midwest assns. for phys. edn. of coll. women, Am. Assn. U. Profs., Mortar Board. Pi Lambda Theta, Alpha Chi Omega. Home: 11 Hampshire Court Bolingbrook IL 60439 Office: 1212 E 59th St U Chgo Chicago IL 60637

MULVEHILL, SISTER M. CRESCENTIA, hosp. adminstr.; b. Spangler, Pa., July 7, 1917; d. Walter James and Adelaide Theresa (Ager) Mulvehill; B.A., Carlow Coll., 1949; M.Ed., Duquesne U., 1955; M.B.A., George Washington U., 1965. Joined Congregation Sisters of St. Joseph, 1934; tchr. Sacred Heart Sch., Altoona, Pa., 1936-45; mistress of novices St. Josephs Novitiate, Baden, Pa., 1948-63; adminstrv. resident Johns Hopkins Hosp., Balt., 1964-65; asst. adminstr. Georgetown U. Hosp., Washington, 1965-67; adminstr. St. Joseph's Hosp., Pitts., 1967-73; exec. dir. South Hills Health System, Pitts., 1974—. Area chmn., United Fund, Pitts., 1971-72. Bd. dirs. St. Pius Residence, Pitts., 1971—. Named one of ten outstanding Pitts. women by Pitts. Post Gazette, 1970. Mem. C. of C., Am. Coll. Hosp. Adminstrs., Am. Hosp. Assn., Pa. Hosp. Assn., Pitts. Inst. Legal Medicine, Cath. Hosp. Assn., George Washington U. Alumni Assn., Hosp. Services Conf. Home: 2112 Sidney St Pittsburgh PA 15203 Office: 2117 Carson St Pittsburgh PA 15203

MULVEY, MARY CROWLEY (MRS. GORDON F. MULVEY), ednl adminstr.; b. Bangor, Me.; d. Michael Joseph and Ann Loretta (Higgins) Crowley; B.A., U. Me., 1930; M.A., Brown U., 1953; Ed.D., Harvard, 1961; m. Gordon F. Mulvey, 1940. Tchr., dir. drama and music Berwick Acad., South Berwick, Me., 1930-32, Madawaska (Me.) High Sch., 1935-38; tchr. Latin, math., Elmhurst Acad., Providence, 1946-48, 50-56; tchr. math., Classical High Sch., Providence, 1957-59; guidance counselor Hope High Sch., Providence, 1959-61, 63-65; supr. adult edn. Providence Sch. Dept., 1965—; dramatics coach, supr., personnel dir. Universal Producing Co., N.Y.C., 1932-35; lectr. U. R.I. extension, Providence, 1963—; cons. and lectr. on adult edn., gerontology, women, for various colls. and nat. orgns.; dir. adult basic edn. Tchr. Trainer Inst. U. Me., summer 1967. Adminstr. Div. Aging R.I., 1961-63; cons. PHA, HHFA (now U.S. Housing and Urban Devel. dept.), R.I., 1963-65; conducted series Edn. Later Maturity, sta. WJAR-TV, 1957, also lectr. radio and TV programs adult edn., gerontology; mem. nat. adv. com. White House Conf. Aging, 1958-61; chmn. R.I. Com. Aging, 1953-64; pres. Sr. Citizens Edn. and Research Center, Washington, 1963-68; mem. tech. rev. com. tng. grants Adminstrn. Aging, U.S. Dept. Health, Edn., Welfare, 1965-70; mem. Nat. Task Force on Edn., White House Conf. on Aging, 1971, chmn. sub-com.; participant nat. sem. innovation edn., U.S. Office Edn. and Kettering Found., Hawaii, summer, 1967; dir. Providence Sr. Aides Project, 1968—, Model Cities Adult Basic Edn. Project, 1972—; Mem. R.I. Council Continuing Edn., 1972—; mem. R.I. Manpower Planning Council, 1973—, Commn. to Study R.I. Tax Reform, 1973—, Gov.'s Task Force to Monitor Nursing Home Inspections, 1973—; dir. confs., programs, workshops, orgns. adult edn., aging; active pub. relations fields Medicare, Social Security, sr. citizens housing. Active R.I. campaigns Kennedy, 1960, Johnson, 1964, Humphrey, 1968. Bd. dirs. Providence Model Cities Edn. Coalition, 1969-71. Fellow Gerontological Soc.; mem. Ind. Schs. Assn. R.I. (sec., treas. 1951-71), Nat. Council Sr. Citizens (co-founder, bd. dirs. 1961—), New Eng. Gerontological Assn. (co-founder, pres. 1955-57, 1955—), Adult Edn. Assn. (exec. bd. R.I. chpt., R.I. legislative chmn. 1966-69, mem. planning com. nat. pilot inst. edn. for aging 1966-67, chmn. sect. on edn. for aging 1969—), Am., R.I. personnel and guidance assns., Nat. Assn. Pub. Continuing and Adult Edn. (sec. R.I. chpt.), Am. Assn. U. Women, Nat. Council Aging, U. Me. Alumnae Assn. (past pres. R.I. chpt.), Internat. Reading Assn. (mem. com. Reading for the Aging. 1969-72), New Eng. Assn. Measurement and Evaluation in Guidance, Harvard Grad. Sch. Edn. Alumni, Assn. Providence Pub. Sch. Staff and Adminstrs., R.I. Women Educators, Providence Tchrs. Union, Pi Lambda Theta, Delta Delta Delta. Club: Soroptimists (gerontology research fellow 1957, 59, 61). Contbr. articles to profl. jours. and directories. Home: 95 Plymouth Rd East Providence RI 02914 Office: Dept Pub Schs 396 Smith St Providende RI 02908

MUMBY, GAY KAREN (MRS. DEAN RICHARD MUMBY), real estate broker; b. Borger, Tex., May 2, 1944; d. Earl Coburn and Wanda Maxine (Stottlemyre) Cunningham; student Grossmont Coll., 1970, U. Cal. Extension, 1971; m. Dean Richard Mumby, Mar. 8, 1962; children—Lisa Gay, Laura Ann. Real estate salesman Mark Realty, La Mesa, Cal., 1968-70; propr., broker Colony Realty, El Cajon, Cal., 1970-72; broker Del Cerro Realty, San Diego, 1972—. Mem. Children's Hosp. Aux., San Diego, Cal., 1973—. Mem. Republican Women's Club. Mem. La Mesa Bd. Realtors. Cal., Nat. real estate brokers assns. Home: 6005 Wenrich Dr San Diego CA 92120 Office: 6349 Del Cerro Blvd San Diego CA 92120

MUMFORD, EMILY HAMILTON, educator; b. Cape Girardeau, Mo.; d. Barney A. and Dola (Stolzer) Hamilton; B.A., U. Tulsa, 1941; M.A., Columbia, 1958, Ph.D., 1963. Shopping editor Family Circle Mag., 1951-58; research asst. Bur. Applied Social Research Columbia, 1958-59; lectr., adviser Hunter Coll., N.Y.C., 1960-61; lectr. to nurses Columbia-Presbyn. Sch. Nursing, 1960; asst. in psychiatry, N.Y. Psychiat. Inst., Columbia-Presbyn. Med. Center; asso. prof. sociology Mt. Sinae Sch. Medicine; research asso. Mt. Sinai Hosp., N.Y.; asso. cons. sociology St. Luke's Hosp.; prof. sociology Lehman Coll., also Grad. Center, City U. N.Y., 1973—; prof. Downstate Med. Sch., State U. N.Y., 1974—; vis. prof. sociology New Coll., Sarasota, Fla., 1965. NIH research grantee, 1965; Commonwealth Fund Grant-in-Aid, 1968; NIH teaching grantee, 1969; Milbank Meml. Fund travel grantee, 1969. Fellow Am. Pub. Health Assn.; mem. Ladies Aux. Am. Psychiat. Assn. (past chmn. dist. br.), William Alanson Whyte Inst. Psychiatry and Psychoanalysis (past chmn. theatre benefit), Am., Eastern sociol. assns., World, Am. assns. pub. opinion research, Am. Assn. U. Profs. Author: Sociology in Hospital Care; Interns: From Students to Physicians; also articles. Home: 360 E 72d St New York City NY 10021

MUMFORD, MARY SHACKELFORD (MRS. JAMES G. MUMFORD), occupational therapist; b. Martinsville, Va., May 26, 1938; d. John Armstrong and Margaret (Dillard) (Spencer) Shackelford; B.A., Mary Baldwin Coll., 1961; Occupational Therapist, Tufts U., 1963-65; M.S., Boston U., 1972; m. James G. Mumford, Dec. 18, 1970; 1 dau., Margaret Lee. Lectr., Tufts U., Boston Sch. Occupational Therapy, 1969-72; staff therapist Mass. Mental Health Center, Boston, 1965-69. Mem. bd. Washington Cathedral Assn., 1972—, Mariner's House, 1973—. Mem. Mass. Assn. Occupational Therapy (membership chmn. 1967-69). Clubs: Duxbury (Mass.) Yacht; Somerset, Harvard (Boston). Home: 174 Marshall St Box 1428 Duxbury MA 02332

MUNCY, LYSBETH WALKER, educator; b. Providence, Apr. 29, 1910; d. William Mabley and Mabel (Walker) Muncy; B.A., Vassar Coll., 1931; postgrad. (Inst. Internat. Edn. fellow 1934-35) U. Berlin, 1934-35; M.A., Brown U., 1938, Ph.D., 1943; Alice Freeman Palmer fellow, German Fedn. U. Women fellow for research in Germany on Prussian History, 1956-57. Instr. Mt. Holyoke Coll., 1942-43; instr. history and govt. Sweet Briar (Va.) Coll., 1943-47, asst. prof., asst. dean, 1947-51, asso. prof., 1952-57, prof., 1957—, chmn. dept. history, 1959-60, 64-70, chmn. div. social studies, 1966-70, Charles A. Dana prof. history, 1973—. Recipient Excellence in Teaching award Sweet Briar, 1970. Mem. German Fedn. U. Women (hon. mem. Berlin chpt.), Am. Assn. U. Women, Am., So. hist. assns., Va. Social Sci. Assn. Conglist. Author: The Junker in the Prussian Administration under William II, 1888-1914, 1944. Address: Sweet Briar Coll Sweet Briar VA 24595

MUNDY, ANN KATHLEEN (MRS. THOMAS GORDON MUNDY), journalist; b. Tulsa; d. William Stephen and Margaret Evelyn (Mokler) Phinney; B.S., Okla. State U., 1970; m. Thomas Gordon Mundy, Oct. 14, 1972. Reporter, writer women's dept. Okla. Publ. Co., Oklahoma City, 1970—. Freelance writer Orbit mag., 1973—. Mem. Oklahoma County Assn. Mental Health, 1971—. Bd. dirs. Okla. Soc. Prevention Blindness, 1973—. Recipient Appreciation certificates for articles on handicapped, 1970, children with learning disabilities, 1972 from Mayor Oklahoma City. Mem. Women in Communications (pres. 1974—), Delta Delta Delta. Republican. Home: 2728 NW 26th St Oklahoma City OK 73107 Office: PO Box 25125 Oklahoma City OK 73125

MUNDY, DOROTHY JEAN, psychologist; b. St. Louis, July 17, 1930; d. John C. and Mrs. Mundy; B.S., St. Louis U., 1951; M.S., 1952; Ph.D., Catholic U., 1960. Instr. psychology Rosemont Coll., Pa., 1952-53; clin. psychologist Columbus (O.) State Hosp., 1953-55; intern Catholic U. Guidance Clinic, VA Tb Hosp., Balt., 1955-58; head guidance, instr. psychology Marymount Coll., Tarrytown, N.Y., 1948-60, asst. prof., 1960-64; sch. psychologist Marymount Secondary Sch., Tarrytown, 1963-64; book editor Am. Catholic Psychol. Assn., 1964-66; asso. prof. psychology L.I. U., Bklyn., 1964-74, prof., 1974—; sr. clin. psychologist St. Vincents Hosp., Manhattan, N.Y., 1964-73. Mem. Am. Psychol. Assn,, Am. Assn. U. Profs., Sigma Xi. Home: 105 W 13th St New York City NY 10011 Office: Flatbush Av Brooklyn NY 11201

MUNGER, ARLENE LORRAINE MCFILLEN (MRS. PAUL FRANCIS MUNGER), educator, psychologist; b. Whitehouse, O., Oct. 31, 1921; d. Glenn C. and Edith (Sasse) McFillen; B.Ed., U. Toledo, 1957; M.Ed., U. N.D., 1958; Ph.D., U. Toledo, 1972; m. Paul Francis Munger, May 7, 1942; children—Paul David, Peter George. Tchr., Ottawa Hills (O.) Elementary Sch., 1956-57, Valley Elementary Sch., East Grand Forks, Minn., 1959-61; clin. psychologist Div. Children and Youth, N.D. Welfare Dept., Grand Forks, 1961-63; tchr., bldg. supr. Univ. Schs., Ind. U., Bloomington, 1963-67, psychometrist, 1967-69; testing and research Monroe County Community Schs., Bloomington, 1969—; asst. prof. dept. ednl. psychology Ind. U., 1969—. Mem. N.E.A., Ind. Edn. Assn., Am., Ind. personnel and guidance assns., Nat. Assn. Sch. Psychologists, Am., Ind. psychol. assns., Pi Lambda Theta (v.p. 1962), Phi Kappa Phi, Kappa Delta Pi, Psi Chi. Home: 115 Lexington Rd Bloomington IN 47401

MUNGER, MARY ALICE COOK (MRS. JOHN ANTHONY MUNGER), civic worker, polit. worker; b. Denver, May 14, 1928; d. Joseph Edward and Alice (Spencer) Cook; B.A., U. Colo., 1950; m. John Anthony Munger, Apr. 28, 1951. With Mountain Bell Telephone Co., Denver and Pueblo, Colo., 1950-55. Mem. Colo. Bd. Health, 1965—, chmn. legislative com., 1968-71, pres., 1974—; mem. Colo. Air Pollution Variance Bd., 1970-71, 73—; treas. Brighton (Colo.) Community Hosp. Aux., 1963. Republican precinct committeewoman, Brighton, 1962-64; vice chmn. Adams County Rep. party, 1964-65; mem. Colo. Rep. Central Com., 1965-69; Colo. vice chmn. Rep. party, 1971-73. Bd. dirs. United Way, Adams County, 1963-70, county campaign chmn., 1965, 67, Denver met. chmn., 1970, exec. com. Met. bd. trustees, 1970-73; bd. dirs. House of Neighborly Service, 1966-69. Recipient Liberty Bell award Adams County Bar Assn., 1973. Mem. Colo. Pub. Health Assn., Am. Contract Bridge League, P.E.O. (chpt. pres. 1971-72), Pi Beta Phi, Psi Chi, Delta Kappa Gamma (hon.). Home: 25 S 17th Av Dr Brighton CO 80601

MUNGER, MARY VIRGINIA, engr.; b. East Hartford, Conn., June 23, 1918; d. Allyn Robins and Emily (Dwyer) Munger; B.A. with honors, St. Joseph Coll., 1939. Tchr. jr. and sr. high schs., Hartford, Conn., 1941-45; asst. computer, engring. asst. Pratt & Whitney Aircraft, East Hartford, 1945-50, sound engr., 1950-55, sr. engr., 1955-69, asst. project engr., 1969—. Pres. Class of 1939, St. Joseph Coll., West Hartford, 1964—, dir. alumnae council, 1969-74, chmn. awards com., 1973-74, pres., 1974—; chmn. book selection com. Cath. Lending Library of Hartford, 1966-71. Trustee St. Joseph Coll. Mem. Soc. Women Engrs. (exec. com. 1961-63, sr., mem. council of sect. reps. 1967—, nat. bylaws chmn. 1958-59, 60—, conv. chmn. 1970), Acoustical Soc. Am., Conn. Joint Fedn. (treas. 1973—), Council Cath. Women, D.A.R. (chmn. jr. group 1947-50), Soc. Mayflower Descs, Ladies of St. Joseph, St. Frances Hosp. Aux., Kappa Gamma Pi. Clubs: Zonta (dir. 1972-74) Catholic Graduates (dir. 1951-53, 64-65) (Hartford). Home: 271 S Marshall St Hartford CT 06105 Office: 400 Main St East Hartford CT 06108

MUNITZ, LENORE BLOOM (MRS. MILTON K. MUNITZ), educator; b. N.Y.C., Apr. 29, 1921; d. Frank and Jennie Bassin (Hurwitz) Bloom; B.A. (N.Y. State Regents scholar 1937), N.Y. U., 1940, M.A. (university scholar), 1941; Ph.D., Bryn Mawr, 1948; postgrad. Smith Coll., 1941-42; m. Milton K. Munitz, Dec. 22, 1946; children—Charles Stephen, Andrew Samuel. Trustee fellow Smith Coll., 1941-42; instr. Syracuse U., 1944-45; asst. philosophy Bryn Mawr Coll., 1942-43, resident fellow, 1943-44; instr. N.Y. U., N.Y.C., 1946-49; lectr. philosophy Swarthmore Coll., Pa., 1956-57, Westchester Community Coll., Valhalla, N.Y., 1948-60, 61-62; prof. philosophy Briarcliff Coll., Briarcliff Manor, N.Y., 1962—, also dean students, dir. acad. advising. Mem. Phi Beta Kappa. Mem. Jewish religion. Home: Marlborough Rd Scarborough NY 10510 Office: Briarcliff Coll Briarcliff Manor NY 10510

MUNK, BARBARA DOROTHEA, physician; b. Berlin, Germany, June 26, 1925; d. Fritz and Hildegard (Pohlman) Munk; M.D., U. Hamburg Med. Sch., 1953. Came to U.S., 1955, naturalized, 1970. Intern, Norwalk (Conn.) Hosp., 1955-56; resident psychiatry N.Y. U., Bellevue Hosp. Med. Center, 1956-59; fellow in child psychiatry Bklyn. Psychiat. Centers, 1961-63; med. dir. East Bklyn. Mental Health Clinic, 1963-69; chief psychiatrist comprehensive child health program Bklyn. Jewish Hosp., 1969—; practice medicine, specializing in psychiatry, N.Y.C., 1961—; mem. staff Gracie Sq. Hosp.; clin. asst. prof. N.Y. U. Bd. dirs. Puerto Rican Family Inst., 1967—. Diplomate Am. Bd. Psychiatry and Neurology. Mem. A.M.A., Am. Psychiat. Assn., N.Y. Council Child Psychiatry, Am. Assn. U. Women. Home and Office: 45 W 10th St New York City NY 10011

MUÑOZ, MARIA OLIVIA MENA (MRS. RAUL MUÑOZ, JR.), ednl. adminstr.; b. Houston, Dec. 18, 1930; d. Juan Gordoa and Esther (Jiménez) Mena; student Universidad de Mexico, summer 1949; B.A., U. Houston, 1952, M.A., 1963; m. Raul Muñoz, Jr., July 12, 1953; children—Juan Raúl, Patricia Anne. Tchr., Rio Grande City (Tex.) Pub. Schs., 1952-59; tchr. Houston Pub. Schs., 1959-61, fgn. lang. supr., 1961-69, dir. fgn. lang. instrn., 1969—. Lectr. Spanish, Rice U., Houston, 1965-69; cons. summer lang. instr. Dept. Health, Edn. and Welfare; summer vis. prof. various colls., univs. Charity chmn. Ladies Aux. of Sembradores de Amistad, 1972-74. Mem. Am. Assn. Tchrs. Spanish and Portuguese (nat. pres. 1970, mem. nat. exec. bd. 1965-68, 71-73), S. Central Modern Lang. Assn., Am. Council on Teaching Fgn. Langs., Tex. Assn. for Bilingual Edn., Tex. Fgn. Lang. Assn., Houston Council Edn., Tex. Elementary Prins. Assn., Houston Area Tchrs. Fgn. Lang. (pres. 1963), L'Alliance Francaise de Houston, Inst. Hispanic Culture (chpt. chmn. student activities, 1970-73), Pi Delta Phi, Sigma Delta Phi. Roman Catholic. Author: (with Thomas Kelly, Dorothy Judd) Español: Lengue y Cultura, 1969. Office: 3830 Richmond Av Houston TX 77018

MUNROE, ISABEL ALEXANDRA, univ. dean; b. Edmonto, Alta., Can., July 10, 1914; d. Alexander Russel and Eva Jane (Hamilton) Munroe; B.A., U. Alta., 1935; diploma, Montreal Sch. Social Work (now McGill Sch. Social Work), 1937. Social worker Alta. Guidance Clinics, 1938-42; with Canadian Children's Service Overseas Service, Eng., 1942-45; Exeter County Council Psychiatric Service for Evacuated Children, Bristol Child Guidance Clinic, Canadian Govt. Dependent's Allowance program Canadian Govt. Family Allowance br. Dept. Nat. Health Welfare Can., 1946; family counselor St. Paul (Minn.) Family Service, 1949-52; field instr. McGill U. Sch. Social Work, 1952-57; case cons. Edmonton Family Service Assn., 1957-68; dean women U. Alta. (Edmonton, Can.), 1968—. Bd. mem. Alta. Coll., Edmonton. Mem. Canadian Inst. Internat. Affairs, Alta. (pres. 1960-62), Canadian (dir. 1940-42, pres. (Montreal br. 1955-57) assns. social workers. Home: 13911 102d Av Edmonton AB T5N 0P5 Canada Office: 200 Pembina Hall University Alberta Edmonton AB T6G 2E1 Canada

MUNROE, MARY LOU SCHWARZ (MRS. ROBERT E. MUNROE), ednl. adminstr.; b. Denver, Nov. 18, 1927; d. John Anthony and Lutie A. (Benefiel) Schwarz; B.A. (Estelle Hunter scholar), U. Denver, 1949, M.A. in Guidance, 1970, Doctorate in Instrnl. Specialist, 1973; m. Robert E. Munroe, Nov. 20, 1948; children—Robert M., Carol E., John E. Dir. Jr. and Collegiate Great Books Program, Archdiocese of Denver, 1961-71, leader tng. staff, 1963-71, archdiocesan dir. grade and high sch., 1966-71; undergrad. counselor Sch. Edn. U. Denver, 1971-74. Feature writer Register, Denver, 1963-71; lectr., workshop dir. Loretto Heights Coll., 1966, regional tng. centers for religion tchrs., 1967—. Mem. steering com. Cinema Critique Series of Denver, 1967; mem.-at-large Bd. Cath. Edn. of Denver Met. Area, 1969—, pres., 1974-75; mem. Denver Met. Adv. Com. Cath. Edn., 1968-69. Named Woman of Year Archdiocese Denver Edn. Assn., 1971. Mem. Cath. Edn. Guild, Mortar Bd., Ednl. Forum Colo. (charter), Phi Beta Kappa, Kappa Delta Pi, Delta Kappa Gamma, Phi Delta Kappa, Delta Gamma. Author: Counseling the Parishioner, 1967. Home: 3715 Southern Mission Pkwy Aurora CO 80013

MUNROE, SHIRLEY ANN, hosp. adminstr.; b. Mpls., Mar. 31, 1924; d. Laurance John and Esther (Tuttle) Munroe; pre-nursing certificate La Sierra Coll., Arlington, Cal., 1943; R.N., Glendale Sanitarium and Hosp. Sch. Nursing, 1946; postgrad. U. Cal. at Los Angeles Extension, 1953-55, Los Angeles City Coll., 1948-51; certificate U. Cal. at Santa Cruz extension, 1971; m. Stanley G. Fjeistrom, Dec. 26, 1954 (div. June 1957). Chief nurse, office mgr. for Roger W. Barnes, R. Theodore Berman, Los Angeles, 1946-51; bus. mgr. Bolander Clinic and Emergency Hosp., Van Nuys, Cal., 1951-56, Mendocino Med. Center, Ukiah, Cal., 1956; adminstr. Hillside Community Hosp., Ukiah, 1956—, sec., 1956—; mem. adv. and evaluation com. Ukiah Dist. Sch. Vocational Nursing, 1965—; faculty U. Cal. extension at Berkeley, Basic Adminstrn. Hosp. Adminstrs. Program 1966—. Asst. dir. pub. relations alumni postgrad. assembly Loma Linda U., Los Angeles, 1949-55; dir. pub. relations world meeting Aerospace Med. Assn., Los Angeles, 1953; chmn. re-edn. nursing com. Cal. Dept. Employment, 1962; cons. lectr. nurse aide edn., adult education Willits, Ukiah high schs., 1962; chmn. Career Project for Sr. High Sch. Girls, 1962-64; mem. Mendocino-Lake adv. com. Regional Med. Program, 1969—; mem. vocational edn. adv. com. Ukiah Unified Sch. Dist., 1970—. Dir., sec. Observatory Investment Co., Ukiah, 1957-67. Soloist, Presbyn. Ch., Ukiah, 1956-69, Ukiah Oratorio Soc., 1958-65. Co-chmn. edn. com. Mendocino County br. Am. Cancer Soc., 1961-62, bd. dirs., 1961—, pres., 1963-65; mem. Ukiah Nursery Sch. Planning Com., 1961-62; mem. steering com. Am. Heart Assn., Mendocino County br. Cal. Heart Assn. Chmn. trustees Tri-County Pre-Payment Medi-Cal Pilot Project, State of Cal., 1969-71; trustee Nor Coa Health, 1967—, 1st v.p. 1969-71, pres., 1971-72, chmn. South Planning council, 1972—; mem. Mendocino-Lake counties council, 1966—; bd. dirs. Mendocino County chpt. A.R.C., 1968-70; bd. dirs. Hosp. Service Cal., 1970—, rep., 1970—. Recipient certificate of commendation Cal. Bd. Nurse Examiners, 1946; Civic Participation award, named Outstanding Women in Professions, Cal. Fedn. Bus. and Profl. Women's Clubs, 1965; Woman of Achievement award Soroptimist Club of Ukiah, 1965; Outstanding Service award Mendocino-Lake br. Am. Cancer Soc., 1963, 64, 65, Notable Service award, 1968. Mem. Am., Cal. (membership com. 1960-61; legislative liaison 1960—, panel hosp. peer rev. adminstrs. 1968—; mem. ins. com. 1971—) hosp. assns., Redwood Empire Hosp. Conf. (ins. com. 1957-59, exec. com. 1968—, 1st v.p. 1968, pres. 1969), Hosp. Council No. Cal. (bd. dirs. 1968—, chmn. com. on program and edn. 1968-70), Assn. Western Hosps. (edn. research found. council 1963—), Glendale Sanitarium and Hosp. Sch. Nursing Alumni Assn. (pres. Glendale 1947-48), Bus. and Profl. Women's Club (exec. bd. 1957-61, pres. 1959-60, 3d v.p. 1960-61, career advancement com. 1961-62, chmn. personal devel. com. 1962-64, music chmn. Redwood Empire dist. 1960-61), Bus. and

Profl. Women's Club (mem. bd. 1962-65). Republican. Mem. Seventh-day Adventist Ch. (soloist, supt. children's edn. 1961-64, supt. youth div. 1964-65, dir. pub. relations 1967—, chmn. finance com. 1967—). Clubs: Cultus Women's (pres. Ukiah 1960-61, 2d v.p. 1961-62), Soroptimist (service com. Ukiah 1961-62, music chmn. 1962-63, service com. 1964—; editor bull. 1965-66, dir. 1970-73). Home: 398 Washington Av Ukiah CA 95482 Office: 333 Laws Av Ukiah CA 95482

MUNSON, LUCILLE MARGUERITE (MRS. ARTHUR E. MUNSON), realtor; b. Norwood, O., Mar. 26, 1914; d. Frank and Fairy (Wicks) Wirick; R.N., Lafayette (Ind.) Home Hosp., 1937; A.B., San Diego State U., 1963; student Purdue U., Kan. Wesleyan U.; m. Arthur E. Munson, Dec. 24, 1937; children—Barbara (Mrs. Charles Papke), Judith (Mrs. Robert Andrews), Edmund Arthur. Staff and pvt. nurse Lafayette Home Hosp., 1937-41; indsl. nurse Lakey Foundry & Machine Co., Muskegon, Mich., 1950-51, Continental Motors Corp., Muskegon, 1951-52; nurse Girl Scout Camp, Grand Haven, Mich., 1948-49; owner Munson Realty, San Diego, 1964—. Home: 1327 Torrey Pines Rd LaJolla CA 92037 Office: 729 San Fernando Pl San Diego CA 92109

MUNSON, MARIE OWETA CHRISTEAN BENNETT (MRS. CRAIG D. MUNSON, JR.), employment agy. exec.; b. Claremore, Okla., Apr. 1; d. Fred R. and Myrtle (Rutherford) Christean; student So. Methodist U., 1943; m. William Franklin Bennett, Jr., Dec. 8, 1938 (dec. Apr. 1962); children—William Franklin, Mark Allen, Robert Christean; m. 2d, Hal R. Colter, Feb. 10, 1966 (div. Oct. 1970); m. 3d, Craig D. Munson, Jr., July 1, 1973. Owner, mgr. Bennett Assos., Odessa, Tex., 1949-54; co-owner with husband Bennett Employment, Inc., Odessa, 1954-62, owner, mgr., Odessa and Midland, Tex., 1962—; pres. Bennett Employment, Inc., Lubbock, Tex., 1965-69; br. mgr. Kelly Services, Inc., Detroit, 1958—; registered rep. Waddell & Reed, Kansas City, Mo., 1962-69, Kelly & Morey, Inc., Denver, 1969—; area mgr. Goals, Inc., Amarillo, Tex.; pres. Nat. Tng. & Testing, Inc., Odessa and Midland, 1964-69, Bennett Munson, Inc., Dallas, DBA Cloud Employment Co., Dallas. Mem. adv. bd. Salvation Army, 1970—. Bd. dirs. Better Bus. Bur. of Permian Basin, 1972—. Recipient awards including Gold Citizen of Year award Nat. Conf. Kelly Service, Inc., 1962, 63, 72. Mem. Nat. Personnel Cons. Assn., St. John's Episcopal Bus. Women, Nat. Employment Assn., Presdl. Room Mus., Midland C. of C., Internat. Platform Assn., Altrusa Internat. Home: 3730 Blossom Lane Odessa TX 79760 Office: 210 W 5th St Odessa TX 79760 also Midland Tower Midland TX 79701 also 32614 Coastsite Dr Bay Club Rancho Palos Verdes CA 90274

MUNTER, PAMELA OSBORNE, educator, psychologist; b. Santa Monica, Cal., Mar. 27, 1943; d. Eric John and Frances Margo (Dellinger) Osborne; B.A., U. Cal. at Berkeley, 1964; M.A., Cal. State U. at Northridge, 1966; M.A., Cal. State U. at Los Angeles, 1969; Ph.D., U. Neb., 1972; m. Leo J. Munter; Aug. 2, 1970; 1 son, Aaron Leonard. Instr. Cal. State U. at Northridge, 1967-69; postdoctoral intern Mendota State Hosp., Madison, Wis., 1972-73; asst. prof. Portland (Ore.) State U., 1973—; pvt. practice clin. psychology, Beaverton, Ore., 1973—. Cons. to schs. in community psychology. NSF grantee, 1970; Neb. Sch. for Alcohol Studies grantee, 1971. Mem. Am., Ore., Portland psychol. assns., Ore. Acad. Profl. Psychologists, Soc. for Personality Assessment, Western Psychol. Assn. (com. on status of women). Democrat. Jewish religion. Cons. editor Jour. Personality Assessment. Editor Ore. Psychologist. Contbr. articles to profl. jours. Home: 18060 SW Salit Ridge Aloha OR 97005 Office: 3800 SW Cedar Hills Blvd Beaverton OR 97005

MUNTZ, MARGARET EMELINE (MRS. RALPH WESLEY MUNTZ), librarian; b. Cin., Apr. 28, 1915; d. Charles Frederick and Luella (Hatherley) Mills; A.B. in Math., Social Studies, Coll. Wooster, 1936; M.S. in Library Sci., Case Western Res. U., 1964; postgrad. Inst. for Advanced Librarianship, Western Mich. U., summer 1967, Loughborough Coll. Edn., 1968, Kent State U., 1969; m. Ralph Wesley Muntz, May 20, 1939; children—Donna Luella (Mrs. Bertram Bastock), Charles William, Marilyn (Mrs. John Kent Chidester), Marlene Anne. Resident tchr. math., social studies Hudson (O.) Country Day Sch., 1936-37; clk. J.C. Virden Coll., Cleve., 1936-37; cataloguer Firestone Tire and Rubber Co., Akron, O., 1938-39; asst. librarian Cleve. Heights High Sch., 1960-62; sec. Laurel Sch., Shaker Heights, O., 1958-60; librarian Hilltop Sch., Beachwood, O., 1962-68; coordinator libraries Beachwood Bd. Edn., 1968-71; head librarian Mayfield High Sch. Libraries, Mayfield, O., 1971-72; librarian Warrensville High Sch., Warrensville Heights, O., 1972-73. Mem. P.T.A., Prospect Sch., sec., 1946-47. Recipient Hilltop P.T.A. award, 1967. Spiritual Frontiers fellow, 1973—. Mem. Am. (rep. Ohio state del. assembly Dallas 1971), Ohio (mem. scholarship com. 1967-69) library assns., Nat., Ohio edn. assns., Women's Nat. Book Assn., Ednl. Media Council Ohio, Ohio Assn. Sch. Librarians (pres. 1970-71), North East Ohio Tchrs. Assn. Republican. Author: (with Robert McMurry) Summary of Audiovisual Workshop, Hilltop School, 1967. Home: 105 Meadow Hill Lane Chagrin Falls OH 44022

MUNZER, MARION PAULINE, librarian; b. Grand Rapids, Minn., June 16, 1923; d. Emil and Helen (Stenzel) Munzer; A.B., State U. N.Y., 1945, B.S. in L.S., 1946; M.A., Cornell U., 1953. Librarian, Greenville (N.Y.) Rural Sch., 1946-48; periodicals librarian Russell Sage Coll., Troy, N.Y., 1948-50, asst. cataloger, 1950-51, head cataloger, 1951-57, reference librarian, 1958-65; exchange librarian, sr. cataloger U. Queensland, Australia, 1957-58; librarian, univ. coll. sect. State U. N.Y., Albany, 1965-67, head tech. services, 1967-70, supr. specialized collections, 1970-72, curator spl. collections, 1972—. Mem. Am. Assn. U. Profs., Am., N.Y. library assns. Contbr. articles to profl. publs. Home: 26 Greenway South Albany NY 12208

MURAKAMI, MOMOKO, librarian; b. Los Angeles, Mar. 12, 1931; d. Edward Noboru and June Kisa (Kaimura) Murakami; B.A., U. Wash., 1953, M.L. in Librarianship, 1954. Librarian I, reference in br. libraries cataloging Chgo. Pub. Library, 1954-57; cataloger, acquisitions librarian U. Cal. Sch. Law Library, Los Angeles, 1957-69, head tech. processes, 1969—. Mem. Am., Cal. library assns., Am. Assn. Law Libraries. Home: 3429 Hillcrest Dr Los Angeles CA 90016 Office: 405 Hilgard Av Los Angeles CA 90024

MURASAKI, ELLEN SPEYER, psychotherapist; b. Frankfurt, Germany, Jan. 30, 1930 (came to U.S. 1940, naturalized 1946); d. Louis and Lucy (Marx) Speyer; B.S. cum laude, N.Y.U., 1952-56; M.S.W., U. So. Cal., 1961; student U. Cal. at Berkeley, 1958-59; Ph.D., Colo. Christian U., 1973; div.; children—Kiyoshi John, Erika Kimiyo. Asst. personnel dir. YMCA Nat. Bd., N.Y.C., 1954-56; child welfare worker Dept. Social Service, Phoenix, 1956-60; psychiat. social worker Vista Del Mar, Los Angeles, 1961-64; practice of psychoatherapy, Arcadia, Cal., 1964-70; partner Murasaki-Samuel Counseling Service, Monterey Park, Cal., 1970—, exec. dir. Santa Anita Family Service, Monrovia, Cal., 1968—; field work instr. U. So. Cal., 1970—, instr. continued edn., 1974—. Cons., Pleasant View Convalescent Hosp., 1969-74. Supr., trainer Los Angeles Counseling Center, 1969-70; chmn. devel. council Pinal County Council, Girl Scouts Am., 1957-58. Mem. Nat. Assn. Social Workers, Clin. Assn. Social Workers, Family and Marriage Counselors Assn., Group Psychotherapy Assn., Am. Arbitration Assn., Los Angeles Psychoanalytic Assn. (asso.), Am. Acad. Pschotherapists. Home: 1355 Doremus Rd Pasadena CA 91105 Office: 616 N Garfield Blvd Monterey Park CA 91754

MURATA, ALICE KISHIYE, psychologist, educator; b. Los Angeles, Oct. 19, 1940; d. Teruo and Hanako (Takamiya) Murata; B.S., U. Ill., 1962; M.A., Northwestern U., 1963, Ph.D., 1969. Asst. dean students State U. N.Y. at Cortland, 1965-67; coordinator Counseling Lab., Northwestern U., 1967-69; dir. counseling services, asst. prof. edn. Elmhurst (Ill.) Coll., 1969-74, counseling cons., 1974—. instr. counselor edn. dept. Northeastern Ill. U., 1973-74, asso. prof. counselor edn., 1974—. Mem. Nat. Assn. Women Deans and Counselors, Am. Personnel and Guidance Assn., Am. Psychol. Assn., Am. Assn. for Higher Edn. Office: Northeastern Ill U Counselor Edn Dept Bryn Mawr Av at St Louis Av Chicago IL 60625

MURDOCH, ALICE BLANCHARD (MRS. JOHN WALES MURDOCH), former educator; b. Lake City, Minn., Mar. 4, 1894; d. Arthur Blanchard and Nora Mae (Ingham) Grannis; certificate Chgo. Art Inst., 1915; diploma Winona State Tchrs. Coll., 1924; B.S., U. Minn., 1928, M.A., 1934; postgrad. Columbia; m. John Wales Murdoch, Dec. 28, 1943; stepchildren—Helen (Mrs. Alfred Hyslop), Cynthia (Mrs. James McConnon), George Baldwin. Tchr. pub. schs., Ia., Minn., 1915-21; tchr., supr. teaching, State Normal Sch., Winona, Minn., 1920-22; teaching prin., Albert Lea, Minn., 1922-24; tchr., supervising tchr. Winona State Tchrs. Coll., 1924-27, 37-44; dir. post high sch. tchr. tng. dept., Chisholm, Minn., 1927-30; tchr., supr. teaching demonstration sch. Duluth State Tchrs. Coll., 1931-36. Mem. Lake City Pub. Library Bd., 1954—, v.p. bd., 1964—; guardian Campfire Girls, 1925-27. Mem. Wabasha County (life, curator 1964—), Minn. State hist. socs., Old Settlers Assn. (v.p. 1956), Lake City Aux. Am. Legion, Pi Lambda Theta (life), Delta Kappa Gamma (life). Mem. Order Eastern Star (worthy matron 1955-56). Contbr. articles to various jours. Home: 210 W Lyon Av Lake City MN 55041

MURILLO-ROHDE, ILDAURA MARIA (MRS. ERLING ROHDE), counselor, therapist; b. Panama, Republic of Panama; d. Amalio Murillo and Ana Etanislaa Diaz de Murillo; B.S., Columbia, 1951, M.A., 1953, M.Ed., 1969; Ph.D., N.Y. U., 1971; m. Erling Rohde, Sept. 19, 1959. Came to U.S., 1945, naturalized, 1953. Staff nurse Bellevue Psychiat. Hosp., N.Y.C., 1950-51, instr., 1951-52, supr., 1952-53; asst. dir., acting dir. nursing service and edn. Wayne County Gen. Hosp., Eloise, Mich., 1954-56; chief nurse psychiat. div. Elmhurst Gen. Hosp., N.Y.C., 1957-58; dir. nursing service and edn. Menorah Hosp and Home, Bklyn., 1958-59; chief nurse psychiat. div. Met. Hosp.-N.Y. Med. Coll. Center, N.Y.C., 1961-63; psychiat. cons. to Govt. Guatemala, WHO, 1963-64; asso. prof., chmn. dept. mental health-psychiat. nursing Grad. Sch. Nursing, N.Y. Med. Coll., N.Y.C., 1964-69; dir. undergrad. mental health-psychiat. nursing integration program N.Y. U., N.Y.C., 1970-72; prof. City U. N.Y., 1972—. Bd. dirs. N.Y. chpt. Internat. House; sec. Joint Council for Mental Health, N.Y.C.; chmn. adv. bd. Parents Without Partners. Fellow Am. Orthopsychiat. Assn.; mem. Am. Nurses Assn., Nat. League for Nursing, Council Nurse Researchers, Am. Assn. Suicidology, Nat. Council Family Relations, Am. Assn. Marriage and Family Counselors (N.Y. regional pres. 1973-75, dir. mem. exec. bd. N.Y. div. 1972), UN Assn. U.S.A., Sigma Theta Tau. Democrat. Home: 300 W 108th St New York City NY 10025

MURIO, JAY, soprano; b. Bastrop, La.; d. John Wesley and Julia A. (Tomlinson) McMurtry; A.B., Ark. Coll.; Mus.M., Am. Conservatory Music, 1931; M.A., U. Chgo. 1933; m. Alex Brunner (dec.); m. 2d, J. M. Sainz, 1941 (dec.); m. 3d, Ben Bartlett, 1948. Writer feature stories and editorials 1929—; as singer appeared at Merrie England, Century of Progress Expn., Chgo., 1934, Tex. Centennial, 1936, concerts Latin Am., 1937-40, throughout U.S., 1942—; sang with Chgo. Civic Opera, Nat. Opera of Mexico; tour in U.S., Latin Am.; owner dairy and cattle farms in Wis. Mem. Nat. League Am. Pen Women, English Speaking Union, U.D.C., Nat. Soc. Arts and Letters (pres. Chgo. 1966-68; mem. nat. bd.), Ill. Opera Guild (dir.), Delta Omicron, Methodist. Contbr. feature stories to Baker's Weekly Chicago, 1928. Author: El Siglo Pitagorico y Vida de Don Gregorio Guadanaby Antonio Enriguez Gomez, as a Source of a Journey From This World to the Next and Johnathan Wild by Henry Fielding. Has recorded Indian and folk music sung by natives in Mexico. Address: 530 Home Av Oak Park IL 60304 also care of HJ McMurtry PO Box 244 Oak Park IL 60303

MURPHEY, VERA EDNA RANDLE (MRS. PAUL BRYAN MURPHEY), educator; b. O'Donnell, Tex., Nov. 5, 1919; d. John Peyton and Lydia Edna (DuPuy) Randle; B.S., N.M. State U., 1941; M.A., Eastern N.M. U., 1960; Ed.D., Okla. State U., 1968; m. Paul Bryan Murphey, May 24, 1941; children—Patricia Gail (Mrs. C. Richard Donovan), Michael Bryan. Statis. clk. War Dept., Washington, and Detroit, 1941-46; kindergarten tchr. Eastern N.M. U., Portales, 1953-55; tchr. home econs. Portales Jr. High Sch., 1955-59; mem. faculty Eastern N.M. U., 1959, asso. prof. home econs., 1967-72; prof., 1972—, dept. chmn., 1968—. Vice pres., program chmn. L.L. Brown PTA, Portales, 1961-62. Recipient Pres.' Outstanding Faculty award Eastern N.M. U., 1972. Mem. Am., N.M. (chmn. univ. sect. 1968-69, treas. 1972-74, pres. elect 1974-76) home econs. assns., Nat., N.M. (chmn. higher edn. sect. 1964-65), edn. assns., Am. Dietetics Assn., Am. Assn. U. Women (br. pres. 1966-67), Internat. Platform Assn., Altrusa Internat. (rec. sec. 1971-72, v.p., program coordinator, del. dist. conf. 1972-73, pres. Portales 1973-74), Delta Kappa Gamma (corr. sec. Phi chpt. 1965-67, publicity chmn. 1969-71 pres. 1974-76), Omicron Nu, Phi Upsilon Omicron; hon. mem. N.M. Future Homemakers Am. Home: 161 Yucca Dr Portales NM 88130 Office: Eastern NM Univ Portales NM 88130

MURPHREE, GWENDOLYN CRIBBS (MRS. HAROLD EDWIN MURPHREE), civic worker; b. Houston, May 13, 1921; d. Walter Lee and Lady Lois (Weller) Cribbs; B.A., Rice U., 1942; postgrad. U. Tex., 1941, U. Houston, 1952-53; m. Harold Edwin Murphree, Jr., Feb. 5, 1942; children—Sandra, Patricia (Mrs. Philip W. Smith), Harold Walter. Pres. League Women Voters, Dickinson, Tex., 1956-58, mem. Tex. State Bd., 1958-64, Ind. State Bd., 1965-68, mem. nat. bd., 1968-72, nat. v.p., 1970-72; mem. Tex. Gov.'s Com. for Mental Health, 1963-64. Bd. dirs. Galveston County (Tex.) A.R.C., Human Relations Council, 1961-64. Methodist. Home: PO Box 7084 Sunny Isle Christiansted St Croix VI 00820

MURPHY, ANNE HUNT BOOTH, found. officer; b. Washington, Conn., Dec. 31, 1896; d. Earle Buckingham and Mariette Elizabeth (Seeley) Booth; student Oberlin Coll., 1913-15, Secretarial Sch., New Haven, 1915-16, Columbia U., 1925-26, 50-51, 54-55; m. Edward F. Murphy, June 23, 1934 (div. June 1941); 1 son, Edward Booth; 1 adopted son, Edward Booth. Asst. to Prof. Fred. R. Fairchild, 1917; with U.S. Rubber Co., 1917-22; sec. to Edward John Noble, Greenwich, Conn. and N.Y.C., 1922-27, financial sec., 1927-58; sec. Edward John Noble Found., Greenwich and N.Y.C., 1940-58, trustee, sec., 1958-71, treas., 1966—. Republican. Conglist. Mem. D.A.R. Club: Thousand Islands (dir.; v.p. 1950—, treas. 1950—) (Alexandria Bay, N.Y.). Home: Horse Heaven Rd Washington CT 06793 Office: 32 E 57th St New York City NY 10022 also Meml Plaza Washington Depot CT 06794

MURPHY, ANNE MARIE, dir. univ. libraries; b. N.Y.C., July 25, 1926; d. Timothy D. and Mary A. (Murphy) Murphy; A.B., Coll. Mt. St. Vincent, 1948; B.L.S., Pratt Inst., 1950. Asst. br. librarian N.Y. Pub. Library, N.Y.C., 1951-54; asst. librarian pub. services Fordham U., 1954-56; asso. librarian, 1956-70, dir. libraries, 1970—. Mem. Am., Cath. library assns. Home: 2441 Webb Av New York City NY 10468 Office: Fordham U Library Bronx NY 10458

MURPHY, BETTY JANE SOUTHARD (MRS. CORNELIUS F. MURPHY), govt. ofcl.; b. East Orange, N.J.; d. Floyd Theodore and Thelma (Casto) Southard; A.B., Ohio State U., 1952; postgrad. Alliance Franciase and U. Sorbonne (Paris), 1952-53; J.D., Am. U., 1958; m. Cornelius F. Murphy May 1, 1965; children—Ann Southard Murphy, Cornelius Francis Murphy, Jr. Corr., free-lance journalist Europe and Asia, 1953-54, U.P.I., Washington, 1955-56; pub. relations counsellor Capitol Properties, Inc. of Columbus (O.), Washington, 1956-58; admitted to D.C. bar, 1958; atty. Applelate Cts. br. NLRB, Washington, 1958-59; practiced in Washington, 1959—; mem. firm McInnis, Wilson, Munson & Woods and predecessor firm, 1959-70; gen. partner Wilson, Woods & Villalon, 1970-74; dep. asst. sec. labor, wage-hour adminstr., Washington, 1974—; adj. prof. law Am. U., 1972—. Mem. adv. com. on rights and responsibilities of women to sec. Dept. Health, Edn. and Welfare, 1972-74. Chmn. adv. bd. visitors Mary Baldwin Coll.; trustee Am. U.; nat. bd. Med. Coll. Pa. Mem. Am., Fed., Inter-Am. (editor Newsletter 1960-69; Silver medal 1967) bar assns., Bar Assn. D.C., World Peace Through Law Center, Internat. Soc. for Labor Law and Social Legislation, Am. U. Alumni Assn. (dir. 1964-65, sec. law sch. 1965-66, pres. 1966-69, chmn. bd. govs. law sch. alumni 1969—), Kappa Beta Pi, Delta Delta Delta. Republican. Episcopalian. Mem. Order Eastern Star. Home: 4105 Necostin Way Annandale VA 22003 Office: Dept Labor Washington DC 20004

MURPHY, GERALDINE JOANNE, educator; b. Cambridge, Mass., Apr. 13, 1920; d. Timothy Francis and Mary Louise (Murphy) Murphy; A.B. summa cum laude, Regis Coll., 1941; M.A., Radcliffe Coll., 1942, Ph.D., 1960. Tchr. pub. and pvt. schs. Mass., 1944-54; teaching fellow Harvard, Cambridge, Mass., 1955-56, research asso., 1960-61; asst. prof. Wesleyan U., Middletown, Conn., 1957-60, asso. prof., 1962-70, prof. English, 1970—. Cons. Am. Ednl. Pubs., 1970—. Author: The Study of Literature, 1968; A Momentary Stay, 1972. Contbr. articles and revs. to profl. jours. Office: 285 Court St Middletown CT 06457

MURPHY, HARRIET SEARCY (MRS. GREER MURPHY), social sci. analyst; b. Tuscaloosa, Ala., Mar. 3, 1917; d. George Harris and Mary (Persinger) Searcy; B.A., U. Ala., 1938; postgrad. Smith Coll., 1938-39; m. Greer Marechal Murphy, Aug. 29, 1940; children—Greer Marechal, Douglas Adams. Interviewer Alley Dwelling Authority, Washington, 1940-42; tech. editor tech. information div. Library of Congress, Washington, 1949-52; social sci. analyst lab. socio-environmental studies Nat. Inst. Mental Health, 1954-64; asso. specialist Inst. Human Devel., U. Cal. at Berkeley, 1971. Mem. women's com. Community Psychiat. Clinic, Bethesda, 1965—, Nat. Symphony, 1970—. Trustee Green Acres Sch., Bethesda, 1959-61; bd. dirs. Washington Guitar Soc., 1973—. Mem. Am. Sociol. Soc. (asso.), Phi Beta Kappa. Club: Potomac Appalachian Trail. Contbr. articles to profl. jour. Home: 7401 Ridgewood Av Chevy Chase MD 20015

MURPHY, JANE M. (MRS. ALEXANDER H. LEIGHTON), educator; b. Denver, Oct. 9, 1929; d. Rex L. and Marie (Stevens) Murphy; B.A., Phillips U., 1951; Ph.D., Cornell U., 1960; m. Alexander H. Leighton, July 30, 1966. Adminstrv. asst., research asso. Dept. Sociology and Anthropology, Cornell U., Ithaca, N.Y., 1951-63, asst. prof. Med. Sch., 1965; asst. prof. Harvard Sch. Pub. Health, Boston, 1966-69, asso. prof. anthropology, 1970—. Fellow Am. Anthrop. Assn.; mem. Cardinal Key, Phi Beta Kappa, Sigma Xi. Home: 20 Chestnut St Boston MA 02108 Office: 677 Huntington Av Boston MA 02115

MURPHY, JANET A. (JONNE) FURMAN (MRS. RAY T. MURPHY), radio-TV exec.; b. White Plains, N.Y., July 1, 1914; d. Eugene A. and Esther M. (Patterson) Furman; B.S., Skidmore Coll., 1935; m. Ray T. Murphy, Dec. 31, 1937 (dec. Jan. 1970); children—Stephen Dexter, Kent Christopher. Personnel asst. Dancer-Fitzgerald-Sample, N.Y.C., 1937-39; office mgr., sec. Newspaper-Radio Com., N.Y.C., 1939-44; estimator MBS, N.Y.C., 1944; sales asst. Storer Broadcasting Co., N.Y.C., 1947-49; office mgr., saleswoman Robert Meeker Assos., N.Y.C., 1949-53; timebuyer Victor & Richards, N.Y.C., 1953-57; broadcast supr. Lawrence C. Gumbinner Agy., N.Y.C., 1957-63; media group supr. Batten, Barton, Durstine & Osborn, N.Y.C., 1963-66; dir. sales services Radio Advt. Bur., N.Y.C., 1966-71; v.p., sr. asso. Vitt Media Internat. Inc., N.Y.C., 1971-74; owner Jonne Murphy & Co. broadcast consultants, 1974—. Mem. Broadcast Pioneers, Internat. Radio and TV Soc., Internat, Platform Assn., Am. Mgmt. Assn., Am. Assn. Ret. Persons. Address: 72 Chatterton Pkwy White Plains NY 10606

MURPHY, JANET GORMAN (MRS. JOHN MURPHY), ednl. adminstr.; b. Holyoke, Mass., Jan. 10, 1937; d. Edwin Daniel and Catherine Gertrude (Hennessey) Gorman; B.A., U. Mass., 1958, postgrad., 1960-61, Ed.D., 1974; M.Ed., Boston U., 1961; m. John Murphy, Aug. 5, 1961; Tchr. English and history John J. Lynch Jr. High Sch., Holyoke, Mass., 1958-60; tchr. English, Chestnut Jr. High Sch., Springfield, Mass., 1961-63; instr. English and journalism Our Lady of Elms Coll., Chicopee, 1963-64; mem. staff Mass. State Coll. System, Boston, 1964—, dir. devel., 1971—. Active fund-raising campaign Am. Cancer Soc., Heart Fund. Mem. campaign staff Robert F. Kennedy Presdl. Campaign, 1968. Recipient John Gunther Tchr. award N.E.A., 1960, award Women's Opportunity Com., Boston Fed. Exec. Bd., 1973; name one of 10 Outstanding Young Leaders of Greater Boston Area, Boston Jr. C. of C., 1973. Mem. Nat. Assn. Women Deans and Counselors, Univ. Women's Assn., N.E.A., Am. Colls. and Univs., Mass. Soc. for Univ. Edn. of Women (chmn. membership com. 1971, 72), Mass. Women's Polit. Caucus, U. Mass. Alumni (dir. 1970—, mem. exec. bd. 1973—), U. Mass. Women's Alumni (mem. exec. com. Boston br. 1966). Home: 26 Waldorf Rd Newton Highlands MA 02161 Office: 53 State St Boston MA 02109

MURPHY, JUANITA FERN, educator, sociologist, nurse scientist; b. Granite, Okla., May 24, 1930; d. Benjamin Franklin and Katherine Pauline (Salinger) Murphy; A.B., Okla. Bapt. U., 1955; M.S., Case Western Res. U., 1961, Ph.D., 1967. Dir. nursing service Okla. Gen. Hosp., Clinton, 1957-59; asst. dir. nursing service Highland View Hosp., Cleve., 1960-62; asst. chmn. dept. nursing edn., asso. prof., program dir. Grad. Nurse Scientist Tng. Program, U. Kan., Kansas City, 1966-71, asso. prof. dept. sociology 1966-71; dean, prof. Coll. Nursing Ariz. State U. at Tempe, 1971—. Mem. Am. Sociol. Assn., Am., Ariz. State nurses assns., Am. Assn. Colls. Nursing (v.p.), Alpha Kappa Delta, Sigma Theta Tau. Home: 1922 E Manhatton Dr Tempe AZ 85282

MURPHY, KATHLEEN LOUISE, educator; b. Fall River, Mass., Apr. 5, 1924; d. John Thomas and Agnes Genevieve (Murphy) Murphy; B.A., St. John's U., 1954; M.F.A., Fordham U., 1959, M.S. in Edn., 1961, Ph.D., 1965. Tchr. elementary schs., Queens, N.Y.,

1946-50; tchr. secondary schs., Bklyn., also Queens, 1950-61; faculty St. John's U., Fordham U., 1961-64; supr. guidance services, high sch. level Diocese of Bklyn., 1964-69; prof. counseling psychology Sch. Edn., Boston Coll., Chestnut Hill, Mass., 1969—. Mem. Am. Personnel and Guidance Assn., Assn. Counselor Edn. Supervision, Nat. Vocational Guidance Assn., Fordham Personnel and Guidance Assn. (pres. 1967-69), Bklyn. Diocesan Guidance Assn. (pres. 1964-66). Author: (with others) Being and Becoming, group guidance series for high schs., 1970. Home: 5118 Washington St West Roxbury MA 02132 Office: McGuinn Hall Sch Edn Boston Coll Chestnut Hill MA 02167

MURPHY, KATHRYN MARGUERITE, archivist; b. Brockton, Mass.; d. Thomas Francis and Helena (Fortier) Murphy; A.B. in History, George Washington U., 1935, M.A., 1939, M.L.S., 1950; postgrad. Catholic U. Am., 1966. With Nat. Archives and Records Service, Washington, 1940—, supervisory archivist Central Research br., 1958-62, archivist, 1962—. Lectr. colls., socs. in U.S., 1950—. Founder, pres. Nat. Archives lodge Am. Fedn. Govt. Employees, 1965—. Recipient commendation Okla. Civil War Centennial Commn., 1965; named hon. citizen Oklahoma City, Mayor, 1963. Mem. A.L.A., Soc. Am. Archivists (joint com. hosp. libraries 1965—), Phi Alpha Theta (hon.). Home: 1500 Massachusetts Av NW Washington DC 20005 Office: 7th and Pennsylvania Avs NW Washington DC 20408

MURPHY, LOIS BARCLAY (MRS. GARDNER MURPHY), psychologist; b. Lisbon, Ia., Mar. 23, 1902; d. Wade Crawford and May (Hartley) Barclay; A.B., Vassar Coll., 1923; B.D., Union Theol. Sem., 1928; Ph.D., Columbia, 1937; certificate Topeka Psychoanalytic Inst., 1960; m. Gardner Murphy, Nov. 27, 1926; children—Alpen G., Margaret (Mrs. Fred A. Small). Mem. faculty Sarah Lawrence Coll. Faculty, Bronxville, N.Y., 1928-52; mem. faculty grad. program clin. psychology Coll., City N.Y., 1947-51; research psychologist Menninger Found., Topeka, 1952-71. Cons. to orgns., agys.; lectr. Bank St. Coll. for Tchrs., N.Y.C., 1937-42; cons. B.M. Inst. Child Devel. and Mental Health Ahmedabad, India, 1950-60, Children's Hosp. of Washington, 1967-71; instr. Topeka Psychoanalytic Inst., 1964-69; prof. Child devel. George Washington U. Med. Sch., 1969—; lectr. Head Start Program, Kan. State U., 1964; mem. com. early childhood care reconsidered Nat. Inst. Mental Health, 1964-66. Mem. White House Task Force on Early Child Care, 1967. Recipient awards including Children's Service award Toy Mfrs. U.S., 1962. Fellow N.Y. Acad. Scis., Am. Orthopsychiat. Assn., Nat. Assn. Edn. Young Children, Soc. Personality Assessment, Soc. Psychol. Study Social Issues, Topeka Psychoanalytic Soc., Assn. Childhood Edn. Author books including: Personality in Young Children, 1956; The Widening World of Childhood, 1962. Editorial bd. Childhood Edn., 1970—, Internat. Early Children, 1971—. Home: Ashland NH 03217

MURPHY, LORETTA MARIE, educator; b. Joliet, Ill., Mar. 14, 1906; d. Charles and Elizabeth Angela (Dolan) Murphy; A.B., U. Ill., 1940; M.A., U. Chgo., 1951, certificate advanced study reading, 1956; M.S., Ill. State U., Normal, 1974. Tchr. rural schs., Manhattan, Ill., 1926-27; tchr. primary grades Rockdale (Ill.) pub. sch., 1927-32; tchr. 1st grade, pub. schs. Joliet, Ill., 1935-71; tchr. English as 2d lang. Sch. Dist. 204, Joliet Twp., evenings 1966-69; instr. reading and study skills Lewis U., Lockport, Ill., evenings 1960-65. Vol. 1st aid instr. A.R.C., 1941-66. Mem. N.E.A., Ill. Edn. Assn., Nat. Assn. Sch. Psychologists, Nat. Soc. Study Edn., Council Exceptional Children. Roman Catholic. Home: 415 N Larkin Av Joliet IL 60435

MURPHY, MARGARET ANN, assn. exec.; b. Boston, Jan. 4, 1929; d. Martin Joseph and Mary Josephine (Maloney) Murphy; B.A., Manhattanville Coll., Purchase, N.Y., 1950. Dir. pub. relations Carney Hosp., Boston, 1950-52, Children's Museum, Jamaica Plain, Mass., 1952-54; instr. English, Newton (Mass.) Coll., 1954-55; dir. pub. relations Nat. Student Assn., 1955-58; editor pub. relations dept. Prudential Ins. Co., Boston, 1958-60; dir. pub. relations Bachrach, Inc., photographers, 1960-62; asst. press sec. to Gov. Endicott Peabody of Mass., 1963-64; pub. relations cons. Mass. Registry Motor Vehicles, 1965; dir. pub. relations Boston Hosp. Women, 1966-70, Mass. Nurses Assn., 1970—. Mem. Pub. Relations Soc. Am., New Eng. Hosp. Pub. Relations Assn. (past sec.), Am. Soc. Hosp. Pub. Relations Dirs. Home: 50 Wellesley Park Dorchester MA 02124 Office: 20 Ashburton Pl Boston MA 02108

MURPHY, MARIANNE CECILIA, educator; b. Oak Park, Ill., Sept. 11, 1937; d. William Francis and Marie Catherine (Garvey) Murphy; A.B., Mundelein Coll., 1960; M.Ed., Loyola U., 1963, postgrad. 1972—; postgrad. (NSF fellow), DePaul U., 1964-67; postgrad. (NSF fellow), Utah State U., 1968. Tchr. math. Roosevelt High Sch., Chgo., 1960-67, chmn. dept., 1961-67, asst. sr. advisor, 1964-67; instr. math., edn. Mundelein Coll., Chgo., 1967-73, dir. student teaching, 1971—, asst. prof. edn., 1973—. N. Central Assn. visitor for evaluation of secondary schs. Tri-Hi Y Sponsor YMCA, 1963-67. Mem. Art Inst. Chgo., Mundelein Coll. Alumnae Assn. (v.p. 1970-72, pres. 1972—), Nat. Council Tchrs. of Math, Ill. Assn. for Tchr. Edn. in Pvt. Colls., Am. Assn. Colls. of Tchr. Edn., Ill. Dirs. Student Teaching, Aquin Guild (exec. bd. 1965, sec. 1966-68), Am., Ill. bar assns. (student mem.), Chgo. Council Lawyers (student mem.), Chgo. Council Fgn. Relations, Alpha Delta Kappa, Phi Alpha Delta. Club: Women's Math. (membership chmn. 1966-67) (Chgo.). Home: 165 N Kenilworth Av Oak Park IL 60301 Office: 6363 Sheridan Rd Chicago IL 60660

MURPHY, MARIBETH LOGAN (MRS. MELVIN L. MURPHY), educator; b. Topeka, June 5, 1921; d. Harry Russell and Leila (James) Logan; student Washburn U., 1939-41, U. Colo., 1941-42; B.A., U. Denver, 1943; M.A., San Diego State Coll., 1965; Ph.D., U.S. Internat. U., 1969; postgrad. So. Ore. Coll., 1955, Portland State U., 1955-57, U. Hawaii, 1966; m. Melvin L. Murphy, Dec. 31, 1941; children—John Lawrence, Russell Andrew, Mary Lenora. Tchr. pvt. schs., Portland, Ore., 1954-57; tchr. Santee (Cal.) Elementary Sch. Dist., 1959-65, guidance cons., sch. psychologist 1965—. Cons. Headstart, 1965, 68; instr. U. Cal. at San Diego, 1969-72. Mem. Am., Cal., San Diego (dir. 1969-73), Foothills (pres. 1968-69) personnel and guidance assns., Am., Cal. sch. counselors assns., Cal. Assn. Measurement and Evaluation in Guidance, N.E.A., Cal., Santee tchrs. assns., Cal. Assn. Sch. Psychometrists and Psychologists, Sigma Alpha Iota, Alphi Phi. Author: Murphy Inventory of Values. Editor: Doctoral Soc. Jour., 1969-70; editorial staff Elementary Sch. Guidance and Counseling Jour., 1968—. Contbr. articles in field to profl. jours. Home: 5283 Countryside Dr San Diego CA 92115 Office: Santee Edn Center Box 220 Santee CA 92071

MURPHY, MARION FISHER (MRS. RAYMOND EDWARD MURPHY), author; b. St. Paul, Oct. 7, 1902; d. William Richard and Nina Florence (Finch) Fisher; B.A., U. Wis., 1925, M.A., 1930; postgrad. U. Ky., 1927-28; m. Raymond Edward Murphy, May 22, 1926; 1 son, Patric Alan. Tchr., Pa. State U., University Park, intermittently 1932-45, Keene (N.H.) State U., 1964-65. Mem. Nat. League Am. Pen Women (state pres., 1964-66, nat. auditor, 1970-72), Assn. Am. Geographers. Author: Pennsylvania: A Regional Geography, 1937, Pennsylvania Landscapes, 1938, 3d edit., 1974; (with Stephen B. Jones) Geography and World Affairs, 1950, 3d edit., 1971; (with others) In The Eastern Hemisphere, 1971; also hist. and geog. articles. Home: 1299 Briarwood Av Deltona FL 32763

MURPHY, MARJORIE MARY PICOT (MRS. DONALD LAWRENCE MURPHY), assn. exec.; b. Cambridge, Mass., July 8, 1926; d. Charles Alexander and Agatha Mary (De Grace) Picot; grad. high sch.; m. Donald Lawrence Murphy, Jan. 4, 1947; children—Elaine McMahon, Steven D., Bryan F., Cheryl Madden. Sec. to credit mgr. Household Finance Co., Malden and Boston, 1945-50; credit mgr. Leed's Furriers, Boston, 1947-49; aquatic dir. Wakefield (Mass.) YMCA, 1957-63; dir. Bear Hill, Wakefield and Camelot Swim Clubs, Boxford, Mass., 1964-65; aquatic dir. Danvers (Mass.) YMCA, 1963-67, phys. dir., 1967-74, asso. exec. dir., 1973-74; aquatic commr. YMCA N.E. region, mem. nat. operating council on aquatics, 1974; now women and girls dir. YMCA, Summit, N.J. Dir. Danvers schs. physically, mentally handicapped, kindergarten swim program, after 1965; water safety trainer Town Wakefield, 1957-63; dir. various pvt. and fund raising water shows, 1957—; mem. conf. staff Council Nat. Cooperation in Aquatics U.S., 1971-74. Dist. chmn. March of Dimes, Wakefield, 1959-60; vol. various fund drives; chmn. N.E. region Synchronized Swim Commn., 1968—; mem. exec. com. N.E. region Girl Leaders Sch., 1966, dir., 1973; v.p. St. Marys High Sch., 1969-70; mem. Pres.'s Council on Phys. Fitness and Sports, 1972, 74; mgr. St. Joseph's Mothers Assn., 1962-64. Recipient Distinguished Service to Aquatics award Nat. YMCA Operating Council on Aquatics, 1973. Mem. N.E. Dist. Phys. Dirs. Soc. (pres. 1968), Nat. Phys. Edn. Soc. (sec. 1973—). Home: Namotur Tower 373 E Main St Apt 415 Somerville NJ 08876 Office: 67 Maple St Summit NJ 07901

MURPHY, MARY ANN FOOTE (MRS. DAVID E. MURPHY), educator; b. Fairbury, Neb., Jan. 2, 1947; s. Eugene Aldin and Marian Dorothy (Shafer) F.; student No. Colo. U., 1965-66; B.A., Kearney State Coll., 1969; M.A., Purdue U., 1971; postgrad. Ohio U., 1973; m. David E. Murphy, May 27, 1972. Mem. faculty Marshall U., Huntington, W.Va., 1971—, prof. speech, 1971—, dir. forensics, 1972—. Tournament coordinator Marshall U., 1972-74, mem. pub. address planning com., 1971-74. Named one of top ten outstanding tchrs. speech, Purdue U., 1971. Mem. Speech Communication Assn. W.Va. (co-exec. sec. 1973-74), W.Va. Intercollegiate Speech Assn., W.Va. Speech Assn., Intercollegiate, Nat., Am. forensic assns., Central States Speech Assn. Baptist. Home: 1949 16th St Rd Huntington WV 25701

MURPHY, MARY DORREDELL DALTON (MRS. JIM GORDON MURPHY), librarian; b. Lawrence, Kan., Dec. 31, 1917; d. William B. and Margery (Bowersock) Dalton; A.B., U. Kan., 1939; B.S., Columbia, 1940; m. Jim Gordon Murphy, June 20, 1941; children—Michael Sean, Donald Evan, Neil Gordon. Acquisitions asst. U. Kan. Library, Lawrence, 1940, periodicals librarian, 1941; hdqrs. librarian Johnson County Library, Shawnee Mission, Kan., 1961-66, dir. in-service tng. 1966-68; reference librarian Lawrence (Kan.) Pub. Library, 1968—; reference librarian, cons. N.E. Kan. Library System, Lawrence, 1968—. Mem. A.L.A., Kan., Mountain Plains library assns., League of Women Voters, Gamma Phi Beta. Conglist. Home: Lake Dabinawa McLouth KS 66054 Office: 707 Vermont St Lawrence KS 66044

MURPHY, MARY FRANCES DE PETRO (MRS. GREGORY HOWARD MURPHY), coll. adminstr.; b. Bradford, Pa., Mar. 5, 1946; d. John Paul and Lucy Marie (Barranti) DePetro; B.A. cum laude, Newton (Mass.) Coll. of Sacred Heart, 1968; postgrad. Babson Coll., 1974—; m. Gregory Howard Murphy, June 17, 1972. Urban intern U.S. Dept. Housing and Urban Devel., Washington, 1968-69, program asst. elderly and handicapped housing, 1969-70, program analyst federally assisted housing programs, 1970, urban intern coordinator, Boston, 1970-72; asst. dir. admissions Newton Coll. of Sacred Heart, 1972, dir. alumnae affairs, 1972—, asst. dir. devel., 1972-74, dir. devel., 1974—. Rep. regional interagency youth task force Dept. Housing and Urban Devel., 1971-72. Vol. worker various local charitable orgns. Mem. Nat. Assn. Housing and Redevel. Ofcls., Am. Alumni Council, Asso. Alumni Sacred Heart, YWCA, Phi Alpha Theta. Club: Newton College Alumnae (Boston). Home: 54 Hartford St Natick MA 01760 Office: 885 Centre St Newton MA 02159

MURPHY, SISTER MARY NADINE, educator; b. Waucoma, Ia., June 22, 1933; d. Charles Thomas and Madeline Elizabeth (McGovern) Murphy; A.B., Clarke Coll., 1954; M.S., Purdue U., 1964, Ph.D., 1965. Joined Sisters of Charity, 1954; instr. dept. biology Mundelein Coll., Chgo., 1959-66, asst. prof. biology, 1966-70, asso. prof., 1970—, chmn. dept. biology, 1966—. Higher Edn. commr. Sisters of Charity, 1973—; cons. evaluator North Central Assn. NSF fellow, 1961-64, Shell Merit fellow Stanford, summer 1970; Am. Council Edn. fellow Acad. Adminstrn. Internship program, 1974-75. Mem. Am. Soc. for Microbiology, A.A.A.S., Sigma Xi. Address: 6363 Sheridan Rd Chicago IL 60660

MURPHY, MARY PATRICIA, journalist; b. Kalispell, Mont., Aug. 8, 1947; d. James Emmett and Sylvia Josephine (Brassett) Murphy; student U. Pacific, 1965-66; B.A. with high honors, U. Mont., 1969; postgrad. U. Wash., 1973. Urban renewal model cities reporter Ind. Record, Helena, Mont., 1969-70; newswoman A.P., Helena, 1970, Omaha, 1970-71, Seattle, 1971-72, 1973—. Mem. Women in Communications, Kappa Tau Alpha, Sigma Delta Chi, Alpha Lambda Delta, Phi Kappa Phi. Home: 154 Valley Seattle WA 98109 Office: 201 Boren N Seattle WA 98111

MURPHY, MARY TERESA JOSEPH, chemist, educator; b. Hartford, Conn., Sept. 10, 1928; d. James Joseph and Lucy Anne (Jackman) Murphy; B.S., St. Joseph Coll., 1950; M.A., Wesleyan U., 1956; Ph.D., Fordham U., 1965; postgrad. U. Cal. at San Diego, 1963-65, U. Glasgow, Scotland, 1966-67. Chemist Naugatuck Chem. div. Uni-Royal Co., Naugatuck, 1950-51; chemist Travelers Ins. Co. Hartford, 1951-54; chemist Monsanto Chem. Co., Springfield, Mass., 1956-58; prof. St. Joseph Coll., West Hartford, Conn., 1965—. Cons. NASA, 1965—, Conn. Geol. Survey, 1967—, Kan. Geol. Survey, 1968—. Teaching award Am. Cyanamid Corp., 1962. Nat. Acad. Sci. fellow, 1966, NASA fellow, 1967. Mem. Am. Chem. Soc., A.A.A.S., Geochem. Soc. Author: (with Eglington, Geoffrey) Organic Geochemistry, 1969. Address: 1678 Asylum Av W Hartford CT 06117

MURPHY, MAUREEN CARTWRIGHT (MRS. MICHAEL VINCENT MURPHY), educator; b. Bklyn., Oct. 14, 1937; d. Maurice Edward and Claire Constance (Darcy) Cartwright; B.A., St. Joseph's Coll., 1960; M.S., Fordham U., 1967; Ph.D., N.Y. U., 1972; m. Michael Vincent Murphy, Dec. 27, 1972. Tchr. secondary schs., N.Y.C., 1960-69; lectr. instr. English edn. Bklyn. Coll., 1969-71, asst. prof., 1971—, secondary curriculum coordinator, 1972—. Cons. performance-based and competency-based tchr. edn. programs. Recipient grant Danforth Found., 1973, innovative grant Bklyn. Coll., summer 1973. Mem. A.A.A.S., Am. Ednl. Research Assn., Nat. Council Tchrs. English, Nat. Council Women U.S., Nat. Soc. for Study Edn., N.Y.C. Assn. Tchrs. English, N.Y. State English Council. Home: 939 82d St Brooklyn NY 11228

MURPHY, MIRIAM (CATHERINE), artist, educator; b. Anoka, Minn.; d. Frank and Emily (Green) Murphy; B.A., U. Ore., 1936; M.F.A., U. Wash., 1950; postgrad. Art Students League, N.Y., 1946, Nat. U., Tokyo and Sophia U., Tokyo, 1961; research in Mus. Europe, 1964. Instr. Holy Names Coll., Spokane, Wash., 1938-45; asst. prof. Marylhurst Coll., Portland, Ore., 1945-60, chmn. art dept., 1950-60, prof. art, 1972—; prof., chmn. art dept. Ft. Wright Coll., Spokane, 1960-66; prof. art Seattle Community Coll., 1967-68; prof. art S.W. State Coll., Marshall, Minn., 1968-72. One-man shows Portland (Ore.) Art Mus., 1954, Linfield Coll., McMinnville, Ore., 1956, Coos Bay (Ore.) Gallery, 1959, Willamette U., Salem, 1960, 65, Marylhurst Coll., Portland, 1951, Unitarian Gallery, Seattle, 1967, Friends Gallery, Seattle, 1968, Anderson Gallery, Seattle, 1968, Louvre Gallery, Seattle, 1971; exhibited in group shows Artist Tchrs. of Inland Empire, 1960-66, Artist of Ore., 1936-60, N.W. Artists Show, 1964, Inland Empire Northwest, 1960-62, Art Center, Albany, N.Y., 1971; Talent VI Minn. Mus., St. Paul, 1971. Carnegie fellow, 1937; grantee for study, Asia, 1961, Europe, 1964, 69. Mem. Coll. Art Assn. Office: Marylhurst Coll Marylhurst OR 97036

MURPHY, MOTHER MARY BENEDICT, educator; b. Bklyn., July 15, 1903; d. Andrew John and Mary Louise (Gavin) Murphy; diploma Virgil Conservatory Music, N.Y.C., 1923; B.A., Marymount Coll., Tarrytown, N.Y., 1928, M.A., 1931; postgrad. Catholic U. Am., 1953-54; Ph.D., Columbia, 1957; postgrad. Xavier U., Cin., 1959; diploma in Portuguese Lang., Lit. and Culture, Coimbra U., Portugal, 1960. Instr. English, French, Latin, music Marymount Acad., Los Angeles, Marymount Acad., Tarrytown, N.Y., 1923-32; instr. English, Latin, philosophy Colegio Sacre-Coeur de Marie, Rio de Janeiro, 1932-42, Sao Paulo, 1942-45; instr. Colegio Sacre-Coeur de Marie, Belo Horizonte, Brazil, 1945-51, also dean, registrar, asst. superior; instr. edn. Marymount Coll., Tarrytown, 1951-61, chmn. edn. dept., dir. tchr. tng., 1951-61, asso. prof. edn., 1968-69; dir. instnl. research Marymount Coll. of Va., Arlington, 1969-72; ednl. cons. Marymount Coll., Palos Verdes Estates, Cal.; edn. editor New Cath. Ency., Cath. U. Am., 1961-65, contbr. sects., 1967; Fulbright lectr. Xavier U. and Ateneo de Manila U., Philippines, 1966-67, Manila (P.I.), U., 1967; translator for World Bank, Internat. Transl. Center, Berlitz. Mem. supt.'s adv. bd. Bd. Edn., N.Y.C., 1955-61. Recipient Brasilia Gratiam Refert award Brazilian Ministry Edn., 1961. Mem. Nat. Council Univ. Research, Assn. Instnl. Research, Am. Translators Assn., Nat. Cath. Edn. Assn., Nat. Cath. Audio-Visual Edn. Assn. (past sec.), Cath. Coll. Council Tchr. Preparation (past sec.), Kappa Delta Pi. Contbr. sects. to New Catholic Ency., 1967. Address: Marymount College of Virginia 2807 N Glebe Rd Arlington VA 22207

MURPHY, SISTER ROSEANNE, educator; b. San Rafael, Cal., Aug. 5, 1932; d. George Edward and Rose Margaret (Corcoran) Murphy; R.N., St. Joseph's Coll. Nursing, 1953; B.A., Mt. St. Mary's Coll., 1959; M.A., Stanford, 1962; Ph.D., U. Notre Dame, 1965. Joined Sisters of Notre Dame de Namur, 1953, provincial councillor, 1970—; tchr. Notre Dame High Sch., Belmont, 1956-58, 59-60; faculty Coll. Notre Dame, Belmont, 1960-62, 65—, asso. prof., dept. sociology, 1965—, also trustee. Mem. Am. Social Assn., Assn. for Sociology of Religion (exec. council 1972-74). Contbr. articles to profl. jours. Address: College Notre Dame Belmont CA 94002

MURPHY, ROSEMARY, actress; b. Munich, Germany (parents U.S. citizens); d. Robert D. and Mildred (Taylor) Murphy; ed. in Paris, France and Kansas City, Mo. Theatrical appearances include Look Homeward Angel, 1958, Night of the Iguana (World premier at Spoleto (Italy) Festival of Two Worlds), 1959, Period of Adjustment, 1961, King Lear, 1963, Any Wednesday, 1964-66, Delicate Balance, 1966, Week End, 1968, Butterflies Are Free, 1970-71; motion picture appearances include To Kill a Mockingbird, 1962, Any Wednesday, 1966, Butterflies are Free, 1970-71, Ace Eli and Roger of the Skies, 1971, Ben, 1971, You'll Like My Mother, 1972. Appeared on TV in Secret Storm, 1970. Nominated for Tony award, 1961, 64, 66; recipient award Motion Picture Arts Club, 1966, Variety Poll award, 1961, 67, Blue Ribbon award 1962. Address: 220 E 73rd St New York City NY 10021

MURPHY, SHARON BOEHM, physician; b. Chgo., Oct. 19, 1943; d. Edwin Reith and Estelle Elizabeth (Stiel) Boehm; B.S. with honors, U. Wis., 1965; M.D. cum laude, Harvard, 1969; m. Frank L. Murphy, Dec. 7, 1968; 1 son, James Edward. Intern, then resident pediatrics U. Colo. Med. Center, 1969-71; postdoctoral trainee pediatric hematology and oncology Children's Hosp., Phila., 1971-73; part-time asso. coll. physician student health dept. Bryn Mawr Coll., 1971-73; research asso. in hematology St. Jude Children's Research Hosp., Memphis, 1973—. Mem. Phi Beta Kappa, Alpha Omega Alpha. Home: 1270 Elmview Lane Memphis TN 38116 Office: St Jude's Research Hospital 332 N Lauderdale Memphis TN 38101

MURPHY, SHARON MARGARET (MRS. JAMES E. MURPHY), educator; b. Milw., Aug. 2, 1940; d. Adolph Leonard and Margaret Ann (Hirtz) Feyen; student Divine Savior Jr. Coll., 1957-59; B.A. cum laude, Marquette U., 1965; M.A. (Jo Caldwell Meyer scholar), U. Ia., 1970; Ph.D., 1973; m. James Emmet Murphy, June 28, 1969; children—Shannon Lynn, Erin Ann. Mem. Sisters Divine Savior, 1957-68; tchr. St. Therese Grade Sch., Schofield, Wis., 1959-61, St. Joseph Grade Sch., East Bristol, Wis., 1961-63, Divine Savior High Sch., Milw., 1963-68; instr., dir. pubis. Kirkwood Community Coll., Cedar Rapids, Ia., 1970-71; instr. U. Ia., Iowa City, 1971-72; asst. prof. mass communications U. Wis., Milw., 1973—. Curriculum coordinator literacy project, inner city Milw., 1968—; coordinator journalism seminars Urban High Schs., U. Ia., 1969-72. Named Outstanding Young Educator, Jr. C. of C., Wauwatosa, Wis., 1966; recipient Distinguished Service award Cath. Sch. Press Assn., 1966, Outstanding Tchr. Adviser award Sch. Journalism, Wis. Journalism Tchr.-Adviser Council, 1968, Journalism Achievement awards Wall St. Jour. Newspaper Fund, 1967, 68, 69. Mem. Journalism Edn. Assn. (chmn. nat. curriculum commn., 1969—), Women in Communications (Outstanding Student Adviser award, 1972), Assn. Edn. in Journalism. Roman Catholic. Editor (with Don Wigal): Screen Experience: An Approach to Film, 1969, 2d edit, 1974. Author: (with others) Laboratory Manual for Jounalism in the Mass Media, 1970; Other Voices: Black, Chicano and American Indian Press, 1974. Editor, Worldwide Mag., 1967-68. Contbr. to profl. jours. Home: 3309 N Hackett St Milwaukee WI 53211

MURPHY, SHERRIE CAROL, advt., publicity exec.; b. Port Chester, N.Y., Feb. 6, 1937; d. Charles and Helen Jane (D'Alton) Murphy; B.A. with honors in Philosophy and History, U. Toronto, 1959. Asst. to account exec. Batten, Barton, Durstine & Osborn, Advt., N.Y.C., 1961-62; advt. mgr. Walker & Co. Pubs., N.Y.C., 1965-68; advt. mgr. Praeger Pubs., N.Y.C., 1968-71, dir. advt., publicity, 1971—. Bd. Alumni Assos. U. Toronto. Recipient Alumni prize for Philosophy U. Toronto, 1959. Mem. Pubs. Advt. Club (bd. dirs.), Pubs. Publicity Assn., Asia Soc. Clubs: Weschester Sports, Dessoff Choirs. Home: 401 E 74th St New York City NY 10021 Office: 111 4th Av New York City NY 10003

MURPHY, SHIRLEY ROUSSEAU (MRS. PATRICK J. MURPHY), author; b. Oakland, Cal., May 20, 1928; d. Otto Francis and Helen (Hoffman) Rousseau; A.A., San Francisco Art Inst., 1951;

m. Patrick J. Murphy, Aug. 5, 1951. Interior decorator Bullocks, Los Angeles, 1952-55; tchr. decorative art San Bernardino (Cal.) Valley Coll., 1956-59; documents asst. and mus. asst. Canal Zone Library and Mus., Panama Canal Zone, 1964-67; painter, sculptor exhibiting in one man shows Instituto Panameno de Arte, 1964, Richmond Mus., Cal., 1963, Light House Gallery, Hermosa Beach, Cal., 1960, Cherry Gallery, San Bernardino, 1960, Ash Grove Gallery, Los Angeles, 1959, Ojai Valley Art Center, Ojai, Cal., 1959, Whittier (Cal.) Art Assn., 1958, San Bernardino Valley Coll., 1958, Jack Carr Gallery, South Pasadena, 1957; exhibited in group shows at Comara Gallery, Los Angeles, 1961, Huysman Gallery, Los Angeles, 1961, Quey Gallery, Tiburon, Cal., 1963, Pasadena Art Mus. Annual, 1958, Los Angeles County Mus. Annuals, 1957, 59, Cal. Water Color Soc. Annuals, 1957, 59, Oakland Mus. Sculptor's Annual, 1959, LaJolla Art Center Annual, 1961, Richmond Mus. Annual, 1962, Los Angeles Art Assn., 1957, 59, Oakland /Rental Gallery, 1962, San Francisco Mus. Rental Gallery, 1961, 64, Marin Rental Gallery, 1961, 68, Richmond Mus. Rental Gallery, 1962, San Francisco Art Inst., 1964 (all in Cal.), Denver Annual, Las Vegas (Nev.) Annual, Tucson (Ariz.) Annual: author children's books, 1967—. Mem. San Francisco Art Inst., Cal. Water Color Soc., Marin Soc. Artists, San Francisco Women Artists. Author: White Ghost Summer, 1967, The Sand Ponies, 1967, Elmo Doolan and the Search for the Golden Mouse, 1970, (with Patrick J. Murphy) Carlos Charles, 1971; Poor Jenny, Bright as a Penny, 1974. Address: 1620 Stonecliff Dr Decatur GA 30033

MURPHY, SUSAN ANN, advt. exec.; b. N.Y.C., May 16, 1945; d. Stewart Frances and Mary Loretta (Abernathy) Murphy; B.A. in English, State U. N.Y., Stony Brook, 1966. Asst. media dir. Deltakos div. J. Walter Thompson Co., N.Y.C., 1966-70; media dir., account exec. Grey Med. Advt. Inc., N.Y.C., 1970—. Mem. Am. Assn. Advt. Agys. (chmn. com. on pharm. media comparability 1974), Pharm. Advt. Club. Home: 141 E 56th St New York City NY 10022 Office: 777 3d Av New York City NY 10017

MURPHY, WINIFRED LEE SCHMALE (MRS. OWEN JAMES MURPHY), TV producer, dir.; b. San Francisco, Aug. 6, 1931; d. John Joseph and Ida Loretta (Drady) Schmale; A.A., San Francisco City Coll., 1951; B.A., San Francisco State U., 1954; m. Owen James Murphy, July 28, 1962; children—Dana Catherine, Megan Elisabeth. Sales sec. KJBS Radio, San Francisco, 1952; with KQED-TV, Pub. TV, San Francisco, Cal., 1954—, sr. producer-dir., 1959—; radio-TV cons. Inner Light Found., Novato, Cal., 1972; writer weekly column Marin Suburban Newspapers, 1963—. Recipient Ohio State U. award for creativity in network category, 1957, Emmy for documentary Am. Acad. TV Arts and Scis., 1972. Republican. Roman Catholic. Address: 43 Fowler Ct San Rafael CA 94903

MURR, SANDRA MICHAEL see Michael, Sandra Dale.

MURRAY, AUDREY MADELEINE (MRS. CECIL COLEMAN), health service adminstr.; b. Innisfail, Alta., Can., Aug. 31, 1918; d. Albert and Fern Gertrude (Brandt) Conn; R.N., Galt Sch. Nursing, Alta., 1941; B.S. in Nursing, U. Wash., 1964; m. Cecil Coleman, Oct. 3, 1969. Staff nurse Vancouver (B.C., Can.) Gen. Hosp., 1943-45, head nurse Jewish Gen. Hosp., Montreal, Que., Can., 1949-53, Calgary (Alta.) Hosp., 1955-56; instr. Jewish Gen. Hosp., 1953-55; instr. St. Paul's Hosp., Vancouver, 1957-59, coordinator, 1959-62, asst. dir. Sch. of Nursing, 1962-69, dir. hosp. nursing service, 1969-70, dir. nursing, 1970—. Clin. instr. U. B.C., 1958—, clin. cons., Sch. Nursing programme, 1972—. Chmn. adv. com. Vancouver City Coll. Mem. Registered Nurses Assn. B.C., Sigma Theta Tau. Home: 1101-1575 Beach Av Vancouver BC V6G 1Y5 Canada Office: 1981 Burrard Vancouver BC Canada

MURRAY, BLANCHE ALMA, recreation coordinator; b. Baldwin, Fla., Mar. 3, 1916; d. Lewis and Ida (Green) Murray; grad. high sch. Recreation worker WPA, Jacksonville (Fla.) Recreation Dept., 1940-42, playground dir., 1942-50, supr. arts and crafts, 1950-67; coordinator pilot study recreation and creative activities Fla. Commmn. on Aging, 1967—. Chmn. arts and crafts div. Greater Jacksonville Agrl. and Indsl. Fair, 1956. Cons. arts and crafts Duval County council Campfire Girls, 1954—; co-chmn. Fla. Fedn. Sr. Citizens Clubs, 1967—; recreation cons. Cathedral Found., 1967—; mem. com. on aging Community Planning Council Jacksonville Area, Inc., 1967—; mem. Fla. Council on Aging; chmn. adv. bd. career and adult edn. Fla. Jr. Coll. Bd. dirs. Greater Jacksonville Fair Assn., 1957—. Recipient Eve award, 1967, 70. Fellow Nat. Parks and Recreation Assn.; mem. Fla., Nat. recreation assns., Jacksonville C. of C. (com. leisure time activities for aging 1960-67), Fla. Fedn. Fairs, So. Parks and Recreation Assn. Methodist. Mem. Order Eastern Star. Home: 9322 Illinois St Jacksonville FL 32208 Office: Cathedral Towers 601 N Newnan St Jacksonville FL 32202

MURRAY, CAROL ORLOWSKY (MRS. GENE MURRAY), accounting co. exec.; b. Cin., July 14, 1929; d. Joseph Adamovich and Carol Frances (Brown) Orlowsky; M.B.A., George Washington U., 1950; m. Gene Murray, Mar. 1, 1958; children—Charles Innes, David Innes, Philip, Eugene, Joan. Vice pres. Gene Murray Advt., N.Y.C., 1958-61; advt. dir. Am. Surety, N.Y.C., 1961-63; dir. communications Touche Ross & Co., N.Y.C., 1963-73; publs. adminstr. Financial Acctg. Standards Bd., Stamford, Conn., 1973—. Mem. Advt. Women N.Y., Internat. Assn. Bus. Communicators, N.Y. Assn. Indsl. Editors, Mayflower Soc. Club: Overseas Press (N.Y.C.). Home: Litchfield Way Alpine NJ 07620 Office: High Ridge Park Stamford CT 06905

MURRAY, FLORENCE KERINS (MRS. PAUL F. MURRAY), judge; b. Newport, R.I., Oct. 21, 1916; d. John X. and Florence (MacDonald) Kerins; A.B., Syracuse U., 1938; LL.B., Boston U., 1942; student R.I. Coll., Edn., 1942, Ed.D. (hon.), 1956; LL.D., Bryant Coll., 1956, R.I. U., 1963, Mt. St. Joseph Coll., 1972; m. Paul F. Murray, Oct. 21, 1943; 1 son, Paul F. Admitted to Mass., R.I. bars; pvt. law practice with husband, under name Murray & Murray, Newport, R.I., 1947; asso. justice R.I. Superior Ct., 1956—; first woman judge State of R.I.; staff, faculty adviser Nat. Coll. state Judiciary, 1971-72. Mem. Gov.'s Jud. Council, R.I. Alcohol Adv. Council Com., Adv. Council on Mental Health, Nat. Adv. Com. on Women in Service; chmn. Newport Sch. Com.; state senator, R.I., 1948-54, bd. dirs., mem., sec. R.I. Physicians Service; dir., sec. R.I. Blue Shield; chmn. R.I. Nat. Endowment Humanities com., 1972. Bd. dirs. YMCA, Newport. Served as lt. col., WAC, World War II. Recipient Legion of Merit, Army Commendation Ribbon, Arents Alumni Award, Syracuse U., 1956, Carroll Award, R.I. Inst. Instrn., 1956; Regina medal, Salve Regina Coll., 1962; Alumni award Boston U., 1965. Mem. Am. Legion (judge adv. post 7, mem. nat. exec. com.), Am. Assn. U. Women (chmn. state edn. com., 1954-56), Bus. and Profl. Woman's Club (past state v.p., past pres. Newport, past pres. nat. legislative com.), Alpha Chi Omega, Kappa Beta Pi. Club: Quota (past gov. internat., past pres. Newport). Home: 2 Kay St Newport RI 02840 Office: Court House Providence RI 02903

MURRAY, GERTRUDE ELLEN (MRS. RICHARD E. SENGHAS), physician; b. Boston, June 22, 1929; d. Leo Joseph and Gertrude E. (Magee) M.; B.S., Simmons Coll., 1950; M.D., Harvard, 1954; m. Richard E. Senghas, Jan. 3, 1955; children—Catherine, Ellen, Margaret, Richard, John, Peter, Ann. Intern, St. Luke's Hosp., Cleve., 1954-55; resident Cleve. Met. Gen. Hosp., 1957-58; civilian physician Dept. Army, Yokohama, Japan, 1956; coll. physician Simmons Coll., Boston, 1958-65, Wellesley (Mass.) Coll., 1965—. Mem. Mass., Middlesex West Dist. (sec. 1970—) med. socs. Home: 44 Front St Hopkinton MA 01748 Office: Wellesley Coll Infirmary Wellesley MA 02181

MURRAY, HELEN MAE GODSEY (MRS. FRANK GRAHAM MURRAY), educator; b. Lynchburg, Va., Aug. 12, 1920; d. Herbert Braxton and Ruby (Moore) Godsey; A.B., Lynchburg Coll., 1942; M.Ed., U. Va., 1962; diploma in advanced grad. studies, U. Va., 1968; m. Frank Graham Murray, Dec. 22, 1942; children—Frank Graham, Janet Lee. Parish worker Meth. Ch., Washington, 1942-44; asst. dir. South Richmond (Va.) Bapt. Goodwill Center, 1944; asst. dir. Lynchburg (Va.) Bapt. Goodwill Center, 1945, dir., 1945-46; tchr. Child Care Center, Inc., Lynchburg, 1946-47, asst. dir., 1947-48; tchr. pub. schs., Lynchburg, 1953-61, guidance dir., 1961-65, dean-guidance coordinator, 1965-66, asst. prin., 1966-68, guidance coordinator, 1966-70; guidance coordinator Dunbar High Sch., Lynchburg, 1970-71, asst. prin. instrn., 1971—; dir. Lynchburg Learning Center, 1970-71; extension instr. U. Va. Sch. Continuing Edn., Roanoke Center, 1965-67, Lynchburg Regional Center, 1967—, Patrick Henry Coll., 1967. Vis. instr. Lynchburg Coll., summer 1972; cons. alternative schs. workshop Va. Assn. Sch. Execs., 1973. Mem. Va. (pres. guidance dept. dist. F 1966-67, parliamentarian 1973-74), Lynchburg (chmn. instrn. com. 1973-74, chmn. career edn. workshop 1974) edn. assns., N.E.A., Am. Personnel and Guidance Assn., Am. Sch. Counselors Assn., Nat. Congress Parents and Tchrs., Assn. Supervision and Curriculum Devel., Va. Assn. Supervision and Curriculum Devel., Am. Assn. U. Women (chmn. edn. com. 1970-72), Bapt. Bus. Women's Fedn. (Lynchburg area chmn. 1959-61, community missions chmn. 1969-70), Va. (chmn. 1962-67), Va. (bd. mem. 1968-70), Lynchburg Area (pres. 1968-70) personnel and guidance assns., Kappa Delta Pi, Delta Kappa Gamma (scholarship chmn. 1968-70; parliamentarian 1972—). Baptist. Home: 4512 Greenwood Dr Lynchburg VA 24502 Office: Dunbar High Sch Polk St at 12th Lynchburg VA 24504

MURRAY, JO BUMBARGER (MRS. CECIL LAWRENCE MURRAY), journalist; b. Laurinburg, N.C., Oct. 8, 1945; d. Paul William and Sara Nowell (Ward) Bumbarger; newspaper reporter Courier-Post, Camden, N.J., 1967-68; writer Del. River Port Authority mag., Camden, 1968-69; reporter, news editor Sierra Vista (Ariz.) Herald-Dispatch, 1970-71; reporter Oakland (Cal.) Tribune, 1972—. Recipient award for best news story in Phila. area during 1968 Phila. chpt. Sigma Delta Chi, award for best pub. service reporting in N.J. in 1968, N.J. chpt. Sigma Delta Chi. Mem. Women in Communications. Home: 2325 Leimert Blvd Oakland CA 94602 Office: 620 Las Junta Martinez CA 94553

MURRAY, JOSEPHINE LEE, pediatrician; b. N.Y.C., Jan. 8, 1921; d. Henry Alexander and Josephine Lee (Rantoul) Murray; A.B. cum laude, Radcliffe Coll., 1944; M.A., Sarah Lawrence Coll., 1954; M.D., N.Y. U., 1961. With O.S.S., Washington, London, Stockholm, 1944-46; research asst. Inst. Human Relations Yale, 1947-48, Harvard Psychol. Clinic, 1949-51; intern Duke Hosp., Durham, N.C., 1961-62; resident Mary Hitchcock Hosp., Hanover, N.H., 1962-63; resident Children's Hosp., Boston, 1963-64, pediatric fellow in psychiatry (Nat. Inst. Mental Health grantee), 1964-65; staff pediatrician Judge Baker Guidance Center, Boston, 1965—. Mem. vis. com. Harvard Health Services, 1968—; exec. com. Planned Parenthood League Mass.; bd. dirs. Boston Mus. Sci., Marlboro Music, Cantata Singers, Boston Indsl. Mission, Center Club Found.; U.S. sec. World Wildlife Fund. Home: 22 Lowell St Cambridge MA 02138 Office: 295 Longwood Av Boston MA 02115

MURRAY, JULIE KAORU (MRS. JOSEPH EDWARD MURRAY), occupational therapist; b. Wahiawa, Oahu, Hawaii, Nov. 18, 1934; d. Gijun and Edna Tsuruko (Taba) Funakoshi; B.A., U. Hawaii, 1956; certificate in occupational therapy U. Puget Sound, 1958; m. Joseph Edward Murray, July 15, 1961; children—Michael, Susan, Leslie. Therapist, Inst. Logopedics, Wichita, Kan., 1958; sr. therapist Hawaii State Hosp., Kaneohe, 1959; part-time therapist Centre County Center for Crippled Children and Adults, State College, Pa., 1963; vice-chmn. adv. bd. Hosp. Improvement Program East Ore. State Hosp., Pendleton, Ore., 1974. Dir. Ashland League Women Voters, 1967-71, v.p., 1970; mem. Ashland Park and Recreation Bd., 1972-73. Office Vocational Rehab. grantee, 1957. Mem. Am., Ore., Hawaii (sec. 1960) occupational therapy assns., Am. Civil Liberties Union, League Women Voters (dir. Pendleton), Common Cause Center Study Democratic Instn. Democrat. Address: 3805 SW Valley View Dr Pendleton OR 97801

MURRAY, KAREN JANE, social work administr.; b. Chgo., Mar. 19, 1928; d. James Dean and Sigrid (Gjovaag) Murray; B.A., St. Olaf Coll., 1949; M.S.W., U. Minn., 1959; m. Gjerruld Rude, Aug. 20, 1950 (div. Apr. 1959). Supr. child welfare Santa Clara County (Cal.) Welfare Dept., San Jose, 1959-61; supervising psychiat. social worker Santa Clara County Health Dept., San Jose, 1961-65, dir. psychiat. social work, 1965—. Field work instr. U. Cal., Sch. Social Welfare, Palo Alto, 1964-65; cons. social work Cal. Dept. Pub. Health, 1969—; mem. profl. adv. com. Cal. State Social Work and Marriage Counselor Qualifications Bd., 1968-69; mem. adv. council staffing standards Cal. Dept. Mental Hygiene, 1971—. Mem. exec. com. Comprehensive Mental Health Planning Santa Clara County, 1965-68; mem. adv. com. Youth Services Bur. Project Santa Clara County, 1969—; rev. cons. Nat. Inst. Mental Health; mem. Mental Health Commn. Bay Area, 1969—; chmn. Mental Health Task Force Reorgn. Santa Clara County, 1971—. Bd. dirs. Home Kare Agy., San Jose. Fellow Soc. Clin. Social Work (charter); mem. Nat. Assn. Social Workers (chpt. pres. 1964-67, statewide chmn. com. profl. devel. and social work Cal. council 1968—), Am. Civil Liberties Union, Am. Friends Service Com. Club: Zonta (bd. dirs., v.p.). Home: 205 Elmwood Ct Los Gatos CA 95030 Office: 2220 Moorpark Av San Jose CA 95128

MURRAY, L. CAROL, museum registrar; b. Miami, Fla., Aug. 24, 1946; d. Eugene X. and Janet Marie (Cordray) Murray; A.A., Miami Dade Jr. Coll., 1966; B.A., Fla. Atlantic U., 1969; M.F.A., Syracuse U., 1972. Asst. registrar Lowe Art Mus., U. Miami, 1969-70; registrar H.F. Johnson Mus. Art, Cornell U., Ithaca, N.Y., 1972—; curatorial research asst. Syracuse U., 1970-71; spl. projects dir. Lowe Art Center, Syracuse U., 1971-72; grad. teaching asst. Syracuse U., 1971-72. Recipient Miami Dade Jr. Coll. art scholarship and award of merit, 1964-66; Edward Marshall Boehm fellow, Syracuse U., 1970-71. Mem. N.E. Museums Conf. Editorial and research asst. African Art Speaks Yoruba, 1971, Karl Schrag, A Catalogue Raisonne of the Graphic Works, 1939-1970, 1971. Office: HF Johnson Mus of Art Cornell Univ Ithaca NY 14850

MURRAY, LANE (JOYCE ELAINE STONE) (MRS. THOMAS FRANCIS MURRAY), educator; b. Celina, Tex., Nov. 6, 1921; d. Esibbious Jefferson and Elise (Porter) Stone; B.A., Tex. Tech. Coll., 1942; M.Ed., Sam Houston State Tchrs. Coll., 1952; Ed.D., U. Houston, 1962; m. Dr. Thomas Francis Murray, Dec. 16, 1941; children—Stone Thomas, Joyce Elaine, Mark Vincent. Secondary sch. English and Spanish tchr., Barstow, Tex., 1942-43; job analyst U.S. Govt., Rome, N.Y., 1944-47; journalism and English tchr. secondary schs., Huntsville, Tex., 1954-58; exec. v.p. Essential Edn., Huntsville, 1957—; also asst. prof. edn., coordinator student teaching, Tex. A. and M. U., College Station, 1960-69, dir. instructional media lab., 1968-69; supt. schs. Windham Sch. Dist., Tex. Dept. Corrections, 1969—. Dir. Guidance Filmstrips (Houston). Dep. county clk. Walker County, Tex., 1952-54. Recipient blue ribbon award Am. Film Festival, 1962, red ribbon award, 1972. Mem. Am. Assn. Sch. Adminstrs., N.E.A., Am. Correctional Assn. (dir.), Correctional Edn. Assn. (v.p.), D.A.R., Kappa Delta Pi. Roman Catholic. Author: Preparation of Manuscripts for Reproduction by Diazo, 1962; The Development of a Secondary-Level Student Teaching Handbook for the University of Houston, 1962. Author filmstrip series: (with Dr. Thomas Murray) The Student Council in Action, 1957; Getting Ready for College, 1957; Getting Ready for High School, 1958; The Physical Education Series, 1960; The Library Series, 1959; The Group Guidance Series, 1961. Documentary (with Dr. Thomas Murray) 16 mm film, color, sound Tattoo My Soul; Make Straight My Mind, 1971. Home: PO Box 968 Huntsville TX 77340 Office: Windham School Dist Texas Dept Corrections Box 99 Huntsville TX 77340

MURRAY, LEE (MRS. GEORGE C. MURRAY), broadcaster; b. Dowagiac, Mich., Aug. 15, 1920; d. Jerry and Betty (Ross) Lane; student Friends Sem., N.Y.C., 1934-36; student Vassar Coll., 1936-37; m. George C. Murray, Dec. 23, 1939; children—William, Robert, Richard. Owner-dir. Puppeteer's Workshop, Utica, N.Y., 1945-48; moderator women's show sta. WKTV-TV, 1948-50; producer children's TV program WKNX-TV, Saginaw, Mich., 1952-53; copy writer Parker Advt. Agy., Saginaw, 1953-54; women's dir. woman's TV program WNEM-TV, Bay City, Mich., 1956-57; women's dir. WJIM-TV, Lansing, Mich., 1957-58; moderator women's show WJRT-TV, Flint, Mich., 1958-59; women's dir. radio sta. WJR, Detroit, 1959-66; syndicated radio 31 Mich. Stas., 1966-73; co-owner Murray Bernardi Assos., advt. agy., Detroit, 1973—. Pres. Birmingham Assn. Academically Talented Children, 1968-69; pub. relations cons. Wayne U. Women, 1969-71; mem. United Found. Speaker's Bur., 1968-71, chmn., 1970. Bd. dirs. Greater Mich. Found., 1973-74. Named Detroit Advt. Woman of the Year, 1970. Mem. Mich. Advt. Industry Alliance (bd. mem., sec. 1971-73), Am. Women in Radio and TV (pres. 1965-67), Women in Communication. Club: Women's Advertising (pres. 1970-73), Detroit Press. (Detroit). Home: 1418 Wrenwood Dr Troy MI 48084 Office: 1700 N Rosevere St Dearborn MI 48128

MURRAY, MARGUERITE ELIZABETH MIRIAM, clin. psychologist; b. St. Joseph, Mo., Aug. 3, 1911; d. Martin Roy and Marguerite E. (Wolfe) Murray; student Kansas City Jr. Coll., 1928-30; B.A., U. Kan., 1933, M.S., 1935; student U. Minn., 1936-38. Clin. intern Menninger Clinic, Topeka, 1945-46; psychoanalytic tng., Seattle, 1948-53, 55; state child psychologist State Children's Bur., Bismarck, N.D., 1938-44; chief psychologist Wash. State Mental Health Dept., Seattle, 1944-45; clin. psychologist Psychoanalytic Clinic, Seattle, 1946-55; pvt. practice clin. psychology, Seattle, 1955-57, La Jolla, Cal., 1957—. Instr. U. Minn., 1937-38; teaching cons. U. Wash., 1947; tchr. Evelyn Woods Dynamic Reading Inst., San Diego, 1966—; cons. psychologist Headstart Program, 1966—. Mem. San Diego Mental Health Assn., 1957—, Social Service League, La Jolla, Cal., 1960—. Asiatic arts com. San Diego Fine Arts Gallery, 1964—; mem. Bismarck Little Symphony, 1941-44, Seattle Philharmonic Orch., 1944-57; violinist La Jolla Civic Orch., 1958—, San Diego County Symphony, 1969—, U. S.D. Symphony, 1972—. Bd. mem. La Jolla Civic-U. Orch., 1958-64, 68—. Mem. Internat. Council Psychologists, Am., Cal., San Diego, Western psychol. assns., San Diego Clin. Psychology Assn. (sec. 1960-64, treas. 1968), Am. Orthopsychiatric Assn., N.Y. Acad. Sci., Nat. Research Council for Child Devel., World Fedn. for Mental Health, Los Angeles Soc. for Psychoanalytic Psychology. Home: 7444 Miramar Av La Jolla CA 92037 Office: 1030 Pearl St La Jolla CA 92037

MURRAY, MARIE JANE MARCHIGIANI, broadcasting exec.; b. Bedford Hills, N.Y.; d. Angelo and Frances (Scerrati) Marchigiani; student Hakes Coll., 1943-45, Union Coll., Schenectady, 1960; m. John Herbert Murray, Aug. 30, 1957 (dec. Mar. 1973); 1 dau., Patti Anne. Office mgr. Asburn Bros., Culver City, Cal., 1947-55; treas.'s asst. M. TenBosch, Inc., Pleasantville, N.Y., 1955-57; with Gen. Electric Broadcasting Co., Inc., Schenectady, 1962—, exec. asst. 1964—. Troop leader Girl Scouts Am., Schenectady, 1969-71. Recipient scholarship Women's Club, Bedford Hills, N.Y., 1943; also numerous awards in journalism. Mem. Am. Women in Radio and TV (nat. v.p. 1973—), Nat. Assn. Real Estate Bds., Schenectady Women's Press Club, Mike and Camera Assn. (pres. 1965-71). Altar Rosary Soc. Home: 1526 Phoenix Av Schenectady NY 12308 Office: 1400 Balltown Rd Schenectady NY 12309

MURRAY, MARY ANN, editor; b. N.Y.C., Aug. 27, 1943; d. James Francis and Rose Regina (Myers) Murray; grad. high sch. Sec to prodn. mgr. Blakiston div. McGraw Hill, N.Y.C., 1961-64, asst. to editor, medicine and dentistry, 1965-70, asst. to editor-in-chief Blakiston Publs., 1971-72, asst. to publisher, 1973—, also mng. editor Jour. Nursing Education, 1971—. Office: McGraw Hill 1221 Av of Americas New York City NY 10020

MURRAY, MARY ELIZABETH, educator; b. Mt. Savage, Md.; d. Michael and Catherine (Cunningham) Murray; student Frostburg State Tchrs. Coll., 1925-27; A.B., U. Md., U. 1929, M.A., 1930; postgrad. U. Cal. at Berkeley, summer 1938; postgrad. Cath. U., summers 1933, 58, 59, postgrad. London Sch. Econs., Eng., 1967. Tchr. journalism, history Allegany High Sch., Cumberland, Md., 1930-59; asso. prof. history, econs. Frostburg (Md.) State Coll., 1959—; reporter Cumberland (Md.) Daily News, 1945-46. Mem. Gov.s Adv. Com. for Sesqui-Centennial of Star-Spangled Banner; mem. Archdiocesan Council Clergy, Religious and Laity. Mem. and sec. senate Md. State Colls. Recipient State Newman award, 1967, Pro Ecclesia et Pontifice medal Pope Paul VI, 1971. Mem. Md. Scholastic Press Assn. (organizer; dir. 1946), Columbia Scholastic Press Assn., Columbia Advisers Assn. (pres. 1948-50), Am. Assn. U. Women (state chmn. status of women 1961-63), Md. Tchrs. Assn. (mem. exec. bd. 1959-60), Cath. Daus. Am. (Md. regent 1960-66, nat. dir. 1968-70, nat. 2d vice regent 1970-72), Sacred Heart Aux., N.E.A., Internat. Platform Assn., Delta Delta Delta, Phi Kappa Phi. Contbr. articles to profl. jours. Home: Mount Savage MD 21545 Office: Frostburg State Coll Frostburg MD 21532

MURRAY, MARY PATRICIA (MRS. JAMES F. DIFFLEY), phys. therapist; b. Milw., July 27, 1923; d. Joseph Michael and Edna (Ehlers) Murray; B.A. cum laude, Ripon Coll., 1944; registered phys. therapist, Mayo Clinic Sch. Phys. Therapy, 1956; M.A., Marquette U., 1956, Ph.D., 1961; m. James F. Diffley, July 6, 1963. Phys. therapist Curative Workshop Milw., 1945-48; with VA Center, Wood, Wis., 1948—, supr. research and edn., phys. therapy, 1959-64, chief kinesiology research lab., 1964—. Asso. prof. Med. Coll. Wis. at Milw., 1967—; mem. applied physiology study sect. NIH, 1972—; mem. acad. standards com. Sch. Phys. Therapy, Marquette U., Milw., 1971. Recipient Marian Williams Research award Am. Phys. Therapy Assn., 1967, 1st place sci. exhbn. award, 1965; Teaching award Marquette U., 1967. Mem. Am. Phys. Therapy Assn. (chmn. research com., 1972-73), Am. Congress Rehab. Medicine, Sigma Xi. Contbr.

to profl. jours. Home: 10523 N Pine Tree Circle Mequon WI 93092 Office: Kinesiology Research Lab VA Center Wood WI 93193

MURRAY, MAYDAWN, educator; b. Evanston, Ill., Apr. 21, 1935; d. Leslie Fife and Eleanor Emma (Cook) Murray; student Monmouth Coll., 1953-55; B.S. in Speech, Northwestern U., 1957, M.A. in Elementary Speech Edn., 1963. Prodn. asst. sta. WTTW, Chgo., 1956-57; with radio-TV dept. Campbell-Mithun Advt. Agy., Chgo., 1957-60; asst. radio-TV prodn. dir. John Shaw Advt. Agy., Chgo., 1960-62; creative drama tchr. Evanston pub. schs., 1963—. Cons. creative drama to dept. program devel. for gifted children, State of Ill., 1969-72; cons. tchr. curriculum Young Artists Studio, Art Inst., Chgo., 1973. Mem. Nat., Ill. edn. assns., Am., Children's theatre assns., Phi Beta, Delta Zeta. Recording Courageous Journeys, 1968. Office: 1314 Ridge Evanston IL 60201

MURRAY, OZEMA LACEY (MRS. LESLEY MURRAY), librarian; b. Vernon, Ala.; d. Arthur Andrew and Anilo Mary (Hankins) Lacey; student Stillman Coll., 1939-41; B.S., Ala. State Coll., 1950, M.Ed., 1954, postgrad., 1967-68; M.S. in Library Media, Ala. A. and M. U., 1972; m. Lesley Murray. Elementary tchr. Springfield Sch., Fernbank, Ala., 1941, Rush Chaple Sch., Fernbank, 1942, Mt. Ollie Sch., Millport, 1943, Temple Star Sch., Vernon, 1944-50, Lamar County Tng. Sch., Vernon, 1950-67, Sulligent (Ala.) Consol. Sch., 1967-68; high sch. librarian Lamar County High Sch., Vernon, 1968—. Active Fayette County Progressive League. Mem. A.L.A., N.E.A., Southeastern Library Assn. Mem. Order Eastern Star. Home: Route 1 Box 67 Vernon AL 35592 Office: Lamar County High Sch Vernon AL 35592

MURRAY, PATRICIA ELLEN, editor; b. Bangor, Me., Feb. 18, 1932; d. Gerald Joseph and Isabelle Mae (Dimitri) Murray; B.A., Newton Coll. of Sacred Heart, 1954. With office pub. Simmons Coll., Boston, 1954; reporter Waltham News Tribune, Waltham, Mass., 1954-56, sales prospector, 1961-64, regional editor, 1961-64; publicity dir. Newton Coll., Newtonville, Mass., 1956-61; reporter Braintree (Mass.) Sunday News, 1962-68, news editor, 1964-68, editor, 1968-70; editor Asso. Newspapers, Stoughton, Mass., 1970—, editor-in-chief Franklin Pub. Co., Rockland, Mass., Bull. Pub. Co., Stoughton, 1974—; corr. Boston Globe, 1968-70. Mem. Mass. Gov.'s Commn. Status of Women, 1974. Home: 354 Washington St Braintree MA 02184 Office: 9 Pearl St Stoughton MA 02072

MURRAY, PATRICIA SOPHIA, psychologist; b. Newark, Feb. 27, 1930; d. Alexander Blair and Sophia Thompson (Cameron) Murray; B.A., Montclair State Coll., 1951, M.A., 1956; Ed.D., Rutgers U., 1963. Tchr., counselor North Arlington (N.J.) High Sch., 1951-55; tchr. Oceanside (N.Y.) Sr. High Sch., 1955-58; counselor Lakeland Regional High Sch., Wanaque, N.J., 1958-62; psychol. intern. N.J. Tng. Sch. Sch., Totowa, 1961, Diagnostic Center, Menlo Park, N.J., 1962; psychologist Kinnelon (N.J.) Pub. Schs., 1962-65, dir. spl. services, 1965—; tchr. evening div. Montclair State Coll., Upper Montclair, N.J. Mem. Am., N.J. psychol. assns., Am. Personnel and Guidance Assn., Am. Sch. Counselors Assn., N.J. Assn. Sch. Psychologists, N.J. Edn. Assn., Am. Ednl. Research Assn. Home: 265 Main St Ridgefield Park NJ 07660 Office: Kinnelon Rd Kinnelon NJ 07405

MURRAY, THELMA E(NID), govt. edn. ofcl.; b. N.Y.C.; d. Henry and Marie Louise (D'Emanuele) Murray; M.A., Tchrs. Coll., Columbia, 1963. Rehab. counselor N.Y. State Edn. Dept., Div. Vocational Rehab., Albany, 1947-60, unit supr., 1960-65, tng. dir., 1965-74, area supr. Office Vocational Rehab., 1974—. Bd. dirs. Girls Club Albany, Albany County Mental Health Assn. Mem. Am., Capital Dist. (pres.-elect 1972-73) personnel and guidance assns., Am. Soc. Pub. Adminstrs., Am. Soc. Tng. and Devel., Nat. Rehab. Assn., Internat. Soc. Welfare of Disabled. Club: Soroptimist (pres. 1966-68, 72-73). Office: 99 Washington Av Albany NY 12210

MURSET, SUSIE JENKINS, pub. relations exec.; b. Buda, Ill., Oct. 11, 1912; d. William and Florence (Aruup) Murset; R.N., St. Luke's Hosp., Chgo., 1934. Pvt. duty nurse various Chgo. hosps., 1934-67; propr. Band Box Beauty Salon, St. Luke's Hosp., Chgo., 1937-41; with Nan Miller & Assos., Inc., pub. relations, Chgo., 1963—, sec., corporate v.p., 1963—, also dir.; with Intercomco Internat., Inc., Chgo., 1971—, sec.-treas., v.p., 1971—, dir., 1971—. Mem. Am., Ill., 1st Dist. nurses assns., Chgo. Assn. Commerce and Industry. Home: 1444 Cullom St Chicago IL 60613 Office: 55 E Washington St Chicago IL 60602

MUSE, DOROTHY ELEANOR (MRS. RICHARD S. MUSE), librarian; b. Arnold, Pa., Sept. 11, 1925; d. Edward Dutill and Hannah Margaret (Austin) Sourwine; student Grove City Coll., 1945-47; B.A., M.S. in Library Sci., U. Pitts., 1967; m. Richard S. Muse, Jan. 30, 1948; children—William R., Marsha Anne, Edward S. Tchr. English, Tarentum (Pa.) Jr. High Sch., 1947-49; tchr. lang. arts, English, George Washington Jr. High Sch., New Castle, Pa. 1957-64; dir. Carnegie Pub. Library of Parkersburg and Wood County, Parkersburg, W.Va., 1968—. Tchr. library sci. courses W.Va. U. Grad. Extension, Parkersburg, 1968-71. Mem. Am., W.Va. library assns., Am. Assn. U. Women, Altrusa (state chmn. intellectual freedom com.). Democrat. Presbyn. Home: 903 Westview Dr Belpre OH 45714 Office: 725 Green St Parkersburg WV 26101

MUSE, FRANCES MCDOWELL, librarian; b. Waverly Hall, Ga., Nov. 15, 1913; d. Paul M. and Lila Agnes (McDowell) Muse; A.A., certificate in piano, Andrew Coll., 1932; B.A., Emory U., 1934, A.B. in L.S., 1936. Tchr. pub. schs., Fulton County, Ga., 1934-35; librarian Thomson (Ga.) High Sch., 1936-37; asst. in charge reserves Emory U. Library, Atlanta, 1937-41, asst. circulation and reference librarian, acting head documents, 1943-45; asst. librarian, cataloger U.S. Waterways Experiment Sta., Vicksburg, Miss., 1941-42, South Atlantic Div. Engring. Office, Atlanta, 1942-43; asst. in circulation and cataloging Ga. Inst. Tech. Library, Atlanta, 1945-46; librarian LaGrange (Ga.) Meml. Library, 1946-47, Emory U. Sch. Bus. Adminstrn., Atlanta, 1947-57, Ga. Power Co., Atlanta, 1957-59; head reference dept. Ga. State U. Library, Atlanta, 1959—. Mem. vis. com. So. Assn. Colls., 1968-69. Mem. Ga. Library Assn. (mem. documents com. 1965-71). Home: 423 Emory Dr NE Atlanta GA 30307 Office: 104 Decatur St SE Atlanta GA 30303

MUSGRAVE, ANNE SIGHTLER (MRS. GEORGE WILMER SAMSON MUSGRAVE), lawyer, clubwoman; b. Montgomery, Ala.; d. Septimus Bonham and Mary Frances Boykin (Freeman) Sightler; grad. George Washington U. Law Sch., 1930; m. George Wilmer Samson Musgrave, June 21, 1919 (dec. Aug. 1947). Admitted to D.C. bar, 1929; practiced in Washington and Md., 1929-69; sr. mem. firm Musgrave & Sightler, 1929-48; individual practice, 1948—. State regent D.A.R., 1949-52, nat. v.p. gen., 1952-55, hon. life v.p. gen., 1967—; sr. nat. hon. v.p. gen. Children Am. Revolution, 1962-68, 72—; nat. chmn. bylaws D.A.R., 1953-56, 62-74; pres. Md. div. U.D.C., 1963-65. Chmn. Citizen's Com. for Nat. Reemployment Service for Prince George's County, 1933-42; mem. Prince George's County Welfare Bd., 1941-54, chmn., 1952-54; co-organizer Laurel (Md.) C. of C., 1946; bd. dirs. U.S.O., 1941-43. Trustee Kate Duncan Smith D.A.R. Sch., Grant, Ala. Recipient Spl. citation Children of Am. Revolution, 1957. Mem. Am., Md., Prince George's County bar assns., Am. Judicature Soc., Nat. Assn. Women Lawyers, Bar Assn. D.C., Women's Bar Assn. D.C., Md., Prince George's County (recording sec. 1954-60, 65-68) hist. socs., Soc. Preservation Md. Antiquities, Soc. Preservation Va. Antiquities, D.A.R., Daus. Colonial Wars, Daus. Am. Colonists, Descendants Colonial Clergy, Flag House Assn., Am. Legion Aux., Am. Assn. U. Women, Prince George's County Fedn. Women's Clubs (pres. 1934-36), Laurel C. of C. (hon.), Kappa Beta Pi. Clubs: Woman's (Laurel, Md., Lake Wales, Fla.). Address: Route 3 Box 587 Lake Wales FL 33853

MUSGRAVE, JEAN EVA MEITZEL (MRS. JAMES MUSGRAVE), museum ofcl.; b. Lyndhurst, N.J., Mar. 8, 1921; d. Harry William and Eva Elizabeth (Brady) Meitzel; grad. high sch.; m. James Edward Musgrave, Apr. 10, 1943 (dec.); children—Linda (Mrs. James Grippe), Wendy, Nancy. With Title Guarantee & Trust, Bronx, N.Y., 1939-40, Goodyear Tire & Rubber Co., N.Y.C., 1941-42, Compton Advt., N.Y.C., 1942-44, Kudner Advt., N.Y.C., 1944-46; sec. Goshen C. of C., 1968—; registrar Hall of Fame of the Trotter, Goshen, N.Y., 1965—. Home: 10 Fleetwood Dr Goshen NY 10924 Office: 240 Main St Goshen NY 10924

MUSGROVE, ANNA MAE KELLER (MRS. RAYMOND ARLINGTON MUSGROVE), museum curator; b. Davistown, Pa., Oct. 29, 1900; d. Harry Logan and Mary Belle (Albright) Keller; student Peterson Bus. Coll., Scottdale, Pa., 1920, Pa. State U., 1959; m. Raymond Arlington Musgrove, Mar. 3, 1921; 1 dau., Mary Ann (Mrs. Jerome C. Sharish). Curator Henry Clay Frick Meml. Museum, West Overton, Pa., 1960—. Mem. Gen. Com. for Centennial of Scottdale (Pa.), 1974. Mem. D.A.R., Women's Soc. World Service (pres. 1961). Methodist (coordinating chmn. history and records com. 1974—). Club: Women's Culture (Connellsville, Pa.). Home: 108 Dubois St Scottdale PA 15683

MUSGROVE, MARTHA ALICE LINDSEY (MRS. CHARLES WILLIAM MUSGROVE), journalist; b. Orlando, Fla., June 18, 1941; d. Harry Lee and Alice Martha (Williams) Lindsey; B.S. in Journalism, Northwestern U., 1963, M.S. in Journalism, 1964; m. Charles William Musgrove, Aug. 21, 1965; children—Charles David, William Joseph. Reporter Atlanta Jour., 1962; Vero Beach (Fla.) Bur. chief Miami Herald, 1964-68, staff writer, West Palm Beach, Fla., 1968-71; mng. editor Palm Beach (Fla.) Daily News and Palm Beach Life, 1971-72, editor, 1972-74; editorial writer Palm Beach Post, 1974—. Instr. journalism Nat. High Sch. Inst., Northwestern U., 1963. Recipient Freedoms Found. medal, 1959. Mem. Women in Communications (regional dir. 1970, nat. legislative chmn. 1971), Fla. Soc. Newspaper Editors (chmn. 1st amendment com. 1973-74, sec.-treas. 1974-75), Palm Beach C. of C., Vero Beach Bus. and Profl. Woman's Club. Clubs: Beach, Poinciana. Office: PO Box 1176 265 Royal Poinciana Way Palm Beach FL 33480

MUSHKIN, SELMA J. (MRS. ISRAEL SAUL WEISSBRODT), educator; b. Centerville, N.Y., Dec. 31, 1913; d. Rueben and Rachel (Rosenberg) Mushkin; B.A., Bklyn. Coll., 1934; M.A., Columbia, 1935; Ph.D., New Sch. Social Research, 1956; m. Israel Saul Weissbrodt, Aug. 7, 1939; children—David, Amy, Ellen Lucile. Chief div. financial studies Social Security Adminstrn., Washington, 1937-49; economist Pub. Health Service, Washington, 1949-60; Adv. Commn. Intergovernment Relations, Washington, 1961-64; dir. state-local finances project George Washington U., Washington, 1963-68; dir. research studies in state and local finance Urban Inst., Washington, 1968-70; prof. econs., dir. Pub. Services Lab. Georgetown U., Washington, 1970—. Formerly research prof. Johns Hopkins U.; cons. to govt. agys. Recipient Econs. award Bklyn. Coll., 1934, Alumni award Bklyn. Coll., 1963. Fellow Am. Pub. Health Assn.; mem. Internat. Inst. Pub. Finance, Am. Polit. Sci. Assn., Nat. Acad. Pub. Adminstrn. Club: Nat. Economist. Author: (with John Cotton) Functional Federalism, 1969; Editor: Economics of Higher Education, 1962; Public Prices for Public Products, 1972; Services to People: State and National Urban Strategies, 1973; Recurrent Education, 1974. Home: 3620 Prospect St NW Washington DC 20007

MUSIAL, HELEN THERESE, personnel exec.; b. Detroit, Aug. 11, 1918; d. John and Nellie Musial; B.B.A. summa cum laude, U. Detroit, 1953; M.B.A., Wayne State U., 1956. Sec., Nash Motors div., Nash-Kelvinator Corp., 1938-42; sec., personnel research and statis. analysis, supr., personnel asst. Gen. Motors Corp., now mgr. women's career planning; apptd. mem. Inst. for Certifying Secs., 1957-60. Recipient Phi Gamma Nu Scholarship Key, 1953. Pres. Gen. Motors Girls' Club, 1968-69, Certified profl. sec. Mem. Nat. Secs. Assn. Internat., Personnel Women of Detroit, Internat. Assn. of Personnel Women, Sigma Iota Epsilon, also Phi Gamma Nu Alumni, U. Detroit Alumni, Wayne State U. Alumni. Home: 28840 Bella Vista Dr Farmington MI 48024 Office: Gen Motors Bldg Detroit MI 48202

MUSIL, MARGARET HOOKER KIRKLAND (MRS. RALPH A. MUSIL), educator; b. Essex, Conn., Oct. 5, 1915; d. Henry Burnham and Helen (Mays) Kirkland; student Mills Coll., 1935-37; M.S. in Early Childhood Edn., Bklyn. Coll., 1962; M.R.E., Bibl. Sem. N.Y., 1962; m. Ralph A. Musil, June 5, 1937; children—Marjorie Anne, Robert Kirkland. Tchr. Tudor City Sch., N.Y.C., 1937-42; tchr. Nassau County Sch. Religion, 1952-62, (dean 1964), summer leadership schs. United Presbyn. Ch. U.S., 1953-60, 64, Bergen Council of Chs., N.J., 1958-63, Queens Fedn. Chs., N.Y., 1957-63, Protestant Council of N.Y., Bklyn. div., 1960-64; N.Y.U. Sch. of Edn. dept. of religion, 1964-65; dir. Hudson View Gardens Nursery Sch., N.Y.C., 1942-44; dir. religious edn. children Nassau Council Chs. of Christ, 1956-61, v.p., 1961-62; mem. bd. Christian edn. N.Y.C. Assn. Congl. Christian Chs., 1954-57, 58—; dir. religious edn. Congl. Ch. of Rockville Centre, N.Y., 1965-71; adj. prof. edn. C.W. Post Center L.I.U., 1972—; instr. protestant council N.Y., Manhattan Div. Sch. Religion, 1965; mem. com. on ch. and econ. life Nat. Council Chs. Dept. Social Justice, 1967—; mem. New Dimensions Commn. Ch. Women United—Ecumenical Assembly, 1967. Life mem. Woodycrest Five Points Child Care, N.Y.C.; mem. women's planning com. Internat. Christian U., Japan; mem. seminar in human relations sponsored by Nat. Conf. Christians and Jews, 1960. Recipient award for services to blind Indsl. Home for Blind, Bklyn., 1957; Centennial citation Wilson Coll., 1969. Mem. N.Y. State Assn. for Edn. Young Children, Magna Charter Dames, D.A.R. (chpt. dir. 1955-61, chmn. approved schs., 1951-58, chmn. chpt. good citizens com. 1965-65), Met. Assn. United Ch. Christ (chmn. children's work com. 1963—, rec. sec. 1967-71, bd. dirs. 1967—; alt. del. nat. synod 1969; mem. N.Y. Conf. Commn. on Edn. 1971—), Nassau Council Chs. (chmn. dept. religious edn. children 1953-65), Nat. Doll and Toy Collectors Club. Club: Garden City Community. Contbr. articles in field to profl. jours. Home: 69 Kenwood Rd Garden City NY 11530

MUSKIE, JANE F. GRAY (MRS. EDMUND S. MUSKIE), wife of U.S. senator; b. Waterville, Me., Feb. 12, 1927; d. Millage Guy and Myrtie (Jackson) Gray; grad. high sch., Waterville, 1945; m. Edmund S. Muskie, May 29, 1948; children—Stephen Oliver, Ellen, Melinda, Martha, Edmund S. Hon. mem. numerous civic, social service orgns. Democrat. Clubs: Democratic Wives, 500. Home: 5409 Albia Rd Washington DC 20016

MUSSELMAN, RUTH BURKEY (MRS. NORMAN BEACHY MUSSELMAN), civic worker, state ofcl.; b. Lamar, Mo.; d. William Edward and Martha (Whaley) Burkey; student Stephens Coll., 1918-19; teaching certificate Kan. U., 1921; student Okla. Bapt. U., 1948-51; m. Norman Beachy Musselman, Apr. 29, 1923; 1 son, Norman Burkey. Art supr. Pub. Schs., Coffeyville, Kan., 1921-22; real estate salesman Sooner Real Estate Investment Co., Shawnee, Okla., 1954-61. Mem. Gov.'s Com. on Supreme Ct., 1964, Commn. on Exec. Mansion, 1965, Okla. Bd. Edn., 1966-72, Okla. Bd. Vocational-Tech. Edn., 1966-72, Shawnee Diamond Jubilee Commn.; pres. Hawthorne Federated Study Club. Pres. Pottawatomie County Federated Republican Womens Club, 1968. Sec., bd. dirs. Okla. Newspaper Found., Womens Vol. League; bd. dirs. Shawnee Little Theatre, Shawnee Community Concerts, Tulsa Civic Opera Assn. Donor Norman Beachy Musselman Meml. award for outstanding newspaper journalism, 1965. Adv. mem. M.B.L.S. Mem. D.A.R., Am. Legion Aux., Huguenot Soc. Founders Manakin (Okla. bd., youth dir.), Okla. Heritage Assn., P.E.O., Alpha Chi Omega, Delta Phi Delta. Presbyn. Club: Shawnee Country. Author: Beachnuts, News Beams and Stardust, 1965. Home: 1618 N Union St Shawnee OK 74801

MUSSER, ELLYN ZUNKER (MRS. GENE H. MUSSER), physician; b. Chgo., July 25, 1937; d. Albert August and Fern (Wiesbach) Zunker; B.S. with honors, Loyola U. (Chgo.) 1958; student Sch. Medicine, U. Ill., 1958-60; M.D., U. Miami, 1962; m. Gene H. Musser, June 22, 1972. Intern Grady Meml. Hosp., Atlanta, 1962-63, resident, 1963-65; practice medicine, specializing in pediatrics, Marietta, Ga., 1965—; mem. staff Kennestone Hosp., Marietta, Henrietta Egleston Hosp. for Children, Northside Hosp., Crawford W. Long Hosp., Atlanta. Fellow Am. Acad. Pediatrics; mem. A.M.A., Am. Med. Women's Assn. (treas. Atlanta chpt. 1969-72, pres. 1974—), Med. Assn. Ga. Home: 9145 Huntcliff Trace NE Atlanta GA 30338 Office: 277 Pat Mell Rd SE Marietta GA 30060

MUSSER, NECIA ANN, librarian; b. Grand Rapids, Mich., Nov. 25, 1928; s. Milton and Gladys Alva (Fairbanks) Musser; B.A., U. Mich., 1950, M.A., 1952, M.A. in L.S., 1953, Ph.D., 1967. Reference librarian U. Mich. at Ann Arbor Library, 1953-61; catalog librarian Mich. Technol. U. Library, Houghton, 1961-62; with Western Mich. U. Library, Kalamazoo, 1962—, head collection devel., 1967—. Mem. A.L.A., Phi Beta Kappa, Phi Kappa Phi. Home: 5251 Solvel St Kalamazoo MI 49004

MUSSER, RUTH D., ret. educator; b. Balt.; d. Joel C. and Beulah May (Buck) Dunbracco; A.B., Goucher Coll., 1917; M.S. in Pharmacology U. Md., 1931; m. Neil B. Musser, June 6, 1919; 1 dau., Ruth Ellen (Mrs. Ronald L. Wiggins). Instr. pharmacology U. Md. Sch. Medicine, 1930-60, asst. prof., 1960-66. Active Girl Scouts Am., 1933-36, USO, 1941-45. Mem. Md. Hist. Soc., D.A.R. (asst. treas. Md. 1967-70), U.S. Daus. War of 1812 (pres. Md. 1970—, nat. librarian), Nat. League Am. Pen Women (nat. treas. 1968-70), Colonial Dames XVII Century, Magna Charta Dames, Colonial Soc., Ams. Royal Descent, Nat. Soc. Daus. Founders and Patriots, Jamestowne Soc., Sigma Xi, Delta Delta Delta. Republican. Methodist. Club: Ice (Balt.). Author: (with Joseph G. Bird) Modern Pharmacology and Therapeutics, 1958, 2d edit., 1961, supplements 1959, 60, 62, 63; (with Betty Shubkagel) Pharmacology and Therapeutics, 1965, (with John J. O'Neill) 4th edit., 1969. Contbr. articles to mags. and jours. Home: Wyman Park Apts 3925 Beech Av Baltimore MD 21211

MUSTILLO, LINA BACCARI (MRS. DOMINIC ANTHONY MUSTILLO), pianist, composer; b. Newport, R.I., Oct. 13, 1905; d. Pasquale and Albina (Palaia) Baccari; studied composition with Hugo Norden, A. Custer, music analysis with Dr. Giebler; m. Dominic Anthony Mustillo, Oct. 6, 1924; 1 dau., Alice (Mrs. Anthony Vincent Orabone). Piano performance Radio Sta. WJAR, Providence, 1927; organist, choir dir. Holy Ghost Ch., Attleboro, Mass., 1930-35; tchr. piano, accordian, marimba, organ, guitar Mustillo Music Sch., Attleboro, 1935-60. Dir. mus. radio program Attleboro council Girl Scouts U.S.A., 1937; chmn. Mother's March of Dimes, Attleboro, 1956. Recipient citation for music in hosps. R.I. Fedn. Music Clubs, 1959. Mem. R.I. Fedn. Music Clubs (state chmn. music in hosps. 1958-60), Italian Women's Sons of Italy (1st venerable Attleboro 1940), Daus. of Isabella (dir. glee club Attleboro 1950-51), Profl. Womens Club Boston. Clubs: Chopin (Providence); Chaminade (pres. Attleboro 1932-33, 38-40). Composer pseudonym Mauria: (piano solos) Etude Intervalle, 1966, Triphon, 1967, A Thought, 1969.

MUSTRIC, FLORENCE, pub. relations exec.; b. Columbus, O., Nov. 2, 1939; d. Theodore and Mary Mustric; A.B., Oberlin Coll., 1961, M.A., 1962; M. Music Cleveland Inst. Music, 1967. Writer, sr. editor World Pub. Co., Cleve., 1966-68; pub. relations dir. Fairview Gen. Hosp., Cleve., 1968—. Mem. Cleve. Orch. Chorus, 1968—; pub. relations adv. com. United Torch Services, Cleve., 1972—. Recipient various local and state awards for writing and editing. Mem. All-Ohio Conf. Editors and Communicators (chmn. 1974), Internat. Assn. Bus. Communicators (pres. Cleve. chpt. 1972-73), Cleve. Oberlin Alumni Assn., Greater Cleve. Hosp. Assn. (pub. relations subcom. 1972—). Club: City (Cleve.). Home: 21981 Elizabeth Cleveland OH 44126 Office: 18101 Lorain Av Cleveland OH 44111

MUTERT, RUTH PAULINE JOERLING (MRS. LESTER MUTERT), educator; b. Marthasville, Mo., Oct. 31, 1924; d. Hugo and Emma (Stegen) Joerling; B.S. cum laude, U. Mo., 1966, M.A., 1967, Ph.D., (grad. fellow), 1970; m. Lester Fred Mutert, Oct. 24, 1946; children—Melissa Ann, Dinah Ruth. Sec. to dist. mgr. Liberty Mut. Ins. Co., St. Louis, 1942-46; clk. to Warren County rep. Mo. Ho. Reps., Jefferson City, 1946-47; editor jour. Agr. Edn. Dept., Jefferson City, 1947-48; testing officer Army Edn. Center, Toul, France, 1961-62; prof. speech and dramatic art Stephens Coll., Columbia, Mo., 1970-73, internat. program U. Mo., 1974—. Mem. Speech Communication Assn., Am. Ednl. Theatre Assn., Central States Speech Assn., Am. Assn. U. Profs., Pi Lambda Theta. Mem. Order Eastern Star. Home: 2605 Summit Rd Columbia MO 65201

MUUS, MARGARET PFEFFER (MRS. MAGNER JOHN MUUS), civic worker; b. Fargo, N.D., Apr. 18, 1918; d. John George and Mary Genevieve (Flynn) P.; B.S., N.D. State U., 1939; postgrad. Moorhead State Coll., 1939; LL.B., U. N.D., 1941; m. Magner John Muus, Aug. 17, 1945; children—Mary Louise (Mrs. Arlo Tonnesen), John Einar, Laura Anne, Paul Magner, Carl James, Martha Mae. Admitted to N.D. bar, 1942, since in pvt. practice. Vice pres. Muus Lumber Co., Minot, N.D., 1963—. Reception com. chmn. Operations Prognosis Com. Council, Inc., 1972—; active YMCA, YWCA; vol. Easter Seal Soc., 1972-73; vol. saleswoman U.S. Savs. Program, 1964-70; life mem. P.T.A., 1967—, local pres., 1968; bd. dirs. Girl Scouts Council, 1962-68; mem. activities com., sci. chmn. Bishop Ryan High Sch., Minot, 1969-72. Served with USMCR, 1942-45. 2d place winner, Singer Co. Regional Sewing competition, 1960; elected Mrs. N.D., 1960, finalist Mrs. America pageant, 1960. Mem. Am. Legion, V.F.W., D.A.V. Roman Catholic. Clubs: Minot Country, Elk. Home: 500 8th Av SE Minot ND 58701

MUZUMDAR, AMMU MENON (MRS. HARIDAS THAKORDAS MUZUMDAR), educator; b. Kavasseri, Kerala State, India, July 30, 1919; d. Raghava and Chinnammu (Nair) Menon; B.A. with honors, Annamalai U., India, 1940; M.A., U. Chgo., 1950; Dr. Social Welfare, Columbia, 1960; m. Haridas Thakordas Muzumdar, June 1, 1960. Came to U.S., 1963. Supt., Avvai Home and Orphanage, Madras, India, 1941-42; lectr. econs. Central Coll. for Women, Nagpur, India, 1945-48; sr. lectr. Faculty Social Work, Maharaja Sayajirao U. of Baroda (India), 1951-57, prof., dean Faculty of Social Work, 1960-63; prof. social sci. and social work U. Ark. at Pine Bluff (formerly Ark. Agrl., Mech. and Normal Coll.), 1963-73; prof. social work U. Ark., Little Rock, 1973—. Dir. Social Edn. Organizers Tng. Centre, Samiyala, Baroda, 1960; head mental hygiene and psychiat. clinic S.S. Gen. Hosp., Baroda, 1960-63; supr. Fetehganj Kalyan Kendra (Fatehganj Welfare Centre), Baroda, 1960-63. Adv. bd. S.E. Ark. Mental Health Center, Pine Bluff. Recipient Internat. Peace Scholarship for Women, P.E.O., U.S.A., 1957-59; fellowship Asia Found., 1959-60. Mem. Acad. Certified Social Workers, Nat. Assn. Social Workers, Internat. (mem.-at-large U.S. com. 1969-73), Ark. confs. social welfare, Council Social Work Edn., Am., Southwestern sociol. assns., Southwestern Social Sci. Assn., Assn. Asian Studies, Ark. Mental Health Assn., League Women Voters (asso.). Author: Social Welfare in India: Mahatma Gandhi's Contributions, 1964. Home: 58 Maryton Park Cove Little Rock AR 72204

MYER, ELIZABETH GALLUP, librarian; b. Hyde Park, Mass.; d. Otto John and Edith (Geer) Myer; student Conn. Coll., 1930-32; A.B., Barnard Coll., 1935; B.S. in L.S., Simmons Coll., 1940; M.A., Brown U., 1947; European study tour Wayne State U., 1956. Asst. Providence Pub. Library, 1935-39; supr. W.P.A. Library Project, R.I., 1940-42; librarian Phoebe Griffin Noyes Meml. Library, Old Lyme, Conn., 1946; bookmobile librarian Enoch Pratt Free Library, Balt., 1948-50; reference librarian Morrill Meml. Library, Norwood, Mass., 1950-53; tchr., librarian Newton (Mass.) pub. schs., 1953-57; supr. pub. library services in rural areas R.I. Dept. State, 1958-64; dir. R.I. Dept. Library Services, 1964—. R.I. exec. dir. Nat. Library Week, 1959; mem. sch. library adv. com. to R.I. Bd. Edn., 1959-63; mem. R.I. Legislative Commn. Libraries, 1962-64; sec. New Eng. Library Bd., 1973—; exec. bd. New Eng. Library Information Network, 1973—; bd. govs. New Eng. Document Conservation Center, 1973—. Exec. bd. Narragansett council Camp Fire Girls, 1969-70; mem. adv. bd. U. R.I. Grad. Library Sch., 1962-64, 70—. Served from ensign to lt., USNR, 1942-45. Mem. Assn. State Library Agys. (bd. 1965-67; chmn. standards revision com. 1968-69), A.L.A., Conn., R.I. (pres. 1962-64), New Eng. (regional planning com. 1965-66, 69-70, chmn. state library services sect. 1969-71, mem. adv. council 1969-70, mem. nominating com. 1970) library assns., Barnard Coll., Brown U., Simmons Coll. alumnae assns., D.A.R., R.I. Hist. Soc., R.I. Audubon Soc. Episcopalian. Contbr. articles to profl. periodicals. Home: 3 Sunset Dr Barrington RI 02806 Office: 95 Davis St Providence RI 02908

MYERS, ALPHA BLANCHE SCOGGIN, educator; b. St. Louis, Sept. 27, 1912; d. Mirt A. and Grace L. (Calvert) Scoggin; B.S., S.E. Mo. State Coll., 1938; B.L.S., George Peabody Coll. for Tchrs., 1945; Ed.D., Rutgers U., 1972; m. Clifton T. Barber, Nov. 19, 1938 (div. Sept. 1945); m. 2d, William S. Myers, Oct. 20, 1947 (div. May 1955). Tchr. elementary sch., De Soto, Mo., 1932-37; tchr. high sch., Salem, Mo., 1937-38; library asst. St. Louis Pub. Library, 1939-42, 43-44; asst. reference librarian Washington U., St. Louis, 1942-43; reference librarian Med. Coll. Ala., Birmingham, 1946-47; sr. and prin. librarian Newark Pub. Library, 1947-59; head librarian Montclair (N.J.) High Sch., 1959-70; asso. prof. library sci. William Paterson Coll., Wayne, N.J., 1970-72, St. John's U., Queens, 1972-73, Kean Coll., Union, N.J., 1973—. Vis. lectr. library sci. U. Md., 1962-63, 67-71, 73; adj. prof. Newark State Coll., 1972; tchr. Nat. Defense Edn. Act Inst., U. Minn., 1965, N.J. Oratorio Soc., 1963; teaching fellow Rutgers U. Grad. Sch. Edn., 1967-68. Mem. Am., N.J. (chmn. reference sect. 1962-64) library assns., Staff Orgns. Round Table (chmn. 1953-55), Kappa Delta Pi. Dmocrat. Mem. Order Eastern Star. Author: (with Sara Temkin) Your Future in Library Careers, 1973. Contbr. articles to profl. jours. Home: 26 Chadwick Dr Nutley NJ 07110 Office: Kean Coll NJ Union NJ 07083

MYERS, BETTY JUNE, parasitologist; b. Ashland, O., Apr. 18, 1928; d. Clarence Wendell and Eldora (Root) Myers; B.A., Ashland Coll., 1949, B.S., 1949; M.A., U. Neb., 1951; Ph.D., McGill U., 1958. Lab. teaching asst. biology and art Ashland Coll., 1947-49, instr. biology, 1951-52; grad. research asst. biology and zoology U. Neb., Lincoln, 1949-51; NIH research asst. Inst. Parasitology, McGill U., Montreal, Que., Can., 1952-54, grad. asst. parasitology, 1953-55, research asst., 1955-57, research asso., 1957-59, asst. prof., 1959-64; asst. found. scientist S.W. Found. for Research and Edn., San Antonio, 1964—. Instr. grad. biology Incarnate Word Coll., San Antonio, 1968-69; adj. asso. prof. microbiology U. Tex. Med. Sch., San Antonio, 1972—; cons. parasitologist fisheries FAO, 1957—. Mem. pres.'s sci. adv. bd. Ashland Coll., 1958—; adv. bd., primate parasite registry Cal. Primate Research Center, Davis, 1971—. Fellow Royal Soc. Tropical Medicine and Hygiene; mem. A.A.A.S., Am. Microscopical Soc. (pres. 1974), Am. Soc. Mammalogists, Am. Soc. Parasitologists (council mem.-at-large 1973—), Am. Soc. Tropical Medicine and Hygiene, Arctic Inst. N. Am., Helminthological Soc. Washington, Soc. for Systemic Zoology, Sci. Research Soc. Am., Southwestern Assn. Parasitologists (officer 1967-73, pres. 1971-73), Sigma Xi, Sigma Delta Epsilon. Contbr. articles to profl. jours. Home: 138B Av Del Rey San Antonio TX 78216 Office: Southwest Found Research and Edn Box 28147 San Antonio TX 78224

MYERS, BEVERLEE ANN REARDAN, state govt. ofcl.; b. Berkeley, Cal., Oct. 14, 1930; d. Harmon Huntington and Helene Anna (Ouer) Reardan; A.B., Washington U., St. Louis, 1951; M.P.H., U. Mich., 1962; m. Duane Sigurd Myers, Jr., Sept. 20, 1952. Lab. research asst. various instns., 1952-57; program dir., local chpt. exec. N.M. Heart Assn., 1957-61; pub. health adviser USPHS, HEW, Rockville, Md., 1965-67, dep. dir. div. health care sers. Community Health Service, Health Services and Mental Health Adminstrn., 1968-69, dep. dir. panel on effectiveness Sec.'s Task Force on Medicaid and Related Programs, 1969-70, asst. adminstr. for resource devel. Health Services and Mental Health Adminstrn., 1971-72, asso. adminstr. program planning and evaluation, 1972-73; dep. commr. for med. assistance dept. social services State of N.Y., Albany, 1973—. Recipient Superior Service award Dept. Health, Edn. and Welfare, 1969. Fellow Am. Pub. Health Assn. (mem. governing council; mem. program devel. bd., sec. med. care sect. 1966-69, chmn. 1972-73; mem. council personal services, chmn. 1971; mem. Delta Omega, Phi Kappa Phi. Author: A Guide to Medical Care Administration, Vol. I: Concepts and Principles, 1965; also contbr. numerous articles to profl. jours. Mem. editorial bd. Med. Care, 1966-69, 72—. Home: 206 Chatham Ct East Greenbush NY 12061 Office: 1450 Western Av Albany NY 12203

MYERS, CAROLINE CLARK (MRS. GARRY CLEVELAND MYERS), mag. exec.; b. Morris, Pa., July 14, 1887; d. Charles Edgar and Elizabeth (Boyd) Clark; grad. Bloomsburg State Tchrs. Coll., 1905; student Ursinus Coll., 1907-08, Juniata Coll., 1912-13, Merrill Palmer Sch., Detroit, 1930-31, Tchrs. Coll., Columbia, summers 1931-34; m. Garry Cleveland Myers, June 26, 1912 (dec. 1971); children—Jack E., Elizabeth (Mrs. Kent L. Brown), Garry C. (dec.). Laura Spellman Rockefeller scholar, 1930; dir. parent edn. and family life Cleve. Welfare Fedn., 1931-41; instr. family life and child devel. Cleve. Coll., Western Res. U., 1931-41; leader pub. forums U.S. Office Edn., 1937; instr. U. Wash., Seattle, summers 1938-41; instr. Ore. State U., 1942; asso. editor Children's Activities, 1941, 46; co-founder, mng. editor Highlights for Children, Honesdale, Pa., also v.p.; dir. Highlights for Children, Inc., 1946—, chmn. bd., 1970—. Co-chmn. Community Fund campaign Wayne County Meml. Hosp., 1947, bd. dirs., 1946—. Recipient Distinguished Service award Bloomsburg State Tchrs. Coll., 1953, B'nai B'rith Citizenship citation, 1971. Mem. Nat. Council-Family Relations. Co-author: Myers Mental Measure, 1920; Language of America, 1921; My Work Book in Arithmetic, 1926; Homes Build Persons, 1950; Your Child and You, 1969; compiler, editor handbooks Highlights for Children. Contbr. articles and chpts. to profl. publs. Home: Milanville PA 18443 Office: 803 Church St Honesdale PA 18431

MYERS, DARNEAL JOHNSON (MRS. IVY JAMES MYERS), occupational therapist; b. Lexington, Ky., Dec. 28, 1940; d. Granville and Nannie Craig (Watson) Johnson; B.S., Hampton Inst., Va., 1962; postgrad. Columbia, 1964-66, 73; m. Ivy James Myers, Dec. 26, 1965; children—Ivan Dean, Lisa Darneal. Playground supr. Lexington (Ky.) Recreation Dept., summers 1959-63; instr. phys. edn., health and dance Portsmouth (Va.) Pub. Sch. System, 1962-64; occupational therapist East Orange (N.J.) VA Hosp., 1966-68; co-adj. instr. workshops for activity dirs. Rutgers U. Extension Div., 1973; also tchr.-cons. Participated in tng. group tchr.-cons. under Health, Edn. and Welfare grant awarded to Am. and N.J. Nursing Homes Assn., 1972-73. NSF fellow, 1963; Nat. Rehab. Assn. fellow, 1964. Mem. Am., N.J. (exec. bd. mem. 1969—, job placement chmn. 1970-72, pres. 1972—) occupational therapy assns., Orgn. Affiliate Presidents Am. Occupational Therapy Assn., Delta Sigma Theta.

MYERS, DORIS EVELYN MINTER (MRS. DELBERT GLENN MYERS), home economist; b. Pine Forest, Tex., Mar. 16, 1915; d. Emmitt Bascom and Ruby Odell (Bryarly) Minter; B.S., East Tex. State U., 1945; M.S., Tex. Woman's U., 1964; m. Delbert Glenn Myers, Sept. 22, 1948 (dec. July 1952); children—Margaret (Mrs. Valter Thomas Gleason), Ruby (Mrs. Morris Enon Morrow). Primary tchr. Bethel Ind. Sch., Como, Tex., 1935-37; prin. Lindenau (Tex.) Ind. Sch., 1944-45; tchr. sci. and geography Cuero (Tex.) Jr. High Sch., 1945-46; tchr. Sulphur Springs (Tex.) Ind. Schs., 1946-48, Robstown (Tex.) Ind. Schs., 1948-54; extension county home demonstration agt. Lavaca County, Hallettsville, Tex., 1954-59; extension agt. in mgmt., College Station, Tex., 1959-60; extension area home mgmt. specialist, College Station, 1960-66; extension home mgmt. specialist Tex. Agrl. Extension Service, Tex. A. and M. U., College Station, 1966—. Mem. Am., Tex. (chmn. family econs.-home mgmt. sect. 1970-72), Houston Area, Brazos County home econs. assns., Am. Council of Consumer Interest, Assn. for Consumer Research, Nat. Home Mgmt. Assn., Tex. Consumer Assn., Elec. Women's Round Table, Inc., Bus. and Profl. Women's Club, Epsilon Sigma Phi, Phi Sigma Alpha. Methodist (mem. ofcl. bd. 1968-74, health and welfare rep. 1971-75). Mem. Order Eastern Star. Contbr. chpts. to books. Home: 710 Garden Acres Bryan TX 77801 Office: System Bldg Tex Agrl Extension Service Texas A and M University College Station TX 77843

MYERS, EDNA MILDRED, ret. supt. schs.; b. Quinlan, Okla., Jan. 26, 1908; d. Charles P. and Laura (Duncan) Mock; A.B., Northwestern State Coll., Alva, Okla., 1949; M.Ed., Phillips U., Enid, Okla., 1953; postgrad. U. Colo., Okla. A. and M. Coll.; m. Ralph C. Myers, July 29, 1933. Tchr. pub. schs. (including rural area) 28 years; county supt. of schs. Woodward County, Okla., 1953-73. Pres. county supt. dept. N.W. Dist. Okla. Edn. Assn., 1953-54; mem. Okla. Edn. Policies Commn. Audio-visual coordinator for 4-H Club camps, Carnegie Library Reading Programs, hosp. and adult edn., ch. schs. Organized Woodward County Future Tchrs. Club, Northwestern Okla. Pioneer Women, also Woodward County (Okla.) Tchrs. State dir. Okla. Heart Assn.; pres. Woodward County Tb Assn.; sec., dir. Mental Health Assn., 1962—; state rep. Spl. Unit on Aging; chmn. Survey for State Okla. Services to the Retarded; dir. N.W. Okla. Guidance Center, 1970—; pres. local br. Am. Cancer Soc.; treas. Woodward County Salvation Army; v.p. N.W. Okla. Regional Tb and Respiratory Disease Assn.; regional rep. Okla. Lung Research. Recipient Outstanding 4-H Leader award, 1951, Carl Puckett award humanitarian services Okla. Tb and Respiratory Disease Assn., 1971. Mem. N.E.A. (life), Am. Assn. of Sch. Adminstrs. (state membership chmn.), C. of C., Woodward Bus. and Profl. Women's Civic Club (past pres.), Dist. Five County Officers' Assn. (pres. 1960—), N.W. Vocational Rehab. Dept. (exec. bd.), Kappa Kappa Iota (past pres. Alpha Chi chpt.). Methodist. Mem. Rebekah, Royal Neighbor. Club: Toastmistress (pres. Woodward). Home: 512 16th St Box 907 Woodward OK 73801 Office: Courthouse 1600 Main St Woodward OK 73801

MYERS, ELISABETH PERKINS (MRS. JOHN HOLMES MYERS), author; b. Grand Rapids, Mich., July 22, 1918; d. Edward Foote and Lili (Zimmermann) Perkins; A.B., Vassar Coll., 1940; m. John Holmes Myers, Aug. 24, 1940; 1 son, Thomas Perkins. Author: Katharine Lee Bates, 1961; F.W. Woolworth, 1962; George Pullman, 1963; Singer of Six Thousand Songs, 1965; Maria Tallchief, 1966; Edward Bok, 1967; Jenny Lind, 1968; Angel of Appalachia, 1968; Rutherford B. Hayes, 1969; Benjamin Harrison, 1969; South America's Yankee Genius, 1969; William Howard Taft, 1970; Langston Hughes, 1970; Andrew Jackson, 1970; Frederick Douglass, 1970; Mary Cassatt: A Portrait, 1971; Madame Secretary: Frances Perkins, 1972; David Sarnoff, 1973; John D. Rockefeller, 1973. Mem. Soc. Midland Authors, Children's Reading Round Table (Chgo. pres. 1967-68), Nat. Soc. Arts and Letters, Women's Nat. Books Assn., Women in Communications (chpt. pres. 1970-71), Psi Iota Xi. Club: Women's Press of Indiana. Home: Heritage Woods Rural Route 12 Box 211 Bloomington IN 47401

MYERS, FRANCES, artist; b. Racine, Wis., Apr. 16, 1936; d. Stephen G. and Bernadette (Gales) Myers; B.S., U. Wis., 1958, M.S., 1959, M.F.A., 1964. Works exhibited Curwen Galleries, London, Eng., Gallery Graphic Arts, N.Y.C., Van Straaten Gallery, Chgo., Haslem Gallery, Washington, U.S. Pavilion World's Fair, Osaka, Japan, Paris Biennale Prints Musse d'Art Moderne, Paris, 1970; represented permanent collections including Met. Museum Art, N.Y.C., Victoria and Albert Museum, London, Art Inst. Chgo., Library Congress, Chgo. Art Inst., USIS and others; tchr. intaglio printmaking St. Martin's Sch. Art, London, 1965-66, Birmingham (Eng.) Coll. Art, 1965-66. Co-dir. Mantegna Press, Hollandale, Wis. Wis. Arts Council grantee, 1973, Nat. Endowment Arts graphics fellow, 1974-75. Address: Route 1 Hollandale WI 53544

MYERS, JEAN KIKUE (MRS. WILLIAM S. MYERS), advt. and pub. relations exec.; b. Papaikou, Hawaii, Oct. 19, 1937; d. Sakae and Irene Hamae (Sato) Takaaze; ed. U. Hawaii; m. William S. Myers, Dec. 20, 1958. Mortgage servicing Bank of Hawaii, Honolulu, 1958-63; radio personality radio sta. KNDI, Honolulu, 1958-62; advt. and pub. relations exec. W.S. Myers & Assos., Inc., Honolulu, 1963—. Mem. Reorgn. Commn. City and County of Honolulu, 1973. Mem. Advt. Agy. Assn. Hawaii. Clubs: Honolulu Advertising, Honolulu Press. Home: 1124 Mokapu Blvd Kailua HI 96734 Office: Ward Plaza Suite 240 Honolulu HI 96814

MYERS, JOAN HELEN FLECK (MRS. RICHARD ALEXANDER MYERS, JR.), mag. editor; b. Balt., Nov. 26, 1934; d. A. Charles and Madeline (Block) Fleck; B.S., Temple U., 1957; m. Richard Alexander Myers, Jr., Oct. 12, 1965; children—Kevin, Deborah, Cheryl, Laura Michele. Sports reporter Balt. News-Post and Sunday Am., Balt., 1953-54; advt. copywriter Julius Gutman's Dept. Store, Balt., 1953; editor Union News, Internat. Ladies Garment Workers Union, Phila., 1955-57, Amalgamated News, Amalgamated Clothing Workers Am., Phila., 1957-58, Your Health, AFL Med. Center, Phila., 1958-60; pub. information dir. Girl Scouts of Central Md., Balt., 1960-64; editor Newsletter for Girl Scout profl. workers Girl Scouts U.S.A., N.Y.C., 1964-65, asso. editor Girl Scout Leader, 1965-72, editor, 1972-73, editor-in-chief, 1973—; features editor Am. Girl mag. Girl Scouts U.S.A., 1965-69. Bd. mgrs. Sch. Bus. and Pub. Adminstrn., Temple U., Phila., 1958-60. Mem. Pub. Relations Soc. Am. (chpt. sec. 1963-65), Women in Communications, Delta Zeta. Lutheran. Home: 197 Dartmouth Av Fair Haven NJ 07701 Office: 830 3d Av New York City NY 10022

MYERS, JUDITH LENDING (MRS. STANLEY MYERS), librarian; b. N.Y.C., Aug. 15, 1929; d. David and Rose (Kaplan) Lending; B.A., U. Richmond, 1950; M.S., Columbia U., 1966; m. Stanley Myers, Dec. 28, 1952; children—Rose-Ellen, Ronald. Librarian, Lillian Morgan Hetrick Library, N.Y. Med. Coll., 1966—. Mem. Am., Med. library assns. Home: 47-30 61st St Woodside NY 11377 Office: Fifth Av and 106th St New York City NY 10029

MYERS, LETITIA JANE SHARRITS (MRS. DONALD WILLIAM MYERS), journalist; b. Lima, O., Oct. 20, 1929; d. Edward Christopher and LaNiece (Shaffer) Sharrits; student Northwestern Coll. Commerce, 1947-48, Ohio No. U., 1961-62; m. Donald William Myers, Jan. 8, 1949; children—Susan (Mrs. Jerry McCormick), Christopher, Sara, James. Women's writer Lima News, 1961-68, asst. state editor, 1965-66, edn. writer, 1966-67, bus. editor, 1967-68; Troy (Mich.) news editor, woman's editor Birmingham (Mich.) Eccentric, 1968-69; staff writer Detroit News, 1969—. Recipient various editorial, feature and news writing awards A.P., Suburban Newspaper Found., Suburban Press Assn.; J.C. Penney-U. Mo. award, 1969. Mem. Women in Communications, Mich. Press Women. Club: Altrusa (Birmingham). Home: 3570 Paddington St Troy MI 48084 Office: 925 E Maple Rd Birmingham MI 48011

MYERS, MARGARET ANN, advt. exec.; b. Lancaster, Pa., Aug. 3, 1942; d. Bernard John and Anna Mary (Palmer) M.; student Hood Coll., 1960-62. Retail advt. staff Hager & Bros., Lancaster, 1963-64; sr. writer advt. John Wanamaker, Phila., 1964-67; writer, creative dir. N.W. Ayer, Phila., 1970, v.p., 1971-74; partner, v.p., creative dir. Tyson & Partners, Inc., Phila., 1974—. Lectr., Cheyney State Coll., 1972-73, Moore Coll. Art, Phila., 1972. Mem. Fashion Group. Republican. Roman Catholic. Home: 1305 Hopkinson House Philadelphia PA 19106 Office: 2011 Walnut St Philadelphia PA 19103

MYERS, MARILYN BEMIS, arts council ofcl.; b. Tulsa, Oct. 2, 1930; d. Ralph M. and Gretchen E. (Stark) Bemis; student Okla. State U., 1948-49; B.F.A., U. Okla., 1953; m. Morris Thurman Myers, Mar. 26, 1951 (div. Oct. 1972); children—Valerie (Mrs. Samuel Lee Autry), Margo, Adrian. Interim dir. Okla. Art Center, Oklahoma City, 1971-72, asst. to dir., 1972-74; dir. Arts Council, Oklahoma City, 1974—. Treas. Jr. League Oklahoma City, 1967-68; sec. Oklahoma City Arts Council, 1969-70, mem. exec. com., 1969—. Precinct sec.-treas. Rep. party, Oklahoma City, 1973-74. Trustee Okla. Sci. and Arts Found., 1969—, v.p., 1969-71. Recipient By-Liners award for arts Am. Women in Radio and TV, 1971. Mem. Kappa Kappa Gamma. Home: 1224 Mulberry Lane Oklahoma City OK 73116 Office: 1426 NE Expressway Oklahoma City OK 73111

MYERS, MARILYN GLADYS (MRS. PAUL F. MOTZKUS), pediatrician; b. Lyons, Neb., July 17, 1930; d. Leonard Clarence and Marian N. (Manning) Myers; B.A. cum laude, U. Omaha, 1956; M.D., U. Neb., 1959; m. Paul F. Motzkus, July 24, 1957. Intern, Orange County Gen. Hosp., Orange, Cal., 1959-60, resident pediatrics, 1960-62; fellow hematology-oncology Orange County Gen. Hosp., Orange, and Los Angeles Children's Hosp., 1962-64; practice medicine, specializing in pediatrics, hematology, oncology, Orange County, Cal., 1961—; dir. outpatient dept. Children's Hosp. of Orange County, Orange, 1964-72, chief dept. hematology-oncology, 1972—. Diplomate Am. Bd. Pediatrics. Fellow Am. Acad. Pediatrics; mem. Orange County Med. Assn., Orange County, Los Angeles pediatric socs. Home: 13601 Wheeler Pl Tustin CA 92680 Office: 1109 W LaVeta St Orange CA 92668

MYERS, MARY FRANCES, graphic arts co. exec.; b. Sweetwater, Tex., Aug. 26, 1914; d. James Earl and Berta Mae (Connaway) Wood; grad. Sweetwater High Sch., 1932; m. Clem Crellan Myers, Nov. 28, 1936 (dec. 1971); children—Nancy (Mrs. Bill E. Simmons), Janice (Mrs. Robert Sivley). Owner, mgr. CC Printing Co., Colorado City, Tex., 1951—. Mem. Nat. Fedn. Ind. Bus., C. of C. Baptist. Club: Colorado County. Home: 1305 Oak Colorado City TX 79512 Office: 154 Walnut Colorado City TX 79512

MYERS, MARY HORTENSE POWNER (MRS. STANLEY M. MYERS), journalist; b. Indpls., July 15, 1913; d. Walter Joseph and Stella (Smith) Powner; B.S., Butler U., 1953; m. Stanley M. Myers, Apr. 27, 1947; 1 son, Mark Powner. Asst. editor The Old Trail News, 1934-42; from newsman to asst. bur. chief Internat. News Service, Indpls., 1942-58; statehouse corr., polit. writer Ind. bur. U.P.I., Indpls., 1958—. Mem. State Traffic Safety Adv. Com. Bd. dirs. Marion County Muscular Dystrophy Found. Recipient of the Frances Wright award for outstanding contbn. to journalism from Ind., 1960. Mem. Nat. Fedn. Press Women (pres. 1962-65; received achievement award 1966), Edn. Writers Assn., Marion County Mental Health Assn., Women in Communications (pres. Indpls. alumnae 1957-58; nat. headliner award 1967), Sigma Delta Chi (pres. Ind. prof. chpt. 1973-74). Methodist. Clubs: Woman's Press of Ind. (pres. 54-56), Zonta (Indpls.). Author: (with Ruth Burnett) Carl Ben Eielson, Young Alaskan Pilot, 1961; (with Robert Thompson) Robert F. Kennedy, The Brother Within, 1962; (with Ruth Burnett) Cecil DeMille, Young Dramatist 1963, Vilhjalmur Stefansson, Young Arctic Explorer, 1966; Edward R. Murrow, Young Newscaster, 1969; Vincent Lombardi, Young Football Coach, 1971. Home: 7839 W 56th St Indianapolis IN 46254 Office: 113 N Capitol St Indianapolis IN 42604

MYERS, MATTIE MAE JONES (MRS. MANUEL CARL MYERS), community organizer; b. Tampa, Fla.; d. Norman and Frances (Bell) Jones; student Fla. A. and M. U., 1941-42; m. Manuel Carl Myers, July 27, 1954; children—Gwendolyn Frances, Emanuel Carl. Mem. staff Gt. Lakes Mut. Life Ins. Co., Detroit, 1949-52; with Afro Am. Life Ins. Co., Tampa, 1941-44; pres., exec. dir. Ralph J. Bunche Council, Inc., Detroit, 1964-68; pres. Ralph J. Bunche Community Council, Inc., Detroit, 1960—; pres., exec. dir. Ralph J. Bunche Homes, Inc., Detroit, 1964—, Ralph J. Bunche Homes, Inc. of Elmwood; pres. Martin L. King Non-Profit Housing Corp. Exec. bd. mem. housing Mich. Consol. Homes; exec. bd. mem. Detroit Neighborhood Conservation and Improved Housing, 1961—; chmn.

Fed. Housing Minority Sub-Com., Detroit, 1966—; exec. bd. Mayor's com. Keep Detroit Beautiful; bd. dirs., treas. Neighborhood Instnl. Adv. Council, 1966—; region v.p., br. bd. mgmt. YWCA; v.p. United Community Services. Mem. Southeastern Mich. Transp. Authority, 1967—, vice chmn., 1972. Bd. dirs. Health Edn. Adv. Com.; asst. sec. Detroit Council Orgns., 1968—; mem. exec. bd., mem. adminstrn. com. Met. Detroit Citizens Devel. Authority. Named 1 of Detroit's top 10 profl. working women, 1971. Mem. Eastside C. of C., Nat. Womens Speakers Bur., Internat. Platform Assn., Detroit Urban League (mem. bd.). Baptist. Democrat. Home: 2233 Iroquois St Detroit MI 48214 Office: 1930 E Lafayette St Detroit MI 48207

MYERS, MICHELE TOLELA (MRS. GAIL E. MYERS), govt. ofcl.; b. Rabat, Morocco, Sept. 25, 1941; d. Albert and Lilie (Abecassis) Tolela; B.A., U. Paris (France), 1962; M.A., U. Denver, 1966, Ph.D., 1967; m. Gail E. Myers, Dec. 20, 1968. Came to U.S., 1964. Asst. to marketing dir. Thomson-Houston, Paris, 1962-64; teaching asst. U. Denver, 1965-67; asst. prof. Manchester Coll., North Manchester, Ind., 1967-68; asst. prof. speech—communication and sociology Monticello Coll., Godfrey, Ill., 1968-71; asst. prof. communications Lewis and Clark Community Coll., 1970-71; dir. tng. U.S. Office Edn., Drug tng. and Resource Center, Trinity U., San Antonio, Tex., 1972—. Cons. communication and leadership tng. Mem. Inst. Gen. Semantics, Speech Communication Assn., Internat. Communication Assn. Author: (with husband) The Dynamics of Human Communication, 1973. Contbr. articles to profl. jours. Home: 139 Oakmont Ct San Antonio TX 78212

MYERS, NORMA JANE MCKAY, psychologist; b. Springfield, Mass., Aug. 27, 1928; d. Claude Carson and Norma Alice (Scott) McKay; student Heidelberg Coll., 1945-47; student Bliss Bus. Coll., 1947-48; B.S., Bowling Green State U., 1960, M.S., 1963; m. W. Howard Myers, Sept. 15, 1947 (div. 1969); children—Virginia (Mrs. Jerry Stidham), Carl. Tchr. elementary schs. Port Clinton, O., 1955-63; reading specialist Elyria (O.) City Schs., 1964-65; intern sch. psychologist Tiffin (O.) City Schs., 1965-66; sch. psychologist Fremont (O.) City Schs., 1966—. Tchr. in child devel. and psychology Michael J. Owens Tech. Coll., Perrysburg, O., 1972—; cons. to sch. systems in reading and psychology. Bd. dir. Sandusky County Mental Health Assn., 1972-74. Mem. Nat. Orgn. Women, Fremont Bus. and Prof. Women (v.p. 1972-73), Maumee Valley Sch. Psychologist Assn. (pres. 1970-71), Nat. Assn. Sch. Psychologists, O. Sch. Psychologists Assn. Home: 1139 N Byrneal Dr Port Clinton OH 43452 Office: 211 S Park Av Fremont OH 43420

MYERS, PATRICIA ELAINE, city ofcl.; b. Lorain, O., June 18, 1936; d. Walter Benjamin and Elaine Dean (Poor) Day; student Syracuse U., 1973; student Internat. Sch. Design, 1971; m. James Albert Myers, Feb. 6, 1954 (div. Aug. 1973); children—Pamela, Debra, Elaine. Sec., Underwood Corp., Lorain, 1954-56; clk. of council, Office City Clk., Amherst, O., 1968—; interior designer Consultation Design, Amherst, 1972—. Former mem. Amherst Hosp. Aux. Mem. Internat. Inst. Municipal Clks., Ohio Municipal Clks. Assn. (sec. 1973-75), Amherst Women's League (hon. mem.; pres. 1966-68), Ohio Municipal League, Allied Bd. Trade. Republican. Mem. Ch. of Christ. Home: 512 N Main St Amherst OH 44001 Office: 206 Main St Amherst MA 44001

MYERS, PATRICIA IRENE, speech pathologist, educator; b. Goodland, Kan., May 15, 1929; d. William Bryan and Roxanna (Harris) Myers; B.A., Tex. Coll. Arts and Industries, 1951; M.Ed., U. Tex., 1954, Ed.D., 1963. Speech pathologist pub. schs., Gonzales and Harlingen, Tex., 1952-56; tchr. exceptional children Tex. Rehab. Center, Gonzales, 1956-60; asst. prof. edn. La. State U., New Orleans, 1963-64; asso. prof. speech Our Lady of the Lake Coll., San Antonio, 1964-71, prof. communication disorders, also chmn. dept., 1970-73; dir. spl. edn. Edn. Service Center, Region XX, San Antonio, 1973—. Cons. speech and hearing Project Head Start. Mem. Am. Psychol. Assn., Am. Speech and Hearing Assn., Council Exceptional Children (div. bd. govs. 1970—, pres.-elect 1973-74). Author: (with others) Methods For Learning Disorders, 1969. Contbr. to profl. jours. Home: 3939 Fredericksburg Rd San Antonio TX 78201

MYERS, SARA FAY LEE (MRS. HOMER LEE MYERS), librarian; b. Shepherdsville, Ky., Sept. 13, 1915; d. Robert Edward and Lucille Inez (Magruder) Lee; A.B., Western Ky. U., 1938; M.S., Catherine Spalding Coll., 1958; m. Homer Lee Myers, Dec. 23, 1938; children—Jon Victor, Janet Fay (Mrs. David Newell Daniel). Tchr., Shepherdsville, 1933-57; head librarian Fairdale High Sch., 1958—. Recipient Distinguished Citizen award City of Louisville and Jefferson County, 1972. Mem. Nat., Ky. edn. assns., Jefferson County Tchrs. Ednl. Assn., Am., Ky. library assns., Ky. Sch. Librarians Assn. Club: Bullitt County Homemakers (county pres. 1956-57) (Shepherdsville). Methodist (youth dir. 1969—). Home: Ky 1526 Brooks KY 40109 Office: 1001 Fairdale Rd Fairdale KY 40118

MYERSON, BESS, TV performer; b. N.Y.C., July 16, 1924; d. Louis and Bella Myerson; B.A., Hunter Coll., 1945; Dr. Pub. Service, Seton Hall U., 1972; L.A.D., L.I.U., 1972; 1 dau., Barbara C. Piano soloist Carnegie Hall, N.Y.C., 1946; began profl. career Sta. WOR-TV, N.Y.C., 1947-51; mistress ceremonies The Big Payoff, CBS-TV, 1951-59; comml. hostess Philco Playhouse, NBC-TV, also Jackie Gleason Show, CBS-TV, 1954-55; TV commentator Miss Am. Pageant, ABC, 1954-68; co-commentator Tournament of Roses, 1960-68; panelist I've Got a Secret, CBS, 1958-68; news staff Mut. Broadcasting Co., 1961-62; commr. Consumer Affairs for City N.Y., 1969-73; syndicated columnist; contbg. editor Redbook mag.; vis. prof. Hunter Coll. Lectr. on The Distaff Side, maj. U.S. cities, 1964-68. Greater N.Y. chmn. Bonds for Israel, 1965-70. Chmn. Hunter Coll. Centennial Fund, N.Y.C., 1964—. Trustee Friends of Music N.Y.C. Jr. High Schs., League Sch. Seriously Disturbed Children; bd. dirs. Pub. Broadcasting Service, Fund for City N.Y., America in 3d Century. Recipient Outstanding Achievement award Hunter Coll., 1955; Presdl. medal, 1970; named Woman of Year, Anti-Defamation League, 1965; fellow Met. Mus. Art. Ford Found. grantee. Office: 1270 Av of Americas New York City NY 10020

MYHRE, JANET MARLENE KLIPPEN (MRS. PHILIP C. MYHRE), mathematician, educator; b. Tacoma, Sept. 24, 1932; d. Leif C. and Thelma G. (Fenney) Klippen; B.A. summa cum laude, Pacific Lutheran U., 1954; M.A., U. Wash., 1956; Ph.D., U. Stockholm (Sweden), 1968; m. Philip C. Myhre, June 12, 1954; 1 dau., Karin. Research engr. Boeing Co., 1956-58; instr. math. Harvey Mudd Coll., 1961-62; prof. math. Claremont (Cal.) Men's Coll., 1961—. Pres., Math. Analysis Research Corp., Claremont, 1973—. Guest prof. Eidgenossische Technische Hochschule, Zurich, Switzerland, 1971-72, U. Stockholm, 1971-72; cons. U.S. Navy, 1968—. Mem. Am. Statis. Assn., Inst. Math. Statistics, Sigma Xi. Assoc. editor Technometrics. Contbr. articles to profl. jours. Home: 4239 Via Padova Claremont CA 91711

MYKUT, MARGARET AMELIA CLARK (MRS. JOHN S. MYKUT), social worker; b. Seattle, May 12, 1923; d. George S. and Inza (Knapp) Clark; B.A., U. Ore., 1942; M.S.W., U. Wash., 1944; m. John S. Mykut, Sept. 9, 1940; children—Michael John (dec.), Matthew Clark. Clin. asso. dept. pub. health and preventive medicine U. Wash., Seattle, 1951-54, clin. instr., 1954-59, clin. asso. prof., 1959-63, instr. Sch. Social Work, 1951-56, asst. prof., 1956-59, clin. asso. prof., 1959—, clin. asso. prof. dept. psychiatry, 1963—; dir. social service dept. U. Wash. Hosp., 1959—; dir. social service Univ. Hosps., 1969—; project dir. Nat. Inst. Mental Health supported Mental Health Tng. Program. Bd. dirs. King County Anti-Tb, Seattle, Nat. Arthritis Found.; participant N.Y. Acad. Scis. Interdisciplinary Communication Program, 1966. WHO fellow, 1962. Mem. Assn. Am. Med. Coll., Nat. Conf. Social Work, Nat. Assn. Social Workers, Anti-Tb League, Alpha Kappa Delta. Contbr. articles to profl. jours. Home: 16235 38th NE Seattle WA 98155 Office: U Wash Hosp Seattle WA 98105

MYLANDER, MAUREEN ROOT, writer; b. Honolulu, July 16, 1937; d. Willard George and Eunice (Murray) Root; B.A., George Washington U., 1959; m. Walter Charles Mylander III, Nov. 21, 1964. Information specialist Office Army Surgeon Gen., Washington, 1959-61; information officer NIH, Bethesda, Md., 1961-65, also reporter World Wide Med. News Service, N.Y.C., 1964; editor U. Cal. Med. Center, San Francisco, 1965-66; sr. editor Per/Se Mag., Stanford, Cal., 1967-68; Washington editor Smith mag., N.Y.C., 1969-70; free-lance writer, 1960—. Class agt. George Washington U., 1969—. Bread Loaf Writer's fellow, 1974. Mem. Am. Newspaper Women's Club, Am. Med. Writer's Assn., Mortar Bd., Pi Delta Epsilon, Pi Beta Phi. Club: Nat. Press. Author: The Generals: Making It, Military Style, 1974. Home: 1845 Beulah Rd Vienna VA 22180

MYRES, SANDRA LYNN, historian, educator; b. Columbus, O., May 17, 1933; d. George Yeagley and Adria Lucile (Stockdale) Swickard; B.A. in Biology, Tex. Tech. U., 1957, M.A. in History, 1960; Ph.D. in history, Tex. Christian U., 1967; m. Charles E. Myres, July 2, 1953 (div. Aug. 1973). Instr. Schreiner Inst., Kerrville, Tex., 1960-61, Arlington (Tex.) State Coll., 1963-67; asst. prof. history U. Tex. at Arlington, 1967-70, Walter Prescott Webb Meml. lectr., 1968, asso. prof., 1970—, also dir. Tex. Com. for the Humanities and Pub. Policy, 1974—. Sheriff Ft. Worth Corral of Westerners, 1970-71. Mem. Soc. Southwest Archivists (v.p. 1971—), Soc. for Hist. Archaeology, Orgn. Am. Historians, Western History Assn. (program chmn. 1975), Tex. State Hist. Assn. (program chmn. 1975), Western Writers Am., Inc., Phi Alpha Theta. Democrat. Episcopalian. Author: Saddlemaker, 1961; The Ranch in Spanish Texas, 1969; Force Without Fanfare, 1968; One Man, One Vote, 1970; Cavalry Wife, 1974. Co-editor: Essays on the American West, 1969; Essays on U.S. Foreign Relations, 1974. Home: 3033 E Park Row No 119 Arlington TX 76010

MYRICK, JOANN, psychologist; b. Terrell, Tex., Aug. 25, 1936; d. James Leonard and Lois (Corbin) Myrick; B.S., U. Tex., 1959; M.S., U. Wis., 1972. Social worker Potter County Juvenile Probation Dept., Amarillo, Tex., 1959-60, Travis County Juvenile Ct., Austin, 1960-63; counselor, asst. to exec. sec. Alpha Gamma Delta Fraternity, Indpls., 1963-66; social worker Logansport (Ind.) State Hosp., 1969-70; sch. psychologist Stoughton (Wis.) Pub. Schs., 1972—. Atty. gen. Tex. Adv. Com. for Children and Youth, 1961-63. Asst. adminstrv. dir. Tex. Inst. on Children and Youth, 1961, adminstrv. dir., 1962, mem. bd. dirs., 1962-65. Mem. Nat. Assn. Sch. Psychologists, Am., Wis., Dane County psychol. assns., Wis. Sch. Psychol. Assn., Am. Personnel and Guidance Assn., Council on Exceptional Children, Psi Chi, Alpha Gamma Delta (province pres. 1966-68, nat. council 1968-70). Democrat. Episcopalian. Home: 1006 Progressive Lane Monona WI 53716 Office: PO Box 189 Stoughton WI 53589

NACHAMIE, SUSAN SCHIFFRES, psychologist; b. N.Y.C., May 8, 1942; d. Stanley Saul and Sarah (Horowitz) Schffres; A.B. magna cum laude, Vassar Coll., 1963; Ph.D., Columbia, 1969; m. Benjamin A. Nachamie, June 16, 1963; children—Stanley Judah, Allison Eve, Stephen David. Tchr. N.Y.C. Bd. Edn., 1963—; ind. research research adj. Columbia, 1969—. Mem. exec. bd. Parents Assn. Columbia Grammar and Prep. Sch., N.Y.C., 1973—. Pres. Hillel, Vassar Coll., 1962-63, Sisterhood of Jewish Temple, Ft. Riley, Kan., 1966-67; class of 1963 alumnae fund chmn. Vassar Coll., 1970-75. N.Y. State Regents Teaching fellow, 1963-66, Klingenstein Teaching fellow, 1963, 65, NSF summer fellow, 1965. Mem. Am., N.Y. State psychol. assns., Women's Aux. Med. Soc. State N.Y., Grad. Faculties Alumni Columbia, N.Y. Zool. Soc., Phi Beta Kappa. Club: Vassar (N.Y.C.). Contbr. article to profl. jour. Address: 1175 York Av New York City NY 10021

NACHMAN, GAIL RUTH, psychiat. social worker; b. Washington, Sept. 27, 1945; d. Zell Jack and Eva B. (Barke) Nachman; B.A., U. Md., 1967; M. Social Work, U. Md., 1973. Caseworker, Prince George County Dept. Social Services, Adelphi, Md., 1967-70; caseworker Great Oaks Center, Silver Spring, 1970-71, psychiat. social worker, 1973—. Field instr., undergrad. social work program U. Md., 1973-74. Mem. Am. Assn. Mental Deficiency. Office: 12001 Cherry Hill Rd Silver Spring MD 20904

NACHOD, GRACE REBECCA, ophthalmologist; b. Jenkintown, Pa., Mar. 25, 1917; d. Julius Ernest and Ruth Naomi (Fueller) Nachod; B.S., Ursinus Coll., 1938; M.D., Med. Coll. Pa., 1943; diploma in ophthalmology U. Pa., 1945. Intern Hosp. Med. Coll. Pa., Phila., 1943-44; practice medicine specializing in ophthalmology, Phila., 1945—; asst. surgeon Wills Eye Hosp., Phila., 1958—; mem. staff Children's Hosp., Phila., Pa. Hosp.; clin. instr. Hosp. Med. Coll. Pa., Phila., 1945-58, asst. prof. ophthalmology, 1960—. Instr. physiologic optics U. Pa. Grad. Sch. Medicine, Phila., 1945-58; chief ophthalmologist Pa. Sch. for Deaf, Phila., 1945—. Diplomate Am. Bd. Ophthalmologists (asst. examiner 1970-73). Fellow Coll. Physicians and Surgeons Phila.; mem. A.M.A., Pa., Phila. County med. socs., Am. Acad. Ophthalmology and Otolaryngology, Am. Assn. Ophthalmologists, Franklin Inst. Republican. Episcopalian. Club: Sunnybrook Golf (Plymouth Meeting, Pa.). Home: 3024 W Queen La Apt A 2-A Philadelphia PA 19129 Office: 5501 Greene St Philadelphia PA 19144

NACHTIGALL, LILA EHRENSTEIN, physician; b. N.Y.C., Feb. 23, 1934; d. Irving and Adele Pearl (Holzer) Ehrenstein; A.B., Bklyn. Coll., 1955; M.D., N.Y. Med. Coll., 1960; m. Richard Henry Nachtigall, Dec. 24, 1957; children—Margaret, Lisa, Ellen. Intern Bellevue Hosp., N.Y.C., 1960-60, resident 1961-64; instr. medicine N.Y. U. Med. Center, 1964-66, asst. prof. obstetrics and gynecology, 1966-74, asso. prof., 1974—, dir. endocrinology Goldwater div., 1966—, dir. Gynecology-Endocrinology Out Patient Dept., 1973—; vis. lectr. Booth Meml. Hosp., Lenox Hill Hosp. Chmn. fund-raising Bank St. Coll. Sch. Children, 1969-74. Recipient Karl Harpuder award in phys. medicine N.Y. Med. Coll., 1960. Mem. A.M.A., Am. Med. Women's Assn., Soc. Study Reprodn., Am. Fertility Soc., Endocrine Soc. Research developed test for estriol determination in human plasma. Home: 355 Riverside Dr New York City NY 10025 Office: 566 1st Av New York City NY 10016

NACOL, MAE, lawyer; b. Beaumont, Tex., June 15, 1944; d. William Samuel and Ethel (Bowman) Nacol; B.A. in Behavioral Scis., Rice U., 1965; B.A., South Tex. Coll. Law, 1969; children by previous marriage—Shawn Alexander Russell, Catherine Regina Russell. Admitted to Tex. Bar, 1969, since practiced in Houston. Diamond buyer and appraiser Nacol's Jewelry, Houston, 1961—; v.p. Environmental Fibers of Tex., Inc., Houston, 1973—, dir., 1973—, diamond cons. for jewelry stores and ins. cos., 1961—. Recipient Mayor's Recognition award, Houston, 1972. Ford Found. fellow, 1965. Mem. Am., Tex., Internat., Fed., Houston (chmn. candidates com. 1970—, chmn. membership com. 1971—, chmn. lawyer's referral com. 1972—), bar assns., Tex. Trial Lawyers Assn., Nat. Assn. Women Lawyers, Am. Judicature Soc., Jewelers Bd. Trade, Nat. Assn. Secondary Materials Inst., T.A.P.P.I. Home: 6012 Memorial Dr Houston TX 77007 Office: 2000 W Loop S Houston TX 77027

NADA, ETHEL YAEKO (MRS. HERBERT YUKIO NADA), hotel exec.; b. Kealia, Kauai, Hawaii, Dec. 18, 1935; d. Charles Soichi and Dorothy Namiko (Eno) Nakagawa; student Honolulu Bus. Coll., 1953-54; m. Herbert Yukio Nada, Mar. 14, 1956. Gen. mgr. Breakers Hotel, Honolulu, 1954—. Mem. Hawaii Hotel Assn., Travel Women Hawaii (mem. chmn. 1969-70). Home: 1715 Ala Aolani Honolulu HI 96819 Office: 250 Beachwalk Honolulu Hawaii 96815

NADDY, SISTER MARIE GREGORY, ednl. adminstr.; b. Ireland, Dec. 31, 1917; d. Peter and Margaret (Bookle) Naddy; came fo U.S., 1935, naturalized, 1945. B.A., Marymount Coll., 1942; M.A., U. Cal. at Los Angeles, 1949; postgrad., U. So. Cal., 1955. Tchr. Marymount Sch., N.Y.C., also Corvallis (Cal.) High Sch., 1941-44, tchr. Marymount Sch., Los Angeles, 1944-51, prin., 1946-51; dean Marymount Coll., Los Angeles, also Palos Verdes Peninsula, Cal., 1951-64, acad. dean, 1964-74, now dir. admissions and records, Palos Verdes Peninsula. Recipient Kellogg grant for study higher edn., U. Cal. at Los Angeles, 1968. Mem. Nat. Soc. for Study Edn. Address: 6717 W Palos Verdes Dr S Palos Verdes Peninsula CA 90274

NADEL, CHARLOTTE, physician; b. Bucharest, Rumania, Jan. 1, 1924; d. Solomon and Mathilda (Friedman) Iosef; came to U.S., 1964; naturalized, 1969; M.D., Faculty Medicine Bucharest, 1949; m. Ignat Nadel, Mar. 24, 1945. Intern Columbus Hosp., N.Y.C., 1965; resident psychiatry Kings County Hosp., Downstate Med. Center, 1966-69; attending physician dept. psychiatry Kings County Hosp. Center, 1971—; fellow Liaison Service, Downstate Med. Center, 1969-71, instr. psychiatry, 1969-71, clin. asst. prof. psychiatry, 1972—. Diplomate Am. Bd. Psychiatry and Neurology. Mem. Am. Psychiat. Assn., Am. Psychosomatic Soc., N.Y. Acad. Scis. Home: 681 Clarkson Av Brooklyn NY 11203 Office: 808 New York Av Brooklyn NY 11203

NADELSON, CAROL COOPERMAN (MRS. THEODORE NADELSON), psychiatrist; b. N.Y.C., Oct. 13, 1936; d. Hyman and Diana (Newman) Cooperman; B.A. magna cum laude, Bklyn. Coll., 1957; M.D. (fellow pediatrics, summer 1959; fellow psychiatry, summer 1960), U. Rochester, 1961; m. Theodore Nadelson, July 16, 1965; children—Robert, Jennifer. Intern medicine U. Rochester-Strong Meml. Hosp., 1961-62; resident psychiatry, teaching fellow psychiatry Mass. Mental Health Center, Boston, 1962-64; fellow psychiatry Beth Israel Hosp., Boston, 1964-66, asst. in psychiatry, 1966, asso. in psychiatry, 1970-72, asso. psychiatrist, 1972—, dir. med. sch. edn. in psychiatry, 1974—; career tchr. Harvard Med. Sch. Boston, 1967-69, instr. psychiatry, 1969-72, asst. prof., 1972—; asst. in psychiatry Children's Hosp. and Med. Center. Cons. Peace Corps, 1966-68; mem. steering com. Day Care, Harvard, 1970; cons., panelist, lectr. in field. Mem. Mass. Gov.'s Commn. Status of Women. Recipient Rush award U. Rochester, 1961. Mem. Boston Aquarium, Boston Zool. Soc., Children's Mus., Mus. Fine Arts. Bd. dirs. The Children's Center, Inc., 1971—, pres., 1970-71; bd. dirs. Pregnancy Counseling Service, now v.p. Mem. Am. Psychiat. Assn. (sec. No. New Eng. dist. br. 1971—; mem. task force on women), Mass. Psychiat. Soc. (pres. elect 1974), Assn. for Acad. Psychiatry, Am. Med. Women's Assn. (sec. New Eng. br.), Mass. Med. Soc., Nat. Orgn. for Women, Mass. Orgn. for Repeal of Abortion Laws, Am. Civil Liberties Union, Ams. for Democratic Action, Physicians for Social Responsibility, Group for Advancement Psychiatry (com. on family), Phi Beta Kappa, Alpha Omega Alpha. Editorial bd. Psychiat. Opinion. Contbr. articles to profl. jours. Home: 30 Amory St Brookline MA 02146 Office: Beth Israel Hosp Boston MA 02115

NADER, LAURA, anthropologist, educator; b. Winsted, Conn., Sept. 30, 1930; B.A., Wells Coll., 1952; Ph.D. in Anthropology, Radcliffe Coll., 1961; m. Norman Milleron, 1962; 1 son, 2 daus. Faculty anthropology U. Cal. at Berkeley, 1960—, asso. prof., 1965—; fellow Center Advanced Study in Behavioral Sci., 1963-64. Mem. cultural anthropology com. Nat. Inst. Mental Health, 1968—, chmn., 1968-71; mem. Social Sci. Research Council, 1968-72; adv. com. NSF, 1971—; NRC rep. behavioral div. Nat. Acad. Scis., 1969-71, 73—; mem. Carnegie Council on Children, 1972—. Trustee Law and Soc. Assn., 1967—, Center for Study Responsive Law, 1968—. Mem. Soc. Women Geographers, Am. Anthrop. Assn. Author: Talea and Juquila: A Comparison of Zapotec Social Organization, 1964; co-author: Conflict Resolution in Two Mexican Communities, 1963. Editor: Law in Culture and Society, 1969. Contbr. articles to profl. jours. Research in ethnography of law. Office: Dept Anthropology Univ Cal Berkeley CA 94720

NADLER, ESTELLE (MRS. JULIUS NADLER), civic worker, social worker; b. Balt., Oct. 15, 1912; d. Henry and Pauline (Katz) Davis; student U. Cal. at Los Angeles, 1926-28; B.A., Mills Coll., 1930; M.A., U. So. Cal., 1931, M.S. in Social Work, 1939; m. Julius Nadler, Dec. 14, 1942; 1 dau., Mindel (Mrs. Joseph Spiegel). Case worker, case supr. State Cal., Los Angeles, 1932-39; information analyst OWI, Dept. Agr., Washington, 1940-43; field supr. A.R.C., Los Angeles, 1944-45. Bd. dirs. United Way, San Fernando Valley, 1968-72, mem. agy. operations, 1968-69, budget, 1969-70, mem. regional budget com., 1972—; chmn. women's div. United Jewish Welfare Fund, San Fernando Valley, 1964; bd. dirs. Women's Conf. Jewish Fedn. Council, San Fernando Valley, 1962—; v.p. women's div. Jewish Fedn. Council Los Angeles, 1966; v.p. Jewish Family Service Los Angeles, 1970-73, Los Angeles Hillel Council, 1969—, Jewish Fedn. Council San Fernando Valley, 1965-73; bd. dirs. Jewish Fedn. Council Los Angeles, Am. Jewish Com., B'nai B'rith Youth Orgn., Los Angeles; chmn. standards and planning Jewish Family Service Los Angeles, 1969-73; mem. adult edn. com. Valley Beth Shalom, Encino, Cal., 1970-72; mem. adv. bd. Los Angeles Jewish Home for Aged, 1972; mem. corporate women's com. United Way, Los Angeles, 1973—. Recipient Community Service award Jewish Fedn. Council San Fernando Valley, 1968; Spl. Recognition award United Way San Fernando Valley, 1967; Ann Manion Schlarb award for outstanding vol. San Fernando Valley United Way, 1970; recipient Nat. Hillel Key, Los Angeles Hillel Council, 1972. Registered social worker, Cal. Mem. Acad. Certified Social Works, Nat. Assn. Social Workers, Am. Assn. U. Women, Los Angeles Mills Coll. Alumnae League, U. So. Cal. Alumni Assn., Pi Delta Phi, Alpha Kappa Delta. Address: PO Box 2178 Toluca Lake Station North Hollywood CA 91602

NADLER, HEDDA CAROL (MRS. DAVID G. NADLER), pub. relations exec.; b. N.Y.C., June 15, 1944; d. Julius Louis and Julia (Nemzer) Cohen; B.B.A., Coll. City N.Y., 1965 ; m. David George Nadler, Oct. 3, 1965; 1 dau., Laura Lee. Sec., Irving L. Straus Irving L. Straus Asso., Inc., N.Y.C., 1965, office mgr., 1966, asst. treas., 1967-69, v.p., 1969—. Home: 1200 Warburton Av Yonkers NY 10701 Office: 475 Park Av S New York City NY 10016

NADLER, RITA KOSLOW (MRS. JACK NADLER), lawyer; b. Paterson, N.J., June 2, 1931; d. Nathan and Sarah (Levine) Koslow; B.A., Smith Coll., 1952; U. Geneva (Switzerland), 1950-51; J.D., U. Chgo., 1955; m. Jack Nadler, Mar. 22, 1953; children—Jennifer, Matthew, Evan. Admitted to Ill. bar, 1955, N.J. bar, 1958; asso. Legal Aid Soc., Jewish Family and Community Service, Chgo., 1956-57; clk. Cole Berman & Belsky, Paterson, 1958, asso., 1958-60; asso. Shavick, Stern, Schotz, Steiger & Croland, Paterson, 1961—. Legal counsel Smith Coll. Club, Montclair, N.J., 1965—. Mem. exec. com. Montclair Dems. for Good Govt., 1963-67. Bd. dirs. League Women Voters Montclair and Glen Ridge, N.J., 1967-69, P.T.A., Edgemont Sch., Montclair, N.J., 1967-69. Trustee Kind Meml. Day Care Center, Newark, 1971—, Far Brook Sch., Short Hills, N.J., 1972-73. Mem. Passaic County Bar Assn. Home: 175 S Mountain Av Montclair NJ 07042 Office: 125 Ellison St Paterson NJ 07505

NAES, ESTELLE BERTHA, educator, ednl. adminstr.; b. St. Louis; d. Anthony and Mary (Cordes) Naes; B.S. in Nursing. St. Louis U., 1936. M.S. in Nursing Edn., 1949, Ph.D., 1962. Dir. dept. nursing edn. St. Louis U., 1949-60; dir. research U. Tenn., Memphis, 1963-64; research cons. State U. N.Y., Buffalo, 1964-65; prof. nursing U. Akron (O.), 1966—, dean of nursing, 1967—. Cons. in nursing. Mem. Little Hoover Commn. Summit County, 1969—. Bd. dirs. Northeast Ohio Regional Med. Program. Mem. Nat. League Nursing, Am. Nurses Assn., Ohio Heart Assn., Bus. and Profl Women's Club. Home: 77 Fir Hill Akron OH 44304

NAGAR, SARLA DEVI (MRS. MURARI LAL NAGAR), curator; b. Uttar Pradesh, India, Mar. 26, 1926; d. Ishwar Das and Satya (Wati) Sarin; M. Hindi Lit., Agra U., 1950; M.A., Columbia U., 1956; M.A., U. Mo., 1968; m. Murari Lal Nagar, Feb. 28, 1951; children—Hari W., Siddhartha. Came to U.S., 1966. Asst. curator Calico Mus. Textile, Ahmedaad, 1964-65; tchr. Sreyas High Sch., Ahmedabad, 1965-66; asso. curator S. Asian art Mus. Art and Archaeology, U. Mo., Columbia, 1969—. Contbr. articles to profl. jours. Home: 1405 St Christopher Columbia MO 65201 Office: Museum of Art and Archaeology University Missouri Library Conley Av Columbia MO 65201

NAGEL, MABEL HUDSPETH, lumber exec.; b. Berryville, Ark., July 7, 1903; d. Joseph D. and Minerva (Robinson) Hudspeth; student N.M. State Coll., 1929-31; m. George Henry Nagel, May 26, 1931 (dec. May 1968); children—Georgia Mae (Mrs R. T. Jenkins), James Henry. Co-owner, operator Nagel Lumber & Timber Co., Winslow, Ariz., 1950-65; pres. Nagel Lumber Co., Inc., 1963—, Acme Lumber Co., 1966—, Nagel Devel. Corp., 1970—; pres. Rincon Cattle Corp., 1960-71; sec. Four Corners Devel. Corp., 1966-70. Mem. Winslow City Council, 1950-54; mem. Sitgreaves Nat. Forest Adv. Com., 1952-62; police commr. Winslow, 1953-54; sec. Winslow Planning and Zoning Commn., 1954-56; pres. Winslow Youth Council, 1955-57; vice chmn. Winslow Devel. Commn., 1958-64; mem. lumber div. Ariz. Water Resources Div., 1958-71; mem. Ariz. indsl. adv. com. rural housing FHA, 1971-73; mem. Ariz. Forest Industry Com., 1962-68, Ariz. Arts and Humanities Council, 1969-74; mem. Navajo County Planning and Zoning Commn., 1971—. Chmn. Navajo County March of Dimes women's div., 1958-59; rep. corrs. Fgn. Soroptimist Sister Club, Antwerp, Belgium, 1962-65, mem. fgn. exchange student com., 1961-64; chmn. water devel. com. Navajo County Devel. Council, bd. dirs., 1963-73; mem. Gov.'s Adv. Council Navajo County Welfare, 1964-66, Apache-Navajo County chmn. Statewide Art Mus. League, 1962-65, adv. bd. Winslow Meml. Hosp., 1957-66; bd. dirs. Bapt. Children's Home, 1959-60; bd. dirs. Ariz. Acad., 1964-68, sec., mem. exec. com. 1965-67; sec. bd. dirs. Indsl. Devel. Endeavor Assn., 1964-66, bd. dirs., 1974—. Named Woman of Year Bus. and Profl. Women's Club, 1954-55. Mem. S.W. Pine Assn. (dir. 1963-64), Nat., Ariz. (rep. Navajo County 1963-72) reclamation assns., Ariz. Press Women (v.p. 1967-68), Navajo County Hist. Soc. (rec. sec. 1972-73, pres. 1973-74), Am. Assn. Ret. Persons (pres. Winslow chpt. 1972-74), C. of C. (dir. 1965, 60, 62). Clubs: Writers (sec.-treas. 1960-64), Winslow Women's, Soroptimist (pres. 1961-62). Feature writer, photographer and news corr. Home: 708 W Maple St Winslow AZ 86047 Office: Box 972 Winslow AZ 86047

NAGLE, CLAIRE WALLER, lawyer; b. New Brunswick, N.J., July 13, 1925; d. Clifford Albert and Eunice (Waller) Nagle; A.B., Douglass Coll., Rutgers U., 1946; J.D., N.Y.U., 1949. Admitted to N.J. bar, 1950; asso. law firm Hicks, Kuhlthau, Thompson & Molineux, New Brunswick, 1950-57; partner law firm Kuhlthau, Nagle, Griggs & Goddard and predecessor firms, 1957—. Mem. N.J. Bd. Higher Edn., 1973—. Trustee YWCA, 1959-64; trustee Rutgers, The State U., 1964—, mem. bd. govs., 1967—, chmn., 1973—; trustee Middlesex Gen. Hosp., 1964-70, Rutgers U. Alumni Faculty Center, 1965-71, E. Jersey Old Town, 1972—. Mem. Am., N.J., New Brunswick bar assns., Am. Assn. U. Women, N.J. Hist. Soc., Asso. Alumnae Douglass Coll. Inc. (dir. 1947-55, 64-70). Republican. Conglist. Home: Middlebrook Rd Bound Brook NJ 08805 Office: 24 Kirkpatrick St New Brunswick NJ 08903

NAGLE, JUSTINE TERESA, advt. exec.; b. N.Y.C., Feb. 3, 1936; d. Nicholas J. and Marguerite P. (Battle) Nagle; student Pace Coll., 1954-59, Cornell Labor Coll., 1972—; m. Edward Dillon, Sept. 14, 1957 (div. May 1964); children—Justine, Stacy. Asst. prod. Geyer Advt., 1954-56, coordinator Rose Marie Reid Bathing Suits, 1956-57; advt. dir. Temas Mag., N.Y.C., 1957-63; with Commerce Advt., N.Y.C., 1963—, v.p., account exec., 1969—; owner, pres. Elgan Communications, N.Y.C. Mem. Advt. Womens Club, Conservation Club, Met. Opera Guild, Mus. Natural History, Mus. Art. Republican. Clubs: Belle Harbor Yacht, N.Y. Athletic (asso.), Gaslight. Home: 301 E 47th St New York City NY 10017 also 537 Beach 130 St Belle Harbor NY 11694 Office: 8 W 40th St New York City NY 10018

NAHEMOW, LUCILLE DAVIS, psychologist; b. N.Y.C., July 7, 1933; d. William and Flora (Fisher) Davis; B.S. in Psychology, 1955, M.A., in Psychology, 1957; Ph.D. in Social Psychology (Univ. fellow, Nat. Inst. Mental Health fellow), Columbia, 1963; m. Martin David Nahemow, 1952 (div. 1966); children—Katharine, Barbara. Teaching fellow Bklyn. Coll., 1955-57, grad. instr., 1963-64; research assoc. Hunter Coll. Ednl. Clinic, 1958-59; sr. scientist biometrics research N.Y. State Dept. Mental Hygiene, Columbia Coll. Phys. and Surg., 1959-66; dir. psychol. research Lincoln Hosp., Albert Einstein Coll. Medicine, 1967-68; research assoc., mem. doctoral faculty environmental psychology program City U. N.Y., 1968-71; sr. scientist Phila. Geriatric Center, 1971—; adj. asso. prof. N.Y. U., N.Y.C., 1972—; project dir. N.Y. State Health Dept., 1973—. Mem. grad. faculty Pratt Inst., 1967-68, City U. Grad. Center, 1968-71, Sarah Lawrence Coll., 1971-72. Mem. Am., Eastern psychol. assns., Gerontological Soc., Soc. for Psycho. Study Social Issues, A.A.A.S., Piagetian Soc., Nat. Caucus on Black Aged, Grey Panthers, Sigma Xi, Psi Chi, Alpha Kappa Delta. Contbr. articles to profl. jours. Home: 601 W 115th St New York City NY 10025

NAHM, HELEN, educator; b. Augusta, Mo., Aug. 17, 1901; d. Alfred and Katherine (Heffern) Nahm; A.B., U. Mo., 1926, D.Sc. (hon.), 1961; M.S., U. Minn., 1939, Ph.D., 1946; L.H.D., U. Cin., 1968; LL.D., U. Cal. San Francisco Med. Center, 1969; D.Sc. (hon.), U. Fla. at Gainesville, 1971. Head nurse U. Hosp., Columbia, Mo., 1926-27; instr. nurses Scott and White Hosp., Temple, Tex., 1927-30; asst. instr. U. of Mo. Sch. of Nursing, 1931-34; supt. Blosser Children's Home, Marshall, Mo., 1934-35; dir. Sch. Nursing, U. Mo., 1935-41, Hamline-Asbury Sch. of Nursing, St. Paul, Minn., 1942-45, Nursing Edn. div. Duke U., 1946-50; dir. Nat. Nursing Accrediting Service, 1950-53; dir. div. nursing edn. Nat. League for Nursing, 1953-58, v.p., 1959—; dean U. Cal. Sch. Nursing, 1958-69, ret.; Carnegie vis. prof. Coll. Nursing, U. Hawaii, spring 1962. Mem. N.C. Com. on Standardization Schs. of Nursing, 1947; v.p. Minn. League of Nursing Edn., 1943-45. Recipient citation of merit in nursing U. Mo. Alumni Orgn., 1966; M. Adelaide Nutting award Nat. League Nursing, 1967; Outstanding Achievement award U. Minn., 1968. Mem. Am. Nurses Assn., Nat. League Nursing (dir. div. nursing edn. 1953—, 1st v.p. 1959), Pi Lambda Theta, Psi Chi, Phi Delta Kappa. Democrat. Christian. Contbr. articles on nursing sch. evaluation and nursing edn. to profl. jours. and publs. Home: 55 Chumasero Dr San Francisco CA 94127

NAHMIAS, BRIGITTE BUCHMANN, physician; b. Kiel, Germany, June 30, 1932; came to U.S. 1948, naturalized 1956; d. Erich and Klara Hildegard (Futing) Buchmann; B.A., George Washington U., 1954, M.D., 1957; m. Andre J. Nahmias, June 9, 1956; children—Cynthia Angela, David Eric, Edward Andre. Rotating intern USPHS Hosp., S.I., N.Y., 1957-58; research fellow pulmonary function and diseases Emory U. Sch. Medcine and Grady Meml. Hosp., Atlanta, 1958-60; jr. asst. resident, then sr. asst. resident 5th and 6th med. services Boston City Hosp., 1960-61, 62-63; Samuel A. Levine fellow Mass. Heart Assn. at Boston U. Sch. Medicine and Mass. Meml. Hosp., 1961-62; dir. Albert Steiner Meml. Emphysema Clinic St. Joseph's Infirmary, Atlanta, 1967—; asst. medicine Boston U. Sch. Medicine, 1961-63; faculty guest lectr. dept. respiratory therapy Sch. Allied Health Scis., Ga. State U., 1970—; clin. asst. prof. pulmonary disease Emory U. Sch. Medicine 1972—. Bd. dirs. Planned Parenthood Assn. Atlanta, 1966-68. Chmn. Cliff Valley Sch. Bd., 1968-69; precinct del. DeKalb County Democratic Party, 1971. Diplomate Nat. Bd. Med. Examiners, Am. Bd. Internal Medicine. Columbian Women scholar, 1954-57; Zonta Club scholar, 1955-57; Oaklawn grantee, 1956-57. Mem. Am., Ga. thoracic socs., Med. Assn. Ga., Am., Ga. heart assns., Am. Med. Women's Assn., New Eng. Diabetes Assn., Smith Reed Russell Soc., Kane King Soc., Iota Sigma Pi. Contbr. articles to profl. jours. Home: 859 Vistavia Circle Decatur GA 30033 Office: 265 Ivy St NE Atlanta GA 30303

NAIMAN, ADELINE, editor, ednl. adminstr.; b. Boston, Oct. 27, 1925; d. Joseph and Jennie (Samuel) Lubell; A.B. cum laude, Radcliffe Coll., 1945; m. Mark Lewis Naiman, July 3, 1947; children—Joris, Alaric, Kieron. Editor Little-Brown & Co., Boston, 1945-48, J.B. Lippincott Co., Phila., 1953-57, Beacon Press, Boston, 1964-66; with Edn. Devel. Center, Newton, Mass., 1965—, editor-in-chief elementary sci. study, 1965—, dir. publns., 1970—, asst. to pres., 1971—, mgmt. council, 1972—. Mem. Mass. Adv. Council Bilingual Edn. Mem. Radcliffe Coll. Alumnae Assn., Lincoln Land Trust, Mass. Audubon Soc., DeCordova Museum, Mass. Inst. Tech. Matrons. Club: Radcliffe (Boston). Author articles, poetry. Home: Moccasin Hill RFD 1 Lincoln MA 01773 Office: 55 Chapel St Newton MA 02160

NAISMITH, GRACE AKIN, writer, editor; b. Ft. Collins, Colo., Nov. 20, 1904; d. A. I. and Nellie (Taylor) Akin; student William Woods Coll., 1920-22, D.Sc., 1969; student U. Colo., 1922; m. John Naismith, 1922; children—James A., Stuart D.; m. 2d, Edward Pierce, 1943; m. 3d, John Devlin, Nov. 23, 1960. Reporter, Rocky Mountain News, 1929-30; information and edn. specialist U.S. Dept. Agr. 1936; editor, writer med. subjects Reader's Digest, N.Y.C., 1938—. Mem. Nat. Assn. Sci. Writers, Soc. Mag. Writers, Overseas Press Club (gov.), Theta Sigma Phi, Alpha Phi. Author: Private and Personal, 1966. Contbr. articles to popular mags. Home: Westview Lane South Norwalk CT 06854 Office: 51 East 42d St New York City NY 10017

NAKAMURA, TOYOKO SHIMIZU (MRS. ALBERT KENICHI NAKAMURA), librarian; b. N.Y.C., Sept. 9, 1918; d. Sojiro and Tomiko (Niwa) Shimizu; B.S., Beaver Coll., 1939; M.L.S., U. Hawaii, 1966; m. Albert Kenichi Nakamura, Dec. 28, 1942; children—Kimi (Mrs. Richard Fukuda), Andrew Tadahiko, Matthew Munehiko. Sch. librarian Hokulani Sch., 1964-65, Linekona Sch., 1965-66, Anuenue Sch., Honolulu, 1964-65, 66—. Bd. dirs. YWCA, 1960. Mem. Am. Assn. Univ. Women, A.L.A., Internat., Am., Hawaii (pres. elect 1972-73) assns. sch. librarians, Pacific Assn. Communication and Tech., Hawaii Council Tchrs. English, Hawaii Assn. Supervision and Curriculum Devel., Hawaii Library Assn., Alpha Delta Kappa. Office: 2530 10th Av Honolulu HI 96816

NAKASORA, CHIYEKO EVELYN, social worker; b. Redwood City, Cal., Mar. 6, 1938; d. Hiroji and Tomiko (Uriu) Nakasora; A.B. in Social Welfare, San Francisco State Coll., 1960; M.S.W., U. Hawaii, 1962. With Santa Clara County (Cal.) Welfare, 1962-65; child welfare supr. San Francisco County Dept. Social Services, 1967-68; social service cons. Cal. Dept. Social Welfare, San Francisco, 1965-67, 68—, now with community care facilities licensing sect. Cal. Health Dept., Berkeley. Mem. Acad. Certified Social Workers, Nat. Assn. for Edn. Young Children. Democrat. Address: 2151 Berkeley Way Berkeley CA 94704

NALDER, REBECCA A. (MRS. NED N. NALDER), state legislator; b. Ogden, Utah, Sept. 2, 1931; d. Dell H. and Sarah (Kershaw) Adams; B.S., Utah State U., 1953; m. Ned N. Nalder, Aug. 19, 1955; children—Adam, Nathan, Eric. Tchr., Davis County (Utah) Schs., 1953-70. Mem. Layton (Utah) City Planning and Zoning Commn., 1969-71; mem. Utah Ho. of Reps., 1971—. Mem. Chi Omega. Democrat. Mem. Ch. of Jesus Christ of Latter-day Saints. Address: 144 Dixie Av Layton UT 84041*

NALLS, THELMA RENTZ (MRS. CHARLIE CHESTER NALLS), hosp. adminstr.; b. Newton, Ga., Apr. 4, 1929; d. Alvin Robert and Clara Bell (Powell) Rentz; B.S. in Nursing, Fla. State U., 1961; M.S. Edn., State Coll. Ark., 1973; m. Charlie Chester Nalls, June 7, 1947; 1 son, Jimmy Donald. Pub. health nurse, Bainbridge, Ga., 1961-63; pub. health dist. supr., Thomasville, Ga., 1963-64, pub. health dist. nursing dir., 1964-68; dir. nursing Bainbridge State Hosp., 1968—, Southwestern State Hosp., Thomasville, 1968—. Mem. Am. Nurse Assn., Am. Acad. Health Assn., Am. Assn. Mental Deficiency, Ga. Nursing Assn., Ga. Hosp. Assn. (co-chmn. nursing sect. program com. 1972-73, mem. ednl. com. 1972-73), Thomas County Mental Health Assn. (adviser to mental health bd. 1972-73), Ga. Pub. Health Assn. (v.p. nursing sect. 1967-68), Ga. Soc. for Health Manpower Edn. and Tng., Gadsden County Assn. for Retarded Children (pres. 1973-74), Alcohol and Drug Problem Assn. Home: PO Box 396 Havana FL 32333 Office: Southwestern State Hospital Thomasville GA 31792

NAMKOONG, JOAN YOUNGCHA, marketing, pub. relations exec.; b. Honolulu, Feb. 19, 1949; d. Peter Tark and Marie (Choi) Namkoong; student U. Puget Sound, 1967-68; B.A. in Advt. with honors, U. Wash., 1970. Pub. relations dir. Sheraton-Waikiki Hotel, Honolulu, 1971-72; advt. mgr. Hawaii Observer, Honolulu, 1973; marketing exec. Innovative Media, Honolulu, 1973—. Commr., Commn. on Children and Youth, 1972-73. Bd. dirs. YMCA, Honolulu, 1972—. Mem. Women in Communications (v.p. 1973-74). Home: 1333 Heulu St Honolulu HI 96822 Office: 837 Cooke St Honolulu HI 96813

NANAGAS, VERONICA NAVARRETE, anesthesiologist; b. Manila, Philippines, Jan. 2, 1944; d. Victor Teodoro and Amparo Barron (Navarrete) Nanagas; M.D., U. Philippines, 1967. Came to U.S., 1967. Intern, Carney Hosp., 1967-68, U. Philippines-Philippines Gen. Hosp. Med. Center, 1966-67; resident anesthesia Tufts-New Eng. Med. Center, 1968-71, fellow cardiovascular and pediatric anesthesia, 1971-72, instr. anesthesiology, 1972-74, asst. prof., 1974—. Diplomate Am. Bd. Anesthesiology. Mem. Am. Soc. Anesthesiology, Mass. Soc. Anesthesia. Home: 8 Fayette St Boston MA 02116 Office: 171 Harrison Av Boston MA 02111

NANCE, ELEANOR GLENN HANOVER (MRS. JOSEPH MILTON NANCE), artist, librarian; b. McGregor, Tex., Mar. 18, 1920; d. Hiram Howard and Edith Glenn (Crain) Hanover; B.A., Mary Hardin-Baylor Coll., 1941; m. Joseph Milton Nance, Mar. 19, 1944; children—Jeremiah Milton, Joseph Hanover, James Clifton. Arts and crafts counselor summer camps, 1941, 42; art. tchr. elementary, high schs., Tex., 1941-43; prodn. illustrator Consol.-Vultee Aircraft Corp., Ft. Worth, 1943-44; draftsman, instrument repair specialist USAAF, Bryan, Tex., 1944-46; pvt. art tchr., substitute tchr. Bryan and College Station Pub. Schs., 1952-65; book illustrator, 1955—; librarian Tex. A. and M. U., 1965—. Tchr. kindergarten St. Thomas Episcopal Ch., College Station, Tex., 1951-56; organizer, dir. Jr. Mus. Natural History, Bryan, Tex., 1960-62, bd. dirs., 1969—, sec., 1970—; v.p. Crockett Elementary Sch. P.T.A., 1959-60; organizer, dir. College Station Summer Recreational Arts and Crafts Program, 1949, 50; art counselor Arrowmoon (Tex.) dist. Boy Scouts Am., 1958—; mem. Brazos County Hist. Survey Com., 1968—, sec., 1969—; dir. arts and crafts Camp Olympia, Trinity, Tex., 1971—; fine arts council Tex. A. and M. U., 1974—. Mem. D.A.R. (chpt. librarian 1968—), Daus. Republic Tex. (chpt. pres. 1963-65), Nat. League Am. Pen Women (treas. Brazos Valley br.), Am. Assn. U. Women, U.D.C. (pres. 1968-71), Kappa Pi, Pi Gamma Mu, Sigma Tau Delta. Episcopalian (pres. women's group 1959). Clubs: Art (pres. 1952), Poetry Soc. (pres. 1959-60) (Bryan-College Station): Women's Social (reporter 1962) (Tex. A. and M. U.) Contbr. poems, articles, stories, illustrations to mags., books. Illustrator: Becoming Physically Educated in the Elementary Schools, 1969. Home: 1403 Post Oak Circle College Station TX 77840 Office: Tex A and M U Library College Station TX 77843

NANCE, ETHEL RAY (MRS. CLARENCE A. NANCE), assn. exec.; b. Duluth, Minn., Apr. 13, 1899; d. William H. and Inga (Nordquist) Ray; grad. Duluth Bus. Coll., 1919; student Columbia, 1925, Hampton Inst., 1942, U. Cal. at Berkeley, 1955, 68, San Francisco State Coll., 1958, Mankato State Coll., 1969; m. Clarence A. Nance, Aug. 3, 1944; children—Thatcher P., Glenn R. Supr. Center Activities and Employment Service, Kansas City Urban League, 1923; asst. to editor Opportunity mag. Nat. Urban League, N.Y.C., 1924-25; asso. head resident Phyllis Wheatley Settlement House, Mpls., 1926-28, bd. dirs., pres. aux., 1936-37; condr. unemployment survey Mpls. Urban League, 1936; condr. housing survey Settlement House, Mpls., 1937; adminstrv. asst. to dean edn. Hampton (Va.) Inst., 1940-43; dep. clk. U.S. Dist. Ct., Seattle, 1944-45; asst. dir. race relations Fed. Housing Authority, Seattle, 1944-45; research asst. to Dr. W.E.B. DuBois, cons. to U.S. Delegation to UN, San Francisco, 1945, now asso. dir., head research dept. San Francisco Am. Hist. and Cultural Soc. Bd. dirs. No. Cal. Com. on Africa, 19—. Mem. Fellowship Ch. of All Peoples. Editor Newsletter Christian Friends for Racial Equality, 1944-45; women's editor Timely Digest, Mpls., 1931; editor Council for Minority Rights, Seattle, 1944. Home: 4173 Army St San Francisco CA 94131 Office: 680 McAllister St San Francisco CA 94102

NANCE, MARGRETTE ZULEIKA GRUBBS (MRS. JOSEPH TURNER NANCE), educator, writer, civic worker; b. Dallas, Sept. 24, 1917; d. Ernest and Carolyn (Roberts) Grubbs; B.S., U. Tex., 1942, M.F.A., So. Meth. U., 1969; m. Joseph Turner Nance, Aug. 23, 1945; children—John Joseph, Mary Carolyn. Writer, dir., broadcaster Greek Round-Up, 1940-42; tchr. Allen Jr. High Sch., Austin, Tex., 1943-44; speech tutor U. Tex., 1944-45; speech instr. So. Meth. U., 1946-47; substitute tchr. Dallas Ind. Sch. Dist., 1955-69; actor role Mrs. Stevenson, Sorry Wrong Number, So. Meth. U., KERA-TV, 1962, author tv script univ. tv workshop. Dallas, Panhellenic Assn., KRLD-TV, 1954, 55; writer columns various newspapers, Dallas, 1963-67. Team capt. United Fund, 1969; vol. specialist A.R.C., 1969; season ticket sales com. mem. Dallas Symphony Orch. League, 1966-68, membership com., 1968—; mem. woman's com. Dallas Theater Center, 1967-70, 72—; mem. Soc. Prevention Cruelty to Abandoned and Neglected Children, 1966—, Dallas Summer Musicals Guild, 1967—, Dallas Mus. Fine Arts, 1966—; dir. Spl. Care Sch. Handicapped Children, 1965-66; mem. Preston Hollow P.T.A., 1955-56; exec. v.p. George B. Dealey P.T.A. 1961-62; mem. com. Benjamin Franklin P.T.A., 1962-63. Dir. Hillcrest Estates Assn., 1960-62. Mem. Dallas Council World Affairs Woman's Group, Tex. Ex-Students Assn. (4th v.p. 1960-61), Tex. State Assn. City Panhellenics (sec. 1957-58), Am. Assn. U. Women, U.D.C., Freedoms Found. at Valley Forge, Dallas Chamber Music Soc. (sponsor), Delta Zeta, Pi Lambda Theta. Republican. Methodist. Clubs: Northwood, Lancers (charter), Mothers' So. Meth. U. (4th v.p., rep. 1968-70), Dallas Lawyer Wives, Tex. Fine Arts Soc., Dallas Federation of Womens (historian 1968-69, chmn. fine arts dept. 1969-70), Austin (Tex.) Womans; Internat. Chateau Sainte Anne, Am. Womans (Brussels, Belgium). Address: 11525 E Ricks Circle Dallas TX 75230

NANCE, SONYA SUE (MRS. JOHN BOYD NANCE), educator; b. Wichita, Kan., Aug. 30, 1945; d. Grant Delbert and Genevieve Virginia (Almack) Silknitter; B.S., U. Kan., 1967; postgrad. Wichita State U., 1968; m. John Boyd Nance, Dec. 22, 1968; 1 son, Devon Everett. Tchr. sophomore English, basic English, drama I, stagecraft, designer sets for plays Washington High Sch., Kansas City, Kan., 1967-69; tng. supr. May Co., Cleve., 1969-71; tchr. make-up, wardrobe and speech Barbizon Sch. Modeling, Cleve., 1970-72; tchr. freshman English, speech I and II, stagecraft, dir. plays Rocky River (O.) High Sch., 1971-73. Counselor for vol. drug drop-in center, 1970-72. Mem. Sigma Kappa. Mem. Christian Ch. (deaconess, study chmn. Christian Women's Fellowship, 1972-73, chmn. World Outreach Fellowship 1972-73). Home: 4941 Upton Ct Denver CO 80239

NANCE, VIRGINIA MUMFORD (MRS. ROBERT LLOYD NANCE), extension agt., home economist; b. Raleigh, N.C., June 27, 1934; d. Garey Gardner and Fannie (Cooper) Mumford; A.A. Mars Hill Jr. Coll., 1953; B.A. cum laude, Meredith Coll., 1955; postgrad. Winthrop Coll., 1961-62, Coll. William and Mary, 1973—; m. Robert Lloyd Nance, July 8, 1956; children—Patti Louisa, Robert Lloyd, Allen Howard. Asst. home demonstration agt. N.C. Agrl. Extension, Iredell County, 1955-56; home econs. editor N.C. Agrl. Extension Service, Raleigh, 1956-58; home econs. research asst. Winthrop Coll., Rock Hill, S.C., 1961-64; dir. homemaking edn. N.C. Coop. Extension, Charlotte, 1966-68; extension agt. Va. Poly. Inst. Coop. Extension, York County, 1969—. Recipient Joe Wise Cup award Rock Hill Jr. C. of C., 1960. Mem. Nat., Va. assns. extension home economists, Va. Extension Service Assn., Adult Edn. Assn., Am., Va. home econs. assns. Home: 106 Braddock Rd Williamsburg VA 23185 Office: PO Box 492 Yorktown VA 23490

NANNINGA, ANN, univ. adminstr.; b. Conway, Ark., June 14, 1912; B.A., Mary Hardin Baylor Coll., 1930; M.A. in Counseling, Guidance, U. N.M., 1960; husband dec.; 2 children. English, history tchr., Cedar Springs High Sch., 1930-33; tchr. Coleman Pub. Grade Sch., 1930-38; English tchr. Albuquerque Pub. Schs., 1954-56, counselor, 1956-59; now prof. edn., dean of women, N.M. Highlands U., Las Vegas. Mem. N.M. Adminstrv. Women in Edn., N.M., Am. personnel guidance assns., N.M., Nat. assns. of women deans and counselors, Am. Assn. Higher Edn., Am. Assn. U. Women. Home: 834 Highlands Dr Las Vegas NM 87701 Office: NM Highlands Univ Las Vegas NM 87701

NAPIER, GRACE DONKERSLOOT, educator; b. Clifton N.J.; d. Martin and Carrie (Van Wageninge) Donkersloot; B.A., Douglas Coll., 1944; M.A., N.Y.U., 1945; Ed. M., Temple U., 1959, Ed.D., 1968, student U. Mich., summer 1948, George Peabody Coll., summer 1953, Syracuse U., summer 1956, U. Minn., 1960-61; m. Charles S. Napier, Aug. 21, 1946 (div. Dec. 1967). Tchr., house-parent Royer-Greaves Sch. for Blind, Paoli, Pa., 1945-48; ednl. counselor N.J. State Commn. for Blind, Newark, 1948-60; instr. Syracuse (N.Y.) U., summers 1957-66; prof. spl. edn. U. No. Colo., Greeley, 1966—. Denver. Mem. Am. Assn. U. Women, United Methodist Women, Internat. Platform Assn., Am. Bus. Women's Assn., Assn. for Edn. Visually Handicapped, Council for Exceptional Children, N.E.A., Internat. Communication Assn., Delta Kappa Gamma, Phi Delta Gamma, Pi Lambda Theta. Methodist. Author: (with others) Handbook for Teachers of the Teachers of the Visually Handicapped, 1974; contbg. author: Education of the Exceptional Child, 1972; The Visually Handicapped Child in School, 1973. Home: 802 20th St Greeley CO 80631

NAPIER, KATHLEEN BENTLEY, editor; b. Oak Park, Ill., May 19, 1933; d. Thomas Douglas and Mary Ellen (Bentley) Napier; B.A., Carleton Coll., 1955; m. William Hogan, Sept. 6, 1958 (div. May 1969). Mgmt. interim Women's Bur. U.S. Dept. Labor, Washington, 1955-56, editorial asst., 1956-57; editorial asst. Soc. Automotive Engrs., N.Y.C., 1957—, mng. editor, gen. publs. dept., 1960-67, mng. editor publs. div., 1968—. Active in neighborhood groups involved in housing and other projects. Home: 318 W 100th St New York City NY 10025 Office: 2 Pennsylvania Plaza New York City NY 10001

NAPIER, VELMA STENNETT (MRS. WILLIAM S. NAPIER), librarian; b. Ellisville, Miss., Jan. 22, 1918; d. Edgar E. and Martha (Bradshaw) Stennett; B.S., Livingston State Coll., 1953; M.S., U. So. Miss., 1967; m. William S. Napier, July 3, 1937; children—William Darrell, Edgar C. Tchr., Mobile County Pub. Sch. Systems, Mobile, Ala., 1949-57, librarian, 1957-65; cataloger Mobile (Ala.) Coll., 1965, head librarian, 1966—, Mem. A.L.A., Ala., Southeastern library assns., Delta Kappa Gamma. Club: Woman's (Mobile). Home: Rural Route 1 Box 209 Semmes AL 36575 Office: Mobile College PO Box 13220 Mobile AL 36613

NAPOLEON, SARA JANE, therapist; b. N.Y.C., Apr. 3, 1944; d. Louis Nicola and Clare (Chianelli) Napoleon; B.A., Mt. Mercy Coll., 1966; M.S., So. Ill. U., 1970. Acting recreation dir. Dixmont State Hosp., Glenfield, Pa., 1966-68; psychologist Grubstake Inc., Pitts., 1970-71; counselor Ft. Sam Houston Alcohol and Drug Rehab. Center, San Antonio, 1971-74. Pvt. practice psychology, Pitts., 1970-71; cons. Halfway House of San Antonio, 1973—. Mem. Am. Psychol. Assn. Home: 1415 Victoria St Apt 914 Honolulu HI 96822

NARCISSE, AUGUSTA RUTH MCSWAIN (MRS. CALVIN BELDON NARCISSE), educator; b. Dothan, Ala.; d. Waymon and Robbie Christine (Bryson) West; B.S., Tuskegee Inst., M.Ed., 1952; postgrad. Boston U., 1955—, M. Reading, U. Ariz., 1969; m. Calvin Beldon Narcisse, Dec. 2, 1966; children—Robbie Ethel Blanche, Calvinetta Christine. Tchr. English Newville Rosenwald Jr. High Sch.; elementary tchr., Dothan, Ala., 1953-57; jr. high sch. tchr. Permasen Am. Sch., 1958-59; high sch. substitute tchr. Baumholder Am. Sch., 1959-60; tchr. English, Carmichael Jr. High Sch., Sierra Vista, Ariz., 1960-65; communication techniques tchr., bi-dialectal English tchr. Buena High Sch., Sierra Vista, Ariz., 1965—; prof. English Cochise Coll., evenings 1966-67. Mem. Ariz. Reading Council. Founder, dir. Huachuca-Vista drug program, Sierra Vista, Huachuca, Ariz., 1970—; founder, chmn. Sierra Vista Internat. Visitors, 1965-70; mem. Ariz. Gov.'s Commn. on Status Women, 1967; gen. chmn. Sierra Vista (Ariz.) 10th Anniversary, 1965—; mem. Nat. Commn. on Status Women, 1967-69; pres. Cochise County Council on Continuing Edn. for Women, 1967-69; founder IALAC, Inc. Bd. dirs., program chmn. YWCA, 1963-64. Recipient Certificate of Outstanding Community Service, certificate of Outstanding Community Service for Internat. Students, U. Ariz., 1965, Mayor's award Sierra Vista, 1966, Outstanding Program award, Nat. Fedn. Bus. and Profl. Women's Clubs, Inc., named Outstanding Woman of Year, Huachua Bus. and Profl. Women's Club, Inc. Mem. N.E.A. (life), Am. Assn. U. Women, Nat., Huachuca fedns. bus. and profl. women's clubs, Nat. Assn. Negro Bus. and Profl. Women's Club, Ariz. Edn. Assn., Buena Classroom Tchrs. Assn., N.A.A.C.P., U. Ariz. Alumni Assn. (life), Alpha Kappa Alpha, Alpha Delta Kappa. Democrat. Baptist (Sunday Sch. tchr.). Home: 124 Kayetan Dr NE Sierra Vista AZ 85635 Office: 4001 Fry Blvd NE Sierra Vista AZ 85635

NAREHOOD, MARY BELLE LONTZ (MRS. S.D. NAREHOOD), author; b. Williamsport, Pa., Mar. 25, 1936; d. Charles Theodore and Hattie Cole (Fertig) Lontz; B.S. in Elementary Edn., Bloomsburg State Coll., 1958; B.S. in Secondary Edn., Bucknell U., 1963; m. S.D. Narehood, Sept. 3, 1971. Tchr., Penns Creek, Pa., 1958-60, Dewart, Pa., 1960-61, Mentoursville, Pa., 1961-63. Recipient medal of appreciation S.A.R., 1969, D.A.R., 1970, Daus. of the War of 1812, 1970, Daus. Am. Colonists, 1970, Mem. Sons and Daus. of Pilgrims, North Central Pa. Archaeology Soc. (pres. North Central chpt. 1958-59), Ind. Soc. Pioneers. Methodist. Author: The Narehood Family, 1971; The Ruhl Family, 1972; The Davisson/Davidson Family, 1972; Index to Otzinachson or a History of the West Branch Valley, 1963; Tax List of Northumberland, Union, Snyder Countie Pennsylvania, 1967; Wills of Centre County, Pennsylvannia, 1800-1853, 1970; The Berkheimer Family, 1972; Index to History of Northumberland, Huntingdom, Mifflin, Centre, Union, Columbia, Juniata and Clinton Counties, Pennsylvania, 1970; Miller Family of Union County, Pennsylvania, 1970; Grimes Family of Berks, Centre Counties, Pennsylvania, 1970; Crouse Family of Centre County, Pa., 1970; Earlywine Family of Virginia, Kentucky, Ohio, Indiana, 1970; Hoover Family of Lancaster County, and Union County, Pa., 1970; Our German, Pilgrim and Quaker Ancestors, 1968; Tombstone Inscriptions of Union County, Pennsylvania, 1967; Union County, Pa., 1865-1965, 1966. Editor, Pa. Genealogy Mag., 1967-73. Home: 412 Vine St Milton PA 17847 Office: 608 Broadway Milton PA 17847

NARINS, RHODA SCHARF (MRS. DAVID J. NARINS), physician; b. N.Y.C., Dec. 2, 1941; d. Louis and Sydelle Scharf; B.A., Barnard Coll., 1961; M.D., N.Y.U., 1965; m. David J. Narins, June 30, 1962; children—Jonathan William, Valerie Whitman. Resident dermatoloty N.Y.U. Med. Center, 1966-68, chief resident, 1969, instr., 1968-70; cons. dermatology Phelps Meml. Hosp., North Tarrytown, N.Y., Dobbs Ferry Hosp.; pvt. practice medicine, specializing in dermatology, Tarrytown, N.Y., 1969—; asst. prof. dermatology Bronx Municipal Hosp. Center and Albert Einstein Coll. Medicine. Diplomate Am. Bd. Dermatology. Mem. Am. Acad. Dermatology, Am. Assn. Dermatologic Surgery, Greater N.Y., Westchester, Atlantic dermatologic socs. Home: 245 Fox Meadow Rd Scarsdale NY 10583 Office: 200 S Broadway Tarrytown NY 10591

NARISS, EDNA, librarian; b. Granite City, Ill., Oct. 20, 1930; d. John W. and Penelope (Graham) Nariss; B.A., Washington U., St. Louis, 1951; M.S. in L.S., U. Tex. at Austin, 1952. Asst. librarian reference dept. Madison County Library, 1952-56, librarian reference dept., 1956-60; head librarian Amalgamated Plastics Co., 1960—. Mem. A.L.A. Episcopalian. Contbr. articles to profl. jours. Address: 3244 S Oak Park Av Berwyn IL 60402

NARUSIS, REGINA GYTÉ FIRANT (MRS. BERNARD V. NARUSIS), lawyer; b. Kaunas, Lithuania, Oct. 12, 1936; d. Victor and Eugenia S. (Cesnavicius) Firant; brought to U.S., 1949, naturalized, 1955; B.A., U. Ill., 1957, J.D., 1959; m. Bernard V. Narusis, June 19, 1959; children—Victor John, Ellen Marie. Admitted to Ill. bar, 1960; partner Narusis & Narusis, Cary, Ill., 1961—; city atty., City of McHenry (Ill.), 1973—; village atty., Fox River Grove, Ill., 1967-73; asst. state's atty., McHenry County, Ill., 1968—, head juvenile div., 1968—; mem. McHenry County Bd. Health, Woodstock, Ill., 1964—, Dist. 46 Sch. Bd., McHenry County, 1964—; mem. McHenry County, Welfare Services Com., 1968—. Mem. adv. com. Bert H. Boerner Meml. Trust, Woodstock, 1972—. Mem. Ill., McHenry County (bd. govs.) bar assns., Women's Bar Assn., Am. Judicature Soc., Nat. Dist. Attys. Assn., Kappa Beta Pi. Address: 213 W Lake Shore Dr Cary IL 60013

NARVID, ETHEL GALLAY, city ofcl.; b. N.Y.C., Dec. 25, 1916; d. James and Manya (Helfant) Gallay; student Hunter Coll., 1933; m. Ben Norman Narvid, Feb. 22, 1941 (div. 1965); children—Michael, Natalie. With U.S. Mil. Govt., Munich, Germany, 1946-48; field rep. for Councilman James C. Corman, Los Angeles, 1956-60; dist. rep. for Congressman James C. Corman, Los Angeles, 1960-69; asst. to pres. Coro Found., Los Angeles, 1969-70; finance dir. Cal. Democratic Com., 1970-72; campaign mgr. Bradley for Mayor, Los Angeles, 1972-73; adminstrv. coordinator Office of Mayor, City of Los Angeles, 1973—. Mem. community relations com. Jewish Fedn. Council Greater Los Angeles, 1961, mem. urban affairs commn., 1972. Mem. exec. com. Cal. Dem. Com., 1958. Mem. Anti-Defamation League (regional bd. 1971). Home: 2616 Hollyridge Dr Hollywood CA 90068 Office: Mayor's Office City Hall Los Angeles CA 90012

NASCA, JUNE ACHILLE (MRS. SALVATORE NASCA), chem. co. exec.; b. N.Y.C., June 19, 1920; d. Peter F. and Clara (Schwencke) Achille; grad. pub. high sch.; m. Salvatore Nasca, Feb. 14, 1942; children—Thomas Peter, Peter Anthony. Sec.-treas. Nasca Compound, Inc., Oceanside, L.I., N.Y., 1959—. Committeewoman 64th election dist. Dem. Party, Nassau County, 1954—. Recipient certificate of Merit, D.I.B. Mem. women's com. Nassau chpt. Boys Town of Italy, Inc. Club: Zonta (pub. relations chmn. L.I. 1963). Home: 2346 Windsor Rd Baldwin NY 11510 Office: 33 Saratoga Blvd Island Park NY 11558

NASH, ELIZABETH IVES, securities co. exec.; b. W. Chazy, N.Y., Aug. 5, 1909; d. Alfred Peabody and Eleanor Collista (Stoughton) Ives; student bus. colls.; m. Maynard Nash, Dec. 7, 1929; 1 son, Paul Ives. Sec., treas., dir. Maynard Nash, Inc., contractor, Stamford, Conn., 1950-68; stock broker asst. v.p. Hardy, Hardy & Assos., Sarasota, Fla., 1961—. Mem. Phila., Balt., Washington stock exchanges. Bd. dirs., sec. First Step, Inc. Mem. Mut. Fund Council, Internat. Financial Planners. Club: Field (Sarasota). Home: 3936 Shell Rd Sarasota FL 33581 Office: 3640 S Tamiami Trail Sarasota FL 33579

NASH, EVA L. WEEKES (MRS. EMILE C. NASH), social worker; b. Atlantic City, July 25, 1925; d. Ulric Oscar and Viola (Henderson) Weekes; A.B., Howard U., 1945; M.S.W., U. Pitts., 1959; student U. Chgo., 1945-46; m Emile C. Nash, Aug. 17, 1946; children—Michele L., Sharon E. Clin. social worker Freedmens Hosp., Washington, 1961-64, Child Guidance Clinic, D.C. Pub. Health, Washington, 1964-67; supervisory social worker Devel. Services Center, D.C. Pub. Health, Washington, 1967-69; Model Cities health planner Exec. Office D.C. Govt., Washington, 1969; community services officer Housing and Urban Devel., Washington, 1969-72; program coordinator Adminstrn. on Aging, Dept. Health, Edn. and Welfare, 1972—. Cons., Group Counseling Program in model sch. div. secondary schs. Co-chmn. spl. services com. D.C. Citizens for Better Pub. Sch. Edn., 1966—; pres. N.W. Settlement House Aux., 1972—. Bd. dirs. D.C. Planned Parenthood, 1962-68, mem. exec. bd., 1965-66, mem. council Met. Washington, 1973. Mem. Nat. Assn. Social Workers, Acad. Certified Social Workers, Am. Orthopsychiat. Assn., N.A.A.C.P. (steering com. D.C. Legal Def. Fund 1973—). Urban League, Delta Sigma Theta, Circle-Let's Inc. (D.C. pres. 1963-65). Home: 4307 18th St NE Washington DC 20018

NASH, JUNE CAPRICE BOUSLEY, anthropologist, educator; b. Salem, Mass., May 30, 1927; d. Joseph and Mary Josephine (Salloway) Bousley; B.A., Barnard Coll., 1948; M.A., U. Chgo., 1953, Ph.D., 1960; m. Manning Nash, Sept. 21, 1951 (div. Sept. 1966); children—Eric, Laura. Lectr. S.E. Jr. Coll., Chgo., 1961-62; asst. U. Chgo., summer 1962; asst. prof. social sci. dept. Chgo. Tchrs. Coll. N., 1962-64; asst. prof., dept. anthropology Yale U., 1964-68; asso. prof. anthropology N.Y. U., 1968-72; prof. City Coll., 1972—. Cons. Guggenheim grant award, Nat. Endowment Humanities. Recipient Guggenheim award, 1970. Fellow Am. Anthropol. Assn. (exec. bd.), mem. Am. Ethnol. Soc., Latin Am. Studies Assn., Social Scis. Research Council (com. Latin Am. studies). Author: Social Relations in Amatenango del Valle: An Activity Analysis, 1969; In the Eyes of the Ancestors: Belief and Behavior in a Maya Community 1970. Contbr. articles to profl. jours. Home: 100 Bleecker St New York City NY 10012

NASH, KATHERINE (MRS. ROBERT NASH), sculptor, educator; b. Mpls.; d. Carl Wilhelm and Elizabeth (Peterson) Flink; student Mpls. Sch. of Art, 1928; B.S., U. Minn., 1932; student Walker Art Center Sch., 1940-46, U. Neb., 1949-51; D.F.A., Doane Coll., Crete, Neb., 1964; m. Robert Nash, Mar. 21, 1934. Exhibited at Bryant Park N.Y., Sculptor's Guild N.Y., Walker Art Center, Mpls., Neb. Centennial, Joslyn Art Mus., Sheldon Gallery Lincoln, Brussel's World Fair, Whitney Mus., Joslyn Art Mus., Omaha, 1952-57; asst. prof. U. Neb., 1947-52; prof. sculpture U. Minn., 1963—; vis prof. San Jose Coll., Cal., 1961-62; represented in permanent collections Walker Art Center, Kan. State U., Joslyn Art Mus., Lincoln (Neb.) Artists Guild, Neb. Art Assn., Sheldon Mus., Lincoln, Neb., U. Minn. and others. State of Minn. Arts Council grantee, U.S. State Dept. U. Minn. grad. grantee, 1964-73. Participant Embassy Art Program, Computer Art Exhbns., Eng., Germany, Switzerland, U.S., Sao Paolo, Buenos Aires, Santiago Chile, others. Mem. Mid-Am. Coll. Art Assn., Minn. Soc. Sculptors (hon.), Artists Equity Assn. (hon., pres. Minn. chpt.), Computer Arts Soc., Am. Assn. U. Profs., Sculptor's Guild, Coll. Art Assn., Internat. Inst. Arts and Letters, Delta Phi Delta. Episcopalian. Home: Box 784 Route 3 Excelsior MN 55331 Office: Studio Art Dept U Minn Minneapolis MN 55455

NASH, MARY BURT (MRS. WILLIAM NASH), lawyer; b. Little Rock, Ark., June 17, 1912; d. William Burt and Orriette (Morris) Brooks; B.S., Northwestern U., 1931; M.A., U. Ia., 1932; LL.B., Ark. Law Sch., 1934; m. William Nash, Jan. 7, 1937; children—David William, Morris Brooks. Admitted to Ark. bar, 1934; referee Pulaski County Juvenile Ct., 1956—. Mem. Ark. Com. on Crime and Law Enforcement; vice chmn. exec. bd. Ark. Com on Status of Women, 1968-70. Trustee So. State Coll., Magnolia, Ark., 1952-63, sec. bd. trustees, 1961-63; bd. dirs. Nat. Interfrat. Found., Big Bros. Pulaski County. Recipient Alumni award Little Rock U., 1952; Alumni Merit award Northwestern U., 1963. Named woman of the Year Ark., 1964. Mem. Am. Bar Assn., Nat. Panhellenic Conf. (treas. 1957-59, sec. 1959-61, chmn. 1961-63), Nat. Council Juvenile Ct. Judges, Nat., Ark. (pres. 1967-69) assns. women lawyers, Am. Assn. U. Women (past state pres., legislative program com. 1955-61), Nat. Assn. Women Deans and Counselors, Interfrat. Research and Adv. Council (trustee 1961-63), Daus. Am. Colonists (past state regent), D.A.R., Dames of the Court of Honor (past state pres.), P.E.O., Delta Kappa Gamma, Alpha Xi Delta (past nat. pres., nat. council 1951-71). Presbyn. Club: Altrusa. Home: 410 Fairfax Av Little Rock AR 72205 Office: Juvenile Ct Juvenile Adminstrn Center 3201 W Roosevelt Rd Little Rock AR 72204

NASH, MYRTLE CORLISS, clin. psychologist; b. Long Island City, N.Y., Mar. 7, 1915; d. Augustin Pride and Hazel (Keene) Corliss; A.B., Swarthmore Coll., 1937; M.A., Bryn Mawr Coll., 1938, Ph.D., 1950; m. Thomas Nash, July 18, 1943; 1 son, Patrick Corliss. Teaching fellow psychology dept. Bryn Mawr (Pa.) Coll., 1938-39, 48-49; catalogue order office mgr. Montgomery Ward, various locations, 1940-43; interviewer YMCA Vocational Service Center, N.Y.C., 1946; research asso. Union Coll., Schenectady, 1949-52; asst. prof. psychology Drake U., Des Moines, 1952-54; asso. prof. psychology Southwestern U. Memphis, 1954-62; asso. prof. psychology Converse Coll., Spartanburg, S.C., 1962-67; prof. psychology Keuka Coll., Keuka Park, N.Y., 1967-71; clin. psychologist Spartanburg (S.C.) Mental Health Center, 1971—. Mem. Am., Southeastern psychol. assns., Phi Beta Kappa. Home: 134A Oakwood St Spartanburg SC 29302 Office: 149 Wood St Spartanburg SC 29303

NASH, ROSE FREEDMAN, linguist; b. Chgo.; d. Joseph B. and Anna (Savitsky) Nash; Mus.B., Northwestern U., 1950; postgrad. Vienna (Austria) Conservatory Music, 1956-57; M.A., Middlebury Coll., 1960; Ph.D., Ind. U., 1967; pvt. study with Ernst Bloch; 1 son, Carl. Lectr. linguistics Ind. U., Bloomington, 1960-62, asst. to editor Research Center in Anthropology, Folklore and Linguistics, 1962, teaching asso. dept. linguistics, 1966-67; sei. linguist Vietnamese sect. Fgn. Service Inst., Dept. State, Washington, 1966; asst. prof. linguistics Inter Am. U., San Juan, P.R., 1967-69, asso. prof., 1969—; asso. prof. research series U. Cal. at Santa Barbara, 1973-74. Research travel grant to U.S.S.R., Program for Intercultural Communication, 1963; Nat. Def. Edn. Act Title VI lang. fellow, 1963-66; research grantee Am. Council Learned Socs., 1967; sr. scholar under USSR cultural exchange program, 1970; guest researcher U. Edinburgh, 1970; Nat. Endowment for Humanities fellow, 1973-74. Mem. Acoustical Soc. Am., Am. Assn. Tchrs. Slavic and E. European Langs., Am. Assn. U. Profs., Assn. Machine Translation and Computational Linguistics, Internat. Linguistic Circle N.Y., Linguistic Soc. Am., Modern Lang. Assn., Tchrs. English to Speakers Other Langs. Author: A Multilingual Lexicon of Linguistics and Philology: English, Russian, German, French, 1968; Turkish Intonation, An Instrumental Study, 1973; Comparing Spanish and English, 1975. Editor, Readings Spanish-English Contrastive Linguistics. Contbr. articles to profl. jours. Home: Villas del Mar Isla Verde PR 00913

NASH, RUTH COWAN (MRS. BRADLEY D. NASH), journalist; b. Salt Lake City, Utah; d. William Henry and Ida (Baldwin) Cowan; A.B., U. Tex., 1923; m. Bradley D. Nash, June 30, 1956. Tchr. pub. high sch., San Antonio, 1924-27; reporter San Antonio Evening News, 1928, United Press, 1929; corr. A.P., Chgo., 1929-40, Washington, 1940-43, 45-56, war corr., North Africa, Gt. Britain, Europe, 1943-45, retired, 1956; free lance journalist, 1956—; asst. to undersec. of health edn. and welfare, 1958-61. Cons., Pub. relations dir., women's div., rep. Nat. Com., Washington; mem. Def. Adv. Com. on Women in the Services, 1958-61. Clubs: Mem. Women's Nat. Press (pres. 1947-48), Overseas Press, Am. Newspaper Women's; Writer and Press (London). Home: High Acres Farm Harpers Ferry WV 25425

NASH, WINIFRED HELENA, educator; b. Boston; d. James and Katherine (Herrity) Nash; B.S., Boston U., 1920, M.A., 1927, Ph.D., 1931; summer study Oxford U., Harvard; Litt.D., Calvin Coolidge Coll., 1953. Mem. English dept. High Sch. Practical Arts, 1921-28; head English dept. Dorchester High Sch. for Girls, 1940-47; English dept. Roxbury Meml. High Sch. for Girls, 1928-40, headmaster, 1947-57, headmaster emeritus, 1957—; clk. of corp and trustees Warren Instn. for Savs., Boston, 1958-68, corporator, 1956-69. Mem. N.E. regional com. High School Tchrs. Fellowship program, Ford Fund for Advancement Edn., 1954-55. Mem. New Eng. Assn. Tchrs. English (pres. 1938, editor English Leaflet 1940-47, hon life mem.), Am. Assn. U. Women (chmn. com. higher edn. Boston 1958-60, chmn. Ryder scholarship com. 1959-61), Nat. Council Tchrs. English, High Sch. Head Masters Assn. (pres. 1954-56), Boston U. Women's Council (editor The Council Window 1962-64, bd. dirs. 1968, mem. com. publs. 1962—), New Eng. Women's Press Assn., Am. Security Council. Co-editor: Literature We Like, Literature We Appreciate. Contbr. articles to profl. jours. Home: 1025 Hancock St Quincy MA 02169

NASON, DORIS ELNORA, educator; b. North Girard, Pa., Apr. 25, 1913; d. Roy B. and Emma (Dean) Nason; student Edinboro State Coll., Pa., 1930-32; B.S. in Edn., Boston U., 1947, M.Ed., 1948, Ed.D., 1951. Elementary tchr. Union Twp., Pa., 1932-35, Union City, Pa., 1935-42, Millcreek Twp., Pa., 1942-43, 45-47; Link Trainer instr. USN, Sanford, Fla., 1943-45; teaching fellow elementary edn. Boston U., 1948-50, lectr. edn., summers 1948-50; asst. prof. edn. U. Conn., 1950-61, asso. prof. edn., 1961-70, prof., 1970—, acting dir. reading-study center, 1969-72, dir., 1972—; dir. Reading Resources Network Center in Conn., 1970—; cons., lectr. in field. Mem. Conn. State Adv. Council Right to Read. Mem. Am. Ednl. Research Assn., Nat. Soc. Study Edn., Conn. Assn. Reading Research, N.E.A., Assn. Higher Edn., Nat. Council Tchrs. English, Nat. Conf. Research English, Internat., New Eng. (mem. exec. bd., 1964-68, pres. 1966-67, pres. Eastern Conn. council 1974-75) reading assns., Internat. Platform Assn., Pi Lambda Theta. Author (with Robert Norris, Herbert Tag and Richard Neville) Foundations for Elementary School Teaching, 1963. Editor: Teacher Education Quar., 1957-58. Editorial bd. 1952-66. Contbr. articles to profl. jours. Home: 29 Agnes Dr Manchester CT 06040

NASSANEY, JEAN CLARE HOSTERT KEISTER (MRS. JOSEPH NASSANEY), lawyer; b. Warren, O., Aug. 28, 1931; d. Peter John and Anna Helen (Brennan) Hostert; student Glendale Coll., 1949-50, (scholar) Queen of Angels Coll. Nursing, Los Angeles, 1951-53; J.D. cum laude (scholar), Southwestern U., 1966; m. Joseph Nassaney, June 25, 1973; 1 son, John Francis. Clk., Glendale (Cal.) Municipal Ct., 1954-59; asst. to dist. atty. City of Pasadena (Cal.), 1959-60; exec. sec. firm Schell & Delamer, Los Angeles, 1960-61; receptionist D.C. Ct. Appeals, 1961-62; legal sec. firm Mepham & Foglia, Los Angeles, 1962-66, mem. firm, 1967-68; admitted to Cal. bar, 1967, U.S. Supreme Ct. bar, 1973; researcher, writer firm Irmas & Rudder, Beverly Hills, Cal., 1967-68; mem. firm Labowe & Ventress, Los Angeles, 1968-74; practiced in Sherman Oaks, Cal., 1974—. Treas., Campfire Girls. Mem. Italian Catholic Fedn. (v.p.), Catholic Daus. Am. (sec.), Patrons Italian Culture (sec.), Beta Sigma Phi (treas.). Clubs: Emblem; Altrusa (treas. Sunland-Tujunga, Cal.). Office: 4645 Van Nuys Blvd Suite 5 Sherman Oaks CA 91403

NASSIF, HELEN G., lawyer; b. Jessup, Ia.; d. George and Edith (Skaff) Nassif; B.A., Coe Coll., 1945; LL.B., George Washington Law Sch., 1948. Admitted to Ia. bar, 1948; lawyer U.S. Ct. Customs and Patent Appeals, Washington, 1945-67, reporter of decisions, 1967—, disbursing officer, 1971—. Mem. Internat., Am., Washington bar assns., Nat. Assn. Women's Lawyers, Women's Bar Assn. D.C., World Peace through Law Center, Clubs: Nat. Press, Am. Newspaper Women's (Washington). Home: 10401 Grosvenor Pl Rockville MD 20852 Office: 717 Madison Pl NW Washington DC 20439

NATHAN, CAROL, educator; b. Akron, O., June 9, 1933; d. Ernest Duke and Carolyn Elizabeth (Ash) Nathan; student Pratt Inst., 1951-53; B.S., N.Y. U., 1958; M.A., U. So. Cal., 1968. Staff occupational therapist Newington (Conn.) Children's Hosp., 1958-60, asst. dir. occupational therapy, 1960-66; supr. clin. edn. Ind. U. Med. Center, Indpls., 1967-68; asst. prof., dir. occupational therapy Ind. U., Indpls., 1968-71, asso. prof., dir. occupational therapy, 1971—; tchr., cons. occupational therapy and allied health. Chmn. adv. com. Profl. Exam. Services for Devel. Proficiency Exam., 1973—. Mem. Am. (nat. chmn. occupational therapy accreditation com. with A.M.A. 1970-73, chmn. council edn. 1973—, mem. nat. bylaws com. 1970-71), Ind. (pres. 1970-72, mem. bylaws com. 1970-72) occupational therapy assns., Nat. Assn. U. Profs., Am. Soc. Allied Health Professions (editorial bd. Jour. 1972), Methodist. Club: Altrusa (chmn. publicity com. 1969-70). Editorial bd. Am. Jour. Occupational Therapy, 1970-72. Home: 826 Chapelwood Blvd Indianapolis IN 46224 Office: 1232 W Michigan St Indianapolis IN 46202

NATHAN, THEODORA NATHALIA (MRS. CHARLES NATHAN), journalist; b. N.Y.C., Feb. 9, 1923; d. Bennett and Salcha (Ralska) Nathan; B.A., U. Ore., 1971; m. Charles Nathan, June 6, 1942; children—Paul Steven, Lawrence Eugene, Gregory. Owner, ins. agt. Valley Ins. Agy., North Hollywood, Cal., 1947-53; mgr. Chase Music Co., Sun Valley, Cal., 1953-60; owner, interior decorator Mrs. Charles Interiors, La Habra, 1961-68; copy desk editor Ore. Daily Emerald, Eugene, 1970-71; weekly columnist, reporter Valley News, also free-lance TV producer, hostess, writer, radio commentator KVAL-TV, Eugene, 1971-72. Pub. relations dir. U. Ore. Women's Recreation Assn., 1971-72, Ore. Women's Polit. Caucus, 1972-73. Vice presidential candidate Libertarian Party, 1972, mem. nat. jud. com., 1972—, dir. Ore., 1972—. Nat. adv. bd. Speak Out!, 1972-73. Mem. Women in Communications (chpt. pres. 1972-73). Clubs: Eu-hane Toastmistress, Metro Civic (Eugene). Home: 2251 McMillan St Eugene OR 97405

NATRELLA, MARY GIBBONS (MRS. JOSEPH V. NATRELLA), statistician; b. Scranton, Pa., Sept. 23, 1922; d. Frank William and Blanche Esther (O'Keefe) Gibbons; A.A., Keystone Jr. Coll., 1940; B.A., U. Pa., 1942; m. Joseph V. Natrella, May 4, 1946; children—Aileen M., Elizabeth S. Mathematician, U.S. Army Ordnance Dept., Phila., 1942-45; statistician Bur. Ships, USN, Washington, 1945-50, Nat. Bur. Standards, Washington, 1950—. Lectr. Nat. Bur. Standards Grad. Sch., 1963. Mem. Am. Statis. Assn., Am. Soc. for Quality Control, Inst. Math. Statistics. Home: 25 N Floyd St Alexandria VA 22304 Office: Statis Engring Lab Nat Bur Standards Washington DC 20234

NAUERT, PATRICIA SIEMINSKI (MRS. C. RANDOLPH NAUERT), mus. ofcl.; b. N.Y.C., Aug. 7, 1946; d. Eugene Burton and Sara (Allee) Sieminski; B.A., New Coll., 1967; postgrad. N.Y. U., 1970-71; m. C. Randolph Nauert, Sept. 16, 1972. Asst. to registrar Mus. Modern Art, N.Y.C., 1967-70, spl. asst. to registrar, Mies Van Der Rohe Archive archivist, cataloger film dept., 1970-71; registrar Los Angeles County Mus. Art, 1971—. Registrar, Fedn. Black History and Arts, 1973. Grantee Nat. Mus. Act, 1974. Mem. Am. Assn. Museums. Christian Scientist (mem. youth com. 1972—). Home: 2119 Estrella Av Los Angeles CA 90007 Office: 5905 Wilshire Blvd Los Angeles CA 90036

NAUGHTON, ALICE SONJA JOHNSON, nursing adminstr., educator; b. Morristown, N.J., June 30, 1929; d. Fletcher and Edna (Ferguson) Johnson; diploma Freedmen's Hosp. Sch. Nursing, 1951; B.S., Catholic U. Md., 1959; M.S., U. Md., 1963; Ph.D., Catholic U. Am., 1974; m. Ezra Naughton, May 26, 1956. Staff nurse, team leader Freedmen's Hosp. USPHS, Washington, 1951-55, 58, supr. psychiat., med.-surg. and emergency units, 1961-62; supr. Psychiat. Inst. D.C. Gen. Hosp., 1958-59; pub. health nurse D.C. Dept. Pub. Health, 1959-61; instr. psychiat. nursing U. Md. Sch. Nursing, 1963-65, asst. prof., 1965-66, asst. prof., chmn. dept. psychiat. nursing, dir. master theses, 1966-69; curriculum cons. Howard U. Sch. Nursing, 1968-69, asso. dean, 1969—; dir. nursing Howard U.-Freedmen's Hosp., Washington, 1969—; lectr. in field. Mem. Am. Assn. U. Profs., Nat. League Nursing, Am. Soc. Tng. and Devel., Am., D.C. (dir. 1972-74) nurses assns., Am. Soc. Hosp. Nursing Adminstrs., D.C. Mental Health Assn., U. Md. Nurses, Catholic U. Am., Freedman's Hosp. Sch. Nursing alumni assn., Sigma Theta Tau, Phi Kappa Phi . Contbr. articles to profl. jours. Home: 510 N St SW Apt N327 Washington DC 20024

NAUMANN, DOROTHY ETHEL, physician; b. Syracuse, N.Y., Mar. 18, 1915; d. Carl William and Louise Margaret (Lynch) Naumann; M.D., Syracuse U., 1940. Intern, resident Ellis Hosp., Schenectady, 1940-42; indsl. physician Gen. Electric Co., 1942-43; univ. physician Syracuse U., 1944-50, 52-63; asso. prof. health and preventive medicine, 1952-63; physician VA, 1951-52; examining physician YWCA, Schenectady, 1940-43, Syracuse, 1947-63; asst. physician in medicine, Syracuse Meml. Hosp., mem. courtesy staff in medicine U. Hosp. of Good Shepherd, 1944-63; asst. prof. community health scis. Duke, 1963—, dir. student health, 1972—. Sec. Student Health Research Found., Inc.; med. adviser for health edn. dept., dir. YWCA; treas. Loan Closet for Sick Room Equipment Com., 1960-63; mem. council Service Clubs of Syracuse, sec. council, 1962-63. Selected mem. Ct. of Honor for Delta Zeta Woman of the Year, 1954; Orchid award YM-YW Bldg. Fund Campaign, 1954. Mem. A.M.A., Profl. Women's League (pres. 1955-56, 62-63), Coll. Health Assn., Am. Soc. Microbiology, Am. Acad. Family Physicians, Am. Assn. U. Women, Syracuse U. Alumni Assn., Durham-Orange County N.C. med. socs., P.E.O., Alpha Epsilon Iota, Sigma Delta Epsilon, Delta Zeta (alumnae chpt. treas.). Mem. Order Eastern Star. Clubs: Altrusa (pres. 1970-72), Duke University Faculty. Home: 2404 Tampa Av Durham NC 27705 Office: Box 6635 College Station Durham NC 27708

NAUMER, CAROLYN PALMER (MRS. HELMUTH JACOB NAUMER), mus. ofcl.; b. Muskogee, Okla., Oct. 26, 1941; d. William Henry and Lizzie Lou (Ross) Palmer; student William Woods Coll. for Women, 1959-60, Okla. U., 1960-62, Tex. Christian U., 1966-67; m. Helmuth Jacob Naumer, Oct. 9, 1966; children—Kyrsten Anne, Tanya. Exec. sec. Mus. Sci. and History, Ft. Worth, 1963-66, Kimbell Art Found., Ft. Worth, 1966-71; adminstrv. sec. Kimbell Art Mus., Ft. Worth, 1971—. Active numerous civic activities. Mem. Jr. League Ft. Worth, Delta Delta Delta. Presbyn. Home: 6355 Waverly Way Fort Worth TX 76116 Office: Will Rogers Rd Fort Worth TX 76107

NAUMOFF, MARY ELIZABETH HULL (MRS. ALEXANDER V. NAUMOFF), lawyer; b. Champaign, Ill., Dec. 8, 1927; d. Frank Leroy and Elizabeth Ellen (Fritchey) Hull; B.S. in Law, U. Ill., 1949, J.D., 1951; m. Alexander V. Naumoff, July 30, 1949; children—Mitchell A., Andrew J., Elizabeth E., Nancy A., Thomas H., Alexander V., Mary L., Barbara S., Christina M., Paul A., Rebecca J. Admitted to Ohio bar, 1952, since practiced in Barberton; mem. firm Naumoff and Naumoff. Mem. Barberton Bd. Edn., 1964-71, pres., 1967. Mem. Akron Bar Assn. Methodist (past supt., sr. high sch. teacher Sunday Sch., chmn. commn. on edn.). Home: 519 Parkview Av Barberton OH 44203 Office: 489 W Park Av Barberton OH 44203

NAVAS, ELIZABETH STUBBLEFIELD, interior designer; b. Coffeyville, Kan., June 29, 1895; d. Elmer E. and Carrie (Drake) Stubblefield; student Columbia; m. Rafael Navas, June 23, 1917. Interior designer, art critic and collector. Trustee, Estate of Louise C. Murdock; hon. trustee Am. Fedn. Arts. Recipient Resolution of Honor and commendation for outstanding cultural contbn. and service to Wichita Art Mus. and City and Citizens of Wichita. Mem. D.A.R., Met. Mus. Mcpl. Art Soc. N.Y. Author: Biography of Louise C. Murdock. Home: 250 E 63d St New York City NY 10021

NAY, MARY SPENCER (MRS. LOU BLOCK), educator; b. Crestwood, Ky., May 13, 1913; d. Benjamin Franklin and Edna M. (Stringer) Nay; student Art Center Assn. Sch., Louisville, 1937-40, Cin. Art Acad., 1941; B.A., U. Louisville, 1942, M.A., 1960; m. Lou Block, Mar. 17, 1951; children—Malu, Fayette. Dir. Art Center Assn. Sch., 1944-49; project supr. Nat. Youth Adminstrn., Louisville, 1938-40; instr. art U. Louisville, 1941-59, asst. prof., 1959-64, prof., Belknap Campus, 1970—. Sec. bd. dirs. Jr. Art Gallery, 1950-55; bd. dirs. Ky. Arts and Crafts Guild, 1963-65, mem. standards com., 1967-70. Recipient Purchase award Ky. State Fair, 1954, 58, 60, Ashland Oil Co. (Ky.), 1945, 50, 58, Tri-State Art Exhibit, 1952, 56, 58. Mem. Am. Assn. U. Profs., Provincetown Art Assn., Ky. Art Edn. Assn. Club: Arts (Louisville). Home: 207 S Galt Av Louisville KY 40206

NAYLOR, HARRIET HOYT CORE (MRS. GEORGE NAYLOR IV), vol. services adminstr.; b. White Plains, N.Y., Dec. 4, 1915; d. Arthur Leslie and Henrietta (Bedford) Core; student N.Y. Sch. Social Work, 1937-39, U. Chgo., 1939-40; A.B., Barnard Coll., Columbia, 1937, M.A., 1963; m. George Naylor IV, July 31, 1939; children—Margery Bedford (Mrs. Peter Van Inwagen), Elizabeth Beekman, George Dustin. Vol., nat. trainer, mem. regional, personnel coms. Girl Scouts U.S.A., 1951-60, tng. adviser, 1960-62; tng. cons. nat. bd. YWCA, 1962-67; dir. vol. service N.Y. State Dept. Mental Hygiene, 1967-71; dir. ednl. devel. Nat. Center Vol. Action, Washington, 1972-74, dir. N.E. region, 1971-72; dir. Office Vol. Devel. Dept. Health, Edn. and Welfare, 1974—; cons. vol. adminstrn. and devel. Instr., Sch. Community Services, Va. Commonwealth U., 1973—. Chmn. N.Y. State Gov.'s Interdepartmental Com. Vols., 1968-71. Fellow Am. Assn. Vol. Services Coordinators (v.p. 1971-73); mem. Am. Soc. Dirs. Vol. Services, Am. Soc. Pub. Adminstrn., Adult Edn. Assn., Am. Assn. U. Women, Assn. Vol. Action Scholars, Coop. Edn. Assn., Assn. Vol. Burs., YWCA. Author: Volunteers Today, 1967; Leadership for Vol. Services in Social Work Practice, 1969; also articles in field of vols., rehab., mental health. Editorial bd. Jour. Assn. Vol. Action Scholars, 1971. Home: Box 261 Rhinebeck NY 12572 also 2701 16th St S Arlington VA 22204

NAYLOR, PHYLLIS REYNOLDS, author; b. Anderson, Ind., Jan. 4, 1933; d. Eugene Spencer and Lura Mae (Schield) Reynolds; diploma Joliet Jr. Coll., Ill., 1953, B.A. in Psychology, Am. U., 1963; m. Rex Vaughn Naylor, May 26, 1960; children—Jeffrey, Michael. Tchr. elementary sch., Hazelcrest, Ill., 1956; asst. exec. sec. Montgomery County (Md.) Edn. Assn., 1958-59; editorial asst. N.E.A. Jour., Washington, 1959-60. Mem. Council for a Livable World, N.A.A.C.P., Common Cause, Zero Population Growth, SANE, Author's Guild, Children's Book Guild Washington. Independent. Unitarian. Author numerous short stories and books, including: To Make a Wee Moon, 1969; Making It Happen, 1970; Wrestle the Mountain, 1971; No Easy Circle, 1972; To Walk the Sky Path, 1973; An Amish Family, 1974. Home: 9910 Holmhurst Rd Bethesda MD 20034

NAZARETIAN, ANGELINE, educator; b. Fairfield, Ala., Apr. 29, 1928; d. O. Jeane and Alice (Yarchalk) Nazaretian; B.S., Ala. Coll., 1950; M.A., U. Ala., 1958. Tchr. girls' phys. edn., sci. Graysville (Ala.) Jr. High Sch., 1951-55; dir. girls' phys. edn. McAdory High Sch., McCalla, Ala., 1955-58; dir. health, phys. edn. Athens (Ala.) Coll., 1958—. First aid, water safety chmn. Limestone County chpt. A.R.C., Athens, 1938—; chmn. Athens-Limestone Heart Fund, 1966, United Givers Fund Drive, 1966; charter mem., pres. Athens Humane Soc., Athens Beautification Program; mem. state bd. Ala. Heart Assn.; active Girl Scouts Am. Named Alumnus of Year Ala. Coll., 1968. Mem. Jefferson County Tchrs. Assn., Am., Ala. (honor award 1968), Jefferson County assns. health, phys. edn. and recreation, Ala. Edn. Assn., N.E.A., Jefferson County Classroom Tchrs. Assn., Am. Camping Assn., Am. Assn. U. Women, Am. Assn. U. Profs., Athens Bus. and Profl. Women, So., Nat. assns. phys. edn. coll. women, C. of C. Zeta Tau Alpha, Pi Delta Epsilon, Kappa Delta Pi, Kappa Delta Kappa, Delta Psi Omega, Pi Tau Chi, Delta Kappa Gamma. Presbyn. Mem. Order Eastern Star. Home: 212 N Beaty St Athens AL 35611

NEAD, LENA CARR (MRS. JOHN E. NEAD), lawyer; b. Ezel, Ky.; d. William Emery and Roena Clarke (Havens) Carr; B.C.S., D.C. Coll., 1928; M.C.S., Southeastern U., 1930, LL.B., 1936; m. John E. Nead, Dec. 24, 1926. Admitted to D.C. bar, 1939; adjudicator Gen. Accounting Office, Washington, 1950-71; pvt. practice law, Washington, 1971—. Mem. Nat. Assn. Women Lawyers, Women's Bar Assn. of D.C. Home: 3533 Ordway St NW Washington DC 20016 Office: 401 Munsey Bldg 1329 E St NW Washington DC 20004

NEAL, ARMINTA PEARL, museum ofcl.; b. El Paso, Tex., Aug. 12, 1921; d. John Robert and Edith Pearl (Aldridge) Neal; B.A., U. Cal. at Los Angeles, 1943; student Los Angeles Art Center Sch., 1946-47; postgrad. U. Denver, 1948-49, 69—. Tech. illustrator Douglas Aircraft, Los Angeles, 1943-44; preparator Denver Art Mus., 1948-49; exhibit preparator Colo. State His. Soc. Mus., Denver, 1949; exhibit designer, curator Denver Mus. Natural History, 1950—. Exhibit cons.; lecture-demonstrator on exhibits for univs., profl. workshops, seminars. Mem. adv. council to Smithsonian Instn. for Nat. Mus. Art, 1973—. Served with WAC, 1944-46. Recipient award of merit Am. Assn. Conservation Information, 1970; Profl. of Year award Mountain-Plains Mus. Conf., 1973. Mem. Am. Anthrop. Assn., Internat. Congress Museums (active com. 1973—), Soc. for Anthropology of Visual Communications, Am. Assn. State and Local History, Am. Assn. Museums, Mountain Plains Museum Conf., Colo.-Wyo. Museum Assn. (dir. 1972-73). Episcopalian. Illustrator: Cherokee Dance and Drama (Frank Speck and Leonard Broom), 1951; The Ways of Mankind (Walter Goldschmidt), 1954; First Came The Family (Ruth Underhill), 1958; Ruffles and Drums (Doris Samford), 1967. Home: 4960 W Oregon Pl Denver CO 80219 Office: Denver Museum Natural History City Park Dever CO 80205

NEAL, BERNIECE ROER (MRS. HARRY EDWARD NEAL), free-lance writer; b. Elsinore, Mo., July 26, 1914; d. William Coade and Edna Odessa (Casteel) Raymer; student pub. schs.; m. George L. Roer, Aug. 13, 1938 (dec. June 1964); children—George William, Michael Leo; m. 2d, Harry Edward Neal, July 15, 1965. Tchr., lectr. creative writing, U.S., 1955—; tchr., lectr. creative writing abroad in writers confs. for Georgetown U., Washington, 1970—; tchr. article writing Writer's Digest Sch., 1973—. Recipient 1st pl. award in article writing Mo. Writers Guild, 1964, in mag. article writing Va. Press Women, 1970. Mem. Soc. Mag. Writers, Nat. Fedn. Press Women. Author: How to Write Articles, 1963. Contbr. articles, short stories to a variety publs. including: N.Y. Times, Woman's Day, Washington Post, Washington Star-News, St. Louis Post-Dispatch, Girl Talk, Better Homes and Gardens, The Writer, Holiday Inn, Optimist Internat., Toledo Blade, Charlotte Observer, Christian Sci. Monitor, Chgo. Tribune, Balt. Sun. Address: 210 Spring St Culpeper VA 22701

NEAL, EMILY GARDINER (MRS. ALVIN W. NEAL), author; b. N.Y.C.; d. John deBarth and Rebekah (McLean) Gardiner; student David Mannes Coll. Music, 1926-30; m. Alvin W. Neal, Mar. 12, 1931; children—Rebekah McLean (Mrs. Frank Kennedy), Diana Harrell (Mrs. William G. Galbreath). Newspaper work, 1944-46; feature writer Redbook, McCall's, Reader's Digest, and others; counselor, lectr.; mem. staff P.Hs. Pastoral Inst. Episcopalian. Author: A Reporter Finds God, 1956; God Can Heal You Now, 1958; The Lord is Our Healer, 1961; In the Midst of Life, 1963; Father Bob and his Boys, 1963; Where There's Smoke, 1967; The Healing Power of Christ, 1972. Home: 2533 Pioneer Av Pittsburgh PA 15226

NEAL, FRANCES POTTER, librarian; b. Strong, Ark., Oct. 27, 1905; d. Finis and Lucy Letetia (Richardson) Potter; B.S. in Edn., U. Ark., 1945; M.A., U. Denver, 1949; m. Karl Neal, Apr. 25, 1931. Tchr. pub. schs., El Dorado, Ark., 1924-31; librarian Warren (Ark.) Elementary Sch., 1941-47; circulation librarian, reference librarian Ark. Library Commn., 1947-51, exec. sec., librarian, 1952—. Recipient Progressive Farmer Woman of Year award, 1956, Ark. Woman of Year, Dem. award, 1957. Mem. A.L.A., Ark. (pres. 1950, councilor to A.L.A. 1951-72), Southwestern (pres. 1964-66) library assns., Am. Assn. U. Women, Bus. and Profl. Women's Club (2d v.p. Little Rock 1956, Pfeifer Cup 1957), Kappa Delta Pi, Delta Kappa Gamma. Home: 108 Brown St Little Rock AR 72205 Office: 506 1/2 Center St Little Rock AR 72201

NEAL, GEORGIANNE DAVIS (MRS. JAMES THOMAS NEAL), newspaper exec.; b. Indpls., Nov. 25, 1930; d. Herschel Ewing and Ruth (Fifer) Davis; A.B., Radcliffe Coll., 1951; postgrad., U. London, summer 1951; m. James Thomas Neal, June 3, 1953; children—Anne deHayden, Andrea Davis. Writer, asst. woman's editor Indpls. News, 1951-55; v.p. Noblesville (Ind.) Daily Ledger, 1967—. Moderator community interview series Pub. TV, Indpls., 1972; Bd. dirs. Park-Tudor Sch. Found., 1970—, Marion County Child Guidance Clinic, 1964-73, Central Ind. council Camp Fire Girls, 1964-67, Orchard Sch. Found., 1968-70; trustee Methodist Hosp., Indpls., 1974—. Mem. Christamore Aid Soc., Soc. of Ind. Pioneers, Jr. League (pres. 1962-64). Republican. Methodist. Clubs: Radcliffe of Ind. (pres. 1954-56), Indianapolis Woman's. Home: 7670 E 126th St Noblesville IN 46060

NEAL, MARY JULIA, educator, author; b. Auburn, Ky., Aug. 15, 1905; d. Presley Taylor and Nettie Lou (Pace) Neal; student Bethel Womans Coll., 1923-25; B.S., Western Ky. U., 1931, M.A., 1933; postgrad. U. Mich., 1943-45, U. Denver, summer 1965, Syracuse U., summer 1967. Instr. English, Western Ky. U., Bowling Green, 1934-41, dir. Ky. Library and Mus., 1964-72; dean of residence Kingswood-Cranbrook, Bloomfield Hills, Mich., 1944-46; asso. prof. English, Florence (Ala.) State Coll., 1946-64. Spl. lectr. Shaker Exhibit, Phila. Mus. Art; participant Hancock (Mass.) Shaker Conf., 1969, Shaker Bicentennial Conf., Cleve., 1974. Mem. South Atlantic Modern Lang. Assn., Manuscript Soc., Am. Studies, A.L.A., Sigma Tau Delta, Chi Delta Phi. Author: Shakers: By their Fruits, 1947; The Journal of Eldress Nancy, 1963; The Shaker Image, 1974. Home: 1523 Park St Bowling Green KY 42101

NEAL, PATRICIA ANN HOUGH (MRS. CHARLES BODINE NEAL, III), civic worker; b. Hartford, Conn., Feb. 12, 1935; d. Perry Tyler and Althea Florence (Goodale) Hough; student Duke U., 1953-56; A.B., Am. U., 1959; m. Charles Bodine Neal III, Dec. 31, 1955; children—Katharine, Constance, Charles Bodine IV, William. Mem. Durham County Sch. Bd., 1969—, vice chmn., 1971, chmn., 1972—; mem. N.C. Study Commn. on Relations between Profl. Employee Assns. and Sch. Bds., 1973-74. Chmn. Durham County Young Republicans, 1966-68; vice chmn. 4th Congl. Dist. Rep. Party, 1968-70. Mem. Nat. (fed. relations network 1973—), N.C. (dir. 1972—) sch. bd. assns. Home: 3442 Rugby Rd Durham NC 27707

NEALIN, PATRICIA LORETTO, broadcasting exec.; b. Chgo., Oct. 19; d. Daniel Edward and Elizabeth Therese (Hallisey) Nealin; B.A., Mundelein Coll., 1949. With WGN Continental Broadcasting Co., Chgo., 1952—, film editor, asst. film dir., then dir. films, 1960-74, mgr. films, 1974—, mem. editorial bd., 1971—, chmn. editorial bd., 1974—; dir. WGN World Travel Services, 1973—. Mem. Broadcast Pioneers, Am. Women in Radio and TV (past dir. at large; past nat. sec.-treas., pres. 1974—), Sigma Delta Chi, Kappa Gamma Pi. Club: Chicago Headline. Home: 3040 Hartzell St Evanston IL 60201 Office: 2501 W Bradley Pl Chicago IL 60618

NEARING, JEWELL HARRIET HARDWICKS (MRS. GEORGE L. NEARING), educator; b. Chgo., June 27, 1924; d. William and Catherine (Johnson) Hardwicks; B.A., U. Ill., 1946, Ph.D. in Spl. Edn. (U.S. Office Edn. fellow), 1974; M.A., Chgo. State U., 1963; m. George L. Nearing, June 16, 1946; children—Ronald, Diane. Probation officer Family Ct., Chgo., 1950-55; tchr. elementary and primary schs., Chgo., 1955-67; coordinator team activities Tchr. Corps, Cycle II, Consortium Colls. and Univs., Chgo., 1967-69; faculty Roosevelt U., Chgo., 1969-73; asso. prof. spl. edn. Chgo. State U., 1974—. Mem. Delta Sigma Theta. Baptist. Home: 9050 S Parnell St Chicago IL 60620

NEAT, SISTER CHARLES MARIE, educator; b. Albany, N.Y.; d. Charles Joseph and Mary (Houseweller) Neat; B.A., Coll. of St. Rose, 1935; M.A., Cath. U. of Am., 1946, Ph.D., 1954. Tchr. St. Ann's Acad., Albany, N.Y., 1935-36; prof. German, Coll. of St. Rose, 1939—, chmn. dept. fgn. langs., 1969-74. Panelist many ednl. confs.,

1969—. Recipient Fulbright Fellow, 1956. Mem. Am. Assn. Tchrs. German. (v.p. Hudson Valley chpt. 1965-68, sec.-treas. 1971-74), Modern Lang. Assn., N.E. Conf. Lang. Tchrs., Am. Assn. U. Profs., (sec. coll. chpt. 1966-68), N.Y. State Modern Lang. Tchrs. Assn., Am. Council on Teaching Fgn. Langs., Intercontinental Biog., Assn., N.Y. State Assn. Fgn. Lang. Tchrs., Assn. Depts. Fgn. Langs., Delta Epsilon Sigma, Alpha Mu Gamma. Address: Coll of St Rose Albany NY 12203

NEDLER, SHARI EVANS, psychologist, educator; b. N.Y.C., May 19, 1929; d. Nathan and Etta (Ulman) Evans; B.A., Smith Coll., 1950; M.S., Trinity U., 1964; Ph.D., U. Tex., 1972; m. Irvin Nedler, Dec. 11, 1951; children—Michael, Karen, Donald. Psychologist, Pre-sch. Program for Spanish Speaking Children, 1964-67; early childhood specialist Southwest Ednl. Devel. Lab., 1968-69, dir. early childhood program, 1969-74; faculty U. Colo., Denver, 1974—. Cons., Tex. Edn. Agy., 1970, Follow Through Program, 1971; mem. faculty U. Tex., 1972-73. Mem. Task Force on Early Childhood Edn., 1972. Mem. Am. Psychol. Assn., Am. Ednl. Research Assn., Soc. for Research in Child Devel., Nat. Assn. for Edn. Young Children. Author: (with Brophy and Good) Teaching in the Preschool, 1974; also chpts. in books. Home: 460 S Marion Pkwy Denver CO 80209

NEDVED, VIRGINIA AUTY (MRS. HOWARD JAMES NEDVED), civic worker; b. Melrose, Mass., May 28, 1930; d. Clarence and Viva Althea (Palmer) Auty; student Westbrook Jr. Coll., 1947-48; B.S. Edn., Tufts U., 1952; diploma occupational therapy Boston Sch. Occupational Therapy, 1952; postgrad. Keene Coll., 1964-66, Rivier Coll., 1971—; m. Howard James Nedved, Apr. 18, 1953; children—Lee Jay, Linda Kay. Occupational therapist Cushing VA Hosp., Framingham, Mass., 1952-53, Johns Hopkins Hosp., Balt., 1953-54; supr. occupational therapy Bedford (Mass.) VA Hosp., 1954-57; dir. occupational therapy Manchester (N.H.) Rehab. Center, 1963-64; prin., tchr. Mt. Hope Sch. for Retarded Children, Nashua, N.H., 1964-66; occupational therapist Manchester Rehab. Center, 1967. Cons., leader Girl Scouts U.S.A., 1967—; active fund drives local charitable orgns. Bd. dirs. YWCA, Nashua, 1970-73. Mem. Am. Occupational Therapy Assn., Am. Assn. Univ. Women (sec. 1971), Nashua Assn. Retarded Children. Mem. United Ch. Christ. Club: College (Nashua). Book rev. editor N.H. Personnel and Guidance Jour., 1972—. Home and office: 297 Dunstable Rd Nashua NH 03060

NEE, SISTER MARY COLEMAN, ednl. adminstr.; b. Taylor, Pa., Nov. 14, 1917; d. Coleman James and Nora Ann (Hopkins) Nee; B.A., Marywood U., 1939, M.A., 1943; M.S. (NSF fellow 1957-59), U. Notre Dame, 1959, postgrad., 1959-62. Tchr. Scranton (Pa.) Pub. Schs., 1939-41, Marywood Sem., Scranton, 1943-55; faculty Marywood Coll., Scranton, 1959-68, asso. prof., 1962-68, pres., 1970—. Chmn. Presidents of Ind. Colls. in Northeast Pa., 1972-73. Mem. Math. Assn. Am., N.E.A., Am. Council Edn., Am. Assn. Colls., Pa. Assn. Colls. and Univs., Commn. for Ind. Colls. and Univs., Am. Assn. Higher Edn., Nat. Cath. Edn. Assn. Address: Marywood Coll Scranton PA 18509

NEEDLES, DOROTHY-JANE GOULDING (MRS. GEORGE WILLIAM NEEDLES), theatrical cons., writer; b. Toronto, Ont., Can., Nov. 26, 1923; d. Arthur and Dorothy (Massey) Goulding; student Toronto Tchrs. Coll., 1941-42; m. George William Needles, Feb. 5, 1946; children—Jane, Arthur, Daniel, Reed, Laura Ann. With Toronto Children Players, 1933-59; writer, composer, broadcaster Kindergarten of the Air, CBC, 1947-56; youth editor Audubon mag., Toronto, 1949-58; editor Canadian Short Stories, CBC, 1955-71; play-acting cons. Etobicoke Bd. Edn., Toronto, 1967—; owner, operator Globe Hotel Restaurant, Rosemont, Ont., 1971—. Mem. Council of Drama in Edn. (v.p. 1971-73), Canadian Scottish Terrier Breeders (v.p. 1969-73). Author: Dorothy-Jane's Book, 1949; Dorothy-Jane's Other Book, 1952; Master Cat and Other Plays, 1953; Margaret, 1967; We're Doing a Play, 1969; Play-Acting in the Schools, 1970. Home: 234 Cortleigh Blvd Toronto ON H5N 1P7 Canada Office: Globe Hotel Restaurant Rural Route 1 Rosemont ON Canada

NEEL, ALICE, artist; b. Merion Square, Pa., Jan. 28, 1900; d. George Washington and Alice (Hartley) Neel; student Phila. Sch. Design for Women, 1924-28; D.F.A. (hon.), Moore Coll. Art, Phila., 1971; m. 1925; children—Richard, Hartley. One-man shows at Pinacotheka Gallery, N.Y.C., 1944, A.C.A. Gallery, N.Y.C., 1950, 51, 59, Reed Coll., 1962, Graham Gallery, N.Y.C., 1963-66, 68, 70, 73, Dartmouth, 1964, Fordham U., Maxwell Gallery, San Francisco, 1967, Langman Gallery, Jenkintown, Pa., 1974, Summit Mus., 1974; exhibited group shows Kornblee Gallery N.Y.C., 1962, Zabriskie Gallery, N.Y.C., 1962, Byron Gallery, N.Y.C., 1964, Mus. Modern Art, 1964, Penthouse Mus. Modern Art, 1964, Norfolk Mus. Arts and Scis., 1966, U. N.C., 1966, World House Galleries, N.Y.C., 1966, Gallery Modern Art, 1968, Nightingale Gallery, Toronto, Ont., Can., 1969; Bloomsburg (Pa.) State Coll., 1972, Sch. Visual Arts, 1972, Cultural Center, N.Y.C., 1972, Focus Show, Phila., 1974. retrospective exhbn. Moore Coll., Phila., 1971, Whitney Mus., 1974; represented in permanent collections Mus. Modern Art, Dillard Inst., Ludgen, Robert Mayer, Whitney Ann., Balt. Mus., and numerous other pvt. collections. Recipient award Longview Found., 1962; Nat. Inst. Arts and Letters, 1969; Benjamin Altman Purchase prize Nat. Acad. Design, 1971; Childe Hassam purchase award, 1972. Address: 300 W 107th St New York City NY 10025

NEEL, ELIZABETH UHLMANN (MRS. BRENT ALLEN NEEL), physician; b. Grand Rapids, Mich., May 26, 1942; d. Hubert Julius and Alice Amelia (Williams) Uhlmann; B.S., Mich. State U., 1964; M.D., U. Mich., 1968; m. Brent Allen Neel, Aug. 28, 1971. Intern, Highland Gen. Hosp., Oakland, Cal., 1968-69; resident pediatrics Kaiser Found. Hosp., Oakland, 1969-71; gen. practice medicine, San Jose, Cal., 1971—; mem. staff San Jose Hosp., Student Health Service, Cal. State U., San Jose. Mem. Am., Cal. med. assns., Santa Clara County Med. Soc. Home: 11073 Bel Aire Ct Cupertino CA 95014 Office: Student Health Service Cal State U San Jose CA 95192

NEELEY, MARY SIMPSON (MRS. JOSEPH ROBERT NEELEY), librarian; b. Kansas City, Mo., Sept. 24, 1912; d. Claude Mitchell and Sarah Elizabeth (Burks) Simpson; B.S., So. Meth. U., 1933; M.L.S., Tex. Woman's U., 1962; m. Joseph Robert Neeley, June 19, 1937; children—Claudia (Mrs. Edward C. Plog Jr.), Sarah (Mrs. Joseph Michael Metschan), Joseph Robert. Elementary tchr., Paris, Tex., 1934-35; phys. edn. tchr., Gladewater, Tex., 1935-37, Bishop, Tex., 1956-61; circulation librarian Tex. A. and I. U., Kingsville, 1961-63; librarian Gallia Acad. High Sch., Gallipolis, O., 1964—. Mem. Ohio, Gallipolis, S. Eastern Ohio edn. assns., Ohio Assn. Sch. Librarians, Beta Phi Mu, Gamma Phi Beta. Home: Rural Route 1 Sandy Heights Point Pleasant WV 25550 Office: 340 4th St Gallipolis OH 45631

NEELY, BETTY HONNOLD, educator; b. Oklahoma City, Mar. 17, 1918; d. Charles Edgar and Marie (Clark) Honnold; student U. Okla., 1934-35; A.B., Smith Coll., 1938; M.Ed., U. Okla., 1952; postgrad. Central State Coll., 1950-51; U. Cal. at Berkeley, 1955-60; m. Ralph Neely, Apr. 27, 1940 (div. Apr. 1949); 1 son, Phillip H. Stenographer, Douglas Aircraft Co., Oklahoma City, 1943-44; asst. to dean women, panhellenic counselor Ohio State U., Columbus, 1952-54; asst. dean students U. Cal., Berkeley, 1954-60, asso. dean students, 1960-62, asso. dean students, dean of women, 1962-73, dir. student activities, 1973—. Mem. adv. bd. Univ. YWCA, 1963-71. Mem. Cal. Assn. Women Deans and Vice Prins. (exec. bd. 1964-66), Nat. Assn. Women Deans and Counselors (v.p. 1968-70), Colonial Dames of Am., Jr. League Oakland, Kappa Alpha Theta, Kappa Delta Pi, Pi Lambda Theta. Club: Womens Faculty (pres., dir. 1966-68). Home: 7609 Potrero Av El Cerrito CA 94530 Office: Sproul Hall U Cal Berkeley CA 94720

NEELY, FLORENCE ELIZABETH, educator; b. Bushnell, Ill., Sept. 13, 1920; d. Ralph Bilyeu and Frances Louzella (McCrary) Neely; A.A., Ellsworth Coll., 1940; A.B., U. Ia., 1942, M.S., 1944; Ph.D., U. Ill., 1951. Instr. plant sci. Vassar Coll., Poughkeepsie, N.Y., 1951-52; asst. prof. biology U. Mo., Kansas City, 1952-60; faculty Augustana Coll., Rock Island, Ill., 1960—, prof. biology 1973—. Cons. environmental inventories U.S. C.E., 1972-74. Mem. Am. Assn. Univ. Women, A.A.A.S., Bot. Soc. Am., Pan Am. Round Table, Sigma Xi, Phi Beta Kappa. Methodist. Home: 2320 1/2 37th St Rock Island IL 61201

NEELY, ISABEL MACDONALD (MRS. STUART MCALISTER NEELY), former editor; b. Glen Ridge, N.J., Feb. 22, 1933; d. Donald and Laura Van Iderstine (Holmes) Macdonald; B.S. in Edn., Tufts Coll., 1955; diploma in occupational therapy Boston Sch. Occupational Therapy, 1955; m. Stuart McAlister Neely, Jan. 26, 1963; children—Ann Mackenzie, Jane Stuart, Donald Kirk. Staff occupational therapist Phila. Gen. Hosp., Phila., 1955-56; editor Biol. Abstracts, Phila., 1956-64. Mem. Am. Occupational Therapy Assn., Jr. League York (bd. mem. 1971-72), Hist. Soc. York County. Republican. Presbyn. Clubs: Wynfield (York, Pa.); Red Lion (Pa.) Country. Home: 2024 Crescent Rd York PA 17403

NEELY, WANDA FAIRYE (MRS. DONALD ROLAND FLEISCHMAN), ophthalmologist; b. Casa Grande, Ariz., Mar. 1, 1930; d. Unice Roscoe and Reedye Irene (Lambert) Neely; student Baylor U., 1948-50, M.D., 1955; student U. Ariz., 1950-51; m. Samuel Pieper, Jr., Jan. 1. 1953 (div. Feb. 1961); children—Wanda Lynne, Melanie Ruth, Cheryl Yvonne; 1 adopted son, Frankie Rodriquez; m. 2d, Donald Roland Fleischman, July 3, 1963; stepchildren—Ida Ann Fleischman Tunison, Margaret Lucille. Intern, Baylor U. Coll. Medicine, Houston, 1955-56, rotating resident ophthalmology, 1958-61; gen. practice medicine, Guam, 1956-58; practice ophthalmology, San Mateo, Cal., 1961-63, Los Gatos, Cal., 1963-68, San Jose, Cal., 1968—; mem. staff Los Gatos-Saratoga Community Hosp., O'Connor, Good Samaritan hosps., San Jose, Campbell (Cal.) Community Hosp. Vice pres. Found. to Aid Mentally Ill Children, 1968-69. Bd. dirs. Santa Clara County Status of Women Ad Hoc Com., 1967—, charter sec. 1973—; adv. bd. Cassette Tape Library for Blind, 1972—. Mem. A.M.A., Cal., Santa Clara County (chmn. humanities com. 1970, 72) med. socs., Am. Acad. Ophthalmology and Otolaryngology, Contact Lens Assn., Peninsula Eye Soc., Cal. (mem. council 1973-74), San Jose (sec. 1969, v.p. 1970) Christian med. socs., Nat. Assn. for Female Execs., Am. Rose Soc., Nat. Wildlife Fedn., Wilderness Soc., Common Cause, Sierra Club, Zonta (local pres. 1970, 71, dist. nomination chmn. 1971). Baptist. Home: 14420 Blossom Hill Los Gatos CA 95030 Office: 2505 Samaritan Dr Room 510 San Jose CA 95124

NEEMAN, RENATE L., educator, occupational therapist; b. Hildesheim, Germany, Feb. 18, 1926; came to U.S., 1946; naturalized, 1952; d. Eduard and Erna Frieda (Koopmann) Berg; student Hunter Coll., N.Y.C., 1946-48; B.S. in Occupational Therapy, N.Y. U., 1951; postgrad. U. Geneva, Switzerland Med. Sch., 1958-59; Ed.M. in Health Edn., State U. N.Y. at Buffalo, 1972; m. Moshe Neeman, May 15, 1960; children—Jenifer S., Edward E., Alisa G., Henry J. Supr. children's recreation service Hosp. for Joint Disease, N.Y.C., 1951-52; staff occupational therapist Farm Colony Hosp., S.I., 1952-54, VA Center, Bath, N.Y., 1954-55, VA Hosp., Buffalo, 1955-61; dir. occupational therapy Cantalician Center Workshop, Buffalo, 1969—; faculty dept. occupational therapy State U. N.Y. at Buffalo Sch. Health Related Professions, 1969-72; dir. perceptual-motor devel. program Cantalician Center for Learning, Buffalo, 1970—; research prof. Niagara U., Niagara Falls, N.Y., 1971—. Research grantee United Health Found. Western N.Y., Buffalo, 1970-73. Fellow Royal Soc. Health; mem. Am. Occupational Therapy Assn., Brit. Assn. Occupational Therapists, Am. Assn. Mental Deficiency, A.A.A.S., A.A.H.P.E.R., Council Exceptional Children, N.Y. Acad. Scis., Nat. Rehab. Assn. Contbr. articles to profl. jours. Home: 5 Sedgemoor Ct Williamsville NY 14221

NEF, EVELYN STEFANSSON, author, editor, specialist polar regions; b. N.Y.C., July 24, 1913; d. Jeno and Bella (Klein) Schwartz; student pub. schs.; m. William Britton Baird, 1932 (div. Feb. 1938); m. 2d, Vilhjalmur Stefansson, Apr. 10, 1941 (dec. 1962); m. 3d, John Ulric Nef, Apr. 21, 1964. Librarian Stefansson Polar Library, N.Y.C., 1941-52, Stefansson Collection, Baker Library, Dartmouth, 1952-63; lectr. polar studies program Dartmouth, 1960-61; adminstrv. officer Am. Sociol. Assn., Washington, 1963-64; research writer, docent Corcoran Art Gallery, Washington, 1969-70; free lance writer book reviews, newspaper articles for N.Y. Times Book Review and Washington Post; has made radio and television appearances; writer newsletter Washington Opera Soc., 1967-70. Mem. women's bd. Washington Opera Soc., 1967-69, Smithsonian Assos., 1971—; mem. women's bd. Nat. Ballet Soc., 1967—, chmn., 1967; treas. John U. and Evelyn Nef Found.; mem. vis. com. U. Chgo. Library. Mem. Soc. Women Geographers (v.p., chmn. Washington group 1969-72, nat. pres. 1972—), Arctic Inst. N.A., Author: Here Is Alaska, 1943, rev. edits., 1959, 73; Within the Circle, 1945; Here Is the Far North, 1957, Editor, contbr. to Polar Notes, 1960-63. Editor in chief: Delacorte Great Explorer Series (Beyond the Pillar of Heracles by Rhys Carpenter, 1966; South from the Spanish Main by Earl Hanson, 1967; Silk, Spices and Empire by Owen and Eleanor Lattimore, 1968; West and By North by Louis B. Wright and Elaine Fowler, 1971; The Moving Frontier by Louis B. Wright and Elaine W. Fowler, 1972; editor, contbr. Eleanor Holgate Lattimore, 1895-1970. Address: 2726 N St NW Washington DC 20007

NEFF, BONITA JEAN DOSTAL, communications scientist; b. Grinnell, Ia., Aug. 16, 1942; d. Lester Ernest and Mary Margaret (Hudnut) Dostal; B.A., U. No. Ia., 1964, M.A., 1966; Ph.D., U. Mich., 1973; m. Gregory Pall Neff, Apr. 27, 1974. Tchr. West High Sch., Waterloo, Ia., 1964-66; speech and communications teaching fellow U. Mich., Ann Arbor, 1966-69; instr. mass communications Wayne State U., Detroit, 1971; lectr. speech communications Eastern Mich. U. Ypsilanti, 1969-72; communications research project dir. Effective Feedback Inc., Ann Arbor, Mich., 1973—. Cons. for edn. Turnkey Systems, Washington, 1974—. Publicity dir. Am. Youth Hostel, Ann Arbor, 1973—, leader Detroit council, houseparent Foote Hostel, Milford, Mich., 1974—. Mem. Nat. Honorary Forensic Soc., Purple Key, Delta Sigma Rho-Tau Kappa Alpha. Home and office: 508 E Ann St Ann Arbor MI 48108

NEFF, FRANCINE IRVING (MRS. EDWARD J. NEFF), polit. party ofcl.; b. Albuquerque, Dec. 6, 1925; d. Edward Hackett and Georga (Henderson) Irving; A.A., Cottey Coll., 1946; B.S., U. N.M., 1948; m. Edward John Neff, June 7, 1948; children—Sindle, Edward Vann. Div. and precinct chmn. Republican Party, Albuquerque, 1966-71; mem. Bernalillo County exec. bd. Rep. Party, 1968-70, central com., 1967—; mem. Rep. State Central Com., 1968—, Rep. State Exec. Bd., 1970—; state adviser Teenage Reps., 1967-68; Rep. nat. committeewoman N.M., 1970—; treas. U.S., 1974—. Campaign coordinator Congressman Lujan, 1970; N.M. chmn. Women for Nixon-Agnew, 1968; mem. exec. com. Rep. Nat. Com., 1972—; del. Nat. Rep. Conv., 1968, 72. Leader Camp Fire Girls, 1957-64; den mother Cub Scouts, 1964-65; pres. Inez P.T.A., 1961. Mem. P.E.O. (pres. Albuquerque chpt. 1963-64), Albuquerque City Panhellenic Assn. (pres. 1959-60), Alpha Delta Pi, Sigma Alpha Iota, Phi Kappa Phi, Pi Lambda Theta, Phi Theta Kappa. Episcopalian. Home: 1509 Sagebrush Trail SE Albuquerque NM 87123

NEFF, HELEN MARGARET OSTERHOLM, writer, editor; b. Superior, Wis.; d. Albin N. and Ellen (Julien) Osterholm; student U. Omaha, 1925-27, U. Cal. at Berkeley, 1929-30; A.B., Washington U., St. Louis, 1933, Rensselaer Poly. Inst.-Tech. Writers' Inst. 1962; m. Carroll Forsyth Neff, Feb. 1, 1930 (div. 1957); children—Charlotte (Mrs. Walter R. Newman), Carroll Forsyth. Sch. reporter Omaha World-Herald, 1923-27; sec. Swedish vice consul, Omaha, 1927-29; case worker St. Louis Relief Adminstrn., 1935-36; med. writer dept. surgery Emory U. Sch. Medicine, Atlanta, 1951-55; writer-editor Center for Disease Control (formerly Nat. Communicable Disease Center), USPHS, Atlanta, 1955—, chief, editorial sect. Information Office, 1960-72, pub. information specialist, 1972—. Bd. dirs., editor newsletter Druid Hills Civic Assn., 1949-70. Fellow Am. Med. Writers Assn. (nat. sec. 1967-70); mem. Am. Pub. Health Assn., A.A.A.S., League Women Voters, Internat. Platform Assn. Methodist. Contbr. articles to profl. jours. Home: 400 Princeton Way NE Atlanta GA 30307 Office: Center for Disease Control Atlanta GA 30333

NEFF, LUCINDA BELLE, exec., genealogist; b. Colchester, N.Y.; d. Lewis Bennett and Jennie Lela (Rutherford) Neff; A.B. cum laude, Syracuse U., 1906. Tchr. pub. high schs., Middleburg, N.Y., 1906-08. Rockville Centre, N.Y., 1908-11, Muskogee, Okla., 1911-21; office mgr., law clk. Neff & Neff, Tulsa, 1925-63. Dep. gov. Gen. Soc. Mayflower Descs., 1957—, editor Mayflower Quar., 1961-64, acting sec. gen., 1962, Okla. sec., 1951—, editor Okla. Mayflower Newsletter, 1951—, compiler Okla. brochure, 1973; organizing sec. Elder William Brewster Descs. Soc., 1963; Tulsa parliamentarian D.A.R., 1955-57, Okla. lineage research chmn., 1962-64; Okla. organizing pres. Nat. Soc. Women Descs. Ancient and Hon. Arty Co., 1964-66, organizing sec. nat. soc. 1965-68; organizing sec. Oil Capitol unit Nat. Assn. Parliamentarians, 1956-58, pres., 1958-60. Recipient Mayflower cup for improving Mayflower Quar., 1963. Mem. Am. Assn. U. Women, Soc. Genealogists (London), New Eng. Historic Genealogic Soc., Okla. Hist. Soc., Colonial Dames XVII Century, Descs. Colonial Clergy, Pilgrim Soc., Magna Charta Dames, Plimoth Plantation, Genealogy Club Am. (life). Republican. Researcher in Eng. and Holland on Mayflower passengers, 1961, 65. Home: 1316 S Trenton Av Tulsa OK 74120

NEFF, MARY CAROLYN, univ. adminstr.; b. Memphis, July 23, 1914; d. Henry W. and Mary (Butler) Neff; B.S., Western Res. U., 1945. Adminstrv. asst. to dean, dir. student relations Cleveland Coll., Western Reserve U., 1943-46; met. dir. bldg. services YWCA, Cleve., 1946-49; devel. officer Cleve. Coll., Western Res. U., 1949-51; adminstrv. asst. to v.p. for devel. Western Res. U., 1951-55, adminstrv. asst. to pres., 1955-59, sec. of univ., 1959-67; sec. of univ. Case Western Res. U., Cleve., 1967—. Mem. manpower planning com. Welfare Fedn., Cleve., 1945-69; trustee Cleve. Friends of Music, 1953-69; sec. U. Circle Devel. Found., Cleve., 1958-70. Home: 2330 Euclid Heights Blvd Cleveland Heights OH 44106 Office: 2040 Adelbert Rd Cleveland OH 44106

NEFF, WINIFRED COBBLEDICK (MRS. CARROLL FORSYTH NEFF), social service cons.; b. Oakland, Cal.; d. Charles F. and Nell M. (Connor) Cobbledick; A.B., U. Cal. at Berkeley, 1938, M. Social Welfare (USPHS Mental Health fellow 1948-49), 1949; m. Carroll Forsyth Neff, May 4, 1957. Field rep. Alameda County Welfare Commn., 1939-40; field work supr., sch. social welfare U. Cal., 1940-41, research asst. bur. pub. adminstrn., 1942-43; field work rep. Children's Home Soc. of Cal., 1941-42, dir. No. dist., 1943-59, Golden Gate dist., 1959-65; exec. dir. Home Vis. Services Contra Costa County (name changed to Home Health & Counseling Services 1966), 1965-68; social service cons., family and marriage counselor, 1968—. Chmn. South Pacific regional conf. Child Welfare League Am., 1957. Bd. dirs. Minority Adoption Recruitment of Children's Homes (MARCH) San Francisco, 1956-59, Concord Coordinated Services Project, 1966-68. Mem. Nat. Assn. Social Workers, Am. Assn. Social Workers (vice chmn. Eastbay chpt. 1944), Acad. Certified Social Workers. Author: Wartime Nurseries, 1943. Co-author: The Legislature of California, 1943. Home: 1099 Keeler Av Berkeley CA 94708 also Av Tonanzintla 40 Col LaPaz Pue Mexico

NEIDIG, MRS. CLARENCE P. (RUTH S. NEIDIG), educator, sorority ofcl.; b. Cin., Oct. 1, 1894; d. Charles E. and Mary (Webb) Sorin; student U. Cin., 1915-16, 17-18, 35-36, Simmons Coll., 1916-17; m. Clarence P. Neidig, Nov. 3, 1921. Supr. home econs. Carey (O.) High Sch., 1918-21; nat. treas. Pi Kappa Sigma, 1925-27, nat. pres., 1927-47, chmn. endowment and scholarship trust fund, 1947-59; del. Nat. Panhellenic Conf., 1947, also speakers bur., 1947-59; coll. com. and social standards com., 1955-59, interfrat. research adv. com., 1953—. Mem. Nat. Conf. Coll. Frats. and Sororities, 1955-59. Mem. Nat. Assn. Women Deans and Counselors, Am. Assn. U. Women (Cin. edn. chmn. 1934-40), Salvation Army Women's Aux., Alumnae Assn. U. Cin., Home Econs. Alumnae Assn., P.E.O., Pi Kappa Sigma, Sigma Kappa (past council mem.). Republican. Presbyn. Clubs: Woman's (past dir., past officer), Town (past dir.), Travel (Cin.). Contbr. articles to nat. fraternity and sorority mags. Home: 5300 Hamilton Av Cincinnati OH 45224

NEIDIGH, PANSY MILLS, artist, former educator; b. New Ross, Ind., Apr. 1, 1904; d. Isaac Hamilton and Martha Alice (Utterback) Mills; A.B., Central Normal, Danville, Ind., 1927; student John Herron Art Sch., 1930-34; M.A., Columbia, 1942, postgrad. 1953, U. Fla., 1955; m. Claude V. Neidigh, Aug. 16, 1946 (dec. 1973). Faculty Ia. State Tchrs. Coll., summers 1943-47; art supr. Richmond (Ind.) city schs., 1938-56; faculty Earlham Coll., Ind. U. Extension, 1947-53, art supr., faculty Leesburg (Fla.) Sr. High Sch., 1955, 1960-66, instr. art, 1962-66, ret. Mem. com. on art edn. Mus. Modern Art, N.Y.C., 13 yrs.; exhibited Nat. Arts Club, N.Y.C., Richmond (Ind.) Art Gallery, Butler Art Inst., Youngstown, O., Hoosier Salon, Indpls., Ia. State Tchrs. Coll., Cedar Falls, Art Assn., Leesburg, Fla., 1956-66, Fla. Fedn. Arts, 1958-66; judge for art activities; lectr. Recipient 1st prize Tchrs. Coll. exhibit Columbia, 1942; Sweepstake Tri Color award; Fedn. Art award, Leesburg, Fla., 1961. Mem. Nat. Art Edn. Assn., Fla. Art Edn. Assn., Southeastern Arts Assn., Brown County Hist. Assn., Western Arts Edn. Assn., N.E.A., Ind. (pres. art tchrs. sect. 1939, 54), Fla. tchrs. assns., Hoosier Hills Art Guild, Leesburg Art Assn., Delta Kappa Gamma, Sigma Delta Pi. Mem. Christian Ch. Clubs: Altrusa (pres. Richmond Chpt. 1944-45); Woman's of

Richmond (Ind.) (art chmn. art program, mem. exec. bd. 1942-45). Author articles art mags. Home: 260 Elnor St Morgantown IN 46160

NEIDLE, ENID ANNE (MRS. HERBERT KAUFMAN), physiologist; b. N.Y.C., Apr. 6, 1924; d. Marks and Cecilia (Feldmann) Neidle; A.B., Vassar Coll., 1944; Ph.D., Columbia, 1949; m. Herbert Kaufman, Dec. 18, 1949; children—Edward Neidle, Margaret N. Asso. dept. pharmacology Jefferson Med. Coll., 1949-50; instr. dept. biology Bklyn. Coll., 1950-54; instr. to prof. dept. physiology and pharmacology Coll. Dentistry, N.Y. U., 1955—, also prof. grad. faculty. Cons. Group Health Ins. Inc., N.Y.C. Prin. Investigator USPHS. Mem. Am. Physiol. Soc., Am. Assn. Dental Schs., Internat. Assn. Dental Research, Harvey Soc., A.A.A.S., N.Y. Acad. Scis., Sigma Xi. Club: Brooklyn Vassar. (past pres.). Bd. editors: Jour. Dental Edn. Contbr. articles to profl. jours. Home: 271 Hicks St Brooklyn NY 11201 Office: 342 E 26th St New York City NY 10010

NEIGHT, THOMASINE IRELAND, ednl. adminstr.; b. Kingston, N.Y., Nov. 9, 1929; d. Thomas Robertson and Patricia (Gilmore) Ireland; student Western Reserve U., 1946-47, N.Y. U., 1950-56; B.A. in Art and Edn., Rivier Coll., Nashua, N.H., 1970, M.Ed. in Couseling, 1973; 1 son, David. Mem. pub. relations staff N.Y. U., 1952-56; newswriter, pub. relations Rivier Coll., 1962-67; dir. pub. relations, evening div. student counselor, New Eng. Aero. Inst. and div. Daniel Webster Jr. Coll., Nashua, 1970—. Free lance advt., pub. relations cons., 1970—. Mem. N.H. Personnel and Guidance Assn. (editorial bd., mem. research com.), N.H. Sch. Counselors Assn., Mensa. Home: 21 Dublin Av Nashua NH 03060 Office: University Dr Nashua NH 03060

NEIL, JESSIE PRUITT, civic worker; b. Pasadena, Cal., Oct 20, 1927; d. Cecil D. and Jessie (Parsons) Pruitt; B.A., U. So. Cal., 1950; m. Edmund R. Neil, Mar. 24, 1956; children—Edmund R. II, Jessica R., Richard William. Dir. design Leland Gardens Bldg. Corp., 1950-56; sales dir. Washington Sq. Bldg. Corp., 1950-1952; pres. Barrett Devel. Corp., 1951-72; sec. Reliance Bldg. Corp., 1951-68; self-employed home designer, 1953; sec. So. Counties Escrow, 1956-73; pres. Futuramic Homes, Inc., 1956-68. Founder Cardiac League Guild of Huntington Meml. Hosp., 1963, pres., 1966, 67, pres. Women's Council, 1967; v.p. San Marino League, 1968-72; v.p. docent council Pasadena Mus. Modern Art, 1969, pres. docent council, 1971-72, mem. membership council, ex-officio trustee, 1971-72. Asso. U. So. Cal; patron Pasadena Art. Mus.; hon. life mem. Arcadia Meth. Hosp.; mem. Costume Council Los Angeles County Mus. Recipient graphics award Pasadena Arts Council, 1968. Republican. Mem. Fellows Pasadena Art Mus., Docent League So. Cal., Delta Zeta. Home: 301 Hermosa St South Pasadena CA 91030

NEIL, JOSEPHINE, librarian; b. Nashville, Nov. 9, 1917; d. Albert Bramlett and Josephine (Pendleton) Neil; B.S., George Peabody Coll., 1939, B.S. in L.S., 1940; postgrad. U. Chgo., 1949. Command librarian Hdqrs. U.S. Army Forces Antilles, San Juan, P.R., 1951-53, Hdqrs. Area Command, So. Area Command, Hdqrs. U.S. Army, Europe, Bremerhaven, Heidelberg, Stuttgart, Germany, 1953-61; Navy regional librarian, Charleston, S.C., 1961—. Chmn. medal of honor archives adv. com. Freedoms Found., Valley Forge, Pa., 1966—; mem. adv. com. S.C. Am. Revolution Bicentennial Commn. Mem. English Speaking Union, Nat. Audubon Soc., Nat. Trust Historic Preservation, Am. (dir. armed forces library sect. 1969-72), Southeastern, S.C. (mem. nat. library week planning com. 1967, mem. adv. com. on Southeastern states coop. survey 1972, v.p., pres.-elect 1973—) library assns., Navy League, S.C. Hist. Soc., Carolina Art Assn., Preservation Soc. Charleston, Charleston Natural History Soc., Am. Patriot Reading Club, Pi Gamma Mu, Kappa Delta Phi, Sigma Delta Pi. Baptist. Clubs: Carolina Bird, Carolina Shell. Home: 111 Queen St Charleston SC 29401 Office: Naval Base Charleston SC 29408

NEILAND, BONITA JUNE (MRS. KENNETH A. NEILAND), educator; b. Eugene, Ore., June 5, 1928; d. Herbert F. and Ann L. (Lattin) Miller; B.S., U. Ore., 1949; M.A., Ore. State U., 1951; diploma rural sci. U. Coll. of Wales, 1952; Ph.D., U. Wis., 1954; m. Kenneth A. Neiland, Dec. 21, 1955. Instr., U. Ore., Eugene, 1954-55; instr., asst. prof. gen. extension div. Ore. State System Higher Edn., Eugene, 1955-60; faculty U. Alaska, Fairbanks, 1961—, prof. botany, 1970—, head dept. land resources and agrl. scis., 1970—. Fellow A.A.A.S.; mem. Nat. Wildlife Fedn., Ecol. Soc. Am., Brit. Ecol. Soc., Arctic Inst. N. Am., Soil Conservation Soc., Sigma Xi, Phi Beta Kappa, Phi Kappa Phi. Home: PO Box 10095 Fairbanks AK 99701

NEILL, ELDEVA MAE WYATT (MRS. C. GORDON NEILL), banker; b. Blue Springs, Mo.; d. Orville Lee and Nannie Lee (Burrus) Wyatt; grad. certificate in comml. banking Am. Inst. Banking, 1955, also grad. certificates investment banking, savs. banking and trusts; m. C. Gordon Neill, May 14, 1942. Asst. mgr. accounting dept. City Nat. Bank & Trust Co. Kansas City (Mo.), 1943-47; v.p. Grand Av. Bank, Kansas City, 1947-66, v.p., 1966—. Pres. NETH Commn.; originator Mayor's Women's Prayer Breakfast; mem. sr. adv. com. Women's Anti-Crime Crusade. Bd. dirs. Shamrock House. Recipient Jean Arnoit Reid award for scholarship and leadership in banking and civic activities Nat. Assn. Bank Women, 1955. Mem. Am. Inst. Banking (life, pres. Kansas City chpt. 1962-63), Kansas City Bus. and Profl. Women (dir., past pres.), Women's C. of C. (mem. health and welfare com. 1965—, dir.), Nat. Assn. Bank Women, Bank Adminstrs. Inst. Democrat. Baptist. Clubs: Zonta (chmn. program com. 1965—, dir. 1968—, pres. 1970) (Kansas City, Mo.); Sunset Hill School Zee (charter, chmn.). Home: 3400 Chippewa Dr Kansas City MO 64116 Office: Grand Av Bank Crown Center Kansas City MO 64141

NEILL, NANCY M., civic worker; b. St. Louis, Oct. 19, 1916; d. Samuel Alfred and Ruth (Young) Mitchell; ed. pvt. schs.; m. Robert Neill, Aug. 5, 1939; children—Robert Neill III, Nancy Lee. Pres. woman's aux. Mo. Hist. Soc., 1954-55, trustee soc., 1959—; chmn. city div. United Fund St. Louis, 1957; pres. Jr. League St. Louis, 1952-53, Endgewood Children's Center, 1956; v.p. Washington U. Child Guidance Clinic, 1959—, Ranken Jordan Home Convalescent Children, 1960—, Merc. Library Assn., 1965—; mem. council lay advisers Washington U., St. Louis, 1959—; dir. Woman's Exchange St. Louis, 1954—, Family-Children's Center, St. Louis, 1956—. Named Woman of Achievement for Community Welfare, St. Louis, 1959. Mem. Mo. Mt. Vernon Ladies Assn. (vice regent 1966—). Democrat. Episcopalian. Home: 20 N Kings Hwy St Louis MO 63108

NEILSON, ELIZABETH ANASTASIA, educator, assn. exec.; b. West Medford, Mass.; d. William H. and Anastasia (Mahony) Neilson; diploma Tufts U., 1933; B.S. in Edn., Boston U., 1934; M.Ed., 1945, Ed.D., 1957. Tchr. pub. schs., Medford, Mass., 1934-43; became instr. State Coll., Lowell, 1944, prof. edn. and chmn. dept. health and phys. edn., until 1972; dir. continuing edn. Am. Sch. Health Assn., 1972—. Asst. prof. Boston Coll., 1953-54; vis. prof. Boston U., 1960, 62, 63, Ind. U., Utah State U., Union Coll., Barbourville, Ky. Del. 6th Internat. Conf. Health, Madrid, Spain, 1965; cons. Mass. and Albany; mem. Mass. commn. White House Conf. on Nutrition; cons. Mass. Adv. Council Sch. Health Curriculum; cons. Heath Glick and Norwin, N.Y.; chmn. health maj. program Lowell State Coll. Recipient distinguished service award Am. Sch. Health; honor award Mass. Assn. Health and Phys. Edn.; Boston Bouvé Coll. alumni citation Northeastern U., 1974. Fellow Am. Sch. Health Assn. (governing council 1963-66, pres.; chmn. study coms.), Royal Soc. Health (Eng.), Am. Pub. Health Assn., A.A.H.P.E.R.; mem. Am. Coll. Health Assn., Mass. Assn. Health, Phys. Edn. and Recreation, Royal Soc. Promotion Health Eng., Internat. Union Health Edn., Bus. and Profl. Women's Club, New Eng. Health Assn., Mass. Tchrs. Assn., League Cath. Women, Pi Lambda Theta. Author: Sch. Health Series, grades 1-8, 1966; Health Program, 1968; Laidlaw Health Series K-12. Home: PO Box 531 Jackson NH 03846

NEILSON, SANDRA LYNN, swimmer; b. Burbank, Cal., Mar. 20, 1956; d. Francis Charles and Elsie Erika (Hutschenreuter) Neilson; student El Monte (Cal.) High Sch., 1970-74. Swimmer El Monte Aquatics, 1966-72; winner 1st place 100 meter freestyle U.S. Nat. Championships, Pullman, Wash., 1971, Pan Am. Games, Cali, Colombia, 1971, 3 Gold medals in swimming Olympic Games, Munich, Germany, 1972. Recipient Helms Hall of Fame Athlete of Year award, 1973; set Am. record for 100 meter freestyle, 1972, new Olympic record for 100 meter freestyle, 1972, also new world records for 400 meter freestyle and medley relay. Home: 10104 Asher St El Monte CA 91733

NEIMARK, ANNE ELIZABETH LOEB (MRS. PAUL NEIMARK), writer; b. Chgo., Oct. 3, 1935; d. Robert M. and Anita (Bronner) Loeb; student U. Chgo., 1940-44; grad. Francis W. Parker Sch., Chgo., 1953; postgrad., Bryn Mawr Coll., 1953-55; m. Paul Neimark, June 13, 1955; children—Jill, Todd, Jeff. Writer numerous stories and articles for children's publs., including Highlights for Children, also for ednl. pubs., including Ency. Brit., Sci. Research Assos.; mem. editorial staff Curriculum Innovations, Inc., Highwood, Ill., 1973—. Author: Touch of Light, The Story of Louis Braille (1st prize in juvenile lit. in Midwest, Friends of Am. Writers 1970). Home: 920 Ridgewood Place Highland Park IL 60035

NELIUS, SIGRID JOHANNA VON RENNER (MRS. ALBERT ARNOLD NELIUS), physician; b. Pirna, East Germany, Mar. 22, 1924; d. Sigmund Georg and Susanne Hertha (Schmidt) von Renner; M.D., U. Munich (Germany), 1949; m. Albert Arnold Nelius, June 19, 1955; 1 son, Alexander Stefan von Renner. Came to U.S., 1953, naturalized, 1960. Intern pathology U. Munich, 1949-50, resident medicine, 1950-52; staff physician medicine 98th Gen. Hosp., U.S. Army, Munich, 1952-53; rotating intern St. Thomas Hosp., Nashville, 1953-54, resident medicine, 1954-56; resident medicine Watts Hosp., Durham, N.C., 1961-62; staff physician medicine John Umstead Hosp., Durham, 1962-67, unit dir. med.-surg. unit, 1967-73; faculty dept. community health scis. Duke U. Med. Center, 1973—. Mem. A.M.A., Med. Soc. State N.C., Durham Orange County Med. Soc. Address: 3112 Sprunt St Durham NC 27705

NELLE, SUSAN VAYLLE, coll. adminstr.; b. Aurora, Ill., July 6, 1942; d. Bruce Fraser and Doris Marie (Parmer) Harris; B.A., U. of Ams., 1966; M.Ed., U. Wash., 1970, postgrad. (Nat. Def. Edn. Act fellow), 1970—; m. Glen Austin Nelle, 1963 (div. 1971); children—Margot, Janis, William. Grad. teaching asst. U. Wash., Seattle, 1971; project dir. Ednl. Habilitation Project, Wash. State Bd. for Community Coll. Edn., Olympia, 1972-73; dir. Office Instl. Research and Devel., Seattle Central Community Coll., 1974—. Partner nelle & hamberg, consultants. Mem. Nat. Task Force on Higher Edn. and Criminal Justice. Mem. Am. Psychol. Assn. Home: 34915 29th St S Auburn WA 98002 Office: 1718 Broadway Seattle WA 98122

NELMARK, RUTH VIRGINIA IVERSON, pub. relations exec.; b. Deming, N.M., Aug. 5, 1922; d. Conrad Martinius and Lily (Ellingson) Iverson; student U. Minn., Duluth, 1941, Mpls., 1947, Glen Lake Bus. Tng. Sch., 1949; m. Charles E. Nelmark, Apr. 2, 1950 (div. 1959); 1 son, Gary Warren. Pvt. sec. to pres.-owner Textile Maintenance Services, Inc., Mpls., 1958-59; adminstrv. asst. N. Central Electric Assn., Mpls., 1959-61; asst. to registrar Mpls. Inst. Arts, 1961-62; exec. sec. to bd. dirs. Franklin Creamery, Inc., Mpls., 1962-63; adminstrv. asst. nat. sales, pub. relations WDGY Radio, Storz Broadcasting Co., Mpls., 1963-64; pub. relations coordinator Kenneth G. Patton Agy. (name changed to The Patton Agency), Phoenix, 1964-65, pub. relations dir. radio, TV 1966-67, pub. relations account exec., dir. electronic media, 1968-71; asso., v.p., account exec. Joanne Patton Ralston and Assos., 1971—. Mem. Mpls. Soc. Fine Arts, 1961-63; com. chmn. Aquatennial Queen's Rev. Luncheon, 1962-63; mem. bus. women's div. Women's Assn. Mpls. Symphony Orch., 1963-64; com. chmn. Mpls. Aquatennial Assn., 1963-64; dir. Womens div. Mpls. C. of C., 1964. Recipient Lulu award Los Angeles Advt. Womens Ann. Achievement Awards Competition for Women in Advt. and Pub. Relations, 1967, (2) 1968, (2) 1969, (2), 1970, (2), 1971, (2), 1973; 1st pl. awards (2) Ariz. Press Women, 1968, (2) 1969, (1), 1970, (1), 1970; 1st pl. award (2) Nat. Fedn. Press Women, 1968, (1) 1969; 1st pl. award Best Pub. Relations Photo of 1971, Pub. Relations Jour.; Certificate of Appreciation, U.S. Marine Corps Recruiting Service, 1971. Mem. Pub. Relations Soc. Am. (dir. 1973—), Ariz. Press Women, Nat. Fedn. Press Women, Nat. Acad. Television Arts and Scis. (bd. govs. 1969-71, 2d v.p. 1971-73), Delta Beta Gamma. Methodist. Clubs: Phoenix Press, Kiva. Home: 1949 E Orange Dr Phoenix AZ 85016 Office: Suite 2000 3003 N Central Av Phoenix AZ 85012

NELMS, DOROTHY LEE, advt. co. exec.; b. Oxford, N.C., May 13, 1925; d. Lonnie and Effie Dorothy (Lee) Nelms; B.A., U. N.C., 1946. With Lindsey & Co., Richmond, Va., 1946-58, Liller, Neal, Battle & Lindsey, Atlanta, 1958-66; with Burton, Campbell & Kelley, Atlanta, 1966—, v.p., media dir., 1970—. Mem. Atlanta Media Planners Assn., Atlanta Broadcast Executives Club. Club: Ansley Golf (Atlanta). Home: 1582 Walthall Court NW Atlanta GA 30318 Office: 1800 Peachtree Rd NW Atlanta GA 30309

NELSEN, NANCY MARY ANN ALELIUNAS (MRS. JAMES M. NELSEN), sporting goods co. exec., pub. relations dir.; b. Chgo., Feb. 26, 1947; d. Walter and Genevieve (Furgal) Aleliunas; grad. Moser Secretarial Sch., 1966; m. James M. Nelsen, Sept. 27, 1970. With E.H. Weiss & Co., Chgo., 1966-70; media dir. A. Eicoff & Co., Chgo., 1972—; pres. Jock Shop Inc., Chgo., 1973—. Home: 5117 N Natoma St Chicago IL 60656 Office: 520 N Michigan Av Chicago IL 60611

NELSON, ALIX ROBIN (MRS. GERALD B. NELSON), journalist; b. N.Y.C., Oct. 15, 1938; d. George P. and Shirley (Polykoff) Halperin; B.A. (N.Y. State Regents scholar), Vassar Coll., 1960; postgrad. (Univ. fellow), Columbia, 1962-63; m. Gerald B. Nelson, July 23, 1961; children—Shawn Elizabeth, Corin Alexandra. Asst. editor Simon & Schuster, Inc., N.Y.C., 1960-61, publicist, 1967-69, sr. editor, 1969-71; freelance journalist for various newspapers, mags. and orgns., including N.Y. Times, Ms, Newsday and Catalyst, 1971—. Theatre and book reviewer Channel 3, Nantucket, Mass., 1973. Mem. Women Strike for Peace, N.Y.C., 1966-67. Author Raggedy Ann and Andy series Bobbs-Merrill, Inc. Home and office: Squam Rd Nantucket MA 02554

NELSON, AMERICA ELIZABETH, pediatrician; b. Chgo., Apr. 9, 1932; d. Lorenzo Raymond and Blanche Juanita (Crawford) Nelson; A.B. in English, U. Mich. at Ann Arbor, 1952, M.S. in Zoology, 1954; postgrad. Tenn. State U., 1952-53, U. Chgo., 1955-56; M.D., Howard U., 1961; M.P.H., U. Ill., 1973. Intern Hahnemann Med. Sch. and Hosps., Phila., 1961-62; resident pediatrics Michael Reese Hosp., Chgo., 1962-63, U. Mich. at Ann Arbor, 1964; practice medicine specializing in pediatric cardiology, Detroit, 1963; practice medicine specializing in pediatrics with father, Baldwin, Mich., 1964-71; pediatrician Tice Clinic, U. Ill., Cook County Hosp., 1965, 66; pediatrician Mile's Sq. Health Center, Chgo., 1967; pediatrician Infant Welfare Soc., Chgo., 1968; cons. pediatrician, child devel. Kalamazoo Child Guidance Clinic, 1969-70, coordinator drug abuse program, 1969-70; med. dir. Chgo. Residential Manpower Center, 1971-72; pediatrician, child devel. Dyslexia Meml. Inst., Chgo., 1972—; lectr. U. Ill. at Chgo. Circle, 1972-73; clin. instr. U. Ill.-Presbyn.-St. Luke's Hosp.; asst. prof. Mental Retardation Inst. N.Y. Med. Coll., 1974; cons. in field. Mem. Am. Acad. Sci., Chgo. Pediatric Soc., Pi Lambda Theta. Contbr. articles to profl. jours. Home: PO Box 34 Baldwin MI 49304 also 505 N Lake Shore Dr Apt 803 Chicago IL 60611

NELSON, ARLENE KAM CHOY WONG (MRS. LYLE EMERSON NELSON), social worker; b. Honolulu, Sept. 29, 1924; d. Leong and Kam Hing (Ing) Wong; B.A., U. Utah, 1946; M.Social Sci., Simmons Sch. Social Work, 1948, postgrad., 1955-56; m. Lyle Emerson Nelson, June 10, 1956; children—Andrea Lai Wah, Von Jan Wah. Med. social worker Bur. Sight Conservation, Honolulu, 1948-51, Bur. Crippled Children, Dept. Health, Honolulu, 1951-61, mental retardation div., Honolulu, 1963-67, crippled children services children health service div., 1967—. Del., World Congress Ophthalmalogy, London, 1950, Internat. Social Work Conf., Paris, France, 1950. Mem. Nat. Assn. Social Workers (sec. Hawaii chpt. 1950), Hawaii Pub. Health Assn. (sec. 1950-51). Home: 2112 Damon St Honolulu HI 96822 Office: 3663 Maunalei Av Honolulu HI 96816

NELSON, AUDREY MAY, rheumatologist; b. Austin, Minn., Apr. 1, 1940; d. Glen Stanley and Clara May (Torgerson) Nelson; B.A., U. Minn., 1962, B.S., 1963, M.D., 1965. Intern medicine N.C. Meml. Hosp., Chapel Hill, 1965-66; resident medicine, rheumatology trainee Mayo Grad Sch. Medicine, 1966-71; cons. Mayo Clinic, Rochester, Minn., 1972—; instr. Mayo Med. Sch., 1972—. Recipient Phillip S. Hench Scholarship award Mayo Found., 1971. Mem. A.C.P., Am. Rheumatism Assn., Phi Beta Kappa, Alpha Omega Alpha. Home: 2105 Valkyrie Dr NW Rochester MN 55901 Office: 200 1st St SW Rochester MN 55901

NELSON, BARBARA LORRAINE (CZURLES) (MRS. DONALD J. NELSON), educator; b. Buffalo, June 26, 1936; d. Stanley Albert and Marie Lillian (Wyatt) Czurles; student Medill Sch. Journalism, Northwestern U., 1954-56; B.S., Syracuse U., 1958; M.Ed. in Ednl. Adminstrn., U. Hawaii, 1973; m. Donald J. Nelson, Dec. 29, 1962. Feature writer and photographer Honolulu Advertiser, 1959; asst. editor Sunday mag. Honolulu Star-Bull., 1959-61; dir. youth careers program Evang. Lit. Overseas, Wheaton, Ill., 1961-62; tchr. English and home econs. Hawaii Bapt. Acad., Honolulu, 1963-68, chmn. dept. English, 1965-68, elementary prin., 1970-71; secondary prin., 1968-73; tchr. English Punahou Acad., Honolulu, 1973—. Curriculum writer So. Bapt. Sunday Sch. Bd., Nashville, 1972-73. Mem. exec. bd. Hawaii Bapt. Conv., 1972-75, Girl Scout Council of the Pacific, v.p., 1973-74. Recipient D.A.R. Citizenship award, 1954; named Outstanding Young Woman of Hawaii, 1970. Mem. Internat. Platform Assn., Nat. Assn. for Supervision and Curriculum Devel., Women in Communications, Honolulu Chorale, Chi Omega Alumni Assn., Omicron Nu. Baptist (music dir. 1970—). Club: Polynesian Gem and Mineral. Home: 45-233 Koa Kahiko St Kaneohe HI 96744 Office: 1601 Punahou St Honolulu HI

NELSON, BETTY JANE BRIGHT (MRS. CHESTER C. NELSON), social work adminstr.; b. Easton, Md., Oct. 31, 1923; d. Charles T. and Nellie (Robinson) Bright; A.A., St. Mary's Jr. Coll., 1942; LL.B., U. Balt., 1950; M.S.W., U. Pa., 1960; m. Chester C. Nelson, Apr. 26, 1952. Classification counsellor Md. Reformatory for Women, Jessup, 1944-51; admitted to Md. bar, 1951; sec. to asso. judge Ct. of Appeals of Md., Annapolis, 1951-52; individual practice law, Cambridge, Md., 1952-57; social work supr. social service dept. Eastern Shore State Hosp., Cambridge, 1957-68; project dir. continuing edn. program for social workers in mental health Md. Dept. Mental Hygiene, Balt., 1968-70; regional dir. Md. Drug Abuse Adminstrn., 1970-72; health planner Health Planning Council Eastern Shore, Cambridge, Md., 1972—. Field instr. schs. social work, 1961-68. Mem. Citizens Adv. Com., Cambridge, 1964—; bd. dirs. Eastern Shore Council Alcoholism, 1964-71, v.p., 1969-71. Mem. Acad. Certified Social Workers, Nat. Assn. Social Workers, Nat. Conf. Social Welfare, Am. Pub. Health Assn. Episcopalian (mem. diocesan council 1972—). Home: 705 Travers St Cambridge MD 21613 Office: PO Box 776 Cambridge MD 21613

NELSON, BETTY JEAN MINTON (MRS. STANLEY NELSON), med. writer, editor; b. Muncie, Ind., Oct. 2, 1923; d. Robert Samuel and Pauline (Clevenger) Minton; m. Peter Haakon Skrefstad, Nov. 20, 1944 (div. Oct. 1963); 1 dau., Sonja (Mrs. Jacques Kaszemacher); m. 2d, Stanley Nelson, June 26, 1966. Asst. to research dir. N.Y. U. Research Service, Goldwater Meml. Hosp., N.Y.C., 1947-57; reporter Med. News, N.Y.C., 1957-61; pharmacy editor Drug News Weekly, N.Y.C., 1961-63; med. reporter Antibiotic News, N.Y.C., 1963-67; med. editor Urologic Soundings, N.Y.C., 1962-70, Geriatric Times, N.Y.C., 1967-70; exec. editor Chronic Disease Mgmt., 1971-72; editor Urologic Procs., 1972; sci. editor Nat. Multiple Sclerosis Soc., 1972-74; editor Surgery in the 70s, 1973—; sr. editor Urology Times, 1974—. Columnist, Mobile Home jour., 1960-61; free lance writer various med. pubs. Mem. Nat. Assn. Sci. Writers, Am. Med. Writers Assn., A.A.A.S. Contbg. editor Hosp. Practice, 1966-72. Home: 372 Pacific St Brooklyn NY 11217

NELSON, CATHERINE JANE STAFFORD (MRS. GEORGE H. NELSON), ednl. adminstr.; b. Saginaw, Mich., Mar. 19, 1916; d. Walter J. and Alma (Phelps) Stafford; B.A., Central Mich. U., 1937, M.A., 1958; m. George H. Nelson, Aug. 30, 1936 (dec.); children—Geoffrey A., Paul Stafford. Tchr., Dow Pvt. Sch., Midland, Mich., 1935-36; tchr. Rosebush (Mich.) Pub. Schs., 1936-40, Mt. Pleasant (Mich.) Pub. Schs., 1950-65; instr. English, Central Mich. U., Mt. Pleasant, 1965-66; mem. faculty Northwood Inst., Midland, Mich., 1966—, instr. English, 1966-68, asst. prof., 1968-70, student personnel dir., 1970—. Pres., Central Mich. U. Lab. Sch. P.T.A., Mt. Pleasant, 1952-53, sec., 1950-51; patron Midland Little Theatre, 1966—, Midland Music Soc., 1966—. Named Hon. Homecoming Queen, Northwood Inst., 1970, Outstanding Tchr. of Year, 1971. Mem. Mich. Personnel and Guidance Assn., Nat. Council English Tchrs., Nat., Mich. assns. woman's deans and counselors, Central Mich. University Faculty Dames (pres. 1946-47), Northwood Women's Library Assn., Mt. Pleasant Community Hosp. Aux. Club: Northwood Town and Campus (Midland). Home: 601 Crescent Dr Mt Pleasant MI 48858 Office: Northwood Inst Cook Rd Midland MI 48640

NELSON, CHLOE MATHILDA, occupational therapist; b. Sedgwick, Colo., Oct. 27, 1914; d. Ture Albert and Carrie Eva (Powers) Nelson; B.S., Colo. A. and M. Coll., 1936; certificate occupational therapy Colo. State U., 1952. Tchr. vocational home econs. Burwell (Neb.) High Sch., 1936-38, Le Mars (Ia.) High Sch.,

1938-40, Idaho Springs (Colo.) High Sch., 1940-42; occupational therapist U. Colo. Med. Center, Denver, 1952—, supr. dept., 1962—, instr. occupational therapy, 1963-69. Vice pres. Coal Creek Canyon Improvement Assn., 1971-73. Served with USNR, 1943-45. Mem. Am., Colo. occupational therapy assns., World Fedn. Occupational Therapy, Nat. Wildlife Fedn. Home: Route 2 Box 735 Golden CO 80401 Office: 4200 E 9th Av Denver CO 80220

NELSON, CHRISTINE AUDREY, occupational therapist; b. Hartford, Conn., Apr. 30, 1937; d. Carl Evert and Gladys Miriam (Kinell) Nelson; B.S. in Occupational Therapy, Coll. William and Mary, 1959; M.S. in Child Devel., U. Wis., 1963; Ph.D. in Human Devel., U. Md., 1973. Staff therapist Sunland Tng. Center, Gainesville, Fla., 1960-62; occupational therapist Central Wis. Colony and Tng. Sch., Madison, 1962-65; Balt. League for Crippled Children and Adults, 1965-67; pvt. practice occupational therapy, Balt., 1967—. Cons. Hamburg (Pa.) State Sch. and Hosp., 1966-67, Polk (Pa.) State Sch. and Hosp., 1968, Va. State Sch., Lynchburg, 1966, Coop. Sch. Fairfax (Va.), 1972-73, No. Va. Treatment Center, Falls Church, 1972—, Balt. Health Dept., 1969—, Children's Guild, Inc., Balt., 1967—, Brooklane Psychiat. Center, Hagerstown, Md., 1970-73, Prince George County (Md.) Pub. Schs., 1970-71. Mem. Am., Md. occupational therapy assns., Internat. Bobath Alumni Assn. (dir. 1970-71). Home: 8315 Roanoke Av Apt 6 Takoma Park MD 20012 Office: 211 W Lombard St Baltimore MD 21201

NELSON, CONSTANCE BURKHARDT, clin. psychologist; b. Franklin, Ind., Oct. 13, 1917; d. Carl Alonzo and Haidee (Forsythe) Brukhardt; A.B., William Jewell Coll., 1938; M.A., U. Minn., 1952; Ph.D., U. Mo. at Kansas City, 1958; postgrad. U. Chgo., 1939, 68, Columbia, 1953, Boston U., 1955, 57; m. Louis O. Nelson, June 16, 1940; children—Nancy Jane (Mrs. Nancy Sayeedi), Constance Ruth (Mrs. H. Dean Bresnahan). With Kansas City VA Hosp. and Mental Hygiene Clinic, 1957-62; chief psychologist children's div. Colo. State Hosp., Pueblo, 1962-63; asst. dir. psychology dept. N.D. State Hosp., Jamestown, 1963, dir. psychology dept., 1963-66; coordinator tng., unit psychologist St. Cloud (Minn.) VA Hosp., 1966-67; clin. psychologist VA Hosp. and Mental Hygiene Clinic, Denver, 1968—. Mem. faculty William Jewell Coll., 1943-44, 46-49, 52-55; lectr. psychology U. Kansas City, 1950, 55-57; teaching asst. U. Minn., 1950-51, clin. asso. prof. psychology, 1966-67; lectr. Coll. St. Teresa, Kansas City, 1959-60; from lectr. to asso. prof. psychology St. John's U., Collegeville, Minn., 1966-67; adj. asso. prof. psychology Loretto Heights Coll., Denver, 1968-70. Mem. Colo. Commn. Status of Women, 1969—. Vol. mental health cons. Denver Pub. Schs., 1968-69. Recipient citation for achievement William Jewell Coll., 1961. Diplomate clin. psychology Am. Bd. Profl. Psychology. Fellow Soc. for Personality Assessment; mem. Am., Colo. (sec. 1968-69, dir. 1969-71, Rocky Mountain psychol. assns., Internat. Rehab. Assn., A.A.A.S., Am. Soc. Clin. Hypnosis, Am. Group Psychotherapy Assn., Assn. Fed. Profl. and Adminstrv. Women (chmn. Denver region 1972-74), Am. Assn. Pastoral Counselors (affiliate), Nat. League Nursing (affiliate), Am. Assn. U. Profs., Am. Assn. U. Women, Psi Chi, Pi Gamma Mu. Club: Denver Zonta. Editor: Internat. Psychologist, 1973-74. Home: 2472 S Kearney St Denver CO 80222 Office: VA Hosp 1055 Clermont St Denver CO 80220 also 145 E Centennial Englewood CO 80110

NELSON, DOROTHY W. (MRS. JAMES F. NELSON), univ. adminstr., lawyer; A.B. in Polit. Sci. (with honors), U. Cal. at Los Angeles, 1950, J.D., 1953; LL.M., U. So. Cal., 1956; m. James F. Nelson; children—Franklin, Lorna. Admitted to Cal. bar; now dean, prof. law, Univ. So. Cal., Los Angeles. Mem. Judicial Process Task Force, Cal. Council Criminal Justice; co-chmn. panel President's White House Conf. on Children, 1970; adv. com. Nat. Center for State Cts. Bd. dirs. Council on Legal Edn. for Profl. Responsibility, Constnl. Rights Found. Named Univ. Cal. at Los Angeles Law Alumnus of the Year, 1967, Los Angeles Times Woman of the Year, 1968; recipient Univ. Cal. at Los Angeles Alumni Professional Achievement award, 1969. Fellow Am. Bar Fedn.; mem. Am. Judicature Soc. (dir.), Continuing Edn. of the Bar (gov. bd.), Am. Assn. U. Women, Am. Bar Assn. (sect. jud. adminstrn., chmn. com. edn. jud. adminstrn., sect. family law), State Bar Cal. (com. legal edn., com. continuing legal edn.), Legion Lex, U. Cal. at Los Angeles Alumni Assn., Law Alumni Assn., Phi Beta Kappa. Mem. Baha'i World Faith (mem. nat. spiritual assembly, nat. treas. Baha'is U.S.). Author: Judicial Administration and the Administration of Justice, 1974. Contbr. articles on law to profl. jours. Office: Univ So Cal Univ Park Los Angeles CA 90007

NELSON, ELIZABETH, educator; b. Birmingham, Ala.; d. John and Mary (Dunigan) Nelson; B.S., Ala. State Tchrs. Coll., 1939; M.S., Wayne State U., 1948; postgrad. N.Y. U., U. Heidelberg, Mich. State U., U. Md., U. Paris, U. Neuchatel (Switzerland). Tchr., Jefferson County (Ala.) pub. schs., 1939-45; tchr. George Washington Carver Sch., Ferndale, Mich., 1945-55, prin., 1955-58, curriculum coordinator, 1959; tchr. Bad Kreuznach (Germany) Elementary Sch., U.S. Army, 1962; tchr. Vassincourt (France) Am. Elementary Sch. Overseas Dependents Schs., Dept. Def., U.S. Army, 1963-65, Verdun (France) Am. Elementary Sch., 1966; tchr. SHAPE Internat. Elementary Sch., NATO SHAPE Support Groups Sect., SHAPE, Belgium, 1967—. Recipient award for contbns. to edn. and people of Mich., State of Mich., 1955. Mem. Nat., Overseas edn. assns., N.A.A.C.P., League Women Voters, Zeta Phi Beta. Address: SHAPE American Elementary School APO NY 09088

NELSON, ELIZABETH ANNE DANIEL, constrn. co. exec.; b. Birmingham, Ala., Jan. 16, 1916; d. Robert Thomas and Emogene (Thomas) Daniel; student Randolph Macon Woman's Coll., 1933-35; m. Jack R. Nelson, Feb. 4, 1954 (div.); 1 dau., Diane Daniel Rennie. Payroll clk. Birmingham Ordnance Dist., 1942-45; sec. Rapistan Co., Birmingham, 1965-67; with Vulcan Materials Co., Birmingham, 1967—, sales forecast analyst, 1971—. Social column writer English, Guatemala City, Central Am., 1950-52; owner, tchr. The Cotillion, Culpeper, Va., 1957-65. Leader Girl Scouts Am., Culpeper, 1956-58; transp. chmn. women's com. Birmingham Symphony Orch., 1969-73; mem. ladies' aux. Culpeper Meml. Hosp., 1958-65. Mem. Am. Marketing Assn. (chpt. sec. 1968-70), Alpha Omicron Pi. Episcopalian (mem. altar guild 1970—). Club: Birmingham Country. Home: 2510 Mountain Brook Circle Birmingham AL 35223 Office: Office Park Circle Birmingham AL 35223

NELSON, EMMIE, assn. exec.; b. Euharlee, Ga.; d. Frank Elihugh and Elizabeth (Williams) Nelson; B.S., U. Ga., 1924; postgrad. Cornell U., Colo. State U.; M.Ed., U. Md., 1956. Home demonstration agt., Augusta, Ga., 1924-37; asst. state 4-H leader, U. Ga., 1937-45; field rep. Nat. 4-H Service Com., Inc., Chgo., 1945—; cons. Recipient citation for service U.S. Dept. Agr., 1951. Mem. Am., Ga. home econs. assns., Home Economists in Bus., Elec. Womens Round Table, Inc., Assn. So. Agrl. Workers, Etowah Creative Arts Council, Phi Upsilon Omicron. Contbr. articles to periodicals. Home: Route 1 Cartersville GA 30120 Office: Nat 4-H Service Committee 150 N Wacker Dr Chicago IL 60606

NELSON, ESTHER MARION, educator; b. Mpls.; d. Victor and Ellen (Martin) Nelson; B.S., U. Ore., 1926; M.A., Columbia, 1929, Ph.D., 1939, postdoctoral research, 1946-48; postgrad. U. Heidelberg (Germany), 1934; postdoctoral Harvard, summer 1940, N.Y. U., 1942. Instr. English, edn. State U. N.Y. Coll. Edn., Oneonta, 1931-43; educator U.S. Naval Operating Base, Guantanamo Bay, Cuba, 1948-50; from asso. prof. to prof. secondary edn. U. Houston, 1950—. Asso., Nat. Survey Edn. Tchrs. U.S., 1931-35; del. Christian Endeavor World Conv., Budapest, Hungary, 1935. Served in WAC, 1943-46. Mem. Am. Assn. U. Women, Am. Assn. U. Profs., N.E.A., Nat. Soc. for Study Edn., Assn. Higher Edn., Tex. State Tchrs. Assn., Nat. Geog. Soc., Internat. Platform Assn., Nat. Assn. for Doctors in U.S.A., Am. Legion, UN Assn. U.S.A., Nat. Audubon Soc., Nat. Wildlife Fedn., Wilderness Soc., Smithsonian Instn., U. Houston Women's Assn., Am. Mus. Natural History (nat. asso.), Intercontinental Biog. Assn. (life), Kappa Delta Pi, Pi Lambda Theta, Alpha Lambda Delta, Alpha Sigma Omicron. Republican. Presbyn. Clubs: Nat. Travel, University Oaks Civic. Author: Analysis of Content of Student Teaching Courses in State Teachers Colleges, 1939. Editor FEASC Intelligence Bull., 1944-45. Contbr. to various ednl. publs. Home: 4432 Wheeler St Houston TX 77004

NELSON, HARRIET LAVERNE SCHERBARTH (MRS. WARREN NELSON), ednl. adminstr.; b. Milw., Aug. 9, 1924; d. Harry Charles and Frances Louise (Molitor) Scherbarth; B.S., U. Wis., 1945, postgrad., 1963-72; m. Warren Nelson, Aug. 11, 1945; children—James, Jo Ann (dec.), Janice (Mrs. George Winget), John, Jack, Jerry. Tchr., Luth. Sch. for Deaf, Detroit, 1945-46; pvt. tutor speech and hearing, 1950-57; supr. speech and hearing dept. So. Wis. Colony and Tng. Sch. for Mentally Retarded, Union Grove, 1957—, asst. prin., 1973—. Cons., Health and Social Services Hometrainers. Leader 4-H Club, 1967-69; area chmn. Am. Cancer Soc. Fund Drive, 1967-72. Mem. Am. Assn. Mental Deficiency (Wis. membership chmn. 1972—), Wis. Speech and Hearing Assn., Women's Soc. Christian Service (pres. 1952-54). Mem. Order Eastern Star (past matron, trustee 1970—). Home: 1323 High St Union Grove WI 53182 Office: So Wis Colony Union Grove WI 53182

NELSON, HAZEL FOWLER (MRS. BOWEN CRESTON NELSON), writer; b. Mulhall, Okla., May 16, 1905; d. Oscar Frederick and Belle Virginia (Lowe) Fowler; B.A., U. Okla., 1927; postgrad. U. Wis., 1928; m. Bowen Creston Nelson Oct. 26, 1941; 1 dau., Creston Annette. Tchr. journalism, English, sponsor publs. Chickasha (Okla.) High Sch., 1927-30; reporter Norman (Okla.) Transcript, 1930-37; feature writer Okla. City Times, 1937-41; mil. editor Miami (Fla.) Herald, 1942-45; officer Nelson Mortgage Co., Inc., Miami, 1941-69, sec., dir., 1942-69; now free-lance writer. Mem. bd. Children's Service Bur., Miami, 1952; v.p. Franklin Bush chpt. U. Miami Women's Cancer Assn., 1961, pres., 1970. Recipient silver award Miami's Fgn. War Brides for assistance through newspaper series, 1946. Mem. Soc. So. Families, Fla. Hist. Assn., Internat. Platform Assn., Women in Communications (pres. U. Okla. chpt. 1927, Miami chpt. 1952-53). Democrat. Mem. Christian Ch. (pres. women's fellowship 1963-64). Home: 10255 SW 53d Av Miami FL 33156

NELSON, HELEN EWING (MRS. NATHAN NELSON), consumer advocate; b. Boulder County, Colo., Oct. 19, 1913; d. Delton Ralph Hodgson and Edith (Abbott) Ewing; B.A., U. Colo., 1935; M.A., Mills Coll., 1936; m. Nathan Nelson, Oct. 2, 1942. Asst. chief labor statistics and research Cal. Dept. Indsl. Relations, 1950-59; consumer counsel Cal. Gov.'s Office, Sacramento, 1959-66; asso. dir. research and devel. Center for Consumer Affairs, U. Wis. Extension, Milw., 1969-71, dir. center, 1971—, asso. prof., 1971-74, prof., 1974—. Past pres., Consumer Fedn. Am.; pres. Consumer Research Found.; sec. Nat. Center for Consumer Legal Services; mem. Gov.'s Coordinating Council for Consumer Affairs; Wis. Dept. Agr. Consumer Council, Wis. Health Policy Council, Wis. Ednl. Congress on the Aging, dir. Mutual Service Ins. Co. Bd. dirs. Consumers Union, Nat. Consumer Law Center, Wis. Health Care Rev., Inc., Wis. Consumers League, Center for Pub. Representation, Wis. Blue Cross Rate Rev. Com.; pub. gov. Am. Stock Exchange. Mem. Am. Econs. Assn., Am. Statis. Assn., Am. Assn. U. Women, League Women Voters, Am. Council Consumer Interest, Am. Arbitration Assn., Assn. for Consumer Research, Group Health Assn. Am. Editor: Consumers Organize for Health Care; Consumers Organize for Health Care; A Short History of Consumer Credit Legislation: An Introduction to Consumer Viewpoints on the Uniform Consumer Credit Code; Consumer Policy on Food Labeling. Address: 1260 N Prospect Av Milwaukee WI 53202 also 929 N 6th St Milwaukee WI 53203

NELSON, IRENE BURI (MRS. GEORGE E. NELSON, JR.), broadcasting exec.; b. Kenosha, Wis., Mar. 17, 1922; d. Philip and Genevieve Julia (Garay) Buri; grad. Patricia Stevens Fashion and Charm Sch., Chgo., 1942; spl. courses Gateway Tech. Inst., Kenosha, Radio Workshop, Milw., 1949; m. George E. Nelson, Jr., Sept. 15, 1951. With radio sta. WLIP AM-FM, Kenosha, 1947—, fashion editor, 1947—, women's dir., 1947—. Bd. dirs. Kenosha Homemakers Health Aid Service, 1969-72; bd. dirs., pub. relations dir. Kenosha unit Am. Cancer Soc., 1973—. Recipient Helping Hand award Kenosha affiliate Wis. Hairdressers and Cosmetologists, 1969, certificate of appreciation, Kenosha Jr. C. of C., 1972. Mem. Am. Women in Radio and TV (Wis. pres. 1965-66, publicity dir. 1968—), A.F.T.R.A. (Kenosha sec.-treas. 1948—), St. Catherine's Hosp. Aux., Am. Cancer Soc. Clubs: Gateway Technical Homemakers (hon. mem.), Catholic Woman's (Kenosha). Home: 929 52d St Kenosha WI 53140 Office: WLIP-AM-FM 625 57th St Kenosha WI 53140

NELSON, JANE GRAY (MRS. ROBERT M. NELSON), curator, librarian; b. Kankakee, Ill., Oct. 10, 1928; d. Donald and Antoinette (Holmes) Gray; B.A., Rockford Coll., 1950; M.L.S., U. Cal. at Berkeley, 1963, M.A., 1971; m. Robert M. Nelson, Sept. 1, 1951; 1 dau., Deborah. Asst. librarian Giannini Found., U. Cal., Berkeley, 1967; head librarian, asst. curator ancient art Fine Arts Mus. San Francisco, 1971—. Mem. Am. Inst. Archaeology, Soc. for Promotion Hellenic Studies, Art Librarians N. Am., Bronte Soc. Home: 2241 Sacramento St San Francisco CA 94115 Office: Fine Arts Museums of San Francisco MH de Young Meml Mus San Francisco CA 94118

NELSON, JANET WAGNER (MRS. TED NELSON), writer, photographer; b. Detroit, Nov. 29, 1930; d. Robert Ray and Isabelle (Taylor) Wagner; B.A., Mich. State U., 1953; m. Ted Nelson, July 10, 1963. Editorial trainee Better Homes & Gardens, Des Moines, 1953-54; with Mich. Bell Telephone Co., Detroit, 1954-56, Am. Tel. & Tel., N.Y.C., 1956-60; staff writer Good Housekeeping, N.Y.C., 1960-63; articles editor Parade mag., N.Y.C., 1963-64; mng. editor Ski mag., N.Y.C., 1964-68; free-lance writer-photographer, Croton-on-Hudson, N.Y., 1968—. Exhibited photographs in one-man show at Garrison (N.Y.) Art Center, 1973. Recipient Sch. Bell award N.E.A., 1964. Mem. Eastern Ski Writers (dir.). Author: How to Ski, 1962; Biking for Fun and Fitness, 1970. Home: Finney Farm Croton-on-Hudson NY 10520

NELSON, JEAN ELLEN, librarian; b. Los Angeles, Feb. 9, 1928; d. Harry Abor and Agnes May (Kissane) Olson; B.A., Cal. State Coll. at Los Angeles, 1965; M.A. in L.S., U. So. Cal., 1966, postgrad., 1968—; m. William Gabriel Nelson, Jan. 1, 1946 (div. Jan. 1970); children—William B., Lawrence P., Carl D., Warren D. Young adult librarian Whittier Pub. Library, Cal., 1966-68, librarian Whittwood br., 1968-72; city librarian San Bruno (Cal.) Pub. Library, 1972-74, Fullerton (Cal.) Pub. Library, 1974—. Mem. Am. Assn. U. Women (area chmn. internat. relations 1971-72, 73-74), A.L.A., Cal. Library Assn., No. Cal. (dir.), So. Cal. pub. library execs., World Affairs Council No. Cal., Peninsula Hosp. Aux. Club: Fullerton Soroptimist. Home: 9403 S Klinedale Av Downey CA 90240 Office: Fullerton Public Library Fullerton CA 92632

NELSON, KARIN D. BECKER (MRS. PHILLIP G. NELSON), pediatric neurologist; b. Chgo., Aug. 14, 1933; d. George and Sylvia Valery (Dermansky) Becker; M.D., U. Chgo., 1957; m. Phillip Gillard Nelson, Mar. 20, 1955; children—Sarah Elizabeth, Rebecca Judith, Jennifer Becker, Peter Tobias. Intern Phila. Gen. Hosp., 1958-59; resident neurology U. Md. and George Washington U. hosps., 1962; registrar to outpatients Nat. Hosp. Nervous Diseases, Queen Square, London, Eng., 1963; pvt. practice pediatric neurology, Washington, 1967—; attending neurologist Children's Hosp. D.C., 1971—; med. officer neurol. perinatal research br. Nat. Inst. Neurol. Diseases, 1963—; asso. prof. neurology George Washington U. Sch. Medicine, 1972—. Profl. adv. bd. Epilepsy Found. Diplomate neurology and child neurology Am. Bd. Psychiatry and Neurology. Mem. Am. Acad. Neurology, Child Neurology Soc. (exec. bd.), D.C. Med. Soc., Alpha Omega Alpha. Home: 5524 Charles St Bethesda MD 20014 Office: 7550 Wisconsin Av Bethesda MD 20014

NELSON, KATHERINE SHAW (MRS. AUBREY WAYNE NELSON), author; b. Hanover, N.H., Feb. 27, 1926; d. Angus and Dolina (MacAskill) Shaw; B.A., Syracuse U., 1948; m. Aubrey Wayne Nelson, Oct. 1, 1950; children—Rae Katherine. Reporter, Claremont (N.H.) Daily Eagle, 1943-44, Manchester (N.H.) Union Leader, 1945; writer CIA, Washington, 1948-51; free-lance writer specializing in cookery, travel, women's subjects for nat. mags., including Gourmet, Woman's Day, House and Garden, 1962—; writer article series Washington Post, 1973—. Mem. Md. Democratic Club. Club: Syracuse Alumni (Washington). Author: Pasta: Plain and Fancy, 1971; Magic of Mushroom Cookery, 1971; Yogurt Cookery: Good and Gourmet, 1972; The Eastern European Cookbook, 1973; Soups, Stews and Ritzy Ragouts, 1974. Address: 5214 Abingdon Rd Washington DC 20016

NELSON, LINDA ANNE AURAND (MRS. WILLIAM GEORGE NELSON, IV), psychologist, educator; b. Governor's Island, N.Y., Aug. 1, 1938; d. Henry Spiese and Elizabeth Muir (Steele) Aurand; student Swarthmore Coll., 1955-58; B.S. with honors, Washington U., 1968; M.S. (Nat. Def. Edn. Act fellow), St. Louis U., 1970, Ph.D., 1971; m. William George Nelson, IV, June 12, 1957; children—William George V, Henry Aurand, Thomas Lane, David Steele. Instr. psychology Harris Tchrs. Coll., St. Louis, 1971-73; asst. prof. psychology Lindenwood Coll., St. Charles, Mo., 1973—, chmn. psychology dept., 1974—. Mem. Nat. Conf. Use On-Line Computers in Psychology. Mem. Am. Psychol. Assn., Am. Assn. Univ. Profs., Sigma Xi. Home: 1121 Westmoor Pl Town and Country MO 63131 Office: Lindenwood Coll St Charles MO 63301

NELSON, LOGAN V. (MRS. FRANK B. NELSON), civic worker; b. Shelbyville, Ky., Oct. 23, 1912; d. Benjamin S. and Elizabeth L. (Hickman) Van Meter; A.B., U. Ky., 1935; m. Frank Buckner Nelson, Sept. 21, 1940; children—Anne Buckner, Elizabeth Logan, Bolling Gordon III. Receptionist, sec. Louisville Paper Co., 1935-38, Seagram's, 1938-40; sec. Pitts. YWCA, 1941-42. Co-chmn. Allegheny County fund-raising campaign for WQED, 1969. Bd. dirs. Fedn. Girls Sch. Socs., pres. 1969-73; bd. dirs. Harmarville Rehab. Center, pres. 1969, 70, sec., 1973—, co-chmn. pub. relations and fund-raising com., program and facilities planning com., exec. com.; mem. Women's Assn. Pitts. Symphony Soc. Mem. Internat. Platform Assn., Western Pa. Golf Assn., U. Ky. Alumni Assn. (pres. Pitts. area 1963-64), Allegheny Children and Youth Service Council, Hosp. Assn. Pa., Nat. Rehab. Assn., Alpha Gamma Delta. Presbyn. Clubs: St. Clair Country (chmn. Women's Golf Assn. 1960, 64, womens golf champion 1960, 64, 66), Perennial Garden (treas. 1963—), Twentieth Century, South Hills College (dir. 1959-60), Pittsburgh Garden Center (hospitality co-chmn. 1963-64). Home: 1160 Bower Hill Rd Pittsburgh PA 15243

NELSON, LORRAINE LAVINGTON (MRS. ROBERT LEE NELSON), social worker; b. Denver, July 10, 1918; d. Leon Edward and Marjorie Adele (Dixon) Lavington; B.A., Denver U., 1943; postgrad. Brown Sch. Social Service, Washington U., St. Louis, 1942-43; m. Robert Lee Nelson, Apr. 15, 1948; children—Robert Leon, Thomas Lee. Red Cross aid 14th Gen. Hosp., Eng., 1943-44; social worker Dept. Pub. Welfare, Denver Co., 1944-45; child care worker Day Care Center for Working Mothers, Denver, 1945-46; social worker Springfield (Md.) State Hosp., 1952-62; social worker Colo. State Hosp., Pueblo, 1962-66; mental retardation group social worker Colo. State Home and Tng. Sch., Pueblo, 1966—. Recipient V.F.W. service awards. Mem. V.F.W. Aux. (post pres. 1970-71, 73—, dist. pres. 1973—), Pi Beta Phi. Episcopalian (del. to state diocese 1969). Home: PO Box 11269 1813 Yakima Pueblo CO 81001 Office: 1330 W 17th St Pueblo CO 81003

NELSON, MARGARET D., designer; b. Springfield, Mass.; d. Andrew and Grace (Fiske) Nelson; grad. (scholar) Parsons Sch. Design N.Y., 1933; m. Richard L. Sandfort, May 1943 (div. July 1950); 1 dau., Linda Nelson Sparrow. Designer, decorator, N.Y.C., 1933-40; head decorating dept. Neiman Marcus, Dallas, 1940-41; free lance home furnishings designer and decorator, 1941—; mgr. interior design studio J.L. Hudson Co., Detroit; now stylist, v.p. Strohelm & Romann, N.Y.C. Has been active fund raising coms. Salvation Army, Southbury (Conn.) Tng. Sch.; mem. N.Y. State Council Women; mem. jury A.I.D. Internat. Design Awards; sec. to adv. bd. Cooper-Hewitt Museum of Decorative Arts. Recipient Trail Blazer award Nat. Home Fashions League, 1956, Resources Council award, 1973. Mem. Am. Soc. Interior Designers (past dir. N.Y. chpt.; recipient Internat. Design award 1965), Color Assn. U.S., Nat. Home Fashions League (past pres., adv. council), Decorators Club (2d v.p.), Nat. Council Women U.S. Home: 333 E 34th St New York City NY 10016 Office: 155 E 56th St New York City NY 10022

NELSON, MARGARET ELIZABETH KLEMMER (MRS. PAUL NELSON), hotel exec.; b. St. Clair, Mich., Oct. 18, 1920; d. Louis E. and Anna (Adamson) Klemmer; student Eastern Mich. Coll. Commerce, 1938-40; m. Paul Nelson, Jan. 27, 1945; children—Kathryn Anne, Susan Elizabeth. With St. Clair Inn, 1943—, successively desk clk., asst. mgr., resident, sales mgr., 1943-60, gen. mgr., 1960-66, v.p., mng. dir., 1966—, also dir. Bd. dirs. March of Dimes, St. Clair Art Assn. Mem. Southeastern Mich. Tourist Assn., Mich. (dir.), Am. hotel assns., Hotel Sales Mgmt. Assn. Clubs: Women's City, St. Clair Formal Dance, St. Clair River Dance, Women's Assn. St. Clair River Country. Home: 130 Meldrum Circle St Clair MI 48079 Office: 500 N Riverside St St Clair MI 48079

NELSON, MARGARET L. MOGENSEN (MRS. CHARLES DEAN NELSON), journalist; b. Eau Claire, Wis., May 13, 1947; d. Martin T. and Catherine L. (Burke) Mogensen; B.A., Wis. State U., 1969; m. Charles Dean Nelson, Jan. 17, 1970. Reporter, The Paper, Oshkosh, Wis., 1969; editorial asst. Marsh & McLennan, Inc., ins. brokers, Chgo., 1970-71; publs. mgr. Michael Reese Med. Center, Chgo., 1971-73; editorial dir. Nat. Easter Seal Soc., Chgo., 1973—; free lance writer Los Angeles Times Syndicate, 1973—. Coordinator women's rights com. and communications task force Hyde

Park-Kenwood Community Conf., Chgo. Mem. Internat. Assn. Bus. Communicators, Indsl. Editors Assn. Chgo., Nat. Orgn. Women. Home: 5419 S University Av Chicago IL 60615 Office: 2023 W Ogden St Chicago IL 60612

NELSON, MARGARET VIOLA (MRS. SAMUEL JOHNSON), physician; b. Elbow Lake, Minn., Mar. 2, 1941; d. Elmer Lawrence and Roxy Viola (Ellison) Nelson; B.A., U. Minn., 1962, B.S., 1966, M.D., 1966; m. Samuel Buchanan Johnson, Aug. 31, 1969; 1 son, Bertram. Intern Orange County Med. Center, Orange, Cal., 1966-67; resident internal medicine U. Wis. at Madison, 1967-70, instr., 1970-72, asst. clin. prof., 1972—, physician Student Health Service, 1970—; cons. VA Hosp., Madison. Mem. Am. Soc. Internal Medicine. Home: 890 Woodrow St Madison WI 53711 Office: 1552 University Av Madison WI 53705

NELSON, MARIE POOLE COLEMAN (MRS. BENJAMIN NELSON), psychoanalyst; b. Cleve., Aug. 3, 1915; d. Charles E. and Rose L. (Hofstetter) Poole; student Theodor Reik Inst., 1951; m. Benjamin Nelson, Nov. 30, 1959; 1 son, James S. Miller. Psychoanalytic research asso. N.Y. Infirmary Women and Children, N.Y.C., 1945-48; practice psychoanalysis, Smithtown, N.Y., 1946—; staff research asso. in psychiatry Assn. Am. Med. Colls., N.Y.C., 1951-53; sr. supr. Theodor Reik Clinic, N.Y.C., 1957-59; asso. chief dept. psychology Stuyvesant Polyclinic, N.Y.C., 1959-63; mng. editor Psychoanalytic Rev., N.Y.C., 1957-67; dir. Smithtown Cons. Center, 1968-71; founding fellow, mem. faculty Center for Modern Psychoanalytic Studies, N.Y.C., 1971—; mem. faculty Jamaica Center for Psychotherapy, 1967—; guest faculty Cal. Grad. Inst., Los Angeles, 1973—. Mem. Nat. Psychol. Assn. Psychoanalysis, N.Y. Soc. Clin. Psychologists, Nat. Accreditation Assn. in Psychoanalysis (co-founder). Author: (with D. Ruhe and A. Nichtenhauser) Films in Psychiatry, Psychology and Mental Health, 1953; Paradigmatic Psychotherapy, 1962; (with J. A. M. Meerloo) Transference and Trial Adaptation, 1965; Roles and Paradigms in Psychotherapy, 1968. Editor: Self in Process Series, 1975—. Contbr. articles to profl. jours. Office: 65 South Av Smithtown NY 11787

NELSON, MARTHA LAURIE RUSHING (MRS. CARL REID NELSON), writer; b. Merigold, Miss., Jan. 19, 1923; d. Ira Columbus and Myrtis Louise (Felder) Rushing; student Delta State Coll., 1940-42, Miss. Coll.; 1947-49, Southwestern Bapt. Theol. Sem., 1950-52; m. Carl Reid Nelson, May 15, 1943; children—Patricia (Mrs. Gary Alton James), Nancy (Mrs. James Liner), Rebecca (Mrs. L. Kent Payne, Jr.). Adminstrv. asst. to pub. relations dir. Am. Optometric Assn., St. Louis, 1966-69; free-lance writer articles for various publs., including Empire, Moody Monthly, 1969—. Conf. leader, speaker Woman's Missionary Union Aux. to So. Bapt. Conv., 1970—, other women's groups; speaker Broadman's Minister's Tape Plan, 1974. Mem. Nat. League Am. Pen Women (Denver sec. 1972-74), Colo. Press Women, Denver Woman's Press Club. Republican. Author: The Christian Woman in the Working World, 1970; A Woman's Search for Serenity, 1972; On Being A Deacon's Wife, 1973. Contbg. author: The Marriage Affair, 1971; Broadman Devotional Annual, 1972. Home: 821 Dogwood Av Littleton CO 80121

NELSON, NANCY ELEANOR, pediatrician; b. El Paso, Apr. 4, 1933; d. Harry Hamilton and Helen Maude (Murphy) Nelson; B.A. magna cum laude, U. Colo., 1955, M.D., 1959. Intern Case Western Res. U. Hosp., 1959-60, resident, 1960-63; practice medicine specializing in pediatrics, Denver, 1963-70; asst. prof. U. Colo. Sch. Medicine, Denver, 1970—. Mem. Am. Acad. Pediatrics, A.M.A. Home: 1265 Elizabeth Denver CO 80206 Office: 4200 E 9th Av Denver CO 80220

NELSON, PATRICIA ANN, health planner; b. St. Paul, Sept. 17, 1944; d. John Walter and Eileen Jeanette (Norrgran) Nelson; B.S. with distinction, U. Minn., 1966; M.P.H., U. Mich., 1969; M.S. in Social Adminstrn., Case-Western Res. U., 1971. Occupational therapist C.T. Miller Hosp., St. Paul, 1966-68, coordinator occupational therapy, 1968; caseworker Center for Human Services, Cleve., 1971-73; planning asso. Met. Health Planning Corp., Cleve., 1973—. Mem. Am. Pub. Health Assn., Acad. Certified Social Workers, Am. Occupational Therapy Assn., Nat. Assn. Social Workers. Office: 908 No Ohio Bank Bldg Cleveland OH 44113

NELSON, SHARI LEE DENNIS (MRS. RODNEY ELLSWORTH NELSON), lawyer; b. Los Angeles, July 30, 1938; d. Leland Bennett and Martha (Stoner) Dennis; B.A. magna cum laude, U. So. Cal., 1959, LL.B (Los Angeles Lawyers Wives scholar 1961-62), 1962; postgrad. U. Cal. at Los Angeles, 1968; m. Rodney Ellsworth Nelson, Aug. 15, 1964. Admitted to Cal. bar, 1963; asso. Gibson, Dunn & Crutcher, Los Angeles, 1962-65, Beardsley, Hufstedler & Kemble, Los Angeles, part-time, 1965-67; individual practice law, Los Angeles, 1965-70; mem. firm Nelson, Liker & Merrifield, Los Angeles, 1970—. Mem. State Bar Cal., Greater Los Angeles Zoo Assn., U. So. Cal., U. Cal. at Los Angeles, Westlake (dir. 1968—) alumni assns., Order of Coif, Phi Beta Kappa, Phi Kappa Phi, Delta Delta Delta. Address: 606 S Olive St Los Angeles CA 90014

NELSON, SUSAN CAROLYNNE, occupational therapist; b. Ontonagon, Mich., Mar. 23, 1932; d. Walter F. and Audrey C. (Peltier) Kerseg; B.S., U. Minn., 1953; m. David W. Nelson, Feb. 20, 1960; children—Barbara, Ross. Staff therapist Hines (Ill.) VA Hosp., 1953, Mary Free Bed Hosp., Grand Rapids, Mich., 1954; dir. occupational therapy Grand Rapids Assn. Blind, 1954-57; evaluator Rehab. Inst., Portland, Ore., 1958-60; dir. adult edn. Christian Edn. Center, Portland, 1968-71; cons. Crestview Hosp., Portland, 1970; cons. Clark Care Centers, Vancouver, Wash., 1971-74; cons. mentally retarded program Beaverton (Ore.) Sch. Dist., 1972-74, developmental specialist, 1974—. Bd. dirs. Edwards Activity Center for Retarded, Beaverton. Mem. Am., Ore. (chmn. legislative com. 1972-74) occupational therapy assns., World Fedn. Occupational Therapists, Am. Assn. Mental Deficiency, Kappa Delta. Address: 726 NW Skyline Crest Portland OR 97229

NELSON, THEODORA SOPHIA, educator; b. Phillips, Neb.; d. Johannes Andrew and Emma S. (Neander) Nelson; student York Coll., 1932; B.S. cum laude in Edn., Kearney State Coll., 1942; M.S., U. Ill., 1946; Ed.D. (Delta Kappa Gamma Rho State scholar 1956), U. Neb., 1959. Tchr. rural schs., Hamilton County, Neb., 1932-35; tchr. pub. schs., Aurora, Neb., 1936-40, Norfolk, 1940-41, Dannebrog, 1942-45; mem. faculty Kearney (Neb.) State Coll., 1946—, prof. math., 1961—. Mem. N.E.A., Am. Assn. U. Profs., Neb. Acad. Sci., Am. Assn. U. Women (treas. 1948-52, sec. 1946-47, 63-64, v.p. 1949-50, 59-60), Neb. (treas. 1948-52), Kearney State Coll. (pres. 1960-61) edn. assns., Am. Math. Assn., Nat. Council Tchrs. Math. (pres. Neb. sect. 1950-51, 59-60, 64-65), Delta Kappa Gamma (Neb. area rep. scholarships, chpt. pres. 1964-66, parliamentarian 1970-72), Pi Mu Epsilon, Kappa Mu Epsilon (charter; corr. sec. 1958-66). Mem. Evang. Free Ch. Am. (sec. 1970, treas. 1957-61, financial sec. 1961-69). Home: 622 W 25th St Kearney NE 68847

NELSON, VIRGINIA LEE (MRS. CARL J. NELSON), editor; b. Oakland, Ia., June 5, 1910; d. Rupert I. and Blanche (Allen) Lee; B.A., U. Ia., 1931; m. Carl J. Nelson, Aug. 4, 1934 (dec. Aug. 1966); 1 dau., Meredith (Mrs. Jon P. Hedrich). Researcher, Gallup Research Service, Chgo., 1931-34; with Carl J. Nelson Research Service, Chgo., 1940-73, owner, 1966-73. Mem Women in Communications. Author, editor Loyally, 1965. Editor: The Adelphean, Alpha Delta Pi, 1946-53, Northbrook Profile, Northbrook League Women Voters, 1951. Home 200 Ocean Lane Dr Key Biscayne FL 33149

NEMEC, JACQUELINE EVE, psychiatrist; b. Passaic, N.J., Dec. 11, 1937; d. Alois Joseph and Josephine Mary (Vican) Nemec; B.A. in Biology, N.Y. U., 1959; M.D., Woman's Med. Coll. Pa., 1963. Intern Mountainside Hosp., Montclair, N.J., 1963-64; resident Phila. Psychiat. Center, 1964-67; fellow in psychiatry Payne Whitney Clinic-Cornell Med. Sch., 1963; practice medicine specializing in psychiatry, Phila., 1967—; staff psychiatrist Community Mental Health Center Phila. Psychiatric Center, 1967-71; staff psychiatrist Student Health Center Temple U., Phila., 1969—; mem. staff Phila. Psychiat. Center; clin. instr. psychiatry Temple Med. Sch., Phila., 1970-72; cons. Thomas Jefferson U. Sch. Medicine, 1972—. Mem. Am. Assn. for Adolescent Psychiatry, Am. Med. Women's Assn. Home: 200 N Wynnewood Av Wynnewood PA 19096 Office: Beekman Pl Belmont Av Philadelphia PA 19131

NEMEYER, CAROL ANMUTH (MRS. SHELDON NEMEYER), assn. exec.; b. N.Y.C., Jan. 29, 1929; d. Archie Arnold and Betty Anmuth (Rosalin) Anmuth; student Queens Coll., 1945-46, Berea Coll., 1946-48; B.A., L.I. U., 1949; M.L.S., Columbia, 1962, D.Library Sci. (Higher Edn. Act fellow), 1971; m. Sheldon Nemeyer, Sept. 23, 1950. Reference, cataloging librarian McGraw-Hill, Inc., N.Y.C., 1962-64, asst. librarian, 1964-68; sr. asso. Assn. Am. Pubs., Inc., N.Y.C., 1971—. Research dir. Nat. Book Com., N.Y.C., 1971; cons. Library of Congress, 1971. Recipient Esther J. Piercy award A.L.A., 1972; Officers grant Council on Library Resources, Inc., 1970-71. Mem. Am. (mem. council 1973—), N.Y. library assns., Spl. Libraries Assn., Am. Soc. for Information Sci., N.Y. Tech. Services Librarians (v.p. 1973-74, pres. 1974—), Beta Phi Mu (chpt. pres. 1969-70). Author: Scholarly Reprint Publishing in the United States, 1972; (with Cora Paul Bomar and M. Ann Heidbreder Guide to the Development of Educational Media Selection Centers, 1973. Contbr. articles to profl. jours. Home: 415 W 23d St New York City NY 10011 Office: One Park Av New York City NY 10016

NEMIR, ROSA LEE (MRS. ELIAS J. AUDI), physician; b. Waco, Tex., July 16, 1905; d. David and Emma Shakir (Damyanos) Nemir; A.B., U. Tex., 1926; M.D., Johns Hopkins U., 1930; D.Sc. (hon.), Colgate U.; m. Elias J. Audi, July 24, 1934; children—Elaine Katherine (Mrs. Daniel L. Macken), Alfred J., Robert N. Instr. pediatrics N.Y. U. Med. Coll., 1933-39, asst. prof. 1939-50, asso. prof., 1950, prof. 1958—, asso. prof. pediatrics Postgrad. Med. Coll., 1950-53, prof. 1953—; lectr. Bellevue Sch. Nursing, 1934-49; asst. vis. pediatrician Bellevue Hosp., Children's Med. Service, 1937-46, asso. vis. pediatrician, 1946-60, vis. pediatrician, 1960—, dir. Children's Chest Service, 1960, dir. Children's Chest Clinic, 1961; attending pediatrician Univ. Hosp., 1950—; attending pediatrician Gouverneur Hosp., 1950-59, cons., 1959-61; vis. prof. Microbiology Coll. Phys. and Surg., Columbia U. Coll. Medicine, 1958-59; cons. staff N.Y. Infirmary, 1954-66, dir. pediatric edn. 1966-72, attending pediatrician, 1967-72; med. dir. Judson Health Center, N.Y.C., 1946-66, trustee, 1963-74. Bd. dirs. Univ. Hosp., Greater N.Y. chpt. A.R.C.; mem. med. bd. Irvington House of Cardiac Child, Irvington-on-Hudson, 1951-57; bd. dirs. Am. Middle East Rehab., 1964-70, mem. med. com., 1971—; bd. dirs. Bklyn. Kindergarten Soc., Willoughby House Settlement, Women's Com. for Boston Symphony Orch., Bklyn., Am. Ped. Soc., Friends Sch. (chmn. program com.); mem. com. for debutante cotillion Xmas Ball for N.Y. Infirmary; mem. bd. intercollegiate br. YMCA, 1954-59, vice-chmn. Med. Students Club, 1954-56, chmn., 1959-60; mem. panel of expert examiners of N.Y.C. Personnel, 1951, 54-55. Recipient citations for 25 and 35 years service N.Y. U. Med. Sch.; named Woman of Year, Women's Med. Soc. N.Y. State, 1973; decorated officer Order of Cedars, Republic of Lebanon, 1968. Diplomate Am. Bd. Pediatrics. Fellow Am. Coll. Chest Physicians (chmn. com. cardiopulmonary diseases in children 1973); mem. Am. Acad. Med. Scis., A.M.A., Am. Thoracic Soc., Am. Women's Med. Assn. (1st v.p. 1960-61, chmn. student loan fellowship and grants com. 1961, pres. 1964, Elizabeth Blackwell award 1970), Med. Women's Internat. Assn. (v.p. N.Am. 1970), N.Y. Acad. Medicine, Soc. for Pediatric Research, Am. Pediatric Soc., Am. Acad. Pediatrics, Am. Soc. Adolescent Medicine. Contbr. articles on pneumonia, Tb, nutrition, virology, chest diseases to profl. jours. Home: 7 Monroe Pl Brooklyn NY 11201 Office: NYU Medical Center 550 1st Av New York City NY 10016

NEMIRO, BEVERLY MIRIUM ANDERSON (MRS. JEROME NEMIRO), writer; b. St. Paul, May 29, 1925; d. Martin and Anna Mae (Oshanyk) Anderson; student Reed Coll., 1943-44; B.A., U. Colo., 1947; postgrad. U. Denver; m. Jerome Morton Nemiro, Feb 10, 1951; children—Guy Samuel, Lee Anna, Dee Martin. Tchr., Seattle pub. schs., 1945-46; fashion coordinator, dir. Denver Dry Goods Co., 1948-51; free lance fashion model, 1951-58; fashion dir. Denver Market Week Assn., 1952-53; moderator TV program Your Preschool Child, 1955-56; free lance writer gen. articles and cookery books articles, 1958—; tchr. U. Colo. at Denver, 1970—. Active Denver Art Museum, Denver Zool. Found., Denver Lyric Opera Guild, Denver Symphony Group, Children's Hosp. Assn.; pres. Denver Jr. Symphony Guild, 1959-60. Recipient Top Hand award Colo. Authors' League, 1969, 72; named one of Colo.'s women of year, Denver Post, 1964. Mem. Colo. Authors League (dir. 1969—), Denver Women's Press Club, Authors Guild, Authors League Am., U. Denver Woman's Library Assn., Colo. Women's Coll. Library Assn., Kappa Alpha Theta. Author: The Complete Book of High Altitude Baking, 1961; Colorado a la Carte, 1963; The Lunch Box Cookbook, 1965; Colorado a la Carte, Series II, 1966; Where to Eat in Colorado, 1967; The High Altitude Cookbook, 1969; The Busy People's Cookbook (Better Homes and Gardens Book Club selection 1971), 1971. Contbr. articles periodicals, newspapers. Home: 476 Westwood Dr Denver CO 80206

NEMMER, MARY CHRISTINE, educator; b. Milw., June 8, 1912; d. Louis and Emma H. (Paulmann) Nemmer; B.S., Loyola U., Chgo., 1942; M.S., Marquette U., 1947; Ph.D., St. Louis U., 1953. Tchr. elementary and secondary schs., Chgo., also Milw., Winsted, Minn.; mem. faculty, biology dept. Alverno Coll., Milw., 1943—, chmn. biology dept., 1961-67, asso. prof. microbiology, 1958—, serials and sci. reference librarian, 1970—. Mem. Am., Wis. library assns., Am. Soc. Microbiology. Address: 3401 S 39th St Milwaukee WI 53215

NEMSER, CINDY HELLER (MRS. CHARLES NEMSER), editor, author, critic; b. Bklyn., Mar. 26, 1937; d. William and Helen (Nelson) Heller; B.A., Bklyn. Coll., 1958, M.A. in English, 1964; M.A. in Art History, N.Y. U., 1966; m. Charles Nemser, Dec. 16, 1956; 1 dau., Cathy. Tchr., N.Y.C. Sch. System, 1958-64; curatorial intern Mus. Modern Art, N.Y.C., 1966; pub., editor Feminist Art Jour., 1972—; contbg. editor Art Mag., 1972—; art critic Changes, 1972. Guest lectr. N.Y. U., U. Wis., Pratt Inst., R.I. U., others; cons. Phila. Focuses on Women in Visual Arts; curator exhbn. In Her Own Image, Fleisher Art Meml., Phila., 1974, Woman's Work-Am. Art: 1974, Mus. Phila. Civic Center. Mem. Coll. Art Assn. (coordinator sessions on women and the art world). Author: Art Talk: Conversations with Women Artists, 1975. Contbr. to Artform, Art in America, Art Jour., others. Home: 41 Montgomery Pl Brooklyn NY 11215

NEMY, ENID (MRS. S. RALPH COHEN), journalist; b. Winnipeg, Man., Can.; d. Benjamin and Frances (Horowitz) Nemy; student United Coll., U. Man., 1943; m. S. Ralph Cohen, Aug. 31, 1951. Came to U.S., 1963. With Canadian Press News Service, 1943-48; feature broadcasting Canadian Broadcasting Corp., 1943-48; parliamentary reporter Bermuda Mid-Ocean News, Hamilton, 1948-50; reporter, feature writer N.Y. Times, N.Y.C., 1963—. Home: 1040 Park Av New York City NY 10028 Office: NY Times 229 W 43rd St New York City NY 10036

NENZEL, PATRICIA HIGH (MRS. CHARLES W. NENZEL), retail store exec.; b. Rocky Mount, N.C., Jan. 30, 1931; d. Robie Jackson and Elizabeth (Bullouck) High; student Va. Commonwealth U., nights 1952-53; m. Charles W. Nenzel, May 31, 1958. Buyer Miller & Rhoads Dept. Store, Richmond, Va., 1955-58; buyer Flair Inc., Richmond, 1960-68, mdse. mgr., 1968-72, v.p., 1972—. Mem. Am. Bus. Women's Assn. (v.p. Hugenot chpt. 1972). Club: Willow Oakes Country (Richmond). Home: 4544 Arrowhead Rd Richmond VA 23235 Office: 5th and Grace Sts Richmond VA 23219

NESBIN, ESTHER WINTER (MRS. ANTHONY T. NESBIN), librarian; b. Denver, Aug. 5, 1910; d. Oscar A. and Helen (Schmandt) Winter; B.A., U. Buffalo, 1931; m. Anthony T. Nesbin, Sept. 21, 1946 (dec. Sept. 1957). Library reference asst. Grosvenor Library, Buffalo, 1931-42; instr. library sci. U. Buffalo, 1939-42; librarian Temple of Jewelled Cross, Los Angeles, 1942-46; librarian, instr. library sci. Palomar Coll., San Marcos, Cal., 1947-65, head dept. library sci. 1962-65, dir. library services, 1965-68, asst. dean instrn. library services, 1969—. Cons., Palo Verde Jr. Coll. Library, 1957, Monterey Jr. Coll. Library, 1958, Camp Pendleton Law Library, 1964. Mem. Cal. State adv. com. Library Tech. Program, 1967—. Mem. Cal. Library Assn., Cal. Assn. Sch. Libraries, Delta Kappa Gamma, Palomar Cactus and Succulent Soc. (pres. 1958-60). Club: Escondido Garden. Home: PO Box 102 San Marcos CA 92069

NESBIT, PHYLLIS SCHNEIDER (MRS. PETER N. NESBIT), lawyer; b. New Kirk, Okla., Sept. 21, 1919; d. Vernon Lee and Irma Mae (Biddle) Schneider; B.S. in Chemistry, U. Ala., 1948, LL.B., 1958; m. Peter N. Nesbit, Sept. 14, 1939. Draftsman, Drydock & Shipbldg. Co., Mobile, Ala., 1942-45; tech. sec. B. F. Goodrich Co., Tuscaloosa, Ala., 1949-55; sec. Ala. Bus. Research Council, University, 1955-58; admitted to Ala. bar, 1958; partner firm Wilters, Brantley & Nesbit, Robertsdale, Ala., 1958—; judge Municipal Ct., Daphne, Ala. Sec., Daphne Civic Assn., 1962—; treas. Joint Legislative Council Ala., 1972-73. Mem. Ala. State Bar, Baldwin County Bar Assn. (pres. 1967-68), Nat. Assn. Women Lawyers, Ala. Women's Lawyers Assn. (pres. 1966-67), Ala. Municipal Judges Assn. (pres. 1970-73), Am. Judicature Soc., Bus. and Profl. Womens Club (pres. 1974-75), Gamma Sigma Epsilon. Mem. Order Eastern Star (worthy matron 1963-64). Home: 411 Church St Daphne AL 36526 Office: Wilters Brantley & Nesbit Box 555 Robertsdale AL 36567

NESBITT, MARGOT LORD, real estate broker, fine arts appraiser; b. Tonbridge, Kent, Eng., Feb. 13, 1927; d. Douglas G.R. and Octave (Waghorne) Lord; came to U.S., 1930, naturalized, 1937; B.A. in English Lit., U. Okla., 1950, B.F.A. in Art History, 1970, M.A., 1974; m. Charles Nesbitt, June 6, 1948; children—Nancy Margot, Douglas Charles, Carolyn Jane. Real estate broker, appraiser fine arts, Oklahoma City, 1968—. Mem. Okla. Arts and Humanities Council, 1971—; mem. women's com. Olka. City Symphony, 1964—; life mem. Okla. Art Center, women's bd., 1962-63. Bd. dirs. Okla. Found. for Disabled. Mem. English Speaking Union, Okla. Hist. Soc., Hist. Preservation Oklahoma City, Am. Soc. Appraisers (sr.), Kappa Alpha Theta (pres. alumni chpt. 1962-64, Okla. chmn. Theta Link 1965-66). Democrat. Episcopalian (treas. assemblies 1971-72, mem. women's bd. 1971-72, treas. altar guild 1972-73). Clubs: Connoisseur (pres. 1956-57); Early American Glass (treas. 1973-74). Address: 1703 N Hudson St Oklahoma City OK 73103

NESBITT, ROSEMARY SINNETT (MRS. GEORGE R. NESBITT), educator; b. Syracuse, N.Y., Oct. 12, 1924; d. Matthew A. and Mary Louise (Kane) Sinnett; B.S. magna cum laude, Syracuse U., 1947, M.A., 1952; m. George R. Nesbitt, June 18, 1955; children—Mary, Anne, George R., Elizabeth. Instr. speech Wells Coll., Aurora, N.Y., 1949-52, Syracuse U., 1952-57; asso. prof. speech and theatre State U. N.Y. at Oswego, 1965—, dir. children's theatre, 1969—. Cons., lectr. pub. schs., N.Y., 1965—. Bd. dirs. Oswego YMCA, 1964-65, Newman Found., 1970-71, Oswego Heritage Found., 1963-69; mem. exec. bd. Syracuse Diocese Cath. Edn., 1968-71. Recipient Avila award Cath. Action, Syracuse U. Thomas More Found., 1956; N.Y. State Yorker award, 1969, Distinguished N.Y. State Author's award Friends of Reading of Syracuse Pub. Library, 1970, State U. N.Y. Chancellor's award for distinguished teaching, 1973. Mem. Oswego County Hist. Soc. (dir. 1970-71), Zonta Club, Am. Assn. U. Women, Alpha Psi Omega, Alpha Epsilon Rho, Zeta Phi Eta. Author: The Great Rope, 1968; Colonel Meacham's Giant Cheese, 1971. Home: 119 W Fourth St Oswego NY 13126

NESLER, SALLY SUTHERLAND (MRS. JOEL THOMAS NESLER), social worker; b. Mayfield, Ky., Aug. 29, 1946; d. Jack Foster and Hazel Eura (Brooks) Sutherland; student Transylvania Coll., 1964-65; B.A., U. Ky., 1968; M.A., Murray State U., 1971, postgrad., 1972—; m. Joel Thomas Nesler, Dec. 23, 1968; 1 son, Joel Thomas. Social worker Western Ky. Regional Mental Health Adv. Bd., Mayfield, 1969-70; social worker J.U. Kevil Mental Health-Mental Retardation Found., Mayfield, 1970-71, vocational evaluator, 1972—; tchr. Graves County Sch., Mayfield, 1971-72. Chmn. health and welfare Mayfield-Graves County Jr. Welfare League, Inc., 1973. Bd. dirs. Graves County Young Dems., 1973. Trustee Ellen Foster Meml. Scholarship Fund, Mayfield. Mem. Am. Assn. Mental Deficiency, Mayfield-Graves County Assn. for Retarded Children, Ky., Western Ky. personal and guidance assns., Nat., Ky. rehab. assns., Ky. Assn. Vocational Evaluators and Work Adjustment Specialists, Delta Delta Delta. Mem. Christian Ch. Home: Rural Route 6 Mayfield KY 42066 Office: South 10th St Mayfield KY 42066

NESMITH, WANDA KAY CRAWFORD (MRS. QUINTON NESMITH), ednl. adminstr.; b. Alamo, Ga., Dec. 25, 1951; d. Carl Joseph and Johnnie Ruth (Gillis) Crawford; A.A. summa cum laude, Brewton Park Coll., 1971; m. Quinton NeSmith, July 25, 1969. Bus. mgr. Brewton Park Coll., Mt. Vernon, Ga., 1969—. Methodist. Home: Route 2 Glenwood GA 30428 Office: Brewton Parker Coll Mount Vernon GA 30445

NESOM, EVE, architect; b. San Angelo, Tex., May 18, 1932; d. Charles Scott and Willie Leone (Flippen) Nesom; student U. Tex. at Arlington, 1949-51; B.Arch., Tex. Technol. U., 1955. Architect with firm Kern Smith, Carlsbad, N.M., 1955-57, Robert Alexander, Dallas, 1957-58, George L. Dahl, Dallas, 1958-62, 68-69, VA, Washington, 1962-64, Austin Co., Houston, 1965-68, Wheeler & Stefoniak, Dallas, 1969; with Pratt, Box, Henderson & Partners, Dallas, 1969—, asso., coordinating architect, 1973—. Home: 3320 Hudnall #176 Dallas TX 75235 Office: 3526 Cedar Springs Rd Dallas TX 75219

NESS, EVALINE (MRS. ARNOLD A. BAYARD), artist; b. Union City, O.; d. Albert and Myrtle Woods (Carter) Michelow; student Muncie State Tchrs. Coll., Art Inst. Chgo., Art Students League, N.Y.C., Corcoran Art Sch., Accedemia di Belle Arti, Rome, Italy; m. Arnold A. Bayard, Nov. 25, 1959. Mag., advt. and fashion illustrator, 1950-60; illustrator children's books, 1960—. Faculty, Parsons Sch. Design, N.Y.C. Recipient 1st prize for painting Corcoran Art Gallery. Author, illustrator: Pavo and the Princess; Exactly Alike; Josefina February; Gift for Sula Sula; Double Discovery, 1965; Sam, Bangs and Moonshine, 1967 (Caldecott award); The Girl and the Goatherd; Do You Have The Time, Lydia?; Yeck Eck. Address: 2160 Ibis Isle Rd Palm Beach FL 33480

NESTER, VIRGINIA EVELYN, social worker; b. London, Ky., Aug. 3, 1941; d. Ralph K. and Ella (Johnson) Nester; student Sue Bennett Jr. Coll., 1960-61; A.B., U. Ky., 1964; M.Ed., U. Louisville, 1968, M.S. in Social Work, 1974. Vocational counselor Dept. Econ. Security, Div. Employment Service, Corbin, Ky., 1965-67, counseling technician, Frankfort, Ky., 1967-69; field rep. Ky. Commn. on Children and Youth, Frankfort, 1969-72, asst. dir., 1972-74; asst. dir. Office for Council Affairs Dept. Human Resources, 1974—. Mem. Am. Personnel and Guidance Assn., Ky. Personnel and Guidance Assn., Ky. Welfare Assn., Council of So. Mountains, Nat. Council Social Welfare, Nat. Children's Lobby, Common Cause, Alpha Delta Pi. Club: Alumni (U. Louisville). Home: 970-3 Leawood Sq Frankfort KY 40601 Office: State Capitol Annex Frankfort KY 40601

NETHERTON, JEAN CAROL MCINTYRE (MRS. CLIFFORD L. NETHERTON), ednl. adminstr.; b. Chgo., Mar. 22, 1932; d. Robert Andrew and Ruth Virginia (Forbes) McIntyre; B.S., U. Ark., 1953; M.S., U. Ill., 1955; Ph.D., Mich. State U., 1966; m. Clifford L. Netherton, June 17, 1967. Tchr., Portage (Ind.) Twp. Schs., 1953-54; instr. Ala. Coll., Montevallo, 1954; grad. asst. U. Ill., Urbana, 1954-55; instr. Mich. State U., East Lansing, 1955-67; asst. prof. U. Md., College Park, 1967-68; asso. prof. phys. edn. No. Va. Community Coll., Annandale, 1968-70, coordinator instructional services, 1970—. Sec. Adv. Com. of Deans of Instrn., 1972-74. Mem. Nat. Assn. Ednl. Broadcasters, Am. Assn. Higher Edn., Assn. Communications and Ednl. Tech., Assn. for Supervision and Curriculum Devel., A.A.H.P.E.R. Home: 448 Springvale Rd Great Falls VA 22066 Office: 8333 Little River Turnpike Annadale VA 22066

NETHERTON, NAN (ANN LOUISE) ROHRKE (MRS. ROSS DEWITT NETHERTON, JR.), PSEUDONYM ANNE BULLARD), historian; b. Chgo., July 30, 1925; d. Lloyd Ernest and Helen (Bullard) Rohrke; Ph.B., U. Chgo., 1947; m. Ross DeWitt Netherton, Jr., May 10, 1947; children—David Ross, Richard Bruce, Nancy Patricia. Supr., Ford, Bacon & Davis, Oak Ridge, 1944-45, Carbide & Carbon, Oak Ridge, 1945-46; service rep. Ill. Bell Telephone Co., Chgo., 1946-48; columnist, feature writer Fairfax-Falls Church Sun-Echo, 1952-55; with Globe Newspapers, Fairfax County, Va., 1957-59; salesman Lord & Taylor, Falls Church, Va., 1965; historic research supr., Div. Planning, Fairfax, Va., 1969—; feature writer Va. Cardinal, Vienna, 1971—. Pres. Symphony Womens Assn., 1968-69; del. Old Dominion Symphony Council, 1967-69; sec. Pimmit Hills Citizens Assn., 1953-54; sec. Fairfax County Fedn. Citizens Assns., 1954-56. Bd. dirs., sec. Freedom Park, Inc., 1954-55; bd. dirs. Fairfax County Cultural Assn., 1965, Fairfax County Symphony Orch., 1964-68. Recipient cup award as citizen of yr. Washington Evening Star, 1957. Mem. Soc. Archtl. Historians, Am. Assn. for State and Local History, Pioneer Am. Soc., Nat. Trust for Historic Preservation, Fairfax Heritage Soc., Hist. Soc. Fairfax County. Author: (with E.L. Templeman) Northern Virginia Heritage, 1966; (with Ross DeWitt Netherton, Jr.), Green Spring Farm, 1970. Editor: Civic-Government Handbook, Fairfax County Fedn. Citizens Assn., 1957, Community and Arts Directory, Fairfax County Cultural Assn., 1965. Home: 7703 Erie St Annandale VA 22003 Office: 4100 Chain Bridge Rd Fairfax VA 22030

NETZER, LANORE A., educator; b. Laona, Wis., Aug. 27, 1916; d. Henry N. and Julia M. (Niquette) Netzer; B.S., Oshkosh State Tchrs. Coll., 1943; M.S., U. Wis., 1948, Ph.D., 1951. Tchr. one room rural sch. Goldhorn Sch., Pound, Wis., 1935-36; tchr., prin. Goldfield Graded Sch., Pound, 1936-39, Spruce (Wis.) Grade Sch., 1939-41; tchr. McKinley Elementary Sch., Neenah, Wis., 1943-46; critic tchr. Oshkosh (Wis.) State Tchrs. Coll., 1946-48; instr., supr. student teaching Milw. State Tchrs. Coll., 1950-56; asso. prof. edn. U. Wis.-Milw., 1956-63; prof. ednl. adminstrn. U. Wis.-Madison, 1963—. Active Wis. U. Hosps. Vol. Service. Mem. Am. Assn. Sch. Adminstrs., Am., Wis. assns. edn. research devel., Nat., Wis. (exec. bd. 1953-56) assns. for student teaching, Nat., Wis. edn. assns., Nat., Wis. elementary sch. prins. assns., Wis. Alumni Assn., Phi Beta Sigma, Kappa Delta Pi, Pi Lambda Theta. Author: Industry Aids for Use in Schools, 1951; (with others) Supervision of Instruction: A Phase of Administration, 1965, 71; Interdisciplinary Foundations of Supervision, 1970; Education, Adminstration and Change, 1970; (with Glen G. Eye) School Administration and Instruction, 1969. Contbr. articles to profl. jours. Home: 3009 University Av Madison WI 53705

NEUBERGER, KATHERINE (MRS. HARRY H. NEUBERGER), mem. Republican Nat. Com.; b. N.Y.C., Apr. 30, 1907; d. Samuel and Elsie (Wallach) Kridel; B.A., Barnard Coll., 1927; postgrad. Columbia, 1932-33; LL.D., Montclair State Coll., 1972, Monmouth Coll., 1973; m. Harry H. Neuberger, Mar. 7, 1929; children—Susan (Mrs. Donald M. Wilson), Joan (Mrs. Henry M. Woodhouse). Vice pres., bd. mgrs. N.J. Reformatory for Women, 1940-57; mem. N.J. Law Enforcement Council, 1952-57, chmn., 1954-57; mem. N.J. Bd. Higher Edn., 1970—, vice chmn., 1972—; Trustee Fairleigh Dickinson U., 1973—; bd. dirs. Monmouth County Orgn. Social Service, 1937-59, Family Service Soc, Monmouth County, 1959—; chmn. Home Service Corps, Monmouth County chpt. A.R.C., 1940-46; bd. dirs. Assn. Aid Crippled Children, 1949—. Pres. N.J. Fedn. Republican Women, 1957-61, mem. exec. bd. Nat. Fedn., 1959-61; now mem. Rep. Nat. Com. for N.J. Mem. Am. Assn. U. Women. Episcopalian. Club: Cosmopolitan (N.Y.C.). Home: 628 Middletown-Lincroft Rd Lincroft NJ 07738 Office: 28 W State St Trenton NJ 08608

NEUBERGER, MIRIAM, civic worker; b. Treves, Germany, Apr. 22, 1920; d. Max and Ella (Schapira) Goldstein; student U. Berne, (Switzerland), 1946; diploma Sch. Modern Photography, N.Y.C., 1947; diploma Ecole Photo et Cinema, Paris, 1951; m. Kurt J. Neuberger, Nov. 29, 1951; children—Orah, Daliah. Came to U.S., 1937, naturalized, 1944. Auditor, Grayson Shops Inc., N.Y.C., 1939-44; auditor, interpreter, translator, intelligence analyst Nurenberg Trials, 1944-46; free-lance photographer, Europe and Middle East, 1949-52; art cons., 1966. Br. editor Israel chmn., treas. Women's League Conservative Judaism No. Cal., 1967—; v.p. United Synagogue Youth Commn., 1965-69; pres. sisterhood Congregation Ner Tamid, 1972-73; vice pres. Women's Overseas Service League, 1973; chmn. UNICEF, 1968-72. Served with WAC, 1944-46. Mem. Women's Army Corps Vets. (dir. 1958—). Mem. B'nai B'rith Women (dir. 1973—, v.p. 1974-75), Internat. Order Foresters. Address: 4018 Pacheco St San Francisco CA 94116

NEUBERT, MARY ELLEN, chemist; b. Jeannette, Pa., Apr. 28, 1939; d. Walter Henry and Georgianna (Wagner) Neubert; B.S., U. Pitts., 1961; Ph.D., U. Rochester, 1968. Jr. research chemist Bristol Labs., Syracuse, N.Y., 1961-63, sr. research chemist, 1968-71; research asso. dept. biol. chemistry Wash. U. Sch. Medicine, St. Louis, 1971-72; postdoctoral fellow, liquid crystal inst. Kent State U., (O.) 1972-74, research asso., 1974—. Mem. Am. Chem. Soc., Chem. Soc. (London), Sigma Xi. Contbr. articles in field to profl. jours. Home: 811 Hollywood Circle Cuyahoga Falls OH 44221 Office: Liquid Crystal Institute Kent State University Kent OH 44242

NEUFELD, DOROTHY HARBIN (MRS. MARION C. NEUFELD), home economist; b. Farmers Branch, Tex., Apr. 24, 1926; d. Elom Edwin and Sallie Mae (Long) Harbin; B.S. in Home Econs. Edn., Tex. Tech. Coll., 1950; postgrad. Okla. State U., 1952-54, Colo. State U., 1954-56; M.S. in Family Econs., Kan. State U., 1964; m. Marion C. Neufeld, Nov. 23, 1956. Home service adviser Southwestern Pub. Service Co., Plainview, Tex., Clovis, N.M. and Guymon, Okla., 1950-51; county extension home demonstration agt. Tex. Coop. Extension Service, Post, 1951-52, Vega and Channing, Tex., 1955-56, Okla. Coop. Extension Service, Guymon, 1952-55; county extension home economist Kan. Coop. Extension Service, Larned, Iola and Garden City, 1957-62, area home mgmt. specialist, 1962-69, area extension home economist, 1969—; asst. prof. home econs. Kan. State U., 1965-73, asso. prof., 1973—. Mem. Kan. Extension Home Economist Assn. (treas. 1960-62), Kan. Home Econs. Assn. (sec. 1965-67), Bus. and Profl. Womens Club, Am. Assn. U. Women, Concerned Citizens for Aging, Epsilon Sigma Phi. Home: Box 941 Garden City KS 67846 Office: 1501 Fulton Terrace Garden City KS 67846

NEUFELD, EVELYN MAY (MRS. HERMAN NEUFELD), educator; b. nr. Saskatoon, Sask., Can., June 10, 1931; d. John and Elizabeth (Ewert) Gossen; came to U.S., 1956; naturalized, 1961; B.A., San Jose State U., 1961; M.A., U. Cal. at Berkeley, 1968, Ed.D., 1972; m. Herman Neufeld, Aug. 25, 1951; 1 son, Dean William. Tchr., Santa Clara, Cal., 1961-69; asso. prof. dept. elementary edn. San Jose (Cal.) State U., 1969—. Tchr. lab sch. U. Cal. at Berkeley, 1965; European Study Tour dir., 1972; cons. in Piagetian philosophy and early childhood edn., 1964—. Bd. dirs. Frances Gulland Children's Center, San Jose, 1972—. Mem. Nat. Council Tchrs. Math., Cal. Math Council., Internat. Reading Assn., Nat. Assn. Edn. of Young Children. Author: (with James S. Lucas) Picture Graphs; Think and Color; Number-Blox; Developing Number Experiences: also chpt. in Psychological Foundations, 1974. Home: 14187 Sobey Meadows St Saratoga CA 95070 Office: Dept Elementary Education San Jose State University San Jose CA 95192

NEUFELD, HERMINIA MARTINEZ banker; b. Havana, Cuba, Nov. 21, 1944; d. Carlos Manuel and Amelia Herminia (Santana) Martinez; student Salem Coll., 1961-62; B.A. with honors, Am. U., 1965; M.S. in Fgn. Service (Univ. fellow), Georgetown U., 1967; student Nat. U. Mexico, summers 1963, 64. Came to U.S., 1960, naturalized, 1972. Prof. Spanish, George Mason Coll. U. Va., Fairfax, 1967-68; researcher internat. trade div. and indsl. econ. div. Internat. Bank for Reconstrn. and Devel. (World Bank), Washington, 1967-69, economist econs. indsl. devel. div., 1969-71, loan officer C.Am. div. and Caribbean dept., 1971-72, C.Am. div., Latin Am. and Caribbean regional office, 1972-73, Mexico and Venezuela div., Latin Am., Caribbean regional office, 1973—. Mem. Am. Econ. Assn., Soc. for Internat. Devel., Brookings Instn. Latin Am. Discussion Group. Contbg. author Economic Growth of Colombia: Problems and Prospects, 1972. Home: 3000 Spout Run Pkwy Arlington VA 22201 Office: 1818 H St Washington DC 20433

NEUGARTEN, BERNICE LEVIN, educator; b. Norfolk, Neb., Feb. 11, 1916; d. David L. and Sadie (Segall) Levin; B.A., U. Chgo., 1936; M.A., 1937, Ph.D., 1943; m. Fritz Neugarten, July 1, 1940; children—Dail Ann, Jerrold. Research asst. dept. edn. U. Chgo., 1937-39; fellow Am. Council on Edn., 1939-41; instr. psychology Englewood Coll., Chgo., 1941-43; sr. guidance editor Nat. Forum. Inc., Chgo., 1945-46; research asso. Com. on Human Devel., U. Chgo., 1948-50, asst. prof., 1951-60, asso. prof., 1960-64, prof., 1964—, chmn., 1969-73. Mem. Council U. Chgo. Senate, 1968-71, 72—, chmn. council com. on univ. women, 1969-70. Mem. tech. com. research and demonstration White House Conf. on Aging, 1971; tech. adv. com. on aging research Dept. Health, Edn. and Welfare, 1972-73. Fellow A.A.A.S., Am. Psychol. Assn. (council reps. 1967-69, 73—), Am. Social Assn., Gerontological Soc. (pres. 1968-69, Kleemeier award for research in aging 1971); mem. Sigma Xi, Pi Lambda Theta. Author: (with R. J. Havighurst) American Indian and White Children: A Social-Psychological Investigation, 1955; Society and Education, 1957, rev., 1974, Personality in Middle and Late Life, 1964; co-author: Adjustment to Retirement, 1969; Social Status in the City, 1971. Editor: Middle Age and Aging, 1968. Asso. editor Jour. Gerontology 1958-61, Human Devel., 1962-68. Contbr. chpts. to books, articles to profl. jours. Home: 5801 Dorchester Av Chicago IL 60637

NEUHALFEN, SISTER CELINE MARIE, hosp. adminstr.; b. Hartington, Neb., Jan. 23, 1932; d. Anthony J. and Veronica E. (Gubbels) Neuhalfen; B.S. in Edn., Alverno Coll., 1964; M.B. in Adminstrn., Xavier U., 1967. Tchr., Madonna Sch., Richland Center, Wis., 1954-61, St. oniface Sch., Elgin, Neb., 1961-64; adminstr. Waupun (Wis.) Meml. Hosp., 1967—. Bd. dirs. Beaver Dam (Wis.) Community Hosp.; pres. bd. dirs. Wis. Conf. Cath. Hosps., Madison, 1973-74; pres. adv. bd. Operating Room Assts., Park Maraine Tech. Instn., Fond du Lac, Wis., 1971-74; dir. area bd. Wis. Heart Assn., Madison, 1973-74, St. Joseph Parish Council, Waupun, 1973-74, Health Agy. Council Provincal Bd., Milw., 1968-74. Mem. Am. Coll. Hosp. Adminstrs., Am., Wis., Cath. hosp. assns. Club: College (Waupun, Wis.). Home: 617 W Main St Waupun WI 53963 Office: 620 W Brown St Waupun WI 53963

NEUHOFER, SISTER M. DOROTHY, librarian; b. St. Joseph, Fla., June 19, 1931; d. Joseph Peter and Helen Frances (Barthle) Neuhofer; B.S. in Edn. magna cum laude, Barry Coll., 1964; M.A. in L.S., Rosary Coll., 1965. Tchr. elementary grades Fla. parochial schs., 1951-59; tchr., prin. Epiphany Cath. Sch., Venice, Fla., 1959-63; reference librarian St. Leo (Fla.) Coll., 1965-67, dir. readers' Services library, 1967—; prioress Holy Name Priory, 1972—. Mem. Am., Fla., Cath. (chmn. book week com. Fla. unit 1968-70) library assns., Am. Benedictine Acad. (sec. library sect. 1969-71; chmn. library sect. 1972—; dir. 1972—). Editor: Library World St. Leo Coll., 1965-69, Union List Cath. Periodicals, 1968. Home: Holy Name Priory San Antonio FL 33576 Office: St Leo Coll Library St Leo FL 33574

NEUMAN, DEANNE ELAINE, editor; b. Webster City, Ia., June 20, 1945; d. Bernard John and Palma Merle (Lande) Neuman; B.A. with honors in Journalism and Polit. Sci., U. Ia., 1967. Asst. editor Internat. Trade Reporter, publ. Bur. Nat. Affairs, Inc., 1967-68, mng. editor, 1968—. Mem. Women in Communication, Inc. Democrat. Club: Nat. Press (Washington). Contbg. editor Biomed. News, 1971—, Grolier Ency. Year Book, 1971, 72. Home: 2853 Ontario Rd NW Washington DC 20009 Office: 1231 25th St NW Washington DC 20037

NEUMAN, FAY ZENO (MRS. PAUL NEUMAN, JR.), former advt. and public relations exec.; b. N.Y.C., July 29, 1946; d. David and Helen (Schell) Zeno; B.F.A., Hunter Coll., 1967; m. Paul Neuman, Jr., June 13, 1972. Copywriter, Cin. Enquirer, 1969-71; dir. pub. relations L.M. Sive & Assos., Inc., Cin., 1971-72; advt. and publicity copywriter Clopay Corp., Cin., 1972-74. Recipient Drummer award for best sales aid Bldg. Supply News mag., 1973, award for merchandising Krafts Foods, 1970, Addy awards 5th dist. Am. Advt. Fedn., 1970, marketing citation Mattel Co., 1969, award Stouffer Co., 1971, low cost cookery-campaign award Hunt-Wesson Foods, 1970, promotional award Advt. Execs. Assn. Ohio Daily Newspapers, Ohio Classified Clinic, 1970. Home: 560 Winters Lane Cold Spring KY 41076

NEUMAN, NANCY ADAMS MOSSHAMMER (MRS. MARK DONALD NEUMAN), civic leader; b. Greenwich, Conn., July 24, 1936; d. Alden Smith and Margaret (Mevis) Mosshammer; B.A., Pomona Coll., 1957; M.A., U. Cal. at Berkeley, 1961; m. Mark Donald Neuman, Dec. 23, 1958; children—Deborah Adams, Jennifer Fuller, Jeffrey Abbott. Pres. Lewisburg (Pa.) area League women Voters, 1967-70; bd. dirs. League Women Voters Pa., 1970—; mem. Pa. Gov.'s Commn. on Mortgage and Interest Rates, 1973, Pa. Commonwealth Child Devel. Com., 1974—. Bd. dirs. Housing Assistance Council, Inc., Washington, 1974—, Nat. Council on Agrl. Life and Labor, 1974—. Home: RD 1 Box 132 Lewisburg PA 17837

NEUMANN, CHARLOTTE GRANTZ (MRS. ALFRED K. NEUMANN), physician; b. N.Y.C., July 20, 1929; d. William and Adele (Glotzer) Grantz; A.B., Harvard, 1950, M.D., 1954, M.P.H., 1960; m. Alfred Kurt Neumann, Sept. 11, 1959; children—Frederick, Peter, Daniel. Intern Children's Hosp. Med. Center, Boston, 1954-55; resident, 1955-56; resident Bellevue Hosp., N.Y.C., 1956-57; practice medicine, specializing in pediatrics, Los Angeles; mem. staff U. Cal. at Los Angeles Hosp., asst. prof. pediatrics, dir. ambulatory div. Cons. Bur. Nutrition State Cal., 1971-72, NIH, 1972-74. Mem. Am. Acad. Pediatrics, Ambulatory Pediatric Soc., Los Angeles Pediatric Soc. Home: 520 20th St Santa Monica CA 90402 Office: Dept Pediatrics U Cal Los Angeles CA 90024

NEUMANN, ELIZABETH MABON, psychologist; b. Boston, Mar. 6, 1931; d. Robert Leonard and Vivian Virginia (Hines) Mabon; B.S. in Social Sci. (Social Sci. scholar 1964), Cal. Poly. U., Pomona, 1964; M.A., U. Cal. at Riverside, 1967, Ph.D., 1971; m. Harry James Neumann, Apr. 15, 1967; children—Dana Marr Smith (Mrs. Ronald E. Hermison), Terry Leann Smith, Vivian Rae Smith, Virgina Lynn Smith (dec.). Pvt. presch. tchr., 1954-61; research asst. U.S. Navy creativity project Cal. State Poly. Coll., 1963-65; survey supr., then psychometrist Riverside sch. study on desegregation, 1966-67; dir. psychol. services Riverside County Head Start, 1968-70; asst. prof. Chaffey Community Coll., Alta Loma, Cal., 1970-72; fellow Child Clin. psychology affiliated program U. So. Cal. and Children's Hosp., Los Angeles, 1972-73; dir. presch. program handicapped children Claremont Colls.-Casa Colina Hosp., Pomona, 1973—; vis. lectr. edn. Claremont Grad. Sch., 1974—; cons., individual practice in field. Mem. Cal., Am., Los Angeles County psychol. assns., Cal. Marriage, Family and Child Counselors, Mem. United Ch. Christ. Co-editor monographs. Home: 685 Sebastopol St Claremont CA 91711 Office: 255 E Bonita St Pomona CA 91767

NEUMANN, JOSEPHINE TRZCINSKI (MRS. STANLEY C. NEUMANN), assn. exec.; b. Hamilton, Ont., Can., Mar. 19, 1916; d. Walter and Stella (Sosnowski) Trzcinski; grad. high sch.; m. Stanley C. Neumann, Sept. 3, 1941; children—Michael, Timothy. Came to U.S., 1921, naturalized, 1940. With Gen. Motors Corp., Detroit, 1946-49; exec. sec. Garden City (Mich.) C. of C. Active numerous civic orgns.; chmn. Garden City Hist. Commn., 1969—. Mem. Garden City Bus. and Profl. Women's Club. Home: 29747 Rush St Garden City MI 48135 Office: 29207 Ford Rd Garden City MI 48135

NEUMANN, SISTER MARY MARGUERITE, educator; b. West Bend, Wis.; d. Edmund Christian and Christina (Becker) Neumann; B.S., Mundelein Coll., 1942; M.S., State U. Ia., 1943; Ph.D., St. Louis U., 1954. Joined Sisters of Charity, 1932; asst. prof. chemistry Mundelein Coll., 1943-50, 1953-57; prof. chemistry, chmn. dept. Clarke Coll., 1957—. Recipient Research award NSF. Mem. Ia. Acad. Sci., Am. Chem. Soc., Albertus Magnus Guild, Midwest Assn. Chemistry Tchrs. Liberal Arts Colls., Am. Assn. U. Women pres.-elect local br., Am. Assn. U. Profs., Ia. Acad., Sigma Xi. Club: Dubuque. Research medicinal chemistry. Home: Clarke Coll Dubuque IA 52001

NEUMAYER, ELEANOR MAY, ret. biologist; b. Grand Island, Neb., Aug. 20, 1910; d. Robert and Harriet M. (Clendenin) Neumayer; B.A., Grand Island Coll., 1931; M.S., Ia. State U., 1932. Tchr. secondary schs., Farwell, Neb., 1933-37, Lexington, Neb., 1937-38, Pontiac, Ill., 1938-43; parasitologist U.S. Dept. Agr. Research Center, Beltsville, Md., 1943-45; biologist E. I. du Pont de Nemours & Co., Inc., Newark, Del., 1945-69, sr. research biologist, 1969-71. Mem. A.A.A.S., Sigma Delta Epsilon, Episcopalian. Contbr. articles to profl. jours. Research in parasitology, med. entomology, virology. Home: Apt 12 C 25 Marvin Dr Newark DE 19711

NEUMEISTER, BETTY LAURA, bus. exec.; b. Cleve., Apr. 6, 1915; d. Alex William and Laura (Schmidt) Neumeister; student pub. schs., Cleveland Heights, O. Sec., Goggle Parts Co., Inc., 1947, name changed to Flexo Products, Inc. 1954, Westlake, O., 1933—. Mem. Cleve. Women's Advt. Club, Edgewater Bus. and Profl. Women's Club (sec. 1959-60). Club: Zonta (treas. Cleve. 1958-60). Home: 408 Pellett Dr Bay Village OH 44140 Office: 24864 Detroit Rd Westlake OH 44145

NEVELSON, LOUISE, sculptor; b. Russia; d. Issac and Minna Sadie (Smolerank) Berliawsky; ed. Rockland, Me., Europe, Mexico; studied with Hans Hoffman, Germany, 1931; husband dec.; 1 son, Myron Nevelson. One-man shows Janis Gallery, The Bienniel, Venice, Italy, 1963, Martha Jackson Gallery, Pace Gallery, also numerous U.S. museums, in Germany, London, Paris, Rome and South America, 1962-63; permanent exhbns. Whitney Mus. Art, Bklyn. Mus., Newark Mus., Carnegie Inst., Sara Robi Found., Brandeis U., Birmingham Mus., Houston Mus., Riverside Mus., Mus. of Modern Art, N.Y.U. Mus., Neb. Mus., Walker Art Center, Queens Coll.; also numerous pvt. collections. Recipient of 1st award United Soc. Artists, 1959; award Chgo. Inst., 1959; Ford Found. gift for Tamarind Workshop, Norfolk Mus., 1963. Mem. Fedn. Modern Painters and Sculptors (v.p.), Artists Equity (pres.), Am. Abstract Artists, Sculptors Guild (exec. bd.). Address: 29 Spring St New York City NY 10012

NEVEU, WILMA BARBRE, librarian; b. Rayne, La., Feb. 25, 1926; d. John Wilmer and Sylvia (Campbell) Barbre; B.A., U. Southwestern La., 1946; B.L.S., La. State U., 1947; m. Durwood Herbert Neveu, Apr. 4, 1948; children—Margaret (Mrs. Bernard E. Lambert), Kathryn Lenain. Cataloger, asst. librarian Lafayette Pub. Library, 1947-48; instr., asst. librarian Sandel Library N.E. La. U., 1960-64; br. librarian New Orleans Pub. Library, 1964-66; head circulation, res.

Library Tulane Med. Sch., 1966-69; asst. regional br. librarian New Orleans Pub. Library, 1969-71; chief librarian VA Hosp. Library, New Orleans, 1971—. Mem. membership com. So. Regional Med. Library Assn. Conv., 1967. Mem. Am., La., Southwestern, Med. library assns., Greater New Orleans Library Club. Home: 508 Elsie Lane River Ridge LA 70123 Office: 1601 Perdido St New Orleans LA 70146

NEVILL, DOROTHY DOBBINS (MRS. GALE ERWIN NEVILL, JR.), ednl. adminstr.; b. Houston, Aug. 9, 1935; d. Nolan Daniel and Fay (Griesenbeck) Dobbins; B.A. with honors (Max Autry and Hohenthal scholars), Rice U., 1957; M.A. (USPHS trainee), U. Fla., 1968, Ph.D. (Grad. Council fellow), 1971; m. Gale Erwin Nevill, Jr., Sept. 4, 1954; children—David Erwin, Robert Nolan. Asst. prof. psychology U. Fla., Gainesville, 1971—, coordinator counseling activities Office Acad. Affairs, 1972-73, asst. dean acad. affairs, 1973—, also cons. Center for Creative and Optimal Design. Cons., psychology service VA, Gainesville. Mem. State Commn. United Ministries to Higher Edn., Fla., 1972-73, bd. dirs. Center for United Ministries, 1972-74, treas., 1973-74. Mem. Am., Southeastern, Fla. (research award 1969) psychol. assns., Am. Ednl. Research Assn., Am. Assn. Higher Edn., Phi Beta Kappa, Psi Chi, Phi Kappa Phi. Home: 3415 NW 13th Av Gainesville FL 32605

NEVILLE, EMILY CHENEY (MRS. GLENN NEVILLE), author; b. Manchester, Conn., Dec. 28, 1919; d. Howell and Anne (Bunce) Cheney; A.B., Bryn Mawr Coll., 1940; m. Glenn Neville (dec. 1965); children—Emily Tam, Glenn H., Dessie, Marcy, Alec. Feature writer, N.Y. Mirror, 1941-42. Author: It's Like This, Cat, 1963 (John Newbery award 1964); Berries Goodman, 1965; the 17th Street Gang, 1966, Traveler From A Small Kingdom, 1968; Fogarty, 1969. Address: Keene Valley NY 12943

NEVILLE, MARGARET M., educator; b. Chgo., Mar. 27, 1907; d. Edward and Johanna (Morgan) Neville; A.B., DePaul U., 1929, M.A., 1930; M.A., Northwestern U., 1939; Ph.D., Loyola U., Chgo., 1950. Mem. faculty English dept., DePaul U., Chgo., 1930—, prof. English, 1960—, chmn. dept. English, 1966-73. Mem. Am. Assn. U. Profs., Modern Lang. Assn., Nat. Council Tchrs. of English. Roman Catholic. Home: 7223 N Claremont Av Chicago IL 60645

NEVILLE, MARY C., govt. ofcl.; b. Mo., Apr. 16, 1920; A.B., Mt. St. Scholastica Coll., 1940; M.S., U. Mich., 1946; Ed.D., Am. U., 1972. Tchr. high sch., 1940-42; supr. student tchrs. math. No. Ill. U., 1942-49; asst. prof. Eastern Mich. U., 1949-50, 51-61; tchr. edn. adviser ICA (named changed to AID 1961), Salisbury, Southern Rhodesia, 1961-63; edn. officer, Lusaka, Zambia, 1963-67; edn. adviser, Lagos, Nigeria, 1967-72; chief higher edn. br., Saigon, 1972—. Address: US AID/ED APO San Francisco CA 96243

NEVIN, EVELYN COOK (MRS. WILLIAM FERGUSON), author, editor; b. Council Bluffs, Ia., Feb. 22, 1910; d. Benjamin Franklin and Nellie Mae (Dorton) Cook; student Wash. State U., 1929-33, N.Y. U., 1949; m. John H. Nevin, Sept. 9, 1934 (dec. Dec. 5, 1950); m. 2d, William B. Ferguson, Apr. 9, 1954. Author: The Lost Children of the Shoshones, 1946; Sign of the Anchor, 1947; Underground Escape (selected for James Weldon Johnson Meml. Collection in Countee Cullen br. N.Y.C. Library), 1949; Captive of the Delawares, 1952; The River Spirit and the Mountain Demons, 1965; The Extraordinary Adventures of Chee Chee McNerney, 1971. Contbr. short stories to Jack and Jill, Boys' Life and ednl. textbooks. Asso. editor: Jack and Jill, 1946; editor Stories, Trailblazer, 1950-61. Home: Route 3 Box 1074 Rainier OR 97048

NEW, ANNE LATROBE (MRS. JOHN CLINTON TIMMERMAN), civic worker; b. Evanston, Ill., May 10, 1910; d. Charles Edward and Agnes (Bateman) New; A.B., U. S.C., 1930; m. John Clinton Timmerman, Sept. 30, 1933; 1 dau., Jan Latrobe (Mrs. Harris Griffith Abbott). Editorial asst. Pictorial Rev. mag., N.Y.C., 1930-32; copy dept. J. Walter Thomson, Co., N.Y.C., 1932-33; sub-editor Cosmopolitan mag., N.Y.C., 1933-37; with pub. relations div. Girl Scouts U.S.A., N.Y.C., 1937-57, asst. dir. div. 1943-46, dir. 1946-47, coordinator pub. information services, 1947-57; dir. pub. information and edn. Nat. Recreation Assn., N.Y.C., 1957-63, spl. asst. to exec. dir., 1963-65, spl. asst. to exec. v.p., 1965-66; asst. to gen. dir. Internat. Social Service, Am. br., 1966-68; cons. community relations Nat. Accreditation Council for Agys. Serving Blind and Visually Handicapped, N.Y.C., 1969-73, dir. devel., 1973—; cons. on planning, devel. and pub. relations to local and nat. health and welfare agys., 1968—. Mem. pub. relations and fund raising adv. com., Nat. Assn. for Retarded Children, 1956; dist. capt. Community Chest, Mamaroneck, N.Y., 1961, bd. dirs., 1965-69, chmn. tng. com., 1966; bd. dirs. Mamaroneck United Fund, 1967-70; mem. tng. com. Westchester United Fund, 1967-68. Mem. Mamaroneck and Westchester County Democratic Coms., 1963-68. Mem. Assn. Fund Raising Dirs. (sec. 1970—, v.p. 1972-73 dir.), Women Execs. in Pub. Relations, Pub. Relations Soc. Am. (dir. N.Y. chpt. 1958-60, chmn. speakers bur. 1963-64, accredited 1966, chmn. edn. com. N.Y. chpt. 1971-72), (sec. 1962-63), Phi Beta Kappa, Chi Delta Phi. Home: 235 S Barry Av Mamaroneck NY 10543 Office: National Accreditation Council for Agencies Serving Blind and Visually Handicapped 79 Madison Av New York City NY 10016

NEW, MARIA IANDOLO, physician; b. N.Y.C., Dec. 11, 1928; d. Loris and Esther (Giglio) Iandolo; B.A., Cornell U., 1950; M.D., U. Pa., 1954; m. Bertrand Latimer, June 4, 1949; children—Erica Maria, Daniel Loris, Antonia Silva. Intern Bellevue Med. 3d Div., 1954-55; resident pediatrics N.Y. Hosp., 1955-57; instr. Cornell Med. Center-N.Y. Hosp., N.Y.C., 1958-63, cons., 1959-63, pediatrician, out-patient dept., 1959-63, coordinator speech and hearing program, 1958-62, asst. prof., asst. attending pediatrician, 1963-68, asso. prof., asso. attending pediatrician, 1968-71, prof., attending pediatrician, 1971—, dir. Pediatric Metabolism and Endocrinology Clinic, 1964—, dir. Pediatric Clinic Research Center, 1964—, div. head pediatric endocrinology, 1964—; career scientist Health Research Council City N.Y., 1964—; vis. physician Rockefeller U., 1971; sr. med. cons. City N.Y. Bur. Handicapped Children. Moderator Acad. Assembly N.Y. Hosp.-Cornell Med. Center. Bd. dirs. Rebekah Harkness Found.; trustee Found. for Internat. Child Health. NIH, USPHS fellow, 1957-68, 58-62, 62-64; USPHS, NIH grantee, 1965—. Mem. A.A.A.S., Am. Diabetes Assn., Am. Pediatric Soc., Am. Acad. Pediatrics, Am. Soc. Nephrology, Am. Soc. Pediatric Nephrology, Endocrine Soc., Harvey Soc., N.Y. Diabetes Assn. (council mem. council clin. soc.), N.Y. Acad. Scis., Soc. Pediatric Research. Asso. editor: Metabolism, 1970—. Home: 435 E 70th St New York City NY 10021 Office: 525 E 68th St New York City NY 10021

NEWALD, CORA REGINA GEIGER (MRS. CARL NEWALD), civic worker; b. Buffalo; d. Charles and Cora (Lannen) Geiger; student U. Buffalo, 1921-23, Cleve. Coll. Western Res. U., 1939-41; m. Carl Newald, July 27, 1940. Advt. writer, account exec. Batten Barton Durstine & Osborn, Buffalo, Cleve., 1931-40, Lang, Fisher & Stashower, Inc., Cleve., 1941-56, Marschalk Co., Cleve., 1961-67; free-lance writer and pub. relations, Cleve., 1967-72. Pub. relations cons. Jewish Family Service Assn. Cleve., 1970-72. Mem. pub. relations com. Welfare Fedn. Cleve., 1948-56, 61-63, chmn. foster home recruiting com., 1962-63. Bd. dirs. Little Theatre P.R., 1957-59; trustee Karamu House, 1950-57, 61-72. Named Advt. Woman of the Year, Women's Advt. Club, 1961, recipient Pres. Trophy, 1968; recipient 2d Nat. award for community service Advt. Fedn. Am., 1968. Mem. Women's Nat. Book Assn. (pres. Cleve. chpt. 1956-57, 67-69), Women's Advt. Club (pres. 1943-45), Cath. Interracial Council, Council on World Affairs, Gamma Alpha Chi. Club: Women's City (dir. 1965-66) (Cleve.). Home: 12700 Fairhill Rd Shaker Heights OH 44120

NEWBERG, DOROTHY BECK (MRS. WILLIAM C. NEWBERG), civic worker; b. Detroit, May 30, 1919; d. Charles William and Mary (Labedz) Beck; student Detroit Conservatory Music, 1938; m. William C. Newberg, Nov. 3, 1939; children—Judith Anne (Mrs. John Robert Bookwalter), Robert Charles, James William, William Charles. Trustee Detroit Adventures, 1967-71, originator A Drop in Bucket Program for talented inner-city children. Trustee, Franklin-Wright Settlements, Meadowbrook Gallery, Oakland U.; bd. dirs. Your Heritage House. Recipient Heart of Gold award, 1969; Mich. vol. leadership award. Mem. Birmingham Soc. Women Painters, Bloomfield Art Assn. (dir. 1960-62, trustee 1965-67). Presbyn. (deaconess). Home: 4310 Vernor Ct Bloomfield Hills MI 48013

NEWBY, LILIAN ANN LOGAN (MRS. JAMES R. NEWBY), journalist; b. Amarillo, Tex., Aug. 31, 1942; d. Gleig and Lilian Linnie (Stubbs) Logan; B.A., U. Okla., 1964; m. James R. Newby, Nov. 13, 1966. Gen. assignment reporter Shawnee (Okla.) News-Star, 1964-65; police-courthouse reporter Daily Ardmoreite, Ardmore, Okla., 1965-66; wire editor Union-Bull., Walla Walla, Wash., 1966-67; state news and met. news desk Oklahoma City Times-Daily Oklahoman, 1967-70; polit.-legislative reporter statehouse Tulsa Tribune, 1970—. Lectr. to high sch. and univ. journalism groups, various women's and polit. orgns. Mem. media com. Okla. Bar, 1971—. Mem. Women in Communications (chpt. pres. 1970-72), Sigma Delta Chi (chpt. pres. 1973—), Gamma Phi Beta. Mem. Ch. of Christ. Home 5141 E 45th St Tulsa OK 74135 Office: 315 S Boulder Tulsa OK 74102

NEWBY, MARTHA REDMON (MRS. JONATHAN D. NEWBY III), ednl. adminstr.; b. Kansas City, Mo., Oct. 26, 1926; d. Theron Alfred and Bertha Little (Jackson) Redmon; grad. nurse Kansas City Gen. Hosp., 1948; B.S., U. Neb., 1963; M.A., Ariz. State U., 1970; m. Jonathan D. Newby III, July 3, 1948; children—Jonathan D. IV. Psychiat. nurse, Omaha, 1963-68; dir. nursing Valley of Sun Sch. for Retarded Children, Phoenix, 1970-73; coordinator continuing edn. for allied health profls. Maricopa County Community Coll. Dist., Phoenix, 1973—. Mem. Western Interstate Commn. for Higher Edn. Mem. Adult Edn. Assn. U.S.A., Mountain Plains Adult Edn. Assn., Am. Assn. Higher Edn., Ariz. Adult Edn. Assn. (pres. 1971, 72), Ariz. Nurses Assn. (dist. 2d v.p. 1971-73, sec. 1973—), Pi Lambda Theta. Mem. Order Eastern Star. Home: 8231 E Sells Dr Scottsdale AZ 85251 Office: 903 N 2d St Phoenix AZ 85004

NEWCOMB, CAROLYN JONES (MRS. ROBINSON NEWCOMB), educator; b. Brookfield, O., June 14, 1901; d. Thomas Anthony and Emily (Joy) Jones; A.B., Oberlin Coll., 1923; postgrad. Columbia, 1925, 29; m. Robinson Newcomb, June 29, 1929; children—Anthony Mead, Sarah Robinson (Mrs. Austin Lamont). Tchr. high schs., Youngstown, O., 1923-29; orientation and practice tchr. Remedial Edn. Center, Washington, 1953-54; remedial teaching Episcopal High Sch., Alexandria, Va., 1955-56, St. Stephens Sch. for Boys, 1957-58; diagnostician tutor tng. program, chmn. tng. com. Kingsbury Center, Washington, 1959-71, bd. dirs., 1966-68, cons., lectr., 1971—. Group leader Camp Fire Girls, Falls Church, Va., 1946-53; tng. chmn. Met. Area Bd., Washington, 1947-53. Home: 1328 Beulah Rd Vienna VA 22180

NEWCOMB, VIRGINIA LYNN THATCHER (MRS. JEFFREY LYNN NEWCOMB), educator; b. Milw., Oct. 25, 1948; d. Franklyn Trumpff and Carol Jean (Lewis) Thatcher; B.S. in Edn. cum laude, U. Wis.-Whitewater, 1970, M.S. in Teaching in Communication and Theatre, 1974; m. Jeffrey Lynn Newcomb, June 26, 1971. Tchr. speech, drama and acting Whitewater High Sch., 1970—, dir. forensics and drama, since 1970—. Guest speaker in field. Mem. Wis. Theatre Assn. (exec. bd. secondary theatre div.), Wis. High Sch. Forensic Coaches Assn., Wis. Secondary Sch. Theatre Assn., So. Lakes Speech Conf. (sec.), Phi Kappa Phi, Zeta Phi Eta. Coach, dir. winning forensic teams, plays. Home: 216 Jefferson St Fort Atkinson WI 53528 Office: 401 Elizabeth St Whitewater WI 53190

NEWELL, BARBARA WARNE, coll. pres.; b. Pitts.; d. Colston E. and Frances (Corbett) Warne; B.A., Vassar Coll., 1951; M.A., U. Wis., 1954, Ph.D., 1958; LL.D., Central Mich. U., Williams Coll.; L.H.D., Trinity Coll.; D.Lit., Northeastern U.; m. George V. Thompson, June 15, 1954 (dec. 1954); m. 2d, George S. Newell, June 9, 1956 (dec. 1964); 1 dau., Elizabeth Penfield. Govt. intern NLRB, 1948; research, teaching asst. U. Wis., 1951-54, asst. to chancellor, 1965-67; research, teaching asst., asso. U. Ill., 1954-59; asst. prof., asso. prof. econs. Purdue U., 1959-64; asst. to pres., asso. prof. econs. U. Mich., Ann Arbor, 1967-71, acting v.p. student affairs, asso. prof., 1968-70; asso. provost grad. studies and research, prof. econs. U. Pitts., 1971-72; pres. Wellesley (Mass.) Coll., 1972—. Sec. Community Action Commn., Madison, Wis., 1965-67; chmn. Nat. Commn. on Med. Care for Women, 1970-72; adviser to bd. trustees Wesleyan U., Middletown, Conn., 1970-71. Bd. dirs. Community Welfare Council, 1965-66, Brookings Inst., Carnegie Endowment for Peace, Am. Council on Edn.; trustee U. Pitts.; bd. overseers Boston Symphony Orch. Wells fellow, 1951. Mem. Club: Seven College (past pres. Champaign, Ill., past dir. Lafayette, Ind.). Author: Chicago and the Labor Movement, 1961; (with Lawrence Senesh) The Pulse of the Nation, 1961; Our Labor Force, 1962. Contbr. articles to profl. jours. Home: Wellesley Coll Wellesley MA 02181

NEWELL, DOROTHY JAMES (MRS. JOHN S. NEWELL, JR.), journalist; b. Brockton, Mass., May 9, 1928; d. Locke LeBaron and Katharine Brown (Alger) James; student Eastern Nazarene Coll., Quincy, Mass., 1945-46, Met. Jr. Coll., Kansas City, Mo., 1952-53; m. John Scott Newell, Jr., 1944; children—John Scott III, Kerry James, Thomas Mark, Herbert Lee, Scott Robert. Asst. editor, religion and social editor, also staff reporter Butler County News Record, Zelienople, Pa., 1955-63; religion editor, environmental reporter Patriot Ledger, Quincy, 1963—; dir. news service Pitts. Nazarene Dist., 1955-63, New Eng. Nazarene Dist., 1963—; mem. news staff Nazarene Gen. Assemblies, 1960, 64, 72. Bd. dirs. Quincy corps Salvation Army, The Way, street ministry for youth. Recipient award spot news in weekly Pa. News Pubs. Assn., 1963; Faith and Freedom award for journalism, 1973; citation New Eng. Methodist Conf., 1963. Mem. Religion Newswriters Assn. (past sec.). Mem. Ch. of Nazarene (past steward). Home: 4 Driftway Weymouth MA 02191 Office: 13 Temple St Quincy MA 02169

NEWELL, GLADYS ELIZABETH, former educator; b. Ticonderoga, N.Y., Aug. 31, 1908; d. Charles R. and Elizabeth (Ives) Newell; A.B., State U. N.Y. at Albany, 1930, M.A., 1935. Tchr., Corinth (N.Y.) High Sch., 1930-33, Bethlehem Central High Sch., Delmar, N.Y., 1933-45; supr. social studies Bethlehem Central Schs., Delmar, 1946-71. Mem. N.Y. State Regents Com. on Exams., 1950-53, N.Y. Social Studies Council Curriculum Com., 1961-63, N.Y. Mental Health Planning Commn., 1963-64. Bd. dirs. State U. N.Y. at Albany Benevolent Assn.; adv. com. N.Y. delegation White House Conf., 1955. Recipient Bus. and Profl. Women Outstanding Citizen award Tri-Village area, 1953; State Coll. Alumni Bertha E. Brimmer award for outstanding teaching, 1955; Citizenship Conf. Outstanding Tchr. award Syracuse U., 1962; Distinguished Alumnus award State U. at Albany, 1969. Mem. N.Y. State Tchrs. Assn. (dir. 1950-62, pres. 1966-67), Eastern Zone Bethlehem Central (a founder, past pres.), Albany Supervisory Dist. (past pres.) tchrs. assns., N.E.A. (rep. of N.Y. State Tchrs. Assn. at tchr. edn. and profl. standards meetings), N.Y. State (past pres.), Capital Dist. (past pres.), Nat. councils for social studies, League Women Voters (past pres. Albany County), Nat. Council on Crime and Delinquency (Albany County bd. dirs.), UN Assn. U.S.A. (past chpt. dir.), World Affairs Council (past dir. Albany), Am. Assn. U. Women, Bus. and Profl. Women's Club, State Adv. Com. Statewide Planning Vocational Rehab., Delta Kappa Gamma. Methodist. Club: Ticonderoga College. Contbr. articles profl. jours. Home: 17 John St Ticonderoga NY 12883

NEWELL, VIRGINIA SHAW, former educator; b. Eau Claire, Wis., Jan. 15, 1901; d. La Forrest and Caroline (Wingen) Newell; student Eau Claire State Tchrs. Coll., 1919-21; B.A., U. Wis. at Madison, 1924; postgrad. Northwestern U., 1941; M.A., Cath. U. Am., 1951. Tchr., Eau Claire (Wis.) Sr. High Sch., 1924-43; tchr., drama dir. Adams (Wis.) Friendship High Sch., 1951-54, tchr. drama and forensic dir., 1963-70; tchr. Westfield (Wis.) High Sch., 1954-55; tchr., drama dir. Medford (Wis.) High Sch., 1955-57; tchr., drama dir. Marinette, Wis., 1957-63. Vol. Am. Cancer Soc.; mem. Adams County Community Arts Assn., Adams County Assn. for Retarded Children. Pres., Adams County Assn. Republican Women, 1969-73; co-ordinator Re-election of Congressman William A. Steiger, 1970, publicity chmn. Adams County Rep. Party of Wis., 1972. Served to lt. Womens Res., USCG, 1943-46. Mem. Am. Assn. U. Women, Internat. Platform Assn., Nat. Travel Club, Nat., Wis. ret. tchrs. assns., Roche-a-Cri Recreation, Delta Kappa Gamma. Roman Catholic. Home: PO Box 173 Adams WI 53910

NEWELL-MORRIS, LAURA LIVINGSTON (MRS. ARVAL ALEXANDER MORRIS), educator; b. Whitehall, N.Y., May 16, 1933; d. Walter J. and Grace A. (Clute) Newell; B.A., U. N.M., 1954; M.A., Northwestern U., 1957; Ph.D. (USPHS fellow), U. Wash., 1967; m. Arval Alexander Morris, Oct. 13, 1969; 1 son, Arval Harold. Acting asst. prof. dept. anthropology and pediatrics U. Wash., Seattle, 1966-67, asst. prof., 1967-70, asso. prof. dept. anthropology, 1970—, research affiliate Regional Primate Research Center, 1966—, research asso. dept. orthodontics, 1970—. Mem. Am. Assn. Phys. Anthropologists, Soc. Human Biology, A.A.A.S., Internat. Primatol. Assn., N.Y. Acad. Sci. Author: Human Populations, Genetic Variation and Evaluation, 1971. Home: 11335 Lakeside NE Seattle WA 98125

NEWER, DOROTHY LOEB (MRS. BERNARD S. NEWER), newspaperwoman; b. N.Y.C., Jan. 20, 1912; d. David S. and Eva (Emanuel) Loeb; B.S., N.Y.U., 1930; student Maxwell Grad. Sch. of Syracuse U., 1931-33, N.Y. Sch. Social Work, 1934; m. Bernard S. Newer, June 28, 1939 (dec. 1963). Social worker Onondaga (N.Y.) County Dept. Welfare, 1933-37, Syracuse Jewish Social Service Bur., 1938-47; migration worker United Service for New Americans, N.Y.C., 1948-49; research worker Community Chest and Council Syracuse, 1963-65; bus. editor Syracuse Post-Standard, 1965—. Mem. Nat. Assn. Social Workers, Nat. Acad. Social Workers, Theta Sigma Phi. Club: Syracuse Press. Home: 126 Hall Av Syracuse NY 13205 Office: Herald Bldg Clinton Sq Syracuse NY 13201

NEWLIN, MARGARET RUDD, poet, critic; b. N.Y.C., Feb. 27, 1925; d. James Harold and Marie (McLaughlin) Rudd; B.A., Bryn Mawr Coll., 1947; Ph.D. (Am. Assn. Univ. Women fellow, Am. Philos. Soc. fellow), U. Reading (Eng.), 1951; m. Nicholas Newlin, Apr. 2, 1956; children—James, David, Robert, Thomas. Mem. staff admissions dept. Bryn Mawr Coll. (Pa.), 1948, mem. faculty, 1953-54, editor poetry sect. Alumnae Bull., 1974—; mem. faculty Harcum Jr. Coll., Bryn Mawr, 1953-54, Washington Coll., 1955-56. Recipient M. Carey Thomas essay award, Gerould award Bryn Mawr Coll., 1947, Greenwood prize English Poetry Soc., 1969, 71. Mem. poetry socs. Am., London. Author: (criticism, under name Rudd) Divided Image, 1953, Organized Innocence, 1956; (poems, under name Newlin) The Fragile Immigrants, 1971, Day of Sirens, 1973. Home: Shipley Farm Secane PA 19018

NEWLON, ELOISE FISHER, librarian; b. Walton, W. Va., May 15, 1913; d. Romeo H. and Icy (Howell) Fisher; student Ohio U., 1929-31; A.B., W. Va. U., 1934, A.M., 1938; B.S. in L.S., Columbia U., 1948; m. William G. Newlon, July 23, 1943, (dec. Sept. 1950). Tchr, librarian Roane County Schs., Walton, W. Va., 1935-43; catalog librarian W. Va. U., 1945-54, Cleve. Pub. Library, 1954-56; asst. librarian Morris Harvey Coll., 1956-66, acting librarian, 1958-61; coordinator library services Kanawha County Schs., Charleston, W.Va., 1966-72; coordinator multi-media Kanawha County Schs., 1972—. Mem. Am., W.Va. library assns., Nat., W.Va. edn. assns., Assn. Ednl. Communications and Tech. Methodist. Mem. Order Eastern Star. Home: 1938 Bona Vista Dr Charleston WV 25311 Office: 200 Elizabeth St Charleston WV 25311

NEWMAN, BARBARA MAE, educator; b. Rockford, Ill., July 16, 1932; d. Greene Adam and Emma Lorene (Fields) Newman; student Rockford Coll., 1961-67; A.A., Rock Valley Coll., 1971; B.S. in Edn. with honors, No. Ill. U., 1973. With Dept. Army, Stuttgart, Germany, 1954-56; typist, internat. div. Electric Storage Battery Co., N.Y.C., 1956-58; sec. Fed. & State Tax Record Systems, Rockford, 1959-60, exec. sec. Rockford Art Assn., 1961-70; substitute tchr. Rockford Bd. Edn., 1973—. Water safety instr. A.R.C., Rockford, 1966-71. Grantee, Ill. State Scholarship Commn., 1970-73; named Woman of Year Forest City chpt. Am. Bus. Women's Assn., 1966. Mem. Council for Exceptional Children, Assn. for Edn. of Visually Handicapped, Am. Bus. Women's Assn. (pres. 1967, v.p. 1969). Home: 1918 Bruner St Rockford IL 61103

NEWMAN, CLAIRE POE (MRS. ROBERT J. NEWMAN), real estate co. exec.; b. Jacksonville, Fla., Dec. 12, 1926; d. Leslie Ralph and Gertrude (Criswell) Poe; student Fla. State Coll. for Women, 1944-45, Tulane U., 1971-73; m. Robert Jacob Newman, July 3, 1948; children—Leslie Claire, Robert, Christopher David. Co-owner Vineyards in Burgundy, France; v.p., dir. Carrollton Realty Co. of New Orleans, 1956—. Mem. various coms. New Orleans Mus. Art. Bd. dirs. Women's com. New Orleans Philharmonic Symphony Assn., 1961-65, chmn. orch. relations com., 1961-63; chmn. New Orleans Easter Seal Drive, 1963; La. trustee Nat. Soc. Crippled Children and Adults, 1963-65. Mem. Women's Aux. C. of C., New Orleans Soc. Archeol. Inst. Am. (v.p. 1972—), Sigma Kappa. Club: Metairie Country, Kitzbuehel (Austria) Golf, Golden Skibook (Kitzbuehel), Pass Christian (Miss.) Yacht; Ski (Arlberg). Home: 1111 Falcon Rd Metairie LA 70005 also Tiemberg Kitzbuehel Austria

NEWMAN, CONSTANCE BERRY (MRS. THEODORE NEWMAN), govt. ofcl.; b. Chgo., July 8, 1935; d. Joseph Alonzo and Ernestine (Siggers) Berry; B.A., Bates Coll., Lewiston, Me., 1956, LL.D. (hon.), 1972; B.S.L., U. Minn., 1959; m. Theodore Newman, July 25, 1959. Personnel specialist, Washington, 1962-67; research analyst Nat. Adv. Commn. on Civil Disorders, 1967; research analyst Commn. on Polit. Activity of Govt. Personnel, 1967; chief Midwest sect., migrant div., Office Econ. Opportunity, 1967-69; spl. asst. to sec. health, edn. and welfare, 1969-71; dir. VISTA, ACTION, Washington, 1971-73; commr. Consumer Product Safety Commn., Washington, 1973—. Recipient Bates Key, 1956; named Outstanding Young Woman of Am., 1969. Mem. Urban Rehab. Corp., Washington Literacy Council, Soc. Personnel Adminstrn., N.A.A.C.P., Council Black Appointees. Home: 7924 16th St NW Washington DC 20012 Office: Consumer Product Safety Commn Washington DC 20207

NEWMAN, CYNTHIA STAIR DALRYMPLE (MRS. CARSON BORU NEWMAN), travel agy. exec.; b. Mpls., Mar. 24, 1922; d. John Stewart and Bernice (Barber) Dalrymple; student Smith Coll., 1939-42; LL.B., U. Va., 1944; m. Edward Zimmerman, Sept. 25, 1943 (div. 1958); children—Robert Hamill, Nancy Stair, Pamela Barber; m. 2d, Carson Boru Newman, May 16, 1958 (dec. 1966); children—Tracy Stewart, Christopher Carson. Admitted to Va. bar, 1944; atty. UNRRA, 1944-46; dir. Nat. Rep. Open Forums, 1946-48; asst. to campaign dir. Rep. Senatorial Com., 1948-50; owner, pres. Waters Travel Service, Washington, 1963—; sec. state Commonwealth of Va., Richmond, 1970-74. Rep. nat. committeewoman for Va., 1956-57, 68—; vice chmn. Rep. Party of Va., 1962-68, state finance chmn., 1959-62; del. Rep. Nat. Conv., 1956, 68, 72, alternate, 1952, 60. Bd. dirs. Nat. Capitol Area YWCA, Washington, 1966-68, Nat. Symphony Orch., 1953-60. Club: Washington Soroptimist (past dir.). Home: 3535 Half Moon Circle Falls Church VA 22044 Office: Water's Travel Service 888 17th St NW Washington DC 20006

NEWMAN, HELEN WILSON (MRS. ROBERT E. NEWMAN), public relations cons., writer; b. Middletown, N.Y., July 20, 1916; d. John H. and Hildred J. (Anderson) Wilson; student Columbia; m. Robert E. Newman, Mar. 29, 1947. Radio-TV dir. Barber & Drullard, Inc., Buffalo, 1957-70; dir. student recruitment, dir. pub. relations Rosary Hill Coll., Buffalo, 1970-73; free-lance advt. and pub. relations cons., writer, Buffalo 1973—. Mem. speakers bur. Buffalo Pub. Schs., 1972—. Served with WAC, 1943-46. Mem. Advt. Women of Buffalo (pres. 1962-63, dir. 1973-74, Ad Woman of Year award 1963). Contbr. articles to profl. trade mags. and newspapers. Address: 947 Delaware Av Buffalo NY 14209

NEWMAN, LORETTA MARIE, musician, educator, psychologist; b. Kansas City, Mo., July 29, 1911; d. Norman Earl and May (Cook) Newman; Mus.B. cum laude, U. Rochester, 1933; M.A. in Edn., U. Kansas City, 1943; M.A. in Psychology, Cal. State U. at Long Beach, 1957; postgrad. U. Wis., U. Mich., U. So. Cal., Nat. Music Camp, Interlochen, Mich. Mem. Eastman Symphony Orch., 1930-34; asst. condr. Women's Symphony, Rochester, 1932-34; instr. violin and viola David Hochstein Sch. Music, Rochester, 1932-34; instr. orch. and bands Kansas City (Mo.) Pub. Schs., 1934-43; instr. Grad. Sch. and Music Clinic, U. Wis., 1935-40; head music dept. Phineas Banning High Sch., 1943-49; condr. All-Harbor High Sch. Symphony, 1945-49; mgr. All So. Cal. Jr. and Sr. High Schs. Orchs. and Band, 1944-49; dean women Arrowbear Music Camp, 1944-52; cons. psychologist Learning Center, El Segundo, 1953-62, Sch. for Exceptional Children, Redondo Beach, Cal., 1958-59, Norair div. Northrup Co., 1966. Developer, dir. Los Angeles Harbor Coll. Reading Center, 1953—; sec. Western States Coll. Reading Assn., 1966—; reading cons. Los Angeles City Schs., 1956—; designer Reading Center, West Los Angeles Coll., 1965; lectr., judge, moderator many music and reading confs. civic affairs, 1935—. Cons. Cal. Bd. Edn. for Community Coll. Reading Centers and programs on fed. grants, 1965—. Treas., South Del Amo Pacific Co-op Apts., Inc., 1965-69; sec. Will Rogers Research Found., 1965-69. Social service worker Ch. Sons of God, 1963—. Mem. Cal. Psychology Assn., Cal. Tchrs. Assn., Los Angeles Harbor Coll. Faculty, Western Coll. Reading Assn. (sec. 1967-70), P.T.A. (life), Nat. Music Camp Alumni (life), Sigma Alpha Iota (life), Psi Chi. Author: Building Basic College Reading Skills, 3d edit., 1972; College Reading and Study Improvement, 3d printing, 1967. Home: 3210 Merrill Dr Torrance CA 90503 Office: Los Angeles Harbor Coll Wilmington CA 90744

NEWMAN, LOUISE BROWN, home economist; b. Poteet, Tex., Oct. 2, 1916; d. Jasper Allee and Zula May (Brown) Newman; B.S. in Home Econs., U. Okla., 1938, postgrad., 1940; postgrad. Tex. Tech. U., 1943, U. Ark.-Regional Summer Sch., 1951, 58, Colo. A. and M., 1953. Instr. vocational home econs. Okeene (Okla.) High Sch., 1938-41; instr. home econs. Moore (Tex.) High Sch., 1941-42; instr. vocational home econs. Devine (Tex.) High Sch., 1943-44; county home demonstration agt. Haskell, Tex., 1944-48; county home demonstration agt. Tex. Agrl. Extension Service, Alice, 1949-71. Recipient Distinguished Service award Nat. Home Demonstration Agts. Assn., 1963; Meritorious Service award Tex. Agrl. Extension Service, 1971; named Outstanding Woman of Yr. Beta Sigma Phi, 1963; Outstanding Woman Bus. and Profl. Women's Club, 1964. Mem. Am., Tex. home econs. assns., County Home Demonstration Agts. Assn. Tex. (dir. 1952), Bus. and Profl. Women's Club Alice (pres. 1951, 58), Am. Assn. U. Women, Delta Kappa Gamma (pres. Beta Pi chpt. 1953-54), Epsilon Sigma Phi. Methodist (Wesleyan Service Guild). Home: 1206 Rose Dr Alice TX 78332

NEWMAN, NANCY BLITZSTEN (MRS. MORTON W. NEWMAN), public relations exec.; b. Chgo., May 22, 1931; d. Harry and Alice Eleanor (Karno) Blitzsten; student Cape Cod Theatre Sch., 1948-50; B.A., B.S., U. Chgo. Coll., 1952; m. Morton William Newman, Apr. 21, 1962. Film cons., nat. directory safety films editor Nat. Safety Council, Chgo., 1952-57; staff writer Chgo. Sun-Times and Chgo. Daily News, 1958-64; asst. dir. pub. relations U. Chgo. Hosps. and Clinics, 1964-66; asst. dir. community relations Michael Reese Hosp. and Med. Center, Chgo., 1966-71; pub. relations dir. Ravenswood Hosp. Med. Center, Chgo., 1971-72; asst. v.p., account supr. Beveridge Kraus Robbins & Manning Inc., Chgo., 1972—. Cons. Bus. Screen Mag. and Jack Lieb Prodns., Chgo., 1957-58. Mem. Publicity Club Chgo. (1st v.p. 1972-74), Pub. Relations Soc. Am., Am. Soc. Hosp. Pub. Relations Dirs., Am. Hosp. Assn., Arts Club Chgo., Welfare Pub. Relations Forum Chgo. (Helen Cody Baker award 1966). Contbr. Panorama mag. Chgo. Daily News. Home: 433 W Briar Pl Chicago IL 60657 Office: 75 E Wacker Dr Chicago IL 60601

NEWMAN, NANCY MARILYN, ophthalmologist; b. San Francisco, Mar. 16, 1941; d. Fred and Marion (Solomon) Newman; A.B. with distinction, with honors in Psychology, Stanford U., 1962, M.D., 1967. Intern Mt. Auburn Hosp., Cambridge, Mass.; resident in ophthalmology Washington U., St. Louis, 1968-71; fellow in neuro-ophthalmology depts. ophthalmology and neurol. surgery U. Cal. Med. Sch., San Francisco, 1971-72; fellow Inst. Visual Scis., San Francisco, 1971-72; asst. prof. neuro-ophthalmology and gen. ophthalmology Pacific Med. Center, 1972—; asst. clin. prof. U. Cal. at San Francisco, 1972—, San Francisco Gen. Hosp., 1972—. NIH spl. fellow; NSF, NIH, USPHS fellow, 1961-71; recipient 1st prize Poetry Soc. Cal., 1957; award of merit Atlantic Mag. Creative Writing Contest, 1958. Mem. Assn. for Research in Ophthalmology, Sierra Club. Author: Eye Movement Disorders. Contbr. articles to profl. jours. Home: 138 San Felipe St San Francisco CA 94127

NEWMAN, PEGGY JO, physician; b. Hollis, Okla., Feb. 8, 1926; d. Jess Allan and Eula B. (Jackson) Newman; B.A., Stephen F. Austin State U., 1944; M.D., Southwestern Med. Found., 1948. Surg. intern Albany (N.Y.) Hosp., 1948-49; resident in medicine and surgery New Eng. Hosp., Boston, 1949-51; resident in gen. practice St. Mary's Infirmary, Galveston, Tex., 1951-53; gen. practice medicine, Burnet, Tex., 1953—; med. dir. coronary care unit Sheppard Meml. Hosp., Burnet, 1969—; research fellow, asst. prof. pharmacology Tufts Coll. Med. Sch., 1949-51; Fellow Am. Coll. Angiology, Am. Acad. Family Physicians (charter); mem. Lampasas-Burnet-Llano Tri-County Med. Soc. (sec.-treas. 1954-62, 74, pres. 1966), Am., Tex. med. assns., Am., Tex. heart assns., Tex. Acad. Family Physicians (sci. program com. 1968-70, membership com. 1974—), Am. Acad. Family Practice (charter). Baptist. Home: 511 Hamilton Creek Dr Burnet TX 78611 Office: Hwy 29 W Burnet TX 78611

NEWMAN, RITA ROSLYN (MRS. PHILIP NEWMAN), psychiatrist; b. Jersey City, Apr. 2, 1936; d. Morris and Yetta (Marcus) Smilowitz; B.A., Barnard Coll., 1957; M.D., Woman's Med. Coll. Pa., 1961; m. Philip Newman, June 29, 1959; children—Lorraine, Stephen, Michael, Jennifer. Intern, Brookdale Hosp., Bklyn., 1961-62; resident Kings County Hosp., Bklyn., 1962-63, Hillside Hosp., Glen Oaks, Cal., 1963-65; pvt. practice psychiatry, West Orange, N.J., 1966-71, Short Hills, N.J., 1971-73; cons. Jewish Counseling Service, Newark, 1966-67; cons. N.J. Rehab. Commn., 1966—; staff St. Barnabas Med. Center, Livingston, N.J., dir. in-service psychiat. edn.; staff Babies Hosp. unit United Hosps., Children's Hosp., Newark. Vis. psychiatrist Manchester (Eng.) Royal Infirmary, 1965-66. Diplomate Am. Bd. Neurology and Psychiatry. Mem. N.J. Med. Soc. Am., N.J. neuropsychiat. assns., N.J. Woman's Med. Assn. (pres. elect), Am., N.J. women's med. assns., Royal Coll. Psychiatrists, Los Angeles Internat. Fern Soc. Office: 1046 S Orange Av Short Hills NJ 07078

NEWMAN, RUTH EINSIDLER (MRS. PHILIP CHARLES NEWMAN), psychologist; b. N.Y.C., Feb. 13, 1918; d. Louis and Marie (Ernst) Einsidler; B.A., Hunter Coll., 1938; M.S., N.Y. U., 1940; M.A., City U. N.Y., 1953; Ph.D. (Columbia scholar 1961-62, Nat. Inst. Mental Health fellow 1962-63), Columbia, 1963; m. Philip Charles Newman, Dec. 12, 1944; children—Michael Jonathan, Barbara Judith, Constance Jael. Sales mgr. Sears, Roebuck and Co., 1940-43; pres. Newman Assos., 1950—, Fgn. Studies Inst., Ridgewood, N.J., 1973—; practice as psychologist, 1963—; staff psychologist Colgate-Palmolive Co., 1970-71, Comprehensive Community Mental Health Clinic, 1970-71, Meadowbrook Hosp., 1970-71. Cons. to govts. U.S., numerous fgn. countries, 1944-60; vis. prof., P.R., 1944-45, Pa. State Coll., 1949-50, Pakistan, 1953-56, Rutgers U., 1968-73. Am. Assn. Univ. Women and N.J. State fellow, 1964-65; Wenner-Gren Anthropological Found. grantee, 1964-65. Mem. Am. Psychol. Assn., Internat. Council Psychologists. Contbr. articles to profl. jours. Office: Foreign Studies Inst PO Box 275 Ridgewood NJ 07451

NEWMAN, RUTH MAY GALLERT (MRS. JAMES R. NEWMAN), psychologist; b. N.Y.C.; d. Ernest Ezra and Belle (Cohen) Gallert; B.A., Rutgers, U., 1937; M.A., George Washington U., 1950; Ph.D., Md. U., 1956; postgrad. Washington Sch. Psychiatry, 1950; m. James R. Newman, July 27, 1940 (dec. July 1966); children—Jeffrey Frederick, Brooke Anne (Mrs. Andrew Hecht). Psychologist Georgetown Day Sch., Washington, 1949-52; dir. edn., child research br. NIH, 1954-60; dir. Sch. Research Program, Washington Sch. Psychiatry, 1960-66, dir. Inst. for Ednl. Service, 1966-67; dir. group therapy Hillcrest Children's Center, Washington, 1967—. Cons. to D.C. Sch.-Pupil Personnel Service, 1967—; cons. to clinics, schs. Meyer Found. grantee, 1963-66, NIH research grantee, 1960-63, 71-72. Mem. exec. com. Washington Sch. Psychiatry, 1962—. Fellow Am. Orthopsychiat. Assn. (v.p.); mem. Am. Psychol. Assn., Am. Assn. U. Profs., Am. Group Psychotherapy, Am. Civil Liberties Union, Better Edn. Group, Assn. Profs. George Washington Med. Sch., Assn. Profs. U. Md. Med. Sch. Author: (with others) Conflict in the Classroom, 1965; Psychological Consultation in the Schools: A Catalyst for Learning, 1967; Groups and Schools, 1974. Home: 2761 Brandywine St NW Washington DC 20008 Office: 1325 W St NW Washington DC 20009

NEWMAN, SARAH HERMAN (MRS. SIMON NEWMAN), orgn. exec.; b. Austria, Mar. 26, 1907; d. Israel and Mary (Gruber) Herman; came to U.S., 1912, naturalized, 1923; A.B., Goucher Coll., 1926; m. Simon M. Newman, Aug. 17, 1930; children—Paul H., Minna (Mrs. James Nathanson), Mark. Exec. dir. Nat. Consumers League, Washington, 1962-72, v.p., 1972—; dir. Consumers Fedn. Am., 1967—. Chmn. D.C. Minimum Wage and Indsl. Safety Bd., 1967—; mem. Citizens Adv. Council D.C., 1964-66; mem. bd. Washington home rule com. D.C. League Women Voters, 1955. Home: 1411 Hopkins St NW Washington DC 20036

NEWMAN, SHIRLEE PETKIN, author-editor; b. Boston, Feb. 16, 1924; d. Israel Perry and Ida (Goldstein) Petkin; adult edn. courses Boston, Cambridge, Mass.; m. Jackson J. Newman, June 25, 1946; children—Paula Fay, Jeffrey Alan. Publicist, advt. copywriter, account exec., Los Angeles, San Francisco, N.Y.C., before 1946, then freelance writer, juvenile writer formerly asso. editor Child Life magazine; tchr. juvenile writing Boston Center Adult Edn., 1962. Mem. Authors Guild, Authors League Am. Author: Liliuokalani, Last Queen of Hawaii, 1960; Yellow Silk for May-Lee, 1961; Folk Tales of Latin America, 1962; Folk Tales of Japan, 1963; (with Diane Sherman) About the People Who Run Your City, 1963; The Shipwrecked Dog, 1964; Marian Anderson, Lady from Philadelphia, 1966; The Story of Lyndon B. Johnson, 1967; Mary Martin on Stage, 1969. Contr. fiction, non-fiction, photog. work to: Am. Girl mag., Calling All Girls, Jack and Jill, Scholastic Publs., The Instr., Grade Tchr., My Weekly Reader, Sci. Research Assos., Reading Labs. Home: 34 Roosevelt Rd Newton Centre MA 02159

NEWMAN, SHIRLEY ANN MILLER (MRS. RICHARD J. NEWMAN), pub. relations exec.; b. Canton, Ill., June 26, 1929; d. Charles and Pearl Laura (Solomon) Miller; B.S., U. Ill., 1950; m. Richard J. Newman, June 27, 1948; children—David, Carol, Jeffry. Editorial asst. Coll. Agr., U. Ill., Urbana, 1950-51; copy chief, v.p. Richard Newman Assos., Inc., Champaign, Ill., 1957—, acting pres., 1963-67; field rep. Ill. Sesquicentennial Commn., Chgo., 1966-68; dir. information Lincoln Heritage Trail Found., 1969—, Conquistadores Trail Found., 1973—; sec. Newsome Center, Inc., Champaign, 1965—. Recipient Silver medal Am. Advt. Fedn., 1972. Mem. Champaign C. of C. (bd. dirs. 1974—), Theta Sigma Phi. Jewish religion (v.p. Sisterhood 1963-64). Clubs: Advertising and Sales (dir. 1968—), Soroptimist (dir. 1969-71) (Champaign). Home: 17 Fields East Champaign IL 61820 Office: 702 Bloomington Rd Champaign IL 61820

NEWMAN-GORDON, PAULINE (MRS. SYDNEY A. GORDON), educator; b. N.Y.C., Aug. 5, 1925; d. Bernard and Eva (Horowitz) Newman; B.A., Hunter Coll., 1947; M.A., Columbia, 1948; doctorate, U. Paris, 1951; m. Sydney A. Gordon, Sept. 13, 1959. Instr. French, Wellesly (Mass.) Coll., 1952-53; instr., asst. prof., asso. prof. French lit. Stanford U., Cal., 1953-69, prof. French lit., 1969—. Mem. Am. Assn. Tchrs. of French, Modern Lang. Assn., Phi Beta Kappa, Sigma Tau Delta, Pi Delta Phi. Author: Marcel Proust et l'Existentialisme, 1953; Un Romancier perigordin: Eugene Le Roy et son temps, 1957; Corbiere, Laforgue et Apollinaire ou le rire en pleurs, 1962; Helene de Sparte; la fortune du mythe en France, 1969; Dictionnaire des Idees dans l'oeuvre de Marcel Proust, 1969. Home: 1163 Brucito Av Los Altos CA 94220 Office: Dept French and Italian Stanford U Stanford CA 93405

NEWMAR, JULIE CHALANE, actress; b. Hollywood, Cal.; d. Donald Charles and Helene (Jesmer) Newmeyer; student U. Cal. at Los Angeles Actress appearing in Seven Brides for Seven Brothers, Silk Stockings, Little Abner, For Love or Money, Marriage-Go-Round, Stop the World, I Want to Get Off, Damn Yankess, Irma La Douce, McKenna's Gold. Recipient Antoinette Perry award. Mem. Actor's Studio. Office: care L J Gang 521 Fifth Av New York City NY 10017

NEWMARK, MARILYN (MRS. LEONARD J. MEISELMAN), sculptor; b. N.Y.C., July 20, 1928; d. Edward Ellis and Mabel (Davies) Newmark; student Adelphi Coll., 1945-47, Alfred U., 1949; m. Leonard J. Meiselman, Mar. 15, 1952; children—Mindy Kim, Mark C. Sculptor, specializing in horses, equestrian figures, dogs in sporting scenes; exhibited in group shows at N.A.D., Nat. Arts Club, Nat. Art Mus. of Sport (all N.Y.C.), James Ford Bell Mus., Wis., Smithsonian Instn., Washington; represented in permanent collections at Harvey Firestone (O.), Whitney Stone (Va.), Ogden Phipps (N.Y.), A.B. Hancock Jr. (Ky.), Charles Scribner (N.J.), Peggy Agustus (Va.), Morgan Firestone (Can.), A. Werk Cook (Mass.). Recipient Anna Hyatt Huntington award, 1970, 71, 72, Gold medal, 1973; award Council Am. Artists Socs., 1972, 73; John Newington award, 1973; N.A.D. Ellin P. Speyer award, 1974. Fellow Nat. Sculpture Soc., Am. Artists Profl. League (Gold medal 1974); mem. Allied Artists Am., Pen and Brush Club, Soc. Animal Artists (jury of admissions 1972-75), Nat. Steeplechase and Hunt Assn., Am. Fox Hound Club, Nat. Sculpture Soc. (council 1973-76), Nassau Suffolk Horsemans Assn. (dir.). Clubs: Catherine Lorillard Wolfe Art (jury of admissions N.Y.C. 1972-74); Smithtown Hunt, Past Meadow Brook Hunt (L.I., N.Y.). Address: Woodhollow Rd East Hills NY 11577

NEWSOM, ANN JOHNSON DOUGLAS (MRS. L. MACK NEWSOM, JR.), journalist, educator; b. Dallas, Jan. 16, 1934; d. J. Douglas and R. Grace (Dickson) Johnson; B.J. cum laude, U. Tex., 1954, B.F.A. summa cum laude, 1955, M.J., 1956; m. Mack Newsom, Jr., Oct. 27, 1956; children—Michael Douglas, Kevin Jackson, Nancy Elizabeth, William Macklemore. Gen. publicity State Fair Tex., 1955; advt. and promotion Newsom's Women's Wear, 1956-57; publicity Auto Market Show, 1961; lab. instr. radio-tv news-writing course U. Tex., 1961-62; local publicist Tex. Boys Choir, 1964-69, nat. publicist, 1967-69; asst. prof. journalism Tex. Christian U., 1969—; pub. relations dir. ann. Gt. S.W. Boat Show, 1966-72; pub. relations cons., writer, 1965—; pub. relations Horace Ainsworth Co., Dallas. Mem. Mortar Bd. Alumnae, Women in Communications (nat. pub. relations dir. 1969-71), Delta Delta Delta. Baptist. Home: 4237 Shannon Dr Fort Worth TX 76116 Office: Dept Journalism Tex Christian U Fort Worth TX 76129

NEWTON, ABBA VERBECK, educator; b. Ballston Spa, N.Y., Feb. 19, 1908; d. Samuel S. and Sarah (Verbeck) Newton; A.B. magna cum laude, Mt. Holyoke Coll., 1929; M.A., U. Chgo., 1931, Ph.D., 1933. Instr., Am. Internat. Coll., Springfield, Mass., 1934-38; prof. math. Hartwick Coll., Oneonta, N.Y., 1938-43; vis. asst. prof. Smith Coll., 1943-44; asst. prof. math. Vassar Coll., Poughkeepsie, N.Y., 1944-50, asso. prof., 1950-57, prof., 1957-73, prof. emeritus, 1973—; prof. Wesleyan Grad. Summer Sch. for Tchrs., 1965, 66; vis. research fellow Princeton, 1971. Trustee St. Margaret's Sch., Waterbury, Conn., 1965-70. Vassar faculty fellow, 1951, 66; NSF fellow, 1958-59. Mem. Math. Assn. Am., Am. Math. Soc., Am. Assn. U. Profs., Phi Beta Kappa, Sigma Xi. Episcopalian. Club: Adirondack Mountain (Poughkeepsie). Reviewer math. books for CHOICE, 1964-66, 70—. Home: 17 Kingston Av Poughkeepsie NY 12603

NEWTON, AUDREY EVELYN, educator; b. Bradford, Ill., Apr. 12, 1925; d. Glenn A. and Averil (Leadley) Newton; B.S., Bradley U., 1946; postgrad. U. Ill., summers 1949, 60; M.S., U. Wis., 1955; postgrad. Va. Poly. Inst., summer 1959; Ph.D., Ohio State U., 1967. Home service adviser Central Ill. Light Co., Peoria, 1946-47; tchr. homemaking Wyoming (Ill.) Community High Sch., 1947-53; teaching asst. clothing and textiles U. Wis., Madison, 1954-55; tchr. clothing Madison Vocational Sch., 1954-55; asst. prof. clothing, textiles and related arts U. Vt., Burlington, 1955-63, chmn. div., 1957-63; chmn. textiles, clothing and design U. Neb., Lincoln, 1965—. Mem. Coll. Agr. and Coll. Home Econs. Library Com., 1966-73, chmn. 1973. Recipient Distinguished Teaching award U. Neb., 1970. Mem. Nat. Retail Research Assn., Nat. Soc. Interior Designers, Am. (rehab. com. 1971-73), Neb. (1st v.p. 1974) home econs. assns., Assns. Coll. Profs. of Textiles and Clothing (pres. 1975), Omicron Nu, Phi Upsilon Omicron. Club: Altrusa (pres. 1970-71; dist. com. chmn. 1972-74). Home: 3505 S 31st St Lincoln NE 68502

NEWTON, COSETTE FAUST (MRS. FRANK HAWLEY NEWTON), museum ofcl., writer; b. Kemp, Tex., July 18, 1889; d. Edwin Michael and Sue (Noble) Faust; certificate Denton Normal Coll., 1906, Sam Houston Normal Sch., 1907; B.A., B.S., Poly. Coll. Ft. Worth, 1911; M.A., U. Tex., 1912; Ph.D., Radcliffe Coll., 1916; M.S., U. Chgo., 1923, J.D., 1924; M.D., Baylor U., 1923; B.E., M.E., Columbia Coll. Expression Chgo., 1924; J.S.D., N.Y. U., 1925; certificate Sorbonne, 1927; m. Frank Hawley Newton, June 14, 1918. Tchr. pub. schs., Baird, Tex. 1907-08; head dept. English, Mexia (Tex.) High Sch., 1912-13; asst. prof. English, So. Meth. U., Dallas, 1917-18, asso. prof., dean of women, 1918; pres. Miramir Mus., Dallas, 1963—. Mem. Nat. League Am. Pen Women, Nat. Poetry Soc., Poetry Soc. Tex., Kappa Alpha Theta, Zeta Phi Eta. Mem. Order Eastern Star. Author: (with Stith Thompson) Old English Poems, 1918; Rainbow-Hued Trail Around the World, 1932; Relatives in Rhyme at Christmas Time, 1938; Around the World in Rhyme, 1939; Kinship Songs, 1939; Dark Interval, 1941; War-Blown, 1941; Songs for Singers, 1942; S.S. Miramar Verses; The Great American "Accident", 1951; Macarthur's Hour, 1951; Romance of A Rosebud; Garden Songs. Contbr. to periodicals and anthologies including: Kaleidograph Press, Expns. Press, Southwester, Crown Publs., Poetry Digest, Corpus Christi Chronicle. Address: 2217 Cedar Springs St Dallas TX 75201

NEWTON, DOROTHY MAY FAIRBANK (MRS. ROBERT E. NEWTON), civic worker; b. St. Louis, Mar. 26, 1919; d. Alfred and Abby Jane (Downing) Fairbank; A.B. Vassar Coll., 1940; m. Robert Eugene Newton, Jan. 31, 1942; children—Peggy D., Gary Fairbank. Sec. Metro-Goldwyn-Mayer, St. Louis, 1941-42. Mem. bd. Monterey Peninsula Community Chest, 1957-66, v.p., 1960-61, pres., 1962; mem. bd. Monterey Peninsula Community Council, 1962-64, 66, v.p., 1966; mem. bd. Monterey Peninsula Council Girl Scouts, 1953-60, v.p. 1958-59; mem. bd. League Women Voters Monterey Peninsula, 1963-67, v.p., 1964-65, 66-67; homes, patron chmn. Am. Field Service, Carmel chpt., 1966-71; chmn. Monterey Bay Area Vassar Coll. Capital campaign, 1971; mem. book com. Harrison Meml. Library, Carmel, 1971—. Mem. aux. Community Hosp. Monterey

Peninsula, pres., 1973. Mem. Phi Beta Kappa. Presbyn. Home: Pen-y-Bryn 3810 Whitman Circle Carmel CA 93921

NEWTON, INDIA ALIDA, librarian; b. Cortland, N.Y., Apr. 30, 1911; d. Earle Williams and Anna (Moore) Newton; student Simmons Coll., 1928-30; B.S., N.Y. State Coll., 1933; postgrad. Columbia, 1935; M.S., Syracuse U., 1940; M.A., San Jose State Coll., 1960. Bus. tchr., pub. schs., Truxton, N.Y., 1933-35, Chittenango, N.Y., 1935-38, Mineola, N.Y., 1938-39; asst. mgr. 76 Ranch, Wilcox, Ariz., 1939; social sec., Hollywood, Cal., 1940; script sec., Hollywood, 1941; owner, mgr. Triangle T Ranch, Dragoon, Ariz., 1943-44; area supr. A.R.C. Overseas Clubmobile, France and Germany, 1945-46; club dir. Spl. Services, Dept. Army, Japan, 1948-50; head librarian Shasta Coll., Redding, Cal., 1955—. Recipient award Am. Nat. Red Cross, 1946, certificate of award Shasta Coll., 1968. Mem. Am. Assn. U. Profs. (chpt. sec.-treas. 1966-68), Am. Assn. U. Women (past fellowship chmn., corr. sec. 1973-74), Cal. Library Assn. Home: 940 Redbud Dr Redding CA 96001

NEWTON, KATHY M. WIESER (MRS. MICHAEL J. NEWTON), broadcasting co. exec.; b. Rapid City, S.D., Jan. 5, 1948; d. Joe J. and Ella Mae (Keiser) Wieser; B.S., S.D. State U., 1972; m. Michael J. Newton, May 31, 1969. Family page editor Estherville (Ia.) Daily News, 1969; media and prodn., mgr. The Company, advt. agy., Fargo, N.D., 1972-73; promotion dir. Sta. KXJB-TV, Fargo, 1973—. Mem. Women in Communication, Kappa Tau Alpha, Phi Upsilon Omicron. Home: 1846 S 14 1/2 St Fargo ND 58102 Office: 4000 W Main St Fargo ND 58102

NEWTON, MARGARET ELIZABETH, wood co. exec.; b. Muskogee, Okla., Sept. 1; d. Herbert E. and Margaret E. (Robins) Newton; Asso. A.B., Christian Coll. Columbia, Mo.; A.B., So. Meth. U.; M.A., U. Tex. Formerly sec. Arnold Tie & Timber Co., Muskogee, asst. treas. Lyles & Buckner, Inc., Muskogee; now sec., treas. Southwestern Wood Preserving Co., Muskogee. Active various community drives. Bd. dirs. Muskogee Goodwill, Muskogee Community Concert Assn. (sec.). Mem. Am. Assn. U. Women, Muskogee Pan-Hellanic Assn., Woman's Soc. Christian Service (dist. and conf. treas. youth sect.), Gamma Phi Beta (treas.). Methodist (rec. sec. Okla. Conf. Bd. Missions, mem. Gen. Bd. Global Ministries). Club: Soroptimist (pres. Muskogee). Home: 619 E Okmulgee Muskogee OK 74401 Office: PO Box 23 Muskogee OK 74401

NEWTON, MARGARET RONALDS (MRS. ANSON PIERSON NEWTON), artist; b. Vincennes, Ind., May 3, 1920; d. Francis Spring and Grace Anne (McFadden) Ronalds; student Coll. William and Mary, 1937-41, Rutgers U., 1941; B.A., U. Ill., 1942; student New Sch., 1970-71; m. Anson Pierson Newton, Sept. 9, 1942; children—Pamela S. (Mrs. Francis Scott Renna), Ronalds S. Operator Grey Barn Gallery, Morristown, N.J., 1954-64; pvt. tchr. painting, 1960-70; art therapist Morristown Meml. Hosp., 1968-72; one-man shows at Argus Gallery, Highgate Gallery, Somerset Gallery; exhibited in group shows at Newark Mus., Morris Mus. Art and Scis., Trenton Mus. (all N.J.), Scranton (Pa.) Mus., Nat. Acad., N.Y.C.; represented in permanent collections Newark Mus., Morris Mus. Arts and Scis. Recipient Patricia Murphy award Nat. Assn. Women Painters, 1959, many others. Mem. Am. Art Therapy Assn., Nat. Assn. Women Artists, Hunterdon Art Assn. (dir. 1957-60), Artists Equity (membership bd. 1973), Morris County Art Assn., Jr. League, Kappa Kappa Gamma. Home: Ansmar Cottage James St Morristown NJ 07960

NEWTON, MARIANA, educator; b. Long Beach, Cal., Aug. 4, 1938; d. Ernest LeRoy and Celia May (Merrill) Newton; A.A., Cottey Coll., 1958; B.A., U. Redlands, 1960, M.A., (William R. Parker Found. scholar), 1963; Ph.D., Northwestern U., 1969. Speech pathologist Pineland Hosp., Pownal, Me., 1960-61, Cal. Elks Maj. Project (rehab. physically handicapped children), 1961-68; asst. prof. speech pathology U. N.C. at Greensboro, 1969—, dir. Speech and Hearing Center, 1970—. Mem. governing bd. Inst. Child and Family Devel. U. N.C. at Greensboro; pres. Cottey Coll. Alumnae Exec. Bd., 1973—; mem. adv. bd. Greensboro Assn. for Children with Learning Disabilities, 1973—. Mem. Am. (legislative councilor 1973—), N.C. (pres. 1972-73) speech and hearing assns., Nat. Rehab. Assn., A.A.A.S., Am. Assn. Mental Deficiency, Am. Acad. for Cerebral Palsy, N.C. Rehab. Assn., P.E.O. (pres. chpt. A 1973—). Home: 2405 B Patriot Way Greensboro NC 27408

NEYHART, LOUISE PAULINE (MRS. CARL NEYHART), author; b. Amboy, Ill., Jan. 30, 1905; d. Frederick Stuyvesant and Lillian Marie (Fitchner) Albright; student Lake Forest Coll., 1922-24; diploma Nat. Coll. Edn., 1925; m. Carl Herbert Neyhart, Sept. 24, 1927; 1 son, Frederick Albright. Tchr. Freeport (Ill.) Pub. Schs., 1925-28, substitute tchr., 1928-55; author: Henry's Lincoln, 1945; Henry Ford Engineer, 1950; Giant of the Yards, 1952. Mem. Ill. Community Coll. Bd., 1970—. Trustee Highland Community Coll., 1966-70, v.p., 1965-69; bd. dirs., charter mem. Highland Community Coll. Found., 1963-70; trustee Freeport Pub. Library, 1965—, v.p., 1970, pres., 1972—; mem. citizens com. U. Ill., 1970—. Recipient Alumni Achievement award Nat. Coll. Edn., 1972. Mem. P.E.O., Beta Sigma Phi (hon. life). Home: 1309 W Lincoln Blvd Freeport IL 61032

NEYLAN, MARGUERITE MARY (MRS. WILLIAM J. KELLEY), pediatrician; b. N.Y.C., May 19, 1916; d. James Joseph and Marguerite May (Freese) Neylan; A.B., Cornell U., 1937; M.D., N.Y. Med. Coll., 1942; m. William J. Kelley, July 6, 1946. Intern Norwegian Lutheran Deaconess Hosp., Bklyn., 1942-43; asst. resident Boston Floating Hosp., 1943-44, chief resident, 1944-45, now mem. pediatric staff; admitting physician Boston Dispensary, 1945-50; now practice medicine, Brookline, Mass.; mem. courtsey staff Boston Hosp. Women, St. Margaret's Hosp., Boston; mem. pediatric staff St. Elizabeth's Hosp., Boston; clin. instr. Tufts U. Med. Sch., 1945—. Mem. A.M.A., Am. Acad. Pediatrics, New Eng. Pediatric Soc., St. Luke's Guild Catholic Physicians. Home: 624 Newton St Chestnut Hill MA 02167 Office: 1018 Beacon St Brookline MA 02146

NEYMAN, PAULA (MRS. DANIEL NEYMAN), pediatrician; b. Breslau, Poland; came to U.S. 1947, naturalized 1949; d. Goerg and Lisa (Getzowitz) Getzowitz; B.A. magna cum laude, Hunter Coll., 1953; M.D., N.Y. U., 1957; m. Daniel Neyman, May 5, 1950; children—Sarena, Freyda. Intern Bellevue Hosp. III div. pediatrics, N.Y.C., 1957-58; resident pediatrics Jacobi Hosp., Bronx, N.Y., 1958-60, now mem. staff; practice medicine specializing in pediatrics, Bronx, 1960—; clin. asst. prof. pediatrics Albert Einstein Coll. Medicine, 1967—. Active various coms. Westchester Day Sch., Mamaroneck, N.Y. Fellow Am. Acad. Pediatrics; mem. Bronx Pediatric Soc., Soc. for Pediatric Ambulatory Services, Am.-Israeli Med. Assn., Phi Beta Kappa. Office: 2110 Barnes Av Bronx NY 10462

NEZELEK, ANNETTE EVELYN (MRS. EDWARD NEZELEK), constrn co. exec.; b. Chgo., Feb. 16, 1921; d. Frank and Susan (Linstra) Van Howe; B.A. in History magna cum laude, Hofstra U., 1952; M.A. in Am. History, State U. N.Y. at Binghamton, 1966; m. Edward L. Nezelek, Apr. 3, 1961. Editorial asst. Salute Mag., N.Y.C., 1946-48; asso. editor Med. Econs., Oradell, N.J., 1952-56; nat. mag. publicist Nat. Mental Health Assn., N.Y.C., 1956-60; exec. dir. Diabetes Assn. So. Cal., Los Angeles, 1960-61; corporate sec., v.p., editor, pub. relations dir. Edward L. Nezelek, Inc., Johnson City, N.Y., 1961—. Substitute tchr. high schs., Binghamton, N.Y., 1961-63. Bd. dirs. Broome County Mental Health Assn., 1961-65, Fine Arts Soc., Roberson Center for Arts and Scis., 1968-70, Found. Wilson Meml. Hosp., Johnson City, N.Y., 1972—, Found. State U. N.Y. at Binghamton; trustee Broome Community Coll., 1973—. Mem. Am. Assn. U. Women, Am. Med. Writers Assn., League Women Voters (dir. Broome County 1969-70), Alumni Assn. State U. N.Y. at Binghamton (dir. 1970—), Am. Acad. Polit. and Social Sci., Alpha Theta Beta, Phi Alpha Theta, Phi Gamma Mu. Clubs: Binghamton Garden, Binghamton Monday Afternoon, Acacia Garden. Editor newsletter Mental Health Assn., 1965-68, newsletter Unitarian-Universalist Ch., weekly 1967-71, History of Broome County Meml. Arena, 1972. Home: 22 Hamton Rd Binghamton NY 13903 Office: 76 Pratt Av Johnson City NY 13790

NICHOL, BETTY BARBARA STAPLETON (MRS. WILLIAM F. NICHOL), artist; b. N.Y.C., Apr. 1, 1921; d. Edward Joseph and Elizabeth Gertrude (Gallegher) Stapleton; student N.Y. U., 1942-45, Art Students League, 1960-65; pvt. study with Leo Manso, Rudolf Baranik, Edgar Whitney, others; m. William F. Nichol, Sept. 11, 1948; children—Betsy, Richard. Exhibited one-man shows at N. Shore Unitarian Ch. Gallery, Stewart Russell Gallery, Adelphi U.; exhibited in group shows at Bergen County (N.J.) Mus., Nat. Acad. Galleries, N.Y.C., C.W. Post Coll., Adelphi U.; tchr. art N.Y.C. Adult Edn. program, also pvt. lessons; lectr. art history radio sta. WEVD, 1972, pvt. orgns. Recipient awards for art. Mem. Island Art Guild (pres. 1966-67), Nat. Assn. Women Artists, Manhasset Art Assn. (sec. 1969-72). Home: 42054 235th St Douglaston NY 11363 Studio: Douglaston Pkwy Douglaston NY 11363

NICHOL, RUTH ARLINE (MRS. WILLIAM EDISON NICHOL), assn. exec.; b. Des Moines, Oct. 7, 1918; d. Charles Green and Ida Clara (Treiber) Ellis; B.S., Neb. Wesleyan U., 1940; postgrad. Denver U., 1960; m. William Edison Nichol, Nov. 29, 1941; children—James Charles, Linda (Mrs. Walter William Harsch Jr.). Tchr. Pierce High Sch., 1940-41; with radio sta. WOW, Omaha, 1941-42; tchr. Scottsbluff (Neb.) High Sch., 1960-63. Mem. Scottsbluff Planning Commn., 1968-72. Mem. Scottsbluff Bd. Edn., 1963—. Recipient Neb. Distinguished Service award for community and state Neb. Schoolmasters Club, 1969. Mem. Am. Assn. U. Women, Neb. Congress of Parents and Tchrs. (pres. 1965-68), Neb. State Sch. Bds. Assn. (pres. 1972-73). Methodist. Elk. Home: 617 E 26 St Scottsbluff NE 69361

NICHOLAS, DONNA LEE, ceramic artist, educator; b. South Pasadena, Cal., Mar. 30, 1938; d. George H. and Dorothy L. (McMannamy) Nicholas; B.A. cum laude, Pomona Coll., 1959; M.F.A., Claremont Grad. Sch. and U. Center, 1966. Ceramics instr. C.S. Mott Community Coll., Flint, Mich., 1966-69; asso. prof. art Edinboro (Pa.) State Coll., 1969—. Exhibited in one-woman shows, including Edward Sherbeyn Gallery, Chgo., 1970, Erie (Pa.) Art Gallery, 1974; two-woman show Shirokiya Dept. Store, Tokyo, Japan, 1964; numerous group shows including: Nitten Exhbn., Tokyo, Nagoya, Osaka, and Kyoto, (Japan) museums of art, 1961; Miami (Fla.) Nat. Ceramics Exhbn. (purchase prize and hon. mention), 1965; Craftsmen U.S.A. '66, Los Angeles (Cal.) County Mus.; Cranbrook Acad. Art, Bloomfield Hills, Mich., 1967; 27th Ann. Ceramic Invitational, Scripps Coll., Claremont, Cal., 1971; Mus. Contemporary Crafts, N.Y.C., 1972; Charleston (W.Va.) Art Gallery (achievement award, 1972; Cal. State U. at San Luis Obispo (1st prize), 1972; 9th Ann. So. Tier Arts and Crafts Show, Corning (N.Y.) Mus. (two jury awards), 1972; Ceramics Internat. '73, Alta. (Can.) Coll. Art, Calgary; Claythings/East Coast Invitational, Moore Coll. Art, Phila., 1974; vis. artist Penland (N.C.) Sch. Crafts, 1971; vis. asso. prof. Scripps Coll., 1974. Bd. dirs. Edinboro Lakeside Assn., 1973—. Archie Bray Found. grantee, 1967. Mem. Coll. Art Assn., Am. Craftsmen's Council. Home: Box 150 Edinboro PA 16412

NICHOLAS, MARY CORNELIA BURKE, govt. ofcl.; b. Tuskegee, Ala.; d. Walter Spurgeon and Ruth (Freeland) Burke; B.A. with honors, U. Wis.; children—Tracy Christine, Scott Cardozo. Asst. editor Am. City Mag., N.Y.C., 1948; asst. city planner N.Y.C. Dept. City Planning, 1950-53; spl. asst. N.Y.C. Housing and Redevel. Bd., 1960-65; exec. asst. N.Y.C. Mayor's Housing Policy Bd., 1962-66; exec. asst. in housing Office of Mayor, N.Y.C., 1964-66; dept. asst. Region I adminstr. U.S. Dept. Housing and Urban Devel., Region 1, N.Y.C., 1966-70; dep. dir. N.Y. State Commn. on Powers of Local Govt., 1970-73; regional economist Region II, Dept. Housing and Urban Devel., N.Y.C., 1974—. Mem. Manhattan Adv. Com. to N.Y. Urban League, 1966—; sponsor Ebony Fashion Fair, 1966—. Bd. dirs. Riverdale Children's Assn., 1966-68, Friends of Channel 13, 1972—, N.Y. Jazz Repertory Co., 1973—. Mem. Nat. Council Women of U.S. (2d v.p. 1970-72), Coalition of 100 Black Women (exec. com. 1972—), Phi Kappa Phi. Sigma Delta Pi. Democrat. Home: 201 E 21st St New York City NY 10010 Office: 26 Federal Plaza Room 3541 New York City NY 10007

NICHOLS, EDITH JUNE (MRS. ROBERT LEO NICHOLS), educator; b. Franklin, Neb., June 26, 1917; d. Benjamin Harrison and Lillian May (Brethouwer) Bos; A.B., San Diego State U., 1961, M.A., 1965; postgrad. Claremont Grad. Sch., 1966-67; Ed.D., U. Cal. at Los Angeles, 1971; m. Robert Leo Nichols, Oct. 11, 1936 (dec. Jan. 1959); children—Roberta (Mrs. William Richard Dorow), Patricia (Mrs. Huel Jay Oldham). Elementary sch. tchr. La Mesa-Spring Valley Sch. Dist., La Mesa, Cal., 1961—, Maryland Av. Elementary Sch., 1970—. Chmn., Gray Lady Red Cross Vols., Memphis, 1954-56. Mem. Nat. Council for Tchrs. Math., Am. Ednl. Research Assn., Assn. for Childhood Edn. Internat., Pi Lambda Theta. Home: 2655 Littleton Rd El Cajon CA 92020 Office: 4750 Date Av La Mesa CA 92041

NICHOLS, EDNA CLARICE (MRS. FRANK T. NICHOLS), communications co. exec.; b. Daviess County, Mo., May 19, 1916; d. Sanford Joseph and Clarice Modena (Roberts) Briner; grad. Chillicothe Bus. Coll., 1933; m. Frank T. Nichols, Oct. 30, 1936; 1 son, Alan Franklin. Sec., revenue accountant Inter-County Telephone Co., Gallatin, Mo., 1934-37; sec. C.D. Brandom, Atty., Gallatin, 1940-44; sec. to pres. Lakeland Telephone Co., Bolivar, Mo., also Inter-County Telephone Co., Albany, Mo., 1951—, sec., asst. treas., 1962—; corporate sec. Telecom Engrs., Inc., Columbia, Mo., also Lake Press, Inc., Stockton, Mo., 1968—, corporate sec. Columbia Service Bur., Inc., 1962—, corporate dir., 1962—. Mem. Nat. Secs. Assn. (rec. sec. 1970-71, membership chmn. 1969-70). Baptist (ch. clk. and sec. 1964-66). Republican. Home: 1806 Parklawn Dr Columbia MO 65201 Office: 200 E Walnut Columbia MO 65201

NICHOLS, JEANNETTIE DOORNHEIN, painter, educator; b. Holland, Mich., July 27, 1906; d. Jacob Lenard and Caroline (Hauk) Doornhein; B.A.E., Art Inst. Chgo., 1934; m. Charles Martin Nichols, Apr. 21, 1941; 1 dau., Jean Lawson. Art supr. Belvidere Pub. Schs., 1929-31; tchr. comml. art Crane Evening Sch., Chgo., 1933-36; tchr. art Chgo. pub. schs., 1933-71, art dept. head 1948-71. Exhibited Pa. Nat. Acad., Phila., Chgo. Asso. Galleries, Mandels Art Gallery, Conrad Hilton Hotel, 1952, Ind. State Fair, 1954, Artists Equity, Gary Artists League, Internat. Artists Exhibit, N.Y.C., 1959, Phoenix, 1959, W.A.A. Mpls. Art Gallery, 1964, 65, and others; one-man shows Waukazoo, Holland, Mich., 1952, Cottage Studios, Chgo., 1953, Gary (Ind.) Hotel, 1957, Crespi Gallery, N.Y.C., 1959, Kriegart Art Gallery, Lombard, Ill., 1971-74; group shows Sherman Hotel Art Gallery, Chgo., 1960, Gary Artists League, Gary Gallery; exhibited in juried shows at 57th St. Art Fair, Chgo., also Gary Music and Arts Am., Chesterton (Ind.) Art Fair, 1961-74, Weatherspoon Gallery, U. N.C., 1969; represented permanent collections Albrecht Art Mus., St. Joseph, Mo., others. Recipient 1st prize enamel on copper Gary Craftsman Guild, 1955; 2d prize mixed-medium Chesterton Ann., 1955; 3d prize water color Gary Artists League, 1955; 1st, 2d, 3d Purchase awards South Bend Art Center, 1956, Tri Kappa award, 1967, other prizes. Fellow Internat. Inst. Arts and Letters (life); mem. Art Educators Chgo. (pres. 1961, bd. mem.), Artist Equity, Gary Artists League (past pres., 1st v.p. 1963), Art Inst. Alumni Assn., Western Arts Assn., N.E.A., Nat. Art Edn. Assn., Chgo. Tchrs. Union, Porter County Arts and Crafts Assn. (pres. 1963). Author article profl. mag. Home and studio: 2800 Deep Ford Dr Woodbridge VA 22191

NICHOLS, JENNIE BARTON (MRS. R. HEWITT NICHOLS), dietitian; b. Stueben County, N.Y., Jan. 16, 1916; d. Revere Stephen and Cora (Yoder) Barton; B.S., Keuka Coll., 1935; diploma West Penn Hosp. Sch. Dietetics, 1936; m. Richard Hewitt, Nichols, Oct. 2, 1943; children—Richard Hewitt, Peter Barton. Asst. dietitian Presbyn. Hosp., Pitts., 1936-37, dir. dietetics, 1937-43; asst. dietitian Providence Hosp., Washington, 1944-45; teaching dietitian Garfield Hosp., Washington, 1945-46; dietitian Mid Atlantic Regional office Slater Food Services Mgmt., Balt., 1959-64; hdqrs. dietitian ARA Slater Sch. and Coll. Services, Phila., 1964—; home economist Agrl. Research Service, U.S. Dept. Agr., Hyattsville, Md., 1971—. Nutrition chmn. Howard County br. A.R.C., 1950—. Mem. women's bd. Montgomery City Gen. Hosp., 1956-59; mem. steering com. Vocational High Sch., Howard County. Mem. Am. (legislative chmn. 1944-48), D.C., Md. (dir. pub. relations, 1948-51) dietetic assns., Howard County Pub. Health Assn. (sec. 1955-57), Am., Md., D.C. home econs. assns., Am. Assn. U. Women (rec. sec. Md. div. 1968-70). Home: Box 108 Clarksville MD 21029

NICHOLS, KATHERINE CAMERON (MRS. CARLILE NICHOLS), educator; b. Knoxville, Tenn., Jan. 18, 1915; d. Donald Field and Katherine (Knight) Cameron; B.S., U. Tenn., 1938, M.S., 1942; student Columbia, summer 1945; m. Carlile Nichols, June 24, 1950. Tchr., Leadwood (Mo.) High Sch., 1938-41; asst. prof. Flora McDonald Coll., Red Spring, N.C., 1942-45; asso. prof. home econs. Centre Coll., Danville, Ky., 1945-50, 54-63, dean women, 1963—, asso. prof. art, 1963-73, prof. art, 1973—. Head residental drives March of Dimes, 1955, United Community Fund, 1954, A.R.C., 1953. Bd. dirs. March of Dimes, 1954-60; bd. dirs. Cancer Soc., 1953-60, treas., 1958-60. Mem. Am. Assn. U. Women, Nat., Ky. assns. women deans and counselors, Nat. Soc. Interior Designers, Delta Kappa Gamma. Presbyn. (deacon). Clubs: Danville Garden, Amanda Rodes Book. Home: 141 N 5th St Danville KY 40422

NICHOLS, MARIE HOCHMUTH, educator; b. Dunbar, Pa., July 13, 1908; d. Alexander and Mary (Flydell) Hochmuth; A.B., U. Pitts., 1931, M.A., 1936; Ph.D., U. Wis., 1945; m. Alan Nichols, Aug. 18, 1960. Instr. Mt. Mercy Coll., Pitts., 1935-39; mem. faculty U. Ill. at Urbana, 1939—, prof. speech, 1958—; vis. prof. U. So. Cal., summers 1957, 67, 69; lectr. La. State U., summer 1960; vis. prof. U. Hawaii, 1962. Mem. Speech Assn. Am. (administrv. council 1960—, pres. 1969), N.E.A. Author: Rhetoric and Criticism, 1963. Editor: History and Criticism of American Public Address, Vol. III, 1955; American Speeches, 1954; Quar. Jour. Speech, 1962-65. Home: 502 W Main St Urbana IL 61801

NICHOLS, MARTHA ARNOLD (MRS. EVERETT NICHOLS), coll. dean; b. Columbus, O., Oct. 26, 1916; d. Alfred A. and Phyllis L. (Loos) Arnold; A.B., Goucher Coll., 1938; M.A., Syracuse U., 1942; m. Everett Nichols, Dec. 20, 1947; children—Stephen A., Jonathan S. Tchr. sci., sports Roland Park Country Sch., Balt., 1938-40; asso. dean students Goucher Coll., Towson, Md., 1947-48, dean students, 1948—. Chmn. coll. program A.R.C., Towson, Md., 1968. Bd. dirs. Children's Aid and Family Service Soc., 1973—. Mem. Nat. Assn. Women Deans, Adminstrs. and Counselors (sec. 1969-71, mem. adv. bd. 1972—), Deans of Women (v.p. Md. regional asso. 1946-48, sec., Md. regional asso. 1948-50). Home: 710 Mildam St Towson MD 21204

NICHOLS, MYRTLE M. (MRS. NORRIS NICHOLS), printing and pub. co. exec.; b. Marion, Md., Aug. 1, 1908; d. Alonzo Lee and Susan (Bozman) Murrell; grad. Md. Tchrs. Coll., Columbia. Asst. personnel dir. Waverly Press, Inc., also The Williams & Wilkins Co., Balt., 1945-51, dir. personnel, 1952-57, v.p. personnel, 1958—, v.p. community relations, 1971-74, also dir., past mem. exec. com. Mem. com. on econ. problems of aging Md. Conf. Social Welfare, 1953-71, dir., 1972—; employment com. Gov.'s Commn. on Aging, 1959-70; chmn. Balt. City Com. Employment of Handicapped, 1953; mem. Mayor's Task Force, Balt.; mem. adv. com. Balt. Mayor's Office of Manpower Resources, 1972—. Bd. dirs. Md. Conf. of Social Concern, Assn. Ind. Coll. Md., Commerce and Industry Combined Health Appeal. Mem. Assn. Personnel Women Md. (past pres.). Address: 1111 Park Av Baltimore MD 21201

NICHOLS, RELIEF AURILLA, educator; b. Brookville, Me.; d. Benjamin Thomas and Caddie E. (Jones) Nichols; grad. Eastern State Normal Sch., Me., 1926; B.S., U. Me., 1949, M.Ed., 1953, postgrad., 1960. Tchr. various schs., Me., 1920-47; mem. faculty Aroostock State Tchrs. Coll., 1949; instr. English, lit. Higgins Classical Inst., Charleston, 1949-55; mem. faculty Washington State Coll., Machias, Me., 1955—, head English dept. until 1970. Trustee, Brooksville Pub. Library. Mem. Brooksville Hist. Soc., Nat., Hancock County (pres.) ret. tchrs. assns., Four Town Nursing Assn., New Eng. Coll. English Assn., Am. Assn. U. Profs., Shakespeare Soc., Delta Kappa Gamma, Kappa Delta Pi, Phi Kappa Phi. Conglist. (deaconess). Mem. Rebekah Lodge. Clubs: Scribblers, Federated Women's. Poems published in mags. including Yankee Mag., newspapers. Home: Willowhurst Brooksville ME 04617

NICHOLS, VERA KOCH (MRS. MERRILL L. NICHOLS), occupational therapist, educator; b. Menno, S.D., May 28, 1907; d. Henry Ernest and Susan (Blumer) Koch; B.A., No. U. Ia., 1930; M.A., State U. Ia., 1945; certificate in occupational therapy State U. Ill., 1946; postgrad. summers Art Inst. Chgo., 1933, 38, Syracuse U., 1946, 50; m. Merrill L. Nichols, May 25, 1946. Tchr. 8th grade Rural Sch. 23, Hutchinson County, S.D., 1925-27; tchr. art and English, Jr. High Sch., Newton, Ia., 1930-33, high sch. art tchr., elementary supt., 1933-34; high sch. art tchr., elementary supt., Waterloo, Ia., 1934-38; high sch. art tchr. Sioux Falls, S.D., 1938-44; elementary art tchr., Syracuse, N.Y., 1946-57; high sch. art tchr., Syracuse, 1957-69; occupational therapist VA Psychol. Day Care Center, Syracuse, 1970. Vol. work as occupational therapist VA Hosp., Syracuse, 1969—. Presbyn. (deacon 1954-57, 73—). Order Eastern Star. Address: 712 N Highland Av East Syracuse NY 13057

NICHOLS, WANDA DOVE (MRS. WILLIAM HAYDEN NICHOLS), educator; b. Hotchkiss, Colo., Mar. 8, 1926; d. Jess Titus and Margarette Elaine (Cotten) Dove; A.A., Compton Coll., 1945;

B.A., Fresno State Coll., 1948; M.A., San Fernando Valley State Coll., 1969; m. William Hayden Nichols, Mar. 23, 1957; (dec. May 1971); children—Gail, Gregory, Carol. With United Air Lines, Honolulu, San Francisco, Los Angeles, 1950-55, Rand Corp., Santa Monica, Cal., 1956-57; tchr. performing arts Jefferson High Sch., Portland, Ore., 1970—, program leader, 1974—. Mem. Am. Theatre Assn., Secondary Sch. Theatre Assn. (regional dir.), Ore. Theatre Arts Assn. (sec. 1973), Empathy, Delta Psi Omega. Home: 3744 N Overlook Blvd Beaverton OR 97227 Office: 5210 N Kerby Portland OR 97217

NICHOLSON, DOROTHY ANN, geographer; b. Phila., July 5, 1932; d. John Lewis and Amanda (Sykes) Nicholson; student Rhodes U. Coll., Grahamstown, South Africa, 1950; B.S., Kent State U., 1954; M.A., Northwestern U., 1956. Jr. engr. Goodyear Aerospace Corp., Akron, O., 1956-59; cartographic researcher Nat. Geog. Soc., Washington, 1962—, mem. Duke-Nat. Geog. Soc. expdns. to search for Civil War ironclad Monitor, 1973-74. Recipient St. Elizabeth's Hosp. Vol. Service Award, 1966. Carnegie Corp. scholar. in African studies, 1955-56. Mem. Assn. Am. Geographers (sec.-treas. Middle Atlantic div. 1972, sec. 1973-74, nat. treas. 1974, editor Middle Atlantic div. Newsletter 1972-74, Am. Geog. Soc., A.A.A.S., Gamma Theta Upsilon, Gamma Phi Beta. Home: 5304 Worthington Dr Washington DC 20016 Office: 17th and M Sts NW Washington DC 20036

NICHOLSON, EDNA ELIZABETH, ret. pub. health ofcl.; b. Redwood Falls, Minn., Dec. 23, 1907; d. Ernest Crawford and Alma (Bordeaux) Nicholson; A.B., U. Mich., 1930, M.S. in Pub. Health, 1931, certificate in social work, 1931. Nat. Tb Assn. fellowship in social research 1930-31; med. social work A.R.C., U.S. Naval Hosp., Great Lakes, Ill., 1931-33; asst. dir. med. relief service, Cook County Bur. of Pub. Welfare, Chgo., 1933-35; instr. in social aspects of nursing Cook County Sch. of Nursing, asst. dir. social service, Cook County Hosp., Chgo., 1935-37; dir., med. relief service Chgo. Relief Adminstrn., 1938-42; vis. lectr. Sch. of Hygiene and Pub. Health, U. Mich., 1939; cons. on med. assistance, bur. of pub. assistance, Fed. Security Agency, 1942-44; dir. Central Service for the Chronically Ill, Inst. of Medicine, Chgo., 1944-54; exec. dir. Inst. Medicine of Chgo., 1955-64; supr., med. assistance specialist Med. Services Adminstrn., Dept. Health, Edn. and Welfare, 1964-71; spl. lectr. program in hosp. adminstrn. Northwestern U. 1945-60; tech. adviser Commn. on Chronic Illness, 1949-56. Recipient Cancer Care award Nat. Cancer Found., 1955. Mem. Am. Pub. Health Assn., Nat. Assn. Social Workers, Phi Beta Kappa, Delta Omega, Sigma Kappa. Author: Terminal Care for Cancer Patients, 1950; Surveying Community Needs and Resources for Care of the Chronically Ill, 1950; The Nurse and Chronic Illness; Planning New Institutional Facilities for Longterm Care, 1956; A Comprehensive Community Plan for Meeting the Problems of Chronic Illness, 1959. Contbr. to profl. jours. Home: 5017 Brookdale Rd Washington DC 20016

NICHOLSON, KATHLEEN FARMER, librarian; b. Syracuse, N.Y., May 20, 1924; d. Thomas Patrick and Birgitta Kathleen (Moran) Farmer; B.A., Manhattanville Coll., 1945; M.L.S., Syracuse U., 1968; m. Robert E. Nicholson, Sept. 2, 1944; children—Therese (Mrs. Philip Ellsworth), Robert E., John A., Thomas F., Birgitta K. Librarian bus. and indsl. dept. Syracuse (N.Y.) Pub. Library, 1968-69, main circulation dept., 1969—. Sec. Parent's Group for Emotionally Disturbed Children, 1959-60; active mem. Jr. League Syracuse, 1946-65, sustaining mem., 1965—. Trustee Assn. for Help Retarded Children, Syracuse chpt., 1956-58. Mem. Internat. Fedn. Cath. Alumnae (v.p. 1963-65), Duchesne Circle (pres. 1968-69), Beta Phi Mu. Republican. Roman Catholic. Home: 208 Clairmonte Av Syracuse NY 13207 Office: 335 Montgomery St Syracuse NY 13202

NICHOLSON, NANCY VIOLA SNIDER, educator; b. Lachine, Mich., May 28, 1923; d. John William and Edna (Mills) Snider; B.A., U. Mich., 1946, M.A., 1947, Ph.D., 1962; m. Fred Nicholson, May 24, 1967 (div. Oct. 1968). English instr. Ia. State Tchrs. Coll., Cedar Falls, 1947-48; instr. Alpena (Mich.) Community Coll., 1953-54; asst. prof. U. N.Y. State Tchrs. Coll., Cortland, N.Y., 1955-56; instr. supr. Columbia Tchrs. Coll., Afghanistan, 1956-57; instr. Tufts U., Medford, Mass., 1957-60; asso. prof. Clarion State Coll., Clarion, Pa., 1963-66; asso. prof. Wis. State U., La Crosse, 1966-67; lectr. Eastern Mich. U., Ypsilanti, 1967-69; prof. English, So. U., Baton Rouge, 1969-71; lectr. English, Central Mich. U., Mt. Pleasant, 1972; asst. prof. U. Isfahan (Iran). Seminar dir. Ford Found., U. Pitts. summer 1964. Founded library in South India, 1954, social work in India, 1954. Mem. Hindustani Assn. U. Mich. (pres. 1954), Modern Lang. Assn., Coll. English Assn., Am. Assn. U. Profs., Am. Assn. U. Women. Contbr. articles in field to profl. jours. Home: Lachine MI 49753

NICHOLSON, NATALIE NEILL, librarian; b. Middletown, R.I., Jan. 3, 1910; d. John and Louisa Bancroft (Barker) Nicholson; S.B., Simmons Coll., 1932; postgrad. (Carnegie fellow), Rutgers U., 1958. Asst., Kirstein bus. br. Boston Pub. Library, 1932-37; librarian grad. sch. engring. Harvard U., Cambridge, Mass., 1937-54; reference librarian Mass. Inst. Tech., Cambridge, 1954-56, exec. asst. to dir. of libraries, 1956-58, asso. dir. libraries, 1958-72, acting dir., 1972-73, dir. libraries, 1973—. Recipient Ann. Alumni Achievement award Simmons Coll. Sch. Library Sci. Alumni Assn., 1972. Mem. A.L.A., Nat., Boston, Spl. library assns., Am. Soc. for Information Sci. Home: 37 Wendell St Cambridge MA 02138

NICHOLSON, NELLIE RUTHRAUFF (MRS. GEORGE A. NICHOLSON), civic worker; b. Circleville, O., Apr. 24, 1884; d. John Mosheim and Sarah Ellen (Morrison) Ruthrauff; A.B., Wittenberg Coll., 1903; student Baker U., 1908-09; m. George Albert Nicholson, Jan. 30, 1907; children—George Albert, Ruth (Mrs. George Fox Trowbridge), Florence Isabelle (Mrs. Charles Overton Stilwell). Tchr., Ariz., Ill., 1904-06; sec., treas. Kusa, Okla. unit Okmulgee County Council Def., 1917-18; chmn. women's div. for liberty loan No. half Okmulgee County, 1917-18; mem. Women's Community Council, Kansas City, Mo., 1921-22; treas. Kansas City Conservatory Music, 1923-24; chmn. women's golf com. Mission Hills Club, Kansas City, 1924-27; mem. bd. dirs. YWCA, Kansas City, 1921-24; dir., sec. v.p. Consumer's League of Kansas City, 1923-30; bd. dirs. Women's City Club, Kansas City, 1923-26; vice chmn. of Daphne Recreation Bd. Named Republican Women of Year Rep. Women Ala., 1971. Mem. Am. Assn. U. Women (v.p., fellowship chmn.), D.A.R. (vice regent Ecor Rouge chpt. 1959-61), Kansas City Art Inst., Nat. Soc. Colonial Dames Am., Birmingham Hist. Soc., Birmingham Art Assn., Birmingham Opera Assn., Mobile Hist. Soc., Mobile (Ala.) Art Assn., Mobile Opera Guild, Met. Opera Guild, Mobile Symphony Aux., Eastern Shore Art Assn., Delta Delta Delta. Episcopalian. Clubs: Highland Book, Daphne Women's Study, Daphne Republican Study (pres. 1967-68). Home: 1019 O'Neal Rd PO Drawer K Daphne AL 36526

NICHOLSON, ODAS, lawyer; b. Pickens, Miss., Mar. 25, 1924; d. George and Tempie (Johnson) Nicholson; student Wilson Jr. Coll., 1944; Ph.B., DePaul U., 1946, J.D., 1947. Admitted to Ill. bar, 1948; asso. Brown, Brown, Cyrus & Green, Chgo., 1948-51; partner Wilson, Calhoun & Nicholson, Chgo., 1951-56; practice law, Chgo., 1956-66; trial atty. Supreme Life Ins. Co., Chgo., 1966-73. Pres. Joint Negro Appeal, Chgo., 1959-62; v.p. Chgo. Youth Centers, 1970—. Del. Sixth Ill. Democrat Constl. Conv., 1969-70, sec. conv. 1969-70. Trustee Women's Bar Found. Ill., 1973-74. Recipient Joint Negro Appeal award for outstanding service, 1963; Omega Gamma Pi, Outstanding service award, 1970; award of recognition Asso. Judges Assn., 1971; Pub. Service award Cook County Bar Assn., 1971; Ann. Merit award Beatrice Caffrey Youth Service, Inc., 1973. Mem. Am., Chgo. Cook County bar assns., Nat. Assn. Women Lawyers, League Women Voters, World Peace Through Law Center, Bus. and Profl. Women's Club, Women's Bar Assn. Ill. (pres. 1973-74), Alpha Kappa Alpha. Home: 5300 South Shore Dr Chicago IL 60615 Office: 536 S Clark St Chicago IL 60605

NICHOLSON, WILLA DEAN, home economist; b. Fairview, Okla., Aug. 30, 1917; d. Justice Clarence and Charle Marie (Floyd) Nicholson; B.S., Okla. State U., 1939, M.S., 1953. Asst. extension home economist Okla. State U., Bryan County, Durant, 1939-40; extension home economist Marshall County, Madill, 1940-42, Texas County, Guymon, 1943-44; food specialist extension div. Okla. State U., Stillwater, 1944-45; tchr. vocational home econs., Fairview, Okla., 1947, El Reno, Okla., 1947-53; extension home economist Woodward County, Woodward, Okla., 1953-59; extension home economist Garfield County, Enid, Okla., 1959—. Mem. adv. com. St. Mary's Hosp., Phillips U. Mem. Okla. Edn. Assn., Nat., Okla. (v.p.) home econ. assns., Bus. and Profl. Womens Club, Delta Kappa Gamma, Epsilon Sigma Phi. Presbyn. Mem. Order Eastern Star. Home: 1931 Mosher Dr Enid OK 73701 Office: Box 1229 Enid OK 73701

NICHTERN, CLAIRE JOSEPH, theatrical producer; b. N.Y.C.; d. Fred and Rebecca (Brumer) Joseph; student N.Y.U., 1951-52; m. Sol. Nichtern, June 4, 1944 (div. 1968); children—Judith (Mrs. Donald Gelfer), David. Casting Dir. Phoenix Theatre, 1955-58, prodn. coordinator, 1959-60; asst. to gen. mgr. Playwrights Co., N.Y.C., 1958-59; producer The Banker's Daughter, N.Y.C., 1961-62, Luv, N.Y.C., 1964—, producer The Typists and the Tiger, N.Y.C., 1962-63, co-producer, London, Eng., 1964-65; producer Jimmy Shine, Broadway, 1968-69; dir. admissions, producer-in-residence Am. Acad. Dramatic Arts, 1970-73; co-producer The Trial of Abraham Lincoln, Los Angeles, 1971; asso. dir. Waltz of the Toreadors at Circle-In-the-Square. Recipient Antoinette Perry award Am. Theatre Wing, 1965. Mem. League N.Y. Theatres, Assn. Theatrical Press Agts. and Mgrs., ANTA. Home: 61 W 9th St New York City NY 10011

NICKEL, KAREN LOUISE (MRS. PHILLIP ARNOLD NICKEL), chemist; b. Trail, B.C., Can., Feb. 22, 1939; d. Theodore Waldemar and Marianne Geraldine (Kirk) Sahlstrom; came to U.S., 1940, naturalized, 1963; student Pacific Luth. U., 1957-59; B.S., Ore. State U., 1961; M.S., Kan. State U., 1966, Ph.D., 1968; m. Phillip Arnold Nickel, Aug. 30, 1959; children—Mark Phillip, Jamie Louise. Research asso. Sci. Research Inst., Corvallis, Ore., 1961-63; grad. research asst. Kan. State U., Manhattan, 1964-68, instr. chemistry, 1968-69; analytical chemist Burroughs Corp., Westlake Village, Cal., 1969-71; clin. chemist, reference lab. div. Abbott Labs., Newbury Park, Cal., 1971—. Instr., Cal. Luth. Coll., 1970—. Mem. Am. Chem. Soc., Am. Assn. Clin. Chemists, Sigma Xi, Iota Sigma Pi. Home: 137 Verde Vista Thousand Oaks CA 91360 Office: Reference Laboratory 1011 Ranch Conejo Blvd Newbury Park CA 91320

NICKEL, MILDRED LUCILLE, library adminstr.; b. Brazil, Ind., Feb. 13, 1912; d. John and Ethel (Beaton) Nickel; A.B., Ind. State U., 1932; B.L.S., U. Ill. 1941; M.A., Mich. State U., 1967. Tchr. Vigo County (Ind.) Schs., 1932-35, Worthington (Ind.) High Sch., 1935-37; librarian Argo (Ill.) High Sch., 1937-41, Lyons Twp. High Sch. and Jr. Coll., LaGrange, Ill., 1941-50; dir. sch. libraries Ill. Dept. Pub. Instrn., Springfield, 1950-58; dir. sch. libraries dep. schs. U.S.A.F., Europe, Weisbaden, Germany, 1958-60; dir. libraries Lansing (Mich.) Sch. Dist., 1960—; vis. instr. U. Mich., 1962, Drexel Inst., 1964, U. Wis., 1965, Fla. State U., 1966, U. Ky., 1969; mem. adv. com. The Bro-Dart Found., 1965—. Mem. Am. (mem. council 1949-52, 68-72, nominating com., 1952-53), Mich. (chmn. planning com. 1966-67), Ill. (pres. 1953-54) library assns., Internat., Am. (chmn. standards com. 1960-66, treas. 1963-64, nominating com. 1967-68) Ill. (pres. 1953-57) assns. sch. librarians, Am. Assn. U. Women, Bus. and Profl. Women's Club, Women's Nat. Book Assn., Delta Kappa Gamma, Beta Phi Mu. Author: Let's Find Out About a Book, 1971; Steps to Service, 1974. Editor: Planning School Library Quarters, 1950. Contbr. articles in field to profl. periodicals. Home: 2715 Senate Dr Lansing MI 48912 Office: 519 W Kalamazoo St Lansing MI 48933

NICKERSON, BETTY ELIZABETH SMITH, orgn. exec.; b. Ft. Scott, Kan., June 26, 1922; d. Clarence Thomas and Helen (Smiley) Smith; student Goucher Coll., 1944-45; B.A., U. Utah, 1948; M.A., U. Man., 1966; postgrad. (Brit. Council fellow, Indian Cultural Council fellow) McGill U.; m. Mark Nickerson, July 25, 1942; children—Stephen Paul, Michael Thomas, Marki. Information officer OPA, Balt., 1942-44; TV broadcaster Canadian Broadcasting Corp., Winnipeg, Man., 1954-63; dir. All About Us/Nous Autres, children's cultural exchange, Ottawa, Ont., Can., 1972—. Mem. Nat. Canadian UNICEF Com., 1966-74. Can. Council Travel grantee, 1972; Local Iniatives Program grantee, 1973-74; Sec. of State (Can.) Devel. grantee, 1974—. Mem. Canadian Authors Assn., Internat. Soc. for Edn. through Art, Man. Home and Sch. Assn. (exec. com. 1959-62), Phi Beta Kappa. Author: How the World Grows Its Food, 1965; Celebrate the Sun, 1969; Chi: Letters from Biafra, 1970. Home: 240 Wilbrod St Ottawa ON K1N 6L6 Canada Office: Box 375 Sta A Ottawa ON Canada

NICKERSON, GERTRUDE SAMPSON, editor; b. Turner, Me., July 18, 1914; d. Charles Fobert and Rosa May (Willard) Sampson; grad. high sch.; m. Kenneth Lloyd Nickerson, May 14, 1943 (div. Feb. 1947); 1 son, William L. Employee, dept. store credit office, Portland, Me., 1931-35; with Burnham & Morrill div. William Underwood Co., Portland, 1935—, exec. sec., 1942—, editor co. newspaper, 1957—. Bd. dirs. St. Joe the Provider. Mem. Internat. Assn. Bus. Communicators. Mem. Order Eastern Star. Home: 225 Evans St South Portland ME 04106 Office: 1 Bean Pot Circle Portland ME 04104

NICKERSON, RUTH, sculptor; b. Appleton, Wis., Nov. 23, 1905; d. Robert Wellington and Kate Mary (Ellis) Nickerson; ed. Simcoe Collegiate Inst., 1921-23, Nat. Acad. Schs., 1928-32; m. Edmund Greacen, Jr., Dec. 30, 1935; children—Elizabeth Ruth, Barbara Eleanor. Works represented in Newark Mus., Cedar Rapids, (Ia.) Art Assn., New Brunswick (N.J.) P.O., Leaksville (N.C.) P.O., children's br. Bklyn. Pub. Library, New Rochelle (N.Y.) City Hall, Grasslands Hosp., Valhalla, N.Y., Montclair (N.J.) Mus. Art, Interchurch Center, N.Y.C. Mem. White Plains Civic Arts Commn., 1948-60. Recipient Nat. Arts Club medal, 1933; Saltus Gold medal N.A.D., 1933; Montclair Mus. medal, 1936; Am. Artists Profl. League medal, 1937; Guggenheim fellow, 1946-47. Fellow Nat. Sculpture Soc.; mem. Grand Central Gallery, N.A.D. (academician), Westchester Art Soc., Audubon Artists. Address: 106 Woodcrest Av White Plains NY 10604

NICKLAS, NANCY ANNE, assn. exec.; b. Milw., Nov. 12, 1942; d. Elmer J. and Marjorie A. (Hinkle) Nicklas; B.A., U. Denver, 1964. Women's phys. edn. instr., acting dean women Otero Jr. Coll., La Junta, Colo., 1964-67; adult edn. dir. Girl Scouts U.S.A., Milw. area, 1967-73, exec. dir. Indian Waters council, Eau Claire, Wis., 1973—. Mem. Eau Claire Coordinating Council, 1973—, Milw. Council for Adult Learning, 1971-73. Mem. Nat. Orgn. for Women, Assn. Girl Scout Profl. Workers. Club: Zonta Internat. (Eau Claire). Home: Rural Route 6 Box 129 Chippewa Falls WI 54729 Office: 415 1/2 Graham Eau Claire WI 54701

NICKOLSON, IRENE N. THOMAS (MRS. NICHOLAS D. NICKOLSON), investment broker; b. Worcester, Mass., Mar. 25, 1929; d. Charles A. and Anna C. (Savas) Thomas; asso. degree accounting, Becker Jr. Coll., Worcester, 1950; m. Nicholas D. Nickolson, July 4, 1954; 1 son, Charles N. With Joseph B. Cohan & Assos., C.P.A.'s, Worcester, 1971-72; clk. Main Lunch of Worcester, 1948—; head bookkeeper Dapol Plastics Co., Worcester, 1952-54; bookkeeper Alan Corp., Worcester, 1959-64; registered rep., office mgr., cashier Bancroft Securities Co., 1964-67; propr. Nickolson Securities, Worcester, 1967—, Diversified Bus. Services, Worcester, 1973—; registered prin. Brokers Diversified, Inc., Worcester, 1973; pres. Charles Corp., real estate, 1950—; office mgr., bookkeeper Graceform, Inc., 1974—. Mem. Nat. Assn. Securities Dealers, Securities Investor Protection Corp., Nat. Assn. Accountants, Worcester Bus. and Prfol. Women's Club, Philoptochos Soc. Home: 34 Longfellow Rd Worcester MA 01602 Office: 615 Main St Worcester MA 01608

NICODEMUS, JOAN BOTSFORD BAIN (MRS. CHARLES LESLIE NICODEMUS), artist, lumber co. exec.; b. Manila, Philippines; d. Jarvis Johnson and Edith (Ralston) Bain; student Tulane U., 1928, 29, Pitts. Art Inst., 1929, Alaska Sch. Mines, 1931, Corcoran Sch. Art, 1940, 41; pvt. study art Robert Graham, John Lenhardt, Wayman Adams; m. Harold A. Kurstedt, Mar. 6, 1931 (div. 1936); 1 dau., Edith Ralston (Mrs. Edward Mitchell Belcher) (dec. 1974); m. 2d, Charles Leslie Nicodemus, Oct. 9, 1942 (dec. 1970). Exhibited one-man shows James Lee Meml. Art Acad., Memphis, 1941, Overton Park, Memphis, 1947; exhibited in group shows including Corcoran Art Gallery, 1941, Brooks Meml. Mus., 1941, 42. Instr., James Lee Meml. Art Acad., 1941-42; pvt. instr. art, 1942-49; v.p. Bain-Nicodemus Lumber Yard, 1944-49; sec., pres. Jackson Apts. (Miss.), 1952—; partner Nicodemus Plywood & Lumber Co., Phoenix, 1961-73; instr. art, Phoenix, 1973—. Mem. Internat. Platform Assn. Republican. Address: 328 E Bethany Home Rd Phoenix AZ 85021

NICOLL, MRS. JEANNE ABBOTT, retail co. exec.; b. Memphis, Aug. 21, 1927; d. William George and Ida Lorena (Yeates) Abbott; student U. Tenn., 1945-46, Southwestern at Memphis, 1946-47; m. Vincent Mitchell Botto, June 25, 1947; children—Stephanie Ann, Vincent Steven; m. 2d, Russell David Nicoll, Apr. 1, 1966. Talent, news dir., then asst. mgr. radio sta. WHER, Tri-State Broadcasting Co., 1957-62, women's dir., 1964-66; dir. advt. and pub. relations Security Am. Life Ins. Co., 1962-64; women's dir. radio sta. WIOD, Cox Broadcasting, 1966-67; pub. service dir. WTVJ, Wometco Enterprises, Miami, Fla., 1967-72; spl. events dir. Jordan Marsh of Fla., Miami, 1972—. Ann. mem. United Fund. Bd. dirs. Heart Assn. Greater Miami, Big Bros. and Big Sisters of Greater Miami. Mem. Miami Ballet Soc. (charter), Miami C. of C. (mem. com. total employment), Crippled Children's Soc., Council Continuing Edn. of Women, Am. Women in Radio and TV, Fla. Pub. Relations Assn. (2d v.p.), Women in Communications (dir.; pres.). Home: 1200 Tallwood Av Hollywood FL 33021 Office: Jordan Marsh 1501 Biscayne Blvd Miami FL 33132

NIDA, JANE BOLSTER (MRS. DOW HUGHES NIDA), librarian; b. Chgo., July 19, 1918; d. Chalmer A. and Elsie R. (Sonderman) Bolster; B.A., Aurora (Ill.) Coll., 1942; B.S. in L.S., U. Ill., 1943; m. Dow Hughes Nida, Sept. 1, 1946; 1 dau., Janice Beth (Mrs. Robert M. Michaels). Circulation librarian Aurora Pub. Library, 1943-44, reference librarian, 1946; acting recreation dir. A.R.C., Eng., France, 1944-46; order librarian Ohio U., Athens, 1947; head librarian Falls Church (Va.) Pub. Library, 1951-54; asst. dir. Arlington County Dept. Libraries, Arlington, Va., 1954-57, dir., 1957—. Mem. Va. Adv. Legislative Council, Com. To Revise State Library Laws, 1968-69. Mem. Women's Joint Congl. Com., 1968—; vol. Am. Cancer Soc., 1971—; bd. dirs. Arlington Am. Cancer Soc., 1974—; mem. exec. com. Regional Adv. Group, Va. Regional Med. Program, 1971—. Bd. dirs. Cultural Laureate Found. Recipient Meritorious Service award A.R.C., World War II. Mem. Am. Assn. U. Women, A.L.A., D.C., Va. (pres. 1969-70) library assns., Arlington Hist. Soc. Baptist. Home: 4907 29th St N Arlington VA 22207 Office: 1015 N Quincy St Arlington VA 22201

NIDETCH, JEAN, weight reducing orgn. exec.; b. Bklyn., Oct. 12, 1923; d. David and May (Rodin) Slutsky; grad. high sch.; m. Mortimer Nidetch, Apr. 20, 1947; children—David, Richard. Founder Weight Watchers Internat., Inc., Great Neck, N.Y., also Los Angeles. Cons. N.Y. State Assembly on Mental Hygiene Com., 1968; adviser Joint Legislative Com. on Child Care Needs, N.Y. Sate Legislature. Pres. Weight Watchers Found. Recipient Internat. Speakers award Sales Promotion Execs. Assn.; named Hon. Ky. Col., Ark. Traveler, Hon. Adm. Great Navy Nebraska; named Man of Yr., L.I. Advt. Club, 1972. Mem. Washington Sq. Bus. and Profl. Womens Club, A.F.T.R.A. Author: Jean Nidetch: Weight Watchers Cookbook, 1966; The Story of Weight Watchers, 1970; Weight Watchers Program Cookbook, 1973. Home: 12002 Benmore Terrace Los Angeles CA 90049 Office: 10880 Wilshire Blve Los Angeles CA 90024

NIDEY, HAZEL PEARL (MRS. FLOYD NIDEY), motel exec.; b. Thompsonville, Ill., May 1, 1914; ed. pub. schs.; m. Floyd Nidey, Dec. 22, 1932; children—Donald, Karen (Mrs. Marvyn Halverson), Faith (Mrs. Mike Villhauer), Daniel. Mgr., Rebel Motel, Iowa City, Ia., 1969—. Methodist. Home: Apt 1 712 Carriage Hill St Iowa City IA 52240 Office: 336 Clinton St Iowa City IA 52240

NIEBALL, MARY LOUISE ROY, librarian; b. Odessa, Tex., Feb. 28, 1929; d. Tom and Angela Roy; A.A., Odessa Coll., 1956; B.S., Sul Ross State Coll., Alpine, Tex., 1959; M.L.S., Tex. Woman's U., 1963; M.A., U.S. Internat. U., 1971; postgrad. Ariz. State U., Cal. Western U., San Diego, now Tex. Woman's U.; m. Paul R. Nieball, Aug. 19, 1950; children—Paul Jay, Jon Roy. Library clk. Ector County Library, Odessa, 1944-49; asst. librarian Odessa Coll. Library, 1950-51, 64-67, head librarian, 1967—; librarian Shannon Sch. of Nursing, San Angelo, Tex., 1951-52; supr. asst. and audio visual librarian Ector County Library, 1953-58; serials clk. U. Tex. Library Sch., Austin, 1956; cataloguer Sul Ross State Coll. Library, Alpine, 1959; sch. librarian Sam Houston Elementary Sch., Odessa, 1959-62, Gonzales Elementary Sch., Odessa, 1963-64; cons. on sch. libraries. Mem. Am. Assn. U. Women, League Women Voters, Odessa C. of C., Am., Southwest, Tex. library assns., Tex. State, Ector County tchrs. assns., Tex. Jr. Coll. Tchrs. Assn., Permian Hist. Assn., Phi Theta Kappa, Kappa Delta Pi, Sigma Tau Delta, Alpha Delta Kappa. Home: 3733 Dover Dr Odessa TX 79760 Office: PO Box 3752 Odessa TX 79760

NIEBAUER, RUBY RUTH DAY, educator; b. Ontario, Wis., Dec. 11, 1910; d. Calvin B. and Mary (Haney) Day; B.S., U. Wis., 1946, M.S., 1947, postgrad., 1960-61; postgrad. U. Cal., 1953-55; m. H.J.

Niebauer, June 24, 1936 (dec. Aug. 1940); children—Ruth Ann, Mary Jo. Elementary classroom tchr., prin., Westmont, Ill., 1930-32; tchr. art pub. schs., Madison, Wis., also supr. student tchrs. U. Wis., 1934-46; head art dept. U. Wis. at Menominie, 1947-49; asst. prof. edn., supr. art San Diego State Coll., 1949-55; asst. prof. home econs. Mich. State U., 1955-58; producer ednl. films The Creative Craft series, CBS and Ency. Britannica Films, 1953—, also films for Visual Edn. Cons., Madison, Wis., Encore Visual Edn., Burbank, Cal.; asst. prof. art U. Mich., Ann Arbor, 1960; researcher dept. edn. U. Wis., Madison, 1960-61; asst. prof. edn., researcher, cons. U. Wis. Milw. campus, 1962-64; asst. prof. home econs. So. Ill. U., 1964-65; asso. prof. home econs. Western Ky. U., 1965-68; chmn. textiles and design, prof. Sch. Home Econs., U. Ky., 1968-70. Recipient internat. awards for films, Venice (Italy) Internat. Film Festival, 1955, Edinburg, Scotland, Eng., 1955, several nat. film awards, 1955-57. Fellow Internat. Inst. Arts, Letters and Scis.; mem. Nat. Soc. Interior Design, Internat. Platform Assn., Nat. Art Assn., Am. Assn. U. Women, N.E.A., Nat. Home Econs. Assn., Nat. Edn. Communications and Tech., Am. Assn. U. Profs., Phi Delta Gamma, Pi Lambda Theta, Phi Upsilon Omicron. Home: 314 Northlawn Av East Lansing MI 48823

NIEDERER, BETTINA SIMON (MRS. JAMES NIEDERER), pediatrician; b. N.Y.C., Jan. 2, 1939; d. Howard and Mina (Lewiton) Simon; B.A., Vassar Coll., 1959; M.D., N.Y. U., 1963; m. James Niederer, May 25, 1963; children—Alison, John. Intern Phila. Gen. Hosp., 1963-64, resident, 1964-66, asst. attending physician, 1968—; dir. pediatric clinic, 1970—; fellow in genetics and endocrinology St. Christopher's Hosp., Phila., 1966-68; sr. instr. pediatrics Hahnemann Med. Coll., 1968—. Mem. Wynnefield Residents Assn., 1967—. Mem. Phila. Pediatric Soc. Home: 2328 N 50th St Philadelphia PA 19131 Office: Phila Gen Hosp 34th and Civic Center Philadelphia PA 19104

NIEHOFF, MRS. MARCELLA LETTS, business exec.; b. Chgo., Oct. 9, 1897; d. Adolph Ludwig and Bernadine (Wein) Letts; student Holy Angels Coll., 1915-17; m. Conrad Erich Niehoff, Aug. 18, 1920 (dec. July 1957); 1 dau., Mary Anne (Mrs. Hellmuth Kirchschlager). Sec., treas. C. E. Niehoff & Co. Chgo., 1923-57, pres., chmn. bd., 1957—. Chmn. women's bd. House of Good Shepherd, Chgo.; pres. Holiday Home, Williams Bay, Wis.; v.p. Mental Health Soc. Greater Chgo. Inc.; bd. lay trustees Loyola, bd. dirs. Stritch Sch. Medicine of Loyola U., Resurrection Hosp., Alexian Hosp. Bd., Central Service for the Chronically Ill.; bd. dirs. Water Safety Patrol, Lake Geneva (Wis.) Civic Assn. Bd. dirs. Woman's Nat. Rep. Club, Chgo. Clubs: Woman's Athletic, Lake Shore (Chgo.); Big Foot Country, Lake Geneva Country (Lake Geneva, Wis.); Germania. Home: 179 Lake Shore Dr Chicago IL 60611 also Country Estate Williams Bay WI 53191

NIELSEN, ELENA FROLOVA (MRS. ANDERS JORGEN K. NIELSEN), journalist; b. Copenhagen, Denmark; d. Vasilij P. and Ekatarina (von Lichine) Froloff; Cand. phil. U Copenhagen, 1936; ballet tng. J. Moller Inst., 1923-36, Ballet Arts Studio, Met. Opera Ballet Sch., 1947-48; m. Anders Jorgen K. Nielsen, May 29, 1948. Came to U.S., 1946, naturalized, 1966. Actress, solo dancer Central Theatre, Oslo, Norway, 1940-46; dir. Internat. Ballet Sch. for UN Children, 1949-54; assisted in TV prodns. involving UN children for the UN, 1950-56; fgn. corr. Danish and Norwegian publs., 1955—, fgn. editor World Wide Features, Inc., 1965-67, U.S. editor Arktuell of Norway, 1967-69, N.Y., Washington and UN editor Reflex News mag., Denmark, also Aktuell, Norway, 1969-71, U.S., UN editor Billedbladet and Nordisk Pressefoto, 1971—. Mem. Fgn. Press Assn. (chmn. stage and screen com. N.Y.; sec. gen. N.Y. and Washington 1970, 71, life mem.), Internat. Platform Assn., Danish-Am. Assn., UN Corrs. Assn. Home: 2 Bedford St New York City NY 10014 Office: Room 310 Press Sect UN New York City NY 10017

NIELSEN, HELEN BERNIECE, author; b. Roseville, Ill., Oct. 23, 1918; d. Niels C. and May (Christensen) Nielsen; student Chgo. Art Inst., 1931-33. Author: The Kind Man, 1951; Gold Coast Nocturne, 1951; Obit Delayed, 1952; Detour, 1953; Woman on the Roof, 1954; Borrow the Night, 1955; The Crime is Murder, 1956; False Witness, 1957; The Fifth Caller, 1959; Sing Me A Murder, 1960; Woman Missing and Other Stories (anthology), 1962; Verdict Suspended, 1964; After Midnight, 1966; A Killer In The Street, 1967; Darkest Hour, 1968; Shot on Location, 1971; The Severed Key, 1973; also short stories and novelettes, teleplay. Mem. Cal. Democratic Council, 1955—, past sec. 22d council, del. council 1955, 56, 57; del. Dem. State Conv.; pres. Adlai Stevenson Democratic Club, 1957. Mem. Am. Civil Liberties Union, N.A.A.C.P. Club: Hollywood Hills Democratic. Home: 2622 Victoria Dr Laguna Beach CA 92651

NIELSEN, MARJORIE LONIEN (MRS. ANDREW T. NIELSEN), coll. adminstr.; b. Faribault, Minn., Apr. 30, 1926; d. John Peter and Marie Frances (Hanagraaf) Lonien; A.A., Everett Community Coll., 1946; B.A., Seattle U., 1967; m. Andrew T. Nielsen, July 3, 1948; children—Drew Andrew, Mary. With Everett (Wash.) Community Coll., 1946—, registrar, 1969—. Bd. dirs. Pilchuck Area Campfire Girls, 1972—. Mem. Am. Assn. of Registrars, Pacific Coast, Wash. Community Coll. assns. registrars, Wash. Council High Sch. Coll. Relations (treas. 1971). Home: 4521 Crescent St Everett WA 98203

NIELSEN, RUBY WARP (MRS. LAVERN W. NIELSEN), museum ofcl.; b. Minden, Neb., Dec. 4, 1911; d. Julius Nickolas and Ella (Benson) Warp; grad. high sch.; m. LaVern W. Nielsen, Dec. 28, 1936; children—Larry, Patricia (Mrs. Joe Dufort), LaMoyne. Sec., Warp Pub. Co., Minden, Neb., 1927-36; clk. George Ball Seed Co., West Chicago, Ill., 1954-65; co-mgr. Harold Warp Pioneer Village, Minden, Neb., 1968—. Address: 900 N Brown St Minden NE 68959 Office: Harold Warp Pioneer Village Minden NE 68959

NIELSON, BONNIE JEAN (MRS. RICHARD PATRICK NIELSON), aluminum co. exec.; b. Cleve., July 27, 1948; d. Albert Nicholas and Irene Sophia (Balint) Petery; B.S., Bowling Green State U., 1970; m. Richard Patrick Nielson, Aug. 15, 1970. Staff asst. writer United Appeal and United Torch Dr. of Greater Cleve., 1970-71, asso. pub. relations writer, 1971-72; editor Alcan Corps U.S.A., Alcan Aluminum Corp., Cleve., 1973—. Mem. Internatl. Assn. Bus. Communicators (v.p. membership 1973-74), Women in Communications. Home: 12900 Lake Av Lakewood OH 44107 Office: 100 Erieview Plaza Cleveland OH 44114

NIEMCZYK, ROSALIE WALSH, ednl. counselor; b. Amityville, N.Y., Sept. 15, 1938; d. Aloysius John and Virginia Marion (McGunnigle) Walsh; B.S., State U. N.Y. at Albany, 1960; M.S., L.I. U., 1969; m. Francis Leon Niemczyk, Nov. 23, 1963. Tchr. bus. edn., Spanish, Bethpage (N.Y.) Sr. High Sch., 1960-69, guidance and career counselor, 1969—. Mem. edn. com. Three Village Sch. Dist., Stony Brook, N.Y., 1973—; pres., founder Ladies' Village Improvement Soc. Setaukets (N.Y.), 1967—, mem. edn. com., 1973—; mem. Civic Assos. Setaukets; mem. Mother Theresa chpt. St. Charles Hosp. Aux., Port Jefferson, N.Y., 1969—. Committeewoman, Conservative party, 1968-70. Mem. Assn. Community-Univ. Cooperation State U. N.Y. at Stony Brook, Am. Assn. U. Women, L.I. Personnel and Guidance Assn., Soc. Preservation L.I. Antiquities; Suffolk County (dir.) Humane Soc., Three Village, Bethpage-Farmingdale hist. socs., Am. Vocational Assn., Cath. Daus. Am. (grand regent ct.), Royal Soc. Prevention Cruelty to Animals (London), Antivisect. League, Soc. for Preservation Mustangs and Burros, Friends of Animals. Club: Three Village Garden. Developer Career Research Centres in high schs. Home: 11 Mills Lane East Setauket NY 11733 Office: Bethpage Pub Schs Cherry Av Bethpage NY 11714

NIEMEYER, IRIS MARIE (MRS. LOUIS JOHN NIEMEYER), real estate broker; b. Pulaski, Wis., Aug. 20, 1927; d. Oscar Knut and Elsie Augusta (Griepp) Olson; student Orange Coast Coll., 1964-67; m. Louis John Niemeyer, Oct. 12, 1946; children—Sandra Joy (Mrs. Steven D. McIntyre), Judith Ann (Mrs. Charles A. Troftgruben), David Alan, Valerie Jean. Real estate salesman N. Tustin (Cal.) Realty, 1965-70; real estate broker Red Carpet Realtors, Tustin, 1970—. Pres., Red Hill Luth. Elementary Sch. Parents Guild, Tustin, 1967. Recipient Women of Year award Red Hill Luth Ch., 1964. Mem. East Orange County Bd. Realtors, Women's Council Realtors (pres. 1973, treas. state chpt. 1974—, local dir.), Cal. Real Estate Assn. (state dir.), Am. Luth. Ch. Women (pres. 1963). Mem. Order Eastern Star. Club: Toastmistress (charter pres. Santa Ana, Cal. 1971). Home: 1641 Bullard Lane Santa Ana CA 92705 Office: 18352 Irvine Blvd Tustin CA 92680

NIEMI, JANICE BAILEY (MRS. PRESTON NIEMI), judge; b. Flint, Mich., Sept. 18, 1928; d. Richard Jesse and Norma Ann (Bell) Bailey; A.B., U. Wash., 1950, J.D., 1967; postgrad. U. Mich., 1950-52; certificate Hague Acad. Internat. Law, The Hague, Netherlands, 1954; m. Preston Niemi, Feb. 4, 1953; children—Ries, Patricia. Admitted to Wash. bar, 1968; asso. firm Powell, Livengood, Dunlap & Silvernale, Kirkland, Wash., 1968; staff atty., office mgr. Legal Services Center, Seattle, 1968-71; judge Seattle Dist. Ct., 1971-72, King County Superior Ct., Seattle, 1973—. Mem. Central Area Sch. Council, Seattle, 1969-71; mem. Lawyers Com. for Civil Rights under Law, 1970-71; mem. Seattle Downtown Coordinating Com., chmn. blvd. task force 1973—; mem. Council on Planning Affiliates Legislative Com., 1973—; mem. Criminal Justice Coordinating Council, 1971-73. Bd. dirs. Allied Arts Bd., 1971—. Recipient Woman of Year award Past President's Assn., 1972; Matrix Table Woman of Year award Women in Communication, 1973. Mem. Am., Wash., Seattle-King County bar assns., Superior Ct. Judges Assn., N.Am. Judges Assn., Municipal League, Urban League, Bus. and Profl. Women's Club. Home: 1061 E Blaine St Seattle WA 98102 Office: King County Court House 3rd and James St Seattle WA 98104

NIEMI, VIRGINIA G. KINNEY (MRS. PAUL A. NIEMI), corp. exec.; b. Duluth, Minn., Dec. 30, 1924; d. George D. and Grace B. (Smalley) Kinney; student U. Minn., 1956, San Diego Bus. Coll., 1960, Mesa Coll., 1964-65, San Diego State U., 1964-68, U. Cal. at San Diego, 1969-72, certificate indsl. relations, 1972; M.B.A., Nat. U., San Diego, 1974; m. Paul A. Niemi, Sept. 23, 1944; children—Pamela Kaye (Mrs. Patrick Eugene Boehmke), Rebecca Jo (Mrs. Paul Roger Spickler). Nurse, St. Francis Hosp., Superior, Wis., 1951-52; nurse, personnel adminstr. Elliott Packing Co., Duluth, 1953-58; indsl. relations sec. Cubic Corp., San Diego, 1959-66; personnel mgr. Spectral Dynamics Corp., San Diego, 1966—. Keyman, United Community Services, San Diego, 1966-70; mem. San Diego Indsl. Recreation Council, 1966—, mem. exec. com., 1970-71; adv. council San Diego Community Coll. Mem. Personnel Mgmt. Assn. San Diego (sec. 1971-72, v.p. 1974), Kearney Mesa Bus. Assn., Am. Soc. Personnel Adminstrn., Am. Soc. Indsl. Security, Amigos de Ser (sec.-treas. 1974). Mem. Seventh-day Adventist Ch. Home: 1556 Plover St San Diego CA 92114 Office: 8911 Balboa Av San Diego CA 92112

NIEMINEN, SUSAN ALICIA, mus. curator; b. Denver, Mar. 20, 1946; d. Matt Alexander and Fern Evelyn (Humrich) Nieminen; B.A., Macalester Coll., 1968; postgrad., Cooperstown U., 1968-69. Manuscript calendarer Western Bus. History Research Center, Denver, 1968; photo librarian State Hist. Soc. Colo., Denver, 1969-70; asst. to the dir., 1970-73; curator Georgetown (Colo.) Soc., 1973—; preservation cons. Western Interpretive Services, Sheridan, Wyo., 1973—. Mem. State Hist. Soc. of Colo., Victorian Soc. in Am., Georgetown Hist. Soc. Baptist. Home: 4801 E 9th Av Denver CO 80220 Office: PO Box 657 Georgetown CO 80444 also PO Box 6467 Sheridan WY 82801

NIEMOTH, JILL LAWRENCE (MRS. EARL JOHN NIEMOTH), public relations co. exec.; b. Canton, O., Nov. 9, 1942; d. Richard Eugene and Lois Ireland (Huston) Lawrence; B.S., Northwestern U., 1964; m. Earl John Niemoth, Sept. 12, 1964; children—Kara Lawrence and Lara Lawrence (twins). Architecture and maintenance editor Institutions Mag., Chgo., 1964-65; asst. to pres. Lynn Davis Employment Service, Chgo., 1965-66; account exec. Theodore R. Sills, Inc., Chgo., 1966-69; dir. pub. information Sch. Dist. 202, Evanston, Ill., 1969-73; pres. Create Communications, Inc., Evanston, Ill., 1973—. Cons. Sch. Dist. #65, Evanston, 1971-72, Nat. Inst. Farm and Land Brokers, 1970—, Real Estate Securities and Syndication Inst., 1973—, Rust-Oleum Corp., Evanston, 1973—, Ill. Assn. Realtors, 1974—. Mem. North Shore Pub. Relations Club, Jr. League, Women in Communication, Spiritual Frontiers Fellowship, Pi Beta Phi, Republican. Club: Touhy Tennis (Skokie, Ill.). Home and office: 2801 Lincoln St Evanston IL 60201

NIENALTOWSKI, MARGARET LOUISE, constrn. co. exec.; b. Detroit, Aug. 16, 1932; d. Charles and Emma Victoria (Lyle) Colbus; grad. high sch.; m. Walter J. Nienaltowski, July 11, 1953 (div. July 1964); children—Paul W., Fay M. Sec., Ryan Industries, Detroit, 1950-51; exec. sec. Squibb Corp., Detroit, 1951-53; sec. Carl F. Beckwith & Son, Detroit, 1953-55, Walt's Resilient Tile, St. Clair Shores, Mich., 1953-62; sec. May & Schlaffer Roofing, Detroit, 1955-56; with Armstead Constrn. Co., Melvindale, Mich., 1964—, corporate sec., dir. 1967—, v.p., 1970—. Lutheran. Office: 4041 Martel Melvindale MI 48122

NIES, JUDITH, polit. writer; b. Boston, Sept. 23, 1941; d. Charles Raymond and Lillian Agnes (Farrell) Nies; B.A., Tufts U., 1962; M.A., Johns Hopkins, 1965; certificate French lang., U. Paris, 1964; m. J. Hugh McFadden, Oct. 28, 1967; 1 dau., Cristina Alexandra. Editor Washington Legislative Newsletter Women's Internat. League Peace and Freedom, 1966-68, dir. Washington office, 1966-68; cons. to ten Democratic congressmen, 1968-70; speechwriter Hon. Don Fraser, U.S. Congressman, Washington, 1971—. Dir. Project on Fellowships and Founds., Women's Equity Action League, 1970—. Mem. Women's Internat. League Peace and Freedom (internat. asso.), Am. Polit. Sci. Assn. (women's caucus 1971-72). Co-editor: American Militarism, 1970; War Crimes and the American Conscience, 1970. Contbr. articles to Ms., Progressive mag. Home: 3100 Macomb St NW Washington DC 20008

NIEVES, ANITA STEINER (MRS. CARLOS NIEVES), lawyer; b. Bklyn., Jan. 22, 1944; d. Samuel and Clara (Haas) Steiner; B.A., Hunter Coll., 1964; J.D. (Rose Hoffer scholar), Bklyn. Law Sch., 1968; m. Carlos Nieves, Nov. 22, 1970. Admitted to N.Y. bar, 1968; staff atty. Harlem Assertion of Rights, N.Y.C., 1968-71; asso. firm Kreindler, Relkin, Olick & Goldberg, N.Y.C., 1971; law sec. to Judge Marro, Civil Court of N.Y., N.Y.C., 1971-74. Mem. N.Y. Womens Bar Assn. Home: 325 Short Hill Lane Fairfield CT 06430

NIEVES-RIVERA, SYLVIA, occupational therapist; b. Manati, P.R., Jan. 20, 1947; d. Fernando and Rosa (Rivera) Nieves; B.S. in Occupational Therapy, U. P.R., 1969; m. Jaime Caballero Alvarez, June 14, 1969; children—Sylvia N., Jaime O. Occupational therapist Mental Health Center, Arecibo, P.R., 1969-71, dir. day care service, 1971-73; occupational therapist, dir. day care service Manati Mental Health Center, 1973—, also dir. outpatient clinic. Mem. Am., P.R. occupational therapy assns. Home: C-6 Victor Pares Urb San Salvador Manati PR 00701 Office: 113 McKinley St Manati PR 00701

NIGAGLIONI, OLGA CRUZ JIMENEZ (MRS. JOSE E. NIGAGLIONI), state legislator; b. Rio Piedras, P.R., July 31, 1933; d. Manuel Cruz Horta and Dolores Jimenez; B.Social Sci., U. P.R., 1954, LL.B. cum laude, 1957; m. Jose E. Nigaglioni, Sept. 11, 1971; 1 dau., Olga Isabel. Admitted to P.R. bar, 1957; legal counsel Pub. Works Dept. San Juan, P.R., 1957-58, P.R. Housing Corp., San Juan, 1957-58; dist. judge at large, San Juan, 1958-60; spl. dist. atty., San Juan, 1960-62; spl. dist. atty. P.R. Justice Dept., San Juan, 1963-64; pvt. practice, 1964-68; mem. P.R. Ho. of Reps., 1968—, majority alternate floor leader, chmn. judiciary com., 1972—. Pres., El Rosario Camp for Disadvantaged Children, Mayagirez, P.R., 1964—. Recipient award for polit. achievement Exchangetts, 1969; award of achievement Nu Sigma Beta, 1969; Most Outstanding Young Women of Year award Jr. C. of C., 1972. Mem. Am., P.R. (Achievement award 1969), bar assns., Am. Judicature Soc., Bus. and Profl. Women's Club, U. P.R. Alumni Assn., Kappa Beta Pi. Club: Zonta. Home: 313 Navarra St Rio Piedras PR 00923 Office: Capitol San Juan PR 00902

NIGHSWANDER, MARY FLUHRER (MRS. STERLING H. NIGHSWANDER), theatre dir.; b. Seoul, Korea, Sept. 7, 1907 (parents Am. citizens); d. Arthur Garner and Sarah Harvey (Nourse) Welbon; B.A., Maryville Coll., 1928; postgrad. Am. Acad. Dramatic Art, 1929; M.A., U. Wis., 1948; m. George B. Fluhrer, Apr. 17, 1929 (dec. Jan. 1941); children—Barbara (Mrs. William Greener), Roy Sylvester, Sally Mae (Mrs. Dennis Sissel); m. 2d, Sterling H. Nighswander, Sept. 2, 1954. Stock rep. Profl. Theatre Companies, 1929-40; operator Fluhrer Dramatic Studio, Davenport, Ia., 1941-71; dir. Davenport Jr. Theatre, Inc., 1951—. Dir. Region 6 Children's Theatre Conf., 1957-59; exec. dir. Broadway Theatre League, Davenport, 1960—. Mem. Am. Theatre Assn., Am. Assn. Univ. Women. Home: Blackhawk Trail Rural Route 3 Davenport IA 52804 Office: 236 W Central Park Davenport IA 52805

NIGHTINGALE, JANICE TULCHIN, pediatrician; b. N.Y.C., Jan. 7, 1921; d. Lewis and Selma (Danson) Tulchin; B.A. cum laude, Hunter Coll., 1942; M.D., N.Y. Med. Coll., 1945; m. Edward Joel Nightingale, Feb. 10, 1946; children—Lewis David, Margaret Jane. Intern Jewish Hosp., Bklyn., 1945-46, resident, 1947-48; resident in pediatrics Willard Parker Hosp., 1946-47, Mt. Sinai Hosp., N.Y.C., 1949; practice medicine specializing in pediatrics, Scarsdale, N.Y., 1950—; mem. attending staff White Plains Hosp. Home and office: 161 Boulevard Scarsdale NY 19583

NILES, DORIS KILDALE (MRS. ARTHUR D. NILES), educator; b. Eureka, Cal., July 26, 1903; d. Alfred Walter and Laura (Peterson) Kildale; A.B., Stanford U., 1926; M.A., 1927; Ph.D., 1931; postgrad. Harvard, 1930; m. Arthur D. Niles, Mar. 11, 1938; children—Katey (Mrs. Niles Walker), Malcolm A., Margaret (Mrs. John C. Rice), James Alfred. Teaching asst. dept. botany Stanford U., 1927-28, Ariz. State Coll., 1932, Humboldt State Coll., Arcata, Cal., 1928-45, 55-58; asso. prof. U. Cal. Extension at Davis, 1958—. Mem. Cal. Acad. Scis., N.Y. Acad. Scis., Phi Beta Kappa, Sigma Xi, Sigma Delta Pi, Pi Lambda Theta. Club. Sierra. Home: PO Box 307 Loleta CA 95551 Office: U Cal Extension Davis CA 95616

NILSEN, ELLI, lawyer, accountant; b. Chgo.; d. John and Anna (Nilsen) Hallenberg; B.C.S. cum laude, Southwestern U., 1948, J.D. cum laude, 1955. Self-employed pub. accountant, 1949-53; self-employed C.P.A., Los Angeles, 1953—; admitted to Cal. bar, 1956; individual practice law, Los Angeles, 1956—. Served with WAC, 1943-45. Mem. State Bar Cal., Cal. (pres. 1965), Am. (dir., membership chmn. 1964-66) assns. atty.-C.P.A.'s, So. Cal. Women Lawyers (pres. 1959), Iota Tau Tau (past supreme dean). Mem. Ch. Religious Sci. (trustee). Home: 360 S Kenmore Av Los Angeles CA 90020 Office: 3750 W 6th St Los Angeles CA 90020

NILSON, ELIZABETH LOGAN (MRS. GEORGE ALBERT NILSON), lawyer; b. Pitts., July 18, 1942; d. Kenneth Melvin and Helen Elizabeth (Hughes) Logan; B.A., Denison U., 1964; LL.B., Yale, 1967; m. George Albert Nilson, Jan. 1, 1966; 1 son, Scott Logan. Summer intern Rep. Policy Com., Ho. of Reps., Washington, 1963; summer intern, civil rights div. Dept. Justice, Washington, 1964; adminstrv. asst. Greater Balt. Com., Urban Policy Group, 1967-68; cons. urban affairs Strategic Planning Corp., Balt., 1968-69; admitted to Md. bar, 1969; asso. Sachs & Baron, Balt., 1971-72; asso. Frank, Berstein, Conaway & Goldman, Balt., 1972—. Mem. Third Dist. Citizens, Balt., Citizens Planning and Housing Assn., Balt. Mem. Am., Md. bar assns., Balt. Zool. Soc., Nat. Wildlife Fedn., Am. Mus. Natural History, Sierra Club, Mortar Bd., Crossed Keys, Phi Beta Kappa, Pi Delta Epsilon, Pi Sigma Alpha, Phi Alpha Theta. Democrat. Presbyn. Club: Women's Nat. Democratic. Home: 4412 Norwood Rd Baltimore MD 21218 Office: 1300 Mercantile Bank and Trust Company 2 Hopkins Plaza Baltimore MD 21201

NILSSON, BIRGIT, soprano, opera singer; b. Karup, Sweden; d. Nils P. and Justina (Paulsson) Svenson; student Royal Musical Acad., Stockholm; LL.D., Andover U.; m. Bertil Niklasson, Sept. 10, 1948. Appeared on state of Wienna, La Scala, Covent Garden, Bayreuth, Stockholm, Buenos Aires, Chgo., San Francisco, and Met. Opera, N.Y.C. operatic roles performed include Brunnhilde, Isolde, Elisabeth, Venus, Elsa, Senta, Aida, Lady Macbeth, Amelia, Tosca, Turandot, Franciulla del West, Elekra, Salome, Marschallinn, Fidelio, Donna Anna. Hon. mem. Royal Mus. Acad. London, Royal Mus. Acad. Stockholm, Vienna State Opera, others. Address: PO Box 527 Stockholm I Sweden

NIMS, MARY ELIZABETH NAUGLE (MRS. MARSHALL NIMS), educator; b. Boise, Ida., Jan. 8, 1914; d. Johnson Edward and Meta (Boeck) Naugle; B.A., U. Denver, 1935; M.A., 1964; m. Marshall Grant Nims, Aug. 23, 1933; children—Barbara Grant (Mrs. Ronald Welss), Julie Boeck (Mrs. Craig Johnson), Peter Dwight, Christopher Grant. Asst. dir. Adult Edn. Council Met. Denver, 1965-69, exec. dir., 1969—. Vol. A.R.C., 1941-44; vol. Christian edn. dir. Women's Aux. Epis. Diocese Colo., 1952-58; mem. Bishops Epis. Diocesan Bd., 1952-58; mem. adult edn. council Met. Denver, 1964-65. Mem. Republican Precinct Com., 1953-65. Mem. Denver alumni bd. U. Colo., 1960-64, Adult Edn. Assn. U.S.A. (mem. exec. com.), Mountain Plains Adult Edn. Assn. (bd. dirs., pres. 1973-74), Colo. Assn. for Continuing Adult Edn., Adult Edn. Council Met. Denver, Friends Denver Pub. Library, Denver Art Museum, Pi Beta Phi. Home: 3409 S Race St Englewood CO 80110 Office: 1100 Acoma St Denver CO 80204

NIN, ANAIS, author; b. Paris, France; d. Joaquin and Rosa (Culmell) Nin; student Cite Universitaire, Paris; D.F.A., Phila. Coll. Art, 1973. Author: D.H. Lawrence, A Study, 1932; (prose poem) House of Incest, 1934; Winter of Artifice, 1939; Under a Glass Bell, 1944;

Ladders to Fire, 1946; Children of the Albatross, 1947; Four Chambered Heart, 1950; Spy in the House of Love, 1954; Collages, 1964; Diary of Anais Nin, First Volume 1930-34, 1966, Diary Vol. II, 1934-39 (Daughter of Mark Twain), 1967; Novel of the Future, 1968; Diary Vol. III, 1969 (Prix Sevigne), Diary Vol. IV, 1971, Diary Vol. V, 1974. Lectr., readings at numerous colls.; readings at Living Theatre, Am. Playwright Theatre; also TV appearances. Mem. Nat. Inst. Arts and Letters. Address: care Gunther Stuhlmann 65 Irving Pl New York City NY 10003

NISBETT, GAY GOLDEN (MRS. JOSEPH LURYL NISBETT), librarian; b. McMinnville, Tenn., July 2, 1923; d. Benjamin F. and Charlotte (Byars) Golden; student David Lipscomb Coll., 1940-42; B.A., Harding Coll., 1946; M.A., George Peabody Coll., 1950; m. Joseph Luryl Nisbett, Oct. 23, 1965; 1 son, Joseph Andrew. Asst. librarian Abilene (Tex.) Christian Coll. Library, 1950-62; tchr., librarian Centertown High Sch., McMinnville, Tenn., 1962-63; asst. librarian Middle Tenn. State Coll., Murfreesboro, 1963-65; librarian Columbia Christian Coll., Portland, Ore., 1965—. Mem. Ore. Library Assn. Mem. Ch. of Christ. Home: 4359 NE Flanders St Portland OR 97213 Office: 200 NE 91st St Portland OR 97220

NISSENSON, NORMA, psychologist; b. Frankfort, Ky., Nov. 18, 1917; d. Jacob and Pearl (Klass) Rosen; B.S. magna cum laude, Northwestern U., 1938, M.A. in Psychology with honors, 1948, postgrad., 1949-50; m. Marc Nissenson, July 6, 1940; children—Carol, Mary. Exec. dir. Career & Counseling Service (formerly B'nai B'rith Vocational Service), Highland Park, Ill., 1946-52, psychologist, 1952—. Vice pres. Nissenson Assos. Ltd., cons., divorce conciliation, Highland Park, 1970—; dir. project Operation HEP, 1966-70; cons., lectr. in field. Mem. adv. council Ill. Commn. Human Relations, 1965-73; civilian rep. from Ill. to Nat. Conf. Alcohol and Drug Abuse, 1972; active local League Women Voters, Girl Scouts, P.T.A. Mem. Am. Assn. Marriage and Family Counselors (clin.), Am., Ill. psychol. assns., Internat. Counseling Services, Am. Acad. Psychotherapists, Acad. Psychologists in Marital Therapy, Nat. Vocational Guidance Assn. Home: 966 Princeton Av Highland Park IL 60035 Office: 1971 2d St Highland Park IL 60035

NISSLEY, ELEANOR STEFFENS, polit. party worker; b. N.Y.C.; d. Emil William and Gertrude (Urchs) Steffens; student Skidmore Coll., B.S., N.Y. U.; m. Warren W. Nissley, Jr.; children—James Edward, Virginia Gale, Peter Bradford, Debra Lou. Tchr., Tucson, 1949. Pres. Bergen County (N.J.) Women's Republican Club, 1962-68; committeewoman Bergen County Rep. Party, 1965—; mem. exec. com. N.J. Rep. Central Com., 1971—; del., mem. platform com. Rep. Nat. Conv., 1968; active numerous campaigns. Sec. Bergen County Mental Health Bd.; 3d v.p. Family Counseling Service Ridgewood, N.J.; mem. lay devel. bd. Organizing Council Coll. Profl. Psychology; adv. bd. Spl. Services Bergen County. Bd. dirs. Bergen County Health and Welfare Council. Recipient Over The Top award Ridgewood Community Chest. Mem. Valley Hosp. Aux., Paramus Hist. Soc., League Women Voters. Presbyn. Clubs: Women's, College (Ridgewood). Address: 145 Phelps Rd Ridgewood NJ 07450

NISTENDIRK, VERNA RUTH, librarian; b. Wright City, Mo., Aug. 12, 1907; d. Henry W. and Susie E. (Thoroughman) Nistendirk; B.S., S.E. Mo. State Coll., 1929; B.L.S., George Peabody Coll. Tchrs., 1933; M.L.S., Columbia, 1944. Tchr. pub. schs., Blodgett, Mo., 1925-28; librarian N. Kansas City (Mo.) Sch., 1929-38; br. librarian Kansas City Pub. Library, 1938-43, extension librarian, 1943-45; regional librarian Boonslick Library, Sedalia, Mo., 1952-56; dir. library devel. Fla. State Library, Tallahassee, 1956-69; librarian Leon, Jefferson and Wakuiia County Libraries, Tallahassee, 1969-73; exec. sec. Fla. Library Assn., 1973—. Mem. steering com. Fla. Library Study Commn., 1971-72; treas. League Women Voters, Tallahassee, 1970-72; mem. Am. Civil Liberties Union, 1969—, Urban League, 1969—, Mental Health Assn., 1969—. Mem. Am. (pres.-elect pub. relations sect. library adminstrn. div. 1972—), Fla. (pres. 1967-68), Southeastern library assns., Lemoyne Art Found., UN Assn., Pilot Club, Delta Kappa Gamma. Home: 2862 WW Kelly Rd Tallahassee FL 32301

NISWONGER, JEANNE DUCHATEAU (MRS. JOSEPH K. NISWONGER), wildlife biologist, writer; b. Indpls.; d. Simon Nicholas and Portia (Reeves) Du Chateau; A.B., Miami U., Oxford, O.; postgrad. Washington Sch. Psychiatry; m. Joseph K. Niswonger; children—Kenneth Arnold, Laura Elaine, Nancy Jo. Research asso. U.S. Dept. Health, Edn. and Welfare W.Va. Dept. Health, Charleston, 1943-45; research biologist Bio-Research Inst. Fla. So. Coll., Lakeland, 1958-61; corr. Tampa (Fla.) Tribune, 1960-70. Mem. bd. dirs. Polk Pub. Museum; dir. pub. relations Polk County Council Parents and Tchrs.; pres. Fla. chpt. Nature Conservancy. Mem. Fla. Audubon Soc. (mem. adv. bd. 1960-72), Lake Region Audubon Soc. (pres. 1960-65), Am. Assn. U. Women (br. sec. 1962-64), Wildlife Soc., Wilderness Soc., Am. Soc. Mammalogists, Am. Assn. Zool. Parks and Aquariums, Izaak Walton League, Fla. Wildlife Fedn., Nat. Wildlife Fedn., Am. Museum Natural History, Fla. Zool. Soc., Defenders of Wildlife, Nat. Parks and Conservation Assn., Womans Aux. Fla. Med. Assn. Asso. editor Fla. Medaux, 1963-65; editor Lake Region Naturalist, 1959-69; asst. editor Fla. Naturalist, 1964-70; editor Fla. Wilderness Calendar, 1964-67. Home: 305 W Beacon Rd Lakeland FL 33803

NIX, ALICE PEARL, educator; b. Choestoe, Ga., Dec. 12, 1912; d. Columbus H. and Lillie (Henson) Nix; A.B., Piedmont Coll., 1940; M.Ed., U. Ga., 1946, Ed.D., 1959; postgrad. U. N.C., 1948, U. Tenn., 1950. Elementary tchr. White County Schs., Cleveland, Ga., 1930-31, 32-34, 36-40, secondary tchr., 1940-45, curriculum cons., 1945-47; dir. guidance, tchr. edn. Truett-McConnell Coll., Cleveland, Ga., 1947-57; counselor, instr. U. Ga., Athens, 1958-59; faculty West Ga. Coll., Carrollton, 1959—, prof. psychology, dir. psychoeducational services, 1966—. Mem. Carroll County Mental Health Bd., 1972—. Named Woman of Year, Beta Sigma Phi, 1973. Fellow Ga. Psychol. Assn.; mem. Am., Southeastern psychol. assns., Ga. Assn. Edn., Bus. and Profl. Women's Club (pres. 1973—), League Women Voters (pres. 1966-69), Delta Kappa Gamma (pres. 1964-66), Kappa Delta Pi. Baptist (dir. women's missionary work 1971—, Sunday sch. tchr. 1959—). Home: 229 Griffin Carrollton GA 30117

NIX, MAE FRANCES, coll. librarian; b. Donaldson, Ark., Feb. 10, 1925; d. John Wiley and Carrie Octavia (Hughes) Nix; B.A., Henderson State Coll., 1948; M.A., George Peabody Coll. for Tchrs., 1954. Librarian, tchr. pub. schs. Ark., 1944-54; librarian Pub. Library of Camden and Ouachita County, Ark., 1954-57, Hall High Sch., Little Rock, 1957-65, Hendrix Coll., Conway, Ark., 1965—; instr. library sci. State Coll. Ark., Conway, 1965. State pres. Ark. Bapt. Bus. Women, 1956-57; mem. Eastern dist. Ark. Selective Service Bd., 1971—. Mem. Am. Assn. U. Women, Am., Ark., Southwestern library assns., Ark. Status of Women (mem. com. 1971—), Delta Kappa Gamma. Home: 314 Western Av Conway AR 72032

NIXON, MARNI, soprano; b. Altadena, Cal., Feb. 22; d. Charles Nixon and Margaret (Wittke) McEathron; student Los Angeles City Coll., 1947-49, Stanford U. Opera Workshop, 1949, U. So. Cal. Opera Workshop, 1950-51; m. Ernest Gold, May 22, 1950 (div. 1970); children—Andrew Maurice, Martha Alice, Melani Christine; m. 2d, L.F. Fenster, July, 1971. Child actress Pasadena (Cal.) Playhouse, 1940-45; soloist Roger Wagner Chorale, 1947-53; appeared with New Eng., Los Angeles opera cos., Ford Found. TV Opera, 1948-63; appeared as Eliza Doolittle in revival My Fair Lady, N.Y.C., 1964, Sister Sophia in Sound of Music, motion picture, 1964; appeared with San Francisco Spring Opera, 1966, Seattle Opera, 1971—; dir. vocal faculty Cal. Inst. Arts; dir. opera workshop Cornish Sch., Seattle; appeared in classical recitals with symphonic orchs., London, Israel, Dublin, BBC-TV, U.S.A., Can., N.Y. Philharmonic, Los Angeles Philharmonic, Buffalo Symphony orchs.; classical and musical comedy recs. for Columbia, Capital, RCA Victor, Ednl. records; TV appearances include Hollywood Palace, Tonight Show, Jack Paar, also night clubs. Named Hostess with the Mostest for being voice of actresses in motion pictures Time Mag., 1964; named Every Composers Favorite Singer, Sat. Rev. Lit., 1966; recipient Gold Record (Song from Mary Poppins, Disneyland Records). Address: 7323 Mercer Terrace Dr Mercer Island WA 98040

NIXON, PHYLLIS RUTH JONES (MRS. EUGENE RAY NIXON), librarian; b. Springfield, Mass., Mar. 10, 1920; d. Wilfred Fuller and Dorothy Maud (Elwin) Jones; B.A. magna cum laude, Mt. Holyoke Coll., 1941; M.A., Brown U., 1944; M.S. in L.S., Drexel U., 1962; m. Eugene Ray Nixon, June 10, 1945; children—Cynthia (Mrs. David Alan DuBose), Emily. Cons. linguistics Army Services Forces, N.Y.C., 1944-45; librarian Eleutherian Mills Hist. Library, Greenville, Del., 1962-63; head librarian Del. Art Mus., Wilmington, 1965—. Mem. Del. Library Assn., Art Libraries North Am., Phi Beta Kappa. Presbyn. Home: 36 Springhouse Lane Media PA 19063 Office: 2301 Kentmere Pkwy Wilmington DE 19806

NIXON, THELMA CATHERINE (PAT) RYAN (MRS. RICHARD MILHOUS NIXON), wife of former Pres. of U.S.; b. Ely, Nev., Mar. 17, 1912; grad. cum laude, U. So. Cal., 1937, L.H.D., 1961; m. Richard Milhous Nixon, June 21, 1940; children—Patricia (Tricia) (Mrs. Edward Finch Cox), Julie (Mrs. Dwight David Eisenhower). X-ray technician, N.Y.C., 1931-33; tchr. comml. courses high schs., Cal., 1937-41; govt. economist, 1942-45. Promoter world-wide humanitarian service, volunteerism in U.S. Named among most admired women George Gallup poll, 1957, 68, 69, 70, 71; named Nation's Ideal Housewife Homemakers Forum, 1957; decorated grand cross Order of Sun for relief work at time of earthquake, 1971 (Peru); grand cordon Most Venerable Order of Knighthood Pioneers (Republic of Liberia), 1972. Address: San Clemente CA 92672

NIYEKAWA-HOWARD, AGNES MITSUE (MRS. IRWIN JAY HOWARD), psycholinguist, educator; b. Tokyo, Japan, May 9, 1924; d. Zensaku and Kano (Niyekawa) Niyekawa; came to U.S., 1949, naturalized, 1960; B.A., Tokyo Woman's Christian Coll., 1945; B.A., U. Hawaii, 1952; M.A., Bryn Mawr Coll., 1954; Ph.D., N.Y. U., 1960; m. Irwin Jay Howard, Dec. 23, 1966; children (by previous marriage)—Erik Calogeras, Meagan Calogeras. Research asso. Research Center for Human Relations, N.Y. U., N.Y.C., 1959-61; postdoctoral research fellow N.Y. State Psychiat. Inst., N.Y.C., 1961-63; asst. prof. ednl. psychology U. Hawaii, Honolulu, 1964-67, asst. researcher Edn. Research and Devel. Center, 1965-67, prof. human devel., 1971-73, chmn. dept. East Asian langs., 1973—; asso. prof. psychology in edn. Northeastern U., Boston, 1968-69; sr. fellow Inst. Advanced Projects, East-West Center, Honolulu, 1969-70, coordinator culture learning program, 1970-71. Cons. Internat. Evaluation of Ednl. Achievement Project, 1966—; mem. Bilingual Task Force for Am. Samoa, 1972. USPHS fellow, 1961-63, Am. Council of Learned Socs. fellow, 1962, Japan Soc. for Promotion of Sci. fellow, 1972; U.S. Office of Edn. grantee, 1965-67, Am. Council of Learned Socs. grantee, 1967-68, Nat. Inst. Mental Health grantee, 1968-70. Mem. Am., Japanese psychol. assns., Am. Ednl. Research Assn., Assn. for Asian Studies. Author: A Study of Second Language Learning, 1968. Home: 500-2003 University Av Honolulu HI 96814

NIZIOL, URSULA MARIA, psychologist; b. Chorzow, Poland, Mar. 16, 1925; d. Augustyn and Hildegarda (Buchala) Krzewica; came to U.S., 1949, naturalized, 1949; B.S. in Edn., Tex. Western Coll., 1964; M.Ed., U. Tex., 1966; Ed.D., N.M. State U., 1970; m. Joseph E. Niziol, Dec. 1945 (div. Dec. 1964); children—John, Julianna (Mrs. J. de la Cruz), Maria, Charles, Christine (Mrs. R. Grant), George. Tchr. El Paso (Tex.) Ind. Sch. Dist., 1964-68; counselor Tex. Rehab. Commn., El Paso, 1968-69; psychologist El Paso Rehab. Center, 1969-72, El Paso Guidance Center, 1972—. Individual practice psychol. counseling, El Paso, 1970—. Pres. Human Relations Inst., El Paso, 1974—. Leader Niagara Falls council Girl Scouts Am., 1955-59; mem. Steering Com. El Paso Community Coll., 1969; adv. bd. Jr. League, El Paso, 1970-74. Mem. adv. bd. United Cerebral Palsy Center, 1973—; bd. dirs. El Paso Epilepsy Assn., sec., 1973—. Mem. Am. Psychol. Assn., Am. Acad. for Cerebral Palsy, Council for Exceptional Children, Assn. for Retarded Children, Nat. Rehab. Assn., Assn. for Children With Learning Disabilities, El Paso Concert Assn., Phi Alpha Theta, Kappa Delta Pi. Home: 6305 Pino Real El Paso TX 79912 Office: 1900 N Oregon El Paso TX 79902

NOAR, GERTRUDE, educator, author; b. Phila.; d. Arnold and Amalia (Bernheimer) Noar; B.S., U. Pa., 1919, M.A., 1922. Tchr. elementary and sr. high schs., Phila., 1914-31; prin. Gillespie Jr. High Sch., Phila., 1931-51; nat. dir. edn. Anti-Defamation League, N.Y.C., 1951-66; self employed cons. tchr. edn., N.Y.C., 1967—. Mem. N.E.A., Assn. for Supervision and Curiculum Devel., Assn. Childhood Edn. Internat., UN Assn. N.Y., Nat. Ret. Tchr. Assn. Mem. B'nai B'rith. Author: Freedom to Live and Learn, 1948; The Junior High School Today and Tomorrow, 1961; The Teacher and Integration, 1966; Teaching and Learning the Democratic Way, 1963; What Research Says About Teaching the Disadvantaged, 1967; Sensitizing Teachers To Ethnic Groups, 1972; Individualized Instruction: Every Child a Winner, 1972; Individualized Instruction for the Mentally Retarded, 1974; also numerous pamphlets. Home: 500 E 77th St New York City NY 10021

NOBLE, ALMA NEASE, educator; b. Coolville, O., June 16, 1901; d. John Myron and Inez (Brown) Noble; A.B., Wittenberg Coll., 1924; A.M., Columbia, 1930; Ph.D., Ohio State U., 1938; A.M., Western Res. U., 1942; postgrad. U. Wis., 1959. Tchr. pub. high schs., New Vienna, O., 1924-25, Copley, O., 1925-28, Bath, O., 1928-29, Troy, O., 1930-34; head lang. dept. Ashland (Ky.) Jr. Coll., 1938-41; asst. prof. French, Latin, Marshall U., Huntington, W.Va., 1941-43, asst. prof. French, 1943-45, head dept., 1943-64, asso. prof., 1945-69, prof. emeritus, 1973—; asso. prof. French, Morris Harvey Coll., Charleston, W.Va., 1969-72, acting head dept. modern langs., 1970-72. Recipient plaque Marshall U., 1966, alumni citation Wittenberg U., 1971, certificate meritorious service, Morris Harvey Coll. 1972, Mem. Am. Assn. Tchrs. French (pres. W.Va. chpt. 1947-48), Modern Lang. Tchrs. Assn. Central States (pres. W.Va. chpt. 1955-56, sec. French sect. 1960-61, chmn. French sect. 1961-62, 2d v.p. 1968-69), Modern Lang. Assn. Am., Nat. Ret. Tchrs. Assn., Nat. Fedn. Modern Lang. Tchrs. Assns., Am. Guild Organists, Eta Sigma Phi, Pi Delta Phi, Delta Kappa Gamma. Presbyn. Mem. Order Eastern Star. Home: 301 W 10th Av Huntington WV 25701

NOBLE, GEORGIANA THOMAS (MRS. ROBERT NOBLE, JR.), occupational therapist; b. Chgo., Sept. 17, 1922; d. Fayette M. and Hazel E. (Muir) Thomas; student Morgan Park Jr. Coll., 1940-42; B.S., U. Chgo., 1945; certificate in occupational therapy Richmond Profl. Inst., 1946; postgrad. Northwestern U., 1946-47, U. Chgo., 1949-50; m. Robert Noble, Jr., Aug. 17, 1945 (div. Dec. 1963); children—Robert James III, Thomas Fayette. Staff occupational therapist VA Hosp., Chgo., Cleve., 1946-48; dir. occupational therapy U. Chgo.-Children's Hosp., 1948-50; asst. dir. adjunctive therapy Psychosomatic and Psychiat. Inst., Chgo., 1965-70; supr. occupational therapy Psychosomatic and Psychiat. Inst., Chgo., 1963-70; dir. activities U. Chgo. Clin., 1970-71; dir. activities and day care Evanston (Ill.) Hosp., 1971—. Mem. Practioners Study Group Evanston Mental Health Bd., Chgo. Area Conf. Partial Hospitalization, 1971-73. Mem. Ill. Group Psychotherapy Soc., Am. Occupational Therapy Assn. Club: Quadrangle (U. Chgo.). Home: 5466 Everett St Chicago IL 60615 Office: 2650 Ridge Av Evanston IL 60201

NOBLITT, KATHERYN MARIE MCCALL (MRS. ALBERT SPENCER NOBLITT), composer, piano tchr.; b. Marion, N.C., Feb. 10, 1909; d. Clifton Reid and Joseph Julia Lillian (Gruber) McCall; Mus.B. summa cum laude, Greensboro Coll., 1930; m. Albert Spencer Noblitt, June 19, 1934; 1 son, Jerry Spencer. Tchr. piano, various locations, N.C., 1930-48, Roanoke, Va., 1948—; pvt. sec., med. sec., Roanoke, Va., 1948-59; co-pastor, ind. Christian worker with husband, 1934—. Mem. Roanoke Music Tchrs. Assn., Roanoke Valley Music Tchrs. Assn., Va. Music Tchrs. Assn., Music Tchrs. Nat. Assn., A.S.C.A.P., Internat. Platform Assn., Am. Guild Authors and Composers, Am. Piano Tchrs.' Assn. Composer numerous piano and vocal solos and suites, ensembles, including, Waltz Mood, 1957, Jack Frost Surprised Me!, 1958, March of the Americans, 1961, Twinkling Keys, 1961, The Wind-Up Donkey, 1974. Home: 4848 Cove Rd NW Lot 1 Roanoke VA 24017

NOCERA, MARY ELIZABETH, ednl. TV adminstr.; b. Syracuse, N.Y.; d. Dante Anthony and Marie (Giangiobbe) Nocera; Mus.B., Syracuse U., 1951, Mus.M., 1958; M.A., Coll. Communication Arts, Mich. State U., 1967. Tchr. East Syracuse (N.Y.) Sch. Dist., 1951-56, East Islip (N.Y.) Sch. Dist., 1956-62, Ithaca (N.Y.) City Sch. Dist., 1962-65; sch. services coordinator Edn. Television Council Central N.Y., WCNY-TV, Syracuse, 1966-68, dir. sch. services, 1968-70, dir. instrnl. services, 1970—. Instructional TV cons. Recipient Nat. Def. Edn. Act assistantship, 1965. Mem. Nat. Assn. Ednl. Broadcasters, Women in Communications. Contbg. author: Televised Music Instruction, 1973. Office: WCNY-TV/Channel 24 Old Liverpool Rd Liverpool NY 13088

NOCHLIN, LINDA, educator; A.B., Vassar Coll.; M.A., Columbia U.; Ph.D., N.Y.U. Prof. art Vassar Coll., Poughkeepsie, N.Y., 1952-53, 54-55, 56-58, 59-62, 63—. Office: Dept Art Vassar Coll Poughkeepsie NY 12601

NOCHMAN, LOIS WOOD KIVI (MRS. MARVIN NOCHMAN), educator; b. Detroit, Nov. 5, 1924; d. Peter K. and Annetta Lois (Wood) Kivi; A.B., U. Mich., 1946, A.M., 1949; m. Harold I. Pitchford, Sept. 6, 1944 (div. May 1949); children—Jean (Mrs. William Horiszny), Joyce Lynn (Mrs. Joyce Whipple); m. 2d, Marvin A. Nochman, Aug. 15, 1953; 1 son, Joseph Asa. Tchr. adult edn., Honolulu, 1947, Ypsilanti (Mich.) High Sch., 1951-52; spl. instr. English, Wayne State U., Detroit, 1953, 54; tchr. Highland Park (Mich.) Coll., 1950-51, instr. English, 1954—. Mem. exec. bd. Highland Park Fedn. Tchrs., 1963, 64, 65, 66, 71, 72, mem. 1st bargaining team, 1965-66, 73 del. to Nat. Conv., 1964, 71, 72, 73, pres. rep. higher edn. to Mich. Fedn. Tchrs. Exec. Com., 1972, 73; mem. faculty adv. com. Gov.'s Commn. on Higher Edn., 1973—. Tchr. Baha'i schs., Davison, Mich., 1954, 55, 58, 59, 63, 64, 65, 66, Beaulac, Que., Can., 1960, Greenacre, Me., 1965; sec. local spiritual assembly Baha'is, Ann Arbor, 1953, sec., Detroit, 1954, chmn., 1955; mem. nat. com. Baha'is U.S., 1955-68; sec. Davison Bahai Sch. Com. and Council, 1956, 58, 63, 64, 65, 66, 67, 68. Mem. Am. Assn. U. Profs., Modern Lang. Assn., Mich. Council Tchrs. English, Mich. Coll. English Assn., Am. Fedn. Tchrs., Am. Civil Liberties Union, Internat. Platform Assn., Am. Acad. Polit. and Social Scis., Women's Equity and Action League, Alpha Lambda Delta, Alpha Gamma Delta. Contbr. poems mags. Home: 25227 Parkwood Huntington Woods MI 48070 Office: Highland Park Coll Highland Park MI 48203

NOCK, MARY L., state senator; b. Green Hill, Md.; grad. Beacom Bus. Coll., Wilmington, Del.; m. Mem. Md. Ho. of Dels., 1947-55; mem. Md. Senate, 1955—, chmn. edn. com., 1959—, mem. legislative council, 1953-54, 59—, senate pres. pro tem, 1959—. Mem. So. Regional Edn. Bd., 1959—; mem. Gov.'s Com. on Structure and Governance of Edn. Mem. bds. Peninsula Gen. Hosp., Edn. Commn. of States. Recipient citation Christian Citizenship Nat. Council Chs. of Christ, 1953, Eleanor Roosevelt Achievement award, 1958. Mem. Md. Congress Parents and Tchrs. (hon. life), Nat. Order Women Legislators, Quota Internat. (hon.), Delta Kappa Gamma (hon.). Mem. Order Eastern Star. Address: 914 Camden Av PO Box 488 Salisbury MD 21801

NODA, GRACE TERUKO UEDA, educator; b. Kauai, Hawaii, Oct. 1, 1920; d. Junsaburo and Mine (Takahashi) Ueda; B.S. in Edn., U. Hawaii, 1946; M.A., Ohio State U., 1969, Ph.D. (Univ. fellow), 1973; m. Daniel Sueo Noda, Aug. 25, 1945; 1 dau., Shannon Sumi (Mrs. Steven Douglas Carroll). High sch. tchr. Dept. of Edn., Honolulu, 1946-53, 56-59, 59-64, 65-71, dist. tchr., 1972—; supr. intern tchrs. U. Hawaii, Honolulu, 1953-56, supr. beginning tchrs. 1964-65. Vice pres. precinct, Honolulu, 1970-71. Coe fellow in Am. history, 1961, Coro fellow, 1962. Mem. Hawaii Edn. Assn. (dir. 1962-65), N.E.A. (improvement instrn. and profl. devel.), Hawaii Council for the Social Studies (pres. 1964-65), Hawaii Classroom Tchrs. Assn. (pres. 1966—), Hawaii State Tchrs. Assn. (dir. 1970-72), Hawaii Community Edn. Assn. (pres. 1974—). Home: 360 G Haleloa Pl Honolulu HI 96821 Office: 4680 Kalanianaole Hwye Honolulu HI 96821

NOE, FRANCES ELSIE (MRS. ROBERT DAVIES), physician; b. Beacon Falls, Conn., May 23, 1923; d. Alfred and Edith (Carlson) Noe; B.A., Middlebury Coll., 1944; M.N., Yale, 1947; M.D., U. Vt., 1954; m. Robert Davies, June 16, 1956; children—Kenneth Roger, Ralph Eric. Intern, Mary Hitchcock Meml. Hosp., Hanover, N.H., 1954-55; fellow cardiovascular research Mich. Heart Assn., 1955-56; resident Henry Ford Hosp. Pulmonary div., Detroit, 1956-57; fellow cardiopulmonary research Wayne State U. Coll. Medicine, 1957-58, instr. anesthesia dept., 1958-61, asst. clin. prof. anesthesia dept., 1961-65; asso. staff div. research Sinai Hosp. of Detroit, 1965-71, chief pulmonary physiology sect., 1971—. Mem. Sigma Xi. Contbr. articles in field to profl. jours. Home: 1601 Kirkway Bloomfield Hills MI 48013 Office: Sinai Hosp Detroit MI 48235

NOEL, CHRIS, actress; b. West Palm Beach, Fla., July 2, 1941; d. Dave Henry and Helen Louise (Truax) Botz; grad. high sch.; m. Roger Hanes, July 31, 1974. Owner, instr. Sch. Charm and Modeling, Lake Park, Fla., 1958-59; model Palm Beach (Fla.) Model Agy., 1951-59; cover girl and model, N.Y.C., 1959-63; hostess radio show A Date with Chris, Armed Forces Radio Service, 1966-71; motion pictures include Soldier in the Rain, 1964, Looking for Love, 1964, Honeymoon Hotel, 1964, For Singles Only, 1965, Glory Stompers, 1970, Get Yourself a College Girl, 1965, Joy in the Morning, 1965, Girl Happy, 1965, Wild Wild Winter, 1966, Beach Ball, 1966, The

Fourth Reich, 1971; numerous TV appearances, including Tonight Show, Merv Griffin Show, Mike Douglas Show, Bob Hope Presents, My Three Sons, What's My Lines, Bewitched, Love on a Rooftop, Password, Smother's Brothers, Hollywood Palace; rec. artist Sundance label. Home: 2100 Wilco St Midland TX 79701

NOEL, IDELLA MARIE (MRS. JAMES PARKER NOEL), editor; b. Prowers County, Colo., Aug. 5, 1925; d. Robert Ellsworth and Audra Ethelene (Compton) Cochran; B.A., U. No. Colo., 1946; postgrad. (King fellow), U. Colo., 1958; m. James Parker Noel, Dec. 22, 1946; children—Junita (Mrs. Richard P. Johannes), J. Bert. Elementary tchr., Springfield, Colo., 1943-45; editor, pub. Platteville (Colo.) Herald & La Salle Leader, 1947—. Recipient award Colo. Press Assn., 1968-72, Spl. Recognition plaque for community service Platteville Bus. Club, 1971. Mem. Colo. Press Women (pres. 1968), Nat. Newspaper Assn., Colo. Press Assn., Weld County Pubs. Assn., Sigma Delta Chi. Club: Platteville Business. Methodist. Home: 414 Grand Av Platteville CO 80651 Office: 309 Marion Av Platteville CO 80651

NOEL, NONA LOVELLA STAHL (MRS. HARLAN M. NOEL), lawyer; b. Lake Charles, La., Mar. 30, 1940; d. Haines and Harriet Vernona (Mose) Stahl; B.A., Grinnell Coll., 1961; M.S., Ind. U., 1963, J.D., 1968; m. Harlan M. Noel, June 4, 1967; children—Morgan, Amelia. Admitted to Ind. bar, 1968; dean of women St. Josephs Coll., Rensselaer, Ind., 1968-70; mem. firm Noel and Noel, Hammond, Ind., 1968—. Bd. dirs. Hammond Community Sch., 1969—. Mem. Natl. Assn. Women Deans and Counselors, Am. Bar Assn., Am. Assn. U. Women (pres. Calumet area 1972-74), Bus. and Profl. Women's Club (pres. 1972). Club: Altrusa (Hammond). Home: 35 Indi Illi Park Hammond IN 45320 Office: 5313 Holman Av Hammond IN 46324

NOETHER, EMILIANA P. (MRS. GOTTFRIED E. NOETHER), educator; b. Naples, Italy; d. Guglielmo and Bianca (Dramis) Pasca; A.B., Hunter Coll., 1943; M.A., Columbia U., 1944, Ph.D., 1948; m. Gottfried E. Noether, Aug. 1, 1942; 1 dau., Monica Gail. Instr. history Douglass Coll., 1947-50, asst. prof. history, 1950-52; research asso. Center for Internat. Studies, Mass. Inst. Tech., 1952-54; lectr. Regis Coll., 1959-63, asso. prof. history, 1963-64, prof. history, 1964-66; prof. history Simmons Coll., 1966-68; prof. history U. Conn., Storrs, 1968—. Italian sect. editor Am. Hist. Rev., 1958—. Am. Assn. U. Women fellow, 1946-47, 62-63; fellow Radcliffe Inst., 1961-62; Sr. Fulbright scholar to Florence, Italy, 1965-66; Am. Philos. Soc. research grantee, summer 1970. Mem. Am. Hist. Assn., Acad. Polit. Sci., Soc. for Italian Hist. Studies (chmn. prize award and citation com. 1968), Am. Assn. U. Women, Pi Gamma Mu. Author: Seeds of Italian Nationalism, 2d edit., 1969. Co-editor, contbr. Modern Italy: A Topical History Since 1861, 1974. Contbr. articles to profl. jours. Office: Wood Hall U Conn Storrs CT 06268

NOGLE, BEATRICE CARRICK, city ofcl.; b. Sapulpa, Okla., Dec. 14, 1916; d. William Charles and Kathryn (Meily) Carrick; student Dodd Coll.; m. Jules Edgar Nogle, Feb. 4, 1951; children—Mary Kathryn (Mrs. Peter L. Clifford), Barbara Ann Nesmith. Sec. to pres., bookkeeper Ogilvie Hardware Co., Shreveport, La., 1942-49; sec. to pres. Temple-White Co., Diboll, Tex., 1949-51; sec.-accountant, sales office sec., legal office sec., sec. to pres., chmn. bd. and exec. v.p. Temple Industries, Inc., Diboll, 1951-72; mem. Diboll City Council, 1970—. Mem. Lufkin (Tex.) Republican Women's Club. Home: 601 Carter Dr Diboll TX 75941

NOKES, JACQUELINE WHITE (MRS. ANDREW GREY NOKES), ednl. services co. exec.; b. Salt Lake City, Feb. 9, 1929; d. James Owen and Edna Amelia (Hansen) White; student U. Cal. at Los Angeles, 1946-49, U. Utah, 1949-50; m. Andrew Grey Nokes; children—Patricia (Mrs. James Kerbs), Laurence Paul, Andrew James, Anthony Grey. Romper room tchr. KSL-TV, Salt Lake City, 1957-59, hostess, producer Midday TV program, 1960-64, 74; now asst. to pres. KSL, Inc., Salt Lake City. Mem. Gov.'s Com. for Employment of Handicapped, 1969; chmn. Utah Soc. for Prevention of Blindness, 1971-73. Bd. dirs., women's chmn. United Cerebral Palsy, 1965-66. Recipient Shield award Delta Gamma, 1973, award Utah Civic Young Men's Assn., 1972, award for patriotic programs Freedoms Found., 1969. Mem. Am. Women in Radio and TV (nat. v.p. 1968-69). Home: 2075 Lincoln Lane Salt Lake City UT 84117 Office: 145 Social Hall Av Salt Lake City UT 84111

NOLAN, AGNES FOLK (MRS. RICHARD NOLAN), real estate co. exec.; b. N.Y.C.; d. William J. and Agnes (Sikora) Gilligan; B.A., Trinity Coll., 1952; LL.B., Columbia, 1955; m. Richard Nolan, Jan. 31, 1959; children—Anthony, Christopher, Timothy, Mariana. Admitted to N.Y. bar, 1957; atty. Calwalader, Wickersham & Taft, N.Y.C., 1955-60; asst. gen. counsel Karper Roth Corp., N.Y.C., 1960-62; pres., real estate broker Whitbread-Nolan, Inc., N.Y.C., 1962—. Home: 271 Central Park New York City NY 10024 Office: 600 Madison Av New York City NY 10022

NOLAN, BERNADETTE JOSEPHINE, assn. exec.; b. Chgo., July 7, 1933; d. Bernard Francis and Josephine Dorothea (Jankowski) Nolan; grad. high sch. Adjustment clk., typist Continental Ill. Nat. Bank & Trust Co., Chgo., 1951-53; typist Hanover Ins. Co. Chgo., 1953-54; sec. appraisers div. Multiple Listing Service and Chgo. Realtor-Traders Club Chgo. Real Estate Bd., 1954-61; legislative sec., exec. editor Cal. Real Estate Assn., Los Angeles, 1961-63; exec. sec. Pomona Valley Bd. Realtors, Pomona, Cal., 1963-64; exec. dir. Am. Indsl. Real Estate Assn., Los Angeles, 1965—; mgr. apt. bldg., Los Angeles, 1967—; field research corr. World Wide Research, Mineola, N.Y., 1970-72. Vol., U.S.O., 1953-55. Adminstrv. asst. Republican precinct orgn., 1969-70; state finance chmn. Com. to Re-elect Gov. Ronald Reagan, 1970; active Pres. Richard Nixon 1972 campaign. Mem. Am. Bus. Women's Assn. (Woman of Year 1972-73), So. Cal. Soc. Assn. Execs. Clubs: International Traders, Executive and Professional (Encino, Cal.). Home: 2214 Glendale Blvd Los Angeles CA 90039 Office: 5670 Wilshire Blvd Los Angeles CA 90036

NOLAN, BETTY, savs. and loan exec.; b. Omaha, July 28, 1916; d. Thomas James and Margaret Regina (FitzPatrick) Nolan; student pub. schs. With Guarantee Mut. Life Ins. Co. of Omaha, 1936-62, supr. investment dept., 1952-62; asst. v.p., personnel dir., mng. officer nation wide lending dept. Comml. Savs. & Loan, Omaha, 1962-73, v.p., 1973—. Mem. Personnel Assn. Omaha, Council Real Estate Women, Omaha C. of C. (dir. women's div. 1966-68). Club: Field (life hon.) (Omaha). Home and Office: care Comml Savs and Loan Assn PO Box 1103 Omaha NE 68132 care Comml Savs and Loan Assn PO Box 1103 Omaha NE 68132

NOLAN, JEANNETTE COVERT (MRS. VAL NOLAN), author; b. Evansville, Ind., Mar. 31, 1897; d. Charles Grant and Grace Louise (Tucker) Covert; grad. high school, Evansville; Litt.D., Ind. U., 1967; m. Val Nolan, Oct. 4, 1917; children—Val, Alan, Kathleen (Mrs. Alan H. Lobley). Reporter, spl. feature writer Courier Jour., Evansville, 1915-16; now writer adult and juvenile fiction and biography. Mem. Woman's Press Club Ind., Nat. Fedn. Am. Presswomen, Ind. Hist. Soc., Ind. War History Commn., Ind. Lincoln Found., Ind. Acad., Theta Sigma Phi (hon. life), Psi Iota Xi (hon.). Democrat. Author: Barry Barton's Mystery, 1932; Second Best, 1933; The Young Douglas, 1934; New Days, New Ways, 1936, English edit., 1937; Red Hugh of Ireland, 1938; Hobnailed Boots, 1939; Where Secrecy Begins, 1939; The Gay Poet, 1940; Profile in Guilt, 1941; The Story of Clara Barton and the Red Cross, 1941; James Whitcomb Riley, 1941; The Little Giant, The Story of Stephen A. Douglas and Abraham Lincoln, rev. edit., 1964; Final Appearance, 1943; Hoosier City, 1943; O. Henry, 1943; Treason at the Point, 1944; Patriot in the Saddle, 1945; I Can't Die Here, 1945; Gather Ye Rosebuds, 1946; Florence Nightingale, 1946; This Same Flower, 1948; Andrew Jackson, 1949; John Brown, 1950; La Salle, 1951; (with Horace Gregory and James T. Farrell) Poet of the People, 1951; The Story of Ulysses S. Grant, 1952; Abraham Lincoln, 1953; The Victory Drum, 1953; George Rogers Clark, 1954; The Story of Joan of Arc, 1954; Martha Washington, 1954; Sudden Squall, 1955; A Fearful Way to Die, 1956; Benedict Arnold, 1956; Dolly Madison, 1958; Spy for the Confederacy, 1960; John Marshall, 1962; The Shot Heard Round the World, 1963; John Hancock, Friend of Freedom, 1966; Belle Boyd, Secret Agent, 1967; Yankee Spy, 1970; Indiana, 1970; Aaron Burr, 1972; Getting to Know the Ohio River, 1973. Columnist, Lines with a Hoosier Accent, Indpls. Star, 1943-44. Address: 25 Northview Dr Indianapolis IN 46208

NOLAN, MARGARET JULIA MALEY (MRS. WILLIAM NOLAN), occupational therapist; b. Chgo., July 24, 1935; d. Joseph Patrick and Lucille Mary (Bruxer) Maley; B.S., Mt. Mary Coll., 1957, certificate in occupational therapy, 1958; postgrad. U. Rochester, 1958-59; m. William Nolan, June 11, 1960; children—Catherine, Michael, Kerry, Jennifer. Staff therapist, sr. therapist Rochester (N.Y.) State Hosp., 1958-64; cons. occupational therapist Brightonian Nursing Home, Brighton, N.Y., 1969-72; cons. Wedgewood Nursing Home, Spencerport, N.Y., 1972—. Co-chmn. community luncheon in honor Susan B. Anthony, 1971, chmn., 1972; chmn. Rose Day Distbn. to Rochester Area Nursing Homes, 1974. Mem. Am., N.Y. State (legislative chmn. 1963, com. mem. for convs. 1959, 65, 73) occupational therapy assns., Rochester Fedn. Women's Clubs (del. 1968-69, 3d v.p. 1972-73, alternate del. 1973-74, exec. dir. 1974—), Police Wives Aux. (sec. 1967-68, treas. 1969), Women's League (v.p. 1973), Bowling League. Roman Catholic (chmn. Christmas bazaar 1974). Address: 14 McCleary Rd Spencerport NY 14559

NOLAND, INIS PEGGY (MRS. THOMAS C. NOLAND), lawyer; b. Arnegard, N.D., May 8, 1931; s. Floyd and Evelyn Grace (Calkins) Van Allen; B.S., Van Norman U., 1964, LL.B., 1966; m. Thomas C. Noland, Nov. 2, 1968; children by previous marriage—Winifred (Mrs. Paul Edmonds), Roberta (Mrs. John Berry), Warren Wagner, David Wagner; adopted children—Thomas Russell, John Patrick, Jerre K. Admitted to Cal. bar, 1967; county pub. defender, Inyo County, 1967-68; individual practice of law, Beverly Hills, Cal., 1967, Lone Pine, Cal., 1968—. Speaker various women's groups So. Cal. Mem. Women Lawyers Assn., Aircraft Owners and Pilots Assn., Cal. State Bar, Inyo County Bar Assn., Lone Pine C. of C. (dir. 1968), Bus. and Profl. Women's Club, Mensa. Club: Mount Whitney Golf (Lone Pine). Home: 1091 S Main St Lone Pine CA 93545 Office: 101 N Main St Lone Pine CA 93545

NOLAND, MARY RUTH, artist, poet; b. Triune, Tenn., Jan. 8, 1919; d. Thomas Granville and Fannie Mae (Anderson) Coleman; student writing Ariz. State U., 1950; pvt. art study; m. Robert Irvin Noland, Jr., Mar. 28, 1937; 1 dau., Marjorie Ann Maurer. Exhibited one woman shows Capitol City Bank, Nashville, 1965, Parthenon Gallery, Nashville, 1966, David Lipscomb Coll., Nashville, 1967. Exhibited at Dept. Interior Gallery, Washington, Phoenix Art Mus., Salt Palace, Utah, others; tchr., demonstrator for galleries. Reader statewide poetry contest Ariz. Dept. Pub. Instrn., 1969, judge, 1970; mem. Ariz. Mother of Year Com., 1970. Recipient numerous prizes. Mem. Nat. League Am. Pen Women (nat. art bd. 1972—, historian Phoenix br. 1972—), Ariz. Poetry Soc. (historian 1969-70, rec. sec. 1970), Ariz. Artist Guild, World Poetry Soc., Internat. Platform Assn., Intercontinental Biog. Soc., Bus. and Profl. Women's Clubs. Mem. Ch. of Christ. Home: 4211 E Roma Phoenix AZ 85018

NOLEN, BARBARA (MRS. DAVID FALES STRONG), editor; b. Ardmore, Pa., Dec. 19, 1902; d. John and Barbara (Schatte) Nolen; A.B. cum laude, Smith Coll., 1924; M.A. in History, Stanford, 1925; m. David Fales Strong, June 14, 1927; children—Stephen Lewis, Deborah Louisa. Asst. to children's book editor Macmillan Co., 1926-27; children's book reviewer Washington Sunday Star, 1954-63, Children's Digest, 1963-70, Young Miss, 1966-70, Humpty Dumpty, 1967-70; editor children's books Century Co., 1931-32; editor Story Parade mag., 1936-54; lectr. children's lit. George Washington U., 1954-56, Am. U., 1959-61; dir. workshops in writing for children George Washington U., 1953-61. Cons. Workshops in Preparation Ednl. Materials, ICA, Washington, 1958, Lima, Peru, 1960; chmn. Action Com. D.C. Sch. Libraries, 1960-62. Adv. bd. Conn. Demonstration Elementary Sch. Library Project; sec. Morris Bldg. Com. for a Library and Hist. Soc. Bd. dirs. Morris Pub. Library, 1969—. Recipient award for com. services D.C. Edn. Assn., 1962, Am. Assn. Sch. Librarians, 1962. Mem. Children's Book Guild of Washington (charter), Morris Hist. Soc. (sec.). Author: (with Delia Goetz) Writers Handbook for the Development of Educational Materials, 1959; Ethiopia, 1971. Editor: Fun and Frolic, 1942; Luck and Pluck, 1942; Merry Hearts and Bold, 1942; The Brave and Free, 1942; Do and Dare, 1951; Spies, Spies, Spies (anthology), 1965; Africa is People (anthology), 1967; Ethiopia, a First Book, 1971; Africa is Thunder and Wonder, 1972; Mexico Is People, 1973. Address: Trotta Lane Morris CT 06763

NOLL, ESTHER ELIZABETH GOULD (MRS. JOHN O. NOLL), psychologist; b. Hurley, Wis., Feb. 19, 1922; d. John E. and Hulda Katherine (Harper) Gould; B.A., U. Wis., 1947; M.S., U. Ill., 1952; Ph.D., U. Pitts., 1955; m. John O. Noll, Feb. 2, 1952; children—Thomas John, Julia Margaret. Clin. psychologist Child Guidance Center, Dayton, O., 1956; asso. dir. Adolescent Treatment Program, Dayton State Hosp., 1956-58; clin. psychologist Mental Health Centers, Moscow and Lewiston, Ida., 1963-65; pvt. practice, Pullman, Wash., 1962-65; psychologist Peace Corps Tng. Center, U. Wis., Milw., 1966; asso. dir., chief psychologist Child Evaluation Center, U. N.D., Grand Forks, 1969—. Cons., Ednl. Services Center, Grand Forks, 1967-69. Mem. Am., N.D. psychol. assns., Soc. Pediatric Psychology. Democrat. Home: 803 24th Av S Grand Forks ND 58201 Office: Box 8212 Univ Sta Grand Forks ND 58201

NOLTE, JUDITH ANN, mag. editor; b. Hampton, Ia., Sept. 17, 1938; d. Clifford P. and Sigrid M. (Johnson) Nolte; B.S., U. Minn., 1960; M.A. in English, N.Y. U., 1965; m. Randers H. Heimer, May 7, 1971. Tchr. English, Middletown (N.Y.) High Sch., 1960-62, High Sch. of Commerce, N.Y.C., 1962-64; merchandising editor Conde Nast Publs., N.Y.C., 1964-69; editor-in-chief Am. Baby mag., N.Y.C., 1969—. Mem. Mortar Bd., Delta Gamma. Home: 344 W 72d St New York City NY 10023 Office: 575 Lexington Av New York City NY 10022

NONKEN, DORIS ELIZABETH LUNDIN (MRS. RAY OLUF NONKEN), coll. dean; b. Goodland, Kan., Sept. 5, 1915; d. Eric Olaf and Lena (Johnson) Lundin; A.B., Kan. Wesleyan Coll., 1937; spl. courses Syracuse U., 1962, 63; M.A., Colo. State U., 1966; postgrad. Kan. State U., 1955-56, Colo. U., 1961, Ft. Hays Kan. State Coll., Kan. State Coll., 1969-72; m. Ray Oluf Nonken, June 1, 1941 (dec. Jan. 1966); children—Karen (Mrs. Robert Pinkall), Linda (Mrs. Robert Bouse), Diane (Mrs. Martie Floyd). Tchr. English and Latin, Manhattan, Kan., 1937-41; tchr. Graber elementary sch., Hutchinson, Kan., 1955-62; reading specialist pub. schs., Hutchinson, 1962-69; dir. study skills center Jr. Coll., Gt. Bend, Kan., 1969-71; dean community services Garden City (Kan.) Community Jr. Coll., 1971—. Evening and summer faculty Sterling (Kan.) Coll., 1966-71. Local dir. humanities project Kan. Com. Humanities, 1973, 74. Mem. Community Concert Bd., 1945-69. Mem. Internat. Reading Assn., Am. Assn. U. Women, Kan. Tchrs. Assn. (v.p. 1968), Delta Kappa Gamma. Methodist. Club: Kansas Dinner. Home: 909 Harding St Garden City KS 67846 Office: Garden City Community Jr Coll Garden City KS 67846

NONKEN, JUNE MARIE AMSDEN (MRS. HARRY NONKEN), psychologist; b. Ogdensburg, N.Y., Aug. 16, 1920; d. Percy A. and Kathryn (Darmody) Amsden; A.B., Columbia, 1942; M.A., Tulsa U., 1956; Ph.D., George Peabody Coll., 1965; m. Donald B. Good, June 12, 1943, (dec. Feb. 1953); 1 dau., Deborah B. (Mrs. Joe D. Johnson); m. 2d, Harry Nonken, Nov. 23, 1968; 1 stepson, Norman L. Pyschometrist, psychologist Tulsa Pub. Schs., 1954-59; teaching asst. staff psychologist Child Guidance Center, George Peabody Coll., 1959-61; clin. psychology intern U. Tex. Med. Sch., Galveston, 1961-62; instr. dept. psychiatry U. Tex. Med. Sch., 1963-64, chief psychologist div. child psychiatry, 1965-66; chief psychologist Community Guidance Center of Bexar County, San Antonio, 1966-71; asso. prof., dir. clin. tng. Trinity U., 1968-69, asso. prof. ednl. psychology, 1971—; asst. clin. prof. U. Tex. Med. Sch., San Antonio, 1967-72; sec. bd. Nonkens, Inc., San Antonio, 1969—. Ednl. cons. Alamo Hts. Ind. Sch. Dist., Judson Ind. Sch. Dist., Children's Center San Antonio, others. Bd. dirs. Tulsa chpt. Mental Health Assn., 1954-59, San Antonio Assn. Retarded Children, 1968-69, Friends Sch., San Antonio; adv. bd. Carmelite Day Care Center, San Antonio, 1973—. Mem. Am., Tex., Southwestern psychol. assns., Am. Orthopsychiat. Assn., Psi Chi. Republican. Presbyn. Home: 5411 Pawtucket Rd San Antonio TX 78230 Office: 715 Stadium Dr San Antonio TX 78284

NOONAN, ARDYCE ARLENE, coll. dean; b. Wolbach, Neb., Apr. 18, 1937; d. Archie Edward and Carrie Alena (Hansen) Nelson; B.A., Kearney State Coll., 1966; M.S., Chadron State Coll., 1969; postgrad. Miss. State U., 1970-71; m. Donald Noonan, Sept. 29, 1956 (div. Jan. 1971); children—Norene, Camela. Tchr. pub. schs., Neb., 1954-68; tchr., counselor Pine Ridge Job Corps, Chadron, Neb., 1969; asso. dean student services N.E. Community Coll., Norfolk, Neb., 1970—. Mem. Am., Neb. (sec. 1973-74, dir. 1973-74) personnel and guidance assns., Nat. Assn. Univ. Adminstrs., Nat. Assn. Student Personnel Adminstrs., Cornhusker Sch. Counselors Assn., Neb. Tech. and Community Student Personnel Adminstrs. (sec. 1973-74), Nat. Assn. Women Deans and Counselors. Home: 1220 Verges St Norfolk NE 68701

NOONAN, JULIA FRANCES, illustrator; b. Naugatuck, Conn., Oct. 25, 1946; d. Francis Michael and Mary Charlotte (Richardson) Noonan; B.A. with honors in graphics, Pratt Inst., 1968; m. Russell G. Poggensee, Oct. 2, 1971. Illustrations pub. in mags. including Redbook, Harper's Bazaar, Ladies Home Jour., N.Y. mag. Author, illustrator: The Best Thing To Be, 1971. Illustrator: The Throme of the Erril of Sherill (Patricia McKillip), 1973; Peter's Pocket (Judi Barrett), 1974; The Magic Three of Solatia (Jane Yolen), 1974. Address: 164 Crown St Brooklyn NY 11225

NOONAN, MARY ELLEN KUBIK (MRS. JAMES STEPHEN NOONAN), public relations exec.; b. Cedar Rapids, Ia., June 10, 1942; d. William John and Vlasta Ruth (Kvetensky) Kubik; B.A. in Biology (scholar), Beloit Coll., 1964; M.A. in Counseling Psychology, Ohio State U., 1966; m. James Stephen Noonan, June 20, 1966. Counselor, dir. residence hall Ohio State U., Columbus, 1964-66, also dean women's staff, 1964-66; asst. to dir. indsl. relations Indsl. Nucleonics Corp., Columbus, 1966-69, asst. mgr. pub. relations, 1969-72, mgr. pub. relations, 1972—. Mgmt. adviser Jr. Achievement, Columbus, 1969-70. Trustee, Univ. Dist. Orgn., Inc., Columbus, pres., 1972-73. Mem. Pub. Relations Soc. Am. (publs. chmn. 1974—), Delta Gamma. Office: 650 Ackerman Rd Columbus OH 43202

NOONAN, SISTER PASCHALA, hosp. adminstr.; b. Quincy, Mass., Aug. 15, 1918; d. Leo Patrick and Helen Gene (Gurney) Noonan; A.A., St. Catharine Jr. Coll., 1937; B.A., DePaul U., 1945; R.N., St. Rose Sch. Nursing, 1948; journalism fellow Creighton U., 1959. Obstet. supr. St. Catherine Hosp., McCook, Neb., 1948-59; asst. prof. sociology and journalism St. Catharine (Ky.) Jr. Coll., 1960-66; adminstr. St. Catherine Hosp., McCook, 1966-74, Community Hosp., McCook, 1974—. Mem. gen. council Dominican Sisters, St. Catherine, Ky., 1960-66, mem. governing bd., 1972—; chmn. Neb. Bd. Health, 1971-73, chmn. search com., 1967-68; chmn. steering com. Mental Health Assn., McCook, 1967-68. Recipient Builder's award C. of C., 1972; Mary Roberts award for nurse writers Am. Jour. Nursing, 1960; Diana award Epsilon Sigma Alpha, 1971; named Neb. Nurse of Year, Neb. Nurses Assn., 1959; Women of Year, Bus. and Profl. Women's Club, 1968. Mem. Neb. Nurses Assn. (1st v.p. 1969-70), Nat. Student Nurses Assn. (resource jr. cons. 1959-69), Nat. League Nursing (resource jr. cons. 1960). Address: Community Hosp 1301 E H St McCook NE 69001

NORA, AUDREY FAYE HART (MRS. JAMES J. NORA), physician; b. Picayune, Miss., Dec. 5, 1936; d. Allen J. and Vera Lee (Ballard) Hart; B.S., U. Miss., 1958, M.D., 1961; m. James J. Nora, Apr. 9, 1966; children—James J., Elizabeth H. Intern, U. Wis. Med. Sch., Madison, 1961-62, resident, 1962-64; fellow pediatric hematology Baylor Coll. Medicine, Houston, 1964-66, instr. dept. pediatrics, 1966-70, asst. prof., 1970-71; clin. asst. prof. pediatrics U. Colo., Denver, 1971—; practice medicine specializing in pediatric hematology-oncology, Houston, 1966-70, genetics, Denver, 1971—; mem. staff Denver Children's Hosp., also dir. genetics sect. Diplomate Am. Bd. Pediatrics. Mem. Western Soc. Pediatric Research, Am. Soc. Human Genetics, Am. Fedn. for Clin. Research, Internat. Dermatoglyphics Soc., Teratology Soc. Contbr. articles to profl. jours. Home: 6135 E 6th Av Denver CO 80220 Office: 1056 E 9th Av Denver CO 80218

NORBECK, MILDRED EVELYN, missionary, educator; b. Sugar Grove, Pa., Feb. 18, 1904; d. Charles August and Olivia (Otander) Norbeck; A.B., Greenville Coll., 1925; Th.B., God's Bible Sch. and Coll., 1943. Ordained as minister of Gospel, 1945; missionary evangelist, pastor, tchr. Free Meth. Ch., Breathitt County, Ky., 1923-38; evangelist Ky., Tenn. confs., 1925-38, Ga., Fla. confs., 1939-40; pastor, Fla., 1941-45; missionary West Indies Bible Mission, Haiti, 1945-48; founder, supt. Haiti Inland Mission, Inc., 1949-64; founder, dir. Great Commn. Crusaders, Inc., 1960—. Mem. Nat. Assn. Evangs., World Evang. Fellowship, W.C.T.U. Haiti. Author: The Lure of the Hills, 1931; The Challenge of the Hills, 1947; 1st Edition of New Testament and Psalms In Creole lang., 1951; Genesis, 1955; The Haitian Challenge and You, 1965. Co-pub. Christian Perfection, 1960, The Old Man, 1972 (both in Haitian). Editor: The Call from Haitian Hills, 1948-64, Christian Action, 1965—. Editor periodical L'Action Chrétienne, 1970—. Pioneer 3 Christian gospel missions in Haiti. Home: PO Box 55 Intercession City FL 33848 Office: PO Box W-30 Port-au-Prince Haiti

NORDALE, MARY ANITA, lawyer; b. Fairbanks, Alaska, Apr. 8, 1934; d. Alton Gerald and Katherine (Driscoll) Nordale; B.A., Gonzaga U., 1957; J.D., George Washington U., 1966. Admitted to D.C. bar, 1967, Alaska bar, 1969; mem. staff U.S. Senator E.L. Bartlett, Washington, 1960-68; asst. U.S. atty., Fairbanks, Alaska, 1968-69, asst. dist. atty., 1969-70; br. counsel Small Bus. Adminstrn., Fairbanks, 1970-72; pvt. practice law, Fairbanks, 1972—. Mem. Central Dist. Dem. Com., Fairbanks, 1973. Mem. bd. Fairbanks Rehab. Assn., Inc., 1970—, pres., 1971-73; mem. bd. Compas, Fairbanks, 1971—, Fairbanks chpt. Alaska Retarded Children's Assn., 1973—. Mem. Fed., Am., D.C., Alaska, Tanana Valley bar assns., Am. Judicature Soc. Club: Soroptimist (Fairbanks). Home: PO Box 1671 Fairbanks AK 99707 Office: 1919 Lathrop St Fairbanks AK 99701

NORDIN, VIRGINIA DAVIS (MRS. KENNETH DAYTON NORDIN), lawyer, educator; b. Royal Oak, Mich.; d. George L. and Eva B. (Barber) Davis; A.B., The Principia, 1956; J.D., Harvard, 1959; m. Kenneth Dayton Nordin, Sept. 26, 1965; children—Dayton Davis, Kendra Evalyn. Instr. pub. speaking Tufts U., Medford, Mass., 1957-59; law clk. Frederick G. Hamley, U.S. Ninth Circuit Court Appeals, San Francisco, 1959-60; admitted to Cal. bar, 1960, N.Y. bar, 1961, Mich. bar, 1967; asst. sec., house counsel Marine Transport Lines, Inc., N.Y.C., 1960-62; mem. firm Reid & Priest, N.Y.C., 1962-64; asst. legislative counsel Christian Sci. Com. on Publ., Boston, 1964-66; research atty., research div. Neighborhood Legal Service Centers, Office Econ. Opportunity, Detroit, 1967; faculty U. Mich., Ann Arbor, 1968-74, chmn. commn. for women, office of the pres., 1971-74, dir. Inst. for Adminstrv. Advancement, 1973—, asst. prof. higher edn., 1974; asst. prof. ednl. adminstrn., U. Wis., Madison, 1974—. Cons. program planning com. Presidents Commn. on Mental Retardation, 1970-73. Bd. dir. YWCA, Cambridge, Mass., 1965-67. Mem. State Bar Mich. (council mem., sec. corp., finance and bus. law sect. 1968-74), Profl. Women's Caucus. Home: 2846 Whippoorwill Lane Ann Arbor MI 48103 Office: 1025 W Johnson St Madison WI 53705

NORDSTRAND, NATHALIE ELIZABETH JOHNSON, artist; b. Woburn, Mass., Nov. 6, 1932; d. Edward N. and Ruth (Peterson) Johnson; A.A., Bradford Jr. Coll., 1952; B.A., Barnard Coll., Columbia, 1954; pvt. art studies with Jay Connaway, Don Stone, Roger Curtis; m. Robert I. Nordstrand, Jan. 12, 1962. Artist oils and watercolor; works exhibited Nat. Acad. Galleries (N.Y.C.), Springfield Mus. Fine Arts, Hammond Mus., North Salem, N.Y.C., Bhulabha Meml. Inst., Bombay, India, Copley Soc. at Boston Symphony Hall, Hermann Fine Arts Center, Marietta, O., Am. C. of C., Hong Kong, others; one man show Rockport (Mass.) Art Assn., 1969; research asso. Gerontology Age Center of New Eng., Boston, 1955-64; clk. corp., dir. Johnson Bros. Greenhouses, Inc., Woburn, 1958—; partner Sullivan-Nordstrand Gallery, Rockport, Mass. Mem. planning bd. North Suburban Art Festival, 1963-68. Recipient numerous awards in nat. and regional competition, 1961—. Mem. Acad. Artists Assn. (Watercolor award 1973), Am. Artist Profl. League (Gold medal 1971), Hudson Valley, North Shore (dir. 1964-67), Rockport, So. Vt. art assns., Copley Soc., Reading Art Assn. (charter, program chmn., Pres.'s award 1973), Am. Watercolor Soc., Allied Artists Am. (Watercolor award 1973), Boston Watercolor Soc., Guild Boston Artists, Internat. Platform Assn. Methodist. Address: 384 Franklin St Reading MA 01867

NORFOLK, VEDA BROOKS, civic worker; b. Baton Rouge, Dec. 5, 1929; d. Laurence Waddill and Neveda Vivian (Stokes) Brooks; B.A., La. State U., 1950; postgrad. U. Miami (Fla.), 1951; m. William Alvin Norfolk, July 27, 1951; children—Veda Lynn, Claire Brooks, William Alvin, Nancy Ann. Dist. mgr. U.S. Census, Baton Rouge, 1970; chmn. horizons com., mem. exec. com. Baton Rouge Bicentennial Commn., 1972—. Mem. bd. Audubon council Girl Scouts U.S.; founder Baton Rouge Goals Congress; pres. Jr. League Baton Rouge, 1967-68. Mem. bd. Nat. Fedn. Republican Women, La. Fedn. Rep. Women; pres. East Baton Rouge Parish Rep. Women, 1969, also mem. exec. com.; mem. Rep. Polit. Action Council, East Baton Rouge Parish; mem. Rep. state central com. Bd. dirs. United Givers, La. Arts and Sci. Center, Community Vol. Bur, Baton Rouge Speech and Hearing Found., Found. Hist. La. (pres. 1974-76). Mem. Chi Omega (pres. alumnae 1962). Episcopalian (pres. ch. women 1972-74). Club: Bocaqe Racquet. Address: 3855 Churchill Av Baton Rouge LA 70808

NORMAN, BEVERLY JEAN, public relations co. exec.; b. Kansas City, Kan., Oct. 13, 1931; d. George Albert and Helen Margaret (Neisler) Reeder; B.S., U. Mo., 1953, postgrad., 1953-54. Asst. pub. relations dir. United Campaign, Kansas City, 1953-55; account exec. Jim McQueeny Assos., Kansas City, 1955-57; partner Fennell, Quinn, & Gibson, Kansas City, 1957-62; owner Beverly Norman Pub. Relations, Kansas City, 1962—. Dir., Pierce Sch. Interior Design, Kansas City, Mo., 1969—. Mem. Pub. Relations Soc. Am. (pres. Kansas City chpt. 1971, nat. assembly del. 1973—), Am. Women in Radio and TV (pres. Kansas City chpt. 1962-63), Women's C. of C. (dir. 1958-61), U. Mo. at Kansas City Alumni Assn., Nat. Assn. Home Builders, Gamma Alpha Che (pres. 1972-73). Presbyn. Soroptimist. Home: 8038 Halsey St Lenexa KS 66215 Office: 4601 Madison St Kansas City MO 64112

NORMAN, ELVA PAULINE KUYKENDALL (MRS. ISAAC DANIEL NORMAN), journalist; b. Waxahachie, Tex., Jan. 18, 1911; d. Thomas Calvin and Laura (Martin) Kuykendall; B.J., Mary Hardin-Baylor Coll., 1930; postgrad. U. Mo., 1964-66; m. Isaac Daniel Norman, Aug. 30, 1931; children—John Kuykendall, Eric Jesse, Thomas Daniel. Publicity dir. St. Louis YWCA, 1944-64; pub. relations dir. St. Louis County Library, 1955-64; editor The Suburban Educator, 1964-72, dir. pub. relations St. Louis Suburban Tchrs. Assn., 1964-72; teaching asst. University City Adult Evening Sch., 1959-72. Mem. bd. Univ. City Youth Center (Wigwam), 1956-57, University City Adult Evening Sch., 1950-72; bd. mgrs. Washington U. campus YM-YMCA, 1972—; nat. pub. relations chmn. Nat. Fedn. Garden Clubs Conv., St. Louis, 1959; local press relations chmn. Nat. Library Assn. Conv., St. Louis, 1964; mem. state com. Nat. Library Week, 1965; mem. communications adv. bd. University City Sch. Dist., 1973—; vol. various local social agys; chmn. pub. relations St. Louis Journalism Found. Dinner, 1970-72. Recipient award for mag. editing-writing Mo. and Nat. Press Women, 1965, 68-72; award for news story Ednl. Press Assn., 1966, award for series, 1969, award for spl. edition, 1971. Mem. Nat. Sch. Pub. Relations Assn., Ednl. Press Assn., Indsl. Press Assn., Am. Women in Radio and Television, Nat., Mo. press women, Mo. Tchrs. Assn., N.E.A., Pub. Relations Soc. Am. (accredited), Delta Kappa Gamma (hon.), Theta Sigma Phi (pres. St. Louis chpt. 1937, 48, 53-55, scholarship chmn. 1968-72, nat. pub. relations dir. 1959-61), Pi Gamma Mu. Baptist. Club: St. Louis Press. Photo editor, sect. editor Bi-Centennial St. Louis Guidebook. Contbr. articles to various publs., newspapers. Home: 7407 Melrose Av University City St Louis MO 63130

NORMAN, FRANCES M. ALEWINE (MRS. GEORGE I. NORMAN, JR.), bus. investments co. exec.; b. Anderson, S.C., Feb. 15, 1932; d. Frank Marion and Ollie (Fendly) Alewine; student Anderson Coll., 1948-49; m. George I. Norman, Jr., Feb. 5, 1954; children—George Irving III, Theodore Van Norman, Eric Anthony, Jonathan Francis. Dir., pres. Intermountain Land Devel. Co., Denver; dir. Med. Enterprises, Inc., Denver; v.p. George I. Norman Broadcasting, Inc., Salt Lake City, 1960-61, Comml. Properties, Inc., Salt Lake City, Real Estate, Inc., Salt Lake City. Docent, lectr. Salt Lake Art Inst., 1968—. Baptist. Clubs: Cottonwood Country, Salt Lake Tennis, Fort Douglas, Hidden Valley Country, Ambassador Athletic. Home: 2501 Olympus Dr Salt Lake City UT 84117 Office: 4751 Holladay Blvd Salt Lake City UT 84117

NORMAN, PATRICIA JOYCE BROWNSON (MRS. RALPH EDWARD NORMAN), journalist; b. Ann Arbor, Mich., July 6, 1930; d. William Thomas and Mildred Marie (Corson) Brownson; B.A. in Journalism, U. Mich., 1951; m. Ralph Edward Norman, June 23, 1951; children—Ralph Edward, Pamela, Mary, Nancy, William, Janet, Linda, Amy, Barbara. Writer Washtenaw Post-Tribune, Ann Arbor, 1944-49, Mich. Daily, Ann Arbor, 1949-51; editor R.C. Allen Bus. Machines, Grand Rapids, Mich., 1951-52; writer Akron Beacon Jour. and Canton Repository, Canton, O., 1965-72; writer Hoover Co., North Canton, O., 1967-69; staff writer Akron Beacon Jour., 1972—. Instr. journalism Walsh Coll., Canton, 1967. Republican precinct committeewoman, pollworker North Canton Jr. Woman's Club, 1963-65. Recipient Nat. award Nat. Fedn. Press Women, 1969, state awards, 1969-73; state awards Ohio Newspaper Women's Assn., 1970-73. Mem. Women in Communications, Ohio Press Women, Ohio Newspaper Women's Assn., Alpha Xi Delta (alumnae pres. 1962-64). Republican. Roman Catholic. Address: 814 Woodside Av SE North Canton OH 44720

NORRELL, GWENDOLYN, educator; b. Eudora, Ark., Nov. 12, 1919; d. Greene and Sylvia (Reed) Norrell; B.S., George Peabody Coll. for Tchrs., 1942; M.A., Columbia, 1945; Ed.D., U. Colo., 1957. Tchr. Eudora Pub. Schs., 1942-44; mem. faculty Mich. State U., East Lansing, 1945—, prof. psychology, 1965—, asst. dir. counseling center, 1964—. Mem. Am., Mich. psychol. assns., Am. Personnel and Guidance Assn. Home: 2928 Kenwick St Lansing MI 48912 Office: Counseling Center Mich State U East Lansing MI 48823

NORRIS, BARBARA JEAN (MRS. ROBERT BREWER NORRIS), pub. relations co. exec.; b. San Francisco, Nov. 19, 1937; d. Reid Harper and Barbara (Smith) Lockhart; A.B., Vassar Coll., 1958; m. Robert Brewer Norris, July 4, 1959; 1 dau., Barbara Reid. Asst. to bur. chief Life mag., Washington, 1960-62; legislative asst. U.S. Ho. of Reps., 1962-63; press asst. to Mrs. Hubert Humphrey, 1964; speechwriter, press aide Dem. Nat. Com., 1964-66; campaign mgr. Humphrey-Muskie campaign, Washington, 1968; v.p. Cochran/Norris, Inc., Washington, 1969-70, Daniel J. Edelman, Inc., Washington, 1970—. Bd. dirs. Jr. League of Washington, 1968-71, sec., 1970-71; bd. dirs. Friends of Juvenile Ct., 1969-71, Morgan Ecology, 1969-70. Mem. Am. Women in Radio and TV, Vassar Coll. Alumni Assn. (dir.). Clubs: Vassar (dir. 1968-70), Women's Nat. Democratic (Washington). Home: 3312 Cathedral Av NW Washington DC 20008 Office: 1730 Pennsylvania Av NW Washington DC 20006

NORRIS, DOROTHY E. KOCH, educator; b. Mineral Ridge, O., Jan. 12, 1907; d. Bruno Richard and Ida (Maggs) Koch; A.B., Oberlin Coll., 1930; M.A., Tchrs. Coll. Columbia, 1940, postgrad. summers 1936, 40, 60, 61; m. Paul Norris (dec. Jan. 1958). Dir. phys. edn. for girls, instr. of elementary sci. and health, Berea (O.) High Sch., 1930-35; instr. health and phys. edn. U. Tenn., 1936-39, asst. prof., 1939-41; cons. on dance Tenn. State Sch. Deaf, 1939-41; asst. prof. of dance specialization Boston U. Coll. Phys. Edn. for Women, Sargent, 1941-45, asso. prof. health and phys. edn., 1945-49, prof. health and phys. edn., chmn. dance minor, 1949-59, dir. modern dance group, 1941-59; prof. health, phys. edn. and recreation State U. Coll., Buffalo, 1959—; tchr. modern dance Creative Arts Conf. for Colls. N.E., 1948. Mem. exec. com. and dance com., chmn. ednl. exhibit N.E. Folk Festival, 1947, chmn. ednl. exhibit, 1947-50. Mem. A.A.H.P.E.R. (dance chmn. So. dist., mem. legislative bd., chmn. com. to compile victrola recordings of dance for nat. sect. dance 1949), N.Y. State Tchrs. Assn., N.Y. State Assn. Health, Phys. Edn. and Recreation, Eastern Assn. Phys. Edn. for Coll. Women, N.E.A., Oberlin Coll. Alumni Assn., Pi Lambda Theta, Kappa Delta Pi. Author: (with Reva P. Shiner) Keynotes to Modern Dance, 1965, rev. edit., 1969. Author manuals and articles on phys. edn. Home: Apt 3 2691 Elmwood Av Kenmore NY 14217

NORRIS, FERN ELIZABETH, law librarian; b. Clinton County, Ind., Feb. 15, 1904; d. Jerome and Lucy Ellen (Weidner) Duenk; student pub. schs.; spl. courses Purdue U., Ind. U.; studied voice; 1 son, Max S. Reporter, Supreme and Appellate Cts., State of Ind., 1945-59; dir. attendance div. Ind. Dept. Edn., 1953-62; law librarian, financial sec. Supreme Ct. Ind., 1963—. Active Nat. Found., Boy Scouts Am.; assisted in drives for dental clinic for Roberts Sch. for Crippled Children, an organ for Knightstown Home. Mem. Ind. Ho. of Reps., 1951; mem. 11th Dist. Republican Com., 1940-44; pres. Ind. Women's Rep. Club, 1948-61. Mem. Nat. League of Am. Pen Women (pres. Indpls. 1954-56, Ind. pres. 1956-68, nat. auditor 1958-60), Am. Legion Aux. (pres. local unit 1936, dist. pres. 1937, v.p. Ind. 1939), Indpls. Bus. and Profl. Women's Club, (v.p. 1970—), Internat. Travel Study Clubs (pres. Isle of Capri chpt.; Artman Council 1940-41, hon. pres. 1957—), Phi Beta. Clubs: Altrusa (pres. Indpls. 1969—), Woman's Department (Indpls.). Home: 5140 N Delaware St Indianapolis IN 46205 Office: State Capitol Indianapolis IN 46204

NORRIS, FLORA CREECH, broadcasting co. ofcl.; b. Raleigh, N.C., May 23, 1923; d. Herbert Burns and Minnie Huntt (Ransom) Norris; student St. Mary's Jr. Coll., 1941, Peace Jr. Coll., 1942-43, Washington Sch. Fashion Modeling, 1944; corr. courses Internat. Accountants Soc., 1957-58. Continuity writer WPTF, Raleigh, 1943-44; traffic mgr. WWDC, Washington, 1944-45; sec., asst. traffic mgr. WRC-NBC, Washington, 1945-46; sec., asst. bookkeeper LWV, Washington, 1947-48; traffic mgr. radio sta. WNAO, Raleigh, 1949-51, broadcaster, 1950; sec. Colonial Life & Accident Ins. Co., Raleigh, 1952, Wachovia Bank & Trust Co., Raleigh, 1952-54, Williams & Wall, C.P.A.'s, Raleigh, 1954-55; sec., accounting clk. Andrew Johnson Hotel, Raleigh, 1962-63; sec. N.C. Hwy. Commn., 1964; employment counselor Snelling & Snelling, Raleigh, 1965; office mgr., sales coordinator WTVD, Raleigh, 1965—. Vol. worker Heart Fund, A.R.C., United Fund. Mem. Am. Women in Radio and TV, Wake County Dem. Women, Wake County Hist. Soc., D.A.R. (chpt. rec. sec. 1971-72). Democrat. Episcopalian. Home: 605-A Smedes Pl Raleigh NC 27605 Office: PO Box 1326 Raleigh NC 27602

NORRIS, FRANCES SOCHOR, physician; b. Endicott, N.Y., Aug. 17, 1932; d. John Francis and Frances (Mikus) Sochor; B.A., Harpur Coll., 1954; M.D., Women's Med. Coll., 1958; m. Henry Jason Norris, Apr., 1961; children—Robin, Dolly, Henry Jason II. Rotating intern Maimonides Hosp., Bklyn., 1958-59; resident pathology Mallory Inst. Pathology, Boston, 1959-61, U. Minn., 1961-63; asst. pathologist endocrine pathology br. Armed Forces Inst. Pathology, Washington, 1963-64, cardiovascular pathology br., 1964-65; med. dir. Md. Med. Labs., 1967; surg. pathologist Doctors Hosp., Washington, 1967-69; pvt. practice pathology, Chevy Chase, Md., 1969—. Panelist, Food and Drug Adminstrn. Com. on OTC Drugs, 1971—; med. dir. div. licensing and certification Md. Dept. Health and Mental Hygiene, 1973—. Pres. Women's Equity Action League, 1971-72, chmn. com. med. edn. and med. practice. USPHS grantee, 1962. Mem. Am. Pub. Health Assn., Am. Med. Women's Assn., Washington Soc. Pathologists, Internat. Acad. Pathologists. Contbr. articles profl. jours. Home: 4 E Lenox St Chevy Chase MD 20015 Office: 301 W Preston St Baltimore MD 21201

NORRIS, JEAN DYON, publisher for blind; b. Chgo.; d. Ralph Oliver and Margaret Elizabeth (Boyle) Dyon; A.A., Santa Monica (Cal.) Jr. Coll., 1938; children—John Dyon, David Raymond, Kenneth Edward. Founder, Twin Vision Pub. div. Am. Brotherhood for Blind 1961, dir., 1961—; program coordinator Kinesthetic Teaching Aids, Am. Thermoform Corp., 1964; tech. adviser TV prodn. Vol., Boy Scouts Am. Asso. mem. Nat. Fedn. Blind of Cal. Mem. Order Eastern Star. Club: Pacific Palisades Jr. Women's (past pres.). Home: 4504 Stern Av Sherman Oaks CA 91403 Office: 18440 Oxnard St Tarzana CA 91356

NORRIS, MILDRED WELLS (MRS. WALTER THOMAS NORRIS, JR.), lawyer, judge; b. Ovett, Miss., Aug. 2, 1913; d. Whit Hix and Margaret Irene (Hudson) Wells; student Miss. State Coll. for Women, 1930; m. Walter Thomas Norris, Jr., June 22, 1940. Admitted to Miss. bar, 1947; asso. firm Roach & Jones, McComb, Miss., 1947-51, Pittman & Pittman, Hattiesburg, Miss., 1955-60; practiced in Brookhaven, Miss., 1951-55, Hattiesburg, 1955—; city judge Hattiesburg Municipal Ct., 1961-65, 73—. Mem. Hattiesburg Area Indsl. Devel. Bd., Miss. Gov.'s Commn. on Status of Women. Bd. dirs. YWCA, Hattiesburg. Mem. Interstate Assn. Commns. on Status of Women (1st v.p.), Miss. Fedn. Bus. and Profl. Women's Clubs (past pres.). Democrat. Mem. Ch. of Christ. Author: Bees Don't Sting — People Do, 1960. Home: 1315 Camp St Hattiesburg MS 39401 Office: PO Box 1633 Hattiesburg MS 39401

NORRIS, VIRGINIA GRACE OAKLEY, educator, civic worker; b. Los Angeles, Jan. 14, 1928; d. Earl James Taylor and Florence Marian (Ashley) Oakley; A.A., U. Cal. at Los Angeles, 1946, B.A., 1948; m. Robert Matheson Norris, Jan. 5, 1952; children—Donald Oakley, James Matheson, Elizabeth Anne. Tchr. art Anaheim (Cal.) Union High Sch., 1949-51; home and hosp. tchr. Santa Barbara (Cal.) City Schs., 1963—; instr. adult edn. div. Santa Barbara City Coll., 1972—. Dir. Arboleda Park Improvement Assn., 1960—, pres., 1965; mem. adv. com. Santa Barbara County Library, 1964-68, 70-73, Friends of Goleta Valley Library, 1965—; Goleta Valley Gen. Plan adv. com., 1973—. Mem. Spinners and Weavers of South Australia, Rep. Women, South Australian Country Women's Assn., U. Cal. at Los Angeles Alumni Assn. (life), Santa Barbara Weaver's Guild, Chi Omega, Pi Lambda Theta. Conglist. Club: University of California Faculty Women's (dir. 1967-70). Home: 4424 Nueces Dr Santa Barbara CA 93110 Office: Santa Barbara High Sch Dist 720 Santa Barbara St Santa Barbara CA 93101

NORSTRAND, IRIS MARIE FLETCHER (MRS. SEVERIN A. NORSTRAND), physician; b. Bklyn., Nov. 21, 1915; d. Matthew E. and Violet (Anderson) Fletcher; B.A., Bklyn. Coll., 1937, M.A., 1965; M.D., L.I. Coll. Medicine, 1941, Ph.D. in Biochemistry, 1972; m. Severin A. Norstrand, May 20, 1941; children—Virginia Helene, Thomas Fletcher, Lucille Joyce. Intern, Montefiore Hosp., Bronx, N.Y., 1941-42; asst. resident neurology N.Y. Neurol. Inst., 1944-45; practice medicine specializing in neurology, Bklyn., 1947-52; resident psychiatry Bklyn. VA Hosp., 1952-54, resident neurology, 1954-55, chief staff neurologist, VA Hosp., 1955—; attending neurologist Kings County, Univ. hosps., Kingsbrook Jewish Med. Center, Bklyn.; clin. asso. prof. neurology State U. Coll. Medicine, Downstate Med. Center, Bklyn. Physician adviser Spl. Bd. Health, Edn. and Welfare of N.Y. Presbytery, 1964-69. Fellow Am. Acad. Neurology; mem. Bklyn. Neurol. Soc. (pres. 1970-71), Am. Assn. Neuropathologists (asso.), Am. Psychiat. Assn., N.Y. Neurol. Soc., Internat. Soc. Psychoneuroendocrinology, Internat. soc. for Neurochemistry, Bklyn. VA Hosp. Med. Soc. (pres. 1973—), Sigma Xi, Needlework Guild. Home: 7624 10th Av Brooklyn NY 11228 Office: Bklyn VA Hosp 800 Poly Pl Brooklyn NY 11229

NORTH, FLORA D'ILLE (MRS. MORGAN NORTH), pub. co. exec.; b. Tomsk, Siberia, Mar. 5, 1917 (father Am. citizen); d. Arthur Leonard and Olga Ivanovna (Karpova) d'Ille; student U. Cal. at Berkeley, 1936-38; m. Morgan North, May 7, 1938; children—Morgan Evan, Ellen Barbour. A founder, partner Howell-North Press, Berkeley, 1938-61; pres. Howell-North Books, Inc., Berkeley, 1961—. Mem. Republican Women's Club, Berkeley. Recipient Merit award Conf. Cal. Hist. Socs., 1971, Book Design awards Rounce and Coffin Club. Mem. Am. Assn. State and Local History, Western Hist. Assn., Cal. (Achievement award 1972), Alameda County hist. socs., Western Book Pubs. Assn., Oakland Art Assn. Republican. Clubs: Claremont, Town and Gown (pres. 1957), Highlands (Berkeley). Home: 73 Alvarado Rd Berkeley CA 94705 Office: 1050 Parker St Berkeley CA 94710

NORTH, FLORENCE MANGUM (MRS. RICHARD LOOMIS NORTH), lawyer; b. Nephi, Utah, Jan. 7, 1908; d. Richard Allen and Fannie Belle (Price) Mangum; LL.B., Southwestern U., 1934; m. Richard Loomis North, Oct. 4, 1937; children—Richard, Linda, Marilyn (Mrs. Alika Kenneth Warren). Admitted to Cal. bar, 1935; research atty. Dist. Court of Appeal of Cal., Los Angeles, 1941-47; probate examiner Los Angeles Superior Court, 1947-49; superior court commr., judge pro tempore, 1949-69; mem. firm Conroy and North, Los Angeles, 1973—. Mem. Ch. of Jesus Christ of Latter-day Saints. Soroptomist. Contbr. articles in field to profl. jours. Home: 4222 Colbath Av Sherman Oaks CA 91403 Office: 6363 Sunset Blvd Suite 718 Los Angeles CA 90028

NORTH, HELEN FLORENCE, educator; b. Utica, N.Y., Jan. 31, 1921; d. James H. and Catherine (Debbold) North; A.B., Cornell U., 1942, M.A., 1943, Ph.D., 1945. Instr. Rosary Coll., River Forest, Ill., 1946-48; asst. prof. Swarthmore (Pa.) Coll., 1948-53, asso. prof., 1953-62, prof., 1962, chmn. dept. classics, 1959—, Centennial prof. classics, 1966-73, William R. Kenan, Jr. prof. classics, 1973—; asso. prof. Barnard Coll., N.Y.C., 1954-55; Martin classical lectr. Oberlin Coll., 1972. Sec. adv. council Sch. Classical Studies, Am. Acad., Rome, 1960—. Trustee, Am. Acad. Rome, LaSalle Coll. Recipient prize scholarship Am. Acad. in Rome, 1942-43. Am. Council Learned Socs. grantee, 1944, 1945; Mary Isabel Sibley fellow, 1945-46; Fulbright fellow, 1953-54; Ford fellow, 1953-54; Guggenheim fellow, 1958-59; Danforth grantee, 1962; Am. Assn. U. Women fellow, 1963-64; Am. Council Learned Socs. fellow, 1971-72; sr. fellow Nat. Endowment for Humanities, 1967-68; Harbison prize for distinguished teaching Danforth Found., 1969; Charles J. Goodwin award of merit Am. Philol. Assn., 1969. Mem. Classical Assn. Atlantic States, Am. Philol. Assn. (dir. 1968, 1st v.p. 1973-74), Cath. Commn. on Intellectual and Cultural Affairs (chmn. 1968-69), Phi Beta Kappa, Phi Kappa Phi. Author: Sophrosyne: Self-Knowledge and Self-Restraint in Greek Literature, 1966. Editor (with Anne King) Of Eloquence; Studies in Ancient and Mediaeval Rhetoric (Harry Caplan), 1970. Translator: Second Defense (John Milton), 1966. Home: 604 Ogden Av Swarthmore PA 19081

NORTH, KATHRYN K. KEESEY (MRS. EUGENE C. NORTH), ret. educator; b. Columbia, Pa., Jan. 25, 1916; d. Isaac and Elizabeth (French) Keesey; B.S., Ithaca Coll., 1938; M.A., N.Y. U., 1950; m. Eugene C. North, Aug. 18, 1938. Dir. music Cairo (N.Y.) Central Sch. Dist., 1938; music edn. cons. Argyle (N.Y.) Central Sch. Dist., 1939; dir. gen. music curriculum Hartford (N.Y.) Central Sch. Dist., 1939; mem. staff Del. Dept. Pub. Instrn., Dover, 1943; dir. music edn. Herricks (N.Y.) Pub. Schs., 1944-71; ret., 1971. Vis. lectr. Ithaca Coll., summers 1959, 60, 62-65, Fairleigh-Dickinson U., Rutherford, N.J., summer 1966, Albertus Magnus Coll., New Haven, summer 1968; instr. Adelphi Coll., 1954-55, Sch. Edn., N.Y.U., 1964-65. Mem. Music Educators Nat. Conf., N.E.A., N.Y. State Sch. Music Assn., N.Y. State Tchrs. Assn., Nassau Music Educators Assn. (exec. bd. 1947-58), N.Y. State Council Adminstrs. Music Edn. (chpt. v.p. 1967-68), Herricks Tchrs. Assn. (pres. 1948), Sigma Alpha Iota. Mem. Order Eastern Star. Home: 1645 Calle Camille La Jolla CA 92037

NORTHCOTT, WINIFRED HALLOCK NIES (MRS. JOHN PETERSEN NORTHCOTT), educator; b. N.Y.C., May 11, 1917; d. Edwin Winfred and Maud Huntington (Peet) Nies; B.A., Conn. Coll. for Women, 1938; M.A., Columbia, 1939, Ednl. Specialist certificate, 1966; Ph.D., U. Minn., 1971; m. John Petersen Northcott, Dec. 21, 1940; children—Hallock, Heather. Tchr. of deaf Lexington Sch., N.Y.C., 1939-42, Mpls. Pub. Schs., 1947-49; dir. Presch. Program, Mpls. Hearing Soc., 1955-65; coordinator Mpls. Pub. Sch. Program, 1967-68; faculty St. Cloud (Minn.) State Coll., U. Minn., 1968—; State cons. Minn. Dept. Edn. Hearing Impaired Programs, St. Paul, 1966-69, Presch. Programs for Handicapped, 1969—; pvt. practice, cons. ednl. programs for hearing impaired Nat. Adv. Com. on Handicapped Health, Edn. and Welfare, 1973. Pres., Council on Edn. of Deaf, 1974—; del. White House Conf. on Children, 1970; pres. League Women Voters, St. Louis Park, 1955-56; mem. Sch. Bd., 1956-71. Trustee Children's Health Center and Hosp., Mpls., U.S. Nat. Com. for Early Childhood Edn., Conn. Coll., 1961-66. Recipient Outstanding Alumni award Conn. Coll., 1968. Grantee, Bur. Edn. for Handicapped, 1969—. Mem. Alexander Graham Bell Assn. for Deaf (dir.), Council on Edn. of Deaf (pres.), Minn. Speech and Hearing Assn. (exec. council), Phi Beta Kappa, Pi Lambda Theta. Editor: The Hearing Impaired Child in a Regular Classroom: Preschool, Elementary, Secondary Years, 1973. Contbr. articles to profl. jours. Home: 4510 Cedarwood Rd Minneapolis MN 55416 Office: 550 Cedar St St Paul MN 55101

NORTHCUTT, BRENDA SUE SKIBINSKI (MRS. JERRY ALLEN NORTHCUTT), newspaper editor; b. McLeansboro, Ill., Feb. 17, 1949; d. Charles Edward and Roberta Kent (Ritchey) Skibinski; A.A., Rend Lake Jr. Coll., 1969; B.S., So. Ill. U., 1971; m. Jerry Allen Northcutt, Nov. 7, 1971. News editor The Daily News, Memphis, 1972-73; women's page editor Bartlesville (Okla.) Examiner-Enterprise, 1973—. Mem. Women in Communications, So. Ill. U. Alumni Assn. Baptist. Home: 205 Spring Rd Bartlesville OK 74003 Office: 300 E Frank Phillips Blvd Bartlesville OK 74003

NORTHCUTT, HELENE LOUISE BERKING (MRS. CHARLES PHILLIP NORTHCUTT), artist, educator; b. Hannibal, Mo., July 6, 1916; d. Robert Stanley and Alice Lee (Adkisson) Berking; Student Christian Coll., Columbia, Mo., 1932-33; B.S., U. Mo., 1939, A.M., 1940, Ed.D., 1959; m. Charles Phillip Northcutt, June 4, 1938; children—John Berking, Francois Lee. Art tchr., supr. Oakwood High Sch. and Elementary Sch., 1937-39; tchr. jr. high sch. U. Mo. Lab. Sch., 1939-40; tchr. elementary art, Memphis, Mo., 1941; county fine arts supr., Ralls County, Mo., 1941-42; tchr. art high sch., Columbia, Mo., 1943-44; tchr. art jr. high sch., Hannibal, Mo., 1951-54; supr. art Ralls County Reorganized Sch. Dist. VI, New London, 1954-56; vis. prof. U. Upper Ia., 1956; instr. U. Mo., 1956-57; prof. art Eastern Mont. Coll. unit U. Mont., Billings, 1957—; vis. prof. art U. B.C., Vancouver, 1965. Cons. in curriculum in art edn.; cons. environmental edn., cons. on Indian edn., early childhood exhibits designs and paintings. State dir. Am. Art Week, Am. Artists Profl. League, 1963-65; exhibit chmn. E.M.C. Gallery Fine Arts; program chmn. Becky Thatcher council Girl Scouts, 1946-48. Bd. dirs. United Christian Campus Ministry. Recipient scholarship Delta Kappa Gamma, 1956-57; Nat. Press award Gen. Fedn. Women's Clubs, 1951; named Outstanding Honor Grad. U. Mo., 1968. Mem. Nat. Soc. Coll. Profs., Mont. Edn. Assn. (past pres. Eastern Faculty unit; v.p. dept. higher edn. 1966-68, dept. pres. 1968-70) Am. Assn. U. Profs., Nat., Mont. (sec. 1967-69) art edn. assns., Am. Assn. U. Women (past chpt. pres.), Mont. Early Childhood Edn. Assn., Gen. Fedn. Women's Clubs (local past pres.), Pacific Art Assn., Delta Kappa Gamma (past chpt. pres.), Delta Phi Delta, Kappa Delta Epsilon. Methodist. Club: Eastern Montana College Faculty (Billings, Mont.). Author: Creative Expression, 1964; Competency base Module-Methods and Materials, 1974. Contbr. to publs. in field. Home: 4505 Rimrock Rd Billings MT 59102

NORTON, BARBARA LINDSEY, assn. adminstr.; b. Globe, Ariz., Aug. 19, 1916; d. Harold Lee and Helen Prettyman (Ross) Norton; A.B., Radcliffe Coll., 1938. Adminstrv. asst. OWI, Washington, 1944-46; dir. publicity Radcliffe Coll., Cambridge, Mass., 1947-50; dir. pub. relations YWCA, Boston, 1950-59, also bd. dirs., chmn. personnel com., 1970-72, dir. pub. relations, N.Y.C., 1959-65; exec. sec. Radcliffe Alumnae Assn., Cambridge, Mass., 1965—. Mem. Am. Alumni Council, Cambridge League Women Voters, Publicity Club (sec. 1963-65). Club: Radcliffe (N.Y.C. and Boston). Home: 48 Shepard St Cambridge MA 02138 Office: 10 Garden St Cambridge MA 02138

NORTON, CYNTHIA CLARE FRIEND (MRS. JOHN WILLIAM NORTON), educator; b. Shelburne Falls, Mass., Aug. 18, 1940; d. John Bronson and Rosalie Beatrice (Johnson) Friend; B.A., Smith Coll., 1961; Ph.D., Boston U., 1967; m. John William Norton, Apr. 20, 1968. Research asso. U. N.H., Durham, 1967-68; postdoctoral fellow, med. schs. Dartmouth Coll., 1968-69, Yale, 1969-71; faculty U. Me., Augusta, 1971—, asst. prof. biology, 1971—. Trustee Theatre at Monmouth (Me.). Recipient Innovative Teaching grant U. Me., 1971. Mem. Am. Soc. Microbiology, Am. Soc. Limnology and Oceanography. Home: PO Box 63 East Vassalboro ME 04935 Office: Dept Biology U Me Univ Heights Augusta ME 04330

NORTON, FAY-TYLER MURRAY (MRS. JAMES ADOLPHUS NORTON), psychologist, educator; b. Baton Rouge, La., Oct, 21, 1925; d. Aaron Bernard and Fay (Tyler) Murray; B.A., La. State U., 1945; student U. Havana, summer 1944; postgrad. U. Tex., 1946-47, Radcliffe Coll., 1948; Ph.D., Fla. State U., 1958; m. James Adolphus Norton, Mar. 4, 1945; 1 dau., Diana Maurine (Mrs. Stephen Robert Haptonstahl). Adminstrv. research asst. Fla. State U., 1954-56; research psychologist Cleve. Soc. for Blind, 1959-62; prof. psychology Cuyahoga Community Coll., Cleve., 1964—, head dept. behavioral scis., 1964-73; adj. prof. Mershon Center, Ohio State U., Columbus, 1973—. Bd. dirs. Columbus Area Internat. Program, 1973-74. Mem. Am. (chairperson 1971-74, mem. ad hoc com. on 2-year coll. of ednl. and tng. bd.), Ohio, Midwestern, Southeastern psychol. assns., Ohio Assn. Two Year Colls. (dir. 1971—), Am. Assn. U. Profs., League Women Voters (dir. Shaker Heights chpt.), Sigma Xi, Sigma Alpha Iota, Mu Sigma Rho, Kappa Kappa Gamma. Democrat. Baptist. Contbr. numerous articles on teaching psychology and tng. psychologists to profl. jours. Home: 325 Blandford St Worthington OH 43085 Office: Mershon Center Ohio State University 199 W 10th St Columbus OH 43201 also Cuyahoga Community College Cleveland OH 44115

NORTON, FRANCES JACOBSON, educator; b. Dallas, June 19, 1914; d. Hans Bruno and Therese (Rubin) Jacobson; A.B., U. Mo. at Kansas City, 1938, M.A., 1940; postgrad. (NSF fellow) U. Mich., summer 1959; Ph.D., U. Ia., 1961; m. Clyde DeWitt Norton, Mar. 27, 1946 (dec.); children—Barbara Therese, Robert DeWitt. Trainer and supr. personnel counselors Western Electric Co., Chgo., 1942-46; instr. psychology Cornell Coll., Mt. Vernon, Ia., part-time 1946-60; teaching asst., research asst. U. Ia., 1958-61; asst. to asso. prof. psychology U. Wis.-Stevens Point, 1961-66; prof. psychology Guilford Coll., Greensboro, N.C., 1966—, chmn. dept., 1968-69, 70-73. Mem. League Women Voters (pres. Mt. Vernon chpt. 1940, dir. Ia. chpt. 1950), Am. Assn. U. Profs. (pres. Guilford Coll. chpt. 1973-74), Am. Psychol. Assn., Am. Civil Liberties Union, Common Cause, Soc. for Psychol. Study Social Issues. Democrat. Mem. Soc. of Friends. Contbr. articles to profl. jours. Home: 1104 Montpelier Dr Greensboro NC 27410

NORTON, HARRIET RUTH SARTWELL (MRS. WILLIAM TREMAINE NORTON), educator; b. Mooers, N.Y., Mar. 2, 1916; d. Edwin and Cora (Rodden) Sartwell; A.B., Houghton Coll., 1936; M.A., Syracuse U., 1947; student U. Buffalo, summer 1959, U. Cal. at Berkeley, 1960-61; m. William Tremaine Norton, Apr. 7, 1955; children—Stanley Glen, Robert Allen. Tchr., Sardinia (N.Y.) High Sch., 1937-39; prin. Kingswood Sch., Springfield, Va., 1939-40; preceptress Waterport (N.Y.) High Sch., 1940-41; tchr. South Otselic (N.Y.) Central Sch., 1941-44, Phoenix (N.Y.) High Sch., 1944-45, Sherburne (N.Y.) Central Sch., 1945-53; asst. prof., supr. Latin, Milne Sch., State U. N.Y. at Albany, 1953-63, asso. prof., chmn. Latin edn., Sch. Edn., 1963-71, prof., chmn. Latin edn., 1971—. Mem. Eastern Zone Latin Tchrs. Assn. (sec. 1953-55, pres. 1974—), Classical Assn. Empire State (exec. council 1964—), N.E. Conf. on Teaching Fgn. Langs., N.Y. Fedn. Fgn. Lang. Tchrs., N.Y. Tchrs. Assn., Faculty Assn. State U. N.Y., N.E.A., Am. Assn. U. Profs., Am. Philol. Assn. Republican. Methodist. Author: (monograph with Charles Graber) Colloquamur Latine cum pueris puellisque: Latin in the Middle School, 1968. Contbr. articles to profl. publs. Home: 24 Palma Blvd Albany NY 12203

NORTON, MARIE A. MCKENNEY (MRS. JOHN C. NORTON), psychiat. social worker; b. Troy, N.Y.; d. Henry J. and Anna (McCarthy) McKenney; A.B., Pembroke Coll., Brown U., 1944; M.S., Boston U., 1956; student Simmons Coll., 1965-66; m. John C. Norton, Dec. 22, 1947; children—John W., Mark S. Claims adjuster Health Edn. and Welfare, Providence, 1948; social worker Providence Welfare Dept., 1948-51; adoption and homefinding caseworker R.I. Child Welfare Services, Providence, 1951-57; caseworker R.I. Hosp. Social Service Dept., Providence, 1962-70 sr. psychiat. social worker, 1970—. State mental health chmn. R.I. Congress Parents and Tchrs., 1968-72, chmn. children's emotional health project, 1972-73. Mem. Nat. Assn. Social Workers, Acad. Certified Social Workers, Internat. Congress Social Psychiatry, British Assn. Social Psychiatry, Internat., Am. group psychotherapy assns., Northeastern Soc. Group Psychotherapy, Am. Acad. Human Services. Home: 104 Legion Way Riverside RI 02915 Office: Social Service Dept RI Hosp Providence RI 02902

NORTON, VIRGINIA SKEEN (MRS. JOHN H. NORTON, JR.), civic worker; b. Atlanta, June 1, 1907; d. Lola Percy and Rebecca (Baldwin) Skeen; A.B., Agnes Scott Coll., 1928; student Columbia U., 1934-35; m. John Hughes Norton, Jr., Dec. 16, 1938; children—Virginia Skeen, John Hughes III. With personnel dept. Retail Credit Co., Atlanta, 1929-31, sec. to v.p., gen. mgr. Davison-Paxon, Co., Atlanta, 1931-34; with Aluminium Ltd., N.Y.C., 1935-41, sec. to pres., 1937-41; sec. to pres. Colonial Williamsburg, Inc., N.Y.C., 1943-44. Mem. bd. North Shore Assos. Chgo. Commons, 1951-54, Infant Welfare Soc. Chgo., 1953-54; bd. dirs. Catherine Morrill Day Nursery, Portland, Me., 1956-59; mem. Me. div. Nat. Farm and Garden Soc., 1956-59. Mem. Greenwich Hosp. Aux. Episcopalian. Address: 49 Foreside Rd Cumberland Foreside ME 04110

NORVELL, SUSAN HAMILTON, public relations exec.; b. Charleston, S.C., Aug. 20, 1949; s. Harold Hamilton and Cecile Marie (Zielinski) Norvell; B.A. in English cum laude, Coll. of Charleston, 1971. Photographer, Historic Charleston Found., Charleston, 1970; reporter, photographer Charleston Evening Post, 1971; editor, photographer, gen. mgr. Berkeley Democrat, Moncks Corner, S.C., 1971-74; pub. relations specialist Seabrook Island Co., Inc. (S.C.), 1974—. Free-lance photographer, journalist, Charleston, 1974—. Mem. Ansonborough Soc., Sigma Alpha Phi, Alpha Kappa Gamma, Chi Omega. Home: 64R Hasell St Charleston SC 29401 Office: Seabrook Island SC 29407

NORWITZ, RUTH JOANNE SCHAEVITZ (MRS. BERNARD BENJAMIN NORWITZ), engring. co. exec.; b. Youngstown, O., Sept. 24, 1918; d. Harry Gerson and Anne (Finkel) Schaevitz; grad. high sch.; m. Bernard Benjamin Norwitz, May 20, 1935; children—Naomi (Mrs. Robert Y. Hilbronner), Steven B. Free-lance accountant, 1935-56; with Schaevitz Engring., Pennsauken, N.J., 1956—, comptroller, 1973—, asst. sec., asst. treas., 1960—. Mem. B'nai B'rith Women. Jewish religion. Home: 1420 S Cooper River Plaza Pennsauken NJ 08109 Office: PO Box 505 Camden NJ 08101

NORWOOD, LINDA STEWART, writer; b. Waukegan, Ill., Feb. 23, 1943; d. Coy P. and Dorothy M. (Perkins) Stewart; B.A., Baylor U., 1964; m. Larry C. Norwood, Feb. 27, 1965; 1 dau., Heather Cade. Asst. editor Tenneco Oil Co., Houston, 1964-65; mng. editor Cotton Digest, also Gulf Coast Lumberman, Houston, 1965-67; copywriter Star Advt. Agy., Houston, 1968; staff writer, asst. dir. pub. relations-publns. Loyola U., New Orleans, 1969-71; free-lance writer, 1973—; part-time editor Fitzgerald Advt. Agy., New Orleans, 1973—. Mem. Women in Communications (v.p. 1970). Address: 349 Millaudon St New Orleans LA 70118

NOTHWANG, AILEEN VIRGINIA BRIMER (MRS. CHARLES H. NOTHWANG), librarian; b. Wilson, Okla., June 4, 1922; d. Eugene Lee and Lilly (Causey) Brimer; B.S., U. Okla., 1943; M.L.S., U. Ore., 1971; m. Charles H. Nothwang, Aug. 3, 1944; children—Louis Eugene, Jack Craig. Sch. librarian, tchr. Engligh, pub. high sch., Shidler and Wilson, Okla., 1943-45; tchr. Grant Union High Sch., John Day, Ore., 1958-62, Mt. Vernon (Ore.) High Sch., 1953-58; tchr., dir. instrnl. materials center Coquille (Ore.) High Sch., 1962-72; dir. library services Otero Jr. Coll., La Junta, Colo., 1972-74. Dir. local activities Centennial of Ore., John Day, 1956. Mem. adv. bd. pre-sch. program Willamalane Park Recreation Dist., Springfield, Ore., 1950-52. Mem. Nat., Ore. (trustee 1961-62), Grant County (pres. 1959-60) edn. assns., Am. Assn. U. Women, A.L.A., Bus. and Profl. Women (charter), Delta Kappa Gamma, Beta Phi Mu. Club: Faculty Women's. Home: 2181 Meade North Bend OR 97459 Office: North Bay School North Bend OR 97459

NOTOPOULOS, JANYCE EVELYN, city adminstr.; b. Sewickley, Pa., July 8, 1939; d. John Anast and Katherine (Gianakos) Notopoulos; B.S., Carnegie Inst. Tech., 1961; M.S., Ind., U., 1963. Asst. dean women U. Md., 1963-66; dir. coll. services Bell Ednl. Services, Washington, 1966-68; dir. devel. Mt. Vernon Coll., Washington, 1968-74; spl. asst. to chmn. D.C. City Council, Washington, 1974—; dir. Hexagon, Inc. Dir. Washington Carnegie Clan, 1967—; admissions counselor Carnegie Melion U., 1968—; mem., chmn. com. D.C. Commn. Acad. Facilities, 1971—. Mem. Council Student Personnel Assns., Capital Area Personnel and Guidance Assn. (sec. 1967-68), Nat. Assn. Fund Raisers, Am. Assn. Jr. Colls., Nat. Com. on Two-Year Colls. (alumni council), Higher Edn. Group Washington, Am. Alumni Council, Am. Coll. Pub. Relations Assn., Edn. Writers Assn., Delta Delta Delta. Greek Orthodox. Home: 3327 N St NW Washington DC 20007 Office: District Bldg 14th and E Sts Washington DC 20004

NOTTERMAN, REBECCA FELDSHER, physician; b. N.Y.C., Mar. 18, 1925; d. Abraham and Tanya (Cohen) Feldsher; R.N., Bellevue Sch. Nursing, 1945; M.D., N.Y.U., 1952; m. Joseph Melvin Notterman, Aug. 10, 1947; children—Daniel A., Abby F. Intern, Bellevue Hosp., N.Y., 1952-53, intern pediatrics, 1953-54; fellow pediatrics N.Y. Hosp., 1954-55, asso. attending pediatrician, 1973—; instr. pediatrics Cornell Med. Sch., 1955-69, asst. clin. prof., 1969-73, asso. clin. prof., 1973—; pvt. practice medicine, specializing in pediatrics, Hightstown, N.J., 1955—. Cons. Nat. Found. Birth Defects Clinic, Trenton, N.J., 1963—; dir. medicine Millstone Sch., 1958—; med. dir. East Windsor Sch., Hightstown, 1965-71; attending pediatrics Princeton Hosp., N.J., 1956—; dir. Poison Control Center, 1962-70; mem. health dept. East Windsor Twp., N.J., 1960-66; mem. med. adv. com. Planned Parenthood, Mercer County, N.J., 1965—. Recipient Outstanding Woman Grad. award N.Y.U. Coll. Medicine, 1952. Diplomate Am. Bd. Pediatrics. Fellow Am. Acad. Pediatrics; mem. Am. Women's Med. Assn., Mercer County Component Med. Soc., Alpha Omega Alpha. Democrat. Jewish religion. Author article. Home: Feldsher Rd Hightstown NJ 08520 Princeton Rd Profl Bldg Hightstown NJ 08520

NOURSE, JOAN THELLUSSON (MRS. PHILIP E. NOURSE), educator, author; b. N.Y.C., Feb. 17, 1921; d. Charles Francis and Mary Agnes (Fitzpatrick) Thellusson; B.A. (N.Y. State scholar), Manhattanville Coll., 1942; M.A., Fordham U., 1944, Ph.D. (scholar), 1948; m. Philip E. Nourse, Feb. 6, 1954; children—William Philip, Kathleen M. Editorial asst. Woman's Day Mag., N.Y.C., 1943-44, True Detective Mag., 1947-48; instr. Hunter Coll., N.Y.C., 1948-52; exec. asst. Comics Code Authority, N.Y.C., 1952-54; asso. prof. English, Seton Hall U., South Orange, N.J., 1958-69, prof., 1969—. Drama critic Catholic News, 1952—, Tablet, 1953—, Cath. Transcript, Hartford, Conn., 1954—, Evangelist, Albany, N.Y., 1953—, Advocate, Newark, 1955—, Monitor, Trenton, N.J., 1954—, L.I. Cath., 1962—, Cath. Universe-Bulletin, Cleve., 1966-74. Mem. Nat. Council Tchrs. of English, Modern Lang. Assn., Outer Critics Circle (mem. nominating com. for awards 1956—). Author: (with A.A. Norton) A Christian Approach to Western Literature, 1961; (with A.A. Norton) Literary Craftsmanship, 1962; Monarch Studies of My Antonia, 1964, The Crucible, 1965, Death of a Salesman, 1965, Major Barbara, 1966; (with Philip E. Nourse) The Happy Family (play), 1967; Lib Comes High (play), 1971. Home: 780 Riverside Dr New York City NY 10032 Office: Seton Hall University South Orange NJ 07079

NOVACK, EVE, advt. agy. exec.; b. Antwerp, Belgium, Apr. 21, 1939; d. Frederick and Hanny (Wassermann) Novack; came to U.S., 1946; naturalized, 1951; A.A.S., Packer Collegiate Inst., 1958; B.A., Hunter Coll., 1960; postgrad. U. Nev., 1963-65. Registered broker-dealer SEC, N.Y.C., 1959-62; advt. space sales rep. Vanderbilt Enterprises, Reno, 1962-65; account exec. Century Advt. Agy., N.Y.C., 1966-67; account exec. Diener & Dorskind, Inc., N.Y.C., 1967-71, v.p. long range planning and sales devel., 1969-71; pres. Novack Devel. Corp.; account exec., exec. v.p. Manister and Assos., Inc., 1971-73; account exec., exec. v.p. Bernard Hodes Advt., Inc., N.Y.C., 1973—. Mem. Soaring Soc. Am., Data Processing Mgmt. Assn. Contbr. articles to profl. jours. Home: 300 E 74th St New York City NY 10021 Office: 711 Fifth Av New York City NY 10022

NOVAK, ELAINE ADAMS, educator; b. West Milton, O., July 3, 1922; d. Edwin Booth and Isabel (Mast) Adams; A.B., Marshall U., 1943; postgrad. Cath. U. Am., 1945-46, Am. Acad. Dramatic Arts, 1946-47, Am. Theatre Wing, 1948—; A.M., Columbia, 1950; Ph.D. (Simon Lazarus scholar), Ohio State U., 1963; m. Svetomir Novakovic (name changed to Novak), 1952 (div.); children—Edwin, Debra Ann. Numerous positions in profl. Theater, N.Y.C., 1946-52; writer WSAZ-TV, Huntington, W.Va., 1953-56; mem. faculty Marshall U., Huntington, 1956—, prof. speech, 1968—, also play dir., 1960—. Dir. plays and musicals for Huntington Community Players, Mus. Arts Guild, Woman's Club, Jr. League, Girl Scouts Am., various chs., intermittently, 1957—. Served with USNR, 1943-46. Recipient Benddum Research grant, 1964. Mem. Am. Theatre Assn., W.Va. Speech Assn. (pres. 1965-67), Marshall U. Alumni Assn. (dir.), Conglist. Contbr. articles to profl. jours. Home: 1606 5th Av Huntington WV 25703

NOVAK, RUTH FRANCES VINCENT (MRS. NICHOLAS NOVAK), educator, psychologist; b. Los Angeles, Mar. 23, 1909; d. Fred Ezekiel and Almira (Smith) Vincent; A.A., Los Angeles Jr. Coll., 1934; B.A., U. Cal. at Los Angeles, 1937, M.A., 1938; postgrad. Claremont Grad. Sch., 1942-43, 61-62, U. So. Cal., 1946-49, San Diego State Coll., 1961, Colo. State Coll., 1964, Cal. State Coll. at Los Angeles, 1963, 65, Mich. State U., 1966-68; m. Nicholas Novak, June 30, 1950 (dec. Mar. 1965). Field sec. Camp Fire Girls, Los Angeles, 1931-37; asst. clin. psychologist Childrens Hosp., Los Angeles, 1938; tchr. Ontario (Cal.) City Schs., 1939-41, Conora (Cal.) City Schs., 1941-43; tchr., counselor Glendale (Cal.) City Schs., 1947-50; instr. Imperial Valley Coll., El Centro, Cal., 1957-60; coordinator counseling, student activities Imperial Valley Coll., Imperial, 1961-63, dean counseling, 1963-72; adminstrv. cons. Maharishi Internat. U., 1972—. Bd. dirs. Camp Fire Girls, Imperial County, Cal., 1951-57, Nat. Council Camp Fire Girls, 1954-56, A.R.C., 1953-55. Served to capt. WACS, 1943-47. Mem. Imperial Valley Guidance Council (pres. 1963), Cal. Jr. Coll. Assn. (sect. dir., sec. 1961-64), Cal. Counseling and Guidance Assn., Nat. Personnel and Guidance Assn., Nat. Vocational Guidance Assn., Imperial-San Diego Counties Jr. Coll. Counselors Assn. (sec. 1966-68), Cal. Community Coll. Counselors Assn. (sec. 1969-70), Na., Cal. assns. women deans and counselors, Cal. Tchrs. Assn., N.E.A., Am. Assn. U. Women, Cal. Personnel and Guidance Assn. (mem. senate 1969-70), Tau Alpha Epsilon, Psi Chi, Pi Gamma Mu, Pi Lambda Theta, Delta Kappa Gamma (chpt. pres. 1966-68), Delta Zeta, Theta Upsilon. Presbyn. Mem. Order Eastern Star (Worthy Matron 1960). Club: Soroptimist. Home: 1245 Len Rey Av El Centro CA 92243 Office: 1015 Galey Av Los Angeles CA 90024

NOVELLI, MARGUERITE, automotive co. exec.; b. Detroit, Mar. 20, 1938; d. Domenic and Carina (Faricelli) N.; grad. East Commerce High Sch., Detroit, 1955. Stenographer Gen. Motors Corp., Detroit, 1956-60, sec., 1960-62, exec. sec., 1962-72, asst. corporate sec., 1972—, also sec., dir. 14 U.S. subsidiary cos. of Gen. Motors. Sec. bd.

regents, sec. exec. com. Gen. Motors Inst., Flint, Mich. Club: Nomads (dir.) (Detroit). Home: 16074 Hauss St East Detroit MI 48021 Office: Gen Motors Corp 8-217 GM Bldg Detroit MI 48202

NOVER, NAOMI GOLL, journalist, writer, educator; b. Buffalo; d. B.B. and Rebecca (Shane) Goll; student U. Buffalo; B.S., Buffalo State Tchrs. Coll., 1934; M.A. George Washington U., 1951; m. Barnet Nover, June 28, 1934. Editorial asst. Buffalo Times, 1931; tchr. pub., pvt. schs. Buffalo, Park Sch., Snyder, N.Y., D.C.; music critic Denver Post at Goethe Festival, Aspen, Colo., 1949, mem. Washington bur., author Washington Dateline column Denver Post, 1952-72; editor Nover News Bur., Washington, 1972—, also mag. articles; nationally syndicated column and features, 1962—; writer on mission to Europe, Portland Oregonian; writer, dir. plays produced in Buffalo; participated radio and TV plays. Christened S.S. Syosset, Balt., 1945. Active civic and philanthropic activities including Red Cross, U.S. Treasury War Bonds (recipient award pin), Community Chest (past chmn. Kalorama area 3 teams, originated Embassy participation teams), Girl Scout Council (chmn. produced program at Pan Am. Union), Women's Hosp. Bd. of George Washington U. Hosp., Columbian Women of George Washington U. (past chmn. program com.); originated Goodwill Embassy Tour (lst jr. hostess com. chmn.). Mem. Congl. Press Galleries U.S. Capitol. Recipient Silver Eagle Girl Scouts. Mem. Am. Assn. U. Women, State Dept. Corrs. Assn., White House Corrs. Assn., Nat. League Am. Pen Women, Nat. Trust Historic Preservation, Pi Lambda Theta (past corr. ofcl. publ.). Clubs: National Press, Washington Press, American Newspaper Women's, Welcome to Washington; Wychmere Harbor (Cape Cod, Mass.). Home: 3001 Veazey Terrace NW Washington DC 20008 Office: Nat Press Bldg Washington DC 20045

NOVINA, TRUDI (MRS. CHARLES E. COAKLEY), pub. relations exec.; b. Bklyn., Dec. 8; d. Isidor and Lilian (Greenberg) Novina; B.A., Bklyn. Coll., 1950; m. Leo H. Papazian, June 24, 1956 (dec. 1964); children—Lyssa D., Gregory M.; m. 2d, Charles E. Coakley, Apr. 27, 1968. Reporter, N.Y. World Telegram & Sun, N.Y.C., 1950-54, asst. woman's editor, 1954-57, home furnishings editor, 1957-60; free-lance writer, 1960-64; account exec., dir. home fashions publicity Donald Degnan Assos., N.Y.C., 1964-69; mgr. home furnishing publicity Allied Chem. Corp., N.Y.C., 1969—. Mem. Am. Inst. Interior Designers, Nat. Home Fashions League (chpt. v.p. 1972-73), Fashion Group. Club: Overseas Press (N.Y.C.). Editor: House and Garden Decorating Book, 1965. Contbr. articles to various mags. Home: 34 W 89th St New York City NY 10024 Office: 1 Times Square New York City NY 10036

NOVINGER, VIRGINIA BARRETT, editor; b. Aurora, Ill., Dec. 7; d. Edward K. and Ethel P. (Black) Barrett; student Northwestern U.; m. Tracy W. Novinger, July 22, 1939; children—Walter B., Melinda (Mrs. Steven M. Green), Richard T. Writer, editor Field Enterprises Ednl. Corp., Chgo., 1960-61; editor publs. Jewel Food Stores, Melrose Park, Ill., 1969—. Mem. Elmhurst (Ill.) Hist. Commn., 1970—. Recipient numerous merit awards for writing. Mem. Women in Communications, Children's Reading Round Table, Indsl. Editors Assn. Chgo., Internat. Assn. Bus. Communicators. Author: Round Trip for Johnny, 1951; Tommy-On-Time, 1952; Skip Sees the Signs, 1953; Peppy Pepi, 1965; That's Our Cleo, 1966; also articles. Editor Story Mag., Elmhurst Meml. Hosp.; writer, editor Environs mag.; woman's editor Press Publs., Elmhurst, 1958-60. Home: 310 S Kenilworth Av Elmhurst IL 60126 Office: Jewel Food Stores 1955 W North Av Melrose Park IL 60160

NOVOTNY, GERALDINE BERTHA, state ofcl., gerontologist; b. N.Y.C., Oct. 15, 1913; d. Jerry and Bertha Ann (Strnad) Novotny; B.A. U. Wis., 1949; M.S., Boston U., 1951. Sec., U. Conn., Storrs, 1933-41, departmental asst., 1941-43, asst. editor, publs. editor, 1950-60, specialist gerontology, 1960-67; dir. Windham Area Sr. Center, Willimantic, Conn., 1967; cons. State Dept. on Aging, Hartford, Conn., 1967—. Adviser, Conn. Council of Sr. Citizens, Inc., 1967—. Bd. dirs. Windham Community Meml. Hosp. Served with Women's Res., USMC, 1943-45. Fed. scholar, 1969. Mem Nat. Inst. Sr. Centers (chmn. tng. com. 1974), Nat. Council on Aging, Conn. Soc. Gerontology (editor 1973—, dir. 1964-67), Women in Communications, Conn. Recreation and Park Assn., Gerontological Soc., Am. Assn. U. Profs., Mental Health Assn. Conn. (exec. bd. eastern chpt. 1969—), Zonta (adv. bd. 1973-74), Czechoslovak Soc. Am. Contbr. articles to profl. publs. Home: Fisher Hill Rd Willington CT 06265 Office: 90 Washington St Hartford CT 06115

NOWAK, JEAN M., govt. ofcl.; b. Sheboygan, Wis.; d. Raymond Carleton and Leila (Stephen) McDuffie; student Lake Forest Coll., 1935-38; B.A., U. Wis., 1939; m. Francis Jefferson Nowak, Dec. 28, 1940 (div. Apr. 1966); children—Francis Jefferson, Nancy Jean, Robert Craig. Asso. editor North Chgo. Tribune, 1938-40; information specialist State of Ill., Springfield, 1940-41; free lance writer, pub. relations cons., Ill., Wis., 1941-51; radio-TV chief Am. Nat. Red Cross, Alexandria, Va., 1951-56, pub. edn. adviser, Washington, 1956-59; dir. information div. Indian Health, Dept. Health, Edn. and Welfare, Washington, 1959-72; dep. dir. pub. information Small Bus. Adminstrn., 1972—. Mem. pub. relations com. Girl Scouts U.S.A., Met. Area Council, Washington. Recipient award USPHS, 1968. Mem. Am. Assn. U. Women (dir.), Am. Women in Radio and TV, Am. Newspaper Women's Club, Washington Press Club (dir.). Episcopalian. Home: 3223 Volta Pl NW Washington DC 20007 Office: 1441 L St NW Washington DC 20416

NOWELS, MARTHA ELLEN, advt. exec.; b. Detroit; d. Russell Wasson and Grace (Rink) Nowels; student Wheaton Coll., Norton, Mass., 1943-45; B.A., U. Ariz., 1947. Advt. dir. Nowels Lumber & Coal Co., Rochester, Mich., 1947-49; rental agt. San Manuel Devel. Corp. (Ariz.), 1949-51; pres. Nowels Advt., Tucson, 1951—. Lectr. Bldg. Materials Inst., Purdue U., 1960-61. Chmn. profl. mems. The Jr. League of Tucson, Inc., 1965-66, sustaining adviser to profls., parliamentary advisor 1966—. Mem. Advt. Agy. Council Tucson (sec.-treas.), Internat. Platform Assn., Pi Beta Phi. Clubs: Tuscon Press (Tucson). Home: 2801 N Columbia Tucson AZ 85705 Office: Lawyers Title Bldg Tucson AZ 85701

NOWLIS, HELEN HOWARD (MRS. VINCENT NOWLIS), psychologist; b. Cranston, R.I., Sept. 22, 1913; A.B., Brown U., 1934, A.M., 1936, hon. Sc.D., 1967; Ph.D. in Psychology, Yale, 1939; m. Vincent Nowlis, 1938; 3 children. Asst. psychologist, child devel. clinic, Yale, 1935-36, inst. human relations, 1936-39; instr. psychology, Smith Coll., 1939-40, U. Conn., 1942-43, Conn. Coll. for Women, 1943-44; research asso. U. Ia., 1946-51; vis. research prof. U. Rochester, 1951-60, prof., 1960-71, asso. dean students, also fgn. student adv., 1961-65, dean, 1965-67, cons. student affairs, 1967-71; dir. drug edn., health, nutrition program U.S. Office Edn., Washington, 1971—. Dir. drug edn. project Nat. Assn. Student Personnel Adminstrs., 1966-68; cons. drug abuse study group Nat. Inst. Mental Health, 1967-71. Fellow Psychology Assn.; mem. Group Adv. Psychiatry, (coll. student com. 1967-69), Am. Coll. Neuropsychopharmacology, Soc. Psychol. Study Social Issues, Coll. Personnel Assn., Assn. Student Personnel Adminstrs. Author: Drugs on the College Campus, 1967. Contbr. articles in field to profl. jours. Office: US Dept Education Div Drug Edn Health and Nutrition Washington DC 20202

NOXON, MARGARET WALTERS (MRS. HERBERT RICHARDS NOXON), club woman; b. Detroit, Dec. 16, 1903; d. George Alexander and Ethelwyn (Taylor) Walters; grad., Liggett Sch. for Girls, Det., 1922; life teaching certificate Wayne State U., 1925; student Columbia Tchrs. Coll., 1939-40; m. Herbert Richards Noxon, July 15, 1926 (dec. Aug. 4, 1971). Bd. dirs. Coll. Club, Detroit, 1925-30. Mem. Coll. Club, Summit N.J., 1941—; historian D.A.R., N.Y.C., 1943-46, vice regent, 1946-49; dir. New Eng., Women, 1961-64; dir. Woodycrest-Five Points Child Care, 1961—; bd. dirs. A.R.C., Summit, N.J., service com. chmn. uniforms and insignias, 1943-45; v.p. N.Y. Infirmary Aux., N.Y.C., 1948-58; bd. dirs., 1959—. Recipient award for meritorious personal service A.R.C., 1945. Mem. Grand Jury Assn. N.Y. County, D.A.R. (dir. 1950—), St. David's Soc. State N.Y., English-Speaking Union, Daus. Am. Colonists, Am. Assn. U. Women Southampton Colonial Soc., Alpha Sigma Tau. Republican. Presbyn. Clubs: Southampton Bath and Tennis (Southampton, N.Y.); City Gardens (dir. 1963-68, mem. adv. com. 1968-74, dir. 1974—), York (bd. govs.) (N.Y.C.). Home: 1100 Madison Av New York City NY 10028

NOYES, ETHEL MARIE LINGELBACH (MRS. FRED WINSLOW NOYES, JR.), restaurant exec.; b. Towne of Smithville, N.J.; d. Christopher Doughty and Caroline Marie (Priebs) Lingelbach ; grad. high sch.; m. Fred Winslow Noyes, Jr., Mar. 20, 1945. Creator, owner Historic Smithville (N.J.) Inn, 1952—; creator, owner Quail Hill, Lantern Light, Village Shops, Smithville Airfield; dir. South Jersey Gas Co. Mem. Gov.'s Commn. on Study Status Women in N.J., 1965—; mem. Gov.'s Conf. on Natural Beauty, 1966-67; sec. Noyes Found.; bd. dirs. So. N.J. Devel. Council; bd. govs. Atlantic City Med. Center; mem. N.J. Historic Sites Council, 1968—; chmn. Atlantic County Heritage Commn., 1971. Named Woman of Year N.J. Travel and Resort Assn., 1966, Woman of Influence, Internat. Toastmistresses Am., 1969. One of 10 Outstanding bus. women in N.J., N.J. Mfrs. Assn., 1963; recipient New Good Neighbor award N.J. Mfrs., 1967, Inter-Racial award for service in human relations Tropicana Federated Charity Club, 1968, Distinguished Achievement award So. N.J. Devel. Council, 1972. Mem. D.A.R., N.J. Travel and Resort Assn., Nat., N.J. restaurant assns., Club: Zonta (Atlantic City). Home: Port Republic NY 08241 Office: Route 9 Towne of Smithville Smithville NJ 08201

NOYES, MARY HOLLEY (MRS. ROBERT WALLACE NOYES), ednl. adminstr.; b. Stockton, Cal., June 1, 1921; d. Franklin Maynard and Nadine (Burnett) Holley; B.A., U. Cal. at Berkeley, 1942; certificate in indsl. mgmt. Stanford, 1943; M.A. in Guidance and Counseling, George Peabody Coll., 1962; m. Robert Wallace Noyes, May 30, 1942; children—Martha (Mrs. George A. Warfel), Paul David. Research asst. Inst. for Mental Retardation and Intellectual Devel., George Peabody Coll., Nashville, 1963-64; research asst. spl. edn. U. Hawaii, Honolulu, 1965-70; vocational counsellor Chapel Hill (N.C.) High Sch., 1970-73; sch. psychologist Bound Brook (N.J.) High Sch., 1973—. Mem. Am. Psychol. Assn., Council for Exceptional Children, Zonta. Home: Box 208A Basking Ridge NJ 07920 Office: Bound Brook High School Bound Brook NJ 08860

NUESE, CANDACE MAIRIE, city ofcl.; b. Marshall, Minn., Mar. 24, 1926; d. Francis Ferdinand and Alexina Marie (Pilotte) Nuese; B.A., Coll. of St. Catherine, 1953; M.A., Gonzaga U., 1963. Tchr. secondary schs. and colls. asso. with Sch. Sisters Notre Dame, Minn. and Washington, 1953-71; tchr. Upward Bound Projects, Southside Chgo., Ft. Valley State Coll., Ga., Central State Coll., Wilberforce, O., summers 1969-71; asst. dir. personnel dept. and pub. service careers City of Lawton (Okla.), 1971—. Cons. Minn. Sch. Dist. 77, 1969-70; tchr. curriculum workshop racial relations, 1969; coordinator workshops tchrs. Indian and Black studies, Mankato, Minn., 1969-71. Mem. Mankato Charter Commn., 1970-71. Chairwoman Blue Earth County Democratic-Farmer-Labor Party, 1970-71, mem. state central com., 1970-71, women's vice chairwoman, Mankato, 1969-70. Mem. Nat. Assn. Social Studies Tchrs., Am. Inst. Discussion (chpt. sec. 1973), Sch. Sisters of Notre Dame, League Women Voters (local program chmn. 1972, v.p. 1974). Roman Catholic. Home: 530 Glendale Dr Lawton OK 73501 Office: 103 S 4th St Lawton OK 73501

NUGENT, VIRGINIA HAYES (MRS. GEORGE ROBERT NUGENT), civic worker; b. Weehawken, N.J., July 17, 1917; d. William Henry Hayes and Jennie Virginia (Mayer) Hollopeter; A.B., Barnard Coll., 1938; postgrad. U. Cin., 1951-53, 59-61, W.Va. U., 1961-69; m. George Robert Nugent, July 3, 1947; children—Dana, Robert, Leslie, Barnes, Courtney. Advt. asst. Borden Co., N.Y.C., 1941-44; adminstrv. asst. to v.p. personnel relations CBS, N.Y.C., 1944-47; research asst. Office of Naval Research Project, Kenyon Coll., Gambier, O., 1947-49; research asst. Cin. Med. Sch., 1951-53; sec. dept. endocrinology Duke Med. Center, 1955-57. Mem. water resources com. League Women Voters, Durham, N.C., 1957-58; unit sec. League Women Voters, Cin., 1959-60; mem. Rockefeller Task Force on Land Use and Urban Growth, 1972-73; mem. W.Va. U. Pres.'s Task Force on New Students-New Options, 1973; mem. Council of State Govt.'s Task Force on Natural Resources, Land Use Information and Tech., 1973—; mem. W.Va. Bd. Regents Task Force on Non-traditional Study, 1973—; mem. Council State Govt. Task Force on Land Use, 1973-74, Interstate Com. on Land Use and Natural Resource for Commn. on Future of South, 1973—. Bd. dirs., bull. editor, 1960-61; bd. dirs. League Women Voters W.Va., 1962-64, chmn. fgn. policy, 1962-64, v.p., 1963-69, also chmn. human resources and vocational edn., pres., 1969-72; bd. dirs., chmn. fgn. policy League Women Voters, Morgantown, W.Va., 1964-66; bd. dirs. League Women Voters U.S., 1972—, land use chmn., Monongalia County Council Social Agys., 1973—; sec. bd. dirs. Monongalia Community Opportunity Council, 1966-69, bd. dirs., 1969-70; mem. vis. com. Appalachian Center W.Va., U., 1970-73; mem. adv. bd. W.Va. U. Office Radio, TV and Motion Pictures, 1972—. Mem. citizens' adv. commn. to W.Va. Legislature, 1970-71. Recipient Merit award W.Va. Vocational Assn., 1969. Mem. Women's Aux. Monongalia County Med. Soc., Psi Chi. Unitarian. Contbr. various articles to newspapers. Home: 760 Mountain View Pl Morgantown WV 26505

NUNAMAKER, ANNE WAGGONER, ednl. cons.; b. Shelbyville, Tenn., June 17, 1934; d. Lemuel Augustus and Margaret (Sory) Waggoner; B.A., Middle Tenn. State U., 1955, M.A., 1959; postgrad. U. Miami, 1957, Case Western Res. U., 1960, U. Ia., 1962, Mich. State U., 1965; Edn. Specialist, George Peabody Coll., 1973. Tchr. English, speech and journalism South Jr. High Sch., Garden City, Mich., 1955-56, Stranahan High Sch., Ft. Lauderdale, Fla., 1956-60, Cleveland Heights (O.) High Sch., 1960-69; tchr. WVIZ-TV, Cleve., 1967-69; asst. prof. journalism Middle Tenn. State U., Murfreesboro, Tenn., 1969-72; ednl. cons. The Tennessean, daily newspaper, Nashville, 1973—. Recipient fellowship Newspaper Fund, 1962, distinguished adviser award, 1964. Mem. Nat. Council Coll. Publs. Advisers, Assn. for Edn. in Journalism, Creative Edn. Found., Nat. Council Tchrs. English, Columbia Scholastic Press Advisers Assn. (v.p. 1965-66), League Women Voters, Am. Civil Liberties Union, Delta Kappa Gamma, Theta Sigma Phi. Office: 1100 Broadway Nashville TN 37202

NUNN, MARIE LOUISE DOWNS, writer; b. Chico, Cal., May 23, 1905; d. James Raymond and Louise (Larson) Downs; grad. Heald's Bus. Coll., 1925; B.A., San Jose State U., 1945; postgrad. U. Cal. at Berkeley, 1956-57; L.H.D., U. Free Asia, Pakistan, 1974; m. L.H. Dahlgren, Jan. 24, 1927; 1 son, Raymond L. Dahlgren; m. 2d Wallace E. Shields, Mar. 3, 1939 (dec. 1954); m. 3d, F. William Nunn, May 6, 1956 (dec. Sept. 1961). Various secretarial positions; writer articles for various mags., including The Gallery, Am. Collector, Western Collector, Antique Trader; writer poetry in publs. including Poet, Janus, Modern Haiku, Haiku Highlights, Dragonfly, Good Deeder, Mount Hermon Log, Pacifica, Swordsman, also anthologies. Sec. bd. dirs. Tb and Respiratory Disease Assn., 1969-73. Recipient Highby Meml. award; Nat. D.A.V. award, 1955; award for writing promoting Christmas seals sales, 1970, 71, 72. Mem. Am. Assn. U. Women, Nat. League Am. Pen Women, World Poetry Soc. Nat. Writers Club, Cal. Writers, Smithsonian Instn., San Francisco Museum Soc., Northwest Writers, Cal. Writers, Cal. Poetry Soc., Chaparral Poets, Santa Cruz County Geneal. Soc., Edwin Markham Poetry Soc., Ky. (1st place award 1974), Ill. poetry socs., Ina Coolbrith Circle, P.T.A. (life). Mem. Order Eastern Star. Author: Rumbling Wagon Wheels, 1974. Address: 362 Horizon Way Pacific CA 94044

NUNNALLEE, RUTH BURNETTE (MRS. MILTON T. NUNNALLEE), music educator; b. Omega, Okla.; d. Earl J. and Katie (Richert) Burnette; B.A., Northwestern State Coll., Okla., 1932; M.Ed., Howard Payne Coll., 1957; certification in supervision N. Tex. State Coll., Denton, 1958; m. Charles H. Parson, Dec. 4, 1933 (dec. June 1973); m. 2d, Milton T. Nunnallee, June 28, 1974. Tchr., Arnett, Okla., 1930-31, High Sch., Gray, Okla., 1931-32, Boise City, Okla., 1932-33, Wilmore, Kan., 1934-35; tchr. vocal and instrumental music Lambert (Okla.) High Sch., 1936-38; English and music tchr. Capron (Okla.) High Sch., 1938-42; choral dir. Seymour (Tex.) High Sch., 1943-44, jr., sr. high schs., Vernon, Tex., 1945-56; asst. prof. edn. Howard Payne Coll., Brownwood Tex., 1956-57; coordinator music Abilene (Tex.) Pub. Schs., 1958-74, now ret. Music cons. in Manhattanville Music Curriculum Program, 1967-70. Recipient Vernon Jr. C. of C. Distinguished Community Service award, 1948. Mem. Bus. and Profl. Womens Club, Music Guild of Abilene (past pres.). Mem. Christian Ch. Home: 1648 Glenhaven Dr Abilene TX 79603

NURENBERG, CAROL ANN, educator; b. Roxbury, Mass., Nov. 27, 1946; d. Israel and Pearl (Katz) Nurenberg; B.A., U. Fla., 1968; M.A. (fellow), Columbia, 1970. Tchr. English, Oceanway (Fla.) Sch., 1969; dir. theatre Annhurst Coll., Woodstock, Conn., 1970—, theatre mgr., 1970—, dir. theatre prodns., 1970—, instr. theatre arts, 1970—. Condr. theatre workshops area secondary schs., 1970—; mng dir. Woodstock Playhouse, 1972—; mem. Woodstock Players, 1970—; mem. Woodstock Area Arts Council, 1971—. Mem. Univ. and Coll. Theatre Assn. Office: Rural Route 2 Annhurst Coll Woodstock CT 06281

NURSE, CROSBY LLEWELLE GRANT (MRS. WILLIAM NURSE), hosp. exec.; b. Glace Bay, N.S., Can., Apr. 23, 1928; d. Walter Cyril and Llewelle Isette (Estwick) Grant; R.N., New Waterford (N.S.) Gen. Hosp., 1949; student St. Francis Xavier U., Sydney, N.S., 1967—; m. William Nurse, Sept. 27, 1952; children—Charlotte (Mrs. George Brown), David. Staff nurse, relief supr. New Waterford Gen. Hosp., 1949-50, staff nurse, 1951-53; staff nurse, charge nurse Univ. Heights Hosp., Bronx, N.Y., 1950-51; mem. staff St. Rita Hosp., Sydney, 1953—, dir. nursing service, 1967—. Mem. Am. Soc. Hosp. Nursing Service Adminstrs., Registered Nurses Assn. N.S. Home: Grand Lake Rd Rural Route 4 Sydney NS B1P 6G6 Canada Office: 409 King's Rd Sydney NS B1S 1B4 Canada

NUSBAUM, LORETTA WILLENE HINSON (MRS. GEORGE MAXWELL NUSBAUM), writer, govt. ofcl.; b. Carthage, Mo., June 30, 1915; d. Clifton Leon and Lola Fern (Sanders) Hinson; grad. high sch.; m. George Maxwell Nusbaum, June 19, 1937. Owner Drug Sundries Store, Bern, Kan., 1940-43; postal clk. U.S. Post Office, Bern, 1954—. Speaker Internat. Platform Assn., Cleveland Heights, O., 1970—; pres. Am. Postal Workers Union, Bern, 1964—. Pres. Nemaha County Council Women's Clubs, 1956-57, Bern Reading Club, 1971—. Recipient numerous awards from lit. publs., including Internat. Platform Assn., 1971, World Poetry Soc., 1972, Am. Penwomen, 1973. Mem. Internat. Platform Assn., Am. Postal Workers Union, Kan. Authors, Epsilon Sigma Omicron. Methodist (mem. council ministeries 1970—). Author: These I Love, 1967. Asst. editor Modern Haiku, 1969—, editor, 1974—. Contbr. numerous poems to various publs. Home: PO Box 144 Bern KS 66408 Office: US Post Office Bern KS 66408

NUSS, VIRGINIA DEL JAMES (MRS. ROBERT WILLIAM NUSS), city ofcl.; b. Wichita Falls, Tex., Mar. 22, 1928; d. Albert William and Amanda Marie (Korsemyer) James; student Midwestern U., 1945-46; m. Robert William Nuss, June 1, 1946; children—R. Stephen, Karen (Mrs. James M. Salp), Mark David, Heidi Marie. Real estate salesman Norwood Realty, Wichita Falls, 1958; stenographer Jeffs Ins. Co., Anderson, Cal., 1959; dep. city clk. City of Anderson, 1960-69, city clk., 1969—. Home: 1341 Pinon Av Anderson CA 96007 Office: 1887 Howard St Anderson CA 96007

NUTLEY, GRACE STUART (MRS. CYRIL ARTHUR NUTLEY), educator; b. Alameda, Cal.; d. Samuel Vernon and Marie Belle (Eubank) Stuart; B.E., U. Wash. 1922; M.A., N.Y. U., 1938, Ph.D., 1945; m. Cyril Arthur Nutley, Aug. 22, 1925; 1 dau., Jean Margaretta (Mrs. Dudley Ives Ferris). Asso. prof. English, Pratt Inst., 1936-46, U. State N.Y., 1938-46; instr. English, N.Y. U., 1944-46; asso. prof. English, Bklyn. Coll., 1946—; lectr. adult edn. YWCA, Bklyn., 1935-50, Federated Women's Clubs, 1952—, N.Y. Times & Herald Tribune Lecture Bur., 1952-58, Friends of UN, 1957—; Smith-Mundt prof. English, State Dept., Philippines, 1950-52; Fulbright lectr. Annamalai U., India, 1959-61; tchr. English, Japan, Taiwan, Manila, 1967. Recipient Fulbright grant as lectr., 1959-61, 67-68, Am. Specialist grant 1964, 67, 68. Fellow Am. Studies Assn.; mem. Mem. Friendly Vistors (pres. 1956-59), Am. Assn. U. Women (chmn. art com. 1953-55, dir. 1954-57). N.Y. Coll. English Assn. (pres. 1954-55, dir. 1955-59), Pan Pacific S.E. Asia Women's Assn. (nat. pres. 1963-67, internat. v.p. 1968—), Asia Soc. (mem. Burma council 1962-72). Am. Assn. U. Profs., Modern Lang. Assn., Coll. English Assn. (nat. chmn. com. on acad. status of women 1968-72), Nat. Council Tchrs. English, Coll. Conf. Composition and Communication, Nat. Council Women, Assn. Higher Edn., Adult Edn. Assn. U.S.A., Am. Acad. Polit. and Social Sci., UN Assn. U.S.A. (pres. N.W. Maricopa County chpt. 1970—, pres. Ariz. div. 1972—), Internat. Platform Assn., Kappa Delta, Mortar Bd., Pi Lambda Theta (pres. N.Y. chpt. 1955-57, dir. 1957-59). Clubs: Foreign Service; Pilot (pres. N.Y. 1955-56, dist. gov. 1958-59). Contbr. articles profl. jours. Home: 9407 109th Dr Sun City AZ 85351

NYREN, DOROTHY ELIZABETH SMITH, librarian; b. Portland, Me., Sept. 29, 1927; d. Johann and Ethel Rita (Mullaney) Smith; B.A., Boston U., 1952, M.A., 1954; M.L.S., Simmons Coll., 1960. Dir. Young Library, Daytona Beach, Fla., 1955-57; town librarian Concord (Mass.) Free Pub. Library, 1959-64; chief librarian Northbrook (Ill.) Pub. Library, 1965-69; coordinator adult services Bklyn. Pub. Library, 1970, chief Central Library, Bklyn., 1971—.

Mem. A.L.A. (councillor 1972—), Pub. Library Assn. (mem. exec. bd. 1973—); chmn. group 1 1972). Author: Modern American Literature, 1960, 4th edit., 1969; Modern Romance Literature, 1968. Office: Bklyn Pub Library Grand Army Plaza Brooklyn NY 11238

NYSTROM, BRUNHILDE GISELA WAGNER (MRS. LEONARD CLARK NYSTROM), city ofcl.; b. Chgo., Jan. 14, 1926; d. Jacob Frank and Martha Sophie (Aichele) Wagner; B.E., Chgo. State U., 1949; postgrad. Drake U., 1951-52, So. Methodist U., 1955, 63; m. Leonard Clark Nystrom, Apr. 24, 1948; children—Donald Paul, Barbara Ann, Warren Frank. Tchr. Perkins Elementary Sch., Des Moines, 1950-52; mem. Mesquite (Tex.) City Council, 1972—. Pres. Dallas Osteo. Hosp. Guild, 1960-61. Named Woman of Yr., Mesquite Elks Club, 1973. Mem. Aux. Tex. Osteo. Med. Assn. (dist. pres. 1967-68), Ladies Aux. Mesquite Elks Club (parliamentarian 1969-70), Woman's Soc. Christian Service (life). Methodist. Home: 1213 Majors Dr Mesquite TX 75149 Office: City Hall PO Box 137 Mesquite TX 75149

NYSWANDER, MARIE, psychiatrist, psychoanalyst; b. Reno, Mar. 13, 1919; d. James and Dorothy (Bird) Nyswander; pre-med. student Sarah Lawrence Coll.; M.D., Columbia; psychoanalytical tng. N.Y. Med. Coll.; m. Leonard Robinson. Intern, Meadowbrook Hosp., L.I., N.Y., 1944-45; served as lt. (j.g.) USPHS, at Pub. Health Service Hosp., Lexington, Ky., 1945-46; resident in psychiatry Bellevue Hosp., 1947-48, jr. psychiatrist, 1948-49; practice medicine, specializing in psychiatry, also psychoanalysis, N.Y.C., 1950—; asst. clin. prof. psychiatry N.Y. Med. Coll. Met. Hosp. Center; dir. narcotics office East Harlem Protestant Parish. Conducted Narcotic Addiction Research Project, N.Y.C., 1955, research clinic for musicians supported by Newport Jazz Festival, 1957; now conducting research project on rehab. of addicts utilizing synthetic narcotic methadone as substitute for heroin Rockefeller Inst. and Manhattan Gen. Hosp.; chmn. research com. Mayor's Adv. Bd. on Narcotics Addiction, N.Y.C., 1959; cons. to numerous programs concerned with drug addiction. Author: The Drug Addict as a Patient, 1956; also numerous articles in med. jours. Address: 1225 Park Av New York City NY 10028

OAKES, FRANCES LOUISE ETHERIDGE (MRS. FRANK EDWIN OAKES), educator, reading cons.; b. Lyndon, Ky., Feb. 27, 1914; d. John Alexander and Frances Emma (Orr) Etheridge; B.A., U. Rochester, 1936, M.A., 1937; Ph.D., Fla. State U., 1955; m. Frank Edwin Oakes, Feb. 27, 1944; children—Frances Barbara, Charles Edwin. Owner Etheridge Tutoring Center, Rochester, N.Y., 1937-42; supply officer U. South Africa, 1942-46; reading specialist, Prince George County, Md., 1947-48; grad. asst. Fla. State U., 1951; instr. U. Ala., 1952-55; chmn. developmental reading and communications dept. Kendall Coll., Evanston, Ill., 1955-59; reading cons. Seabury-Western Theol. Sem., 1958-59; reading cons. Flint, Mich., 1959—. Mem. League Women Voters (pres. Flint 1963-65), Am. Assn. U. Women (2d v.p.) Flint C. of C., Flint Inst. Arts, Internat. (pres. Chgo. council 1958-59, Flint council 1960-61), Mich. reading assns., Nat. Platform Assn., Nat. Wildlife Fedn., Nat., Mich. edn. assns., Phi Theta Kappa, Theta Alpha Epsilon. Democrat. Episcopalian. Club: Zonta. Home: 805 Blanchard Av Flint MI 48503 Office: 428 Stevens St Flint MI 48503

OAKES, ROSALYN, state ofcl.; b. Balt., Mar. 30, 1925; A.B. Radcliffe Coll., 1947; M. Ed., Smith Coll., 1957, M.A. in Psychology, 1967; 1 son, 2 daus. Chmn. Vt. State Housing Authority, 1969—; rep. Brattleboro Town Meeting, 1957-67. Trustee, Brattleboro Music Center, Vt.; bd. dirs. New Eng. Program in Tchr. Edn., 1970—. Radcliffe Inst. fellow, 1973-74. Mem. Vt. Psychol. Assn. Address: Guilford VT 05301

OAKLEY, ADELINE DUPUY, educator; b. Cleve., Sept. 14, 1914; d. Arthur Oliver and Laura Veronica (Mondoux) Dupuy; B.Ed., Bridgewater (Mass.) State Coll., 1962, postgrad. 1967—; M.L.S., Simmons Coll., Boston, 1964; m. Kenneth Holbart Oakley, July 20, 1935; children—Kenneth Nelson, Judith (Mrs. Gene F. Mazenko). Psychiat. nursing asst. Brockton (Mass.) VA Hosp., 1955-61; circulation librarian Canton (Mass.) Pub. Library, 1962; tchr.-librarian Bridgewater-Raynham Regional High Sch., 1962-63, Catherine Laboure Sch. Nursing, Boston, 1963-67; part-time prof. library sci. U. Mass. extension, 1966-67; prof. library sci. Bridgewater State Coll., 1967—, asst. dir. Title 11-B Inst., summer 1968; prof. library sci. Regis Coll., summers 1970, 73, Trenton State Coll., summer 1971; cons. in field. Pres. Poughkeepsie (N.Y.) P.T.A., 1947; family life chmn. Dutchess County (N.Y.) Home Bur., 1949-50; mem. Friends of Library, Randolph, Mass., 1965-66. Bd. dirs. Poughkeepsie Vis. Nurse Assn., 1947. P.T.A. scholar, Vassar Coll., summer 1947. Mem. Am., Catholic (chmn. health sci. sect. 1971-72, v.p. New Eng. unit 1970), Mass. (edn. com. 1971—) library assns., Simmons Coll. Sch. Library Sci. Alumni Assn. (chmn. nominating com. 1970, chmn. alumni day com. 1971, chmn. continuing edn. com. 1972, dir. 1973—), Women's Nat. Book Assn. (v.p. chpt. 1974—), Pi Lambda Theta. Home: 24 Reynolds Av Randolph MA 02368 Office: Library Sci Dept Bridgewater State Coll Bridgewater MA 02324

OAKLEY, CAROLYN COBB (MRS. ROBERT CARROLL OAKLEY), librarian; b. Wilson, N.C., Nov. 5, 1946; d. Raymond Earl and Edna Gay (Hardison) Cobb; B.S., East Carolina U., 1969, M.Ed., 1970; m. Robert Carroll Oakley, Nov. 25, 1971. Cataloger, N.C. Dept. Community Colls., Raleigh, 1970; dir. library Vance-Granville Tech. Inst., Henderson, N.C., 1970—. Mem. Am. Assn. U. Women (treas.), N.C. (dir. resources and tech. services sect. 1973—), Southeastern library assns. Club: Henderson Junior Woman's. Home: 1111 Dabney Dr Henderson NC 27536 Office: 406 Chestnut St Henderson NC 27536

OAKLEY, MARGARET MARY FRANCIS (MRS. HAROLD EUGENE OAKLEY), anesthesiologist; b. Granite City, Ill., June 29, 1934; d. Oscar David and Eulalia Mary (Krill) Francis; B.S., U. Ill., 1955; M.D., St. Louis U., 1959; m. Harold Eugene Oakley, May 24, 1958; children—Laura Diane, Linda Claire, Brian Christopher, Lisa Margaret. Intern, St. John's Mercy Hosp., St. Louis, 1959-60; resident Washington U.-Barnes Hosp., St. Louis, 1960-63; chief anesthesiology Shriner's Hosp. for Crippled Children, St. Louis, 1963—; courtesy staff St. Joseph Hosp., Kirkwood, Mo., 1969—. Picnic booth chmn. Villa Duchesne, 1964, Wright Sch., 1973-74; pack treas. Cub Scouts, 1973. Diplomate Am. Bd. Anesthesiology, Am. Coll. Anesthesiology. Mem. Internat., Am., Mo., St. Louis (sec. 1970) socs. anesthesiologists, Mo., St. Louis med. socs. Club: St. Joseph Academy Mother's (St. Louis). Home: 407 Steepechase St St Louis MO 63131

OAKLEY, MARY MARTHA, advt. agy. exec.; b. Peoria, Ill., Oct. 1, 1933; d. Frederic R. and Alice Marie (Dolan) Oakley; B.A., Bradley U., 1954; postgrad. Mich. State U., 1954-56, Ill. State U., 1957. Prodn.-continuity dir. Radio Station WIRL and WAAP, Peoria, 1957-59; copywriter Arbingast and Becht Advt., Peoria, 1961-63; asst. creative dir. Evans-Work & Costa, advt., Springfield, Ill., 1963-64; copywriter Robert Lichty Co., Bloomington, 1964-65; pub. aid visitor State of Ill., Peoria, 1965-66; with Burdon Advt., Inc., Peoria, 1966—, v.p., creative dir., 1967—. Publicity work for various local civic groups and orgns. Bd. dirs. A.R.C., Central Ill. Youth Symphony, Girl Scouts U.S.A. Recipient numerous local, regional and nat. advt. awards. Mem. Ill. Art League (dir. 1974—), Cornstock Theatre, Peoria Hist. Soc. (dir.), Peoria Symphony, Amateur Mus. Club, Peoria Advt. and Selling Club, Lakeview Art Center Community Chorus, Chi Omega. Club: Catholic Alumnae (dir.). Home: 1339 N Glenoak St Peoria IL 61601 Office: 809 Central Bldg Peoria IL 61602

OAKMAN, BARBARA FRANCES HOEN (MRS. JAMES RUSSELL OAKMAN, SR.), educator; b. San Rafael, Cal., Apr. 19, 1931; d. Richard and Margaret Florence (Gould) Hoen; A.B., San Francisco State Coll., 1953, M.A., 1954; postgrad. Sacramento State Coll., 1968-69, U. Ariz., 1969-70; m. James Russell Oakman, Sr., June 18, 1960; children—James Russell, Stella Margaret, Frances Rosemary. Tchr., Sisters of the Holy Name, Los Gatos, Cal., 1954-59; reading cons. Irvington Sch. Dist., Fremont, 1959-62; reading specialist Pittsburg (Cal.) Sr. High Sch., 1962-66, American River Coll., Sacramento, 1966-68, Pima Community Coll., Tucson, 1969—. Cons., Indian Health Service, 1971—. Mem. Western Coll. Reading Assn. (mem. newsletter editorial bd. 1971), Beta Sigma Phi. Mem. Ind. Order Foresters. Author: Countdown to Successful Reading, 1971; Aids to Learning, 1973. Home: 7114 E Sylvane Dr Tucson AZ 85710

OATIS, BOBBIE NELL, coll. dean; b. Silver Creek, Miss., Nov. 10, 1934; d. Samuel and Fannie Dae (Clark) Oatis; B.S., Jackson State Coll., 1957; M.A., Ohio State U., 1965. Tchr., Pilate Vocational High Sch., 1957-62; guidance counselor Easom High Sch., 1962-67; asso. dean student affairs for women Jackson (Miss.) State Coll., 1967—. Mem. pub. edn. com. Am. Cancer Soc., 1973—; mem. Miss. Women Cabinet Pub. Affairs, 1970—; active United Givers Fund, Heart Fund, Boy Scouts Am. Bd. dirs. Middle Miss. council Girl Scouts Am., 1972—. Mem. Am. Assn. U. Women (sec. Jackson br. 1973—, state coordinator corp. rep.), Nat. Assn. Women Deans, Adminstrs. and Counselors, Nat. Council Negro Women (mem. bd. Miss. sect. 1969—). Baptist. Home: PO Box 17085 Jackson MS 39217

OATMAN, JESSIE MARIE, accountant; b. Corpus Christi, Tex., May 5, 1917; d. Duke and Nettie (Griffin) Oatman; student Coll. Arts and Industries (now Tex. Women's U.), 1937. Various stenographic, secretarial positions, 1937-41; accountant Am. Smelting & Refining Co., Corpus Christi, 1942-53, metal accountant, 1953-54, cost accountant, 1955, chief accountant, 1955-74, accounting mgr., 1974—. Chmn. information and registration disaster preparedness and relief com. Corpus Christi chpt. A.R.C., 1960-61. Mem. Nat. Assn. Accountants (dir. Corpus Christi chpt. 1967-68, treas. 1968-69). Club: Altrusa (v.p. 1958-59, pres. 1959-60, 67-69, treas. 1960-62, 64-66, dir. 1966-67, 69-70) (Corpus Christi, Tex.). Author: Arcs of Thought (poetry), 1969. Home: 630 Texas St Corpus Christi TX 78404 Office: PO Box 810 Corpus Christi TX 78403

OBEAR, MARGARET FEALY (MRS. DONALD WOOD SMITH), physician; b. Washington, July 23, 1935; d. William Gray and Margaret Gertrude (Fealy) Obear; A.A., B.A., George Washington U., 1954, M.D., 1955-58; m. Donald Wood Smith, Nov. 27, 1964; 1 dau., Christina Margaret Wood. Intern, George Washington U. Hosp., 1958-59, resident, 1959-60; resident ophthalmology Stanford, 1960-63; practice medicine, specializing in opthalmology, N.Y.C., 1964-67; clin instr. Stanford, 1967-70; asst. clin. prof. Cornell U., N.Y.C., 1967—; asso. surgeon Manhattan Eye Ear and Throat Hosp., N.Y.C., 1964—. Heed Found. fellow, 1963-64. Mem. Am. Acad. Ophthalmology and Otolaryngology, Am. Soc. Opthalmic Plastic and Reconstructive Surgery (pres. 1972-73), A.M.A., Am. Women's Med. Soc., Pan Am. Ophthalmology Assn. Home: 500 E 83d St New York City NY 10028 Office: 655 Park Av New York City NY 10021

OBENHAUS, MARION P. (MRS. VICTOR OBENHAUS), social worker; b. Norwich, Conn., Feb. 1, 1914; d. Richard F. and Laura (Nielsen) Pendleton; B.A., Conn. Coll. For Women, 1936; grad. Columbia U. Sch. Social Work, 1938; m. Victor Obenhaus, July 30, 1938; children—Constance (Mrs. Arnold Goldberg), Helen (Mrs. Richard Halverson), Mark D. Social worker Cumberland Plateau, Pleasant Hill, Tenn., 1938-41; research Project on Aged, Chgo. Theol. Sem. Congl. Chs., 1949-51; asso. dir. Dept. Social Welfare, Ch. Fedn. Chgo., 1954-57, dir., 1957-61; asso. dir. Chgo. Child Care Soc., 1961-63, exec. dir., 1963—. Mem. child and family adv. council Welfare Council Met. Chgo., 1964-66; mem. execs' adv. council Child Welfare League Am., 1967—; chmn. Ill. Task Force on Pub.-Voluntary Planning for Children, 1972—; exec. council Council Health & Welfare Services United Ch. of Christ, 1967, bd. dirs. Bd. Homeland Ministries, 1967-72; mem. Gov.'s Commn. on 1970 White House Conf. on Children and Youth. Bd. dirs. Hyde Park Neighborhood Club, Chgo., 1952-54, Community Fund Chgo., 1956-59, 66-70, Child Care Assn. Ill., 1966—, Planned Parenthood. Mem. Nat. Assn. Social Workers. Home: 5549 Woodlawn Av Chicago IL 60615 Office: 5467 University Av Chicago IL 60615

OBEREMBT, CONSTANCE LEA MERRIMAN, educator; b. Mitchell, S.D., Oct. 22, 1945; d. Vern L. and Mildred M. (Hague) Merriman; student S.D. State Coll., 1963-64; B.A. with honors in drama Dakota Wesleyan U., 1967; M.Ed., U. N.D., 1970; m. Allan Bernard Oberembt, Aug. 12, 1967. Tchr. English, Spearfish (S.D.) High Sch., 1967-68; tchr. speech and English, Sturgis (S.D.) High Sch., 1968-69; instr. speech U. N.D., Grand Forks, 1969-70; tchr. speech and drama, dir. speech activities Central High Sch., Grand Forks, 1970—. Dir. children's theatre Grand Forks Park Bd., summer 1970; judge local contests Miss Am. Pageant, 1966—. Mem. Nat., N.D., Grand Forks (rep. to assembly 1974-75) edn. assns., Central States, N.D. speech assns., N.D. English Assn., Am. Assn. U. Women, Mrs. Jaycees, Sigma Tau Delta, Theta Alpha Phi. Methodist. Home: 2015 S 20th St Grand Forks ND 58201 Office: Central High Sch Grand Forks ND 58201

OBERMAYER, JUDITH HIRSCHFIELD (MRS. ARTHUR S. OBERMAYER), real estate adminstr.; b. Pittsburgh, May 7, 1935; d. Morris Hyman and Rose (Rabkin) Hirschfield; B.S., Carnegie Inst. Tech., 1956; A.M., Radcliffe Coll., 1957; Ph.D., Harvard, 1963; m. Arthur S. Obermayer, June 23, 1963; children—Henry Mark, Joel Bruce, Marjorie Hannah. Instr. math. Wellesley Coll., 1960-63, asst. prof., 1963-66; bookkeeper, accountant Moleculon Research Corp., Cambridge, Mass., 1972-73; adminstr. Tech. Realty Trust, Newton, Mass., 1972—, trustee, 1969—. Mem. admissions council Carnegie Mellon U., 1970—. Bd. dirs. Freeport House, Inc., Newton. NSF fellow, 1956-60. Mem. Am. Math. Soc., Am. Math. Assn., Nat. Orgn. for Women, Women's Polit. Caucus, Action for Children's Television, Common Cause, Newton Mental Health Assn., Am. Civil Liberties Union, Ams. for Dem. Action, League Women Voters (Newton budget chmn. 1972-73, Newton 1st v.p. 1973—, Mass. budget chmn.). Home: 239 Chestnut St Newton MA 02165

OBERSTAR, HELEN ELIZABETH WEISS (MRS. EDWARD CHARLES OBERSTAR), cosmetics mfg. co. exec.; b. Ottawa, Ill., Aug. 29, 1923; d. Milton Edward and Helen (Herrick) Weiss; student Antioch Coll., 1939-41; B.S., Monmouth Coll., 1943; postgrad. N.Y. U., 1944-45, Northwestern U., 1946-48; m. Edward Charles Oberstar, Feb. 3, 1945. Asst. food technologist Standard Brands, Inc., N.Y.C., 1943-45; chemist Miner Labs., Midwest div. A.D. Little, Inc., Chgo., 1946-50; research chemist, supr. Toni Co. div. Gillette Co., Chgo., 1951-65; group leader Shulton, Inc., Clifton, N.J., 1965-71; sect. mgr. Consumer Research Center, Am. Cyanamid Co., Clifton, N.J., 1972—. Mem. Soc. Cosmetic Chemists (house chmn. midwest chpt. 1963-64). Patentee in field. Home: 26 MacLeay Rd Montville NJ 07045 Office: 697 Route 46 Clifton NJ 07015

OBERT, GENE MADALENE SAULSBURY (MRS. PAUL M. OBERT), nurse; b. Oklahoma City; d. Claude and Elizabeth (Young) Saulsbury; R.N., St. Anthony Hosp. Sch. Nursing, 1947; B. Nursing Arts, Okla. U., 1947; m. Paul M. Obert, Apr. 27, 1947; children—Mary (Mrs. James Leita), Jeanne, Paul, Elizabeth, Catherine. Supr. nurses Wesley Hosp., Oklahoma City, 1948; directress nursing McCurdy Hosp., 1948-50; dir. Red River Med. Center Corp., Victoria, Tex., 1968-72. First aid instr. A.R.C., 1958—. Bd. dirs. Fine Arts Assn., Victoria. Republican. Roman Catholic. Mem. Tex. Mem. Profl. Nurses Assn., Victoria-Calhoun-Goliad Tri-County Med. Aux. Club: Victoria Country. Home: 303 Tampa St Victoria TX 77901 also Rockport TX Office Box 3784 Victoria TX 77901

OBLINGER, JACKIE PERO (MRS. JOHN PHILLIP OBLINGER), TV producer, actress; b. Wilkes-Barre, Pa., Sept. 16, 1929; d. John W. and Rachel (Herbert) Pero; B.S., Bluefield Coll., 1947; spl. student Va. Poly. Inst.; student Conover Sch. TV and Modeling, N.Y., Shelter Mgmt. Sch., U.S. Dept. Def., Marshall U., 1966—; grad. Morris Harvey Coll., 1966; M.A. in Communication Arts, Marshall U., 1972; m. John Phillio Oblinger, Dec. 6, 1947; children—Michael John Pero, Phillip Frederick Stephen, Mark Llwellyn. Woman's program dir. radio sta. WHIS, Bluefield, W.Va., 1952-55, WHIS-TV, 1955-60, WCHS-TV, Charleston, W.Va., 1960—, mem. news staff; producer, dir., master of ceremonies Woman's Whirl, The Jackie Oblinger Show, Contact 8; club speaker; free-lance fashion commentator, feature writer, and comml. announcer; mem. faculty Speech Dept., Morris-Harvey Coll.; faculty W.Va. Career Coll., Charleston, exec. dir., 1974—. Formerly mem. state adv. com. Nat. Found. Infantile Paralysis; mem. golden jubilee com. Va. Fedn. Women's Clubs; bd. dirs. W.Va. Multiple Sclerosis Soc., United Fund, Bluefield Symphony, So. Appalachian council Girl Scouts Am.; bd. dirs., program chmn. P.T.A.; bd. dirs., pub. relations vol. W.Va. Dept. Civil Def.; ofcl. chaperone Miss. W. Va.; adv. bd. Japanese Christian U. Selected W.Va. Daughter of Year, West Va. Soc. of Washington, 1959-60. Mem. Bapt. Bus. Women's Fedn., Am. Women in Radio and Television, Am. Speech Assn., Delta Kappa Gamma. Baptist (mem. bd. Christian edn.). Clubs: Press (Charleston, W.Va.); Kanawha Players; Kanawha Valley Junior Woman's (charter); Quota (Bluefield, W.Va.); Arcadian. Home: 1799 Huber Rd Charleston WV 25314 Office: WCHS-TV 1111 Virginia Av E Charleston WV 25301

OBLINGER, JOSEPHINE KNEIDL HARRINGTON (MRS. WALTER L. OBLINGER), state ofcl.; b. Chgo., Feb. 14, 1913; d. Thomas William and Margaret (Kneidl) Harrington; B.S., U. Ill., 1933; LL.B., U. Detroit, 1943; L.H.D., Sioux Empire Coll., 1966; m. Walter L. Oblinger, Apr. 27, 1940; 1 son, Carl D. Tchr. Lanphier High Sch., Springfield, Ill., 1951-62; clk. Sangamon County, assessor Capitol Twp., Springfield, 1962-69; asst. dir. Ill. Dept. Registration and Edn., Springfield, 1970—; exec. dir. Gov.'s Com. on Voluntary Action, 1970-73; asst. to the pres. Lincoln Land Community Coll., 1973—. Sec. Springfield and Sangamon County Community Action, 1965-70, pres., 1970—; mem. finance com. Child and Family Service, Springfield, 1965-71; mem. Sangamon County planning com. United Community Services, 1971—; mem. Urban League, 1955—, Nat. Com. for Day Care of Children, 1960—; bd. dirs. Nat. Center for Voluntary Action, 1971—. Officer, Republican Women's Luncheon Club, 1959—, pres., 1963—; chmn. Sangamon County Rep. com., 1965—; 1st v.p. Ill. Fedn. Rep. Women, 1972; del. Rep. Nat. Conv., 1972. Del. to White House Conf., 1960. Bd. dirs., pres. Sangamon County Council on Alcoholism and Drugs. Mem. Ill. Assn. County Clks. and Recorders (pres.), Am. Bus. Women's Assn., Am., Ill., Sangamon County bar assns., N.A.A.C.P. (exec. bd.), U. Ill. Alumni Assn., Nat. Assn. Counties, Nat. Assn. Recorders and Clks., Ill. Fedn. Tchrs. (pres. 1959-63, parliamentarian, 1963—), Sangamon County Hist. Soc., P.E.O., Am. Assn. Vol. Services Coordinators (chmn. pub. policy com.), Kappa Delta Pi, Sigma Delta Pi, Delta Delta Delta. Clubs: Riverton (Ill.) Women's; Altrusa (pres. 1968—, dir.) (Springfield, Ill.). Home: Rural Route 1 Sherman IL 62684 Office: 3865 S Sixth St Springfield IL 62703

OBOLENSKY, MARILYN WALL (MRS. SERGE OBOLENSKY), metals co. exec.; b. Detroit, Aug. 13, 1929; d. Albert Fraser and Christine (Frischkorn) Wall; student Duschesne Jr. Coll., 1947; m. William Zeder Breer, 1947; children—Albert F. Wall and Carl Breer II (twins). m. 2d, Serge Obolensky, June 3, 1971; Chmn. bd. Wall-Colmonoy Corp., Detroit, 1959-61, dir., 1961-65, sec., 1961—. Bd. dirs. Heart and Lung Found., N.Y.C. Republican. Roman Catholic. Club: Bathing Corporation (Southampton, N.Y.). Home: 525 Park Av New York City NY 10022

OBRE, SALLY ANN MURPHY (MRS. PAUL LIPPINCOTT OBRE), beauty cons.; b. Quincy, Mass., Sept. 10, 1932; d. Phillip Weber and Mary Catherine (White) Murphy; B.A., Ind. U., 1954; m. Paul Lippincott Obre, Feb. 22, 1962; 1 son, David Robert. Merchandising editor Glamour mag., N.Y.C., 1961-64; fashion editor Ingenue mag., N.Y.C., 1965-69; beauty editor Ladies Home Jour., N.Y.C., 1969-74; now free lance beauty cons. Mem. N.Y. Fashion Group. Democrat. Episcopalian. Home: 24 E 81st St New York City NY 10028 Office: 641 Lexington Av New York City NY 10028

O'BRIEN, ANNA BERARDI (MRS. DANIEL J. O'BRIEN), lawyer; b. Milford, Mass., Jan. 4, 1920; d. Frank and Jennie M. (Crescenzi) Berardi; A.B., Boston U., 1941, J.D., 1943; m. Daniel J. O'Brien, Dec. 11, 1948; children—Anna Marie, Daniel Joseph. Admitted to Mass. bar, 1943, U.S. Dist. Ct., 1945, U.S. Supreme Ct., 1970; practiced in Mass., 1943—, now practicing in Milford. Mem. Milford Sch. Com., 1947-53, chmn., 1950-51; town counsel, Milford, 1950-52; mem. Milford Finance Commn., 1962-73; mem. Milford Zoning Bd., 1969—, chmn., 1969-72. Mem. Milford Town Republican Com., 1943—. Recipient award Boston U. Sch. Law, 1972. Mem. Am. Legion Aux., Daus. Italy, Mass., Worcester County, Milford bar assns., Mass. Trial Lawyers Assn., Mass. Women Lawyers Assn., Kappa Beta Pi, Theta Phi Alpha. Rotarian. Club: Catholic Woman's (Milford). Home: Congress Terrace Milford MA 01757 Office: 262 Main St Milford MA 01757

O'BRIEN, AUDREY O'BRIEN, educator; b. N.Y.C., May 16, 1921; d. John Henry and Ida Gertrude (Neumann) O'Brien; B.A., Hunter Coll., 1942; M.S., Fordham U., 1943; Ph.D., Columbia, 1960; m. Harold Joseph O'Brien, Aug. 18, 1956. Instr. to asst. prof. speech pathology Fordham U., N.Y.C., 1943-59; asso. prof., chmn. dept. St. John's U., N.Y.C., 1960-65, prof., 1966-67; prof. speech pathology Trenton (N.J.) State Coll., 1967—. Mem. Am. Speech and Hearing Assn., Internat. Assn. Logopedics and Phoniatrics, Internat. Phonetic Assn., Internat. Soc. Phonetic Scis., Am. Dialect Soc., Am. Assn. Univ. Profs. Author: (monograph) Speech and Hearing Services in the Republic of Ireland, 1973; Directory of Speech and Hearing Clinic Facilities in the Counties of Kings and Queens, 1965. Office: Dept

Speech Pathology and Audiology Trenton State Coll Trenton NJ 08625

O'BRIEN, BARBARA RUTH, home economist; b.Wakefield, Mass., June 21, 1923; d. Joseph Leo and Margaret Helena (Ryan) O'Brien; B.S., U. Mass., 1944, Colo. A. and M. U., 1951, Brown U., 1967. Tchr., Petersham (Mass.) High Sch., 1944-45; asso. agt. Bristol County Extension Service, Segreganset, Mass., 1945-47, head home economist, 1947—. Pres., bd. dirs. Taunton (Mass.) Vis. Nurse Assn. Mem. Council on Aging, Raynham; bd. dirs., rec. sec. Raynham Human Services Assn. Recipient Distinguished Service award Nat. Assn. Extension Home Economists, 1959, Achievement award Epsilon Sigma Phi, 1968. Mem. Am. Assn. U. Women (v.p. 1961), Nat. Assn. Extension Home Economists (sec. 1970-72), Am., Mass. (dir. 1965—), Southeastern Mass. (pres. 1967-73) home econs. assns. Roman Catholic (chmn. parent edn. 1969-70). Club: Quota (v.p. 1970—) (Taunton). Home: 390 White St Raynham Center MA 02767 Office: Center St Segreganset MA 02773

O'BRIEN, BEREA JOAN, nursing home adminstr.; b. Bowmanville, Ont., Can., Aug. 20, 1933; d. Raymond E. and Ruby (Ward) Hutchinson; R.N., Peterborough (Ont.) Civic Hosp., 1955; m. Patrick D. O'Brien, Nov. 19, 1957; 1 dau., Deirdre. Operating room nurse Peterborough Civic Hosp., 1956; theatre nurse London (Eng.) Clinic, 1956-59; operating room supr. Espanola Central Hosp., 1959-61; nurse intensive care unit Northwestern Hosp., 1961-69; nursing dir., then adminstr. Cheltenham Nursing Home, Downsview, Ont., 1969—. Mem. Ont. Coll. Nurses. Mem. Yorkview Progressive Conservative Assn. Address: 195 Exbury Rd Downsview ON M3M 1R9 Canada

O'BRIEN, CORNELIA SMITH (MRS. JOHN BAYLEY O'BRIEN), orgn. exec.; b. Rome, N.Y., July 9, 1899; d. Lyle Avery and Esther (Capron) Smith; grad. Scudder Sch., N.Y.C.; m. John Bayley O'Brien, Apr. 29, 1936. Staff asst. A.R.C., 1939-42; nat. chmn. press relations D.A.R., 1942-47, author Press Relations Guide, 1942, rev. 1945, editor Press Digest, 1946-48, nat. chmn. transportation, 1947-50, originator, dir. 1st tour of nat. bd. to approved schs., 1948, mem. nat. resolutions com. 1942-57, asso. editor D.A.R. Motion Picture Revs., 1952-54; nat. treas. Nat. Soc. Women Descs. of Ancient and Honorable Arty. Co., 1947-50, nat. auditor, 1950-53, 1st v.p., 1953-56, nat. pres., 1956-59, hon. nat. pres. for life, 1959—, edited History and Lineage Book, 1959, compiled triennial yearbooks, 1953, 56, 59, 62, 65, parliamentarian, 1960, 62-65; 1st v.p. Nat. Chairmans Assn., 1953-55; state councillor Nat. Soc. Daus. Founders and Patriots Am., 1951-54, 62-65, 69-72, nat. chmn. restoration of records, 1952-55; surety Nat. Soc. Daus. of Barons of Runnemede, 1950-53, 57-59, treas., 1953-56, pres. 1959-62, compiled and edited yr. books, 1960, 61, 62, nat. chmn. restoration records 1962-68, hon. pres. for life, 1962—. Mem. Order Arms. Armorial Ancestry (1st v.p. 1958-61, auditor 1967-71), Order First Fams. of Va., Nat. Soc. Descs. Colonial Clergy, Nat. Soc. Mayflower Descs., Huguenot Soc. Am., Nat. Soc. Colonial Dames, N.Y. Hist. Assn., Nat. Presidents Assn., Order of Crown in Am. (councillor 1962—), Nat. Trust for Historic Preservation, Soc. Third Street Music Sch. Settlement (N.Y.C.), English Speaking Union, Rome (N.Y.) Hist. Soc., Central N.Y. Community Arts Council, Smithsonian Instn. Clubs: Sorosis (treas. 1968-71, auditor 1972—), Woman's Press (N.Y.C.); Colonial Dames (Washington). Home: 25 Parkview Av Bronxville NY 10708

O'BRIEN, DALLAS SUSAN JANE, architect-planner; b. Dallas, Aug. 13, 1942; d. Jack Dallas and Jane (Childs) O'Brien; B.Arch., Tex. Technol. U., 1966; postgrad. U. Tex., 1969—. Designer, Preston M. Geren, architect and engr. and assos., Fort Worth, 1966-69, sr. designer, 1970-73, design asso., 1973—; teaching asst. U. Tex. at Austin Sch. Architecture, 1969-70. Recipient Jesse H. Jones Scholarship, 1965. Mem. A.I.A. (mem. com. on central bus. dist. planning and design 1973-74), Am. Inst. Planners, Nat. Council Archtl. Registration Bds., Regional Sci. Assn., Metropolitan Assn. Urban Designers and Environmental Planners, Urban Land Inst., Tex. Soc. Architects, Kappa Kappa Gamma, Alpha Lambda Delta. Author vol. of poetry. Home: 1709 E Park Row Arlington TX 76010 Office: 1125 Electric Service Bldg Fort Worth TX 76102

O'BRIEN, ELLEEN MCCANN (MRS. JAMES A. O'BRIEN), editor; b. Chelsea, Mass., June 22, 1909; d. Peter F. and Edith (Wyllie) McCann; B.A., Wellesley Coll., 1931; m. James A. O'Brien, June 2, 1939; children—James A., Frederick James. Newspaper reporter, feature writer, woman's editor Boston Record-Am., Honolulu Advertiser, 1931-40; editor Paradise of the Pacific, monthly mag., Honolulu, 1942-54; editor Tongg Pub. Co., Honolulu, 1956-59, Paradise of the Pacific, 1960-62; currently editor of Here's Hawaii; now state information specialist Dept. Planning and Econ. Devel., Hawaii. Chmn. adv. com. first Aloha Week in Hawaii; pub. relations dir. Hawaii chpt. World Brotherhood. Recipient award U.S. Treasury, 1957, 73. Mem. Pub. Relations Women of Honolulu, Women in Communications. Author: Hawaiian Words and Phrases, Kauai Handy Guide, Hawaii Handy Guide, Hawaiian Host and Hostess. Home: 1753 Halekoa Dr Honolulu HI 96821 Office: PO Box 2359 Kamamalu Bldg Honolulu HI 96804

O'BRIEN, ETHEL HIERONYMUS, physician; b. Jeffersontown, Ky., Feb. 8, 1901; d. Herman E. and Julia A. (Zellich) Hieronymus; A.B., U. Louisville, 1930, M.D., 1933; m. George T. O'Brien, May 16, 1939. Intern Louisville Gen. Hosp., 1933-34, Worcester (Mass.) State Hosp., 1936-37; resident Inst. Human Relations, New Haven, 1937-38; sr. psychiatrist Central State Hosp., Lakeland Ky., 1938-42, Fairfield State Hosp., Newtown, Conn., 1942-43; pvt. practice psychiatry, Waterbury, Conn., 1943-46; psychiatrist Jefferson County (Ky.) Juvenile Ct., Louisville and Jefferson County Children's Home, 1947-55, Community Service Div., Dept. Mental Health Ky., Louisville, 1955-64; part-time psychiatrist No. Ky. Mental Health Clinic, Covington, 1957-71, Louisville Comprehensive Care Center, 1971-72; psychiatrist Circuit Ct., Louisville, 1965—, Jefferson County Jail, 1965-72; cons. psychiatrist Children's Mental Health Unit and Hosp., Lakeland, Ky., 1955-62; asso. instr. Dept. Psychiatry U. Louisville Med. Sch., 1950—. Mem. A.M.A., Ky., World med. assns., Am., Ky. psychiat. assns., Jefferson County Med. Soc., Am. Med. Woman's Assn., World Fedn. Mental Health. Home: 2519 Cherokee Pkwy Louisville KY 40204

O'BRIEN, GRACE WILHELMINA EHLIG (MRS. LOUIS J. O'BRIEN), psychologist, adminstr., co-owner travel bur.; b. Los Angeles, Aug. 27, 1922; d. Max Carl and Janette (Rentchler) Ehlig; A.A., Pasadena City Coll., 1942; A.B., U. Cal. at Los Angeles, 1944; postgrad. Riverside City Coll., 1946; postgrad. Cal. State Coll. at Los Angeles, 1954-70, M.A. in Guidance, 1964; m. Louis J. O'Brien, Nov. 8, 1947; children—Carol Jean, Lawrence John, Perry Lewis. Tchr., Perris (Cal.) Union High Sch., 1945-46; tchr., counselor, psychometrist Los Angeles City Schs., 1946-66, cons. counselor, sch. psychologist Elementary Secondary Edn. Act, Edn. and Guidance program, 1966-68; head counselor Garden Gate Opportunity Sch., 1968-73; vice prin. Markham Jr. High Sch., 1973, Belvedere Jr. High Sch., 1974; asst. prin. Garfield High Sch., 1974—; co-owner, asst. mgr. Golden State Travel Bur., Pasadena, Cal., 1954—. Den mother chmn. Cub Scouts, 1964-66. Recipient spl. service award Boy Scouts, 1964. Mem. U. Cal. at Los Angeles Alumni Assn., Sr. High Asst. Prins. Assn., Los Angeles Assn. Sch. Adminstrs., Cal. Counselors and Guidance Assn., Domestic Internat. Travel Tour Orgn., Pi Lambda Theta, Chi Delta Phi. Presbyn. (supt. Sunday sch. 1953-54). Home: 3880 Shadow Grove Rd Pasadena CA 91107 also 3615 E Foothill Blvd Pasadena CA 91107 Office: 5101 E 6th St Los Angeles CA 90022

O'BRIEN, HARRIET ELLEN, concert mgr.; b. Troy, N.Y.; d. Michael Henry and Mary Frances (Brannen) O'Brien; B.A., Smith Coll., 1921; postgrad. Boston U., 1922. With advt. dept. Chandler's (now Condrad-Chandler), Boston, 1923-25; research writer Walton Advt. Co., Boston, 1925-31; owner, operator Harriet E. O'Brien Assos., publicity counselors, Boston, 1932—; exec. dir. Boston Opera Assn., 1958—; mgr. Boston seasons Metropolitan Opera, 1958—; cons. North Shore Community Arts Found., Beverly, Mass. Mem. Boston Press Club (charter), Publicity Club Boston (charter), Internat. Assn. Concert Mgrs. Author: Paul Revere's Own Story, 1929; Smith College Today, 1926. Contbr. articles to profl. publs. Home: 72 Chestnut St Boston MA 02108 Office: Boston Opera Assn 420 Boylston St Boston MA 02116

O'BRIEN, KATHARINE ELIZABETH, writer; b. Amesbury, Mass.; d. Martin William and Catherine (Higgins) O'Brien; A.B., Bates Coll., 1922; M.A., Cornell U., 1924; Ph.D., Brown U., 1939; D.Sc. in Edn. (hon.), U. Me., 1960; L.H.D., Bowdoin Coll., 1965. Chmn. math. dept. Coll. of New Rochelle, 1925-36; head math. dept. Deering High Sch., Portland, Me., 1940-71; lectr. math. U. Me., Portland, 1962-73, Brown U., summers 1962-65, 67. Speaker at profl. meetings; cons. calculus books. Mem. Math. Assn. Am., Poetry Soc. Am. (poetry judge 1972—), Internat. Platform Assn., Bates Key, Soc. Bowdoin Women, N.Y. Acad. Scis., Phi Beta Kappa, Sigma Xi. Club: Portland College. Author: Sequences (math. enrichment series), 1966; Excavation and Other Verse, 1967. Contbr. articles and book revs. to various profl. jours., poetry and light verse to mags. and newspapers, including Saturday Rev., Christian Sci. Monitor, N.Y. Herald Tribune, Ladies' Home Jour., Sci. Monthly. Home: 130 Hartley St Portland ME 04103

O'BRIEN, KATHERINE LORD, librarian; b. Ellisburg, N.Y., Oct. 22, 1907; d. Thomas and Lena (Brown) O'Brien; B.A. magna cum laude, Wells Coll., 1928; B.L.S., Columbia, 1931. Library asst. Albany Pub. Library, 1929-30; with N.Y. Pub. Library, 1931—, successively spl. positions, asst. librarian Central Circulation br., librarian Riverside Br., Richmond Regional librarian, 1931-54, prin. librarian Donnell Library Center, 1955-59, coordinator of adult services, 1959-67; chief Mid-Manhattan Library, 1967—; cons. N.Y. State Bur. of Adult Edn., 1946-47 lectr. librarianship Pratt Inst. Library Sch., also Rutgers U. Grad. Sch. Library Service. Mem. Am. (past chmn. adult services standards devel. com.), N.Y. State (past pres. adult services div.) library assn., N.Y.C. Library Club (past pres.). Democrat. Episcopalian. Author articles in field. Home: 400 Central Park W New York City NY 10025 Office: 8 E 40th St New York City NY 10016

O'BRIEN, KATHRYN ROSE BUTTICE, mathematician; b. Chgo., Feb. 26, 1936; d. Gaetano T. and Mary (Perzia) Buttice; B.S., Marquette U., 1958, M.S., 1960; candidate Ph.D., Ill. Inst. Tech., 1966; m. Neil Edward O'Brien, Sept. 17, 1960; 1 dau., Mary Catherine. With Ill. Inst. Tech. Research Inst., 1959-66, asst. mathematician, 1959-62, research mathematician, 1962-66; cons. mathematician Missile and Space div. Gen. Electric Co., 1966-68; dir. faculty Computer Programming Inst. No. Ill., Inc., 1966-70; pres., gen. mgr. Dido, Inc., Joliet, Ill., 1970—. Mem. Soc. Indsl. and Applied Math., Data Processing Mgmt. Assn., Am. Math. Soc., Pi Mu Epsilon, Sigma Pi Sigma. Contbr. to sci. jours. Home: 811 Junie Ct Joliet IL 60435 Office: 1013 Dawes Av Joliet IL 60435

O'BRIEN, SISTER MARY CONSILIA, educator; b. Jersey City; d. Thomas Francis and Julia (Ritter) O'Brien; B.S., Fordham U., 1936; M.A., Catholic U. Am., 1937, Ph.D., 1939; certificate in theology Theol. Inst. for Sisters, Providence Coll., 1951; M.A., St. Xavier's Theol. Inst., Chgo., 1957. Tchr. elementary sch., 1930-36; supr. schs. Dominican Sisters of Newburgh, N.Y., 1939-48; tchr. religion secondary sch., part-time theology prof. Mt. St. Mary Tchr.-Tng. and Normal Sch., 1948-54; prof. philosophy, theology, sociology and psychology Mt. St. Mary Liberal Arts Coll. for Women, 1954-60, prof. philosophy and theology, 1960-70; founder Center for Devel. Learning and Reading, 1954, dir., 1954-72, now emeritus; reading cons., 1960—. Pres. Am. Acad. for Human Devel., 1969—, bd. dirs., 1970—; cons in psychology Dallas Acad., 1970—; mem. adv. bd. Periwinkle Prodns., 1971; cons. in edn., lang. arts East Syracuse-Minoa (N.Y.) Sch. Dist., 1968—; cons. learning disabilities pub. sch. dist., Ossining, N.Y.; cons. N.Y. Insts. for Child Devel., N.Y.C., 1971—; mem. com. certification and examination reading thcrs. Tchr. Edn. and Certification div. N.Y. State Dept. Edn.; mem. N.Y. State adv. council Rockefeller Bros. Fund Project. Trustee Mt. St. Mary Liberal Arts Coll. Mem. Internat. Reading Assn., Nat. Assn. Children with Learning Disabilities, Assn. Cath. Coll. Tchrs. Sacred Doctrine. Mem. bd. cons. editors Academic Therapy Publs., San Rafael, Cal., 1971—, Jour. Learning Disabilities, Chgo. Address: Mt St Mary Newburgh NY 12550

O'BRIEN, MARY LOIS SOUTHALL (MRS. JOHN EDMUND O'BRIEN), coll. adminstr.; b. Sunnyside, L.I., N.Y., Dec. 9, 1929; d. Thomas Henry and Susan Frances (Burke) Southall; B.S., Coll. St. Rose, 1951; M. Ed., Towson State Coll., 1971; postgrad. Cath. U., 1971-72; m. John Edmund O'Brien, June 9, 1951; children—Michele, Julia, Catherine, John, Bart, Gregory. Tchr., Merchants and Bankers Bus. Sch., 1951-55, N.Y.C. Pub. Schs., 1953-55, Browne's Bus. Coll., Lynbrook, L.I., 1957-59, Lynbrook (L.I.) Adult Edn., 1958-59; lectr., instr. Villa Julie Coll., Stevenson, Md., 1970-71, counselor, coordinator student activities, 1971-72, counselor/coordinator placement, 1972-73, coordinator student personnel services, 1973-74, dean of students, 1974—. Religious edn. instr. Immaculate Conception Parish, Md., 1971-72, 73-74; mental health counselor trainee Phipps Clinic, Johns Hopkins Hosp., 1972-73. Mem. Balt. League Internat. Visitors, 1966-69, Balt. Neighborhoods, 1971-72; co-chmn. edn. com. Balt. chpt. Women's Internat. League for Peace and Freedom, 1973; del. Pub. Edn. Nominating Conv. Balt. County, 1973; active various community drives; Cana chmn. Family Life Bur., 1966-68. Mem. Md. Personnel and Guidance Assn., Md. Assn. Community and Jr. Colls., Adult Student Personnel Assn. Republican. Roman Catholic. Home: 809 Providence Rd Towson MD 21204 Office: Valley Rd Stevenson MD 21153

O'BRIEN, MARY NELSON FIRTH (MRS. BRIAN O'BRIEN), psychiat. occupational therapist; b. Hope, Eng., Feb. 22, 1910; d. Edward Loxley and Julia Tuck (Morgan) Firth; came to U.S., 1914, naturalized, 1934, diploma in Occupational Therapy, Columbia, 1948, B.S., 1949; M.A. in Edn., N.Y. U., 1950; M.A. in Italian Lang. and Culture, Middlebury Coll. Modern Lang., 1950; m. Brian O'Brien, Apr. 14, 1956; 1 stepson, Brian. Asst. occupational therapist Hallbrooke Sanitarium, Greens Farms, Conn., 1948-50; chief therapist pediatrics dept. Univ. Hosp., Balt., 1951; chief therapist Neurol. Inst., Milan, Italy, 1951-52; chief occupational therapist, Ospedale Mayer Hosp., Florence, Italy, 1952-53; cons. occupational therapy, Woodstock, Conn., 1953—. Fulbright grantee, 1951-53. Mem. Am. Occupational Therapy Assn., Am. Assn. Tchrs. Italian, Nat. Soc. Colonial Dames Am. (Conn. br. mem. Gunston Hall com. 1965-73, area chmn. Gunston Hall com. 1973-74). Clubs: New Haven Lawn, Petit Cercle Francais. Address: Box 62 Green Rd North Woodstock CT 06257

O'BRIEN, ORIN YNEZ, double bassist; b. Los Angeles, June 7, 1935; d. George J. and Marguerite G. (Churchill) O'Brien; student U. Cal., Los Angeles, 1953-54; Adelaide Reckford scholar, Juilliard Sch. Music, 1954-57. Mem. N.Y.C. Ballet Orch., 1956-66; first permanent woman mem. N.Y. Philharmonic, N.Y.C., 1966—; mem. Saidenberg Little Symphony; extra bass Met. Opera Orch., 1961-66; faculty YMHA, N.Y.C., 1967-71, Manhattan Sch. Music, 1969—. Mem. Soroptimist Fedn. Home: 200 W 58th St New York City NY 10019 Office: c/o NY Philharmonic Broadway at 65th St New York City NY 10023

O'BRIEN, PADDY GUNN, gallery ofcl.; b. Surrey, Eng., Oct. 13, 1929; d. Frederick Norman and Dorothy Mary (Proctor) Gunn; M.Ed. diploma, Reading (Eng.) U., 1948-51; student Academie de la Section d'Or, Paris, 1955-56; m. Richard D. O'Brien, Aug. 1951 (div. Feb. 1958). Art gallery asst. London (Ont.) Pub. Library and Art Mus., 1952-63, registrar, 1963-73, curator, 1973—. Recipient Seagram trophy for best set design Dominion Drama Festival, 1963. Mem. Canadian Assn. Mus. Dirs., Ont. Assn. Art Galleries (treas. 1973), Ont. Soc. Artists. Home: 1265 Richmond St N Apt 1603 London ON Canada Office: London Public Library and Art Museum 305 Queens Av London ON N6B 1X2 Canada

O'BRIEN, SALLY ANN, marketing exec.; b. Elmira, N.Y., Mar. 13, 1929; d. Francis J. and Katharine (McCarthy) O'Brien; A.B., Coll. St. Rose, 1951; M.B.A., N.Y.U., 1960. Jr. statistician, statistician, sr. analyst market research dept. Colgate-Palmolive Co., Inc., N.Y.C., 1951-62, sect. head market research, 1962-64, mgr. market research, 1964-68, dir. market research, 1968—. Mem. Am. Marketing Assn., Confraternity Christian Doctrine Tchrs., Coll. St. Rose Alumni Assn. N.Y.-L.I. (pres. 1956-60), Catholic Daus. Am. Roman Catholic. Home: 199 Stokes Av Freeport NY 11520 Office: 300 Park Av New York City NY 10022

O'BRIEN, THERESA MARIE MANDL (MRS. CHARLES EMIL O'BRIEN), historian; b. Glenwood Springs, Colo., Apr. 15, 1895; d. Carl and Marie (Reindl) Mandl; student pub. schs.; m. Charles Emil O'Brien, Apr. 18, 1913 (dec. Apr. 1948); children—Dorothy May (Mrs. Dale Harvey Wells), Mazie Juanita (Mrs. Charles August Gabarde). With Vienna City Laundry, Leadville, Colo., 1928-45, 65-68, Crestone Merc. Bus. (Colo.), 1947-48; owner Leadville Art Shop, 1949-51; with Vendome Hotel, Leadville, 1951-61; tourist guide, historian Tabor Opera House Mus., Leadville, 1958—. Mem. Neighbors of Woodcraft. Home: 326 W 7th St Leadville CO 80461 Office: 326 W 7th St Leadville CO 80461

O'BRYANT, MATHILDA BRUGH, librarian, educator; b. Logan, W.Va., Apr. 2, 1918; d. Rex and Katie Virginia (Layman) Brugh; B.A., Mary Baldwin Coll., Staunton, Va., 1939; B.S. in L.S., Drexel Inst. Tech., 1940; M.A., U. Mich., 1944; m. Albert H. O'Bryant, May 23, 1944 (div Aug. 1968); children—Alice-Anne, Daniel. Head cataloger Brandeis U., Waltham, Mass., 1955-56; chief cataloger State U. of N.Y., Oneonta, 1957-61, Union Coll., Schenectady, N.Y., 1961-62; head catalog dept. Princeton, (N.J.), 1962-67; head of acquisitions U. Louisville Library, 1967-73, asso. prof., 1967-73; chief cataloger, asst. prof. Queens Coll., Flushing, N.Y., 1973—. Mem. Am., Ky., N.Y., City Univ. N.Y. library assns., Am. Assn. U. Profs., Speed Art Mus., Mary Baldwin Coll. Alumnae Assn. (trustee 1963-67). Democrat. Presbyn. (Sunday sch. tchr. 1958-73). Club: Altrusa. Home: 69-10C 188th St Apt 1C Flushing NY 11365

O'BRYON, MARTHA SEFFER, editor; b. Peoria, Ill., June 20, 1918; d. James Henry and Lillian Louise (Court) Seffer; A.B., Knox Coll., Galesburg, Ill., 1939; m. Leonard Leon O'Bryon, June 17, 1939; children—Leonard, Michael, Colleen (Mrs. Ray Melone), Patrick, Laura, James, Nora. Tchr. Am. history Humphries Coll., Stockton, Cal., 1961; editor Pacific Historian, publn. U. Pacific, Stockton, 1968—. Mem. Cultural Heritage Bd. Pres. San Joaquin Area Camp Fire Girls, 1963. Recipient Seton award Camp Fire Girls, 1963, Gulick award, 1964. Mem. Am. Assn. U. Women, Nat. League Am. Pen Women (pres. 1969-71), Stockton Poetry Soc., Delta Zeta. Episcopalian. Editor monographs. Home: 3027 N Pershing St Stockton CA 95204 Office: 3601 Pacific Av Stockton CA 95204

OBST, EMILY VIRGINIA TURK (MRS. HAROLD A. OBST), architect; b. Norfolk, Va., Dec. 18, 1918; d. Morris Stettiner and Diana (Umstadter) Turk; A.B., Barnard Coll., 1939; B. Arch., Columbia, 1944; m. Harold A. Obst, Nov. 8, 1943; children—Anthony, Mary Diana, James Hagen. Architect, Bur. Yards and Docks, USN, Key West Fla., 1944; designer, draftsman Kahn and Jacobs, N.Y.C., 1945; pvt. practice architecture as partner E. and H. Obst, architects, Palm Beach, Fla., 1948—; draftsman N.Y. dist. Corps Engrs., U.S. Army, 1942-43. Bd. dirs., mem. exec. com. Fla. Lung Disease Assn.; v.p. Am. Lung Assn. S.E. Fla., Fla. Episcopal Coll. Registered architect, Fla. Mem. A.I.A. (corporate mem.; corr. mem. nat. com. on religious architecture; chmn. Palm Beach chpt. Beaux Arts Ball 1965), Fla. Assn. Architects, Am. Assn. U. Women (past dir. Palm Beach br.), League Women Voters (past dir. Palm Beach). Episcopalian (pres. Woman's Aux. 1953, 57). Prin. works include: Base Operations Bldg., Palm Beach AFB, 1952, Air Police Bldg., Palm Beach AFB, 1952, Palm Beach AFB Bakery, 1952, residences Dr. and Mrs. J.R. Skyer, Palm Beach, 1954, Dr. and Mrs. B.F. Altman, Palm Beach, 1952, residences of Judge and Mrs. C.E. Chillingworth and Judge and Mrs. James Knott, Palm Beach County; Congress Av. Office Bldg., 1959, West Palm Beach Social Security Adminstrn. Bldg., 1961; Palmcrest Convalescent Center, 1964, Palm Beach County Juvenile Detention Center, Lake Clarke Gardens, John Leonard High Sch., Golfview Jr. High Sch.; Palm Beach Habilitation Center, 1968. Past chmn. com. on architecture Episcopal Diocese of S.E. Fla.; supervising architect for Palm Beach and Okeechobee counties Fla. Div. Hotels and Restaurants; former vice chmn. Fla. Council Clean Air. Contbr. articles on fgn. architecture to Fla. Architect; on architecture to Your Church. Home: 7512 West Lake Dr Lake Clarke Shores West Palm Beach FL 33406 Office: 324 Royal Palm Way Palm Beach FL 33480

O'BYRNE, MARJORIE ANNE HINNERS (MRS. JOHN COATES O'BYRNE), journalist, educator; b. N.Y.C., May 3, 1919; d. Frank Albin and Marie Josephine (McCloskey) Hinners; B.A. in English and Journalism, Syracuse U., 1941, postgrad., 1942-43; postgrad. U. Ia.; m. John Coates O'Byrne, Apr. 28, 1945; children—Kathleen Marie, Stephen Francis, Margret Ann, Mary Erin. Writer, Harper's Bazaar, 1940; reporter, columnist Syracuse (N.Y.) Post Standard, 1941-43; editor Women's Wear Daily, 1943-44; copywriter Filene's, Boston, 1946-47, Alden's, Iowa City, 1951-53, Killian's, Cedar Rapids, Ia., 1953-55; asst. in pub. Simmons Coll., Boston, 1947-48, dir. intern program in communications, 1973—; instr. pub. relations and mass communications U. Ia., 1950-51, 52, instr. rhetoric, 1960-65; reporter Evanston (Ill.) Rev., 1967-69; lectr. Medill Sch. Journalism, Northwestern U., Evanston, 1967-72; community relations dir. Bloomingdale's, Chestnut Hill, Mass.,

1973—. Instr. journalism Syracuse U., 1942-43; lectr. Boston U. Sch. Pub. Communications, 1973—. Pres., Johnson County Democratic Women, 1960. Mem. Women in Communications (dir. region 3, 1970-71, pres. Boston chpt. 1974-75), Soc. Profl. Journalists, Advt. and Publicity Club of Boston. Club: Press (Chgo.). Home: 141 Plymouth Rd Newton Highlands MA 02161 Office: Bloomingdale's Chestnut Hill MA 02167 also Sch Public Communications Boston University Boston MA 02115

OCH, LOUISE MARIA (MRS. JOSEPH L. H. OCH), tile co. exec.; b. Augsburg, Germany, Nov. 24, 1914; d. Martin and Maria (Schott) Scharz; came to U.S., 1928, naturalized, 1935; R.N., Cornell U., 1935; m. Joseph L. H. Och, July 10, 1940. Head nurse Cornell Med. Center, N.Y.C., 1935-38; supr. Alton Rd. Hosp., Miami, Fla., 1938-40; indsl. nurse charge first aid Opa Locka AFB, Miami, Fla., 1940-44; pub. health nurse Dade County Health Dept., Miami, 1946-49; owner, mgr. Continental Tile Co., Miami, 1952-70, v.p., 1970—. Mem. Miami Opera Guild, Miami Mental Health Soc., Friends of the University Library, U. Miami, Miami Builders Exchange, Women in Constrn. Clubs: Snapper Creek Lakes, The Vizcayans, Coral Reef Yacht. Runaway Bay, Jockey; (Miami); Ocean Reef (Key Largo). Home: 10343 NE 6th Av Miami Shores FL 33153 Office: 7014 NE 4th Ct Miami FL 33138

OCHOCINSKI, SISTER RAPHAEL MARIE, nurse, adminstr., educator; b. Buffalo; d. Francis and Catherine (Sikorski) Ochocinski; B.S., State U. N.Y. at Buffalo, 1964; postgrad. Saint Bonaventure U., 1967. Nurse, Mount St. Mary's Sch. of Nursing, Niagara U., Niagara Falls, N.Y., 1936; instr. Red Cross nursing St. Gerards Health Center, Maternal Care and Well Baby Clinic, Toronto, Ont., 1939-44; pub. health U. Toronto, 1940-41; child nursing care St. Rita's Home for Children, Buffalo, 1944-46, adminstr., 1958-66; exec. sec. Catholic Settlement Day Nursery, Toronto, Ont., 1946-55; lectr. Villa Maria Coll., Buffalo, 1965-66; dir. Cantalician Center for Learning, Cantalician Center Workshop, 1969—. Mem. Council for Exceptional Children, Div. on Mental Retardation, 1961; mem. adv. com. on Mental Retardation for Erie County, 1965; mem. planning com., dept. continuing edn. Sch. Nursing, State U. N.Y. at Buffalo, 1970. Fellow Am. Assn. on Mental Deficiency; mem. Guild of Catholic Psychiatrists (asso.), U. Buffalo Alumni Assn., Nat. Catholic Edn. Assn., Nat. Rehab. Assn., N.Y. State Assn. for Retarded Children, Mental Health Assn. Erie County. Address: 3233 Main St Buffalo NY 14214

O'CONNELL, LINDA JEANNE PEARSON (MRS. THOMAS A. O'CONNELL), banker; b. Mpls., Aug. 14, 1947; d. Harry Walter and Delores J. (Just) Pearson; B.A., U. Minn., 1969; m. Thomas A. O'Connell, June 14, 1969. With Northwestern Nat. Bank of Mpls., 1969—, asst. v.p., 1973—. Mem. Nat. Assn. Bank Women (mem. minority lending com. 1973-74), Am. Bankers Assn., Delta Delta Delta, U. Minn. Alumni Assn., Phi Delta. Home: 4825 Townes Rd Edina MN 55424 Office: 7th and Marquette St Minneapolis MN 55480

O'CONNELL, MARGARET JANE PHELAN (MRS. DANIEL O'CONNELL), librarian; b. Niagara Falls, N.Y., May 1, 1930; d. William Francis and Hilda Mary (Clements) Phelan; A.B., Mercyhurst Coll., 1951; postgrad. State U. N.Y., 1951; M.S., Columbia, 1956; m. Daniel O'Connell, Aug. 9, 1958; 1 son, Daniel. Librarian, Alden (N.Y.) Central Sch., 1951-53, Hicksville (N.Y.) Sr. High Sch., 1953-59; librarian West Islip Pub. Schs., West Islip, N.Y., 1960—, dir. sch. libraries, 1963-68. Lectr., St. John's U., N.Y.C., 1957-58. Mem. N.Y. United Tchrs., Nat., West Islip tchrs. assns., Suffolk County Media Specialists, Cath. Daus. Am. (grant regent Hicksville 1956-57). Clubs: Long Island Traditional Jazz (Babylon, N.Y.); Long Island Model A (Welleston Park, N.Y.). Home: 123 Haynes St West Islip NY 11795 Office: Bayview Sch Snedecor Av West Islip NY 11795

O'CONNOR, ELINOR PATTERSON, lawyer; b. Bay City, Mich., Apr. 20, 1929; d. Frank Clark and Agnes (Murphy) Patterson; A.B., U. Mich., 1950; J.D., Seton Hall U., 1970; m. John C. O'Connor, Oct. 28, 1950 (div. Oct. 1967); children—Christine, Valerie, Amy, Christopher Criffan. Editorial asst. Silver Burdett Pub. Co., subsidiary Time, Inc., Morristown, N.J., 1964-65; asst. publicity mgr. Worthington Corp., 1965-67; dir. devel. and pub. relations Children's Aid and Adoption Soc. N.J., 1967-68; admitted to N.J. bar, 1970; practiced in Newark, 1970, Morristown, 1971, Springfield, 1972, Hackettstown, 1972—; partner Mulligan & Jacobson, N.Y.C., 1973—. Atty., Hackettstown Planning Bd., 1973—, Green Twp. (N.J.) Zoning Bd., 1973—, Blairstown Twp (N.J.) Zoning Bd., 1973—; mcpl. prosecutor Blairstown Twp., 1974—. Mem. Am., Warren County, Morris County bar assns., Assn. Bar City N.Y., Selden Soc., Kappa Alpha Theta. Republican. Home: Panther Valley Hackettstown NJ 07840 Office: 425 Washington St Hackettstown NJ 07840

O'CONNOR, SISTER GEORGE AQUIN, coll. pres.; b. Astoria, N.Y., Mar. 5, 1921; d. George M. and Joana T. (Loughlin) O'Connor; B.A., Hunter Coll., 1943; M.A., Catholic U. Am., 1947; Ph.D. (Nat. Inst. Mental Health fellow), N.Y. U., 1964. Mem. faculty St. Joseph's High Sch., 1944-45; mem. faculty St. Joseph's Coll., Bklyn., 1946—, chmn. social sci. dept., 1966-69, prof. sociology and anthropology, 1966—, pres., 1969—. Mem. Regents Regional Coordinating Council for Postsecondary Edn., 1973-76. Fellow African Studies Assn., N.Y. Acad. Scis.; mem. Council Higher Ednl. Insts. N.Y.C. (dir. 1973-76), Bklyn. Instl. Council (trustee 1972—), Bklyn. C. of C. (dir. 1973-76), Alpha Kappa Delta. Author: The Status and Role of West African Women: A Study in Cultural Change, 1964. Home: 245 Clinton Av Brooklyn NY 11205

O'CONNOR, HELEN MARIE MURPHY, govt. ofcl.; b. Butler, Pa.; d. Thomas Michael and Helen Marie (Grant) Murphy; B.S., in Sci., Villa Maria Coll., 1938; m. Thomas B. O'Connor, Nov. 17, 1942 (dec. Apr. 1954). Teletype operator Calvert Distilling Co., Balt., 1939; receptionist, telephone, teletype operator Daugherty Refinery, Petrolia, Pa., 1940-42; legal sec. Carney, O'Connor & Carney, Erie, Pa., 1943-45; clk.-in-charge divisional office U.S. Dist. Ct., Erie, 1954—. Mem. Fed. Ct. Clk.'s Assn. (chmn. resolutions com.), Erie County Assn. Lawyers' Wives, Aux. Erie Maennerchor, Kappa Gamma Pi. Club: Zonta. Home: 210 W 6th St Erie PA 16507 Office: US Ct House Erie PA 16501

O'CONNOR, JEAN KATHERINE, pub. relations exec.; b. Chester, Pa., Aug. 7, 1936; d. Arthur D. and Margaret A. (Hawkins) O'Connor; B.A., Am. U., 1958. Account exec. Roy Blumenthal, pub. relations, N.Y.C., 1964; asso. Edward Thomas Assos., pub. relations, N.Y.C., 1964-67; v.p. Ruder & Finn, internat. pub. relations, N.Y.C., 1967—; dir. Woodstock Communications, Inc.; speaker, lectr. in field. Mem. Publicity Club N.Y. (media chmn. 1967-70), Theta Sigma Phi. Clubs: Jockey, Racquet, Palm Bay, La Gorce Country (Miami, Fla.); North Hempstead (N.Y.) Country. Home: 45 Sutton Pl S New York City NY 10022 Office: 110 E 59th St New York City NY 10022

O'CONNOR, JEAN SMITH (MRS. GERALD FRANCIS O'CONNOR), author; b. nr. Hamlin, W.Va.; d. Oscar French and Florence (Adkins) Smith; grad. W.Va. Bus. Coll.; m. Gerald Francis O'Connor, Aug. 3, 1929; children—Joan Florence (Mrs. Alfred James Dickerson, Jr.), Peggy Frances (Mrs. Lanny J. Pixley), Geraldine Phyllis (Mrs. Philip James Barrons). Mem. editorial staff Echoes of W.Va., Charleston, 1952-56; v.p., sec.-treas. Line Creek Coal Corp., Charleston, 1962-66. Mem. W.Va. Poetry Soc. (state pres. 1968-69), Poetry Soc. Va., Acad. Am. Poets (affiliate), Nat. League Am. Pen Women (state pres. 1964-66, nat. poetry chmn. 1970-72), Cath. Daus. Am., Huntington Poetry Guild. Democrat. Roman Catholic. Club: St. Agnes Garden. Author: The Quiet Hills, 1963. Home: Apt 4K Plaza E 4300 N Ocean Blvd Fort Lauderdale FL 33308

O'CONNOR, KATHERYN LUCILLE (MRS. MARIO S. CIOFFARI), physician; b. Providence, May 11, 1920; d. James W. and Rhea C. (Fillian) O'Connor; A.B., Brown U., 1942; M.D., Woman's Med. Coll. Pa., 1946; m. Thomas H. Chapman, July 13, 1947 (dec. 1966); 1 son, Michael John; m. 2d, Mario S. Cioffari, Aug. 14, 1969. Intern, Meth. Hosp., Phila., 1946-47, resident medicine, 1947-48; resident medicine Woman's Coll. Hosp., Phila., 1948-49, fellow medicine, 1950-51; resident medicine Herman Kiefer Hosp., Detroit, 1949-50, asst. dir. out-patient clinic, 1951-52; county med. examiner Wayne County (Mich.), 1952-59; pvt. practice medicine, specializing in internal medicine, Detroit, 1951—, Southfield, Mich., 1972—; staff physician Mt. Carmel Hosp., Detroit, 1951—, dir. diabetes clinic, 1970—; courtesy staff Sinai Hosp., Detroit, 1954—; instr. medicine Wayne U. Sch. Medicine, Detroit, 1955—. Mem. Am., Mich. (chmn. camp com. 1952-61, 70-72) diabetes assns., Am., Mich. heart assns., Woman's Med. Assn. Mich., Am., Mich., Wayne County med. assns., Assn. Internal Medicine, Sigma Xi, Zeta Phi. Home: 345 Arlington Rd Birmingham MI 48009 Office: 20411 W 12 Mile Rd Southfield MI 48076

O'CONNOR, SISTER MARY CONSOLATA, coll. pres.; b. Waterbury, Conn.; d. John Joseph and Nora (Perkinson) O'Connor; B.A., St. Joseph Coll., 1939; M.A., Cath. U. Am., 1951, Ph.D., 1955. Tchr. St. Peter's Sch., Hartford, Conn., 1942-46, Cathedral Sch., Hartford, 1946-50; tchr. St. Joseph Coll., West Hartford, Conn., 1954-67, dean students, 1954-58, acad. dean, 1958-69, pres., 1969—. Mem. exec. com. Conn. Council Higher Edn., 1971—, v.p., 1973—; sec. Greater Hartford Consortium for Higher Edn., 1972—. Trustee Soc. for Savs. Mem. Am., New Eng. hist. assns., Nat. Catholic Edn. Assn. (mem. exec. com. New Eng. unit). Home and office: 1678 Asylum Av West Hartford CT 06117

O'CONNOR, MARY SCRANTON, advt. agy. exec.; b. New Haven, May 9, 1942; d. James Thomas and Mary Elizabeth (Scranton) O'Connor; B.A., Manhattanville Coll., 1964. Reporter Hartford (Conn.) Times, 1964-65, women's editor, 1965-68; pub. relations account exec. Wilson, Haight & Welch, Inc., Hartford, 1968-71, mgr. pub. relations, 1971-72, v.p., dir. pub. relations, 1972—. Pub. relations adv. com. Greater Hartford chpt. A.R.C., 1968-70; mem. community relations task force Greater Hartford Voluntary Action Center, 1971—. Mem. Pub. Relations Soc. Am. (chpt. membership chmn. 1972), St. Joseph Acad. Alumnae (publicity chmn. 1969-71). Home: 221 Main St Farmington CT 06032 Office: Wilson Haight & Welch Inc 100 Constitution Plaza Hartford CT 06103

O'CONNOR, MAUREEN FRANCES, city councilwoman; b. San Diego, July 14, 1946; d. Jerome J. and Frances Mary (Shinnick) O'Connor; B.A. in Psychology, San Diego State Coll., 1969. Tchr., counselor Rosary High Sch., San Diego, 1969-72; mem. San Diego City Council, 1971—. Hon. co-chmn. Cystic Fibrosis Found., 1972; chmn. Community Service Club San Diego, 1970-72. Exec. bd. Muscular Dystrophy Assn., 1960—. Recipient Citation of Merit, Muscular Dystrophy Assn. Am., 1964-72. Home: 5015 Santa Cruz St San Diego CA 92106 Office: City Hall 202 C St San Diego CA 92101

O'CONNOR, OLLIE MAE GRAY (MRS. DONALD R. O'CONNOR), educator; b. Iuka, Miss., Nov. 1, 1916; d. Timothy B. and Ollie Edna (Heagerty) Gray; B.S., Millsaps Coll., 1939; M.A., Cal. State U. at Long Beach, 1968, postgrad. at Arcata, 1972; postgrad. U. Cal. at Los Angeles, 1969-72, at Santa Barbara, 1973, U. Utah, 1971; m. Donald R. O'Connor, June 9, 1942; children—B. Patrick, Kathleen (Mrs. Joel Blumhagen), Sheila (Mrs. Ira Chaffin). Tchr. math. secondary schs., Miss., 1939-42; instr. math., physics East Central Coll., Decatur, Miss., 1942-43; tchr. math., sci. Las Vegas, Nev., 1953-59, Claremont, Cal., 1959-65, Long Beach, 1965—. Active Girl Scouts U.S.A., 1960-65, United Fund, 1955-65. Recipient Pan-Hellenic award, Outstanding Woman Grad., Millsaps Coll., 1939; Flower Arranging award Las Vegas Garden Club, 1957-59; Original Clothing Design award, Cal. Sewing Group, 1965. Mem. Tchrs. Assn. Long Beach (sec. polit. action com. 1971-74), Cal. Tchrs. Assn., N.E.A., Nat. Council Tchrs. Math., Am. Assn. U. Women, Am. Assn. UN, Federated Women's Clubs, Women's Soc. Christian Service (hon. life). Methodist (hon. pres. women's club 1973). Home: 5532 Ravia St Lakewood CA 90713 Office: 1830 W Columbia St Long Beach CA 90810

O'CONNOR, ROSA (MRS. GERALD JEREMIAH O'CONNOR), writer; b. Clarksburg, W.Va., Aug. 30, 1918; d. Steve and Susan (Pastor) Huger; A.B., Salem Coll., 1940; M.S. (fellow), Northwestern U., 1945; m. Gerald Jeremiah O'Connor, Apr. 25, 1959. Research writer, opinion polls Oral Hygiene Mag., Evanston, Ill., 1943-44; asst. editor CAL Mag., Chgo., 1945-53; writer, publicity, promotion Regina Travel Bur., Chgo., 1956; free lance writer 1956—. Tchr. Chgo. Pub. Schs., 1956-64; owner/writer Chgo. Tchrs. Rev. Sch., 1959-61. Recipient Distinguished Service award Women in Communications, 1971. Mem. Women in Communications, Chgo. Press Club, Third Dist. Literary Forum, Salem Coll. Alumni Assn. of Chgo. (pres. 1961-74). Roman Catholic. Clubs: Chicago Press, Hungarian, Northwestern (Chgo.). Home: 201 E Walton Pl Chicago IL 60611

O'CONNOR, SANDRA ANN FURTICK (MRS. ROBERT EMMETT O'CONNOR), lawyer; b. Louisville, Feb. 4, 1943; d. Robert Wade and Cleo Charleen (Romines) Furtick; A.B., Ind. U., 1964, LL.B., 1966, J.D., 1967; m. Robert Emmett O'Connor, July 13, 1968; children—Kelly Ann, Robert Wade. Tax and ins. mgr. McCormick & Co., Inc., 1966-67; admitted to Md. bar, 1967, since practiced in Balt.; asst. state's atty., trial capt., Balt., 1967-71, chief felony div. States Atty's. Office, Balt., 1971-74; fed. pub. defender for Md., 1974—. Bd. dirs., mem. exec. com. Jr. Achievement. Recipient nat. citation V.F.W., 1974. Mem. Am., Md. bar assns., Nat. Dist. Attys. Assn. (mem. legislative com. 1972-74), Ind. U. Alumni Assn., Delta Delta Delta. Clubs: Country, Rolling Road Country (Balt.). Home: 1907 Tadcaster Rd Baltimore MD 21228 Office: 204 Court House Baltimore MD 21202

O'CONNOR, SANDRA DAY (MRS. JOHN J. O'CONNOR III), state senator; b. El Paso, Tex., Mar. 26, 1930; d. Harry A. and Ada Mae (Wilkey) Day; B.A. with great distinction, Stanford, 1950, LL.B., 1952; m. John Jay O'Connor, III, Dec. 20, 1952; children—Scott, Brian, Jay. Admitted to Cal. bar, 1952, Ariz. bar, 1957; dep. county atty. San Mateo County, Cal., 1952-53; civilian atty. Quartermaster Market Center, Frankfurt/Main, West Germany, 1954-57; pvt. practice, Maryvale, Ariz., 1959-60; adminstrv. asst. Ariz. State Hosp., 1965; asst. atty. gen. Ariz., 1965-69; mem. Ariz. Senate, 1969—; mem. Legislative Council, 1969—; chmn. State, County and Municipal Affairs Com., 1970-71; mem. Probate Code Revision Com., 1970-72; mem. Ariz. Adv. Council on Intergovernmental Relations, 1970—. Dir. First Nat. Bank Ariz. Pres. Jr. League Phoenix, 1965-66; mem. Maricopa County Juvenile Ct. Study Com., 1968-69; mem. Ariz. Personnel Commn., 1968-69; mem. Gov.'s Com. on Mental Health, 1964—; mem. Gov.'s Com. on Marriage and Family Problems, 1961-62; mem. Maricopa County Bd. Adjustments and Appeals, 1961. Bd. dirs., sec., mem. exec. com. Ariz. Acad.; bd. dirs. Golden Gate Settlement, 1960-62; trustee Phoenix Country Day Sch., 1969-70; v.p., trustee Heard Mus. Mem. Maricopa County Bar Assn. (chmn. lawyer's referral plan 1964-65), State Bar Ariz., State Bar Cal., Order of Coif. Home: 3651 E Denton Lane Paradise Valley AZ 85253 Office: Ariz State Senate Capitol Bldg Phoenix AZ 85007

ODA, MARGARET KURISU (MRS. GLENN K. ODA), educator; b. Wailea, Hakalau, Hawaii, Mar. 26, 1925; d. Satoru and Satoyo (Kurisu) Kurisu; B.S., U. Hawaii, 1947, counselors certificate, 1954, vice prin. certificate, 1957, prin. certificate, 1962, adminstr.'s certificate, 1967; M.A., Mich. State U., 1950; m. Glenn K. Oda, Jan. 25, 1947; 1 dau., Marjorie A. S. Instr. Mich. State U., 1947; counselor Hilo (Hawaii) Intermediate Sch., 1951-53, 54-57, vice prin., 1957-64; tchr. Northeastern Jr. High Sch., Kalamazoo, 1953-54; instr. theory of math. U. Hawaii, 1963; prin. Hakalau-Honomu-Pepeekeo Sch., 1964-65; curriculum specialist secondary edn. Leeward Dist. Dept. Edn., 1965-66; dir. elementary edn. Dept. Edn., Hawaii, 1967-68, dir. gen. edn., 1968—. Mem. Hawaii County Children and Youth Com., 1960-64, sec., 1962-64; instr. Hilo Hongwanggi Tchr. Tng. Class, 1960-65. Yale Center for Edn. fellow, 1973. Mem. Nat. Assn. Secondary Sch. Prins., Nat. Assn. Sch. Adminstrs. Assn. Supervision and Curriculum Devel., N.E.A., Pi Mu Epsilon. Home: 1088 Waiholo St Honolulu HI 98621 Office: PO Box 2360 Honolulu HI 96803

O'DANIEL, MARY KATHLEEN, occupational therapist; b. Evansville, Ind., Nov. 1, 1937; d. Bernard Melvin and Elizabeth Margaret (Brune) O'Daniel; B.A., St. Mary-of-the-Woods Coll., 1961; postgrad. (NSF grantee) Holy Cross Coll., 1966, Ball State U., 1973—; B.S., in Occupational Therapy with highest honors, Ind. U., 1971. Mem. Order Sisters of Providence 1956-69; tchr., St. John the Bapt. Grade Sch., Ft. Wayne, Ind., 1961-63, Cheverus High Sch., Malden, Mass., 1963-67, Washington (Ind.) Cath. High Sch., 1967-69; occupational therapist Community Hosp., Indpls., 1971-73, La Rue D. Carter Hosp., 1973—. Instr., Ind. U., Bloomington, 1972. Mem. Am., Ind. (placement chmn. 1973—) occupational therapy assns. Home: 2514 E 17th St Indianapolis IN 46218 Office: 1315 W 10th St Indianapolis IN 46202

O'DAY, MARIE ESTELLE (MRS. MARCUS D. O'DAY), librarian; b. Portland, Ore., Apr. 21, 1911; d. Anthony John and Alice Estella (Morrow) Parenti; B.A., Reed Coll., 1938; M.A., Simmons Coll., 1966; m. Marcus Driver O'Day, June 23, 1935 (dec. 1961); children—Jane Antoinette (Mrs. Gordon Doerfer), Marcia Dianne (Mrs. Stuart Landau). Library asst. Hanscom Air Force Library, Bedford, Mass., 1962; with Robbins Library, Arlington, Mass., 1962—, readers adviser, 1962-64, librarian Young Adults Dept., 1964—; book reviewer Arlington Advocate and for local radio, 1968—. Mem. A.L.A. (book selection com., materials com. 1971—), Mass. Library Assn. (membership com. 1965), Young Adult Coop. Book Rev. Group (steering com. 1970—). Baptist (missionary soc. pres. 1955-57). Editor (with Emily Cross) Young Adult Cooperative Book Review Group of Mass., 1970—. Home: 642 Pleasant St Belmont MA 02178 Office: 700 Massachusetts Av Arlington MA 02174

ODDEN, CONSTANCE (ODELLE), scientist, educator; b. Osage, Ia.; d. Hans Andreas and Olena C. (Maakestad) Odden; B.A. in Chemistry, St. Olaf Coll., 1927; M.S. in Bacteriology, U. Ia., 1940. Tchr. pub. schs., Bellingham, Minn., 1927-29; med. technologist to physicians, Mpls., 1930-37; research fellow Ia. U., 1938-40; bacteriologist Minn. Dept. Health, Mpls., 1940-58; chief bacteriologist, Duluth, 1943-46; instr. Mankato State Coll., 1958-61, asst. prof. microbiology, 1962—, coordinator allied health programs, 1968—. Am. Scandinavian Found. fellow to Danish Serum Inst., 1950-51. Fellow A.A.A.S., Am. Pub. Health Assn.; mem. Henrici Soc. for Microbiologists, Am. Soc. for Microbiology, Am. Assn. U. Women, Minn. Acad. Sci., N.E.A., Royal Soc. Health, Sigma Delta Epsilon. Lutheran. Research in field. Home: 518 S 4th St Mankato MN 56001

ODDO, GENEVIEVE FILOMENA (MRS. PAUL C. ODDO), pub. co. exec.; b. Bklyn., Apr. 14, 1917; d. Alfred and Celeste (Quadrino) Grillo; student Bklyn. Mus. Sch. Settlement, 1947-52; m. Paul C. Oddo, Dec. 7, 1946; children—Paul C., Charles Warren, Warren Alfred. Exec. sec. Firmenich & Co., N.Y.C., 1940-46; mng. editor Oddo Pub. Co., Fayetteville, Ga., 1964—, now also exec. v.p. Recipient Bronze medal Roosevelt Meml. Spanish Tchrs. Assn., N.Y.C., 1934. Mem. A.L.A., Am. Booksellers Assn. Club: Flat Creek Country. Home: PO Box 68 Beauregard Blvd Fayetteville GA 30214 Office: Storybook Acres Box 68 Fayetteville GA 30214

O'DEA, MARIE, advt. exec.; b. Norfolk, Va., Nov. 12, 1900; d. Nicholas Francis and Nora (Tyers) O'Dea; student Johns Hopkins, 1919-20; A.B., George Washington U., 1923, M.A., 1923; postgrad. Columbia, 1926. Lab. asst. U.S. Dept. Agr., Washington, 1918-19; chemist Balt. Butterine Co., 1919-20, sales promotion mgr., corporate sec., 1926-34; instr. chemistry George Washington U., 1923-26; partner O'Dea Co., 1934-36; sales promotion mgr. Rennert Hotel, Balt., 1936-37; free-lance writer, 1937-40; asso. editor Herald-Argus weekly paper, Catonsville, Md., 1940-43, editor, 1943-65, asso. editor Catonsville Times & Herald-Argus, 1966-70; advt. mgr. Charles A. Skirven, Inc., realtor, Balt., 1967—. Mem. Md. Gov.'s Juvenile Delinquency Commn., 1940; founder Catonsville Fourth July celebrations, 1947; mem. Catonsville Sr. High Park Project; mem. publicity com. Balt. A.R.C. Mem. Nat. League Am. Pen Women (pres. br. 1972-74), George Washington U. Alumni Assn., Iota Sigma Chi, Phi Mu, Pi Delta Epsilon. Democrat. Roman Catholic. Clubs: Soroptimist (charter pres. br. 1951-53), Women's Advertising (pres. 1933-34). Home: 906 Frederick Rd Catonsville Baltimore MD 21228 Office: 700 Frederick Rd Catonsville Baltimore MD 21228

ODELL, JOAN ELIZABETH, lawyer; b. Jo Davies County, Ill., May 3, 1932; d. Peter Emerson and Olive Isabelle (Bonnet) Odell; A.B. cum laude, U. Miami, Fla., 1956, J.D., 1958. children—Dominique Rosalyn, Nicole Laurienne (adopted). Admitted to Fla. bar, 1958, trial atty. U.S. SEC, 1959-60; asst. state atty., Dade County, Fla., 1960-64; asst. county atty., Dade County, 1964-70; county atty., Palm Beach County, Fla., 1970-71; regional counsel U.S. Environmental Protection Agy., Region IV, Atlanta, 1971-73; asso. gen. counsel U.S. Environmental Protection Agy. Washington, 1973—. Bd. dirs. Mental Health Assn. Palm Beach County. Named Outstanding Young Woman in Am., 1965. Mem. Fed., Fla., Dade County, Palm Beach County bar assns., Nat. Assn. County Civil Attys. (sec.-treas.), Fla. Assn. County Attys. (dir.), Am. Assn. U. Women. Home: 2539 S Bayshore Dr Miami FL 33133 Office: Waterside Mall 401 M St SW Washington DC 20460

ODELL, LOIS DOROTHEA, biologist, educator; b. Watertown, N.Y., Sept. 25, 1915; d. Joseph Davis and Pearl Lois (Rees) Odell; A.B., State U. N.Y., Albany, 1940; M.A., Cornell U., 1945, Ph.D.,

1951; postgrad. Syracuse U., 1946-47. Tchr. pub. schs., Washingtonville and Altmar, N.Y., 1941-43; teaching asst. biology Cornell U., Ithaca, N.Y., 1943-47; faculty Towson (Md.) State Coll., 1947—, prof. biology, 1962—. Environmental cons. Md. Wildlands Com., 1971—; organizer Nature Mus. of Cylburn Park, Balt., 1961, bd. dirs., 1961-70. Mem. A.A.A.S., Md. Acad. Scis., Natural History Soc. Md., Md. Ornithol. Soc., Cylburn Wildflower Preserve and Garden Center Orgn., Pi Lambda Theta, Phi Kappa Phi, Sigma Delta Epsilon. Home: 76 Cedar Av Towson MD 21204

O'DELL, LYNN MARIE LUEGGE (MRS. NORMAN D. O'DELL), librarian; b. Berwyn, Ill. Feb. 24, 1938; d. George Emil and Helen Marie (Pesek) Luegge; student Lyons Township Jr. Coll., La Grange, Ill., 1957; student N. Ill. U., Elgin Community Coll., U. Ill.; m. Norman D. O'Dell, Dec. 14, 1957; children—Jeffrey, Jerry. Sec. Martin Co., Chgo., 1957-59; librarian, Carol Stream (Ill.) Pub. Library, 1964—. Exec. com. Du Page County Library System, 1967, 68, 71—. Active Carol Stream unit Central DuPage Hosp. Aux. Named Woman of Year, Wheaton Bus. and Profl. Woman's Club, 1968. Mem. A.L.A., Ill. Library Assn. Club: Carol Stream Woman's (sec. 1968, 1st v.p. 1969). Lutheran (organist). Home: 182 Yuma Lane Carol Stream IL 60187 Office: 397 Blackhawk Dr Carol Stream IL 60187

ODETTA, folk singer, actress; b. Birmingham, Ala., Dec. 31, 1930; d. Reuben and Flora (Sanders) Holmes; music student Los Angeles City Coll.; m. Dan Gordon, May 1, 1959. Mem. chorus Finian's Rainbow, 1949, then on tour, San Francisco; folk singer (nightclubs) Tin Angel, San Francisco, Blue Angel, N.Y.C., Gate of Horn, Chgo., (film) Cinerama Holiday; appeared in concert engagements in U.S. and Can., including Chgo., Boston, Toronto, Vancouver, Town Hall, N.Y.C., 1959; TV spls. Tonight with Belafonte, 1959, Parable in the Park, 1960; recital Carnegie Hall, N.Y.C., 1960; featured singer Newport (R.I.) Folk Festival, 1960; motion picture appearance in Sanctuary, 1960; recording artist for Tradition Records, Vanguard, Active various fund raising drives. Recipient Sylvania award, 1959. Mem. Am. Fedn. Musicians, Am. Guild Variety Artists. Conglist.

ODLAND, LURA M(AE), coll. dean; b. Morgantown, W.Va., Nov. 22, 1921; d. Theodore E. and R. Elizabeth (Aamodt) Odland; B.S., U. R.I., 1943, D.Sc., 1970; M.S., U. Conn., 1945; Ph.D. (fellow 1947-50) U. Wis., 1950. Inst. foods and nutrition U. Conn., 1945; nutritionist com. on food composition, food and nutrition bd., NRC, 1945-47; asst. U. Wis., 1947-50; asso. prof. Mont. State Coll. and Agrl. Expt. Sta., 1950-55; adminstr. State Expt. Stas. div. U.S. Dept. Agr., Washington, 1955-59; dean Coll. Home Econs., U. Tenn., 1959—, dir. home sci. under ICA in India, 1959-62. Rep. of U.S. Dept. Agr. to Internat. Congress of Nutrition, 1957, 1966. Fellow A.A.A.S., Am. Pub. Health Assn.; mem. Am. Inst. Nutrition, Am. Chem. Soc., Am. Home Econs. Assn., Tenn. Edn. Assn., Am. Dietetic Assn., Tenn. Home Econs. Assn. (pres. 1964-66), Inst. Food Technologists, Sigma Xi (chpt. pres. 1965-66), Phi Kappa Phi, Omicron Nu. Author numerous tech. publs. Office: Coll Home Econs U Tenn Knoxville TN 37916

ODOM, CLAUDIA ALICE BEACH (MRS. TROY JOHNSTON ODOM), social worker; b. Little Rock, Nov. 28, 1913; d. Ernest Edward and Sara Alice (Tanner) Beach; B.A., Tex. Woman's U., 1935; M.S.W., Tulane U., 1940, M.P.H., Sch. Medicine, 1968; m. Sylvain Clement Bouche, Sept. 2, 1938 (dec. Dec. 1942); m. 2d, Robert L. Pye, June 24, 1944 (div. 1950); m. 3d, Troy Johnston Odom, Aug. 2, 1957. Intern med. social work Michael Reese Hosp., Chgo., 1936; social case worker Orleans Parish Dept. Pub. Welfare, 1936-40; med. social worker New Orleans Charity Hosp., 1941-44; med. social cons. La. vocational rehab. div. La. Dept. Edn., 1944-45; hosp. service case supr. Am. Nat. Red Cross, 1946; med. social worker, instr. Tulane U. Sch. Medicine, New Orleans, 1947-67, asst. prof., 1967—, asst. prof. Sch. Pub. Health and Tropical Medicine, 1967-73, asso. prof., 1973—, chmn. alumni activities, also coordinator Sch. Pub. Health and med. alumni, 1967—, cons. Sch. Social Work, 1962-64. Cons. VA Hosp., New Orleans, 1961; pres. temporary inter-assn. council all social work assns., New Orleans, 1954-55. Co-ordinator Tulane U. Alumni Fund drive, 1963-66, recipient plaque, 1964; charter mem., bd. dir. Met. New Orleans Council on Aging, 1965-73; corporate mem. New Orleans Area Health Planning Council, 1968; mem. Mayor's Task Force on Aging, 1971-72; adv. bd. Golden Age Home Care. Recipient Am. Cancer Soc. award, 1965, Heart Assn. award, 1954, Nat. Assn. Social Workers award, 1966. Mem. Am. (charter; mem. exec. bd. social work sect. 1970—, pres. elect 1973-74), La. (charter) pub. health assns., Nat. Assn. Social Workers (charter mem.; pres. med. social work sect. 1961-69, chpt. pres. 1957-59, nat. del. 1960-61, mem. nat. com. on regional inst. programs, chmn. regional inst. program subcom. on publs.; co-chmn. So. regional inst. 1971, bd. dirs. 1972—), Acad. Certified Social Workers (charter mem.). Am. Assn. Med. Social Workers (inst. chmn. 1955), Am. Assn. U. Profs., Assn. Am. Med. Colls., Nat. Rehab. Assn., La. Tb and Respiratory Disease Assn., La. Conf. Social Welfare, Tulane Med. Internat. Club (treas. 1964-65), La. Assn. for Mental Health. Co-designer course for sr. med. students Tulane Med. Sch. Home: 711 Bourbon St New Orleans LA 70116 Office: 1430 Tulane Av New Orlens LA 70112

ODOM, ELLEN PAYNE ODOM (MRS. JAMES M. ODOM), civic worker; b. Blossburg, Ala., July 5, 1906; d. Turner Ashby and Annie Ellen (Ancell) Payne; A.B. summa cum laude, Judson Coll., 1923-26; M.A., U. Ala., 1931; B.S., Howard Coll., 1932; m. James Malcolm Odom, Aug. 25, 1935. Tchr. French, Spanish, Italian, Judson Coll., 1926-30; U. Ala., 1930-31; head dept. romance langs. Norman Coll., Norman Park, Ga., 1933-35. Chmn. Colquitt County March of Dimes, 1953; sec. Colquitt County Civic Music Asns., 1959-65; mem. adv. bd. Ga. Extension Service, 1957-63; dir. Ga. Tb Assn., mem. exec. com., 1963-66, sec., 1965-66; trustee Colquit-Thomas Regional Library, 1963-71, mem. regional bd. of trustees, 1964-71; bd. dirs. Moultrie YMCA; pres. Colquitt County Tb Assn., 1961-62; adviser 4-H Club, 1936—, state adviser 1961-62. Mem. 2d Congl. Dist. Dem. Exec. Com., 1965-66. Recipient Colquitt County Woman of Year, 1961. Mem. Friends of Library, League Woman Voters, U.D.C. (parliamentarian Ga. div. 1958—, exec. bd., 1948—, v.p. 1968-70), Huguenots (nat. corr. sec. 1948-49), D.A.R. Club: Woman's (pres. 1957-58). Author: A History of the Library of Moultrie, Ga., 1966. Home: Odomfarms RFD 5 Moultrie GA 31768

ODOM, SUSAN ANNETTE GREGG (MRS. BENJAMIN SCOTT ODOM), physician; b. Chgo., Jan. 13, 1944; d. Ashley Mandle and Rose (Matoush) Gregg; B.S., U. Ida., 1964; M.D., Washington U., St. Louis, 1968; m. Benjamin Scott Odom, June 21, 1969. Intern pediatrics Children's Hosp., Los Angeles, 1968-69; resident pediatrics St. Louis Children's Hosp., 1969-70; chief resident pediatrics St. Joseph's Hosp., Phoenix, 1970-71; head. pediatric residency program Ariz. State Crippled Children's Hosp., Phoenix, 1971—. Mem. Phi Kappa Phi, Pi Beta Phi. Home: 10815 N 45th Pl Phoenix AZ 85028 Office: 200 N Curry Rd Tempe AZ 85281

O'DONNELL, SISTER ANNE COLUMBA, educator; b. Bklyn., Jan. 7, 1922; d. Charles and Margaret (Doherty) O'Donnell; B.A., Manhattan Coll., 1950; M.A., St. Johns U., 1957; postgrad. Cath. U., 1953, Columbia, 1965. Tchr., Cath. schs., Bklyn., 1941-56; tchr. Latin, Mary Louis Acad., Jamaica, N.Y., 1956-59; itinerant tchr. visually handicapped children Cath. Schs., Bklyn. and Queens, 1959-62, coordinator itinerant program for visually handicapped, 1962—. Mem. Am. Fedn. Cath. Workers for Blind (dir. 1966-70), N.Y. State Fedn. Workers for Blind (dir. 1963-69), Nat. Cath. Edn. Assn. (sec. 1972-74), Assn. for Edn. Visually Handicapped, Nat. Aid to Visually Handicapped, Nat. Braille Assn. (dir. 1969-74, v.p. 1974—), Council for Exceptional Children, Council for Edn. Partially Seeing, Council Adminstrs. Spl. Edn. Home: 137-21 Brookville Blvd Rosedale NY 11422 Office: 345 Adams St Brooklyn NY 11201

O'DONNELL, SISTER MIRIAM TERESA, educator; b. Bronx, N.Y.; d. Jeremiah and Ita (Ryan) O'Donnell; B.A., Hunter Coll., 1937; M.A., Columbia, 1956; L.H.D., Loyola Coll., 1973. Joined Order of Sisters of Mercy of the Union, 1942; statis. clk. Western Electric Co., N.Y.C., 1937-42; tchr. St. Mary High Sch., Wilkes-Barre, Pa., 1944-55; tchr., chmn. dept. math. Coll. Misericordia, Dallas, Pa., 1955-64, pres., 1964-66, 1967—; provincial councilor Sisters of Mercy, Scranton Province, 1963-66; asst. provincial, 1966-70. Chmn. Northeastern Pa. Ind. Colls., 1969-70. Bd. dirs., mem. exec. com. Commn. Ind. Colls. and Univs., Pa. Assn. Colls. and Univs., 1971-74. Mem. Am. Assn. Physics Tchrs., Math. Assn. Am. Address: College Misericordia Dallas PA 18612

O'DONNELL, RUTH MIKELL, univ. ofcl.; b. Billings, Mont., Apr. 29, 1941; d. Gustave Roeser and Ruth Marian (Fritzen) O'Donnell; B.A., U. Colo., 1963; Ph.D., U. Md., 1973. Asso. dir. judiciary office U. Md., College Park, 1967-70; dean women Ida. State U., Pocatello, 1970-72; asso. dean students Ia. State U., Ames, 1973—. Mem. Ida. Commn. on Women's Programs, 1970-72. Mem. Nat. Assn. Women Deans, Adminstrs. and Counselors, Nat. Assn. Student Personnel Adminstrs., Am. Assn. Higher Edn. Home: 4329 Lincoln Swing Apt 27 Ames IA 50010

ODOR, DOROTHY LOUISE, educator, anatomist; b. Washington, May 25, 1922; d. Edbert Franklin and Onie (Wrenn) Odor; B.A., cum laude, Am. U., 1945; M.S., U. Rochester (N.Y.), 1948, Ph.D., 1950. Instr. dept. anatomy Sch. Medicine U. Wash. 1950-56; asst. prof. dept. anatomy Sch. Medicine U. Fla., 1956-60, asso. prof., 1960-61; asst. prof. dept. anatomy Bowman Gray Sch. Medicine, Winston-Salem, N.C., 1961-65, asso. prof., 1965-69; asso. prof. Med. Coll. Va., Commonwealth U., Richmond, 1969-73, prof., 1973—. Mem. Am. Assn. Anatomists, Am. Soc. Cell Biology, A.A.A.S., Soc. for Study Reprodn., Am. Inst. Biol. Scis., So. Soc. Anatomists, Reticuloendothial Soc., Va. Acad. Scis., N.Y. Acad. Sci., Am. Assn. U. Profs., Sigma Xi. Republican. Baptist. Club: Pilot. Contbr. articles to profl. jours. Home: 8704 Queensmere Pl Richmond VA 23229

O'DRISCOLL, MARGARET MILLAR (MRS. JAMES O'DRISCOLL), real estate broker; b. Hollywood, Cal., Aug. 2, 1925; d. Russell Hartney and Marion Scott (Macarthur) Millar; student U. Cal. at Los Angeles, 1942-44; children—William Russell Walker, Elizabeth Howland (Mrs. John Flint Locke), Hiram Scott Walker; m. 2d, James O'Driscoll, Oct. 17, 1970. Salesman, Carol Smart Real Estate, Del Mar, Cal., 1966-68, Bernard & Asso., Solana Beach, Cal., 1968-70; owner Town and Country Real Estate, Rancho Santa Fe, Cal., 1970—; pres. Peggy O'Driscoll Enterprises, Inc. Mem. publicity com. Rancho Santa Fe Republican Women, 1950-58. Clubs: Rancho Santa Fe Garden (publicity chmn. 1965-74), Rancho Santa Fe Women's Golf (founding mem.). Home: PO Box 457 Rancho Santa Fe CA 92067 Office: PO Box 44 Rancho Santa Fe CA 92067

ODZIOMEK, CECILIA MARIE, advt. agy. exec.; b. Chgo., Sept. 21, 1929; d. John and Mary (Minkalis) Odziomek; student Northwestern U., 1953-56. With Compton Advt., Inc., Chgo., 1950-71, v.p., 1965-71, asso. media dir., 1968-71; v.p., media dir. Arthur & Wheeler, Inc., Chgo., 1971—. Mem. Am. Women in Radio and TV (chpt. v.p. 1973-74). Home: 6222 N LeMai St Chicago IL 60646 Office: 166 E Superior St Chicago IL 60611

OEFINGER, MYRTLE OEFINGER (MRS. ROY D. OEFINGER), editor; b. San Antonio, Apr. 7, 1917; d. Barney Roy and Mamie (Perrin) Heath; student Westmoorland Coll., 1935, Milam Secretarial Sch., 1936; m. Roy Donald Oefinger, Dec. 7, 1937 (dec. Oct. 1949); children—Janet Frances, Roy Donald, Cheryl Ann. Sec. Frost Nat. Bank, 1936-39, 50-53; staff writer San Antonio Express and News, 1953-54, sch. editor, 1954-55, women's editor, 1955—. Bd. mgrs. N.W. br. YMCA. Recipient 1st pl. award Tex. woman's div. Associated Press Managing Editors Assn., 1958, 62, 66; Headliner award Theta Sigma Phi, 1963. Mem. S.W. Research Found. Forum, Women's Soc. Christian Service (life), Theta Sigma Phi (past pres.). Methodist. Mem. Order Eastern Star. Club: Zonta. Home: 918 Alexander Hamilton Dr San Antonio TX 78228 Office: Av E and 3d Sts San Antonio TX 78206

OEHLER, NELLIE JOAN (MRS. DENNIS ELMER OEHLER), county extension agt.; b. Coos Bay, Ore., June 30, 1942; d. Henry and Alida Margaretha (DeHaan) VanCalcar; B.S., Ore. State U., 1964; m. Dennis Elmer Oehler, Aug. 14, 1971. Del., Internat. Farm Youth Exchange to Jamaica, 1964-65; county extension agt. Linn and Benton counties (Ore.), 1965—; asst. prof. home econs. Ore. Sate U., Corvallis, 1971—; mem. State Foods and Nutrition Extension Devel. Com., 1970-72, State Internat. Devel. Com., State Judges Tng. Sch. Com., 1969—, State Extension Youth Agts. Tng. Com., 1973—, State Extension Nutrition Edn. Com., 1973—. Chmn. dist. 4 Gov.'s Commn. on Children and Youth, 1970—; youth com. Linn County chpt. A.R.C., 1971-72; mem. adv. council Ore. State U. Sch. Home Econs., 1969-71. Mem. Ore. Assn. Extension Home Economists (treas., 1968-69), Am., Ore. home econs. assns., Nat. Assn. Extension Home Economists, Ore. Nutrition Council, Nat., Ore. Intern. farm youth exchange (pres. Ore., 1968-69), Ore. Extension Assn., Morning Star Grange, Ore. State U. Home Econs. Alumni Assn. (treas. 1971-72). Clubs: Yamhill County Jersey Cattle; State Jersey Cattle Ore. Contbr. articles to bulletins in field. Home: 839 W 4th St Albany OR 97321 Office: PO Box 765 Albany OR 97321

OEHLHAFFEN, CAROL ANN, educator; b. Benton Harbor, Mich., Jan. 5, 1939; d. Nelson John and Marie Elizabeth (Rupp) Oehlhaffen; student Nazareth Coll., 1957-58; B.S., Western Mich. U., 1962, M.A., 1966. Occupational therapist Marion County Gen. Hosp., Indpls., 1962-63; occupational therapist Bronson Hosp., Kalamazoo, 1963; tchr. spl. edn. Ann J. Kellogg Sch., Battle Creek, 1966-70, Howe Orthopedic Sch., Green Bay, Wis., 1970—. Mem. Am., Wis. occupational therapy assns., Nat., Wis., Green Bay edn. assns. Home: 1077 Raleigh St Green Bay WI 54304 Office: 1567 Deckner Av Green Bay WI 54301

OELRICH, MARGARET HAZEL MALMBORG (MRS. CARL M. OELRICH), hosp. adminstr.; b. Chgo., Jan. 28, 1927; d. Paul A. and Myrtle E. (Matson) Malmborg; student Wheaton Coll., 1945-46; B.S., Western Mich. U., 1949; m. Carl M. Oelrich, Oct. 22, 1949; 1 son, Paul. Asst. dir. occupational therapy North Shore Health Resort, Winnetka, Ill., 1949; staff occupational therapist Kalamazoo (Mich.) State Hosp., 1950; staff occupational therapist Pacific State Hosp., Pomona, Cal., 1953-55, coordinator vol. services, 1955-60; dir. occupational therapy City of Hope Med. Center, Duarte, Cal., 1960-72, dir. rehab., 1972—, coordinator home health service, 1971—. Lectr. Los Angeles City Coll., 1968—, Pasadena (Cal.) City Coll., 1971-72, Cal. Nursing Schs., Los Angeles, 1972; clin. asso. occupational therapy dept. Sargent Coll. Allied Health Professions, Boston U. Recipient Pres. Citation, City of Hope, 1971. Mem. Am. Arbitration Assn. (mem. nat. panel 1969—), Cal. State Personnel Bd. (mem. panel of interviewers 1969), Am., So. Cal. occupational therapy assns., So., Cal., San Jose schs. councils, Los Angeles Western Alumni Assn. (dir. 1969—). Home: 800 W 1st St Apt 1405 Los Angeles CA 90012 Office: 1500 E Duarte Rd Duarte CA 91010

OELS, HELEN CLAIRE, physician; b. Phila., Apr. 13, 1931; d. Ernest Joseph and Helen Claire (Murphy) Oels; B.S. magna cum laude, Chestnut Hill Coll., 1953; M.D. magna cum laude, Med. Coll. Pa., 1957; Ph.D., Mayo Grad. Sch. Medicine, U. Minn., 1970. Intern, Phila. Gen. Hosp., 1957-58; resident in pathology Harlan Meml. Hosp., 1961-63, Mayo Grad. Sch. Medicine, 1963-69; pvt. practice medicine, specializing in gen. practice, Whitesburg, Ky., 1960-61; fellow, resident pathology Mayo Clinic, Rochester, Minn., 1963-69; asso. prof. microbiology and immunology Temple U. Med. Sch., Phila., 1969—, asst. prof. pathology, 1969—. NIH postdoctoral fellow, 1958-60; recipient Career Devel. award NIH, 1971—; NIH grantee, 1970-73. Diplomate Am. Bd. Pathology Mem. A.M.A., Pa., Philadelphia County med. socs., Coll. Physicians of Phila., Am. Soc. Clin. Pathologists, Phila. Pathology Soc., Am. Soc. Microbiology, Sigma Xi, Alpha Omega Alpha. Contbr. articles to profl. jours. Home: Box 146A Sumneytown PA 18084 Office: Dept Pathology Allentown Gen Hosp Allentown PA 18102

OESTMANN, MARY JANE, nuclear and radio chemist; b. Chgo., May 22, 1924; d. Charles E. and Harriet E. (Stoltenberg) Oestmann; A.B. with honors, Denison U., 1946; M.S., U. Wis., 1948, Ph.D., 1954. Vis. research scientist Inst. for Atomic Energy, Kjeller, Norway, 1954-55; vis. chemist A.B. Atomenergi, Stockholm, Sweden, 1955-56; vis. lectr. chemistry State U. Ia., Ia. City, 1957; prin. chemist radioisotopes and radiation div. Battelle Meml. Inst., Columbus, O., 1957-60, sr. chemist, 1960-61; asso. chemist internat. inst. nuclear sci. and engring. Argonne Nat. Lab., Chgo., 1961-65, office of coll. and univ. coop. 1965-67, asso. chemist liquid metal fast breeder reactor program office, 1967-70, asso. chemist Center for Environmental Scis., 1971; environmental analyst, project mgr. Directorate of Licensing, AEC, Washington, 1971—. Recipient Distinguished Alumni citation Denison U., 1971. Fellow Am. Inst. Chemists (exec. council Chgo. sect. 1969-71); mem. Instrument Soc. Am. (sr.), Inst. Environmental Scis. (sr.), Midwest Soc. Health Physics, Am. Nuclear Soc. (sec. isotopes and radiation div. 1966-72, vice chmn. 1972-73, chmn. 1973—, sec. environmental scis. tech. group 1970-72, treas. 1972—), Am. Soc. for Testing and Materials (chmn. speakers bur. 1962-66, E-10 com. 1961—), Am. Chem. Soc. (chmn. ladies program Chgo. sect. 1967-68), Health Physics Soc., Soc. Applied Spectroscopy (program chmn. nuclear spectroscopy sessions at nat. meeting, 1967, 68, 70), A.A.A.S., Ill., Wis. acad. arts, Letters, and Sci., N.Y. Acad. Sci., Atomic Indsl. Forum, Chgo. Gas Chromatography Discussion Group, Open Lands Project, Internat. Platform Assn., Am. Mus. Natural History, Am. Scandinavian Found., League Women Voters, Bus. and Profl. Women's Club, Am. Assn. U. Women, Ill. Audubon Soc., Smithsonian Assos., Phi Beta Kappa (exec. com. Chgo. area), Sigma Xi, Iota Sigma Pi, Sigma Delta Epsilon. Clubs: Sierra; Toastmistress (v.p. 1969-70, sec. 1973—). Contbr. articles in nuclear and environmental sci. to profl. jours. Home: 4857 Battery Lane Apt 502 Bethesda MD 20014 Office: AEC Washington DC 20545

O'FERRELL, EILEEN MARIE (MRS. ARTHUR HELWIG), physician; b. Cuyahoga Falls, O., Apr. 13, 1915; d. Francis an[d] Catherine (Lutz) O'Ferrell; R.N., City Hosp., Akron Sch. Nursin[g] 1933; B.S., U. Cin., 1949; M.D., Ohio State U. Coll. Medicine, 195[4] m. Arthur Helwig, Mar. 25, 1961. Staff nurse Akron City Hosp 1936-39, Longview State Hosp., 1939-50, Ohio State U. Hosp 1950-54; intern. Christ Hosp, 1954-55; practice medicine, specializin[g] in family medicine, Cin., 1955—; mem. staff Christ Hosp., Goo[d] Samaritan Hosp., Children's Hosp., Deaconess Hosp., St. Franc[is] Hosp.; asst. dir. Mt. Auburn Health Center, 1969-72; med. dir. We[st] End Health Center, Cin., 1968-72. Trustee Health Planning Ass[n.] Hamilton County. Named Woman of the Year, Cin. Enquirer, 197[0] Mem. Am., Ohio med. assns., Cin. Acad. Medicine, Am., Ohio acad[s.] family practice, Southwestern Ohio Soc. Family Physicians, Am. So[c.] Physicians and Surgeons, Am. Med. Women's Assn. (mem. financ[e] com. 1969-72, chmn. resolutions com. 1971—), Med. Women['s] Internat. Assn., Acad. Parapsychology and Medicine. Diplomate Am Bd. Family Practice. Office: 3233 Westbourne Dr Cincinnati OH 45211

OFFERLE, MILDRED GLADYS GOODELL (MRS. MARTIN ADOLPH OFFERLE), educator; b. Barnum, Minn., Jan. 3, 1912; d. John Sprague and Lilian Caroline (Ortman) Goodell; grad. Duluth Tchrs. Coll., 1932; B.S., Mankato State Coll., 1966; certificate Famou[s] Writers Sch., 1963; m. Martin Adolph Offerle, Aug. 31, 1938; 1 dau. Caroline. Tchr., Mapleton, Minn., 1932-33, Barnum, Minn., 1933-38 Madelia (Minn.) Elementary Sch., 1964—. Recipient Golden Eagle Scout award, 1930. Mem. N.E.A., World Poetry Soc Intercontinental, Rep. Centro Studi E Scambi Internazionali, Nat. Poetry League, League Minn. Poets, Minn. Edn. Assn., Madelia Tchrs. Assn. Club: Sorosis (Madelia). Author: Crystal Wells, 1950; The Long Cry, 1960; Moods and Thoughts, 1970. Home: 105 3d St Madelia MN 56062 Office: 216 Main St Madelia MN 56062

OFFORD, LENORE GLEN (MRS. HAROLD OFFORD), author, book reviewer; b. Spokane, Wash., Oct. 24, 1905; d. Robert A. and Catherine (Grippen) Glen; B.A., Mills Coll., 1925; postgrad. U. Cal., 1925-26; m. Harold R. Offord, Sept. 17, 1929; 1 dau., Judith. Mystery book reviewer San Francisco Chronicle, 1950—. Author: Murder on Russian Hill, 1938; Cloth of Silver, 1939; Angels Unaware, 1940; The Nine Dark Hours, 1941; Clues to Burn, 1942; Skeleton Key, 1943; The Glass Mask, 1944; My True Love Lies, 1947; The Smiling Tiger, 1949; Enchanted August, 1956; Walking Shadow, 1959; collaborated in The Marble Forest, 1951; The Girl In The Belfry, 1957. Mem. Mystery Writers Am., Crime Writers Assn. Eng. Home: 641 Euclid Av Berkeley CA 94708

O'GARA, MARY LOUISE REESE (MRS. FRANCIS BARTLY O'GARA), writer; b. Red Oak, Ia., Aug. 11, 1938; d. Charles Arthur and Alice (Hayes) Reese; student Grinnell Coll., 1956-57, U. Neb., 1958-61, summers 1965, 66; B.A., U. Neb., 1966; postgrad. Augustana Coll.; m. Francis Bartly O'Gara, July 7, 1962. Copy editor Lincoln (Neb.) Jour., 1960-61; reporter-photographer Ogden (Utah) Standard-Examiner, 1963-64; owner retail bus., Davenport, Ia., 1968-72; salesman Success Motivation Inst., Davenport, 1971-73; free-lance writer contbg. to Family Circle, Lady's Circle, others. Mem. Women in Communications (legislative com. 1973-74), Women's Equity Action League (Ia. pres. 1972-73, 74—, mem. state bd. 1972—), League Women Voters (Ia. tax chmn. 1973), Mystery Writers Am., Nat. Orgn. Women, Mensa, P.E.O., Nat. Women's Polit. Caucus, Kappa Tau Alpha. Address: 1000 Blythwood Pl Apt A-10 Davenport IA 52804

OGATA, WINIFRED F., social worker; b. Paia, Maui, Hawaii; d. Hikoshiro and Masu (Okawara) Ogata; B.A., U. Hawaii, 1949; M.A., Ind. U., 1956. Sight conservation worker Bur. Sight Conservation, Honolulu, 1949-54; social worker State Dept. Pub. Welfare, Honolulu,

1956-57, Hawaii State Hosp., Kaneohe, 1957-62, Diamond Head Mental Health Clinic, Honolulu, 1962-64; sr. social worker Lanakila Mental Health Clinic, Honolulu, 1964—; field work supr. U. Hawaii Sch. Social Work, 1959—. Mem. Nat. Assn. Social Workers, Acad. Certified Social Workers, Hawaii Pub. Health Assn., Internat. Platform Assn. Home: 5871 Haleola St Honolulu HI 96821 Office: 1027 Hala Dr Honolulu HI 96817

OGDEN, ANN (MRS. ALVIN C. OGDEN), editor; b. Kansas City, Mo., Aug. 30, 1932; d. Audley W. and Leona R. (Locke) Porter; B.S. in Tech. Journalism, Kan. State U., 1954; M.A. in Secondary Edn. (univ. fellow), U. Mo., 1968; m. Alvin C. Ogden, May 29, 1954; 1 dau., Karen. Society editor Lyons (Kan.) Daily News, 1954-56; asst. editor Rose Publs., Shawnee Mission, Kan., 1962-63; instr. U. Mo., Kansas City, 1964-67; asst. editor Kansas Alumni, U. Kan., Lawrence, 1967-68; asst. editor Vol. Leader and Trustee, Chgo., 1969-72; owner Ogden Editorial Services, Oak Park, Ill., 1973—. Tchr. journalism Bishop Miege High Sch., Shawnee Mission, 1966-67. Recipient award Rose Publs., 1962, Gen. Excellence award Kan. Press Assn., 1962, Kan. PTA Story award, 1962-63. Mem. Women in Communications (mem. nat. resolutions com. 1973, pres. Chgo. chpt. 1973-74, historian-archivist Chgo. chpt. 1971-72, mem. procedures manual com. Chgo. chpt. 1971-72, mem. career conf. com. Chgo. chpt. 1971, mem. vol. bur. com. Chgo. chpt. 1971). Home and office: 328 S Ridgeland Av Oak Park IL 60302

OGG, JACQUELINE POLEY (MRS. RICHARD ANDREW OGG, JR.), educator, choreographer; b. Boulder, Colo., Nov. 27, 1917; d. Cyrus Watt and Mildred Margot (MacNutt) Poley; student Pasadena Playhouse Sch. of Theatre, 1935-38; A.A., Pasadena Jr. Coll., 1939; B.A., Stanford, 1942, M.A., 1945; m. Richard Andrew Ogg, Jr., July 25, 1942 (dec. 1962); children—Andrew Ian, Sharon Yvonne, Anthony Cyrus Gordon. Tchr. dance Pasadena (Cal.) Playhouse, 1938-40; tchr. contemporary dance Stanford U., 1943-44; tchr. adult edn., creative dramatics and dance Castilleja Sch., Palo Alto, 1945-48; instr. dance and drama San Francisco State Coll., 1948-49; instr. dance Ecole de Ballet de Pourtales Geneva, Switzerland, 1952-58; choreographer Geneva English Drama Soc., Switzerland, 1960-63; tchr. contemporary dance Ballet de la Suisse Romand, 1962, Centre de Danse Classique, Cannes, France, 1962-63; asst. prof. Colo. State U., Ft. Collins, 1963-68; asso. prof. movement and dance, choreographer drama dept. U. Alta., Edmonton, 1968—. Dir. Dance Theatre Group, San Francisco, 1953-58; choreographer San Francisco Dance League, 1953-58, Bauff Sch. Fine Arts, Bauff, Alta., 1972-74; founder, co-artistic dir. Alta Contemporary Dance Theatre, 1972—. Mem. Am. Theatre Assn. (chmn. sect. period movement 1968), Am. Dance Guild (chmn. nat. conv. movement and dance for theatre 1972), Canadian Assn. Univ. Tchrs., Dance Notation Bur., Com. on Research in Dance, Orchesis, Phi Beta Kappa, Alpha Psi Omega. Home: 16227 128th St Edmonton AB Canada

OGILVIE, ELISABETH M(AY), author; b. Boston, May 20, 1917; d. Frank Everett and Maude (Coates) Ogilvie; student pub. schs. Author: High Tide at Noon, 1944; Storm Tide, 1945; The Ebbing Tide, 1947; My World Is An Island, 1949; Rowan Head, 1949; The Dawning of the Day, 1954; Whistle For A Wind, 1954; Blueberry Summer, 1956; No Evil Angel, 1956; The Fabulous Year, 1958; The Witch Door, 1959; How Wide the Heart, 1959; Becky's Island, 1961; Call Home the Heart, 1962; A Woman's Reputation, 1962; Turn Round Twice, 1962; There May Be Heaven, 1964; Ceiling of Amber, 1964; Masquerade at Sea House, 1965; The Seasons Hereafter, 1966; Waters on a Starry Night, 1968; The Pigeon Pair, 1968; Bellwood Come Abroad and Bring Your Dory!, 1969; The Face of Innocence, 1970; A Theme for Reason, 1970; Weep and Know Why, 1972; Strawberries in the Sea, 1973; Image of a Lover, 1974. Mem. Foster Parents' Plan, Inc. Recipient N.E. Woman's Press Assn. award for fiction, 1946. Mem. Mystery Writers Am., Nature Conservancy. Republican. Baptist. Address: Gay's Island Pleasant Point ME 04563

OGLE, LOUISE GODFREY, composer, musician; b. Knoxville, Tenn., Mar. 8, 1892; d. Elmore Myrick and Helen (Scruggs) Godfrey; student U. Tenn., summers 1911-13; pvt. studies with A. K. Virgil, A. L. Manchester, Bessie E. Godfrey, others; diploma Sherwood Music Sch., Extension, 1942; m. Ernest Addington Ogle, June 5, 1914. Tchr. piano, organist, poet; pvt. studio music, Asheville, N.C., 1916—. Composer (piano): The Laughing Brook, 1943, Trees at Night, 1944, Spring Magic, 1945, Scented Showers, 1946, Little Indian Scout, 1953, Mother's Lullaby, 1953, Dance With Me, 1954, Dancing with the Breeze, 1955, Ghosts and Goblins; (2 pianos) On A Bright Day, 1959; (organ) Interlude in D Flat, 1949, Song of Hope and Adoration; (anthem) My Voice Shalt Thou Hear, 1950; In Remembrance, organ solo, 1964, others. Mem. Federated Music Clubs (extension chmn. N.C. bd. 1939, chmn. jr. composers contest 1968), Am. Musicol. Soc., Nat. Guild Piano Tchrs. (audition judge), Nat. League Am. Pen Women (pres. N.C. 1946-48; nat. music chmn. 1964-66, state music chmn. 1968-70). Methodist. Clubs: Asheville Music (pres. 1936-37). Musicians Am. Author: (poetry) (with Marie Smith Inzer, Edith Deaderick Erskine) Clouds, Chords and Calico (rev. edit), 1944. Home: 6 Caledonia Rd Asheville NC 28803

OGLESBEE, HARRIET BARKLEY (MRS. TOM W. OGLESBEE, JR.), librarian; b. Statesville, N.C., Sept. 27, 1939; d. Harry E. and Beatrice (Gainey) Barkley; A.B. in Elementary Edn., Erskine Coll., 1961; M.S. in Library Sci., Fla. State U., 1967; m. Tom W. Oglesbee, Jr., Dec. 30, 1972. Tchr. elementary sch., Beaufort, S.C., 1961-64, Greensboro, N.C., 1964-65, Iredell County, N.C., 1965-66; asst. reference librarian Savannah (Ga.) Pub. Library, 1968-70; librarian, asst. prof. Limestone Coll., Gaffney, S.C., 1970—. Mem. Am. Assn. U. Women, A.L.A., S.C., Southeastern library assns., Jr. Mems. Round Table. Presbyn. Home: Route 2 Box 458-A Gaffney SC 29340

OGLESBY, CLAIRE CRAIG (MRS. ROBERT OGLESBY), business exec. ; b. Logansport, Ind., Oct. 20, 1917; d. Everard Granville and Clare (Fischer) Delgado; A.B. cum laude, Butler U., 1938; m. Robert Oglesby, Aug. 30, 1958. Translator in Spanish, asst. to mgr. S. Am. div. Eli Lilly & Co., Indpls., 1938-40; reservation and ticket mgr. Trans World Airlines, Indpls., 1940-46; founder, owner, pres., gen. mgr. Travel, Inc., Washington, 1946-61; regional v.p. Fugazy Travel Bur., Inc., 1961-66; owner Oglesby Enterprises, Inc., 1966-69; dir. tour and travel Southeastern div. Hiltons Hotels Corp., 1969—; cons. in travel to Quota Internat., Inc. Adm. of Am. Airlines. Mem. Nat. Assn. Life Underwriters, Nat. Fedn. Bus. and Profl. Women's Clubs, Chi Omega; ambassador mem. Trans World Airlines. Presbyn. Clubs: Quota (dir.) Washington, D.C.); Clipper of Pan American World Airlines, Nat. Association Executives of Washington. Author: Beginning Spanish, 1938. Home: 4201 Cathedral Av NW Washington DC 20016 Office: Hilton Hotels Corp Washington DC 20009

O'GRADY, SISTER DOREEN GABRIELLE, coll. pres.; b. Tuam, Ireland, Jan. 12, 1917; d. Patrick Thomas J. and Margaret Mary (O'Donoghue) O'Grady; diploma (King's scholar) St. Mary's Tchr. Coll., 1940; B.A., Catholic Tchrs. Coll., 1951; M.Ed., Boston Coll., 1961; Ed.D., Laurence U., 1972. Came to U.S., 1947, naturalized, 1952. Prin., St. Luke Sch., West Barrington, R.I., 1958-65; mem. adminstrv. council Sisters of Cross and Passion, Wakefield, R.I., 1965-68; mem. faculty Mt. St. Joseph Coll., Wakefield, 1965—, pres., 1970—, dir. tchr. edn., 1969—, trustee, 1970—. Mem. New Eng. Bd. Higher Edn. Mem. Am. Assn. Higher Edn., Am. Assn. U. Women, World Future Soc., R.I. Assn. Tchrs. Educators, Nat. Catholic Edn. Assn. Address: Mt St Joseph Coll Tower Hill Rd Wakefield RI 02879

O'GRADY, SISTER ELEANOR, ednl. adminstr.; b. Phila., Sept. 27, 1932; d. Joseph M. and Nora Theresa (Gallagher) O'Grady; B.A., Alvernia Coll., 1963; M.A., Catholic U. Am., 1971. Joined Bernardine Sisters St. Francis, 1958; tchr. La Reine High Sch., Washington, 1963-67, St. Mary High Sch., Greenwich, Conn., 1967-70; registrar, dir. admissions Alvernia Coll., Reading, Pa., 1970—. Mem. Am. Assn. Collegiate Registrars and Admissions Officers, Middle States Assn. Collegiate Registrars and Officers of Admission, Nat. Assn. Coll. Admissions Counselors. Address: Alvernia College Reading PA 19607

O'GRADY, LILLIAN MARY QUINLAN (MRS. VALENTINE M. O'GRADY), social worker; b. Chgo.; d. Norbert A. and Lillian (Johnson) Quinlan; A.B., St. Xavier Coll., 1937; M.S.W., Loyola U., Chgo., 1943; postgrad. U. Chgo., 1954-56, 68-69, U. Ill., 1958-64, U. No. Ill., 1965—; m. Valentine M. O'Grady, Aug. 30, 1939; children—Thomas J., John J., Mary Jo. Sr. caseworker Chgo. Welfare Dept., 1938-39, Ill. Pub. Aid, 1939-40; sr. interviewer, tng. dir. Ill. Employment Serivce, 1940-42, sr. social worker Municipal Ct. of Chgo., 1948-50; sr. social worker Blue Island (Ill.) Pub. Schs., 1953-62, 63—; social work cons. Park Lawn Sch. for Retarded Children, 1965—; supr. social work Chgo. Foundlings Homes, 1962-63; pvt. practice social work, Chgo., 1963—. Program dir. Blue Island Area Youth and Family Council, 1953—, So. Area Counselors, 1961-63, speaker, chmn. Worth Twp. Tchrs. Inst., 1959-60; sect. del. White House Conf. on Children, 1960; chmn. Ill. Inst. for Sch. Social Workers, 1961-62, 67-68, 69-72; mem. bd. for social work-human devel. Moraine Valley Community Coll., 1968-70. Licensed real estate broker, Ill. Mem. Acad. Certified Social Workers, Nat., Ill. edn. assns., Ill. Welfare Assn., St. Xavier Coll., Loyola U. Alumnae, Am. Assn. U. Women, Nat. Assn. Social Workers (chmn. schs. council). Contbr. articles to profl. jours. Home: 2941 W 102d Pl Chicago IL 60642 Office: 2515 W 123d St Blue Island IL 60406

O'HALLORAN, (LAVERNE M.) KATHLEEN (MRS. JOHN R. O'HALLORAN, JR.), realtor; b. Laurium, Mich., Nov. 15, 1921; d. Joseph Wilfred and Della K. (Gervais) Shaffer; student Fond Du Lac Comml. Coll., 1938-40, Fresno City Coll., 1965-66; m. John Richard O'Halloran, Jr., July 15, 1942; children—Sheila Ann (Mrs. Leonard Stoll), Gregory, Michael, Maureen, Sean, Margaret. Co-owner Hamlin Hotel, San Francisco, 1946-48, Lazy F Guest Ranch, Ellensburg, Wash., 1948-50; broker Cal-Real Realtors, Fresno, 1965—. Charter mem. Infant of Prague Adoption Agy. Aux., 1954—, sec., 1955; mem. Mayor's Com. for Community Devel., 1963-64; pres. Sacred Heart Mothers Club, 1959; pres. Cal. Citizens for Decent Lit., 1961-63, Central Cal. Citizens for Decent Lit., 1959-64. Precinct chmn. Goldwater campaign, 1964; chmn. Fresno County United Republicans Cal., 1962; area coordinator Clean Campaign Ballot Initiative, 1966; candidate Fresno City Council, 1961. Mem. Fresno Bd. Realtors, Nat. Assn. Real Estate Bds. Roman Catholic. Home: 3503 N Bond St Fresno CA 93726 Office: 4841 N 1st St Fresno CA 93726

OHANESIAN, SYLVIA, coll. dean; b. Haverhill, Mass., Aug. 11, 1934; d. V. Charles and Queenie (Tarpinian) Ohanesian; B.S., Simmons Coll., 1956; M.S. in Edn., Ind. U., 1958. Asst. dean women Bucknell U., Lewisburg, Pa., 1958-61; asst. dean women U. Vt., 1961-63; asst. dean students Douglass Coll., New Brunswick, N.J., 1963-65; asst. dean students Beaver Coll., Glenside, Pa., 1965-69; dean of women, asso. dean students Rider Coll., Trenton, N.J., 1969-73, dean residential life, asso. dean students, 1973—. Bd. dirs. exec. com. Phila. Coll. Bound Corp., 1966-69, Mercer County council Girl Scouts Am., 1970-71, Planned Parenthood Assn. Mercer Area, 1972—. Mem. Nat. (past treas., com. chmn.), Pa. (past editor, chmn. publs.), N.J. assns. women deans and counselors, Alpha Lambda Delta (hon.), Phi Chi Theta (hon.).

O'HANLON, PHILOMENA GERTRUDE, sch. adminstr.; b. Berwind, W.Va., Oct. 15, 1924; d. Frank Orr and Margaret Ann (Cumming) O'Hanlon; B.A., Chestnut Hill Coll., 1946; M.A., Villanova U., 1961. Tchr. English, Harding Jr. High Sch., Phila., 1948-55, Fels Jr. High Sch., 1955-57, N.E. High Sch., 1957-69; head English dept. High Sch. Dist., Phila., 1969-73; curriculum specialist Sch. Dist. Phila., 1973—. Vis. lectr. Holy Family Coll., Phila., 1971. Mem. Nat. Council Tchrs. English, Am., Pa., Phila. (editor newspaper 1964-65) fedns. tchrs., Women in Edn., Chestnut Hill Alumnae Assn. (pres. Phila. chpt. 1956-58). Roman Catholic. Author: Archive 75, 1965. Home: 1741 Vista St Philadelphia PA 19111 Office: 21st St South of Pkwy Philadelphia PA 19103

O'HARA, SISTER ANN MARGARET, coll. adminstr.; b. Louisville, Dec. 22, 1937; d. Edwin Thomas and Margaret Mary (Schwartz) O'Hara; B.A., St. Mary-of-the-Woods Coll., 1960; M.S., Ind. U., 1969. Tchr., St. Francis Xavier Sch., Wilmette, Ill., 1960-63; tchr., chmn. bus. dept. Chartrand High Sch., Indpls., 1963-67; dir. student personnel, chmn. bus. div. Immaculata Coll. Washington, 1967—. Pres., Council Women Religious Archdiocese Washington, 1973—. Mem. Archdiocesan Self Study (sec. Washington 1970-73). Indpls. Archdiocesan Bus. Edn. Assn. (pres. elect 1966-67), Delta Pi Epsilon. Address: 4300 Nebraska Av NW Washington DC 20016

O'HARA, SISTER MARY L(OUISE), educator; b. Indpls., May 28, 1923; d. James H. and Louise (Triska) O'Hara; B.A., Coll. of St. Catherine, 1946; M.A., Cath. U. Am., 1948, Ph.D., 1956; student U. Louvain (Belgium), 1952-53. Asso. prof. Coll. St. Catherine, 1956-63, prof. philosophy, 1964—; research fellow Yale Divinity Sch., 1967-68, vis. Scholar Union Theol. Sem., Summer 1968. Mem. Commn. for Ecumenism, Archdiocese of St. Paul, Mpls., 1969-72, mem. pastoral council, 1972—, mem. exec. com., 1973—. Mem. Minn. Philos. Soc. (pres. 1963-64), Am. Cath. (regional pres., 1959), Am. philos. assns., Metaphys. Soc., Phi Beta Kappa, Pi Gamma Mu. Author: Consciousness and Bodiliness. Contbr. articles in field to profl. jours. Home: 8650 Russell Av S Minneapolis MN 55431

O'HEARON, DORIS MARIE, librarian; b. Duluth, Minn., Feb. 28, 1928; d. Harvey Ernest and Eva Delores (Mayer) O'Hearon; B.A., Aquinas Coll., 1963; M.A., Rosary Coll., 1967; postgrad. Central Mich. U., 1964, Drake U., 1969, No. Ill. U., 1970. Tchr., sch. librarian Marywood Dominican Sisters, Grand Rapids, Mich., 1949-65; asst. librarian Thornridge High Sch., Dolton, Ill., 1965-66; librarian, tutor Bateman Sch., Chgo., 1966-68; reference librarian, instr. Aurora (Ill.) Coll., 1967-71; dir. Nat. Safety Council Library, Chgo., 1971-73; librarian Yorkville (Ill.) Sch. Dist. 115, 1973—; established, directed several grammar sch. libraries, Ill. Sch. Dist. 127, 1966. Mem. Am., Ill., Cath. library assns., Internat. Inst. Children's and Popular Lit., Friends of Am. Writers. Regional editor Library Scene, 1969—. Book reviewer Sch. Library Jour., 1969-71. Home: 42 Oak Terrace Ct Batavia IL 60510 Office: Game Farm Rd Yorkville IL 60560

O'HERN, EDNA M., sociologist; b. Hammond, Ind.; d. Dennis E. and Catherine (Nowak) O'Hern; B.A., in English Lit., St. Xavier Coll., Chgo., 1941; M.A. in Polit. Sci., Cath. U. Am., 1949, Ph.D. in Sociology, 1956. Sociology faculty mem. St. John Fisher Coll., Rochester, N.Y., 1954-62, St. John's U., Bklyn., 1962-64, U. Windsor (Ont., Can.), 1964-67; prof. St. Francis Coll., Bklyn., 1967—, head dept. sociology, 1968—. Served as lt. USNR, 1943-46. Fellow Am. Sociol. Assn.; mem. Am. Assn. U. Profs. Contbr. articles to revs. and jours. Home: 225 Adams St Brooklyn NY 11201

O'HERN, JANE SUSAN, psychologist, educator; b. Winthrop, Mass., Mar. 21, 1933; d. Joseph Francis and Mona (Garvey) O'Hern; B.S., Boston U., 1954, Ed.D., 1962; M.A., Mich. State U., 1956. Teaching asst. Mich. State U., 1955-56; instr. Mercyhurst Coll., Erie, Pa., 1954-55; instr. Hofstra Coll., Hempstead, N.Y., 1956-57; instr. State Coll. at Salem and Boston, 1957-60; teaching fellow Boston U., 1960-62, asst. prof., 1962-67, asso. prof. edn. 1967—, coordinator of assessment Peace Corps Tng. Program, summer 1966, chmn. dept. counselor edn., 1972—; vis. counselor Mich. State U., summers 1959-61; vis. prof. U. Md., summer 1963, Kent State U., summer 1965; cons. Raytheon Co., Gen. Electric Co., Singer Corp. Dir. Nat. Def. Edn. Act Counseling Inst., Boston U., summer 1964; dir. Edn. Professions Devel. Act Inst. in Sch. Mental Health, 1971—. Fellow Mass. Psychol. Assn.; mem. Am. Personnel and Guidance Assn., Assn. Counselor Educators and Suprs. (past pres. North Atlantic region), Pi Lambda Theta. Author: (with Litwack and Holmes) Critical Issues in Student Personnel Work, 1965. Home: 191 Jamaicaway Tower Boston MA 02130 Office: 765 Commonwealth Av Boston MA 02115

OHL, HAZEL MCNITT (MRS. WAYNE CLIFFORD OHL), librarian; b. Trent, Mich., May 23, 1910; d. George Edward and Effie (Nelson) McNitt; student Hiram Coll., 1928-32; m. Wayne Clifford Ohl, Feb. 10, 1934. Librarian, Moses Cleaveland Jr. High Sch., Cleve., 1936-37; asst. librarian Portage County (O.) Pub. Library, Hiram, 1938-40, 45-46, librarian, 1940-44; asst. librarian bookmobile, 1949-56; librarian Breaden br. Youngstown (O.) Pub. Library, 1957-61; librarian Struthers (O.) Pub. Library, 1961-66; head gen. reference div. Youngstown Pub. Library, 1967—. Dir. Project NOLA, 1972-73. Mem. Ohio Library Assn., Soc. Ohio Archivists, Pub. Librarians Assn. Youngstown. Home: 6116 Glenwood Av Youngstown OH 44512 Office: 305 Wick Av Youngstown OH 44503

OHLIGER, GLORIA ANN, pub. information specialist; b. Brownsville, Tex., 1925; d. Frederick and Evangeline (Anzaldua) Ohliger; student George Washington U., 1945-46. Editor women's page Washington Daily News, 1963-70; pub. information specialist Bur. Mint, Dept. Treasury, Washington, 1970—. Recipient Spl. award for excellence Treasury Dept., 1973. Home: 1330 New Hampshire Av NW Washington DC 20036 Office: Bur Mint Dept Treasury Washington DC 20220

OHLSON, ANNETTA KATRINA DIEKHOFF, librarian; b. Ann Arbor, Mich., Oct. 31, 1912; d. Tobias Johann and Julia Catherine (Schacht) Diekhoff; B.A., U. Mich., 1933, A.B. in L.S., 1934; m. John Edward Ohlson, Feb. 5, 1934 (dec. 1966); children—John Edward, Linda Frances, Anne Catherine (Mrs. Edwin Lee Reese). Asst. librarian Detroit News Catlin Meml. Library, 1951-55; librarian Nat. Bank of Detroit, 1955—. Mem. Spl. Libraries Assn., Women's Econ. Club, Kappa Delta. Presbyn. Home: 15541 Garfield Av Allen Park MI 48101 Office: Box 116A Detroit MI 48232

OHMERT, HAZEL MARY, educator; b. Washington, Cal., Mar. 20, 1890; d. Joseph Alfred and Amy Burton (Hippert) Ohmert; B.A., U. Nev., 1912; M.A., U. Ore., 1944. Tchr. county sch., Smith, Nev., 1912-13; vice prin. secondary sch., Winnemucca, Nev., 1913-19; welfare worker Gen. Fedn. Women's Club unit AEF, France, 1919; tchr. Washington High Sch., Portland, Ore., 1919-38, dean of girls, vice prin., to 1955; dean of women Multnomah Jr. Coll., Portland, 1955-67. Vol. tutor fgn. students Portland (Ore.) State Coll., 1972. Active Republican polit. campaigns. Mem. Women's Overseas Service League, Delta Delta Delta. Methodist. Home: 222 SW Harrison St Apt 7C Portland OR 97201

OHRWALL, EMILY MARION (MRS. STEPHEN COCHRAN OHRWALL), recreation adminstr., art gallery adminstr.; b. Bonifay, Fla.; d. James Alvin and Marquerite (Swindle) Holland; B.A. in Art, U. Cal. at Davis, 19—; M.A. in Recreation Adminstrn., Chico State U., Cal., 1971; m. Stephen Cochran Ohrwall, Apr. 3, 1971. Asst. to dir. Meml. Union Art Gallery, U. Cal. Davis, 1965-69, dir. cultural recreation programs, 1970—, mem. com. for Arts and Lectures, 1972-74. Mem. Assn. Coll. Unions Conf. (chmn. region XV 1968), Cal. Parks and Recreation Soc. Home: 2807 Catalina Davis CA 95616 Office: Cultural Recreation Programs Meml Union Craft Center Art Gallery U Cal Davis CA 95616

O'KEEFE, ELLEN MARIA WIERDAK (MRS. JAMES JOSEPH O'KEEFE), coll. adminstr.; b. Chgo., May 24, 1941; d. Andrew James and Helen May (Mancuso) Wierdak; B.A., St. Mary-of-the-Woods Coll., 1963; M.A., Cath. U. Am., 1965; m. James Joseph O'Keefe, July 4, 1969. Asst. prof. speech and drama Immaculata Coll. Washington, 1963-69; asst. prof. speech and drama Elizabeth Seton Coll., Yonkers, N.Y., 1969-72, dir. community ednl. services, 1972—. Mem. lay bd. Little Sisters Assumption Family Health Care Center, N.Y.C., 1970—. Bd. dirs. Contemporary Living Program, St. Vincent's Sch. Nursing. Home: 361 W 51st St New York City NY 10019 Office: 1061 N Broadway Yonkers NY 10701

O'KEEFE, ROBERTA FLEETWOOD, poet; b. Brownwood, Tex., Dec. 28, 1903; d. Robert Edward and Nettie (Hall) Fleetwood; grad. high sch.; m. Sidney Wayne O'Keefe, Dec. 2, 1928; 1 son, Robert Franklin (dec.). Mem. Poetry Soc. Tex. (area councilor 1966—). Presbyn. Author: Moods and Monologues, 1966. Home: 2802 Hughes St Amarillo TX 79109

O'KEEFFE, GEORGIA, artist; b. Sun Prairie, Wis., Nov. 15, 1887; d. Francis and Ida (Totto) O'Keeffe; student Sacred Heart Acad., Madison, Wis., 1900, Chatham (Va.) Episcopal Inst., 1902-04, Art Inst. Chgo., 1904-05, Art Students' League (N.Y.C.), 1907-08, U. Va., summer 1912, Columbia, 1914-16; D.F.A., William and Mary Coll., 1938; Litt.D., U. Wis., 1942, Mills Coll., 1951; D.F.A., U. N.M., 1964; m. Alfred Stieglitz, Dec. 11, 1924. Illustrator for advt. cos., 1909; supr. art, pub. schs., Amarillo, Tex., 1912-14; instr. art, U. Va., summers, 1913-16; head art dept., West Tex. State Normal Coll., Canyon, 1916-18; has confined activities to painting, 1918—. Became one of group sponsored by Alfred Stieglitz; paintings first exhibited by him at 291, N.Y.C., 1916-17, Anderson Galleries, 1923-25. Ann. one-man shows at Intimate Gallery, An Am. Pl. till 1946 (N.Y.C.); retrospective exhbn. Art Inst. Chgo., 1943; Mus. Modern Art, N.Y.C., 1946, Worcester (Mass.) Art Mus., 1960, Amon Carter Mus., 1966, Mus. Fine Arts, Houston, 1966, Whitney Mus. Am. Art, 1970; Art Inst. Chgo., 1971; San Francisco Mus. Art, 1971; represented in large museums and galleries throughout U.S. Recipient Creative Arts award Brandeis U., 1963; Gold medal for painting Nat. Inst. Arts and Letters. Mem. Nat. Inst. Arts and Letters, Am. Acad. Arts and Letters, Am. Acad. Arts and Scis. Home: Biquiu NM 87510

OKES, IMOGENE ESTA, govt. ofcl.; b. Terre Haute, Ind.; d. Vernor J. and Ethlyn (Willis) Okes; B.S., Ind. State U., 1944; M.A., Am. U., 1960. Clk., editor, librarian U.S. Fgn. Service, China and Norway, 1945-52; groupworker, pub. relations rep. Internat. Inst., Fresno, Cal., 1955-56; research asso. Spl. Operations Research Office, Am. U., Washington, 1957-61, Inst. for Def. Analyses, Washington, 1962-63; adult edn. specialist U.S. Office Edn., Washington, 1965—. Guest lectr. Fgn. Service Inst., U.S. Dept. State, Washington, 1961-62; instr. Ginling Girls Coll., Nanking, China, 1947; co-chmn. for arrangements Nat. meeting Assn. Asian Studies, Washington, 1964. Program chmn. YWCA Internat. Womens Club, Nanking, China, 1947. Mem. Am. Assn. U. Women (sec., mem. bd. Washington br. 1969-71), A.A.A.S., Am. Sociol. Assn., Am. Statis. Assn., Inst. Mgmt. Scis. (bd. dirs. Washington chpt. 1970—), Adult Edn. Assn. (pres. Greater Washington br. 1973-74), Assn. for Ednl. Data Systems, Am. Ednl. Research Assn., Assn. Instnl. Research, Operations Research Soc. Am., Am. Polit. Sci. Assn., Am. Acad. Polit. and Social Scis., Assn. Asian Studies, Mongolia-Tibet Soc. Author: Psychological Operations-Afghanistan-Project PROSYMS, 1961; Effective Communication by Americans with Thai, 1961; Participation in Adult Edn., 1969, Initial Report, 1971; Adult Edn. in Pub. Edn. System, 1968-69, 1969-70, States Summaries, 1974. Home: 5480 Wisconsin Av Chevy Chase MD 20015 Office: US Office Edn Washington DC 20202

O'KOREN, MARIE LOUISE, ednl. adminstr.; b. Eveleth, Minn., Mar. 10, 1926; d. Joseph J. and Theresa (Markovich) O'Koren; diploma U. Minn. Sch. Nursing, 1946; B.S. in Nursing, Long Beach State Coll., 1957; M.S. in Nursing, U. Ala., 1958, Ed.D. (Nat. League for Nursing doctoral fellow, Bixler scholar), 1964. Staff nurse, asst. supr. operating room Seaside Meml. Hosp., Long Beach, Cal., 1947-57; faculty U. Ala., Birmingham, 1958—, asst. dean, chmn. grad. program, asso. prof. nursing, 1964-67, asst. dean, chmn. grad. program, prof. nursing, 1967-69, asso. dean, chmn. grad. program, prof. nursing, 1969, dean, prof. nursing, 1970—. Mem. Am. Assn. U. Profs., Am. Assn. Deans for Coll. and U. Schs. Nursing, Assn. for Suprs. and Curriculum Devel., World Edn. Fellowship, Jefferson County Mental Health Soc., Am., Ala. nurses assns., Nat., Ala. leagues for nursing, Sigma Theta Tau, Sigma Chi Nu, Delta Kappa Gamma, Kappa Delta Pi. Home: 2650 Chandalar Lane Birmingham AL 35244 Office: Univ Station U Ala Sch Nursing Birmingham AL 35294

OKOSHI, EUGENIA SUMIE, artist; b. Seattle; d. Masanari and Ryoko (Fukuda) Ushiyama; student Seattle U., 1954-56, Henry Frye Mus., Seattle, 1957-59. Exhibited abstract paintings and prints in internat. shows; represented in collections Miami Mus. Modern Art, Lowe Gallery, U. Miami, also pvt. collections; tchr. flower arrangement Ikkenobo Sch. Mem. Burr Artists, Japanese Artists Assn. N.Y., Westbeth Graphic Workshop. Studio: 463 West St New York City NY 10014

O'KRENT, HELEN KAISER (MRS. THEODORE J. O'KRENT), floor covering co. exec.; b. Evansville, Ind., Aug. 15, 1907; d. Arthur and Anna (Goldstein) Kaiser; student Evansville Coll., 1926; m. Theodore J. O'Krent, Oct. 9, 1927; children—Arthur, Anita. (Mrs. William Kramer). With O'Krent Floor Covering Corp., San Antonio, 1937—, sec.-treas., 1957—. Charter pres. San Antonio chpt. B'nai B'rith Women, 1944; pres. Mother's Club of Community Talmud Torah, 1946; v.p., program chmn. Rodfei Sholom Sisterhood, 1960-61; mem. bd., chmn. social action and Israel affairs com. Agudas Achim Sisterhood, 1972-73; mem. charter planning com. Golden Manor Nursing Home, 1957, sec.-treas., 1955; mistress ceremonies ann. banquet Pioneer Women's Orgn., 1967-71; pres. Meadowood Garden Club, 1966-67; mem. women's com. Nat. Conf. Christians and Jews, 1971, speaker Brotherhood Week, 1972-73; mem. Haddassah, 1938—, chmn. Bible study group, San Antonio, 1956-74; lectr. on Israel to chs., schs. and clubs, 1970—. Named Mother of Year, Hebrew Free Loan Assn. and Jewish Community Center, San Antonio, 1947; recipient Ima certificate San Antonio chpt. Hadassah, 1974. Home: 2306 Briarwood St San Antonio TX 78209 Office: 300 San Pedro St San Antonio TX 78212

OKUN, LILIAN, radio and TV producer, script writer, author; b. N.Y.C.; d. David and Henrietta (Sadovitch) Okun; student Am. Acad. Dramatic Arts, Columbia. Actress in Broadway plays including The Spider, The Trial of Mary Dugan, Lysistrata; others asst. studio mgr. radio sta. WOR, 1933-37; dir. Your Personal Problems WJZ, 1937-38; writer, producer Sydney Moseley, news commentator, 1938-43, Let's Listen to a Story for radio, 1943—, Young Book Reviewers WPIX-TV, radio, 1958—; prod. Your Lions Share Program, WNYC-TV, Focus on Books, Channel 31, Between the Lions, WNBC radio; producer It's Fun To Read program Channel 31; reviewer children's books N.Y. Times children's book sect., 1962. Cons. radio and TV, N.Y. Pub. Library, also TV series Nat. Council P.E. Ch., 1960—; mem. Emmy Award com. sponsored by Television Acad. Arts and Crafts, 1967-68. Recipient Peabody award, 1962. Mem. Am. Women in Radio and Television, Women's Nat. Book Assn., Writers Guild East, Broadcast Pioneers (sec.), Broadcasters' Found. (sec.), Nat. TV Acad. Arts and Scis. Author: Let's Listen to a Story, 1959. Address: 307 E 44th St New York City NY 10017

OLANSKY, MARIAN FREEHAFER (MRS. SIDNEY OLANSKY), pediatric allergist, educator; b. Washington, Nov. 2, 1918; d. Charles Edwin and Leah Catherine (Parson) Freehafer; B.A., George Washington U., 1940, M.D., 1944; m. Sidney Olansky, Oct. 13, 1945; children—Leann (Mrs. Charles Lucius Cope Jr.), Alan Joseph, David Charles, Ad Sidney. Intern, D.C. Gen. Hosp., Washington, 1944-45, resident in pediatrics, 1945-46; fellow pediatric allergy Duke U. Sch. Medicine, 1946-47, mem. faculty, 1955-59; faculty Emory U. Sch. Medicine, Atlanta, 1959—, asst. prof. pediatrics, 1969—, instr. internal medicine, 1959—. Fellow Am. Acad. Pediatrics; mem. Southeastern Med. Assn., Am. Med. Women's Assn., Fulton County (Ga.) Med. Soc., Phi Beta Kappa. Home: 3275 Majestic Circle Avondale Estates GA 30002 Office: Emory University Clinic Atlanta GA 30322

OLD COYOTE, ELNORA ALISON STENERSEN (MRS. JOHN M. OLD COYOTE), educator; b. Ft. Lupton, Colo., Mar. 6, 1922; d. Bennet Almer and Doris (Campbell) Stenersen; diploma Eastern Mont. Normal Sch., 1941; B.S., Mont. State Coll., 1950, M.S., 1957; Ed.D., Harvard, 1966; m. John Melvin Old Coyote, Sept. 12, 1970; adopted children—John Winston Wright, Jean Corinne Wright. Rural tchr., Mont., 1941-44; jr. high sch. tchr., Livingston, Mont., 1944-47; elementary tchr., Bozeman, Mont., 1950-55; instr. to asso. prof. elementary edn. Mont. State U., 1955—; curriculum coordinator Title VII Bilingual Edn. Program, Crow Indian Reservation, 1970-75; writer poetry, short stories and articles. Mem. Gov.'s Commn. on Status of Women, 1971-75. Elizabeth Stroh fellow, 1960-66. Mem. Mont. Inst. Arts, Wilderness Soc., Mont. Press Women, Nat. Fedn. Press Women, Nat. Sci. Tchrs. Assn., Phi Kappa Phi, Delta Kappa Gamma. Co-author: Introduction to Physical Sciences, 1970. Editor: (with H.G. Merriam and Ida Donahue) Seed in the Soil, 1963. Home: Box 415 Crow Agency MT 59022

OLDENBURG, ADELE LOUISE, librarian; b. Cleve., Feb. 11; d. Arthur Louis and Theresa M. (Mangan) Oldenburg; B.A., Bowling Green (O.) State U., 1948; M.S., Fla. State U., 1964; M.A., U. South Fla., 1974. With Internat. Minerals & Chem. Corp., 1955-62; asst. dir. Lakeland (Fla.) Pub. Library, 1962-69; reference librarian Polk Community Coll., Winter Haven, Fla., 1969—. Adviser, Winter Haven Pub. Library, 1970, J.B. Stuart Library, 1968. Mem. Southeastern, Fla. library assns., Am. Assn. U. Women (v.p. Lakeland 1968), Lakeland Symphony Guild, Oral History Assn., Sierra Club (sec.), Humane Soc. Polk County, Sanibel-Captiva Conservation Found., Fla. Assn. for Media in Edn., Nat. Ret. Tchrs. Assn., Sigma Tau Delta, Phi Kappa Phi, Chi Omega. Republican. Contbr. to Values in Conflict, A Text Reader in Social Problems. Home: 1317 Candyce St Lakeland FL 33801 Office: 999 Av H NE Winter Haven FL 33880

OLDENDORF, YVETTE MARIE BOE, state ofcl.; b. Bismarck, N.D.; d. Norman Ronnie and Martha Lucey (Gunville) Boe; B.A. (scholar), Macalester Coll., 1961; M.A. (Reader's Digest scholar, Euland fellow, Shevland fellow), U. Minn., 1966; m. John Phillip Oldendorf, June 20, 1964; 1 son, Brian Powell. Instr., Met. State Jr. Coll., Mpls., 1966-67; asst. dir. Higher Edn. Low Income Persons, Mpls., 1967-69; coordinator common market programs Minn. State Coll. Bd. Office, St. Paul, 1969-73; dir. esthetic environment programs State of Minn., St. Paul, 1973—. Bicentennial project coordinator Women Historians Minn., 1973. Asso. chairperson Senate Dist. 52, Democratic Farmer Labor Party, 1970-74, co-chairperson constl. commn., 1972-74, issues and program coordinator Feminist Caucus, 1973; del. Dem. Nat. Conv., 1972; co-chmn. 1st Congl. Dist. McGovern campaign, 1972; met. coordinator Minn. Women's Polit. Caucus, 1972—. Mem. Women's Equity Action League. Home: 421 Ruby Dr West St Paul MN 55118 Office: State Capitol Bldg St Paul MN 55155

OLDFIELD, RUTH LATZER (MRS. DANIEL G. OLDFIELD), tech. writer, editor; b. N.Y.C., June 2, 1922; d. Frederick and Bessie (Cohen) Latzer; grad. electronics engring. course RCA Insts., 1942; m. Daniel G. Oldfield, June 2, 1950; children—Elizabeth I., Frederic M. Jr. engr. Industry Service div. RCA Labs., N.Y.C., 1942-45; tech. writer Hazeltine Electronics Corp., N.Y.C., 1945; instr. mathematics Am. TV Labs., Los Angeles, 1946-47; tech. editor John F. Rider, N.Y.C., 1947-50, mng. editor, 1949-50; copy editor F. E. Compton & Co., Chgo., 1951-52; tech. editor Stemar Co., Chgo., 1952-54; free-lance tech. writer and editor, Chgo., 1954—; supr. communications courses Britannica Schs., Chgo., 1962-66; pub. relations counsel tech. dept. Gardner, Jones & Cowell, Chgo., 1965—, asst. dir. trade-tech. services, 1966-72; pres. R.L. Oldfield & Assos., 1972—. Phys. scis. cons. Children's Sci. Ency., Children's Press, 1961-62. Mem. Inst. Elec. and Electronics Engrs. (charter Chgo. chpt., chmn. profl. tech. group on engring. writing and speech, exec. editor Scanfax 1961—, mem. nat. adminstrv. com. profl. tech. group on engring. writing and speech), Soc. Women Engrs., Soc. Tech. Communications (sr. chmn. Chgo. nominating com. 1963-64), Soc. Programed and Automated Learning (chmn. membership com. 1963-64), Am. Women in Radio & TV, 1971—. Author: Radio-Television and Basic Electronics, 1956; The Practical Dictionary of Electricity and Electronics, 1959; Albert Einstein, Man of Science, 1964; People of Destiny: Albert Einstein, 1968. Contbr. to Above and Beyond, The Ency. of Aviation and Space Sciences, 1968. Home and office: 1200 Madison Park Chicago IL 60615

OLDHAM, PHYLLIS VIRGINIA KIDD, librarian; b. Lafayette, Ind., Mar. 19, 1926; d. Hulbert Haven and Grace Ellene (Doup) Kidd; B.S., Purdue U., 1948, M.S., Butler U., 1966; children—Stephen Kidd. Tchr. English, Jefferson High Sch., Lafayette, Ind., 1950; tchr., librarian Tudor Hall Sch., Indpls., 1954-70; librarian Park Tudor Sch., 1970—. Dist. dir. People-to-People Student Ambassador Program, 1970—. Mem. Marion County Librarians Assn. (pres. 1969-72), Ind. Sch. Librarians Assn., Kappa Delta Pi, Pi Beta Phi. Club: La Sertoma (dist. gov. 1969-70) (Indpls.). Home: 7015 Warwick Rd Indianapolis IN 46220 Office: 7200 N College St Indianapolis IN 46240

OLDHAM, VIRGINIA ALDRIDGE (MRS. M. BRENT OLDHAM), economist; b. Adsit, Va.; d. Zebedee and Jennie (Ridley) Aldridge; B.A., Howard U., 1959; m. Archie W. Johnson, Sept. 4, 1937 (dec. Sept. 1939); m. 2d, M. Brent Oldham, Aug. 27, 1949; 1 son, Brent Aldridge. Elevator operator Woodward and Lothrop Dept. Store, 1940-42; clk. War Dept., 1942-43, War Manpower Commn., 1943; accounting clk. OPA, 1943-46, financial analyst, 1946-47; payroll clk. Dept. Labor, 1947-51, 1953-55; statis. clk. NPA, 1951-52, clk., 1953-54; statis. clk. Bur. Comml. Fisheries, Dept. Interior, 1956-58, industry economist, 1958-64, economist Bur. Indian Affairs, 1964-66; staff asst. Field Operations Service Personnel (all Washington); staff asst., recruit specialist, employee counselor, part-time human relations instr. mgmt. and systems service VA, Washington, 1966-72, dep. fed. women's program coordinator, 1970—, personnel mgmt. specialist, 1972-73; equal opportunity specialist Office Asst. Adminstr. for Personnel, 1973—. Coordinator Fed. Savs. Bonds Program, 1969-73. Mem. invitations and tickets com. Presdl. Inaugural, 1965, 69, 73; mem. Hospitality and Information Service, Washington, 1964—; rep. Parents Council Washington, 1964-65. Mem. League Women Voters, Ams. for Democratic Action (v.p. Washington chpt. 1962, mem. exec. bd. 1959), Nat. Council Negro Women, Am. Econ. Assn., Pub. Personnel Assn. Clubs: Howard U. Faculty Wives, Howard U. Women's. Author: (with others) New England Groundfish Situation Reports, 1962, 63. Research on relative position fishing industry in domestic economy, 1961; on early rehab. housing program Am. Indians in 1930's, 1964. Home: 4325 20th St NE Washington DC 20018 Office: VA 810 Vermont Av NW Washington DC 20420

OLDS, FLORA ANNE CONNER, museum ofcl.; b. Rochester, Pa., Nov. 10, 1926; d. Samuel Grant and Elizabeth Adelia (Sharp) Conner; student Nat. Sch. Art, 1945-47, Parsons Sch. Design, 1947-48; m. Frederick Albert Olds, Sept. 3, 1949; children—Kathleen, Laura (Mrs. Thomas Towler), Erich, Lucinda. Layout artist Yukon (Okla) Rev.; designer, sales Jack's Flowers, Weatherford, Okla.; owner Olds' Gallery Western Art, Weatherford; now exhibits deisgner Okla. Hist. Soc., Oklahoma City, also Okla. Territorial Mus., Guthrie, Okla. Mem. Guthrie C. of C. (chmn. hist. preservation com.), Gamma Phi Beta. Home: 623 Castleton St Edmond OK 73034 Office: Okla Territorial Museum 402 E Oklahoma St Guthrie OK 73044

OLDS, LEILA CALISTA, educator; b. St. Cloud, Minn.; d. Charles S. and Nellie (Hodgson) Olds; student Wheaton (Ill.) Coll., 1932-34; B.Ed., St. Cloud State Coll., 1936; M.A., Hartford Sch. Religious Edn., 1952; B.D., Hartford Theol. Sem., 1954; Ph.D., U. St. Andrews (Scotland), 1961. Tchr. math. and speech Pipestone (Minn.) Pub. Schs., 1936-38, Community Sch., Teheran, Iran, 1938-43; tutored high sch. subjects Am. Legation, Kabul, Afghanistan, 1943-44; engrs. asst. Caterpillar Tractor Co., Peoria, Ill., 1945-46; tchr. gen. sci. Faribault (Minn.) Pub. Schs., 1946-50; asso. in edn. 1st Congl. Ch., Glastonbury, Conn., 1951-54; asst. prof. religious edn. Macalester Coll., St. Paul, 1954-56; prof. religion, chmn. dept. religion and philosophy Defiance (O.) Coll., 1956-60, prof., 1965—. Cons. religious edn. John S. Welles fellow Hartford Theol. Sem., 1956-58. Mem. Am. Assn. U. Profs., Soc. for Bibl. Lit. and Exegesis, Am. Acad. Religion, Am. Assn. U. Women, Religious Edn. Assn., Assn. Profs. and Researchers in Religious Edn. Home: 231 Harding St Defiance OH 43512

O'LEARY, VIRGINIA KYLE BOOTH (MRS. DANIEL B. O'LEARY), journalist; b. Washington, Jan. 8, 1928; d. Kyle and Helen (Sutton) Booth; student George Washington U., Washington, 1944-46; m. Philip Warren, Jr. (dec.); children—Joseph B., Virginia Kyle, Philip C.S., Timothy P.M., Mary M., Ruth N., Kathleen; m. 2d, Daniel B. O'Leary, Nov. 12, 1967. Reporter, Alexandria (Va.) Gazette, 1943-50, women's editor, religious news editor, asst. city editor, 1961-64; columnist N. Va. Free Press, 1948-49; women's editor, city editor No. Va. Sun., 1964-66; pub. relations dir. Arlington Red Cross, 1966; pub. relations dir. Alexandria Hosp., 1966-68; spl. writer Alexandria (Va.) Gazette, 1968-73, Women's editor, 1973—. Bd. dirs. Nat. capital area chpt. March of Dimes, 1961-67. Mem. Nat. League Am. Pen Women, No. Va. News Assn., Va. Press Women, Chi Omega. Home: 428 Monticello Blvd Alexandria VA 22305

OLENDER, TERRYS T. (MRS. EDWARD GLICK), lawyer, author; b. San Francisco; d. Julius and Mollie Olender; B.A., U. Cal. at Berkeley; postgrad. U. So. Cal. Law Sch.; m. Edward Glick, May 26, 1952. Admitted to Cal. bar, 1932, Fed. bar, 1932; practiced law in Los Angeles, 1933-41, 50—, San Francisco, 1942-49; dep. dist. atty. Los Angeles County, 1933-38; fgn. corr. Overseas News Agy., Mediterranean area, 1949-50; land subdivider, developer, 1955—; program coordinator radio and TV, producer, 1959—; feature columnist, editorial writer Citizen News, 1971—, also Athens (Greece) Daily Post; guest numerous interview and panel shows. Del. of Internat. Fedn. Women Lawyers to ECOSOC, Geneva, 1962. Mem. mayor's adv. com. Juvenile Delinquency and Narcotic Committees; pres.'s com. to Maintain Hotel Rent Control, San Francisco, 1948; an organizer, liaison officer No. Cal. br. Am. Christian Palestine Com., 1947-49, liaison officer, Los Angeles, 1950-59. Founder, pres. Olender Found.; trustee Inst. Cancer and Blood Research. Recipient joint awards Los Angeles Bd. Suprs. and Los Angeles City Council, 1961; Western mem. adv. bd. U.S. Wheelchair Sports Fund; sponsor Cal. Wheelchair Athletic Club. Named Women of Year, Zionist Orgn. Am., 1964; recipient award Israel Found. for Handicapped Children, 1968; named Woman of Achievement, Cal. Press Women, 1968. Mem. Los Angeles Bar Assn., So. Cal. Women Lawyers, International Federation of Women Lawyers, also mem. Acad. Television Arts and Scis. (judge Emmy awards Los Angeles area 1964), Radio and TV Women So. Cal., Nat., Cal. fedns., press women, Profl. Writers League, World Affairs Council, Am. Bar Assn., Cal. State Bar, Brit. Anti-Slavery Soc., Nat. Assn. Women Lawyers, Am. Women Radio and Television, UN Assn. U.S.A. (dir. Los Angeles). Democrat. Clubs: Greater Los Angeles Press, Hollywood (Cal.) Foreign Press. Author: For The Prosecution: Miss Deputy D.A.; Delitto Prequidizio; My Life in Crime (autobiography, 1st prize Cal. Press Women Writing contest 1967), 1966. Legal tech. adviser motion picture The Long Rope, 1961. Contbr. articles newspapers, mags.; feature columnist Los Angeles Daily Jour.; syndicated column, Hollywood Oddities, World Union Press. Address: 450 N Rossmore Av Los Angeles CA 90004

OLEON, SALLY JOY, ednl. adminstr.; b. Pitts.; d. William and Lillian (Schlesinger) Oleon; A.B., U. Pitts., M.Ed., Ph.D., 1958. Research asst. Grad. Sch. Pub. and Internat. Affairs, U. Pitts., 1958-60; sr. scientist mgmt. research projects, Washington, 1960-61; analyst Adv. Commn. on Intergovtl. Relations, 1961-63; asst. to v.p. George Washington U., Washington, 1963-65, asst. professorial lectr., 1961-65; spl. asst. Am. Council on Edn., 1965-66; Washington intern in edn., 1965-66; program officer Ford Found., 1966-69, Research Found. City U. N.Y., 1969-73; dir. office grant coordination Queensborough Community Coll., City U. N.Y., 1973—. Cons. Ford Found., Moton Found., 3 M Co. Mem. Am. Soc. for Pub. Adminstrn. (chpt. bd. 1963-66), Am. Polit. Sci. Assn., Am. Assn. Higher Edn., N.Y. Acad. Scis., Nat. Council Univ. Research Adminstrs., UN Assn. U.S.A., Mortar Bd., Pi Sigma Alpha, Pi Lambda Theta, Phi Delta Gamma. Author: Records Essential for Identification, 1961; Changing Patterns in Continuing Education for Business, 1967; (with A. Richter) Performance of Urban Functions: Local and Areawide, 1963; (with A. Manvel) Factors Affecting Voter Reaction to Governmental Reorganization in Metropolitan Areas, 1962. Home: 340 E 64th St New York City NY 10021 Office: Queensborough Community Coll Bayside NY 11364

OLHEISER, SISTER MARY DAVID, educator; b. Dickinson, N.D., Jan. 13, 1918; d. Rudolph and Magdalene (Goetz) Olheiser; student Coll. of St. Benedict, St. Joseph, Minn., 1936-37; B.A., Holy Names Coll., Spokane, Wash., 1942; M.A., St. Louis U., 1952; Ph.D., Boston Coll., 1962. Elementary sch. tchr., Tacoma, 1942-50; faculty Coll. of St. Benedict, 1950-69, prof. edn., chmn. dept., 1962-69, also mem. ednl. policies com., continuing edn. com., acad. dean, 1972-73, v.p. acad. affairs, dean faculty, 1973—; chmn. joint dept. edn. Coll. St. Benedict and St. Johns U., Collegeville, Minn., 1969-72, also chmn. tchr. edn. com.; ednl. cons., Winnipeg, Man., Can. Recipient Distinguished Achievement award Boston Coll. Grad. Sch., 1962, Invitational grant Nat. Conf. Health, Edn. and Welfare Task Force, Houston, 1971. Mem. Order of St. Benedict, Nat. Soc. Study Edn., Internat. Reading Assn., Am. Assn. Higher Edn., Nat. Catholic Edn. Assn. (instl. rep.), N.E.A. (instl. rep.), Am. Assn. for Coll. Tchr. Edn. (instl. rep.), Minn. Tchr. Edn. Council (instl. rep.). Author: Sister-Teacher Interest Scale, 1963. Home: Coll of St Benedict St Joseph MN 56374

OLIVARI, IRENE MARIA, educator; b. N.Y.C., Aug. 18, 1917; d. Prospero and Rita (Dodici) Olivari; B.A., Hunter Coll., 1930; M.S. in Ednl. Psychology, Fordham U., 1950, Ph.D. in Ednl. Psychology, 1958. Tchr. elementary schs., N.Y.C., 1945-60, supr., 1962-72; mem. faculty dept. edn. Lehman Coll., Bronx, N.Y., 1974—, prof., 1974—. Mem. Corpus Christi Sch. Bd., 1973—; vol. St. Luke's Hosp., N.Y.C. Recipient award for leadership and service Doctorate Assn. N.Y. Educators, 1973. Mem. Internat. Reading Assn., Am. Assn. Sch. Adminstrs., Nat. Council Adminstrs. Women in Edn., Am. Assn. U. Women (dir. 1972—), Doctorate Assn. N.Y. Educators (pres. 1971-73), Audubon Soc., Columbians. Home: 80 La Salle St New York City NY 10027 Office: Lehman College Bedford Park Blvd W Bronx NY 10468

OLIVE, BETSY ANN, librarian; b. Fuquay Springs, N.C., June 9, 1923; d. Burrell Raymond and Virginia Paschall (Wood) Olive; A.B., Duke U., 1945: degree L.S. U. N.C., 1955; postgrad. Cornell U., 1957-61. Several bus. positions in bank, law offices and retailing, 1945-53; asst. librarian documents dept. U. N.C. Library, 1953-55; with Grad. Sch. Bus. and Pub. Adminstrn. Library, Cornell U., Ithaca, N.Y., 1955—, librarian, 1965—, coordinator pub. services Cornell Libraries, 1972—. Mem. A.L.A., Spl. Libraries Assn., Med. Librarians Assn., Am. Soc. Information Sci. Author: Management: A Subject Listing of Recommended Books, Pamphlets and Journals, 1965. Compiler (with others) Executives Guide to Information Sources, 1965, Encyclopedia of Business Information Sources, 1970. Home: 121 N Sunset Dr Ithaca NY 14850

OLIVEN, CAROL CARDE (MRS. MELVIN NORMAN OLIVEN), educator; b. Boston, Feb. 19, 1943; d. Freeland Harold and Marybelle (Finger) Carde; B.A., Wellesley Coll., 1964; M.A., U.

Ia., 1966, Ph.D., 1971; m. Melvin Norman Oliven, July 11, 1964; children—Kenneth Norman, Everett James. Research asst. Bur. Bus. and Econ. Research, Iowa City, 1964-66; instr. econs. U. Ia., Iowa City, 1964-68; asst. prof. econs. Kirkwood Community Coll., Cedar Rapids, Ia., 1967-69; asst. prof. econs. Coe Coll., Cedar Rapids, 1969-73; dir. service planning Am. Coll. Testing Program, 1973—. Cosip grantee NSF, 1969, 72. Fellow Ia. Acad. Sci. (chmn. econs. sect. 1971-72); mem. Am., Midwest econ. assns., Omicron Delta Epsilon, Beta Gamma Sigma. Unitarian. Club: University Physics Wives (pres. 1970-71) (Iowa City). Author: Some Fiscal Effects of Regional Integration: Latin America, 1971; The Structure and Development of The Medical Industry, 1972. Home: 441 Lexington Av Iowa City IA 52240 Office: Am Coll Testing Program Box 168 Iowa City IA 52240

OLIVER, EDITH, theatrical reviewer; b. N.Y.C., Aug. 11, 1913; d. Samuel and Maude (Biow) Goldsmith; grad. Horace Mann Sch., N.Y.C., 1931; student Smith Coll., 1931-33. Author radio program Take It Or Leave It, 1940-52; mem. editorial staff New Yorker mag., 1947—. Off-Broadway reviewer, 1961—. Office: New Yorker Mag 25 W 43d St New York City NY 10036

OLIVER, EDNA PARTIN, city ofcl.; b. Cleveland, Tex., Apr. 20, 1908; d. Robert Wade and Letha Jane (Stetson) Partin; student Lee Coll., 1943; m. Coy Oliver, Aug. 22, 1925. Mgr., bookkeeper McDowell's Grocery, Baytown, Tex., 1936-43; supr. bookkeeping Peoples State Bank, Baytown, Tex., 1944-46; city clk., City of Baytown, Tex., 1946—. Mem. Nat. Secs. Assn. (pres. San Jacinto chpt. 1963). Mem. Assembly of God Ch. Club: Pilot (Baytown). Home: 709 Beecher St Baytown TX 77520 Office: 2401 Market St Baytown TX 77520

OLIVER, JEAN WEST, assn. exec.; b. Jasper, Ala., Dec. 8, 1920; d. John Mason and Lillie Lorene (O'Rear) West; student Del Mar. Coll., 1962; m. Benson Gordon Oliver, Mar. 6, 1937; children—Gloria Diane (Mrs. Joe David Maxey), John Gordon, James Moreland. Exec. sec. Nueces County Med. Soc., Corpus Christi, Tex., 1960—. Med. librarian Meml. Med. Center, 1960-71, art coordinator, 1964-70. Active P.T.A., 1945-68, Boy Scouts Am., 1957-60; vol. Am. Cancer Soc., 1971—. Mem. Am. Assn. Med. Execs., Les Amies du Vin. Clubs: Aurora Study (San Benito, Tex.); Corpus Christi Press, Junior Woman's, Woman's, Knife and Fork, Petroleum. Home: 430 Peerman Pl Corpus Christi TX 78411 Office: 2606 Hospital Blvd Corpus Christi TX 78405

OLIVER, MARY WILHELMINA, law librarian, educator; b. Cumberland, Md., May 4, 1919; d. John Arlington and Sophia (Lear) Oliver; A.B., Western Md. Coll., 1940; B.S. in Library Sci., Drexel Inst. Tech., 1943; J.D., U. N.C., 1951. Asst. circulation librarian N.J. Coll. Women, 1943-45; asst. in law library U. Va., 1945-47; asst. reference, social sci. librarian Drake U., 1947-49; research asst. Inst. Govt., U. N.C., 1951-52, asst. law librarian, 1952-55, asst. prof. law, law librarian, 1955-59, asso. prof. law, law librarian, 1959-69, prof. law and library sci., law librarian, 1969—; admitted to N.C. bar, 1951. Mem. Am. Assn. Law Libraries (v.p., pres.-elect 1971, pres. 1972-73) Spl. Libraries Assn., Am., N.C. bar assns., Assn. Am. Law Schs., Am. Soc. Legal History, Law Alumni Assn. U. N.C., Internat. Assn. Law Libraries, Seldon Soc., Order of Coif. Home: Box 733 Chapel Hill NC 27514

OLIVER, PEGGY ANN (MRS. JEFFERSON W. OLIVER, JR.), educator; b. Monterey, Cal., May 31, 1945; d. Carl W. and Neola Elizabeth (Cox) Clark; B.A., Ida. State U., 1972, postgrad. 1973-74; m. Jefferson W. Oliver, Jr., Apr. 11, 1964; children—Susan Lee, Angela Lynn. Dir. youth activities USAF Karamursel AFB, Turkey, 1964-65; sec. CIT Finance Corp., Biloxi, Miss., 1965-67; grad. asst. Ida. State U., Pocatello, 1971-72; debate coach Snake River High Sch., Blackfoot, Ida., 1972-73; tchr. Bonneville High, Idaho Falls, Ida., 1973—. Asso. students Ida. State U. scholar, 1968-73. Mem. Nat., Ida. edn. assns. Republican. Mem. Ch. of Jesus Christ of Latter-day Saints. Home: 694 Melrose Dr Idaho Falls ID 83401

OLIVER, SYLVIA ELLEN BASSETT (MRS. WILLARD CHELSEA OLIVER), librarian; b. South Bend, Ind., Mar. 24, 1921; d. Clark and Lillian (Geer) Bassett; B.S., S.W. Tex. U., 1942; M.L.S., U. Mo., 1969; m. Willard Chelsea Oliver, Jan. 10, 1942; children—Jeffrey David, Jill Jeanette (Mrs. James Pilkington). Tchr., Moberly (Mo.) Jr. High Sch., 1954-55, Westran High Sch., Huntsville, Mo., 1955-58, Springfield Twp. Jr. High Sch., Michigan City, Ind., 1958-59; dir. Little Dixie Regional Library, Moberly, 1962-73; librarian Moberly Area Jr. Coll., 1973—. Founder, mem. exec. com. Randolph County Council Social Agys., Moberly, 1973—. Bd. dirs. Randolph County United Fund. Mem. Am. (councilor 1974—), Mo. (exec. bd. pub. relations com. 1970-73, exec. bd. outreach round table 1971-73) library assns., Mo. Assn. Social Welfare (bd. dirs. E. Central div. 1973—). Baptist. Clubs: Lioness (pres. Huntsville, Mo. 1973-74); Altrusa (pres. Moberly, Mo. 1974-75). Home: Route 2 Huntsville MO 65259

OLIVERIO, MARY ELLEN (MRS. BERNARD H. NEWMAN), educator; b. Fairmont, W.Va., Jan. 17, 1926; d. Luigi and Elizabeth (LaCova) Oliverio; A.B., B.S., Fairmont State Coll., 1947; M.A., Columbia, 1949, Ph.D., 1954; m. Bernard H. Newman, Dec. 26, 1964. Tchr., Fairview (W.Va.) High Sch., 1947-48; instr. Marshall U., Huntington, W.Va., 1949-51; asst. prof. edn. Tchrs. Coll., Columbia, 1954-57, asso. prof., 1957-61, prof., 1961-73. Ednl. cons. to schs. and job corps for girls; speaker at many confs. and workshops; cons. Ministry Edn., Lima, Peru, 1964. Bd. dirs. Girl Scouts U.S., 1966-74; trustee Manpower Edn. Inst. Mem. Nat. Bus. Edn. Assn. (pres. research found. 1960-61), Inst. Certifying Secs., Eastern Bus. Tchrs. Assn. (exec. bd. 1966-69). Author: (with Bowman) Shorthand Dictation Studies, 1965; (with Agnew and Meehan) Secretarial Office Practice, 8th ed., 1972; Clerical Office Procedures, 1973; International Business Communications in English, 1974. Editor: Business Education Quarterly, 1958-60. Contbr. articles to profl. pubs. Home: 106 Morningside Dr New York City NY 10027 also Via Pola 4 Milano Italy

OLLER, ANNA KATHRYN, educator; b. Waynesboro, Pa., July 1, 1916; d. Daniel G. and Blanche (Ruthrauff) Oller; A.B., Juniata Coll., 1938; B.S., Drexel Inst. Tech., 1939; M.S., U. Ill., 1951; Ph.D., U. Mich., 1963. Researcher, U. Ill., 1949-50, teaching fellow, 1950-51; instr. Fla. State U., 1951-52; asst. prof. Grad. Sch. Library Sci., Drexel U., Phila., 1952-54, asso. prof., 1955-67, acting dean, 1967-68, prof., asso. dean, 1969—; vis. prof. Pa. State U., summers 1947-49, 51, Emory U., summer 1953, U. Mich., summer 1954. Asst. librarian Huntingdon County Library, 1939-40, librarian, 1942-45; cataloguer Juniata Coll. Library, 1940-42; librarian Adams County (Pa.) Library, 1945-47; asst. extension librarian Pa. State Library, 1947-49. Trustee, Juniata Coll., Huntingdon, Pa., 1969-72. Mem. Am. (mem. subscription books com. 1963-69, 73—, chmn. Isadore Mudge Citation Jury 1967-68), Pa. library assns., Am. Assn. Library Schs., Germantown Hist. Soc., Hist. Soc. Pa., Am. Assn. U. Profs., Am. Soc. Information Sci., Beta Phi Mu (pres. 1974—). Contbr. articles to profl. jours. Home: 706C Alden Park Manor Philadelphia PA 19144

OLMER, JANE CHASNOFF (MRS. FRANCOIS JEAN OLMER), information handling, computer specialist; b. St. Louis; d. Jacob and Julia (Linenthal) Chasnoff; B.A., Wellesley Coll., 1934; M.S., Washington U., 1937; postgrad Sorbonne (Paris), 1936; m. Francois Jean Olmer, Aug. 2, 1937 (dec. 1966). Tchr., Am. Sch., Paris, France, 1937-39; editor Paris newsletter, radio broadcaster, Paris, 1939-41; cons. statistician May Co., Cleve., Morristown, N.J., 1942-52; analytical statistician USN Electronics Supply Office, Great Lakes, Ill., 1954-55, supervisory analytical statistician, 1955-56, specialist trainee, 1956, mathematician, 1956-59, math. statis., 1959-61; sr. mathematician mem. staff dir. Data Processing Center, Johns Hopkins U. Applied Physics Lab., Silver Spring, Md., 1961—. Mem. SHARE, 1964—, mgr. text information processing retrieval project, 1965-73; mem. Wellesley Expt. in Mutual Understanding, 1962—, co-chmn., 1970—. Recipient Superior Accomplishment award U.S. Navy, 1961. Mem. League Women Voters, Data Processing Mgmt. Assn. (chpt. dir. 1965-67), Assn. for Computing Machinery, Alliance Francaise de Washington, Phi Beta Kappa, Sigma Xi, Pi Mu Epsilon. Clubs: Federal Toastmistress (pres. 1965, club. rep. 1966), Wellesley of D.C. Contbr. articles to profl. jours. Home: 2510 Virginia Av NW Washington DC 20037 Office: 8621 Georgia Av Silver Spring MD 20910

OLMSTED, AUDREY JUNE PERRYMAN (MRS. RICHARD RAYMOND OLMSTED), educator; b. Sioux Falls, S.D., June 5, 1940; d. Leslie Thomas and Dorothy Lucille (Else) Perryman; B.A., U. No. Ia., 1962, M.A., 1963; Ph.D., Ind. U., 1971; m. Richard Raymond Olmsted, Jan. 31, 1963. Teaching fellow Ind. U., Bloomington, 1963-66; instr. speech dept. Coll. Liberal Arts, Boston U., 1968-72, asst. prof., 1972—. Mem. Speech Communication Assn., Delta Sigma Rho. Home: 28 Lawrence St Boston MA 02116

OLMSTED, ELIZABETH HIATT (MRS. JOHN M.H. OLMSTED), librarian; b. Topeka, Kan., Oct. 9, 1919; d. Lyman Ray and Isabel Paul (March) Hiatt; student State Tchrs. Coll., Dickinson, N.D., 1936-38, U. N.D., 1938-39; Mus.B., Eastman Sch. Music, 1940; M.A., U. Minn., 1946, B.S. in L.S., 1950; certificate (fellow) Sch. Library and Information Services, U. Md., 1968; m. John M.H. Olmsted, Dec. 20, 1951 (div. May 1955); 1 dau., Jane Isabel. Tchr. high sch. English and music, N.D. and Ida., 1940-43; invoice clk. U. Minn., Mpls., 1943-44; clk. Century Book Store, Mpls., 1944-46; music librarian Mpls. Pub. Library, 1946-51; head music librarian Ohio State U., Columbus, 1954-58, Oberlin (O.) Coll. Conservatory Library, 1958-74. Tchr. music bibliography Case Western Res. U., Cleve., 1969; tchr. music library Kent State U., summer 1969. Mem. Music Library Assn. (v.p. 1968-69, editor, Catalog of Printed Music 1953-72, Distinguished Service citation 1974). Home: RD 2 Peasley Rd Amherst OH 44001

OLNEY, MARY BELLE, pediatrician; b. Chgo., Jan. 12, 1908; d. Clyde Charles and Augustha May (Spaulding) Olney; A.B., U. Cal., 1928, M.D., 1933. Intern, San Francisco County Hosp., 1932-33; resident U. Cal. Hosp., 1933-35, U. Chgo., 1935-36; practice medicine, specializing in pediatrics, San Francisco, 1936—; mem. staff St. Luke's Hosp., San Francisco Gen. Hosp., U. Cal. Hosp.; clin. prof. pediatrics faculty U. Cal. at San Francisco, 1936—; exec. dir. Diabetic Youth Found., 1936—. Home: 1651 8th Av San Francisco CA 94122 Office: 1128 Irving St San Francisco CA 94122

OLSEN, FLORENCE JOHANNA, machinery mfg. exec.; b. Bklyn., July 3, 1924; d. Samuel Matthew and Bertha Eva (Woodruff) Olsen; B.S., N.Y. U., 1943, postgrad., 1943-45. Research asst. Outdoor Advt., Inc., N.Y.C., 1943-44; media research Batten, Barton, Durstine & Osborne, N.Y.C., 1944-48; copy research v.p. Bur. Advt., Am. Newspaper Pubs. Assn., 1948-65; sec. corp., charge advt. Kensol-Olsen Mark, Inc., Melville, N.Y., 1965—; v.p. charge advt. Whiley-Kensol, 1972—. Nurses aide, motor corps driver A.R.C., 1940-45; asso. Lincoln Center Performing Arts, 1965—. Mem. Met. Opera Guild, Internat. Platform Assn., Am. Advt. Fedn., Advt. Women N.Y. Republican. Club: N.Y. University Alumni (N.Y.C.). Contbr. articles to profl. jours. Home: 896 Lincoln Av Baldwin NY 11510 Office: 40 Melville Park Rd Melville NY 11746

OLSEN, INGRITH DEYRUP (MRS. SIGURD M. OLSEN), educator; b. Englewood, N.J., Dec. 22, 1919; d. Alvin S. and Edith (Henry) Johnson; A.B. summa cum laude, Barnard Coll., 1940; Ph.D., Columbia, 1944; m. Sigurd M. Olsen, Dec. 28, 1962. Mem. faculty Columbia U., N.Y.C., 1942-64, prof. dept. zoology, 1958-64; research prof. zoology U. Wash., Seattle, 1964-69, prof. zoology, 1969—. Fulbright fellow, 1953-54, Guggenheim fellow, 1953-54. Fellow N.Y. Acad. Scis.; mem. Am. Physiol. Soc., Am. Soc. Zoologists, Am. Soc. Cell Biology, Soc. Gen. Physiologists, Harvey Soc. Mem. writing teams also coms. high sch. biology programs Biol. Scis. Curriculum Study, 1960—. Home: 6542 55th Av NE Seattle WA 98115

OLSEN, MARY JUDITH, occupational therapist; b. Waseca, Minn., Apr. 19, 1940; d. Milo Burton and Teckla Ruth (Sommerstad) Olsen; B.S. in Occupational Therapy (Minn. Occupational Therapy Assn. scholar, Minn. Dept. Health, Edn. and Welfare scholar), Coll. St. Catherine, St. Paul, 1962; M.S. in Counseling and Guidance, U. N.D., 1971. Occupational therapist Rochester (Minn.) State Hosp., 1963-66; instr., coordinator Occupational Therapy Assts. Sch., Bd. Edn., Duluth, Minn., 1966-68; instr. U. N.D., Grand Forks, 1968-71; chief occupational therapist Bivins Rehab. Center, High Plains Baptist Hosp., Amarillo, Tex., 1972—. Mem. exec. bd. Home Delivered Meals, Inc., Grand Forks, 1969-71. Mem. Nat. Rehab. Assn., Am. Assn. Univ. Women, Am., Tex. Occupational Therapy assns. Episcopalian. Home: 3453 Amherst St Apt 408 Amarillo TX 79109 Office: 1600 Wallace Blvd Amarillo TX 79106

OLSEN, SANDRA ENDICOTT WEBBER (MRS. FRANK VERNE OLSEN), occupational therapist; b. Seattle, Jan. 27, 1937; d. Carl Endicott Edwards and Catharine Thayer (Marple) Webber; B.S. in Occupational Therapy, U. Puget Sound, 1958; certified Am. Occupational Therapy Assn., 1960; m. Frank Verne Olsen, June 8, 1958; children—Frank Verne, Bradley, Marcella, Rebecca. Evaluator, instr. Goodwill Industries, Tacoma, 1959-60; staff occupational therapist Good Samaritan Hosp. and Rehab. Center, Puyallup, Wash., 1966-67, dir. occupational therapy, 1970-74; dist. occupational therapist Bethel schs., 1974—; occupational therapy cons. Puyallup Manor Nursing Home, 1966-67, Valley Terrace Nursing Center, Puyallup, 1968-69. Active P.T.A., 1964—; adviser Tri Hi Y, 1964-65. Named Club Woman of Year, Jr. Women's Club, 1969. Mem. Am. (clin. rep. 1971—, steering com. Council on Edn. 1974—), Wash. (recruitment rep. 1966, del.-at-large 1971, treas. 1974-74) occupational therapy assns., Wash. State Prevention of Blindness (mem. visual screening team 1966-68), Pi Beta Phi Alumni (house chmn. 1962). Presbyn. (tchr. 1967-70). Home: 816 4th Av SW Puyallup WA 98371 Office: 407 14th Av SE Puyallup WA 98371

OLSEN, THEODORA EGBERT PECK (MRS. SEVERT ANDREW OLSEN), artist; b. Union, N.J., Sept. 6, 1909; d. Edward Egbert and Theodorea G. (Tucker) Peck; student N.Y. Sch. Design, 1928-29, Pratt-Phoenix Sch. Design, N.Y.C., 1929-32, Coll. City N.Y., 1955; m. Ray Sheldon Wilbur, Sept. 8, 1933 (dec. 1966); 1 dau., Margaret Anne (Mrs. Prudhomme); m. 2d, Severt Andrew Olsen, July 17, 1967; stepchildren Arlene Christine, Severt Eugene. Exhibited at Contemporary Gallery, Newark, 1932, S.I. Mus., 1947-65, N.Y.C. Fedn. Women's Clubs exhibit, 1961, Island Art Center Gallery, New Dorp, S.I., 1961, 33d N.J. Exhbn., Montclair Art Mus., 1964, Summit (N.J.) Art Center, 1965; outdoor shows at Sailors Snug Harbour, S.I., 1956-63, Greenwich Village, N.Y.C., 1961-64, Southhampton and Westhampton (L.I.) Beach, 1964, Summit Art Center, N.J., 1967, Spring Festival Arts, Staten Island, 1968; represented in permanent collection at Wagner Coll., S.I.; prin. works include View From Guild Hall, Show Case, Variation on Theme VIII, Long Island Expressway, Seed Pods, Emergence from Chrysalis. Cons., lectr., pvt. tchr., 1934—; tchr. painting YWCA, S.I., 1968-72. Active fund-raising Richmond Mem. Hosp., 1946-54, com. to beautify halls Tottenville (S.I.) High Sch., 1958-60. Recipient S.I. Mus.-Wagner Coll. Purchase award, 1958—; Julius Weisglass award S.I. Mus., 1960, 65; 1st prize and Honorable mention N.Y.C. Fedn. Women's Clubs competition, 1961. Founder, hon. life mem. S. Shore Artists Group (pres. 1946-47, 49-61, 2d v.p. 1965-66); mem. S.I. Inst. Arts and Scis., S.I. Hist. Soc. Women's Aux., S.I. Hist. Soc., Pratt-Phoenix Sch. Design, Alumni (jury awards 1949), Epsilon Nu Sigma. Clubs: Prince Bay Women's (pres. 1969-71); Coast Guard Officer's Wives. Home: 72 Bayview Av Prince Bay NY 10309

OLSHER, LAURA NANCY FEISS, drama educator; b. Evanston, Ill., Mar. 24, 1927; d. Sidney Laurence and Frances (Rosenberg) Feiss; B.A., Northwestern U., 1944; M.A., U. Cal. at Los Angeles, 1968; postgrad. (Shubert fellow) U. Cal. at Davis, 1969-70; children—Janet Prest, Alice, David. Children's program dir. Sta. KPFK-FM, 1960-61; star radio program for children The Magic Basket, Sta. KMLA-FM, Los Angeles, 1961-63; writer, dir., actress program for children Magic Basket, Stage Soc. Theater, Los Angeles, 1961-63; tchr. English as a 2d lang. and pub. speaking Los Angeles Adult Edn., 1963-67; tchr. Coll. of Holy Names, Oakland, Cal., summers 1968—; tchr., books and storytelling for children U. Cal. at Los Angeles Edn. Extension, 1963—; TV actress, animated voices for TV and radio programs and commls. including Disney, also recs., 1961—; tchr. English as 2d lang. Los Angeles Community Adult Sch., 1970—; tchr. books and storytelling for children U Cal. at Irvine Extension, Pierce Jr. Coll. Extension, 1970—; writer radio scripts Heartbeat Theatre, 1970—. Actress as Laura of Lindyland storyteller, Lindy Opera House Children's Theatre, 1963-64; guest lectr. oral communication So. Cal. Coll., 1969—; drama cons. Glendale Arts Impact Project, 1970-72; lectr. theater arts dept. U. Cal. at Los Angeles, 1972-73; mem. drama subcom. Statewide Fine Arts and Humanities Framework Com., 1969—. Recipient award for excellence in children's programming Nat. Assn. for Better Radio and Television, 1961; various playwriting awards, 1969-70. Mem. Am., Children's theater assns., So. Cal. Theater Assn. (bd. advisers 1973—). Author plays: The Time for Living, 1972; Behind Each Face, 1972; The Fifth Victim, 1973; film Love's Beginning. Address: 1541 N Poinsettia Pl Los Angeles CA 90046

OLSON, BERNICE CAROL JONSON (MRS. ARTHUR E. OLSON), lawyer; b. Quincy, Wash., June 12, 1914; d. Axel Ernest and Karen Olea (Gilbertson) Jonson; J.D., U. Wash., 1936; m. Arthur E. Olson, Dec. 5, 1949; children—Thomas, Marshall, Gerald, Ralpha, Eric, Mark. Admitted to Wash. bar, 1936; practiced in Seattle. Bd. dirs. Ballard Gen. Hosp., Seattle. Mem. Am., Wash. bar assns., Nat. Trial Lawyers Assn., Am. Judicature Soc., Ballard Comml. Club, Bus. and Profl. Club. Mem. Order of Eastern Star. Home: 7737 34th St NW Seattle WA 98107 Office: 1734 NW Market St Seattle WA 98107

OLSON, BONNIE WAGGONER BRETERNITZ (MRS. O. DONALD OLSON), civic worker; b. North Platte, Neb., May 30, 1916; d. Floyd Emil and Edith (Waggoner) O.; A.B., U. Chgo., 1947; m. O. Donald Olson, May 17, 1944; children—Pamela Lynne, Douglas Donald. Dep. clk. Dist. Ct., Lincoln County, Neb., 1940-42; advt. researcher Burke & Assos., Chgo., 1942; contbg. newspaper columnist Chgo. Herald-Am., 1943; social worker A.R.C., Chgo., 1942-44; exec. sec. Econometrica, Cowles Commn. for Research in Econs., Chgo., 1945-47. Col., Chgo. Maternity Center Fund Drive, 1953; mem. Colo. Springs Community Council, 1956-58, chmn. children's div., 1956-58, mem. exec. bd., 1956-58, mem. budget com., 1957-58; mem. Colorado Springs Charter Assn., 1956-60, mem. exec. bd., 1957-59, sec., 1958; chmn. El Paso County P.T.A., Protective Services for Children, 1959-61; chmn. women's div. fund drive A.R.C., 1961; mem. League Women Voters, 1957—, mem. state children's law com., 1961-63; chmn. ad hoc com. El Paso County Citizens' Com. for Nat. Probation and Parole Survey, Juvenile Ct. Procedures and Detention, 1957-61; mem. children's adv. com. Colo. Child Welfare Dept., 1959-63, chmn., 1961; del. White House Conf. on Children and Youth, 1960, 70; sec. Citizens Ad Hoc Com. for Comprehensive Mental Health Clinic for Pikes Peak Region, 1966—; mem. Colorado Springs Human Relations Commn., 1968-71; sustaining mem. Symphony Guild, 1970-72, Fine Arts Center, 1957—; bd. dirs. Pikes Peak Mental Health Center, 1964-67. Recipient Lane Bryant Ann. Nat. Awards citation, 1961; alumni citation for pub. service U. Chgo., 1961. Mem. Am. Acad. Polit. and Social Sci., Council on Religion and Internat. Affairs. Episcopalian. Clubs: Quadranglar, University (Chgo.); Broadmoor Golf, Garden of the Gods, ENT Officers Wives (hon.) (Colorado Springs). Home: 31 Broadmoor Av Colorado Springs CO 80906

OLSON, BURNEY KATHARINE MCAULEY (MRS. RUSSELL H. OLSON), social worker; b. Holly Springs, Miss.; d. Angus Malcolm and Van Burney (Deaton) McAuley; student Superior State Tchrs. Coll., 1931-32, Miss. Synodical Coll., 1932-33; B.S., U. Minn., 1936; M.S. in Social Work, U. Tenn., 1957; m. Russell Howard Olson, Aug. 9, 1938. Caseworker Children's Bur., Memphis, 1953-56, 57-61; caseworker Hope Cottage, Children's Bur., Dallas, 1961-64, dir. child care services, Dallas, 1964-74, staff supr., 1974—. Mem. Nat. Assn. Social Workers, Nat. Foster Parents Assn., Chi Omega. Presbyn. Home: 10564 Royal Club Lane Dallas TX 75229 Office: 2301 Welborn St Dallas TX 75219

OLSON, CYNTHIA ANNE (MRS. RONALD ERIC OLSON), psychologist; b. Columbus, O., July 29, 1941; d. Lewis A. and Marguerite Ann (Stevens) Paul; student Coll. of Emporia, 1959-61; B.S., Emporia Kan. State Coll., 1963, M.S., 1964; postgrad. U. Kan., 1969, 72, 74, U. Mo., 1970-71; m. Ronald Eric Olson, June 5, 1965; 1 son, Benjamin Eric. With Lindsborg (Kan.) Pub. Schs., 1964-66; sch. psychologist DeSoto (Kan.) Unified Sch. Dist. 232, 1966—. Mem. health adv. council DeSoto Pub. Schs. 1969-72; mem. Sunflower (Kan.) Coordinating Council, 1967—; mem. adv. council Johnson County Mental Health Center, Greater Kansas City, Kan., 1971—; mem. Drug Edn. Council, DeSoto, 1971-72; participant Gov.'s Conf. on Drug Abuse, 1970, team facilitation, 1972. Mem. Nat., Kan. edn. assns., Nat. (nat. membership com. co-chmn. 1971-72, mem. exec. bd. 1970-72, regional West Central dir. 1970-72), Kan. (mem. exec. bd. 1966—, pres. 1974-75) assns. for sch. psychologists, Jaycee Jaynes (pres. 1971-72), Beta Sigma Phi. Episcopalian. Home: PO Box 411 900 W 9th St DeSoto KS 66018 Office: PO Box 119 Sunflower KS 66019

OLSON, DORISE EVELYN (MRS. RAUL J. MINA-MORA), artist; b. N.Y.C., June 8, 1932; d. Athur C. and Anna (Carlson) Olson; student Art Student's League, L.I. Art League, Woodstock, N.Y., Traphagen Sch. Design, N.Y.; m. Raul J. Mina-Mora, Oct. 27, 1967.

One-man shows at Caravan House Galleries, Lord & Taylor's Galleries, Nat. Art League, Wickford Art Gallery; exhibited in group shows at Bklyn. Mus., Nat. Arts Club, Nat. Acad., Nat. Acad. Fine Arts, Parrish Art Mus., 1970, 72, Pacem in Terris Gallery, 1972; represented in pvt. collections. Demonstrator watercolor for various schs. and pvt. clubs. Recipient award Bus. and Profl. Women's Club, N.Y.C., 1967; gold medal Knickerbocker Artists, 1968; Hydenryk award Catherine Lorillard Wolfe Art Club, 1969; 1st place award in watercolor Bklyn. Mus. competition, 1966, 67, 69, Windsor and Newton award, Nat. Arts League Gold medal, 70, Grumbacher award 1971. Mem. Am. Artists Profl. League, Allied Artists Am., Catherine Lorillard Wolfe Art Club, Nat. Soc. Painters in Casein and Acrylic, Knickerbocker Artists, Audubon Artists. Address: 106-20 Shore Front Pkwy Rockaway Park NY 11694

OLSON, EDNA HOWARD (MRS. LAWRENCE CARROLL OLSON), librarian; b. nr. Dawsonville, Ga.; d. William Stevens and Esty (Dooley) Howard; B.C.S., Ga. State U., 1950; M.Librarian, Emory U., 1955; m. Lawrence Carroll Olson, Mar. 4, 1939 (dec. Oct. 1953); children—Lawrence Howard, Wayne Carroll, Edna Margaret. Librarian, Ga. Agrl. Expt. Sta., 1949—. Trustee, chmn. bd. trustees Flint River Regional Library, Griffin, Ga. Mem. Internat. Assn. Agrl. Librarians and Documentalists, Am., Southeastern, Ga. (sec. 1961-63) library assns., Am. Library Trustees Assn., Delta Mu Delta. Baptist. Home: 733 E College St Griffin GA 30223 Office: Ga Agrl Expt Sta Experiment GA 30212

OLSON, ELIZABETH ANNE, social worker; b. Milw., Dec. 24, 1914; d. Christian M. and Anna Marie (Joecks) Olson; B.A., Milw. Downer Coll. (now part of Lawrence U.), 1936; M.A., U. Chgo., 1949. Tchr. langs. Minocqua (Wis.) High Sch., 1936-38, Janesville (Wis.) High Sch., 1938-42; field rep. Midwestern area A.R.C., also dir. service to mil. families, dir. tng., St. Louis, 1944-72, loaned to Hawaii chpt. as acting dir. disaster and service to mil. families, 1962-63, loaned to League Red Cross Socs., Geneva, Switzerland as cons. on staff tng. and assisting African Nat. Red Cross socs., 1969, 70, 72, asst. dir. disaster nat. hdqrs., Washington, 1972-73, nat. dir. personnel tng. and devel., 1973—. Trainer, cons. various community and profl. groups, sch. systems. Vice chmn. com. on adminstrn., vol. trainer met. bd. YWCA, St. Louis, 1958-70; chmn. personnel and program coms. YM-YW Inter-Campus Bd., 1967-70; active various coms. and task forces related to vol. work in Inner City; class chmn. alumni fund raising for Lawrence U., U. Chgo., 1967—. Mem. Am. Soc. Tng. and Devel. (dir. St. Louis chpt. 1967, mem. nat. manpower com. 1969-71), Nat. Assn. Social Workers, Assn. Certified Social Workers, Internat., Nat. confs. social welfare, Adult Edn. Assn., Common Cause. Episcopalian (treas. 1967-72). Club: Zonta (St. Louis, 1st. vice chmn. 1970). Home: 2401 H St NW Washington DC 20037 Office: 17th and D Sts NW Washington DC 20006

OLSON, GLORIA ANN SONDRA, army officer; b. Rome, N.Y., May 7, 1928; d. John Stanley and Mary (Pardi) Olson; B.S., State U. N.Y., Oswego, 1951; M.S., Syracuse U., 1953; certificate advanced pub. relations U. Wis., 1965. Commd. 2d lt. U.S. Army, 1954, advanced through grades to lt. col., 1972; chief of TV, Def. Information Sch., Fort Benjamin Harrison, Ind., 1965-67; dep. chief radio-TV news br. Dept. Def. Pub. Affairs Office, Directorate of Information, Washington, 1967-68; spl. staff officer Gen. Creighton W. Abrams, also dep. chief of command information Mil. Assistance Command, Vietnam, 1968-69; WAC recruiting coordinator, chief WAC br., 1st recruiting dist., Ft. Meade, Md., 1970-72; information officer Hdqrs. Dept. Army, Washington, 1972—. Decorated Bronze Star medal, Air medal, Meritorious Service medal, Joint Service Commendation medal with 2 oak leaf clusters, Army Commendation medal with 2 oak leaf clusters; name Woman of Yr., Writers League, 1970. Mem. Am. Women in Radio and TV, Alpha Psi Omega. Club: Potomac (Md.) Boxer. Home: 243 Shore Dr Crownsville MD 21032 Office: OCINFO-PPD Room 2E637 Pentagon Washington DC 20310

OLSON, HERTHA OLIVIA GJERLOFF (MRS. HOWARD WILBER OLSON), advt. exec.; b. Marquette, Neb., Aug. 8, 1911; d. Carl Samuel and Jennie (Feddersen) Gjerloff; grad. high sch.; m. Howard Wilber Olson, Oct. 28, 1934; 1 dau., Susan Ann (Mrs. Theodore Kretzer). With advt. staff Grand Island (Neb.) Ind., 1944-47; with Miller & Paine, Lincoln, Neb., 1956—, mgr. advt. dept., 1962—. Mem. Am. Women in Radio and TV, Goodwill Industries Aux., Women's Div. C. of C., P.E.O. Mem. Order Eastern Star. Home: 643 W Lakeshore Lincoln NE 68524 Office: 13th and O Sts Lincoln NE 68501

OLSON, ILYNE MCJIMSEY (MRS. KENNETH VERDERE OLSON), educator; b. Kerrville, Tex., Apr. 16, 1919; d. Albertus and Laura (Wilson) McJimsey; B.J., U. Tex., 1941, postgrad., 1953; postgrad. U. Tenn., 1963, Incarnate Word Coll., 1967; m. Kenneth Verdere Olson, June 21, 1942; children—Daniel Verdere, Sharon Kathlyne (Mrs. Wilson James Ramsey, Jr.), John Laurence. Advt. copywriter Sears Roebuck & Co., 1941-42; advt. mgr. Stowers Furniture, San Antonio, 1942-43; tchr., St. Michael Episcopal Sch., Dallas, 1965-66; tchr. Alamo Heights Sch. Dist., San Antonio, 1966-68, N.E. Ind. Sch. Dist., San Antonio, 1968-69; tchr. history W.T. White High Sch., Dallas Ind. Sch. Dist., 1970-72; tchr. journalism Alief Ind. Sch. Dist., Houston, 1972—. Creator ednl. games Internat. Travel Mate, Addison, Tex., 1971, Kenworthy Ednl. Service, Buffalo, 1974; owner, I.M. Olson-Ednl. Games, 1973—. Mem. Women in Communications, Sigma Delta Chi. Home: 6407 Redding Rd Houston TX 77036 Office: Box 42263 Houston TX 77042

OLSON, JANE VIRGINIA, editor; b. Chgo., Dec. 14, 1916; d. Oscar Wilford and Mary (Bowles) Olson; B.A., U. N.M., 1939; m. William M. Gooden, Feb. 16, 1955 (div. 1957). Copy editor Atlantic Monthly mag., Boston, 1942-46; copy editor Vogue mag., N.Y.C., 1946-49; tech. editor Ill. Geol. Survey, Urbana, 1949-55; sci. and social sci. editor Yale U. Press, New Haven, 1958-69; editor Am. Scientist mag., New Haven, 1969—. Mem. League Women Voters. Home: 130 Everit St New Haven CT 06511 Office: 345 Whitney Av New Haven CT 06511

OLSON, JUDITH LUELLEN HAZARD JOHNSON (MRS. KENNETH PAUL OLSON), educator; b. Alamosa, Colo., Mar. 13, 1938; d. Claude Howard and Lenora Luellen (Ainsworth) Hazard; B.A., U. Colo., 1964; postgrad. U. Denver, 1973—; m. Kenneth Paul Olson, Nov. 12, 1965; 1 son (by previous marriage), Glen Edward Johnson. Writer, editor newspapers, Colo., Tex., 1964-68; self-employed in pub. relations and advt., Colorado Springs, Colo., Fort Worth, 1968-73; instr., El Paso Community Coll., Colorado Springs, Colo., 1973—. Editorial cons. Century Sch. Book Press, San Francisco, 1965-66. Publicity chairwoman, coordinator YWCA, 1968-70. Mem. Nat., Colo. edn. assns., Women in Communications, Colorado Springs Ad Club, D.A.R., El Paso Community Coll. Faculty Assn., ITM Club, Theta Sigma Phi. Republican. Episcopalian. Author: Deadline for Tim, 1967. Home: Box 215 Manitou Springs CO 80829 Office: El Paso Community Coll Colorado Springs CO 80922

OLSON, LAURA MAXINE, UN ofcl.; b. Baker, Ore., June 16, 1927; d. Arthur Vard and Retta Belle (Mercer) Olson; B.S., U. Ore., 1949. Line-up editor True Detective mag., N.Y.C., 1949-50; promotion writer N.Y. Herald Tribune Syndicate, writer N.Y. Herald Tribune Newsservice, 1950-52; counsellor for women U. Ore., 1952-53; news editor Cottage Grove (Ore.) Sentinel, 1953-54; reporter, polit. writer Roseburt (Ore.) News-Rev., 1954-56; research asst. to U.S. rep., 1957-60; press asst. to U.S. senator, 1961-62; asst. legislative asst. to U.S. senator, 1962-65, legislative asst., 1966-68; spl. cons. population problems U.S. Senate Operations Subcom. on Fgn. Aid Expenditures, 1965-68; head information office Nat. Endowment for Humanities, 1968-70; chief clearing house and information service UN Econ. and Social Commn. for Asia and Pacific, 1970—, chmn. staff assn., 1971-73, co-editor staff bull., 1973-74, co-chmn. staff assn. welfare com. Mem. Women in Communication, Delta Delta Delta. Democrat. Episcopalian. Club: Royal Bangkok Sports. Home: McKenzie Hwy Leaburg OR 97401 Office: UN ESCAP Population Div Bangkok Thailand

OLSON, LILLY CORRINE JOHNSON (MRS. LOREN KEITH OLSON), civic leader; b. Proctor, Minn.; d. Christ and Ragna (Carlson) Johnson; B.S., U. Wis., Stout, 1934; postgrad. U. Wis., 1935; m. Loren Keith Olson, July 31, 1937; children—Douglas Keith, Loren Keith. Tchr. Model Progressive Sch., Williams Bay, Wis., 1935-37, U. Wis., Stout, Menomenie, Wis., 1938. Mem. League Republican Women D.C. (1st v.p. 1969-71, bd. dirs. 1969-73). Mem. Ind. Agy. Wives Assn. (corr. sec. 1963), Achievement Rewards for Coll. Scientists, World Affairs Forum, Am. Assn. U. Women, Friends of Kennedy Center, Salvation Army Aux., Lawyers Wives of D.C., P.E.O. (treas. 1968-70). Conglist. Clubs: Washington (bd. govs., mem. exec. com., treas. 1971-72, pres. 1972—), International Neighbors (sec.-treas. 1966, pres. 1970-71), Capitol Speakers (bd. dirs. 1971-72). Home: 5335 Falmouth Rd Washington DC 20016

OLSON, MARJORIE KATHLEEN, advt. agy. exec.; b. Wataga, Ill., Dec. 16, 1920; d. Olof Serenius and Anna Mae (Hegstrom) Olson; student Brown's Bus. Coll., 1939-40. Sec., Knox Finance Corp. Webster Ins. Agy., Galesburg, Ill., 1940-42; sec. to officer-in-charge U.S. C.E., Peoria, Ill., 1942-46; office asst. Neighborhood House, Peoria, Ill., 1946; media supr. Charles Ruppman Advt. Inc., Peoria, Ill., 1946-74; now staff marketing dept. Indsl. div. Caterpillar Tractor Co. Mem. Delta Theta Tau (chmn. province 1961-62, 66-67, chmn. nat. philanthropy com. 1972-73). Republican. Lutheran. Home: 1121 NE Perry Av Peoria IL 61603

OLSON, MATTIE ELLA MCQUAIG (MRS. ROLAND WAYNE OLSON), advt. exec.; b. Ft. Sam Houston, Tex., Dec. 2, 1939; d. Allen David and Mattie Elizabeth (Bass) McQuaig; B.S., Miss. State Coll. for Women, 1961; postgrad. U. Ala., summer 1959; M.S., Ia. State U., 1963; m. Roland Wayne Olson, Mar. 13, 1965; children—Lars David, Elizabeth Erika. Co-head Columbus (Miss.) bur. Memphis Comml. Appeal, 1959-60; grad. asst., tchr. dept. tech. journalism Ia. State U., Ames, 1961-63; statewide pub. relations coordinator Nat. Rural Electric Co-op. Assn., Washington, 1963-68, mgr. nat. advt. program, 1968-74, asst. pub. relations dir., 1972-74; dir. advt. Maurer, Fleisher, Zon & Anderson, Inc., 1974—. Mem. bd. Nat. Rural Electric Co-op. Assn. Fed. Credit Union, 1966, 67. Pres. Georgetown Co-op. Nursery Sch., 1972-73. Writer Rural Ams. for Johnson-Humphrey, 1964. Mem. Nat. Rural Electric Co-op. Editorial Assn., Women in Communications, Advt. Club Washington. Home: 2931 28th St NW Washington DC 20008 Office: 1120 Connecticut Av NW Washington DC 20036

OLSON, REVA DEVERAUX, real estate broker; b. Driggs, Ida., Mar. 11, 1923; d. Arthur and Hildred (Wilcock) Deveraux; student Long Beach City Coll., 1964-67, U. Cal. at Los Angeles, 1967-70, U. Cal. at Irvine, 1970-71; m. Warren A. Mathews, Aug. 3, 1941 (div. Mar. 1953); children—Brent, Sharman, Shana; m. 2d, LeRoy A. Olson, Aug. 6, 1959 (div. Feb. 1967). In real estate bus., 1953—; v.p. Tech. Edn. Press, Seal Beach, Cal., 1966-68; owner Reva Olson, realtor, Los Alamitos, Cal., 1971—. Mem. Nat. Assn. Realtors, Nat. Inst. Real Estate Bds., Cal. Real Estate Assn., Los Alamitos, Long Beach chambers commerce, Internat. Meditation Soc. Home: 9131 Marina Pacifica Dr N Long Beach CA 90803 Office: 3682 Katella Av Los Alamitos CA 90720

OLSON, RUE EILEEN (MRS. RICHARD L. OLSON), librarian; b. Chgo., Nov. 1, 1928; d. Paul H. and Martha M. (Fick) Meyers; student Herzl Jr. Coll., 1946-48, Northwestern U., 1948-50, Ill. State U., 1960-64; m. Richard L. Olson, July 18, 1964; children—Catherine, Karen. Accountant Ill. Farm Supply Co., Chgo., 1948-59; asst. librarian Ill. Agrl. Assn., Bloomington, 1960-66, librarian, 1966—. Mem. area com. Nat. Library Week, 1971, 74, area steering com., 1972. Mem. Am., Ill., McLean County (pres. 1970-71) library assns., Spl. Libraries Assn. (sec. Ill. 1970-72 chmn. ins. div. 1973-74, mem. adv. council agenda com. 1972-74), Internat. Assn. Agrl. Librarians and Documentalists, Am. Soc. Information Sci., Am. Mgmt. Assn. Home: 103 Radliff Rd Bloomington IL 61701 Office: 1701 Towanda Av Bloomington IL 61701

OLSON, RUTH ANN (MRS. JEFFREY W. OLSON), artist; b. Oak Park, Ill., May 19, 1948; d. Robert H. and Emma Jane (McLallen) Beeby; B.A., Bennington Coll., 1970; m. Jeffrey W. Olson, June 20, 1970. Jr. designer Jeanne Hartnett Interiors, Chgo., 1969; interior designer Stix, Baer & Fuller, St. Louis, Mo., 1970-72; sec. Helman Gallery, St. Louis, 1972, Greenberg Gallery, St. Louis, 1972-73; exhibited in group shows Emden Gallery, St. Louis, 1974, Berenson Gallery, Bay Harbor Islands, Fla., 1973, Bennington (Vt.) Coll., 1970. Mem. Womens Art Center, St. Louis, 1972-73. Home: 5250 N Kenmore Chicago IL 60640

OLSON, SANDRA JANE FORBES (MRS. RONALD WAYNE OLSON), physician; b. East Chgo., Ind., Jan. 8, 1938; d. James C. and Mabel (Newman) Forbes; B.S., Purdue U., 1959; M.D., Northwestern U., 1963; m. Ronald Wayne Olson, Sept. 2, 1967; children—Ronald Wayne, Kirsten Ann. Intern Chgo. Wesley Meml. Hosp., 1963-64; resident neurology Northwestern U., 1965-68; practice medicine specializing in neurology, Chgo., 1969—; asso. attending physician neurology Chgo. Wesley Meml. Hosp., 1969; asst. electroencephelographer, asst. prof. dept. neurology Northwestern Med. Sch., 1969—, fellow in electroencephelography. Diplomate in neurology Am. Bd. Psychiatry and Neurology, Am. Bd. Electroencephalography. Mem. Chgo. Neurol. Soc., Am. Acad. Neurology, Am. Electroencephalography Soc., Sigma Xi, Psi Iota Xi, Pi Beta Phi, Alpha Omega Alpha. Home: 220 E Walton St Chicago IL 60611 Office: 251 E Chicago St Chicago IL 60611

OLSON, SUSAN RAYNOR, educator; b. Utica, N.Y., June 20, 1945; d. Alton Randolph and Mildred Pauline (Heil) Raynor; B.A., Rollins Coll., 1966; M.A., U. Ga., 1967; Ph.D., Ohio State U., 1972; m. Richard M. Olson, June 3, 1972. Instr. speech Marshall U., 1967-69; teaching asso. broadcasting Ohio State U., 1969-72; project dir. ednl. communications for nursing edn. Riverside Sch. Nursing, Columbus, O., 1972-74; asst. prof. telecommunications U. Ky., 1974—; chmn. nursing edn. tech. City of Columbus; sponsor workshops Inst. Media and Individualized Instruction, 1973-74. Mem. Nat. Assn. Ednl. Broadcasters, Am. Assn. U. Women, Internat. Communications Assn., Assn. Ednl. Communication Tech., Speech Communication Assn., Rollins, Ohio State U. alumni assns., Kappa Kappa Gamma. Home: 109 Desha St Lexington KY 40502

OLSRUD, LOIS CHRISTINE, librarian; b. Havre, Mont., Sept. 21, 1930; d. Oscar Ludwig and Marguerite Pernella (Martinson) Olsrud; B.A., Concordia Coll., 1952; postgrad. U. Minn., summers 1954-56, 60, 64; M.A., Ind. U., 1966. Librarian, Princeton (Minn.) Pub. Schs., 1952-54, Havre (Mont.), High Sch., 1954-57, West Jr. High Sch., Great Falls, 1957-65; reference librarian U. Ariz., Tucson, 1966—. Supr. summer sch. session, Sandefjord, Norway, 1963; Treas., Tucson Area Library Council, 1973-74. Del., Mont. Edn. Assn. Del. Assembly, 1963-65. Mem. Com. on Status Univ. Women. Mem. Am., Southwest, Ariz. (sec. 1970-71), U. Ariz. (v.p. 1967-68) library assns., Am. Assn. U. Profs., Ariz. Coll. Assn., Delta Kappa Gamma (sec. 1974-74), Beta Phi Mu. Lutheran. Home: 969 N Jones Blvd Tucson AZ 85716

OLSSON, NELLA MAE (MRS. MAXWELL D. OLSSON), editor; b. Bloomington, Ind., June 30, 1919; d. Henry Alfred and Carrie (Noel) Livingston; grad. high sch.; m. Maxwell D. Olsson, Oct. 17, 1937; children—Rhonda (Mrs. Bruce A. Harris), Mark T. With Ind. Univ. Alumni Assn., Bloomington, 1954-57; women's editor Daily Herald-Telephone, Bloomington, 1958—, Sunday Herald-Times, Bloomington, 1966—. Bd. dirs. Hoosier Hills Art Guild, 1962-66, Altrusa Inc., 1968-70. Mem. Nat. League Am. Pen Women (Ind. state pres. 1972—), Nat. Soc. Arts and Letters (dir. pub. relations Bloomington chpt. 1970—), Nat. Fedn. Women's Clubs (hon. mem. Monroe County chpt.), Women's Press Club Ind. (1st Pl. award state newspaper supplement 1973), Women in Communications, Nat. Fedn. Press Women, Indpls. Hoosier Salon Art Assn., Brown County Art Assn., Delta Theta Tau. Mem. Christian Ch. Mem. Order Eastern Star. Home: 3204 Colfax Dr Bloomington IN 47401 Office: 1900 S Walnut St Bloomington IN 47401

OLTMAN, RUTH MARIE, educator, psychologist; b. Cleve.; d. Rudolph Carl and Ida (Schroeder) Oltman; A.B., Oberlin Coll., 1934; M.A., Western Res. U., 1951, Ph.D., 1961. Contact rep. VA, Cleve., 1946-51 adminstrv. asst. (personnel) Navy Finance Center, Cleve., 1951-55; counselor, psychologist Vocational Guidance and Rehab. Services, Cleve., 1955-62; dean of women Baldwin-Wallace Coll., Berea, O., 1962-69; asst. dir. program higher edn. Am. Assn. U. Women, Washington, 1969-74; dean grad. program Hood Coll., 1974—; lectr. in psychology Cleve. Coll. of Case-Western Res. U., 1952-53, Baldwin-Wallace Coll., 1962. Served as lt. WAVES, 1942-46. Mem. Am. Psychol. Assn., Nat. Assn. Women Deans, Adminstrs. and Counselors, Am. Personnel and Guidance Assn., Zonta, Phi Delta Gamma. Methodist. Office: Hood Coll Frederick MD 21701

OLTMANNS, MILDRED VOGES (MRS. HERMAN JOHNSON OLTMANNS), museum ofcl.; b. Worthing, S.D., Nov. 19, 1907; d. George Herman and Arminta Ellen (Wood) Voges; A.B., U. S.D., 1929, M.A., 1933; postgrad. George Peabody Coll. for Tchrs., 1938; m. Herman Johnson Oltmanns, May 1, 1948; 1 dau. by previous marriage, Marilyn Kay Bacon (Mrs. Paul Wendell Wilderson III). Sr. lab. asst. U. S.D., 1928-29; tchr. sci. and English, prin. Lebanon (S.D.) High Sch., 1929-32, Worthing High Sch., 1934-37; acting prof. natural sci. So. State Coll., Springfield, 1937; tchr. sci. and English, Jackson (Minn.) Sr. High Sch., 1939-42; instr. radio operating Air Force Tech. Tng. Sch., Sioux Falls, 1942-45; registrar Sioux City (Ia.) Pub. Museum, 1964—. Vice pres. P.T.A., Sioux City, 1952-53; mem. Woodbury County Am. Revolution Bicentennial Commn., 1973—. Precinct del. Woodbury County Rep. Conv., 1951-52; clk. of elections, 1951-55. Mem. Am. Assn. U. Women (chmn. writers group 1952), Episcopal Church Women (sometimes sec. or treas.), Phi Sigma (treas. 1928-29). Home: 3255 Stone Park Blvd Sioux City IA 51104 Office: 2901 Jackson St Sioux City IA 51104

OLZENDAM, HARRIETT STEELE, lawyer; b. Dover, N.H., Aug. 5, 1914; d. Enoch Ned and Lena Marion (Steele) Olzendam; B.A., Wellesley Coll., 1936; M.A., Trinity Coll., 1942; J.D. with distinction, U. Conn. Sch. Law, 1946. Admitted to Conn. bar, 1946, Fed. Dist. bar, 1948; with The Travelers Ins. Co., Hartford, Conn., 1937—, chief contract underwriter, 1951-61, asst. sec., 1961-69, sec., 1969—. Mem. residence com. YWCA, Hartford, Conn., 1964—, dir., 1971—, sec., 1972-74, v.p., 1974—. Mem. Am., Hartford County bar assns., Am. Judicature Soc., Wellesley Coll. Alumnae Assn., U. Conn. Sch. Law Alumni Assn., Trinity Coll. Alumni Assn. Republican. Conglist. Clubs: Wellesley, Quota (corr. sec. Hartford 1970—). Home: 2012 Blvd West Hartford CT 06107 Office: One Tower Sq Hartford CT 06115

O'MALLEY, CORNELIA LEARY (MRS. LOUIS JOSEPH O'MALLEY), lawyer; b. Cin., Aug. 14, 1906; d. Jeremiah Daniel and Anna Bell (Cooney) Leary; student St. Mary's Coll., Notre Dame, Ind., 1926; LL.B., U. Cin., 1929; m. Louis Joseph O'Malley, Oct. 17, 1936; children—Owen L., Charles J., Louis F., Cornelius C., Ann E., James D. Admitted to Ohio bar, 1930, Mass. bar, 1940; practiced in Cin., 1930-41, Boston, Cohasset, Mass., 1940—. Mng. partner Grey Ledges Partnership, Cohasset, 1967—. Cons. on parliamentary procedure to orgns., 1930—. Mem. Inst. Parliamentary Law, Mass. Assn. Women Lawyers (dir. 1954-56), Phi Delta Delta (internat. v.p. 1932-36). Address: 375 Jerusalem Rd Cohasset MA 02025

O'MALLEY, SISTER EMANUELA, educator, poet; b. Mercier, Kan., July 23, 1914; d. Edward F. and Gertrude (Coleman) O'Malley; A.B., Marymount Coll., 1957; M.A., Syracuse U., 1970; postgrad. De Paul U., U. Ia. Joined Sisters of St. Joseph, Concordia, Kan., 1932; tchr. intermediate grades, Kan., Neb., Ill., 1936-67; faculty English dept. Marymount Coll., Salina, Kan., 1967—, asst. prof., 1970—. Treas., mem. exec. bd. Kan. Alliance for Arts in Edn., 1974—. Mem. adv. com. Workshop Publs., N.Y.C., 1972. Mem. Poetry Soc. Am., Kan. Authors Club (state pres. 1972-74), Midwest Chaparral (Kan. poet of year award 1973). Contbr. articles and short stories to various publs. Contbr. poems to Commonweal, Kan. Quar., America, Spirit, Negro Digest, Sawanee Rev., also others. Home: Marymount Coll Salina KS 67401

O'MALLEY, MARGARET GALVIN, judge; b. Chgo., July 25, 1917; d. Patrick J and Margaret ('Connor) Galvin; student St Xavier's Coll., 1935-36; LL.B., DePaul U., 1940, J.J.D., 1972; children—Patrick, Mary, James, Margaret. Admitted to Ill. bar, 1940; pvt. practice, Chgo., 1940-48; legal dept. Dept. of Welfare, City of Chgo., 1948-51; asst. states atty., Cook County, 1951-53; referee Family Ct. of Cook County, 1953-64; magistrate Circuit Ct. of Cook County, 1964-70, asso. judge, 1970-71, judge, 1971—. Mem. Mayor's Adv. Com. on Juvenile Delinquency, 1958-59; mem. Ill. Commn. on Children, 1971. Dir. Fedn. Women, 1957-64, ward committeewoman, 1957-64. Bd. dirs. Joanne Merge Meml. Fund. Mem. Women's Bar Assn. Ill., Nat. Assn. Women Lawyers, Cath. Lawyers Guild, Am., Ill., Chgo. bar assns., Women's Share in Pub. Service, Kappa Beta Phi. Home: 5232 W Crystal St Chicago IL 60651

O'MALLEY, MARY CAROL, coll. adminstr.; b. Port Huron, Mich., Dec. 23, 1941; d. Vincent Joseph and Mary Gazelle (Urban) O'Malley; B.A., Marygrove Coll., 1963. Asst. controller Manley, Bennett, McDonald & Co., Detroit, 1963-71; dir. alumni relations Marygrove Coll., Detroit, 1971—. Mem. Universite Internacional (sec. Detroit chpt. 1973—), Am. Assn. U. Women, Am. Alumni

Council. Home: 23039 Brook Forest Rd Novi MI 48050 Office: 8425 W McNichols St Detroit MI 42821

O'MALLEY, SISTER MARY THERESE, educator; b. Chgo., Apr. 19, 1933; d. Patrick John and Norah Imelda (O'Malley) O'Malley; B.A., U. Neb., 1955; M.A., Catholic U. Am., 1963; Ph.D., Columbia, 1971. Joined Dominican Sisters of Sinsinawa, Wis.; prof. math. Rosary Coll., River Forest, Ill., 1968—. NSF fellow, summers 1958-62. Mem. Am. Math. Soc., Math. Assn. Am., Nat. Council Tchrs. Math., Am. Assn. U. Profs., Sigma Xi. Home: 7900 W Division St River Forest IL 60305

O'MARA, JULIE (MRS. ROBERT T. WALL), metals co. exec.; b. St. Louis, Sept. 14, 1946; d. Lawrence Charles and Edna Julia Alice (May) O'Mara; B.S., U. Mo., 1969; m. Robert T. Wall, Mar. 31, 1973. Pub. relations supr. Whirlpool Corp., Benton Harbor, Mich., 1969-72, supr. marketing communications, 1972-73; writer, program designer, cons. Response & Assos., Chgo., 1971—; mgr. communications Marmon Group, Chgo., 1973—. Youth activities chmn. United Fund, 1971. Mem. Women in Communications, Inc. (newsletter editor Chgo. chpt. 1973-74, v.p. programs 1974—), Am. Assn. U. Women, Internat. Transactional Analysis Assn., Pub. Relations Soc. Am., Indsl. Editors Assn., Nat. Orgn. Women. Home: PO Box 333 Chicago Heights IL 60411 Office: 39 S LaSalle St Chicago IL 60603

O'MEARA, MAE GOLDEN (MRS. JEREMIAH P O'MEARA), artist; b. Weehawken, N.J., Mar. 5, 1900; d. Hugh and Mary (McGinn) Golden; student St. Francis Acad., Art Students League, Bklyn. Mus. Art Sch.; pvt. instrn.; m. Jeremiah P. O'Meara, Oct. 2, 1918 children—Jeremiah Daniel, Margaret (Mrs William Green). Instr. art Douglaston (N.Y.) Art League, 1945-50, O'Meara Studios, Flushing, N.Y., 1956-57, Bayside Tall Oaks, 1950-56, Art League L.I. (past pres.), 1950-57, Kew Gardens Art Center, 1953-57, Great Neck Women's Club, 1954-61; exhibited in group shows at Nat. Collection Fine Arts, Mus., Washington, Jersey City Mus., Riverside Mus., Gallery 21, Butler, Art League L.I., others. Mem. com. art edn. Mus. Modern Art, N.Y.C. Mem. Queens Bot. Gardens Art Festival, 1948-58; music and art chmn. Flushing Council Women's Orgns. 1952-55; one of founders, treas. Art Alliance of Women, Flushing, N.Y., 1957-61, pres. 1963-65; founder Flushing Art Center, instr., 1957. Mem. Am. Artists Profl. League, Bklyn. Mus. Art, Sch. Alumni Assn., Painters and Sulptors Soc. N.J., Flushing Art League (past pres.), East Hampton Guild Hall, South-Hampton Parrish Mus. Club: Catherine Lorillord Wolf Art. Address: 4017 149th Pl Flushing NY 11354

OMER, SHIRLEY JEAN, newspaper editor; b. Sanborn, Ia., Sept. 22, 1927; d. Samuel Milham and Minnie Floy (Finchum) Omer; student pub. schs., Sanborn. Long distance operator Northwestern Bell Telephone Co., 1946-48; enumerator U.S. Census Bur., 1952-54; partner Omer Cafe, 1950-54; partner O'Brien County Bell Newspaper, Primghar, Ia., 1955-67, owner, editor, 1967—; partner Peterson (Ia.) Patriot Newspaper, 1966-67, owner, editor, 1967—. Instr. linotype Ia. Vocational Rehab., 1960-65. Mem. Primghar Town Council, 1972—. Recipient award Mississippi Valley Assn., 1960. Mem. Primghar C. of C. (pres. 1973), Paullina Women's Bowling League, Baum-Harmon Hosp. Aux. Home: 620 12th St Primghar IA 51245 Office: O'Brien County Bell Newspaper 612 15th St Primghar IA 51245

O'MORCHOE, PATRICIA JEAN RICHARDSON (MRS. CHARLES CHRISTOPHER CREAGH O'MORCHOE), histologist, cytopathologist, educator; b. Halifax, Yorkshire, Eng., Sept. 15, 1930; d. Alfred Eric and Florence Patricia (Pearson) Richardson; B.A., Dublin (Ireland) U., 1953, M.B., B. Ch., B.A.O., 1955, M.A., 1966, M.D., 1966; m. Charles Christopher Creagh O'Morchoe, Sept. 15, 1955; children—Charles Erie Creagh, David James Creagh. Came to U.S., 1961. Intern, Halifax Gen. Hosp., 1955-57; instr. physiology Trinity Coll., Dublin, 1958-59, lectr., 1959-61, 63-68; instr. cytopathology Johns Hopkins, Balt., 1961-62, 68-70, asst. prof. pathology, 1973-74; research asso. in pathology Harvard, Cambridge, Mass., 1962-63; asst. prof. anatomy U. Md., Balt., 1970-74; asso. prof. pathology Loyola U. Stritch Sch. Medicine, Maywood, Ill., 1974—. Mem. Am. Soc. Cytology. Contbr. articles to med. jours. Office: Dept Pathology Loyola U Stritch Sch Medicine 2160 S 1st Av Maywood IL 60153

ONDIK, HELEN MARGARET, crystallographer; b. N.Y.C., Dec. 25, 1930; d. Louis and Helen (Nagy) Ondik; B.A., Hunter Coll., 1952; M.A., Johns Hopkins, 1954, Ph.D., 1957. Crystallographer, Nat. Bur. Standards, Washington, 1958—. Recipient Fulbright grant U. Amsterdam, 1957-58, Silver medal award U.S. Dept. Commerce, 1971. Mem. Am. Crystallographic Assn., Am. Chem. Soc., A.A.A.S., P.E.O., Phi Beta Kappa, Iota Sigma Pi, Sigma Xi. Baptist. Editor: (with J.D.H. Donnay) Crystal Data Determinative Tables, Vol. 1, 1972, Vol. 2, 1973. Home: 2737 Devonshire Pl NW Washington DC 20008 Office: Nat Bur Standards Washington DC 20234

ONDRIK, LOUISE WILLIAMS (MRS. ANTHONY FRANCIS ONDRIK), journalist; b. Knoxville, Tenn., July 31, 1926; d. Elisha and Grace Gertrude (Humphrey) Williams; B.S., Ind. U., 1967, M.A., 1971; m. Anthony Francis Ondrik, June 16, 1946; children—Michael Anthony, Richard Steven, Daniel Keith. Tchr. pvt. kindergarten, Kokomo, Ind., 1959-62; sch. reporter, edn. editor Kokomo Tribune, 1962-66; high sch. journalism tchr., publs. adviser, Kokomo, 1967-73; free-lance writer, Kokomo, 1973—. Den mother Cub Scouts Meshingomesia council Boy Scouts Am., 1956-61; chpt. pres. P.T.A., 1957-58; mem. Coordinating Council Fine Arts, Kokomo, 1965—, editor newsletter, 1967-68; county co-chmn. UNICEF, 1972-73. Recipient John E. Stempel Fellowship, Ind. U., 1970. Mem. N.E.A., Ind. State, Kokomo tchrs. assns., Ind. High Sch. Press Assn. (pres. 1973, mem. exec. bd. 1974), Women in Communications, Beta Sigma Phi. Mem. Christian Ch. Home: 722 Westminster Lane Kokomo IN 46901

O'NEAL, MARY JO (MRS. EDWIN JAMES O'NEAL), home economist; b. Clayton, N.M., June 25, 1931; d. Roy Leonard and Myrtice Etta (Williams) Kennedy; B.S., N.M. State U., 1953; postgrad. Colo. State U., summers 1959-62, 67, 69; m. Edwin James O'Neal, Dec. 5, 1970; children—(from a previous marriage) Jacquetta Ann Carlton, Jo Lynn Carlton, Janelle Kay Carlton. Asst. home agt. Coop. Extension Service, N.M. State U., Lovington, 1953-55, county home agt., 1955-70; county home agt. N.M. State U., Deming, 1970—. Tchr. foods and clothing classes at night sch., Hobbs, N.M., 1964. Mem. N.M., Am. home econs. assns., N.M., (v.p. 1962-63), Nat. (Distinguished Service award 1968), extension home economists assns., C. of C. (women's div.), Bus. and Profl. Women's Club. Baptist. Home: 1521 Kipling Dr PO Box 1194 Deming NM 88030 Office: County Extension Service Deming NM 88030

O'NEIL, ELIZABETH PENDLETON, ednl. adminstr.; b. Stockton, Cal., Apr. 20, 1935; d. Broughton and Doris M. (Baldridge) Pendleton; B.A., U. Cal. at Berkeley, 1956; m. Miles Alan Cobb, Dec. 22, 1956 (div. July 1971); children—Jennifer, Melissa, Mary; m. 2d, John R. O'Neil, Dec. 24, 1973. Asst. dir. admissions Mills Coll., Oakland, Cal., 1956-60, dir. admissions, 1971—; asst. dir. ednl. opportunity program U. Cal., Berkeley, 1968-70, dir. Morabito 49er Fund, San Francisco Found., 1968-71. Voting rep. Coll. Entrance Examination Bd., 1971—. Bd. dirs. Wright Ins., Berkeley, 1970-71, Alameda County Vol. Bur., 1969-70, Neighborhood House, N. Richmond, Cal., 1968-71; mem. community edn. opposition bd. San Francisco Consortium, 1969-71; mem. projects bd. Jr. League Oakland, Cal., 1966-69. Recipient Rosalie M. Stern award U. Cal., 1968, award San Francisco Found., 1970. Mem. Nat. Assn. Coll. Admissions Officers (nat. del. 1972—), Pacific Assn. Coll. Registrars and Admissions Officers, Delta Gamma. Home: 2995 Dwight Way Berkeley CA 94704 Office: Mills College Oakland CA 94613

O'NEIL, MARGARET STUHLER, ins. agy. exec., govt. ofcl.; b. Edgartown, Mass., May 31, 1921; d. John and Meriam C. (Earl) Stuhler; student pub. schs.; m. John O'Neil, Nov. 19, 1940 (div. Aug. 1967); children—Margaret (Mrs. Joseph Serpa, Jr.), Sharon (Mrs. George A. Willoughby), Kathryn (Mrs. Antone A. Bettencourt, Jr.), Richard J., Stephen J., Elizabeth J., J. Michael, Peter W. Owner Vose Ins. Agy., Edgartown, 1956—; secretarial asst. Anna B. Flynn Real Estate Agy., Edgartown, 1964-68, real estate broker, 1968—; asst. treas. County of Dukes, Mass., 1961-68, treas., 1969—. Chmn. Am. Cancer Crusade Dr., Edgartown, 1964-69, A.R.C. Dr., 1957-61; pres. P.T.A., Edgartown, 1960-61. Sec. Martha's Vineyard chpt. Nat. Found., 1957—; asst. treas. Marine Research Found., Edgartown. Mem. Mass. County Treas. Assn. (sec. 1972—), Mass. Ind. Ins. Agts. and Brokers, Mass. Assn. Contributory Retirement Systems (exec. bd. 1974—), Am. Legion (post pres. 1971-74). Clubs: Zonta (v.p. 1968-71, pres. 1971-73), Edgartown Mothers (pres. 1954-55), St. Elizabeths Guild (pres. 1969-70). Home: State Rd Edgartown MA 02539 Office: Main St Edgartown MA 02539

O'NEIL, SISTER MARY AGNES, hosp. adminstr.; b. Bridgeport, Conn., Sept. 12, 1926; grad. St. Vincent's Hosp. Sch. Nursing, 1947; B.S., St. Joseph's Coll., Emmitsburg, Md., 1952; M.A., Boston Coll., 1960; LL.D., Sacred Heart U., 1973. Staff nurse St. Vincent's Hosp., Bridgeport, 1947-48; joined Daus. of Charity of St. Vincent de Paul, 1948; 3d directress Sisters of Charity Sem., St. Joseph's Provincial House, Emmitsburg, Md., 1952-54; supr. nursing Carney Hosp., Boston, 1954-57, dir. nursing service, 1957-60, adminstrv. asst., 1960-61; dir. nursing St. Vincent's Hosp., Jacksonville, Fla., 1961-63; asst. adminstr. St. Mary's Hosp., Troy, N.Y., 1963, adminstr., 1963-69, bd. govs., 1962-69; adminstr. St Vincent's Hosp., Bridgeport, 1969—, trustee, mem. adv. bd., 1971—; mem. steering devel. com. St. Vincent's Fund Drive, 1971. Mem. exec. agy. United Community Services, 1963-69; mem. adv. bd. Neighborhood Youth Corp., 1965-69; bd. dirs. Hudson Valley Community Coll. Sch. Nursing, 1964-69; v.p. bd. Seton Day Nursery, Troy, N.Y., 1963-69; bd. dirs. Am. Cancer Soc., Bridgeport, 1969, 71-72, mem. exec. com., 1972-73, mem. service com. 1972-73; mem. Mental Health Council, 1972-73; mem. right to life com. Family Life Bur., 1971; mem. comprehensive planning agy. United Fund, 1971; mem. joint conf. com. St. Joseph's Manor; mem. Greater Bridgeport Mental Health Council, 1970, mem. exec. com., 1971-72; mem. Regional Hosp. Assembly, 1970; mem. Regional Med. Program Conf., Yale U., 1970, Research Task Force on Nurses for Change, Grad. Sch. U. Bridgeport, 1970; bd. dirs. Hosp. Coop. Services, 1970, Bridgeport unit Am. Heart Assn., 1969-70, St. Joseph's Home for Convalescent and Aged, 1969-70, Hosp. Coop. Soc., 1971-72, New Eng. Hosp. Conf., 1971-72. Mem. Am. Coll. Hosp. Adminstrs., Local Hosp. Adminstrs. Council, Alcoholism Study Group, Am. Nurses Assn., Nat. Council Catholic Nurses, Am., Conn. hosp. assns., Cath. Hosp. Assn. (exec. com. New Eng. council), Bridgeport Cath. Nurses Assn., Conn. Hosp. Assn., Bridgeport C. of C. Address: St Vincent's Hosp 2820 Main St Bridgeport CT 06606

O'NEILL, ANNE FRANCES, mathematician, educator; b. Troy, N.Y., Aug. 21, 1915; d. Dennis Patrick and Sarah Anne (Strong) O'Neill; B.A., Vassar Coll., 1938; M.A., Radcliffe Coll., 1939, Ph.D., 1942. Instr. math. Smith Coll., Northampton, Mass., 1942-47, asst. prof. math, 1947-52; asst. prof. math Wheaton Coll., Norton, Mass., 1952-54, asso. prof., 1954-60, prof., 1960—. NSF faculty fellow U. Cal. at Berkeley, 1961-62. Mem. Am. Math. Soc., Math. Assn. Am., Am. Statis. Assn., Am. Assn. U. Profs., Phi Beta Kappa, Sigma Xi. Author: (with N.H. McCoy and R.E. Johnson) Introduction to Mathematical Analysis, 1962. Home: PO Box 264 7 Pine St Norton MA 02766

O'NEILL, EMMA LOUISE ERDMAN (MRS. EDWARD A. O'NEILL), civic worker; b. Honolulu, Nov. 7, 1906; d. John Pinney and Marion (Dillingham) Erdman; B.A., Vassar Coll., 1928; m. Charles J. Henderson, May 25, 1929 (dec. Sept. 1960); children—Harold Erdman, Charles Belknap II; m. 2d, Edward A. O'Neill, Mar. 13, 1972. Pres., Jr. League of Honolulu, 1931-32; chmn. Christmas seal campaign Tb Assn., 1937; chmn. Punahou Centennial Pageant, 1941; chmn. women's div. Community Chest, 1941; mem. mgmt. com. U.S.O. Victory Club, also chmn. vol. hostesses Army-Navy YMCA, 1942-45; pres. Honolulu Community Theatre, 1946-47, 49-51; mem. Mayor's Com. for Civic Auditorium, 1950-56; bd. dirs. Honolulu Theatre for Youth, 1955-58, 69-70, Hawaii Mission Children's Soc., 1968—, Hawaii Found. for Am. Freedoms, 1972—. Mem. Daus. of Hawaii (regent 1952-55), Honolulu Acad. Arts, Oahu League Republican Women, Navy League U.S. (life), Outdoor Circle. Club: Garden (2d v.p. 1966-67, treas. 1970-72) (Honolulu). Home: 3965 Noela Pl Honolulu HI 96815

O'NEILL, HELEN MARIE, social worker; b. Rochester, N.Y., Feb. 8, 1928; d. Emmet J. and Lucy U. (Michel) O'Neill; B.A., Nazareth Coll., 1949; M. Social Service, U. Buffalo, 1960. Caseworker, Monroe County Dept. Social Services, Rochester, N.Y., 1949-56, casework supr., 1956-71, dir. social services delivery, 1971—. Mem. adv. com. Children's Rehab. Center. Bd. dirs. Rochester (N.Y.) Neighbors. Mem. Acad. Certified Social Workers, U. Buffalo, Nazareth Coll. alumni assns. Home: 68 Holmes St Rochester NY 14613 Office: 111 Westfall Rd Rochester NY 14620

O'NEILL, MARGARET MOFFETT (MRS. FRANCIS JOHN O'NEILL), educator, civic worker; b. Kenton, Del., Nov. 14, 1900; d. Michael E. and Margaret Jane (Martin) Moffett; B.A., U. Del., 1922; m. Francis John O'Neill, Oct. 2, 1924 (dec. Mar. 1961); children—Francis John, Margaret Jane (Mrs. John Robert Jacobs). High sch. tchr., Smyrna, Del., 1922-24, 43-51, Wilmington, Del., 1924-25; prin. high sch., Smyrna, 1951-53. Bd. dirs. Catholic Press, Inc. Mem. Smyrna Sch. Bd., 1954-65, pres., 1956-65; mem. Kent County Planning Bd., Dover, 1964; bd. dirs. Del. Soc. for Crippled Children, Wilmington; v.p. Women's Aux. Hosp. for Mentally Retarded, 1960-64; mem. Conn. Com. Human Rights, 1963; mem. White House Conf. on Youth, 1960; mem. Gov.'s Com. on Children and Youth, 1965—; mem. County Planning and Zoning Bd., 1970—. Recipient Outstanding Citizens award Smyrna Lions Club, 1952; named Del. Mother of the Year, 1964. Mem. Del. Sch. Bds. Assn. (pres.), Old Bohemia, Duck Creek (pres. 1969) hist. socs., Nat. Congress Parents and Tchrs., N.E.A., State Fedn. Women's Clubs (internat. chmn.), Del. Edn. Assn., Alumnae Assn. U. Del., Alpha Tau (hon.). Club: Twentieth Century (1st v.p. 1962-64). Home: Rural Route 300 Smyrna DE 19977

O'NEILL, VIRGINIA LOWERY (MRS. THOMAS JOSEPH O'NEILL), social worker; b. N.Y.C.; d. Charles Pemberton and Mary (Carr) Lowery; B.A., Hunter Coll.; M.S.W., Columbia, 1946; m. Thomas Joseph O'Neill, 1 dau., Virginia. Formerly social worker Columbia, also Vanderbilt Clinic, N.Y.C., E. Harlem Settlement House; formerly supr. Bd. Child Welfare, dir. Bur. Tng., N.Y.C. Dept. Welfare, adminstr. Ft. Green Welfare Center, asst. dir. Bur. Pub. Assistance; dir. Bur. Spl. Services, Dept. Welfare, 1956-71, exec. dir. Adult Counseling Service for Older Persons, 1955; dep. asst. commr. Dept. Social Services, N.Y.C., 1972—; lectr. social welfare policy grad. sch. Social Work, Rutgers U.; faculty mem. Tng. Inst. on Sr. Centers, U. Okla., 1966—. Cons. Comeback, N.Y.C., 1960, Vacations for Aging, 1959—; oral examiner N.Y. State Civil Service Commn., 1965; leader Inst. on Aging of Ga. Commn. on Aging, 1966, mem. Gov.'s Tech. Review Com.; profl. adv. com. Nat. Arthritis Found. Bd. dirs. Hodson Community Center, N.Y.C., mem. nat. roster of interviewers Council on Social Work Edn. Recipient N.Y.C. Pub. Service award for outstanding profl. achievement in community welfare, 1963. Mem. Nat. Assn. Social Workers, Acad. Certified Social Workers, Am. Pub. Welfare Assn. (mem. nat. com. on aging, sec. adminstrn. of services for aging). Author publs. in field. Home: 15 Sherwood Dr Plainview NY 11803 Office: 250 Church St New York City NY 10013

O'NEILL, WINIFRED, clothing co. exec.; b. N.Y.C., Feb. 23, 1912; d. James H. and Matilda W. (Roeck) O'Neill; grad. high sch. With Manhattan Industries, Inc., N.Y.C., 1930—, asst. sec., 1969—. Home: 81-15 35th Av Jackson Heights NY 11372 Office: 1271 Av of Americas New York City NY 10020

ONESTO, SERENE FRANCES (MRS. JOSEPH E. ONESTO), univ. ofcl.; b. Chgo., Aug. 28, 1926; d. Harold and Bessie Blanche (Lorber) Panama; B.A., DePauw U., 1948; M.S., Ill. Tchrs. Coll., 1966; doctoral candidate No. Ill. U.; m. Joseph E. Onesto, Aug. 27, 1961. Classroom tchr. Chgo. Bd. Edn., 1960-65, tchr., librarian, 1965-67; asst. prof. library sci., head instructional materials center Chgo. State U. West Center, 1967-73, head client services office Instructional Media, 1973—. Mem. Ill. Curriculum Council. Mem. Am. Assn. U. Profs., Nat., Ill. edn. assns., Am., Ill. library assns., Ill. Assn. Sch. Librarians, Assn. Edn. Communication Tech., Ill. Audio-visual Assn., Chicago Library Club, Delta Kappa Gamma, Phi Delta Kappa. Home: 1055 D Peterson Park Ridge IL 60068 Office: 95th and King Dr Chicago IL 60628

ONGANIA, ANN LAURIEN DUNCAN (MRS. LESTER ONGANIA), realtor; b. Lynn, Mass., July 29, 1931; d. Harry Angus and Yvonne Elizabeth (Pepin) Duncan; A.A., Los Angeles City Coll., 1951; m. Lester Ongania, June 17, 1951; children—Richard, Douglas, Laurien. With Century 21 Real Estate, Canoga Park, Cal., 1965—, v.p., 1970—, gen. mgr., 1971—. Mem. San Fernando Valley Bd. Realtors (dir. 1974-76). Home: 7110 Fullbright Av Canoga Park CA 91306 Office: 7616 Topanga Canyon Canoga Park CA 91304

ONGKEKO, LOURDES ASTRAQUILLO (MRS. HERMIE T. ONGKEKO), editor; b. Laoag City, Philippines, Aug. 19, 1928; d. Isabelo Palacio and Juanita Donato (Justo) Astraquillo; B.S., U. Philippines, 1950; M.A., U. So. Cal., 1968; m. Hermie T. Ongkeko, Feb. 14, 1952; children—Ralph A., Gilda A., Geraldine A. Asso. editor Today, Dept. Nat. Defense, Philippines, 1954-60; mem. editorial staff Manila (Philippines) Daily Bull., 1949-53; mng. editor Sociology and Social Research, U. So. Cal., Los Angeles, 1966—; columnist, regional editor Philippine News, 1971—. Literary chmn. Los Angeles Met. Dist., 1972—; v.p. Filipino Community Action Services, Inc., 1972—. Recipient Maria Clara award Los Angeles Philippines Women's Club, 1971-72, Mayor Yorty award, 1973, Award of Honor Club Filipino Los Angeles, 1973. Mem. Women in Communications, Daus. Isabella (pub. relations officer 1950-55), Philippine-Am. C. of C. (bd. mem. 1972). Club: Philippine Women's (pres. 1972-73) (Los Angeles). Home: 527 Casitas St Monterey Park CA 91754 Office: U So Cal Los Angeles CA 90007

ONOFARO, MARY FRANCES ELAINE, ednl. adminstr.; b. Elkins, W.Va., Sept. 15, 1947; d. Ross and Carmela (Gallo) Onofaro; B.A. magna cum laude, U. Pitts., 1968; M.Ed. with honors, Ind. U. Pa., 1969; postgrad. W.Va. U., 1969-72. Asst. prof. sociology West Liberty State Coll., Wheeling, W.Va., 1972; dir. student personnel services W.Va. No. Community Coll., Wheeling, 1972—. Mem. student affairs adv. com. W.Va. Bd. Regents, Charleston, 1972—; mem. Greater Wheeling (W.Va.) Community Devel. Council, 1969-73. Mem. W.Va. Assn. Financial Aid Adminstrs. (sec. 1973-74), Nat., Midwestern assns. financial aid adminstrs., Nat. Assn. Student Personnel Counselors and Adminstrs., W.Va., Am. personnel and guidance assns., Nat. Assn. Women Deans, Nat. Council Social Scis., W.Va. Assn. Colls. and Univs., League Women Voters, Phi Theta Kappa, Phi Lambda Theta, Beta Sigma Phi. Home: 4 Sigma Av Wheeling WV 26003 Office: 87 15th St Wheeling WV 26003

OPARIL, SUZANNE, physician; b. Elmira, N.Y., Apr. 10, 1941; d. Stanley and Anna (Penkova) Oparil; A.B., Cornell U., 1961; M.D., Columbia, 1965. Intern Presbyn. Hosp., N.Y.C., 1965-66, asst. resident, 1966-67; sr. resident medicine Mass. Gen. Hosp., Boston, 1967-68; fellow research, clin. and teaching cardiac unit Mass. Gen. Hosp., 1968-71; asst. prof. medicine U. Chgo., 1971—. NIH spl. fellow, 1968-71. Diplomate Am. Bd. Internal Medicine. Mem. Am. Fedn. Clin. Research, Am. (established investigator 1973—, med. adv. bd. council for hypertension research 1973—), Ill. (research com. 1973—), Chgo. (research com. 1973—) heart assns., Phi Beta Kappa, Phi Kappa Phi, Alpha Omega Alpha. Mem. editorial bd. Circulation Research, 1974—. Contbr. articles to profl. jours. Home: 5401 S Hyde Park Blvd Chicago IL 60615 Office: 950 E 59th St Chicago IL 60637

OPATOW, LORNA, marketing research cons.; b. Phila.; d. Elias and Frances (Schoenfeld) Opatow; B.A., U. Pa., 1952; M.B.A., Temple U., 1955. Research dir. Good Housekeeping mag., N.Y.C., 1956-59, Hearst Mags., N.Y.C., 1959-63; pres. Opatow Assos., Inc., marketing research cons., N.Y.C., 1963—. Bd. dirs. Vols. of Shelters, Inc., N.Y.C., 1973-74. Mem. Nat. Home Fashions League (chpt. pres. 1969-71), Am. Marketing Assn. (sec. 1958-60), Advt. Women N.Y. (v.p. 1961-63), World, Am. assns. opinion research, Consumer Research Assn., Advt. Women in Radio and TV, Am. Sociol. Assn., Am. Psychol. Assn. Home: 320 E 52d St New York City NY 10022 Office: 527 Madison Av New York City NY 10022

OPIE, RUTH ROBERT (MRS. FRANCIS M. OPIE), banker; b. Whitehall, Mont., Dec. 31, 1916; d. Alex W. and Rubie E. (Maxwell) Robert; A.A., U. Minn., 1936; postgrad. Butte Bus. Coll., 1936-37; m. Francis M. Opie, Aug. 5, 1937; children—Roberta (Mrs. Lawrence Dapp), Everett T., Janice M. (Mrs. Howard C. Hunt), James A. Asst. cashier Whitehall State Bank, 1934-50, asst. cashier, 1959-62, dir., 1960—, v.p., 1962-65, exec. v.p., 1965-72, pres., 1972—; bookkeeper, teller Western Mont. Bank, Missoula, Mont., 1951-55; asst. cashier Security Bank, Butte, (Mont.) 1955-59; pres., dir. Security Bank Three Forks (Mont.); agt. Robert Ins. Agy., Whitehall, Sheridan. Pres., Council Catholic Women, 1960-62; county chmn. Nat. Found. Infantile Paralysis, 1960-65. Mem. Whitehall C. of C. (past pres.). Address: Whitehall MT 59759

OPPEDAHL, ALISON OWEN (MRS. JOHN F. OPPEDAHL), librarian; b. Burlington, Vt., Oct. 3, 1939; d. Eivion and Dorothy May (Arkley) Owen; B.A., Bishop's U., 1960; M.L.S., U. Cal. at Berkeley,

1966; m. John F. Oppedahl, Dec. 30, 1971. Asst. acquisitions librarian Harvard U. Library, Cambridge, Mass., 1966-68; reference librarian Hamtramck (Mich.) Pub. Library, 1968-70; librarian Detroit Free Press, 1970—. Mem. Spl. Libraries Assn., Am. Soc. Information Scientists. Club: Detroit Press. Home: 908 Trombley Grosse Pointe Park MI 48230 Office: 321 W Lafayette Detroit MI 48231

OPPENHEIM, CAROL, journalist; b. Chgo., May 6, 1936; d. Nathan M. and Helen (Freshman) Oppenheim; B.A., U. Mich., 1957. Reporter Chgo. Am., 1957-62; adminstrv. asst. New Haven Redevel. Agy., 1962-66; asst. city editor Chgo. Today, 1968-72; reporter Chgo. Tribune, 1972—. Office: 435 N Michigan Av Chicago IL 60611

OPPENHEIM, IRENE GARTNER, educator; b. N.Y.C., July 26, 1928; d. Samuel and Bessie (Gersten) Gartner; B.S. (Anita Brady scholar, Laura Steele scholar, Home Econs. scholar), Pratt Inst., 1949; M.A., Sch. Edn., N.Y. U., 1957, Ph.D., 1961; m. Don Bruce Oppenheim, June 22, 1949; children—Ellen, Wendy Lee, Barbara Joan. Tchr. pub. schs., N.Y.C., 1949-50, Newark Adult Sch., 1954-55, pub. schs., Irvington, N.J., 1957-59; asst. prof. home econs. Montclair State Coll., Upper Montclair, N.J., 1959-63; asst. prof. home econs. Sch. Edn., N.Y. U., N.Y.C., 1963-65, asso. prof., 1965-69; cons. consumer edn. N.J. Dept. Edn., 1969-72; cons. pub. service adv. com. FDA, 1964, 65; cons. com. on low income family Dept. Health, Edn. and Welfare, 1964; mem. com. on hazardous substances to children Am. Standards Assn., 1964, 65, 66; pres. Am. Council on Consumer Interests, 1964-65. Bd. dirs. N.J. Consumers League, 1962-64. Recipient Founders Day award N.Y.U., 1961. Mem. Am. Home Econs. Assn. (tech. cons. 1965-67). Clubs: Princeton Skating, Springdale Golf. Author: The Family As Consumers, 1965; Management of the Modern Home, 1971; The Young Consumer. Home: 40 Van Dyke Rd Princeton NJ 08540

OPPENHEIM, MARY GERBER (MRS. NORMAN W. OPPENHEIM), lawyer; b. Chgo., Dec. 6, 1912; d. Benjamin and Henrietta (Pabenwitz) Gerber; student U. Ill., 1930-31; B.S., DePaul U., 1932, J.D., 1934; m. Norman W. Oppenheim, Oct. 11, 1942. Admitted to Ill. bar, 1934; tchr., Chgo. Bd. Edn., 1934-42; atty. immigration and naturalization dept. U.S. Dept. Justice, Chgo., 1943-47; partner Korshak, Rothman, Oppenheim & Finnegan, Chgo., 1962—; pres. Windy City Liquors Distributors, Inc., Chgo., 1971—. Mem. Ill. Bar Assn., Decologue Soc., Woman's Bar Assn. Ill. Home: 400 E Randolph St Chicago IL 60601 Office: 69 W Washington St Suite 1717 Chicago IL 60602

OPPENHEIM, NANCY J. PETRY (MRS. STEPHEN G. OPPENHEIM), artist, actress; b. Akron O., Sept. 6, 1928; d. Clarence E. and Elsie Hanna (Peck) Petry; student Cleve. Sch. Art, 1948, 49, Columbia, 1950-51, Queens Coll., 1955, 56, Cooper Union, 1956-59; m. 1946 (div. Nov. 1954); m. 2d, Stanley Lawrence Brown, July 4, 1959 (dec. Sept. 1964); children—S. Randall, Brynn Elise, Todd Wellerson; m. 3d, Stephen G. Oppenheim, 1967. Fashion artist Higbee's, Cleve., 1948-50; arts crafts tchr. Beth El and nursery sch. tchr., N.Y.C., 1953-55; free-lance artist, 1956-59; TV comml. actress, N.Y.C., 1958, 59, Hollywood, Cal., 1960—; v.p. Jerob Corp., Los Angeles, 1959-62; v.p. Trafalgar Importers, Ltd., Beverly Hills, 1963-65; affiliated Studio Gallery, 1963-65, Method Art Corp., Hollywood 1965—; head Nancy Brown Enterprises, 1966—; v.p. Stephen Oppenheim, A.I.A. Orgn., 1972—. Pres. Beverly Hills (Cal.) Community Art League, 1962-64; program speaker Los Angeles Goals, 1967. Mem. Women's Arch. League (v.p. 1969, pres. So. Cal. chpt. 1970, pres. Cal. council 1972), Am. Fedn. TV and Radio Artists, Screen Actors Guild, Internat. Platform Assn., Profl. Women Assn. Hollywood Bowl Los Angeles Symphony. Exhibited in group shows Beverly Hills Community Art League, 1962, 63, 64, Albany (N.Y.) Profl. Artists Shows, 1952; numerous paintings in pvt. collections. Address: 2330 W Live Oak Dr Hollywood CA 90028

OPPENHEIMER, CHRISTINE BACKUS (MRS. MAX OPPENHEIMER, JR.), poet; b. Marseilles, France, July 9, 1920; d. Alexander Hamilton and Wilhelmina Emily (Litzenberger) Backus; B.A., U. Cal. at Los Angeles, 1942; m. Max Oppenheimer, Jr., Oct. 14, 1942; children—Edmund M., Carolyn C. Tchr., Montebello (Cal.) Sr. High Sch., 1942-45; poems pub. in jours., periodicals and anthologies, including N.Y. Times, Mass. Rev., Bitterroot, Poetry Out of Wisconsin, Spring Anthology (London), Poet; pvt. instrn. poetry and self-expression, 1959—. Leader Jr. Red Cross, Montebello, 1943-45; press corr., troop leader Appilachicola council Girl Scouts Am., 1959-64; vol. worker Heart Fund, Cancer Crusade, March of Dimes, 1965-70. Bd. dirs. YWCA, Iowa City, 1963, pres. bd., 1964-67. Recipient Bronze and Silver medals Centro Studi Scambi Internat., Rome, Italy, 1969-71, 1st prize trophy and awards Cal. Olympiad of Arts, 1964, 68, gold medal Pres. of Philippines, 1969, other prizes and awards. Mem. Nat. League Am. Pen Women, Acad. Am. Poets, Avalon Internat., Wis. Fellowship of Poets, Internat. Com. Centro Studi Scambi Internat., Internat. Platform Assn., Fellowship of Reconciliation, Save the Redwoods (life), U. Cal. at Los Angeles (life), Chautauqua Corp., Chautauqua Art Assn., Chautauqua Poets, Shakespeare Club. Author: Building the Bridge (book of poetry), 1964. Antiques dealer Arcade Antiques, 1970—. Home: PO Box 309 Fredonia NY 14063

OPPENHEIMER, EVELYN B., radio commentator, literary agt., book reviewer, writer; b. Dallas, Oct. 20, 1907; d. Louis and Gertrude (Baum) Oppenheimer; Ph.B., Chgo., 1929; pvt. study in Europe (Rome, Florence, Paris, London). Book reviewer Chgo. Evening Post, 1929-30; feature writer Chgo. Journal, 1930-31; Southwest lecture tour annually, 1936—; book reviewer WRR, Dallas, KMEO, Phoenix, KDFC, KIBE, San Francisco, KPOL, Los Angeles; instr. book rev. techniques Tex. Technol. U., 1957, U. Tex., 1958, 60, U. Cal. at Los Angeles, 1958, U. Dallas, 1959, Amarillo Coll., 1960. Mem. Archaeol. Inst. Am., Phi Beta Kappa. Author: Legend and Other Poems, 1951; Finance Fashioned for Women, 1957; Book Reviewing For An Audience, 1962; Introduction to Heroes of Texas, 1964; The Articulate Woman, Public Speaking Fashioned For Women, 1968; Texas in Color, 1971; co-author: Red River Dust, 1968. Address: 4505 Fairway Dallas TX 75219

OPPENHEIMER, JANE MARION, biologist, historian, educator; b. Phila., Sept. 19, 1911; d. James Harry and Sylvia (Stern) Oppenheimer; B.A., Bryn Mawr Coll., 1932; Ph.D., Yale, 1935. Sterling fellow Yale, 1935-36, Am. Assn. U. Women fellow, 1936-37; research fellow embryology U. Rochester, 1937-38; faculty Bryn Mawr Coll., 1938—, successively instr., asst. prof., asso. prof., 1938-53, prof. biology, 1953-74, prof. History of Sci., 1974—, acting dean grad. sch., 2d semester, 1946-47; vis. prof. biology Johns Hopkins U., 1966-67, Brown U. summers, 1967-73; exchange prof. Faculty of Scis., U. Paris, 1969. Mem. history life scis. study sect. NIH, 1966-70. Recipient Guggenheim Meml. Found. fellowship, 1942-43, 52-53, Rockefeller Found. fellowship, 1950-51, NSF postdoctoral fellow, 1959-69. Fellow A.A.A.S. (sec. sect. L 1955-58); mem. Am. Soc. Zoologists (treas. 1957-59, chmn. div. devel. biology 1967, pres 1973), Am. Assn. Anatomists, History of Sci. Soc., Am. Assn. History Medicine (council mem. 1972-74), Internat. Soc. Developmental Biology, Am. Soc. Naturalists, Soc. for Developmental Biology, Am. Assn. U. Women, Internat. Acad. History Sci. (corr.), Internat. Soc. History Medicine. Author: New Aspects of John and William Hunter, 1946; Essays in history and embryology and biology, 1967; co-author: Foundations of Experimental Embryology, 1964, 2d edit., 1974. Asso. editor Jour. Morphology, 1956-58, Quar. Rev. Biol., 1963-64; mem. editorial bd. Am. Zoologist, 1965-70, Jour. History of Biology, 1968-74, Quar. Rev. Biology, 1968—; editorial cons. developmental biology Biol. Abstracts, 1970-73. Office: Biology Bldg Bryn Mawr Coll Bryn Mawr PA 19010

OPPENHEIMER, SELMA LEVY (MRS. REUBEN OPPENHEIMER), artist; b. Balt.; d. William and Beatrice (Stern) Levy; A.B., Goucher Coll., 1919; student Md. Inst., 1920-22; m. Reuben Oppenheimer, June 26, 1922; children—Martin J., Joan (Mrs. Stanley Weiss). Exhibited in group shows at Balt. Mus. Art, 1935-61, also invitational exhbn., 1968, Peale Mus., 1938-66, Phila. Art Alliance, 1940, So. State, 1947, Hagerstown Mus. Fine Arts, Pa. Acad., 1938, Chgo. Art Inst., 1952, Phillips Meml. Gallery, 1938, Corcoran Gallery, 1941-47, 51, 56, 57, 60, Va. Mus. Fine Arts, 1938, Ringling Mus. Art, 1960, Cal. Palace Legion Honor, San Francisco, 1938, Mus. Modern Art, N.Y.C., 1933, Smithsonian Instn., 1956, N.A.D., N.Y.C., 1938-66, Royal Acad. Galleries, Edinburgh, Scotland, 1963, Royal Birmingham (Eng.) Soc. Artists Galleries, 1963, Johns Hopkins Med. Residence Hall, 1961, Goucher Coll., 1965, Jewish Community Center Retrospective Exhibit, 1967; with traveling exhbn. U.S., 1963-65, Scotland (Edinburg), 1964, France, 1965; represented in permanent collection Balt. Pub. Schs., Loyola Coll. Chmn. art com. Jewish Community Center, Balt., 1958-65, bd. dirs., 1958-64; corr. sec. Balt. br. Council Jewish Women; publicity chmn. Md. Fedn. Women's Clubs; sec.-treas. Balt. Art Festival; vice chmn. artists com. Balt. Mus. Art, 1950, artists com., trustee, 1961-72, chmn. classical arts accessions com., 1969—. Recipient medal Md. Inst., 1933, Balt. Mus. Art, 1935, 38, Balt. Water Color Club, 1959, award oil painting Nat. Assn. Women Artists, 1952, 60, 65, purchase award Loyola Coll., 1967. Mem. Nat. Assn. Women Artists, Artists Equity Assn. (past pres. Md. chpt.), Am. Fedn. Arts, Balt. Watercolor Club. Clubs: Hamilton Street (Balt.); Suburban (Pikesville, Md.). Address: 7121 Park Heights Av Baltimore MD 21215

OPPLIGER, E. SUE, social worker; b. Lincoln, Kan.; d. Edwin and Eleonore (Tiemann) Oppliger; student Valparaiso U., 1945-47; B.A., Kan. U., 1949; M.S.W., Tulane U., 1953. With social service dept., pediatrics div. Stanford U. Hosp., San Francisco, 1949-51; clin. social worker Charity Hosp. Social Service Dept., New Orleans, 1953-55, New Orleans Regional Mental Health Center, 1955-60; coordinator Community Involvement Program, Shreveport (La.) Mental Health Center, 1960-73; dir. family and community services Northwest State Sch., Bossier City, La., 1973—; field work instr. Tulane U., 1957-60, La. State U., 1960-68. Cons., Caddo-Bossier Assn. for Retarded Children, 1961—; chmn. state-wide community participation com. La. Dept. Hosps., 1970; cons. La. Nursing Home, 1970-73. Bd. dirs. Caddo-Bossier Council on Alcoholism, 1970—; League Women Voters Shreveport, Open Ear, Multiple Sclerosis Soc. No. La., Caddo-Bossier Vol. Sers. Bur., Nat. Center for Voluntary Action, Washington; v.p. bd. dirs. Project Accept Alcoholism Program. Chmn. mental health vocational employment com. Community Council Caddo-Bossier Parishes, 1968-71, pres. Human Relations Council, 1970-72; chmn. People's Housing Coalition; mem. pub. Affairs Research Council. Mem. Nat. Assn. Social Workers (chpt. pres. 1963-64), La. Conf. Social Welfare (pres. 1965-67), La. Assn. Retarded Children (dir. 1964-70, sec. 1968-70), N.W. La. Health Careers Council, Am. Civil Liberties Union, La. Assn. Mental Health (dir. 1967—, regional v.p. 1968—, chpt. dir. 1966—), Am. Assn. Vol. Services Coordinators, Internat. Platform Assn., Nat. Orgn. for Women (dir. Shreveport-Bossier chpt.). Club: Zonta. Home: 322 College St Shreveport LA 71104 Office: 5401 Shed Rd Bossier City LA 71010

O'PRAY, BARBARA LYNNE, physician; b. Tampa, Fla., June 8, 1943; d. Raymond Francis and Edna Katrina (Sandgren) O'Pray; A.B., Ripon Coll., 1964; M.D., Med. Coll. Pa., 1968. Intern, Med. Coll., Va., 1968-69, resident pediatrics, 1969-71; fellow adolescent medicine Children's Hosp. Med. Center, 1971-73, asst. in medicine, 1973—; fellow adolescent medicine Harvard Med. Sch., Boston, 1971-73, clin. instr. pediatrics, 1973—. Mem. Am. Acad. Pediatrics. Home: 94 Howard Gleason Rd Cohasset MA 02025 Office: Dept Medicine Mass Institute Technology 77 Massachusetts Av Cambridge MA 02139

OPSAHL, JEANETTE CLARA, physician, research scientist; b. Bemidji, Minn., Dec. 29, 1916; d. Jens J. and Clara Matilda (Swanson) Opsahl; B.Sc., B.Edn., U. Minn., 1940, M.Sc., 1942; Ph.D. (Alexander Browne Coxe Meml. fellow) Yale, 1950; M.D. (Damon Runyon clin. research fellow), U. Alta., Can., 1954. Intern Univ. Hosp., Edmonton, Alta., 1954-55; resident Peter Bent Brigham Hosp., Boston, 1955-58, mem. staff, 1973—, physician to Sch. Nursing, 1960-61; mem. staff Harvard Med. Sch., Cambridge, Mass., 1955-62; pvt. practice specializing in internal medicine, Boston, 1962—; research fellow dept. physiology Yale Sch. Medicine, New Haven, 1952-55; clin. investigator Damon Runyon Cancer Research Found., Edmonton, Alta., 1955-63; civilian scientist Office Naval Research, Dept. Navy, Washington, also overseas, 1950-62; med. coordinator Project Hope, 1959-60; cons. bur. employees' compensation U.S. Dept. Labor, Boston, 1963-64; U.S. Dept. Interior Water Pollution and Evaluation and Standardization of Water Quality Control, 1968-69, Arthur D. Little, Inc., Cambridge, 1964—. Served to lt. USNR, 1955-63. Mem. A.M.A., Canadian Med. Assn., Mass., Conn., Norfolk Dist., New Haven County med. socs., Endocrine Soc., Am. Soc. Biol. Chemists, A.A.A.S., U.S. Naval Inst., Am. Med. Writers Assn., Sigma Xi, Alpha Epsilon Iota. Asst. to editor Jour. A.M.A., 1961-62, mng. editor Archives of Dermatology, A.M.A., 1961-62. Contbr. numerous articles to profl. jours. and publs. Address: Copley Plaza Hotel 138 St James Av Boston MA 02116

O'QUINN, CLEODIA LYNDON, missionary, community organizer; b. Ark., Oct. 16, 1925; d. Lucius C. and Exorter Cleodia Lyndon (Anderson) Dawkins; diploma Herzl Jr. Coll., Chgo.; married; 1 son, Milton Lafayette. Tchr. Montefiore Soc. Adjustment Sch.; founder, dir. O'Quinn's Fine Arts Sch.; tchr. leadership adult vols. Boy Scouts Am.; operator O'Quinn's Royal Gladiators and Drum and Bugle Corp. Recipient numerous citations for civic work. Mem. League Women Voters, Am. Legion Aux. Address: 121 Central Park Av Chicago IL

ORAVEC, LEE MORGAN (MRS. BRUCE J. ORAVEC), mus. curator; b. Boston, Aug. 1, 1946; d. Jay Lewis and Margaret (Lee) Morgan; B.A., Wellesley Coll., 1968; M.A., U. Mich., 1970; m. Bruce J. Oravec, June 15, 1968. Asst. curator Brockton (Mass.) Art Center, 1972-73, curator, 1973—. Mem. Am. Assn. Mus., Coll. Art Assn., Wellesley Coll. Club, Phi Beta Kappa. Democrat. Home: 8 Stonybrook Rd Medfield MA 02052 Office: Oak St Brockton MA 02401

ORCHARD, MARGARET JEAN, health services adminstr.; b. Burbank, Cal., May 29, 1926; d. Harland Alexander and Margaret (Delp) Orchard; A.A., U. Cal. at Los Angeles, 1946; B.S., U. So. Cal., 1949, certificate in Occupational Therapy, 1950, M.Pub. Adminstrn., 1969, certificate in Health Adminstrn., 1970. Occupational therapist Winter VA Hosp., Topeka, 1950-51, Brentwood VA Hosp., Los Angeles, 1951-52; dir. occupational therapy Orthopaedic Hosp., Los Angeles, 1952-60; chief occupational therapist St. John's Hosp., Santa Monica, Cal., 1960-63; head occupational therapist Los Angeles County Harbor Gen. Hosp., Los Angeles, 1966-68; lectr., adminstrv. asst. U. So. Cal., Los Angeles, 1968; tech. adviser So. Cal. Comprehensive Health Planning Assn., Los Angeles, 1969; rehab. coordinator Northridge (Cal.) Hosp. Rehab. Center, 1970-72; asst. dir. Coordinating Council for Edn. in Health Scis., San Diego, 1972; health planner Comprehensive Health Planning Council Los Angeles County, 1972-73; exec. dir. Orange County-Long Beach Health Consortium, Inc., Irvine, Cal., 1974—. Lectr., cons. Cal. univs., 1951—. Bd. dirs. Westwood Community Meth. Mental Health Center, Los Angeles, council Los Angeles County Art Mus. Office of vocational rehab. grantee, 1956; USPHS grantee, 1969; Cal. Dept. Pub. Health grantee, 1970. Mem. Am. Pub. Health Assn., Nat. Rehab. Assn. (pres. elect. 1968), So. Cal. Assn. Rehab. Med. Dirs. and Coordinators, World Fedn. Occupational Therapists, Am., So. Cal. (coms. del. 1970, dir., pres. 1958) occupational therapy assns., U. So. Cal. Alumni Assn. (life), Alpha Omicron Pi. Republican. Methodist. Contbr. articles to profl. jours. Home: 220 Promontory Dr West Newport Beach CA 92660 Office: 2021 Business Center Dr Suite 204 Irvine CA 92664

ORCUTT, ROBERTA KIEFER (MRS. RICHARD GATTON ORCUTT), librarian; b. Los Angeles, July 29, 1929; d. Frank Vincent and Laura Ellen (Roberts) Kiefer; A.B., U. Cal. at Los Angeles, 1950; B.L.S., U. Cal. at Berkeley, 1951; m. Richard Gatton Orcutt, June 23, 1951; children—Deborah, Caroline, Lawrence. Jr. librarian Cal. Dept. Pub. Health, 1951-52, U.S. Dept. Agr. Library, Washington, 1952; asst. head phys. scis. libraries U. Cal. at Berkeley, 1953-55; asst. acquisitions librarian U. Fla. Library, 1967-68; asst. reference librarian U. Nev. at Reno, 1968-70; librarian Desert Research Inst., Reno, 1970—. Mem. Am., Nev. library assns., Phi Beta Kappa, Phi Kappa Phi, Alpha Phi. Home: 985 Munley Dr Reno NV 89503 Office: Desert Research Inst Library Sage Bldg Stead Campus Reno NV 89507

ORDEN, SUSAN R. (MRS. ALEX ORDEN), sociologist; b. N.Y.C., Jan. 25, 1920; d. Oscar and Bella (Beyer) Rabinowitz; B.A., Hunter Coll., 1940; M.A., Am. U., 1950; m. Alex Orden, Dec. 8, 1946; children—Ruth (Mrs. Gabriel Leitner), David, Jeanne. Economist, WPB, Washington, 1942-46; statistician Harvard Bus. Sch., Cambridge, Mass., 1947-48; sociologist Nat. Opinion Research Center, Chgo., 1963-72; asso. dept. community health and preventive med. Northwestern U. Med. Sch., Chgo., 1973—. Mem. Fifth Ward Citizens Com., Chgo., 1968—; v.p. U. Chgo. Lab. Sch. Parents Assn., 1968. Mem. Am. Sociol. Assn., Am. Econ. Assn., Hyde Park League Women Voters, (chmn. 1965). Home: 5715 S Kenwood Av Chicago IL 60637 Office: 303 E Chicago Av Chicago IL 60611

O'REILLY, INEZ LOUISE, mus. curator; b. Parkhill, Ont., Can., Apr. 24, 1922; d. Elson Frederick and Kathleen (Kenny) David; student U. B.C., 1970—; m. John Windham O'Reilly, May 20, 1967; children—Thomas Frederick Whiffin, David Elson Whiffin. Curator, owner Point Ellice House Mus., Victoria, B.C., Can., 1967—. Served with RCAF, 1940-45. Mem. English Speaking Union (v.p. 1973-74, Craigdarroch Castle Soc. (mem. exec. council 1967—), B.C. Hist. Soc., Monarchish League Can., B.C. Museums Assn., Oral History B.C. Provincial Mus., Psysic Research B.C. Home: 2616 Pleasant St Victoria BC Canada

OREN, ANNE WINSLOW, social worker, educator; b. Winnipeg, Man., Can., Nov. 29, 1909; d. Carmi and Charlotte (Sletto) Winslow; came to U.S., 1910; B.A., U. Minn., 1931, Ph.D., 1957; M.A., U. Chgo., 1942; m. Donald Smith Oren, Apr. 7, 1951; children—John, Mary. Adminstrv. sec. to dir. Minn. Dept. Pub. Welfare, St. Paul, 1933-39; hosp. field dir. A.R.C., 1942-44; research analyst Social Security Bd., Mpls., 1944-45; supr. social services Wash. State Dept. Pub. Welfare, Lewis and Whatcom counties, 1945-47; asso. prof. social work U. Minn., 1947-66, prof., 1966-72, ret.; pvt. practice as psychotherapist, 1972—. Mem. exec. com. Minn. Council on Social Work Edn., 1950-54, 57-60; program chmn. Minn. Welfare Conf., 1951; dir. Mpls. Travelers Aid, 1956—; mem. adv. bd. Youth Action, Inc., Edina, Minn. Mem. Am. Assn. U. Profs., Acad. Certified Social Workers, Nat., Am. (chpt. chmn. 1948-50) assns. social workers, Nat. Council Social Work Edn., Am. Civil Liberties Union, Friends of Inst. of Arts, Urban League. Presbyn. Club: Minneapolis Woman's. Home: 5317 Hollywood Rd Edina MN 55436

ORENS, ELAINE FRANCES COHEN (MRS. PERRY ARNOLD ORENS), artist; b. N.Y.C., July 18, 1929; d. Louis and Jennie (Diamond) C.; B.A., Hunter Coll., 1951; m. Perry Arnold Orens, Dec. 26, 1953; children—Matthew Lee, Jonathan Brett, Emily Risa. One man shows Adelphi U.; exhibited in group shows Heckscher Mus., Hunterdon Art Center, Bklyn., N.A.D., Jesse Bresser Mus., Alpena, Mich., Larsen Gallery, Brigham Young U., Queens Coll., Nassau Community Coll., Bergen County (N.J.) Mus., Asso. Am. Artists, N.Y.C. Recipient William Graf Scholarship, Hunter Coll., 1953, Pratt Printmaking award Suburban Art League, 1968, Jeffrey Childs Willis award Nat. Assn. Women Artist, 1971. Mem. Nat. Assn. Women Artists. Home: 121 Shoreward Dr Great Neck NY 11021

ORES, CELIA NEWTON, pediatrician; b. Dubienka, Poland, May 5, 1928; d. Paul and Ita (Wesnstein) Newton; M.D., U. Bern (Switzerland), 1956; m. Richard Ores, Jan. 17, 1954 (div. Aug. 1971); children—Pauline, David, Michelle. Came to U.S., 1950, naturalized, 1955. Intern, Brookdale Med. Center, Bklyn., 1956-57, resident, 1957-60; resident Babies Hosp., Columbia-Presbyn. Med. Center, 1960-62; practice medicine, specializing in pediatrics, N.Y.C., 1962—; attending pediatrician Babies Hosp., Columbia Presbyn. Med. Center, N.Y.C., 1961—; instr. pediatrics Columbia U. Med. Sch., 1962-72, asst. prof. clin. pediatrics, 1972—. Contbr. articles to profl. jours. Home: 254 Christie Heights St Leonia NJ 07605 Office: 3975 Broadway New York City NY 10032

ORFANOS, MINNIE, librarian; b. Hinsdale, Ill., Dec. 10, 1921; d. Antonious George and Catherine (Lekatsos) Orfanos; Ph.B., Northwestern U., 1954; M.A. in L.S., U. Mich., 1958. Library clk. Chgo. Pub. Library, 1940-43; library asst. Dental Sch. Library, Northwestern U., Chgo., 1943-45, asst. librarian, 1945-50, acting librarian, 1950-52, librarian, 1952—. Condr. dental library survey Assn. Canadian Faculty of Dentistry, 1970. Pres. governing bd. and Council Midwest Regional Med. Library and Information Services, 1974. Recipient Merit award Am. Coll. Dentists, 1967. Mem. Med. Library Assn. (dental group chmn. 1952, exchange com. 1964, chmn. exchange com. 1965—, mem. nominating com. 1970-71; exec. com. Midwest group 1965—, chmn. nominating com. 1970, cons. to coms., pres. Midwest group 1968), Sigma Phi. Contbr. articles to profl. publs. Home: 45 Wilmette Av Glenview IL 60025 Office: 311 E Chicago Av Chicago IL 60611

ORGAN, (AVIS) JOYCE CULPEPPER (MRS. RALEIGH RALPH ORGAN), librarian; b. Floresville, Tex., Apr. 6, 1912; d. Darius Ivan and Elfie May (Spencer) Culpepper; student Our Lady of the Lake Coll., San Antonio, 1956-57; m. Raleigh Ralph Organ, June 9, 1938. With Lackland AFB Library System San Antonio, 1950—, librarian Officer Tng. Sch. Library, 1959—. Mem. Bexar County

Library Assn., Cath. Library Assn., Tex. Watercolor Soc. (corr. sec.), San Antonio Art League, River Art Group, San Antonio Conservation Soc., Nat. Audubon Soc., Wilderness Soc., Nat. Parks and Conservation Soc., Nat. Forests Soc., Air Force Assn., Smithsonian Instn. Editor, writer, compiler River Art Group bull. 1955-68. Home: 518 E Mayfield Blvd San Antonio TX 78214 Office: Forbes Hall Medina Annex Lackland AFB San Antonio TX 78214

ORICK, ADELE KASPER (MRS. WILLIAM L. ORICK), computer programmer; b. Amsterdam, N.Y., Oct. 9, 1922; d. Anthony and Antonina (Shaules) Kasper; A.B., N.Y. State Coll. for Tchrs., 1946, M.A., 1953; postgrad. Columbia, 1947; m. William L. Orick, Aug. 21, 1948; children—Karen Marie, Sheila Kathryn. Secondary math. tchr., Whitehall, N.Y., 1946-47, Chatham, N.Y., 1947-48; 7th grade arithmetic tchr., Mechanicville, N.Y., 1956-57; computer programmer Gen. Electric Co., Schenectady, 1957—. Unitarian (mem. social action council 1971-72). Office: Gen Electric Co Schenectady NY 12345

ORLOFF, ETHELROSE, ednl. adminstr.; b. Spokane, Wash., Mar. 16, 1917; d. George Frederick and Eva Josephine (Rodes) Orloff; A.A., Los Angeles City Coll., 1937; postgrad. George Pepperdine Coll., 1937-38; B.A., U. Cal. at Santa Barbara, 1940; M.A., Columbia U., 1951. Tchr. Santa Monica (Cal.) High Sch., 1941-46; adminstr. Los Angeles City Coll., 1946-62; tchr. psychology Citrus Coll., Azusa, Cal., part-time, 1960-61; adminstr. East Los Angeles Coll., 1962—. Dir. Beverly Pines Camp, Blue Jay, Cal., 1944-45. Mem. Am. Assn. U. Women, Bus. Profl. Women, Cal. Assn. Woman Adminstrs. and Counselors, Nat. Assn. Women Deans and Counselors, Delta Kappa Gamma. Home: 834 Glenn Alan Av West Covina CA 91791 Office: 5357 E Brooklyn Av Los Angeles CA 90022

ORLOSKY, ELIZABETH ALMA BROWN (MRS. JOHN DAVID ORLOSKY), educator; b. Angola, Ind., Apr. 13, 1920; d. Harold Fenimore and Vesta Pearl (Lautzenhiser) Brown; B.A. cum laude, DePauw U., 1942; M.A., Ball State U., 1962; postgrad. Western Mich. U., 1960, Ind. U., 1966; m. John David Orlosky, Sept. 11, 1948; children—Mary Ann, Patricia Alma. Tchr., Walkerton (Ind.) High Sch., 1942-43, Fairmount (Ind.) High Sch., 1943-44, Rochester (Ind.) High Sch., 1944-48; owner, operator Beth Orlosky Program Bur., Angola, Ind., 1948-56; faculty Tri-State Coll., Angola, 1956—, prof. speech, dir. forensics, 1967—. Trustee Carnegie Pub. Library, Angola, Ind., 1967—. Mem. Speech Communication Assn., Am. Forensic Assn., Central States, Ind. speech assns., D.A.R., Bus. and Profl. Women (pres. 1966-67), Delta Sigma Rho, Delta Kappa Gamma, Psi Iota Xi. Contbr. poetry to various publs. Home: 213 S Kinney St Angola IN 46703

ORMISTON, MARY BETH, assn. exec., TV hostess; b. Grinnell, Ia., Apr. 18, 1948; d. Eldon K. and Mary Jane (Bramer) Ormiston; B.S. in Speech and Theater, U. No. Ia., 1970. Asst. phys. dir. Black Hawk County YMCA, Waterloo, Ia., 1970, program, aquatic dir., 1971-72, phys. dir., 1973—; hostess Today with Beth, Channel 7, Waterloo, 1972—; membership and pub. relations dir. Radio Show YMCA, Sta. KXEl, Waterloo, 1973—. Instr. police sci. and adult edn. dept. Hawkeye Inst. Tech. Vol. probation officer Black Hawk County, 1971-73; merit badge counselor Boy Scouts Am., Waterloo, 1972-74, instr. water safety, 1971-74; Bremer county water safety instr. YMCA, Waterloo, 1971-72, membership campaign dir., 1972-73; pres. Mid-Ia. Swim League, 1973. Mem. Ia. Soc. Phys. Dirs., Assn. Profl. YMCA Dirs., Assn. Bus. Women Am. Methodist. Home: 1149 Dixon Dr Apt 2 Waterloo IA 50702 Office: 154 W 4th St Waterloo IA 50704

ORMSBY, JEANNE LOUISE, restaurant exec.; b. Detroit, Sept. 6, 1926; d. Irwin Duffield and Lucille Florence (Cooke) Ormsby; A.B., Case Western Res. U., 1949. Trainee, The Hubbell Advt. Agy., Cleve., 1949-51; staff asst. pub. relations dept. United Appeal, Cleve., 1951-55; pub. relations dir. Luth. Hosp., Cleve., 1955-56, St. John's Hosp., Cleve., 1956-62; community relations dir. Cuyahoga County Library System, Cleve., 1962-68; account exec. Dix & Eaton Advt. and Pub. Relations Agy., Cleve., 1969; editorial dir. Stouffers Restaurants & Inns, Cleve., 1969—. Pub. relations cons. Pickands Mather & Co., Cleve., 1968; founder, first chmn. tech. adv. com. on pub. relations Cleve. Hosp. Council, 1958; chmn. pub. relations workshop Welfare Fedn. Cleve., 1961; pub. relations chmn. bd. mem. Cleve. council Camp Fire Girls, 1960-66, YWCA, Cleve., 1965—; mem. pub. relations com. Welfare Fedn., 1965-66. Mem. Pub. Relations Soc. Am. (pres. Greater Cleve. chpt. 1966). Club: Zonta (pres. 1972-74) (Cleve.). Editor Ohio Library Assn. Bull., 1963. Home: 4550 Van Epps Rd Cleveland OH 44131 Office: 1375 Euclid Av Cleveland OH 44115

ORNISH, NATALIE GENE MOSKOWITZ (MRS. EDWIN PAUL ORNISH), film co. exec.; b. Galveston, Tex., Feb. 15, 1926; d. George I. and Bess (Shapiro) Moskowitz; B.A., Sam Houston State Coll., 1943; M.S., Northwestern U., 1945; m. Edwin Paul Ornish, Nov. 6, 1949; children—Laurel Ann, Dean Michael, Steven Andrew, Kathy April. Editor, A.P., Omaha, 1945-46; with pub. relations dept. Rogers & Smith Advt. Co., Dallas, 1947; dir. publicity Galveston Pleasure Pier, 1948-49; contbg. editor Galveston Isle Mag., 1948-49; pres. Dallas Records Co., 1957—, Dallas Records Pub. Co., 1967—, Creative Child Prodns., Dallas, 1973—; dir., Natwin Co., Dallas, Sherry Lane Investment Corp., Dallas. Mem. Dallas Motion Picture Classification Bd., 1965-69; mem. speakers bur. Dallas Ind. Sch. Dist., 1972. Pres., Dallas Ballet Theatre Women's Com., 1972-73. Bd. dirs. Dallas Civic Ballet Women's Guild, 1972-73. A.S.C.A.P., Information Film Producers Am. Author: Bridge is Child's Play, 1973. Producer ednl. films The Circus Horse-a Ballet, Learning to Dive. Address: 7146 Currin Dr Dallas TX 75230

ORNSTEN, FRAYDA LYNN, educator; b. Denver, Mar. 17, 1936; d. Ben and Anne (Katchen) Blumberg; B.S. in Bus. Edn., U. Denver, 1965, M.A. in Spl. Edn., 1968; spl. curriculum workshops Kan. State Tchrs. Coll., 1969, Western State Coll., 1970, U. No. Colo., 1970-73; m. Bruce Stephen Ornsten, Dec. 25, 1971; children—Arlan Murray Harris, Richard Alan Harris. Cons. pub. schs., Aurora, Colo., 1969-70; tchr., spl. educator, Denver, 1965-68; spl. educator Jefferson County (Colo.) Schs., 1970-71; operator Lab. for Educationally Handicapped, Jefferson County Schs., Arvada, Colo., 1971-73; learning disabilities specialist Profl. Psychiat. and Guidance Clinic, Denver, 1973-74; dir. The OK Center, Denver, 1974—. Co-dir. curriculum devel. in spl. edn. Colo. Dept. Edn., 1969-71; mem. Colo. Title III Adv. Council, 1971-74. Trustee Babi Yar Park Found. Mem. Council Exceptional Children (membership chmn. 1969-70, workshop chmn.), Nat., Colo. edn. assns., Am. Assn. Mental Deficiency. Democrat. Jewish religion. Home: 1670 Zenobia St Denver CO 80204 Office: 2999 S Colorado Blvd 114 Denver CO 80222

OROSZ, BARBARA JEAN, librarian; b. Glendale, Cal., Aug. 5, 1939; d. Bert George and Elizabeth Ann (Simay) Orosz; B.S. in Chemistry, Immaculate Heart Coll., Los Angeles, 1961; M.L.S., U. So. Cal., 1967. Asst. research chemist Union Oil Co. of Cal., Brea, 1961-64, head librarian, 1964—. Mem. adv. bd. U. So. Cal. Sch. of Library Sci., 1970-73; library tech. adv. com. Community Coll. Dist. North Orange County, Cal., 1971—. Mem. Spl. Libraries Assn. (treas. petroleum div. 1972—), Geosci. Information Soc., Am. Soc. for Information Sci., Iota Sigma Pi, Delta Epsilon Sigma. Home: 201 E Chapman St Placentia CA 92670 Office: PO Box 76 Brea CA 92621

O'ROURKE, JACQUELYN WARREN, public relations cons.; b. Gettysburg, Pa., Sept. 28, 1937; d. Elmer Willard and Gladys May (Palmer) Warren; B.A., U. Miami (Fla.), 1958; postgrad. Am. Inst. Pub. Relations, Chgo., 1970; m. T. Nelson O'Rourke, Mar. 17, 1973. Publicity asst. Fla. Power & Light Co., Miami, 1960-62, publicity rep., 1962-73, supr. employee communications, 1972-73, editor Sunshine Service News, 1970-73; prop. Jacque O'Rourke Pub. Relations, Daytona Beach, Fla., 1973—. Recipient Best Feature Story award Fla. Mag. Assn., 1966, Gen. Excellence award for internal mag., 1966, 67, 70, 71, Best Picture Story award, 1967, Gold Quill award Am. Assn. Indsl. Editors, 1970. Mem. Am. Women in Radio and TV, Women in Communications (pres. Miami 1967-68, co-chmn. nat. conv. 1971), Delta Delta Delta. Office: 625-13 N Halifax Av Daytona Beach FL 32018

O'ROURKE, RUTH ANN (MRS. JAMES P. O'ROURKE), coll. adminstr.; b. Dubuque, Ia., Oct. 31, 1937; d. Alfred A. and Anselma (Fessler) Buenker; B.A. in English cum laude, Clarke Coll., 1959; m. James P. O'Rourke, July 25, 1970. Tchr. high sch. Saydel Community Sch. Dist., Des Moines, 1959-63; admissions counselor Clarke Coll., Dubuque, 1963-70, dir. admissions, 1972—. Newspaper Fund fellow, Wall St. Jour., 1960. Mem. Ia. Assn. Coll. Admissions Counselors (sec.-treas. 1972-74). Home: 1717 Kane St Dubuque IA 52001 Office: Clarke College Dubuque IA 52001

ORR, AILENE COOK, hosp. adminstr.; b. York, Me., Apr. 15, 1913; d. Fred Rae and Ella Florence (Moulton) Cook; student Mass. Gen. Hosp. Sch. Nursing, 1934; B.S. in Nursing, St. Anselm's Coll., 1963; M.S. in Nursing Service Adminstrn., Boston U., 1964, certificate advanced study adminstrn. and supervision, 1971; m. Joseph J. Paterno, Aug. 9, 1935; children—Kenneth John, Joseph J.; m. 2d, Clement W. Orr, May 15, 1971. Pvt. duty nurse Mass. Gen. Hosp., Boston, 1934-37, team leader, 1955; med.-surg. charge nurse Laconia (N.H.) Hosp., 1955-58, night supr., 1958-62, instr., dir. inservice edn., 1963; dir.-coordinator inservice tng. Laconia State Sch. and Tng. Center, 1964-67, dir. child care and nursing, 1967-71. Chmn. planning Central N.H. Home Care Services, Laconia, 1971; sec. N.H. Home Care Services, Inc., Concord, 1972-74. Dept. Health, Edn. and Welfare grantee, 1963—, 64. Mem. Mass. Gen. Hosp. Alumnae Assn., Altrusa. Rebekah, Odd Fellow. Author: The Therapeutic Care and Training of Exceptional Children, 1970, Instructor's Guide, 1970. Address: RFD #4 Roberts Rd Laconia NH 03246 also Imperial Harbor Bonita Springs FL 33923

ORR, EVELYN PRICHARD (MRS. JAMES C. ORR, JR.), ednl. adminstr.; b. Lebanon, Tenn., Dec. 15; d. Joe Blythe and Katherine Evelyn (Webster) Prichard; A.B., Cumberland U., 1937; M.Ed., U. Chattanooga, 1960; m. James C. Orr, Jr., June 1, 1937; children—Nancy (Mrs. John B. Winkler), Jon Blythe. Tchr. high sch., Wilson County, Tenn., 1937-39; prin. elementary sch. Roane County 1939-41; elementary tchr., Hamilton County, Chattanooga, 1948-58, reading coordinator, 1960-65, sch. psychologist, supr. psychol. services, 1965—; reading tchr. U. Chattanooga Reading Clinic, 1958-60. Bd. dirs. Hamilton County Children Learning Disabilities. Mem. Tenn. Assn. Psychology in Schs. (pres. elect 1973-74), Internat. Reading Assn. (pres. Tenn. 1968-69), Hamilton County Assn. Childhood Edn., Delta Phi Omega, Delta Kappa Gamma. Methodist. Home: 3114 Greenwich Av Chattanooga TN 37415 Office: 317 Oak St Chattanooga TN 37403

ORR, JOAN, state senator; b. Cedar Rapids, Ia., Feb. 10, 1923; d. Joseph Urvin and Gail Helen (Gauby) Yessler; B. Music Ed., Oberlin Coll., 1946; postgrad. Chgo. Tchrs. Coll., U. Ia., 1949-51; m. Carl Orr, Nov. 26, 1947. Former tchr., Chgo., Cedar Rapids; operator dairy, Grinnell, Ia., until 1966; mem. Ia. Senate, 1970, 72—. Mem. League Women Voters. Address: 10 Merrill Park Circle Grinnell IA 50112

ORR, JUANITA OLSON, state legislator; b. Danville, Wash., Jan. 12, 1917; d. Antone M. and Bertha (Bergay) Olson; student Levina Coll. Credit, 1939, Behnke Walker Bus. Coll., 1942-45, Portland State U., 1963; m. Robert Orr, Mar. 4, 1942. Sec-treas. also tax cons. property mgmt. Imperial Collections, Inc., Portland, 1959-66; mem. Ore. Ho. of Reps., 1954—, chmn. financial affairs com., 1961-63, vice chmn., legislative counsel coms. Natural Resources, Food, Dairying, 1963-65, mem. coms. Health and Welfare, Per Diem, 1965—; tax cons.; sec. State of Ore. Interim Com. on Social Problems, 1962—. Del. Democratic Nat. Conv., 1964, mem. rules com. Mem. Lake Grove (Ore.) Water Bd. Mem. Ore. Hist. Soc., Jane Jefferson Woman's Club of Clackames County (Ore.) (founder), Ore. Grange, Farmer's Union, Research Club, Lake Oswego (Ore.) Women's Club, V.F.M. Aux. (pres. Oswego chpt. 1964-66), Farm Bus., Animal Defenders League, President's Club. Lady Elkette. Sponsor passage various laws including the Battered Baby Bill for protection of children, 1963. Home: 15348 SW Parker St Lake Grove OR 97034 Office: 15868 1/2 SW Parker St Lake Oswego OR 97035

ORR, LEONA CHARLOTTE AMEN (MRS. FOSTER RAY ORR), constrn. co. exec.; b. Proctor, Colo., Sept. 23, 1914; d. Henry and Mary Katherine (Uhrich) Amen; grad. Mercy Hosp. Nursing Sch., 1936; m. Foster Ray Orr, Mar. 9, 1937; children—Judith Rae (Mrs. Merrill Turner Ham), John Foster, James Henry. Pvt. duty nurse, Denver, 1936-48; sec.-treas. F. R. Orr Constrn. Co., Inc., Denver, 1948—; dir. Union Bank & Trust, Denver. Active Craig Rehab. Hosp. Aux., Littleton, Colo. Mem. Mercy Alumni Assn. Clubs: Columbine Country (Littleton, Colo.); Athletic (Denver). Home: 6191 S Franklin St Littleton CO 80121 Office: 4414 Vine St Denver CO 80216

ORR, SISTER MARY MARK, librarian; b. Beattie, Kan., Mar. 1, 1900; d. Thomas John and Julia (Kraemer) Orr; A.B., U. Kan., 1928, M.A., 1931; B.S. in L.S., U. Ill., 1933; postgrad. Universidad Nacional de Mexico, 1944; Workshop in archival mgmt. Truman Library, Independence, Mo., 1959. Tchr. rural schs., Marshall County, Kan., 1918-22; prin. pub. sch., Home, Kan., 1922-24; tchr. Annunciation High Sch., Denver, 1928-30, Immaculata High Sch., Leavenworth, Kan., 1930-32; asst. librarian, St. Mary Coll., Leavenworth, Kan., 1933-36, head librarian, 1936-72, spl. collections librarian, 1972—; chmn. program and exhibits ann. Bible Weeks, 1943—. Mem. Am., Kan., Catholic (award Midwest unit) library assns., Cath. Bibl. Assn., Met. Opera Guild, Delta Epsilon Sigma. Contbr. chpt. to The Beattie Story, 1970. Book editor Poise, 1943-44; contbr. to profl. jours. Home: St Mary Coll Leavenworth KS 66048

ORSINI, MARGARET WARD (MRS. GIAN NAPOLEONE GIORDANO ORSINI), physiologist, educator; b. Le Roy, N.Y., Mar. 18, 1916; d. Harold Butler and Florence Maria (Chapman) Ward; B.A. in Zoology with honors, Mt. Holyoke Coll., 1937; Ph.D. (Simon Henry Gage fellow), Cornell U., 1946; postdoctoral (Nat. Cancer Institute fellow) U. Wis., 1949-52; m. Gian Napoleone Giordano Orsini, July 29, 1949. Technician, U. St. Louis Sch. Medicine, 1937-38; technician, pathology lab. Manhattanville Coll. Sacred Heart, N.Y.C., 1938-40, asst. in biology, 1940-42; instr. Duke U., Durham, N.C., 1946-49; project asso. U. Wis., Madison, 1952, research asso., 1953-69, asst. prof. anatomy, 1970-72, asso. prof., 1972-73, prof., 1973—. Invited lectr. U. London (Eng.), 1968. NSF grantee, 1953-58; NIH grantee, 1958—. Fellow N.Y. Acad. Scis., A.A.A.S.; mem. Soc. for Study of Reprodn. (dir. 1972-74), Am. Assn. for Lab. Animal Sci., Am. Assn. Anatomists, Am. Inst. Biol. Sci., Am. Soc. Animal Sci., Am. Soc. Zoologists, Internat. Soc. Devel. Biologists, Soc. Endocrinology, Soc. for Exptl. Biology and Medicine, Soc. for Study Devel. and Growth, Soc. for Study Fertility, Am. Fertility Soc., Endocrine Soc., Internat. Sec. for Research in Reprodn., Phi Kappa Phi (pres. Madison chpt. 1969-70). Contbr. articles to profl. jours. Home: 1815 Adams St Madison WI 53711

ORT, LORRENE LOVE (MRS. VERGIL K. ORT), educator; b. Sedalia, Mo., Apr. 17, 1918; d. James Owen and Alma (Hirschfelt) Love; Mus.B., Oberlin Coll., 1939; M.A., Ohio State U., 1950, Ph.D., 1955; m. Vergil K. Ort, Nov. 1, 1941. Tchr., supr. Napoleon (O.) Pub. Schs., 1939-42, 46-51; dir., tchr. Feleti Meml. Tchr.-Tng. Sch., Pago Pago, Tutuila, Am. Samoa, 1951-53; related arts coordinator Ohio State U. Lab. Sch., Columbus, 1954-55; instr. Coll. Edn., Ohio State U., Columbus, 1955-56; prof. asst. prof. edn. Bowling Green (O.) (O.) State U., 1956-61, asso. prof., 1961-65, prof., 1965—, grad. prof., 1970—, dir. student teaching and profl. lab experiences, 1956-70. Mem. N.E.A., Ohio Edn. Assn., Am. Assn. U. Women, Assn. Supervision and Curriculum Devel., Nat. Council Tchrs. English, Mortar Bd., Pi Lambda Theta, Kappa Delta Pi (pres. 1970-72). Author: (with Don C. Rogers and Mary C. Sera) My Word Book, 1966, 2d edit., 1970, 3d edit. (with Eunice Wallace), 1974. Home: 29 Parkwood Dr Bowling Green OH 43402

ORTH, MARY CATHERINE, advt. exec.; b. Burlington, Ia., Jan. 23, 1939; d. Leonard L. and Helen M. (Fleming) Orth; student Marquette U., 1958-59. With Cedar Rapids (Ia.) Gazette, 1959—, classified advt. sales dept., 1961-67, display advt. sales dept., 1967-68, nat. advt. sales dept., 1968—. Mem. housing com. YWCA, 1970. Mem. Cedar Rapids Advt. Club, 1969-70. Club: Elmcrest Country (Cedar Rapids). Office: 500 Third Av SE Cedar Rapids IA 52401

ORTIZ, SILVIA, advt. co. exec.; b. Havana, Cuba; d. Ezequiel and Adoracion (Villanueva) Ortiz; Ph.D. and Arts, U. Havana, 1954, M. Advt., 1956; student Iranzo Conservatory Music, 1944-51. Copywriter, Publicidad Alvarez Perez, Havana, 1959-60; creative dir. Internat. Marketing & Advt. Corp., San Juan, P.R., 1961-67; creative dir. Spanish Advt. & Marketing Services, Inc., N.Y.C., 1967-74; pres. Spanish Ideas, Inc., N.Y.C., 1974—. Cons. marketing and research, P.R., 1964-67. Mem. Cultural Cuban Center. Recipient El Mundo Newspaper Advt. award; Internat. Film Festival award, 1973. Mem. Spanish Inst. Home: 40-05 Hampton St New York City NY 11373 Office: 663 Fifth Av New York City NY 10022

ORTIZ, VIRGINIA KATHRYN FIGY (MRS. FRED CHAVEZ ORTIZ), home economist; b. Morenci, Mich., Apr. 14, 1921; d. Charley and Adeline Genevieve (Newell) Figy; B.A., Albion Coll., 1942; M.A., Siena Heights Coll., 1965; m. Fred Chavez Ortiz, Dec. 2, 1965; children—Charles Scott, Charlyn Kathryn (Mrs. Larry MacFarland), Tamara (Mrs. Garfield Perry), Vandria Scott. Tchr. pub. sch. Mich., 1942-61; tchr. English, home econs. Bur. Indian Affairs, 1961-68; home economist Mich. State U. Extension, Lapeer, 1968—. Vice chmn. Citizen's Probation Council, 1970—. Bd. dirs., mem. exec. bd. Thumb area Office Econ. Opportunity, 1971—. Recipient Quest for Quality fellowship Kellogg Found., 1971; Distinguished Service award Extension Home Economists Mich., 1971. Mem. Bus. and Profl. Women (pub. relations chmn. Lapeer County chpt. 1969-70), Nat., Mich. assns. extension home economists, Am., Mich. assns. home economists, County Assn. Home Economists, Zeta Tau Alpha. Club: Delphian (Lapeer). Home: 1683 Madeline Dr Lapeer MI 48446 Office: Fed Bldg Lapeer MI 48446

ORTIZ-CASTRO, DYANA LETICIA, lawyer; b. San Juan, P.R., Sept. 1, 1937; d. Alvaro and Maria I. (Castro) Ortiz; B.A. magna cum laude, U. P.R., 1958, LL.B., 1962; m. Julio E. Gonzalez Carlo, Mar. 19, 1965 (div. Mar. 1968). Admitted to P.R. bar, 1963; law clk. P.R. Supreme Ct., 1963; judge Dist. Ct. Mayaguez, 1963-68; pvt. law practice, Old San Juan, 1968—. Dir., adviser Divers Inc., Well Corp., ROB Corp., Antox P.R., Inc., AFAB Corp. (all San Juan). Pres. Animal Protection Com. of P.R., Inc., 1972—. Mem. P.R. Bar Assn. (gov. 1971-72, sec. bd. govs. 1972—). Home: 1669 Georgina St Pio Piedras PR 00926 Office: SPO Box 4648 Old San Juan PR 00905

ORTNER, SANDRA PHYLLIS, occupational therapist; b. N.Y.C., Jan. 17, 1934; d. Jacob M. and Hilda M. (Moskowitz) Goodman; B.S. in Occupational Therapy, N.Y. U., 1955; postgrad. Columbia, 1971, N.Y. U., 1973; m. Herbert Ortner, Jan. 23, 1955; children—Patricia, Andrew, William. Occupational therapist Park Town House Nursing Home, N.Y.C., 1953-54, Mt. Sinai Hosp., N.Y.C., 1955-56, Bird S. Coler Hosp. and Home, Welfare Island, N.Y., 1957, Health Conservation Unit, N.Y.C., 1957-60; dir. occupational therapy Inst. for Muscle Disease, N.Y.C., 1960-61; occupational therapist Rockefeller Univ. Hosp., N.Y.C., 1966-67; cons. in occupational therapy DeWitt Nursing Home, N.Y.C., 1971—. Lectr., Hunter Coll., 1958, 59. Mem. Am. Occupational Therapy Assn., Orton Soc., League Women Voters, John Jay Park Improvement Assn. (vice chmn. 1962-69). Office: 211 E 79th St New York City NY 10021

ORTON, DIANE ELLEN BREAKELL (MRS. RICHARD ALBERT ORTON), coll. dean; b. Nyack, N.Y., Nov. 24, 1945; d. Lawrence Frank and Mildred Anne (Gerhard) Breakell; A.B., Clark U., 1967; m. Richard Albert Orton, June 21, 1969. Personnel asst. Restaurant Assos. Industries, Boston, 1967-70; vocational instr., rehab. counselor Paul Dever Sch., Taunton, Mass., 1970-71; asst. dean students for career planning and placement Wheaton (Mass.) Coll., 1971—. Mem. Eastern Coll. Personnel Officers, New Eng. Assn. Sch. Coll. and U. Staffing. Home: 96 Walnut St Plainville MA 02762 Office: Wheaton Coll Norton MA 02766

ORTON, JUNE FRANCES LYDAY, educator; b. Newton, Ia.; d. Joseph Hiram and June (Lumbert) Lyday; A.B., Vassar, 1917; M.S.S., Smith Coll., 1920; postgrad. N.Y. Sch. Social Work of Columbia, 1949-50, State U. Ia., 1924-27, Merrill Palmer Sch., Detroit, 1928, Coll. City N.Y., 1948-49, Wake Forest U., 1959, U. N.C., 1962; m. Samuel T. Orton, July 16, 1928 (dec. Nov. 1948); stepchildren—Samuel T., Sarah P., Mary F. Chief psychiat. social worker Recorders Ct., Detroit, and Ia. Psychopathic Hosp., 1921-25; coordinator lang. research program Ia. Psychopathic Hosp., 1925-27; clin. asst. to Dr. Samuel T. Orton, pvt. practice and research in children's lang. disorders, N.Y.C., 1928-48; dir. Graylyn Lang. Clinic, Bowman Gray Sch. Medicine of Wake Forest U., 1950-57, Orton Reading Center, Winston-Salem, N.C., 1957-72; spl. lectr., cons. Learning Disability Center, Salem Coll., Winston-Salem, 1972—; cons. ednl. testing; remedial lang. therapist. Recipient Samuel T. Orton award Orton Soc., Inc., 1969. Mem. Internat. Reading Assn., Orton Soc. (pres. 1949-60), Am. Assn. Univ. Women, League Women Voters, YWCA, Phi Beta Kappa, Delta Kappa Gamma. Club: Vassar (N.C.). Author: A Guide to Teaching Phonics, 1964. Editor, Orton Soc. bull., 1950-62. Contbr. articles profl. jours. Home: 2655 Forest Dr NW Winston-Salem NC 27104

OSBORN, DOLORES JEAN, educator; b. Hillsboro, Ill., Apr. 8, 1935; d. Jacob Henry and Annie Myrtle (Davidson) Osborn; student So. Ill. U., 1953-54; B.S., Eastern Ill. U., 1956; postgrad. San Jose (Cal.) State Coll., 1960, U. Cal. Berkeley, 1960; M.A., Colo. State Coll., 1963, postgrad., 1966-67; Ed.D., U. No. Colo., 1970. Tchr. bus. Wesclin Sr. High Sch., Trenton, Ill., 1956-58; sec. Lyon Van & Storage Co., San Leandro, Cal., 1958-60; tchr. bus. Hayfork (Cal.) High Sch., 1960-65; asst. prof. bus. edn. Central Wash. State Coll., Ellensburg, 1965, now asso. prof. Mem. Nat., Wash., Central Wash. (pres.) bus. edn. assns., Ellensburg Bus. and Profl. Women's Club (pres.), Am. Assn. U. Profs., Kappa Delta Pi, Pi Lambda Theta, Delta Pi Epsilon (past pres. Alpha Alpha chpt.). Home: 1209 Vuecrest Ellensburg WA 98926

OSBORN, JUNE ELAINE (MRS. JAY MILFORD LEVY), pediatrician, microbiologist; b. Endicott, N.Y., May 28, 1937; d. Leslie A. and Dora W. (Wright) Osborn; B.A., Oberlin Coll., 1957; M.D., Western Res. U., 1961; m. Jay Milford Levy, Feb. 28, 1966; children—Philip I., Ellen D. and Laura A. (twins). Pediatric intern Harvard Hosps., 1961-62, resident, 1962-64; postdoctoral fellow Johns Hopkins Hosp., 1964-65, U. Pitts., 1965-66; practice medicine specializing, in pediatrics, Madison, Wis., 1966—; mem. staff Univ. Hosps., St. Mary's Hosp.; instr. depts. pediatrics and med. microbiology U. Wis. Med. Sch., Madison, 1966-67, asst. prof., 1967-70, asso. prof., 1970—. Bd. dirs. Stetler Research Fund for Women Physicians. NIH grantee, 1969, 72, Nat. Multiple Sclerosis Soc. grantee, 1971. Fellow Am. Acad. Pediatrics; mem. Infectious Diseases Soc. Am., Soc. Pediatric Research, Am. Assn. Immunologists. Contbr. articles to profl. jours. Home: 1120 Merrill Springs Rd Madison WI 53705

OSBORN, MARJORIE MARIE, marketing div. mgr.; b. Indpls., Apr. 20, 1924; d. Ira H. and Lela (Colvin) Osborn; student DePauw U., 1942-44, Ohio Wesleyan U., 1944-45, Wright State U., 1968-70. Dept. asst. mgr. Rike Kumler Co., Dayton, O., 1945-54; statistician Electric Motor div. A. O. Smith Corp., Tipp City, O., 1954-56; statistician market research Mead Corp., Dayton, 1956-66, market research analyst, 1966-68, bus. economist, 1968-70; sr. marketing planning analyst Nat. Cash Register Co., Dayton, 1970-73; registered rep. Waddell & Reed, Inc., 1973—. Trustee Kettering (O.) and Suburban Sr. Citizens. Mem. Am. Marketing Assn. (treas. 1963-66, dir. 1965-66, mem. nat. indsl. directory com. 1965-66), Internat. Assn. Financial Planners, Am. Econ. Assn., Nat. Assn. Bus. Economists, Chi Omega. Presbyn. Club: Pilot International (dist. chmn. pub. relations 1966-68, dir. exec. bd. Kettering 1960-62, 64-66, mem. community service com., liaison sr. citizens project 1965-68). Contbg. Author: Administrative Control and Executive Action, 1961. Home: 5417 Landau Dr Kettering OH 45429 Office: Waddell and Reed 1563 E Dorothy Lane Dayton OH 45429

OSBORN, VELVA JEANNE, educator; b. Revere, Mo., Apr. 25, 1918; d. Earl Orlando and Zola Esther (Christy) Osborn; B.S., Kan. State Tchrs. Coll., 1939; M.A., U. Chgo., 1944; Ph.D., U. Ill., 1965. Br. librarian Kansas City (Kan.) Pub. Library, 1939-42; cataloger Chgo. Tchrs. Coll., 1942-44; reference librarian Columbia, 1945-52; reference librarian Midwest Inter-Library Center, 1952-53; head catalog dept. Western Ill. U., Macomb, 1954-67; asso. prof. No. Ill. U., DeKalb, 1967-71; prof. U. Ia., Iowa City, 1971—. Mem. N.E.A., Am. Civil Liberties Union, Assn. Am. Library Schs., Am., Ia., Ill. library assns. Contbr. articles to profl. jours. Home: 1434 Franklin St Iowa City IA 52240

OSBORNE, JULIA LOU, state ofcl.; b. Columbus, O., Nov. 2, 1950; d. John Benson and Betty Lou (Russell) Osborne; B.A. in Journalism cum laude, Ohio State U., 1971, M.A. in Journalism, 1973. Teaching asso. dept. speech Ohio State U., Columbus, 1972, Sch. Journalism, 1972-73, research asso. Center for Vocational and Tech. Edn., 1973; pub. information officer div. mental retardation and devel. disabilities Ohio Dept. Mental Health and Mental Retardation, Columbus, 1973—. Mem. Women in Communications, Kappa Tau Alpha, Sigma Delta Chi. Democrat. Home: 609 1/2 City Park St Columbus OH 43206 Office: 65 S Front St Columbus OH 43215

OSBORNE, NANCY FONTAINE, educator; b. Paces, Va., Apr. 12, 1908; d. William W. and Martha (Wayte) Osborne; A.B., U. Richmond, 1931; M.A., Columbia, 1933, Ph.D., 1945; diplome Sorbonne, 1933. Faculty Averett Coll., Danville, Va., summer 1935; French faculty Anderson (Ind.) Coll., 1943—, chmn. fgn. lang. dept., 1957—. Active Community Concert Assn., Anderson, 1962—. Mem. Modern Lang. Assn., Nat. Fedn. Modern Lang. Tchrs., Ind. Tchrs. French, Urban League. Club: Altrusa. Home: 500 1/2 College Dr Anderson IN 46011

OSBORNE, ORPHA NADINE, coll. adminstr.; b. Princeton, Ill., Oct. 25, 1921; d. George James and Ethel Precious (Bowman) Osborne; B.A., Walla Walla Coll., 1948, postgrad., 1951-56. Sec. Schwabacher Bros., Inc., Seattle, 1942-44; sec. in registrar's office Walla Walla Coll., College Place, Wash., 1948-51, asst. registrar, 1951-58, asso. registrar, 1959-62, registrar, 1963—. Cons., bd. higher edn. Gen. Conf. of Seventh Day Adventists, 1971. Mem. Am., Pacific Coast assns. collegiate registrars and admissions officers. Home: 105 E Whitman Dr College Place WA 99324

OSBORNE, RUTH SHATTUCK WRIGHT (MRS. BRADFORD ALLEN OSBORNE), librarian; b. Avon, N.Y., July 30, 1914; d. Jasper Heman and Ethel Mary (Shattuck) Wright; student U. Vt., 1932-35; B.S., Simmons Coll., 1936; postgrad. Columbia, 1938; m. Bradford Allen Osborne, Nov. 1, 1940; children—John Wright, Martha (Mrs. Joseph F. Zeman, Jr.), Allen Wright. Asst. head reference dept.-bus. and tech. Yonkers (N.Y.) Pub. Library, 1936-41; head librarian Bethel Park (Pa.) Pub. Library, 1956-61; with Charlotte (N.C.) Pub. Library, 1962—, head bus.-sci.-tech.-U.S. documents reference sect., 1973—. Cons. So. Piedmont com. N.C. Environmental and Edn. Network, 1973-74. Mem. N.C. (chmn. printed resources com., pub. library sect. 1973-75), Mecklenburg (membership chmn. 1973-74) library assns., Charlotte Women's Caucus, Charlotte C. of C. (mem. task force com. 1972-74), Pub. Library of Charlotte and Mecklenburg County Staff Orgn. (pres. 1964-65), Pi Beta Phi. Home: 434 Blairmore Dr Charlotte NC 28211 Office: 310 N Tryon St Charlotte NC 28202

OSBURN, HARRIET SISSON, librarian; b. Marshall, Minn.; d. Burl Neff and Bernice (Bravinder) Osburn; B.S., Millersville (Pa.) State Coll., 1945; M.A., Columbia, 1949; M.S. in Library Sci., Drexel Inst., 1955. Librarian, West York (Pa.) Pub. Schs., 1945-48, N.Y. Pub. Library, 1949, Bellport (N.Y.) Union Free Sch., 1949-52, Alexis I. du Pont Jr.-Sr. High Sch., Wilmington, Del., 1952-55; librarian Am. Edn. Publs., Inc. (name changed to Xerox Edn. Publs.), Middletown, Conn., 1955-60, head librarian, 1960—. Mem. Am. Library Assn., Spl. Libraries Assn., Altrusa Internat., Beta Phi Mu. Home: 404 Pine St Middletown CT 06457 Office: 245 Long Hill Rd Middletown CT 06457

OSGOOD, CONSTANCE, social worker, sociologist; b. Boston, Aug. 12, 1916; d. Gardner and Nellie (Cowan) Osgood; B.A., Lindenwood Coll., 1937; M.S.W., U. Kan., 1958, Ph.D., 1969. Research dir. Council Social Agys., Kansas City, Mo., 1947-49; with Inst. for Community Studies, Inc., Kansas City, 1949—, sr. scientist, program dir. for social services, 1965—. Instr. grad. dept. social work U. Kan., part-time 1961-68; research prof. dept. sociology U. Mo. at Kansas City. Mem. Am. Sociol. Assn., Nat. Assn. Social Workers. Club: Women's City (Kansas City, Mo.). Home: 8830 Riley St Overland Park KS 66212 Office: 2 W 40th St Kansas City MO 64111

OSLADIL, NADINE ROSE, pub. relations exec.; b. Albany, Cal., July 9, 1944; d. Anthony Dennis and Kathleen Marie (Dignan) Osladil; student U. Mich., 1962-63; B.A., Wayne State U., 1967. Newspaper reporter Parker Publs., Highland Park, Mich., 1966-67; hosp. pub. relations cons. Louis Graff Asso., Ann Arbor, Mich., 1968-70; pub. relations dir. Grace Hosp., Detroit, 1970—. Mem. Mich., S.E. Mich. (sec. 1971-72) hosp. pub. relations assns., Women in Communications (treas. 1970-71, dir. 1972—). Club: Detroit Press. Home: 22916 Gary Lane St Clair Shores MI 48080 Office: 4160 John R St Detroit MI 48201

OSMAN, MARY ELLA WILLIAMS (MRS. JOHN OSMAN), jour. editor; b. Honea Path, S.C., June 15, 1913; d. Humphrey Bates and Jennie Louise (Williams) Williams; student Coll. William and Mary, Ga. State Coll. for Women, Richmond Profl. Inst.; A.B., Presbyn. Coll., 1939; B.S. in L.S., U. N.C., 1944; m. John Osman, Oct. 22, 1936. Asst. librarian Presbyn. Coll., Clinton, S.C., 1936-38, Union Theol. Sem., Richmond, Va., 1938-44; sr. cataloger, asst. librarian Southwestern Coll., Memphis, 1944-52; asst. test cities project Ford Found. Fund for Adult Edn., N.Y.C., 1952-57, asso. dir. office of information, 1957-61, exec. asst. to pres., sec. to bd. dirs., 1960-61; asst. librarian A.I.A., Washington, 1962-68, asst. editor AIA Jour., 1969-72, asso. editor, 1972—. Mem. Chi Delta Phi, Kappa Delta. Republican. Presbyn. Contbr. to various mags. Home: 2500 Que St NW Washington DC 20007 Office: AIA 1735 New York Av Washington DC 20006

OSOFSKY, BARBARA LANGER (MRS. ABRAHAM J. OSOFSKY), mathematician, educator; b. Beacon, N.Y., Aug. 4, 1937; d. Theodore William and Shirley Babbett (Alpert) Langer; B.A., Cornell U., 1959, M.A. (Gen. Electric fellow), 1960; Ph.D., Rutgers U., 1964; m. Abraham J. Osofsky, Aug. 31, 1958; children—Deena, Laura, Samuel. Teaching asst. Cornell U., 1959; instr. Douglass Coll., 1961-63; asst. prof. Rutgers U., New Brunswick, N.J., 1964-67, asso. prof., 1967-71, prof. math., 1971—; mem. Sch. Math., Inst. for Advanced Study, Princeton, N.J., 1967-68; prin. lectr. NSF Regional Conf., Washington, 1971. NSF postdoctoral fellow, 1967-68. Mem. Am. Math. Soc. (mem. proceedings editorial com.), Math. Assn. Am., Conf. Bd. Math. Scis. (council mem. at large, 1972-74), Am. Assn. U. Profs., Phi Beta Kappa, Sigma Xi, Phi Kappa Phi. Contbr. articles profl. jours. Office: Dept Math Rutgers U New Brunswick NJ 08903

OSOL, VIRGINIA LEBO (MRS. ARTHUR OSOL), assn. exec., artist; b. Phila., Feb. 21, 1908; d. Frank Clayton and Amelia (Howell) Lebo; student Phila. Coll. Pharmacy and Sci., 1926-29; m. Arthur Osol, Dec. 28, 1928. Editorial asst. Dispensatory of the U.S.A. and other reference works, 1934—. Mem. Nat. League Am. Pen Women, Aux. Woman's Hosp. of Phila., Auxiliary Phila. Orch., Women's Club of Phila. Coll. Pharmacy and Sci. (pres. 1945-49), Profl. Panhellenic Assn. (pres. Phila. Area, 1956-60), Republican Women of Pa., Phila. Art Alliance (profl. mem.), Woodmere Art Gallery, Pa. Acad. Fine Arts (profl. mem.), Lambda Kappa Sigma (national pres. 1940-46, nat. editor 1942-52, bus. mgr. 1952-54, nat. hon. adviser 1954-68). Club: Peale. One-man shows Bala-Cynwyd Women's Club, Women's University Club, Panoras Gallery (N.Y.), Twentieth Century Club of Lansdowne, Women's City Club, Phila., Annie S. Kemerer Mus., Bethlehem, Pa.; exhibited group shows Phila. Art Alliance, Woodmere Art Gallery, Phila. Sketch Club (100th Ann. Exbn. award), Wayne Art Center. Home: 128 Colwyn Lane Bala-Cynwyd PA 19004

OSORIO, CARMEN, educator; b. San Juan, P.R.; d. Lino and Maria L. (Travecier) Osorio; ; B.S., L.I. U., 1954; M.S.W., Fordham U., 1957. Caseworker, Cath. Charities N.Y., N.Y.C., 1954-55, ct. cons., ct. rep. Manhattan Family Ct., 1957-62; social worker, therapist, community organizer Lower Eastside Information Center, Moblzn. for Youth, N.Y.C., 1962-64; instr. Albert Einstein Coll. Medicine, Yeshiva U., Lincoln Hosp. Mental Health Services, N.Y.C., 1964-67; community mental health rep., narcotic addiction Bur. Accreditation and Contract Services, N.Y. State Narcotic Addiction Control Commn., N.Y.C., 1967-71, sr. field rep. Office Pub. and Pvt. Agy. Affairs, 1971-72; asst. prof. Fordham U. at Lincoln Center Grad. Sch. Social Service, N.Y.C., 1972—. Bd. dirs. Puerto Rican Family Inst., N.Y.C.; bd. dirs. Puerto Rican Ednl. Projects, treas., 1971—; bd. dirs. Puerto Rican Bd. Guardian, treas., 1972—. Fellow Am. Orthopsychiat. Assn.; mem. Acad. Certified Social Workers, Nat. Assn. Social Workers, Nat. Conf. Social Welfare, World Fedn. Mental Health, Nat. Conf. Christians and Jews, A.A.A.S., Assn. Spanish Speaking Cath. Social Workers (pres. 1960-70), N.Y. Assn. Puerto Rican Social Workers (pres. 1965-68); UN Assn. U.S., Council on Social Work Edn. Home: 1342 Morrison Av Bronx NY 10472 Office: 113 W 60th St New York City NY 10023

OSSIP, BOBBI ANN, educator; b. Cumberland, Md., Aug. 1, 1938; d. George and Jeanne Susan (Rosenstein) Ossip; B.A., U. Pitts., 1960, M.Litt., 1962; postgrad. Barry Coll., Miami, Fla., 1967-68, U. Mont., 1971; A.A., Miami-Dade Community Coll., 1972. Receptionist, Conn. Gen. Life Ins. Co., Pitts., 1960-62; pub. relations Nat. Union Ins. Co., Pitts., 1962-63; pub. relations Diplomat Hotel, Hollywood, Fla., 1964; pub. relations Hume, Smith & Mickleberry Advt. Agy., Miami, 1964; sr. asso. prof. Miami-Dade Community Coll., 1964—, acad. adviser, 1969—, dir. recruitment, 1973—. Class agt. U. Pitts. Alumni Giving Fund, 1966—; chmn. fund raising projects Childrens Center, 1968-71. Named to U. Pitts. Hall of Fame, 1960. Mem. Fla. Personnel and Guidance Assn., Fla. Assn. Community Colls., Am. Assn. Community and Jr. Colls., Mortar Board, Phi Sigma Sigma (nat. pub. relations chmn. 1969-73, editor nat. mag. 1968-73), Grand Archon (nat. pres. 1973—). Clubs: Pitt (Miami), Phi Sigma Sigma Alumnae Greater Miami (treas.). Contbr. articles profl. jours. Home: PO Box 402553 Miami Beach FL 33140 Office: 11380 NW 27th Av Miami FL 33167

OSSOFSKY, HELEN JOHNS (MRS. ELI OSSOFSKY), physician; b. Phila., Dec. 7, 1921; d. William Calloway and Gertrude (Schindele) Johns; A.B., Mt. Holyoke Coll., 1943; student Women's Med. Coll. Pa., 1950-52; M.D., Johns Hopkins, 1954; m. Eli Ossofsky, Aug. 8, 1950, (dec. Oct. 1950). Research asso. Johns Hopkins Sch. Hygiene and Pub. Health, 1957-59; asst. prof. Georgetown U. Sch. Medicine, 1959-66, asso. prof. pediatrics, 1966—; supervisory med. officer D.C. Dept. Pub. Health, 1959-62, med. cons. div. mental retardation, 1967—; child psychiatry consultation practice, McLean, Va., 1966—. Cons., Inst. Child Health and Human Devel., NIH, Bethesda, Md., 1962-63; cons. in med. tng. div. chronic diseases USPHS, 1964-65, Va. Assn. Children with Learning Disabilities; lectr. Catholic U. Sch. Cardiovascular Nursing, 1959—; mem. adv. council Cybernetic Research Inst. Mem. Med. Soc. D.C., A.M.A., Am. Heart Assn., Washington Psychiat. Soc., Am. Psychiat. Assn., Johns Hopkins Med. and Surg. Assn., Phi Beta Kappa. Author: Tumors of the Eye and Adnexa in Infancy and Childhood, 1962; also articles in profl. jours. Address: 1333 Merrie Ridge Rd McLean VA 22101

OSTENSO, GRACE LAUDON (MRS. NED ALLEN OSTENSO), govt. ofcl.; b. Tomah, Wis., Sept. 15, 1932; d. Charles Christian and Ruby Gertrude (Lamb) Laudon; B.S., Stout State U., 1954; M.S., U. Wis., 1960, Ph.D., 1963; m. Ned Allen Ostenso, June 29, 1963. Asst. dir. dietetics Peter Bent Brigham Hosp., Boston, 1955-59; research asst. U. Wis., Madison, 1959-63, asst. prof. foods and nutrition, 1963-67; asso. editor tech. Ency. Brit., Chgo., 1967-69; with Food and Nutrition Service, U.S. Dept. Agr., Washington, 1970—, dir. nutrition and tech. services, 1973—. Cons., Army Med. Specialist Corps, Office Surgeon Gen., Washington, 1969—. Recipient Alumni Distinguished Service award Stout State U., 1970. Fellow A.A.A.S., Royal Soc. Health; mem. Am. Dietetic Assn., Am. Pub. Health Assn., Inst. Food Technologists, Soc. for Advancement of Food Service Research, Nutrition Today Soc., Omicron Nu. Home: 2871 Audubon Terrace NW Washington DC 20008 Office: 500 12th St SW US Dept Agr Washington DC 20250

OSTERKAMP, ANNEMARGRET LEWENZ (MRS. F. EMILE OSTERKAMP), social worker; b. Dresden, Germany, Sept. 4, 1910; d. Hans Leo and Ella Henriette (Arnhold) Lewenz; came to U.S., 1938, naturalized, 1948; vocational certificate U. Pa. Sch. Social Work, 1951; m. F. Emile Osterkamp, Apr. 15, 1942; 1 son, George. Caseworker, Children's Aid Soc. Montgomery County, Norristown, Pa., 1951-54; supr. Child Study Center, Pa. Hosp., Phila., 1954-56; supr. Eastern Pa. Psychiat. Inst., Phila., 1956-62; chief social worker Center for Child Guidance, Phila., 1962-64; unit dir. Charles Peberdy Child Psychiatry Clinic, Hahnemann Med. Coll. and Hosp., Phila., 1964-74, chief child psychiat. social worker children's services, 1974—, asst. prof., 1971—. Counselor, counseling service, family relations com. Phila. Yearly Meeting of Friends, 1958—. Mem. corp. Friends Hosp., Phila., 1970, Foulkeways at Gwynedd, Phila., 1967. Fellow Am. Orthopsychiat. Assn.; mem. Nat. Assn. Social Workers, Nat. Conf. Social Welfare, Internat. Conf. Social Welfare, Acad. Certified Social Workers, Women's Internat. League for Peace and Freedom, Women's Nat. League for Peace and Freedom. Mem. Soc. of Friends. Author papers in field. Home: 333 W Johnson St Philadelphia PA 19144 Office: 314 N Broad St Philadelphia PA 19102

OSTERWEIL, SUZANNE LESSER, artist; b. N.Y.C., June 22, 1940; d. Fredrick and Lillian (Simon) Lesser; B.S., Pratt Inst., 1961, M.S. in Art Edn. (Sch. Art League scholar, Deans scholar), 1964; postgrad. City U., 1963-67, (Nat. Edn. Def. Act Title I fellow) N.Y. U., 1963-69, Pace U., 1970, Pratt Graphic Center, 1972-74. Exhibited one-woman show paintings, prints Alonzo Gallery, N.Y.C.; exhibited art in group shows at Alonzo Gallery, Avnet-Hechlinger Gallery, Avanti Gallery, Nat. Assn. Women Artists nat. and internat. shows, USIA Traveling Graphics, Nat. Assn. Artists in Casein and Acrylics Shows, Hunterdon Art Center Print Show, Pratt Graphic Center; tchr. fine arts, chairwoman dept. James Madison High Sch., Bklyn., 1963-70, Bklyn. Mus., summer 1969; licensed supr. art, N.Y.C.; free lance graphic designer, 1968-70. Recipient prize for painting Nat. Assn. Women Artists, 1972, prize for graphics, 1973. Mem. Nat. Assn. Women Artists (graphic jury 1974-75), N.Y. State Art Tchrs. Assn. Home: 60 E 9th St New York City NY 10003 Studio: 80 1/2 Jane St New York City NY 10014

OSTFELD, BARBARA MOLEN, psychologist; b. N.Y.C., Nov. 17, 1945; d. Sam and Sarah (Lifshitz) Molen; B.A., N.Y.U., 1965; M.S. Rutgers U., 1967, Ph.D., 1969; m. Leonard S. Ostfeld, Aug. 22, 1965; 1 son, Robert Jonathan. Asst. prof. edn. psychology Rutgers U., 1968-70; developmental psychologist, project cons. Curriculum Devel., Inc., N.Y.C., 1971; postdoctoral fellow clin. psychology Children's Psychiat. Center Monmouth County (N.J.), 1971—; dir. Center for Infancy and Early Childhood, Rutgers U., 1972-73, psychol. cons., 1973—. N.Y. State Regents fellow, 1965; recipient Founders Day award N.Y.U., 1966. Mem. Am., N.J. psychol. assns., Am. Assn. for Care Children in Hosps., Phi Beta Kappa, Sigma Xi, Psi Chi, Delta Phi Alpha. Contbg. editor Day Care and Early Edn., 1973—. Contbr. chpts. to Day Care Staff Development Program (Brian Sutton-Smith, ed.), 1971. Contbr. articles profl. Jours.

OSTFELD, RUTH V. (MRS. ADRIAN M. OSTFELD), assn. exec.; b. South Bend, Ind., June 26, 1925; d. Alexander and Olga (Spiegler) Vogel; student Ind. U., 1943-45; B.S. in Occupational Therapy, Milw.-Downer Coll., 1947, certificate in occupational therapy, 1948; m. Adrian M. Ostfeld, Dec. 31, 1950; children—Barbara (Mrs. Frederick Herman), Richard, Robin. Occupational therapist Ypsilanti (Mich.) State Hosp., 1948-50, Topeka State Hosp., 1950; dir. dept. occupational therapy St. Louis State Hosp., 1951-52; pres. League Women Voters, Elmhurst, Ill., 1965-67, pres. Du Page County, Ill., 1967-68, treas. Conn., 1969-71, dir. Conn., 1971-73, 2d v.p. Conn., 1973—, v.p. Conn. edn. fund 1973—. Mem. Jewish Community Council, 1973—. Polling place election ofcl., North Haven, Conn., 1969—; mem. Democratic Town Com., North Haven, 1974—. Bd. dirs. Conn. Citizens for Jud. Modernization, North Haven Coordinating Council. Home: 17 Marlborough Road North Haven CT 06473 Office: League of Women Voters of Conn 60 Connolly Pkwy Hamden CT 06514

OSTRIN, LILLIAN SHULMAN (MRS. SOLOMON PHILIP OSTRIN), psychologist; b. N.Y.C., Sept. 10, 1925; d. Louis and Fannie (Selsky) Shulman; B.A., Rutgers, 1949; M.A., N.Y. U., 1951; Gen. Elementary Teaching certificate Newark State Coll., 1952; m. Solomon Philip Ostrin, Oct. 18, 1949; children—Elaine, Lynn. Tchr. Burnett St. Sch., Newark, 1952-55; psychol. externe Child Study Center, Newark State Coll., Union, N.J., 1967-68; psychol. externe dept. spl. service Irvington (N.J.) Pub. Schs., 1968; psychologist Kenilworth (N.J.) Pub. Schs., 1968—. Union County committeewoman Republican party, 1966-69. Mem. League Women Voters (pres. 1963-65, 3d v.p. Livingston 1971-73), Mental Health Assn. Union County (pres. Newark 1973—), Kenilworth Tchrs. Assn. (pres. 1973-74), N.J. Edn. Assn., N.E.A., Union County Sch. Psychologists (treas. 1973), Nat. (charter), N.J. assn. schs. psychologists. Jewish religion. Office: 426 Boulevard Kenilworth NJ 07033

OSTROM, ERNA DOROTHEA BENKE, financial exec.; b. Chgo., Feb. 2, 1927; d. Frederick and Adele (Belke) Benke; student Blair Sch. Finance; m. Eugene Walter Ostrom, May 8, 1948; children—Susan Jean, Eugene Frederick. Head accounts receivable dept. Bankers Life & Casualty Co., Chgo.; head cost accounting dept. Roofing Machinery Mfg. Co.; exec. sec., bookkeeper, Des Plaines (Ill.) Hefter Constrn. Co.; comptroller Acme Tool and Specialties Co., Des Plaines, Ill. Camp dir. YMCA; Scuba instr. Me. Adult Evening Edn. Mem. Purchasing Mgmt. Chgo. (membership chmn.), Order Eastern Star. Club: Soroptimist (Des Plaines, Ill.). Home: 1401 S Western Av Park Ridge IL 60068 Office: 55 E Bradrock Dr Des Plaines IL 60018

OSTROM, SUSAN MCWHIRTER, realtor, newspaper columnist, civic worker, clubwoman; b. Greencastle, Ind., Aug. 28, 1888; d. Felix T. and Luella (Smith) McWhirter; student Vassar Coll., 1907-08; A.B., De Pauw U., 1909; m. Henry Evan Ostrom, Apr. 29, 1910 (div. Apr., 1951); children—Ethel Mary (Mrs. Theodore Clay Pilcher), Henry Felix. With Clyde Realty Co., Indpls., 1948—; sec. Ostrom Realty and Constrn. Co., Indpls., 1912-50; columnist Indpls. News, 1913-63; dir. pub. relations and information div. Ind. Dept. Pub. Instrn., 1942-47. Sec., Indpls. Council Federated Ch. Women, 1931-35; charter mem.

Meth. Hosp. White Cross Guild, 1933—; hon. mem. commn. ecumenical mission and relations United Presbyn. Ch. U.S., 1966; chmn. Marion Co. women's div. Ind. War Finance Com., 1942-47; vice-chmn., incorporator Monument Circle Easter Sunrise Carol Service, 1935-61; mem. Indpls. Anti-Crime Crusade. Del., Ind. Republican Conv., 1946; bd. dirs. Indpls. Women's Rep. Club, 1963-64. Recipient Frances Wright award outstanding contbn. to journalism 1958, Women in Communications, Gold medallion 50 yrs.-in-journalism, 1963; awards (2) Ind. Fedn. Women's Clubs, 1963; Distinguished Service certificate of honor Gen. Fedn. Women's Clubs, 1972; 50 year service pin Indpls. Newspapers, Inc., 1963. Mem. Ind. Fedn. Clubs (adv. council 1913-63; hon. mem. state officers clubs 1958—), Nat. W.C.T.U. (adv. bd. 1913-20), Nat. League Am. Pen Women (v.p. Indpls. br. 1960-62), Soc. Ind. Pioneers (publicity chmn. 1963-65), Ind. Hist. Soc., Ind. Vassar Alumnae Club (sec. 1935-37), DePauw U. Alumni Assn., Indpls. Women's Dept. Club (charter mem. 1912, dir. 1965-67, recognition award 1973), Woman's Press Club Ind. (charter mem. 1913, sec. 1921-23, emblem locket 1973), D.A.R., Epsilon Sigma Omicron, Kappa Alpha Theta (pres. Indpls. alumnae chpt. 1918-19). Presbyn. (sec. ch. circle 1965-67). Address: 3777 N Meridian St Apt 304 Indianapolis IN 46208

OSTRY, SYLVIA (MRS. BERNARD OSTRY), govt. ofcl.; b. Winnipeg, Man., Can.; d. Morris Jack and Betsy (Stoller) Knelman; B.A., McGill U., 1948, M.A., 1950; Ph.D., Cambridge and McGill U., 1954; LL.D., York U., U. N.B., 1971, McGill U., 1972, U. Western Ont., 1973, McMaster U., 1973, U. B.C., 1973; m. Bernard Ostry, Sept. 21, 1956; children—Adam, Jonathan. Research officer Oxford (Eng.) U. Inst. Statistics, 1955-58; asst. prof. McGill U., Montreal, Que., Can., 1958-62; asso. prof. econs. U. Montreal, 1962-64; dir. spl. manpower studies Dominion Bur. Statistics, Ottawa, Ont., Can., 1964-69; dir. Econ. Council of Can., Ottawa, 1969-72; chief statistician Govt. of Can., Ottawa, 1972—. Mem. Am., Canadian, Royal econ. assns., Am. Statis. Assn. Contbr. articles to profl. jours. Home: Rural Route 2 Aylmer Rd Alymer East PQ Canada Office: Statistics Can RH Coats Bldg Tunney's Pasture Ottawa ON K1A 0T6 Canada

OSTWALD, VENICE ELOISE VARNER, educator, librarian; b. Denver, July 19, 1928; d. Earl Robert and Madeline (Shoemaker) Varner; B.A., U. Colo., 1946; M.S., U. So. Cal., 1954; m. Leonard F. Ostwald, 1954 (div.). Sch. librarian, Long Beach, Cal., 1954-61; asst. prof. librarianship U. Ore., 1961-63; dir. libraries and audio-visual Hillsborough (Cal.) Pub. Schs., 1963-65; adminstrv. asst. to dir., research and devel. librarian San Jose State U., 1965-67; instrn. specialist, dir. independent studies DeAnza Coll., Cupertino, Cal., 1967—. Bd. dirs., founder Singles in Service. Asso. Women Students Scholarship grantee, U. Colo., 1949. Mem. N.E.A., Am., Cal. library assns., Cal. Assn. Sch. Librarians (community coll. chmn. 1970-71), Cal Tchrs. Assn., Beta Phi Mu, Kappa Delta. Contbr. articles to profl. jours. Song lyricist Part of Me, Oasis, Peru, Caliente, Esclava, Huayno Cucurumba. Home: 1373 Phelps St Apt 13 San Jose CA 95117 Office: De Anza Coll Learning Center Cupertino CA 95117

O'SULLIVAN, MARY JO EDMOND (MRS. WAYNE MICHAEL O'SULLIVAN), coll. adminstr.; b. Wayland, N.Y., Oct. 26, 1944; d. Robert Lewis and Mary Regina (Bricks) Edmond; B.A. cum laude, St. Bonaventure U., 1966; M.S., State U. Coll., Buffalo, 1972; m. Wayne Michael O'Sullivan, Apr. 3, 1971. Tchr., East Seneca Elementary Sch., West Seneca, N.Y., 1966-67; geriatric caseworker Cath. Charities, Buffalo, 1967-68; dir. admissions Trocaire Coll., Buffalo, 1968—. Mem. Am. Assn. Collegiate Registrars and Admissions Officers, N.Y. State Assn. Jr. Colls., Western N.Y. Coll. Personnel Assn., Western N.Y. Consortium for Vets. Affairs (mem. com. registrars and admissions officers 1972—). Home: 3266 Seneca St Bldg 11 Apt 12 West Seneca NY 14224 Office: 110 Red Jacket Pkwy Buffalo NY 14220

O'SULLIVAN, PEGGY VIRGINIA, educator; b. Cascilla, Miss., Aug. 19, 1928; d. Frank O'Sullivan and Mary Virginia (Leftwich) O'Sullivan Dobbs; A.A., Stephens Coll., 1949; B.S. in Journalism, So. Meth. U., 1951, M.A., 1958; postgrad. (Wall St. Jour. fellow) U. Tex., 1961, Memphis State U., 1970-72. Dir. pub. relations Memphis City Beautiful Commn., 1951-52; asst. alumnae sec., mng. editor Stephens Coll. Alumnae News, Columbia, Mo., 1952-54; tchr. English, St. Mary's Episcopal Sch., Memphis, 1954-55, tchr. English, pubs. adviser, 1962—; tchr. English, journalism Highland Park High Sch., Dallas, 1959-62. Mem. Assn. for Preservation Tenn. Antiquities, 1970—, Memphis Better Films Council, 1970—. Dallas Times Herald grantee Tex. A. and M. U., 1959; others. Named Outstanding Tchr., St. Mary's Episcopal Sch., 1965. Mem. Women in Communications (dir. Memphis chpt.), Gamma Alpha Chi, Delta Delta Delta. Episcopalian. Home: 375 N Highland Memphis TN 38122

OSWALD, BETTY ROBINSON (MRS. ROBERT H. OSWALD), former coll. adminstr.; b. Biloxi, Miss., Nov. 30, 1928; d. William Washington and Viola (Collins) Robinson; B.A., Miss. Coll., 1950; M.A., U. Ala., 1965, postgrad. 1966; m. Robert H. Oswald, July 23, 1966; children by previous marriage—Glenn Dismukes, Pamela Jean Dismukes. Music tchr., Gulfport, Miss., 1950-54; tchr. elementary sch., Mobile, Ala., 1955-59, speech and debate, 1959-64; faculty U. S. Ala., Mobile, 1964-69; dir. instructional TV Miss. Gulf Coast Jr. Coll., Gautier, 1969-72; legal asst. firm Robert H. Oswald, Atty., Pascagoula, Miss., 1972—. Chmn., Mobile United Fund, 1963-65. Mem. S. Miss. Festival Art (vice chmn. 1971—), Internat. Platform Assn., N.E.A., So. Speech Assn., Speech Com. Am., Alpha Omicron Pi, Delta Kappa Gamma. Mem. Opti-Mrs. Home: 4412 Scarlet Oak St Gautier MS 39553 Office: PO Box 189 Markland Bldg Pascagoula MS 39567

OSWALD, ELEANOR ELAINE HOOK (MRS. VINCENT ELMER OSWALD), mfg. co. exec.; b. Somerfield, Pa.; d. James Samuel and Olive (Bowman) Hook; B.S., Carnegie-Mellon U., 1935; m. Vincent Elmer Oswald, July 17, 1937; 1 dau., Gretchen (Mrs. Isaac John Haviland). Tchr. Brownsville (Pa.) Sr. High. Sch., 1935-37; tchr. adult edn., Monongahela, Pa., 1949-51; sec.-treas. Mfg. & Repair Co., Pitts., 1952—. Mem. women's assn. Pitts. Symphony Soc., 1958—; sponsor South Hills Child Guidance Center, 1958; pres. South Side Hosp. Aux., 1969-71, bd. dirs., 1971-73. Mem. D.A.R., Daus. Am. Colonists, League Women Voters, Pitts. Athletic Assn. Clubs: Pittsburgh College; Twentieth Century, Mt. Lebanon Women's, St. Clair Country (Pitts.); Chautauqua (N.Y.) Yacht. Home: 954 Osage Rd Pittsburgh PA 15243 Office: 2025 Milford Dr Pittsburgh PA 15102

OTENASEK, MILDRED, Dem. nat. committeewoman; b. Balt., Feb. 6, 1914; d. Frank and Josephine (Kuchar) Busick; A.B., Coll. Notre Dame Md., 1936; Ph.D. in Polit. Economy, Johns Hopkins, 1939; m. Frank J. Otenasek, June 9, 1937. Asso. prof. econs. Trinity Coll., Washington, 1940-54; prof. polit. economy Mt. St. Agnes Coll., Balt., 1954-56; lectr. econs., also polit. sci. Notre Dame Coll. Md., 1956-64, asso. prof., 1964-73, prof., 1973—. Vice chmn. Md. Dem. Central Com., 1946-56; Dem nat. committeewoman for Md., 1956—; del. nat. convs., 1956, 60, 64, 68, 72; pres. United Dem. Women's Clubs Md., 1955-57. Civilian cons. 2d Army Hdqrs.; mem. adv. bd. Cath. Charities Balt.; mem. bd. Citizens Planning and Housing Assn. Balt., Nat. Conf. Christians and Jews Balt.; mem. Port Balt. Com., 1954-56; chmn. women's div. various charitable drives in Md. Mem. Cath. Commn. Intellectual and Cultural Affairs, Cath., Am. econ. assns., Am. Assn. U. Women, Internat. Fedn. Cath. Alumnae (chmn. legislation Md. chpt.; past pres. Balt. circle), YWCA (past mem. bd. Internat. Center), Delta Epsilon Sigma. Home: 4000 N Charles St Baltimore MD 21218

OTERO, JACQUELYN KAY (MRS. GEORGE GILBERT OTERO), historian; b. Albert Lea, Minn., Nov. 4, 1937; d. Kenneth W. and Virginia (Lowry) Hillman; student U. Ia., 1956-58; B.A., U. N.M., 1960, M.A., 1962; m. George Gilbert Otero; children—Kevin Antonio, Jeffrey Alan. Programmer, Gen. Programmed Teaching Corp., Albuquerque, 1962; free lance historian, free lance editor State of N.M. Archives and U. N.M. Press, 1964—; librarian, bibliographer Peace Corps Tng. Center, U. N.M., 1962-63; archivist State Records Center and Archives, Santa Fe, N.M., 1963-64. Mem. N.M. Hist. Soc., Soc. Am. Archivists, Western History Assn., Albuquerque Dirt Gardeners, Phi Alpha Theta. Author: Constitution of the United States, 1962. Editor: How a Bill Becomes a Law, 1962. Address: 1620 San Cristobal Rd SW Albuquerque NM 87104

OTOMO, AIKO, sch. adminstr.; b. Lahaina, Maui, Hawaii, Nov. 27, 1923; d. Kei and Suma (Asahina) Otomo; B.E., U. Hawaii, 1947, 5th year diploma, 1948; M.A., N.Y.U., 1956. Grade sch. tchr. Hawaii Dept. Edn., 1948-51, asst. intern supr., 1951-55, intern supr., 1956-57, adminstrv. intern, 1963-64; instr. edn. U. Hawaii, Honolulu, summers, 1953, 55; supervising tchr. Univ. Elementary Sch., Honolulu, 1957-63; tchr. Japanese, 1959-60; vice prin. Kalihi Waena Sch., Honolulu, 1964, curriculum specialist elementary Leeward Sch. Dist. Oahu, 1964-67, dep. dist. supt., 1969—; chief program planner Dept. Edn. Hawaii, 1968-69. Mem. N.E.A., Assn. for Supervision and Curriculum Devel. (charter Honolulu), Nat. Council Social Studies, Nat. Soc. for Study Edn. Home: 780 Amana St Apt 502 Honolulu HI 96814 Office: 94-366 Pupupani St Waipahu Oahu HI 96797

O'TOOLE, JEANNE MARIE, educator; b. Chgo., Sept. 18, 1924; d. Dennis Joseph and Eleanor Marie (Fleming) O'Toole; B.A., Mt. Mary Coll., 1946; M.A., St. Xavier U., 1966; Ph.D., Loyola U., Chgo., 1972. Supr., Hartford Accident and Indemnity Co., Chgo., 1946-53; supr. personnel Carson Pirie Scott & Co., Chgo., 1953-57; tchr., Evergreen Park Sch. Dist., 1957-69; lectr., Loyola U., Chgo., 1969—. Chmn. ednl. planning Beverly Area Planning Assn., 1973—; mem. finance com. Christ the King Sch. Bd., 1973—, pres. bd., 1974—; mem. exec. adv. bd. Loyola U., Chgo., 1972—, chmn. grad. sch. fund raising drive, 1973, v.p. Chgo. Alumnae Assn., 1974. Recipient Fellowship, Loyola U., 1970. Mem. P.T.A. (life), Am. Assn. U. Profs., Am. Ednl. Studies Assn., Council Basic Edn., History Edn. Soc., Delta Kappa Gamma. Republican. Roman Catholic. Club: Big Sand Lake (Phelps, Wis.). Home: 9636 S Oakley St Chicago IL 60643

O'TOOLE, LELA, coll. dean; b. Thomas, Okla., Sept. 9, 1909; d. Edmund B. and Emma (Williams) O'Toole; B.S. in Edn., Okla. State U., 1935; B.S. in Home Econs. Edn., 1939, M.S. in Home Econs. Edn., 1941; Ph.D., Ohio State U., 1949. Elementary, secondary sch. tchr., Okla., 1929-34, 35-40; dist., state supr. home econs. edn., Okla, 1940-47; prof. home econs. edn. Okla. State U., 1949-50, dean div. home econs., 1951—; program specialist home econ. edn. U.S. Office Edn., 1950-51; dir., tchr. first home econs. summer sch., Norway, 1954; leader ednl. study home econs., Pakistan, 1957; cons. to Govt. Pakistan and Ford Found. on five year plans for colls. for home econs.; group leader, speaker numerous confs.; mem. pres.'s Nat. Council Vocational Edn., 1967; mem. home econs. commn. Nat. Assn. State Univs. and Land Grant Colls., 1972—. Recipient Centennial Achievement award Ohio State U., 1970. Mem. Internat. Fedn. Home Econs. (exec. com. 1965—, v.p. 1969—), Nat., Okla. (edn. assn.), Am. (pres. 1969-70), home econs. assns., Nat. Assn. Land-Grant Colls. and State Univs., Mortar Bd., Phi Kappa Phi, Omicron Nu, Phi Upsilon Omicron, Kappa Delta Pi, Pi Lambda Theta, Delta Kappa Gamma. Club: Altrusa. Contbr. articles profl. jours., bulls. Home: 1820 Arrowhead Pl Stillwater OK 74074

OTT, BETTY STEINHAUER, radio broadcasting exec.; b. Newport, Ky., July 9; d. Walter Valentine and Agatha (Hagemeyer) Steinhauer; student Miami U., Oxford, O., 1929; A.B., Cleve. Marshall Law Sch., 1934; m. David Ott, June 12, 1928; 1 dau., So. Ann. Broadcaster, dir. community affairs WXEL-TV, WJW-TV, WGAR-Radio, WCLV (all Cleve.), 1950—. Creator, Garden for the Blind, 1965. Bd. dirs. Cleve. Sight Center. Mem. Cleve. Women's Advt. Club, Zeta Tau Alpha (nat. pres. 1934-37), Alpha Chi (nat. pres. 1967), Western Res. Hist. Soc. Mem. Order Eastern Star. Club: Zonta (Cleve.). Home: Box 55 Music St Novelty OH 44072 Office: WCLV Penthouse East Terminal Tower Cleveland OH 44113

OTT, HARRIETT HOY DEANE (MRS. FORREST WILLIAM OTT), educator; b. Hannibal, Mo., Nov. 22, 1912; d. John Maxwell and Ethel (Hoy) Deane; A.A., Christian Coll., 1932; B.S., Central Mo. State, 1935, M.A., U. Mo. at Kansas City, 1952; specialist degree Central Mo. State U., 1970; m. Forrest William Ott, June 25, 1936; children—Dee Ann (Mrs. Edwin Herde), Janie (Mrs. Bill Frank), Matthes, Novella (Mrs. Allen L. Perrin). Tchr. rural schs., Cass County, Mo., 1933, Harrisonville, 1935-36, Archie (Mo.) High Sch., 1947; prin. Freeman (Mo.) High Sch., 1948-49; headmistress Barstow Sch. for Girls, Kansas City, Mo., 1952-53; prin. Lee's Summit (Mo.) Grade Sch., 1953-74, now ret. Active Girl Scouts U.S.A. Mem. Lee's Summit Hosp. Bd. Mem. Internat. Reading Assn. (pres. Lee's Summit council), N.E.A., Jackson County Elementary Prins. Delta Kappa Gamma. Democrat. Mem. Order Eastern Star. Contbr. articles to profl. jours. Home: 228 S McClendon Dr Lee's Summit MO 64063

OTT, LORETTA KEOUGH (MRS. CARLYLE G. OTT), ednl. adminstr.; b. Murphysboro, Ill., Aug. 6, 1926; d. George Alfred and Mayabelle Eloise (Snoddy) Keough; B.S., So. Ill. U., 1948, M.S. in Edn., 1951; m. Carlyle G. Ott, Nov. 21, 1948; 1 dau., Carla Eloise. Asst. to dean women So. Ill. U. at Carbondale, 1948-51, asst. dean women, 1951-57, asst. dean students, dean women, 1957-65, asst. to univ. dean students, 1965-67, asst. dean students, 1967-71, asso. dean students, asst. prof., 1971—, acting dean student life, 1974—. Mem. Am. Personnel and Guidance Assn., Am. Coll. Personnel Assn., Nat., Ill. (pres. 1972-74) assns. women deans, adminstrs. and counselors, Pi Omega Pi, Phi Kappa Phi (pres. 1973-74), Alpha Lambda Delta, Phi Lambda Pi, Delta Kappa Gamma. Christian Scientist. Home: 1206 W Freeman St Carbondale IL 62901 Office: Dean Students Office So Ill U Carbondale IL 62901

OTTEN, ANNA VON KUTSCHIG (MRS. KLAUS W. OTTEN), educator; b. Nestemice, Czechoslovakia; d. Karl and Emma (Tschinkel) von Kutschig; B.A., Waterloo Coll., 1953; M.A., U. Western Ont., London, 1954, Ph.D., 1958; m. Klaus W. Otten, June 13, 1958. Asst. prof. Antioch Coll., Yellow Springs, O., 1956-62, asso. prof. French and German, 1962-70, prof., 1970—, chmn. dept. fgn. langs., 1962-64, 68-70. Mem. Intercultural Assn. of Southwestern Ohio (pres.). Contbr. articles in field to profl. jours. Home: 1925 Trebein Rd Xenia OH 45385 Office: Antioch Coll Yellow Springs OH 45387

OTTENBERG, MIRIAM, journalist; b. Washington, Oct. 7, 1914; d. Louis and Nettie (Podell) Ottenberg; student Goucher Coll, 1931-33; B.A., U. Wis., 1935. With Neisser-Meyerhoff Advt. Agy., Chgo., 1935-36, Akron (O.) Times-Press, 1937; reporter Washington Star-News, 1937—. Trustee Fed. Woman's Award, Washington. Recipient Pulitzer prize in journalism, 1960; Washington Newspaper Guild grand award (Bill Pryor Meml. award), 1960, 63; U. Wis. award for distinguished service to journalism, 1961; Central High Sch. certificate of distinction, 1961; Nat. Headliners award for outstanding pub. service in investigative reporting of consumer fraud, 1969. Mem. Washington Press Club (pres. 1964-65), Mystery Writers Am., Women in Communications, Sigma Delta Chi. Author: The Federal Investigators, 1962. Home: 2939 Van Ness St NW Washington DC 20008 Office: Washington Star-News 225 Virginia Av SE Washington DC 20061

OTTING, SISTER AGNES, hosp. adminstr.; b. Lingen Ems, Germany, Dec. 12, 1940; d. Heinrich M. and Alvina (Feldman) Otting; came to U.S., 1959, naturalized, 1964; B.S. in Nursing, Coll. of St. Catherine, St. Paul, 1966; M.Hosp. Adminstrn., U. Minn., 1968. Adminstr., St. Joseph Hosp., Arcadia, Wis., 1968-71, St. Francis Hosp., Shakopee, Minn., 1971—. Mem. Sisters Senate, Archdiocese of St. Paul; coordinator, treas. Sisters of St. Francis, 1971—. Bd. dirs. St. Joseph Hosp., Arcadia, St. Mary's Assn. Mem. Shakopee C. of C., Nat. Sisters Vocational Conf., Sigma Theta Tau. Address: St Francis Hosp Shakopee MN 55379

OTTINGER, CAROL BLANCHE, educator; b. Batesville, Ark., Dec. 25, 1933; d. Edgar Guy and Lucy Pearl (McLendon) Ottinger; B.S.E., Ark. Coll., 1954; M.S., Okla. State U., 1960, Ed.D., 1969; postgrad. Tulane U., 1961, Stanford, 1962. Tchr. Cossett (Ark.) High Sch., 1954-56, Jonesboro (Ark.) High Sch., 1956-58, Claremore (Okla.) High Sch., 1960-63; prof. math. Miss. U. for Women, 1963—, chmn. dept., 1974—. Shell merit fellow, 1962. Mem. Nat. Council Tchrs. Math., Math. Assn. Am. (vice chmn. Miss.-La. sect. 1969-70), Pi Mu Epsilon. Methodist. Home: 900 5th Av S Columbus MS 39701

OTTO, JOANN EAGAN (MRS. ROBERT EMIL), state ofcl.; b. Kansas City, Mo., Jan. 22, 1927; d. John William and Marian Morrow (Konantz) Eagan; B.A., B.S., Tex. Woman's U., 1949; M.S., So. Ill. U., 1964; m. Robert Emil Otto, Oct. 7, 1950; children—Robert Emil, Kevin Mark, Michael Chas. Staff therapist Independence (Ia.) Mental Health Center, 1950-51; staff therapist for criminally insane Spring Grove State Hosp., Catonsville, Md., 1951-52; dir. rehab. therapies Crownsville State Hosp., Annapolis, Md., 1952-54; staff therapist Ill. Dept. Mental Health, Anna, 1957—, program coordinator, 1967-73, sub-region coordinator developmentally disabled, 1974—. Instr., So. Ill. U. at Carbondale, 1967-74. Sec., A-J Teen Town Bd., 1970-71. Mem. adv. bd. Employment Tng. Center, So. Ill. U., 1968-74. Mem. Nat. Occupational Therapy Assn., Nat. Ill. rehab. assns., Nat. Rehab. Counseling Assn., Ill. Pub. Health Assn., Egyptian Assn. for Mental Retardation, Drug Abuse and Alcoholism Council So. Ill., Ill Rehab. Counseling Assn. (sec. 1967, dir. 1969-70). Home: 803 N Main St Anna IL 62906 Office: 1000 N Main St Anna IL 62906

OTTO, LUCY ANNE, microbiologist; b. Saginaw, Mich., Apr. 30, 1927; d. Franz Stephen and Lucy (Brooks) Otto; student Rutgers Coll. S. Jersey, 1954-56; A.B. in Chemistry and Bacteriology, Douglass Coll., 1958; M.S. in Bacteriology, U. So. Cal., 1962, postgrad. U. Cal. at Los Angeles, 1972-74. Lab. technician St. Anthony's Hosp., Amarillo, Tex., 1950, Bronx (N.Y.) Hosp., 1954; research microbiologist Magna Corp., Anaheim, Cal., 1962-63, N.Am. Aviation, Apollo project, Torrance, Cal., 1963-64, VA, Long Beach, Cal., 1964-66; microbiologist FDA, Los Angeles, 1966—. Served with WAC, 1950-53. Mem. Am. Soc. Microbiology, Soc. Gen. Microbiology, Biol. Photographers Assn., A.A.A.S., Inst. Food Technologists, Phi Sigma (sec. Los Angeles chpt. 1960), Iota Sigma Pi. Roman Catholic. Home: 12061 Candy Lane Garden Grove CA 92640 Office: 1521 W Pico Blvd Los Angeles CA 90015

OTZEN, HELEN CLARK, bus. exec.; b. Cando, N.D.; d. George C. and Birgit (Myrland) Clark; B.A., Lawrence Coll., 1916; m. John Otzen (dec. Oct. 1950); 1 son, John Myrland. Owner, pres. Otzens Importers, Chgo., 1935—. Trustee Hadley Sch. for Blind, 1961—. Mem. Am. Assn. U. Women, Nat. Home Fashion League, P.E.O. (chpt. pres. 1950-52). Club: Soroptimist (Chgo. pres. 1959-61). Home: 500 E Fairview St Arlington Heights IL 60005 Office: Mdse Mart Chicago IL 60654

OUBRE, JUANITA BERNICE HUREL (MRS. HAYWARD L. OUBRE), educator; b. New Orleans, Nov. 27, 1925; d. Orlando Earnest and Geneva Marion (Gash) Hurel; B.A., Dillard U., 1943; M.A., U. Ia., 1948; m. Hayward L. Oubre, Jan. 2, 1945; 1 dau., Amelie Geneva. Asst. prof. Ala. State Coll., Montgomery, 1949-65; asst. prof. speech and theatre Winston-Salem (N.C.) State U., 1965—; cons. Ednl. Facilities Labs., Inc., N.Y.C., 1971—; dir. fed. insts.; lectr. various ednl. instns. and govt. agys. Information specialist Nat. Council Negro Women, Bd. dirs. YWCA, Winston-Salem; cons., mem. bd. dirs. Greater Charlotte Dance Guild, 1970—. Mem. Nat. Assn. Dramatic and Speech Arts (pres. 1970-73), Council Arts Nat. Orgns. Execs. (a founder), Partnership for Arts, Am. Theatre Assn., U.S. Inst. Theatre Tech. Home: 2422 Pickford Ct Winston-Salem NC 27101 Office: EH 101 Winston-Salem State U Winston-Salem NC 27101

OUELLETTE, IRENE THERESE, advt. agy. exec.; b. New Bedford, Mass., Aug. 27, 1946; d. Francis George and Marie Rosaria Gisele (Tardi) Ouellette; student Holyoke Community Coll. Office employee Eastern Etching & Mfg. Co., Chicopee, Mass., 1964-66; clk.-steno U. Mass., Amherst, 1966-67; office mgr. Black & Musen, Inc., East Longmeadow, 1967—. Home: 263 Dwight St Extension Springfield MA 01105 Office: 145 Shaker Rd East Longmeadow MA 01028

OUJESKY, HELEN MATUSEVICH (MRS. FRANK PETER OUJESKY), educator; b. Fort Worth, Aug. 14, 1930; d. Steve and Lillie (Krivanek) Matusevich; B.A., B.S. (scholar), Tex. Woman's U., 1951, Ph.D., 1968; M.A., Tex. Christian U., 1965; m. Frank Peter Oujesky, Dec. 27, 1951; children—Michael, David, Christopher. Tchr., Tech. High Sch., Fort Worth, 1951-63; asst. prof. biology Tex. Women's U., Denton, 1968-72; asso. prof. div. earth and life scis. U. Tex., San Antonio, 1973—. Instl. Research grantee Tex. Woman's U., 1968-70. Mem. Am. Inst. Biol. Scis., A.A.A.S., Am. Assn. U. Profs., Tex. Assn. Coll. Tchrs., Radiation Research Soc., Am. Soc. Microbiology, Soc. Indsl. Microbiology, Tex. Acad. Sci., N. Tex. Biol. Soc., Tex. Assn. Radiation Research, Tex. Assn. Microbiology, Slovanske Podporujici Jednoty Statu Tex., Sigma Xi, Phi Sigma, Iota Sigma Pi, Beta Beta Beta. Contbr. articles to profl. jours. Home: 604 Skyforest Dr San Antonio TX 78232 Office: 4242 Piedras Dr E San Antonio TX 78284

OULTON, SARAH CHRISTINE EILEEN MACKINNON (MRS. WILLARD RUSSELL OULTON), museum ofcl.; b. Coleman, P.E.I., June 7, 1911; d. James Artemas and Annie Floy (Gorrill) MacKinnon; diploma applied arts Mt. Allison Ladies Coll., 1932; m. Willard Russell Oulton, Sept. 5, 1935; children—William Russell, David James, Ian Robert. Photographer, researcher bldgs. in Alberton area; researcher Island families; dir. mapping and transcribing of cemeteries, 1973; founding mem. bd. P.E.I. Heritage Found., 1970—; founder, curator Alberton Mus., P.E.I., 1965—. Mem. West Prince C. of C., Alberton Handcraft Guild, MacLeod Soc. P.E.I., Alberton Tignish Tourist Assn., Canadian Mus. Assn. Heritage Can. Anglican. Home: Alberton PE Canada Office: Alberton Mus Poplar St Alberton PE Canada

OUTHIER, BETTY RUTH, lawyer; b. Woodward, Okla., Sept. 11, 1947; d. Robert Elmer and Ethel Mae (Castiller) Outhier; B.A., Oklahoma City U., 1969; J.D., Vanderbilt U., 1972. Admitted to Okla. bar, 1972; atty. Tulsa County Legal Aid Soc., 1972-73; asst. U.S. atty. Dept. Justice, Eastern Dist. Okla., Muskogee, 1973—. Reginald Heber Smith Community Lawyer fellow Howard U., 1972-73. Mem. Am., Okla., Tulsa, Muskogee County bar assns., Okla. Trial Lawyers Assn., Okla. Women Lawyers Assn., Bus. and Profl. Women's Club, Gamma Phi Beta. Republican. Methodist. Club: Soroptomist (Muskogee). Home: PO Box 355 Muskogee OK 74401 Office: PO Box 1099 Muskogee OK 74401

OUTLAR, FLORENCE BEATON (MRS. JESSE OUTLAR), librarian; b. Waycross, Ga., Dec. 17, 1920; d. Evrette Monroe and Anna Joe (Johnson) Beaton; B.S., Oglethorpe U., 1960; M.Ed., Auburn U., 1964, postgrad., 1964-67; m. Jesse Outlar, Oct. 12, 1946; children—Barry Thomas, Jan Louise. Librarian DeKalb County Bd. Edn., Atlanta, 1960—; dir. Outlar Internat. Tours. Named 5th Dist. Ga. Homemaker of Year, 1960; Merith Mother of the Year, Ga. Mothers Assn., 1966. Mem. Delta Kappa Gamma. Club: North Clairmont Woman's (pres. 1970-72) (Atlanta). Home: 2947 Delcourt Dr Decatur GA 30033 Office: 1131 Briar Vista Terrace Atlanta GA 30024

OVERALL, MARY ANN (MRS. MAURICE ALLEN OVERALL), speech therapist; b. Oak Park, Ill., Jan. 1, 1943; d. Harvey Thomas and Eula Inez (Greer) Morris; student Okla. State U., 1961-62; B.A., Tulsa U., 1965, postgrad., 1966-68; m. Maurice Allen Overall, June 28, 1966; Speech therapist Enid (Okla.) State Sch., 1965-66; speech therapist Hissom Meml. Center, Sand Springs, Okla., 1966-69, supr., 1969—. Mem. Am. Assn. Mental Deficiency, Tulsa Assn. Speech Pathology and Audiology, Okla., Tulsa speech and hearing assns., Kappa Delta. Home: 7839 S Gary Place Tulsa OK 74114 Office: PO Box 310 Sand Springs OK 74063

OVERMAN, FRANCES ELIZABETH HENSON, writer, civic worker; b. Eddyville, Ky.; d. John Napoleon and Ida Belle (Koon) Henson; student Union U., 1930-32; A.B., Murray State U., 1937; postgrad. Northwestern U., 1940, U. Wis., 1941, 44; m. Ralph Theodore Overman, June 30, 1945 (div. Jan. 1968); children—Ralph Theodore, Ann Frances. Tchr. elementary schs., Ballard County, Ky., secondary schs., LaCenter, Cadiz, Maysville, and Benton, Ky., 1937-44; tchr. Oak Ridge Schs., 1944-45, 57-59; free lance writer; contbr. to Fact and Fiction, Internat. (Oak Ridge). Active Cub Scouts, Brownies; adviser Y-Teens; active Oak Ridge Civic Music Assn., Oak Ridge Community Playhouse, Oak Ridge Community Art Center. Recipient Community Service award, 1972. Fellow Intercontinental Biog. Assn.; mem. Internat. Platform Assn., League Women Voters, Centro Studi E Scombi Internazionali (internat. com. fine arts 1970-71), Internat. Acad. Leonardo Da Vinci, Tau Kappa Alpha. Contbr. articles to profl. jours. Address: 109 Pelham Rd Oak Ridge TN 37830

OVERSTREET, BONARO WILKINSON, author, lectr.; b. Geyserville, Cal., Oct. 30, 1902; d. Edward and Margaret Elizabeth (Bonar) Wilkinson; A.B., U. Cal., 1925, teacher's certificate, 1926; m. Harry Allen Overstreet, Aug. 23, 1932. Research asso. Am. Assn. Adult Edn., 1939-40; instr. adult edn. Claremont County, Cal., summer, 1940, Mills Coll., Cal., summer, 1941, U. Mich. Extension Service, 1945-46, 49, U. Cal. extension div., 1948. Mem. Am. Assn. for Adult Edn., Sigma Delta Pi, Phi Beta Kappa, Theta Sigma Phi. Clubs: Nat. Press, International (Washington). Author: Poetic Way to Release, 1931; Footsteps on the Earth, 1934; Search for a Self, 1938; Brave Enough for Life, 1941; (with H.A. Overstreet) Town Meeting Comes to Town, 1938; Leaders for Adult Education (Am. Assn. Adult Edn.), 1940; American Reasons, 1943; Courage for Crisis, 1943; Freedom's People, 1945; How to Think About Ourselves, 1948; Understanding Fear: in Ourselves and Others, 1951; The Mind Alive (with H.A. Overstreet), 1954; Hands Laid Upon the Wind, 1956; The Mind Goes Forth 1956, What We Must Know About Communism, 1958 (with H.A. Overstreet); The War Called Peace; (with H.A. Overstreet); Krushchev's Communism 1961, The Iron Curtain, 1963; The Strange Tactics of Extremism, 1964; The FBI in Our Open Society, 1969. Contbr. to jours. Home: 3409 Fiddler's Green Falls Church VA 22044

OVERTON, HELEN PARKER (MRS. SAMUEL WATKINS OVERTON), civic worker; b. Memphis, Dec. 30, 1920; d. William and Pearl (Pinkston) Parker; m. Samuel Watkins Overton, Sept. 3, 1952; children—Helen Parker, Napoleon Hill. Exec. sec. Memphis State U., 1941-43, Chgo. and So. Air Lines, 1943-46, Memphis Bd. Edn., 1948-50; dir. women's program Sta. WHBQ-TV, Memphis, 1950-52. Pres., Beethoven Club, 1960-66, 72—, Mid-South Opera Guild; dir. auditions Mid-South region Met. Opera, 1960-71, mem. nat. council, 1960-71; chmn. Tenn. Arts Commn. Bd. dirs. Memphis Acad. Arts, Memphis Opera Theatre, Arts Appreciation, Tenn. Arts Commn. Mem. Sigma Alpha Iota, Alpha Gamma Delta. Clubs: Memphis Country (Memphis). Home: 5476 Collingwood Cove Memphis TN 38117

OVERTON, JANE VINCENT HARPER (MRS. GEORGE W. OVERTON, JR.), educator; b. Chgo., Jan. 17, 1919; d. Paul Vincent and Isabel (Vincent) Harper; A.B., Bryn Mawr Coll., 1941; Ph.D., U. Chgo., 1950; m. George W. Overton, Jr., Sept. 1, 1941; children—Samuel, Peter, Ann. Research asst. U. Chgo., 1950-52, asst. prof. biology, 1952-64, asso. prof., 1964-72, prof., 1972—. NIH and NSF research grantee, 1965—. Contbr. articles to profl. jours. Research embryology and cell biology. Home: 1368 E 57th St Chicago IL 60637

OVITZ, CAROL JANE, stock and commodity broker; b. Rockford, Ill., Nov. 19, 1942; d. John William and Virginia (Noyes) Ovitz; B.A., Smith Coll., 1964. With Mitchell, Hutchins & Co., Inc., N.Y.C., 1965-73, asst. v.p., 1969-73; ind. mem. Chgo. Bd. Trade, 1973—. Mem. Bd. Trade City of Chgo., 1969—. Pres. Infant Welfare Soc., 1970-71. Clubs: Soroptimist, Commodity, Smith (Chgo.). Home: 300 N State St Chicago IL 60610 Office: 2 First National Plaza Chicago IL 60670

OWEN, ANGELA MARIA JAFFÉ (MRS. SIDNEY OWEN), music educator; b. Berlin, Germany, July 12, 1928; d. Werner and Gertrud Minna (Noetzel) Jaffé; came to U.S., 1947, naturalized, 1953; Mus.B., Boston Conservatory, 1952, certificate in conducting, 1953; Mus.M., Boston U., 1953, Ph.D., 1957; m. Sidney Owen, June 21, 1958; children—Bruce Dieter, Leslie Reneé. Instr. solfege South End Music Sch., Boston, 1951-53; dir. band and instrumental music Oxford (N.C.) Pub. Schs., 1953-54; supr. instrumental music Weymouth (Mass.) Pub. Schs., 1956-59; instr. music appreciation, music theory and recorder Cubberley Adult Sch., Palo Alto, Cal., 1962—; instr. recorder and violin Community Sch. Music and Arts, Mountain View, Cal., 1968—; instr. music appreciation and recorder Menlo-Atherton (Cal.) Adult Sch., 1970—; instr. music history Foothill Coll., Los Altos, Cal., 1974—. Dir. Mid-Peninsula Recorder Orch., 1967—; den mother Cub Scouts, 1969-71; music badge adviser Girl Scouts U.S.A., 1972-74; merit badge adviser Boy Scouts Am., 1973—; sec. Palo Alto Youth Recitals, 1972-74; recreation chmn. P.T.A., 1972-74; mem. City of Palo Alto Arts Forum Planning Com., 1973, Adv. Com. for City/Schs. Joint Music Activities, 1973-74. Mem. Am. Recorder Soc. (co-recipient 1st place composition award Miami chpt. 1972), Cal. Council for Adult Edn., Pi Kappa Lambda. Methodist. Club: Sierra (Loma Prieta, Cal.). Contbr. to publs. Composer: Theme and Variation for 3 recorders, 1972. Editor, arranger various publs. of recorder music. Home: 246 Walter Hays Dr Palo Alto CA 94303

OWEN, ANN ORENE HAY (MRS. KERMIT Q. OWEN), rd. machinery distbg. co. exec.; b. Bandera, Tex., Dec. 24, 1917; d. George Douglas and Rosa Mae (Porter) Hay; grad. Draughon's Bus. Coll., 1935; student San Antonio Coll., 1961-65; m. Kermit Q. Owen, Dec. 24, 1937; children—Bobbe (Mrs. Brad Crawford), Keith, Cathy (Mrs. Jim R. Nix). Legal sec. firm Fagan Dickson, 1936-37; mgr. Advance Distbg. Co., San Antonio, 1936-37; asst. to prin. Harlandale High Sch., 1950-54; sec. Hi-Way Machinery Co., 1955; sec. Girard Machinery & Supply Co., San Antonio, 1956, sec.-treas., 1957—, also dir. Mem. Exec. Secs., Inc. Baptist. Home: 818 W Harding Blvd San Antonio TX 78221 Office: 3428 Roosevelt St San Antonio TX 78221

OWEN, FLORENCE ANDREW HULINGS (MRS. LEO MATTHEW OWEN), writer; b. Denver; d. Willis James and Florence (Andrew) Hulings; student U. Cal. at Los Angeles, 1947-50; m. Donald Charles Bayer, (dec.); 1 dau., Jayne Andrew (Mrs. Roger Clark Hartwig); m. 2d, Leo Matthew Owen, Sept. 19, 1952; 1 dau., Kathleen Caldwell. Newspaper reporter Los Angeles Herald-Express; radio continuity writer, dir. continuity CBS-KROY, Sacramento; advt.-pub. relations writer Hodgson Advt. Agy., Sacramento; 1953-54; advt. dir. Bon Marche, Ransohoffs, Sacramento; owner, pres. Owen Advt. Agy., Sacramento; free-lance writer under name France Owen short stories and articles for various Catholic Herald, Modern Maturity, MainLiner, Nat. Parks, Southland, Sunset; Vista, others. Cons. pub. relations and advt., 1952-70; tchr. mag. article and fiction writing, advt. and pub. relations, communications Adult Edn. Program, Sacramento, 1971-74; lectr. in field. Recipient writing awards Writer's Digest 1967, 68, 70, 72. Mem. Cal. Writers Club, Internat. Platform Assn. Author: History of Buffum's, 1962, also tech. books.

OWEN, HELEN LERENE HAWORTH (MRS. ALFRED J. OWEN), coll. ofcl., b. Spokane, Wash., Nov. 15, 1913; d. John M. and Nellie M. (McLeod) Haworth; B.S. in Nursing, U. Wash., 1936, certificate in pub. health, 1938, postgrad., 1944-69; postgrad. Wash. State U., 1965-66; m. Alfred J. Owen, Jan. 3, 1941; children—Carl, Thomas M. Dir., health edn. U.S. Army Air Corp., Galene, Wash., 1942-45; vol. Seneca Indian Reservation, Quaker Bridge, N.Y., 1945-53; instr. practical nursing Spokane Trade Sch., 1953-68; adminstr. health occupations dept. Spokane Community Coll., 1968—. Mem. Wash. State Bd. Practical Nurse Examiners, 1968-74, chmn., 1968-73; mem. Comprehensive Health Planning Ednl. Com., Spokane, 1972; mem. Task Force on Aging, Spokane, 1973; mem. Home Health Services Adv. Com., Spokane, 1973; vol. Health Outreach Clinic, Spokane, 1972. Mem. Assn. for Higher Edn. N.E.A., Am., Spokane (chmn. ednl. com. 1942) nurses assns., Am. Vocational Assn., Spokane Pub. Health Nurses Assn. (pres. 1944-45). Club: Social. Home: E 1920 S Riverton St Spokane WA 99202 Office: E 3404 Mission Av Spokane WA 99207

OWEN, JANICE MARIE JONES (MRS. FREDRICK ANTON OWEN), editor, photographer, univ. ofcl.; b. Cin., May 1, 1948; d. Morris Alton and Edna Margueritte (Pharis) Jones; B.S. in Journalism, Bowling Green State U., 1970; m. Fredrick Anton Owen, Dec. 27, 1971; 1 son, Eric William. Gen. assignment reporter Reading (Pa.) Eagle, 1970-71; asst. editor Pub. Communications Office, Colo. State U., Ft. Collins, 1972-74. Free-lance photographer, Ft. Collins, 1972—; occasional lectr. on photography to area groups. Recipient 1st place award Am. Assn. Agrl. Coll. Editors. Mem. Women in Communications. Republican. Methodist. Home: 641 Whedbee St Fort Collins CO 80521

OWEN, JEAN CHLOE WIVEL (MRS. ROGER D. OWEN), psychiatrist; b. Two Rivers, Wis., Feb. 22, 1941; d. Charles Carroll and Ruth Agnes (Drager) Wivel; B.S., U. Wis., 1963, M.D., 1966; m. Roger D. Owen, Feb. 24, 1968; 1 son, David Neal. Intern, U. Ore., Portland, 1966-67, psychiat. resident, 1967-70; practice medicine, specializing in psychiatry, Portland, 1970-72, Santa Barbara, Cal., 1972—; psychiat. cons. Ore. Drug Treatment and Tng. Project, 1970-72, Multnomah Mental Health Clinic, Portland, Ore., 1970-72; psychiatrist Santa Barbara County Mental Health Services, 1972—. Mem. Ore. Med. Assn., Am. Psychiat. Assn., Santa Barbara Psychiat. Soc., Am. Civil Liberties Union, Phi Beta Kappa, Alpha Omega Alpha. Home: 1636 Hillcrest Dr Santa Barbara CA 93103 Office: 4444 Calle Real Santa Barbara CA 93105

OWEN, JERRIE ANN MUSSON, drama dir., playwright; b. Chgo., Dec. 9, 1930; d. Clettis V. and Evelyn (Estey) Musson; student Northwestern U., 1949-54; 1 son, Richard Glenn. Appeared in theatre and stock prodns. including Wizard of Oz, Lady in the Dark, Once in a Lifetime; on tour with Northwestern Univ.'s Children's Theatre, 1948-56; drama dir. Northwestern U., Chgo., 1956-65; pres. Little Theatre Assos., Elmwood, Ill., 1962—. Instr., dir. theatre and music depts. Triton Coll., River Grove, Ill., 1973—; pvt. drama coach profl. actors, Chgo., 1972—. Founder teen age drama group Elmwood Park (Ill.) Youth Commn., 1967, dir., 1967—; author, dir. plays Cub Scouts, Elmwood Park, 1966—; resident dir. Children's Theatre, Oak Park/River Forest Civic Theatre, 1972—. Recipient awards, citations including 1st pl. trophy Best Magic Act for Women, Internat. Magigals, 1965. Mem. Am. Ednl. Theatre Assn., Internat. Platform Assn., Internat. Magigals Inc. (internat. sec. 1963-65, corr. sec. Chgo. assembly 1951-53, internat. v.p. 1973—). Author: (children's plays) The Silver King Dragon, 1955; The Princess of the Golden Palace, 1956; Kingdom of Clowns, 1958; Santa and the Magic Shoes, 1963; The Flight of the Rainbow Witches, 1969. Co-editor Backstage with Magigals, 1961-63. columnist, 1961-63. Home: 7923 Westwood Dr Elmwood Park IL 60635

OWEN, KATHERINE PATRICIA CRAWFORD, librarian; b. Montclair, N.J., Jan. 27, 1925; d. Frank W. and Gertrude (Haller) Crawford; B.A., Caldwell Coll., 1972; m. R.F. Owen (div. 1956). Asst. librarian Hoffmann-LaRoche, Inc., Nutley, N.J., 1944-45; asst. librarian Winthrop Labs., N.Y.C., 1946-56; chief librarian Warner-Lambert Research Inst., Morris Plains, N.J., 1957-72, mgr. library services, 1972—. Mem. ad hoc adv. com. drug literature program Nat. Library Medicine, 1966. Mem. Spl. Libraries Assn., Pharm. Mfrs. Assn. (mem. lit. subcom. steering com. 1971—). Mem. United Methodist Ch. Home: Regional Rd RD 1 Annandale NJ 08801 Office: 170 Tabor Rd Morris Plains NJ 07950

OWEN, LOCKIE ELOISE (MRS. JAMES THOMAS OWEN), city ofcl.; b. Waurika, Okla., Dec. 24, 1920; d. Miller and Annie Olive (Bone) Sparkman; grad. high sch.; m. James Thomas Owen, Apr. 12, 1942; 1 son, James Richard. With City of Gainesville, Tex., 1938—, now city sec. Treas. Aux. Gainesville Meml. Hosp. Christian Scientist. Club: Soroptimist (past pres.). Home: 814 E Broadway Gainesville TX 76240 Office: 200 S Rusk St Gainesville TX 76240

OWEN, MARY STEELE, educator; b. Indpls., Oct. 23, 1913; d. Perceval W. and Meta (Steele) Owen; A.B., Franklin Coll., 1936; A.M., Ind. U., 1944; Ph.D., Ind. U., 1956, postgrad. U. Chgo., summers, 1937, 38. Tchr. Martin Boots Jr. High Sch., 1937-40, Marion High Sch., 1941-43 (both Marion, Ind.); teaching asst. Ind. U., 1943-44, counselor staff dean of women, 1944-46; instr. history Butler U., Indpls., 1946-48; asso. prof. Franklin (Ind.) Coll., 1948-54, prof. history, 1954-71, dir. advanced studies, 1963-67, chmn. social sci., and history depts., 1967-68 (recipient outstanding faculty award 1961, 64); vis. prof. history Sam Houston State U., Huntsville, Tex., 1969-70, prof. history, 1971—, dir. dept. history, 1972—. Mem. Am. Assn. U. Profs. (pres. Ind. chpt. 1961), Am. Assn. U. Women, Women's Study Club (sec. 1960), Am., Miss. Valley, Ind. hist. assns., Delta Kappa Gamma, Kappa Kappa Kappa, Phi Alpha Theta, Pi Beta Phi, Alpha, Pi Delta Phi. Episcopalian (sr. warden vestry). Author: The American Frontiersman, An Analysis Based on Contemporary French Travel Accounts. Home: Parkwood Pl Apts 2720B Apt 104 Huntsville TX 77340 also 75 W Herriott St Franklin IN 46131

OWENS, BETTY JANE (MRS. WILLIAM I. OWENS), dermatologist; b. Huntington, Ind., Oct. 9, 1917; d. Claude H. and Edith Irene (Fulton) Brechner); A.B., U. Cin., 1939, M.D., 1942; postgrad. U. Mich., 1943-46; m. William I. Owens, June 5, 1942; children—William Brechner, Jane Ann, Sara Katherine. Intern Cin. Gen. Hosp., 1942-43; resident U. Mich. Hosp., 1943-46; practice medicine specializing in dermatology, Middletown, O., 1949—; mem. staff Middletown Hosp. Address: 6737 Hamilton-Middletown Rd Middletown OH 45042 Office: Middletown Fed Savings & Loan Bldg Middletown OH 45042

OWENS, BILLIE AUSTIN (MRS. WILLIAM DAN OWENS, JR.), librarian; b. Tipton, Okla., Nov. 28, 1921; d. William McDaniel and Vilena Forest (Gray) Austin; B.A., North Tex. State Tchrs. Coll., Denton, 1942; m. William Dan Owens, Jr., July 15, 1942; children—William Dan III, Diana (Mrs. Floyd Scott May, Jr.), Robert Austin. High sch. librarian, Joinerville, Tex., 1942-44; mem. library bd. Wichita Free County Library, Iowa Park, Tex., 1964-67; asst. librarian Sheppard AFB, Tex., 1961-65, adminstrv. librarian, 1965—, fed. women's program coordinator, 1974—. Mem. A.L.A. (past com. chmn.), Soc. Am. Archivists, D.A.R., Daus. of Colonists, Assos. Nat. Archives (charter), Fed. Librarians Assn. (charter). Baptist. Home: 903 Kiowa St Box 452 Burkburnett TX 76354 Office: Base Library FL 3020 SSL Sheppard Air Force Base TX 76311

OWENS, BLANCHE ELIZABETH, ednl. adminstr.; b. nr. Crowley, Colo.; d. Robert L. and Jessie E. (Frazee) Owens; A.A., Compton Jr. Coll., 1937; B.S., U. Cal. at Los Angeles, 1940, M.S., 1949; Ph.D., State U. Ia., 1956. Tchr. pub. schs., Pueblo, Colo., 1942-43, 46, Wichita, Kan., 1946-52; supr. schs., Wichita, 1952-57; dir. ednl. television, Wichita, 1957-60; coordinator ednl. television No. Ill. U., DeKalb, 1960-68, 70-72, prof. edn., 1972—; dir. utilization and program planning Dept. Instructional TV. and Radio, Office Supt. of Pub. Instrn., Springfield, Ill., 1968-70; dir. Los Angeles Bd. Ednl. Recreation Dept., Los Angeles City Recreation Dept.; cons. Midwest Program Airborne Television Instrn. Purdue U. Served with USAAF, 1943-46; now col. USAF Res. Mem. N.E.A., Ill. Edn. Assn., Assn. Higher Edn., Ill. Assn. Supervision and Curriculum Devel., Nat. Assn. Ednl. Broadcasters, Ill. Assn. Audio-Visual Edn., Assn. For Better Radio and Television, Photog. Soc. Am., Ill. Ednl. Television Council, Pi Lambda Theta. Baptist. Club: Altrusa International. Contbr. articles to profl. jours. Home: Rt 1 Box 64B Sycamore IL 60178

OWENS, ELISABETH ANN, educator, lawyer, 1919; A.B. in Econs. summa cum laude, Smith Coll., 1940; student U. Chgo.; LL.B., Yale, 1951. Economist. Office Price Adminstrn., Reciprocal Trade Agreements Program, Bur. of Budget, UNRRA, for seven years; with Harvard Law Sch., Cambridge, Mass., 1956—, lectr. internat. tax law, 1964, prof., 1972—, research dir. Internat. Tax Program. Contbr. articles in field to profl. publs. Address: Sch of Law Harvard Univ Cambridge MA 02138

OWENS, ELIZABETH TYSON (MRS. JOHN M. OWENS, JR.), journalist; b. Norristown, Pa., Sept. 18, 1924; d. William Henry and Ella Mae (Slough) Tyson; A.B., Ursinus, 1945; m. John M. Owens, Jr., Jan. 5, 1946; children—Gail Elizabeth, Jacquelyn Edith. Gen. reporter, Norristown (Pa.) Times Herald, 1945-47; asso. editor Sharp & Dohme Pharms., Phila., 1947-49; pub. specialist Lit Bros. Dept. Store, Phila., 1949-50; pub. relations dir. YWCA, Phila., 1950-51; dir. consumer pub. Arndt Advt. Co., Phila., 1951-53; writer, Phila., 1954-62, Denver, 1963—. Sec., dir. Walnut Hills (Colo.) Civic Assn., 1970-72; water safety instr. A.R.C., Phila., Denver, 1945-72; dir. YWCA Water Show, Phila., 1960, 61. Mem. Denver Women's Press Club, Englewood Bus. and Profl. Women (chmn. pub. relations 1972-73), Women in Communications, Tri Hi (sec. Jarre Canyon 1973-74). Home: 19 Oak Valley Rd Sedalia CO 80135 Office: PO Box 84 Sedalia CO 80135

OWENS, ETTA MAE HARRIS (MRS. GEORGE W. OWENS), rehab. exec.; b. Pontotoc, Miss., Apr. 30, 1911; d. Jesse Seale and Viola (Abernathy) Harris; student Blue Mountain Coll., 1928-31; B.S., U. So. Miss., 1940; M.Ed., Miss. State U., 1967, ednl. specialist, 1971; postgrad. U. Miss., 1941; m. George W. Owens, Dec. 20, 1937. Tchr. elementary sch., Ecru, Miss., 1931-34; county supr. adult edn., Pontotoc, 1934-37; sec. to registrar U. So. Miss., Hattiesburg, 1938-40, instr., 1940-42; instr. Itawamba Agr. High Sch., Fulton, Miss., 1944-46; counselor Rehab. Div. for Blind, Pontotoc, Miss., 1955-66, supr., 1967—. Mem. Nat. Rehab. Assn. (chpt. sec. 1963-70, 73-74, divisional dir. 1968-71, nat. chmn. awards com. 1971-72, pres. Miss. adminstrv. and supervisory practices unit 1973-74), Am. Assn. Workers for Blind (nat. dir. 1969-72), Miss. Assn. Workers Blind (pres. 1969-72), Miss. Womens Cabinet Pub. Affairs, Am., Miss. heart assns., Rehab. Assn. Miss. (sec. 1973-74), Miss. Fedn. Womens Clubs (chmn. 1958—). Baptist. Clubs: Pontotoc Womens, Miss. Women's (officer 1937-44, 62-70). Home: 210 Brooks St Pontotoc MS 38863 Office: Box 149 Pontotoc MS 38863

OWENS, EVALYN BERGSTRAND, former educator; b. Danville, Ill., Sept. 9, 1907; d. John Ivard and Esther (Jernberg) Bergstrand; B.S., U. Minn., 1928, grad. student 1939-41; M.S., Ia. State Coll., 1936; m. Emery E. Owens, Dec. 1948. Nutritionist, Nassau County (L.I.) Com. Tb and Pub. Health, 1928-29, Freeport (L.I.) pub. schs., 1929-30; tchr. home econs., Frederic, Wis. 1930-32, Waupaca (Wis.) High Sch., 1932-35; teaching grad. asst. in home econ., Iowa State Coll., 1935-36; instr. home mgmt., child devel. Mich. State Coll., 1936-39, asst. prof., 1941-42; instr. in home econ., U. Minn., 1939-40; dean home econ., U. Conn., 1942-49; instr. home mgmt., child devel. Ia. State Coll. summer 1937, acting head home mgmt. dept., summer 1938-39. Exec. com. Family Service Agy. Waukesha County; mem. Waukesha County Council Child Welfare, Social Agys. Council.

Mem. Bd. vistors U. Wis., 1950-60; mem. U.S. Dept. Agrl. Research Adv. com., 1954-60. Recipient outstanding achievement award, U. Minn., 1956. Mem. Am. (treas. 1952-54), Tex. home econ. assns., Am. Assn. U. Women, Omicron Nu, Phi Upsilon Omicron, Pi Lambda Theta, Iota Sigma Pi, Kappa Alpha Theta. Club: Altrusa. Address: 919 S Silver Lake St Oconomowoc WI 53066 Winter 212 N 40th St McAllen TX 78501

OWENS, GRACE MARIE ELLIOTT (MRS. WARREN RUSSELL OWENS), occupational therapist; b. Salem, Ore., Nov. 20, 1914; d. Carl Hodge and Mildred E. (Packer) Elliott; student Westminster Coll., 1935; grad. Phila. Sch. Occupational Therapy, 1937; m. Warren Russell Owens, Feb. 20, 1942; children—Mildred Margaret (Mrs. Kenneth Demaree), Mary Lucile Wright. Occupational therapist State Hosp., Binghamton, N.Y., 1937-43, 60—. Cons. occupational therapy River-Mede, Binghamton, 1967-70. Mem. Am., N.Y. State (vice chmn. Central dist. 1970) occupational therapy assns. Home: 51 Rush Av Binghamton NY 13903 Office: 425 Robinson St Binghamton NY 13901

OWENS, IVY MAY, cosmetic mfr.; b. Rockdale, Tex., Mar. 9, 1913; d. Claude Ross and Alice Belle (Blackmon) Dodson; extension student U. Wis., 1942-43; div.; 1 dau., Jeannette (Mrs. J. Edd Lovvorn). Sr. accountant C.P.A. firms, Madison, Wis., 1942-43; sec.-treas. Flynn Investment Co., Rio Grande Bldg. & Loan Assn. and F.L. Flynn Ins. Agy., Harlingen, Tex., 1944-66; organizer, owner Aloe Cosmetic Co. (formerly Ivec Industries), Aloe Vera products, Houston, 1965—; operator bookkeeping and tax service, 1967—. Mem. Am. Contract Bridge League (master). Home: 4102 Aruba St Houston TX 77055 Office: 1514 Foley St Houston TX 77055

OWENS, LANORA RAY, advt. exec.; b. Oklahoma City, Oct. 19, 1931; d. Vivian Ray and Ruth (Smith) Owens; B.A., Central State Coll., 1957. Continuity writer Radio Sta. KECK, Odessa, Tex., 1951, TV Sta. KMID, Midland, Tex., 1952, announcer, 1952; writer, announcer daily show KTOK, Oklahoma City, 1953; with advt. dept. John A. Brown Store, Oklahoma City, 1954; writer Country Club Publications, Oklahoma City, 1955; staff announcer Radio Sta. KTOK, Oklahoma City, 1956; tchr. N.W. Classen High Sch., Oklahoma City, 1957; asso. editor Country Club Publ., Oklahoma City, 1958-62; editor Petroleum Club News, Oklahoma City, 1962-63; writer Lowe Runkle Co., Oklahoma City, 1964-69, v.p., 1969—; account exec. Kerr-McGee Co., Oklahoma City, 1967; asst. account. exec. Okla. Gas & Electric, Oklahoma City, 1968. Bd. dirs. Central State Coll. Alumni, 1970—, Oklahoma County Mental Health Assn., 1971—. Home: 3000 Hemingford Lane Oklahoma City OK 73120 Office: 1800 Liberty Tower Oklahoma City OK 73102

OWENS, MARTHA ARMISTEAD (MRS. JOSEPH JAMES OWENS, JR.), librarian; b. Washington, Jan. 12, 1930; d. Robert Benjamin and Olivia Catherine (Boughton) Armistead; Mus. B., Madison Coll., 1951; library certification William and Mary Coll., 1969; postgrad. U. Va., 1970-71; M.S. in Edn., Old Dominion U., 1973; m. Joseph James Owens, Jr., Nov. 29, 1952; children—Joseph James III, Jeffrey Laurence, Kathryn Martha. Tchr. mus. and chorus Broad Creek Jr. High Sch., Norfolk County, Va., 1951-53; tchr. Norfolk County and Virginia Beach City, Va., 1951-72; librarian Virginia Beach Schs., 1966-74, tchr. English, 1961-74; librarian Lynnhaven Jr. High Sch., Virginia Beach, 1974—. Recipient State Research grant, 1970-72. Mem. Am., Va. library assns., N.E.A., Norfolk Panhellenic Assn., Va. Edn. Assn., Am. Assn. U. Women, Kappa Delta Pi, Alpha Sigma Alpha. Presbyn. Home: 1712 S Woodhouse Rd Virginia Beach VA 23454 Office: Lynnhaven Jr High Sch Virginia Beach VA 23456

OWENS, NORA FAYE MOOREHEAD (MRS. SAM D. OWENS), psychologist; b. Jackson, Miss., Dec. 25, 1946; d. James Arlis and Doris Wenona (Hill) Moorehead; B.S., Miss. State U., 1967, M.A., 1968, Ph.D., 1972; m. Sam D. Owens, July 20, 1973. Spl. edn. tchr., Tuscaloosa, Ala., 1968-69; vis. instr. Miss. State U., 1971; psychologist Anderson County Sch. Dists. I and II, Belton, S.C., 1971-72; psychologist Jackson Mental Health Center, 1972—. Vis. instr. Clemson (S.C.) U., 1972; vis. instr. Univs. Center, Jackson, 1972—; sch. cons., 1972—; individual practice psychology, 1973—. Mem. Miss., Southeastern, Am. psychol. assns., Phi Kappa Phi. Home: 270 Melrose Dr Jackson MS 39211 Office: 969 Lakeland Dr Jackson MS 39211

OWENS, NORMA PRANCELL (MRS. JAMES H. OWENS, JR.), educator; b. Thedford, Neb., Jan. 14, 1924; d. Charles and Rosetta (Meehan) Speese; A.B., San Francisco State Tchrs. Coll., 1952; M.A., N.Y.U., 1956, Ed.D., 1968; m. James H. Owens, Jr., June 30, 1946. Mem. faculty div. nursing edn. N.Y. U., N.Y.C., 1955—, asso. prof. biophys. pathology, 1970—, also dir. biophys. pathology sect., 1972-74. Cons., adviser Am. Cancer Soc., 1965—, bd. dirs., chairperson N.Y.C. div. nurses adv. com., 1973-74; mem. edit. consulting bd. MEDCOM, N.Y.C., 1968-70; mem. med.-surg. nursing film com. Am. Jour. Nursing, 1969—. Founding pres., community liaison S.I. Council Civil Rights, 1958-64; mem. Anti-Poverty com. Coordinating Com. S.I., 1967-69, neighborhood adv. com. Mayor's Task Force, 1966-69, S.I. adv. bd. Urban League Greater N.Y., 1964-67, various coms. N.A.A.C.P., 1951-66; editor newsletter S.I. League Better Govt., 1966; mem. Congress Racial Equality, 1958-66, Women's Civic and Polit. Union S.I., 1954—. Mem. Sch. Bd., Richmond, N.Y., 1962-70, sch. bd. rep. to student council Susan Wagner High Sch., 1968-70. Title II grantee, 1961, Sigma Theta Tau scholar, 1968; recipient Honors Scholar Founders Day award N.Y. U., 1969, Alexander's Salute to Women of Achievement award, N.Y.C., 1972, Woman Achievement award Brown Bombers Assn., Staten Island, 1970, Alumnae Distinguished Achievement award Gregory Sch. Nursing, 1973. Mem. N.Y.U. Alumni Fedn. (bd. dirs.), Am. Nurses Assn. Inc., Nat. League Nursing, N.E.A., Sch. Edn. Nurse Alumni Assn., Am. Assn. U. Profs., Nat. Assn. Fgn. Student Advisers, N.Y. Soc. Exptl. Study Edn., Pi Lambda Theta, Sigma Theta Tau, Delta Sigma Theta, Lambda Kappa Mu. Lutheran. Author: (with others) Nursing Care of the Cancer Patient, 1972. Editor: Primer on Cancer for Nurses, 1966. Home: 510 King St Staten Island NY 10312 Office: 429 Shimkin Hall NY Univ Washington Square New York City NY 10003

OWENS, RUTH JOHNSON (MRS. WYATT OWENS), Dem. nat. committeewoman. Personal sec. to Gov. Folsom of Ala., 1955-58. Mem. Dem. Nat. Comm. from Ala., 1960—; del. Dem. nat. conv., 1968. Home: 1208 Vista Lane Birmingham AL 35203*

OWENS, RUTH PARRY, physician; b. Muncie, Ind., Dec. 28, 1929; d. Thomas Roger and Marie (Williams) Owens; A.B., Miami U., Oxford, O., 1952; M.D., Western Res. U. (now Case Western Res. U.), 1961. Intern Univ. Hosps. Cleve., 1961-62, resident, 1963-64; resident Colo. Med. Center, Denver, 1962-63; mem. staff Univ. Hosp.; instr. pediatrics Case Western Res. U. and Hosp., Cleve., 1967-69, sr. instr., 1969-71, asst. prof., 1971—, instr. in pediatrics in psychiatry, 1969—. Trustee Diabetes Assn. Greater Cleve. Pediatric Endocrinology and Metabolism fellow Oglebay Found., 1964-67. Mem. No. Ohio Pediatrics Assn., Am. Assn. Child Care in Hosps., Ambulatory Pediatrics Assn. Home: 2385 Overlook Rd Cleveland Heights OH 44106 Office: 2103 Adelbert Rd Cleveland OH 44106

OWLES, ELIZABETH JOYCE, archaeologist; b. Restin, Peru, Aug 4, 1925; d. George Ernest and Faith (Allen) Owles; Classics degree, Univ. Coll., London, 1950, postgrad. diploma, 1952. Excavated in Jericho, Chios, also Italy, 1954-58; archaeologist Ipswich (Eng.) Mus., 1958—; lectr. Workers Edn. Assn., 1965—. Hon. editor group 7, Council Brit. Archaeology. Fellow Soc. Antiquaries London; mem. Suffolk Inst. Archaeology (council). Author articles. Home: Bramford Lodge Bramford nr Ipswich England Office: The Museum High St Ipswich Suffolk England

OWYANG, JUDITH FRANCINE, art critic; b. Sacramento, Feb. 9, 1940; d. Mervyn Tai and Esther Lorraine (Yen) Owyang; B.A. in Art History, U. So. Cal., 1969. Art critic, art editor Santa Monica (Cal.) Evening Outlook, 1970—. Mem. Am. Assn. U. Women. Home: 2030 S Sherbourne Dr Apt 11 Los Angeles CA 90034 Office: 1540 3d St Santa Monica CA 90401

OXTOBY, LILLIAN ROSEN (MRS. TOBY EWING OXTOBY), educator; b. Portland, Me., Feb. 12, 1926; d. Benjamin and Bella (Kaufman) R.; B.S., Coll. City N.Y., 1949; M.A., Columbia, 1952; m. Toby Ewing Oxtoby, Aug. 3, 1952; 1 step-son, John, 1 son, Kenneth. Child welfare program specialist Cal. State Dept. Social Welfare, Los Angeles, 1953-56; dir. East Tremont Child Care Center, N.Y.C., 1961-70; guest lectr. Lehman Coll., 1968-73; asst. prof. edn. N.Y.C. Community Coll., 1970-71, chmn. child care-early childhood edn. program., 1971—; vis. prof. Fordham U., 1973—. Bd. dirs. East Tremont Child Care Center, Urban Child Devel. Center, Clinton Pre-Sch. Mem. Profl. Day Care Dirs. Assn. (pres. 1967-69), Nat. Assn. Social Workers, Assn. Childhood Edn. Internat., Nat. Assn. Edn. Young Children, Nat. Froebel Found., East Tremont Neighborhood Assn. Author: Day Care It's Implication on Divorce and Separation. Producer, dir. film East Tremont Welcomes You, also slide and sound presentation on day care. Home: 170 West End Av New York City NY 10023 Office: 300 Jay St Brooklyn NY 11201

OZICK, CYNTHIA, author; b. N.Y.C., Apr. 17, 1928; d. William and Celia (Regelson) Ozick; B.A. cum laude with honors in English, N.Y. U., 1949; M.A., Ohio State U., 1950; m. Bernard Hallote, Sept. 7, 1952; 1 dau., Rachel Sarah. Author: Trust, 1966; The Pagan Rabbi and Other Stories, 1971; (novellas) An Education, 1972, Usurpation, 1974; fiction, poetry, essays, criticism, reviews, translations in numerous periodicals and anthologies; anthologies include Martha Foley's Best American Short Stories, 1970, 1972; tchr. lit. Ohio State U., 1949-51, N.Y. U., 1964-65, Chautauqua Fiction Workshop, 1966; Elly Stolnitz Meml. lectr. Ind. U., 1972; O'Connor prof. Colgate U., 1973; delivered America-Israel address on Cultural Affairs at Weizmann Inst., Rehovot, Israel, 1970. Nat. Endowment for the Arts fellow, 1968. Recipient Edward Lewis Wallant award for fiction, 1972; B'nai B'rith Jewish Heritage award for fiction, 1972; Jewish Book Council award for fiction, 1972; Nat. Acad. Arts and Letters-Nat. Inst. Arts and Letters award for lit., 1973; O. Henry 1st prize, 1974; nominee Nat. Book award, 1972; Myrtle Wreath award for lit. Hadassah, 1974. Judge fiction category Nat. Book award, 1974. Mem. Phi Beta Kappa. Office: care Alfred A Knopf Co 201 E 50th St New York City NY 10022

OZONOFF, IDA FRANKLIN (MRS. JACOB B. OZONOFF), artist; b. LaCrosse, Wis., July 27, 1904; d. Meyer and Tillie (Selznik) Franklin; grad. Milw. State Tchrs. Coll., 1924; student Milw. Downer Coll., 1958, 59, U. Wis. at Milw., 1960-63; m. Jacob B. Ozonoff, July 25, 1926 (dec. Oct. 1957); children—Maer B., Ethel (Mrs. Alan S. Lieberthal), David M. Tchr. pub. schs., Milw., 1924-29, tchr. spl. edn., 1958-61; one-man shows Bradley Galleries, Milw. U. Sch., Jewish Community Center, Bank of Commerce, Abilene (Tex.) Fine Arts Mus., Rahr Civic Center and Mus., Manitowoc, Wis., 1972, Cardinal Stritch Coll., Milw., 1972, Charles Allis Art Library, Milw., 1972, others; exhibited in group shows N.A.D. (N.Y.C.), Erie County Tech. Inst. (Buffalo), Wayland Acad. (Beaver Dam. Wis.), Walker Art Center (Mpls.), Wright Art Center (Beloit, Wis.), Smithsonian Instn. (Washington), Soc. of Four Arts (Fla.), Allied Artists, N.Y.C., U. Wis. Alumni Art Invitational, 1972, Wis. Women in Arts, Milw., 1972—, numerous others; represented in permanent collections Smithsonian Instn., Oshkosh Pub. Schs., Milw. Jour. Collection, Milw. Pub. Sch. System, Milw. Bank of Commerce, U. Wis., Internat. div. First Nat. Bank, Mpls., Knutson Cos., Mpls., First Nat. Bank St. Paul, Gateway Transp. Co., LaCrosse, Wis., Fingerhut Corp., Mpls. Recipient Benjamin Altman award N.A.D., 1968. Mem. Milw. Art Center Collectors Gallery, Wis. Painters and Sculptors (dir.), Internat. Platform Assn. Home: 5165 N Marlborough Dr Milwaukee WI 53217

PAARFUS, BARBARA DIANE LEIDHOLDT, educator; b. Hartford, Conn., Apr. 29, 1936; d. Louis Frederick and Helen (Christenson) Leidholdt; B.A., Gettysburg Coll., 1957; M.A., Temple U., 1958; m. Edward Charles Paarfus, Mar. 28, 1967 (div.); children—Edward Charles III, Virginia Marsden, Murray Thompson, Richard Mahlon. Grad. asst. Psychology Clinic, Temple U., Phila., 1957; tchr., Overbrook Sch. for the Blind, Phila., 1958-60; guidance counselor Henrico County Sch. Bd., Richmond, Va., 1960-61; staff psychologist Med. Coll. Va., Va. Commonwealth U., Richmond, 1961-65, instr. psychiatry, 1965-68, clin. instr. psychiatry, 1968-73; sch. psychologist for vocational rehab. Richmond Sch. Bd., 1973—. Cons. psychologist Fredericksburg Area Mental Hygiene Clinic, 1966; actress community and summer theaters Haverford Twp., Pa., 1954-55, Sandston, Va., 1963, 64, Richmond, 1964, 65, 66, 67, 68, Chester, Va., 1970. Active Dept. Recreation and Parks, United Givers Fund, Heart Fund, Cystic Fibrosis, Va. Mus. Bd. dirs. Shakespeare Players, Inc. Recipient Cappy award for best actress Community Actors Playhouse, 1963. Mem. Am., Richmond Area psychol. assns., Am. Group Psychotherapy Assn., Va. Assn. Sch. Psychologists, MidAtlantic Group Psychotherapy Assn., Nat. Wildlife Fedn., Chi Omega, Psi Chi, Alpha Psi Omega. Home: 4610 Bromley Lane Richmond VA 23226

PABLO, NARCISA CALZADA (MRS. RAMON L. ALCALA, JR.), physician; b. Manila, Philippines, July 7, 1938 (came to U.S. 1963); d. Tomas M. and Luisa G. (de la Calzada) Pablo; A.A. with honors, Letran Coll., Philippines, 1957; M.D., U. Santo Tomas, Philippines, 1962; m. Ramon L. Alcala, Jr., Jan. 8, 1967. Intern, St. Barnabas Med. Center, N.J., 1963-64; med. resident Bklyn. Cumberland Med. Center, 1964-65, Misericordia Hosp., N.Y.C., 1965-66; fellow renal and electrolyte sect., dept. medicine, Brookdale Hosp. Center, Bklyn., 1967-70, Nat. Kidney Found. fellow, 1968-69, asst. attending in medicine and renal sect., asst. attending in community health, 1972—. Mem. N.Y. Soc. Nephrology, Am. Soc. Nephrology, Am. Fedn. Clin. Research, Internat. Soc. Nephrology, Philippine Med. Assn. Contbr. articles to profl. pubs. Home: 429-15 Franklin Turnpike Mahwah NJ 07430 Office: Brookdale Hospital Center Brooklyn NY 11212

PACE, MARGARET ANN, sch. prin.; b. Camp Rucker, Ala., Aug. 7, 1943; d. Lawrence James and Nettie Zell (Elswick) Pace; B.A., Marshall U., 1965, M.A., 1971; M. Ed., U. Va., 1968. Tchr. educable mentally handicapped Lincoln Sch., Wheeling, W.Va., 1965-67; tchr. Mercer County Bd. Edn., W.Va., 1968-69; prin. Park Ungraded High, Bluefield, W.Va., 1969—. Bd. dirs. Mercer County Fellowship Home, sec. treas., 1973; bd. dirs. Mercer County Opportunity Workshop for Handicapped, sec., 1972-74. Recipient Spl. Olympic Appreciation award Princeton Jr. C. of C., 1970; named W.Va. Educator of Year Jr. C. of C., 1971. Mem. Nat., Mercer County, W.Va. edn. assns., Nat., W.Va. (pres. 1972-74), Mercer County assns. for retarded children, Am. Assn. on Mental Deficiency, Mercer County Secondary Prins. Assn. (sec. treas. 1972-73), Nat. Secondary Prins. Assn., Council for Exceptional Children (W.Va. membership chmn. 1969-71, sec. 1968-69, rep. to nat. bd. govs. 1971-73), Delta Kappa Gamma. Roman Catholic. Clubs: Wheeling Jr. Women's, Princeton Jr. Women's, Princeton Elks Country; Quota. Home: 106 Circle Dr Princeton WV 24740 Office: 104 Park St Bluefield WV 24701

PACE, MARIE SLADE, librarian; b. Meansville, Ga., Aug. 19, 1915; d. Joseph Samuel and Odessa (Maddox) Slade; B.S., Ga. State Coll. Women, 1934; postgrad. Library Sch. Emory U., summer 1949; m. Daniel Boone Pace, June 24, 1950; children—Virginia (Mrs. Jonathan Thomas Crenshaw), Joseph Robert. Tchr. elementary sch. Thomaston, Ga., 1934-36, Douglas, Ga., 1936-40, math., high sch., Thomaston, 1940-45; spl. service librarian Fort McPherson, Atlanta, 1945-46; tchr. math. high sch., Griffin, Ga., 1946-49, sch. librarian, 1950-56, tchr. math., 1956-60; regional dir. library services State Ga., Griffin, 1949-50; tchr. math. jr. high sch., Melbourne, Fla., 1960-61, librarian, 1961—. Sponsor, leader Girl Scouts, Eau Gallie, Fla., 1962-69. Methodist (tchr.). Home: 453 Penguin Dr Satellite Beach FL 32937 Office: 4100 Duke St Melbourne FL 32901

PACHMUSS, TEMIRA A., educator; b. Skamja, Estonia, Dec. 24, 1927; d. Johannes Eduard Andreas and Helene (Trediakova) Pachmuss; B.A. with honors U. Melbourne, 1954, M.A., 1955; Ph.D., U. Washington, 1959. Came to U.S. 1955, naturalized, 1966. Instr. U. Mich., 1958-59, U. Colo., 1959-60, U. Ill., 1960-61; asst. prof. U. Ill., 1961-64, asso. prof. Russian lit., 1964-68, prof., 1968—. Fulbright-Hays Research fellow, 1964, Am. Philos. Soc. grantee, 1965, 67, 69, travel grantee Center for Russian Lang. and Area Studies, U. Ill., Urbana, 1962, 64, 66, 68, 70, 72, 73, 74, Am. Council Learned Socs. grantee, 1971, 73. Mem. Assn. Russian-Am. Scholars in U.S.A., Am. Assn. for Slavic and E. European Tchrs., Estonian Learned Soc. Am., Internat. Dostoevsky Soc., Nat. Slavic Honor Soc. (hon.), Phi Kappa Phi. Author: F.M. Dostoevsky: Dualism and Synthesis of the Human Soul, 1963; Zinaida Hippius: An Intellectual Profile, 1971; Z.N. Hippius: Collected Poetical Works 1899-1945, 1972; Intellect and Ideas in Action: Selected Correspondence of Zinaida Hippius, 1972; Zinaida Hippius: Selected Works, 1972; Zinaida Hippius: Collected Dramatical Works, 1972. Contbr. articles to profl. jours. Home: 2013 Vawter St Urbana IL 61801

PACK, CLAIRE, automotive exec.; b. N.Y.C., Oct. 19, 1924; d. Paul and Sarah (Trieb) Pack; student N.Y. U., 1941, Delahanty Bus. Sch., 1940. With U.S. Signal Corps, Bklyn. and Phila., 1941-47; with Allegheny Body Co., Inc., Phila., 1947—, bookkeeper, 1947-55, comptroller, 1955-65, treas., 1965—. Cons. Gerald Stevens Advt., Phila., 1971—. Sec., treas. Ahavas Chesed Congregation, Phila., 1958-59; v.p. Sisterhood B'nai Jeshurun, AC, Phila., 1966-67. Mem. League Women Voters, Truck Body and Equipment Assn. Home: 551 Carpenter Lane Philadelphia PA 19119 Office: 1633 N 6th St Philadelphia PA 19122

PACK, PHOEBE KATHERINE FINLEY (MRS. ARTHUR NEWTON PACK), civic worker; b. Portland, Ore., Feb. 2, 1907; d. William Lovell and Irene (Barnhart) Finley; student U. Cal. at Berkeley, 1926-27; B.A., U. Ore., 1930; m. Arthur Newton Pack, June 11, 1936; children—Charles Lathrop, Phoebe Irene. Layman referee Pima County Juvenile Ct., Tucson, 1958—; dir. Kress Nursing Sch., Tucson, 1957—, Pima County Assn. for Mental Health, 1958—, Ariz. Assn. for Mental Health, Phoenix, 1963—. Mem. Mt. Vernon Ladies Assn. Union (state vice-regent, 1962—), Alpha Phi. Home: PO Box 50166 Tucson AZ 85703

PACKARD, LOLITA JEAN PROVOST, automobile dealership exec.; b. Winooski, Vt., July 26, 1922; d. Eugene and Blanche Lydia (Mongeon) Provost; m. 1940 (widow); children—Juanita (Mrs. Don Cordero), Roberta Jean (Mrs. Frank Hogancamp). File clk. Civil Service Commn., Panama, C.Z., 1942, chief accountant U.S. Navy, West Bank Naval Sta., Panama, 1942-45; office mgr. Clippering Chevrolet Co., Covina, Cal., 1945-49, Bob Estes Lincoln-Mercury, Inglewood, Cal., 1949-50; bus. mgr., corporate sec. Vel's Parnelli Jones Ford, Torrance, Cal., 1954—; sec. R & D Engring.-Devel. Co.; bus. mgr. Jim Cook Assos., Jones-Miletich Land Co., Miletich-Jones Land Co.; internal auditor Ontario Motor Speedway, Colt Investment Co. Home: 21107 Ladeene Av Torrance CA 90503 Office: 20900 Hawthorne Blvd Torrance CA 90503

PACKARD, MARJEAN PHILLIPS (MRS. CHARLES A. PACKARD), former sch. adminstr.; b. New Vienna, O.; d. Harley M. and Nancy Ann (Johnson) Phillips; student Miami U., 1920-22; B.S., Wilmington (O.) Coll., 1944; M.Ed., U. Miami, 1954; m. Charles A. Packard, Sept. 7, 1927; 1 son, Charles Edgar. Tchr. Cin. pub. schs., 1922-27; saleswoman William Ruggles Real Estate, Evanston, Ill., 1936-38; tchr. Pine Crest Prep. Sch., Ft. Lauderdale, Fla., 1939-51; prin. Pine Crest Elementary Sch., 1951-73, now ret. Pres. Broward County Panhellenic, 1947-48. Mem. Ft. Lauderdale Art Center, Ft. Lauderdale Symphony Soc., Ft. Lauderdale Community Concert Assn.; past bd. dirs. Broward County Girl Scouts, Pine Crest Prep. Sch. Marjean Packard Learning Center named in honor. Mem. Hist. Soc. Ft. Lauderdale, Inc., Friends of Library at Ft. Lauderdale, P.E.O. (pres. chpt. X 1947-48), Nat. Elementary Sch. Prins., Am. Assn. U. Women, Fort Lauderdale C. of C. (Citizen of Month June 1973), Zonta of Ft. Lauderdale (pres.), Internat. Platform Assn., Delta Kappa Gamma (pres. Xi chpt. 1959-62, state pres. 1965-67, mem. internat. adminstrv. bd., regional dir. 1968-70), Sigma Kappa. Presbyn. (past deacon, trustee). Club: Lauderdale Yacht. Contbr. to Jour. of Fla. Edn., Nat. Elementary Prins. Letter. Home: 124 Isle of Venice Box 2105 Fort Lauderdale FL 33303

PACKHAM, MARIAN AITCHISON (MRS. JAMES LENNOX PACKHAM), educator; b. Toronto, Ont., Can., Dec. 13, 1927; d. James and Clara Louise (Campbell) Aitchison; B.A., U. Toronto, 1949, Ph.D., 1954; m. James Lennox Packham, June 25, 1949; children—Neil, Janet. Sr. fellow dept. biochemistry U. Toronto, 1954-58, lectr., 1958-63; research asso. dept. physiol. scis. Ont. Vet. Coll., Guelph, 1963-65; research asso. blood and cardiovascular disease research unit U. Toronto, 1965-66, lectr., 1966-67, asst. prof., 1967-72, asso. prof. dept. biochemistry, 1972—. Vis. asst. prof. dept. pathology McMaster U., Hamilton, Ont., 1967—. Med. Research Council Can. grantee. Mem. Canadian Biochem. Soc., Canadian Soc. for Clin. Investigation, Canadian Hematology Soc., Am. Soc. Hematology, Am. Soc. for Exptl. Pathology, Am. Heart Assn. (council on thrombosis), Internat. Soc. on Thrombosis and Haemostasis. Contbr. articles to profl. jours. Home: 65 Glengowan Rd Toronto ON M4N 1G3 Canada

PACKWOOD, GEORGIE ANN OBERTEUFFER (MRS. ROBERT W. PACKWOOD), wife of U.S. senator; m. Robert W. Packwood, Nov. 25, 1964; 1 son, William Henderson. Wife U.S. senator from Ore. Home: 6215 Lakeview Dr Falls Church VA 22041*

PADAWER-SINGER, ALICE MARIE (MRS. LEWIS SINGER), research and lectr. psychology; b. Paris, France, Dec. 16, 1922; d. Izak and Rose (Zucker) Padawer; A.B., N.Y. U.; M.A., Columbia, 1960, Ph.D., 1964; m. Lewis Singer, Dec. 17, 1945; children—Andrew Neil, Rickie Laura. Lectr. Bklyn. Coll., 1962; fellow Columbia, 1963; research asst. 1964-65, sr. research staff Bur. Applied Social Research, 1968—; research instr., sr. investigator Albert Einstein Coll. of Medicine, 1965-66; research asso. N.Y. U., 1966—; lectr. Bklyn. Coll., 1965-66; prof. L.I. U., Bklyn., 1966—; dir. Free Press-Fair Trial project; cons. in behavioral research, Research Found. N.Y. U.; lectr. on research methods and exptl. design; cons. to research projects Berkeley U., Cal.; cons. N.Y. State Dept. Edn., N.Y.C. Bd. Edn., Bar Inst. N.J. Mem. exec. com Zionist Orgn. Am., 1964—. Mem. A.A.A.S., Am. Assn. Pub. Opinion Research, N.Y. Acad. Scis., Soc. for Psychol. Study Social Issures, Am. Psychol. Assn., Assn. for Applied Psychoanalysis, Am. Psychology-Law Soc. (pres.-elect). Home: 130 E 67th St New York City NY 10024 Office: Zeckendorf Campus, Long Island U Brooklyn NY 11201 also Bureau Applied Social Research Columbia 605 W 115th St New York City NY 10025

PADBERG, SISTER HARRIET ANN, educator; b. St. Louis, Nov. 13, 1922; d. Harry J. and Marie Louise (Kilgen) Padberg; A.B. with honors, Maryville Coll. Sacred Heart, 1943; Mus.M., U. Cin., 1949; M.A., St. Louis U., 1956, Ph.D., 1964; postgrad. Pius X Sch. Liturgical Music, 1957-59, Am. U., U. Okla., Stanford. Elementary and secondary tchr. math. and music, Cin., 1946-47, St. Charles Mo., 1947-49, Grand Coteau, La., 1949-52, St. Louis, 1956-58; instr. Coll. Sacred Heart, Grand Coteau, 1947-48, asst. prof., 1951-54; asst. prof. math. and music Maryville Coll. Sacred Heart, St. Louis, 1956-64, asso. prof., 1964-68, prof., 1968—; tchr. Manhattanville (N.Y.) Coll., 1965, Lindenwood Coll., St. Charles, 1970—. Mem. adv. panel evaluation proposals for sci. equipment NSF, 1968; cons. coll. music curriculum com. Manhattanville Music Curriculum Project, 1970. Judge St. Louis Post-Dispatch Sci. Fair, 1970-74. Mem. Am. Assn. U. Profs., Nat. Council Tchrs. Math., Math. Assn. Am., Am. Math. Soc., Assn. for Computing Machinery, Mo. Math. Assn. for Advancement of Tchr. Tng., Nat. Cath. Music Edn. Assn., Mo. Council Tchrs. Math., Mo. Acad. Scis., Albertus Magnus Guild, Sigma Xi, Pi Mu Epsilon, Delta Epsilon Sigma. Roman Catholic (mem. archdiocesan commn. sacred liturgy, music and art 1972-75). Home: 13550 Conway Rd St Louis MO 63141

PADBERG, NANCY A. MORRISON (MRS. THOMAS LORENZ PADBERG), social worker; b. Cary, N.C., Nov. 30, 1937; d. Murph John and Anita (Parks) Morrison; student U. N.C. Womans Coll., 1955-57; B.A., Fla. State U., 1959; M.A., U. Chgo., 1962; postgrad. Smith Coll., 1964; m. Thomas Lorenz Padberg, June 23, 1968; 1 dau., Suzanne Nicole. Social worker Manteno (Ill.) State Hosp., 1963-66; child welfare worker West Palm Beach and Martin counties, West Palm Beach, Fla., 1959-60; social worker Jacksonville (Ill.) State Hosp., 1962-63; instr. Jane Adams Grad. Sch. Social Work, U. Ill., Chgo., 1966-68; instr. social work grad. students U. Cal. at Los Angeles, 1968-69; profl. writer, research, Pitts., 1969-71; clin. social worker U. Cal. Los Angeles Hosp. and Center for Health Scis., 1971—; pvt. practice psychotherapy and childbirth edn. Mem. Nat. Assn. Social Workers (state rec. sec. 1966-67), Nat. Conf. Social Welfare, Council Social Work Edn., Zeta Tau Alpha. Republican. Episcopalian. Home: 12511 Rosy Circle Los Angeles CA 90066

PADGETT, JOANN EVELYN (MRS. BOB JOE PADGETT), occupational therapist; b. Oklahoma City, Sept. 29, 1932; d. Basil Lawrence and Edna Francis (Wright) Anderson; B.S., U. Kan., 1954; m. Bob Joe Padgett, Oct. 8, 1955; children—Tracy Lea, Lawrence Wesley. Mem. occupational therapy staff Central State Griffin Meml. Hosp., Norman, Okla., 1954-55, dir. occupational therapy, 1955-57; dir. occupational therapy Meth. Hosp., Houston, 1957; staff therapist Cerebral Palsy Center, New Orleans, 1958; clinic supr. VA Hosp., Houston, 1958-61. Vol. worker motor devel. act, visual perception program in pub. schs., nurses clinics; active P.T.A. and Parent Tchr. Orgn., 1969-73. Recipient Superior Performance award VA, 1960. Mem. Am., Tex., S.E. Dist. occupational therapy assns., Houston Tennis Assn. (tournament chmn., youth coach, dir. 1973—), Gamma Phi Beta Alumni. Home: 7815 Leader St Houston TX 77036

PADGETT, ROSE, educator; b. Bradford, Yorkshire, Eng.; d. George Charles and Polly (Winterburn) Padgett; B.S., No. Univs., Leeds, Manchester, Eng., 1933; M.S., U. Tenn., 1951; Ph.D., Purdue U., 1955. Came to U.S., 1950, naturalized, 1956. Tchr., Bradford (Yorkshire) Edn. Com., 1934-42; civil def. and aux. nurse Air Raid Precaution, 1939-45; vol. nurse Officer of St. John of Jerusalem, 1939-49; tchr. Skipton Girls High Sch., Bradford, 1942-49; exchange tchr. Kingswood (W.Va.) High Sch., 1948-49; asso. prof. U. Tenn., summer 1951; instr. Purdue U., 1950-55, asst. prof. textiles and clothing, 1955-62; asso. prof. So. Ill. U., Carbondale, 1962-69, prof., 1969—, chmn. dept. clothing and textiles, 1962—. Mem. English-Speaking Union, Am. Assn. U. Profs. (chpt. sec. 1960-62), Am. Chem. Soc., Am. Textile Chemists and Colorists, Am. Standards for Testing Materials, Am. Home Econs. Assn., Internat. Silk Assn., Textile Inst. Manchester (Eng.) (licentiate) Internat. Platform Assn., Am. Soc. for Testing Materials, Sigma Xi, Phi Lambda Theta, Omicron Nu, Sigma Delta Epsilon (pres. 1956-57, liaison officer 1958-62). Author: Textile Chemistry and Testing in the Laboratory, 1956; also articles in profl. jours. and mags. Research on insect damage to textiles, interior furnishings, consumer problems, environmental degradation to textiles. Home: 204 Brook Lane Carbondale IL 62901

PADYKULA, HELEN ANN, scientist, educator; b. Chicopee, Mass., Dec. 27, 1924; d. Stanley and Pauline (Dabrowska) Padykula; B.S. magna cum laude, U. Mass., 1946; M.A., Mt. Holyoke Coll., 1948; Ph.D., Harvard, 1954. Grad. asst. zoology Mt. Holyoke Coll., 1946-48; instr. zoology Wellesley Coll., 1948-50, prof. biol. scis., 1964—; tchr. asst. in embryology Marine Biol. Lab., 1948-49; research fellow in anatomy Harvard, 1951-53, instr, 1953-55, asso. in anatomy, 1955-59, asst. prof. anatomy, 1959-64; Anne Louise Barrett fellow, 1950-51, Benjamin White Whitney fellow, 1950-51, Nat. fellow Am. Assn. U. Women, 1951-52; sr. research fellow NIH, 1959-64; cons. USPHS, 1968-72, spl. research fellow, 1971-72; vis. investigator Ian Clunies Ross Lab., Australia, 1971; vis. prof. dept. anatomy McGill U., 1972. Mem. sci. adv. com. Muscular Dystrophy Assns. Am., 1972—; mem. bd. sci. counsellors Nat. Eye Inst., 1972—. Recipient Distinguished Achievement award Radcliffe Grad. Soc., 1971. Mem. Internat. Soc. Cell Biology, Internat. Soc. Developmental Biology, Am. Soc. Cell Biology, Soc. Study Devel. and Growth, Am. Soc. Zoologists, Am. Assn. Anatomists (exec. com. 1973—), Histochem. Soc., Phi Beta Kappa, Phi Kappa Phi, Sigma Xi. Contbr. articles in field. Am. editor Histochemie, 1970—; asso. editor Am. Jour. Anatomy, 1971—. Home: 184 Wellesley Av Wellesley Hills MA 02181 Office: Lab Electron Microscopy Wellesley Coll Wellesley MA 02181

PAETRO, MADELINE JEAN ELLIS (MRS. SAMUEL P. PAETRO), librarian; b. N.Y.C., Jan. 25, 1922; d. Max and Hannah (Moore) Ellis; B.S. in Edn., U. Miami (Fla.), 1944; M.S. in L.S. with honors, Columbia, 1957; m. Samuel P. Paetro, Feb. 14, 1942; children—Maxine A., Anthony S. Tchr. pub. schs., Dade County, Fla., 1951-53, librarian, 1954-66, coordinator, 1966-68, supr., 1968—; prof. library sci. U. Miami (Fla.), 1957—; summer faculty Sch. Library Sci., Columbia, 1970-72. Mem. Zonta Internat., Alpha Delta Kappa, Delta Phi Epsilon, Phi Lambda Pi. Home: 6820 Gratian St Coral Gables FL 33134 Office: 1410 NE 2d Av Miami FL 33132

PAGANELLI, DOLORES FLORA, physician; b. N.Y.C., Apr. 6, 1928; d. Armand and Elizabeth (Ferzaco) Paganelli; A.B. cum laude, Hunter Coll., 1949; M.D., State U. N.Y., 1954. Intern, Flushing (N.Y.) Hosp. and Dispensary, 1954-55; resident obstetrics and gynecology, St. Catherine's Hosp., Bklyn., 1955-58; practice medicine specializing in obstetrics and gynecology, Bklyn., 1958—; attending staff obstetrics and gynecology St. John's Queens Hosp., Elmhurst, N.Y., 1965-72; attending staff obstetrics and gynecology Greenpoint Hosp., Bklyn., 1958-72; now asso. dir. intern/resident edn. Catholic Med. Center of Bklyn. and Queens. Diplomate Am. Bd. Obstetrics and Gynecology. Fellow A.C.S., Bklyn. Gynecol. Soc., Am. Coll. Obstetricians and Gynecologists; mem. N.Y., Kings County med. socs., Internat. Narcotics Officers Enforcement Assn. Home: One Westminster Dr White Plains NY 10604 Office: 50 Bushwick Av Brooklyn NY 11211 also 89-18 56th Av Elmhurst NY 11373

PAGE, ANTOINETTE H. EDGETT, newspaper publisher, author; b. Moscow, Ida., July; d. Clarence Mills and Ruby (Slee) Edgett; student pvt. schs.; m. Holland Page, Jr., Aug. 17, 1947 (div. 1954). Aviation columnist Flight Mag., Dallas, 1940-45; aviation editor Valley Times, San Fernando, Cal., 1945-47; columnist Aviation News Beacon, Los Angeles, 1945; contbg. editor Bus. Girl, Dallas, 1944-46, Women in Aviation, XC News, Ft. Worth, 1945-52; pub. Cross Country News, Ft. Worth, 1952—. Vol., chmn. house com. Austin YWCA, 1950-53; vol. Austin State Mental Hosp., 1950-54. Recipient Woman of Year in Aviation award, 1960; James J. Strebig award Aviation-Space Writers Assn., 1962; Fairfield award citation for air safety writing, 1962-65; citation and awards Flight Safety Found., Inc.; named adm. Am. Airlines, hon. chief Sycamore Indian Tribe. Mem. Ft. Worth Press Club, Aviation-Space Writers Assn., Tex. Aviation Assn., Tex. Pvt. Fliers Assn., Hump Pilots Assn., Womens Aero. Assn., Am. Helicopter Assn., Air Force Assn., Ninety Nines, Whirly-Girls, Theta Sigma Phi. Club: Turtle. Home: Box 9661 Fort Worth TX 76107 Office: Meacham Field Fort Worth TX 76106

PAGE, BEVERLY JEAN ANDERSEN, TV sta. exec., author; b. Chgo., May 5, 1926; d. Edward and Margaret (Rankin) Andersen; A.A., North Park Coll., Chgo., 1946; B.S., U. Ill., Urbana, 1948; m. Clarence Page, Nov. 21, 1948 (dec. Aug. 1954); children—Carol Lynn (Mrs. John Ritter), Edward Andersen. Owner, Mayfair, Hillside, Ill., 1952-57; promotion dir. Goldblatt's, Chgo., 1957-62; copy chief Aldens Shoppers World, Chgo., 1962-64; advt. coordinator Polk Bros., Chgo., 1964-65; pub. relations dir. Fashion Fair Co., Cin., 1965-67; promotion publicity dir. WLW-Radio, Cin., 1967-69, WXEX-TV, Richmond, Va., 1969—; pres. Beverly Page Advt., Richmond. Cons. on Scandinavian cooking Gourmet Soc. of Cin., originator, dir. Coffee House, Cin., 1966-69; owner Kitchen Skills Internat., Ltd., Page One Advt. Bd. advisers sub com. for Cin. Mag., 1969-71; publicity dir., trustee Cin. Rosie Reds; bd. dirs. Upper Room Coffee House, 1970—. Named Woman of Year, Cin. Enquirer, 1968. Mem. Pub. Relations Soc. Am., Cin. Scandinavian Soc. Author: Shopper's Cost Chopper, 1973; The Nifty Thrifty Book, 1974. Home: 900 Pump Rd No 32 Richmond VA 23229

PAGE, GERALDINE, actress; b. Kirksville, Mo., Nov. 22, 1924; d. Leon and Pearl (Maize) Page; student Goodman Theatre Dramatic Sch., Chgo., 1942-45; studied acting and voice at Herbert Berghof Sch., N.Y.C. Played in stock at Lake Zurich, Ill., Marengo, Ill., Woodstock, Ill., 1944-52; appeared in Summer and Smoke in Greenwich Village, 1952; mem. cast NBC Best Plays radio series, 1953, Summer Smoke, Ethan Frome, Glass Menagerie; TV shows, A Christmas Memory, 1966, Barefoot in Athens, 1966, A Thanksgiving Visitor. Broadway plays Mid-summer, 1953, The Immoralist, 1954, The Rainmaker, 1954-55 (London, 1956-57), Separate Tables, 1957-58, Sweet Bird of Youth, 1959-60, Strange Interlude, 1963, The Three Sisters, 1964, P.S. I Love You, 1964, The Great Indoors, 1966, Black Comedy, 1967; appeared role of supporting actress in motion picture Hondo, 1953; appeared in motion picture Sweet Bird of Youth, 1962, Summer and Smoke, 1961, Toys in the Attic, 1963, Dear Heart, 1964, Monday's Child, 1966, You're a Big Boy Now (nominated for Acad. award for best performance by supporting actress), 1967, The Happiest Millionaire, 1967, Whatever Happened to Alice, 1969, Beguiled, 1971, The Day of the Locust, 1974. Nominated for the best performance by a supporting actress in Hondo, Acad. Motion Picture Arts and Scis., Theatre World award winner, season 1952-53; N.Y. Drama Critics award, season 1952-53; Donaldson award, also Theatre Time award, season 1952-53; Sarah Siddons Soc. plaque award for actress of the yr.; Cinema Nuova Gold plaque, Venice, 1961, Golden Globe, foreign press award, 1962, best actress Nat. Bd. Rev. Motion Pictures, 1961, Cue mag., 1961, Donatello award for best actress, 1963 (all for film Summer and Smoke); 2 Emmy awards. Mem. Actors Equity Assn., Screen Actors Guild, Am. Fedn. TV-Radio Artists, Phi Beta. Office: care Stephen Draper 37 W 57th St New York City NY 10019

PAGE, HELEN MAE HAMMER (MRS. MARIUS CURT PAGE, JR.), radiologist; b. Scales Mound., Ill., Nov. 20, 1941; d. Elmer George and Margaret (Kendall) Hammer; grad. St. Mary's Sch. Radiologic Tech., 1961; student music U. Wis. at Sauk County campus; m. Marius Curt Page, Jr., Sept. 22, 1962; children—Michael Charles, Robin Joan. Asst. to chief technologist St. Mary's Ringling Hosp., Baraboo, Wis., 1961-62, chief technologist, 1962, asst. to chief technologist St. Clare's Hosp., Baraboo, Wis., 1963-65; radiologist Med. Assos. Baraboo, 1968—. Observer Ontario Cancer Found., Ottawa, Ont., Can., 1961. Ward co-chmn. St. Mary's Ringling Manor Bldg. Fund, 1967; dir. St. Joseph's Guitar Choir; asst. treas. Sauk County Assn. for Mental Health, 1966—. Mem. Am. Registry of Radiologic Technologists, Am., Wis. socs. radiologic technologists. Roman Catholic (v.p., program chmn. Our Lady of Grace Sodality, pres. 1969). Club: Baraboo Country (asst. handicap chmn. 1968—). Contbr. articles to profl. jours. Home: 410 1st St Baraboo WI 53913

PAGE, TONY, publisher; b. Moscow, Ida., July 11, 1910; d. Clarence Mills and Ruby (Slee) Edgett; grad. pvt. schs.; m. Holland Page, Jr., 1947 (div. 1954). Staff, Flight mag., Dallas, 1940-45; aviation editor Valley Times, San Fernando, Cal., 1945-47; writer Cross Country News, Austin, Tex., 1947-52; owner, pub. XC News, Fort Worth, 1954—. Named Woman of Year in Aviation, Woman's Aero. Assn., 1960. Mem. Nat. Aero. Assn., Hump Pilots Assn., Aviation/Space Writers Assn. (Sherman Fairchild merit certificate award 1962-65, James J. Strebig Meml. Trophy award 1962), Whirly Girls, Ninety Nines, Ft. Worth Press Club. Home: PO Box 9661 Fort Worth TX 76107 Office: Meacham Field Fort Worth TX 76106

PAGEL, BETTY LOU HUNLEY, ednl. adminstr.; b. Cheyenne, Wyo., May 31, 1920; d. Jesse Newton and Gretchen Nickel (McCall) Hunley; B.A. with honors, U. Wyo., 1952, M.Ed., 1956; m. Willis George Pagel, Nov. 1, 1942 (div. Aug. 1949); 1 dau., Judith Carrol. Tchr. elementary grades, Burns, Wyo., 1940-42; tchr. Corlette Sch., Cheyenne, 1949-54, prin., 1965-66; coordinator elementary grades Laramie County Sch. Dist. 1, Cheyenne, 1954-65; supr. elementary edn. Laramie County Sch. Dist #1, Cheyenne, 1966—. Bd. dirs. Laramie County Cancer Soc. Recipient Gold Key award Wyo. Edn. Assn., 1969, Wyo. Tchr. of Yr. award Wyo. C. of C., 1957. Mem. Nat., Wyo. (pres. 1967-68) edn. assns., Internat. Reading Assn., Assn. for Supervision and Curriculum Devel., Assn. Childhood Edn. Internat., Nat. Elementary Sch. Prins., Am. Assn. Sch. Adminstrs., Wyo. Press Women (sec. 1973-75), D.A.R. (chpt. regent 1972-74, state sec. 1974-76). Mem. Order Eastern Star. Home: 304 E 5th Av Cheyenne WY 82001 Office: 253 Prairie Av Cheyenne WY 82001

PAIGE, NORMA ZELAZO (MRS. SAMUEL PAIGE), lawyer, bus. exec.; b. Lomza, Poland (parents Am. citizens); d. Morris and Edith (Kachorek) Zelazo; student U. Mo., 1940-42; B.A., N.Y. U., Washington Sq. Coll., 1944; J.D., 1946; m. Samuel Paige, June 23, 1945; children—Martin, Holly, Madelyn. Admitted to N.Y. bar, 1946; since practiced in N.Y.C., mem. firm Paige and Paige, 1948—; pres., dir. Astronautics Domestic Internat. Sales Corp., 1974—; v.p., dir. Astronautics Corp. of Am., Milw., also Torrance, Cal., 1959—; dir. Astronautics C.A. Ltd., B'nei-Brak, Israel. Mem. N.Y. Womens Bar Assn. (pres. 1959-60). Office: One World Trade Center Suite 3853 New York City NY 10048 also 907 S 1st St Milwaukee WI 53204 also 2416 Amsler St Torrance CA also 8 Hayarakim Pl Bnei Brah Israel

PAILLOU, MARY LOUISE CAROL BOEHME, city ofcl.; b. St. Louis, Apr. 18, 1930; d. Erwin Waldemar and Margaret Catherine (Coibion) Boehme; student Harris Tchrs. Coll., 1947-49; m. Maurice E. Paillou, June 22, 1951 (div. May 1966); children—Michelle Louise, Michael Louis. Legal sec. Gravely, Lieder & Woodruff, St. Louis, 1951-57, 1965-71; stenographer-reporter City Webster Groves, Mo., part-time, 1958-71; sec. Dept. Environmental Services, City Webster Groves, Mo., 1971-72, city clk., 1972—. Vice pres. Webster Groves Municipal Employees Credit Union, 1972-73, sec., 1973-74. Mem. Municipal Clks. Assn. (sec.-treas. 1974), Mo. Clks. and Finance Officers Assn., Beta Sigma Phi. Episcopalian. Home: 33 S Maple Av Webster Groves MO 63119 Office: 4 East Lockwood Av Webster Groves MO 63119

PAINE, DALE, broadcasting exec.; b. Washington, Apr. 10, 1943; d. John Liston and Pauline (Crapo) Paine. Media buyer McCann-Erickson, N.Y.C., 1962-65, Foote, Cone, Belding, N.Y.C., 1965-66; mgr. research H-R Television, N.Y.C., 1966-68; v.p. sales devel. and research WPIX, Inc., N.Y.C., 1968-74; v.p. sales devel. and research Top Market TV, Inc., N.Y.C., 1974—. Chmn., N.Y. Stas. Research Com., 1973. Mem. Radio and TV Research Council, Nat. Acad. TV Arts and Scis., Am. Women in Radio and TV, Internat. Radio and TV Soc., Mensa. Home: 444 E 86th St New York City NY 10028 Office: 437 Madison Av New York City NY 10022

PAINE, ROBERTA MARY, mus. ofcl.; b. Los Angeles, Oct. 2, 1925; d. Edward Harris and Josephine (Speakman) Paine; student Principia Jr. Coll., 1943-45; A.B., Barnard Coll., 1947; postgrad. Inst. Fine Arts, N.Y. U., 1947-48; M.A., Bryn Mawr Coll., 1953. Curatorial asst. N.Y. Hist. Soc., N.Y.C., 1947-50; asso. mus. educator Met. Mus. Art, N.Y.C., 1953—. Cons. arts, Jr. Leagues N.Y., N.J., Conn. Mem. Assn. Am. Museums. Democrat. Clubs: Sandy Bay Yacht (Rockport, Mass.); Bryn Mawr (N.Y.C.). Author: Looking at Sculpture, 1968; Looking at Architecture, 1974; also 14 booklets on art history, Met. Mus., 1954—. Home: 240 E 76th St New York City NY 10021 Office: Met Mus Art New York City NY 10028

PAINTER, ANN FORBES, educator; b. Balt., Sept. 12, 1935; d. Sidney and Nivea (Forbes) Painter; B.A., Middlebury Coll., 1957; M.L.S., Rutgers, 1960, Ph.D., 1963. Instr., Rutgers U., 1961-63; data processing systems analyst Nat. Bur. Standards, Washington, 1963-64; staff asst. tech. service Nat. Agrl. Library, Washington, 1964-65; asst. prof. grad. library sch. Ind. U., 1965-68, asso. prof., 1968-70; asso. prof. grad. library sch. Drexel U., Phila., 1970-73, prof., 1973—. Cons. on cataloging, classification and reclassification of information and materials. Mem. Am., Pa. library assns., Am. Soc. Information Sci. (sec. 1969-70), Am. Nat. Standards Inst., Com. on Sci. and Tech. Information (task group on library programs 1967-71). An Analysis of Duplication and Consistency of Indexing, 1963; Role of the Library in Relation to Information Handling Activities, 1968; Reader in Cataloging and Classification, 1972. Home: PO Box 281 Narberth PA 19072 Office: Grad Sch Library Science Drexel U Philadelphia PA 19104

PAINTER, CHARLOTTE, writer; b. Baton Rouge; d. L.E. Painter and Dillie Womack; M.A. (creative writing fellow), Stanford, 1962; m. Thomas Voorhees, Apr. 28, 1962 (dec. June 1963); 1 son, Thomas Gregory. Fellow Radcliffe Inst., Cambridge, 1964-66; faculty, U. Cal. at Berkeley, 1972-73, U. Cal. at Santa Cruz, 1967, Stanford, 1966-71; poetry and short stories pub. in lit. and popular mags., including The New Yorker, Mass. Rev., Yardbird, Mediterranean Rev. Nat. Endowment of Arts fellow, 1972. Author: Who Made the Lamb, 1965; Confession from the Malaga Madhouse, 1971. Co-editor Revelations, Diaries of Women, 1974. Home: 372 63d St Oakland CA 94618 Office: care Lynn Nesbit Internat Famous Agy 1301 Av of Americas New York City NY 10019

PAINTER, EDITH PRATT (MRS. CLYDE A. PAINTER), coll. ofcl.; b. Weymouth, Mass., Sept. 19, 1925; d. Charles E. and Mildred (Graham) Pratt; B.A., Tufts U., 1947; M.A., Columbia, 1948; Ed.D., U. No. Colo., 1964; m. Clyde A. Painter, Dec. 27, 1952; children—Scott Douglas, Brett Alan. Asst. dean women Meredith Coll., Raleigh, N.C., 1948-50; asst. dean students New Paltz (N.Y.) State Coll., 1950-51; Spl. Services recreation dir. Ft. Monmouth, N.J., 1951-52; exec. dir. South Shore council Camp Fire Girls, Quincy, Mass., 1952-58; dean women Boise (Ida.) Coll., 1958-61; dean women Youngstown (O.) U., 1961-70, asso. dean of students, 1970-72, asso. prof. psychology, 1964-72; v.p. Russell Sage Coll., Troy, N.Y., 1972—. Bd. dirs. Mental Health Assn., 1964—. Mem. Nat. Assn. Women Deans and Counselors, Am. Psychol. Assn., Phi Beta Kappa, Delta Kappa Gamma. Office: Russell Sage College Troy NY 12180

PAINTER, FRANCES JUANITA WOODS (MRS. HOWARD LEE PAINTER), sales exec.; b. Lewistown, Ill., July 6, 1916; d. Harley Francis and Emma Grace (Bandle) Woods; grad. high sch.; m. Howard Lee Painter, Feb. 11, 1939; children—Judith Lee (Mrs. William Jones), David Kent. Salesman, Marshall Field & Co., Oak Park, Ill., 1957-65, sales mgr. book sect., 1965-70, sales mgr. toy dept., 1970—. Leader, Girl Scouts, Canton, Ill., 1952-56, neighborhood chmn. leaders, 1953-55; leader 4-H Club, 1953-56. Home: 1127 S Ridgeland St Oak Park IL 60304 Office: 1144 Lake St Oak Park IL 60302

PAINTER, HELEN WELCH (MRS. WILLIAM ISAAC PAINTER), educator; b. Covington, Ind.; d. Charles Victor and Rebecca Anne (Huffer) Welch; A.B., Ind. U., 1935, M.A., 1936, Ed.D., 1941; m. William Isaac Painter, Aug. 9, 1933. Grad. asst., Ind. U., 1938-40, sch. psychologist Univ. Sch., Ind. U., 1938-42, tchr. English, 1941-42, instr. Shurtleff Coll., Alton, Ill., 1944-45; prof. edn. U. Akron (O.), 1945-67; prof. elementary edn. Kent (O.) State U., 1967—; vis. prof. N.M. Highlands U., Las Vegas, summer 1938, Colo. Coll., Colorado Springs, summer 1963, Ohio State U., Columbus, summer 1965, Kent State U., summer 1966, State Dept. Edn., Hawaii, 1968. Dir. Nat. Def. Edn. Act Inst. for Advanced Study English Kent State U., summer 1968. Cons. pub. schs., univ. workshops; dir. P.T.A. Workshops, 1953-67. Mem. N.E.A., Ohio Edn. Assn., English Assn.

Ohio, Nat. Council Tchrs. English (nat. dir. 1962-64), Ohio Internat. Reading Assn., (state pres. 1965-66), Internat. Reading Assn., Am. Assn. U. Profs., Delta Kappa Gamma, Pi Lambda Theta, Kappa Delta Pi, Alpha Epsilon, Alpha Sigma Lambda, Eta Sigma Phi. Author: Poetry and Children, 1970. Editor: Reaching Children and Young People Through Literature, 1971. Contbr. articles in field to profl. jours. Home: 88 Monroe Av Cuyahoga Falls OH 44221 Office: Kent State U Kent OH 44242

PAINTER, JOANN ELLEN DAUBENSPECK (MRS. DOUGLAS PARKER PAINTER), ednl. adminstr.; b. Erie, Pa., Aug. 9, 1929; d. Paul Grant and Beatrice Ellen (Johnson) Daubenspeck; B.S., Pa. State U., 1952; M.Ed., Gannon Coll., 1969; postgrad. Case Western Res. U., 1970-71; m. Douglas Parker Painter, June 12, 1954; children—David, Susan, Sally, Polly. Tchr. bus. edn., sec. sch. bd., Harbor Creek, Pa., 1952-55; dir. guidance and placement Villa Maria Coll., Erie, Pa., 1969-73, dir. student personnel services, 1973—, dir. Career-Counseling Center for Adult Women, 1972—. Mem. Am. Personnel and Guidance Assn., Am. Coll. Personnel Assn., Nat. Assn. Women's Deans and Counselors, Am. Assn. U. Women. Club: Kappa Kappa Gamma Alumnae. Office: 2551 West Lake Rd Erie PA 96505

PAINTER, LORENE JANET HUFFMAN (MRS. HANLEY HAYES PAINTER), educator; b. nr. Hickory, N.C., Aug. 16, 1932; d. Horace Clifton and Jennie (Lineberger) Huffman; A.B., Lenoir Rhyne Coll., 1953; M.A., Appalachian State U., 1957; postgrad. U. N.C. at Greensboro; m. Hanley Hayes Painter, June 11, 1950; children—Charles Nathan, Janet Fern. Tchr., Taylorsville (N.C.) Sr. High Sch., 1953-54, Coll. Park Jr. High Sch., Hickory, 1954-59; asst. prof. edn., supr. student teaching Lenoir Rhyne Coll., Hickory, 1959—, co-ordinator curriculum lab., contbr. to 4-1-4 coll. calendar and gen. edn. innovation, 1969, 70, 71, editor, contbr. to tchr.-edn. curriculum revision, 1967, 68, 69; secondary curriculum cons. Catawba County Schs., 1973-74. Judge various ednl. contests. Vol. worker Am. Cancer Soc., Heart Fund, 1960—, Optimist Oratoricals. Bd. dirs. North State Acad., Hickory, 1974—; adv. bd. Catawba County Multi-Handicapped Children's Center, 1973—. Mem. N.E.A., N.C. Assn. Edn., Assn. for Supervision and Curriculum Devel., So. Assn. Secondary Schs. and Colls. (evaluator secondary English depts. for accreditation 1959—), Assn. Tchr. Educators, Delta Kappa Gamma, Pi Kappa Delta. Mem. Advent Christian Ch. Author: Guide To Secondary Student Teaching, 1968, revised 1970; Guide To Curriculum Laboratory, 1965, rev. edit., 1974. Contbr. articles to profl. jours. Home: 1137 11th St Circle NW Hickory NC 28601

PAINTING, MARJORIE BERNICE (MRS. JOHN A. PAINTING), hotel exec.; b. Bklyn., Mar. 22, 1922; d. Daniel and Margaret (Traynor) O'Donnell; student Hunter Coll., 1943, Community Coll., 1967; m. John A. Painting, Jan. 20, 1951; 1 son, John. Tchr. parochial elementary schs., Bklyn., L.I., 1957-61, 65-67; owner-mgr. Hotel Phoenicin, N.Y.C., 1961-65; adminstrv. asst. Americana Hotel, 1967; exec. housekeeper, dir. William Sloane House YMCA, N.Y.C., 1968-74, dir. marketing and guest services, coordinator sr. citizen program, 1974—. Mem. Deborah Heart Assn., Cath. Daus. Am., Ancient Order Hiberians, Assn. Profl. Dirs. YMCA, Nat. Exec. Housekeepers Assn. Home: 635 Leonard St Brooklyn NY 11272 Office: 356 W 34th St New York City NY 10001

PAISLEY, MIRIAM ROSE JUNGBLUT (MRS. JOHN CALVIN PAISLEY), poet; b. Balt., Jan. 8, 1920; d. William Christian and Madeline Marie (Sommerfeld) Jungblut; grad. YWCA Bus. Coll., 1937; certificate Famous Writers Sch., 1973; m. John Calvin Paisley, Apr. 16, 1949; 1 son (by previous marriage), Ronald William Bounds. Sec., Johns Hopkins, Balt., 1947-51; with Balt. Urban Renewal and Housing Agy., 1960-62; with publs. dept. Balt. City Pub. Schs., 1962-68, with radio-TV dept., 1968-70; with Northwood-Appold United Meth. Ch., Balt., 1970-72; legal-med. sec. Lady Baltimore Office Services and Able Temporaries, Balt., 1972-74; sec. U. Md. Sch. Pharmacy, 1974—. Poems pub. in The Co-Ed Triangle Newsletter, 1947, 48, Sad Sad America, 1967, Gato mag., 1969, Patterson High Sch. Clipper, 1969, Clover Book of Poetry Collection of Verse, Vol. III, 1970, Dance of the Muse, anthology, 1970, Yearbook of Modern Poetry, 1971, The Oriole, Md. Poetry Soc., Vol. 1, 2, 4, 1971-73, The Best of Gato, 1971, Internat. Who's Who in Poetry Anthology, 1973, The Other Side of Poetry, 1974, others. Dir. Balt. Mt. Vernon Players, 1963-69, Religious Drama Group, 1970-73. Mem. Nat. Fedn. State Poetry Socs., Md. Poetry Soc. (rec. sec. 1972-74), Women's Internat. League for Peace and Freedom, Fellowship of Reconciliation, Deutsche Damen Chor, Clover Poetry Assn., Soc. Lit. Designates Washington. Methodist (worship and drama chmn. Council on Ministries). Author: The Literary Urge, 1966, rev. edit., 1969. Playwright: Saddlebag to Satellite, 1970; From Riches to Religion, 1972. Editor, contbr. Potpourrie of Poets' Expressions, 1974. Home: 1525 E 35th St Baltimore MD 21218

PAISNER, CLAIRE (MRS. JULIEN SERGE DOUBROVSKY), editor; b. Boston, Apr. 10, 1933; d. Philip and Hilda (Benjamin) Paisner; B.A. cum laude, Cornell, 1955; M.A., Harvard Sch. Internat. Relations, 1958; postgrad. Inst. de Sciences Politiques, Paris, 1962-66; m. Julien Serge Doubrovsky, June 17, 1956; children—Renee, Catherine. Instr. polit. sci. Mt. Holyoke Coll., South Hadley, Mass., 1961-62; exec. editor N.Y. Voice, N.Y.C., 1969—. Recipient Community award Ministerial Council on Race Relations, 1973; Journalism awards Nat. Newspaper Pubs. Assn., 1970, 71, 74. Mem. Nat. Assn. Media Women, Bus. and Profl. Women, Urban League, N.A.A.C.P. Home: 138-17 78th Rd New York City NY 11367 Office: 89-48 162d St New York City NY 11432

PAK-CHONG, GERTRUDE CHONG (MRS. PETER A. PAK-CHONG), educator; b. Honolulu; d. Meu Yuen and Abbie (Ho) Chong; B.Ed., U. Hawaii, 1941; M.A., Colo. State Coll., 1942; postgrad. U. Chgo., Gregg Bus. Coll., 1942-43; m. Peter A. Pak-Chong, June 25, 1949. Tchr., Ben Parker Sch., 1945-46; counselor Castle High Sch., 1950-58 (both Kaneohe, Hawaii); tchr. Aiea (Hawaii) Intermediate Sch., 1946-49, Kailua (Hawaii) Intermediate Sch., 1949-50; counselor Dole Intermediate Sch., Honolulu, 1959-60, Kalani High Sch., Honolulu, 1960—. Gen. partner Waimanalo Investments, Kailua, 1958—; dir. Delta Investments, Inc., Honolulu. Group leader Chinese Refugee Drive; Palolo Men's Home, 1962. Mem. Eastern Bus. Tchrs. Assn. (chmn. membership 1950-51), Nat., Hawaii, Oahu edn. assns., Am. Personnel and Guidance Assn. (chmn. membership Hawaii 1960-61), Hawaii Sch. Counselors Assn. (chmn. membership 1958, conf. 1959), Assn. Coll. Admissions Counselors, Asso. Chinese U. Women (legislative chmn., auditor, v.p. 1961, pres. 1962), Te Chih Sheh Alumni (v.p. 1960, pres. 1961, 71-72), Pi Lambda Theta (rec. sec. Hawaii Alumnae chpt. 1966-67, corr. sec. 1971-72). Home: 354 Uluniu St Kailua HI 96734

PALADIN, VIVIAN ALMA (MRS. JACK R. PALADIN), editor; b. Glasgow, Mont., Aug. 4, 1918; d. Hans G. and Clara (Haugen) Hilden; student U. Mont., 1939-41; m. Jack R. Paladin, Feb. 7, 1946; 1 dau., Elizabeth Ann (Mrs. R.A. Tobosa). Linotype operator Glasgow Courier weekly, 1935-39; linotype operator-reporter Cut Bank (Mont.) Pioneer Press weekly, 1941-44; local news editor Havre (Mont.) Daily News, 1946-50; linotype operator-proofreader Bergen Evening Record, Hackensack, N.J., 1950-53; with Mont. Hist. Soc., Helena, 1956—, editor Mont. mag. of Western History, 1966—. Mont. Post newsletter, 1963—. Mem. pub. information br. Gov.'s Commn. on Crime Control, 1972-73. Recipient 1st pl. award for publ. edited by a woman Nat. Assn. Press Women, 1965-72, Meritorious Achievement award Lewis and Clark Trail Heritage Found., 1972; Spl. award for publ. in field Western art, Nat. Cowboy Hall of Fame, 1971; named Woman of Achievement, Mont. Press Women, 1967. Mem. Am. Assn. State and Local History, Western History Assn. Lutheran. Author: Buffalo Bones to Sonic Boom, 1962, Rendezvous of Western Art, 1972, 73, 74. Home: 5550 N Montana Av Helena MT 59601 Office; 225 N Roberts St Helena MT 59601

PALAZZO, DORIS JUNE (MRS. GERALD LUBIN), dermatologist; b. New Castle, Pa., May 23, 1929; d. John Rudolph and Bernice Louise (Angeloni) Palazzo; B.A., U. So. Cal., 1950; M.D., Med. Coll. Pa., 1954; m. Gerald I. Lubin, Oct. 18, 1954; children—Judith, Theresa, Diana, Stephen. Intern Queen Angeles Hosp., Los Angeles, 1954-55; resident U. Cal. at Los Angeles, 1956-57, U. Soc. Cal. County Hosp., 1957-58, Long Beach VA Hosp., 1959-60; physician Los Angeles City Health Dept., 1961-63; dermatologist Los Angeles County Health Dept., 1961—; instr. U. So. Cal. Sch. Medicine, 1966—. Diplomate Am. Bd. Dermatology. Fellow Am., Met. dermatol. assns.; mem. Los Angeles Med. Assn. Home: 2743 Lake Hollywood Dr Los Angeles CA 90068 Office: Los Angeles County Health Services N Hollywood Dist 5300 Tujunga Blvd North Hollywood CA 91601

PALCIC, MARIE EUGENIE (MRS. A. PATRICK PALCIC), realtor; b. Nyack, N.Y., Sept. 7, 1935; d. Hugh Allen and Marion Frances (Zeck) Keahon; student Rosemont Coll., 1954-56; B.A., Fairleigh Dickinson U., 1960; m. A. Patrick Palcic, June 4, 1960; children—Patric M.K., Christopher, Hugh Anthony. Social worker, County Rockland, N.Y., 1960-61; exec. asst. polit. sci. research Hudson Inst., Harrison, N.Y., 1961-63; realtor Scott Realtors, New Paltz, N.Y., 1965—. Pres., Welcome Wagon Club, 1971-72; v.p. P.T.A., 1973-74; den mother Cub Scouts, 1971—; v.p. Am. Field Service, New Paltz, 1973-74. Mem. Am. Assn. U. Women. Roman Catholic. Club: U.S. Trotting Assn. Home: 500 S Ohioville Rd New Paltz NY 12561 Office: 157 Main St New Paltz NY 12561

PALEN, JENNIE MAY, author; b. Samsonville, N.Y.; d. Frank and Mary (Every) Palen; B.C.S. summa cum laude, N.Y. U., 1919. Report reviewer, prin. Haskins & Sells, C.P.A.'s, N.Y.C., 1918-49; accountant, editor, researcher, lectr. accountancy, 1950—; editor Prentice-Hall Publs., N.Y.C., 1963-66; instr. accountancy Baruch Coll., N.Y.C., 1957-62; author: Moon Over Manhattan (poems), 1949; Report Writing for Accountants, 1955; Good Morning, Sweet Prince (poems), 1957; Stranger, Let Me Speak (poems), 1964; Ency. Accounting Forms and Reports, vol. 1, 1964; poems pub. Sat. Eve. Post, N.Y. Herald Tribune, Good Housekeeping, Christian Sci. Monitor, Voices, Lyric, Laurel Rev., others; compiler, editor, contbr. Ency. Auditing Techniques, 1966; contbr. articles to profl. jours. Recipient Greenwood prize Poetry Soc. (London), 1968; others. C.P.A., N.Y. Mem. Am. Woman's Soc. C.P.A.'s (pres., 1946-47), Pen and Brush Club (pres. 1970-72), Bklyn. Poetry Circle (pres. 1959-65), Womens Press Club N.Y.C., Am. Inst. C.P.A.'s, N.Y. State Soc. C.P.A.'s, Poetry Soc. Am., Beta Gamma Sigma. Club: Query. Poetry editor Pen Woman, 1962-64. Home: 26 E 10th St New York City NY 10003

PALERMO, ELLEN ANNE, speech pathologist; b. Bklyn., Mar. 14, 1947; d. Augustine Joseph and Eleanor Frances (McManus) Palermo; B.S. in Edn., St. John's U., 1968; M.A., Coll. City N.Y., 1969; postgrad. Tchrs. Coll. Columbia, 1970—. Speech clinician Shield Inst. for Retarded Children, Flushing, N.Y., 1969-70, speech supr., 1970-72, dir. spl. hearing and lang. program Developmental Evaluation Clinic, 1974—; dir. speech and hearing program Assn. Children with Mentally Retarded Devel., Bklyn., 1972-74. Vol., Spl. Olympics, N.Y.C., 1970-71; mem. Queens Residential Care Com. for Mentally Retarded, N.Y.C., 1972-73. Mem. Council Exceptional Children, Am. Speech and Hearing Assn., Am. Assn. Mental Deficiency. Office: 144-61 Roosevelt Av Flushing NY 11354

PALIANI, MARY ANN, librarian; b. Rochester, N.Y., Jan. 31, 1935; d. Angelo and Madeline (Serpico) Paliani; B.A. in Biology, U. Rochester, 1956; M.L.S. in Library Sci., Syracuse U., 1960; postgrad. Justus Liebig U., 1964-65. Lab. technician U. Rochester Med. Center, Rochester, N.Y., 1956-58; librarian trainee Rochester Pub. Library, 1958-59, reference librarian, 1960-62; army library supr. U.S. Army Spl. Services Br., Giessen, Germany, 1962-64; ref. librarian N.Y. Pub. Library, N.Y.C., 1965-68; library supr. Rocky Flats div., Dow Chem., Golden, Colo., 1968-74, supr. information services, 1974—. Mem. Colo. Council Library Devel., 1973-75. Recipient N.Y. State Librarians Tng. grant, 1959. Mem. Spl. Libraries Assn. (chpt. pres. 1970-71) vice chmn., chmn. elect nuclear sci. div. 1973-75, Am. Soc. Information Sci. (sec.-treas. 1972), Soc. Tech. Communication (chpt. sec. 1973-74). Club: Colo. Mountain (Boulder). Home: 3250 O'Neal Circle #16B Boulder CO 80302 Office: PO Box 938 Golden CO 80401

PALIN, ROBERTA ANN (MRS. JOHN F. PALIN), psychologist; b. Kendallville, Ind., Sept. 19, 1930; d. Robert Leslie and Annie Janet (Davis) Isbell; B.A., Valparaiso U., 1969; M.A., Western Mich. U., 1971; m. John F. Palin, June 10, 1951; children—Daniel, Renee. Psychologist Grand Rapids (Mich.) pub. schs., 1972-73; psychol. cons. Indpls. pub. schs., 1973-74. Prohibition officer and cons. St. Joseph County Juvenile Ct., South Bend, Ind., 1971-72. Mem. Am., Mich. psychol. assns., Bromeliad Soc., Am. Orchid Soc. Home: 7048 East 65th St Indianapolis IN 46256

PALLADINO, MADALINE, lawyer; b. Allentown, Pa., May 5, 1924; d. Joseph and Angelina (Trentalange) Palladino; A.B., U. Pa., 1944; J.D., Columbia, 1947. Admitted to N.Y. bar, 1948, Pa. bar, 1949, since practiced in Allentown; asst. solicitor City of Allentown, 1952-56; solicitor Lehigh County Recorder of Deeds, 1952; solicitor Lehigh County Register of Wills, 1956-59, 65—. Chmn. Lehigh County chpt. A.R.C., 1956-58; mem. exec. com. Lehigh Valley Community Chest, 1956-58; asst. dist. atty., Lehigh County, 1960-64; exec. com. Lehigh Valley Guidance Clinic; bd. dirs. Civic Little Theatre Allentown, YWCA, Baum Art Sch.; pres. Girls Club Allentown, 1967-69. Mem. exec. com. Lehigh County Rep. Com.; pres. Lehigh County Council Rep. Women, 1961-63; mem. Young Reps. of Lehigh County. Bd. assos. Muhlenberg Coll., treas., 1973—; adv. bd. Allentown campus Pa. State U., pres., 1972—. Mem. Am. Assn. U. Women (pres. 1958-60), Am., Pa. (sec. treas. Conf. County Legal Jour. Officers 1961-68, chmn. 1970-72, chmn. pub. relations com.), Lehigh County (sec.-treas.) bar assns., Alumni Assn. Columbia, U. Pa. Alumnae Assn. Bus. and Profl. Women's Club, Phi Beta Kappa. Clubs: Quota (pres. Allentown, 1953-54), Woman's (Allentown). Home: 226 N 27th St Allentown PA 18104 Office: Commonwealth Bldg Allentown PA 18101

PALLEN, LUCILE CALVERT (MRS. VINCENT PALLEN), educator; b. Columbus, Ind.; d. Truman B. and Luna B. (Owen) Calvert; student Ball State Tchrs. Coll.; B.A., Lake Forest Coll., 1927; M.A., Northwestern U., 1929; postgrad. Columbia, 1945-46; m. Vincent Pallen, July 7, 1945. Asso. prof. speech, dir. univ. theatre DePauw U., Greencastle, Ind., 1929-41; prof. speech, dir. univ. theatre Butler U., Indpls., 1941-45; prof. speech, radio Good Council Coll., White Plains, N.Y., 1946-47; voice, diction instr. N.Y. U., N.Y.C., 1948-51; instr. speech Union Theol. Sem., N.Y.C., 1956-58; asso. prof. speech, C.W. Post Coll. of L.I. U., Bklyn., 1960—, dir. Reading Theatre, 1961—. Lectr. on theatre; tour as platform artist; profl. actress stage, screen, TV. Mem. Am. Assn. Univ. Profs., Speech Communication Assn., Nat. Collegiate Players, Am. Ednl. Theatre Assn., Actors' Equity Assn., Screen Actors Guild, Am. Fed. TV and Radio Artists, Am. Nat. Theatre Acad., Phi Beta, Gamma Phi Beta. Mem. Christian Ch. Address: 1 Christopher St New York City NY 10014

PALLESEN, LORRAINE LAVON SYSEL (MRS. CHARLES M. PALLESEN, JR.), civic worker; b. Crete, Neb., July 23, 1935; d. Edward and Marie H. (Soukup) Sysel; R.N., St. Elizabeth Sch. Nursing, 1956; A.B., Doane Coll., 1959; M.A., U. Neb., 1962, postgrad. 1963-69; m. Charles M. Pallesen, Jr., June 30, 1963; children—Michael, Edward. Med., surg. instr. St. Elizabeth Sch. Nursing, Lincoln, Neb., 1960-61; part-time instr. ednl. psychology U. Neb. at Lincoln, 1962-63, part-time instr. history, philosophy, 1965-69; instr. psychology dept. Towson State Coll., Balt., 1963-65. Mem. Mayor's Com. on Urban Design, Lincoln, 1971-73; bd. dirs. Citizens for Environmental Improvement, Lincoln, 1970-72; bd. dirs. Jr. League of Lincoln, 1972-74, chmn. environmental panorama, 1971-72; chmn. Community Research, 1972-73, corr. sec. 1973-74, exec. com. 1973-74, community edn. chmn., 1974-75; mem. bd. Prescott Sch. P.T.A., 1973-75, projects co-chmn., 1973-74; co-chmn. headdress parade 1973-74. Bd. dirs. Lincoln Symphony Guild, 1971—, also Symphony Headdress Ball, 1973; bd. dirs. Lincoln Playhouse Guild, 1973—. Mem. Am. Assn. Univ. Women (bd. dirs. 1970-71, pres. 1972-73), Am. Psychol. Assn., Nat. Soc. for the Study of Edn., Cardinal Key, Pi Lambda Theta, Alpha Psi Omega, Tau Beta Sigma, Omega Psi Theta (alumni pres. 1972-73). Conglist. (bd. deaconesses 1972-75). Rotary Ann (pres. 1974-75). Address: 2727 Royal Court Lincoln NE 68502

PALLOTTA, JOHANNA ANTOINETTE (MRS. MICHAEL J. STEPHEN), physician; b. Boston, May 7, 1937; d. John and Antoinette (Lanni) Pallotta; B.S. in Chemistry magna cum laude, Boston Coll., 1958; M.D., N.Y. Med. Coll., 1962; m. Michael J. Stephen, Aug. 13, 1966; children—Jacqueline, Antonia, Elizabeth, Michael John. Intern, St. Elizabeth's Hosp., Boston, 1962-63; resident internal medicine N.Y. Med. Coll., Met. Hosp. Med. Centers, 1963-64, Bronx VA. Hosp., 1964-66; fellow endocrinology Yale Med. Sch., 1966-67; instr. internal medicine Harvard, 1967-70, asst. prof., 1970—; asst. in medicine Beth Israel Hosp., Boston, 1967-69, asso., 1969-71, asst. physician, 1971—, dir. endocrinology clinic, 1967—; dir. Radioimmunoassay Lab., 1971—. Vol. Cath. Med. Mission Bd., Africa, 1971; tutor med. scis. Harvard Med. Sch., 1972. Diplomate Am. Bd. Internal Medicine. Fellow A.C.P., mem. New Eng. Diabetes Soc., Nat. Orgn. for Women, Alpha Omega Alpha. Home: 35 Robinson St Cambridge MA 02138 Office: 330 Brookline Av Boston MA 02215

PALM, LEAH, occupational therapist; b. Everett, Mass., Apr. 23, 1938; d. Joseph and Christine Josephine (Boudreau) Palm; student Brown-Mackie Sch. Bus., Salina, Kan., 1956-57; B.S., U. Kan., 1966; occupational therapy clin. affiliation certificate Walter Reed Army Med. Center, 1966; M.A., Our Lady of Lake Coll., 1973. Commd. 2d lt. U.S. Army, 1965, advanced through grades to capt., 1967; staff therapist Brooke Army Med. Center, Ft. Sam Houston, 1966-68; asst. clinic chief Madigan Army Med. Center, Tacoma, 1968-70, Inst. Surg. Research, Ft. Sam Houston, Tex., 1970-72; personnel counselor Health Services Command, Army Med. Specialist Corps, Ft. Sheridan, Ill., 1973—. Mem. Am. Occupational Therapy Assn., Am. Burn Assn., Council for Exceptional Children, Alumni Assn. U. Kan. Home: 32 Washington Blvd Mundelein IL 60060 Office: AMEDD Procurement Bldg 142 Fort Sheridan IL 60037

PALM, NANCY DALE (MRS. WILLIAM M. PALM), polit. worker; b. Nashville, Apr. 14, 1921; d. Dillard Young and Mary (Bishop) Dale; B.A., Vanderbilt U., 1942; m. William M. Palm, July 4, 1942. Pub. relations sec. Harris County Med. Soc., Houston, 1951-58. Mem. Houston Civic Music Assn., 1948-73. Active numerous Republican polit. activities, 1952—, del. nat. conv., 1972, chmn. Harris County Rep. party, 1968—. Named One of Ten Outstanding Women in Tex. Politics, 1972. Mem. Am. Assn. U. Women (v.p. Houston chpt. 1950-51), Internat. Relations Study Group. Home: 612 E Friar Tuck Houston TX 77024 Office: 2626 Westheimer Houston TX 77006

PALM, NANCY J., real estate mgmt. co. exec.; b. McKeesport, Pa., Dec. 3, 1938; d. Walter Vaughn and Nellie Jane (Sullivan) Leech; student Mt. San Antonio Coll., 1969-70; div.; 1 dau., Tiffany Lane. Corporate sec. U.S. Filter Corp., Newport Beach, Cal., 1965-71; pres. Jaquar Research Corp., Los Angeles, 1971—; cons. in field. Author: Resident Managers Handbook. Home: 1818 Thayer Av Apt 207 Los Angeles CA 90024 Office: 12330 Santa Monica Blvd Los Angeles CA 90025

PALM, ROSE, psychologist; b. Emmen, Holland, Apr. 17, 1912; d. Karel Palm and Selma J. (Windmuller) Palm; A.B., Gymnasium, Kampen, Holland, 1930; M.A., U. Amsterdam, 1934, Ph.D., 1938. Chief psychologist State Hosp., Apeldoorn, Holland, 1938-40; cons. psychologist Apeldoorn, Child Guidance Clinic, 1940-41; lectr. Montessori Tchrs. Tng. Coll., Amsterdam, Holland, 1941-42; psychologist N.Y. State Tng. Sch. for Boys. Warwick, N.Y., 1944-45, Jewish Bd. of Guardians, N.Y.C., 1945-47; research psychologist Columbia U. and Josiah Macy Found., 1947-48; sr. research psychologist N.Y. State Dept. of Mental Hygiene, 1948-53; instr. Hunter Coll., 1949-51; psychol. cons. Family Service Community Service Soc., N.Y.C., 1951-53; lectr. L.I. U., 1951-54; bd. dirs., faculty mem. Inst. Psychoanalytic Tng. and Research, 1961-65; pvt. practice, 1966—. Panel Psychologist N.Y. State Dept. Edn., 1967—, vocational rehab. div., 1966—. Certified N.Y. State Dept. Edn.; diplomate Am. Bd. Examiners in Clinic Psychology. Fellow Am. Psychol. Assn.; mem. N.Y. State Psychol. Assn. (exec. bd. 1960-63), Internat. Platform Assn. Mem. editorial staff Excerpta Medica. Holland, 1956—. Address: 263 West End Av New York City NY 10023 Office: 133 E 73d St New York City NY 10021

PALMER, AGNES MAE HIGH (MRS. DANIEL DAVID PALMER), sculptress, chiropractor, clubwoman; b. Lancaster, Pa.; d. David and Elizabeth (Futerer) High; D.C., Palmer Coll., 1938; m. Daniel David Palmer, June 27, 1943; children—Bonnie Joan (Mrs. Thomas D. McCloskey, Jr.), Jenny Wren (Mrs. Kermit S. Sutton II), Vickie Anne. Private practice as chiropractic dr., West Chester, Pa., 1938-43. Sculptress, since 1967—; important works include Portraits Robert Kennedy, D.D. Palmer, I and II, Bonnie, Jenny, Vickie, Philip D. Adler. Singer popular music and opera 1938—. Mem. St. Luke's Hosp. Aux., Davenport, Naples (Fla.) Community Hosp. Mem. Internat. Chiropracters Assn., Nat. (asso.), State duplicate bridge leagues, Daus. of Nile, Tri-City Symphony Assn., Broadway Theatre League, League Women Voters, Ia. Fedn. Music Clubs, Nat. Fedn. Music (life), Sigma Phi Chi. Mem. Order Eastern Star. Clubs: Saint Katherine's Mothers (pres.), Town (Davenport), Lend-A-Hand,

Quota, Music Students, Etude, Davenport, Davenport Country, Union League (Chgo.), Naples Music, Naples Garden, Eldorado Country, Royal Poinciana Golf, Rock Island Arsenal Golf, Davenport Country, Crow Creek Country. Home: 5 Forest Rd Davenport IA 52803

PALMER, BEVERLY BLAZEY, educator, psychologist; b. Cleve., Nov. 22, 1945; d. Lawrence Edwin and Mildred Marie (Schlecht) Blazey; B.A. in Psychology, U. Mich., 1966; M.A. in Counseling, Ohio State U., 1969, Ph.D., 1972; m. Richard Cletus Palmer, June 24, 1967. Research asst. psychiatry Ohio State U., 1966-68; high sch. tchr. Southwestern city schs., Grove City, O., 1967-69; adminstrv. asso. Ohio State U., 1969-70; research psychologist medicine Nat. Center Health Services Research and Devel., 1971-74; counseling adminstr. Harbor Free Clinic, San Pedro, Cal., 1971-73; asst. prof. clin. psychology Small Coll., Cal. State Coll., Dominguez Hills, 1973—. Precinct dir. 4th City campaign Palos Verdes Peninsula, 1973. Recipient proclamation Los Angeles County Bd. Suprs., 1972; Beautiful Activist award Germaine Monteil and the Broadway, 1972. Mem. Am. Psychol. Assn., Am. Personnel and Guidance Assn., Assn. Counselor Edn. and Supervision, Assn. Humanistic Psychology, Nat. Orgn. Women. Contbr. articles to profl. jours. Home: 6736 Los Verdes Dr Palos Verdes Peninsula CA 90274 Office: 1000 E Victoria St Dominguez Hills CA 90747

PALMER, CATHERINE GARDELLA (MRS. ROBERT MEAD PALMER), educator; b. N.Y.C., Apr. 28, 1924; d. Alfred and Eva (Cella) Gardella; A.B., Hunter Coll., 1947; M.A., Smith Coll., 1949; Ph.D., Ind. U., 1953; m. Robert Mead Palmer, May 29, 1954; children—Christopher, Eve, Ann. Research asst. Smith Coll., 1949; research asso. Ind. U., 1953-55, instr., 1955-60, asst. prof., 1960-65, asso. prof., 1965-70, prof., 1970—. Mem. A.A.A.S., Genetics Soc. Am., Am. Soc. for Human Genetics, Am. Soc. for Cell Biology, Tissue Culture Assn., Genetics Soc. Can., Sigma Xi. Home: 7801 Holly Creek Lane Indianapolis IN 42640

PALMER, DOROTHY ANN SMARDACK (MRS. H. PHILLIP PALMER), coll. adminstr.; b. Chgo., Jan. 12, 1941; d. Bruno Alexander and Lena (Warnell) Smardack; B.A., Grinnell Coll., 1962, secondary certificate, 1965; m. H. Phillip Palmer, Aug. 4, 1963; children—Jennifer Ann, Daphne Anne. Secondary tchr. Malosa Secondary Sch., Malawi, Central Africa, 1962-63, Grinnell, Ia., 1968; alumni exec. sec. Grinnell Coll., 1971—. Pres., Youth Council, Grinnell, 1969-72; mem. Recreation Commn., Grinnell, 1971-73. Mem. Am. Alumni Council, P.E.O. (chmn. Ia. scholarship com. 1972-73), Grinnell Coll. Alumni Assn. (sec. bd. dirs. 1967-71). Mortar Bd. Democrat. Episcopalian (mem. Ia. diocesan campus ministry com. 1972—).

PALMER, DOROTHY GRACE SIMPSON (MRS. JOHN ALLEN PALMER), psychiat. social worker; b. Lansing, Mich., Sept. 30, 1914; d. John Milton and Grace (Fownes) Simpson; student Denison U., 1932-34; A.B., Kalamazoo Coll., 1936; M.S.W., George Warren Brown Sch. Social Work, Washington U., 1938; m. John Allen Palmer, June 8, 1940; children—John Allen, David Simpson, William Brewster. Caseworker Kalamazoo Emergency Relief, 1936, Family Soc., Phila., 1938-51, 43; exec. sec. Civic League, Kalamazoo, 1943-44; psychiat. social worker Social Service Dept. N.J. State Hosp., Greystone Park, 1959-72, asst. social work supr.; chief psychiat. social worker Morristown (N.J.) Meml. Hosp., 1972—. Field practice instr. Grad. Sch. Social Work, Rutgers U., New Brunswick, N.J., 1962-64; field instr. Grad. Sch. Social Work, Fordham U., N.Y.C., 1973—. Mem. Nat. Assn. Social Workers, Acad. Certified Social Workers, Kalamazoo Coll. Nat. Alumni Assn. (sec.-treas. 1956), Chi Omega. Episcopalian. Home: 15 N Star Dr Morristown NJ 07960 Office: Morristown Meml Hosp Morristown NJ 07960

PALMER, ELIZABETH WOOD (MRS. THEODORE ALVIN PALMER), lawyer; b. San Bernardino, Cal., May 12, 1910; d. George McClaren and Lena Octavia (Stewart) W.; A.B., U. Cal. at Los Angeles, 1932; J.D., U. Cal. at Berkeley, 1935; m. Theodore Alvin Palmer, Dec. 31, 1938; children—Theodore Andrew, Susan Elizabeth (Mrs. John Gary Brady). Admitted to Cal. bar, 1935; with trust dept. Bank of Am., Los Angeles, 1936-37; with legal dept. Metro-Goldwyn-Mayer, Los Angeles, 1937-39; with U.S. Dept. Justice, Los Angeles, 1942-43; dep. atty. gen. State of Cal., San Francisco, 1943-71, sr. asst. atty. gen., 1971—. Named Woman of Achievement, San Francisco Bus. and Profl. Women, 1964. Mem. State Bar Cal. (mem. adminstrn. justice com. 1973—), Assn. Pub. Welfare Attys. (dir. Western region 1970-73), San Francisco Bar Assn., Queen's Bench, Union Sq. Bus. and Profl. Women (pres. 1966-67), Sigma Kappa Alumnae (scholarship adviser 1950-56). Clubs: Ms. (San Francisco); Montclair Women's (pres. 1953-54) (Oakland, Cal.). Home: 13850 Skyline Blvd Oakland CA 94619 Office: State Bldg San Francisco CA 94102

PALMER, EMMA ANN BENEDETTO (MRS. HAROLD CHARLEY PALMER), educator; b. Pittsburg, Kan., July 25, 1910; d. John Baptista and Maria (Rodes) Benedetto; B.S., Pittsburg State Coll., 1932, postgrad., 1932; M.S., Kan. U., 1958; postgrad. Ia. U., 1934, U. S.D., 1960; m. Harold Charley Palmer, Aug. 11, 1935; children—Harold C., Cecilia Maria (Mrs. Lawrence Muff). Health supr., high sch. phys. edn. tchr. Cherryvale Pub. Schs., 1932-35; tchr. health and phys. edn. Chanute (Kan.) Pub. Schs., 1942-52; mem. faculty Benedictine Coll., Atchison, 1953—, prof. health and phys. edn., 1958—, chmn. dept., 1954—, mem. governing bd. Camp dir., instr. Girl Scouts U.S., Chanute, summers, 1945—; instr., trainer first aid A.R.C., 1940—; trainer water safety Atchison (Kan.) area, 1965—. Named Outstanding Kan. Phys. Edn. Tchr. Kan. Assn. for Health and Phys. Edn., 1969. Mem. A.A.H.P.E.R., N.E.A., Nat., Central assns. phys. edn. coll. women, Internat. Assn. Health and Phys. Edn., Am. Assn. U. Women, Kan. Assn. Health, Phys. Edn. and Recreation (regional rep. 1965-69), Bus. and Profl. Club, Alumni Assn. Kan. U., P.E.O., Delta Kappa Gamma (pres. 1968, 70), Kappa Delta Pi, Sigma Sigma Sigma. Republican. Methodist (youth dir., religious tchr., bd. dirs.). Clubs: Zonta International (pres. 1958-60), Bellevue Country. Home: 1704 N 2d St Atchison KS 66002

PALMER, HELEN HANSSEN (MRS. ARTHUR MACDONALD PALMER), librarian; b. New Orleans, June 19, 1911; d. Soren Christian and Petra (Olsen) Hanssen; B.A., La. State U., 1956, M.A., 1960, M.S., 1961; m. Arthur Macdonald Palmer, June 19, 1934; 1 dau., Patricia Jean (Mrs. Wade Noland Thomas). Librarian, La. State U., Baton Rouge, 1961—, head sci. div., 1961—. Author: (with Dyson) American Drama Criticism, 1967, European Drama Criticism, 1968, English Novel Explication, 1973. Home: 3753 Hyacinth Av Baton Rouge LA 70808

PALMER, IRENE MARY SABELBERG, nurse; b. Franklin, N.J., May 28, 1923; d. John Joseph and May (Heiser) Sabelberg; B.S., N.J. Tchrs. Coll., 1945; M.A., N.Y. U., 1951, Ph.D., 1963. Operating room nurse Jersey City Med. Center, 1945; clin. instr. Paterson (N.J.) Gen. Hosp., 1946-47; ednl. dir. Overlook Hosp., Summit, N.J., 1948-49, Lynn Hosp., Mass., 1950-51, Cooper Hosp., Camden, N.J., 1951-53, Glenn Dale Hosp., Md., 1956; dir. nursing service and edn. Glenn Dale Hosp., Md., 1956-61; asso. clin. prof. nursing Georgetown U., Washington, 1960-61; asso. chief Nursing Service for Research, VA Hosp., San Francisco, 1963-64; research nurse cons. Dept. Health, Edn. and Welfare, San Francisco, 1964-66; asst. dean, asso. prof. Sch. Nursing, U. Colo., Denver, 1966-68; dean, prof. Sch. Nursing, Boston U., 1968—. Served to capt. Nurse Corps, AUS, 1953-56. Mem. Am., Colo. (dir. 1967-69), Mass. (dist. dir., mem. legislative com.) nurses assns., Nat. League Nursing, Am. Assn. Colls. Nursing (treas.), Sigma Theta Tau, Pi Lamba Theta. Contbr. articles in field to profl. jours. Home: 7 Knight Rd Framingham MA 01701 Office: 635 Commonwealth Av Boston MA 02215

PALMER, JUDY, pediatrician; b. Denver, Apr. 1, 1942; d. Raymond E. and Ruth J. (Fengel) Palmer; student Sierra Coll., 1961-62, U. Cal. at Davis, 1962-65; B.S., U. Cal. at San Francisco, 1967, M.D., 1969. Intern St. Christopher's Hosp., Phila., 1969-70, resident, 1970-71, fellow pediatric pulmonary and infectious disease, 1971-73; instr. pediatrics Temple U., Phila., 1973; asso. prof. Hahnemann Med. Coll., 1974—. Mem. Sierra Club. Home: 932 Rumsey St Cody WY 82414 Office: Hahnemann Med Coll Philadelphia PA 19102

PALMER, LIMA JUSTINE HOWARD (MRS. HAROLD BROOKS PALMER), county ofcl.; b. Paris, Tenn., Feb. 20, 1923; d. Billie Edward and Cordia Mai (Gray) Howard; grad. exec. sec. Toler's Bus. Coll., 1949; m. Harold Brooks Palmer, Nov. 25, 1951 (dec. Oct. 1973); children—Harriet, Morna, Michael. Treas. Afro-Am. Co., Paris, 1967; magistrate County Ct. of Henry County, 1972—. Mem. Ambulance Bd. Henry County, 1973; mem. Sanitation Bd. Henry County, 1972-74; mem. Beer Bd. Henry County, 1972—; Dem. youth adviser, 1972-73. Served with WAC, 1942-46. Mem. N.A.A.C.P. (county pres. 1968-69), Tenn. Black Elected Ofcls. and Apptd. Ofcls. (chmn. steering com. 1973-74). Methodist. Home: 403 Rison St Paris TN 38242

PALMER, MARGARET EVANGELINE WILLIS (MRS. WILLIAM J. PALMER), civic and religious edn. worker; b. Marysville, Cal.; d. Elbridge Root and Mary (Hyde) Willis; student U. So. Cal., 1909-10, Cal. State Normal Sch., San Francisco, 1910-12; m. William J. Palmer, July 22, 1915; children—John Willis (dec.), Ruth Elizabeth (Mrs. Howard B. Douglas), William Stanley. Tchr., Cal. Pub. Schs., 1912-15. Pres., Women's Guild kindred socs. Meth. Ch., intermittently 1929-65; sec. Cancer Research Support Group, U. Cal., Los Angeles, 1955-63; sec. Women's Aux. Meth. Hosp., Los Angeles, 1955-63; mem. Operation Moral Upgrade. Mem. Entre Nous Alumnae U. So. Cal. (pres. 1956—), P.E.O. (chpt. sec. 1960), Pres.'s Circle (U. So. Cal.), Sierra Club, Gen. Alumni U. So. Cal., Pi Beta Phi. Republican. Methodist. Clubs: Westwood Hills Women's (Los Angeles), Mother's (Pi Beta Phi, pres. 1941—), Westwood Hills Camera (hon. life). Home: 1850 Alice St Oakland CA 94612

PALMER, MARILYN RUSHING (MRS. ELIGE G. PALMER), bank auditor; b. Troy, Ala., Dec. 11, 1926; d. Joseph Ernest and Elizabeth (Rushton) Rushing; student LaSalle Extension U., 1970; m. Elige G. Palmer, June 8, 1946; children—Ann (Mrs. James Curtis Byrd), Jerry Wayne. With Comml. Bank, Andalusia, Ala., 1944—, now internal auditor. Baptist. Club: Pilot (pres.). Home: 505 Montezuma St Andalusia AL 36420 Office: 200 Church St Drawer 1298 Andalusia AL 36420

PALMER, MARY MAXINE, clergywoman; b. Harrison, Ark., Jan. 8, 1926; d. Earl and Dorothy (Speer) Jones; A.B., Tex. Christian U., 1947, M.A., 1952; m. Ralph Thomas Palmer, Aug. 30, 1948; children—Angella Marie, Carol Celeste. Ordained to ministry Christian Ch., 1947; minister Christian edn. St. Charles Av. Christian Ch., New Orleans, 1947-48; missionary Christian Chs., also Disciples of Christ in Christian edn., churchmanship, No. Honshu, Japan, 1952-56; field work, tchr., writer, lectr. United Christian Missionary Soc., Indpls., 1956-70; mem. Tex. com. World Outreach, 1972—; mem. Hi-Plains area bd. Christian Ch. in Tex., 1973—; cons. Hi-plains area Christian Women's Fellowship. Home: 2404 Comanche Pampa TX 79065 Office: 1633 N Nelson Pampa TX 79065

PALMER, NANCIE BROWN (MRS. HAROLD C. PALMER), civic worker; b. Milw., Oct. 12, 1917; d. Victor Lawrence and Harriet (Zens) Brown; ed. Vassar Coll., 1935-37; m. Thomas S. Nichols, Nov. 4, 1939; 1 son, Thomas S., Jr.; m. 2d, George J. Stewart, July 9, 1947; children—George James, Jr., Victor E., Caroline H.; m. 3d, Harold C. Palmer, July 10, 1974. Pres. Day Care Council N.Y., Inc., N.Y.C., 1960-70, chmn. bd., 1970—. Vol. many bds. including N.Y. Jr. League, Travelers Aid-Internat. Social Services, Am. Br. and Day Care and Child Devel. Council Am.; sec. Community Council Greater N.Y.; vice chmn. Day Care Alliance, Nat. Council Orgns. for Children and Youth; cons. day care throughout N.Y. and elsewhere. Mem. adv. com. N.Y.C. Commr. Social Service Mayor's Early Childhood Devel. Task Force, 1969; chmn. State Adv. Com. Day Care, 1970-73; chmn. Family Day Care Careers Program, 1966-68, Riverdale Childrens Assn., 1955-72; trustee Ednl. Alliance, N.Y.C., 1966; pres. State Welfare Conf., 1973; state del. White House Conf. Children, 1960, 70; mem. N.Y.C. Council Against Poverty, 1965-67. Recipient Sustaining Mems. award N.Y. Jr. League, 1970. Author: A Handbook for Citizens Concerned with Day Care Programs, 1971. Contbr. articles to profl. jours. Home: 79 E 79th St New York City NY 10021 Office: 205 E 42d St New York City NY 10017

PALMER, PAIGE (MRS. ARTHUR FREEMAN), television personality; b. Akron, O., Jan. 17; d. Paul and Katharine (Grisbraun) Rohrer; degree in Phys. Edn., U. Akron, postgrad. in Fashion and Home Econs.; m. Arthur Freeman, Apr. 18, 1964; children—Richard Rohrer Roush, Paul Allen Roush, Perry Nelson Brown. Asst. dir. Richard Hudnut Success Sch., N.Y.C., 1942; dir. teen cosmetic line Tone, Helena Rubenstein, 1943; dir. retail promotion Cohn-Hall-Marx, N.Y.C., 1944; mng. dir. Dorothy Ferrier Sch. Fashion and Modeling, Beverly Hills, Cal., San Francisco, Los Angeles, San Diego, 1946, also fgn. fashion editor Californian Mag., 1946; presented 1st woman's program on fashions and fabric, exptl. television N.Y.C., 1947; originator 1st women's television program WEWS, Cleve., 1948—, syndicated columnist Fashion'n Figure, 1970—; travel editor Traveling Times, Healthways Mag. Digest, The Reporter, Akron. Bd. dirs. Goodwill Industries, Cleve. Recipient numerous awards, including FRANY Fashion award, Nat. Golden Slipper award, A.F.T.R.A. award, Best of Industry award Cleve. Press Club, Patroness of Arts award Cleve. Artists, Nat. Arthritis and Rheumatism Found. award, March of Dimes award, Nat. Heart Assn. award, Meritorious Service award Goodwill Industries, Service award Salvation Army; mentioned in Congl. Record for work in phys. fitness; decorated Lion medal Premier Nickolai Bulganin, 1957, Confrerie des Compagnons de Bordeaux, Confrerie du Diament Noire et du Vin de Cahors, Confrerie de St. Vincent, French govt, 1970. Mem. Am. Women in Radio and TV (pres. Western Res. chpt. 1968—), Overseas Press Club, Fashion Group, Acad. TV Arts and Scis., Cleve. Press Club. Author: Fitness Is A Family Affair; Woman and Her Concerns for Being a Woman; A Pain in the Back and How To Get Rid of It. Home: 2750 N Revere Rd Bath OH 44210 Office: WEWS-TV 3001 Euclid Av Cleveland OH 44115

PALMER, PATRICIA JANE, manuscripts librarian; b. Chgo., July 16, 1936; d. Rex Bishop and Catharine (Baum) Palmer; student Pomona Coll., 1954-56;; B.A., U. Wash., 1958; postgrad. George Washington U., 1962. Med. sec. for drs., Seattle, 1960-61; archives asst. Library of Congress, 1961-63, archivist, 1963; asst. manuscripts librarian Stanford Libraries, 1963-67, manuscripts librarian, 1967—. Mem. Soc. Am. Archivists, Soc. Cal. Archivists (ad hoc organizing com. 1971, temporary steering com. 1971-72, chmn. by-laws com. 1971-72), Cal. Library Assn., Manuscripts Soc., Alpha Gamma Delta. Author: Contract and Finance Company, 1969, Frederick Steele, Forgotten General, 1971. Editor microfilm edit. David Starr Jordan Papers, 1969. Office: Stanford U Libraries Stanford CA 94305

PALMER, RUTH KATHRYN PRETTY (MRS. RICHARD M. PALMER), civic worker; b. St. Louis, Apr. 22, 1909; d. Royden Keith and Sophia Dorothea (Risch) Pretty; B.A., U. Ill., 1930; jr. high teaching certificate Chgo. Tchrs. Coll., 1931; m. Richard M. Palmer, July 29, 1933; children—Patricia P., Richard Keith. Caseworker Unemployment Relief, 1931-32; tchr., Chgo. Sch. System, 1932-35. Chmn. City Panhellenics Com., Nat. Pahnellenic Conf., 1969—. Bd. dirs. Kenilworth United Fund, 1958-60. Mem. Alpha Delta Pi (Nat. Panhellenic Conf. del. 1965-73), Alpha Lambda Delta. Clubs: Westmoreland Country (Wilmette, Ill.); Neighbors, Clippers, Garden Kenilworth (Ill.). Home: Route 2 Green Hills Mill Spring NC 28756

PALSER, BARBARA F(RANCES), educator; b. Worcester, Mass., June 2, 1916; d. George Norman and Cora (Munson) Palser; B.A., Mt. Holyoke Coll., 1938; M.A., 1940; Ph.D., U. Chgo., 1942. Instr. botany U. Chgo., 1942-45, asst. prof., 1945-51, asso. prof., 1951-60, prof., 1960-65; asso. prof. Rutgers U., 1965-66, prof., 1966—, faculty fellow 1969-70; vis. prof. Duke, 1962. Erskine Fellow U. Canterbury, Christchurch, New Zealand, 1969. Fellow A.A.A.S.; mem. Bot. Soc. Am. (sec. 1970—), Internat. Soc. Plant Morphologists, Torrey Bot. Club (pres. 1968), N.J. Acad. Sci., Wilderness Soc., Am. Forestry Assn., Nat. Parks Assn., Am. Inst. Biol. Scis., Phi Beta Kappa, Sigma Xi. Asso. editor Bot. Gazette, 1950-59, editor, 1960-65. Bot. adviser Ency. Brit., 1957-59. Contbr. articles to profl. jours. Home: 18 Charlotte Dr Somerville NJ 08876 Office: Rutgers U New Brunswick NJ 08903

PALUSZNY, MARIA JANINA (MRS. ANTONI PALUSZNY), child psychiatrist; b. Warsaw, Poland, Apr. 16, 1939; d. Joseph and Janina (Gallot) Domaszewski; A.B., Wayne State U., 1960; M.D., U. Mich., 1962; m. Antoni Paluszny, July 16, 1960; children—Mark, Tadeus and Kristina (twins). Intern St. Joseph's Mercy Hosp., Ann Arbor, Mich., 1962-63; resident Neuropsychiat. Inst., Ann Arbor, 1963-65; resident Children's Psychiat. Hosp., Ann Arbor, 1965-67, resident V, instr., 1967-68, asst. dir. out patient service 1968-73; program dir. for child psychiatry Inst. for Study of Mental Retardation and Related Disabilities, U. Mich. at Ann Arbor, 1973—; instr. dept. psychiatry, 1968-71, asst. prof., 1971—; cons. Downriver Child Guidance Clinic, Dearborn, Vocational Rehab. Center, Wyandotte. Diplomate Am. Bd. Psychiatry and Neurology, also splty. in child psychiatry. Fellow Am. Acad. Child Psychiatry; mem. Am. Psychiat. Assn., Mich., Washtenaw County med. socs. Contbr. articles to profl. pubs. Home: 939 Forest Rd Ann Arbor MI 48105 Office: 130 S 1st St Ann Arbor MI 48108

PAMILLA, JEANNE ROSE, orthopedic surgeon; b. N.Y.C., Apr. 2, 1943; d. Salvatore Charles and Josephine Serafina (Di Gregorio) Pamilla; B.S., St. John's U., 1964; M.D. (Alpha Omega Alpha fellow), Woman's Med. Coll. Pa., 1968. Intern, Lenox Hill Hosp., N.Y.C., 1968-69, gen. surg. resident, 1969-70, orthopaedic surg. resident, 1970-73; fellow in pediatric orthopedics and cerebral palsy Hosp. for Spl. Surgery, Cornell Med. Center, N.Y.C., 1973-74, sr. fellow, 1974-75; instr. surgery Cornell Med. Sch., 1973—. Recipient Physician's Recognition award, 1971, 73. Mem. Am. Med. Women's Assn., Am. Acad. Cerebral Palsy, Alumnae Assn. Woman's Med. Coll. Pa. Editor: IATRIAN, yearbook Woman's Med. Coll. Pa., 1968. Home: 77-17 62d St Glendale NY 11227 Office: Hosp Special Surgery 535 E 70th St New York City NY 10021

PANAJOTOVIC, ELENA MARIA KAHN (MRS. ILIJA PANAJOTOVIC), film prodn. co. exec.; b. Cuba, May 21, 1941; d. Werner Anselm and Lotte Elsa (Meyer) Kahn; came to U.S., 1957, naturalized, 1967; B.A., Occidental Coll., 1962; M.L.S., U. Cal. at Los Angeles, 1963; m. Ilija Panajotovic, Jan. 27, 1963; children—Eric, Sonja. Asst. reference librarian Occidental Coll., Los Angeles, 1963-68; v.p. Noble Prodns., feature film producing co., Los Angeles, 1968—. Address: 1615 Crest Dr Los Angeles CA 90035

PANCOAST, ADELAIDE GOFF BIRCKHEAD (MRS. OMAR B. PANCOAST JR.), ency. co. exec.; b. Balt., Jan. 24, 1916; d. Lennox and Mary (Albert) Birckhead; B.A., Vassar Coll., 1938; postgrad., Columbia, 1939-40; m. Omar B. Pancoast, Jr., June 24, 1939; children—Howard W., Omar B. III, Taylor A., Joanna R. Salesman, World Book Ency., Field Enterprises Ednl. Corp., Chgo., 1953, area mgr., 1954-56, dist. mgr., 1956-58, 73—, regional mgr., 1958-72. Mem. Soc. of Friends. Club: Soroptimist (Upper Montgomery County, Md.). Home: 16501 Blackrock Rd Germantown MD 20767 Office: Honeywell Bldg Suite 603 7900 West Park Dr McLean VA 22101

PANEK, JERI HERNDON, pub. relations exec.; b. Salt Lake City, June 15, 1939; d. Norman C. and Geraldine E. (Griffin) Herndon; ed. U. Utah; 1 son, Brad. Pub. relations asst. Univac, Salt Lake City, 1961-69; dir. communications U. Utah, Salt Lake City, 1969-73; coordinator communications Sperry-Univac, Salt Lake City, 1973-74; electronic data processing communications coordinator Singer Bus. Machines Internat. Div., 1974—. Mem. Pub. Relations Soc. Am. (chmn. membership com., editor newsletter 1968—), Assn. Computing Machinery (mem. conf. and symposia com. 1972-74). Home: Av Van Becelaere 26A 1170 Brussels Belgium Office: Singer Bus Machines Rue de la Loi 120 1040 Brussels Belgium

PANESSA, BARBARA JEAN, educator; b. Yonkers, N.Y., Feb. 21, 1947; d. John Alfred and Rose (Brue) Panessa; B.A., N.Y. U., 1968, M.S., 1971, Ph.D. (teaching fellow), 1974. Tchr. anatomy, physiology St. Vincent's Hosp., N.Y.C., 1969-72, sr. instr. pathology, genetics, sci. of addiction Sch. Nursing, 1973-74, asst. prof., 1974—. Tchr. scanning electron microscopy, x-ray microanalysis NSF Hofstra U. Sch. Microscopy, 1973; vis. Prof. Instituto di Zoolozia Universita di Siena, Siena, Italy, summer 1974; cons. Gen. Telephone & Electronics, Bayside, N.Y., 1972, Stuffer Chem. Co., Dobbs Ferry, N.Y., 1973, Esso Research & Engring., Linden, N.J., 1973. N.Y. State Regents scholar, recipient Student award for excellence in electron beam research Electron Probe Analysis Soc. Am., 1972. Mem. N.Y. Soc. Electron Microscopists (treas.); Electron Microscope Soc. Am., Bot. Soc. Am., Electron Probe Analysis Soc. Am., Am. Soc. Cell Biology, Biophys. Soc. Am. Editor: Thin Section Microanalysis. Home: 4 Washington Square Village New York City NY 10012 Office: St Vincents Hosp 158 W 12th St New York City NY 10011

PANKEY, MARY ANN BLACK (MRS. BILLY JOE PANKEY), city ofcl.; b. Fouke, Ark., Mar. 20, 1942; d. Murray Bennett and Hope Virginia (Collins) Black; grad. high sch.; m. Billy Frank Ward, Dec. 24, 1960 (div. May 1970); children—Steve Alan, Dale Lee; m. 2d, Billy Joe Pankey, May 18, 1972; stepchildren—Paulette, Debbie Jo, Joseph M., Sandra Kay, Gary Lynn. Secretarial position Southwestern Bell Telephone Co., Houston, 1960-61, Am. Motors Corp., Houston,

1962-63, S.P. R.R., Houston, 1964-65, Red River Army Depot, Texarkana, Tex., 1966-67; sec. to personnel and purchasing City of Texarkana (Ark.), 1969-72, city clk.-treas., 1972—. Mem. Assn. Ark. Municipal Ct. Clks. (sec.-treas.), Internat. Inst. Municipal Clks. (mem. records mgmt. com. 1973—), Ark. Municipal League. Home: Route 2 Box 149 Fouke AR 71837 Office: PO Box 2711 Texarkana AR 75501

PANNELL, LOLITA, educator; b. Millburn, N.J., May 10, 1912; d. Edwin Durward and Mary Katharine (Goltra) Pannell; Ph.B., Brown U., 1934; M.A., Kan. U., 1947, Ph.D., 1950. Asst. phys. dept. Essex County Hosp., Cedar Grove, N.J., 1934-39; bacteriologist Strong Meml. Hosp., Rochester, N.Y., 1939-41, Meadowbrook Hosp., West Hemstead, N.Y., 1941-43; asst. in diagnostic bacteriology, virology, hematology, Kan. U., 1947-50; asst. prof. bacteriology and immunology Jefferson Med. Coll., Phila., 1950-54; asst. prof. bacteriology Med. Coll. S.C., Charleston, 1954-57, asso. prof. bacteriology, 1957-67, prof., 1967—. Served from ensign to lt. USNR, 1943-47. NIH grantee, 1955-62, 66-73; S.C. Heart Assn. grantee, 1963-66. Mem. Am. Pub. Health Assn., A.A.A.S., Am. Soc. for Microbiology, N.Y. Acad. Scis., Sigma Xi. Home: 224 Molasses Lane Mount Pleasant SC 29464 Office: 80 Barre St Charleston SC 29401

PANNWITT, BARBARA SEMPLE (MRS. FRED J. PANNWITT), ednl. adminstr.; b. Stamford, Conn., Mar. 31, 1917; d. Clarence Carleton and Perle P. (Gibson) Semple; A.B., Coll. White Plains, 1936; M.S., Sch. Journalism Columbia U., 1937; postgrad. Loyola U., Chgo., 1955, Northwestern U., 1963-64, Northeastern U., 1967; m. Fred J. Pannwitt, Feb. 12, 1941; children—Monica (Mrs. Henry S. Bradsher), Elizabeth (Mrs. Pannwitt Coleman). Mem. pub. relations staff J. Walter Thompson Co., N.Y.C., 1937-39, St. Regis Hotel, N.Y.C., 1939-41; cons., writer Adult Edn. Assn. U.S., Chgo., 1945-50; tchr. English, Evanston (Ill.) High Sch., 1955-73, chmn. dept. English, 1966-73, dir. pub. information services, 1973—. Named Creative Writing Honor Roll Tchr., Scholastic Mag., 1959-73; recipient award Zonta Internat., 1973. Mem. Ill. Edn. Assn., N.E.A., Nat. Council Tchrs. English, Ill. Assn. Tchrs. English, Ill. Assn. Tchr. Educators (pres., 1969-72), Women in Communications, League Women Voters, Delta Kappa Gamma. Author: The Art of Short Fiction, 1964; (with John Ogden, Jr.) Inward Vision: Imaginative Writing, 1971; (with others) Contemporary English, books 7, 8, 10, 11, 12. Home: 833 South Blvd Evanston IL 60202 Office: Evanston Twp High School 1600 Dodge Av Evanston IL 60204

PANOS, ANN PHILLIPS, cerebral palsy educator; b. Berlin, Md., Aug. 19, 1946; d. Edward Percy and Margaret Ann (Gunby) Phillips; B.S. in Occupational Therapy with honors, Va. Commonwealth U., 1968; M.S. in Learning Disabilities, Coll. St. Rose, 1973, M.A. in Reading, 1973; m. Philip James Panos, June 3, 1972. Staff occupational therapist Sunnyview Rehab. Center, Schenectady, 1969-70, Rome (N.Y.) State Sch., 1970-71; instr. Utica (N.Y.) Coll., 1970-72; cons. Genesee Nursing Home, Utica, 1971; tchr., dir. children excluded from pub. schs., Troy, N.Y., 1972-73; prin. Cerebral Palsy Treatment and Ednl. Facility, Albany, N.Y., 1973—; cons. occupational therapy rehab. Fred Sammons, Inc. of Chgo. for Middle N.Y. State area, 1974—. Mem. Council Exceptional Children, Assn. Tchrs. Mentally Handicapped, Am., N.Y. State (chairperson publicity Capital dist., treas. 1974) occupational therapy assns., Albany Jaycees (sec., treas. 1974), United Cerebral Palsy Women's Aux. Home: 439 Myrtle Av Albany NY 12208 Office: 314 S Manning Blvd Albany NY 12208

PANTOJA, ANTONIA, educator; b. San Juan, P.R., Sept. 13, 1922; d. Conrado and Luisa (Acosta) Pantoja; diploma Normal Sch., U. PR., 1942; B.A., Hunter Coll., 1952; M.S.W., Columbia, 1954; Ph.D., Union Grad. Sch., 1973. Dir. adult div. Union Settlement, N.Y.C., 1954-56; dir. community relations div. N.Y.C. Commn. Human Rights, 1956-62; exec. dir. Aspira of Am., Inc., N.Y.C., 1962-66; asst. prof. Columbia Sch. Social Work, 1966-67; exec. v.p. P.R. Forum, N.Y.C., 1967-68; pres. Pantoja Assos. in P.R., San Juan, 1968-69; exec. dir. Puerto Rican Research and Resources Center, Washington, 1969-73; chancellor Universidad Boricua, Washington, 1973; asso. prof. social policy San Diego State U., 1973—. Pres., Pub. House, Research for Urban Edn., N.Y.C., 1967-72, cons. U.S. Office Edn., 1966-73; planner, founder, 1st chancellor U. Boricua, Washington, 1973—. Mem. Study Commn. on Undergrad. Edn. and Edn. of Tchrs., 1972—, Steering Com. Nat. Urban Coalition, Washington, Citizens Com. for Pub. TV, Gov. P.R. Council on Puerto Ricans in U.S., N.Y.C., N.Y. State Constl. Conv., Albany; planner, founder bd. dirs. Aspira of Am., N.Y.C., v.p., 1970—; planner, founder Puerto Rican Forum; mem. bd. selectors Am. Inst. for Pub. Service, 1973—. Leopold Schepp Found. grantee, 1950-52; Antoinette Cannon fellow, 1953; John Hay Whitney Opportunity fellow, 1954. Author: (with others) Events in the History of Puerto Rico, 1967. Home: 6204 Madeline St San Diego CA 92115

PAOLUCCI, BRIDGET RIZZO (MRS. U. C. PAOLUCCI), producer and broadcaster; b. Detroit, Nov. 18, 1932; d. Frank and Dora (Lenzini) Rizzo; B.A., Manhattanville Coll., 1953; M.A., U. Mich., 1958; m. U. C. Paolucci, Oct. 7, 1961; children—Anne Marie, John Christopher. Copywriter, J.L. Hudson Co., Detroit, 1953-55; producer-dir. WDTR-WTVS, Detroit, 1955-59; writer-dir. Tng. Films, Inc., N.Y.C., 1959-60, became project supr. 1960; free-lance writer and broadcaster Canadian Broadcasting Corp. and Radio Italia, Rome, 1960-61; producer WNDT, N.Y.C., 1961-62; producer-broadcaster Canadian Broadcasting Corp., 1962—; free-lance producer-broadcaster, BBC, 1972. Recipient of Fulbright scholarship in radio and TV Italy, 1960-61, Nat. Assn. Edn. Broadcasters scholarship, 1955, U. Mich. fellowship in speech, 1956. Mem. Am. Women in Radio and TV (treas. Detroit chpt. 1957-58), Manhattanville Coll. Alumnae Assn. (nat. bd., chmn. publs. 1968-71, founder, chmn. Mornings at Manhattanville 1971—). Author: This is Washington, 1964; also articles. Editor Italian Heritage mag. Home: 22 Euclid Av Mount Vernon NY 10552

PAP, LUCIA TAMAR FISCHER (MRS. GEORGE S. PAP), physician, med. writer; b. Buenos Aires, Argentina, Feb. 13, 1933; d. Abraham and Sarah (Gersenovich) Fischer; came to U.S., 1958, naturalized, 1964; M.D., U. Buenos Aires, 1956; m. George S. Pap, Aug. 7, 1958; children—Claudia Linda, Charles Adrian. Intern, W. Suburban Hosp., Oak Park, Ill., 1958-59; pediatric research fellow Baylor U., Houston, 1960-61; trainee allergy, U. Ill., Chgo., 1962-64, clin. instr. medicine, allergy, 1965-69, clin. asso. in medicine, 1969-71; practice medicine specializing in allergy, Rockford, Ill., 1964—; mem. staffs Rockford Meml., Swedish-Am., St. Anthony hosps., Rockford; clin. asst. prof. medicine and allergy Rockford Sch. Medicine, U. Ill., 1973—. Pres., Rockford Hadassah, 1968. Ketty Mirelman med. research scholar, 1957-58. Recipient prizes for childrens and adults stories. Diplomate Am. Bd. Allergy and Immunology. Mem. Ill., Winnebago County med. socs., A.M.A. (Physician's Recognition award 1969), Chgo. Soc. Allergy, Am. Acad. Allergy, Am. Coll. Allergists. Editor: No. Ill. Med. Jour. Contbr. stories, articles to publs.

PAPAC, ROSE JEANNETTE (MRS. JAMES J. FISCHER), hematologist, oncologist; b. Montesano, Wash., Oct. 18, 1927; d. Stephen and Katherine (Broderick) Papac; student Reed Coll., 1945-46; B.S., Seattle U., 1949; M.A., St. Louis U., 1953; m. James J. Fischer, Aug. 20, 1970. Intern St. Louis U. Hosp., 1953-54; resident Stanford Hosps., San Francisco, 1954-56; with Cancer Research Inst., U. Cal. at San Francisco, 1958-63; asst. clin. prof. Yale Sch. Medicine, 1962—. Dir. med. adv. com. Conn. div. Am. Cancer Soc., 1970-72. Mem. Am. Soc. Hematology, Am. Assn. Cancer Research, N.Y. Acad. Scis. Home: RFD 3 River Rd Killingworth CT 06417 Office: Dept Medicine Yale Sch Medicine New Haven CT 06520

PAPAIOANOU, HELEN ANTOINETTE, physician; b. Springfield, Mass., July 21, 1928; d. John Xenophone and Susie Assunta (Raverta) Papaioanou; B.S., Bates Coll., 1949; M.D., Boston U., 1953; M.S., U. Mich., 1968. Intern Boston City Hosp., 1953-55, fellow child psychiatry, 1956-57, resident Univ. Hosp.-U. Mich. Med. Center, Ann Arbor, 1955-56; chief pediatrics McDowell (Ky.) Meml. Hosp., 1957-58; fellow allergy U. Mich., 1966-68; practice medicine specializing in pediatrics, Westfield, Mass., 1959-66, in pediatric allergy, Grosse Pointe Woods, Mich., 1966—; mem. staffs St. John's Hosp., Detroit, Children's Hosp. of Mich., Detroit; pres. Westfield Child Guidance Center, 1964. Trustee Bates Coll., 1965-70, 71—. Recipient outstanding women's award Westfield Bus. and Profl. Women's, 1964. Diplomate Am. Bd. Pediatrics, Am. Bd. Allergy and Immunology. Mem. Am. Acad. Pediatrics, Am. Acad. Allergy, A.M.A., Mich. Allergy Soc. (exec. com. 1971—). Methodist (chmn. social concerns commn. 1964-66). Home: 10103 Cadieux Rd Detroit MI 48224 Office: 20361 Mack Av Grosse Point Woods MI 48236

PAPAJ, MARIANNE LOUISE ELIZABETH, editor; b. Buffalo, July 4, 1941; d. William Edward and Mary Theresa (Grabowski) Papaj; B.A., State U. N.Y., Buffalo, 1965. Librarian, E. High Sch., Buffalo, 1965-66; res. asst. Columbia Bus. Sch. Library, N.Y.C., 1967-68; acquisitions librarian, archivist St. Mark's Library, Gen. Theol. Sem., N.Y.C., 1967-72; asst. editor Paulist Newman Press, N.Y.C., 1972-73; asso. editor Dendron Publ. Inc., N.Y.C., 1973—. Vis. archivist Edinburgh (Scotland) Theol. Tng. Coll., 1968, 69; vis. lectr. State U. N.Y., Buffalo, 1972. Mem. Book League N.Y. Office: 1865 Broadway New York City NY 10023

PAPANDREAS, MARY JOHNIENE, scenic and costume designer; b. Morgantown, W.Va., May 22, 1952; d. John George and Madeline Louise (Jones) Papandreas; B.F.A. in Drama, W.Va. U., 1974. Advt. designer TV sta. Teleprompter cable channel 10, Morgantown, 1971—; graphic designer drama dept. div. publicity W.Va. U., Morgantown, 1971—. Coordinator drama workshop Kennedy Youth Center, Morgantown, 1970, 71. Bd. dirs. Town and Country Players, Playhouse of Possibilities, children's theatre workshop. Mem. Internat. Alliance Theatrical Stage Employees, Am. Theatre Assn. (mem. div. Children's Theatre Assn.), Nat. Collegiate Players (pres. 1973-74). Home: 24 Lincoln Av Morgantown WV 26505 Office: 333 High St Morgantown WV 26505

PAPANEK, HELENE (MRS. ERNST PAPANEK), physician, psychiatrist; b. Vienna, Austria, June 10, 1901; d. Samuel and Marie (Bernstein) Goldstern; M.D., U. Vienna, 1925; certificate Postgrad. Center Mental Health, 1951; m. Ernst Papanek, June 27, 1925 (dec. 1973); children—Gustav, George. Intern, resident Vienna City Hosp., 1925-29; asst. physician advancing to chief physician Pvt. Sanitarium for neurotic and psychotic patients Vienna, 1929-38; physician, psychiat. adviser OSE Homes for Children, Montmorency, France, 1938-40; intern Lebanon Hosp., N.Y.C., 1942-43; pvt. practice, 1943—; lectr. mental hygiene N.Y.C. Health Dept., 1948-50; supervising psychiatrist and staff lectr. Postgrad. Center for Mental Health, 1951—; exec. dir. of Alfred Adler Inst., N.Y.C., 1951—; adj. psychiatrist emeritus Lenox Hill Hosp., N.Y.C., 1956—; dir. group therapy dept. Alfred Adler Mental Hygiene Clinic, 1945-73; cons. VA, 1966—. Fellow Am. Group Psychotherapy Assn., Assn. Advancement Psychotherapy, Am. Soc. Adlerian Psychology, Am. Psychiat. Assn.; mem. Inst. Study Drug Addiction (research adv. panel; editorial bd.), N.Y. Soc. Clin. Psychiatry, Soc. Ethical Culture, Am. Assn. Marriage and Family Counselors, N.Y. Acad. Scis., Schilder Soc. Contbr. chpts. to books; articles to profl. jours. Mem. editorial bd. Individual Psychologist, Jour. Individual Psychology, Internat. Jour. of the Addictions. Address: 1 W 64th St New York City NY 10023

PAPANEK, MIRIAM ANNA LEWIN, psychologist; b. Berlin, Germany; d. Kurt and Gertrud (Weiss) Lewin; B.A., Swarthmore Coll., 1952; M.A., Harvard, 1955, Ph.D., 1957; children—Susan, Michael, Deborah. Research asso. Center Sociopsychol. Research Harvard Med. Sch., 1957-59; lect. sociology and anthropology N.Y. U., 1960; research sychologist The Fieldston Sch., Riverdale, N.Y., 1961-63; research supr. developmental research div. Ednl. Testing Service, Princeton, N.J., 1966-68; mem. faculty dept. psychology Sarah Lawrence Coll., Bronxville, N.Y., 1968-70, asst. prof. Manhattanville Coll., Purchase, N.Y., 1970, chmn. dept. psychology, 1972-74. Contbr. articles profl. jours. Address: 15 Temple Rd Dobbs Ferry NY 10522

PAPANGELIS, PATRICIA JEAN (MRS. CHARLES PAPANGELIS), editor; b. Gibson County, Tenn., Sept. 16, 1932; d. Henry Clay and Mollie Elizabeth (Clayton) Cuthbertson; student Fox Bus. Sch., 1951, Am. Inst. Banking, 1951-53, Art Inst. Chgo., part-time 1955-56; m. Charles Papangelis, May 23, 1953; children—Dena, Stacy. Sec., Live Stock Nat. Bank, Chgo., 1951-53; with Pubs. Devel. Corp., Chgo., 1953-54; with Playboy Enterprises, Inc., Chgo., 1954-59, 62—, adminstrv. editor, 1972—. Home: 551 Roscoe Chicago IL 60657 Office: 919 N Michigan Av Chicago IL 60611

PAPIER, ROSE L. (MRS. WILLIAM BERNARD PAPIER), social worker; b. St. Mary's O., Nov. 29, 1912; d. Harry Locum and Mollie Hattie (Menovitz) Locum; B.S., Ohio State U., 1940, M.A., 1942; m. William Bernard Papier, Aug. 1, 1937; children—Jeffre Harlan (dec.), Cheri Maia. Grad. mem. research staff sch. social adminstrn. Ohio State U., 1941-42, teaching asst. in econs., 1945; occupational analyst USES, 1944-45. Mem. budget com. Franklin County Community Chest; central state com. Ohio Sesqui-Centennial Commn.; vice chmn. United Appeals for Franklin County chmn. women's div., 1956; campaign chmn. Columbus Symphony Orch., 1957-58; research dir. Gov.'s Commn. on Aging, 1959-61; sec. Ohio Commn. Aging, 1961-63; planning cons. on aging Ohio Dept. Mental Health and Mental Retardation, 1963-65, coordinator div. adminstrn. on aging, 1965-73, coordinator state geriatric centers and community services, 1973—. Del. White House Conf. on Aging, 1961, 71, co-chmn. Ohio delegation, 1971. Named 1 of 10 outstanding women of Columbus, 1956. Mem. of League Women Voters (v.p. Franklin County 1950-51), Nat. Rehab. Assn., Acad. Certified Social Workers, Scholaris Alpha Kappa Delta. Author: Unemployment Compensation Experience of Beneficiaries in Columbus, Ohio, 1939-40 (Ohio State U.), 1943. Co-author: After Unemployment Benefits—What? 1946. Editor: Ohio's Senior Citizens; Industrial Pension and Insurance Plans for Senior Citizens. Home: 1023 S Remington Rd Bexley OH 43209 Office: State Office Bldg Columbus OH 43215

PAPIER, SYLVIA GINSBURG (MRS. HARRY PAPIER), pub. relations exec.; b. Charleston, S.C., May 31, 1913; d. Gus and Molley (Eisenberg) Ginsburg; student Coll. of Charleston, 1928-29; B.A., U. S.C., 1931; m. Harry Papier, June 19, 1954; children—Stanley Cheren, Carol (Mrs. Harris Goodman). Dir. pub. relations YM & YWHA, Miami, 1951, Mt. Sinai Hosp., Miami Beach, 1952-54, Somerset Hosp., Somerville, N.J., 1954-61, Mt. Sinai Med. Center, Miami Beach, Fla., 1961—. Speaker, panelist various regional and nat. meetings. Recipient service plaque Greater Miami chpt. K.P., 1970, Women's Cancer League Miami Beach, 1970-72; MacEachern nat. award for publs. Somerset Hosp., 1960; plaque for publs. Fla. Hosp. Assn., 1968, 69, 71, 72. Mem. Pub. Relations Soc. Am., Am. Hosp. Assn. Pub. Relations Dirs. (charter), Fla. Hosp. Assn., Fla. (dir. 1970-72), South Fla. (charter mem., pres. 1968-69) hosp. pub. relations assns. Home: 6039 Collins Av Miami Beach FL 33140 Office: 4300 Alton Rd Miami Beach FL 33140

PAPIN, LOUELLA HELEN (MRS. JOSEPH MARK PAPIN), newspaper editor; b. Rouses Point, N.Y., Feb. 11, 1911; d. Albert Henry and Emma Alice (Dragon) Gebo; student Plattsburgh Bus. Inst., 1931; m. Joseph Mark Papin, July 8, 1934; children—Michael, Gary, Michele. Supr. finishing dept. Ayerst Labs., Inc., Rouses Point, 1934-38; with The North Countryman, The Press Republican and The Banner, Rouses Point, 1945—, office mgr., 1967-68, editor North Countryman (now part of Denton Publs.), 1968—. Chmn., Am. Cancer Soc. Fund Dr., Rouses Point, 1962-72. Mem. Champlain Valley Bus. and Profl. Women's Club, Champlain Home Bur., Stony Point Assn. (sec.-treas. 1970—). Roman Catholic. Home: Stony Point Rouses Point NY 12979 Office: 100 Lake St Rouses Point NY 12979

PAPP, PEGGY, health service adminstr.; b. Salt Lake City, Feb. 20, 1928; d. Heber and Vera (Weiler) Bennion; B.A., U. Utah, 1951; postgrad. Hunter Coll., Sch. Social Work, 1961; m. Joseph Papp, Oct. 27, 1951 (div. 1974); children—Miranda, Anthony. Family counselor Community Service Soc., N.Y.C., 1961-62; psychiat. caseworker St. Lukes Child Guidance Clinic N.Y.C., 1962-65; tng. supr. family therapy, dir. community programs Nathan Ackerman Family Inst., N.Y.C., 1965—. Faculty mem. family studies sect. Albert Einstein Sch. Medicine, N.Y.C., 1972—. Asso. dir. Center for Family Learning, New Rochelle, N.Y.C., 1973—. Fellow Am. Orthopsychiat. Assn., Am. Group Psychotherapy Assn. Home: 1199 Park Av New York City NY 10025 Office: 149 E 78th St New York City NY 10021

PAPPALARDO, NANCY ARLENE (MRS. VINCENT PAPPALARDO), constrn. co. exec.; b. Danville, Ill., Aug. 31, 1934; d. Curt and Rosie (Rosenberger) Taylor; student U. Miami, 1952-53; B.B.A., U. Ill., 1956; m. Vincent J. Pappalardo, June 11, 1965; 1 son, Tom Zeppelin. Tchr. North Palm Beach (Fla.) Elementary Sch., 1963-65; sec.-treas. Fairway Home, Inc., Palm Beach Gardens, Fla., 1965—, Pappalardo Constrn. Co., 1965—, Yorkshire Properties, Inc., 1965—, Fairhaven Properties, 1965—, Tanglewood Mgmt. Inc., 1965—. Mem. Chi Omega. Republican. Presbyn. Club: P.G.A. Womens Golf Assn. (Palm Beach Gardens). Home: 4278 Hickory Dr Palm Beach Gardens FL 33403 Office: 10800 N Military Trail Palm Beach Gardens FL 33403

PAPPAS, EVELYN ANTOINETTE ROMANO (MRS. JOHN G. PAPPAS), real estate broker; b. Tuckahoe, N.Y.; d. Michaelangelo and Katherine (Golia) Ramano; grad. Our Lady Of Victory Bus. Coll., 1926; m. John G. Pappas, Nov. 24, 1927; children—Kathrene (Mrs. John Davis), Helene (Mrs. Ronald Parker). Exec. sec. Kollner's Food Co., Jamaica, N.Y., 1940-46; supr. Home Ins. Co., Los Angeles, 1947-57; active real estate, 1957—. Sec. real estate edn. adv. com. Pasadena (Cal.) City Coll., 1968—; organizer, charter pres. La Canada chpt. Women's Council Realtors, 1962; chmn. salesman div. La Canada Bd. Realtors, 1963. Named Women of Year, W. Coast Title Co., 1966; recipient testimonial Bd. Suprs. County Los Angeles, 1971, Recognition of merit Gov. R. Reagan, 1971. Mem. Women's Council Realtors (nat. pres. 1971, pres. Cal. 1969), Cath. Daus. Am. (pres. past grand regents Archdiocese Los Angeles 1967-68). Home: 342 W Olive St Monrovia CA 91016 Office: 2115 Huntington Dr San Marino CA 91108

PAPPAS, LEAH AGLAIA, dist. ct. clk.; b. Ogden, Utah, Mar. 23, 1936; d. George Thomas and Maria (Harmaes) Pappas; student U. Utah, 1954-57, 62-63; B.A., Coll. St. Mary of Wasatch, 1959. Tchr., Bishop Gorman High Sch., Las Vegas, 1959-64, Whitesboro High Sch., Marcy, N.Y., 1965-66, J.D. Smith Jr. High Sch., Las Vegas, 1967-69; dist. ct. clk., legal sec. office of dist. atty., Las Vegas, 1972—. Alternate del. Democratic Nat. Conv., 1968; supr. Edward Kennedy's hdqrs. for re-election to U.S. Senate, Boston, 1970. Mem. Greek Orthodox Ch. Home: 1323 Marilyn Dr Ogden UT 84403

PAPPIN, CHARLENE PATRICIA, educator; b. Chgo., Mar. 23, 1939; d. Charles John and Irene Mary (Schultz) Pappin; A.A., Wright Jr. Coll., 1958; A.B., Mundelein Coll., 1960; postgrad. DePaul U., 1961, Columbia, 1963-73, M.A., 1966, Ed.D., 1973. Instr. math. Madonna High Sch., Chgo., 1960-64, instr., chmn. math. dept., 1964-66; instr. math. Wright Coll., City Colls. Chgo., 1966-69, asst. prof., 1969-73, asso. prof., 1973—. Math. instr. Pestalozzi-Froebel Tchrs. Coll., Chgo., 1968, Nat. Coll. Edn., urban campus, Chgo., 1971-72; math. cons. Archdiocese Chgo. Sch. Bd., 1965-66. Mem. Nat. Council Tchrs. Math. (chmn. hospitality com. conv. 1972), Math. Assn. Am., Sch. Sci. and Math. Assn., Inc., Am. Fedn. Tchrs., Ill. Council Tchrs. Math., No. Ill. Math. Assn. Community Colls. (corr. sec. 1971-72), Women's Math. Club Chgo. and Vicinity (pres. 1970-71, chmn. nominating com. 1971-72), Chgo. Cath. Sci. Tchrs. Assn. (math. sect. chmn. 1968-69, council mem. 1968-69), Kappa Delta Pi, Pi Lambda Theta, Phi Delta Kappa. Author: Arithmetic (complete course), 1970; Progress Tests in Arithmetic, 1970; Computational Arithmetic (complete course), 1972; Progress Tests in Computational Arithmetic, 1972; A Descriptive Study of Implementation of Specific Programmed Materials for Junior College Arithmetic Students, 1973. Home: 2832 N Monitor Av Chicago IL 60634 Office: Math Dept Wright Coll 3400 N Austin Av Chicago IL 60634

PAQUETTE, SISTER G., hosp. adminstr.; b. La Reine, Que., Can., June 9, 1923; d. William and Alice (Blouin) Paquette; B.A., U. Ottawa, 1956, B.Sc. Com., 1959. Tchr. grade schs., Rouyn, Que., 1944-45, Alfred, Ont., Can., 1945-46, Ottawa, Ont., 1947-59; various adminstrv. positions Ottawa Gen. Hosp., 1959-68, exec. dir., 1968—. Fellow Am. Coll. Hosp. Adminstrs.; mem. Hosp. Financial Mgmt. Assn. Address: 43 Bruyere St Ottawa ON Canada

PARADEE, MARY JANE HOWARD (MRS. DANIEL PARADEE), clubwoman, civic worker; b. Pitts., July 15, 1929; d. Milton Albert and Mildred (Henderson) Howard; student Kan. State U., 1950; m. Daniel Paradee, Dec. 26, 1948. State jr. dir. Wis. Fedn. Women's Clubs, 1962-64, jr. internat. chmn., 1964-66, internat. projects chmn., 1964-66, printing chmn., 1966-72, treas., 1972-74; v.p. Dodge County Fedn. Women's Clubs, 1964-66, pres., 1966-68; 2d v.p. 2d Dist. Fedn. Womens Club, 1973-74, 1st v.p., 1974—; sec. lay adv. Com. for Joint Sch. Dist. 7 on Assets and Liabilities in Wis.; mem. (1st woman) Hustisford Village Bd., 1966—; treas., dir. Hustisford Indsl. Devel. Corp. Mem. D.A.R. (Americanism com. Milw. chpt. 1971—), Women's Aux. to Am. Vet. Med. Assn. (v.p. student loans 1962-66, pres. 1971-72), Am. Council for Better Broadcasts (tres. Wis. 1963-66), Dodge County Vet. Med. Assn. (sec.-treas. for men's assn. 1960-66, 67—), Marsh Service League (charter pres. 1970-72). Sec. County Bd. for the Day Care Services for Mentally Retarded,

1964-69. Presbyn. (ruling elder; mem. dept. missions Presbytery of Milw. 1969—). Home: Box 373 Hustisford WI 53034

PARAGAMIAN, HELEN, librarian; b. Braddock, Pa., May 10, 1919; d. Hamo and Adeline (Kirkyasharian) Paragamian; B.S., Simmons Coll., 1941. Children's librarian Shute Meml. Library, Everett, Mass., 1941-49, asst. librarian, children's librarian, 1949-56; head librarian Pine Manor Jr. Coll., Chestnut Hill, Pa., 1956—, instr. children's lit., 1956-57. Mem. Women's Nat. Book Assn. (sec. 1958-60, treas. Boston chpt. 1973—), A.L.A., New Eng., Mass. library assns., Assn. Colls. and Research Libraries (chmn. constn. and by-laws com., jr. coll. libraries sect. 1961-63, sec. in coll. libraries sect. 1965-66), Round Table of Children's Librarians (treas. 1951-53), Librarians of Small Colls. Greater Boston Area (pres. 1971—). Republican. Methodist. Editorial bd. Books for Junior College Libraries. Home: 26 Lodge Rd Belmont MA 02178 Office: 400 Heath St Chestnut Hill MA 02167

PARAMESWARAN, PRISCILLA (MRS. VENKETACHALAM PARAMESWARAN), pub. affairs exec.; b. Alwaye, India, Dec. 27, 1937; d. Merad and Felcy (Fernandoe) D'Cruz; Intermediate cum laude Kerala U., 1956; B.A. with honors Presidency Coll., Madras U., 1959; M.A., Fordam U., 1963, Ph.D., 1970; m. Venketachalam Parameswaran, Jan. 28, 1967; 1 son, Prem. Came to U.S., 1961, naturalized, 1974. Lectr. English, asst. dean Fatima Coll., Quilon, India, 1959-61; program specialist Inst. Internat. Edn., N.Y.C., 1967-68; editorial control officer UN, N.Y.C., 1969; prof. English Co-Operative Coll. Centre State U. N.Y., Yonkers, 1970-74; pub. affairs specialist IBM, Armonk, N.Y., 1974—. Recipient numerous awards, Kerala U., 1956. Mem. Modern Lang. Assn., Tagore Soc. U.S.A., Am. Assn. U. Women, (sec. 1973, UN del. 1973), UN Assn. U.S.A. (dir. internat. cultural centers for youth 1972). Club: Village (Scarsdale, N.Y.). Contbr. articles to profl. jours. Home: 141 Bradley Rd Scarsdale NY 10583

PARAS, HELEN, lawyer; b. Sacramento, Nov. 15, 1928; d. Steve and Calliope (Nikakis) Paras; A.A., Sacramento Jr. Coll., 1947; B.A., U. Cal. at Berkeley, 1951; tchr. certificate Sacramento State Coll. and San Francisco State Coll., 1961; J.D., McGeorge Coll. of Law and Humpreys Coll. Law, 1970. Social worker child welfare div. Sacramento County Welfare Dept., 1951-57; tchr. elementary sch. Sacramento City Unified Schs., 1957-73; admitted to Cal. bar, 1971; individual practice law, Sacramento, 1971—; atty., sec.-treas. Omega Produce, 1973—, Capital Produce, Inc., 1972-73. Mem. Sacramento, Cal. tchrs. assns., N.E.A., Sacramento County Bar Assn. Republican. Greek Orthodox. Address: 1001 Los Molinos Way Sacramento CA 95825

PARATORE, ANNE ESTHER, educator; b. Johnstown, Pa., July 17, 1944; d. James Joseph and Helen Nancy (DiBartola) Rizzo; B.A. in Edn., Slippery Rock State Coll., 1966; M.Ed., Indiana (Pa.) U., 1971; m. Edward Paratore, Aug. 25, 1969; 1 dau., Lisa. Tchr., Greater Johnstown Schs., 1966-68; asst. supr. recreation Pa. Rehab. Center, Johnstown, 1967-68; instr. phys. edn. U. Pitts., Johnstown, 1968—. Mem. A.A.P.H.E.R., Alpha Xi Delta, Alpha Psi Omega. Club: Windber Country. Home: 109 Wedgewood Dr Johnstown PA 15904

PARCH, GRACE DOLORES, librarian; b. Cleve., May 15; d. Joseph Charles and Josephine Dorothy (Kumel) Parch; B.A., Case Western Res. U., 1946, postgrad., 1947-50; B.L.S., McGill U., 1951; postgrad. Newspaper Library Workshop, Kent State U., 1970, Cooper Sch. Art, 1971-72, API Newspaper Library Seminar, Columbia U., 1971. Publicity librarian, Spl. Services U.S. Army, Germany, 1951; post librarian, USAF, Italy, 1952, base librarian, 1953-54; br. librarian Cleveland Heights (O.) Pub. Library, 1954-62; asst. head reference div. Va. State Library, Richmond, 1964; dir. Twinsburg (O.) Pub. Library, 1965-70; dir. newspaper library Cleve. Plain Dealer, 1970—. Cons., Cath. Library Assn., 1961-64; mem. home econs. adv. com. Summit County, 1969, books/job com., 1968; mem. adv. com. Union Guide of Ohio Newspapers, 1971-74. Recipient John Cotton Dana award A.L.A., 1967, Pub. Relations Council award A.L.A., 1972. Mem. McGill U. Alumnae Assn. (sec., 1973—), A.L.A. (rep. on joint com. with Cath. Library Assn. 1967-70), Cath. Library Assn. (co-chmn. 1960-63), Spl. Libraries Assn. (chmn. publicity 1972-73), Ohio Library Assn., Am. Soc. Indexers, Cleve. Mus. Art, Assn. Coll. and Research Librarians, Women's Nat. Book Com. Roman Catholic. Contbr. articles Akron Beacon Jour., N. Summit Times, Twinsburg Bull., Bedford Times Register, Plain Dealer. Author: Where In the World But in the Plain Dealer Library, a manual, 1970. Home: 688 Jefferson St Bedford OH 44146 Office: 1801 Superior Av Cleveland OH 44114

PARDUN, PATRICIA JANE SMITH (MRS. WALTER GLEN PARDUN), polit. party ofcl.; b. Independence, Ia., Oct. 23, 1925; d. Allen and Myra Marguerite (Mattice) Smith; student U. Dubuque, 1943-44, U. Ia., 1944-46; m. Walter Glen Pardun, Nov. 13, 1943; children—Paulette (Mrs. Stanley L. Brossman), Anthony Allen, Pamela (Mrs. Bruce N. Dunlap). Precinct committeeman Harrison Twp., Benton County, Ia., 1956-72; county vice chmn. Republican party, Benton County, Ia., 2d. dist. vice chmn. Rep. party 2d Congl. dist., 1959-62; pres. Benton County Rep. Women's Club, 1960-62; state program chmn. Ia. Fedn. Rep. Women, 1962-64; 4th dist. vice chmn. 4th Congl. dist., 1964-67; state co-chmn. Rep. Party Ia., 1966-74; del. Rep. Nat. Conv., 1968, 72, mem. Nat. Rules Commn., 1972. Active A.R.C., Am. Cancer Soc.; sec. bd. Brandon Consol. Sch. Dist., 1953-56; pres. Brandon P.T.A., 1954-55; mem. care rev. com. Extended Care Center People's Meml. Hosp., Independence, 1974—. Mem. Ia. Hist. Soc. Presbyn. Clubs: Wapsipinicon Golf (Independence); First Republican Ladies (founder 1973). Home: Route 4 Golf Club Rd Independence IA

PAREL, CRISTINA P., statistician, educator; b. Quezon City, Philippines, July 24, 1917; d. Baldomero Parel and Barbara Perlas-Parel; B.S.E. in Math., U. Philippines, 1935; M.S. in Math, U. Mich., 1949, Ph.D. in Math. Statistics (U. Philippines fellow), 1958. Instr. math. U. Philippines, Manila, 1937-41, asst. prof. math., 1949-57, asso. prof. statistics, 1958-63, prof. statistics, 1964—; lectr. math. U.S. Army Sch., Manila, 1946-47. Cons. nat. surveys, 1967—. UNESCO fellow, 1971, 73. Fellow Am. Statis. Assn., Philippine Assn. for Advancement Sci.; mem. Philippine Statis. Assn. (pres. 1966-67, 1968-69), Philippine Social Sci. Council (pres. 1973-74, mem. exec. bd. 1970—), Internat. Statis. Inst. Author: (with others) Introduction to Statistical Methods, 1966; (with others) Mathematics: A New Approach, 1968. Home: 35 Maginhawa St University of Philippines Village Diliman Quezon City Philippines Office: PO Box 479 Padre Faura Manila Philippines

PARENTEAU, SHIRLEY LAUROLYN (MRS. GEORGE WILLIAM PARENTEAU), writer; b. Garibaldi, Ore., Jan. 22, 1935; d. Howard Paul and Olive (Stanbrough) Brunson; grad. high sch.; m. George William Parenteau, Oct. 9, 1954; children—David William, Scott Lane, Cherie Gaye. Freelance writer of outdoor material appearing in outdoor, travel and boating mags., 1961—; writer Outdoor Wife, newspaper column, 1972—. Mem. Dem. Women's Club, Elk Grove, Cal., 1972—. Mem. Cal. Writers Club. Democrat. Conglist. (deaconess 1972-74, historian 1973-74). Home: PO Box 336 9805 Hunt Rd Elk Grove CA 95624

PARHAM, MARJORIE BROWER (MRS. HARTWELL H. PARHAM), publisher; b. Batavia, O., Feb. 12, 1918; d. James Branson and Estella May (Harvey) Brower; student Wilberforce U., 1935-37, U. Cin., 1937-39, Chase Sch. Bus., 1947-48; m. Hartwell H. Parham, Sept. 18, 1965; m. William Matthew Spillers; div. June 1946; 1 son, William Matthew. Clk., VA, Cin., 1946-61; pres. Porter Pub. Inc., Cin., 1963—. Mem. Citizens Sch. Com., 1967—, N.A.A.C.P., 1965—, Cin. Ci-Centennial Com., 1973—, Riverfront Devel. Com., 1973—, A.R.C., 1970—. Bd. dirs. Cin. Opportunites Industrialization Center; trustee Cin. Tech. Coll. Named Bus. Woman of Year, Iota Phi Lambda, 1970; Outstanding Woman in Communications, Women in Communications, 1973. Episcopalian. Home: 4503 Sunnyslope Terrace Cincinnati OH 45229 Office: 863 Lincoln Av Cincinnati OH 45206

PARHAM, RUBY INEZ MYERS (MRS. JEWELL A PARHAM), educator; b. Tamaha, Okla., Nov. 4, 1914; d. Ola T. and Bursha Bell (Culver) Myers; B.S. in Edn., Northeastern State Coll., 1940, M.Teaching, 1955; m. Rufus K. McCollum, Dec. 31, 1937 (dec. Oct. 1966); m. 2d, Jewell A. Parham, June 10, 1973; stepchildren—Bill, Donal E., Ann (Mrs. Jim Garrett), Garry. Tchr. rural schs., Haskell County, Stigler, Okla., 1934-38, Adair County, Stilwell, Okla., 1946-50, Cherokee County, Tahlequah, Okla., 1939-46, 50-66; tchr. Westville (Okla.) Jr. High Sch., 1966—. Recipient Oklahoma Bankers award, 1965. Mem. Nat., Okla. edn. assns., Am. Legion Aux., Northeastern State U. Alumni Assn. (life), Nat. Wildlife Assn., Kappa Kappa Iota (royal high lady Tahlequah, Okla., 1953-55), Delta Kappa Gamma. Republican. Baptist. Rebekah (noble grand 1959-60, jr. noble grand 1960-61, lodge dep. 1961-63, musician). Home: 215 S College St Tahlequah OK 74464 Office: Westville High Sch Westville OK 74965

PARIS, DOROTHY, artist; b. Boston; d. David and Sarah L. (Fritz) Paris; student Columbia U. Extension, 1920, Am. Acad. Dramatic Art, 1921, Academie De La Grande Chaumiere, Paris, 1926, Honolulu Acad. Art, 1945; U. Hawaii, 1945, Art Students League, 1947, with Hans Hoffman, 1948; m. William Elton Brock (dec.); 1 dau., Dorothy (Mrs. Bagley). One-man shows at Galerie Zak, Paris, 1950, Van Dieman-Lilienfeld Galleries, N.Y.C., 1951, Barzansky Galleries, N.Y.C., 1954, Bodley Gallery, N.Y.C., 1959; exhibited in group shows at Whitney Mus., N.Y.C., Mus. Modern Art, Tokyo, Japan, Mint Mus., Hickory Mus., Museum Des Belles Arts, Argentina, Mus. Fine Arts, Mexico, Everhart Mus., Messillon Mus., Art Inst. Zanesville, Evansville Mus., Wesleyan Coll., Ga. Mus. Art, Columbus Mus., U. Miami, Auburn U., Art League of Huntsville (Ala.), Sheldon Swope Mus. Art, World's Fair, 1965; others; represented in permanent collections Evansville (Ind.) Mus., Joe and Emily Lowe collection at U. Miami, Peabody Mus., Nashville, Dallas Mus., Phoenix Art Mus., Mus. Fine Arts, Little Rock, Mus. Modern Art, Miami, Sheldon Swope Mus. Art, Colby Coll., Brandeis U., Birmingham Mus Art, Notre Dame U., Witty Meml. Mus., San Antonio, Akron Art Inst., Jewish Mus. of Hebrew Union Coll., Cin., Cornell U., Oakland Mus. Art, Norfolk Mus., U. Minn., Butler Inst. Am. Art, Purdue U., Musee de Cognac (France), Musee de Cannes (France), others. Recipient award Honolulu Acad. Art Mus., 1946, Fla. Internat. Art Exhbn., 1952, Nat. Women's Ann. show, 1953, Jersey City Mus., 1957, Bklyn. Soc. Artists, 1958. Fellow Albert Gallatin Assos. of N.Y. U.; mem. Am. Soc. Contemporary Artists (exec. bd. 1960—, 1st v.p. 1965-67, pres. 1967-69, chmn. publicity 1969-72, award 1970), Nat. Assn. Women Artists (exec. bd. 1960—, 1st v.p. 1972-74, chmn. exhbns. 1972-74), Conf. Am. Artists (treas. 1971), Internat. Assn. Art (sec. U.S. com. 1969-72). Address: 88 7th Av S New York City NY 10014

PARIS, JANET FRESCH (MRS. MAURICE THATCHER PARIS), librarian; b. Balt., July 29, 1911; d. George Oliver and Jane (Grady) Fresch; B.A., Wilson Coll., 1933; B.S. in L.S., Drexel Inst. Tech., 1934; M.L.S., Columbia, 1940; m. Maurice Thatcher Paris, June 19, 1943; 1 dau., Katrina Van Buskirk Douglass. Cataloger, Enoch Pratt Free Library, Balt., 1934-41; cataloger, descriptive cataloging div. Library of Congress, Washington, 1941-52; cataloger N.Y. Pub. Library Reference Div., 1953-56; instr. library sci. Nazareth Coll., Louisville, 1956-60; cataloger in charge book catalog project Montgomery County (Md.) Dept. Pub. Libraries, Gaithersburg, 1960-66; cataloger S.C. State Library, Columbia, 1966-68; dir. Georgetown County Meml. Library, Georgetown, S.C., 1968—. Recipient Superior Accomplishment award Library of Congress, 1950. Mem. Southeastern, S.C. library assns., Georgetown County Hist. Soc. Democrat. Episcopalian. Home: Wicklow Hall Plantation Georgetown SC 29440 Office: PO Drawer D Georgetown SC 29440

PARIS, KATHERINE LEE WALLACE, mus. ofcl.; b. Kansas City, Mo., Feb. 6, 1930; d. Julian Lee and Eva Katherine (Wright) Wallace; A.A., Stephens Coll., 1947; B.A., Carnegie-Mellon U., 1950, M.A., 1950; m. John Lyn Paris, Dec. 29, 1950; children—Nicole, Christopher, Deirdre. Docent, William Rockhill Nelson Gallery Art, Kansas City, 1961-68, adminstr. tour programs, 1968-69; registrar, curator decorative arts Columbus (O.) Gallery Fine Arts, 1970—, coordinator mus. studies, 1971—. Mem. Am. Assn. Museums, Midwest Museums Conf., Women's Music Club. Author exhbn. handbooks. Home: 4374 Stinson Dr W Columbus OH 43214 Office: 480 E Broad St Columbus OH 43215

PARISH, BARBARA LU SHIRK (MRS. HARLIE ALBERT PARISH, JR.), writer; b. Lincoln, Kan., Nov. 28, 1942; d. Henry Lee and Effie Iola (Rohe) Shirk; B.A. in English, Fort Hays State Coll., 1964; M.A. in English, U. Mo., 1966, M.A. in L.S., 1968; m. Harlie Albert Parish, Jr., Aug. 30, 1964. Library asst. U. Mo., Columbia, 1966-68; cataloger, instr. library sci. U. Louisville, 1968-69, sec. Library Faculty, 1969, instr. library sci., reference librarian, part-time, 1971; free lance writer, Louisville, 1972—. Mem. Nat. Fedn. State Poetry Socs., Ky. State Poetry Soc., Louisville Writers Club, Women's Internat. Bowling Congress. Republican. Methodist. Home: 7904 Avanti Way Louisville KY 40291

PARISH, FRAEDA PHYLLIS (MRS. SANFORD PARISH), producer; b. Rochester, N.Y., Nov. 17, 1930; d. Benjamin Norman and Mollie Pearl (Schenfeld) Aronovitz; B.S., Cornell, 1952; M.A., State U. N.Y. at Binghamton, 1973; m. Sanford Parish, June 29, 1952; children—Jeffrey, Beth, Richard, Linda, Barbara. Dir. adult activities Jewish Community Center, Binghamton, 1967-68; cons. Plaza Travel Bur., Binghamton, 1968—; box office mgr., research asst., Dept. Theatre State U. N.Y. at Binghamton, 1971—, co-dir. Lion's Pride Theater Workshop for Youth, dir. children and youth theater. Mem. Broome County Com. for Performing Arts Theater, 1968-70. Mem. Am. Theater Assn., Mortar Bd., Phi Kappa Psi. Author: (with A.C. Brooks and E. Harris) Max Reinhardt Bibliography, 1973. Asso. editor Max Reinhard Catalogue, 1973, Max Reinhardt: A Fest Schrift, 1973. Home: 529 Midvale Rd Binghamton NY 13903 Office: Dept Theatre State Univ NY Binghamton NY 13901

PARK, AGATHA CHAIKYUNG LEE (MRS. PAUL HANYOUNG PARK), dermatologist; b. Seoul, Korea, Feb. 4, 1938; d. Kwan Hee and Chin Bae (Kim) Lee; M.D., Yonsei U. Coll. Medicine (Korea), 1963; m. Paul Hanyoung Park, June 5, 1965; 1 dau., Grace. Came to U.S., 1963, naturalized, 1969. Intern South Side Hosp. of Pitts., 1963-64; resident dermatology Northwestern U. Med. Center, Chgo., 1964-67; practice medicine specializing in dermatology, Granite City, Ill., 1970-73, Ferguson, Mo., 1973—; cons. staff Christian Hosp., Florissant, Mo., St. Elizabeth Hosp., Granite City, Ill. Mem. A.M.A., Am. Acad. Dermatology, Chgo. Med. Soc. Home: 7204 Landmark Ct Hazelwood MO 63042 Office: 111 Church St Ferguson MO 63135

PARK, CLARA JUSTINE CLAIBORNE (MRS. DAVID ALLEN PARK), educator; b. Tarrytown, N.Y., Aug. 19, 1923; d. Robert Watson and Virginia Spotswood (McKenney) Claiborne; B.A. magna cum laude, Radcliffe Coll., 1944; M.A., U. Mich., 1948; m. David Allen Park, Aug. 18, 1945; children—Katharine, Rachel, Paul, Jessica. Teaching asst. English, U. Mich., Ann Arbor, 1946-48; faculty English dept. Berkshire Community Coll., Pittsfield, Mass., 1960-72; vis. lectr. English, Williams Coll., Williamstown, Mass., 1972. Recipient award Nat. Assn. for Mental Health, 1969. Mem. New Eng. Coll. English Assn. (dir.). Author: The Siege, 1967. Editor: Nat. Soc. Autistic Children Newsletter, 1968-72. Contbr. articles to mags., jours. Home: 20 Hoxsey St Williamstown MA 02167

PARK, DOROTHY GOODWIN DENT (MRS. ROY HAMPTON PARK), broadcasting exec.; b. Raleigh, N.C.; d. Walter Reed and Mildred (Goodwin) Dent; student Peace Jr. Coll., 1925-33; A.B., Meredith Coll., 1936; m. Roy Hampton Park, Oct. 3, 1936; children—Roy Hampton, Adelaide Hinton (Mrs. Charles August Gomer III). Vice pres., sec., dir. Roy H. Park Broadcasting of Va., Inc., Sta. WTVR-TV-AM-FM, Richmond, 1965—, Roy H. Park Broadcasting of Tri-Cities, Inc., Sta. WJHL-TV Johnson City, Tenn., 1964—, Roy H. Park Broadcasting of Tenn., Inc., Sta. WDEF-TV-AM-FM, Chattanooga, 1963—; sec., dir. Park Broadcasting, Inc., Ithaca, N.Y., 1942—, Roy H. Park Broadcasting, Inc., Sta. WNCT-TV-FM, Greenville, N.C., 1962—, Roy H. Park Radio, Inc., Sta. WNCT-AM, Greenville, 1963—, Park Outdoor Advt., Inc., Ithaca, 1964—, Park Displays, Ithaca, 1964—, Park Found., Inc., Greenville, 1966—, Cobb House of Rock Hill, S.C. Inc., 1967—, Roy H. Park Broadcasting of Midwest, Inc., Sta. WNAX-AM, Yankton, S.D., Sta. WEBC-AM, Duluth and Sta. KRSI-AM, KFMX-FM, St. Louis Park, Minn., 1968—, Roy H. Park Broadcasting of Roanoke, Inc., Sta. WSLS-TV, 1969—, KWJJ, also KJIB-RM, Portland, Ore., 1973—, Roy H. Park Broadcasting of Utica-Rome, N.Y., Inc., Sta. WUTR-TV, 1969—, Windup, Inc., Ithaca, 1970—, sec., dir. Park Newspapers, Inc., Ithaca, 1972—, RHP Newspapers, Inc., Ithaca, 1973—, Roy H. Park Broadcasting of Birmingham (Ala.), Inc., Sta. WBMG-TV, 1973—, RHP, Inc., Ithaca, 1945—, Park Newspapers Va., Inc., 1973—; dir. Park Outdoor Advt. of Scranton-Wilkes-Barre, Inc., Park Newspapers of Ga., Inc., 1972—. Bd. visitors Peace Coll., Raleigh, 1968—. Mem. D.A.R. (1st vice regent 1955-57), Daus. Am. Colonists, Nat. Soc. Magna Charta Dames, Sovereign Colonial Soc. Ams. Royal Descent, Desc. Knights of Garter, Colonial Order of Crown, Service League Ithaca, League Women Voters. Presbyn. Clubs: Garden (Ithaca), Ithaca Woman's. Home: 205 Devon Rd Ithaca NY 14850 Office: Terrace Hill Ithaca NY 14850

PARK, HELEN O'BOYLE (MRS. EDWARD CAHILL PARK), archtl. historian; b. Sayre, Pa., Feb. 17, 1925; d. John Aloysius and Mary Immaculata (Duffy) O'Boyle; B.A., Smith Coll., 1948; M.A., Radcliffe Coll., 1959; m. Edward Cahill Park, July 28, 1951. Fellow 1st Seminar for Hist. Adminstrs., Colonial Williamsburg, 1959; adminstrv. asst. Essex Inst., 1956-58. Mem. Cal. Museum Sci. and Industry, Los Angeles County Mus. Art, U. Cal. at Los Angeles Art Council, Essex Inst. Mem. Soc. Archtl. Historians, Soc. Archtl. Historians So. Cal. (pres. 1973-74), Nat. Trust for Historic Preservation, League Women Voters. Author: A List of Architectural Books Available in America Before The Revolution, 1973. Home: 932 Ocean Front Santa Monica CA 90403

PARK, ISABELLE SPRINGER (MRS. DAVID EUGENE PARK), club Woman; b. El Paso, Tex., Nov. 9, 1895; d. Thomas Hanson and Mary Louise (Rogers) Springer; certificate Ethical Culture Sch., N.Y.C., 1915; m. William J. Millard, June 9, 1917; children—William J., Mrs. Elizabeth Malley; m. 2d, David Eugene Park, Sept. 26, 1931; 1 son, David Eugene. Vice pres., sec. Am. Woman's Club, Buenos Aires, Argentina, 1932-36, v.p., Bogota, Colombia, 1937-38; charter mem. Campo Allegro Library, Caracas, Venezuela, 1939; pres. Am. unit Venezuela Red Cross, Caracas, 1940-42; mem. bd. Harris County unit Am. Cancer Soc., Houston, 1958-62, sec.; mem. bd. Pan Am. Round Table, Houston, 1959-60, asso. state dir. Tex., 1967—; mem. Woman's com. Nat. Found. Poliomyelitis, N.Y.C., 1948-49. Mem. Am. Inst. Mining, Metall. and Petroleum Engrs. Women's Aux. (mem. bd. 1946-52, v.p.), D.A.R. (mem. bd. N.Y.C. chpt. 1955-57, bd. Houston chpt. 1961-66), Daus. Republic Tex. Home: 1800 N Stanton St El Paso TX 79902

PARK, MARY CATHRYNE, educator; b. Bellefonte, Pa.; d. J. Theodore and Lucie Catherine (Coons) Park; B.A. with maj. honors (Judge Horace Stern scholar), U. Pa., 1939, A.M. (Frances Bennett scholar, univ. scholar), 1942, Ph.D., 1947. Market research analyst Scott Paper Co., Chester, Pa., 1944-47; asst. prof. English, speech Anderson (Ind.) Coll., 1947-50; asso. prof. English and German, Catawba Coll., Salisbury, N.C., 1950-52; asso. prof. English, Stetson U., DeLand, Fla., 1952-55; asso. prof. English, Fla. So. Coll., Lakeland, 1955-60; prof. English Brevard Community Coll., Cocoa, Fla., 1960—, chmn. div. social scis.; creator TV series preventive medicine, Humanities series, 1962-64. Lectr., cons. in field. Pres., Brevard County div. Am. Cancer Soc.; mem. budget and finance com. Brevard County United Fund. Bd. dirs. Fla. Cancer Soc., Brevard County Community Services Council, Council on Aging. Mem. Am. Assn. U. Women (founder, pres. Salisbury and Lakeland chpts.), Modern Lang. Assn. (life), South Atlantic Modern Lang. Assn. (chmn. 1955, 58), Am. Studies Assn., Southeastern Am. Studies Assn., English Speaking Union, Fla., Indian River (pres. 1963) anthrop. assns. Home: 450 Norwood St Merritt Island FL 32952 Office: Brevard Community Coll Cocoa FL 32922

PARK, MERLE FLORENCE, ballerina; b. Salsbury, S. Rhodesia, Oct. 8, 1937; ed. Elmhurst Ballet Sch., Royal Ballet Sch.; m. James Monahan, 1965; 1 son; m. 2d, Sidney Bloch, 1971. Joined Saddler's Wells Ballet (now the Royal Ballet), 1954, 1st solo role, 1955; repertoire includes Facade, In the Night, Pineapple Poll, Sleeping Beauty, Coppelia, Les Sylphides, Mamzelle Angot, La Fille Mal Gardee, Romeo and Juliet, Giselle, The Nutcracker, Shadowplay, A Wedding Bouquet, Laurentia, The Dream, Triad, La Bayadere, Swan Lake, Anastasia, Firebird, Walk to the Paradise Garden, Dances at a Gathering, Don Quixote, Deux Pigeons, Serenade, Scene de Ballet, Les Rendezvous, Mirror Walkers, Symphonic Variations, Daphnis and Chloe, Elite Syncopations, others. Decorated comdr Brit. Empire; recipient Adelaine Genee medal, other certificates and medals. Office: care The Royal Ballet Convent Garden London WC2 England

PARK, NORMA LEE, retail co. exec.; b. Granville, O., Sept. 7, 1932; d. Lester Eugene and Viola Irene (Weekly) Baumann; B.A., Kent State U., 1950; postgrad U. Utah, 1953-54; m. Hugh Winston Park, Sept. 7, 1952 (div. Jan. 1966); 1 dau., Vanessa Kay. Performer, writer Aunt Fran and Lee, WBNS-TV, Columbus, O., 1951-52; producer, performer At Home with Lee, KLS-TV, Salt Lake City, 1953-56; free-lance writer, 1956-59; exec. asst. L'Oreal of Paris, N.Y.C.,

1963-65; free-lance writer, N.Y.C., 1965-67; copy chief Lane Bryant, Inc., N.Y.C., 1967-70; sales promotion dir. Peck & Peck, N.Y.C., 1970-74, Wm. Hengerer Co., Buffalo, 1974—. Judge for Clio Awards, 1971, 72, 73. Recipient Seklemian Merit award Retail Advt. Week, 1969, 70, 71. Mem. Nat. Retail Mchts. Assn. (dir. 1971—), Fashion Group. Home: 559 Lafayette Av Buffalo NY 14222 Office: 465 Main St Buffalo NY 14205

PARK, SUE WORTHINGTON (MRS. JAMES M. PARK), banker; b. Beebe, Ark., Feb. 22, 1907; d. Finley Dick and Matilda Frances (Hickman) Worthington; student Central Coll., Conway, Ark., 1924-26; m. James Marvin Park, Sept. 15, 1928 (dec.); children—James Marvin, Joseph Worthington. Bookkeeper, Bank of Cabot, Ark., 1939-42, asst. cashier, 1942-52, cashier, 1952-56, v.p., cashier, 1956-71, pres., 1971—. Mem. Nat. Assn. Bank Women (regional v.p. 1959-60), Cabot C. of C. Home: 118 S Lincoln St Cabot AR 72023 Office: Bank of Cabot 113 Main St Cabot AR 72023

PARK, VIRGINIA RAY, educator, dentist; b. Phila., July 27, 1920; d. Matthew and Caroline (Obenland) Park; D.D.S., U. Pa., 1942; m. Theodore L. Merolla, Apr. 29, 1945 (div. Feb. 1953); children—Todd Park, Richard Park. Practice dentistry, Royersford, Pa., 1942-46; mem. faculty dept. restorative dentistry U. Pa. Sch. Dental Medicine, Phila., 1951—, asst. prof. restorative dentistry, 1965—, dir. course dental assisting, 1956-69; vis. dentist Children's Heart Hosp. Phila., 1956-57, dentist, cons., 1963-67, active staff, 1967—. Examiner certifying bd. Am. Dental Assts. Assn., 1963. Mem. Am. Dental Assn., Pa. State, Philadelphia County (mem. dental assts. com. 1960—) dental socs., U. Pa. Women's Dental Soc. (founder 1952, pres. 1963-67), Assn. Am. Women Dentists (dist. chmn. 1967, editor News Letter 1968—, pres. 1970-71), Pa. Assn. Dental Surgeons (mem. exec. com. 1967—, pres. 1973-74), Internat. Assn. Dental Research, Acad. Stomatology, Omicron Kappa Upsilon (chpt. pres. 1958, 69-70, chpt. sec.-treas. 1966-67, 71—). Club: University Pa. Women's Faculty (mem.-at-large 1959-60, 67-68). Author: (with J. R. Ashman) A Textbook For Dental Assistants, 1966. Home: 1081 Beverly Rd Jenkintown PA 19046 Office: 4001 Spruce St Philadelphia PA 19104

PARKAS, IVA RICHEY (MRS. GEORGE EDUARDO PARKAS), educator, curator; b. Comanche County, Tex., June 28, 1907; d. Andrew Jackson and Pearl Lucretia (Kennedy) Richey; grad. Wayland Coll., 1927; B.A., Tex. Tech. U., 1935; M.Litt., U. Pitts., 1950; postgrad. U. Cal. at Los Angeles, 1960, Pa. State U., 1961, U. Cal. at Berkeley, 1962, Duquesne U., 1963, Carnegie-Mellon U., 1968; m. George Eduardo Parkas, May 5, 1945; 1 stepson, Rex Allen Beene. Curator, historian Fort Pitt Blockhouse, Pitts., 1946-52, now asst. curator, historian; tchr. U.S. history Pitts. pub. schs., 1953-72. Del. White House Conf. on Children and Youth, Washington, 1960, 70. Bd. dir. Arts and Crafts Center of Pitts. Henry Clay Frick Ednl. fellow, Nat. Defense Edn. Act grantee; Greater Pitts. Air Force Squadron scholar. Mem. Nat. (life), Pa. edn. assns., Am. Assn. U. Women (pres. Pitts. br. 1974—), Hist. Soc. Western Pa., Western Pa. Council for the Social Studies (pres. 1969-71), U. Pitts. Alumni Assn. (dir.), D.A.R., Delta Kappa Gamma, Phi Alpha Theta. Contbr. articles on hist. subjects to newspapers, mags. Home: 5520 Fifth Av Pittsburgh PA 15232

PARKE, KATHRYN EMMA, librarian; b. Fairport, N.Y., Feb. 12, 1915; d. Howard B. and Emma L. (Grant) Parke; B.A., Smith Coll., 1936; B.L.S., State U. N.Y. at Albany, 1941; M.L.S., U. Ill., 1946. Librarian, tchr. English high schs., N.Y., 1936-41, 42-44, Mitchell Coll., New London, Conn., 1941-42; asst. librarian Green Mountain Coll., Poultney, Vt., 1945-47, State U. N.Y. Coll. at Geneseo, 1947-51; head librarian State U. N.Y. Agrl. and Tech. Coll., Cobleskill, 1951-73. Guest Norwegian Folk-Coll. Tchrs'. Assn. at centennial celebration Norwegian folk-colls. Trustee Capital Dist. Library Council, Schenectady, 1965-70. Mem. Am., N.Y., Hudson-Mohawk (pres. 1964-66, dir. 1966-68) library assns. Mem. Soc. Friends. Author: Norway's Folk-High-Schools, 1963. Contbr. articles to ednl. jours. Address: Box 729 Cobleskill NY 12043

PARKE, MARGARET BITTNER (MRS. ROGER I. PARKE), educator; b. Mauch Chunk, Pa.; d. Oscar H. and Laura (Rader) Bittner; student Bloomsburg State Tchrs. Coll., 1923, Pa. State Coll., 1927; M.A., Columbia, 1930, Ed.D., 1945; Arts D. of Oratory honoris causa, Staley Coll., 1959; m. Roger I. Parke, Dec. 24, 1937. Tchr. pub. schs., Pa., 1919-26, N.Y., 1928-29; tchr. dir. guidance and research Eastchester N.Y., 1929-37; jr. research asst., research asso. N.Y.C. pub. schs., 1937-51; asso. prof., prof. Bklyn. Coll., 1951-71. Recipient Fulbright award to U. Sydney, 1960; Distinguished Alumna award Pa. State U., 1972; Distinguished Service award Bloomsburg State Coll., 1973. Mem. N.E.A., Nat. Conf. on Research English, Nat. Council Tchrs. English, Assn. Tchrs. Reading Internat., Nat. Council Adminstrv. Women in Edn., Woman's Nat. Book Assn., D.A.R., Am. Assn. U. Women, Pi Lambda Theta, Kappa Delta Pi. Club: Women's Press (N.Y.C.). Author: Young Readers Dictionary, 1955; My First Book to Read, 1957; My Second Book to Read, 1957, Young Readers Color Picture Dictionary, 1958; Picture Dictionary for Primary Grades, 1960; Getting to Know Australia, 1962; The Practice Workbooks of Writing I, II, III; Young Readers Dictionary Workbook, 1963; Your Child Can Learn to Read, 1968; Vocabulary Workbook, 1970; also bulls., articles in field. Home: 1655 Flatbush Av Brooklyn NY 11210

PARKER, AILEEN WEBBER, ednl. adminstr.; b. Thompsonville, Ill., July 21, 1922; d. Alexander and Nellie Mae (Isaacs) Webber; B.S. in Edn., So. Ill. U., 1954, M.S. in Edn., 1957; Ph.D., Ind. U., 1961; m. Kenneth Lee Parker, Nov. 29, 1941; 1 dau., Shirley Faye Mrs. Edwin Neves). Asso. prof. edn. So. Ill. U., Carbondale, 1960-67; adminstr. spl. edn. Marion (Ill.) Community Unit No. 2, 1967—. Mem. Ill. Adminstrs. Spl. Edn. (pres. 1973-74), Council Exceptional Children (chpt. pres. 1973), So. Ill. Psychol. Assn. (pres. 1967), Phi Lambda Theta. Mem. Order Eastern Star. Contbr. articles to various publs. Home: 605 W St Louis West Frankfort IL 62896 Office: 113 S Russell St Marion IL 62959

PARKER, ALBERTA W. (MRS. WALTER W. HORN), physician; b. Bakersfield, Cal., Nov. 1, 1917; d. James H. and Laura (West) Parker; B.A., U. Cal. at Berkeley, 1938, M.P.H., 1963; M.D., U. Cal. at San Francisco, 1942; m. Walter W. Horn, Apr. 14, 1949; children—Michael, Peter, Rebecca. Intern U. Cal. Hosp., San Francisco, 1941-42, asst. resident 1942-43; resident Presbyn. Hosp., N.Y.C., 1943-45; practice medicine specializing in pediatrics, Berkeley, 1945-49; dir. maternal and child health Berkeley City Health Dept., 1948-55, asst. health officer, 1958-66; chief Bur. Crippled Children's Services, Alameda County Health Dept., 1955-58; lectr. pub. health U. Cal. Sch. Pub. Health, 1958-69, clin. prof. community health, 1969—, asso. dean Sch. Pub. Health, 1971-72; cons. Office Econ. Opportunity, Washington, 1967-73. Diplomate Am. Bd. Pediatrics. Mem. Am. Pub. Health Assn., Phi Beta Kappa, Delta Omega. Home: 339 Western Dr Richmond CA 94801 Office: Earl Warren Hall School Public Health U Cal Berkeley CA 94720

PARKER, AUDREY MAURINE, ednl. adminstr.; b. Des Moines; d. Leslie Garfield and Lura Margaret (Wallace) Parker; B.A., Occidental Coll., 1928; M.A., Columbia, 1946, Ed.D., 1956. Tchr., R.D. White Sch., Glendale, Cal., 1928-43; asso. dean students Bethany (W.Va.) Coll., 1947-49; dean women Ohio Wesleyan U., Delaware, O., 1949-63; asso. dean students Cal. Western U., San Diego, 1963-71; asst. to dean Grad. Sch., United States Internat. U., San Diego, 1971—. Served with USNR, 1943-46. Mem. League Women Voters, Am. Assn. U. Women, Pilot, Internat., Nat., Cal. assns. women adminstrs. and counselors. Republican. Presbyn. Home: 617 Tarento Dr San Diego CA 92106 Office: 10455 Pomerado Rd San Diego CA 92131

PARKER, BERTHA MORRIS, author; b. Rochester, Ill., Feb. 7, 1890; d. Homer Darius and Margaret Elizabeth (Lawrence) Parker; student Oberlin Coll., 1908-09; student Columbia U., 1909; S.B., U. Chgo., 1914, S.M., 1923. Tchr. pub. schs., Springfield, Ill., 1909-12, 14-16; tchr. sci. U. Chgo. Lab. Schs., 1916-55, chmn. dept., 1940-55. Cons. Rosenwald Fund, 1935; adviser Columbia Sch. of Air, 1935-38; cons. Field Enterprises, Inc., Golden Press, Western Pub. Co., Inc.; research asso. Field Mus. Natural History, 1955—. Mem. Central Assn. Sci. and Math. Tchrs. (chmn. elementary sect. 1933-34), Nat. Council on Elementary Sci. (pres. 1935-36, editor Sci. News Notes 1934-38), Nat. Assn. for Research in Sci. Teaching (asso. editor Sci. Edn. 1938-45), Phi Beta Kappa, Sigma Delta Epsilon. Methodist. Author numerous books, monographs on sci. edn., including The Golden Treasury of Natural History, 1952, rev. edit., 1968; The Golden Book of Science, 1956, rev., 1963; The Golden Book Encyclopedia, vols. I-XVI, 1959, rev., 1969; The Golden Book of Facts and Figures, 1962; Nature Wonderland, 1963; Wonders of Science, 1963; The Fifty States, 1965; books in Basic Sci. Edn. Series, 1941-66; Rockets and Missiles, 1961; Satellites and Space Travel, 1961; Out Into Space, 1965; Creatures of the Past, 1965; Travel Aloft, 1965; Stream of Life, 1967; Achievements of Civilization series, 1932-33, Merrigold Activity Books, 1964-65; Science and Us, 1969; Plants, Animals, and Us, 1969; (with Alice F. Martin) Exploring Chemistry I, II, Exploring Geology, 1970, Dinosaurs, 1973; Rocks and Minerals, 1974. Contbr. numerous articles to jours., mags., encys. Prepared film strips on sci. subjects, 1947-62. Home: 1700 E 56th St Chicago IL 60637

PARKER, BONNIE ELIZABETH KERR, author; b. Detroit; d. Rosmer Pettis and Evelyn (Hauer) Kerr; student Wayne State U., 1961-63; children—Judith Lynne, Holly Shannon. Book reviewer Scrivener Mag. Mem. Cath. Poetry Soc. Am., Detroit Women Writers, Ida. Poets and Writers Guild, N.H., Mich., Lansing poetry socs., Am. Poetry Fellowship Soc., Composers, Authors and Artists of Am. (state pres. 1965—). Author: Dark Tigers of My Tongue, 1957; Season of the Golden Dragon, 1961; Leopard on a Topaz Leash, 1962; A Pride of Lion-Noons, 1964; Seed of the Wild Stallion, 1969; Morning of the Unicorn, 1970. Editor: Legend Mag. Contbr. poems to anthologies. Address: 39213 Gloucester St Westland MI 48185

PARKER, DONA SCOTT (MRS. ROBERT E. PARKER), lawyer; b. Highland Park, Mich., Sept. 30, 1943; d. Donald Hill and Shirley Jean (Myers) Scott; B.A., U. Mich., 1965; J.D., U. Detroit, 1970; m. Robert E. Parker, June 27, 1969; 1 son, Robert Scott. Law clk. to circuit judge, Howell, Mich., 1969-70, Mich. atty. gen., 1970-71; research atty. Ct. Appeals Mich., 1970-71; admitted to Mich. bar, 1971; with McGivney & Parker, Brighton, Mich., 1971; sr. partner Parker & Parker, Howell, 1973—; pres., chief exec. officer Parker Abstract & Title Co., Howell; dir. 1st Nat. Bank Howell. Mem. U. Mich. Alumni Assn., Kappa Beta Pi, Kappa Kappa Gamma. Republican. Clubs: Cheumung Hills Country (Howell); Ann Arbor Towne. Home: 415 W Grand River Av Howell MI 48843 Office: 704 E Grand River Av Howell MI 48843

PARKER, DORRIS R. (MRS. FRANK PARKER), bank exec.; b. Pasadena, Cal., Sept. 25, 1925; d. Albert Ernest and Martha (Christian) Holtz; student U. So. Cal., 1962, Am. Inst. Banking, 1946-56; m. Frank M. Parker, Oct. 29, 1943. Typist, Loyalty Group Ins. Co., Los Angeles, 1943; typist Bank Am., Baldwin Park, Cal., 1945-46, 46-50, teller, 1950-57, loan interviewer, 1957-60, pro-asst. cashier spl. tng. program, Los Angeles, 1960-62, asst. cashier gen. lending officer Midway Center br., Elmonte, Cal., 1962-66, mgr. Eastland br., Covina, Cal., 1966-69, mgr. Rowland Heights (Cal.) br., 1969—. Mem. adv. bd. San Gabriel Valley YWCA, Covina, 1969—; vol. Am. Cancer Soc. Campaign, 1973. Mem. Baldwin Park Bus. and Profl. Women's Club (charter; treas. 1958-60, v.p. 1960-61, pres. 1961-62, chmn. various coms., recipient Woman of Year award 1972, Woman of Achievement award 1973), Nat. Assn. Bank Women. Club: Altrusa Covina-West Covina (sec. 1967-68, pres. 1968-69, dir. 1969—, chmn. various coms.). Home: 126 N Mangrove Av Covina CA 91722 Office: 19036 E Colima Rd Rowland Heights CA 91745

PARKER, EDNA JEAN, journalist; b. Akron, O., June 26, 1935; d. Murray Stephen Parker and Vera Darlene (Rigdon) Brown; student Mexico City Coll., 1954; B.A. in Journalism, Ohio State U., 1955; B.A. in Secondary Edn., U. Akron, 1962; M.A., U. Alaska, 1971; postgrad. Kent State U., 1962, 70. Tchr. secondary schs. Summit County, O., 1959-60; reporter, editor Akron Beacon Jour., 1961-69; writer univ. news service U. Alaska, Fairbanks, 1970-71; freelance writer United Features Syndicate, N.Am. Pubs. Assn., Plain Dealer, Grit, others, 1971—; writer Sun Newspapers, Cleve., 1972—. Lectr. journalism U. Akron, 1971—. Pres., Hillcrest Recreation Center, Inc., Akron, 1965—. Recipient Best Oil and Gas Reporting award Am. Assn. Petroleum Landmen, 1972; numerous other awards. Mem. Ohio Press Women (pres. 1969-70), Nat. Fedn. Press Women (regional dir.), Ohio Newspaper Women's Assn. (bd. mem. 1967-69), Women in Communications (chpt. pres. 1973—), Ohio Hist. Soc., Delta Zeta. Episcopalian. Mem. Order Eastern Star. Address: 74 Maplewood Av Akron OH 44313

PARKER, ELNOR COLES (MRS. IVAN WILLIAM PARKER), univ. press editor; b. Ann Arbor, Mich., Oct. 5, 1914; d. Walter Peter and Helena Emmeline (Nimtz) Coles; B.A. summa cum laude (Phillips scholar 1933-35), U. Mich., 1936, tchrs. certificate, 1936; m. Ivan William Parker, June 26, 1939; children—William Walter, James and Gerald (twins). Proofreader, Edwards Bros., Ann Arbor, 1932-35; asst. to the registrar U. Mich., Ann Arbor, 1936-40, asso. editor ofcl. publs., 1960-67, editor Mich. Index to Labor Union Periodicals, bur. indsl. relations Sch. Bus. Adminstrn., 1967-69; asst. editor U. Mich. Press, 1957-60, asso. editor, 1969-72, editor, 1972—. Active P.T.A., Cub Scouts Am. Mem. Phi Beta Kappa, Alpha Lambda Delta, Phi Kappa Phi, Phi Tau Alpha, Alpha Gamma Sigma. Methodist (sec. enlistment 1970—, chmn. pastor-parish relations com. 1974—). Clubs: Sara Browne Smith Alumnae (v.p. 1955-56), University Michigan Faculty Women's. Author: (with Burley F. Lamb and Ivan W. Parker) Who's Who in the Lyon Family, 1972. Home: 1111 Woodlawn St Ann Arbor MI 48104 Office: U Mich Press 615 E University St Ann Arbor MI 48106

PARKER, ETHEL MAX (MRS. CEDRIC M. PARKER), assn. exec.; b. Sheboygan, Wis.; d. Mayer and Jennie (Zion) Max; B.A., U. Wis., 1928, M.A., 1951; m. Cedric M. Parker, Aug. 19, 1951. Tchr. elementary sch., Cudahy, Wis., Sheboygan, 1921-25; columnist, feature writer Capital Times, Madison, Wis., 1926-33; tchr. secondary schs. and adult edn., pub. schs. Sheboygan, 1934-49; dir. pub. information A.R.C., Madison, 1952-66; vol. pub. information cons. Wis. Capital div. A.R.C., Madison, 1966—, sec., 1972—. Chmn. pub. policy com. for establishment of child treatment center Wis. Mental Health Assn., 1958-59. Recipient Writers Cup Theta Sigma Phi, 1961. Mem. Women in Communications, Wis. Acad. Scis., Arts, and Letters (life), Wis. Alumni Assn., Am. Assn. U. Women, Women in Communications, Pi Lambda Theta. Club: Madison Press. Home: Rural Route 3 Box 320 Madison WI 53711 Office: 1202 Ann St Box 603 Madison WI 53711

PARKER, GAIL THAIN, coll. pres.; b. Chgo., Feb. 8, 1943; d. Richard Janness and Jane (Noyes) Thain; A.B., Radcliffe Coll., 1964; Ph.D., Harvard, 1969; m. Thomas David Parker, June 9, 1964; 1 dau., Julia Thain. Asst. prof. Harvard, 1969-72; pres. Bennington (Vt.) Coll., 1972—. Trustee Amherst Coll. Woodrow Wilson fellow, 1964-65, Charles Warren Center fellow, 1972-73, Rockefeller Found. fellow, 1972-73, Radcliffe Inst. fellow, 1972-73. Mem. Phi Beta Kappa. Author: The Oven Birds, 1972; Mind Cure in New England, 1973. Address: Bennington Coll Bennington VT 05201

PARKER, GENEVIEVE FISH (MRS. E.M. PARKER), mus. ofcl.; b. Punxsutawney, Pa., Sept. 25, 1903; d. John Charles and Ollie Jane (Van Dyke) Fish; grad. high sch.; m. E.M. Parker, June 21, 1923; children—Earl M., Walter E. (dec.). Cashier, J.H. Fink Co., Punxsutawney, Pa., 1920-23; curator E.M. Parker Indian Mus., Brookville, Pa. 1925—. Mem. Jefferson County Hist. and Geneal. Soc., Dames of Malta Lodge. Mem. Order Eastern Star. Home and office: 247 E Main St Brookville PA 15825

PARKER, GWENDOLYN LOUISE ROTHLEIN, educator; b. Newark, Aug. 4, 1932; d. Earl Carl Clifford and Gertrude Louise (Selander) Rothlein; B.S. in Nursing, Coll. Mt. St. Vincent, N.Y.C., 1954; certificate in occupational therapy N.Y. U., 1962, M.A., 1968; m. William Burdick Parker, Dec. 29, 1970. Staff nurse St. Vincent's Hosp. and Med. Center, N.Y.C., 1954-55, asst. head nurse, 1957-59, night asst. adminstr., 1960-62; chief occupational therapy St. Joseph's Hosp., Yonkers, N.Y., 1962-68; cons. occupational therapy N.Y. State Dept. Health, Albany, 1968-70; head occupational therapy Wilton (N.Y.) State Sch., 1970-71; asst. prof. occupational therapy programs U. Western Ont., London, 1971—. Cons. community programs, homes for spl. care, mental retardation centers; mem. geriatric adv. com. Faculty of Medicine, U. Western Ont., 1973. Grantee Ministry No. Devel. and Indian Affairs, 1974. Mem. Am. (chmn. spl. interest group on aging, liaison U.S. Senate Com. Aging 1966-68, mem. council on practice 1966-68, regional council on practice planning com. 1966-69, registration com. 1969), N.Y. State (chmn. com. nominations 1970-71) occupational therapy assns., Canadian, Ont. (pres. London br. 1972—) socs. occupational therapists, World Fedn. Occupational Therapists. Contbr. to profl. publs. Home: Williamsfield Pelee Island Norimo ON Canada

PARKER, JANET ALENE (MRS. GEORGE L. POPKY), physician; b. Jersey City, Apr. 1, 1932; d. William A. and Esther (Taggart) Parker; A.B., Hood Coll., 1954; M.D., Woman's Med. Coll. Pa., 1958; m. George L. Popky, June 2, 1964; children—Deborah Ruth, Donna Harrell, Jennifer Babette. Intern Episcopal Hosp., Phila., 1958-59; resident radiology Temple U., Phila., 1959-62; fellow Am. Cancer Soc., 1962-64; fellow radiation therapy Royal Victoria Hosp., 1963; radiation therapist Germantown Hosp., Phila., 1964-71; dir. radiation therapy and nuclear medicine Hosp. Med. Coll. Pa., 1971—; asst. prof. radiology Temple U. Health Scis. Center, 1967—; asso. prof. radiology Med. Coll. Pa., 1971—. Diplomate Am. Bd. Radiology, Am. Bd. Nuclear Medicine. Mem. Soc. Therapeutic Radiologists, Am. Coll. Radiology, Radiol. Soc. N.Am., Soc. Nuclear Medicine, A.M.A., Alpha Omega Alpha. Home: 3134 W Coulter St Philadelphia PA 19129 Office: Hosp of Med Coll of Pa Philadelphia PA 19129

PARKER, JEAN R., educator; b. Lebanon, N.H., Dec. 4, 1927; d. Aurel Courtney and Helen (Roberts) Parker; B.A., Middlebury Coll., 1949; M.A., Cornell U., 1956; student Radcliffe Coll., summer 1958. Research asst. Jackson Meml. Lab., Bar Harbor, Me., 1949-50; asst. Admissions Office Dartmouth Coll., Hanover, N.H., 1950-53; grad. resident Cornell U., Ithaca, N.Y., 1953-54, head resident, 1954-58, adminstrv. asst. Office Dean of Women, 1957-58; asst. editor Coop. Grange League Fedn. Exchange, Inc., Ithaca, N.Y., 1958-59; adminstrv. aide to dean Dartmouth Med. Sch., Hanover, 1959-60; asst. to dir. Dartmouth Coll. News Service, Hanover, 1960-62, asst. dir., 1962, mng. editor proposed faculty jour. 1965, asst. Dartmouth Coll. News Service, 1965-67; editorial asst. Agrl. Research Mag., U.S. Dept. Agr., Washington, 1962-63, mng. editor, 1963-64; program officer, staff Com. on Internat. Exchange Persons, Washington, 1964-65; asst. dean women U. Me., Orono, 1968-69, asst. dean student activities and orgns., 1969-70; free lance writer, 1970—. Vol. neighborhood work, Alternate del. Adams-Morgan Community Council, Washington, 1964-65. Bd. dirs., mem. staff Community Coffeehouse, Hanover, 1966-67. Mem. Nat. Assn. Women Deans, Adminstrs. and Counselors, Am. Personnel and Guidance Assn., Sigma Kappa. Home: Etna Rd Lebanon NH 03766

PARKER, KARLA VAN OSTRAND (MRS. JAMES C. PARKER), civic leader; b. South Haven, Mich., Nov. 30, 1894; d. Charles Harry and Ray (Delamere) Van Ostrand; grad. Western State Normal (now Western Mich. U.), 1915. LL.D., 1960; m. James C. Parker, Sept. 17, 1919; children—Nona Rae (Mrs. Charles Donald O'Connor), Carlene Alice (Mrs. Robert E. Vander Klipp). Tchr. Mich. schs., 1915-23; began parent-teacher work, 1928; state pres. Mich. Congress Parents and Tchrs., 1942-45, regional v.p. Nat. Congress Parents and Tchrs., 1945-48. 1st v.p., 1955-58, pres., 1958-61, chmn. Congress Publs., orgn. publn., 1948-54; active Camp Fire Girls, 1930-58, pres. nat. council, 1946-49, Dir. Community Cannery, Grosse Pointe Farms, Mich., sponsored by Dept. Agr. and Mich. State U., World War I; mem. Mich. Youth Commn., 1950-68; mem. Gov.'s Adv. Com. on Recreation, 1966-69; sec. Grand Rapids Pub. Recreation Assn., 1939-65. Recipient spl. award Mich. Recreation and Parks Assn., 1968; swimming pool Ottawa Hills High sch. named Karla V. Parker Natatorium, 1973. Mem. Mich. Council Adult Edn. (pres. 1952-53), Nat. Council Adult Edn., YWCA. Nat. Congress Parents and Tchrs. (pres. 1958-61), Delta Kappa Gamma. Republican. Christian Scientist. Contbr. articles nat. periodicals; author juvenile fiction. Address: 131 E Candlewyck Dr Kalamazoo MI 49001

PARKER, KATE HARDING BATES (MRS. FRANK KNIGHT PARKER), lawyer; b. Corsicana, Tex.; d. William David and Kate (Broocks) Bates; student U. Tex., 1919; LL.B., South Tex. Coll. of Law, 1940; m. Frank Knight Parker, Nov. 24, 1943. Tchr. elementary sch., Toby, 1917-19, Smithville, Tex., 1920-21; clk. County Clk.'s office, Austin, Tex., 1921; legal sec. to Judge Gaines, 1922-23, Fogle & Gentry, attys., Houston, 1923-25, law dept. Gulf Oil Corp., 1925-43; admitted to Tex. bar, 1940. Mem. State Bar of Tex., Houston Bar Assn., Tex. Hist. Assn. (patron), Washington County (Ark.) Hist. Soc., Magna Charta Dames (regent E. Tex. colony 1963-65, councillor, round table Tex. div. 1963-65, 65-67), Colonial Dames XVII Century, Americans of Royal Descent (life), Dames of Ct. of Honor, Daus. of Republic of Tex. (corr. sec. 1953-55, registrar 1961-62, registrar gen. 1967-69, chmn. nominating com. 1969-71, chpt. parliamentarian 1969-71), Colonial Order Crown (life), U.D.C., D.A.R. Home: 302 S Congress St San Augustine TX 75972 Office: PO Box 371 San Augustine TX 75972

PARKER, MARCELINE L., educator; b. Johnston County, N.C.; d. Osborne B. and Ophelia (Weaver) Langston; A.B., East Carolina U., 1946, M.A., 1953, postgrad., 1962; postgrad. N.C. State U., 1970; m. D. Eugene Parker, Dec. 25, 1939 (div. 1967); children—M. Jean (Mrs. William Cobb), Donna Anne, Betty Sue, Barry. Tchr. elementary classroom Johnston County, N.C., 1937-60, elementary prin., 1960-62; asst. prof. edn. and dir. elementary student teaching Campbell Coll., Bules Creek, N.C., 1962—, asst. dir. curriculum lab., 1962—; cons. early childhood edn., 1970; cons. for inservice tchr. program, 1966-67. Mem. N.E.A., N.C. Edn. Assn., Assn. Higher Edn., Assn. Student Tchrs., Nat. Council Adminstrv. Women in Edn., Nat. Social Studies Council, Assn. Tchr. Edn., Assn. U. Profs. Teaching Reading, Internat. Council Tchr. Edn. Episcopal Ch. Woman. Episcopalian. Clubs: Cambell College Women's. Author: Handbook for Student Teachers, 1963, rev. edit., 1972. Home: Box 156 Bules Creek NC 27506

PARKER, MARGARET ELISABETH KOSCIELNY, artist; b. Tallahassee, Aug. 13, 1940; d. John Peter and Ida (Hooten) Koscielny; student Tex. Woman's U., 1958-59; B.A. in Art History, U. Ga., 1963, M.F.A., 1967. Instr. art Jacksonville (Fla.) Pub. Schs., 1962-64; instr. art history Jacksonville Episcopal High Sch., 1967-69; instr. art Jacksonville U., asst. to dir. Cummer Gallery of Art, Jacksonville, 1969-74; exhibited one-man shows Jacksonville Art Mus., 1967, San Jose Barnett, 1968; exhibited in group shows U. Ga. Traveling Print Exhbn., 1963, 66-68, Island Art Center, St. Simon's Island, Ga., 1964, Jacksonville U., 1964-66, Loch Haven Art Gallery, Orlando, Fla., 1964, Jacksonville Art Mus., 1964-68, Southeastern Print and Drawing competition, Jacksonville, 1964-66, St. Petersburg Jr. Coll., 1965, Fla. State Fair Competition, Tampa, 1965, Piedmont Invitational, Atlanta, 1966, U. Ga., 1966, 67, LeMoyne Art Found., Tallahassee, 1966, Ga. Art Mus., Athens, 1967, Am. Drawing, Phila., 1968, Graphics Gallery, Jacksonville, 1970, Heath Gallery, Atlanta, 1968-70, Art Sources, Jacksonville, Jacksonville Art Mus., others; represented in permanent collections Jacksonville Art Mus. Sch. Resource Library, U. Ga., Ga. Art Mus.; represented in pvt. collections; commd. various corps. including John Portman Assos., Atlanta, 1970, Alpert Enterprises, Atlanta, 1971. Instr., Jacksonville U., 1967, Jacksonville Art Mus., 1968; guest lectr. to numerous orgns., 1969—. Visual arts chmn. Jacksonville Arts Festival, 1970; mem. devel. com. Action Plan for Arts, Jacksonville, 1972-73; mem. adv. bd. Arts Festival Jacksonville Council Arts, 1972-73; co-organizer, originator Art Celebration, 1973-74; exhibited 1st free non-mus. affiliated exhbn. in Jacksonville Art Celebration, Nat. Art Workers Community. Home: 1254 Belvedere Av Jacksonville FL 32205

PARKER, MARION DEAN HUGHES, pub. relations cons.; b. Greenwich, Conn.; d. Walter A. and Marion K. (Dean) Hughes; B.A., U. Cal. at Los Angeles, 1942; m. Conkey P. Whitehead, Nov. 14, 1939 (dec. Nov. 1941); m. 2d, Willard Parker, Oct. 5, 1942 (div. 1951); 1 son, Walter van Eps. Actress appearing in Broadway prodns., New Faces, Three Waltzes, I Must Love Someone, on tour in The Women, The Man Who Came to Dinner, Lady in the Dark; various night club engagements; appeared in motion picture All About Eve; TV appearances; owner, mgr. Marion Parker's Guys & Dolls, Scottsdale, Ariz., 1951-59; mng. dir., purchasing agt. shipboard gift and accessory shops Am. Export Lines, 1960-64; dir. spl. events Internat. Telephone & Telegraph, N.Y.C., 1965-66; exec. dir. Assn. Operating Room Nurses, N.Y.C., 1966-68; pres. Care-Ring Service, N.Y.C., 1968—; asst. to v.p. in charge devel. Bennett Coll., Millbrook, N.Y., 1970; pub. relations cons., 1970—. Mem. Women's Nat. Rep. Club, N.Y.C., Manhattan East Rep. Club, N.Y.C. Mem. Assn. Exec. Dirs., Am. Assn. U. Women. Address: 301 E 78th St New York City NY 10021

PARKER, MARJORY EVA WINSTON (MRS. THOMAS LEE PARKER), lawyer; b. Santa Barbara, Cal., Sept. 2, 1926; d. Chester Parker and Lois Genevieve (Warner) Winston; B.A., U. Wash., 1949; LL.B., Georgetown U., 1965; m. Thomas Lee Parker, Sept. 1, 1967. Commd. 2d lt. USAF, 1951; personnel officer continental U.S., Europe, 1951-61; admitted to Cal. bar, 1966, U.S. Supreme Ct. bar, 1972; dep. atty. gen. Cal., Sacramento, 1966—. Mem. Internat. Oceanographic Found., Underwater Soc. Am., Am. Bar Assn., Nat. Assn. Women Lawyers, Nat. Assn. Dist. Attys., Nat. Orgn. for Women, Queen's Bench, Aircraft Owners and Pilots Assn., Sierra Club, Alpha Gamma Delta, Kappa Beta Pi. Democrat. Episcopalian. Club: Commonwealth. Office: 555 Capitol Mall Suite 550 Sacramento CA 95814

PARKER, MARY EVELYN DICKERSON (MRS. W. BRYANT PARKER), state ofcl.; b. Fullerton, La., Nov. 8, 1920; d. Racia E. and Addie (Graham) Dickerson; B.A., Northwestern State Coll., 1941; diploma of social welfare, La. State U., 1943; m. W. Bryant Parker, Oct. 31, 1954 (dec. May 1965); children—Mary Bryant, Ann Graham. Social worker, Allen Parish, La., 1941-42; personnel adminstr. War Dept., Camp Claiborne, La., 1943-47; editor Oakdale (La.) Jour., 1947-48; exec. dir. La. Dept. of Commerce and Industry, Baton Rouge, 1948-52; with Mut. of N.Y., Baton Rouge, 1952-56; chmn. State Bd. of Pub. Welfare, Baton Rouge, 1950-51; commr. La. Dept. of Pub. Welfare, Baton Rouge, 1956-63; commr. Div. of Adminstrn., State of La., Baton Rouge, 1964-67; state treas. State of La., Baton Rouge, 1968—. Chmn. White House Conf. on Children and Youth, 1960; pres. La. Conf. of Social Welfare, 1959-61. Nat. Democratic Committeewoman, 1948-52. Bd. dirs. Womans Hosp., Baton Rouge. Baptist. Home: 9321 Hill Trace Av Baton Rouge LA 70809 Office: PO Box 44154 Capitol Sta Baton Rouge LA 70804

PARKER, MARY LANGSTON, physician; b. Inverness, Fla., Nov. 14, 1924; d. Bernard G. and Jarda (Johnson) Langston; B.S., Fla. State Coll. for Women, 1946; M.S., Fla. State U., 1949; M.D., Washington U., St. Louis, 1953; m. Charles W. Parker, June 13, 1953; children—Keith, Charles, Katherine, Christine, Sandra. Intern St. Louis Children's Hosp., 1953-54; resident metabolism Washington U., St. Louis, 1960-62, dir. health services, 1971—, asst. prof. pediatric endocrinology, mem. staff St. Louis Children's Hosp., Barnes Hosp., St. Louis. Home: 307 S Forest St Webster Groves MO 63119 Office: Health Services Washington U St Louis MO 63110

PARKER, PAMELA ANTOINETTE MATTHEWS (MRS. CECIL MAURICE PARKER), phys. therapist; b. Washington, June 8, 1949; d. Charles Wilbur and Charlotte LaVerne (Banks) Matthews; B.S., Boston U., 1971; m. Cecil Maurice Parker, Aug. 21, 1971. Phys. therapist dept. human resources D.C. Gen Hosp., Washington, 1971—; speaker Nat. Med. Assn. Careers Program. Active United Givers Fund Campaign, 1971. Bd. govs. Nat. A.R.C. Mem. Am. Phys. Therapy Assn., Am. Legion Aux., Delta Sigma Theta. Home: 3912 Southern Av SE Washington DC 20020 Office: 19th and Massachusetts Av SE Washington DC 20003

PARKER, RENA (MRS. L. L. PARKER), mayor; b. Cheyenne, Wyo., June 2, 1918; d. Rowley C. and Eloise Leslie (Fletcher) Ellsworth; B.S., cum laude, U. Wyo., 1939; m. Leland L. Parker, Oct. 2, 1945; children—Barry Lee, Karen Eloise, Warren Roy, Linda Louise. Sec. U. Wyo., 1939-42; statistician Wyo. Welfare Dept., Cheyenne, 1942-43; economist Rivers and Harbors Bd., Army Engrs., Washington, 1943-46; apptd. mem. Corona (Cal.) City Council, 1963, elected mem., 1964-72, mayor, 1966-72. Corona rep. So. Cal. Assn. Govts. 1965-72, mem. exec. com., 1965-71; Corona rep. Transp. Assn. So. Cal., 1965-67; mem. Local Agy. Formation Com., 1968-72, chmn., 1970-72; chmn. Riverside County Transp. Commn., 1972—; mem. Cal. Atty. Gen.'s Task Force for Environment, 1973—. Organizer Co-op. Nursery Sch., Corona, 1958; chmn. United Fund Drive, 1962, pres., 1974; chmn. Hosp. Bond Drive, 1963; active P.T.A., ch. work 1955-72; active Boy Scouts Am., 1955-65. Bd. dirs. San Gorgonio council Girl Scouts U.S.A., 1965-74. Named Citizen of Year, C. of C., 1967. Mem. Corona Women Voters, Friends of Library, Am. Assn. U. Women. Club: Woman's Improvement (Corona). Home: W Ontario St Corona CA 91720 Office: 812 Washburn St Corona CA 91720

PARKER, ROSE MARIE NORWOOD (MRS. JOHN A. PARKER, JR.), librarian; b. Durham, N.C., Sept. 12, 1942; d. Shellie Vernon and Minnie Estelle (Holt) Norwood; B.A. (Va. State Library fellow), U. N.C., 1966, M.S. in L.S., 1967; student Old Dominion Coll., 1960-64; m. John Albert Parker, Jr., May 29, 1970. Acting head children's dept. main library Norfolk (Va.) Pub. Library, 1966, library extension activities, 1967, acting head children's dept., 1967, library extension activities, 1968-70, head children's dept., 1970—; condr. storytelling workshops. Mem. Va., Southeastern library assns., Nat. Story League. Christian Scientist. Home: 601 Baldwin Av Norfolk VA 23517 Office: 301 E City Hall Av Norfolk VA 23510

PARKER, ROSE (MRS. SAM PARKER), civic worker; b. St. Paul, Aug. 9, 1911; d. John Algot and Mary Rein (Paukner) Hogquist; m. Sam Parker, Nov. 5, 1950; 1 son, Dean Ethan. Operations mgr. Duluth-Chgo. Freight Lines, 1937-40; claim agt., bookkeeper Moland Bros. Trucking Co., Duluth, Minn., 1940-46; treas. Duluth Air Lines, 1946-47; auditor Hotel Duluth, 1947-50; co-owner Parker Co. Mem. Sr. Citizens Bldg. Center Adv. Com. Pres. Duluth Bus. and Profl. Women's Club, 1948-49, B'nai B'rith Women's Auxiliary, 1955-57; League Women Voters, Rice Lake, Wis., 1959-62, Rice Lake P.T.A., 1959-60, Elks Ladies Aux., Rice Lake Golf Club Aux.; sec. Civic Concert Assn., 1963-68; dir. Girl Scout Camp Assn., Rice Lake Scholarship Found.; chmn. Barron County of Gov.'s Com. to Keep Wis. Clean and Beautiful; sec. bd. trustees U. Wis., Barron County Center; mem. Citizens Adv. Council to Mayor; pres. Fortnightly Womens Club. Mem. Internat. Platform Assn. Address: 823 Lake St Rice Lake WI 54868

PARKER, SANDRA ANN, educator; b. Batavia, N.Y., June 14, 1943; d. Warren Howard and Agnes Ella (Shiltz) Parker; B.A., N.Y. State U. at Geneseo, 1965; M.A. (fellow), Western Res. U., 1967, Ph.D. (fellow), 1968; postgrad. St. Hilda's Coll., Oxford, Eng., 1967, Universidad Iberoamericana, Mexico City, Mexico, 1963. Asst. prof. English Hiram (O.) Coll., 1968—. Recipient Research grants, Hiram Coll., 1963, 73. Mem. Am. Assn. U. Profs., Nat. Council Tchrs. English, Modern Lang. Assn., English Speaking Union, Western Res., Aurora hist. socs. Democrat. Roman Catholic. Home: 59 E Garfield St Aurora OH 44202 Office: PO Box 306 Hiram OH 44234

PARKER, SARAH ELIZABETH, lawyer; b. Charlotte, N.C., Aug. 23, 1942; s. Augustus and Zola Elizabeth (Smith) Parker; student Meredith Coll., 1960-62; A.B., U. N.C. at Chapel Hill, 1964, J.D., 1969. Admitted to N.C. bar, 1969; tchr. Middle East Tech. U., Peace Corps, Ankara, Turkey, 1964-66; asso. firm Cansler, Lassiter, Lockhart & Eller, Charlotte, 1969—. Mem. pub. affairs com. YWCA, 1970-71. First vice pres. Democratic Women's Club, 1972, pres., 1973; mem. organizational steering com. Charlotte Women's Polit. Caucus, 1971; mem. exec. bd. Mecklenburg County Dem. party, 1973. Mem. 26th Jud. Dist., N.C., Am. bar assns. Episcopalian. Editorial staff N.C. Law Rev., 1968-69. Home: 3912 Hough Rd Charlotte NC 28209 Office: North Carolina National Bank Bldg Charlotte NC 28202

PARKER, SUSAN WISLER (MRS. JOSEPH WALTER PARKER), occupational therapist; b. Columbia, Pa., July 12, 1946; d. Charles Root and Charlotte Mary (Snell) Wisler; B.A., Emory U., 1968; certificate U. Utrecht (The Netherlands), 1967; M.S., Va. Commonwealth U., 1971; m. Joseph Walter Parker, Dec. 26, 1970; 1 dau., Elisabeth Ann. Staff occupational therapist VA Hosp., Richmond, Va., 1971—. Pres., VA Youth Adv. Com., 1972. Mem. Am., Va. occupational therapy assns., Chi Omega, Pi Delta Epsilon. Republican. Episcopalian. Home: 5805 Signal Hill Rd Mechanicsville VA 23111 Office: 1201 Broadrock Rd Richmond VA 23249

PARKER, VIRGINIA, librarian; b. Brookhaven, Miss., Oct. 10, 1916; d. Elmer Clifford and Amelia (Sebastian) Parker; B.A., Newcomb Coll. of Tulane U., 1937; B.S. in L.S., La. State U., 1942. Library asst. Wayne U. Coll. Medicine, 1942-43; library staff mem. Detroit News, 1943-46; librarian Am. Cancer Soc., New Orleans, 1946-49; asso. librarian U. Tex. Med. Br. at Galveston, 1956-57; librarian Tex. Med. Center Library, Houston, 1957-67; librarian Health Scis. Library, Queen's U., Kingston, Ont., 1967—, asst. prof. Faculty of Medicine, 1967—. Mem. Med. Library Assn., Audubon Soc., Phi Beta Kappa, Phi Kappa Phi, Beta Phi Mu, Phi Mu. Mem. Unitarian Ch. Author articles on med. history. Asso. editor Bull. of Med. Library Assn., 1951-54, 71-74. Home: 237 Bath Rd Kingston ON K7M 2X8 Canada

PARKER, VIRGINIA MARGUERITE MOULTON (MRS. LAWRENCE CRAIG PARKER), ednl. adminstr.; b. Livermore Falls, Me., Jan. 17, 1912; d. Clement Richmond and Myrtle (Marston) Moulton; A.B., Bates Coll., 1933; postgrad. So. Conn. State Coll., 1963-64; m. Lawrence Craig Parker, May 12, 1934; children—Lawrence Craig, Judith A. (Mrs. John E. Cole III). Sec. to newspaper editor and pub., Lewiston, Me., 1933-38; sec. to pres. U. New Haven, West Haven, Conn., 1953-54, adminstrv. asst. to pres., 1954-55, dir. div. spl. studies, 1955—. Pres., Branford Mus. Art Soc., 1957-58; mem. residence com. New Haven YWCA, 1964—. Mem. Am. Assn. U. Women. Mem. Ch. of Christ. Club: Quota (v.p. 1969, dir.) (New Haven). Home: 137 Hotchkiss Grove Rd Branford CT 06405 also Whitingham VT 05361 Office: 300 Orange Av West Haven CT 06516

PARKIN, ANNE GOULDING, ednl. adminstr.; b. Pitts., Feb. 4, 1949; d. William Metcalf and Helen Mar (Goulding) Parkin; diploma Winchester-Thurston Sch., Pitts., 1966; B.A., Hood Coll., 1970. Admissions counselor Hood Coll., Frederick, Md., 1970-71; asst. dir. admissions, financial aid officer Briarcliff Coll., Briarcliff Manor, N.Y., 1971—, now dir. admissions. Class agt. Hood Coll., Frederick, Md., 1970. Mem. Coll. Entrance Exam. Bd., Coll. Scholarship Service Assembly, N.Y. State Financial Aid Adminstrs. Assn., Winchester-Thurston Sch., Hood Coll. alumnae assns. Home: 330 S Broadway Apt G-7 Tarrytown NY 10591 Office: Briarcliff Coll Briarcliff Manor NY 10510

PARKIN, EVELYN HOPE, med. social worker; b. Owatonna, Minn.; d. Wilbur L. and Verta (Cowles) Parkin; B.A., Carleton Coll., 1931; postgrad. U. Minn., 1939-41. Pediatric social worker, instr. field work U. Minn. Hosps., 1941-45; pediatric med. social worker, supr. Med. Social Service Dept., Mayo Clinic, Rochester, Minn., 1946-53, dir. Med. Social Service Dept., 1953—. Dir. Minn. Heart Assn., 1959-64; mem. nat. com. Am. Heart Assn., 1958-62. Mem. voting Staff Mayo Clinic, 1972—. Treas. Young Republican League Rochester, 1962; sec. Olmsted County Rep. Com., 1953-55, dir. YWCA, Rochester, Minn., 1953-54; sec. bd. dirs. Mayo Clinic Credit Union, 1958-65, 65-68. Mem. Nat. Assn. Social Workers (mem. exec. com. Minn. sect. 1964-65), Minn. Welfare Conf. (sec. 1954), Am. Assn. U. Women (asst. treas. 1953-54), Am. Hosp. Assn., Soc. Hosp. Social Work Dirs. Presbyn. Clubs: Mayo Clinic Women's (pres. 1950-52), Carleton College Alumni. Home: 502 15th Av SW Rochester MN 55902 Office: Mayo Clinic Rochester MN 55902

PARKINS, NORMA JEAN HUFFMAN (MRS. RUSSELL MYRON PARKINS), banker; b. Macomb, Ill., Apr. 18, 1930; d. Ezra Lee and Jessie Irene (Smith) Huffman; grad. high sch.; m. Russell Myron Parkins, June 6, 1948; children—Randall Lee, Rex Alan. Bookkeeper Union Nat. Bank, 1960-66; bookkeeper, teller First Nat. Bank, 1966-70, asst. cashier, 1970— (both Macomb); owner/operator Miniature Golf & Golf Driving Range, Macomb, 1969—. Mem. Nat. Assn. Letter Carriers Aux. (treas. 1966-72), Am. Legion Aux. Mem. Christian Ch. Club: Jolly Housekeepers Household Science (Colchester, Ill.). Home: Rural Route 4 Macomb IL 61455 Office: First Nat Bank 804 W Jackson St Macomb IL 61455

PARKINSON, JOAN LIDDELL (MRS. RALPH THOMAS PARKINSON), educator; b. Rockford, Ill., Oct. 2, 1926; d. Geroge Turner and Arlene (Pratt) Liddell; B.A., Maryville Coll., 1947; M.A., U. Ky., 1956; student George Peabody Coll., 1964, U. N.C., 1965, 71-74; m. Ralph Thomas Parkinson, May 21, 1947 (dec. May 1955); children—Judith, Ralph Thomas. Tchr. pub. schs., Orange County, N.C., 1947-48, Limestone, Tenn., 1948-49, Washington, 1949-51, Berea Coll. Training Sch., Berea, Ky., 1956-57, Statesboro, Ga., 1958-60, Memphis, 1960-63; asst. prof. edn. Lenoir Rhyne Coll., Hickory, N.C., 1963—; grad. asst. U. N.C., 1971-74. Cons., Comprehensive Sch. Improvement Program, Burke County, N.C., Tchr. Aide Program, Shelby, N.C. Alumni bd. Maryville Coll.; bd. dirs. Child Devel. Council, Hickory. Mem. N.E.A., N.C. Assn. Educators (chpt. pres. 1967-71), Assn. Childhood Edn. Internat., Nat. Assn. Edn. Young Children, Am. Assn. U. Profs., Assn. Student Teaching, Delta Zeta (chpt. dir. 1965-69), P.E.O. Presbyn. Home: Route 4 110 Warren Way Chapel Hill NC 27514

PARKS, ARLIE MARIE MULLER, educator; b. N.Y.C., June 1, 1937; d. Walter Nicholas and Mary Frances (Pernicka) Muller; B.S. in Elementary Edn. and Speech Edn. (Faculty Dames scholar), State U. Coll., Fredonia, N.Y., 1959; M.A. in Speech, Pa. State U., 1962; postgrad. U. Pitts., 1963-65, Temple U., 1968, Elmira Coll., 1969, Edinboro State Coll., 1969, U. Hawaii, 1970, Fla. State U., 1971; m. Vaughn Parks, Mar. 7, 1964 (div.). Instr. speech Shippensburg (Pa.) State Coll., 1961-63; tchr. speech, drama, English, Wilkinsburg High Sch., Pitts., 1963-65; cooperating tchr. student tchrs. U. Pitts., 1963-65; tchr. Meadowland Nursery Sch. and Kindergarten, Jenkintown, Pa., 1966; asst. prof. speech Mansfield (Pa.) State Coll., 1966-71, asso. prof., 1971—. Recipient Certificate of Appreciation Jr. C. of C., 1970. Doctoral grantee Delta Kappa Gamma, 1972. Mem. Nat. Fedn. Bus. and Profl. Women, Am. Assn. U. Women, Pa. High Sch. Speech League (coll. rep. exec. bd. 1967-71), Am. Assn. U. Profs., Internat. Soc. for Gen. Semantics, Inst. for Gen. Semantics, Speech Communication Assn. Pa., Council for Rhetoric and Pub. Address, Oral Interpretation Council, Speech Edn. Council (at-large, chmn.), Internat. Communication Assn., Am. Ednl. Research Assn., Internat. Platform Assn., Gamma Theta Nu (founder). Home: PO Box 443 Mansfield PA 16933

PARKS, EDNA DORINTHA, educator; b. Wakefield, Mass., Oct. 7, 1910; d. Thomas Fulton and Lillian Estelle (Mansfield) Parks; Mus.B., Yale, 1935; M.A., Boston U., 1944, Ph.D., 1957. Tchr. music Wakefield Pub. Schs., 1937-47; instr. music, coll. organist Western Coll. for Women, Oxford, O., 1947-48; mem. staff music dept. Green Mountain Coll. Poultney, Vt., 1948-56; vis. lectr. Wheaton Coll., Norton, Mass., 1957, asst. prof. music, 1957-61, asso. prof., 1961-64, prof. music, 1965—, chmn. music dept., 1962-66. Named One of Outstanding Educators Am., 1974. Mem. Music Library Assn., Am. Musicological Soc., Coll. Music Soc. (nat. sec. 1972-74). Author: The Hymns and Hymn Tunes Found in the English Metrical Psalters, 1966; Early English Hymns: An Index, 1972. Contbr. articles, book revs. to profl. jours. Home: 212 Forest St Winchester MA 01890 Office: PO Box 267 Norton MA 02766

PARKS, EVELYN AUGUSTA, trade assn. exec.; b. Pitts., Jan. 6, 1927; d. Ralph E. Wagner and Evelyn E. (Gettings) Gaudian; student Pa. State U., 1947-50, Ikeda U. Fine Art, Japan, 1953, 54, U. Nuremberg (Germany) Art, 1960-61, Inst. Orgn. Mgmt., Syracuse U., 1969; m. Robert H. Parks, Aug. 8, 1946 (div. Mar. 1963); children—Diane Renee, Martin Hill. With Nat. Assn. Cemeteries, Arlington, Va., 1961—, writer, asst. editor trade jour., office mgr., 1965—, exec. asst. to exec. v.p., 1968-73; exec. asst. to exec. v.p. Nat. Assn. Indsl. Parks, 1973—. Mem. Fairfax Hunt, English Speaking Union, Hist. Soc. Fairfax County, Navy League U.S., S.C. Soc., Internat. Platform Assn., Ladies Oriental Shrine, Beta Sigma Phi. Episcopalian. Club: Arts (Washington). Home: 1240 Providence Terrace McLean VA 22101 Office: 1800 N Kent St Arlington VA 22009

PARKS, EVELYN LOUISE, librarian; b. Seven Springs, N.C., Feb. 27, 1910; d. William Leon and Nellie (Kornegay) Parks; A.B., N.C. Coll. Women, 1932, A.B., 1933. Librarian, Farm Life Sch., Vanceboro, N.C., 1933-34, Central Jr. High Sch., Greensboro, N.C., 1934-37, Stanley County Library, Albemarle, N.C., 1937-41, Pack Meml. Library, Asheville, N.C., 1941-43; trustee, cons. Mich. State Library, Lansing, 1943-49; librarian May Meml. Library, Burlington, N.C., 1949-63; regional dir. Central N.C. Regional Library, Burlington, 1963—. Mem. Am. (pub. relations com. 1953-54), Southeastern (chmn. pub. library sect. 1959-61), N.C. (chmn. pub. library sect. 1965-67) library assns., League of Women Voters of N.C. (sec. 1953-54, dir. 1963-65), Women's div. Alamance County C. of C. Club: Burlington Business and Professional Women (dir. 1973). Home: Towne House Graham NC 27253 Office: 342 S Spring St Burlington NC 27215

PARKS, JUANITA GREENE (MRS. THOMAS M. PARKS), artist; b. El Reno, Okla., Oct. 5, 1909; d. John Thomas and Claudia Lewella (Wallace) Greene; B.Art Edn., Chgo. Art Inst., 1932; M.F.A., Peabody Coll., 1958; postgrad. Boston Mus. Sch. Art, U. Chgo., Art Student's League N.Y.C.; pvt. study with Robert Brackman, Jerry Farnsworth, Ivan Olinsky, Xavier Gonzalez, George Bridgman, Reginald Marsh, Elliot O'Hara; m. Julian P. Williams, Aug. 24, 1932 (dec. Mar. 1958); children—Ann Parker (Mrs. James Thomas High), Juanita Jean (Mrs. Bruce O. Watkins), Julia Wallace (Mrs. W. Kenneth Parks); m. 2d, Thomas M. Parks, June 6, 1966. Exhibited one-man show at Lynn Kottler Gallery, N.Y.C., Parthenon Galleries, Nashville; exhibited in group shows at Chgo. Art Inst., Atlanta High Mus., Ark. Fine Arts Center, Brooks Meml. Gallery, Memphis, Mystic (Conn.) Art Gallery, Parthenon Galleries, Nashville, Cheekwood Galleries Fine Art, Nashville, Memphis Biennial Exhbn., Memphis, Conn. Woman's Watercolor Festival, Tenn. Artists Exhbn., Cheekwood, others; represented in permanent collections Ark. Fine Arts Center, Parthenon Gallery, Mystic Art Gallery, Atlanta High

Mus., Brooks Meml. Art Gallery, many pvt. collects; art instr. in design Memphis Acad. Arts, 1938-40; art dir. Watkins Inst., sch. adult edn., Nashville, 1945-73; established 1st out-of-town circulating gallery program, Nashville, 1950; pvt. art instr., 1950-74; vis. instr. Tenn. Colls.; art lectr. to art socs., also civic groups, 1945-68; judge various art exhbns., 1945-74; founder ann. Tenn. All State Artists Exhbn., 1950. Recipient honors, awards from various orgns. including Conn. Woman's Watercolor Festival, 1954, Tenn. Art League, 1958-68, Tenn. State Fair, 1948, 58, 60, 62, 67, Art Inst. Alumni Exhbn., 1963, Ark. Delta Fine Arts Exhbn., 1959, Mystic Art Gallery, 1959, Central S. Exhbn., 1968. Mem. Nat. Assn. Women Artists, Tenn. (charter founder, 1st v.p. 1960—), Memphis art leagues, Memphis Acad. Art (dir. 1940-58), Mystic Art Assn., Tenn. Watercolorists, Soc. for Preservation Antiquities of Tenn., Phi Sigma Alpha. Author: Drawing Fundamentals for the Beginner, 1968. Home: 4514 Beacon Dr Nashville TN 37215 Office: Watkins Inst 6th and Church Sts Nashville TN 37219

PARKS, MARY JUNE WILLS (MRS. BURGESS SPURLOCK PARKS), ins. agt.; b. Pleasureville, Ky., Aug. 7, 1926; d. Clyde Gano and Bertha (Hall) Wills; student U. Ky., 1944-45, Murray State U., 1946-47; m. Burgess Spurlock Parks, June 14, 1949. Tchr. music Shelby County (Ky.) Schs., 1948-51; asso. Porter & Lucas, Georgetown, Ky., 1961-64; rep. Investors Heritage Life Ins. Co., Frankfort, Ky., 1961—. Recipient Nat. Assn. Life Ins. Cos. awards, 1969-73. Mem. Woman's Assn. Georgetown Coll. (life), Sigma Alpha Iota. Mem. Christian Ch. Club: Scott County Woman's (pres. 1958-59) (Georgetown). Home: 910 Crosshill St Frankfort KY 40601 Office: 200 Capital Av Frankfort KY 40601

PARKS, MURIEL MINA, ednl. adminstr.; b. Outlook, Sask., Can., Apr. 19, 1917; d. Robert Mills and Edna May (Sabin) Parks; A.A., Gogebic Community Coll., 1938; B.Ed., Western Ill. U., 1940; M.A., Northwestern U., 1943. Came to U.S., 1918. Tchr. English Evanston (Ill.) Twp. High Sch., 1940-43, student activities sec., liason with P.T.A., 1952-55; registrar Evanston Twp. Community Coll., 1946-52; registrar U. Nev. at Las Vegas, 1955—. Hosp. recreation worker A.R.C., New Guinea and Philippine Islands, 1943-45. Mem. P.E.O., Delta Kappa Gamma. Home: 2009 Howard Av Las Vegas NV 89105 Office: University Nevada 4505 S Maryland Pkwy Las Vegas NV 89154

PARMER, OPAL ELIZABETH, clin. psychologist; b. Hungtington, W.Va., Feb. 15, 1920; d. George Roy and Mary Alice (Jamison) Belchar; A.B., East Carolina Coll., 1947; M.Ed., Temple U., 1950; postgrad. U. Toledo, 1950-63, Ohio State U., 1969-74; summer workshop student Case Western Res. U., 1965; m. Robert L. Parmer, June 30, 1951. Instr. Lee Coll., Cleveland, Tenn., 1945-46; supr. Reading Lab. Sch. Temple U., summers 1946-49; reading tchr. Maumee Valley Day Sch. and Ottawa Hills Sch., Toledo, 1948-51; tchr. Marion City Sch., 1951-56; psychologist Columbus (O.) Schs., 1956-63; supervising psychologist Sangamon County schs., Springfield, Ill., 1963-66, Pickaway County (O.) schs., 1967-67; clin. psychologist Juvenile Diagnostic Center, Columbus, 1967-71, Diocesan Guidance Center, Columbus, 1971-73, Interfaith Counseling Center and Columbus schs., 1973—; legislative cons. in field, 1972. Mem. women's aux. Mt. Carmel Hosp., Columbus. Named Tchr. of Year, Maumee Valley Sch., 1947. Mem. Am., Ohio (award outstanding service to psychology 1972), Central Ohio (dir.) psychol. assns., Ohio, Central Ohio edn. assns., Ohio, Central Ohio sch. psychologists, Council Exceptional Children, Am. Psychiat. Assn. Children, Pi Lambda Theta, Pi Delta Gamma. Methodist (pres. Weslyan Women 1971-74). Contbr. articles to profl. jours. Home: 4034 Pegg Av Columbus OH 43214

PARNELL, DIANA RUTH DEANGELIS (MRS. FRANCIS WILLIAM PARNELL, JR.), physician; b. Tacoma, Wash., May 18, 1940; d. Fulvio Garibaldi and Ruth (Nordlund) DeAngelis; B.S., Pa. State U., 1961; M.D., Georgetown U., 1965; m. Francis William Parnell, Jr., Feb. 27, 1965; children—Cheryl Lynn, John Francis, Kathleen Diana, Alison Anne. Intern, Univ. Hosps., Madison, Wis., 1965-66, resident in dermatology, 1966-69; practice medicine, specializing in dermatology U. Wis. Student Health Service, Madison, 1969-70; pvt. practice dermatology, Greenbrae, Cal., 1970—. Clin. instr. dermatology U. Wis. Med. Sch., 1969-70, U. Cal. at San Francisco Med. Sch., 1971—. Diplomate Nat. Bd. Med. Examiners, Am. Bd. Dermatology, Mem. A.M.A., Cal., Marin County med. assns., Am. Acad. Dermatology, San Francisco Dermatol. Soc., Delta Delta Delta. Roman Catholic. Home: 80 Corte Precita Greenbrae CA 94904 Office: Ross Valley Med Clinic 1350 S Eliseo Dr Greenbrae CA 94904

PARR, LUCY CHAMBERLAIN (MRS. ROBERT EMMET PARR), author; b. Kanab, Utah, July 25, 1924; d. Eustace Josiah and Geneva (Esplin) Chamberlain; grad. high sch.; m. Robert Emmet Parr, May 21, 1945. Writer articles, verse, numerous stories appearing in mags., including Highlights for Children, The Instr., Jack and Jill, Newstime, The Children's Friend. Republican. Mem. Ch. of Jesus Christ of Latter-day Saints. Author: Pioneer and Indian Stories, 1969; Family Christmas Stories, 1973. Home: 452 Westminster Av Salt Lake City UT 84115

PARR, MARY LAVINIA YOHANNAN (MRS. WENDELL R. PARR), educator; b. Cleve., June 21, 1927; d. Shlemon and Jemima (Blackford) Yohannan; A.B., Coll. of Wooster, 1948. M.L.S., Western Res. U., 1949; postgrad. Tchrs. Coll., 1957-61, New Sch., 1960-61. Columbia, 1968-69; m. Wendell R. Parr, Oct. 1, 1949. Children's librarian Cuyahoga County Library, Cleve., 1949-50; head librarian Willard (O.) Meml. Library, 1950-51; sec. Supt.'s Office Luna County Bd. Edn., Deming, N.M., 1951-52; cost analyst Miller Paper Co., Syracuse, N.Y., 1952-53; librarian extension div. San Antonio Pub. Library, 1953-54; asst. library dir. Newark State Coll., Union, N.J. 1955-62; adj. Drexel Inst. Tech. Phila. 1961-62; asst. prof. Villanova (Pa.) U., 1962-63; asso. prof. Pratt Inst., Bklyn., 1963-69; asso. prof. library sci. St. John's U., Jamaica, N.Y., 1969-73, chmn. library sci., 1972-73; head program devel. D.C. Pub. Library, 1973—. Mem. A.L.A., Woman's Nat. Book Assn., Am. Assn. U. Profs., Internat. Relations Round Table (treas. 1969-71), N.J., N.Y. library assns., N.Y. Library Club. Home: 63 Essex Av Montclair NJ 07042 Office: Martin Luther King Meml Library 901 G St NW Washington DC 20001

PARR, PHYLLIS ANN GRAHAM (MRS. JAMES THEODORE PARR), educator; b. Princeton, Ind., Dec. 4, 1937; d. James Edward and Opal Beatrice (Miller) Graham; B.S.E., Oakland City Coll., 1959; M.A., Ind. U., 1961, Ph.D., 1964; m. James Theodore Parr, Sept. 3, 1966; 1 son, Graham Allen. Asst. prof. math. Ind. State U., Terre Haute, 1964-66; asst. prof. math. U. Ill., Urbana, 1966-71; asso. prof. math. Ill. Wesleyan U., Bloomington, 1971-73; asst. prof. math. Ill. State U. at Normal, 1973—. Vol. adult edn. program, Champaign, Ill., 1971. Mem. Am. Math. Soc., Math. Assn. Am., Univ. and Coll. Women Ill. (pres. 1973-74), Sigma Xi. Episcopalian. Home: 2109 Peirce Av Bloomington IL 61701

PARRILLO, MARIANNE JOAN, lawyer; b. Chgo., Mar. 20, 1948; d. James Rosario and Hazel Marie (Phillips) Parrillo; B.S. in Psychology, U. Ill., 1967; J.D., Loyola U., Chgo., 1970. Admitted to Ill. bar, 1970; asst. corp. counsel City of Chgo., 1971—. Gen. counsel for Chgo. Commn. on Human Relations. Mem. Am., Ill., Women's bar assns. Home: 2948 S Emerald Chicago IL 60616 Office: Room 511 City Hall Chicago IL 60607

PARRIS, JUDITH ANN HEIMLICH (MRS. ADDISON W. PARRIS), polit. scientist; b. Columbus, O., June 5, 1939; d. William F. and Mary (Eitel) Heimlich; A.B. cum laude, Smith Coll., 1961; M.A., Columbia, 1963, Ph.D., 1967; m. Addison W. Parris, Oct. 12, 1968. Reporter Housing and Urban Affairs Daily, Washington, 1961-62; press asst. Senator George A. Smathers, Washington, 1962; policy planning research asst. Small Bus. Adminstrn., Washington, 1963-65; research asst. Brookings Instn., Washington, 1966-68, research asso., 1968—; professorial lectr. Am. U., 1970. Pres.'s fellow Columbia U., 1965-66. Mem. Am., Washington Area polit. sci. assns. Democrat. Author: (with others) Congress Urban Problems, 1969; The Convention Problem, 1972; (with Wallace S. Sayre) Voting for President, 1970; (with Richard C. Bain) Convention Decisions and Voting Records, 2d edit., 1973. Home: 3105 Northampton St NW Washington DC 20015 Office: 1775 Massachusetts Av NW Washington DC 20036

PARRIS, PEGGY BALDWIN (MRS. JACK A. PARRIS), art center adminstr.; b. Hebron, Neb., July 23, 1934; d. Donald J. and Edith W. (Butcher) Baldwin; student U. Richmond, 1952-53, U. Dayton, 1953-54; B.F.A. with distinction, U. Neb., 1956; postgrad. Mich. State U., 1961; m. Jack A. Parris, Aug. 18, 1956; children—Christopher, Andrew, Timothy, Patrick. Asst. to dir. U. Neb. Art Gallery, Lincoln, 1956-57; edn. dir. Sioux City (Ia.) Art Center, 1971, asst. dir., 1972, acting adminstr., 1972, dir., 1972—. Instr., Morningside Coll., Sioux City, 1972. Bd. dirs. Briar Cliff Coll., Sioux City. Mem. Siouxland Council Arts and Scis., Midwest Museums Conf. (adv. council), Am. Assn. Museums, Sioux City Artists Group, Chi Omega. Home: 3105 Viking Dr Sioux City IA 51104 Office: 513 Nebraska St Sioux City IA 51101

PARRISH, EVE JANET, ednl. adminstr.; b. Milw., Feb. 17, 1943; d. Wilfred Orville and Fleurette Hope (Matthes) Parrish; B.A. with honors (Woodrow Wilson fellow), U. Wis., 1964; A.M., U. Pa., 1967, Ph.D. (Hyneman fellow), 1969. Asst. prof. ancient studies U. Md. Baltimore County, Balt., 1969—, dir. spl. sessions, 1972—. Served to lt. (j.g.) USNR, 1964-66; now lt. comdr. Res. Mem. Am. Philol. Assn., Sigma Epsilon Sigma, Eta Sigma Phi, Phi Alpha Theta, Phi Kappa Phi. Home: 4000 N Charles St Baltimore MD 21218

PARRISH, JAN TELLANDER, clin. psychologist; b. Evanston, Ill., Sept. 28, 1929; d. Frederic and Rose Evelyn (Mazur) Tellander; B.A., U. Miami, M.S., 1964, Ph.D. (NSF fellow), 1967. Staff psychologist Henderson Clinic, Ft. Lauderdale, Fla., 1969-70; staff psychologist Community Mental Health Services Clinic, Miami, Fla., 1969-70; individual practice clin. psychology, 1969—; instr. U. Miami; lectr. civic groups. Mem. Am., Dade County psychol. assns., Common Cause, Am. Civil Liberties Union. Office: 1492 S Miami Av Miami FL 33130

PARRISH, JEAN JACOB, educator; b. Huron, S.D., July 27, 1922; d. Paul Emile and Anna (Dominian) Jacob; B.A., U. Ill., 1943; M.A., Radcliffe Coll., 1950, Ph.D., 1961; m. Stephen Maxfield Parrish, Feb. 26, 1945 (div. 1969); children—Madeleine, Anne. Adminstrv. asst. to chief French Purchasing Mission of Telecommunications, Washington, 1945-46; mem. UN Secretariat, Dept. Pub. Information, Lake Success, N.Y., 1946-48; co-founder Mandrake Book Store, Cambridge, Mass., 1948-49; teaching asst. Harvard, 1952-54; part-time instr. Cornell, 1955-61, instr., 1961-64, asst. prof., 1964-66, asso. prof. Romance lit., 1966-72, chmn., 1966-70; prof., chmn. dept. comparative lit. Rutgers U., New Brunswick, N.J., 1972-74, chmn. langs. and lit., 1974—. Mem. Modern Lang. Assn., Mortar Bd., Bronze Table, Phi Beta Kappa, Phi Kappa Phi. Contbr. articles to profl. jours. Home: 88 Mountain Av Princeton NJ 08540

PARRISH, JEMIMA BUCHANAN (MRS. A. LEONARD PARRISH), artist, poet; b. Jasper, Ala.; d. John H. and Anne (Tubb) Buchanan; student pub. schs.; m. A. Leonard Parrish, Aug. 17, 1926; 1 son, David Buchanan. Exhibited in group shows at Birmingham (Ala.) Art Mus., Buchanan Hall Gallery, Samford U. (Birmingham), Atlanta Art Assn., Fine Arts Center (Lynchburg, Va.), Dayton (O.) Art Inst., Emerson Mus. Art (Syracuse, N.Y.), Miami (Fla.) Museum Modern Art, Smithsonian Instn., Norton Gallery (West Palm Beach, Fla.), Des Moines (Ia.), Denver Art Museum, Municipal Art Gallery, Los Angeles, La Grange (Ga.) Sidewalk Show; represented in permanent collections at Jackson, Miss., Ashville, N.C., Birmingham, Knoxville, Tenn. Mem. Nat. League Am. Pen Women (Ala. art chmn. 1968-70, 72—), Acad. Am. Poets, Ala. Writers Conclave, Ala. State Poetry Soc., Ala. Art League. Club: Quill. Author: New American Poetry, 1945; Testament of Faith, 1942. Home: 1426 24th St N Birmingham AL 35234

PARROTT, MARY EMILY, coll. dean; b. Mullins, S.C., Dec. 26, 1946; d. Ralph Emerson and Louise (Fowler) Parrott; A.B. in Psychology, U. S.C., 1969, M.Ed. in Higher Edn., 1971. Edn. counselor E. Carolina U., Greenville, N.C., 1971; asst. dean residence life, adj. faculty U. S.C., Columbia, 1971—. Vol. Columbia Community Center, 1967—; active YWCA. Mem. Nat., S.C. (coll. chmn. 1973) assns. women deans, counselors and adminstrs., Nat. Assn. Student Personnel Adminstrs. (task force womens' concerns 1973, mem. regional research and programs com.), Am. Personnel and Guidance Assn., Am. Assn. Higher Edn., Am. Assn. U. Women, Am., So. coll. personnel assns., League Women Voters. Home: 4215 Bethel Church Rd Columbia SC 29206

PARRY, ANN (MRS. NICHOLAS PARRY), real estate broker; b. Greensburg, Pa., Aug. 16, 1916; d. Myer and Dora (Goodman) Liebman; student Pierce Jr. Coll., 1962-63; m. Nicholas L. Parry, Dec. 6, 1933; children—Patricia Ann (Mrs. Stanley D. Rand), Joyce Marlene (Mrs. Edwin Zabel), Darryl J., Douglas J. Various real estate positions, 1966-68; owner Ann Parry Real Estate, Tarzana, Cal., 1968—. Home: 5461 Newcastle Encino CA 91316 Office: 18159 Ventura Blvd Tarzana CA 91356

PARRY, BETTY WIDDER (MRS. HUGH J. PARRY), pub. relations cons.; b. N.Y.C., Jan. 5, 1927; d. Jacob and Blanche (Gardner) Widder; B.A., Queens Coll., 1948; postgrad. New Sch. Social Research, 1958-59; m. Milton J. Brawer, Sept. 11, 1949 (div. Feb. 1960); children—Stephen, Roberta; m. 2d, Hugh J. Parry, Mar. 10, 1961; children—John Weston (stepson), Brian Michael. Social worker N.Y.C. Dept. Welfare, 1949-51; social research interviewer Columbia, Nat. Opinion Research Center, J. Walter Thompson, Inc., 1955-58; research analyst Young & Rubican, Inc., 1958-59, Bur. Social Sci. Research, Child Rearing Study, Health Welfare Council, Washington, 1961-63; pub. relations cons. Betty Parry Assos., Chevy Chase, Md., 1964—. Cons. pub. relations State U. N.Y., Kindler Found., Washington Music Tchrs. Assn., Friday Morning Music Club Found. Active civil rights orgns.; dir. pub. relations Washington Chamber Orch., 1964; dir. lit. arts Jewish Community Center of Greater Washington, 1971-73; dir. poetry and lit. series Textile Mus., Washington, 1973—. Mem. Am. Assn. Pub. Opinion Research, Am. Sociol. Assn. Address: 4814 Falstone Av Chevy Chase MD 20015

PARRY, NANCY, physician, surgeon; b. Salt Lake City, Dec. 20, 1940; d. Nathaniel Edmunds Parry and Dortha Nell (Harris) Miller; B.S., U. Utah, 1963; M.D., U. Cal. at Irvine, 1967. Rotating intern Latter-day Saints Hosp., Salt Lake City, 1967-68; practice gen. medicine, Anaheim, Cal., 1968—; chmn.. gen. practice dept. Anaheim Meml. Hosp., 1971-73, Good Samaritan Hosp. Orange County; mem. staffs West Anaheim (Cal.) Community Hosp., Martin Luther Hosp., Garden Park Hosp. Mem. adv. com. Orange County Regional Planned Parenthood, 1971-72. Chmn. med. adv. bd. Anaheim Counseling Center; mem. med. adv. bd. So. Cal. Coll. Med. and Dental Assts. Mem. Am. Acad. Gen. Practice, Am. Coll. Emergency Physicians, Orange County, Cal. med. assns., A.M.A. Home: 1459 James Way Anaheim CA 92801 Office: 1720 W Ball Rd Anaheim CA 92804

PARRY, NORMA JEAN STEBLETON (MRS. EVAN J. PARRY), counselor; b. Britt, Ia., Nov. 9, 1920; d. Joseph R. and Vida S. (Robbins) Stebleton; student U. Ia., 1938-40, M.A., 1969; B.A. cum laude, Coe Coll., 1963; postgrad. Roosevelt U., Chgo., summer 1964; m. Evan J. Parry, Sept. 21, 1940; children—Susan (Mrs. Douglas Nohlgren), Robert. Caseworker Linn County Dept. Social Services, Cedar Rapids, Ia., 1964-66, supr. Linn County Work Experience project, 1966-68; counselor St. Luke's Hosp. Sch. of Nursing, Cedar Rapids, 1969—. Mem. Am. Personnel and Guidance Assn., Am. Coll. Personnel Assn., Nat. Assn. Women Deans and Counselors. Presbyn. Home: 2515 Franklin Av NE Cedar Rapids IA 52402 Office: St Lukes Hosp Sch of Nursing Cedar Rapids IA 52402

PARSELL, MIRIAM ANN, librarian; b. Newark, Feb. 3, 1920; d. Henry and Edna Blanche (Dey) Parsell; student Western Md. U., 1945-46, Scarritt Coll. for Christian Workers, 1946-48; M.L.S., Rutgers U., 1967-68. Ordained to ministry Methodist Ch. as deaconess, 1948; dir. Christian edn. First Meth. Ch., Waterbury, Conn., 1948-51, St. James Meth. Ch., Phila., 1952-60; field worker, woman's div. Christian service Meth. Ch., N.Y.C., 1960-65; librarian United Mission Library, Meth.-Presbyn. chs., N.Y.C., 1968—. Home: 2055 Center Av Fort Lee NJ 07024 Office: 475 Riverside Dr New York City NY 10027

PARSON, MARY JEAN, TV exec.; b. Houston, July 26, 1934; d. Guy Virgil and Ursula (Clark) Parson; B.A., Birmingham-So. Coll., 1956; M.F.A., Yale, 1959. Dir. spl. projects ANTA, 1959-60; producer The Sap of Life, off-Broadway, 1961; mgr. John Brown's Body, off-Broadway, 1961; bus. mgr. Mineola Playhouse, 1962; asst. to pres. Nat. Performing Arts, 1963; dir. prodn. exhibits Better Living Center, N.Y. World's Fair, 1964-65; unit mgr. ABC Network TV, 1965-67; supr. program unit mgrs. ABC-TV, 1968; mgr. program controllers ABC News, 1969; asso. dir. planning ABC, Inc., 1970-73, asso. dir. employee relations, 1973—. Free-lance writer U.P.I., 1962; founder Mineola Sch. of Theatre for Children, 1962—; tchr. Am. Acad. Dramatic Arts and John Robert Powers Sch., 1961-62; author, asso. producer Ala. Gala in Washington 1966, Ala. Sesquicentennial, 1969; Minstrels to Mods, 1971. Named Outstanding Young Woman Am., 1966, Foremost Woman in Communications, 1969. Mem. Inst. for Advanced Studies in Theatre Arts, Playwright's Unit Actors Studio, ANTA, Am. Women in Radio and Television (dir., treas., pres. N.Y.C. chpt), Mus. Arena Theater Assn., Ala. Hist. Soc., Yale Drama Alumni (exec. com.), Phi Beta Kappa, Phi Sigma Iota, Alpha Psi Omega, Mortar Bd., Zeta Tau Alpha. Home: 490 Cumberland Av Teaneck NJ 07666 Office: 1330 Av of Americas New York City NY 10019

PARSONNET, MIA, physician; b. Vienna, Austria, Jan. 19, 1924 (came to U.S. 1939, naturalized 1944); d. Oser and Sabina (Huebscher) Eimer; B.A., U. Cal. at Los Angeles, 1943; M.D., Med. Coll. Pa., 1951; m. Victor Parsonnet, June 22, 1950; children—Jeffrey, Brian, Julie. Intern Newark Beth Israel Med. Center, 1951-52, now mem. staff, dir. spl. treatment unit Newark Beth Israel Med. Center; fellow medicine N.Y. U.-Bellevue Hosp., 1952-53; resident medicine Newark City Hosp., 1963-65; mem. staff Coll. Medicine and Dentistry N.J., Newark, Martland Hosp., Newark. Home: 113 Sagamore Rd Millburn NJ 07041 Office: 201 Lyons Av Newark NJ 07112

PARSONS, DORENE MAY HULSE (MRS. JOSEPH EDWARD PARSONS), editor, pub., publicist; b. Port Jervis, N.Y., Mar. 20, 1914; d. Frank Seymour and Edna M. (Elliott) Hulse; student Hunter Coll., 1932; grad. Collegiate Secretarial Inst., N.Y.C.; m. LeRoy Vincent Reilly, Dec. 1932 (dec. Dec. 1933); m. 2d, Joseph Edward Parsons, Apr. 16, 1952; 1 dau., Ethel Virginia. N.Y.-Hollywood star columnist, feature star writer Hart Publs., London, Eng., 1935; free-lance writer Hollywood fan mags., 1936; columnist, staff feature writer Encinian Newspaper, Encino (Cal.) News, 1941; West Coast Hollywood editor teenage movie mags. Press. & TV News Corp., 1953; Hearst corr., photographer, women's soc. editor, Orange County sect. Los Angeles Examiner, 1961-66; commentator KGGK-FM Startime, Orange County, U.S.A., 1963; columnist Showtime Mag., 1962; free-lance writer, photographer Orange County newspapers, 1955—; West Coast Hollywood editor Celebrity Publs., Playgirl Mag., Anaheim, Cal., 1965—; publicist, pub. relations dir. Rebel Randall Prodns., Hollywood, 1952; owner Orange County Publicity Bur., 1969-74; feature writer Melodyland Messenger, newspaper, 1970—. Publicity, press dir. John Tracy Clinic For Deaf Children, 1963-64; Cal. adviser Youngkwang Orphanage Children's Home, Pusan, Korea, 1965-66; dir. publicity, press Orange County Children's Theatre Assn., Tustin Playhouse, Jamestown Village, 1966, prodn. asst. to producing dir., owner Orange County Acad. of Children's Theatre, 1966; Cal. dir. publicity, asst. Nat. Shut-In Soc., 1971—. Bd. dirs. Anaheim-Orange County Psycho-Cybernetics Personality Groups for Melvin Powers. Club: Soroptimist (past publicity dir. Garden Grove). Mem. Nat. League Am. Pen Women (publicity chmn., corr. sec. Orange County 1970-72, pres. Garden Grove br. 1972-74, editor-pub. Pen and Palette Cal. South publ. 1970—, state chmn. speakers bur. 1970-74), Cal. Press Women, Nat. Fedn. Press Women, Orange County Acad. Astrology, Women United Internat. (pres. chpt. 1974). Club: Francis X. Bushman Sr. Citizen Futurama (publicity chmn. 1973-74). Address: PO Drawer 3759 Anaheim CA 92803

PARSONS, ELIZABETH CHAMPLIN, psychologist; b. Jefferson, N.Y., Jan. 9, 1932; d. John Raymond and Edith Louise (Hobert) Champlin; B.S., Wilkes Coll., 1953; M.S., Pa. State U., 1959; m. Edward T. Parsons, Dec. 22, 1951 (dec. 1972); children—Claudia Louise, Catherine Eve; m. 2d, Robert E. Cutter, June 29, 1974. Psychologist, Indiana County (Pa.) Guidance Center, 1960-62; psychologist Family Counseling Center, Kenosha, Wis., 1962-71, psychologist, adminstr., 1971—; counseling psychologist Taylor Children's Home, Racine, Wis., 1964-68; part-time psychologist Racine Mental Health Clinic, 1971-72; personnel cons. Johnson Wax Co., Racine, 1970-71. Mem. adv. com. spl. edn. Kenosha, 1970-72, Outpost Youth Counsellor Program, Kenosha, 1972—; steering com. Kenosha Youth Service Bur., 1973—. Mem. Assn. Mental Health Adminstrs., Com. Mental Health Edn.; asso. mem. Am., Wis. psychol. assns. Home: 5217 Durand Av Racine WI 53406 Office: 1202 60th St Kenosha WI 53140

PARSONS, ESTELLE, actress; b. Lynn, Mass.; d. Eben and Elinor (Mattson) Parsons; grad. Oak Grove Sch. for Girls, Vassalbord, Me., 1945; A.B. in Polit. Sci., Conn. Coll. Women, 1949; postgrad. law sch. Boston U., 1949-50; m. Richard B. Gehman, Dec. 19, 1953 (div. Aug. 1958); children—Martha and Abbie (twins). Actress plays Happy Hunting, N.Y.C., 1956, Jerry Herman's Nite Cap, N.Y.C., 1958, Beg, Borrow or Steal, N.Y.C., 1959, Three Penny Opera, N.Y.C., 1960, Mrs. Dally has a Lover, N.Y.C., 1962, Next Time I'll Sing to You, N.Y.C., 1963, In the Summer House, N.Y.C., 1964, Ready When You Are, C.B., N.Y.C., 1965, Malcolm, 1966; movie Bonnie and Clyde 1966, with East Wind and Galileo, Lincoln Centre Repertory Co., N.Y.C., 1967; movie Rachel, Rachel, 1967; We Bombed in New Haven, Yale Repertory Co., New Haven, 1967; The Seven Descents of Myrtle, N.Y.C., 1968; movies Don't Drink the Water, 1969, I Never Sang for My Father, 1970, I Walk the Line, 1970, Watermelon Man, 1970, Two People, 1972; Broadway play And Miss Reardon Drinks a Little, 1971. Recipient Promising Personality award, Theatre World, 1962-63; Village Voice Off-Broadway award for distinguished performances in In the Summer House and Next Time I'll Sing to You, 1963-64; Acad. award Best Supporting Actress for Bonnie and Clyde, 1968; medal of honor for outstanding achievement Conn. Coll., 1969. Address: 505 West End Av New York City NY 10024

PARSONS, IRENE, govt. ofcl.; b. North Wilkesboro, N.C.; d. Everett T. and Martha (Minton) Parsons; B.S. in Bus. Edn. and Adminstrn., U. N.C., 1941; M.S. in Pub. Adminstrn., George Washington U., 1965; LL.D. (hon.), U. N.C., 1967. Tchr, high sch., Roanoke Rapids, N.C., 1941-42; rep. U.S. Civil Service Commn., Norfolk, Va., 1942-43; with VA, Washington, 1946—, dir. personnel, 1961-65, asst. adminstr., 1965—, spl. asst. to adminstr. vets.' affairs, 1974—. Mem. exec. com. Pres. Study Group on Careers for Women. Alumni trustee U. N.C. Served as lt. USCGR, 1943-46. Recipient Fed. Woman's award for Outstanding Achievement by Women in Fed. Service, 1966, Amvets Silver Helmet award as civil servant of year, 1971, Career Service award Nat. Civil Service League, 1972, Alumni Achievement award George Washington U., 1973. Mem. Assn. Federal Woman's Award Recipients (chmn. 1972—). Office: Veterans Adminstrn Washington DC 20420

PARSONS, JOANNE HELEN, health service exec.; b. Tarentum, Pa., July 31, 1942; d. Joseph Bernard and Helen Florence (Wangler) Parsons; student Allegheny Valley Hosp. Sch. Nursing, 1960-61. Co-head booking dept. Union Nat. Bank of Pitts., Tarentum, Pa., 1962-65; clk. specifications of quality control Allegheny Ludlum Industries, Research Center, Brackenridge, Pa., 1966-70; clk. Medicare ins. Allegheny Valley Hosp., Natrona Heights, Pa., 1971—. Mem. Western Pa. Harness Horse Assn. (sec. 1965-67), U.S. Trotting Assn., Western Pa. Colt Stakes (sec. 1967-68), Mem. First Ch. of God (com. sec. devel. and orgn. new ch. bldg. 1971—). Home: 838 9th Av Brackenridge PA Office: Carlisle S Natrona Heights PA 15065

PARSONS, MARGARET A., med. entomologist; b. Atlanta, July 21, 1933; d. Paul Prentice and Mildred Fay (Rummel) Parsons; B.S., U. Mass., 1956, M.S., 1964. Research asst. dept. entomology U. Mass., Amherst, 1956, teaching fellow, 1956-57; research asst. Mass. Coop. Wildlife Research Unit, Amherst, 1956, research cons., 1960; asst. chief, USPHS and Mass. Dept. Pub. Health, Taunton, 1957, 58-59; profl. asst., dept. entomology and plant pathology U. Mass., 1960, tech. asst., dept. zoology, 1959-61; civilian entomologist 3d U.S. Army Med. Lab., Ft. McPherson, Ga., 1962-63; med. entomologist Nat. Communicable Disease Center, Atlanta, 1963-65, Ohio Dept. Health, Columbus, 1965—. Cons., Dr. Charles T. Collins, Cal. State Coll., Long Beach. Mem. Am., Ohio (pres. 1970-72) mosquito control assns., Nat. Wildlife Fedn., Audubon Soc., Am., Eastern, Inland bird-banding assns., Wildlife Disease Assn., Am. Soc. Parasitologists, Am. Entomol. Soc., Am. Inst. Biol. Scis., Entomol. Soc. Washington, Am. Quarter Horse Assn., Appaloosa Horse Assn., Research and Engring. Soc. Am. (asso.), Sigma Xi. Contbr. articles to profl. jours. Home: RFD 1 Lucas OH 44843 Office: 1571 Perry St PO Box 2568 Columbus OH 43216

PARSONS, PATRICIA FOWLER, coll. dean; b. Montclair, N.J., Mar. 1, 1943; d. Amos Franklyn and Constance Woodruff (Fowler) Parsons; student Bowling Green State U., 1961-63; B.A., Conn. Coll., 1965; M.A., Claremont Grad. Sch., 1970, Ph.D., 1974. Asst. dean of students San Bernardino Valley Coll., San Bernardino, Cal., 1971-73; dean of students Crafton Hills Coll., Yucaipa, 1973—. Mem. Am. Psychol. Assn., Nat. Assn. Student Personnel Adminstrs., Nat. Assn. Women Adminstrs., Deans and Counselors, Cal. Personnel and Guidance Assn., Assn. Humanistic Psychology, Am. Assn. U. Women. Home: 859 N Mountain St Upland CA 91786 Office: 11711 Sand Canyon St Yucaipa CA 92399

PARTCH, ELIZABETH KATHERINE (MRS. RODNEY L. PARTCH), journalist; b. Bloomington, Neb., Mar. 16, 1922; d. Roy Cornelius and Bessye Agnes (Kelly) Petersen; B.F.A., U. Neb., 1942; m. Rodney L. Partch, Sept. 6, 1944; children—Sue, Ted. Tchr. art, English, Latin, Eldon, Ia., 1942-43, Bird City, Kan., 1952-59; editor Bird City Times, 1963-73, columnist, 1973—. Owner, Bette's Pl. ceramic studio, 1973—. Pres., P.T.A., 1954-56; 4H Club community leader, 1953-63. Mem. Democratic Twp. Com., 1969-72. Mem. U. Womens Club, Am. Assn. U. Women, Delta Phi Delta. Clubs: Nautilus, Kanred Home Demonstration Unit. Home: Rural Route 1 Bird City KS 67731 Office: Hale Pub Co Bird City KS 67756

PARTIN, JANICE ELIZABETH, psychologist; b. Nacogdoches, Tex., Jan. 28, 1947; d. William Robert and Mamie Louise (Brown) Partin; B.A., Tex. Woman's U., 1969, M.A., 1971. Tchr. pvt. sch. Children's Devel. Center, Dallas, 1969-70; psychol. examiner Region 10 Edn. Service Center, Richardson, Tex., 1970-72, asso. sch. psychologist, 1972—. Psychol. cons. adv. bd. East Dallas Head Start. Mem. Am., Southwestern, Tex. psychol. assns.

PARTINGTON, SUSAN TROWBRIDGE (MRS. JAMES HENRY MARSHALL PARTINGTON), writer; b. Milw., Oct. 21, 1924; d. John Calvin and Elsa (Gumz) Trowbridge; student U. Wis., 1941-42, U. Wash., 1943-44; m. James Henry Marshall Partington, Feb. 22, 1954; children—Marshall, Bartholomew. Creative dir. John Robert Powers Enterprises, N.Y.C., 1949-53; spokeswoman fashion, homemaking TV women's interest talk shows, home service programs, 1960—. Lectr. color dynamics in home decorating; fashion show commentator. Clubs: York (gov. N.Y.C. 1971—); Edgartown (Mass.) Yacht. Author: Beauty and Charm the Model's Way, 1969; (with John Robert Powers) The Powers Way to Teenage Beauty, Charm and Popularity, 1962. Author, editor column Art, Antiques and Architectures, Westchester mag., 1970—. Editor, collaborator: (with John Robert Powers) How To Have Model Beauty, Poise, and Personality, 1960. Collaborator: Debby Drake's Way to a Perfect Figure and Glowing Health, 1961; (with Betty Cornell) So You're Going To Be A Teen, 1964; Arlene Dahl's Always Ask A Man, 1965. Adv. bd. Clarke Sch. for Deaf, Conn. br. Humane Soc. U.S. Home: 2 Sutton Pl S New York City NY 10022 also 251 Merrain Rd Palm Beach FL 33480 Office: 200 E 42d St New York City NY 10017

PARTON, MARGARET ANNE, writer; b. San Francisco; d. Lemuel F. and Mary (Field) Parton; B.A. with honors, Swarthmore Coll., 1937; m. E.V.B. Britter, Oct. 30, 1948; 1 son, Lemuel (dec. Jan. 1969); m. 2d, Alfred Rodman Hussey, Mar. 30, 1963 (dec. Nov. 1964). Reporter, book critic, N.Y. Herald Tribune, 1943-55, fgn. corr. Japan and India, 1946-52; asso. editor, staff writer Ladies' Home Jour., 1955-63; freelance writer articles and books, pub. in various mags., including Saturday Rev., Ladies' Home Jour., McCall's, Women's Day, 1963—. Recipient Sidney Hillman award Sidney Hillman Found., 1963; award N.Y. Newspaper Women's Club, 1949, 52, 54, 56, English-Speaking Union, 1950, N.Y. Newspaper Guild, 1955. Mem. P.E.N., Newswomen's Club N.Y., Silurians, Author's League, Phi Beta Kappa. Democrat. Mem. Soc. of Friends. Club: Overseas Press. Author: Laughter on the Hill, 1945; The Leaf and the Flame, 1959; Journey Through a Lighted Room, 1973. Address: Box 577 Palisades NY 10964

PARTRIDGE, DOROTHY GARRETSON, author; b. Phila., Mar. 20, 1917; d. LeRoy and Jessie (Fox) Garretson; A.B., Bryn Mawr Coll., 1938; postgrad. Temple U., 1939-42, U. Pitts, 1940-41; m. H. Kelsey Partridge, Jr., Oct. 12, 1968. Intern tchr. Germantown Friends Sch., Phila., 1938-39; tchr. Sewickley (Pa.) Acad., 1939-41, Stevens Sch., Phila., 1941-43; editor Sharp & Dohme, Inc., Phila., 1943-45; editor Phila. Mag., C. of C. Greater Phila., 1945-49; mng. editor Etude, Theodore Presser Co., 1949-51; sr. editorial asst. Sun Oil Co., Phila., 1952-66, editor, 1966-67, mgr. corporate publs., 1970-73. Pub. relations com. Phila. council Girl Scouts, 1961-70; mem. Phila. Art Alliance. Recipient silver award oil information com. Am. Petroleum Inst., 1954, gold award, 1956. Mem. Assn. Desk and Derrick Clubs of N.A. (chmn. press. room conv. N.Y.C. 1955), Phila. Indsl. Editors Assn. (chmn. steering com. 1943-44, mem. exec. com. 1944-46, 48-49, chmn. program com. 1946-47, chmn. nominating com. 1948), Am. Petroleum Inst. (chmn. Phila. women's activities com. 1952-53, sec. 5 county Phila. area exec. com. 1957-60), Bryn Mawr Coll. Alumnae Assn., Phila. Orch. Assn. (mem. jr. com. exec. bd. 1954-63), C. of C. Greater Phila. Women's Indsl. Com. (program chmn. 1954-55; vice chmn. 1955-56, chmn. 1956), Theta Sigma Phi. Clubs: Soroptimist (corr. sec. 1952-53, first v.p. 1960-62, pres. 1962-63, dir.), William Penn Desk and Derrick (chmn. publicity com. 1952-53, dir. 1953-55, chmn. by-laws com. (1955, chmn. Am. Petroleum Inst. ladies com. 1957, chmn. nominating com. 1957, chmn. program com. 1959). Author articles in field. Home: The Benson East Jenkintown PA 19046

PASCALE, FRANCES CLAIRE, educator; b. New Haven, July 15, 1940; d. Frank Arthur and Clare Theresa (Colella) Pascale; B.A., Albertus Magnus Coll., 1962; M.A., Bryn Mawr Coll., 1964; postgrad. Fairfield U., 1965-67, Wesleyan U., 1967-68, U. Minn., 1968, San Jose State Coll., 1970-71, Cath. U., 1972, N.Y. U., 1970—. Teaching asst. math., statis. asst. Bryn Mawr Coll., 1962-64; tchr. math. North Haven (Conn.) High Sch., 1964-67; instr. math. Albertus Magnus Coll., New Haven, 1967-70, asst. prof., 1970-74, asso. prof., 1974—, chmn. dept., 1971—. Instr. math. Quinnipiac Coll., 1964-67, asst. prof., 1970-71. Vol. Recording for the Blind, 1970-71. NSF grantee, 1968, 70, 71, 72, 73. Mem. Math. Assn. Am., Nat. Council Tchrs. Math., Am. Statis. Assn., Assn. Women in Math., Caucus Women in Statistics, Am. Assn. U. Profs., Kappa Gamma Pi. Home: Apt C4 21 Plaza Terrace Hamden CT 06514

PASCALE-KITE, JANE FAY (MRS. JOSEPH H. KITE, JR.), physician; b. New Haven, May 20, 1932; d. John Adam and Madeline J. (Pompano) Pascale; B.A., Mt. Holyoke Coll., 1954; M.D., U. Chgo., 1959; m. Joseph H. Kite, Jr., Aug. 6, 1970. Intern anatomical pathology Yale New Haven Hosp., 1959-60, asst. resident anatomical pathology, 1960-61, asst. resident clin. pathology, 1961-62, NIH trainee clin. pathology, 1962-63, dir. serology immunology lab., asst. attending clin. pathology, 1968-69; NIH spl. fellow Yale Med. Sch. Dept. Microbiology, 1963-64, Institut de Recherches Scientifiques sur le Cancer, Paris, France, 1964-66; asst. in pathology Mass. Gen. Hosp., Boston, 1966-68; attending pathologist E.J. Meyer Hosp., Buffalo, N.Y., 1969—; asst. in pathology Harvard Med. Sch., 1966-68; asst. prof. clin. pathology Yale Med. Sch., 1968-69; clin. asst. prof. pathology State U. N.Y. at Buffalo, 1969—. Diplomate Nat. Bd. Med. Examiners, Am. Bd. Pathology in anat. and clin. pathology. Fellow Coll. Am. Pathologists, Am. Soc. Clin. Pathologists; mem. A.M.A. Home: 108 Chasewood Lane East Amherst NY 14051 Office: E J Meyer Meml Hosp Dept of Pathology 462 Grider St Buffalo NY 14215

PASCH, DOROTHY FRANCES, ednl. cons.; b. Toledo; d. Albert F. and Mary (Helwig) Pasch; student Toledo U., 1924-25; A.B., Ohio State U., 1928, A.M., Northwestern U., 1938. Tchr. elementary schs. Toledo, 1929-39, high sch., 1939-42; dir. Toledo Nursery and Extended Sch. Services, 1942-45; supr. spl. edn. Toledo Bd. Edn., 1945-54; dir. spl. edn. Toledo Pub. Schs., 1954-66, dir. office Ednl. Innovation and Planning, 1966-70; ednl. cons., 1970—; staff mem. U. Colo. Western Interstate Conf. on Higher Edn., 1961; summer workshop coordinator Colo. State Coll., 1962, 63, 64; vis. lectr. U. Cin., summer, 1951; summer sch. staff Ohio State U., Southburg (Conn.) Tng. Sch., 1955; Toledo U., 1956, Rainier State Sch., Buckley, Wash., 1957-59. Pres. Council Adminstrs. of Spl. Edn. in local Sch. Systems in U.S. Former bd. dirs. Toledo Day Nursery; mem. local Rehab. Com.; bd. dirs. Family Life Program, 1957, Hearing and Speech Center. Recipient spl. edn. award Nat. Council Adminstrs. Spl. Edn. Fellow Am. Assn. Mental Deficiency (v.p. ednl. sect., mem. planning bd.); mem. Ohio Soc. Crippled Children, State Assn. Tchrs. Mentally Deficient, Internat. Council Exceptional Children (governing bd.), Nat., Ohio edn. assns., Northwestern Ohio Lung Assn. (sec.), Am. Assn. U. Women, Zeta Tau Alpha. Club: Zonta Internat. Contbr. chpt. in field to bull. Home: 1211 Brigitte Dr Toledo OH 43614

PASCHER, FRANCES (MRS. ABRAM KANOF), physician; b. N.Y.C., June 5, 1905; d. Mendal Joel and Tobe (Dubester) Pascher; student Columbia, 1922-24; M.D., L.I. Coll., 1928; m. Abram Kanof, June 28, 1931; children—Elizabeth (Mrs. Ronald Levine), Margaret (Mrs. Carl Norden). Intern Montefiore Hosp., N.Y.C., 1928-29; intern Jewish Hosp. of Bklyn., 1929-31, resident, 1931-32; pvt. practice dermatology, Bklyn., 1935-66; attending dermatologist U. Hosp. Bellevue Med. Center, N.Y.C., 1945—; asso. vis. dermatologist N.Y. U. Med. Center, 1949—; vis. dermatologist, 1968-72; asso. prof. clin. dermatology N.Y. U., 1945-57, prof. clin. dermatology, 1957-72, prof. emeritus, 1972—; mem. com. pharmacy and formulary Univ. Hosp., 1960-72, chmn., 1971-72; chmn. formulary com. N.Y. Skin and Cancer Unit, 1950-72; clin. prof. dermatology U. N.C., Chapel Hill, 1973—; cons. dermatol. Talbot Perkins Adoption Service. Vice pres. Friends of N.Y. U. Med. Library. Diplomate Am. Bd. Dermatology and Syphilology. Fellow N.Y. Acad. Medicine, Am. Acad. Dermatology and Syphilology, Soc. Investigative Dermatology, Dermatology Found.; mem. A.M.A., Dermatological Soc. Greater N.Y. (pres. 1956), Modern Mus., Jewish Mus., Met. Mus., N.Y. Zool. Soc., Audubon Soc., Nat. Parks Assn., Nat. Assn. Standard Med. Vocabulary (cons.); hon. mem. Cuba, Brazil, Venezuela, Israeli derm. socs. Mem. B'nai B'rith (mem. Jewish hist. com.). Contbr. numerous articles profl. jours. Editor: Dermatologic Formulary of Skin and Cancer Unit, N.Y. U. Medical Center, 1952, 2d edit. 1957; adv. editor Jour. Investigative Dermatology, 1952-60. Prod. film on dermatologic allergy. Address: 1715 Nottingham Rd Raleigh NC 27607

PASCOE, ELIZABETH JEAN, editor; b. Cloquet, Minn.; d. Truman Archie and Mary Floride (Vos) Pascoe; B.S. in Journalism, U. Wis. Sr. asso. editor Med. Econs., Oradell, N.J., 1960-61, 66-67; researcher Time mag., N.Y.C., 1961-66; writer-editor Woman's Day, N.Y.C., 1967-70; writer, N.Y.C., 1970—; Right Now editor McCall's, N.Y.C., 1973—. Democrat committeewoman N.Y. County, 1973. Mem. Soc. Mag. Writers. Home: 45 W 10th St New York City NY 10011 Office: McCall's Mag 230 Park Av New York City NY 10017

PASKEY, MAY ANNETTE (MRS. CLARENCE MICHAEL PASKEY), librarian; b. Kirkville, Ia., Dec. 29, 1897; d. Christian Herman and Mindy (Newell) Schmitz; B.A., Coll. St. Teresa, 1923; degree in L.S., Moorhead State Coll., 1953; m. Clarence Michael Paskey, June 26, 1927; children—Vincent Michael, Ronald Christian. Prin. high sch., Waubun, Minn., 1923-29, instr. high sch., 1941-53, librarian, 1953-63; librarian Carnegie Pub. Library, Detroit Lakes, Minn., 1963—. Mem. Cath. Daus. Am. (2d vice regent 1970-72). Elkette. Club: Country Club Bridge Assn. (Detroit Lakes). Home: 220 E Willow St Detroit Lakes MN 56501 Office: 1000 Washington Av Detroit Lakes MN 56501

PASNIK, MARION GROSS (MRS. JOEL PASNIK), ednl. adminstr.; b. Bronx, N.Y., Nov. 20, 1922; d. Joseph and Rose (Botfan) Gross; B.B.A., Coll. City N.Y., 1943; M.A., N.Y. U., 1945; Ed.D., Columbia, 1968; m. Joel Pasnik, Oct. 30, 1943; children—Alan, Diane, Amy. Tchr. bus. high sch., N.Y.C., 1943; accountant Seidman and Seidman, N.Y.C., 1944; buyer, Chas. Buchman Resident Buying Office, N.Y.C., 1945-47; tchr. pub. schs., Roslyn and Great Neck, N.Y., 1957-65; ednl. facilities standards coordinator N.Y.C. Pub. Schs., 1965—; adj. prof. Ednl. Facilities Planning N.Y. U., 1970—; cons. Ednl. Facilities Lab., N.Y.C.; conv. lectr. Assn. Sch. Bus. Ofcls. Mem. Am. Assn. Sch. Adminstrs., N.Y. Assn. Sch. Bus. Ofcls., Council Ednl. Facilities Planners, Assn. Sch. Bus. Ofcls. U.S. and Can., Kappa Delta Pi. Home: 32 Pine Dr N Roslyn NY 11576 Office: 110 Livingston St Brooklyn NY 11201

PASS, BEVERLY CLAIRE, pediatrician; b. New Britain, Conn., Dec. 22, 1937; d. Leonard Andrew and Mary Helene (Zack) Pass; B.S. cum laude, Jackson Coll., 1958; M.D., Tufts U., 1962; m. John Martin Pierce, Apr. 26, 1962; children—John Pierce, Leonard A., Brian T. Intern New Britain Gen. Hosp., 1962-63; resident pediatrics Boston City Hosp., 1965-67; practice medicine specializing in pediatrics, Winsted, Conn., 1968—; active staff Winsted Meml. Hosp., chief pediatrics, 1972—; sch. physician Colebrook, Conn., 1969—; guest lectr. N.W. Conn. Community Coll. Cons. Headstart Program. Mem. exec. com. March Dimes, 1969—, med. adv. com., 1969—. Mem. Winchester Bd. Edn., 1971—. Diplomate Am. Bd. Pediatrics. Fellow Am. Acad. Pediatrics; mem. Conn. Med. Soc. Democrat. Home: Colebrook Rd Winsted CT 06098 Office: 71 Spencer St Winsted CT 06098

PASSMORE, MILDRED REBECCA, pediatrician; b. Huntley, Ill., Sept. 19, 1912; d. Charles Lucius and Mattie Pearl (Prickett) Passmore; B.A., U. Wichita, 1942; M.D., Kan. U., 1946. Intern Jackson Park Hosp., Chgo., 1946-47; resident in pediatrics Hotel Dieu and Charity Hosp., New Orleans, 1954-56; research fellow pediatric hematology La. State U., 1956-58; practice medicine specializing in pediatrics, Wichita, Kan., 1947-54, Winfield, Kan., 1958-63, Roanoke, Va., 1963—; mem. staffs Roanoke Meml. Hosp., Community Hosp. Roanoke Valley. Diplomate Am. Bd. Pediatrics. Fellow Am. Acad. Pediatrics; mem. Roanoke Acad. Medicine, Va. Pediatrics Soc., Va. Med. Soc. Lutheran. Home: 4450 Northridge St NE Roanoke VA 24012 Office: 1701 Grandin Rd SW Roanoke VA 24015

PASSOVOY, SUSAN JANE, lawyer; b. Stockton, Cal., Apr. 10, 1946; d. Aaron and Ann (Hackman) Passovoy; B.A., Stanford, 1967; J.D., U. Cal. at Berkeley, 1971. Admitted to Cal. bar, 1972; asst. legal counsel Trimont Land Co., San Francisco, 1971-73; project counsel, staff planner Flower Mound New Town Ltd., Dallas, 1973-74; practice law, San Francisco, 1974—. Sec., New Town Found., 1973-74. Mem. Am., Cal., San Francisco bar assns., Common Cause. Clubs: Barristers (San Francisco); Sierra. Office: 111 Sutter St San Francisco CA 94104

PASTERNAK, EUGENIA, instn. adminstr.; b. Ukraina, Jan. 18, 1919; d. Mychail and Maria (Okonska) Nowakiwsky; student philosophy, Goethe U., Germany, 1945-47; certificate Shaw Bus. Coll., Toronto, Ont., Can., 1956; diploma McMaster U., 1971; m. Eugene Pasternak, July 19, 1944. Came to Can., 1948, naturalized, 1955. Tchr., prin. jr. coll., Galitzia, Ukraina, 1939-42; exec. relief coms., also A.R.C. during and after World War II; exec. Multoblitz Photog., Toronto, 1955-57; accountant Legal Humenick and Rodmanko, Toronto, 1958-63; pres. Ukrainian Home for Aged, Toronto, 1961-73; dir., adminstr. Ivan Franks Home, Toronto, 1964—. Mem. Ont. Inner Group Com.; commnr. for taking affidavits Province Ont. Recipient medal and scroll Ukrainian Canadian Com., 1962. Address: 767 Royal York Rd Toronto ON M8Y 2T3 Canada

PASTOR, LUCILLE ELIZABETH, artist, mfg. co. exec.; b. Waterbury, Conn., Sept. 7, 1920; d. Thomas and Francis (Russo) Pastor; student Waterbury Art Sch., 1946-49, U. Conn., 1953-56, U. Bridgeport, 1957, Paier Sch. Art, 1966-67. Asst. bookkeeper Diamond Ginger Ale Co., Waterbury, 1941-42; comptometer compilations clk. U.S. Dept. Interior, Washington, 1942-43; sec., asst. mgr. Pastor Stop-Watch Co., Waterbury, Conn., 1943-70, owner, 1970—; bookkeeper, accountant Maurice Gelman, C.P.A., Waterbury, 1953-59; bookkeeper, typist Maurice Donovan, ins. agt., Waterbury, 1959-60; bookkeeper, accountant Waterbury Club, 1960-63; office sec., bookkeeper Waterbury Truck Service, Inc., 1966-70; bookkeeper Allied Airco Services, Waterbury, 1970. Exhibited in one-man shows at Conn. Light & Power Co., Waterbury, Conn. State Unemployment Office, Waterbury; exhibited in group shows at Stony Creek Library, Washington Art Gallery, Guildford Art League, Meriden Arts and Crafts Assn., Torrington Art Assn., Brookfield Center. Recipient 3d prize, oil painting A&W exhibit Bethlehem Fair, 1952, 1st prize, 1954, 1st prize, jr. exhibit, 1954; 3d prize, oil painting Bethlehem State Fair Art Exhibit, 1961; 3d prize, oil painting Cheshire Grange Fair Art Exhibit, 1965, 1st prize, watercolor painting, 1968. Mem. Artists and Writers of Conn. (1st v.p. 1961-62), Cheshire Art League (sec. 1961), Waterbury Arts Council (gen. co-chmn. 1962 Arts Festival), Pub. Relations Soc. Am. (chpt. hospitality chmn. 1964), Bus. and Profl. Women's Club (membership chmn. 1968-73), Washington (Conn.) Art Assn., Guilford Art League, Meriden Arts and Crafts Assn., Torrington Artist Assn. Address: 94 Ledgeside Av Waterbury CT 06708

PASTORFIELD, J. CLAIRE (MRS. JAMES A. PASTORFIELD), real estate broker, builder; b. Brockway, Pa.; d. James and Teresa (Falco) Biondi; student Fairleigh-Dickinson U., 1957-58; m. James A. Pastorfield, Sept. 28, 1940 (dec. Nov. 1967); 1 son, James Markley. Real estate broker, Wood-Ridge, N.J., 1943—, Fire Island, N.Y., 1943-54; ins. agt., Wood-Ridge 1945—; builder partner Clayne Homes, Inc., Wood-Ridge, 1950—. Exhibited art in shows at Ocean Beach, Fire Island, N.Y., Wood-Ridge Library, The Barn, Ridge-Wood. Recipient several awards for art works. Mem. Fire Island (sec. 1949-54), Ridgewood art assns., Psychic Register

Internat., Internat. Platform Assn. Address: 223 Hackensack St Wood Ridge NJ 07075

PATCH, ETHEL LEE, coll. ofcl.; b. Henrico County, Va., Jan. 19, 1938; d. Ralph Lee and Mary Alice (Winston) Patch; B.S. in Bus. Edn., Radford Coll., 1960, M.S. in Edn., 1965. Tchr. bus. James Wood High Sch., Winchester, Va., 1960-64, guidance counselor, 1964-65; coordinator guidance Frederick County Jr. High Sch., Winchester, 1965-67; counselor Central Va. Community Coll., Lynchburg, 1967-69, coordinator admissions and records, 1969—. Mem. Am., Va. (membership chmn. 1973-74), Lynchburg personnel and guidance assns. Home: 1609A Wards Ferry Rd Lynchburg VA 24502

PATCH, GERTRUDE KEILEY, coll. pres.; b. Bklyn., Oct. 28, 1926; d. Roderick Stanley and Gertrude (Keiley) Patch; B.A., Lone Mountain Coll., 1947, M.A., 1953; Ph.D., Stanford, 1957. English tchr. Sheridan Rd. Convent, Chgo., 1950-53, Convent Sacred Heart, Lake Forest, Ill., 1953-54; instr. English San Francisco Coll. Women, 1956-58; prof. English, San Diego Coll. Women, 1958-65, dir. grad. sch., 1962-65; chmn. dept. English, San Francisco Coll. Women (name now Lone Mountain Coll.), 1965, pres., 1966—. Trustee San Francisco Consortium. Mem. Assn. Am. Colls. (chmn. Commn. Religion 1974-75), Kappa Gamma Pi. Address: Lone Mountain Coll San Francisco CA 94118

PATCHETT, ISABEL STEDMAN (MRS. EDWARD PATCHETT), statistician; b. Hartford, Conn., July 2, 1924; d. Lewis H. and Margaret M. (Wilson) Stedman; B.S., U. Conn., 1951; M.B.A., U. Hartford, 1965; m. Edward Patchett, June 14, 1947; 1 son, Lewis. Supr. group dept. Travelers Ins. Co., Hartford, 1952-65; marketing research analyst Royal Typewriter Co., Hartford, 1965-68; econ. statistician Scovill Mfg. Co., Waterbury, Conn., 1968—. Regional marketing dir. Quest Adventures, Inc. retail travel agy., Atlanta, 1972-73. Campaign mgr. Republican candidate for congress, Farmington, Conn., 1961; mem. Rep. Town Com., Farmington, 1962-64. Mem. U. Conn. Alumni Assn. (treas., 1960-63), U. Hartford Alumni Assn., Am. Marketing Assn. (treas., 1970-71), League Women Voters. Episcopalian. Mem. Order Eastern Star. Home: 146 W Avon Rd Unionville CT 06085 Office: 99 Mill St Waterbury CT 06720

PATCHIN, NAOMI RUTH, assn. exec.; b. Highland Park, Mich., Feb. 18, 1935; d. DeForest Ira and Esther Mary Alice (Schnepper) Patchin; student Andrews U., 1953-54; B.S., Columbia Union Coll., 1957; M.P.H. (USPHS trainee), U. Mich., 1962. Pub. health nurse, Oakland County, Mich., 1957-61; coordinator, instr. pub. health nursing Columbia Union Coll., Takoma Park, Md., 1962-65; staff, bur. research and edn. Am. Hosp. Assn., Chgo., 1965-69; dir. patient care services Conn. Hosp. Assn., New Haven, 1969-70; dir. sect. on nursing, asst. dir. health manpower Am. Med. Assn., Chgo., 1970—. Cons. nursing Modern Hosp. publication McGraw-Hill Inc., 1972-73. Fellow Am. Pub. Health Assn.; mem. Am. Nurses Assn., Nat. League for Nursing, Art Inst. Chgo., Smithsonian Instn. Clubs: Internationale (Washington); Admirals (N.Y.C.). Home: 2800 N Lake Shore Dr Apt 3514 Chicago IL 60657 Office: American Medical Association 535 N Dearborn St Chicago IL 60610

PATCHIN, ZELMA, univ. dean; b. Hobart, Okla., Dec. 30, 1909; d. Henry E. and Mary I. (Brown) Patchin; B.S., U. Okla., 1932; M.S., Okla. State U., 1939. Homemaking tchr. Sentinal (Okla.) High Sch., 1933-38; prof. home econs. U. S.W. La., Lafayette, 1939-50; dean of women Okla. State U., Stillwater, 1951—. Mem. Nat. Assn. Deans of Women, Am. Personnel and Guidance Assn., Am. Assn. U. Women, Mortar Bd., Alpha Xi Delta, Omicron Nu. Club: Altrusa. Home: 1924 W 10th St Stillwater OK 74074

PATE, ANNIE BERENICE, city govt. ofcl.; b. McKee's Rocks, Pa., Feb. 1, 1907; d. Sydney Verner and Edna Elizabeth (Dewrose) Todd; grad. high sch.; m. Waldo Hays Pate, May 14, 1927; children—Roberta Lee (Mrs. Donald T. Bowden), Carolyn Jean (Mrs. Clarence J. Kooi). Pathologist technician Stanford Lane Med. Sch., San Francisco, 1930-34; lab. technician, office nurse to Dr. Waldo H. Pate, Alturas, Cal., 1935, 43-44; exec. sec. Cal. Indian Commn., 1968-69; tchr. Cal. Indian culture, 1955—; councilman City of Auburn, Cal., 1966-67, 70-73, mayor, 1970, 72. Pres. Sacramento Valley div. League Cal. Cities, 1972-73; mem. spl. bldg. commn. Auburn Area Recreation Dist., 1959-60; bd. dirs. Placer County Health Council, 1970-72, Placer County Hist. Soc., 1971-74; Placer County Hist. Museum Found., 1972-74. Recipient resolution of commendation Cal. Senate, 1970; named to Book of Golden Deeds, Auburn Exchange Club, 1974. Mem. Nat., Cal. assns. parliamentarians, V.F.W. (past pres.), Auburn Fedn. Women's Club (past pres.), Auburn Bus. and Profl. Women's Club (Woman of Achievement award 1974). Mem. Order Eastern Star (past worthy matron), White Shrine Jerusalem (past worthy high priestess). Home: 135 S McDaniel Dr Auburn CA 95603 Office: 1103 High St Auburn CA 95603

PATE, CHRISTINE VETTER (MRS. WILLIAM CRAIG PATE), lawyer; b. San Diego, Sept. 27, 1943; d. William Paul and Ethel Marguerite (Waters) Vetter; student U. Vienna (Austria), 1963-64; B.A., U. Cal., Berkeley, 1965; postgrad. U. Cal. Hastings Coll. Law, 1965-66; J.D. cum laude, U. San Diego, 1969; m. William Craig Pate, Oct. 30, 1966; children—William Christopher, Bryan Laughlin. Admitted to Cal. bar, 1970; atty. Higgs, Jennings, Fletcher & Mack, San Diego, 1970-71, Jennings, Engstrand & Henrikson, San Diego, 1971—. Mem. Am., San Diego County bar assns., Lawyers Club San Diego (dir.), Alpha Gamma Delta. Republican. Roman Catholic. Club: Soroptimist (La Mesa). Home: 1144 Glorietta Blvd Coronado CA 92118 Office: 2022 Camino del Rio N San Diego CA 92108

PATE, MARGARET FARHA (MRS. STANTON STANLEY PATE JR.), pub. relations and advt. exec.; b. Wichita, Kan.; d. Merhige Samuel and Saidy (Mattar) Farha; student William Woods Jr. Coll., 1932-34, U. Mo., 1934-37; m. Stanton Stanley Pate, Jr., Feb. 28, 1944. With Griffith Amusement Co., intermittently 1931-40, U.S. Recruiting and Induction Hdqrs., 1941-45; founder, partner (with husband) The Pate Orgn., pub. relations and advt., Oklahoma City, 1947—. Mem. Okla. Med. Research Found. Recipient award Oklahoma City C. of C., 1957; Spl. award Gov. of Okla., 1960; awards for authorship and design of printed publs.; William Woods Coll. Centennial Alumna award distinction, 1970. Mem. Oklahoma City C. of C. (nat. affairs com., distinguished visitors com.), Internat. Platform Assn., Okla. Press Assn., Phi Beta Kappa. Episcopalian. Rotary Ann. Clubs: Oklahoma City Press, Oklahoma City Golf and Country. Author: The Immutable Images of Oklahoma; Oklahoma City—Apogee of Action. Home: 6409 Avalon Lane Oklahoma City OK 73102 Office: The Pate Orgn 6403 NW Grand Blvd Oklahoma City OK 73116

PATE, MARGERY, banker; b. Fort Gaines, Ga., July 19, 1922; d. James Travis and Amy Estelle (Craft) Pate; grad. high sch. Clk., Baker County Bank, Newton, Ga., 1943-49, cashier, 1949-50; utility clk. First Nat. Bank & Trust Co., Macon, Ga., 1950-60; asst. cashier Ga. Bank & Trust Co., Macon, 1960-63, asst. v.p., 1963-71, v.p. (1st woman), asst. trust officer, 1971—. Treas., Aid for Leukemia Stricken Children Am., Macon, 1960—; mem. Quota Club of Macon, 1960-69, trustee, 1961-65, treas., dir., 1963-65; chmn. Bibb County appeal Easter Seal Soc., 1972, mem. service com. 7th div. Ga., 1972—; mem. Entertainment and Registration Com. for Organizational meeting, 1966, chmn. group six, 1969-70, now bd. dirs. Ga. Easter Seal Soc. Mem. Ga. Bankers Assn. (women's com.), Am. Inst. Banking, Nat. Assn. Bank Audit and Control (dir. 1962-63), Nat. Assn. Bank Women. Home: 3089 Highpoint Dr Macon GA 31204 Office: 515 Mulberry St Macon GA 31202

PATE, MARTHA B. LUCAS, educator; b. Louisville, Nov. 27, 1912; d. Robert H. and Gertrude (Lasch) Lucas; A.B., Goucher Coll., Balt., 1933, LL.D., 1946; A.M., George Washington U., 1935; Ph.D., U. London, 1940; LL.D., Ala. Coll., 1946, Atlanta U., 1972; L.H.D., U. Louisville, 1950, Smith Coll., 1971; m. Maurice Pate, Oct. 1961 (dec. 1965). Asso. prof. philosophy and religion, dean of students U. Richmond (Va.), 1941-44; asso. dean Radcliffe Coll., 1944-46; pres., prof. philosophy of religion Sweet Briar Coll. (Va.), 1946-50; exec. dir. office of univ. and coll. relations Inst. Internat. Edn., 1961-62; chmn. Coll. and Sch. div. United Negro Coll. Fund, 1962—, bd. dirs., 1967—; bd. dirs. Fgn. Policy Assn., 1963—; bd. dirs. Rec. for the Blind, 1962—, chmn. planning and devel. com., 1963—. Mem. nat. selections com. for Fulbright Scholarships, 1948-50, U.S. del. UNESCO Prep. Conf. of U. Reps., Utrecht, Holland, 1948, 4th Gen. Conf. UNESCO, Paris, 1949; mem. Adv. Council for Jr. Year in France, 1947-50; mem. bd. dirs. Assn. Am. Colls., 1949-50, v.p. So. U. Conf. and chmn. com. on improvement of coll. teaching, 1949-50; 2d vice chmn. Am. Council on Edn., 1949-50; mem. adv. council on health careers United Hosp. Fund; adv. council Columbia U. Sch. Social Work, 1967—, chmn. nominations com., 1970—; mem. U.S. Nat. Adv. Commn. on Internat. Edn. and Cultural Affairs, 1970—; mem. Nat. Com. on U.S.-China Relations, 1971—; pub. mem. USIA, 1973. Trustee N.Y. Med. Coll. 1967—, Fund for Peace, 1967—, N.Y. Sch. Psychiatry, 1971—, Fund for Theol. Edn., Inc., 1969—; bd. dirs. Westchester Med. Center Found., 1969—; trustee L.I. U., 1969—, chmn. acad. policies com. 1970—; trustee Pierce Coll., Athens, Greece, 1962-69, chmn. acad. affairs com., 1962-69, hon. trustee, 1969—; alumnae trustee Goucher Coll., 1968-71. Decorated chevalier French Legion of Honor; recipient George Washington U. Alumni Citation, 1947. Fellow Soc. Religion in Higher Edn.; mem. Am. Philos. Assn., Nat. Inst. Social Scis., Council on Religion and Internat. Affairs (trustee 1968—, chmn. 60th anniversary com. 1970—), Acad. Religion and Mental Health, Phi Beta Kappa. Clubs: Faculty (New Haven); Vassar, Cosmopolitan (N.Y.C.). Episcopalian. Author: (with others) Religious Faith and World Culture, 1951. Lectr. on ednl. philosophy and civic affairs. Home: Godstow RFD 1 West Redding CT 06896 Office: 330 E 49th St New York City NY 10017

PATE, VIRGINIA FORWOOD (MRS. EDWARD WETTER), broadcasting exec.; b. Havre de Grace, Md., Aug. 10, 1919; d. Walter F. and Bennita (Charshee) Forwood; B.A., Coll. William and Mary, 1940; m. Jason Thomas Pate, Dec. 6, 1941 (dec. 1960); children—J. David, V. Kennon, Barbara W.; m. 2d, Edward Wetter, Apr. 7, 1972. With Standard Oil Co. Pa., 1940-41; pub. relations with Irwin & Leighton, contractors and constrn., 1941-42; v.p. Chesapeake Broadcasting Corp., Havre de Grace, 1955-60, pres., gen. mgr., 1960—; sec. Cash Loan Co., 1960—, WKEN, Inc., 1956-58. Treas., past pres. Havre de Grace Coop. Kindergarten; former dir. pub. relations Susquehanna council Girl Scouts U.S.A.; past dir. Harford County Heart Assn., Harford County Cancer Soc.; dir., past chmn. Harford County Com. on Employment Physically Handicapped; chmn. 150 anniversary celebration St. John's Ch., Havre de Grace. Mem. Harford County (Md.) Bd. Edn., 1959-69, v.p., 1960-66, pres., 1966-69; exec. sec. Md. Assn. Bds. Edn., 1962, pres., 1964; adv. bd. Harford Jr. Coll., 1958—, trustee, 1959-69, community v.p., 1960-66, chmn., 1966-69; mem. Nat. Com. for Support Pub. Schs. Mem. Am. Women Radio and TV (past pres. Md., nat. chmn. industry news com., area v.p. 1966-68, nat. pres. 1970-71), Md.-D.C.-Del. Broadcasters Assn. (edn. chmn. 1960-66, sec.-treas. 1964-65, v.p. 1965-66, pres. 1966-67), P.T.A. (past pres., sec. Havre de Grace, past v.p. pres.'s conf.), Nat. Assn. Broadcasters (radio code bd. 1966-67, Md. chmn. future of broadcasting com. 1971—), Chi Omega. Democrat. Episcopalian (vestry 1968—). Home: 1000 Chesapeake Dr Havre de Grace MD 21078 Office: WASA/WHDG Radio Box 97 Havre de Grace MD 21078

PATEL, COOMI DHUN (MRS. DHUN B. PATEL), occupational therapist; b. Bombay, India, Oct. 25, 1937; d. Darabsha M. and Dolat D. (Patel) Pavri; intermediate sci. degree (Youths' Own Union scholar), Bombay U., 1958; diploma occupational therapy Nagpur Med. Sch., 1961; m. Dhun B. Patel, June 18, 1967; 1 son, Malcolm. Came to U.S., 1964, naturalized, 1973. Chief occupational therapist B.D. Petit Parsee Gen. Hosp., Bombay, India, 1961-62, St. George's Hosp., Bombay, 1962-64; occupational therapist Rochester (Minn.) State Hosp., 1964-65; staff occupational therapist Creedmoor State Hosp., N.Y.C., 1965-68, sr. occupational therapist, 1970-72; cons. occupational therapist Hudsonview Nursing Home, Yonkers, N.Y., 1970—, Ro-Fay Nursing Home, Bronx, 1972—, Williamsbridge Manor Nursing Home, Bronx, 1971—. Lady Meherbai Tata Trust Fund scholar, 1964. Mem. Am. Occupational Therapy Assn., Zoarastrian Assn. N.Y., Theosophists Lodge Bombay. Home: 32 Twin Lakes Dr Monsey NY 10952 Office: Hudsonview Nursing Home 65 Ashburton Av Yonkers NY 10701

PATERAKIS, ANGELA GREGORY (MRS. GEORGE A. PATERAKIS), educator; b. Oak Park, Ill., June 1, 1932; d. Kostas and Sophia (Spiliotou) Gregory; B.Art Edn., Sch. Art Inst. Chgo., 1954; M.A. (U. Ill. fellow), U. Ill., 1955; m. George A. Paterakis, July 31, 1958. Tchr. art Oak Park Elementary Schs., 1955-60; instr. Sch. Art Inst. Chgo., 1961-63, asst. prof., 1963-64, asso. prof., also chmn. div. tchr. edn., 1963-70. Cons. and juror Nat. Scholastics Art awards, 1962; art juror U. Ill. Extension Services, Chgo. area, 1964—; cons. film series Sch. Art Inst. Chgo., 1963. Mem. Fine Arts Adv. Com. on Legislation, Springfield, Ill., 1964, Oak Park-River Forest chpt. Infant Welfare, 1962-71. Mem. N.E.A. (life), Nat. Art Edn. Assn. (editor Art at the Secondary Level 1972), W. Regional Art Assn., Ill. Art Edn. Assn. (governing council 1963-65, 2d v.p. 1966, pres. 1971), Ill. Arts Council (adv. panel 1968-69), Delta Phi Delta. Contbr. articles on children and art edn. to profl. jours. Co-editor Sculpture '67. Home: 1230 Lathrop Av River Forest IL 60305

PATERSON, EILEEN, physician; b. Bklyn., Oct. 16, 1939; d. John Alexander and Frances Marie (Rabito) Paterson; B.A., Wilson Coll., 1961; M.D., Woman's Med. Coll., 1965. Intern, Highland Hosp., Rochester, N.Y., 1965-66; resident radiology U. Rochester Med. Sch., 1966-69; radiation therapist Strong Meml. Hosp., Rochester, 1969—; instr. radiology U. Rochester, 1969-70, asst. prof. radiology, 1970—. Home: 7251 Coy Rd Livonia NY 14487 Office: Strong Memorial Hosp Rochester NY 14611

PATERSON, LAURENE OLIVE, research co. exec.; b. London, Ont., Can., Apr. 6, 1916; d. Thomas and Christina (Chapman) Paterson; student U. Western Ont., 1934-38; M.A., Wayne U., 1946. Came to U.S., 1945, naturalized, 1947. Chemist, dir. research R.P. Scherer Co., Detroit, 1945-49; pres. Drug Research, Inc., Adrian, Mich., 1950—. Recipient outstanding inventors award Mich. Bar Assn., 1963. Patentee in field. Home: 5581 W US Hwy 223 Adrian MI 49221 Office: 1219 E Church St Adrian MI 49221

PATERSON, PATRICIA GARLETZ (MRS. ROBERT E. PATERSON), educator; b. Preston, Minn., Mar. 10, 1908; d. John Ross and Josephine (Hubbard) Garletz; A.B., Hamline U., 1930; M.A., U. Minn., 1937; summer study U. Minn., U. Wis., U. Cal. at Los Angeles, Harvard, U. So. Cal.; m. Robert E. Paterson, Dec. 21, 1945 (dec. Nov. 1946). Asst. prof. phys. edn. Hamline U., St. Paul, 1931-66, asso. prof., 1966-72, prof., 1972—; instr. adult edn. St. Paul Pub. Schs., 1958-61. Coll. adviser St. Paul chpt. A.R.C., 1939—; state council Minn. Health and Tb Assn., 1960—. Mem. A.A.H.P.E.R., Am. Assn. U. Profs., Nat. Assn. Phys. Edn. for Coll. Women (pub. relations chmn. 1970-71), Minn. Assn. for Health, Phys. Edn. and Recreation (past pres., mem. exec. bd., historian 1961—), Delta Kappa Gamma. Methodist. Home: 861 Aldine St St Paul MN 55104

PATMAN, CARRIN MAURITZ (MRS. WILLIAM NEFF PATMAN), polit. worker; b. Houston, Mar. 1, 1932; d. Fred and Carrin (Foreman) Mauritz; B.A. with honors in Philosophy and English, U. Tex., 1954; m. William Neff Patman, Sept. 5, 1953; 1 dau., Carrin Foreman. Past pres. Jackson County-Mauritz Meml. Hosp. Aux. Democratic precinct chmn., Ganado, Tex., 1960-62; mem. Tex. Dem. Exec. Com., 1964-66, 72—, mem. subcom. on rules; mem. Tex. Dem. Reform Commn., 1969-70; mem. Dem. Nat. Com., 1969-72; del. Dem. Nat. Conv., 1972, mem. permanent conv. rules com.; mem. Commn. Del. selection and Party Structure, 1972—. Past bd. dirs. Jackson County United Fund, Ganado P.T.A. Hon. mem. Delta Kappa Gamma. Methodist (past bd. dirs. ch.). Club: Senate Ladies of Tex. (past pres.). Address: PO Drawer A Ganado TX 77962

PATON, MARY MARGARET, corp. exec.; b. St. Louis, Feb. 18, 1918; d. William L. and Margaret (Brown) Paton; student pub. schs. Clk. typist Dun & Bradstreet, St. Louis, 1935-36; clk. typist, sec. Wm. A. Streub, Inc., Clayton, Mo., 1936-44, sec. to pres., 1947-53, corp. sec., 1950—, buyer, 1963—, supr. restaurant operations, 1953-72; with U.S. Civil Service, Army Air Base, Tonopah, Nev., 1944-46; sec. Parkside Realty Co., Clayton, 1950—; pres. Pro-Mir Garments, Ltd., St. Louis, 1971—. Presbyn. Home: 8845 Burton Av St Louis MO 63114 Office: 8282 Forsyth Blvd Clayton MO 63105

PATRAM, SARAH LEE, nursing educator; b. Rocky Mount, N.C., Jan. 22, 1922; d. John Lyons and Emma (Spoon) Patram; diploma Petersburg Hosp. Sch. Nursing, 1943; A.B., Bridgewater Coll., 1947; B.S. in Nursing Edn., U. Va., 1952; M.S. Nursing, Cath. U. Am., 1959. Coll. nurse Bridgewater (Va.) Coll., 1943-45, 46-47; night supr. Petersburg (Va.) Hosp., 1945-46, instr-supr. obstetrics, 1947-50; pvt. duty nursing, Petersburg, 1950-51; dir. nursing service Randolph Hosp., Inc., Asheboro, N.C., 1952-53; dir. Burlington (N.C.) City Sch. Practical Nursing, 1953-55; sr. instr. coordinator Schs. Practical Nursing, Miners Meml. Hosp. Assn., Harlan, Ky., 1955-57, dir. Sch. Practical Nursing, Williamson, W.Va., 1958-62; asst. dir. nursing service in charge inservice edn. Meml. Med. Center, Williamson, 1962-64; asso. prof. chmn. dept. nursing edn. Marshall U., Huntington, W.Va., 1964—. Instr.-trainer Home Nursing courses, A.R.C. mem. adv. com. Home Health Agy., Huntington, W.Va., Sch. Practical Nursing Cabell County Career Center. Bd. dirs. W.Va. Health Planning Fund; chmn. Hupp Meml. Ednl. Fund. Mem. Am., Ky., W.Va. nurses assns., Nat. League for Nursing, Petersburg Hosp. Sch. Nursing Alumnae Assn., So. Regional Edn. Bd. Council on Collegiate Nursing, Am. Assn. U. Women, Am. Assn. U. Profs., U. Va., Cath. U. alumni assns., Nat. Audubon Soc. Home: Prichard Bldg Huntington WV 25722

PATRICK, ANN GARRICK (MRS. THOMAS MAXIE PATRICK), banker; b. Easley, S.C., Sept. 30, 1937; d. James Edwin and M. Ruth (Black) Garrick; B.S. in Bus. Edn., Lander Coll., 1959; m. Thomas Maxie Patrick, June 7, 1959; 1 son, Thomas David. Transit clk. S.C. Nat. Bank, Greenville, 1959-60, analysis clk., bookkeeper, supr., 1962-68; tchr. Greenville County Sch. Dist., 1960; with First Piedmont Bank & Trust Co., Greenville, 1968—, operations officer, 1970—, mgr. personnel, 1970—. Active fund drives United Fund, Greenville County; pres. P.T.A., 1968-69, sec., 1971-72, 2d v.p., 1973-74. Mem. Am. Inst. Banking (instr. principles bank operations Greenville chpt. 1971—, treas. 1969, pres. 1972—), Bank Adminstrv. Inst. (voting rep. 1970—), Nat. Assn. Bank Women (vice-chmn. Piedmont Group). S.C. Bankers Assn., Greenville Personnel Assn. Baptist. Club: Zonta. Home: 11 Hardwick Dr Greenville SC 29611 Office: First Piedmont Bank & Trust Co PO Box 3028 Greenville SC 29602

PATRICK, JUDITH TAPPER (MRS. KIRK A. PATRICK), physician; b. Dayton, O., Apr. 24, 1938; d. Ralph W. and Marjorie (Johnson) Tapper; B.S., Ohio State U., 1960; M.D., Tulane U., 1964; m. Kirk A. Patrick, Feb. 13, 1964; children—Kirk A. III, Kelly. Intern Charity Hosp. of La., New Orleans, 1964-65, resident, 1968-71; practice medicine specializing in dermatology, Baton Rouge, 1971—. Mem. La., Baton Rouge med. socs., Am. Acad. Dermatology, La. Dermatology Soc. Home: 721 Kenilworth Pkwy Baton Rouge LA 70808

PATRICK, RUTH (MRS. CHARLES HODGE), limnologist, diatom taxonomist; b. Topeka, Kan.; d. Frank and Myrtle (Jetmore) Patrick; B.S., Coker Coll., 1929; M.S., U. Va., 1931, Ph.D., 1934; D.Sc., Beaver Coll., 1970, PMC Colls., 1971; LL.D., Coker Coll., 1971; D.Sc., Phila. Coll. Pharmacy and Sci., 1973; m. Charles Hodge IV, July 10, 1931; 1 son, Charles V. Asso. curator microscopy Acad. Natural Scis., Phila., 1939-48, curator Leidy Micros. Soc., 1937-48, curator limnology, 1948—, chmn. dept limnology, 1948-73, holder Francis Boyer Research Chair, 1973—, also chmn. bd. trustees; prof. biology dept. U. Pa., 1970—; leader Catherwood Amazon Expdn. to headwaters of Amazon River, 1955; U.S. del. to Internat. Limnological Congress, 1953; mem. Internat. Com. on Nomenclature of Algae, 1949-59. Mem. subpanel on water blooms Pres.' Sci. Adv. Com., 1965; mem. panel on water resources and water pollution Gov.'s Sci. Adv. Com., 1965, mem. panel on pollution, 1967-68; mem. nat. tech. adv. com. on water quality requirements for fish, and other aquatic life and wildlife Dept. Interior, 1967-68; mem. citizen's adv. council Pa. Dept. Environmental Resources, 1971-73; mem. hazardous materials adv. com. Environmental Protection Agy., 1971-74; mem. Pa. Gov.'s Sci. Adv. Com., 1972; mem. adv. council Electric Power Research Inst., 1973—, NSF, 1973—. Bd. dirs. Environmental Planning and Information Center Pa.; trustee Aquarium Soc. Phila., 1951-58, Lacawac Sanctuary Found. Recipient Distinguished Dau. of Pa. award, 1952; Richard Hopper Day meml. medal Acad. Natural Scis., 1969; Gimbel Phila. award, 1969; Gold medal YWCA, 1970; Lewis L. Dollinger Pure Environment award Franklin Inst., 1970; Pa. award for excellence in sci. and tech., 1970; Eminent Ecologist award Ecol. Soc. Am., 1972. Fellow A.A.A.S.; mem. Nat. Acad. Scis. (nominating com. 1973-74), Bot. Soc. Am. (mem. Darbarker prize com. 1956—, merit award 1971), Phycological Soc. Am. (pres. 1954), Internat. Limnological Soc., Internat. Soc. Plant Taxonomists, Am. Soc. Plant Taxonomy, Am. Soc. Limnology and Oceanography, Pa. Zool. Soc., Colonial Dames Am., Soc. Study Evolution, Water Resources Assn. Del. River Basin (dir.), Am. Soc. Naturalists, Ecol. Soc. Am., Smithsonian Instn. (adv. council), Am. Inst. Biol. Scis., Internat. Phycol. Soc., Soc. Sigma Xi. Presbyn. Author: (with Dr. C.W. Reimer) Diatoms of the United States, Vol. I, 1966. Contbr. articles in field to profl. jours. Office: Acad Natural Scis Philadelphia PA 19103

PATRICK, SUSANN JANE (MRS. ANTHONY J. PATRICK), physician; b. Jackson, Mich., Oct. 31, 1940; d. Francis Robert and Dorothy Eleanor (Fedor) McOsker; B.S. magna cum laude, Mary Grove Coll., Detroit, 1962; M.D., U. Mich., 1966; m. Anthony J. Patrick, Sept. 2, 1967. Intern St. Luke Hosp., Saginaw, Mich., 1966-67; emergency physician Gen. Hosp., 1967-68; practice gen. medicine, Baldwin, Mich., 1968-69, Battle Creek, Mich., 1969—; mem. staff Leila Post Hosp., Battle Creek; mem. staff chief gen. practice Community Hosp., Battle Creek, 1971-72. Mem. Am. Acad. Gen. Practice, Mich. Med. Soc. Author: (with Anthony J. Patrick) Drug Abuse in Industry, 1972. Home: 319 Lakeshore Dr Battle Creek MI 49017 Office: 729 Capital St SW Battle Creek MI 49010

PATROVSKY, PHYLLIS CALDWELL (MRS. STANLEY P. PATROVSKY), bishop; b. Mitchell, S.D., Jan. 2, 1929; d. Edward and Margaret (Adams) Caldwell; D.D., Los Angeles U., 1972; m. Stanley P. Patrovsky, Dec. 27, 1947; children—Edward Bruce, Brian Neal. Ordained to ministry First Ch. of God the Father, 1970; adminstr. Tainan (Taiwan) Vocational Sch., 1970-73, Tainan Sem., 1970-73; pastor Village Brimm, Taiwan, 1970-73; dir. San Gabriel Valley sect. 1st Church God the Father, Covina, Cal., 1970—, bishop, 1972—. Spl. asst. to sec. Office Madame Chaing Kai Chek, Tainan, 1972-73. Named Minister of Year in Ch., 1973. Club: Covina Women's. Author: In the Beginning, 1972; Mountain People in Taiwan, 1973; Lord Buddha in Taiwan, 1973. Home: 725 E Hurst St Covina CA 91723

PATRY, MAURITA ANN, health service adminstr., pyschologist; b. Toledo, May 25, 1941; d. Maurice and Nita Irene (Arnold) Patry; B.A., Hiram Coll., 1964; M.A., U. Akron, 1970. Spl. edn. tchr. Medina (O.) Pub. Schs., 1963-64; home tng. cons. Retarded Children's Program, Cuyahoga County Children Welfare Dept., Cleve., 1964-67, mental retardation social worker, 1967-69; sch. psychologist intern Cleve. Pub. Schs., 1969-70, psychologist, 1974—; program psychologist, adminstrv. asst. Cuyahoga County Bd. Mental Retardation, Cleve., 1970-72; case mgmt. supr. Ohio div. Mental Retardation and Developmental Disabilities, Cleve., 1972-74. Mem. Profl. Adv. Bd. Information and Referral Service for Retarded, 1973—, Cuyahoga East Spl. Edn. Project Governing Bd., 1972—. Mem. Council for Exceptional Children (governing bd. 1972-73), Am. Assn. Mental Deficiency, Ohio Profl. Assn. for Retarded Children Cleve. Assn. Sch. Psychologists (spl. edn. com. 1972—), Child Welfare League. Address: 118 E Lafayette Rd Medina OH 44256

PATTEN, EILEEN DUNLEVY (MRS. GRANT ALEXANDER PATTEN, JR.), hosp. pub. relations exec.; b. Paterson, N.J., Sept. 9, 1923; d. Robert Patrick and Julia A. (Hennessy) Dunlevy; A.B., Coll. New Rochelle, 1944; postgrad. Columbia, 1946-47; m. Grant Alexander Patten, Jr., Sept. 30, 1950; children—Kathleen Burke, Margaret Alexandra. Mem. guest relations staff WOR Radio, N.Y.C., 1944-45; corr. A.P., N.Y.C., 1945-48; women's editor Ridgewood (N.J.) newspapers, 1948-51; panelist, moderator Community Action interview program WPAT, N.Y., N.J., Conn., 1946-48; dir. community relations Valley Hosp., Ridgewood, N.J., 1960—. Adviser Bergen County Cath. Youth Orgn., 1966-68. Chmn., Women's Campaign for Congressman William B. Widnall (Rep.-N.J.), 1950-54. Bd. dirs. regional A.R.C., 1950-59. Recipient various awards N.J. Press Assn., 1948-51. Fellow Am. Acad. Hosp. Pub. Relations, Am. Soc. Hosp. Pub. Relations Dirs. (nat. membership panel 1970-72); mem. Am., N.J. hosp. assns., Nat. Pub. Relations Council (regional panel 1972-73), Nat. Fedn. Press Women, Women in Communications, Advt. Club N.J., Coll. New Rochelle Alumnae (chpt. v.p. 1957-61). Home: 597 Rock Rd Glen Rock NJ 07452 Office: Valley Hosp Linwood Av Ridgewood NJ 07451

PATTEN, EVELYN TILDEN (MRS. WILBERT HOWE PATTEN), mfg. co. exec.; b. Detroit, July 28, 1899; d. Bert Olin and Mary Abby (Mayo) Tilden; diploma Trenton State Model Sch., 1917; B.A., Wellesley Coll., 1921; B.S., Columbia, 1928; M.A., Bread Loaf Sch. English, 1927; m. Wilbert Howe Patten, Nov. 11, 1947; 1 step son, Robert Ross. Pres. Pattern-Machine & Foundry Corp., Trenton, N.J., 1970—. Mem. Wellesley Coll. Alumnae Assn., Chatham (Mass.) Hist. Soc. Home: 40 Eggerts Rd Trenton NJ 08638 Office: 3rd and Schenck Sts Trenton NJ 08611

PATTERSON, ALICE LITTLETON (MRS. CHESTER A. PATTERSON), ret. bus. exec.; b. Ipava, Ill., Nov 19, 1907; d. Marion Stanley and Frances Estelle (Moslander) Littleton; grad. high sch.; m. Chester Arthur Patterson, Sept. 17, 1929 (dec. June 1954); children—Stuart (dec. Feb. 1959) and Wallace (twins), Nancy (Mrs. Nancy Patterson Allmon). Pres. Patterson Pub. Co., Chgo., 1955-69, chmn. bd., 1961-69 (merged with Indsl. Pub. Co., Cleve., 1969); exec. editor Indsl. Pub. Co., 1969-74. Pres., Women of Rotary Club Chgo., 1939-40, mem. 1929—. Mem. precinct election bd. Chgo., 1941-50. Recipient several awards from motel, hotel, restaurant and assns., 1951-72; named hon. citizen Fla., 1962, Ky. col. by Gov. Ky., 1966, Hon. lt. col. a.d.c, Gov. Ga., 1966. Mem. Nat. Assn. Travel Orgns., N.Y. Restaurant Assn., Motel Assn. Am., United Airline 100,000 Mile Club. Author: Let's Begin At the Beginning, 1959. Extensive world travel on behalf of tourism and motel bus., hotel and restaurant; lectr. and organizer workshops at various univs. in these areas. Home: Harrison AR 72601

PATTERSON, AMY WOODBURY (MRS. JOHN GILMOUR PATTERSON), trust co. exec.; b. Shrewsbury, Vt., Nov. 18, 1914; d. George Asahel and Blanche Matilda (LaFrance) Woodbury; student Burlington Bus. Coll., 1934; m. John Gilmour Patterson, Sept. 4, 1943. Sec., Max L. Powell, Atty., 1934-36; cashier Gen. Motors Acceptance Corp., 1936-43; transit clk., teller, asst. treas., asst. v.p., then v.p. Chittenden Trust Co., Burlington, Vt., 1943—. Treas. Vt. Heart Assn., Chittenden County, 1966—. Mem. Vt. Banking Assn., Nat. Assn. Bank Women, Bus. and Profl. Women (past treas.). Mem. Order Eastern Star. Club: Altrusa (dir.) (Burlington). Home: 16 Circle Dr South Burlington VT 05401 Office: 2 Burlington Sq Burlington VT 05401

PATTERSON, ANN EILEEN, coll. librarian; b. Marquette, Mich., Oct. 5, 1913; d. George Andrew and Ellen Bridget (McCarthy) Patterson; A.B., No. Mich. U., 1934; A.B. in L.S., U. Mich., 1941, A.M. in L.S., 1943. Tchr., Iron Mountain (Mich.) Pub. Schs., 1934-39, Grosse Ile (Mich.) Pub. Schs., 1939-40; librarian Mercy Coll., Detroit, 1941-42, U. Mich., Ann Arbor, 1942-52; acquisitions librarian U. Mont., Missoula, 1952-53; reference librarian Detroit Pub. Library, 1953-65, No. Mich. U., Marquette, 1966-67; catalog librarian Lake Superior State Coll., Sault Sainte Marie, Mich., 1967—. Mem. Am. Assn. U. Profs., A.L.A., U. Mich. Alumni Assn., Sault Internat. Naturalists Club. Democrat. Roman Catholic. Home: 1300 14th St W Sault Ste Marie MI 49783

PATTERSON, AUDREY HAGEN (MRS. JAMES BERTCH PATTERSON), hotel owner; b. N.Y.C., June 10, 1942; d. Winston Henry and Christine Ramsay (Hoguet) Hagen; Ecole d'Interprètes, U. Geneva (Switzerland), 1962; student Goethe Inst., Munich, Germany, 1962-63; m. James Bertch Patterson, Jan. 13, 1967; 1 dau., Lucy Trotter. Formerly engaged in advt., pub. relations, travel promotion; former dir. tourism Trinidad and Tobago Tourist Bd.; formerly asso. Stephen Goerl Assos., Homerica, Inc.; owner with husband, mgr., chef Chester Inn (Vt.), 1968—. Included in America's Best Restaurant Recipes, N.Y. Times, 1973. Home and office: Chester Inn Chester VT 05143

PATTERSON, CLARISSA MAY HAYFIELD (MRS. MERRILL B. PATTERSON), coll. dean; b. Killingly, Conn., Jan. 18, 1932; d. Clarence Eugene Winsor and Alma Irene (Carroll) Hayfield; B.S., Bryant Coll., 1953; M.A., Columbia, 1955; profl. diploma R.I. Coll./U. Conn., 1966; Ed.D., Laurence U., 1972; m. Merrill B. Patterson, Aug. 13, 1955. Asst. in admissions office Columbia Tchrs. Coll., N.Y.C., 1954-55; faculty Bryant Coll., Smithfield, R.I., 1955—, prof. secretarial and office edn., tchr. edn., 1972—, chmn. office edn. dept., 1968-72, dean acad. instrn., 1972—. Cons. Coop. Planning for Efficiency Project, 1966-67; coordinator Govt. Grant for Opportunities Industrialization Center Project, 1969-70; affirmative action officer Office for Civil Rights Action Program, 1973—, chmn., v.p. search com., 1973-74. Mem. Acad. Mgmt., Nat. Bus. Edn. Assn., Acad. Affairs Adminstrs., Eastern Assn. Coll. Deans and Advisers of Student, Bus. and Profl. Women (dir. chpt.). Contbr. articles to profl. jours. Office: Bryant Coll Smithfield RI 02917

PATTERSON, D(ELLA) JEANNE HAYS (MRS. JAMES PATTERSON), ednl. adminstr.; b. Billings, Mont., Nov. 7, 1934; d. Leonard C. and Grace M. (Chamberlin) Hays; student U. Mont., 1952-54; B.S. in Bus., U. Colo., 1956; M.B.A., Ind. U., 1960, D.B.A., 1967; m. James M. Patterson, July 3, 1964; children—James Marshall, Julia Marie. Sr. research asso. Bur. Bus. Research Sch. Bus., Ind. U., Bloomington, 1968-71, chmn. undergrad. div., asso. prof. Sch. Pub. and Environmental Affairs, 1972—; lectr. Loyola U., Chgo., spring 1967. Cons. for econ. devel. study Youngstown, O., cons. City Planning Assos., Ind., 1967. Dir. resource devel. internship project Midwestern Adv. Com. on Higher Edn. Council State Govts., 1971—; mem. exec. bd. Nat. Center for Pub. Service Internships, 1972—. Mem. Am. Econ. Assn., Am. Finance Assn., Am. Soc. Pub. Adminstrs. (sec.-treas. Ind. Chpt. 1973—), Ind. Econ. Forum (pres. 1974), Am. Polit. Sci. Assn., Kappa Alpha Theta. Author: The Local Industrial Development Corporation, 1967; (with Bonser et al.) Business Taxation in Indiana, 1967; (with Jack Wentworth) Business Taxation, 1970. Home: 2431 N Dunn St Bloomington IN 47401

PATTERSON, (ELEANOR) JANE, educator; b. Fort Morgan, Colo., June 14, 1915; d. Harry Taplin and Ellen Leona (Warner) Patterson; B.A., U. Denver, 1938; M.A., U. No. Colo., 1947; Ed.D., N.Y. U., 1955. Tchr. pub. schs. Pueblo, Colo., 1938-43; instr. health and phys. edn. Eastern Ore. Coll., LaGrande, 1947-48; asst. prof. Eastern Wash. Coll., Cheney, 1948-53; supr., dir. elementary sch. phys. edn. Houston Ind. Sch. Dist., 1955-67; asso. prof. health and phys. edn. U. Houston, 1967-73, prof., 1973—. Cons. Beaumont (Tex.) Center for Mentally Retarded, 1971-72, Migrant Schs. Inst., McAllen, Tex., 1967-69, pub. schs. Houston, Beaumont, Livingston, Tex. and Lafayette, La. Vice chmn. recreation informal edn. Com. Community Council, 1961-65, Houston Program Com. YWCA, 1966-68; mem. phys. edn. com. Bd. Edn. Houston Ind. Sch. Dist., 1968-72. Served with WACS, 1943-46. Delta Psi Kappa research scholar, 1955; recipient Founders Day award N.Y. U., 1955. Mem. Tex. (pres. 1970-71, honor award 1971), Nat. assns. health, phys. edn. and recreation, Nat. Assn. Phys. Edn. Coll. Women, Gamma Phi Beta. Contbr. 7 films on elementary sch. phys. edn., 1961-65. Home: 3914 Ascot Lane Houston TX 77018

PATTERSON, ELIZABETH CHAMBERS (MRS. ANDREW PATTERSON, JR.), educator; b. Clarksville, Tex.; d. Clifton Ayres and Eva Ellen (Smith) Chambers; B.A., U. Tex., 1937, M.A., 1940; postgrad. Mt. Holyoke Coll., 1938-39, U. Mich., summer 1938, Oxford U., 1966-67, Somerville Coll. Oxford, 1972; m. Andrew Patterson, Jr., June 6, 1940; children—Ellen Clifton (Mrs. Jonathan C. Brown), Andrew Muir, Elizabeth L., Katharine C. Teaching asst. dept. chemistry U. Tex., 1937-38; teaching asst. dept. physiology Mt. Holyoke Coll., South Hadley, Mass., 1938-39; instr. chemistry U. Tex. at Arlington, 1940-41; research asst. dept. chemistry U. N.C., at Chapel Hill, 1942-44; prof. phys. scis. Albert Magnus Coll., New Haven, 1948, 58—, chmn. dept. phys. scis., 1970—. NSF fellow, 1963, Sci. Faculty fellow, 1967; Am. Philos. Soc. grantee. Mem. Am. Phys. Soc., Am. Assn. Physics Tchrs., A.A.A.S., Conn. Acad. Arts and Scis., History of Sci. Soc., Brit. Soc. for History of Sci., Phi Beta Kappa, Sigma Xi. Clubs: New Haven Lawn; North End, Saturday Morning (New Haven). Author: John Dalton and the Atomic Theory, 1970. Editor Somerville papers, 1967—. Contbr. articles to profl. jours. Home: 175 East Rock Rd New Haven CT 06511

PATTERSON, FRANCES MARIE LEE (MRS. JOHN B. PATTERSON), civic worker; b. Denver, May 1, 1934; d. Francis Xavier and Helen Ruth (Kerns) Lee; B.A., Loretto Heights Coll., 1956; postgrad. Ohio State U., 1956-57; m. John B. Patterson, Jan. 25, 1958; children—John Lee, Kathleen Marie. Tchr., Notre Dame High Sch., San Jose, Cal., 1958-59; tchr., costumer designer Baldwin-Wallace Coll., Berea, O., 1965-67, Cabrillo Coll., Aptos, Cal., 1967-70; legal sec., office mgr. Hulland & Robinson, Attys., West Covina, Cal., 1971-73; legal sec., Bakersfield, Cal., 1973—. Sec. West Covina La Puente Youth Soccer Orgn., 1972-73. Mem. Am. Theatre Assn., Cal. Edn. Theatre Assn., Childrens Theatre Conf., Speech Communications Assn., Nat. Notaries Assn., Legal Secs. Assn. Bakersfield. Home: 2214 Alturas Dr Bakersfield CA 93305 Office: 1112 Truxtun Av Bakersfield CA 93301

PATTERSON, JOYCE RAYE, religious assn. exec.; b. St. Joseph, Mo., Dec. 8, 1930; d. Perry William and Fredda F. (Crouse) Patterson; A.B., Nat. Coll., Kansas City, Mo., 1952; postgrad. Scarritt Coll., 1957. Dir. youth work Kan. Conf., Meth. Ch., Baldwin, 1952-56; exec. dir. Wesley Community Center, St. Joseph, Mo., 1957-70, Wesley/Cath. Service, St. Joseph, Mo., 1970—. Mem. Commn. on Deaconess and Home Missionary Service, 1968—, pres., 1973; mem. adv. com. community center dept. Bd. Missions, United Meth. Ch., 1968-72, dist. sec. ecumenical affairs, 1970—, mem. conf. bd. Mo. West Conf., 1966—, del. S. Central Jurisdicitonal Conf., 1968-72, sec. Evanston regional com. woman's com. Bd. Missions, 1970—; cons. Black Citizens for Progress, 1968-69. Mem. St. Joseph Community Planning Council, 1967-69; mem. Mayor's Adv. Com., 1966—; mem. St. Joseph Adv. Council on Aging, 1971—; mem. ABCD Regional Planning Council, Comprehensive Health Planning sect., 1971—; mem. planning com. White House Conf. on Aging, 1971-72; mem. Mo. Gov.'s Adv. Com. on Aging, 1973. Bd. dirs. Econ. Opportunity Corp. Mem. Nat. Fedn. Settlements, Nat. Assn. Social Welfare, Nat. Conf. Cath. Charities, Child Welfare League Am., Mo. Assn. Social Welfare, South Central Jurisdiction Deaconess and Home Missionary Assn. (pres. 1971). Home: Rural Route 4 St Joseph MO 64503 Office: 200 Cherokee St St Joseph MO 64504

PATTERSON, MARGOT TRUMAN, educator; b. Grand Rapids, Mich., May 1, 1918; d. Lewis R. and Caroline L. (Auwers) Truman; B.A., U. S.D., 1941, M.A., 1947; postgrad. U. Mo., 1949-53, U. So. Cal., summer 1948, N.Y. U., summer 1949, U. Mich., summer 1954; m. H.F. (Pat) Patterson, Sept. 11, 1953 (dec. Mar. 30, 1965); children—Christopher, David Francis II. Instr. U. S.D., Vermillion, 1944; tchr. Stephens Coll., Columbia, Mo., 1946-55; asst. prof. extension edn. U. Mo., Columbia, 1966—, program cons. Acad. Support Center, 1975—. Appeared women's program TV sta. KOMU, Columbia, 1953-54; cons. Mo. Commn. on Status of Women, 1965-66, Mo. Assn. Social Welfare, 1969-70; organizer, chairperson Community Congress, Columbia, 1969-70. Mem. Mo. Ho. of Reps., 1965-66; v.p. Democratic Women's Club, 1959-63. Bd. dirs. Community Day Care, Columbia, 1965-73. Mem. Adult Edn. Assn. U.S. (chairperson continuing edn. for women sect. 1973-75), Legislative Women's Club, Tau Kappa Alpha, Pi Lambda Theta, Alpha Epsilon Rho. Home: 109 W Burman Rd Columbia MO 65201 Office: Acad Support Center 505 E Stewart Rd Columbia MO 65201

PATTERSON, MARION LOUISE, photographer; b. San Francisco, Apr. 24, 1933; d. Morrie Leslie and Esther Elizabeth (Parker) Patterson; A.B. cum laude, Stanford, 1955; postgrad. Cal. Sch. Fine Arts, 1956-58; M.A., Cal. State U., 1971. Free-lance photographer, including expdns. in C.Am., 1956—; with Best's Studio, Yosemite, 1958-61; asst. to photo editor Sunset mag., Menlo Park, Cal., 1961-64; communications cons. Projects to Advance Creativity in Edn., Redwood City, Cal., 1966-68; instr. photography Foothill Coll., Los Altos, also De Anza Coll., Cupertino, 1968—. Exhibited photographs in one-man shows including San Francisco Mus. Art, 1965, Oakland Mus., 1966, Focus Gallery, San Francisco, 1971, Monterey (Cal.) Mus. Art, 1971, Photo-Arts, Cupertino, 1973, Gallery 115, Santa Cruz, 1973; exhibited in group shows George Eastman House, Rochester, N.Y., Ind. U., Bloomington, 1959, Friends of Photography, Carmel, Cal., 1970, 71, 73, Bay Area Regional Graphics, 1973, others; represented in permanent collections at Mass. Inst. Tech., Oakland Mus., also pvt. collections. Exec. dir. Croner Found., 1969—. Mem. Am. Craftsmen's Council, Cal. Acad. Scis., Friends of Photography, Common Cause. Democrat. Mem. Universal Life Ch. (minister 1968—). Contbr. photographs, articles to numerous publs. Home: 1745 Croner Av Menlo Park CA 94025 Office: PO Box 842 Menlo Park CA 94025

PATTERSON, MARY MARGARET (MRS. DAVID S. PATTERSON), journalist; b. Fairmont, W.Va., July 12, 1944; d. H. Sutton and Columbia R. (Rosetta) Sharp; B.A. cum laude, Ohio State U., 1966, M.A., 1967; m. David S. Patterson, June 15, 1968. Writer, editor Project Africa newspaper, Columbus, O., and Pitts., 1968; writer Ohio State U. News and Information Service, Columbus, 1968-69; writer, editor Ohio State Regional Med. Program, Columbus, 1969; staff asso. Am. Hosp. Assn., Chgo., 1969-70; feature writer Chicago Today newspaper, 1970; edn. writer The Houston Chronicle, 1971-74. Free lance writer, 1970—. Instr. news writing W.Va. U., Parkersburg Center, 1968, Ohio State U., summer, 1968, U. Houston, 1972, 74—. Recipient first prize Newspaper Fund, Inc., 1966, first prize in W.Va. President's Com. for Hiring Physically Handicapped Essay Contest, 1962. Univ. fellow Ohio State U., 1966-67. Mem. Women in Communications (pres. coll. chpt. 1966), Sigma Delta Chi, Kappa Tau Alpha. Mem. Unitarian Ch. Home: 3029 Bluebonnet Blvd Houston TX 77025

PATTERSON, MILDRED L(UCRETIA), asso. dist. judge; b. Guthrie, Okla., July 30, 1912; d. Columbus W. and Lydia K. (Cash) Patterson; student Okla. City Coll. Law, 1941-45. Legal sec. bookkeeper, underwriter, 1931-51; admitted to Okla. bar, 1945; head law book dept. Co-Operative Pub. Co., Guthrie, 1951-54; asst. editor Ofcl. Session Laws of Okla., 1951, editor, 1953-55, 57, 59, 61; asst. editor New Ins. Laws of Okla., 1951; county judge Logan County, Guthrie, 1955-69; asso. dist. judge Logan County, 1969—. Pres. bd. dirs. Guthrie Community Chest Fund, 1957-58; asso. mem. Gov.'s Com. on Futherance of Employment for Physically Handicapped, 1957, 58—; Pres.' Com. on Handicapped. Trustee I.O.A. Ranch for Boys, Perkins, Okla.; mem. nat. council U.S.O. Mem. Okla. Assn. Juvenile Ct. Judges (sec. 1964), Am. Legion Aux., Nat. Council of Juvenile Ct. Judges, Okla. Juvenile Officers Assn., Bus. and Profl. Women's Club (past pres.), Am. Life Assn. (dir.), Okla. Assn. Women Lawyers (state sec.), Okla. County Officers Assn. (dist pres.), Iota Tau Tau. Mem. Christian Ch. Mem. Order Eastern Star, Daus. of Nile. Home: 215 N Elm St Guthrie OK 73044 Office: Courthouse Guthrie OK 73044

PATTERSON, PHOEBE BUMGARNER (MRS. ASHBY METCALFE PATTERSON), civic worker; b. Millers Creek, N.C.; d. George Washington and Mary Elizabeth (Nichols) Bumgarner; R.N., Baron Erlanger Hosp. Sch. Nursing, 1920; student U. Chattanooga, 1922, 36-37; m. Ashby Metcalfe Patterson, Dec. 27, 1926 (dec. Jan., 1972); 1 dau., Elizabeth. Supr. patients Baroness Erlanger Hosp., 1920, night supt., 1922-23; record librarian, 1925-26; supt. nurses Newell Hosp., Chattanooga, 1924; became owner, operator Phoebe's Antiques & Museum, Chattanooga, 1959—. Founder, Care and Share Inc., 1959, pres., 1960-62, chmn. bd., 1962—; pres. Garden Club of Riverview, 1939-41, hon. pres., 1965; pres. Chattanooga-Hamilton County Council Garden Clubs, 1941-43; v.p. Tenn. Fedn. Garden Clubs, 1943-45; a founder Chattanooga Rose Soc.; lectr. astronomy, 1945—, wild flowers and ornithology, 1938-70; founder Chattanooga Early Am. Glass Club, 1963; past counselor Chattanooga and E. Tenn. area Tenn. Poetry Soc. Mem. Nat. Assn. Dealers in Antiques, Soc. Philatelic Ams., Nat. Early Am. Glass Club, Chattanooga Audubon Soc. (a founder, hon. life mem.), Am. Poetry League, D.A.R., Am. Numis. Assn. Methodist (pres. Woman's Soc. Christian Service 1944-46, 52-53). Contbr. poetry to various publs. Home: 1614 Shady Circle Chattanooga TN 37405

PATTERSON, POLLY REILLY (MRS. W. RAY PATTERSON), ret. communications co. exec., civic worker; b. Wilkinsburg, Pa.; d. Thomas L. and Margaret (Coughey) Reilly; grad. high sch.; m. W. Ray Patterson, Sept. 2, 1943. With Bell Telephone Co. of Pa., Pitts., 1925-71, beginning as clk., successively various mgmt. positions, 1935-64, staff asso. pub. relations staff, 1965-71; dir. Chatham Village Homes, Inc., 1973—. Asst. treas. Allegheny County Soc. for Crippled Children, 1962-66, v.p., 1966-70; bd. dirs. Jr. Achievement, Inc. of S.W. Pa., 1950-71, Pitts. YWCA, 1964-72, Pa. Soc. Crippled Children and Adults, 1960-68. Named One of Pitts.'s Ten Outstanding Women, Pitts. Sun Telegraph, 1959, Pitts. Advt. Woman of Year, 1958; recipient Crystal Prism award Am. Advt. Fedn., 1972. Mem. Pitts. Bus. Women's Clubs (dir. 1946—), Altrusa Internat., Pitts. Advt. Club (v.p., sec. 1929-69). Home: 402 Olympia Rd Pittsburgh PA 15211

PATTERSON, SARAH FRANCES, lawyer; b. Atlanta, Aug. 19, 1945; d. Francis and Kathleen (Elmore) Patterson; student Furman U., 1963-65; A.B., Atlantic Christian Coll., 1967; J.D., U. N.C., 1971; certificate comparative law, London Polytechnic, 1970. Admitted to N.C. bar, 1971; advt. mr. Belk Tyler Co., Wilson, N.C., 1967-68; asst. dist. atty. 7th Solicitional Dist., Wilson, 1971—. Mem. Am. Bar Assn., Nat. Dist. Atty's Assn., U. N.C. Alumni Assn. (life), Phi Mu. Democrat. Home: 305 Raleigh Rd Wilson NC 27893 Office: PO Box 261 Wilson NC 27893

PATTERSON, VIRGINIA MARIE, physician; b. Dallas, Sept. 23, 1917; d. Leiland Augustus and Marie Elnore (Hilliard) Norrell; A.B., Tex. State Coll. Women, 1939; B.S., U. Ill., 1947, M.D., 1949; m. John V. Patterson, Dec. 20, 1952 (div. Oct. 1961); 1 son, John V. III. Intern, St. Barnabas Hosp., Mpls., 1949-50; practice medicine, Brunswick, Ga., 1953-55; resident radiology DePaul Hosp., Norfolk, Va., 1955-57; resident U. Ill. Hosp., 1958, asst. radiologist, 1959-65, asso. radiologist, 1965—, chief nuclear medicine sect., 1959; asso. prof.

radiology U. Ill., 1965—; cons. radiologist Chgo. State Tb Sanitorium, 1962-63; cons. nuclear medicine Delnor Hosp., St. Charles, Ill., 1973—. Served to lt. USNR, 1950-53. Diplomate Am. Bd. Radiology, Am. Bd. Nuclear Medicine. Mem. Am. Coll. Nuclear Medicine (charter), Soc. Nuclear Medicine, Am. Coll. Radiology, A.M.A., Am. Med. Women's Assn., D.A.R. Pilgrim Colony, Nat. Soc. New Eng. Women, Nat. Geneal. Soc., New Eng. Hist. Geneal. Soc., Alpha Omega Alpha. Baptist (trustee 1967-70). Office: 840 S Wood St Chicago IL 60612

PATTISON, ROSE MARY, ednl. adminstr.; b. Elana, W.Va., Mar. 5, 1919; d. William Hunter and Roxie Gay (Sibert) Smith; B.S. in Home Econs., W.Va. U., 1941; M.A. in Higher Edn., Ohio State U., 1965; postgrad No. Ill. U., 1972-73; children by previous marriage—George Edgar, Kay Louise (Mrs. Fred Meister), Carol Anne (Mrs. John Stegmiller). Instr., Ohio State U., 1959-65; supr. adult basic edn. Ohio Dept. Edn., Columbus, 1965; dir. adult basic edn. Ind. Dept. Pub. Instrn., Indpls., 1966-69; dir. div. adult edn. Black Hawk Coll., Moline, Ill., 1969-73; asst. to vice chancellor Ohio Bd. Regents, Columbus, 1973—. Cons. examiner commn. insts. high edn. N.Central Assn. Colls. and Secondary Schs., 1971—, U.S. Office Edn. Regional Tng. Inst., U. Ia., 1971. Mem. Rock Island County Welfare Council (chmn. div. aging 1971-72, chmn. com. edn. 1972-73), Rock Island County Migrant Council (mem. adv. com. 1973, del. White House Conf. Aging, 1971, U.S. rep. to Internat. Seminar on Problems Adult Edn., Salzburg, Austria, 1966, 70, to N.Am. Conf. Adult Edn.; Montreal, Que., Can., 1967. Recipient Alfred J. Wright award Ohio State U., 1964; Ill. State 4-H Alumni award, 1973. Mem. Nat. Assn. for Pub. Continuing and Adult Edn. (sec.-treas. 1967-73, mem. legislative com. 1971-72, chmn. publs., 1973-74, liaison to com. internat. aspects adult and correctional edn. 1972-73, curriculum devel., 1971-73, publs. 1972-73, correctional edn., 1972-73, pres. elect 1974-75), Nat. Council State Dirs. Adult Edn., N.E.A., Adult Edn. Assn. U.S.A. (Ind. rep. nat. conf. 1968, del. assembly, 1968, exec. com. commn. aging 1972-73, editor Ind. newsletter 1967-69, mem. Ill. legislative com. 1971-72), Am. Assn. Jr. Colls., Child Conservation League (Ohio legislative chmn. 1952, regional pres. 1953), Altrusa, Alpha Xi Delta, Phi Upsilon Omicron. Author: (with Joseph C. Payne) Evaluation Tools for Adult Education, 1968; To See in Not to Know, 1966. Contbr. articles to profl. jours. Home: 4559 Arlingate Dr Columbus OH 43220 Office: Ohio Bd Regents 30 E Broad St Columbus OH 43215

PATTON, ALMEDA JANE VANDIKE, librarian; b. Elberon, Ia., May 17, 1914; d. Frank Allen and Clara Marie (Tarvestad) VanDike; student Culver Stockton Coll., U. Ia., 1931-36, B.S., Fla. State U., 1957, M.S., 1967; m. John Henry Patton, Feb. 20, 1937 (div.); children—Jon, Judith (Mrs. John Lotas), Joanna. Librarian, Springfield (Fla.) Elementary Sch., 1956-57, Bay County Pub. Library, Panama City, Fla., 1957—; dir. N.W. Regional Library System, Panama City, 1960—. Mem. Fla. Right-to-Read Council, 1973-74. Work-study grantee Fla. State Library, 1965-66. Mem. Am. Assn. U. Women (edn. chmn. 1961-66), Am., Southeastern, Fla. (standards com. 1969—) library assns., Audubon Assn. (program chmn. 1971-72), Panama Art Assn. (program chmn. 1972), C. of C. (pub. affairs com. 1967), World Future Soc. Clubs: Woman's (chmn. edn. com. 1962-66), Country (Panama City). Home: 1613 Dewitt St Panama City FL 32401 Office: 25 W Government St Panama City FL 32401

PATTON, ALTA CHAPMAN, lawyer; b. Livingston, Ala., Mar. 3, 1912; d. William Wayne and Anna (Chapman) Patton; A.B., U. Ala., 1932; LL.B., Jones Lab. Sch., 1949. Social worker, Sumter County, Ala., 1933-35, chief clk. Probate Office, 1935-39; stenographer Ala. Dept. Agr. and Industries, Montgomery, 1939-41, Office Ala. Atty. Gen., 1941-46; accounts examiner VA, Montgomery, 1946-48; admitted to Ala. bar, 1948; legal analyst Legis. Reference Service Ala., Montgomery, 1948—. Mem. Ala. Bar, Ala. Women Lawyers, Ala., Sumter County hist. socs. Episcopalian. Home: 3010 Cloverdale Rd Montgomery AL 36106 Office: State Capitol Montgomery AL 36104

PATTON, BESS EVELYN WHITEHEAD (MRS. JAMES GRAHAM PATTON), business exec., civic worker, clubwoman; b. Hattiesburg, Miss., Sept. 18, 1913; d. Charles Oliver and Bessie (Vining) Whitehead; student Miss. Woman's Coll., 1931-32; A.A., Sunflower Jr. Coll., 1934; student corr. course N.Y. Sch. Interior Design; m. James Graham Patton, Mar. 10, 1935; 1 dau., Betty Graham (Mrs. Richard Carrington Stockett, Jr.). Free lance interior decorator, 1950-55; co-owner (with husband), operator Stratton Hotel, Winona, Miss., 1958-60, Wisteria Apts., Winona, 1957-70; sec.-treas. Arvonia Realty Co., Inc., Jackson, 1961—; co-owner, sec.-treas., editor Hammond (La.) Vindicator, Inc., 1966-67; co-owner, sec.-treas. Franklin Printers Inc., Jackson, 1968-69; co-owner (with husband) Standard Printing Equipment of Baton Rouge (La.), 1964—. Sec. Baton Rouge chpt. D.A.R., 1966-69, 1st vice regent, 1969-71; membership chmn. Isaac Monet chpt. Colonial Dames of Seventeenth Century, 1969-71, pres., 1973-75. Active various community drives. Presbyn. (asso. circle leader women of ch. 1969-70). Mem. La. Arts and Scis. Clubs: Federated Woman's, Euphemian (pres. 1967-68, publicity chmn. 1969-70), Woman's (bd. mgrs. 1965—, chmn. stock 1968—), Found. for Hist. La., Baton Rouge Music. Writer weekly column pub. various newspapers, 1967—. Home: 666 Sherwood Forest Blvd Baton Rouge LA 70815

PATTON, BETTY CAROLYN BURNETT (MRS. CLERMONT CLINTON PATTON), editor; b. nr. Memphis, Tex., Nov. 27, 1935; d. Blufford Isaac and Ara Faye (Dennis) Burnett; grad. high sch.; m. Clermont Clinton Patton, Nov. 27, 1954; children—Susan Carolyn, Dwight Clinton. Advt. mgr. Deming (N.M.) Newspapers, 1965-67; editor, Pecos Valley News, 1968; soc. editor Carlsbad (N.M.) Current-Argus, 1968—; dir. Eddy County Abstract Co. Leader Luna council Girl Scouts U.S., 1960-68. Bd. dirs. United Fund, bd. dirs., sec. Carlsbad Assn. Retarded Children. Mem. N.M. Press Assn. (recipient E. H. Shaffer award 1970), Carlsbad Area Art Assn. Methodist. Club: Woman's (Carlsbad). Home: 1010 Irvin St Carlsbad NM 88220 Office: 101 W Mermod St Carlsbad NM 88220

PATTON, ELDA CLAYTON, physician; b. Hartford, Ky.; d. Clayton Lunsford and Lena Rivers (Miller) Patton; B.A., U. Evansville (Ind.), 1942, Hum.D. (hon.), 1971; M.A., Columbia, 1950; M.D., U. Padua (Italy), 1959. Tchr. pub. schs., Ind., 1930-33, 38-43, N.J., 1950, N.Y., 1953-54; translator, interpreter U.S. Fgn. Service, Buenos Aires, Argentina, 1945-47; intern N.Y. Polyclinic Hosp., N.Y.C., 1959-60; resident Central Islip (N.Y.) State Hosp., 1960-62; sr. psychiatrist Manhattan State Hosp., N.Y.C., 1962-65; supervising psychiatrist Lower Manhattan Narcotic After Care Clinic, N.Y.C., 1965-67; asst. to met. unit chief, Kirby Manhattan State Hosp., 1970-72, head out-patient services, 1972—; practice medicine specializing in psychiatry, N.Y.C., 1961—; mem. staff Gracie Sq. Hosp., N.Y.C.; supervising psychiatrist Bayview Rehab. Center, N.Y.C., 1967-70; cons. Puerto Rican Family Inst., 1967—, med. dir., 1974—. Mem. drug-abuse sub-com. Pub. Health Com., N.Y. County Med. Soc., 1965—. Mem. A.M.A., Am. Psychiatry Assn., Am. Womens Med. Soc., Womens Med. Soc. N.Y. State. Home: 25 Leroy St New York City NY 10014 Office: 4 E 89th St New York City NY 10028

PATTON, ELIZABETH HYDE, librarian; b. Charleston, S.C., Aug. 6, 1917; d. Samuel Black and Elizabeth Allen (Easley) Hyde; B.S., Coll. Charleston, 1938; M.S., Columbia, 1961; m. William David Patton, Aug. 22, 1940 (dec. 1962); children—John Davidson, Lucy Hyde. Librarian, U. New Haven, 1958-66; librarian in charge Free Pub. Library, New Haven, 1966—. Mem. Am., Conn. library assns., Film Co-op. Conn. (chmn. 1974), Beta Phi Mu. Home: 135 Clifford St Hamden CT 06517 Office: 133 Elm St New Haven CT 06510

PATTON, FRANCES ANNE (MRS. EARL R. PATTON), lawyer; b. Cleve., Jan. 14, 1917; d. Peter Mathew and Frances Helen (Lovrenic) Basar; student John Marshall Coll., Cleve., 1934-35, John Carroll U., 1935-37; LL.B., Columbus U., Washington, 1940, LL.M., 1941; m. Earl Richard Patton, Apr. 20, 1945 (div. Oct. 1963); 1 son, John Michael. Admitted to U.S. Dist. Ct. for D.C., 1940, U.S. Ct. Appeals, D.C. Circuit, 1940, U.S. Supreme Ct., 1944; with Dept. Interior, Washington, 1938—, chief, br. mineral leasing appeals Bur. Land Mgmt., Washington, 1962-64, chief, br. mineral appeals, 1964-70, spl. asst. to dir. Office Hearings and Appeals, Office Sec., Arlington, Va., 1970—. Recipient Superior Performance award, 1966, Meritorious Performance award Dept. Interior, 1968. Mem. Unified Bar D.C., Women's Bar Assn. D.C., Fed. Bar Assn., Am. Judicature Soc., Phi Alpha Delta. Home: 3725 Macomb St NW Washington DC 20016 Office: Office Hearings and Appeals Dept Interior 4015 Wilson Blvd Arlington VA 22203

PATTON, JOAN ANTHONY, librarian; b. Los Angeles, Jan. 19, 1934; d. Normand Anthony and Barbara Estelle (Clegg) Schneider; A.A., Tenn. Wesleyan U.; B.S., U. Tenn., 1955; M.L.S., Rutgers U., 1964; m. Roy Lee Patton, Dec. 22, 1955. Librarian, media specialist McMinn County High Sch., Athens, Tenn., 1955, Memphis pub. schs., 1956, Daniel Boone Joint Sch. Dist., Birdsboro, Pa., 1956, Wyomissings Hills (Pa.) Sch., 1957; tchr., librarian Harding Twp. Sch., New Vernon, N.J., 1958—; mem. faculty Summer Inst. Library Service, Ind. U., 1966. Mem. Am., N.J. library assns., Nat., N.J., Morris County, Harding Twp. (pres. 1969-70) edn. assns., N.J. Sch. Library Assn. (legislative chmn. 1965, pres. 1968-69, recruitment chmn. 1974), Morris County Sch. Librarian's Assn. (pres. 1965-66). Home: Box 647 RD 5 Flemington NJ 08822 Office: Harding Twp Schs Lee's Hill Rd New Vernon NJ 07967

PATTON, JUNE LORRAINE HYATT (MRS. DALLAS C. PATTON), lawyer, broker; b. Kansas City, Mo., May 19, 1937; d. Jesse Walton and Lucille Virginia (Powell) Hyatt; B.A. in Psychology, U. Mo., 1960; LL.B., U. Kansas, 1964; m. Dallas Clarence Patton, Apr. 19, 1963; children—Cassandra Carrie, Tiffany Alice. Jr. securities analyst Continental Research Corp., Kansas City, Mo., 1960-61; admitted to Kan. bar, 1964, Ia. bar, 1969; law clk. Wagner, Leek & Mullins, Shawnee Mission, Kan., 1962-63, atty., 1964-65; practiced in Roeland Park, Kan., 1964-65, Winterset and Des Moines, Ia., 1969—; June Lorraine H. Patton, atty. at law, 1969—; pres. J.L.H. Patton & Co., computer broker, cons., Des Moines, 1970—. Sec. non-profit Corp. for Restoration and Improvement Winterset Community Area, 1973—. Mem. Am., Ia., Polk County bar assns. Mem. Order Eastern Star. Home: 520 W Court Winterset IA 50373 Office: Municipal Airport Terminal Des Moines IA 50321

PATTON, LEONA PEARL, museum ofcl.; b. Connellsville, Pa., May 31, 1916; d. John George and Martha Jane (Gregg) Fenton; night student Fleming Bus. Coll., Uniontown, Pa., 1936-38; m. Harry Blaine Patton, Dec. 14, 1955. Sec. to dir. Uniontown C. of C., 1936-48, asst., sec., 1948-49; officer mgr. The Furniture Outlet Subsidiary Household Furniture Co., Uniontown, 1949-55; with records mgmt. U.S. Dept. Navy, 1956-57; mem. staff West Point Mus., U.S. Mil. Acad., N.Y., 1959—, adminstrv. asst., 1962—. Recipient Superior Performance award West Point Mus. Republican. Methodist (adminstrv. bd.). Home: 2 Schneider Av Highland Falls NY 10928 Office: West Point Museum US Mil Acad West Point NY 10996

PATTON, MARTHA LEE FORGY (MRS. GILBERT LEE PATTON), author; b. Mt. Vernon, Ind.; d. Horace Eugene and Martha Lee (McGrew) Forgy; B.A., Ind. Porter Sch. Commerce, 1930; m. Gilbert Lee Patton, Apr. 23, 1943; 1 son, Gilbert Lee. Telegraph editor-staff writer Evansville (Ind.) Press, 1930-35; writer-commentator radio sta. WGBF (NBC), Evansville, Ind., 1935-36; assignment writer Macfadden Publs., N.Y.C., 1936-50; mgr. advt. Winter Park (Fla.) Sun Heartald, 1959, editor, 1960, mng. editor, 1962-70; assignment writer Whitestone Publs., N.Y.C., 1970-73; free lance Fawcett Publs., Christian Adv., ghost lectrs. for judges and attys., 1936-50. Mem. Nat. Fedn. Press Women, Nat. League Am. Pen Women (Fla. publicity chmn. 1970, 74), Internat. Platform Assn., Artists' League Orange County, Fla. Fedn. Art, Albin Polasek Art Assn., D.A.R. Presbyn. Mem. Order of Eastern Star. Author: Around the World Tour, 1932; The Closing Net, 1944; A Little Boy and God, 1954; The Destiny of One, 1968. Home: 1541 Sunnyside Dr Maitland FL 32751

PATTON, NANCY JOAN DONALDSON, state ofcl.; b. Chanute, Kan., Nov. 2, 1938; d. George W. and Mildred J. (McKinney) Donaldson; student Chanute Jr. Coll., 1956-57, Kan. U., 1957-59; children—Tonnie Gay, Julia Renée, Laura Beth. Receptionist, legal sec. Mountain Fuel Supply Co., Wichita, Kan., 1958-59; sec. to mgr. sales promotion dept. Hallmark Cards, Kansas City, Mo., 1959-60; sec. to account exec. Foote, Cone & Belding, San Francisco, 1960-62; legal sec. Pence & Millett, attys. at law, Laramie, Wyo., 1962-67; sec. to Gov. Stan Hathaway of Wyo., Cheyenne, 1967-72; dir. Communications Services Div. Wyo. State Dept. Edn., 1972—. Bd. dirs. Nat. Assn. State Edn. Dept. Information Officers. Home: 914 Hillcrest St Cheyenne WY 82001 Office: Capitol Bldg Cheyenne WY 82001

PATTON, ROSEZELIA ANNE (MRS. WALTER B. PATTON), ednl. adminstr.; b. Cin., Sept. 25, 1934; d. Robert Lloyd and Rosezelia (Bradshaw) Leahr; student, U. Colo., 1953-54, Miami U., 1962-63, Western Coll., 1970-72; m. Walter B. Patton, Sept. 6, 1958; children by previous marriage—Councill Harris, Rebecca L. Harris. Trade book buyer Du Bois Bookstore, Oxford, O., 1962-69; registrar Western Coll., Oxford, 1969-74; records analyst Sch. Edn. Miami U., Oxford, 1974—. Bd. dir. Mental Hygiene, 1966-69. Mem. Bus. and Profl. Womens Club, Oxford Fedn. Womans Clubs. African Methodist. Home: 520 S Main St Oxford OH 45056 Office: Room 203 McGuffey Hall Miami U Oxford OH 45056

PAUGH, MINNIE ELLEN, librarian; b. Virginia City, Mont., Apr. 7, 1919; d. George E. and June (Buhite) Paugh; M.Ed., U. Mont., 1952; M.L.S., U. Denver, 1961. Tchr. history, Laurel, Mont., 1942-47, Havre, Mont., 1947-52, Glasgow, Mont., 1954-56, Whitefish, Mont., 1956-60; spl. collections librarian Mont. State U. Library, Bozeman, 1961—. Mem. Am. Assn. U. Women, Am. Assn. U. Profs., Am., Mont. (sec. 1971-72), Pacific Northwest (bibliography com. 1968-74, authors com. 1968-74) library assns., Am. Assn. for State and Local History, Bozeman History Group (chmn. 1964-74), Delta Kappa Gamma (chpt. sec. 1970-72). Mem. Order Eastern Star. Home: 510 W Story St Bozeman MT 59715 Office: Montana State University Library Bozeman MT 59715

PAUL, CHRISTA-ELIZABETH (MRS. MARTIN PAUL), educator; b. Stargardt, Germany, Dec. 27, 1924; d. Louis and Else Ida (Frank) Noll; B.A., Temple U., 1966, M.A., 1970; m. Martin Paul, June 9, 1960. Came to U.S., 1953, naturalized, 1958. With periodicals div. Temple U. Library, Phila., 1955-58, dir. fgn. lang., English and anthropology lab., 1958-67; asst. prof. German lang. and lit. Phila. Coll. Pharmacy and Sci., 1967—, mem. faculty council, 1970—. Ednl. cons. Chester Electronics (Conn.), 1962-67. Mem. Modern Lang. Assn., Am. Assn. Tchrs. German, Am. Assn. U. Profs., Nat. Assn. Lang. Lab. Dirs., Pa. Modern Lang. Assn., Delta Phi Alpha. Home: 718 Lombard St Philadelphia PA 19147

PAUL, EVE WEINSCHENKER (MRS. ROBERT DAVID PAUL), lawyer; b. N.Y.C., June 16, 1930; d. Leo I. and Tamara (Sogolow) Weinschenker; B.A., Cornell U., 1950; J.D., Columbia, 1952; m. Robert David Paul, Apr. 9, 1952; children—Jeremy Ralph, Sarah Elizabeth. Admitted to N.Y. bar, 1952, Conn. bar, 1960; asso. mem. firm Botein, Hays, Sklar & Herzberg, N.Y.C., 1952-54, Bernard D. Cahn, 1954-56; research asso., adv. com. practice and procedure N.Y. State Temporary Commn. on Cts., 1957; individual practice law, Stamford, Conn., 1960-70; staff atty. Legal Aid Soc., Family Ct. Br., Manhattan, 1970-71; staff atty. legal analysis project Planned Parenthood, N.Y.C., 1971-72; asso. mem. firm Greenbaum, Wolff & Ernst, N.Y.C., 1972—. Exec. sec. Commn. Inquiry Bd. Edn. N.Y.C., 1961; mem. Stamford (Conn.) Planning Bd., 1967-70. Mem. Assn. Bar City N.Y., N.Y. County Lawyers Assn., Conn., Stamford bar assns., Nat. Assn. Women Lawyers, Phi Beta Kappa, Phi Kappa Phi. Club: Cornell. Editor: Columbia Law Rev., 1951-52. Home: 500 E 77th St New York City NY 10021 Office: 437 Madison Av New York City NY 10022

PAUL, GWENDOLYN HOPE (MRS. JAMES EDWARD PAUL), educator; b. nr. Forest City, N.C., July 7, 1933; d. Leonard T. and Cleo (Vassey) Hope; B.S., Limestone Coll., 1955; M.Ed., U. Ga., 1970; m. Sherman Ray Ellington, June 14, 1957 (div. Nov. 1967); children—Stephen Ray, Alice Lynn, Carol Ann.; m. 2d, James Edward Paul, May 17, 1968. Tchr. phys. edn. Gastonia (N.C.) City Schs., 1955-57; tchr. Cherokee County Schs., Gaffney, S.C., 1957-59, Forest Park (Ga.) Sr. High Sch., 1960-66; tchr. safety edn. U. Ga., Athens, 1966-67; DeKalb Jr. Coll., Decatur, Ga., 1966-67; counselor Huie Elementary Sch., Forest Park, Ga., 1966-71; counselor Pebblebrook High Sch., Mableton, Ga., 1971—. Chmn. Cystic Fibrosis Dr., Clayton County (Ga.), 1961—; leader Girl Scouts of Am., 1951-53; organizer Old Mill Trace-Terrell Mill Homeowners Assn., 1973; mem. civic group com. Bumbry Elementary Sch. Community Improvement Program. Named Woman of Yr., Forest Park, 1961. Mem. N.E.A., Ga., Clayton County edn. assns., Ga. Sch. Counselor Assn., Am. Personnel and Guidance Assn., Ga. Drivers Edn. Assn. (treas. 1966-67), Chi Beta Phi, Alpha Delta, Beta Sigma Phi (pres. 1962-66). Democrat. Baptist. Club: Terrell Mill Estates Garden (pres. 1973). Home: 1410 Glenwood Ct SE Marietta GA 30060

PAUL, LYNN (MRS. HERMAN PAUL), lawyer; b. Bklyn., Dec. 13, 1924; d. Samuel and Harriet (Namm) Pines; B.A., U. Cal. at Los Angeles, 1946; LL.B., Blackstone Coll. Law, 1956; m. Herman Paul, Aug. 18, 1945; children—Jay, Peter, Roy, Glen. Admitted to Cal. bar, 1958, practiced in Bell Gardens. Tchr. law Bell Gardens Sr. High Sch. Adult Div., 1960—. Mem. Bell Gardens City Council, 1961-68; mayor Bell Gardens, Cal., 1961-62, 66-67; elected to Central Democratic Com., Los Angeles County, 1962—. Mem. S.E. Dist. Bar Assn., Women Lawyers Bar Assn., Iota Tau Tau. Address: 6141 Clara St Bell Gardens CA 90201

PAUL, MIMI, ballet dancer; b. Nashville, Feb. 3, 1943; d. Norman and Marguerite (Pahud) Paul; student Holton Arms, Washington, 1955-59; m. M. Avedon, May 14, 1967. With N.Y.C. Ballet, 1960—, soloist, 1963-66, prin. dancer, 1966-68, prin. dancer with ballet theatre, 1968—. Home: 155 W 68th St New York City NY 10023

PAUL, PHYLLIS OSTRUM, physician; b. Phila., June 9, 1926; d. Samuel B. and Rose (Shay) Ostrum; B.A., Temple U., 1946; M.D., Hannemann Coll., 1950; m. Gerson S. Paul, June 24, 1951; 1 dau., Sindy Michelle. Intern Hahnemann Hosp., Phila., 1950-51, now mem. staff; practice medicine specializing in internal medicine, Phila., 1951-54, 55-56, USAF Hosp., Elmendorf Air Force Base, Anchorage, Alaska, 1951—; mem. staff Phila., Albert Einstein Med. Center, Oxford Hosp., Rolling Hill Hosp., John F. Kennedy Meml. Hosp.; instr. medicine Hahnemann Med. Col., 1951-58; sec., treas. Gyneco Products, Inc., Bay Pharm. Co., Inc., 1962—. Diplomate Nat. Bd. Med. Examiners. Mem. A.M.A., Pa. State, Phila. County med. socs., Am. Geriatric Soc., Pa. Thoracic Soc., Am. Acad. Gen. Practice, Nat. Steeplechase and Hunt Assn., Am. Horse Show Assn., Pa. Horse Breeders Assn. Home: 1710 Woodland Rd Abington PA 19001 also 29 N Overbrook Av Longport NJ Office: 2001 Knoor St Philadelphia PA 19149

PAUL, VERA LEE MEYER (MRS. GEORGE ALLEN PAUL), fraternity exec.; b. Cin., June 8, 1929; d. Herbert Christian and Frieda (Stutie) Meyer; B.A., U. Cin., 1951; m. George Allen Paul, Dec. 15, 1951; children—Mark Hanna II, Don Christian. Instr. Coll. Design, Art and Architecture, U. Cin., 1951-53; with Alpha Chi Omega, Cin., 1951—, chmn. U. Cin. adv. bd., 1951-63, province pres., 1963-67, nat. social devel. chmn., 1966-70, nat. membership dir., 1970—; wedding cons., Cin., 1972—. Mem. Com. 100, U. Cin. Active Boy Scouts Am., P.T.A. Mem. Nat. Wildlife Fedn., View Place Civic Assn., U. Cin. Alumnae Assn., Alpha Lambda Alpha, Alpha Chi Omega. Republican. Author: Alpha Chi Omega Social Guide, 1970. Address: 520 Wellesley Av Cincinnati OH 45224

PAULEY, GAY (MRS. JOHN L. SEHON), women's editor; m. John L. Sehon. Began newspaper career with Huntington (W.Va.) Daily Advertiser; with U.P.I., N.Y.C., 1943—, successively dist. and police reporter, polit. and state-house writer, bur. chief, 1943-53, became editor women's news activities, 1953, also editor spl. page News and Features for Women; now women's editor U.P.I.; news broadcaster Mutual Network, 1957-64; regular panelist WOR-TV news show, 1964-66; also lecture tours. Mem. N.Y. Newspaper Women's Club (v.p.), Theta Sigma Phi (nat. headliner award 1965). Office: 220 E 42d St New York City NY 10017

PAULI, LYDIA LYGIA BOKS (MRS. BENNO PAULI), physician; b. Vladisvostok, Russia; d. Alois and Tatiana (Sapilov) Boks; B.S., Gymnasium, Czechoslovakia; M.D., U. Graz, Austria, 1950; m. Benno Pauli, Oct. 11, 1952. Rotating intern St. Johns Episcopal Hosp., N.Y.C., 1950-51; pediatric intern Johns Hopkins Hosp., Balt., 1951-53, asst. resident, 1953-54, fellow in pediatrics, 1954-57, asso. Epilepsy Clinic, 1955-57, asso. dir., 1957-73, cons. convulsive disorders for comprehensive health care, 1967-70; instr. pediatrics Johns Hopkins Sch. Medicine, Balt., 1957-63, asst. prof., 1963—, asso. dir. Samuel Livingston Epilepsy Diagnostic and Treatment Center, 1973—. Cons. on convulsive disorders Md. Dept. Health, 1957—; cons. Md. Dept. Vocational Rehab., 1957—. Bd. dirs. Chesapeake Assn. for Epilepsy. Recipient 1st prize of exhibit Am. Acad. Neurology, 1962, Gold award Am. Psychiat. Assn., 1967. Mem. A.M.A., N.Y. Acad. Scis., Am. Pub. Health Assn., Am. Epilepsy Soc., Md. Soc for Research, Balt. Med. and Chirurg. Soc.; asso. Am. Acad. Neurology, Am. Acad. Pediatrics, Balt. Neurol. Soc.

Research and publs. on exptl. anti-convulsive drugs, heredity in epilepsy, socio-econ. aspects and employment in epilepsy. Contbg. author: Comprehensive Textbook of Psychiatry, 1967. Home: 6651 Loch Hill Rd Baltimore MD 21239 Office: 1039 St Paul St Baltimore MD 21202 also CMSC-POPS Johns Hopkins Hosp Baltimore MD 21205

PAULINE, SISTER MARGARET, educator; b. Boston, Aug. 29, 1907; d. Arthur Parkhurst and Pauline (Fottler) Young; A.B., Trinity Coll., 1928; M.A., Boston Coll., 1939; Ph.D., Boston U., 1947; summer study U. Madrid, 1957. Instr. Spanish Emmanuel Coll., 1938-40; asst. prof., 1940-47, prof., chmn. dept. Spanish and Portuguese, 1947—. Mass. adv. com. of Fgn. Langs., 1963; dir. Northeast Conf. on Fgn. Langs., 1964—. Decorated Cruz y Orden de Isabel la Catolica. Mem. Modern Lang. Assn., Tchrs. Spanish and Portuguese, N.E. Modern Lang. Assn. (v.p. 1958), Am. Council Tchrs. Fgn. Langs. Author: Nuestra Senora de Guadalupe, 1951; Three Poems of Machado in Context, 1969. Home: 400 Fenway Boston MA 02115

PAULL, MARY ANN, advt. co. exec.; b. Chgo., May 15, 1927; d. Jerry and Mary (Maschek) Saffron; student Wright Jr. Coll., 1947, Elmhurst Coll., 1949, Northwestern Bus. Sch., 1950; m., Jan. 12, 1974. Account exec. Arthur Meyerhoff, Chgo., 1959-63, Geyer-Oswald Co., Chgo., 1963-68, Barickman Advt. Co., Chgo., 1968-70, I/Mac Inc., Chgo., 1970—. Home: 3230 S Maple Av Berwyn IL 60402 Office: 1058 W Washington Blvd Chicago IL 60607

PAULSEN, LYDIA RANSIER (MRS. F. ROBERT PAULSEN), civic worker; b. Tuscon, Apr. 3, 1920; d. Charles D. and Lydia (Broadbent) Ransier; student U. Ariz., 1937-41; m. Frederick H. Lowry, June 29, 1941; children—Linda (Mrs. Dennis D. Romley), Margo; m. 2d, F. Robert Paulsen, Nov. 1, 1969. Chief employee relations, civilian personnel Davis-Monthan AFB, Ariz., 1943-45; asst. dir. project CREATES, 1967-68; coordinator four agys. Community Mental Health Center, 1968-69; planning asso. community resources project U. Ariz. Coll. Edn., 1968-70; cons. Ariz. Dept. Pub. Health, Ariz. Pub. Schs., 1967—. Mem. Ariz. Bd. Crippled Children's Services, 1961—, chmn., 1966; mem. Ariz. Adv. Council Edn. Act of 1965, 1966—, chmn., 1970—; mem. state adv. com for facility for delinquent girls, 1965-67; mem. regional planning conf. and survey com. Nat. Inst. Mental Health, 1968-70; panelist annual meeting Am. Orthopsychiat. Assn., 1970; referee Pima County (Ariz.) Junvenile Ct., 1957—; mem. adv. bd. Children's Evaluation Center So. Ariz., 1965-68, chmn. steering com., 1966-67; mem. Ariz. Blue Shield Bd., 1973; bd. dirs. Girls Living Centers, Inc., 1960-65, pres., 1964; chmn. researchers Am. Cancer Soc. Research Study, 1960-65; bd. dirs. United Community Campaign, 1952-54, gen. chmn. residential div., 1951; chmn. coordinating com. Tuscon-Southern Counties Mental Health Services, Inc., 1967-69, pres. bd. dirs., 1969—; bd. dirs. Tuscon Child Health Guidance Clinic, 1953-59, 61-66, pres., 1953-54, v.p., 1966; bd. dirs. Tuscon Community Council, 1966-69, sec., 1968-69; bd. dirs. YWCA, 1952-54, v.p., 1954, sec., 1952-53; bd. dirs. Tuscon Art Center, 1955-57, 59-51, 65-66, sec., 1957, 64-65; bd. dirs. Tuscon Art Center League, 1965-68, chmn., 1965-66; active fund drives A.R.C., Tuscon Med. Center; bd. dirs. Family Service Agy., 1954-59, sec., 1956; bd. dirs. Social Service Exchange, 1954-59, 58-59, Council of Social Agcy., 1950-52; bd. dirs. Palo Verde Found Psychiat. Hosp., 1968-70; bd. visitors St. Luke's-in-the-Desert, 1962—. Named Tuscon Woman of the Year, 1967; recipient Pinel award for outstanding contributions by a non-psychiatrist in field of mental health, Ariz. Psychiat. Soc., 1966-67. Mem. Nat. Assn. State Adv. Council Chmn. (council, exec. com. 1970—), Jr. League of Tuscon (bd. dirs. 1956-60, v.p. 1958-59, pres. 1959-60, mem. sustaining group bd. 1966-67, 70-71), Tuscon Council Garden Clubs, Pima County Mental Health Assn. (charter), U. Ariz. Alumni Assn. (bd. dirs. Tuscon 1965—), Tuscon Symphony Women's Assn., Catalina Jr. Women's Club (bd. dirs. 1948-51, sec. 1949-50, treas. 1950-51). Episcopalian. Clubs: Tuscon Desert, Patio Garden (pres. 1955-56). Home: 2801 N Indian Ruins Tucson AZ 85715

PAULSHOCK, BERNADINE ZIEGLER (MRS. MARVIN PAULSHOCK), physician; b. Bethlehem, Pa., Feb. 28, 1928; d. Louis C. and Ruth (Meyers) Ziegler; B.A., U. Pa., 1944, M.D., 1951; m. Marvin Paulshock, June 17, 1951; children—Craig, Dale, Sharon. Intern, Del. Hosp., Wilmington, 1951-52, resident 1952-55; practice medicine specializing in internal medicine, Wilmington Med. Center, 1955—, chief. sect. on endocrinology and metabolism dept. medicine, 1972—, asso. program dir. dept. family practice, 1972—; clin. asst. prof. medicine Jefferson Med. Coll., Phila., 1971—. Diplomate Am. Bd. Internal Medicine. Fellow A.C.P.; mem. Newcastle County Med. Soc. (exec. bd. 1971—), Phi Beta Kappa. Sr. asso. editor: Del. Med. Jour., 1968—; editorial bd. Patient Care, 1972—. Home: 1306 Marsh Rd Wilmington DE 19803 Office: 1202 Jefferson Wilmington DE 19801

PAULSON, CARLA LEPORTE (MRS. J.P. PAULSON), editor; b. Sioux City, Ia., Jan. 15, 1948; d. Lawrence Charles and Dolores Margaret (Kelso) Leporte; B.A. in Journalism and Mass. Communications, U. Minn., 1971; m. J.P. Paulson, June 1, 1974. Copywriter, Powers Dept. Store, Mpls., 1971; mag. editor Decathlon Athletic Club, Bloomington, Minn., 1971-73; editor comml. div. mag. Honeywell Corp., Mpls., 1973—. Free lance writer, 1971—. Mem. Women in Communications, Internat. Assn. Bus. Communications, Arrowhead Soc., Minn. Alumni Assn. Home: 5234 Blackfriars Lane Minnetonka MN 55343 Office: Honeywell Plaza Minneapolis MN 55408

PAULSON, LOUISE HILL (MRS. BELDEN HENRY PAULSON), author; b. Summit, N.J., May 19, 1928; d. William Scott and Mary Elizabeth (Dietrich) Hill; student Vassar Coll., 1946-48; B.A., Oberlin Coll., 1950; m. Belden Henry Paulson, Jan. 9, 1954; children—Eric Belden, Steven Benjamin. Dir. admissions Expt. in Internat. Living, Putney, Vt., 1950-52; social worker Casa Mia Social Center, Naples, Italy, 1952-53; head student employment, counselor U. Chgo. Personnel Office, 1954-56; writer, researcher Psy-Bionics Center, 1971—; v.p., sec., exec. dir. Psy-Bionics Ednl. and Research Found., 1974—. Co-chmn. 1st and 2d Ann. Psychic-World Confs., 1972, 73. Cellist, Milw. Civic Symphony Orch., 1962—; bd. mem. Hartford Av. Sch. P.T.A., 1969-70. Mem. U. Milw. Women's League (chmn. modern dance group 1969-71), Wis. Soc. Psychical Research (dir. 1972-73). Conglist. Author: (with Belden Henry Paulson) The Searchers, 1966. Home: 2602 E Newberry Blvd Milwaukee WI 53211

PAULUS, NORMA JEAN PETERSEN (MRS. WILLIAM G. PAULUS), state legislator; b. Belgrade, Neb., Mar. 13, 1933; d. Paul Emil and Ella Marie (Hellbusch) Petersen; LL.B., Willamette Law Sch., 1962; m. William G. Paulus, Aug. 16, 1958; children—Elizabeth, William Frederick. Sec. to Harney County Dist. Atty., 1950-53; legal sec., Salem, Ore., 1953-55; sec. to chief justice Ore. Supreme Ct., 1955-61; admitted to Ore. bar, 1962; of counsel Paulus and Callaghan, Salem, mem. Ore. Ho. of Reps., 1971—, mem. judiciary com., environmental and land use com., profl. responsibility com., criminal law revision com., Rep. floor leader. Fellow Eagleton Inst. Politics, 1971. Mem. Salem Human Relations Commn., 1967-70, Marion-Polk Boundary Commn., 1970-71. Recipient Golden Torch award Bus. and Profl. Women Ore., 1971, Distinguished Service award City of Salem, 1971. Mem. Nat. Order Women Legislators, Nat. Soc. State Legislators (dir. 1971-72), Ore. State Bar. Home: 3090 Pigeon Hollow Rd S Salem OR 97302 Office: House of Representatives State Capitol Salem OR 97310

PAULY, HERTA HILDEGARD, educator; b. Berlin, Germany (came to U.S. 1933, naturalized 1940); d. Georg and Hermine Caroline (Correns) Pauly; student Pomona Coll., 1940-41; M.A., Claremont Coll., 1943; Ph.D., Columbia, 1952. Instr. Vassar Coll., Poughkeepsie, N.Y., 1948-49; asst. prof. Upsala Coll., East Orange, N.J., 1949-54, asso. prof., 1954-59, prof. dept. philosophy, 1959—; vis. prof. U. Fla., 1965-66. Mem. East-West Philosopher's Conf., Hawaii, 1959, 64, 69. Mem. Am. Philos. Assn., Am. Soc. Aesthetics. Contbr. articles to profl. jours. Office: Dept Philosophy Upsala Coll East Orange NJ 07019

PAUST, JOAN CAROL, anesthesiologist; b. Milw., July 3, 1940; d. Clyde M. and Doris Marie (Hall) Paust; B.S. in Zoology, U. Chgo., 1962; M.D., U. Wis., 1967. Intern Columbia Hosp., Milw., 1967-68; resident in anesthesia U. Wis. Hosps., Madison, 1968-70; asst. prof. anesthesiology U. Wis., Madison, 1970-72; asst. clin. prof. anesthesiology Yale, 1972—. Diplomate Am. Bd. Anesthesiology. Fellow Am. Coll. Anesthesiology; asso. fellow Am. Coll. Obstetricians and Gynecologists; mem. A.M.A., Internat. Anesthesia Research Soc., Am., Wis. heart assns., Soc. Obstet. Anesthesiologists and Perinatologists, Conn. State Med. Soc., New Haven County, New Haven med. assns., Am., Conn. socs. anesthesiologists, Am. Med. Women's Assn. Home: 320 Manley Heights Orange CT 06477

PAUTLER, MARGARET ORLOU, chem. co. exec.; b. St. Louis, Apr. 12, 1932; d. Ermin Anthony and Margaret Ruth (Bleines) P.; B.S., Fontbonne Coll., 1954; M.S. in Commerce, St. Louis U., 1969. Distbr. shoes Edison Bros. Stores, Inc., St. Louis, 1954-55; librarian Krupnick & Assos. advt., St. Louis, 1955-60, asst. media mgr., 1960-62; information specialist, project specialist Monsanto Co., St. Louis, 1962—. Cons., Morex, Inc., Maryland Heights, Mo., 1971—. Mem. Am. Marketing Assn. (sec. 1967-68), Spl. Libraries Assn. (program chmn. 1959-61). Roman Catholic. Home: 9810 Whitcomb Lane Affton MO 63123 Office: 800 N Lindberg Blvd St Louis MO 63166

PAVAN, BARBARA NELSON (MRS. ROBERT JOHN PAVAN), sch. prin.; b. Bklyn., July 2, 1932; d. Francis Edward and Blanche Nadine (Snouffer) Nelson; student Bennington Coll., 1950-52; A.B., Adelphi Coll., 1958; M.S., State U. Coll. N.Y. at New Paltz, 1962; Ed.D. (teaching fellow), Harvard, 1972; m. Robert John Pavan, Aug. 23, 1952; children—Michael John, John David. Tchr. prekindergarten, Syosset, N.Y., 1958-59; tchr. elementary sch., Hicksville, N.Y., 1960-67; lectr. edn. Queen's Coll., N.Y.C., 1967-68; prin. Franklin Elementary Sch., Lexington, Mass., 1972—. Cons. nongrading, individualized instrn., open space, team teaching, pub. schs. N.Y., Mass., N.H., Me., 1970-72. Mem. Mass., Nat. assns. elementary sch. prins., Nat., Mass. assns. supervision and curriculum devel., Mass. Tchrs. Assn., Lexington Edn. Assn., N.E.A., Nat. Soc. Study Edn., Psi Chi, Phi Delta Kappa, Pi Lambda Theta. Home: 6 Wessex Rd Newton Centre MA 02159 Office: 7 Stedman Rd Lexington MA 02173

PAVELKA, MARGARET STRAWSER, nurse adminstr.; b. Edgar, Neb., Feb. 8, 1924; d. Cecil R. and Lois (Peters) Strawser; R.N., Bryan Meml. Hosp., 1946; B.S., Neb. Wesleyan U., 1946; M.S. in Psychiat. Nursing, U. Neb., 1958, candidate for Ph.D. in Adult Continuing Edn., 1974; m. Albert W. Pavelka, May 20, 1947 (dec.); children—Ronald E., Leonard E., Richard L., Sandra Sue. Served as ednl. dir. Hastings Regional Center, Ingleside, Neb., 1946-53, acting dir. nursing, 1952; asst. dir. nursing edn. Mary Lanning Hosp., Hastings, 1953-56; dir. nurses Glenwood (Ia.) State Sch., 1957-60; dir. nursing Bryan Meml. Hosp., Lincoln, Neb., 1960-71; exec. dir. Neb. Bd. Nursing, 1974—. Mem. adv. coms. Lincoln Tech. Coll., Mental Health Technicians, Operating Room Technicians. Chmn. bd. dirs. Lincoln Area Heart Assn., 1974-75. Named Dist. Nurse of Year, 1966. Mem. Neb. Bd. Nursing, 1962-69, chmn., 1967-68; chmn. Neb. Hosp. Schs. Nursing Com.; mem. Mental Health Congress Neb., 1963; regional chmn. Task Force Study Mental Retardation; mem. Neb. Heart Assn. (coronary care com., bd. dirs.). Chmn. Neb. Nurses Com. on Counseling and Placement. Mem. Nat. League for Nursing (dir.), Am. Nurses' Assn., Dist. Nurses Assn. (pres. 1950-51, chmn. legislation com., chmn. membership com., profl. practice steering com.), Am. Assn. for Mental Deficiency, Adult Edn. Assn., Am. Acad. Polit. and Social Sci., Internat. Platform Assn., Delta Zelta (candidate for Woman of Year 1963), Pi Kappa Delta. Methodist. Address: 2126 S 48th St Lincoln NE 68506

PAWLACZYK, JEANNE ALICE DEMLER (MRS. EDWARD C. PAWLACZYK), occupational therapist; b. Buffalo, Jan. 26, 1919; d. Frank C. and Violet E. (Burley) Demler; certificate of proficiency, occupational therapy, U. Buffalo, 1961; B.S. in Occupational Therapy, State U. N.Y., 1971; m. Edward C. Pawlaczyk, Sept. 21, 1940; children—Camillia (Mrs. Robert Izzo), Michael, Edward Jr. China designer Banks Ceramics Co., Buffalo, 1942-44; freelance artist, 1945-57; occupational therapist Buffalo State Hosp., 1958-62; occupational therapist West Seneca (N.Y.) State Sch., 1963-68, chief occupational therapist, 1969-71, mental hygiene treatment team leader, 1971—. Clin. instr. occupational therapy State U. N.Y., Buffalo, 1963-71, Erie Community Coll., Buffalo, 1968-71. Troop leader Girl Scouts U.S.A.; instr. multi-media 1st aid A.R.C., 1972—. Recipient grant Crossroads Hosp., Indps., 1960. Mem. Am. Occupational Therapy Assn., Hamburg Antique Study Group, Contemporary Hist. Vehicle Assn. Roman Catholic. Home: 4904 Abbott Rd Hamburg NY 14075 Office: 1200 East and West Rd West Seneca State Sch West Seneca NY 14224

PAWSON, PANSY, social worker; b. Granite, Okla., May 31, 1916; d. Thomas T. and Louise (Hindert) Pawson; Mus. B., Okla. Coll. for Women, 1938; M.S.S., Smith Coll., 1947. Caseworker, Dept. Pub. Welfare, State Okla., various locations, 1941-43; intake worker VA Mental Hygiene Clinic, Oklahoma City, 1947-52; social worker VA Hosp., Topeka, Kan., 1952-53; social worker Bur. Indian Affairs, Ft. Berthold, N.D., 1953-55, asst. area social worker, Juneau, Alaska, 1955-58; supervisory social worker VA Hosp., St. Louis, 1958-61; asst. area social worker Bur. Indian Affairs, Mpls., 1961-64, social worker, Nevada Agy., Stewart, 1964-69; social worker Hopi Indian Agy., Keams Canyon, Ariz. 1969—. Field instr. VA Hosp., St. Louis, 1958-61. Fellow Assn. Applied Anthropology; mem. Nat. Assn. Social Workers, Accredited Social Workers, Carson City Bus. and Womens Assn. (pres. 1968). Presbyn. Home: Box 154 Keams Canyon AZ 86034 Office: Hopi Indian Agy Keams Canyon AZ 86034

PAXTON, ALICE ADAMS (MRS. JAMES L. PAXTON, JR.), artist designer; b. Hagerstown, Md., May 19, 1914; d. William Albert and Josephine (Adams) Rosenberger; student Peabody Inst. Music, Balt., 1937-38; grad. Parson's Sch. Design, N.Y., 1940; studied portrait painting with J. Laurie Wallace, 1944-46; studied with Augustus Dunbier, 1947-48, Sylvia Curtis, 1949, Milton Wolsky, 1950, Frank Sapousek, 1951; m. James Love Paxton, Jr., June 26, 1942; 1 son, William Allen III. Free-lance work archtl. renderings and interior design for various N.Y. interior decorators, 1937-40; interior designer, spl. furnishings designer and muralist Orchard and Wilhelm, furniture store, Omaha, 1940-42; designer interior Chapel Boys' Town, Neb., 1942; tchr. art classes Alice Paxton Studio, Omaha, 1957-64; dir. Paxton-Mitchell Co., Omaha; tchr. mech. drawing, archtl. rendering, mech. perspective Parson's Sch. Design, N.Y., 1937-40; exhibited at one-man show of Archtl. Renderings, Washington County Mus. Fine Arts, Hagerstown, 1944; exhibited group shows at Joslyn Mus., Omaha, 1943, 44, Ann. Exhbn. Cumberland Valley Artists, Hagerstown, Md., 1945; represented permanent collections at No. Natural Gas Co. Bldg., Omaha, Swanson Found., Omaha, also pvt. collections. Vol. designer, decorator recreation room Omaha Blood Bank, A.R.C., 1943, recreation room Creighton U., 1943, lounge psychiat. ward Lincoln (Neb.) Army Hosp., 1944; planner color coordinator Children's Hosp., Omaha, 1947, painted murals, 1948, decorated dental room, 1950; also numerous other vol. profl. activities for civic orgns., hosps., clubs, chs., also community playhouse. Co-chmn. camp and hosp. coms. A.R.C., 1943-45, county com. select and send gifts servicemen, 1943-46; mem. Ak-Sar-Ben Ball com., Omaha, 1946-48; judge select Easter Seal design, Joslyn Mus., 1946; mem. council Girl Scouts Am., Omaha, 1943-47; spl. drs. chmn. Jr. League, Omaha, 1947-48, chmn. Jr. League Red Cross, fund dr., 1947-48; bd. dirs., vol. worker Creche, Omaha, 1954-56; chmn. Jr. League Community Chest Fund Dr., 1948-50; co-chmn. Infantile Paralysis Appeal, 1944. Recipient three teaching scholarships Parson's Sch. Design, 1937-40; presdl. citation A.R.C. activities, 1946; 1st prize Ann. Midwest Show Joslyn Mus., 1943; painted and decorated straw elephant bag which was presented to Mrs. Richard Nixon, 1960. Contbr. articles and photographs Popular Home mag., 1958. Mem. Asso. Artists Omaha (charter), Jr. League Omaha. Republican. Episcopalian. Clubs: Omaha, Omaha Country, Omaha Press. Home: 3623 Jackson St Omaha NE 68105 Office: Alice Paxton Studio 3623 Jackson St Omaha NE 68105

PAXTON, JUANITA WILLENE, univ. dean; b. Birmingham, Ala., Oct. 30, 1930; d. William and Elizabeth (Davis) Paxton; A.B., Birmingham-So. Coll., 1950; M.A., Mich. State U., 1951; Ed.D., Ind. U., 1971. Dormitory dir. Tex. Technol. Coll., 1951-53; counselor Counseling Center, Mich. State U., summer 1952; asst. dean students State U. Coll. Edn., Fredonia, N.Y., 1953-56, asso. dean students, 1956-57; asst. dean of women U. N.M., 1957-63; dean of women East Tenn. State U., 1963—. Chmn. East Tenn. Edn. Assn. Guidance Dept., 1967-68. Mem. N.M. Assn. Women Deans and Counselors (v.p. 1958), N.M. Council Adminstrv. Women in Edn. (sec. 1960), Am., Watauga (sec. 1966-67, pres.-elect 1967-68) personnel and guidance assns., Am. Coll. Personnel Assn., Nat., Tenn. (v.p. 1964-66, pres. 1966-68) assns. women deans and counselors, Am. Assn. U. Women (pres. Johnson City br. 1966-68), Tenn. Personnel and Guidance Assn. (legislative com. 1968), Am. Assn. Higher Edn., Assn. Counselor Educators and Suprs., Intermountain Psychol. Assn., So. Coll. Personnel Assn., East Tenn., Tenn. edn. assns., So. Assn. Counselor Educators and Suprs., Alpha Chi Omega, Pi Lambda Theta, Delta Kappa Gamma (pres. chpt. 1974-76). Methodist. Office: Box 2017 East Tennesee State U Johnson City TN 37601

PAYETTE, VIRGINIA MARGARET ELLIS (MRS. WILLIAM COLIN PAYETTE), syndicated columnist; b. Los Angeles; d. Dwight M. and Kathryn (Smith) Ellis; B.A., U. So. Cal., 1942; m. William Colin Payette, Aug. 5, 1951; children—Kathryn Susan (Mrs. James Edward McDougal), Bruce Donald. Morgue asst. Los Angeles Herald Express, 1942-44; reporter, rewriteman, Hollywood corr. U.P.I., Los Angeles, 1943-51; syndicated columnist United Feature Syndicate, Inc., N.Y.C., 1969—. Mem. Newspaperwomen's Club N.Y.C., Phi Beta Kappa, Phi Kappa Phi, Theta Sigma Phi, Sigma Delta Chi. Home: 4 Bacon Ct Bronxville NY 10708 Office: 220 E 42d St New York City NY 10017

PAYNE, GLENNA TOLBERT (MRS. RICHARD T. PAYNE), state ofcl., pub. relations exec.; b. New Tazewell, Tenn., Dec. 3, 1944; d. Thomas Glenn and Cassie Lee (Whitaker) Tolbert; A.B. in Radio-TV, Ind. U., 1967, M.A., 1973, now student Law Sch.; m. Richard T. Payne, Sept. 13, 1969. Statehouse reporter sta. WLWI-TV, Indpls., 1968-71; adminstrv. asst. Bur. Motor Vehicles, Indpls., 1971-72; information dir. drug abuse div. Dept. Mental Health, Indpls., 1972—. Mem. Women's Council Channel 20. Recipient Casper award Indpls. Community Service Council, 1969, Ind. News Photographers Team Filming Spot News award, 1970. Bd. dirs. Hoosier Heartland Repertory Theater. Mem. Women in Communications, Hancock County Mental Health Assn., Hancock County Assn. for Retarded Children, Greenfield Country Club Women's Assn., Mortar Bd. Alumnae Assn., Ind. U. Alumni Assn., Kappa Kappa Kappa. Home: Route 1 Box 46 Greenfield IN 46140 Office: Room 202 State Office Bldg Indianapolis IN 46204

PAYNE, JUNE PATRICIA, editor; b. Albuquerque, May 20, 1930; d. Stanley Thomas and Effie (Pierce) Payne; B.A., Ariz. State U., 1952. Asso. editor, art dir. Ariz. Beverage Jour., 1952-64; reporter state desk Ariz. Repub., Phoenix, 1964; editorials asst. acad. publs. Ariz. State U., Tempe, 1964—. Freelance photographer Ariz. Hwys. mag., 1971-72. Mem. Ariz. Press Women (state pres. 1961-62), Women in Communications, Photog. Soc. Am., Phoenix Press Club. Home: 4733 E Cambridge St Phoenix AZ 85008 Office: Bur Publs Ariz State U Tempe AZ 85281

PAYNE, LAVETA MAXINE, educator; b. Lebanon, Kan., Feb. 20, 1916; d. Verne Hobart and Flossie (Whitaker) Payne; B.A., Union Coll., 1940; M.A., U. Neb., 1943, Ph.D., 1952; B.A., Atlantic Union Coll., 1966. Tchr. pub. schs., Smith County, Kan., 1934-36, Lincoln, Neb., 1940-41; tchr. Shenandoah Valley Acad., New Market, Va., 1941-46, Platte Valley Acad., Shelton, Neb., 1946-50, U. Neb. Extension Div., 1950-51; asso. prof. edn. Columbia Union Coll., Takoma Park, Md., 1951-59, Newbold Coll., Bracknell Berkshire, Eng., 1955-57; prof. edn., chmn. div. Atlantic Union Coll., South Lancaster, Mass., 1959-66; prof. edn., psychology So. Missionary Coll., Collegedale, Tenn., 1966—; Newbold curriculum cons. Mem. Nat., Tenn. edn. assns., Am., Tenn. psychol. assns., Nat. Soc. for Study Edn., A.A.A.S., Am. Assn. U. Profs., D.A.R. Mem. Seventh-day Adventists. Author: Called to Teach, 1969; Your Career in Secondary Education, 1971; A Guide for Better Teaching in Secondary Schools, 1973. Home: Pierson and Suhrie Dr Collegedale TN 37315

PAYNE, LELIA EMILY CLEMENT (MRS. ALBERT S. PAYNE), librarian; b. Walker County, Ga., Oct. 10, 1920; d. William M. and Leona L. (Davis) Clement; student Maryville Coll., 1937-38; A.B., Shorter Coll., 1958; M.L.S., Emory U., 1963, diploma for Advanced Study in Librarianship, 1970; m. Albert S. Payne, Aug. 4, 1940; children—LeAnn (Mrs. Strom), William Lawsha. English tchr. Model Sch., 1958-59; children and young people's librarian Tri-County Regional Library, 1959-64, acting dir., 1964, dir., 1965—. Instr. Rome Off-Campus Center, U. Ga. System, 1965-70. Mem. Stay and See Ga. Com., 1969; mem. steering com. Civic Center, 1971—. Health Edn. Welfare Insts. grantee, 1968-69. Mem. Internat. Platform Assn., Am. Assn. U. Women, S.E., Ga. (govtl. relations chmn. 1970-71, 72-73) library assns., Ga. Assn. Educators, Floyd County Assn. Educators, Bus. and Profl. Women's Club, Farm Bur. (program com. 1969-70), Atlanta Hist. Soc., Rome Area C. of C. (ednl. com. 1968-71, mem. fine arts com., 1973, dir. 1974). Home: PO Box 567 Rome GA 30161 Office: 606 W 1st St Rome GA 30161

PAYNE, MARGARET JUNE BUTTIMER (MRS. MORLEY ELDON PAYNE), owner rest home; b. Salmon Beach, N.B., Can., May 25, 1919; d. Allen and Ada Pearl (Knowles) Buttimer; student pub. schs.; m. Morley Eldon Payne, July 15, 1940; children—Lillian Grace Pearl (Mrs. Raymond Joseph Russell), Marjorie Frances (Mrs. Rodney Hubert Sealy), George Allen, Dorothy Edna (Mrs. Donald Ramsey), Margaret June. Owner, operator Paynes Rest Home for Sr. Citizens, Bathurst, N.B., Can., 1964—. Mem. United Ch. of Can. Home: Box 585 Rural Route 1 Bathurst NB E2A 3Y5 Canada

PAYNE, MARY ANN, physician; b. Frederick, Md., Aug. 29, 1913; d. Irving Joseph and Blanche Virginia (Stark) Payne; A.B., Hood Coll., 1935; M.A., U. Wis., 1941, Ph.D., 1943; M.D., Cornell U., 1945. Intern N.Y. Hosp., N.Y.C., 1945-47, resident, 1947-49, now mem. staff; research fellow N.Y. Hosp., Cornell U. Med. Coll., 1949-50; practice medicine specializing in internal medicine, N.Y.C., 1950; mem. staff Drs. Hosp., N.Y.C.; dir. 66th St. Lab., N.Y.C., 1967—; asso. prof. clin. medicine Cornell U. Med. Coll., 1957—. Diplomate Am. Bd. Internal Medicine. Mem. A.C.P., A.M.A., Am. Assn. Study Liver Disease, Endocrine Soc., N.Y. Acad. Medicine, N.Y. Acad. Sci., N.Y. State, N.Y. County med. socs., N.Y. Gastroenterology Soc., Citizen's Union. Home: 53 E 66th St New York City NY 10021 Office: 260 E 66th St New York City NY 10021

PAYNE, MARY LIBBY BICKERSTAFF (MRS. BOBBY RAY PAYNE), state ofcl., lawyer; b. Gulfport, Miss., Mar. 27, 1932; d. Reece O. and Emily A. (Cook) Bickerstaff; student Miss. State Coll. Women, 1950-52; B.A. cum laude, U. Miss., 1954, LL.B., 1955; m. Bobby Ray Payne, Dec. 20, 1955; children—Reece Allen, Glenn Russell. Admitted to Miss. bar, 1955; partner Bickerstaff & Bickerstaff, Gulfport, 1955-57; employee Guranty Title Co., Jackson, 1957; asso. Henley, Jones & Henley, Jackson, 1958-61; free-lance research and brief writing, 1962-63; individual law practice, Brandon, 1963-68; exec. sec. Miss. Judiciary Commn., 1968-70; chief research and drafting div., ho. mgmt. com. Miss. Ho. of Reps., 1970-72; asst. atty. gen., 1972—. Instr. bus. law Miss. Coll., Clinton, 1956-57; v.p., dir. First Finance Corp. of Rankin County, 1964-68; legislative draftsman Miss. Ho. of Reps., 1964-68. Chmn. Pearl-McLaurin Water Investigative Com., 1967; counsel Rankin County Christian Action Com., 1968. Mem. steering com. Rankin County campaign United Drys, 1966. Mem. Miss. State Bar (co-chmn. lawyers placement com. 1965, mem. bd. bar commrs. 1965-67, 71-72), Rankin County Bar Assn. (sec. 1965, v.p. 1966-67, pres. 1968), Am. Assn. U. Women (chpt. legislative chmn. 1956), P.T.A. (sec. Pearl-McLaurin 1966, parliamentarian 1967, pres. 1968, 69), Miss. Congress Parents and Tchrs. (exec. bd. 1972—), Am. Judicature Soc., Scribes. Home: 3617 Wilcox Dr Pearl MS 39208 Office: Gartin Justice Bldg Jackson MS 39205

PAYNE, MILDRED YOUNGER (MRS. SPAFFORD O. PAYNE), educator; b. Adamsville, Tenn.; d. John Robert and Winifred (Carothers) Younger; A.B., Athens (Ala.) Coll., 1939; M.A., Murray State Coll., 1952; m. Spafford O. Payne, Nov. 27, 1928; 1 son, James Franklin. Tchr. Athens Elementary Sch., 1933-39; instr. Latin and Bible, Athens Coll., 1939-41; tchr. lang. and lit. Weakley County Pub. Schs., Greenfield, Tenn., 1943-54; asst. prof. English and edn. U. Tenn., Martin, 1954-70, asso. prof. English, after 1970, now prof., chmn. dept. speaker and cons. for Asso. Collegiate Press, Chgo., 1964. Mem. folk art panel Tenn. Arts Commn., 1968; dir. Nat. Folk Festival, 1969. Recipient Outstanding Tchr. award Pi Sigma Phi, 1969; Max King award Phi Sigma Kappa, 1969; Distinguished Service award Pi Kappa Alpha, 1970; Outstanding Tchr. award U. Tenn., 1971. Mem. Nat. Council Tchrs. English (dir. Tenn.; recorder Am. lit. sect., Hawaii 1967), Tenn. Philol. Assn. (pres. 1970-71), Tenn. (pres. 1967-69), Ky. folklore socs., South Central Modern Lang. Assn., Tenn., W. Tenn. edn. assns., Sigma Tau Delta, Kappa Delta Pi, Phi Mu, Pi Sigma Phi, Alpha Psi Omega, Phi Kappa Phi (U. Tenn. scholar). Author: (non-fiction) Mounds In The Mist, 1968; Payne's Lectures on Milton's Poetry, 1971; In the Eighteenth Century, Swift, Addison and Steele, 1972; (poetry) Prolegomena; Western Culture: Renaissance-Romanticism, 1973; Western Culture: Realism-Multanimity, 1973. Contbr. articles in field to profl. jours. Home: 216 Oxford St Martin TN 38237

PAYNE, PHYLLIS (BONNIE) MARY (MRS. ROBERT G. PAYNE), advt. exec.; b. Manchester, N.H., Sept. 19, 1943; d. Paul Wilbert and Ruth Marie (White) Armstrong; B.A., U. N.H., 1966; m. Robert G. Payne, Sept. 3, 1966. Editor, Fideler Publ. Co., Grand Rapids, Mich., 1968-70; librarian, prodn. asst. Norman, Navan, Moore & Baird, Inc., advt., Grand Rapids, 1970—, mem. creative plans bd., 1973—. Mem. Women's Advt. Club Grand Rapids (pres., 1972-73), Alpha Xi Delta. Home: 1226 Thomas St SE Grand Rapids MI 49506 Office: 40 Pearl St NW Grand Rapids MI 49502

PAYNE, PRISCILLA COBB (MRS. WILLIAM J. PAYNE, JR.), ednl. adminstr.; b. Cin., Mar. 25, 1908; d. Ernest Codman and Bertha Browning (Barnes) Cobb; B.S., Tufts U., 1930; M.Ed., State Coll. Boston, 1960; m. William T. Doran, Jr., Aug. 20, 1932 (div. Oct. 1948); children—Joanna Lee (Mrs. William D. Bradshaw, Jr.), Peter Cobb, Priscilla Alden (Mrs. Hossein Dastmalchian); m. 2d, William J. Payne, Jr., June 19, 1952 (dec. Sept. 1966). Employment exec. personnel R.H. Macy & Co., N.Y.C., 1930-33; tchr. Dana Hall Schs., Wellesley, Mass., 1956-61; dir. social service Rogerson House, Jamaica Plain, Mass., 1961-64; asso. dir. Learning Disabilities Found., Inc., Wellesley, 1964—. Mem. Am., Mass. personnel and guidance assns. Unitarian-Universalist. Home: 38 Fuller Brook Rd Wellesley MA 02181 Office: Prides Crossing MA 01965

PAYNE, RHODA (MRS. DONALD PAYNE), drama dir.; b. N.Y.C., June 14, 1934; d. Abraham and Ida (Ulano) Wasserman; B.Sc. (fellow), Julliard Sch. Music, 1955; Ph.D., Case Western Res. U., 1971; m. Donald Payne, June 24, 1956; children—Bruce, Ellen. Drama dir. Cleve. Jewish Community Center, 1972—. Actress, dir., prodn. mgr., tchr. Lake Erie Opera Theater of Cleve. Orch., Karamu, Cleve. Playhouse, Cleve. State U., Cuyahoga Community Coll., Case Western Res. U., Kent (O.) State U. Repertory Co., Cape Cod Light Opera Soc., Falmouth, Mass., Rochester (N.Y.) Community Theater. Asso. mem. Royal Coll. Music, London, Eng., 1957. Home: 3440 Avalon Rd Shaker Heights OH 44120 Office: 3505 Mayfield Rd Cleveland OH 44118

PAYNICH, MARY LOUISE, nurse-sociologist; b. Copper City, Mich.; d. George Acacie and Justine (Chopp) Paynich; R.N., U. Mich. Sch. Nursing, 1934, B.S., Sch. Pub. Health, 1944; M.S., Cath. U. Am., 1953, Ph.D., 1961. Staff nurse U. Mich. Hosp. and Health Service, Ann Arbor, 1934-39; health counselor Longfellow Camp for Boys, Annapolis, Md. summer 1939; pub. health staff nurse Md. Health Dept., Balt., 1940-42; pub. health nurse and field tchr. Kellogg Found., Battle Creek, Mich., 1944-47; nursing cons. Am. Nat. Red Cross, 1947-51; asst. prof. Cath. U. Am., Washington, 1952-56; research asso., supr. N.M. Health Dept., Santa Fe, 1961-63; research cons., asst. prof. Mercy Coll. of Detroit, 1963-64; asso. prof., U. S.C. Sch. Nursing, Columbia, 1964-67; prof., chmn. pub. health nursing dept. sch. nursing, Med. Coll. Va., Richmond, 1967-70, now asso. prof. Nazareth Coll., Kalamazoo; engaged in writing, Paw Paw, Mich. Lt. comdr. USPHS, Res. Fellow USPHS; mem. Am. Sociol. Assn., Am. Nurses Assn., Am. Assn. U. Profs., Am. Assn. U. Women, Am. Acad. Polit. and Social Sci., Nat. League for Nursing, Am. Acad. Scis., Sigma Theta Tau, Pi Gamma Mu. Contbr. articles to profl. jours. Home: Route 3 Paw Paw MI 49079 Office: Nazareth Coll Kalamazoo MI 49074

PAYNTER, SISTER MARY, educator; b. Madison, Wis., May 23, 1931; d. Arthur John and Jane (O'Neill) Paynter; B.A., Rosary Coll., 1952; M.A., U. Wis., 1953, Ph.D., 1965; postgrad Sorbonne, U. Paris, 1953-54. Asso. prof. English, Rosary Coll., River Forest, Ill., 1956-70, acad. dean, 1964-70; prof. English Edgewood Coll., Madison, Wis., 1970—. Mem. Modern Lang. Assn., Am. Assn. U. Women, Am. Assn. Higher Edn. Am. Conf. Acad. Deans. Home: Dominican Edn Center Sinsinawa WI 53824

PAYSON, JOAN WHITNEY, civic worker; b. N.Y.C., Feb. 5, 1903; d. Payne and Helen (Hay) Whitney; grad. Miss Chapin's Sch., 1921; student Barnard Coll.; hon. degree Hofstra Coll.; m. Charles S. Payson, July 5, 1924; children—Sandra (Lady George Weidenfald), Payne (Mrs. Henry B. Middlton), Lorinda (Mrs. Vincent de Roulet), John. Partner Payson & Trask, N.Y.C., 1947—, Country Art Gallery, 1953—; co-owner Greentree Stable, 1945—, Greentree Stud, Inc., 1945—. Gov. Soc. N.Y. Hosp.; trustee North Shore Hosp., Manhasset, L.I. (past pres.), United Hosp. Fund, Asso. Hosps., The Met. Mus. Art, N.Y.C., Lighthouse, St. Mary's Hosp., Palm Beach, Fla.; pres. Helen Hay Whitney Found.; pres. N.Y. Met. Baseball Club, Inc. Mem. Jr. League N.Y. Clubs: Colony, Women's City, Women's Nat. Republican (N.Y.C.). Home: Manhasset NY 11030 Office: 748 Madison Av New York City NY 10021

PAYTON, CAROLYN ROBERTSON, psychologist; b. Norfolk, Va., May 13, 1925; d. Leroy Solomon and Bertha Marie (Flanagan) Robertson; B.S., Bennett Coll., 1945; M.S., U. Wis., 1948; Ed.D., Columbia, 1962; m. Raymond Rudolph Payton (div. Feb. 1951). Asst. prof. psychology Howard U., Washington, 1959-64, dir. univ. counseling service, 1970—; dep. dir. to dir. Peace Corps, Eastern Caribbean, 1966-69. Cons. psychologist, 1970—. Mem. adv. council Spl. Services for Disadvantaged Students, Counseling Resources Center. Bd. dirs. Nat. Capital Area Big Bros. Peace Corps nominee for Fed. Woman's award, 1968. Nat. Inst. Mental Health grantee, 1961-64. Mem. Am. psychol. Assn. (vice chairwoman com. on sci. and profl. ethics and conduct, 1971-74), Am. Personnel and Guidance Assn., D.C. Psychol. Assn. Black Psychologists, Common Cause, Pi Lambda Theta, Kappa Delta Pi, Sigma Delta Epsilon. Office: 4th and Howard Pl NW Washington DC 20001

PAYTON, MILDRED BERNICE BRIGHT, educator; b. Ruthfordton, N.C., Mar. 30, 1918; d. John William and Lollie Angeline (Lynch) Bright; B.S., A. and T. Coll., 1939; LL.B., N.C. Central U., 63; M. Teaching, East Central State Coll., 1967; m. Earl Lenion Payton, June 9, 1936 (div. 1946); 1 dau., Majorie Carol (Mrs. Juan Otto Lawson). Tchr. home econs. Louisburg (N.C.) pub. schs., 1939-44; home econ. agt. N.C. Agrl. Extension Service, Franklin County, 1944-47, Chatham County, 1947-59; women's editor The Carolina Times, Durham, N.C., 1962; peace corps vol., Turkey, 1963-65; team leader Nat. Tchr. Corps, Ada, Okla., 1966-67; tchr. black history and polit. sci. Ada pub. schs., 1967-70; tchr. bus. law, organizer black heritage seminar Okla. State U., Stillwater, 1970-72; asso. prof. law, asso. dir. center for health law N.C. Central U., Durham, N.C., 1973—. Chmn. Law Day, U.S.A., Pontotoc County, Okla., 1968. Organizer, bd. dirs. Chatham County (N.C.) Colored Fair, Inc., 1950; bd. dirs. Lee-Chatham Credit Union, 1954-59. Mem Memn. N.C. State Bar, Nat. Assn. Women Lawyers (N.C. del. 1964-66), N.A.A.C.P. (state chmn. edn. com. 1969-72, organizer Pontotoc County chpt. 1969), Phi Alpha Delta, Zeta Phi Beta. Author: Lay O' the Land, 1954 (book of poetry). Home: 1008 S Benbow Rd Greensboro NC 27406 Office: NC Central U Durham NC 27707

PAYTON, SALLYANNE, lawyer, govt. ofcl.; b. Los Angeles, May 18, 1943; d. Nolan Hartford and Georgia Mae (Williams) Payton; B.A. in English, Stanford, 1964, LL.B., 1968. Social caseworker Cal. Bur. Pub. Assistance, Los Angeles, 1964-65; admitted to Cal. bar, 1969, D.C. bar, 1969; practiced in Washington; asso. firm Covington & Burling, Washington, 1968-71; staff asst. to U.S. Pres. Domestic Council, White House, Washington, 1971-73; chief counsel Urban Mass. Transp. Adminstrn. Dept. Transp., 1973—. Mem. Commn. Orgn. Govt. of D.C., 1971—. Bd. visitors Stanford Sch. Law, 1971-73; trustee Stanford. Mem. State Bar Cal. Home: 1863 Kalorama Rd NW Washington DC 20009 Office: Urban Mass Transp Adminstrn Dept Transp Washington DC 20590

PCHELKIN, HILDEGARD ELISABETH WOLFF (MRS. V. N. PCHELKIN), librarian; b. Oberstein, Nahe, West Germany, Jan 8, 1914; d. Wilhelm and Elvira F. (Hahn) Wolff; diploma in philology Friedrich Wilhelm U., 1937; grad. library sci. Fla. State U., 1953; m. V. N. Pchelkin, Oct. 3, 1950; children—Richard B., Caspari. Came to U.S., 1938, naturalized, 1944. Library asst. Air Univ. Library, Maxwell AFB, 1944-48, information specialist, translator, 1948-50; tech. librarian Chemstrand Co. div. Monsanto Chem. Co., Pensacola, Fla., 1953-68; tech. librarian Monsanto Textiles Co., Pensacola, Fla., 1968-73, heading all Textiles Div. Tech. Libraries and Information Centers, mgr. library systems, 1973-74, now ret.; lectr. on Pensacola Sci. Seminar for Superior Students, 1961—; established med. library Escambia Gen. Hosp., 1962-63. Mem. bd. Santa Rosa County Library, N.W. Fla. Regional Library, 1974—. Mem. League Women Voters (dir. Pensacola 1961-62), Am. Assn. Textile Technologists, Fla. Library Assn., Spl. Libraries Assn., Am. Chem. Soc., Am. Soc. Testing and Materials. Home: 22 Highpoint Dr Gulf Breeze FL 32561 Office: Box 12830 Pensacola FL 32575

PEABODY, MARGARET VAN BUREN MASON (MRS. PAUL E. PEABODY), civic worker; b. Green Bay, Wis., Aug. 15, 1898; d. George Grant and Marion (Peak) Mason; student Miss Spence's schs.; m. Samuel Sloan Colt, Jan. 12, 1918 (div. Sept. 1945); children—Marion (Mrs. Maclean Williamson), Catherine (Mrs. David W. Yandell), Richard Colt; m. 2d, Paul E. Peabody, Jan. 25, 1947. Dep. commr. A.R.C. Commn. to Gt. Britain, 1942-45; nat. dir. vol. services A.R.C., 1945-47; mem. Pres. Hwy. Safety Com., 1953, Pres. Assay Commn., 1958. Mem. Nat. Republican Finance Com., 1958—. Trustee, Miss Spence's Sch., N.Y.C., 1936-40, Bennet Coll., 1957-70, Millbrook Sch. for Boys, Millbrook, N.Y., 1969—. Mem. Nat. Council Women, League Women Voters, English Speaking Union, Am, Overseas Assn., Colonial Dames Am. Club: Colony (N.Y.C.). Home: Millbrook NY 12545

PEACOCK, BENETA JANE, pediatrician; b. Sioux City, Ia., Dec. 7, 1923; d. Kenneth Cleland and Beneta (Whitehead) Peacock; B.A., Mary Baldwin Coll., 1946; postgrad. George Washington U., 1959-61; M.D., N.Y. U., 1965. Intern Duke Med. Center, Durham, N.C., 1965-66; resident pediatrics Children's Hosp. D.C., 1966-68, staff pediatrician comprehensive health care program, 1968—, dir. child health center, 1971—; practice medicine specializing in pediatrics, Washington, 1966—; clin. instr. pediatrics George Washington U. Med. Sch., 1968-73, asst. prof. dept. child health and devel., 1973—. Diplomate Am. Bd. Pediatrics. Fellow Am. Acad. Pediatrics; mem. Ambulatory Pediatric Assn., D.C. Pub. Health Assn. Home: 11733 Flints Grove Lane Gaithersburg MD 20760 Office: 2125 13th St Washington DC 20009

PEACOCK, IRENE LOUISE, health service adminstr., occupational therapist; b. Wyoming, O., Feb. 19, 1916; d. Howard William and Serene Elka (Allan) Peacock; B.S. in Occupational Therapy, Wayne U., 1949, M.S. in Edn., 1956. Dir. dept. of occupational therapy Receiving Hosp., Detroit, 1949-51; instr. occupational therapy U. Pa. Sch. Aux. Med. Services, Phila., 1951-56; dir. dept. occupational therapy Richmond (Ind.) State Hosp., 1956—. Propr., dir. Pet Haven Cemetery, Wayne County, Ind.; breeder, exhibitor pure-bred cocker spaniels. Served with AUS, 1944-46. Mem. Am., Ind. occupational therapy assns., Mental Health Assn. Wayne County. Episcopalian. Clubs: Dayton Kennel, Richmond Kennel (founder 1970), Whitewater Valley Kennel (founder 1965), American Spaniel. Home: 353 Grace Dr Richmond IN 47374 Office: Richmond State Hospital Richmond IN 47374

PEAK, RITA PAULEY (MRS. ARCHIE L. PEAK), educator; b. Danville, W.Va., Jan. 25, 1918; d. Arnold J. and Vinnie (Miller) Pauley; A.B., Concord Coll., W.Va., 1941; M.A., George Peabody Coll., 1953; postgrad. Marshall U.; adminstrv. supervisory certificate W.Va. U.; m. Archie L. Peak, June 11, 1946; 1 son, George Thomas III. Tchr., Ward Jr. High Sch., Kanawha County, W.Va., 1941-43, Roosevelt Jr. High Sch., Kanawha County, 1945, Danville (Ky.) High Sch., 1946, Leewood Jr. High Sch., Kanawha County, 1948, Roosevelt Jr. High Sch., 1949-52, Decota Elementary Sch., 1952-54, Spring Hill Jr. High Sch., 1954, Horace Mann Jr. High Sch., 1955-58; gen. supr. elementary schs., art cons. Kanawha County, 1958-60, art coordinator, 1960—. Recorder Kanawha Cultural Council; mem. council Rhododendron State Art Festival. Mem. W.Va. Gov.'s Travel Council. Bd. dirs. Owens Center for Art. Mem. Nat., W.Va. (past pres.), Kanawha County (past pres.), Eastern art edn. assns., Eastern Arts Assn., Nat., W.Va. edn. assns., W.Va. Assn. for Supervision and Curriculum Devel., Internat. Soc. for Edn. Through Art, Women in Marines Assn., Cardinal Key Soc., Morris Harvey Coll. Women Builders, Internat. Platform Assn., Delta Kappa Gamma (corr. sec.). Home: 866 Chappell Rd Charleston WV 25304 Office: 200 Elizabeth St Charleston WV 25311

PEAKS, MARY JANE (MRS. ROBERT MALCOLM POLK), orthodontist; b. N.Y.C., Aug. 19, 1916; d. Archibald Garfield and Emilie Henrietta (Stauderman) Peaks.; D.D.S., U. Pa., 1939; orthodontic certificate Columbia, 1974; m. Robert Malcolm Polk, Sept. 29, 1942; children—Robert, Mary Moneen (Mrs. Frank Froster Gilmore), Eileen. Pvt. practice dentistry specializing in orthodontics, N.Y.C., 1939-52, Garden City, N.Y., 1950—. Fellow Royal Soc. Health; mem. Am. Assn. Orthodontists, Am. Dental Assn., Am. Soc. Composers, Authors, Publishers, N.Y. Soc. Orthodontists, N.Y. Assn. Professions, Soroptimist Internat., Am. Guild Authors and Composers, Songwriters Hall of Fame. Composer: I Told A Lie, 1954. Home: 152 W 11th St New York City NY 10011 Office: 520 Franklin Av Garden City NY 11530

PEAL, JANET MARJORY, educator; b. N.Y.C., Sept. 4, 1917; d. George Hamilton and Jane Marie (Lee) Peal; A.B., Caldwell (N.J.) Coll., 1949; M.A., Catholic U., 1957; Ph.D. in Philosophy, St. John's U., 1968. Tchr., St. Mary Sch., Dover, N.J., 1937-50, Mt. St. Dominic Acad., 1950-54, St. Mary's High Sch., Rutherford, N.J., 1954-57; mem. faculty Caldwell Coll., 1957—, prof. philosophy, 1968—, chmn. dept., 1968—; superior St. Philip's Convent, Clifton, N.J., 1971—. Mem. Sisters of St. Dominic (chpt. del., mem. diocesan council). Home: 797 Valley Rd Clifton NJ 07013 Office: Caldwell College Caldwell NJ 07006

PEARCE, ANN PHILIPPA, writer, editor; b. Gt. Shelford, Cambridgeshire, Eng.; d. Ernest Alexander and Gertrude Alice (Ramsden) Pearce; M.A., with honours, Girton Coll., Cambridge U., 1942; m. Martin J. G. Christie, May 9, 1963 (dec.); 1 dau. Script writer, producer sch. broadcasting dept. BBC, 1945-58; editor ednl. dept. Oxford U. Press., 1959-60; free-lance writer, broadcaster, producer BBC, 1961—; children's book editor Andre Deutsch Ltd., 1961-67. Mem. Soc. Authors. Author: (children's books) Minnow on the Say, 1954; Tom's Midnight Garden (Carnegie medal 1959), 1958; Mrs. Cockle's Cat, 1961; A Dog So Small (Spring Book Festival award 1963), 1962; (with Sir Harold Scott) From Inside Scotland Yard, 1963; The Strange Sunflower, 1966; (with Sir Brian Fairfax-Lucy) The Children of the House, 1968; The Elm Street Lot, 1969; The Squirrel Wife, 1971; Beauty and the Beast, 1972, What the Neighbors Did and Other Stories, 1972. Address: care Kestrel Books Penguin Books Ltd Harmondsworth Middlesex England

PEARCE, CHARLOTTE ALLYNE GARNETT (MRS. MELVIN MARCUS PEARCE), educator; b. Tahoka, Tex., Feb. 21, 1925; d. Ed Turnley and Alma Daisy (Webb) Garnett; B.A., Eastern N.M. U., 1967; M.A., Tex. Tech. U., 1972; m. Melvin Marcus Pearce, June 10, 1942; children—Michael, Thomas, Stevan, Tanis, Philip, Greg. Tchr., Heizer Jr. High Sch., Hobbs, N.M., 1967-71, faculty English, Spanish, N.M. Jr. Coll., Hobbs, 1971-72, counselor, prof. Spanish, 1973—. Organizational leader 4-H Clubs, 1957-73. Named Outstanding 4-H leader in N.M., 1967. Mem. Delta Kappa Gamma. Mem. Ch. of Christ. Home: Star Route A Box 19 Hobbs NM 88240

PEARCE, DOROTHY ANDREE DE LORENZO, civic worker; b. N.Y.C., Mar. 22, 1927; d. Andrew John and Margaret (Robilotti) De Lorenzo; B.A., Barnard Coll., 1947; m. Charles W. Pearce, Apr. 2, 1955; children—Charles W., Andrew Francis, Margaret Elizabeth. Research asst. cardiac catherization lab. Bellevue Hosp., 1948-50, Cornell Med. Coll., 1950-55; exec. research librarian Shell Chem. Co., 1955-57. Thrift shop rep. Soc. N.Y. Hosp. Women's Aux., 1959-60; bd. govs. New Orleans Opera House Assn. Women's Guild, 1965—, social hostess, 1966—, historian, 1969—; chmn. uptown subscription com., 1967-69, mem. children's concerts com., 1964-66; mem. tour com. New Orleans Springs Fiesta Assn., 1966-67; mem. opera orientation com. New Orleans Opera House Assn., 1964—, registrar, hostess, 1965—; active New Orleans Symphony Previews, 1968—; mem. fund raising com. De Paul Hosp. Women's Aux., 1968—; vol. Crippled Children's Hosp. Guild, 1965-66; mem. La. Council for Performing Arts, 1967—; mem. Gallier Hall Women's Com., 1967; mem. bd. Community Concerts Assn., New Orleans; mem. fund raising com. Hotel Dieu Women's Aux., 1968—. Bd. dirs. Mercy Hosp. Women's Aux., 1965—, pres., 1970; bd. dirs. Sara Mayo Hosp. Guild, 1964—, chmn. hospitality com., 1967—; bd. dirs. Orleans Parish Med. Soc. Women's Aus., 1969—, Vis. Nurses' Assn., 1971—; chmn. A.M.A. edn. and research fund com., 1969—. Mem. New Orleans Garden Soc. (chmn. Christmas decorations 1969—), Fgn. Relations Assn., Am, Assn. U. Women, La. Landmark Soc. Republican. Roman Catholic. Club: New Orleans Country. Home: 6145 St Charles Av New Orleans LA 70118

PEARCE, JOSEPHINE ANNA, educator; b. Ottawa, Ont., Can., Dec. 3, 1918; d. Joseph A. and Esther E. (Mott) Pearce; A.B., U. Wash., 1940; M.A., Stanford, 1942; postgrad. U. N.C., 1942-44; Ph.D., U. Mo., 1955. Lectr. Victoria Coll., U. B.C., 1945-46; instr. U. Miami (Fla.), 1946-49, U. Mo., Columbia, 1949-55; asst. prof. English

Bradley U., Peoria, Ill., 1955-58, asso. prof., 1958-64, prof., 1964—. Recipient Putnam award Bradley U., 1963. Mem. Modern Humanities Research Assn., Renaissance Soc. Am., Modern Lang. Assn., Phi Kappa Phi. Research on Shakespeare's English history plays. Contbr. articles, papers to profl. meetings. Home: 9422 N Northview Rd Peoria IL 61614

PEARCE, MARY MCCALLUM (MRS. CLARENCE A. PEARCE), artist; b. Hesperia, Mich., Feb. 17, 1906; d. Archibald and Mabel (McNeil) McCallum; A.B., Oberlin Coll., 1927; student John Huntington Inst., 1929-34, Cleve. Inst. Art, 1935-37, 54, Dayton Art Inst., 1946-49; m. Clarence A. Pearce, June 30, 1928; children—Mary Martha (Mrs. William B. Robinson), Thomas McCallum. One man shows at Cleve. Women's City Club, 1959, Cuyohoga County Library, 1965, Cleve. Orch., 1967, Cleve. Playhouse Gallery, 1968, 71, Woman's City Club Cleve., 1969, Brechsville County Library, 1969; exhibited in group shows at Oberlin Art Mus., Akron Art Inst., Grand Rapids (Mich.) Art Gallery, Dayton (O.) Art Inst., Smithsonian Instn., Birmingham Mus. Art, Am. Watercolor Soc., Cleve. Mus. Art, Watercolor U.S.A., Springfield, Mo., many others; represented in pvt. collections; tchr. art, supr. pub. schs. Mayfield Heights, O., 1927-28, Maple Heights, O., 1928-30, Chagrin Falls, O., 1938-39. Named best woman artist, Ohio Watercolor Soc., 1955; recipient Bush Meml. award Columbus Gallery Fine Arts, 1962, Wolfe Watercolor award, 1971; nat. 1st prize, drawing, Nat. League Am. Penwomen, 1966, 68; Littlehouse award Ala. Watercolor Soc., 1967, Merit award Longboat Key Art Center, Sarasota, Fla., 1973. Mem. Nat. League Am. Penwomen (treas. 1962), Am. (asso.) Mich., Ala. watercolor socs. Republican. Conglist. Home: 5400 Ocean Blvd Siesta Key Sarasota FL 33581

PEARL, DORIS DICKOV (MRS. NORMAN H. PEARL), psychotherapist; b. N.Y.C., May 19, 1932; d. Al and Rose (Gabel) Dickov; student State U. N.Y., Albany, 1950-51; A.B., U. Vt., 1955; postgrad., Syracuse U., 1963-67, Coll. City N.Y., 1970-71; m. Norman H. Pearl, Nov. 18, 1951; children—Douglas Craig, Andrea Lynn. Asst. tchr. Community Nursery Sch., Dewitt, N.Y., 1960-61, tchr., 1961-62; psychol. research asst. dept. pediatrics Upstate Med. Children's Center, Syracuse, N.Y., 1964-65; grad. asst. counselor Syracuse U. Counseling Center, 1966-67; staff psychotherapist Bronx (N.Y.) Consultation Center, 1971—. Vol. reading tchr. White Plains (N.Y.) Schs., 1970-71. Mem. P.T.A. bd. Highlands Jr. High Sch., 1968-70, mem. White Plains curriculum study com., 1970-71; chmn. White Plains com. fund raising Planned Parenthood, 1971-73. Mem. Am. Psychol. Assn. (asso.), Westchester Ethical Humanist Soc., Am. Assn. for Abolition Involuntary Mental Hospitalization (platform chmn. 1974—). Home: 102 Hillair Circle White Plains NY 10605 Office: 941 Burke Av Bronx NY 10605

PEARLMAN, BARBARA, fashion illustrator; b. N.Y.C., Apr. 25, 1938; d. Henry and Edith (Stein) Pearlman; grad. Parsons Sch. Design, N.Y.C., 1960; m. Charles B. Yulish, Aug. 22, 1973. Illustrator, Neiman-Marcus, Dallas, 1961; free-lance illustrator, Europe, 1962-64, U.S., 1964—; lectr., tchr. Parson Sch. Design, 1971—; artist Galey & Lord div. Burlington Industries, 1964-74. Recipient award Soc. Illustrators. Work pub. in U.S. and European mags., also books. Address: 2259 Edsall Av Bronx NY 10463

PEARLMUTTER, DEANNE RUTH, educator, nurse; b. Bay Shore, N.Y., Sept. 12, 1939; d. David and Bess (Berliner) Pearlmutter; B.S. cum laude (Regents scholar), Syracuse U., 1962; M.Ed., Columbia, 1967, Ed.D., 1973. Pub. health nurse Suffolk County Health Dept., Riverhead, N.Y., 1962; various staff positions, research asso. Mt. Sinai Hosp., N.Y.C., 1963-70; faculty Pa. State U., University Park, 1972, Hunter Coll., N.Y.C., 1973; asso. prof. Cornell U.-N.Y. Hosp. Sch. Nursing, N.Y.C., 1973—. Nat. Inst. Mental Health trainee, 1965-67, 70-73. Mem. Am. Nurses Assn., Am. Orthopsychiat. Assn., Am. Nurse Assn. Council of Nurse Researchers. Home: 230 E 71st St New York City NY 10021 Office: 1320 York Av New York City NY 10021

PEARSON, BETSY DECELLE (MRS. WELTON DENNIS PEARSON), educator; b. Geromont, Liege, Belgium; d. Leon Gabriel and Camille Mignolet (Francois) De Celle; student Sisters of the Cross, Liege, Ecole Superieure de Demoiselles, Liege, Bus. Sciences, Liege, Institut d'Education Physique, Liege; intern in re-edn. St. Laurent Mil. Hosp., 1943-44; M.A., U. Tenn., 1968; postgrad. Vanderbilt U., 1969; m. Welton Dennis Pearson, Apr. 24, 1946; 1 dau., Elisabeth Leone. Came to U.S., 1948. Moniteur Institut d'Education Physique, Liege, Belgium, 1940-41, professeur, 1942-43; asso. prof. Institut des Sciences Sociales, Liege, Belgium, 1942-45; collaborator Laboratoire de Biometrie Experimentale, Liege, 1942-45, Sorbonne, 1962, Nat. Def. Edn. Act Inst., 1965; chmn. lang. dept. Chattanooga High Sch. Vol. tchr. Talented Youth Program and Frye Inst.; mem. Opera Assn.; active Community Concerts, Heart Assn., United Fund, A.R.C.; treas. Newcomers Club, 1949; founder L'Amicale Francaise, Chattanooga, 1952. Served with Army of Liberation, 1940-45. Decorated Medaille de la Resistance (Belgium); recipient Mieux Doues Scholarship, Liege, 3 yrs. Mem. N.E.A., Tenn. Edn. Assn., Am. Assn. U. Women, Internat. Platform Assn. Clubs: Metropolitan, Music (mem. bd. 1958-59). Home: 938 McCallie Av Chattanooga TN 37403

PEARSON, CHARLOTTE DANDRIDGE (MRS. EDWARD ALPHONSO PEARSON), univ. adminstr.; b. Lexington, Va., Aug. 27, 1932; d. Frank McKutcheon and Naneen (Galvin) Dandridge; B.S., Va. State Coll., 1954; M.A., Hampton Inst., 1973; m. Edward Alphonso Pearson, Feb. 23, 1957. Sec. to dir. pub. relations Hampton (Va.) Inst., 1955-57, accounting clk., 1957-66, personnel officer, 1966—. Mem. Coll. and Univ. Personnel Assn. (regional dir. 1973, nat. sec.-treas. 1973), Kappa Delta Pi. Home: 1279 Old Buckroe Rd Hampton VA 23668

PEARSON, GLADYS ELIZABETH (MRS. JAMES MARION PEARSON), cons.; b. Mpls., May 5, 1930; d. Johan Anderson and Anna Elizabeth (Swanson) Westberg; B.S. in Occupational Therapy with highest honors (Audubon Soc. scholar, State Coll. scholar, Tb Assn. scholar, Rehab. Services Adminstrn. scholar), U. Minn., 1967; m. James Marion Pearson, Dec. 25, 1970; 1 dau. by previous marriage, Laurie (Mrs. Harold Kalvig). Asso. dir. occupational therapy Kenny Rehab. Inst., Mpls., 1967-68, dir. prevocational dept., 1968-71; asso. dir. Minn. Alcohol and Drug Authority, St. Paul, 1971-74; project mgr., cons. Unco, Inc., Washington, 1974—. Cons. orgn., planning to state, fed. govts., 1971—; cons. Nat. Inst. on Alcohol Abuse and Alcoholism, Washington, 1974—. Mem. Am. (nominating com. 1970), Minn. (sec. 1969-70) occupational therapy assns., Nat., Minn. (sec. 1970-71, 71-72) rehab. assns., Internat. (chmn. registration conf. 1970), Minn. (sec.-treas. 1971-72) assns. rehab. facilities, Vocational Evaluation and Work Adjustment Assn., Rehab. Counseling Assn. Minn., Minn. Assn. for Children with Learning Disabilities, Nat. Assn. for State Drug Abuse Program Coordinators (vice chmn. 1972-73), Alcohol and Drug Problems Assn. N.Am. (co-chmn. nominations 1972-73), Minn. Welfare Assn. Methodist. Home: 4710 Bethesda Av Bethesda MD 20014 Office: 815 15th St NW Washington DC 20005

PEARSON, JOYCE A. ZIEGLER (MRS. WAYNE E. PEARSON), physician; b. Pottstown, Pa., Jan. 5, 1929; d. Amos B. and Bertha (Schlegel) Ziegler; B.S., Dickinson Coll., 1950; M.D., Johns Hopkins, 1954; m. Wayne E. Pearson, June 19, 1954; children—Steven Wayne, Eric Alan, Carol Jayne. Intern, research fellow U. Ill. Research and Edn. Hosp., Chgo., 1954-57; practice medicine, Wilmington, Del., 1958-62; clin. asst. Del. Hosp., Wilmington, 1962-65; physician Mental Health Clinic, Charlotte, N.C., 1965-67; med. dir. Alcoholism Services, Wilmington Med. Center, 1968—. Mem. A.M.A., New Castle County Med. Soc., Am. Acad. Gen. Practice. Unitarian. Home: 109 Hackney Circle Wilmington DE 19803 Office: Alcoholism Services 505 W 13th St Wilmington DE 19801

PEARSON, LESLEY AGNES JOAN (MRS. LOUIS JOSEPH FRIDENBERG), advt. exec.; b. Aberdeen, Scotland, May 27, 1918; d. Gerald Hamilton Jeffery and Mary Agnes (Mackenzie) Pearson; came to U.S., 1924; student Drexel Inst., 1936-37; m. Louis Joseph Fridenberg, July 3, 1945 (dec. Jan. 1970). Free-lance advt. cons., Phila., 1941-49; sales promotion dir. Dewees Splty. Store, Phila., 1949-64; chief all fashion advt. Gimbels Stores, Phila., 1964—; instr. fashion merchandising Temple U., 1961, 63. Chmn. splty. stores div. United Fund, 1960. Mem. Phila. Club Advt. Women, Fashion Group. Home: 1801 J F Kennedy Blvd Philadelphia PA 19103 Office: Chestnut-Market 8th and 9th Sts Philadelphia PA 19105

PEARSON, LOIS HILL (MRS. LAMBERT O. PEARSON), pub. relations exec.; b. Victoria, Tex., July 14, 1914; d. John Howard and Lucille (Lane) Peters; B.A., Rice U., 1935; m. Lambert O. Pearson, Nov. 22, 1960; 1 son, Rodney Hill. Editorial asst. to dir. WAC, Washington, 1942-44; research analyst in mil. intelligence Far East div. U.S. Army, Washington, 1944-45; asso. editor Med. Arts Pub. Co., staff writer Book of Health, Houston, 1950-55; dir. pub. relations St. Luke's Episcopal Hosp., Houston, Tex. Children's Hosp., Houston, Tex. Heart Inst., Houston, 1954—. Recipient Anson Jones award Tex. Med. Assn., 1961. Mem. Tex. Hosp. Assn., Women in Communications. Home: 5630 Reamer St Houston TX 77035 Office: 6621 Fannin St Houston TX 77025

PEARSON, LOUISE MARY (MRS. NELS K. PEARSON), mfg. co. exec.; b. Inverness, Scotland, Dec. 14, 1919 (parents Am. citizens); d. Louis Houston and Jessie M. (McKenzie) Lenox; grad. high sch.; m. Nels Kenneth Pearson, June 28, 1941; children—Lorine (Mrs. Ronald Walters), Karla. Dir. Wauconda Tool & Engring. Co., Inc., Algonquin, Ill., 1950—. Reporter Oak Leaflet, Crystal Lake, Ill., 1944-47, Sidelights, Wilmette, Ill., 1969-72. Active Girl Scouts U.S.A., 1955-65. Recipient award for appreciation work with Girl Scouts, 1965. Clubs: Antique Automobile of Am. (Hershey, Pa.); Veteran Motor Car (Boston); Classic Car of Am. (Madison, N.J.). Home: 125 Dole Av Crystal Lake IL 60014

PEARSON, MARGARET GEORGINA (MRS. BERNARD BRINE), physician; b. Calgary, Alta., Can., May 19, 1922; d. Stanley Cecil and Mary Shaw (Dundas) Pearson; R.N., Calgary Gen. Sch. Nursing, 1944; B.S., U. Alta., 1950, M.D., 1952; m. Bernard Brine, Aug. 2, 1958 (dec. Oct. 1959). Intern, U. Alta. Hosp., Edmonton, 1952-53, Hosp. for sick children, Toronto, Ont., Can., 1955-57, Hamilton (Ont.) Gen. Hosp., 1957-58, War Meml. Children's Hosp., London, 1958-59; resident Royal Coll. Physicians and Surgeons, 1959; practiced medicine, Lethbridge, Alta., 1953-55; specializing in pediatrics in Calgary, 1959—; mem. staffs Calgary Gen. Hosp., 1959—, Alta. Children's, Holy Cross, Grace hosps., Calgary, 1960—. Clin. dir. Neuromuscular Handicapped Clinic, Calgary, 1964—; poison service officer, So. Alta., 1960—. Mem. Can., Calgary, Dist. Med. socs., Can., N. Pacific, Alta. pediatric socs. Mem. United Ch. Can. Mem. Order Eastern Star. Clubs: Calgary Professional, Calgary Golf and Country. Home: 35 4915 8th St SW Calgary AB T2S 2P1 Canada Office: 305 906 8th Av SW Calgary AB T2P 1H9 Canada

PEARSON, MARGARET JEAN ROYALL (MRS. GEORGE BERNARD PEARSON), artist; b. Austin, Tex., July 5, 1931; d. Nathaniel and Margaret (Hay) Royall; student Abbott Art Sch., 1943-47, Corcoran Art Sch., 1948-49; B.F.A., U. Tex., 1953; m. George Bernard Pearson, May 1, 1965; 1 dau., April Michelle. Artist, illustrator Stacy Advt. Agy., Dallas, 1953, Ferguson Advt. Agy., Dallas, 1954, Chance Vought Aircraft, Dallas, 1954-58, Collins Radio Co., Dallas, 1959-65. One-man show Mother Frances Hosp., Tyler, Tex., 1968; exhibited in group shows including Witte Mus., San Antonio, 1959, 61, 64, 66, 67, 68, Nat. Acad. Gallery, N.Y.C., 1964, 66, 68, Dallas Mus. Fine Art, 1961, 62, Oklahoma City Art Center, 1962, Fairfield (Conn.) U., 1968, Stamford (Conn.) Mus. Fine Art, 1968, New Canaan (Conn.) Art Exhibit, 1968, 69; works included in Am. Watercolor Soc. traveling exhibit, 1966. Recipient various awards Southwestern Watercolor Soc., 1964, 65, 67; 2d prize watercolor New Canaan Art Exhibit, 1972. Mem. Southwestern, Tex. watercolor socs., Rowayton (Conn.) Art Center, Alpha Phi. Episcopalian. Clubs: Cotillion, Slipper. Home: 72 Woodway Ridge Lane New Canaan CT 06840

PEARSON, MARILYN, state legislator; Formerly writer, Stratford (Conn.) Times Sentinel; now mem. Conn. Ho. of Reps. Pres., Stratford Community Arts Council, 1965-72; pres. Children' Theater at Stratford, 1964-74, pres. workshop, 1966-68; programming chmn. Shakespeare Guilde, 1965-66; rep. dir. Stratford Red Cross, 1967-68; treas. Sterling House Community Center, 1964-66, council mem. 1964-68. Formerly clk. Stratford Town Council. Named Outstanding Clubwoman, Stratford Jr. Woman's Club, 1971, outstanding legislator Coll. Young Reps. of Conn., 1969-70; Pub. Service award Kidney Found. Conn.; spl. award State Employees Conn., 1973. Mem. Conn. Order Women Legislators (pres.). Club: Stratford Junior Woman's (founder 1967). Home: 605 Light St Stratford CT 06497

PEARSON, MARY EARL (MRS. REX KENNETH PEARSON), newspaper editor; b. Medicine Hat, Alta., Can., May 7, 1921; d. John and Mary (Young) Earl; came to U.S., 1923, naturalized, 1942; student Ft. Hays Kan. State Coll., 1939-42, B.A., 1969; m. Rex Kenneth Pearson, Mar. 6, 1943; children—Mary Gay (Mrs. Randal Lee Menscer), Thomas Rex. News editor Ellis (Kan.) Rev., weekly newspaper, 1963-69, editor, 1970—. Mem. Ellis Library Bd., 1952-62, Ellis Recreation Commn., 1950-65, Ellis Dist. Sch. Bd., 1960-61. Vice pres. Ellis County Republican Women, 1961. Recipient award, state writing contest Kan. Press Women, 1970-72, award contest news/feature div., 1971, 72; mem. Nat. Fedn. Press Women (award nat. writing contest 1973), Kan. Press Women, Kan. Press Assn., C. of C., Alpha Sigma Alpha. Conglist. Mem. Order Eastern Star. Home: 124 W 10th St Ellis KS 67637 Office: 1018 Washington St Ellis KS 67637

PEARSON, PHYLLIS MARTIN, musician; b. N.Y.C., Oct. 9, 1940; d. Leonard and Edythe (Sher) Martin; student Bennington Coll., 1957-60; B.S. in Sociology, Columbia, 1964; m. Harry W. Pearson, Jr., Feb. 10, 1966; children—Nels, Nina Rachel; 1 stepson, Nicholas. Instr. piano and percussion Bennington Coll., 1969—; tympanist Vt. State Symphony Orch., 1969—; dir. VSSO Percussion Ensemble, 1972—; staff percussionist Composers Conf., Johnson, Vt., 1973—; pianist, percussionist Berkshire Chamber Ensemble, Williamstown, Mass., 1974; organist, pianist, percussionist various chs., theatre cos., orchs., choral socs., 1960—; organist North Bennington Congl. Ch., 1968-73. Owner Coffee Express, food service, Bennington, 1972—. Address: Bennington College Bennington VT 05201

PEARSON, ZADIE RUTH, elementary sch. librarian; b. Quanah, Tex., Jan. 28, 1915; d. James Leonard and Sylvia Grace (Motley) Willis; B.A., U. Tex., 1936; M.Ed., Tex. Women's U., 1952; m. Fred William Pearson, July 18, 1936; children—Fred Leonard, Robert Wayne. Tchr., Kermit (Tex.) Ind. Sch. Dist., 1943-52, elementary sch. librarian, 1952—. Active local Am. Heart Assn., Am. Cancer Soc. Named Tchr. of Year in Kermit schs., 1962. Mem. N.E.A., Am., Tex. library assns., Tex. Tchrs. Assn., Tex. Classroom Tchrs. Assn., Delta Kappa Gamma. Methodist. Home: 701 Hejupe St Kermit TX 79745 Office: Elementary Sch S Mulberry St Kermit TX 79745

PEASLEE, CHARLOTTE HOFFMAN, mag. editor; b. N.Y.C. July 13, 1931; d. Edmund Witherbee and Emily (Delafield) Peaslee; student Radcliffe Coll., 1949-52; B.J., U. Mo., 1958. Reporter, Paterson (N.J.) Morning Call, 1958; editorial asst. Electronic and Appliance Specialist, N.Y.C., 1958-60, Palmerton Pub. Co., N.Y.C., 1960-61; asst. editor in charge prodn. Sci. Digest, Hearst Mag. div., N.Y.C., 1964-69; writer Consol. Edison Co., N.Y.C., 1964-69; tech. editor Nat. Elec. Mfrs. Assn., N.Y.C., 1969-70; free-lance writer, copy editor, 1970-71; mng. editor Lady's Circle mag. Lopez Publs., N.Y.C., 1971—. Mem. Women in Communications, Nat. Orgn. for Women (N.Y. exec. v.p. 1972, dir. 1973), Kappa Tau Alpha, Kappa Alpha Mu. Club: Overseas Press (N.Y.C.). Home: 165 E 72d St New York City NY 10021 Office: 21 W 26th St New York City NY 10010

PEATEE, MARJORIE CONRAD (MRS. ROGER A. PEATEE), physician; b. Phila., Jan. 24, 1922; d. William H. and Sue E. (Jackson) Conrad; B.S., U. Pa., 1943; M.D., Hahnemann Med. Coll., 1946; m. Roger A. Peatee, Jan. 29, 1966. Intern Meml. Hosp., Wilmington, Del., 1946-47; practice gen. medicine, Wilmington, 1947-66, Bowling Green, O., 1966—. Mem. Am., Ohio acads. family physicians, Wood County Med. Soc. Republican. Methodist. Mem. Order Eastern Star. Home: 1138 Clark St Bowling Green OH 43402 Office: 15819 BG Rd W Bowling Green OH 43402

PEATTIE, LISA REDFIELD (MRS. WILLIAM A. DOEBELE), educator; b. Chgo., Mar. 1, 1924; d. Robert and Margaret Lucy (Park) Redfield; student Swarthmore Coll., 1941-43; M.A., U. Chgo., 1950, Ph.D., 1968; m. R.E. Peattie, June 26, 1943 (dec. Dec. 1962); children—Christopher, Sara, Miranda, Julia Peattie; m. 2d, William A. Doebele, Jan. 15, 1972. Research asso. Bank St. Coll. Edn., N.Y.C., 1957-62; staff anthropologist Guayana project Mass. Inst. Tech.-Harvard Joint Center for Urban Studies, Venezuela, 1962-64; prof. urban studies Mass. Inst. Tech., Cambridge, 1965—. Author: The View from the Barrio, 1968. Contbr. articles to profl. jours. Home: 271 Lowell Av Newton MA 02160 Office: Mass Inst Tech Cambridge MA 02139

PECILLO, JEANETTE MARIE (MRS. STEVEN PECILLO), statistician; b. Darby, Pa., Sept. 1, 1947; s. John and Mary (Socha) Szwec; B.A., Temple U., 1969; M.S., Villanova U., 1973; m. Steven Pecillo, July 18, 1970. Statis. cons. fabrics and finishes dept. Marshall Lab., E.I. duPont de Nemours & Co., Inc., Phila., 1969—. Instr. statistics Community Coll. Phila., part-time 1973—. Mem. Women's Polit. Caucus, 1972—. Mem. Am. Statis. Assn. Club: Society Hill. Home: 413 Pine St Philadelphia PA 19106 Office: 3500 Grays Ferry Av Philadelphia PA 19146

PECK, ANNE ELLIOTT ROBERTS (MRS. ROBERT GRAY PECK 3RD), educator, journalist; b. N.Y.C., Dec. 17, 1935; d. James Ragan and Jane Ziegler (Elliott) Roberts; B.A. with honors in English, Wellesley Coll., 1957; M.A. with honors in Comparative Lit., Columbia, 1966; m. George Linn Davis, May 29, 1955 (div. Aug. 1967); children—James Roberts, Elliott Britton, George Linn, William Vaughn; m. 2d, Robert Gray Peck 3d, Oct. 24, 1969; children—Andrew Adams, Matthew Canfield, Roberts. English tchr. The Masters Sch., Dobbs Ferry, N.Y., 1963-65; sports feature writer Westchester-Rockland newspapers, White Plains, N.Y., 1969—; corr., daily column Knickerbocker News-Union Star, Capital Newspapers, Albany, N.Y., 1971-73. Mem. art com. Schenectady Mus. Art and Sci. Bd. dirs. Scarsdale (N.Y.) Jr. League, 1960-61, Greenacres Sch. P.T.A., 1968-69, Planned Parenthood League, Schenectady, N.Y. State Legislative Forum, 1971-73. Recipient prize Coll. Bd. Contest Mademoiselle mag., 1954; Prix de Paris, Vogue mag., 1957. Mem. D.A.R. (Harvey Birch chpt.), Scarsdale Woman's Club, Am. Assn. U. Women (dir. Schenectady 1971-73), N.Y. State Women's Press Club (Capital dist. br.), Jr. League Phila. (edn. com.). Republican. Episcopalian (dir. women's group). Clubs: Schenectady Curling, Mohawk Golf (Schenectady); Shenorock Shore (Rye, N.Y.); Wellesley Alumnae (Phila.). Home: 100 Steeplechase Rd Devon PA 19333

PECK, JEAN MARIE, librarian; b. Buffalo, Nov. 15, 1925; d. Charles Lazalere and Irene Belle (Henry) Peck; B.S., U. Buffalo, 1956; M.S., Syracuse U., 1961. Staff nurse N.Y. Hosp., 1946-47, Millard Fillmore Hosp., Buffalo, 1948, Cedars of Lebanon Hosp., Los Angeles, 1949, Dartmouth Coll. Infirmary, 1949-50, VA Hosp., Buffalo, 1951-54; nursing service supr. Buffalo Gen. Hosp., 1956-60; librarian supr. Mich. State U., 1961-66, U. Cal. at Berkeley, 1966—. Mem. Nat. Audubon Soc., Sierra Club, Point Reyes Bird Obs., A.L.A., Cal. Library Assn., Beta Phi Mu. Episcopalian. Home: 135 Windsor Av Kensington CA 94708 Office: Library U Cal Berkeley CA 94720

PECK, KATHRYN BLACKBURN (MRS. HARLAN C. PECK), author; b. Jacksonville, Ill., July 9, 1904; d. Charles Edmund and Mary Amelia (Cary) Blackburn; ed. pub. schs., also spl. tutoring; m. Harlan Charles Peck, Aug. 23, 1919; children—Marlin E., Lillian (Mrs. Calvin Mathews), Dolores (Mrs. M. Alsobrook). Author: Golden Windows, 1942; Along the Winding Pathway, 1947; In Favor with God and Man, 1952; Better Primary Teaching, 1957; Up in the Jumby Tree, 1960; Mother Memories, 1960; Every Day and Sunday, 1959; God Made the Lovely, Lovely World, 1960; I Too Can Sing, 1961; Candles in the Dark, 1964; You Can Be a Happy Shut-In, 1965; Joy in the Morning, 1969, also Bible sch. textbooks and ch. sch. materials. Tchr. Christian Service Tng. groups, Mo., Kan., Colo., Ind., Fla., Cal., Nev. Home: 1704 W O'Brien Rd No 413 Lees Summit MO 64063

PECK, MARY ANN EKSTROM (MRS. PAUL SANFORD PECK), designer, artist, horse and dog breeder, civic worker; b. Hibbing, Minn., Apr. 12, 1920; d. Edwin Carl and Ethel Sophia (Salmonson) Ekstrom; grad. Hockaday Jr. Coll., 1939; degree in costume design and illustration Parson's N.Y. Sch. Fine and Applied Arts, 1939-42; m. Paul Sanford Peck, Feb. 14, 1943 (dec. Mar. 1964); children—Carl Sanford, Randal Nelson. Fashion coordinator coll. attire Neiman Marcus Co., Dallas, 1937-42; dir. Nueces Transp. Co., Corpus Christi, Tex., 1945-64, exec. v.p., 1964-67; dir. Nueces Mack Truck Co., Nueces Truck & Equipment Leasing Co., 1950-64, exec. v.p., 1964-67; breeder saddle horses, showing and training Arabians, and Am. Saddlebreds Show Ponies and Walking Horses, 1959—; owner Fairmount Farms, Inc., Corpus Christi, 1964—, breeder greyhound dogs. Donated (with father) and worked on building Carmelite Day Nursery, 1966; established perpetual fund for underprivileged boys YMCA, 1965; Vol. work Jr. League, 1940-60, now asso.; vol. decorator and designer for clubs and charities,

1945-53; pres. Charity League, 1960; charter mem. Gulf Coast Charity Horse Show, 1964, sec., 1964-65, v.p., 1967; chmn. Buccaneer Day Parade, 1959. Named hon. dep. sheriff Nueces County, 1949, Friend of Ct., 1949. Mem. Profl. Horseman's Assn. Am. Saddlebred Futurity Assn., Am. Horse Shows Assn., Nat. Coursing Assn., Las Donas de la Corte (charter), Order de Pineda (v.p. 1947, steering com. 1966). Democrat. Episcopalian. Clubs: Am. Cotillion (charter), Corpus Christi Country. Home: 401 Coral Pl Corpus Christi TX 78411

PECK, RUTH BOYER (MRS. THEODORE A. PECK), author; b. San Diego; d. Harvey K. and Jean (Cook) Boyer; certificate in pub. health nursing U. Wash., 1929; m. Morris R. Scott, June 8, 1929 (dec. 1965); children—Jean (Mrs. Howard Shipley), Carol (Mrs. C.T. Ireland); m. 2d, Theodore A. Peck, Oct. 14, 1972. Free lance mag. article writer, 1947—; author, originator Hope through Research series pamphlets NIH, Bethesda, Md., 1957-73. Recipient certificate of merit Dept. Health, Edn. and Welfare, 1970, 72, 73. Mem. D.A.R., Nat. Assn. Sci. Writers, Soc. Magazine Writers, Hymn. Soc. Am. (life), Washington Press Club. Author: Magnificent Pursuit, 1974. Home: 210 E Fairfax St Apt 421 Falls Church VA 22046

PECK, ZULA MARION SKEEN, state employee; b. Little Rock, Oct. 14, 1913; d. Frank and Tulcie Mabel (Jamison) Skeen; student McKenzie Bus. Sch., Tarpon Springs, 1930-31; m. Walter Welch Coleman, June 2, 1932 (div. 1938); 1 dau., Marion Laurel (Mrs. Francis Carroll Steinhice), Wire editor, polit. reporter Asso. Press, Nashville, 1942-44, wire editor, London, Eng., 1945-46; acting chief photo div. OWI, London, 1944-45; dep. dir. pub. relations office Office Mil. Govt. for Germany, 1946-49; pres. and publs. officer U.S. State Dept., Berlin, Germany, 1949-53; reporter Chattanooga Times, 1953-65; dir. pub. information Tenn. Dept. Mental Health, Nashville, 1965-72; staff aide to gov. Tenn., Nashville, 1972—. Pres., dir. Hixson Pike Fire Dept., Inc., 1955—. Recipient awards from various local state and national groups and orgns. Mem. Pub. Relations Soc. Am., Smithsonian Assos. Republican. Home: 6712 Currywood Dr Nashville TN 37205 Office: 1025 Andrew Jackson Bldg Nashville TN 37219

PECKENS, GLORIA ESKE (MRS. RUSSELL G. PECKENS), educator; b. Columbus, O., Apr. 5, 1926; d. Louis Henry and Eula Marguerite (Peague) Eske; B.S. in Edn., U. S.D., 1951; M.A. (Fed. fellow), Tex. Woman's U., 1966; m. Russell G. Peckens, May 30, 1949; 1 dau., Tina Marguerite. Tchr. elementary and secondary pub. schs., S.D., Mont., Colo., 1949-55; tchr. spl. edn. for mentally retarded Balt. Schs., 1956-57, Johnson City (Tex.) City Schs., 1958-63, Tex. State Instn. for Retarded, Denton, 1963-64; Lewisville, Tex., 1964-65; asst. prof. spl. edn. U. Guam Coll. Edn., Agana, 1968—. Mem. State Level Adv. Council, Guam, 1969-71, Gov.'s Task Force on Mental Health and Mental Retardation, Guam, 1971—. Recipient Meritorious Service award to edn. Guam Tchrs. Assn., 1972. Mem. Assn. on Mental Deficiency, Council for Exceptional Children (pres. Guam chpt. 1969-71), Sigma Alpha Iota. Democrat. Lutheran. Address: Box EK U Guam Agana GU 96910

PECKUS, JOLANTA ALDONA DRASUTIS (MRS. SARUNAS PECKUS), physician; b. Kaunas, Lithuania, Nov. 30, 1935; d. Pranas and Aldona Birute (Vegele) Drasutis; came to U.S., 1948, naturalized, 1954; B.A. magna cum laude, Western Res. U., 1957; M.D., U. Heidelberg, 1963; m. Sarunas Peckus, Sept. 6, 1958; children—Linas, Darius. Intern Euclid-Glennville Hosp., Cleve., 1963-64; emergency room physician Highland Park (Ill.) Hosp., 1966-69; emergency physician, unit adminstr. Med. Emergency Service Assos., Elmhurst, Ill., 1969—; emergency physician St. Elizabeth's Hosp., Chgo., Northwest Community Hosp., Arlington Heights, Ill., St. Francis Hosp., Blue Island, Ill.; emergency physician, adminstr. emergency dept. St. Anne's Hosp., Chgo., 1972—. Vol. camp physician Lithuanian Boy Scout and Girl Scout camps, 1973-74. Mem. A.M.A., Am. Coll. Emergency Physicians, Am. Med. Women's Assn., Am. Lithuanian Med. Assn., Ill., Chgo. med. socs., Phi Beta Kappa. Office: 111 N Addison St Elmhurst IL 60126

PEDEN, IRENE CARSWELL (MRS. LEO J. PEDEN), elec. engr., educator; b. Topeka, Kan., Sept. 25, 1925; d. Jay Horton and Lena (Anderson) Carswell; B.S., U. Colo., 1947; M.S., Stanford, 1958, Ph.D., 1962; m. Leo J. Peden, Aug. 28, 1962; step-daus., Jefri Lyn, Jennifer. Jr. engr. Delaware Power &Light Co., 1947-49; jr. engr. Stanford Research Inst., 1949-50, research engr. antenna research group, 1950-52, 1954-57; research engr. Midwest Research Inst., 1952-54, research asst. Hansen Microwave Lab., Stanford, 1958-61; acting instr. elec. engr. Stanford, 1959-61; asst. prof. elec. engring. U. Wash., Seattle, 1961-64, asso. prof., 1964-71, prof., 1971—, asso. dean, 1973—. Mem. nat. adv. drug com. Food and Drug Adminstrn., 1971—; adv. council Sch. Engring., Stanford, 1972—. Mem. Space Physics Bd. Nat. Acad. Scis., 1974. Recipient Soc. of Women Engrs. Shining Star award, 1964-65; Golden Lyre award for community service Iota Iota alumnae chpt. Alpha Chi Omega, 1968, Nat. Achievement award, 1972; named Woman of Achievement, Seattle Theta Sigma Phi, 1966; Woman of Year, Seattle sect. Quota Internat., 1971, Distinguished Contbn. to Edn. Seattle Fedn. Women's Clubs, 1971. Fellow I.E.E.E. (chmn. Seattle sect. 1965-66, vice chmn. 1967-68, membership and transfers com. 1966-69, com. on profl. opportunities for women 1971—, edn. com. group on antennas and propagation 1971—, editorial bd. procs. 1965-70); sr. mem. Soc. Women Engrs. (chmn. Pacific Northwest sect. 1967-68, nat. achievement award 1973); mem. A.A.A.S., Am. Geophys. Union, N.Y. Acad. Sci., D.A.R., Morter Bd. (hon. mem. Tolo chpt.), Sigma Xi, Tau Beta Pi. Home: 8752 Sand Point Way NE Seattle WA 98115

PEDEN, KATHERINE GRAHAM, bus. exec.; b. Hopkinsville, Ky., Jan. 2, 1926; d. William E. and Mary (Gorin) Peden; grad. pub. schs. Ky. With radio station WHOP, Hopkinsville, Ky., 1944-64; pres. radio sta. WNVL, Nicholasville, Ky., 1962-71; indsl. cons., real estate broker, 1968—. Mem. personnel bd. Commonwealth Ky., 1960-63; commr. commerce State Ky., 1964-68; mem. Gov.'s Cabinet, 1964-68; mem. Pres.' Commn. on Civil Disorders, 1967-68; Democratic nominee for U.S. Senate, 1968. Trustee Bus. and Profl. Women's Found., 1958-62; bd. dirs. Ky. Derby Festival, Jefferson County Riverport Authority. Recipient Woman of Year award, Hopkinsville, Ky., 1951. Mem. Ky. Fedn. Bus. Profl. Women's Clubs (pres. 1955-56, 1st v.p. nat. fedn. 1960-61, pres. nat. fedn. 1961-62), Am. Indsl. Devel. Council, Indsl. Devel. Research Council, Louisville C. of C. (dir.). Mem. Christian Ch. (deaconess 1956-59, 60-64). Home: 2118 S Virginia St Hopkinsville KY 42240 Office: Citizen's Plaza No. 2306 Louisville KY 40208

PEDERSEN, ELLINOR ELLEN, librarian; b. Vindbyholt, Denmark, June 2, 1925; d. Hans Peder and Ane (Nygaard) Pedersen; came to U.S., 1951; bus. certificate Sir George Williams U., 1954; B.A., Boston U., 1959; M.L.S., Simmons Coll., 1962. Asst. to head of circulation Harvard Bus. Sch. Library, Boston, 1960-62; asst. to head acquisition dept. Harvard Law Sch. Library, Cambridge, 1962-64; asst. librarian Harvard Grad. Sch. Edn. Library, Cambridge, 1964-66; librarian Fisher Jr. Coll. Library, Boston, 1966—. Recipient various fellowships and grants. Mem. Mass. Library Assn., Fgn. Press Assn. (asso.). Author: (with G. Gansing) Danske Nationalretter, 1949, Verdens morsomste mand, Victor Borge, 1956. Home: 24 Prescott St Apt 25 Cambridge MA 02138 Office: 118 Beacon St Boston MA 02116

PEDIGO, JUNE HILL, med. illustrator; b. Wisconsin Rapids, Wis., Aug. 26, 1923; d. Myron and Eva (Wagner) Hill; B.F.A., Ohio U. (Athens, O.), 1945; m. Louis S. Pedigo, June 18, 1952 (div. 1959); m. 2d, George E. Hiscott IV, June 11, 1967. Med. illustrator, acting dir., dept. med. illustration La. State U. Sch. Medicine, New Orleans, 1946-53; asst. dir. dept. med. art, photograph and visual edn. Michael Reese Hosp., Chgo., 1953-56; med. artist Presbyn.-St. Luke's Hosp., Chgo., 1956-58; free-lance med. illustrator, Chgo., 1958—; work permanently exhibited Hinsdale Health Mus. (Ill.), cons. prior to opening of mus., 1956-58. Chmn., Bells for Independence Day, Evanston, Ill., 1970-71. Mem. Assn. Med. Illustrators, D.A.R. (nat. def. chmn. Ft. Dearborn chpt. 1966-68, 1st vice regent 1968-70, 72-74). Illustrator: Biovue Modern Biology Series, Chemistry and Physiology, 1967, Living with your Ulcer, 1971, Living With Your Bad Back, 1972; Living With Your Bronchitis and Emphysema, 1972; Living With Your Eye Operation, 1974. Research writer on Flexichrome process. Address: 1745 Spruce St Highland Park IL 60035

PEEBLES, ANNE DOBIE, civic worker; b. Stony Creek, Va., July 7, 1922; d. William Dunn and Mary (Dobie) Peebles; A.B., Coll. William and Mary, 1944; postgrad., U. Va., 1946-47. Tchr. U.S. history, govt. pub. schs., Sussex County, Va., 1945-47. Mem. State Bd. Edn. Va., 1958-70, pres., 1968-70; woman's chmn. U.S. Savs. Bonds for Va., 1959—; mem. Va. Twin Trailers Study Commn., 1969-71, Gov.'s Com. to Employ Handicapped, 1947-60, Gov.'s Adv. Com. on Va. Economy, 1947-60, State Edn. Assistance Authority, 1959-72; mem. steering com. White House Conf. on Children and Youth, 1960; exec. com. Va. YMCA, 1969—; mem. Va. Adv. Legislative Council, 1969—; 1971 Cancer crusade chmn. Va. Co-chmn. Democratic campaign Harrison-Godwin-Button for gov., lt. gov. and atty. gen. Va., 1959; co-chmn. Dem. campaign Godwin-Pollard-Button for gov., lt. gov. and atty. gen. Va., 1965; campaign co-ordinator for Sen. Harry F. Byrd, 1970; woman's chmn. Godwin for Gov., 1973. Sec., trustee Va. div. Am. Cancer Soc.; trustee Patrick Henry Hosp., Va. Council on Health and Med. Care, Va. YMCA, John Tyler Community Coll.; trustee Va. Woman's Forum, 1972; mem. Southeastern regional bd. Salvation Army. mem. liaison com. for continuing edn. for nurses Med. Coll. Va., now mem. exec. com. Recipient medallion Soc. of Alumni Coll. William and Mary, 1969. Mem. Dirs. Soc. of Alumni Coll. William and Mary (sec.), Va. Fedn. Womens Clubs (pres. 1958-60), Delta Kappa Gamma. United Methodist (bd. edn.). Club: Colony (Richmond). Home: Dunnlora Carson VA 23830

PEELER, ELIZABETH FISKE BOGGESS, civic worker; b. Louisville; d. Walter Fisk and Elizabeth Fiske (Jones) Boggess; B.A., Wellesley Coll.; m. Joseph David Peeler; children—Stuart Thorne, Joyce Woodson (Mrs. Joseph Kinnear Morford II). Mem. bd. various coms. Jr. League, Los Angeles; pres. Las Madrinas Debutante Ball, Los Angeles; founder Jr. Philharmonic Com., Los Angeles; charter mem. costume council Los Angeles County Mus. Art, Asso. Music Centre of Los Angeles, Otis Art Inst., Los Angeles; mem. Los Angeles bd. Nat. Soc. Colonial Dames Am.; trustee Marlborough Sch. Clubs: Wellesley (Los Angeles), Hancock Park Garden (founder); Town (Pasadena). Home: 131 N June St Los Angeles CA 90004

PEET, RUTH HARRIS, physician; b. Prattville, Ala., Jan. 13, 1921; d. Mitchell L. and Annie (Jacobs) Harris; A.B., Howard Coll. (Sanford U.), 1942; M.D., Bowman Gray Sch. Medicine Wake Forest U., 1945; m. Ben E. Peet, Apr. 6, 1948 (dec. Jan. 1968); children—Charles M., Martha V., Judith (Mrs. James F. Fredrick). Intern Watts Hosp., Durham, N.C., 1945-47; physician Cerro de Pasco Co. (Peru), 1951-53; practice gen. medicine, Flat Rock, Ala., 1954-73, Scottsboro, Ala., 1973—; physician Well-baby Clinic Jackson County Health Dept., Scottsboro, Ala., family planning program, Head-start and Migrant Sch. program in area; mem. Jackson County Mental Health Bd. Mem. Am. Assn. U. Women, Music Study Club. Baptist (tchr. Sunday sch. 1968—). Home: 517 Scott St Scottsboro AL 35768 Office: 302 Martin St Scottsboro AL 35768 35966

PEGAU, RUTH MOYER (MRS. ERNEST E. PEGAU), library cons.; b. Fairfield, Ia., Dec. 12, 1920; d. Ralph Hart and Esther (Wilson) Moyer; B.A. cum laude, Parsons Coll., 1941; postgrad. Cal. State U., 1962-64, Pepperdine U., 1968-70; M.L.S., Immaculate Heart Coll., 1965; postgrad. Chapman Coll., 1967-68, U. Cal. at Irvine, 1967, U. Cal. at Riverside, 1967-68; m. Ernest E. Pegau, June 18, 1942; 1 dau., Mary (Mrs. David E. Crawford). Tchr., Laurel, Ia., 1941-42, Corpus Christi, Tex., 1942-43, Brawley, Cal., 1943-44, Woodbridge, Va., 1958-59, Tustin, Cal., 1963-64, Temple City, Cal., 1968-69; lectr. Cal. State U., Long Beach, 1967-70; library cons. Mook & Blanchard, La Puente, Cal., 1971—. Mem. Cal., Orange County sch. library assns., Orange County Sch. Librarians (pres. 1968), Young Adult Reviewers, Theta Alpha Phi, Alpha Gamma Delta. Democrat. Editor: Jay Alden Prodns., 1972—. Contbr. book reviews to profl. jours. Home: 13061 Wreath St Tustin CA 92680 Office: 546 Hofgaarden St La Puente CA 91744

PEGG, ELIZABETH MARGARET (MRS. ALAN FRANCIS PEGG), harness racing judge; b. Oak Park, Ill., Oct. 13, 1948; d. Delbert Kemrie and Margaret Della (Schlotthauer) Dunlop; B.S. in Journalism, Northwestern U., 1970; m. Alan Francis Pegg, Mar. 18, 1972. Reporter, photographer Lerner Newspapers, Chgo., 1964-71; adminstrv. asst. Ill. Racing Bd., Chgo., 1971-73; racing judge East Moline Downs, Ill., 1973—. Asst. state steward Ill. Racing Bd., Chgo., 1973—. Mem. Women in Communications (Chgo. publicity chmn. 1972), U.S. Trotting Assn., Alpha Gamma Delta. Lutheran. Contbg. editor: Where the Fun Is USA, 1969. Home: 3638 7 1/2 St East Moline IL 61244

PEGRAM, ANNE (MRS. FRED PEGRAM), ceramist; b. Lenoir, N.C.; d. William Julius and Harriet (Garrision) Dula; student Davenport Coll., Lenoir, N.C., 1934-36, Miss Hardbargers Sch., Raleigh, N.C., 1936-38. Vice pres. Pegram's of Lenoir, N.C., 1948—; pres. Anne's Ceramics & Crafts, 1965—; exhibits Caldwell County Hist. Soc. Arts and Craft Show, Lenoir, yearly, 1960—, Charlotte (N.C.) Festival in the Park, 1964, Blowing Rock (N.C.) Crafts, 1967; permanent exhibit at Vance Place Mus., Asheville, N.C.; teaching cons. for Lenoir Recreation Commn., 1966. Mem. N.C. Room com. Richmond Confederate Mus., 1967. Mem. D.A.R. (registrar 1963-64, chpt. organizing regent 1969), U.D.C. (past pres.), Lenoir Little Theatre. Democrat. Methodist. Clubs: Numismatic, Lenoir Country; Lenoir Womans, Cedar Rock Country. Home: 412 Kentwood Lenoir NC 28645

PEINEMANN, EDITH, violinist; b. Mainz, Germany, Mar. 3, 1940; d. Robert and Hildegard (Rohde) Peinemann; pvt. student of father, also Max Rostal; student Guildhall Sch. Music, London. First prize. debut Internat. Concours, Munich, Germany, 1956; soloist Berlin, Czech, London philharmonic archs., also others; U.S. debut, 1962; tours with leading orchs. U.S., 1962—. Recipient Plaquette Jsaye, Liege, 1961. Home: 54 Hegibachstrasse Zurich Switzerland Office: care Columbia Artists Mgmt, 165 W 57th St New York City NY 10019

PEINS, MARYANN, educator, speech pathologist; b. South Amboy, N.J.; d. Rudolph Manning and Marie (Hanke) Peins; B.A., Montclair State Coll., 1947; M.A., U. Denver, 1948; M.A., N.Y. U., 1960; Ph.D., Pa. State U., 1958. Asst. prof. speech and coll. counselor, Office of Counseling Services N.Y. U., Washington Sq. Coll., 1948-58; asso. prof. speech and dir. Speech and Hearing Center, So. Conn. State Coll., New Haven, 1958-61; prof. speech pathology Douglass Coll., Rutgers U., 1961—; dir. speech and hearing clinic, Middlesex Rehab. Hosp., North Brunswick, N.J., 1961—; speech cons. Speech and Hearing Clinic at Roosevelt Hosp., Menlo Park, N.J., 1964—; adj. prof. psychiatry N.J. Coll. Medicine and Dentistry, 1974—. Mem. Am., N.J. (pres.) speech and hearing assns., Council Exceptional Children, Speech Assn. Eastern States, Phi Kappa Phi, Kappa Delta Pi. Contbr. articles in field to profl. jours. Home: 5 Christie St Edison NJ 08817 Office: 135 George St New Brunswick NJ 08901

PEIRSOL, BETTY LOUISE (MRS. JAY BERNARD HOFFMAN), physician; b. Rochester, Pa., June 2, 1928; d. Dilworth Roy and Emma Hazel (Amsler) Peirsol; B.S., Geneva Coll., 1949; M.D., U. Pitts., 1955; m. Jay Bernard Hoffman, Apr. 20, 1963; children—David, Danny. Intern Columbia Hosp., Pitts., 1955-56; practice gen. medicine, Turtle Creek, Pa., 1956-62; resident surgery McKeesport (Pa.) Hosp., 1962-67, now mem. staff, dir. emergency services, 1969—; practice gen. surgery, Murrysville, Pa., 1967—; mem. staffs Magee Women's Hosp., Pitts. Home: Skyline Ranch 3440 School Rd Murrysville PA 15668 Office: 3205 Sardis Rd Murrysville PA 15668

PELL, KATHERINE (KAY) DUNWOODY (MRS. KALMAN LOUIS PELL), state ofcl.; b. Lafayette, Ind., Apr. 15, 1914; d. Benjamin F. and Della (Siefers) Dunwoody; B.S. with distinction, Purdue U., 1936; M.S., Wellesley Coll., 1938; postgrad. in law and polit. sci., U. Ida.; m. Kalman Louis Pell, Sept. 5, 1940; children—Larry, John. Dir. community recreation, Moorestown, N.J., 1938-40, Reading, Pa., 1940-42, U.S.O. (YWCA), Washington, 1942-44, community recreation, Moscow, Ida., 1951-53; county assessor, Moscow, Ida., 1957-61; registered investment rep., Lewiston, Ida., 1961-67; exec. dir. Community Action Agy., Inc., 1967-71; dir. Ida. Dept. Spl. Services, 1971—. Research asst. Bur. Pub. Affairs Research U. Ida., Moscow, 1962-66; mem. adv. com. Ida. Council on Aging, 1969-71. State committeewoman Democratic party, Latah County, Ida., 1953-57, 1961-66; state chmn. Operation Support, Pres. Johnson and Kennedy's Programs, 1961-66, Ida. del. Dem. Nat. Conv., 1964. Mem. Am. Assn. U. Women, Ida. Community Action Agy. Dirs. Assn. (state pres. 1968-70), League Women Voters, Sigma Xi. Democrat. Methodist. Author: (with William O. Lewis) Handbook for Elected Officials in Idaho, 1963, Salaries and Fringe Benefits in Idaho Municipalities, 1964; (with H. Sydney Duncombe) Idaho Municipal Salaries, 1966, Handbook for Idaho County Officials, 1966. Home: 1429 Euclid Av Boise ID 83706 Office: Idaho Dept Special Services Statehouse Boise ID 83707

PELL, SUSAN MYRA PATTERSON (MRS. JOHN THOMAS PELL), speech and hearing therapist; b. Wheeling, W.Va., July 19, 1943; d. Ralph Emerson and Dorothy May (Dueker) Patterson; B.S., W. Va. U., 1964, M.A., 1970; postgrad. U. Md., 1964-65; m. John Thomas Pell, May 30, 1964; 1 son, John Patrick. Lang. specialist, coordinator speech and hearing program Head Start, Howard County, Md., 1965-66; speech and hearing therapist for orthopedically handicapped Pitts. Pub. Schs., 1966-67; speech therapist Easter Seal Program and pub. sch. system, Marion County, W.Va., 1967-68; speech and hearing therapist Prince Georges County (Md.) Pub. Schs., 1970—, tchr. deaf pre-sch. children, 1970-71, now therapist several schs. in system. Bd. dirs. Marion Assn. for the Retarded, 1967-68. Mem. Nat., Prince George's edn. assns., Alpha Sigma Eta, Pi Beta Phi. Presbyn. Home: 7616 Den Meade Av Oxon Hill MD 20022

PELLE, MILLICENT BRASS, ins. co. exec., lawyer; b. N.Y.C., Nov. 14, 1924; d. Louis M. and Anne (Folb) Brass; A.A., Green Mountain Jr. Coll., 1942; LL.B., Bklyn. Law Sch., 1947; m. C. Dana Bossart; children by previous marriage—Donna Susan, Anthony Harris. Admitted to N.Y. bar, 1948, Fla. bar, 1952, U.S. Supreme Ct. bar, 1958; mgr. dist. atty. office Kings County, N.Y., Bklyn., 1947-50; dir. Womens div. Miami (Fla.) Jewish Fedn., 1950-54; asst. dir. Nat. Conf. Christians and Jews, Miami, 1954-58; individual practice law, Miami, 1958-61; mem. firm Orr, Weiss & Simon, Miami; v.p., counsel and mgr. Am. Title Ins. Co., Miami, 1961—. Mem. Fla., Dade County Bar assns. Home: 19601 NW 4th Av Miami FL 33169 Office: 150 SE 3rd Av Miami FL 33131

PELLETIER, EDITH J. TERCASIO (MRS. GEORGE PELLETIER), business exec.; b. N.Y.C.; d. John and Rose (Graziosa) Tercasio; grad. high sch.; m. George Pelletier, Apr. 27, 1927; 1 dau., Anne (Mrs. Joseph De Cristofaro). Rep., Elizabeth Arden, 1930-32; sales rep. Reefer & Galler, 1932-45; established (with husband) Columbia Loose Leaf Corp., N.Y.C., 1945, exec. sec., treas., 1945—. Mem. Arcana, St. Johns U. Ladies Aux. Home: 198-06 Romeo Ct Holliswood New York City NY 11423 Office: 50-02 5th St Long Island City NY 11101

PELLETTIER, IDA CAROLYN (MRS. JOHN RITCHIE PELLETTIER), physician; b. St. Catharines, Ont., Can., July 19, 1944; d. Harold W.M. and Ida Alice (Empringham) Smith; M.D., Queen's U., 1969; m. John Ritchie Pellettier, Aug. 17, 1968; 1 son, Malcolm Brock Ritchie. Intern Toronto (Ont., Can.) Western Hosp., 1969-70; staff U. Guelph (Ont.) Health Service, 1970—, asst. dir., 1974—; family practice medicine, Guelph, 1973—. Dir. Biggar's Frosted Foods, Vineland, Ont. Bd. dirs. Planned Parenthood Guelph Birth Control Clinic, 1973—, v.p., 1972—. Mem. Can. Med. Assn., Family Planning Fedn. Can. Home: 125 Stuart St Guelph ON N1E 4S7 Canada Office: 2 Quebec St Guelph ON N1H 2T3 Canada

PELLOW, RITA BOLL, clin. psychologist; b. Pitts., Nov. 15, 1925; d. Raymond A. and Stella (Henson) Boll; B.S. in Psychology, U. Pitts., 1964, M.S., 1966, Ph.D., 1970; m. James A. Pellow, Jan. 20, 1948; children—James A. III, Michael, David, Lisa. With Clin. Psychology Center, U. Pitts., 1966-67; intern in psychology Pitts. Child Guidance Center, 1967-68; staff psychologist, 1968-69; staff psychologist Allegheny County Intermediate Unit, Pitts., 1970—. Mem. Am., Pa., Pitts. psychol. assns., Phi Beta Kappa, Sigma Xi. Home: 105 Oak Park Pl Pittsburgh PA 15243

PELLOWSKI, ANNE, librarian; b. Pine Creek, Wis., June 28, 1933; d. Alexander P. and Anna (Dorava) Pellowski; B.A., Coll. St. Teresa, 1955; M.S., Columbia, 1959. Childrens librarian, storytelling and group work specialist N.Y. Pub. Library, N.Y.C., 1957-66; dir. information Center on Childrens Cultures, N.Y.C., 1967—. Cons. numerous internat. agys. Fulbright fellow, 1955-56. Mem. A.L.A. (mem. council 1969-72), Soc. Internat. Devel. Roman Catholic. Author: The World of Childrens Literature, 1968; numerous articles in profl. jours. Mem. internat. jury Hans Christian Andersen award, 1969-70. Office: 331 E 38th St New York City NY 10016

PELOQUIN, PHYLLIS C. COOK (MRS. J. CAMILLE PELOQUIN), state ofcl.; b. Woonsocket, R.I., May 6, 1928; d. Reuben Ballou and Alice (Carr) Cook; student R.I. Coll., 1958, Cath.

Tchrs. Coll., 1960-64, U. R.I., 1960-68; m. J. Camille Peloquin, Feb. 5, 1949; children—J. Camille, Linda (Mrs. Robert Clayton), Ronald, Theodore A. Spinner, Blackstone Cotton Mill (Mass.), 1942-46; stitcher Finkelstein's, Woonsocket, 1946-50; tchr. Holy Family Sch., Woonsocket, 1958-67, Grove St. Sch., Woonsocket, 1967; asst. curator archives R.I. State Archives, Providence, 1967—. Active worker local charitable orgns. Sec. Lincoln Dem. Town Com., 1964-73; pres. Lincoln Dem. Women's Club, 1960-74; sec. Manville Dem. Dist. Com., 1966-74; women's state coordinator campaign for Gov. Nieth, 1968. Rebekah. Home: 16 Jane St Providence RI 02904 Office: Room 314 State House Smith St Providence RI 02903

PELSWICK, ROSE, writer, artist. Motion picture reviewer and interviewer N.Y. Jour.-Am., 1937-66; author of short stories, articles and radio scripts; radio and TV appearances. Mem. N.Y. Film Critics (co-founder), Am. Newspaper Guild. Clubs: Nat. Arts, Overseas Press. Home: 67 Park Av New York City NY 10016

PELUSO, PAULINE SMITH (MRS. WALTER A. PELUSO), modeling agy. exec.; b. Amarillo, Tex., Mar. 22, 1933; d. Jack Lane and Eurapha (Williams) Smith; student Amarillo Bus. Coll., 1944, Amarillo Jr. Coll., 1951-52, Los Angeles City Coll., 1953; m. Walter A. Peluso, May 31, 1946; children—Andrew, Joy (Mrs. Peter Mader), Cynthia. With publicity dept. Columbia Studios, Hollywood, Cal., 1965; columnist Critique, Sherman Oaks, Cal., 1967-73, Valley Publs., Encino, Cal., 1969-70; agt. Variety Artist Agy., Hollywood, 1970-71; talent agt. 20th Century Artists, North Hollywood, 1972-73; talent agt. Dorothy Shreve Agy., Sherman Oaks, 1968-72; dir. Hugh Hefner's Playboy Model Agy., Los Angeles, 1973—, asst. sec., mem. bd. dirs., 1973—. Chmn. Heart Fund Drive, Granada Hills, Cal., 1972. Mem. Am. Fedn. TV and Radio Artists, Screen Actors Guild. Home: 10435 Haskell St Granada Hills CA 91345 Office: 8560 Sunset Blvd Los Angeles CA 90069

PELYCH, THELMA ALBERTA MCCARTHY (MRS. JOSEPH M. PELYCH), city ofcl.; b. Hornell, N.Y., Apr. 13, 1926; d. Gerald Francis and Thelma E. (Thomas) McCarthy; grad. high sch.; m. Joseph M. Pelych, Nov. 20, 1948; children—Kathleen, Michael, Patricia, Joseph. Clk., Erie R.R., Hornell, N.Y., 1944-49, Erie Lackawanna Ry. Co., Hornell, 1957-66; chamberlain City of Hornell 1967—. Mem. city and county Democratic Coms., 1960-71. Mem. N.Y. State Soc. Municipal Finance Officers (dir.), Hornell Bus. and Profl. Women's Club (2d v.p. 1971—), Ladies of Columbus. Home: 27 Glen Av Hornell NY 14843 Office: 108 Broadway Hornell NY 14843

PENALBA, ALICIA, sculptor; b. San Pedro, Buenos Aires, Argentina, Aug. 9, 1918; d. Santiago Perez and Maria de los Remedios Penalba; diplomada de Dibujo y Pintura, Escuela Superior de Bellas Artes, Buenos Aires, 1946; lre medaille etrangere de Gravure, Ecole Superieure des Beaux Arts de Paris, 1949; student Academie de la Grande-Chaumiere, 1949-51; m. Amadeo Binci, June 25, 1939 (div.). One man exhbns. include: Galerie du Dragon Paris, 1957, Mus. Haus Lange, Krefeld, 1959, Galerie Claude Bernard, Paris, France, 1960, Otto Gerson Gallery, N.Y.C., 1960, Galerie Charles Lienhard, Zurich, Switzerland, 1961, Sixth Biennial of Sao Paulo (Brazil), 1961, Museu de Arte Moderna, Rio de Janeiro, 1962, Devorah Sherman Gallery, Chgo., 1962, Rijks museum Kroller-Muller Otterlo and Stedelijk Van Abbemuseum Eindhoven (Netherlands), Stadtisches Mus. Leverkusen, Schloss Morsbroich (Germany), 1964, Galerie Creuzevault, Paris, France, 1965, Galeria Bonino, N.Y.C., 1966, The Phillips Collection, 1966, Galerie Pauli, Lausanne, 1967, Musee d'Art Moderne de Paris, 1968, Nuovo Carpine, Roma-Toninelli, Milano, 1969; group exhbns. include: Salon de Mai, Paris, 1952, Salon de la Jeune Sculpture, Paris, 1952-57, Biennale d'Anvers, 1953-55, 61, Realities Nouvelles, 1955-58, 63, Ecole de Paris au Japon, 1956, Musee d'Angers, 1956, Musee de Tours, 1957, Kunstgewerbe-museum, Zurich, 1957, exposition internationale Musee Rodin, Paris, 1957, hommage a Brancusi, Galerie Suzanne de Coninck, Paris, 1957, Musee de Charleroi, 1958, Kunsthalle de Recklinghausen, 1958, Guggenheim Mus., 1958, 62, Fine Arts Gallery, N.Y., 1959, Biennale Triveneta, Padova, 1959, Documenta II, Kassel, 1959, 64, Rotterdam Kunstring, 1960, Currier Gallery Art, Manchester, N.H., 1960, Musee de St. Etienne, 1960, 6th Biennale de Sao Paulo (1st internat. prize sculpture), 1961, Museu de Arte Moderna, Rio de Janeiro, 1961, Festival dei Due Mondi, Spoleto, 1962, Mus. des 20. Jahrhunderts, Vienna, 1962, Meisterwerke der Plastik, Mus. des 20. Jahrhunderts, Vienna, 1964, Pitts. Internat. Exhbn., Carnegie, Inst., 1964, Hessisches Landesmuseum Darmstadt, 1964, Mus. Boymans van Beuningen, Rotterdam, 1965, Biennale Trirenata, Padova, 1965, 8ths Tokyo Biennale, 4th Carrara Biennale, 1965, Phillips Collections, Washington, Karmeliter Kloster, Frankfurt/Main, Sonsbeek Park, Arnheim, DeCordova Mus., Lincoln, Mass., Palazzo Ducale, Venice, 2d Salon des Galeries-Pilotes, Musee Cantonnal des Beaux Arts, Lausanne, Stadtisches Mus., Leverkusen, Landesmus. Kassal, Musee de Grenoble, 1966, Pa. Acad. Fine Art, 1967, Kunstmuseum Basel, 1967, Found. Maeght St. Paul de Vence, 1968, Musee de Lyon, Museo Civico, Bologna, Musee de St. Germain-en-Laye, Hakone Biennale Anvers, 1969; rep. permanent collections Musee Moderne, Paris, Musee de Tourcoing, Musee d'art et d'Industrie, St. Etienne, France, Cleve. Mus. Art, Mus. des 20 Jahrhunderts, Vienna, Isaac Delgado Mus. Art, Middleheim Park, Mus. Art, Carnegie Inst., Pitts., Rijksmuseum Kroller-Muller Otterlo, Stedlijk Van Abbemuseum Eindhoven, Stadtiches Mus. Leverkusen, Museu de Arte Moderna, Rio de Janeiro, Musee municipal d'Art Moderne, Paris, Albright-Knox Art Gallery, Buffalo, St. Gall St., Dallas Mus. Fine Art, Staatsgalerie Stuttgart, Phillips Collection, Washington, Hakone Open Air Mus., others; also pvt. collections. Decorated knight French Order Arts et Lettres. Mem. de la Ligue Francaise contre la vivisection. Address: 24 rue du Rio-de-Sicile Paris 4 France

PENCE, FERN MCCOMB, social worker, state ofcl.; b. Ft. Wayne, Ind., Oct. 27, 1908; d. Hubert James and Addie (Schorr) McComb; A.B., Ind. U., 1930; M.A. (Commonwealth fellow), U. Chgo. Sch. Social Service Adminstrn., 1945; m. Robert G. Pence, Feb. 3, 1933 (div. Dec. 1941). Supr. pub. assistance cons. Ind. Dept. Pub. Welfare, Indpls., 1943-46; dir. social services St. Joseph County Dept. Pub. Welfare, South Bend, 1946-49. Cleve. Rehab. Center, 1952-56; exec. dir. Children's Day Care Assn., Ft. Wayne, 1949-52; dir. welfare Am. Joint Distbn. Com., Casablanca, Morocco, 1956-58; supr. pub. assistance field staff Fla. Dept. Pub. Welfare, Jacksonville, 1959-61, program dir. to organize and dir. U.S. Cuban Refugee Assistance Program in Dade County (agt. for fed. govt.), Miami, 1961-62, welfare program supr. for pub. assistance field service and statewide Cuban refugee assistance program, Jacksonville, 1962-70, supr. sub-profls. and vols. Cuban refugee service program and repatriated Am. program, 1970-73; asst. chief, Bur. Adult Services Fla. Div. Family Services, 1974—. Mem. state adv. com. facilities and workshops Fla. Dept. Edn.; pub. assistance cons. Greater Boston Health and Welfare Survey, 1948-49; cons., condr. insts. Child Welfare League Am., 1949-55; speaker nat. program Nat. Soc. for Crippled Children, Nat. Conf. Social Work, 1951—; condr. grad. insts. pub. welfare adminstr. Western Res. U. Sch. Applied Social Scis., Cleve., 1949-50, faculty med. social work dept., 1955; sec.-treas. Fla. Council on Aging, 1963-64, sec., 1967—, citation for outstanding service, 1972, adv. com. Fla. In-Step Project; del. White House Conf. on Aging, 1972. Recipient Scroll of Friendship, City of Miami, 1962. Mem. Nat. Assn. Social Workers, Acad. Certified Social Workers, Internat. Conf. Social Work, Nat. Conf. Social Work, Theta Sigma Phi, Phi Mu. Democrat. Episcopalian. Home: 479 Tabor Dr Jacksonville FL 32216 Office: PO Box 2050 Jacksonville FL 32203

PENDERGAST, KATHLEEN FLORENCE KELLEHER (MRS. WILLIAM EDWARD PENDERGAST), educator; b. Ellensburg, Wash., Jan. 8, 1919; d. Cornelius Joseph and Margaret Marie (McLaughlin) Kelleher; B.A., Central Wash. State Coll., 1941; M.A., U. Wash., 1952; m. William Edward Pendergast, Aug. 14, 1943 (dec. Nov. 1967). Tchr., speech pathologist Port Townsend (Wash.) Pub. Schs., 1940-42; speech pathologist Seattle Pub. Schs., 1942-61, supr. lang., speech and hearing, 1961—; instr. U. Wash., Seattle, 1961. Cons. to research com. Cal. Speech and Hearing Assn., 1971-72. Fellow Am. Speech and Hearing Assn.; mem. Western Speech Assn. (pres. 1957), Wash. Speech and Hearing Assn. (pres. 1965), Council Exceptional Children, Zeta Phi Eta, Kappa Delta Pi. Author: (with S. Dickey, J. Selmar, A. Soder) Photo Articulation Test, 1965; Building Good Speech, 1971. Cons. editor: Lang., Speech, and Hearing Services in Schs., 1971—, Jour. Speech and Hearing Disorders, 1974—. Home: 3816 E Madison St Seattle WA 98112

PENDERGRASS, MARGARET ELIZABETH, librarian; b. Springfield, Ill., Aug. 9, 1912; d. Ulysses Grant and Susie Katherine (Huston) Pendergrass; B.S. in L.S., Hampton Inst., 1934. Br. librarian Greenville (S.C.) Pub. Library, 1934-41; army librarian, Ft. Custer, 1941-43, Camp Ellis, Ill., 1943-45, Camp Miles Standish, Mass., 1945-46, Camp Kilmer, N.J., 1946-49; cataloger juvenile books Ill. State Library, Springfield, 1950-57, head juvenile dept., 1957-70, asst. reference librarian, head children's Book Reviewing Center, 1970—. Bd. dirs. Springfield Urban League, also mem. housing com., personnel com.; bd. dirs. Springfield chpt. N.A.A.C.P. Mem. World Federalists (dir. Springfield chpt. 1962—), A.L.A., Ill. Library Assn. (pres. children's sect. 1957-58) James Weldon Johnson Study Guild (pres., sec.), Cath. Library Assn., Springfield Library Club, Menelik Assembly, Order Golden Circle. Baptist (chmn. bldg. fund, pres. Missionary Soc). Contbr. articles to profl. jours. Home: 2001 S 11th St Springfield IL 62703 Office: Ill State Library Centennial Bldg Springfield IL 62756

PENDLETON, LAURIE CRAGG (MRS. C. BRIAN PENDLETON), marketing exec.; b. Washington, May 28, 1945; d. Richard Edwards and Dorothy (Shawhan) Cragg; B.A., Northwestern U., 1967; m. C. Brian Pendleton, May 20, 1972. Psychol. research analyst Allstate Ins. Co., Northbrook, Ill., 1968-70; project supr. Marsteller, Inc., Chgo., 1970-74; marketing research mgr. corporate planning dept. Internat. Harvester, Chgo., 1974—. Guest lectr. market research various univs. and assns. Mem. jr. bd. Lawrence Hall, sch. for boys., Chgo., 1973—. Mem. Am. Marketing Assn. (chmn. career conf. 1975—), Indsl. Psychologists Assn. Chgo., Jr. League Chgo., Nat. Orgn. Women, Alliance Francaise, Chgo. Council on Fgn. Relations. Alpha Delta Pi. Club: Woman's Athletic. Home: 1300 Ritchie Ct Chicago IL 60610 Office: Internat Harvester 401 N Michigan Av Chicago IL 60611

PENDLETON, PATRICIA RUTH (MRS. BENJAMIN FRANKLIN PENDLETON), health service adminstr.; b. Berea, Ky.; d. Paul Donald and Ruth Hilda (Coyle) Muncy; B.S., U. Louisville, 1957, M.S. in Social Work, 1959; postgrad Columbia, 1962-63; m. Benjamin Franklin Pendleton, May 17, 1947. Psychiat. social worker Bingham Child Guidance Clinic, Louisville, 1959-63, chief social worker, 1967-69; adminstr. adolescent unit Central State Hosp., Louisville, 1963-64; chief social worker Region Eight Waverly Community Mental Health Center, Louisville, 1969-72; dir. River Region South Jefferson Mental Health Center, Louisville, 1973—. Nat. Inst. Mental Health grantee, 1958, 59, 63. Mem. Nat. Assn. Social Work, Acad. Certified Social Workers, Ky. Welfare Assn., Kappa Delta Pi, Phi Kappa Phi. Home: 9818 Meadow Valee Dr Louisvelle KY 40222 Office: 1901 Outer Loop Louisville KY 40219

PENDLEY, EVELYN HOGE (MRS. WALTER O. PENDLEY), author; b. Rome, Ga., June 24, 1918; d. Edward Herman and Caroline (Bostick) Hoge; A.B., Berry Coll., 1938; M.A., Emory U., 1941; spl. study Shorter Coll., Converse Coll., Winthrop Coll.; m. Walter O. Pendley, Nov. 14, 1943; children—Joyce Bernadette, Lee Hoge. Tchr. pub. high sch., Ga., 1939-41, 45; sec. to treas. Emory U., 1942-43; instr. English, Memphis State Coll., 1949-50; instr. Berry Coll., Mt. Berry, Ga., 1959-62, asst. prof. English, asst. coll. supr. student tchrs., 1962—; med. sec. to Dr. Pendley, 1954—. Pres. Open Door Home Bd., Rome, Ga., 1953-55. Mem. Rome Symphony Orch., Berry Alumni Council, Am. Assn. U. Women, Women's Auxiliary to Med. Assn. Ga., Ga. Writers Assn., Am. Poetry League, South Atlantic Modern Lang. Assn., Nat. Council Tchrs. English, Am. Assn. U. Profs., Soc. Study So. Lit. Presbyn. Club: Three Rivers Garden. Author: Sketches of the Life of Martha Berry, 1945; Mountain Top Moments, 1953; Growing Pleasures, 1956; Angel Wings, 1957; A Golden Chain (poems), 1962; Sixty Years of Education for Service, 1964; A Lady I Loved, 1966; Open Before Christmas, 1967; (poetry) As One. Home: Sequoia Acres Rome GA 30161 Office: Berry Coll Mount Berry GA 30149

PENFIELD, HANNAH WILLIAMS GRIFFITH, personnel exec.; b. Stow Creek, N.J., Aug. 16, 1918; d. Charles Frederick and Hannah Lillian (Griffith) Williams; student Cumberland County Coll., 1971; m. William G. Penfield, Sept. 2, 1936; 1 son, Glen A. With R.J. Ritter Co., food processor, Bridgeton, N.J., 1943—, personnel mgr., 1972—. Active local A.R.C., P.T.A. Mem. election bd. Cumberland County Democratic Com. Mem. Bowling Proprietor's Assn., Women's Traveling League (pres., rep. Bowl O Drome). Episcopalian (treas. women's aux.). Home: 30 Burt St Bridgeton NJ 08302 Office: P.J. Ritter Co S Laurel St Bridgeton NJ 08302

PENFIELD, JANET HARBISON (MRS. THORNTON B. PENFIELD), ednl. adminstr.; b. East Orange, N.J., Apr. 19, 1916; d. Harold Richardson and Evangeline Frances (Dalrymple) German; A.B., Smith Coll., 1937; postgrad. Princeton Theol. Sem., 1958; m. E. Harris Harbison, Sept. 25, 1937 (dec. 1964); children—John Harris, Helen (Mrs. Ervand Abrahamian), Margaret; m. 2d, Thornton B. Penfield, Jan. 3, 1970. Asso. editor Presbyn. Life mag., Phila., 1959-72; adminstrv. asst. for devel. Princeton (N.J.) Theol. Sem., 1972—. Mem. nat. bd. and world council YWCA, 1948-60, mem. exec. com. nat. bd., 1955-60. Mem. Women in Communications. Presbyn. (delegation Consultation on Ch. Union 1962—). Adv. bd. Theology Today, 1974—. Contbr. to various publs. Home: 30 Galbreath Dr E Princeton NJ 08540

PENN, FLOY LIVINGSTON (MRS. C. J. PENN), educator, cons.; b. nr. Six Mile Run, Pa.; d. Charles A. and Sarah (Whited) Livingston; B.S., Cal. State Coll., 1933; M.Ed., U. Pitts., 1938, Ph.D., 1953; m. Calvin J. Penn, Mar. 14, 1942 (dec. 1968). Tchr. pub. sch., Allegheny County, Pa., 1922-29; classroom tchr. Mt. Lebanon, Pa., 1929-38, remedial tchr., 1938-48, pub. sch. psychologist, 1948-54, dir. instrn., 1954-70; ednl. cons. Nat. Drug Abuse TV Project, 1970-71; dir. spl. services Washington County Bd. Edn., 1971-72, coordinator spl. services, Intermediate Unit I, 1972; exec. dir. Wesley Inst., 1972—. Curriculum com. Ednl. TV Sta. WQED, Pitts., 1957-70, chmn., 1968-70. Lectr. U. Pitts., summer 1963. Pres. Western Pa. chpt. Council Exceptional Children, 1949-57; scholarship com. United Mental Health Services, Pitts., 1960-68; edn. com. Sch. of Nursing, South Side Hosp., Pitts., 1957-70. Trustee South Hills Child Guidance Center, 1957-68; bd. dirs. Wesley Inst., pres., 1972; bd. dirs. Meth. Home, Mt. Lebanon, 1974—. Mem. Am. Assn. U. Women, Assn. for Supervision and Curriculum Devel., Nat. Soc. for Study Edn., N.E.A., Pa. State Ednl. Assn., Am., Pa., Pitts. psychol. assns., Adminstrv. Women in Edn. (pres. Pitts. 1959-61), Pitts. Doctoral Assn. of Educators (treas. 1966—), Cum Laude Soc., Pa. P.T.A., Delta Kappa Gamma (sec. 1956-58), Pi Lambda Theta. Methodist (adminstrv. council). Club: South Hills College, Pittsburgh College. Editor Scribe, 1964-66. Home: 2675 Strathmore Lane Bethel Park PA 15102

PENNER, GLORIA ELAINE (MRS. ROBERT PENNER), broadcasting exec.; b. N.Y.C., Apr. 17, 1931; d. Jack and Ethel (Gold) Stern; B.A., Bklyn. Coll., 1952; postgrad N.Y. U., 1952; M.A., Syracuse U., 1955; m. Robert Penner, Dec. 26, 1954; children—Stevenson R., Bradley A. Prodn. asst. NBC-TV network news, Today Show, Washington, 1959-61; commentator radio sta. KULA, Honolulu, 1961; chief speechwriter Dillingham for U.S. Senate, Honolulu, 1962; publicist Hawaii Ho. of Reps., Honolulu, 1963-64; dir. community relations KPBS-TV, San Diego, 1969-71, dir. pub. affairs, 1972, dir. TV program devel., 1973—. Bd. dirs. Alvarado Hosp., San Diego, 1973—. Recipient Corp. for Pub. Broadcasting Spl. Recognition Devel. award, 1972. Mem. Nat. Acad. TV Arts and Scis. (gov. 1973), Women in Communications (Matrix award 1973), Nat. Assn. Ednl. Broadcasters. Club: San Diego Press. Home: 4546 Cresta Verde Lane Bonita CA 92002 Office: KPBS-TV San Diego State University San Diego CA 92115

PENNEY, ANNETTE LORENA CULLER, journalist, pub. relations specialist; b. Cordele, Ga., July 1, 1916; d. Jake Phillip and Maude (Burke) Culler; grad. bus. adminstrn. South Ga. Coll., 1941, George Washington U., Am. U.; m. Robert Adam Penney, Aug. 7, 1963. Asst. mgr. Waycross (Ga.) div. Diana Stores Corp., 1940-42; with pub. relations dept. Hecht Co., Washington, 1945-46; newspaper corr. Fairchild Publs., Washington staff, 1946-61; free-lance writer and pub. relations specialist, 1961—; spl. press aide to dir. Pub. Housing Adminstrn., 1964-66; dir. pub. affairs and press information, spl. asst. to pres. Steadman Security Corp., Washington, 1967-70; v.p. Paul Glass Pub. Relations Co., San Francisco, 1972—. Tchr. home fashions merchandising Am. U. Author: Dirksen: The Golden Voice of The Senate, 1968; contbr. column This Generation for Chgo. Tribune and N.Y. News Syndicate, 1966-67, San Francisco Chronicle, San Mateo Times, 1971-72. Mem. Home Fashions League (pres. 1951-52, v.p. 1961-62). Internat. Platform Assn., Va. Press Women, Salvation Army Womens Aux. Clubs: Women's National Press (v.p. 1957-58), Am. Newspaper Women's (v.p. 1970-71). Home: PO Box 154 Upperville VA 22176

PENNIMAN, GWENDOLEN BROOKS, writer, actress, artist; b. Lincoln Neb.; d. Harrington and Florence (Brooks) Emerson; A.B. in Speech, San Jose State Coll., 1944, A.B. in English, 1951; postgrad. Stanford, 1947; L.H.D., Free U. Asia, 1968; m. Arthur Webb Penniman, Mar. 8, 1921; children—Beatrice Brooks Frazier (div.), Arthur Brooks. Played leads in Western motion pictures, Okla. and Cal. for Reliance, Lubin and Universal cos.; leads in various touring and stock plays; appeared on Broadway with Douglas Fairbanks, Warner Oland and others; chmn. founder Cal. Olympiad of Arts, 1955; inaugurated Children's Fgn. Lang. program, 1958; directed, wrote, taught dramatics in San Diego, San Francisco, San Jose, Cal., 1921-41; dir. Lyrie Players In a Mandarin's Garden, at Villa Montalva Renaissance Greek Theatre, Saratoga, for 2d Olympiad of Arts, 1960, The Boy Shakespeare, 1964, Phaedre, 1968-69, The Secret Bread, 1971; exhibited sculptures and paintings at Los Gatos Art Assn. Juried shows, Montalvo Gallery, others; columnist The Saratoga (Cal.) News, 1956—. Pres. Quadrennial Contests in the Arts, 1963-68. Recipient Montalvo Lit. awards, poetry prizes, 1938, 39, 52, 56, 62; 1st prize for traditional sculpture Los Gatos Art Assn., 1954. Pres. Macapagal, gold medal awards and Carta award also Pres. Marcos gold laurel crown and gold medal United Poets Laureate Internat., 1965. Mem. Nat. League Am. Pen Women, Am. Assn. U. Women (chmn. lang. courses, 1958, 1961-62, 65-67), Internat. Platform Assn., Edwin Markahm Poetry Soc. (pres. 1931-34), Casual Arts Club (pres. founder 1955), Saratoga Contemporary Artists, Montalvo Assn. Christian Scientist. Club: Stanford. Author: (poetry) The Eagle-Mexico and California, Poems of Japan, 1964; (prose) Goona Goona; also articles and stories in newspapers and mags., poems in anthologies A Years Harvest, 1931; The Laureate's Wreath, 1934; Contemporary American Women Poets, 1936. Contbg. The Poet Bland and Sixteen Specimen Poems, 1943. Editor, contbr.: The Laureate's Wreath, 1934; Thirty-Three Love Sonnets, 1950; A Day at Montalvo, Anthology, 1964; The Winged Pegasus, 1965; Apollo 11 Anthology, 1971; Apples from Hesperides, 1971; Hail, Rising Sun, 1972. Home: 22100 Mount Eden Rd Saratoga CA 95070

PENNINGTON, LEA GIBLYN, psychologist; b. Freeport, N.Y., June 9, 1935; d. Leo Frederick and Edna (Decker) Giblyn; B.A. in Sociology, Hofstra U., 1957; M.S. in Sch. Psychology, U. Wis., 1960; m. Leonard W. Pennington, Jr., Dec. 26, 1969. Playground asst. Freeport Pub. Schs., 1951-52, playground instr., 1953-57, tchr., 1957-59, psychologist, 1960-61; tchr. Madison (Wis.) Pub. Schs., 1961-63, psychologist, 1963—, psychologist spl. lang. clinic, summers 1967-72. Mem. Nat., Wis. edn. assns., Nat., Wis. assns. sch. psychologists, Madison Tchrs. Assn., Alpha Delta Kappa, Pi Delta Epsilon, Phi Epsilon. Home: 6309 Landfall Dr Madison WI 53705 Office: 545 W Dayton St Madison WI 53703

PENNINGTON, LILLIAN BOYER (MRS. R. CORBIN PENNINGTON), author; b. Harrisburg, Pa., Apr. 2, 1904; d. Lynn Hutchinson and Eva Jane (Liggett) Boyer; State Normal Sch. diploma Shippensburg State Coll., 1926; postgrad Manhattan Sch. Music, 1937-39, Nat. Acad. Sch. Fine Art, 1963-66; m. R. Corbin Pennington, Dec. 28, 1926; 1 son, Corbin. Tchr., Ickesburg, Pa., 1922, Windsor, Colo., 1926, Closter, N.J., 1927-33, 35-37, Fieldston Sch., N.Y.C., 1943, Riverdale Country Sch., N.Y.C., 1947-58, 60-63; author, 1930—. Mem. Nat. League Am. Pen Women (art chmn. Pikes Peak br. 1969-70), Am. Watercolor Soc. (asso.), Photog. Soc. Am. (recipient photography awards 1971—), Altrusa Club, Columbine Camera Club, Pikes Peak Camera Club, Pueblo, Colorado Springs (sec. 1970-72) art guilds, Palmer Lake, Pikes Peak (v.p. 1969-70) artist assns., Miniature Art Soc. Author: Choo Choo Train, 1958: Treasure House of Bedtime Stories, 1963: Reading for Beginners, 1963: SNAFU the Littlest Clown, 1972: Contbr. articles to profl. sch. pubs. Home and studio: 900 Saturn Dr Colorado Springs CO 80906

PENTA, IRENE PLATT (MRS. WALTER E. PENTA), nurse, club woman; b. Concord, N.H., Jan. 2, 1920; d. Frank Bishop and Ida Louisa (Cable) Platt; student Portland Jr. Coll., 1939; R.N., Dr. Drummond's Hosp. Nursing Sch., Portland, Me., 1942; m. Walter E. Penta, Sept. 25, 1943; 1 son, Donald Platt. Nurse, Me. Med. Center, Portland, 1942-43, Mercy Hosp., Portland, 1943, Boston City Hosp., 1943-44, Beth Israel Hosp., Boston, 1944, Mass. Gen. Hosp., Boston, 1944, Deaconess Hosp., Boston, 1943, Meth. Hosp., Dallas, 1944-45, Med. Arts, Dallas, 1944-45, So. Bapt. Hosp., Dallas, 1944-45, Sec., Woman's Auxiliary Me. Med. Assn., Portland, 1955-56, v.p., 1956-57, pres.-elect, 1957-58, pres., 1958-59, bd. dirs., 1955—, chmn.

internat. health-womans aux. 1967—; v.p. Ladies of Kiwanis, Portland, 1958, pres., 1959, bd. dirs., 1957—; active Hosp., Auxiliary Me. Med. Center; mem. organizational com. Tri-State Health Careers Research Group, Portland, 1960-61; rural health chmn. region one, Woman's Auxiliary to A.M.A., 1960-65, Me. internat. health chmn. Mem. Me. Nurses Assn., Dr. Drummonds Hosp. Alumni Assn. (pres. 1964-66), Internat. Platform Assn., Wives Wing of Aerospace Med. Assn., Nat. Soc. Daus. of Founders and Patriots Am., Nat. Soc. Women Descs. of Ancient and Honorable Arty. Co. (v.p. Me. chpt. assts. 1972—). Conglist. (pres. Jr. Guild 1956). Club: Woodfords (Portland). Home: 316 Woodford St Portland ME 04103

PENTLAND, SUE-BYRD (MRS. ROBERT PENTLAND, JR.), ballerina; b. Sioux City, Ia., Mar. 25, 1928; d. Edgar O. and Mabel (French) Hill; student Ark. U., 1943; m. Ernest Edward Roberts, June 10, 1944 (dec. Sept. 1960); 1 son, William-Hill; m. 2d, Robert Pentland, Jr., Jan. 25, 1967. Formerly prima ballerina Miami Ballet; tchr. acad. classical ballet technique St. Stephen's Episcopal Day Sch., Coconut Grove, Fla., 1959-62. Active U.S.O. prin. dancer, soloist The Iham Follies for crippled children, 1953-61. Recipient gold medal U.S.O.; Queen of Hearts award Variety Internat. Club, 1971, Great Gal award, 1972. Mem. U.D.C., Dance Masters Am., Dance Educators Am., Internat. Platform Assn. So. Democrat. Episcopalian. Clubs: Miami Woman's (perpetual mem., chmn. ballet, drama and music div. fine arts dept., 1958-60, 61-62), Hibiscus Garden; University of Miami Woman's. Home: 2800 N Surf Rd Hollywood Beach FL 33020

PENTZ, KLARA N. (MRS. JOHN A. PENTZ), artist; flower arrangement exhibitor; b. Balt., Dec. 8, 1907; d. Frederick and Martha (Geisser) Nordenholz; student McCoy Coll., 1926; m. John A. Pentz, Apr. 11, 1930; 1 dau., Klara Barbara (Mrs. Jacques Donald Bambling). Nat. Council judge amateur flower shows, 1961—. Recipient Lucy Benton Silver Bowl for outstanding arrangement in Md. contest, 1959, 62, 64, 65; nat. award winner Sterling Bowl Rose Arrangment Tournament, 1960, Am. Camellia Soc. nat. flower arrangement contest, 1960, 61, 64; other blue ribbons and awards in club, dist., city and state contests; photos of arrangements pub. in competitive calendars, 1962, 64, 66, 67; best-in-show award for oil painting, state-wide contest, Timonium Fair, Md., 1969. Mem. Acad. Arts Easton (Md.), Tchrs. Assn. Sogetsu Sch. Japanese Flower Arranging, Md. Rose Soc., Ikebana Internat., Star-Spangled Banner Flag House Assn., Rehoboth Art League, Chesapeake Bay Maritime Mus., Hist. Soc. Talbot County. Episcopalian. Clubs: Talbot County Garden, St. Michaels Woman's. Home: The Grove Church Neck St Michaels MD 21663

PEPPARD, JANE COLLINS (MRS. DAVID G. PEPPARD), charitable orgn. exec.; b. Bucyrus, O., June 17, 1924; d. Gilbert Charles and Marie A. (Harrison) Collins; student Ga. State Coll. for Women, 1944-45, Cin. Coll. Commerce, 1946-48; m. David G. Peppard, Dec. 31, 1945; children—Keith, Marsha, Ann, Marianne. Dir., officer John Q. Shunk Assn., Marion, O., 1948—, exec. sec. to philanthropist John Q. Shunk, Bucyrus, 1948-59; exec. dir. United Way of Marion County, Marion, 1967—. Mem. women's bd. Marion Gen. Hosp., Mid-Ohio Health Planning Fedn.; mem. River Valley Bd. Edn., Marion Council Alcohol and Drugs, Marion County Home Health Nursing Service; bd. of bldg. comm. Marion Area Counseling Center. Served with Women's Res., USNR, 1943-45. Recipient Community Services award Marion County AFL-CIO, 1973, Outstanding Citizens award United Way of Marion County, 1974. Club: Altrusa. Home: 1201 Timber Lane Marion OH 43302 Office: 320 W Center St Marion OH 43302

PEPPER, ADELINE ELIZABETH, author, photographer; b. Madison, Wis.; d. John William and Emmeline (Able) Pepper; B.A., U. Wis. Med. writer A.M.A., A.C.S.; asst. advt. mgr. Mead Johnson & Co., Evansville, Ind., publicity dir. Com. on Care of Children in Wartime, Evansville, 1945; radio advt. writer Knox Reeves, Inc., Mpls.; pub. relations Pa. R.R. Centennial, 1946; advt. writer L. W. Frohlich Agy., N.Y.; med. advt. writer and designer E. R. Squibb & Sons, Ciba Pharm.; owner Pep, Inc., advt. service, 1956—. Mem. Authors League Am., Am. Med. Writers Assn., Phi Kappa Phi. Author: Tours of Historic New Jersey (N.J. Tercentary medal 1964), 1965, rev. edit., 1973; N.J. vol. Fodor's Guide to the U.S.A., 1966; The Glass Gaffers of New Jersey and Their Creations (award N.J. Assn. Tchrs. English 1972, award of Merit Am. Assn. State and Local History 1972), 1971. Contbr. articles on travel, history, and decorative arts to mags. and maj. met. newspapers. Address: 430 W 7th St No 2J Plainfield NJ 07060

PEPPER, RUTH MOORMAN MCANULTY (MRS. HENRY MORRIS PEPPER), librarian; b. Marianna, Ark., Apr. 25, 1913; d. Hiram Clark and Gussie Z. (Hobbs) McAnulty; B.A., Bethel Coll., 1934; postgrad. U. Ala., Huntsville, 1967-69, Ala. A. and M. U., 1969-71; m. Henry Morris Pepper, Sept. 5, 1934; children—Beverly Ann (Mrs. Paul B. Brown), John Clark. With Cumberland Presbyn. Denominational Center, Memphis, part-time, 1951-57; library asst., information desk Memphis Pub. Library, 1959; organizer, librarian East Side Cumberland Presbyn. Ch., Memphis, 1952-59; organizer, librarian Scottsboro Cumberland Presbyn. Ch. Library, Scottsboro, Ala., 1961—, Scottsboro Jr. High Sch. Library Media Center, Scottsboro, 1962—; tchr. math. Pisgah (Ala.) High Sch., 1961-62. Pres. Conv. Cumberland Presbyn. Women of Cumberland Presbyn. Ch., 1968. Mem. Ala. Library Assn. (chmn. sch. library div. 1971), Ala. Instrnl. Media Assn. (dir. 1974), Bethel Coll. Alumni Assn. (charter mem., pres. Memphis 1952). Contbr. articles to various publs. Home: 215 S Kyle St Scottsboro AL 35768 Office: 305 S Scott St Scottsboro AL 35768

PEQUIGNOT, MILDRED ANNE, realtor; b. Fort Wayne, Ind., Oct. 13, 1911; d. Henry C. and Anna May (Isenbarger) Pequignot; student Internat. Bus. Coll., 1935; LL.B., LaSalle U., 1957; postgrad. Famous Writers' Sch., 1972, Life Underwriters' Tng. Sch., 1962-63. Legal sec. Fruechtenicht Law Office, 1930-57; self-employed as realtor, insuror, tax cons., Fort Wayne, Ind., 1954—; owner Multiple Listing Assn., Inc., 1962-72. Treas. Fort Wayne and Allen County Humane Soc., 1947-57, pres., 1972—; mem. Humane Commn. operating Humane Shelter, 1960-64; treas. Northeastern Ind. Kennel Club, Inc., 1972-73. Mem. Ft. Wayne Bd. Realtors, Nat. Secs. Assn. (parlimentarian Twasi chpt. 1942-57), Soc. Real Estate Appraisers, Ind. Mut. Ins. Agts. Contbr. column Kennel Rev. Home: 6616 Lower Huntington Rd Fort Wayne IN 46809 Office: 3704 S Calhoun St Fort Wayne IN 46807

PER, CAROLYN ANN FENTIN (MRS. SHELDON DAVID PER), journalist; b. Malden, Mass., Sept. 1, 1949; d. Arthur and Ruth L. (Swirsky) Fentin; B.A., Syracuse U., 1971; m. Sheldon David Per, Aug. 22, 1971. Reporter woman's pages Burlington County Times, Willingboro, N.J., 1972—. Recipient 1st place award in sports writing N.J. Daily Newspaperwomen's Assn., 1972, 1st place award food, fashions etc., 1973, 2d place gen. features, 1973. Mem. Women in Communications, Orgn. for Rehab. Through Tng. Home: 3026 Hallowell Ct Cornwells Heights PA 19020 Office: Burlington County Times Route 130 Willingboro NJ 08046

PERATIS, KATHLEEN MARY, lawyer; b. Long Beach, Cal., July 21, 1944; d. James Theoharris and Mae Maxine (Papadakis) Peratis; A.B. (university scholar) magna cum laude, U. So. Cal., 1966, J.D. (university scholar), 1969; m. Francis E. Jones, Jr. Dec. 12, 1970. Admitted to Cal. bar, 1970; practiced in Los Angeles, 1970-74; asso. firm O'Melveny & Myers, Los Angeles, 1969-73; asso. firm Bodle, Fogel, Julber, Reinhardt, Rothschild, Los Angeles, 1973-74; dir. women's rights project Am. Civil Liberties Union, N.Y.C., 1974—; lectr. equal rights amendment U. Cal., 1971. Incorporator Women's Center Legal Program, Los Angeles, 1970—; mem. Council of Lawyers, Los Angeles, 1969—; mem. City Atty.'s Adv. Commn. Labor Relations, 1973—, chairperson subcom. sex discrimination, 1973; participant Ford Found. Select Conf. Feminist Litigators, N.Y.C., 1973. Officer lawyer com. Democratic primary candidate George Brown for U.S. Senate, 1969-70. Mem. State Bar Cal., Am., Los Angeles County bar assns., Am. Civil Liberties Union (women's right com. 1971—), Nat. Orgn. Women (legal com. 1971—), Phi Beta Kappa, Phi Kappa Phi. Contbr. articles profl. jours. Home: 155 W 68th St New York City NY 10023 Office: 22 E 40th St New York City NY 10016

PERCY, SUSAN FARRAN, editor, state ofcl.; b. Atlanta, Mar. 1, 1944; d. Paul Carrol and Martha (Briggs) Farran; A.B. in Journalism cum laude, U. Ga., 1966; m. George Winchester Percy III, Dec. 21, 1965. Tchr. English New Orleans, 1966-68; women's editor, staff writer West Bank Guide, Gretna, La., 1968-70; free lance writer, 1970-71; news dir. WTNT Radio, Tallahassee, 1971; staff writer Fla. Dept. Commerce, 1971-72, asst. mng. editor, 1972-74, mng. editor, 1974—. Mem. equal employment opportunity com. Fla. Dept. Commerce. Bd. dirs. Ants, Inc., conservation group. Recipient La. Press Assn. awards for best feature story and community service, 1969, citations Jefferson Parish (La.) Community Action Program, 1969, 70. Mem. Women in Communications, Sierra Club (publicity dir. Big Bend group Fla. chpt. 1971-73, dir. 1973—), Phi Beta Kappa, Phi Kappa Phi, Kappa Tau Alpha. Democrat. Home: 1832 Jackson Bluff Rd Tallahasse FL 32364 Office: Collins Bldg Tallahassee FL 32304

PEREIRA, SARAH MARTIN, educator; b. Cleve.; d. Alexander H. and Mary (Brown) Martin; A.B., Ohio State U., 1931; M.A., Western Res. U., 1935; Ph.D., Ohio State U., 1942; m. Charles R. Eason, Sept. 1, 1937 (div. June 1942); m. 2d, Jose Rodriguez Pereira (dec. June 1959); 1 son, Carlos Martin. Instr. Spanish, French Shaw U., Raleigh, N.C., 1931-39, Miner Tchrs. Coll., Washington, 1941-45; part-time asso. prof. French Howard U. Grad. Sch., Washingtin, 1943-45; part-time lectr. Spanish Cleve. Coll., Western Res. U., Cleve., 1946-49; asso. prof. Spanish, French Fenn Coll., Cleve., 1946-52; prof. romance langs., Spanish-French and head dept. W.Va. State Coll., Institute, W.Va., 1953-58; prof. Spanish and French, Tenn. A. and I State U., Nashville, 1958-62; prof. Spanish and Portuguese, D.C. Tchrs. Coll., Washington, 1962—, also chmn. div. fgn. langs., 1971—. Mem. Am. Assn. Tchrs. Spanish, Portuguese, Am. Assn. Tchrs. French, Am. Assn. U. Profs., N.E.A., Am. Assn. Higher Edn., Phi Beta Kappa, Sigma Delta Pi, Kappa Delta Pi, Pi Lambda Beta. Mem. Bahai Faith (mem. aux. bd. Hands of W. Hemisphere 1953-64, nat. spiritual assembly 1958—, continental bd. counsellors N.Am.). Address: DC Tchrs Coll Washington DC 20009

PERELMANN, DORA (DEBORAH), composer, condr., concert pianist; b. St. Petersburg, Russia; d. Savely and Maria (Tiger) Perelmann; studied piano with Felix Blumenfeld, M. Rosenthal; conduting with Max Steinberg, F. Weingartner, E. Von Sauer, Alexander Glazounoff, L. Nacolaieff; grad. top honors, artists' diploma St. Petersburg (Russia) Conservatory Music; student State Acad. Music, (Vienna) honor scholarship in conducting Mozarteum Acad., Salzburg, 1936-37; master piano course with Egon Petri, Berlin; student Juilliard Sch. Music, Curtis Inst. Music, Columbia Tchrs. Coll., N.Y. U. Came to U.S., naturalized, 1933. Conducting debut State Acad. Music, Vienna, 1935; numerous piano recitals, Israel; piano debut Tel Aviv, Israel, also guest condr. and piano soloist with local symphony orch. in all-Beethoven program; concert appearances Europe and Orient as piano soloist, guest condr., composer; also radio and TV network appearances U.S.; Am. debut as composer, piano soloist, condr. Symphony of the Air, Carnegie Hall, N.Y.C., 1960; presented world premiere 2 original symphonic works, Tone Poem for coloratura soprano and orchestra, Piano Concerto (winner Am. Composers competition, 1942); asso. condr. opera N.Y. Operatic Soc.; concert pianist Met. Opera, Ballet Theater Co., N.Y.C.; organized all-girl orch., N.Y.C.; guest condr. Phila. Nat. Youth Orch. Composer: (ballet) The Nightingale and the Rose, Night Violet's Dream; (piano) Vision Victorieuse (Distinguished Am. Contemporary Composers series), also chamber music, symphonic works, vocal and piano compositions. Home: 350 Central Park W New York City NY 10025 Office: care Celebrity Artists Service Mgmt 29 W 57th St New York City NY 10019

PEREZ-REYES, MARIA GISPERT, psychiatrist; b. Barcelona, Spain, Nov. 20, 1929 (came to U.S. 1956, naturalized 1971); d. Jose and Montserrat (Cruells) Gispert; B.S., Academia Hispano Mexicana, 1945; M.D., Universidad Nacional Autonama de Mexico, 1952; m. Mario Perez-Reyes, July 23, 1952; children—Arthur, Edward, Nuria. Gen. practice medicine Fortin, Mexico, 1952-56; intern pediatrics N.C. Meml. Hosp., Chapel Hill, 1960, Watts Hosp., Durham, N.C., 1960-61; resident psychiatry N.C. Meml. Hosp., Chapel Hill, 1961-63, fellow child psychiatry, 1963-65, fellow, instr., 1965, instr., 1966-68, asst. prof., 1968-72, asso. prof., 1972—; dir. outpatient child psychiatry clinic N.C. Sch. Medicine, Chapel Hill, 1970-72, NIMH grantee, 1971—. Diplomate with splty. child psychiatry, Am. Bd. Psychiatry and Neurology. Fellow Acad. Child Psychiatry, mem. Am. Psychiat. Assn., Am. Assn. Psychiat. Clinics for Children, A.M.A., N.C. Med. Assn., Am. Orthopsychiat. Assn. Home: 808 Christopher Rd Chapel Hill NC 27514 Office: NC Meml Hosp Manning Dr Chapel Hill NC 27514

PERGANDE, MARY JUDE O'MALLEY (MRS. FRED W. PERGANDE), interior designer; b. Chgo., Oct. 28, 1936; d. John Patrick and Genevieve Catherine (Sullivan) O'Malley; B.S., Rosary Coll., 1958; m. Fred W. Pergande, Dec. 27, 1958; children—Michael, Christine, John, Joan, Stephen. Owner, Jude Pergrande Interiors, Green Bay, Wis., 1971—. Mem. com. Girl Scouts U.S.A., 1968-70; co-v.p. St. John Home-Sch., 1969-71. Mem. Rosary Coll. Alumnae (area pres. 1967-71). Address: 920 Allouez Terrace Green Bay WI 54301

PERING, KATHERINE LUNDSTROM, geochemist; b. Pago, Pago, Samoa, Sept. 5, 1941; d. Alfred Eugene and Kathryn (Haines) Lundstrom; B.S. in Chemistry, U. Alaska, 1963; M.S. in Chemistry, U. Cal. at Berkeley, 1965; Ph.D. in Geology, Stanford, 1972; m. Richard Durand Pering, Sept. 19, 1965; children—Celine, Trevor. Research chemist Ames Research Center, NASA, Moffett AFB, Cal., 1965-72; research analytical geochemist Stanford, 1972-73; research geochemist U.S. Geol. Survey, Menlo Park, Cal., 1973—. Mem. Am. Chem. Soc., N.Y. Acad. Scis., Geochem. Soc., Sigma Xi. Contbr. articles to profl. jours. Mem. team analyzing lunar samples for organic compounds; co-discoverer biogenic organic matter in meteorites. Home: 2377 Ramona St Palo Alto CA 94301 Office: US Geol Survey 345 Middlefield St Menlo Park CA 94025

PERKIN, ETHEL MURPHY (MRS. FRANK SCOTT PERKIN), clubworker; b. Chgo., July 21, 1916; d. John F. and Ethel (Howden) Murphy; student Highland Park Jr. Coll., 1935-37; A.B. in English Edn., Wayne U., 1939; m. Frank Scott Perkin, Feb. 27, 1942 (dec. Nov. 1973); children—Linda Josephine, John Francis, Sandra Ethel. Tchr. elementary English, lit., gen. lang., Detroit, 1941-45; personnel counselor women Plymouth plant Chrysler Corp., Detroit, 1943; asst. sec., dir. Murphy Ventures Corp., Grosse Pointe, Mich., 1956—. Chmn. membership Harper Hosp. Aux., Detroit, 1951, chmn. publicity, 1961; treas. Maire Sch. P.T.A., Grosse Pointe, 1960-62, mem. P.T.A. Council, 1960-62; mem. bd. Mich. Humane Soc.; 2d v.p. Women's City Club of Detroit, 1969-71, bd. dirs., 1964—, nominating com., 1972—; mem. women's aux. Wayne County Med. Soc., 1942—; mem. women's com. Grosse Pointe Symphony Orch.; life mem. Women's assn. Detroit Symphony Orch.; mem. women's div. Project Hope. Mem. Detroit Hist. Soc. (life) Internat. Platform Assn., Art Founders' Soc., Archives Am. Art, Detroit, Friends Pub. Library, Grosse Pointe, Am. Assn. U. Women, Detroit Rev. Club (pres. 1974-75), Liggett Sch. Parents Assn. (bd. 1965-66), Alpha Gamma Delta. Club: Colony Town. Address: 1709 Shore Club Dr St Clair Shores MI 48080

PERKINS, ANN, educator; b. Chgo., Apr. 18, 1915; d. Joseph Atwood and Grace Marie (Hardman) Perkins; A.B., U. Chgo., 1935, A.M., 1936, Ph.D., 1940. Research asst. U. Chgo., 1942-49; research asso. Yale, 1949-58, lectr. in archaelogy, 1955-65, editor, Dura-Europos Publs., 1958-65; prof. art U. Ill., Champaign, 1965—. Guggenheim fellow, 1954-55. Mem. Archeol. Inst. Am., Coll. Art Assn., Deutsches Archaologisches Institut. Author: The Comparative Archaelogy of Early Mesopotamia, 1949; The Art of Dura-Europos, 1973. Home: 1009 W Clark Champaign IL 61820

PERKINS, ANNA REBECCA (MRS. JAMES MANLIUS PERKINS), dietician; b. Haverhill, Mass., Nov. 23, 1919; d. Edwin Herbert and Anna Belle (Hubbard) Moulton; student Framingham Tchrs. Coll., 1938-41; B.S., U. N.H., 1942; m. James Manlius Perkins, Jan. 30, 1946; children—Helen Anne (Mrs. Richard Robert French), Harry Moulton. Therapeutic dietician Hale Hosp., Haverhill, 1942-45; lectr. food values for P.T.A. and field dietetics Haverhill High Sch., 1941; instr. diets for spl. patients to vol. hosp. workers, 1943-44; instr. therapeutic diets Profl. Womens Club of Boston, 1968—. Chmn. social service com. Florence Crittenton League, 1948-51; mem. Leisure Hour, Haverhill, 1947-52; life mem. Hale Hosp. Aux., 1972; mem. Community Club of Newton, 1968-69, Friends of Jackson Homestead, 1969; bd. dirs. Haverhill Day Nursery, 1948-51, Childrens Aid Soc., 1951-52, Worcester Womens Club, 1955-56. Mem. Huguenot Soc. Mass. (state historian 1966-68, asst. treas. 1968-70), Daus. of Founders and Patriots (councillor 1967-70, chpt. publicity chmn. 1970-73), Daus. Colonial Wars (lady of council 1966-69, state chmn. hospitality 1968-71 Mass.), D.A.R. (treas. chpt. 1962-68, regent 1968-74), Mass. Soc. Children Am. Revolution (sr. state chmn. motion pictures com. 1958-60), Nat. Soc. Women Descs. of Ancient and Hon. Arty. Co. (aide 1968-71), Soc. Descs. Colonial Clergy, Bunker Hill Monument Assn., Wedgewood Soc., Boston Browning Soc., Haverhill Hist. Soc., Womens Ednl. and Indsl. Union, Duston-Dustin Family Assn., Dames of Ct. of Honor (heredity life mem. Mass. chpt. 1970, pres. chpt. 1974—). Conglist. (co-chmn. unit Womens Guild Haverhill, publicity chmn. Womens Assn. Newton). Clubs: 100 (U. N.H.); Haverhill College (treas. 1947-48), Whittier, Octagon Art of Haverhill (hon.); Boston College (v.p. 1967-69, dir. 1969-72); Farm and Garden; Social Science (auditor 1972—); Capitol Hill (Washington). Home: 172 Hunnewell Av Newton MA 02158

PERKINS, DOROTHY ANDERSON (MRS. L.T. PERKINS), assn. exec.; b. Weiser, Ida., Aug. 13, 1926; d. Ross William and Josephine Stanford William (Gwilliam) Anderson; student Inst. for Orgn. Mgmt., U. Colo., 1969-74; m. L.T. Perkins, Nov. 16, 1948; children—Larry Taylor, Michael A., Drew A., Nancy. Sec., Ida. State Police, Boise, 1947-48, Ida. Supt. Pub. Instrn., Boise, 1953-56; sec. Casper (Wyo.) Area C. of C., 1962-63, adminstrv. sec., 1963-69, asst. mgr., 1969-72, exec. mgr., 1972—. Mem. Wyo. C. of C. Execs. (pres. 1972-74), Mountain States Assn. (dir.), Nat. Secs. Assn. (pres. 1970-71). Mem. Ch. of Jesus Christ of Latter-day Saints (organist, tchr., youth leader, choir dir.). Home: 1581 Nottingham St Casper WY 82601 Office: PO Box 399 Casper WY 82601

PERKINS, GERTRUDE HALL (MRS. ROBERT LEE PERKINS, SR.), journalist; b. Frederick, Okla., June 27, 1923; d. Thomas Ethridge and Lorena Merle (Cotton) Hall; student Frederick Jr. Coll., 1941-42, Southwestern State Coll., Weatherford, Okla., 1942-43; m. Robert Lee Perkins, Sr., June 7, 1942; children—Robert Lee, Merry Helen (Mrs. Lawrence Bland Nulty), Merrle Hollie. With Radio KOMA, Oklahoma City, 1943-44, U.P.I., Oklahoma City, 1944-45; reporter Frederick (Okla.) Daily Leader, 1948-51, news editor, 1958-67, advt. mgr., 1967-70, feature and news writer, women's editor, 1970—. Home: 911 S 12th St Frederick OK 73542 Office: 304-06 W Grand St Frederick OK 73542

PERKINS, GLORIA SUE OKES (MRS. EVERETT DAN PERKINS), editor; b. Hannibal, Mo., Jan. 5, 1932; d. Guy Chalmer and Vera Irene (Hanson) Okes; B.J., U. Mo., 1953; postgrad. U. Ill., 1963; m. Everett Dan Perkins, June 20, 1953; children—Keith Stuart, Michael Okes. Editor, Webster Groves (Mo.) News-Times, 1953-54; pub. relations dir. St. Louis County Library System, 1955; editor The Jonquil, Loveland, Colo., 1969—. Pub. relations vol. YWCA, Rockford, Ill., 1955-56. Recipient prize for individual achievement in spl. writing Theta Sigma Phi, 1953. Mem. Penpointers, Kappa Tau Alpha, Theta Sigma Phi, Delta Tau Kappa. Mem. Evangelical Free Ch. (sec. governing bd. 1971—). Home: 201 Annabel Lane Fort Collins CO 80521 Office: Box 359 Loveland CO 80537

PERKINS, IDA VIRGINIA, govt. ofcl.; b. Howard, Ga., Apr. 5, 1920; d. Eugene Hugh and Mattie J. (Vanlandingham) Perkins; A.B., La Grange Coll., 1940; M.S. in Hygiene, Harvard, 1950. Various positions from lab. technician to bacteriologist Ga. Dept. Pub. Health Lab., Atlanta, 1940-53; serologist WHO, Paraguay, 1953-56; lab adviser ICA, El Salvador, 1956-60, Venezuela, 1960-61, AID, Tegucigalpa, Honduras, 1961-63; microbiologist NIH, Nat. Cancer Inst., Accra, Ghana, 1964-68, microbiologist, project officer, Burkitt's tumor project, 1968—. Mem. Am. Soc. Microbiologists, Am. Pub. Health Assn., State and Provincial Pub. Health Lab. Dirs. Conf. Office: Accra Dept of State Washington DC 20521

PERKINS, JAYNE MARGUERITE REYNOLDS (MRS. CLINTON RAYMOND PERKINS), bus. exec.; b. St. Louis, Mar. 12, 1913; d. Walter Elbert and Bertha (Crowe) Reynolds; student Washington U., St. Louis, 1930-33, U. Cal., Berkeley, 1939-40; m. Reason Day Hardesty, Apr. 14, 1936 (dec., 1950); m. 2d, Clinton Raymond Perkins, June 17, 1952. Bookkeeper, Nat. Ammonia Co., St. Louis, 1930-36; asst. to Mr. Hardesty in design and devel. programs for Gen. Motors Inst. Tech., 1936-50; co-owner hotels, motels, apts., mgr. real estate properties, tng. of personnel, setting up accounting programs and ins. analysis, 1952—; pres. N.W. Home Furnishings Mart, Inc.; v.p. Blair House, Inc.; sec.-treas. Magnolia Bayshore Devel. Co. Honor guest Matrix Table, Seattle, 1968, 69, 70, 71, 72, 73. Trustee, pres. First Hill Improvement Club. Mem. Seattle

Apt. Owners and Operators (trustee), Nat. Home Fashions League, Bldg. Owners and Mgrs. Assn., Seattle C. of C., Assn. Wash. Industries. Home: 500 Wall St Seattle WA 98109

PERKINS, LUCY ANN, social worker; b. Louisville; d. Emmitt and Alice (Williams) Perkins; B.A., U. Louisville, 1944; M.S.W., Atlanta U., 1946; postgrad. Western Res. U., 1948-51, Coll. William and Mary, 1956-57. Sr. caseworker Cuyahoga County Child Welfare Bd., Cleve., 1947-52; sr. worker in charge dist. office Family Service Soc., Hartford, Conn., 1952-56; casework supr. Friends Assn. for Children, Richmond, Va., 1956-57; caseworker supr. Family Service and Travelers Aid, Inc., Utica, N.Y., 1957-63; casework supr. Wiltwyck Sch. for Boys, N.Y.C., 1963-65; chief psychiat. social worker Chgo. State Hosp., also Children and Adolescent Services Reod Zone Center, 1965-70; dir. Soundview Community Mental Health Center, Albert Einstein Coll. Medicine of Yeshiva U., dept. psychiatry, Bronx, NY., 1970—. Cons., lectr., supr., project demonstrator Marcy (N.Y.) State Hosp., 1958-63. Mem. Nat. Assn. Social Work, Am. Orthopsychiat. Assn., Social Work Vocational Bur., Conf. Social Welfare, Zeta Phi Beta. Home: 15700 Arlington Av Riverdale NY 10471 Office: Soundview Community Health Center Albert Einstein College Medicine Yeshiva U Dept Psychiatry Bronx NY 10461

PERKINS, MARGARET NELSON KAYE (MRS. WILLIAM ROBERTSON PERKINS, JR.), artist-painter; b. Topeka, Sept. 7, 1904; d. James Philip and Frances (Nelson) de Bevers Kaye; student art, Florence, Italy, 1922-24; grad. N.Y. Sch. Fine and Applied Art, 1927; spl. student Randolph-Macon Woman's Coll., 1946-48; m. William Robertson Perkins, Jr., Oct. 1, 1938; 1 dau., Sarah Frances (Mrs. Ronald Smither). One-man shows Lynchburg Art Club, 1961, Myrtle Beach, S.C., 1967; 2-man show Randolph-Macon Woman's Coll., 1948; exhibited in group shows Va. Mus. Fine Arts, Nat. Biennial Am. League Am. Pen Women, others. Pres., Lynchburg Art Center, 1955-56. Recipient 1st prize Lynchburg Civic Art, 1949, 55, Va. Fed. Women's Clubs, 1955, 58, Va. Biennial Nat. League Am. Pen Women, 1963. Mem. D.A.R., Archeol. Inst. Am., Assn. for Preservation Va. Antiquities, Historic Lynchburg Found., L'Alliance Francaise de Lynchburg, N.E. Hist. Geneal. Soc., Mayflower Soc. (treas. Va. 1954-72), Nat. League Am. Pen Women (v.p. Lynchburg br. 1966-67, art chmn. Va. 1970-71, chmn. selected art exhbn. 1971). Clubs: Antiquarian (v.p., program chmn. 1970-71), Garden of Virginia, Lynchburg Art. Illustrated booklet Christmas in Colonial Virginia, 1957. Home: 3116 Rivermont Av Lynchburg VA 24503

PERKINS, MILDRED ROSE SUE TAYLOR (MRS. EDSON L. MISENER, JR.), dentist; b. San Bernardino, Cal., July 31, 1926; d. Mertus L. and Myrtle Rose (Lamb) Taylor; student Fresno State Coll., 1949-52; D.D.S., U. Cal. at San Francisco, 1956; m. Robert E. Perkins, 1946 (div. 1956); m. 2d, Edson L. Misener, Jr., July 13, 1957. Practice dentistry, San Francisco, 1956-58, San Diego, 1958—. Instr., U. Cal. Coll. Dentistry, San Francisco, 1956-58. Mem. Assn. Women Dentists, Am. Dental Assn., So. Cal., San Diego County dental socs., Upsilon Alpha. Republican. Home: 3535 Lowell Way San Diego CA 92106 Office: 1802 Cable St San Diego CA 92107

PERKINS, PRISCILLA CROSWELL, educator; b. Glens Falls, N.Y., Oct. 26, 1940; d. James Croswell and Evangeline Pearl (Beougher) Perkins; B.A. magna cum laude, Bryn Mawr Coll., 1962; Ph.D., U. Cal. at Berkeley, 1967. Instr. dept. geology Boston Coll., 1967-68, asst. prof., 1968-72; vis. asst. research geologist Inst. Geophysics, U. Cal. at Los Angeles, 1972-73; vis. asst. prof. dept. geology U. Cal. at Davis, 1973-74. Exec. sec. Lake Powell Research Project, 1971—; cons., vis. staff mem. Los Alamos Sci. Lab., 1972—. Mem. Com. on Minority Participation in Earth Sci. and Mineral Engring., U.S. Dept. Interior, 1972—. NSF fellow, 1962-66. Fellow Geol. Soc. Am.; mem. Am. Geophys. Union, Geol. Soc. London, Assn. Earth Sci. Editors, A.A.A.S., Am. Assn. U. Profs., Soc. Mayflower Descs., Sierra Club, Appalachian Mountain Club. Editor: Lake Powell Research Project Bull., 1973—. Contbr. articles to profl. jours. Office: Inst Geophysics U Cal at Los Angeles Los Angeles CA 90024

PERLBERG, ZELMA, educator; b. Balt.; d. Philip and Ida (Gumnitzky) Perlberg; B.A., U. Md., 1952, M.A., 1954, postgrad., 1960-66; postgrad. Johns Hopkins, 1960. Social worker Balt. Dept. Welfare, 1953-54; tchr. spl. edn. Balt. Dept. Edn., 1954-59, counselor emotionally disturbed, educable, mentally retarded adolescents, Balt., 1959—. Mem. Am. Orthopsychiat. Assn., Nat. Assn. Sch. Counselors, N.E.A., Md. Personnel and Guidance Assn. Office: School 17 200 E North Av Baltimore MD 21202

PERLMAN, EVELYN BERNICE, psychologist; b. Boston, Dec. 8, 1928; d. Joseph and Anna (Wallace) Kushner; A.B., Bates Coll., Lewiston, Me., 1949; M.A., Radcliffe Coll., 1950; grad. student psychology Boston U., 1951-54; m. Sumner Earl Perlman, June 23, 1956; children—Andrew Jay, Walter Lew, Gary David. Therapeutic tutor and tester Browne and Nichols Sch., Cambridge, Mass., 1951-54; psychologist Mass. Youth Service Bd., Lancaster Sch. Girls, 1954-56, Quincy (Mass.) pub. schs., 1956-58; part-time psychologist, psychol. counseling dept. Arlington (Mass.) pub. schs., 1960—. Chairperson study group League Women Voters, Waltham, Mass., 1957-58, corr. sec., 1956-57; pre-sch. program chairperson Lexington (Mass.) P.T.A., 1960-62. Mem. Mass. Sch. Psychologists Assn. (charter), Mass. (chairperson child devel. group 1971-72), Am. psychol. assns., Women's Am. ORT (dir., chairperson study groups 1965-69). Co-author: K-Q Kindergarten Questionnaire. Home: 10 Tyler Rd Lexington MA 02173 Office: 23 Maple St Arlington MA 02174

PERLMAN, HELEN HARRIS (MRS. MAX S. PERLMAN), social worker, educator; b. St. Paul; d. Lazar and Annie (Schwartz) Harris; B.A., U. Minn., 1926; M.S. (Commonwealth fellow), Columbia, 1943; D.Litt., Boston U., 1974; m. Max S. Perlman, Aug. 16, 1935; 1 son, Jonathan Harris. Social caseworker, supr. Jewish Family Service, Chgo., 1927-35; supr., adminstr. Jewish Family Service, N.Y.C., 1935-40; supr., lectr. Columbia Sch. Social Work, N.Y.C., 1940-45; asst. prof. U. Chgo., 1945, prof., 1949-53, 54-71, Samuel Deutsch Distinguished Service prof. emeritus. Vis. lectr., U. Cal. at Berkeley, U. Hawaii, U. Hong Kong, others, 1950—; cons., tng. and standards br. Nat. Inst. Mental Health, 1955-58; mem. adv. bd. neurology and psychiatry VA, 1958-63; mem. bd. Nat. Council on Social Work Edn., 1957-60. Recipient Distinguished Achievement award Bd. Regents, U. Minn., 1967. Fellow Am. Orthopsychiat. Assn. (bd. dirs.); mem. Am. Assn. U. Profs., Nat. Assn. Social Workers, Am. Civil Liberties Union, Phi Beta Kappa. Author: Social Casework: A Problem-Solving Process, 1957; So You Want To Be A Social Worker, 1962; Persona: Social Role and Personality, 1968. Editor: Helping: Towle on Social Work, 1969; Perspectives in Casework, 1971. Editorial bd. Social Service Rev., 1946—, Social Work, 1972—. Contbr. articles to profl. jours. Home: 1321 E 56th St Chicago IL 60637

PERLMAN, ROSE LERNER (MRS. SOL PHILLIPS PERLMAN), lawyer; b. Dunafoldvar, Hungary, Oct. 11, 1894; d. Daniel and Pauline (Blumenthal) Lerner; LL.B., U. Pa., 1917; A.B., 1938; m. Sol Phillips Perlman, Mar. 13, 1923; children—Theodore Dsmurl Lerner, Joan Ellen (Mrs. Marshall H. Fisher). Admitted to N.J. bar, 1923; partner firm Perlman and Lerner, Trenton, N.J., 1920—; under sheriff Mercer County, N.J., 1923-25; rent atty. OPA, Mercer County, N.J., 1947-49. Vice Pres. Trenton Credit Assn. Pres. Women's Democratic Club. Trustee Mercer County Sr. Citizens; bd. dirs. Mercer County Tb and Health Assn., 1935—, pres., 1957-59. Mem. Mercer County Bar Assn. N.J., Vis. Nurses Assn. (dir.), U. Pa. Alumnae Assn., Zonta Internat. (dir.). Club: College. Home: 206 Cornwall Av Trenton NJ 08618 Office: 143 East State St Trenton NJ 08608

PERLMANN, GERTRUDE ERIKA, educator; b. Reichenberg, Czechoslovakia, Apr. 20, 1912; d. Walter and Elise (Gibian) Perlmann; D.Sc., German U. Prague, 1936. Fellow, Biol. Lab., Carlsberg Found. Copenhagen, Denmark, 1937-39; research asst. dept. phys. chemistry Harvard Med. Sch., Boston, 1939-41, research fellow medicine 1945; research fellow medicine Mass. Gen Hosp., Boston, 1941-45; vis. investigator Rockefeller Inst., N.Y.C., 1945-47, asst., 1947-51, asso., 1951-57, asst. prof., 1957-58, asso. prof. biochemistry, 1958-72, prof., 1972—. Mem. Am. Chem. Soc., Am. Soc. Biol. Chemists, Am. Biophys. Soc. Brit. Biochem. Soc., Harvey Soc. Home: 155 E 93d St New York City NY 10028 Office: 66th St and York Av New York City NY 10021

PERMAR, ELISE JOHNS (MRS. EDWARD ANDREW PERMAR, JR.), editor; b. N.Y.C., Aug. 25, 1918; d. Victor Harold and Elise (Perron) Johns; student N.Y. State Tchrs. Coll., New Paltz, 1934-37, N.Y. U., 1937-40, U. South Miss., 1956-56; m. Edward Andrew Permar, Jr., Nov. 19, 1940; children—Pamela (Mrs. Harold Hubbard), Andrew, Matthew. Tchr., Cedar Knolls Sch., Whippany, N.J., 1937, Southside Elementary Sch., Dover, N.J., 1938-40; free lance writer, 1957—; corr. Fairchild Publs., N.Y.C., 1960-66; women's editor Brunswick (Ga.) Daily News, 1966-70; editor Women's World, Brunswick, 1970-71; owner, editor Islander, St. Simons Island, Ga., 1972—. Episcopalian. Mem. Order Eastern Star. Home: 520 Wesley Oaks Circle St Simons Island GA 31522 Office: PO Box 539 St Simons Island GA 31522

PERNA, DORIS, physician; M.D., Med. Coll. Pa., 1962. Intern, Cedars of Lebanon Hosp., Los Angeles, 1962-63, resident 1963-65, adj., child psychiatry; fellow in child psychiatry Reiss-Davis Child Study Center, Los Angeles, 1965-67; practice medicine, specializing in child psychiatry, Beverly Hills, Cal., 1967—; asst. in psychiatry Mt. Sinai Hosp., Los Angeles; asso. attending child psychiatry Cedars-Sinai Med. Center, chairperson house staff rights com.; asst. prof. psychiatry U. Cal. Neuropsychiat. Inst., Los Angeles. Cons., Crippled Children's Soc., Los Angeles County Dept. Mental Hygiene. Asso., Smithsonian Instn.; patron Los Angeles County Mus. Art. Diplomate Am. Bd. Psychiatry and Neurology, Nat. Bd. Med. Examiners, Am. Bd. Child Psychiatry. Mem. A.M.A., Cal., Los Angeles County, Beverly Hills Dist. med. assns., Am., So. Cal. (chmn. com. on referral) psychiat. assns., Los Angeles Soc. Child Psychiatry, Am., So. Cal. (sec. 1971, v.p. 1972), Los Angeles socs. adolescent psychiatry, Am. Acad. Child Psychiatry, Los Angeles Pediatric Soc., Am. Med. Woman's Assn., Med. Coll. Pa. Alumni Assn. Contbr. articles to profl. jours. Office: 465 N Roxbury Dr Beverly Hills CA 90210

PERNA, RITA, retail chain exec.; B.A., New Rochelle Coll.; M.A., Columbia. Art instr. high sch., coll.; stylist Alden's, Chgo., catalog co.; asst. fashion coordinator Spiegel's Chgo., catalog co.; fashion coordinator Abraham & Straus, 1946; with Montgomery Ward, Chgo., 1954—, nat. fashion coordinator, now asst. v.p. Mem. Trends, Inner Circle, Fashion Group (pres.), Round Table, Nat. Council of Women, Sales Exec. Club. Office: NY Apparel Office Montgomery Ward 393 7th Av New York City NY 10001

PERNOTTO, SISTER ANDREA, educator; b. Youngstown, O., Dec. 23, 1941; d. Anthony James and Veronica (Kology) Pernotto; B.S., Youngstown State U., 1964; postgrad. Notre Dame U., 1967; M.A. in Spl. Edn., M.A. in Spl. Religious edn., Cardinal Stritch Coll., 1973. Tchr. mentally retarded children and adults Mahoning County Sch. for Mentally Retarded, Youngstown, 1971—, dir. ecumenical spiritual enrichment program, 1969—. Cons. spl. religious edn. for handicapped St. Rose Parish, Diocese Youngstown, 1971—, cons. parents newly born infants who are handicapped, 1969—. Joseph P. Kennedy, Jr. grad. scholar, 1969-70, Joseph P. Kennedy, Jr. grantee, 1971; Internat. Order of Alhambra scholar, 1968—. Mem. Am. Assn. Mentally Retarded, Nat. Cath. Edn. Assn., Nat., Ohio assns. retarded children, Profession Assn. Retarded. Club: Behavioral Science (Riverside, N.J.). Home: 61 E Main St Girard OH 44420 Office: 4801 Woodridge Dr Youngstown OH 44515

PERRA, BETSEY JANET BARTON (MRS. ANDREW JOSEPH PERRA), home economist; b. Warwick, R.I., Jan. 15, 1932; d. Rowland Benjamin and Ruth Viola (Powell) Barton; B.S., U. R.I., 1953, M.A., 1974; m. Andrew Joseph Perra, Sept. 1, 1951; children—Andrew B., Bruce W., Deborah R., Stephen C., Victoria E. Home economist U. R.I. Coop. Extension Service, Cranston, 1965—, home econs. cons. dept. social and rehabilitative services, 1965—. Vice-pres. P.T.A., Conimicut, R.I., 1966-67; asst. roundtable commr. Cub Scouts, Narragansett council Boy Scouts Am., 1969-71. Recipient Silver Fawn, Boy Scouts Am., 1971. New Eng. (pres-elect), Ct.-R.I. (sec. 1970-72) assns. extension home economists, R.I. Extension Service Assn. (treas. 1973-74, chmn. food stamp nutrition com. 1971—). Methodist. Mem. Order Eastern Star. Home: 1429 Centerville Rd Warwick RI 02893 Office: 600 New London Av Cranston RI 02920

PERRIGO, LUCIA (MRS. HOWARD B. MEYERS), hotel exec.; b. Chgo.; m. Howard (Howdee) B. Meyers, 1946. With pub. relations dept. Warner Bros., Chgo.; film critic Chgo.'s Am. (formerly Herald-Am.); dir., exec. asst. to mgmt. Ambassador Hotels, Chgo. Producer (with husband) travel films. Address: Ambassador Hotels N State and Goethe St Chicago IL 60610

PERRIN, ELLEN COSER (MRS. JAMES MARC PERRIN), physician; b. N.Y.C., Nov. 11, 1943; d. Lewis Alfred and Rose (Laub) Coser; A.B., Columbia, 1964; M.D., Case-Western Res. U., 1968; m. James Marc Perrin, June 7, 1968; children—Andrew Jonathan, Eric Benjamin. Intern, Strong Meml. Hosp., Rochester, N.Y., 1968-69; resident Children's Hosp. D.C., Washington, 1969-71; chief resident pediatrics, 1970-71; asso. dir. pediatric ambulatory services Strong Meml. Hosp., U. Rochester Sch. Medicine, 1971—, also asst. prof. pediatrics. Recipient Maynard Cohen award Children's Hosp. D.C., 1970. Office: Strong Meml Hosp 260 Crittenden Blvd Rochester NY 14620

PERRIN, ELLEN HAYS, coll. adminstr.; b. Buckhannon, W.Va.; d. Charles Gilbert and Geraldine Sexton (Hays) Perrin; B.S. in Music Edn., Duquesne U., 1946; M. Edn., U. Pitts., 1952, postgrad., 1971—. Tchr. music West Mifflin (Pa.) Dist. Schs., 1947-61, counselor, 1961-64; dean of women Slippery Rock (Pa.) State Coll., 1965-70, asst. to v.p. for student affairs, 1970-72, dir. counseling and career services, 1972—, dean of students, 1974—. Mem. supts. adv. com. West Mifflin Dist. Schs., 1955-60; steering com. Fgn. Affairs Forum, 1959-60. Mem. com. on edn. Gov.'s Commn. on Status of Women, 1965-66. Mem. Pitts. Bicentennial Assembly, 1958-59. Mem. N.E.A., Pa. Edn. Assn. (pres. West Mifflin br. 1962-64, exec. com. west region 1963-64, v.p. assn. ind. sch. dists. Allegheny County 1963-64), Am. Assn. U. Women (pres. Pitts. br. 1958-62, Pa. div. chmn. status of women 1962-63, chmn. cultural interests 1963-64, area rep. for edn. 1964-66, chmn. edn. projects for state div., chmn. topic of study 1967-69, fellowship award named in her honor 1970), Nat., Pa. (parliamentarian 1969-72, 2d v.p. 1972—), Western Pa. (sec. 1970-71) assns. women deans and counselors, D.A.R. (conservation chmn. local chpt. 1959-62, chpt. chaplain 1963-65), Pa. Assn. Student Personnel Adminstrs. (membership chmn. 1972), Zonta Internat., Alpha Phi (local alumnae dir. 1955). Presbyn. Clubs: South Hills College (Pitts.); Women's (chmn. edn. com. 1970-72) (Slippery Rock). Home: 140 Longue Vue Dr Mt Lebanon Pittsburgh PA 15228 Office: Slippery Rock State Coll Slippery Rock PA 16057

PERRIN, GAIL, editor; b. Boston, Oct. 14, 1938; d. Hugh and Helen (Baxter) Perrin; B.A., Wellesley Coll., 1960. Copy girl Washington Daily News, summers 1954-57, reporter, 1958, 1960-61, acting women's editor, food editor, 1961-62, rewrite reporter, 1963-65; reporter Honolulu Star Bull., 1959; women's editor Boston Globe, 1965-71, asst. met. editor, 1971-74, food editor, 1974—. Mem. Washington Press Club. Home: 27 Rolling Lane Weston MA 02193

PERRIN, HELEN JOYCE, physician; b. Oskaloosa, Ia., Mar. 23, 1915; d. Leslie R. and May E. (Hendrix) Perrin; B.S., Ia. Wesleyan Coll., 1935; postgrad., U. Ia., 1936-37, M.D., 1941. Intern, Santa Barbara (Cal.) Gen. Hosp; 1941-42; resident St. Elizabeth's Hosp., Washington, 1942-44; practice medicine, specializing in psychiatry, Des Moines, 1945-54, Long Beach, Cal., 1954-64; individual and group cons. practice for adults and children, 1970—; asst. clin. prof. psychiatry and child psychiatry U. Cal. Coll. Medicine, Irvine, 1965—; mem. cons. staff Meml., St. Mary's, Community hosps. Diplomate Am. Bd. Psychiatry and Neurology. Fellow Am. Psychiat. Assn.; mem. A.M.A., Los Angeles Soc. Child Psychiatry, Pi Kappa Delta, Beta Beta Beta, Alpha Psi Omega. Club: Los Angeles Athletic. Author: Portraits: Word Pictures of Fellow Travelers in the South Pacific, 1964, Happiness Doctor, 1965. Home: The Lafayette 140 Linden Av Long Beach CA 90802

PERRIN, JANE CAROL SCHUTTER (MRS. EUGENE PERRIN), pediatrician; b. Syracuse, N.Y., Dec. 3, 1930; d. Claude Alvin and Ethelyn Vernon (Nelke) Schutter; B.S., Syracuse U., 1952; M.S., U. Wis., 1954; M.D., Harvard, 1957; m. Eugene Victor Perrin, Mar. 31, 1956; children—Daniel, Miriam, Adam, Joshua. Pediatric intern Children's Hosp. Med. Center, Boston, 1957-58; resident N.Y. Hosp.-Cornell Med. Center, N.Y.C., 1958-59, Children's Hosp. Med. Center, Cin., 1960-61; practice medicine specializing in pediatrics, Cin., 1961-66, Cleve., 1967-74, Detroit, 1974—; dir. comprehensive care program Children's Hosp. Mich., 1974—; cons. Hamilton County Diagnostic Clinic, Cin., 1961-66; asst. med. dir. Comprehensive Care Program, Cleve. Met. Gen. Hosp., 1967-69, asso. med. dir., 1969-72, co-dir., 1973-74; asst. prof. pediatrics Case Western Res. U. Sch. Medicine, 1969-74; asso. prof. Wayne State U. Sch. Medicine, 1974—; chmn. med. staff Health Hill Hosp., 1972-74. Chmn. intake and review Help Home for Retarded, 1970-73. Fellow Am. Acad. Pediatrics; mem. Ambulatory Pediatric Assn., No. Ohio Pediatric Soc. (com. for handicapped children 1971-74), Phi Beta Kappa, Kappa Alpha Theta. Home: 26318 Dundee Huntington Woods MI 48070 Office: Childrens Hosp of Mich 3901 Beaubien Blvd Detroit MI 48201

PERRIN, SARAH ANN (MRS. JAMES FRANK PERRIN), lawyer; b. Neoga, Ill., Dec. 13, 1904; d. James Lee and Bertha Frances (Baker) Figenbaum; LL.B., George Washington U., 1941, J.D., 1964; m. James Frank Perrin, Dec. 24, 1926. Admitted to D.C. bar, 1942; asso. atty. Mabel Walker Willebrandt, law office, Washington, 1941-42; atty. various fed. housing agencies, 1942-69, asst. gen. counsel FHA, Washington, 1959-60, asst. gen. counsel Dept. Housing and Urban Devel., Washington, 1960-69; sec. Nat. Housing Conf., Washington, 1970—; research cons. housing and urban devel., Palmyra, Va., 1970—. Acting sec. Nat. Housing Research Council, Washington, 1973—. Bd. dir. Nat. Housing Conf., 1972—. Mem. Am. Bar Assn., Fed. Bar Assn., Women's Bar Assn. of D.C. (pres. 1959-60), Nat. Assn. Women Lawyers, Phi Delta Delta, Fluvanna County Hist. Soc. (pres. 1973-75). Presbyn. Mem. Order Eastern Star. Home: Solitude Plantation Palmyra VA 22963

PERRY, BARBARA FISHER (MRS. ERNEST GENE PERRY), author, childrens theatre exec.; b. N.Y.C., Dec. 10, 1940; d. David and Regina (Mandel) Fisher; B.A., Hunter Coll., 1962; m. Ernest Gene Perry, Sept. 23, 1967; 1 son, Athelantis. Fund raising cons. N.Y. State Council on the Arts, 1967—; exec. dir. Children's Theatre, Ten Penny Players, Inc., N.Y.C., 1968—. Cons. Poppet Puppets, 1970-71, Bil Baird, 1967-68. Bd. dirs. Am. Internat. Sculptor's Symposium, 1971—. Sec., Artist Tenants Assn., N.Y.C., 1962-64; sec. Met. Council on Housing, N.Y.C., 1963-65; treas. 799 Greenwich St. Tenants Corp., N.Y.C., 1972—. Mem. Dem. County Com., 1963-65, W. Village Dem. Com., 1972—. Mem. Dramatists Guild, Authors Guild. Episcopalian. Author: Care Without Care, 1972. Address: 799 Greenwich St New York City NY 10014

PERRY, BERTHA FRANCES WININGER (MRS. RALPH GRAHAM PERRY), savs. and loan exec.; b. Stanhope, Ia., Aug. 4, 1924; d. Harry Alfred and Rose (Bockwoldt) Wininger; grad. Capital City Comml. Coll., 1943, Am. Savs. and Loan Inst., 1970; m. Ralph Graham Perry, Feb. 12, 1949; children—Steven Ralph, Debra Kay. Gen. office girl Jewel Tea Co., Des Moines, 1943-50; bookkeeper, Ardan Wholesale Co., Des Moines, 1952-57; v.p., sec. Scandia Savs. & Loan Assn., Des Moines, 1957—. Mem. Soc. Savs. and Loan Controllers (pres. Des Moines chpt. 1963), Am. Savs. and Loan Inst. (pres. Des Moines chpt. 1964-65), Des Moines Women's C. of C. (v.p. 1970-71), Adminstrv. Mgmt. Soc. Club: Golf and Country (Ankeny, Ia.). Home: 522 Ash Dr Ankeny IA 50021 Office: 518 E Locust St Des Moines IA 50309

PERRY, BONITA LYNN, psychologist; b. Detroit, Oct. 9, 1944; d. John J. and Jane G. (Skulnick) Perry; B.S., Wayne State U., 1966; M.A., Mich. State U., 1967, Ph.D., 1971. Consumer psychologist Nat. Analysts, Phila., 1971—, also supr. undergrad. student interns from Temple U. Named Outstanding Teaching Asst., Mich. State U., 1970. Mem. Am. Psychol. Assn., Internat. Communication Assn., Am. Assn. for Pub. Opinion Research. Office: 400 Market St Philadelphia PA 19106

PERRY, DENISE KATHLEEN, editor; b. Sevierville, Tenn., Jan. 21, 1947; d. William Arthur and Elizabeth Sawers (Haden) Perry; B.S., U. Md., 1969. News editor Queen Anne's Record-Observer, Centreville, Md., 1969; reporter Chester River Press, Chestertown, Md., 1969, acting editor, 1970; acting editor Record-Observer, Centreville, Md., 1970-71, exec. editor, 1971-73; news editor Star-Democrat, Easton, Md., 1973—; co-editor Waterman's Gazette, Annapolis, Md., 1974—. Mem. Women in Communications, Sigma Delta Chi. Home: 210 Prospect Av Easton MD 21601 Office: PO Box 600 Easton MD 21601

PERRY, EDITH DICKERSON (MRS. HERMAN HILARY PERRY), banker; b. Nashville, Sept. 19, 1923; d. William Rom and Edna (Lassiter) Dickerson; student Watkins Inst., 1968, U. Tenn.,

1965-66, Peabody Coll. for Tchrs., 1967-68; m. Herman Hilary Perry, Aug. 22, 1946. Sec. to head trust dept. First Am. Nat. Bank, Nashville, 1942-67, asst. trust officer, 1967-72, trust officer, 1972—. Mem. Estate Planning Council, Nashville, 1968—. Recipient Exec. Woman of the Year award Nat. Women Execs., Nashville, 1971. Mem. Nat. secs. Assn. Internat. (past officer Nashville chpt.; internat. nominations com. 1968-69; award 1967), Nat. Assn. Bank Women, Am. Inst. Banking. Club: Old Hickory Country (Old Hickory, Tenn.). Home: 100 Meadowlake Dr Hendersonville TN 37075 Office: First Am Nat Bank First Am Center Nashville TN 37237

PERRY, ELIZABETH GRACE, physician; b. Teaneck, N.J., Jan. 5, 1937; d. Edward Frederick and Marjorie Grace (Johnstone) Grueninger; B.A., U. Rochester, 1958; M.D., N.Y. Med. Coll., 1962; m. Clark William Perry, June 16, 1962; children—Linda Joy, Edward William, Jeanette DuBois. Intern, Holy Name Hosp., Teaneck, attending anesthesiologist, 1965—, anesthesiologist, 1969—; resident Columbia-Presbyn. Med. Center, N.Y.C.; practice medicine specializing in anesthesiology and respiratory therapy, Teaneck, 1965—; dir. dept. respiratory therapy, 1969—. Mem. adv. com. respiratory therapy Bergen Community Coll. Diplomate Am. Bd. Anesthesiology. Fellow Am. Coll. Anesthesiologists. Mem. A.M.A., N.J., Bergen County med. socs., Am., N.J. socs. anesthesiologists. Home: 174 W Saddle River Rd Saddle River NJ 07458 Office: 190 Moore St Hackensack NJ 07602

PERRY, ERMA JACKSON MCNEIL (MRS. IRVING C. PERRY), journalist; b. Winthrop, Mass.; d. Hooper Martyn and Henrietta D. (Jackson) McNeil; B.S., Boston U., 1936; m. Irving C. Perry, Apr. 29, 1939; children—Dorothy Gayle (Mrs. T. Jeffrey Toy), Irving C., III. With Phila. Daily News, 1954-56; feature writer Phila. Inquirer, 1956; Phila. Bull., 1963—; syndicated writer Copley News Service, San Diego, 1967—; free-lance feature writer numerous mags., newspapers, including Holiday, Lady's Circle, N.Y. Times, Ford Times, Am. Artist, Christian Sci. Monitor, Better Homes & Gardens; v.p. Arkwright-Boston Ins. Co. Mem. women's com. Internat. House, 1951-56; mem. Friends Social Order Com., 1956-66; mem. Friends Prison Service Com., 1965-67. Trustee, Phila. Center for Older People, 1960-67; mem. bd. Quaker Women, 1964-69. Named hon. citizen of Tex., 1972, winner nat. article writing contest, 1971, 72. Mem. Bucks County Writers (treas. 1965-66, pres. 1970), Phila. Pub. Relations Assn., Soc. Am. Travel Writers. Mem. Soc. Friends. Clubs: Jenkintown (Pa.) Womens (sec. 1964-66) Manufacturer's Golf and Country (Oreland, Pa.); North Conway (N.H.) Country. Contbr. articles to mags. Home: 134 Greenwood Av Jenkintown PA 19046 also West Side Rd North Conway NH 03860

PERRY, HELEN GUEST WASHBURN (MRS. THOMAS WHIPPLE PERRY), librarian; b. N.Y.C., July 1, 1928; d. Robert Collyer and Helen Blackwell (Mulford) Washburn; A.B., Keuka Coll., 1950; M.S., Simmons Coll., 1952; m. Thomas Whipple Perry, June 19, 1951; children—Sarah, Taft, Charles. Reference librarian Harvard Bus. Sch., 1950-54, 61-62; head librarian Houghton Mifflin Co., Boston, 1966—. Leader Bay Path council Girl Scouts Am., 1963-66; mem., vice-chmn. Watertown Sch. Bldg. and Survey Com., 1969-73; mem. Town Meeting, 1959-64, 70—. Mem. Watertown (Mass.) Democratic Town Com., 1962—. Trustee Watertown (Mass.) Free Pub. Library, 1961—, chmn., 1972—; bd. dirs. Beaverbrook Guidance Clinic. Mem. League Women Voters (dir. 1958-61), Am., Mass. library assns., Spl. Libraries Assn. (chmn. edn. sect. 1973-74). Home: 64 Russell Av Watertown MA 02172 Office: 1 Beacon St Boston MA 02107

PERRY, HOPE CRAIG, pediatrician; b. Atlanta, Aug. 4, 1929; d. Frederick Stephen and Peggy (Lathem) Craig; B.A. (Sigma Xi fellow), Smith Coll., 1950; M.D., Columbia, 1954; m. Roger Hobart Perry, May 18, 1957; children—Elizabeth, Stephen. Intern Cin. Gen. Hosp., 1954-55; resident N.Y. Hosp., N.Y.C., 1955-57; Nat. Found. fellow microbiology N.Y. Hosp., 1957-58; mem. staff Sage Hosp., Ithaca, N.Y., 1968—; pediatrician Tompkins County Health Dept., Ithaca, 1959—. Physician univ. health services, Cornell U., Ithaca. Diplomate Am. Bd. Pediatrics. Home: 151 N Sunset Dr Ithaca NY 14850 Office: Gannett Clinic Cornell U Ithaca NY 14850

PERRY, JACQUELIN, orthopedic surgeon; b. Denver, May 31, 1918; d. John F. and Tirzah (Koruptkat) Perry; B.Ed., U. Cal. at Los Angeles, 1940; M.D., U. Cal. at San Francisco, 1950. Intern Children's Hosp., San Francisco, 1950-57; resident U. Cal., 1951-55; orthopedic surgeon Rancho Los Amigos Hosp., Downey, Cal., 1955—, chief Kinesiology, 1968, chief stroke service, 1971—, asso. chief surg. services, 1972—; asso. prof. surgery (orthopedic) U. So. Cal., 1969-72, prof., 1972—; Packard Meml. lectr. U. Colo., 1970; guest speaker 3d Mary McMillan Lecture by Phys. Therapy Curriculum Western Res. U., Cleve., 1965. Cons. USAF. Served as phys. therapist WAC, 1941-46. Named Woman of Yr. for Medicine in So. Cal., Los Angeles Times, 1959. Mem. Am. Acad. Orthopedic Surgeons, Am., Western orthopedic assns., A.M.A., Cal., Los Angeles County med. assns., Am. Phys. Therapy Assn. (hon., Golden Pen award 1965), Scoliosis Research Soc., LeRoy Abbott Soc., Pan-Pacific Surg. Assn., Am. Acad. Cerebral Palsy. Home: 12319 Brock Av Downey CA 90242 Office: 7601 Imperial Hwy Downey CA 90242

PERRY, JOAN PONDER (MRS. CURTIS LAWRENCE PERRY), advt. agy. exec.; b. Birmingham, Ala., Jan. 19, 1941; d. Hubert Alexander and Sybil (York) Ponder; grad. high sch.; m. Curtis Lawrence Perry, June 21, 1958; children—Michael C., Christine. Exec. sec. to pres. Royal Cup Coffee, Inc., Birmingham, 1958-62; adminstrv. exec. Frank M. Taylor, advt., Birmingham, 1962-73; pres. Perry-Hoyle Advt., Inc., Birmingham, 1973—. Mem. pub. information com. A.R.C., 1968-71, chmn. Christmas blood donor campaign, 1969-70. Recipient award Birmingham Ad Club, 1963, Outstanding Service award A.R.C., 1970. Mem. Am. Marketing Assn., Exec. Secs., Inc., Am. Women in Radio and TV (local pres. 1967-69, So. area membership chmn. 1972, dir. at large nat. bd. 1973—), Birmingham Area C. of C. Clubs: Birmingham Press, Birmingham Ad. Home: 909 Reedwood Lane Birmingham AL 35235 Office: 3928 Montclair Rd Birmingham AL 35213

PERRY, JULIANNE SHOTWELL (MRS. JAMES CLINE PERRY), ednl. adminstr.; b. Clinton, Mo., Aug. 10, 1945; d. William Chester and Carolyn Frances (Veatch) Shotwell; B.S., Central Mo. State U., 1967; M.Ed., U. Mo., 1969; postgrad. So. Ill. U., 1970, U. Minn., 1972; m. James Cline Perry, May 31, 1969. Elementary Spanish tchr., Prairie Village, Kan., 1967-68; research asst. U. Mo., Columbia, 1968-69; dir. student activities and testing, counselor, asst. instr. Spanish, E. Central Jr. Coll., Union, Mo., 1969—, dir. women's program, 1973. Mem. Adult Basic Edn. Adv. Bd., Union, Mo., 1970-71, Profl. Counseling Center Adv. Bd., 1972. Mem. Mo. Guidance Assn., Am. Coll. Personnel Assn., Am. Personnel and Guidance Assn., Mo. Assn. Jr. Colls., Cwens, P.E.O., Alpha Lambda Delta, Alpha Phi Delta, Kappa Delta Pi, Sigma Sigma Sigma. Presbyn. (elder 1971-73). Club: East Central Junior College Faculty Women. Author: (with John Ferguson and William Grimsley) Survey of Adult Basic Education in Missouri, 1969. Home: Route 1 Box 192H Washington MO 63090 Office: Box 529 Union MO 63084

PERRY, MARCELLA ELLEN DONOVAN, banker; b. Yorktown, Ind.; d. James Garfield and Elizabeth (Jones) Donovan; student Rice Inst., 1922-24; m. Glenn Arthur Perry, Nov. 10, 1930 (div. 1958); 1 dau., Gayle Donovan (Mrs. Fredric Milam Saunders). Owner Donovan Dance Studio, Houston, 1932-54; sec.-treas. Heights Savs. Assn., Houston, 1954-61, pres., 1961—; chmn. bd. dirs. 1st Pasadena State Bank, Almeda-Genoa Bank. Del. Democratic Nat. Conv., 1960, 64; mem. State Dem. exec. com. 6th Senatorial Dist. Tex.; mem. state adv. bd. Small Business Adminstrn., 1965-67, mem. nat. adv. bd., 1969-70; sec. Harris County (Tex.) Grand Jury Assn., 1965-72; port commr. Port of Houston Authority of Harris County, 1973—; vice chmn. Am. Revolution Bicentennial Commn. of Tex.; pres. Allegro Ballet of Houston, 1966; mem. Houston-Harris County Economic Opportunity Bd., 1965; mem. Exec. Res. Office Emergency Planning; chmn. Houston Municipal Art Commn., 1971-72. Chmn. bd. regents Tex. Woman's U., 1973—. Mem. Nat. Assn. Bank Women (chmn. Houston 1965-66, regional v.p., 1965-66), Harris County Savs. and Loan League (pres. 1969). Home: 1132 Shelterwood Dr Houston TX 77008 Office: PO Box 7483 Houston TX 77008

PERRY, MARY-FRANCES FOLEY (MRS. BERNARD J. PERRY), former electronics exec.; b. Holyoke, Mass., Oct. 21, 1925; d. Francis Joseph and Katharyne (Driscoll) Foley; student U. N.H., 1943-45; B.A., Notre Dame Coll., 1961; m. Bernard J. Perry, Oct. 21, 1944; children—Mary-Frances (Mrs. William B. Sterndale), Paula (Mrs. Richard F. Wadleigh, Jr.), Susan E. (Mrs. Gary C. LaPointe), Bernard J. Treas., dir., R.C.L. Electronics, Inc., Manchester, N.H., 1962-69. Mem. adv. com. vocational edn. Manchester Sch. Bd. Chmn. bd. trustees Notre Dame Coll.; mem. governing bd. Sacred Heart Hosp.; mem. adv. com. N.H. Coll. and Univ. Council; incorporator, trustee Catholic Med. Center. Home: 1080 Montgomery St Manchester NH 03102

PERRY, REVA ANDERSON (MRS. JOHN OWEN PERRY), coll. adminstr.; b. Rutland, Vt., Dec. 13, 1941; d. Henry Oscar and Helen Mable (Scribner) Anderson; Rutland Bus. Coll., 1961; m. John Owen Perry, Dec. 18, 1964; 1 dau., Linnea Kay. Sec. to registrar and dean of coll. Castleton State Coll., Castleton, Vt., 1961-69, registrar, 1969—. Registrar Selective Service Local Bd. 11, Rutland, 1964—, mem. bd., 1973—. Home: RFD Chittenden VT 05737 Office: Castleton State College Castleton VT 05735

PERRY, ROSALIE SANDRA, state ofcl.; b. Little Rock, May 31, 1945; d. John William and Rosalie (Baer) Perry; Mus.B. with honors, U. Ark., 1967; M.A., U. Tex., 1969, Ph.D., 1971. Information specialist U. Tex. Office Financial Aid, Austin, 1968-70; exec. dir. dept. planning Office Ark. State Arts and Humanities, Little Rock, 1971—. Recipient gold medals Nat. Biennial Piano Rec. Festival, 1957, 59. Mem. Phi Beta Kappa, Alpha Lambda Delta, Sigma Alpha Iota. Democrat. Author: Charles Ives and The American Mind, 1974. Home: 8112 Westwood St Little Rock AR 72204 Office: 404 Train Station Sq Little Rock AR 72201

PERRY, SOPHIE LIVADAS (MRS. GEORGE E. PERRY), physician; b. Athens, Greece, June 10, 1929 (came to U.S. 1954, naturalized, 1957); d. Spyros P. and Irene (Katalanou) Livadas; M.D., U. Athens, 1954; m. George E. Perry, Oct. 4, 1953; children—Clio Irene, Constance Maria. Intern, Greenpoint Hosp., Bklyn., 1954-55; resident pathology Met. Hosp., N.Y.C., 1956-57, St. Clare's Hosp., N.Y.C., 1957-58, VA Hosp., N.Y.C., 1959-61; asst. pathologist St. Elizabeth (N.J.) Hosp., 1961-62; asso. pathologist St. Mary Hosp., Hoboken, N.J., 1962; pathologist, D.C. Gen. Hosp., Washington, 1962-67, acting dir. labs., 1967-68, dir. labs., 1968—; clin. instr. pathology Georgetown U. Sch. Medicine, 1963—; clin. asst. prof. pathology Howard U. Sch. Medicine, 1967—. Dir. Sch. Certified Lab. Assts., 1967—. Diplomate Am. Bd. Pathology. Fellow Coll. Am. Pathologists, Washington Soc. Pathologists. Home: 6100 Eastview St Bethesda MD 20034 Office: DC Gen Hosp 19th and Massachusetts Av SE Washington DC 20003

PERSHING, RUTH WHIPPLE (MRS. IRVING KIMBALL PERSHING), educator; b. Saugatuck, Mich.; d. Harold Clifford and Leah (Durham) Whipple; student Mich. State U., 1947-49; B.S., Western Mich. U., 1953, M.A., 1957, postgrad. (Vocational Rehab. Adminstrs. trainee), 1960-61, Specialist in Edn., 1969; m. Irving Kimball Pershing, Feb. 17, 1962; 1 dau., Bonnie Kimball. Chief occupational therapy Detroit Cerebral Palsy Center, 1953-56; asst. prof. occupational therapy Tex. Woman's U. Sch. Occupational Therapy, Denton, 1957-60, asso. prof., 1961-72, prof., 1972—, asst. dir. occupational therapy, 1957-60, dir., 1961—. Served with USAAF, 1945-47. Mem. Am., Mich., Tex., World Fedn. occupational therapy assns., Am. Assn. U. Women, Am. Assn. U. Profs., Tex. Assn. Coll. Tchrs., Assn. Schs. Allied Health, Am. Legion, Am. Legion Aux., Ft. Worth Soc. Crippled Children and Adults, Pi Theta Epsilon. Mem. Order Eastern Star. Club: Soroptimist (Denton). Home: 409 Woodland St Denton TX 76204

PERSON, RUTH FINLEY (MRS. EVERT BERTIL PERSON), newspaper exec.; b. San Francisco, Nov. 27, 1916; d. Ernest Latimer and Ruth (Woolsey) Finley; student U. Cal. at Berkeley, 1935-36; m. Evert Bertil Person, Jan. 26, 1944. Vice pres. Press Democrat Pub. Co., Santa Rosa, Cal., 1946-73, sec., 1973—; v.p. Finley Broadcasting Co., Santa Rosa, 1946-73, sec.-treas., 1973—, sec.-treas. Finley Ranch & Land Co., Santa Rosa, 1952—. Concert pianist San Francisco Symphony, 1961, Santa Rosa Symphony, others. Pres. Santa Rosa Symphony League, 1958-59; mem. Ballet Guild. Mem. Cal. Newspaper Pubs. Assn. (women's pres. 1970-71), Alpha Phi, Phi Beta. Clubs: Etude, Saturday Afternoon, Santa Rosa Golf and Country (Santa Rosa); San Francisco Musical, Metropolitan, St. Francis Yacht (San Francisco). Home: 1020 McDonald Av Santa Rosa CA 95404 Office: PO Box 569 Santa Rosa CA 95402

PESEK, KATHERINE ELIZABETH, nurse; b. Jourdanton, Tex., Mar. 5, 1927; d. John Thomas and Elizabeth Georgia (Kallus) Pesek; diploma Santa Rosa Div. of Nursing of Incarnate World Coll., 1948. Staff nurse Shotts Meml. Hosp., Poteet, Tex., 1948-49, adminstr., 1949-55; with Pleasanton (Tex.) Hosp. and Clinic, 1955—, adminstrv. cons., 1973—, also supr. surgery dept. Cons. Retama Manor #1, Pleasanton, Geriatrics Inc., Greeley, Colo. Mem. Am., Tex. nurses assns., Tex. Hosp. Assn. Republican. Roman Catholic. Home: 415 Oakhaven St Pleasanton TX 78064 Office: 310 W Oaklawn Rd Drawer P Pleasanton TX 78064

PESICKA, LELAH LILLIE WEEKS (MRS. RALPH PESICKA), newspaper editor; b. Climbing Hill, Ia., Apr. 2, 1917; d. Irvin and Ada E. (Haakinson) Weeks; student pub. schs.; m. Ralpha Harlan Pesicka, Jan. 10, 1943; children—Patsy (Mrs. James Woolery), William, Ralph Harlan, Edna (Mrs. Ken Bunn), Linda (Mrs. Ole Keehner), Richard. Sec., Ziebach County Extension Office, Dupree, S.D., 1963-69; editor, office mgr. West River Progress, Dupree, 1969—. Pres., County Republican Women's Club. Mem. Am. Legion Aux. (pres. 1964-66). Episcopalian (chmn. Women's Guild 1970). Club: Lonetree Extension (pres. 1959-61). Home: Box 175 Dupree SD 57623 Office: Box 237 Dupree SD 57623

PESMEN, SANDRA ZUCKERMAN (MRS. HAROLD W. PESMEN), reporter; b. Chgo., Mar. 26, 1931; d. Benjamin S. and Emma M. (Lipschultz) Zuckerman; B.S. in Journalism, U. Ill., 1952; m. Harold W. Pesmen, Aug. 16, 1952; children—Bethann, Curtis. Reporter Radio News Service, Chgo., 1952-53, Lerner Chgo. North Side Newspapers, 1953-68, Chgo. Daily News, 1968—. Recipient Golden Key award Ill. Mental Health Assn., 1966-71, Inst. Psychoanalysis award, 1971-72, Ill. State Med. Soc. feature writing award, 1973. Mem. Chgo. Newspaper Guild. Club: Chicago Press. Home: 2811 Fern St Northbrook IL 60062 Office: 401 N Wabash Av Chicago IL 60611

PETCHENIK, EDNA, lumber co. exec.; b. Chgo., July 28, 1931; d. Allen and Ida (Crofts) Petchenik; B.A., Ia. State U., 1953. Sec., Guilford Lumber Co., Chgo., 1954-57, asst. office mgr., 1957-63, office mgr., 1963-68, asst. to pres., 1968—. Chmn. local chpt. Camp Fire Girls; active Cancer Crusade. Mem. Nat. Assn. Bus. and Profl. Women, D.A.R., Delta Delta Delta. Republican. Methodist. Mem. Order Eastern Star. Address: 335 Lincolnwood Rd Highland Park IL 60035

PETER, LILY, plantation operator, writer; b. Marvell, Ark.; d. William Oliver and Florence (Mobrey) Peter; B.S., Memphis State U., 1927; M.A., Vanderbilt U., 1938; grad. student U. Chgo., 1930, Columbia, 1935-36; L.H.D. (hon.), Moravian Coll., Bethlehem, Pa., 1965. Owner, operator plantations, Marvell, Ratio (both Ark.); writer poetry, feature articles pub. in S.W. Quarterly, Am. poetry Mag., Etude, Silhouettes, Am. Weave, others; mem. staff S.W. Writers Conf., Corpus Christi, Tex., 1954—, sponsor Ark. Writers' Conf. Chmn. Poetry Day in Ark., 1953—. Hon. trustee Moravian Music Found; mem. nat. council Met. Opera Assn., N.Y.C.; bd. dirs. So. Ginners Assn., Nat. River Acad., Helena, Ark., Ark. State Festival Arts. Recipient Moramus award, Friends of Moravian Music, 1964; Distinguished Alumni award Vanderbilt U., 1964; named Ark. Democrat Woman of Year, 1971; Liberty Bell award Phillips County Bar Assn., 1971; Kenneth Beaudoin Gemstone award, 1967; named poet laureate of Ark., 1971. Mem D.A.R. (hon. state regent), Nat. League Am. Pen Women, Ark. Authors and Composers Soc. (Gold Cup of Achievement 1965), Poets' Roundtable Ark. (C.C. Allard award 1962), Poetry socs. of Tenn., Tex., Ga., Okla. (Gold Cup 1967), Sigma Alpha Iota. Democrat. Methodist. Clubs: Pacaha (Helena, Ark.); Woman's City (Little Rock, Ark.). Author: The Green Linen of Summer, 1964; The Great Riding, 1966; The Sea Dream of the Mississippi, 1973. Home: Route 2 Box 69 Marvell AR 72366

PETERMANN, MARY LOCKE, biochemist; b. Laurium, Mich., Feb. 26, 1908; d. Albert Edward and Anna (Grierson) Petermann; A.B., Smith Coll., 1929, D.Sc., 1966; Ph.D., U. Wis., 1939. Postdoctoral fellow U. Wis., 1939-42, 44-45, profl. asst. com. med. research NDRC, 1942-44; research chemist Meml. Hosp., N.Y.C., 1945-46; asso. Sloan-Kettering Inst. Cancer Research, N.Y.C., 1946-60, asso. mem., 1960-63, mem., 1963-73, mem. emeritus, 1973—; prof. Sloan-Kettering div. Grad. Sch. Med. Scis., Cornell U., 1966-73, prof. emeritus, 1973—. Recipient Sloan award in cancer research, 1963; Garvan medal, 1966. Fellow N.Y. Acad. Sci.; mem. Am. Soc. Biol. Chemists, Biophys. Soc., Am. Assn. Cancer Research. Republican. Presbyn. Author: The Physical and Chemical Properties of Ribosomes, 1964. Contbr. articles to profl. jours. Home: 315 E 56th St New York City NY 10022 Office: 425 E 68th St New York City NY 10021

PETERS, ANN DEHUFF (MRS. RICHARD MORSE PETERS), pediatrician; b. Augusta, Ga., Mar. 22, 1915; d. John David and Elizabeth Mary (Willis) DeHuff; B.A. cum laude, U. N.M., 1936; B.S., Simmons Coll., 1937, M.S., 1938; M.D. cum laude, Washington U., St. Louis, 1946; m. Richard Morse Peters, Oct. 12, 1946; children—Joan, Deborah, Barbara, Richard Morse. Caseworker, Children's Bur. of Indpls. Orphan Asylum, 1938-42, case supr., in child placement and adoption, 1942-43; intern obstetrics and gynecology Johns Hopkins Hosp., Balt., 1946-47; med. research asst. Children's Bur., Washington, 1947-49; fellow in neuropsychiatry and preventive medicine Washington U. Sch. Medicine, St. Louis, 1949-51, instr., 1951-52; mem. pediatrics faculty, U. N.C. at Chapel Hill, 1953-69, asso. prof. maternal and child health Sch. Pub. Health, 1960-69; lectr. child devel. San Diego State U., 1971-72, 74—; clin. asso. prof. pediatrics U. Cal. at San Diego, 1971—; pediatric cons. San Diego Children's Health Center, 1970-72; research pediatrician Neuropsychiat. Inst., U. Cal. at Los Angeles, 1974—. Chmn. task force on health and sanitation Nat. Study on Day Care Licensing, 1971-72; cons. to com. on infant and presch. child Am. Acad. Pediatrics, 1970-72. Bd. dirs. Cal. Children's Lobby, 1971—. Fellow Am. Pub. Health Assn. (chmn. com. on day care 1962-68), Am. Orthopsychiat. Assn. (mem. task force on early childhood programs 1971, chmn. ad hoc commn. on current issues in day care 1973—), mem. Soc. for Research in Child Devel., Nat. Assn. for Edn. of Young Children (chmn. commn. on health 1973—), Day Care and Child Devel. Council Am. (dir. 1971—), San Diego Pediatric Soc. Home: 1010 Muirlands Vista Way La Jolla CA 92037

PETERS, BEULAH MARJORIE (MRS. WILLIAM PETERS), real estate broker, educator; b. Chgo., Sept. 25, 1917; d. George H. and Margaret G. (Schneider) Schumacher; certificate in Real Estate, Victor Valley Coll., 1973; m. Frank Lanser, Sept. 28, 1940 (dec. Aug. 1954); children—Vivian (Mrs. H.A. Stafford Jr.), Yvonne (Mrs. Wayne Fox), Valerie (Mrs. John Deems), Frank G., Jack F., Jill Marie; m. William Peters, Dec. 16, 1961 (dec. Aug. 1972). Salesman, V.A. Cornish Realty, Victorville, Cal., 1965-69; broker, owner Tri-Valley Realty Co., Victorville, 1969—. Instr., Victor Valley Coll., 1972—, mem. real estate adv. com., 1970-72. Mem. Victor Valley Bd. Realtors (pres. 1972), Cal. Real Estate Assn. (state dir.), Santa Maria (pres. 1952-53), Victor Valley (pres. 1971-72) bus. and profl. women's clubs, Victor Valley Altrusa Club (v.p. 1973-74). Home: 15700 Rimrock Rd Apple Valley CA 92307 Office: 14741 7th St Victorville CA 92392

PETERS, CAROL BEATTIE TAYLOR (MRS. FRANK ALBERT PETERS), mathematician; b. Washington, May 10, 1932; d. Edwin Lucius and Lois (Beattie) Taylor; B.S., U. Md., 1954, M.A., 1958; m. Frank Albert Peters, Feb. 26, 1955; children—Thomas, June, Erick. Group mgr. Tech. Operations, Inc., Arlington, Va., 1957-62, sr. staff scientist, 1964-66; supervisory analyst Datatrol Corp., Silver Spring, Md., 1962; project dir. Computer Concepts, Inc., Silver Spring, 1963-64; mem. tech. staff Informatics Inc., Bethesda, Md., 1966-67, now tech. dir. software systems Mem. Assn. Computing Machinery, Operations Research Soc., I.E.E.E. Computer Group. Home: 12321 Glen Mill Rd Potomac MD 20854 Office: 6000 Executive Blvd Rockville MD 20852

PETERS, DOROTHY MARIE, educator; b. Sutton, Neb., Oct. 23, 1913; d. Sylvester and Anna (Olander) Peters; A.B. with high distinction, Neb. Wesleyan U., 1941; M.A., Northwestern U., 1957; Ed.D., Ind. U., 1968. Tchr. Neb. pub. schs., 1931-38; caseworker Douglas County Assistance Bur., Omaha, 1941; hosp. field dir., gen. field rep. A.R.C., 1941-50; social worker Urban League, Meth. Ch., Planned Parenthood, Washington, 1951-53; asst. prin., dir. guidance, Manlius (Ill.) Community High Sch., 1953-58; dean of girls, guidance dir. Woodruff High Sch., Peoria, Ill., 1958-66; lectr. edn.-Bradley U.,

Peoria, 1959—; coordinator counseling and evaluation Peoria Pub. Sch. System, 1966-68, dir. pupil services, 1968-72, dir. youth service programs, vol. program cons. Central Ill. chpt. and Heart of Ill. div. A.R.C., Peoria, 1973—. Bd. dirs, home service com. disaster com. Peoria chpt. A.R.C., 1958—; staff counselor, bd. dirs. Ct. Counselor Program; mem. Human Resources Council, City of Peoria; mem. Tri County Comprehensive Health Planning Com.; Sec. Coordinating Com. for Parent Edn.; rep. on Ill. Commn. on Children; rep., liaison, mem. adv. panel Project-Action Now for Children and Youth Nat. Com. for Children and Youth. Mem. Peoria Edn. Assn. (v.p. 1962-64), Ill. Guidance and Personnel Assn. (v.p. Area 8, 1963-64), N.E.A., Ill. Edn. Assn. (del. 1962-64), Am. Personnel and Guidance Assn., Am. Sch. Counselors Assn., Nat. Assn. Women Deans and Counselors (exec. bd. 1972—), Ill. Vocational Guidance Assn. (dir.), Ill. Assn. Women Deans and Counselors (sec.), Am. Assn. U. Women, Phi Kappa Phi, Psi Chi, Pi Gamma Mu, Pi Lambda Theta, Delta Kappa Gamma (scholarship com.), Alpha Gamma Delta. Clubs: Pilot, Willow Knolls Country, Creve Couer. Home: 3307 N Missouri Peoria IL 61603 Office: 3202 N Wisconsin St Peoria IL 61603

PETERS, ESTHER DORR BROWN (MRS. KENNETH WILLIAM PETERS), radio commentator, newspaper editor; b. Germantown, Pa.; d. Everett Henry and Ruth Dalton (Leeds) Brown; student Bryn Mawr Coll., 1934-35; m. Frank J. Oehlschlaeger, May 12, 1936 (div. Sept. 1954); children—Anne Louise, Frank Kirchhoff, Everett Henry Brown; m. 2d, Kenneth William Peters, Oct. 30, 1954 (dec. Nov. 1970); 1 dau., Susan. Ency. research and writer Kendall Morton Assos., N.Y.C., 1937-40; womens program dir., commentator Radio Sta. WLNH, Laconia, N.H., 1954-62, 64-68, women's program dir., sales mgr., 1968—; editor columnist Laconia News, 1963-68. Gen. chmn. Gilford (N.H.) Sesquicentennial, 1962; mem. Gilford Sch. Bd., 1957-63, chmn., 1960, 63; mem. Gilford Planning Bd., 1954-57, Gilford Conservation Commn., 1964-68, 72—. sec., 1964-67; sec. Gilford Civil Def. Adv. Com.; incorporator, Lakes Region Gen. Hosp., 1957—; dir. Lakes Region Clean Water Com.; bd. dirs. Save the Mill Soc. Mem. N.H. Assn. Hist. Socs. (v.p. 1963-65), N.H. Archaeol. Soc., Bus. and Profl. Womens Club (v.p.), N.H. Fedn. Womens Clubs, C. of C. Episcopalian (vestrywoman). Clubs: Womans (pres. 1963-65), Altrusa (pres. 1968-70, internat. bd. 1972—), Emblem. Home: RD 2 Cotton Hill Laconia NH 03246 Office: Sta WLNH Parade Rd Laconia NH 03246

PETERS, EUNICE SARAH BATES LOWERY (MRS. WILLIAM J. PETERS), artist; b. Chelsea, Mass., Oct. 18, 1906; d. William Edgar and Eunice Hall (Fergusson) Lowery; grad. Famous Artists Sch., Mind Psi-Genics; M. Psycho-Cybernetics, Am. Inst. Motivational Sci.; m. William J. Peters, June 3, 1927 (dec. June 1967); children—Eunice L. (Mrs. Ben C. Harrington), William J. Exhibited in group shows at Pasadena Soc. Artists, San Gabriel Soc. Arts. Sec., dir. Trail Chem. Corp., El Monte, Cal., 1947. Mem. Pasadena Arts Council, Pasadena Artists Assn., San Gabriel Fine Arts and Culture Assn., Pasadena Artists, Nat. League Am. Pen Women (pres. Pasadena br. 1972-74), Composers and Artists (Pasadena br.). Home: 1315 Montery Pl San Marino CA 91108 Office: 9904 Gidley St El Monte CA 91731

PETERS, FRANCES ELIZABETH, librarian; b. Phila., Nov. 25, 1915; d. Alexander and Sarah Mower (Scott) Peters; B.S. in Edn., U. Pa., 1936, M.A. in Latin (Univ. fellow), 1938; B.S. in L.S., Drexel Inst. Tech., 1940; M.L.S., Drexel U., 1966. Br. librarian Free Library of Phila., 1951-52, 57-62, asst. in office of work with adults, 1953-57, asst. in art dept., 1945-48, asst. in extension div., 1941-45; librarian Holiday mag. Curtis Pub. Co., Phila., 1948-51; asst. librarian Pedagogical Library, Sch. Dist. Phila., 1962-63; librarian Cheltenham High Sch., Wyncote, Pa., 1963-66, Community Coll., Temple U., Phila., 1966-67; asst. librarian Holy Family Coll., Phila., 1967; librarian Pa. Coll. Podiatric Medicine, Phila., 1968—. Mem. Spl. Libraries Assn., Am. Assn. U. Women, English-Speaking Union, Classical Assn. Atlantic States, Phila. Classical Assn., Hist. Soc. Pa., Am. Classical League, Am. Soc. for Information Sci., Cruiser Olympia Assn., Assn. Colls. Podiatric Medicine, Pi Lambda Theta, Eta Sigma Phi, Beta Phi Mu, Phi Delta Gamma, Phi Kappa Phi. Republican. Baptist. Soroptimist. Home: 3634 Midvale Av Philadelphia PA 19129 Office: Charles E Krausz Library Pa Coll Podiatric Medicine 8th St at Race St Philadelphia PA 19107

PETERS, GERTRUDE JANE, motel owner; b. Albia, Ia., Aug. 3, 1907; d. Joseph Alva and Maggie (Hoogendorn) Miller; student Pa. Sch. Commerce, 1925. Order desk clk. Carr & Young Millwork Co., Des Moines, Ia., 1925-28, Hieb Radio, 1929-31; office mgr. Midwest Timmerman Co., Des Moines, 1932-34; bookkeeper Winston Newell Co., Des Moines, 1935-37, Nat. Assn. Credit Men, Des Moines, 1938-40, Railway Express, Dayton, O., 1941-46; legal sec. Allen Whitfield, Des Moines, 1947-52; owner Dairy Queen, Waseca, Minn., 1953-54; owner Tall Corn Motel, Shenandoah, Ia., 1955—. Mem. Altrusa Club, Bus. and Profl. Women, Am. Motel Assn., Ia. Restaurant Assn. Home and office: Junction Hwy 2 Hwy 59 Hwy 48 Shenandoah IA 51601

PETERS, JOANN, lawyer; b. Cotulla, Tex., Nov. 25, 1933; d. Joe J. and Lulu (Philips) Peters; B.S. in Chemistry, N. Tex. State U., 1955; J.D., So. Meth. U., 1961. Chemist Southwestern Med. Sch., U. Tex., Dallas, 1955-56; with VA Hosp., McKinney, Tex., 1955; research biochemist Scott and White Research Found., Temple, Tex., 1956; chemist Socony Mobile Oil Co., Dallas, 1956-60; admitted to Tex. bar, 1961; claims atty. Rio Grande Nat. Life Ins. Co., Dallas, 1961-62; practice law, Dallas, 1962—; now partner firm Welz, Anderson and Peters, Dallas; counsel Educators Auto Ins. Co., Mid-South Ins. Co., Jefferson Ins. Co., 1964-65; gen. counsel Mutual Security Life Ins. Co., Fort Worth, 1965-67. Chmn. legacy com., counsel Met. Dallas chpt. Nat. Found. March Dimes, 1966—. Bd. dirs. Dallas County Assn. Mental Health, Golf Execs., Ltd., Dallas; bd. dirs., chmn. polit. action task force Women for Change. Mem. Am., Dallas (sec.-treas. criminal bar sect. 1966—), Dallas Jr. (speaker's bur., chmn. 1965—, trial by jury chmn. 1965—), Dallas County Criminal bar assns., State Bar Tex., Dallas Assn. Plaintiffs Attys., Am., Tex. trial lawyers assns., Bus. and Profl. Women's Club (pub. affairs chmn. Dallas club 1965—, dist. rep. women in govt. com. Tex. fedn. 1965—, civic participation chmn. 1966, 69-70, Dallas pres. 1971-72, dist. membership chmn. 1972—), Golf Execs. (membership chmn. 1970-71, v.p. 1971-72), Am. Bus. Women's Assn. (charter pres. Tanda chpt. 1966—, woman of year), Nat. Assn. Women Lawyers, Tex. Women's Polit. Caucus, Women's Equity Action League, Kappa Beta Pi (v.p. 1960), Alpha Chi. Democrat. Club: Zonta (parliamentarian 1970-71) (Dallas). Home: 3217 Rotan Lane Dallas TX 75229 Office: 2720 Fairmount Dallas TX 75201

PETERS, LAURI, actress; b. Detroit, July 2, 1943; d. Harold Carl and Emily Laura (Caldwell) Peterson; grad. High Sch. Performing Arts, 1958; student Quintanos Sch. Young Profls., 1961, Columbia, 1961; ballet tng. Am. Sch. Ballet, N.Y.C., Ballet Russe Cleve., Ballet Arts, N.Y.C.; drama tng. Sanford Meisner, N.Y.C., Tamara Day Kabhanova, N.Y.C.; voice tng. John Mace Studio, N.Y.C.; m. Jon Voight, Apr. 29, 1961 (div. Mar. 1969). Appeared with N.Y.C. Ballet, 1957; Broadway appearances include Say Darling, 1958, First Impressions, 1958, Sound of Music, 1958-60, Cradle Will Rock, 1964, A Murder Among Us, 1963; off-Broadway appearances Seagull, 1966; roles in repertory theatre include Juliet in Romeo and Juliet, San Diego Shakespeare Theatre, 1973, Hilda in Masterbuilder, Olivia in Twelfth Night Tyrone Guthrie Theater, Mpls., 1968-69; Sandra in a Thousand Clowns, Alice in You Can't Take it With You at Man. Theater, 1968-70, Rebecca West in Rosmersholm, also Olivia in Twelfth Night, McCarter Theatre, Princeton, 1973-74, Margaret in Cat on Hot Tin Roof, also Julie in Miss Julie, Theatre Co. of Boston, 1974; films include Mr. Hobbs Takes a Vacation, 1961; Summer Holiday, 1962, For Live of Ivy, 1968; also summer stock; TV appearances Bell Telephone Hour, Dave Garroway Spl., What's My Line, Camera Three, Ghost Story, Search, others. Recipient Daniel Blum Theatre World award, 1959-60; Tony award nomination, 1959-60. MEM. A.F.T.R.A., Screen Actors' Guild, Actors' Equity. Author: After Goodbye, 1971. Home: 345 Riverside Dr New York City NY 10025

PETERS, MARY ANNE JONES (MRS. GERALD O. PETERS), lawyer; b. Clearwater, Fla., Sept. 28, 1922; d. Milton H. and Irene (Baskin) Jones; student Fla. State U., 1940-42, Am. U., 1963-65; J.D., Am. U., 1967; m. Gerald O. Peters, Feb. 7, 1943; children—Judith Lynn (Mrs. David Childs), Gerald Owen, Andrew Howard. Pvt. practice law, Tucson. Mem. legal adv. com. Pima County Juvenile Ct., 1973—; legal adviser to bd. Cerebral Palsy Found. So. Ariz., 1972—. Bd. dirs. Cerebral Palsy Found. Mem. Am., Ariz., Va. Pima County bar assns., Am. Civil Liberties Union, Am. Assn. U. Women, Tucson Symphony Women's Assn., Kappa Delta Pi, Alpha Gamma Delta. Democrat. Methodist. Club: Lakeside Officers (Ft. Huachuca, Ariz.). Home: 6202 San Bernardino Tucson AZ 85715 Office: 177 N Church St Tucson AZ 85701

PETERS, MARY CATHERINE (MRS. LAWRENCE E. USDROWSKI), radiologist; b. Denver, Aug. 23, 1940; d. John George and Alfreda Patricia (Dillon) Peters; B.S., St. Louis U., 1962; M.D., Loyola U., 1966; m. Lawrence E. Usdrowski, Aug. 31, 1972; children—Kate Marie, Brian Lawrence. Intern St. Francis Hosp., Evanston, Ill., 1966-67, resident, 1967-70; practice medicine specializing in radiology, Del Fava & Asso., Evanston, 1970—; mem. staff St. Francis Hosp., Evanston, 1970—. Mem. Am. Coll Radiology. Home: 101 Sterling Lane Wilmette IL 60091 Office: 355 Ridge Av Evanston IL 60202

PETERS, MERCEDES, psychotherapist; b. N.Y.C.; B.S., L.I. U., 1945; postgrad. Columbia, 1944-45; M.S., U Conn., 1953; tng. in therapy Am. Inst. Psychotherapy and Psychoanalysis, 1960-70. Social worker various agys., pub. instns., 1945-63; staff affiliate psychotherapist Community Guidance Service, 1960—; pvt. practice psychotherapy, Bklyn., 1961—. Fellow Am. Orthopsychiat. Assn.; mem. Nat. Assn. Social Workers, League Women Voters, N.A.A.C.P. Office: 106 Pierrepont St Brooklyn NY 11201

PETERS, MILDRED GOLDENBERG (MRS. VICTOR S. PETERS), lawyer; b. Chgo., Nov. 29, 1923; d. Jacob S. and Esther (Williams) Goldenberg; A.B., U. Chgo., 1944, J.D., 1949; m. Victor S. Peters, July 13, 1946; children—Scott, James F. Admitted to Ill. bar, 1952; interviewing atty. Legal Aid Bur., Chgo., 1963-66; mem. firm Peters & Peters, Northfield, Ill., 1966—. Mem. Fed. defender panel No. Dist. Ill., Chgo., 1966—. Village trustee on Village Council, Winnetka, Ill., 1972—; mem. plan commn. Village of Winnetka, Ill., 1973—; sec. Winnetka (Ill.) Caucus Com., 1965. Mem. Chgo. Bar Assn., Woman's Bar Assn. Chgo., U. Chgo. Law Sch. Alumni Assn. (dir. 1971—). Home: 1205 Sunset Rd Winnetka IL 60093 Office: 550 Frontage Rd Northfield IL 60093

PETERS, PATRICIA ANN, banker; b. Santa Monica, Cal., Sept. 17, 1943; d. John Dennis and Dorothy Amanda (Tydeman) Peters; B.A. magna cum laude and with distinction, Cornell U., 1965; M.A. in Econs., Stanford, 1966. With Morgan Guaranty Trust Co., N.Y.C., 1966—, asst. treas., 1968-70, asst. v.p., 1970-73, v.p., 1973—. Mem. Phi Beta Kappa. Club: Mid-America (Chgo.). Home: 311 E 71st St New York City NY 10021 Office: 23 Wall St New York City NY 10015

PETERS, ROBERTA, soprano, operatic singer; b. N.Y.C.; d. Sol and Ruth (Hirsch) Peters; ed. privately; Litt.D., Elmira College, 1967; Mus.D., Ithaca Coll., 1968, Westminster Coll., 1974, m. Bertram Fields, Apr. 10, 1955; children—Paul Adam, Bruce Eric. Made Met. Opera debut as Zerlina in Don Giovanni, also appears in Rigoletto, The Magic Flute, The Barber of Seville, The Marriage of Figaro, Den Rosenkavalier, Cosi Fan Tutte, Lucia, Orfeo, Tales of Hoffman, Masked Ball, Die Fledermaus, Don Pasquale, Gianni Schicchi, La Sonambula; appeared in Cin. Opera, Pitts. Opera, San Antonio Opera, Tulsa Opera, Hartford Opera Co., also concert tours, appearances with symphony orchestras in Chgo., Cin., Pitts., Minn., others; appeared in motion pictures Tonight We Sing, Barber of Seville; frequent appearances on radio and TV, sang at Royal Opera House Convent Garden, London, Eng., Deutsche Oper Berlin, Stuttgart Opera; concert tours in U.S., and many European countries; debut State Opera in Vienna, Salzburg Festival; command performance for King of Norway; debuts in concert and opera houses West Germany; TV appearances in West Germany, Austria, France, Italy; debut Kirov Opera, Leningrad, 1972, Bolshoi Opera, Moscow, 1972. Recipient Bolshoi medal, 1972; named Woman of Yr. Fedn. Women's Clubs, 1964. Author: (with Louis Biancolli) Debut at the Met, 1967. Address: care Hurok Concerts 1370 Av of Americas New York City NY 10019

PETERS, RUTH DORIS, pediatrician; b. N.Y.C., July 31, 1930; d. Emil John and Beatrice Sofia (Saxon) Peters; A.B., Hunter Coll., 1958; M.D., Woman's Med. Coll. Pa., 1962; adopted daus., Ann Bridget, Kathleen Kimberly. Intern, Nassau County Med. Center, East Meadow, N.Y., 1962-63, resident, 1963-64; resident N.Y. Hosp.-Cornell Med. Center, N.Y.C., 1964-65; practice medicine, specializing in pediatrics, Hicksville, N.Y., 1965—; pediatrician East Nassau Med. Group, Hicksville, 1965—; jr. attending staff, pediatric endocrine clinic Nassau County Med. Center, also Babies Hosp., Columbia-Presbyn. Hosp., 1973—; pediatrician Hope Ship, Natal, Brazil, 1972. Mem. exec. com. Split Rock Sch. P.T.A., Syosset, N.Y., 1971-72. Smith, Kline & French fgn. fellow, India, 1961. Diplomate Am. Bd. Pediatrics. Fellow Am. Acad. Pediatrics; mem. Nassau County Med. Soc., Nassau County Pediatric Soc., Phi Sigma. Office: 350 S Broadway Hicksville NY 11801

PETERSEN, CAROL MARGARET (MRS. GEORGE CLIVE HOOK), lawyer; b. Highland Park, Ill., Dec. 30, 1940; d. Edward Hjalmar and Beryl LaRue (Shindoler) Petersen; student DePauw U., 1958-59; B.S., U. Ill. at Urbana, 1962; M.A., Stanford, 1963, J.D., 1966; m. George Clive Hook, May 11, 1968. Admitted to Cal., Ill. bars, 1967; practiced in Chgo., 1967—; asso. firm Schiff Hardin & Waite, Chgo., 1966-72, partner, 1973—. Recipient citation Leadership Council for Met. Open Communities, Chgo., 1970. Mem. Am., Ill., Chgo (vice chmn. younger members sect. 1971-73) bar assns., Women's Bar Assn. Ill. (sec. 1969-70, dir. 1969-72), Stanford Law Soc. Midwest (v.p. 1971-72), Chgo. Council Lawyers, Phi Beta Kappa. Home: 2650 Lakeview Chicago IL 60614 Office: Schiff Hardin & Waite 231 S LaSalle St Chicago IL 60604

PETERSEN, GAIL MARIE, advt. co. exec.; b. Fertile, Minn., Oct. 7, 1940; d. Jurgen Hans and Norma Luella (Hendricks) Petersen; B.S. in Journalism, Northwestern U., 1962. Catalog copywriter Sears, Roebuck and Co., Chgo., 1962-64; copywriter E.H. Weiss & Co., Chgo., 1964-67; copywriter J. Walter Thompson Co., Chgo., 1967, group head, 1968, asso. creative dir., 1971-73, v.p. asso. creative dir., 1973—. Office: 875 N Michigan Av Chicago IL 60611

PETERSEN, HAZEL MIRIAM, bus. woman; b. Oleander, Cal., Oct. 17, 1915; d. Maurice and Lydia (Petersen) Petersen; student Dana Coll., Neb., 1933, 34, Fresno State Coll., 1934-36. Asst. cashier S. H. Kress & Co., 1936-42; payroll mgr. Valley Express Co., Valley Motor Lines, Inc., 1942-69; claims mgr. Imperial Truck Lines, Inc., Los Angeles, 1969-70; N.C.R. supr. Urich Oil Co., Whittier, Cal., 1970—. Pvt. tchr. voice, piano, 1936-65. Mem. Am. Guild Organists, Am. Bus. Women's Assn., Smithsonian Assos., Choral Condrs. Guild, Internat. Platform Assn. Lutheran. Club: Christian Bus. and Profl. Women. Home: Apt A 6311 S Comstock Whittier CA 90601 Office: 12920 E Whittier St Whittier CA 90607

PETERSEN, NANCY KAY (MRS. KENNETH WILLIAM PETERSEN), broadcasting co. exec.; b. Hollywood, Cal., May 9, 1943; d. Cyril James and Virginia (Van Norden) Woodbridge; B.A., Cal. State U. San Diego, 1965; m. Kenneth William Petersen, Jan. 28, 1968. With pub. relations Braille Inst. Am., Los Angeles, 1967-68; audience promotion radio sta. KFI, Los Angeles, 1968-69; editorial researcher KNBC/Channel 4, Burbank, Cal., 1969—. Mem. Alpha Gamma Delta. Home: 1725 N Niagara St Burbank CA 91506 Office: KNBC/Channel 4 3000 W Alameda Av Burbank CA 91523

PETERSON, A.E.S. (MRS. CARL U. PETERSON), artist; b. Northampton, Mass., June 30, 1908; d. Albert Hobart and Louise Josephia (Lenardson) Sanderson; pvt. study painting; m. Carl U. Peterson, May 1, 1937. Exhibited one-man shows Attleboro (Mass.) Mus., Providence (R.I.) Water Color Club, Providence Art Club, Newport (R.I.) Art Assn.; exhibited group shows N.A.D., Nat. Arts Club, N.Y.C., Riverside Mus., N.Y.C., Bristol (R.I.) Art Mus., Attleboro Art Mus.; represented in permanent collections Nat. Shawmut Bank, Boston, R.I. Hosp. Trust Co., Providence, Grant Capital Mgmt. Corp., Providence, Tillinghast-Stiles Co., East Providence. Recipient Am. Watercolor Soc. awards, 1968; Nat. Soc. Painters in Casein medal, 1968, awards, 1970, 73; Audubon Artists award, 1969, Nat. Art League awards (2), 1969; Painters and Sculptors Soc. N.J. award, 1970, medal, 1973; awards Allied Artists Am., 1970, Catharine Lorillard Wolfe Art Club, 1970, Greater Fall River Art Assn., 1970; gold medal Catharine Lorillard Wolfe Art Club, 1971; awards Greater Fall River Art Assn., 1971, Allied Artists Am., 1973, others. Mem. Am. Watercolor Soc., Nat. Soc. Painters in Casein and Acrylic (dir. 1970—, chmn. traveling exhbns. 1971—), Allied Artists Am., Painters and Sculptors Soc. N.J., Catharine Lorillard Wolfe Art Club, Nat. Assn. Women Artists, Nat. Art League, Providence Art Club (mem. ladies adv. bd. 1965-68), Providence Water Color Club (treas. 1962-70, rec. sec. 1971—), Attleboro Mus., Bristol Art Mus., Internat. Platform Assn. Home and studio: 27 Holbrook Av Rumford RI 02916

PETERSON, AGNES F., research instn. exec.; b. Berlin, Germany, Mar. 8, 1923; d. Hermann O. L. and Ruth (Seckels) Fischer; B.A., U. Toronto, 1945; M.A., Radcliffe Coll., 1949; m. Louis J. Peterson, Dec. 22, 1954. Research asst. Nat. Film Bd. Can., Ottawa, Ont., 1945-48; library asst. Cal Hist. Soc., 1949-52; circulation and reference asst. Hoover Instn. War, Revolution and Peace, Stanford, 1952-54, acting curator Central and Western European collection, 1954-59, curator Central and Western European collection, 1959—. Mem. Am. Hist. Assn., Conf. Group on German Politics, Soc. for French Hist. Studies, Cal. Hist. Soc. Compiler: (with Grete Heinz) Guide to Hoover Instn. Microfilm Collection, 1964; (with Gabor Erdelyi) German Periodical Publications, 1967; (with Grete Heinz) The French Fifth Republic: Establishment and Consolidation, 1958-1965, 1970; Western Europe, 1970; (with Grete Heinz) The French Fifth Republic: Continuity and Change, 1966-1970, 1974. Contbr. reviews to Library Journal. Home: 362 Yerba Buena Av Los Altos CA 94022 Office: Hoover Institution Stanford Univ Stanford CA 94305

PETERSON, ANN, marketing cons., former sch. adminstr.; b. Boston, Feb. 19, 1928; d. Edwin Thomas and Ethel (Asnault) Peterson; B.S., Simmons Coll., 1949; M.B.A., Boston U., 1971. Chemist, Otis Clapp & Son, Boston, 1949-50; chemist, tracer lab. Harvard Sch. Pub. Health, Boston, 1950-51, sec., technician, 1951-61; adminstrv. asst. Mass. Inst. Tech., Cambridge, 1961-69; adminstrv. asst. Boston U., 1969-71; dir. admissions Katharine Gibbs Sch., Boston, 1971-72, dir. Katharine Gibbs Sch., Boston, 1972-74; marketing cons., 1974—. Mem. nat. alumni council Boston U., 1973—, mem. alumni awards com., 1972, 73. Mem. Am. Acad. Polit. and Social Scis., Pan Am. Soc. New Eng., Mass. Assn. Bus. Schs. (dir. 1973-74), Mass. Personnel and Guidance Assn., Greater Boston Personnel and Guidance Assn., Greater Boston C. of C., Beta Gamma Sigma. Club: Executives (Boston). Address: Princess Anne Bus Coll 2924 N Lynnhaven Rd Virginia Beach VA 23452

PETERSON, BARBARA PRESTON (MRS. KERMIT SVEIN PETERSON), civic worker; b. Kenmare, N.D., July 19, 1928; d. Harry Earl and Althea Frances (Hurd) Preston; student U. N.D., 1946-49; m. Kermit Svein Peterson, Aug. 28, 1949; children—Stefan, Sarajane, Seth, Sabin. Del. Republican Nat. Conv., 1968; corr. sec. N.D. Rep. Women's Fedn., 1972-74. Bd. dirs. Mouse River Theatre, 1972-73, Minot Symphony Assn., 1974—, Lake Metigoshe Assn., 1974. Presbyn. (bd. ruling elders). Home: 1508 7th Av NW Minot ND 58601

PETERSON, BETTY ANN (MRS. WALLACE B. PETERSON), newspaper photographer and writer; b. Waco, Tex., July 12, 1929; d. James Herbert and Verna Elsie (Jones) Guthrie; student U. Tex., 1948-49, Rosenberg Coll. (Switzerland), 1949; m. Wallace Bennett Peterson, Nov. 27, 1952; children—Wallace Bennett, Kenneth J., David W., Kathryn V., Ronald L., Nancy A. Soc. writer and photographer Aurora (Colo.) Sun Newspaper, 1972—, also dir. Mem. Colo. Democratic Exec. Com., 1968-69; chmn. Arapahoe County Senatorial Dist. 22, 1968; del. county and state convs., 1974. Recipient award Camp Fire Girls, 1973. Clubs: Cherry Creek Women's (charter), Eleanor Roosevelt (charter) (Aurora). Home: 2420 S Lima St Denver CO 80232 Office: 1585 Chester St Aurora CO 80010

PETERSON, ELEANOR MARIE, ednl. adminstr.; b. Spokane; d. Carl A. and Eda (Johnson) Peterson; B.A., Wash. State U., 1933; M.A., Columbia, 1942, Ph.D., 1953. High sch. tchr., Manson and Spokane, 1933-44; counselor Spokane pub. schs., 1946-52; dir. spl. services Spokane Pub. Schs., 1952-66, asst. supt. schs., 1966—. Instr., vis. lectr. U. Wash., 1960, Central Wash. State Coll., 1958, Whitworth Coll., 1956-66. Mem. adv. bd. Salvation Army, 1960—; bd. dirs. Riverview Terrace and Med. Center Named Spokane Woman of Achievement, 1966. Served with USNR, 1944-46. Mem. Am., Wash. psychol. assns., Am., Wash. State (sec. 1961) personnel and guidance assns., Nat., Wash. (pres. 1962) assns. woman deans and counselors, N.E.A., Nat., Wash. assns. sch. adminstrs., Nat. Assn. Pupil Personnel Adminstrn., Nat. Council for Exceptional Children, Phi Beta Kappa,

Pi Lambda Theta, Delta Kappa Gamma. Club: Zonta (pres. Spokane 1955). Author: Aspects of Readability in the Social Studies, 1953; Successful Living, 1956, rev. edit., 1968. Home: 1919 W Glass St Spokane WA 99205 Office: 825 W Trent St Spokane WA 99201

PETERSON, ELLEN WELCH, educator; b. Charlotte, N.C., Dec. 5, 1923; s. Shelby Walker and May Yancey (Long) Salisbury; B.S., U. Ga., 1945; M.S., Appalachian State U., 1965. Tchr. pub. schs., Ky., Fla., 1945-48; with Comml. Credit Corp., N.Y.C., 1949; with Ferro Spl. Labs., Los Angeles, 1950; tchr. Lynnwood, Cal., 1955; owner children's camp, Bogota, Colombia, 1957-62; tchr. Hosler Sch., Largo, Fla., 1962-65; with Edison Community Coll., Ft. Myers, Fla., 1965—, dir. guidance and counseling, 1967—. Mem. Am. Personnel and Guidance Assn., Nat. Assn. Women Deans, Adminstrs. and Counselors. Home: PO Box 2422 Fort Myers Beach FL 33931 Office: College Pkwy Fort Myers FL 33901

PETERSON, ESTHER EGGERTSEN (MRS. OLIVER PETERSON), consumer adviser; d. Lars E. and Annie (Nielsen) Eggertsen; A.B., Brigham Young U., 1927; M.A., Columbia, 1930; LL.D., Smith Coll., 1963, Bryant Coll., Carnegie Inst. Tech., Montclair Coll. 1964; hon. degrees Hood and Mercyhurst Colls., 1966, Northeastern U., Western Coll. for Women, U. So. Utah, Mich. State U., U. Mich., U. Utah; m. Oliver A. Peterson, May 28, 1932; children—Karen Kristine, Eric Niels, Iver Echart, Lars Erling. Tchr., Br. Agr. Coll., Cedar City, Utah, 1927, Winsor Sch., Boston, 1930-36; asst. dir. edn. Amalgamated Clothing Workers, N.Y.C., 1939-44, dir. edn., Washington, 1945-48, 69—; legislative rep. Indsl. Union Dept., AFL-CIO 1958-61; dir. women's bur. Dept. Labor, Washington, 1961-64, asst. sec. labor for labor standards, 1961-69; spl. asst. to Pres. for consumer affairs, 1964-67; chmn. Pres.'s Com. Consumer Interests, 1964-67; exec. vice chmn. Pres.'s Commn. on Status Women, 1963-65; exec. vice chmn. Interdeptl. Com. on Status Women, 1963-65, vice chmn., 1965—; adviser U.S. delegation ILO Conf., Geneva, Switzerland, 1961, 64; mem. White House Conf. on Food, Nutrition, and Health, 1969; consumer adviser Giant Food, Inc., Landover, Md., 1970—. Active YWCA. Worked with Swedish and Belgium trade unions and Internat. Confedn. Free Trade Unions, 1944-56; hon. chmn. Nat. Com. Household Employment. Mem. Consumer Fedn. Am. (v.p. 1969), Am. Assn. U. Women, Am. Newspaper Women's Club (asso.), League Women Voters, Am. Home Econs. Assn. (hon.), Nat. Consumer League, Inst. Am. Democracy, Bus. and Profl. Womens Club, Women's Africa Com. Phi Chi Theta (hon.). Clubs: Women's Nat. Democratic (pres. 1969-70), Nat. Capital Democratic. Contbr. articles in field. Home: 7714 13th St Washington DC 20012 Office: 815 16th St NW Washington DC 20006

PETERSON, FREDDIE-NADINE, surgeon; b. Varna, Ill., June 26, 1911; d. Enoch Fred and Edna Munn (Ledwith) Peterson; B.S., Northwestern U., 1933, M.B., 1939, M.D., 1940; 1 adopted dau., Valerie Anne. Intern, Milw. County Gen. Hosp., 1939-40; surg. resident Passavant Meml. Hosp., Chgo., 1940-41, Milw. Children's Hosp., 1941-43; plastic surgery, preceptor Milw., 1943-47; resident Milw. Children's Hosp., 1955-56; practice medicine, specializing in plastic and reconstructive surgery, Milw., 1947-53, also specializing in pediatrics, Wayland, Mass., 1959—; med. fellow Children's Med. Center, Boston, 1956-58. Instr. oral medicine Marquette U. Dental Sch., Milw., 1945-50; pediatric investigator NIH maternal infant health program Boston Lying-In Hosp., 1958-64; head civilian def. program for physicians Milwaukee County Med. Soc., 1947-53; founder, mgr. DuPont Creche and Youth Centre for Fgn. Missions, Kingston, Jamaica, Brit. W.I., 1954-55; mem. staff, dir. pediatric emergency service Newton-Wellesley Hosp.; mem. staff lying-in div. Boston Hosp. for Women, Boston Children's Med. Center Oconomowoc (Wis.) Meml. hosps.; physician Wayland pub. schs., 1962-68 pediatrician, surgeon Hartland Clinic (Wis.), 1971—. Served as sr. surgeon, med. dir. USPHS Res., 1965. Diplomate Am. Bd. Plastic Surgery, Am. Bd. Pediatircs; mem. A.M.A., Wis., Waukesha County med. socs., New Eng. Pediatric Soc., Delta Delta Delta. Republican. Clubs: Alumni of Boston, Children's Hosp.; Milwaukee Athletic; Wayland Swimming and Tennis. Home: 6151 Sand Beach Rd Oconomowoc WI 53066 Office: Oconomowoc WI 53066

PETERSON, HELEN JENNIE MORGAN, state ofcl.; b. Hastings, Neb., June 21, 1914; d. Julian Brown and Florence (Loghry) Morgan; B.A., Neb. Wesleyan U., 1945; m. Hollis M. Johnson, Nov. 9, 1933 (dec. Feb. 1947); children—Gregg Morgan, Stephanie Jane (Mrs. Donald John Elder); m. 2d, Russell E. Peterson, Nov. 6, 1948 (div. Jan. 1963); children—Hjordis Marie (Mrs. Ronald Johnson), Douglas Emil Peterson. With Torrington (Wyo.) Telegram, 1935-38; with Hardin (Mont.) Tribune-Herald, 1938-73, pub., 1947-73, editor, 1959-73; mem. Mont. State Tax Appeal Bd., Helena, 1973—. Chmn. Hardin Camp Fire Council, 1952; bd. dirs., chmn. pub. relations Custer Battle Re-enactment, 1964-73; sec. Gov.'s Task Force on Indian problems, 1969-70. Recipient Mont. 4-H Alumni Recognition award, 1963. Mem. Mont. Press Assn. (pres. 1967, chmn. exec. com. 1968, dir., life mem.), Nat. Press Women, Pi Kappa Delta, Phi Gamma Mu. Home: B-10 Park Av Apts Helena MT 59601 Office: State Tax Appeal Bd Helena MT 59607

PETERSON, HELEN MAY STONE (MRS. ARTHUR H. PETERSON), author; b. Binghamton, N.Y., May 12, 1910; d. George Fordyce and May (Cox) Stone; A.B., Oberlin Coll., 1932; M.S.S., Smith Coll., 1933; m. Arthur H. Peterson, July 7, 1934; children—George E., Arthur H. Social worker Community Service Soc., N.Y.C., 1934-36, Bur. Mental Hygiene, Conn. State Dept. Health, Hartford, Conn., 1936-39. Home service worker A.R.C. Tompkins County (N.Y.), 1941-42; den mother Cub Scouts, Ithaca, N.Y., 1954-59. Bd. dirs. N. and W. Side Settlement Houses, Ithaca, 1948-51. Mem. Nat. Assn. Social Workers. Clubs: Agrl. Circle (pres. 1955-56), Campus (pres. 1957-58) (Cornell U.). Author: Henry Clay, 1964; Jane Addams, 1965; Abigail Adams, 1967; Roger Williams, 1968; Electing Our Presidents, 1970; Susan B. Anthony, 1971; Sojourner Truth, 1972; Give us Liberty! The Story of the Declaration of Independence, 1973; The Making of the U.S. Constitution, 1974. Address: 223 Highgate Rd Ithaca NY 14850

PETERSON, KAREN IDA, research co. exec.; b. Rahway, N.J., Dec. 30, 1939; d. Sigurd Thage and Harriet Erma (Pearson) Peterson; B.A., Wellesley Coll., 1961. Research asst. Opinion Research Corp., Princeton, N.J., 1961-63, Interpublic Group of Companies, N.Y.C., 1963-65; with Oxtoby-Smith, Inc., N.Y.C., 1965—, v.p., 1970—, mem. mgmt. com., 1970—. Lectr. marketing research Am. Mgmt. Assn., 1973—. Mem. Am. Marketing Assn. (co-chmn. N.Y. chpt. marketing research workshop 1973). Club: N.Y. Wellesley Coll. (dir. 1971-73). Home: 354 W 23rd St New York City NY 10011 Office: 150 E 58th St New York City NY 10022

PETERSON, MARGARET ANN SCHAWDE (MRS. JOSEPH F. PETERSON), ednl. adminstr.; b. Dodgeville, Wis., May 29, 1927; d. Herman and Wilma L. (Murrish) Schawde; B.A. in Journalism, U. Wis., 1948; m. Joseph F. Peterson, June 22, 1948; children—Charles J., Alan A., Richard S. Librarian, faculty asst. Sch. Journalism, U. Wis. at Madison, 1948-49; free-lance writer, editor, designer, Kiel and Muscoda, Wis., 1949-65; office supr. M. B. Victora Ins. Agy., Muscoda, 1963-65; librarian, publs. coördinator St. Joseph's Hosp. Sch. Nursing, Marshfield, Wis., 1965-66; pub. information coordinator U. Wis. Center System, Marshfield-Wood County campus, Marshfield, and continuing edn. agt. U. Extension, Marshfield, 1966-71, community relations rep. Mid-State Tech. Inst., Marshfield, Stevens Point and Wisconsin Rapids, Wis., 1971—. Dir. Title 1 Fine Arts Project for Central Wis., 1966-67. Publicity chmn. Marshfield Four Score Com., 1967. Bd. dirs. Marshfield council Camp Fire Girls, 1967—, Marshfield Art Com.; adv. council Sunburst Youth Homes, 1972—. Recipient Writing awards Wis. Press Women, 1968, 69, 70, 71, 72, 73, Am. Assn. U. Women (Wis.) Short Story project, 1972, Nat. Merit award, 1973. Mem. Am. Assn. U. Women (Marshfield historian 1968—, dir. 1973—), Marshfield Bus. and Profl. Women (pres. 1972-74), North Wood County Hist. Soc. (writers group chmn. 1973—), U. Wis. Alumni Assn., Women's Action Council Marshfield (founding chmn. 1972), North Wood County Brotherhood Com. (chmn. 1973), Delta Kappa Gamma. Methodist. Clubs: Women's (Marshfield); Central Wis. Press. Editor: Marshfield Centennial Commemorative History, 1972. Office: Mid-State Vocational Tech and Adult Edn Dist Wisconsin Rapids WI 54494

PETERSON, MARTHA, coll. pres.; b. Jamestown, Kan., June 22, 1916; d. Anton R. and Gail (French) Peterson; A.B., U. Kan., 1937, M.A., 1943, Ph.D., 1959; postgrad. Northwestern U., Columbia U.; L.H.D., Chatham Coll., 1968, Med. Coll. Pa., 1970, Molloy Coll., 1971, Mundelein Coll., 1972, Pace Coll., 1974; LL.D., Columbia U., 1968, Douglass Coll., 1968, Hofstra U., 1969, Austin Coll., 1972, Hamilton Coll., 1974. Instr. U. Kan., 1942-46, asst. dean women, 1946-52, dean women, 1952-56; dean women U. Wis., 1956-63, asst. to pres., 1963, univ. dean for student affairs, 1963-67; pres. Barnard Coll., N.Y.C., 1967—. Dir. Dry Dock Savs. Bank, Exxon, Met. Life Ins. Co. Mem. exec. com. Commn. Ind. Colls. and Univs. Assn. Colls. and Univs. N.Y., 1969—; mem. adv. council presidents Assn. Governing Bds. Univs. and Colls.; chmn. Empire State Found. Ind. Liberal Arts Coll. Trustee Chatham Coll., Pitts., 1965—, Coll. Entrance Exam. Bd.; bd. overseers Bowdoin Coll. Recipient Distinguished Alumni award, U. Kan., 1968, medalist award N.Y. Acad. Pub. Edn. Mem. Am. Council Edn. (student personnel commn. 1956-59, chmn. exec. com. 1971—), Nat. Assn. Women Deans and Counselors (exec. bd. 1959-61, pres. 1965-67), Intercollegiate Assn. Women Students (nat. adviser 1953-55, 59-61.) Am. Personnel and Guidance Assn., Am. Arbitration Assn. (dir.), Phi Beta Kappa, Sigma Xi, Mortar Bd., Pi Lambda Theta, Phi Kappa Phi. Office: Barnard College New York City NY 10027

PETERSON, MAXINE WAUSON (MRS. CARROLL V. PETERSON), city ofcl.; b. Tokio, Tex., Jan. 1, 1932; d. Archie and Clara Belle (Winkler) Wauson; R.N., Beth El Sch. Nursing, 1953; m. Carroll V. Peterson, Mar. 14, 1954; children—Trent, Terryl, Laurel, Janet. Office nurse Colorado Springs, 1953-54; nurse Gen. Hosp., Mpls., 1954-56, U. Ia. Hosp., Iowa City, 1959-60; city councilwoman, Durango, Colo., 1973—. Mem. Durango City Planning Commn., Animas Regional Planning Commn., Recreation and Conservation Devel. Council. Bd. dirs. Colo. Health Planning Council. Mem. League of Women Voters, Colo. Municipal League, San Juan Ecol. Soc. Home: 622 3d Av Durango CO 81301 Office: Box 872 Durango CO 81301

PETERSON, MILDRED OTHMER, lectr., writer, librarian, civic leader; b. Omaha, Oct. 19, 1902; d. Frederick George and Freda Darling (Snyder) Othmer; student U. Neb., U. Ia., U. Chgo., Northwestern U.; m. Howard R. Peterson, Aug. 25, 1923 (dec. Feb. 1970). Asst. Central High Sch. Library, Omaha, 1915-19; asst. Tech. High Sch. Library, 1919-20; asst. purchasing agt. Met. Utilities Dist., 1920-21; asst, U. Neb. library, 1921-23; tchr. piano, Harlan, Ia., 1924-26; dir. pub. relations and gen. asst. Des Moines Pub. Library, 1928-35; broadcaster weekly book programs WHO and other Ia. radio stas.; columnist, writer Mid-West News Syndicate, Des Moines Register and Tribune, editor Book Marks, 1929-35; writer for Drug Topics, Drug Trade News and others, for No. Ill., 1935; editor Adelphean of Alpha Delta Pi, 1938-39; writer and spl. asst. A.L.A., 1935—, Chgo. Tribune, 1941—; lectr. on travel, fgn. jewelry and internat. relations, 1940—; lectr. S.S. Rotterdam of Holland Am. Line, 1971. Del. 1st Assembly Librarians of Americas, Washington, 1947. Chgo. chmn. India Famine Relief, 1943. A founder, pres. Pan. Am. Bd. Edn., 1955-58, Internat. Visitors Center, 1954-58; rep. Chgo. at State Dept. Founding Conf. on Community Services to Fgn. Visitors, Washington, 1957; mem. Mayor's Com. on Chgo. Beautiful. Cited by Chgo. Sun and Ill. Adult Edn. Council; recipient scholarship in Latin-Am. field U. Chgo. and Coordinator Inter-Am. Affairs, U.S. Govt., 1943. Bd. dirs. YWCA. Recipient world understanding merit award Chgo. Council Fgn. Relations, 1955; named Woman of Year for U.S. and Can. by Alpha Delta Pi, 1955; recipient Distinguished Service award Hospitality Center, 1958; Distinguished Service medal U. Neb., 1963; Ambassador of Friendship award Am. Friendship Club, 1963; Merit award YWCA; Civic Salute WMAQ Radio, Chgo., 1965; Distinguished Service award Pan-Am. Bd. Edn., 1966, also founders award, 1968; Laura Hughes Lunde Meml. award Citizens of Greater Chgo., 1968; Uruguayan medal, 1952; Internat. Eloy Alfaro medal, 1952, medal Order of Carlos Manuel de Cespedes, 1956 (Cuba); medal Order of Vasco Nunez de Balboa (Panama), 1956; Internat. Friendship award Girls Scouts of Philippines, 1971, Outstanding Service award Orgn. Am. States, 1971, Distinguished Service award Internat. Travelers Assn., 1971. Fellow Am. Internat. Acad. (life mem.); mem. Nat. Council Women U.S., Pan-Am. Bd. Edn., U.S. Capitol, Ill., Neb., Chgo. hist. socs., Chgo. Natural History Mus., Citizenship Council Met. Chgo., Oriental Inst., Am. Heritage Council, Am., Ill. library assns., Friends Chgo. Pub. Library, Chgo. Opera Guild, Chgo. Hort. Soc., Marquis Biog. Soc., Am. Security Council, Chgo. Zool. Soc., Mus. Contemporary Art, Crossroads Student Center, Hyde Park Neighborhood Club, Hyde Park-Kenwood Community Conf., Internat. House Assn., Japan-Am. Soc. Soc. Woman Geographers, Ill. Partners of Ams. (gov.'s com. Sao Paulo, Brazil), Council Fgn. Relations (speakers bur.), Pan Am. Council (a founder, distinguished service award 1966), Library Internat. Relations (consular ball com.), U. Neb. Alumni Assn. (past pres. local chpts.), U. Neb. Found., Chgo. Symphony Orch. Soc., Chgo. Art Inst., U. Chgo. Service League (dir.) Am. Legion Aux. (mem. of state boards of Ia. and Ill.), Am. Assn. U. Women, League Women Voters, Children's Benefit League, United Negro Coll. Fund Bd., Renaissance Soc., Peruvian Arts Soc., Hispanic Soc. Chgo., Chgo. Acad. Scis. (woman's bd.) Chgo. Chamber Orch. Assn., John G. Shedd Soc., Internat. Platform Assn., Alpha Delta Pi (past pres. local alumnae chpts.), Xi Delta. Mem. Order Eastern Star. Clubs: South Shore Country, College, Quadrangle, Ill. Athletic, University of Chicago Dames, Iowa Authors; Pan Am Airways Clipper; United Airlines 100,000 Mile; Lakeside Lawn Bowling, Hyde Park Neighborhood. Contbr. newspapers, periodicals, encys. and yearbooks. Visited and photographed with husband 118 fgn. countries. Travels and lectrs. on fgn. countries. Unofcl. attendant numerous internat. confs. Address: 5834 Stony Island Av Chicago IL 60637

PETERSON, MODENA HODGES, physician; b. Cumberland, Miss., June 25, 1903; d. Key Rushing and Donna (Walker) Hodges; B.A., U. Miss., 1929, B.S., 1934; M.D., U. Tenn., 1938; m. Paul F. Peterson, June 4, 1929; 1 son, Paul Key. Intern Asbury Hosp., Mpls., 1938-39; physician Blue Mountain (Miss.) Coll., 1939-50; resident Sedgwick Hosp., Wichita, Kan., 1950-51; mem. staff Miss. State Hosp., Whitfield, 1951-74, now ret. Mem. A.M.A., Miss. Women's Med. Assn., Am., Miss. psychiat. assns., Capitol Bus. and Profl. Club, Va., and So. geneal. socs., Alpha Epsilon Iota. Home: Wesson MS 39191

PETERSON, NADEEN ANN, advt. agy. exec.; b. McKeesport, Pa., Dec. 3, 1934; d. Michael James and LaVerna Peal (Long) Powell; student U. Fla., 1952-53; m. Robert Glenn Kilzer, Dec. 24, 1966; 1 son, Douglas Robert Kilzer. Copywriter, Ellington & Co., N.Y.C. 1961-64; v.p., asso. creative dir. Tatham-Laird, N.Y.C., 1964-65; v.p., asso. creative dir. Foote, Cone & Belding, Inc., N.Y.C., 1966-69; v.p., sr. asso. creative dir. Norman, Craig & Kummell, N.Y.C., 1969; sr. v.p., creative dir. D'Arcy-MacManus-Intermarco, Inc., N.Y.C., 1970-72; partner, sr. v.p., dir. creative services Lord, Geller, Federico, Peterson, Inc., N.Y.C., 1972-74; v.p., dir. creative workshop Kenyon & Eckhardt, Inc., N.Y.C., 1974—. Home: 15 W 81st St New York City NY 10024 Office: 200 Park Av New York City NY 10017

PETERSON, NANCY ANN, editor; b. St. Paul, Mar. 11, 1943; d. Robert Francis and Genevieve Alice (Schoenecker) Peterson; A.A., Hibbing Jr. Coll., 1963; B.A., Marquette U., 1966. Pub. relations asst. United Community Services, Milw., 1966-67; asso. univ. editor Marquette U., Milw., 1967-69; asst. editor St. Paul Cos., Inc., 1970-72; writer-editor Center for Ednl. Devel., U. Minn., Mpls., 1972—. Mem. Women in Communications (pres. Milw. chpt. 1968-69, chmn. progress of women com. Mpls.-St. Paul chpt. 1972—), Kappa Tau Alpha. Home: 1947 Grand Av St Paul MN 55105 Office: 317 Walter Library U Minn Minneapolis MN 55455

PETERSON, PATRICIA MARIE, educator; b. Albany, N.Y., Apr. 14, 1926; d. Eric L. and Anne (McMichael) Peterson; B.S., State Tchrs. Coll., Cortland, N.Y., 1948, M.S., 1952; postgrad. U. Colo., 1958; Ph.D., U. So. Cal., 1967. Supr. elementary and jr. high phys. edn. Hudson (N.Y.) Pub. Schs., 1948-49; tchr. Delmar (N.Y.) Grade Sch., Bethlehem Central Sch. Dist., 1949-52; phys. edn. instr. Cazenovia (N.Y.) Jr. Coll., 1952-55; asst. prof. phys. edn., women's ski coach U. Vt., Burlington, 1955-60; instr. phys. edn. Smith Coll., Northampton, Mass., 1960-66; prof., chmn. dept. women's health and phys. edn. State U. N.Y., Coll. Arts and Sci., Oswego, 1967—. mem. Nat. Ski Hall of Fame and Hist. Com., U.S. Ski Edn. Found., 1967—; asst. leader U.S. Collegiate Sports Council Ski Team, 1972. Mem. Internat. Assn. Ski Instrn., Eastern Ski Assn., Far West Ski Assn., A.A.H.P.E.R. (eastern dist. chmn. div. girls and women's sports 1962-65), Nat., Eastern (sec. 1971-73) assns. phys. edn. coll. women, Gen. Alumni Assn. U. So. Cal. (univ. scholarship alumni interview chmn. Albany and Upper N.Y. State 1971—), North Am. Soc. Sport History. Home: 28 Harris Av Albany NY 12208 Office: State U Coll Oswego NY 13126

PETERSON, PHYLLIS KATHRYN SMITH (MRS. SUMNER W. PETERSON), stock broker; b. Edmonton, Alta., Can.; d. Frank M. and Edna (Malone) Smith; grad. New Eng. Conservatory Music, 1942; A.B., Am. U., 1953; m. Sumner W. Peterson, Sept. 4, 1942; children—Phyllis S., Peri S. Came to U.S., 1937, naturalized, 1945. Registered rep. Sade & Co. (mem. N.Y. Stock Exchange), Washington, 1961—, gen. partner, 1963—. Mem. Phila.-Balt.-Washington, Am. stock exchange. Trustee, chmn. finance com. Am. U., Washington. Mem. Air Force Aid Soc., Air Force Assn. Episcopalian. Clubs: Army-Navy Country (Arlington, Va.); Army-Navy (Washington). Home: 2744 Quebec St Arlington VA 20007 Office: 905 16th St NW Washington DC 20006

PETERSON, SARA JANE GODSHALL (MRS. JAMES CLEMENT PETERSON), research analyst; b. Washington, Jan. 24, 1946; d. Melvin William and Bertha Fredericka (Bier) G.; B.A., Gettysburg Coll., 1966; postgrad. Syracuse U., 1971; m. James Clement Peterson, Sept. 14, 1969; 1 dau., Rebecca Sue. Math. statistician Current Medicare Survey, Office Research and Statistics, Social Security Adminstrn., Dept. Health Edn. and Welfare, Balt., 1966-70; research asso. Greater Delaware Valley Regional Med. Program, Haverford, Pa., 1970; program analyst Syracuse (N.Y.) U. Research Corp., 1970-73; research analyst, program developer People's Equal Action for Community Effort, Inc., Syracuse, 1973—. Mem. community witness and World mission coms. Iroquois Assn. Am. Bapt. Chs., 1970—. Mem. Am. Pub. Health Assn. Democrat.

PETERSON, SHIRLEY ANN KAISER, state ofcl.; b. Stuart, Neb., Mar. 12, 1935; d. Leon Leonard and Pearl Cecilia (Zahradnicek) Kaiser; student Graceland Coll., 1954-55; m. Charles Roland Peterson, Jan. l, 1953; children—Barbara, Brenda, Belinda, Charles Roland II, Clifton, Blythe. Mem. Atkinson (Neb.) Sch. Bd., 1961-70; mem. Neb. Bd. Edn., since 1971—. Mem. Precinct Election Bd., 1965-71; pres. Holt County Fedn. Republican. Women, 1971—; sec. Neb. Fedn. Rep. Women, 1973—. Mem. Ch. of Jesus Christ of Latter-day Saints (treas. local ch. 1959-64). Club: Extension (Atkinson) (pres. 1966—). Address: Amelia NE 68711

PETHERICK, FLORENCE RUBY (MRS. HAROLD PETHERICK), educator; b. Leominster, Mass.; d. Albert Samuel and Anna (Merrifield) Ruby; A.B., Calvin Coolidge Coll., 1942; A.M., Boston U., 1945, Ph.D., 1954; m. Harold Petherick, Oct. 11, 1926; 1 dau., Ann (Mrs. Charles Ludeking). Instr., Fisher Jr. Coll., 1952-55; prof. Suffolk U., Boston, 1956—, chmn. dept. humanities, 1970—. Mem. Am. Assn. U. Profs., Pi Gamma Mu. Home: 98 Union Bridge Rd Duxbury MA 02332 Office: 41 Temple St Boston MA 02114

PETIONI, MURIEL MARJORIE (MRS. MALLALIEU S. WOOLFOLK), physician; b. Trinidad, B.W.I., Jan. 1, 1914; d. Charles Augustin and Rosa (Allen) Petioni; B.S., Howard U., 1934, M.D., 1937; m. Mallalieu S. Woolfolk, June 6, 1942; 1 son, Charles M. Came to U.S., 1919, naturalized, 1925. Intern, Harlem Hosp., N.Y.C., 1937-39; coll. physician Wilberforce U., Xenia, O., 1939-40, Ala. State Tchrs. Coll., Montgomery, 1940-42, Bennett Coll., Greensboro, N.C., 1942-45, Hampton (Va.) Inst., 1945-46; practice medicine, specializing in family medicine, N.Y.C., 1950—; chief gen. practice staff Mt. Morris Hosp., 1955-64; mem. staff Harlem Hosp., 1962—. Med. adminstr. United Harlem Drug Detoxification Service, 1970-71; med. adviser Narcotic Program Council Harlem's Smaller Chs., 1970-71; mem. med. adv. com. on Headstart, 1967—; mem. med. adv. com. on Medicaid, 1967—. Bd. dirs. Bergen County council Girl Scouts U.S., Morrisania Youth and Community Service Center Inc. Named Woman of the Year, Morrisania Youth Community Service Center, 1969; recipient Hon. award N.Y. Council Smaller Chs., 1970, Elks, 1970. Mem. N.Y.C. Dept. Health Sch. Physicians, Nat. Med. Assn., Am. Acad. Gen. Practice, Drs. Assn. N.Y.C. (gov.), N.A.A.C.P., Howard U. Alumni Assn., Delta Sigma Theta. Mem. Order Eastern Star, Elk. Home: 114 W 131st St New York City NY 10027

PETITT, KATHLEEN OVERBEY (MRS. GERALD WILLIAM PETITT), advt. co. exec.; b. Fairborn, O., Nov. 10, 1947; d. George Douglas and Margaret Kathleen (Roberts) Overbey; B. Journalism, U. Mo., 1969; postgrad. Hunter Coll., 1972—; m. Gerald William Petitt, May 13, 1972. Jr. writer pub. relations Cunningham & Walsh, Inc., N.Y.C., 1969-70; account exec. and chief copy writer R & L Advt. Co., N.Y.C., 1970-71; account exec. Kert Advt. Co., Toronto, Ont., Can., 1972-73; account exec. Needham & Grohmann Inc., N.Y.C.,

1971-72, 73—. Mem. Assn. Nat. Advertisers, Women in Communications. Republican. Presbyn. Contbr. travel articles to newspapers, mags. Home: 160 Waverly Place New York City NY 10014 Office: 30 Rockefeller Plaza New York City NY 10020

PETLUCK, ANN S., social work adminstr., lawyer; b. N.Y.C., Apr. 17, 1908; d. Joseph and Alice (Serber) Petluck; B.Sc. (Elliott F. Shepard Scholar 1927-28), N.Y.U., 1928, LL.B., 1929, LL.M., 1930; M.S. in Social Work, Columbia, 1942; m. Meyer Poses, June 19, 1932. Admitted to N.Y. bar, 1930; pvt. practice, N.Y.C., 1931-33; caseworker Bklyn. sect. Nat. Council Jewish Women, 1934-36, caseworker, then supr. nat. coordinating com., 1936-42; dir. migration services Nat. Refugee Service and United Service for New Ams., including liaison work with govt. orgns., 1942-51; asst. exec. dir. United Service for New Americans, 1951-54; dir. U.S. operations of United Hias Service, 1954-64; dep. regional rep. to UN High Commn. for Refugees, 1964-68; exec. dir. Assn. Jewish Family and Children's Agys., 1972-73; cons. on refugee matters. Lectr. law Grad. Sch. Social Work Adelphi Coll., 1952-60; U.S. agys. rep. to Internat. Refugee Orgn. conf. on specialists, Gwatt, Switzerland, 1948; chmn. resettlement tech. com. Am. Council Vol. Agys., 1948-54, 56-64; mem. bd. Am. Immigration and Citizenship Conf., 1959-64, 68—; bd., chmn. legislative com. Nat. Council Naturalization and Citizenship, 1958-60; mem. bd. Internat. League Rights of Man. Mem. Am. Bar Assn., Assn. Immigration and Nationality Lawyers, Nat. Assn. Women Lawyers, Internat. Conf. Social Work, Nat. Conf. Jewish Communal Services, Internat. League for Rights of Man (dir.), Eclectic, Internat. Platform Assn., Alpha Epsilon Phi, Tau Kappa Alpha. Home: 441 E 20th St New York City NY 10010

PETRI, HILDA NEIHARDT, lawyer; b. Bancroft, Neb., Dec. 6, 1916; d. John G. and Mona (Martinsen) Neihardt; A.B., U. Neb., 1937; J.D., U. Mo., 1963; m. Albert J. Petri, Apr. 18, 1942; children—Gail Evalyn (Mrs. William Toedebusch), Robin Neihardt, Coralie Joyce. With Consulate of Switzerland, St. Louis, 1937-42, admitted to Mo. bar, 1963; mem. firm Petri, Tofle & Oxenhandler, Columbia, Mo., 1963—; asso. dir. devel. Stephens Coll., Columbia, 1973—. Mem. Rock Bridge Meml. Park Bd., 1967—. Bd. dirs. Wayne State Found., Neihardt Found. Served with WAVES, 1944-45. Mem. Mo. Bar, Am. Judicature Soc., Boone County Bar Assn. (sec. 1970-72). Club: Quota (Columbia). Home: Route 5 Box 249A Columbia MO 65201 Office: 110 N 8th St Columbia MO 65201 also Stephens Coll Columbia MO 65201

PETRICK, ARLINE C., nurse, educator; b. Webster, Mass., May 20, 1927; d. George Rudolph and Louise (Neuhaus) Petrick; B.S., Boston U., 1952, M.S., 1960. Asst. dir. nursing Ring Sanatorium, Arlington, Mass., 1952-53; supr. Mass. Mental Health Center, Boston, 1955-58; asso. prof., coordinator child psychiat. nursing program Boston U., 1959-69; asst. prof., coordinator child psychiat. nursing program U. Md., Balt., 1969-71; dir. nursing Harbor Mental Health and Mental Retardation Area, Erich Lindemann Mental Health Center, Boston, 1971—. Mem. Am. Nurses Assn., Nat. League Nursing, Am. Orthopsychiat. Assn., Sigma Theta Tau. Contbr. articles to profl. jours. Home: 100 Prospect Av Revere MA 02151 Office: Govt Center Boston MA 02103

PETRIE, ASENATH SCHONFELD, med. psychologist; b. London, Eng., Nov. 29, 1914, came to U.S., 1957; d. Victor and Rachel (Sternberg) Schonfeld; B.Sc., London U., 1936, Ph.D., 1954. Research psychologist Neuroses Center for Allied Forces, Mill Hill Emergency Hosp., London, 1944-47; vis. research psychologist St. George's and Atkinson Morley hosps., 1947-51; dir. Rockefeller Project, Inst. Psychiatry, London, 1952-56; med. research psychologist Mattapan Chronic Disease Hosp., Boston City Hosp., 1956-69; asso. dept. surgery Harvard Med. Sch., 1957-70; sr. research fellow Health Edn. Council, London, 1970-73; fellow Inst. for Study Pathology of Behavior, Chgo., 1973—; cons. dept. orgn. and health care Hadassah Med. Orgn., Jerusalem, 1973—. Cons. Ednl. Testing Service, 1971—. Cons. U. Chgo. Med. Sch., 1962-68, NIH, 1965-69, U. Cal. Med. Sch. at San Francisco, 1965-66, Pitts. Sch. Pub. Health, 1965-70, E. I. DuPont de Nemours & Co., 1968-69; vis. tchr. Kings Coll., 1948-49, U. Cal. Med. Sch., 1965-66, Stanford, 1966-67. Worker evacuation London, 1939-44; adminstr. relief work refugee camps, Europe and Asia, 1942-47. NIH grantee, 1958-65, Founds. Fund for Research in Psychiatry grantee, 1957, Israel Zangwill Fund grantee, 1970, Population Council grantee, 1971, Rockefeller fellow, 1943-47; Fulbright fellow U. Pa., 1951-52; Lasker fellow, 1957-58. Author: Personality and Frontal Lobes, 1952; Individuality in Pain and Suffering, 1967. Inventor perceptual reduction and augmentation meter. Address: 30 Hurley St Belmont MA 02178

PETRIE, ELIZABETH M. (MRS. DONALD A. PETRIE), civic worker; b. Camden, N.J.; d. Walter Eugene and Janet (Harbage) Murphy; LL.D., Drexel Inst. Tech., 1964; L.H.D., Ursinus Coll., 1965; LL.D., Temple U., 1972; m. Donald A. Petrie, Sept. 12, 1973; children from previous marriage—Theodore A. Hallstrom II, Janet Hallstrom (Mrs. Scurria). Past pres. Phila. League Women Voters; exec. dir. Phila. br. Fgn. Policy Assn., 1947-49, World Affairs Council Phila., 1946-52; chmn. Bd. Trade and Convs., Phila., 1952-54; bd. mgrs. Savs. Fund of Germantown, 1971-73; dir. Blue Cross Phila., 1959-73. Mem. Phila. Bd. Pub. Edn., 1957-71, Pa. Bd. Pub. Edn., 1963-71. Vice pres. Phila. Museum Art; trustee Phila. Coll. Art. Unitarian. Club: Cosmopolitan (Phila).

PETRIE, MILDRED MCCLARY TYMESON (MRS. GEORGE W. PETRIE III), writer; b. South Stukely, Que., Can., Sept. 26, 1912; d. Rodney H. and Sayde M. (Lanphear) McClary; A.B., Atlantic Union Coll., 1933; A.M., Boston U., 1947; postgrad. Harvard, 1966, U. Wis., 1971; m. Ralph A. Tymeson, Oct. 20, 1935; m. 2d. George W. Petrie III, Jan. 1, 1967. Author: American Authors, 1940; The Norton Story, 1953, rev. edit. 1960; Men of Metal, 1954; Rural Retrospect, 1956; The Book of Quaboag, 1960; Old As The Hills, 1960; As Far West As The Sunset, 1962; Two Towers, The Story of Worcester Tech, 1965; This Is Worcester, 1965; Paul Revere, 1965; Worcester Centennial, 1948; But One Lamp, 1970; Worcester Bankbook, 1956, rev. edit. 1966; The Lancastrian Towns, 1967; writer articles and poetry for numerous mags. Mem. Gov.'s Com. for Marquette-Jolliet Tercentenary, 1973. Mem. Author's Guild, Nat. League Am. Pen Women (br. pres. 1964-66), Univ. League, Am. Assn. U. Women. Conglist. (mus. dir. 1940-48). Home: 4573 Northlake Dr Sarasota FL 33580 also 1170 Mt Mary Dr Green Bay WI 54302

PETRIE, YVONNE ELAINE, fashion editor; b. Hammond, Ind., Nov. 29, 1927; d. Harold Francis and Elizabeth (Nuttall) Petrie; student U. Chgo., 1946-47, Ind. U., 1948-49, U. Mich., 1957; m. Charles L. Nevins, Apr. 25, 1959; children—Noel, Charles. Reporter women's dept. Hammond (Ind.) Times, 1948-53; reporter, fashion editor, columnist Detroit News, 1953—; commentator fashion shows, speaker clubs, Detroit. Recipient 1st prize women's page feature div. Theta Sigma Phi (Ind.), 1949; J. C. Penney-U. Mo. fashion reporting award, 1963, spl. award, 1973; Headliner award Detroit chpt. Women in Communication, 1964; Mich. Women's Press Club award, 1970; 2 awards U.S. Men's Fashion Assn., 1972. Mem. Fashion Group Detroit (regional dir. 1961-62), Women in Communications, Sigma Delta Chi. Clubs: Detroit Yacht, Detroit Press. Home: 1353 Nicolet Pl Detroit MI 48207 Office: 615 W Lafayette St Detroit MI 48231

PETRIKO, MARY HARTENIAN (MRS. JAMES E. PETRIKO), village ofcl.; b. Shirkieville, Ind., Dec. 19, 1922; d. Frank and Frances (Sporcic) Mahnic; grad. high sch.; m. James E. Petriko, Oct. 17, 1970; children (by previous marriage)—Kenneth M. Hartenian, Lawrence R. Hartenian. Clerical position Nahigian Bros., Chgo., 1939-41; clerical position Village of Riverdale (Ill.), 1965-67, dep. village clk., 1967-69, village clk., 1969—. Mem. Thornton Twp. High Sch. Supt. Adv. Bd., 1968; v.p. P.T.A., Riverdale, 1964-65. Bd. dirs. United Fund Riverdale, 1968—, pres., 1967. Lutheran (supt. Sunday sch. 1957-63, mem. ch. council 1968-73, pres. Altar Guild 1957-59, pres. Ladies Soc. 1963-65). Home: 14325 Edbrooke Av Riverdale IL 60627 Office: 142d St and Stewart Av Riverdale IL 60627

PETROS, SOPHIE KARIPIDES (MRS. THOMAS S. PETROS), home economist, dir. pub. relations; b. Canton, O., Nov. 4, 1932; d. Constantine N. and Martha (Sideropoulos) Karipides; student Ohio State U., 1950-52; B.S. in Journalism, Northwestern U., 1954; m. Thomas S. Petros, Jan. 10, 1960; 1 son, Dean. Tchr. home econs. St. Charles Borromeo Environment House, Chgo., 1958; publicity-promotion asst. Toni Co., Chgo., 1954-55; TV account exec. Yardis Advt. Co., Phila., 1955-56; TV writer, demonstrator Crestline Co., Chgo., 1957; home service rep. Peoples Gas Light & Coke Co., Chgo., 1957-62; dir. pub. relations and advt., sec. Dial On Corp., Milw., 1962—; condr. gourmet cooking show WISN-TV, Milw., 1971—; free-lance food demonstrator; free-lance television commls., 1956—. Chmn., Hope for Hope Fund, Canton, 1954. Recipient debate award Nat. Forensic League, 1950. Mem. Am. Fedn. Television and Radio Artists, Am. Home Econs. Assn., Home Econs. in Bus., Northwestern U. Alumni Assn., Theta Sigma Phi, Alpha Xi Delta. Mem. Greek Orthodox Ch. Clubs: Pilot, St. Constantine and Helen Women's. Author: Sophie Kay's Step-by-Step Cook Book, 1972. Home: 15325 Westover Rd Elm Grove WI 53108 Office: 4747 S Howell Av Milwaukee WI 53207

PETT, AMY JANE, newspaper editor; b. Chgo., Jan. 27, 1943; d. Saul and Leanore (Green) Pett; B.A., Goddard Coll., 1965. Teaching intern Franconia (N.H.) Coll., 1965-66; asst. editor Great Neck (N.Y.) Record, 1969-70; editor Port Washington (N.Y.) News, 1970—, writer women's column, 1972—. Exhibited original embroideries in shows Embroiderer's Guild U.S. Biennial exhibit, N.Y.C. Vice pres. North Shore Open Sch., Port Washington, 1973-74, chmn., 1974—. Recipient awards for embroidery. Office: Port Washington News 270 Main St Port Washington NY 10050

PETTIGREW, KAREN DREIER (MRS. HUGH MCCLELLAND PETTIGREW), statistician; b. Billings, Mo., Oct. 5, 1938; d. Avery Lewis and Frances Alline (Williams) Dreier; student S.W. Mo. State Coll., 1956; A.A., Stephens Coll., 1958; A.B., George Washington U., 1960, M.A., 1964; m. Hugh McClelland Pettigrew, Sept. 9, 1961; children—Lynne Elizabeth, Anne Louise. Research math. statistician Nat. Inst. Mental Health, Bethesda, Md., 1961—. Mem. Am. Statis. Assn., League Women Voters, Biometric Soc. Club: Stephens College Alumnae Northern Virginia. Home: 9118 Friar's Rd Bethesda MD 20034 Office: NIH Bethesda MD 20014

PETTIGREW, MILDRED MAXINE WILLIAMS (MRS. JAMES BRISCOE PETTIGREW), city ofcl.; b. Adamsville, Tenn., Oct. 24, 1916; d. Albert Sidney and Hattie Lena (Majors) Williams; grad. high sch.; m. James Briscoe Pettigrew, Sept. 6, 1935; children—Jimmy Max, Joe Wain. Mgr., accountant Pettigrew Motor Co., Adamsville, 1961-74; commr. parks and recreation City of Adamsville, 1967-73. Democrat. Methodist (pres. United Meth. Women 1961-62, 1971-72; dist. chmn. Christian social relations Women's Soc. Christian Service 1968-72; mem. adminstrv. bd. 1969-72). Home: S Magnolia St Adamsville TN 38310 Office: Main St Adamsville TN 38310

PETTIJOHN, JULIA IVANS (MRS. BRUCE A. PETTIJOHN), lawyer; b. Bklyn., Jan. 27, 1918; d. Peter A. and Wanda (Szwaba) Ivans; A.B., U. Ala., 1941; J.D., Fordham U., 1944; m. Bruce A. Pettijohn, May 10, 1944; 1 dau., Celeste Ann. Admitted to N.Y. bar, 1946, U.S. Supreme Ct. bar, 1961; partner Pettijohn & Pettijohn, Harrison, N.Y., 1946-58, sr. partner, 1953-58; individual practice law, Slingerlands, N.Y., 1958—. Acting rec. clk. Westchester County Land Records Office, 1952; asst. atty. N.Y. State Bd. Equalization and Assessment, 1971. Republican dist. leader Country Club Dist., Harrison, N.Y., 1953-57. Mem. Nat. Assn. Women Lawyers, Am. Assn. U. Women. Club: Westchester Country. Address: 12 Carstead Dr Slingerlands NY 12159

PETTYCREW, JACQUELINE LOUISE PATTERSON, newspaper exec.; b. Chgo., Mar. 16, 1932; d. John William and Marguerite Rose (Letz) Patterson; A.A., Phoenix Coll., 1951; m. Kay Eugene Pettycrew, Sept. 14, 1951 (div. Nov. 1965); children—David Kay, Richard Douglas. With Republic and Gazette, Phoenix Newspapers, Inc., 1950-68, research mgr., 1970—; promotion dir. Thomas Mall, 1969. Mem. Am. Marketing Assn. (pres. 1972-73), Am. Statis. Assn., Sales and Marketing Execs. Internat., Phoenix Execs. Club. Contbr. articles to various publs. Home: 2518 E Meadowbrook St Phoenix AZ 85016 Office: PO Box 1950 Phoenix AZ 85001

PETTYJOHN, ANGELIQUE PERRINS (DOROTHY PERRINS), actress; b. Los Angeles, Mar. 11, 1943; d. Richard Lee and Maia Irene (Enke) Perrins; student Utah State U., 1962-64; m. Otho Pettyjohn, May 11, 1966 (div. Feb. 1968). Legal sec., 1961-62; dancer Las Vegas, 1964-66; appeared in films including Heaven with a Gun, 1969, Clambake, 1968, Tell Me That You Love Me, Junie Moon, 1970, Childish Things, 1967, Salute L'Artiste, 1973; appeared in TV shows including Get Smart, Star Trek, Girl from UNCLE, Batman, It Takes a Thief; dancer, commedienne Barry Ashton's Show, Silver Slipper, Las Vegas, 1970-72; dancer, singer Paris cabaret, 1973-74. Address: PO Box 12073 East Las Vegas NV 89112

PEUGH, SARAH LOUISE PEARSON (MRS. WALTER STEPHEN PEUGH, SR.), columnist, bridal cons.; b. Houston, Miss., Oct. 4, 1924; d. Edd Monroe (dec.) and Mattie (Shivers) (dec.) Pearson; student Trevecca Coll., 1941-43, Miss. state Extension, 1964, Auburn U., 1970, student Itawamba Jr. Coll., 1970; m. Walter Stephen Peugh, Sr., Dec. 20, 1947; children—Sarah (Mrs. T.W. Franks), Mary Jo, Steve, Jr., Bob. Clk., teller First Nat. Bank, Phila. and San Diego, 1944; owner Town House Restaurant, Aberdeen, Miss., 1952-62; owner, cons. Wedding Services, Aberdeen, Miss., 1969—. Columnist Aberdeen Examiner, 1970-74; Aberdeen News Herald, 1974—. Exec. sec. A.R.C., Aberdeen, 1972-73, bd. dirs. 1973—. Named Aberdeen Most Outstanding Woman Jr. Aux. Charity Ball, 1972. Mem. Aberdeen C. of C., Miss. Press Women, Nat. Fedn. Press Women, Internat. Platform Assn., Miss. Poetry Soc., Am. Legion, Tombigbee. Clubs: Woman's (pres. 1973-74), Home and Garden Gourmet (founder) (Aberdeen). Editor The Glencoe Story, 1967. Contbr. poetry to various publs. Address 205 Hillcrest St Aberdeen MS 39730

PEVEY, PEGGY PAGE (MRS. WILLIAM PEVEY), former probate judge; b. Wheeler County, Tex., Feb. 8, 1915; d. James Amos and Madge D. (Clay) Page; student Amarillo Jr. Coll., 1930-31; student West Tex. State U., 1933-34; m. William L. Pevey, Apr. 25, 1935; 1 son, William L. Sec., Elliott & Waldron Abstract Co. Inc., Lovington, N.M., 1957—; probate judge Lea County, Lovington, 1968-72. Mem. Lovington Women's Club, Lovington C. of C., Lovington Bus. and Profl. Womens Club (sec. 1963-64), Lea County Legal Secs. (pres. 1968-69), Altrusa Club (charter). Episcopalian (treas. ch. 1970, 71). Mem. Order Eastern Star (matron 1940-41). Home: 1103 W Av N Lovington NM 88260 Office: Box 817 Lovington NM 88260

PEYSER, MINNA POST, cons. firm exec.; b. N.Y.C., May 17, 1922; d. Philip Mansfield and Ann Urdong (Nadler) Kayden; student U. Pa., 1939-40; B.A., U. Cal. at Los Angeles, 1943, postgrad., 1943-44; postgrad. Columbia, 1950-54, George Washington U., 1963-64, U. Me., 1965, City U. N.Y., 1967-69; m. Seymour M. Peyser, Feb. 27, 1949 (div.); children—Andrea, Jill, Michael. Dir. social service Univ. Religious Conf. U. Cal. at Los Angeles, 1943-44; dep. probation officer Los Angeles County Probation Dept., 1944-45; exec. sec., exec. dir. Nat. Citizens Polit. Action Com., Los Angeles and So. Cal., 1945-46; interior designer, decorator, Beverly Hills, Cal., 1947-48; exec. sec. ad hoc com. to lift ban on The Nation mag., N.Y.C., 1948-50; exec. dir., project dir. research and curriculum devel. Bill of Rights program Civil Liberties Ednl. Found., Inc., N.Y.C., 1956-62; exec. dir., sec.-treas. Nat. Assembly on Teaching the Principles of the Bill of Rights, Washington, 1962-64; cons. Nat. Def. Edn. Act Civics Insts., Media Insts. U.S. Office Edn., Washington, 1966; founder, asso. dir. Center Research and Edn. Am. Liberties, sr. research asso. Columbia, 1965-67; cons. pub. policy and ednl. innovation, N.Y.C., 1967-70; cons. to pres. for planning and devel., mem. faculty Coll. Human Services, N.Y.C., 1968-69; head Minna Post Peyser & Assos., cons. firm, N.Y.C., 1971—. Sr. asso. Network Project, Columbia, 1970—; asso. dir. Energy Inst., N.Y.C., 1974—; lectr. in field. Organizing exec. Nat. Service Center Orgns. Scientists, Scholars and Profls. concerned with Pub. Issues, 1969-70. Pres. P.T.A., Greenburgh, N.Y., 1956-57, legislative chmn. Westchester County (N.Y.) exec. com., 1957-58. Democratic committeewoman, Greenburgh, 1952-63; mem. Woman's Nat. Dem. Club, Washington, 1963—. Mem. Nat. Council Social Studies, Am. Polit. Sci. Assn., Am. Orthopsychiat. Assn., Assn. for Humanistic Psychology, World Future Soc., Am. Humanist Soc., Pi Lambda Theta, Alpha Epsilon Phi. Club: Women's City (N.Y.C.). Author: (with Harriet Pilpel) The Legal Rights of Married Working Women, 1965. Editor: A Bibliography of Civil Rights and Civil Liberties, 1962; A Program for Improving Bill of Rights Teaching in the United States, 1963; Report of Colo. Law Sch. Seminar on Sch. Curricula for Instrn. on Bill of Rights, 1964. Contbr. articles to profl. jours., newspapers, mags. Address: 320 Central Park W New York City NY 10025 also N View Estates Lake Oscawana Putnam Valley NY 10579

PEYTON, RUTH MARGARET, educator; b. Balt., Oct. 19, 1933; d. Robert Edwin and Ruth (Austin) Peyton; B.A. in History, Coll. William and Mary, 1955; M.A. in Art History (scholarship), Northwestern U., 1959, postgrad., 1964—. Mus. aid Nat. Gallery Art, Washington, 1956-57; registrar Albright-Knox Art Gallery, Buffalo, 1960-62; instr. art history U. Va., Charlottesville, 1962-64; instr. Northwestern U., summer 1965, instr. evening div., 1966; instr. art history, curator univ. art gallery Colgate U., Hamilton, N.Y., 1967-68; asst. prof. dept. art Western Ill. U., Macomb, 1970—; interne at Albright-Knox Art Gallery on grant from N.Y. State Council on Arts, 1968-70. Mem. Coll. Art Assn. Am., Am. Assn. U. Profs., Nat. Trust for Historic Preservation, McDonough Arts Council (exec. bd.), Delta Delta Delta. Episcopalian. Home: care of Dr Robert Peyton 108 Ruelle San Antonio TX 78209 Office: Western Ill U Dept Art Macomb IL 61455

PEYTON, SARAH MARGARET, physician; b. Crisfield, Md., Dec. 29, 1895; d. William John and Margaret Edith (Adams) Peyton; A.B., Goucher Coll., 1916; M.D., Johns Hopkins, 1923. Intern New Eng. Hosp. for Women and Children, Boston, 1923-24; physician Playground Athletic League Md., 1924-25; gen. practice medicine, Crisfield, 1925—; mem. staff McCready Meml. Hosp., Crisfield, chief physician, 1970. Mem. welfare bd. Somerset County, Md., 1963-69. Named Citizen of Year, Crisfield C. of C. 1940. Mem. A.M.A., Am. Acad. Family Physicians, Md. Hist. Soc., Md., Crisfield med. assns., Phi Beta Kappa, Delta Delta Delta. Democrat. Methodist (trustee 1966-70). Club: Women Civic (pres. 1946-48) (Crisfield). Address: 33 W Main St Crisfield MD 21817

PEZENIK, DOROTHY PHYLLIS (MRS. ALFRED JOEL PEZENIK), occupational therapist; b. N.Y.C., Nov. 14, 1926; d. Charles Max and Ceil (Mast) World; student U. Toronto, 1944-46, diploma in Occupational Therapy, 1949; m. Alfred Joel Pezenik, Feb. 16, 1960. Staff therapist Goldwater Meml. Hosp., Roosevelt Island, N.Y., 1950-56, sr. therapist, 1956-61, chief therapist, 1961-67, sr. occupational therapist, 1967—. Cons. occupational therapy St. John's Episcopal Home for Aged and Blind. Mem. Am., Can. occupational therapy assns., Alpha Epsilon Phi. Author: (with M. Lee, M. Dasco) Wheelchair Prescription, 1967. Home: 532 W Walnut St Long Beach NY 11561 Office: Goldwater Meml Hosp Roosevelt Island New York City NY 10017

PFAFF, CONSTANCE A., librarian; b. St. Louis, July 9, 1910; d. Albert F. and Mary Ann (Thielen) Pfaff; B.S. in Bus. Adminstrn., U. Mo., 1944, postgrad., 1952; postgrad. Washington U., St. Louis, 1946. Student asst. circulation dept. St. Louis Pub. Library, 1926-28, asst. circulation dept., 1928-29, asst. in circulation dept. U. Mo. Library, Columbia, 1929-41; librarian William Woods Coll., Fulton, Mo., 1941-44; librarian Baylor U. Coll. Dentistry, Dallas, 1944-45; research librarian Fed. Res. Bank St. Louis, 1945—. Mem. Spl. Libraries Assn. (mem. student loan com. 1950-51, scholarship and student loan com. 1954-56, nominating com. 1968-69, research com. 1969-72, pres. St. Louis chpt. 1950-51, asst. chmn. union list serials com. St. Louis chpt. 1959-62, chmn. nominating com. St. Louis chpt. 1970-71, 71-72, chmn. employment com. St. Louis chpt. 1973—), Am. Inst. Banking, Downtown Activities Unltd. Home: 40 Plaza Square St Louis MO 63103 Office: PO Box 442 St Louis MO 63166

PFEFFER, CYNTHIA ROBERTA, psychiatrist; b. Newark, May 22, 1943; d. Edward I. and Ann C. (Chinich) Pfeffer; B.A., Douglass Coll., 1964; M.D., N.Y.U., 1968. Intern, pediatrics Bellevue Hosp., N.Y.C., 1968-69; resident psychiatry Jacobi Hosp., N.Y.C., 1969-71, fellow child psychiatry, 1971-73; clin. instr. child psychiatry Bronx Municipal Hosp. Center, 1973—, N.Y. U. Med. Center, 1973—. Mem. Am. Psychiat. Assn., Am. Soc. Adolescent Psychiatry, Am. Med. Womans Assn., Phi Beta Kappa, Sigma Xi. Home: 343 E 30th St New York City NY 10016 Office: 955 Park Av New York City NY 10028

PFEFFER, SUSAN BETH, writer; b. N.Y.C., Feb. 17, 1948; d. Leo and Freda (Plotkin) Pfeffer; B.A., N.Y. U., 1969. Free-lance writer novels, reviews, articles, 1970—; lectr. children's lit.; instr. Orange County Community Coll., Middletown, N.Y., 1972. Bd. dirs. New Country Theater, Ridgebury, N.Y., 1972. Author: Just Morgan, 1970; Better Than All Right, 1972; Rainbows and Fireworks, 1973; The Beauty Queen, 1974; Whatever Words You Want to Hear, 1974. Home: 14 S Railroad Av Middletown NY 10940 Office: care Curtis Brown Ltd 60 E 56th St New York City NY 10022

PFEIFER, ELLEN CLAIRE (MRS. DANIEL M. POLVERE), journalist; b. St. Louis, June 23, 1947; d. George Edwin and Audrey Louise (McIntosh) Pfeifer; student U. Colo., 1964-65; B.S. in Journalism, Northwestern U., 1968; postgrad. U. So. Cal., 1968-70; m. Daniel M. Polvere, Apr. 8, 1973. Asst. music critic Boston Globe, 1970-72; music critic Boston Herald-Am., 1972—. Participant Rockefeller Found. Project Tng. Music Critics, 1969-71; Rockefeller fellow, 1969-71. Home: 33 Monument Sq Charlestown MA 02129 Office: 300 Harrison Av Boston MA 02106

PFEIFER, LUANNE MALSIE (MRS. JAMES WAYNE PFEIFER), journalist; b. Tampa Bay, Fla., Nov. 27, 1928; d. Willard George and Mary Theresa (Tierney) Malsie; B.S., Seattle U., 1950; m. James Wayne Pfeifer, Aug. 13, 1955; children—Kathleen, Dianna, Michael. Ski editor Santa Monica Evening Outlook, 1958-67; writer, columnist Los Angeles Times, 1968-69; staff writer Ski Mag., Malibu, Cal., 1969—; sr. editor World Travel mag., 1972-73. Recipient W.B. Barry award for outstanding news coverage U.S. Ski Assn. 1967; Harold Hirsch award for excellence in ski journalism nationally, 1968. Mem. U.S. Ski Writers Assn., Ski Writers Assn. So. Cal., Malibu Hist. Soc., Far West Ski Assn., Am. Soc. Mag. Writers. Roman Catholic. Clubs: Yacht (Malibu), Junior League. Home and office: 3224 Malibu Canyon Rd Malibu CA 90265

PFEIFER, SUSAN ELIZABETH (MRS. ANASTASIOS C. SOUTZOS), lawyer; b. Frederick, Md., Dec. 10, 1943; d. Charles Ernest and Catherine Virginia (Sanbower) Pfeifer; B.A., Am. U., 1964, J.D., 1967; m. Anastasios C. Soutzos, Nov. 16, 1969. Law clk. firm Fulbright, Crooker, Freeman, Bates & Jaworski, Washington, 1964-68; admitted to Md. bar, 1967, D.C. bar, 1968; mem. firm Richey & Clancy, Chevy Chase, Md., 1968-71, Clancy & Pfeifer, Chevy Chase, Md., 1971—. Mem. Am., Md., D.C. bar assns., Am. Judicature Soc., Kappa Beta Pi (dean 1968, vice dean 1972). Home: 11812 Hunting Ridge Ct Potomac MD 20854 Office: 5454 Wisconsin Av Chevy Chase MD 20015

PFEIFFER, ASTRID ELIZABETH, utility co. exec.; b. N.Y.C., Nov. 15, 1934; d. Ernest Franz and Alice (Strobel) Pfeiffer; B.A., Cornell U., 1955; J.D. cum laude, Wayne State U., 1967; m. Edmund Lee Gettier III, May 28, 1956 (div. Feb. 1966); children—Evan, Elizabeth, Edmund Lee IV, Sheila, David. Mng. editor Detroit Inst. Arts, 1962-67; admitted to Mich. bar, 1968, N.Y. bar, 1969; atty. J.P. Mattimoe, Detroit, 1967-68, Chubb & Son, Inc., N.Y.C., 1969-70, Cadwalader, Wickersham & Taft, N.Y.C., 1971-73; atty., corporate sec. Fla. Power & Light Co., Miami, 1973—. Mem. Am., N.Y. bar assns., Am. Soc. Corporate Secs. Home: 9615 Coral Way Miami FL 33165 Office: 4200 W Flagler St PO Box 013100 Miami FL 33101

PFEIFFER, MILDRED CLARA JULIA, physician, health services adminstr.; b. Phila., Aug. 16, 1910; d. Emil and Natalie Marie (Doehler) Pfeiffer; B.S. in Biology, U. Pa., 1933, M.D., 1936, M.P.H., 1945. Intern Phila. Gen. Hosp., 1936-38, resident in internal medicine, 1938-39; practice medicine, specializing in internal medicine, Phila., 1939-52; dir. Chronic Diseases and Planning Evaluation and Research Pa. Dept. Health, Harrisburg, 1952—; chief medicine Women's Hosp. Phila., 1939-52; mem. staffs Phila. Gen. Hosp., Grad. Hosp. U. Pa., Drs. Hosp.; asst. clin. prof. medicine, gastroenterology and proctology Women's Med. Coll. Pa., 1939-52, dir. student health services, 1940-46, instr. biostatistics, dir. dept. oncology, 1948-52, vis. prof. pub. health, 1952-56. Mem. Bd. Health Lower Merion Twp., 1962—. Governing mem. Arthritis Found., pres. Central Pa. chpt., 1965-68. Recipient Distinguished Service citations Nat. Arthritis Found., 1969, Pa. Heart Assn., 1959, Drexel Inst., Phila., 1953. Diplomate Am. Bd. Internal Medicine. Fellow A.C.P. (life), Am. Coll. Chest Physicians, A.A.A.S. (life); mem. Am. Med. Women Assn. (sec. 1944-46), Am. Soc. Planning Ofcls., Am. Pub. Health Assn., Royal Soc. Health, Royal Soc. Medicine, Internat. Soc. Internal Medicine, Grad. Women in Sci., Am. Soc. Pub. Adminstrn., Am. Proctologic Soc., Nat. Rehab. Assn., Gerontologic Soc., Am. Geriatrics Assn., Adult Edn. Assn., Am. Acad. Polit. and Social Scis., Alpha Omega Alpha, Delta Phi Alpha, Zeta Phi. Club: Quota (v.p. 1967-68) (Harrisburg). Contbr. articles to med. jours. Home: 358 Valley Rd Merion Station PA 19066 Office: Pa Dept Health PO Box 90 Harrisburg PA 17120

PFISTER, LOIS KNAPP (MRS. ALFRED PFISTER), pediatrician; b. Washington, July 8, 1938; d. George Edwin and Doris Estelle (Carlton) Knapp; B.S. in Chemistry, Gustavus Adolphus Coll., 1957; postgrad. Am. U., summers 1956, 57; M.D., George Washington U., 1961; m. Alfred Karl Pfister, June 4, 1961; children—Alfred Karl III, Constance Carlton, Philip George. Intern George Washington U. Hosp., Washington, 1961-62; resident in pediatrics N.C. Bapt. Hosps., Winston-Salem, 1962-63; resident pediatrics Charleston (W.Va.) Meml. Hosp., 1962-64, pediatrician Pediatric Clinic, 1969—; pediatrician Kanawha County Well Child Clinic, 1969—, USPHS Hosp., Shiprock, N.M., 1966-68; pediatric cons. Raleigh-Boone Med. Center, Whitesville, W.Va., W.Va. Health Dept. Consultation and Mental Evaluation Clinic. Asst. dir. vaccination project, Charleston, 1964-66. Mem. Kanawha County Med. Soc., Kanawha County Med. Soc. Women's Aux., W.Va. Med. Assn., W.Va. Pub. Health Assn. (pub. relations com. 1969). Lutheran. Home: 794 Echo Rd South Charleston WV 25303 Office: Charleston Meml Hosp 3200 Noyes Av SE Charleston WV 25303

PFLUEGER, MARGARET LOIS, librarian; b. Franklin Furnace, O., Apr. 12, 1916; d. John Henry Luther and Anna Caroline (Pauschert) Pflueger; B.A., Capital U., 1937; M.A., Ohio State U., 1940; B.L.S., U. Chgo., 1944. Library asst. Columbus (O.) Pub. Library, 1942-43; librarian Metall. Lab., U. Chgo., 1944-45; cataloger Army Library, U.S. Dept. Def., Washington, 1945-48; various positions U.S. AEC, Oak Ridge, 1948-72, chief, reference br. tech. information center, 1972—. Mem. Am. Soc. for Information Sci., Spl. Libraries Assn. (pres. Oak Ridge chpt. 1958-59). Democrat. Lutheran. Home: 140 N Beverly Circle Oak Ridge TN 37830 Office: US Atomic Energy Commission Division Technical Information PO Box 62 Oak Ridge TN 37830

PFLUGH, ELIZABETH MARIE (MRS. WILLIAM R. PFLUGH), city ofcl.; b. Glenfield, Pa., May 24, 1920; d. William Herman and Erna Dorothea (Kloppenburg) Doerper; student Duffs Bus. Coll., 1938-40; m. William Miller, June 21, 1940 (div. July 1948); 1 dau., Carol Jean; m. William R. Pflugh, Sept. 22, 1948; 1 dau., Joanne B. Pflugh. Bookkeeper, Mauro Hudson Garage, Sewickley, Pa., 1940-45; bookkeeper advt. Pitts. Post-Gazette, 1945-47; office mgr. Dapper Dan Club, 1947-52; office mgr. Sewickley Borough, Pa., 1957—, borough sec., 1962—. Mem. Southwestern Pa. Municipal Secs. Assn., Pa. Local Govt. Secs. Assn., Pitts. Ballet Theatre Guild, Women Civic Club (corr. sec. 1952). Mem. Order Eastern Star. Home: Box 168 S McCoy Pl Sewickley PA 15143 Office: Municipal City Hall Bldg Thorn St Sewickley PA 15143

PHAIR, MARY IDA (MRS. ROBERT LYNN PHAIR), librarian; b. Amarillo, Tex., Oct. 23, 1920; d. Luther Dorman and Alice Henrietta (Harkey) Knight; B.A., U. Cal. at Los Angeles, 1962; M.A. with honors, U. So. Cal., 1963; m. Robert Lynn Phair, Nov. 8, 1941; children—Robert Lynn, Randall Clinton. Librarian, South Pasadena (Cal.) High Sch., 1963—. Mem. adv. bd. U. So. Cal. Sch. Library Sci., 1970-72, Pasadena City Coll. Library, 1970. Mem. Cal. Congress P.T.A. (hon.), Delta Kappa Gamma. Home: 1244 Brunswick South Pasadena CA 91030 Office: 1401 Fremont St South Pasadena CA 91030

PHARIS, MARY MARGARET EVANS (MRS. DAVID BUNSEN PHARIS), psychiat. social worker; b. Milw., July 3, 1938; d. Silas MaAfee and Lorraine (McManamy) Evans; student Stanford U., 1956-58; B.S. with sr. honors, U. Wis., 1960; M.A. (Univ. fellow 1961-62), U. Chgo., 1962; m. David Bunsen Pharis, Aug. 6, 1966; children—Christopher Eugene, Michael Jonathon. Caseworker Scholarship and Guidance Assn., Chgo., 1962-66; social work supr., psychiat. services Michael Reese Hosp., Chgo., 1966-68, coordinator student program, psychiat. social work dept., 1967-68; spl. services social worker Lab. Sch., Evanston, Ill., 1968-69; pvt. practice, 1970—; instr. MacMurray Coll., 1972-74, Ill. Coll., 1972-74. Therapist dept. clin. services Family Ct. of Cook County, 1964-66; field work instr. U. Chgo. Sch. Social Service Adminstrn., 1966-68, Smith Coll. Sch. Social Work, Northampton, Mass., 1967-68; cons. Loretto Hosp., Chgo., 1969, Ill. Law Enforcement Commn., 1970. Bd. dirs. Jacksonville Area Council on Alcoholism, Morgan County Big Bro.-Big Sister Assn. Recipient Lindsey Barbee fellowship Am. Assn. U. Women, 1960-61, Nat. Inst. Mental Health fellow, 1974—. Mem. Nat. Assn. Social Workers, Acad. Certified Social Workers, Ill. Soc. Clin. Social Work (sec., dir.), League Women Voters, Gamma Phi Beta. Club: Service of Milw. Contbg. editor: Clin. Social Work Jour., 1972—. Contbr. to profl. jours. Address: 13412 Lois Lane Austin TX 78759

PHELAN, HELEN M., psychologist; b. Utica, N.Y., Nov. 17, 1913; d. William N. and Anna M. (Jordan) Phelan; B.S., Syracuse U., 1939, M.A., 1946. Editor univ. bulls. Syracuse U., 1943-46; clin. psychologist, travelling child guidance clinics N.Y. State Dept. Mental Hygiene, 1946-58; sch. psychologist Syracuse City Sch. Dist., 1958-73. Mem. Sch. Psychologists Upstate N.Y., UN Assn. (rep. Central N.Y. 1973-74). Clubs: Soroptimists (chmn. publicity 1970-71, dir. 1971-73), Catholic Women's. Research and publs. in field. Home: 1067 W Genesee St Syracuse NY 13204

PHELAN, MARY CLAIRE WALSH (MRS. WILLIAM THOMAS PHELAN), librarian; b. East Cleveland, O., Jan. 27, 1943; d. William Ignatius and Clara Florence (Streisel) Walsh; B.A., Ursuline Coll. Women, 1965; M.A. (Spl. libraries Assn. scholar 1965-66; U.S. Nat. Library Medicine scholar 1966-67), U. Chgo., 1967; m. William Thomas Phelan, Dec. 14, 1968. Sci. reference librarian Abbott Labs., North Chicago, Ill., 1967-68; biology librarian U. Chgo., 1968-70; spl. sci. bibliographer U. Man., Winnipeg, Man., Can., 1971-74. Swimming instr. A.R.C., 1957-62. Mem. Am. Soc. Information Sci., A.L.A., Spl. Libraries Assn., Med. Library Assn. Roman Catholic. Address: 6 Jonathan Lane Chelmsford MA 01824

PHELAN, MARY KAY (MRS. MARTIN DUPONT PHELAN), author; b. Baldwin City, Kan.; d. Thomas LeGrand and Adah (Shafer) Harris; A.B., DePauw U., 1935; M.A., Northwestern U., 1937; m. Martin DuPont Phelan, Aug. 14, 1937; children—Richard Harris, Jerry DuPont. Advt. copywriter Marshall Field & Co., Chgo., 1937-42. Mem. P.E.O., Alpha Chi Omega. Republican. Episcopalian. Author: The White House, 1962; The Circus, 1963; Mother's Day, 1965; Mr. Lincoln Speaks at Gettysburg, 1966; The Fourth of July, 1966; Election Day, 1967; Four Days in Philadelphia, 1776, 1967; Midnight Alarm, 1968; Probing The Unknown (The Story of Dr. Florence Sabin), 1969; The Story of the Great Chicago Fire, 1971; Martha Berry, 1972; Mr. Lincoln's Inaugural Journey, 1972; The Story of the Boston Tea Party, 1973. Home: 2524 Lorton Av Davenport IA 52803

PHELAN, PEARL CAREN LIPSIE (MRS. RICHARD H. PHELAN), psychologist; b. Forsyth, Ga., Nov. 9, 1927; d. William Thomas and Mary Grace (Rowland) Tyler; B.A., U. Md., 1967, M.Ed., 1968, Ph.D., 1973; m. Richard H. Phelan, Aug. 11, 1973; children—Michael, William, Caren Ann Lipsie. Counselor, St. Elizabeths Hosp., Washington, 1968-70, unit supr. dept. vocational rehab., 1970-72; behavioral scientist Ft. Sam Houston, Tex., 1972-74; unit dir. San Antonio State Hosp., 1974—. Rehab. cons. Community Workshop and Halfway House, Washington. Mem. Am., Tex. psychol. assns., Am. Personnel and Guidance Assn., San Antonio Group Psychotherapy Assn., Nat. Rehab. Counselors Assn., Kappa Delta Pi. Democrat. Home: Route 1 Box 168 WW San Marcos TX 78666 Office: Bldg 17 San Antonio State Hosp San Antonio TX 78223

PHELPS, BETTY JEANE POTTENGER (MRS. CHARLES PUTERBAUGH PHELPS), civic worker; b. Warsaw, Ind., Oct. 20, 1921; d. Royal and Erba Ermal (Hinkson) Pottenger; A.B., Manchester Coll., 1943; registered Occupational Therapist, Washington U., St. Louis, 1952; m. Charles Puterbaugh Phelps, June 5, 1955; children—Carl James, Rebecca Susan. Tchr., Richland Center Sch., Rochester, Ind., 1943-44, Lakeview Sch., Tulia, Tex., 1944-45; staff therapist, student supr. Indpls. Gen. Hosp., 1953; dir. occupational therapy James O. Parramore Hosp., Crown Point, Ind., 1954-55. Vol. worker Meals-on-Wheels, 1972-73; active fund-raising drives United Fund, March of Dimes, Cancer Fund. Mem. Am. Occupational Therapy Assn., Universal Esperanto Assn., Esperanto League N.Am., Common Cause. Democrat. Presbyn. Home: 18 E 2d St Peru IN 46970

PHELPS, CHARLOTTE P. DEMONTE, economist, educator; b. East Orange, N.J., Jan. 26, 1933; d. Robert William and Marian (Page) DeMonte; B.A., Radcliffe Coll., 1955; M.A., Yale, 1956, Ph.D., 1961; m. Edmund Strother Phelps, Jr., Sept. 28, 1957 (div. Dec. 1969). Instr., Conn. Coll., New London, 1961; research asst. Mass. Inst. Tech., Cambridge, 1962-63; research staff economist Cowles Found. and Econ. Growth Center, Yale, New Haven, 1963-65; research Social Sci. Research Council, Com. on Econ. Stablzn., New Haven, Phila., 1965-68; research asst. prof. dept. econs. Temple U., Phila., 1967-69, asso. prof. dept. econs., 1969—. Lectr., Cheltenham Twp. Adult Sch., 1971; vis. prof. dept. econs. Stanford, summer 1972. exec. producer film Women and Work in the Age of Aquarius, 1970. Mem. tech. adv. com. Phila. Day Care Council, 1970-72. Mem. Am. Assn. U. Profs., Am. Econ. Assn., Pa. Acad. Art, Phila. Mus. Art. Club: Radcliffe (dir. 1973-74) (Phila.). Contbr. articles to profl. jours. Home: Hopkinson House Washington Sq Philadelphia PA 19106 Office: Dept Econs Temple U Philadelphia PA 19122

PHELPS, EDITH BLAKESLEE, edn. cons.; b. Worcester, Mass., June 23, 1917; d. George Hubbard and Edna (Day) Blakeslee; grad. Smith Coll., 1938; postgrad. history Clark U., 1938-39; Litt.D. (hon.), Emerson Coll., 1973; m. William Griswold Phelps, Sept. 5, 1941 (dec.); children—Judith (Mrs. John Felton), Lisa (Mrs. Laurence J. Brengle III), Catherine. Head history dept. Riverdale Country Sch. Girls, 1939-43; instr. history, cadet tng. detachment USAAF, Coll. Ida., 1943-44; lectr. Council Fgn. Affairs, Boston, 1946-51; head history dept. Concord Acad., 1958-59, asst. headmistress, 1959-63; prin. Dana Hall Sch., Wellesley, Mass., 1963-73; edn. cons. Nat. Assn. Ind. Schs., 1973-74; nat. exec. dir. Girls Clubs Am., Inc., 1974—. Chmn. com. Smith Coll. Day Sch., 1962-65; mem. vis. com. student affairs Mass. Inst. Tech. Corp., 1965-68; mem. Commn. Ind. Schs., 1960-68, chmn., 1965-68, v.p., 1967-69, mem. exec. com., 1965—, pres., 1969-70. Trustee Brimmer-May Sch., 1960-63, Smith Coll., 1974—, Middlesex Sch., 1973—. Recipient Smith medal, 1971. Mem. Nat. Assn. Ind. Schs. (dir. 1965-68; mem. ednl. practices com. 1968—), Nat. Assn. Prins. Schs. for Girls, Headmistresses Assn. East. Contbr. articles to profl. jours. Home: 200 E 66th St New York City NY 10021 Office: 133 E 62d St New York City NY 10021

PHELPS, EDNA MAE (MRS. JOE ELTON PHELPS), Democratic nat. committeewoman; b. Tulsa, June 12, 1920; d. William Harold and Nedda Pearl (Jerome) Hough; B.A., Okla. State U., 1942; postgrad. Okla. U., 1965, Okla. Coll. Liberal Arts, 1963; m. Joe Elton Phelps, Sept. 10, 1942; children—Ronald Jerome, Joelton Mark. News editor, Okla. Live Stock News, 1942-45; mem. pub. relations dept. Tulsa C. of C., 1945-47; mem. Okla. Fedn. Democratic Women, 1966—, pres., 1967-71; del. Dem. Nat. Conv., 1968 (mem. credential coms.), 1972; Okla. mem. Dem. Party's Nat. Charter Commn., 1972—; Dem. nat. committeewoman from Okla., 1973—; chmn. Okla. Election Bd., 1969—; precinct chmn. or co-chmn., 1960-70. Mem. adv. bd. Seminole Jr. Coll., 1972—. Trustee, Seminole Pub. Library, 1955—. Mem. Theta Sigma Phi, Kappa Kappa Phi. Episcopalian. Club: Modern Literature (Seminole). Home: 916 Lee St Seminole OK 74868 Office: State Capitol Bldg Oklahoma City OK 73105

PHELPS, ELOISE WARD (MRS. ORVA LEWIS PHELPS), librarian; b. Rosehill, N.C., July 28, 1911; d. Oscar Lee and Berta (Page) Ward; A.B., U. N.C. at Greensboro, 1931; M.A., U. N.C. at Chapel Hill, 1940; m. Orva Lewis Phelps, July 19, 1941; children—Robert Ward, Kathryn Lee. Tchr., librarian Currituck County (N.C.) schs., 1931-35; librarian Thomasville (N.C.) Pub. Library, 1935-36; librarian High Point (N.C.) High Sch., 1936-37; dean students, 1937-39; dean women Lamar (Colo.) Jr. Coll., 1940-41, 1942-43; counselor Pueblo County (Colo.) high Sch., 1956-66; reference librarian So. Colo. State Coll., 1966-67, head reference librarian, 1967—. Tchr. library sci., N.C. Coll., Durham, summers 1938-39, instr. counseling U. Colo., summer 1941. Mem. Am. Field Service Ams. Abroad Com., 1963-64, chmn., 1965. Bd. dirs. Pueblo County Mental Health, Spanish Peaks Guidance Center, Pueblo Youth Center; adv. bd. Upward Bound. Mem. Colo. Council High Sch. Coll. Relations (bd. mem. 1963-65), Colo. Counselors Assn. (mem. bd. 1963-65) Colo. Edn. Assn. (del. state assembly 1964, 65), Am. Personnel and Guidance Assn., Am. Sch. Counselors Assn., N.E.A., Pueblo County Edn. Assn., Am. Assn. U. Women, Colo. Assn. Women Deans and Counselors, Internat. Toastmistresses (pres. Pueblo club 1952-53), Columbian P.T.A. (v.p. 1952-54), Am., Mountain Plains, Colo. library assns., League Women Voters (chmn. library com., mem. exec. bd.), Pueblo Area Librarians (pres.), Elkette Bowling League (pres.), Am. Assn. Sch. Librarians, Assn. Coll. and Research Libraries, Delta Kappa Gamma. Democrat. Conglist. (diaconate). Home: 1604 Claremont Av Pueblo CO 81004 Office: 2200 Bonforte Blvd Pueblo CO 81001

PHELPS, FLORA L(OUISE) LEWIS (MRS. C. RUSSELL PHELPS), editor, anthropologist; b. San Francisco, July 28, 1917; d. George Chase and Louise (Manning) Lewis; student U. Mich. A.B. cum laude, Byrn Mawr Coll., 1938; A.M., Columbia, 1954; m. C(lement) Russell Phelps, Jan. 15, 1944; children—Andrew Russell, Carol Lewis, Gail Bransford. Acting dean Cape Cod Inst. Music, East Brewster, Mass., summer 1940; asso. social sci. analyst, U.S. Govt., 1942-44; co-adj. staff instr. anthropology Univ. Coll., Rutgers U., 1954-55; mem. editorial bd. Americas, Pam Am. Union, Washington, 1960—, sr. editor, 1963-71, editor English edition, 1971—. N.J. vice chmn. Ams. Democratic Action, 1950; mem. Dem. County Com. N.J., 1948-49. Mem. Am. Anthrop. Assn., Anthrop. Assn. Washington, Am. Ethnol. Soc., A.A.A.S., Soc. Woman Geographers, Woman's Nat. Dem. Club. Author articles anthropology, art, architecture, edn. Office: Gen Secretariat OAS Washington DC 20006

PHELPS, FLORENCE LOUISE HARLLEE (MRS. JOHN C. PHELPS, JR.), social worker; b. Dallas; d. Norman Washington and Florence (Coleman) Harllee; A.B., Howard U., 1925; M.S.W., Atlanta U., 1949; M.Ed., N. Tex. State U., 1958; postgrad. summers U. Tex., 1954, U. Ill., 1959, So. Meth U., 1963, N. Tex. State U., 1964; m. John C. Phelps, Jr.; children—Norma Belle (Mrs. George Barratt), Lucy Pearl (Mrs. Albert Simeon Patterson). Social worker City County Dept. Pub. Welfare, Dallas, 1936-41; sch. social worker Dallas Ind. Sch. Dist., 1941-71; asst. prof. Grad. Sch. Social Work, U. Tex. at Arlington, 1971-72. Instr., acting dir. Wiley Coll. Extension Sch., Dallas, 1955; dir. C.E.M.A. Financial Corp.; Dallas; cons. spl. case and adoptions Hope Cottage, Children's Bur., summer 1961. Chmn., Community Round Table on Social, Health and Welfare Problems, 1962-64; bd. dirs. Opportunity Indsl. Center, Dallas, 1969-70, Vis. Nurse Assn., Dallas, 1970-73; pres. vis. Tchrs. Dallas. Mem. Nat. Assn. Social Workers (Social Worker of Year-Dallas chpt. 1973), Acad. Certified Social Workers, Vis. Tchrs. Assn. Tex., Tex. United Community Services (dir. 1970-73), League Women Voters, United Meth. Women, Iota Phi Lambda (Woman of Year-Dallas chpt. 1973), Alpha Kappa Alpha. Home: 2804 Magna Vista Dr Dallas TX 75216

PHELPS, JANICE IRENE KELLER NIELSON (MRS. DONALD G. PHELPS), pediatrician; b. Tacoma, Sept. 4, 1932; d. Harold Curtis and Eunice Marie (Huseby) Keller; B.S. in Basic Med. Sci., U. Wash., 1953; M.D., Northwestern U., 1957; m. Eugene R. Nielson, 1961 (div. 1971); children—Peter Harold, Howard Anders, Julia Eunice; m. 2d, Donald Gayton Phelps, 1972. Intern, Harborview Med. Center, Seattle, 1957-58; resident in pediatrics U. Wash., Seattle, 1958-60; practice medicine specializing in pediatrics, Seattle, Issaquah, North Bend (all Wash.), 1960-67; med. dir. Echo Glen Children's Center, Snoqualmie, Wash., 1967-72; clin. asst. prof. pediatrics U. Wash. Med. Sch., 1969-72; staff physician U. Md. Student Health Center, 1972-73; dir. Dist. Ct. Diagnostic Team, Rockville, Md., 1973—. Med. officer County Well Baby Clinics, 1971-72. Lectr. on adolescents, delinquency and sex edn. to parent, tchr. and bus. groups; instr. sex edn. to teenagers. Sandoz Labs. grantee to study Mellaril vs Placebo in emotionally disturbed children, 1971-72. Mem. King County Med. Soc., Seattle, N. Pacific pediatric socs., Wash. Med. Assn., Wash. Pediatric Assn. (chmn. youth com. 1971-72), Soc. for Adolescent Medicine. Home: 8603 Hidden Hill Lane Potomac MD 20854

PHELPS, JOANNE MCEWEN, psychologist; b. Wichita, Kan., Oct. 2, 1923; d. Harold Daniel and Evelyn (Rorabaugh) McEwen; B.A., U. Tex., 1944; postgrad. Toke-Coburn Sch. for Fashion Careers, 1945; M.A., So. Meth. U., 1963; m. Robert White Phelps, June 12, 1947; children—Carol, Chris, Halley. With mdse. office Harper's Bazaar, 1945-46, Martha Grigsby, Inc., 1946-49, Neiman-Marcus Co., 1949-50; psychologist YMCA Community Guidance, 1963-72, Reading Clinic and Psychol. Service, So. Meth. U., 1962-69, Scottish Rite Hosp. Crippled Children, Dallas, 1966—. Bd. dirs. Planned Parenthood Dallas, Family Day Care Assn. Dallas, Women's Council Dallas. Mem. Am., Tex. psychol. assns., Jr. League Dallas. Club: Dallas Women's. Home: 6031 St Andrews Dr Dallas TX 75205 Office: 2201 Welborn St Dallas TX 77211

PHELPS, MARY, educator; b. San Francisco, Aug. 28, 1933; d. William Harrington and Laura (McKenna) Phelps; B.A. summa cum laude, U. San Francisco, 1961; postgrad. U. San Francisco, (NSF grantee) 1962, San Jose (Cal.) State Coll., 1962-63; M.A., St. Louis U., 1967, Ph.D., 1974. Tchr. Presentation High Sch., San Francisco, 1956-62, San Jose, 1962-64; lectr. U. San Francisco, 1963-65; research asst. translation and analysis of manuscripts Vatican Microfilm Library, 1965-66, 67-69, sec. Guidance Center, 1970-72; asst. St. Louis U., 1966-74; asst. prof. philosophy U. Nev., Las Vegas, 1974—; instr. U. Mo. at St. Louis, 1970-72. Mem. Am. Assn. U. Profs., Medieval Acad. Am., Am. Philos. Assn. Address: Dept Philosophy U Nev Las Vegas NV 89154

PHELPS, MARY POWELL ELLIOTT (MRS. WILLIAM B. PHELPS), librarian; b. Lexington, Ky., May 27, 1911; d. James Nathan and Marie Louise (Powell) Elliott; student Sweet Briar Coll., 1928-30; B.A., U. Ky., 1932, M.S. in L.S., 1959; m. William Baldwin Phelps, Nov. 13, 1933; children—Mary (Mrs. Herbert Lomas), David B. (dec.). Asst. head acquisitions dept. U. Ky. Library, Lexington, 1959-62; dir. U. Ky. Agr. Library, 1962-65; head acquisitions State U. N.Y., Stony Brook, 1965-68; dir. Lexington (Ky.) Pub. Library, 1968—; guest lectr. U. Ky. Library Sci. Sch., 1968—. Bd. dirs. Blue Grass Trust for Historic Preservation, Northside Neighborhood Assn. Mem. Am., Ky. library assns., U. Ky. Alumnae Assn. Home: 432 W 2d St Lexington KY 40508 Office: 251 W 2d St Lexington KY 40507

PHELPS, NAN DEE HINKLE (MRS. ROBERT PHELPS), artist; b. London, Ky.; d. John W. and Lula May (Weaver) Hinkle; ed. Cin. Art Acad. m. Robert Phelps, Apr. 9, 1926; children—Alma (Mrs. Norman Lamb), Wilmarie (Mrs. Robert P. Pfroerer), Donna (Mrs. Hans Beer), Paul R., Robbie. One man shows at Galerie Etienne, N.Y.C., Cin. Mus.; exhibited in group shows at Paula Insen, N.Y.C., Galerie St. Etienne, Copley Soc., Bos., Pallette Club, Hamilton, O., Trinidad, numerous others Ohio area; represented in permanent collections at Ford Motor Co., Pulaski (Va.) C. of C., U. Dayton, Miami U., Oxford, O., other schs., numerous pvt. collections; executed murals in churches and residences. Mem. Copley Soc. Club: The Brush Easel (Hamilton, O.) Address: 1721 Green Wood Av Hamilton OH 45011

PHELPS, PATSY RUTH, pediatrician; b. Earle, Ark., May 3, 1923; d. Charley Idol and Nettye Lee (Ricketts) Phelps; grad. St. Joseph Hosp. Sch. Clin. Lab. Diagnosis, Memphis, 1943; B.S., U. Miss., 1949; M.D., U. Va., 1953. Autopsy bacteriologist Johns Hopkins Hosp., Balt., 1946, intern in pediatrics, 1953-54, fellow in pediatric cardiology, 1954-55, pediatric resident, 1955-56; chief pediatric resident Charity Hosp., New Orleans, 1956; practice medicine specializing in pediatrics, Raceland, La., 1957—; mem. staff St. Anne Gen. Hosp., Raceland, Terrebonne Gen. Hosp., Houma, La., St. Joseph's Hosp., Thibodaux, La. Served with Hosp. Corps, WAVES, 1945. Mem. Lafourche Parrish Med. Soc. (pres. 1970). Home: Sako Dr Raceland LA 70394 Office: PO Box 340 Raceland LA 70394

PHELPS, WAYNE ARNITA BYNUM (MRS. SAM PERRY PHELPS), civic worker; b. Jackson, Tenn., Aug. 26, 1919; d. William Edward and Clara Bynum; A.B., Birmingham-So. Coll., 1941; m. Sam Perry Phelps, Dec. 13, 1941; children—Janice Arnita (Mrs. John Parks Dukes), Lynn Karen (Mrs. Lenard Carl Kelley). Pres., Birmingham Panhellenic Assn., 1949-50; pres. Jackson Elementary Sch. P.T.A., 1953-54, Birmingham council, 1960-61; pres. Birmingham Bd. Edn., 1966-68; dist. 5 chmn. Combined Service Ty. Service to Mil. Families Birmingham chpt. A.R.C.; pres. intra-state parliamentary unit 1967-69; mem. Tuscaloosa field adv. council Southeastern Ednl. Lab.; sec. Meth. Bd. City Missions, Birmingham, 1963-67, vice chmn., 1967-69. Vice pres. 5th dist. Ala. Sch. Bd., 1971-72. Bd. dirs. Birmingham area chpt. A.R.C., Health Council Birmingham and Jefferson Council, Community Centers, Eva Comer Home, 1969—; Mem. Nat. (life), Ala. (life) congresses parents and tchrs., Nat. Assn. Parliamentarians, Delta Kappa Gamma, Delta Zeta (Woman of Year Birmingham 1964). Methodist (pres. Woman's Soc. Christian Service, 1962-64, supt. youth dept. 1963-71). Home: 1205 16th Way SW Birmingham AL 35211

PHETTEPLACE, BETTY HELENA (MRS. JOSEPH ARTHUR PHETTEPLACE), curator; b. Sterling, Ill., Dec. 24, 1916; d. Thomas and Oral (Leland) Shelkey; grad. high sch.; m. Joseph Arthur Phetteplace, June 25, 1936; 1 adopted son, Larry Charles. Curator, Phetteplace Mus., Wauzeka, Wis., 1956-74. Lapidary tchr. State Youth Camp, Lomira, Wis., 1949-54. Mem. Midwest Fedn. Mineralogical and Geol. Socs. Methodist. Home: Wauzeka WI 53826 Office: Phetteplace Museum 115 Inlay Av Wauzeka WI 53826

PHILBROOK, ROMA ROBESON, hotel exec.; b. Liberty, Mo., Dec. 6, 1909; s. James Andrew and Blanche (Maughmer) R.; A.A., Kansas City Jr. Coll., 1929; B.S. summa cum laude, Northwestern U., 1947; m. Clarence Edward Philbrook, Oct. 5, 1929 (div. Oct. 1945). Accountant, U. Chgo. Clinics, 1934-42; asst. to asst. supt. Wesley Meml. Hosp., Chgo., 1943-47; adminstrv. asst. Florence Hotel, Missoula, Mont., 1948-49; mgr. Asilomar Conf. Grounds, Pacific Grove, Cal., 1949—. Mgmt. cons. on property devel. for confs., govt. and pvt. firms. Mem. Monterey Peninsula Hotel Assn. (pres. 1966-67, treas. 1964-65, 72—), Bus. and Profl. Womens Club. Club: Quota (charter). Home and office: Asilomar Conference Grounds PO Box 537 Pacific Grove CA 92950

PHILLIP, LEE (MRS. WILLIAM J. BELL), TV performer; b. Chgo.; d. James A. and Helen Phillip; B.S., Northwestern U., 1950; m. William J. Bell, Oct. 23, 1954; children—William J., Bradley P., Lauralee Kristen. Under contract CBS-TV, Chgo., 1954—, appearing currently on WBBM-TV shows, Lee Phillip Show. Mem. Mayor's Spl. Com. for a More Beautiful City, 1957—, Chgo. Maternity Center, United Cerebral Palsy; mem. Def. Adv. Com. for Women in Service, 1970—, chmn. pub. relations com., 1972. Trustee Chgo. Northwestern U. Hosp. Named outstanding woman of radio and TV, McCall's mag., 1957, 58, 64; voted top favorite feminine personality TV Guide Poll, 1956; award Top Woman's TV Show, Chgo. Federated Advt. Club, 1956; Chgo. Emmys for best performer female, best sales person 1960, 61, 62, 63, 64, 65, 66; Media Person of Year, 1960; 1 of Chgo.'s 10 best dressed women, 1960; One of World's 10 Best Coiffured Women, Helene Curtis Guild, 1967; Golden Mike award Am. Women In Radio and Television, 1968; I Will award City Chgo., 1971; TV Broadcaster of Year, 1972; DuPont-Columbia award for Rape of Paulette, 1973; Ill. Med. Soc. award, 1973; Cambridge U. award, 1973. Mem. Fashions Group, Am. Women in Radio and Television, Chgo. Unlimited, Nat. Acad. Television Arts and Scis. (Outstanding achievement award 1971-72), Delta Delta Delta. Home: 209 E Lake Shore Dr Chicago IL 60602 Office: 630 N McClurg Ct Chicago IL 60611

PHILLIPS, AILEEN BALL (MRS. HIRAM PHILLIPS), banker; b. Pinsonfork, Ky., May 5, 1922; d. Francis Marion and Myrtle (Coburn) Ball; attended Am. Inst. Banking, Williamson, W.Va., 1953, 54; m. Hiram Phillips, Feb. 19, 1944; 1 son, Paul David. With Matewan Nat. Bank, W.Va., 1942-72, asst. cashier, 1952-60, cashier, 1960-63, v.p., 1963-72, sec. bd., 1964-72; exec. v.p. Gilbert (W.Va.) Bank & Trust, 1972—; exec. sec. Matewan Ins. Agy., 1963—; pres. Hatfield-McCoy Ford, Williamson, W.Va., 1969—. Mem. Appalachian Regional Hosp. Aux., 1965—. Dir., sec., treas. Matewan Park Bd., 1970. Mem. Nat. Assn. Bank Women (chmn. W.Va. group 1967-69), Matewan Bd. Trade (treas. 1967—), Club: Matewan Woman's (pres. 1970-72). Home: Box 387 Matewan WV 25678 Office: Box 8 Matewan WV 25678

PHILLIPS, ANN COLE (MRS. RALPH B. NEUBERGER), artist; b. N.Y.C., Mar. 12, 1911; d. Samuel and Sophia (Weill) Cole; student Nat. Acad. Art, 1932-35, Art Students League, 1935-38, New Sch., 1948; pvt. study with Jose Clemente Orozco, Mexico, 1940-43, Jacques Villon, Paris, 1946; m. Phillip W. Phillips, Dec. 15, 1934 (dec.); 1 son, Calman Peter. One man shows at VenDome, Schaeffer, Andre Weil Gallery, Paris, France, Chase Gallery, others; exhibited in group shows at Whitney and Riverside museums, N.A.D., Pa. Acad., Petrides Gallery, Paris, France, Massillon Museum, Chase Gallery, Molton Gallery, London, Eng., Bodley Gallery, N.Y.C., Towntown Gallery, New Orleans, Hamilton Gallery, London, N.Y. Cultural Center Museum, Wroxton Coll., Eng., Fairleigh Dickinson U., Rutherford, N.J.; represented in permanent collections at Union Coll., Ga. Museum, Columbia, S.C. Nat. Acad., Pa. Acad., Whitney Museum, Cornell U., Phoenix Art Mus., museums at Basie, Lugamo, Switzerland. Art lectr. St. Marys Coll., Notre Dame, Ind., Laura Musser Art Museum, Muscatine, Ia., Fairleigh Dickinson U., Rutherford, N.J.; chmn. arts and skills A.R.C., Governors Island, Fort Joy, 1942-45; mem. aux. bd. N.Y. Philharmonic Orch., 1963—. Recipient Karasink award, Nat. Assn. Women Artists, 1954; Grumbacher prize N.A.D., 1955; Lehman award N.Y. Soc. Women Artists, 1956, Livingston award, 1974. Mem. Art Students League (life), Nat. Assn. Women Artists, N.Y. Soc. Women Artists, Artists Equity, Women's Internat. Art Club (Eng.), Internat. Contemporary Artists (London), English Speaking Women. Unitarian. Club: Women's City (A.R.C. chmn. 1955—). Home: 190 E 72 St New York City NY 10021 Office: 401 E 87 St New York City NY 10028

PHILLIPS, BARBARA WHARTON (MRS. GEORGE PERLE), sculptor; b. London, Eng., Feb. 9, 1918; d. Henry G. M. and Zillah (Wharton) Phillips; student Slade Sch. Art. U. London 1936-39, pvt. student Henry Moore, 1938; m. James H. Massey, 1939 (dec. Oct. 1942); 1 son, Max Henry; m. 2d, George Perle, Aug. 13, 1958; children—Katherine, Annette. Came to U.S., 1951. Worked and exhibited in Eng. until 1950; one-man shows including Zwemmer Gallery, London, 1948, Ellen Donovan Gallery, Phila., 1952, Art Alliance, Phila., 1955, Crocker Mus., Sacramento, 1960, Heritage Gallery, Los Angeles, 1962, Little Gallery, Phila., 1963, Alice Nash Gallery, N.Y., 1966, Ithaca Coll., 1968, Phoenix Gallery, N.Y.C., 1973, Queens Coll., 1973; exhibited group shows including London Artists, 1939, Yorkshire Artists, 1946, 47, Phila. Mus., 1957, Cal. Palace Legion of Honor, San Francisco, 1959, Hecksher Mus., Huntington, L.I., 1962, N.Y. World's Fair, 1964, Silvermine Guild Artists, 1964. Tchr. sculpture, Phila., 1952-58, Fleisher Art Meml., 1953-58, North Shore Community Art Centre, L.I., 1961-67; lectr. Phila. Mus. Art, 1956; executed orb and sceptre heads St. John's Ch., St. Johns Wood, London, 1944, play sculpture design City of Phila., 1954, two wood columns Rosenfield House, Phila., 1961; represented in numerous pub. and pvt. collections, U.S.A. and U.K. Vol. worker Turn Towards Peace, 1961-63; mem. Women's Strike for Peace, 1961-65. Recipient sculpture prizes Slade Sch., 1939, London Artists, 1949, Germantown Festival, 1956, Cal. Crafts, 1959, Kingsley Ann., Cal., 1961, Hecksher Mus., 1962, Audubon Artists, 1963, Suburban Art League, 1964, N.J. Ann., 1965. Yaddo fellow, 1952, 66; Huntington Hartford fellow, 1957, 61; MacDowell Colony fellow, 1958, 59, 69. Mem. Profl. Artists Guild, Nat. Assn. Women Artists. Home: 114 82d Rd Kew Gardens NY 11415

PHILLIPS, BONNALEE HAYDEN (MRS. RICHARD E. PHILLIPS), owner crafts shop; b. Ottumwa, Ia., Feb. 25, 1925; d. John Harrison and Iva Sylvia (Riggs) Hunt; student pub. schs., Famous Writers Sch.; m. Kenneth E. Hayden, June 12, 1942 (dec. Sept. 1962); children—Paul K., Philip K., Priscilla K.; m. 2d, Richard E. Phillips, Nov. 3, 1963; 1 dau., Linda L. Owner, Bonnalee's Novelties, Illiopolis, Ill., 1970—. Pres., P.T.A., 1968-69. Mem. Nat. League Am. Pen Women (state pres. 1968-70), Internat. Platform Assn., Nat. Assn. Women's Clubs (pres. local br. 1970). Mem. Ch. Disciples of Christ. Mem. Order Eastern Star (matron 1961-62). Author: Flowercraft, 1958; Beads, Bangles, Bracelets, 1971; Beading with Bonnalee, 1972. Contbr. articles to Sunshine mag., newspapers and poetry publs. Home and office: Rural Route 1 Box 188 Illiopolis IL 62539

PHILLIPS, BONNIE RAYE CAMPBELL (MRS. HOWARD OLEN PHILLIPS), orgn. exec.; b. Clinton, Ark., Apr. 24, 1924; d. George Carrol and Mary Magdeline (Harper) Campbell; grad. high sch.; m. Howard Olen Phillips, July 27, 1946; children—Karol (Mrs. John Givens), Daniel Olen. Bookkeeper, First Nat. Bank, Binger, Okla., 1942-45; office mgr. Cottrell Jewelry, Cushing, Okla., 1945-46; bookkeeper, teller Farmer's Nat. Bank, Cushing, 1946-47; receptionist, bookkeeper, colorist Phillips Portrait Studio, Ponca City, Okla., 1951-66; exec. dir. Nat. Multiple Sclerosis Soc., Tulsa, 1966-68, United Way of Ponca City, Okla., 1968—. Active various charitable orgns. Republican. Mem. Disciples of Christ. Club: Soroptimist (publicity chmn. Ponca City 1973-74). Home: 715 Monument St Ponca City OK 74601 Office: 202 E Central St Ponca City OK 74601

PHILLIPS, DORIS HOLT, club woman, educator; b. Hartford, Conn., Aug. 14, 1911; d. Sidney E. and Olive (Holt) Phillips; A.A., Colby Coll.-N.H., 1931; grad. Pratt Inst., 1934; student N.Y. U., 1933; student extension course Columbia, 1945; student U. Guadalajara (Mexico), summer 1945. Tchr. Coll. of Conn., 1950, summer 1952, Hillyer Coll., 1955. Tchr. arts and crafts Orange (N.J.) High Sch., 1934-37; technician New London (N.H.) Players, 1934; tchr. arts and crafts Hall High Sch., West Hartford, Conn., 1937-57, Conrad High Sch., West Hartford, 1957-58. Mem. town budget com., New London, 1963-65. Mem. Am. Assn. Ret. Persons, Am. Dog Owners Assn., Arthritis Found., New London Hist. Soc. (dir. 1961-68), Colby Coll.-N.H. Alumni Assn. (sec. 1952-55, dir. 1958-62), New London Hosp. Ladies Aid (pres. 1961-62), N.H. Federated Garden Clubs (dist. dir. 1964-66), Dog Writers Assn. of Am. (award 1966), Norwegian Elkhound Assn. of Am. (sec. 1964-72, dir. 1974—), Hist. Soc. of Early Am. Decoration, League of Women Voters, Elkins Ladies Benevolent Soc. Clubs: New London Garden (dir. 1961-73), Colby Junior College (alumnae council 1957-72, 73—), Appalachian Mountain, Lakes Region Kennel (dir. 1960-63, 65-68, v.p. 1969, pres. 1970-71, dir. 1973—). Editor: Pawprint, 1962-73; N.H. Barks, 1974—. Home: Elkins NH 03233

PHILLIPS, DORIS JEAN STURGIS (MRS. CAREY W. PHILLIPS, JR.), physician; b. Birmingham, Ala.; d. Franklin and Bethal (Crow) Sturgis; A.B., Samford U., 1946; M.D., Med. Coll. Ala., 1950; postgrad. Washington U., St. Louis, 1952-54; m. Carey W. Phillips Jr., Sept. 14, 1951 (dec.); children—Anne Sturgis, Paula Beth, Jean Carey. Intern, U. Hosp., Birmingham, 1950-51; resident St. Louis Children's Hosp.; practice medicine specializing in pediatric allergy, Birmingham; mem. staff Children's Hosp., Birmingham; asso. clin. prof. pediatrics Med. Coll. Ala., Birmingham, 1954—. Mem. Women's Aux. Birmingham Symphony Arlington Hist. Soc., A.M.A., Ala., Jefferson County med. socs., So. Med. Assn., Am. Acad. Pediatrics, Am. Coll. Allergists, Am. Acad. Allergy, Jefferson County Pediatric Soc., Med. Progress Assembly, D.A.R., Delta Zeta. Home: 2930 Carlisle Rd Birmingham AL 35213 Office: 924 S 18th St Birmingham AL 35205

PHILLIPS, EDYTH D. YEATES (MRS. GENE ALAN PHILLIPS), physician; b. San Francisco, Dec. 19, 1934; d. Arthur Talbot and Ruth Marie (Johnson) Yeates; student Pacific Union Coll., 1952-54; B.A., San Francisco State Coll., 1958; M.D., Loma Linda U., 1961; m. Gene Alan Phillips, Feb. 12, 1966; children—Quinn Edward, Troy Cameron, Cherie Renee. Intern, Loma Linda U. Med. Center, Cal., 1961-62, resident, 1962-63; resident U. Wash., Seattle, 1963-67; interim dir. Child Psychiatry Clinic, Seattle, 1967-68; practice medicine, specializing in child psychiatry, Seattle, 1968—; staff psychiatrist dept. behavioral scis. Children's Orthopedic Hosp. and Med. Center. Recipient Outstanding Women of Am. award, 1968. Mem. Am. Psychiat. Assn., Wash. State, King County med. assns., Loma Linda U. Alumni Assn. 7th-Day Adventist. Home: 9026 SE 60th St Mercer Island WA 98040 Office: 4800 Sand Point Way NE Seattle WA 98105

PHILLIPS, EUGENIE ELVIRA (MRS. TOWNSEND W. ANDERSON), physician; b. N.Y.C.; d. Randolph Arthur and Maude (Blackman) Phillips; A.B., Hunter Coll., 1940; M.D., Meharry Med. Coll., 1944; m. Townsend W. Anderson, June 12, 1946 (dec. Feb. 1961); children—Eugenie V., Randolph C. Intern Harlem Hosp., N.Y.C., 1944-45; resident Margaret Hague Maternity Hosp., Provident Hosp., Balt., 1945-47; practice medicine, specializing in obstetrics-gynecology, Balt., 1947—; mem. staff Provident, Bon Secours hosps.; sch. physician Coppin State Coll.; asst. sch. physician Morgan State Coll. Mem. Am. Med. Womens Assn., Obstetrical and Gynecol. Soc. Md., Nat. Med. Assn., Med. and Chirurg. Faculty Md., So., Md. State, Monumental, Balt. City med. assns., Am. Fertility Soc. Office: 1612 Edmondson Av Baltimore MD 21223

PHILLIPS, FRANCES MARIE, educator; b. Hale Center, Tex., Nov. 8, 1918; d. Clyde C. and Ada (Stutzman) Phillips; B.A., W. Tex. State Coll., 1940, M.A., 1946; Ph.D. (Univ. fellow), U. N.M., 1956; postgrad. (Fulbright scholar), U. London, 1954-55. Tchr. pub. schs. Channing, Miami, Tex., Palisade, Colo., Tucumcari, N.M., 1940-46; supr. State Tchrs. Coll. Campus High Sch., Wayne, Neb., 1947-51; instr. U. Md. Overseas Program, Eng., 1955; grad. asst. N. N.M., 1955-56; asst., asso. prof. history Sul Ross State Coll., Alpine, Tex., 1956-60, prof. history, dean grad. div., 1962-71; dir. baccalaureate programs, coordinating bd. Tex. Coll. and Univ. System, Austin, 1971—; asst. prof. Mankato (Minn.) State Coll., 1960-62. Mem. Tex. Bd. Examiners for Tchr. Edn., 1972—. Chmn. bd. Wesley Found., Carlsbad Dist., 1962-66. Mem. Am. Assn. U. Women, Am. Hist. Assn., Orgn. Am. Historians, N.M. Hist. Soc., N.E.A., Assn. Tex. Grad. Schs. (2d v.p. 1967-68, pres. 1969-70), Tex. Tchrs. Assn., Alpha Chi, Phi Kappa Phi, Phi Alpha Theta, Delta Gamma Kappa. Democrat. Methodist (mem. N.M. Conf. Bd. Edn., 1965-71, ch. ofcl. bd.). Research in Anglo-American relations, 1954-56, 1962. Home: 8700 Millway Dr Austin TX 78758 Office: PO Box 12788 Capitol Station Austin TX 78711

PHILLIPS, GLADYS WILBER (MRS. LESTER EUGENE O'DAY), lawyer; b. Aberdeen, Wash., June 30, 1912; d. James Marston and Ernestine Ethel (Wilber) Phillips; B.A., U. Wash., 1936, LL.B., 1936; m. Lester Eugene O'Day, Feb. 14, 1947. Admitted to Wash. state bar, 1937, U.S. Dist. Ct. Wash., 1939; individual practice law, Aberdeen, 1937—. Mem. adv. bd. St. Joseph Hosp., Aberdeen, 1973. Mem. Wash. Ho. of Reps., 1951. Mem. Grays Harbor, Wash., Am. bar assns., Am. Judicature Soc., Am. Trial Lawyers Assn., Grays Harbor Rose Soc. (pres. 1972-73). Republican. Presbyn. (mem. session 1971-72). Home: 2 Copland Rd Aberdeen WA 98520 Office: Finch Bldg Aberdeen WA 98520

PHILLIPS, HELEN CECILIA, historian; b. Bridgeton, N.J., Aug. 27, 1903; d. Hugh Joseph and Ellen (Uhland) Phillips; B.Litt., Coll. St. Elizabeth, 1923, diploma in edn., 1923, LL.D., 1969; M.A., Columbia, 1944; certificate Oxford U., 1947; certificate Harvard, 1958. Extensive hist. research in Europe and U.S.; tchr. Cath. schs., Red Bank, N.J., 1923-28; mgr. Gambinossi and Cecchi, sch. for craftsmen, Florence, Italy, 1929-43; tchr. pub. schs., Rumson, N.J., 1943-46, head dept. social studies Rumson Country Day Sch., 1946-49; chief Museum and Hist. Office, Ft. Monmouth, N.J., 1952-67, dir. U.S. Army Signal Corps Museum, 1954-67; conducted research in hist. studies, 1943-44; compiled book History of Rumson, 1944, Ft. Monmouth History and Place Names, 7 edits., 1954-61; History of Red Bank, 1970. Adv. com. Twin Lights Corp., 1965—. Fellow Co. Mil. Historians; mem. Am. Hist. Assn., Am. Mil. Inst., Nat. Trust for Historic Preservation, Nat. Trust for Eng. and Scotland, Soc. Am. Archivists, Armed Forces Communications and Electronics Assn., Am. Assn. Museums, Am. Assn. State and Local History, N.J., Monmouth County (trustee), Twinlights hist. socs., Assn. U.S. Army (asso.). Donated Phillips Rare Book Library to Coll. St. Elizabeth, 1967. Home: 146 Maple Av Red Bank NJ 07701

PHILLIPS, JEAN M. MAHONY (MRS. PAYTON GRAY PHILLIPS), psychologist, educator; b. Portland, Me., Oct. 8, 1927; d. Daniel Patrick and Ethel (Stevens) Mahony; B.A., U. Okla., 1957; Ed.M., Boston U., 1962, Ed.D., 1964; m. Payton Gray Phillips, Jan. 27, 1945 (div. 1966); 1 son, Patrick Gray. Elementary sch. tchr., East Stoneham, Me., 1946-47; therapist Okla. Speech and Hearing Clinic, Oklahoma City, 1956; elementary tchr., Natrona County, Wyo., 1957-58; psychometrist Wyo. Dept. Edn., 1958; spl. edn. tchr. jr. high and high sch., Corcoran, Cal., 1958-60; lectr. psychology U. Alaska, College, 1960-61; asst., then asso. prof. psychology No. Mich. U., Marquette, 1964-70, dir. counseling center, 1965-70; staff psychologist, then sr. psychologist, dept. psychol. services Prince George's County Bd. Edn., Upper Marlboro, Md., also supr. dep. psychol. services; trainee, then trainer Nat. Drug Edn. Program for State of Md.; pvt. practice; tng. program S. Shore Guidance Center, Quincy, Mass., 1962-63; diagnostic cons. Upper Peninsula Child Guidance Center, Cath. Social Services Cuban program, K.I. Sawyer AFB, Gwinn, Mich., Vocational Rehab. Office, county probate ct., pub. schs.; cons. Loudon County (Va.) Sch. System, U.S. Office of Edn. Pres. Community Social Services Orgn.; mem. Zone 3 Health Planning Council-Mental Health Com.; mem. adv. council to Probate Ct.; mem. adv. com. on women in services Dept. Def., 1971—; mem. mental health adv. com., Prince Georges County, 1973—. Adv. bd. Bowie Involvement Program for Parents and Youth, 1972—; med. adv. bd. Raphael House, Washington, 1973—. Nat. Def. Edn. Act. fellow, 1961-64. Mem. A.A.A.S., Am. Assn. Mental Deficiency, Am., D.C. psychol. assns., Council Exceptional Children (past sec.-treas. Kings County, Cal.), Found. for Exceptional Children (charter), Phi Beta Kappa, Alpha Lambda Delta, Kappa Delta Pi, Pi Lambda Theta. Episcopalian. Address: 6423 Carriage Dr Alexandria VA 22310

PHILLIPS, JOAN KARIN ROSENFIELD, coll. adminstr.; b. Chgo., May 27, 1932; d. Ben and Vivien Dorothy (Federman) Rosenfield; student Northwestern U., 1950-51, U. Wis., 1951, U. Ill., 1953-54; B.A. in Communication Arts, Columbia Coll., 1970; M.A. in Cultural Studies, Governors State U., 1973, M.A. in Human Learning and Devel., 1974; 1 son, Lee Michael. Tchr., performing artist, piano, voice, folk guitar, Chgo., 1962—; exec. mgr. Chgo. offices Boys Town of the Desert, 1966-69; asst. registrar Columbia Coll., Chgo., 1969-70, dir. admissions, fgn. student adviser Columbia Coll., Chgo., 1970—. Coordinator, Learning Exchange, Evanston, 1973; founder, dir. Center for Human Relations, New Directions, Chgo., 1973—; human relations cons. Communications Labs., 1974—. Mem. Nat. Assn. Women Deans, Adminstrs. and Counselors, Ill. Assn. Coll. Admissions Counselors, Assn. for Humanistic Psychology, Am. Humanist Assn., Nat. Assn. Fgn. Student Affairs, Am., Ill. assns. collegiate registrars and admissions officers, Oasis, Midwest Center for Human Potential.

PHILLIPS, JOSEPHINE MCKEEBY, educator; b. Montague, N.J., May 16, 1914; d. Walter and Sara (Cole) McKeeby; A.B. with honors, Montclair State Coll., 1935, M.A., 1941; postgrad. Newark Coll. Engring., 1942; Ed.D., Columbia, 1962; m. Edwin Robert Phillips, July 18, 1943 (div. Nov. 1948); 1 son, Edwin Robert. Tchr. pub. schs., N.J., 1935-42; asst. prof. math. dept. Longwood Coll., 1948-51; instr. Montclair State Coll., 1951-53; arithmetic editor D. C. Heath & Co., Boston, 1953-60; specialist in edn. U. Ill., 1962-70; prof. U. Cin., 1970—. Cons. to educators, U.S., Fiji, Japan, Iran, 1960—. Served to lt. (j.g.) USCG Women's Res., 1943-44. Mem. Nat. Council Tchrs. Math., Sch. Sci. and Math. Assn., Kappa Delta Pi. Author: (with others) Learning to Use Arithmetic, 1962, Teaching Modern Mathematics in the Elementary School, 1967, Motion Geometry, 1969, Algebra Problems, 1972, Paper-Folding Geometry, 1974, others. Elementary math. editor Sch. Sci. and Math., 1969—; contbg. editor The Instructor, 1966-72. Contbr. articles to profl. jours. Home: 621 McAlpin Av Cincinnati OH 45220

PHILLIPS, LEILA DOUGLAS (MRS. DONALD FREDERICK PHILLIPS), journalist; b. Nashville, May 7, 1925; d. Richard and Louise Ingram (Moore) Douglas; B.A. magna cum laude, Vanderbilt U., 1945; m. Donald Frederick Phillips, Dec. 11, 1954; children—Donald Frederick, Leila Douglas, Louise Byrd. Reporter Nashville Banner, 1945—; editor Tenn. Arts Commn. newsletter, Nashville, 1971—. Bd. dirs. Nashville Children's Theatre, 1958—. Mem. Internat. Assn. Theatre for Children and Youth (mem. com. fourth world congress 1972), Am., Southeastern theatre assns., Polk Meml. Assn., Hermitage Assn., Nat. Soc. Colonial Dames of Am. in Tenn., Jr. League Nashville, Am. Ednl. Theatre Assn. (mem. bd. children's theatre conf. 1967-72, co-editor Children's Theatre Rev., 1967-72), Phi Beta Kappa, Kappa Alpha Theta, Phi Sigma Iota, Episcopalian (mem. bd. women of the ch. 1965-67). Contbr. articles to mags. Address: 6104 Jocelyn Hollow Nashville TN 37205

PHILLIPS, LESLIE GORDON, lit. agt., lectr.; b. Omaha, Neb.; d. Ben S. and Rose (Green) Gordon; student U. Omaha, Northwestern U.; m. Lionel F. Phillips, Sept. 7, 1935 (dec.). Editing, collaboration, research for Sherman Rogers, speaker and mag. writer, 1931; research dir. Jackson Babbitt, Inc., N.Y.C., 1932; speeches on prohibition issue, 1932; co-founder, research and orgn. dir. Nat. Recovery Crusade, 1933-34; research dir. The Crusaders, Inc., N.Y.C., 1935; co-founder, exec. sec. The Am. Factfinders Inst., Inc. N.Y.C., 1936; editorial work Country Home Mag., Crowell Collier Publs., N.Y.C., 1937, free-lance publicity research, pub. relations work, 1937-74; v.p., dir. research Broadcast Editorial Reports, N.Y.C., 1959-63; lectr. in field, editorial cons. Club: Overseas Press. Co-author: The New Crusade-1000 Years of Liquor Legislation, also numerous pamphlets, scripts. Contbr. numerous articles to jours. and mags. Address: 2023 Preuss Rd Los Angeles CA 90034

PHILLIPS, MADGE, educator; b. DuBois, Pa., Mar. 29, 1925; B.A., Keuka Coll., 1947; M.S. (Amy Morris Homans fellow), Wellesley Coll., 1951; Ph.D., U. Ia., 1960. Dir. teenage dept. Bridgeport (Conn.) YWCA, 1947-49; chmn. phys. edn. Grinnell Coll., 1951-59, chmn. div. phys. edn., 1958-59; asst. prof. U. Cal. at Santa Barbara, 1959-64; asso. prof. Wash. State U., Pullman, 1964-71, prof., chmn. women's phys. edn. U. Neb., Lincoln, 1971—, chmn. phys. edn. and recreation, 1974—. program dir., head counselor New Eng. Camps. Mem. A.A.H.P.E.R., Am. Acad. Phys. Edn., Nat. Assn. Phys. Edn. for Coll. Women (v.p.), Am. Coll. Sports Medicine, Am. Assn. U. Profs., League Women Voters, Altrusa, Delta Kappa Gamma, Pi Lambda Theta. Contbr. articles to profl. jours. Home: 1520 Circle Dr Lincoln NE 86506

PHILLIPS, MARCELLA LINDEMAN (MRS. JAMES F. PHILLIPS), physicist; b. Cumberland, Ia., Jan. 15, 1901; d. Frank and Marie (Marley) Lindeman; grad. Highland Park Coll., 1917; B.A., State U. Ia., 1921; M.S., 1922; m. James F. Phillips, June 27, 1927; children—Laura Marley, Frederica Lindeman (Mrs. Ulric Henry Weil). Asst. physicist State U. Ia., 1919-22; instr. Hunter Coll., N.Y.C., 1924-25; physicist Gen. Electric Co., Nela Park Lab., Cleve., 1925-27, Thomas and Hochwalt Lab., Dayton, O., 1930-31; prof. physics Adamson U., Manila, 1937-39; physicist Carnegie Inst., 1940-42, Nat. Bur. Standards, Washington, 1942-51, Mass. Inst. Tech., 1951-53; cons. physicist Mass. Inst. Tech., Am. Car & Foundry Industries Internat. Tel. & Tel. Electro-Physics Lab., Columbia, Md., Comite Consultativ Internat.-Radio, Union Radio Sci. Internat., 1953—. Mem. Am. Phys. Soc., Am. Geophys. Union, Washington Philos. Soc., Washington Acad. Sci., I.R.E. (chmn. wave propagation com. 1956-62, chmn. standards subcom.), Acoustical Soc. Am., Sigma Xi. Contbr. profl. publs. Address: 2510 Virginia Av NW Washington DC 20037 also Buenavista 16 Cronista Benitez Inglott Las Palmas de Gran Canaria Spain

PHILLIPS, MARGARET JOSEPHINE, educator; b. Sandusky, O., Mar. 19, 1943; d. Armenio and Lidia (Arduini) Phillips; B.S., Bowling Green State U., 1965; M.A., George Washington U., 1969; postgrad. Firelands Coll., part-time. Tchr. 6th grade Randolph Village Elementary Sch., Landover, Md., 1965-68, tchr. learning disabilities, 1968-69; tchr. 6th grade Bataan Elementary Sch., Port Clinton, O., 1969-70; tchr. learning disabilities Portage Elementary Sch., Gypsum, O., 1970—. Mem. Port Clinton (exec. bd. 1970—), N.W. Ohio, Ohio edn. assns., George Washington U. Gen. Alumni Assn., Council for Exceptional Children, Ohio Assn. for Children with Learning Disabilities, Bowling Green State U. Found., Delta Kappa Gamma. Democrat. Roman Catholic. Home: 311 11th St Port Clinton OH 43452 Office: Portage Elementary Sch Lake St Gypsum OH 43433

PHILLIPS, MARGARET LOUISE (MRS. EDWIN J. STEINAM), physician; b. Carrollton, Ill., June 30, 1923; d. Eugene Martin and Cora Belle (Ellis) Phillips; B.A., U. Ill., 1944; R.N., U. Minn., 1948; M.D., Northwestern U., 1952; m. Edwin J. Steinam, Sr., July 12, 1958; children—Susan Jane, Patricia Louise. Penhellenic adviser State U. Ia., 1944-45; intern Chgo. Wesley Meml. Hosp., 1952-53, resident internal medicine 1953-55; practice medicine specializing in internal medicine Chgo., 1955-63, Woodstock, Ill., 1963—; asso. dept. internal medicine Northwestern U. Med. Sch., 1955-63; attending staff internal medicine Chgo. Wesley Meml. Hosp., 1955-63; attending staff Meml. Hosp. McHenry County, 1963—. Diplomate Am. Bd. Internal Medicine. Mem. Chi Omega. Home: PO Box 412 Woodstock IL 60098 Office: 13707 W Jackson St Woodstock IL 60098

PHILLIPS, MARIAN MAXINE, educator; b. Chgo., Sept. 8, 1919; d. Charles Buchanan and Edith (Johnson) Wright; student Chgo. Art Inst., 1959-63; B.A., U. Chgo., 1963; M.S., U. So. Cal., 1965; postgrad. U. Cal. Los Angeles, 1967-70, Peperdine U., 1966-67, Cal. State U., 1966-67, San Diego State Coll., 1971, U. Oslo, 1968; m. Herman L. Phillips, July 3, 1954 (dec. Feb. 1965); 1 dau., Carolyn Frances Stradford (Mrs. Ivan Hardy). Tchr. educationally handicapped Los Angeles Unified Schs., 1964-67, tchr. physically handicapped mentally retarded, 1967-69, cons. and resource tchr., 1969—. Tchr. and cons. to parents of handicapped children. Mem. Mayor's Council for Internat. Visitors and Sister Cities, 1969-71. Recipient Tchr. of Year award Council of Exception Children, 1969, certificate of Merit Los Angeles Urban League, 1970, Recognition Service award, U. So. Cal., 1971, Recognition award Council for Exceptional Children, 1973. Mem. Cal. State Fedn. Councils for Exceptional Children (sec.), Nat. Assn. Coll. Women (pres.), Am. Assn. Mental Deficiency, Cal. Assn. Neurol. Handicapped Children, Exceptional Children's Found., Am. Assn. for Mental Deficiency, Cal. Assn. Neurol. Handicapped, Phi Delta Kappa, Delta Sigma Theta, Pi Lambda Theta. Home: 7411 Dalton Av Los Angeles CA 90047 Office: Salvin School 1925 Budlong Av Los Angeles CA 90007

PHILLIPS, MARJORIE, artist, mus. dir.; b. Bourbon, Ind., Oct. 25, 1894; d. Charles Ernest and Alice (Beal) Acker; student Classical Sch. for Girls, N.Y.C., Miss Fuller's Sch., Ossining, N.Y., Art Students League, N.Y.C.; D.F.A. (hon.), Smith Coll., 1973; m. Duncan Phillips, Oct. 8, 1921; children—Mary Marjorie, Laughlin. Painter, dir. Phillips Collection, Washington, ret., 1972. Paintings exhbt. at Century of Progress, N.Y. World's Fair, Golden Gate Expn., Mus. Modern Art, Am. Exhbn. in Paris, Art Inst. Chgo., Pa. Acad., Carnegie Inst., Whitney Mus., Mus. Legion of Honour, Edward Root Art Center, Utica, N.Y., London, Eng., 1973; one-woman retrospective exhbt. Marlborough Fine Art, London, 1973; represented in permanent collections Whitney Mus., Boston Mus. Fine Arts, Yale Mus., The Phillips Collection, Corcoran Gallery Art, pvt. collections; one-man shows include Kraushaars, Durand Ruel, Bignou, Durlacher Bros., Sam Gillian, Jack Youngerman, Clifford Still; painting included in loan exhbn. to Tate Gallery, London, 1946; assisted with loan exhbns. and directed decorating Annex Phillips Gallery. Recipient award of merit Pa. Mus. Sch. Art. Author: Duncan Phillips and his Collection, 1971. Home: 2101 Foxhall Rd NW Washington DC 20007

PHILLIPS, MARY MARGARET CLARKESON (MRS. BRUCE L. PHILLIPS), mathematician; b. Albany, N.Y., Aug. 9, 1946; d. John and Helen Margaret (Falcon) Clarkeson; B.A., Conn. Coll., 1968; postgrad. U. Md., 1969, George Washington U., 1970-71; m. Bruce L. Phillips, June 7, 1969; 1 son, Brian Lee. Mathematician, Dept. Defense, Ft. Meade, Md., 1968-72; programmer Gen. Electric Research and Devel. Center, Schenectady, 1972—. Joseph F. Joseph asst. Conn. Coll., 1967-68. Mem. Math. Assn. Am., Am. Assn. U. Women, Phi Beta Kappa. Home: 707 Crescent Village Apts Vischers Ferry Rd Elnora NY 12065 Office: Gen Electric Research and Devel Center Schenectady NY

PHILLIPS, MARY VIOLA, educator; b. Vandergrift, Pa., Jan. 12, 1913; d. Andrew Jay and Ophelia Florence (Hilty) Phillips; B.S., U. Pitts., 1936, M.A., 1940; Ed.D., Columbia, 1964. Tchr. elementary and sr. high sch. New Kensington Pub. Schs., 1940-57; vis. prof. U. Pitts., 1954-56, instr., 1957-59, asst. prof., 1959-63, asso. prof. geography and edn., 1963-73, prof. geography, 1973—. State curriculum cons., 1960-72; judge, Buhl Planetarium Ann. Geography Show, Pitts., 1957-70. Active United Fund. Recipient Nat. awards Jour. Geography, 1952, 58, Albert J. Nystrom Meml. fellowship Assn. Am. Geographers, 1961-62. Mem. Soc. Woman Geographers, Internat. Geog. Union, Am. Assn. U. Profs., Assn. U. Women, Assn. Am. Geographers, Am. Geog. Soc., Nat. (pres. 1958), Pa. (pres. 1956-57) councils geog. edn., Phi Alpha Meta, Delta Kappa Gamma, Pi Lambda Meta, Kappa Delta Pi. Author: Textbook-World Geography, 1960; Biography-Edith Putnam Parker, 1964; Physical Geography, 1966; Manual for Geography Earth and Man, 1969; Film-Physical Maps, 1969. Asso. editor Jour. Geography, 1955-65. Office: Geography Dept Mervis Hall U Pitts Pittsburgh PA 15213

PHILLIPS, MILDRED EVALYN, educator, pathologist; b. N.Y.C., May 21, 1928; d. Fitzgerald and Kathleen Irene (Miller) Phillips; B.A., Hunter Coll., 1946; M.D., Howard U., 1950. Intern, Kings County Hosp., N.Y.C., 1950-52; resident pathology Mt. Sinai Hosp., N.Y.C., 1952-54; fellow surg. pathology Columbia-Presbyn. Med. Center, N.Y.C., 1954-55; instr. pathology Downstate Med. Center, Bklyn., 1955-56; instr. pathology N.Y. U. Med. Center, N.Y.C., 1957-58, asst. prof., 1958-65, asso. prof., 1965-73; asso. prof. dept. pathology State U. N.Y., Stonybrook, 1973—. John Blumentahl fellow, Nat. Med. fellow, 1953, John Polacheck fellow, 1962, Black Women's Community Devel. Found. fellow, 1963. Mem. Am. Assn. Pathologists and Bacteriologists, Am. Soc. for Exptl. Pathology, Am. Assn. for Cancer Research, Harvey Soc. Contbr. numerous sci. papers to profl. lit. Home: 541 E 20th St New York City NY 10010 Office: Dept Pathology State U NY Stonybrook NY 11790

PHILLIPS, PEGGY (MRS. BAXTER E. BURRIS), pub. relations exec., coll. adminstr.; b. Marengo, Ill.; d. Eugene and Maude (Hoit) Neubauer; student Alderson Jr. Coll., 1926-27, Stephens Coll., 1927-28, U. Mo., 1928-30; A.A. (hon.), Christian Coll., Columbia, Mo., 1964; m. J. Webster Phillips, May 4, 1930 (dec.); 1 dau., Peggy Ann (Mrs. Vernon Lyle Jennings); m. 2d, Baxter Emmet Burris, Dec. 29, 1972. Reporter, feature writer Fairmont (W.Va.) Times, 1924-26, Columbia (Mo.) Missourian, 1928-29, Columbia Daily Tribune, 1942-45; dir. news bur. Stephens Coll., 1945-58; asso. dir. 50th anniversary Sch. Journalism, U. Mo., Columbia, 1958-59; dir. pub. relations Christian Coll., Columbia, 1959-64; coordinator resources and research Am. Alumni Council and Am. Coll. Pub. Relations Assns., Washington, 1964-66; publicity chmn. Nat. Cherry Blossom Festival, Washington, 1966-67; dir. pub. information Cedar Crest Coll., Allentown, Pa., 1967—. Free lance writer, editor. Named hon. alumna Christian Coll., Cedar Crest Coll. Mem. Am. Coll. Pub. Relations Assn. (nat. program dir. 1956-57, 1st place award for ednl. news and features 1961), Nat. Fedn. Press Women (v.p. membership 1959-61, 3 1st place awards 1972), Mo. Press Women (pres. 1958-59), Pa. Women's Press Assn., Lehigh Valley Pub. Relations Club (pres. 1973-74), Women in Communication (nat. v.p. mems.-at-large 1959-61, pres. Washington chpt. 1965-66). Clubs: Pa. Press (Bethlehem); Women's of Allentown; Am. Newspaper Women's (Washington). Co-author: Places, 1972. Editor: Entertaining in the White House, 1966. Contbr. chpts. to books, articles to newspapers, mags. Home: De Olde Haus 1365 Main St Orefield PA 18069 Office: Cedar Crest College Allentown PA 18104

PHILLIPS, ROSALIND ANN (MRS. PAUL WAYNE PHILLIPS), lawyer, state ofcl.; b. Columbia, Mo., Oct. 5, 1941; d. Roswell Latimer and Helen Frances (Jenkins) Wayne; A.B., U. Mo., 1962, B.S. in Med. Scis., 1963, J.D., 1969; m. Paul Wayne Phillips, Dec. 12, 1970; 1 dau., Laura Wayne. Med. technologist Am. Soc. Clin. Pathologists, U. Colo. Med. Center, Denver, 1964-65, St. Vincent Hosp., N.Y.C., 1965-67, St. Luke's Hosp., Kansas City, Mo., 1967-69; admitted to Mo. bar, 1969, U.S. Supreme Ct. bar, 1973; practiced in Kansas City, 1968-70, Jefferson City, 1971—; law clk., asso. firm McLaughlin and Vanet, Kansas City, 1968-70; counsel div. ins. State Mo., Jefferson City, 1971—. Mem. Mo., Cole County bar assns., Common Cause, Am. Soc. Clin. Pathologist, Phi Delta Theta. Democrat. Episcopalian. Club: Dianna's Federated Women's (finance chmn. 1973—). Home: 134 West Circle Dr Jefferson City MO 65101 Office: 11th Floor Jefferson State Office Bldg Jefferson City MO 65101

PHILLIPS, ROSE MARY DEROSA (MRS. EMIL R. PHILLIPS), city ofcl.; b. New Rochelle, N.Y., Feb. 18, 1918; d. Carl and Lucy (Cioffari) DeRosa; student Syracuse U., 1968-69; m. Emil Ralph Phillips, Sept. 28, 1941; children—Emil Ralph, Barbara (Mrs. Thomas E. Pope), John R., Catherine. Employed with City of New Rochelle (N.Y.), 1935—, city clk., 1964—; real estate broker, operator agy. Trustee Police Pension Fund, City of New Rochelle, 1964—, trustee Fire Pension Fund, 1964—. Mem. N.Y. State Assn. City and Village Clks. (sec. 1933—). Republican. Club: Soroptimist (pres. 1958-60) (New Rochelle, N.Y.). Home: 450 Beechmont Dr New Rochelle NY 10804 Office: 515 North Av New Rochelle NY 10801

PHILLIPS, SHIRLEY ANNE BAYER (MRS. ANDY PHILLIPS), hosp. adminstr.; b. Bidwell Twp., Ont., Can., Oct. 3, 1936; d. Charles Grant and Florence Teressa (McCulligh) Bayer; grad. high sch.; m. Andy Phillips, Feb. 25, 1955; children—Eunice Anne, Frances Kimberley, Sherry Diana, Timothy Andrew, Trevor Leonard Grant. Laundry aide St. Joseph's Gen. Hosp., Little Current, Ont., 1964-69, laundry supr., 1969—. Home: Sheguiandah Manitoulin Island ON P0P 1W0 Canada Office: Box 460 Little Current ON P0P 1K0 Canada

PHILLIPS, THELMA LEE MCDANIEL (MRS. PAUL PHILLIPS, JR.), librarian; b. nr. Rock Hill, S.C., Mar. 27, 1924; d. Adam Theodore and Maggie Lee (Falls) McDaniel; A.B., N.C. Coll., 1945; B.L.S., U. Chgo., 1946; m. Paul Phillips, Jr., Aug. 10, 1947; children—Paula Lorraine (Mrs. Dwight Wilkinson), Elaine Freddye, Paul III, Janet Yvonne. Reference librarian Tuskegee (Ala.) Inst., 1946-50; hosp. librarian Vets. Hosp., Tuskegee, 1950-52; vol. cons. Pioneer Meml. Library, Fredericksburg, Tex., 1958-63, chmn. library bd., 1963-65, county librarian, 1966-73; librarian, St. Mary's High Sch., Fredericksburg, Tex., 1965-66; coordinator brs. and community services Arlington (Tex.) Pub. Library, 1973—. Mem. Tex. Library Systems Act Adv. Bd., 1969-74; mem. Tex. Gov's. Conf. on Libraries, 1966; mem. steering com. 2d Tex. Gov.'s Conf. on Libraries, 1973-74. Active P.T.A., Girl Scouts U.S., Boy Scouts Am. Mem. Am. Assn. U. Women, Jack and Jill of Am., Am., Tex. (dist. sec.-treas. 1968-69, mem. library devel. com. 1967-69, named Tex. Librarian of Year 1971 chmn. scholarship selection com. 1973—, v.p. pub. library div. 1973—), Multi-County (pres. 1969-71) library assns., C. of C., Alpha Kappa Alpha. Methodist. Club: Toastmistress (Fredericksburg). Home: 1700 Meadowlane Terrace Fort Worth TX 76112 Office: 101 E Abram St Arlington TX 76010

PHILLIPS, VIRGINIA ESTELLE, librarian; b. Florence, Ala., Feb. 13, 1921; d. Mace Hawkins and Vergia Marie (Broadfoot) Phillips; B.S., State Tchrs. Coll., Florence, 1943; B.L.S., Peabody Coll., 1946. Tchr. pub. schs., Lauderdale County, Ala., 1940-42; lab. asst. Am. Lava Corp., Chattanooga, 1943-45; librarian Chattahoochee (Fla.) Pub. Schs., 1946-50, Southwestern La. Inst., Lafayette, 1950-51, U. Ala., Tuscaloosa, 1951-54; editor Air U. Library, Maxwell AFB, Ala., 1954-69, chief documents systems br., 1969—. Recipient Sustained Superior Performance award Air U. Library, 1958. Mem. Ala. (rep. coll., univ. and spl. libraries div. 1962-63), Southeastern library assns., Spl. Libraries Assn. (chmn. chpt. membership com. 1957-58, archivist 1963-69). Methodist. Club: Junior Womans (pres. 1946-48) (Chattahoochee). Editor: Air U. Library Index to Military Periodicals, 1954-69; compiler Air University Abstracts of Research Reports, 1957-68. Home: 3382 F McGehee Rd Montgomery AL 36111 Office: Air University Library Maxwell AFB AL 36112

PHILLIPS, YVONNE, educator; b. Newellton, La., Jan. 6, 1926; d. Jesse Moore and Jeanette (Hundley) Phillips; B.A., Northwestern State U. La., 1947; M.A., La. State U., 1950, Ph.D., 1953. Mem. faculty Northwestern State U., Natchitoches, La., 1947-69, prof. geography 1958-69, head social sci. dept., 1954-67; dir., prof. La. Studies Inst., 1967-69; prof. geography Western Carolina U., Cullowhee, N.C., 1969—, asst. vice chancellor for acad. affairs, 1973—. Mem. Assn. Am. Geographers, Am. Geog. Soc., Am. Assn. U. Women, Phi Kappa Phi (chpt. treas. 1951-53), Phi Alpha Theta (chpt. pres. 1946-47), Kappa Delta Pi (chpt. pres. 1946-47). Editor La. Studies, 1962-69. Contbr. articles to publs. Home: PO Box 2141 Cullowhee NC 28723

PHILLIS, JUDITH ANN, psychologist; b. Uniontown, Pa., Mar. 22, 1942; d. Earl Horton and Eleanor Irene (Blossor) Phillis; B.S., Carnegie-Mellon U., 1964; M.A., U. Fla., 1967, Ph.D., 1969. Research asst. Craig House for Children, Pitts., 1964-65; NIH fellow Communication Scis. Lab., U. Fla., 1970-71; staff clin. psychologist Alachua County Mental Health Service, Gainesville, Fla., 1971-72; coordinator children's programs N. Central Fla. Community Mental Health Center, Gainesville, 1972—. Chmn. prevention com. Gainesville chpt. Mental Health Assn., 1974. USPHS trainee, 1965-68. Mem. Am. Psychol. Assn. Contbr. articles to profl. jours. Office: 606 SW 3d Av Gainesville FL 32601

PHILPOTT, EMALEE ISOLA EWING (MRS. EARL RUSSELL PHILPOTT), librarian; b. Charlotte, N.C., Dec. 19, 1921; d. David Weldon and Ada (Gilliam) Ewing; A.B., Coll. William and Mary, 1942; postgrad. George Washington U., 1945-47; M.Ed., U. Ariz., 1955; postgrad. U. N.C., 1968; m. Earl Russell Philpott, Apr. 8, 1950. Profl. asst. to librarian Hollins (Va.) Coll., 1942-43; librarian Corey Meml. Library, Oceana (Va.) Pub. Schs., 1943-44; post librarian Army Library Service, Camp Pendleton, Va., 1944; hosp. librarian Ft. Story (Va.) Canvalescent Hosp., 1944-45; post librarian Camp Pickett, Va., 1945; profl. reference librarian Gen. Reference and Bibliography Div., Library of Congress, Washington, 1945-47; cataloger Indsl. Coll. Armed Forces, Nat. War Coll., Ft. Leslie J. McNair, Washington, 1947-48; chief of libraries Engr. Research and Devel. Labs., Ft. Belvoir, Va., 1948-50; sec., tchr. Spanish, history, social studies Duncan (Ariz.) Union High Sch., 1950-52; librarian, English tchr. Pima (Ariz.) pub. schs., 1952-55; librarian Thatcher (Ariz.) High Sch., 1955—; jr. partner Philpott & Son, wholesale distbrs., Duncan, Ariz., 1950—; asso. in edn. dept. Library sci. Ariz. State U., Tempe, summer 1961, 66, 67; librarian, dir. Instrnl. Materials Center. Attended NDEA Inst. U. N.C., summer 1968. Mem. Ariz. Adv. Council on Libraries, 1971—. Merit badge counselor Graham County council Boy Scouts Am., 1952—. Mem. Am. Assn. U. Women (br. arts chmn. 1959-64), A.L.A. (life), N.E.A., Ariz. Edn. Assn., Ariz. Library Assn. (chmn. state recruitment com. 1958-60, editor Ariz. Librarian 1960-62, pres. 1963-64, state policy chmn., 1964-65; state policy chmn. sch. libraries div. 1965-66; chmn. SLAA adv. com.) Student Library Assn. Ariz. (founder; state sponsor 1969-70, 71-73), Dept. Audio Visual Instruction, Assn. Ednl. Communications and Tech. (nat. legislative com. 1970—), Internat. Platform Assn., Ariz. Assn. Audio Visual Edn. (state legis. com.), Beta Sigma Phi. Methodist. Mem. Order Eastern Star (worthy matron). Contbr. articles to profl. jours. Home: PO Box 233 Duncan AZ 85534 Office: Thatcher High Sch Thatcher AZ 85552

PHINNEY, BARBARA E., govt. ofcl.; b. Lynn, Mass.; d. William Edwin and Avis (Wright) Phinney; B.A., Wellesley Coll., 1937; M.A., George Washington U., 1947; postgrad., Am. U. Field dir. Cambridge

(Mass.) Girl Scouts, Inc., 1937-41; asst. dir. Girl Scouts of D.C., Inc., 1941-43; asst. chief personnel adminstrn. services to Armed Forces Am. Nat. Red Cross, 1943-45, asso. chief, 1945-46; asst. dir. service VA hosps., A.R.C., Washington, 1946-48, dep. dir., 1948-52, dir., 1952-60; personnel dir. Girl Scouts of U.S.A., N.Y.C., 1960-68; personnel staffing specialist U.S. Civil Service Commn., 1968—. Mem. Phi Beta Kappa, Phi Delta Gamma, Phi Sigma Alpha. Episcopalian. Home: 4000 Cathedral Av NW Washington DC 20016 Office: 1900 E St NW Washington DC 20415

PHIPPS, RUTH LUCILLE SCHOMIG, bus. exec.; b. Batavia, Ill.; d. Michael George and Angeline (Lindholm) Schomig; B.E., No. Ill. U., 1935; M.S., No. State Coll., Aberdeen, S.D., 1962; m. Irwin F. Thomle, Dec. 25, 1942 (dec.); children—Robert Michael, Richard Lindholm; m. 2d, Horace T. Phipps, Nov. 25, 1971. Tchr. art La Moille (Ill.) Coummunity Schs., 1935-37, Pontiac (Ill.) Elementary Schs., 1937-39; dir. art elementary schs., La Grange, La Grange Park and Congress Park, Ill., 1939-42; supr. art Batavia High Sch. and elementary schs., 1947-49; tchr. Des Moines North High Sch., 1958; dir. art Aberdeen City Schs., 1959-71; now sec.-treas. Phipps-Schockey, Inc. Vice pres. Aberdeen Boys Club. Mem. Kappa Delta Pi, Kappa Pi. Club: Zonta. Home: 407 S Jackson St Batavia IL 60510

PIAZZA, MARGUERITE, opera singer; b. New Orleans, May 6, 1926; d. Albert William and Michaela (Piazza) Luft; Mus.B., Loyola U. of South; Mus.M., La. State U.; Mus.D. (hon.), Christian Bros. Coll., 1973; m. William J. Condon, July 15, 1953 (dec. Mar. 1968); children—Gregory, James, Shirley, William J., Marguerite, Anna; m. 2d, F.H. Bergthodt, Nov. 8, 1970. Soprano, N.Y.C. Center Opera, 1948, Met. Opera Co., 1950; TV artist, Show of Shows, NBC, 1950-54; pres. Dunbar Transfer & Storage Co., Memphis. Dir. Found. World Literacy, Nat. Conf. Christians and Jews, St. Jude Found.; nat. chmn. Soc. Cure of Epilepsy; nat. crusade chmn. Am. Cancer Soc., 1971. Bd. dirs. Memphis Symphony Orch. Recipient Sesquicentennial medal for Carnegie Hall Concert, 1952; service award Chgo. Heart Assn., 1956, Fedn. Jewish Philanthropies of N.Y., 1956; named Outstanding Italian-Am. Woman of Year, AMITA, 1968; Italian-Am. of Yr. Chgo. Marie Alelaide Soc., 1973. Mem. Woman's Exchange, Italian Am. Cultural Soc., Beta Sigma Omicron, Phi Beta. Roman Catholic. Clubs: Memphis Country, Memphis Hunt and Polo. Home: 1720 Central Av Memphis TN 38104

PICCIANO, JACQUELINE LUCILLE CHAMBERS (MRS. EUGENE M. PICCIANO), librarian; b. Los Angeles, July 19, 1928; d. Frank Booth and Margaret Mary (Metzler) Chambers; B.A., Trinity Coll., 1950; M.S., Catholic U., 1952; m. Eugene M. Picciano, Dec. 31, 1955; children—Louis, Eugene, Stephen, Michael. Work fellow catalog dept. Catholic U. Library, 1950; reference librarian Armed Forces Med. Library, Washington, 1950-55; librarian VA Regional Office, N.Y.C., 1955-56; Hoffmann-LaRoche, Inc., Nutley, N.J., 1956-57; Acad. Medicine, N.J. Library, Bloomfield, 1960-71; Am. Jour. Nursing Co., Inc., N.Y.C., 1971—; asst. editor Internat. Nursing Index, N.Y.C., 1971-72, editor, 1973—. Indexer, Biol. Coordination Center, NRC and Inst. for Advancement Med. Communication, 1950-68. Mem. Am. Assn. U. Women (fellowship chmn. Bloomfield br. 1971, 2d v.p. 1972-73), Assn. Hosp. and Inst. Libraries (bd. mem. at large 1968-71, chmn. com. on orgn. 1972—), A.L.A., Med. (chmn. recruitment com. 1971—, chmn.-elect N.Y. regional group 1973-74), N.J. (past chmn. reference sect.) library assns. Democrat. Roman Catholic. Contbr. articles to profl. jours. Home: 502 Essex Av Bloomfield NJ 07003 Office: 10 Columbus Circle New York City NY 10019

PICHETTE, KATHRYN B. HOYE (MRS. LUCIEN O. PICHETTE), educator; b. New Bedford, Mass., Aug. 31, 1922; d. Frederic J. and Laura A. (Powers) Hoye; B.S., Mass. State U., 1944; postgrad. Boston U., 1944-46, Oxford U. (Eng.), summer 1961; M.A., U. Tex., 1959; Ph.D., U. Colo., 1968; m. Lucien O. Pichette, Jan. 12, 1946; children—Marie Louise (Mrs. Ben Wathen Smith, III), Anne Terese (Mrs. R. Kent Brown), Jeanne Ellen (Mrs. Michael Bussey), Lucien O., Christine Anne. Tchr. pub. schs., Mass., 1944-46, Ysleta, Tex., 1956-60, Arvada, Colo., 1960-61; instr. English, Regis Coll., Denver, 1961-63, asst. prof., 1963-67; asso. prof. English, Colo. Western Coll., Montrose, 1967-69, prof., 1969-71; faculty div. continuing edn. U. Colo., 1971-74; free lance writer. Dir., tchr. lang. arts Colo. Migrant Council Program, Montrose, 1968-69. Mem. Colo. Council on Arts and Humanities, 1965-67; mem. Com. on Minority Problems City Montrose, 1968-69; project dir. Delta-Montrose Nutrition Program for Older Ams., 1973—. Mem. civil rights commn. Colo. Democratic Party, 1974. Mem. Am. Assn. U. Women (state area rep. for edn. 1972-74), Montrose Arts Council (dir.), Colo. Humanities Council, Magic Circle Players (dir.), Montrose County Hist. Soc., Kappa Delta Pi, Delta Kappa Gamma. Roman Catholic. Home: 737 S Townsend St Montrose CO 81401

PICI, FLORENCE DONATIELLO (MRS. GIOVE PICI), hardware co. exec.; b. Gerardo and Frances (Cianicullo) Donatiello; grad. high sch.; m. Giove Pici, Nov. 18, 1945; children—Jo Ann, Giove, Michael, Francine. With Pella Products of No. N.J., Fairfield, 1962-67; comptroller Howard Hardware Products, Bloomfield, 1970—. Treas. Unico Nat., service orgn., 1974—, chpt. pres. 1965; troop cons. West Essex council Girl Scouts U.S.A.; pres. P.T.A., Belleville, N.J., 1955. Mem. Nat. Secs. Assn. (program chmn. 1968-69, recipient Lamp of Learning award). Home: 45 Watsessing Av Belleville NJ 07109 Office: 38 Davey St Bloomfield NJ 07003

PICK, ANNE GILBERT DANIELSON, developmental psychologist; b. Sycamore, Ill., Jan. 1, 1938; d. Clifford T. and Marjorie E. (Gilbert) Danielson; B.A., Smith Coll., 1959; Ph.D., Cornell U., 1963; m. Herbert L. Pick, Jr., Dec. 28, 1961; children—Cynthia Gilbert, Karen Danielson, Gretchen Eichel. Asst. prof. Macalester Coll., 1963-66; lectr. Makerere U. Coll., Uganda, 1969-70; fellow Center for Advanced Study in Behavioral Scis., Stanford, 1972-73; asst. prof. Inst. Child Devel. U. Minn., Mpls., 1966-68, 70-71, asso. prof., 1971-73, prof., 1973—. Fellow Am. Psychol. Assn.; mem. Soc. for Research in Child Devel. (sec. 1973—). Home: 1603 Northrop St St Paul MN 55108 Office: Inst Child Devel Univ Minn Minneapolis MN 55455

PICK, RUTH HOLUB (MRS. ALFRED PICK), physician; b. Carlsbad, Czechoslovakia, Nov. 13, 1913; d. Arthur and Paula (Lenk) Holub; M.D., German U. of Prague (Czechoslovakia), 1938; m. Alfred Pick, M.D., May 28, 1938. Came to U.S., 1949, naturalized, 1954. Resident Priessnitz Hosp., Grafenberg, Czechoslovakia, 1938, Hosp. Veleslavin, Prague, 1945-47; extern in pathology State Hosp., Motol, Prague, 1948; research fellow cardiovascular dept. Michael Reese Hosp., Chgo., 1949-50, research asso., 1951-58, asst. dir. cardiovascular dept., 1958-71, prof. pathology and medicine, chief exptl. atherosclerosis sect. Cardiovascular Inst., 1971—; established investigator Am. Heart Assn., 1958-64. Mem. Am. Heart Assn. (fellow council on arteriosclerosis, council on circulation), Am. Fedn. Clin. Research, Am. Physiol. Soc., A.A.A.S., Central Soc. for Clin. Research, Chgo. Heart Assn. Contbr., co-author articles in field pub. sci. jours., publs. Home: 601 E 32d St Chicago IL 60616 Office: 2900 S Ellis St Chicago IL 60616

PICKENS, LYNNE ROBERSON, librarian; b. Savannah, Ga., Sept. 17, 1944; d. Cecil Roberson and Linda Jean (Marlor) Pickens; B.A., Lewis and Clark Coll., 1966; M.Librarianship, Emory U., 1967. Children's librarian Upham's Corner br. Boston Pub. Library, 1967-68; children's librarian Central Library, Atlanta Pub. Library, 1968-71, head children's dept., 1971—. Mem. A.L.A., Southeastern, Ga. (vice chmn. children's and young people's sect. 1971-73), Met.-Atlanta (pres. 1973-74), library assns., Atlanta Pub. Library Staff Assn. (pres. 1969-71). Episcopalian. Home: 3700 Buford Hwy Apt 71 Atlanta GA 30329 Office: 126 Carnegie Way NW Atlanta GA 30303

PICKETT, BETTY RUTH HORENSTEIN (MRS. JAMES MCPHERSON PICKETT), psychologist; b. Providence, Feb. 15, 1926; d. Isadore S. and Etta (Morrison) Horenstein; A.B., Pembroke Coll. in Brown U., 1945; M.S., Brown U., 1947, Ph.D., 1949; m. James McPherson Pickett, Mar. 10, 1952. Asst. prof. psychology U. Minn., Duluth Br., 1949-51, U. Neb., 1951; lectr. psychology U. Conn., 1952; profl. asso. Bio-Scis. Information Exchange, Smithsonian Instn., Washington, 1953-58; exec. sec. behavioral scis. study sect., div. research grants NIH, Bethesda, 1958-59, exec. sec. expt. psychology study sect., 1959-62; cons. Nat. Inst. Mental Health Research Grants, Health, Edn., Welfare region 1, Boston, 1962-63; exec. sec. research career program Nat. Inst. Mental Health, Bethesda, 1963-66, chief cognition and learning sect., behavioral scis. research br., 1966-68, dep. dir. div. extra mural research programs, 1968—. Mem. Am., Eastern psychol. assns., Psychonomic Soc., Assn. of Women in Sci., Phi Beta Kappa, Sigma Xi. Contbr. articles in field to profl. jours. Home: 2561 Waterside Dr NW Washington DC 20008 Office: Nat Inst Mental Health Rockville MD 20852

PICKETT, LAUREL ANNE FRANKLIN (MRS. WILLIAM FREDERICK PICKETT), educator; b. Pocotello, Ida., Oct. 1, 1929; d. Harrison Grant and Mary Glee (Smith) Franklin; B.S. with highest honors, Wash. State U., 1948, B.Ed., 1951; M.S., U. Wash., 1966, Ed.D., 1973; m. William Frederick Pickett, Dec. 22, 1951; children—Cynthia Dawn, William Benoit. Tchr., Camas (Wash.) High Sch., 1948-51, Vancouver (Wash.) High Sch., 1950-55, Hudsons Bay High Sch., Vancouver, 1955-57; with Franklin High Sch., Seattle, 1957—, head home econs., 1961—. Sponsor Campfire Girls, Bellevue, Wash., 1958-63. Recipient Fulbright fellowship to Holland, 1952. Mem. Bus. and Profl. Women's Assn. (ednl. chmn. 1952-53), Wash. Edn. Assn., N.E.A., Seattle Tchrs. Assn. (mem. exec. bd. 1972—), Nat. Women's Deans and Counselors, Am. Ednl. Research Assn., Seattle Dept. Heads Assn. (v.p. 1971—), South Home Econs. Tchrs. Assn. (treas. 1962, 65, pres. 1963-64), Phi Kappa Phi, Mu Beta Beta, Phi Lambda Theta, Omicion Nu. Clubs: Saddle (Kirkland, Wash.); Interline (Seattle); Community (Bellevue, Wash.). Home: 16636 SE 26th St Bellevue WA 98008 Office: 3013 Mt Baker Blvd S Seattle WA 98144

PIE, VIRGINIA HUGHES (MRS. ROBERT S. PIE), orgn. pub. relations exec.; b. Charlottesville, Va., Jan. 30, 1935; d. Roy L. and Virginia Belle (Thomas) Hughes; student Stratford Jr. Coll., 1953-55, U. N.C., 1955-56; m. Robert Scollins Pie, Feb. 16, 1957; 1 son, Robert Scollins. Continuity mgr. radio sta. WEZI, Richmond, Va., 1958-59, dir. pub. information Am. Nat. Red Cross, Richmond, 1959-62, Eastern area dir. radio-TV, 1962-64, dir. information services, 1964-66, asst. dir. community relations, 1966-68, dir. community relations, Balt., 1968-73; dir. pub. relations United Way of El Paso, 1973—. Exec. dirs.'s communications adv. council Md. Tb and Respiratory Disease Assn., 1970-72. Mem. Pub. Relations Soc. Am. (accredited, pres. Balt. chpt. 1971-72, program chmn. Rio Grand chpt. 1973), Md. Assn. Communicators (pres. 1971-72), El Paso Press Assn. (asso.). Home: 776 Somerset Dr El Paso TX 79912 Office: 2112 Murchison Dr El Paso TX 79902

PIEDEM, MARGARET STANEK, educator; b. N.Y.C., Dec. 8, 1920; d. John and Katherine (Krajcirik) Stanek; B.A., Hunter Coll., 1941; postgrad. Ore. State U., 1960; M.B.A., Rutgers U., 1961, postgrad., 1970—; postgrad. Mich. State U., 1962, 64, Princeton, 1963, San Jose State Coll., 1970; m. Andrew Piedem, Sept. 13, 1942 (dec. 1958); 1 dau., Cathleen Lynn. With Tchrs. Ins. & Annuity Assn., N.Y.C., 1941-42; with Beneficial Finance Corp., Newark, 1942-43; with OSRD, N.Y.C., Washington, 1943-46; statistician tissue assn. div. Am. Pulp and Paper Assn., N.Y.C., 1946-48; statistician Am. Cyanamid Co., Inc., Bound Brook, N.J., 1950-59; tchr. Bridgewater Twp. Bd. Edn., Raritan, N.J., 1959-61; chmn. dept. math. Franklin Twp. Bd. Edn., Somerset N.J., 1961-68; asso. prof. math Somerset County Coll., North Branch, N.J., 1968—, sec. faculty assns., chmn. senate, 1972-73; tchr. math to socially deprived coll. candidates Upward Bound Project, Fla. A. and M. U., summer 1965. Rep. N.J. Council Community Coll. Faculty. Mem. Am. Assn. U. Women (past treas.), Central Jersey Math. League, N.J. Heart Assn., N.E.A., Nat. Council Tchrs. Math., N.J. Edn. Assn., N.J. Tchrs. Math. Assn., Assn. Dept. Chmn. Secondary Schs., Hunter Coll., Rutgers U. alumni assns., Phi Beta Kappa, Pi Mu Epsilon, Beta Gamma Sigma. Home: 135 N 7th Av Manville NJ 08835 Office: Somerset County Coll North Branch NJ 08812

PIEL, ELEANOR JACKSON (MRS. GERARD PIEL), lawyer; b. Santa Monica, Cal., Sept. 22, 1920; d. Louis Harris and Blanche Melicint (Virden) Jackson; student U. Cal. at Los Angeles, 1936-39; B.A., U. Cal. at Berkeley, 1940, LL.B., 1943; postgrad. U. So. Cal., 1940-41; m. Gerard Piel, June 24, 1955; 1 dau., Eleanor Jackson. Admitted to Cal. bar, 1943; N.Y. bar, 1957; law clk. U.S. Dist. Ct., San Francisco, 1939, 44; dep. atty. gen. State of Cal., 1944; clk. U.S. Senate Civil Service Com., 1945; legal adviser Supreme Command Allied Powers, Japan, 1945-48; practice law in Los Angeles, 1948-55 atty. Legal Aid. Soc., N.Y.C., 1957-58; practice in N.Y.C., 1957—. Cons., English in Action, 1973—. Trustee N.Y. U. Med. Center, 1967—. Mem. Assn. Bar. City N.Y. (mem. spl. com. to revise criminal code 1970—, com. on penology 1971—, grievance com. 1973—), Assn. for Study of Abortion (dir. 1967—). Clubs: Cosmopolitan, Women's City. Home: 320 Central Park West New York City NY 10025 Office: 36 W 44th St New York City NY 10036

PIELOCH, PAULINE ANNA, physician, educator; b. N.Y.C., Apr. 28, 1925; d. Boleslaw and Maryanna (Andrzejczyk) Pieloch; student Kings County Hosp. Sch. Nursing, 1942-45; B.S. cum laude, Hunter Coll., 1952; postgrad., Columbia, 1957-58, Berne (Switzerland) U., 1958-61; M.D., State U. N.Y. Downstate Med. Coll., 1964. Intern, King's County Hosp. Med. Center, N.Y.C., 1964-65; resident anesthesia L.I. Jewish Hosp., 1965-66; resident anesthesia State U. N.Y., Upstate Med. Center, 1966-68, asst. prof. anesthesiology, 1968-72, asst. clin. prof. anesthesiology, 1972—; asso. attending anesthesiologist Cortland (N.Y.) Meml. Hosp., 1972—, med. dir. respiratory care dept., 1973—, chmn. respiratory therapy, infections control coms., 1973—. Served to capt. Nurse Corps, AUS, 1953-56. Diplomate Am. Bd. Anesthesiology. Fellow Am. Coll. Anesthesiologists; mem. Am., N.Y. State socs. anesthesiologists, Internat. Anesthesia Research Soc., N.Y. Acad. Sci., Alpha Omega Alpha. Home: 2914 Ridge Rd RFD 1 McGraw NY 13101

PIELOU, EVELYN C. HANCOCK (MRS. D.P. PIELOU), educator; b. Bognor, Eng.; d. John Barff and Dorothy (Holmes) Hancock; came to Can., 1948, naturalized, 1956; B.Sc., U. London, 1950, Ph.D., 1962; m. D.P. Pielou, June 22, 1944; children—Ruth (Mrs. George Shapka), Richard, Frank. Research scientist Canadian Govt., 1963-68; prof. biology Queen's U., Kingston, Ont., Can., 1969-71; Killam research prof. biology Dalhousie U., Haifax, N.S., Can., 1971—. Vis. prof. dept. statistics N.C. State U., 1968, Sch. Forestry, Yale, 1969. Fellow A.A.A.S.; mem. Ecol. Soc. Am., Am. Statis. Assn., Biometric Soc., Am. Soc. Naturalists. Author: An Introduction to Mathematical Ecology, 1969. Contbr. articles to sci. jours. Home: 6755 Jubilee Rd Halifax NS Canada Office: Dalhousie U Halifax NS Canada

PIENIADZ, DOROTHY MIERZWA (MRS. EDWARD WALTER PIENIADZ), educator; b. Buffalo, May 12, 1924; d. Louis J. and Rose C. (Janik) Mierzwa; B.S., State U. N.Y. at Buffalo, 1945; M.A., Columbia, 1947, Ed.D., 1953; postgrad. Boston U., spring 1970; m. Edward Walter Pieniadz, Aug. 23, 1969. Tchr., Tonawanda, N.Y., 1945-46, Goshen, N.Y., 1946-48; supr. student tchrs. State U. N.Y. at Potsdam, 1948-51; dir. student life Tchrs. Coll., Columbia, 1951-53; dean students Glassboro (N.J.) State Coll., 1954-56, R.I. Coll., 1956-69; prof. edn. R.I. Coll., 1970—. Pres. bd. dirs. Narragansett Council Campfire Girls, R.I., 1969-72; sec. bd. dirs. Family Service R.I., Inc., 1971-73, Fed. Hill Settlement, 1969—; exec. bd. Big Sister Assn. R.I., 1967—; vice chmn. bd. dirs. R.I. Council Community Service, 1971-73, mem. group work and recreation com., 1968—. Fgn. fellow Kappa Delta Pi, 1953-54. Mem. N.E.A., Assn. Higher Edn., Internat. Council Tchr. Edn., Eastern States Assn. Tchr. Edn. (pres. 1963), Kappa Delta Pi, Pi Lambda Theta. Club: Zonta (pres. 1958-60). Home: 73 Erie St Providence RI 02908

PIERCE, ANNA GRACE, research physician; b. Fayette City, Pa., Mar. 19, 1921; d. Charles Leslie and Margaret Helen (Bainbridge) Pierce; A.B., Allegheny Coll., 1942; M.D., Temple U., 1945. Intern, Chester (Pa.) Hosp., 1945-46; resident Women's Med. Coll. Hosp., Phila., 1947-49, Aultmann Hosp., Canton, O., 1949-50; practice medicine specializing in obstetrics and gynecology, Canton and Akron, O., 1950-61; with Bur. Medicine, FDA, Washington, 1963-65; with dept. research and statistics D.C. Health Dept., Washington, 1966-67; with clin. research dept Hoffmann-LaRoche, Inc., Nutley, N.J., 1967-71; asso. dir. clin. research Ortho Research Found., Raritan, N.J., 1971-73, dir. med. research therapeutics, 1973—. Diplomate Am. Bd. Obstetrics and Gynecology. Mem. Am. Med. Writers Assn., Am. Fertility Soc., D.C. Med. Soc. Home: 29 Indiana Rd Somerset NJ 08873 Office: Ortho Research Found Raritan NJ 08869

PIERCE, ARLEEN CECILIA, chemist; b. N.Y.C.; d. John T. and Isabel (Wesly) Pierce; B.S., Queens Coll., 1959; Ph.D., U. Pa., 1962. Sr. research chemist Allied Chem. Corp., 1962-66; asst. prof. Douglass Coll. Rutgers-The State U., 1966-68; prof., chmn. dept. chemistry, dean faculty Unity Coll. (Me.), 1968-72; head chemist N.E. Lab. Services, Me., 1972-74; cons. Recipient E. Fahs Smith Meml. Scholarship, 1961-62, W.T. Taggart Scholarship, 1961-62. Mem. Am. Inst. Chemists, Am. Chem. Soc., Sigma Xi. Contbr. articles to profl. jours. Patentee in field. Home: RFD 2 Lubec ME 04652

PIERCE, DOLPHINE WESLEY, psychologist; b. Chgo.; d. Joseph Henry and Annie Belle (Watkins) Wesley; B.Ed., Chgo. Tchrs. Coll.; M.Ed., Ill. State Coll., 1962; M.S., Chgo. State U., 1968; m. Rivers S. Pierce. Tchr. educable mentally handicapped and regular elementary sch. children Chgo. Bd. Edn., to 1967, chmn. counseling dept., 1967-69, psychologist, 1969—. Pres. Emerald Av. Community Orgn., 1974; vol. Mental Health Assn. Greater Chgo., 1970—. Bd. dirs. Center Pre-Sch. Edn., 1970—. Mem. Ill. Psychol. Assn., Nat., Chgo. assns. sch. psychologists, Assn. Children with Learning Disabilities, Ill., Chgo. councils children with learning disabilities, N.A.A.C.P. (life), Phi Delta Kappa, Zeta Phi Beta. Mem. United Ch. Christ (bd. Christian edn.). Office: 8310 S St Lawrence Av Chicago IL 60619

PIERCE, DOROTHY KOCH, assn. exec.; b. New Haven, Mo., Oct. 24, 1918; d. Frederic August and Erna Frederica (Schwamb) Koch; B.J., U. Mo., 1947, postgrad., 1954-55, Washington U., 1955, George Washington U., 1957-59; m. Cornell David Pierce, Jan. 11, 1941 (div. Aug. 1954). Tchr. rural schs. Franklin County, Mo., 1937-40; tchr. journalism, English, Sullivan and St. Clair High Sch., Franklin County, 1947, 52-54; asst. instr. journalism U. Mo., Columbia, 1955; asst. editor Christian Bd. Publs., St. Louis, 1955-56; editorial asst. to Patent, Trademark and Copyright Found., George Washington U., Washington, 1957-59; asst. to editor N.E.A., Washington, 1959—. Mem. Women in Communications, N.E.A., Edn. Press Assn. Am., U. Mo. Alumni (sec. Washington chpt. 1961-63), Kappa Alpha Mu. Republican. Presbyn. (elder 1959-65, clk. of session 1962-65, chmn. Christian edn. 1960-64, Sunday sch. tchr. 1958-66). Home: 2705 30th St SE Washington DC 20020 Office: 1201 16th St NW Washington DC 20036

PIERCE, ETHEL TAYLOR (MRS. EDWARD A. PIERCE), pharmacist; b. Grayling, Mich., July 27, 1910; d. Floyd L. and Elizabeth V. (Bunting) Taylor; B.S., Ferris Inst., 1938, Ph.G., 1932; M.Pharmacy (hon.), Mass. Coll. Pharmacy, 1973; m. Edward A. Pierce, Apr. 29, 1939. Pharmacist, Central Drug Store, Grayling, 1934-35, L.F. Hamlin, Inc., Binghamton, N.Y., 1935-36, 1937-41, Nichols Meml. Hosp., Battle Creek, Mich., 1936-37, People's Drug Stores, Washington, 1945-46, Liggett Drug Co., Pittsfield, Mass., 1946-48; chemist Office Censorship, Cristobal, C.Z., 1941-44, Washington, 1944-45; chief pharmacist South Shore Hosp., South Weymouth, Mass., 1948—. Commr. Bd. Registration in Pharmacy, 1972—. Mem. exec. council Abington Girl Scouts U.S.A., 1947-49; mem. Abington Bd. Health, 1954—, chmn., 1955-57, 73-74, 74-75. Mem. Abington Republican Town Com., 1949—. Mem. D.A.R. (mem. Am. Indian Com. chpt. 1950—; regent 1960-62, 63-65), Am. Pharm. Assn. (del. Pan Am. congresses 1951, 54, 57, alternate del. 1960), Internat. Fedn. Pharmacy (del. 1962, 66), Mass. Cos. Hosp. Pharmacists (pres. 1953; chmn. legislative com. 1957-67, mem. exec. com. 1958-67), S. Shore Pharm. Assn. (v.p. 1966-67, pres. 1967-68), Ferris Inst. Alumni Assn., Am. Soc. Hosp. Pharmacists, Mass. State Pharm. Assn. (rec. sec. 1967-75), Nat., Mass. assns. sanitarians, Southeastern Mass. Assn. Bds. Health, Internat. Fedn. Pharmacy (asso.), New Eng. Historic Geneal. Soc. Boston, Am. Coll. Apothecaries, Royal Soc. Health Gt. Britain, Mass. Coll. Pharmacy, Acad. Gen. Practice Pharmacy. Mem. Order Eastern Star, Trinity Shrine (high priestess 1968-69), White Shrine Jerusalem (high priestess 1952-53, 1954-55, 1968, 72). Club: Abington Woman's. Home: 19 Pearl St North Abington MA 02351 Office: South Shore Hosp 50 Fogg Rd South Weymouth MA 02190

PIERCE, FLORENCE MARIE MCLAUGHLIN (MRS. WILLIAM AVERY PIERCE), pub. co. exec.; b. N.Y.C., June 6, 1920; d. Thomas James and Bertha (Fenz) McLaughlin; student Eastman Bus. Sch., 1937, Rutgers, 1966-67, N.Y. U., 1967-68; m. William Avery Pierce, June 4, 1938; children—Barbara (Mrs. Simeon Semco), Susan (Mrs. Galen Denton). Sec., John W. Marquand, N.Y.C., 1937; cashier, bookkeeper Gen. Pub. Loan Corp., N.Y.C., 1938; test examiner Ednl. Record Bur., N.Y.C., 1951-53; sec. Parents Mag., Inc., Bergenfield, N.J., 1953-63, fulfillment supr., 1963-66, personnel mgr., 1966-70; with New Am. Library, Inc., 1970—, personnel dir., office mgr. N.Y.C., 1972—, No. asst. to state project chmn. Ranch Hope, N.J. Fedn. Women's Clubs, Alloway, 1969-70, state project chmn. Camp Merry Heart, Hackettstown, 1970-72. Bd.

dirs. Consortium of Pubs. for Equal Opportunity, N.Y.C., 1970-73. Mem. Am. Soc. Personnel Adminstr., Personnel Mgmt. Assn. Bergen County (sec. 1971-73), Bergenfield C. of C. Presbyn. (asst. Sunday sch. supt. 1953-60). Clubs: Bergenfield Womans (bd. govs. 1957-73; financial sec. 1972-73); X Club (sec. State N.J. 1972-73). Home: 347 New Bridge Rd New Milford NJ 07646 Office: 1301 Av of Americas New York City NY 10019

PIERCE, GRACE WAGNER, polit. party worker; b. Coatesville, Pa., May 9, 1926; d. Jacob and Grace Anne (Wallace) Wagner; student Goldey Coll., 1944, Wesley Jr. Coll., 1970, 73; pupil art Howard Schroder, Loren Kohut, Lon Fluman; m. W. Lemar Pierce, Dec. 15, 1945; children—Linda Lee (Mrs. Walter T. Dolan), Barry Wallace, Susan Butler. Sec.-treas. Pierces Pharmacies, Inc., Dover, Del., 1962—. Republican committeewoman 29th dist. Kent County, Del., 1966-69; chmn. vols. Kent County Rep. campaign, 1968; del. Rep. Nat. Conv., 1968; program chmn. Del. Fedn. Rep. Women, 1968-69; vice chmn. Kent County Rep. Com., 1969-72, vice chmn. edn. com., 1973—; pres. Fedn. Rep. Women Del., 1970-72; Rep. committeewoman 31st dist. Kent County, 1973—; chmn. Kent County campaign Gov. R.W. Peterson, 1972; candidate Del. Ho. of Reps., 1974. Pres. jr. bd. Kent Gen. Hosp., 1960-62; work with presch. children Capitol Green Community Center, 1970-71; chmn. East Coast Environmental Leadership Conf., 1974; mem. women's study com. Del. Tech. and Community Coll. Bd. dirs. Kent Gen. Hosp., 1971—, Delawareans for Orderly Devel., exec. bd. Watch Our Waterways. Mem. Rehoboth Art League, Palmer Home. Club: Maple Dale Country (Dover). Address: 535 American Av Dover DE 19901

PIERCE, GRETCHEN NATALIE HULT (MRS. HOWARD W. PIERCE), paper co. exec.; b. Eugene, Ore., July 7, 1945; d. Nils B. and Jewel B. (Bauman) Hult; B.A., U. Ore., 1966; m. Howard W. Pierce, Dec. 26, 1970. Research analyst Boise Cascade, Portland, Ore., 1966-69; mgr. Corporate Information Center, Boise, Ida., 1969-71, mgr. price adminstrn., 1971—. Mem. Am. Marketing Assn., Spl. Libraries Assn., Am. Soc. Information Sci. Home: Route 1 Eagle ID 83616 Office: 1 Jefferson Sq Boise ID 83728

PIERCE, LORETTA MAE (MRS. CLAYTON A. PIERCE), real estate broker; b. Montrose, O., Mar. 20, 1910; d. Harry B. and Mary Ann (Ley) Stein; student, Akron Bus. Coll., 1928; Chgo. Sch. Interior Decorating, 1960; grad. Real Estate Inst., 1969; m. Clayton A. Pierce, Nov. 10, 1933 (dec.). Clerical positions Ohio Edison Co., Kent, 1928-36; adminstrv. asst. to pres. Braun & Co., Los Angeles, 1936-59, sec., treas. 1956-59; real estate salesman Bud's Realty, Hemet, Cal., 1959; real estate broker Maury C. Coleman, San Jacinto, Cal., 1960; sales mgr. Divine's Real Estate, San Jacinto and Hemet, 1962-65; owner, real estate broker Loretta Pierce Realtor, Hemet, 1965—. Pres., St. Joseph Med. Center Guild, Burbank, Cal., 1951-52; mem. Hemet (Cal.) Hosp. Aux., 1960—. Bd. dir. Ramona United Way, 1972-73. Named Woman of Year, Bus. And Profl. Womens Club, 1968; recipient James Vincent Francisco Achievement award Hemet Real Estate Bd., 1968. Mem. Nat. Assn. Realtors, Nat. Inst. Real Estate Brokers, Nat. Inst. Farm and Land Brokers, Cal. Real Estate Assn. (regional v.p. 1971, state dir. 1963, 66-68, dir. at large 1970-71), Hemet-San Jacinto Bd. Realtors (pres. 1967), Womens Council of Realtors (pres. Hemet-San Jacinto chpt. 1974), Bus. and Profl. Womens Club (treas. 1973), C. of C. Club: Zonta Internat. (v.p. Hemet 1973). Home: 41283 Merriwood Dr Hemet CA 92343 Office: 40598 Florida Av Hemet CA 92343

PIERCE, MARGARET HUNTER, govt. ofcl.; b. Weedsport, N.Y., June 30, 1910; d. Thomas Murray and Ruby (Sanders) Hunter; B.A., Mt. Holyoke Coll., 1932; J.D., N.Y.U., 1939; m. John R. Pierce, Nov. 4, 1950 (div. May 1959); 1 dau., Barbara Hunter. Admitted to N.Y. bar, 1941, D.C. bar, 1958; atty. Office Alien Property Custodian, Washington, 1942-43, 45, Office Solicitor, Dept. Labor, 1943-45, NLRB, 1946, 47-48; atty.-adviser U.S. Ct. Claims, 1947-48, 48-59, reporter of decisions 1959-68; commr. U.S. Indian Claims Commn., 1968—. Mem. Nat. Assn. Govt. Lawyers, D.C. (ct. claims com., 1958—, military law com. 1967—), Fed. (Indian Law com. 1955—), Am., Womens bar assns. Club: Zonta (Washington). Home: 3829 Garfield St NW Washington DC 20007 Office: 1730 K Street NW Washington DC 20006

PIERCE, MARGARET K. (MRS. WALTER MORGAN PIERCE), club woman; b. Washington, Dec. 20; d. John Daniel and Ellen (O'Brien) Kelliher; student pub. and parochial schs.; m. Walter Morgan Pierce, Sept. 27, 1951; step-children—Walter Morgan, L. Staples. Past v.p. Miami chpt. Pearl S. Buck Found.; chmn. Miami Heart Ball, 1968, Ballet Ball, 1969, Opera Ball, 1970-73. Bd. dirs. Miami Ballet Soc.; trustee Opera Guild Greater Miami; chmn. Debutante Ball Com., 1972-74; mem. women's aux. Miami Heart Inst., mem. aux. bd. Humane Soc. Mem. Vizcaya, Young Patronesses of Opera (pres. 1962-63), Theatre Arts League (pres. 1960-61, 61-62, dir.), Miami Art Center. Republican. Presbyn. Clubs: Surf, La Gorce Country, Bankers (Miami Beach); Beach Colony, Palm Bay, Miami Arts Center (Miami); Farmington Country (Charlottesville, Va.); South Miami Riding; Round Meadow (Christiansburg, Va.). Editor, pub. Social Engagement Book for Opera Guild, 1966, 67, 68, 69, 72, 73. Home: 5955 Pine Tree Dr Miami Beach FL 33140

PIERCE, MARTHA JANE DURGY, advt. agy. exec.; b. Dunkirk, N.Y., Oct. 29, 1925; d. Herbert Walter and Mildred Selina (Williams) Durgy; grad. high sch.; m. William Hastings Pierce, Sept. 1, 1948 (div. June 1961); children—Pamela Jane Tison, Patricia Ann. Women's program dir., broadcaster WSIR Radio, Winter Haven, Fla. 1956-63; women's program dir. WTWB Radio, Winter Haven, 1963-64; account exec. Pearson Clark Sawyer, advt. and pub. relations, Lakeland, Fla., 1964-72; co-owner The Happy Place in Dixieland Mini Mall, Lakeland, 1972; owner Jane Pierce & Assos., pub. relations and advt., Lakeland, 1973—. Pub. relations counsel United Cerebral Palsy Assn., Lakeland, 1968; publicity chmn. Polk County March of Dimes campaign, 1971. Polk County Republican coordinator U.S. senatorial campaign, 1962, Fla. gubernatorial campaign, 1962. Named Polk County Advt. Woman of Year, Polk Advt. Fedn., 1969, 73, Silver Medal award, 1974. Mem. League Women Voters, Epsilon Sigma Alpha (charter). Club: Quota (charter mem. Winterhaven). Home: 1042 Cumberland Av Lakeland FL 33801 Office: PO Box 2389 Lakeland FL 33803

PIERCE, NANNETTE CHRIST, psychologist; b. Niagara Falls, N.Y., May 19, 1942; d. Herbert Noble and Ruthe Ann (Miller) Christ; B.A. in Clin. Psychology, U. Tulsa, 1966; M.A. in Counseling, Ariz. State U., 1968; m. Kyle K. Pierce, June 14, 1969; stepchildren—Kyle Kay, Cameron Brigham. Counselor, supr. Ariz. State Hosp., Phoenix, 1966-68; supr. Warm Springs (Mont.) State Hosp., 1969-72; service worker Child Protective Services Ariz. Dept. Econ. Security, Tucson, 1973-74. Psychol. cons. Warm Springs schs., 1971-72. Mem. Am. Psychol. Assn. Address: 2417 Iris Rd NW Albuquerque NM 87104

PIERCE, PAULINE BURCHARD DAY (MRS. HAROLD CLIFTON PIERCE), curator; b. Chgo., Nov. 28, 1917; d. Lawrence Atherton and Emily Blair (Holmes) Day; grad. Hockaday Sch., 1935; student So. Meth. U., 1935-38; m. Canterbury Brooke Pierce, Dec. 20, 1942 (dec. 1944); m. 2d, Harold Clifton Pierce, Nov. 2, 1946; children—Lillyan Brooke, Charles, Lawrence. Bridal cons. Lord & Taylor, N.Y.C., 1940-42, asst. buyer, 1944-46; bridal cons. Bachrach Photographers, N.Y.C., 1943-44; part-owner, mgr. Stork Shop, Knoxville, Tenn., 1946; curator, adminstr. hist. room Stockbridge (Mass.) Library, 1967—. Mem. bd. Episcopal Diocese Western Mass., Westboro, 1960-63. Mem. Berkshire County Hist. Soc. (dir.), Soc. Am. Archivists, New Eng. Archivists, Pi Beta Phi. Clubs: Lenox (Mass.) Garden; Great Barrington Garden. Home: PO Box 122 Great Barrington MA 02130 Office: Stockbridge Library Stockbridge MA 01262

PIERCE, PONCHITTA ANNE, journalist; b. Chgo., Aug. 5, 1942; d. Alfred Leonard and Nora (Vincent) Pierce; B.A. cum laude, U. So. Cal., 1964; student Cambridge (Eng.) U., summer 1962. Asst. editor Ebony, N.Y.C., 1964-65, asso. editor, 1965-67, N.Y. editor, 1967-68; N.Y. editorial bur. chief Johnson Pub. Co., 1967-68; spl. corr. CBS News, 1968-71; contbg. editor McCall's mag., N.Y.C., 1971—; co-host Sunday show Sta. WNBC-TV; editorial cons. Phelps Stokes Fund, 1971—. Mem. Manhattan Adv. com. N.Y. Urban League; del. WHO Conf. on Food, Health and Devel., Geneva, Switzerland, 1973. Trustee Freedom from Hunger Found., bd. dirs. African Student Aid Fund. Recipient award Penney-Mo. Mag. Awards Contest, 1967, N.Y. Urban League John Russwurm award 1968. Mem. Am. Fedn. TV and Radio Artists, Am. Women in Radio and TV, Women in Communications (chpt. pres. 1964, Nat. Headliner award 1970), Mortar Bd. (chpt. editor 1964). Home: 780 Madison Av New York City NY 10021 Office: WNBC-TV 30 Rockefeller Center New York City NY 10019

PIERLOT, LUCILLE GEORGETTE, communications cons.; b. Boston, Aug. 12, 1928; d. George Eugene and Elsa Anna (Wilberding) Pierlot; B.F.A., Carnegie-Mellon U., 1950; m. Joseph A. Taylor, Aug. 25, 1965; 1 dau., Emily. Actress, N.Y.C. and Hollywood, 1950-60; editor Overseas Press Bull., N.Y.C., 1960-64; Midwest pub. relations dir. Time, Inc., Chgo., 1964-65; partner Taylor & Pierlot, communications cons., Boston and Austin, Tex. 1965—. Coordinator, Media 3 Americas internat. communications seminars, Austin, 1971—. Speechwriter, researcher mayoral campaign John V. Lindsay, N.Y.C., 1965. Mem. Pub. Relations Soc. Am. (chpt. dir. 1972-74), Nat. Acad. TV Arts and Scis., Women in Communications (nat. pub. relations dir., editor nat. mag. Matrix 1971—). Republican. Club: Chicago Press. Editor Tex. Town and City mag., 1972—. Address: 3905 Balcones Dr Austin TX 78731

PIERMAN, HARRIET JANE LEESTMA (MRS. GEORGE EUGENE PIERMAN), nurse; b. Sturgis, Mich., Sept. 16, 1918; d. George and Mary (Koekkoek) Leestma; R.N., Blodgett Meml. Hosp., 1939; m. George Eugene Pierman, Aug. 2, 1947; children—Gail (Mrs. John Berzins), Douglas, Susan. Nurse, B.M. Hosp., Grand Rapids, Mich., 1940, Evang. Luth. Hosp., Cleve., 1948-49, Penrose Hosp., Colorado Springs, Colo., 1960-61, Calhoun County Health Dept., Battle Creek, Mich., 1970—. Mem. Battle Creek Community Chorus, 1970; art league Battle Creek (Mich.) Civic Art Center, 1970-73; box office Battle Creek Civic Theater, 1971-73. Served with Nurses Corps, AUS, 1941-47. Mem. First Presbyn. Women Assn. (pres. 1971-73), Women's Overseas Service League (v.p. 1971-73). Club: Gogouac Garden (pres. Battle Creek 1971-72). Home: 191 Rebecca Rd Battle Creek MI 49015 Office: Calhoun County Health Dept Battle Creek MI 49017

PIERS, MARIA WEIGL (MRS. GERHART PIERS), child psychologist; b. Vienna, Austria, May 17, 1911; d. Karl I. and Elsa (Pazeller) Weigl; student U. Vienna, 1932-37; Ph.D., U. Basel, 1939; postgrad. Northwestern U., 1942; m. Gerhart Piers, July 20, 1938; children—Margaret Maria, Matthew Jakob. Came to U.S., 1939, naturalized, 1944. Staff mem. Vienna Dept. Pub. Welfare, 1934-38; social worker Ill. Soc. Mental Health, 1940-42, Assn. for Family Living, 1941-50; faculty Rockford Coll., 1950-51; prof. Chgo. Med. Sch., 1949-52, Chgo. Inst. for Psychoanalysis, 1959-62; lectr. U. Chgo., 1959—; star About People, Children Growing, ednl. TV stas., 1958—; child expert ABC-TV, 1965—; dean Erikson Inst. for Early Childhood Edn., 1966—. Chmn. aid to dependent children com. Mental Health Soc., Chgo. Mem. Am. Assn. Social Workers, Royal Soc. Health. Author: How To Work with Parents, 1952; Growing Up With Children, 1966; Wages of Neglect, 1969. Editor: Play and Development, 1972. Contbr. articles to profl. jours. Home: 5811 Dorchester Av Chicago IL 60637 Office: 1525 E 53d St Chicago IL 60615

PIERSOL, JUDY ALICE GREGERSON (MRS. THOMAS B. PIERSOL), civic worker; b. Madison, S.D., July 17, 1940; d. Russell Kanouse and Mary Alice (Hoisington) Gregerson; student extension courses No. S.D. State Coll., 1967; m. Thomas B. Piersol, Sept. 27, 1958; children—David Dean, Dale Thomas. Adminstrv. asst. S.D. Republican Central Com., Pierre, 1964-73, S.D. Easter Seal Soc. for Crippled Children and Adults, Pierre, 1973—. Sec., S.D. Developmental Disabilities Council, 1971-73. Treas., P.T.A., Pierre, 1966. Sec., treas. S.D. Young Republicans, 1964-69, chmn., 1969-71. Named Outstanding Young Republican Woman, S.D. Young Rep. League, 1969, Nat. Young Rep. Fedn., 1971. Mem. Nat. Sec. Assn. (corr. sec. 1971-72, pres. 1974—). Club: Toastmistress (2d. v.p. 1971-72) (Pierre). Home: 900 W Pleasant Dr Pierre SD 57501 Office: PO Box 297 Pierre SD 57501

PIERSON, ANNE BINGHAM (MRS. RICHARD NORRIS PIERSON, JR.), physician; b. N.Y.C., June 9, 1929; d. Woodbridge and Ursula Wolcott (Griswold) Bingham; A.B., Vassar Coll., 1951; M.D., Columbia U., 1955, M.P.H., 1972; m. Richard Norris Pierson, Jr., July 10, 1954; children—Richard Norris III, Olivia Tiffany, Alexandra deForest, Cordelia Stewart Comfort. Substitute intern Am. U. Hosp., Beirut, Lebanon, 1955; rotating intern Lenox Hill Hosp., N.Y.C., 1955-56; gen. practice medicine Seventh Day Adventist Hosp., Taipei, Taiwan, 1957; cons. gynecologist Continental Ins. Co., N.Y.C., 1958-69; clin. asst. obstetrics and gynecology clinics Englewood (N.J.) Hosp., 1965-68; asst. outpatient dept. obstetrics and gynecology St. Luke's Hosp. Center N.Y.C., 1965-70; physician Contraception Counselling and Edn. Clinic, Cowell Hosp., U. Cal. at Berkeley, 1971; asst. clin. prof. obstetrics and gynecology Sloane Hosp., Columbia-Presbyn. Med. Center, N.Y.C., 1972—. Bd. dirs. Planned Parenthood of Bergen County, 1962—, mem. med. adv. com., 1964—, med. dir., 1966—; mem. nat. med. adv. com. World Fedn. Planned Parenthood, 1966-69. Mem. subcom. on open spaces Englewood Planning Bd., 1968-69; mem. Conservation Commn., 1969-70; asst. troop leader Girl Scouts U.S.A., Englewood, 1968-69. Mem. Am. Assn. Planned Parenthood physicians, Bergen County Med. Soc., Jr. League. Club: Northern N.J. Vassar. Office: Internat Institute for Study Human Reproduction 78 Haven Av New York City NY 10032

PIERSON, PEGGY JOYCE (MRS. KENNETH E. PIERSON), horse show judge; b. Pickneyville, Ill., July 13, 1931; d. Harold and Elizabeth (Morgenstern) Margenthaler; m. Kenneth E. Pierson, Aug. 18, 1970; 1 dau., Ann. Owner, breeder, trainer Shetland and Hackney ponies, also Standardbred trotting and pacing horses, Pinckneyville; judge various horse shows in U.S. including Eastern States, Springfield, Mass., Pin Oaks Charity, Houston, A-Z, Phoenix, Ill., Ohio, and Mich. State Fairs. Mem. Am. Horse Shows Assn., U.S. Trotting Assn. Home: 802 E St Pinckneyville IL 62274

PIERSTORFF, LOLA ROSE, educator; b. Maiden Rock, Wis., Jan. 27, 1917; d. Charles F. and Lelah (Ragan) Pierstorff; B.E., Whitewater (Wis.) State Tchrs. Coll., 1938; B.L.S., U. Wis., 1941, M.L.S., 1952. High sch. librarian, Huron, S.D., 1941; librarian Edn. Library, U. Wis., Madison, 1942-54, edn. reference librarian U. Wis. Meml. Library, 1954-57, asst. prof. curriculum and instrn. dept., 1957—, dir. library services Instructional Materials Center, 1957—. Co-founder Lewis Carroll Shelf award given annually by U. Wis., 1958—; mem. credit com. U. Wis. Credit Union, Madison, 1971—; mem. exec. com. Mineral and Lapidary Club, Madison (Wis.) Community Center, 1960—. Mem. N.E.A. (student adviser 1950-60), Am., Wis. (sec. 1956) library assns., Wis. Edn. Assn. Council (local pres.), Assn. for Supervision and Curriculum Devel., Assn. for Ednl. Communications and Tech., Pi Lambda Theta. Co-editor Wis. Dirs. Ednl. Materials Centers Newsletter, 1960—. Home: 113 Alden Dr Madison WI 53705

PIETRANTONI, JEANETTE MARY, educator; b. Syracuse, N.Y., May 9, 1936; d. Gene Anthony and Jennie Mary (Cianfrocca) Pietrantoni; B.A., State U. N.Y. Albany, 1958; M.A., Syracuse U., 1964. Tchr. English, Syracuse City Sch. Dist., 1958-65, Lincoln Jr. High Sch., 1968—; tchr. Peace Corps, Kenya, East Africa, 1966-67. Del. profl. convs. Mem. N.E.A., Am. Fedn. Tchrs., N.Y. State United Tchrs., N.Y. State English Council, Syracuse Tchrs. Assn. (1st v.p. 1972—). Editor: STA News, 1969—. Home: 227 Lemoyne Av Syracuse NY 13208 Office: 941 James St Syracuse NY 13203

PIETRASANTA, ALEXANDRA MARY, art gallery adminstr.; b. Nice, France, Mar. 16, 1936; d. Vittorio and Alexandra (Troubetzkoy) Pietrasanta; came to U.S., 1949, naturalized, 1957; diploma Brera Acad. Fine Arts, Milan, Italy, 1967; B.A., Trinity Coll., 1958. Pub. relations information officer Mus. Modern Art, N.Y.C., 1958-59; office mgr. Rapho Guillumette Pictures, Inc., N.Y.C., 1959-60; head of research World House Galleries, N.Y.C., 1961-63; asst. mgr. Graphics 1 & 2, N.Y.C., 1970-71; v.p. Peter Rose Gallery, N.Y.C., 1971—. Home: 16 E 98th St New York City NY 10029 Office: 340 E 52d St New York City NY 10022

PIGG, (MARY) EVELYN HOEY, psychologist; b. Garden City, Mo., Nov. 20, 1914; d. Claude Clifton and Emily Mae (Hawkins) Hoey; B.S. in Edn., Central Mo. State Coll., 1945; postgrad. U. Denver 1959, Tex. Coll. Arts and Industry, 1961, (Nat. Def. Edn. Act grantee) U. Miami (Fla.), 1967, Sam Houston State Coll., 1973; M.Ed., U. Tex., 1963; m. Marvin Charles Pigg, June 2, 1950; (div.); 1 dau., Laura Mae. Chmn. dept. bus. edn. high sch., Harlingen, Tex., 1955-61; sch. counselor, Georgetown, Tex., 1962-65; secondary sch. counselor, Austin, Tex., 1965—; individual practice psychology, Austin, Tex., 1971—. Cons., Warm Springs Found., Crippled Children, Gonzales, Tex., 1972. Mem. N.E.A., Am., Tex. personnel and guidance assns., Am., Tex. psychol. assns., Am. Sch. Counselors Assn., Central Tex. Sch. Counselors, Austin Assn. Tchrs., Am. Assn. U. Women, Alpha Phi Delta, Kappa Delta Pi. Democrat. Roman Catholic. Home: 1900 B Glen Allen Austin TX 78704 Office: 1211 E Oltorf Austin TX 78704

PIGGOTT, LUCILLE CORNELIA JOHNSON (MRS. BERT C. PIGGOTT), ednl. adminstr.; b. Alton, Ill., Apr. 11, 1925; d. Cyrus Leroy and Jennie Cornelia (Keene) Johnson; B.S. in Bus. Edn. summa cum laude, N.C. Agrl. and Tech. State U., 1954; M.Ed. in Bus. Edn., U. N.C., Greensboro, 1964; m. Bert C. Piggott, Aug. 20, 1949; 1 son, Bert C., Jr. Statis. clk. Supreme Life Ins. Co., Chgo., 1945-49; stenographer Office of Pres., N.C. Agrl. and Tech. State U., Greensboro, 1954-60, sec. to dean acad. affairs, 1960-64, dean of women, 1964-71, asso. dean student affairs, 1971-73, dean student affairs for student orgns. and devel., 1973—. Mem. Nat. (sec.), N.C. (v.p. 1968-70, pres.) assns. women deans and counselors, N.C., So. coll. personnel assns., N.C. Personnel and Guidance Assn., Jack and Jill Am., Inc., Holidays Inc., Delta Kappa Gamma, Alpha Kappa Alpha, Delta Pi Epsilon, Pi Omega Pi, Alpha Kappa Mu. Democrat. Presbyn. Home: 801 Cambridge St Greensboro NC 27406

PIJAN, MARGARET EMMA, pediatrician; b. Chgo., Apr. 30, 1916; d. Leopold Henry and Emma Meta (Menzel) Pijan; student North Park Coll., 1934-36; B.S., Loyola U., 1938, M.D., 1941; M.S., U. Ill., 1969. Intern Swedish Covenant Hosp., Chgo., 1941-43, now mem. staff; resident Children's Meml. Hosp., Chgo., 1943-45, fellow, 1953-55; fellow U. Minn., Mpls., 1953-55; pediatrician Child Devel. Clinic, Children's Meml. Hosp., 1957-66; med. dir. Loyola U. Guidance Center, Chgo., 1969—. Instr., sch. social service adminstr. U. Chgo., 1963-65; asso. Northwestern U. Med. Sch., 1961-66. Recipient Sr. Med. Traineeship award in mental retardation, Dept. Health, Edn. and Welfare, 1966-67. Mem. Chgo. Pediatric Soc., Am. Acad. Pediatrics, A.M.A., Chgo. Med. Soc., Am. Med. Women's Assn. Co-author: Brain Damage and Behavior, 1965. Office: 1043 W Loyola St Chicago IL 60626

PIKE, DIANE KENNEDY (MRS. JAMES ALBERT PIKE), author; b. Norfolk, Neb., Jan. 24, 1938; d. George Edward and Arlene Alice (Wyant) Kennedy; B.A. in Elementary Edn. with distinction, Stanford, 1959; M.A. in English with honors, Columbia, 1964; m. James Albert Pike, Dec. 20, 1968 (dec.). Missionary, tchr. Crandon Inst., Montevideo, Uruguay, 1959-62; tchr. English Willow Glen High Sch., San Jose, Cal., 1964-65; dir. youth and children's work First United Meth. Ch., Palo Alto, Cal., 1965-67; exec. dir. New Focus Found., Santa Barbara, Cal., 1967-69; group facilitator, 1972—; lectr. Bd. dirs., pres. Bishop Pike Found., Santa Barbara, 1969-72, The Love Project, San Diego, 1972—. Mem. Common Cause, Am. Soc. for Psychical Research, Order of Fransisters and Franbrothers, P.E.O., World Future Soc., Women's Internat. League for Peace and Freedom, Am. Acad. Polit. and Social Sci., Fellowship of Reconciliation, Clergy and Laymen Concerned about Vietnam. Democrat. Methodist. Author: (with James A. Pike) The Other Side, 1968; Search, 1970; (with R. Scott Kennedy) The Wilderness Revolt, 1972; (with Arleen Lorrance) Channeling Love Energy, 1974. Editor: New Focus, 1969-72; (with Arleen Lorrance) The Seeker Newsletter, 1972—. Contbr. articles to mags. Address: 4470 Orchard Av San Diego CA 92107

PIKE, LILLIAN FRANCES WILSON (MRS. JIMMIE MASON PIKE), state ofcl.; b. Newton, N.C., Apr. 23, 1928; d. Austin and Bertha AnnaLyza (Garrett) Wilson; A.A., Pfeiffer Jr. Coll., 1948; B.A., U. N.C., 1950; m. Jimmie Mason Pike, Apr. 6, 1963; 1 dau., Beverly Inez. Field cons., news editor N.C. Tb Assn., Raleigh, 1950-60; alcoholism communications and information specialist N.C. Dept. Mental Health, Raleigh, 1960-73, editor Inventory, 1960-73; sec.-treas. Pike's Electronics Services, Raleigh, 1966—; alcoholism program coordinator Orange-Person-Chatham Mental Health Center, Chapel Hill, 1973—. Mem. Alcoholism Profls. N.C. (chmn. awards com. 1969-71, Distinguished Service award 1972). Methodist. Editor: Manual on Alcoholism for Social Workers, 1965. Home: 1433 Chester Rd Raleigh NC 27608 Office: 310 W Franklin St Chapel Hill NC 27514

PIKE, RUTH E(LSIE) (MRS. LAWRENCE LEONARD PIKE), recreation ofcl.; b. Wymore, Neb., Mar. 21, 1906; d. George Frederick and Elsie Mae (Miller) Schad; A.B. in Journalism, U. Neb., 1926, M.A. in Sociology, 1931; m. Lawrence Leonard Pike, Mar. 30, 1927. Editor, Extension Publs., U. Neb., Lincoln, 1926-42; supr. employee relations Office of Censorship, San Antonio, 1942-43; chmn. dept. sociology Trinity U., San Antonio, 1943-45, editor Univ. Publs., 1943-45; specialist in social problems U. Colo., Boulder, 1945-48, editor Colo. Municipalities, 1945-48; research asso. Wash. State U., Pullman, 1948-50; supr. pub. information Wash. State Parks and Recreation Commn., Seattle, 1950-62; adminstrv. asst. (pub. relations) urban renewal office Office of Mayor, Seattle, 1962-64; staff U.S. Bur. Outdoor Recreation, Seattle, 1964-68, asst. to regional dir., 1968—. Exec. dir. Wash. White House Conf. on Children and Youth, 1959-61; mem. Gov.'s com. White House Conf. on Children and Youth, 1970. Recipient Luther Halsey Gulick award Camp Fire Girls, 1969; Ernest Thompson Seton award, 1967, Appreciation award Am. Camping Assn., 1970. Mem. Am. (Mr. Chmn. award 1969, Distinguished Fellow award 1973, mem. exec. com. 1973), Wash. (Honor Fellow award 1967) recreation and park socs., Nat. Recreation and Park Assn. (trustee 1974-77), Women in Communications (pres. Seattle profl. chpt. 1962-63). Home: 3527 Wallingford Av N Seattle WA 98103 Office: 1000 2nd Av Seattle WA 98104

PIKE, TERESA MARIA DE HOSPODAR (MRS. NATHAN R. PIKE), lectr., artist; b. Nagy Mihaly, Austria; d. John and Mary (Tasko) de Hospodar; student N.A.D., 1923-24, Drake Bus. Coll., 1925-26; m. Nathan R. Pike, Aug. 18, 1937. Came to U.S., 1912, naturalized, 1944. Oneman shows, including Art Center, N.Y.C.; exhibited in group shows, including Am. Artists Profl. League, Nat. Arts Club, Salamagundi Club, Nat. League Pen Women; represented in pvt. collections. Lectr. on hist. antiquities, glass, also primitive, ancient and Early Am. lighting; catalouger, appraiser fine arts. Chmn. fund raising Westchester Mental Hygiene Assn., 1953-57; mem. Friends of Greenwich Library, Glenville Community League. Recipient various prizes for paintings. Mem. Nat. League Am. Pen Women (Conn. publicity chmn., New Eng. regional editor Pen Woman 1962-64, Conn. art chmn. 1958-60, 66-68, nat. scrapbook chmn. 1964-66, nat. chmn. pre-teen age stories 1968-70, state pres. 1972-74), Am. Artists Profl. League (1st v.p. N.Y. State chpt. 1962-64). Clubs: Boston College; Greenwich Woman's. Author: Fairy Lamps and How to Make Them, 1955; How to Collect Early American Glass, 1964; Ballet In Porcelain, 1965. Contbr. articles to Conn. and N.Y. newspapers. Address: Twas a Farm Soundview Ridge 7 Woods Av Glenville CT 06830

PILARSKI, LAURA PATRICIA, journalist; Niagara Falls, N.Y., Dec. 10, 1926; d. Joseph and Mary (Pytko) Pilarski; B.A. magna cum laude, Syracuse U., 1948; postgrad. U. Wis.-Milw., 1958-59; spl. courses Warsaw (Poland) U., 1962-63. Gen. news reporter Milw. Jour., 1949-60; asst. to corr. A.P., Warsaw, 1962-63; free-lance corr., 1963-65; chief corr. McGraw-Hill World News, Zurich, Switzerland, 1965—. Recipient award Milw. Press Club, 1957. Mem. Assn. de la Presse étrangère en Suisse, Overseas Press Club Am., Phi Beta Kappa, Theta Sigma Phi. Roman Catholic. Home: 2245 Welch Av Niagara Falls NY 14303 also Kornelius-strasse 1 8008 Zurich Switzerland

PILDES, ROSITA STEPHAN (MRS. ROBERT PILDES), pediatrician; b. Buenos Aires, Argentina, July 18, 1929; d. Samuel and Shirley (Chaden) Stephan; came to U.S., 1940, naturalized, 1954; M.D. with honors, U. Ill., 1953; m. Robert Pildes, June 14, 1953; children—Richard, Ellyn. Intern, Cook County Hosp., Chgo., 1953-54; resident pediatrics Michael Reese Hosp., Chgo., 1954-56, dir. ambulatory pediatrics, 1957-63; asso. newborn nursery U. Ill., Chgo., 1965-67; dir. neonatology Cook County Children's Hosp., Chgo., 1967—; asso. prof. pediatrics U. Ill. Coll. Medicine, Chgo., 1967-73, prof. pediatrics, 1973—. Mem. maternal and child health adv. com. City of Chgo., 1970-73. Mem. Am. Diabetes Assn., Am. Acad. Pediatrics, Soc. for Pediatric Research, Am. Pediatric Soc., Midwest Soc. for Pediatric Research, Chgo. Pediatric Soc., Alpha Omega Alpha. Office: 700 S Wood St Chicago IL 60612

PILGRIM, GENEVA HANNA (MRS. WALTER N. PILGRIM), educator; b. Paynesville, Minn., Nov. 25, 1914; d. George A. and Regula (Figi) Hanna; B.A., Hamline U., St. Paul, 1937; M.A., Northwestern U., 1941, Ph.D., 1946; m. Walter N. Pilgrim, July 3, 1965. Tchr. English, St. Clair and Worthington, Minn., 1937-40; tchr. English and social studies, Des Moines, 1940-43; tchr. Evanston Twp. High Sch., 1943-44; asst. prof. edn. Ohio State U., 1945-50; prof. English edn. U. Tex., Austin, 1950—; cons., summer teaching Tex. schs., William and Mary Coll., Northwestern U., U. Ga., Tchrs. Coll. Columbia. Recipient Teaching Excellence award Students Assn., U. Tex., Austin, 1961, U.S. Office Edn. grant Prospective Tchrs. of Disadvantaged, 1968-70, U. Tex. Research grant, 1970-71. Mem. Nat. Council Tchrs. English (dir.), Conf. English Edn., Am. Ednl. Research Assn., Assn. Supervision and Curriculum Devel. (dir.), N.E.A., Am. Assn. U. Women, Delta Kappa Gamma, Pi Lambda Theta. Democrat. Methodist. Author: Learning and Teaching Practices in English, 1966; (with Mariana McAllister) Books, Young People, and Reading Guidance, 1968. Home: 709 E 46th St Austin TX 78751

PILGRIM, MARY JANE, social worker; b. Youngstown, O.; d. Frederick Henry and Geneva (Jones) Pilgrim; student Wittenberg U., 1938-40; B.S., Western Res. U., 1942; M.A., Ohio State U., 1949; postgrad. Boston U., 1954-55. Social worker Youngstown Family Service and Youngstown Community Corp., 1950-52; dir. social services Mahoning County Tb Sanitarium, Youngstown, 1952-54; social worker Youngstown Child Guidance Center, 1955-58, dir. social services Child and Adult Mental Health Center, 1964—; chief social worker Athens County Mental Health Center, Athens, O., 1958-59; social work supr. Family Service, Warren, O., 1959-61; chief social worker Norfolk (Va.) Mental Health Center, 1961-62, Athens Mental Health Center, 1962-64. Cons. home sch. visitation program, 1966—; guest lectr. Youngstown State U. Mem. adv. bd. Soc. for Blind, Youngstown, 1969-70. Mem. Nat. Assn. Social Workers (vice chmn. 1967-68, sec.-treas. 1951-53), Acad. Certified Social Workers, Ohio Mental Health Forum, Kappa Delta Alumni Assn. Baptist. Club: Quota. Home: 92 Buena Vista Av Youngstown OH 44512 Office: 1001 Covington Av Youngstown OH 44510

PILIKOWSKI, ANNE CECILE, librarian, nurse; b. Prince Albert, Sask., Can., Feb. 3, 1924; d. William and Josephine (Klamantoski) Pilikowski; R.N., Holy Family Hosp., Prince Albert, 1947, R.R.L., 1960. Asst. dir. med. records Holy Family Hosp., Prince Albert, 1960-71; chief record librarian Norfolk Gen. Hosp., Simcoe, Ont., Can., since 1971-73; record librarian Victoria Hosp., London, Ont., 1973—. Mem. Ont. Health Record Assn., Canadian Assn. Med. Records Librarians. Address: 500 Gordon Av Apt 902 London ON N6J 2V8 Canada

PILLAERT, E(DNA) ELIZABETH, mus. curator; b. Baytown, Tex., Nov. 19, 1931; d. Albert Jacob and Roseline Nettie (Kelly) Pillaert; B.A., U. St. Thomas, 1953; M.A., U. Okla., 1963; postgrad. U. Wis., 1962-67, 70-73. Asst. curator archaeology Stovall Mus., Norman, Okla., 1959-60, edn. liaison officer, 1960-62; research asst. U. Okla., Norman, 1962; research asst. U. Wis., Madison, 1962-65, curator osteology U. Wis. Zool. Mus., 1965—, head curator, 1967—. Cons. archaeol. faunal analysis, 1965—. Mem. Am. Assn. Museums, Okla. Anthrop. Soc. Home: 216 N Prairie St Stoughton WI 53589 Office: Zoological Museum University of Wisconsin Madison WI 53706

PILLANS, JUDITH ANN HART (MRS. CHARLES PALMER PILLANS III), educator; b. Charleston, S.C., Nov. 7, 1940; d. Felder Pat and Jean Graves (Norris) Hart; B.A., U. S.C., 1962; M.S., Fla. State U., 1963; m. Charles Palmer Pillans III, July 6, 1963; children—Charles Palmer IV, Helen Hart. Children's librarian Jacksonville (Fla.) Pub. Library, 1963-64, chief children's services, 1967-69, coordinator library oral and visual experience, summer 1972; regional children's librarian Santa Fe Regional Library, Gainesville, Fla., 1964-66; recruiter Fla. State Library, Tallahassee, 1969, 70; tchr. Scott Mill Lake Kindergarten, Jacksonville, 1973—. Pres. fund Friends of Jacksonville Pub. Library, 1972-73; mem. Jacksonville Symphony Guild, Women's Guild Jacksonville Children's Mus. Bd. dirs. Family Consultation Service. S.C. State Library Bd. scholar, 1963. Mem. Fla. Library Assn. (editor Fla. Libraries quar. jour. 1969-71, chmn. recruitment com. 1970, chmn. sch. and children's div. 1967-68), A.L.A., Jacksonville Bar Aux. (2d v.p. 1973-74), Chi Omega, Beta Phi Mu. Methodist. Club: Lakewood-San Jose Junior Woman's (charter mem. Jacksonville, pres. 1971-72). Home: 2957 Amellia Dr Jacksonville FL 32217

PILLON, NANCY HARGIS BACH, educator; b. Jackson, Ky., July 28, 1917; d. Grannis and Evelyn (Crawford) Bach; student Lees Jr. Coll., 1934-36; B.A., Western Ky. State U., 1939; M.S. in Library Sci., U. Ky., 1957, Ed.D., 1967; m. Richard Walsh Pillon, Oct. 6, 1950 (div.); 1 son, Richard Crawford. Librarian Breathitt County High Sch., Jackson, Ky., 1939-42, tchr., librarian, 1952-60; instr. library sci. No. Ill. U., Dekalb, 1960-65; asst. prof. library sci. U. Ky., Lexington, 1965-69; asso. prof. library sci. Ind. State U., Terre Haute, 1969—, acting chmn. dept. library sci., 1971. Chmn. conf. Indian Sch. Library Suprs., 1969-73; mem. Ind. State Com. Certification Sch. Librarians, 1971—. Served with USNR, 1942-50. Mem. A.L.A., Am. Assn. Library Schs., D.A.R. (chpt. regent 1958-60). Democrat. Presbyn. Home: 2375 Ohio St Terre Haute IN 47803

PILLOTE, FLORENCE ANN HATTERY (MRS. JOHN F. PILLOTE), pediatrician; b. Celina, O., July 28, 1936; d. Sidney Dillon and Mary Edith (Coil) Hattery; A.B., Ind. U., 1958, M.D., 1961; m. John Franklin Pillote, June 30, 1962; children—Katherine Elaine, Cynthia Louise, Mark, Kurt. Intern, Harper Hosp., Detroit, 1961-62; resident Children's Hosp. of Mich., Detroit, 1962-64; practice medicine specializing in pediatrics, Marquette, Mich., 1964—; chief pediatrics St. Luke's Hosp., Marquette, 1968-73, St. Mary's Hosp., Marquette, 1968-73. Home: 26 Lakeview Dr Marquette MI 49855 Office: 1414 W Fair Av Marquette MI 49855

PILLSBURY, ELIZABETH ANN, sch. psychologist; b. Milw., July 20, 1915; d. Frank Lewis and Bessie Eastman (Lewis) Pillsbury; B.S., Milw.-Downer Coll., 1937, Occupational Therapist, 1938; M.S., U. Wis., 1947. Occupational therapist Milw. Childrens Hosp. and Convalescent Home, 1938-40, dir. occupational therapy, 1940-43; occupational therapist Gaenslen Sch., Milw. Pub. Schs., 1943-48, sch. psychologist, 1948-65, clin. psychologist Child Study Center, 1965-72, sch. psychologist cons. to mental retardation programs, 1972—. Mem. adv. com. United Assn. Retarded Children, Milw.; active various civic orgns. Bd. dir. Hearing Soc. Fellow Am. Assn. Mental Deficiency; mem. Am. Assn. U. Women, Wis. Sch. Psychol. Assn., Learning and Behavioral Disability Assn., Am. Occupational Therapy Assn., Am. Psychol. Assn., Delta Kappa Gamma, Pi Lambda Theta. Home: 425 W Willow Court Milwaukee WI 53217 Office: 5225 W Vliet St Milwaukee WI 53208

PILSNER, JOYCE MARION, health services adminstr.; b. N.Y.C., Jan. 30, 1925; d. Sol and Estelle (Schaffle) Mayersohn; A.B., Hunter Coll., 1944; M.A., Columbia, 1946; m. Harry Pilsner, Dec. 20, 1947; 1 dau., Toby Jane. Tchr., N.Y.C., 1945-67; research asso. Inst. Community Studies, Sarah Lawrence Coll., Bronxville, N.Y., 1968-69, asst. to dean faculty, dir. edn., 1968-70; research asso., field coordinator Consortium on Community Crises, Cornell U., Ithaca, N.Y., 1970-71; adminstrv. dir. Riverdale Mental Health Clinic, Bronx, N.Y., 1971—. Group discussion leader Urban Systems Staff Devel. Center, Yonkers, N.Y., 1970. Del., memberships chmn., corr. sec. Riverdale Community Council; mem. dist. bd. Comprehensive Health Planning Agy.; mem., sec. sub-regional com. Bronx Fedn. Mental Health and Mental Retardation Agys. Mem. Riverdale Mental Health Assn. (dir. 1965-71, chmn. pub. relations, editor newsletter), UN Assn. (dir. Riverdale chpt., chmn. publicity), Am. Assn. U. Women, League Women Voters, Am. Orthopsychiat. Assn., Assn. Adminstrs. Mental Health and Mental Retardation Facilities (dir. 1974—). Home: 4721 Delafield Av New York City NY 10471 Office: 2736 Independence Av New York City NY 10463

PIMSLEUR, MEIRA GOLDWATER (MRS. SOLOMON PIMSLEUR), cons. editor, bibliographer; b. N.Y.C., Sept. 8, 1904; d. Michael and Ada Rose (Levenson) Goldwater; B.A., Hunter Coll., 1946; postgrad. Columbia Sch. Library Service, 1946-48; m. Solomon Pimsleur, July 8, 1925; children—Paul, Joel Leon. With Columbia 1929-73, cataloger, 1942-47, head acquisitions dept. Law Library, 1947-73; cons. editor, bibliographer Oceana Publs., Inc., Dobbs Ferry, N.Y., 1973—. Indexer, compiler, bibliographer, lectr. law library problems to library assns. Mem. Am. Assn. Law Libraries, Assn. Law Libraries Greater N.Y., Assn. Law Libraries Upstate N.Y., Common Cause, Phi Beta Kappa. Jewish religion (mem. sisterhood). Home: 535 W 110th St New York City NY 10025 Office: 75 Main St Dobbs Ferry NY 10522

PIMSLEUR, SUSAN, artist rep.; b. N.Y.C.; d. Isaac and Giselle (Wishik) Pimsleur; evening student N.Y.C. Coll., 1927-30; student Hunter Coll., N.Y. U., 1938-40; m. children—Richard, Michael Westley. Dir. Hampton Center of Contemporary Arts, Inc., 1963—; personal rep. and artists' mgr. of ballet, jazz stars and theater prodns., 1949—; owner Hampton Arts Theatre, 1958—; produced art festivals, also prodns. for Boston, Montreal, L.I. Mem. Asso. Councils of Arts, Internat. Assn. Concert and Festival Mgrs., Lioness of Islips. Home: 120 Elder Rd Islip NY 11751 Office: 119 W 57th St New York City NY 10019

PINCHOT, ANN (MRS. BEN PINCHOT), author; b. N.Y.C., Nov. 23, 1918; d. Barnet and Diana (Kulick) Kramer; m. Ben Pinchot, Mar. 19, 1939; 1 dau., Susan. Free lance writer, 1941—; editor trade div. Prentice Hall, Engle Wood Cliffs, N.J., 1962-67. Author: (with G.L. Hall) Jacqueline Kennedy, A Biography; (with Lillian Gish) Mr. Griffith, The Movies and Me; The Manchasers; (with M. Deans) Weep No More My Lady, The Story of Judy Garland, 1972; (with M. Franklin, M. Krauthamer, A. Razzak Tal) The Heart Doctors' Heart Book, 1974. Home: 88 Maltbie Av Stamford CT 06902

PINCK, JOAN BRAVERMAN (MRS. DAN CHANNING PINCK), coll. adminstr.; b. Lowell, Mass., Feb. 27, 1929; d. Edwin and Esther (Goodman) Braverman; A.B., Radcliffe Coll., 1950; m. Dan Channing Pinck, Aug. 26, 1951; children—Anthony, Jennifer, Alexandra, Charles. Acad. counselor Pine Manor Jr. Coll., Chestnut Hill, Mass., 1969-70, dean studies, 1970-72, acad. dean, 1972, dir. Open Coll., 1971—; dir. first year report program Harvard Bus. Sch., Boston, 1972-74, dir. adminstrv. appts. and policies, 1974—, also lectr. bus. adminstrn. Radcliffe Inst. Fellow, 1967-68, 68-69. Mem. Womens Equity Action League (pres. Mass. chpt. 1972-74), Radcliffe Coll. Alumnae Assn. (dir. 1971-74), Soc. Radcliffe Inst. fellows (dir. 1972—), Nat. Assn. Bank Women (adv. bd. endl. found.). Home: 48 Clark St Belmont MA 02178 Office: Baker 432 Harvard Business School Boston MA 02163

PINCKNEY, CATHERINE LARKUM (MRS. EDWARD R. PINCKNEY), author, consumer reporter; b. N.Y.C.; d. Edward S. and Isolde (Illian) Larkum; student N.Y. U., 1942-44, 48, Syracuse U., 1946-48, New Sch. for Social Research, 1949, U. Cal. at Berkeley, 1969-70; m. Edward R. Pinckney, Sept. 18, 1944; 1 dau., Cathey Lee. Writer various stories Ben Casey, tv series; co-writer daily and Sunday column Mirror of Your Mind pub. in U.S., fgn. newspapers, 1967—; book reviewer Parade of Books, 1965—. Mem. Writers Guild Am., Author's League. Author: The Fallacy of Freud and Psychoanalysis, 1964; Medical Encyclopedia of Common Illnesses, 1962; Granny's Hillbilly Cookbook, 1966; The Cholesterol Controversy, 1973; A Consumer's Guide to Common Medical Dilemmas, 1975. Contbr. articles to publs. Office: Box P Beverly Hills CA 90213

PINCOCK, CAROLYN SNYDER, pediatrician; b. Kingston, N.Y., Oct. 9, 1910; d. Howard E. and Carrie (Bortz) Snyder; student U. Wis., B.A., George Washington U., 1931, M.D., 1934; m. Glen Pincock, June 6, 1934; children—David, Diane R., Douglas G. Intern Jr. Kingston (N.Y.) Hosp., 1933, George Washington U. Hosp., Washington, 1934-35; resident Children's Hosp., Washington, 1935-36; pvt. practice pediatrics, Silver Spring Md., 1936—; mem. staff Children's Washington, Montgomery Gen., Holy Cross, Washington Adventist, Suburban, Mem. Comprehensive Health Planning Bd., 1973-74. Bd. dirs. Cynthia Warner Sch., Easter Seal Soc. Montgomery County. Recipient Togetherness award McCall's mag., 1957, certificate of distinction Central High Sch. Medicine, 1957. Mem. A.M.A., Am. Med. Women's Assn. (Med. Women of Year award 1956, pres.-elect), D.C., Montgomery County (pres. 1970), George Washington U. med. socs., D.A.R., Alpha Epsilon Iota, Chi Sigma Gamma. Home: 14602 Edelmar Dr Silver Spring MD 20906 Office: 1944 Seminary Rd Silver Spring MD 20910

PINCUS, FLORENCE VOLKMAN, clin. psychologist; b. Bklyn., July 6, 1916; d. Herman and Anne (Fox) Sadowsky; B.A., Bklyn. Coll., 1936; M.S.S., New Sch. for Social Research, 1938; m. Jacob Volkman, Oct. 6, 1939 (div. May 1963); children—Erika Ann (Mrs. Thomas Duncan), Toby Alice; m. 2d, Alexis Pincus (div. Apr. 1974). Personnel technician War Dept., Washington, 1940-42, ct. psychologist Richmond, Va., 1942-45; sch. psychologist Bur. Child Guidance, N.Y.C., 1953-59; staff psychologist Hillside Hosp., Glen Oaks, N.Y., 1959-64; psychologist Speech and Hearing Center, Queens Coll., 1964—; chief psychologist Community Mental Health Program, Chgo.; psychologist Bklyn.-S.I. Mental Health Center, 1971—; gen. practice psychotherapist and psychoanalyst, 1958—; psychol. cons. Anti-Poverty Program, 26 Head-Start Centers, Miss., summer 1965; cons. Emory U. Med. Sch., Atlanta, 1971—. Mem. nat. steering com. Psychologists for Social Action. Bd. dirs. Vietnam Era Vets. Nat. Resource Project. Fellow Inst. Practising Psychotherapists; mem. Am. Psychol. Assn., N.Y. Soc. Clin. Psychologists (exec. bd.), Address: 145 4th Av New York City NY 10003

PINE, CHARLOTTE WEIKINGER (MRS. JAMES ALEXANDER PINE), lawyer; b. Wurzburg, Germany, Nov. 22, 1921; d. Frank Christof and Wally (Friedrich) Weikenger; came to U.S., 1923; naturalized, 1931; B.S., U. Md., 1943, LL.B., 1945; m. James Alexander Pine, Mar. 4, 1944; children—James Alexander, Frank Carlton, Mary Frederick, Nancy Lee. Admitted to Md. Bar, 1945; since practiced in Baltimore County; mem. firm Pine & Pine, Towson, Md., 1945—. Chmn. March of Dimes, Balt. County, 1955-60, Cancer Crusade, 1961-65; pres. Balt. County Chpt. Am. Cancer Soc., 1966-67; chmn. Balt. Councty United Fund, 1968. Mem. Phi Delta Delta, Kappa Kappa Gamma. Home: Thornhill Baldwin MD 21013 Office: 607 Baltimore Av Towson MD 21204

PINEDA, ELIZA LAOANG (MRS. BERNARDO G. PINEDA), psychiatrist; b. Camiling, Tarlac, Philippines, Feb. 9, 1930; d. Julio C. and Marciana (Concepcion) Laoang; M.D., U. Santo Tomas, 1955; m. Bernardo G. Pineda, Jan. 21, 1956; children—Grace Lynn, Michelle, Duane. Intern, St. Clare's Hosp., Schenectady, N.Y., 1957-58; resident in psychiatry Traverse City (Mich.) State Hosp., 1959-63; practice medicine specializing in psychiatry, Manila, Philippines, 1963-66, Burlington, Ia., 1969—; tchr. health edn. and guidance and counseling Nat. Tchrs. Coll., Philippines, 1964-66; staff psychiatrist Mental Health Inst., Mt. Pleasant, Ia., 1966-69; med. dir. Henry County Mental Health Center, Mt. Pleasant, 1971; mem. med. staff Meml. Hosp. Burlington, Ia. Mem. Des Moines County Med. Soc., Women's Aux. Med. Soc. Burlington. Rotary Ann. Club: Golf (Burlington). Home: 2917 Garden St Burlington IA 52601 Office: Reipe Peterson Bldg Burlington IA 52601

PINEDA, IRENE BASILIO (MRS. ANDREW J. STIBER), physician; b. Philippines, Aug. 5, 1939; d. Saturnino C. and Consalacion B. (Basilio) Pineda; A.A., U. St. Tomas, 1957, M.D., 1962; m. Andrew J. Stiber, Mar. 30, 1968; children—Jonathan A., Jason A. Intern, St. Clare Hosp., Schenectady, 1963-64; resident Bellevue and U. Hosp., N.Y.C., 1965-68; asst. dir. gynecare Bellevue Hosp., 1971—; clin. instr. N.Y.U. Sch. Medicine, 1973—. Jr. fellow Am. Coll. Obstetricians and Gynecologist. Home: 48 Ash St Englewood Cliffs NJ 07632 Office: 200 E 36th St New York City NY 10016

PINEDA, MARIANNA, artist, sculptor; b. Evanston, Ill., May 10, 1925; ed. Bennington Coll., U. Cal. at Berkeley, Columbia; m. Harold Tovish. Exhibited in one-man shows Slaughter Gallery, 1951, Walker Art Center, 1952, Swetzoff Gallery, 1953, 64, De Cordova, Lincoln, Mass., 1954, Honolulu Acad. Art, 1970, Alpha Gallery, Boston, 1970, 72, Newton (Mass.) Coll., 1972, Bumpus Art Gallery, Duxbury, Mass., 1974; exhibited in group shows Mus. Modern Art, 1957, 60, Chgo. Art Inst., 1957, 60, Albright Gallery, Buffalo, 1948, Boston Arts Festival, 1957, 58, 60, U. Ill., 1957, 61, Pitts. Internat., 1960, N.E., Sculpture Exhbns., Boston, 1968, 69. De Cordova Mus., Mass., 1966-72; tchr. sculptutre Newton (Mass.) Coll.; represented in permanent collections Addison Gallery Am. Art, Boston Mus. Fine Arts, Dartmouth, Wadsworth Athenaeum, Hartford, Walker Gallery, Munson, Williams, Proctor Inst., Williams Coll., State of Hawaii, Fogg Mus. Harvard, Radcliffe Coll., others. Scholar Radcliffe Inst., 1962-64. Home: 164 Rawson Rd Brookline MA 02147

PINGATORE, ROSARI ANTOINETTE FOTI (MRS. ANTHONY PINGATORE), educator; b. Westfield, N.Y., June 4, 1921; d. Salvatore Paul and Margaret (Lotempio) Foti; B.E., State U. Coll. Fredonia, 1942; spl. edn. certificate Kent State U., 1970; M.S., St. John Coll., 1972; m. Anthony Pingatore, Sept. 22, 1951; children—Frances, Toni-Marie. Tchr. rural schs., N.Y. State, 1942-44; tchr. Charlotte Sidway Sch., Grand Island, N.Y., 1944-47; mgr. Childcraft div. Field Enterprises, Pitts., 1947-52; tchr. trainable retarded Cuyahoga County, Cleve., 1962; supr. trainable classes Murray Hill Sch., also William Brett Schs., Cleve., 1964-67; tchr. intermediate class educable mentally retarded Mayfield (O.) Center, 1970-71; tchr. primary educable mentally retarded Mayfield Sch. Dist., 1971; elementary cons. educable mentally retarded Lake and Geauga Counties, 1971-72; tchr. children with learning disabilities and behavior disorders Mapledale Sch., Wickliffe, O., 1972—. Leader

Girl Scouts, 1966-68; mem. Ohio Citizens Com. for Spl. Edn., 1972—; mem. adv. com. Explorer Troop of Retarded Children, 1973—; pres. Greater Cleve. Friends and Parents of Slow Learners, 1963-65, Garfield Heights Friends and Parents of Slow Learners; v.p. Hillcrest Friends of Library, 1970-71; mem. adv. bd. spl. edn. dept. Notre Dame Coll., Cleve., 1972—. Mem. Council Exceptional Children, N.E. Ohio (mem. bd.), Cleve. assns. children with learning disabilities. Home: 6756 Bonnie View Rd Mayfield Village OH 44143

PINHEIRO, JANE SEYMOUR (MRS. JOSEPH COELHO PINHEIRO), artist; b. Denver, Sept. 29, 1907; d. Rugley Dunlap and Nellie (Flick) Seymour; normal diploma U. Utah, 1925; m. Joseph Coelho Pinheiro, Sept. 25, 1930. One man shows at Santa Barbara Mus. Natural History, San Diego Mus., Los Angeles County Mus., N.Y. Bot. Gardens, Bowers Mus., S.W. Mus., Hunt Mus., others; exhibited in group shows at Los Angeles County Fair, others; represented in permanent collections at Carnegie Inst. Tech., Cleve. Garden Center, Theodore Payne Found., others. Chmn. state parks com. Cal. Joshua Trees State Park, 1954-57. Bd. dirs. 50th Dist. Agrl. Assn., 1960-70, So. Cal. chpt. Nature Conservancy, 1963— (1st v.p. 1969—), Antelope Valley chpt. A.R.C., 1970—; bd. dirs. Desert Protective Council, 1964—, treas., 1964-72; bd. dirs. Antelope Valley Dist. Hosp., 1953-57; mem. adv. bd. dirs. Theodore Payne Found., 1960—. Recipient Merit award Cal. Conservation Council, 1965, award of merit Desert Protective Council, 1971, Outstanding Citizens of Year award Elks Lodge, 1972, Distinguished Service citation Cal. Conservation Hall of Fame, 1974. Mem. Antelope Valley Allied Arts Assn. (hon. life), Antelope Valley Hosp. Guild (life), Quartz Hill C. of C. (past pres.). Democrat. Unitarian. Clubs: Quartz Hill Woman's (past pres.), Lancaster Women's (past pres.), Zonta. Home: 4819 W Av M Quartz Hill CA 93534

PINHEIRO, MARILYN LAYS (MRS. JOSE GONCALVES DE ARAUJO PINHEIRO), educator, health services adminstr.; b. Brockton, Mass., Apr. 18, 1924; d. Alan Fletcher and Ruth (Wilbar) Lays; B.A., Boston U., 1945; M.S., Case Western Res. U., 1957, Ph.D., 1969, postgrad. (NIH fellow), 1969-71; m. Jose Goncalves de Araujo Pinheiro, July 21, 1946; children—Edwin, Angela (Mrs. James J. Miller). Speech therapist and audiologist Inst. Neurology, Rio de Janeiro, Brazil, 1957-60; dir. clin. audiology Clinica do Prof. Jose Kos, Rio de Janeiro, 1958-65; research asst. and instr. Case Western Res. U., Cleve., 1969; cons. in audiology Cleve. Hearing and Speech Center, 1970-71; asso. prof. neurosci. Med. Coll. Ohio, Toledo, 1971—, dir. hearing and speech services, 1971—. Adj. prof. Bowling Green State U., 1971—, U. Toledo, 1974; cons. neuroaudiology Family Learning Center, Toledo, 1973—. Mem. Am., Ohio Speech and Hearing assns., Aphasiology Assn. Ohio (mem. exec. com., 1972—, area rep. 1972—), Soc. Neurosci., Acoustical Soc. Am., Assn. for Children with Learning Disabilities (mem. exec. bd. 1973—), Phi Beta Kappa. Club: Quota. Contbr. articles to profl. jours. Home: 1255 S Byrne Rd Toledo OH 43614

PINKHAM, ELEANOR HUMPHREY (MRS. JAMES HANSEN PINKHAM), univ. librarian; b. Chgo., May 7, 1926; d. Edward Lemuel and Grace Eleanor (Cushing) Humphrey; A.B., Kalamazoo Coll., 1948; M.S. in L.S. (Alice Louise LeFevre scholar), Western Mich. U., 1967; m. James Hansen Pinkham, July 10, 1948; children—Laurie Sue, Carol Lynn. Pub. services librarian Kalamazoo Coll., 1967-68, asst. librarian, 1960-70, library dir., 1971—. Vis. lectr. Western Mich. U. Sch. Librarianship, 1970—. Chmn., Pretty Lake Vacation Camp for Underprivileged Children, Kalamazoo, 1966. Mem. A.L.A., Mich. Library Assn., Am. Assn. U. Profs., Beta Phi Mu, Delta Kappa Gamma. Presbyn. (elder 1969—). Club: Service (Kalamazoo). Home: 2519 Glenwood Dr Kalamazoo MI 49008 Office: 1200 Academy St Kalamazoo MI 49001

PINKNEY, GERTRUDE GOLDSMITH (MRS. IRVING PINKNEY), librarian; b. Bklyn., Sept. 15, 1916; d. Morris and Celia (Weiss) Goldsmith; B.A., U. Mich., 1936, B.A. in Library sci., 1937; m. Irving Pinkney, Aug. 19, 1951; children—Henry S., Alfred E. Organizer, head Municipal Ref. Library, Detroit, 1944-49; chief, Reference Bibiog. Loan Service, U.S. Bur. Budget Library, Washington, 1942-44, 1949-51; asst. librarian Nat. Indsl. Conf. Bd. Library, N.Y.C., 1952-53; chief Municipal Ref. Library, Detroit Pub. Library, 1968—. Cons. Oakland County Planning Commn., 1969; lectr. Univ. Center Adult Edn., Detroit, 1972-73. Mem. Mayor's Citizen Study Team for Consumer Edn. and Protection, 1969; mem. Wayne County Commn. Juvenile Justice, 1973—. Mem. Council Planning Librarians, Spl. Libraries Assn. Club: Women's Economic (Detroit). Author article So You Want to Start a Municipal Reference Library, 1973. Home: 10725 Borgman Av Huntington Woods MI 48070 Office: 1004 City County Bldg Detroit MI 48226

PINKNEY, HELEN LOUISE, museum curator; b. Decatur, Ill., May 4, 1911; d. Charles DeWitt and Anna (Fisk) Pinkney; grad. Sch. Dayton Art Inst., 1940. Librarian, registrar collections Dayton Art Inst., 1936-45, curator, librarian, 1945-59, librarian and curator textiles, 1959—. Tchr. textile design Sch. Dayton Art Inst., 1945-46. Mem. Am. Assn. Museums, Spl. Libraries Assn. Home: 37 Stoddard Av Dayton OH 45405 Office: 405 W Riverview Av Dayton OH 45401

PINSKER, ESSIE LEVINE (MRS. SIDNEY PINSKER), advt., pub. relations exec.; b. N.Y.C.; d. Harris and Sophia (Feldman) Levine; B.A., Bklyn. Coll., 1940; postgrad. Columbia, 1950-51, N.Y. U., 1952-53, 72-74, New Sch. for Social Research, 1954-56, Art Students League, 1955-56; m. Sidney Pinsker, June 15, 1941; children—Susan Harris, Seth Howard. Buyer Ohrbachs, N.Y.C., 1942-44, Arkwright, Inc., N.Y.C., 1944-49; sportswear editor Women's Wear Daily, N.Y.C., 1953-59; press dir. Am. Symphony Orch., N.Y.C., 1962-64; with Essie Pinsker Assos., Inc., N.Y.C., 1960—, pres., 1968—. Exhibited sculpture in group shows at Allied Artists Am. 61st ann. exhbn., Knickerbocker Artists 23d and 24th ann. exhbns., Met. Life Village and Town Art Show, Fashion Group Art Show (all N.Y.C.), also N. Shore Community Arts Center, Manhasset, N.Y., Huntington (N.Y.) Twp. Art League Ann. Exhbn. fashion cons. Claire Lang Assos., 1959-60; lectr., instr. Fashion Inst. Tech., 1962-65. Guest editor Teen Merchandiser, 1946-47, Infants and Childs Rev., 1947-48; travel editor, fashion and beauty editor Woman Golfer, 1969-70. Home: 8 Peter Cooper Rd New York City NY 10010 Office: 110 W 40th St New York City NY 10018

PINTER, ELIZABETH LOUISE (MRS. ANTHONY S. PINTER), ednl. writer; b. Weleetka, Okla., Mar. 13, 1924; d. Harry Paul and Nellie Dunlap (Adamson) Lees; A.B., U. Okla., 1945; M.S., Columbia, 1946; postgrad. U. Cal. at Berkeley, U.S. Internat. U., Azusa Pacific Coll., San Diego State U.; m. Anthony S. Pinter, Sept. 25, 1956; children—Stephanie Ann, Claudia Louise. With Study Abroad, Inc., 1950-70, exec. dir., 1952-70; dir. communications Escondido (Cal.) Elementary Educators Assn., 1970—; ednl. cons. Escondido (Cal.) Union Sch. Dist., 1970—. Free lance writer and lectr; cons. on sch. book fairs to various schs. Chmn. acad. council San Pasqual High Sch., Escondido, 1972-74. Mem. Women in Communications, Am. Assn. U. Women, League Women Voters, Phi Beta Kappa. Mem. Order Eastern Star. Home: 2636 Loma Vista Dr Escondido CA 92025

PIORE, NORA KAHN (MRS. EMANUEL R. PIORE), economist, educator; b. N.Y.C., Nov. 28, 1912; d. Alexander and Sara (Rosenbaum) Kahn; B.A., U. Wis., 1933, M.A., 1934; m. Emanuel R. Piore, Aug. 26, 1931; children—Michael Joseph, Margot Debrah (Mrs. Joseph Onek), Jane Anne (Mrs. Robert H. Gilman). Economist U.S. Senate Com. on Labor and Pub. Welfare, 1950-53; program analyst N.Y. State Interdepartmental Com. on Low Incomes, N.Y.C., 1957-58; spl. asst. to commr. N.Y.C. Dept. Health, 1955-62, dir. Urban Med. Econs. Research Project, 1960-68; asso. prof. econs. Urban Research Center, Hunter Coll., N.Y.C., 1962-71; Belding Scholar Assn. Aid of Crippled Children, 1968-71; prof. health econs. Sch. Pub. Health, Columbia, 1971—, also asso. dir. Center for Community Health Systems; mem. vis. com. Harvard Med. Sch. Mem. Nat. Adv. Health Council, USPHS, N.Y.C. Health Research Council. Trustee Madison Felicia Settlement House Assn. N.Y.C.; Manhattan adv. council N.Y. Urban League; mem. tech. adv. council Planned Parenthood-World Population. Health Research Council career scientist award N.Y.C., 1962-66. Fellow Am. Pub. Health Assn. (med. care sect. council); mem. Am. Econs. Assn., Indsl. Relations Research Assn., Am. Acad. Polit. and Social Sci., Phi Beta Kappa. Club: Women's City (trustee) (N.Y.C.). Contbr. articles to profl. publs. Home: 115 Central Park W New York City NY 10023 Office: 630 W 168th St New York City NY 10032

PIORKOWSKI, GERALDINE KOMOSA, clin. psychologist; b. Chgo., Apr. 10, 1936; d. Adolph E. and Helen (Malec) Komosa; student Mundelein Coll., Chgo., 1954-56, Loyola U., Chgo., 1956-57; B.S., U. Ill. at Urbana, 1958, A.M. (fellow), 1961, Ph.D., 1964; m. Frank M. Piorkowski, Jan. 24, 1959; children—Paul, Michael, Julie. Psychology intern VA Hosp., Danville, Ill., 1961-62; instr. U. Ill., 1963; clin. psychologist Springfield (Ill.) Mental Health Center, 1964-65; clin. psychologist Ill. State Psychiat. Inst., Chgo., 1967-69; lectr. in psychology Loyola U., Chgo., 1965-68; chief psychologist Plainfield (N.J.) Consultation Center, 1969-70; clin. asst. prof. psychology N.J. Coll. Medicine and Dentistry, Newark, 1970-73; clin. psychologist Ill. State Psychiat. Inst., Chgo., 1973—. Cons. psychologist Ill. State Tng. Sch. for Girls, Geneva, 1965-66. Mem. Drug Adv. Council, Summit, N.J., 1972-73. Nat. Inst. Mental Health fellow, 1960-61. Mem. Am., N.J., Midwestern psychol. assns., Phi Beta Kappa. Contbr. articles to profl. publs. Home: 925 Chestnut Av Wilmette IL 60091 Office: 1601 W Taylor St Chicago IL 60612

PIPER, JULIA LUCILE MARKHAM (MRS. JAMES CALVERT PIPER), ch. worker; b. Parsons, Kan., July 4, 1913; d. Howard Crawford and Rhoda (Bartlett) Markham; B.A., U. Kan., 1935; hon. doctorate Coll. Emporia (Kan.), 1964; m. James C. Piper, Oct. 20, 1935; children—Mark, John, Paul, Gordon. Del. 3d Assembly World Council Chs., New Delhi, India, 1961; mem. Commn. on Evangelism United Presbyn. Ch., 1963-65, mem. Nat. Commn. on Religion and Race, 1964-65, program chmn. Nat. Exec. Com., 1958-61, exec. com. Commn. Ecumenical Mission and Relations, mem. Gen. Council, 1967-71; governing bd. Nat. Council Chs., 1972—. Pres. Parsons (Kan.) Bd. Edn., 1962-63; speaker Protestant Women of Chapel, U.S. Armed Forces, Europe, Africa, 1965; 1st pres. League Women Voters, 1959-61; chancellor's asso. U. Kan. Republican precinct com. woman. Bd. dirs. Kan. Delta Dental Ins. Plan. Mem. N.A.A.C.P., Farm Burs., United Ch. Women (nat. v.p. 1971—, bd. mgrs. exec. com.), U. Kan. Alumni Assn. (bd. dirs.), Mortar Board, Phi Beta Kappa, Gamma Phi Beta, Theta Sigma Phi. Dir. Presbyn. Life, natl. mag. Home: 1423 Morgan St Parsons KS 67357

PIPER, SUSAN GREENBERG (MRS. ROBERT GORDON PIPER), pub. relations exec.; b. N.Y.C., July 17, 1949; d. Herbert and Rosalie Marian (Brown) Greenberg; B.S., Northwestern U., 1971; m. Robert Gordon Piper, Mar. 21, 1971. Pub. relations asst. L.I. Jewish Med. Center, New Hyde Park, N.Y., 1969, Grant Hosp., Chgo., 1971; free lance pub. relations cons., San Diego, 1971-72; with KPBS Stas., San Diego, 1972-73; pub. relations Hollywood Presbyn. Med. Center, 1973-74, dir. pub. relations, 1974—. Bd. dirs. U. Cal. at San Diego Hosp. Aux., newsletter editor, 1972-73. Mem. Women in Communications (pres. elect chpt. 1973-74, chmn. nat. com. interships 1974—), League of Women Voters (voters service chmn. 1973), Pub. Relations Club of San Diego, So. Cal. Indsl. Editors Assn., Sigma Delta Chi. Editor: KPBS Guide, 1972—, Horizon Quar., 1974—. Home: 3703 Arbolada Rd Los Angeles CA 90027 Office: 1300 N Vermont St Los Angeles CA 90027

PIPES, JOYCE ELMYRA GRAGG, educator; b. Boone, N.C., Nov. 27, 1927; d. William Roy and Myra (Shook) Gragg; B.S., Appalachian State U., 1948, M.A., 1962; postgrad. U. N.C., Greensboro, 1967-70; m. Charles Duane Pipes, Dec. 23, 1950 (div. Dec. 1961); 1 son, Richard Sherman. Tchr. various schs., N.C., Ariz., Mich., 1948-52, 53-54, 56-58, 59-60; grad. teaching fellowship Appalachian State U., Boone, N.C., 1961-62; prof. phys. edn. Wingate (N.C.) Coll., 1962—. Mem. A.A.H.P.E.R., N.C. Assn. Health, Phys. Edn. and Recreation, Nat., So. (state membership chmn. 1963) assns. phys. edn. coll. women. Home: 206 Faculty Dr Wingate NC 28174

PIPITONE, PHYLLIS LUIS (MRS. S. JOSEPH PIPITONE), psychologist, educator; b. Chgo., Oct. 28, 1929; d. Max and Julia Antionette (Walkey) Luis; student Chgo. Conservatory Music, 1941, Chgo. Tchrs'. Coll., 1946, Peabody Conservatory Music, 1948, So. Meth. U., 1951; B.A., U. Akron, 1965, M.A., 1967; Ph.D. (Nat. Inst. Mental Health grantee), Kent State U., 1974; m. S. Joseph Pipitone, Aug. 28, 1948; children—Guy, Daniel, Paul. Pvt. practice psychologist, Akron, O., 1967-72; psychologist, instr. Kent (O.) State U., 1970—. Instr. piano and theory Music Acad., Chgo., 1946-47. Mem. Council for Exceptional Children, Am. Psychol. Assn., Am. Soc. Psychologists Assn., Am. Soc. for Psychical Research, Kent PSI Research Group, Mensa, Tuesday Mus. Club, Weathervane Theatre Women's Bd. Home: 560 Winslow Av Akron OH 44313

PIPKIN, SARAH BEDICHEK (MRS. ALAN C. PIPKIN), educator; b. Deming, N.M., Apr. 25, 1913; d. Roy and Lillian Lee (Greer) Bedichek; B.A., U. Tex., 1933, Ph.D., 1936; m. Alan Collins Pipkin, Sept. 6, 1938; children—Alan Collins, Roy B., George P. Rockefeller Found. fellow Univ. Coll., London, Eng., 1937-38; asso. prof. biology N. Tex. State Coll., Arlington, Tex., 1938-43; Rockefeller grantee, lectr. Am. U. of Beirut (Lebanon), 1946-49; research asso. Howard U., Washington, 1957-59, asso. prof. zoology, 1966-68, prof., 1968—; research asso. Gorgas Meml. Lab., Panama, 1959-64, Johns Hopkins U., Balt., 1964-66. Recipient grant NIH, 1959-68, 71-72, NSF, 1968-70, 73-74. Mem. Genetics Soc. Am., Am. Genetic Assn., Entomol. Soc. Washington, Am. Soc. Naturalists, Soc. for Study Evolution, A.A.A.S., Am. Inst. Biol. Scis., Soc. Exptl. Biology and Medicine, Phi Beta Kappa, Sigma Xi. Contbr. articles to profl. jours. Home: PO Box 66 Simpsonville MD 21150 Office: PO Box 138 Adminstrn Bldg Howard U Washington DC 20001

PIQUETTE, JULIA CAMILLA, educator; b. Chgo., Jan. 24, 1927; d. Walter N. and Laura E. (Wetzel) Piquette; B.S., Northwestern U., 1948, M.A., 1952, Ph.D., 1963. Tchr. Horlick High Sch., Racine, Wis., 1948-51; asst. dir., dean of girls Nat. High Sch. Inst. in Speech, teaching fellow Northwestern U., Evanston, Ill., 1951-52; instr. English and Speech State U. N.Y. Coll. at Buffalo, 1952-54, asst. prof. speech and English, 1954-59, asso. prof. speech, 1960-64, prof., 1964—, chmn. dept. speech and theatre, 1972—. Cons. State Edn. Dept., Albany, N.Y., 1955. Mem. Speech Communication Assn., N.Y. State Speech Assn., (mem. exec. council 1956-58), Am. Assn. U. Profs., Eastern Communication Assn., Zonta Internat., Delta Kappa Gamma (pres. chpt. 1974-76). Home: 174 Hedstrom Dr Buffalo NY 14226 Office: 1300 Elmwood Av Buffalo NY 14222

PIRTLE, IVYL LEORA FLEMING (MRS. J. MAX PIRTLE), educator; b. nr. Ottumwa, Ia., Jan 11, 1906; d. Barton Earl and Lillie (Roberts) Fleming; student Ia. State Coll., 1931; B.A., U. Fla., 1944; M.A., Fla. State U., 1951; m. J. Max Pirtle, Sept. 17, 1938. Tchr. elementary schs., Ia., 1924-39; tchr. Grace Stern Pvt. Sch., Miami Beach, Fla., 1939-40; tchr. elementary schs., Indiantown, Fla., 1940-43; tchr. primary grades, Stuart, Fla., 1943-50; demonstration tchr. Fla. State U., Tallahassee, summer 1949; tchr. Palmetto Sch., West Palm Beach, 1950-55; supr. elementary edn. Palm Beach County, 1955-65, dir. library services, 1965-70. Mem. Fla. steering com. Nat. Def. Edn. Act, 1958-68. Trustee Jr. Mus. Palm Beach County, 1960-63. Recipient certificate of appreciation for service to edn. Fla. State Dept. Edn., 1969. Mem. Assn. Childhood Edn. Internat. (br. pres. 1953-55, primary edn. com., 1954-56), Fla. Assn. Sch. Librarians (area chmn. 1959-62), N.E.A., Fla. Edn. Assn. (state chmn. dept. suprs. 1959-60; citation for meritorious service Dept. Suprs. 1968), Assn. Supervision and Curriculum Devel., Delta Kappa Gamma (chpt. pres. 1955-59), Kappa Delta Pi, Phi Kappa Phi, Club: Zonta. Contbr. articles profl. jours. Home: 340 Nottingham Blvd West Palm Beach FL 33405

PISANO, MARIANNA CICILIA LAROCCO (MRS. SAL PISANO), educator; b. N.Y.C., Jan. 21, 1926; d. Gus and Lena (Curreri) LaRocco; B.A., Hunter Coll., 1950; M.S., Bklyn. Coll., 1970; m. Sal Pisano, Jan. 24, 1953; children—Lucianna, Louis. With Sterling Nat. Bank, N.Y.C., 1943-47, Am. Bowling Congress, N.Y.C., 1947-48, Castleton China Co., N.Y.C., 1949-50, others; primary tchr. Seaford (L.I., N.Y.) Schs., 1951-60; primary tchr., gifted children Sands Point (L.I.) Sch., 1965-66; tchr. mentally retarded children N.Y.C. Sch. System, 1967—. Tchr. evening recreation program Seaford Schs., 1955-56. First v.p. Seaford Schs. P.T.A., 1956-57. Mem. Am. Assn. Mental Deficiency, N.Y. State Assn. Tchrs. Children with Retarded Mental Devel., Cath. Tchrs. Assn., Bklyn. Coll. Alumni Assn., Hunter Coll. Alumni Assn. Home: 235 Ocean Pkwy Brooklyn NY 11218

PISCEVICH, MARGO DEE, lawyer; b. Kimberly, Nev., Apr. 6, 1947; d. Joe and Lydia (Stocking) Piscevich; B.S., U. Utah, 1969, J.D., 1971. Researcher, Am. Bar Assn., Salt Lake City, Utah, 1969-70; clk. to justice supreme ct. Utah, Salt Lake City, 1970-71; admitted to Nev. Bar, 1971; dep. atty. gen., Carson City, Nev., asst. counsel Dept. Hwys., 1971—. Dir. Denee, Inc., Reno. Vol., ski instr. Reno Recreation Dept., 1971—. Bd. dirs. Washoe County Legal Aid Soc. Mem. State Bar Nev. (civil and appellate practice com. 1973-74), Washoe County Bar Assn., Barristers Club. Home: 1480 Lillian Way Reno NV 89502 Office: 1263 S Stewart St Carson City NV 89701

PITCHER, CHARLES ANDREWS HOLCOMBE (MRS. SARGENT PITCHER, JR.), lawyer; b. Baton Rouge, Dec. 22, 1916; d. Charles Andrews and Rachel (Jones) Holcombe; student Ward-Belmont Jr. Coll., 1934; B.A., La. State U., 1937, LL.B., 1942, J.D., 1970; m. Sargent Pitcher, Jr., Sept. 2, 1936; children—Frances H. (Mrs. George C. Crosby), Olive M. (Mrs. David L. French), Charles S. IV, Rachel A. (Mrs. John Gayden Morgan). Admitted to La. bar, 1942; spl. asst. atty. gen., Baton Rouge, 1952-56; 3rd asst. dist. atty., 1961-72; mem. firm Pitcher & Pitcher, Baton Rouge, 1950-60, Pitcher & French, Baton Rouge, 1973—. Mem. La., E. Baton Rouge bar assns., D.A.R., Colonial Dames of 17th Century, La. Geneal. and Hist. Soc., Phi Delta Delta, Kappa Kappa Gamma. Democrat. Methodist. Editor: La. Geneal. Register, 1968-72. Home: 14111 Old Hammond Hwy Baton Rouge LA 70815 Office: 345 Grandpre St Baton Rouge LA 70802

PITCHER, GLADYS, music editor, composer, arranger; b. Belfast, Me., Dec. 11, 1890; d. Elbridge S. and Emma B. (Pitcher) P.; student Belfast high sch., grad. with hons. New Eng. Conservatory Music, 1911, postgrad., 1911-12; spl. work in orchestration and composition Frederick S. Converse, 1922. Tchr. theory and harmony high sch., Chelsea, Mass., 1912-13; mem. music dept. and acting dean of women Beloit (Wis.) Coll., 1917-19; harmony dept. Am. Inst. Normal Methods, Auburndale, Mass., summers 1922-25; tchr. pub. sch. music, Passaic, N.J., 1920-21, Bennington, Vt., 1922-24, Manchester, N.H., 1924-25; editorial staff C.C. Birchard and Co., Boston, 1925-46, editor-in-chief, 1946-57; free-lance composer, arranger and editor, 1957—. Chmn. Boston Bookbuilders, 1941-42, Bookbuilders Workshop, 1950-52; mem. bd. mgrs. Boston Port and Seamen's Aid Soc., 1958-63. Mem. Am. Musicol. Soc., Nat. Music Educators Assn., Mass., Me. music educator's confs., Plimoth Plantation, Victoria Soc. of Me. Women, Pi Kappa Lambda, Alpha Chi Omega. Republican. Conglist. Clubs: Belfast Business Women's, Travellers' of Belfast (Me.)(pres. 1966-68). Author: A Singing School, series music books for children. Composer, arranger many works for chorus. Cons. This Is Music series, music textbooks. Address: 1 Northport Av Belfast ME 04915

PITCHFORD, EUGENIE BALLARD, assn. exec.; b. Paia, Maui, Hawaii, Apr. 13, 1916; d. Harold Ivan and Gladys Ogier (Stanford) Pitchford; student U. Hawaii, 1933-37. Columnist Honolulu Advertiser, 1952-53; advt. account exec. Peterson Asso., Honolulu, 1953-58; exec. sec. Hawaii Hotel Assn., Honolulu, 1963—; owner Hawaiian Flag Products, Honolulu, 1953—. Bd. dirs. Napili Kai Found., 1972—. Mem. Friends of the Library of Hawaii. Clubs: Travel Women Hawaii (pres.), Outrigger Canoe (editor monthly pub., 1959-61) (Honolulu). Author: Hawaiian Time, 1950; Young Folks Hawaiian Time, 1955. Pub. musical album: Hawaiian Time, 1972. Home: 1800 B Vancouver Dr Honolulu HI 96822 Office: 2270 Kalakaua Av 907 Honolulu HI 96815

PITCHFORD, HARRIET DAY, librarian; b. Canton, Miss.; d. Sterling G. and Lidie (Hunnicutt) Pitchford; B.S., Miss. So. U., 1935; M.A., George Peabody Coll., 1959; postgrad. Columbia, summers 1961, 64, 66. Tchr. elementary sch., Miss., 1935-41; librarian Main Post Library, Camp Van Dorn, Miss., 1941-43, Camp Roberts, Cal., 1943-47, Camp Zama, Japan, 1947-49, Ft. Benning, Ga., 1949—, Vietnam, 1970-71. Mem. Am. Assn. U. Women, UN Assn. of Am. Club: Altrusa (pres. 1967-68, v.p. 1972-73) (Columbus, Ga.). Home: 115 Matheson Rd Columbus GA 31903 Office: PO Box 1972 Ft Benning GA 31905

PITMAN, DOROTHY ELIZABETH, educator; b. Newnan, Ga., Apr. 30, 1922; d. Jason D. and Ida Bell (Noland) Pitman; A.B., Mary Hardin-Baylor Coll., 1952; M.A., U. N.C., 1958, Ph.D., 1960. Sec. to gen. mgr. Alcoma Coop., Lake Wales, Fla., 1941-47; sec. to pres. Mary Hardin-Baylor Coll., Belton, Tex., 1950-52; counselor for women Mercer U., Macon, Ga., 1953-55; asst. prof. sociology Austin Coll., Sherman, Tex., 1959-60; asso. prof. sociology Carson-Newman Coll., Jefferson City, Tenn., 1960-64; prof. sociology, chmn. dept. Ga. Coll. Milledgeville, 1964—. Mem. Am. Sociol. Assn., Am. Assn. U. Women (br. pres. 1966-69, state pres. 1971-73), Ga. Conf. Social Welfare, Am. Assn. U. Profs., Ga. Gerontology Soc., Ga. Sociol and Anthrop. Assn. (pres. 1968-69), So. Sociol. Soc., Pi Gamma Mu,

Delta Kappa Gamma. Baptist. Home: PO Box 668 Georgia Coll Milledgeville GA 31061

PITMAN, NAOMI KIME (MRS. THERON PITMAN), med. educator; b. Luther, Mont., June 22, 1908; d. Samuel Henderson and Rose Anna (Mooney) Kime; student Andrews U., 1926-28, Walla Walla Coll., 1929-31; M.D., Loma Linda U., 1936; M.S., 1964; m. Theron Pitman, July 26, 1937 (dec.); children—Linda Lee, Tui Devere. Tchr., Balt. Jr. Acad., 1928-29; intern Los Angeles County Hosp., 1935-36; resident City Maternity, Los Angeles, 1936, San Luis Obispo Gen. Hosp., 1936-37; gen. practice medicine, pub. health clinics, Los Angeles, Fresno, 1937-42; resident pediatrics Fresno Gen. Hosp., 1942-43; physician, instr. nursing sch. Chulamani Hosp., Bolivia, 1943-46; dir. Guayaremarin Hosp., Bolivia, 1946-48; resident pediatrics White Meml. Hosp., Los Angeles, 1948-50; physician examiner Los Angeles City Schs., 1950-51; pediatrician Madison (Tenn.) Sanitarium, 1951-59; asst. prof. pediatrics Loma Linda U., Sch. Medicine, Cal., 1959-61, asso. prof. pediatrics, 1961-73. Vis. prof., Tanzania, 1961, New Guinea, 1964, Afghanistan, 1972, Autonomous U. Guadalajara (Mexico), 1973—. Diplomate Am. Bd. Pediatrics, Nat. Bd. Med. Examiners. Fellow Am. Acad. Pediatrics; mem. Am., Cal. med. assns., San Bernardino County Med. Soc., Los Angeles Pediatric Soc., Western Soc. for Pediatric Research, Pub. Health Assn. of Seventh-day Adventists, U.S.-Mexican Border Pub. Health Assn., Am. Acad. Pediatrics (mem. newborn com. 1962, Dist. XII com. 1972). Mem. Adventists Ch. Address: 1839 Rio Colatlan Los Aguilas Jalisco Mexico

PITMAN, PENNY LOU, furniture co. exec.; b. Wentzville, Mo., Mar. 27, 1946; d. Clifton Elton and Matilda Catherine (Schierbaum) Pitman; A.A., Christian Coll., 1965; B.S., Northwestern U., 1967. Pub. relations dir. Childrens Press, Chgo., 1967-69; sales and promotion mgr. U. Mo. Press, Columbia, 1969-71; advt. mgr. Falcon Products, Inc., St. Louis, 1972—. Mem. Cherokee Lake Assn. (sec. 1972-73), Jr. Advt. Club, Women in Communications. Home: 330 McDonough St St Charles MO 63301 Office: 9387 Dielman Ind Dr St Louis MO 63132

PITNER, N(ELVA) KATHRYN, govt. ofcl.; b. Morrison, Ill., Oct. 30, 1944; d. Gordon Harrelson and Ava Dorothy (Monier) Pitner; student Hamilton Coll., 1964-65; B.A., Colo. Coll., 1966; M.A., U. Colo., 1968; postgrad. U. Denver, 1972—. Reporter, Council Bluffs (Ia.) Nonpareil, newspaper, 1968-69; tchr. French, Council Bluffs Dept. Adult Edn., 1969; employee devel. specialist, co-dir. communication of office skills inst. Denver Regional Tng. Center, U.S. Civil Service Commn., Denver, 1970-73; regional tng. officer, employee devel. specialist U.S. Dept. Housing and Urban Devel., Denver, 1973—. Mem. Am. Soc. Tng. and Devel., Nat. Orgn. Women, Women in Communications. Home: 627 C St NE Apt #A Washington DC 20002 Office: Dept Housing and Urban Devel West Tng Center Loretto Heights Coll 3001 S Federal Blvd Denver CO 80236

PITRE, LULA LEE OSGOOD (MRS. HAROLD FRANCIS PITRE), social worker; b. Denham Springs, La., Mar. 11, 1919; d. William Oscar and Clara (Rheams) Osgood; B.S., La. State U., 1939, certificate social work, 1948; m. Harold Francis Pitre, June 6, 1942; children—Lee Frances Lorene, Jane Claire Velyn. Caseworker, Livingston Paris Dept. Pub. Welfare, Livingston, La., 1939-42; dir. East Feliciana Parish Welfare Dept., Clinton, La., 1943-48; supr. East Baton Rouge Parish Welfare Dept., Baton Rouge, 1949-50, dir., 1950-64; exec. asst. La. Dept. Pub. Welfare, 1964-65, welfare adminstrv. coordinator, 1965-72, dir. services to family and children, 1972—; exec. dir. Mental Health Assn. for Greater Baton Rouge, 1972—. Cons. Gov.'s Com. on Status of Women. Adv. bd. Salvation Army. Vice chmn. La. com. White House conf. Children and Youth, 1968. Recipient Charles E. Dunbar, Jr. Career Service award, 1961. Mem. Nat. Assn. Social Workers, Am. Pub. Welfare Assn. (nat. v.p., membership com. 1958, chmn. planning com. S.W. region 1960, mem bd.), La. Conf. Social Welfare (pres. region VII, 1962-63), La. State U., La. State U. Sch. Social Welfare (v.p. 1962-63) alumni assns., Alpha Delta Pi Mothers. Baptist. Clubs: Denham Springs County; Soroptimist (pres. 1963-64) (Baton Rouge). Home: Route 6 Box 238 Denham Springs LA 70726 Office: PO Box 64585 Baton Rouge LA 70806

PITRONE, JEAN MADDERN (MRS. ANTHONY PITRONE), author; b. Ishpeming, Mich., Dec. 20, 1920; d. William Courtney and Gladys Mae (Beer) Maddern; ed. Ishpeming pub. schs.; m. Anthony Pitrone, Oct. 26, 1940; children—Joseph, Jill (Mrs. William Zick), Anthony Peter, Joyce (Mrs. Patrick Hawkins), John, Janet, Julie, Jane, Cheryl. Freelance writer short fiction and articles pub. in various mags. and newspapers, including Chgo. Tribune, Redbook, Catholic Digest, Detroit News, 1950—; asso. editor Writers Digest mag., 1969—. Mem. Women's Nat. Book Assn. Detroit Women Writers, Theta Sigma Phi. Democrat. Roman Catholic. Author: Trailblazer: Negro Nurse in American Red Cross (1st place award Friends of Am. Writers 1970), 1969; The Touch of His Hand, 1970; Chavez: Man of the Migrants, 1971. Address: 8244 Riverview Dearborn Heights MI 48127

PITTMAN, BERTIE, microbiologist; b. Quincy, Fla., Aug. 28, 1932; d. William Bertis and Kathryn (Grubb) Pittman; B.S., Fla. State U., 1954, M.S., 1957. Med. bacteriologist VA Hosp., Birmingham, Ala., 1957-58; research microbiologist Nat. Center for Disease Control, Atlanta, 1958—. Mem. Am. Soc. Microbiology (sec., treas. Southeastern br. 1966-67), Research Soc. Am. Episcopalian. Contbr. numerous articles to profl. jours., papers to profl. symposia. Research methodology leading to devel. more rapid, accurate diagnosis bacterial infections; establishment techniques and procedures for use in quality control testing of fluorescent antibody reagents. Home: 4041 Flintridge Dr Stone Mountain GA 30083 Office: 1600 Clifton Rd Atlanta GA 30333

PITTMAN, ELIZABETH DAVIS, judge; b. Council Bluffs, Ia., June 3, 1921; d. Charles F. and Mabel (Adams) Davis; student U. Neb., 1938-40; B.S., Creighton U., 1944, LL.B., 1947; LL.D., Creighton U., 1973; m. Arthur Basil Pittman, Dec. 25, 1942 (div. 1957); 1 dau., Antoinette Marguerite. Admitted to Neb. bar, 1948; mem. firm Davis & Pittman, Omaha, 1948—; now judge. Aux. faculty John F. Kennedy Coll. Mem. Omaha Bd. Edn., 1951. Mem. Soc. Liberal Arts Joslyn Mus., Omaha; mem. Ia.-Neb. Fedn. Settlement; formerly pres. Nat. Fedn. Settlements; mem. Omaha Urban League Guild, Omaha YWCA, Woodson Center Settlement House, Omaha; bd. dirs. Nat. Assembly on Social Policy and Devel., Nat. Conf. Social Work. Recipient award of merit Omaha Urban League, 1948; United Community Services Career award, 1963; citizenship award B'nai B'rith, 1965; award of merit Women Lawyers of Neb., 1971; Myrtle Wreath award Omaha chpt. Hadassah; named Woman of Year, Omaha Bus. and Profl. Women, 1971. Mem. N.A.m. Trial Judges Assn., Am. Judicature Soc., Am., Neb., Omaha bar assns., N.A.A.C.P. (dir. Omaha), Omaha Urban League (dir.), Omaha Women Lawyers Guild (pres. 1953), Links, Inc. (chpt. pres.), Gamma Pi Epsilon, Alpha Kappa Alpha (basilous Omaha 1949), Phi Delta Gamma (hon.). Democrat. Episcopalian (del. gen. conv. 1949). Elk. Home: 976 N 25th St Omaha NE 68131 Office: Interim City Hall Omaha NE 68102

PITTMAN, MARIE ESTELLA MCGHEE (MRS. LOUIE CLARK PITTMAN), univ. librarian; b. Mt. Olive, Miss., Apr. 17, 1923; d. Neal and Maggie (Minor) McGhee; B.S., N.C. Central U., 1952; M.S. in L.S. (univ. scholar), Atlanta U., 1959; postgrad. N.C. Agrl. and Tech. U., 1967—; m. Louie Clark Pittman, Mar. 10, 1940 (dec. May 1963); children—Louie Clark, Joyce Lavonne. Library asst. N.C. Central U., Durham, 1952-57, asst. catalog librarian, 1958-59, music librarian, 1959-64; asst. prof., head catalog librarian, N.C. Agrl. and Tech. State U., Greensboro, 1964-69, asst. prof. library edn., 1969-72, head circulation librarian, 1972—. Chmn., Guilford County (N.C.) Com. Black and African Arts and Culture, 1972—. Mem. Am., N.C. library assns., Guilford Library Club, Am. Assn. Univ. Profs., Am. Assn. Univ. Women, Delta Sigma Theta (May Week 1972, rec. sec. 1959-64, 70-72). Democrat. Methodist. Home: 415 B Lindsay St Greensboro NC 27401

PITTS, ELAINE RUTH HALLEAD (MRS. PAUL ELBERT PITTS), co. exec.; b. Chgo., June 20, 1917; d. Harry Albert and Ethel Mae (Waring) Hallead; student Ill. Inst. Tech., 1948-49, Art Inst. Chgo., 1947-48; m. Paul Elbert Pitts., Aug. 25, 1945. Packaging engr. Aldens, Inc., Chgo., 1943-46; sr. packaging engr. Spiegel, Inc., Chgo., 1946-52; mgr. package engrng. Sperry & Hutchinson Co., Chgo., 1953-59, mgr. consumer relations, N.Y.C., 1959-70, dir. consumer affairs, N.Y.C., 1970, v.p. corporate relations, 1970—. Lectr., Mass. Inst. Tech., U. Wis., Purdue U., U. Cal. at Los Angeles, Ill. Inst. Tech., U. Ill. Nat. adv. bd. Distributive Edn. Clubs Am., 1962—, vice chmn., 1964, chmn., 1965. Mem. Secs. Guild Chgo. Boys Clubs (pres. 1963), Bus. and Profl. Women's Club, Soc. Packaging and Handling Engrs. (chpt. pres. 1957, nat. chmn. bd. 1966-67), Office Edn. Assn. (dir.), Soc. Women Engrs. (exec. com. 1968-69), Am. Women Radio and TV (v.p. 1969-70, pres. 1973-74), Pub. Relations Soc. Am., U.S. C. of C. Consumer affairs com.). Home: 77 E 12th St New York City NY 10003 Office: 330 Maddison Av New York City NY 10017

PIXLEY, EMILY CHANDLER (MRS. HENRY H. PIXLEY), educator; b. Knoxville, Tenn., Aug. 19, 1904; d. David Sanders and Mayme (McCoy) Chandler; B.A., Randolph-Macon Woman's Coll., 1926; M.S., U. Chgo., 1927, Ph.D., 1931; m. Henry H. Pixley, Sept. 8, 1931; children—Dorothy Anne (Mrs. Joel A. Rothschild), David Chandler, Richard Henry. Instr. St. Xavier Coll., Chgo., 1927-30, prof., chmn. math. dept., 1930-36; instr. Wayne State U., Detroit, part-time, 1936-42, full time 1942-45, asst. prof., 1945-48; asst. prof. U. Detroit, 1948-50, asso. prof., 1950-55, prof., 1955-73, prof. emeritus, 1973—, acting chmn. dept. math., summers 1963-69, 68-69. Mem. Am. Math. Soc., Math. Assn. Am., Phi Beta Kappa, Sigma Xi. Home: 20194 Briarcliff St Detroit MI 48221

PLACE, ANGELA MOORE (MRS. HERMANN G. PLACE), civic worker; b. Flushing, N.Y., Oct. 19, 1897; d. John Bassett and Helen (Toland) Moore; B.A., Bryn Mawr Coll., 1919; m. Hermann G. Place, June 11, 1921; children—Angela (Mrs. Cochran B. Supplee), John Bassett Moore, Hermann Curtis. Vice chmn. adv. council U.S. Nat. Arboretum, 1949-70; bd. mgrs., v.p. N.Y. Bot. Garden, 1958-69; vice chmn. Nat. Trust for Historic Preservation, 1958—. Mem. Hort. Soc. N.Y., Inc. (dir., sec.), Garden Club Am. (pres. 1947-50), Colonial Dames Am., Nat. Soc. Colonial Dames, Daus. of Cin., Order Colonial Lords of Manor. Club: Colony. Home: Millbrook NY 12545 also 45 E 62d St New York City NY 10021

PLACE, DIANE MCLANE (MRS. TYRUS WILSON PLACE), govt. ofcl.; b. Detroit; d. Arthur Miller and Harriet (Evans) McLane; B.A., Wayne State U., 1961, student Consumer Edn., 1971; m. Tyrus Wilson Place, Mar. 4, 1939; 1 son, Tyrus Wilson. Consumer communicator Market Opinion Research Corp., 1950-55; coordinator Coop. Consumer Panel Study, Wayne State U.-Mich. State U., 1955-61; news editor Shamie Publs., Mich., 1960-62; home econs. specialist Mich. State U. Extension. Wayne County, 1963; consumer cons. FDA, U.S. Dept. Health, Edn. and Welfare, 1964—. Attended Presdl. Office Consumer Affairs Conf. for Gt. Lakes Region, 1964. Pres., Detroit Bd. Health, 1963, 67, 71; mem. Wayne County Bd. Suprs., 1963, 67; mem. City-County Mental Health Com., 1963-64; mem. Art Founder's Soc., 1957—. Precinct del. Mich., Wayne County Republican convs., 1947-48; dir. West Bloomfield Twp. Rep. Com., 1952-55. Recipient citation U.S. Dept. Health, Edn., Welfare, 1969, citation Detroit C. of C., 1971, citation for nomination to Fed. Women's award U.S. Food and Drug Adminstrn. Commn., Headliner award Women of Wayne State U., 1972. Mem. Am., Mich. home econs. assns., Consumer Alliance of Mich., Women in Communications, Am., Mich. pub. health assns., Assn. Food and Drug Ofcls. U.S. Clubs: Detroit Press, Women's City (chmn. membership com.) (Detroit). Contbr. articles, pamphlets to profl. jours., govt. publs. Home: 1322 Nicolet Pl Detroit MI 48207 Office: 1560 E Jefferson St Detroit MI 48207

PLACE, IRENE (MRS. DAROLD PLACE), educator, author; b. Omaha, Jan. 27, 1912; d. Paul and Magdeline (Krance) Glazik; B.A., U. Neb., 1932; M.A., Columbia, 1933; Ed.D., N.Y. U., 1947; m. Darold Place, Aug. 11, 1940. Instr. Briarcliff Jr. Coll., Briarcliff Manor, N.Y., 1933-36, Marshall Coll., Huntington, W.Va., 1936-37; asst. prof., bus. tchr. tng. dept. head U. Toledo, 1937-43; asso. prof. Grad. Sch. Bus. Adminstrn. U. Mich., 1943-66; prof. Sch. Bus., Portland State U., 1966—. Bd. dirs. Portland YWCA. Recipient Distinguished Service award System and Procedures Assn., 1968. Mem. Nat. Secs. Assn. (hon.), Nat. Bus. Edn. Assn., Western Bus. Edn. Assn., Ore. Bus. Edn. Assn., Am. Vocational Assn., Zonta Internat. (past pres. Portland), Kappa Delta, Phi Chi Theta, Alpha Sigma Alpha, Delta Pi Epsilon, Pi Lambda Theta. Clubs: Portland City, Portland Presidents. Author: Careers in Management; Filing and Records Management, 1966; Office Management, 1971; Collegiate Secretarial Procedures, 1972; Filing Fundamentals, 1973. Contbr. articles to profl. jours., yearbooks. Home: 13550 SW Berthold St Beaverton OR 97005

PLACEK, KAROLINA BEIN, physician; b. Warsaw, Poland; d. Jan Feliks and Helena (Dobrejcer) Bakowski; M.D., Acad. of Medicine (Warsaw) 1950. Came to U.S., 1950, naturalized, 1954. Dir. Well Baby Clinic, Casablanca, Morocco, 1950-52; intern Hosp. for Joint Diseases, N.Y.C., 1952-54; resident, fellow in psychiatry N.Y. U., Bellevue Psychiat. Hosp., 1954-58; staff psychiatrist Union County Psychiat. Clinic, Elizabeth, N.J., 1958-59; practice psychoanalytic psychotherapy for adults, children and adolescents, Newark, 1957—; mem. staff Clara Maas Hosp.; candidate Columbia Psychoanalytic Inst. and panel psychiatrist Child Care Assn., N.Y.C., 1959-62; med. dir. N. Essex Child Guidance Clinic, Belleville, N.J., 1962-66, Jewish Counseling and Service Agy. Newark, 1966—; tchr. psychiatry N.J. Med. Sch., Columbia Psychiat. Inst. Cons. N.J. Sch. System. Diplomate psychiatry Am. Bd. Psychiatry and Neurology. Mem. A.M.A., Am. Psychiat. Assn., Assn. for Advancement Psychiatry, N.J. Med. Assn., N.J. Neuropsychiat. Assn. Contbr. articles to profl. jours. Home: 312 Harding Dr South Orange NJ 07079

PLACHY, JUNE WILDER (MRS. FREDRIC RICH PLACHY), educator; b. LaGrange, Ga., Apr. 13, 1929; d. Ernest Lee and Seba Merle (Summerlin) Underwood; B.A., LaGrange Coll., 1951; M.Ed., U. N.C., 1960; Ed.D., Okla. State U., 1969; m. Fredric Rich Plachy, Mar. 22, 1968. Grad. asst., instr. math. Okla. State U., Stillwater, 1963-69; tchr. math. Brown High Sch., Atlanta Bd. Edn., 1957-63, Bibb County Bd. Edn., Ga., 1955-57; prof. math. Agnes Scott Coll., Decatur, Ga., 1969-72; prof. DeKalb Coll., Decatur, Ga., 1972—, dean evening sch., 1974—. Mem. Am. Math. Soc., Math. Assn. Am., Nat. Council Tchrs. Math., Ga. Council Tchrs. Math., Metro-Atlanta Math. Club. Club: Tara Golf and Country (Jonesboro, Ga.). Home: 3654 Idle Creek Dr Decatur GA 30034 Office: DeKalb Coll Decatur GA 30034

PLAGA, EMMA GEORGE WOOD (MRS. RUDIA PLAGA), educator; b. Pitts., July 13, 1930; d. Benjamin Franklin and Rose (Ware) Wood; B.S., Columbia, 1966, M.A., 1967, profl. diploma in social scis., 1968; m. Jonathan Andrews, May 1957 (dec. Oct. 1956); 1 son, Gregory L.; m. 2d, Rudia Plaga, Nov. 21, 1958; 1 son, Rudia Clayton. Tchr. fundamentals of nursing Providence Hosp., Balt., 1956-58; supr. psychiat. nursing Northport (L.I., N.Y.) VA Hosp., 1958-59; pvt. duty nurse Cancer Meml. Hosp., N.Y.C., 1959-60; staff nurse N.Y. Hosp.-Cornell Med. Center, 1961-62, asst. head nurse, 1962-64, head nurse, 1964-65; edn. coordinator Massive Econ. Neighborhood Devel., Inc., N.Y.C., 1966-67; interviewer Bur. Applied Social Research, Columbia, 1967-68; dir. youth narcotic center Harlem Teams for Self-Help, 1968; lectr., cons. City Coll., City U. N.Y., 1970; coordinator mental retardation program Flower Fifth Av Hosp., N.Y.C., 1969-72; asst. prof. dept. community devel. Livingston Coll., Rutgers U., New Brunswick, N.J., 1972—. Fellow Am. Inst. for Group Counselling; mem. Am. Soc. for Tng. and Devel., Internat. Soc. for Community Devel., Am. Assn. Mental Deficiency, Am. Assn. for Nat. Edn. Assn., Acad. Arts and Sci., Common Cause, N.A.A.C.P., Urban League, Alpha Psi Omega, Alpha Tau Delta. Home: 70 W 95th St New York City NY 10025 Office: Dept Community Devel Livingston Coll Rutgers U New Brunswick NJ 08903

PLAIN, ELEANOR, librarian; b. Aurora, Ill.; d. Frank G. and Jennie (Guinang) Plain; A.B., U. Mich., 1925, A.B. in Library Sci., 1936; M.A., U. Chgo., 1950. Gen. asst. Aurora Pub. Library, 1931-34, asst. reference librarian, 1934-36, head cataloger, 1937-39, head librarian, 1939—; asst. cataloger, instr. library sci. Ind. State Tchrs. Coll. at Terre Haute, 1936-37. Mem. adv. council librarians U. Ill. Grad. Sch. Library Sci. at Urbana, 1964-67. Vice pres. Fox Valley Animal Welfare League, 1972—. Mem. Am. (exec. sec. pub. libraries div. 1948-51; chmn. pub. libraries div. archives com. 1951-52, jury on citation trustees 1953-56, chmn. subcom. classification and pay plans 1954-57, chmn. council nomination com. 1956-57, subcom. standards small libraries 1960-62, mem. standards com. 1963-69, chmn., 1967-68; dir. 1965-69, mem. council 1954-58, 65-69), Ill. (legislative chmn. 1947; v.p. 1947-48, pres. 1948-49; citation 1963), Pub. (chmn. subcom. on costs pub. library service 1968-69) library assns., Am. Assn. U. Women, Ill., Aurora (treas. 1943-56, v.p., dir. 1956—) hist. socs., D.A.R., League Women Voters, Beta Phi Mu, Chi Omega. Home: 305 W Downer Pl Aurora IL 60506 Office: Aurora Pub Library 1 Benton St Aurora IL 60504

PLAISTED, GLENNA WADE, ednl. adminstr.; b. Belfast, Me., Feb. 1, 1938; d. Donald H. and Ora D. (Wade) Plaisted; B.A., Boston U., 1958. Tchr., English, Kent Hill Prep. Sch., Me., 1958-59, North Phoenix High Sch., 1959-60, Monroe (Conn.) High Sch., 1960-63, Plymouth (Mass.)-Carver High Sch., 1963-67; chmn. new English curriculum Telstar High Sch., Bethel, Me., 1967; founded Pinehenge Sch., Waterford, Me., 1968, dir., 1968-72, also pres. bd. dirs.; founder, dir. Riley Country Day Sch., Glen Cove, Me., 1972—. Cons. English various schs. Mem. Community Concert Assn., 1953-69, Bd. Plymouth Library Assn., 1965-67, Ford Forum, 1964—, New Eng. Anti-Vivisection Soc., 1963—. Mem. Nat., Me. (speaker conv. 1970), Plymouth (sec. 1965-67, scholarship com. 1965-67) tchrs. assns., New Eng. Tennis Assn., Nat. Council English Tchrs., Beta Sigma Phi. Republican. Home: Box 51 Glen Cove ME 04846

PLAMONDON, SISTER MARIE ANNE, dietitian; b. Plamondon, Alta., Can., Jan. 2, 1918; d. John Baptiste and Marie Elizabeth (Duperron) Plamondon; dietary technician course No. Alta. Inst. Tech., 1966-67. Head dietary dept. Lac La Biche (Alta.) Gen. Hosp., 1958-68, 70-73. Mem. Catholic Women League. Home: PO Box 100 Lac La Biche AB T0A 2C0 Canada Office: Lac La Biche Gen Hosp Lac La Biche AB T0A 2C0 Canada

PLANK, ADALINE JANE, occupational therapist; b. Pitts., Jan. 25, 1914; d. William Bertolet and Helen Josephine (Beck) Plank; A.B., Wellesley Coll., 1936; certificate Phila. Sch. Occupational Therapy, 1938; postgrad. N.Y. U., 1960, Northwestern U., 1961, U. Cal. at Los Angeles, 1962. Staff therapist Harrisburg (Pa.) State Hosp., 1938-41, Presbyn. Hosp., N.Y.C., 1941-49; supr. occupational therapy Mt. Sinai Hosp., N.Y.C., 1949-50; dir. occupational therapy Inst. Logopedics, Wichita, Kan., 1950-60; head gen. occupational therapy State Hosp. for Crippled Children, Elizabethtown, Pa., 1960—. Asst. in children's prosthetics research N.Y. U., 1960—. Mem. Am., Eastern Pa. occupational therapy assns., Morgantown-Caernarvon Hist. Soc. Episcopalian (asst. treas. 1971—). Club: Wellesley (Reading, Pa.). Aphasia editor Am. Jour. Occupational Therapy, 1953-60. Home: Morgantown PA 19543 Office: State Hosp for Crippled Children Elizabethtown PA 17022

PLANK, DARLENE HELEN, occupational therapist; b. Milw., Aug. 28, 1946; d. LeRoy Edward and Ruth Helen (Colley) Plank; B.S. in Occupational Therapy, Colo. State U., 1968. Sr. occupational therapist, activity therapist Ft. Logan Mental Health Center, Denver, 1969—. Owner, operator Darcy's Ltd., Denver, 1973—. Mem. Am. Occupational Therapy Assn., Inst. Personal Relations, Gamma Phi Beta. Home: 3035 S Eaton St Denver CO 80227 Office: 3520 W Oxford St Denver CO 80236

PLANK, EMMA NUSCHI SPIRA (MRS. ROBERT PLANK), ednl. cons.; b. Vienna, Austria, Nov. 11, 1905; d. Emil and Doris (Langbein) Spira; came to U.S., 1938, naturalized, 1944; M.A., Mills Coll., 1947; m. Robert Plank, Sept. 17, 1932. Tchr., Montessori Elementary Sch., Vienna, 1923-30, dir., 1930-38; tchr. Presidio Hill Sch., San Francisco, 1939-43, dir., 1943-46; dir. spl. project Am. Friends Service Com., Vienna, 1948-50; faculty Case Western Res. U. Sch. Medicine, Cleve., 1951-73, asso. prof., 1963-73, prof. emeritus, 1973—. Dir. child life and edn. program Cleve. Met. Gen. Hosp., 1955-72, cons., 1972—; cons. to various ednl. agys. Recipient Grace Owen award Mills Coll., 1947; Medal of City of Vienna, 1949; Montessori Centennial medal, 1970. Fellow Am. Orthopsychiat. Assn.; mem. Nat. Assn. for Edn. Young Children (chmn. health commn. 1969-71), Midwestern Assn. for Nursery Edn. (pres. 1961-62), No. Ohio Pediatric Soc., Assn. for Care of Children in Hosps. (pres. 1969-70), Am. Assn. Child Psychoanalysis. Author: Working with Children in Hospitals, 1971. Contbr. articles to profl. publs. Home: 2387 Overlook Rd Cleveland OH 44106 Office: Cleve Met Gen Hosp 3395 Scranton Rd Cleveland OH 44109

PLANTAMURA, SISTER FRANCES MICHAEL, hosp. adminstr.; b. Lawrence, Mass., Jan. 31, 1920; d. Michael and Mary Frances (Bianchi) Plantamura; R.N., St. John's Hosp. Sch. Nursing, 1940; B.S. in Nursing Edn., Cath. U. Am., 1942; M.A. in Edn., N.Y. U., 1945. Adminstr., Sacred Heart Hosp., Pensacola, Fla., 1959-65; dir. Catherine Laboure Sch. Nursing, Boston, 1965-67; adminstr. Providence Hosp., Washington, 1967-69; adminstr., pres. bd. trustees

Carney Hosp., Boston, 1969—. Mem. adv. com. on nursing edn. Commonwealth of Mass. Bd. Higher Edn., 1969—; mem. provider appeals com. Blue Cross Assn., 1970-72. Fellow Am. Coll. Hosp. Adminstrs.; mem. Am., Mass. (dir.), New Eng., Greater Boston (dir.), Cath. (chmn. council on assn. relations and devel. 1971-74, dir. New Eng. council) hosp. assns., Nat. League Nursing, Am. Nurses Assn. Address; Carney Hosp 2100 Dorchester Av Boston MA 02124

PLANTE, INGE KATHARINE RUDLOFF (MRS. MARC ALBERIC PLANTE), physician; b. Leipzig, Germany, Sept. 20, 1929; d. Erich A. and Hildegard (von Kienitz) Rudloff; grad. U. Wuerzburg, German, 1949; fellow Ursinus Coll., 1951-52; D. Medicine and Surgery U. Munich, 1955-3m. Marc Alberic Plante, December 28, 1957 (dec. Feb. 1967); children—Sabrina, Michele Andree, Marc Rudloff. Came to U.S., 1955, naturalized, 1960. Resident psychiatry N.J. Psychiat. Hosp., Trenton, 1956-58, asst. med. dir., 1970-73, med. dir., chief exec. officer Trenton Psychiat. Hosp., 1973—. Mem. A.M.A., Am. Psychiat. Assn. Contbr. articles on med. research to tech. jours. Address: Sta A Trenton NJ 08625

PLATT, DORIS HUBBARD, educator; b. Elgin, Ill., Aug. 14, 1914; d. Frank James and Georgia (Hubbard) Platt; B.A., Beloit Coll., 1935; M.A., U. Wis., 1945, Ph.D., 1947. Ad writer Chgo. Daily News, 1935-37; tchr. French, English, Mooseheart (Ill.) High Sch., 1937-41; tchr. Freeport High Sch., 1941-44; instr. English dept. U. Wis., 1947-48; research asso. State Hist. Soc. of Wis., 1948-55, editor Badger History mag., 1955-62, dir. sch. services, radio and TV coordinator, 1961-65, supr. mus. edn., 1965—. Cons. WHA and WHA-TV, U. Wis. sta. on Sch. of Air programs; own radio program Wis. Then and Now, 1959-61, Wis. Writers, 1961-64, History Highlights, 1964-65; tv programs Pioneer Wis., 1958-60, Born on the Prairies, 1961-63, Wisconsin Windows, 1963-65; cons. TV programs Wisconsin Outdoors, When Our State Was Young, radio program The Way It Was; mem. edn. com. Madison Citizens Cable Council. White House Conf. planner Gov.'s Advocacy Com. on Children and Youth. Mem. Wis. Council for Social Studies (exec. council), Nat. Assn. Ednl. Broadcasters, State Hist. Soc. Wis., Am. Hist. Assn., Wis. Council for Better Broadcasts, Orgn. Am. Historians, Wis. Acad. Scis., Arts and Letters, Am. Assn. for State and Local History (exec. council 1973—), Nat., Madison (v.p.) Audubon socs., Phi Delta Gamma (pres. 1956), Phi Lambda Theta (pres. 1954), Phi Sigma Iota, Ka Ne, Phi Beta Kappa. Democrat. Conglist. (deacon). Author: Wisconsin Reader, 1960; Wisconsin, a Student's Guide to Localized History, 1965; History for Young People, 1966. Editor: Youthful Outlook column in History News. Home: 4723 Sheboygan Av No 204 Madison WI 53705 Office: 816 State St Madison WI 53706

PLATT, DOROTHY MANSFIELD (MRS. JOHN W. PLATT), sch. psychologist; b. West Haven, Conn., Apr. 10, 1920; d. Raymond E. and Mary (Tierney) Mansfield; B.S., New Haven State Tchrs. Coll., 1941, M.A., 1957; postgrad. So. Conn. State Coll.; m. Harold E. Morgen, July 17, 1943 (dec. Nov. 1957); children—Christopher Pedersen, Jennifer Pedersen; m. 2d, John W. Platt, Sept. 21, 1968 (dec. 1974). Tchr., Bd. Edn., Guilford, Conn., 1941-46, Orange, Conn., 1946-47, Milford, Conn., 1952-53, West Haven, 1953-62; psychol. examiner Bd. Edn. West Haven, 1962-71, dir. pre-sch. program, 1966—, asst. supr. spl. edn., 1971-72; acting dir. Reading and Communication Skills Center, West Haven, 1972—. Bd. dirs. Clinton (Conn.) Improvement Assn., 1971—; bd. dirs., pres. Provisional League Women Voters, 1973—. Mem. N.E.A., Conn. Edn. Assn., Conn. So. Conn. State Coll. Alumni Assn. Contbr. to profl. publs. Home: 25 Kelseytown Rd Clinton CT 06413 Office: Blake Adminstrn Bldg 25 Ogden St West Haven CT 06516

PLATT, ETHEL FRIEDMAN (MRS. DAVID PLATT), physician; b. Phila., Dec. 27, 1916; d. Alexander and Rebecca (Kramer) Friedman; B.S., U. Pa., 1937; M.D., Woman's Med. Coll. Pa., 1941; m. David Platt, June 16, 1940; 1 son, Richard. Intern, Frankford Hosp., Phila., 1941-42; practice medicine specializing in family medicine and obstetrics, Wilmington, Del., 1942—; mem. sr. attending staff Wilmington Med. Center. Diplomate Am. Bd. Family Practice. Mem. A.M.A., Med. Soc. Del., New Castle County Med. Soc., Am., Del. acads. family physicians, Del. Acad. Medicine, B'nai B'rith Women, Hadassah. Home: 5 Mahaffy Dr Wilmington DE 19809 Office: 1100 S Broom St Wilmington DE 19805

PLATT, LOIS IRENE, physician; b. Oil City, Pa., May 23, 1908; d. Hugh Ashley and Myrtle (Dolby) Platt; A.B., Goucher Coll., 1931; M.D., U. Md., 1946. Tchr. pub. schs., Baltimore County, Md., 1931-42; intern, resident Garfield Meml. Hosp., 1946-47; cancer trainee Nat. Cancer Inst., NIH, 1947-49; practice medicine specializing in pathology, Washington, 1949—; clin. instr. pathology George Washington U., 1949-54, asst. prof., 1954-66, asso. prof., 1966-73, emeritus, 1973—; prof. biology Gallaudet Coll., 1966—; cytologist Cancer Clinic, 1949—; cons. VA; dir. Sch. Cytotech. dept. pathology George Washington U. Hosp., 1963—; dir. Employment and Counselling Service of No. Va., 1959-64. Trustee D.C. div. Am. Cancer Soc., recipient Appreciation award, recipient St. George medal, 1972. Mem. A.M.A., Am. Med. Women's Assn., Am. Soc. Cytology, A.A.A.S., N.Y. Acad. Sci., Smithsonian Instn. Assos. Episcopalian. Club: Soroptimist of Arlington (Va.). Contbr. articles to profl. pubs. Home: 3500 Perry St Fairfax VA 22030

PLATZ, ELIZABETH ALVINA, clergywoman; b. Pitts., Aug. 29, 1940; d. Victor Byron and Merna Beatrice (Webb) Platz; B.A., Chatham Coll., Pitts., 1962; B.D., Lutheran Theol. Sem., Gettysburg, Pa., 1965. Lay asso. Luth. Campus Ministry, U. Md., 1965-70; ordained to ministry Luth. Ch., 1970; campus pastor Luth. Campus Ministry, U. Md., College Park, 1970—. Home: 4313 Knox Rd College Park MD 20740 Office: Memorial Chapel U Md College Park MD 20742

PLAUT, BERTA GERTRUD, librarian; b. Ludwigsburg, Germany, June 20, 1898; d. Jakob and Julie (Spiegelthal) Plaut; B.L.S., Columbia, 1943. Came to U.S., 1938, naturalized, 1944. Asst., Deutsches Ausland-Instut, Stuttgart, Germany, 1921-24; intern library sci. Columbia Libraries, 1942-43; research asso. Tice & Lnych, N.Y., 1944-45; cataloguer U.S. Nat. Library of Medicine, 1945-46; head librarian Temple Emanu-El, N.Y., 1946-49; cataloguer N.Y. Pub. Library, 1949-52, incunabula Bryn Mawr Coll. Library, 1952-53; cataloguer W.Va. U. Library, and Arthur S. Dayton Collection of Rare Books, 1953-63, sr. catalogue librarian. Mem. Am., W.Va., Spl. library assns., A.A.A.S., Bibliog. Soc. Am., Am. Assn. U. Women, Columbia Sch. Library Service Alumni Assn., Morgantown Art Assn., UN Assn. U.S.A., Bibliographical Soc. U. Va. Centro Studi e Scambi Internzionali: (Rome, Italy), Intercontinental Biog. Assn., Internat. Platform Assn., Smithsonian Assos., Nat. Hist. Soc., Am. Assn. Ret. Persons, Friends of Morgantown Pub. Library. Club: Women's Music. Address: 236 S High St Morgantown WV 26505

PLAUTH, BARBARA HARTLEY GREENE (MRS. WILLIAM HENRY PLAUTH, JR.), physician; b. Bklyn., Oct. 21, 1936; d. Carl Hartley and Anna Earl (Purdy) Greene; B.A., Vassar Coll., 1958; M.D., Johns Hopkins, 1962; m. William Henry Plauth, Jr., Aug. 5, 1961; children—Anna Earl, William Henry III. Intern, Johns Hopkins Hosp., Balt., 1962-63, resident, 1964; resident Beth Israel Hosp., Boston, 1964-65, fellow endocrinology, 1965-66; fellow endocrinology Childrens Hosp. Med. Center, Boston, 1967-69; clin. asst. U. Health Services Harvard, Cambridge, Mass., 1969-71; asst. prof. dept. medicine Emory U., Atlanta, 1971—. Mem. Jr. League Boston. Home: 1350 W Wesley Rd NW Atlanta GA 30327 Office: Grady Meml Hosp 80 Butler St SE Atlanta GA 30303

PLAYER, THELMA B., librarian; b. Owosso, Mich.; d. Walter B. and Grace (Willoughby) Player; B.A., Western Mich. U., 1954. Reference asst. USAF Aero. Chart & Information Center, Washington, 1954-57; reference librarian U.S. Navy Hydrographic Office, Suitland, Md., 1957-58; asst. librarian, 1958-59; tech. library br. head U.S. Navy Spl. Project Office, Washington, 1959-68, Strategic Systems Project Office, 1969—. Mem. Spl. Libraries Assn., Am. Soc. for Information Sci., D.C. Library Assn., Am. Assn. U. Women, English-Speaking Union, Washington Performing Arts Soc., Nat. Trust for Historic Preservation, Nat. Cathedral Assn., Smithsonian Assos., Asso. Nat. Archives. Episcopalian. Home: 2025 38th St SE Washington DC 20020 Office: Dept Navy Washington DC 20376

PLEASANT, MARILYN LEE LAWRENCE (MRS. LAWRENCE WAYNE PLEASANT), newspaper exec.; b. Neoga, Ill., Dec. 10, 1934; d. Raymond Francis and Sylvia Baker (Figenbaum) Lawrence; m. Lawrence Wayne Pleasant, June 10, 1955; children—Daniel Lee, Timothy Wayne, Andrew F. Owner (with husband), editor, pub. Dolores (Colo.) Star, 1960—; owner Dove Creek (Colo.) Press, 1961-73. Bd. dirs. Dolores Pub. Library. Home: 142 E Montezuma St Cortez CO 81321 Office: Box 644 Dolores CO 81323

PLEASANTS, BARBARA LANE, data processor; b. Atlantic City, Sept. 13, 1936; d. Henry Bridge and Geneva Elizabeth (Banks) Lane; B.S. with highest honors (scholar), Hampton Inst., 1959; postgrad. George Washington U., 1970; div.; children—Charles, Michael, Linda. Mathematician, U.S. Weather Bur., Washington, 1959-62; research asso. Tech. Operations, Inc., Ft. Monroe, Va., 1963-67; computer systems analyst Dept. Army, Ft. Monroe, Va., 1967—. Mem. Jack and Jill of Am. (local pres. 1973—), Zeta Phi Beta. Methodist. Home: 1173 Old Buckroe Rd Hampton VA 23663 Office: Hdqrs TRADOC Fort Monroe VA 23651

PLECHNER, SOPHIE LOUISE COPPERSMITH (MRS. WALTER W. PLECHNER), cosmetics co. exec.; b. Newark, Mar. 1, 1903; d. Frederick Martin and Theresa (Pinner) Coppersmith; B.S., Rutgers U., 1923; M.A., Columbia, 1927; Ph.D., 1929; m. Walter W. Plechner, Oct. 26, 1929; 1 son, Richard F. Tchr., East Rutherford (N.J.) High Sch., 1923-26; research chemist Bristol Myers, Hillside, N.J., 1929-31; cons. Consumers Research, N.Y.C., 1931-33; research chemist Carter-Wallace, Inc., Cranbury, N.J., 1943-68, mgr. tech. services, 1968—. Mem. tech. adv. com. for poison prevention packaging U.S. Consumer Product Safety Commn., 1974—. Recipient Alumnae Service award Douglass Coll., 1948, Distinguished Achievement award, 1973. Mem. Cosmetic, Toiletries and Fragrances Assn. (chmn. sci. sect. 1953), Soc. Cosmetic Chemists (medal award 1965, pres. 1961). Patentee in field. Home: 62 Oak Av Metuchen NJ 08840 Office: Half Acre Rd Cranbury NJ 08512

PLEDGER, JACQUELYN ERNALEE (MRS. ARTHUR P. SKWERSKI), pub. relations exec.; b. Chgo., Mar. 20, 1937; d. Jack Moss and Gladys (Ricks) Pledger; B.S., Purdue U., 1959; M.A., Ind. U., 1964; m. Arthur P. Skwerski, July 19, 1969; 1 son, Peter Kenneth. Substitute tchr. Bloomington (Ind.) Met. Sch. System, 1960-61; editor, author ednl. filmstrips Soc. for Visual Edn., Chgo., 1961; editor primary textbooks Benefic Press, Chgo., 1961-63; editor Gas News, Peoples Gas Light & Coke Co., Chgo., 1963-66, pub. relations specialist, 1966-70; pres. Jackie Pledger & Assos., Chgo., 1970— Active Girl Scouts U.S.A. Mem. Women in Communications (pres. Chgo. chpt. 1970-71). Baptist. Address: 3123 N Keating Av Chicago IL 60641

PLEIN, JOY BICKMORE, educator; b. Logan, Utah, Nov. 10, 1925; d. Harvard Tarry and Claire (Barber) Bickmore; B.S., Ida. State U., 1947; M.S., U. Wash., 1952, Ph.D., 1956; m. Elmer M. Plein, Aug. 30, 1952. Pharmacist, Heinz Apothecary, Salt Lake City, 1947-49; lectr. Seattle Pacific Coll., 1954-59, 61-65; writer, asst. editor Am. Hosp. Formulary Service, 1959-66; lectr. pharmacy U. Wash., Seattle, 1966-72, asso. prof., 1972-74, prof., 1974—. Mem. reference panel Am. Hosp. Formulary Service, 1969—; mem. panel on rev. dentifrices and dental care agts. FDA, 1973—. Mem. Am., Wash. (pres. 1965-66) socs. hosp. pharmacists, Am. Pharm. Assn., Drug Information Assn., Women's Research Group U. Wash., Sigma Xi, Rho Chi, Phi Sigma. Author: (with husband) Fundamentals of Medications, 1967, 2d edit., 1974. Contbr. articles to profl. jours. Home: 5122 NE 75th St Seattle WA 98115

PLETCHER, VERA EDITH CROSBY (MRS. BLAINE F. PLETCHER), educator; b. Plainview, Neb., Nov. 6, 1916; d. William Edward and Lula (Partridge) Crosby; student U. Kan., 1947-51; B.S. cum laude, Kan. State U., 1956, M.A. (Mueller scholar 1958-59), 1960; postgrad. Pa. State U., 1967; m. Blaine F. Pletcher, Sept. 9, 1936; children—Patricia Louise (Mrs. James E. Carlson), Janet Sue, Sharon Lee. Tchr. elementary schs., Kan., 1935-37, 44-54, secondary schs., Kan., 1956-57; mem. faculty Kan. State U., Manhattan, 1959-67, instr. history and social scis., 1962-67; instr. Manhattan Sr. High Sch., 1966-69, head social service dept., 1969-74, dir. advanced placement and ind. study, 1974—. Counselor, Wamego Rural High Sch., 1959-62; instr. U. Kan. Ind. Study Center, 1965-70; Mem. Riley County Bicentennial Com. Nat. Def. Edn. Act grantee, 1960, 67; Nat. Edn. grant, 1969. Named Woman of Year, Rho chpt. Phi Delta Gamma, 1967; recipient Meritorious Teaching award Nat. Council Geog. Edn., 1971. Mem. N.E.A., Kan. State Tchrs. Assn., Kan. Assn. Women Deans and Counselors (sec.-treas. 1962-64), Am. Personnel and Guidance Assn., Kan. State Alumni Assn., Kan. State Hist. Soc. (bd. dirs. 1972—), Am. Hist. Assn., Bus. and Profl. Women, Nat. Hist. Soc. (charter), Phi Kappa Phi, Phi Alpha Mu, Phi Alpha Theta, Delta Kappa Gamma, Phi Delta Gamma (chpt. pres. 1966, 72, nat. treas. 1966-68, nat. rep. 1968-70, nat. conv. chmn. 1972-74). Mem. Christian Ch. Mem. Order Eastern Star, Jobs Daus. (guardian 1971-74). Home: Route 5 Manhattan KS 66502

PLETSCH, MARIE ELEANOR (MRS. LUDWIG BREILING), plastic surgeon; b. Walkerton, Ont., Can., May 3, 1938; d. Ernest John and Olive Wilhemina (Hossfeld) Pletsch; M.D., U. Toronto, 1962; m. Ludwig Philip Breiling, Aug. 25, 1967; children—John Philip, Michael Robert. Intern Cook County Hosp., Chgo., 1962-63, resident in gen. surgery, 1963-64; resident in gen. surgery St. Mary's Hosp., San Francisco, 1964-66; resident in plastic surgery St. Francis Hosp., San Francisco, 1966-69; practice medicine specializing in plastic surgery, Santa Cruz, Cal., 1969—. Home: 100 Las Lomas St Aptos CA 95003 Office: 550 Water St Santa Cruz CA 95060

PLITT, JEANNE GIVEN, librarian; b. Whitehall, N.Y., Aug. 27, 1928; s. Charles Russell and Anna Marie (Noyes) Given; student St. Lawrence U., 1945-47; A.B., U. Md., 1940; postgrad. Am. U., 1960-61; M.S. in L.S., Cath. U. Am., 1968; m. Ferdinand Charles Plitt, Jr., Jan. 19, 1952; children—Christine, Marie, Charles Randolph. Library asst. Spl. Services div. U.S. Army, 1949-51; tchr. secondary schs., Md. and Va.; reference librarian Alexandria (Va.) Library, 1967-68, asst. dir., 1968-70, dir., 1970—. Chmn. librarians' tech. com. Council Govts., Washington, 1971-72. Active Little Theatre Group, Alexandria. Recipient Alexandria pub. service award, 1964, 74. Mem. Va. Library Assn., P.T.A., U. Md., Cath. U. alumni assns., Alexandria Assn., Urban League. Roman Catholic. Club: Zonta (sec. chpt. 1972-73, dir. 1973-74). Office: Alexandria Library 717 Queen St Alexandria VA 22314

PLOCHMANN, CAROLYN GASSAN (MRS. GEORGE KIMBALL PLOCHMANN), painter; b. Toledo, May 4, 1926; d. Edward Paul and Elizabeth Mildred (Hale) Gassan; B.A. cum laude, Toledo Mus. Art, Sch. Design and U. Toledo, 1947; M.F.A. (George W. Stevens fellow), State U. Ia., 1949; m. George Kimball Plochmann, Jan. 28, 1950; 1 dau., Sarah Kimball. Supr. art Allyn Tng. Sch., So. Ill. U. at Carbondale, 1949-50; exhibited in one man shows So. Ill. U. at Carbondale, 1952, Toledo Mus. Art, 1955, 65, Bergstrom Mus., Neenah-Menasha, Wis., 1959, Evansville Mus. Arts and Sci., Ind., 1962, Vanderbilt U., Nashville, 1963, St. Louis Gallery, 1966, Gallery in the Square, Neiman-Marcus, Ft. Worth, 1966, 68, Witte Mus., San Antonio, 1968; exhibited in group shows Escuola Nacional de Artes Plasticas, Mexico City, 1963, Carnegie Inst., Pitts, 1943, City Art Mus. St. Louis, 1953, 54, 57, Cin. Art Mus., 1958, Dayton (O.) Art Inst., 1958, Nat. Council Chs., 1960, Am. Soc. Ch. Architecture, 1964, Finkel Gallery, 1965, Brooks Meml. Art Gallery, 1969, State U. Ia., 1956, Weyhe Gallery, N.Y.C., 1968, Pa. Acad. Fine Arts, 1969, Ill. State Mus., Springfield, 1973; represented in permanent collections So. Ill. U., Carbondale, Toledo Fedn. Art Soc., Seldon Rodman Collection, Oakland, N.J., Tupperware Art Mus, Orlando, Fla., Butler Inst. Am. Art, Youngstown, O., Ted Leyhe Collection, Oshkosh, Wis. Recipient numerous awards and prizes in art competition. Mem. Silvermine Guild Artists, Woodstock Art Assn., Phila. Water Color Club, Toledo Fedn. Art Socs. Contbr. articles and illustrations to profl. jours. Home: Route 1 Carbondale IL 62901 Office: Kennedy Galleries 20 E 56th St New York City NY 10022

PLOCKELMAN, CYNTHIA HOLLEY, librarian; b. West Palm Beach, Fla., June 22, 1938; d. Raymond Henry and Grace (Holley) Plockelman; B.A., Fla. State U., 1960; M.A., Emory U., 1961. Spl. librarian Central and So. Fla. Flood Control Dist. Library, West Palm Beach, Fla., 1963—. Vol. chmn. library Jr. League Palm Beaches, 1967-70, chmn. hist. tapes project, 1972-73; mem. Civic Music Assn., 1968—. Bd. dirs. Nelle Smith Residence for Girls, 1971-73. Mem. Spl. Libraries Assn. (pres. Fla. 1974—, Fla. employment chmn. 1970), Fla. Library Assn., Am. Assn. U. Women (br. treas. 1963-65), Am. Malacological Union, Cal. Malacozool. Soc., Internat. Graphic Arts Soc., Everglades Audubon Soc. (Nature Trail project), Episcopalian. Republican. Club: Palm Beach County Shell (editor Seafari 1965-72, exec. council 1963-64, 65-73). Home: 311 Franklin Rd West Palm Beach FL 33405 Office: PO Box V West Palm Beach FL 33402

PLOG, ROSE MARIE (MRS. GERALD SCHNEIDER PLOG), civic worker; b. Gate City, Va., June 25, 1918; d. William T. and Lucinda (Jones) Bellamy; student Sch. Nursing, U. Tenn., 1938-41; m. Gerald Schneider Plog, Oct. 31, 1941 (dec. Apr. 1967); children—Michael Bellamy, Martha Ann. Leader, Girl Scouts U.S.A., Martin, Tenn., 1956-61; cub scout leader Boy Scouts Am., Martin, 1953-56; pres. Martin P.T.A., 1960—. Dir. First Fed. Savings and Loan, Martin. Mem. Am. Legion Aux., Zeta Tau Alpha (adviser Delta Mu chpt.). Methodist. Mem. Order Eastern Star (del. to grand chpt. 1959—, past matron). Home: 337 S McComb St Martin TN 38237

PLONA, SISTER MARY LAETITIA, nurse administr., educator; b. Gardner, Mass., Dec. 31, 1906; d. Alexander and Alexandra (Wiski) Plona; B.S. in Nursing Edn., Catholic U. Am., 1946; M.S., Boston Coll., 1963. Dir. nursing service St. Joseph Hosp., Bangor, Me., 1947-54; dir. sch. practical nursing Okla.-Blackwell Gen. Hosp., 1954-55; infirmarian Our Lady of Angels Infirmary, Enfield, Conn., 1955-57; dir. nursing service St. Joseph Hosp., Bangor, 1957-66, adminstr., 1958-60, 62-64, dir. Sch. Practical Nursing, 1963-72, coordinator program in diploma nursing, 1973—, trustee. Mem. Am., Me. (dir.) nurses assns., Sigma Theta Tau. Contbr. articles to profl. jours. Address: 297 Center St Bangor ME 04401

PLOTKIN, NATHALIE (MRS. NORMAN PLOTKIN), music critic, performer; b. N.Y.C., Sept. 8, 1924; d. Joseph Meyer and Rebecca (Nemirowsky) Chasick; B.A., Queens Coll., 1945; M.A., Claremont Grad. Sch., 1970; m. Norman Plotkin, July 1, 1951; children—David, Fredric, Lawrence. Tchr. recorder All Saints Sch., Carmel, Cal., 1970—; violist Monterey Peninsula Symphony, 1971—; music critic Monterey Peninsula Herald, 1973—. Mem. Am. Recorder Soc. Home: 20 Twin Oaks Dr Monterey CA 93940

PLOTT, ELIZABETH ANN ROGINSON (MRS. THOMAS EDWARD PLOTT), hosp. adminstr.; b. Niagara Falls, N.Y., Jan. 14, 1930; d. Frederick Raymond and Elizabeth (Collins) Roginson; B.A., Oberlin Coll., 1949; M.S.W., U. Cal. at Los Angeles, 1953; R.N., Chaffey Coll. Sch. Nursing, 1964; m. Thomas Edward Plott, Sept. 8, 1958; children—Thomas, Elizabeth, Sarah, Jennifer. Dep. counselor mental health Los Angeles County Dept. Mental Health, 1953-56; adminstr. Los Angeles Sanitarium, 1956-58; social worker Plott Nursing Home, Ontario, Cal., 1959-70; co-owner, adminstr. Waterman Convalescent Hosp., San Bernardino, Cal., 1964—; cons. social work Upland (Cal.) Convalescent Hosp., 1964-70. Mem. Nat. Assn. Social Workers. Home: 1415 Dillson Rd San Bernardino CA 92404 Office: 1850 N Waterman Av San Bernardino CA 92404

PLUMB, BARBARA LOUISE BROWN, editor; b. Pitts., Apr. 22, 1934; d. Earle Alfred and Louise (Graham) Brown; student Denison U., 1951-53; B.A., Cornell U., 1955; m. William Lansing Plumb, Oct. 8, 1955 (div.); 1 son, Christian Chamberlain. Editorial asst. Womans Day, 1955; copywriter Eves Advt. Agy., 1955, Walker Scott Dept. Store, 1956-57; tchr. English, Brit. Sch. of Milan, 1957-59; asst. editor Interiors Mag., 1959-60, asso. editor, 1961-62; reporter N.Y. Times, N.Y.C., 1962-70; architecture and environment editor Am. Home Mag., N.Y.C., 1970-73; editor Charles Scribner's Sons, N.Y.C., 1973—. Home: 108 E 86th St New York City NY 10028 Office: 597 Fifth Av New York City NY 10017

PLUMB, GERALDINE HOLLADAY (MRS. HYLON T. PLUMB), ednl. adminstr.; b. Salt Lake City, Jan. 17, 1916; d. John Willard and Lillian (Zabriskie) Holladay; B.S. in Home Econs., U. Utah, 1937; M.A. in Edn. Exceptional Children, San Francisco State Coll., 1965; postgrad. Marianne Frostig Sch. Ednl. Therapy, 1969; Ed.D., U. Ida., 1974; m. Hylon T. Plumb, Aug. 30, 1937; children—Hylon, Robert, Carla (Mrs. Charles Byers), Sheri (Mrs. Dennis Grenda). Tchr. home econs., English, Utah Schs., 1937-38; tchr. exceptional children Boise (Ida.) Schs., 1962-66, tchr., dir. work experience programs exceptional student, 1963-66, supr. spl. edn., 1966-70, coordinator fed. programs, 1970—; instr. U. Ida. Continuing Edn. Center, Boise, 1970. Mem. ad hoc com. Certification Tchrs. in Ida., mem. Ida. ad hoc com. vocational rehab. dept., 1966—; del. Whitehouse Conf. Children and Youth, Washington, 1970. Chmn. pub. relations com. Booth Meml. Hosp., Boise, 1969-72. Mem., vice chmn. Boise Pub. Sch. Bd., 1956-62; pres. Ida. Unified Edn. Council, 1970. Bd. dirs. Gem Haven Sch. Retarded Children. Recipient Woman of the Year award Altrusa Club, Boise, 1952. Mem. Ida. Assn. Retarded Children, Council Exceptional Children, (Ida. br.), Sch. Trustees Assn. (past officer), Ida. Conf. Social Welfare (pres.

1962-63), Am. Assn. U. Women, Ida. Congress P.T.A. (pres. 1969-71), Alpha Delta Kappa, Phi Delta Kappa. Ladies of the Nile. Home: 120 Mobley Dr Boise ID 83702 Office: Boise Schs 1207 Fort St Boise ID 83702

PLUMMER, AGNES FOLEY (MRS. WESLEY F. PLUMMER), printing co. exec.; b. St. Augustine, Tex., Nov. 9, 1909; d. Hugh and Mary Willie (Sims) Foley; student Lamar U., 1970-73; m. Wesley F. Plummer, Mar. 24, 1934 (dec. June 1970); children—Beverly (Mrs. Gordy), Frances (Mrs. Paul Hugh Crozier Jr.), Carolynn (Mrs. Dessommes), Wesley F., Mary Sandra (Mrs. James McCoy), Patrick Foley. Owner, Beaumont Printing & Lithographing Co. (Tex.), 1935—. Mem. Neches River Festival, Beaumont, 1959—, Cancer Crusade, Beaumont, 1969-70, Beaumont Civic Opera, 1971—, Cath. Hermitesses, 1968—; pres. Am. Little League Aux., 1952-53. Bd. dirs. Better Bus. Bur., 1971—. Mem. Sabine Area Advt. Fedn., Nat. Council Cath. Women, C. of C. Clubs: Houston Litho; Soroptimist, Beaumont Knife and Fork, Pinewood County (Beaumont, Tex.). Office: 200 Pearl St Box 3088 Beaumont TX 77704

PLUMMER, BEVERLY JEANETTE (MRS. JOHN F. PLUMMER), author; b. Chgo., Dec. 6, 1918; d. Ray and Mary Irene (Burns) Watson; grad. high sch.; m. John F. Plummer, Apr. 18, 1941; children—John F. III, Christopher, Roxanne. Writer articles to various mags., newspapers including Christian Sci. Moniter, Chgo. Sunday Mag., Chgo. Sun Times, Parents, Woman's Day and Venture, 1960—; author Enriched Presents, 1974. Author: Give Every Day a Chance, 1970. Home: 630 Grove St DeKalb IL 60115

PLUMMER, MRS. MILDRED YATES, lawyer; b. Port Arthur, Tex., Feb. 21, 1921; d. Calder Emmet and Edith Olive (Coe) Yates; A.A., Lamar Coll., 1940; A.B. cum laude, Baylor U., 1942; LL.B., Tulane U., 1948 (J.D. 1969); m. Herbert Aden Plummer, July 8, 1943; children—Pati Edith-Yates, Paula Coe-Yates. Tchr. English, Thomas Jefferson Sr. High Sch., Port Arthur, Tex., 1942-43; with Gulf Oil Corp., 1943-46; admitted to Tex. bar, 1949, U.S. Supreme Ct. bar; practiced law, Port Arthur, 1949—. Past pres. Port Arthur Symphony Club; past legislation chmn. Service League Port Arthur; pvt. practice specializing in real property, probate domestic relations law, maritime collections; owner Port Arthur's Insurers. Recipient Outstanding Club Family award Tex. Fedn. Women's Clubs, 1958, poet laureate, 1960-62, pres. Magnolia dist. Bd. dirs. Beaumont Civic Ballet Co. Mem. State Bar Tex., D.A.R. (chpt. regent 1969-71), Daus. Republic Texas (state parliamentarian 1965-66, local pres.), Tex. Fedn. Music Clubs (past legislation chmn. 4th dist.), Bus. and Profl. Women's Club (local pres. 1969-70), Alpha Delta Kappa, Beta Pi Theta, Kappa Delta Pi, Alpha Chi, Sigma Tau Delta, Pi Kappa Delta, Phi Delta Delta, Kappa Delta. Presbyn. Clubs: Griffing Garden, Port Arthur Country Club, Department (past pres.); Past Presidents Symphony (pres. 1969-71). Home: 4200 Griffing Dr Port Arthur TX 77640 Office: 305 Dryden Pl Port Arthur TX 77640

PLUMRIDGE, KATHRYN MARIE, ednl. adminstr.; b. Buffalo, June 23, 1944; d. Robert Frank and Mary Margaret (Anetzberger) Plumridge; B.S., Boston U., 1966; M.B.A., U. Mass., 1970. Systems engr. IBM, Worcester, Mass., 1966-67; job analyst Worcester County Nat. Bank, 1967-68; registrar Williamsport (Pa.) Area Community Coll., Williamsport, Pa., 1971—. Rep., Model UN, N.Y.C., 1966. Mem. Am. Assn. Collegiate Registrars, Soc. Advancement Mgmt. Episcopalian (social chmn. 1961; v.p. 1962). Home: 91 Roderick Rd Williamsport PA 17701 Office: 1005 W 3d St Williamsport PA 17701

PLUNKETT, BERNADETTE JUDITH TELGARSKY (MRS. THOMAS WILLIAM PLUNKETT), writer; b. Johnstown, Pa., Aug. 7, 1932; d. Paul Stephen and Judith Ann (Kvorjak) Telgarsky; B.A. magna cum laude, Coll. Misericordia, 1954; m. Thomas William Plunkett, Jan. 3, 1959; children—Thomas William, Mark J., Michael P. Exec. sec. Nat. Council Cath. Youth, Nat. Cath. Welfare Conf., Washington, 1954-59; free-lance writer articles pub. in various newspapers and mags., 1963—; women's editor Dearborn Heights (Mich.) Leader, 1964-66, feature story editor, 1966-69; spl. writer news and feature stories Detroit News, 1970—. Publicity chmn. Mich. Coll. Tuition Grant, 1967-68; cons. high sch. and univ. career guidance days, 1964—; panelist arts festivals U. Mich. Alumni and Dearborn Community Arts Council, 1969, 70, 71, 72; chmn. hist. exhibit Dearborn Heights 10th Anniversary, 1973; Dearborn Heights rep. to United Community Services, 1969-71; asst. Dearborn Heights Mayor's Youth Com. on Narcotics, 1969-70. Mem. Nat. Conf. Cath. in Youth Serving Agys. (charter mem., corr. sec. 1958), Citizens for Ednl. Freedom. Roman Catholic (pres. Confrat. Christian Mothers 1972-73). Home: 6645 Amboy Dearborn Heights MI 48127

PLUNKETT, CONNIE RENÉE BERG (MRS. THOMAS SEWELL PLUNKETT), city ofcl.; b. Woodward, Okla., July 1, 1946; d. Eric Wilhelm and Regena May (Black) Berg; B.A., Wesleyan Coll., 1968; m. Thomas Sewell Plunkett, June 7, 1967. Tchr., Bowdon (Ga.) High Sch., 1968-69; asst. advt. mgr. Carroll Pub. Co., Carrollton, Ga., 1969-70; city councilwoman Carrollton, 1973—. Vice chmn. Democratic party State Ga., 1973—, mem. state exec. com., 1971—; mem. Dem. Credentials Com., 1972; del. Nat. Dem. Conv., 1972; mem. Nat. Dem. Charter Commn., 1973—, Nat. Dem. Com., 1973. Bd. dirs. A.R.C., Carrollton; trustee Oak Mountain Acad., Carrollton. Baptist. Club: Garden (Carrollton). Home: West Club Dr Carrollton GA 30117 Office: City Hall Carrollton GA 30117

PLUNKETT, IRMA MARGARET (MRS. JOSEPH A. PLUNKETT), educator; b. East Orange, N.J., July 1, 1914; d. Patrick Henry and Mary Elizabeth (Dempsey) Lawless; B.S. in Edn., Seton Hall U., 1964; postgrad. William Paterson Coll., 1969-72; m. Joseph A. Plunkett, Jan. 21, 1939; children—Edward, Susan (Mrs. John Rosenberger), John, Joseph, Michael. Tchr. elementary sch. St. Catherine of Siena, Cedar Grove, N.J., 1960-64; tchr. Woodmont Sch., Montville Twp., N.J., 1964—. Mem. Nat. Soc. for Study Edn., Montville Tchrs. Assn., Nat., N.J. edn. assns. Roman Catholic (sec. Rosary soc. 1960-61). Club: Catholic. Home: 612 Ridge Rd Cedar Grove NJ 07009 Office: Woodmont School Montville NJ 07045

POATS, ELLA GRAYSON, ednl. adminstr.; b. Clemson College, S.C., Aug. 23, 1911; d. Thomas Grayson and Anna Laura (Mell) Poats; B.A. magna cum laude, Converse Coll., 1933; M.A., Emory U., 1948. Tchr. Gray Court-Owings Sch., Gray Court, S.C., 1933-34; tchr. Spartanburg (S.C.) City Schs., 1934-43, adminstrv. asst., 1943-47, asst. to supt., 1948-53, coordinator instrn., 1953-73, asst. supt., 1973—; mem. Defined Minimum Program Adv. Com. for S.C. Dept. Edn., 1974—. Mem. Task Force Model Cities, Spartanburg, 1971-72; mem. S.C. Edn. Survey Com., 1947-48; mem. numerous other curriculum revision coms. Adv. bd. S.C. Ednl. TV, 1966-67; bd. dirs. Spartanburg Speech and Hearing Clinic, 1969-71, Spartanburg Mental Health Center, 1955-57, Spartanburg Cancer Assn., 1949-50; bd. dirs. Spartanburg Jr. League, 1948-51. Mem. N.E.A., S.C. Edn. Assn., Am. Assn. Sch. Adminstrs., Spartanburg Jr. League, 1971-72; mem. S.C. rose socs. Episcopalian. Home: 909 Brentwood Dr Spartanburg SC 29302 Office: PO Box 970 Spartanburg SC 29301

PODOLSKY, CHARLOTTE, educator; b. Boston, June 16, 1930; d. Joseph and Etta (Weiner) Podolsky; B.S. (Jewish Women's Coll. Club scholar, Shapiro Found scholar), State Coll. Boston, 1951; M.S., Coll.

City N.Y., 1960; Ph.D. (Univ. scholar), N.Y. U., 1964. Tchr. retarded children Boston Pub. Schs., 1951-57, Hempstead (N.Y.) Pub. Schs., 1957-61; instr., teaching fellow ednl. psychology dept. N.Y. U., 1962-64; asst. prof. ednl. psychology and spl. edn. U. Minn., Mpls., 1964-66; asst. prof. spl. edn. Hofstra U., Hempstead, N.Y., 1966-70, asso. prof., 1970—, program coordinator mental retardation, 1966-73, chairperson dept. spl. edn., rehab., 1973—; fellow psychotherapy L.I. Consultation Center, N.Y., 1967-69, staff psychotherapist, 1969-72; pvt. practice as psychotherapist, 1969—. Cons. spl. edn. dist. 8 liaison com. on spl. edn. N. Shore L.I. Pub. Schs. Dists., 1969—. Office Edn.-Fed. fellow in leadership tng. in mental retardation, 1961-63. Recipient Tomlinson Meml. award for outstanding achievement in field psychology N.Y. U., 1969. Mem. Am. Assn. Mental Deficiency, Council for Exceptional Children (state membership chmn. 1968-71), Am. Ednl. Research Assn., Am. Psychol. Assn., Am. Assn. U. Profs., Assn. for Children with Learning Disabilities, Asso. editor Exceptional Children, 1968—. Script writer, dir., editor films of unrehearsed classroom instrn. of retarded children Mpls. Ednl. TV, 1965-66. Home: 50 Alpine Way Huntington Station NY 11746 Office: Dept Spl Edn and Rehab Hofstra U Hempstead NY 11550

PODVIN, SISTER CATHERINE MARIE, coll. adminstr.; b. Saginaw, Mich., Sept. 20, 1920; d. Armedose Charles and Marie Magdalena (Danziesen) Podvin; B.S., Siena Heights Coll., 1952; M.A., DePaul U., 1963; postgrad., Providence Coll., 1967-69. Various secretarial postitions, Saginaw, Mich., 1938-46; tchr., Mich. and Ill., 1948-68; registrar Siena Heights Coll., Adrian, Mich., 1969-74; chmn. bus. dept. Aquinas Dominican High Sch., Chgo., 1974—. Chmn. Siena Heights Plant and Mgmt. Com., Adrian, 1972—. Mem. Am., Mich. (mem. registrars practices com. 1972—) collegiate registrars and admissions officers. Writer poems. Address: Aquinas Dominicas High Sch 2121 E 72d St Chicago IL 60649

POE, ELIZABETH HOLT (MRS. FRANK WILSON POE), librarian; b. Phila.; d. Alan Edward and Laura (Cowell) Holt; B.S. in Edn., Temple U., 1940; B.L.S., Drexel Inst. Tech., 1950; postgrad. Wake Forest Coll. Sch. Law, 1946-50, U. Ill. Coll. Law, 1950-52; m. Frank Wilson Poe, Aug. 26, 1961. Asst. law librarian Temple U. Law Sch., 1942-43, acting law librarian, 1943-46; law librarian Wake Forest Coll. Sch. Law, 1946-50; asst. law librarian U. Ill. at Urbana, 1950-52; law librarian U. Neb., 1952-53; law librarian Nev. State 'Library, Carson City, 1953-57; law librarian State Library Pa., 1957—. Am. Assn. Law Libraries rep. Council Nat. Library Assn. on Library Work as Career, 1959-65, chmn. exhibits com., 1964-67, chmn. recruitment com., 1967-69, chmn. com. law library service to prisoners, 1971-73, mem. exec. bd., 1973—, rep. to Am. Correctional Assn. council, 1972—. Mem. Am. Assn. U. Women (v.p. Nev. div. 1957), Pa. Library Assn. Contbr. articles to profl. jours. Home: 358 Beverly Rd Camp Hill PA 17011 Office: 316 Education Bldg Harrisburg PA 17126

POFF, PHYLLIS ROSALIN GRATZ (MRS. RICHARD B. POFF), judge; b. Waterloo, Ind., Dec. 26, 1930; d. Pliny David and Rosa (Muйерfer) Gratz; student Ind. U., 1948-51; LL.B., John Marshall Law Sch., 1953; m. Richard B. Poff, Aug. 11, 1962; 1 dau., Michelle Marie. Admitted to Ind. bar, 1953; individual practice law, Auburn, Ind., 1954—; judge Auburn City Ct., 1967—; county atty. DeKalb County, 1960-64; town atty. Waterloo, Ind., 1960-64. Mem. Am., Ind., DeKalb County (pres. 1970) bar assns., Auburn C. of C.

POGASH, HARRIET ILENE, retail trade exec.; b. N.Y.C., Sept. 25, 1941; d. Milton M. and Dorothy C. (Cohen) Pogash; B.A., Barnard Coll., 1963. Advt. copywriter Montgomery Ward, N.Y.C., 1963-65, asst. buyer fashions, 1966-69, asst. sales mgr. 1970-72, nat. retail sales mgr., 1973—. Mem. Mus. Modern Art N.Y.C., Mus. of N.Y.C., N.Y. Cultural Center, Friends of Central Park, Mus. Natural History, Equity Library Theatre, N.Y.C. Mem. Riverside Democratic Club. Mem. Barnard Alumnae Assn. Office: 393 7th Av New York City NY 10001

POGREBIN, LETTY COTTIN, mag. editor, author; b. N.Y.C., June 9, 1939; d. Jacob and Cyral (Halpern) Cottin; B.A. cum laude with spl. distinction in English and Am. lit., Brandeis U., 1959; m. Bertrand B. Pogrebin, Dec. 8, 1963; children—Abigail and Robin (twins), David. Vice pres. Bernard Geis Assos., book pubs., N.Y.C., 1960-70; columnist The Working Woman column Ladies Home Jour., 1971—; editor Ms. mag., N.Y.C., 1971—. Cons. Women's Action Alliance, 1971—; cons. Free to Be, You and Me projects, 1972—. Mem. N.Y. County Dem. Com., 1973—. Bd. dirs. Ms. Found., Action Children's Television. Recipient award Phila. Publicity Assn., 1970, Theta Sigma Phi, 1971, Myrtle Beach (S.C.) Bus. and Profl. Women's Club, 1972. Mem. Nat. Orgn. Women, Nat. Women's Polit. Caucus, Women's Equity Action Alliance, Am. Civil Liberties Union. Author: How To Make It In A Man's World, 1970. Contbr. articles to N.Y. Times and other publs. Office: Ms Mag 370 Lexington Av New York City NY 10017

POGUE, MARY ELLEN (MRS. L. WELCH POGUE), youth and community worker; b. Fremont, Neb., Oct. 27, 1904; d. Frank E. and Mary (Coe) Edgerton; B.F.A., U. Neb. 1926; studied violin with Harrison Keller, Boston, 1926-28, Kemp Stillings Master Class, N.Y.C., 1939-40; m. L. Welch Pogue, Sept. 8, 1926; children—Richard Welch, William Lloyd, John Marshall. Mem. Potomac String Ensemble, 1948—. Vice chmn. Montgomery County (Md.) Victory Garden Center, 1946-47; pres. Bethesda Community Garden Club, 1946-48; mem. bd. Montgomery County YWCA, 1946-50, 52-55; bd. govs., historian William Bradford Compact, 1966—. Mem. Mayflower Soc. (dir. D.C. 1955), Nat. Geneal. Soc., Columbia Hist. Soc., League Women Voters, Epis. Policy Assn. (council 1969—), Capital Speaker's, P.E.O. (pres. D.C. chpt. 1957-59), Mortar Bd. (pres. D.C. alumni 1966-67), Delta Omicron Music. Democrat. Methodist. Editor: Favorite Menus and Recipes of Mary Edgerton of Aurora, Neb. (cookbook), 1963; Edgerton-Coe History, 1965. Home: 5204 Kenwood Av Chevy Chase MD 20015

POHALA, MARY JOSEPHINE, research scientist; b. Swoyerville, Pa.; d. Felix William and Josephine (Buchek) Pohala; B.S., Bucknell U., 1944; diploma Geisinger Med. Center Sch. Med. Tech., 1945; M.S., U. Pa., 1955; postgrad. Rutgers U., 1956-62. Supr. clin. labs. Monmouth Med. Center, Long Branch, N.J., 1945-47; bacteriologist Syracuse (N.Y.) Meml. Hosp., 1947-50; supr. plasma processing lab. A.R.C. Blood Bank, Wilkes-Barre, Pa., 1950-53; asso. scientist ORTHO Research Found., Raritan, N.J., 1955-64, sr. scientist, 1964—. Recipient Research award ORTHO Diagnostics, 1973. Mem. N.Y. Acad. Sci., Am. Assn. Blood Banks, Am. Soc. Clin. Pathologists, Am., N.J. socs. med. technologists, Am. Heart Assn. (council on thrombosis), A.A.A.S., Am. Assn. U. Women, Am. Med. Writers Assn., Phi Sigma. Contbr. articles to profl. jours. Home: 82 E Cliff St Somerville NJ 08876 Office: ORTHO Research Found Route 202 Raritan NJ 08869

POHL, MARGARET LOUISE, former educator; b. N.Y.C., Nov. 22, 1915; d. Charles Andrew and Mabel (Harrigan) Pohl; B.A., N.Y. U., 1936; R.N. Bellevue Sch. Nursing, 1939; M.A., Columbia, 1952, Ed.D., 1963. Asst. sci. instr. Bellevue Sch. Nursing, N.Y.C., 1939-42; dir. edn. Met. Hosp. Sch. Nursing, N.Y.C., 1942-52; instr. nursing edn. Hunter Coll. City U. N.Y., N.Y.C., 1952-65, asst. prof. dept.

nursing edn., 1966-71. Mem. nursing adv. com. Beth Israel Sch. Nursing, N.Y.C., 1958-67; mem. review panel Nursing Research, 1963—, abstractor current research articles Am. Nurses' Found., 1963—. Mem. Nat. League Nursing (chmn. com. undergraduate edn. dept. baccalaureate and higher degree programs 1960-68), Am. Nurses' Assn., Am. Assn. U. Profs., Phi Beta Kappa, Sigma Theta Tau, Kappa Delta Pi. Author: Teaching Function of Nursing Practitioner, 1968. Home: 20 Barberry Lane Sea Cliff NY 11579

POHL, MARJORIE ELAINE CONLEY (MRS. RICHARD WALTER POHL), pub. relations exec.; b. Norfolk, Va.; d. Harry Delmar and Elsie Veletta (Wilson) Conley; A.B., U. Pa., 1940; M.S., 1942; postgrad. Hardin-Simmons Coll., 1944, Ia. State U., 1958-68; m. Richard Walter Pohl, Aug. 15, 1941; children—Katharine (Mrs. Larry Max McMillin), Richard Wilson, Ann Marie (Mrs. John E. Ullman). Dir. Jr. Cultural Series, Ames, Ia., 1962-68; free-lance proof reader Ia. State Press., 1970-71; pub. relations Central Ia. council Camp Fire Girls, Inc., Des Moines, 1973—. Tchr. English, Country Day Sch., San Jose, Costa Rica, 1969, Ia. State U., 1958-60; substitute tchr., Ames (Ia.) Pub. Schs., 1969-74. First v.p. Community Theatre, 1966-67. Bd. dirs. Camp Fire Girls, 1965—, pres. bd., 1967-68, 69-70. Mem. Am. Assn. U. Women (pres. Ames 1962-64; 1st v.p. Ia. state 1966-68), Nat. League Am. Pen Women, Pi Lambda Theta, Gamma Chi, Alpha Xi Delta, Phi Sigma Alpha. Methodist. Republican. Home: 1501 Carroll Av Ames IA 50010 Office: Camp Fire Girls Inc 700 Hawley Welfare Bldg Des Moines IA 50309

POIANI, EILEEN LOUISE, educator; b. Newark, Dec. 17, 1943; d. Hugo F. and Eileen Louise (Crecca) Poiani; A.B., Douglass Coll., New Brunswick, N.J., 1965; M.S., Rutgers U., 1967, Ph.D. in Math., 1971. Teaching asst., summer instr. math. Rutgers U., 1966-67; asst. counselor Douglass Coll., 1969-70; instr. St. Peter's Coll., Jersey City, 1967-70, asst. prof. math., 1970-74, asso. prof., 1974—, dir. centennial vis. lectr. program, 1971-73; dir. middle states self study, 1974—; programmer Bell Tel Labs., Whippany, N.J., summer 1964, Nat. Newark and Essex Bank, summer 1965. Mem. centennial council St. Peter's Coll., 1972. Louis Bevier fellow Rutgers U., 1965-66; named Danforth Asso. Discussion leader Nutley Ecumenical Com., 1971-72. Mem. Am. Math. Soc., Assn. Math. Tchrs. N.J., Am. Assn. U. Profs., Math. Assn. Am. (asso. sec.-treas. N.J. sect. 1971—, nat. film projects adv. com. 1973-75), Nutley Hist. Soc., Douglass Coll. Alumnae Assn. (class pres. 1970—, long-range planning com. 1972—), Pi Mu Epsilon (nat. councillor 1972-76, moderator local chpt. 1968—), Phi Beta Kappa (coll. rep. 1973-74). Home: 49 Carrie Ct Nutley NJ 07110 Office: Dept Math Saint Peter's Coll Jersey City NJ 07306

POINDEXTER, BETTY LOU, educator; b. Cleburne, Tex., July 20, 1930; d. Curtis and MaryLou (Doby) Poindexter; B.S., Tex. Woman's U., 1951, Ph.D., 1963. Elementary, jr. high sch. tchr., Cleburne, Tex., 1951-57; grad. asst. Tex. Woman's U., Denton, 1958-63; faculty Ga. Coll., Milledgeville, 1963—, prof. health, phys. edn., recreation, 1968—. Ga. Coll. rep. Ga. Univ. System Adv. Council for Health and Phys. Edn., 1969-70; condr. dance workshops, classes, Tex., Ark., Ga., Fla., 1959-69; appeared solo performances modern dance, Ga., 1963-68. Recipient scholarships dir. Jacob's Pillow, 1961, 62. Mem. A.A.H.P.E.R., So. Dist. Health, Phys. Edn. and Recreation, Nat., So. assns. phys. edn. coll. women, Ga. Edn. Assn., Ga. Assn. Health, Phys. Edn. and Recreation (chmn. dance sect. 1971-72), Ga. Coll. Tchr. Edn. Council, Ga. Tchr. Edn. Council, Sigma Alpha Iota, Pi Lambda Theta. State of Ga. editor Dance Newsletter, 1969-70. Home: 1671 Pine Valley Rd Milledgeville GA 31061

POINDEXTER, GAMMIEL GRAY (MRS. GERALD GLENN POINDEXTER), lawyer; b. Baton Rouge, La., Sept. 22, 1944; d. James Austin and Lee Ethel (Forrest) Gray; A.B., U. Ind., 1965; J.D., La. State U., 1969; m. Gerald Glenn Poindexter, Sept. 4, 1971; 1 son, John Langston Royal. Admitted to La., D.C. bars, 1969, Va. bar, 1971; staff atty. Solicitor's Office, U.S. Dept. Labor, 1968-70; staff atty. Legal Aid Soc. Baton Rouge, 1970-71; dep. dir. Neighborhood Legal Aid Soc., Richmond, Va., 1971-73; mem. firm Greene & Poindexter, Inc., Petersburg, Va., 1973—. Mem. Gov.'s Commn. on Status of Women, 1973—, Surry County Bi-Centennial Com., 1973—. Bd. dirs. Richmond YWCA. Constance Baker Motley law scholar Herbert Lehman Found. of N.A.A.C.P. Legal Def. and Ednl. Fund, 1967-68. Mem. Alpha Kappa Alpha. Home: Route 1 Box 239 Surry VA 23883 Office: 212 Sycamore St Petersburg VA 23803

POINDEXTER, HALLY BETH WALKER (MRS. ROBERT WILLIAM POINDEXTER), educator; b. Houston, Oct. 21, 1927; d. John House B. and Elizabeth Inez (Hall) Walker; B.A., Rice U., 1947; M.A., U. No. Colo., 1950; B.S., U. Houston, 1949; postgrad. Baylor Coll. Med., 1966; Ed.D., Columbia, 1957; m. Robert William Poindexter, July 20, 1946; children—Hally Beth, Pamela Walker. Asst. prof. Rice U., 1949-55, prof., 1965, asso. dean students, 1967-69; asst. prof. Columbia Tchrs. Coll., 1955-60, asso. prof., 1960-65; prof. health and phys. edn. U. Houston, also Rice U., 1969—; vis. prof. Tsuda Coll., Tokyo, Japan, 1964-65. Dist. adviser Girl Scouts, Far East, 1964-66; cons. Vols. Pub. Schs., also numerous sch. systems programs phys. edn. atypical children. Recipient Hugh Scott Cameron award Rice U., 1968. Mem. Am., Tex. assns. health, phys. edn. and recreation, So., Nat. assns. phys. edn. coll. women, Am. Coll. Sports Medicine, Soc. Psychology Sport and Phys. Activity. Author: (Maryhelen Vannier) Team and Individual Sports for Girls and Women, 1960; Physical Activities for College Women, 1964: (with C.L. Mushier) Coaching Competitive Team Sports for Girls and Women, 1973. Home: 10907 Candlewood St Houston TX 77042 Office: U Houston Dept Health and Physical Edn Holman St Houston TX 77004

POKORNY, LEITHIA MURRAY, librarian; b. Coopers Plains, N.Y., Nov. 2, 1918; d. John James and Clistia Bertha (Stickler) Murray; B.S., State U. N.Y. at Geneseo, 1940; postgrad. St. Lawrence U., State U. N.Y. at New Paltz; m. William Fletcher Pokorny, June 20, 1945; children—Laurian Lee, Kim Ann. Librarian, Painted Post High Sch., 1940-42, State U. N.Y. at Potsdam, 1942-46; cons. librarian Clarkson Coll. Tech., 1942-46; head librarian, 1946-47; asso. prof., head main circulation desk Hunter Coll., 1947-51; coordinator libraries Half Hollow Hills Schs., Melville, N.Y., 1957-70, library chmn., 1970—. Cons., charter mem. Half Hollow Hills Community Library. Lt., Civil Air Patrol, 1942-45. Recipient blood donation award Canadian Red Cross, 1943. Mem. N.Y., Suffolk library assns., Suffolk Sch. Librarians Assn. (pres. 1968), N.E.A., N.Y., Half Hollow Hills (exec. bd. 1958-60, 69-70) tchrs. assns., Suffolk Ednl. Communications Council. Episcopalian (chmn. library com. ch. women). Home: 1 Rupert Pl Melville NY 11746

POKRAS, SHEILA FRANCES GRABELLE (MRS. NORMAN MARTIN POKRAS), lawyer; b. Newark, Aug. 5, 1935; d. Moses Joseph and Pauline (Goldberg) Grabelle; B.S. in Secondary Edn., Temple U., 1957; LL.B. cum laude, Pepperdine Sch. Law, 1969; m. Norman Martin Pokras, Sept. 11, 1954; children—Allison, Andrea, Laurence. Tchr. jr. high sch., Phila., 1957; tchr., counselor Newark Pub. Schs., 1957-59; admitted to Cal. bar, 1970; mem. firm Levin & Pokras, Long Beach, Cal., 1970-73; individual practice law, Long Beach, 1973—. Mem. Lakewood City Council, 1972—, Los Angeles County Regional com. for Mental Retardation, 1973—. Recipient Torch of Liberty award B'nai B'rith Anti-Defamation League, 1972.

Mem. League Women Voters (dir. 1963), Anti-Defamation League Los Angeles County (mem. bd.), Am., Bar Assn., State Bar Cal., Am. Assn. U. Women, Amicus Pepperdine Alumnus Assn. (treas. 1974-75), Greater Lakewood C. of C., Democrat. Hadassah (local chmn. Am. affairs 1963-64). Club: Pilots. Home: 3960 Bouton Dr Lakewood CA 90712 Office: 4311 E Carson St Long Beach CA 90808

POLAN, NANCY MOORE (MRS. LINCOLN MILTON POLAN), artist; b. Newark, O.; d. William Tracy and Francis (Flesher) Moore; A.B., Marshall U., 1936; m. Lincoln Milton Polan, Mar. 28, 1934; children—Charles Edwin, William Joseph Marion. One-man shows Charleston Art Gallery, 1961, 67, 73, Greenbrier, 1963, Huntington Galleries, 1963, 66, 71, N.Y. World's Fair, 1965, W.Va. U., 1966, Carroll Reese Mus., 1967; exhibited in group shows Am. Watercolor Soc., Allied Artists of Am., Nat. Arts Club, 1968, 69, 70, 71, 72, 73, Pa. Acad. Fine Arts, Opening of Creative Arts Center W.Va. U., 1969, Internat. Platform Assn. Art Exhibit, 1968-69, 72, 73, Allied Artists W.Va., 1968-69, Joan Miro Graphic Exhbn., Barcelona, Spain, 1970, XXI Exhibit Contemporary Art, La Scala, Florence, Italy, 1971, Rassegna Internazionale d'Arte Grafica, Siena, Italy, 1973, others. Mem. internat. com. Centro Studi e Scambi Internazionale, Rome, Italy, 1968, spl. rep., 1970. Recipient Norton Meml. award 3d Nat. Jury Show Am. Art, Chautauqua, N.Y., 1960; Purchase prize, Jurors award, Watercolor award Huntington Galleries, 1960, 61; Nat. Arts Club for watercolor, 1969, many others. Mem. D.A.R., Allied Artists W.Va., Internat. Platform Assn., Allied Artists Am. (asso.), Tri-State Arts Assn., Composers, Authors and Artists of Am., Sunrise Found., Mus. Natural History, Am. Fedn. Arts, Nat. Arts Club, Leonardo da Vinci Acad. (Rome), Sigma Kappa. Episcopalian. Address: 2 Prospect Dr Huntington WV 25701

POLAND, KATHRYN ELEANOR, state legislator; b. Portland, Ore., Oct. 12, 1919; d. James Francis and May Vesta (Jones) Kennedy; student U. Wash., 1937-38, 40, Moravian Coll. for Women, 1938-39; m. Bill Merle Poland, Jan. 1, 1949 (div. Aug. 1972); children—Patrick Kennedy, Kathleen (Mrs. Theodore Carlsen), Shannon Elizabeth. Chief clk. Treas.' Office, Ter. Alaska, 1940-43; sec. Wage and hour div., 1944-45, accountant Dept. Taxation, 1947-48; accountant Juneau Cold Storage (Alaska), 1946-47; cannery accountant King Crab, Inc., Kodiak, Alaska, 1958-64; travel agt., Kodiak, 1965; accountant Kodiak Fisheries and Columbia Wards Fisheries, Kodiak, 1966-70; apptd. to Alaska State Senate, 1970, re-elected, 1971. Precinct sec. Democratic Party, Kodiak, 1958-69; del. Dem. dist. conv., 1958, 66; del. Alaska Dem. conv., 1966, 70. Mem. Pioneers of Alaska Aux., Alaska Fedn. Natives, Kodiak Area Native Assn., League Women Voters. Roman Catholic. Home: PO Box 45 Kodiak AK 99615

POLCARI, ANN LINDA, librarian, educator; b. N.Y.C., Feb. 19, 1943; d. Victor Benjamin and Janet (Slesinger) Polcari; B.A., Queens Coll., 1963; M.L.S., U. Pitts., 1968. Library asst. Purdue U. Libraries, 1963-65; bibliographer computer sci. dept. Pa. State U., 1966-67; ref. librarian U. Conn., 1968—, instr. library research methods, 1971—. Mem. Conn., New Eng. library assns., Beta Phi Mu. Home: 30 Weeks Trailer Park Storrs CT 06268

POLCINO, ANNA MARGARET, psychiatrist; b. Phila., July 24, 1924; d. Joseph and Carmella (Toto) Polcino; A.B., Immaculata Coll., 1948; M.D., Women's Med. Coll. Pa., 1955. Intern, St. Francis Hosp., Pitts., 1955-56; R.C. missionary Med. Mission Sisters of Phila., 1949—; staff Holy Family Hosp., Karachi, West Pakistan, 1959-68, Holy Family Hosp., Dacca, East Pakistan, 1965-66; resident surgery St. Agnes Hosp. and Hahnemann Med. Coll. Hosp., Phila., 1956-59; resident psychiatry Worcester (Mass.) State Hosp., 1969-72; psychiat. dir., co-founder Cons. Center for Clergy and Religious, Worcester, 1970—; co-founder House of Affirmation, Whitinsville, Mass., 1972—; psychiat. dir. Valley Adult Counseling Service, Whitinsville, Mass., 1971-72, Green Island Neighborhood Opportunity Center, Worcester, 1969-71. Recipient award Amita, Inc., 1965. Mem. A.M.A., Am. Psychiat. Assn., Worcester Psychiat. Soc. Home and office: 120 Hill St Whitinsville MA 01588

POLCYN, MARGARET LOUISE WALTER (MRS. FRANK POLCYN), pub. relations exec.; b. Cleve., Apr. 15, 1928; d. George Edward and Margaret Agnes (Hyson) Walter; student Bowling Green U., 1947; B.B.A., Cleve. State U., 1951; m. Frank Robert Polcyn, Aug. 13, 1949; children—Laura, F. Michael, Thomas, Stephen. Personnel asst., house organ editor Sterling-Lindner-Davis, Cleve., 1951-52; asst. to treas. Patterson-Sargent Co., Cleve., 1952-54; pub. relations coordinator North Allegheny Sch. Dist., Pitts., 1966-71; credit mgr. Honeybee & Piccadilly Stores, St. Louis, 1972-73; pub. relations dir., dir. continuing edn. Notre Dame Coll., St. Louis, 1973—. St. Louis area dir. Nat. Coll. Adv. Service, 1973; coordinator adult edn. course for women in communication Parkway Sch. Dist., 1973. Mem. Coalition for Environment, St. Louis, 1973—. Recipient Nat. award for excellence in sch. pub. relations Sch. Mgmt. mag., 1968, Nat. award in sch. pub. relations, 1969. Mem. Am. Coll. Pub. Relations Assn., Women in Communications. Episcopalian. Home: 1520 Windridge Dr Des Peres MO 63131 Office: 320 E Ripa Av St Louis MO 63125

POLEK, MITTIE PLYMALE JOHNSON, real estate and ins. broker; b. Barnes, Ark., Nov. 12, 1905; d. John Anderson and Margaret Amelia (Honaker) Plymale; ed. pub. schs., spl. real estate courses; m. Joseph E. Polek, Feb. 25, 1952; 1 son by previous marriage, Albert. Fed. govt. employee, 1943-56; real estate salesman, Robert Barry Realtor, Grandview, Mo., 1956-57; partner Johnson-Polek Realtors, Belton, Mo., 1957—, notary pub. Jackson County. Licensed real estate broker, Mo., Ark., Kan., Okla. Midwest Mo. Bd. Realtors (dir., pres. 1969), Am. Bus. Women's Assn. Episcopalian. Mem. O.E.S. Club: Pilots (Ft. Smith). Home: 6206 E 149th St Grandview MO 64030 Office: PO Box 67 Belton MO 64012

POLENZ, JOANNA MAGDA UBERALL (MRS. DARYL LOUIS POLENZ), physician; b. Cracow, Poland, Oct. 20, 1936; d. Mieczyslaw and Erna (Goldberger) Uberall; M.D., U. Sydney (Australia), 1961; m. Daryl Louis Polenz, July 8, 1962; children—Teresa Ann, Daryl Philip, Elizabeth Sophia. Came to U.S., 1961. Intern, Bklyn. Hosp., 1961-62; resident Mt. Sinai Inst. Psychiatry, N.Y.C., 1962-65, fellow psychiatry, 1965-66, research fellow, 1966-67; med. dir. Tappan Zee Mental Health Clinic, Phelps Meml. Hosp., North Tarrytown, N.Y., 1967-71, dir. dept. psychiatry, 1971—; instr. psychiatry Mt. Sinai Sch. Medicine, 1966-67. Diplomate Am. Bd. Psychiatry and Neurology. Mem. A.M.A., Am. Psychiat. Assn., Group Psychotherapy Assn., N.Y. Acad. Scis. Home: Willowcrest Dr RFD 2 Katonah NY 10536 Office: 1133 Pleasantville Rd Briarcliff Manor NY 10510

POLICH, KATHERINE ROTHERHAM, librarian; b. Fresno, Cal., Mar. 8, 1940; d. Oswald and Katherine Alexander (Strother) Rotherham; student Fullerton Jr. Coll., 1958-59; B.A., U. Cal., 1962; M.S. in L.S., U. So. Cal., 1965; M.A. in history, U. N.M., 1969. Cataloger Zimmerman Library of U. N.M., 1965-67; librarian Imperial Valley Campus of San Diego State U., 1969—; research Archivo General del la Nación, Mexico City, 1968, Bancroft Library, 1969. Mem. A.L.A., United Profs. of Cal., Cal. Library Assn., Soc. Librarians, Am. Civil Liberties Union. Mem. Movement of Spiritual Inner Awareness. Home: PO Box 1298 Calexico CA 92231

POLIER, JUSTINE WISE (MRS. SHAD POLIER), judge; b. Portland, Ore., Apr. 12, 1903; d. Stephen S. and Louise (Waterman) Wise; B.A., Barnard Coll., 1924; LL.B., Yale, 1928; m. Leon Arthur Tulin, June 14, 1927 (dec. Dec. 1932); 1 son, Stephen W.; m. 2d, Shad Polier, Mar. 26, 1937; children—Trudy H. Festinger, Jonathon W., Michael W. (dec.). Admitted to Conn. bar, 1928, N.Y. bar, 1929; referee Workman's Compensation, N.Y. Dept. Labor, 1929-34; asst. corp. counsel N.Y.C., 1934-35; judge Domestic Relations Ct., N.Y.C., 1935—, N.Y. State Family Ct., until 1973; dir. Juvenile Justice project Children's Def. Fund, 1973—. Cons., Office Civilian Def., 1941-42. Del. White House Conf. on Children and Youth, 1960; mem. bd. N.Y. Sch. for Nursery Years; mem. Foster Care Commn., N.Y.C.; v.p. Citizens Com. for Children; chmn. Louise Wise Services; mem. N.Y. State Com. on Children; mem. joint commn. Inst. Juvenile Adminstrn.-Am. Bar Assn. Bd. dirs. Field Found., World Ch. Peace Union; pres. Wiltwyck Sch. for Boys; adv. council judges Nat. Council on Crime and Delinquency; bd. visitors Antioch Sch. Law; chmn. N.Y. Family Ct. Com.-Mental Health Services. Mem. Pub. Affairs Com. Recipient Isaac Ray award Am. Psychiat. Assn. Fowler Harper fellow Yale Law Sch. Fellow Am. Orthopsychiat. Assn.; mem. Eleanor Roosevelt Inst., Am. Jewish Congress (hon. pres. women's div., chmn. exec. com.), World Jewish Congress (exec. com.). Author: Everyone's Children, Nobody's Child; A View From The Bench; The Rule of Law and the Role of Psychiatry, 1968. Home: 175 E 64th St New York City NY 10021 Office: 135 E 22d St New York City NY 10021

POLIFRONI, MARGUERITE OWINGS (MRS. VINCENT JOSEPH POLIFRONI), educator; b. Brest, France, Apr. 22, 1918; came to U.S., 1924, naturalized, 1941; d. Chloe Belle Owings; B.A. in Social Service Adminstrn., U. Chgo., 1940, postgrad., 1940; M.A., Pacific Oaks Coll., 1968; m. Vincent Joseph Polifroni, Feb. 14, 1942; children—Adele Marie (Mrs. Charles Pineda), Mary Katherine, Francis Joseph Jr. caseworker Bur. Pub. Welfare, Denver, 1941-42; caseworker Family Soc., Pitts., 1942-43, Child and Family Service, Elmira, N.Y., 1943-45; head tchr. Pacific Oaks Children's Sch., Pasadena, Cal., 1956-63, acting dir., 1963-64, dir., 1964-66, asso. dir., 1966-69, dir. community services, 1967-69; dir. credential program Pacific Oaks Coll., Pasadena, 1968-70, asst. dean faculty, 1969-70, dean faculty, 1970-73, mem. faculty 1973-74, coordinator credential programs, 1974—. Mem. Cal. Gov.'s Adv. Com. to Pre-Sch. Edn. Programs, 1966-67; ednl. cons. Project Head Start, 1965-69; mem. home econs. dept. adv. com. Cal. State Coll. at Los Angeles, 1968-70; mem. accrediation teams Cal. Dept. Edn., 1970-72; mem. early childhood edn. adv. coms. Pasadena Unified Sch. Dist., 1973, Hamilton Primary Schs., 1973. Mem. Nat. Assn. for Edn. Young Children, Assn. for Childhood Edn. Internat. (corr. sec., state exec. bd. 1971-73, nat. publs. com. 1972—), Cal. Council on Edn. Tchrs. (exec. bd. 1972—), Pacific Ackworth Assn., Cal. Profs. Early Childhood Edn. (exec. bd 1974—), Pi Lambda Theta, Delta Phi Upsilon. Contbr. articles to profl. jours. Home: 3637 Canyon Crest Rd Altadena CA 91001 Office: 714 W California Blvd Pasadena CA 91105

POLIN, CLAIRE (MRS. MERLE SCHAFF), musician; b. Phila.; d. Josef and Celia (Dolgien) Polin; B.Mus., Phila. Conservatory of Music, 1948, M.Mus., 1950, D.Mus., 1955; postgrad. Temple U., Juilliard Sch. Music, Dropsie Coll., Gratz Coll., Berkshire Music Center; m. Merle Schaff, June 3, 1956; children—Josef Bruce E., Gabriel Jacob G. Faculty, Phila. Conservatory-Phila. Mus. Acad., 1955-65; faculty Rutgers U., 1957—, dir. Univ. Exchange Concerts, 1960—. Free-lance flutist, 1955—; PanOrphic Duo, Europe, spring 1966; vis. lectr. U. Wales, 1966, Leverhulme fellow, 1968-69; vis. lectr.-composer-performer Gt. Britain, France, Israel, 1969 recipient award-commn. Ga. State Brass Symposium, 1970; Faculty Study award Rutgers U., 1973-74. Mem. Am. Assn. U. Profs., Am. Soc. U. Composers, Soc. for Ethnomusicology, Am. Music Center, Phila. Art Alliance, Am. Musicol. Soc., Composers Guild Gt. Britain, Bibliotheque Internationale de Musique Contemporaine, Welsh Guild, A.S.C.A.P., Delta Omicron (awards 1953, 59). Author: Music of the Ancient Near East 1954; Gift of Jubal, 1954; with Wm. Kincaid) 5-volume Flute Method; also articles on Welsh, Jewish and Early Am. music. Compositions include; Third String Quartet, 1961; Second Symphony (commd. by Korean Symphony Orch.), 1964; No-Rai, 1964; Welsh Bardic Odes, 1959; Gilgamesh for string orchestra, 1960; Antigone for string quartet, 1960; No Man is an Island, SATB and piano, 1964; Pentalogue for 4 brasses and harpsichord, 1967; Structures for Solo Flute, Summer Settings for harp, 1967; Consecutivo for 5 players; At Cader Idris for brass quintet (Am. Brass Symposium award 1970), 1969; Makimono for 5, 1969-71 (versions I, II); Synaulia for 5, 1969; Margoa for solo flute, 1970; De Spei, TTB, 1970; The Journey of Owain Madoc for brass quintet, piano and percussion (commd. by N.Y. Brass Quintet), 1971; Infinito for saxophone, soprano, chorus, narrator-dancer, 1972; Aderyn Pur for flute, Saxophone, tape, 1972; Eligmos Archaios for solo harp, 1973; Procris for flute and tuba, 1973; Biblical Madrigals SSATB, 1973. Home: Dragon Hill Baird and Heath Rds Merion PA 19066 Office: Rutgers U Camden NJ 08102

POLING, BERENICE MAE COTA (MRS. SAMUEL FLETCHER POLING), lawyer; b. Medicine Lake, Mont., May 15, 1914; d. Lute Lyle and Lena Mae (Boruff) Cota; student Ind. U., 1933-35, LL.B., Ind. Law Sch., 1938; m. Samuel Fletcher Poling, May 25, 1941. Admitted to Ind. bar, 1938; practiced in Indpls., 1938—; mem. firms McDonald and Poling, 1938-71, Patrick and Patrick, 1971—; atty., Marion County Plan Commn., Bd. Zoning Appeals, 1943-52; referee, hearing judge Marion County Juvenile Ct., Indpls., 1953—. Atty. bd. trustees Fire Pension Fund, City Indpls., 1958—, Indpls. Dist. Ch. Nazarene, 1954—. Mem. Ind., Indpls. (bd. mgrs. 1960-61) bar assns., Iota Tau Tau. Republican. Mem. Christian Ch. (mem. adminstrv. bd. 1963-65). Rotarian. Home: 5610 Carrollton St Indianapolis IN 46620 Office: 810 King Cole Bldg Indianapolis IN 46204

POLIVKA, JOAN MARGARET HICKEY (MRS. RUSSELL WILLIAM POLIVKA), assn. exec.; b. Manitowoc, Wis.; d. James S. and Mary Agnes (Kelly) Hickey; student Lawrence U., 1945-47; B.S., U. Wis., 1949, postgrad., 1957-58; postgrad. Oxford (Eng.) U., 1955, U. Coll., Dublin, Ireland, 1964; m. Russell William Polivka, Aug. 29, 1959. With Merathon Corp. (name now Am. Can Co.), Menasha, Wis., 1939-46; field dir., camp dir. Girl Scouts Am., Wis., 1946-47, 49-51; pub. relations asst. to pres. Miller Brewing Co., Milw., 1951-57; community relations coordinator Internat. Inst. Milwaukee County, 1957-59; founder mem., exec. dir. Mpls. People to People, 1963-72. Nat. pub. relations chmn. Nat. Assn. Fgn. Student Affairs, 1966-68, regional chmn., 1970; co-founder, bd. chmn. Peace Corps Service Council Minn., 1969—; mem. women's adv. com. Minn. State Dept. Human Rights, 1969—, mem. com. on UN Internat. Women's Year; co-founder, chmn. internat. affairs com. Mpls. Commn. Human Relations, 1972—. Mem. Minn. Women's UN Rally Bd., 1966-72; mem. U. Minn. World Affairs Bd., 1966—; mem. U. Minn. Internat. Center Bd., 1962-63; founding com. mem. Minn. State-Wide Hospitality Com., 1969—; charter mem. Irish Am. Cultural Inst., 1965—; mem. internat. relations bd. Macalester Coll., St. Paul, 1967—; Minn. rep. Sister Cities Internat., now pres. Minn. Council; mem. planning com. State Dept. Briefings, 1961-62, mem. State Dept. Adv. Com. Internat. Orgns., 1972—. Pub. relations com. Am. Cancer Soc., Milwaukee County, 1957-59; founding com. mem. Milw. Chamber Music Series, 1954; founder Action Service Council Minn., 1972—. Bd. dirs. March of Dimes, 1961-62, hon. dir., 1960—; bd. dirs. Milw. Repertory Theatre, 1954—. Recipient Medalla Primera Class of Order of Bernardo O'Higgins, Govt. Chile, 1967. Mem. Am. Assn. U. Women (mem. fgn. policy com. 1970-71), Mpls. League Cath. Women (mem. bd. 1965-70), Am. Fedn. Advt. (mem. bd. Milw. 1954-59), Phi Beta. Club: Woman's (Mpls.); Zonta Internat. (status of women chmn. 1970-72) (Mpls.). Home: 405 W Minnehaha Pkwy Minneapolis MN 55419 Office: Syndicate Bldg Minneapolis MN 55402

POLIZZI, BARBARA ANN SCHULTZ, banker; b. Chgo., Aug. 18, 1928; d. Clyde H. and Isabelle (Riker) Schultz; B.A. with distinction, De Pauw U., 1950; m. Glenn L. Flint, Aug. 28, 1950 (div. Jan. 1960); 1 dau., Diane L.; m. 2d, James J. Polizzi, May 4, 1974. Accounting clk. Union Starch & Refining Co., Columbus, Ind., 1950-52; financial mgmt. Irwin Mgmt. Co., Columbus, Ind., 1955-59; trust asst. No. Trust Co., Chgo., 1959-60, divisional asst., 1960-65, asst. sec., 1965-70, 2d v.p., 1970-72, v.p., 1972—. Mem. Am. Inst. Banking, Chgo. Council Fgn. Relations, Delta Zeta. Club: Chicago Pony (sec. 1968-70; dir. 1968-70). Home: 159 Cottage Hill Elmhurst IL 60126 Office: 50 S La Salle St Chicago IL 60690

POLK, ANITA E. LEWIS, assn. exec.; b. Birmington, Ala., Sept. 20, 1928; d. John Henry and Emmie (Garlington) Lewis; B.A., Spelman Coll., 1946; postgrad. Case Western Res. U.; certificate (Ford Motor Co. scholar), U. Manchester, Eng., 1972; m. Oct. 7, 1957 (div. 1961); 1 dau. Stacey Emmie G. Lewis. Cleve. editor, Pitts. Courier, Cleve., 1954-57; women's editor, feature and fashion writer Cleve. Call and Post, Cleve., 1957-66, also Cleve. Plain Dealer, Johnson Pub. Co.; dep. dir. Greater Cleve. Manpower Advancement Program, Cleve., 1966; dir. community relations Urban League Cleve., Cleve., 1966-69, dep. dir., 1970—; founder Poly Tech Engring. Inc. Free-lance writing and advt.; dir. Modern Homemakers, Cleve., 1957-65. Pub. relations cons. industry, community, state and local polit. campaigns. Bd. dirs. Great Lakes Inst., Glenville Neighborhood Community Center; bd. trustees Mt. Zion Jr. League. Recipient numerous awards from civic orgns. Mem. Am. Acad. Polit. and Social Scis., Cleve. Press Club, Women's Advt. Club, N.A.A.C.P., Media Women, Olivet Instl. Bapt. Ch., Women's City Club, Am. Judicature Soc., Pub. Relations Soc. Am., Women's Civic League, Tau Gamma Delta. Home: 1076 E 98th St Cleveland OH 44108 Office: Grad Sch Case Western Res U 2065 Abington Rd Cleveland OH 44108

POLK, BONNIE WHITE (MRS. JOHN W. POLK), govt. ofcl.; b. Haverhill, Mass., July 8, 1943; d. Ned and Shirlee (Euster) White; B.S., Simmons Coll., 1965; m. John W. Polk, Nov. 30, 1968; 1 son, Daniel W. Editor, Food and Nutrition mag. and newsletter Food and Nutrition Service, U.S. Dept. Agr., Washington, 1971-73, asst. dir. information, 1973-74, br. chief programs, 1974—. Mem. Arlington County (Va.) Consumer Protection Commn., 1972—. Recipient Blue Pencil award Fed. Editors Assn., 1971, certificate of merit Food and Nutrition Service, 1973, Superior Service award U.S. Dept. Agr., 1973. Mem. Women in Communications. Home: 516 N Jackson St Arlington VA 22201 Office: Information Div Food and Nutrition Service US Dept Agr Washington DC 20250

POLK, GENE-ANN (MRS. EDWIN CLAY HORNE), pediatrician; b. Roselle, N.J., Oct. 3, 1926; d. Charles Carrington and Olive Mae (Bond) Polk; student Howard U., 1944-45; B.A., Oberlin Coll., 1948; M.D., Women's Med. Coll. Pa., 1952; M.P.H., Columbia U., 1968; m. Edwin Clay Horne, Aug. 23, 1952; children—Carol Anne, Edwin Christian. Intern Sydenham Hosp., N.Y.C., 1952-53; resident Harlem Hosp., N.Y.C., 1953-55; practice medicine specializing in pediatrics, Englewood, N.J., 1959-67; sch. physician, Englewood, 1963-67; dir. pediatric ambulatory care services Harlem Hosp. Center, N.Y.C., 1968—; asso. prof. clin. pediatrics Columbia, 1968—. Mem. adv. bd. Bergen County Youth Orch., 1969—, Adult Sch. Englewood, 1968—. Diplomate Nat. Bd. Med. Examiners. Fellow Am. Acad. Pediatrics; mem. Bergen County, N.J. med. socs., Nat. Med. Assn., Am. Med. Women's Assn., Alpha Kappa Alpha. Home: 374 Miller Av Englewood NJ 07631 Office: Harlem Hosp Center 136th and Lenox Av New York City NY 10037

POLKING, KIRK ANN, editor; b. Covington, Ky., Dec. 21, 1925; d. Henry and Mary (Hull) Polking; student Am. U., 1944, Evening Colls., Xavier U., U. Cin., 1945—. Editorial asst. Modern Photography mag., Cin., 1948-50; asst. circulation mgr. Farm Quar., Cin., 1950-52, circulation mgr., 1952-57; free-lance writer, 1957-62; editor Writer's Digest, Cin., 1963-73; dir. publs. devel. F & W Pub. Co., Cin., 1973—. Lectr. various univs. Recipient Nat. Headliner award Women in Communications, 1970. Mem. Nat. League Am. Pen Women (Ohio pres. 1970-73), Authors League. Author: 4 children's books, 1963-68; The Private Pilot's Dictionary and Handbook, 1974. Home: 5450 Beechmont Av Cincinnati OH 45230 Office: 9933 Alliance Rd Cincinnati OH 45242

POLLACK, HARRIET SCHULGASSER (MRS. JOSEPH POLLACK), educator; b. N.Y.C., Mar. 23, 1925; d. David and Minna (Rabinowitz) Schulgasser; B.A., Hunter Coll., City U. N.Y., 1945, M.A., 1962; Ph.D., Columbia, 1967; m. Joseph Pollack, Oct. 23, 1943; children—Deborah, Amy. Lectr. Hunter Coll., N.Y.C., 1962-64; instr. State U. N.Y., Stonybrook, 1966-67; asso. prof., chmn. dept. govt. John Jay Coll., City U. N.Y., N.Y.C., 1967-73, prof. govt., 1973—. Mem. Phi Beta Kappa. Author: (with Alexander B. Smith) Crime and Justice in a Mass Society, 1971. Home: 82-36 215th St Queens Village NY 11427 Office: John Jay Coll City U NY New York City NY 10010

POLLACK, ISOBEL TOMSON KOGEL (MRS. SIMEON POLLACK), pediatrician; b. Bklyn., Jan 21, 1933; d. Marcus David and Fannie Irene (Tomson) Kogel; A.B., Vassar Coll., 1953; M.D., Columbia, 1957; m. Simeon Pollack, Feb. 26, 1956; children—Deborah, Marianne, Shoshannah, Richard, Russell. Intern, Bronx (N.Y.) Municipal Hosp. Center, 1957-58, resident pediatrics, 1958-60; pediatrician Washington Health Dept., 1961-65, Lincoln Hosp., Bronx, 1965-71; chief pediatrics, med. dir. No. Med. Group, 1971—; asst. clin. prof. pediatrics Albert Einstein Coll. Medicine, Bronx, 1971—. Diplomate Am. Bd. Pediatrics. Fellow Am. Coll. Pediatrics. Home: 8 Jordan Rd Hastings on Hudson NY 10706 Office: 115 Dreiser Loop Bronx NY 10475

POLLACK, JOAN DIEHL (MRS. EUGENE L. POLLACK), scientist; b. Long Island City, N.Y.; d. Franklin and Lu (Murphy) Diehl; A.B., Barnard Coll., 1953; M.A., Columbia, 1959, Ph.D., 1963; m. Eugene L. Pollack, June 16, 1962; children—Steven Diehl, Linda Catherine. Lab. asst. Columbia U. Electronics Research Labs., 1953-55, jr. psychologist, 1955-58; research asst. IBM Research Center, Yorktown Heights, N.Y., 1959; staff psychologist Dunlap & Assos., Inc., Stamford, Conn., 1960; asst. psychology Columbia U., 1959-62; asst. research zoologist U. Cal., Los Angeles, 1963-70. Mem. Am., Western psychol. assns., Human Factors Soc., A.A.A.S., Sigma Xi, Psi Chi. Contbr. articles to profl. jours. Home: 30214 Cartier Dr Palos Verdes Peninsula CA 90274

POLLARD, FRANCES MARGUERITE, educator; b. Florence, Ala., Oct. 7, 1920; d. Lorenzo Marquis and Carrie (Mayfield) Pollard; grad. Selma Jr. Coll., 1938; B.S., Ala. State Coll., 1941; M.S. in L.S., Western Res. U., 1949, Ph.D., 1963; postgrad. Columbia, 1952-54. Tchr. elementary sch., Waterloo, Ala., 1938-39, Marengo County Tng. Sch., Thomaston, Ala., 1941-42, Sterling High Sch., Sheffield, Ala., 1942-43; library asst. Enlisted Men's Library 2, Fort McClellan, Ala., 1943-46, Ala. State Coll., Montgomery, 1946-48; student aide, childrens room Sterling br. Cleve. Pub. Library, 1948-49; asst. librarian Ala. State Coll., 1949-61, head librarian, 1961-63; adminstrv. asst. Booth Library, Eastern Ill. U., Charleston, 1963-70, prof. library sci., head library sci. dept., 1970—. Mem. Ill. Library Adv. Council on Library Devel., 1967—. Mem. Nat., Ill. edn. assns., Am., Ill. library assns., Am. Acad. Polit. and Social Sci., Soc. for Applied Anthropology, Am. Sociol. Assn. (asso.), Am. Assn. U. Profs., Am. Assn. U. Women, Alpha Kappa Alpha. Author: (with others) Major Problems in Education of Librarians, 1954. Home: 1330 A St Charleston IL 61920

POLLERT, IRENE ELIZABETH, nursing educator; b. Brownstown, Ind., Oct. 10, 1926; d. Albert and Lillie W.C. (Fenneberg) Pollert; student St. John's Coll., 1949-50, (H.A. Hanser Meml. scholar 1953) Luth. Hosp. Sch. Nursing, 1950-53; B.S., Washington U. 1955, M.S. (NIH fellow), 1958, postgrad., 1966, 67-68. Head nurse Luth. Hosp., St. Louis, 1954-57; research asst. Washington U., 1958-60; staff nurse VA Hosp., St. Louis, 1960-61; coll. health nurse St. John's Coll., 1961-62; instr. Ind. U. Sch. Nursing, 1962—. Named Outstanding Student Nurse of Year, Mo. State Nurses Assn., 1953. Mem. Am. Nurses Assn., Nat. League Nurses, Am. Coll. Health Assn., Gerontological Soc., Nat. Soc. Study Edn. Lutheran. Home: 700N Alabama St Indianapolis IN 46204 Office: 1100 W Michigan St Indianapolis IN 46202

POLLITT, GERTRUDE STEIN, social worker; b. Vienna, Austria, Sept. 12, 1919; d. Julius and Sidoni (Brauch) Stein; came to U.S., 1949, naturalized, 1951; B.A., Roosevelt U., 1954; M.A., U. Chgo., 1956; certificate Chgo. Inst. Psychoanalysis, 1963; m. Erwin P. Pollitt, Jan. 13, 1951. Resident social worker Anna Freud, Essex, Eng., 1944-45; dep. dir. UN, U.S. Zone, Germany, 1945-48; psychiat. social worker Jewish Children's Bur., Chgo., 1955-63; pvt. practice as psychiat. social worker, Glencoe, Ill., 1961—. Cons., Winnetka Community Nursery Sch., 1962-63, North Shore Congregation Israel Nursery Sch., 1966-69. Fellow Am. Orthopsychiat. Assn.; mem. Nat. Assn. Social Workers (chmn. pvt. practice com. 1967-70), Nat. Assn. Clin. Social Workers, Menninger Found., Acad. Certified Social Workers. Author articles in field. Home: 481 Oakdale Av Glencoe IL 60022 Office: 695 Venron Av Glencoe IL 60022

POLLITT, MARY TODD BELKNAP, realtor; b. Lansing, Mich., Apr. 7, 1918; d. Leslie Howard and Mary Louise (Todd) Belknap; B.S., Mich. State U., 1940; grad. Grad. Realtors Inst. of U. Mich., 1969; m. William Ryder Pollitt, Aug. 3, 1946 (div. May 1970); children—Mary (Mrs. Richard Hahin), Kathryn (Mrs. John W. Chemacki). Salesman Pearl & Larsen, Grand Ledge, Mich., 1958-59, George P. Bomersheim, Grand Ledge, 1960-63, Ingham Home Realty, Lansing, 1963-64; salesman Simon Real Estate, Lansing, 1964-67, broker, 1968-69, v.p., 1968-69; broker, v.p., closing officer Furman-Dey Realty Co., Lansing, 1970-73; v.p., closing officer State Wide Real Estate Service of Lansing, 1973—. Pres. Grand Ledge PTA Area Council, 1957-58; active Grand Ledge Girl Scouts, 1956-61. Recipient distinguished service award, Mich. Congress Parents and Tchrs., 1958. Mem. Nat. Assn. Real Estate Bds. (treas. Lansing womans council 1967), Real Estate Alumni of Mich., Lansing Bd. Realtors. Republican. Episcopalian. Home: 317 W Scott St Grand Ledge MI 48837 Office: 3519 S Cedar St Lansing MI 48910

POLLIZZE, BERNADETTE ANNA, petroleum co. exec.; b. Phila., Apr. 9, 1937; d. Anthony and Lillian (Severino) Tavani; grad. high sch.; m. James Pollizze, Sept. 1, 1962. Bookkeeper, C.P. Bonnetti Inc., gen. contractor, Phila., 1954-58, Metco Mfg. Co., tool and die mfrs., Phila., 1958-59; with Pa. Petroleum Products Co., Phila., 1959—, export mgr., 1968—, ins. mgr., 1969—; real estate sales, 1974—. Mem. Women's Traffic Club Phila. (speaker chmn. 1970, placement chmn. 1974). Home: 609 N Glassboro Rd Woodbury NJ 08097 Office: 25 Shunk St Philadelphia PA 19148

POLLOCK, MARION BEST, educator; b. Youngstown, O., Oct. 6, 1914; d. Alexander and Sybil Melissa (O'Connor) Best; A.B., Miami (O.) U., 1937; M.S., U. Cal. at Los Angeles, 1962, Ed.D., 1966; 1 son, Thomas Gordon. Caseworker, City of Cin. Dept. Social Welfare, 1938-40; prodn. mgr., writer John Guedel TV Prodns., 1951-61; dir. vols. TB and Health Assn., 1962-63; health educator Fullerton (Cal.) Union High Sch., 1963-64; asso. prof. health sci. Cal. State U., Long Beach, 1964—. Cons. Govt. Argentina Dept. Pub. Health, Buenos Aires, 1971; asst. dir. Sch. Health Edn. Study, Washington, 1968-70. Assn., 1972. Fellow Royal Soc. Health, Am. Pub. Health Assn., Am. Sch. Health Assn. (Distinguished Service award 1972), Soc. Pub. Health Educators; mem. Am. Ednl. Research Assn., A.A.H.P.E.R., Pi Lambda Theta. Author: (with D. Oberteuffer, O. Harrelson) School Health Education, 1972; (with Oberteuffer) Health Science and the Young Child, 1974. Home: 1760 Hanscom Dr South Pasadena CA 91030 Office: Cal State U Long Beach CA 90804

POLLOCK, NANCY REIBEN, actress; b. Bklyn., Feb. 10, 1907; d. Philip and Rachel (Gelbrass) Reiben; ed. U. Havana, N.Y.U., Columbia; m. Herbert H. Pollock, Feb. 10, 1925; children—Doris (Mrs. Alvin Greenberg), Patricia Lee (Mrs. Elliott M. Brown). Appeared professionally, Havana, Cuba, 1925-27, Mexico City, 1927-29, Spain, 1929-35; appeared in summer stock, off-Broadway, then Broadway; appeared in Diamond Lil, 1949, One Bright Day, 1952, In the Summer House, 1953, Middle of the Night, 1956-58, Period of Adjustment, 1960, Counting House, 1962, Have I Got a Girl for You, 1963, A Dream of Swallows, 1963, Pictures in the Hallway, 1964, After the Fall, 1965, Cherry Orchard, 1966, Sabrina Fair, 1967, Ceremony of Innocence, Joe Egg, 1968, The Wrong Way Light Bulb, 1969, 6 Rooms River Vu; film appearances include The Last Angry Man, 1959, Go Naked in The World, 1960, The Pawnbroker, 1964, Such Good Friends, 1971, 72, Holding On, 1972; also appeared on TV daytime serials and other shows. Address: 98 Riverside Dr New York City NY 10024

POLOW, NANCY BETH GROSS, speech pathologist; b. N.Y.C., Feb. 11, 1946; d. Jack and Shirlee (Hirshleifer) Gross; B.S., N.Y. U., 1967; M.A., Seton Hall U., 1968; Ph.D., Fordham U., 1974; m. Peter Maurice Polow, Sr., May 16, 1970; 1 son, Peter Maruice. Speech therapist Cerebral Palsy Rehab. Inst. of N.J. Orthopedic Hosp., Orange, 1967-68; instr. Miami-Dade Jr. Coll., 1968-70; speech therapist Title I Program, 1970, Millburn and Short Hills, N.J., elementary schs., 1970-71, Child Devel. Services Nursery Sch., Chatham, N.J., 1972-73, summer sch., West Caldwell and Caldwell, N.J., 1972; pvt. practice speech therapy, 1971-73; instr. William Paterson Coll., 1974—. Certified speech pathologist. Mem. Am., N.J. speech and hearing assns., Myofunctional Therapy Assn., Sigma Alpha Eta, Kappa Gamma Chi. Home: 667 Brentwood Dr South Orange NJ 07079

POLSON, ALMA IRENE, educator, author; b. Princeton, Ill.; d. Frank William and Ellen Christine (Eckstrom) Polson; A.B., Augustana Coll., Ill., 1948; M.A., Northwestern U., 1954; postgrad. U. Birmingham, Eng., 1951, U. Ill. 1956, 59-60, U. Neb., 1962, 64, U. Vt., 1967, 70, De Paul U., Chgo., 1964-65, Am. Conservatory of Music, 1964-67, 71-72, Elmhurst Coll., 1956, Middlebury Coll., 1957, 66. Tchr. journalism United Twp. High Sch., East Moline, Ill., 1948-53; tchr. English, York Community High Sch., Elmhurst, Ill., 1954-57; librarian, tchr. French, Sangamon and Menard counties schs., 1959-63; tchr. Harvard (Ill.) Community High Sch., 1963-64; tchr. English, Gage Park High Sch., Chgo., 1965—. Tchr., counselor Mary Coll. French Camp, Bottineau, N.D., 1958; solo vocalist chs., Burlington, Vt. and Chgo., 1970, Gage Park High Sch., 1972. Mem. adv. council Central States Conf. on Teaching of Fgn. Langs.; active YMCA. Mem. Nat. Council Tchrs. English, Am. Assn. U. Women (chmn. creative writing study group 1962), Nat. League Am. Pen Women, Nat., Ill. edn. assns., Poets and Patrons Chgo., Springfield Versewriters Guild (v.p. 1961-62), Delta Kappa Gamma. Lutheran. Clubs: Elmhurst Ski, Illini Ski, Oak Park Ski. Author: It's Fun to Ski, 1973. Contbr. articles, poems to various publs. Home: 4559 S Washtenaw Chicago IL 60632

POLSON, BILLIE MAE, librarian; b. St. Louis, Nov. 6, 1932; d. William Alton and Willa Mae (Craven) Polson; B.A., U. Nev., 1954; M.S. in L.S., U. So. Cal., 1956. Children's librarian Los Angeles Pub. Library, 1956-59; chief catalog librarian James Dickinson Meml. Library of U. Nev., 1959-64, acting librarian, 1965-65, head catalog dept., 1964—. Dir. Nat. Library Week for Nev., 1968. Recipient recognition award, Nev. Centennial Year, 1964. Mem. A.L.A., Mountain Plains (dir. 1967-68), Nev. (pres. 1972-73, dir. 1974) library assns., Am. Assn. U. Women (treas. Las Vegas br. 1963), Am. Assn. Univ. Profs. Club: Las Vegas Faculty Women's. Home: 1420 E Helm Dr Las Vegas NV 89119

POLUS, ELIZABETH ALICE HART (MRS. ALLAN RICHARD POLUS), puppeteer; b. Detroit, Aug. 10, 1939; d. Charles King and Alice (Mather) Hart; student Cal. Poly. Inst., 1957-58; Indonesian Shadow puppetry with Oemetrpo, Mills Coll., summers 1969-71. A.S. in Theatre-Tech., Cabrillo Community Coll., 1973; m. Allan Richard Polus, Sept. 20, 1958; children—Patricia Alaina, Ann Elizabeth, Julie Suzanne. Owner, puppeteer Folk Puppet Theatre, Boulder Creek, Cal., 1970—. Tchr. puppetry YWCA, Santa Cruz, Cal., 1969; Boulder Creek Recreation Dept., 1973, Boulder Creek Elementary Sch., 1973-74. A.R.T.S. artist program Santa Cruz County Bd. Edn., Santa Cruz County council Arts, 1972-74. Mem. Puppeteers of Am., San Francisco Bay Area Puppeteers Guild (treas. 1967-71, sec. 1973), Cabrillo Players (treas. 1973). Methodist. Author: how to puppetry pamphlets. Address: 14755 Two Bar Rd Boulder Creek CA 95006

POMERANTZ, RHODA SOLOMON, physician; b. Phila., May 6, 1937; d. Alexander and Bertha (Joffe) Silverstein; A.B., U. Pa., 1958; M.D., Woman's Med. Coll. Pa., 1963; m. Marc Abraham Pomerantz, Aug. 14, 1958; children—Lauren Eve, Susan Leigh. Med. intern Rush Presbyn.-St. Luke's Med. Center, Chgo., 1963-64, med. resident, 1964-66, med. resident sect. community medicine, 1968-69, med. dir. ambulatory care services, 1969-72, dir. sect. geriatrics, dept. medicine, 1972—, attending physician ANCHOR, 1971—; asst. prof. Rush Med. Coll., 1971—; practice medicine specializing in internal medicine, Vista, Cal., 1967; attending physician Mile Sq. Health Center, Chgo., 1969-72; project dir. Johnston R. Bowman Geriatric Center, 1972—. Pres. Circle Sq. Assn., Chgo., 1971-72, 73-74, treas., 1972-73. Recipient Alpha Omega Alpha award Woman's Med. Coll. Pa., 1959, John Stewart Rodman Meml. prize, 1962, Am. Soc. Clin. Pathologists Bausch and Lomb medal, 1962, Am. Med. Women's Assn. award achievement, 1963, Rush med. award Presbyn.-St. Luke's Hosp., 1964. Diplomate Am. Bd. Internal Medicine. Mem. A.M.A., A.C.P., A.A.A.S., Am. Pub. Health Assn., Phi Beta Kappa, Alpha Omega Alpha, Pi Delta Phi, Pi Mu Epsilon, Alpha Epsilon Delta. Home: 829 S Loomis St Chicago IL 60607 Office: 1753 W Congres Pkwy Chicago IL 60612

POMEROY, DINAH CAMPBELL (MRS. FLETCHER J. POMEROY), lawyer; b. Seattle, Jan. 19, 1942; d. Alexander Duncan and Kathryn Benson (Donehoo) Campbell; B.S., U. Ore., 1963; J.D., U. Wash., 1967; m. Fletcher J. Pomeroy, Dec. 26, 1969. Admitted to Wash. bar, 1967; asst. atty. gen. State Wash., Seattle, 1967—. Mem. Am., Wash. State, King County bar assns. Home: 3637 122d NE Bellevue WA 98005 Office: 1266 Dexter Horton Bldg Seattle WA 98101

POMEROY, FRANCES MUIR (MRS. HUGH R. POMEROY), civic worker; b. Farmington, Wash., June 23, 1902; d. Alexander and Margaret A. (Beattie) Muir; tchrs. diploma U. Cal. at Los Angeles, 1924; m. Hugh R. Pomeroy, Jan. 21, 1923 (dec. July 1961); 1 dau., Helen (Mrs. Denis E. Sullivan). Pres., Roosevelt P.T.A., Hollydale, Cal., 1930-31, Coordinating Council Tujunga, Cal., 1938-39, San Fernando Valley Hist. Soc., 1958-63; dir. ch. vacation sch., Tujunga, 1935-42, North Hollywood, 1946-49; writer, producer dramas for children, 1938-49; leader in preservation Hon. John S. McGroarty home for historic recreation and cultural center, Los Angeles, 1953; pub. relations chmn. Lankershim Pioneers, North Hollywood, Cal., 1947-64; historian Meth. Ch., North Hollywood, 1944—; dir. jr. ch. history and landmarks chmn. North Hollywood Woman's Club, 1949—; pres. Wesleyan Service Guild, 1972, 73. Author: Catholic School Plays, 1941. Home: 11332 Otsego St North Hollywood CA 91601

POMFRET, ANNA (MRS. DAVID BUCKLEY POMFRET), physician; b. Dublin, Ireland, Mar. 7, 1941, (came to U.S., 1964, naturalized, 1967).; d. Terence and Nancy (Morrissey) Rafferty; M.B., B.Ch., B.A.O., U. Coll., Dublin, Ireland, 1965; m. David Buckley Pomfret, Mar. 31, 1964; children—Mark, Bruce, Scott, Heidi. House physician Chelsea (Mass.) Soldiers' Home, 1965-66; resident phys. medicine and rehab. Tufts New Eng. Med. Center, Boston, 1967-70; cons. physiatrist New Eng. Med. Center, Boston, 1971—; asst. prof. phys. medicine and rehab. Tufts U. Med. Sch., Boston, 1971—. Med. tng. grantee Radcliffe Inst., Cambridge, Mass., 1969, 70. Mem. New Eng. Rheumatism Soc., New Eng. Soc. Phys. Medicine and Rehab., Mass. Med. Soc. Home: 49 Pine St Wellesley Hills MA 02181 Office: 185 Harrison Av Boston MA 02111

POMPEY, HATTIE RUTH, librarian; b. Quincy, Fla., May 9, 1923; d. Joseph W. and Mary Lee (Oliver) Keys; A.A., Fla. Normal Coll.; A.B., Fla. A & M U., 1945; B.L.S., Atlanta U., 1948; postgrad. Syracuse U.; m. C. Spencer Pompey, Aug. 27, 1948; 1 dau., Cheryl Zaneta. Formerly tchr. jr. high sch., librarian Carver High Sch.; now librarian Hagen Road Sch., Lake Worth, Fla. Mem. Democratic Exec. Com., 1971-73. Mem. A.L.A., United Tchrs., Fla. Assn. Media Edn., Palm Beach County Classroom Tchr. Assn. (sec. 1968), Alpha Kappa Alpha (basileus 1964). Clubs: F.J. Bright Woman's (past pres.), Naciremas (financial sec.). Home: Box 1533 Delray Beach FL 33444 Office: 10439 Hagen Rd Lake Worth FL 33460

POMRANKA, JEANNE MARGARET (MRS. CLARENCE ALBERT POMRANKA), editor; b. Kewanee, Ill., Feb. 19, 1917; d. Alphonse Thomas and Elizabeth Mary (Hagerty) Van Coutren; student No. Ill. State Tchrs. Coll., 1934-36; m. August E. Carlson, Aug. 6, 1937 (dec. Apr. 1958); children—Donald E., Richard C., Dianne (Mrs. Norman Bennett), Neil M.; m. 2d, Clarence Albert Pomranka, Sept. 25, 1955; 1 son, Stephan J. Processor, David C. Cook Pub. Co., Elgin, Ill., 1941-42; asso. editor Aspire mag., Denver, 1963-68, editor, 1968—. Mem. Divine Sci. Fedn. Internat. Home: 21 S Eaton St Lakewood CO 80226 Office: 1819 14th Av Denver CO 80218

PONDER, CATHERINE VIRGINIA COOK (MRS. ROBERT STEARNS), clergywoman; b. Hartsville, S.C., Feb. 14, 1927; d. Roy Charles and Kathleen (Parrish) Cook; student U. N.C. Extension, 1946, Worth Bus. Coll., 1948; B.S. in Edn., Unity Ministerial Sch., 1956; m. R.K. Ponder, June 24, 1961; 1 son, Richard; m. 2d Robert Stearns, June 19, 1970. Ordained to ministry Unity Ministers Assn., 1957, Unity Sch. Christianity, 1958; minister Unity Ch., Birmingham, Ala., 1956-61; founder, minister Unity Ch., Austin, Tex., 1961-69, San Antonio, 1969-73, Palm Desert, Cal., 1973—. Pres. Prosperity Inst., Inc., San Antonio, 1971—; pres. Unity Ch. Worldwide, Palm Desert, 1973—, bd. trustees, 1973—. Mem. Assn. Unity Chs., Inc., Internat. New Thought Alliance, Internat. Platform Assn. Clubs: Bermuda Dunes Country (Palm Springs, Cal.). Author: The Dynamic Laws of Prosperity, 1962; The Prosperity Secret of the Ages, 1964; The Dynamic Laws of Healing, 1966; The Healing Secret of the Ages, 1967; Pray and Grow Rich, 1968; (with others) The Parker Prosperity Program, 1967. Office: 73-875 Hwy 111 Palm Desert CA 92260

PONSELLE, ROSA MELBA, soprano; b. Meriden, Conn., Jan. 22, 1897; d. Benjamin and Maddalena (Conti) Ponzillo; protege Enrico Caruso; Mus.D. (hon.) Peabody Conservatory Music, 1957; m. Carlo A. Jackson, Dec. 13, 1936 (div.). With Met. Opera Co., N.Y.C., 1918-37; operatic performances include Norma, La Traviata, Carmen, La Forza del Destino, Il Trovatore, Aida, La Gioconda; also appeared in revivals of Don Giovanni, La Vestale, L'Africaine, Don Carlos, other grand opera; voice, operatic coach; recorded. Artistic dir. Balt. Civic Opera Co., 1950—. Named Italian-Am. of Year, 1957; named to Hall of Fame, 1968; decorated comdr. Order of Merit Republic of Italy, 1969. Home: Villa Pace Valley Rd Stevenson MD 21153 Office: 11 E Lexington St Baltimore MD 21202

PONSETI, HELENA PERCAS, educator; b. Valencia, Spain, Jan. 17, 1921; d. Nicolas and Ana (Babenco) Percas; came to U.S., 1940, naturalized, 1950; B.A., Barnard Coll., 1942; M.A., Columbia, 1943, Ph.D., 1951; m. Ignacio V. Ponseti, 1961. Instr., dir. Spanish House, Russell Sage Coll., Troy, N.Y., 1943-45; lectr. Columbia, 1945-47, Queens Coll., 1946-48; asst. prof. modern fgn. langs. Grinnell (Ia.) Coll., 1948-54, asso. prof., 1954-57, prof., 1957—, chmn. elect dept. modern langs., 1956-60, Roberts hon. prof. modern fgn. 1961-62, Richards endowed professorship modern fgn. langs., 1963, chmn. Spanish, Russian depts., 1964-65. Mem. Modern Lang. Assn. Am. (chmn. Latin-Am. sect. 1959-60), Am. Assn. U. Profs. (chpt. pres. 1955-56), Am. Assn. Tchrs. Spanish and Portuguese, Hispanic Inst. U.S., Instituto Internacional de Literatura Iberoamericana (mem. editorial staff Revista Iberoamericana 1959-61), Instituto de Cultura Hispanica (Madrid). Author: La Pcesia Femenina Argentina (1810-1950), 1958; Cervantes y su concepto del arte, 1974. Home: 110 Oak Ridge Av Iowa City IA 52240 Office: Grinnell Coll Grinnell IA 50112

PONZINI, DIANA FRANCIS, advt. agy. exec.; b. N.Y.C., Nov. 25, 1937; d. Louis Joseph and Anna Francis (Nicolazzi) Ponzini; B.A., Hunter Coll., 1961. Comptroller Camer Glass, Inc., N.Y.C., 1955-61; comptroller Peter Mehlich Orgn., N.Y.C., 1961-69, pres., 1969—; exec. v.p. Lubar Southard Inc., N.Y.C., 1967—. Home: 140 E 52d St New York City NY 10022 Office: 145 E 52d St New York City NY 10022

PONZO, TERESE MARIE, ednl. adminstr.; b. Chgo., Jan. 16, 1919; d. Salvatore John and Marie Concetta (Principe) Ponzo; student DePaul U., 1939-42; B.S., Northwestern U., 1948, M.A., 1954. Dir. Spalding Sch., 1942-49; tchr. educable mentally handicapped children Evergreen Park (Ill.) Elementary Sch., 1949-69; dir. Learning Resource Center, Evergreen Park, 1969—; mem. faculty Morine Valley Community Coll., Palos Hills, Ill. Dir. spl. camps for cerebral palsied child, 1969-70, for trainable children, 1969-70. Mem. St. Patricia Sch. Bd., Hickory Hills, Ill., 1972—. Mem. Am. Assn. Mental Deficiency, Council Exceptional Children, Council Children Learning Disabilities, Children with Behavioral Disorders, Mental Retardation P.T.A. Office: 94th and Sawyer Sts Evergreen Park IL 60642

POOL, MARILYN MYERS (MRS. JOSEPH HAROLD POOL), theatre dir.; b. Fresno, Cal., Nov. 2, 1934; d. Laurence B. and Asa (Griggs) Myers; B.A., Stanford, 1955, postgrad., 1955-56; postgrad. U. Tex., 1957-60, W. Tex. State U. summers 1962, 63; m. Joseph Harold Pool, Dec. 28, 1955; children—Pamela Elizabeth, Victoria Anne, Catherine Marcia. Pvt. tchr. drama, speech, acting, directing, speech correction, Amarillo, Tex., 1960—; free-lance radio and TV actress, 1960-70; asst. mng. dir. Amarillo Little Theatre, 1964-66, mng. dir., 1966-68; mng. dir. Horsehoe Players, touring profl. theater, 1969—; actress, multi-media prodn. Palo Duro Canyon, 1971. Pres., Tex. Non-Profit Theatres, 1972—; 1st v.p. High Plains Center for Performing Arts, 1969—. Adv. mem. Tex. Constnl. Revision Commn., 1973—; mem. adv. council U. Tex. Coll. Fine Arts, 1969-72. Bd. dirs. Amarillo Ballet Theatre, YMCA Motivation of People, Tex. Panhandle Heritage Found. Recipient certificate of appreciation Woman of Year, Amarillo Bus. and Profl. Women's Club, 1966; Best Actress award for Hedda Gabler role Amarillo Little Theatre 1965, Best Dir. award for Rashomon, 1967. Travel fellow Am. Assn. U. Women, 1973. Mem. Am. Community Theatre Assn., S.W. Theatre Conf. (dir.), Tex. Theatre Council (dir.), Am. Assn. U. Women (br. pres. 1973—), D.A.R. (chpt. chaplain 1971—), C. of C. (fine arts council), Desk and Derrick (chmn. house com. 1961-62), U.S. Judo Assn., Symphony Guild, Art Alliance, Amarillo Law Wives Club (2d v.p. 1974—). Disciples of Christ. Home: 2410 Teckla St Amarillo TX 79106 Office: Box 7563 Amarillo TX 79109

POOL, MARY JANE, mag. editor; b. La Plata, Mo.; d. Earl Lee and Dorothy (Matthews) Pool; B.A., Drury Coll., 1946. Staff Vogue Mag., N.Y.C., 1946-69, asso. mdsing. editor, 1948-57, promotion dir., 1958-66, exec. editor, 1966-69, editor-in-chief, 1970—. Bd. govs. Fashion Group, Inc., N.Y.C. 1967—; trustee Drury Coll. Mem. Am. Soc. Mag. Editors. Episcopalian. Office: House and Garden 350 Madison Av New York City NY 10017

POOL, TAMAR DE SOLA (MRS. DAVID DE SOLA POOL), lectr., writer; b. Jerusalem, Israel; d. Haim and Eva (Cohen) Hirshenson; brought to U.S. 1904; B.A., Hunter Coll., 1913; internat. travel scholar U. Paris, 1913-14, Columbia, 1914-17; m. David de Sola Pool, Feb. 6, 1917. Dir. Children's Story Hour—Hoboken Pub. Library, 1909-13; tutor Lycee Lamartine, 1914, instr. French, Latin, Greek, Hunter Coll., 1914-17; faculty adviser Menorah Soc., 1915-17; lectr. pub. affairs, Zionism, lit. and religion, 1912—. Mem. mgmt. bd. Youth Aliyah, World Zionist Council, Young Judea. Founder, sometime chmn. Am. Mothers Com. selecting ann. Am. Mother of Yr.; del. Zionist Congresses; rep. Youth Aliyah to Cyprus, Morocco, Tunisia, France, Eng. Mem. bd. Nat. Council Women U.S., United Negro Coll. Fund; chmn. bd. Sisterhood of Spanish and Portuguese Synagogue of N.Y.; pres. N.J. Woman Suffrage Assn., 1915-17;

founding mem. Council Vol. Agys. for Fgn. Service; pres., now hon. pres. Sifriot-Am. Com. for Youth Libraries in Israel and U.S.; chmn. Henrietta Szold Found. Child Welfare; organizer Hebrew U. Hadassah Med. Sch.; bd. govs. Hebrew U., Jerusalem; world pres. Henrietta Szold Centennial. Named Outstanding Woman of Achievement, Women's Internat. Expn., 1954. Mem. Am. Assn. U. Women, Hunter Coll. Alumni Assn. Hadassah (pres. N.Y. chpt. 1930-35, nat. pres. 1939-43, editor mag., hon. life v.p.), Phi Beta Kappa. Author: (hist. drama) The Spirit of '76; Israel and the United Nations; (with David de Sola Pool) An Old Faith in the New World, 1955; Is there An Answer?: An Inquiry Into Some Human Dilemmas, 1966; (hist. novel) The Triple Cord; also numerous articles and monographs. Translator: (with David de Sola Pool) The Passover Haggadah. Office: 8 W 70th St New York City NY 10023

POOLE, ELEANOR RUTH, hosp. adminstr.; b. Wendell, N.C., Nov. 11, 1942; d. Chester Claude and Annie Lorene (Jones) Poole; B.S., East Carolina U., 1964, M.Ed. (Clara B. Burdette scholar), 1966; postgrad. N.C. State U., 1966, 68. Instr., Mt. Olive (N.C.) Coll., 1965-66; personnel analyst N.C. Personnel Dept., Raleigh, 1966-74, editor Career newsletter, 1966-74; personnel dir. Dorothea Dix Hosp., Raleigh, 1974—. Campaign asst. United Fund, 1969-70. Mem. Pub. Personnel Assn. (N.C. treas. 1971-72, v.p. 1972-73), Internat. Personnel Mgmt. Assn. (N.C. pres. 1973-74, mem. exec. bd. 1974—), State Information Officers Assn. (sec. 1970-71), N.C. State Employees Assn., Alpha Phi, Tau Sigma. Democrat. Baptist. Home: Route 2 Wake Forest NC 27587 Office: McBryde Hall Dorothea Dix Hospital Raleigh NC 27611

POOLE, JILLIAN HANBURY, civic worker, fund raiser; b. London, Eng., Aug. 11, 1930; d. Anthony H.R.C. and Una (Rawnsley) Hanbury; ed. Cambridge Sch., Weston, 1944-48; B.A., George Washington U., 1952; m. Richard Armstrong Poole, Nov. 2, 1957; children—Anthony Hanbury, Colin Rawnsley. With Nat. Planning Assn., 1952-55; with Ridder Publs., Inc., 1955-57; govt. liaison asst. Matson Nav. Co., Washington, 1957-59; exec. dir. Nat. Cathedral Assn., Washington, 1960-64; dir. Washington Cathedral Fund, 1966-69; mgr. devel. Corcoran Gallery Art, Washington, 1969-71; dir. devel. John F. Kennedy Center, Washington, 1972—; asst. to chmn., dir. devel. Kennedy Center Prodns., Inc., 1973—. Exec. dir. United Givers' Fund hdqrs., Washington, 1971. Bd. dirs. McLean Citizens Assn., 1972, 2d v.p., 1973. Mem. Nat. Assn. Fund Raisers (dir. 1967, 70), Am. Alumni Council, Pub. Relations Soc. Am. Home: 817 Mackall Av McLean VA 22101 Office: JF Kennedy Center Washington DC 20566

POOLE, LILLIAN SANDRA, librarian; b. New Orleans, June 23, 1938; d. Marvin Eldridge and Lillian (Drott) Poole; B.A., Mary Washington Coll., 1960; M.S., La. State U., 1961. Reference librarian Kansas City (Mo.) Pub. Library, 1960-62; acquisitions librarian Park Coll., 1962-64; pub. library cons. Mich. State Library, 1964-65; cataloger U. Mo., 1965-66, head of acquisitions, 1966-68; reference librarian Kansas City (Kan.) Pub. Library, 1968—. Pres., bd. dirs. Towers Homes Assn. Mem. A.L.A. Episcopalian. Clubs: Challenger Camera, German American Citizens. Home: 1323 N 77th St Kansas City KS 66112 Office: 625 Minnesota Av Kansas City KS 66101

POOLE, LORENA BEL, poet; b. Horatio, Ark., Feb., 1904; d. Theodore Osceola and Mary Alice (Gray) Poole; grad. high sch. Writer, file clk. Magnolia Petroleum, 1926-27; operator calculating machinery Doyle Wholesale, Little Rock; poetry pub. in Ark. Gazette, Ft. Smith, other papers, anthologies. Address: Route 1 Horatio AR 71842

POOLE, LUCILLE BUCHANAN (MRS. HUGH D. POOLE), savs. and loan exec.; b. Jacksonville, Fla., Jan. 19, 1926; d. Arthur T. and Myrtle M. (Roberts) Buchanan; grad. high sch.; m. Hugh D. Poole, Aug. 5, 1972; children by previous marriage—Charle A. Greene, Charlene D. (Mrs. Joe M. Breazeale). Teller, First Fed. Savs. & Loan Assn., Jacksonville, 1956-65, br. mgr., 1965-72, collection mgr., 1972—. Named Woman of Year, Am. Bus. Women, 1969. Mem. Am. Bus. Women (pres. Bold City chpt. 1967), Am. Savings and Loan Inst. (chpt. pres. 1972). Home: 56 W 44th St Jacksonville FL 32208 Office: 300 W Adams St Jacksonville FL 32202

POPE, DONNA KOLNIK, state legislator; b. Cleve., Oct. 15, 1931; d. John Emil and Marie Josephine (Thiel) Kolnik; ed. pub. schs., adult evening classes; m. Raymond Pope, Oct. 21, 1950; children—Candace (Mrs. George Evans), Cheryl Ann. Supr. Cuyahoga County Bd. Elections, also Parma ward leader, 1966-72; precinct committeeman, 1966—; mem. Rep. State Central Com., 1966-72; rep. Ohio Gen. Assembly, 1972—; mem. Cuyahoga County Rep. Exec. Com., House ways and means, state govt. coms., Nat. Legislative Com. on Sci. and Tech., Gov.'s Task Force on Health Care, spl. study com. health care costs Legislative Service Commn., Parma Women's Rep. Club. Active P.T.A., Greater Cleve. Citizens League. Named an outstanding woman legislator in nation, Eagleton Inst. Politics of Rutgers U., 1972. Mem. Nat. Soc. State Legislators, Nat. Orgn. Women Legislators, Internat. Platform Assn., Am. Bus. Women's Assn., Nat. Travel Club. Roman Catholic. Home: 3915 Longwood Av Parma OH 44134 Office: State House Columbus OH 43215

POPE, DOROTHY HAMPSON (MRS. EDWARD HOPKINS POPE), editor; b. Providence, Dec. 28, 1905; d. George Robert and Ellen (Senior) Hampson; A.B. cum laude, Brown U., 1927; postgrad. Duke, 1939-41; m. Herbert Arnold Clark, Oct. 13, 1928; children—Janice (Mrs. William Moffitt) and Joyce (Mrs. George Johnson) (twins); m. 2d, Edward Hopkins Pope, Oct. 19, 1941. Mng. editor Jour. Parapsychology, Duke, 1942-64, editor, 1964—, editor Parapsychol. Bull., 1946-58; editor Parapsychology Press, Durham, N.C., 1966—. Mem. Parapsychology Assn., A.A.A.S., Phi Beta Kappa. Republican. Episcopalian. Contbr. articles to profl. jours. Home: 3405 Windsor Way Durham NC 27707 Office: Found for Research on Nature of Man Box 6847 College Station Durham NC 27708

POPE, GEORGIA HELEN (MRS. LELAND D. POPE), retail trade exec.; b. Watonga, Okla., Jan. 13, 1932; d. Arnold J. and Fern D. (Neal) Prickett; student U. Okla., 1950-52; student U. N.M., 1959, No. Ariz. U., 1960; m. Leland Dean Pope, June 1, 1952; children—Christy Lee (Mrs. B. Butler), Julie Beth. Tchr. Gallup McKinley County (N.M.) pub. schs., 1958-60; agt. Nat. Old Line Ins. Co., Gallup, 1961-65, dist. gen. agt., 1965-71; propr., mgr. Pants Rack store, Gallup, 1971-73, Jane's Fashions store, Gallup, N.M., 1973—. Mem. Republican N.M. Central Com., 1966-70; chmn. Republican Com., McKinley County (N.M.), 1968-69. Mem. Soroptimist Club, N.M. Retailers Assn. (past pres.), Epsilon Sigma Alpha (dir.). Methodist (sec. Sunday sch. 1960-68). Mem. Order Eastern Star (past matron 1965). Club: Gallup Country. Home: 510 Julie Dr Gallup NM 87301 Office: 122 West Coal Gallup NM 87301

POPE, LILLIE BELLIN (MRS. MARTIN POPE), ednl. psychologist; b. N.Y.C., June 22, 1918; d. Isidore and Annie (Chusid) Bellin; B.A., Hunter Coll., 1937; M.S., Coll. City N.Y., 1941; Ph.D., N.Y. U., 1969; m. Martin Pope, June 27, 1946; children—Miriam, Deborah. Psychologist div. pediatric psychiatry Bklyn. Jewish Hosp., 1954-63; dir. bur. instrn. and tng. Job Orientation In Neighborhoods, N.Y.C. Anti-poverty Agy., 1964-65; dir. psycho-ednl. center Coney Island Hosp., Bklyn., 1965—. Faculty, N.Y. U. Grad. Sch. Edn., 1968-72; adj. prof. City U. N.Y.C., 1973—, Yeshiva U., 1973—; cons. various psychol., ednl. anti-poverty agys. Adv. bd. Nat. Affiliation for Literacy Advancement, 1969—. Nat. Inst. Mental Health fellow, 1966-67; study grantee United Cerebral Palsy of Queens, 1968. Diplomate Am. Bd. Prof. Psychologists. Fellow Am. Orthopsychiat. Assn.; mem. Am. Psychol. Assn., Am. Assn. Mental Deficiency, Internat. Reading Assn., Assn. for Children with Learning Disabilities, Council for Exceptional Children. Author: Guidelines to Teaching Remedial Reading, 1967; Issues in Urban Education and Mental Health, 1971; Psycho-Educational Evaluation of the Pre-School Child, 1972; Tutor's Sampler, 1973. Contbr. articles to profl. jours. Office: Coney Island Hosp 2601 Ocean Pkwy Brooklyn NY 11235

POPE, MARION LEOLA (MRS. LYLE JAMES POPE), ednl. adminstr.; b. Carleton, Neb., Jan. 1, 1907; d. Walter Alonzo and Maude (Zeller) Gilbert; student Colo. State Coll., 1937-39, U. Tenn., 1963; diploma Nat. Bus. Sch., 1936, Lewis Hotel Tng. Sch., 1961; m. Lyle James Pope, June 24, 1925; 1 dau., Leola Lyla (Mrs. Donald Meade Shepherd). Bookkeeper, Texaco Co., Longmont, Colo., 1944-45; asst. buyer Webb's Dept. Store, Glendale, Cal., 1945-48; asst. to cataloguer U. Colo., Boulder, 1948-56; clk., switchbd. operator Alexander Hotel, Oak Ridge, 1957-59; adviser U. Tenn., Knoxville, 1960-69; dean women Lincoln Meml. U., Harrogate, Tenn., 1971—. Mem. Wartime Foods Com., Boulder County, Colo., 1938-43; treas. Haxtun (Colo.) Sch. Bd., 1928-29. Mem. Epsilon Sigma Omicron. Methodist. Clubs: Faculty Women's, Business and Professional Women's, Federated Women's. Address: Lincoln Meml U Harrogate TN 37752

POPE, MARY ANN IRWIN (MRS. RICHARD CORAINE POPE), artist; b. Louisville, Mar. 8, 1932; d. James Cecil and Margaret Edwina (Taylor) Irwin; student Cooper Union, 1952; m. Richard Coraine Pope, Nov. 26, 1954; children—Neil, Taylor, Trent. One man shows at Birmingham So. U., A & M U., Huntsville, Ala.; exhibited in group shows at Birmingham Mus., Mint Mus., Charlotte, N.C.; travelling exhibit Art Train; represented in permancent collections at Nat. Coll. Fine Arts, Mint Museum N.C.; draftsman Army Map Service, Louisville, 1951-54; fashion artist Byck's Louisville, 1956-60; free lance fashion artist, Louisville, 1960-65. Bd. dirs. Huntsville Art League Museum Assn., Huntsville, Ala., 1966-72. Mem. Ala. Watercolor Soc., Birmingham Art Assn., Huntsville Art League, Cal. Watercolor Soc. Address: 1705 Greenwyche Rd SE Huntsville AL 35801

POPE, SHARON KAY, edn. adminstr.; b. Kansas City, Mo., Dec. 27, 1944; d. Allen David and Mildred M. (Wilcox) Pope; B.S. U. Mo., 1966, M.Ed., 1967, Ph.D. (edn. Profession Devel. Art fellow), 1971; m. Robert Callis, Sept. 4, 1971. Adminstrv. asst. Dean Students Office, U. Mo., Columbia, 1967-68, asst. dir. student affairs women, 1968-69, counseling psychologist, asst., prof. edn., 1970-73, coordinator extended services, 1973—; mem. staff Edn. Professions Devel. Act Inst., Columbia, 1969-70. Mem. Am. Coll. Personnel Assn. (chmn. Commn. 4 1974-76), U. Mo. Columbia Edn. Alumni Assn. (dir. 1968—, chmn. membership 1969-70), Mortar Bd., Delta Gamma. Home: 1548 Towne Dr Columbia MO 65201 Office: 106 Read Hall Univeristy of Missouri Columbia Columbia MO 65201

POPE, VIRGINIA ANN VOSS (MRS. ROBERT RUSSELL POPE JR.), educator, clubwoman; b. Fruithurst, Ala., Aug. 26, 1934; d. Chester P. and Margaret (Branham) Voss; B.A., Jacksonville State U., 1955, B.S., 1972; postgrad. U. Grenoble, 1956; m. Robert Russell Pope, Jr., Dec. 21, 1957; children—Pamela Marchet, Patrice Voss, Robert Russell III. Tchr., Cleburne County Bd. Edn., Heflin, Ala., 1956-62, Humpty Dumpty Sch., Heflin, 1962-64; pvt. French classes, 1957—; substitute high sch. tchr., 1964—. Pres., v.p., sec. Lit. Club, 1959—; pres., v.p. Wesleyan Service Guild, 1959—; co-chmn. Mothers March Dimes, 1962; pres., v.p. Spade and Trowel Garden Club, 1964—; pres. Mothers Club, 1964—; neighborhood chmn., troop leader Cottaquilla council Girl Scouts U.S.A., 1965—, bd. dirs., 2d v.p. council, 1968—; active Hort. Soc., 1964-68; membership chmn. P.T.A., 1967—; fair chmn. Cleburne County Arts and Crafts League. Bd. dirs. Teen, Inc. Recipient French Govt. award, 1955; named Cleburne County Woman of Year, 1966, Outstanding Young Woman of Heflin, 1971. Mem. Ala. Edn. Assn., Am. Assn. Tchrs. French, Jacksonville Alumni Assn., Delta Kappa Gamma (v.p. 1968-70). Author Fruithurst: Alabama's Vineyard Village, 1971. Home: 202 Lakeview Dr Heflin AL 36264

POPIEL, ELDA STAVER (MRS. CHARLES POPIEL), educator; b. Scandia, Kan., June 9, 1915; d. Emil A. and Mae R. (Johnson) Isaacson; R.N., Research Hosp. Sch. Nursing, 1935; B.S., Coll. St. Teresa, 1955; M.S., U. Colo., 1959; m. Allan P. Staver, 1933 (dec. 1948); children—David Allan; m. 2d, Charles Popiel, Nov. 28, 1957; step-children—Harold L., Robert Alan. Head nurse Research Hosp., Kansas City, 1935-36; sch. nurse Roseland Sch. Dist., Johnson County, Kan., 1941-55; pub. health nurse Johnson County Health Dept. 1948-49, head nurse U. Kan. Med. Center, Kansas City, summers 1950-55; teaching fellow U. Colo. Sch. Nursing, 1957-58, non-clin. coordinator, faculty adviser freshman students, 1958—, dir. continuation edn., asst. dean, prof.; cons. in field; project dir. intensive courses in leadership devel. for nurses in N.M., Wyo., and Colo. Council mem. Western Council Higher Edn. in Nursing; mem. com. continuation edn., Nursing div. Health, Edn., Welfare, Washington; mem. Task Force for Tng. for Leadership in Continuing Edn., Washington; cons. continuing Edn. for Nurses Program, Anchorage, also U. No. Colo., Greeley. Den mother Cub Scouts Am., 1943-46; health, welfare chmn. P.T.A., 1942-55; cons. Campfire Girls Program in Health and First Aid, 1946-55; sponsor Campus Corps. Caps and Capes, 1958—. Mem. Kan. Sch. Health Assn., Am. Assn. U. Women, Colo. Nurses Assn. (pres. 1969-70), Johnson County Mental Health Assn., Colo. League for Nursing, Am. Assn. U. Profs., Colo. Mental Health Assn., Denver Tb Soc., Colo. Assn., Am. Nursing Home Assn., Colo. Heart Assn., Adult Edn. Assn., Colo. Health Careers Council, Sigma Theta Tau (chapter counselor). Unitarian. Contbr. articles to profl. jours. Home: 3918 E Evans Av Denver CO 80210 Office: 4200 E 9th Av Denver CO 80220

POPKIN, MARY O'ROURKE (MRS. ROY S. POPKIN), pub. relations exec.; b. Milw., Oct. 24, 1932; d. James A. and Leah M. (Anvoots) O'Rourke; B.S., Marquette U., 1954; m. Roy S. Popkin, June 26, 1971. Advt. dir. Manpower, Inc., Milw., 1956-65; pub. relations dir. Greater Milw. chpt. A.R.C., 1965-71, D.C. chpt., 1971-73; specialist pub. relations Am. Nat. Red Cross Blood Program, Washington, 1973—. Mem. Women in Communications. Home: 17628 Sequoia Dr Gaithersburg MD 20760 Office: Am Nat Red Cross 17th and E Sts NW Washington DC 20006

POPPEL, LOUISE FISH (MRS. EUGENE HERBERT POPPEL), assn. adminstr.; b. Phila., Sept. 24, 1943; d. J. Joshua and Sylvia (Noble) Fish; B.S., Temple U., 1965; m. Eugene Herbert Poppel, June 20, 1965. Staff pub. relations writer Maurie H. Orodenker Advt. Agy., Phila., 1965-66, Fedn. Jewish Agys., Phila., 1967-74; pub. relations dir. Kravco, Inc./The M.A. Kravitz Co., Inc., King of Prussia, Pa., 1974—; owner Louise Poppel Advt. Agy., Phila., 1971—. Mem. Am. Jewish Congress, Women in Communications (corr. sec. Phila. chpt. 1972—). Home: 326 S 19th St Philadelphia PA 19103 Office: 160 King of Prussia Plaza King of Prussia PA 19406

POPPELL, ESTHER ALMIRA (MRS. JAMES GIDEON POPPELL), lawyer; b. Balt., Sept. 7, 1898; d. Nelson Thomas and Mary Virginia (Brown) McCourtney; student Fla. State U., 1942-43, U. Fla., 1944, U. Miami, 1945; m. James Gideon Poppell, Jan. 23, 1923. Admitted to Fla. Bar, 1933; practiced in Miami, 1933—; mem. firm Morehead & Pallot, 1933-41, Pallot, Poppell, Goodman & Shapo, Miami, 1951—. Founder, Biscayne Fed. Savings & Loan, Miami, 1955, sr. v.p., 1971—, sec., 1956—. Examiner, Fla. Indsl. Commn., 1941-44; mem. Bd. Miami Housing Authority, 1961-65. Mem. Am., Fla. Bar assns., Am. Judicature Soc., Nat., Fla. (pres. 1953-54) assns. women lawyers, Am. Trial Lawyers Assn., Biscayne Bus. and Profl. Womens Club (pres. 1954-55, dist. dir. 1957-58), D.A.R. (regent 1971-73), U.S. Daus. of 1812, Smithsonian Inst., Mem. Order Eastern Star. Clubs: Miami Woman's, Carol Gables Country. Home: 3228 SW 3rd St Miami FL 33135 Office: 1504 Alfred DuPont Bldg Miami FL 33131

POPRICK, MARY ANN, psychologist; b. Chgo., June 25, 1939; d. Michael and Mary (Mihalcik) Poprick; B.A., De Paul U., 1960, M.A., 1964; Ph.D., Loyola U. (Chgo.), 1968. Intern psychology Elgin (Ill.) State Hosp., 1961-62; staff psychologist, 1962; staff psychologist Ill. State Tng. Sch. for Girls, Geneva, 1962-63, Mt. Sinai Hosp., Chgo., 1963-64; lectr. psychology Loyola U. at Chgo., 1964-67; asst. prof. Lewis U., Lockport, 1967-70, asso. prof., 1970—, chmn. dept., 1968-72 (on leave 1972-73); postdoctoral intern in clin. psychology Ill. State Psychiat. Inst., Chgo., 1972-73; pvt. clin. practice in assn. with Paul P. David, M.D., Riverdale, Ill., 1973—. Co-chmn. commn. on personal growth and devel. Congregation of 3d Order St. Francis of Mary Immaculate, Joliet, 1970-71. Mem. Am., Ill., Midwestern psychol. assns., Am. Assn. U. Profs., A.A.A.S., Psychologists Interested in Religious Issues, Kappa Gamma Pi, Psi Chi (sec. 1964-65, pres. 1965-66). Home: 547 Marquette Av Calumet City IL 60409 Office: Lewis Univ Lockport IL 60441

POR, FRIEDA, physician; b. Eperjes, Hungary, Sept 18, 1896, (came to U.S., 1938, naturalized, 1944); d. Bernat and Rosa (Grossmann) Boehm; M.D., U. Vienna, 1923; m. Leo Por, Dec. 20, 1925 (div. Sept. 1933). Tng. pediatrics Carolinen Kinderspital, Vienna, Austria, 1923-24; researcher, bacteriology and serology State Serotherapeutic Instn., Vienna, 1925; staff 1st Med. U. Hosp., Vienna, 1925-30; head endocrine dept. Sonntagh Sanatorium, Novy Smokovec, High Tatra, Czechoslovakia, 1930-32; tng. heart and circulatory diseases, then staff mem. Herzstation, Vienna, 1932-34; asst. in medicine Sanatorium Gutenbrunn, Baden, nr. Vienna, head dietetic dept., 1934-38; practice medicine specializing in internal medicine, Brookline, Mass., 1940—; mem. staff New Eng. Hosp. for Women and Children; asso. physician Beth Israel Hosp., Boston. Fellow Am. Acad. Family Physicians; mem. Am. Med. Women's Assn., Am. Physician Fellowship Assn., Am. Med. Assn., Mass., Norfolk med. socs., Mass. Heart Assn. Address: 9 Sewall Av Brookline MA 02146

PORADA, EDITH, educator; b. Vienna, Austria, Aug. 22, 1912; d. Alfred and Catherine (Magnus) Porada; Ph.D., U. Vienna, 1935; Litt.D., Smith Coll., 1967. Instr. art history Queens Coll., Flushing, N.Y., 1950-58; mem. faculty Columbia, N.Y.C., 1958—, prof. art history, archaeology ancient Nr. East, 1964—. Hon. curator seals and tablets Morgan Library, 1956—. Guggenheim fellow, 1950, Bollingen Found. fellow, 1947-49, Am. Council Learned Socs. grant, summer 1960. Fellow Am. Acad. Arts and Scis.; mem. Am. Oriental Soc., Am. Inst. Archaeology, Deutsche Orientgesell schaft. Club: New York Oriental (N.Y.C.) Author: Seal Impressions of Nuzi, 1947; Corpus of Ancient Near Eastern Seals in North American Collections, 1948; The Art of Ancient Iran, 1965; Tchoga Zanbil IV: La Glyptique, 1970. Address: Dept Art History and Archaeology Columbia Univ New York City NY 10027

PORADA, ELIZABETH ANTONIA, lawyer; b. Northampton, Mass., Sept. 1, 1933; d. Joseph Valentine and Antonia Elizabeth (Malinowski) Porada; A.B., Radcliffe Coll., 1955; J.D., Boston U., 1958; LL.M., Harvard, 1961. Research librarian, lectr. law Boston Coll. Law Sch., Chestnut Hill, Mass., 1958-60; admitted to Mass. bar, 1958; practiced in Northampton, 1961—; spl. asst. atty. gen. Commonwealth of Mass., 1961-62; trustee Nonotuck Savs. Bank, Northampton. Town counsel Town of Hatfield, 1962—, Town of Hadley, 1964—, Town of Worthington, 1968— (all Mass.). Dir. Hampshire County (Mass.) United Fund, 1967-71. Mem. Hatfield Democratic Town Com., 1968—. Bd. dirs. Children's Aid Soc. and Family Service Hampshire County, Occupational and Vocational Developmental Center for the Handicapped. Mem. Am., Hampshire County (sec., treas. 1971-72) bar assns., Am. Judicature Soc., Northampton C. of C. (past dir.), Nat. Orgn. for Women. Club: Quota (pres. Northampton 1969-71). Home: 28 Elm St Hatfield MA 01038 Office: 76 Gothic St Northampton MA 01060

POREMSKI, VALERIE TARANOVICH (MRS. BERNARD B. POREMSKI), hotel exec.; b. Proctor, Vt., Jan. 25, 1919; d. William V. and Christine S. (Speck) Taranovich; student Bishop DesGoes Briard Sch. Nursing, 1936-37; m. Bernard B. Poremski, Nov. 24, 1938; children—Bernard W., Rosemary J. (Mrs. Charles Rogers). Foreman, Killington Mfg. Co., Rutland, Vt., 1950-57; supt. Cornish Wire Co., Rutland, 1956-57; owner, mgr. Trakenseen Hotel-Motel Edgewater Inn, Lake Bomoseen, Vt., 1957—. Pres. P.T.A., Florence, Vt., 1948. Mem. Am. Legion Aux. Home: 183 State St Rutland VT 05701 Office: 30 Lake Bomoseen VT 05732

PORONSKY, MARY ELIZABETH, savs. and loan exec.; b. Chgo., Oct. 31, 1924; d. Albert B. and Helen (Maxian) Tabola; student DePaul U., 1942-43; grad. Am. Savs. and Loan Inst., 1947; m. John A. Poronsky, Oct. 20, 1946; children—Mary Beth, John A., Albert B., Pamela Ann, Janine Marie, Paul M., Christopher J. With Damen Savs. & Loan Assn., Chgo., 1937—, exec. officer, 1942—, pres., 1961—. Roman Catholic. Home: 9532 S Leavitt St Chicago IL 60643 Office: 5100 S Damen Av Chicago IL 60609

PORRES, NORMA ESTEVEZ (MRS. FELIPE DOMINGO PORRES), physician; b. Havana, Cuba, Oct. 29, 1923; d. Jose Antonio and Ofelia Maria (Valdes-Roig) Estevez; B. Arts and Scis., Instituto 3, Havana, 1943; M.D., U. Havana, 1950; postgrad. Tex. Tech. U., 1961-64; m. Felipe Domingo Porres, Nov. 18, 1951; children—Felipe Gonzalo, Norma Isabel. Came to U.S., 1951, naturalized, 1957. Pediatric intern Hosp. de Infancia, Havana, 1950-51; rotating intern Springfield (O.) City Hosp., 1951-52; resident pediatrics in Robert B. Green Hosp., San Antonio, 1953; resident in gen. practice All Saints Hosp., Ft. Worth, 1954-55; gen. practice medicine, Lubbock, Tex., 1958—; dir. City County Welfare Clinic, Lubbock City County Health Dept., 1958; infirmary physician Tex. Tech. U., 1963, asst. clin. prof., 1972-73; mem. active staff St. Mary of Plains Hosp.; active staff Methodist Hosp., chmn. family practice staff, 1970; physician Lubbock Well Baby Clinic, Lubbock Presbyn. Clinic. Med. cons. Tex. Rehab. Agy., Lubbock, 1969—; adviser Tex. Bank, Lubbock; founder, 1st pres. Planned Parenthood of Lubbock, 1962, 63, 69, 71, also physician; mem. Lubbock Head Start Council, 1971—; adviser to bd. dirs. Lubbock Assn. Med. Assts., 1971-72. Bd.

dirs. Lubbock Welfare Clinic, 1958-63, Lubbock Cancer Soc., 1968-69, Lubbock Tb Assn., 1959. Co-recipient Citizen of Year award South Plains chpt. Nat. Assn. Social Workers, 1973. Mem. Am., Tex. (sec.-treas. South Plains chpt. 1972-73) acads. family practice, A.M.A., Tex. Med. Assn. (com. health of poor 1973), Panhandle Dist., Lubbock-Crosby Garza (chmn. welfare com. 1969-70, 72-73) med. socs. Club: Altrusa (pres. Lubbock 1969-71, chmn. internat. relations com. dist. 9, 1972-74). Home: 4804 18th St Lubbock TX 79416 Office: 4005 24th St Lubbock TX 79410

PORRO, CATHERINE REBOK, psychologist; b. Harrisburg, Pa., Nov. 1, 1921; d. Norman Z. and Edna (Rexroth) Rebok; B.A., U. Cal. at Los Angeles, 1961, M.A., 1965, Ph.D., 1967; m. Emo D. Porro, June 7, 1941 (div. Aug. 1971); children—Jeffrey D., Jennifer M. Asst. prof. Cal. State U., Northridge, 1967-70; individual practice clin. psychology, Encino, Cal., 1970—; exec. dir. Coldewater Counseling Center, 1972—; staff psychologist Met. State Hosp., Norwalk, Cal., 1972—. Cons., Bel Air (Cal.) Counseling Center, 1970—; tchr., student adviser Coll. Oriental Studies Grad. Sch., 1973—. Mem. Am., Cal. psychol. assns., Gestalt Therapy Inst. Los Angeles. Home: 4549 Wortser Av Studio City CA 91604 Office: 11400 Norwalk Blvd Norwalk CA 90650

PORTER, DOROTHEA WILHELMINA FOUNTAINE (MRS. JOHN E. PORTER), realtor; b. Savannah, Ga., July 18, 1914; d. Noah Adam and Ada Wilhelmina (Galovitz) Fountaine; R.N., St. Joseph's Sch. Nursing, 1935; m. John E. Porter, Jan. 29, 1937; children—John Emerson, James K., Camilla Gabrielle (Mrs. James R. Ford). Sec.-treas. Butler, Cooper, Knight & Porter, Inc., 1962, Cooper, Knight & Porter, Inc., 1964-65; v.p. Knight & Porter, Inc., 1965-66; pres., Porter Realty, Inc., Savannah, 1966—. Bd. govs. Ga. Realtor Inst. Named Outstanding Citizen of Savannah, Savannah C. of C., 1959, Savannah Realtor of Yr., 1973. Mem. Aux. Med. Assn. Ga. (state pres. 1963-64, exec. bd. 1963-72), Savannah Real Estate Bd. (sec.-treas. 1969-72, dir. 1969-72, pres. 1973—), Nat. Inst. Real Estate Brokers, Nat. Assn. Real Estate Bds. Clubs: Women's, Federated Women's (dir. 1958-62) (Savannah). Home: 1231 Bacon Park Dr Savannah GA 31406 Office: 5105 Paulsen St Savannah GA 31405

PORTER, E. LOUISE H(OFFEDITZ), psychologist, educator; b. York, Pa., Aug. 10, 1910; d. F.A.R. and Carrie L. (Foreman) Hoffeditz; B.A., Pa. State U., 1931, M.S., 1932; Ph.D., U. Neb., 1935; m. Robert M. Porter, June 12, 1937; 1 son, Douglas M. Research fellow Tng. Sch., Vineland, N.J., 1935-36; asst. headmistress Girls Latin Sch., Balt., 1936-37; instr. psychology Beaver Coll., 1939, U. Del., 1939-41; with Southbury (Conn.) Tng. Sch., 1943-56, recreation leader, 1943-44, cottage life asst., 1944-46, psychologist, 1946-47, registrar, 1947-52, research asso. 1952-56; research asso. Rainier Sch., Buckley, Wash., 1956-59; engaged in pvt. practice, 1959—; psychol. cons. Mesa Coll., Grand Junction, 1961—; cons. in mental retardation, 1961—; mem. Colo. Com. Designing Edn. for Future; adv. bd. Mesa County Mental Health Assn.; bd. dirs. Western Colo. Center for the Arts, adv. com. div. health programs Mesa Coll.; founder, bd. dirs. Greenbelt, Inc.; bd. dirs. Hist. Mus. and Inst. Western Colo., Bookcliff Council Arts and Humanities. Recipient award Mesa County Mental Health Assn. Certified psychologist, Colo. Fellow Am. Psychol. Assn.; mem. Am. Assn. Mental Deficiency (life), Colo. Assn. Retarded Children, Am. Assn. U. Women, League Women Voters, Council Exceptional Children (past pres. Rainier chpt.), Sigma Xi, Alpha Lambda Delta, Psi Chi (nat. sec.-treas. 1935-40), Alpha Omicron Pi. Conglist. Home: State Home and Tng Sch Grand Junction CO 81501

PORTER, EDITH JANE, educator; b. Steubenville, O., May 23, 1924; d. Frank Seeley and Edith Helene (Bothe) Porter; A.B., Ohio U., 1946. M.Ed., 1957; Ph.D., Ohio State U., 1969. Profl. exec. Allegheny County and Steubenville Area councils Girl Scouts U.S.A., 1945-51; elementary tchr. Cross Creek Local Sch. Dist., 1951-56, teaching prin., 1956-58; elementary tchr. Steubenville Pub. Schs., 1958-62; asst. prof. edn. Bethany Coll., 1962-66; teaching asso. Ohio State U., 1966-69; asst. prof. edn. U. Del., Newark, 1969-73, asso. prof., 1973—. Chmn. Block Wardens, Steubenville, 1950-53. Improvement of Instrn. grantee U. Del., 1972. Mem. Am. Assn. U. Women (pres. Steubenville br. 1958), D.A.R. (regent Steubenville chpt. 1964-65), Nat. Soc. Study Edn., Nat. Conf. Research in English, Internat. Reading Assn., Nat. Council Tchrs. English, Jean Piaget Soc., Assn. Childhood Edn. Internat., Kappa Delta Pi, Delta Kappa Gamma. Mem. Order Eastern Star. Club: Pilot (lt. gov. Dist. 10, 1953). Research editor Elementary English, 1972—. Contbr. articles to profl. jours. Home: 606 Apple Rd Newark DE 19711

PORTER, HELEN VINEY (MRS. LEWIS MORGAN PORTER, JR.), lawyer; b. Logansport, Ind., Sept. 7, 1935; d. Charles Lowry and Florence Helen (Kunkel) Viney; A.B., Ind. U., 1957; J.D., U. Louisville, 1961; m. Lewis Morgan Porter, Jr., Dec. 26, 1966; children—Alicia Michelle, Andrew Morgan. Admitted to Ind. bar, 1961, Ill. bar, 1961, U.S. Supreme Ct. bar, 1971; atty., office chief counsel Midwest regional office Internal Revenue Service, Chgo., 1961-73; asso. regional atty. Equal Employment Opportunity Commn., Chgo. Litigation Center, 1973-74. Bd. dirs. Profl. Orgn. Women for Equal Rights. Fellow Am. Bar Found.; mem. Nat. Assn. Women Lawyers (pres. 1973-74), Fed. (pres. Chgo. chpt. 1974-75), Ill. State (assembly del. 1972-75) bar assns., Women's Bar Assn. Ill. (pres. 1972-73). Club: City of Chicago (bd. dirs. 1974-77). Home: 225 Maple Row Northbrook IL 60062

PORTER, JEAN HASLER (MRS. CHARLES HUNT PORTER), ednl. adminstr.; b. Buffalo, Jan. 29, 1922; d. Henry Louis and Ida May (Otto) H.; B.A., U. Buffalo, 1941; M.L.S., State U. N.Y. at Geneseo, 1951; m. Charles Hunt Porter, Feb. 9, 1945; 1 son, Charles Henry II. Librarian, tchr. English, Castile (N.Y.) High Sch., 1941-46; librarian Lydonville (N.Y.) Central Sch., 1949-54, tchr. English, 1949-51, tchr. French, 1952; librarian Newfane (N.Y.) Central Sch., 1954-62; ednl. communications dir. Orleans-Niagara Counties Bd. Coop. Ednl. Services, Sanborn, N.Y., 1962—. Cons. N.Y. State Edn. Dept., 1966—; dir. Library and Instrnl. Resources and Tech. Services Center Innovative ESEA Title III Project, 1966-69. Mem. A.L.A., N.Y. State Library Assn. (pres. 1971-72), N.Y. State Ednl. Communications Assn., N.Y. State Tchrs. Assn. (chmn. library sect. Western zone 1958-59, chmn. library sect. Northwestern zone 1966-67), Niagara-Orleans Area Assn. Sch. Librarians (pres. 1960-62), Sole Niagara County Supervisory Dist. Ednl. Assn. (pres. 1959-61), Delta Kappa Gamma (pres. 1974—). Contbr. articles to profl. jours. Home: 3739 Hartland Rd Gasport NY 14067 Office: 4124 Saunders Settlement Rd Sanborn NY 14132

PORTER, JENNY LIND, educator, poet; b. Fort Worth, Sept. 3, 1927; d. Drue Jackson and Josephine (Jones) Porter; B.A., Tex. Christian U., 1948, M.A., 1949; Ph.D., U. Tex., 1955, postgrad. 1955-56; D. Humane Letters (hon.), U. Free Asia, (Pakistan), 1970. Instr. U. Tenn. at Knoxville, 1958-59; asst. prof. West Tex. State U., Canyon, 1959-61; asst. prof. S.W. Tex. State U., San Marcos, 1961-64; chmn. dept. English Huston-Tillotson Coll., Austin, Tex., 1968—. Mem. Internat. Good Neighbor Council, Austin, 1972—. Named Poet Laureate of Tex., Tex. State Legislature, 1964, 65; recipient gold medal for poetry and humane activities, Govt. Philippines, 1970, gold medal for poetry, Leonardo da Vinci Acad., Rome, 1972. Mem. Am. Assn. U. Women (chpt. pres. 1968-69), Poetry Soc. Am. (Alice Fay di Castanda award 1970), Poetry Soc. Austin, Poetry Soc. Tex., Coll. Conf. Tchrs. English, Poets Laureate Internat., Leonardo da Vinci Acad. (Rome), The Rosicrucian Order. Club: Austin Woman's Symphony League. Condr. program on poetry, poets, writers Bookcase, KLRN-TV, 1963-64. Author: The Lantern of Diogenes, 1954; Azle and the Attic Room, 1957; The Witch Poesy, 1960 (books of poetry); On the Trellis of Memory (with Elithe Hamilton Kirkland), 1971. Articles, translations from French and Italian poems pub. in nat. and internat. periodicals including The Ladies Home Jour., Seventeen, Folio, Prairie Schooner, The N.Y. Times, The Personalist of USC, Wings, This is TCU, The Tex. Churchman, St. Anthony Messenger, The Classical Journal, The Golden Year Anthology of the Poetry Soc. Am., The Diamond Anthology of the Poetry Soc. Am., Tex. P.T.A., Surf, Stars and Stone, Tex. in Color, A Tex. Anthology. Home: 1713 Wethersfield Rd Austin TX 78703 Office: Huston-Tillotson Coll Austin TX 78702

PORTER, JOAN, county ofcl.; b. Kennedy, Ala., Mar. 31, 1947; d. Charles Alon and Geneva (Cork) Porter; B.S. in Elementary Edn., U. Ala., 1969, M.A. in Guidance and Counseling, 1970. Residence hall dir. U. Ala., 1969-70; residence hall counselor U. No. Ia., 1970-72; adminstrv. asst. Ala. Regional Council Govts., 1972; coordinator Scottsboro (Ala.)-Jackson County Child Devel. Center, 1973—. Mem. Nat. Assn. Women Deans, Adminstrs. and Counselors, Nat. Assn. Student Personnel Adminstrs., League Women Voters, Am. Assn. Univ. Women, Nat. Orgn. for Women. Home: 1506 S Broad St Scottsboro AL 35768 Office: Route 2 Box 470 Scottsboro AL 35768

PORTER, KAREN LYNNE, physician; b. Baton Rouge, La., May 18, 1942; d. Paul Burton and Jo Reeks (Rogillio) Porter; B.S., La. State U., 1964, M.D, 1967; m. Herbert R. Alexander, Sept. 1, 1973. Intern, Charity Hosp. La., 1967-68; fellow dept. dermatology Tulane U., 1968-69; resident Charity Hosp., 1969-72; practice medicine specializing in dermatology, New Orleans, 1971—; mem. staff St. Bernard Gen., Mercy, Sara Mayo hosps. (all New Orleans). Mem. Am. Acad. Dermatology, La. Dermatology Soc., Orleans Parish, La. med. socs., Alpha Delta Pi. Republican. Presbyn. Home: 813 Barracks St New Orleans LA 70116 Office: 3801 Canal St New Orleans LA 70119

PORTER, KATHERINE ANNE, writer; b. Indian Creek, Tex., May 15, 1890; d. Harrison Boone and Mary Alice (Jones) Porter; student in various pvt. schs.; D.Litt., Women's Coll., U. N.C., 1949; L.H.D., U. Mich., 1954; D.Litt., Smith Coll., 1958, Wheaton Coll., 1961, LaSalle Coll., 1962, Rutgers U., 1966; L.H.D., U. Md., 1966; m. Eugene Dove Pressly, Mar. 11, 1933 (div. Mar. 1938); m. 2d, Albert Russel Erskine, Jr., April 19, 1938 (div. 1942). Writer-in-residence, lectr. Leland Stanford U., 1949; guest lectr. U. Chgo., 1951; with English dept. U. Mich., 1953-54; Fulbright lectr. U. Liege, Belgium, 1955; Ford Found. grant in lit., 1959-61; Dept. State grant USIA lectr. Am. lit., Mexico, Trinidad, 1960, Asia, 1964; Regents' lectr. U. Cal., 1961. Mem. Pres.'s Commn. on Presdl. Scholars, 1964. Recipient Guggenheim fellowship for creative writing, 1931, 38; Book-of-the-Month Club award, 1937; first annual gold medal for lit. Soc. for Libraries of N.Y.U., 1940, for Pale Horse, Pale Rider; Ann. prize lit. work Tex. Inst. Lit., Dallas, 1950; Emerson-Thoreau medal Inst. Arts and Scis., 1962; 1st prize O'Henry Short Stories, 1962; Nat. Book award for fiction, 1966; Pulitzer award for fiction, 1966. Vice pres. Nat. Inst. Arts and Letters, 1950-52, Gold medal for fiction, 1967. Author: Flowering Judas, 1930; Hacienda, 1934; Noon Wine, 1937; Pale Horse, Pale Rider, 1939; The Itching Parrot (translation from Spanish), 1942; Preface to Fiesta in November (South American short stories), 1942. The Leaning Tower, Book of Short Stories, 1944; The Days Before, 1952; Ship of Fools, 1962; Collected Short Stories, 1965; A Christmas Story, 1967. Fellow Regional Am. Lit., Library of Congress, 1944. Contbr. book reviews and short stories to mags.; compiler, translator of French Song Book, 1933. Address: care Atlantic Monthly Press Boston MA 02101

PORTER, MARGARET EUDINE PRESTON (MRS. BERNARD HARDEN PORTER), pub. co. exec.; b. Rio Vista, Cal., June 1, 1905; d. James Henry and Mary Ann (McHugh) Preston; student U. Cal., Berkeley, 1935, Munson Bus. Coll., 1937; m. Bernard Harden Porter, Aug. 27, 1955. Dir. Bern Porter Books, Rockland, Me., 1955—, Bern Porter, Inc., Rockland, 1955—. Bd. dirs. Inst. Advanced Thinking, Rockland, 1959—. Cons. Small Bus. Adminstrn., 1968, Internat. Exec. Service Corp., 1968; corr. World Field Research, 1967—. Address: PO Box 17 Rockland ME 04841

PORTER, MAXIENE HELEN GREVE (MRS. DALE R. PORTER), civic worker; b. Los Angeles; d. Henry Chris and Meyerl (Dixon) Greve; student U. So. Cal., 1928; m. Wellington Denny Palmer, Nov. 18, 1929 (dec. Mar. 1933); children—Virginia (Mrs. William H. Stanhagen), Wellington Denny; m. 2d, Dale R. Porter, May 17, 1941. Accounting clk. Inglewood, Cal. Sch. System, 1948-51; dep. tax collector City of San Luis Obespo, Cal., 1963-65; accounting clk. San Luis Obispo County Schs., 1965-66; asst. innkeeper Holiday Inn, Darien, Conn., 1967, Alexandria, Va.; innkeeper Holiday Inn, Falls Church, Va., 1973—; asst. gen. mgr. Darien Motor Lodge Assos.; sec.-asst. treas. Seven Fountains Corp. Officer, Native Daus. Golden West, 1953—, state pres., 1959-60; chmn. various coms. Cal. Fedn. Womens Clubs, 1960-63; v.p. Bus. and Profl. Women, 1936-37; sec. Inglewood Coordinating Council, 1945-47, pres., 1947-48; pres., various other offices West Ebell Club, Los Angeles, 1947, 60-63; mem. pub. relations com. YWCA, Fairfax County, Va., 1967-68, Fairfax Hosp. Aux., 1967-68, spl. pub. com. Smithsonian Assn., 1967-68; sec.-treas. Pinecrest Citizens Assn., 1968, v.p., 1974; chmn. finance com. Va. Commn. Status of Women, 1973-75. Treas. Greater Falls Church Republican Womens Club, 1968-70, v.p., 1973-74; treas. Va. Fedn. Rep. Women, 1968—; vice-chmn. Va. Nixon Inaugural Com., 1968-69; treas. Va. Women for Nixon, 1968; mem. Fairfax County Nixon for Pres. Com., co-chmn. Fairfax County Ladies for Lin—Gov.'s Campaign, 1969; mem. Fairfax County Republican Com., 1968—, dist. chmn., 1974—. Mem. Fairfax County C. of C. (mem. legislation, edn., polit. activities coms. 1973-74), Nat. Trust for Historic Preservation, Nat. Hist. Soc., Va., Metro (mem. program com., v.p. 1972-73) motel assns., Am. Mgmt. Assn., Fairfax Cultural Assn. (membership com. mem. 1969—). Toastmistress Club: Pinecrest Garden. Lutheran. Home: 6436 Elmdale Rd Alexandria VA 22312

PORTER, OLGA LYONS (MRS. DONALD ROY PORTER), retail corp. exec.; b. New Orleans, Apr. 17, 1920; d. Theodore Hart and Yvonne (Labatt) Lyons; student New Orleans Secretarial Coll., 1937-38; m. Donald Roy Porter, July 8, 1938; children—Donald Roy, Jr., Theodore L., Cecil (Mrs. Wayne Williamson), Sharon (Mrs. Walter Jung III), Stephen L., Marcus, Andrew J. Mgr. Don Porter's Men Wear, New Orleans, 1939-50; agt. L.G. Balfour Co., New Orleans, 1940-51; mgr. Black Warrior Farms, Gallion, Ala., 1941-65; with Relco, Inc., Gallion, 1959—, gen. mgr., sec., treas., 1961—. Dir. Ala. Dairy Assn., Montgomery, 1956-57; dir., sec., treas. West Ala. Co-op., Demopolis, Ala., 1955-64. Chmn. Margengo County (Ala.) March of Dimes, 1949-55; program chmn. Demopolis P.T.A., Demopolis, 1947-48, Inaugarating Beauty Pageant, Demopolis, 1949-55, Halloween Carnival, Demopolis. Chmn., Hale County Republican party, 1951-54. Named County Mother of Year City of Demopolis, 1950; Outstanding Citizen, Key Club, 1953. Episcopalian. Clubs: Country, Luncheon (organizer 1952—), Silhouette (pres. 1964), Music Study (all Demopolis); Home Demonstration (pres. Gallion 1953-54). Home: Black Warrior Farms Gallion AL 36742 Office: Box 1 Porter's Rd Gallion AL 36742

PORTER, PARA BEATRICE WRIGHT (MRS. ANDREW W. PORTER), educator; b. Malone, Tex., Jan. 14, 1915; d. James Thomas and Margaret Jane (Wells) Wright; grad. cum laude, Hillsboro Jr. Coll., 1935; B.S., M.S., N. Tex. State U., 1938; postgrad. U. Houston, 1945, U. Tex., 1950, East Tex. State U., 1971; Ph.D., Baylor U., 1960; m. Andrew W. Porter, Dec. 23, 1935; children—Drue Annelle (Mrs. William O. Burt, Jr.), James Patrick. Tchr. elementary sch., Leroy, Tex., 1938-39, High Sch., Malone, 1939-43, Conroe, Tex., 1943-48, Avalon, Tex., 1948-49, Dawson, Tex., 1952-54, Hillsboro, Tex., 1954-61; supr. Hill County Schs., Hillsboro, 1949-51; asso. prof. edn., dir. student teaching, head secondary edn. dept. La. Coll., Pineville, 1961-62; asst. prof. edn. East Tex. State U., Commerce, 1962-66; asst. prof. edn., supr. student tchrs. Baylor U., Waco, Tex., 1966-71; supt. Bosqueville Ind. Sch. Dist., 1971-72; supr. McLennan County Schs., Waco, 1972. Tex. state adv. com. Tex. Assn. Edn. Young Children, 1969-70. Mem. Tex. State Tchrs. Assn. (sec. 1958), N.E.A., Internat. (lectr., panelist 1967, 69, 71), Centex reading assns., Assn. Childhood Edn., Internat. (resource person, group leader 1966, 68, 70), Nat., Tex. assns. edn. young children, Am. Assn. Higher Edn., Nat. Council Tchrs. Math., Assn. Supervision and Curriculum Devel., So. Assn. Children Under Six, Tex. Assn. Improvement Reading, Tex. Soc. Tchrs. Edn., Elementary Kindergarten Nursery Edn., Internat. Platform Assn. Baptist. Author: What to Teach in Reading: Practical Activities, 1970; co-author Practical Ideas and Activities for Pre-School Enrichment Programs, 1966. Contbr. articles to profl. jours. Home: 1616 S 9th St Waco TX 76706

PORTER, PRISCILLA MANNING, ceramic and glass products artist; b. Balt., Feb. 1, 1917; d. William Hamilton and Amy Russell (Manning) Porter; B.A. in Sci., Bennington Coll., Vt., 1940. Tchr. sci. and math. pvt. schs., N.Y.C., 1943-53; tchr. ceramics and glass dept. edn. Museum Modern Art, N.Y.C., 1952-61; tchr. courses in fused glass Brookfield (Conn.) Craft Center, 1961-66, Worcester (Mass.) Craft Center, 1964-66; craftsman of fused glass, 1966—; represented in permanent collection Corning Mus. Glass, New Britain Mus. of Art. Pres. Washington Vis. Nurse Assn., 1970-72. Mem. Phila. Art Alliance, Soc. Conn. Craftsmen, Washington Art Assn. (mem. art and exhbn. com. 1961—), Artist-Craftsmen N.Y. (award of merit 1968). Republican. Address: Plumb Hill Rd Washington CT 06793

PORTER, S(YLVIA) F(IELD), writer; b. Patchogne, L.I., N.Y., June 18, 1913; d. Louis and Rose (Maisel) Feldman; B.A. magna cum laude, Hunter Coll., 1932; postgrad. Grad. Sch. Bus. Adminstrn., N.Y.U.; hon. degrees, Bryant Coll., Hood Coll., Western Coll. for Women, Bates Coll., Catawba Coll., Russell Sage Coll., Tufts U., Ft. Lauderdale U., U. Portland, Allegheny Coll.; m. Reed R. Porter, 1931; m. 2d, Sumner Collins, 1943. Editor weekly news letter Reporting on Govts.; asso. N.Y. Post, 1935—, now financial columnist writing syndicated daily column, monthly column Ladies Home Jour. Mem. Phi Beta Kappa. Author: How To Make Money in Government Bonds; If War Comes to the American Home; Sylvia Porter's Annual Income Tax Guide; co-author: How To Live Within Your Income; Managing Your Money. Home: 2 Fifth Av New York City NY 10011 Office: 30 E 42d St New York City NY 10017

PORTER, VIRGINIA PILLOW (MRS. GEORGE H. PORTER), anesthesiologist; b. Buffalo, July 31, 1933; d. Chester M. and Estelle (Wise) Pillow; A.B., Duke, 1954, M.D., 1958; m. George H. Porter, Apr. 5, 1958; 1 dau., Virginia Mapp. Intern, Duke Hosp., 1958-59; resident anesthesiology Peter Bent Brigham Hosp., Boston, 1958-59; instr. Harvard Med. Sch., 1960-61; asst. prof. George Washington U. Sch. Medicine, 1961-64; anesthesiologist, Oshsner Med. Center, New Orleans, 1964—. Mem. Phi Beta Kappa. Home: 1330 Eleonore St New Orleans LA 70115 Office: 1516 Jefferson Hwy New Orleans LA 70121

PORTNER, MILDRED CHAFFIN (MRS. STUART PORTNER), govt. ofcl.; b. Ithaca, Mich., June 2, 1911; d. Perry Francis and Helen M. (Belding) Chaffin; student U. Mich., 1939-40; m. Stuart Portner, June 24, 1939; children—James Perry, Julie. Adminstrv. asst. Mich. Hwy. Dept., Lansing, 1929-30, Mich. Securities Commn., 1930-33; bus. mgr. Works Progress Adminstrn., Lansing and Detroit, 1935-39; asso. Reports Analysis, Detroit, 1939-40; dir. personnel People's Dept. Store, 1940-42; sec. library Library of Congress, Washington, 1946—. Mem. A.L.A., D.C. Library Assn., Soc. Am. Archivists, Soc. Personnel Adminstrn., Capital Hill Assn., Mich. State Club. Episcopalian. Home: 2500 Virginia Av NW Washington DC 20037 Office: Library of Congress Washington DC 20540

PORTTEUS, ELNORA MARIE MANTHEI (MRS. PAUL PORTTEUS), librarian; b. Rosendale, Wis.; d. H. R. and Anna M. (Kentop) Manthei; student Oshkosh State Coll., 1937-39; B.S., U. Wis., 1941; M.A., Kent State U., 1954; m. Paul Portteus, Oct. 19, 1942; children—Carrie Jo (Mrs. J.P. Thomas), Lane Paul, Andre Eugene. Librarian, tchr. Racine-Kenosha Normal Sch., 1942; library asst. Fed. Res. Bank of Cleve., 1943; asst. librarian Indsl. Relations Counselors N.Y., 1947-48; librarian Findlay (O.) City Schs., 1948-58; asst. prof. dept. library sci. Kent State U., 1958-65; directing supr. ednl. media services Cleve. Bd. Edn., 1965—. Cons., Coop. Ednl. Services, Columbus, 1956—; adv. bd. H.W. Wilson Standard Catalogue Series. Dir. NDEA Inst., 1965. Mem. adv. bd. library tech. program Cuyahoga Community Coll., adv. bd. Sch. Library Sci. Kent State U. Chmn. Findlay Council Youth Serving Agys., 1954-56. Recipient 1st place Ency. Britannica Sch. Library, 1967; Distinguished Alumna award, Kent State U., 1967. Mem. Am. Assn. U. Women, Am. (chmn. adv. com. Midwest Program on Airborn TV Instrn. 1964-68; John Cotton Dana Publicity award, 1967, 70, 1st v.p., pres. 1972-74), Ohio (pres. 1957-58) assns. sch. librarians, Ohio Library Assn. (chmn. book examination center com. 1964-65, chmn. scholarship com. 1965-67; Ohio Librarian of Yr. 1972), Ohio Edn. Assn., A.L.A., Order Eastern Star, Beta Phi Mu, Delta Kappa Gamma. Contbr. articles to profl. jours.; reviewer Library Jour. Jr. Books. Home: 7357 West Lake Blvd Kent OH 44240 Office: 10600 Quincy Av Cleveland OH 44106

POSEY, SUSANN MARIE FRIDINGER (MRS. WILLIAM ROBERT POSEY), educator; b. Waynesboro, Pa., Aug. 4, 1946; d. John William and Zelma Louise (Black) Fridinger; B.A. in Edn., Shippensburg State Coll., 1968; postgrad., 1969; postgrad. Western Md. Coll., 1968-69, Coppin State Coll., 1970-71, Am. U., 1972-73; m. William Robert Posey, June 20, 1969; 1 son, Brian William. Librarian, tchr. Victor Cullen Sch., Sabillasville, Md., 1967-73, head tchr., 1973-74; now employed Grove Mfg. Co., Shady Grove, Pa. Part-time coordinator library services Md. State Dept. Juvenile Services Balt., 1972-73. Mem. com. for inservice tng. Dept. Juvenile Services Md., 1969-73. Mem. Md., Cumberland Valley library assns., St. John's Ladies Guild, Gamma Y Gradale (v.p. 1972-75). Moose. Home: Route 4 Box 308A Waynesboro PA 17268

POSNER, KATHLEEN WEIL-GARRIS (MRS. DONALD POSNER), educator; b. Cheam, Surrey, Eng., Apr. 7, 1934; d. Kurt Hermann and Charlotte (Garris) Weil; A.B., Vassar Coll., 1956; postgrad. U. Bonn (Germany), 1956-57; M.A., Radcliffe Coll., 1958; Ph.D., Harvard, 1965; m. Donald Posner, June 25, 1962. Prof. fine arts N.Y. U., 1963—. Fulbright grantee, 1957. Mem. Coll. Art. Assn. Am. (dir.), Renaissance Soc. Am., Am. Assn. U. Women, Am. Assn. U. Profs., Istituto per la Storia dell'arte Lombarda, Phi Beta Kappa. Home: 37 Washington Square W New York City NY 10011 Office: 1 E 78th St New York City NY 10021

POSNER, MARY MCCLEARY (MRS. ALAN KENT POSNER), pub. relations exec.; b. Kansas City, Mo., Mar. 21, 1939; d. Glenn Avann and Julia Porter (Quinby) McCleary; student Ohio Wesleyan U., 1957-59; A.B., U. Mo., 1961; M.A., Ind. U., 1962; postgrad. N.Y. U., 1966-70; m. Alan Kent Posner, Dec. 27, 1965. Pub. relations supr. long lines div. Am. Tel. & Tel. Corp., N.Y.C., 1962-68; v.p., Harshe-Rotman & Druck, N.Y.C., 1968-74, sr. v.p., 1974—. Mem. N.Y. dist. adv. council U.S. Small Bus. Adminstrn., 1972-74. Sec.-treas. Women's Nat. Republican Club, 1971-73. Bd. dirs. Ohio Wesleyan U. Mem. Internat. Pub. Relations Assn., Delta Delta Delta. Home: 673 King St Chappaqua NY 10514 Office: 300 E 44th St New York City NY 10017

POST, ANNABEL DOROTHY, editor; b. Sumner, Wash., Dec. 15, 1922; d. Leslie Wallace and Mildred June (Bothwell) Post; B.S., U. Washington, 1945. Tchr. home econs. pub. high sch. Vashon, Wash., 1944-46, Everett, Wash., 1946-50; staff home economist Woman's Home Companion mag., N.Y.C., 1950-53, asso. food editor, 1954-56; food editor Sunset Mag., Menlo Park, Cal., 1957—. Cons. editor for Sunset Books. Mem. Am., Cal., Bay Dist. home econs. assns., Home Economists in Bus. (mem. nat. and San Francisco chpts. 1951—). Home: 1747 Alma St Palo Alto CA 94301 Office: Sunset Magazine Menlo Park CA 94025

POST, ANNE BRETZFELDER (MRS. JOSEPH POST), artist; b. St. Louis; d. Ira L. and Belle (Schlesinger) Bretzfelder; B.A., Bennington Coll., 1938; m. Joseph Post, Mar. 1, 1942; children—David, Thomas. Exhibited Toledo Mus. Art, St. Louis Mus. Art, Bennington Mus. Art, J.B. Neumann Gallery, N.Y.C., Soc. Ind. Artists, N.Y.C., and St. Louis; rep. Mo. at Contemporary Arts Exhibit, N.Y. Worlds Fair; exhibited Mus. of State U. N.J., N.Y.U., So. Vt. Art Assn., Sculpture Center, N.Y.C., Art World Gallery, Boston, Artists Little Gallery, N.Y.C., Gallery Beyond Blue Door, L.I., Klotz-Makowiecki, Stuttgart, Germany, Twentieth Century Gallery, Williamsburg, Va., Cooper Union Mus. Gallery; represented in permanent collections Bennington Coll. Fine Arts, Wellesley Coll., Norfolk (Va.) Mus., Israel Mus., Jerusalem Israel, Sawdust Gallery, N.Y.C., U. Chgo. Dept. Fine Arts, accept (N.Y. Council on Alcholism) Greenwich House, N.Y.C., Artista Gallery, L.I., La Maison Francaise, N.Y.U.; represented in pvt. collections in U.S., Japan, Eng., Europe; retrospective exhibit, N.Y.C., 1960, traveling exhibit, N.J., 1960. Tchr. army hosps., W.Va., Tex. settlement house, People's Art Center, St. Louis. Home: 29 Washington Sq W New York City NY 10011

POST, ELIZABETH LINDLEY (MRS. WILLIAM G. POST), author; b. Englewood, N.J., May 7, 1920; d. Allen L. and Elizabeth (Ellsworth) Lindley; grad. high sch.; m. William G. Post, Aug. 5, 1944; children—Allen C., William G., Lucinda Ann, Peter L. Dir., Emily Post Inst., 1965—; author syndicated newspaper column Doing the Right Thing, 1966—. Republican. Episcopalian. Author: Emily Post's Book of Etiquette for Young People, 1968; Wonderful World of Weddings, 1970; Please Say Please, 1972. Revised Emily Post's Etiquette, 1965, 69, 75. Home: North Hill Farm Waterbury Center VT 05677 Office: 6 E 45th St New York City NY 10017

POST, MARGARET MOORE (MRS. H. JOHN POST), journalist; b. Plainfield, Ind., Aug. 16, 1909; d. Robert Wans and Virginia (Rupe) Stephenson; student U. Mich., 1926-27, Butler U., summer 1929; A.B., La. State U., 1930; L.H.D., Franklin Coll., 1973; m. Everett Laurence Moore, Dec. 4, 1932 (dec. Mar. 1952); children—Jo Ann (Mrs. David E. Long), Sue Ellen (Mrs. M. Stanton Evans); m. 2d, H. John Post, June 27, 1970. Editor, The Reveille, La. State U. newspaper, 1929-30; reporter Logansport (Ind.) Press, 1930-32; editor Mooresville (Ind.) Times, 1933-38; columnist Indpls. Star, 1932-42; head journalism dept. Franklin Coll., 1942-51; copy editor Indpls. News, 1952-53; pub. relations Indpls. Star and Indpls. News, 1952-68; polit. writer Indpls. News, 1968—. Tchr. journalism Ind. U. at Indpls., 1954-55; tchr. creative writing N. Central High Sch., Indpls., 1962-63. Mem. Mayor's Manpower Commn., 1964—, Indpls. Community Service Council, 1960—, Indpls. Parent-Tchr. Council 1965—, Soc. for Intensified Edn., 1965—, Gov.'s Criminal Justice Planning Agy., 1969—, Nat. Adv. Commn. on Criminal Justice Standards and Goals, coordinator Indpls. Anti-Crime Crusade; speaker on How To Fight 1971—, Pres.'s Commn. on Crime Prevention, 1972; Crime at White House, 1968. Bd. dirs. News Camp for Children, Indpls., 1954-60, Settlements Camping, Inc., 1959—, Concord Center Settlement House, 1959—, Nat. Soc. for Prevention of Blindness, 1954—, United Cerebral Palsy Ind., 1960—. Named Ind. Mother of Year, 1956-66. Mem. Ind. Woman's Press Club (pres. 1942-44), Indpls. Press Club, Am. Acad. Polit. and Social Sci., U.S. C. of C. (crime control panel 1959—), Nat. Council Women (woman of conscience award 1968), Ind. Acad., Ind. Forum, Indpls. C. of C., Gen. Fedn. Women's Clubs (law enforcement chmn. 1968—), Bus. and Profl. Women's Club, Nat. Fedn. Bus. and Profl. Women's Clubs, Nat. League Am. Pen Women, Theta Sigma Phi (nat. sec. 1947-53, nat. headliner 1968), Delta Kappa Gamma. Republican. Quaker religion. Clubs: Altrusa; Delta Gamma Social Sorority Mothers (pres. 1955-56). Author: (with M. Stanton Evans) The Law Breakers (Book of Month Club Selection), 1968. Home: 5343 N Arlington Av Indianapolis IN 46226 Office: 307 N Pennsylvania St Indianapolis IN 46206

POSTELL, PATRICIA LUCK (MRS. PAUL E. POSTELL), librarian; b. New Orleans, Mar. 17, 1911; d. William Theophile and Eugenie Patten (Grosch) Luck; A.B., Ursuline Coll., 1932; B.S. in L.S., La. State U., 1933; m. Paul E. Postell, Dec. 24, 1935; children—Paul Everett, Patricia (Mrs. Julian C. Roberts), Kathleen (Mrs. Donald D. Stephens), Virginia (Mrs. Roy Y. Gaylor, Jr.), Rebecca (Mrs. Ronald E. Jones), Mark W. Librarian, Xavier U., New Orleans, 1933-36; asst. librarian La. Library Commn., Baton Rouge, 1937-40; librarian St. Margaret's Hosp., Montgomery, Ala., 1949-51; acting librarian Oak Ridge Pub. Library, 1957-60, dir., 1960—. Mem. Am., Tenn., Southeastern library assns., Oak Ridge Hist. Assn. (dir.). Roman Catholic. Home: 502 Michigan Av Oak Ridge TN 37830 Office: Oak Ridge Pub Library Civic Center Oak Ridge TN 37830

POSTON, ALICE MARIE, educator; b. Boiling Springs, N.C., Jan. 25, 1940; d. Hoyle and Genie Lee (Davis) Poston; B.S., N.C. Central U., 1963, M.S., 1968; postgrad. Columbia, 1968-69. Head dept. phys. edn. Inbordin High Sch., Enfield, N.C., 1963-65; instr. to asst. prof. dance and statistics Bowie State Coll., Md., 1965—, head dept. phys. edn., 1967-68. Chmn. dance com. div. girls and women's sports State of Md.; pres. bd. dirs. Prince Georges Dance Theatre; talent cons. Md. Correctional Prison Camp (Jessups). Recipient award, Md. Correctional Camp Center, 1974. Mem. Bowie Fine Arts Soc. (dir. 1973-74), A.H.P.E.R., Md. Assn. Phys. Edn. and Recreation, Md. Tchrs. Assn., Md. Council for Dance. Author: Manual for Beginning Statistic Students, 1972. Home: 2501 25th St SE Washington DC 20020 Office: Bowie State College Bowie MD 20715

POSWISTILO, MARGARET HOLLAND (MRS. FRANK S. POSWISTILO), lawyer; b. Phila., Feb. 14, 1926; d. Daniel Edward and Kathleen (Mills) Holland; B.A., Rosemont Coll., 1947; M.A., U. Pa., 1949; LL.B., Temple U., 1953; m. Frank S. Poswistilo, Jan. 14, 1956; children—Kathleen, Margaret, Susan, Marianne, Stephen. High sch. tchr., Phila. Pub. Schs., 1949-56; admitted to Pa. bar, 1954; atty. City of Easton (Pa.), 1956-70; pvt. practice law, Easton, part-time 1956—, asst. pub. defender Northampton County, 1972—. Chmn., Easton Charter Study Commn., 1969-70. Democratic telephone campaign chmn. nat. congl. campaign, 1962, 68. Mem. Northampton County Bar Assn., Am. Assn. U. Women, Lawyers Wives. Roman Catholic. Address: 204 N 13th St Easton PA 18042

POTE, DORIS R., lawyer, educator; b. Mass.; d. Guy S. and Margaret E. (Lyons) Pote; A.B. cum laude, Radcliffe Coll.; J.D, Suffolk U., 1967; postgrad. Harvard Law Sch., 1972. Treas., Conant Littleton Co., Littleton, Mass., 1950-62; asst. to v.p. 1st Realty Co., Boston, 1962-67; admitted to Mass. bar, 1967; registrar, asso. prof. law Suffolk U. Law Sch., Boston, 1967—. Trustee Consumer Affairs Found., Inc., Boston, 1972—. Mem. Am., Mass. (chmn. consumer affairs subcom. 1972—) bar assns., Mass. Assn. Women Lawyers (pres. 1972-73), Phi Beta Kappa. Home: 46 Clinton Rd Brookline MA 02146 Office: 41 Temple St Boston MA 02114

POTEET, FRANCES THERESA RIHA (MRS. EUGENE ADAMS POTEET), govt. ofcl.; b. Omaha, Aug. 1, 1921; d. James August and Marie Magdeline (Svoboda) Riha; student U. Mo., 1955-56; student U. Kan., 1947-50; student Omaha U., 1938-40; m. Eugene Adams Poteet, Feb. 9, 1963; 1 dau., Riha Maria Linde Rushlau. Asst. comptroller Westminster Enterprises Ltd., St. Louis, 1960-64; mem. staff Mo. State Council on Arts, 1965-73; cons. Nat. Endowment for Arts, 1969—, regional coordinator, 1973—. Mem. adv. panel on dance Nat. Council on Arts, 1969-72. Mem. adv. panel Mo. Dept. Edn., 1968—; mem. adv. com. St. Louis chpt. Young Audiences, Inc., 1968—. Bd. dirs. St. Louis Symphony Soc., 1971—, Arts and Edn. Council Grater St. Louis, 1974—. Mem. Nat. Assn. Regional Ballet (dir. 1969—), N.Am. Assembly State and Provincial Arts Councils (mem. exec. com. 1970-73), Music Educators Nat. Conf. (mem. study com. 1970), Asso. Councils on Arts, Am. Symphony Orch. League, Am. Nat. Theatre Assn. Home: 7440 Somerset St St Louis MO 63105 Office: 7440 Somerset St Louis MO 63105

POTENZA, DAISY MCKASKLE (MRS. JULIUS ORIAN POTENZA), newspaperwoman; b. Houston, Mar. 5, 1906; d. George Washington and Dora Amy (Crump) McKaskle; student Sinclair Bus. Coll., 1925, Massey's Bus. Coll., 1924-26, U. Houston; m. Julius Orian Potenza, Sept. 26, 1928; 1 dau., Marjorie Ann (Mrs. William L. Hale) (dec.). With Houston Chronicle, 1926—, adminstrv. asst. to editor-in-chief, 1930—. Exec. sec. Houston Endowment, Inc., 1968-69. Mem. Nat., Tex. press women, Women in Communications, Press Club Houston (hon. life). Democrat. Methodist. Club: Farm and Ranch. Home: 2405 San Felipe Rd Houston TX 77019 Office: 801 Texas Av Houston TX 77002

POTTER, BARBARA ANN, mag. pub. exec.; b. Chgo., Apr. 19, 1945; d. John Francis and Mignonne Elinor (Huffman) Burke; student U. Chgo., summers 1964, 65; B.A. (Univ. scholar), Purdue U., 1967; Programmer, data processing Time, Inc., Chgo., 1967, interviewer, personnel dept., 1967-69, asst. employment mgr., personnel dept., 1969-70, dept. head, mag. subscriber relations, 1970-72, mem. adminstrv. staff, 1972—; mng. dir. Ron Nielsen Photography, Nielsen Communication Team, Four Quarters, Chgo., 1973—. Vol. worker Children's Meml. Hosp., 1969-72, Rehab. Inst. Chgo., 1973—. Mem. Women in Communications (2d v.p. membership 1974-75, chmn. hospitality com. 1973-74), Chgo. Press Club, Purdue Alumni Assn., Mortar Bd., Zeta Tau Alpha. Presbyn. Club: Canyon. Home: 175 E Delaware St Chicago IL 60611 Office: 541 N Fairbanks Ct Chicago IL 60611

POTTER, CAROL ANN, lawyer, educator; b. New Orleans, Sept., 1943; d. Roger N. and Lucille (Coffman) Potter; B.A., U. Ia., 1965; M.A. (Woodrow Wilson fellow), U. Cal. at Berkeley, 1967; J.D., Boalt Hall Sch. Law, 1971. Instr., U. Hawaii, Honolulu, 1968-69; admitted to Cal. Bar, 1972; asst. prof. bus. law San Diego State U., 1971-72, 73—; asst. prof. legal studies U. Mass., Amherst, 1972-73. Mem. Am., Cal. bar assns., Sierra Club, Am. Civil Liberties Union, Phi Beta Kappa.

POTTER, ELOISE FRETZ (MRS. JAMES MCCONNELL POTTER, JR.), editor; b. Norfolk, Va., Feb. 17, 1931; d. James B. and Lillian Doreatha (Rackley) Fretz; student Meredith Coll., 1949-50; m. James McConnell Potter, Jr., June 12, 1950; children—James Brian, David Theodore, Crystal Lillian, Patricia Eileen. Editor, Chat, Tryon, N.C., 1963—. Methodist. Club: Carolina Bird (Tryon). Home: PO Box 277 Zebulon NC 27597

POTTER, FAY ANN ALDRIN, art gallery dir.; b. Dayton, O., June 12, 1928; d. Edwin Eugene and Marion Gladys (Moon) Aldrin; B.S., Hood Coll., Frederick, Md., 1950; m. Stanley C. Potter, Sept. 9, 1950 (div.); children—Dana Ross, Tom Carleton, Holly Manchester. Asso. Carl Solway Gallery, Cin., 1968-73; asso. dir. William Sawyer Gallery, San Francisco, 1973—. Asst. Urban Walls Project, Cin., 1972-73; pres. Hyde Park P.T.A., Cin., 1965-66. Mem. Alpha Psi Omega. Club: Cincinnati Garden. Home: 63 Barbaree Way Tiburon CA 94920 Office: 3045 Clay St San Francisco CA 94115

POTTER, JACQUELINE RILEY (MRS. ERNEST ELLIOTT POTTER), advt. agy. exec.; b. Joplin, Mo., Dec. 8, 1929; d. Perry Cromwell and Lorraine Crystal (Hammons) Riley; A.A., U. Cal. at Berkeley, 1949, U. Ill., 1951; m. Ernest Elliott Potter, Feb. 4, 1951; children—Jamey Neal, Lisa Gail. Tchr., Ludlow (Ill.) Pub. Sch., 1951-52; jr. copywriter Spiegel's Co., Chgo., 1952-53; continuity editor KSWM Radio, Joplin, 1953-54; advt. copywriter Carthage Marble Corp. (Mo.), 1953-62, advt. mgr., 1962-67; pres. Jacqueline Potter Advt. Agy., Carthage, 1967—. Mem. Citizen's Commn. Carthage, 1972—. Bd. dirs. Carthage Pub. Library. Recipient Advt. Excellence award Archtl. Record, 1965. Mem. Carthage Type Writers' Guild (v.p. 1973—), Shakespeare Soc., P.E.O. Methodist (chmn. commn. edn., mem. adminstrv. bd. 1965-67, pub. chmn. bldg. com. 1973—). Contbr. poems, articles to mags. Address: 608 W Highland St Carthage MO 64836

POTTER, LEONA JOHNSTON (MRS. HAROLD L. BOYD), county welfare dir.; b, Creekside, Pa., Aug. 31, 1907; d. Joseph M. and Belle (McHenry) Johnston; grad Ind. Normal Sch., 1927; student Las Vegas Normal U., summer 1933; courses Carnegie Inst. Techn. Sch. Social Work, summer 1945, U. Pitts. Grad. Sch. Social Work, 1956-57; m. Edgar D. Potter, July 16, 1932 (div.); m. 2d, Harold L. Boyd, Oct. 9, 1972. Tchr. Creekside pub. schs., 1927-30, Papago Indian Reservation, Sells, Ariz., 1931-33; caseworker, supr., Indiana County (Pa.) Bd. Assistance, 1934-54, exec. dir., 1954-68, ret. 1968. Cons. asso. Community Research Assos., N.Y.C. Recipient Ind. Jaycees award for distinguished Service, 1966. Mem. Daus. Am. Colonists, Indiana County Hist. Soc., Indiana County Tourist Promotion Bur. (hon. life), Sierra County (N.M.) Hist. Soc. (sec.). Lutheran. Clubs: Truth or Consequences (N.M.) Women's Soroptimist, Hot Springs Woman's. Home: Box 78 Route 2 Hillsboro NM 88042

POTTER, LOIS SHEFTE (MRS. ALBERT A. POTTER), educator, speech cons.; b. Volga, S.D., Dec. 15, 1924; d. E.K. and Laura (Johnson) Shefte; B.A., Yankton Coll., 1946; postgrad. U. S.D., 1947; M.A., U. Ia., 1950; Ph.D., U. Wis., 1959; m. Albert A. Potter, June 18, 1960; 1 son, Lee; 1 stepson, Donald. Tchr., Redfield (S.D.) High Sch., 1946-47, Yankton (S.D.) High Sch., 1947-49; instr. speech pathology, speech cons. U. No. Ia., Cedar Falls, 1950-53, asst. prof., cons., 1954-59, asso. prof., 1959-72, prof., 1972—; diagnostician, speech therapist U. Wis. Hosps., Madison, 1953-54. U.S. Office Edn. grantee, 1956, summers 1958, 1959; Am. Speech and Hearing Found. grantee, 1959. Mem. Am., Ia. speech and hearing assns., Council for Exceptional Children, Ia. Council for Exceptional Children, Central States Speech Assn., Nat. Council Tchrs. English, Assn. for Student Teaching, Phi Lambda Theta, Sigma Alpha Eta. Contbr. articles to profl. jours. Office: Dept Teaching Malcolm Price Lab Sch U No Ia Cedar Falls IA 50613

POTTER, LOUISE FRANCES, educator; b. Ware, Mass., Oct. 10, 1920; d. Harris James and Ethel Rosamond (Howard) Potter; B.S., U. Mass., 1942; M.A., Smith Coll., 1944; Ph.D., U. Wis., 1947. Instr., U. Wis., Madison, 1946-47, Smith Coll., Northampton, Mass., 1947-49; faculty Vassar Coll., Poughkeepsie, N.Y., 1949-60, asso. prof., 1955-60; prof. Windham Coll., Putney, Vt., 1962-63; asso. prof. div. natural scis. Elmira (N.Y.) Coll., 1963-65, prof., 1965—. Cons. Schering Corp. Chmn. adv. com. Ret. Sr. Vol. Program, 1973—. Bd. dirs. Coop. Extension Chemung County, 1968-74, mem. program com., 1974—. Ford Found. fellow, 1953-54; sr. faculty fellow NSF, 1959-60, research grantee, 1951-61. Fellow A.A.A.S.; mem. Am. Chem. Soc., Am. Soc. Microbiology, Am. Pub. Health Assn., Soc. Gen. Microbiology, N.Y. Acad. Scis., Bus. and Profl. Women, Sigma Xi. Home: 850 Hofman St Elmira NY 14901

POTTER, SALLY NEIDERT (MRS. WYATT POTTER), librarian; b. Rochester, N.Y., Apr. 10, 1925; d. Frank and Ethel (Ross) Neidert; B.S., State U. N.Y. at Brockport, 1945; M.L.S., Syracuse U., 1967; m. Wyatt Potter, July 2, 1946; children—Lynette (Mrs. Wayne Tuttle), Allan F., Douglas R. Tchr. English, Holley (N.Y.) Pub. Schs., 1945-46; substitute tchr. Liverpool (N.Y.) Central Sch. Dist., 1957-63; jr. high sch. librarian, Liverpool, 1963-65; trainee Liverpool Pub. Library, 1965-67; tech. service librarian Onondaga Community Coll., Syracuse, N.Y., 1967—, media librarian, 1972, acting chmn. library dept., 1970-71, asso. prof., 1973—. Field adviser tech. service projects Syracuse U. Sch. Library Sci., 1971-74, alumni rep. to curriculum com., 1971-72. Trustee, v.p. Liverpool Pub. Library, 1958-62. Mem. A.L.A., N.Y. Library Assn., Syracuse U. Sch. Library Sci. Alumni Assn. (pres. 1973-75), Beta Phi Mu. Home: 222 Buckley Rd Liverpool NY 13088 Office: Coulter Library Onondaga Community Coll Syracuse NY 13215

POTTMYER, ALICE ANN ALLRED (MRS. JAMES J. POTTMYER), editor; b. Rapid City, S.D.; d. Berten Wendell and Alice (Worthington) Allred; B.S., Brigham Young U., 1960; m. 2d, James J. Pottmyer, Apr. 17, 1971; 1 dau., Laura Marie. Brigham Young U. corr. to Salt Lake Tribune, 1959-60; pub. relations asst. Lawrence Jeppson Assos., Washington, 1960-61; publs. editor Am. Vets. Nat. Hdqrs., Washington, 1961-65; dir. publs. Nat. Soc. Pub. Accountants, Washington, 1965-70; mng. editor phys. therapy Am. Phys. Therapy Assn., Washington, 1970-72; freelance editor, 1972—. Publicity chmn. D.C. Theatre Festival, Dept. Recreation, Washington, 1967. Bd. dirs. Hollyday House of Adams-Morgan, Inc., Washington. Mem. Soc. Nat. Assn. Publs. (dir. 1968-70; sec. 1971; treas. 1972). Mem. Ch. of Jesus Christ of Latter-day Saints. Home: 5540 N 32d St Arlington VA 22207

POTTS, GENEVIEVE GRACE, sch. librarian; b. Wetumka, Okla., Feb. 3, 1937; d. Robert Houston and Helen Ruth (La Shier) Potts; B.A., N.M. Highlands U., 1959, postgrad., 1961, 71; M.A., U. Denver, 1962-63; postgrad. U. N.M., 1960, 64, 71, 73, Our Lady of Lake Coll., 1966, Utah State U., 1972, Adams State Coll. Colo., 1972. Tchr. Gallup-McKinley County Schs., Gallup, N.M., 1959-62, librarian John F. Kennedy Jr. High Sch., 1963—. Mem. Am. Assn. U. Women (pres. 1973—), Delta Kappa Gamma (chpt. pres. 1970-71). Presbyn. Home: PO Box 874 926 Cerrito Dr Gallup NM 87301

POU, EMILY HOTCHKISS (MRS. JOHN WILLIAM POU), univ. dean; b. Pitts.; d. Leonard B. and Thelma (Jennings) Hotchkiss; B.S., Ga. State Coll. for Women, 1948; M.S., U. Wis., 1962, Ph.D., 1964; m. Robert Earl, Aug. 25, 1955 (div. June 1958); 1 son, David Michael; m. 2d, John William Pou, Oct. 6, 1973. Extension home economist U. Ga., Athens, 1955-56, U. Ariz. Tucson, 1956-61; fellow U. Wis., Madison, 1961-63; asso. prof. edn. N.C. State U., Raleigh, 1964-67, prof. edn. and state leader of tng., 1967-71; dean Sch. Home Econs., U. Ga., Athens, 1971—. Mem. Adult Edn. Assn. of U.S., Ga. Adult Edn. Assn., Am., Ga. home econs. assns., So. Assn. Home Econs. Adminstrs., Assn. Adminstrs. Home Econs. (exec. bd.), Ga. Nutrition Council, Acad. Outstanding Tchrs., Phi Upsilon Omicorn, Omicron Nu, Delta Kappa Gamma. Author: (with E. J. Boone, E. H. Quinn) Curriculum Development in Adult Basic Education, 1967. Cons. editor Adult Edn. jour. Home: 175 Baxter Dr K-8 Athens GA 30601

POULIOT, SISTER YVONNE, hosp. adminstr.; b. Berlin, N.H., Feb. 14, 1916; d. Wilfrid Joseph and Eva M. (Morin) Pouliot; B.A., Rivier Coll., Nashua, N.H., 1966. Tchr. Norway House, Man., 1940-43; accountant, clk. Flin Flan (Man.) Gen. Hosp., 1943-48, gen. bursar, 1958-60; tchr. St. Theresa Parish, Man., 1943-58; asst. gen. Sisters of Charity, 1960-66, superior gen., 1966-72; personnel dir., bus. mgr. St. Anthony's Gen. Hosp., The Pas, Man., Can., 1972—. Home: 67 1st St The Pas MB R9A 1K4 Canada Office: Box 240 The Pas MB Canada

POULSON, JENNIEV JORGENSEN, educator; b. Provo, Utah; d. Mads and Melinda (Baum) Jorgensen; B.S., Brigham Young U., 1933; M.S., Ia. State U., 1954, Ph.D., 1964; postgrad. Cornell U., 1957; m. William Lavern Smith, Aug. 11, 1927 (dec. June 1929); children—Lavern J., Joseph Lorain; m. 2d, M. Wilford Poulson, June 12, 1936 (div. 1941); 1 dau., Jennie Lin (Mrs. John Ray Strong). Home econs. tchr. Jordan Sch. Dist., Union, Utah, 1933-36; med. sec. Utah State Hosp., Provo, 1942-46; social worker Utah County Welfare Dept., 1947; county home agt. Utah State U., Utah County, 1947-58; asst. state supr. home econs. programs extension services, 1958-61; chmn. dept. housing and home mgmt., asso. prof. Brigham Young U., Provo, 1963-69, prof. family econs. and home mgmt., 1969-74, emeritus, 1974—. Chmn., Western Regional Coll. Tchrs. Home Mgmt. and Family Econs. Conf., 1971. Mem. Utah County Civil Def. Bd., 1956-58; mem. planning com. Utah County Homemakers' Roundup, 1967-72; bd. mem. Utah County Community Action Program, 1968-70, mem. exec. council, 1970-71; chmn. Provo City Beautification Com., 1974. Named Moapa Valley High Sch. Alumnus of 1964. Mem. Utah Home Econs. Assn. (past pres. elect),

Am. Home Econs. Assn., Nat. Council Family Relations, Am. Sociol. Assn., Utah and Nat. Acad. Arts and Scis., Ia. State U. Home Econs. Alumni Assn., Provo City C. of C. (dir. women's div. 1970-71, dir. 1973—, pres. women's div. 1973, exec. com. women's div. 1974), Phi Kappa Phi, Gamma Phi Omicron, Omicron Nu, Alpha Kappa Delta, Epsilon Sigma Phi, Sigma Xi. Clubs: Provo (pres. 1969-70); Altrusa Internat. Home: 1223 Aspen Av Provo UT 84601

POUNCEY, LORENE, librarian, educator; b. North Little Rock, Ark., Oct. 18, 1921; d. Amos Joseph and Mamie (Price) Pouncey; student Delmar Coll., 1940-42; B.A., U. Tex., 1946; B.L.S., U. Cal, at Berkeley, 1947; postgrad. U. Ill., 1949-50; M.A., U. Houston, 1963. Cataloger, Henry E. Huntington Library and Art Gallery, San Marino, Cal., 1947-49, U. Ill. Library, Urbana, 1949-51; bibliographer Johns Hopkins U. Library, Balt., 1952-53; bibliographic asst. map div. Library of Congress, Washington, 1954-55, gifts and exchange div., 1955-56; catalog librarian, asst. prof. U. Houston, 1956-61, asst. catalog librarian, 1961-71, asso. prof., 1961—, rare book cataloger, 1972—. Served as 1st lt. USAF, 1951-52. Mem. Bibliog., Soc. Am., Bibliog. Soc. (London), Tex. Library Assn., Tex. Assn. Coll. Tchrs., Poetry Soc. Tex., S. Central Renaissance Conf. Presbyn. Home: 2815 Jarrard Houston TX 77005

POUND, MARY ELIZABETH, univ. librarian; b. Houston, June 9, 1932; d. Joseph Horace and Ruth (Robinson) Pound; B.A., Rice U., 1954; M.L.S., U. Tex., 1957. Serials cataloger U. Tex. at Austin Library, 1955-70, chief catalog librarian, 1970-73, head librarian serials unit, 1973—. Mem. Am. (mem. at large cataloging and classification sect. 1970-73), Southwestern (chmn. tech. services sect. 1970-72), Tex. library assns., Beta Phi Mu. Asst. editor for serials Library Resources and Tech. Services, 1969—; editor Tex. Library Jour., 1965—. Home: 9212 Hunters Trace E Austin TX 78758

POUR-EL, MARIAN BOYKAN (MRS. AKIVA POUR-EL), mathematician, educator; b. N.Y.C.; d. Joseph and Mattie (Caspe) Boykan; Ph.D., Harvard, 1958; m. Akiva Pour-El; 1 dau., Ina. Asst. prof. math. Pa. State U., 1958-62, asso. prof., 1962-64; asso. prof. math. U. Minn., Mpls., 1964-68, prof., 1968—. Mem. Inst. Advanced Study, Princeton, N.J., 1962-64; lectr. in field. Nat. Acad. Sci. grantee, 1966. Mem. Am. Math. Soc., Assn. for Symbolic Logic, Math. Assn. Am., Phi Beta Kappa, Sigma Xi, Pi Mu Epsilon, Sigma Pi Sigma. Research and publs. in math. logic, analog computer, women in sci. Home: 1389 Keston St St Paul MN 55108 Office: Dept Math U of Minn Minneapolis MN 55455

POWELL, ANICE CARPENTER (MRS. ROBERT WAINWRIGHT POWELL), librarian; b. Moorhead, Miss., Dec. 2, 1928; d. Horace Aubrey and Celeste (Brian) Carpenter; student Sunflower Jr. Coll., 1945-47, Miss. State Coll. Women, 1947-48; B.S., Delta State Coll., 1961, M.L.S., 1974; m. Robert Wainwright Powell, July 19, 1948; children—Penelope Elizabeth, Deborah Alma. Librarian, Sunflower (Miss.) Pub. Library, 1958-61; instr. English, Isola (Miss.) High Sch., 1961-62; coordinator Sunflower County Library, 1962—. Mem. adv. council State Instl. Library Services, 1967-71; chmn. pub. library category Sunflower County Merit Program, 1973—. Chmn. Miss. Heart Assn., Sunflower, 1963-72. Mem. A.L.A., Miss. (sect. chmn. 1965, treas. 1970, vice chmn. N.W. region 1972, fed. relations coordinator 1973-74, legislative com. 1973-74, intellectual freedom com. 1974), Southeastern library assns., Kappa Delta Pi. Methodist. Home: Box 387 Sunflower MS 38776 Office: Box 428 Sunflower MS 38778

POWELL, BARBARA JOAN, psychologist; b. Williamsville, Ill., June 30, 1933; M.A., George Washington U., 1960; Ph.D., Washington U. (St. Louis), 1964. Research psychologist Galesburg (Ill.) State Research Hosp., 1964-67; dir. psychol. service Malcolm Bliss Mental Health Center, St. Louis, 1967—. Contbr. articles to profl. jours. Home: 120 Edgemore Dr Lexington KY 40503 Office: 1420 Gratten St St Louis MO 63104

POWELL, BEATRICE HOPPER, librarian; b. Russell County, Ky., May 18, 1910; d. Ivy L. and Corinna (Nelson) Hopper; B.S., Western State U., 1949, M.A., 1960; m. Curtis J. Powell, June 18, 1935. Tchr., Russell County Schs., 1935-41, Balt., 1942, Ky., 1946-49; sec. Civil Service Commn., Balt., 1944; head librarian Russell County High Sch., 1952-60; librarian Russell Springs Elementary Sch., 1960—. Mem. Ky. Edn. Assn., N.E.A. (life), Ky. Library Assn., Ky. Assn. Sch. Librarians, Russell County Ednl Assn. (founder 1955, pres.), Future Tchrs. Club Middle Cumberland Dist. (founder, dir. 1966), Bus. and Profl. Woman's Clubs (charter mem., membership chmn. 1973-74), United Methodist Women (charter mem., officer, com. chmn.), Kappa Kappa Iota, Delta Kappa Gamma, Rebekah (past state officer, dist. pres.), Ky. Folklore Soc. (pres. 1973-74). Contbr. articles to ednl. and folklore publs., also newspapers. Home: PO Box 276 Russell Springs KY 42642

POWELL, BETTY LOUISE SUDEK (MRS. THOMAS POWELL), editor, publisher; b. N.Y.C., Mar. 6, 1932; d. Rudolph Ferdinand and Anna (Poborsky) Sudek; student New Sch. for Social Research, 1951-52, N.Y. U., 1952-53; m. Thomas Powell, Oct. 10, 1952. Hort. writer 1952-63; feature writer Organic Gardening mag., Emmaus, Pa., 1960-62; co-owner, advt. mgr. Organic Gardeners Supply Center, N.Y.C., 1959-62; co-mgr. Lager & Hurrell Orchid Nursery, Summit, N.J., 1962-64; editor Bull. Hort. Soc. of N.Y., N.Y.C., 1964-66; co-owner, exec. editor Avant Gardener, Hort. Data Processors, pubs., N.Y.C., 1968—; hort. cons., 1958—; lectr., tchr. on orchids, 1959—; exhibitor Internat. Flower Show, N.Y.C., 1958—. Recipient numerous trophies and awards for major flower show exhibits, 1958—. Mem. Greater N.Y. Orchid Soc., Am. Orchid Soc., Hort. Soc. N.Y. Originator editor Orchidata, Greater N.Y. Orchid Soc., Inc., 1960-64. Address: 238 E 82nd St New York City NY 10028

POWELL, DORIS MEDLEY, banker; b. Stockport, O., June 19, 1921; d. J. Bryan and Gladys Mae (Parsons) Medley; grad. Ohio Sch. Banking, Ohio U., 1963, Ohio Sch. Instalment Credit, Kent State U., 1967; m. William Leon Powell, Aug. 19, 1944; 1 son, Richard O'Bryan. Sec. Wright-Patterson Field, Dayton, O., 1942-43; loan officer Citizens Nat. Bank, McConnelsville, O., 1950—, asst. cashier, 1973—. Pres., Morgan County Bd. Edn., and Morgan Local, 1970, 73, 74, v.p., 1971, 72. Served with WAC, AUS, 1943-45; PTO. Decorated Philippine Liberation, Asiatic Pacific campaign medals, 3 Bronze Stars, World War II victory medal; recipient Scholarship award to Central States Sch. Banking, Madison, Wis., 1971. Mem. Nat. Secs. Assn. (Sec. of Year award Morgan Raiders chpt. 1970, chpt. pres. 1971), Morgan County Mental Health Assn. (treas. 1966), Pennsville P.T.A. (sec. 1963), Ohio Bankers Assn. (mem. woman's activities 1971, chmn. 1974), Pennsville Community Meml. Day Assn. (sec. 1963—), Ohio Sch. Bds. Assn., Ohio Sch. Banking Alumni Assn., Kent State Ohio Sch. Instalment Credit Alumni Assn., Nat. Assn. Bank Women, Am. Legion. Democrat. Methodist. Mason (sec. Woman's Shrine Club 1973); mem. Order Eastern Star, Women's Oriental Shrine N.Am. Home: Route 1 Stockport OH 43787 Office: Box 329 McConnelsville OH 43756

POWELL, ELIZABETH BALAS (MRS. NORBORNE BERKELEY POWELL), physician, educator; b. McKeesport, Pa., Oct. 22, 1914; d. Paul Steven and Lillian (Krisson) Balas; B.S., U. Pitts., 1936; M.D., Duke, 1938; m. Norborne Berkeley Powell, Dec. 18, 1939; children—Norborne Berkeley, Barbara Key. Intern Duke Hosp., Durham, N.C., 1938-39; resident Charity Hosp. of La., New Orleans, 1939-41; practice medicine, specializing in pathology, Houston, 1942—; pathologist Jefferson Hosp., Bapt. Hosp., Birmingham, Ala., 1942, Meml. Hosp., Houston, 1942-45, instr., asst. prof. pathology Baylor U. Sch. Medicine, 1945-71, asso. prof., 1971—. Diplomate in pathologic anatomy and clin. pathology Am. Bd. Pathology. Mem. Am., Tex. med. assns., Am. Soc. Cytology, Tex. Soc. Pathologists, Harris County Med. Soc., Alpha Omega Alpha. Presbyn. Contbr. articles to med. jours. Home: 2410 Avalon Pl Houston TX 77019

POWELL, ELIZABETH FLORIS, librarian; b. Columbia, Mo., July 9, 1916; d. Franklin Morris and Ora May (Smith) Sapp; B.S., U. Mo., 1938, postgrad., summer 1952; m. Hampstead Rowe Powell, Dec. 25, 1938; children—Betty (Mrs. James B. Thurman), Ronald Rowe, Judith Ann. Librarian Mississippi County Library, Charleston, Mo., 1951—. Club: Athena Study. Home: Hillsdale Av Charleston MO 63834 Office: Mississippi County Library Charleston MO 63834

POWELL, ELIZABETH PARKER (MRS. DAVID GEORGE POWELL), civic worker; b. Denver, Dec. 5, 1938; d. Everett Humphreys and Clare (Davis) Parker; B.A., Smith Coll., 1960; M.A., Fletcher Sch. Law and Diplomacy, 1962; student L'Institute des Etudes Francaises de Tourraine (France), 1962; postgrad. Babson Coll., Wellesley, Mass.; m. David George Powell, Sept. 21, 1963; children—Parker Davis, Clare Madeline, Elizabeth Everett. Govt. Intern U.S. senator Gordon Allott, Washington, summer, 1959; mem. Wellesley Town Meeting, 1973—, sec. com. to study needs and requirements Wellesley Free Library. Nat. alumnae chmn. devel. fund com. Abbot Acad., Andover, Mass., 1970-73, dir. Boston Abbot Club, 1971-73; provisional and finance com. Jr. League of Boston; capt. Heart Fund. 1964-65; solicitor Planned Parenthood, 1964-66; womens bd. Inst. Cancer Research, Phila., 1966-70; resource com. Mayor's Office Cultural Affairs, Boston; bd. mgrs. Jr. League Phila., 1967-70, dir. Smith Coll. Club, Phila., 1968-70; dir. Wellesley (Mass.) Smith Coll. Club, 1971—, v.p. Class of 1960, v.p., 1973-75; mem. exec. com. Wellesley P.T.A.; mem. alumni council Phillips Acad. Andover, Mass., 1973—. Mem. Nat. Assn. Parliamentarians, Nat. Soc. Colonial Dames, Mass. Women's Squash Racquets Assn. Republican. Episcopalian. Club: Acorn (Phila.). Home: 109 Edmunds Rd Wellesley Hills MA 02181

POWELL, ERNESTINE BREISCH, lawyer; b. Moundsville, W.Va., Feb. 16, 1906; d. Ernest Elmer and Belle (Wal-lace) Breisch; student Dayton YMCA Law Sch., 1929; m. Roger K. Powell, Nov. 15, 1935; children—R. Keith (dec.), Diane L.D., Bruce W. Admitted to Ohio bar, 1929; tax analyst tax dept. Wall, Cassell & Groneweg, Dayton, O., 1929-31; pvt. practice law, 1931-40; gen. counsel for Dayton Jobbers amd Mfrs. Assn., 1931-41; mem. firm Powell, Powell and Weimer Columbus, O., 1944—. Ohio chmn. Nat. Woman's Party, Washington, 1950-51, nat. chmn., 1953, hon. nat. chmn. Pres. vol. activities com. Columbus State Sch., 1960-61, trustee, 1957-59. Mem. Nat. Assn. Women Lawyers, Am., Ohio, Columbus bar assns., Nat. Soc. Arts and Letters (pres. Columbus chpt. 1963-64), Nat. Lawyers Club (charter mem.). Co-author: Tax Ideas, 1955; Estate Tax Techniques, 3 vols., 1955-74. Editor-in-chief: Women Lawyers Jour., 1943-45. Home: 103 Charleston Av Columbus OH 43214 Office: 17 S High St Columbus OH 43215

POWELL, FREDA GIBSON (MRS. W.T. POWELL), educator; b. Atlanta, Tex., Dec. 9, 1906; s. Frederick Proby and Alma Lucille (Hunter) Gibson; B.S., Sul Ross State U., 1937, M.A., 1945; postgrad. Columbia, 1952, (Danforth fellow), 1954, U. Tex., 1963-64, U. Birmingham (Eng.), 1964; m. W.T. Powell, June 27, 1928. Asso. prof., chmn. dept. drama Sul Ross State U., Alpine, Tex., 1945-54, Odessa (Tex.) Coll., 1959-67, Tarrant County Jr. Coll., Ft. Worth, 1967-72; guest prof. U. Tex., Austin, summers 1965-57, N. Tex. State U., Denton, 1973; exec. dir. Carillon Theatre, Ft. Worth, 1969-72. Speaker for various civic, profl. groups, service clubs, lit. groups, chs., youth orgns. Fellow to Shakespeare Inst., Stratford-Upon-Avon, Eng., 1965. Recipient citation Tex. Ednl. Theatre Assn., 1973. Mem. Am. Theatre Assn. (com. on standards 1968-71), Tex. Ednl. Theatre Assn. (dir. 1965-72, exec. sec.-treas. 1968-71), Alpha Psi Omega, Alpha Chi, Kappa Delta Pi. Home: 4411 Bellaire Dr S Fort Worth TX 76109

POWELL, GERALDINE WEST (MRS. WILLIAM J. POWELL), artist; b. Pitts.; d. Charles Howard and Helen (Baker) West; student Carnegie Inst. Tech., 1919-21, U. Pitts., 1921-22; studied with Frank du Monde, Revington Arthur, Jerry Farnsworth; m. William John Powell, Mar. 7, 1929 (dec. Feb. 1971); 1 son, William John. Exhibited Carnegie Art Gallery, 1942, 47, Newcomb Macklin Galleries, N.Y.C., 1947, 48, Norwell, Mass., 1949-50, Duxbury (Mass.) Art Assn., 1964, Bumpus Gallery-Duxbury Library, 1969, one-man show at Duxbury Playhouse, 1952. Formerly active in civic work, Pitts., chmn. Sanibel Island (Fla.) Shell Show, 1941, 42. Mem. Assn. Artists Pitts., Fedn. Girls Schs. (sec. Pitts. 1925-30), Winchester Alumnae Assn. (pres. 1927-29), Briarcliff Alumnae Assn. (pres. 1926-28), D.A.R. (regent Pitts. chpt. 1938-40), Western div. Pa. Fedn. State Garden Clubs (v.p. 1937-39). Republican. Unitarian. Clubs: Duxbury Yacht, Garden. Home: Box 151 Washington St Duxbury MA 02332

POWELL, JOANN, coll. counselor; b. Sharon, Pa., July 28, 1934; d. John Lawrence and Evelyn Pauline (Brest) Powell; B.S. in Edn., Youngstown U., 1956; M.S. in Edn., Westminster Coll., 1960; Ph.D., Northwestern U., 1970. Tchr. bus. Hartford (O.) Sch. Dist., 1956-60, Badger (O.) Sch. Dist., 1960-61; instr. bus. edn. Youngstown (O.) U., 1961-67; asst. dean students Northwestern U., Evanston, Ill., 1968-71; counselor William Rainey Harper Coll., Palatine, Ill., 1971-74, dean counseling, 1974—. Mem. Am., Ill. assns. women deans, adminstrs. and counselors, Am., Ill. personnel and guidance assns., Am. Psychol. Assn., Zeta Tau Alpha. Contbr. articles to profl. jours. Office: Harper College Roselle Rd Palatine IL 60067

POWELL, LENORE EILEEN MAGILL, educator; b. Loami, Ill., July 28, 1920; d. Samuel Rufus and Ethel Lenore (Thompson) Magill; B.S., Mary Washington Coll., Fredericksburg, Va., 1941; M.Ed., U. Ill., 1962; m. children (by previous marriage)—Michael Graham, Arlene Magill, Kay Lenore, Stephen Charles. Tchr. country sch., Ill., 1941-43; Springfield, Ill., 1959-64; regional cons. Ill. Dept. Spl. Edn., Springfield, 1964-66; dir. Instructional Materials Center for Handicapped Children and Youth, Springfield, 1966-71; dir. Title I Elementary and Secondary Edn. Act, State of Ill., 1971-72; field supr. Christian Children's Fund, Inc., Buenos Aires, Argentina, 1972—. Pres. Springfield chpt. Ill. Council for Exceptional Children, 1961-62, coordinator student activities, 1963-67, pres., 1968-69; mem. exceptional child com. United Community Services, 1961-63; tech. cons. Ill. Activities for 1970 White House Conf. on Children and Youth; dir. Camp for Educable Mentally Handicapped Children, Camp Walter Scott, Effingham, Ill., 1967; mem. adv. bd. S.Am. East territory Salvation Army. Served to lt. (j.g.) USNR, 1943-46. Mem. Assn. Educators Homebound and Hospitalized Children (editor Newsletter 1965-68). Methodist (mem. ofcl. bd.). Home: 24 Alberta Lane Springfield IL 62704 Office: Christian Children's Fund Inc Lavalle 445 Buenos Aires Argentina

POWELL, LILLIAN FRANCES, educator, musician; b. Big Springs, Tex., Oct. 2, 1937; d. Ira Milton and Margaret Elizabeth (Anderson) Powell; Mus.B., N. Tex. State U., 1959; Mus.M., Mich. State U., 1961. Elementary music specialist Odessa (Tex.) Pub. Schs., 1959-60; grad. asst. Mich. State U., Lansing, 1960-61, mem. faculty, 1961-63; elementary music specialist Lansing Pub. Schs., 1961-63, elementary, secondary music specialist, 1964-68; music coordinator U.S. Army Dependent Mil. Schs., Germany, 1963-64; music specialist Met. Nashville Schs., 1968—; studio tchr., exec. producer WDCN-TV Ednl. TV, Nashville, 1968—; owner, head Music Unlimited pub., rec., Nashville, 1968—. Performing artist civic orgns., clubs, profl. groups, 1959—; rec. artist, 1968—. Recipient Most Promising Profl. Artist award Am. Guild Mus. Artists, Mich. State U., 1961. Mem. Nat. Acad. Rec. Arts and Scis. (bd. govs.), Nat., Tenn. edn. assns., Met. Nashville Ednl. Assn., Nat. Music Educators Assn., Nat. Assn. Ednl. Broadcasters, So. Ednl. Communications Assn., Pi Kappa Lambda, Sigma Alpha Iota, Delta Kappa Gamma. Mus. compositions include Hum and Strum, 1966; Everyone Sing, 1969; Music Box, 1970; Tune Town, 1970; Music Land, 1971; Sound Shop, 1971; Sing Out America, 1972; Rhythm Road, 1972; How to Enjoy Making Music, 1973. Home: Grassland Estates Bobby Dr Franklin TN 37064 Office: WDCN-TV PO Box 12555 Nashville TN 37212

POWELL, MARCIA LEONORA, pub. relations cons.; b. Opelika, Ala.; d. Clyde LeRoy and Marcia Leonora (Stowe) Powell; A.B., U. Ga., 1962; postgrad. N.Y. Sch. Interior Design, 1968-69, New Sch. for Social Research, 1970. Club editor Phoenix Gazette, 1962-64; asst. account exec. Edward Gottlieb & Assos., Ltd., N.Y.C., 1964-65; pub. relations specialist Parsons-Jurden Corp., N.Y.C., 1965-66; eastern editor Irving-Cloud Pub. Co., N.Y.C., 1966-67; housing editor Dun-Donnelley Pub. Co., N.Y.C., 1967-73; owner Marcia Powell Enterprises, 1973—. Mem. editorial adv. com. Assn. Home Appliance Mfrs., 1967—. Chmn. minority media advt. conf., urban task force, Black Heritage Assn., 1970-71; mem. Project Head Start Cultural Program, 1966—. Recipient awards Ariz. Press Women, 1963, 64; Am. Laundry Mfrs. Assn. awards, 1972, 73. Mem. Elec. Women's Round Table (N.Y pres. 1969-70), Am. Home Econs. Assn., Home Economists in Bus., Nat. Acad. Television Arts and Scis., Nat. Home Fashions League, Designer's Lighting Forum, Nat. Press Women, Women in Communications (N.Y. pres. 1969-70), Alpha Xi Delta (pub. relations dir. 1965-67; cons. 75th Anniversary Conv. 1968), Sigma Delta Chi. Address: 160 W 73d St New York City NY 10023

POWELL, MARY LOUISE WELLS (MRS. ELTON GEORGE POWELL), psychologist, educator; b. Asheville, N.C., July 7, 1935; d. John Kendall and Beatrice (Rice) Wells; A.B., U. N.C., 1957, M.S., 1964, postgrad., 1965—; m. Elton George Powell, June 21, 1969. Tchr. Myers Park High Sch., Charlotte, N.C., 1957-58; editorial research asst. Time, Inc., N.Y.C., 1959-60; recreation and program dir. Spl. Services U.S. Forces Europe, Germany and France, 1960-62; resident adviser undergrad. women U. N.C. at Chapel Hill, 1963-64, research asso. and asst. to project coordinator State/Fed. Inst. for Profl. Devel., 1964-66; asst. prof. indsl. personnel psychology Appalachian State U., Boone, N.C., 1967—. Nat. Def. Edn. Act fellow, 1966. Mem. Am., N.C., Southeastern psychol. assns., Am., N.C. personnel and guidance assns., Am., N.C. coll. personnel assns., Nat. Vocational Guidance Assn., Am. Assn. Univ. Profs., Am. Assn. U. Women, Nat. Orgn. Women, Pi Delta Phi. Home: 114 Oak St Apt 8 Boone NC 28607 Office: 331 Duncan Hall Appalachian State University Boone NC 28607

POWELL, MARY MARTIN, orthopedic surgeon; b. Fredericksburg, Va., Jan. 26, 1926; d. Samuel Peter and Dorothy Vaughan (McCormick) Powell; B.S., U. Va., 1945; M.D., U. Tenn., 1949; m. Stuart Hayes Lewis, Oct. 23, 1954; children—Dorothy, Caroline, Margaret, Judith. Intern Balt. City Hosps., 1950-51; resident surgery Med. Coll. Va., 1951-52; resident radiology Johns Hopkins Hosp., 1952-54; resident orthopedic surgery Hahnemann Hosp., Phila., 1957-58, Shriner's Hosp. Crippled Children, Phila., 1958-59; practice medicine specializing in orthopedic surgery, Abington, Pa., 1959-61, Bryn Mawr, Pa., 1961—; mem. staff Bryn Mawr Hosp., Presbyn. Hosp., Phila. Diplomate Am. Bd. Orthopedic Surgery. Fellow Am. Acad. Orthopedic Surgeons. Home: 1721 Mt Pleasant Rd Villanova PA 19085 Office: 888 Glenbrook Av Bryn Mawr PA 19010

POWELL, NANCY MARY ROLICK (MRS. ORLO ALLEN POWELL), physician; b. Hartford, Conn.; d. John and Esther (Nydza) Rolick; A.B., U. Conn., 1956; M.D., Yale, 1960; m. Orlo Allen Powell, June 4, 1960; children—Allen Orlo, John Richard, Mary Esther. Rotating intern Hartford Hosp., 1960-61, resident in anesthesiology, 1961-64; asso. in anesthesia Middlesex Meml. Hosp., Middletown, Conn., 1964-66; internist Rocky Hill (Conn.) State Vets. Hosp., 1967—; dir. med. services Central Conn. Regional Center, Meriden, 1970—. Mem. P.T.A., Wethersfield, Conn., 1967-70. Mem. Am. Soc. Anesthesiology, Conn. State Med. Soc., Hartford County Med. Assn., Phi Beta Kappa. Club: Zonta Internat. Home: 473 Wolcott Hill Rd Wethersfield CT 06109

POWELL, NINA REEVES (MRS. LYNN BANKS POWELL III), realtor; b. Elk City, Okla., Sept. 1, 1933; d. J.B. and Dessie Omega (Hill) Sanders; student U. N.M., 1951, Miss Prathers Sch. for Girls, 1952, U. Mo., 1965; m. Eugene Everett Reeves, Mar. 7, 1953 (div. Nov. 1965); children—Lynn, Laura, Lisa; m. 2d, Lynn Banks Powell III, June 22, 1970; 1 dau., Susan. Pvt. sec. J. Korber Co., Albuquerque, 1952, AEC Archives, Albuquerque, 1953, Beneficial Finance Co., Columbia, Mo., 1953-56; city clk., Caruthersville, Mo., 1970-72, with Garden Homes, Bradenton, Fla., 1972—. Vol. asst. to high sch. guidance counselor, Caruthersville, 1966-67; tchr. kindergarten Presbyn. Ch. Sch., Caruthersville. Active in campaign for election Gov. Warren Hearnes, Mo., 1962. Mem. P.E.O. Presbyn. Home: 8260 Alderwood Dr Sarasota FL 33580 Office: 5840 26th St W Bradenton FL 33505

POWELL, RUTH MARIE ASH (MRS. HOWARD FRANCIS POWELL), real estate broker; b. Lincoln, Neb., Sept. 16, 1912; d. Grant Ulicious and Sarah Jane (Reeder) Ash; R.N., Mo. Meth. Hosp., 1935; m. Howard Francis Powell, Dec. 25, 1941; children—Patricia (Mrs. Richard Dulaney), Jane (Mrs. James Goddard). Supr. surg. floor Mo. Meth. Hosp., St. Joseph, 1935-36; supt. nurses Pomona Valley Hosp., Pomona, Cal., 1937-40; supt. Miner's Hosp., Nevada City, Cal., 1940-43; x-ray technologist St. Bernardines Hosp., San Bernardino, Cal., 1943-44; med. dir. Dunne & Dunne Placement, Los Angeles, 1944-45; real estate saleswoman Don Lingo Realty, La Crescenta, Cal., 1956-64; owner-broker Ruth Powell Real Estate, La Crescenta, 1964—. Named Realtor of Year, La Crescenta Bd. Realtors, 1971. Mem. Cal. Real Estate Assn. (state dir. 1971, 72-73), Bd. Realtors La Crescenta (pres. 1972), La Crescenta C. of C. (dir. 1968-71, pres. 1973). Home: 4952 Cecilville St La Crescenta CA 91214 Office: 3541 Foothill Blvd La Crescenta CA 91214

POWER, HELEN MARY BLACKBURNE (MRS. KENNETH T. POWER), univ. ofcl.; b. Rochester, N.Y.; d. William Hugh and Kathryn (Maher) Blackburne; A.B., U. Rochester, 1927, Litt.D. (hon.), 1971; Litt.D., Nazareth Coll., 1964; L.H.D., Keuka Coll.,

1968; LL.D., Hobart Coll., 1970, St. John Fisher Coll., 1974; m. Kenneth T. Power, Sept. 29, 1927; children—Kenneth T., William B., Bruce D. Bd. regents State U. N.Y., Albany, 1964—, chmn. regent's legislative com., 1968—. Mem. Community Planning Com. on Nursing Edn., Rochester, 1967—; active A.R.C. Mem. Monroe County Republican Com., 1950; sec. N.Y. State Fedn. Rep. Women's Clubs, 1942-44. Pres. bd. trustees Judy Weis Meml. Ednl. Fund, 1963—; bd. dirs. Monroe County Mental Health. Recipient awards including Helen Power Internat. grant Am. Assn. U. Women, 1958. Mem. Am. Assn. U. Women (br. pres. 1952-53, div. v.p. 1958-69), Fedn. Women's Clubs, (Rochester pres. 1963-64), Delta Kappa Gamma (hon.). Republican. Clubs: Seventh Judicial District Past Presidents (hon.), Monroe County Past Presidents (hon.), Susan B. Anthony (hon.). Home: 16 Southern Pkwy Rochester NY 14618

POWER, HELEN WOLLACK (MRS. RICHARD WILSON POWER), educator; b. Chgo., Oct. 9, 1935; d. Fred and Ella (Bass) Wollack; A.B., U. Chgo., 1955; M.A., Washington U., St. Louis, 1965, Ph.D., 1966; m. Richard Wilson Power, Mar. 10, 1956; children—Carla Emily, Nicholas Evan Doan. Reporter, San Diego Ind., 1957-59; lectr., Washington U., St. Louis, 1965, 72—, Pars Coll., Tehran, Iran, 1971-72, USIS, Iran, 1972. Mem. Modern Lang. Assn., Phi Beta Kappa. Home: 7515 Buckingham Dr St Louis MO 63105

POWER, SARAH GODDARD (MRS. PHILIP H. POWER), govt. ofcl.; b. Detroit, June 19, 1935; d. Wendell Converse and Katherine (Russel) Goddard; B.A., Vassar Coll., 1957; M.A., N.Y.U., 1965; m. Philip H. Power. Asst. to exec. dir. Asso. Alumnae Vassar Coll., 1957-58; personal asst. to Gov. Nelson A. Rockefeller, 1959-63; exec. dir. N.Y.C. Commn. for the UN and for The Consular Corps, 1966-69; exec. dir. U.S. UN-N.Y.C. Host Country Adv. Com., N.Y.C., 1969-72; co-chairperson Mich. program Nat. Endowment for Humanities; asst. chairwoman U. Mich. Commn. for Women, 1973—. Trustee Elizabeth N. Arnstein Fund, Power Found. Mem. UN Assn. (mem. UNESCO exec. com.). Democrat. Home: 12 Ridgeway W Ann Arbor MI 48104

POWER, VIRGINIA WING (MRS. GEORGE WILLIAM POWER), civic leader, former advt. exec.; b. Roswell, Ga., Apr. 13, 1906; d. J. Bartow and Hattie (Suddath) Wing; A.B., Agnes Scott Coll., 1926; m. George William Power, June 16, 1928. Feature writer, advt. writer Atlanta Georgian, 1926-28; copy writer, account exec., assisted in re-orgn. Power and Condon Advt., 1946-57, cons., 1957—; dir. Target Printing and Lithographing Co., Chattanooga, Designers, Inc., Chattanooga, Kyle Lake Farms, Inc. Apptd. to Tenn. Commn. on Aging, 1963, chmn., 1965-68; chmn. planning com. Tenn. region conf., 1959; mem. Nat. Council on Aging, 1958, Nat. Assn. State Units on Aging (dir. 1969-71); co-founder, 1st pres. Sr. Neighbors Chattanooga; chmn. aging sect. Chattanooga Council Community Forces, 1957-59; mem. adv. com. Tenn. Dept. Pub. Welfare, 1964-65; mem. adv. com. Chattanooga-Hamilton County Health Dept., 1964-70; chmn. adv. com. on home care, 1970—; Tenn. del. White House Conf. on Aging, 1961, 71; chmn. com. on implementation White House Conf. resolutions Tenn. Commn. on Aging, 1972-73. Trustee St. Barnabas retirement apts. and nursing home complex, 1964—; bd. dirs. Chattanooga YWCA, 1951-57; bd. dirs., v.p. Chattanooga Family Service Agy., 1949-55. Served with overseas hosp. div. A.R.C., 1943-45, also in charge of unit 46th Field Hosp.; ETO. Recipient citations for services to aging, local and state authorities, 1962, 66; recipient award of merit for community service Nat. Council on Aging, 1967. Episcopalian (edn. chmn. women's div. 1963-65). Clubs: Jr. League (mem. bd.; editor 1935-37), Tennis (pres. 1947-48) (Chattanooga); Reflection Riding (dir. 1965—). Research, publs., spl. reports on aging. Home: 1418 Winding Way Chattanooga TN 37405 Office: Tenn Commn on Aging S & P Bldg 306 Gay St Nashville TN 37201

POWERS, ANNE, author; b. Cloquet, Minn., May 7, 1913; d. John Patrick and Maud (Lynch) Powers; student U. Minn., 1932-33; m. Harold A. Schwartz, Aug. 22, 1938; children—Weldon, Lynn. Author: The Gallant Years, 1946; Ride East, Ride West, 1947; No Wall So High, 1949; The Ironmaster, 1951; The Only Sin, 1953; The Thousand Fires, 1957; Ride With Danger, 1958; No King But Ceasar, 1960. Instr. creative writing Coll. Journalism Marguette U., Milw. Received ann. award for best gen. book submitted, Nat. Fedn. Press Women, 1946; matrix citation for fiction writing, Theta Sigma Phi, 1951. Mem. Allied Authors, Fictioneers, Sigma Kappa. Roman Catholic. Club: Shorewood Woman's (Milw.). Author: (fictionized biography) Rachel, 1973. Home: 3800 N Newhall St Milwaukee WI 53211 Office: care Bobbs-Merrill Co Inc 1720 E 38th St Indianapolis IN 46218

POWERS, ANNIE FLORENCE (MRS. HOUSTON MELTON POWERS), ednl. adminstr.; b. Sallis, Miss., Sept. 26, 1921; d. Sydney Sallis and Alice Clayton (Smith) Owen; grad. Holmes Jr. Coll., 1940; B.S. in Secretarial Sci. and Bus. Edn., Miss. State Coll. for Women, 1942; m. Houston Melton Rowers, Sr., Dec. 27, 1948; children—Houston Melton, Alice Virginia. Stenographer, Miss. River Commn., Vicksburg, 1942; tchr. Holmes Jr. Coll., Goodman, Miss., 1942-45; dir. placement, instr. dept. econs. and bus. Belhaven Coll., Jackson, Miss., 1945—. Vis. instr. Delta State Coll., Cleveland, Miss., 1946, 47, Draughon's Bus. Coll., Jackson, 1948-50, 52, Amarillo (Tex.) Coll., 1944. Corp. sec. Miss. Bapt. High Schs., Inc., 1971—; pres. French Elementary Sch. P.T.A., Jackson, 1959-60; active Boy Scouts Am., 1960-61. Trustee Jackson Met. Library Commn. Baptist. Home: 4216 Richmond Circle Jackson MS 39209

POWERS, BARBARA LEA ROBERDEE (MRS. JOHN JOSEPH POWERS), newspaperwoman; b. Cedar Rapids, Ia., June 20, 1936; d. Clarence Burdette and Carol Marie (Paxson) Roberdee; B.A., State U. Ia., 1958; m. John Joseph Powers, Apr. 8, 1961; children—Julie Marie, Molly Ann. News reporter Morning Democrat, Davenport, Ia., 1958; feature writer, home furnishings editor Phoenix Gazette, 1960-61; home furnishings editor Chgo. Daily News, 1962-64; free-lance writer, 1964-65; home editor Post-Tribune, Gary, Ind., 1965—. Mem. Nat. Home Fashions League, Ind. Press Women, Nat. Fedn. Press Women, Nat. Soc. Interior Design (press mem.). Home: 28 Hackberry Lane Glenview IL 60025 Office: 1065 Broadway Gary IN 46402

POWERS, COLETTE URSULA EMIN (MRS. JAMES H. POWERS), data processor; b. Georgiaville, R.I., Oct. 14, 1922; d. Leander Francis and Bertha Christina (Andrews) Emin; Ed.B., R.I. Coll. Edn., 1942; M.A., Tchrs. Coll. Columbia, 1946; grad. U. Mass. Sch. Edn., 1965; student IBM Schs., 1962, 66, 70; m. James Harrison Powers, July 16, 1949. Tchr., I.S. Cook Sch., Geog, R.I., 1942-43, R.I. Assn. Blind, Providence, 1943-44, R.I. Sch. for Deaf, Providence, 1944-45, Lexington Sch. Deaf, N.Y.C., 1945-49, Franklin County Hearing League, Greenfield, Mass., 1951-62, Mass. State Dept. Edn. Extension, Greenfield, 1961-62; teaching prin. Montague Center (Mass.) Sch., 1951-62; cons. data processing dept. Town Amherst (Mass.) Pub. Schs., City Northampton High Sch., Westfield State Tchrs. Coll., 1962-65; mgr. electronic data processing dept. Wheaton Coll., Norton, Mass., 1965—. Dir. Franklin County Hearing League, Greenfield, 1960-62. Instr. Americanization, Smithfield, R.I., 1943-45; sect. warden Civil Def., Smithfield, 1941-42; leader Girl Scouts U.S.A., Smithfield, R.I., 1942-43; troop adviser Boy Scouts Am., Montague, 1958-62. Recipient Grad. Assistantship award U. Mass., 1963-65. Mem. Am. Hearing Soc., Mass. Edn. Data Processing Assn., Nat. Assn. Coll. and U. Bus. Officers, Coll. and U. Machine Records, R.I. Coll. Edn., Columbia, U. Mass. alumni assns., St. Xavier Acad. Alumnae Assn. Roman Catholic. Home: Perry Circle Norton MA 02766

POWERS, DOROTHY ROCHON (MRS. ETHRIDGE ELWOOD POWERS), journalist; b. Erskine, Alta., Can., Oct. 9, 1921; d. Clarence G. and Edna (Waterbury) Rochon; came to U.S., 1924, naturalized, 1958; B.A. cum laude, U. Mont., 1943; m. Ethridge Elwood Powers, Nov. 19, 1945. Gen. assignment reporter Spokesman Rev., Spokane, 1943-45, reporter, 1947-54, columnist, 1954-66, feature writer, 1966—, editorial writer, 1969—; editor Maryville (Tenn.) Enterprise, 1946; reporter Clarksville (Tenn.) Leaf-Chronicle, 1946. Vis. prof., lectr. U. Mont., 1962. Republican nominee U.S. Congress, 1966; exec. sec. Rep. State Central Com., 1966; Rep. state committeewoman, 1966; pres. Spokane County Women's Rep. Club, 1963. Mem. adv. bd. Sch. Nursing, Deaconess Hosp., Spokane, 1967—; bd. dirs. Spokane Community Concert Assn., Ednl. Loan Found. Recipient Nat. Ernie Pyle Meml. award, 1959, Nat. Headliners Club award, 1958, Distinguished Alumni award U. Mont., 1960, Washington Press Women 1st place award for editorial writing, 1971, 73, Nat. Fedn. Press Women award, 1971, 73; Catherine O'Brien Journalism award, 1973; Sigma Delta Chi Distinguished Journalism 1st place award, 1973. Mem. Spokane Press Club (pres. 1960), Women in Communications (Nat. Headliner award 1959, nat. 2d v.p. 1964), Delta Kappa Gamma (hon.). Club: Zonta (pres. 1959). Home: W 2340 1st Av Spokane WA 99204 Office: Monroe and Riverside Spokane WA 99210

POWERS, ELAINE LOUISE SLEEPER (MRS. JAMES ALTON POWERS), town ofcl.; b. Lisbon, Me., Mar. 22, 1925; d. Charles Myrick and Eva Beatrice (Coolidge) Sleeper; grad. with honors Ecole' St. Bernadette, 1942; certificate Stonehill Coll., 1960; postgrad. Mass. Inst. Tech., 1963-64; m. James Alton Powers, July 11, 1942; 1 son, James Michael. Clk. of town treas. and town collector, East Bridgewater, Mass., part-time, 1957; clk. Bd. Assessors, East Bridgewater, 1958-59; asst. clk., East Bridgewater, 1960-70, town clk., 1971—; clk. Bd. Registrars, East Bridgewater, 1960—; justice of peace, East Bridgewater, 1960—; news, advt. corr. Brockton Enterprise Times, 1970—; mem. Charter Commn., East Bridgewater, 1973—. Mem. East Bridgewater Republican Town Com., 1972—; mem. Tri Town Republican Woman's Club, 1967—; mem. Plymouth County Republican Club, 1973—. Mem. Brockton Bus. and Profl. Woman's Club (auditor 1968—), Brockton Enterprise Corr. Assn., Tri County City, Mass., New Eng. city and town clks. assns., Internat. Inst. Municipal Clks. Methodist (trustee 1970). Home: 99 Cook St East Bridgewater MA 02333 Office: 137 Central St East Bridgewater MA 02333

POWERS, GEORGIA M. (MRS. JAMES L. POWERS), state legislator; b. Springfield, Ky., Oct. 29, 1923; d. Ben and Frances (Walker) Montgomery; student Louisville Municipal Coll., 1940-42; m. James L. Powers; 1 son, William F. Supr. IBM Data Processing div. U.S. Census Bur., 1959-62; asst. hosp. adminstr., Louisville, Ky., 1966; mem. Ky. State Senate, 1968—. Mem. Gov.'s Adv. Council on Mental Retardation, 1967-68. Dist. chmn. Jefferson County Democratic Exec. Com., 1964-66; chmn. Blume for Congress campaign, 1966; del. Dem. Nat. Conv., 1968. Bd. dirs. Louisville area chpt. A.R.C., 1970-72. Recipient Kennedy-King Meritorious award Ky. Young Dems., 1968; Achievement award Zion Bapt. Ch., 1968; certificate of appreciation Ky. Sch. Bds. Assn., 1968. Mem. YWCA, N.A.A.C.P., Urban League. Presbyn. Address: 733 Cecil Av Louisville KY 40211

POWERS, GERTHA JOHNSON (MRS. EARL RICHARD POWERS), banker; b. Waterloo, N.Y., Nov. 17, 1925; d. Jay Henry and Gertha Adele (Kuney) Johnson; student Rochester Bus. Inst., 1944-45; grad. So. La. State U. Banking Sch., 1973; m. Earl Richard Powers, Feb. 17, 1946 children—Earl William, Elaine (Mrs. Richard Thomas Ferguson). Statis. accountant, purchasing agt. U.S. Dept. Army Seneca Ordnance Depot, Romulus, N.Y., 1951-57; information, rebate clk. First Nat. Bank, St. Petersburg, Fla., 1961-63; mgr. loan dept. So. Bank of St. Petersburg, 1963-67; asst. cashier First State Charter Bank, St. Petersburg, 1967-69, cashier, 1969-74, v.p., cashier, 1974—, operations officer, 1967—. Mem. Am. Inst. Banking (gov., women's rep. St. Petersburg 1963-71), Nat. Assn. Bank Women (nat. scholarship award 1970). Republican. Methodist. Home: 8280 60th St N Pinellas Park FL 33565 Office: First State Charter Bank PO Box 12469 St Petersburg FL 33733

POWERS, JANE BIDDLE (MRS. WILBUR E. POWERS), librarian; b. Ann Arbor, Mich., July 11, 1915; d. Thomas Israel and Clemma Lydia (Mills) Biddle; A.B., U. Mich., 1936, B.S. in L.S., 1937; m. Wilbur Emmett Powers, June 18, 1939 (dec. June 1967); children—Carol Ann (Mrs. Leonard Allen Wood), Robert Emmett. Asst. librarian River Rouge (Mich.) Pub. Library, 1938-39; sr. librarian Hamilton Twp. Pub. Library, Trenton, N.J. 1959-64, dir., 1964—. Mem. Hamilton Twp. League Women Voters, 1968—. Mem. A.L.A., N.J. Library Assn. Am. Assn. U. Women, Hamilton Twp. Hist. Soc. Office: Apt 1 1780 Klockner Rd Trenton NJ 08619

POWERS, JEANNE AUDREY, clergywoman; b. Mankato, Minn., July 5, 1932; d. Philip Raymond and Florence Margaret (Jones) Powers; B.S., Mankato State Coll., 1954; postgrad. Princeton Theol. Sem., 1955-56, St. Andrews U., Scotland, 1958-59, S.T.B., Boston U., 1958. Ordained to ministry Meth. Ch., 1958; campus minister Wesley Found. U. Minn., St. Paul, 1959-64; mem. conf. program staff United Meth. Ch., Mpls., 1964-67; minister Univ. United Meth. Ch., Mpls., 1967-69; sec. for missionary personnel Bd. Missions, United Meth. Ch., N.Y.C., 1969-73, asst. gen. sec. ecumenical and interreligious concerns div. Bd. Global Ministries, 1973—; rec. sec. United Meth. Commn. Status and Role of Women, 1972—. Danforth Grad. fellow, 1954-55; Lucinda Bidwell Bebee fellow, 1958-59; recipient Distinguished Alumnus award Boston U. Sch. Theology, 1970. Home: 501 W 123d St New York City NY 10027 Office: 475 Riverside Dr New York City NY 10027

POWERS, KATHRYN LAWYER (MRS. JAMES LOCKHART POWERS), lawyer; b. Jacksonville, Fla., Oct. 7, 1945; d. John Hooper and Grace Ann (Medlin) Lawyer; B.A. cum laude (fellow), Vassar Coll., 1967; J.D. with honors (fellow), U. Fla., 1969; m. James Lockhart Powers, Aug. 31, 1968; 1 son, Dylan Hooper. Admitted to Fla. bar, 1970; atty. Office Gen. Counsel, SEC, Washington, 1969-71, Powers & Powers, Jacksonville, Fla., 1971-73, Mahoney, Hadlow, Chambers & Adams, Jacksonville, 1973—. Mem. law center council U. Fla. Law Center, 1972—. Mem. Mayor's Commn. on Status of Women, 1973—, Area Planning Bd. Adv. Commn., 1972—. Bd. dirs. Community Planning Council; bd. dirs., pres. Women's Center for Reproductive Health, Jacksonville. Mem. Am., Fla., Jacksonville bar assns., League Women Voters, Am. Assn. U. Women, Nat. Orgn. for Women, Order of Coif, Phi Kappa Phi. Democrat. Unitarian. Club: Baymeadows (Jacksonville). Home: 1418 Avondale Av Jacksonville FL 32205 Office: 100 Laura St Jacksonville FL 32202

POWERS, (LUCY) LINDLEY, educator; b. Albany, N.Y., Aug. 19, 1926; d. William Tibbits and Winifred (Lispenard) Powers; A.B., Smith Coll., 1948; M.A. in Speech, U. Wis., 1963, M.F.A. in Theater Directing, 1963, Ph.D. in Speech (E.B. Fred fellow), 1968; postdoctoral Espiscopal Theol. Sch., 1972—, Weston Coll. Sch. Theology, 1974—; m. Davis Spencer, Mar. 5, 1949 (div. 1961); children—Eleanor Tibbits (Mrs. Robert R. Tupper, Jr.), Joseph Allen Powers Spencer. Children's librarian N.Y.C. Pub. Library, 1948-49; tchr., Racine, Wis., 1959-61; dir. drama program Wis. 4-H Clubs, also research asst. U. Wis., 1961-64; instr. U. Wis., 1964-65, 66-67, teaching asst. Sch. Music, 1965-66; asst. prof. drama Bridgewater (Mass.) State Coll., 1968-69; asso. prof., dir. grad. study theatre edn. Emerson Coll., Boston, 1969-71, asso. prof. fine arts, 1971—, adviser creative service interdisciplinary program, 1974—. Condr. community and conv. workshops in theatre arts. Bd. dirs., mem. adminstrv. com. Ch. Home Soc., Boston. Mem. Am. Theatre Assn., Speech Communications Assn., Am. Assn. Univ. Profs., Internat. Platform Assn., Iona Community (asso. mem.), Dobbs (dir., mem. exec. com. 1949-57, editor bull., 1949-57), Smith alumnae assns., Shakespeare Club Boston, Phi Beta. Author drama ednl. materials. Episcopalian (lay reader). Home: 63 Atlantic Av Boston MA 02110 Office: 148 Beacon St Boston MA 02116

POWERS, MALA, actress; b. San Francisco, Dec. 20, 1931; d. George Evart and M. Dell (Thelen) Powers; student U. Cal. at Los Angeles; pupil Michael Chekhov; m. M. Hughes Miller, May 17, 1970; 1 son by previous marriage, Toren Michael Vanton. Motion picture appearances include Cyrano de Bergerac, 1950, Outrage, Edge of Doom, Yellow Mountain, Bengazi, Tammy, Daddy's Gona A'Hunting; stage prodns. include Absence of a Cello, 1964-65, Hogan's Goat, Night of the Iguana, Bus Stop, Far Country, The Rivalry; also starred radio and TV prodns. including Lux Radio Theater, This is Your FBI, Cisco Kid, Hazel, Man from Uncle, G.E. Theater, Bonanza, Ironside, Perry Mason, Owen Marshall; co-star with Anthony Quinn in The Man and the City, 1971-72; lectr. in field. Entertainer troops, U.S.O., Korea, 1951-52; chmn. So. Cal. Mother's com. March of Dimes, 1972-74. Mem Acad. Motion Picture Arts and Scis. (mem. fgn. film com.), Nat. Acad. TV Arts and Scis., ANTA (v.p., exec. com. 1974—). Editor The Secret Seven and the Grim Secret; The Secret Seven and the Old Fort Adventure, 1972. Mem. Unity Sch. Christianity. Home: 4317 Forman Av North Hollywood CA 91602 Office: 1270 Av of Americas Suite 2212 New York City NY 10020

POWERS, MARCIA JOAN, journalist; b. Ottawa, Ont., Can., May 21, 1938; d. Harold Matthew and Jessie Urma (Goudie) Powers; student parochial sch. Sec., Dept. Transp., Ottawa, 1955-56; with Pub. Printing and Stationery, Hull, Que., 1956-57; with Ottawa Jour., 1957—, ch. editor, 1969—. Exec. sec. Can. Mng. Editors Conf., 1967-70. Roman Catholic. Club: Nat. Press of Can. Home: 2045 Carling Av Ottawa K2A IG5 ON Canada Office: 365 Laurier Av W Ottawa K1G 3K6 ON Canada

POWERS, MARGARET PAULINE SERRITELLI (MRS. RAYMOND ALLEN POWERS), editor; b. Chgo., May 16, 1947; d. Thomas and Stella Maria (Tomburrano) Serritelli; A.A., Pasadena City Coll., 1967; B.A., Cal. State Coll. at Los Angeles, 1970; m. Raymond Allen Powers, Feb. 1, 1969. Woman's editor Post-Advocate, Alhambra, Cal., 1969—. Mem. Alhambra Coordinating Council. Bd. dirs. San Gabriel Community Boys Club. Recipient award LaChime Bus. and Profl. Woman's Club, 1970, award San Gabriel Valley Pilot Club, 1970, award San Gabriel Valley Symphony Assn. Women's Com., 1971, Ring of Truth award Copley Newspapers, 1971, Outstanding Young Women of Am. award, 1971. Mem. So. Cal. Press Club, Alhambra Day Nursery Assn. Club: Soroptimist (v.p. 1971-72) (Alhambra, Cal.). Office: 512 Cortez Rd Arcadia CA 91006

POWERS, MARY GRIFFIN (MRS. JOSEPH POWERS), educator; b. Hartford, Conn., Nov. 24, 1932; d. James J. and Deborah (O'Neil) Griffin; B.S., Central Conn. State Coll., 1955; M.A., U. Mass., 1957; Ph.D., Brown U., 1963; m. Joseph Powers, Jan. 19, 1957; children—Deborah Jane, Janet Elizabeth. Instr. dept. sociology U. Mass., Amherst, 1957-58; teaching asst. Brown U., Providence, 1959-61; survey statistician-demographer U.S. Bur. of Census, Washington, 1962-65; asst. prof. dept. sociology and anthropology Fordham U., Bronx, N.Y., 1965-67, asso. prof., 1967-72, prof., 1972—, chmn. dept., 1972-75. Mem. Am., Eastern sociol. assns., Am. Statis. Assn., Population Assn. Am., Internat. Union for Sci. Study Population, Am. Assn. U. Profs., Am. Assn. U. Women. Contbr. articles to profl. jours.

POWERS, MARY RITA, mathematician; b. Norwich, Conn., Aug. 4, 1920; d. George Shea and Ellen Regina (Foley) Powers; B.A., Conn. Coll., 1942; M.A. in Math., U. Cal. at Los Angeles, 1955. Mathematician, U.S. Army Aberdeen (Md.) Proving Ground, 1942-46, digital computing div. USN Underwater Systems Center, New London (Conn.) Lab, 1946—. Mem. Assn. for Computing Machinery, Fed. Profl. Assn., Conn. Coll. Alumni Assn. (mem. finance com. 1971—, pres. New London chpt. 1964-66), Council Catholic Women (pres. Norwich dist. 1962-64, treas. 1957-59, treas. Norwich Diocesan Council 1964-66). Contbr. articles on underwater acoustics to profl. jours. Home: 7 Cliff Pl Norwich CT 06360 Office: Fort Trumbull New London CT 06320

POWNALL, HILDA PAULINE CLARK (MRS. FRANK L. POWNALL), motel exec.; b. Light, Va., July 19, 1908; d. Lee V. and Redella F. (DeHaven) Clark; student pub. schs., Siler, Va.; m. Frank L. Pownall, Aug. 3, 1933 (dec. Aug. 1961). Owner, operator Wheatland Motel, Martinsburg, W.Va. Mem. W.Va. Hotel-Motel Assn. (dir. 1972—), Berkley County Hist. Soc. (treas. 1972—). Mem. Order Eastern Star. Home: 1193 Winchester Av Martinsburg WV 25401 Office: 1193 Winchester Av Martinsburg WV 25401

POWSNER, RHODA MOSCOVITZ (MRS. EDWARD R. POWSNER), physician; b. N.Y.C., Oct. 4, 1930; d. David J. and Anna (Felenstein) Moscovitz; B.A., Adelphi Coll., 1949; M.D., Yale, 1953; m. Edward R. Powsner, June 8, 1950; children—Seth, Rachel, Ethan, David. Intern, Wayne County Gen. Hosp., Eloise, Mich., 1953-54, resident, 1954-55; resident City of Detroit Receiving Hosp., 1955-56, Dearborn (Mich.) VA Hosp., 1956-57; research asso. pediatric cardiology U. Mich., 1957-59; asst. chief chest physician VA Hosp., Ann Arbor, Mich., 1961-63; practice medicine specializing in cardiology, Ann Arbor, 1963—; mem. staffs St. Joseph Mercy Hosp., Ann Arbor; chief coronary care unit Beyer Hosp., 1967-71; cons. cardiology Saline (Mich.) Hosp., Beyer Meml. Hosp., Ypsilanti, Mich.; instr. dept. internal medicine U. Mich., 1971—. Diplomate Am. Bd. Internal Medicine. Fellow A.C.P., Am. Coll. Chest Physicians, Am. Coll. Angiology; mem. Washtenaw County Med. Soc. (exec. council 1971—). Contbr. articles to profl. pubs. Office: 2350 Wastenaw Av Ann Arbor MI 48104

POYNER, WINIFRED ANN, nursing educator; b. Palestine, Tex., Sept. 29, 1935; d. Earnest Eldon and Opal Arline (Grantham) Poyner; nursing diploma N.W. Tex. Hosp., Amarillo, 1957. Nurse charge orthopedic operating room Parkland Meml. Hosp., Dallas, 1957-59; supr. operating room D.M. Cogdell Meml. Hosp., Synder, Tex.,

1959-61, part-time supr. operating and recovery room, 1969-73; pvt. office and hosp. nurse, Snyder, 1961-73; dir., coordinator vocat. nursing program Western Tex. Coll., Snyder, 1973—. Mem. Snyder City Council from Place 2, 1970-74. Bd. dirs. Scurry County Workshop Mentally Retarded, Scurry County Cancer Soc. Mem. Nat. Assn. Operating Room Nurses, Tex. Tchrs. Assn., Tex. Jr. Coll. Tchrs. Assn. Home: 3605 Hill Av Snyder TX 79549

POZNANSKI, ELVA ORLOW (MRS. ANDREW K. POZNANSKI), physician; b. Glendale, Cal., Dec. 18, 1933; d. Eric and Alta (Franklin) Orlow; student Pasadena City Coll., 1950-52, U. So. Cal., 1952-53; M.D., McGill U., 1957; m. Andrew K. Poznanski, Feb. 2, 1957; children—Diana, Suzanne. Intern Henry Ford Hosp., Detroit, 1957-58; resident Lafayette Clinic, Wayne State U., Detroit, 1958-62, clin. instr. psychiatry, 1962-67, clin. asst. prof., 1967-68; practice medicine, specializing in child psychiatry, Huntington Woods, Mich., 1962-68; instr. psychiatry U. Mich., Ann Arbor, 1968-70, asst. prof., 1970-73, asso. prof., 1973—; mem. staff Children's Meml. Hosp., Detroit, 1962-66, Beaumont Hosp., 1965-68. Diplomate Am. Bd. Psychiatry and Neurology (examiner 1967-69), Am. Bd. Child Psychiatry. Fellow Am. Psychiat. Assn., Am. Acad. Child Psychiatrists; mem. Mich. Soc. Neurologists and Psychiatrists. Home: 2662 Salisbury Lane Ann Arbor MI 48103 Office: Children's Psychiatric Hosp U Mich Ann Arbor MI 48104

PRADO, GLORIA FERNANDEZ, educator; b. Santa Clara, Cuba, Sept. 12, 1920; d. Obdulio Jose and Maria Severa (Diaz de Velis) Fernandez; grad. Havana (Cuba) Tchr. Coll., 1940; postgrad. Havana U., 1948; M.A., Dallas State Coll., 1972; m. Jose V. Prado, Nov. 15, 1947; 1 dau., Deborah Lynne. Came to U.S., 1960, naturalized, 1965. Tchr. elementary sch., Cuba, 1940-47; charge psychopedagogy lab. Annex Sch. Edn., Havana U., 1947-59; pvt. tutor mentally retarded children, N.Y.C., 1960-66; head tchr. North Dade Children's Center, Miami, Fla., 1966-68; tchr. trainable mentally retarded Rowland Unified Sch., Rowland Heights, Cal., 1968-70; tchr. trainable mentally retarded Villacorta Sch., La Puenta, Cal., 1970—. Recipient certificate appreciation North Dade Children's Center, 1967, Casa Alegre Hosp., La Puente, 1970. Mem. Am. Assn. Mental Deficiency, Cal. Assn. Neurologically Handicapped Children, Council Exceptional Children, Royal Soc. London. Democrat. Roman Catholic. Address: 7937 E 4th St Downey CA 90241

PRAGER, ALICE HEINECKE, music exec.; b. N.Y.C., Aug. 2, 1930; d. Paul and Ruth (Collin) Heinecke; grad. Russell Sage Coll., 1951; postgrad. N.Y.U.; m. George L. Drescher. With SESAC, Inc., N.Y.C., 1946—, now pres.; pres. The Personal Touch, Inc. Asso. trustee Hamptons Hosp. and Med. Center. Named hon. citizen, Tenn., Fla. Mem. Radio and Television Execs. Soc., Internat., Am. (adv. bd.) women in radio and television, A.I.M., Nat. Acad. Rec. Arts and Scis., Broadcast Pioneers, Advt. Women N.Y. (dir.), Gospel and Country Music Assn. (life). Club: Zonta. Home: 300 Central Park W New York City NY 10024 Office: Coliseum Tower 10 Columbus Circle New York City NY 10019

PRANKE, EUGENIE IRMA, physiotherapist; b. Wapella, Sask., Can., Oct. 5, 1936; d. Gustave and Amanda (Kossman) Pranke; diploma physiotherapy U. Alta. Staff physiotherapist Victoria Hosp., London, Ont., 1959-60, Moncton (N.B.) City Hosp., 1960-62; staff therapist Christian Med. Coll. Hosp., Vellore, South India, 1962-67; with Grande Prairie (Alta.) Municipal Hosp., 1968—, supr. physiotherapy, 1968—. Office: 10409 98th St Grande Prairie AB Canada

PRASAD, ARYABALA RAY (MRS. ANANDA S. PRASAD), physician; b. Cuttack, India; d. Birkishore and Saraswati (Pattanayak) Ray; M.B., B.S., Patna (India) U., 1951; M.S., U. Minn., 1958; m. Ananda S. Prasad, Jan. 9, 1952; children—Rita Rochelle, Sheila, Ashok, Nivedita Audrey. Came to U.S., 1952, naturalized, 1968. Resident obstetrics and gynecology St. Paul's Hosp., Dallas, 1952-53, St. Barnabas Hosp., Mpls., 1953-55; resident surgery Mt. Sinai Hosp., Mpls., 1955-56; resident pathology St. Joseph Hosp., St. Paul, 1956-57; teaching asst. physiology U. Minn., 1957-58; vis. staff physician Nemazee Hosp., Pahlevi U., Shiraz, Iran, 1958-61, in charge obstetrics service, 1959-61; physician Planned Parenthood Clinic, Detroit, 1965-71; mem. staff St. Joseph, Pontiac Gen. hosps. Mem. Detroit Founders Soc. Detroit Inst. Arts, Detroit Internat. Inst. Home: 4710 Cove Rd Orchard Lake MI 48033 Office: 435 Hickory St Milford MI 48042

PRATT, ANN B(OGUE) (MRS. RICHARD F. PRATT), psychologist, educator; b. Austin, Tex., May 6, 1929; d. William John and Gladys Margaret (Bogue) Reilly; A.B., Antioch Coll., 1952; M.A. in Psychology, U. Minn., 1961, Ph.D. in Psychology, 1970; m. Richard F. Pratt, Aug. 13, 1965; children from previous marriage—Douglas Owen Cornog, Clay Ian Cornog. Psychometrist U. Chgo., 1962-63; guidance counselor Michael Reese Hosp. Sch. of Nursing, Chgo., 1963-70; asst. prof. psychology Elmhurst (Ill.) Coll., 1970-72; asst. prof. psychology Capital U., Columbus, O., 1972—. Cons. on learning, motivation and ednl. measurement for Chgo. and Columbus area schs. of nursing, 1968—. Mem. Community Resources Bd., Westerville (O.) P.T.A. Mem. Am., Ohio psychol. assns., A.A.A.S., Am. Ednl. Research Assn. Home: 477 Delaware Court Westerville OH 43081 Office: 215 Learning Center Capital University Columbus OH 43209

PRATT, CAROL ISAACS, educator; b. Faith, S.D., Dec. 15, 1931; d. William McKinley and Belle Rosella (Higgins) Isaacs; B.S. in Edn., Black Hills State Coll., 1954; M.A., U. S.D., 1959; postgrad. La. State U., 1969-74. Tchr. theatre and vocal music Faith (S.D.) High Sch., 1954-56, Gettysburg (S.D.) High Sch., 1956-58, Lemmon (S.D.) High Sch., 1959-61; dir. theatre Aberdeen (S.D.) High Sch., 1961-66, Chadron (Neb.) State Coll., 1966-69; asst. prof. theatre and speech U. Southwestern La., Lafayette, 1971-72; now grad. asst. La. State U., Baton Rouge. Mem. Nat. Collegiate Players, Props and Liners (life, pres. 1953-54) Speech Communication Assn., Zeta Phi Eta, Sigma Kappa. Methodist. Home: Box 54 Faith SD 57626 Office: Dept Speech La State U Baton Rouge LA 70803

PRATT, ELEANOR PARSONS (MRS. ELEANOR PARSONS), mus. ofcl.; b. Stonington, Conn., Mar. 13, 1915; d. John Rushmore and Ella (Woodruff) Parsons; student U. N.M., 1966-69; m. Philip Marlow Pratt, Apr. 21, 1940; children—Elizabeth, Adam Scott, Deborah Ruth. Apprenticeship, Lab. Anthropology, Mus. N.M., Santa Fe, 1960-66; asst. curator Maxwell Mus. Anthropology, Albuquerque, 1969-70; librarian Philmont Scout Ranch and Explorer Base, Cimarron, N.M., 1970, dir. Museums, 1973—. Mem. profl. tech. staff Boy Scouts Am., North Brunswick, N.J., 1955-60; instr. swimming Santa Fe Recreation Dept., 1955-60; cons. pub. relations for Internat. Visitors, U. N.M. Maxwell Mus., 1968-70. Bd. dirs. N.M. Tb Assn., 1953-56, Cimarron (N.M.) Hist. Soc., 1973—. Recipient fellowship Am. Assn. State and Local History, 1973. Mem. Am., N.M. assns. museums, Mountain-Plains Mus. Conf. Address: Philmont Scout Ranch Cimarron NM 87714

PRATT, E(LLEN) MARCELLA MORIN (MRS. GEORGE COLLINS PRATT), designer; b. Trail, B.C., Canada (parents Am. citizens); d. Francis George and Rose Delima (Bousquet) Morin; student extension courses Wash. State Coll.; grad. Normal Coll., Victoria, B.C.; m. George Collins Pratt, Sept. 22, 1946. With art dept. Universal Internat. Pictures 1935-46; now home designer and decorator, Cal., Wash. Mem. Assistance League So. Cal., Canadian Red Cross (life), Coachella Valley Community Concert Assn., Opera Guild Desert, Desert Forum, Eisenhower Med. Aux., Palm Desert, Cal. Republican. Club: Desert Dinner. Home: Box 2133 Laguna Hills CA 92653

PRATT, GERTRUDE VIOLA, educator; b. Boyne City, Mich., Oct. 19, 1899; d. William and Gertrude Helena (Sillaway) Pratt; B.A., Albion Coll., 1921; M.A. (Univ. fellow), U. Mich., 1923, postgrad., summers 1951, 57; postgrad. summers U. Cal. at Berkeley, 1927, U. Wis., 1929, U. Grenoble (France), 1938, McGill U., Montreal, Que., 1941, (Gen. Electric fellow) Purdue U., 1955, U. Hawaii, 1963. Tchr. math. Grand Ledge (Mich.) High Sch., 1921-22; head math. dept. Mt. Clemens (Mich.) High Sch., 1923-42; faculty Central Mich. U., Mt. Pleasant, 1946-69, asso. prof. math., 1946-69, asso. prof. emeritus, 1969—. Summer faculty Bay View U., 1922-24. Served to maj. WAC, AUS, 1942-46. Mem. Am. Assn. U. Women (past pres. Mt. Clemens), League Women Voters (chmn. observers 1971-73), Alpha Chi Omega, Kappa Mu Epsilon, Delta Sigma Rho. Mem. Order Eastern Star. Home: 200 E Gaylord St Mount Pleasant MI 48858

PRATT, JANE JO HARTLEY (MRS. CHANNING LEE PRATT), lawyer; b. Kankakee, Ill., May 19, 1930; d. Herman Roscoe Hartley and Edith (Kerr) Hartley Byrne; A.B. cum laude, Franklin Coll., 1952; LL.B., Ind. U., 1952, J.D., 1967; m. Channing Lee Pratt, Aug. 21, 1955; children—Paula Lee, Steven Hartley, Channing Lee. Sec., H.R. Hartley Assos., Indpls., 1946-49, Ind. State Fair Commn., Indpls., 1950-51; admitted to Ind. bar, 1955, Ill. bar, 1957; admissions counselor Franklin Coll., Ind., 1952; dormitory counselor Ind. U., Bloomington, 1952-53; research asst. Don Rogers, atty., Bloomington, 1953-55; legislative asst. U.S. Congressman, Washington, 1955-56; practiced in Monmouth, Ill., 1958—; mem. firm Love, Beal, Pratt, 1958—, asst. State's Atty., Warren County, Ill., 1964-68. Regional asst. Franklin Coll. Devel. Fund drive, 1967; mem. Monmouth Coll. Concert Lecture Bd., 1960-62, sec., 1960-61, chmn., 1962; mem. Monmouth Hosp. Aux. 1959—, Mon-mouth P.T.A. Council, 1964—; bd. dirs. Warren County YMCA, 1970—, pres., 1974; bd. dirs. Franklin Coll. Alumnae Assn., 1970-74; bd. dirs. Community Meml. Hosp., 1973—, pres., 1974—. Chairwoman Warren County Republican Com., Monmouth, 1962-70; Rep. del. Ill. State Conv. 1962, 64. Mem. Am., Ill. (probate and trust law council), Warren County (pres. 1967-68, sec. 1969-70) bar assns., Am. Judicature Soc., Ill. Fedn. Rep. Women, D.A.R., Talatashar Gt. Books Discussion Group (chmn. 1962-63), Pi Beta Phi. Methodist (ofcl. bd. 1964-66). Home: 415 N 9th St Monmouth IL 61462 Office: 57 SE Public Square Monmouth IL 61462

PRATT, JOAN BERRY (MRS. DAVID E. PRATT), accountant; b. Portland, Ore., Aug. 24, 1942; d. George E. and Charlotte V. (Bernard) Berry; B.C.S., Seattle U., 1964; M.B.A., U. Wash., 1967; m. David E. Pratt, June 12, 1967. Mem. audit staff Haskins & Sells, Seattle, 1964-66; accountant Edwin L. Luoma, C.P.A., Gearhart, Ore., 1968—. Bd. dirs. Clatsop Youth Devel. Assn. C.P.A., Ore., Wash. Mem. Am. Soc. Women Accountants, Am. Women's Soc. C.P.A.'s, Bus. and Profl. Women. Home: PO Box 574 Gearhart OR 97238 Office: 1010 Duane St Astoria OR 97103

PRATT, VIRGINIA LORRAINE, librarian; b. Trenton, Mich., June 15, 1919; d. Harry Grant and Gladys Fern (Harvey) Pratt; B.S. in Bus. Adminstrn., Wayne State U., 1942; B.S. in L.S., U. Denver, 1944; student U. Oslo, summer 1955. Asst. librarian United Aircraft Corp., E. Hartford, Conn., 1944-45; jr. librarian Redwood City (Cal.) Pub. Library, 1945-48; asst. librarian Stanford Research Inst., Menlo Park, Cal., 1948-50, librarian, 1950-57, mgr. library services, 1957—; cons. council rectors univs. Chile, 1957-58. Mem. Spl. Libraries Assn. (pres. San Francisco Bay Region chpt. 1958-59), Am. Soc. Information Sci., Nat. Microfilm Assn., Fedn. Internat. de Documentation, Inst. Mgmt. Sci. Home: 1019 Los Trancos Rd Menlo Park CA 94025 Office: 333 Ravenswood Av Menlo Park CA 94025

PRATT, YVONNE KATHLEEN (MRS. CHARLES ALFRED PRATT), real estate co. exec.; b. St. Boniface, Man., Can., May 18, 1921; d. John Caswell and Priscilla (Guilbault) Davis; U. Man., 1939-40; grad. Real Estate Inst., 1973; m. Charles Alfred Pratt, June 19, 1941; children—Donald, Charles, Arthur. Came to U.S., 1950, naturalized, 1955. Sales lady with realtor, Woodland Hills, Cal., 1967-70; owner Pratt Realty, Inc., Woodland Hills, 1970—. Mem. Internat. Real Estate Fedn., Women's Council, St. Anne's Maternity Hosp., Catholic Big Sisters, Woodland Hills C. of C. Republican. Roman Catholic. Home: 5885 Fitz Patrick Rd Hidden Hills CA 91302 Office: 23013 Ventura Blvd Woodland Hills CA 91364

PRATTER, MARIANNE BUNZL (MRS. PAUL J. PRATTER), chem. co. exec.; b. Vienna, Austria, Dec. 21, 1938; d. Izidor and Cerest (Bleier) Bunzl; came to U.S., 1960; naturalized, 1967; B.S. in Chemistry, Budapest U., Hungary, 1957; M.S. in Chemistry, U. Cal. at Los Angeles, 1962; m. Paul J. Pratter, Dec. 13, 1962; 1 son, Joshua E. Inorganic chemist Eastern div. Research Organic/Inorganic Chems. Corp., Belleville, N.J., 1963-65, adminstrv. dir., 1965-68, pres., 1968—; pres. Western div. Research Organic/Inorganic Chems. Corp., Sun Valley, Cal., 1968—. Mem. Am. Chem. Soc. Home: 50 Rock Spring Rd West Orange NJ 07052 Office: 507-519 Main St Belleville NJ 07109

PRAZAK, JANICE MILDRED ARNDT (MRS. GARY WILLIAM PRAZAK), social worker; b. Owatonna, Minn., June 24, 1940; d. Richard H. and Helen (Loges) Arndt; B.A., Wartburg Coll., 1962; M.S.W., U. Minn., 1964; m. Gary William Prazak, Sept. 6, 1968; children—Lisa Christine, Paul. Social caseworker Mpls. Rehab. Center, 1964-67; project coordinator, 1967-68, dir. social work services, 1968-69, dir. evaluation and program devel., 1970-72; cons. human services, 1972—. Seminar instr. Am. Rehab. Found., U. Va., 1968-69; cons. Commn. on Accreditation of Rehab. Facilities, 1968-72, Inst. for Interdisciplinary Studies, 1970—. Mem. Acad. Certified Social Workers. Home: 8218 W 16th St Minneapolis MN 55426 Office: 123 East Grant St Minneapolis MN 55403

PRAZAK, MURIEL (MRS. JACOB GEFFS), lawyer; b. Chgo., Dec. 6, 1926; d. John and Lydia (Bueker) Prazak; B.A., U. Wis., 1948, LL.B., 1951; m. Jacob Geffs, Sept. 21, 1955; 1 dau., Aileen. Admitted to Wis. bar, 1951; pvt. practice law, Clinton, Wis., 1951-69; mem. firm Prazak & Geffs, Clinton, 1969—. Mem. Wis., Rock County bar assns. Home: Box 2 Clinton WI 53525 Office: 213 Allen St Clinton WI 53525

PRCHAL, DOLORES, coll. adminstr.; b. Vienna, Austria, Sept. 17, 1915; d. Antonin and Maria (Marikova) Sperka; came to U.S., 1952, naturalized, 1957; B.A., San Jose State U., 1966, M.A., 1969; m. Edward M. Prchal, Sept. 3, 1943; 1 dau., Kejka (Mrs. Dennis Collins). Journalist, Czechoslovakia, 1935-39; staff mem. Dept. of Information, Czech Govt. in Exile, London, 1940-42; free lance writer, Czechoslovakia, 1945-50; staff mem. Helen Hay Whitney Found., N.Y.C., 1952-56; library asst. Foothill Coll., Los Altos Hills, Cal., 1958-66, librarian, 1966-71, asso. dean instrn., 1971—, coordinator library technical assisting program, 1967, 72—. Mem. adv. bd. dept. librarian ship San Jose State U., 1972—. Served with WAAF, 1942-45. Mem. Nat. Soc. for Programmed Instrn. (sec. chpt. 1965-66), Cal. Tchrs. Assn., Cal. Library Assn., Cal. Assn. for Edn. Media and Tech., Assn. for Ednl. Communications and Technology, Cal. Sch. Libraries Assn., Pub. Library Execs. of Central Cal. Home: 159 Paso Robles Los Altos CA 94022 Office: 12345 El Monte Los Altos Hills CA 94022

PREBIS, JEAN ELLEN, psychologist, educator; b. Chgo., Sept. 3, 1931; d. Edward John and Virginia (Smietanka) Prebis; B.S. in Occupational Therapy, U. Ill., 1954; M.A. in Human Devel., U. Chgo., 1962, Ph.D. (La Verne Noyes scholar), 1970. Dir. occupational therapy dept. Chgo. State Hosp., 1954-59; instr. psychology U. Chgo. extension div., 1965-66; instr. psychology Calumet campus, Purdue U., Hammond, Ind., 1969-70, asst. prof. psychology Purdue U., Hammond, 1970—, also tng. dir. Human Services, Child Tng. Program, 1971—. Dir. The Bridge, Inc. Cons. in gerontology Wildwood Manor Nursing Home, Gary, Ind., 1970-71. Mem. Ind. Planning Consortium on Child Care, 1972—, Mental Health Planning Commn., Hammond, 1973—, Tri-City Comprehensive Community Mental Health Center, Inc., 1974. USPHS traineeship in gerontology, 1961-63. State of Ill. Employment, Edn. grantee, 1959-61. Mem. Am., Ind. psychol. assns., Am. Occupational Therapy Assn., Ind. Assn. for Edn. of Young Children. Home: Rural Route 1 Box 183 Valparaiso IN 46383 Office: 171st St and Woodmar Hammond IN 46323

PREBLE, BETTY URIE (MRS. ROBERT BRUCE PREBLE), occupational therapist, hosp. adminstr.; b. Toledo, Aug. 9, 1922; d. Arthur William and Edna M. (McKenzie) Urie; B.S. in Zoology, U. Mich., 1947, M.P.H., 1973; certificate occupational therapy, Wayne State U., 1969; m. Robert Bruce Preble, June 21, 1947; children—Elizabeth, Margaret. Chemist, Pure Oil Co., Toledo, 1942-46; research asst. Parke Davis Co., Detroit, 1947-49; staff occupational therapist Sinai Hosp., Detroit, 1969-71; therapist Pub. Health Dept. Lenawee County (Mich.), 1972; dir. occupational therapy dept. Emma L. Bixby Hosp., Adrian, Mich., 1972-74; supr. occupational therapy dept. U. Mich. Hosp., Ann Arbor, 1974—. Mem. Am. Occupational Therapy Assn., Pi Theta Epsilon. Home: 1110 Fairholme Rd Grosse Pointe MI 48236 Office: U Mich Hosp Ann Arbor MI 48104

PREBLE, MABEL GORMLEY (MRS. PARKER E. PREBLE), counselor, city ofcl.; b. Oak Park, Ill., Mar. 1, 1924; d. Arthur Spain and Marguerite Ruth (Fietsch) Gormley; student U. Wis., 1942, U. Colo., 1943; B.A. (scholar), Denver U., 1961; M.S., Colo. State U., 1966; m. Parker E. Preble, July 5, 1945; children—Daniel, Deborah, Pamela, Christine. Staff psychologist Univ. Counseling Center, Colo. State U., Ft. Collins, 1966—. Chmn. Ft. Collins Sr. Citizen Commn., 1967-71; leader Girl Scouts, 1963-67; mem. region 2 Div. of Criminal Justice, Priorities and Steering Com. of Designing Tomorrow Today, 1970—. City councilman City of Fort Collins, 1971—, mayor, 1973—. Mem. Am., Colo. personnel and guidance assns., Colo. Municipal Assn. (mem. legislative com. 1973, mem. resolution com. 1973, mem. nominating com. 1973), League Women Voters, Psi Chi, Kappa Alpha Theta Alumni. Presbyn. Home: 717 Dartmouth Trail Fort Collins CO 80521 Office: C-13 Social Science Bldg Colo State U Fort Collins CO 80521

PREISNER, OLGA K., museum ofcl.; b. Prague, Czechoslovakia, Feb. 15, 1927; d. Karel and Vlasta (Vlasakova) Witt; Ph.D. in Art History and Aesthetics, Charles U., Prague, 1953; m. Rio Preisner, Aug. 21, 1951; 1 dau., Ruth Marie. Came to U.S., 1969, naturalized, 1974. Identification expert Czechoslovakian Adminstrn. Preservation Artistic and Historic Monuments, 1953-57; spl. asso. graphics dept. Nat. Gallery Art, Prague, 1957-64; research asso. Czechoslovakian Inst. Preservation Monuments, 1964-68; registrar Mus. Art, Pa. State U., 1972—. Author: Krivoklat, a Gothic Castle in Bohemia, 1964; Abstract and Imaginative Art in Czechoslovakia, 1966; co-author: New Discoveries of the Gothic Castle Vysoky Chlumec Jaroslav Herout, 1967. Home: 401 Weymouth Circle State College PA 16801 Office: Museum of Art Pa State Univ University Park PA 16802

PREISSER, BERNICE GOLDMAN (MRS. THOMAS E. PREISSER), advt. agy. exec.; b. Pitts., Mar. 18, 1917; d. Maurice and Ethel (Rosenstein) Goldman; student U. Pitts., 1934-36; B.A., U. Wis., 1938; m. Thomas E. Preisser, Apr. 10, 1947 (dec. May 1957); 1 son, Thomas E. III. Copywriter, Grant Advt. Co., Pitts, 1940-45; dir. TV/radio div. May Co., Los Angeles, 1945-50; sr. copywriter Wade Advt. Co., Los Angeles, 1950-54; consumer marketing dir. Ketchum, Macleod & Grove, Pitts., 1954-62; v.p. dir. consumer div. Lando/Bishopric Co., Pitts., 1962—. Dir., Civic Light Opera, Pitts., 1972—. Bd. dirs. Horizon Home, Pitts. Mem. Pitts. Advt. Club (Advt. Woman of Year 1965, v.p. 1955—), Radio-TV Club (dir.), Women in Communications, Press Club. Home: 4927 Wallingford St Pittsburgh PA 15213 Office: 725 Liberty Av Pittsburgh PA 15222

PREJS, GENEVIEVE BARBARA, med. record adminstr., cons.; b. New Britain, Conn.; d. Felix and Eve (Bonczek) Prejs; student Central Conn. State Tchrs. Coll., 1953-54; diploma St. Mary's Hosp. Sch. for Med. Record Librarians, 1956; B.S. in Edn., Boston, 1961; certificate in hosp. adminstrn. St. Louis U., 1970. Med. record librarian New Britain (Conn.) Meml. Hosp., 1953-54; med. record librarian Sancta Maria Hosp., Cambridge, Mass., 1957-66, adminstr., 1966-72; registered rec. adminstr. Bon Secours Hosp., Methuen, Mass., 1972—; cons. Baldpate Hosp., Georgetown, Mass., 1973—, Anlaw Nursing Home, Lawrence, Mass. Recipient commendation Mass. State Senate, 1971, Gov. of Mass., 1972; named First Lady of Day, WRCH, 1971. Mem. Am. Assn. Med. Record Librarians, Am. Acad. Med. Adminstrs., Am., Mass. med. record assns. Office: Bon Secours Hosp Methuen MA 01844

PRENDERGAST, NANCY ALLISON DRENAN (MRS. ROBERT MICHAEL PRENDERGAST), educator; b. Columbus, O., Dec. 26, 1932; d. Marion Crawford and Mabelle Ruth (Hurley) Drenan; B.S., Ohio State U., 1954; M.Ed., Temple U., 1970; m. Robert Michael Prendergast, Sept. 25, 1954; children—Robert Michael, Frank, Suzanne, Beth. Staff therapist, supr. Benjamin Franklin Hosp., Columbus, 1954-56; supr. Ohio Tb Hosp., Columbus, 1956-60, coordinator activities therapy, 1961-67; instr. Ohio State U., Columbus, 1956-67; cons. Ohio Dept. Welfare, 1960-61; asst. prof. Temple U., Phila., 1967-71; asso. prof., chmn. dept. occupational therapy Med. Coll. Ga., Augusta, 1971—. Mem. adv. com. Greater Del. Valley Comprehensive Health Planning, 1970-71; mem. Ga. Gov.'s Conf. on Arthritis, Task Force on Allied Health, 1972—; mem. profl. adv. group Ga. Regional Med. Program, 1972—; cons. to occupational therapy curriculum Towson (Md.) State Coll., 1973; mem. exec. com. Augusta Mental Health Assn. Mem. Am. (council on edn. 1965—, accreditation com. 1973—, continuing certification project 1973—), Ga. occupational therapy assns., Alpha Xi Delta. Editor: Principles of Clinical Education, 1971. Contbr. articles to profl. publs. Home: 1901 Brenda Dr North Augusta SC 29841 Office: Med Coll Ga Augusta GA 30902

PRENTICE, LOIS ANNE, lawyer; b. Bridgeport, Conn., Oct. 23, 1936; d. Samuel Rutherford and Beatrice C. (Minteau) Prentice; B.A. cum laude, U. Bridgeport, 1958; J.D., Columbia, 1963; student Sr.

Dramatic Workshop, N.Y.C., 1958-59. Admitted to Cal. bar, 1965; partner firm Ramsey & Prentice, Oakland, 1965, Belli, Ashe, Gerry & Ellison, San Francisco, 1965-66; pvt. practice, San Francisco, 1967—. Founding dir. Sausalito Art Assn., 1968. E. Everett Cortright scholar, 1954-58; grantee Columbia, 1960. Mem. Cal. Bar Assn., San Francisco Lawyers Club, Criminal Trial Lawyers No. Cal., Am. Trial Lawyers Assn. Club: Commonwealth (San Francisco). Contbr. legal jours. Home: PO Box 105D Sausalito CA 94965 Office: 605 Commercial St San Francisco CA 94111

PREOBRAJENSKA, VERA NICOLAEVNA, composer; b. San Francisco, Apr. 27, 1926; d. Nicolas A. and Tatiana N. (Kasperovich) Preobrajensky; spl. student Mills Coll., 1945-47, U. Cal. at Berkeley, 1945-49; A.A., San Francisco State Coll., 1952, A.B., 1953; M.A. in Mus. Composition, Bernadean U., Las Vegas, 1972, Ph.D. in Musicology, 1973; pvt. study piano and composition with Ernst von Dohnanyi, Dmitre Shostokovich; pvt. study with Darius Milhaud, Ernst Bloch, Roger Sessions, Frederick Jacobi, Alexander Tcherepnin. Concert mgr. Musical Artists of Am., 1959-61; musical stenographer Berkeley Music City Rec. Co., 1964; tchr., arranger songs Skye Music Services, Oakland, Cal., 1964; asst. tchr. women's phys. edn. U. Cal. Extension, Berkeley, 1965-68; classroom pianist for ballet and modern dance U. Cal. at Berkeley campus, 1965-68; writer, arranger orchestration for comml. song writing, 1949—; prof. music extension: corr. studies Bernadean U., 1973—. Asso. composer Am. Music Center N.Y.C., 1956—; mem. Music Performance Regional Arts Council, 1966—. Mem. Contemporary Cal. Composers, Am. Soc. Univ. Composers. Compositions include: Concept of the Egg, dance-comedy score, 1956; The Creation, cantata for chorus, 1970; Hebraic Rhapsodie (Ballet Score), for orch. 1968. Home: 5423 Ygnacio Av Oakland CA 94601

PRESAR, SANDRA EILEEN (MRS. CHARLES IRVIN PRESAR), educator; b. McCutchenville, O., Aug. 18, 1940; d. Ira Gerald and LaVere V. (Healy) Hablitzel; B.S. in Edn., Bowling Green State U., 1962, M.A. in Theatre, 1963; m. Charles Irvin Presar, Oct. 12, 1962; children—Stephanie, Craig, Jennifer, Jeremy. Tchr., Middle Island Schs., L.I., N.Y., 1963; sec. Hall of Free Enterprise, N.Y. World's Fair, N.Y.C., 1964; tchr. kindergarten Lorain (O.) Pub. Sch., 1966-67; instr. speech and dramatic arts W.Va. Wesleyan Coll., Buckhannon, 1968—. Vol., Booth Meml. Hosp., Queens, N.Y., 1964, Boulder Valley (Colo.) Schs., 1973. Mem. Jr. Women's Club Buckhannon (chmn. edn. dept. 1970-72), Sigma Tau Delta, Kappa Sigma Delta, Theta Alpha Phi (sec. 1961-62), Alpha Psi Omega, Pi Kappa Delta. Methodist. Home: 26 Central Av Buckhannon WV 26201

PRESS, AIDA KABATZNICK (MRS. NEWTON PRESS), editor; b. Boston, Nov. 18, 1926; d. Max and Rose Elizabeth (Segal) Kabatznick; A.B. cum laude, Radcliffe Coll., 1948; m. Newton Press, June 5, 1947; children—David, Dina (Mrs. John Weber), Benjamin. Waltham (Mass.) and Watertown corr. Boston Herald-Traveler, 1963-70; publs. asst. Brookline Pub. Schs., 1968-69; cons. Mass. Dept. Mental Health, 1966-72; editor Radcliffe Quar., Cambridge, Mass., 1971—; dir. news, publs. Harvard Grad. Design, 1972—. Pres., Newton (Mass.) Citizens for Edn., 1970-72. Chmn. ward 3 Democratic com., Newton, 1972—; mem. Dem. State Platform Com., 1972—. Recipient 1st prize Sch. Mgmt. mag., 1969. Mem. Am. Alumni Council (publication of distinction award 1974), Am. Coll. Pub. Relations Assn. Contbr. articles to gen. mags., newspapers. Home: 18 Furbush Av West Newton MA 02165 Office: 10 Garden St Cambridge MA 02138 also Gund Hall Cambrige MA 02138

PRESSLER, MARION JOAN, librarian; b. Hollidaysburg, Pa., June 24, 1925; d. Howard Delo and Alice Elizabeth (Buehler) Pressler; B.S., State Tchrs. Coll., Slippery Rock, Pa., 1946; M.L.S., Carnegie Inst. Tech., 1959; certificate of advanced study U. Chgo., 1969. Tchr. high sch., Sandy Lake, Pa., 1946-47; librarian high sch., Phillipsburg, Pa., 1947-49; staff mem. Altoona Mirror, newspaper, 1950-53; tchr. high sch., East Berlin, Pa., 1953-55, Hollidaysburg, 1955-58; librarian Mt. Lebanon Sch. Dist., Pitts., 1959—, chmn. library services, 1971—. Gen. chmn. Council Sch. Librarians, Pitts., 1967-68. Bd. dirs. Hollidaysburg Library. Frick Found. scholar, 1960-63. Mem. Nat., Pa. edn. assns., Mt. Lebanon Edn. Assn., Am., Pa. library assns., Blair County Hist. Soc., Friends of the Library, Altoona Community Theater, Altoona Music League, Sigma Tau Delta, Beta Phi Mu, Pi Lambda Theta, Alpha Psi Omega. Clubs: Blair County Women's, Hollidaysburg Women's. Contbr. articles to profl. jours. Home: Chatham Center Pittsburgh PA 15219 Office: Mount Lebanon School District Moffett St Pittsburgh PA 15243

PRESSMAN, FLORENCE, ednl. adminstr.; b. Boston; d. Sam and Mary (Ross) Pressman; B.S., Simmons Coll., 1958; M.A. in Student Personnel Adminstrn., Tchrs. Coll. Columbia, 1959, postgrad. 1968-70; postgrad. Johns Hopkins, 1959-60. Guidance cons., organizer exptl. human relations program Mass. Soldiers Home, Chelsea, summer 1959; asst. dir. residence Towson (Md.) State Tchrs. Coll., 1959-60; coordinator Melton Research Center, N.Y.C., 1961-71; dep. exec. dir. N.Y. State Optometric Assn., N.Y.C., 1971—. Mem. N.E.A., Am. Personnel and Guidance Assn., Am. Assn. U. Women, N.A.A.C.P., N.Y.C. Pub. Health Assn., Internat. Assn. Optometric Execs., Pi Lambda Theta, Kappa Delta Pi. Democrat. Jewish religion. Club: Manhattan Simmons (sec. 1968-70). Home: 173 E 90th St New York City NY 10028 Office: 250 W 57th St New York City NY 10019

PREST, DOROTHY BOYD, microbiologist, educator; b. Manchester, Mass., July 25, 1920; d. John Lee and Gertrude (Appleton) Prest; B.S., Mass. State Coll., 1942; M.A., Boston U., 1957; Ph.D., U. Ariz., 1966. Med. technologist Salem (Mass.) Hosp., 1942-46, New. Eng. Bapt. Hosp., Boston, 1946-47; chief med. technologist Salem Hosp., 1947-59; bacteriologist Tucson Med. Center, 1959-65; teaching asst. U. Ariz., Tucson, 1963-65, research asst., 1965-66; project asso. U. Wis., Madison, 1966-68; asst. prof. biology Keuka Coll., Keuka Park, N.Y., 1968-73, asso. prof. biology, 1973—. Mem. Am. Soc. for Microbiology, Mycol. Soc. Am., N.Y. Acad. Scis., A.A.A.S., Sigma Xi, Sigma Delta Epsilon, Chi Beta Phi. Episcopalian. Home: Box 178 Keuka Park NY 14478 Office: Biology Dept Keuka Coll Keuka Park NY 14478

PRESTIDGE, LELA FRANCES CHEEK, real estate broker; b. Floyd, N.M., Oct. 2, 1920; d. Hiram and Edyth Ellen (King) Cheek; grad. high sch.; m. Truman E. Prestidge, Sept. 22, 1947; children—Katherayn (Mrs. Fitzpatrick), Barbara Dugan, James E. Saleswoman, broker asso. Willoughby Real Estate, Highland, Cal., 1964-69; owner-realtor Prestidge Real Estate, Highland, 1970—. Mem. Am. Bus. Women's Assn., Highland Area C. of C. (pres. 1970). Home: 6978 N Central Av Highland CA 92346 Office: 27005 Baseline St Highland CA 92346

PRESTON, BETTY (MRS. PHILIP ROBIN OILER), journalist; b. Petoskey, Mich., Feb. 6, 1920; d. Earl Roy and Lillian Pauline (Emrey) Preston; B.A., Mich. State U., 1941; m. Philip Robin Oiler, Nov. 11, 1949. Women's editor Wyandotte (Mich.) News Herald, 1942-44, news editor, 1944-45; editor people sect. Glendale (Cal.) News Press, 1945-73, editor-mgr., 1974—. Bd. dirs. Glendale Community Found., Glendale Family Service. Recipient J.C. Penney awards U. Mo., 1962, 64, 67, 69. Mem. Women in Communications, Zeta Tau Alpha. Home: 4030 Lehman Rd La Crescenta CA 91214 Office: PO Box 991 Glendale CA 91209

PRESTON, ELIZA HOYT, editor; b. Columbia, Mo., Dec. 12, 1936; d. Charles Edwin and Frances Gertrude (Reynolds) Barkshire; A.B., U. Mo., 1955, B.J., 1956, M.A. Reporter, feature writer Daily Republican Times, Ottawa, Ill., 1956-61; asso. editor Irving Cloud Pub. Co., Lincolnwood, Ill., 1961-63; asst. editor Sci. Research Assos., Chgo., 1963-64; instr., pub. editor, extension div. Coll. Agr., U. Mo., Columbia, 1965-73; editor consumer information services Sears, Roebuck & Co., Chgo., 1973—. Chmn. pub. relations com. Boone County (Mo.) Assn. Mental Health, 1970-73. Mem. Am. Assn. Agrl. Coll. Editors, Am. Assn. U. Women, Chgo. Council Fgn. Relations, Kappa Epsilon Alpha, Theta Sigma Phi, Delta Delta Delta, P.E.O. Contbg. editor Mo. Today. Home: 145 Callan Av Evanston IL 60202

PRESTON, EUDORA LUVERNE MACDONALD (MRS. DOUGLAS G. PRESTON), artist; b. Calgary, Alta., Can., May 16, 1906; d. Frank Cameron and Elsie Almeda (Kinney) MacDonald; student U. Wash.; pvt. study; m. Douglas G. Preston, Oct. 8, 1928; children—Doris Jean (Mrs. R. B. Nickerson), David Douglas. One-man shows, Juneau, Fairbanks, Anchorage, Kodiak, Ketchikan (all Alaska), Pasadena, Cal., Seattle, Sumner, Wash., Los Angeles Tower Gallery, Baudon, Gold Beach, Ore.; exhibited in group shows N.Y., Washington, Fairbanks, Juneau, Ashland, Ore.; represented in permanent collections U. Alaska Mus. and Women's Dormitory, First Nat. Bank, Wien Alaska Airlines Office, Alaska Nat. Bank, Nordale Hotel, First Fed. Savs. & Loan Gallery (all Fairbanks), Midnight Sun Broadcasting Co., Anchorage, White House, Washington, Vatican City, Arch-Diocese Anchorage, Alaska, also pvt. collections. Instr. art, oil painting Ladd br. U. Alaska, Fairbanks, U. Alaska Community Coll., also pvt. classes. Mem. adv. council Alaska Bd. Edn., 1961—. Fellow Internat. Inst. Arts and Letters, Intercontinental Biog. Assn.; mem. Nat. League Am. Pen Women (past Alaska pres. and North Pacific regional dir. 1958—), Bus. and Profl. Women (Alaska past v.p.), Pioneer Women of Alaska, Am. Artists Profl. League, St. Augustine Art Assn. Home: Route 1 Box 29-D North Bank Rd Gold Beach OR 97444

PRESTON, LELIA BRUTUS (MRS. ROBERT WENDEL PRESTON), banker; b. Lafayette, Ind., Jan. 10, 1911; d. John Walter and Clara Belle (McFerren) Brutus; grad. Anthony Wayne Inst., 1930; m. Robert Wendel Preston, Aug. 19, 1938; 1 dau., Roberta Sue (Mrs. Larry Duane Rothenberger). Asst. to dir. admissions Culver Mil. Acad., 1930-37; sec. to dist. supr. ICC, 1937-46; officer trust operations Lafayette Nat. Bank, Ind., 1959-72, asst. trust officer, 1972—. Mem. Citizens Lay Com. constrn. high sch., 1969. Named Hon. Girl Scout, Girl Scouts Am., Lafayette, 1956. Mem. Am. Inst. Banking (sec. Lafayette chpt. 1961), Nat. Assn. Bank Women, Alpha Phi Mothers (pres. Purdue U. Chpt. 1968, 69). Club: Cosmopolitan (Lafayette). Home: 1504 Franklin St Lafayette IN 47905 Office: Lafayette Nat Bank 337 Columbia St Lafayette IN 47902

PRESTON, LOYCE ELAINE, educator; b. Texarkana, Ark., Feb. 25, 1929; d. Harvey Martin and Florence (Whitlock) Preston; student Texarkana Jr. Coll., 1946-47; B.S., Henderson State Tchrs. Coll., 1950; certificate in social work La. State U., 1952; M.S.W., Columbia U., 1956. Tchr. pub. schs. Dierks, Ark., 1950-51; child welfare worker Ark. Dept. Pub. Welfare, Clark and Hot Spring Counties, 1951-56, child welfare cons., 1956-58; casework dir. Ruth Sch. Girls, Burien, Wash., 1958-60; asst. prof. spl. edn. La. Poly. Inst., Ruston, 1960-63; asst. prof. Northwestern State Coll., Shreveport, La., 1963-73; asst. prof. La. State U., Shreveport, 1973—. Chpt. sec. La. Assn. Mental Health, 1965-67, Govs. adv. council, 1967-70. Mem. Am. Assn. Univ. Women (dir. Shreveport br. 1963-68), Acad. Cert. Social Workers, Nat. Assn. Social Workers (del. 1964-65, pres.-elect N. La. chpt., state-wide com. 1967-68, pres. 1968-69), La. Conf. Social Welfare, Council Exceptional Children (v.p. La. fedn. 1969-70, pres.-elect 1970-71, pres. 1971-72), La. Tchrs. Assn. Home: 602 Pickwick Pl Shreveport LA 71108 Office: 8515 Youree Dr Shreveport LA 71105

PRESTON, SISTER PATRICIA ANN, ednl. adminstr.; b. Milw., Mar. 11, 1933; d. Charles Francis and Dorothy Catherine (Engman) Preston; B.A. magna cum laude with honors, Bryn Mawr Coll., 1955; M.A. (Wilson fellow), Cath. U. Am., 1961, Ph.D., 1964. Tchr. Christ King Sch., Wauwatosa, Wis., 1955-56; joined Order Sch. Sisters Notre Dame, 1956; part-time instr. Spanish, Mt. Mary Coll., Milw., 1956-59, prof., 1964-71, chmn. Spanish dept., 1970-71, acad. dean, 1971—; tchr. Spanish, Acad. of Our Lady, Chgo., 1959-60; founder, dir. Project Head Start, Council for Spanish Speaking, Milw., 1965-71; founder, dir. Guadalupe Center, Milw., 1966-71. Lectr. various civic, religious groups, 1965—; dir. performing arts program Co-op. Coll. Urban Program for Learning Exchange, 1968-70; cons., developer Milw. Pub. Schs. Bilingual program, 1969—; cons. Renascence Soc., 1966-70; cons.-evaluator North Central Assn. Colls., 1974—. Mem. adv. bd. Wis. State Day Care, Madison, 1967-70; chmn. com. social responsibility of conf. maj. superiors Women of Milw. Archdiocese, 1967-68; task force mem. County Mental Health Planning Com., Milw., 1969-70; mem. adv. bd. Law Enforcement Assistance Act, Milw. Fire and Police Commn., 1970. Chmn. coalition bd. Project Head Start, Milw., 1970-74. Bd. dirs. Council for Spanish Speaking, Milw., Cath. Social Services, Milw. Recipient Hester Ann Corner Prize in lit. Bryn Mawr Coll., 1955; Woodrow Wilson dissertation fellow, 1963-64; Fulbright Summer Seminar fellow to Spain, summer 1966. Mem. Am. Assn. Higher Edn., Am. Conf. Acad. Deans. Author: A Study of Significant Variants in the Poetry of Gabriela Mistral, 1964. Address: 2900 Menomonee River Pkwy Milwaukee WI 53222

PRESTON, PENNY ANN, librarian; b. Toronto, Ont., Can., Nov. 27, 1942; d. Hugh Wilfred and Etta Margaret (Weber) Price; diploma St. Michael's Hosp., Toronto, 1962; married. Asst. med. record librarian Mississauga (Ont.) Hosp., 1962-65, chief med. record librarian, 1965—. Tchr. continuing edn. Sheridan Coll. Mem. Canadian, Ont. health record assns. Home: 830 Westlock Rd Mississauga ON Canada Office: 100 Queensway W Mississauga ON Canada

PRESTWOOD, ANNIE KATHERINE, wildlife parasitologist; b. Lenoir, N.C., July 4, 1935; d. John Howard and Emily Beatrice (Adkins) Prestwood; student Woman's Coll., U. N.C., 1954-56; B.S., N.C. State U., 1960; D.V.M., U. Ga., 1962, M.S., 1964, Ph.D. (Southeastnern Coop. Wildlife Disease Study fellow), 1968. Research asso. Southeastern Coop. Wildlife Disease Study, Coll. Vet. Medicine, U. Ga., Athens, 1966—. Mem. Am., Ga. vet. med. assns., Wildlife Disease Assn., Wildlife Soc. (council 1974—), Am. Soc. Parasitologists. Mem. editorial bd. Jour. Wildlife Mgmt., 1973. Home: Route 2 Athens GA 30601 Office: Coll Veterinary Medicine U Ga Athens GA 30602

PREUSS, ANNE MACDOUGALL (MRS. J.M. PREUSS), editor; b. Mpls., Aug. 28, 1934; d. F.H. and Anne Van Derlip (Reichmann) MacDougall; B.A., Swarthmore Coll., 1956; postgrad. Courtauld Inst. Art, London U., 1956-57; m. J.M. Preuss, Jan. 21, 1961; children—Eric M., Ian M. Editorial asst. Mademoiselle mag., N.Y.C., 1957-59; with Met. Museum Art, N.Y.C., 1959—, asso. editor art publs., 1968-74, editor, 1974—. Mem. com. to administer the Greening of Ruppert, garden plots from vacant lots, 1972-73. Mem. Victorian Soc. Home: 86 Stuyvesant Av Larchmont NY 10538 Office: Met Museum Art 5th Av and 82d St New York City NY 10028

PREVIN, DORY LANGAN, lyricist; b. Rahway, N.J.; d. Michael Joseph and Florence Annastasia (Shannon) Langan; student Am. Acad. Dramatic Art; m. Andre Previn (div.). Began career as jr. writer MGM Studios; writer UPA Animation Studios, 2 years; lyricist for numerous films, including song The Faraway Part of Town from Pepe, 1961, Second Chance from Two for the Seesaw, 1962, Come Saturday Morning from The Sterile Cuckoo, 1969; author Go Go Frug (satirical protest songs), 1967; author English libretto for opera The Impresario (Mozart), 1969; author, performer for record album On My Way to Where, 1970. Lectr. lyric writing course U. Cal. at Los Angeles. Address: 120 El Camino Dr Beverley Hills CA 90212

PREWITT, JUDITH MARTHA SHIMANSKY, mathematician; b. Bklyn., Oct. 16, 1935; d. Charles Theodore and Rebecca (Sanders) Shimansky; student Harvard, 1954; B.A. with high honors, Swarthmore Coll., 1957; M.A. in Math., U. Pa., 1959, postgrad., 1959-62, 65-66; m. Richard Hickman Prewitt III, July 2, 1956; 1 son, David Joshua. Asst. devel. engr. Burroughs Corp., Paoli, Pa., 1956-57, mathematician, 1958; mathematician, analyst programmer Auerbach Corp., Phila., 1961-62; asst. instr. dept. math. U. Pa., Phila., 1960-62, research asst., 1962, instr., 1963, research mathematician, instr. dept. rediology Sch. Medicine, 1962-71; mathematician div. computer research and tech. NIH, Bethesda, Md., 1971—, also coms. on automated cytology and radiologic diagnosis Nat. Cancer Inst.; cons. biomathematics Community Mental Health Center, Hahnemann Med. Coll., also Dept. Radiology, U. Pa. Mem. Sci. Research Soc. Am., Math. Assn. Am., Soc. Indsl. and Applied Math. (past chmn. Del. valley sect., past mem. nat. standing com. on sects.), Assn. Computing Machinery (reviewer computing revs. Rev. Jour.), Internat. Platform Assn., Biomed. Engring. Soc. (charter), I.E.E.E. (sr.), A.A.A.S., Mortar Board, Phi Beta Kappa, Sigma Xi. Research applied math., math. modeling and computer simulation in biology and medicine, pattern recognition and artificial intelligence, automatic analysis of biomed. pictorial data, mathematico-statis. studies tumor growth and therapy optimization, computer models for investment portfolios. Contbr. numerous articles to profl. pubs. Home: 8008 Aberdeen Rd Bethesda MD 20014 Office: Div Computer Research and Tech Nat Insts Health Bethesda MD 20014

PRIBBLE, MARY JO, chemist, educator; b. Macfarlan, W.Va., Jan. 20, 1930; d. Willis and Flora Isabel (Skidmore) Pribble; B.A., Maryville Coll., Tenn., 1952; M.A., Duke, 1957; Ph.D. (NSF Faculty fellow) in Chemistry, La. State U., 1970. Instr. chemistry Marietta (O.) Coll., 1957-59; documentation chemist Ethyl Corp., Baton Rouge, La., 1959-61; instr. chemistry Marshall U., Huntington, W.Va., 1961-63; asst. prof. chemistry Limestone Coll., Gaffney, S.C., 1963-66, asso. prof., 1967-69, prof., chmn. dept. chemistry, 1969-70, prof. chemistry, chmn. div. Sci. and Math., 1970—. Mem. Am. Chem. Soc. (sec., treas. Western Carolina sect. 1973-74), S.C. Acad. Sci., Am. Assn. Univ. Profs., Am. Assn. Univ. Women (pres. Gaffney br. 1966-68), Sigma Xi, Iota Sigma Pi. Home: 700 Lyman St Gaffney SC 29340

PRIBYL, MARY KAY, clin. psychologist; b. Kansas City, Mo., July 14, 1941; d. Walter Brault and Honore Gorman (Walter) Neilsen; B.S., Loyola U., Chgo., 1964; M.A., Northwestern U., 1966, Ph.D., 1967; m. Joseph F. Pribyl, June 26, 1965; children—Stephen, Karen. Asst. prof. Loyola U., 1969-70, lectr. psychology, 1970-72; pvt. practice clin. psychology, Glenview, Ill., 1972—. Mem. Am., Midwestern, Ill. psychol. assns., Sigma Xi, Phi Sigma Tau. Contbr. articles to profl. jours. Home: 1231 Pam Anne Dr Glenview IL 60025 Office: 1029 Pine St Glenview IL 60025

PRICE, CHRISTINE HILDA, author, illustrator; b. London, Eng., Apr. 15, 1928; d. Clair and Hilda (Cumings) Price; student Vassar Coll., 1944-45, Art Students League, 1945-46, Central Sch. Arts and Crafts London, Eng., 1949-51. Mem. Soc. Women Geographers, Art Students League (life), Internat. P.E.N., Nat., Mass. Audubon socs., Authors Guild, Archeol. Inst. Am. Episcopalian. Author: Three Golden Nobles, 1951; The Dragon and the Book, 1953; Song of the Wheels, 1956; David and the Mountain, 1959; Made in the Middle Ages, 1961; Made in the Renaissance, 1963; The Story of Moslem Art, 1964; The Valiant Chattee-Maker, 1965; Cities of Gold and Isles of Spice, 1965; Made in Ancient Greece, 1967; Sixty at a Blow, 1968; Happy Days, 1969; Made in Ancient Egypt, 1970; The City of the Dagger and other tales from Burma, 1971 (with H.H. Keely); Heirs of the Ancient Maya, 1972; Talking Drums of Africa, 1973. Illustrator numerous children's books. Address: RFD 1 Castleton VT 05735

PRICE, HELEN MONA, mgmt. cons. firm exec.; b. Omaha, July 16, 1918; d. Beary Leroy and Ella Grace (Cleasby) Price; student U. Omaha, 1934-35. With Am. Condenser Co., Chgo., 1951-56; with Albert Ramond & Assos., mgmt. cons., Chgo., 1956—, sec.-treas., 1959—, v.p., 1974—, also dir. Club: Altrusa (pres. Chgo. 1967-68). Home: 6538 N Northwest Hwy Chicago IL 60631 Office: Albert Ramond & Assos Inc Tribune Tower Chicago IL 60611

PRICE, JOAN ALECE, educator; b. Phoenix, May 20, 1931; d. Fred V. and Loreen (Ackley) Price; B.S., U. Ariz., 1955; M.S. (Univ. fellow); Springfield (Mass.) Coll., 1956; M.A. (Univ. fellow), Ariz. State U., 1969, Ph.D., 1973. Tchr. physiology S.W. Tex. State Coll.; 1956-57; tchr. English and phys. edn. Wickenburg High Sch., 1957-59, Westfield (Mass.) High Sch., 1960-61, Stafford (Ariz.) High Sch., 1961-62; counsellor Paradise Valley High Sch., 1962-63; free lance writer, Scottsdale, Ariz., 1963-68; prof. philosophy Mesa (Ariz.) Community Coll., 1969—. Lectr. Oriental philosophy, philosophy of Sri Aurobindo, psychology of Carl G. Jung. Author: A Very Special Burro, 1966; also mag. articles on Hopi Indian ceremonies and philosophy, pamphlet on philosophy of Aurobindo. Office: Mesa Community College Mesa AZ 85201

PRICE, JOYCE EVALINE, physician; b. Altoona, Pa., Oct. 27, 1927; d. Ray John and Esther Louise (Corbin) Price; R.N., Jefferson Sch. Nursing, 1949; A.B., Immaculata Coll., 1961; M.D., Jefferson Med. Coll., 1965. With dept. surg. research Jefferson Med. Coll., 1951-58; intern Pa. Hosp., Phila., 1965-66, resident surgery, 1966-70; cardiovascular surg. fellow Jefferson Hosp., Phila., 1970-71; practice medicine, specializing in gen. and vascular surgery, Farmington, N.M., 1972—; mem. staff San Juan Hosp., Farmington. Dir. N.M. Blue Cross-Blue Shield. Mem. com. continuing med. edn. State of N.M. Diplomate Am. Bd. Surgery. Fellow Internat. Coll. Surgeons, S.W. Surg. Congress, Am. Coll. Angiology; mem. A.C.S., A.M.A. (Physicians Recognition award 1970, 72), N.M., Pa., Philadelphia County, San Juan County (past sec.-treas., now pres.) med. socs., Am. Coll. Abdominal Surgeons. Home: 5302 Hill'n Dale St Farmington NM 87401 Office: 304 S Lake St Farmington NM 87401

PRICE, LEAH ZIMRING (MRS. MORRIS PRICE), educator; b. Bklyn., Apr. 25, 1916; d. Frank and Anna (Brenner) Zimring; B.A., Bklyn. Coll., 1937; M.A., Queens Coll., 1957; Ph.D., Adelphi U., 1965; m. Morris Price, July 10, 1938; children—Wayne, Kenneth. Various positions, 1931-54; tchr. Uniondale High Sch., 1954-55, guidance counselor, 1955-61; clin. psychologist VA, N.Y.C., 1962-66;

asst. prof. edn. dept. Lehman Coll., Bronx, N.Y., 1966—. Faculty, Adelphi U., part-time 1964-66; pvt. practice as psychologist, Valley Stream, N.Y., part-time 1966—. Mem. Am., Eastern, Nassau County, N.Y. State psychol. assns., Am. Assn. U. Profs. Home: 144 Albermarle Av Valley Stream NY 11580 Office: Lehman Coll Bronx NY 10468

PRICE, LEONTYNE, concert, opera singer; b. Laurel, Miss., Feb. 10, 1927; d. James A. and Kate (Baker) Price; B.A., Central State Coll. Wilberforce, O., 1949; student Juilliard Sch. Music, 1949-52; studied singing with Florence Page Kimball; D.Mus. (hon.), Howard U., 1962, Central State U., 1968; L.H.D. (hon.), Dartmouth U., 1962, Fordham U., 1969; Dr. Humanities (hon.), Rust Coll., 1968. Appeared as Bess in Porgy and Bess, Vienna, Berlin, Paris, London, under auspices U.S. State Dept., also N.Y.C. and U.S. tour, 1952-54; recitalist, soloist with symphonies, U.S., Can., Australia, Europe, 1954—; appeared concerts in India, auspices State Dept., 1956, 64; soloist Hollywood Bowl, 1955-59, 66, Berlin Festival, 1960; opera singer NBC-TV, 1955-58, 60, 62, 64, San Francisco Opera Co., 1957-59, 60-61, 63, 65, 67, 68, 71, Vienna Staats-opera, 1958, 59-60, 61, Berlin Opera, 1964, Rome Opera, 1966, Paris Opera, 1968; recital Brussels Internat. Fair, auspices State Dept., 1958, Verona Opera Arena, 1958-59, recitals Yugoslavia for State Dept., 1958; recording artist RCA-Victor, appeared Covent Garden, London, 1958-59, 70, Chgo. Lyric Theatre, 1959, 60, 65; soloist Salzburg Festival, 1959, 60, 61, 62, 63, Met. Opera, N.Y.C., 1961-62, 63-70, 72, La Scala-Milana, 1960-61, 63, 67, 68; debut Teatro Colon, Buenos Aires, Argentina, 1969, Hamburg Opera, 1970. Recipient 20 Grammy awards Nat. Acad. Rec. Arts and Scis., 1960-69; citation YWCA, 1961; Spirit of Achievement award Albert Einstein Coll. Medicine, 1962, citation of Merit, N.Y. Singing Tchrs. Assn., 1962; Recipient merit award for role of Tosca in NBC-TV Opera, Mademoiselle mag., 1955; Hon. mem. bd. dirs. Campfire Girls; hon. vice chmn. U.S. nat. com. UNESCO; co-chmn. Rust Coll. Upward Thrust Campaign. Trustee, bd. dirs. Internat. House; mem. adv. bd. Nat. Cultural Center. Presidential medal freedom, 1964; Spingarn Medal, N.A.A.C.P., 1965. Schwann Catalog award for rec. Prima Donna, vol. 1, 1968, also Number 1 in Nation Award, 1968; named Musician of Yr., Mus. Am. Mag., 1961; decorated Order of Merit, Republic Italy, 1965. Fellow Am. Acad. Arts and Scis.; mem. Am. Guild Mus. Artists, Actors Equity Assn., Am. Fedn. TV and Radio Artists, Sigma Alpha Iota, Delta Sigma Theta. Address: 1133 Broadway New York City NY 10010

PRICE, LOIS MATILDA BARTLETT (MRS. CLARENCE LEE PRICE), real estate broker; b. Clarksburg, W.Va., Sept. 10, 1930; d. Flavious Dorsey and Blanche (Hacker) Bartlett; student West Liberty State Coll., 1948-49, Fairmont State Coll., 1949, W.Va. U., 1950, Santa Monica Coll., 1969-74; m. Clarence Lee Price, Dec. 23, 1949; children—Sylvia (Mrs. David Andrew Lowe), Pamela, Melvin, Evelyn. Sec.-treas. C L Properties, Inc., Sant Monica, Cal., 1969-71, pres., 1971-73; salesman Western Real Estate Co., Santa Monica, 1973-74. Leader, Camp Fire Girls, 1962-67, sponsor, 1969-73. Bd. dirs. Meals on Wheels, Santa Monica. Recipient AWAKAN award, 1969. Mem. Santa Monica Bay Dist Bd. Realtors (dir. 1973). Presbyn. (deacon 1973-75, sec. 1973, chancel choir pres. 1973-74, moderator 1974). Home: 2139 Carlyle Av Santa Monica CA 90402 Office: 1407 Montana Av Santa Monica CA 90403

PRICE, LUCILE BROWN (MRS. CHARLES EDWARD PRICE), b. Decorah, Ia., May 31, 1902; d. Sidney Eugene and Cora (Drake) Brickner; B.S., Ia. State U., 1925; M.A., Northwestern U., 1940; m. Maynard Wilson Brown, July 2, 1928 (dec. Apr. 1937); m. 2d, Charles Edward Price, Jan. 14, 1961. Asst. dean women Kan. State U., Manhattan, 1925-28; mem. bd. student personnel adminstrn. Northwestern U., 1937-41; personnel research Sears Roebuck & Co., Chgo., 1941-42, overseas club dir. A.R.C., Eng., Africa, Italy, 1942-45; dir. Child Edn. Found., N.Y.C., 1946-56. Participant 1st Ia. Humanists Summer Symposium, 1974. Del. Mid Century White House Conf. on Children and Youth, 1950; mem. com. on program and research of Children's Internat. summer villages, 1952-53; mem. bd. N.E. Ia. Mental Health Center, 1959-62, pres. bd., 1960-61; mem. Ia. State Extension Adv. Com., 1973—. Trustee Porter House Mus., Decorah, Ia. Mem. Am. Coll. Personnel Assn., (life), Am. Overseas Assn. (nat. bd.; life), Am. Assn. U. Women (life mem., mem. bd. Decorah; chmn. mass media in the past 1965—, area rep. world problems, chmn. study-action group 1973-75), Nat. Assn. Mental Health (del. nat. conf. 1958), Norwegian-Am. Mus. (life), Ia. Soc. for Preservation Historic Landmarks, Winneshiek County Hist. Soc. (life), D.A.R., Common Cause, Pi Lambda Theta, Chi Omega. Home: 508 W Broadway Decorah IA 52101

PRICE, NORMA ANN (MRS. JAMES WILLIAM ESTES), physician; b. Raleigh, N.C., Apr. 12, 1942; d. George Norman and Elizabeth Ann (Cooper) Price; B.S., Miss. Coll., 1964; postgrad. U. Miss., 1963-65; M.D., U. Tenn., 1966; m. James William Estes, Oct. 26, 1968; children—Justin Scott, Crista Laine. Intern, City of Memphis Hosps., 1967-68, resident in internal medicine, 1969-71; practice medicine specializing in internal medicine and hematology, Memphis, 1968-73, in oncology and hematology, Atlanta, 1973—; fellow M.D. Anderson Hosp. and Research Inst., Houston, 1972; fellow in oncology Emory U. Clin. and Hosp., 1972-73. Mem. Alpha Chi. Republican. Baptist. Research in hematology, platelet function in sickle cell disease. Home: 607 Conway Forest Dr NW Atlanta GA 30327 Office: 960 Johnson Ferry Rd NE Atlanta GA 30342

PRICE, RUTH GILL, museum ofcl.; b. Jackson, Miss., Feb. 5, 1901; d. Willis Preston and Lucie Abbie (Gill) Price; student Shorter Coll., 1918-19; spl. student Agnes Scott Coll., 1921. Secretarial positions with various businesses, 1923-42; sec. Ark. Dept. Edn., Little Rock, 1942-46. Tchr. Retirement System of Miss., Jackson, 1946-52; bookkeeper, sec. Miss. Library Commn., Jackson, 1953-55; co-owner, mgr. R. & D. Price, Booksellers, Jackson, 1955-61; resident hostess The Oaks Museum House, Jackson, Miss., 1965—. Recipient Blue Ribbon, Miss. Art Assn. Oil Show, 1947. Baptist. Home: 823 N Jefferson St Jackson MS 39202

PRICE, VIRGINIA ANN, extension home economist; b. Augusta, Ark., July 28, 1938; d. Ben Burks and Edna M. (Harrison) Price; B.S., U. Ark., 1960; M.S., Okla. State U., 1967. Asst. home demonstration agt. Okla. State Co-op. Extension Service, Guthrie, 1960-61, asst. home demonstration agt., Shawnee, 1961-62, home demonstration agt., Nowata, 1962-66, extension home economist, Medford, 1967-72, Tahlequah, Okla., 1972—. Mem. adv. bd. Medford Sr. Citizens, 1968-69; mem. Bicentennial Commn., Cherokee Cultural Arts Council. Bd. dirs. Nowata Library, 1963-66. Recipient N.E. Okla. A. and M. Coll. Rural Youth Leadership award, 1965; Norma Brumbaugh scholar, 1963. Mem. Okla. (sec. 1965, treas., 1969-71), Nat. assns. extension home economists, Am. Home Econs. Assn., Epsilon Sigma Phi, Phi Upsilon Omicron. Methodist. Editor, EHE Reporter, 1974-75. Home: 1004 N Francis St Tahlequah OK 74464 Office: 210 S Water St PO Box 149 Tahlequah OK 74464

PRICHARD, NANCY SAWYER GILBERT (MRS. KENNETH D. PRICHARD), assn. exec.; b. Owosso, Mich., Mar. 9, 1924; d. Morgan Rowland and Helen Morrill (Stone) Gilbert; B.A. cum laude, U. Wash., 1952, M.A., 1954; m. Kenneth D. Prichard, Dec. 9, 1954; 1 son (by previous marriage), Thomas Morgan Davis. Teaching fellow U. Wash., 1952-54; tchr. English and speech St. Nicholas Sch. for Girls, Seattle, 1958-64; prof. English, asst. chmn. humanities div., dir. coll. exploratory program Shoreline Community Coll., Seattle, 1964-69; asst. exec. sec. Nat. Council Tchrs. English, Urbana, Ill., 1969-73, asso. exec. sec., 1973—. Speaker, cons. at nat. and regional confs. on teaching English. Field reader U.S. Office Edn., 1972—. Served with WAVES, 1944-45. Recipient Oral Interpretation award U. Wash., 1952. Mem. Am. Assn. U. Profs., Phi Beta Kappa. Editor: (with J. Strugar, D. Wright, A. Maxwell) Voices, 1970. Contbr. articles on tchr. edn., lit. of Third World. Home: 806 Oakland St Urbana IL 61801 Office: 1111 Kenyon Rd Urbana IL 61801

PRICKETT, MARGARET HARRIS, mayor; b. Mishawaka, Ind.; d. Edward and Myrtle (Jones) Harris; grad. high sch.; m. Ward D. Prickett, Aug. 29, 1929; children—Carolyn (Mrs. Phil Gutman), Joyce (Mrs. Richard Coppens), Marilyn (Mrs. Robert Ehhsagser). Pres., owner Prickett's Supermarket Inc., Mishawaka, 1930—; mayor of Mishawaka, 1964—. Mem. Bus. and Profl. Women's Club. Mem. Order Eastern Star. Home: 2006 Linden Av Mishawaka IN 46544 Office: Mayor's Office City Hall Mishawaka IN 46544

PRIDDY, MARJORIE (MRS. NEWTON D. PRIDDY), former hosp. exec.; b. Cleve.; d. Joseph Patrick and Margaret Haley (Cain) Nealon; R.N., Charity Hosp. Sch. Nursing, 1932; postgrad. Ohio State U.; m. Newton D. Priddy, Dec. 3, 1935 (dec.); children—Marjorie Ann, Dale (foster son). Former owner (with husband) Ravenswood (W.Va.) Hosp. Mem. Ohio Heritage Club, Internat. Platform Assn. Clubs: Senior Women's, DeSales Heights Academy Mother's (past pres.). Address: 136 Washington Ravenswood WV 26164

PRIDE, L. FRANCES, educator; b. Sawyer, Kan., Nov. 29, 1920; d. Roy Henry and Marian Nellie (Sandburg) Pride; B.S., Union Coll., Lincoln, Neb., 1950; M.S., U. Colo., 1956; Ph.D., U. Md., 1967; postgrad. Georgetown, U., 1972-74. Med. head nurse Boulder (Colo.) Meml. Hosp., 1945-48; instr. Union Coll., Lincoln, 1950-55, asst. prof., 1956-60; asso. prof. Columbia Union Coll., Takoma Park, Md., 1960-66, prof., 1967—, head grad. program psychiat. nursing, 1967-74, chmn. gen. studies, 1971-74; asso. dean Sch. Nursing, dir. grad. program in nursing Loma Linda (Cal.) U., 1974—; cons. psychiat. nursing Loma Linda U., 1959, Washington Sanitarium Hosp., 1963, 68-74, N.M. State Hosp., Las Vegas, 1966-67; cons. curriculum revision So. Missionary Coll., Collegedale, Tenn., 1970-72; cons. test constrn. No. Va. Community Coll., Annandale, 1972; cons. curriculum Andrews U., Mich., 1972-74. Mem. speaker's bur. Montgomery County Assn. Mental Health, Md., 1960-65, com. social action, 1968-72. Recipient Pre-doctoral fellow Dept. Health, Edn. and Welfare, 1963-67. Mem. Am., Colo. (sec. ednl. adminstrs. counsellors tchrs. 1958-60), Md. (dir. dist. V 1964-68, 70-72, 2d v.p. 1970-72, chmn. nominating com. 1973) nurses assns., Assn. Seventh-day Adventist Nurses (mem. nominating com. 1972-74, forum editor 1972-74), Am. Ednl. Research Assn., Assn. Adventist Forums, Sigma Theta Tau, Phi Beta Kappa. Contbr. articles profl. jours. Home: 52 Orange Tree Villa 25210 Lawton Av Loma Linda CA 92354

PRIDMORE, PATRICIA ANN, banker; b. Pelzer, S.C., May 10, 1935; d. William Richard and Verna Lee (Fielding) Pridmore; student Draughon's Bus. Coll., Greenville, S.C., 1953. Clk., Gen. Mortgage Co., Greenville, 1953-55; clk. S.C. Nat. Bank, Greenville, 1955-61; trust operations officer Bankers Trust S.C., N.A., Greenville, 1961—. Mem. Nat. Assn. Bank Women. Baptist. Home: 322 Farley Av Laurens SC 29360 Office: PO Box 608 Greenville SC 29602

PRIEFERT, VIRGINIA RUTH (MRS. BURDETTE WILLIAM PRIEFERT), curator; b. Alexandria, Neb., Dec. 14, 1929; d. Max and Ruth Elizabeth (Thomas) Griffin; student Fairbury Jr. Coll., summers 1947-55, U. Neb., 1949-50; m. Burdette William Priefert, Feb. 14, 1951; children—Jack Erwin, Leah Pauline. Tchr., Alexandria, 1954-60; spl. edn. tchr. Thayer County Spl. Edn. Class, Belvidere, Neb., 1962-64; curator Thayer County Mus., Belvidere, 1970—. Sec., Belvidere Community Improvement Program, 1970-75, Thayer County Tchrs. Assn., 1957-58. Mem. Thayer County Hist. Soc. (pres. 1969-72), Delta Kappa Gamma. Presbyn. (pres. womens guild 1968, 71). Clubs: Belvidere Woman's (sec. 1953-55, treas. 1974-75); Better Homemakers Extension (pres. 1958), Sunshine (Belvidere). Home: Rural Route 1 Box 82 Belvidere NE 68315 Office: Thayer County Mus Belvidere NE 68315

PRIEHS, HERMINE SOUKUP (MRS. GEORGE WILLIAM PRIEHS), retail co. exec.; b. N.Y.C., Aug. 30, 1909; d. Albert and Maria (Pischel) Soukup; B.A., U. Mich., 1931; m. George William Priehs, Oct. 27, 1932; Marolyn L. (Mrs. William Pagels), Susan S. (Mrs. Thomas Butterwick). Asst. to residence stypist J.L. Hudson Co., Detroit, 1931-32; buyer Priehs Dept. Store, Mt. Clemens, Mich., 1933-65; treas., dir. J. Priehs Merc. Co., Inc., Mt. Clemens, 1947—; sec., dir. Priehs Realty Co., Inc., 1949—. Asst. sec. U. Mich. Alumni Class of 1931, 1931—. Club: Officers Wives (Selfridge Air N.G. Field, Mt. Clemens). Home: 24805 Crocker Av Mount Clemens MI 48043 Office: 60-66 Macomb St Mount Clemens MI 48043

PRIESING, DOROTHY MCLEMORE (MRS. ELWOOD R. PRIESING), musician, educator; b. Nantucket, Mass., July 31, 1910; d. William Dennis and Elizabeth (Baxter) McLemore; diploma in piano (fellow in composition) Juilliard Sch. Music, 1930, 1934; B.S., Columbia U., 1932, M.A., 1933; m. Elwood R. Priesing, June 11, 1941; 1 son, Richard Baxter. Mem. faculty Keene (N.H.) State Normal Sch., 1935-36, Juilliard Sch. Music, N.Y.C., 1936-39, 43-60, Columbia U., N.Y.C., 1935-39, Shimer Coll., Mt. Carroll, Ill., 1939-41; mem. faculty Montclair (N.J.) State Coll., 1953—, asso. prof. music, 1969—. Adjudicator for piano auditions, lectr., pianist and other work connected with music. Mem. A.S.C.A.P., Sigma Alpha Iota. Author: Language of the Piano; Basic Piano for the College Student. Composer: Three Preludes for Piano; Choral material; also others. Home: 42 Llewellyn Rd Montclair NJ 07042

PRIEST, HELEN MARYANN RUBYOR (MRS. WHAYNE CRAVENS PRIEST), educator, clubwoman; b. Elgin, Ia.; d. Sidney White and Margaret (Schmid) Rubyor; student Coe Coll., 1923-25; B.A., U. Ia., 1929; postgrad. U. Colo., 1930, Northwestern U., 1931, Ky. Wesleyan Coll., 1961; m. Whayne Cravens Priest, June 14, 1936; children—Whayne Cravens, Adrienne Verene (Mrs. John Scott McGaw). Tchr. English, speech, drama Nichols Sch., Evanston, Ill., 1929-36, Ohio County High Sch., Hartford, Ky., 1954—. Mem. Gov.'s Conf. Ky.'s Jud. System, 1968; mem. Ohio County Bicentennial Com., 1973-74. Adviser, women's activities for Ky., Nat. Found. Infantile Paralysis, 1948-54; bd. mem. Ky. Fedn. Music Clubs, 1945—, state pres., 1953-55; Dixie dist. pres. Nat. Fedn. Music Clubs, 1955-57, bd. dirs., 1965—, chmn. jr. clubs achievement. Named Tchr. of Year high sch. students of Ohio County, 1968, Mother of Year Western Ky., 1964; Ky. Col. Mem. Ky. Assn. Communicative Arts, Kappa Alpha Theta. Methodist (mem. adminstrv. bd.). Club: Woman's (Hartford, pres. 1946, 58, 74). Editor Ky. Keynote, 1953—. Home: 101 Mulberry Dr Hartford KY 42347

PRIEST, IVY BAKER, state treas.; b. Kimberly, Utah; d. Orange Decatur Baker; D.Sc., Bryant Coll., Providence, 1953; LL.D., Rider Coll., Trenton, N.J., 1953; L.H.D., Elmira (N.Y.) Coll., 1956; m. Roy Priest (dec. June 1959); children—Roy Baker (dec.), Nancy (Mrs. J. A. Valenzuela), Patricia (Mrs. Pierce Jensen, Jr.); m. 2d, Sidney W. Stevens, 1961 (dec.). U.S. Treas., Washington, 1952-61; treas. State of Cal., 1967—. Asst. chmn. Republican Nat. Com. Bd. dirs. Cal. Easter Seal Soc., Greater Los Angeles Safety Council; trustee Nat. Soc. Crippled Children and Adults. Recipient achievement award for outstanding accomplishment in politics, Womens Nat. Press Club, Woman of Achievement award Am. Fedn. Soroptimist Clubs, 1956. Mem. Bus. and Profl. Women's Club, Women's Advt. Club Washington (hon. life), Beta Sigma Phi, Delta Zeta. Mem. Ch. of Jesus Christ of Latter-day Saints. Club: International Soroptimist. Author: Green Grows Ivy, 1955. Office: State Capitol Sacramento CA 95814

PRIEST, JEAN LORRAINE FISHER (MRS. PAUL R. PRIEST), ednl. sec.; b. Vale, S.D., July 7, 1918; d. Earl and Hazel (Shuck) Fisher; student Hastings Coll., Neb., 1936-38, U. Neb., 1938-40; m. Paul R. Priest, May 6, 1955 (dec.); children—Richard W., Clayton Fisher (by previous marriage), stepchildren—Paula (Mrs. Alden E. Lemmon), Michael Scott. Sec. to dir. student union U. Neb., 1938-40; sec. to dir. U. Denver Coll. Edn., 1942; med. sec. for orthopedic surgeon, Albuquerque, 1952-54; collection mgr. Presbyn. Hosp., 1954-56; exec. sec. to dep. supt. schs., Albuquerque, 1956—. Mem. Albuquerque (pres. 1963), N.M. (pres. 1964), Nat. (pres. 1971-72) assns. ednl. secs., N.E.A., Alliance Assns. Advancement Edn. (sec. 1971—). Home: 8309 Dellwood Rd NE Albuquerque NM 87110 Office: PO Box 25704 Albuquerque NM 87125

PRIEST, RUTH THOMAS (MRS. WESLEY M. PRIEST), ranch exec.; b. Woodstock, N.Y., Nov. 20, 1920; d. Mahlon Apgar and Margaret (Elwyn) Thomas; B.A., N.Y. U., 1941; m. Wesley M. Priest, Jan. 31, 1948; 1 son, Mahlon S. Apprentice technician CBS, N.Y.C., 1942; studio engr. OWI, N.Y.C., 1942-44, NBC, N.Y.C., 1944-45; writer, reporter, announcer Radiodiffusion francaise, Paris, France, 1946; co-editor, writer English page l'Alliance Nouvelle, French weekly, Paris, 1946; sec.-treas. Priest, Inc., Brewster, Wash., 1957—; editor, advt. mgr. Herald-Reporter, Brewster, 1964-68. Mem. Wash. State com. White House Conf. on Children and Youth, 1968. Chmn. Okanogan County Republican Central Com., 1961. Recipient award for outstanding contbn. toward better understanding Wash. Edn. Assn., 1967; 1st place for promotion, 1st place for news story, 2d place display advt. Wash. Press Women, 1968. Mem. Lady Elks. Clubs: Spokane (Wash.), Ruby Arts of Lake Chelan (Wash.). Address: Box 666 Brewster WA 98812

PRIESTER, PATRICIA LEE, statistician; b. Palm Springs, Cal., Dec. 13, 1943; d. Harold F. and Thelma Lee (Hendrickson) Priester; A.B. in Math., Bucknell U., 1965; M.S. in Statistics, Fla. State U., 1967. Statistician, U.S. Census Bur., Suitland, Md., 1967-68, Communications Sattelite Corp., Washington, 1969-70, D.C. Govt., 1970-71, U.S. Postal Service, 1972—. Mem. Am. Statis. Assn., Phi Beta Kappa, Pi Mu Epsilon. Home: 1600 S Eads St Arlington VA 22202 Office: 475 L'Enfant Plaza W SW Washington DC 20260

PRIETO, MARIANA BEECHING, educator; b. Cin., Aug. 6, 1912; d. Charles Train and Sylvia (Beck) Beeching; student Colegio Sagrada Corazon, Havana, Cuba, 1930-32, U. Fla., 1936; teaching certificate U. Miami, 1943; m. Martin Prieto Benitez, Aug. 22, 1939 (dec. May 1974); 1 dau., Nita (Mrs. Ralph Owen Maercks). With WIOD, Miami, Fla., 1960; tchr. Dade County Schs. Adult Edn., 1974—, adult edn. U. Miami, 1974—. Active Friends of Everglades, Gasp Orgn. Mem. Miami Writers Club. Author: When the Monkeys Sombreros, Wore 1971; Raimundo, 1972; Spanish and How, 1973; Fun Jewelry, 1973. Home: 2499 SW 34th Av Miami FL 33145

PRIEVE, SARAH MAE, city ofcl.; b. Ononomowoc, Wis., Oct. 1, 1938; d. Bernard Charles and Phyllis Mae (Roster) Tralle; grad. high sch.; m. Elmer M. Prieve, Nov. 24, 1956 (div. Mar. 1969); children—Mark Edward, Jill Kathleen. Sec. to dir. admissions Shattuck Sch., Faribault, Minn., 1958-63; dep. to county auditor Rice County, Faribault, 1964-68; sec. printing products div. Minn. Mining and Mfg. Co., St. Paul, 1968-71; city clk. City of West St. Paul, 1971—. Adult com. leader Girl Scouts and Boy Scouts, 1972-74. Mem. Minn. Clks. and Finance Officers Assn. (regional v.p. 1973-74, treas. 1974-75). Home: 440 8th Av S South St Paul MN 55075 Office: 1616 Humboldt Av West St Paul MN 55118

PRIMAVESI, MAEDA, hosp. adminstr.; b. Olmuetz, Austria; d. Otto and Maeda (Butschek) Primavesi; pvt. edn.; student Acad. Applied Art, Vienna, Austria; 1 adopted son, Richard. Came to Can., 1948, naturalized, 1973. Children's art tchr. Art Gallery and Mus., Toronto, Ont., Can., 1949-51; tchr. extension courses Ont. Dept. Edn., 1949-51; tchr. Montreal (Que., Can.) Mus. Fine Arts, Montreal Children's Hosp., 1952-61; exec. dir. Children's Convalescent Hosp., Montreal, 1961—, Children's Village, Montreal, 1968—. Home: 3550 Ridgewood Av Montreal PQ Canada Office: 1371 Pine Av W Montreal PQ Canada

PRIMUS, CONSTANCE MERRILL, music tchr.; b. Denver, Aug. 26, 1931; d. Marcellus Samuel and Geraldine Lauren (Robinson) Merrill; student Bucknell U., 1949-50, U. Colo., 1950-52, U. Denver, 1965, Western State Coll., 1972; m. Robert John Primus, Dec. 27, 1952; children—David Merrill, Christopher John. Pvt. tchr. flute, Denver, 1965—; tchr. recorder, adult classes YWCA, also pvt. lessons and classes of children and adults, met. Denver, 1968—; condr. workshops for pub. sch. tchrs. on recorder, 1971—; guest condr. Denver chpt. Am. Recorder Soc., 1971—; mem. Camerata, and other performing chamber music ensembles, 1968-72; presented programs on medieval music and on history of flutes, 1971—. Sec. P.T.A., Lakewood, Colo., 1967. Active worker local Rep. party, 1958-69. Mem. Am. Recorder Soc. (certified tchr.), Sigma Alpha Iota, Tau Beta Sigma, Alpha Chi Omega. Presbyn. Club: Mount Vernon Country (Denver). Address: 13607 W Mississippi Ct Lakewood CO 80228

PRIMUS, MARY JANE DAVIS (MRS. PAUL C. PRIMUS), social worker; b. Marion, Ia., May 31, 1924; d. Lawrence Henry and Verna Leona (Suman) Davis; B.S., Ia. State U., 1950; m. Paul C. Primus, Aug. 23, 1955; children—Kenneth Roy, Donald Karl. Asst. cashier First State Bank, Greene, Ia., 1942-46; tchr. Oskaloosa (Ia.) pub. schs., 1950-52; extension home economist Ia. State U., Oskaloosa-Eldora, 1952-57; homemaker, supr. Ia. Dept. Social Service, Webster City, Ia., 1970—. Substitute tchr. Eldora Pub. Schs., 1966-68; homemaker health aide supr. Mid-Ia. Community Action Office of Econ. Opportunity, 1968-69. Den mother Boy Scouts Am., Steamboat Rock, Ia., 1966-71; leader Girl Scouts Am., Steamboat Rock, 1969-72; mem. Ia. State U. Extension Family Living Council, Hardin County, 1961-65; outreach chmn. Ia. Family and Children Services, 1966-72; field days women's program chmn. Ia. Soil Conservation, 1968. Mem. Am. Home Econs. Assn., Nat. Council Homemaker-Home Health Aide Services, Soil Conservation Soc. Am., Am. Legion, P.E.O. Mem. Ch. of Christ (pres. 1963-65). Mem. Order Eastern Star. Club: Federated Women's (Steamboat Rock). Author: Through the Window, 1973. Contbr. poems to various publs. Office: Box 54 Webster City IA 50595

PRINCE, DOROTHY MAE, educator; b. Charlotte, N.C., Aug. 18, 1931; d. Abraham H. and Susan (Peacock) Prince; A.B., Oberlin Coll., 1953; M.A., Syracuse U., 1954; Ed.D., Ind. U., 1962. Instr., Alcorn

(Miss.) A. and M. Coll., 1954, So. U., Baton Rouge, 1954-55; vis. instr. Atlanta U., summer 1956, 57; asst. prof. N.C. A. and T. State U., Greensboro, 1955-62, prof. edn. and psychology, acting chmn. dept. edn. and psychology, 1966-67, chmn. dept. edn., 1967. Cons. to ednl. media program for coll. and univ. personnel Dept. Health, Edn. and Welfare, Office Edn., Washington; participant Faculty Seminar, Yugoslavia, summer 1972; cons. community mental health tng. program. John Hay Whitney fellow, 1961-62; Ellis L. Phillips Found. fellow, 1964-65. Mem. N.E.A., Am. Assn. U. Profs., Assn. for Ednl. Communications and Tech., N.C. Nat. Council Adminstrv. Women in Edn., Pi Lambda Theta, Delta Sigma Theta. Presbyn. Home: 1803 Curry St Greensboro NC 27406

PRINCE, FRANCES ANNE KIELY (MRS. RICHARD EDWARD PRINCE, JR.), civic worker; b. Toledo, Dec. 20, 1923; d. John Thomas and Frances (Pusteoska) Kiely; student U. Louisville, 1947-49; A.B., Berea Coll., 1951; postgrad. Kent Sch. Social Work, 1951, Creighton U., 1969, U. Neb. at Omaha, 1974; m. Richard Edward Prince, Jr., Aug. 17, 1951; children—Anne, Richard III. Instr. flower arranging Western Wyo. Jr. Coll., 1965, 66. Chmn., Lone Troop council Girl Scouts U.S.A., 1954-57, trainer leaders, 1954-68, mem. state camping com., 1959-61, bd. mem. Wyo. state council, 1966-69; chmn. Community Improvement, Green River, Wyo., 1959, 63-65, Wyo. Fedn. Women's Clubs State Library Services, 1966-69; mem. Wyo. State Adv. Bd. on Library Inter-Co-op., 1965-69; bd. mem. Sweetwater County Library System, 1962—, pres. bd., 1967-68; adv. council Sch. Dist. 66, 1970—; bd. dirs. Opera Angels, 1971, fund raising chmn., 1971-72; bd. dirs. Morning Musicale, 1971—, v.p., 1974—; bazaar com. Children's Hosp., 1970—; docent Joslyn Art Mus., 1970—. Recipient Library Service award Sweetwater County Library, 1968. Mem. Am. Assn. U. Women, New Neighbors League (dir. 1969-71), Ikebana Internat., Symphony Guild, Omaha Playhouse Guild, Am., Neb. library assns., Omaha Council Garden Clubs (1st v.p. 1972, pres. 1973—), Internat. Platform Assn., Nat. Trust for Hist. Preservation, Neb. Flower Show Judges Council, Neb. Fedn. Garden Clubs (2d v.p.). Mem. United Ch. of Christ. Clubs: Intermountain (dir. 1963-69), Garden (dir. 1970-72, pres. 1972—). Home: 8909 Broadmoor Dr Omaha NE 68114

PRINCE, GRACE ROSENE SIMMONS (MRS. JOHN CALVIN PRINCE), dietitian; b. nr. Union City, Tenn., Jan. 4, 1935; d. Dewey Benjamin and Jewel LaVerne (Brown) Simmons; B.S., U. Tenn., 1957, M.S., 1971; m. John Calvin Prince, June 28, 1959 (dec. Apr. 1964); children—Deborah Rosene, Mari Loy. Dietary intern Barnes Hosp., St. Louis, 1958, hosp. adminstrn. intern in dietetics, 1959, adminstrv. dietitian, 1958-60; tchr. Haywood County (Tenn.) Elementary Sch., 1961; extension home economist, Dresden, Tenn., 1964-73; cons. dietitian Medco Facilities Corp., nursing homes, 1973—. Active Easter Seal Soc. Program, 1969-72, Mental Retardation Program, 1969-72; co-chmn. Cerebral Palsy drive, Weakley County, Tenn., 1966; com. chmn. Cancer Drive, Weakley County, 1967-71; com. mem. Heart Fund Drive, 1969-71; active establishment Day Care Centers, Weakley County, 1967-72. Bd. dirs. Tri-State Greater Evansville Area Diabetic Assn., 1973—. Mem. Nat., Tenn. (area fund drive chmn. nat. bldg. fund) home econs. assns., Nat., Tenn. assns. extension home economists, Am., S.W. Ind. (dir. Evansville chpt.) diabetic assns. Baptist. Home: 716 S Kenmore Dr Evansville IN 47715

PRINCE, HELEN WALTER DODSON (MRS. EDMOND L. PRINCE), astronomer, educator; b. Balt., Dec. 31, 1905; d. Henry Clay and Helen (Walter) Dodson; A.B., Goucher Coll., 1927, Sc.D., 1952; M.A., U. Mich., 1932, Ph.D., 1933; m. Edmond Lafayette Prince, Oct. 24, 1956. Asst. statistician Md. Dept. Edn., 1927-31; asst. prof. Wellesley Coll., 1933-45; mem. staff radiation lab. Mass. Inst. Tech., 1943-45; asso. prof. astronomy Goucher Coll., 1945-50; asst. prof. U. Mich., 1947-57, prof., 1957—, asso. dir. McMath-Hulbert Obs., Lake Angelus, Mich., 1962—. Mem. Am. Astron. Soc. (Annie Jump Cannon prize 1954), Internat. Astron. Union, Am. Geophys. Union, Soc. Astrononique de France, Am. Assn. U. Women, Am. Assn. U. Profs., Internat. Sci. Radio Union, A.A.A.S., Phi Beta Kappa, Sigma Xi. Episcopalian. Home: 650 Lake Angelus Shores Pontiac MI 48055 Office: McMath-Hulbert Observatory Lake Angelus Pontiac MI 48055

PRINCE, JUDY LYNN ELLIS (MRS. JOHN LOUIS MACHO), pub. relations exec.; b. Babylon, N.Y.; d. Malcom Judd and Madeline Francis (Eistrat) Ellis; B.S., U. Fla., 1964; postgrad. Institute de Technilogico, Monterrey, Mexico, 1959, U. S. Fla., summer 1961, New Sch. Social Research, 1972, N.Y. U., 1973; m. John Louis Macho, Oct. 20, 1971. Pub. relations dir. WEDU-TV, Tampa, Fla., 1964-65; pub. relations asst. tourist promotion State of Fla. Devel. Com., N.Y.C., 1965-66; account exec. Harshe-Rotman & Druck, pub. relations, N.Y.C., 1966-69; asst. dir. Cigar Inst. Am., N.Y.C., 1969-73; account exec. Daniel J. Edelman, pub. relations, N.Y.C., 1973-74; media specialist Mobil Oil Corp., N.Y.C., 1974—. Free-lance writer, 1972—. Mayor, Land O'Lakes (Fla.), 1964-65. Mem. Am. Women in Radio and TV (treas. 1973-74, exec. v.p. 1974-75), Women in Communications. Club: Publicity (1st v.p. N.Y.C. 1973-74, dir. 1974-76). Home: 60 Sutton Pl S New York City NY 10022 Office: 150 E 42d St New York City NY 10017

PRINCE, KATHERINE E. DE CAROUSO (MRS. JAMES J. PRINCE), artist; b. San Francisco; d. Victor H. and Nina (Majors) de Carouso; student U. Cal. at Berkeley, 1935-36, Laney Coll., 1968-70; m. James J. Prince, May 22, 1937. Exhibited one-woman shows Diablo Gallery, Bates Gallery, Oakland, Cal.; exhibited in group shows Oakland Art Mus., Vet.'s Hall, Guerneville, Freemont Park, Artrium, Santa Rosa, Marin Art and Garden Center, Kentfield; represented in permanent collections Community Ch., Guerneville, Surrey Oakland Mus., also pvt. collections. Docent, Oakland Mus. Chmn. events East Bay Activity Center for Emotionally Disturbed Children, 1955-65. Bd. dirs. East Bay Opera League, 1967-68; bd. dirs. Sonoma County Arts Council, 1972—, v.p., 1973, 74. Mem. Western Sonoma County Art Workshop, Oakland Symphony Guild (dir. 1964-67), Sigma Phi Omega. Episcopalian. Clubs: Redwood Palette Art (pres. 1968-73), River Pot-'n' Trowell Garden (pres. 1968-70), Diablio Country, Northwood Golf. Home: 15320 Paradise Lane Guerneville CA 95446

PRINCE, MADELINE ELLIS, realtor; b. Oakland, Cal., Apr. 8, 1912; d. Thomas and Frances (Jirkowsky) Eistrat; B.A., U. Cal. at Berkeley, 1933, postgrad., 1934; postgrad. Ore. State Coll., 1933, U. Fla., 1964, U. Conn., 1965, U. So. Fla., 1968; m. Ellsworth M. Prince, Feb. 14, 1946 (div. Aug. 1954); 1 dau., Judy Lynn (Mrs. John L. Macho). Tchr., Santa Monica (Cal.), Jr. High Sch., 1935-36; tchr. Los Angeles council Girl Scouts, 1944-46; realtor Madeline E. Prince Realty, Land O'Lakes, Fla., 1950—. Mem. stockholders adv. com. Northside Bank, Tampa, Fla., 1963-73; dir. Landmark Bank North Tampa. Trustee, Univ. Community Hosp., Tampa, 1973—. Named Realtor of Yr., East Pasco County, 1963, Zephyrhills Bd. Realtors, 1969. Mem. Zephyrhills Bd. Realtors (pres. 1969, treas. 1972), East Pasco County Bd. Realtors (pres. 1963). Club: Lutz-Land O'Lakes Womans (dir. 1970-72, historian 1972-74). Office: PO Box 128 Land O'Lakes FL 33539

PRINCE, RUTH EVELYN WHITE (MRS. HARRY HYMRICK PRINCE), educator; b. Whiteville, N.C., July 16, 1921; d. Lloyd McCoy and Emma (Ward) White; student Wilmington Coll. Cosmetology, 1940-41, So. Bapt. Sem., 1970; m. Harry Hymrick Prince, Oct. 18, 1941; children—Harry Hymrick, Stephen White. Beautician, Tabor City Beauty Salon (N.C.), 1941-42; sec. Galveston Dry Docks (Tex.), 1943-44; owner, operator Florist & Gift Shop, Clarkton, NC, 1951-58; supt. missions Bladen Bapt. Assn., Elizabethtown, N.C., 1966—. Mem. Gov.'s. Community Relations Council, Raleigh, N.C., 1967; pink lady Bladen County Hosp., Elizabethtown, 1964-65. Bd. dirs. Vol. Service Guild, Dorothea Dix Hosp., Raleigh, 1968—. Mem. N.C. State Bapt. Supt. Missions (pub. relations dir. 1968), Bapt. Woman's Missionary Union, Internat. Platform Assn. Baptist. Club: Clarkton Woman's (pres. 1966-68). Home: PO Box 662 Clarkton NC 28433 Office: PO Box 62 Elizabethtown NC 28337

PRINCE, VIRGINIA FAYE DIXON (MRS. A. E. PRINCE), educator; b. Big Springs, Mo., July 23, 1919; d. William Marcellus and Cassie Mae (Walker) Dixon; A.A., Hannibal-LaGrange Coll,, 1946; B.A., N.E. La. State Coll., 1956; M.Ed., Southwestern La. U., 1959; postgrad. U. Mo., 1948, U. Hawaii, 1952, 53, So. Ill. U., 1960-64, degree certificate of specialist So. Ill. U., 1969; m. A. E. Prince, June 9, 1949. Sec. to pres. Hannibal-LaGrange Coll., 1946-48; tchr. pub. schs., Center, Mo., 1947-48, Honolulu, 1952-54, Monroe, La., 1954-56, Jennings Mo. 1958—; dietitian Hannibal-LaGrange Coll., 1948-50; sec. to pastor Auckland (New Zealand) Bapt. Tabernacle, 1951-52. Mem. Internat. Reading Assn., Assn. Childhood Edn; N.E.A., Mo., St. Louis tchrs. assns., Am. Bell Assn., Alpha Delta Kappa, Kappa Delta Pi. Republican. Baptist. Mem. Order Eastern Star. Home: PO Box 4015 St Louis MO 63136

PRINCE, VIVIAN CHRISTINE, educator; b. Equality, S.C., July 31, 1908; d. James Chesley and Elsie (Entrekin) Prince; A.B. with honor, Winthrop Coll., 1929; B.L.S., U. N.C., 1940; M.L.S., Columbia, 1948. Tchr., librarian, Gatesville, N.C., 1930-32, Manning, S.C., 1932-36, Pageland, S.C., 1936-38, Kingstree, S.C., 1938-39, Fort Mill, S.C., 1939-41, Rockingham, N.C., 1941-43; cataloger U. Fla., Gainesville, 1943-46, head cataloging dept., 1946-49, head tech. processes, 1950-62; asso. prof. library sci. U. So. Cal., Los Angeles, 1962—. Vis. prof. library sci. U. Cal. at Berkeley, 1959-61, Emory U., 1953, 65, U. N.C., 1962, 64, U. Ill., 1960. Fulbright grantee, 1956-57. Mem. Am. Assn. U. Profs. (chpt. sec. 1954-55), D.A.R., Am. Assn. U. Women, Am. (sec. cataloging sect. 1961-65), Cal. (pres. tech. processes group 1965-66) library assns., Delta Kappa Gamma, Phi Alpha Theta. Democrat. Presbyn. Home: 3028 W 4th St Los Angeles CA 90020

PRINDLE, KAREN, broadcaster; b. Utica, N.Y., Apr. 28, 1938; d. Spencer W. and Dorothy F. (Fairbanks) Prindle; B.S., Ithaca Coll., 1960. Production asst. WNED-TV, Buffalo, 1960-62, producer, dir., 1962-63; asso. producer WNEW-TV, N.Y.C., 1964; asst. dir. WNET, N.Y.C., 1965; producer, dir. WTTW, Chgo., 1965-71; asso. dir. WMAQ-TV, NBC, Chgo., 1972—. Recipient Emmy award Nat. Acad. of TV Arts and Scis., 1967. Mem. Directors Guild of Am. (mem. Chgo. Coordinating com. 1973), Nat. Acad. TV Arts and Scis., Chgo. Women in Broadcasting. Home: 629 W Fullerton Chicago IL 60614 Office: WMAQ-TV Merchandise Mart Chicago IL 60654

PRINS, RUTH BALKEMA (MRS. ROBERT FREDERICK PRINS), actress, sch. adminstr.; b. Sioux City, Ia., Oct. 26, 1920; d. Peter and Oma Lorene (Foster) Balkema; B.A., U. Wash., 1942, M.A., 1952, Doctoral candidate, 1970; m. Robert Frederick Prins, Mar. 21, 1942; children—Robert Peter, Debra Susan. Dir. Childrens Theatre, U. Wash., 1947-52; dir. Seattle Jr. Programs Plays for Children, 1947-52; appearance with Lillian Gish in Mrs. Carlyle, 1948; producer, actress childrens programs KING-TV, Seattle, KGW-TV, Portland, Ore., Telaventure Tales (weekly), 1950-71, Wunda Wunda (daily), 1953-73, Mrs. Alphabet (weekly), KNBC, Los Angeles, 1969-73; tchr. drama, speech, linguistics pvt. kindergarten, Seattle, 1947-64; dir., instr. Ruth Prins Primary Schs., Seattle, 1964—. Producer, actress, writer Compass Rose, ethnic series childrens television programs for NET, 1958-59. Recipient Music and Art Found. award, 1954, 1st award Inst. for Edn. by Radio and TV, 1952, 54, 56, Peabody award for outstanding childrens program in U.S., 1958, Sugar Plum award Wash. Press Women, 1961; named Woman of Achievement, Theta Sigma Phi, 1964. Mem. Nat. Acad. Arts and Scis., Nat. Press Women, N.E.A., Am. Women in Radio and Television, Nat. Council Tchrs. English, D.A.R., Orton Soc., Early Childhood Edn. Internat., Assn. Internat. du Théatre pour L'enfants et La Jeunesse, Phi Mu Gamma. Club: Womens University (Seattle). Address: 4735 W Roberts Way Seattle WA 98199

PRIOR, FAITH KENYON (MRS. A.B. ROLLINS, JR.), educator; b. Vergennes, Vt., Mar. 17, 1920; d. Murray Adams and Alice Josephine (Connell) Kenyon; grad. Pratt Inst., 1939; B.S. magna cum laude, U. Vt., 1943, M.S., 1964; m. Roger W. Prior, Aug. 30, 1941 (div. Apr. 1955); children—Christopher, Katherine (Mrs. Gregory Gaura), Martha; m. 2d, A.B. Rollins, Jr., June 16, 1973. Tchr. home econs. Bradford, Vt., 1943-44, Burlington, Vt., 1955-62; social worker mil. welfare service A.R.C., Chelsea (Mass.) Naval Hosp., 1943-46; translator, writer Biol. Bur., U. Montreal, 1946-50; extension specialist family econs. U. Vt., Burlington, 1962—, asst. prof. home econs., 1967—, founder, chmn. Consumer Information Clearinghouse, 1963—. Dir., Blue Shield Vt.-N.H. Mem. Vt. Gov.'s Emergency Resources Priorities Bd., 1966—, Regional Med. Adv. Bd., 1969—, Vt. Health Planning Adv. Council, 1969—; adviser OEO, Burlington, 1964-68; cons. Pres.'s Com. on Consumer Interest, 1965-68; chmn. consumer adv. council Am. Bankers Assn., 1969-73; mem. adv. com. Bd. Truth in Lending Fed. Res. Bd., 1970—; mem. adv. com. on health Am. Hosp. Assn., 1972—; U.S. del., 1st Internat. Consumer Edn. Conf., The Hague, 1966; mem. edn. com. Internat. Orgn. Consumers Union, 1970—; dir. Credit Union, 1966-69; corporator Burlington Savs. Bank, 1970—; broadcaster Vt. radio stas., TV series WCAX-TV, Burlington, 1962—, Vt. Edn. TV, Winooski, 1969—; columnist Burlington Free Press, 1962—. Bd. dirs. Green Mountain Med. Found., 1971—. Mem. Am. Council on Consumer Information, Am., Vt. home econs. assns., League Vt. Writers, Metric Assn., Phi Beta Kappa, Omicron Nu. Contbr. fiction and non-fiction to nat. mags. Home: Bishop Rd Shelburne VT 05482 Office: 210 Terrill Hall U Vt Burlington VT 05401

PRIOR, MARY ELIZABETH BARBOT (MRS. GRANVILLE TORREY PRIOR), hist. soc. exec.; b. Charleston, S.C., Sept. 5, 1910; d. Joseph Claudius and Ellen L. (Touhey) Barbot; B.A. with high honors, Coll. of Charleston, 1931; M.A., Duke, 1942; m. Granville Torrey Prior, Dec. 27, 1943; 1 dau., Ellen Torrey (Mrs. Joseph Francis Baldacchino, Jr.). Tchr. English and Latin, Memminger High Sch., Charleston, 1935-41; program dir. sta. WTMA, Charleston, 1942-45; tchr. Latin, Ashley Hall Sch. for Girls, Charleston, 1951-53; dir. S.C. Hist. Soc., Charleston, 1956—. Mem. S.C. Tricentennial Com. on Scholarly Activities, 1970, S.C. Com. for Humanities, 1971-74. Mem. Carolina Art Assn., Poetry Soc. S.C. (editor Yearbook 1933, sec.-treas. 1942-46), Charleston Mus., Preservation Soc. S.C., Natural Hist. Soc. Roman Catholic. Editor: S.C. Hist. Mag., 1958-64. Home: 62 Broad St Charleston SC 29401 Office: 100 Meeting St Charleston SC 29401

PRITCHARD, ELIZABETH O'SHEA, educator; b. Cortland, N.Y., Sept. 18, 1934; d. Leo Vincent and Alice Florence (Gibbons) O'Shea; B.S., State U. N.Y., Buffalo, 1956, M.S., 1961. Tchr. physically handicapped, Rochester, N.Y., 1956-61; tchr. mentally retarded, Syracuse, N.Y., 1961-62, Locust Valley, N.Y., 1965-66; tchr. of hard of hearing/deaf, Rochester, 1962-65; asst. prof. phys. handicap State U. N.Y., Buffalo, 1966-69, asso. prof., 1969-73; tchr. learning disabilities Tutu Sch., St. Thomas, V.I., 1973—; cons. Allegheny County, Toronto Pub. Schs., Girl Scouts U.S.A., Assn. for Retarded Children, Cerebral Palsy Assn., Geneva, N.Y. Sec., Council for Exceptional Children. Mem. Am. Assn. for Children With Learning Disabilities, N.E.A., N.Y. State Tchrs. Assn., Council for Exceptional Children. Author: (with others) Aphonic Communication for Cerebral Palsied Children, 1958. Home: Box 728 St Thomas VI 00801 Office: Estate Tutu St Thomas VI 00801

PRITCHARD, LINETA CRAVEN (MRS. WILLIAM FREDERICK PRITCHARD), journalist; b. Raleigh, N.C., July 28, 1943; d. Frederick Thorns and Martha Louise (Kindel) Craven; B.A., Wake Forest U., 1965; m. William Frederick Pritchard, Aug. 26, 1967; children—Allen Russell, Kindel Craven. Promotional copywriter radio sta. WTOB, Winston Salem, N.C., 1966; asst. dir. pub. relations Hennis Freight Lines, 1967; advt. copywriter Carolina Power & Light Co., 1968-69; women's editor The Raleigh Times, 1970-72; partner Maximus, freelance advt. agy., 1969—. Publicity positions for various fund raising orgns. Mem. Raleigh Jr. League. Home: 2100 St James Rd Raleigh NC 27607

PRITCHARD, ZONA BELLE, librarian; b. Huntsville, Tex., Nov. 27, 1913; d. Paxton and Lula May (Overman) Hinson; B.A., Hardin-Simmons U., Abilene, Tex., 1938; M.A., North Tex. State U., Denton, 1955, M.L.S., 1967; m. A.H. Pritchard, Apr. 15, 1933; children—Betty, Joe Charles, James Hinson, John Robert. Elementary sch. tchr., 1934-59; high sch. librarian, Corpus Christi, Tex., 1960-67; librarian H.M. King High Sch., Kingsville, Tex., 1967—. Nat. Def. Edn. Act. scholar, 1965. Mem. Tex. Tchrs. Assn., Tex. (chmn. dist. IV), Coastal Bend library assns., Tex. Assn. Sch. Libraries (chmn. workshop 1973-74), Delta Kappa Gamma. Baptist. Home: 1710 Santa Monica St Kingsville TX 78363 Office: Box 871 Brahma Blvd Kingsville TX 78363

PRITCHETT, BETTY JENSEN (MRS. MORGAN S. PRITCHETT), educator; b. Omaha, Neb., Sept. 14, 1924; d. Lars Peter and Ruth Edith (Norby) Jensen; B.S., Portland State U., 1965; M.B.A., U. Ore., 1966; Ed.D., Ore. State U., 1973; m. Morgan S. Pritchett, June 27, 1944; children—Randall, Robin, Royce Marie (Mrs. Danny Cobb). Retail buyer Rodgers, Inc., Portland, Ore., 1947-62; chmn. bus. div. Mt. Hood Community Coll., Gresham, Ore., 1966-69, dir. evening coll., 1969-71, asso. dean, 1972—. Mem. Ore. Bus. Edn. Council, Portland, 1968-71. Mem. Am., Ore. vocational assns., Ore. Bus. Edn. Assn., Ore. Media Assn., Mt. Hood Community Coll. Womens Assn. Clubs: Portland City, Soroptimist (pres. elect 1974-75) (Portland). Home: 16430 NE Hoyt Portland OR 97230 Office: Mount Hood Community College 26000 SE Stark Gresham OR 97030

PRITCHETT, MARGARET ELAINE (MRS. WILSON PRITCHETT), health agy. exec.; b. Portland, Ore., Oct. 6, 1911; d. John Jacob and Alice May (Smith) Handsaker; B.A., Reed Coll., 1933; m. Wilson Pritchett, June 5, 1937; children—John, David, Margaret (Mrs. Vinson). Caseworker, adminstr. Ore. Pub. Welfare Commn., 1934-40; trainer Girl Scouts, Bay Area, San Lorenzo, Cal., 1959-61; Y-Teen dir., YMCA, Richmond, Cal., 1962-65; exec. dir. Contra Costa Alameda Epilepsy League, Richmond, 1966—, bd. dirs., 1953-66. Mem. Contra Costa County, Alameda County, Area V (Bay Area) developmental disabilities councils. Bd. dirs. Girl Scouts, Waseca, Minn., 1944-47, Richmond, 1947-59; bd. mem., v.p. Contra Costa Community Workshop, Richmond, 1966-73. Fed. Emergency Relief Adminstrn. fellow U. Wash. Sch. Social Work, 1935. Democrat. Methodist (bd. mem.). Home: 6262 Highland Av Richmond CA 94805 Office: 345 22d St Richmond CA 94801

PRITCHETT, SUSIE SANTEE (MRS. E. EDD PRITCHETT), lawyer; b. Houston, Oct. 6, 1941; d. Gwaltney Comer and Delilah Maxine (Watts) Santee; B.S., U. Okla., 1963; M. Teaching, Central State U., 1964; law student Oklahoma City U., 1968-69; J.D., U. Okla., 1972; m. E. Edd Pritchett, Feb. 8, 1969; children—Lesleigh Kristine, E. Edd. Instr., Central State U., Edmond, Okla., 1963-64, Cowley County Community Jr. Coll., Arkansas City, Kan., 1964-65, Inst. Logopedics, Wichita, Kan., 1965-66; asst. editor Ecomony Co. Ednl. Pubs., Oklahoma City, 1967-69; asst. pub. defender Oklahoma County Pub. Defender's Office, 1972-73; asst. U.S. atty. Western Dist. Okla., Oklahoma City, 1973—. Concessions co-chmn. Lyric Theater Guild, 1971—; chmn. family law div. Equal Rights Amendment Seminar, 1972. Asst. editor Okla. Republican News, 1970; precinct chmn. Rep. party, 1970-71. Mem. Am., Okla., Oklahoma County bar assns., Okla. Trial Lawyers Assn. (mem. program com. 1972-73), Okla. Fedn. Bus. and Profl. Women's Clubs (state chmn. penal reform 1973), Okla. Quarter Horse Assn., Iota Tau Tau, Phi Alpha Delta. Home: Route 1 Cashion OK 73750 Office: US Atty's Office Federal Court House Bldg Oklahoma City OK 73102

PRITTS, ROSE MARIE ROZYCKI (MRS. RICHARD WILLIS PRITTS), physician; b. Everson, Pa., Dec. 4, 1940; d. Raymond Lawrence and Stella Loretta (Getek) Rozycki; B.S., Duquesne U., 1962; M.D., Woman's Med. Coll. Pa., 1967; m. Richard Willis Pritts, Dec. 28, 1963; children—Deborah Lynn, Richard Willis. Intern, Westmoreland Hosp., Greensburg, Pa., 1967-68; resident internal medicine St. Francis Gen. Hosp., Pitts., 1968-71; practice medicine, specializing in internal medicine, Greensburg, 1971—; mem. staff Westmoreland Hosp., Jeannette (Pa.) Dist. Meml. Hosp. Mem. A.M.A., A.C.P., Am. Soc. Internal Medicine, Pa. Med. Soc., Westmoreland County Med. Assn. Home: 516 Shogan St Greensburg PA 15601 Office: 559 Shearer St Westmoreland Med Pavilion Greensburg PA 15601

PROCIUK, HELEN SYDNEY SZKOLNY (MRS. STEFAN GEORGE PROCIUK), vocational counselor; b. Terebovla, Ukraine; d. Michael and Hermina Szkolny; came to U.S., 1957, naturalized, 1962; M.S., U. N.C., 1961; m. Stefan George Prociuk, June 6, 1943. Vocational counselor Job Orientation in Neighborhoods, Bklyn., 1962-65, Manpower Devel. Tng. Program, 1965-74; vocational rehab. counselor Office Vocational Rehab., N.Y. State Bd. Edn., 1974—. Recipient Office of Manpower Automation and Tng. award U.S. Dept. Labor, 1965. Mem. Internat. Alliance Women, World Fedn. Ukrainian Women's Orgns. (internat. officer 1958—), Ukrainian Nat. Women's League Am., Am. Personnel and Guidance Assn., Alumni Assn. U. N.C. Home: 50 E 76th St New York City NY 10021

PROCTER, CAROL ANN, musician; b. Oklahoma City, June 26, 1941; d. Leland H. and Alice (McElroy) Procter; student Eastman Sch. Music, 1958-60; Mus.B., New Eng. Conservatory Music, 1963, Mus.M., 1965. Mem. cello sect. Springfield (Mass.) Symphony Orch., Cambridge Festival Orch., Boston, 1961-65; mem. cello sect. Boston Symphony Orch., Boston Pops Orch., 1965—; mem. New Eng. Harp Trio, 1971—. Cellist, Resident String Quartet, Peabody Jr. Conservatory, Lyndonville, Vt., summers 1962-64; Boston Symphony

Orch.-Japan Philharmonic Musician's Exchange program, 1969-70; pvt. tchr. cello, 1962—. Fulbright grantee, 1965; Fromm Found. fellow, Berkshire Music Center, Lenox, 1965. Mem. Mu Phi Epsilon. Office: Symphony Hall Boston MA 02115

PROCTOR, DOROTHEA SABINA HARDY (MRS. PERCY QUAYLE PROCTOR), artist, author; b. Calhan, Colo.; d. James Edson and Louise Catherine (Scheible) Hardy; student U. Tulsa, 1937-57; m. Percy Quayle Proctor, Dec. 9, 1922; 1 son, Edwin Gover III. One-woman show Philbrook Mus., Tulsa; exhibited in group shows Philbrook Tulsa County, Okla. Ann. shows. Publicity chmn. Nat. Poetry Festival, Tulsa, 1967, Opera Guild, 1966-68; mem. Women's Assn. for Tulsa Philharmonic, 1950—. Recipient sculpture award U. Tulsa, 1945, Silver Poetry award Poetry Soc. Okla., 1972. Mem. Poetry Soc. Am., Nat. Fedn. State Poetry Socs., Airs Poetica, Okla. Writers Assn., Tulsa Opera Guild, Tulsa Poets, Women's Alliance Arts Council, Women's Assn. Tulsa Philharmonic, United Poets Laureate Internat., Tuesday Writers (publicity chmn. 1950-60). Republican. Methodist. Author: Poetry—Listening for Absolutes, 1968; The Delight of Being, 1971. Contbr. poetry to anthologies, lit. mags. Home: 1542 E 34th St Tulsa OK 74105

PROCTOR, VILMA, librarian, educator; b. Hamburg, Germany, 1910; d. Wilhelm and Anne (Buck) Prochownick; Ph.D. magna cum laude, U. Hamburg, 1932; B.S. in L.S., Denver U., 1940. Came to U.S., 1934, naturalized 1940. Research asso. dept. biochemistry Harvard Med. Sch., 1934-38; free lance med. research bibliographer, 1938-42; librarian Cal. State Hosp., 1942-46; prof. med. bibliography U. So. Cal., Los Angeles, 1946—, mem. dean's exec. com. Sch. Med. 1956—; mem. Salerni Collegium. Cons. U.S. VA for Med. Library. Mem. Mayor's Bicentennial Celebration Com. Bd. dirs. Med. Library Scholarship Found., Los Angeles. Clara Sachs fellow, 1934-36; Lederle Research fellow, 1936-38. Mem. Am. Assn. U. Profs., Hist. Med. Soc., Med. Library Assn., Hist. Soc. So. Cal., Mus. Assn., Sierra Club. Home: 701 S Harvard Blvd Los Angeles CA 90005 Office: U So Cal Sch Medicine 2025 Zonal Av Los Angeles CA 90033

PROJECTOR, DOROTHY SOUTH (MRS. THEODORE H. PROJECTOR), fed. ofcl.; b. Memphis, Jan. 14, 1923; d. Warwick Payne and Isabel Ruth (Jenkins) South; B.A., Southwestern Coll., Memphis, 1943; M.A., George Washington U., 1951; m. Theodore H. Projector, Jan. 25, 1949. Economist, Fed. Res. Bd., Washington, 1946-49, 51-55, 57-67, U.S. Dept. Labor, Washington, 1967-68; economist Social Security Adminstrn., Washington, 1968—, dir. div. econ. and long range studies, 1970—. Mem. Conf. on Research in Income and Wealth, Nat. Bur. Econ. Research, 1971—. Mem. Am. Econ. Assn., Am. Statis. Assn., Nat. Economists Club Washington. Author: Survey of Change in Family Finances, 1968; (with G.S. Weiss) Survey of Financial Characteristics of Consumers, 1966. Home: 3304 Edgewood Rd Kensington MD 20795 Office: 1875 Connecticut Av NW Washington DC 20201

PROKES, SISTER DOROTHY, theatre dir.; b. Jackson, Minn., Feb. 10, 1920; d. Wesley John and Lillian Catherine (Dostal) Prokes; B.S., Viterbo Coll., 1953; M.A., U. Detroit, 1961; postgrad Marquette U., 1964, 65, Coll. St. Thomas, 1966, U. Ia., 1967; Ph.D. (Univ. honors scholar), N.Y. U., 1971. Joined Order Franciscan Sisters Perpetual Adoration, 1935; Tchr. parochial schs., Wis., 1939-51, 55-61, Ia., 1951-55, 1962-68, Wash., 1963-64; prin. St. Anne Sch., Stanley, Wis., 1955-61, St. Bernard Sch., Breda, Ia., 1962-63, St. Mary High Sch., Guttenberg, Ia., 1965-66; founder, dir. ednl. theatre program CRE-ACT, La Crosse, Wis., 1970-71, Pocatello, Ida., 1972—. Research asst. for teenage performing arts workshop, N.Y., 1969. Bd. dirs. Pocatello Community Players. U.S. del. Brit. Nat. Children's Theatre Festival, 1973. Mem. Am. Theatre Assn., Children's Theatre Conf., Creative Edn. Found., Conf. for Exceptional Children, Assn. for Gifted and Talented, Internat. Assn. Theatre for Children and Young People (U.S. del. to Venice, Italy 1970), Alpha Psi Omega. Home: 583 W Sexton St Blackfoot ID 83221 Office: 920 E Lovejoy St Pocatello ID 83201

PROMBO, MARJORIE PIERCE, physician; b. Ft. Wayne, Ind., Jan. 3, 1916; d. Nikola Carl and Marjorie (Lewis) Pierce; B.S., U. Mich., 1938, M.S., 1939; Ph.D., Northwestern U., 1949, M.D., 1950; m. Stanley J. Prombo, June 19, 1948 (dec. Nov. 1961); children—Carol Ann, Patrick James. Intern, Passavant Meml. Hosp., Chgo., 1950-51; resident Children's Meml. Hosp., Chgo., 1951-53; practice medicine specializing in pediatrics, Homewood, Ill., 1954-69, Olympia Fields, Ill., 1969—; mem. staff St. James Hosp., Chicago Heights, Ill., South Suburban Hosp., Hazelcrest, Ill. Chmn. profl. adv. bd. Parents Without Partners, Olympia Fields, 1967-71. Fellow Am. Acad. Pediatrics. Home: 18446 Dixie Hwy Homewood IL 60430 Office: 3235 Vollmer Rd Flossmoor IL 60422

PRON, ANN BLANCHE, ins. orgn. exec.; b. Scranton, Pa., Mar. 9, 1924; d. Walter Anthony and Mary Constance (Gorgol) Pron. Bookkeeper, student Internat. Corr. Schs., 1942-64. Bookkeeper Sponjnia Home for Aged, also Sponjnia Farm and Dairy, Waymart, Pa., 1964—, adminstr., sec., 1971—. Sec.-treas. youth and ednl. commn. Polish Nat. Union Am., 1963—, v.p., 1971—. Mem. United Girls Sodalities (treas. 1948-52, pres. 1952-69), United Choirs (financial sec. 1943-66, v.p. 1966-73). Mem. Sch. Christian Living (teaching staff 1959—). Home: 627 Cherry St Scranton PA 18505 Office: 1006 Pittston Av Scranton PA 18505

PROPST, ESTHER RUTLEDGE (MRS. RALPH CLYDE PROPST), univ. librarian; b. Demopolis, Ala., July 26, 1914; d. Frank Bellamy and Daisy (Kirn) Rutledge; student Judson Coll., 1931-33; B.A., U. Ala., 1935, M.A., 1959; m. Ralph Clyde Propst, Aug. 30, 1939 (dec. Oct. 1959); children—Dashiell (Mrs. James Trumbull McKay), Elizabeth, Daisy (Mrs. Jonathan Baird Druhl). Tchr. pub. schs., Demopolis, 1935-40, 47-59; acquisition librarian Jacksonville (Ala.) State U., 1959-60; reference librarian U. Ala. Edn. Library, University, 1960-67, head librarian, 1967—, library rep. univ. council, 1970-71, 73-74, mem. univ. parking and traffic com., 1973-75. Mem. Ala. (life, chmn. interllectual freedom 1971, conv. chmn. ann. meeting 1971 com. Southeastern library assns., Kappa Delta Pi, Delta Kappa Gamma, Alpha Gamma Delta. Home: 530-29th Pl Tuscaloosa AL 35401 Office: U Ala Box 2604 University AL 35486

PROSKE, BEATRICE GILMAN (MRS. HERBERT PROSKE), ret. curator; b. Thornton, N.H., Oct. 31, 1899; d. Milan Jeremiah and Alice May (Hazeltine) Gilmen; B.S., Simmons Coll., 1920; m. Herbert Proske, Aug. 19, 1935; 1 dau., Cynthia (Mrs. Edward J. Maestro). Mem. staff Hispanic Soc. Am., N.Y.C., 1920—, asst. curator for sculpture, now curator sculpture emerita. Mem. Hispanic Soc. Am. (hon. corr. sec. 1948; Sorolla medal 1937, Sculpture medal 1953, membership medal 1970), Nat. Sculpture Soc., Real Academia de Bellas Artes de San Fernando (Spain; corr. mem.), Real Academia de Bellas Artes y Ciencias Historicas de Toledo (Spain), Real Academia de Bellas Artes de Santa Isabel de Hungria de Sevilla, Société Francaise d'Archeologie. Author: Gregorio Fernandez, 1926; Hispanic Soc. Catalogue of Sculpture, 2 vols., 1930-32; Brookgreen Gardens Sculpture, vol. 1, 1943, vol. 2, 1955, rev. edit., 1968; Robert A. Baillie, Carver of Stone, 1946; Henry Clews, Jr., Sculptor, 1953; Castilian Sculpture, Gothic to Renaissance, 1951; Pompeo Leoni: Work in Marble and Alabaster in Relation to Spanish Sculpture, 1956; Archer Milton Huntington, 1963; Juan Martinez Montanes, Sevillian Sculptor, 1967. Home: 2 Lincoln Av Ardsley NY 10502 Office: 613 W 155th St New York City NY 10032

PROSKY, PHOEBE SNOVER (MRS. PAUL JOSEPH PROSKY), psychotherapist; b. Phila., Sept. 24, 1942; d. Arthur Lawrence and Phoebe (Young) Snover; B.A., Goucher Coll., 1964; M.S. Columbia, 1966; m. Paul Joseph Prosky, June 24, 1964, Psychiat. social worker, Psychiat. Inst., N.Y.C., 1966-68; mem. staff and faculty Ackerman Family Inst., N.Y.C., 1968-70, 71—. Individual practice psychotherapy, N.Y.C., 1971—. Mem. Am. Orthopsychiat. Assn., Nat. Assn. Social Workers, Integral Yoga Inst., Amateur Chamber Music Players. Contbr. articles and chpts. to profl. jours and books. Home: 310 w 106th St New York City NY 10025 Office: 149 E 78th St New York City NY 10021

PROSNITZ, ELAINE LOIS POLINSKY (MRS. ERIC H. PROSNITZ), educator; b. Jersey City, July 2, 1947; d. Aaron Samuel and Helen Ann (Vogel) Polinsky; B.S. (Mental Retardation grantee), So. Conn. State Coll., 1969; M.S. (U.S. Dept. Edn. fellow), John Tracy Clinic, U. So. Cal., 1970; m. Eric H. Prosnitz, Aug. 23, 1970. Tchr. deaf classes Marlton Sch., Los Angeles, 1970-71, Mary E. Bennet Sch., 1971-73, Taylor Sch. Rehab. Center, Cedar Rapids, Ia., 1973—. Mem. Council for Exceptional Children (pres. student chpt. 1969), Am. Assn. Mental Deficiency, Cal. Assn. Tchrs. and Parents of Hearing Impaired Children, Ia. Speech and Hearing Assn. Jewish religion. Mem. Hadassah. Club: Interns and Residents Wives. Home: 309 N 3d St Hills IA 52235 Office: 720 7th Av SW Cedar Rapids IA 52406

PROSSER, ELEANOR ALICE, educator; b. Pasadena, Cal., Sept. 1, 1922; d. Norman Isbel and Alice Bertha (Austin) Prosser; certificate Pasadena Jr. Coll., 1937-41, 47; A.B., Occidental Coll., 1950; M.A., Stanford, 1957, Ph.D., 1960. Faculty, San Jose (Cal.) State Coll., 1957-66, prof. English, 1965-66; asso. prof. drama Stanford, 1966-68, prof., 1968—. Mem. acting co. Ore. Shakespearean Festival, Ashland, 1952-54. Lilly fellow, 1964-65. Mem. Am. Assn. U. Prof., Shakespeare Assn. Am., Modern Lang. Assn., Am. Theatre Assn., Mediaeval Acad. Am., Malone Soc., Common Cause, Am. Civil Liberties Union, Phi Beta Kappa. Democrat. Author: Drama and Religion in the English Mystery Plays: A Re-evaluation, 1961; Hamlet and Revenge, 1967, rev. edit., 1971. Asso. editor Ednl. Theatre Jour., 1972—. Home: 657 Los Ninos Way Los Altos CA 94022 Office: Stanford U Dept Drama Stanford CA 94305

PROTACIO, ANDREA BEATRIZ, librarian; b. Bklyn., May 24, 1926; d. Gregorio Carlos and Dorothy Ottiwell (Fischer) Joaquino; A.A., U. Philippines, 1948; B.A. with honors in English and Secondary Edn., U. Guam, 1967; M.A. in Library Sci., U. Mich., 1968; m. Arthur Scott Protacio, Jan. 26, 1946; children—Alexander, Cynthia, Iris Rose, Patrick. Librarian, Agat Jr. High Sch., Guam, 1964-67; library cons. Guam Dept. Edn., 1968-71, coordinator ESEA Title II, 1968-71; librarian St. John's Coll., Washington, 1972—. Mem. Am., Guam, D.C. library assns., Am. Assn. U. Women. Author library handbooks. Home: 13654 Kingsman Rd Woodbridge VA 22193 Office: St Johns Coll 2607 Military Rd NW Washington DC 20015

PROTEAU, ROSEANNE VITULLO, pediatrician; b. Chgo., Sept. 26, 1936; d. Ralph N. and Elvira (Liambo) Vitullo; A.B. summa cum laude, Clarke Coll., 1958; M.D., Stritch Sch. of Medicine of Loyola U., Chgo., 1962; m. Paul Joseph Proteau, Sept. 2, 1967; children—Paul Michael, Susan Marie. Intern Resurrection Hosp., Chgo., 1962-63; pediatric resident Presbyn.-St. Luke's Hosp., Chgo., 1963-66; pediatrician Mile Sq. Health Center, Chgo., 1966-73; dir. Birth Defect Spl. Treatment Center Rush-Presbyn.-St. Luke's Hosp., 1973—; med. dir. Misericordia Home for Retarded Children, Chgo., 1972—. Asst. prof. pediatrics and preventive medicine Rush Med. Sch., Chgo., 1972—; mem. Ill. Gov.'s Adv. Council for Developmental Disabilities, 1973—. Bd. dirs. St. Mary's Sch., Riverside, Ill. Diplomate Am. Bd. Pediatrics. Mem. Chgo. Pediatric Soc., Am. Acad. of Pediatrics, Clark Coll. Alumni Club (pres. 1962-63), Kappa Gamma Pi, Delta Sigma Epsilon. Home: 744 Leesley Rd Riverside IL 60546 Office: 2916 W 47th St Chicago IL 60632

PROUDFOOT, ALICE-BOYD MAGRUDER (MRS. THEODORE W. PROUDFOOT), poet; b. Canton, O., Jan. 1, 1921; d. Walter Drane and Alice (Thomson) Magruder; student U. Miami, 1938-40; m. Grant Stockdale, May 30, 1940 (dec.); children—Sally, Ann, Grant, Lee Lawson, Susan; m. 2d, Lee E. Beaird, Jan. 1, 1966 (dec.); m. 3d, Theodore W. Proudfoot, Oct. 6, 1973. Contbr. poetry to Good Housekeeping, Ladies Home Jour., Sat. Eve. Post, Better Homes and Gardens. Pres. Laramore-Rader Poetry Group, Miami, Fla., 1957-58. Mem. Poetry Soc. Am., Nat. League Am. Pen Women, Kappa Kappa Gamma. Author: (poetry) To Ireland With Love, 1964. Home: 10 Courseview Rd Bronxville NY 10708

PROUDFOOT, BERNADETTE AGNES, educator; b. Jersey City, June 22, 1921; d. George Francis and Lillian Agnes (Fay) Proudfoot; B.A., Caldwell Coll., 1952; M.S., Institutum Divi Thomas, 1958; Ph.D., St. Thomas Inst., 1972. Instr. biology Caldwell Coll., 1955-59, asst. prof., 1960-69, asso. prof., 1970-72, prof., 1973—, chmn. dept. natural sci., 1972, now dir. undergrad. research program. Mem. Albertus Magnus Guild, Nat. Sci. Tchrs. Assn., Am. Inst. Biol. Scis., Nat. Assn. Biology Tchrs. Home: Ryerson Av Caldwell NJ 07006

PROULX, MARIE ANTOINETTE, clin. psychologist; b. Newark, Nov. 9, 1921; d. Anthony Paul and Lena Mary (Salerno) Iannarone; A.B., U. Cin., 1962, M.A., 1963; widow; 1 dau., Barbara (Mrs. Jeremy Chandler). Co-owner indsl. electronics equipment co.; staff clin. psychologist Marlboro (N.J.) Psychiat. Hosp., 1968; part-time instr. Monmouth (N.J.) Coll., 1969, Brookdale Coll., 1970. N.J. State fellow psychology, 19—. Fellow N.J. Psychology Assn.; mem. Am., Monmouth-Ocean County psychol. assns., Am. Suicidology Assn., Am. Assn. U. Women, Assn. N.J. Instl. Psychologists, Mensa, Right to Life, Fish, Monmouth Players, Phi Beta Kappa. Home: 431 Spring St Red Bank NJ 07701 Office: Marlboro Psychiat Hosp Marlboro NJ 07746

PROVDA, LOIS MAHARAM (MRS. PAUL PROVDA), educator; b. N.Y.C., Mar. 19, 1942; d. Arthur and Helen Eunice (Keen) Maharam; B.S., Boston U., 1962; M.A., N.Y. U., 1964, postgrad., 1973—; m. Paul Provda, June 5, 1969; 1 son, Asher. Ednl. dir. N.Y. Hosp., Payne Whitney Psychiat. Clinic, N.Y.C., 1964-68; ednl. counselor and remedial reading therapist Sheltering Arms Children's Service, N.Y.C., 1968-69; reading dir. Buckingham Sch., Bklyn., 1969-73; instr. Performance-Based Undergrad. Program for Edn. Tchrs., Bklyn. Coll., 1973—. Ednl. cons. Rye Neck Schs., Adolescent Research Project, Mamaroneck, N.Y., 1968-69, Crowell-Collier Pub. Co., N.Y.C., 1968—; pvt. practice as ednl. therapist specializing in reading disabilities, N.Y.C., 1968—. Mem. Gracie Sq. chpt., Women's Am. Orgn. for Rehab. and Tng., N.Y.C., 1972—; mem. Deborah Heart and Lung Center, 1973—. Recipient Grad. award U.S. Office Edn., Dept. Spl. Edn., 1970. Mem. Internat. Reading Assn., Assn. for Children with Learning Disabilities, Am. Orthopsychiat. Assn. Home: 240 E 82d St New York City NY 10028 Office: Brooklyn Coll Brooklyn NY 11210

PROVENCE, SALLY ANN, educator, pediatrician; b. Wills Point, Tex., Sept. 4, 1916; d. Thomas King and Anvaline (Meredith) Provence; A.B., Mary Hardin Baylor Coll., 1937; M.D., Baylor U., 1941; M.A. (hon.), Yale, 1968. Rotating intern Baylor Hosp., Dallas, 1941-42; resident pediatrics Children's Med. Center, Dallas, 1942-44; pvt. practice pediatrics, Dallas, 1944-46; pediatric cons. Tex. Dept. Health, 1946-47; fellow child devel. Cornell-N.Y. Hosp., 1947-48; instr. Cornell Med. Sch., 1948-49; mem. faculty Yale, 1949—, now prof. pediatrics. Author: Infants in Institutions; Guide for the Care of Infants in Groups. Home: Orchard Av Branford CT 06405 Office: 333 Cedar St New Haven CT 06510

PROVENCHER, KATHLEEN JANE (MRS. ANDRE ARTHUR PROVENCHER), journalist; b. Norwich, Conn., Oct. 29, 1930; d. Daniel Anthony and Theodora Eileen (August) McCarthy; grad. Norwich Free Acad., 1948; m. Andre Arthur Provencher, Nov. 23, 1950; children—John, Jeffrey, Cathy Ann, David, Christine. Bookkeeper, Baltic Mills Co., (Conn.), 1948-51, Torrance Constrn. Co., Norwich, 1953-56; abstract and tax work Town of Sprague, Conn., 1957-60, town nurse, selectmen's sec., 1960-65; corr., photographer Hartford Times Co., 1965-67; reporter, photographer Norwich Bull. Co., 1967-69, journalist, mem. editorial staff, 1969—. Leader, 4-H Boys' Club, Baltic, Conn., 1960-65; publicity leader for County 4-H Program, 1967—. Publicity chmn. Sprague Democratic Women's Club, 1965-69. Bd. dirs. Assn. Retarded Children. Recipient awards A.R.C., 1969, 70, 71, service award Assn. Mentally Retarded Children, 1970, Norwich Woman's City Club, 1971, Sigma Delta Chi, 1972. Mem. Norwich Bus. and Profl. Women's Club, Beta Sigma Phi (Writing award 1972). Democrat. Roman Catholic. Club: Norwich Woman's City. Home: RFD 1 Hanover Rd Baltic CT 06330 Office: 66 Franklin St Norwich CT 06360

PROVENSEN, ALICE ROSE TWITCHELL (MRS. MARTIN PROVENSEN), artist; b. Chgo; d. Jay Horace and Kathryn (Zelanis) Twitchell; student Chgo. Art Inst., 1930-31, U. Cal., at Los Angeles, 1939, Art Students League N.Y., 1940-41; m. Martin Provensen, Apr. 17, 1944; 1 dau., Karen Anna. With Walter Lanz Studios, 1942-43, OSS, 1944-45; exhibited (with Martin Provensen) Balt. Mus., 1954, Am. Inst. Graphic Arts, N.Y., 1959, Botolph Group, Boston, 1964. Books represented in Fifty Books of Year selections Am. Inst. Graphic Arts, 1947, 48, 52. The Charge of the Light Brigade named Best Illustrated Children's Book of Year N.Y. Times, 1964. Co-recipient Gold medal Soc. Illustrators, 1960. Author, illustrator books including Karen's Opposites, 1963; Karen's Curiosity, 1963; What is a Color;, 1967; (with Martin Provensen) Who's In The Egg, 1970; The Provensen Book of Fairy Tales, 1971; Play on Words, 1972; My Little Hen, 1973; Roses are Red, 1973; Our Animal Friends, 1974; illustrator children's books, textbooks. Home: Meadowbrook Lane Clinton Hollow RD Staatsburg NY 12580

PROVITT, EVELYN, state ofcl.; b. Massillon, O., Apr. 27, 1930; d. Alfonzo and Lucresie (Anderson) Provitt; diploma in nursing Good Samaritan Hosp. Sch. Nursing, Zanesville, O., 1953; B.S., Wayne State U., 1960, M.S., 1965. Dir. inservice edn. Northville (Mich.) State Hosp., 1960-62, asso. dir. nursing services, 1962-66; psychiat.-mental health nurse cons. Mich. Dept. Mental Health, Lansing, 1966-67, asst. program devel. and planning, mental retardation services, 1967-68, dept. asst. dir., div. dir. mental retardation services, 1968-70, state coordinator, dir. planning for mental retardation services, 1970—. Mem. adv. council Inst. for Study of Mental Retardation and Related Disabilities, U. Mich., 1968—; mem. state adv. com. for vocational rehab. services Mich. Dept. Edn., 1972—; mem. State of Mich. Council for Developmental Disabilities Services and Facilities Constrn., 1971—; mem. nat. adv. council on services and facilities for developmentally disabled, social and rehab. service Dept. Health, Edn. and Welfare, 1973—. Mem. Am. Assn. Mental Deficiency (mem. social and legislative issues com. 1972—), Nat. Assn. Coordinators State Programs for Mentally Retarded. Home: 501 Rampart Way East Lansing MI 48823 Office: Mich Dept Mental Health 320 Walnut St Lansing MI 48926

PRUE, JUNE PATRICIA, lawyer; b. Somerville, Mass., Sept. 29, 1931; d. Harvey P. and Gertrude M. (Jaycock) Davis; student Northeastern U., 1960-61; J.D., Boston U., 1966. Admitted to Mass. bar, 1966; title examiner's aide Mass. Land Ct., Boston, 1966-70; asst. city solicitor, Newton, Mass., 1971; pvt. practice law, North Reading, Mass., 1972—. Mem. North Reading Community Planning Commn., 1971—, Republican Town Com., 1972—. Mem. Mass., Middlesex County Bar assns., Faneuil Bus. and Profl. Women's Club, Assn. Women Lawyers, Mass. City Solicitors and Town Counsel Assn., Mass. Conveyancers Assn., Boston U. Law Sch. Alumni Assn. Sr. editor: Boston U. Law Review, 1965-66. Home: 13 Redmond Av North Reading MA 01864 Office: 180 Park St North Reading MA 01864

PRUFER, CYNTHIA MUNRO, psychologist; b. Cleve., Jan. 12, 1936; d. Thomas Boston and Lucile Celia (Nadler) Munro; B.A. cum laude, Radcliffe Coll., 1958, M.A., 1960; M.A., Case Western Res. U., 1967; m. Olaf Prufer, Sept. 20, 1958 (div. June 1973); children—Keith, Diana, Kevin. Psychol. intern, research, cons. Headstart, Mental Devel. Center, Cleve., 1966-67; child psychologist Holyoke (Mass.) Mental Health Center, 1967-68; cons. psychologist Soc. for Crippled Children, Cleve., 1971-73; child therapist Cleve. Guidance Center, 1973—. Mem. Am., Cleve. psychol. assns. Home: 2172 Maplewood St Cleveland OH 44118 Office: 2525 E 22d St Cleveland OH 44115

PRUITT, ANNE LORING SMITH (MRS. RALPH L. PRUITT), educator; b. Bainbridge, Ga., Sept. 19, 1929; d. Loring A. and Anne (Ward) Smith; B.S., Howard U., 1949; M.A., Columbia, 1950, Ed.D., 1964; m. Ralph Lewis Pruitt, Feb. 20, 1965; 1 dau., Leslie; stepchildren—Dianne, Pamela, Sharon, Ralph Lewis. Counselor, dean of women's staff Howard U., Washington, D.C., 1950-52; tchr., counselor Hutto High Sch., Bainbridge, Ga., 1952-55; dean of women, dean of students Albany (Ga.) State Coll., 1955-59, Fisk U., Nashville, 1959-61; asst. prof. dept. edn. Case Western Res. U., Cleve., 1963-69, asso. prof. dept. edn., 1969-74, prof., 1974—, dir. counseling Mather Coll., 1969-71. Cons. to Pres.'s Task Force on War on Poverty, 1964; dir. Workshop on Employment Problems of Negro High Sch. Grads., summers 1965-69. Trustee Central State U., Wilberforce, O. 1973—. Mem. Nat. Vocational Guidance Assn. (chmn. commn. on career guidance through curriculum 1968-71), Assn. for Counselor Edn. and Supervision, Am. Coll. Personnel Assn. (sec. 1971-73), Am. Personnel and Guidance Assn., Nat. Assn. Women Deans and Counselors, Ohio Assn. for Counselor Edn. and Supervision (pres. 1966-67), Urban League (trustee Cleve. 1965-71, sec. 1969, chmn. com. on edn. and youth incentives 1968-70, chmn. street acad. project com. 1968-71), Welfare Fedn. Cleve. (manpower planning and devel. commn. 1972), Links, Pi Lambda Theta, Psi Chi, Kappa Delta Pi, Alpha Kappa Alpha. Conglist. Editorial bd. Jour. Coll. Student Personnel, 1969-71. Contbr. articles to profl. jours. Home: 18700 Scottsdale Blvd Shaker Heights OH 44122 Office: Dept Edn Case Western Res U Cleveland OH 44106

PRUSOFF, BRIGITTE AUERBACH (MRS. WILLIAM HERMAN PRUSOFF), educator; b. Berlin, Germany, Oct. 14, 1926; d. Richard Julian and Ella Georgine (Levi) Auerbach; B.A.,

Berea Coll., 1946; M.P.H., Yale, 1967; m. William Herman Prusoff, June 20, 1948; children—Alvin, Laura. Research asso. psychiatry Yale, 1967-71, asst. prof. psychiatry, 1971—. Statis. cons. Addiction Center, N.Y.C., 1970-72. Mem. Biometric Soc., Am. Statis. Assn. Home: 46 DeForest Dr North Branford CT 06471 Office: 100 Park St New Haven CT 06511

PRYOR, ALICE FOLLAND (MRS. ROBERT NEWELL PRYOR), real estate broker; b. Duluth, Minn., Dec. 11, 1928; d. Peter Alfred and Amanda Elise (Longseth) Folland; student Vallejo Jr. Coll., 1946-47; m. Robert Newell Pryor, Aug. 26, 1950; children—Janet (Mrs. Tom Terrell), Jeanne, Edward. Real estate salesman Town & Country Real Estate, Fairfield, Cal., 1966-69; real estate broker Dover Realty, Fairfield, 1969-72; pres., dir. Key Realty, Inc., Fairfield, Cal., 1972—. Chmn., Multiple Listing Service, 1973, pres., 1974. Mem. No. Solano Bd. Realtors (v.p. 1973—, dir.). Home: 2471 Heather Dr Fairfield CA 94533 Office: 1462 W Texas St Fairfield CA 94533

PRYOR, BARBARA BECK (MRS. JOHN GATEWOOD PRYOR, JR.), utilities exec.; b. N.Y.C., Aug. 8, 1945; d. Will R. and Eleanor F. (Keeney) Beck; student Emory U., 1963-65; B.A. in Journalism, U. Ga. 1967; m. John Gatewood Pryor, Jr., July 6, 1968. Advt. copywriter Sears, Roebuck & Co., Atlanta, 1967-69, Ga. Power Co., Atlanta, 1969—. Mem. Atlanta and Dekalb County chpts. Soc. for Prevention of Cruelty to Animals, Ga. Conservancy. Mem. Women in Communications, Phi Kappa Phi, Kappa Tau Alpha, Phi Mu. Office: 270 Peachtree St Atlanta GA 30303

PRYOR, BLANCHE WILSON (MRS. GRANT PRYOR), educator; b. Midway, Utah, Apr. 5, 1910; d. James Brigham and Lota Eliza (Huffaker) Wilson; B.S., Brigham Young U., 1954; M.Ed., U. Ariz., 1968; m. Grant Pryor, May 23, 1934; children—Evva Joan, Jay Floyd. Elementary tchr., Utah, 1930-33, 38-54; tchr. Mary Lynn Elementary Sch., Tucson, 1954-58; spl. edn. tchr. Blenman Sch., Tucson, 1959-63; program asst. supervising city-wide, Tucson, 1963-66; lectr., supr. student tchrs. U. Ariz., 1967-71; supr. homebound and teenage parents Tucson Pub. Schs., 1972—. Pres. Latter-day Saints Youth Programs So. Ariz., 1968-72, area dir. speech, 1965-68, area dir. teenage parents, 1973. Mem. Nat., Ariz., Tucson edn. assns., Ariz. Assn. Retarded Children, Council Exceptional Children (pres. 1966-68); Pi Lambda Theta. Club: Soroptimist (v.p. 1972-73) (Tucson). Home: 100 W Main St Minersville UT 84752 Office: 501 E 6th St Tucson AZ 85705

PRYOR, CAROL GRAHAM, physician; b. Savannah, Ga., Dec. 11; d. Charles Britt and Helen (Hall Smith) Pryor; A.B., Ga. State Coll. for Women; M.D., Med. Coll. Ga., 1947; m. Dr. Louis O. J. Manganiello, June 11, 1950; children—Carol Helen, Victoria. Rotating intern Balt. City Hosp., 1947-48; asst. residency pathology Baroness Erlanger Hosp., Chattanooga, 1948; intern obstetrics City Hosp., Balt., 1949; coll. physician, head health services, prof. health edn. Ga. State Coll. Women, 1949-50; resident obstetrics City Hosp., Balt., 1950-51; asst. resident gynecology U. Hosp., Balt., 1951-52, sr. resident obstetrics and gynecology, Augusta, 1952; pvt. practice obstetrics and gynecology, Augusta, 1952—; chief div. obstetrics and gynecology St. Joseph's Hosp., 1960-61, 71-72, sec. obstetrics staff, 1969-70; splty. privileges St. Joseph's Hosp., U. Hosp., Doctors Hosp., Augusta; instr. obstetrics, gynecology, Med. Coll. Ga. Chmn. health edn. com. Better Health Council of Ga., Atlanta, 1952-54; chmn. Augusta U.S.O. Com. 1961. Mem. Ga. Med. Edn. Bd., 1965-69; mem. Status Women Com., Ga., 1966-72; chmn. Ga. Med. Edn. Bd., 1968-69. Bd. dirs. Augusta Jr. Achievement. Named Med. Woman of Yr., 1961. Diplomate Am. Bd. Obstetrics and Gynecology. Fellow Am. Coll. Obstetrics and Gynecology, A.C.S.; mem. So. Med. Assn., Richmond County Med. Soc. (1st v.p. 1957-59), Am. Assn. U. Women (2d v.p. state 1958-60, chmn. Ga. div. of social and econ. issues 1960-63, state rep. on Ga. Council Mental Health 1960-62, pres. Augusta br. 1958-61, 73-74, nat. membership com. 1961-63, pres. Ga. div. 1963-65), Alumnae Club Ga. State Coll. (pres. Augusta 1955-57, 10th dist. dir. 1961-63), Am. Med. Women's Assn. (pres. br. 51 1962-63, 71-74), A.M.A., Ga. Med. Assn., D.A.R., Royal Soc. Medicine Alpha Epsilon Iota, Delta Kappa Gamma. Club: Iris Garden (publicity chm., 1st v.p. 1958-59, pres. 1959-60, Augusta). Author articles in field. Home: 656 Milledge Rd Augusta GA 30904 Office: 1500 Johns Rd Suite 7 Medical Village Augusta GA 30904

PRYOR, LUCILLE (MRS. CHARLES N. FULTZ), lawyer; b. Monroe County, Ind., Aug. 25, 1910; d. James Levi and Ruth Addie (Judson) Pryor; LL.B., Benjamin Harrison Law Sch., 1936, Ind. U., 1942; m. Charles N. Fultz, Apr. 4, 1954 (dec. Jan. 1965). Sec. trust dept. Union Trust Co., Indpls., 1929-42; admitted to Ind. bar, 1936; with judge adv. gen. tax sect. USN, Washington, 1942-45; practiced law, Indpls., 1946—. Served with USNR, 1942-45. Mem. Am. Soc. Women Accountants, Ind. Soc. Pub. Accountants, Ind., Indpls. bar assns. Indpls. C. of C. Republican. Presbyn. (clk. 1970—). Mem. Order Eastern Star. Club: Athletic (Indpls.). Home: 1637 N Tibbs Av Indianapolis IN 46222

PRYOR, MARGO TUPPER (MRS. THEODORE LOY PRYOR II), journalist; b. Arcadia, Fla., Feb. 7, 1919; d. Perry C. and Lessie Virginia (Williams) Browne; student Fla. State U., 1934, Stetson U., 1939; m. Richard Waring Tupper, May 15, 1942 (dec. 1970); children—Jan (Mrs. Terence Cogley), Richard Landon; m. 2d, Theodore Loy Pryor, Sept. 29, 1973. Editor Belle Glade (Fla.) Herald, 1939-40; reporter, Internat. News Service, Washington, 1941-42; editor A.P., Jacksonville, Fla., 1943-45; research writer NBC, Washington, 1962-63; writer articles for numerous mags., including Redbook, Good Housekeeping, This Week, Parade. Mem. Capital Press Women, Am. Newspaper Women's Club. Democrat. Presbyn. Club: Nat. Press (Washington). Author: No Place To Play, 1966. Address: 2024 Franklin Av McLean VA 22101

PSALMONDS, MARJORIE (MRS. W. GORDON PSALMONDS), educator; b. Taylor, Miss.; d. Fred Winford and June (Wolfe) Varner; B.A., William Jewell Coll., 1943; M.R.E., B.S.M., Southwestern Sem., 1947; M.A., Ariz. State U., 1958; postgrad. Ariz. State U., Columbia, Washington U.; m. W. Gordon Psalmonds, Mar. 23, 1940; 1 child, Jonathan Lowrie. Organist, music dir. 1st Bapt. Chs., Bartlesville, Okla., 1947-50, McAlester, Okla., 1950-51; organist 1st Bapt. Ch., Duncan, Okla., 1951-54; supr. pub. sch. music Murphy Sch,, Phoenix, 1954-60; asso. prof. organ Grand Canyon Coll., Phoenix, 1956-67, asso. prof. music, 1960-71; asst. prof. music Mo. Baptist Coll., St. Louis, 1971—. Am. Guild Organists (past dean Central Ariz. chpt.), Music Educator's Nat. Conf., N.E.A., Delta Kappa Gamma, Sigma Alpha Iota. Baptist. Home: 1095 Charolais Dr Ballwin MO 63011

PTASZYNSKI, PAMELA ANN, educator; b. Chgo., July 24, 1948; d. Sigmund Jerome and Blanche Marie (Stomper) Ptaszynski; B.S., U. Ill., 1970. Tchr. mentally handicapped, West Chicago, 1970-73; presch., 1973—. Dir. religious edn. for exceptional children Sacred Heart Parish, Lombard, Ill., 1971—. Mem. Council for Exceptional Children, Assn. on Mental Deficiency, N.E.A. Roman Catholic. Office: 750 Ingalton St West Chicago IL 60185

PUCKETT, BARBARA CHANDLEY (MRS. ROBERT HUGH PUCKETT), author; b. Kansas City, Kan., Feb. 14, 1935; d. John Stothers and Edythe Raechel (Jones) Chandley; A.A., Stephens Coll., 1955; m. Robert Hugh Puckett, Dec. 23, 1964; 1 dau., Sarah Anne. Reporter, Kansas City (Mo.) Star, 1956-58, asst. soc. editor, 1958-63, asst. women's page editor, 1963-64. Bd. dirs. Terre Haute YWCA, Terre Haute Women's Symphony Assn.; trustee Kansas City Jr. Women's Philharmonic Assn., 1959-60. Recipient Humanities award Stephens Coll., 1955. Mem. Fashion Group, Inc., League Women Voters (dir. Terre Haute 1971-75), Stephens Coll. Alumni Assn. (regional dir. 1959-60), Theta Sigma Phi. Club: Stephens College Dinner (pres. 1959-60) (Kansas City, Mo.), Author: History of the League of Women Voters of Charlottesville-Albemarle, 1966. Home: 110 Berkeley Dr Terre Haute IN 47803

PUCKETT, REBECCA NEWMAN (MRS. FERRILL RUSSELL PUCKETT), journalist; b. New Market, Va., Feb. 27, 1920; d. Edgar Walton and Marguerite Helena (Price) Newman; bus. degree Shenandoah Bus. Coll., Woodstock, Va., 1938; m. Ferrill Russell Puckett, June 3, 1946; children—Patricia (Mrs. William Herman Sessions), Beverly. Teller, Comml. Nat. Bank, Charlotte, N.C., 1941-46; sec. in agronomy dept. N.C. State U., Raleigh, 1946-48, sec. zoology dept., 1948-51; women's editor Orangeburg (S.C.) Times and Democrat, 1969—. Vol. worker Orangeburg chpt. A.R.C., 1960-68; leader Girl Scouts, 1959-65. Mem. Am. Legion Aux. Clubs: Garden, Country, Elks (Orangeburg). Home: 1031 Moore Rd Orangeburg SC 29115 Office: 211 Broughton St Orangeburg SC 29115

PUCKETT, RUBY PARKER (MRS. LARRY WILLARD PUCKETT), dietitian; b. Dora, Ala., Nov. 26, 1932; d. John Franklin and Ethel Victoria (Short) Parker; B.S., Auburn U., 1954; postgrad. U. Fla., 1970—; m. Larry Willard Puckett, July 2, 1955; children—Laurel Lynn, Hollie Kristina. Intern in dietetics Henry Ford Hosp., Detroit, 1955; staff dietitian VA Hosp., Houston, 1955-56; dietitian Matty Hersee Hosp., Meridian, Miss., 1957-58; asst. dir. dietetics U. Miss., Jackson, 1960-61; dir. dietetics Fort Sanders Presbyn. Hosp., Knoxville, Tenn. 1961-63, Waterman Meml. Hosp., Eustis, Fla. 1963-68, J. Hillis Miller Health Center, U. Fla., Gainesville, 1968—. Preceptor, coordinator corr. course for food service suprs. Am. Dietetic Assn., 1965-70; guest lectr. Santa Fe Jr. Coll., 1970-72, U. Fla., 1971-72; tchr. mgmt. systems and philosophies to dietetic interns; mem. adv. com. Fla. State Dept. Edn., 1966-67, Santa Fe Jr. Coll., 1968-69; pres. Field Agy. Nutrition Service, Gainesville, 1970-71; mem. White House Conf. Food, Nutrition and Health, 1969; mem. faculty Fla. Conf. Food Nutrition Health, 1970; Senate Select Com. for Nutrition and Health, 1974. Named Outstanding Dietitian Fla., 1972. Mem. Am. Dietetic Assn. (chmn. AHA-ADA com. 1971), Dietetic Internship Council, Fla. Dietetic Assn. (exec. bd. 1965—, sec. 1968-70, pres. 1973), Hosp. Institutional Edn. Food Service Soc. (founder Fla. chpt. 1965), Gainesville Dietetic Assn. (pres. 1970), Southeastern Hosp. Conf. Dietitians (nominating com. 1969, sec. 1974), Am. Soc. Hosp. Food Service Adminstrs., Royal Soc. Health, Nutrition Edn. Soc. (charter), Pi Lambda Theta, Kappa Delta Pi. Republican. Mem. Ch. Jesus Christ of Latter Day Saints. Club: Pilot (pres. 1967). Editor: (with others) Diet Manual Shands Teaching Hospital, 1971; Study Guide for Food Service Supervisors, 1972, 2d edit., 1974; Guide to Normal Nutrition and Diet Modification Manual, 1973; Preceptors Guide for Food Service Supervisors, 1974. Contbr. articles to profl. jours. Home: 3806 SW 4th Pl Gainesville FL 32607 Office: Box 770 J Hillis Miller Health Center Gainesville FL 32610

PUCKETTE, PANSY MAE, educator; b. Magnolia, Ark., June 13, 1917; d. Thomas Otis and Frances (Wilkerson) Puckette; A.A., So. State Coll., 1936; B.A., Henderson State Coll., 1938; M.A., George Peabody Coll. for Tchrs., 1946; postgrad. U. Ark., Mich. State U. Math. and English tchr. Rison High Sch., Rison, Ark., 1938-41; math. tchr. Blytheville High Sch., Blytheville, Ark., 1941-42, Magnolia High Sch., Magnolia, 1942-47; counselor Magnolia High Sch., 1947-65; guidance dir. Magnolia Pub. Schs., 1965—, staff mem. Elementary and Secondary Edn. Act, Title III, Planning Proposal, 1967-68, dir. career edn. project, 1972—. Mem. Ark. Legislative Council's adv. com. on edn., 1967-68; Ark. Women's Com. on Public Affairs, 1967-69; mem. Ark. Tchr. Retirement System Bd., 1969—; sec. S. Central Ark. Community Action Authority Bd., 1970-74. Mem. Nat., Ark. (pres. 1967-68), Columbia County edn. assns. (past pres.), Am. Personnel and Guidance Assn., Am. Sch. Counselors Assn., Ark. Personnel and Guidance Assn., Ark. Sch. Counselors Assn. (past pres.), Am. Assn. U. Women, League Women Voters, Delta Kappa Gamma (local treas. 1965-68), Kappa Delta Pi. Contbr. articles in field. Home: 1726 Dudney Rd Magnolia AR 71753 Office: PO Box 649 Magnolia AR 71753

PUCKO, DIANE ELIZABETH BOWLES (MRS. RAYMOND JOHN PUCKO), pub. relations counseling co. exec.; b. Wyndotte, Mich., Aug. 15, 1940; d. Mervin Arthur and Bernice Leticia (Shelly) Bowles; B.S. in Sociology cum laude, Bucknell U., 1962; m. Raymond John Pucko, May 22, 1965; children—Todd Anthony, Gregory Bowles. Asst. v.p. pub. relations Edward C. Michener Assos., Inc., Harrisburg, Pa., 1962-65; advt. and pub. relations coordinator Superior Switchboard, Inc., Canton, O., 1965-66; editorial dir. women's services pub. relations group Hutchins Advt., Inc., Rochester, N.Y., 1966-71; prin. Editorial Communications; Concept to Conclusion, Rochester, Elyria, O., 1971—. Mem. adv. bd. Community Savs. Bank, Rochester, 1971-72. Mem. Pub. Relations Soc. Am., Pa. Pub. Relations Soc., Am. Bus. Women's Assn., Am. Soc. for Preventive Dentistry, Phi Beta Kappa, Delta Zeta. Mng. editor Traffic Engring. Mag., 1963-65; asso. editor Practical Pub. Relations, 1971—. Address: 656 University Av Elyria OH 44035

PUGH, ELLEN TIFFANY (MRS. DAVID BENJAMIN PUGH), librarian; b. Cleve., June 2, 1920; d. Clarence Romaine and Margaret May (Williams) Tiffany; A.B., Western Res. U., 1943, B.S. in L.S., 1945; M.A., Northwestern U., 1947; m. David Benjamin Pugh, July 3, 1949. Librarian, Western Res. U., 1943-45, Northwestern U., 1945-47, U. Neb., 1958-63, U. Ore., 1963-65 U. Rochester, 1965-68; tech. services librarian Wash. State U., Pullman, 1969—. Mem. A.L.A., Spokane Writers Guild. Author: Tales From the Welsh Hills, 1968; Brave His Soul, 1970; More Tales From the Welsh Hills, 1971. Home: Apt 15 SW 600 Crestview Pullman WA 99163

PUGH, MARTHA GREENEWALD, lawyer; b. Washington, Feb. 1, 1913; d. Eugene Ludwig and Mary Martha (Curtis) Greenewald; B.A. in Physics, U. Colo., 1934; M.S. in Physics, U. Mich., 1936; J.D., Seton Hall U., 1961; m. Wallace R. Pugh, Aug. 1935 (div. 1946); children—John Clifford, William Wallace. Instr. physics Washington Sq. Coll., N.Y.C., 1941-43; mem. patent staff Bell Telephone Labs., Murray Hill, N.J., 1943-47; patent agt. Gutton Industries, Metuchen, N.J., 1957-58; admitted to D.C. bar, 1964, N.J. bar, 1965; since practiced in Summit, N.J. Vol., Union County Probation, 1972-73, Small Bus. Adminstrn., 1968—, N.J. vols. in Parole, 1972. Mem. Am., N.J. D.C. bar assns., N.J. Assn. on Correction, Am., N.J. patent law assns., Mortar Bd., Sigma Pi Sigma, Pi Beta Phi. Club: Green Mountain (N.J. sect.). Home: 11 New Providence Av Summit NJ 07901

PUGH, NINA NICHOLS (MRS. THOMAS BRYAN PUGH II), lawyer; b. Baton Rouge, Jan. 15, 1925; d. Irby Coghill and Pauline (Wright) Nichols; B.A., La. State U., 1945, LL.B., 1947, M.A., 1963. J.D., 1968; m. Thomas Bryan Pugh II, Jan. 3, 1948; children—Thomas Bryan III, Pauline Wright, Stephen Nichols. Research asso. La. State U. Law Sch., 1955-70, instr. classical langs., 1948-50, 57-58; law clk. La. State Ct. Appeal, First Circuit, Baton Rouge, 1970—. Pres., Jr. League Baton Rouge, 1957-58, Community Services Council, 1964-66, Community Advancement, 1967-69, Baton Rouge Area Council on Alcoholism, 1970, Baton Rouge Area YWCA, 1972-74; v.p. Baton Rouge Youth, 1973-74; chmn. legislative com. Family Relations Council La., 1973-74; mem. Battered Child Com., 1972—; chmn. charter and by-laws com. Baton Rouge Arts Council, 1973-74; sec. Gov.'s. Com. for Employment Handicapped, 1962-65. Bd. dirs. Planning Council United Givers, Community Vol. Bur., Cath. Social Services Agy., Uniting Campus Ministry, Interracial Bus. Council, Univ. Chamber Mus. Soc. Mem. La., Baton Rouge (chmn. youth edn. com. 1972-74) bar assns., Colonial Dames Am., Chi Omega, Phi Delta Delta. Democrat. Methodist (mem. adminstrv. bd. 1955-60, 72—). Home: 2000 Cloverdale Av Baton Rouge LA 70808 Office: 1100 Laurel St Baton Rouge LA 70802

PUGHSLEY, GLORIA STOCKTON (MRS. JAMES PUGHSLEY), city ofcl.; b. Gonzales County, Tex., Jan. 20, 1916; d. Grover and Jhonnie (White) Stockton; student Chgo. U. Coll., 1954; grad. nurse Manley Sch., Chgo., 1951; m. James Pughsley, Oct. 5, 1940 (dec. July 1951). Pub. health nurse City of Chgo., 1951-54, community coordinator, 1960—. Del., Ill. Constl. Conv., 1970. Baptist. Home: 1527 S St Louis Av Chicago IL 60623 Office: City Hall 121 N LaSalle St Chicago IL 60602

PUGMIRE, DOROTHY JEAN, educator; b. Paris, Ida., May 28, 1923; d. Jonathan Rich and Ellen (Budge) Pugmire; B.S., Utah State U., 1948; postgrad. Merrill-Palmer Inst., 1948-49; M.A., U. Mich., 1951; postgrad. Columbia, 1967; Ed.D., U. Md., 1973. Kindergarten tchr., Provo, Utah, 1947-51, Logan, Utah, 1951-52; tchr. Utah State U. Lab. Sch., 1953-54; tchr. Army Dependent Sch., Tokyo, Japan, 1954-55; tchr. elementary edn. Coll. So. Utah, 1955-56; prof. elementary edn. Utah State U., Logan, 1956—. Dir. ednl. Personnel Devel. Act project, 1970-73; dir. Nat. Defense Edn. Act Workshop for tchrs. Indian Children, Blanding, Utah, 1966; Mem. state adv. council on early childhood edn., 1963—. Bd. dirs. Cache County Mental Health Assn., Cache County Migrant Council. Served with WAVES, 1944-46. Fellow Inst. Child Study, U. Md., 1964-65. Mem. N.E.A., Assn. Childhood Edn., Soc. Study Edn., Assn. Edn. Young Children (Utah pres. 1971-72), Assn. Supervision and Curriculum Devel. (Utah pres. 1973-74), U.S. Nat. Commn. Early Childhood, Bus. and Profl. Women, Utah Edn. Assn. Home: 486 E 4th N Logan UT 84321

PULLEN, DORIS LUCK (MRS. PHILIP FLEMING PULLEN), editor; b. Poughkeepsie, N.Y., Jan. 18, 1919; d. Herman Carl and Helen (Corwin) Luck; B.A., Skidmore Coll., 1940; m. Philip Fleming Pullen, Feb. 8, 1941; children—Martha Jo (Mrs. Martha Jo Jenkins), Philip Luck, Amelia Baxter. Reporter, Hudson Valley Sunday Courier, Poughkeepsie, 1940-41; researcher Fortune mag., N.Y.C., 1942-47; reporter Life mag., N.Y.C., 1947-49; corr. Time, Inc., Boston, 1949-60; free lance writer, lectr., 1949-72; lectr. journalism Northeastern U., Boston, 1965-71; exec. staff, dir. dept. publs. Unitarian Universalist Assn., Boston, 1972—, editor-in-chief Unitarian Universalist World, newspaper, 1972—; partner Battle Green Publs., Lexington, Mass., 1959—. Co-founder, staff leader ann. New Eng. Writers Conf., 1969—. Mem. Lexington Celebrations Com., 1959-62, Lexington Bicentennial Com., 1971—. Mem. Women in Communications (Nat. Headliner award 1974), Nat. Orgn. Women, D.A.R., Lexington Hist. Soc. (life), League Women Voters (Lexington v.p. 1952-54). Democrat. Unitarian Universalist. Club: Boston Authors. Author: Lexington, A History of the Massachusetts Town for Young People, 1964; They Nobly Dar'd, 1963; Self-Discovery; Explorations in Life Crises, 1970, rev. 1972. Contbr. to anthology, 1970. Home: 17 Percy Rd Lexington MA 02173 Office: 25 Beacon St Boston MA 02108

PULLEN, PHYLLIS KOUWENHOVEN (MRS. KEATS A. PULLEN, JR.), physician; b. Balt., Feb. 10, 1923; d. Frank Wolfert and Alice Henrietta (Witherell) Kouwenhoven; A.B., Goucher Coll., 1944; M.D., U. Md., 1962; m. Keats A. Pullen, Jr., Jan. 6, 1945; children—Peter K., Paul V., Keats A. III, Andrew W., Victoria F. Intern, U. Md., 1962-63, fellow medicine and arthritis, 1963-64, asst. resident dermatology, 1964-65; practice medicine specializing in gen. medicine, Kingsville, Md., 1965—. Mem. Phi Beta Kappa, Alpha Omega Alpha, Delta Gamma. Republican. Presbyn. Address: Route 1 Box 381 Kingsville MD 21087

PULLMAN, ELIZABETH DODD, occupational therapist; b. Birmingham, Ala., Feb. 26, 1920; d. Thomas McDuffe and Lucy (McEwen) Dodd; B.A., Vanderbilt U., 1941; certificate occupational therapy Va. Commonwealth U., 1955; M.A. in Psychiat. Occupational Therapy, N.Y. U., 1969; m. J. Wesley Pullman III, May 16, 1942; children—J. Wesley IV, Dodd Cooper. Social worker U.S. Employment Service and Welfare Dept., Savannah, Ga., 1941, A.R.C., 1942-47; sr. occupational therapist Rockland State Hosp., Orangeburg, N.Y., 1951-60, cons. Mt. Vernon unit, Bronx unit, Yonkers Hudson unit and Rockland County unit; chief occupational therapy Rockland Psychiat. Center, 1960—; cons. in field. Bd. dirs. consortium occupational therapy edn. Nat. Com. Employment Youth, 1972—; mem. clin. practice council Occupational Therapy Program, Columbia, N.Y. U. and Tufts U.; dir. 3d nat. course Certificate Occupational Therapy Assts., 1960-70. Bd. dirs. Rockland County chpt. Planned Parenthood Assn. Fed. Masters Program Occupational Therapy grantee, 1967-69. Mem. Am., N.Y. State occupational therapy assns., Am. Assn. U. Women (charter pres. Nyack br. 1948), D.A.R. (N.Y. State Am. heritage chmn.), Washington Hdqrs. Assn., Gamma Phi Beta. Home: 52 Oak Tree Rd Tappan NY 10983 Office: Rockland Psychiatric Center Orangeburg NY 10962

PULOS, HELEN J., publishing co. exec.; b. Gunn, Wyo., Aug. 31, 1924; d. John S. and Sylvia Frances (West) Pulos; grad. high sch., Rock Springs, Wyo. Stenographer, Wyo. State Lab., Cheyenne, 1942; with Rock Springs Newspaper, Inc., 1942—, advt. mgr., 1963-71, advt. dir., 1971-73, bus. mgr., 1973—. Sec. Sweetwater County Camp for Girls, Inc., 1949—. Recipient best classified advt. page awards Wyo. Press Assn., 1962, 64, 65, 66, 70, 71. Mem. Wyo. (dir. 1963—), Rock Springs City (pres. 1958-59, 65, 70-71) women's bowling assns., Rock Springs C. of C., Rock Springs Bus. and Profl. Women's Assn. (pres. 1948-51). Democrat. Roman Catholic. Home: 130 L St Rock Springs WY 82901 Office: 215 D St Rock Springs WY 82901

PULSKAMP, SISTER MARY LEO, hosp. adminstr.; b. Hillsboro, N.D., Apr. 3, 1926; d. Jacob G. and Bertha (Mueller) Pulskamp; R.N., St. Andrew's Hosp. Sch. Nursing (N.D.), 1948; B.S. in Dietetics, Fontbonne Coll., 1952. Registered nurse St. Andrew's Hosp., Bottineau, N.D., 1948-49; adminstr. St. Margaret's Hosp., Spring Valley, Ill., 1968—, also sec.-treas. bd. dirs. Bd. dirs. Corporate Bd. Sisters of Mary of Presentation. Address: 600 E 1st St Spring Valley IL 61362

PULVERMACHER, MARIE BARBARA, newspaper editor; b. Sauk City, Wis., Apr. 24, 1919; d. Carl Peter and Theresa Magdalena (Geier) Pulvermacher; B.S., U. Wis., 1942. Reporter, Capital Times, Madison, Wis., 1942-46, copy editor, 1946-55, feature editor, 1955—, editor arts sect., 1970—. Mem. Women in Communications (treas. Madison chpt. 1964-66, pres. 1966-67), Madison Art Assn., Madison Civic Music Assn., U. Wis. Alumni Assn., Friends of Elvehjem Art Center. Club: Madison Press (pres. 1972). Home: 111 W Wilson St Madison WI 53703 Office: Capital Times Box 1030 Madison WI 53701

PUNCHES, DOROTHY HOFFMANN (MRS. GEORGE L. PUNCHES), polit. worker; b. Saginaw, Mich.; d. George J. and Louise M. (Reitter) Hoffmann; grad. Saginaw Coll. Cosmetology, 1931; m. George Louis Punches, Apr. 26, 1931; children—Joan Louise (Mrs. Louis Dulac), Carole Faith (Mrs. William Morgan), George Clayton. Mem. central com. Mich. Republican Com., 1952-57, sec. central com., exec. com., audit and research com., 1952-54, vice chmn. Saginaw County Rep. Com., 1955-57; del., mem. com. on permanent orgn. Rep. Nat. Conv., 1956; pres. Saginaw County Rep. Women's Club, 1954-56, 60-64, sec., 1971—; dir. Federated Rep. Women's Clubs Mich., corr. sec., 1959-61, membership chmn. and rep. to State Central Com.; 1st v.p. Rep. Women's Fedn. Mich., 1963-65; orgnl. dir. Saginaw County Rep. Com., 1962; co-chmn. 8th Congl. Dist. Mich. Citizens for Goldwater and Miller, 1964; county del. Rep. Conv., 1950—, Mich. del., 1952-72. Mem. (first and only Women) Bridgeport Planning Commn., 1963. Bd. dirs. Hartley Nature Camp, Saginaw County; bd. dirs. St. Lukes Hosp. Guild, pres. 1969-70, pub. relations dir., 1971-72; mem. Saginaw County Bd. Canvassers, 1965-67. Mem. Citizen's Action Com. Saginaw County, Saginaw Interracial Com., 1961-62. Pres., v.p., sec. P.T.A. in Saginaw and Flint, 1939-49; bd. dirs. Saginaw council P.T.A.; active Girl Scouts Am., YWCA. Trustee, sec. Saginaw Community Hosp.; bd. dirs. Delta Coll. Mem. St. Lukes Hosp. Assn. (life), Nat. Farm and Garden Club, Nat. Campers and Hikers Assn., East Central Dist. Hosp. Auxs., Mich. Assn. Hosp. Auxs. Lutheran (former mem. choir, Sunday Sch. tchr.). Clubs: Midland Antique, Saginaw Woman's. Home: 3359 S Airport Rd Bridgeport MI 48722

PUNGITORE, VERNA LEAH, librarian; b. Clairton, Pa., Apr. 30, 1941; d. Dominick and Carmella (Enos) Pungitore; A.B., Blackburn Coll., 1963; M.L.S. (Owens fellow 1964-65), U. Pitts., 1965. Readers adviser Youngstown (O.) Pub. Library, 1963-64, br. librarian, 1965-67; reference coordinator Clinton Essex Franklin County Library System, Plattsburgh N.Y., 1967-68; dir. Plattsburg Pub. Library, 1968—. Mem. Clinton County Council of Community Services, 1968—. Mem. N.Y. Library Assn., Ind. Central Libraries Assn. N.Y. (sec.-treas. 1969-72), Plattsburgh Little Theatre Group, Inc. (pres. 1971), Common Cause, Clinton County Hist. Soc., Champlain Valley Bus. and Profl. Women's Club (chmn. civic participation 1971-72). Home: 88 Lafayette St Plattsburgh NY 12901 Office: 15 Oak St Plattsburgh NY 12901

PURCELL, MARY HAMILTON (MRS. WILLIAM PAXSON PURCELL, JR.), club woman, educator; b. Ft. Worth; d. Joseph Hants and Letha (Gibson) Hamilton; B.A., Mary Hardin-Baylor Coll., 1947; M.A., La. State U., 1948; m. William Paxson Purcell, Jr., Dec. 28, 1950; children—William Paxson III, David Hamilton. Instr., dept. speech and dramatic arts Temple U., Phila., 1948-53, 60-61; part-time instr. speech Ellen Cushing Jr. Coll., Bryn Mawr, Pa., 1966—. Pres., Pa. Program for Women and Girl Offenders, 1968-73. Named Outstanding Alumna Mary Hardin-Baylor Coll., 1972. Mem. Am. Assn. U. Women (div. pres. 1968-70, v.p. middle Atlantic region 1973—), Lansdowne-Aldan Home and Sch. Assn. (pres. 1967-68), League Women Voters, Am. Assn. U. Profs., Speech Assn. Am., World Affairs Council Phila., Pi Kappa Delta, Pi Gamma Mu, Delta Sigma Rho, Alpha Psi Omega, Alpha Chi. Democrat. Baptist (deacon). Home: 9 Oak Knoll Dr Wallingford PA 19086

PURCELL, MARY LOUISE GERLINGER (MRS. DALE PURCELL), educator; b. Thief River Falls, Minn., July 17, 1923; d. Charles and Lajla (Dale) Gerlinger; student Yankton Coll., 1941-45, Yale Div. Sch., 1949-50, N.Y. U., summer 1949; M.A. (alumni fellow), Tchrs. Coll. Columbia, 1959, Ed.D., 1963; m. Walter A. Kuyawski, June 9, 1950 (dec. July 1954); children—Amelia Allerton, Jon Allerton; m. 2d, Dale Purcell, Aug. 26, 1962. Teen-age program dir., YWCA, New Haven, 1945-52; dir. program in family relations, asst. prof. sociology Earlham Coll., Richmond, Ind., 1959-62, conf. co-ordinator undergrad. edn. for women, 1962; chmn. div. home and community Stephens Coll., Columbia, Mo., 1962-73, head family life edn. dept. and community life dept., 1973—, dir. continuing edn., 1974—, devel. course The Contemporary Am. Woman, 1962, cons., 1962; vis. prof. Ind. U. Summer Sch., 1970. Cons. student personnel services, Trenton (N.J.) State Coll., 1958-59, 61. Mem. exec. com. Nat. Council on Family Relations, also chmn. film awards com. Mem. Am. Home Econs. Assn. (chmn. family relations child devel. sect. 1967-69, bd. dirs.), Am. Assn. University Women, Groves Conf. Family Life Nat. Council Family Relations (chmn. spl. emphases sect., bd. dirs.), Kappa Delta Pi, Pi Lambda Theta. Presbyn. Contbr. articles in field to coll. bulls. Home: 229 Saint Francis St Fulton MO 65251

PURCELL, REGINA BLIGH, lawyer; b. Mineola, N.Y., May 4, 1934; d. William T. and Loretta R. (Fogarty) Bligh; B.A., St. John's U., 1955, J.D., 1961; postgrad. Stanford, 1963-64; M.S., Fordham U., 1966; m. James L. Purcell, May 31, 1971; 1 son, Daniel P.; stepchildren—Joseph M., Joan E., James L., Catherine A. Tchr., East Meadow, N.Y., Palo Alto, Cal. and Hempstead, N.Y., 1955-64; admitted to N.Y. bar, 1962; atty. Coudert Bros., N.Y.C., 1966-68, Paul, Weiss, Goldberg, Rifkind, Wharton & Garrison, N.Y.C., 1968-70, Simpson, Thacher & Bartlett, N.Y.C., 1970-71; individual practice law, N.Y.C., 1971—. Legal adviser Catholic Charities, Diocese Rockville Centre, N.Y., 1971—. Mem. Fed. Bar Council, Assn. Bar City N.Y. Home: 130 Cherry Valley Av Garden City NY 11530

PURCELL, VERNITA NADINE (MRS. JOHN E. PURCELL), librarian; b. North Bend, Ore., Nov. 1, 1935; d. Delbert Marion and Gertrude Maud (Osgood) Harkins; B.A., Westmont Coll., 1957; M.A., Spl. Libraries Assn. scholar 1959, 60), U. Denver, 1960; m. John E. Purcell, Sept. 24, 1966. Catalog librarian Central Bapt. Theol. Sem. Library, Kansas City, Kan., 1957-62; asst. prof. library sci. So. Ore. Coll., Ashland, 1962-66; head processing center Jackson County Library System, Medford, Ore., 1966—. Mem. Ore., Am., Pacific Northwest (vice chmn. pub. libraries div. 1973-75) library assns., League of Women Voters (pres. 1967-69, 71-73). Presbyn. Home: 920 Wilson Rd Ashland OR 97520 Office: 1915 Hazel St Medford OR 97501

PURCHAS, BILLIE BLISS (MRS. WILLIAM JOHN PURCHAS, JR.), rancher; b. Cumberland, Md., Dec. 28, 1921; d. Clinton Farley and Evelyn Lee (Craig) Bliss; B.S. magna cum laude, Western Mich. U., 1952; m. Kenneth Vander Meulen, Mar. 6, 1941; 1 dau., Billie Lee (Mrs. Donald Orenbuch); m. 2d, Wm. John Purchas, Jr., May 31, 1952. Actress with Kalamazoo Civic Theatre, 1941-42, Grand Rapids (Mich.) Civic Theatre, 1946; med. asst. to L. Paul Ralph, Grand Rapids, 1945-50; practice speech therapy, Grand Rapids, 1952-56; style show commemtator Paul Steketee & Sons, Grand Rapids, 1955-56; now owner, rancher B/B Ranch, Scottsdale, Ariz., breeder Peruvian Paso horses. Press relations D.A.R., Sophie de Marsac chpt. 1954-56; program chmn. Health and Welfare Council, Grand Rapids, 1955-56; program chmn. Shakespeareiana, Grand Rapids, 1955-56; capt. Kent County United Fund, 1955; chmn. Clay Twp., Hamilton County (Ind.) United Fund, 1963; bd. dirs. A.R.C., Hamilton County 1959-63; v.p. Goodwill Service Guild, Indpls., 1960-61, pres., 1961-64; 2d v.p. Nat. Auxs. to Goodwill Industries Am. Inc., 1961-63, rec. sec., 1963-65, pres., 1965-67; bd. dirs. Goodwill Industries Am., 1965-70. Vice chmn. Republican Party, Clay Twp., 1962-63. Mem. Am. Speech and Hearing Assn., Am. Assn. U. Women (program chmn. Grand Rapids 1952-56, chmn. book analysis study group Indpls. 1957-58, chmn. speakers bur. 1958-60, chmn. philosophy study group 1958-59, chmn. N.E. Central Regional Conf., 1964, pres. Indpls. br. 1964-67), Kappa Delta Pi, Club: Woodland Country (chmn. Spring Handicap tournament 1961). Home: B/B Ranch East Asher Hill PO Box 861 Scottsdale AZ 85252

PURDOM, MARTHA ELDA, nutritionist, educator; b. Xenia, O.; d. Charles David and Stella (Smith) Purdom; B.S., Ohio State U., 1933, Ph.D., 1958; M.S., U. Cal., Los Angeles, 1945. Teaching fellow, asso. instr. U. Cal., Los Angeles, 1940-43; asst. prof. foods, nutrition Wash. State U., 1943-44; asso. prof. foods, nutrition, inst. mgmt. Bowling Green (O.). State U., 1944-52; asst. prof. foods, nutrition Mich. State U., 1952-58; nutrition cons. therapeutics Greene Meml. Hosp., Xenia, 1960-62; asso. prof. Sch. Home Econs., N. Tex. State U., Denton, 1962-73, prof., 1973—. Fellow A.A.A.S., Am. Inst. Chemists; mem. Am. Tex. dietetic assns., Am., Tex. home econs. assns., Tex. Nutrition Council, A.A.A.S., Am. Pub. Health Assn., Am. Chem. Soc., N.Y., Tex. acads. sci., Am. Assn. U. Profs., Royal Soc. Health London, Omicron Nu, Phi Mu, Sigma Delta Epsilon. Club: Sigma Xi of North Texas State University (past sec.-treas.). Contbr. articles in field of animal nutrition research to various publs. Office: Sch Home Econs N Tex State U PO Box 13486 Denton TX 76203

PURDY, PATRICIA DOYLE (MRS. ARTHUR C. PURDY), publishing co. exec.; b. Houghton, Mich., Mar. 18, 1922; d. Timothy J. and Florence (Garske) Doyle; student Mich. Tech. U., 1940-43; m. Arthur C. Purdy, May 29, 1968. Mgr. OPA, Houghton, Mich., 1944-46; owner Personal Mailing Service, 1946-50; sales and sales promotion mgr. Ironwood Trailer Coaches, (Mich.), 1950-52; asst. to pres., then v.p. Drake Pub. Co., Chgo., 1952-60; dir. adminstrv. services Hitchcock Pub. Co., Wheaton, Ill., 1960-66, v.p. 1966—, also dir. circulation. Bd. dirs. Bus. Publs. Audit of Circulation, 1973—. Mem. Assn. Indsl. Advertisers, Adminstrv. Mgmt. Assn., Direct Mail Advt. Assn., Chgo. Federated Advt. Club, Women's Advt. Club (v.p. 1963, chmn. speakers bur. 1964, 1st v.p. 1968, pres. 1968-69). Club: St. Charles (Ill.) Country. Home: 965 N 2d Av St Charles IL 60174 Office: Hitchcock Bldg Wheaton IL 60174

PURDY, SUSAN GOLD (MRS. GEOFFREY HALE PURDY), author, illustrator; b. N.Y.C., May 17, 1939; d. Harold A. and Frances (Joslin) Gold; student Vassar Coll., 1957-59, Sorbonne and Ecole des Beaux Arts, Paris, France, 1959-60; B.S., N.Y. U. 1962; m. Geoffrey Hale Purdy, Sept. 29, 1963. Textile designer Wamsutta Mills, N.Y.C., 1961-63; free-lance designer, 1963-64; co-founder, co-dir. Music and Art Day Camp, Wilton, Conn., 1964-66; author, illustrator, 1964—. Mem. Author's Guild and League of Am. Author and illustrator: My Little Cabbage, 1965, If you Have a Yellow Lion, 1966, Be My Valentine, 1966, Christmas Decorations for You To Make, 1965, Holiday Cards for You to Make, 1967, Festivals for You To Celebrate, 1969, Jewish Holidays, 1969; Costumes for You To Make, 1971; Books for You To Make, 1973; illustrator: Suddenly a Witch; contbr. articles to mags., including Good Housekeeping, Ladies Home Jour., Family Circle; tchr. cooking for young people CBS-TV, 1973—, demonstrator crafts various TV programs. Home: PO Box 59 Wilton CT 06897

PURDY, SYLVIA KATSENES (MRS. ROBERT JAMES PURDY III), lawyer; b. Boston, Nov. 9, 1941; d. Arthur Vasilios and Catherine (Cocotas) Katsenes; A.B., magna cum laude, Suffolk U., 1963, LL.B. (Trustees scholar 1963-66), 1966; m. Robert James Purdy III, Aug. 28, 1971. Admitted to Mass. bar, 1966, since practiced in Newton; mem. firm Katsenes and Katsenes. Mem. Mass. Assn. Women Lawyers, Tech. Matrons, Waltham, Weston and Newton Bar Assn. Home: 156 Walpole St Dover MA 02030 Office: 743 Washington St Newtonville MA 02160

PURDY, VIVIAN MILLER (MRS. IRA JAMES PURDY), assn. exec.; b. Ossining, N.Y., Feb. 7, 1915; d. Wilson Phraner and Hazel (Kipp) Miller; R.N., Mt. Sinai Sch. Nursing, N.Y.C., 1936; m. Ira James Purdy, Aug. 4, 1939 (dec. Sept. 1959); children—Kim Ellen (Mrs. Donald Graham), Pamela Jean (Mrs. John Scott). Nurse supr. Mt. Sinai Hosp., N.Y.C., 1938-39; sec. Basketball Hall of Fame, Springfield, Mass., 1959-61; exec. sec. Hampden Dist. Med. Soc., Springfield, 1961—. Exec. dir. Health Care Found. Western Mass., 1972-74. Sec.-treas. Bay State Physicians Polit. Action Com., 1971-73; mem. Bd. Health, Charlton, Mass., 1973; mem. adv. com. Easter Seal Soc., 1967-70; vice chmn. Springfield Meml. Soc., 1970—. Bd. dirs. Vis. Nurse Assn. Springfield, 1967-72, pres., 1970-71. Mem. Springfield C. of C. (dir. 1971-73, pres. women's div. 1970-71), New Eng., Western Mass. (sec. 1970—) pub. health assns., Western Mass. Heart Assn. (dir. 1971—), Am. Assn. Med. Soc. Execs. (mem. com. on membership 1970-72), Springfield Bus. and Profl. Women's Club, Valley Press Club. Club: Zonta (Springfield). Home: Shore Rd Charlton MA 01508 Office: 1414 State St Springfield MA 01109

PURSWELL, EVELYN HOKE (MRS. BOBBY GERALD PURSWELL), city ofcl.; b. Dickinson, Tex., July 14, 1933; d. Charles Eber and Eva Ida (Brasher) Hoke; student Lee Jr. Coll., 1961, U. Ala., 1970, 72, 73; m. Bobby Gerald Purswell, Jan. 25, 1951; children—Terry D., Randall G. Bookkeeper, Hall's Ins. Agy., Dickinson, 1952; office mgr. Tuck Ins. Agy., Baytown, Tex., 1956-58; office mgr. Citizens Ins. Agy., Baytown, 1959-68; city clk. City of Guntersville, Ala., 1970—. Sec.-treas. Dr.'s Recruitment Com. Guntersville. Recipient Accounting award Ala. Soc. C.P.A.'s, 1971. Mem. Ala. Assn. Municipal Clks. and Adminstrs., Epsilon Sigma Alpha. Baptist. Club: Pilot (Guntersville). Home: Rural Route 2 Lakewood Dr Guntersville AL 35976 Office: 341 Gunter Av Guntersville AL 35976

PURUCKER, BETTE JOAN, banker; b. South Bend, Ind., Dec. 6, 1940; d. Forest Lee and Emma Eulalia (Chinn) Purucker; grad. high sch. Bookkeeper, teller, loan dept. teller, asst. cashier, cashier Corydon (Ind.) State Bank, 1958—. Recipient certificate Dale Carnegie Course for Effective Speaking and Human Relations, 1970, Achievement award Corydon Bus. and Profl. Women, 1972. Mem. Nat. Assn. Bank Women (chmn. So. Ind. group 1971-72), Corydon Credit Women Internat. (pres. 1971-73), Harrison County C. of C., Am. Inst. Banking, Phi Beta Psi. Mem. Christian Ch. Home: 143 Beech St Corydon IN 47112 Office: 219 N Capitol Av Corydon IN 47112

PURVIS, LOIS ALLENE (MRS. JAMES PITTMAN PURVIS), newspaper editor; b. Sudan, Tex., Nov. 26, 1929; d. Vernon Francis and Elsie Winifred (Easley) Nivens; student Hardin Simmons U., 1948-49, U. N.M., 1950, Coll. Artesia, 1969-70; m. James Pittman Purvis, July 3, 1953; children—James Daniel, Rebecca Joann, John Easley. Asst. to oil editor and society editor Odessa (Tex.) American, 1955-56; with Encinitas (Cal.) Coast Dispatch, 1960-64; cor. El Paso Times, 1965-68; city editor Artesia (N.M.) Daily Press, 1966-70, editor, 1970-71; regional and Sunday editor Roswell (N.M.) Daily Record, 1971—. Recipient numerous writing awards N.M. Women's Press Assn. and N.M. Press. Assn. Home: 1516 S Kentucky St Roswell NM 88201 Office: 2301 N Main St Roswell NM 88201

PURVIS, MARY BELLE, chemist; b. Greeneville, Tenn., June 12, 1932; d. Silas Wayne and Malcena Elizabeth (Bird) Purvis; B.A., Tusculum Coll., 1953, Tchrs. certificate, 1953; M.A., East Tenn. State U., 1959. Chemistry lab. asst. Tusculum Coll., Greeneville, 1951-53; bill collector, Greeneville, 1954-59; self-employed bookkeeper, Greeneville, 1956-65; organic lab. instr. East Tenn. State U., Johnson City, 1958-59; self-employed chem. lit. researcher, Greeneville, 1959-65; pvt. researcher, Greeneville, 1965—. Asst. leader Girl Scouts Am., 1949-52, 1953-56; instr. water safety A.R.C., 1949-56, instr. first aid, 1952-56, instr. home nursing, 1955-59; rec. sec. Home Demonstration Club Greene County Council, 1968-70, mem. hospitality and fellowship com., 1962-64, chmn. reading program, 1966-68. Named Outstanding Club Woman Union Temple Home Demonstration Club, 1965. Mem. D.A.R. (named outstanding jr. mem. Nat., Tenn. socs., S.E. div. 1965; state chmn. com. 1968-71; co-chmn. com. 1970—; chpt. regent 1964-66, registrar 1972-74), Children Am. Revolution (sr. pres. 1970—), Nat. Soc. So. Dames Am. (state rec. sec. 1967-70), Internat. Fedn. U. Women (life), Am. Assn. U. Women (br. pres. 1972-74), East Tenn. (life), Green County hist. socs., Watauga Assn. Genealogists, Genealogy Club Am. (life), Soc. Descs. Colonial Clergy (life), Nat. Hist. Soc., United Daus. Confederacy, Gen. Fedn. Women's Clubs, Internat. Platform Assn., Alpha Epsilon Delta (life), Bass Anglers Sportsman Soc., Am. Fishing Assn. (life), Smithsonian Assos., Franklin Mint. Presbyn. Clubs: Union Temple Home Demonstration (pres. 1962-64; leader health and safety 1968), Rod and Gun, Fishing of Am., Nat. Travel. Author: A Fungicidal Study, 1959. Address: 426 W Main St Greeneville TN 37743

PURYEAR, RACHELLE MARIE, museum curator; b. Washington, Aug. 27, 1947; d. Reginald Thomas and Martina (Morse) Puryear; B.A., Trinity Coll., 1969; M.A. (Carnegie fellow), Ind. U., 1971. Dir. photo archives Ind. U., Bloomington, 1970-71; head art dept. St. Anne's Sch., Arlington Heights, Mass., 1971-72; curator African art Museum Nat. Center of Afro-Am. Artists, Dorchester, Mass., 1972-74. Instr. African art and culture Career Opportunities Program, Boston State Coll., 1973. Carnegie travel grantee 1971, Nat. Endowment for Arts fellow, 1973. Mem. African Studies Assn. Home: 2606 Myrtle Av NE Washington DC 20018

PURYEAR, RUBY HAMILTON (MRS. MAHLON T. PURYEAR), educator; b. Morganton, N.C., Apr. 13, 1917; d. Edward N. and Margaret Louise (Burnett) Hamilton; B.S., Hampton Inst., 1942; M.A., Columbia, 1949, Ed.D., 1970; postgrad. Colo. Coll. Edn., 1950, New Sch. for Social Research, 1962; m. Mahlon T. Puryear, June 24, 1939; children—Ruby L. (Mrs. Robert W. Hearn), Katherine A. Asst. prof. Morehouse Coll., 1951-61; research asso. Harlem Youth Opportunities, 1962; adj. lectr., research asso. Yeshiva U. Grad. Sch. Edn., 1963-65; asst. prof. Iona Coll., 1970; asso. prof. City U. N.Y., 1971-73; cons. ednl. and developmental psychology, New Rochelle, N.Y., 1973—. Bd. dirs. Westchester Urban League; mem. Westchester Day Care Council. Recipient grant So. Fellowships Fund, 1956. Deans scholar tchrs. Coll., Columbia, 1948. Mem. Am. Psychol. Assn., Assn. Black Psychologists, A.A.A.S., Internat. Council Psychologists, Delta Sigma Theta, Psi Chi, Pi Lambda Theta, Kappa Delta Pi. Home: 33 Vaughn Av New Rochelle NY 10801

PUTERBAUGH, KATHRYN ELIZABETH, corporate exec.; b. Denver, Mar. 5, 1924; d. Frederic John and Cora (Zoph) Puterbaugh; B.A., U. Colo., 1945. Accountant F.J. Puterbaugh & Co., Denver, 1946-49; sec. Herbert Bayer-artist, designer, 1950-51; accountant Himel's, New Orleans, 1951-53; asst. controller Berol Pen Co., 1953-54; office mgr., controller Garratt-Callahan Co., Millbrae, Cal., 1955-65, corporate treas., 1966—, also dir. Mem. com. for dedication Millbrae library, 1961; mem. steering com. People-to-People Program, Millbrae, 1962; mem. Belmont-San Carlos Human Relations Com., 1968—; historian Millbrae Sister City Program, 1962-63; active various community fund drives; judge Bank Am. Youth Achievement Awards, 1973. Mem. San Mateo County (Cal.) Fedn. Republican Women, 1960—. Mem. Nat. Orgn. for Women (charter mem., chpt. v.p. 1966-68). Episcopalian. Clubs: Soroptimist (pres. Millbrae-San Bruno 1965-66, active Southwestern region coms.), Ski (Bear Valley, Cal.). Home: 1220 Alameda de las Pulgas Belmont CA 94002 Office: 111 Rollins Rd Millbrae CA 94030

PUTMAN, MADONNA RUTH, clothing co. exec.; b. Joshua, Tex., Nov. 17, 1927; d. William Earl and Dollye Lee (Maupin) Putman; grad. Durhams Bus. Coll., 1948; student Tex. Christian U., 1949-50. With Williamson-Dickie Mfg. Co., Ft. Worth, 1945—, purchasing agt., 1964—. Baptist (dir. Sunday sch. 1953-59). Home: 3762 Cornish Av Fort Worth TX 76133 Office: 509 W Vickery Blvd Fort Worth TX 76104

PUTMAN, PATRICIA KLEIN (MRS. EDISON W. PUTMAN), univ. dean; b. Omaha, Dec. 6, 1922; d. Leo Byron and Blanche (Monheit) Klein; B.A., U. Cal. at Berkeley, 1944, J.D., 1956; m. Edison W. Putman, Nov. 20, 1944; children—Edison K., Jennifer K. Admitted to Cal. bar, 1956, Hawaii bar, 1960; practice law, Berkeley, Cal., 1956-59; atty. Legislative Reference Bur., Hawaii Legislature, 1960-72; asso. dean. legal and legislative affairs U. Hawaii Sch. Medicine, Honolulu, 1972—, chmn. U. Commn. on status women, 1971—. Cons. Hawaii Regional Med. Program, 1972—, Hawaii Tumor Registry, 1972, Citizens Com. on Constl. Conv., 1968. Mem. legislative com. Hawaii Pub. Health Assn., 1972—; legislative coordinator Spl. Project on Female Offender in Hawaii, 1973—; adviser Hawaii Model Cities and Community Action Programs, 1970—; chmn. health ins. com. State Council for Comprehensive Health Planning, 1972—; mem. Rev. Panel for Health Facilities Expenditures, 1973—, Gov.'s Hwy. Safety Council; mem. law revision projects for penal, penal procedures and probate laws Hawaii Jud. Council, 1967—. Fellow Am. Coll. Legal Medicine; mem. Am., Hawaii bar assns., State Bar Cal., Am. Judicature Soc. (commr. uniform state laws 1963—), Am. Civil Liberties Union, N.A.A.C.P. (dir.), Am. Lung Assn. (Hawaii bd. dirs.), Hawaii Legal Aid Soc. (dir.). Home: 3006 Pualei Circle Honolulu HI 96815

PUTNAM, ALYCE RUTLAND (MRS. J. FRANK PUTNAM), educator; b. Flat Rock, Ala., Dec. 28, 1915; d. William Watson and Martha Frances (Watson) Rutland; student Ala. Coll., 1933-34, B.A., Howard Coll., 1940; M.Ed., Emory U., 1952, postgrad, 1958-60, 62-64; postgrad. U. Ga., 1969-71; m. J. Frank Putnam, Feb. 2, 1935; children—Frances Susan (Mrs. Barry Eugene Duggan), Anne (Mrs. Joseph Key). Dir., The Play Sch., Watertown, Mass., 1945-48; tchr., supervising tchr. DeKalb County Schs., Ga., 1955—; v.p. Utility Services, Decatur, Ga., 1957—. Leader, Girl Scouts Am., 1951-55; active Toney P.T.A., 1955-72. Mem. Assn. Childhood Edn. (pres. local br. 1970-72, treas. Ga. br. 1973—) Nat., Ga. assns. tchr.

educators, Decatur, Ga. edn. assns., Ga. Assn. Tchr. Educators (Ga. mem.-at-large exec. bd. 1971-74), Delta Kappa Gamma (editor chpt. news 1970-74, state scholarship chmn. 1973—, chpt. v.p. 1974—), Holeyville (Ala.) Alumni Assn., Flying Rebels. Methodist. (ch. sch. tchr. 1933-64, supt. ch. sch. kindergarten 1949-64). Home: 2489 Brookcliff Way NE Atlanta GA 30345 Office: 2535 Caladium Dr NE Atlanta GA 30045

PUTNAM, CAROLINE JENKINS (MRS. ROGER LOWELL PUTNAM), civic worker; b. Glymont, Md., Nov. 16, 1892; d. Thomas Canfield and Eleanor (Compton) Jenkins; student Mt. St. Agnes Acad., 1905-07; LL.D., Newton Coll. Sacred Heart, 1967, St. Mary's Coll., 1959, Regis Coll., 1952, St. Michael's Coll., 1956; L.H.D., Am. Internat. Coll., 1950, Manhattanville Coll., 1959; L.H.D. (hon.), Duquesne U., 1969; m. Roger Lowell Putnam Oct. 9, 1919; children—Caroline Canfield, Roger Lowell, William Lowell, Anna Lowell (Mrs. Putnam Finnerty), Mary Compton (Mrs. Charles W. Chatfield), Michael Courtney Jenkins. Mem. Springfield (Mass.) Housing Authority, 1952-62; mem. adv. bd. Mass. Commn. Against Discrimination, Springfield, 1949—; mem. Comm. for Study of De Facto Segregation Pub. Schs. of Mass., 1964-65; mem. Mass. sub-com. under Nat. Commn. on Civil Rights, 1959-64; pres. Catholic Scholarships for Negroes, Inc., 1946—. Mem. Kappa Gamma Phi (hon.). Democrat. Roman Catholic. Home: 101 Mulberry St Springfield MA 01105

PUTNAM, LILLIAN RUSSELL (MRS. ROBERT CONRAD PUTNAM), educator; b. Quincy, Mass., July 30, 1920; d. Robert and Helen (Forbes) Russell; B.S., Bridgewater State Coll., 1942; postgrad. Radcliffe Coll., 1944-45; M.A., Harvard, 1946; Ed.D., Columbia, 1962; m. Robert Conrad Putnam, June 24, 1944; children—Susan (Mrs. Eric Muirhead), Roger Scott. Tchr. pub. schs. Fairhaven, Mass., 1942-43, Quincy, Mass., 1943-44, Tower Sch., Marblehead, Mass., 1946-47; prof. edn. Rutgers U., 1962-63; prof. Keane Coll., Union, N.J., 1964—, dir. reading clinic, 1971—, chmn. reading conf., 1964-73. Cons. 21 communities. Bd. dirs. Model Cities Program, Perth Amboy, N.J., 1971-73, Community Fund Mountain Lakes, 1956-57. U.S. Office Edn. research grantee. Mem. N.J. Reading Tchrs. Assn. (pres. 1970-71), Coll. Reading Assn. (editor clin. column Newsletter), Am. Assn. U. Women (pres., 1960-61). Author: Case Studies for Reading Teachers, 1967. Contbr. articles to profl. jours. Research in reading methods for disadvantaged children. Home: 147 Boulevard Mountain Lakes NJ 07046 Office: Dept Edn Keane College Union NJ 07083

PUTT, ARLENE MAY, nurse educator; b. Quentin, Pa., Mar. 27, 1926; d. Maurice Robert and Mary E. (Bowman) Putt; student Hershey Jr. Coll., 1945; diploma nursing Temple U., 1948, B.S. in Nursing Edn., 1950, M.Ed., 1953; Ed.D., U. Ariz., 1969. Head nurse Jackson Clinic, Temple U., Hosp., Phila., 1948-49; instr. sci. Hahnemann Hosp. Sch. Nursing, Phila., 1950-54; instr. U. Mich. Sch. Nursing, Ann Arbor, 1954-57, asst. prof., 1957-61; asst. prof. Coll. Nursing, State U. Ia., Iowa City, 1961-62; asst. prof. Coll. Nursing, U. Ariz., Tucson, 1962-63, asso. prof., 1963-67, 69-71, prof., 1971—; prin. investigator Conf. to Plan Collaborative Study Fatigue, 1971-73. Nursing cons. VA Hosp., Tucson, 1963-67. Spl. nurse fellow USPHS, 1967-69. Mem. Am. Nurses Assn., Council Nurse Researchers, Nat. League for Nursing, Ariz. Heart Assn., Ariz. Diabetes Assn., A.A.A.S., Ariz. Soc. for Prevention of Blindness, Am. Assn. Higher Edn., Am. Assn. U. Women, Am. Assn. U. Profs., Sigma Xi, Sigma Theta Tau, Pi Lambda Theta. Mem. adv. panel Am. Jour. Nursing, 1967—; book reviewer Choice, publ. Assn. Coll. and Research Libraries, 1967—. Home: 7821 E Elida St Tucson AZ 85715

PUTZEL, CONSTANCE KELLNER (MRS. WILLIAM PUTZEL), lawyer; b. Balt., Sept. 5, 1922; d. William S. and Corinne (Strauss) Kellner; A.B., Goucher Coll., 1942; J.D., U. Md., 1945; postgrad. Goucher Coll., Johns Hopkins, U. Md.; m. William Putzel, Aug. 28, 1945; 1 son, Arthur William. Social worker Balt. Dept. Pub. Welfare, 1945-46; admitted to Md. bar, 1945; atty. New Amsterdam Casualty Co., Balt., 1947; staff atty. Legal Aid Bur., Balt., 1947-49; mem. firm Putzel, Putzel & Danoff, Pikesville, 1950—, sr. partner, 1967—. Mem. Md. Commn. on Status of Women, 1972—, Md. Commn. to Implement Equal Rights Amendment, 1973—. Bd. dirs. Legal Aid Bur., Balt., 1951-52, 71-73. Mem. Am., Md. (gov. 1972-73) bar assns., Women's Bar Assn. (pres. 1951-52), Bar Assn. Balt. City (exec. com. 1970-71), United World Federalists (Balt. chmn. 1967-69, vice chmn. nat. exec. council 1968), League Women Voters (mem. finance adv. com. 1973), Nat. Council Jewish Women, Bipartisan Assn. Responsible Citizenship, World Federalists U.S.A. (dir. 1969—). Jewish religion (sisterhood bd. 1973—). Home: 8207 Springbottom Way Pikesville MD 21208 Office: 600 Reisterstown Rd Pikesville MD 21208

PUUMALA, MARIE KATHERINE BEPKO (MRS. REINO HENDRICK PUUMALA), physician; b. Chgo., Aug. 14, 1904; d. John and Catherine (Zeleznik) Bepko; B.S., U. Ill., 1932, M.D., 1935; m. Reino Hendrick Puumala, Sept. 23, 1932; children—Ricard, Kathleen (Mrs. James Gawboy), Nancy Ann (Mrs. Ka Luomala); adopted children--Dierre, Mark, Dale. Intern, Am. Hosp., Chgo., 1934-35; trainee Elgin (Ill.) State Hosp., 1936; mem. staff Chgo. State Hosp., 1936-37; practice obstetrics, gynecology and pediatrics, Cloquet, Minn., 1937—; mem. staff St. Lukes Hosp., St. Marys Hosp., Cloquet Community Meml. Hosp. Mem. A.M.A., Am. Med. Women's Assn., Med. Women's Internat. Assn., World Med. Assn. (U.S. com.), Pan Am. Med. Women's Alliance, Minn., St. Louis County, Chgo. med. socs., Interurban Acad. Medicine Am. Heart Assn., Am. Assn. U. Women, Nat. Congress Parents and Tchrs., Cloquet C. of C., Nu Sigma Phi, Iota Sigma Pi, Alpha Lambda Delta. Mem. Order Eastern Star. Clubs: Professional Business, Reading Library (Cloquet); Metropolitan Dinner (Ft. Lauderdale, Fla.). Home: 1013 Carlton Av Cloquet MN 55720 Office: 40 12th St Cloquet MN 55720

PYBURN, MARY ETHEL ABERNATHY (MRS. LEROY PYBURN), educator; b. Greenwood, Miss., Sept. 10, 1921; d. Jim Eddie, Sr., and Bettie Jeneva (Thomas) Abernathy; B.S., Kan. State Coll., 1943; postgrad. U. Chgo., 1944; M.S.W., Atlanta U., 1949; B.S., Macalester Coll., 1955; m. Marion Greg Taylor, June 21, 1953; 1 son, Marion Greg; m. 2d, Leroy Pyburn, July 31, 1972. Tchr. Douglas Sch., Kansas City, Kan., 1943-48; vis. tchr., Atlanta, 1948-49; tchr. Lincoln Sch., Kansas City, Kan., 1949-53; family practice case worker St. Paul Family Service, 1953-54; tchr. Madison Sch., Mpls., 1955-74, Greeley Elementary Sch., 1974; tchr. reading adult edn. Mann Sch., Mpls., summer 1967; tchr. Edina (Minn.) Adult Armchair Edn., 1968-70; mem. Minn. Team Action for the Gifted, 1973. Mem. Twin Cities Internat. Program, 1967—; mem. Guidelines for Human Relations Edina Schs., 1972, observor Edina Human Rights Commn. Bd. dirs. Mpls. YWCA, 1953-54, Madison Sch. P.T.A., 1971-72. Mem. League of Women Voters, Kan. Tchrs. Assn (pres. grade tchrs. 1945-47), N.E.A., Minn. Edn. Assn., Assn. Chilhood Edn. Internat. (state pres. 1974). Women in Edn., N.A.A.C.P., Urban League, Alpha Kappa Alpha. Home: 17128 Stowers Av Cerritos CA 90701

PYE, JEWELL GWENDOLYN, educator; b. Cushing, Tex., Feb. 24, 1925; d. Ocie Orum and Nannie Arrena (Goldsberry) Pye; B.S., Stephen F. Austin State U., 1946; M.Ed., U. Houston, 1950, Ed.D., 1963. Tchr., San Angelo (Tex.) pub. schs., 1946-49, Sonora (Tex.) pub. schs., 1950-55, Midland (Tex.) pub. schs., 1959-60; asso. prof. Sul Ross State U., Alpine, Tex., 1955-62; with Angelo State U., San Angelo, Tex., 1962—, prof. phys. edn., 1964—. Mem. Am., Tex. assns. health, phys. edn. and recreation. Democrat. Presbyn. Home: 2011 Guadalupe San Angelo TX 76901 Office: 2601 West Av N San Angelo TX 76901

PYE, ROYACE ANN, psychologist; b. Bryan, Tex., Jan. 28, 1935; d. Edward E. and Doris Louis (Vincent) Zalenski; B.Ed. cum laude, Sam Houston State U., 1958; M.Ed., Tex. A. and M. U., 1966, Ph.D., 1971; m. James Merrill Pye, Aug. 4, 1956; children—Doriann, Lorilynn, James Merrill. Instr., research asso. in psychology Tex. A. and M. U., College Sta., 1967-71; psychologist Brazos Valley Mental Health Center, Bryan, 1971-72; clin. psychologist, dir. day treatment center Rusk (Tex.) Hosp., 1972-74, head dept. rehab. therapies, 1974—. Cons. in behavior modification Tex. Gov.'s Commn. Phys. Fitness, 1972—. Mem. Am., Southwestern psychol. assns., Rusk C. of C., Phi Kappa Phi, Sigma Alpha Iota. Home: Route 1 Rusk TX 75875 Office: Rusk State Hospital Box 318 Rusk TX 75785

PYLE, BEATRICE ALZIRA, educator; b. West Chester, Pa., May 21, 1922; d. Norman James and Audrey (Dilks) Pyle; B.S., Gettysburg Coll., 1944; M.S. in Hygiene and Phys. Edn., Wellesley Coll., 1946; certificate U. Oslo, 1960. Instr. Gettysburg Coll., 1938-40, Vassar Coll., 1946-52; tchr. pub. schs., Winnetka, Ill., 1952-57; asst. prof. phys. and health edn. Miami U., 1957—. Mem. Am. Pub. Health Assn., Royal Soc. Health Can. and Eng., Nat., Ohio edn. assns., A.A.H.P.E.R., Ohio Coll. Assn., Am. Camping Assn., Am. Assn. U. Women, Ohio, Midwest assns. health, phys. edn. and recreation. Author: Small Craft: An Instructional Textbook for Teachers. Home: 119 N Campus Av Oxford OH 45056

PYLE, CLAIRE, librarian; b. Johnstown, Pa., Sept. 17, 1917; d. George G. and Rose (Knauf) P.; A.B. summa cum laude, U. Pitts., 1939, postgrad., 1939-40; grad. diploma Ind. U., Am. Savs. and Loan Inst., 1952; M.L.S., Carnegie Library Sch., 1958. Tchr., Johnstown Sch. Dist., 1939-42; treas. Cambria Savs. & Loan Assn., Johnstown, 1941-57, now dir.; reference librarian Carnegie Library, Pitts., 1958-64, head gen. reference div., 1964-66, head reference dept., 1966-69, head br. services, 1969—. Mem. Am. (mem. reference and subscription books rev. com. 1973-75), Pa. library assns., Beta Phi Mu, Phi Theta Kappa, Pi Lambda Theta. Club: Altrusa. Home: 4733 Centre Av Pittsburgh PA 15213 Office: 4400 Forbes Av Pittsburgh PA 15213

PYLE, KATHERINE PARK (MRS. LUCIEN R. PYLE), club woman; b. Kansas City, Mo., Sept. 13, 1916; d. John Garrett and Kate (McVey) Park; student Kansas City Jr. Coll., 1933-35, U. Ky., 1935-37; tchr.'s certificate Washburn U., 1955; student Washburn U., 1954-55, U. Kan., 1971; m. Lucien R. Pyle, Feb. 3, 1956; children (by previous marriage)—Frances (Mrs. E.B. Wakeman), Oliver Gilliland. Pres. United Presbyn. Women, First Presbyn. Ch., Topeka, 1964, mem. ch. session, 1967-70; pres. Woman's Aux. Shawnee County Med. Soc., 1965-66; co-chmn. Topeka Health Fair, 1967; coordinator Conf. on Young Family, 1973; pres. Woman's Aux. Kan. Med. Soc., 1973-74. Vol. worker Republican party, 1966, 68, 70; vol. chmn. Morris Kay for Gov., 1972. Bd. dirs. Crittenton Home, Topeka, 1958-64. Mem. P.E.O. Clubs: Minerva, U and I (Topeka). Home: 3139 Canterbury Lane Topeka KS 66604

PYLE, WILMA J., educator; b. nr. Red Key, Ind.; d. William F. and Mae E. (Nixon) Pyle; B.S., Ball State U., 1947; M.A., Ohio State U., 1950; Ed.D., Wayne State U., 1964. Tchr. pub. schs., Ft. Wayne, Ind., Grandview Heights, O., Battle Creek, Mich., Pontiac, Mich., 1947-59; prin. Mark Twain Sch., Pontiac, 1959-60; instr. Wayne State U., Detroit, 1960-64; asso. prof. Mercy Coll., Detroit, 1964-65; prof. edn. State Univ. Coll., Fredonia, N.Y., 1965—, chmn. dept. early childhood edn. and elementary edn., 1974—. Author-cons. Scott, Foresman Pub. Co., 1966—; reviewer elementary trade books Nat. Council Tchrs. English, 1966-69. Mem. Nat. Council Tchrs. of English, Internat. Reading Assn., Am. Assn. Sch. Adminstrs., Assn. for Supervision and Curriculum Devel., N.Y. State English Council, Am. Assn. U. Profs., Am. Assn. Higher Edn., Assn. Supervision and Curriculum Devel. Author: First, Second Talking Story Book Box; Reading Systems, 1968-73, also children's poetry anthologies, numerous articles. Home: 21 University Park Fredonia NY 14063

PYTEREK, MARGARET MCNEIL CLYSDALE (MRS. EDWARD PHILIP PYTEREK), educator; b. Peterborough, Ont., Can., June 3, 1948; s. Walter George and Margaret Audrey (Miller) Clysdale; came to U.S., 1950, naturalized, 1968; B.A. cum laude, Bradley U., 1970; M.A., Northwestern U., 1974; children—Anne, Jennifer; m. Edward Philip Pyterek, June 23, 1973. Sec., Chgo. Aerial Industries, part-time 1966-69; with Jewel Home Shopping Service, Barrington, Ill., part-time 1969-70; tchr. kindergarten Glenview (Ill.) Pub. Schs., 1970—. Pvt. tutor, 1968-73. Mem. Drug Edn. Curriculum Com., Glenview 1972-73; v.p. Glenview Theatre Guild, 1973. Mem. Am., Children's theatre assns., Ill. Speech and Theatre Assn., N.E.A., Glenview Edn. Assn., Internat. Reading Assn., Bradley Alumni Assn., Nat. Thespian Soc. (publicity chmn. 1965-66), Gamma Sigma Phi (treas. 1969-70). Democrat. Methodist. Home: 2024 Central Rd Glenview IL 60025 Office: 1333 Greenwood Rd Glenview IL 60025

QUAIL, GERTRUDE LOIS STYCHE (MRS. WALTER FREDERICK QUAIL), rest home adminstr.; b. Wolverhampton, Eng., Mar. 29, 1880; d. Enoch James and Clara (Davis) Styche; edn. pvt. schs. and bus. schs., Eng.; certificate Yale U. Summer Sch. Alcohol Studies, 1948; m. Walter Frederick Quail, Mar. 27, 1920; 1 dau., Gloria (Mrs. Alfred Bullett). Came to U.S., 1920, naturalized, 1928. Secretarial postion, Coventry, Eng., 1910-12; confidential aide Conventry Ordnance Works, 1912-20; pres., adminstr. Warren Meml. Home, Oakfield, N.Y., 1925-37, pres. 1932—; dir. alcohol edn. Allied Forces, Rochester, N.Y., 1932—. Nat. dir. Am. Women's Overseas Service League, 1928, pres. local unit, mem. bd. Drug and Alcohol Council. Republican. Club: Century (Rochester, N.Y.). Home: 240 S Goodman St Rochester NY 14607

QUALEY, ROSELLA EILEEN, educator; b. Donnelly, Minn., Oct. 6, 1917; d. Howard Delmore and Emma Christina (Anderson) Hultgren; B.S., U. Minn., 1939; M.S., U. Wis., 1960; children—Leanne (Mrs. David Skjervold), Terryl K. Home agt., Kandiyohi County, Minn., 1946-54; dist. supr. Home Econs. Extension, U. Minn., St. Paul, 1954-72, prof. Agrl. Extension Service, 1968—, asst. dist. dir. Coop. Extension Service, 1972—. Mem. Am., Minn. (pres. 1969-71, former sec., treas., councilor, v.p.) home econs. assns., Am., Minn. (membership com.) adult edn. assns., Minn. Safety Council (agrl. div. and women's div.), Gamma Sigma Delta, Epsilon Sigma Phi (pres. 1967). Home: 1782 Holton St St Paul MN 55113 Office: U Minn St Paul MN 55101

QUALLS, ELSIE SIMS (MRS. ERNEST C. QUALLS, SR.), educator; b. Woodville, Miss., Jan. 26, 1941; d. John James and Lula (Arbuthnot) Sims; B.S., Alcorn A. and M. Coll., 1962; M.A., Tuskegee Inst., 1970; m. Ernest Cain Qualls, Sr., Dec. 25, 1962; children—Ernest Cain, Elceria Chantelle, Errol Cedric. Tchr., Walthall County Sch. Bd., Tylertown, Miss., 1962—, tchr. spl. edn. Tylertown Elementary Sch., 1962—. Leader, Brownie Scouts, 1963—. Mem. N.E.A., Miss. Tchrs. Assn., Am. Assn. Mental Deficiency, Council for Exceptional Children, N.A.A.C.P. Democrat. Baptist. Home: Route 6 Box 58-A Tylertown MS 39667 Office: 613 Broad St Tylertown MS 39667

QUALLS, MARJORIE CAROL GOULD (MRS. JOHN PAUL QUALLS), home economist; b. Seattle, July 7, 1937; d. Elbert Raymond and Ethel E. (Beieler) Gould; B.A., Wash. State U., 1959; postgrad. Sacramento State Coll., 1960, U. Wash., 1964; m. John Paul Qualls, Mar. 20, 1967; stepchildren—Denise, Michele, John Michael, Lisa. Tchr. home econs. Norte Del Rio High Sch., North Sacramento, Cal., 1959-61, Kirkland (Wash.) Jr. High Sch., 1962-65; home economist S. Central div. Puget Sound Power & Light Co., Renton, Wash., 1965—, adviser co. scholarship winner; service sta. insp. Union Oil Co., No. Cal., No. Nev., summers 1960-61. Profl. cons. Camp Fire Girls; publicity chmn. United Good Neighbor Campaign, Renton, 1969; mgmt. com. East Valley Area YWCA, 1972—; mem. citizens com. Renton (Wash.) Pub. Schs., 1972; mem. Redmond (Wash.) High Sch. Accreditation Com., 1971. Named Bus. Woman of Day KREN Radio, 1968, KIXI Radio, 1972; One of Women of Achievement Seattle Profl. and Alpha chpts. Theta Sigma Phi, 1969; Woman of Achievement, Wash. Fedn. Bus. and Profl. Women's Clubs, 1972. Mem. Am. Home Econs. Assn., Wash. Home Economists in Bus. (past sec., chmn. housing, furnishings and equipment chmn. 1972-73), Internat. Fedn. Home Econs., Elec. Women's Round Table (Service award, past chmn. award Puget Sound chpt. 1969, chmn. Puget Sound chpt., nat. dir. 1970-73, editor nat. newsletter 1972—), N.W. Electric Light and Power Assn. (ladies chmn. spring conf. 1972), Internat. Order Jobs Daus. (chmn. grand session sewing contest 1972). Club: Soroptimist of Renton (pres. 1970-71, mem. extension com. Northwestern region 1972—, chmn. Northwestern regional conf. 1973). Home: 17804 98th Av S Renton WA 98055 Office: PO Box 329 620 Grady Way Renton WA 98055

QUANTIUS, FRANCES WELLS, educator; b. Milw., July 21, 1915; d. Francis Bernard and Frances (Wells) Quantius; B.A., U. Wis., 1937, M.A., 1938, Ph.D., 1943. Instr. econs. Ohio State U., Columbus, 1942-45, asst. prof., 1946-53, asso. prof., 1954-62, prof., 1963—. Research and teaching asst. U. Wis., 1939-42; text book evaluator Dept. Defense, U.S. Govt., 1970—. Numerous speeches to civic orgns., radio and TV appearances on financial subjects. Mem. Am. Finance Assn., Am. Econ. Assn., Columbus Rock and Mineral Soc., Beta Gamma Sigma, Phi Alpha Kappa, Omicron Delta Epsilon. Club: Ohio State U. Faculty. Author: (with others) Economics: Basic Problems and Analysis. Contbr. numerous articles to financial and trade jours. and ednl. publs., also Ency. Brit., Lincoln Library Ency. Home: 1000 Urlin Av Columbus OH 43212

QUARRINGTON, ADELE MARLENE WACHNA, physician; b. Vita, Man., Can., Apr. 24, 1938; d. Walter and Mary (Chalaturnyk) Wachna; grad. Walkerville Collegiate Inst., Windsor, Can., 1956; M.D., Queen's U., 1962; m. A.J. Quarrington, Feb. 6, 1961; children—Jamie, Jonathan, Joan. Intern, Ottawa (Ont., Can.) Civic Hosp., 1962-64, resident radiology, 1965-68, mem. staff radiology, 1968—. Mem. Can., Ont. med. assns., Can. Assn. Radiologists, Queen's U. Alumnae (v.p.), Ottawa Neuroscis. Soc. Home: 5 Eleanor Dr Ottawa ON K2E 5Z8 Canada Office: Ottawa Civic Hosp Ottawa ON Canada

QUAT, HELEN, printmaker, artist; b. Bklyn., Oct. 2, 1918; d. Nathan Daniel and Bess (Nemerov) Shapiro; ed. Skidmore Coll., Art Students League; m. Leon Quat, June 25, 1940; children—Joanna, Daniel. Painter, 1936—; printmaker, 1965—; rep. by Alonzo Gallery (N.Y.C.) and Bermond Art, Ltd. (Lake Success, N.Y.); work rep. collections N.J. State Mus., U. Mass., Nassau Community Coll. MacDowell Colony fellow, 1971—. Mem. Nat. Assn. Women Artists, Graphics Jury (chmn.), L.I. Artists Alliance, Profl. Artists Guild, Women in Fine Arts. Author, illustrator: The Wonderful World of Freezer Cooking, 1964. Home: 16 Elliot Rd Great Neck NY 11021

QUATTLEBAUM, DOROTHY EVELYN CLEWIS (MRS. WALTER EMMETT QUATTLEBAUM, JR.), investment exec.; b. Unadilla, Ga., Nov. 1, 1924; d. Otis Clyde and Mabel (DuPree) Clewis; student Puttman Bus. Sch., 1953, Chipola Jr. Coll., 1962-64; m. Walter Emmett Quattlebaum, Jr., Oct. 19, 1946; children—Walter Emmett III, Amalia Ann. Sec.-treas. Sneads Telephone Co., 1948-55, Cottondale Telephone Co., 1954-55, Grand Ridge Telephone Co., 1954-55; sec.-treas., dir. Tri-County Telephone Co., Inc., Bonifay, Fla., 1955-62; asst. to stock analyst Quattlebaum Investments, Bonifay, 1962—. Methodist (pres. Wesleyan service guild 1957, 58). Address: PO Box 36 Bonifay FL 32425

QUATTLEBAUM, MARGUERITE REBECCA VOGEDING (MRS. CHARLES ALBERT QUATTLEBAUM), librarian; b. Garrett, Ind., Oct. 14, 1909; d. Eugene Frederick and Agnes Estella (Moorhouse) Vogeding; A.B. with distinction, Ind. U., 1931; A.B. in L.S., George Washington U., 1939; m. Charles Albert Quattlebaum, June 1, 1941. With Library of Congress, Washington, 1938—, tech. publs. planning officer subject cataloging div., 1970—. Mem. A.L.A., D.C. Library Assn., George Washington U. Library Sci., Ind. U. alumni assns., L C Profl. Assn., Arlington Ridge Civic Assn., Phi Beta Kappa Assn. Washington, Phi Beta Kappa, Phi Delta Gamma, Eta Sigma Phi, Pi Lambda Theta. Home: 1022 S 26th Rd Arlington VA 22202 Office: Library of Congress Washington DC 20540

QUAY, SHARON RUSSELL (MRS. FRED W. QUAY), coll. adminstr.; b. Sioux Falls, S.D., July 3, 1934; d. Thomas J. and Gwendolyn M. (Kellar) Russell; B.A., Colo. State U., 1956; M.A., Ind. U., 1958; M.L.S., Drexel U., 1974; m. Oscar J. Eichhorn, Jr. (dec. 1971); 1 son, Owen; m. 2d, Fred W. Quay, Feb. 3, 1973. Dir. residence Wis. State Coll., Platteville, 1957-59; asst. dean women Colo. Coll., Colorado Springs, 1959-61; dean women, asst. dean students U. Denver, 1961-66; dir. resident affairs Internat. House, Phila., 1968-72; dir. students personnel Rosemont (Pa.) Coll., 1972—. Republican committee woman, 1961-66, twp. rep. 1966-68. Mem. Nat. Assn. Women Deans and Counselors. Home: 219 Buck Lane Haverford PA 19041 Office: Rosemont College Rosemont PA 19010

QUAYLE, KATHRYN SUZANNE, ednl. adminstr.; b. Detroit, Aug. 4, 1942; d. John Corlette and Elizabeth (Goward) Quayle; B.S., Eastern Mich. U., 1964; M.Ed., Wayne State U., 1966; postgrad. U. Mich., 1966—. Tchr. emotionally disturbed children Wyandotte (Mich.) Pub. Schs., 1964-67; adviser to women's activities Eastern Mich. U., Ypsilanti, 1967-68; asst. to dean of women Oberlin (O.) Coll., 1968-69; tchr., cons. Down River Learning Disability Center, Wyandotte, 1969, diagnostician, cons., 1969—; lectr. U. Mich., spring 1972, supr. grad. internship program, 1971-72. Coordinator pal-vol. program Down River Child Guidance Clinic, 1966-68; sec. human relations commn. Eastern Mich. U., 1967-68. Mem. Nat. Assn. Women Deans and Counselors, Council for Exceptional Children, Council for Children with Behavioral Disorders, N.E.A., Am. Assn. Higher Edn., Mich. Edn. Assn., Asso. Women Students (pres. 1963-64), Adahi, Stoics, Kappa Delta Pi, Alpha Xi Delta. Home: 1529 Davis St Wyandotte MI 48192 Office: 2613 Biddle St Wyandotte MI 48192

QUELER, EVE (MRS. STANLEY QUELER), conductor; b. N.Y.C., Jan. 11, 1936; d. Benjamin J. and Harriet (Hirsch) Rabin; student Mannes Coll. Music, 1953-62, Coll. City N.Y., 1953-55, Hebrew Union Sch. Sacred Music, 1953-54; m. Stanley Queler, Dec. 23, 1956; children—Andrew, Elizabeth. Mem. music staff N.Y.C. Opera Co., 1958-70: asso condr. Fort Wayne (Ind.) Philharmonic, 1970-71; music dir. Opera Orchestra N.Y., 1968—; condr. Lake George Opera Festival, Glen Falls, N.Y., 1971-72, Oberlin (O.) Music Festival, 1972. Guest condr. Paris Radio Orchestra, 1972, Boston Philharmonia, 1972. Recipient Martha Baird Rockefeller Fund for Music award, 1968; named Woman of Year, Washington Sq. Bus. and Profl. Women's Club, 1971; named Musician of Month Mus. Am. Mag., 1972. Research done in Library Paris Opera resulted in 1st performance of previously unknown aria in Rossini's William Tell, 1972. Office: 630 3d Av New York City NY 10017

QUERY, JOY MARVES NEALE (MRS. WILLIAM T. QUERY), educator; b. Worcestershire, Eng., June 18, 1926; d. Samuel and Dorree (Oakley) Neale; came to U.S., 1952; A.B., Drake U., 1954, M.A., 1955; Ph.D., U. Ky., 1960; postgrad. U. Syracuse, 1955-56; m. William T. Query, June 1, 1956; children—Jonathan, Millie, Evan. Tchr. secondary schs., Staffordshire, 1947-52; dep. prin. Smethwich Hall Girls' Sch., Staffordshire, 1948-52; instr. U. Ky., 1956-57, asst. prof., 1960; asso. prof. sociology and psychology, Transylvania Coll., Lexington, Ky., 1961-66; asso. prof. N.D. State U., Fargo, 1966-68, prof. sociology and psychology, 1969—, also chmn. sociology and psychology depts., 1969-70, chmn. sociology and anthropology dept., 1968-73; on sabbatical leave Yale, 1974-75. Field dir. Girl Scouts U.S.A., 1953-55; mem. Lexington Civic Rights Commn., 1960-66, Bd. dirs. Fargo-Moorhead Family Service Agy., 1967-70. Fellow Internat. Assn. Social Psychiatry; mem. Am. Sociol. Assn., Am., N.D. psychol. assns., Am. Assn. U. Profs., Midwestern Sociol. Soc. (dir. 1970-73), Alpha Kappa Delta. Unitarian (bd. mem.). Contbr. articles, papers to profl. jours. Home: 1202 Oak St N Fargo ND 58102

QUESENBERRY, EVELYN PEARL, home economist; b. Warrensburg, Mo., Mar. 22, 1922; d. Ernest T. and Bertha Pearl (French) Hutson; B.S., Central Mo. State Coll., 1943; postgrad. U. Colo., summer, 1948; M.S., U. Wis., 1960, Ph.D., 1968; m. J. Lewis Quesenberry, Apr. 26, 1952 (div. Jan. 1954); 1 dau., Susan Kay. Vocational home econs. tchr. pub. schs., Pleasant Hill, Mo., 1943-47, St. Joseph, 1947-49; county home demonstration agt. Agrl. Extension Service, Frederick, Allegany counties, Md., 1949-52, Monroe County, Ind., 1954-57; asst. 4-H Club work Purdue U., Lafayette, Ind., 1957-65; program dir. home econs., family living, Agrl. Extension Service, U. Minn., St. Paul, 1967—. Recipient fellowship Nat. Extension Center for Advanced Study, U. Wis., 1959, 65. Mem. Am., Minn. home econs. assns., Adult Edn. Assn., Minn. Nutrition Council, Nat. Assn. Land Grant Colls. and Univs. (mem. home econs. commn.), Kappa Omicron Phi, Epsilon Sigma Phi. Methodist. (chmn. edn. commn. 1970-72, lay leader 1973-74). Club: Zonta (program chmn. 1970-71). Home: 2297 Hillside Av St Paul MN 55108 Office: 340 Coffey Hall University of Minnesota St Paul MN 55101

QUICK, ANNABELLE (MRS. JOHN W. QUICK), assn. exec.; b. Greeley, Colo., Oct. 16, 1922; d. Alfred K. and Marie (Frater) Johnson; B.A., Colo. State Coll., 1943; m. Donald W. Macmillan, Mar. 28, 1949 (div. 1951); m. John W. Quick, Nov. 24, 1962. Tchr. music Denver pub. schs., 1948-50; asst. music editor Silver Burdett Co., N.Y.C., 1950-51; export sec. A/B Max Sievert, Sundbyberg, Sweden, 1951-52; conv. and exhibit mgr. Modern Lang. Assn., N.Y.C., 1952-73; dir. confs. and exhibits Spl. Libraries Assn., N.Y.C., 1974—. Translator numerous books from Swedish to English under name Annabelle MacMillan. Mem. Nat. Assn. Expn. Mgrs. (dir. 1970-72, chmn. N.Y. chpt. 1972—), Am. Soc. Assn. Execs., N.Y. Soc. Assn. Execs., Modern Lang. Assn., Am. Fedn. Musicians. Home: 96 Fifth Av New York City NY 10011 Office: 235 Park Av S New York City NY 10003

QUIGG, DOROTHY QUAY, librarian; b. Livermore, Ky., Dec. 2, 1913; d. Quay Corrigan and Ella (Atherton) Quigg; B.A., Western State U., Bowling Green, Ky., 1941; M.S., Cath. U. Am., 1954. Librarian, tchr. English, Rutherford (Tenn.) High Sch., 1941-43; with Library of Congress, 1943-55, editor New Serial Titles, 1952-54; with Naval Ordnance Lab. Library, White Oak, Md., 1955-57; chief, cataloging sect. Dept. Housing and Urban Devel. Library, Washington, 1957—, also editor Urban Vocabulary. Mem. Spl. Libraries Assn., D.A.R. (vice regent 1972—). Republican. Baptist. Home: 3515 N Washington Blvd Arlington VA 22201 Office: 451 7th St SW Washington DC 20410

QUIGLEY, ELIZABETH KERNAN (MRS. DENIS C. QUIGLEY), real estate agt.; b. Warrenton, Va., Feb. 10, 1927; d. George Morgan and Elizabeth (Skinker) Kernan; B.A., Sweet Briar Coll., 1948; postgrad. Cath. U., 1955-56; m. Denis Carroll Quigley, May 19, 1973. Intelligence officer phys. scis. CIA, Washington, 1948-64; sci. research asst., com. sci. and astronautics Ho. of Reps., Washington, 1964-73; real estate agt. Harvey Rosendorf Realtors, Bethesda, Md., 1974—. Vol. worker Jr. Village D.C. Welfare Dist., 1956-57. Mem. Nat. Assn. Female Execs. Inc., Nat. Trust for Historic Preservation, Porsche Club Am. Episcopalian. Contbr. articles to profl. jours. Home: 5112 Saratoga Av Washington DC 20016 Office: Harvey Rosendorf Realtors 5101 River Rd Bethesda MD 20016

QUIGLEY, M(ARIE) CAROLINE, profl. nurse; b. Council Bluffs, Ia.; d. Richard Francis and Marie Christine (Jorgensen) Dunn; diploma Colo. Tng. Sch. Nurses, Denver Gen. Hosp., 1930; B.S., George Peabody Coll. Tchrs., 1936, M.A., 1945. Pvt. duty nurse, 1930; teaching supr. Denver Gen. Hosp., 1931-32; supr. Greenville, S.C. City Hosp., 1932-34; staff nurse Tenn. Dept. Health, 1936-37; supervising nurse McCracken County (Ky.) Health Dept., 1938-40; regional adv. nurse La. Health Dept., 1940-41, cons., asst. dir. pub health nursing, 1943-47; asst. prof. pub. health nursing, George Peabody Coll. Tchrs., 1942-43; counselor, exec. sec. Tenn. Nurses Assn., 1948-53; dir. nursing Mid-State Bapt. Hosp., Nashville, 1953-54; exec. dir. Evansville (Ind.) Pub. Health Nursing Assn., 1955-60; ICA pub. health adviser for W. Pakistan, Iran, 1960-61; cons. nurse, S.C. Bd. Health, 1962-63; sec. cons. Tenn. Board Nursing, 1963-65; dir. nursing Champaign-Urbana (Ill.) Pub. Health Dist., 1966-68; cons. nurse Ill. Health Dept., 1968-74; coordinator home health services fed. programs Ill. Dept. Pub. Health, 1974—; vice pres. Am. Jour. Nursing co., 1957-58. Served from 2d lt. to 1st lt. Army Nurse Corps, 1945-46; lt. col. Res. ret. Fellow Am. Pub. Health Assn.; mem. Am. Nurses Assn., Nat. League Nursing, P.E.O., Kappa Delta Pi. Club: Zonta. Home: 6 Nottingham Dr Chatham IL 62629 Office: Ill Dept Pub Health 1130 S 6th St Springfield IL 62705

QUILTER, JOAN MARY, psychologist; b. Waterbury, Conn., Jan. 12, 1928; d. Thomas George and Sally (Sakocius) Quilter; student Notre Dame Coll., 1945-46, Hunter Coll., 1955-56; B.S., Boston U., 1958, postgrad., 1958-59; M.A., Fairfield U., 1960, postgrad., 1960-62; postgrad. St. John's U., 1968—. IBM operator main office Chase Brass & Copper Co., Waterbury, Conn., 1954-55; tchr. 6th grades St. Jean Baptiste Sch., N.Y.C., 1955-56; tchr. 3d and 6th grades St. Patrick Sch., Stoneham, Mass., 1956-59; tchr. math. Crosby High Sch., Waterbury, Conn., 1959-64; psychol. examiner Middlebury, Watertown and Waterbury (Conn.) Pub. Schs., 1964-68, sch. psychologist, 1968-70; sch. psychologist, dir. spl. services Regional Dist. 15, Middlebury and Southbury, Conn., 1970—. Psychol. examiner Head Start Program, Waterbury, Conn., summer 1965, 66; evaluation summer sch. reading program, Waterbury, Conn., summer 1967. Bd. dirs. Central Naugatuck Valley Mental Health Assn., Central Naugatuck Valley Health and Mental Health Assn. Mem. N.E.A., Am., Conn. psychol. assns., Nat. Conn. assns. sch. psychologists, Am., Conn. personnel and guidance assns., Am., Conn. sch. counselor assns., Am. Ednl. Research Assn., Conn. Assn. Women Deans and Counselors, Pomperaug Edn. Assn., Am. Assn. Mental Deficiency, Council Exceptional Children, Pomperaug Adminstrs. Assn. (sec.-treas.), Conn. Assn. Pupil Personnel Adminstrs., Conn. Assn. for Gifted, Conn. Edn. Assn., Conn. Assn. Suprs. Instrs. Spl. Edn., Am. Assn. U. Women, Delta Kappa Gamma. Club: Quota (Waterbury). Home: 641 Washington Av Waterbury CT 06708 Office: Main St Southbury CT 06488

QUILTY, FLORENCE ELIZABETH MACINNIS (MRS. FRANCIS C. QUILTY), physician; b. Bowdle, S.D.; d. Austin Edward and Ella (Juntilla) MacInnis; student St. Mary's Coll., Notre Dame U., 1920-22; B.S. in Medicine, Marquette U., 1927, Md., 1928; m. Francis C. Quilty, Sept. 8, 1951. Intern, St. Anthony's Hosp., Terre Haute, Ind.; resident Wis. Anti-Tb Assn., 1928-41; dir. Tb Milw. Health Dept., 1941-44; practice medicine specializing in pulmonary diseases, Kansas City, Mo., 1944—; dir. pub. health Tb. div. Tb Out-Patient Dept., Kansas City Gen. Hosp.; mem. staffs St. Mary's, Research Bapt. hosps. (all Kansas City, Mo.); clin. prof. medicine Mo. U., 1964—. Mem. exec. com. State Tb Assn., 1950—, also bd. dirs. Bd. dirs. Heart Assn., Social Health Soc. Recipient Dearholt medal Miss. Valley Tb Conf., 1965. Mem. Women's C. of C. Clubs: Soroptimist, Woman's City. Home: 609 Romany Rd Kansas City MO 64113 Office: 4620 JC Nichols Pkwy Kansas City MO 64112

QUIMBY, DOROTHY WEBB (MRS. LAWRENCE HUGH QUIMBY), librarian; b. Portland, Me., Sept. 1, 1929; d. Philip Raymond and Genevieve (Dunlap) Webb; A.B., Bates Coll., 1951; M.L.S., U. Me., 1967; m. Lawrence Hugh Quimby, Aug. 30, 1952; children—Peter Lawrence, Richard Webb. Head librarian Unity (Me.) Coll., 1966—. Rep. of acad. libraries of Me. to panel counsellors New Eng. Library Bd., 1973—. Mem. Unity Conservation Commn., 1973—. Mem. Am., New Eng., Me. library assns., Me. Audio-Visual Assn., Nature Conservancy, Phi Beta Kappa, Phi Kappa Phi. Methodist. Home: Unity ME 04988

QUINLAN, CLAIRE AGNES, educator; b. Westerly, R.I., Oct., 3, 1929; d. William J. and Mary (Murray) Quinlan; B.A., U. R.I., 1951; M.A., U. No. Colo., 1961, Ph.D., 1964. Tchr. algebra, French, Latin, biology Cambridge High Sch., Jeffersonville, Vt., 1952-53; tchr. English, journalism, phys. edn. Rangely (Colo.) High Sch., 1953-58; tchr. English, social studies Babcock Jr. High Sch., Westerly, R.I., 1958-59; tchr. English, French, Westminster (Colo.) High Sch., 1959-60; instr. psychology U. No. Colo., Greeley, 1963-64, counselor, asso. prof. psychology, asst. dean psychol. services, 1964-69; v.p. for student affairs Jamestown (N.D.) Coll., dean social sci. div., chmn. psychology dept. Mem. Am. Ednl. Research Assn., Am. Personnel and Guidance Assn., Am. Coll. Personnel Assn., Am. Assn. for Higher Edn., N.D. Personnel Deans Assn., Student Personnel Assn. for Tchr. Edn. (past nat. research chmn.). Home: 615 7th Av SE Jamestown ND 58401

QUINLAN, ELAINE BEVERLY BASTEDO (MRS. ROSCOE J. QUINLAN), therapist; b. Chgo., July 13, 1936; d. Raymond W. and Helen M. (Dolak) Bastedo; B.S. in Phys. Therapy, U. Okla., 1958; certificate in Occupational Therapy, U. So. Cal., 1963; m. Roscoe J. Quinlan, Nov. 27, 1968. Staff phys. therapist San Diego County Hosp., 1958-59; phys. therapist Children's Hosp., San Diego, also part time Dr. W.Gordon Smith, Hillside House (both Santa Barbara, Cal.), 1960; phys. and occupational therapist United Cerebral Palsy Assn., San Diego, 1963; rehab. supr. geriatrics unit, chief physical therapist Ariz. State Hosp., Phoenix, 1964-65; asst. program dir. phys. and occupational therapy Easter Seal Soc. Crippled Children and Adults Nev., Inc., Reno, 1965-68; dir. occupational therapy dept. Nev. Mental Health Inst., Reno, also individual practice, Reno, 1968-74; owner Sierra Rehab., Reno, 1974—. Owner (with husband), sec.-treas. B & G Beauty Supply, Inc., Reno, 1972—. Examiner Nev. Bd. Phys. Therapy Examiners. Mem. Am., Cal., Ariz., Nev. (v.p.) phys. therapy assns., Am., Cal., Ariz., Nev. occupational therapy assns., Nev. Pub. Health Assn., Phi Mu. Club: Soroptimists (Reno). Home: 4000 Lakeside Dr Reno NV 89502 Office: 820 S Virginia St Reno NV 89501

QUINLAN, LULA EGAN, journalist; b. Vinita, Okla.; d. James and Vina (Gray) Egan; student U. Tulsa, 1944; m. Harry Francis Quinlan, Apr. 8, 1920 (div. Jan. 1944); children—Harry James, Eileen (Mrs. Durward Wayne Rystrom). Garden editor Tulsa World, newspaper, 1936—; garden columnist Oklahoma City Times, 1945; master of ceremonies Garden Quiz Program Sta. KTUL, Tulsa, 1939-40; editor Okla. Gardener, 1938-40; writer Flower and Garden mag., 1957—, also Madison Coopers Gardening mags., 1937-39, Gardener's Chronicle, 1940-42, Sun Up mag., 1949-51. Bd. dirs. Tulsa Garden Center. Mem. Am. Rhododendron Soc., Am. Hemerocallis Soc. Home: 1724 S Rockford St Tulsa OK 74120 Office: Tulsa World Tulsa OK 74102

QUINLIVAN, MARY ANN, nurse; b. Buffalo, July 31, 1944; d. Thomas Joseph and Gertrude Agnes (Kerwin) Quinlivan; grad. Mercy Hosp. Sch. Nursing, 1965; student Canisius Coll., 1962-63, D'Youville Coll., 1971—. Staff nurse Mercy Hosp., Buffalo, 1965-66; staff nurse West Seneca Developmental Center, West Seneca, N.Y., 1966—, head nurse, 1968—, supervising nurse, 1970—, coordinator interfaith religion classes, 1973-74. Trustee Father John Fund for Mentally Retarded, West Seneca. Mem. Am. Assn. Mental Deficiency. Home: 24 Oschawa St Buffalo NY 14210 Office: 1200 East and West Rd West Seneca NY 14224

QUINN, BETTY NYE HEDBERG (MRS. JOHN F. QUINN), educator; b. Buffalo, Mar. 21, 1922; d. Fritz A. and Alma (Svenson) Hedberg; A.B., Mt. Holyoke Coll., 1941; A.M., Bryn Mawr Coll., 1942, Ph.D., 1944; m. John F. Quinn, Sept. 11, 1950 (dec. Sept. 1963). Instr., asst. prof. classics Vassar Coll., Poughkeepsie, N.Y., 1948-59; dir. pub. relations, 1954-59; asso. prof. classics Mt. Holyoke Coll., South Hadley, Mass., 1959-67, prof., 1967—, chmn. dept. classics, 1959—. Mem. Am. Philol. Assn., Mediaeval Acad., Classical Assn. New Eng. Republican Lutheran. Home: 27 W Parkview Dr South Hadley MA 01075

QUINN, CHRISTINE ANN DANY, editor; b. Dallas, July 16, 1948; d. John Pallai and Grace Vera (Bardarik) Dany; B.A., Trinity U., 1970; M.S., Tex. A. and M. U., 1973; m. Larry A. Quinn, Aug. 22, 1970. Editorial intern Kelly Air Force Base Information Office, San Antonio, 1968; pub. relations asst. Coll. of Geoscis. of Tex. A. and M. U., 1970-71, coordinator environmental quality program, 1971-72, information rep. Office of Information and Publs., 1972-74; writer, editor Farm Credit Adminstrn., 1974—. Mem. Am. Assn. Agrl. Coll. Editors, Women in Communcations, Inc. Presbyn. Research on pollution abatement pub. relations in indsl. corps. Home: 6814 Field Master Dr Springfield VA 22152 Office: 490 L' Enfant Plaza SW Washington DC 20578

QUINN, JANE BRYANT (MRS. DAVID CONRAD QUINN), journalist; b. Niagara Falls, N.Y., Feb. 5, 1939; d. Frank Leonard and Ada (Laurie) Bryant; A.B., Middlebury Coll., 1960; m. David Conrad Quinn, June 10, 1967; children—Matthew Alexander, Justin Bryant. Asso. editor Insider's Newsletter, N.Y.C., 1962-65, editor, 1966-67; sr. editor Cowles Book Co., N.Y.C., 1968; editor-in-chief Bus. Week Letter, N.Y.C., 1969-72, gen. mgr., 1973-74; syndicated financial columnist, 1974—. Bus. news analyst Sta. WPIX-TV, N.Y.C., 1973. Mem. Financial Writers Assn., N.Y. Soc. Newsletter Pubs., Phi Beta Kappa. Editor The Skilled Collector, 1966-68. Home: 7 Berrybrook Circle Chappaqua NY 10514 Office: Washington Post 444 Madison Av York City NY 10020

QUINN, JUDITH MARIAN, ednl. cons.; b. Lewiston, Ida., Jan. 25, 1945; d. Marion Merideth and Dorothy Virginia (Ballard) Holben; B.A. in Edn., Eastern Wash. State Coll., 1968. Instnl. tchr., 1968-70, condr. parent tng. program for multiply handicapped, 1970-73; parent cons. for visually impaired children, Coeur d'Alene, Ida., 1973—. Mem. Wash. Assn. Retarded Children, Am. Assn. Mental Deficiency, Council Exceptional Children. Home: 912 E Maple St Post Falls ID 83854 Office: PO Box 711 Coeur d'Alene ID 83832

QUINN, OLIVE WESTBROOKE, educator; b. Jonesboro, Ark., Aug. 1, 1914; d. Edward Lynn and Clifton (Jones) Westbrooke; A.B., Goucher Coll., 1936; A.M. (Rosenwald fellow), U. Chgo., 1945, Ph.D. (Rosenwald fellow), 1950; m. Edwin Martin Quinn, Dec. 21, 1947 (div. 1961); 1 adopted son, Edward Westbrooke. Profl. photographer, Jonesboro, 1936-40; tchr. Dixie Consol. Sch., Lake City, Ark., 1940-42; tchr. Jonesboro High Sch., 1942-43; asst. prof. psychology, sociology, asso. prof. Southwestern at Memphis, 1945-54; research sociologist Nat. Inst. Mental Health, Bethesda, Md., 1954-58; asso. prof., prof. sociology Goucher Coll., Towson, Md., 1958—, also chmn. dept., dir. Center For Sociol. Study; mem. Bd. Review Patuxent Instn.; vis. scientist Psychol. Lab., Nat. Inst. Mental Health, 1973. Mem. Gov.'s Commn. on Illegitimacy Md., 1961-62; mem. Gov.'s Commn. on Sentencing in Criminal Cases, 1963; chmn. housing com. Human Relations Commn. Baltimore County, 1964-65. Southwestern-Carnegie grantee, 1950; Fulbright scholar Third Summer Inst. in Chinese Civilization, Taiwan, 1964. Mem. A.A.A.S., Am. Sociol. Assn., So. Sociol. Soc., Am. Assn. U. Profs. Democrat. Presbyn. Contbr. articles profl. jours. Home: 800 Range Ct Towson MD 21204 Office: Goucher Coll Baltimore MD 21204

QUINONES, VINIA ROSE JOHNSON (MRS. GILBERT QUINONES), hosp. adminstr.; b. N.Y.C.; D. Herbert and Inez (Hawkins) Johnson; fellow Sch. Advt. Art, 1950; B.A., U. City N.Y., 1956; M.S.W. (univ. and A.R.C. fellows) Adelphi U., 1959; postgrad. N.Y. U., 1970—; m. Gilbert Quinones, Feb. 24, 1963; 1 dau., Liza A. Caseworker, disaster worker Bklyn. chpt. A.R.C., 1958-61; with Arthur C. Logan Meml. Hosp. (formerly Knickerbocker Hosp.), N.Y.C., 1961—, chief psychiat. social worker, dir. social service dept., 1966-71, program planner/evaluator adminstr., 1971, asst. exec. dir., 1971—. Cons. Citizens Action for Neighborhood Devel. Orgn., N.Y.C., 1967—, Brookwood Child Care Center, Bklyn., 1968-72, Groves Counseling Service, N.Y.C., 1970—; field instr. N.Y. U. Grad. Sch. Social Work, 1964-70; guest lectr. Queens Coll., U. City N.Y.; field faculty instr. U. City N.Y., also Barnard Coll., 1962-65; field faculty med. tech. student Manhattan Community Coll., U. City N.Y., 1970-72. Mem. Bd. Higher Edn., N.Y.C., 1974—; chmn. community bd. 9th Borough Manhattan. Bd. dirs. Manhattanville Renewal Assn., Inc., N.Y.C.; bd. dirs. Manhattanville Community Outreach, chmn., 1971—. Dr. Martin Luther King fellow, 1969-70; Inst. Child Mental Health fellow, 1969-70; U.S. Dept. Health, Edn. and Welfare fellow 1970-71. Mem. Acad. Certified Social Workers, Nat. Assn. Social Workers (co-chmn. council mental health 1968-69), Am. Soc. Pub. Adminstrs. (conf. minority pub. adminstrs.), Nat. Assn. Social Welfare, Am. Pub. Health Assn., Council Social Work Edn., Internat. Platform Assn., Nat. Assn. Health Service Execs., Nat. Black Assn. Planners and Adminstrs. (dir., exec. sec.), N.A.A.C.P., Nat. Social Welfare Conf., Am. Acad. Polit. and Social Sci., Am. Pub. Health Assn., Washington Heights-West Harlem-Inwood Mental Health Council, City U. N.Y. Alumni Assn. (mem. com. to study campus disorders 1967-68), Adelphi U. Alumni Assn. Mem. Order Eastern Star (chmn. audit com. Nat. Supreme Grand chpt., 1961). Editorial bd. Comprehensive Health Planning Dist. Manhattan N. Address: PO Box 412 New York City NY 10027

QUINT, MARY D(OROTHEA), manpower cons.; b. Worcester, Mass., Jan. 4, 1913; d. Henry W. and B. Louise (Barrett) Quint; B.S. Edn., Worcester State Tchrs. Coll., 1936; M.L.S., Simmons Coll., 1955; M.S., Boston U., 1972. Librarian, Free Pub. Library, Worcester, 1937-39, Met. State Hosp., Waltham, Hosp., 1939-46; librarian Am. Optical Co., Southbridge, Mass., 1946-52, cons., 1959; supervisory librarian USAF Cambridge Research Center, Geophysics Research Center, Bedford, Mass., 1955-60; librarian U.S. Army Spl. Services, Korea, 1960-61; supervisory librarian Holloman AFB, N.M., Office for Research Analyses Tech. Library, 1961-64; part-time library cons. Liberty Mut., Boston, 1964-66; library information specialist Syracuse (N.Y.) U. Research Center, 1966-68; dir. library careers Onondaga Library System, Syracuse, 1966-71; manpower cons. Ill. State Library, Springfield, 1972—. Cons. State U. N.Y., 1968; profl. cons. Spl. Libraries Assn., 1955-65. Smithsonian asso. Mem. Am., Ill. library assns., Spl. Libraries Assn., Am. Studies Assn., Bus. and Profl. Women, Art Inst. Chgo. Club: Zonta (Springfield). Contbr. articles to profl. jours. Home: 2202 Westchester Blvd Springfield IL 62704 Office: Ill State Library Centennial Bldg Springfield IL 62756

QUIRK, JANE HELEN WAGNER, state govt. ofcl.; b. Eagle River, Wis., Jan. 18, 1915; d. William Walter and Sarah Ann (Carter) Wagner; student Oshkosh State Tchrs. Coll., 1934-35, Am. U., 1944, Chgo. U. Extension, 1948, Purdue U. Extension, 1965, 68; m. Neil A. Hall, Sept. 17, 1934 (div. May 1939); 1 son, Carter Lee (dec.); m. 2d, John J. Quirk, Jan. 25, 1949 (div. Oct. 1955); 1 dau., Sarah Jane. Jr. welfare worker, employee relations counselor Selective Service System, Washington, 1942-46; personnel counselor Western Electric Co., Chgo., 1946-49; exec. sec. speakers bur. Indpls. chpt. A.R.C., 1950-51; editor, personnel dir. Monument Engrng. Co., Indpls., 1952-55; employee publs. mgr. Internat. Tel. & Tel. Kellogg, Chgo., 1960-61; editor Buehler Corp., Indpls., 1955-60, pub. relations mgr., 1961-70; dir. advt. Review Publs., Indpls., 1971-72; placement interviewer Ind. State Employment Service, Indpls., 1973—. Mem. Community Service Council, Indpls., 1968—; mem. women's council Indian Lake Devel. Assn., 1970. Recipient Hon. awards Nat. Found. March of Dimes, 1964-68, certificate of merit United Fund, 1968, 69. Mem. Ind. Indsl. Editors Assn. (Best Newspaper award 1969, pres. 1965), Internat. Council Indsl. Editors (exec. bd. 1964-65), Ind. Mfrs. Assn. (mem. pub. relations com. 1968-70), Indpls. C. of C. Home: 7023 Indian Lake N Dr Indianapolis IN 46236 Office: 141 W Georgia St IN 46204

QUIRK, SISTER MARY RICHARDINE, ednl. adminstr.; b. Milw., June 8, 1908; d. Michael William and Mary Ellen (O'Connell) Quirk; A.B., Clarke Coll., 1945; M.A., Marquette U., 1953; Ph.D., Cath. U. Am., 1965. Tchr. parochial schs., Ill., Colo., Ia., Neb., 1928-47; prin.

St. Francis Xavier Sch., Kansas City, Mo., 1947-50; provincial superior Sisters of Charity Blessed Virgin Mary, Davenport, Ia., 1950-56; coordinator secondary student teaching, edn. dept. Mundelein Coll., Chgo., 1956-58; asso. sec. elementary sch. dept. Nat. Cath. Ednl. Assn., Washington, 1958-64; dir. grad. div. Clarke Coll., Dubuque, Ia., 1965. Charter mem. Nat. Sister Formation Com., Washington, 1954-63; mem. steering com. Criteria for Evaluation Cath. Elementary Schs., 1965; mem. task force on world population edn. Nat. Catholic Ednl. Assn.-Center of Concern, Washington, 1974. Mem. Nat. Cath. Edn. Assn. (1st asso. sec. for elementary edn. 1958-64, chmn. tchr. edn. sect. 1970-71), Council Nat. Orgns. for Children and Youth (mem. exec. com. 1964-66), Nat. Council Tchrs. English (mem. commn. on English curriculum 1964-67), Am. Assn. U. Women. Editorial adv. bd. Cath. Ency. for Sch. and Home, 1958-64. Home: Clarke College 1550 Clarke Dr Dubuque IA 52001

QUISGARD, LIZ BYRD WHITNEY, painter, sculptor; b. Phila., Oct. 23, 1929; d. Kenneth E. and Elizabeth (Warwick) Whitney; grad. Md. Inst. Coll. Art night sch., 1947, grad. day sch., 1949; student Johns Hopkins evening sch., 1952-58; pvt. study Morris Louis, 1958-60; B.F.A. in Painting, M.F.A. in Sculpture, Md. Inst., 1966; m. Joseph C. Spahn, 1968 (div.); children—Kristin, Berit. Five one-woman shows, Balt., 1954-59; one-woman shows Jefferson Place Gallery, Washington, 1960, Key Gallery, N.Y.C., 1960, Emmerich Gallery, N.Y.C., 1962, Goucher Coll., 1966, U. Md., 1969, Gallery 707, Los Angeles, 1974; exhibited group shows Balt. Museum, 1951, 52, 53, 58, Corcoran Gallery Area Show, 1956, 64, Corcoran Biennial Show, 1963, Peale Mus., 1947, 56, Butler Inst. Am. Art, 1957, Provincetown Art Assn., 1955, U. Colo., 1963, Pa. Acad. Am. Ann., 1964, Chgo. Art Inst., 1965, Gallery 707, Los Angeles, 1973, S. Houston St. Gallery, N.Y.C., 1974; represented in permanent collections U. Ariz., U. Balt., Lever House, N.Y.C., pvt. collections; pvt. tchr. painting, Balt., 1955—; mem. staff Met. Sch. Art, 1957-58; now conducting classes Balt. Hebrew Congregation; mem. faculty Md. Inst., Coll. Art, 1965, Goucher Coll., Towson, 1966-68, Balt. Jewish Community Center, 1974—; lectr. colls. and orgns. in Md., Va., W.Va., Pa.; art critic Balt. Sun, 1969-71, Craft Horizons, 1969—, The Paper, 1971—; set designer prodns. at Center Stage, Goucher Coll., Johns Hopkins. East Coast agt. Irvin Grief, Stevenson, Md.; West Coast rep. Gallery 707, Los Angeles. Recipient scholarships Md. Inst., 1947, 48, 49; Balt. Mus. 2d artist prize, 1958; Rinehart fellowship in sculpture, 1964-66; Best in Show award Loyola Coll. Invitational, 1966. Home and studio: 321 Rossiter Av Baltimore MD 21212

QUIST, SUSAN, author; b. Cin., Sept. 10, 1944; d. John David and Kathryn Day (Seitz) Quist; student U. Pitts., 1962-63, U. Cin., 1967-69; 1 dau., Jenny Gibbs. Vol. writing tchr. Pub. Sch. 3, N.Y.C., 1973; participant P.E.N. Prisoner Corr. Program, 1974; coordinator Cherry Valley Writing Project, 1974; farm editor Freeman's Jour., Cooperstown, N.Y., 1974—; poet-in the schs. Pa. Council Arts, 1974. Recipient Emergency grant Am. chpt. P.E.N., 1972, Camaras award St. Lawrence U., 1974. Author: Indecent Exposure, 1974. Contbr. poems and prose to lit. mags. Address: Box 335 Cherry Valley NY 13320

RAAD, VIRGINIA, educator, artist; b. Salem, W.Va., 1925; d. Joseph M. and Martha (Joseph) Raad; B.A., Wellesley Coll., 1947; spl. student New Eng. Conservatory Music, 1947-48; diplome Ecole Normale de Musique, Paris, France, 1948-52; Doctorat de l'Universite (French govt. grantee), U. Paris, 1955. Artist-in-residence, Salem (W.Va.) Coll., 1959-70; musician-in-residence N.C. Arts Council and N.C. Community Colls., 1971-72. Concerts, lectrs. master classes Carleton Coll., Northfield, Minn., Middlebury (Vt.) Coll., Marietta (O.) Coll., Wheeling (W.Va.) Coll., N.Y. Piano Tchrs. Congress, Phillips Gallery Washington, Palm Beach Art Inst., U. Paris, Wellesley (Mass.) Coll., Mt. Mary Coll., Milw., Manhattanville Coll., N.Y.C., Fedn. des Alliances Francaises aux Etats-Unis, Oglebay Park, Wheeling, St. Anselm's Coll., Manchester, N.H., Elmira (N.Y.) Coll., U. Pitts., Bklyn. Music Tchrs. Guild, Ednl. TV Channel 13, Pitts., Community Concerts Morris Harvey Coll., Charleston, W.Va., Seton Hill Coll., Greensburg, Pa., Huntington Galleries, Fordham, Lincoln, Notre Dame univs., Eastern Mennonite, Curry, So. Conn. State, Viterbo Colls., others. U.S. rep. Debussy Collogue, 1962. Am. Council Learned Socs. travel grantee, 1962, named Outstanding W.Va. Woman Educator, Delta Kappa Gamma, 1965. Mem. Societe Francaise de Musicologie, Am. Musicol. Soc. (regional officer 1960-65), Societe Internationale de Musicologie, Am. Assn. U. Profs., Am. Soc. for Aesthetics, Music Tchrs. Nat. Assn. Republican. Roman Catholic. Contbg. author Debussy et l'Evolution de la Musique aux XXe Siecle, 1965. Contbr. articles to profl. jours. Home: 60 Terrace Av Salem WV 26426

RAATTAMA, RUTH JOHANNA (MRS. ALAN FISHER), pediatrician; b. Bovey, Minn., Oct. 2, 1906; d. John Peter and Ida Alina (Blomberg) Raattama; B.A., Carleton Coll., 1928; M.D., Northwestern U. Med. Sch., 1933; M.P.H., Johns Hopkins Sch. Hygiene and Pub. Health, 1953; m. Alan B. Fisher, Mar. 16, 1953; 1 step-dau., Nora. Intern, Albany (N.Y.) Gen. Hosp., 1932-33, Maternal Center, Chgo., 1933, Childrens Meml. Hosp., Chgo., 1934; resident Sea View Hosp., S.I., N.Y., 1935-36, Municipal Contagious Disease Hosp., Chgo., 1936; cons. pediatrics Ill. Dept. Health, Springfield, 1937-41; dir. maternal and child health Ida. Health Dept., Boise, 1941-47, Dept. Health and Hosps., Denver, 1947-65; dir. Brentwood Presch., Denver, 1967—; mem. staff Denver Gen. Hosp., 1947-65; asso. prof. U. Colo. Med. Sch., 1949-65. Mem. adv. com. children and youth Colo. Welfare Dept., 1960-66; mem. Colo. Adv. Com. Family Health Services, 1968—, chmn. com., 1970; v.p., nursery sch. dir. Colo. Assn. Childhood Edn., 1967-68; chmn. exceptional child com. Nat. Congress Parents and Tchrs., 1952-57. Fellow Am. Pub. Health Assn.; mem. Am. Coll. Preventive Medicine, Am. Med. Womens Assn., Rocky Mountain Pediatric Soc. Home: 730 Franklin St Denver CO 80218 Office: 1899 S Irving St Denver CO 80219

RABB, MIRIAM HOWARD GLOVIER, mus. ofcl.; b. Jacksonville, Fla.; d. Mont and Anesta (Abernathy) Glovier; student Stetson U., 1935-36, Lees-McRae Coll., 1936-37, U. Minn., 1949-50, N.C. State U., 1954-55; m. Stuart White Rabb, Jr., June 26, 1939 (div. Feb. 1952). Feature writer Asheville, Winston-Salem and Charlotte (N.C.) newspapers, 1939-41; state editor Columbia (S.C.) Record, 1942-45; pub. relations Naples Co. (Fla.), 1947-49; publicity dir. South Appalachian Hist. Assn., Boone, N.C., 1952-53; state travel editor N.C. Travel and Promotion Div., Raleigh, 1954-68; adminstr. Nat. Trust Historic Preservation, Leesburg, Va., 1968—. Regional v.p. Va. Travel Council, 1972—. Mem. Soc. Am. Travel Writers, Am. Women in Radio and TV, Nat. Steeplechase and Hunt Assn., Am. Forestry Assn., Loudoun Hist. Soc. (dir. 1972—). Episcopalian. Clubs: Soroptimist (Leesburg); Triangle Foxhounds (Durham, N.C.); Loudoun Hunt (Hamilton, Va.). Columnist, Charlotte Observer, 1962-66. Address: Oatlands Route 2 Box 352 Leesburg VA 22075

RABIN, ETHEL BERLEY, artist; b. Rochester, N.Y.; d. Meyer and Sarah (Senderovitsch) Rabin; student Columbia U., 1941-45, Art Students League Paris, France, and Italy, 1946-57. Work exhibited Nat. shows Nat. Acad., Am. Watercolor Soc., Audubon Artists, Knickerbocker Artists, Allied Artists, Nat. Arts Club, Painters and Sculptors League N.J., Am. Artists Profl. League; traveling and group shows Riverside Mus., Rochester Meml. Art Gallery, Dallas Tex. Mus. Fine Art, Fine Arts Gallery (Chgo.), Cleve. Mus. Art, Albright Art Gallery (Buffalo), Corcoran Gallery (Washington), Falmouth Art Assn., Tirca Karlis Gallery, Provincetown, Mass., Donnell Library, N.Y.C., Le Chateau de la Napoule, France, Musee de Cognac, France, Cultural Centre of the Cannes Municipal Casino. Prop. Berley Studios, N.Y.C., 1960—; 10 one-man shows, 1972; designer costumes stages screen and trade, 1930—; included in collections, Jersey City State Coll., Norfolk Mus. Recipient award Nat. Assn. Women Artists (oil), 1962, hon. mention Painters and Sculptors Soc. N.J. (oil), 1965, Sydney Taylor Meml. prize sculpture Knickerbocker Artists, 1965, medal of merit Syndicate Mag., 1965, Grumbacher award Nat. Art Club, 1967, award Municipal Casino, Cannes, France, 1969, gold medal Allied Artists Am., 1970, award Audubon Artists, 1972. Mem. Artists Equity Assn., Provinceton Art Assn., Nat. Assn. Women Artists (award 1973), Cape Cod Art Assn., Art Students League, Am. Water Color Soc. (award 1967), Nat. Assn. Painters in Casein and Acrylic (award 1973), N.Y. Soc. Women Painters, League Present Day Artists, Allied Artists, Audubon Artists. Address: 285 Central Park W New York City NY 10024

RABON, FLORENCE GRAHAM (MRS. WRIGHT COXWELL RABON, JR.), columnist; b. Key West, Fla., July 22, 1906; d. George Barthell and Margaret (McClintock) Graham; B.S. in Social Scis., Fla. State Coll. for Women, 1927; m. Wright Coxwell Rabon, Jr., Dec. 16, 1950; 1 dau., Margaret Eleanor (Mrs. Vannie Gerald Ritchie). Supr., mgmt. analyst USN, Key West, 1941-70; columnist Miami (Fla.) Herald, 1958—. Dep. tax assessor Monroe County (Fla.), 1970—. Mem. Monroe County Democratic Exec. Com., 1971—. Chmn. pub. relations com. bd. dirs. Key West Heart Council, 1963—, Community Concerts Assn., 1953—. Recipient Outstanding Citizen award, Am. Legion, 1958, Meritorious awards, Key West Lions Club, 1965-66, 67, Certificate, Easter Seal Soc., 1972, certificate Bus. and Profl. Woman's Club, 1972. Mem. Nat. League Am. Pen Women, Fla. Pub. Relations Assn. (dir. Fla. Keys chpt.), Key West Art and Hist. Soc., Key West Panhellenic, Woman's Club, Am. Legion Aux., Alpha Kappa Delta, Phi Alpha Theta, Alpha Xi Delta, Beta Sigma Phi (recipient Order of Rose 1964). Episcopalian. Mem. Lion Aux. Home: 1622 Laird St Key West FL 33040 Office: Monroe County Courthouse Key West FL 33040 falso Miami Herald Bur Duval and Catherine Sts Key West FL 33040

RABON, NANCY ANN, physician; b. Burbank, Okla., Nov. 7, 1933; d. Otway Thomas and Corinne (Moore) Rabon; B.A., Okla. Baptist U., 1955; M.D., U. Okla., 1959. Intern, U. Okla. Med. Center, Oklahoma City, 1959-60; resident Sacred Heart Hosp., Yankton, S.D., 1960-61, Good Samaritan Hosp., Cin., 1961-63; practice medicine specializing in obstetrics and gynecology Fayetteville, Ark., 1963—; mem. staffs Washington Gen. Hosp., City Hosp., Fayetteville, Springdale (Ark.) Meml. Hosp., Rogers (Ark.) Meml. Hosp. Diplomate Am. Bd. Obstetricians and Gynecologists. Fellow Am. Coll. Obstetricians and Gynecologists; mem. Am., So. med. assns., Am. Fertility Soc., Ark. State, Washington County (sec. 1967-72). med. socs. Republican. Baptist. Clubs: Altrusa (Fayetteville). Home: 2238 Sheridan St Fayetteville AR 72701 Office: Evelyn Hills Shopping Center Fayetteville AR 72701

RABSTEIN, LOUISE SKLAR (MRS. MELVIN M. RABSTEIN), histopathologist; b. Phila., Sept. 23, 1915; d. Harry and Bessie (Liss) Sklar; D.V.M., Kan. State U., 1934, M.S., 1937; postgrad. (fellow) U. Md., 1937-39; m. Melvin M. Rabstein, Nov. 17, 1939; children—Jeanne (Mrs. Alan Nevin), Susan (Mrs. Thomas Mandel), Linda (Mrs. Steven Brooke). Pvt. vet. practice, Frederick, Md., 1944-64; histopathologist Microbiol. Assos., Inc., Walkersville, Md., 1965—. Mem. Bacteriology Soc. U. Md. (hon.). Contbr. articles to profl. jours. Home: 412 Carroll Pky Frederick MD 21701 Office: Walkersville MD 21793

RACE, ANNETTE ISABELLE RINKER (MRS. GEORGE J. RACE), physician, child psychiatrist; b. Dallas, May 14, 1925; d. Walter A. and Anne (Allen) Rinker; B.S., So. Meth. U., 1946; M.D., U. Tex., 1958; m. George J. Race, Dec. 21, 1946; children—George William Daryl, Jonathan Clark, Mark Christopher, Elizabeth Margaret Rinker. Intern, Baylor U. Med. Center, Dallas, 1962-63, asso. attending staff dept. psychiatry and neurology, 1971—; resident in psychiatry U. Tex. Southwestern Med. Sch., Dallas, 1966-70, clin. asst. prof. psychiatry, asst. prof. psychiatry in obstetrics and gynecology, 1971—, adj. prof. Law Sch., 1974—; dir. mental health So. Meth. U., Dallas, 1970—. Bd. dirs. Dallas unit Am. Cancer Soc. Mem. A.M.A., Tex. Med. Assn., Am. Soc. Adolescent Psychiatry, Am. Acad. Child Psychiatry, Tex. Soc. Child Psychiatry, Am. Coll. Health Assn., Dallas So. Clin. Soc., Am., N. Tex. psychiat. assns., Vis. Nurse Assn. (dir.), Jr. League, Mortar Bd., Kappa Kappa Gamma. Clubs: Dallas County, Chaparral. Home: 3429 Beverly Dr Dallas TX 75205 Office: Health Center So Meth U Dallas TX 75205

RACELY, JUDITH KALLOCH (MRS. EDWARD W. RACELY), occupational therapist; b. Boston, Feb. 21, 1933; d. Elmus Mirriam and Jessie Emmons (Gunderson) Kalloch; B.S., Tufts U., 1956; Occupational Therapist, Boston Sch. Occupational Therapy, 1956; M.A., U. So. Cal., 1958; m. Edward W. Racely, Sept. 1, 1959; children—Peter, Sara. Mem. occupational therapy staff Lemuel Shattuck Hosp., Boston, 1956; head occupational therapy, supr. Children's Hosp., Boston, 1957; head occupational therapy Spastic Children's Cerebral Palsy Center, Pasadena, Cal., 1969; cons. in occupational therapy to hosps., Marin County, Cal., 1962-71; cons. Loma Prieta Center for Mentally Retarded, San Jose, Cal., 1971—. Pres. local group Boyd Children's Mus., San Rafael, Cal., 1968-70. Flower Guild Los Angeles grad. fellow in pediatric occupational therapy U. So. Cal., 1958-59. Mem. Am. Assn. U. Women, Am. Assn. Occupational Therapy. Republican. Home: 95 Reservoir St Atherton CA 94025

RACHLIN, CAROL KING, anthropologist; b. Newark, July 21, 1919; d. Benjamin and Marjorie (King) Rachlin; A.A., Chevy Chase Coll., 1940; B.S., Columbia, 1953. Asst. state archaeologists N.J. State Mus., Trenton, N.J., 1951-53; asso. in spl. research Am. Mus. Natural History, N.Y.C., 1955-58; research asso. Indian Hist. Soc., Indpls., 1954-58; asso. dir. S.W. Research Assos., Oklahoma City, 1960—; anthrop. cons. Okla. Indian Council, Oklahoma City, 1962—; permanent artist-in-residence div. liberal arts Central State U., Edmund, Okla., 1968—; dir. dietary program Okla. Indian Council, asso. prof. N. Am. ethnology U. Okla., 1965-66. Recipient Key and Theta Sigma Pi, 1969. Research fellow Am. Acad. Arts and Scis., Boston 1961; Am. Philos. Soc. research grantee, 1969-70. Fellow Am. Anthropol. Assn. A.A.A.S., Soc. Applied Anthropology; mem. Am. Archeol. Soc., Am. Mus. Assn., Okla. Folkways Soc. (chmn. bd. trustees), Author's Guild. Author: (with Alice Marriott) American Indian Mythology, 1968, American Epic, 1969, Peyote, 1971 (Okie award Okla. Writers Fedn. 1971); Oklahoma-Forty Sixth Star, 1972; Plains Indian Mythology, 1975. Contbr. articles to profl. articles. Home: 1836 NW 56th St Oklahoma City OK 73118

RACHLIN, JOY BARRON (MRS. WILLIAM S. RACHLIN), lawyer; b. Boston, May 5, 1931; d. Samuel, Jr. and Jennie (Loitman) Barron; A.B., Wellesley Coll., 1952; J.D., Boston U., 1955; m. William S. Rachlin, June 17, 1952; children—Faye Barron, Margo Barron. Admitted to Mass. bar, 1957, 1st Fed. Dist. bar, 1958; asso. firm Barron, Feldman and Dunn, Boston, 1957-63; mem. firm Barron, Feldman, Dunn and Rachlin, Boston, 1963-71; asso. firm Barron and Stadfeld, Boston, 1971—. Dir. Home Owners Fed. Savs. & Loan Assn. Bd. dirs. Beth Israel Hosp., Hadassah, Boston, 1957-61. Mem. Mass., Boston bar assns., Mass. Conveyancers Assn. Home: 515 Clinton Rd Chestnut Hill MA 02167 Office: 19 Milk St Boston MA 02109

RACHLIN, SYLVIA NEWBURGER (MRS. ABRAHAM RACHLIN), social work adminstr.; b. Bedford Hills, N.Y.; d. Bernard and Bertha (Travers) Newburger; B.S., N.Y. U., 1937; postgrad. Columbia, 1942-44; certificate Yale U. Sch. Alcohol Studies, 1945; M. Social Service, Fordham U., 1952; m. Abraham Rachlin, July 10, 1949. Exec. v.p. Spl. Social Services, N.Y.C., 1943—; founder, exec. v.p. Myopia Internat. Research Found., N.Y.C., 1963—. Recipient citation for dedicated service Am. Correctional Chaplains Assn., 1960; award for distinguished service to underprivileged N.Y. council Women's Internat. Classified Service Clubs, 1963; N.Y. U. Alumnae Club Key award. Mem. Acad. Certified Social Workers, Nat. Assn. Social Workers, Am. Correctional Assn., Am. Correctional Chaplains Assn., Nat. Council Crime and Delinquency, N.Y. State Welfare Conf., N.Y.C. Fedn. Women's Clubs (dir.), Jr. Women's League N.Y., Hadassah, Garment Congregation Sisterhood (pres.), Fedn. Jewish Women's Orgns. (v.p.), Kappa Delta Pi. Home: 2 Meadowbrook Lane Valley Stream NY 11580 Office: 415 Lexington Av New York City NY 10017

RACHWAL, ESTHER BALDISS (MRS. WALTER J. RACHWAL), savs. and loan exec.; b. Paterson, N.J., Feb. 26, 1924; d. Anthony and Annette (Sella) Baldisserotto; ed. pub. schs., Am. Savs. and Loan Inst., Sherwood Sch. Bus.; m. Walter J. Rachwal, Oct. 11, 1969. With 1st Savs. & Loan Assn. of Fair Lawn (N.J.), 1941-46; with 1st Fed. Savs. & Loan Assn. of Paterson, 1946—, exec. v.p., 1967—. Mem. Women's Assn. of Savs. and Loan Instns. of N.J. (pres.), Passaic County Savs. and Loan League (pres.). Methodist (treas. ch.). Club: Paterson Zonta (corr. sec.). Home: 1289B Valley Rd Wayne NJ 07470 Office: 177 Market St Paterson NJ 07505

RACINES, AUDREY GARDNER (MRS. GUILLERMO I. RACINES), lawyer; b. Allentown, Pa., May 8, 1944; d. Theodore Roosevelt and Margaret Schaeffer (Knoll) Gardner; student Cedar Crest Coll., 1961-63; A.B., George Washington U., 1965, J.D., 1968; m. Guillermo I. Racines, June 6, 1966; 1 son, Theodore Rafael. Admitted to Pa. bar, 1969; partner Gardner, Gardner & Racines, Allentown, 1969—; dist. justice of peace, 1970—. Corr. sec. Young Republicans Lehigh County, 1969. Mem. Am., Pa., Lehigh County bar assns. Mem. United Ch. Christ. Office: 546 Hamilton St Allentown PA 18101

RACITI, DOMENICA GRACE, pub. co. exec.; b. N.Y.C., June 2, 1928; d. Joseph and Marie (DiBiase) Raciti; B.Ed., State U. N.Y., 1948; M.Ed., Columbia, 1953, profl. diploma, 1956. Tchr. first grade, White Plains, N.Y., 1948-53; remedial reading tchr., Bogota, N.J., 1953-55; reading specialist Bd. Coop. Ednl. Services, White Plains, N.Y., 1955-63; lang. arts cons. Northeastern U.S., 1963-65; nat. curriculum coordinator Am. Book Co., 1965-68, dir. marketing services, N.Y.C., 1968-70, exec. editor lang. arts, 1970-73, v.p., dir. marketing, 1973—. Mem. Internat. Reading Assn., Nat. Council Tchrs. English. Office: 450 W 33d St New York City NY 10001

RACITI, KATINA AURELIA (MRS. GEORGE POUDER), pediatrician; b. New Rochelle, N.Y., Jan. 23, 1924; d. Venerando and Bertha (Buchanan) Raciti; B.A., Barnard Coll., 1945; M.D., N.Y. U., 1949; certificate Coll. U. Sch. Continuing Edn., 1967; m. George Pouder, Feb. 9, 1957; children—George, Leonard, Nicholas. Intern, Bellevue Hosp., N.Y.C., 1949-50; resident Bklyn. Methodist Hosp., 1950-51, St. Luke's Hosp., N.Y.C., 1951-53; practice medicine, specializing in pediatrics, New Rochelle, N.Y., 1953-58; pediatrician New Rochelle Dept. Pub. Health, 1956—; sch. physician New Rochelle Dept. Health, 1966—; dep. dir., acting dir. Pub. Health, 1971-73, dist. dir. New Rochelle West County Dept. Health, 1973—. Bd. dirs. Banksville Community House, 1970—. Diplomate Am. Bd. Pediatrics. Fellow Am. Acad. Pediatrics; mem. N.Y. State, Westchester County med. socs., N.Y. Allergy Soc., Handweavers Guild of Westchester County. Episcopalian. Home: Greenwich Rd Bedford NY 10506 Office: New Rochelle Dept Health 30 Church St New Rochelle NY 10804

RACZ, RHONDA, pub. relations exec.; b. N.Y.C., July 1, 1947; d. David and Jeanette (Schneck) Levin; B.A., N.Y. U., 1968; postgrad. N.Y. Sch. Interior Design, 1968-69; m. Michael Racz, Aug. 26, 1965 (div. Aug. 1970). Display dir. Nat. Design Center, N.Y.C., 1968-70, editor Guide to Home Decorating Ideas, 1968-70; pub. relations exec. H. Richard Silver, Inc., N.Y.C., 1970-72; pub. relations account supr. The Rowland Co., Inc., N.Y.C., 1972-74; mgr. pub. relations Clairol, Inc., 1974—. Spokeswoman, Hardwood Inst., N.Y.C., 1970-72. Mem. publicity com. Citizens for Children N.Y., 1972. Mem. Nat. Home Fashions League. Author: 101 Great Decorating Ideas, 1969; 101 Great Kitchen Ideas, 1969. Home: 201 E 37th St New York City NY 10016 Office: 345 Park Av New York City NY 10017

RADABAUGH, MARTHA KATHRYN (MRS. EUGENE EDWARD RADABAUGH), educator; b. Mt. Vernon, O., Oct. 2, 1925; d. Arch August and Verne Elma (Snare) Topp; B.S. in Accounting, Ohio U., 1947, M.A. in Excptl. Children, 1965, Ph.D. (grad. fellow), 1970; m. Eugene Edward Radabaugh, Nov. 28, 1948; children—Julia, Michael, Jeffrey. Tchr., Knox County, O., 1960-64, tchr. supr., 1964-66; tchr., Mt. Vernon, O., 1966-67; asso. prof. spl. edn. Ashland (O.) Coll., 1969—, chmn. dept. spl. edn., 1973—. Sec., Inter-Univ. Council on Mental Retardation, O., 1971-72. Bd. dirs. Ashland County Day Care Center; bd. dirs., cons. Ashland County Diagnostic Center for Developmentally Disabled, 1973—. Mem. Council for Exceptional Children, Assn. Children with Learning Disabilities, Am. Assn. Mental Dgficiency. Author: A Behavioral Curriculum for EMR Students, 1971; Locus of Control and Occupational Adequacy of Educable Mental Retardates, 1970; The Effect of Systematic Instruction in Language Upon Trainable Mentally Retarded Children, 1965. Home: 333 Slaon Av Ashland OH 44805

RADCLIFFE, ELEANOR BASSETT (MRS. ALLEN B. RADCLIFFE, SR.), art gallery ofcl.; b. Phila., Dec. 5, 1919; d. George and Anna (Rowlinson) Bassett; grad. high sch.; m. Allen B. Radcliffe, Sr., Apr. 3, 1941; 1 son, Allen B. Various secretarial positions U.S. Air Force, 1951-66; sec. Freer Gallery Art, Smithsonian Instn., Washington, 1966-67, registrar, 1967—. Formerly active Cub Scouts, A.R.C. Office: Freer Gallery Art Smithsonian Instn Washington DC 20560

RADCLIFFE, EVELYN JUANITA WINDER (MRS. WILLIAM HICKMAN RADCLIFFE, JR.), journalist; b. Independence, Kan.; d. Thomas Milton and Kathleen (Williams) Winder; student U. Cal. at Berkeley, 1938-40; m. William Hickman Radcliffe, Jr., June 7, 1944; 1 son, William Hickman III. Asst. head Coll. Shop John Wanamaker, Phila., 1939; salesgirl, model I. Magnin, San Francisco, 1940-42; personnel interviewer Q.M.C., U.S. Army, Oakland, Cal., 1942-45; employee counselor U.S. Naval Air Sta., Alameda, Cal., 1945-46;

fashion editor, columnist, fashion photographer, Palo Alto, Cal., 1956-69; feature writer Christian Sci. Monitor, San Francisco, from 1958; book reviewer Peninsula Newspapers, Inc., Palo Alto, 1968—. Mem. Nat. League Am. Pen Women, Cal. Writers Club, Fashion Group, Inc. Club: Palo Alto Hills Golf and Country (Palo Alto). Address: 2930 Alexis Dr Palo Alto CA 94304

RADCLIFFE, REDONIA WHEELER (MRS. ROBERT RADCLIFFE), journalist; b. Republican City, Neb.; d. Donnel F. and Lois (Woolman) Wheeler; B.A., San Jose State Coll., 1951; m. Melvyn J. Nunes, 1947 (div. 1949); 1 son, Melvyn D.; m. 2d, Robert C. Radcliffe, 1957. Reporter, women's editor, county editor The Salinas Californian, 1951-59; free-lance writer, Europe, 1959-66; reporter, The Wash. Star, Washington, 1967-72; social editor The Washington Post, Washington, 1972—. Mem. Women's Nat. Press Club, Am. Newspaper Women's Club, Sigma Delta Chi. Office: 1150 15th St NW Washington DC 20005

RADER, MILLICENT CAROLYN, artist; b. Utica, N.Y., May 13, 1936; d. LeRoy Arthur and Irene Anna (Schwenk) Rader; B.F.A., Wichita State U., 1958; M.F.A., Cath. U. Am., 1974; 1 dau., Heather Viola Harris. Sr. tech. illustrator Analytic Services, Inc., Falls Church, Va., 1959-67, cons., 1967-68; co-owner MRRH Studio Gallery, Fairfax, Va., 1970—; corr. Alexandria (Va.) Gazette, 1972; artist-in-residence, bd. dirs. Trident Found., Washington, 1974—; instr. art women's bur. D.C. Dept. Corrections, 1974—; tech. asst. Catholic U., 1974—. Exhibited in group shows Wichita (Kan.) Art Mus., 1957, 58, 59, Mulvane Art Inst., Topeka, 1958, Smithsonian Instn., Washington, 1962-63, Dept. Commerce, Washington, 1966, Delliger Art and Antique Gallery, Alexandria, Va. and Madison, N.Y., 1966—, Salt Palace, Salt Lake City, 1970, Goldman Fine Arts Gallery, Rockville, Md., 1971, 72, Arts Club, Washington, 1973, 74, Art Barn, Washington, 1973, 74, Cath. U. Am., Washington, 1973, 74, Fed. Dept. Interstate Commerce, 1974, Am. Spirit Gallery, Washington, 1974, Regis Coll., Boston, 1974, Salve Regina Gallery, Washington, 1974, Sculpture Garden at Firenze, Washington, 1974, others; represented in permanent collections Holy Name Coll., Wichita State U. Area chmn. March of Dimes, 1970-74. Campaign mgr. Congl. candidate, 1972. Exec. bd. No. Va. Conservation Council, 1973. Recipient best in show award, best portrait, state exhibit Nat. League Am. Pen Women, 1970, also 1st prize in nat. yearbook competition, 1971. Mem. Artists Equity Assn. (bd. mem., pub. relations 1974—), Washington Watercolor Assn. (pres. 1974—), Nat. League Am. Pen Women (br. v.p. 1972-74, state art chmn. 1972-74), D.C. Arts Congress (steering com. visual arts 1974—), Internat. Platform Assn., Nat. Orgn. for Women, Va. Women's Polit. Caucus (mem. state policy council 1972), Mortar Bd., Kappa Pi, Delta Delta Delta. Roman Catholic. Home: 3010 Wisconsin Av NW Washington DC 20016 Office: 4440 Glenn Rose St Fairfax VA 22030

RADICIA, LUCY MARQUERITE (MRS. JOSEPH D. BERALDI), pediatrician; b. Omaha, Oct. 10, 1925; d. Lucian and Agathina (Ponte) Radicia; B.S., Creighton U., 1946, M.D., 1950; m. Joseph D. Beraldi, June 30, 1951; children—Rosemary, Nancy, Anthony, Joanne. Intern, St. Mary's Hosp., Mpls., 1950-51; resident Children's Meml. Hosp., also St. Joseph's Hosp., Omaha; practice medicine, specializing in pediatrics, Council Bluffs, Ia., 1954—; mem. courtesy staff Jennie Edmundson Hosp., Council Bluffs; sec. treas. med. staff Mercy Hosp., Council Bluffs, 1955, 60, 68-70, chief pediatric dept., 1973—. Med. adviser Council Bluffs chpt. Ia. March of Dimes. Mem. A.M.A., Am. Med. Women's Assn., Am. Acad. Pediatrics, Cath. Physicians Guild, Ia. Pediatric Assn., Ia., Pottawattamie County med. socs., Ia. Heart Assn., Creighton Alumni Assn., Alpha Epsilon Iota. Mem. Lionels. Roman Catholic. Home: 601 Forest Dr Council Bluffs IA 51501 Office: 701 Ervin Bldg Council Bluffs IA 51501

RADLOFF, CAROL JEAN KRAMSKY (MRS. CHARLES JOHN RADLOFF III), educator; b. Chgo., June 7, 1945; d. Edward F. and Adeline (Kudrna) Kramsky; B.A., Elmhurst Coll., 1967; M.A., Eastern Mich. U., 1969; m. Charles John Radloff III, June 8, 1968. Tchr., George Rogers Clark High Sch., Whiting, Ind., 1967-68, St. Charles (Ill.) High Sch., 1968-69; dir. theatre N. Shore Country Day Sch., Winnetka, Ill., 1970—. Mem. Am. Theatre Assn., Secondary Sch. Theatre Conf. Home: 1 N Martin St Waukegan IL 60085 Office: 310 Green Bay Rd Winnetka IL 60093

RADMACHER, CAMILLE J., librarian; b. Monmouth, Ill., Apr. 14, 1917; d. Harry M. and Esther (Greenleaf) Radmacher; student Monmouth Coll., 1935-37. With adult dept. Warren County Library, Monmouth, 1937-48, head county librarian, 1948—, exec. dir. Western Ill. Library System, 1965—. Exec. dir. Nat. Library Week in State of Ill., 1959. Mem. Monmouth Coll. Community Concert Lecture Bd., 1967-72; mem. adv. com. Ill. State Library, 1962-72. Mem. Ill. Library Assn. (Ill. Librarian Citation award 1967), Womens Nat. Book Assn., D.A.R. Methodist. Mem. Order Eastern Star. Club: Altrusa (treas. 1968-69). Home: 500 N 1st St Monmouth IL 61462 Office: 60-62 Public Sq Monmouth IL 61462

RADMACHER, MARY, librarian; b. Monmouth, Ill.; d. Harry Maynard and Esther (Greenleaf) Radmacher; B.A., U. Ill., 1945; B.S. in L.S., U. Ill., 1946. Children's librarian Warren County Library, Monmouth, Ill., 1936-41; circulation and reference asst. Warren County Library, Monmouth, Ill., 1941-43; clerical asst. catalog dept. U. Ill. Library, 1943-46; reference asst. Gary (Ind.) Pub. Library, 1946-51, head reference dept. 1951-56; chief librarian Skokie (Ill.) Pub. Library, 1956—. Mem. Fine Arts Commn., Skokie, Ill. Dir., Ill. Regional Library Council, 1971—. Recipient Ill. Librarians citation award, 1970. Mem. Am., Ill. library assns., Children's Reading Round Table, League of Women Voters of Skokie, Art Inst. Chgo. (hon. life), Beta Phi Mu. Home: 1209 Sherwin Av Chicago IL 60626 Office: 5215 Oakton St Skokie IL 60076

RADOMSKI, JEAN TERESA (MRS. THEODORE JOHN RADOMSKI), psychologist; b. Phila., Mar. 18, 1927; d. Leonidas Howard and Thelma Rita (Robbins) Smith II; B.A. magna cum laude, Temple U., 1958, M.A., 1959, Ph.D., 1964; m. Theodore John Radomski, Aug. 1, 1964; children—Linda DiMauro Maher, Alison DiMauro Kavanaugh. Staff psychologist Norristown (Pa.) State Hosp., 1964-66; staff psychologist Friend's Hosp., Phila., 1967-68, chief psychologist, 1968-71; staff psychologist VA Center, Togus, Me., 1971-72, staff psychologist, 1973—, chief psychologist, program dir. Fairfield (Me.) Inst., 1972-73. Mem. Am., Me. psychol. assns. Home: 81 Bay View St Camden ME 04843 Office: VA Center Togus ME 04330

RAEDLER, DOROTHY FLORENCE, theatrical producer, dir.; b. N.Y.C.; d. Charles Conrad and Florence (Radley) Raedler; B.A., Hunter Coll., 1942. Founder, Am. Savoyards, exec. dir., 1952-68, pres. 1952-53; stage dir. operas, operettas throughout U.S., 1948—; prodn. coordinator, stage dir. N.Y.C. Center Gilbert & Sullivan Co., 1961-66; stage dir. N.Y.C. Center Opera Co., 1959-65; dir. V.I. Inst. Arts, 1969-70; asso. dir. V.I. Council on Arts, 1970; owner, dir. St. Croix Sch. Arts, 1970-73; pres., chmn. bd., dir. St. Croix Sch. Arts, Inc., 1973—. Arranged and staged individual concerts throughout U.S., Can.; producer, mgr. mus. prodns., mounted radio and TV performances of Gilbert & Sullivan; lectr.; pres. Am. Gilbert & Sullivan Presentations, Inc., 1966-68, Gilbert & Sullivan Festival Theatre, Inc., 1954-59, Am. Savoyards Investors Corp., 1953-54. Bd. dirs. St. James Sch. Arts, 1963-65. Recipient award Show Bus. mag., 1954. Mem. N.Y. Gilbert and Sullivan Soc. (hon.). Editor: Handbook for Gilbert and Sullivan, 1962. Home: PO Box 1086 Christiansted St Croix VI 00820

RAEF, LAURA GLADYS CAUBLE (MRS. WILLIAM RAEF), writer; b. Walnut Grove, Mo.; d. William Arthur and Edna May (Fox) Cauble; R.N., Burge Hosp. Tng. Sch. for Nurses, 1934; student San Francisco State Coll., 1958, San Mateo Coll., 1961-62; m. William Raef, Jan. 31, 1937; 1 dau., Sharon Ann. Pvt. duty nurse, Springfield, Mo., 1935-36; indsl. nurse Met. Life Ins. Co., San Francisco, 1948-57; free-lance writer, 1958—. Mem. Cal. Writers Club. Author: Symphony in the Sky, 1970; Nurse in the News, 1970; Nurse in Fashion, 1972; Nurse Jan and the Legacy, 1974; short stories pub. in Christian Sci. Monitor, also various love story mags. Address: 965 San Marcos Circle Mountain View CA 94040

RAEFF, LILLIAN, psychologist; b. Vienna, Austria, Nov. 5, 1926; d. Irving I. and Josephine (Licht) Gottesman; came to U.S., 1943, naturalized, 1947; B.S. in Edn., Coll. City of N.Y., 1950, M.A., 1951; Ph.D., Clark U., 1956; m. Marc Raeff, Sept. 24, 1957; children—Anne, Catherine. Instr., Smith Coll., 1954-55; with Worcester (Mass.) Youth Guidance Clinic, 1958-59; staff psychologist Bergen Pines County Mental Hosp., Paramus, N.J., 1961-63, Hackensack (N.J.) Mental Health Consultation Center, 1964-69; dir. clin. services Bergen Center for Psychol. Services, Tenafly, N.J., 1969—, chmn. bd. dirs., 1969—, pres., 1974—. Mem. Am., N.J. psychol. assns. Home: 479 Knickerbocker Rd Tenafly NJ 07670 Office: 30 River Edge Rd Tenafly NJ 07670

RAE-GRANT, NAOMI INGRID PENFOLD, physician; b. Southampton, Eng.; d. Henry Lewis and Gwendolyn (Yorke-Slader) Penfold; student U. London, 1947-49; M.B., B.S., Westminster Hosp. Sch. Medicine, 1952; D.P.M., U. London, 1957; m. Quentin A. F. Rae-Grant, July 9, 1955 (div. June 1966); children—Alexander D., John Paul. Came to U.S., 1958, naturalized, 1964. Intern, Westminster, Royal Southants and Addenbrooke's hosps., Eng., 1953-54; resident Bethlem Royal, Maudsley hosps., London, 1954-58; clin. dir. div. child psychiatry Jewish Hosp., St. Louis, 1960-63; cons. psychiatrist Family and Children's Service Greater St. Louis, Shriners Hosp., Our Lady of Grace Child Center, 1963-65; psychiatrist, div. child psychiatry Psychiat. Inst., U. Md., Balt., 1966-67, asst. dir., 1967-69; cons. Children's Guild, Balt., D.C. Children's Center, Laurel, Md., 1966-69; dir. Children's Services Br., Mental Health Div., Ont. (Can.) Ministry Health, Toronto, 1969-74, now sr. cons.; chief child psychiatry War Meml. Children's Hosp., London, Ont., 1974—. Instr. child psychiatry Washington U., 1959-65; asst. prof. child psychiatry Md. U., 1966-69, asso. prof., 1969; asso. prof. child psychiatry U. Toronto, 1970-74; prof., coordinator child psychiatry U. Western Ont., 1974—. Diplomate Am. Bd. Neurology and Psychiatry. Fellow Am. Orthopsychiat. Assn., Am. Psychiat. Assn., Am. Acad. Child Psychiatry; mem. Royal Coll. Psychiatrists. Home: 38 Anglesey Blvd Etobecoke ON Canada Office: 15 Overlea Blvd Toronto ON Canada

RAEKE, CAROLYN SUE, journalist; b. Harlingen, Tex., July 7, 1944; d. Louis Alfred and Marvel Jane (Reiplinger) Raeke; B.S., Tex. Woman's U., 1966; postgrad. U. N.C., 1966-67, U. Houston Sch. Law, 1969-70. Reporter Houston Post, 1967-72, Washington corr., 1972; Washington corr. Dallas Morning News, 1972—. Trustee, Washington Journalism Center, fellow, 1972. Mem. Women in Communications, Nat. Women's Polit. Caucus. Office: 637 Nat Press Bldg Washington DC 20004

RAFAEL, RUTH KELSON (MRS. RICHARD VERNON RAFAEL), librarian, archivist; b. Wilmington, N.C., Oct. 28, 1929; d. Benjamin and Jeanette (Spicer) Kelson; B.A. with high honors, San Francisco State Coll., 1953, M.A., 1954; M.L.S., U. Cal. at Berkeley, 1968; m. Richard Vernon Rafael, Aug. 26, 1951; children—Barbara Jeanette, Brenda Elaine. Head librarian Congregation Beth Sholom, San Francisco, 1965—; asst. archivist Western Jewish History Center, Judah L. Magnes Meml. Mus., Berkeley, 1968-69, archivist, 1969—. Cons. Regional Oral History Office U. Cal. at Berkeley, 1972; cons. Camp Swig, Saratoga, Cal., 1972, Congregation Sherith Israel, San Francisco, 1972, Brandeis Day Sch., San Francisco, 1973; lectr. ednl. and religious groups. Mem. Library Exhibit com. Cultural Council for Israel 25th Anniversary, 1973. Mem. Cal. Library Assn., Acad. and Research Librarians, Cal. Hist. Soc., Soc. Cal. Archivists, Assn. Jewish Librarians, De Young Soc. and Patrons Art and Music, Friends Library, League Women Voters (chmn. unit publs. 1971). Jewish religion mem. Sisterhood, chmn. book and library com. 1971—. Contbr. articles, book reviews, and poetry to profl. and popular jours. and mags. Address: 2911 Russell St Berkeley CA 94025

RAFFENSPERGER, MARY AMES (MRS. EDWARD COWELL RAFFENSPERGER), pediatrician; b. Columbia, Tenn., May 13, 1913; d. Roger Post and Jessie Harriet (Daniel) Ames; B.A., Agnes Scott Coll., 1934; M.D., U. Tex., 1940; D.Sc., Dickinson Coll., 1965; m. Edward Cowell Raffensperger, Apr. 9, 1949. Rotating intern Jefferson Davis Hosp., Houston, 1940-41, resident pediatrics, 1941-42; asst. pediatric resident Children's Hosp. of Mich., Detroit, 1942-43, chief pediatric resident, 1944-45; chief pediatric resident children's med. services Bellevue Hosp., N.Y.C., 1943-44; chief pediatric dept. Harrisburg Polyclin. Hosp., Harrisburg, Pa., 1947-62, coordinator pediatric residency program, 1954-62; cons. pediatrician State Hosp. for Crippled Children, Elizabethtown, Pa., 1947—; coordinator rehab. services Children's Hosp. of Phila., 1962—, dir. ambulatory services, 1973—; prof. pediatrics U. Pa., 1973—. Mem. med. adv. bd. March of Dimes, Phila. chpt. Nat. Found., 1966-70. Trustee Dickinson Coll., Carlisle, Pa., So. Home for Children, Phila. Diplomate Am. Bd. Pediatrics. Mem. Am. Pediatric Soc., A.C.P., Am. Acad. Pediatrics, Am. Acad. Cerebral Palsy, Am. Assn. Mental Deficiency, Am. Pub. Health Assn., Pa. (chmn. commn. maternal and child health 1958-63), Phila. County med. socs., Pa. Assn. Retarded Children, Phila. Coll. Physicians, Phila. Pediatric Soc. Contbr. articles to profl. jours. Home: 290 St James Pl Philadelphia PA 19106 Office: Children's Hosp 1 Children's Center Philadelphia PA 19146

RAFFERTY, ELIZABETH FRANCES, security analyst; b. Phila., June 17, 1921; d. Joseph Aloysius and Elizabeth Frances (Tourish) Rafferty; A.B., Chestnut Hill Coll., 1943; certificate in bus. adminstrn. St. Joseph's Coll., 1966. Tech. editor aerospace Budd Mfg. Co., stainless steel body stamping, Phila., 1943-46; exec. sec., v.p. pharm. and biol. mfg. Wyeth Labs., Radnor, Pa., 1946-59; sr. investment officer, security analyst, financial editor, dir. publs. Provident Nat. Bank, Phila., 1959—; vis. lectr. econs. evening div. St. Joseph's Coll., 1967-70. Mem. Phila. Financial Analysts Soc., Chestnut Hill Coll. Alumnae Assn. (pres. 1957-63, dir. 1954—). Republican. Roman Catholic. Home: 6625 Greene St Philadelphia PA 19119 Office: PO Box 7648 Philadelphia PA 19101

RAFFES, HELEN FRANCES LEVIN (MRS. ABE RAFFES), librarian; b. N.Y.C., June 4, 1915; d. Max and Eva (Josephson) Levin; B.A. cum laude, Hunter Coll., 1938; M.L.S. cum laude, Pratt Inst., 1959; m. Abe Raffes, Aug. 24, 1941; 1 son, Stanley Bruce. Sch. librarian in secondary schs. Bd. Edn., N.Y.C., 1958-61; children's specialist Queens Borough Pub. Library, Jamaica, N.Y., 1961-73. Cub Scout pack sec.-treas. Queens Council Boy Scouts Am., 1956-58. Recipient N.Y. State scholarship, 1933. Mem. N.Y. State Pub. Library Assn., Phi Beta Kappa, Beta Phi Mu. Club: Queens Botanical Gardens (N.Y.C.). Sci. and polit. studies book reviewer Sch. Library Jour., 1972—. Home: 143-25 41st Av Flushing Queens NY 11355 Office: 89-11 Merrick Blvd Jamaica NY 11432

RAFSKY, JEANNE C. (MRS. NORMAN JASPAN), physician; b. N.Y.C., July 16, 1925; d. Henry A. and Bertha (Fischel) Rafsky; B.A. cum laude, Pembroke Coll. in Brown U., 1945; M.D., N.Y.U., 1949; m. Norman Jaspan, Dec. 22, 1946; children—Michael David, Ronald Howard. Rotating intern Lenox Hill Hosp., N.Y.C., 1949-50, resident medicine, gastroenterology, 1953-54, asst. adjunct gastroenterology, 1954—; asst. medicine U. Hosp., N.Y.C., 1954-58; clin. asst. vis physician Bellevue Hosp. 4th div., N.Y.C., 1954-58; instr. clin. medicine N.Y.U., 1954-58; gastroscopist Grand Central Hosp., N.Y.C. 1956-62; asst. attending radiologist U. Hosp., 1958-67; clin. teaching asst. radiology N.Y.U. Sch. Medicine, 1960-67; gastroenterologist, radiologist Sidney Hillman Health Center; cons. gastroscopist Wickersham Hosp., 1965—. Mem. adv. council to Senate Com. on Health, 1966—. Founder, mem. Digestive Disease Found. Diplomate Nat. Bd. Med. Examiners. Fellow N.Y. Acad. Medicine; mem. Am. Soc. Gastrointestinal Endoscopy, N.Y. County Med. Soc., N.Y. Acad. Sci., A.M.A. Author articles in field. Home: 993 Park Ave New York City NY 10028 Office: 79 E 79th St New York City NY 10021

RAGAN, ELIZABETH HOFFMAN (MRS. HERBERT TOMLINSON RAGAN), wholesale co. exec.; b. Albemarle, N.C., Nov. 11, 1916; d. Joseph Filson and Lilly Bassett (Carter) Hoffman; certificate bus. adminstrn. High Point Coll., 1937; m. Herbert Tomlinson Ragan, Oct. 14, 1939; 1 son, Herbert Tomlinson. Head bond dept. Sunflower Ordnance Works, Hercules Powder Co., DeSota, Kan., 1942-45; sec.-treas. Ragan-Carmichael, Inc., High Point, N.C., 1956—, Staple Products, Inc., High Point, N.C., 1956—, R & C Holding Co., Inc., High Point, N.C., 1956—; trustee Ragan-Carmichael, Inc. Profit Sharing Trust and Pension Trust. Cellist N.C. Symphony, 1932-35. Democrat. Mem. Soc. of Friends (organist, choir dir.). Home: 1001 Oakhurst Av High Point NC 27260 Office: 1116 Ward St High Point NC 27261

RAGANS, SHERRILL WILLIAMS, univ. housing dir.; b. nr. Telfair County, Ga., Apr. 23, 1938; d. Julian David and Mattie Melva (Anderson) Williams; A.B., Tift Coll., Forsyth, Ga., 1958; M.A., U. So. Miss., 1959; postgrad. Fla. State U.; m. James W. Ragans, May 3, 1964. Counselor for women William Carey Coll., Hattiesburg, Miss., 1958-59; counselor to students, asst. dean of women, dir. residence programs, dir. resident student devel. Fla. State U., 1959—; dir. camps for Woman's Missionary Union of Ga., summers. Named an outstanding young woman of Am., 1966. Mem. Am. Personnel and Guidance Assn., Am., So. coll. personnel assns., Common Cause, Am. Coll. and Univ. Housing Ofcls., Tift Coll. Alumni Assn. (pres.-elect), Gamma Sigma Sigma. Baptist. Home: 1305 Parga St Tallahassee FL 32304

RAGGIO, LOUISE BALLERSTEDT (MRS. GRIER H. RAGGIO), lawyer; b. Austin, Tex., June 15, 1919; d. Louis F. and Hilma (Lindgren) Ballerstedt; B.A., U. Tex., 1939; student Am. U., Washington, 1939-40; LL.B., So. Meth. U., 1952; m. Grier H. Raggio, Apr. 19, 1941; children—Grier, Tommy, Kenneth. Intern, Nat. Inst. Pub. Affairs, Washington, 1939-40; area counselor Nat. Youth Adminstrn. in Tex., 1940-41; asst. dist. atty. Dallas County, Tex., 1954-56; partner Raggio and Raggio, 1956—. Dir. attys. fund campaign Dallas Community Chest; dir. Council Social Agys. Dallas, Dallas Women's Council, Red Cross Home Service Com., Linz Award Com.; bd. Dallas Girl Scout Council, Park Cities YMCA Girls com.; sec. Gov.'s Commn. on Status Women, 1970. Recipient Zonta award for distinguished community service, 1970, Woman of Achievement award So. Meth. U., 1971. Mem. Jr. Bar Dallas (v.p.) State Bar Tex. chmn. family law sect.), Am. Bar Assn. (mem. council family law sect. 1968—, vice chmn. sect. 1973-74), League Women Voters (pres. Austin 1945-46), Dallas UN Assn. (mem. bd.), Dallas Fedn. Women's Clubs (dir.), Bus. and Profl. Women's Club (vice chmn. women in govt. com., past pres.), Dallas Bar Assn. (sec.-treas. 1970), Am. Acad. Matrimonial Lawyers (gov. 1973-74), Phi Beta Kappa (pres. Dallas chpt. 1970-71), Kappa Beta Pi. Unitarian. Club: Quota (past pres.). Home: 3561 Colgate St Dallas TX 75225 Office: United Fidelity Bldg Dallas TX 75202

RAGGIO, OLGA, mus. curator; b. Rome, Italy, Feb. 5, 1926 (came to U.S. 1950, naturalized 1955); d. Enrico and Renee (Levine) Raggio; A.B. (Maturita Classica), Italian Liceo Rome, Italy, 1944; Baccalaureat, French Lycee, Rome, Italy, 1945; Litt.D. cum laude, U. Rome, 1949; postgrad. N.Y. U. Inst. Fine Arts, 1950-52. Asst. dept. renaissance, modern art Met. Mus. Art, N.Y.C., 1951-54, asst. curator, 1954-63, asso. research curator, 1963-67, asso. curator, 1967-68, curator, 1968—, now chmn. dept. Western European arts. Asso. univ. seminar on the renaissance Columbia, N.Y.C., 1959—; tchr., lectr., cons. in art history; adj. asso. prof. N.Y. U. Inst. Fine Arts, 1965-68, adj. prof. 1968— guest lectr. Frick Collection. Am. Council Learned Socs. fellow, 1962; also Belgian-Am. Found. fellow. Mem. Coll. Art Assn., Am. Assn. Mus., Renaissance Soc. Am. Author: (with M. Laclotte and S. Beguin) Exposition de la Collection Lehman, 1957; El Patio de Velez Blanco, 1968. Contbr. articles to profl. jours. Address: 64 E 94th St New York City NY 10021

RAGINS, NAOMI (MRS. MARK GOLDSMITH), psychiatrist; b. Chgo., Apr. 23, 1926; d. Oscar B. and Ida (Kraus) Ragins; student U. Ariz., 1943-44; Ph.B., U. Chgo., 1946, B.S., 1947, M.D., 1951; m. Mark Goldsmith, July 31, 1956. Intern, U. Chgo. Clinics, 1951-52; resident U. Pitts. Med. Sch., 1952-55, 56-57, staff psychiatrist Pitts. Child Guidance Center, 1957—, staff psychiatrist Children's Residential Treatment Service of Western Psychiat. Inst. and Clinic, 1957-63, faculty univ. dept. psychiatry 1957—, clin. asso. prof., 1973—; faculty Pitts. Psychoanalytic Inst., 1967—; cons. Carlow Coll., Pitts., 1963—. Mem. A.M.A., Am. Psychiat. Assn., Am. Psychoanalytic Assn., Am. Acad. Child Psychiatry, Am. Orthopsychiat. Assn., Assn. for Child Analysis, Pitts. Psychoanalytic Soc., Pittsburgh Council Child Psychiatry.

RAGLAND, BARBARA GAIL, ednl. adminstr.; b. Angier, N.C., June 4, 1947; d. Roscoe and Elnora (Lawrence) Ragland; B.S., Shaw U., 1969; M.Ed., Coppin State Coll., 1973. Recreation leader City of Balt., 1969-70; asst. dir. pub. relations Coppin State Coll., Balt., 1970-74; publs. officer Fayetteville State U., 1974—. Adminstrv. asst. Coppin State Coll. Devel. Found., 1970-74. Ford Found. fellow, 1972. Mem. Am. Coll. Pub. Relations Assn., Nat. Council for Negro Women, Coppin State Coll. Alumni Assn., Shaw U. Alumni Club (corr. sec. Balt. 1973), Delta Sigma Theta. Home: PO Box 361 Angier NC 27501

RAGLAND, IONE HOPE (MRS. FRED MONROE RAGLAND), ednl. adminstr.; b. Raton, N.M., June 24, 1915; d. Arthur Stuart and Cathern (Pulliam) Crawford; A.A., Eastern N.M. Jr. Coll., 1936; B.A., U. Ariz., 1950, M.Ed., 1960; postgrad. Sam Houston U., 1971, Lamar

U., 1973, U. Tex., 1973-74; m. Fred Monroe Ragland, Apr. 4, 1936 (dec. June 1961); children—Fred Arthur, Charles Dean, Sharon Kay. Elementary tchr. Longs Sch., Roosevelt County, N.M., 1935-36, Fremont Sch., Tombstone, Ariz., 1947-57, Walter J. Meyers Sch., Tombstone, 1957-58; elementary sch. prin. Huachuca City (Ariz.) Sch., 1958-62; elementary tchr. Carmichael Sch., Sierra Vista, Ariz., 1962-66; reading cons. Sierra Vista Pub. Schs., 1966-70; dist. supr. spl. edn., sch. counselor Humble (Tex.) Ind. Sch. Dist., 1970-71, dist. dir. spl. services, 1971—. Mem. Ariz. Assn. Elementary Sch. Adminstrs. (mem. exec. bd. 1960-61), Am. Assn. Sch. Adminstrs., N.E.A., Nat. Council Adminstrv. Women in Edn., Nat. Assn. Elementary Sch. Principals, Ariz. Edn. Assn., Dept. Elementary Sch. Prins., Buena Classroom Tchrs. Assn., Tex. Assn. Vocational Adjustment Coordinators, Greater Houston Area Reading Council, Tex., Humble tchrs. assns., P.T.A., Internat. Reading Assn. Home: 1200 Walnut Lane Humble TX 77338 Office: 219 Main St Humble TX 77338

RAHILL, MARGARET FISH, museum ofcl.; b. Milw., Feb. 21, 1919; d. Joseph B. and Margaret (Scherdan) Schmidt; B.A., U. Wis.-Milw., 1958; m. Frank Rahill, Dec. 16, 1950; children—Mary Fish (Mrs. John Arcuri), Marguerite, Laura. Art editor, critic Milw. Sentinel, 1945-61; pub. relations dir. Milw. Art Center, 1961-62, Layton Sch. Art, 1962-68, Florentine Opera Co., 1962-65, Bel Canto Chorus, 1965-68; librarian in charge Charles Allis Art Library, Milw., 1968—; owner Book Bay, 1961-73; free lance writer. Mem. Milw. Mayor's Beautification Com.; quondam bd. mem. Friends Art of Milw. Art Center and Opera Club; organizing com. Milw. Music Chamber Soc. Recipient Milw. Press Club awards for articles on art and edn., 1955, 57, 59, 60. Mem. Wis. Painters and Sculptors (hon.). Club: Milw. Press. Home: 2633 N Hackett Av Milwaukee WI 53211 Office: 1630 E Royall Pl Milwaukee WI 53202

RAHJA, VIRGINIA HELGA, ednl. adminstr.; b. Aurora, Minn., Apr. 21, 1921; d. Emil and Mae A. (Nevala) Rahja; B.A., Hamline U., 1944; M.F.A., Sch. Asso. Arts, 1966. Asst. prof. art Hamline U., St. Paul, 1943-48; asst. supt. fine arts Minn. State Fair, St. Paul, 1944-48; dir. Hamline Galleries, St. Paul, 1945-48; co-founder Sch. Asso. Arts, St. Paul, Minn., 1948, instr., 1948-49, asst. prof., 1949-50, asso. prof., 1950-51, prof. art, 1951—, dean, 1960-73, dir., 1973—. Mem. Am. Assn. U. Women, Nat. Soc. Interior Designers. Presbyn. Home: 360S Lexington Pkwy St Paul MN 55105 Office: Sch of Asso Arts 344 Summit Av St Paul MN 55102

RAHL, KATHERINE MARY, assn. exec.; b. Wooster, O., May 5, 1913; d. James Blaine and Harriet (Munson) Rahl; B.A., Coll. Wooster, 1935; M.A., N.Y. U., 1939; certificate Charles Morris Price Sch. Advt. and Journalism, 1973. Supr. Wooster pub. schs., 1935-40; instr. U. Chgo., 1940-42; dean women U. Ore., Portland, 1947-48; supr. Ore. Dept. Edn., Salem, 1948-52; asso. dir. edn. Am. Social Hygiene Assn., N.Y.C., 1952-56; exec. sec. Correct Seating Inst., Reading, Pa., 1956-58; dir. health edn. Linden Hall, Lititz, Pa., 1958-61; dir. community service Food Fair Stores, Inc., Phila., 1962-69; dir. pub. relations Planned Parenthood Assn. Southeastern Pa., Phila., 1970—. Active Altrusa Club, 1950—, pres. Phila. chpt., 1964-66, chmn. publicity Dist. II, 1970-72; sec. Phila. Fedn. Women's Clubs, 1970-72, v.p., 1972-74. Bd. dirs. CARE, Eastern Pa. Served to lt. comdr. USNR, 1942-46. Recipient Internat. Relations award CARE, 1969, Carrie May Price award excellence journalism, 1973. Fellow Am. Sch. Health Assn.; mem. Res. Officers Assn. (sec.-treas. chpt. 1962—), Phila. Pub. Relations Assn., Phila. Club Advt. Women, Women in Communications. Episcopalian. Clubs: Poor Richard, Rittenhouse Swim (Phila.); Naval Officers (Bklyn. and Phila.); Chesapeake (Tides Inn, Va.). Editor: Six-Player Field Hockey Guide, 1941; You-in Uniform, 1952. Home: 718 Addison St Philadelphia PA 19147 Office: 1402 Spruce St Philadelphia PA 19102

RAHN, ANASTASIA DALAKLIS (MRS. HILTON H. RAHN, JR.), mus. ofcl.; b. Somerville, Mass., Aug. 3, 1925; d. Dimitrios and Catherine (Mizikou) Dalaklis; grad. Wyndham Sch., Boston, 1944; m. Hilton N. Rahn, Jr., June 27, 1959. Asst. to statistician Dept. Pub. Health and Welfare, Boston, 1957-59; treas., asst. to exec. dir. Historic Bethlehem, Inc. and Kemerer Mus., Bethlehem, Pa., 1966-69; curator, Northampton County Hist. and Geneal. Soc. and Mus., Easton, Pa., 1970—. Lutheran. Clubs: Garden (Bethlehem); Lafayette Coll. Aux. (Easton). Home: 3640 Mark Twin Circle Bethlehem PA 18017 Office: 101 S 4th St Easton PA 18042

RAHO, MARTHA LOUISE, hotel exec.; b. Oneonta, N.Y., July 3, 1934; d. Ralph Daniel and Anna Leona (Kuhlman) Heim; B.A., Pa. State U., 1956; m. Arrigo Raho, Aug. 22, 1962 (div. Jan. 1970); children—Marianna, John Anthony. Promotion writer McGraw-Hill Pub. Co., N.Y.C., 1956-57; publicity asst. Miami Beach (Fla.) Asso. Hotels, 1958; asst. pub. relations dir. Tropical Park, Inc., Coral Gables, Fla., 1959-61; editor Italian Times, Rome, Italy, 1962; asst. editor The Am. Rev. Johns Hopkins Sch. of Internat. Studies, Bologna, Italy, 1963-64; corr. McGraw-Hill World News, Milan (Italy) Bur., 1965; pub. relations account exec. Spiro and Assos., Phila., 1966-68; internal communications and creative supr. Sonesta Internat. Hotels Corp., Boston, 1968-70, pub. relations mgr., 1970-71; dir. advt. and pub. relations Archris Hotel Corp., Boston, 1972; dir. pub. relations Marco Beach Hotel, Marco Island, Fla., 1973—; freelance writer. Mem. Internat. Assn. Bus. Communicators, Mensa, Pub. Relations Soc. Am., Women in Communications. Home: 1940 Indian Hill Marco Island FL 33937 Office: Marco Beach Hotel Marco Island FL 33937

RAILO, BARBARA CAROL, librarian; b. N.Y.C., Apr. 25, 1943; d. Eino Gosta and Vieno Ingrit (Huhtala) Railo; B.A., Smith Coll., 1964; M.L.S., Rutgers U., 1966; student Mannes Coll. Music, 1968-71; M.A., N.Y. U., 1973. Reference and circulation librarian Columbia U., N.Y.C., 1966-68; record librarian N.Y. Pub. Library, N.Y.C., 1969-72; head librarian Mannes Coll. Music, N.Y.C., 1972—. Mem. Am. Musicological Soc., Music Library Assn., N.Y. Library Assn. Office: 157 E 74th St New York City NY 10021

RAILSBACK, BERNICE HICKMAN (MRS. JAMES ERNEST RAILSBACK), educator; b. Mountain Home, Ark.; d. Charles Isaac and America Maria (Lewis) Hickman; student Mountain Home Coll., 1927, 29, Ark. State Coll., summers 1930-31; B.S., Tex. Tech. Coll., 1941; M.S., 1951; m. James Ernest Railsback, June 9, 1932; children—Norman Leighton, Charles Hickman, Phyllis Elaine (Mrs. George A. Carlton). Tchr. pub. schs., Budford, Ark., 1927-28; tchr., girls coach Salem (Ark.) pub. schs., 1929-32, McClung Sch., Slation, Tex., 1933-34; tchr. Hodges Sch., Levelland, Tex., 1939-41; tchr. jr. high sch. math. and reading Levelland Pub. Schs., 1947-54, dir. elementary edn., 1954-70. Chmn. subcom. schs. and colls., dir. Tex. affiliate Am. Heart Assn. Chmn., Democratic Women of Hockley County, 1966. Recipient poetry award S. Plains Writers Assn., 1964, 65; named Woman of Yr., Levelland C. of C., 1969. Mem. Assn. Supervision and Curriculum Devel. (Tex. rep. to nat. bd. 1962-67, state pres. 1966-67, 69-70), Tex., West Tex. (regional pres. 1966-67) assns. supervision and curriculum devel., N.E.A., Tex. Elementary Prins. and Suprs. Assn., Tex. Assn. Instructional Supts. (state pres. 1959-60), Am. Assn. U. Women, Tex. Congress Parents and Tchrs. (life), Internat. Platform Assn., Poetry Soc. Tex., S. Plains Writers Assn., Tex. Assn. for Improvement of Reading, Internat. Reading Assn., Tex. Assn. Edn. Young Children, Assn. for Gifted, Tex. Edn. Agy. (mem. state certification com.), Marigolds, Delta Kappa Gamma. Mem. Order Eastern Star (past worthy matron). Clubs: Levelland Music, Matrons Study. Contbr. to various publs. Home: 307 Sandalwood Lane PO Box 156 Levelland TX 79336

RAINBOW, KATHRYN ADELINE (MRS. WILLIAM EARHART), physician; b. Wheeling, W.Va., Mar. 21, 1921; d. John Henry and Addaline (Holly) Rainbow; B.S., Fort Valley State Coll., 1942; M.D., Meharry Med. Coll., 1948; m. William Earhart, July 29, 1966; children—(by previous marriage) Frederic B., Holly R. Bryant. Intern, Harlem Hosp., N.Y.C., 1948-49; pediatric resident Mercy-Douglas, Children's hosps., Phila., 1949-50, Freedman's Hosp., Washington, Nat. Found. for Infantile Paralysis fellow, 1950-52; Nat. Inst. Mental Health psychiat. residency fellow Menninger Sch. Psychiatry, Topeka, 1962-65, grad. 1965; pvt. pediatric practice, Rocky Mount, N.C., 1952-54; staff physician Lakin State Hosp., W.Va., 1954-60, supt., 1960-62; staff psychiatrist Topeka State Hosp., 1965—, adviser to Psychiat. Aide Orgn., 1969-71. Bd. dirs. The Villages, Topeka, Topeka Assn. Retarded Children. Recipient 5-years Service to Humanity pin Lakin State Hosp., 1961, 25 years service to humanity plaque Meharry Med. Coll., 1973. Mem. Am., Nat., Kan. med. assns., W.Va. (pres. 1961-62), Shawnee County med socs., Am. Med. Women's Assn., Am. Psychiat. Assn., Menninger Sch. Psychiatry Alumni Assn., Mental Health Assn. Shawnee County, N.A.A.C.P., Quota Internat., Links, Alpha Kappa Alpha. Mem. A.M.E. Ch. Home: 2916 Kentucky Av Topeka KS 66605 Office: 2700 W 6th St Topeka KS 66606

RAINE, DOROTHY LILLIAN EWING (MRS. C. MACON RAINE), social work adminstr.; b. San Francisco, Feb. 2, 1918; d. Frank H. and Amy (Currier) Ewing; B.A., U. Cal., Berkeley, 1939, certificate in social welfare, 1940; M.S.W., Western Res. U., 1946; m. C. Macon Raine, Sept. 29, 1946; children—William Woody, Patricia Ann. Social worker Alameda County (Cal.) Welfare Dept., 1940-42; with A.R.C., 1942-51, 58—, hosp. field dir. 107th Gen. Hosp., Eng., 1944-45; field dir. Naval Hosp., Corpus Christi, Tex., 1949-51, 58-70, sr. field dir., 1970—. Bd. mem. Coastal Bend chpt. Mental Health Assn.; v.p. Scurry County (Tex.) chpt. Am. Cancer Soc., 1956-57. Mem. Nat. Assn. Social Workers (sec. sub chpt. 1960-62), Acad. Certified Social Workers, Am. Assn. U. Women (v.p. 1956-57). Presbyn. (charter mem., treas. women of ch. 1956). Home: 473 Palmetto St Corpus Christi TX 78412 Office: ARC Naval Hosp Corpus Christi TX 78419

RAINES, FLEETA LORAINE KINSELL (MRS. W. CARL RAINES), real estate broker; b. Stanley, N.M., May 3, 1915; d. Dillman Clay and Louie Mae (Willingham) Kinsell; student Albuquerque Bus. Coll., 1934; student U. N.M., 1935-36; m. W. Carl Raines, June 17, 1939; children—W. Carl, Dorothy (Mrs. Dale Bystrom). With KGGM Radio, Albuquerque, 1936-39, KROP, Brawley, Cal., 1946-48; self-employed as real estate broker, Modesto, Cal., 1948—. Mem. Planning Commn. City of Modesto, 1973—. Mem. Nat. Assn. Realtors (regional v.p. women's council 1959), Cal. Real Estate Assn. (regional v.p. 1962), Modesto Bd. Realtors (dir. 1961, 69, pres. 1960, pres. women's council 1954, 57, Realtor of Year 1958). Presbyn. (trustee, elder). Mem. Daus. of Nile. Club: Zonta (pres. 1969—). Home: 1003 Wellesley St Modesto CA 95350 Office: 812 14th St Modesto CA 95354

RAINES, KATHARINE ANDREWS (MRS. O.C. RAINES III), physician; b. Kansas City, Mo., Oct. 2, 1942; d. Berneil Walter and Helen Ruth (Jackson) Andrews; B.S., So. Meth. U., 1964; M.D., U. Mo., 1968; m. Marvin Ross Pyron, July 9, 1965; 1 dau., Kate W.; m. 2d, O.C. Raines III, Mar. 1, 1974. Intern, U. Mo. Med. Center, Columbia, 1968-69, resident 1969-71; practice medicine, specializing in internal medicine, Kansas City, Mo., 1971-74, Gulfport, Miss., 1974; lectr. medicine U. Mo. Sch. Medicine, Kansas City, 1971-74. U.S. Govt. grantee, 1966. Mem. A.C.P., Am. Soc. Internal Medicine, Jackson County Med. Soc. Home: 15 Oakwood Dr Gulfport MS 39501 Office: 4500 15th St Gulfport MS 39501

RAINEY, ELLEN LEWIS (MRS. TRACY RAINEY), constrn. co. exec.; b. El Dorado, Ark., July 24, 1924; d. Melvin Walker and Webel Jenny (Molthu) Lewis; grad. high sch.; m. Tracy Rainey, July 8, 1950; children—Debra, Bradford, Patrick. Sec. U.S. Dept. Agr., Ashland, Miss., 1942-43, Barrow-Agee Labs., Memphis, 1943-48, CBS Radio Sales, Memphis, 1948-52; sec., treas. Rainey Bros. Constrn. Co., Inc., Memphis, 1952—; sec., treas. Dawn Crest, Inc., Gowan Dawn Crest, Inc., Whitney Dawn Crest, Inc., Steele Dawn Crest, Inc., Frayser Manor, Inc. (all Memphis). Mem. Memphis City Beautiful Commn., 1959-66, vice chmn., 1960-63; v.p., bd. dirs. Sea Isle P.T.A., 1965-67; mem. adv. bd. Mid-South Fair, 1967—. Treas. Shelby County Democratic Women's Club, 1963, 65; founder Greater Memphis Dem. Women's Club, 1968, pres., 1968-69; bd. dirs. Tenn. Fedn. Dem. Women, 1965-66. Mem. Memphis Home Builders Aux. (2d v.p. 1967-68, treas. 1968-70), Memphis Jaycettes (pres. 1959-60, 1st. v.p. 1954-56). Mem. Internat. Order Kings Daughter & Sons (parliamentarian 1970-72, corr. sec. 1971-72), Opportunity Circle (co-leader 1972-74). Club: Oak Grove-Arkabutla Lake Civic (pres. 1967-70) (Hernando, Miss.). Address: 5347 Knollwood Dr Memphis TN 38117

RAINEY, LAURA JEAN, librarian; b. Benton, Ill.; d. Carl Raymond and Daisy (Stevens) Rainey; B.A., U. Cal. at Los Angeles, 1948, M.A., 1950, M.L.S., 1965. Librarian Braun and Co., pub. relations and mgmt. cons., 1951-57, Foote, Cone and Belding, advt., Los Angeles, 1957-65; catalog librarian Rand Corp., Santa Monica, 1965-66; catalog librarian Sci. Center, Rockwell Internat. Corp., 1966-69, head tech. processing, power systems div., 1969-70, head librarian Rocketdyne div., 1970-74, mgr. Tech. Information Center, 1974—. Mem. Spl. Libraries Assn., Am. Soc. Information Sci., Phi Gamma Mu. Home: 4617 Natick Av Sherman Oaks CA 91403

RAINS, TWYLA JEAN, journalist; b. Fort Worth, Aug. 21, 1951; d. William Marlin and Mildred Lewis (Halve) Rains; B.A., U. Tex., 1973; postgrad. Tex. Christian U., 1973—. Reporter, Fort Worth News Tribune, 1970-71; free lance journalist-photographer local news media-mags., Fort Worth, 1971—. Pres., Young Democrats in Tarrant County, Fort Worth, 1972. Recipient scholarships Theta Sigma Phi, 1969, 70, 71. Mem. Women in Communications, Sigma Tau Delta. Home: 1921 Haltom Rd Fort Worth TX 76117

RAINSFORD, GRETA M., pediatrician; b. N.Y.C., Dec. 28, 1936; d. Maurice George and Gertrude Eleanor (Edwards) Rainsford; B.A., Hunter Coll., 1958; M.D., Howard U., 1962. Intern, resident pediatrics Meadowbrook Hosp., East Meadow, N.Y., 1962-65; pvt. practice ltd. to pediatrics, Hempstead, N.Y., 1965—; asst. attending pediatrics Mercy Hosp., Nassau County Med. Center; clin. instr., dir. sickle cell anemia Nassau County Med. Center. Mem. Hempstead Bd. Edn., 1969— (pres., 1971-72, 73-74). Bd. dirs. L.I. div. Am. Cancer Soc. Mem. Nassau Pediatric Soc., Nassau County Med. Soc. Office: 312 Greenwich St Hempstead NY 11550

RAISBECK, BARBARA WIENER (MRS. GORDON RAISBECK), biologist; b. Arlington, Mass.; d. Norbert and Margaret (Engemann) Wiener; B.S., Boston U., 1951; Ph.D., Brandeis U., 1969; m. Gordon Raisbeck, Dec. 22, 1948; children—Michael Norbert, Lucy Margaret, Alison Jane, Timothy Gordon, James Gregory. Research asst., teaching asst. Brandeis U., Waltham, Mass., 1963-69; research asso. dept. biology Tufts U., Medford, Mass., 1969-71; NRC vis. scientist entomology div. Pioneering Research Labs., U.S. Army Lab., Natick, Mass., 1971-73; asst. prof. biology Northeastern U., Boston, 1973—. Mem. Am. Inst. Biol. Scis., Am. Soc. Zoologists, Tissue Culture Assn., A.A.A.S. Home: 40 Bloomfield St Lexington MA 02173 Office: Dept of Biology Northeastern University Boston MA 02115

RAISFELD, ILENE HOMNICK (MRS. LAWRENCE S. RAISFELD), physician; b. N.Y.C., June 24, 1940; d. Jack and Henrietta (Poverstein) Homnick; M.D., N.Y. U., 1964; m. Lawrence S. Raisfeld, Mar. 16, 1960; children—Robin Gaye, Arthur Adam. Intern, Bellevue Hosp., N.Y.C., 1964-65; resident N.Y.U. Med. Center, N.Y.C., 1965-67; fellow liver disease Mt. Sinai Sch. Medicine, N.Y.C., 1967-69; practice medicine specializing in liver disease and clin. pharmacology, N.Y.C., 1969—; asst. prof. medicine, N.Y.U., Sch. Medicine, 1970—; asst. vis. physician Bellevue Hosp., 1970—; attending physician Univ. Hosp., 1970—; dir. medicine South Shore div. L.I./Hillside Med. Center, Queens; cons. liver disease N.Y. Infirmary, 1971—, Clin. Pharmacology Group, N.Y. U., 1970—. Fellow A.C.P. Contbr. articles to profl. jours. Office: 566 1st Av New York City NY 10016

RAISOR, LEOTA SEARS, real estate exec.; b. Piqua, Kan., Apr. 22, 1927; d. Harold Leland and Alice S. (Kinney) Sears; student Cerritos Coll., 1965; children by previous marriage—Deborah Jean, Melody Dawn. Underwriter, Ohio Casualty Ins. Co., Kansas City, Mo., 1952-55, Marsh & McLennan, Inc., Tulsa, 1956-59; office mgr. Gachman Steel Corp., Norwalk, Cal., 1959-61, Internat. Pipe & Steel, Los Angeles, 1962-63; real estate property mgmt. W.M. Garland Co., Los Angeles, 1963-67, Red Hill Realty, Tustin, Cal., 1967-69; sales mgr. Vision Red Hill Realty, Irvine, Cal., 1969—. Mem. Sales and Marketing Internat. (recipient Distinguished Salesman's award 1972), East Orange County, Newport Harbor-Costa Mesa (recipient Top Lister Unit Sales award 1970) bd. realtors, Nat. Assn. Realtors, Nat. Assn. Female Execs., Am. Bus. Women's Assn. Home: 17392 Sandalwood Irvine CA 92664 Office: 18124 Culver Dr Irvine CA 92664

RAJEC, ELIZABETH MOLNAR (MRS. STEPHEN L. RAJEC), librarian; b. Bratislava, July 23, 1931; d. Lorinc and Tereza (Hinterschuster) Molnar; came to U.S., 1957, naturalized, 1962; B.S., Columbia, 1963; M.L.S., Rutgers U., 1964; m. Stephen L. Rajec, Apr. 5, 1961. Interpreter, Inst. Cultural Relations, Budapest, Hungary, 1951-56; fashion asst. Dress Studio, N.Y.C., 1957-64; librarian City Coll. N.Y., 1964—. Mem. Am. Fedn. Tchrs., Am., N.Y. library assns., Alumni Rutgers U., Delta Phi Alpha. Home: 500 E 77st St New York City NY 10021 Office: 135th St at Convent Av New York City NY 10036

RAKO, SUSAN MANDELL, psychiatrist; b. Springfield, Mass., Sept. 4, 1939; d. Robert and Ann (Melnikoff) Mandell; student Wellesley Coll., 1957-60; B.S., U. Cin., 1961; M.D., Albert Einstein Coll. Medicine, 1966; m. Dr. Jules Rako, June 12, 1960 (div. May 1967); children—Jennifer, Sarah; m. 2d, Barry Zaltman, Sept. 13, 1970. Intern Mt. Auburn Hosp., Cambridge, Mass., 1966-67; resident psychiatry Mass. Mental Health Center, 1967-69; resident child psychiatry Beth Israel Hosp., Boston, 1969-70; pvt. practice ltd. to psychiatry, Brookline, Mass., 1970—; clin. instr. psychiatry Harvard Med. Sch.; staff psychiatrist Mass. Mental Health Center. Democrat. Jewish religion. Research on long term psychotherapeutic treatment of schizophrenic patients. Home: 83 Walker St Newtonville MA 02160 Office: 1101 Beacon St Brookline MA 02146

RAKOWSKA-HARMSTONE, TERESA, educator; b. Poland, Aug. 12, 1927; d. Tadeusz Jan and Jadwiga Rakowski; naturalized, 1955; B.A. with honors, McGill U., 1950; A.M., Radcliffe Coll., 1952; Ph.D., Harvard, 1966; div.; 1 son, Andrew Tadeusz. Research analyst fgn. area studies div. Am. U., 1957-61; instr. dept. polit. sci. Douglass Coll., Rutgers U., 1961-65; asst. prof. Carleton U., Ottawa, Ont., Can., 1966-68, asso. prof., supr. grad. studies, 1968-70, prof., 1974—, dir. Inst. Soviet and East European Studies, 1973—; exec. dir. League Women Voters U.S., 1970-72. Am. Assn. U. Women fellow, 1963-64. Mem. Am. Polit. Sci. Assn., Am. Assn. Advancement of Slavic Studies. Author: Russia and Nationalism in Soviet Central Asia, 1970. Editor: (with A. Bronke) Communist States in Disarray, 1972. Home: 21 Farnham Crescent Ottawa ON Canada

RALEY, SISTER AGNES LUCILE, psychologist; b. Leonardtown, Md., July 3, 1907; d. John Francis and Lucy Roberta (Dawson) Raley; A.B., Boston Coll., 1936, M.A., 1940; Ph.D., Fordham U., 1942. Joined Sisters of Charity of Nazareth, 1925; tchr. Nazareth High Sch., Boston, 1929-39; prof. psychology Spalding Coll. (formerly Nazareth Coll.), Louisville, 1942-72, prof. emeritus, 1972—, dir. Psychol. Services Center, 1973—. Cons. Child Devel. Services System, Louisville Bd. Edn., 1972—. Mem. Ky. Gov.'s Child Welfare Adv. Com., 1963-65; mem. Louisville Mayor's Human Relations Commn., 1963-65. Diplomate, fellow Am. Psychol. Assn.; mem. Ky. Psychol. Assn. (pres. 1964-65), Regional Personnel and Guidance Assn. (pres. 1968). Contbr. articles to profl. jours., New Cath. Ency. Home and office: 851 S 4th St Louisville KY 40203

RALEY, WILHELMINA ALSOBROOK (MRS. JOHN CALVIN RALEY), nurse supr.; b. Statesboro, Ga., Dec. 14, 1940; d. Henry Herman and Wilhelmina (Pool) Alsobrook; student Ga. So. Coll., 1958-60; B.S., Ga. Sch. Nursing, 1963; m. John Calvin Raley, Sept. 3, 1961 (div. July 1972). Pediatric nurse Med. Coll. Ga., Augusta, 1963-65; pub. health nurse Gracewood (Ga.) State Sch. and Hosp., 1965—, nurse supr., 1973—, instr. assigned to Med. Coll. Ga., 1966-67. Mem. Am., Ga. State Nursing assns., Burke County Assn. for Retarded Children (v.p. 1965-67, treas. 1965-73), Am. Assn. Mental Deficiency, Ga. Pub. Health Assn., Med. Coll. Ga. Alumni Assn. Club: Burke Jr. Women's (pres. 1969-70). Home: 2524 Richmond Hill Rd Augusta GA 30906 Office: Gracewood State School and Hospital Gracewood GA 30812

RALLS, KATHERINE, educator, biologist; b. Oakland, Cal., Mar. 21, 1939; d. Alvin Wallingsford and Ruth (McQueen) Smith; A.B., Stanford, 1960; M.A., Radcliffe Coll., 1962; Ph.D., Harvard, 1965; m. Kenneth M. Ralls, June 1958 (div. Sept. 1968); children—Robin, Tamsen, Kristin. Post-doctoral fellow U. Cal. at Berkeley, 1965-67; investigator Rockefeller U., N.Y.C., 1968-70, adj. asst. prof., 1970—; asst. prof. biology Sarah Lawrence Coll., Bronxville, N.Y., 1970—; research zoologist Inst. for Research in Animal Behavior, N.Y. Zool. Soc., 1968—. Mem. Am. Soc. Zoologists, Am. Soc. Mammalogists, Animal Bahavior Soc. Contbr. articles to profl. jours. Home: 915 Kimball Av Bronxville NY 10708

RALSTON, JOANNE SMOOT (MRS. JOSEPH P. RALSTON), pub. relations exec.; b. Phoenix, May 13, 1939; d. A. Glenn and Virginia (George) Smoot; B.A., Ariz. State U., 1960; m. Joseph P. Ralston, May 13, 1972. With Univ. News Bur., Ariz. State U., 1957-60; gen. assignment reporter Ariz. Republic, Phoenix, 1959-62; co-owner, pub. relations dir. Patton Agy., Phoenix, 1962-71; pres., pub. relations dir. Joanne Patton Ralston & Asso., Inc., Phoenix,

1971—. Mem. Samaritan Health Services Task Force on Pub. Affairs and Devel., Phoenix, 1973—; mem. alumni bd. Ariz. State U., 1972—. Recipient awards various orgns., including Los Angeles Advt. Women, Nat. Fedn. Press Women. Mem. Pub. Relations Soc. Am. (counselor 1966—), Phoenix C. of C. (mem. pub. affairs com. 1970—, mem. legislative com. 1971—), Phoenix Press Club (pres. 1970-71), Alpha Phi, Gamma Alpha Chi, Pi Delta Epsilon. Clubs: Phoenix Country, Kiva (Phoenix); White Mountain Country (Pinetop, Ariz.). Home: 371 E Palm Lane Phoenix AZ 85004 Office: 3003 N Central Av Phoenix AZ 85012

RALSTON, MARY AGNES, lectr., writer; b. Caledonia, Ill.; d. William D. and Agnes (Kelly) Ralston; student Rockford Coll., U. Wis. Extension; B.S., Northwestern U. Lectr., free lance writer. Mem. Nat. Assn. Bank Women, Council for Wis. Writers, Am. Assn. U. Women, Indsl. and Ednl. Counselors Assn., Asso. Bus. Writers Am., Wis. Regional Writers Assn., Internat. Platform Assn., Wis. Press Women, Nat. Fedn. Press Women, Nat. Writers Club, Nat. Orgn. Women, Women in Communications, Authors' Guild, Authors' League Am., Kappa Alpha Theta. Club: Zonta. Author: How to Return to Work in an Office, 1973. Contbr. numerous articles to profl., trade jours. Home: 1006 E State St Milwaukee WI 53202

RALSTON, NANCY CAROLINE, educator; b. Indpls., June 2, 1931; d. Glenn B. and Gail C. (Long) Ralston; A.B., DePauw U., 1953; M.S., Ind. U., 1954, Ph.D., 1961. Examiner, Cin. Pub. Schs., 1957-62; asst. prof., asso. prof., prof. psychology and edn. U. Cin., 1962—. Bd. dirs. Sacred Heart Acad., Cin., 1969-71. Recipient Cohen award for teaching excellence U. Cin., 1969. Mem. Am. Psychol. Assn., Am. Assn. U. Profs., Am. Assn. U. Women, Nat. Council on Measurement in Edn., Delta Delta Delta. Author: The Child: Case Studies for Analysis, 1972; The Adolescent: Case Studies for Analysis, 1974. Home: Rural Route 10 Box 292A Bloomington IN 47401

RALSTON, NYNA MAHEALANI, psychologist; b. Kawaiahao, Kauai, Dec. 13, 1924; d. Jesse James and Deborah Kamehaokalani (Mahikoa) Hamic; B.S. (Leahi Hosp. scholar), Baylor U., 1952; B.A., North Tex. State U., 1960, M.A., 1961; m. William Putman Ralston, Jr., Mar. 31, 1951; children—Scrappy (Mrs. Harry Wessel Chillingworth), Deborah Kamehaokalani, William Putman III. Vis. nurse Vis. Nurses Assn., Dallas, 1952-54; emergency nurse Grapevine (Tex.) Hosp., 1954-58; asso. prof. biology North Tex. State U., Denton, 1959-61, research asst. in chemistry, 1959; psychologist research and guidance clinic Dallas Ind. Sch. Dist., 1961-65; sch. psychologist Honolulu Dept. Edn., 1965—. Mem. Gov's Com. on Mental Health, Hawaii, 1973—. Pres. George B. Dealey P.T.A., Dallas, 1964, pres. Lincoln Elementary P.T.A., Honolulu, 1966. Anderson Meml. Hosp. research grantee, 1957-60. Mem. Am., Dallas, Southwestern, Hawaii psychol. assns., Nat. Council for Adminstrs. and Women in Edn., Am. Bus. and Women's Assn. Episcopalian. Mem. Sons and Daus. of Hawaiian Warriors. Home: 2244-A Aulii St Honolulu HI 96817 Office: 1136 California St Wahiawa HI 96786

RAMBO, FLORENCE LASSETER (MRS. OLIN OSBORNE RAMBO), ednl. adminstr.; b. Cordele, Ga., Nov. 28, 1916; d. William Hugh and Florence C. (Jones) Lasseter; A.B., Agnes Scott Coll., 1937; M.Ed., U. Ga., 1961, Ed.D., 1964; m. Olin Osborne Rambo, Oct. 10, 1941 (dec. Mar. 1945); children—Samuel Hugh, Florence Kathryn (Mrs. Joseph Majette Browne). Tchr. English, French, Elberton (Ga.) Schs., 1937-41; elementary tchr., 1946-57; counselor Clarke Jr. High Sch., Athens, Ga., 1958-65; prin. Pattie Hilsman Jr. High Sch., Athens, 1965-68; dir. personnel services Clarke County (Ga.) Sch. Dist., Athens, 1968-71; supr. psychol. services DeKalb County (Ga.) Schs., Decatur, 1971—. Ednl. cons. Mem. Ga., DeKalb County edn. assns., Ga. Assn. Sch. Counselors, Am., Ga. personnel and guidance assns., Ga. Assn. Sch. Psychologists, Am. Sch. Counselor Assn., Pilot Internat., Phi Kappa Phi, Kappa Delta Pi. Home: 444 Landover Dr Decatur GA 30030 Office: 2892 N Druid Hills Rd Atlanta GA 30329

RAMBO, JUDITH LOUISE CRAIN, broadcasting co. exec.; b. Durham, N.C., Feb. 9, 1947; d. James Charlie and Eunice Louise (Grice) Crain; A.B. (Dean's list) in Radio, TV, Motion Pictures, U. N.C., 1968; m. James Everett Rambo, June 3, 1967. Traffic mgr. Ring Radio Co., Atlanta, 1969-71; promotions and prodn. mgr., 1972—; free lance copywriter, free lance voice recorder. Mem. Am. Women in Radio and Television, Ad Club 2, Atlanta Phoenix Cat Soc. (charter, pres. 1973-74). Home: 1270 Biltmore Dr NE Atlanta GA 30329 Office: 3954 Peachtree Rd NE Atlanta GA 30319

RAMBO, SYLVIA HILDA, lawyer; b. Royersford, Pa., Apr. 17, 1936; d. Granville A. and Hilda E. (Leonhardt) Rambo; A.B. cum laude, Dickinson Coll., 1958; LL.B., Dickinson Sch. Law, 1962, J.D., 1968. Admitted to Pa. bar, 1963; atty. trust dept. Bank Del., Wilmington, 1962-63; practice law, Carlisle, Pa., 1963—. Pub. defender, Carlisle, 1972—; adj. prof. law Dickinson Sch. Law, Carlisle, 1973—. Mem. Am., Pa., Cumberland County bar assns., Pa. Trial Lawyers Assn., League Women Voters, Gen. Alumni Assn. Dickinson Sch. Law (treas. 1967). Home: RD 5 Carlisle PA 17013 Office: 27 W High St Carlisle PA 17013

RAME, PIRY (MRS. JACK RAME), artist; b. Czechoslovakia, Nov. 5, 1920; d. Emanuel and Fanny (Schnitzer) Herskovitz; came to U.S., naturalized, 1933; student McDowells Sch. Fashion, 1940, Bklyn. Coll., 1946, Art Students League, 1962; m. Jack Rame, Mar. 9, 1941; children—Rochelle (Mrs. Robert Friedman), Marilyn (Mrs. Jerry Wechsler), Elyse. Exhibited one-man shows at Nassau Community Coll., N.Y. U., U. Mass., Shelter Rock Library, Madison Art Gallery, Priscilla Gallery; exhibited in group shows at Audubon Artists Assn., Allied Artists Assn., Guild Hall Southampton, Silvermine Art Assn., N.A.D., Port Washington Library, N. Shore Art Center, others. Recipient 2d prizes Emily Lowe Found., 1967, Arts Ann., 1962, 1st prize L.I. Artists, 1970, Pres.'s award Audubon Artists, 1970. Mem. Nat. Assn. Women Artists, Profl. Artists Guild, Artists in Am. Workshop. Address: 57 Hayloft Lane Roslyn Heights NY 11577

RAMER, FAYE PADGETT (MRS. MAXWELL RAMER), librarian; b. Darlington, Fla., Mar. 10, 1930; d. Thomas Clayton and Evie Irene (Kirkland) Padgett; B.S., Fla. State U., 1961, M.S., 1966, postgrad., 1973-75; m. Maxwell Ramer, Sept. 14, 1947; children—Clayton Frederick, Philip Gregory, David Maxwell. Tchr. elementary sch., Bay County, Fla., 1959-63; elementary sch. librarian Bay County (Fla.) Schs., 1963-66, jr. high librarian, 1966-71, sr. librarian, Panama City, 1971—. Recipient Appreciation award Fla. Congress Parents and Tchrs., 1970. Mem. Am. Assn. U. Women (local treas. 1963-65), Fla. Assn. for Media in Edn., N.E.A., A.L.A., Assn. Ednl. Communications and Tech., Fla. Edn. Assn., Bay County Sch. Librarians Assn. (pres. 1966-67), Alpha Delta Kappa, Delta Kappa Gamma, Kappa Delta Pi. Baptist. Home: 4625 N Lakewood Dr Panama City FL 32401 Office: 1200 Harrison Av Panama City FL 32401

RAMER, MARY ANNE THERESA, editor; b. Syracuse, N.Y., May 2, 1946; d. Everett William and Mary Elizabeth (Bowman) Ramer; B.A. (Regents scholar), Syracuse U., 1968; M.A. (Herbert Lehman fellow), U. Rochester, 1970, postgrad., 1970-71. Reporter, feature writer Syracuse Herald-Jour., 1967, Rochester Democrat & Chronicle, 1968-69; free-lance writer local and nat. publs., 1969-71; dir. voluntary action center United Community Chest, Rochester, 1971-73; editor creative services Hutchins-Darcy, Rochester, 1973—. Mem. adv. com. Ret. Sr. Vol. Program, Monroe County. Mem. Am. Assn. Vol. Services Coordinator, Am. Soc. for Tng. and Devel., Women in Communications (chpt. project chmn. 1973-74). Home: 51 Westminster Rd Rochester NY 14607 Office: 400 Midtown Tower Rochester NY 14604

RAMEY, MARTHA LOUISE (MRS. JOHN C. RAMEY), city ofcl.; b. Hale Center, Tex., July 15, 1924; d. Hoyt Lafayette and Mary Myrtle (Surratt) Owens; student Compton (Cal.) Jr. Coll.; m. John Clinton Ramey, Apr. 5, 1956; 1 son, Mikel John. Accounting staff, various automobile agencies, Shreveport, La., Bartown, Fla., 1956-61; cashier for finance USAF, Tripoli, 1962-65; sec. Central Base Fund, Barksdale AFB, La., 1967-68, Yokota AFB, Japan, 1969-70; bookkeeper, bus. mgr. Kennedale (Tex.) Sch., 1971-72; city sec. Colleyville, Tex., 1972—. Home: 5700 Oak Top Dr Grapevine TX 76051 Office: 5201 Bransford Rd Grapevine TX 76051

RAMIREZ-IRIZARRY, ANGELA A., surgeon; b. Lajas, P.R., Nov. 19, 1935; d. Enrique and Estela (Irizarry-Castillo) Ramirez-Irizarry; B.A. summa cum laude, Inter-Am. U., San German, P.R., 1956; M.D., U. P.R., 1960; m. Bambran Aravind Adyanthaya, Mar. 1, 1963; 1 son, Aravind Enrique. Intern, U. Pa. Grad. Hosp., Phila., 1960-61; resident Jefferson Med. Coll. Hosp., Phila., 1961-65, Mt. Sinai Hosp., N.Y.C., 1965-68; practice medicine, specializing in plastic and reconstructive and hand surgery, Mayaguez, P.R., 1968—; mem. staffs Mayaguez Med. Center, Hosp. Concepcion, San German, Clinica Espanola, Bella Vista Hosp., Clinica Perea, Mayaguez; head plastic surgery div. gen. surgery dept. Mayaguez Med. Center, 1968—; cons. plastic surgery VA Hosp., San Juan, P.R., Ramey AFB Hosp., Aguadilla, P.R., 1969-73. Diplomate Am. Bd. Plastic Surgery. Fellow A.C.S.; mem. Am. Soc. Plastic and Reconstructive Surgeons, P.R. Med. Assn. (div. plastic surgery), Am. Cleft Palate Assn., Caribbean Soc. Surgery of Hand, Am. Assn. for Surgery of Hand. Roman Catholic. Home: PO Box 426 65th Infantry St No 20 Lajas PR 00667 Office: 19 N Post St PO Box 753 Mayaguez PR 00708

RAMO, VIRGINIA M. SMITH (MRS. SIMON RAMO), univ. trustee; b. Yonkers, N.Y.; d. Abraham Harold and Freda (Kasnetz) Smith; B.S. in Edn., U. So. Cal.; m. Simon Ramo; children—James Brian, Alan Martin. Tchr. high sch., Schenectady, U.S. Army Depot, Schenectady. Nat. co-chmn. annual giving U. So. Cal., 1968-70, trustee, 1971—; vice-chmn. Bd. Overseers Hebrew Union Coll.; bd. dirs. The Muses, Cal. Mus. Sci. and Industry, U. Cal. at Los Angeles Affiliates, Los Angeles County Heart Assn., Friends of Library U. So. Cal.; bd. dirs., v.p. Achievement Rewards for Coll. Scientists Found.; bd. dirs. Les Dames Los Angeles, Women's council Los Angeles Community Ednl. Television; bd. dirs., v.p. Founders Los Angeles Music Center, Blue Ribbon-400 Performing Arts Council, Ramo Found. Mem. U. Cal. at Los Angeles Med. Aux. (dir.), U. So. Cal. Pres. Circle (dir.), Los Angeles Opera Guild, Commerce Assos., Cedars of Lebanon Hosp. Women's Guild (dir. 1967-68).

RAMSAY, ELLA MCELWAIN (MRS. WILLARD ROSS RAMSAY), civic worker; b. Fawn Grove, Pa., June 12, 1904; d. Henry Clay and Mary Agnes (Almoney) McElwain; student extension courses U. Pa., 1924, Pa. State U., 1923; grad. Pa. State Tchrs. Coll., 1926; m. Willard Ross Ramsay, Dec. 24, 1926; children—Mary Louise (Mrs. Ben W. Wolf), Miriam (Mrs. Harry S. Diffenderfer III), Richard W., Larry M. Tchr. pub. schs., Star View, Pa., 1922-23, Mt. Wolf, Pa., 1923-27; co-owner W. R. Ramsay Property & Rentals, 1940—; v.p. W. R. Ramsay Constrn. Co., 1952—; sec. R. W. Ramsay Co., Inc., 1964— (all New Cumberland, Pa.). Chmn. March of Dimes, 1965-67. Recipient Pa. Children of Am. Revolution Grandmothers award, 1961, S.A.R. medal of appreciation, 1965-68; Pa. chptr. D.A.R. Am. Heritage 1st nat. award, 1967. Mem. D.A.R. (dir. 1959-68, chpt. regent 1962-65, South Central dir. 1968-71, sec. state conf. 1961, state dir. 1968-71, Pa. chmn. Washington luncheon 1972—, nat. vice chmn. geneal. record), Daus. Am. Colonists (regent 1962-64, York County Hist. Soc., Hist. Soc. Dauphin County, Huguenot Soc. Pa., Holy Spirit Hosp. Guild, Millersville State Coll. Alumni Assn., Soc. Descs. of Schwenkfeldian Exiles, Friends of Ft. Hunter. Republican. Presbyn. Clubs: New Cumberland Womens, Lions Aux., Harrisburg Civic (dir. 1968—, program chmn. outdoor dept. spl. tree planting project), Harrisburg Garden. Home: Hillcrest Manor New Cumberland PA 17170 Office: Box G New Cumberland PA 17070

RAMSAY, ETHEL MAY DAVIS (MRS. WILLIAM JAMES RAMSAY), educator; b. Salisbury, N.C., June 15, 1905; d. Angier Bryant and Ada Catherine (Taylor) Davis; B.A., Duke, 1926, M.A., 1928; postgrad. U. Tenn., 1958, Columbia Basin Community Coll., 1963; m. William James Ramsay, June 3, 1934; children—Mary, William, Richard, Robert, Frances. Cadet tchr. Durham (N.C.) city schs., 1927-29; tchr. English Kosciusko (Miss.) High Sch., 1929-31, Kingsport (Tenn.) high schs., 1931-34, Coulee City (Wash.) High Sch., 1957-58, Morristown (Tenn.) High Sch., 1958-62; asst. prof. English Tusculum Coll., Greeneville, Tenn., 1962-63; instr. Columbia Basin Coll., Pasco, Wash., 1963-70; Walters State Community Coll., Morristown, 1973-74. Mem. Am. Assn. Ret. Persons, Am. Assn. U. Profs., Nat., Wash. State ret. tchrs. assns., Phi Beta Kappa, Chi Delta Phi, Kappa Delta Pi. Republican. Methodist. Pub. book reviews to pub. catalogues and newspapers. Contbr. poetry to various publs. and anthologies. Address: 504 W Sixth N St Morristown TN 37814

RAMSDEN, NAOMI ROBINSON (MRS. CHARLES ANTHONY RAMSDEN), lawyer; b. nr. Newport News, Va., Oct. 14, 1942; d. Robert Frederick and Hilda (Wallach) Robinson; student U. Paris (France), 1963-64; B.S., U. Cal. at Berkeley, 1965; postgrad. U. Irvine, 1965-66; LL.B., Hastings Coll. Law, 1970; m. Charles Anthony Ramsden, Aug. 30, 1969. Law clk. Hurwitz, Hurwitz, Remer, Newport Beach, Cal., 1969; admitted to Cal. Bar, 1971; practiced in San Francisco, 1971-72, 74—; VISTA vol., staff atty. Legal Aid Soc. San Mateo County (Cal.), 1973-74. Vol. San Francisco Neighborhood Legal Assistance Found. Clin. Program, 1968-69. Mem. Am., San Mateo County bar assns., Cal. Trial Lawyers Assn., Lawyers Club San Francisco, San Francisco Opera Guild, San Francisco Opera Guild Bd. Aux., Sierra Club. Club: San Mateo Duplicate Bridge. Home: 24 W Santa Inez St San Mateo CA 94402 Office: 2221 Broadway Redwood City CA 94063

RAMSETH, LOIS RUTH, food co. exec.; b. Chgo., Dec. 10, 1917; d. Hans S. and Florence M. (Albright) Ramseth; student evening sch. Northwestern U., 1943-45. With Oscar Mayer & Co., Inc., Chgo., 1941—, asst. sec., 1951-71, sec., 1971—. Mem. Am. Soc. Corp. Secs. Home: 1 North Dee Rd Park Ridge IL 60068 Office: 5725 E River Rd Chicago IL 60631

RAMSEY, BERNICE EVA (MRS. WILLIAM L. RAMSEY), real estate broker; b. New Frankfort, Mo.; d. Elza Horton and Lillie Mae (Stalsworth) Allman; grad. high sch.; m. William L. Ramsey, Feb. 27, 1934. Buyer, mgr. Haggarty's Women's Apparel, Los Angeles, 1936-50; owner, real estate broker Bernice Ramsey Real Estate, LaCrescenta, Cal., 1950—. Commr. parks and recreation City of Glendale, Cal., 1964-67. Mem. Nat. Assn. Real Estate (pres. womens council 1961, state chpt. v.p. womens council 1963, state chpt. chaplin 1964), LaCrescenta Bd. Realtors (pres. 1971), LaCrescenta C. of C. Mem. Order Eastern Star. Home: 3300 Henrietta St LaCrescenta CA 91214 Office: 2431 Foothill Blvd LaCrescenta CA 91214

RAMSEY, C. MAURINE, nurse; b. Ft. Worth, Dec. 30, 1915; d. Elvitt Dean and Julia Ruth (Dinkins) Ramsey; Nursing diploma City County Hosp., Ft. Worth, 1939; student Tex. Christian U., 1940-42, Tex. Women's U., 1973-74. Asst. head nurse John Peter Smith Hosp., Ft. Worth, 1939, head nurse, 1939-40; head nurse Swift & Co., Ft. Worth, 1940-44, 46-71; asst. head nurse All Saints Hosp., Ft. Worth, 1971-72; occupational health nurse dept. health, edn. and welfare, USPHS, div. fed. employee health, health unit, Dallas, 1972-74, Ft. Worth, 1974—. Served to 1st lt., Nurses Corps, AUS, 1944-46; CBI. Mem. Am. Nurses Assn., Am. Assn. Indsl. Nurses, Am. Bd. Occupational Health Nurses, Women's Overseas Service League (pres. Ft. Worth unit 1968-70), Tex. Grad. Nurses Assn. (dir. 1948-50), Tex. Assn. Indsl. Nurses, Ft. Worth Area Indsl. Nurses Assn., City County Hosp. Nurses Alumna Assn. (pres. 1942). Home: 4709 Darla Dr Fort Worth TX 76132 Office: 819 Taylor St Room 13A25 Fort Worth TX 76102

RAMSEY, COLLETTE NICKS (MRS. HOBART COLE RAMSEY), civic worker; b. Nashville, Aug. 31, 1918; d. Charles S. and Virginia (Christian) Nicks; m. Hobart Cole Ramsey, Sept. 30, 1936; children—Collette Christian Wynn, Janet Houston Conrad. Founder, pres. Deafness Research Found., N.Y.C., 1958-68, vol. adminstr., dir. programs, fund-raising, 1958-68, chmn. bd., 1968—, chmn. exec. com., 1969-72, founder, cons., 1972—, instrumental in establishing affiliated Centurion Club, 1963. Mem. President's Com. Employment of Handicapped, 1964—; adviser N.J. League for Hard of Hearing, Inc., 1967—; mem. Surgeon Gen.'s Council, Nat. Inst. Neurol. Diseases and Blindness, 1964-67; mem. Nat. Com. Research in Neurol. Disorders, 1962—. Co-committeewoman Republican party, 1950's. Bd. dirs. Nat. Assn. Hearing and Speech Agys., N.J. Hist. Soc., Summit Speech Sch., Alexander Graham Bell Assn. for Deaf, Inc. (hon.); trustee St. Barnabas Med. Center, Livingston, N.J. Recipient Citizens award for Meritorious Service N.Y. Co. Med. Soc., 1962, Ann. citation Am. Triological Soc., 1963, Ann. Achievement award N.J. Acad. Ophthalmology and Otolaryngology, 1963, citation Am. Otological Soc., 1964, Honors citation Alexander Graham Bell Assn. for Deaf, 1965, Distinguished Service award Rotary Club N.Y., 1966, Eleanor Roosevelt award N.Y. League for Hard of Hearing, 1968, Citizen's Award medal Acad. Medicine N.J., 1968, merit award Am. Laryngol., Rhinol. and Otol. Soc., 1972, Recognition award Am. Acad. Opthalmology and Otolaryngology, 1972; named candidate for Great Living Ams. award Nat. C. of C., 1963, Outstanding Woman N.J. Fairleigh-Dickinson U., 1964. Conglist. Contbr. numerous articles, booklets in field of deafness. Office: 366 Madison Av New York City NY 10017

RAMSEY, ELIZABETH see Klagsbrunn, Elizabeth Ramsey

RAMSEY, EVELYN ADAMS (MRS. CHARLIE RAMSEY), ednl. adminstr.; b. Elizabethtown, Ky., Aug. 17, 1918; d. Sellie Preston and Louella (Spencer) Adams; B.A., Blue Mountain Coll., 1939; postgrad. Western Ky. U., 1939; M.S. in L.S., Spalding Coll., 1964; m. Charlie Ramsey, Dec. 31, 1943; children—Charles Leslie, Linda Margaret. Librarian, chief file sect. Armored Bd., Ft. Knox, Ky., 1941-46, editorial asst., 1946-47; librarian Kyoto (Japan) Dependent Schs., 1947, Hardin County Sch. System, Elizabethtown, 1962-71; dir. Hardin County Materials Center, Elizabethtown, 1971—. Mem. Assn. Sch. Adminstrs., Ky. Assn. Ednl. Suprs., Ky. Librarians Assn. Democrat. Baptist. Home: 608 Cherrywood St Elizabethtown KY 42701 Office: 110 S Main St Elizabethtown KY 42701

RAMSEY, MARJORIE ELIZABETH (MRS. CURTIS PAUL RAMSEY), educator, univ. dean; b. Kimball, Minn., May 25, 1921; d. William Emil and Emma Edith (Ryti) Leppa; B.S., St. Cloud State Coll., 1955, M.S., 1957; Ed.D. (Ford Found fellow), George Peabody Coll., 1961; m. Curtis Paul Ramsey, July 18, 1964; children—Rebecca, Cynthia. Tchr., prin., vis. lectr., Minn., 1940-57; asst. prof. St. Cloud State Coll., Minn., 1957-59; supr. edn. Montgomery County, Md., 1961-64; research asso. George Peabody Coll., Nashville, 1964-68; supr. Vanderbilt U., Nashville, 1964-69; asso. prof. early childhood edn. Kent (O.) State U., 1969-73, prof., 1973—, dean student personnel Coll. Edn., 1973—. Mem. Assn. for Supervision and Curriculum Devel., Nat. Assn. for Edn. Young Children, Internat. Reading Assn., Assn. for Childhood Edn. Internat., Delta Kappa Gamma, Kappa Delta Pi. Contbr. articles to profl. jours. Home: 1215 Fairview Dr Kent OH 44240

RAMSEY, ROSLYN WARREN BARSS (MRS. ROBERT H. RAMSEY), social worker; b. Glen Ridge, N.J., Dec. 6, 1924; d. Edward M. and Mary (Scott) Barss; B.A., Westminster Coll., 1947; postgrad., Harvard Grad. Sch. Edn., 1947-48; M.S., Simmons Coll. Sch. Social Work, 1951-53; m. Robert H. Ramsey, Aug. 31, 1952 (dec. Sept. 1963); children—John, Susan. Caseworker, Family Service of Rochester (N.Y.), 1954, Mass. Div. Mental Hygiene, 1955, Family and Children's Service, Richmond, Va., 1963-67; chief psychiat. social worker Ednl. Therapy Center, Richmond, 1967-71; psychiat. social work supr. Va. Treatment Center for Children, Richmond, 1971—. Mem. Nat. Assn. Social Workers (chmn. local council on mental health 1969-71). Presbyn. Home: 1810 Maple Shade Lane Richmond VA 23227 Office: Box IL Richmond VA 23201

RAMSEY, SALLY ANN SEITZ, state ofcl.; b. Columbus, O., Feb. 15, 1931; d. Albert Blazier and Mildred (Dodson) Seitz; B.A., Ohio State U., 1952, M.A., 1955, postgrad., 1963-66; postgrad. St. Mary Coll., Xavier, Kan., 1962; m. Edward Lewis Ramsey, Apr. 11, 1953 (div. Aug. 1962); children—Edward Lewis, Sylvia Ann. Research engr., then sr. research engr. N. Am. Aviation, Inc., Columbus, O. and Downey, Cal., 1962-67; legislative intern State of Ohio, 1964-65; research and information officer Ohio Dept. Urban Affairs, Columbus, 1967-68; adminstrv. specialist Ohio Dept. Devel., Columbus, 1968; asso. planner Div. State Planning, Fla. Dept. Adminstrn., Tallahassee, 1968—. Gray lady A.R.C., 1961-62; den mother Cub Scouts Am., 1964-65. Congl. campaign cons., 1966. Mem. Am. Polit. Sci. Assn., Am. Soc. Pub. Adminstrn., Kappa Kappa Gamma, Pi Sigma Alpha. Home: 2112 Faulk Dr Tallahassee FL 32303 Office: 660 Apalachee Pkwy Tallahassee FL 32301

RAMSEY, VIRGINIA CARRAWAY (MRS. JOSEPH HAWTHORNE RAMSEY), lawyer; b. Birmingham, Ala., Aug. 1, 1922; d. Charles Newton and Frances Ashley (Spaulding) Carraway; A.B., Randolph-Macon Woman's Coll., 1943; J.D., Samford U., 1971; m. Joseph Hawthorne Ramsey, Sept. 17, 1947 (dec. May 1973); children—Joseph Hawthorne, Charles Clark, Frances Virginia. Admitted to Ala. bar, 1971; asst. trust officer First Nat. Bank of Birmingham, 1971—. Mem. Am., Ala., Birmingham bar assns., Estate Planning Council Birmingham, Jefferson County Med. Aux., Birmingham Bar Aux., Phi Alpha Delta. Club: Birmingham Music (treas. 1972, 73).

RAMSEY-KLEE, DIANE M. (MRS. HARRY GRAYDON KLEE), research scientist; b. Duluth, Minn., Nov. 6, 1928; d. William Henry and Mildred (Miller) Ramsey; B.A. cum laude, U. Minn., 1950, M.A.,

1954, Ph.D., 1958; m. Benjamin Franklin Albitz, Aug. 19, 1950 (div. June 1961); m. 2d, Harry Graydon Klee, Dec. 7, 1968. Adminstrv. asst. Project B Am. Psychol. Assn., Mpls., 1954-55; research fellow, dept. psychology U. Minn., Mpls., 1955-58; advanced systems officer C.I.A., Washington, 1958-63; sr. research scientist Astropower Lab., McDonnell Douglas Corp., Newport Beach, Cal., 1963-67; research psychologist Reiss-Davis Child Study Center, Los Angeles, 1967-69; dir. R-K Research and System Design, Malibu, Cal., 1969—; instr. U. Minn., 1955-57, U. Va., 1961-62. Sci. editor Interdisciplinary Communications Program, Smithsonian Instn., Washington, 1968—; cons. research div. Reiss-Davis Child Study Center, Los Angeles, 1966-67, 71—, Community Electrocardiographic Interpretative Service, Denver, 1972, div. health care information systems and tech. Bur. Health Services Research and Evaluation, Rockville, Md., 1969—, Colo. Regional Cancer Center, Denver, 1973-74, Clin. Information Systems Group, U. Ala., Birmingham, 1974, office Information Systems, U. Cal. at San Francisco, 1974—. Mem. A.A.A.S., Am., D.C., Western psychol. assns., Am. Soc. Information Sci., N.Y. Acad. Scis., Phi Beta Kappa. Contbr. articles to profl. jours. Address: 3947 Ridgemont Dr Malibu CA 90265

RAND, AYN, writer, lectr.; b. Leningrad, Russia, 1905; grad. U. Leningrad, 1924; L.H.D. (hon.), Lewis and Clark Coll., 1963; m. Frank O'Connor, 1929. Came to U.S., 1926, naturalized, 1931. Screenwriter, 1932-34, 1944-49; lectr. colls. and univs.; editor, pub. The Objectivist, 1962-71, The Ayn Rand Letter, 1971—. Author: (plays) Night of January 16th, 1935, pub. in book form, 1968; The Unconquered, 1940; (novels) We the Living, 1936, Anthem, 1938; The Fountainhead (novel and screenplay), 1943; Atlas Shrugged, 1957; (non-fiction) For the New Intellectual, 1961; The Virtue of Selfishness, 1965; Capitalism: The Unknown Ideal, 1966; Introduction to Objectivist Epistemology, 1967; The Romantic Manifesto: A Philosophy of Literature, 1969; The New Left: The Anti-Industrial Revolution, 1971. Address: care Ayn Rand Letter 183 Madison Av New York City NY 10016

RAND, HELEN PIERCE (MRS. ROBERT W. RAND), civic worker, artist; b. Coldwater, Mich., Jan. 31, 1926; d. L. Earl and Marjorie (Treacher) Pierce; A.B., U. Mich., 1949; m. Robert W. Rand, Dec. 17, 1949; children—Carl Wheeler II, Richard Pierce. Instr. dentistry U. Mich., 1948-50, translator of Russian, 1951. Exhibited group shows Tower Gallery, Hollywood Park, 1965, Pasadena (Cal.) Pub. Library, 1965, Los Angeles City Hall, 1966, Pacific Art Guild Gallery, Westchester, Cal., 1966, Brand Library Gallery, Glendale, 1966, Occidental Bldg., Los Angeles, 1968, Westwood Art Assn., Los Angeles, 1965-67. Rec. sec. Jr. Philharmonic Com., Los Angeles, 1966—, 1st v.p., liaison rep. to Women for Music Center, 1971-72; rec. sec. Coll. Alumnae Aux. Assistance League, Los Angeles, 1959—. Mem. Women's Aux. Los Angeles County Med. Assn., U. Cal. Los Angeles Med. Faculty Wives (dir., chmn. ways and means 1967-68), Jr. Women Assos. U. Religious Conf., Mother's Club Harvard Sch. (bd. dirs. 1971-72). Home: 521 N Bristol Av Los Angeles CA 90049

RAND, KATHY SUE, pub. relations agy. exec.; b. Miami Beach, Fla., Feb. 24, 1945; d. William Robert and Rose (Lasser) Rand; B.A., Mich. State U., 1965; postgrad. San Francisco State Coll., 1966-67. Tchr. pub. schs., Chgo., 1965-66; asst. editor Lyons & Carnahan, publs., Chgo., 1967-68; mng. editor Cahners Pub. Co., Chgo., 1968-71; pub. relations writer SuperMarket Inst., Chgo., 1972-73; account exec. Pub. Communications, Inc., Chgo., 1973—. Mem. Women in Communications, Am. Civil Liberties Union, Elec. Women's Round Table (chpt. pres. 1971-72), Nat. Orgn. Women (regional dir. 1972—, mem. nat. bd. and exec. com. 1972—), Chgo. Women in Pub. (hon.), Common Cause, Mensa. Home: 502 W Roscoe St Chicago IL 60657 Office: 35 E Wacker Dr Chicago IL 60601

RAND, PATRICIA JUNE, botanist; b. St. Paul, June 6, 1926; d. Frank Lee and Flavia Clara (Otto) Rand; B.S., U. Minn., 1947, M.S., 1953; Ph.D., Duke U., 1965. Teaching asst., instr. U. Minn., Mpls., 1947-53; instr. Hamline U., St. Paul, 1953-58; teaching asst. Duke, 1958-60; instr., asst. prof. U. Ark., Fayetteville, 1961-66; asst. prof. U. Neb., Lincoln, 1966-73; sr. sci. adviser Atlantic Richfield Co., Los Angeles, 1973—. Ecol. cons. U.S. Nat. Park Service, 1960-70, Clark & Mnersen, Lincoln, 1969-72, Mits Kawamoto & Assos., Omaha, 1972-73, Hoskins Western, Sonderegger, Lincoln, 1970-71, W.S. Bur. Reclamation, 1968-72. Mem. Wilderness Park Com., Lincoln, 1968-73, S.E. Neb. Pub. Health Planning Council, 1971-73. Fellow A.A.A.S.; mem. Neb. Environmental Coalition (rec. sec. 1972-73, editor 1972-73), Zero Population Growth (v.p. Neb. chpt. 1970-73), Ecol. Soc. Am., Bot. Soc. Am., Am. Inst. Biol. Scis., S.W. Assn. Naturalists Grad. Women in Sci. (v.p. Iota chpt. 1970-71, nat. v.p. 1973-74, pres. 1974—), Sigma Xi (asso. sec. Neb. chpt. 1970-72). Columnist: Man and His World, Lincoln Jour. and Star, 1969-73. Contbr. articles to profl. jours. Home: 444 S Kingsley Dr Los Angeles CA 90020 Office: Environmental Protection Atlantic Richfield Co 515 S Flower St Los Angeles CA 90071

RANDALL, ANN MATHILDE, occupational therapist; b. Indpls., May 20, 1947; d. Theodore Harold and Emma Lee (Tinsley) Randall; B.S. cum laude, Tufts U., 1969. Staff occupational therapist Cin. Gen. Hosp., 1969-70; staff occupational therapist Riley Hosp. for Children, Indpls., 1970-74, chief occupational therapist Child Devel. Center, 1974—. Mem. Am., Ind. occupational therapy assns., Pi Theta Epsilon, Delta Sigma Theta (chpt. rec. sec. 1973—). Methodist (sec. commn. on Christian social concerns 1972—). Home: 3810 Rookwood Av Indianapolis IN 46208 Office: 1100 W Michigan St Indianapolis IN 46202

RANDALL, ANN MICHELLE KNIGHT (MRS. JULIUS THOMAS RANDALL), educator; b. N.Y.C., Oct. 19, 1942; d. Robert Leon and Ruth Mildred (Bayton) Knight; B.A. (Jesse Noyes Found. scholar), Barnard Coll., 1963; postgrad. N.Y. U., 1963-64; M.S. with honors, Columbia, 1967, postgrad., 1969—; m. Julius Thomas Randall, Nov. 8, 1963; 1 dau., Christine Renee. Claims adjuster U.S. Social Security Adminstrn., N.Y.C., 1963-64; library asst. U.S. Army, Bamberg, Germany, 1964-65; librarian trainee adult services Bklyn. Pub. Library, 1965-67; instr. City U. N.Y., Queens Coll., 1967-69; adj. lectr. Bklyn. Coll., 1969-73, asst. prof. for edn./instructional resources and African-Am. bibliography, 1973—. Lectr. librarianship Columbia, 1970-73, Pratt Inst., 1971-73, Queens Coll., 1972-73, Rutgers U., 1973; cons. R.R. Bowker Pub. Co., Urban Resources Systems, U. Mich., 1973—. Active Girl Scouts Am., YWCA, Bklyn. Recipient Brotherhood award Nat. Council Christian and Jews, 1968. Oratorical Prize, United Order Tents, 1959. Nat. Def. fellow, 1969-72. Mem. A.L.A., Acad. Polit. Sci., N.E.A., Spl. Libraries Assn. (mem. exec. bd. N.Y. documentation group 1969-71), Assn. for Study Negro Life and History, Beta Phi Mu. Contbr. articles to profl. jours. Office: Bklyn Coll Library Midwood Campus Av H City U NY Brooklyn NY 11210

RANDALL, CAROLYN DINEEN (MRS. JAMES D. RANDALL), lawyer; b. Syracuse, N.Y., Jan. 30, 1938; d. Robert Emmet and Carolyn Emily (Bareham) Dineen; A.B. summa cum laude, Smith Coll., 1959; LL.B., Yale, 1962; m. James D. Randall, Sept. 9, 1961; children—James Donald, Philip David, Stephen Edward. Admitted to D.C. bar, 1962, Tex. bar, 1963; practiced in Houston, 1962—; asso. atty. Fulbright, Crooker & Jaworski, Houston, 1962-72; asso. atty. Childs, Fortenbach, Beck & Guyton, Houston, 1972-73, partner, 1973—. Mem. Dallas regional panel Pres.'s Commn. on White House Fellows, 1972-74; mem. Houston dist. adv. council U.S. Small Bus. Adminstrn., 1972—. Mem. women's spl. gifts com. Houston Symphony Soc., 1965—. Trustee, mem. exec. com., treas. Houston Ballet Found., 1967-70. Mem. Phi Beta Kappa. Home: 3829 Chevy Chase Houston TX 77019 Office: PO Box 391 Houston TX 77001

RANDALL, EUDORA PATRICIA, nurse; b. North Bridgeton, Me., Jan. 23, 1930; d. Lewis Calvin and Emily Wilson (Sanborn) Randall; B.S. in Nursing, Boston U., 1960, M.S., 1965. Staff nurse Augusta (Me.) Gen. Hosp., 1951-52, VA Center, Togus, Me., 1952-55; with Me. Dept. Health and Welfare, 1956-73, staff nurse, supv., also pub. health nursing cons., 1973—; dir. nursing Portland (Me.) Health Dept. Mem. Am. Nurses Assn., Am. Pub. Health Assn., Am. Assn. Mental Deficiency, Am. Assn. U. Women, Nat. League Nursing, Royal Soc. Health, Altrusa Internat. Republican. Baptist. Home: RFD 1 Winthrop ME 04364 Office: 389 Congress St Portland ME 04111

RANDALL, LILLIAN PAULA HAEUSSLER, sculptor; b. Plato, Minn., Dec. 21, 1895; d. Carl Herman and Elizabeth Catherine (Scherer) Haeussler; student Ia. State Tchrs. Coll., 1916, Mpls. Inst. Arts, 1923, U. So. Cal., 1938, U. Cal. at Los Angeles, 1938-40, Otis Art Inst., 1963; Ph.D. in Biochemistry, St. Andrews Collegiate Coll., London, Eng., 1959; Ph.D. in Arts and Letters, Internat. Episcopal U., London, 1968; m. John R. Randall, Sept. 11, 1930 (div. 1943). Tchr. country sch., 1916-17; head biochemistry dept. Scripps Clinic, LaJolla, Cal., 1927-30; head biochemistry div. Labs. Huntington Hosp., Pasadena, Cal., 1930-43; head Randall Med. Lab., Pasadena Cal., 1943-63, ret., 1963; tchr. sculpture Pasadena Sch. Fine Arts, 1970; one-man shows Gallery 185, Pasadena, Frank Lang Gallery, Los Angeles, Downstairs Gallery, Pasadena, Taiwan U. Gallery, Cal. Inst. Tech. Gallery; exhibited art in group shows at Jack Carr Gallery, Occidental Coll. Gallery, Los Angeles State U. Gallery, Laguna Beach (Cal.) Art Museum, Riverside Art Gallery, John Nelson Gallery; represented in permanent collections Tournament Roses Bldg., Pasadena, Nat. Audubon Soc., Sacramento, also pvt. collections. Mem. Am. Chem. Soc., Pasadena Soc. Artists, Nat. Audubon Soc. (chpt. pres. 1966-68), Nat. Soc. Psychic Research. Contbr. poetry to Driftwind, Am. Poetry Mag., Poetry of Our Times, Squeezebox. Composer lyrics Seaward, 1928. Address: 441 Ramona Av Sierra Madre CA 91024

RANDALL, MARTHA CLAIRE, writer, editor; b. San Antonio, Oct. 6, 1940; d. Milton Cross and Martha Ruth (Young) Randall; B.S., Trinity U., San Antonio, 1962; postgrad. San Antonio Coll., 1965, 69-70. With Tri-City Pub. Co., San Antonio, 1962; civilian with Kelly AFB, Tex., 1962—, chief pub. relations/community relations div. Office Information, Hdqrs. USAF Security Service, 1972, writer-editor cryptologic dept., 1972—. Recipient 4 certificate recognition USAF, 1972. Mem. Armed Forces Pub. Information Council (v.p. 1970-71), Women in Communications, Council Internat. Relations. Presbyn. Home: 1430 Nacogdoches Rd San Antonio TX 78209 Office: Hdqrs USAF Cryptologic Depot/DAA Kelly AFB TX 78243

RANDALL, MARY ELISABETH DUDLEY (MRS. RICHARD RANDALL), ednl. adminstr.; b. Vanceboro, Me., Dec. 9, 1943; d. Warren Linwood and Elisabeth Holbrook (Davis) Dudley; B.A., U. Me., 1965; m. Richard Randall, June 27, 1964; 1 son, Matthew. Tchr., Winthrop (Me.) Jr. High Sch., 1965-66; registrar, dir. instnl. research and equal opportunity U. Me., Augusta, 1967—. Mem. Am., New Eng. assns. collegiate registrars and admissions officers, Nat. Orgn. Women. Home: Route 1 Bean Rd Readfield ME 04355 Office: U Maine at Augusta University Heights Augusta ME 04330

RANDALL, PRUDENCE BILUTAN (MRS. SALVATORE SERRAINO), editor; b. N.Y.C., Sept. 28, 1939; d. Eugene and Myrtle Harriett (Wright) Bilutan; B.S., Western Res. U., 1960, M.A., 1966; Ph.D., Case Western Reserve U., 1971; m. Salvatore Serraino, July 28, 1973. Coordinator speech and hearing therapy services Mayfield City Schs., Mayfield Heights, O., 1960-62; asst. to dean Mather Coll., Western Reserve U., Cleve., 1962-64; asst. dir. admissions, 1964-66, Ph.D. research fellow, 1966-69; sr. editor Ency. Edn., Crowell, Collier & Macmillan, Inc., N.Y.C., 1969-71; edn. editor Edn. Yearbook, Macmillan, Inc., N.Y.C., 1971—; adj. asst. prof. Baruch Coll. City U. N.Y., 1974. Vol., Meml. Sloan-Kettering Cancer Center, N.Y.C., 1969—; mem. Soc. Meml. Sloan-Kettering Cancer Center, 1972—. Mem. bd. overseers Case Western Reserve U., 1973-76, mem. vis. com. for Western Reserve Coll., 1970—. Mem. Am. Ednl. Research Assn., Am. Ednl. Studies Assn., Nat. Assn. Edn. Young Children, Nat. Assn. Women Deans, Adminstrs. and Counselors, History Edn. Soc., N.Y. Area Alumni Assn. Case Western Res. U. (v.p. 1973-75). Gamma Delta Tau. Republican. Episcopalian. Editor The Folio, 1965-66. Home: 2809 Quinlan St Yorktown Heights NY 10598 Office: 866 3d Av New York City NY 10022

RANDAZZO, CORINNE OHLSEN (MRS. SAMUEL RANDAZZO), ednl. adminstr.; b. Vidalia, La., Sept. 23, 1932; d. Albert Henry and Corinne Louise (Barlow) Ohlsen; B.A., U. Southwestern La., 1954; M.S., La. State U., 1958; postgrad. U. Okla., summer 1966, U. So. Miss., summers 1969, 70; m. Samuel Randazzo, June 17, 1956; 1 dau., Rene Ohlsen. Librarian, Martinville High Sch., St. Martinville, La., 1954-59, Natchez (Miss.) High Sch., 1959-66; library supr. Natchez Pub. Schs., 1966—. Instr. library sci. U. So. Miss., Hattiesburg, 1968-69, U. Okla., 1967-68. Mem. Am., Miss. (v.p. 1971) library assns., Miss. Edn. Assn., Miss. Assn. Sch. Librarians (pres. 1965). Roman Catholic. Home: 103 Carter Vidalia LA 71373 Office: 301 Main St Natchez MS 39120

RANDAZZO, SHIRLEY ANN ZONDORAK, advt. agy. exec.; b. Hackensack, N.J., Jan. 22, 1940; d. Michael James and Ann Constance (Rusin) Zondorak; student Drake U., 1958; m. Angelo Randazzo, Aug. 16, 1958 (div. Nov. 1967); children—Suzanne, Frank Michael. Owner, Randazzo's Floris, Lodi, N.J., 1962-67; asst. internat. mgr. Aircraft Radio Corp., Boonton, N.J., 1967-68; writer Cessna Aviation Co., Wichita, Kan., 1968-69; advt. mgr. Radiation Machinery Corp., Parsippany, N.J., 1969-70; with Ad-Com, Inc., advt. and pub. relations, Boonton, 1970—, exec. v.p., 1971—. Author: (scripts and records) Effects of Gamma Radiation, 1970, Obviousness of Sun Sign Astrology, 1972. Home: 200 Baldwin Rd Parsipanny NJ 07054 Office: 811-B Main St Boonton NJ 07005

RANDEL, LUCILLE MARIE-BERTHE GENDRON (MRS. OGDEN MORRIS RANDEL), artist; b. Cohoes, N.Y., July 4, 1908; d. Delphis and Beatrice (LaFreniere) Gendron; student McGill U., 1926-28; m. Ogden Morris Randel, Jan. 27, 1937; children—Gail Michelle (Mrs. William Richard), Andrea Mai. Statis. clk. N.Y. State Edn. Dept., Albany, Bur. Field Services, N.Y.C., 1928-39; statis. clk. Columbia Tchrs. Coll., 1940-41; one-man shows at Gallery 9, Chatham (N.J.) United Counties Trust-Peoples Trust, YWCA; exhibited in group shows at Allied Artists, Audubon Artists, Nat. Arts Club travelling exhibits; represented in permanent collections at Bell Telephone Labs., Allied Chem. Corp., Union-Camp Paper Co., Summit Trust Co. Art instr. YWCA, Summit, N.J., 1964-67, Millburn Art Center, 1969. Chmn. recreation program, O'Fallon, Ill., 1954-56; A.R.C. Grey Lady occupational therapy Lyons (N.J.) Vet. Hosp., 1958-61; active Urban League, Summit, N.J. Recipient art awards Am. Artist Profl. League, Summit Art Center, Hunterdon County Art Center, Flemington Prize Winners Exhibit, Morris County Art Center, Garden State Watercolor Assn. Mem. Am. Artists Profl. League, Hudson Valley Artists, N.J. Painters and Sculptors Art Assn., Nat. Soc. Painters in Casein-Old Bergen Art Guild, Nat. Arts Club, Allied Artists (asso.), Am. Watercolor Soc. (asso.), Audubon Artists (asso., award), Garden State Watercolor Soc. Roman Catholic. Home: 37 Constantine Pl Summit NJ 07901

RANDOLPH, ELIZABETH GARLAND SCHMOKE (MRS. JOHN DANIEL RANDOLPH), educator; b. Farmville, N.C.; d. John Hagans and Pearl (Johnson) Schmoke; A.B., Shaw U., 1936; M.A., U. Mich., 1945; postgrad. U. N.C., 1964; m. John Daniel Randolph, June 7, 1950 (dec. Dec. 1963). Tchr., English and French, New Hope High Sch., Rutherfordton, N.C., 1936-37; tchr. librarian DuBois High Sch., Wake Forest, N.C., 1937-43, Jordan Sellars High Sch., Burlington, N.C., 1943-44; tchr. English, adminstrv. asst. W. Charlotte (N.C.) High Sch., 1944-58; prin. University Park Elementary Sch., Charlotte, 1958-68; dir. ESEA activities Charlotte-Mecklenburg Schs., 1968-73, adminstrv. asst. for sch. operations, 1973—. Mem. Charlotte Hosp. Authority, Bd. dirs. Charlotte-Mecklenburg Day Care Council, N.C. chpt. Am. Cancer Soc.; bd. mgrs. Charlotte Meml. Hosp. Mem. Am. Assn. U. Women, N.C. Kindergarten Assn. (dir.), N.E.A. (life), Assn. Supervision and Curriculum Devel. (exec. council), Charlotte Bus. and Profl. Womans Club, Links (pres. Charlotte chpt.), N.A.A.C.P., Delta Kappa Gamma, Alpha Kappa Alpha (Mid-Atlantic regional dir. 1964-68, chmn. standards com.). Home: 1616 Patton Av Charlotte NC 28208 Office: Edn Center PO Box 149 Charlotte NC 28201

RANDOLPH, KATHERINE, ednl. adminstr.; b. Cin.; d. Solomon Elbert and Clara (Hollins) Randolph; B.A., Bennett Coll., 1947; postgrad. Cornell U., 1953; M.A., Columbia, 1957; postgrad. State U. N.Y., 1964—. Children's supr. N.Y. State Tng. Sch. for Girls, Hudson, 1949-51, instn. edn. tchr., 1951-52, instn. edn. dir., 1954-56, instn. edn. supr., 1952-54, 56-59, 66-68; dir. Brookwood Annex, Closed Treatment Center, Hudson, N.Y., 1966-68; dir. edn. Bedford Hills (N.Y.) Correctional Facility, 1972—. Cons. in intercultural relations N.Y. State Edn. Dept., 1969—; mem. adv. council Westchester Community Coll.; pres. N.Y. State Tng. Sch. Fed. Credit Union, 1963-69. Mem. Delta Kappa Gamma. Home: 450 Dunham Av Mount Vernon NY 10553 Office: Bedford Hills Correctional Facility 247 Harris Rd PO Box 244 Bedford Hills NY 10507

RANDOLPH, MARY K. (MRS. JENNINGS RANDOLPH), wife of U.S. senator from W. Va.; d. Frank and Gertrude (Scherr) Babb; grad. Potomac State Coll., Beaver Coll.; m. Jennings Randolph, Feb. 18, 1933; children—Jennings Randolph, Frank Babb. Formerly field worker W. Va. Dept. Pub. Health. Home: 4608 Reservoir Rd NW Washington DC 20007

RANGER, LYDIA SUMIKO ASATO, librarian; b. Kailua, Hawaii, Sept. 2, 1927; d. Shuki and Kame (Uezu) Asato; B.A., U. Hawaii, 1958; M.S., U. So. Cal., 1959; m. William R. Ranger, May 29, 1965. Children's librarian Inglewood br. Los Angeles County Library, 1959-60; children's librarian Hawaii State Library System, 1960-69, head State Library for Handicapped, Honolulu, 1969—. Mem. A.L.A., Hawaii Library Assn. Office: 402 Kapahulu Av Honolulu HI 96815

RANIA, MILDRED IRWIN DICK (MRS. JOSEPH JOHN RANIA), genealogist, heraldist; b. Cambridge, Mass., May 29, 1912; d. William James and Margaret (McQuillan) Dick; student Boston U., 1930-31; A.A., San Bernardino Valley Jr. Coll., 1962; B.A., Brantridge Forest Sch., Eng., 1970; m. Joseph John Rania, Sept. 9, 1947; children—Mrs. Grace Guyton, Mrs. Dora Morris. Geneal. research on numerous families, 1955—, including Dick, McQuillan, Irvine, Park, Ewing, Whittaker, Higgins, Gough, Moore, Thompson, Greer, Lindsay, Ker, Adair, Kellett, Dowdeswell, Covert, King. Harris, Adams, Holmes; research on Irish history and local libraries. Supr. San Bernardino County Welfare Dept. Mem. Friends Prospect Park Com. Fellow Augustan Soc. (geneal. rev. editor Augustan), Soc. Antiquaries, Scotland; mem. Scottish Geneal. Soc., Heraldry Soc. (London), Parke Soc. (life), Lincoln Meml. Assos., Ulster-Irish Soc. Cal., Redlands Hort. and Improvement Soc., Instituto Culturals Mexicano-Etiope, Mexicano-Belga, Mexicano-Tunecino, Mexican Japanese Red Cross, Am., Internat. heraldry socs., Order St. Lazarus of Jerusalem (dep. sec. gen. grand priory Am.). Republican. Author: Songs of a Coast Guard Wife, 1957; The McQuillan Family, 1965. Pub. The William Dick Line, 1966, Hound of the North, 1973—. Home: 218 W Fern Av Redlands CA 92373

RANICH, ELSIE, state ofcl.; b. Port Jervis, N.Y., June 5, 1930; d. Arthur Lee and Margaret Rainey (Cameron) Clark; grad. pub. high sch.; children by previous marriage—Terry (Mrs. Gino Prestimonico), Tracy, Shelley, Lorilee. Stenographer, N.Y. Dept. Social Welfare, Otisville, 1957-59; policy writer R.C. Lain, Inc., Port Jervis, N.Y., 1959-61; sr. stenographer N.Y. Exec. Dept. div. for youth, Middletown, 1961—. Owner race horses, Monticello, N.Y., and Goshen, N.Y., 1966—. Mem. U.S. Trotting Assn., N.Y. State Civil Service Employees Assn. Home: 106 Mills Av Middletown NY 10940 Office: Hill Station Box 144 Middletown NY 10940

RANKER, IRENE MAY PLATTS (MRS. JESS RANKER), univ. adminstr.; b. Detroit, Apr. 1, 1924; d. Ralph Hollister and May Etta (MacPherson) Platts; A.A., Harbor Coll., 1964; B.A., Marymount Coll., 1966; M.Ed., Loyola U., 1970; m. Jess Ranker, June 13, 1969; children—Kevin Lance Kelly, Valerie Ann Kelly. Dir. relations with schs. and colls. Cal. State U. at Fullerton, 1966—. Sec. adv. bd. County Mental Health Dept., South Bay, 1970-72. Mem. Am. Assn. U. Women, Pacific Assn. Coll. Registrars and Admissions Officers (mem. exec. com. 1971—). Presbyn. (ruling elder 1966—). Home: 37 Silver Spring Dr Rolling Hills Estates CA 90274 Office: Cal State U Fullerton CA 92634

RANKIN, DONNA LEE CARPENTER, lawyer; b. Pittsfield, Mass., Oct. 14, 1943; d. Thomas James and Donna Louise (Kramer) Carpenter; A.B. cum laude, Oberlin Coll., 1965; J.D., U. Chgo., 1971; m. J.W. Rankin, June 25, 1966. Tchr. Ellis Jr. High Sch., Elgin, Ill. 1965-66, Hirsch High Sch., Chgo., 1966; computer programmer, systems analyst Continental Assn. Co., Chgo., 1966-68; admitted to Ill. bar, 1971, since practiced in Chgo.; asso. firm Hopkins, Sutter, Owen, Mulroy & Davis, 1971—. Mem. Am., Chgo. bar assns., Women's Bar Assn. Ill., Order of Coif, Law Rev., Lawyers for Creative Arts. Episcopalian (substitute ch. organist 1974—). Office: 1 First National Plaza Suite 5200 Chicago IL 60670

RANKIN, MARJORIE EUNICE, educator; b. Troy, N.Y.; d. Alexander and Melissa (Speidel) Rankin; B.S. in Home Econs., Russell Sage Coll., 1939; M.S., Cornell U., 1945. Tchr. home econs. Argyle (N.Y.) Central Sch., 1939-41, Batavia (N.Y.) Jr.-Sr. High Sch., 1941-44; instr. Coll. Home Econs., Drexel U., Phila., 1945-46, asst. prof., 1946-50, asso. prof., 1950-55, prof., 1955—, asst. dean, 1955-62, asso. dean, 1962-63, dean, 1963—. Mem. ednl. adv. com. Wool Bur., Inc., 1954-57. Trustee Community Coll. of Phila., 1971-73. Recipient

Doris L. Crockett distinguished service alumnae award Russell Sage Coll., 1965. Mem. Am. Assn. U. Women (pres. Phila. br. 1966-68), Am. (chmn. textiles and clothing sect., mem. exec. council 1954-56, chmn. agy. mem. unit 1968-70), Pa. (treas. 1959-61, 64-65, pres. 1970-71), Phila. (pres. 1955-56) home econs. assns., N.E.A., Nat. Council Adminstrs. Home Econs., League Women Voters, Omicron Nu, Phi Kappa Phi. Democrat. Christian Scientist. Contbg. author Guide to Modern Clothing, 1962. Home: 2136 Locust St Philadelphia PA 19103

RANKIN, PEGE BETTY (MRS. HERBERT E. RANKIN), educator; b. Twin Falls, Ida., July 23, 1919; d. Marion P. and Margaret (Conway) Betty; B.A., U. Cal. at Berkeley, 1941, tchrs. credential, 1967; postgrad. U. Cal. at Berkeley, Cal. State Coll., Savannah State Coll., San Francisco State Coll.; m. Herbert E. Rankin, June 5, 1941; children—Greg Robert, Todd Conway. Tchr. contract bridge San Francisco Bay area, 1950-69; press officer Oakland (Cal.) Pub. Schs., 1967—; tchr. journalism Skyline High Sch., Oakland, 1967—. Tchr. guide European coll. tours, summers 1970-72. Chmn. div. fund Am. Cancer Soc., 1958; organizer, condr. Mental Health Bridge Charity, 1961; mem. Friends of Herrick Hosp., Friends of Berkeley Library. Wall Street Jour. Newspaper Fund fellow, 1969. Mem. Am. Assn. U. Women, Am. Contract Bridge League, Oakland Press Honor Assn., Women in Communications (scholarship chmn. 1973), Columbia Scholastic Press Assn., Journalism Educators No. Cal., Alpha Chi Alpha. Republican. Methodist. Club: Fannie Hill Ski (San Francisco). Office: 12250 Skyline Blvd Oakland CA 94619

RANKIN, VELDA FRANCES (MRS. RALPH THORTON RANKIN), textile-clothing specialist, educator; b. Spearville, Kan., May 20, 1915; d. Walter Henry and Frances Helen (Hansen) Umbach; B.S., Kan. State U., 1937; M.S., 1966; m. Ralph Thornton Rankin, July 18, 1937; 1 dau., Roberta (Mrs. Dale Mattheis). Tchr. Bucklin (Kan.) High Sch., 1945-52; home economist Kan. State U., Manhattan, 1952-63; clothing and textiles specialist U. Mo., Columbia, 1966—; demonstrator, sales hostess Barlow and Selig Mfg. Co. Oklahoma City, 1937-41. Mem. Gov. Safety Council, 1950-61. Recipient Mental Health grant Kan. Mental Health Inst., 1966, Delta Kappa Gamma scholarship, 1966. Mem. Fashion Group Inc., Am. Assn. U. Women, Am., Mo. home economist assns., Omicron Nu, Epsilon Sigma Phi, Delta Kappa Gamma, Phi Delta Gamma, Gamma Sigma Delta. Club: Soroptimist (pres., 1950-51) (Wellington, Kan.). Author: Clothing World of A Girl, 1969. Home: 908 Fairview Rd Columbia MO 65201

RANNEY, HELEN MARGARET, physician, educator; b. Summer Hill, N.Y., Apr. 12, 1920; d. Arthur C. and Alesia (Toolan) Ranney; A.B., Barnard Coll., 1941; M.D., Columbia, 1947. Intern Presbyn. Hosp., N.Y.C., 1947-48, resident 1948-50; practice medicine, specializing in internal medicine, hematology, N.Y.C., 1954-70; asst. physician Presbyn. Hosp., 1954-60; instr. Coll. Phys. and Surgeons Columbia, 1954-60; asso. prof. medicine Albert Einstein Coll. Medicine, 1960-64, prof. medicine, 1965-70; prof. medicine State U. N.Y., Buffalo, 1970-73; chmn. dept. medicine U. Cal., San Diego, 1973—. Mem. Am. Soc. for Clin. Investigation, Am. Soc. Hematology, Harvey Soc., Am. Assn. Physicians, Nat. Acad. Sci., Inst. Medicine, Phi Beta Kappa, Sigma Xi, Alpha Omega Alpha. Home: 6229 La Jolla Mesa Dr La Jolla CA 92037 Office: Dept Medicine 8110 University Hosp 225 W Dickinson St San Diego CA 92103

RANSDELL, JACQUELINE MCCARTHY (MRS. ERNEST DICKENS RANSDELL), pub. information officer; b. Norfolk, Va., Oct. 5, 1933; d. John Linus and Rosebud (Cowan) McCarthy; A.A., Coll. William and Mary-Va. Polytech. Inst., 1953; A.B. in Phys. Edn., U. N.C., 1955, M.A. in Communications, 1959; m. Ernest Dickens Ransdell, Dec. 12, 1959; children—Jennifer Lynn, Jeffrey Ernest. Hosp. recreation worker A.R.C., Maxwell AFB, Ala., 1955-57; pub. information officer, editor N.C. Dept. Mental Health, Raleigh, 1959-73; chief standards services N.C. Div. Mental Health Services, Raleigh, 1973—. Adv. bd. Raleigh Parks and Recreation Dept., 1972—. Prodn. mgr. N.C. Jour. Mental Health, 1971-73. Presbyn. (Circle chmn. 1971-73). Editor: Resume, 1968-73. Home: 3004 Ruffin St Raleigh NC 27607 Office: 325 N Salisbury St Raleigh NC 27611

RANSDELL, LENA GIBBS (MRS. DENTON T. RANSDELL), ret. librarian; b. Anderson County, Ky., July 26, 1903; d. Ezra and Mary Zella (Moffett) Gibbs; B.S., Spaulding Coll., Louisville, 1959, M.S. in L.S., 1962; m. Denton T. Ransdell, May 26, 1927; 1 dau., Nancy Gene (Mrs. Wayne E. Scott). Elementary sch. tchr. Louisville Sch. Dist., 1945-66; librarian V.H. Engelhard Sch., 1966-72, ret. Mem. Nat., Ky. edn. assns., Ky. Assn. Sch. Librarians, Ky. Library Assn., Ky. Audio Visual Assn., Assn. Childhood Edn., D.A.R., Ky. Hist. Soc. (life), Daus. War 1812, Colonial Dame 17th Century, Daus. and Founders Patriots of Am., Daus. Am. Colonies, Delta Kappa Gamma. Baptist. Club: Filson (life) (Louisville). Home: 124 S Crestmoor Av Louisville KY 40206

RANSMEIER, JUDITH DUNLOP MULLIGAN (MRS. JOHN C. RANSMEIER), lawyer; b. Bklyn., Nov. 8, 1943; d. William Haesloop and Helen Julia (Kliemand) Dunlop; B.A., Bennington Coll., 1966; J.D., Boston U., 1969; m. Edward J. Mulligan, Jr., May 25, 1968 (dec. Apr. 1971); m. 2d, John C. Ransmeier, Feb. 16, 1974. Admitted to N.H. bar, 1969; atty. Office of Atty. Gen., State of N.H., Concord, 1969-71; mem. firm McLane, Graf, Greene & Brown, Manchester, 1971—. Bd. dirs. Merrimack Valley Day Care Service, Concord. Mem. N.H. Bar Assn., League of N.H. Craftsmen (dir. 1971—). Home: 9 Grover St Concord NH 03301 Office: 40 Stark St Manchester NH 03101

RANSOHOFF, BABETTE (MRS. ARTHUR LEE RANSOHOFF), Republican nat. committeewoman; b. N.Y.C., Mar. 25, 1904; d. Martin and Annie (Jackson) Strauss; B.A., Vassar Coll., 1925; m. Arthur Lee Ransohoff, Feb. 10, 1926; children—Martin, Jack, Barbara (Mrs. Howard Burnett). Vice pres. Conn. Soc. for Prevention Blindness; dir. Family and Children's Center; v.p. Stamford Mus. Mem. Republican Nat. Com. from Conn., 1959-65, 72—, vice chmn., mem. exec. com., 1963—. Trustee Ferguson Library; mem. bd. Nat. Soc. Prevention Blindness; mem. Conn. Library Com. Club: Vassar (N.Y.C. and Fairfield County). Home: Wyndover Lane N Stamford CT 06902

RANSOM, MARY ANN, office supply co. exec., musician; b. Sistersville, W.Va., Jan. 25, 1916; d. Lewis Velton and Florence (Clawson) Ransom; student DeSales Heights Acad., 1933-34, Ohio U., 1941-42. With Parkersburg Office Supply (W.Va.), 1934—, office mgr., 1934-42, store mgr., 1942-47, sec.-treas., dir., 1947—; Violinist, Marietta Coll. Symphony Orch., 1963—. W.Va. rep. nat. bd. Women's Med. Coll. Pa., 1953. Trustee Alderson-Broaddus Coll., Phillipi, W.Va., 1971—. Mem. Community Concert Assn. (v.p.), D.A.R., P.E.O. (rec. sec., 1961), Nat. Soc. Arts and Letters. Baptist. Club: Parkersburg Country. Home: 601 10th and One Half St Parkersburg WV 26101 Office: 326 5th St Parkersburg WV 26101

RANSON, MARY KATHLEEN, educator; b. Farmville, Va., Aug. 3, 1915; d. Lee Edward and Nannie Lee (Bowman) Ranson; B.S., Longwood Coll., 1936; M.A., George Peabody Coll., 1941; postgrad. Smith Coll., 1943, William and Mary Coll., 1945, Tchrs. Coll. Columbia, 1950; Ed.D., U. Mo., 1952. Tchr. elementary sch. Spottswood, Va., 1936-40; tchr., asst. county supr. Liberty Acad., Bedford, Va., 1940-42; supervising tchr., instr. edn. Ga. State Coll. for Women, Milledgeville, 1942-43; instr. psychology, counselor reading and study services U. Mo., Columbia, 1947-52; prof. edn. Central Mo. State Coll., Warrensburg, 1952—. Leader, Girl Scouts U.S.A., Farmville, Va., 1935-36; judge Kansas City Sci. Fairs. Served with WAVES, 1943-46. Recipient award Am. Legion, 1928. Mem. Internat. Reading Assn., Mo. Acad. Sci., Am. Psychol. Assn., Am. Assn. U. Women, Am. Assn. U. Profs., Am. Soc. Curriculum Devel., Assn. Student Teaching, Mo. Assn. Social Welfare, Mo. Council Children and Youth, Mo. Assn. Childhood Edn. (pres. 1968-70), Assn. Childhood Edn. (internat. conf. planning com. 1971-73, internat. com. to write action plan for children), Am. Coll. Personnel Assn., Pi Lambda Theta, Psi Chi, Delta Kappa Gamma, Alpha Pi Zeta, Kappa Delta Pi, Alpha Lambda Delta, Alpha Phi Sigma. Clubs: Hot Springs Village Country, Cherokee Village Country. Editorial bd. Jour. Thought, 1966—. Contbr. articles to profl. jours. Home: Hwy 13 S Route 5 Warrensburg MO 64093

RANSON, NANCY S., artist; b. Manhattan, N.Y.C., Sept. 13, 1905; d. Bernard and Ida (Jablonsky) Sussman; grad. Pratt Inst. Art Sch., 1926, B.F.A., 1974; student Art Students League, Bklyn. Mus. Art Sch.; m. Jo Ranson, Jan. 1927 (dec. July 1965); children—Justine (Mrs. Scott Schachter), Ellen Toby (Mrs. Phillip Adams). Exhibited at Am. Water Color Soc., 1940, 42, 43, Nat. Assn. Women Artists, 1943—, Bklyn. Soc. Artists, 1941-62, Am. Soc. Contemporary Artists, 1963—, Tomorrow's Masterpieces, 1943, Artists for Victory, 1944, Critics Choice Show, Grand Central Galleries, 1947, Prize Winner's Show, 1947, Butler Art Inst., 1950, Bklyn. Artists Biennial, Bklyn. Mus., 1950, 54, 56, N.W. Printmakers Internat., 1952, 56, Boston, 1955, Silvermine Guild Ann., 1956, Nat. Mus. of Art, Sydney, Australia, 1956, Nat. Exhibition Contemporary Arts U.S., Pomona, Cal., 1956, N.Y. Soc. Women Artists, 1952—, Am. Color Print Soc., 1952—, Pa. Acad. Fine Art, 1957, Color Prints of The Americas, N.J. State Mus., 1970, other shows; one-woman shows George Binet Gallery, N.Y., 1948, 50, Bklyn. Pub. Library Main Br., 1951, Mexican Govt. Tourist Commn., Radio City, N.Y., 1952, U. Me., 1964; exhibited in group shows in museums and galleries U.S., India, Can., France, Switzerland, Japan, including Artists Equity, Whitney Mus., 1951, others; represented collections at Fogg Mus. Art, Mus. Art, Norfolk, Va., Brandeis U., U. Me., Mexican Govt. Tourist Commn., Mus. City N.Y., Key West Art Hist. Soc., Reading Pub. Mus., Free Library, Phila., also nat. mus., Jerusalem, Israel, New Delhi, India, Tokyo, Japan, Sydney, Australia. Recipient hon. mention Bklyn. Mus., 1946; Nat. Assn. Women Artists Ann., 1952, Clendenin prize, 1953, Medal of Honor in Graphics, 1956, Nat. Acad. Galleries, 1952; popular painting prize Critics Choice Show Grand Central Galleries, 1947; Grumbacher award, Bklyn. Soc. Artists, 1954, 1st prize in graphics, 1955, 58. Presentation Print, Joseph Torch award, 1955, Francesca Wood Award, 1955; 1st prize graphics Nat. Assn. Women Artists, 1958, print and drawing exhbn., 1962, Harold Kovner prize Audubon Artists Ann., 1958, award, 1961; Gramercy prize Nat. Soc. Painters in Casein, 1963; Andrews-Nelson-Whitehead award Am. Soc. Contemporary Artists, 1964, First prize in Graphics, 1970; MacDowell Found. fellowship, 1964. Mem. N.Y. Soc. Women Artists, Nat. Assn. Women Artists (chmn. fgn. exhbns. 1964-67, chmn. admissions 1969-71, chmn. oil jury 1973-75), Bklyn. Soc. Artists (corr. sec. 1948-53, pres. 1954-56), Am. Color Print Soc., Hunterdon County Art Center, Audubon Artists (chmn. awards com. 1958, dir. graphics 1970-73), Nat. Soc. Painters in Casein and Acrylics, Am. Soc. Contemporary Artists (chmn. constitution 1963—, pres. 1969-71, permanent dir.), Internat. Assn. Art (del. U.S. com.). Lecture: Art and Archaeology Around the World. Home and studio: 1299 Ocean Av Brooklyn NY 11230

RANUCCI, MARGUERITE CULLEN, statistician; b. Trenton, N.J., Apr. 12, 1949; d. Eugene Joseph and Mildred Joan (Cullen) Ranucci; B.A., Anna Maria Coll., 1971; postgrad. Trenton State Coll., 1974—. Statis. researcher State Dept. Edn., Trenton, N.J., 1971-73. Worcester student co-chmn. Senator E.M. Kennedy's Senatorial campaign, 1970; active Senator George McGovern Presdl. campaign, Trenton, 1971. Mem. Am. Assn. Mental Deficiency, Common Cause. Democrat. Office: 225 W State St Trenton NJ 08625

RAPHAEL, MARGARET ANN, mathematician; b. N.Y.C., Oct. 28, 1923; d. Walter Davidson and Anna Frances (Sharpe) Raphael; B.A., Immaculate Heart Coll., 1945; M.S., St. Louis U., 1958. Tchr. math. high schs., Long Beach, Cal., 1946-49, 55-57, 59-60, Los Angeles, 1949-51, 52-54, San Luis Obispo, Cal., 1951-52, Downey, Cal., 1954-55; asst. prof. Immaculate Heart Coll., Los Angeles, 1960-67; mathematician Naval Weapons Center, China Lake, Cal., 1967—, coordinator Fed. Women's Program, 1970—. Mem. Math. Assn. Am. Democrat. Roman Catholic. Home: 1027 N Norma St Ridgecrest CA 93555 Office: Code 5124 Naval Weapons Center China Lake CA 93555

RAPHAEL, MARJORIE, nun; b. Bronxville, N.Y., Oct. 17, 1923; d. Donald DuPuy and Marjorie Eudora (MacMonnies) Wysong; B.A., Barnard Coll., 1945. Joined Soc. of St. Margaret, Anglican Ch., 1947; dietician St. Margaret's Nursing Home, Montreal, Can., 1951-54; missionary, Port-au-Prince, Haiti, 1955-62; tchr. art history Coll. St. Pierre, Port-au-Prince, 1962-63; asst. superior Soc. St. Margaret in Am., Boston, 1963-65, mother superior, 1965—. Rep. Missionary Diocese Haiti at triennial Episcopal Churchwomen, 1958, 61; founder Foyer Notre Dame, home for aged underpriviledged, Haiti, 1962; dir. ann. camp conf. for women, Haiti, 1956-60. Address: St Margaret's Convent 17 Louisberg Sq Boston MA 02108

RAPIN, ISABELLE JULIETTE MARTHA (MRS. HAROLD OAKLANDER), physician; b. Lausanne, Switzerland, Dec. 4, 1927; d. Rene and Mary Coe (Reeves) Rapin; Baccalaureat Letters, Gymnase de Jeunes Filles, 1943-46; Swiss Fed. diploma physician, U. Lausanne Med. Sch., 1946-52, Doctorate Medicine, 1955; m. Harold Oaklander, Apr. 5, 1959; children—Anne Louise, Christine, Stephen, Peter. Intern dept. pediatrics N.Y. U., Bellevue Med. Center, 1953-54; resident Columbia-Presbyn. Med. Center, N.Y.C., 1954-57, asst. neurologist, 1957-58; asst. vis. physician in medicine (neurology) Bronx (N.Y.) Municipal Hosp. Center, 1958-63; asso. vis. pediatric neurologist Bronx Mun. Hosp. Center, Montefiore, Lincoln, Morrisania hosps., 1963-69, vis. pediatric neurologist, 1969—; asst. in neurology Columbia, 1957-58; instr. in neurology Albert Einstein Coll. Medicine, 1958-61, instr. in pediatrics, 1960-61, asst. prof. neurology and pediatrics, 1962-67, asso. prof., 1967-72, prof., 1972—. Fellow Am. Acad. Neurology; mem. Assn. Research Nervous and Mental Diseases, Assn. Univ. Profs. Neurology, A.A.A.S., Physician's Forum, N.Y. Acad. Scis., Child Neurology Soc., Internat. Child Neurology Assn., Internat. Neuropsychology Soc., Soc. for Neuroscis. Home: 158-18 Riverside Dr W New York City NY 10032 Office: Albert Einstein Coll Medicine 1300 Morris Park Av Bronx NY 10461

RAPPAPORT, ANNA MARIA (MRS. B. HOWARD RAPPAPORT), actuary; b. New Orleans, Sept. 15, 1940; d. Ludwig and Gertrude (Goldschmidt) Guckenheimer; student U. Chgo., 1956-58; m. B. Howard Rappaport, Sept. 17, 1958; 1 dau., Jennifer. Actuarial asst. N.Y. Life Ins. Co., N.Y.C., 1958-62; sr. v.p. Standard Security Life Ins. Co. of N.Y., N.Y.C., 1962-73, chief actuary, 1962-73; second v.p., asso. actuary Equitable Life Assurance Soc. U.S., N.Y.C., 1973—. Adj. faculty Coll. Ins., N.Y.C., 1966-71. Recipient, Mademoiselle Merit award Mademoiselle mag., 1964, Amita Sister award Amita, 1965. C.L.U. Mem. Soc. Actuaries (gov. 1971-74), Actuaries Club N.Y. (pres. 1974—), Am. Risk and Ins. Assn., Assn. Computing Machinery, Inst. Actuaries (asso.), Am. Acad. Actuaries. Office: 1285 Av of Americas New York NY 10019

RAPPAPORT, DORIS EDA (MRS. JACK DAVID LEVY), physician; b. N.Y.C., Aug. 9, 1916; d. Louis Solomon and Pauline (Levy) Rappaport; B.A., Hunter Coll., 1936; M.D., Woman's Med. Coll. Pa., 1942; m. Jack David Levy, Jan. 5, 1946; children—Ned Louis, Marjorie Ellen. Intern, Women's Med. Coll. Pa., 1942, then resident and chief resident; practice gen. medicine, Teaneck, N.J., 1944—; mem. attending staffs dept. gen. practice Hackensack (N.J.) Hosp., mem. sr. attending staff dept. pediatrics. Vol. Narcotics center, Hackensack. Mem. A.M.A., Bergen County Med. Soc., Alpha Omega Alpha. Home: 1375 Pennington Rd Teaneck NJ 07666 Office: 384 W Englewood Av Teaneck NJ 07666

RAPPAPORT, SANDRA JOYCE (MRS. JORDAN J. FISKE), psychologist, educator; b. Syracuse, N.Y., Sept. 25, 1946; d. Sidney Saul and Helen (Lapides) Rappaport; B.S., Cornell U., 1968; M.Ed., Tufts U., 1969; M.A., Columbia, 1971, Ph.D., 1974; m. Jordan J. Fiske, June 22, 1974. Supervising Sch. psychologist St. Elizabeth's Sch., N.Y.C., 1971—. Instr. clin. psychology Columbia, N.Y.C., 1973. Nat. Inst. Mental Health fellow, 1969-72. Mem. Am. Psychol. Assn., Psi Chi, Omicron Nu. Home: 132 East 35th St New York City NY 10016 Office: St Elizabeth's School 612 West 187th St New York City NY 10033

RAPPAPORT, YVONNE KINDINGER, educator; b. Crestline, O., Feb. 15, 1928; d. Paul Theodore and Florence Iona (Cover) Kindinger; B.S. summa cum laude, Northwestern U., 1949; M.A., Va. Poly. Inst. and State U., 1973; m. Norman Lewis Rappaport; children—Michael, Laura, Hilary, Stephen, Jocelyn. Personnel officer, then cons. and mgmt. analyst USAF, 1953-63; cons. mgmt. analysis, personnel and pub. relations, 1963-67; cons. program devel., instr. U. Va., 1967-70, dir. continuing edn. for women, 1970—; dir., performer theatre, children's theatre, radio and TV, 1953—; cons. in field. Mem. No. Val. Adv. Com. Ednl. Telecommunications, 1971—. Bd. dirs. Home and Sch. Inst., Washington, 1971—. Recipient Meritorious Service award USAF, 1959. Mem. Nat. Assn. Women Deans, Adminstrs. and Counselors (S.E. regional coordinator 1973—), adult edn. assns. U.S. (Nat. Leadership award 1973; chmn. commn. status women in edn. 1972—, dir. 1973—), V. (pres. 1971-73; Recognition of Merit award 1971-73), League Women Voters (state dir. 1968-73, nat. pub. relations com. 1970—), Am. Assn. U. Women, P.T.A., Am. Personnel and Guidance Assn., Nat. Univ. Extension Assn., Assn. Continuing Higher Edn., Am. Bus. Women Assn. (award 1960). Mem. Order Eastern Star. Author handbooks and work books, also radio, TV scripts. Home: 3225 Atlanta St Fairfax VA 22030 Office: Sch Continuing Edn Univ Va Charlottesville VA 22903

RAPPARLIE, EVALYN BARBARA (MRS. DONALD FREDERICK RAPPARLIE), educator; b. Lansing, Mich., Mar. 10, 1931; d. Richard Wilfred and Grace Marie (West) Rogers; student Mich. State U., 1948-50; B.S., Findlay Coll., 1963; M.Ed., Bowling Green State U., 1965; Ed.D., U. Ill., 1968; m. Donald Frederick Rapparlie, Dec. 29, 1950; children—Richard, Linda, Patricia, Elizabeth. Tchr. pub. schs., North Baltimore and Findlay, O., 1961-65; teaching fellow U. Ill., 1965-67; faculty State U. N.Y., Oswego, 1967—, asso. prof., 1969-73, prof., 1973—, mem. Acad. Policy Council, 1969—; cons. Dept. Health, Edn. and Welfare Model Tchr. Tng. Program, Syracuse U. Recipient Research grant U. Ill., 1967. Mem. Internat. Reading Assn., Assn. for Supervision and Curriculum Devel., Ednl. Research N.Y. State, Kappa Delta Pi. Author: (with others) Man in World of Change, social studies series, 1971-72. Home: 8 Edwards Circle Oswego NY 13126 Office: 13 Poucher Hall Oswego NY 13126

RAS, FLORENCE ANN, educator; b. Chgo.; d. Andrew C. and Frances (Lechert) Ras; B.A., Barat Coll.; M.A., Northwestern U., 1962; M.Ed., Fla. Atlantic U., 1968. Tchr., Ft. Lauderdale (Fla.) Oral Sch., 1958-64, asst. dir., 1962-64, dir., 1964—. Instr., Confraternity of Christian Doctrine, 1963-64; tchr. deaf children, West Palm Beach, Fla., 1961. Leader, Girl Scouts U.S.A., Chgo., 1946-47; vol. worker A.R.C., Chgo., 1948-49; chmn. speech reading classes for adults, Broward County, Fla., 1966-68; mem. adv. com. for workshops and facilities State Dept. Edn. Div. Vocational Rehab., 1967-68. Bd. dirs., adviser Young Deaf Adult Club, Ft. Lauderdale, 1967-68. Mem. Alexander Graham Bell Assn., Conv. Am. Instrs. of Deaf, Am., Fla. Broward County (dir. 1965-70, pres. bd. dirs. 1967-68) speech and hearing assns., N.E.A., Barat Coll., Northwestern U. alumni assns. Home: 3124 NE 42d Ct Fort Lauderdale FL 33308

RASCHE, LOIS MUELLER (MRS. RICHARD WRIGHT RASCHE), psychologist; b. Milw., Nov. 30, 1943; d. Herman Gregor and Ora Emma (Dettmann) Mueller; B.S., U. Wis.-Milw., 1965; M.A., U. Tex., 1966, Ph.D., 1969; m. Richard Wright Rasche, Oct. 10, 1970. Postdoctoral intern VA Hosp., Wood, Wis., 1969-71; counselor, asst. prof. So. Ill. U. Counseling Center and dept. psychology, Carbondale, 1970-72, coordinator personal counseling, asst. prof., 1972—; individual practice clin. psychology, Carbondale, 1972—. Campaign worker for Sen. George McGovern presdl. race, 1972. Mem. Am., Ill. psychol. assns., Am. Guidance and Personnel Assn. Club: So Ill. U. Womens. Contbr. articles to profl. jours. Home: Route 4 Carbondale IL 62901

RASCO, JUDITH ANN MCGETTIGAN, pub. relations exec.; b. San Francisco, Oct. 25, 1940; d. Kevin Wiley and Jean (Adelstein) McGettigan; B.A., San Francisco State Coll., 1962, postgrad., 1962-63. Adminstrv. asst. Dept. Health, Edn. and Welfare, San Francisco, 1962-63, pub. health analyst, 1965-67; social worker Yuba County Welfare Dept., Marysville, Cal., 1967-68; dir. pub. information and edn. Greater Omaha Assn. Retarded Children, 1968-71, cons. pub. relations, 1971—; dir. pub. information and edn. Eastern Neb. Community Office Retardation, Omaha, 1971—. Cons. developmental disabilities tech. assistance, 1973—. Chmn. pub. relations com. Mayor's Commn. on Hiring the Handicapped, 1969-72; chmn. media com. Mayor's Commn. on Status of Women, 1972—. Mem. Pub. Relations Soc. Am., Am. Women in Radio and TV (1st v.p. 1972-73), Nat. Assn. Retarded Citizens, Am. Assn. Mental Deficiency, Neb. Assn. Bus. Communicators (2d v.p. 1972-73), Omaha Press Club (pub. relations com. 1969—, press ball com. 1969-73), Omaha Fedn. Advertisers, Alpha Epsilon Rho (charter). Home: 5615 N 105th Plaza Apt 12 Omaha NE 68134 Office: 116 S 42d St Omaha NE 68131

RASEY, JEAN FISCHER, poet; b. Bennington, Vt., Jan. 28, 1893; d. William August and Marguarithe (Winkle) Fischer; student Bennington pub. schs.; m. Clarke Archie Rasey, Sept. 7, 1917; children—Rose Jean (Mrs. Charles C. Crowl), Violet C. (Mrs. Livio Reggi). Co-editor Poem a Day; poet, works pub. Sat. Eve. Post, N.Y. Times, Christian Sci. Monitor, N.J. Jour.-Am., Wall St. Jour., other periodicals; works pub. anthologies. Mem. Nat. League Am. Pen

Women, Cal. Writers Club, Edwin Markham Poetry Soc., Ariz. Poetry Soc. Club: Scottsdale (Ariz.) Woman's. Author: Pictures I Took Myself, 1973. Address: care Dr and Mrs L Raggi 1435 Wake Forest Davis CA 95616

RASKIN, JOAN, physician; b. Balt., Aug. 11, 1930; d. Moses and Rose (Frank) Raskin; B.A., Goucher Coll., 1951; M.D., U. Md., 1955. Intern U. Hosp., Balt., 1955-56, resident, 1956-58, fellow in dermatology, 1958-59; fellow in dermatology U. Minn. Hosps., Mpls., 1959-60; practice medicine, specializing in dermatology, Balt., 1960—; mem. staff South Balt. Gen. Hosp., Sinai Hosp., asso. in medicine U. Md., 1960-63, asst. prof. medicine, 1963-67, asso. prof., 1967—; mem. staff Mercy Hosp. Diplomate Am. Bd. Dermatology and Syphilology. Mem. Am. Acad. Dermatology, A.M.A., Balt. City Med. Soc., Med. and Chirung. Faculty Md., Balt. Dermatol. Soc. (sec. 1962-64), Am. Med. Women's Assn., Soc. Am. Bacteriologists, Women's Med. Soc. Md. (pres. 1962-63), Soc. Investigative Dermatology. Contbr. articles to profl. jours. Research in circulating antibodies in certain dermatoses, others. Home: 6605 Park Heights Av Baltimore MD 21215 Office: 3506 N Calvert St Baltimore MD 21218

RASKIN, JUDITH, soprano; b. N.Y.C., June 21, 1928; d. Harry A. and Lillian (Mendelson) Raskin; B.A., Smith Coll., 1949, M.A. (hon.), 1963; m. July 11, 1948; 2 children. Made operatic debut in Dialogues of the Carmelites, NBC-TV, 1957, N.Y.C. Opera Co. debut in Cosi fan Tutte, 1959, Met. Opera debut as Susanna in Le Nozze di Figaro, 1962; European debut at Glyndebourne Festival Opera in Die Zauberflote, 1963; recital debut in N.Y.C. as Ford Found. winner, 1964; appeared with orchs., N.Y.C., Cleve., Phila., Mpls., Cin.; rec. artist Columbia, London, Decca, RCA Victor records; appeared as Nanetta in Met. Opera prodn. Falstaff, 1964. Address: Metropolitan Opera Co New York City NY 10023

RASMUSON, MARY LOUISE MILLIGAN (MRS. ELMER E. RASMUSON), ret. army officer; b. East Pittsburgh, Pa., Apr. 11, 1911; d. George Vincent and Alice Carmen (Graff) Milligan; B.S., Carnegie Inst. Tch., 1932; M.Ed., U. Pitts., 1940; grad. Adj. Gen. Sch., 1943, Command and Gen. Staff Sch., 1945; LL.D., Carnegie Inst. Tech., 1959; m. Elmer Edwin Rasmuson, Nov. 4, 1961. Asst. to supervising prin. Forest Hills Schs., Pitts., 1932-36, asst. supervising prin., 1936-42. Commd. 2d Lt. Women's Army Aux. Corps, U.S. Army, 1942, advanced through grades to col., 1957, ret. 1962; classification officer Women's Army Aux. Corps Tng. Center, Ft. Des Moines, Ia., 1942, apptd. WAC dir. WAC Tng. Center, 1943-46; gen. staff officer G-1, Dept. Army, Washington, 1946-47; dep. dir. WAC, 1947-52; WAC staff adviser U.S. Army Europe, 1952-56; staff officer Continental Army Command, Ft. Monroe, Va., 1956; dir. Women's Army Corps, Dept. Army, Washington, 1957-62. Bd. dirs. Alaska div. Am. Cancer Soc.; chmn. Anchorage Hist. and Fine Arts Commn.; v.p. Anchorage Fine Arts Mus. Assn.; mem. Alaska Air Pollution Control Bd. Decorated Legion of Merit with oak leaf clusters, recipient alumni merit award Carnegie Inst. Tech., 1951; Distinguished Dau. Pa.; Ala. Commendation medal Gov., 1962. Mem. Am. Assn. U. Women Am. Legion, Bus. and Profl. Women's Club. Clubs: Zonta, Army-Navy, Anchorage Women's; Anchorage Republican Womens; Alaska Native Sisterhood. Address: Box 600 Anchorage AK 99510

RASMUSSEN, ALICE MARIE, educator; b. West Palm Beach, Fla., Jan. 27, 1931; d. John Albert and Marie Ruth (Schick) Rasmussen; B.A., Central Bible Coll., 1954; M.Ed., Women's Coll. Ga., 1963; Ed.D., U. Ga., 1966. Tchr., Sapnish, Miami (Fla.) Jr. High Sch., 1959-62; grad. asst. Women's Coll. Ga., Milledgeville, 1962-63; grad. asst. U. Ga., Athens, 1963-65, asst. prof., 1965-66; asst. prof. modern langs. Oral Roberts U., Tulsa, 1967-69, asso. prof., 1969-72, prof., 1972—, chmn. modern langs. dept., 1968—. Mem. Am. Assn. Tchrs. Spanish and Portuguese (sec. Ga. chpt., 1962-66), Am. Council on Teaching Foreign Langs. (sec. Okla. chpt. 1967), Nat., Okla. edn. assns., S. Central Modern Lang. Assn. (sec. linguistics sect. 1969-73), Okla. Fgn. Lang. Tchrs. Assn. (sec. 1967, cons. 1967), Council Dept. Chmn. Okla. (chmn. 1968, mem. com. tchr. certification guidelines 1968), Central States Conf. Fgn. Lang. Teaching (mem. adv. council 1969). Mem. Ch. Assemblies of God (ordained minister 1953). Home: 8589 S Lewis St Tulsa OK 74136

RASMUSSEN, COLETTE MICHELE (MRS. RICHARD ALLEN RASMUSSEN), physician; b. Paris, France, Mar. 5, 1932; d. Charles Simon and Marie Phoebe (Gestetner) Ullman came to the U.S., 1940, naturalized, 1945; B.A., U. Chgo., 1951, M.D., 1958; B.S., Roosevelt U., 1954; M.P.H., U. Mich., 1962; m. Richard Allen Rasmussen, Oct. 24, 1955; children—Jonathan, Michele. Intern, MacNeal Hosp., Berwyn, Ill., 1959-60; resident Cook County Health Dept., Chgo., 1960-61, chief div. preventive medicine, 1962—; asso. prof. pub. health Loyola U. Sch. Medicine, Maywood, Ill., 1965; asso. prof. U. Ill. Sch. Pub. Health. Diplomate Am. Bd. Preventive Medicine. Mem. A.M.A., Am., Ill. pub. health assns. Home: 1320 E 56th St Chicago IL 60637 Office: 1425 S Racine Av Chicago IL 60608

RASMUSSEN, ELIZABETH LOUISE ARMSTRONG (MRS. PAUL GEORGE RASMUSSEN), clin. psychologist; b. Lawrence, Kan., Oct. 2, 1935; d. Cecil Werner and Marie Louise (Irelan) Armstrong; B.S., Miami U., Oxford, O., 1957; M.S. (Alumni Reserach Found. fellow 1958-59), U. Wis., 1960; postgrad. Syracuse U., 1961-63; Ph.D. in Psychology, U. Okla., 1969; m. Paul George Rasmussen, June 7, 1958; children—Janet Louise, Eric Rolf. Postdoctoral clin. psychology intern U. Okla. Med. Sch., Oklahoma City, 1969-71; postdoctoral clin. psychology fellow Oklahoma City Psychiat. Clinic, 1971-72; pvt. practice clin. psychology, Oklahoma City, 1972—; partner, dir. Adventures: Center for Natural Growth. Mem. Am., Southwestern, Okla. psychol. assns., Am. Assn. U. Women (pres. Oklahoma City br. 1972-74), Phi Beta Kappa. Unitarian (trustee ch. 1970-72, chairperson human sexuality com. 1972—, pres. women's evening alliance 1970-72). Home: 3329 Everett Dr Route 3 Edmond OK 73034 Office: 912 NW 57th St Oklahoma City OK 73118

RASMUSSEN, HELEN MARIETTA GIESE (MRS. HUBERT J. RASMUSSEN), social worker, horse breeder; b. Red Willow, Neb.; d. Henry C. and Nettie (Helm) Giese; A.A., Stephens Coll., 1927; Mus.B., Colo. U., B.Music Edn., 1931; m. Hubert J. Rasmussen, May 1, 1946. Caseworker Denver Dept. Pub. Welfare, 1931-35; caseworker Morgan County Dept. Pub. Welfare, Ft. Morgan, Colo., 1936-39, welfare dir., 1939—. Co-owner, Laurel Dell Morgan Horse Farm. Mem. Morgan County Adv. Com. Pub. Welfare. Recipient longevity service award Colo. Dept. Pub. Welfare, 1961. Mem. Am. Pub. Welfare Assn., Colo. County Welfare Dirs. Assn., Nat. Fedn. Bus. and Profl. Women's Clubs, Circle J Morgan Horse Assn., Rocky Mountain Horse Show Assn., U. Colo. Alumnae Club, U. Colo. Buffaloes, Fort Morgan C. of C., Kappa Alpha Theta, Eta Upsilon Gamma. Republican. Methodist. Mem. Order Eastern Star. Clubs: University (pres. Fort Morgan 1951), Fort Morgan Country. Home: 617 Lincoln St PO Box 712 Fort Morgan CO 80701 Office: PO Box 712 Fort Morgan CO 80701

RASMUSSEN, LOUISE GARNET (MRS. KENNETH PEDERSEN), editor; b. Roundup, Mont., Aug. 27, 1914; d. Alfred William and Rachel Victoria (Johnston) Eiselein; grad. in Journalism, U. Mont., 1937; m. Kenneth Pedersen Rasmussen, Nov. 4, 1944; children—Polly Louise, Eric Neil. With Roundup Record-Tribune, 1937-41, 1952—, editor, 1959—, pub., 1962—. Served with U.S. Navy, 1942-44. Mem. Mont. Press Assn. (dir. 1967-69), Mont. Advt. Service (dir. 1965-69, pres. 1967-68), Roundup C. of C. (dir. 1971), P.E.O. Theta Sigma Phi. Republican. Episcopal. Home: 324 4th St W Roundup MT 59072 Office: 29 Main St Box 747 Roundup MT 59072

RASMUSSEN, PHYLLIS JOANNE, librarian; b. Blair, Neb., June 20, 1942; d. Elmer Michael and Myrtle Martha (Lee) Rasmussen; B.A. magna cum laude, Dana Coll., 1964; M.A., U. Minn., 1966. Librarian Nordsjaellands Central Library, Elsinore, Denmark, 1967-68, Frederiksberg Libraries, Copenhagen, 1968; asst. librarian Dana Coll. Library, 1969-72; cataloger Scandinavian sect. Shared Cataloging div. Library of Congress, Washington, 1972—. Future faculty fellow, Am. Luth. Ch., 1964. Mem. Library Congress Profl. Assn., Am. Scandinavian Found. (v.p. Dana chpt. 1970-71), A.L.A., Library Assn., Soc. Advancement Scandinavian Studies, Am. Assn. Univ. Women, Alpha Chi. Club: Danish (Washington). Home: 3200 Curtis Dr Marlow Heights MD 20031

RASSIGA, ANNE LOUISE, physician; b. Oceanside, N.Y., June 19, 1942; d. William August and Edna Irene (Chickray) Rassiga; A.B. cum laude, Bryn Mawr Coll., 1962; M.D., Harvard, 1966; m. George Bernard Pidot, Jr., Sept. 4, 1962 (div. 1972); m. 2d, Charles Herman Pimlott, Jr., July 5, 1974. Intern, Dartmouth Med. Sch. Affiliated Hosps., Hanover, N.H., 1966-67, resident internal medicine, 1967-69; spl. NIH research fellow in hematology Dartmouth Med. Sch., Hanover, 1969-71, instr. medicine, 1971-72; asst. prof. medicine Case Western Reserve Med. Sch., 1972; mem. staff Hitchcock Med. Clinic, Hanover, N.H., 1971-72; asst. chief sect. hematology VA Hosp., Cleve., 1972—. Mem. med. adv. bd. Upper Valley Planned Parenthood Assn., 1969-72. Fellow A.C.P.; mem. Am. Soc. Hematology, Am. Fedn. Clin. Research. Contbr. to publs. in field. Home: 22 Ridgecrest Rd Chagrin Falls OH 44022 Office: VA Hosp 10701 East Blvd Cleveland OH 44106

RATCLIFFE, MARCIA GRACE, psychic; b. Ogdensburg, N.Y., Mar. 31, 1930; d. Harold Daniel and Elizabeth Edith (Vanier) Ratcliffe; A.A., San Jose City Coll., 1973; m. Frank George Warzek, Mar. 7, 1952 (div. Nov. 1970); children—Michelle Jay, Michael Randal. Legal sec., 1969-74; parapsychology editor Let's Go Mag., 1971-72; program dir. Dr. Milan Ryzl's seminars, 1972, 73; tchr. classes in extrasensory perception. Sponsor 1st ESP Conv., San Jose, Cal., 1970; co-dir. Universal Receivers Assn., 1968—; lectr. metaphysics. Mem. Acad. Parapsychology and Medicine, Universal Receivers Assn. Mem. Unity Ch. Office: PO Box 5535 San Jose CA 95150

RATH, DOROTHY LYDIA, ednl. adminstr.; b. Bklyn., Dec. 13, 1925; d. Christian and Lydia (Pfost) Rath; B.S. in Sociology, Albright Coll., 1949; M.A. in Student Personnel Adminstrn., Syracuse U., 1967; postgrad. (Lutheran Study grantee) U. Wis., 1970. Asst. dean women Syracuse (N.Y.) U., 1966-67; dir. career planning and placement Carthage Coll., Kenosha, Wis., 1967—, women students adviser, 1967—, instr. sociology, 1972—. Dir. vol. services Am. Red Cross, Syracuse, 1960-67. Mem. Wis. Career Planning and Placement Assn. (mem. exec. bd. 1971-73), Wis. Coll. Personnel Assn. (mem. exec. bd. 1973), S.E. Wis. Personnel and Guidance Assn., Wis. Assn. Sch. Personnel Adminstrs. Office: Carthage College 2000 Alford Dr Kenosha WI 53140

RATH, HILDEGARD, artist, author, lectr.; b. Freudenstadt, Germany, Mar. 22, 1909; d. Ernst Adolf and Emma (Katz) Rath; pvt. instrn., 1925, Kunstgewerbeschule, Stuttgart, 1926-27; student Rustinsches Lehrinstitut Potsdam, 1928-30, Akademie Der Bildenden Kunste, Berlin, 1933-37; spl. study with Lotte Laserstein, Berlin, Otto Manigk, Berlin; m. Hermann Gross, June 14, 1946 (div.). Came to U.S., 1948. One-man shows Ausstellung Weissenhof Stuttgart, 1927, Kunsthaus Schaller Stuttgart, 1941, 46, 59, Avant-Garde Gallery, N.Y., 1961, Ligoa Duncan, N.Y., 1967, Galerie Internationale, N.Y.C., 1972, others; group shows throughout U.S., fgn. countries; travel exhibition throughout the United States; represented in numerous museums in U.S. and Europe, also pvt. collections; owner, dir. European Sch. Fine Arts, N.Y.C., 1949-54; lectr. art and artists from prehistoric times to present, 1960-62; history of art Great Neck (N.Y.) Pub. Sch., adult edn. Great Neck, 1960-62, Northshore Art Assn. Roslyn, N.Y., 1960-61; World field research corr., 1967. Recipient Grumbacher award of merit Fla. Internat., 1952; Salon of the Fifty States, N.Y., 1962; Prix de Paris, 1963. Mem. Wurttembergischer Kunstverein Stuttgart, Landesverband Wurttembergischer Kunstler Tubingen (Germany) So. Vt., N. Shore art assns., Artists Equity N.Y., Knickerbocker Artists N.Y., Nat. Assn. Pub. Sch. Adult Educators, Internat. Platform Assn. Episcopalian. Address: 3 Cypress Av Kings Point NY 11024

RATH, ROSEMARY THERESA, health services adminstr.; b. Allentown, Pa., Oct. 10, 1925; d. Edward Thomas and Rose Eugenia (Flaherty) Rath; diploma Sacred Heart Hosp. Sch. Nursing, 1946; B.S. in Nursing Edn., U. Pa., 1955, certificate in pub. health nursing, 1955, M.S. in Nursing, 1963; postgrad. U. N.C., 1963, N.Y. Med. Coll., 1964. Pub. health nurse coordinator Methodist Hosp., Phila., 1955-58, Phila. Dept. Health, 1958-59, Children's Hosp., Phila., 1959-61; psychiat. nurse Pa. Hosp., Phila., 1962-63; pub. health nursing cons. crippled children's sect. N.C. State Bd. Health, Raleigh, 1964-68; dir. information and referral mental retardation program Lehigh County Mental Health Clinic, Allentown, Pa., 1968—. Adv. bd. Lehigh County Community Coll., 1973; chmn. Lehigh County Com. on Employment Handicapped, 1973. Mem. Am. Pub. Health Assn., Am., Pa. (vice chmn. pub. health nurses sect. 1957-68, Phila. dist. 1957-58), Bus. and Profl. Women (sec. 1970-72, v.p. 1972-73), Am. Assn. U. Women. Democrat. Roman Catholic. Soroptomist. Home: 411 Keystone Av Whitehall PA 18052 Office: 523 Hamilton St Allentown PA 18105

RATH, RUTH EMILY NELSON (MRS. GEORGE RATH), counselor; b. Eaton, O., Feb. 25, 1905; d. Victor Redfield and Harriett Clifford (Neal) Nelson; diploma Kearney State Tchrs. Coll.; student U. Wyo., summer 1944; B.S., U. Ore., 1956; M.S., 1958; m. George Rath, Jan. 22, 1944; 1 dau., Betty James (Mrs. Reed James). Adminstr., tchr., Neb., Wyo., 1924-50; with Bur. Reclamation, Casper, Wyo., 1952-54; counselor, program coordinator Eugene (Ore.) Pub. Schs., 1954-71; program coordinator Sr. Opportunities and Services Inc., Eugene, 1971-72, exec. dir., 1972—. Chmn., Guidance and Counseling Workshops, Eugene, summers 1960-70. Bd. dirs. Ore. Council Aging. Mem. N.E.A., Ore., Eugene edn. assns., Emerald Empire Council (dir.), Ore. Personnel and Guidance Assn. Mem. Order Eastern Star. Responsible for initiating home visitation programs in schs. Dist 4J, Eugene. Home: 2950 Ferry Eugene OR 97405 Office: 673 W 10th St Eugene OR 97402

RATH, SONJA FEINGOLD, psychologist; b. The Hague, Netherland, Aug. 10, 1926; d. Leo and Regina (Engellard) Feingold; brought to U.S., 1941, naturalized 1948; A.B., Hunter Coll., 1947; M.A., Clark U., 1948; m. Frederick Rath, Mar. 10, 1950; children—Daniel, Deborah. Research asst. med. genetics Psychiatric Inst., N.Y.C., 1948; psychol. intern N.Y. State Dept. Mental Hygiene, 1949; clin. psychologist Utica (N.Y.) State Hosp., 1950; clin. psychologist Pilgrim State Hosp., Brentwood, L.I., N.Y., 1950-52, sr. clin. psychologist, 1957-58; sr. psychologist Peninsula Child Guidance Center, Cedarhurst, L.I., 1959-68, chief clin. psychologist, 1968-73; pvt. practice psychology, Woodmere, L.I., 1952—. Mem. Am., Nassau County psychol. assns., N.Y. State Soc. Clin. Psychologists, Am. Group Psychotherapy Assn. Address: 391 Yale Av Woodmere NY 11598

RATHBUN, MARGARET LAWRENCE, physician; b. Rochester, N.Y., Mar. 12, 1917; d. Lewis A. and Gladys (Wood) Rathbun; B.A., U. Rochester, 1939, M.D., 1943; M.P.H., Johns Hopkins, 1954; m. Wendell R. Ames, Sept. 21, 1964. Intern Wilson Memorial Hosp., Johnson City, 1943-44; resident St. Louis Children's Hosp., Los Angeles Children's Hosp., 1944-47; pvt. practice pediatrics, Rochester, N.Y., 1947-53; dir. maternal and child health Rochester Health Bur., 1953-56, dep. health officer, 1956-58; dep. county health dir. Monroe County (N.Y.) Dept. of Health, 1958-73, ret., attending physician St. John's Nursing Home, Rochester, 1973—. Diplomate Am. Bd. Preventive Medicine and Pub. Health. Mem. Am., N.Y. State acads. preventive medicine, Rochester Acad. Medicine (treas. 1957-58, 63-65), Monroe County Med. Soc., N.Y. State Pub. Health Assn., Rochester Pediatric Soc. Address: 225 Lanning Rd Heneaye Falls NY 14472

RATHE, JANET JOHNSON, orgn. exec.; b. Portland, Ore., Nov. 22, 1924; d. Samuel Victor and Lucy May (Slade) Johnson; B.S. in Home Econs., Ore. State U., 1947; m. Hjalmar Jacob Rathe, July 9, 1952; children—Karen Marie, Jay Hjalmar, Christ Victor, Eric Alan, Jonn Michael. Writer, make-up editor women's page, The Oregonian, Portland, 1947-51; sec. Easter Seal Agy., Portland, 1951-52; demonstrator Garrett Appliance Co., Eugene, Ore., 1952-54; founding dir. Ore. Consumer League, Portland, 1966, exec. sec., 1967—; host weekly radio program Consumerscoop, 1971—; cons. in field. Mem. resident's Consumer Adv. Council, 1970-72, Ore. Adv. Com. Synthetic Chems. in the Environment, 1969—; bd. dirs. Ore., Multnomah County nutrition councils. Mem. nat. adv. com. Com. to Re-elect the President, 1972; 1st v.p. Portland Met. Republican Women's Club, 1973-74. Recipient Consumer Achievement award Ore. Consumer League, 1969; Achievement award Portland Fedn. Women's Orgns., 1971. Mem. Am. (chmn. consumer interests com. 1973-74), Ore. (dir. 1968-70) home econ. assns., Am. Assn. U. Women (dir. Portland 1971), Women in Communications (pres. Portland 1948), Omicron Nu. Presbyn. Address: 3131 NW Luray Terrace Portland OR 97210

RATHER, SHEILA ELIZABETH BALL (MRS. HAL EVANS RATHER), employment agy. exec.; b. Newcastle-on-Tyne, Eng., Sept. 20, 1930; d. Leonard Henry and Jane Taylor (Mayes) Ball; student Reading (Eng.) U., 1946-47, Royal Acad. Music and Dramatic Art, Eng., 1947-48; asso. Royal Coll. Music, 1947; Licentiate Guildhall Sch. Music and Drama, 1949; m. Hal Evans Rather, Mar. 20, 1958; children—Julian Stephen, Jonathan Massey. Came to U.S., 1962, naturalized, 1964. Prodn. asst. Brit. Broadcasting Co., London, 1953-55; feature editor Asso. TV, London, 1955-60; casting dir. Goodson Todman Enterprises, N.Y.C., 1962-65; exec. v.p. Brook Street Bur. Mayfair, Ltd., N.Y.C., 1965-69, 70—; coordinator placement activities Berkeley Schs., 1969-70. Mem. Brit. Am. C. of C. (v.p. 1968-74, dir. 1968—, membership chmn. 1968—), N.Y. C. of C. Home: 36 Brewster Rd W Massapequa NY 11758 Office: Brook Street Bureau Mayfair Ltd 147 E 50th St New York City NY 10022

RATHMAN, CATHERINE MARY, assn. exec.; b. Jamestown, N.D., Apr. 21, 1908; d. Frank Ernest and Delia Alice (Bailey) Rathman; B.A. cum laude, Jamestown Coll., 1930; M.A., Columbia, 1951; postgrad. U. Cal. at Berkeley, 1945, U. Mont., 1947. Tchr. English and French, LaMoure (N.D.) High Sch., 1930-37; tchr. English, French, social studies Great Falls (Mont.) High Sch., 1937-50, dean of girls, 1950-65; internat. exec. sec. Delta Kappa Gamma Soc., Austin, Tex., 1965—. Mem. Gov.'s Conf. on Children and Youth, 1970, White House Conf. for Children and Youth, Washington, 1970; mem. Mayor's Commn. on Status of Women, Austin, 1970—. Mem. N.E.A., Mont. Edn. Assn., Mont. Dept. Classroom Tchrs. (state sec. 1946-47), Mont. Personnel and Guidance Assn. (state pres. 1951-52), Am. Assn. U. Women. Clubs: Soroptimist, Austin Woman's, Heritage (Austin, Tex.). Home: 119 The Regency 601 W 11th St Austin TX 78701 Office: PO Box 1589 Austin TX 78767

RATNER, LILLIAN GROSS (MRS. HAROLD RATNER), psychiatrist; b. N.Y.C., Aug. 18, 1932; d. Herman and Sarah (Widelitz) Gross; B.A., Barnard Coll., 1953; postgrad. U. Lausanne (Switzerland), 1954-56; M.D., Duke U., 1959; m. Harold Ratner, Feb. 4, 1961; children—Sanford Miles, Marcia Ellen. Intern, Kings County Hosp., Bklyn., 1959-60, resident, 1967-70, fellow in child psychiatry, 1969-70, psychiatrist devel. evaluation clinic, 1970-72; resident Jewish Hosp. Bklyn., 1960-62, fellow in pediatric psychiatry, 1962-63; physician in charge pediatric psychiatric clinic Greenpoint (N.Y.) Hosp., 1964-67; pvt. practice psychiatry, Great Neck, N.Y., 1970—. Clin. instr. psychiatry Downstate Med. Center, Bklyn., 1970-74, clin. asst. prof., 1974—; psychiatric cons. N.Y.C. Bd. Edn., 1972—; mem. med. bd. Camp Sussex, Sussex, N.J. 1963—. Diplomate Am. Bd. Pediatrics, Am. Bd. Psychiatry and Neurology. Fellow Am., Bklyn. acads. pediatrics; mem. Am., Nassau, Bklyn. psychiatric assns., Am. Bd. Child Psychiatry, Bklyn. Pediatric Soc. (sr. mem.), A.M.A., N.Y., Kings County med. socs. Home and office: 55 Bluebird Dr Great Neck NY 11023

RATNER, ROCHELLE ANN, editor; b. Atlantic City, Dec. 2, 1948; d. Herman and Esther (Tischler) Ratner; student New Sch. Social Research, 1968-70. Book review editor East Village Other, N.Y.C., 1969-72; poetry editor Survivor's Manual, N.Y.C., 1971—. Coordinating Council of Lit. Mags. grantee, 1971-72. Mem. Coordinating Council Lit. Mags. Author: Broadside: Variations on a Theme in Blue, 1970; A Birthday of Waters, 1971; False Trees, 1973. Address: 50 Spring St New York City NY 10012

RATTLEY, JESSIE L. M. MENIFIELD (MRS. ROBERT L. RATTLEY), educator; b. Birmingham, Ala., May 4, 1929; d. Alonzo B. and Altona (Cochran) Menifield; B.S. with honors, Hampton Inst., 1951, postgrad. 1957; extension course LaSalle U., 1946; postgrad. IBM Sch., 1959; m. Robert L. Rattley, Aug. 26, 1952; children—Florence Elizabeth, Robin Altona. Tchr., Huntington High Sch., 1951-53; founder pres., owner Peninsula Bus. Coll., Newport News, Va., 1952—. Pres., Peninsula Coordinating Com., 1964—; mem. Newport News City Council, Planning Commn., Redevel. Housing Com., Library Bd. Sec. Mayor's Human Relations Council, Newport News, 1963—; bd. mem. Office Econ. Opportunity, 1966—. Va. Peninsula Chaplaincy Service, 1966—. Recipient awards including Meritorious Service award Eta chpt. Chi Eta Phi, 1965, Legion Honor Freedom citation, Chapel 4 Chaplains Temple U.; named Profl. Woman of Year, Bus. and Profl. Women's Club, Inc., 1961, Outstanding Citizen of Year, Alpha chpt. Omega Psi Phi, 1965, Bus. Woman of Year State of Va., 1962, Bus. Woman of Year, Fedn. Colored Women's Club, Inc., 1962, Woman of Courage for City Newport News, Ch. Women United. Mem. Nat. Council Negro Women, Chi Rho, Alpha Kappa Alpha (chpt. basileus 1962-66, supreme tamiouchos; Annie L. Harbey Achievement award Mid-Atlantic region 1970). Presbyn. (trustee, sec. 1966—). Home: 529 Ivy Av Newport News VA 23607

RATZLAFF, NINA MAY SMITH, librarian; b. nr. Carmen, Okla., May 30, 1917; d. Oliver Herbert and Eva Lela (Henage) Smith; B.A., Anderson Coll., 1941; M.A., Columbia, 1951; postgrad U. Portland, 1959, 60, La Escuela Normal Sch., Saltillo, Mexico, 1961, U. South Fla., 1968; M.S., Fla. State U., 1972; m. Leslie W. Ratzlaff, Aug. 29, 1940; children—Paul Wilmer, Dale Leroy. Missionary, educator Ch. of God, B.W.I., 1941-47, 52-55; jr. librarian Trenton Pub. Library, 1947-50; instr. Warner Pacific Coll., Portland, Ore., 1956-62; instr. Cascade Coll., Portland, 1962-63; tchr. Miami-Norland Sr. High Sch., 1963-64; tchr., librarian Polk County, Fla., 1966-71; librarian Warner So. Coll., Lake Wales, Fla., 1967—. Mem. N.E.A., A.L.A., Fla. Library Assn., Am. Assn. U. Women. Address: Warner Southern College Lake Wales FL 33853

RAUCH, HELENE DORIS COBEN (MRS. HAROLD LEO RAUCH), microbiologist; b. Los Angeles, Oct. 2, 1930; d. Jack Harry and Bella Ruth (Zager) Coben; B.A., U. Cal. at Los Angeles, 1951, Ph.D., 1958; m. Harold Leo Rauch, Nov. 17, 1952; children—Alisa Yvonne, Steven Coben, Paul Evan, Ilana Elizabeth. Bacteriologist Los Angeles County (Cal.) Pub. Health Dept., 1951-52; research asst. zoology dept. U. Cal. at Los Angeles, 1953-54, teaching asst. bacteriology dept., 1955-57; research asso. dept. allergy and immunology Palo Alto Med. Research Found., 1957-60; research asso. dept. medicine, div. infectious diseases Stanford Sch. Medicine, 1960-61, Nat. Multiple Sclerosis Soc. postdoctoral fellow, 1961-64, research asso. dept. med. microbiology, 1964—. Mem. A.A.A.S., Am. Soc. Microbiology, Am. Fedn. Clin. Research, Am. Assn. Immunologists (chmn. com. on status of women), Tissue Culture Assn., Profl. Women Stanford Med. Sch. (council), Sigma Xi. Contbr. articles to profl. jours. Office: Medical Microbiology Dept Stanford U Sch Medicine Stanford CA 94305

RAUCH, JEANNE GIRARD (MRS. MARSHALL ARTHUR RAUCH), textile mill exec.; b. Gastonia, N.C., Sept. 15, 1923; d. Frank Henry and Ida Sadie (Paradies) Goldberg; student Duke U., 1940-41; B.S., Syracuse U., 1944; m. Marshall Arthur Rauch, May 18, 1946; children—Ingrid, Marc, Peter, Stephanie, John. With Pyramid Mills, Bessemer City, N.C., 1959—, v.p., 1963—, also dir.; sec. Rauch Industries. Sec. Rauch Found., Inc., 1965-72. Bd. dirs., United Fund, Gaston, 1970, 71, 72; trustee N.C. Mus. Art, 1973—; mem. county bd., Girl Scouts U.S.A., 1950; mem. occupational adv. bd. Gaston Coll., 1971-73; bd. visitors Sacred Heart Coll., 1971-72; mem. Arts Commn. N.C., 1973—. Mem. Sisterhood Hadassah (pres. 1954-57), Little Theater (1st sec. 1949, 50), Gaston Art Guild (1st pres. 1963, 65), Sir Walter Cabinet (v.p. 1969), N.C. Art Soc. (dist. rep.), Alpha Epsilon Phi, Alpha Epsilon Rho. Democrat. Home: 1121 Scotch Dr Gastonia NC 28052 Office: Box 755 Bessemer City NC 28016

RAULINAITIS, VALERIJA BIRUTE BERZINSKAS (MRS. VICTOR RAULINAITIS), psychiatrist; b. Riga, Latvia; d. Victor and Maria (Norkus) Berzinskas; M.D., U. Vytautas the Great, Kaunas, Lithuania, 1938; m. Victor Raulinaitis, July 20, 1940; 1 dau., Ruta (Mrs. Rimvydas Mulokas). Intern Ia. Luth. Hosp., Des Moines, Ia., 1951; resident Northwestern U. and VA, 1957; staff Children's Hosp., Kaunas, Lithuania, 1941-43, Children's Orphanage, Kaunas, 1943-44; pediatrician Displaced Person Camps, Germany, 1945-49; staff physician, clin. dir. Woodward (Ia.) State Hosp., 1951-54; staff physician VA Hosp., Downey, Ill., 1957-61, chief of staff, 1962-71; dir. VA Hosp., Pitts., 1971-73, VA Hosp., American Lake, Wash., 1973—. asso. dept. psychiatry Northwestern U. Med. Sch., Chgo., 1966—. Bd. mem. Lake County (Ill.) Mental Health Soc., 1964-71, pres., 1966-67; bd. mem. Lake County Council on Alcoholism, 1967-71. Recipient Outstanding Supervisory Employee award in Fed. Govt. Service in Chgo. Met. Area Chgo. Fedn. Exec. Bd. and Fed. Personnel Council Chgo., 1965. Diplomate in psychiatry Am. Bd. Psychiatry and Neurology. Fellow Am. Psychiat. Assn.; mem. A.M.A., Lake County Med. Soc. Club: Pittsburgh Altrusa International (bd. mem. 1969-71). Address: VA Hosp American Lake Tacoma WA 98493

RAUSCH, EMILIE MARIE, educator; b. Poplarville, Miss., June 13, 1944; d. Walter William and Emilie Marie (Stapp) Rausch; B.S., La. State U., 1967, M.A., 1970. Instr. communications, chmn. div. fine arts Meridian (Miss.) Jr. Coll., 1970—, v.p. Faculty Assn., 1973—. Mem. Speech Communication Assn., So. Speech Communication Assn., Miss. Speech Assn., Miss. Edn. Assn., Masquers, Phi Mu, Theta Alpha Phi. Episcopalian. Club: Meridian Singles (chmn. bd.). Home: 4609 Broadmoor Dr Meridian MS 39301 Office: 5500 Hwy 19 N Meridian MS 39301

RAVAL, SUSHILA NAVNIT (MRS. NAVNIT RAVAL), educator; b. Dakor, India, Nov. 21, 1932; d. Purushottam Damodar and Dahiben (Motilal) Pandya; came to U.S., 1955; M.A., Am. U., 1958, Ed.D., 1962; m. Navnit Raval, June 24, 1955; children—Pauravi, Kautilya, Arushi. Research asst. Am. Personnel and Guidance Assn., Washington, 1962-63; asst. prof. N.Y. State U. Coll., New Paltz, 1963-66; prof. ednl. psychology and child psychology Coppin State Coll., Balt., 1966—. Mem. Am. Psychol. Assn. Home: 5816 Narcissus Av Baltimore MD 21215 Office: 2500 West North Av Baltimore MD 21216

RAVE, ELIZABETH JEANNE, educator; b. Mendota, Ill., Dec. 29, 1932; d. Adolph John and Elizabeth Dora (Sauer) Rave; B.S., Ill. State U., 1954; M.A., U. Colo., 1961; Ed.D., U. So. Cal., 1969. Counselor, tchr. English and journalism Crystal Lake (Ill.) Community High Sch., 1954-61; counselor Glendale (Cal.) High Sch., 1961-62; counselor, supr. U. So. Cal., 1962-67; sch. psychologist, Aurora, Ill., 1968; asst. prof. psychology, counseling and guidance U. No. Colo., Greeley, 1968—. Cons. Nat. Orgn. Women Rape Task Force, Greeley. Precinct committeewoman Democratic party, Ill., 1958-61, Colo., 1972-74; mem. county exec. com. Dem. party, 1973-74. Mem. Am. Psychol. Assn., Sch. Psychologists Assn., Women in Psychology, Am. Personnel and Guidance Assn. Home: 1703 19th Av Greeley CO 80631 Office: Dept Psychology Counseling and Guidance U No Colo Greeley CO 80631

RAVEN, CLARA, pathologist; ret. army officer; d. Morris and Lillian (Greenfield) Raven; B.A., U. Mich., 1927, M.S., 1928; postgrad. Duke, 1932-33; M.B., Northwestern U., 1936, M.D., 1938. Intern Women and Children's Hosp., Chgo., 1937-38; resident in pathology Cook County Hosp., Chgo., 1936-37, Chgo. Municipal Contagious Disease Hosp., 1937, Mahoning County (O.) Tb Hosp., 1940; research in bacteriology Herman Kiefer Hosp., Detroit, 1928-29, Mich. Children's Fund Studies, U. Mich., 1929-30, dept. medicine U. Chgo., 1930-31, Northwestern U., 1933-35, U. Liverpool (Eng.), 1938-39, Women's Med. Coll. Pa., 1939-40; instr. pathology U. Ill. Med. Sch., 1936-37; asso. clin. pathologist Women's Med. Coll. Pa., 1939-40; pathologist, dir. labs. Scranton (Pa.) State Gen. Hosp., 1941-43; commd. capt. U.S. Army, 1943, advanced through grades to col.; chief pathologist, dir. labs. U.S. Army Hosp., U.S. and Europe, 1944-47, VA Center, Dayton, O., 1947-51, Japan, 1951-53; pathologist Armed Forces Inst. Pathology, Washington, 1953-55; chief of labs., Ft. Rucker, Ala., 1955-57, Ft. Sill, Okla., 1957-59, ret., 1959, active res., 1959-65; dep. chief med. examiner Wayne County, Detroit, 1959-70, ret., 1970; now mem. Mich. Gov.'s Health Adv. Council, 1973—. Decorated service medals; recipient Northwestern U. Nat. Alumni Merit award, 1963; named Top Working Woman Detroit, 1966. Diplomate Am. Bd. Pathology. Fellow Am. Soc. Pathology and Bacteriology, Am. Soc. Clin. Pathology, Am. Coll. Pathology, Am. Acad. Forensic Scis., Am. Pub. Health Assn., Am. Soc. Tropical Medicine, and Hygiene, Internat. Acad. Pathology, Nat. Assn. Med. Examiners; mem. Am. Med. Writers Assn., A.M.A., Mich., Wayne County, N.Y. acads. scis., Am. Med. Women's Assn., Assn. Mil. Surgeons, Nat. Japanese Pathology Assn., Internat. Platform Assn., Ret. Officers Assn., Res. Officers Assn., Mil. Order World Wars, Nat. Assn. Uniformed Services, Nat. Assn. Fed. Employees, Women's Overseas Service League, D.A.V., Am. Legion, Altrusa Club, Detroit Philos. Soc. (dir.), Internat. Guild Infant Survival (adv. council). Author (with others) Japanese textbook on pathology, 1956. Contbr. articles to profl. publs. Home: 1419 Nicolet Place Detroit MI 48207

RAVEN, JUANITA GARCIA, educator; b. Vacaville, Cal., Feb. 21, 1926; d. Miguel and Mary Caparoos (Caparros) Garcia; B.A., San Francisco State Coll., 1948, M.A., 1955; M.A., San Francisco Coll. for Women, 1965; postgrad. U. Hawaii, 1958, U. Valencia, 1960; m. Richard C. Raven, Feb. 12, 1966 (dec. June 1966). Tchr., George Washington High Sch., San Francisco, 1950, Am. Dependent Sch., Japan, 1951-54; instr. Troop Information and Edn., Japan, 1952-54; adminstrv. asst. Fgn. Broadcasting Information Service, 1955; tchr., Portola Jr. High Sch., San Francisco, 1957, Oakland and Skyline High Sch., Oakland, Cal., 1957—. Mem. Cal. Atty. Gen.'s Vol. Adv. Council. Mem. Cal. Young Republicans, 1955-68; asso. soc. mem. Cal. Rep. State Central Com., 1966-70, mem., 1968—; sec. Cal. Rep. League, 1968, 2d. v.p., 1969, interim dir., 1970-72, pres., San Francisco chpt., 1970—, v.p. No. Cal., 1974; Twin Peaks area chmn. for Rep. Supr. James Mailliard, 1968; asso. mem. San Francisco County Rep. Central Com., 1968-71; mem. steering coms. for Gov. Ronald Reagan, Evelle Younger, Atty. Gen. Cal., Senator George Murphy; San Francisco chmn. Educators for Senator George Murphy, 1968; mem. Oakland Edn. Legislative Com., 1969-73; Bay area co-chmn. Re-election Pres. Nixon, 1972; dinner co-chmn. Flournoy for Gov., 1974. Nat. Def. Edn. Act French lang. grantee U. Hawaii, 1958. Mem. Fgn. Lang. Assn. No. Cal., Cal., Oakland tchrs. assns., Bus and Profl. Women's Club. Clubs: Olympic; Golden Gate Women's Tennis (pres. 1970-71); Presidio Yacht. Home: 120 Fernwood Dr San Francisco CA 94127 Office: 12250 Skyline Blvd Oakland CA 94619

RAVESON, BETTY RICH (MRS. SHERMAN H. RAVESON), columnist; b. Schenectady, June 16, 1913; d. Edwin L. and Florence (Nutree) Rich; A.B., Columbia, 1934; m. Sherman H. Raveson, Apr. 26, 1932. Eastchester editor Herald Statesman, Yonkers, N.Y., 1940-42; night bur. mgr. United Press Assn., Albany, 1942-43; Delray editor, columnist Palm Beach (Fla.) Illustrated, 1959-62; columnist Palm Beach Daily News, Delray Beach News-Jour., 1962-69, Boynton Beach News-Jour., 1966-69, Franklin (N.C.) Press, 1967—; feature writer Palm Beach Life mag., 1962-69, TV commentator, 1964—; exec. editor Palm Beach Voice, 1969-70; editor Mountain Living Mag., 1970—; v.p. Mountain Living, Inc., 1970—. Pub. relations dir. Delray Beach Playhouse, 1959-61. Mem. Bus. and Profl. Women's Club. Presbyn. Clubs: Fla. Women's Press; Fla. Gold Coast Press (outstanding achievement award 1963) (Delray Beach); Quills (Palm Beach); Atlanta Press; N.C. Press. Home: Wayah Valley Rd Franklin NC 28734 Office: PO Box 290 Franklin NC 28734

RAVEY, SISTER RUTH MARY, coll. adminstr.; b. Burlington, Vt., Aug. 21, 1933; d. Henry James and Lena Delia (Shequin) Ravey; student Catholic U. Am., 1956; B.A., Trinity Coll., 1960; postgrad. (Nat. Def. Edn. Act grantee) Boston U., 1967—; M.A., St. Michael's Coll., 1973. Joined Sisters of Mercy, 1951; tchr. Cathedral Grammar Sch., Burlington, 1957-60, Marian High Sch., Barre, Vt., 1960-68, Rice Meml. High Sch., 1968-71; dir. devel. and pub. relations Trinity Coll., Burlington, 1971—. Mem. Women's Polit. Caucus, Diocesan Bd. Edn. (chmn. 1973), Sisters' Senate (v.p. 1973), Sisters Mercy Formation Team. Home and office: Trinity Coll Burlington VT 05401

RAVID, ROSE JUNE (MRS. ALBERT JOSEPH RAVID), psychologist, health service adminstr.; b. Chgo., June 23, 1914; d. Jacob Steven and Adele (Becker) Stein; B.S., Roosevelt U., 1962, M.A., 1964; Ph.D., Ill. Inst. Tech., 1969; m. Albert Joseph Ravid, June 12, 1949; children—Geri (Mrs. Jerry Padzensky), Bruce, Fred. Staff psychologist Washington Blvd. Mental Health Center, Chgo., 1965-68; sr. psychologist Clark-Locust Mental Health Center, Chgo., 1968-72, community coordinator, 1969-73, dep. adminstr., 1973-74; coordinator alcoholism programs for N. Side, Chgo. Cons. to adult agys., Chgo. Mem. Am. Psychol. Assn., Am. Group Psychotherapy Assn. Home: 1342 Monroe River Forest IL 60305 Office: 4200 N Oak Park Av Chicago IL 60634

RAVIN, ROSE STEED, physician; b. Dallas, Jan. 11, 1911; d. Thomas Nelson and Etna (Atkinson) Steed; A.B., summa cum laude, So. Meth. U., 1934; M.D., U. Colo., 1938; m. Abe Ravin, Dec. 27, 1937; children—Thomas, Lenore. Intern, Colo. Gen. Hosp., Denver, 1938-39, N.E. Women and Children's Hosp., Boston, 1939-41; resident U. Colo. Sch. Medicine, 1941-45; asst. prof. dermatology U. Colo., Denver, 1950—; pvt. practice, Denver, 1945—. Recipient Woman of Achievement award So. Meth. U., 1972. Asso. fellow Am. Acad. Dermatology and Syphilology; mem. A.M.A., Rocky Mountain Dermatology Soc. (charter mem.), Colo. Dermatol. Assn. (pres. 1959-61), N.Am. Clin. Dermatologists (charter mem.), Am. Med. Women's Assn. (pres. Rocky Mountain chpt.), Phi Beta Kappa. Home: 45 S Dahlia St Denver CO 80222

RAWALT, MARGUERITE (MRS. HARRY SECORD), lawyer, govt. ofcl.; b. Prairie City, Ill., Oct. 16; d. Charles T. and Viola Bell (Flake) Rawalt; A.B., J.D., George Washington U., 1933, LL.M., 1936; LL.D., Baylor U., 1945; m. Harry Secord, May 1, 1937 (dec. 1963). Admitted to D.C. Bar, 1932, Tex. bar, 1935; tax atty. Office Chief Counsel, Internal Revenue Service, 1933-65, successively spl. and trial atty., chief brief rev. sect., 1933-49, asst. head appeals and civil divs., 1949-59, staff asst. to chief counsel, 1959-63, asst. dir. RL div., 1963-65; prof., lectr. George Washington U., 1973-74. Mem. Pres.'s Commn. on Status of Women, 1961-63, mem. Citizens Adv. Council, 1963-69; mem. D.C. Commn. on Status Women, 1967-69; organizing chmn. Equal Rights Amendment Ratification Council, 1972, vice chmn., 1973—. Mem. nat. bd. Woman's Med. Coll.; chmn. organizing com., 1957, dir. 1957—, Found. Fed. Bar Assn.; founder pres. Bus. and Profl. Women's Found. U.S., 1956. Recipient centennial award Berea Coll., 1955, award of merit D.A.R., 1956; named Profl. Woman of Year, D.C., 1957; recipient Nat. Achievement award Profl. Panhellenic Assn., 1967; Woman of Year award Ladies Home Jour., 1973; Mem. Am. (mem. ho. dels. 1943-44, 45-46, chmn. com. facilities Law Library of Congress 1947-48), Fed. (nat. pres. 1943-44, nat. council 1944—, asso. editor jour. 1944-47), D.C. bar assns., State Bar Tex., Women's Bar Assn. D.C., UN League Lawyers (registrar 1946-47), Nat. Assn. Women Lawyers (nat. pres. 1942-43, first mem. ho. dels.), Nat. Fedn. Bus. and Women's Clubs (nat. pres. 1954-56, nat. legal adviser, v.p. 1946-54, historian 1960-64), Nat. Orgn. for Women (gen. counsel 1966-69), Am. Assn. U. Women, Am. Judicature Soc., D.A.R., Internat. Fedn. Bus. and Profl. Women (dir. 1954-56), Gen. Fedn. Womens Clubs (nat. bd., chmn. status of women 1966-70), Order of Coif, Kappa Beta Pi, Zeta Tau Alpha. Club: Zonta (internat. 2d v.p. 1962-64). Address: 1600 S Joyce St Arlington VA 22202

RAWLS, CAROLINA DEMONTIGNE (MRS. OSCAR G. RAWLS), pub. relations dir.; b. Oshkosh, Wis.; d. Arthur Joseph and Frances (Wever) DeMontigne; B.S., Fla. State U., 1935, postgrad. library sci.; m. Oscar Grieson Rawls, July 16, 1936; 1 dau., Carolina DeMontigne. Librarian, Landon High Sch., Jacksonville, Fla., 1935-36; county supr. sch. libraries, Palo Pinto County, Tex., 1936-37; woman's commentator, radio sta. KARK, Little Rock, 1938-39; advt. layout and copy, editor house organ and serviceman's paper Cohen Bros. Dept. Store, Jacksonville, 1944-46; writer, producer 13 weeks series hist. programs, radio sta. WPDQ, Jacksonville, 1945; commentator radio sta. WOBS, Jacksonville, 1947; fashion commentary, coordination, prodn. (free lance), Jacksonville dept. stores and shops, including 2 fashion movies WMBR-TV, WJHP-TV and city-wide fashion show for C. of C., 1946—; compiler The Jacksonville Story, a history and pictorial record of city, C. of C., 1951; condr. programs WJHP-TV, 1955; asso. editor, feature writer Suntime mag., Jacksonville, 1952-56; pub. relations dir. Guild Players, Inc., 1955-71, bd. dirs., 1st woman trustee, 1956-71. Dir., sec. Ednl. TV, Inc., 1953-56; mem. program planning com. Ednl. TV of Jacksonville, WJCT-TV, 1957-58; dir. Queens Contest, Gator Bowl Assn., 1955-60; pres. Jr. Cotillion of Jacksonville, 1955-56; treas. Sr. Cotillion, 1956-58; publicity dir., mem. bd. Little Theatre of Jacksonville, 1948-54; instr. self-improvement courses YWCA, 1957-58; sec. Jacksonville Council of the Arts, 1957-61; performance chmn. Citywide Arts Festival, 1966-67; coordinator Furchgott's Dept. Store 100th Anniversary Celebration, 1967; 1st v.p. Four Found., Inc., 1971-73, pres., 1973; mem. Jacksonville Bicentennial Commn., 1974-76; membership chmn. Jacksonville Children's Museum, 1974—. Recipient Eve award Fla. Pub. Co., 1971. Mem. P.T.A., Friends of The Library, Friends of Jacksonville Library, Jacksonville, Fla. hist. socs., Panhellenic, Mortar Bd., Garnet Key, Alpha Chi Omega (chmn. nat. pub. relations com.), Phi Kappa Phi, Kappa Delta Pi. Democrat. Episcopalian. Club: Woman's of Jacksonville (2d v.p., civic dir. 1968, 1st v.p., fine arts dir. 1969-71, pres. 1971-73). Home: 1357 Tiber Av Jacksonville FL 32207

RAWLS, ELMYRA MARY (MRS. LESLIE ELEY BUSH), antique dealer; b. Franklin, Va., Apr. 30, 1900; d. Uriah and Nannie Elizabeth (Cotton) Rawls; student Va. Intermont Coll., 1920-21, William and Mary Coll., 1921; m. Leslie Eley Bush, Sept. 24, 1921; children—Jacquelin S., Dorothy Turner, Jeanne Campbell. Owner So. Antique Shop, Richmond, Va., 1936—. Mem. Nat. Antiques Dealers Assn. Baptist. Home: 3911 Brook Rd Richmond VA 23227 Office: 8 E Main St Richmond VA 23219

RAWLS, EUGENIA (MRS. DONALD RAY SEAWELL), actress; b. Macon, Ga.; d. Hubert Fields and Louise (Roberts) Rawls; grad. Wesleyan Conservatory, 1932; student U. N.C., 1933; m. Donald Ray Seawell, Apr. 5, 1941; children—Eugenia Ashley Brook (Mrs. John Joseph Speidel), Donald Brockman. Appeared in numerous Broadway plays including The Children's Hour, 1934, Pride and Prejudice, 1936, The Little Foxes, 1939, 41, Margaret Webster's Shakespeare Company: Guest in the House, 1942, Rebecca, 1945, The Second Mrs. Tanqueray, 1940, The Shrike, 1952, Private Lives, 1949, The Great Sebastians, 1956, First Love, 1961, The Glass Menagerie, 1965, 67, Our Town, 1967; Tallulah, A Memory, Lincoln Center, 1971, London, 1974, Affectionately Yours Fanny Kemble, London, 1974; The Enchanted Kennedy Center, 1973; presented one woman show Fanny Kemble at Arts Theatre, London, 1969; appeared Abbey Theatre, Dublin, Ireland, 1972; toured Europe with one woman show, 1972; recorded talking books for the blind; appeared TV programs, including U.S. Steel, Love of Life. Mem. com. Plays for Living, 1964-67. Rockefeller Found. artist-in-residence, Denver U., 1967-68, U. Tampa, 1970; artist-in-residence U. No. Colo., 1971, 72, 73, Internat. Theatre Inst. Congress, Prague, 1968. Recipient Alumna award U. N.C., 1969, Distinguished Achievement award Wesleyan Coll., 1969, Gold Chair award Central City (Colo.) Opera House Assn., 1973, (with husband) Frederick H. Koch Drama award U. N.C., 1974. Address: 510 E 84th St New York City NY 10028

RAWLS, SHEILA D. KIRSCH (MRS. WALTER C. RAWLS), civic worker; b. Doncaster, Eng.; d. Samuel M. and Pola (Danielska) Kirsch; grad. Harrogate Coll., 1947; grad. La Chatelainie (Neuchatel, Switzerland), 1949; degree in Langs., U. Neuchatel; m. Walter C. Rawls, Jr., June 30, 1954; children—James David, Richard Wayne. Mem. Duval Med. Center Auxiliary. Clubs: Overseas Women's (pres. 1966-70), San Jose Woman's (treas. 1967), Metropolitan Dinner, British-American, Southside Women's Bowling League (pres. 1968-70), Early Birds Women's Bowling League (pres. 1968-70). Home: 6962 Almours Dr Jacksonville FL 32217

RAWSON, ELEANOR STIERHEM, editor; m. Kennett Longley Rawson, Feb. 19, 1954; children—Linda, Kennett Longley. Formerly reporter Atlantic City, N.J.; editorial staff, writer Am. Mag., free-lance writer for radio, mags., newspaper syndicates, fiction editor Today's Woman mag., Collier's mag.; currently v.p., exec. editor David McKay Co., book pubs.; teaching staff Columbia, 1956-57; lectr. Columbia, N.Y.U., New Sch., N.Y. Trustee Suffolk Museum; mem. exec. council Am. Assn. Pubs. Mem. Women's Nat. Book Assn., Stony Brook Found., N.Y. Infirmary Aux., Soc. Meml. Hosp. Women's Aux. Mather Meml. Hospital, P.E.N., Overseas Press Club of Am. Clubs: Old Field (Stony Brook); Women's City (N.Y.). Home: Blueberry Bay Farm 23 Brewster Lane Setauket NY 11733 Office: David McKay Co 750 3d Av New York City NY 10017

RAY, ALICE KUNZ, coll. ofcl.; b. Springfield, Ill., Dec. 19, 1917; d. Frank E. and Mabel C. (Gillespie) Kunz; B.J., U. Mo., 1939; M.A., U. Chgo., 1945; m. Hartley C. Ray, 1957 (div.). Gen. assignment reporter Ill. State Register, Springfield, 1939-42; adoptive placement worker Chgo. Child Care Soc., 1942-45; instr. sociology U. Tex. at El Paso, 1945-46; asst. pub. relations dir. Community Fund of Chgo. and Crusade of Mercy, Chgo., 1946-73; asst. to chmn. fund raising campaign U. Chgo. Sch. Social Service Adminstrn., 1969-73; asso. dir. devel. Berry Coll., Rome, Ga., 1973—. Mem. Pub. Relations Soc. Am. (past officer, dir. Chgo. chpt.). Home: 11 Shorter Circle Rome GA 30161 Office: Mount Berry GA 30149

RAY, BETTY (BLANCHE SMITH RAY), coll. adminstr.; b. Jeffersonville, Ga., July 23, 1920; d. Smith W. and Blanche A. (Cook) Ray; A.B., Wesleyan Coll., 1942. Field rep., disaster case worker A.R.C., Atlanta, 1943-57; dir. pub. relations United Fund, St. Petersburg, Fla., 1957-59, 65-66; advt. copy writer dir. radio and TV prodn., asst. to pres. Griffith Advt., St. Petersburg, 1959-63; with Louis Benito Advt., Tampa, Fla., 1963-65; account exec. Lino and Assos., St. Petersburg, 1966; asst. dir. pub. information Eckerd Coll. St. Petersburg, Fla., 1966-68, dir. pub. information, 1968—. Bd. dirs. South Pinellas chpt. A.R.C., 1969—, vice chmn., 1972—, mem. adv. council, 1972—; Recipient public relations award Fla. Pub. Relations Assn., 1963. Mem. Women in Communications, Am. Coll. Pub. Relations Assn. Episcopalian. Contbr. to profl. publs. Home: 2312 Andalusia Way NE St Petersburg FL 33704 Office: Eckerd Coll PO Box 12560 St Petersburg FL 33733

RAY, DOROTHY FLORENCE STULL, banker; b. Pierceville, Kan., July 1, 1926; d. Charles Mead and Mabel Era (Ward) Douglass; ed. pub. schs., Dodge City (Kan.) Bus. Coll.; m. Lyman F.T. Ray, Feb. 5, 1972; children by previous marriage—Douglass Stull, Brent Stull, Shane Stull. With Valley State Bank, Syracuse, Kan., 1944-45, 1st Nat. Bank of Dodge City, 1945-47; v.p. 1st Nat. Bank in Wichita (Kan.), 1947—. Mem. Wichita C. of C., Nat. Assn. Bank Women, Ins. Women of Wichita (pres. 1971-72). Lutheran. Club: Soroptimist. Home: 623 Highland Park Dr Mulvane KS 67110 Office: PO Box 880 Wichita KS 67201

RAY, DOROTHY JEAN (MRS. VERNE FREDERICK RAY), author; b. Cedar Falls, Ia., Oct. 10, 1919; d. Oscar Theodore and Vina Evelyn (Younker) Tostlebe; B.A. cum laude, U. No. Ia., 1941; postgrad. Radcliffe Coll., 1949-50, U. Alaska, 1952-53, U. Wash., 1954-55; m. Verne Frederick Ray, Feb. 2, 1955; 1 son, Eric Stanley Thompson. Researcher and writer Eskimos of Alaska, Labrador and Umatilla, Cowlitz Indians, 1950-68; cons., asst. to editor publs. Am. Enthnol. Soc., 1958-62, U. Washington Press, 1958—, Alaska mag., Alaska Jour., Assn. Research Libraries, Indian Arts and Crafts Bd.; coordinator Alaska Sci. Conf. Alaska div. A.A.A.S., 1953. Grantee, Arctic Inst. N.Am., 1950, Am. Philos. Soc., 1968, U. Wash., 1954, 55; scholar U. No. Ia., 1954-55. Mem. Soc. Woman Geographers, Wilderness Soc., Am. Name Soc. Author: Artists of the Tundra And The Sea, 1961; Eskimo Masks: Art And Ceremony, 1967; Graphic Arts Of The Alaskan Eskimo, 1969. Contbr. articles to profl. jours. Home: PO Box 586 Port Townsend WA 98368

RAY, GRACE ERNESTINE, writer, educator; b. Bernie, Mo., Jan. 8, 1900; d. Ernest Elmer and Geneva Belle (McElyea) Ray; B.A., U. Okla., 1920, M.A., 1923. Faculty, U. Okla., Norman, 1920-70, prof. journalism, 1953-70, prof. emeritus, 1970—; writer articles appearing in various publs. including Mademoiselle, Sci. Digest, Ford Times, Med. Tribune, Country Gentleman, Western Horseman, Coronet, Okla. Today, Am. Forests, N.Y. Times, Washington Post, Chgo. Tribune, Kansas City Star, San Francisco Chronicle, Dallas News. Faculty research grantee U. Okla., 1962. Mem. Am. Assn. U. Profs., Am. Assn. U. Women, Southwestern Assn. Naturalists, Okla. Ornithol. Soc., Women in Communications (Matrix Table citation as Faculty Woman of Year 1953), Phi Beta Kappa, Kappa Tau Alpha. Author: Early Oklahoma Newspapers, 1928; Wily Women of the West, 1972. Home: 520 W Symmes St Norman OK 73069 Office: 860 Van Vleet Oval Norman OK 73069

RAY, HOPE WALKER (MRS. KENNETH C. RAY), club woman; b. McConnelsville, O., Oct. 11, 1906; d. S. Carlton and Grace (Wells) Walker; student Ohio U., 1940-41; A.B. in Edn., George Washington U., 1958; m. Kenneth C. Ray, June 24, 1931; children—John Walker, Beverly Ann (Mrs. Daniel Klineko). Tchr., Morgan County (O.) schs., 1925-31. Mem. D.A.R. (past regent), Daus. Colonial Wars, Columbian Women George Washington U., Am. Assn. U. Women, Pi Lambda Theta. Republican. Methodist. Mem. Order Eastern Star. Author: (elementary grade workbooks) Number Trails, 1938. Home: 263 E Main St McConnelsville OH 43756

RAY, INEZ POE, librarian; b. Apex, N.C., Mar. 15, 1915; d. Herbert Mont and Nancy Katherine (Andrews) Poe; A.B., Meredith Coll., 1935; A.B., U. N.C., 1938, M.A., 1970; m. Marl Ellis Ray, Aug. 29, 1943; children—Philip Ellis, Karen Inez. Tchr., Norwood (N.C.) High Sch., 1935-37; librarian Farm Security Adminstrn., Raleigh, N.C., 1938-40, Murray State Tchrs. Coll., 1940-42; library cons. N.C. Dept. Pub. Instrn., 1962; librarian Wake Forest High Sch., 1963-65; coordinator curriculum materials center N.C. State U., 1965-74. Leader, Girl Scouts U.S.A., 1955-62. Mem. League Women Voters (pres. Raleigh 1956-59), Chaucer Book Club. Baptist. Home: 3401 Noel Ct Raleigh NC 27607

RAY, JANET MARIE WOLFGANG, clergywoman; b. Hanover, Pa., July 29, 1940; d. Jacob Wilson and Florence Jennie (Bankert) Wolfgang; A.B., Catawba Coll., 1962; B.D., Lancaster Theol. Sem., 1965; m. Harry Forrest Ray, Aug. 27, 1961. Ordained to ministry United Ch. Christ, 1965; co-pastor Lemasters (Pa.) Charge United Ch. Christ, 1965-70; interim pastor Grindstone Hill Charge United Ch. Christ, Lemasters, 1971; asso. pastor Lemasters-Upton Charge United Ch. Christ, 1971—; interim pastor Ft. Loudon-McConnellsburg Charge, United Ch. Christ, 1973-74, Heidelberg United Ch. of Christ, Marion, Pa., 1974—. Substitute tchr. pub. schs., Lemasters, 1965—. Mem. camping com. Pa. Central Conf. United Ch. Christ, 1968-72, sec. bd. dirs. Camp Michaux, 1969-71. Mem. Centennial Com. Lemasters, 1972; chmn. home selection com. Am. Field Service, 1967-71, pres. Mercersburg chpt., 1973-74; mem. Intercamp and Conf. Com., Central Pa., 1971—; mem. nominating com. United Ch. Christ Gen. Synod, 1973—, bd. dirs. Penn Central Conf., 1973—, mem. exec. com. Mercersburg Assn. of Penn Central Conf., 1973—. Bd. dirs. Franklin County Sunday Sch. Assn. Mem. Am. Assn. U. Women (area rep. for internat. relations 1972-74), Soc. Farm Women Franklin County. Home: PO Box 105 Lemasters PA 17231

RAY, MARGOT SMITH (MRS. PHILIP B. RAY), charity exec.; b. Benton, Ill., Jan. 16, 1916; d. O.C. and Cora Alice (Crisp) Smith; B.A. (Noel scholar 1934-37), James Millikin U., 1937; m. Philip B. Ray, Jan. 30, 1938. Tax checker State Ill., Springfield, 1943-46; campaign dir. Community Chest, Wichita, Kan., 1950-53; asst. devel. officer Wichita State U., 1953-57; campaign dir. United Fund Wichita and Sedgwick County, Wichita, Kan., 1957-71, asso. exec. dir., campaign dir., 1971—. City Gray Lady chmn. A.R.C., 1947-50; dir. U.S.O., 1957-68; mem. finance com. YWCA, 1957—; mem. adv. com. Wichita Centennial, 1970-71. Adviser to numerous civic, hosp. and agy. capital fund campaigns. Mem. Alpha Chi Omega. Baptist. Club: Soroptimist (pres. 1960-61) (Wichita). Home: 1626 Womer Dr Wichita KS 67203 Office: 515 Insurance Bldg 212 N Market St Wichita KS 67202

RAY, MAY ELIZABETH CAIN (MRS. HOMER WALLACE RAY, JR.), newspaper pub.; b. Mangum, Okla., Dec. 2, 1927; d. Ralph Emerson and Lessie Elizabeth (Marsh) Cain; grad. high sch.; m. Homer Wallace Ray, Jr., July 23, 1961; 1 son, Mike Wallace. With Vici Beacon, 1945-47, 56-60; co-pub. Yale (Okla.) News, weekly newspaper, 1965—; stringer Tulsa Tribune, 1973—; comml. photographer, 1967—; journalist, 1965—; corr., 1965—. Mem. Bicentennial Heritage '76 Com. for Okla., 1973—. Del. Okla. Dem. Conv., 1969. Mem. Nat. Newspaper Assn., Okla. Press Assn., Okla., Cimarron Valley hist. socs., Yale C. of C. (chmn. retail promotion 1968-73), Beta Sigma Phi, Sigma Delta Chi. Mem. Christian Ch. Mem. Order Eastern Star. Club: All-Sports Booster (Yale, Okla.). Research Okla. history and Jim Thorpe family. Address: Box 307 Yale OK 74085

RAY, NANCY RAY, journalist; b. Geneva, Ill., May 23, 1930; d. Chester Nelson and Mabel Margaret (Gloeckler) Benjamin; B.A. cum laude in Journalism, U. Neb., 1952; M.A. in Econs., Mt. Holyoke Coll., 1956; m. George Webster Ray, Nov. 1, 1958 (div. 1963); children—James Benjamin, Christopher Barton. Reporter Lincoln (Neb.) Star, 1949-53, 56-65; news editor East Denver Jour., 1954; news dir. radio sta. KGMC, Englewood, Colo., 1954-55; reporter San Diego Union, 1965—. Regents scholar, 1948-52, Seacrest scholar, 1953; recipient State Woman of the Year in Journalism award U. Neb., 1958, Best News Story award North San Diego County Press Assn., 1968. Mem. Women in Communications, Phi Beta Kappa, Alpha Lambda Delta, Psi Chi, Pi Beta Phi, Sigma Delta Chi. Democrat. Presbyn. Clubs: North San Diego County Press (v.p.), San Diego Press. Home: 401 9th St Del Mar CA 92014 Office: 350 Camino de la Reina San Diego CA 92112

RAY, MRS. ROBERT D., wife of gov. Ia.; b. Colombus Junction, Ia., May 16, 1928; d. Herbert F. and Eva (Hickman) Hornberger; B.S. in Edn. cum laude, Drake U., 1950; m. Robert D. Ray, Dec. 22, 1951; children—Randi Sue, Lu Ann, Vicki Jo. Tchr. elementary sch., 1950-55. Active United Campaign, Heart Fund, March of Dimes, Easter Seals, Mental Health drives. Mem. Polk County Atty. Wives, Drake Nat. Alumni Assn. (dir. 1970—), Chi Omega. Address: 2900 Grand Av Des Moines IA 50312

RAY, RUTH, violinist; b. Alvin, Ill.; d. Frank H. and Anna L. (Moyer) Ray; student U. Chgo. Am. Conservatory Music, Chgo.; Mus. M., Eastman Sch. Music, U. Rochester, 1941; violin student of Leopold Auer, 6 yrs. Debut Carnegie Hall, N.Y.C., Nov. 4, 1919; appeared as soloist with N.Y. Philharmonic Orch., Nat. Symphony, Chgo. Symphony, Balt. Symphony and Mpls. Symphony orchs., Woman's Symphony Orch. Chgo., U. Chgo. Orch. and in individual recitals throughout U.S. and Can.; recitals in Germany and France, summer 1952, 54, 65, Holland, Germany, Switzerland, summer 1968. Mem. adv. bd., head ensemble dept., Columbia Sch. Music, Chgo., 1924-33; pvt. studio, 1933—; head violin dept., also classes and lectures in mus. hist. and appreciation Bradley Coll. Music, Peoria, 1929-45, Cornell Coll., Mt. Vernon, Ia., 1945-57, string coach U. Chgo., Orch., 1933-38; concertmaster Woman's Symphony Orch., 1927-30. Mem. Am. Assn. U. Profs., Pi Kappa Lambda, Mu Phi Epsilon. Composer short pieces for violin and piano, Midland Tune and My Lord, What a Mournin. Home: 815 Judson Av Evanston IL 60202

RAY, RUTH (MRS. JOHN R. GRAHAM), artist; b. N.Y.C., Nov. 8, 1919; d. Oscar Willard and Marie (Beynon) Ray; student Swarthmore Coll., 1936-38, Barnard Coll., 1938-39, Art Students League, 1939-41; m. John Reginald Graham, Jan. 3, 1948 (dec.); children—Ian, Willard R., Lyle. One-man shows Norlyst Gallery, N.Y.C., 1944, Ferargil, N.Y.C., 1947, 49, Raymond and Raymond, Cal., 1947, Stamford (Conn.) Mus., 1950, Silvermine Guild Artists 1952, Darien (Conn.) Pub. Library, 1958, 59, 63, Grand Central Art Galleries, N.Y.C., 1958, 62, 66, 70, Window Gallery, N.Y.C., 1958; Columbus (Ga.) Mus., 1964, State Nat. Bank, Darien, Conn., Rive Gauche, Denver, Silvermine Guild, Conn., Nat. Art Mus. Sport, N.Y.; 19th one-man show at Marymount Coll., 1968; included in 4 Carnegie Anns., Whitney Ann., 1959, N.A.D., Nat. Assn. Women Artists, Pa. Acad. Ann., 1959, Allied Artists, Audubon Artists, Conn. Acad. Fine Arts, New Haven Paint and Clay Club; represented in Springfield Mus. Fine Arts, Columbus Mus. Art, Fla. So. Coll., Norfolk Mus. Art, N.A.D., Nat. Art Mus. of Sport, also pvt. collections; illustrator books, comml. artist for several bus. firms; radio and TV appearances, N.Y.C. Mem. adv. bd. Nat. Art Mus. Recipient Alger prize Nat. Assn. Women Artists, 1945, Marcia Brady Tucker prize, 1953; popular and purchase prize Springfield Mus. Fine Arts, 1946; purchase prize La Tausca, N.Y., 1946; Julius Hallgarten prize N.A.D., 1948; popular prize Conn. Contemporary Exhbn., 1950; prize Silvermine N.E. Ann., 1953; major award Conn. Acad. Fine Arts, 1953; medal of honor Am. Artists mag., 1956; bronze medal Allied Artists Am., 1957; Mrs. Stanley Simon award Silvermine Guild Artists, 1959; New Haven Paint and Clay, 1960; Allied Artists, 1960, 63; hon. mention Smithsonian Instrn., 1963; 1st profl. prize, Darien, 1967. Mem. Silvermine Guild Artists, Conn. Acad. Fine Arts, Allied Artists Am., Art Students League (life), Grand Central Galleries, N.A.D. (council 1969-72). Presbyn. Clubs: Ox Ridge (bd. stewards) (Darien). Address: 291 Mansfield Av Darien CT 06820

RAYBERN, JUDITH ANN, educator; b. Indpls., July 16, 1939; d. Luell C. Raybern and Evelyn H. (Jacob) Raybern Kane; B.S. in Elementary Edn., Butler U., 1961, M.S. in Elementary Edn. Adminstrn., 1965, postgrad., 1970; Ed.D., Ind. U., 1974. Tchr. Indpls. pub. schs., 1961-70, elementary asst. prin., 1970-72; instr. lang. arts Ind. U., Bloomington, 1972-74, Indpls., 1972-73, Columbus, 1973; asst. prof. edn. DePauw U., Greencastle, Ind., 1974—. Mem. Ind. Gov.'s. Adv. Council, Ind., 1968, Ind. Adv. Council, 1969-71, Ind. Textbook Commn. Lang. Arts, 1968. Mem. Nat. Council Tchrs. English, Internat. Reading Assn., Soc. for Intensified Edn. (treas. 1969-73), Bus. and Profl. Women's Orgn., Nat. Assn. Adminstrv. Women, Ind. Assn. Elementary Principals, Delta Kappa Gamma, Pi Lambda Theta, Delta Delta Delta. Mem. Ch. of Christ. Home: Apt 125 215 Wood St Greencastle IN 46135

RAYBURN, CAROLE ANN (MRS. RONALD ALLEN RAYBURN), psychologist; b. Washington, Feb. 14, 1938; d. Carl Frederick and Mary Helen (Milkie) Miller; B.A., Am. U., 1961; M.A., George Washington U., 1965; Ph.D., Catholic U. Am., 1969; m. Ronald Allen Rayburn, June 18, 1964. Clin. psychology extern D.C. Gen. Hosp., 1962-63; clin. psychologist Spring Grove State Hosp., Catonsville, Md., 1966-68; research psychologist Regional Med. Services of Washington, also lectr. psychology Strayer Coll., Washington, 1969-70; clin. psychologist, instl. care services div. D.C. Children's Center, Laurel, Md., 1970—. Cons. psychologist for community psychologists, Washington, 1966—; psychotherapist, Silver Spring, Md., 1971—; cons. psychologist Julia Brown Montessori Sch., Laurel, 1970—. Mem. Tamarack Triangle Civic Assn., Silver Spring, 1973—. Fellow Md. Psychol. Assn. (com. ethics and profl. standards); mem. Am., D.C. (community affairs com.) psychol. assns., Am., D.C. (mem. task forces on use of drugs, monitoring and evaluation of health programs, instl. care children and adults 1973—) pub. health assns., Am. Orthopsychiat. Assn., Montgomery County Mental Health Assn., Am. Civil Liberties Union, A.A.A.S., Council for Advancement of Psychol. Professions and Scis., Balt. Assn. Cons. Psychologists, Psi Chi. Mem. Seventh-Day Adventist (asst. chairperson community services 1973-74). Home: 1200 Morningside Dr Silver Spring MD 20904 Office: Institutional Care Services Div Laurel MD 20810

RAYMOND, HELEN JAMES, legal sec., journalist; b. Pitts., Sept. 14, 1913; d. Robert Leroy and Elora (Brandon) James; student Sweet Briar Coll., 1931-32, Mary Baldwin Coll., 1932-35; div.; children—Eileen (Mrs. G. Kenneth Corbitt), Helen-Mar (Mrs. Robert Stockton Michener), James Edward, Robert MacPherson, William Brewster. Exec. sec. Keep Am. Out of War Com., Boston, 1937-39; reporter Country Courier, West Brookfield, Mass., 1953-57; sec. Weymouth Art Leather, South Braintree, 1957-60; reporter Hull News Mirror, North Scituate, 1965—, Boston Herald, 1970-72; legal sec., Hingham, Mass., 1969—. Pres. Hull High Sch. P.T.A., 1959-61; mem. state com. Citizens for Participation Politics, 1970-72; chmn. Hull Youth Commn., 1971—; mem. Hull Hist. and Bicentennial Commn., 1973—. Mem. Hull Dem. Town Com., 1972—. Mem. Hull Hist. Soc. (pres. 1970-74). Conglist (supt. primary dept. 1960-62). Home: 74 Kingsley Rd Hull MA 02045 Office: 115 North St Hingham MA 02043

RAYMOND, LOUISE VANDERGRIFT, bus. exec.; b. Bordentown, N.J.; d. Louis J. and Anna (Mills) Vandegrift; B.S., Douglass Coll., 1923; m. Bouvier L. Raymond, Aug. 1, 1929 (div. June 1950). Tchr., Ventnor Pub. Schs., 1927-42; real estate and property mgmt., 1950—; pres., owner Lake Realty, Inc., 1952—, Lake Property Mgmt. Corp., 1961—; pres. Palm Beach Realty Listing Bur., 1969. Mem. C. of C., Nat., Fla. assns. realtors, Palm Beach Bd. Realtors (past pres.), Inst. Real Estate Mgmt., Internat. Real Estate Fedn., Nat. Assn. Real Estate Bds. (v.p. Palm Beach County women's council 1968). Address: 455 Australian Av Palm Beach FL 33480

RAYMOND, MARILYNN A., dietitian; b. Davenport, Ia., Oct. 8, 1941; d. Robert J. and Mae (Roche) Raymond; B.A., Clarke Coll., 1963. Dietetic intern VA Hosp., Hines, Ill., 1963-64; therapeutic dietitian ARA-Hosp. Food Mgmt. Central DuPage Hosp., Winfield, Ill., 1964-65; supervising dietitian Midwest Region ARA-Hosp. Food Mgmt., Chgo., 1965-66, asst. exec. dietitian, Phila., 1966-69, dir. patient services, Phila., 1969-73; v.p. hosp. food mgmt. ARA Food Services Co., Phila., 1973—. Cons., White House Conf. on Food, Nutrition and Health, 1969. Mem. Am., Pa., Phila. (mem. exec. com. 1969-70) dietetic assns., Am., Phila. (mem. exec. com. 1969-70) home econs. assns., Phila. Home Economists in Bus. (treas. 1971-73). Home: 2904 Monterey Ct Springfield PA 19064 Office: Independence Square W 6th at Walnut St Philadelphia PA 19106

RAYMOND, PHYLLIS HALL (MRS. RICHARD L. RAYMOND), coll. adminstr.; b. Phila., Nov. 29, 1932; d. Philip S. and Elizabeth B. (Barr) Hall; student Swarthmore Coll., 1950-53, William and Mary Coll., 1953; B.A. (scholar 1956), Ind. U., 1956; M.A., Swarthmore Coll., 1971; m. Richard L. Raymond, Aug. 16, 1952; children—Richard Lee, David G., Philip H., Jean E. Substitute tchr. Media Friends Sch., Media, Pa., 1968-70; asst. to deans Swarthmore (Pa.) Coll., 1971—. Pres., Upper Providence Aux., Riddle Meml. Hosp., 1961-63; mem. alumni council Swarthmore Coll., 1970-73. Bd. dirs. Media Friends Sch. Mem. Nat. Assn. Women Deans, Adminstrs. and Counselors, Pa. Assn. Women Deans and Counselors. Republican. Mem. Soc. of Friends (mem. religious edn. com., budget and finance com. 1971—). Home: 630 University Pl Swarthmore PA 19081

RAYNER, MARY ANN (POLLY), newspaper editor; b. Bethlehem, Pa.; d. John Joseph and Cecilia M. (Skledar) Rayner; B.A., Moravian Coll., 1953; postgrad. Lehigh U: Gen. reporter, photographer, feature writer Call-Chronicle, Allentown, Pa., family living sect. editor, 1966—, women's editor Morning Call and Evening Chronicle, 1973—. Bd. dirs. Womens Ednl. Liaison div. United Fund, Allentown, Pa.; chmn. nominating com. for bd. dirs. Moravian Coll., 1966, scholarship com., 1972; bd. dirs. Lehigh Valley Mental Health Assn. Recipient citations for outstanding community service, United Fund, Allentown, also numerous other state and nat. awards for writing, Frany award for meritorious and outstanding fashion reporting, 1974. Mem. Am. Assn. U. Women, Nat. Fedn. Press Women, Pa. Womens Press Assn., Women Editors Am. Dailies (charter mem.), Pi Delta Epsilon (v.p.) Clubs: Moravian Coll. Alumnae, Washington Press, Pa. Press. Home: 1130 E 3d St Bethlehem PA 18015 Office: 6th and Linden Sts Allentown PA 18105

RAYWID, MARY ANNE, educator; b. Washington, Oct. 25, 1928; d. Leo and Vivian Eleanor (Thrift) Raywid; A.B., U. N.C., 1949; M.A., U. Ill., 1950, Ph.D., 1959; m. Raymond Lewis Scheele, Mar. 28, 1964; 1 son, Scott Alan. Editor N.E.A., 1950-54; tchr. history and civics Evanston (Ill.) High Sch., 1956-58; prof. philosophy of edn. Hofstra U., 1959—; speaker, author, schools cons. Mem. John Dewey Soc. (pres.), Middle Atlantic Philosophy of Edn. Soc. (past pres.), Am. Ednl. Studies Assn. (exec. council 1970-72), Philosophy of Edn. Soc. (exec. bd. 1972-75). Author: The Ax-Grinders, 1962. Mem. bd. editors of Studies in Philosophy and Edn., 1968—, Jour. of Thought, 1972—. Contbr. articles to profl. jours. Office: Hofstra University Hempstead NY 11550

REA, PAULINE HELEN, civic worker; b. Fremont County, Ia., Mar. 14, 1912; d. Clinton J. and Martha Jane (Barrett) Sanderson; student Tchrs. Coll., Cedar Falls, Ia.; m. Verbyl LeRoy Schnepp, May 21, 1932; 1 son, Danny Lee (dec.); m. 2d, Maurice Gerald Rea, Jan. 26, 1974. Bookkeeper, Schnepp Ford Agy., 1958-61; office mgr., agt. Schnepp Ins. Agy., 1961-70; with County Treas. and Automobile Dept., Sidney, 1971-73. Exec. bd. Fremont County Hist. Soc.; bd. dirs. Fremont County chpt. Ia. Cancer Soc. Pres., Ia. Fedn. Republican Women, 1974-75, membership chmn., 1970-71, 1st v.p., orgn. chmn., 1972-73; pres. 7th Dist. Rep. Women, 1969-71; co-chmn. Fremont County Rep. Central Com., 1960—; twp. committeewoman Rep. party. Address: Rural Route 1 Sidney IA 51652

READ, CLAUDIA MOORE (MRS. CHARLES LEWIS READ), educator; b. Concord, N.C., Mar. 6, 1913; d. Zebulon Morris and Grace (Fisher) Moore; B.S. U. N.C.G., 1934; M.A., N.Y.U., 1942; student U. Va., summer 1964; m. Charles Lewis Read, July 25, 1946. Instr. phys. edn. U. Neb., Lincoln, 1934-38; Fla. State U., Tallahassee, 1938-39; asst. tchr. Doris Humphrey and Charles Weidman Studio, N.Y.U. and Columbia U., N.Y.C., 1939-40; asst., demonstrator Charles Weidman, N.Y.U., 1940-41; guest tchr. New Paltz (N.Y.) Normal Sch., 1941-42; instr. phys. edn. State Tchrs. Coll., LaCrosse, Wis., 1942-44; asst. prof. phys. edn. U. Colo., Boulder, 1944-45; prof. phys. edn. Mary Washington Coll., Fredericksburg, Va., 1945—. Mem. dance subcom. Va. Commn. on Arts and Humanities, 1968-72. Bd. dirs. Va. Mus. Fine Arts, 1956—. Mem. A.A.H.P.E.R., Va. Assn. Health, Phys. Edn. and Recreation, Am. Dance Therapy Assn., Com. on Research in Dance (dir. 1970-73), Dance Notation Bur., Am. Dance Guild, Nat., So. assns. phys. edn. coll. women, Va. Dance Soc. (dir.). Methodist. Home: 1400 Brent St Fredericksburg VA 22401

READ, HELEN APPLETON, art historian; b. Bklyn., 1887; d. Ruel Ross and Mary (Schaumburg) Appleton; grad. Bklyn. Heights Sem.; A.B., Smith Coll., 1908; student Art Students League, 1909-12; m. Charles Albert Read, May 29, 1914; 1 dau., Helen (Edmund K. Trent). Art critic Bklyn. Daily Eagle, 1922-38; contbg. art editor Vogue mag., 1925-31; dir. Portraits, Inc., 1943-57, pres., 1957-74; dir. exhbn. 400 Years of German Painting, 1939, Am. painting sent to Latin Am. capitols, 1943, under auspices coordinator cultural relations between N. Am. and S. Am. Recipient Medal of Honor, Salmagundi Club, 1967; medal Smith Coll., 1968. Lectr. Am. and German art, romantic art, Am. colls. and univs. Mem. Alumnae Assn. Smith Coll., Bklyn. Jr. League (charter). Clubs: Cosmopolitan, Smith College (N.Y.C.). Author: Robert Henri, 1931; Caspar David Friedrich, 1939. Contbr. to art publs. Home: 146 Hicks St Brooklyn NY 11201 Office: 41 E 57th St New York City NY 10022

READ, SUE ELLEN, counselor; b. Houston, Dec. 20, 1942; d. George Edward and Louise B. (Fletcher) Read; B.A., Northeastern State Coll., 1964; M.A. in counseling, Central State Coll., 1971. Counselor Oklahoma City Bd. Edn., 1964-66, 1968-70, Okla. County Child Welfare Unit, 1966-68, Central State U., 1970-71, Heritage Hall Upper Sch., Oklahoma City, 1971—. Active speakers bur. Dem. polit. campaigns. Named outstanding young woman of Oklahoma City, Bus. and Profl. Women's Club, 1970, outstanding young woman of Okla., 1970. Mem. Okla. Speech Assn. (exec. sec. 1967-68), Assn. Women Deans and Counselors, Nat. Assn. Coll. Counselors (assembly del. 1971-72), Nat. Forensic League. Author: Oklahoma City Speech Curriculum Guide K-12, 1970; Oklahoma City Debate Curriculum

Guide 7-12, 1971. Home: 4766 NW 25th St Oklahoma City OK 73127 Office: 3704 N Walker St Oklahoma City OK 73112

READING, JUNE ALLEN (MRS. JAMES E. READING), mus. dir.; b. Chgo., Oct. 23, 1918; d. Thomas Rexford and Lillian Catherine (Brunet) Allen; B.A., U. Minn., 1940; m. James E. Reading, June 27, 1961. Mem. staff Junipero Serra Mus., San Diego, 1957-60; sec. Hist. Shrine Found., 1954-60, acting dir. Whaley House Museum, 1960—. Mem. citizen adv. com. for landmark restoration, San Diego, 1956-60. Mem. San Diego (dir. 1957-68, Meritorious Service award 1960, award Merit 1973), Cabrillo Nat. Monument hist. socs., Conf. Cal. Hist. Socs. (mem. bicentennial com. 1969, nominating com. 1971-72, reports com. 1967-68). Daus. Am. Colonists (regent 1962-74), D.A.R. (registrar chpt.). Author: Consignments to El Dorado, 1972. Contbr. articles and stories to profl. jours. and popular mags. Home: 3447 Dite St San Diego CA 92103 Office: 2482 San Diego Av San Diego CA 92110

READMAN, MARY KATHLEEN (MRS. WILLIAM JOHN READMAN), editor; b. Consort, Alta., Can., Nov. 9, 1933; d. Harold M. and Dorothea M. (Militz) Scott; grad. high sch.; m. William John Readman, July 8, 1953; 1 dau., Carol Elaine. Printer, Consort Enterprise, 1950-57, editor, 1957—. Bd. dirs. Consort Hosp. (v.p. 1966—). Mem. Consort C. of C. (pres. 1973-74). Club: Kinette of Consort. Office: Consort Enterprise Box 129 Consort AB Canada

READY, SISTER MARY CARMEL, librarian, educator; b. Proctor, Vt., Dec. 13, 1907; d. Michael Joseph and Anne Elizabeth (Connor) Ready; A.B., Trinity Coll., Burlington, Vt., 1932; M.A. in English, St. Michaels Coll., Winooski Park, Vt., 1945; M.A. in L.S., Catholic U. Am., 1944. Tchr. English, Cathedral High Sch., Burlington, 1932-43; librarian, asso. prof. English, Trinity Coll., Burlington, 1944-72, prof., 1972—, dir. pub. relations, 1952-58; tchr., lectr. St. Michaels Coll., summers 1946-49, dean women, summer 1952. Mem. Nat. Council Tchrs. English, A.L.A., New Eng., Vt. library assns., Champlain Valley Library Assn. (past pres.), Vt., Chittenden County hist. socs., Vt. Archeol. Soc., Green Mountain Folklore Soc. Author: Short History of Vermont, 1945. Home: Trinity Coll 208 Colchester Av Burlington VT 05401

REAGAN, ANNIE MOODY (MRS. CLARK W. REAGAN), real estate broker; b. Fort Worth, Mar. 7, 1908; d. Clement C. and Ora Bell (Woodby) Moody; student Golden Gate Coll., 1953-55, Coll. Marin, 1954-60, U. Cal. at Berkeley, 1960-61; m. Clark W. Reagan, Oct. 3, 1943 (dec. May 1963); children—Eugene Godwin, Dana T. Employed in secretarial positions, 1928-52; owner Annie M. Reagan Realtor and Ins., San Rafael, Cal., 1952—. Sec. Las Gallinas Valley San. Dist., 1952-64. Mem. Marin County Bd. Realtors (by-laws com. 1972-73, mem. pub. affairs com. 1972-73). Republican. Presbyn. (elder). Mem. Order Eastern Star. Home: 51 Mariner Green Dr Corte Madera CA 94925 Office: 294 N San Pedro Rd San Rafael CA 94903

REAGAN, NANCY DAVIS (MRS. RONALD REAGAN), wife of former gov. Cal.; b. Chgo.; d. Loyal and Edith (Luckett) Davis; student Smith Coll., 1943; m. Ronald Reagan, Mar. 4, 1952; children—Patricia Ann, Ronald Prescott. Mem. Jr. League, Assistance League, Colleagues. Presbyn.

REAGIN, YNEZ MOREY (MRS. CHARLES EDWARD REAGIN), graphoanalyst, educator; b. Flasher, N.D., Mar. 3, 1913; d. Gideon Earl Morey and Margie (Ozbun) Morey Real; B.S., Colo. State U., 1934, postgrad. 1935; postgrad. U. Colo., 1945, 60, U. No. Colo., 1961-64, Western State Coll., 1967-68; m. Charles Edward Reagin, July 10, 1935. Tchr. biology high sch., Sisseton, S.D., 1942-44; tchr. biology, gen. sci., high sch., Pueblo, Colo., 1944-46; tchr. biology Pueblo Jr. Coll., 1946-47; tchr. high sch. Lamar, Colo., 1947-50, tchr. English, 1950-51, sec. to prin., 1952-53; office mgr. Troy Pub. Accountant, Lamar, 1953-55; self-employed with tax work, 1955-58; tchr. English high sch., Canon City, Colo., 1958-59, Women's Correctional Instn., 1967; tchr. psychology Adult Edn. Program, Canon City, 1970—; instr. psychology Internat. Graphoanalysis Congress, Chgo., 1964—; tchr. graphoanalysis, Canon City, 1962—. Organizer Great Books Found. Discussion Group, Canon City, 1961, mem. 1961-66; judge Fremont, Chaffee Counties 4-H Talent Festivals; active self-help groups Colo. State Prison, Colo. Women's Prison. Organizing sec. Jane Jefferson Democratic Club, Canon City, 1963, precinct com. woman, 1960-64, 1968—, sec. precinct caucuses, judge on election bds. Mem. bd. dirs. Entertainment, Inc., 1964-68; certified volunteer Suicide Prevention and Crisis Center, Fremont County, Colo., 1973—. Recipient President's Merit award, Internat. Graphoanalysis Soc., 1969. Mem. Internat., Colo. (charter member 2d v.p. 1971-72), So. Colo. (chmn. 1963-71) Graphoanalysis Socs., Am. Assn. U. Women (pres. 1968-70, treas. 1964-66, state historian 1970-72), Canon City Graphoanalysis Study Group (organizer, chmn. 1962—), Nat. Fedn. Bus. Profl. Women's Club, Delta Zeta, Beta Beta Beta. Mem. Order Eastern Star (worthy matron, 1944-45). Democrat. Methodist. Clubs: Altrusa Internat. (dir. 1970-72, archives chmn., pub. and membership chmn. 1967-72, publicity award Dist. 10, 1972) (Canon City); Internat. Knife and Fork (dir. 1956-67) (Fremont County, Colo.). Contbr. articles to profl. jours. Address: 610 Burrage St Canon City CO 81212 Office: 610 Burrage St Canon City CO 81212

REAGOR, PAMELA ANITA, psychologist; b. El Paso, Tex., May 12, 1944; d. Arthur and Anita Francene (Blum) Reagor; B.A. cum laude, So. Methodist U., 1966; M.A., U. Ill., Urbana, 1968, Ph.D., 1970. Asst. prof. residence program in social ecology U. Cal., Irvine, 1970-72, lectr., 1972-74, asst. clin. prof. psychiatry and human behavior, Coll. Medicine, 1974—; clin. psychologist Orange County Dept. Mental Health, North County region, Fullerton, Cal., 1972—, chief of consultation and tng., 1973—, chief outpatient services, 1973-74, dep. dir., 1974—; pvt. practice, Newport Beach, Cal., 1973—. Cons. Easter Seal Rehab. Center, Orange, Cal., 1971-72. USPHS fellow Neuropsychiat. Inst., U. Cal., Los Angeles, Center for Health Scis., 1969-70. Mem. Am., Western psychol. assns., Am. Civil Liberties Union, Common Cause, Phi Beta Kappa. Democrat. Home: 4951 Paseo Segovia Irvine CA 92664 Office: 232 W Commonwealth Av Fullerton CA 92632 also 881 Dover Dr Suite 36 Newport Beach CA 92660

REAMS, ELINOR PAYNE (MRS. ARTHUR A. REAMS), internat. edn. specialist, cons., ret. govt. ofcl.; b. Dothan, Ala., Apr. 17, 1914; d. Alvin A. and Gladys Wise (Fritter) Payne; A.B. cum laude, Fla. State U., 1935; postgrad. George Washington U., 1940; m. Arthur Arnold Reams, Jan. 11, 1941; 1 dau., Anne Emily. Newspaper work Panama City, Fla., 1935; mgr. Clements Ins. Agy., Miami, Fla., 1935-39; head dept. English Redland High Sch., Dade County, Fla., 1936-40; writer confidential reports Bur. Contract Information, 1940-41; editorial asst. War Dept., 1941; personnel asst. Co-ordinator Information, 1941-42; personnel officer FSA, 1942-43; mgmt. planning analyst O.W.I., 1945; mgmt. planning officer Dept. State, 1945-48, chief deptl. staff U.S. Adv. Commn. Ednl. Exchange, 1948-52, cons. internat. information adminstrn., 1952-53, Bur. Internat. Scientific and Tech. Affairs Dept. State, 1973—; cons. Am. Council Edn., 1955-56, spl. asso. and cons. commn. edn. and internat. affairs 1956-61, also liaison officer with UNESCO relation staff Dept. State; sr. personnel mgmt. officer Dept. State, 1961-62, chief program planning and mgmt. staff, 1962-63; fgn. affairs officer Policy Review and Research Staff, Bur. Ednl. and Cultural Affairs, Dept. State, 1963-65, asst. dir. policy review and coordination staff, 1965-67, sr. policy officer and asst. exec. dir. council on internat. ednl. and cultural affairs, 1967-70; ind. research cons., 1970—; mem. asst. sec. states com. reorgn., 1946; mem. survey mission rev. ednl. exchange activities in Europe and Near East, Dept. State, 1949; Am. Council Edn. rep. 3d gen. conf. Internat. Assn. Univs., 1960. Recipient Meritorious Service award Dept. State, 1964, Superior Service award, 1966, Superior Service Honor award, 1970. Mem. Delta Delta Delta, Phi Kappa Phi, Beta Pi Theta. Democrat. Presbyn. Clubs: Washington Golf and Country, St. Andrews Bay Yacht. Author report profl. jour. Home: 920 West Beach Dr Panama City FL 32401

REARDON, ANNA JOYCE, educator; b. East St. Louis, Ill., Jan. 22, 1910; d. John Leo and Julia Gertrude (Galvin) Reardon; A.B., Coll. St. Teresa, 1930; M.S., St. Louis U., 1933, Ph.D., 1937. Instr. physics and math. Ursuline Coll., New Orleans, 1936-37, Mt. St. Scholastica Coll., Atchinson, Kan., 1937-39, Coll. St. Teresa, Winona, Minn., 1939-40, Loretto Heights (Colo.) Coll., 1940-41; faculty U. N.C., Greensboro, 1941—, asso. prof. physics, 1945-47, prof., 1949—, head physics dept., 1942-65. Cons. physics Moses H. Cone Hosp., Greensboro, 1959-61; chmn. N.C. Com. for High Sch. Physics, 1967—. Mem. Am. Phys. Soc., A.A.A.S., Am. Assn. Physics Tchrs. (regional counselor N.C. 1968-70), Am. Assn. U. Women, N.C. Acad. Sci. (sec. 1952-53, mem. exec. bd. 1970-73), Sigma Xi, Delta Kappa Gamma. Contbr. articles to jours. Home: 1105 Dover Rd Greensboro NC 27408

REARDON, MARTHA BOOTH (MRS. PAUL MICHAEL REARDON), broadcasting adminstr.; b. Sherman, Tex., Sept. 3, 1930; d. James Roy and Maurine (Penland) Booth; B.A. in Speech-Radio, Baylor U., 1952; m. Paul Michael Reardon, Oct. 26, 1968. Sec. to pres., TV traffic mgr., KWTX-TV, Waco, Tex., 1952-63; personal sec. to pres. and owner Couchman Advt. Agy., Dallas, 1963-64; TV traffic mgr. KDFW-TV, Dallas, 1964-68, WPIX-TV, N.Y.C., 1968-73; staff asst. J. Walter Thompson Field Office, Dallas, 1973; TV traffic mgr. Crest Broadcasting Co.-KVRL, Houston, 1974—. Mem. Am. Women in Radio and Television (various offices Dallas chpt. 1964-68), Alpha Epsilon Rho. Home: 2201 Fountain View St Houston TX 77027 Office: 3935 Westheimer Houston TX 77027

REARDON, MARY RUTH WESTER (MRS. FREDERICK D. REARDON), physician; b. Des Moines, Oct. 10, 1922; d. Reuben Axel and Gertrude Theoren (Hazen) Wester; A.B., Vassar Coll., 1944; M.S., Yale, 1945; M.D., Temple U., 1952; m. Frederick D. Reardon, June 29, 1966; stepchildren—Frederick Douglas, Charles L. Intern, Phila. Gen. Hosp., 1952-53; resident in anesthesiology Temple U., 1953-56, asst. prof., 1956-65, asso. prof., 1965-68, prof. anesthesiology, 1968—. Diplomate Am. Bd. Anesthesiology. Mem. A.M.A., Am., Pa. socs. anesthesiologists, Pa. Med. Soc. Home: 748 Millbrook Lane Haverford PA 19041

REASONOVER, FRANCES LOIS, home economist; b. Kemp, Tex., May 25, 1917; d. Charles Edward and Katherine Gilchrist (McDougald) Reasonover; B.S., East Tex. State Tchrs. Coll., 1938; M.A., Tex. State Coll. Women, 1954. Tchr. homemaking Kaufman (Tex.) High Sch., 1938-39; tchr. Edgewood High Sch., San Antonio, 1940-43, Kemp (Tex.) High Sch., 1943-45; home mgmt. supr. Farmers Home Adminstrn., Greenville, Sherman, Tex., 1945-47; county home demonstration agt., Athens, Tex., 1947-49; foods and nutrition specialist Tex. Agrl. Extension Service, College Station, 1950—. Served with WAC, 1943. Recipient Superior Service awards U.S. Dept. Agr., 1971, Tex., 1971. Mem. Am., Tex. home econs. assns., Am. Assn. U. Women, Inst. Food Technologists, Tex. Nutrition Council (pres. 1970—). Author publs. on foods and nutrition. Home: 311 Foch Bryan TX 77801 Office: Extension Service College Station TX 77843

REBECK, NITA MARIE ALLMAN (MRS. JOSEPH REBECK), physician; b. nr. Kingston, Minn., Aug. 19, 1935; d. Charles F. and Louise (Bartsch) Allman; B.A., Clarke Coll., 1957; M.D., Temple U., 1961; m. Joseph Rebeck, Dec. 21, 1963; 1 dau., Ramona. Intern, Miller Hosp., St. Paul, 1961-62; with Permanente Med. Group, Los Angeles, 1962—, partner, 1966—. Diplomate Am. Bd. Family Practice. Fellow Am. Acad. Family Physicians; mem. Am., Cal., Los Angeles County med. assns.; Alpha Epsilon Iota, Kappa Gamma Pi. Home: 3203 Seaclaire Dr Palos Verdes Peninsula CA 90274 Office: 2680 Saturn Av Huntington Park CA 90255

REBELSKY, FREDA ETHEL GOULD (MRS. WILLIAM REBELSKY), educator; b. N.Y.C., Mar. 11, 1931; d. William and Sarah (Kaplan) Gould; B.A., U. Chgo., 1950, M.A., 1954; Ph.D., Radcliffe Coll., 1961; m. William Rebelsky, Jan. 1, 1956; 1 son, Samuel. Counselor, U. Chgo. Orthogenic Sch., 1952-55; research asst. Kenyon & Eckhart, Inc., 1956-58; research asst. Lab. Human Devel., Harvard, 1959-60, teaching asst. psychology dept., 1960-61, instr. edn., 1960-61; research asso. Speech Research Lab., Children's Hosp., 1960-61, Mass. Inst. Tech., 1961-62; asst. prof. Boston U., 1962-68, asso. prof. psychology, 1968-72, prof., 1972—, dir. doctoral program in devel. psychology, 1969—; vis. lectr. Utrecht (Holland) U., 1965-67; Froman prof. Russell Sage Coll., 1972. Recipient grants Office Edn., 1964-65, Boston U. Grad. Sch., 1967-70, Office Econ. Opportunity, 1967—, Nat. Inst. Mental Health, 1974—. Recipient Distinguished Tchr. of Psychology award Am. Psychol. Found., 1970; Harbison award for excellence in teaching Danforth Found., 1971. Mem. A.A.A.S., Soc. for Research in Child Devel. (sec. Boston chpt. 1963-65), Am. Assn. U. Profs. (sec. Boston U. chpt. 1964-65), Am., Eastern, Mass. (chmn. program com. 1962-64) psychol. assns., Sigma Xi, Psi Chi. Author: Child Behavior and Development: A Reader, 1969; Child Behavior and Development, 1970, 2d edit., 1973. Home: 1 Billings Park Newton MA 02158 Office: 64 Cummington St Boston MA 02215

REBHUN, PEARL (MRS. LIONEL REBHUN), artist; b. N.Y.C.; d. Emanuel and Bertha (Purcell) Greenblatt; student Bklyn. Mus. Art, 1955-57, North Shore Community Art Center, Ruth Leaf Graphic Workshop; m. Lionel Earl Rebhun, Mar. 29, 1947; children—Laurence, Andrew, Donald. Exhibited one-man show at Willoughby Wallace Meml. Library, Stony Creek, Conn.; exhibited in group shows at Hecksher Mus., Huntington, N.Y., Wustum Mus. Fine Arts, Racine, Wis., Palazzo Vecchio, Florence, Italy, Pompeiian Pavillion, Naples, Italy, Jesse Bosser Mus., Alpena, Mich., Washington County Mus. Fine Arts, Hagerstown, Md., Howell Gallery, N.Y.C., Shelter Rock Library, Albertson, N.Y. others; represented in permanent collections at Trinity Coll., Hartford, Conn. tchr. etching in pvt. studio, 1970—. Chmn., Lake Success Ann. Art Show, 1969; v.p. Lake Success Civic Assn., 1970-71. Mem. Nat. Assn. Women Artists, Artists in Am. Home: 25 Meadow Woods Rd Lake Success Great Neck NY 11020

REBMAN, VIRGINIA BROOKS WILLRATH, real estate broker; b. Greensboro, N.C., Nov. 21, 1912; d. Thomas Nevada and Minnie Leoma (Bustle) Brooks; student Columbia, 1931-35; m. Theodore F. Willrath Demis, May 1945; m. 2d, Walter H. Rebman, Feb. 14, 1947 (dec.). Personnel dir. N.Am. Phillips Corp., Dobbs Ferry, N.Y., 1945; real estate broker, Sebring, Fla. Mem. Highlands County Art League, Highlands County Dependent and Delinquent Children, Youth Care, Inc., Highlands Gen. Hosp. Aux.; sponsor Heart of Fla. council Girl Scouts Am., 1965-72. Mem. adv. planning bd. City Council Sebring. Recipient award medal of merit for ednl. channel WEDU, 1970, citations Lions Club, 1969, Kiwanis Club, 1969, Lake Placid C. of C., 1969. Mem. Fla., N.C. Press, Fla. Pub. Relations Assn. (dir. chpt.), Highlands Hist. Soc., Sebring C. of C. Presbyn. Clubs: Sebring Golf and Country, Placid Lakes Golf and Country. Address: 154 W Center Av Sebring FL 33870

RECK, CLAIRE YUNGCLAS, civic worker; b. Webster City, Ia., Feb. 6, 1903; d. Henry Theodore and Anna May (Argubright) Yungclas; B.S., Ia. State U., 1924; m. Franklin Mering Reck, Jan. 27, 1926; children—Linda Reck Head, Sarah (Mrs. John E. Wakefield). Tchr. home econs., 1924-26; office mgr. Am. Boy Mag., Airplane Model League Am., 1928-30; field sec. Sigma Kappa, 1927-29; chmn. bd. Detroit council Camp Fire Girls, 1931-40; worked with A.R.C. Canteen, 1942-46; mem. Manchester Twp. Library Bd., 1943—, Manchester Community Chest bd., 1947-70; chmn. Manchester Red Cross Blood Bank, 1957—; mem. Washtenaw County Library Bd., 1962—; sec. Washtenaw County Red Cross Bd., 1966-72; chmn. Manchester Family Service, 1965—. Mem. Omicron Nu, Mortar Bd., Sigma Kappa. Democrat. Home: 665 W Main St Manchester MI 48158

RECK, RIMA DRELL (MRS. RICHARD COLLIN), educator, author, critic; b. N.Y.C., Sept. 29, 1933; d. Jacob and Liza (Maisenberg) Drell; B.A. summa cum laude, Brandeis U., 1954; postgrad. (Fulbright scholar), Universite de Caen and The Sorbonne, 1954-55; Ph.D. (Univ. and Jr. Sterling fellow, Boies scholar), Yale 1960; m. Andrew Joseph Reck, Aug. 30, 1956; m. 2d, Richard Collin. Instr. French, Tulane U., New Orleans, 1958-61; asst. prof. French, comparative lit. U. New Orleans, 1961-64, asso. prof., 1964-68, prof. comparative lit., 1968—. Lectr. before learned socs., 1960-73. Am. Philos. Soc. grantee, 1962, 64, 70, La. State U. research grantee, 1964, Am. Council Learned Socs. grantee, 1968-70; Guggenheim Fellow, 1972-73. Mem. Modern Lang. Assn., South-Central Modern Lang. Assn. (chmn. comparative lit. sect.), Am. Assn. Tchrs. French, Am. Comparative Lit. Assn., Societe des Amies de Georges Bernanos, Societe des Amis de Marcel Proust, Am. Assn. U. Profs., Association des Professeurs Francais en Amerique, Phi Beta Kappa. Author: (with others) Studies in Comparative Literature, 1962, Bernanos, Confrontations, 1966; Literature and Responsibility: The French Novelist in The Twentieth Century, 1969; co-author (under Rima Collin) The New Orleans Cookbook, 1975. Asso. editor The Southern Review, 1963—. Translator French works, 1955-66. Editor: Explorations of Literature, 1966. Contbr. articles to learned jours. and quarterlies. Home: 1309 7th St New Orleans LA 70115

RECKDAHL, JOAN MARIE SCHRAMM (MRS. JEROME RECKDAHL), polit. worker; b. Hutchinson, Minn., Aug. 27, 1936; d. Henry Frederick and Bertha Wilhelmina (Duesterhoeft) Schramm; A.A., Concordia Coll., 1956; B.S., U. Minn., 1959; m. Jerome Reckdahl, Aug. 3, 1958; children—Beth, Keith, Kathryn, Benjamin, Andrea. Tchr., Immanuel Luth. Sch., Mpls., 1959-61; English tchr. Grove City (Minn.) High Sch., 1961-64, 70-71; interviewer Minn. Poll. Meeker County, 1970-72. Chmn. Meeker County Democratic-Farmer-Labor party, 1970—, chmn. subdist. of 6th Congl. Dist., 1972—; mem. 6th dist. exec. com., 1972—, asso. chmn. Minn. Senatorial Dist. 22, 1972—, mem. state central com., 1972—. Mem. Am. Assn. U. Women (pres. Grove City-Atwater br. 1967-69, 71-72). Lutheran. Club: Women's (sec. 1973-75) (Grove City, Minn.). Home: 204 S 3d St Grove City MN 56243

RECKNAGEL, HELEN JOHNSTON (MRS. A. BERNARD RECKNAGEL), educator; b. Stratford, Okla., Sept. 6, 1910; d. Keener Kavanaugh and Wilhelmena (Grosendorf) Kelly; B.S. in Commerce, Okla. State U., 1932; M.B.A., U. Chgo., 1937; Ph.D., N.Y.U., 1953; m. A. Bernard Recknagel, Dec. 23, 1947; 1 dau., Carol Anne. Asst. prof. U. Tulsa, 1933-40; jr. exec. pub. relations dept. N.A.M., 1942-43; asso. prof. Cornell U., 1943-61, prof., 1961—; cons. Hilton Hotels, 1956, 61. Trustee U.S. Travel Data Center. Recipient Editorial Merit award Nat. Assn. Coll. and Univ. Food Service, 1972. Mem. Instnl. Editorial Food Council (nat. treas. 1969-71), Travel Research Assn., Hotel Sales Mgmt. Assn. (research asso. 1954), Tompkins County Hosp. Aux., Nat. League Am. Pen Women, Instnl. Food Editors Council (nat. treas. 1969—), Delta Pi Epsilon (nat. v.p. 1944-46), Phi Kappa Phi. Presbyn. Co-author: Marketing the Fall House, 1972. Editor: Cornell Hotel and Restaurant Adminstrn. Quar., 1960—. Home: Frontenac Rd Trumansburg NY 14886

RECTENWALD, MARGARET BUCK (MRS. THOMAS L. RECTENWALD), ednl. adminstr.; b. Elmira, N.Y., Apr. 30, 1947; d. Seelev Earl and Margaret E. (Bruun) Buck; B.A., State U. N.Y. at Buffalo, 1969, M.Ed., 1971; m. Thomas L. Rectenwald, Aug. 23, 1969. Counseling intern State U. N.Y. at Buffalo, 1970-71, asst. to v.p. student affairs, 1970-71; counselor Barat Coll., Lake Forest, Ill., 1972—. Recipient Nat. award for pub. relations material, 1969, award for outstanding service State U. N.Y. at Buffalo, 1968. Mem. Am. Personnel and Guidance Assn., Am. Coll. Personnel Assn., Nat. Assn. Women Deans, Adminstrs. and Counselors. Home: 461C Nicholson St Fort Sheridan IL 60037 Office: Box 655 Lake Forest IL 60045

RECTOR, RUTH GILL, librarian; b. Liberty, Mo., June 8, 1911; d. James Perry and Elizabeth Lee (Wall) Gill; B.A., William Jewell Coll., 1932; B.S. in L.S., Columbia, 1940; m. Hartman Rector, Feb. 17, 1958. Ref. librarian Mo. Sch. Mines and Metallurgy, 1934-39, U. Kansas City, 1939-40, N.Y. Pub. Library, 1941-42; head librarian Mont. Sch. Mines, 1943; librarian spl. services br. U.S. Army and Air Force, 1944-49; metallurgy librarian Oak Ridge Nat. Lab., 1950; post librarian Ft. McPherson, Ga., and Camp Rucker, Ala., 1951-52; regional demonstration librarian Mo. State Library, Jefferson City, 1952-53; reference librarian Jackson County Library, Independence, Mo., 1954; head librarian Mexico-Audrain County Library, Mexico, Mo., 1955-56, Little Dixie Regional Library, Moberly, Mo., 1956-58; interlibrary loan librarian San Diego (Cal.) Pub. Library, 1962-67; librarian North Clairemont br. San Diego Pub. Library, 1968-70, librarian govtl. ref. library, 1971-73; ret., 1973. Mem. A.L.A., Spl. Libraries Assn. (pres. San Diego chpt. 1970-71). Contbr. articles to newspapers. Home: 3531 Sterne St San Diego CA 92106

REDDICK, NANCY CAROL, advt. co. exec.; b. Dallas, May 11, 1937; d. Walter Grady and Carol Chamberlain (Shands) Reddick; B.F.A., So. Meth. U., 1966. Art dir. Riverside Press, Dallas, 1966; mem. sales promotion staff Southwestern Drug Corp., Dallas, 1966-72, chief pricer, 1972-73; dir. Merritt/Mitchell Assos., Dallas, 1973—, sec., 1973—. Recipient Merit award Truett Labs., Dallas, 1969. Mem. Delta Delta Delta. Republican. Episcopalian. Club: 500 Inc. Editor Southwestern Roundup, Dallas, 1966-72. Home: 4535 Cedar Springs Dallas TX 75219 Office: 1165 Empire Central Dallas TX 75247

REDDIG, GERALDINE B. (MRS. JAMES C. REDDIG), civic leader; b. East Orange, N.J., June 6, 1908; d. George and Cornelia (Hales) Badenoch; B.A., Wellesley, 1929; m. James C. Reddig, Apr. 8, 1933; children—Janice (Mrs. Richard Coggeshall), J. Burr (dec.),

William R., Alan George. Pres., Monroe County League Women Voters, 1961-64; v.p. Rochester Area Ednl. TV Assn., 1961-66, trustee, 1960—; chmn. Citizens Com. to obtain charter for Monroe County, 1964; mem. Monroe County Bd. Ethics, 1970-72. Trustee Rochester Center for Govtl. and Community Research, 1966-72; life trustee Center for Govtl. Research, Inc., 1972—. Recipient Helen Jones Meml. award, 1964; Fed. Women's Clubs Achievement award, 1969, Forman Flair award, 1970. Home: 698 Lake Rd Webster NY 14580

REDDY, HELEN, vocalist; b. Melbourne, Australia, Oct. 25, 1941; d. Max and Stella (Lamond) Reddy; ed. pub. schs.; m. Jeff Wald, Nov. 1, 1966; children—Traci, Jordan. Vocal recs. include Crazy Love, I Don't Know How to Love Him, Peaceful, I Am Woman, Delta Dawn, Keep on Singing, You and Me Against the World, Angie Baby; star NBC Summer Show, 1973. Active Nat. Women's Polit. Caucus, NOW, Women's Center, Alliance for Women in Prison. Recipient Grammy award for writing and rec. I Am Woman, 1973; also numerous gold records, platinum records. Address: 9000 Sunset Blvd Los Angeles CA 90069

REDFIELD, ELAINE M. GRAF (MRS. WILLIAM D. REDFIELD), free-lance writer, critic, interior designer; b. N.Y.C., Dec. 9, 1917; d. Oscar L. and Gertrude (Hauser) Graf; student Wellesley Coll., 1934-37; A.B., U. Cal. at Los Angeles, 1943; m. Edward Mittelman, Apr. 11, 1943 (dec. Oct. 1960). Book reviewer San Francisco Chronicle, 1943-45; sales asst. Asso. Am. Artists, Beverly Hills, Cal., 1947-48; free-lance editorial asst. W.H. Freeman Co., San Francisco, 1953-54; publicity dir. Orange County Philharmonic Soc., 1954-57, dir., 1957-69, adv. bd., 1970—; design cons. and interior designer. Mem. Fullerton Cultural and Fine Arts Com.; mem. Pres.'s Council Chapman Coll.; pres. Music Assos. Cal. State U. at Fullerton, 1970-73, now mem. exec. bd. Bd. dirs. Friends of Library of U. Cal. at Irvine, 1968-70, Orange County Cultural Center, 1974—; exec. bd. Friends of Coll., Cal. State Coll. at Fullerton. Named Woman of Year Fullerton C. of C., 1971—; Woman of Achievement Fullerton Bus. and Profl. Women's Club, 1966. Mem. Am. Soc. Interior Designers, League of Women Voters, Am. Assn. U. Women. Club: Wellesley (pres. 1962-64). Home: 1403 Sunny Crest Dr Fullerton CA 92635

REDGRAVE, LYNN, actress; b. London, Eng., Mar. 8, 1943; d. Michael Scudemore and Rachel (Kempson) Redgrave; ed. Queensgate Sch., London, also Central Sch. Speech and Drama, London; m. John Clark, Apr. 2, 1967; children—Benjamin, Kelly. Theatrical appearances include Midsummer Night's Dream, 1962, The Tulip Tree, 1962, Andorra, Hayfever, Much Ado About Nothing, Mother Courage, Love for Love, all with Nat. Theatre Company of Gt. Britain, 1963-66, Black Comedy (on Broadway), 1967, Zoo Zoo Widershins Zoo at Edinburgh Festival, 1969, The Two of Us, Garrick Theatre, 1971, Slag, Royal Ct. Theatre, 1971, Born Yesterday, 1973, A Better Place at Dublin Gate Theatre, My Fat Friend (on Broadway), 1974; film appearances include Tom Jones, 1963, Girl with the Green Eyes, 1964, Georgy Girl, 1966, The Deadly Affair, 1966, Smashing Time, 1967, Virgin Soldiers, 1969, Last of Mobile Hotshots, 1970, Viva La Muerta, Tua, 1971, Every Little Crook and Nanny, 1972, Everything You Always Wanted to Know About Sex, 1972; The National Health, 1973. Recipient N.Y. Film Critics award, Golden Globe award, I.F.I.D.A. award, also Oscar nomination for best actress, all for Georgy Girl, 1967. Address: care Internat Clients Servicing Inc 205 W 57th St New York City NY 10019 also ICS Inc 256 S Robertson St Beverly Hills CA 90211

REDGRAVE, VANESSA, actress; b. London, Eng., Jan. 30, 1937; d. Michael and Rachel (Kempson) R.; student Central Sch. Speech and Drama, London, 1955-57; m. Tony Richardson, Apr. 28, 1962 (div.); children—Natasha Jane, Joely Kim, Carlo. Prin. theatrical roles include Helena in Midsummer Night's Dream, 1959; Stella in The Tiger and the Horse, 1960; Katerina in The Taming of the Shrew, 1961; Rosaline in As You Like It, 1961; Imogene in Cymbeline, 1962; Nina in The Seagull, 1964; Miss Brodie in The Prime of Miss Jean Brodie, 1966, Susan Thistlewood in Cato Street, 1971; Polly Peachum in The Threepenny Opera, 1972, Viola in Twelfth Night, 1972, Cleopatra in Anthony & Cleopatra, 1973, Gilda in Design for Living, 1974; film roles include Leonie in Morgan-A Suitable Case for Treatment (Best Actress award Cannes Film Festival 1966), 1965; Sheila in Sailor from Gibraltar, 1965; Anne-Marie in La Musica, 1965; Jane in Blow Up; Guinevere in Camelot; Isadora in Isadora Duncan; Clarissa in Charge of the Light Brigade; Flavia in A Quiet Place in the Country, 1969; Andromache in The Trojan Women, 1970; Sister Jean in The Devils, 1970; Mary Stuart in Mary, Queen of Scots, 1971; Mary Daberon in Murder on the Orient Express, 1974. Bd. govs. Central Sch. Speech and Drama, 1963—, Med. Aid to Vietnam, 1965—. Recipient Eve. Standard Drama award, 1961; Variety Club Gt. Britain Best Actress award, 1961, 66; Brit. Guild TV Producers and Dirs. Best Actress award, 1966; comdr. Order Brit. Empire, 1967. Author: Pussies and Tigers, 1964. Address: 18 St Peters Sq London W6 England

REDICK, JOANN PAULINE BOWEN (MRS. RUSSELL DAVID REDICK), realtor; b. Rockford, Ill., July 21, 1940; d. Chester Aden and Verna Mabel (Bokath) Bowan; student Mt. San Antonio Coll., 1957-58, Los Angeles State Coll., 1958-59; m. Russell David Redick, Nov. 25, 1957; children—David, Fredrick, Laura. With Mission Realty, Laguna Beach, Cal., 1965—. Sec. South Coast YMCA, South Orange County, Cal., 1972, chmn., 1973-74; bd. dirs. Laguna Beach Bd. Realtors, 1972, v.p., 1974; bd. dirs. Met. YMCA, Santa Ana, Cal., 1973-74. Named Woman of Year, Met. YMCA, 1973. Home: 3115 Mountain View Dr Laguna Beach CA 92651 Office: 985 S Coast Hwy Laguna Beach CA 92651

REDMAN, GEORGEANN WYNETTE, social worker, educator; b. Coatesville, Pa., June 14, 1943; d. George Washington and Mary (Hoar) Redman; B.A., Pa. State U., 1963; M.S.W., State U. N.Y. at Buffalo, 1965, now postgrad. in ednl. adminstrn. Social caseworker, family life educator Family Service Soc., Buffalo and Erie County, 1965-69; asst. prof. Sch. Social Welfare, State U. N.Y. at Buffalo, 1969-74, project dir. Fed. mental retardation tng. grant, 1969—, asst. to dir. field instrn., 1973—; dir. social services Linwood Bryant Hosp., 1971-74; dir. client services, mgmt., community devel. East Coast A.R.C., 1974—. Cons. on groups to West Seneca (N.Y.) Youth Bd., 1969; mem. adv. bd. Western N.Y. Assn. Children Learning Disabilities, 1972—; mem. adv. bd. for devel. De Veauy Sch., 1972-73. Mem. Nat. Assn. Social Workers (exec. com.), Council on Social Work Edn., Alumni Assn. State U. N.Y. Sch. Social Welfare (v.p. 1968—), Pi Gamma Mu, Alpha Kappa Delta. Home: 141 Briarwood Dr West Seneca NY 14224

REDMON, ANNIE LOUISE ADAMS (MRS. LEROY REDMON), educator; b. Indpls.; d. Theophilus Adolph and Eugenia (Dudley) Adams; B.S., Purdue U., 1946, M.S., 1960, Ph.D., 1970; m. Leroy Redmon, June 28, 1948; 1 dau., Lydia Ann (Mrs. Jones). Tchr. home econs. Roosevelt High Sch., Gary, Ind., 1948-50, Pulaski Sch., Gary, 1951-60, guidance counselor, 1960-62; coll. counselor Tolleston High Sch., Gary, 1962-65; teaching asst. dept. edn., Purdue U., 1959-60, grad. intern in student personnel services, counselor in office dean of women, 1965-66, asst. dir. of admissions 1966-68, adviser black student affairs, 1968-70; asst. prof., adviser Afro-Am. studies dept. ethnic studies U. Cal. at Berkeley, 1970-71; asst. prof. dept. ednl. psychology Cal. State Coll., Hayward, 1971—; clin. psychologist Contra County Hosp., Martinez, Cal., 1971—; asso. prof. psychology John F. Kennedy U., Martinez, Cal., 1972—. Ind. Personnel and Guidance Assn. rep. to Ind. Guidance Adv. Com. Nat. Def. Edn. Act fellow Purdue, summer 1962, U. Pitts., 1964. Bd. dirs. Lafayette United Negro Coll. Fund. Mem. Am. Personnel and Guidance Assn., Am. Psychol. Assn., Am. Assn. U. Women, Internat. Platform Assn., Nat., Ind. (pres. 1969-70) assns. women Deans and Counselors, Kappa Delta Pi, Alpha Kappa Alpha. Club: Commonwealth of Cal. Home: 107 Ardmore Way Benecia CA 94510 Office: Dept Ednl Psychology Cal State College Hayward CA 94501

REED, ALETTE ELIZABETH, lawyer; b. Milw., Mar. 4, 1931; d. Torger Howard and Ruth Elizabeth (Sutfin) Dolan; A.B. cum laude, Boston U., 1952; LL.B., Harvard, 1955; m. John Myers Reed, Dec. 19, 1951; children—Thomas, Emily. Admitted to Mass. bar, 1955; asso. firm Sherin and Lodgen, Boston, 1955-70, partner, 1970—. Mem. Town Meeting, Brookline, Mass., 1965-71; mem. Brookline Sch. Com., 1967—, vice chmn., 1971—. Bd. dirs. Big Sister Assn. Greater Boston, 1960—, pres., 1966-71. Home: 166 Tappan St Brookline MA 02146 Office: 140 Federal St Boston MA 02110

REED, BONNIE JEAN FIELD (MRS. MICHAEL DANA REED), occupational therapist; b. Morris, Minn., Dec. 12, 1942; d. Roy Harold and Harriet (Blaisdell) Field; B.S., U. Minn., 1964; certificate advanced rehab. techniques Rancho Los Amigos Hosp., 1970; m. Michael Dana Reed, Sept. 5, 1964; children—Daniel Lawrence, Benjamin Roy. Staff therapist Abbott Hosp., Mpls., 1964-65; dir. occupational therapy Les Passees Rehab. Center, Memphis, 1965-66; supr. occupational therapy Mesa Vista Hosp., San Diego, 1966-67; staff occupational therapist San Diego County Hosp., 1967-69; dir. occupational therapy U. Hosp., San Diego, 1970-72; dir. occupational therapy Hemet Valley Mental Health, Hemet, Cal., 1973—. Mem. Am., So. Cal., San Diego dist. occupational therapy assns. Home: 180 Canyon Dr No 65 Oceanside CA 92054 Office: 1116 E Latham St Hemet CA 92343

REED, DAPHNE STEVENSON, coll. adminstr.; b. Hartford, Conn.; d. Edward McMurtry and Adele (Vaughan) Stevenson; B.A., Am. U., 1945; M.F.A. (univ. fellow), U. Mass., 1969; children by previous marriage—Bonnie, Laurie, Rory. Artist, L.I., N.Y., also Tucson, Amherst, Mass., 1950-70; instr., dept. theatre arts Mt. Holyoke Coll., South Hadley, Mass., 1970-72, theatre dir. and designer, 1970-72; asst. to dean, coordinator governance activities, Hampshire Coll., Amherst, Mass., 1972—. Staff asst. U. Mass., Boston, 1964-67, theatre dir. and designer, 1969; cons. Mass. Council on Arts and Humanities, 1972—. Mem. Am. Theatre Assn., New Eng. Theatre Conf., Women Adminstrs. New Eng., Mortarboard, Pi Kappa Phi, Delta Gamma. Home: 305 Middle St South Amherst MA 01002 Office: Cole Center Hampshire College Amherst MA 01002

REED, DONNA LOUISE, public relations exec.; b. Wichita, Kan., May 10, 1935; d. Joseph Melvin and Dorothy Yetta (Leben) Kogan; student So. Methodist U., 1952-53, Dallas Coll., 1955-56; m. William Eugene Reed, Feb. 17, 1968; 1 dau., Allison Lynn. Vice pres. pub. relations Preferred Printers, Inc., Dallas, 1960-68; dir. pub. relations Dallas Area Respiratory Health Assn., 1969-71; free-lance pub. relations, Dallas, 1972—. Mem. nat. pub. relations adv. com. Nat. Tb and Respiratory Disease Assn. Recipient Pub. Relations award Nat. Tb and Respiratory Disease Assn., 1970, Gridiron awards Press Club Dallas. Mem. Internat. Assn. Bus. Communicators, Women in Communications (pres. Dallas 1973-74), Dallas Woman's Forum (chmn. jr. aux.), Gamma Alpha Chi (pres. Dallas 1971-72). Mem. Order Eastern Star. Address: 13559 Willow Bend St Dallas TX 75240

REED, ELIZABETH GREY STEWART (MRS. JOHN ERNEST REED), author; b. Port Huron, Mich., May 11, 1914; d. Shirley and Elizabeth (Atkinson) Stewart; student Principia Jr. Coll., 1931-33; B.S., Columbia, 1935; m. John Ernest Reed, June 17, 1939; children—Stewart Borden, Elizabeth Carroll. Mem. staff New Yorker, N.Y.C., 1934-40; asst. account exec. Snow, Bates & Orme, Springfield, Mass., 1940-42. Bd. mgrs. Shurtleff Mission, Westfield, Mass., 1957-61; sec., trustee Westfield Athenaeum, 1954—; bd. dirs. Hampden Dist. Mental Health Clinic, 1968—. Republican. Clubs: Longmeadow (Mass.) Country; Sankaty Head Golf (Siasconset, Nantucket Island, Mass.); Colony. Author: Surrender The Heart, 1947; Young Man of The Year, 1961. Contbr. verse, fiction various nat. publs. Home: 10 Tekoa Terrace Westfield MA 01085

REED, EMELYNE ELY, civic worker; b. Oak Hill, O., Jan. 15, 1912; d. George Leonard and Jessie (Climer) Ely; grad. Office Tng. Sch., 1931; m. Richard A. Reed, May 2, 1943 (div. Mar. 1948); 1 dau., Alice Jane. Steno.-sec. Ohio Nat. Bank, Columbus, 1931-34, Brunson Bank & Trust Co., Columbus, 1934-37, Standard Savs. & Loan Co., Columbus, 1937-43; underwriter Trafford Tallmadge Agy., Columbus, 1943-47; statis. sec. Mead Corp., Chillicothe, O., 1947-65, tech. sec. Central Research Labs., 1965—. Publicity chmn. bd. mgrs. Ohio P.T.A., 1963-66, dir. Dist. 11, 1966-70, 71—, communications chmn., 1970-71; mem. State Library of Ohio Adv. Council for Fed. LSCA Programs, 1971—. Pres. OVAL Council, 1971-73, pres. OVAL trustees, 1973—; trustee Ross County Dist. Library, 1959-69, pres., 1963-69; trustee Ross County Community Action Commn., 1963-71, Chillicothe and Ross County Pub. Library, 1970—, Ross County chpt. Am. Heart Assn. Mem. Am., Ohio (exec. com. 1972-73, sec. 1973—) library trustees assns., P.T.A. (life). Home: Box 165 Londonderry OH 45647

REED, ESTELLA ELIZABETH, educator; b. Acton, Ind.; d. George Harvey and Carolyn Harrison (Noack) Reed; A.B., Ball State U., 1940; postgrad. George Washington U., 1946-47; M.S., Butler U., 1948; Ed.D., Ind. U., 1966. Tchr., Napoleon (Ind.) High Sch., 1940-42, Mt. Comfort (Ind.) High Sch., 1942-43, Center Grove (Ind.) High Sch., 1943-45, 48-49, Franklin (Ind.) High Sch., 1945-46; librarian Mt. Vernon Sem. and Jr. Coll., Washington, 1946-48, 49-50; tchr., Brookville (Ind.) High Sch., 1950-55, Ind. U. Univ. High Sch., Bloomington, 1956-58, East Chicago (Ind.) Pub. Schs., 1955-56, 58-66; prof. edn. dept. Purdue U., Calumet campus, Hammond, Ind., 1966—. Mem. task force Ind. Right to Read Program, 1971. Recipient Internat. grant Delta Kappa Gamma. Mem. Internat. Reading Assn., Am. Assn. Sch. Librarians, Ind. State Tchrs. Assn., Ind. Sch. Librarians Assn., Delta Kappa Gamma, Pi Lambda Theta. Home: 6820 Leland St Hammond IN 46323 Office: 2233 171st St Hammond IN 46323

REED, GEORGIE MARIE (MRS. HARRY JACOB REED), newspaper editor; b. Verona, Pa., Apr. 13, 1909; d. Thomas Alfred and Robina Harvey (Brass) Watterson; grad. Duff's Bus. Coll. 1933; m. Harry Jacob Reed, Dec. 2, 1933; 1 dau., Ann Reed (Mrs. Richard Melvin Kelly). Reporter Advance Leader, Oakmont, Pa., 1933-43, columnist, 1942—, society editor, 1943-52, asst. editor, 1952-60, editor, 1960—. Pres. Advance Leader Christmas Fund., 1973—. Pres. Verona Jr. Woman's Club, 1933-34. Bd. dirs. Salvation Army. Recipient writing awards including First Prize for editorials Pa. Women's Press Assn., 1961, 66, Keystone Press award for columns, 1959. Mem. Pa. Womens Press Assn. (v.p. southwestern dist. 1963), Verona and Oakmont C. of C., Woman's Club of Oakmont (v.p. 1939-43), Allegheny County Fedn. Womans Clubs (dist. v.p. 1944). Author: Betwixt and Between, 1949. Home: 360 Maryland Oakmont PA 15139 Office: 227 Allegheny Av Oakmont PA 15139

REED, GWENDOLYN ELIZABETH, author; b. Louisville, June 27, 1932; d. Henry Morrison and Cecelia (Zawatski) Reed; grad. Louisville Collegiate Sch., 1950; B.A., Radcliffe Coll., 1954. Asso. editor Book of Knowledge, Grolier, Inc., N.Y.C., 1961-63. Author: Lean Out of the Window: An Anthology of Modern Poetry, 1965; Out of the Ark: An Anthology of Animal Verse, 1968; The Sand Lady, 1968; Adam and Eve, 1968; When the Assyrians Came Down from the Trees, 1969; The Talkative Beasts: Myths, Fables and Poems of India, 1969; Bird Songs, 1969; Songs the Sandman Sings, 1969; Beginnings, 1971. Home: 2837 Riedling Dr Louisville KY 40206 Office: Curtis Brown Ltd 60 E 56th St New York City NY 10022

REED, JANET CAROLYN, educator; b. Kingwood, W.Va.; d. W. Scott and Mabel (Stepp) Reed; B.S., W.Va. U., 1936; M.S., Cornell U., 1953. Tchr., Bethany (W.Va.) High Sch., 1936-40; 4-H club agt. Coop. Extension Service, W.Va. U., New Cumberland, 1940-46; county home demonstration agt. Coop. Extension Service, Ohio State U., Steubenville, 1946-49; textiles and clothing specialist Cornell U., Ithaca, 1949-58, U. Del., Newark, 1958—; state leader home econs. Extension Service U. Del., Newark, 1968—. Cons. Celanese Ednl. Adv. Com., 1966-67; adv. council Nat. Assn. Extension Home Economists, 1971-72, Del. Div. Consumer Affairs, 1971—. Mem. Am., Del. (sec. 1961, v.p. 1968-69, pres.-elect 1969-70, pres. 1970-71) home econs. assns., Grange, Council of Consumer Information, Newark Bus. and Profl. Women (v.p. 1966-67), Assn. Adminstrs. Home Econs., Internat. Fedn. Home Economists, Zonta Internat., Mortar Bd., Phi Upsilon Omicron, Kappa Delta Pi, Pi Lambda Theta, Epsilon Sigma Phi (sec.-treas. 1965-66). Club: Cornell Women's (Del.). Home: 7 Kensington Lane Newark DE 19711

REED, KATHLYN LOUISE, univ. adminstr.; b. Detroit, June 2, 1940; d. Herbert Curtis and Jessie Ruth (Krehbiel) Reed; student U. Wis., 1958-61; B.S., U. Kan., 1964; M.A., Western Mich. U., 1966; Ph.D., U. Wash., 1973. Temporary supr., occupational therapist Vis. Nurse Assn., Beloit, Wis., 1964; staff occupational therapist Kan. U. Med. Center, Kansas City, Kan., 1964-65; instr. U. Wash., Seattle, 1967-70; research asso. Child Devel. Center, Seattle, 1972-73; chmn. dept. occupational therapy U. Okla., Oklahoma City, 1973—. Cons. Dept. Health, Edn. and Welfare Pub. Health grant to Ohio State U., 1970-71, NIH grant to Am. Occupational Therapy Assn., 1972-73; acting instr. U. Puget Sound, Tacoma, Wash., 1971. Telephone worker, counselor Open Door Clinic, 1968-72; mem., co-chmn. citizen's bd. Seattle Mental Health Center, 1970-72, mem. exec. bd., 1971-72. Recipient Elmer H. Wilds award Western Mich. U., 1966, Traineeship Dept. Health Edn. Welfare-Rehab. Services Adminstrn., 1970-72. Mem. Council Exceptional Children (chpt. treas. 1970-72), Am. Pub. Health Assn., Assn. Children with Learning Disabilities, Am. (nominating com. chmn. 1972), Okla. (practice chmn. 1973-74, pres. 1974—), Wash. (del. 1968-73) occupational therapy assns. Sigma Kappa, Pi Lambda Theta. Home: 1311 N Meridian Apt 155 Oklahoma City OK 73107

REED, LAURA LOUISE (MRS. MICHAEL REED), occupational therapist; b. Bklyn., Feb. 4, 1945; d. Otho Mills Rassmusen and Charlotte Louise (Emmingham) Rasmussen Gurney; student U. Denver, 1963-65; B.S., Colo. State U., 1967; m. Michael Reed, Sept. 19, 1970. VA trainee, 1965-67; staff occupational therapist Caruth Meml. Rehab. Center, Dallas, 1968-70; chief occupational therapist Easter Seal Soc. for Crippled Children and Adults of Tarrant County, Ft. Worth, 1970-72; occupational therapist Diagnostic and Evaluation Center for Mentally Retarded Children, U. Tex. Health Sci. Center, Dallas, 1972—. Named Woman of Year, Tanda chpt. Am. Bus. Womens Assn., 1970. Mem. Am., Tex. (continuing edn. dist. rep. 1970-72), N.Tex. (sec. 1969-72) occupational therapy assns. Home: 3445 Castle Rock Lane Garland TX 75042 Office: 1935 Amelia St Dallas TX 75235

REED, LOLA STUART, physician; b. Telford, Pa., Feb. 5, 1917; d. Ira Stewart and Elsie Fulmer (Stover) Reed; B.S., Ursinus Coll., 1938; M.D., U. Pa., 1942. Intern, Allentown (Pa.) Gen. Hosp., 1942-43; resident Phoenixville (Pa.) Hosp., 1943-44, Children's Hosp. Phila., 1944-45; practice medicine, specializing in pediatrics, Phoenixville, 1945—; chief of pediatrics Phoenixville Hosp., 1959—, pres. staff, 1961. Mem. adv. bd. Chester County Children's Services, 1959—; permanent chmn. bd. Phoenixville Area Day Care Assn., 1965—; mem. Chester County Com. on Regional Comprehensive Health Planning, 1972—. Pres. No. Central Chester County United Fund, 1971-72. Bd. dirs. No. Chester County Community Nursing Service, 1947-71, chmn. profl. adv. com., 1947-72; bd. dirs. Phoenixville United Fund, 1967—, pres., 1970-71. Presbyn. (elder 1970-73, deacon, 1965-68). Home: 4 McAvoy Lane Phoenixville PA 19460 Office: 620 Valley Forge Rd Phoenixville PA 19460

REED, MARGARET F. (MRS. RICHARD Y. REED), educator; b. Chgo., Mar. 13, 1916; d. Paul C. and Sarah (Pruner) Fox; B.A., U. Chgo., 1938, M.A., 1940, Ph.D., 1951; m. Richard Yates Reed, May 17, 1952; children—Christopher Yates, Sarah Margaret Yates. Personnel work Western Electric Co., Chgo., 1941-43; vocational counselor U. Chgo., 1943-49; counselor for socially maladjusted Bloom Township High Sch., Chicago Heights, Ill., 1951-52; asst. editor Scott Forsman publs., 1952-53; pvt. practice marriage and family counseling, Chgo. and Miami, 1952-64; prof. social work Moorhead (Minn.) State Coll., 1964—, also chmn. dept. social services. Cons. Vols. for Community Service. Bd. dirs. United Community Council. Mem. Am. Psychol. Assn., Am., Nat. assns. marriage counselors, Nat. Assn. Social Workers, Council on Social Work Edn., Minn. Conf. Social Work Edn., Mental Health Assn. Address: 1309 13th St S Moorhead MN 56560

REED, MARTHA SWAIN, editor; b. Houston, Sept. 8, 1930; d. Emmett Conway and Ysleta Evelyn (Spurlock) Swain; student Tex. Christian U., 1948-51, U. Houston, 1951-56; married, children—Rebecca, Ann, Steven. Clk., Humble Oil and Refining Co., Houston, 1951-53; tchr. Rapides Parish Schs., Oakdale, La., 1958-61; asst. editor Oakdale (La.) Jour., 1960-62; women's editor Baytown (Tex.) Sun, 1964-71; owner, Image, pub. relations firm, 1968-71; fashion coordinator, buyer The Cage, Baytown, Tex., 1968-71; editor family living dept. Beaumont (Tex.) Enterprise and Jour., 1972—. Trustee Sterling Municipal Library, Baytown. Recipient Community Service award Baytown Jr. Forum, 1968, citations Girl Scouts Am., 1964-71, United Appeal, 1964-72, March of Dimes, 1971. Mem. Nat. Fed. Press Women (dir. 1969—), Women in Communications, Tex. Press Women (pres. 1970-72). Home: 6312 Ivanhoe Lane Beaumont TX 77706 Office: PO Box 3071 Beaumont TX 77704

REED, MARY KATHERINE STEVENS (MRS. HOWARD LOUIS REED), supt. schs.; b. Crandall, Ind.; d. Albert T. and Mabel (Fellmy) Stevens; B.S., Ind. State U., 1950, M.S., 1952; Ed.D., U. So. Cal., 1965; 1 son, Vernon Lawrence. Elementary and high sch. tchr., Ind., 1943-47; reading cons., Kendallville, Ind., 1947-49; dir. spl. edn., Monticello, Ind., 1949-51; demonstration tchr. Terre Haute (Ind.) city schs., 1951-52; curriculum cons. E. Whittier (Cal.) Sch. Dist. 1952-54;

head reading clinic, reading cons. Long Beach (Cal.) city schs., 1954-57; dir. curriculum Fullerton (Cal.) Elementary Schs., 1957-63; dir. instructional services El Segundo (Cal.) Unified Sch. Dist., 1963-73, supt., 1973—; instr. U. So. Cal., part-time. Cons. Nat. Def. Edn. Act, Orange and Santa Barbara Counties, 1964—; mem. part-time faculty various colls. and univs., 1954—. Mem. Cal. Adv. Com. for Child Devel. Centers, 1967—; mem. lang. arts adv. com. Cal. Dept. Edn., 1966-68, curriculum com. Los Angeles County Regional TV Adv. Com., 1958—; spl. cons. to Gov.'s Commn. Status Women. Named Ky. Col., 1966, El Segundo Woman of Yr., 1967; El Segundo Citizen of Month, El Segundo C. of C., 1973. Mem. Internat. Reading Assn., Assn. for Supervision and Curriculum Devel. (state v.p. 1965-66, nat. dir. 1963—), Cal. Assn. Elementary Sch. Adminstrs. (dir.-at-large So. sect. 1959-62), Assn. of Gifted, Math. Council, Assn. Cal. Sch. Adminstrs. (regional chmn. instrn. and curriculum com.), Nat. Com. for Early Childhood Edn., Los Angeles County Curriculum Assn., Delta Kappa Gamma (chpt. pres. 1962-64, publicity chmn. 1966-68; Chi-state corr. sec. 1963-65, chmn. profl. affairs 1965-67), Delta Epsilon. Methodist (chmn. edn. commn., mem. adminstrv. bd. and pastor-parish relations). Clubs: Bus. and Professional Women's (pres. 1966-67) (El Segundo); Quota (sec. 1965-66, parliamentarian 1967-69) (El Segundo). Author: What Is Man? (Social Sci. Series Grades Kindergarten-4th), 1970; Our Family of Man, A Conceptual Approach to Social Studies, 1972. Home: PO Box 356 El Segundo CA 90245 Office: 641 Sheldon St El Segundo CA 90245

REEDER, JANE BEASLEY, educator; b. Florence, Ala., Feb. 13, 1931; d. William Marvin and Stella (Beasley) Reeder; B.S., East Tenn. State U., 1953; M.S., U. Tenn., 1955; postgrad U. Mich., U. Chattanooga, 1957-64, Cadek Conservatory of Music, Chattanooga, summers 1957-66, U. Tenn., summer 1964, Samford U., summer 1966, U. W.Va., summer 1967, Oberlin Coll., 1968. Dir. instrumental and vocal music West High Sch., Knoxville, Tenn., 1953-57; chmn. dept. music, vocal and orchestral dir. Red Bank High Sch., Chattanooga, 1957-67, also tchr. journalism, adviser sch. newspaper; dir. vocal music, dir. sch. newspaper Ooltewah (Tenn.) High Sch., 1967—, chmn. dept. music, 1969—. Mem. East Tenn. Sch. Band and Orch. Assn., East Tenn. Vocal Assn. (treas. 1956-60), Am. String Tchrs. Assn., Music Educators Nat. Conf., Nat. Sch. Orch. Assn., Nat. Choral Condrs. Guild, Am. Choral Found., Am. Assn. U. Women, Tenn. (chmn. information and study com.), East Tenn., Hamilton County (exec. bd., editor Movements) edn. assns., Tenn. Music Educators Assn., Music Educators Nat. Conf., Freedom's Found., Chattanooga, Knoxville opera assns., Chattanooga Concert Choir, Journalism Edn. Assn., Nat., Columbia scholastic press assns., Tenn. High Sch. Press Assn., Columbia Scholastic Press Assn. Advisers Assn., Alpha Delta Kappa (sgt.-at-arms 1972-74), Delta Omicron, Alpha Omicron Pi. Mem. Christian Ch. Contbr. articles to profl. jours. Home: 4000 Harbor Hills Rd Chattanooga TN 37416 1Office: Ooltewah High Sch Ooltewah TN 37363

REEL, DOROTHY C. (MRS. LOUIS W. REEL), business exec.; b. Trenton, N.J., May 17, 1909; d. Henry Earle and Lizzie (Perrine) Cole; student Orange County Vocational Sch., Orlando, Fla., 1929-30; m. John Perrine de Noyelles, Dec. 31, 1926 (dec. Nov. 1960); 1 son, John Perrine de Noyelles; m. 2d, Louis W. Reel, Nov. 23, 1961. Sec., bookkeeper Maitland Citrus Service Co. (Fla.), 1930, Endion Fruit Co., Maitland, 1930-31; sec. cashier Fla. Pub. Service Co., Winter Park, 1932; with Am. Fire & Casualty Co., Orlando, 1934—, corp. sec., 1953-72, asst. sec., 1972—, mem. exec. com., 1956-66, also dir.; asst. corporate sec., dir. several affiliates, all Orlando; dir. exec. com. Am. Fed. Savs. & Loan Assn. Mem. women's exec. com. Orlando Central Bus. Dist. Mem. Greater Orlando C. of C. Democrat. Methodist. Club: Dubsdread Country. Home: 537 W Stetson Av Orlando FL 32804 Office: PO Box 2753 Orlando FL 32802

REES, ELIZABETH LODGE, physician; b. Berkeley, Cal., Aug. 1, 1914; d. Lesley Arthur and Mary Elizabeth (Nelson) Lodge; A.B., U. Cal. at Berkeley, 1935; M.D., U. Cal. at San Francisco, 1941; m. Rees Bynon Rees, Aug. 8, 1936; children—Daniel Lodge, David Wetterman. Intern, U. Cal. Med. Sch., 1940-41, resident, 1941-43; practice medicine specializing in pediatrics, Castro Valley, Cal., 1947—; mem. staff Children's Hosp. Med. Center, Oakland, Cal., Eden Hosp., Castro Valley, Levine Hosp., St. Rose Hosp., Hayward, Cal.; staff Alameda County Instns.; med. dir. Mineralab. Levine Hosp. Bldg., Hayward; cons. physician Acad. Pediatrics to Cal. Intertribal Council; Mem. Am., Cal., Alameda-Contra Costa County med. assns., Med. Women's Assn., Western Electroencephalograph Soc. Am. Acad. Pediatrics (handicapped child com. 1969—, Indian health com.), Acad. Orthomolecular Psychiatry, Acad. Parapsychology and Medicine, Phi Beta Kappa. The Rosicrucians. Author: (with Steven Get) The Mentally Ill Child, 1956; A Doctor Looks at Toys, 1961. Contbr. articles to med. jours. Address: 5311 Greenridge Rd Castro Valley CA 94546

REESE, BETTY JO SEELIG, librarian; b. Montezuma County, Colo., June 30, 1921; d. Charles Otis and Mary Mildred (Schaaf) Seelig; A.B., Western State Coll. Colo., Gunnison, 1947; postgrad. U. Colo.; M.S. in Librarianship, U. Denver, 1966; m. Donald Wesley Reese, Nov. 20, 1941; children—Sheryl (Mrs. Joseph Clyde Clayton), Robin. Tchr., Cortez, Colo., 1947-49; tchr., librarian, Gunnison, 1949-50; librarian Canon City (Colo.) High Sch., 1950-53; tchr., Easton, Pa., 1954-57; librarian Boulder Valley Sch. Dist., 1958—. Mem. Colo. Assn. Sch. Librarians (sec. 1967), Colo. Library Assn. (pres. sch. div. 1970), A.L.A., N.E.A., Boulder Valley Edn. Assn., Phi Beta Phi. Mem. Christian Ch. Home: 441 Harvard Lane Boulder CO 80303

REESE, CHARLOTTE PAUL, newspaperwoman, author, govt. ofcl.; b. Seattle, May 22, 1916; d. Charles and Alice (Paine) Paul; B.A., Wellesley Coll., 1938; m. Edward Winston Groshell, Aug. 21, 1942 (div. June 1964); children—Hiram Paul, John Paine; m. 2d, Robert W. Reese, Feb. 14, 1966. Asst. to fgn. news editor Chgo. Times, 1940-42; free-lance writer, 1941—; mem. editorial staff Coronet-Esquire mags., 1942-45; editor, co-pub. Snoqualmie Valley Record, North Bend Record, 1949-61; mem. Wash. State Council Children and Youth, 1957-61, Wash. State Bd. Prison Terms and Paroles, 1962-64; mem. U.S. Bd. Parole, 1964—. Mem. Woman's Nat. Democratic Club. Recipient numerous nat. prizes for feature articles, columns, news, books, mag. work from Nat. Fedn. Press Women, Wash. State Press Women, Wash. State Press Club; named Nat. Press Woman of Year, Nat. Fedn. Press Women, 1957. Mem. Am. Assn. U. Women, Nat. Council Crime and Delinquency, Assn. Paroling Authorities, Western Probation, Parole and Correction Assn., Potomac Bus. and Profl. Women's Club, Theta Sigma Phi. Author: Hear My Heart Speak, 1950; Gold Mountain, 1953; Minding Our Own Business, 1955; The Cup of Strength, 1958; And Four to Grow, 1961. Office: HOLC Bldg 101 Indiana Av NW Washington DC 20001

REESE, DELLA (DELLAREESE TALIAFERRO), singer; b. Detroit, July 6, 1932; student Wayne U. Singer in choirs, 1938—; summers with Mahalia Jackson troupe, 1945-49; organized gospel group while student at Wayne U.; club appearances, Detroit, later moved to N.Y.C., joined Erskine Hawkins; solo artist, 1957—, appearing radio shows with Robert Q. Lewis, on TV with Jackie Gleason, Ed Sullivan, others; role in motion picture Let's Rock, 1958; recs. for Jubilee, RCA Victor Records.

REESE, DOROTHY HARMON, educator; b. Fowler, Kan., Feb. 1, 1930; d. Harry Hershel and Edith Clare (Miller) Harmon; B.S. in Secondary Edn., Auburn U., 1967; M.A. in Spl. Edn., U. South Fla., 1973—; children by previous marriage—Edith Jones, Virginia (Mrs. Kent Emory Bryant), Patricia Lee. Dir. Happy House, Albany, Ga., 1963-66; tchr. Silver Sands Sch., Ft. Walton Beach, Fla., 1967-70; instr. Hillsborough County Sch., Tampa, Fla., 1970—. Dir., Okaloosa County (Fla.) Summer Recreation Program, 1969. Bd. dirs. Fla. Epilepsy Found. Mem. Council for Exceptional Children (sec. 1969—), Gulf Coast Epilepsy Found. Author: (with B. Wiley, A. Jensen) Okaloosa County Curriculum Guide for Educable Mentally Retarded, 1969. Home: 3411 B Carlton Arms Dr Tampa FL 33614 Office: 9401 North Blvd Tampa FL 33612

REESE, GLADYS BRADEN (MRS. CARLTON B. REESE), scientist; b. Campti, La., Dec. 2, 1938; d. James Leo and Hattie (Thompson) Braden; B.S., So. U. 1960; postgrad. Miami U. (Ohio), 1960-62; m. Carlton B. Reese, Dec. 23, 1960; children—Michael B., Carla M., Brian A. Student research asst., instr. microbiology So. U., Baton Rouge, 1958-60; grad. teaching asst. Miami U., Oxford, O., 1960-62; microbiologist Nat. Marine Fisheries Service U.S. Dept. of Commerce, Pascagoula, Miss., 1965-67, fishery biologist, 1967—. Mem. Soc. Am. Microbiologists, Am. Fisheries Soc., Beta Beta Beta, Phi Sigma. Contbr. articles to profl. jours. Home: 2006 Eastwood DR Moss Point MS 39563 Office: PO Drawer 1207 Pascagoula MS 39567

REESE, JEAN ALICE ETTER (MRS. JOHN KENNETH REESE), educator; b. Waynesboro, Pa., Nov. 22, 1948; d. George Rennis and Mabel Catherine (Suffocool) Etter; B.S., Shippensburg State Coll., 1970, M.S., 1972; m. John Kenneth Reese, May 22, 1970. Apprentice TV div. Washington County Bd. Edn., Hagerstown, Md., 1970; tchr. English, Central Jr. High Sch., Chambersburg, Pa., 1970—, drama coach, 1970—. Mem. Theatre Assn. Pa. (dir. 1970-73), Alpha Psi Omega. Home: 341 Briar Lane Chambersburg PA 17201 Office: Central Jr High Sch Queen St Chambersburg PA 17201

REESMAN, FRANCES LEE (MRS. KENNETH GEX REESMAN), coll. adminstr.; b. Newton Grove, N.C., Aug. 16, 1921; d. James Marshall and Alese (Wagstaff) Lee; B.S., U. N.C., 1942; M.A., E. Carolina U., 1972; m. Kenneth Gex Reesman, Apr. 27, 1946; children—Ann Price, Susan Lee. Pvt. sec. to commr. agr., Raleigh, N.C., 1942-46; personal sec. Gov. N.C., 1949-51; tour guide, hostess Tryon Palace Restoration, New Bern, N.C., 1953-69; guidance counselor Craven Community Coll., New Bern, N.C., 1969-73, registrar, 1973—, bus. instr., 1967-69. Mem. USO council Craven County, 1970-73. Mem. Student Services Personnel Assn., Carolinas Assn. Collegiate Registrars and Admissions Officers, Alpha Delta Gamma, Kappa Delta Pi. Methodist (ofcl. bd. 1969-71, 74—, pres. Women's Orgn. 1972). Clubs: Golf and Country (New Bern, N.C.); Junior Woman's (Raleigh, N.C.); Federated Women's (v.p., div. chmn. 1959-69) (New Bern, N.C.); Federated Garden (pres. chpt. 1966-69) (New Bern). Home: 4100 Greenwood Rd New Bern NC 28560 Office: PO Box 885 Racetrack Rd New Bern NC 28560

REEVE, LYDIA RYDHOLM, advt. agy. exec.; b. Cleve., Jan. 3, 1925; d. Carl Oscar and Marion Louise (Hager) Rydholm; student Ohio Wesleyan U., 1944-45; B.A., Washington Sq. Coll., N.Y. U., 1948; m. Donald Burkett Reeve, June 16, 1956 (div. Nov. 1962). Media clk. Alfred J. Silberstein, Bert Goldsmith, Inc., advt. agy., N.Y.C., 1948; with Foote, Cone & Belding Advt., Los Angeles, 1949-69, asso. media dir., 1958-65, media dir., 1965-69, v.p. media, 1968; v.p., media dir. Honig-Cooper & Harrington Advt., Los Angeles, 1969—. Bd. dirs. Com. of Profl. Women, Los Angeles Symphony/Hollywood Bowl Assn. Mem. Am. Advt. Fedn. (dir., One of Top Ten Advt. Women in U.S. 1971, sec. Western region 1974-75), Advt. Rev. Council So. Cal. (sec.-treas. 1973—), Hollywood Radio and TV Soc. (dir., sec. 1974-75), Los Angeles Advt. Women (life, pres. 1967-68), Los Angeles Area C. of C. (chmn. pub. relations women's div. 1973-74). Office: 3600 Wilshire Blvd Los Angeles CA 90010

REEVE, MINERVA TABITHA SMITH (MRS. KEITH GRAHAM REEVE), civic worker; b. Indpls., June 10, 1907; d. Franklin Peter and Sophia Pearl Allen (Deatherage) Smith; student U. Ill., 1926-27; m. Keith Graham Reeve, June 9, 1927 (dec. Nov. 1961); children—Patricia Louise (Mrs. Melvin Bruce Haskell), Josephine Ann (Mrs. George Theodore Savas). Owner style shop, Mt. Carmel, Ill., 1939-48; now dean of women's staff, head resident Noble Hall, Auburn (Ala.) U. Pres., P.T.A., Mt. Carmel, 1942-44; mem. Auburn council Girl Scouts U.S.A., 1946-48; a founder Art League, Huntsville, Ala., pres., 1957; adviser, sponsor Auburn U. Dames chpt., 1954; founder U. Dames Chpt. Ferris Inst., Big Rapids, Mich., 1956; patroness to Chi Omega, Auburn, 1946-56; philanthropy chmn. Lee County Nursing Home, 1964—; mem. Lee County Hosp. Aux. 1964—. Recipient Gold medal Appreciation, Ala. S.A.R., 1959. Mem. D.A.R. (regent 1948-50, publicity chmn. 1968-70; chmn. antique show; chmn. Nat. Def. Luncheon), Colonial Dames XVII Century (pres. Ala. 1969—, organizing sec. Ala., chmn. Ala. state conf. 1974), Ala. Magna Charta Dames (historian 1966), Campus Club Auburn U. (v.p. 1948). Mem. Christian Ch. Mem. P.E.O. Sisterhood (v.p. Auburn chpt.). Clubs: Newcomer's (program chmn. 1946), Woman's (chmn. art dept. 1936), Perry Garden (pres. 1948-49) (Auburn). Home: 533 Wrights Mill Rd Auburn AL 36830

REEVES, CAROLINE BUCK (MRS. WILLIAM HARVEY REEVES), author, civic worker; b. St. Louis; d. Philo Melvin and Aletheia (Hall) Buck; A.B., Wellesley Coll., U. Wis., 1928; M.A., Columbia, 1934; m. William Harvey Reeves, Aug. 29, 1931; children—Aletheia Nevius Kerr, H. Van Kirk. Editorial, coll. depts. Henry Holt & Co., pubs., N.Y.C., 1928-31; indsl. economist U.S. Govt., Washington, 1942-45, Rockefeller U., 1970—. Pres. bd. mgrs. Home for Old Men and Aged Couples, N.Y.C., 1955-58, mem. bd. 1951—, sec. bd., 1960-62, trustee, 1969—, mem. com. on aging Fedn. of Protestant Welfare Agys., N.Y.C., 1951-58; mem. hobby show com. Community Council of Greater N.Y., 1955-63; mem. N.Y. Com. Frontier Nursing Service, Inc.; bd. dirs. The Bargain Box, Inc., 1962-69. Mem. Colonial Dames Am., Delta Delta Delta. Clubs: City Gardens, Colony. Author: Impact of War on Tri-City Area, 1917-19, 1943; Impact of World War I on Hampton Roads Area, 1944, Disposition of Surplus Machine Tools by the War Department following World War I, 1944, also articles. Home: 273 Harbor Rd Southport CT 06490

REEVES, MARGARET RUTH, educator, ednl. adminstr.; b. Parkersburg, Ia., Jan. 9, 1922; d. Rudolph and Anne Margaret (Schnucker) Roelfs; B.A., U. No. Ia., 1943; M.S., No. Ill. U., 1961; postgrad. Western Mich. U., 1965-68, Chgo. Music Conservatory, 1958-59; div.; 1 son, Tom. Sec. ins. agy., Washington, 1943-44; sec. dean women U. No. Ia., Cedar Falls, 1944-45; tchr. music and bus., pub. high schs., Emmetsburg, Ia., 1947-49, Belvidere, Ill., 1949-55, elementary schs., 1956-60, also supr., 1956-60; assistantship-guidance No. Ill. U., DeKalb, 1960, instr. music methods, 1961-62, also supr. music interns; counselor Proviso East High Sch., Chgo., 1962-68; asso. prof. psychology Kankakee (Ill.) Community Coll., 1971—, dir. coll. services, 1970—, also choir dir. Pvt. instr. voice, piano, organ, 1934—; asst. personnel dir. Green Giant Co., Belvidere, 1950-52; summer counselor Presbyn. camps, Belvidere, 1953-59. Mem. Kankakee Mental Health Bd., 1969, 70. Bd. dirs. Kankakee Community Coll. Credit Union, pres., 1972—. Mem. Kankakee Faculty Assn. (pres. 1969-71), Am. Assn. Univ. Women, Nat. Assn. Collegiate Admissions Counselors, Nat. Student Personnel Assn., Women's Bus. and Profl. Club, Phi Lambda Theta. Clubs: Zonta, Internat. Service. Home: 1429 Grace St Kankakee IL 60901 Office: Rural Route 1 Box 888 Kankakee IL 60901

REEVES, MILDRED JONES, educator; b. Long Branch, N.J., Feb. 24, 1917; d. S. Walter and Eliza L. (Kyte) Jones; B.A., U. Ky., 1938; M.Ed., U. Fla., 1962; m. Ralph C. Reeves, Apr. 20, 1941 (div. 1962); children—Hillary Ann (Mrs. Frank Schnorrbusch), Courtney Lea (Mrs. James T. Winstead). Asst. to dean women Translyvania Coll., Lexington, Ky., 1939-40; asst. to dean Centre Coll., Danville, 1940-41; with dept. indsl. engring. Tenn. Coal & Iron Co., Birgingham, Ala., 1942-43; tchr. pub. schs., Manatee and Sarasota counties, Fla., 1952-56; sch. psychologist Sarasota County Schs., Sarasota, 1956-65; instr. sociology Manatee Jr. Coll., Bradenton, Fla., 1963-66; specialist psychol. services St. Petersburg Jr. Coll., 1965—; instr. psychology St. Petersburg Jr. Coll., 1966—. Sec., Sarasota County Civic League; mem. research com., steering com. Common Cause, St. Petersburg, 1972—. Bd. dirs. Sarasota County Mental Health Assn., 1960-62. Mem. Am. Personnel and Guidance Assn., Fla. Edn. Research Assn., Fla. Psychol. Assn. (publs. com. 1959-60), Fla. Assn. Sch. Psychologists (sec.-treas. 1961-63, mem. at large exec. com. 1964—), Am. Psychol Assn., Fla., Sarasota County (pres. 1960-61, exec. com. 1961-63) edn. assns., Delta Kappa Gamma (corr. sec. 1957-58). Home: Apt 30 515 Plaza Sevilla Treasure Island FL 33706 Office: 6605 5th Av N St Petersburg FL 33710

REEVES, NANCY GOLDHABER, lawyer, author, educator; b. Phila., Dec. 9, 1913; d. Koppel and Sadie (Finkler) Goldhaber; B.A., Hunter Coll., 1935; LL.B., N.Y.U., 1938, J.D., 1974; m. Edward Alban Reeves, Mar. 3, 1944. Admitted to N.Y. bar, 1940, Cal. bar, 1946; practiced in N.Y.C., 1941-42, Los Angeles, 1953—; mem. legal staff Office Atty. Gen. of Cal., 1945-47; star program A Woman's Place, on ednl. radio; TV lectr. on status of women; designed and taught first coll. course on sociology of women U. Cal. at Los Angeles, 1969, 71; vis. lectr. U. Reading (Eng.), 1971, Claremont Grad. Sch., Cal. State Coll., Los Angeles, U. Cal. at Los Angeles, U. Wis., Chaffey Coll.; feminist-in-residence U. Pitts., 1972, Scripps Coll., 1972. Recipient MacDowell Colony award, 1973, 74. Mem. Fedn. Internationale des Femmes Juristes, Women's Internat. League for Peace and Freedom (nat. bd., pres. Los Angeles br. 1960-62, v.p. Cal. br. 1961-63). Author: Womankind beyond the Stereotypes, 1971 (lit. award State Bar Conv. Cal. 1972). Bd. editors Dialectic: An Ann. of Feminist Thought. Contbr. articles to profl. jours., other periodicals. Home: Santa Monica Shores 2700 Nailson Way Santa Monica CA 90405 Office: 3111 Los Feliz Blvd Los Angeles CA 90039

REEVES, MRS. OLA MAE (MRS. JOSEPH W. REEVES), govt. ofcl.; b. Dora, Ala.; d. Edward L. and Beulah (Isobel) Sargent; student Birmingham-So. Coll., 1936-38, Bryant and Stratton Bus. Coll., Chgo., 1942; m. Joseph W. Reeves, May 23, 1944; children—JoAnn, Joseph W., Nancy. Stewardess Eastern Air Lines, 1943-45; interviewer Mass. Employment Service, Fitchburg, Mass., 1946-51; interviewer, counselor, employment service supr., acting mgr. Alaska Employment Service, Fairbanks, 1951-54, mgr., 1954-56; dep. dir. Employment Security Div. Alaska Dept. Labor, 1956-62; social adminstrn. adviser U.S. Dept. Labor, Bur. Employment Security, Unemployment Ins. Service, 1962-69, supervisory unemployment ins. specialist Manpower Adminstrn. Unemployment Service, 1969—, chief br. of manpower tng. allowances procedural control, spl. assignment unemployment ins. service Bur. Employment Security, 1961-62. Recipient merit award Internat. Assn. Personnel in Employment Security, 1956, Superior Performance award U.S. Dept. Labor, 1967, 73. Mem. Alaska Health, Welfare and Edn. Council, Fairbanks Community Service Council (first sec.-treas.), Bus. and Profl. Women's Clubs, Internat. Assn. Personnel in Employment Security (pres. Alaska chpt. 1955, del. internat. conv. 1955, 57, 58, 59, 70, internat. sec., 1957-59). Home: 10307 Leslie St Silver Spring MD 20902 Office: Manpower Adminstrn Unemployment Ins US Dept Labor Washington DC 20525

REFORD, STEPHANIE MCCANDLESS (MRS. ROBERT W. REFORD), educator; b. St. Louis, Mar. 8, 1934; d. Lee and Mary (Glor) McCandless; B.A. cum laude, Principia Coll., 1956; M.A., U. Washington, 1962; m. Robert W. Reford. Tchr. world history Punahou Acad., Honolulu, 1958-59, 62-63; program specialist Inst. Internat. Edn., N.Y.C., 1960; asst. dean students State U. N.Y., Oswego, 1960-61; exec. dir. Pacific and Asian Affairs Council, Honolulu, 1963-70; project adminstrn. officer UN Inst. Tng. and Research, N.Y.C., 1970-73. Mem. Nat. Com. for Support of Pub. Schs., Washington, 1967. Mem. Nat. Council for Social Studies, UN Assn. (dir. 1966-70), Pan Pacific, S.E. Asian Womens Assn., Hawaii Hist. Soc., Canadian Inst. Internat. Affairs, Royal Ont. Mus. Theta Sigma Phi. Christian Scientist. Home: 12 Metcalfe St Toronto ON M4X 1R6 Canada

REGAN, ELLEN FRANCES (MRS. WALSTON SHEPARD BROWN), ophthalmologist; b. Boston, Feb. 1, 1919; d. Edward Francis and Margaret (Moynihan) Regan; A.B., Wellesley Coll., 1940; M.D., Yale, 1943; m. Walston Shepard Brown, Aug. 13, 1955. Intern Boston City Hosp., 1944; asst. resident, resident Inst. Ophthalmology, Presbyn. Hosp., N.Y.C., 1944-47, asst. ophthalmologist, 1947-56, asst. attending ophthalmologist, 1956—; instr. ophthalmology Columbia Coll. Phys. and Surgs., 1947-55, asso. ophthalmology, 1955-67, asst. clin. prof., 1967—. Mem. Am. Ophthal. Soc., A.M.A., Am. Acad. Ophthalmology, Assn. Research Ophthalmology, N.Y. Acad. Medicine, N.Y. State, Mass. med. socs., N.Y. Diabetic Assn. Clubs: River, Wellesley, York. Home: Tuxedo Park NY 10987 Office: 1 E 71st St New York City NY 10021

REGAN, MARGARET BLACKINGER, educator, nursing exec.; b. Boise, Ida., Jan. 19, 1918; d. William V. and Mollie (Merle) Regan; R.N., St. Joseph's Coll. Nursing, 1944; B.A., San Francisco Coll. Women, 1958; M.Nursing, U. Wash., 1964. Supr. neurology, neuropsychiatry VA Hosp., San Francisco, 1948-50; dir. nursing service Providence Hosp., Seattle, 1962-64; asst. prof. nursing. U. Wash. Sch. Nursing, Seattle, 1964-69; dir. Am. Way King County, 1969-72; dir. nursing Group Health Hosp., Seattle, 1972—. Cons. VA Hosp., Roseburg, Ore., 1965-70, Success Motivation Inst., 1969-71; mem. Wash. Gov's Med. Adv. Council, 1965-70, USPHS Surgeon Gen.'s Emergency Health Preparedness Adv. Com., 1967-70, Wash. State Health Manpower Adv. Council, 1967-70. Mem. nursing services com. A.R.C., Seattle, 1964-70. Served to maj. U.S. Army Nurse Corp, 1950-60; now col. Res. Mem Am. (commn. nursing services 1966-70, council nursing facilitators 1973—), Wash. State (pres. 1964-67, v.p. 1968-70) nurses assns., Am. Mgmt. Assn., Am. Soc. Personnel Adminstrs., Am. Security Council, Wash. Assn. Retarded Children, Sigma Theta Tau. Club: Magnolia Community. Home: 2639 Perkins Lane W Seattle WA 98199

REGAN, MARY MARGARET, librarian; b. Detroit, Jan. 12, 1927; d. Michael Cornelius and Ann Elizabeth (Cusack) Regan; A.B., Marygrove Coll., Detroit, 1949; postgrad. Wayne U., 1950-51, N.Y. U., 1962-63; M.A. in L.S., U. Mich., 1953. Librarian, Control Instrument Co., Bklyn., 1953-55; sr. reference librarian Young & Rubicam, Inc., N.Y.C., 1955-68; supervising librarian, lit. specialist in econ. and pub. affairs div. N.Y. Pub. Library, N.Y.C., 1968—. Co-discussion leader Am. Mgmt. Assn. seminar, 1965. Mem. Murray Hill Com., 1973—. Mem. Spl. Libraries Assn. (pres. N.Y. chpt. 1965-66), Victorian Soc., Bronte Soc., Georgian Soc. Exec. editor: Guide to Special Issues and Indexes of Periodicals, Spl. Libraries Assn. publ., 1962. Home: 36 E 36th St New York City NY 10016

REGAN, OUIDA BAGGETT, constrn. co. exec.; b. Pensacola, Fla., Sept. 6, 1927; d. Thomas Lloyd and Lois (Byrd) Baggett; student Huntingdon Coll., 1945-48; m. James Ronald Regan, June 7, 1946 (div. Oct. 1949); children—Daniel Thomas, Marcia. Pres., owner Baggett Constrn. Co., Pensacola, 1953—. Past chmn. Santa Rosa Island Authority; vice chmn., sec., treas. Fla. Small Bus. Adminstrn. Adv. Council, 1963-64, mem. Southeastern regional adv. council, 1963-64; mem. interim council on econ. devel. Fla. State Agy., 1960-61, chmn., 1960-61; pres. Fiesta Five Flags Com., 1964, now dir.; adv. mem. Girl Scouts U.S.A.; mem. Def. Adv. Com. on Women in Services, 1973—. Dir. Pensacola Oratoria Soc. Bd. Trustee Pensacola Art Assn., Nat. Housing Council; past dir. Pensacola Symphony; bd. dirs. Episcopal Day Sch. Recipient award for service in home bldg. industry, award for service performed as chmn. Fla.'s Devel. Econs. Council, award for outstanding service Fiesta Five Flags Commn. Mem. Fla. (past sec.), W. Fla. (past sec., dir. 1962—; award for outstanding service) home builders assns., Nat. Assn. Home Builders (life dir., exec. com. 1974—), Greater Pensacola C. of C. (v.p., dir.). Episcopalian. Clubs: Pensacola Country, Pensacola Yacht. Home: The Bayshore Pensacola FL 32507 Office: 825 Bayshore Dr Pensacola FL 32507

REGENER, FRANCES ELIZABETH BRADFORD, mayor; b. Coatesville, Pa., Aug. 13, 1918; d. Park William and Helen Elizabeth (Holt) Bradford; ed. pub. schs., Chester County Magistrate Sch.; m. Robert Carl Regener, June 20, 1936; children—Gerald Carl, Helen Carole (Mrs. Max Evans). Judge of elections, Coatesville, 1948-49; policewoman, 1956-59; alderman, City of Coatesville, 1966-72, mayor, 1972—. Mem. Navy Mothers Club; dir. United Charities. Mem. Gov.'s Justice Commn., Chester County Women's Dem. Club. Mem. V.F.W. Aux., Polish Am. Club Aux., West End Fire Co. Aux., Coatesville C. of C., Coatesville Hosp. Aux. Home: 208 Charles St Coatesville PA 19320 Office: 52 S 1st Av Coatesville PA 19320

REGENSBERGER, EDITH ROMANO (MRS. WILLIAM J. REGENSBERGER), psychologist, educator; b. N.Y.C., Aug. 10, 1922; d. Morris and Florence (Weiner) Greenwald; B.A. magna cum laude, Syracuse U., 1943, Ph.D. in Spl. Edn., 1968; m. William J. Regensberger, Mar. 18, 1971. Social worker A.R.C., Syracuse, N.Y., Atlanta, Oakland, Cal. 1944-45; clin. psychologist Psychol. Service Center, Syracuse U., 1947-50, instr. Dept. Spl. Edn., 1957, vis. lectr., 1968—; clin. psychologist Syracuse Cerebral Palsy Clinic, 1948-59; pvt. practice clin. and cons. psychologist, 1947—; dir. DeVillo Sloan Sch. for Retarded Children, 1954-71; dir. spl. edn. Bd. Coop. Ednl. Services, Onondaga and Madison Counties, N.Y., 1971—. Bd. dirs. Consol. Industries Greater Syracuse, Inc. Chmn. Exceptional Children and Youth, Central Div. N.Y. State Congress Parents and Tchrs., 1959-60; mem. scholarship com. Rosamond Gifford Found., Onondaga County chpt. N.Y. State Council on Crime and Delinquency. Commr. edn. Syracuse Pub. Schs., 1962-66; councilman-at-large City of Syracuse, 1970-74. Licensed psychologist, N.Y. Recipient Woman of Achievement in Edn. award Syracuse Post Standard newspaper, Syracuse Fedn. Women's Clubs, 1958. Fellow Am. Assn. Mental Deficiency; mem. Internat. Council Exceptional Children, N.Y. State Tchrs. Assn., Am. (div. clin. psychology), N.Y. State, Central N.Y. (pres. 1971) psychol. assns., Phi Beta Kappa, Psi Chi. Home: 753 James St Syracuse NY 13203 Office: 6820 N Thompson Rd Syracuse NY 13211

REGENSBURG, ALICE BRESCHEL (MRS. CHARLES REGENSBURG), pub. relations exec.; b. N.Y.C., July 13, 1918; d. Gustav and Ann (Doherty) Breschel; student Columbia, 1937-39; m. Charles Regensburg, May 7, 1937; 1 dau., Jill (Mrs. Alan Bomser). Account exec. Lynn Farnol Group, 1953-56, dir. creative services, 1956-59, v.p., 1959-62, pres., 1962—; guest lectr. pub. relations, fashion, food-nutrition, and interior design various univs. Judge Penney-Mo. Journalism Awards, 1970. Mem. Am. Footwear Inst. (dir.), Pub. Relations Soc. Am., Women Execs. Pub. Relations (chmn. 1968-69, dir. 1974—), Am. Women in Radio and TV, Fashion Group, Elec. Women's Roundtable, Shoe Women Execs. (pres. 1967). Clubs: Hemisphere, Raffles (N.Y.C.). Home: 875 Park Av New York City NY 10021 Office: 50 Rockefeller Plaza New York City NY 10020

REHRIG, GERALDINE HAINES, educator; b. nr. Allentown, Pa., Feb. 10, 1923; d. Howard R. and Mabel L. (Haines) Rehrig; A.B., Bryn Mawr Coll., 1942; M.F.A., Yale, 1946. Actress in theatre, film, TV, radio, 1945-64; tchr. Alfred Dixon Speech Systems, Inc., and Speech Center, N.Y.C., 1950-63, Pitts. Playhouse Sch., 1963-66; asst. prof. U. Alta., Edmonton, Can., 1966-69; asst. prof. Pa. State U., University Park, 1970—. Vis. prof. Boston U., 1970. Mem. Actors' Equity Assn., Screen Actors Guild, Am. Fedn. TV and Radio Artists, Am. Theatre Assn., Speech Communication Assn., Can. Speech Assn., Can. Univ. Theatre Assn. Author: Workbook-Vocal Characterization for the Actor, 1970. Home: 5253 Apache Lane Drexel Hill PA 19026 Office: Dept Theatre Arts Pa State Arts Bldg III University Park PA 16802

REHSE, MARGARET SARAH POLLOCK (MRS. LOUIS REHSE), nursing adminstr.; b. St. Williams, Ont., Can., Feb. 8, 1909; d. James and Catherine (McKinnon) Pollock; R.N., Ont. Hosp. Tng. Sch. for Nurses, 1935; m. Louis Rehse, Sept. 6, 1958. Office employee Northway's, Ltd., Toronto, Ont., 1928-32; spl. home nursing Powell-Rouyn Gold Mine, Noranda, Que., Can., 1936; staff nurse St. Joseph Hosp., Flint, Mich., 1937-39, Walkerton Bruce Gen. Hosp., Walkerton, Ont., 1940-41, Ontario Hosp., New Toronto, 1941-45; night supr. Kincardine (Ont.) Gen. Hosp., 1945-55; dir. nursing Hanover (Ont.) Meml. Hosp., 1955—. Mem. R.N. Assn. Ont. Baptist (deacon 1973-74). Home: Rural Route 3 Hanover ON Canada Office: 97 7th Av Hanover ON Canada

REIBMAN, JEANETTE FICHMAN (MRS. NATHAN L. REIBMAN), state senator; b. Fort Wayne, Ind., Aug. 18, 1915; d. Meir and Pearl (Schwartz) Fichman; B.A., Hunter Coll.; LL.B., Ind. U.; LL.D. (hon.), Lafayette Coll., Wilson Coll.; m. Nathan L. Reibman; 3 children. Atty. tax amortization br. U.S. War Dept., Washington; atty. U.S. War Prodn. Bd., 1941-44; mem. Pa. Ho. of Reps., 1954-56, 58-66, sec. com. of welfare, chmn. com. on edn., 1959-62, com. on twps., 1965; mem. Pa. Senate, 1966—. Del. White House Conf. on Problems of Aging, White House Conf. on Children; mem. Gov.'s Citizens Commn. on Basic Edn.; mem. Joint State Govt. Commn. on Decedents' Estates; mem. Pa. Council Arts, Pa. Higher Edn. Assistance Agy. Trustee Lafayette Coll., St. Luke's Hosp. of Bethlehem; bd. dirs. Pa. Higher Edn. Assistance Agy. Named Distinguished Dau. Pa. Mem. Am. Assn. U. Women, League of Women Voters, Family Service, Delta Kappa Gamma, Sigma Delta Tau. Democrat. Home: 514 McCartney St Easton PA 18042

REICH, CAROL MUSSELMAN, educator, city ofcl.; b. Allentown, Pa., June 9, 1943; d. Henry Oliver and Grace Naomi (Wieand) Musselman; B.A. with honors, Wheaton Coll., 1965; Ph.D. in Social Psychology, U. Mich., 1970; m. Peter Allen Reich, June 24, 1967; 1 son, Adam. Research asso. Bd. Edn. for the City of Toronto, Ont., Can., 1970—. Mem. Com. on Selection of Qualified Women for Positions of Responsibility, Toronto Bd. Edn., 1972—. Ont. Ministry of Edn. grantee, 1972-74. Am. Psychol. Assn., Am. Ednl. Research Assn., Assn. of Ednl. Research Officers of Ont. (v.p. 1973-74). Home: 51 Wembley Rd Toronto ON M6C 2G1 Canada Office: 155 College St Toronto ON M5T 1P6 Canada

REICH, ELENORE JULIA CAPPA (MRS. LEWIS MILTON REICH), metal co. exec.; b. White Valley, Pa., Feb. 8, 1925; d. Quinto Theodore and Josephine Mary (Rupnik) Cappa; grad. high sch.; m. Lewis Milton Reich, Oct. 14, 1949; 1 dau., Linda Lou. Sales order corr. Westinghouse Electric Corp., East Pittsburgh, Pa., 1943; office mgr. J. M. Hall, Inc., Murrysville, Pa., 1948-66; purchasing dir. Overly Mfg. Co., Greensburg, Pa., 1968—. Home: 535 Athena Dr Delmont PA 15626 Office: 574 W Otterman St Greensburg PA 15601

REICH, KATHLEEN JOHANNA WEICHEL, librarian; b. Mannheim, Germany, May 1, 1927; d. Robert and Luise Charlotte Helene (Kurowsky) Weichel; diploma Leibniz U., Leipzig, Germany, 1948, Zwischenpruefung, 1950; cand. phil. Gutenberg U., Mainz, Germany, 1950-54; 1 son, Robert Weichel. Came to U.S. 1955, naturalized, 1959. Head tech. processes Orlando (Fla.) Pub. Library, 1955-57; cataloger U. Detroit, 1957-60; head tech. processes Muskegon (Mich.) Pub. Library, 1960-61; head tech. processes Trinity U., San Antonio, 1961-62; adminstr. Book Process Center, Orlando, Fla., 1962-68; bur. chief Fla. Dept. State, Div. Library Services, Winter Park, 1968-71; asst. prof. library services Rollins Coll., Winter Park, Fla., 1971—. Library cons. Ardaman Assos., 1967; cons. Fla. State Library, 1971-72; liaison officer The Rhodes Found. and Danforth Fellowship, 1973. Mem. Am. Assn. U. Profs., Am. Council Tchrs. Fgn. Langs., Fla. Library Assn. (former mem. exec. bd., tech. services roundtable chmn. 1968-69). Club: Am. Water Ski Assn. (Winter Haven). Home: 211 Fawsett Rd Winter Park FL 32789 Office: Rollins Coll Winter Park FL 32789

REICH, ROSALIE RICHMAN (MRS. LEON A. REICH), educator; b. Bklyn., Feb. 28, 1931; d. Sam and Esther (Zwick) Richman; B.A., U. Cal. at Los Angeles, 1952; M.A., Bklyn. Coll., 1955; Ph.D. in English, N.Y. U., 1967; m. Leon A. Reich, July 1, 1951; children—Yaron, Ilan, Leora. Instr., Bklyn. Coll., 1960-67; faculty Staten Island Community Coll., City U. N.Y., 1965—, prof., 1973—, dir. Place Experimenting Center, 1971-74. Recipient Faculty Research award City U. N.Y., 1972, Faculty award State U. N.Y., 1973. Mem. Am. Assn. Univ. Profs., Modern Lang. Assn. Author: Tales of Alexander the Macedonian, 1972. Office: 715 Ocean Terrace Staten Island NY 10301

REICHMANN, JOAN REINHARDT, banker; b. Sheboygan, Wis., Dec. 23, 1928; d. David Jacob and Rosalie (Schmidt) R.; student U. Wis. at Madison, 1946-47; corr. course Am. Soc. Travel Agts., 1959; m. Robert Richard Reichmann, Aug. 6, 1949. With Security Travel Bur., Security First Nat. Bank, Sheboygan, 1948—, asst. mgr., 1961-64, mgr., 1964—. Mem. Sheboygan Bus. and Profl. Women (v.p. 1960). Home: 305 Wisconsin Av Sheboygan WI 53081 Office: Security Travel Bur 603 N 8th St Sheboygan WI 53081

REID, ANITA IRENE LENZ (MRS. RICHARD M. REID, II), physician; b. Milw., July 11, 1941; d. Carl Frederick and Viola Irene (Dunham) Lenz; student Andrews U., Berrien Springs, Mich., 1959-62; B.S., Walla Walla (Wash.) Coll., 1964; M.D., Loma Linda U., 1968; m. Richard M. Reid, II, Aug. 24, 1969; 1 dau., Heather Eileen. Rotating intern Hinsdale Sanitarium and Hosp., (Ill.), 1968-69, emergency medicine, 1969-70; physician student health U. Wyo., Laramie, 1970-71, 72-73; gen. practice medicine, Laramie, 1971-72; practice emergency medicine Fla. Hosp., Orlando, 1973; dir. emergency and outpatient services Walla Walla (Wash.) Gen. Hosp., 1973—. Tchr. emergency nurses' course Community Coll., 1974—; med. cons. Mental Health Center, Walla Walla, 1974—; coordinator emergency med. technician program, Walla Walla, 1974; mem. edn. com. Am. Cancer Soc., 1974. Mem. Am. Coll. Emergency Physicians, A.M.A., Wash. State Med. Assn., Walla Walla Valley Med. Soc. (chmn. emergency com. 1974). 7th Day Adventist. Home: Box 55 Route 1 Walla Walla WA 99362 Office: 933 Bonsella Walla Walla WA 99362

REID, ANNIE THOMPSON, educator; b. Latta, S.C., Oct. 4, 1922; d. Wallace W. and Larkie (Nowling) Thompson; B.S., Simmons Coll., 1943; M.A., Boston U., 1944; postgrad. Harvard, 1944-47, Howard U., 1950-51, George Washington U., 1958-61, U. Pitts., 1971-73; m. Herbert O. Reid, Feb. 13, 1943 (div. June 1964); children—Herbert O., Carlene F. Tchr. pub. schs., Washington, 1956-62, counselor, 1962-63; vis. lectr. D.C. Tchrs. Coll., 1964-66; counseling supr., dep. dir., dir. manpower programs United Planning Orgn., Washington, 1964-66; asst. dir. study racial isolations in pub. schs. U.S. Commn. on Civil Rights, Washington, 1966, dep. dir. research div., 1966-68, cons., 1968-69; asso. prof. Bowie (Md.) State Coll., 1968—, acting chmn. dept. edn., 1970-71, asst. to pres., 1973—, also bd. visitors. Cons., dir. exptl. program in library edn. U. Md. Sch. Library and Information Services, 1968-70; cons. Md. Bd. Edn. Div. Library Devel. and Scis., 1970—. Recipient Nat. Sci. Acad. award for outstanding teaching, 1960; Outstanding Educator Am. award, 1970, 71. Mem. Am. Sociol. Assn., Polit. Sci. Assn., Nat. Assn. Community Devel., Am. Ednl. Research Assn., A.A.A.S. Home: 3147 Adams Mill Rd NW Washington DC 20010 Office: Bowie State Coll Bowie MD 20715

REID, BETTY ADAMS GRANGER, govt. ofcl.; b. Rocky Mount, N.C., Feb. 3, 1924; d. Jesse Louis and Romayne (Smith) Adams; B.A., Hunter Coll., 1946; postgrad. N.Y. U., 1948, Temple U., 1950; div.; children—Betty, Patricia (Mrs. Roy McCurdy), William R. Granger III, Wendy E. Pub., editor Cal. Voice Newspaper, Los Angeles, 1957-59; program dir. Radio Sta. WLIB, N.Y.C., 1959-70; mng. editor N.Y. Amsterdam News, N.Y.C., 1959-70; dir. spl. concerns Office Consumer Affairs, White House, Washington, 1970-71; dir. Office Civil Rights, Gen. Services Adminstrn., N.Y.C., 1971—. Mem. N.Y.C. Mayor's Com. on Child Adoption, 1969-74; mem. N.Y. Gov.'s Com. on Bias in Media, 1969-71; commr. N.Y.C. Mayor's Com. on Pub. Events, 1969-74. Recipient numerous distinguished service awards. Mem. Nat. Council Negro Women (life), N.A.A.C.P., Nat. Urban League, Overseas Press Club. Club: V.I. (Charlotte Amalie). Office: 26 Federal Plaza New York City NY 10007

REID, CHARLOTTE THOMPSON, govt. ofcl.; b. Kankakee, Ill.; d. Edward Charles and Ethel (Stith) Thompson; student Ill. Coll.; pvt. study voice; m. Frank R. Reid, Jr., Jan. 1, 1938 (dec. Aug. 1962); children—Patricia (Mrs. George Lindner), Frank R. III, Edward Thompson, Susan. Mem. staff NBC, Chgo., 1936-39; vocalist Don McNeill's Breakfast Club, 1936-39; mem. 88th-91st congresses from 15th Ill., former dist. mem. com. on interior and insular affairs, also com. on pub. works; mem. House Com. on Appropriations, and subcom.; commr. FCC, 1971—. Home: 183 S 4th St Aurora IL 60505 Office: 1919 M St NW Washington DC 20554

REID, EDITH CECILE (MRS. JOHN LEE EDMONDS), physician; b. Atlantic City, July 26, 1925; d. Christopher and Anne W. (Shackleford) Reid; A.B., Hunter Coll., 1946; M.D., Meharry Med. Coll., 1951; m. John Lee Edmonds, Sept. 7, 1957. Intern, Beth-El Hosp. (now Brookdale Med. Center), Bklyn., 1951-52, chief resident medicine, 1954-55; jr. med. resident Kings County Hosp. Center, Bklyn., 1952-53, sr. med. resident, 1953-54; fellow cardiology Met. Hosp., Flower-Fifth Av. Hosp., N.Y. Med. Coll., 1955-56; individual practice medicine, specializing in internal medicine and cardiology, St. Albans, N.Y., 1957—; clin. asst. cardiology service Met., Bird S. Coler hosps., 1957; clin. instr. medicine, asst. physician Flower Fifth Av. Hosp., N.Y. Med. Coll., 1957; physician Chest Clinic, N.Y.C. Health Dept., 1957-60; asst. vis. physician medicine and cardiology Jamaica (N.Y.) Hosp., 1959-67, asso. attending medicine and cardiology, 1967—; dir. med. service George and Robert Carter Community Health Center, Jamaica, 1968—. Dir., Greater Jamaica Devel. Corp., Vanguard Nat. Bank, Hampstead, N.Y. Mem. med. adv. com. Project Headstart Health Services, N.Y.C. Human Resources Adminstrn., 1968—; mem. health task force N.Y. Urban Coalition, 1970—. Bd. dirs. St. Albans Community Center Headstart. Nat. Heart Inst.-NIH grantee, 1955-56. Fellow Am. Geriatric Soc.; asso. fellow Am. Coll. Chest Physicians; mem. A.M.A., Nat. Med. Assn., Queens Clin. Soc., Inc. (pres. 1967-71, corr. sec. 1971-72), N.A.A.C.P., N.Y. State, Queens County med. socs., N.Y. Heart Assn., Trudeau Soc., N.E. Alumni Nat. Med. Fellowship, Inc. (scholar 1954-55), Delta Sigma Theta. Home: 190-21 Dormans Rd St Albans NY 11412

REID, HELEN WOOD (MRS. JOHN ARTHUR REID), educator; b. Lansing, N.C., May 28, 1918; d. Walter Avery and Etta Ellen (Davis) Wood; grad. West Chester State Tchrs. Coll., 1946; postgrad. U. Del., U. Md., Rutgers U.; m. John Arthur Reid, July 3, 1942; 1 son, Walter Ronald. Elementary tchr. West Brandywine Twp., Pa., 1945-46, Pennsgrove Sch., Pa., 1946-48, North East (Md.) Elementary Sch., 1951-52, Rising Sun (Md.) Elementary Sch., 1952-69, St. Croix (V.I.) Country Day Sch., 1969-73; partner Nottingham Sales and Nottingham (Pa.) Manor Mobile Homes Ct., 1971—; real estate sales person Mattia Realtors, Oxford, Pa., 1974—. Mem. Chester County Republican Com., 1964-69; justice of peace West Nottingham Twp., 1968—. Mem. N.E.A., Magistrates Assn. Episcopalian. Home: Ridge Rd Nottingham PA 19362

REID, HOPE BIDEZ, librarian; b. Hammond, La., Feb. 8, 1929; d. Columbus and Hope Amy (Bidez) Reid; student Randolph Macon Women's Coll., 1947-48; B.A., Newcomb Coll., 1950; B.S. in Library Sci., La. State U., 1952. Head tech processes Miss. Library Commn., Jackson, 1958-61; head reference and circulation dept. Millsaps Coll., Jackson, 1961-63; head librarian Belhaven Coll., Jackson, 1964—. Mem. Miss. Library Assn., Miss. Animal Rescue League. Club: Quota (treas. Jackson chpt. 1973-74). Home: 1546 Devine St Jackson MS 39202 Office: Belhaven College Library Jackson MS

REID, MADELEINE BREINIG (MRS. JOHN F. REID), ednl. adminstr.; b. Mincola, N.Y., Feb. 17, 1916; d. Granville Miller and Beatrice May (Claussen) Breinig Jr.; student Buffalo Sem., 1933, Wellesley Coll., 1933-35; B.J., U. Mo., 1937; m. John F. Reid, Sept. 1, 1939; children—Susan V. (Mrs. James W. Greene II), Johathan B., Christopher B., Nicholas Van Brunt. Prodn. mgr. Horace A. Laney Advt. Agy., Buffalo, 1937-40; prodn. mgr. Moss-Chase Advt. Agy., Buffalo, 1954-58; dir. alumnae affairs and fund raising Buffalo (N.Y.) Seminary, 1964—, trustee, 1960-63. Mem. Erie County Day Care Council, pres. 1970-71, 72-73, Comprehensive Health Planning Council Erie County (mem. exec. com. 1973—, by-laws com. 1972-74, chmn. nominating com. 1972-74, dir. 1973—), Research and Planning Council Western N.Y. (dir. 1973-76), Women in Communication, Grads. Assn. (pres. 1959-61), Buffalo City Panhellenic Assn. (pres. 1964-65), Albright-Knox Art Gallery, Buffalo Zool. Soc., Kappa Alpha Theta (pres. Buffalo chpt. 1956-57, dist. pres. 1960-63). Club: Zonta International (sec. 1968-69, sec. Dist. IV, 1969-72, chmn. Status of Women 1972-74); Buffalo Skating. Editor: Isolationist Impulse (Selig Adler), 1957. Home: 150 Jewett Parkway Buffalo NY 14214 Office: Buffalo Seminary 205 Bidwell Pkwy Buffalo NY 14222

REID, MARGARET GRAGG (NYBERG), librarian; b. Centralia, Ill., July 22, 1909; s. Robert Lacey and Mabel Claire (Ennis) Gragg; B.A., Colo. Coll., 1931; B.S. in L.S., U. Denver, 1936; m. Gustaf H. Nyberg, Oct. 1939 (div. May 1945); m. 2d, N. Stanley Reid, Oct. 22, 1947 (dec. Dec. 1972). Circulation and reference librarian Deering Library Northwestern U., Evanston, Ill., 1937-39; staff U.S. Air Sea Rescue Agy., Washington, 1943-47; reference librarian Colorado Springs (Colo.) Pub. Library, 1947-49, city librarian, 1949-63; library dir. Pikes Peak Regional Library Dist., Colorado Springs, 1964—. Adv. council Colo. State Library Colo. Council Library Devel., 1967-71. Mem. Colo. (pres. 1957-59, exhibits chmn. 1961-66, rep. to A.L.A., 1967-71), Mountain Plains library assns., A.L.A., Nat. League Am. Pen Women, Colorado Springs Fine Arts Center, Urban League, Women's Ednl. Soc. (asso.). Club: Pikes Peak Press. Home: 25 Cragmor Village Colorado Springs CO 80007 Office: Pikes Peak Regional Library Dist Box 1579 Colorado Springs CO 80901

REID, MARILYN JOANNE (MRS. MARLIN DAVID REID, JR.), lawyer; b. Chgo., Aug. 14, 1941; d. Kermit and Newell Azile (Hahn) Neuman; B.A., U. Ill., 1963; J.D., Ohio No. U., 1966; m. Marlin David Reid, Jr., Nov. 26, 1966; children—David William, Nelson Marlin. Admitted Ark. Bar, 1967, Ohio Bar, 1966; asst. trust adminstr. First Nat. Bank, Dayton, O., 1966-67; asso. Sloan & Ragsdale, Little Rock, 1967-69; practice law, Dayton, 1969—. Recipient Am. Jurisprudence Evidence Book award Ohio No. U. Sch. Law, 1965, Am. Jurisprudence Income Tax Book award, 1966. Mem. Am., Greene County, Ohio Bar assns., Beavercreek Jaycettes (v.p. 1971-72, pres. 1972-73), Kappa Beta Phi (pres. 1966), Gamma Phi Beta (alumni group v.p. 1971-73). Lion (v.p. 1974). Office: 3862 Indian Ripple Rd Dayton OH 45440

REID, MILDRED I., author, lectr., literary critic; b. Boston, Apr. 29, 1908; d. Julius and Harriet (Fest) Weinzerl; student Columbia U., 1926-28; m. C. Allan Reid, 1928 (dec. Nov. 1958); 1 son, Robert Allan. Profl. dancer, 1918-25; profl. singer, 1918-49; radio writer, Boston, Pitts., Phila., Chgo., Miami, Fla., 1924-38; began lit. criticism service for writers, 1947, own Chgo. studio, 1947—; owner operator Summer Writers' Colony, Contoocook, N.H., 1947—; tchr. creative writing, Boston, Concord, N.H., Miami Dade Jr. Coll. Mem. Internat. Platform Assn., Nat. League Am. Women, The Authors Guild Inc. Author: Writers: Here's How!, 1940, rev., 1970, 74; Writers: Let's Plot, 1943; rev. 1967, 70, 74; Writers: Help Yourselves!, 1944-61, 68; Writers: Make It Sell!, 1957-68, 71-73; Writers: Try Short Shorts!, 1947; Writers: Learn to Earn, 1948-57, 68; Writers: Why Stop Now?, 1968-72, 74 (accepted as textbooks by many colls. and univs.; two transcribed into Braille, used 19 fgn. countries; all 7 recorded for blind by N.Y. Pub. Library). Author: The Devil's Handmaidens, 1951 (prize winning novel); Over Fool's Hill, 1966; also numerous short stories, articles, plays and poems. Address: (summer) Writers Colony

Penacook Rd Contoocook NH 03229 (winter) Nautical Aire Apts 917 Bucida Rd Delray Beach FL 33444

REID, PATRICIA LYNN, journalist; b. Ventura, Cal., Apr. 7, 1948; d. William Samuel and Helen Frances (Hern) Reid; student U. So. Cal., 1966-69; B.A., Syracuse U., 1970. Editorial asst. Christian Sci. Monitor, Boston, 1970-72, reporter, photographer, Bonita Pub. Co., Montclair, Cal., 1972-73; pub. relations asst. Occidental Coll., Los Angeles, 1973-74. Mem. Women in Communications (v.p. Boston 1972). Home: 835 S Robinhood Lane Redlands CA 92373

REID, SHIRLEY MARIE, ednl. adminstr.; b. Hartford, Conn., June 22, 1927; d. William James and Pearl Madaline (Sproat) Reid; Asso. Sci., Vt. Coll., 1947; B.A., U. Vt., 1958; M.A., U. Conn., 1968. Inspector med. dept. Conn. Mutual Life Ins. Co., Hartford, 1948; office mgr. Automotive Legal Assn., Hartford, 1949-51; mortgage sec. State Savings Bank, Hartford, Conn., 1951-54; admissions counselor Vt. Coll., Montpelier, 1954-56; head resident, U. Vt., Burlington, 1957-58; tchr., counselor Bennington, Middlebury and Rutland (Vt.) Pub. Schs., 1958-70; state cons. Pupil Personnel Services, Montpelier, Vt., 1970—. Mem. Am. (dir. 1974-77), Vt. (pres. 1963-64, mem. exec. com. 1970—) personnel and guidance assns., New Eng. Assn. Measurement and Evaluation in Guidance (mem. exec. com. 1970—), Nat. Vocational Guidance Assn., Am. Sch. Counselor Assn., Assn. Counselor Edn. and Supervision, Nat. Employment Counselor Assn., Assn. for Measurement and Evaluation in Guidance, New. Eng. Personnel and Guidance Conf. (mem. exec. com. 1965—, co-chmn. 1966—), Nat. Assn. Women Deans, Adminstrs. and Counselors. Author: (with James F. Cawley) Handbook for Conference Development, 1969. Editor: The Past, the Present and Trends of New Eng. Personnel and Guidance Conference (Estelle E. Feldman), 1971. Office: State Dept Edn Montpelier VT 05602

REIF, RITA MURPHY (MRS. PAUL REIF), author, columnist; b. N.Y.C., June 12, 1929; d. Henry Vincent and Louise Clarice (Becker) Murphy; B.S., Fordham U., 1950; M.A., Columbia U., 1951; m. Paul Reif, July 2, 1953; children—Leon Leslie, Timothy Mark. With N.Y. Times, N.Y.C., 1948—, reporter, 1956—, antiques columnist, 1972—. Recipient Dorothy Dawe award Am. Furniture Mart, Chgo., 1969, 70, 71, Press award Nat. Soc. Interior Designers, 1971. Author: Living With Books, 1968; The Antique Collector's Guide to Styles and Prices, 1970; Treasure Rooms of America's Mansions, Manors and Houses, 1970. Home: 57 W 58th St New York City NY 10019 Office: New York Times 229 W 43rd St New York City NY 10036

REIFEL, LOUIE ELIZABETH ROGERS (MRS. ALEXANDER F. REIFEL), librarian; b. Curve, Tenn.; d. Henry Ollie and Louie (Dean) Rogers; student Memphis State U., 1931-33; B.S., U. Houston, 1947; M.L.S., U. Tex., 1956, postgrad., 1961-62; m. Alexander F. Reifel, Nov. 18, 1932; children—Rogers Anthony, Patsy Ruth (Mrs. Walter Ray Wesley, Jr.), Michael Dean, Mary Lou (Mrs. Ordine Luke Bordelon), Claudia Frances (Mrs. Kenneth L. Moursund), Catherine Lee (Mrs. Stanley E. Stevens Jr.). Tchr. Adline Ind. Sch. Dist., 1945-49, librarian, 1950-53; librarian Houston (Tex.) Ind. Sch. Dist., 1953-61, cons. library services, 1961-63, supr. library services, 1963-64, acting dir. Instructional Materials Services, 1964—. Part-time instr. Nat. Def. Edn. Act insts., 1966, 67. Dist. chmn. Tex. P.T.A., 1953-54. Mem. A.L.A. (state rep. library adminstrn. div. recruiting com. 1961—, council 1972-73), N.E.A., Southwestern (program planning com. 1972-74), Tex. (chmn. 1962-63, chmn. nominating com. 1973-74) library assns., Am. (chmn. nominating com. 1967-68, dir. region VI 1970-72), Tex. (liaison for Ency. Brit. awards for Tex. 1963-67, chmn. dist. planning com. 1966-68) assns. sch. librarians, Tex. State Tchrs. Assn., Houston Council Edn. (pres. 1972-74), Houston Assn. Supervision and Curriculum Devel., Houston Assn. Sch. Adminstrs., U. Tex. Grad. Sch. Library Sci. Alumni Assn. (pres. 1963-64), Kappa Delta Pi (pres. Houston alumni chpt. 1974-76), Delta Kappa Gamma, Alpha Delta Kappa. Club: Houston Library (pres. 1966-67). Home: 2315 Dryden St Houston TX 77027

REIFMAN, LUCILLE KRAUSS (MRS. ALFRED REIFMAN), govt. ofcl.; b. N.Y.C., June 6, 1921; d. B.B. and L.B. Krauss; A.B. cum laude, City U. N.Y., 1941; Ph.D. candidate Am. U., 1955-61; postgrad. U. Paris, 1961-63; m. Alfred Reifman, July 25, 1942; children—Ann, Katherine, Elizabeth. Asso. prof. Am. U., Washington, 1955-61; vis. lectr. U. Paris, 1961-63; exec. sec. Study Group in Econs. Edn., Orgn. for Econ. Coop. and Devel., Paris, France, 1963-65; chief program analysis NIH, Bethesda, Md., 1965-70; chief office program planning and evaluation Med. Services Adminstrn., Dept. Health, Edn. and Welfare, Washington, 1970-72, asso. commr. Medicaid program, 1972—. Pres. Montgomery County and Potomac Area Fedn. Coop. Nursery Schs., 1954. NSF Faculty fellow. Mem. Pi Mu Epsilon. Author: Systems Analysis and Educational Planning; Health Planning in Developing Nations. Home: 7314 Broxburn Ct Bethesda MD 20034 Office: 330 C St SW Washington DC 20201

REIFSCHNEIDER, MOLLIE BRUNNER (MRS. EDWARD REIFSCHNEIDER), steel vessels mfg. co. exec.; b. Grimm, Russia, Sept. 3, 1907; d. Jacob and Kathryn (Fritzler) Brunner; student Compton Coll., 1950-51; B.A., U. Cal. at Los Angeles, 1952; m. Edward Reifschneider, June 27, 1927 (dec.); children—Elaine J., Darrel, Robert. Chmn. bd. Manchester Tank & Equipment Co., Lynwood, Cal., 1947—. Mem. pub. affairs com. Nat. Liquified Petroleum Gas Assn., 1972—. Asst. dir. Compton Counselling Service, Inc., 1946-56; mem. S.E. Mental Health Service. Bd. dirs. Family Service, Los Angeles, 1962-70; mem. Lynwood Planning Commn., 1965-68. Bd. dirs. Lynwood Youth Employment, 1964—, Welfare Planning Council, 1963-67, S.E. Rio Vista YMCA, Huntington Park, Cal., 1970—, U.S.O., Los Angeles, United Way, Inc., Los Angeles; bd. dirs. S.E. Council Alcoholism and Drug Problems, 1973—, chmn., 1974; pres. Edward Reifschneider Found., 1968—. Recipient Outstanding Service award United Way, Inc., 1963, Outstanding Citizen award Jr. C. of C., 1968; Youth Helping Hand award, 1971. Mem. U.S. (dir. 1968—) Lynwood chambers commerce. Clubs: Soroptimist (pres. 1952) (Lynwood-South Gate); San Moritz (Crestline, Cal.); La Quinta (Cal.); Town Hall (Los Angeles). Office: 2880 Norton Av Lynwood CA 90262

REIFSTECK, ELEANOR MAXINE (MRS. EDWIN EUGENE REIFSTECK), legal sec.; b. Rockwell City, Ia., May 2, 1928; d. Philo Arthur and Margaret Marie Isabel (Lange) Kirk; grad. pub. high sch.; m. Edwin Eugene Reifsteck, Oct. 27, 1946; 1 dau., Luceen Cheryl (Mrs. Danny Alan Bowyer). Abstracter, legal sec. Brower Abstract Co., Rockwell City, 1960—. Asst. curator Calhoun County Mus., Rockwell City, 1965—. Active Girl Scouts Am., 1956-57. Mem. Ia., Calhoun County (pres. 1970, 71) hist. socs., VFW Aux. (sec. 1971—). Lutheran. Home: 525 High St Rockwell City IA 50579 Office: 329 Court St Rockwell City IA 50579

REIKER, HELEN CATHERINE, psychiat. social worker; b. Cape Girardeau, Mo., Sept. 24, 1911; d. Charles and Nadine Nazaria (Wahl) Reiker; A.B. cum laude, St. Louis U., 1938, postgrad., 1938-41; M.S.W., Washington U., St. Louis, 1952. Med./psychiat. social worker VA Regional Office, Fresno, Cal., 1952-53; sr. psychiat. social worker Cal. State Dept. Mental Hygiene Bur. Social Work, Fresno, 1953-66; adoption caseworker Infant of Prague Adoption Services, Fresno, Cal., 1966-67; dir. med. social service Fresno County Gen. Hosp., Fresno, Cal., 1967-69, St. Agnes Hosp., Fresno, Cal., 1969. Mem. Tb Case Finding Com., 1967-69; mem. Battered Child Com., 1967-69; mem. Hemodialysis Com., 1967-69. Bd. dirs. Tb Assn., Fresno, Cal., 1960-65. Served with AUS, 1944-49; ETO. Mem. Nat. Assn. Social Workers, Acad. Certified Social Workers. Club: Young Ladies Institute, Women's Overseas Service League (Fresno). Home: 3342 Clinton No 3 Fresno CA 93703

REILING, SUSAN WALLACE (MRS. FREDERICK E. REILING), curator; b. Denver, Aug. 2, 1940; d. Laird Hemphill and Alison (Rowntree) Wallace; B.F.A., Moore Inst. Art, 1962; M.A., U. Miami, 1972, postgrad., 1973—; m. Frederick E. Reiling, Nov. 21, 1962. Interior designer Richard Plumer Co., Miami, Fla., 1962-63; designer, decorator James Merrick Smith, Miami, 1963-65; self-employed interior designer, Miami, 1965-68; sec. Vizcaya-Dade County Art Mus., Miami, 1968-71, curator decorative arts collection, 1971—. Mem. Am. Assn. Museums, Archaeol. Found., Hist. Assn. (Eng.), English-Speaking Union, Jr. League Miami. Clubs: Biscayne Bay Yacht, Coral Beef Yacht (Miami). Episcopalian. Home: 100 Prospect Dr Miami FL 33133 Office: 3251 S Miami Av Miami FL 33129

REILLEY, JEANNE MARIE, med. librarian; b. Ellwood City, Pa., Dec. 16, 1916; d. Edward Michael and Jeanne Lena (Blandine) Reilley; A.B., Geneva Coll., 1937; B.S., Carnegie Inst. Tech.; Litt.M., U. Pitts., 1946; postgrad. Columbia. Reference librarian Duquesne U., 1938-39; acting librarian St. Francis Coll., Loretto, Pa., 1939-40; hosp. librarian VA, 1940-46, supervising librarian, 1946-49; sr. reference librarian Carnegie Library, Pitts., 1949-51, A.M.A., 1951-55; asst. librarian U. Pitts. Med. Sch., 1955-56; med. librarian VA Hosp., Pitts., 1956-73, chief librarian, 1973—. Mem. A.L.A., Spl. Libraries Assn., Med., Pa. library assns., Friends of Music Library. Home: 6109 Alder St Pittsburgh PA 15206 Office: University Dr C Pittsburgh PA 15240

REILLY, ALICE FIELDS, librarian; b. Denver, Sept. 18, 1911; d. Mark Joseph and Della (Day) Fields; A.B., U. Denver, 1932, B.L.S., 1933; m. John Reilly, Aug. 19, 1942; 1 dau., Jean Day (Mrs. Polsley). Librarian secondary schs., Ft. Morgan, Colo., Lake Forest, Ill., 1933-41; librarian Army posts, 1941-45; head librarian Manhattan (Kans.) Pub. Library, 1949-57; cons. Fla. State Library, 1957-58, Cal. State Library, 1958-60; county librarian Fresno County (Cal.) Free Library, 1960—. Mem. Fresno Cultural Council, 1965-66; pres. Fresno County Dept. Heads Council, 1964. Mem. Nat. Soc. Arts and Letters, Am. Soc. Pub. Adminstrn., Am., Cal. library assns., Adult Edn. Assn., Am. Assn. U. Women, Zeta Tau Alpha. Democrat. Episcopalian. Contbr. articles to library publs. Home: 599 W San Jose St Fresno CA 93704 Office: 2420 Mariposa St Fresno CA 93721

REILLY, EILEEN L., educator; b. Chgo., Feb. 28, 1919; d. James and Ellen (O'Leary) Reilly; A.A., Wright Coll., 1938; B.Ed., Chgo. Tchrs. Coll., 1942; M.Ed., U. Ariz., 1955; postgrad. Loyola U. (Chgo.), 1943-45, Ariz. State U., U. Ariz., 1955-62. Tchr. elementary sch., Chgo. and Buckeye, Ariz., 1942-55; dir. Reading Clinic, Buckeye Elementary Sch., 1956—, dir. guidance dept., 1956—, coordinator, 1966—; instr. Coll. Santa Fe, summers 1965-68. State chmn. Tchr. Edn. and Profl. Standards Commn., 1956; mem. Govs. Adv. Bd. for Edn., 1958-64, Govs. Commn. Formulate Guidelines for Elementary Guidance, 1966-68. Mem. Ariz. Personnel and Guidance Assn. (exec. bd. 1967), Ariz. Sch. Counselor Assn. (exec. bd. 1967—), Ariz. Sch. Psychologists Assn. (sec. 1968-70), N.E.A., Ariz. Edn. Assn., Internat. Reading Assn., Council for Exceptional Children, Spl. Edn. Adminstrs. Assn., Pi Lambda Theta. Home: 503 Edison Av Buckeye AZ 85326

REILLY, ESTHER HUNTINGTON WHITMAN (MRS. JAMES HERBERT REILLY), interior designer; b. Portland, Me., Aug. 19, 1917; d. Charles Huntington and Rachel Jones (Foster) Whitman; B.A., Douglass Coll., 1939; certificate in interior architecture and design Parsons Sch. Design, 1943; m. James Herbert Reilly, Jr., May 18, 1943; children—Diane (Mrs. Joseph English), Rachel, Alison. Asso., Lucille B. Chisholm, interior decorations, Charlottesville, Va., 1949-58; owner, Esther H. Reilly, interiors, Palo Alto, Cal., 1958—. Tchr. interior design U. Va. Extension Service, 1952-53, Santa Clara County (Cal.) Adult Edn., 1959—, De Anza Jr. Coll., Cupertino, Cal., 1969—. Mem. Kappa Pi. Author: At Home with Decorating, 1971. Address: 401 Marlowe St Palo Alto CA 94301

REIN, ANN MONTGOMERY (MRS. DOYLE REIN), journalist; b. Madison, Wis., July 21, 1930; d. Richard Noel and Ruby Helena (Rubbert) Montgomery; B.S. cum laude, Butler U., 1952; m. Doyle Rein, Feb. 4, 1956; children—Richard, Mary. Editor home furnishings Indpls. News, 1953-63, shopping columnist and reporter, 1951-63, asst. women's editor, 1962-63; publicity dir. Catholic Charities of Indpls., 1966-72; mng. editor Hoosier Chef mag., Indpls., 1969-70; staff writer Charlene Hillman Pub. Relations Assos., Indpls., 1972; free lance writer, editor, 1966—. Bd. dirs. Catholic Social Services of Indpls., 1971-72. Mem. Women in Communications (pres. Indpls. chpt. 1972), Indpls. Art Assn., Zeta Tau Alpha, Phi Kappa Phi. Roman Catholic. Address: 60 E Kessler St Indianapolis IN 46220

REIN, CATHERINE AMELIA (MRS. BARRY B. REIN), lawyer; b. Lebanon, Pa., Feb. 7, 1943; d. John and Esther A. (Scott) Shultz; B.A., Pa. State U., 1964; J.D., N.Y. U., 1968; m. Barry B. Rein, May 1, 1965. Admitted to N.Y. bar, 1968; law asso. Dewey, Ballantine, Bushby, Palmer & Wood, N.Y.C., 1968—. Mem. Am., N.Y. bar assns., Assn. Bar City N.Y. (mem. profl. and judicial ethics com. 1973—), N.Y. Law Assos. Council. Episcopalian. Home: 2684 Crest Lane Scotch Plains NJ 07076 Office: 140 Broadway New York City NY 10005

REINACH, JACQUELYN KRASNE, composer, author; b. Omaha, Sept. 17, 1930; d. Clyde and Dorothy (Reuben) Krasne; student Stanford, 1947-49; B.A., U. Cal. at Los Angeles, 1951; m. Anthony M. Reinach, 1953 (div. 1961); children—Barron Anthony, Alan Jay; m. 2d, Harry Wolff, 1969 (div. 1972); m. 3d, Paul B. Morofsky, 1973. With TV prodn. Goodson-Todman Co., N.Y.C., 1952-53; composer-author numerous children's songs for Golden Records; designer games; cons., programming for children; writer children's TV shows Tottle-Fran Allison, Learn at Home, 1960-65; composer, co-author play for mus. theater, 1965-66; co-founder, v.p. Discobook, Inc., 1970—; co-founder Childways, Inc.; founder Operation Saturday; pres. Reinach Prodns. Mem. Child Study Assn. Am., A.S.C.A.P., Dramatists Guild, Council For Basic Edn. Republican. Author: (with others) Looking and Listening, 1966; Naming and Knowing, 1966; Thinking and Imagining, 1966; Carefree Cooking, 1970; author-composer Reading Awareness, 1971. Composer: A Child's Introduction to Reading, Writing and Arithmetic, 1963; Music To Read The Pretenders By, 1969; Liberation, Now, 1970; Letter People Suite, 1972. Address: 8 Barbara Lane Irvington-on-Hudson NY 10533

REINAUER, DOROTHY POLITO, truck stop owner; b. Hawthorne, N.J., May 4, 1923; d. Patrick and Leona (Gantner) Polito; ed. pub. and bus. schs.; m. Charles W. Reinauer, Oct. 1, 1965; children from previous marriage—Susan Marie Mosmann, John Ernest Mosmann. Service rep. Bell Telephone Co., Paterson, N.J., 1945-47; sales clk. B. Altman & Co., 1947-50; sec.-treas. Reinauer Bros. Oil Co., Inc., Mahwah, N.J., 1965—; owner Reinauer Restaurant. Named Am.'s outstanding truck stop man and wife team, Nat. Assn. Truck Stop Operators, 1973. Clubs: High Mountain Golf (Franklin Lakes, N.J.); Ridgewood (N.J.) Country. Home: 821 Pueblo Dr Franklin Lakes NJ 07417 Office: Route 17 Mahwah NJ 07430

REINBOLD, EMMA JANE, educator; b. Green Point, Pa., June 29, 1916; d. Josiah A. and Emma J. (Ditzler) Reinbold; A.B., Lebanon Valley Coll., 1935; postgrad. Pa. State Coll., 1939, 40; M.Ed., Temple U., 1952, Ed.D., 1958; postgrad. U. Del., 1959. Tchr. Mt. Penn High Sch., Reading, Pa., 1939-48; tchr., counselor Reading (Pa.) High Sch., 1948-57; research asso. U. Del., 1957-59; counselor Brandywine High Sch., Wilmington, Del., 1959-64; dir. guidance Alexis I. duPont High Sch., Greenville, Del., 1964—. Adj. lectr. U. Del., 1966—; research asso. Nat. Training Lab., Bethel, Me., 1957; cons. Cecil County (Md.) Bd. Edn., 1952, Phila. Girl Scouts, 1950-51; counselor rep., bd. trustees Wilmington (Del.) Sch. Nursing, 1963-65; mem. counseling and guidance com. Wilmington (Del.) Meml. Hosp., 1962-64. Bd. mgrs. Western br. YMCA, 1966-68. Mem. Nat. Assn. Coll. Admissions Counselors (del. Potomac and Chesapeake chpt. 1971—), Middle States Assn. Colls. and Secondary (com. on sch. and coll. relations 1971—), N.E.A. (life), Am. Sch. Counselor Assn., Am., Del. (mem. adv. com. 1967—, pres. 1962-63) personnel and guidance assns., Del. Assn. Certified Sch. Counselors (organizer 1963, mem. exec. com. 1964—, pres. 1966), Del. Sch. Counselor Assn. (state del. 1970, chpt. pres. elect 1970-71), Delta Kappa Gamma. Home: 13 Chippendale Circle Newark DE 19711 Office: Hillside Rd Greenville DE 19807

REINDL, PAULINE CATHERINE, museum ofcl.; b. Crestline, O., Mar. 9, 1906; d. Lawrence William and Mary (Karl) Reindl; student U. Chgo., 1926. Owner, mgr. Mobile Manor, mobile home park, Crestline, O., after 1961; dir. Shunk Museum, Crestline, 1969—. Pres. Hosp. Guild, Crestline, 1971. Mem. Crestline City Council, 1960-64. Mem. Central Ohio Iris Soc. (sec.-treas. 1962-72), Bus. and Profl. Women (treas. 1969), Crestline Hist. Soc. (pres. 1969—, dir. 1959). Democrat. Roman Catholic (pres. Altar Soc. 1970). Club: Woman's (treas. 1968), Nature Study (treas. 1965-72). Home: 440 North Crestline OH 44827

REINECKE, MARY ELIZABETH, sch. psychologist; b. N.Y.C., Mar. 13, 1941; d. John Jacob and Virginia Elizabeth (Smith) Reinecke; B.A., DePauw U., 1962; M.A., U. Minn., 1964; Ph.D., U. Md., 1972. Research asst. NIH, Bethesda, Md., 1964-66; psychologist, St. John's Child Devel. Center, Washington, 1966-68; psychologist, Prince George's County Pub. Schs., Upper Marlboro, Md., 1968—. Mem. Council Exceptional Children, Nat. Assn. Sch. Psychologists (mem. research com. 1973-74). Home: 2510 Hughes Rd Adelphi MD 20783 Office: Hill Rd and L St Landover MD 20785

REINER, MARY ELISABETH WELLS (MRS. JOHN PAUL REINER), civic worker; b. N.Y.C., Apr. 19, 1931; d. Francis Drake and Ethel Biddle (Pleis) Wells; B.A., Middlebury Coll., 1953; M.A., N.Y. U., 1955; M.A., Columbia, 1960, diploma Russian Inst., 1960; m. John Paul Reiner, July 27, 1961; children—Mary Elisabeth, Clark Biddle Charles. Asst. prof. Russian, govt. Notre Dame Coll., S.I., N.Y., 1960-62; tchr. Marymount Sch. for Girls, N.Y.C., 1973—. Del. 20th Triennial World Conf. Girl Guides and Girl Scouts, Helsinki, Finland, 1969, 21st Triennial Conf., Toronto, 1972; docent Met. Mus. Art, N.Y.C., 1971-72; com. mem. div. programs for aging Community Service Soc., N.Y.C., 1972-73; chmn. UN Hdqrs. Youth Caucus Environment Task Force, 1972—. Bd. dirs. N.Y. Jr. League, 1968-69; non-govtl. del. to UN for World Assn. Girl Guides and Girl Scouts, 1968—. Asso. editor NGO-Unicef Newsletter, 1973—. Address: 151 Av B New York City NY 10009

REINHARDT, JACKIE KAY STERN (MRS. MICHAEL JAMES REINHARDT), journalist; b. San Antonio, Mar. 1, 1942; d. Alfred and Catherine (Rogers) Stern; B.S., (Mabel McLaughlin Beck Journalism scholar) U. Kan., 1964; m. Michael James Reinhardt, Dec. 5, 1969. Reporter, Albuquerque Jour., 1964-65; press asst. U.S. Senator Clinton P. Anderson of N.M., Washington, 1965-66, press sec., 1967-69; reporter Met. div. Los Angeles Times, 1969-70; communications coordinator, editor regional med. programs U. Cal. at Los Angeles, 1970-73; dir. communications for So. Cal., Cal. Regional Med. Program, 1973-74; dir. pub. relations Kidney Found. So. Cal., 1974—. Mem. Assn. Am. Med. Colls., Am. Newspaper Women's Club, U.S. Senate Press Secs. Assn., U.S. Senate Staff Club, Women in Communications (career opportunity chmn., membership v.p. Los Angeles chpt. 1973-75). Home: 2508 Arizona Av Santa Monica CA 90404 Office: 1281 Westwood Blvd Suite 207 Los Angeles CA 90024

REINHERZ, HELEN ZARSKY (MRS. SAMUEL E. REINHERZ), educator, ednl. adminstr.; b. Boston, Aug. 4, 1923; d. Zachary and Anna (Cohen) Zarsky; A.B. magna cum laude, Wheaton Coll., 1944; M.S., Simmons Coll., 1946; S.M., Harvard, 1963, Sc.D., 1965; m. Samuel E. Reinherz, Aug. 29, 1943; 1 son, Ellis. Social worker Newton (Mass.) Family Service, 1946-49, Mass. Gen. Hosp., Boston, 1949-51; supr. psychiat. social work State Hosp., Waltham, Mass., 1958-61; prof. methods research Simmons Coll., Boston, 1965—, dir. research Sch. Social Work, 1968—, cons. Simmons drug tng. program, 1972—. Research cons. Dept. Mental Health, 1970—; lectr. continuing edn. Boston U., 1974; prin. investigator study of adolescent drug abuse, 1971-73. Chmn. Gov.'s Adv. Council Mental Health and Retardation, 1972. Bd. dirs. Family Soc. Malden, 1950-65. Recipient Maida H. Solomon award Simmons Coll. Alumni, 1961; NIH tng. fellow, 1961-65; Grant Found. grantee, 1963, Med. Found. grantee, 1967-69; Fellow Am. Orthopsychiat. Assn.; mem. Acad. Certified Social Workers, Am. Pub. Health Assn., Council Social Work Edn., League Women Voters (dir. 1951-59), Malden Mental Health Assn. (v.p. 1966-68), Harvard Sch. Pub. Health Alumni Assn. (sec. treas. 1965-68), Phi Beta Kappa, Delta Omega. Author: (with H. Wechsler, D. Dobbin) Research in Social Work and Human Services, 1975. Cons. editor Community Mental Health Jour., 1968—. Contbr. articles on mental health to profl. publs. Home: 17 Corey Rd Malden MA 02148 Office: Simmons College School of Social Work 51 Commonwealth Av Boston MA 02116

REINING, PRISCILLA ALDEN COPELAND (MRS. CONRAD C. REINING), anthropologist; b. Chgo., Mar. 11, 1923; d. Kenneth Bayard and Elsie (Weser) Copeland; A.B., U. Chgo., 1945, M.A., 1949, Ph.D., 1967; m. Conrad (Copeland) Reining, June 26, 1944; children—Robert Cushman, Anne Elizabeth, Conrad Copeland. Fellow, E. African Inst. Social Research, Kampala, Uganda, 1951-55; lectr. U. Minn., Mpls., 1956-59, Howard U., Washington, D.C., 1960-65; research asso. Cath. U. Am., Washington, 1966-68, 70—; coordinator Center for Study of Man, Smithsonian Instn., Washington, 1968-70. Cons., lectr. Peace Corps, 1961-63; cons. livestock appraisal mission to Tanzania, Internat. Bank for Reconstrn. and Devel., 1972; cons. West African grain stblzn. program AID, 1973; lectr. Johns Hopkins, evenings 1970-71, 72-73. NSF grantee, 1967. Fellow African Studies Assn., Am. Anthrop. Assn., Washington, E. African acads. scis.; mem. Internat. African Inst., Sigma Xi. Episcopalian. Co-author: Culture and Population Change,

1974. Editor, contbr. Kinship Studies in the Morgan Centennial Year, 1972. Contbr. articles to profl. jours. Home: 3601 Rittenhouse St NW Washington DC 20015 Office: Dept Anthropology Cath U Am Washington DC 20017

REININGHAUS, RUTH BERRY (MRS. ALLAN JOSEPH SMITH), advt. exec.; b. N.Y.C., Oct. 4, 1922; d. Emil William and Pauline Rosa (Lazarik) Reininghaus; student Hunter Coll., 1944-46, 50-52; student Nat. Acad. Design (scholar), 1963, Frank Reilly Sch. Art (Robert Lehman scholar), 1963, N.Y. U. (scholar), 1968, Art Student's League, 1966; m. Allan Joseph Smith, May 28, 1960; children—George J. Morales, Robert Charles Morales. Draftsman, Allied Control Co., Inc., N.Y.C., 1950-54, liason between engring. and prodn., 1954-64, sales engr., 1964-65, supr. drafting dept., 1965-66, internal sales rep. for West Coast area, 1966-68, sales promotion and advt., 1968-69; advt. mgr. Elec. Testing Labs., Inc., N.Y.C., 1969—, staff asst., 1969—. Art instr. Bankers Trust, N.Y.C., 1970—, Kittredge Club for Women, N.Y.C., 1964—; line art illustrator Sound Pub. Co., 1966—. Mem. Am. Artists Profl. League, Allied Artists Am., Hudson Valley Art Assn., Advt. Women N.Y., Musical Box Soc., Alpha Delta Pi. Club: Salmagundi (dir.-at-large) (N.Y.C.). Home: 418 E 88th St New York City NY 10028 Office: 2 E End Av New York City NY 10021

REINMILLER, ELINOR CALMBACH, librarian; b. Oswego, Kan., Aug. 29, 1919; d. William Garfield and Clara Elinor (Bruns) Calmbach; B.A., U. Ia., 1939; B.S. in Library Sci., North Tex. State U., 1947, M.A., 1954. Reference and acquistion librarian U. Tex. Health Sci. Center, Dallas, 1947—. Mem. Spl. Libraries Assn., Southwestern, Tex., Med. library assns., Phi Alpha Theta, Alpha Delta Pi. Home: 2033 W Oak St Denton TX 76201 Office: 5323 Harry Hines Blvd Dallas TX 75235

REINSTEIN, JULIA AGNES BOYER (MRS. VICTOR REINSTEIN), historian, educator; b. Buffalo, Mar. 3, 1907; d. Lee M. and Julia Agnes (Smith) Boyer; B.A., Elmira Coll., 1928; M.A., Columbia, 1942; m. Victor Reinstein, Sept. 28, 1942; stepchildren—Victor, Robert; 1 dau., Julia. Tchr. pub. schs., Tinton, S.D., 1929-31, Deadwood, S.D., 1931-33, Castile, N.Y., 1933-40; tchr. Pine Hill High Sch., Cheektowaga, 1940-42; instr. history dept. U. Buffalo, 1947-48; town historian Town of Cheektowaga, 1952—. Spl. tchr. local history Park Sch., Buffalo, 1960—. Mem. Cheektowaga Pub. Library Bd., 1962—, chmn., 1970-74; mem. Erie County Com. Historic Preservation, 1962—; mem. N.Y. State Conservation Forum, 1943—, sec.-treas., 1949-50; pres. Wyoming County Council Social Studies, 1935-39. Named Citizen of Yr., Cheektowaga Central Sch. Dist., 1962; Cheektowaga Citizen of Yr., 1964; recipient achievement award (with husband) U.S. C. of C., 1964; Service to Mankind award, Sertoma Internat., 1969; Erie County Sesquicentennial award, 1971; Citizen of Year award Cheektowaga C. of C., 1972; commendation Am. Assn. State and Local History, 1972. Mem. A.L.A., N.Y. State Library Trustees Assn., N.Y. State Hist. Assn., Nat. Trust for Historic Preservation, Canal Soc. N.Y. State (charter), Cobblestone Soc. N.Y. (charter), Buffalo and Erie County Hist. Soc., Old Ft. Niagara Assn., Erie County Hist. Fedn. (pres. 1959—), Municipal Historians N.Y. State (pres. 1970-73), Descs. War 1812, D.A.R. Presbyn. Mem. Order Eastern Star. Author-editor: Town of Cheektowaga Historical Atlas, 1966; History of Town of Cheektowaga, 1971. Home: 11 Danforth St Cheektowaga NY 14227 Office: Cheektowaga Town Hall Broadway at Union Rd Cheektowaga NY 14227

REINTJES, VERNA MARONEY (MRS. JOHN WILLIAM REINTJES), clin. psychologist; b. Santa Ana, Cal., Apr. 28, 1923; d. Frank Vernon and Belle (Higgins) Maroney; B.A., Stanford, 1944, M.A., 1945; m. John William Reintjes, Mar. 11, 1950; children—Anne, Christine, Susan, Peter. Psychologist, San Francisco Juvenile Ct., 1945-47; clin. psychologist, Honolulu, 1947-52; clin. psychologist N.C. Bd. Pub. Welfare, 1962-68; clin. psychologist Neuse Mental Health Center, New Bern, N.C., 1967-71, dir. psychol. services, 1971—; practice clin. psychology, Morehead City, N.C., 1962—; psychol. cons. Camp Lejeune (N.C.) Schs., 1966-68. Sec., Carteret County Mental Health Assn., Morehead City, 1963-64, pres., 1966-67, 69-70, bd. dirs., 1967—; mem. exec. com. Carteret County Community Action Com., 1966. Mem. Am., N.C. psychol. assns. Home and office: Route 2 Box 85 Morehead City NC 28557

REINWALD, CLIO SHARPE (MRS. ROYCE ROBERT REINWALD), educator; b. Mehoopany, Pa., Nov. 12, 1915; d. Arthur Butler and Martha (Story) Sharpe; B.S. in Home Econs., State Coll., Mansfield, Pa., 1935; M.S., Cornell U., 1943; postgrad. Pa. State U., U. Pa.; m. Royce Robert Reinwald, June 20, 1942 (dec. Oct., 1942). Tchr. home econs. Laceyville, Meshoppen, Tunkhannock Schs., 1935-46; area supr. home econs. Wyoming, Sullivan counties area, 1946-53; state supr. homemaking edn., and sch. food services, state adviser, hon. mem. Pa. Assn. Future Homemakers Am., 1953-68, coordinator home econs., sch. food servs. and migrant edn., 1956-68; state supr. home econs. Dept. Vocational Edn., Phoenix, 1968—; adv. to Pa. Sch. Food Service Assn. Mem. Govs. Com. Migrant Labor, 1958-66, Pa. Citizens Council; mem. adv. com. State Instnl. Food Service Research Program, 1957-62, Pa. Rural Safety Council, 1955-67, Central Ariz. Coll., Scottsdale Community Coll., Phoenix Coll.; mem. Ariz. Early Childhood Edn. Council, Govs. Adv. Council on Status of Women, 1966-68; mem. adv. com. Pa. Day Care Services; mem. Early Childhood Edn. Council. Mem. Nat., Pa., adult edn. assns., Am. Vocational Assn. (life), Am., Ariz. home econs. assns., Nat. Council on Family Relations, Am. Assn. Secondary Sch. Adminstrs., Am., Pa. sch. food service assns., Nat. Assn. State Suprs. of Home Econs. Edn., Am. Assn. U. Women, Harrisburg Art Assn., D.A.R., Pi Lambda Theta, Kappa Delta Pi. Methodist. Mem. Order of Eastern Star (past matron). Clubs: Home Economics (Harrisburg, Pa.), Altrusa (pres.) (Phoenix). Author publs. in field. Mem. adv. bd. Favorite Recipes Press, Inc. Home: 6329 N 14th St Phoenix AZ 85014 Office: 1535 W Jefferson St Phoenix AZ 85007

REISMAN, BETTY LOU, coll. adminstr.; b. Youngstown, O., Nov. 9, 1941; d. Bernard and Florence Esther (Liebermann) Reisman; B.A., Case Western Res. U., 1963; M.A., Kent State U., 1965. Asst. dean students State U. Coll. at Buffalo, 1965-68; asst. dean student affairs Clarion (Pa.) State Coll., 1968-69; asst. dir. housing, adj. instr. sch. psychology and counseling State U. N.Y. Coll. at Oswego, 1969—. Adviser Hillel Group, 1973. Mem. Am. Coll. Personnel Assn., Am. Coll. and U. Housing Officers, Nat. Assn. Women Deans, Adminstrs. and Counselors, N.Y. Assn. Women Deans, Adminstrs. and Counselors (mem. adv. bd. 1973-75), Sigma Psi. Home: 3475 5th Av Youngstown OH 44505

REISTRUP, JEANNE MOSS (MRS. JAMES REISTRUP), interior designer; b. Glasgow, Mo., Aug. 11, 1905; d. Samuel and Jennie (Easley) Moss; student U. Ill. 1923-27; study in Europe, 1931; m. James Reistrup, July 23, 1931; children—Paul H., John V. Head bur. interior decorating Davidson Bros., Sioux City, Ia., 1928-31; owner firm Jeanne Moss Reistrup, 1933—; also lectr. Tchr. interior decorating YWCA, Catholic U. Active civic work; mem. women's com. Nat. Symphony Orch. Recipient Woman of Achievement award, Sioux City, Ia., 1946. Fellow Am. Inst. Designers (nat. by-laws com., nominating com., chmn. nat. conf., 1953, chmn. exhibit Nat. Housing Center 1959; chmn. bd. govs., corr. sec., chmn. by-laws com., lecture com. D.C. chpt. 1971—); mem. Ia. State Soc. (v.p. 1963-65), Nat., D.C. fedns. music clubs, YWCA, P.E.O., Delta Zeta. Clubs: Fortnighty (past pres.), Morningside Coll. Faculty Women's (past pres.). Author articles in field. Home: 3701 Connecticut Av NW Washington DC 20008

REITH, GERTRUDE LOUISE MCKEAN, educator; b. Stockport, Ia.; d. Herbert Allen and Gertrude (Fickel) McKean; B.A., U. Washington, 1939, M.A., 1940; Ph.D., Clark U., 1963; m. John William Reith, Sept. 5, 1942 (div. Apr. 1965); children—Gertrude Helen (Mrs. John Michael Ferron), John Herbert; m. 2d, Seth Arthur Fessenden, Sept. 19, 1970 (div. Sept. 1971). Sr. cartographer OSS, Washington, 1942-45; asst. prof. U. Washington, 1945-46; mem. faculty Cal. State U., Fullerton, 1961—, prof. geography, 1970—, chmn. dept., 1968-71. Mem. Assn. Am. Geographers, Am. Geog. Soc., Assn. Pacific Coast Geographers, Cal. Council for Geog. Edn., Phi Beta Kappa, Phi Kappa Phi. Home: 1015 Diane St Placentia CA 92670 Office: Geography Dept Cal State U Fullerton CA 92634

REITZ, BEVERLY WALKER (MRS. HAROLD AXTEL REITZ), interior designer; b. Oak Ridge, Mo., Feb. 21, 1901; d. Dix and Ida (Turner) Walker; B.S. in Edn., U. Mo., 1920; postgrad. U. Ill., 1924-25, N.Y. Sch. Interior Design, 1934-35, Parsons Sch. Design, 1935-37; m. Harold Axtel Reitz, June 27, 1931. Tchr. pub. high schs., Ia. 1920-24, Okla., 1926-28, N.J., 1928-38; owner Beverly Reitz Interiors, N.Y.C., 1938—. Mem. Am. Inst. Interior Designers (v.p. N.Y. 1953-55), Decorators Club N.Y. (pres. 1951-53, 66-67), Archtl. League (exec. com. 1967-69), Home Lighting Forum (dir. 1958-60), U.D.C., D.A.R., Victorian Soc., Nat. Trust for Historic Preservation, Municipal Art Soc., Delta Delta Delta. Episcopalian. Contbr. articles to profl. Jours., also mags. Home: 30 E 62d St New York City NY 10021 also Saw Mill Hill Rd Ridgefield CT 06877 Office: 30 3 62d St New York City NY 10021

REITZEL, HILDA MARIE, librarian; b. Pitts., May 9, 1921; d. Harry A. and Mary (Senn) Reitzel; A.B., U. Pitts., 1943, M.A., 1952; B.S. in L.S., Carnegie Inst. Tech., 1945. Asst. med. librarian U. Pitts., 1943-45, asst. reference dept., 1945-52, research librarian, 1952; librarian Mine Safety Appliances Co., 1952-54; head reference dept. U. Pitts., 1954-56; librarian Mine Safety Appliances Co., 1956—. Recipient Pitts. Female Coll. Assn. award, 1942. Mem. Spl. Libraries Assn. (pres. 1958-59), Am., Pa. (editor bull. 1961-72, certificate of merit 1967) library assns., Assn. Coll. and Research Libraries, (Phi Delta Gamma. Club: Library (pres. 1950-51) (Pitts.). Home: Bigelow Apts Pittsburgh PA 15219 Office: 400 Penn Center Blvd Pittsburgh PA 15235

REJAUNIER, JEANNE ALLYN, author; b. Mineola, N.Y., Apr. 19, 1934; d. Edward William and Harriet Belle (Wright) Rejaunier; A.B., Vassar Coll., 1956; postgrad. Sorbonne, Paris, 1955, U. Pisa, Italy, 1955, Goetheschule, Rome, Italy, 1960-61, U. Cal. at Los Angeles, 1963-74, New Sch. for Social Research, 1962. Model, actress, 1956-67; novelist, Los Angeles, 1968—. Recipient writing award Holly (Cal.) C. of C., 1969; Beautiful People, award Can. Film Co., 1972. Mem. Actors Equity, A.F.T.R.A., Screen Actors Guild, Writers Guild Am. West, Authors' League Am. Dramatists' Guild, Literary Guild, Los Angeles Children's Riding Center. Author: Beauty Trap, 1969; Astrology for Lovers, 1970; Motion and the Act, 1972; The Fugitive Wife, 1975. Home and office: 1226 N Havenhurst St Los Angeles CA 90046

REJENT, MARIAN MAGDALEN, physician; b. Toledo, Aug. 12, 1920; d. Casimir Stanley and Magdalen (Szymanowski) Rejent; B.S., Mary Manse Coll., 1946; M.D., Marquette U., 1946; M.P.H., U. Mich., 1960. Intern St. Vincent's Hosp., Toledo, 1946-47; resident pediatrics City Hosp., Cleve., also Children's Hosp., Akron, O., 1947-50; practice medicine specializing in pediatrics, 1950-54; chief div. maternal and child health City of Toledo, 1954-65; dir. pediatrics Maumee Valley Hosp., 1964-70; acting chmn. pediatrics Med. Coll. of Ohio at Toledo, 1970-73, asso. prof. pediatrics, 1970—; adj. prof. pub. health U. Toledo; asso. prof. social medicine Med. Coll. of Ohio at Toledo; mem. staff Med. Coll., Toledo, St. Vincent's, Mercy hosps. Dir. Poison Information Center, Toledo, 1958—. Fellow Am. Pub. Health Assn.; mem. A.M.A., Ohio Med. Assn., Acad. Medicine of Toledo and Lucas County, Am. Acad. Pediatrics, Northwestern Ohio Pediatric Soc., Nat. Council Cath. Women, Greater Toledo Nutrition Council. Club: Quota (Toledo). Home: 631 Woodstock St Toledo OH 43607 Office: PO Box 6190 Toledo OH 43614

RELPH, RITA MARGARET (MRS. JOSEPH S. RELPH), editor; b. Winfield, Kan., Mar. 26, 1929; d. Earnest Avery and Mabel Claire (Cook) Parsons; student Independence Jr. Coll., 1947-48, U. Okla., 1955-58; m. Joseph S. Relph, June 30, 1948; children—Mina (Mrs. Kirk DePerry), Patricia, Joseph S. II, Ross, Virginia, Meredith. Owner, editor, columnist Wilson County Citizen, Fredonia, Kan., 1961—. Chmn., Fredonia Planning Commn., 1973-74; Republican committeewoman, Fredonia, 1963-74. Mem. Bus. and Profl. Women (pres. 1967-68), Nat., Kan. Press assns. Roman Catholic. Author: History of City of Fredonia, 1973; Life of John S. Gilmore, 1973. Producer Escape, CBS-TV, 1967. Home: 632 N 8th St Fredonia KS 66736 Office: 706 Madison St Fredonia KS 66736

REMAR, ELIZABETH MARY, mental health ofcl.; b. West Kirby, Eng., June 16, 1927; d. Alexander Robert and Queen Maya (Shearson) Boyle; came to U.S., 1946, naturalized, 1948; student Lancaster (Eng.) Coll. Art, 1941-43, London U., 1944-46; B.A. Goddard Coll., Plainfield, Vt., 1972, M.A., 1974; divorced; children—Robert, Katy, Lisa, James, Suzy, Michael. Pub. information officer Mass. Assn. Mental Health, 1964-65; vol. supr. Boston State Hosp., 1965-67; chief vol. services Mass. Dept. Mental Health, 1967—; tchr. vols. and citizen participation Quonsigamond Community Coll., Worcester, Mass., 1970; cons. in field. Pres. Assn. Mentally Ill Children, 1968-71, mem. profl. adv. bd., 1973—; founding mem., trustee Samaritans of Boston, 1973—; del. White House Conf. Children and Youth, 1970; founding mem., bd. dirs. Newton (Mass.) Mental Health Assn. and Clinic, 1962-65, League Sch. Boston, 1965-67; founding mem., mem. adv. bd. Warren Camp Disturbed Children, 1960-62; pres. Mass. chpt. Nat. Orgn. Mentally Ill Children, 1959-61. Mem. Internat. Assn. Vol. Edn., Assn. Human Services, Assn. Vol. Action Scholars, Les Amis do Vin. Contbr. papers in field. Home: 661 Commonwealth Av Newton Centre MA 02159 Office: 190 Portland St Boston MA 02114

REMES, LURA DUFF ELLISTON, civic worker, poet; b. Ft. Worth, July 20, 1933; d. Fred Addison and Lura Duff (Elliston) M.; student Duke, 1951-52, U. Tex., 1952-54; m. Eugene Marriot Remes, Apr. 13, 1974; children—Edward Duff Nowotny, George Edward Nowotny, III, Addison Dance Nowotny, Mark Randall Remes. Dir. Sebastian County Mental Health Assn., 1963-69, Ark. Assn. Mental Health, 1966-72; gov. Western Ark. Counciling and Guidance Center, 1969-74; bd. dirs. Spark's Hosp. Guild, 1964-70, 71-73, pres., 1973; bd. dirs. Concert Assn., 1968-72; pres. Ft. Smith Affiliation of the Arts, 1968; co-chmn. arts festivals, 1964, 65, 70; leadership cons. Nat. Assn. Retarded Children, 1968-69; mem. Retardation Com. State Health Planning, 1968-69; area chmn. Council on Children's Emotional Health, 1974. Committeewoman Rep. 3d Congl. Dist., 1962-64, 68-70; charter mem. County Rep. Women, 1961-72; co-chmn. Rep. United Campaign, 1962; sec. Rep. State Conv., 1968; justice of peace, 1973—. Life trustee Old Fort Museum, 1968, pres., 1970-72; mem. adv. bd. St. Edward's Mercy Hosp., 1967-69; trustee, v.p., treas. St. John's Sch. for Children with Learning Disabilities, 1971—; bd. govs. Juvenile Detention Center of Sebastian County, 1974—. Recipient first place lyric poetry award Ark. Arts Festival, 1968; named One of Outstanding Young Women of Am., 1966. Mem. Jr. League Ft. Smith, D.A.R., Delta Delta Delta. Episcopalian (chmn. altar guild 1967, 70, pres. ch. women 1961-62). Founder, designer Ft. Smith Children's Museumobile, 1965; author vol. art enrichment program Ft. Smith Pub. Schs., 1969; author: New Look Trio, 1970, 1972. Home: 2 River Ridge Rd Little Rock AR 72207

REMICK, LEE (MRS. WILLIAM R. GOWANS), actress; b. Boston; d. Frank E. and Margaret (Waldo) Remick; student Barnard Coll., 1953; m. William R. Gowans, 1970; children by previous marriage—Kate, Matthew. Broadway debut in Be Your Age, 1953, other Broadway plays, Anyone Can Whistle, 1964, Wait Until Dark, 1966; toured in Jenny Kissed Me, 1954; motion pictures include A Face in the Crowd, 1956, The Long Hot Summer, 1957, Anatomy of a Murder, 1959, Wild River, 1959, Sanctuary, 1960, Experiment in Terror, 1961, Days of Wine and Roses, 1961, The Wheeler Dealers, 1962, Baby The Rain Must Fall, 1963, Hallelujah Trail, 1965, No Way to Treat a Lady, 1968, The Detective, 1968, Hard Contract, 1969, A Severed Head, 1970, Loot, 1971; Sometimes A Great Notion, 1971; A Delicate Balance, 1973; also performer in numerous TV shows. Address: c/o Ashley-Famous Agy 1301 Av Americas New York City NY 10019

REMINGTON, DEBORAH WILLIAMS, artist; b. Haddonfield, N.J.; d. Malcolm Van Dyke and Hazel I. (Stewart) Remington; grad. Cal. Sch. Fine Arts, 1952; B.F.A., San Francisco Art Inst., 1955. One-man shows Six Gallery, San Francisco State Coll., Dilexi Gallery, San Francisco Mus. Art, Bykert Gallery, N.Y.C., Galerie Darthea Speyer, Paris, France, Obelisk Gallery, Boston, Pyramid Galleries, Washington; exhibited group shows Mus. Modern Art, Whitney Mus., Auckland (New Zealand) Mus., La Jolla Mus., Cin. Mus., San Francisco Mus. Art, De Young Mus., Oakland Mus. Art, Fondation Maeght, St. Paul de Vence, France, Smithsonian Inst., Bklyn. Mus., 1970, Art Inst: Chgo. Mus., 1974, many others; represented in permanent collections Whitney Mus. Am. Art, Auckland Mus., San Francisco Mus. Art, Centre National d'Art Contemporain, Paris, France, Palace of Legion of Honor Mus., Boymans Mus., Rotterdam, Holland, Addison Gallery Am. Art, Andover, Mass., Indpls. Mus., others. Tchr. painting and drawing U. Cal. at Davis, 1962, San Francisco State Coll., 1965, Cooper Union, N.Y.C., 1973—; tchr. painting and drawing San Francisco Art Inst., 1958-65, guest instr., summer 1966. Home: 309 W Broadway New York City NY 10013

REMINGTON, SALLY (MRS. PAUL E. REMINGTON), club woman; b. Louisville, Colo., Dec. 20, 1894; d. Daniel McGregor and Edith M. (Kerr) McNeil; B.A., U. Colo., 1916; m. Paul E. Remington, Dec. 31, 1919. Tchr., Grand Junction, Colo., 1916-18, Frederick, Colo., 1918-19. Mem. Am. Assn. U. Women, Territorial Daus. Colo., Sons of Pioneers, Acacia Aux., Alpha Delta Pi. Republican. Methodist. Clubs: Montclair Women's, Lakewood Country, Denver, University (Boulder). Died July 23, 1974. Home: 350 Ponca Pl Boulder CO 80303

REMMEY, LOUISE AUSTIN, journalist, govt. ofcl.; b. Balt., Sept. 7, 1932; d. Franklin C. and Dorothy (Treide) Austin; A.B., Bucknell U., 1954; Fulbright scholar U. London, 1955; postgrad. U. Tokyo, 1956, Harvard, 1958-59; piano grad. prep. Peabody Conservatory Music, 1950. Researcher Washington bur. CBS News, 1960-71, chief of research, 1962-71; asst. editor program and mag. John F. Kennedy Center for Performing Arts, Washington, 1971-72; cons. Nat. Endowment for Arts, 1972, pub. information specialist, 1973—; free-lance writer music and arts, 1967—; regular contbr. to Balt. Sun, Washington Post, others. Trustee Bucknell U. Fellow Music Critics Inst., Aspen/Santa Fe, summer 1972. Mem. Am. Women in Radio and Television, Radio-Television Corrs. Assn., Am. Hist. Assn., Am. Polit. Sci. Assn., Phi Beta Kappa. Club: Nat. Press. Home: 3806 T St NW Washington DC 20007 Office: Nat Endowment for Arts Washington DC 20506

REMY, JOAN HOLDEN, psychologist, state ofcl.; b. Utica, N.Y., July 3, 1924; d. Gordon Alfred and Frances (Norman) Holden; B.A., Syracuse U., 1947; Ph.D., Adelphi U., 1960; m. Charles M. Remy, Apr. 9, 1947 (div. Sept. 1951). Asst. med. psychologist U. Md., 1956-58; asst. instr., staff psychologist N.Y. Med. Sch., 1963; staff psychologist Children's unit Buffalo State Hosp., 1966-68; instr. psychology and criminology Mohawk Valley Community Coll., Utica, N.Y., 1969-71; clin. psychologist N.Y. State Dept. Mental Hygiene, Marcy (N.Y.) State Hosp., 1968—. Guest lectr. police agys., nursing assns., 1968—; mem. curriculum devel. com., Mohawk Valley Community Coll., 1969-71. Mem. Am. Psychol. Assn. Book reviewer Utica Observer Dispatch. Home: 1015 Park Av Utica NY 13501 Office: March State Hospital Marcy NY 13403

RENAULT, BARBARA JEAN SEELEY (MRS. LAWRENCE RICHARD RENAULT), advt. agy. exec.; b. N.Y.C., Feb. 23, 1934; d. William M. and Margaret Lenore (Ford) Seeley; B.A., Fla. So. Coll., 1956; m. Lawrence Richard Renault, Feb. 2, 1969; 1 dau., Leslie Diane. Tchr. elementary and secondary schs., Lakeland, Fla., 1955-57; soc. editor Collier County News, Naples, Fla., 1950-54; with display advt. dept. Lakeland Ledger, 1952-54; operations mgr. WNOG, Radio, Naples, 1957-62; continuity dir., pub. service dir., asst. prodn. engr. WINZ Radio, Miami, 1962-64; producer Lando/Bishopric Advt., Miami, 1964-73; producer, account coordinator Hume, Smith, Mickelberry Advt., Miami, 1973—. Recipient various 1st pl. awards So. dist. Am. Fedn. Advt., 1964, 66, 67, 68, 72, 73, Big Mike award (3) Miami Broadcasters Assn., 1968. Mem. Am. Women in Radio and TV (charter), Alpha Chi Omega, Cap and Gown, Sigma Tau Delta, Phi Delta Epsilon. Episcopalian. Home: 5725 SW 117th Av Miami FL 33143 Office: 1000 Brickell Av Miami FL 33131

RENBARGER, PAMELA LYNN (MRS. WILLIAM DERRELL RENBARGER), occupational therapist; b. South Bend, Ind., Dec. 3, 1947; d. George William and Marilyn Arlene (McCully) Sink; A.A., Southwestern Mich. Jr. Coll., 1968; B.S., Eastern Mich. U., 1971; m. William Derrell Renbarger, Oct. 20, 1973. Staff therapist Elkart (Ind.) Gen. Hosp., 1971-72; occupational therapist Mich. Rehab. Center for Blind, Kalamazoo, 1972—. Mem. Am. Occupational Therapy Assn., Am. Assn. Workers for Blind, Weavers Guild. Home: Route 3 44th Av Paw Paw MI 49079 Office: 1541 Oakland Dr Kalamazoo MI 49008

RENEKER, BETTY CONGDON (MRS. ROBERT W. RENEKER), civic worker; b. Coffeyville, Kan., Feb. 2, 1913; d. Carl Otto and Eva (Budge) Congdon; student Purdue U., 1930-33; m. Robert W. Reneker, Mar. 2, 1934; children—William Carl, David Lee. State pres. Congl. Christian Womens Fellowship, 1956-59, nat. pres., 1959-62; pres. womens bd. Boy Scouts Am., Chgo., 1966-68, Ridge Service Guild, 1967-69; pres. Fortnightly Club, Chgo.; chmn. John Crerar Library Assos.; sec. women's div. Chgo. Heart Assn.;

chmn. exec. com. Chgo. Theol. Sem.; mem. women's bd. U. Chgo.; mem. exec. bd. Chgo. Area council Boy Scouts Am. Bd. dirs. Community Renewal Soc., Beverly Art Center, Adler Planetarium, John Crerar Library. Mem. United Ch. of Christ. Home: 1300 Lake Shore Dr Chicago IL 60610

RENFER, MARY EMMA (MRS. RUDOLF ALBERT RENFER), educator; b. Dallas, Jan. 23, 1914; d. Benzie Ragsdale and Eloise (Gillespie) Fewell; B.A. magna cum laude, Wheaton (Ill.) Coll., 1935; A.M., So. Methodist U., 1959; Ph.D., U. So. Cal., 1966; m. Rudolf Albert Renfer, Sept. 21, 1935; children—Nancy Marie (Mrs. Robert P. Sturges), Rudolf Albert, Patricia (Mrs. Don G. Wilson). Tchr. English, Tustin (Cal.) Union High Sch., 1961-63; prof. psychology Orange Coast Coll., Costa Mesa, Cal., 1963-70; prof. psychology Mountain View Coll., Dallas, 1970-73, prof., 1973—, counselor, 1970—. Pvt. practice psychology. Mem. Am., Southwestern psychol. assns., Am. Edn. Research Assn. Home: 6706 Lupton Dr Dallas TX 75225

RENFIELD, MARILYN LEWIS, physician; b. Washington, Jan. 2, 1940; d. Leon and Irene (Kitay) Lewis; A.B., Duke, 1961; M.D., George Washington U., 1965; m. Richard Lee Renfield, June 17, 1961; children—Richard Jonathan, Michelle Lisa. Intern, George Washington U. Hosp., 1965-66; resident pediatrics Children's Hosp., Washington, 1967-69, fellow neonatology, 1969-71; asst. prof. pediatrics George Washington U., 1971-73; dir. neonatology George Washington U. Hosp.; practice medicine specializing in pediatrics, Falls Church, Va. Fellow Am. Acad. Pediatrics; mem. Am. Acad. Pediatrics, Med. Soc. Va., Kane-King Obstet. Honor Soc., Smith-Reed-Russel Soc., Phi Beta Kappa, Order of Hippocrates, Alpha Omega Alpha. Home: 2200 Leeland Dr Falls Church VA 22043

RENICH, JILL HELEN TORREY (MRS. FREDERICK CHARLES RENICH), religious orgn. exec.; b. Tsinan, Shantung, N. China, July 29, 1916; d. Reuben Archer and Janet Slade (Mallary) Torrey, Jr.; B.A., Wheaton Coll., 1941; m. Frederick Charles Renich, Oct. 28, 1944; children—Janet (Mrs. Robert Claude Barger), Rosalie, Frederick, Jacqueline. Missionary U.S., China, Australia, 1948—; founder, dir., pres. Winning Women, Inc., Farmington, Mich., 1963—. Producer, speaker radio program Between Us Women, 1963—; sec. Living Life Ministeries, Inc., 1973—; free-lance writer, 1964—. Baptist (mem. library com. 1971-73). Author: So You're A Teenage Girl, 1966; To Have and To Hold, 1972. Home: 36264 Freedom Rd Farmington MI 48024 Office: 34749 Grand River Av Farmington MI 48024

RENNER, MARY LUCILLE (MRS. DARWIN SPRATHARD RENNER), geol. lab. exec., sorority exec.; b. Chico, Tex., Oct. 27, 1916; d. Ernest Lee and Ella Irene (Clark) Barksdale; B.A., So. Meth. U., 1938; m. Darwin Sprathard Renner, Oct. 21, 1944; children—Karl Hertzian, Kathryn Elaine (Mrs. George Philip Morehead), Betty Karolyn. Tchr. Dallas Pub. Schs., 1938-44; control engr. WRR Radio Sta., Dallas, 1942-44; sec.-treas. Geotronic Labs., Inc., Dallas, 1950—; grand v.p. Collegiate chpts. Alpha Delta Pi, 1969—. Active worker for Heart Fund, Lukemia, Muscular Dystrophy, Cancer and March of Dimes drives; active in Girl Scouts, Cub Scouts and Campfire Girls; former mem. Dallas Women's Forum. Sec. Democratic precinct 420, Dallas, 1958-70; del. to Dallas County and Tex. State Dem. Convention 1958-70. Mem. Dallas Geol. and Geophys. Aux., Am. Assn. U. Women, Pro Am. (pres. 1960-61), Dallas City Panhellenic (pres. 1963-64), So. Meth. U. Mothers Club and Alumni Assn., Alpha Delta Pi (province pres. 1964-69), Gamma Sigma. Club: Dallas Public Affairs Luncheon. Presbyn. Home: 1314 Cedar Hill Av Dallas TX 75208

RENNIE, HELEN SEWELL JOHNSON (MRS. LEONARD C. RENNIE), painter; b. Cambridge, Md.; d. Sewell Marvin and Helen Alexander (Skinner) Johnson; student Corcoran Sch. Art, Nat. Acad. Design; m. Leonard C. Rennie, Oct. 3, 1945. Tchr. painting Phillips Gallery Art Sch., Washington, 1930-32; designer, art dir. U.S. Dept. Agr., Washington, 1935-45, U.S. Office Edn., 1947-48, U.S. Dept. Labor, 1946-47, U.S. Dept. Navy, 1948-51; designer, art dir., visual information officer OPS, 1951-53; One-woman shows Bridge Gallery, N.Y.C., 1963, Capricorn Gallery, N.Y.C., 1968, 69; Franz Bader Gallery, Washington, 1954, 58, 62, 66, 72; paintings in collections in U.S. Dept. Commerce, Phillips Gallery, Am. U., Barnet-Aden Collection, U.S. Dept. State, Art in Embassies program. Mem. Soc. Washington Artists, Artists Guild, Artists Equity Assn. Home and studio: 1306 30th St NW Washington DC 20007

RENO, JUNE MELLIES (MRS. EARL CLIFTON RENO), journalist; b. St. Louis, June 17, 1921; d. Oscar Arthursand Winifred Carr (Wagon) Stumpe; A.B., Washington U., St. Louis, 1943; M.A., U. Chgo., 1944; M.S., Columbia U., 1944; m. Earl Clifton Reno, July 14, 1972; children (by previous marriage)—Penny, Tom, Meg (Mrs. Robert Simon), David. Journalist, St. Louis Globe Democrat, 1942, Newsweek, N.Y.C., 1944-45, Pageant Mag., N.Y.C., 1945-46; author, Cornwall Bridge, Conn., 1965—. Instr., N.Y. U., N.Y.C., 1952, New Sch., N.Y.C., 1955-56, Ind. U., 1962; lectr. U. Conn., Bridgeport, 1971-72. Recipient A.M.A. ann. award, 1964; Nat. Soc. Christians and Jews ann. award, 1965; Pulitzer Prize nominee, 1954. Mem. Overseas Press Club, Soc. Mag. Writers, Am. Newspaper Guild, Wilton Riding Club, Green Mountain Horse Assn., Brit. Horse Soc. Mem. Soc. of Friends. Author: Eight Weeks to Live, 1954; Human Sexual Inadequacy (Analysis), 1971; The Horse You Care For, 1973; Kayengha, 1974; Keeper of the Fire, 1974. Home and office: Box 72 Cornwall Bridge CT 06754

RENOUD, DOROTHY OWEN, publishing co. exec.; b. Far Rockaway, N.Y., Aug. 11, 1933; d. Herbert William and Elizabeth (Fischer) Owen; ed. pub. schs., bus. courses; m. David F. Renoud, Jan. 18, 1958; children—David, Douglas. File clk. Reinhold Pub. Co., N.Y.C., 1951-59, sales adminstrv. mgr., 1959-61; asst. to circulation mgr. United Tech. Pub. Co., Garden City, N.Y., 1961-63, circulation dir., 1963—. Mem. Subscription Fulfillment Mgrs. Assn., Nat. Bus. Circulation Council Long Beach Fire Dept. Ladies Aux. Home: 527 West Chester St Long Beach NY 11561 Office: 645 Stewart Av Garden City NY 11530

RENTER, LOIS IRENE HUTSON, librarian; b. Lowden, Ia., Oct. 23, 1929; d. Thomas E. and Lulu Mae (Barlean) Hutson; B.A. cum laude, Cornell Coll., 1965; M.A., U. Ia., 1968; m. Karl A. Renter, Jan. 3, 1948; children—Susan Elizabeth, Rebecca Jean, Karl Geoffrey. Tchr. Spanish, Mt. Vernon (Ia.) High Sch., 1965-67; head librarian Am. Coll. Testing Program, Iowa City, Ia., 1968—. Vis. instr. U. Ia. Sch. Library Sci., 1972—. Mem. Am. Soc. Information Sci., A.L.A., Spl. Libraries Assn., Phi Beta Kappa. Methodist. Home: 1125 29th St Marion IA 52302 Office: Box 168 Iowa City IA 52240

RENTON, VIRGINIA HILL (MRS. MALCOLM J. RENTON), clubwoman; b. Macon, Ill., Nov. 19, 1905; d. Charles B. and Mattie (Bell) Hill; B.A., U. Cal. at Berkeley, 1928, postgrad., 1928-29; postgrad. U. So. Cal., 1930; m. Malcolm J. Renton, Aug. 7, 1944; 1 son, David Malcolm. Tchr. English, math., history Avalon High Sch., Long Beach, Cal., 1929-44. State pres. Cal. Scholarship Fedn., 1939-40, bd. dirs., 1955-61; pres. Catalina Coordinating Council, Avalon, Cal., 1956-62; area chmn. Girl Scouts U.S.A., Avalon, 1956—; sec. Catalina Mus. Soc., 1956-71, pres., 1971—; dist. chmn. A.R.C., Avalon, 1960—; pres. Avalon P.T.A., 1960-62; pres. Catalina Art Assn., 1965-67; co-chmn. fund raising com. Avalon Municipal Hosp.; mem. Gov.'s Conf. on Youth, 1969. Mem. Internat. Platform Assn., Delta Kappa Gamma, Alpha Xi Delta. Republican. Presbyn. Home: Box 91 Avalon Catalina Island CA 90704

RESH, MARY SHERMAN, ednl. cons.; b. Washington, Aug. 14, 1905; d. Aaron and Esther (Zaritsky) Sherman; A.B., George Washington U., 1929, M.A., 1939; postgrad. Md. U., 1940-45, D.C. Tchrs. Coll., 1941-49; m. Frank S. Resh, June 26, 1927 (div. Aug. 1946); 1 dau., Margot (Mrs. Jerome Heckman). Tchr., prin., pub. schs. Washington, 1941-56; program specialist Bur. Vocational-Tech. Edn., U.S. Office Edn., Dept. Health, Edn., Welfare, Washington, 1956-62; spl. asst. to dir., Office Manpower, Automation and Tng., U.S. Dept. Labor, 1962-66, dept. asst. manpower adminstr., 1966-69; ednl. cons., 1969—. Mem. Minimum Wage Bd., Washington, 1942-44; pres. Citizen's Assn., Washington, 1944-46; pres. Research Club, pub. schs. Washington, 1942-43; chmn. joint legislative council, Ednl. Orgns., Washington, 1942-45; v.p. Nat. Council on Hotel and Restaurant Edn., Ithaca, N.Y., 1958-61; internat. pres. Altrusa Internat., Inc., Chgo., 1967-69. Mem. bd. dirs., past pres. Altrusa Internat. Found., Chgo.; trustee MacFarland High Sch. Guidance Clinic, Washington. Mem. Edn. Assn. D.C. (past pres.), N.E.A., (past bd. dirs.), Am. Vocational Assn. (editor women's sect. newsletter, 1956-66; recipient citation for leadership, 1964, award for internat. contribution to women, 1967), Assn. Schs. Allied Health Professions, Practical Nurses Assn. Washington (hon. life). Contbr. articles to profl. publs. Home and office: 4201 Cathedral Av NW Washington DC 20016

RESNIK, REGINA, mezzo-soprano, concert and opera singer; b. N.Y.C., Aug. 30, 1924; d. Sam and Ruth Resnik; B.A., Hunter Coll.; m. Harry W. Davis, July 18, 1946; 1 son, Michael Philip. Mezzo-soprano Met. Opera Co., N.Y.C., Covent Garden Opera, Vienna State Opera, Salzburg Festival, Paris Opera, Staatsoper, Stuttgart, Staatsoper, Hamburg, Leatro Colon, Buenos Aires, Bayreuth Festival. Address: care Met Opera Co Lincoln Center New York City NY 10023*

RESNIKOFF, FLORENCE LISA HERMAN (MRS. GEORGE J. RESNIKOFF), artist; b. Ft. Worth; d. M.I. and E. (Drucaroff) Herman; A.A., Herzl City Jr. Coll., 1939; B.F.A., Cal. Coll. Arts and Crafts, 1967; M.A. in Art, Cal. State U. at San Jose, 1973; m. George J. Resnikoff, Apr. 4, 1943; 1 son, Carl F. One-man exhbns. of jewelry and sculpture in shows at Stanford, Chgo. Pub. Library Art Room, Am. Craft Center, San Francisco, M.R. deYoung Mus., San Francisco, 1973; exhibited in group shows at San Francisco Mus., De Young Mus., Palace of Legion of Honor, Mus. West; travelling jewelry show, Eng., Scotland; jewelry in permanent collection at Oakland Mus., City and County of San Francisco; mem. faculty Cal. State U., San Jose, Cal. State U., San Francisco. Recipient prizes and awards, including prize Richmond Civic Mus., 1965, 69; jewelry prize San Francisco Women Artists, 1968; merit awards (2) San Francisco Art Festival, 1964; sculpture prize and award South Shore Gallery, Chgo., 1963; Nat. Endowment for Arts grantee, 1973. Mem. Cal. Craft Congress (chmn. 1970-71), Metal Arts Guild No. Cal. (charter), Designer-Craftsmen of No. Cal. (treas. 1967—), San Francisco Women Artists (dir. 1968). Address: 5654 Maxwelton Rd Oakland CA 94618 also 5654 Maxwelton Rd Oakland CA 94618

RESTAINO, KATHERINE MARIE (MRS. BERNARD F. DICK), coll. pres.; b. Bklyn., Nov. 14, 1937; d. John Joseph and Katherine Marie (Fischetti) Restaino; B.A., Coll. of White Plains, 1960; M.A. (fellow 1960-63), Fordham U., 1962, Ph.D., 1966; m. Bernard F. Dick, July 31, 1965. Instr. English, Mercy Coll., Dobbs Ferry, N.Y., 1963-66, asso. prof., 1967-70, dir. honors program, 1966-70; asso. prof. English Coll. of White Plains (N.Y.), 1970—, acad. dean, 1970-72, acting pres. 1972-73, pres. 1973—. Mem. Am. Comparative Lit. Assn., Modern Lang. Assn., Kappa Gamma Pi. Home: 989 Wilson Av Teaneck NJ 07666 Office: 78 N Broadway White Plains College White Plains NY 10603

RETHY, KATHARINA (MRS. EMERY I. RETHY), counselor; b. Jimbolia, Rumania, Sept. 4, 1922; d. Johann and Gertrud (Gruber) Kostner; tchrs. diploma, Scoala Normala de Fete, 1941; student U. Vienna, 1942-45; Ph.D., U. Munich, 1949; postgrad. U. Cal. at Berkeley, 1959-60; m. Emery I. Rethy, Jan. 19, 1952; 1 son, Victor Stephen. Came to U.S., 1950, naturalized, 1955. With Catholic Social Service, San Francisco, 1953-60; pvt. practice, asso. East Bay Psychol. Center, Oakland, Cal., 1967—. Mem. Am., Cal. psychol. assns., Am. Assn. Marriage and Family Counselors, Am. Assn. U. Women, U. Cal. Alumni Assn. Home: 3381 West Terrace Lafayette CA 94549 Office: 315 14th St Oakland CA 94612

RETZER, MARY ELIZABETH HELM (MRS. WILLIAM RAYMOND RETZER), librarian; b. Balt.; d. Francis Leslie C. and Edna (Smith) Helm; B.A., Western Md. Coll., 1940; M.A., Columbia, 1946; postgrad. George Washington U., Ind. U., U. Ill., Ill. State U., Bradley U.; Ph.D., Western Colo. U., 1972; m. William Raymond Retzer, June 28, 1945; children—Lesley Elizabeth, Apryl Christine. Mem. faculty Rockville (Md.) Bd. Edn., 1940-47, elementary supr., 1945-47; cons. librarian Bergan High Sch., 1964-67; condr. library sci. course in reference Bradley U., 1966—; librarian Hines Elementary Sch., 1963-66, Roosevelt Jr. High Sch., 1966-69; head librarian Manual High Sch., Peoria, Ill., 1969—. Instr. water safety courses A.R.C., summers, 1940—; pres. women's bd. Salvation Army, 1952-54; pres. Peoria Nursery Sch. Assn., 1953-54; mem. Crippled Children's Adv. Com., Peoria, 1957-60; active various community drives; mem. women's adv. bd. Peoria Jr. Star, 1970-73. Mem. Ill. Valley Librarians Assn. (pres. 1971-72), A.L.A., Ill. Library Assn., Ill. Assn. Sch. Librarians (certification com. 1973—), Nat., Ill., Peoria edn. assns., Am. Assn. U. Women, Internat. Platform Assn. Republican. Presbyn. Mem. Order Eastern Star. Clubs: Ill. State University Administrators, Willowknolls Country. Home: 1317 W Moss Av Peoria IL 61606

REUL, MYRTLE ROSE CROUSE (MRS. PAUL ARTHUR REUL), educator; b. Dooley, Mont., July 3, 1919; d. Z. John and Victoria (Robinson) Crouse; A.B., Albion Coll., 1947, L.H.D., 1967; M.A., Mich. State U., 1952, M.S.W., 1953, Ed.D., 1957, postgrad., 1959-60; m. Paul Arthur Reul, Dec. 24, 1937;children—M. Santa Marie (Mrs. Richard Schoof), Pauline Catherine (Mrs. William Holland). Secondary pub. sch. tchr. Tawas City, Mich., 1947-49; elementary tchr., prin., Jackson, Mich., 1949-51; caseworker Family Service Agy., Jackson, 1951-52; supr. Mich. Children's Aid Soc., Lansing, 1952-54, exec., Jackson, 1957; instr. Sch. Social Work, Mich. State U., East Lansing, 1954-57, asst. prof., 1957-63, asso. prof., 1963-68, cons. Coll. Edn., 1971; prof. U. Ga. Sch. Social Work, Athens, 1968—, also asst. dean. Cons. various fed., state and local agys., 1955—; tech. cons. agrl. labor camp adv. com. Mich. Dept. Health, 1965—; cons. U.S. Gen. Accounting Office, 1971—, Sch. Social Work, U. Ark., 1971—; mem. consortium of cons. Center for Rural Manpower and Pub. Affairs, Mich. State U. and U.S. Dept. Labor. Mem. exec. com. Greater Lansing Youth Council, 1958-62; mem. day care com. Mich. Youth Commn., 1960-66; mem. div. of family Mich. Human Resources Council, 1965-68; chmn. family service, social devel. sect. Gov.'s Goals for Ga. Mem. Am. Assn. U. Profs. (chmn. com. on faculty women's status U. Ga. chpt., v.p. U. Ga. chpt.), Nat. Assn. Social Workers, Nat. Conf. Social Welfare, Council Social Work Edn., Nat. Family Relations Council, Acad. Certified Social Workers, Mich. Sch. Social Work Assn. Republican. Baptist. Author: Parents Plus, 1954; A Survey of the State Wide Michigan Children's Aid Society, 1956; A Practical Approach to Marriage, 1965; Chartbook for Parents: Through the Seas of Adolescence, 1965; Where Hannibal Led Us, 1967; Changing Services for Changing Clients, 1969; Fruit and Vegetable Harvest Mechanizations Manpower Implicatons, 1969; Territorial Boundaries of Rural Poverty, 1974. also short stories. Contbr. articles to profl. publs. Home: 204 Riverside Dr Athens GA 30601

REUMERT, PATRICIA LEE, educator; b. Phoenix, Mar. 17, 1929; d. Edgar Hall and Augusta Marie (Partridge) Lee; B.A., Trinity U., 1949; M.A., U. Houston, 1965; m. Ole Reumert, Nov. 27, 1947; (div. Aug. 1969); children—Robert Lee, Vicki (Mrs. William Smith). Freelance in pub. relations and advt., 1950-59; tchr. pub. schs., Houston, 1959-69; adminstr. sch. TV, KUHT, Houston, 1967-69; instr. English, Tex. So. U., Houston, 1969—. Founder Harris County Center for Retarded, Houston, 1952. Democrat precinct chmn., Houston, 1972. Mem. Women in Communications. Author: The Padre Island Story, 1965. Home: 4040 San Felipe Houston TX 77027

REUTER, ANNA HELEN, drama dir., coach; b. Chgo.; d. George John and Anne Mary (Pollak) Reuter; student Sherwood Mus. Sch., Northwestern U., Pasadena (Cal.) Playhouse, Fordham U. Dir. plays for high schs., univs. and community theatre groups in Chgo. Area. Critic judge for drama festivals in numerous states. Bd. dirs. Chgo. Drama Festival, 1958-68, Catholic Theatre Conf., 1960-68. Recipient Ednl. Theatre award for excellence in directing. Mem. Internat. Thespian Assn., Am. Nat. Theatre Acad., Am., Nat. theatre assns., Ill. Speech and Theatre Assn. Author, dir. numerous original plays.

REUTER, LAUREL J., art gallery ofcl.; b. Devils Lake, N.D., Oct. 17, 1943; d. George Agustus and Evelyn Constance (Hadselford) Wallace; B.A., U. N.D., 1965, B.S., 1967, M.A., 1974. Neighborhood worker Poverty Program, Cedar Rapids, Ia., 1965-66; instr. Upward Bound Program, U. N.D., Grand Forks, 1967-70, founder Univ. Art Gallery, 1971—, dir., 1971—; intern Mus. Adminstrn., Mpls. Inst. Art, 1972-73. Cons. on regional collections; part time instr. univ. classes in native Am. arts and crafts and humanities. Mus. profl. fellow, summer 1973. Mem. Am. Folklore Soc., Am. Assn. Mus., Am. Assn. U. Profs., Coll. Art Assn., Mountain-Plains Mus. Conf. Author catalog: Hallelujah Anyway!, 1974. Home: 321 Princeton St Grand Forks ND 58201

REUTER, NANCY ROGERSON BROWN (MRS. F. TURNER REUTER), real estate broker; b. Boston, Aug. 1, 1923; d. John Freeman and Gladys G. (Pascoe) Brown; student Skidmore Coll., 1941-43; m. F. Turner Reuter, Feb. 14, 1948; children—F. Turner, Diana Shaw, John Adams. Mgr., promoter of antique expositions in major cities on E. coast, 1938-45; mgr. Country Inn, Ossipee Lake, N.H., summers 1938-45; real estate saleswoman, Washington, 1959-68; restorer of houses in Georgetown, Washington, establisher, real estate broker, and pres. Reuter's, Inc., Washington, 1969—. Founder Antiques Center, Middleburg, Va., 1973—, restored early Fed. style house, Middleburg, Va., 1974. Student pilot instr. Civil Air Patrol, N.H., 1942-45. Mem. womens bd. George Washington Univ. Hosp. Served with USMC, 1945-46. Recipient Citizens Assn. award for archtl. and restoration of remodeling of house Palisades Citizens Assn., 1968. Mem. Washington Real Estate Bd., Soc. of Women Geographers. Republican. Episcopalian. Clubs: Evergreen Garden (pres. 1965-67) (Washington); Londoun Hunt Pony Club (dist. commr. 1965-67) (Leesburg, Va.). Home: 4000 52d St NW Washington DC 20016 also Glenstone Farm Aldie VA 22001 Office: 4614 Wisconsin Av NW Washington DC 20016

REUTHER, RUTH ELIZABETH (MRS. J. R. REUTHER), educator, author; b. Gainesville, Tex., Feb. 27, 1917; d. Edwin Jerry and Grace (Patrick) Huffaker; A.A., Gainesville Jr. Coll., 1936; B.S., N. Tex. State Coll., 1938; m. Dr. J. R. Reuther, Jan. 26, 1941; 1 dau., Alma Grace. Tchr. English, Valley View (Tex.) Ind. Sch., 1944-46; tchr. Sam Houston Elementary Sch., 1957-58, tchr. reading and lit., Wichita Falls, Tex., 1958-74, ret. Author: Wife of Four Hobbies, 1956; also articles on visual tng. profl. jours. Mem. Visual Tng. Assts. Congress, Ft. Worth. Mem. Tex. State Tchrs. Assn., Circus Fans Assn. Am., N.E.A., Assn. Childhood Edn., Woman's Forum, Wichita Falls (pres.), Tex. poetry socs., Internat. Reading Assn., Delta Kappa Gamma. Baptist. Mem. Order Eastern Star. Club: Poetry (Wichita Falls). Author: (juvenile) Gray C. Circus Horse, 1970; also short stories. Home: 4450 Phillips Dr Wichita Falls TX 76308

REVERE, ANNE, actress; b. N.Y.C., June, 1907; d. C. T. and Harriette (Winn) Revere; student Wellesley Coll.; m. Samuel Rosen, 1935. Actress motion pictures, including Song of Bernadette, National Velvet, Sunday Dinner for a Soldier, Fallen Angel, Dragonwyck, Gentlemen's Agreement; roles in theatre prodns. Double Door, Children's Hour, Cue for Passion, Toys in the Attic. Recipient Acad. Award as best supporting actress, 1945; Tony award for performance Toys in the Attic, 1960. Home: New York City NY 10027

REVILL, THERESA IRENE NICENKO (MRS. JOHN A. REVILL), realtor; b. Busk, Poland, June 20, 1925; d. Ivan F. and Anna S. (Resnitchenko) Nicenko; came to U.S., 1953, naturalized, 1958; student U. Krakow (Poland), 1941-44, Compton and Cerritos Coll., 1962-65, Real Estate Brokers Lumbleu Sch., 1965; m. John A. Revill, Mar. 8, 1947; children—Corinne, Lorraine Anne. Nurse Brit. Red Cross, Villach, Austria, 1945-47; real estate salesman Rex L. Hogdes Realty, Long Beach, Cal., 1962-64; real estate broker, realtor Viking Realty, Inc., Long Beach, 1964—. Vol. City Hope, Los Angeles, 1958—. Mem. Rep. Woman Assn., Long Beach, Cal., 1973-74. Mem. Nat., Cal. real estate assns. Club: Anglo-American (Long Beach, Cal.). Home: 1065 E Freeland St Long Beach CA 90807 Office: 3748 Atlantic Av Long Beach CA 90807

REVILLON, LEONE, linguist, writer; b. Paris, France, June 24, 1914; d. Theodore Leon and Kate (Vidler) Revillon; grad. Coll. de Groslay, France, 1931-33; m. Fedor de Nikanov, Apr. 16, 1950. Painter, work exhibited Salon de Printemps, Paris, 1933, N.Y.C., 1935-38; mem. jr. editorial bd. mag. So You're Going to Be Married?, 1934-35; mng. dir. Lang Guild, N.Y.C., 1942—; now editorial cons., translator; dir. Trans-Ocean Pub. Relations, Inc., 1959. Mem. Am. Translators Assn. Author: (with Theodore Graesse) Travelers Conversational Grammar, 1954. Home: 55 E 86th St New York City NY 10028 Office: 75 E 55th St New York City NY 10022

REVIS, FRANCES W. (MRS. SIDNEY M. REVIS), educator; b. Colbert, Okla., Dec. 10, 1910; d. Harvey R. and Ophelia (Dane) Williamson; B.S., Southeastern State Tchrs. Coll., 1931; M.A., Tex. State Coll. Women, 1950; Ed.D., Tex. Woman's U., 1958; m. Sidney M. Revis, January 19, 1963. Tchr. home econs. Checotah (Okla.) High Sch., 1931-33; county dir. pub. welfare, Cotton, Logan, LeFlore counties, Okla., 1933-40; tchr. vocational homemaking Colbert (Okla.) High Sch., 1940-57; faculty mem. Southeastern State Coll., 1958—, asst. prof. home econs., 1959-65, asso. prof., 1965-69, prof., head home econs. dept., 1969—. Sec.-treas. western sect., So. Regional Conf. Coll. Food and Nutrition Tchrs., 1957—. Named Outstanding Tchr. Southeastern State U., 1973-74. Mem. Am., Okla. home econs. assns., Okla. Edn. Assn., Am. Assn. U. Profs., Higher Edn. Alumni Council Okla., N.E.A., Am. Assn. U. Women, Am., Okla. vocational assns., Am., Okla. sch. food service assns., Nat. Council Adminstrs. Home Econs., Delta Kappa Gamma. Home: PO Box 70 Colbert OK 74733 Office: Southeastern State Coll Durant OK 74701

REW, CATHERINE MCNARY, educator; b. Salem, Ore., Apr. 15, 1905; d. Wilson Davis and Francis Ednahdel (Hubbard) McNary; A.B., U. Wash., 1927, postgrad., summers 1958, 60, 61, 62; postgrad. Walla Walla Coll., 1954-55, Ithaca Coll., summer 1967, U. Oslo, summer 1969; m. Kenneth G. Rew, Aug. 4, 1933 (div. Sept. 1947); children—Linda Sharon (Mrs. Ronald Ray Davidson), Stuart Brent (dec.), Joan Garrison (Mrs. Bradley Allyn Buswell). Psychiat. social worker Dept. Instns. Cal., Los Angeles, Ukiah, Cal., 1928-31, VA, Ft. Lyon, Colo., 1931-33; dir., tchr. Seguin Sch. for Retarded, Walla Walla, Wash., 1955-57; psychol. services Sch. Dist. No. 140, Walla Walla, 1957-60; dir. spl. edn. Sch. Dist. No. 140, 1959-68, mem. bd. edn., 1969—. Home service chmn. A.R.C., 1953-57; mem. Walla Walla Community Service Council, 1959—; dir. spl. edn. Blue Mountain Soc. for Crippled Children and Adults; mem. com. on mental health and mental retardation Wash. Med. Assn., 1964-65; mem. Wash. State Adv. Council Spl. Edn., 1967—; mem. Walla Walla County Bd. Mental Retardation, 1971—; mem. Blue Mountain Comprehensive Health Planning Council. Mem. nat., state local coms. Republican Party. Bd. dirs., mem. Walla Walla Little Theater, 1957-65; mem. bd. Lillie Rice Activity Center for Handicapped. Mem. Walla Walla Community Concert Assn., Am. Assn. U. Women (sec. 1958-59, v.p. 1959-63, dir. 1958-65), Nat., Washington (chpt. v.p. 1963-65) assns. for retarded children, Am. Assn. on Mental Deficiency, Nat. Assn. for Gifted Children, Council for Exceptional Children (governing bd. Wash. fedn.), Council Adminstrs. of Spl. Edn., Wash. Assn. Adminstrs. Spl. Edn. (sec.-treas. 1967-68, pres. 1969-70, exec. bd.), N.E.A., Wash., Walla Walla edn. assns., Assn. for Childhood Edn., Am. Acad. Polit. and Social Scis., Nat. Soc. Colonial Dames XVII Century (chpt. pres.), Walla Walla Area C. of C. (taxation and legislation com., edn. com.), Allied Arts Council Walla Walla, Carnegie Center for Arts (life), Wash. State Sch. Dirs. Assn. (state resolutions com. 1971—, mem.-rep. to state legislative assembly), Nat. Ret. Tchrs. Assn., Daus. of Nile, Walla Walla Pioneer and Hist. Soc., Internat. Platform Assn., Little Theatre, Daus. Pioneers of Ore.-Wash., Alpha Gamma Delta. Clubs: Altrusa (v.p. 1962-64, pres. 1964-66), Knife and Fork, Walla Walla Art (treas. 1953-54, sec. 1964-65, v.p. 1963-64), Walla Walla Women's Reading. Episcopalian. Home: 234 Whitman St Walla Walla WA 99362

REXFORD, CHERYL ANN, reporter; b. St. Paul, Oct. 3, 1944; d. Lloyd E. and Carlyn E. (Cordes) Rexford; B.A. in Journalism, U. Ariz., 1966. News reporter Ariz. Republic, Phoenix, 1966-73; pub. relations media rep. Good Samaritan Hosp., Phoenix, 1973-74, Desert Samaritan Health Service, 1973-74; news reporter sta. KTAR-TV, Phoenix, 1974—. Adviser, Phoenix Jr. Achievement, 1971-72. Recipient Distinguished Pub. Service award Maricopa County (Ariz.) Bar Assn., 1970. Mem. Ariz. Press Women, Nat. Fedn. Press Women, Big Sisters, Women in Communications, Am. Soc. Hosp. Pub. Relations, Phi Lambda Phrateres (v.p. 1964-65). Mem. Phrateres Internat. Office: KTAR-TV 1101 N Central St Phoenix AZ 85004

REYHER, REBECCA HOURWICH, writer, lectr., educator; b. N.Y.C.; d. Isaac A. and Lisa (Joffe) Hourwich; student Columbia, U. Chgo.; B.A., N.Y. Sch. Social Work; m. Ferdinand Reyher, July 13, 1917 (div. 1934); 1 dau., Faith (Mrs. Melvin Jackson). Woman's suffrage worker for Women's Polit. Union, Nat. Woman's Party, N.Y., Boston, Chgo., and 30 states, 1915-23; feature writer Hearst's Internat. mag., Africa, 1923-24; advt. writer, editor J. Walter Thompson & Co., 1927-29; pub. relations asst. Joseph McKee (pres. bd. aldermen, later mayor), N.Y., 1930-31; cons., adviser Sears, Roebuck & Co., 1931-33; regional dir., profl., service, arts projects Fed. Works Progress Adminstrn., N.Y., N.E., 1935-37; asst. to dir., dir. motion pictures Information Service, W.P.A., 1937-39; exec. sec., mem. bd. dirs. Dominican Rep. Settlement Assn. Inc., 1939-43; weekly broadcast, City Fun with Children, sta. WYNC, N.Y., 1945-49, also radio series Behind the Scenes with U.N., 1946; mem. faculty New Sch. Social Research, N.Y.C., 1963-70. Cons., Internat. Inst. Women's Studies, Washington, 1971—. Mem. flying caravan del. People's Mandate Com. Inter-Am. Peace and Cooperation throughout 17 countries, South and Central Am., 1937. Author: The Stork Run, 1944; Babies and Puppies are Fun, 1944; My Mother is the Most Beautiful Woman in the World, 1945; Zulu Woman, 1948 (paperback edit. 1972); The Fon and His Hundred Wives, 1953. Editor anthology, Babies Keep Coming, 1947. Contbr. articles leading mags. and newspapers. Traveled South and Portuguese East Africa to gather material for books and articles, 1923-24, 24-25, North Africa, Europe, Russia, Near East, 1929. Nigeria, Brit. Cameroons, 1949-50, South Africa, 1950-51, Belgian Congo, Nigeria, Uganda, Kenya, Pakistan, India, Ceylon, Europe, 1957, 13 African countries, 1965, France, 1966. Address: 14 Washington Pl E New York City NY 10003 also Robinhood ME 04670

REYNAL, JEANNE, artist; b. White Plains, N.Y., Apr. 1, 1903; d. Eugene S. and Adele (Fitzgerald) Reynal; m. Thomas Sills, Aug. 1953. Exhibited mosaics in numerous galleries and museums, 1941—; exhibited mosaic sculpture Betty Parson Gallery, 1971, Newport (R.I.) Art Assn., 1971; executed murals State Capitol, Lincoln, Neb., 1965, 66, Our Lady of Fla. Roman Catholic Ch., 1962, S.S. Joachim and Anne Queens Village, L.I., N.Y., 1967, Travellers Club, Hartford, Conn.; travelling exhbn. U.S., 1964-67; film Mosaics, 1968. Tchr. Dord Fitz Gallery, Amarillo, Tex., 1964, Notre Dame U., Ind., 1969. Author: The Mosaics of Jeanne Reynal, 1964, revised, 1969. Address: 240 W 11th St New York City NY 10014

REYNOLDS, CAROLYN MARIE FRLAN (MRS. ARMAND J. REYNOLDS), lawyer; b. Santa Monica, Cal., May 26, 1939; d. Carl Martin and Mary Marie (Cargo) Frlan; student U. So. Cal., 1957-60; LL.B., U. Loyola, Los Angeles, 1963; m. Armand J. Reynolds, Sept. 5, 1965; children—Christopher, Cathleen. Admitted to Cal. bar, 1964; asst. U.S. atty. Central Dist. Cal., Los Angeles, 1964—. Recipient certificate of award Dept. Justice, 1969. Mem. Fed., Los Angeles County bar assns., State Bar Cal., Women Lawyers (bull. editor 1968), Los Angeles Zoo Assn. Democrat. Roman Catholic. Home: 2705 Outpost Dr Los Angeles CA 90068 Office: 312 N Spring St Los Angeles CA 90012

REYNOLDS, DORIS KOOI (MRS. JAMES CREW REYNOLDS), former Republican nat. committeewoman; b. Chgo.; d. Peter and Mary Helen (Brown) Kooi; ed. Lewis Inst., Chgo., and The Castle, Miss Mason's Sch., Tarrytown, N.Y.; m. James Crew Reynolds, Oct. 30, 1923; 1 dau., Crewe Kooi (Mrs. Selmer E. Moeller). Republican State committeewoman, Sheridan County, Wyo., 1936-37; pres. meeting to organize Nat. Fedn. Rep. Women's Clubs, 1937; mem. Rep. Nat. Com., 1937-48; organizer State Fedn. Women's Rep. Study Groups and Clubs of Wyo. (charter mem. Nat. Fedn. Women's Rep. Clubs), 1939; promoted passage of 50-50 Law in Wyo., 1939; mem. rules com. Rep. Nat. Conv., 1940, contests com., 1944, arrangements com., 1948. Mem. state com. Nat. War Fund; local radio chmn., United China Relief; mem. exec. com. and chmn. finance com., Sheridan Youth Center; pres. Sheridan Woman's Club, 1953-54; past pres. Bus. and Profl. Women's Club, Sheridan, past state fedn. parliamentarian, chmn. legislative com.; mem. Sheridan County Meml. Hosp. Aux.; dir. Grand View Addition Co., Bank of Commerce of Sheridan; former v.p., dir. Sheridan Flouring Mills, Inc.; pres., dir. D and D Hardware Co., Sheridan. Mem. Zoning Bd. for City of Sheridan, 1946-49; chmn. Legislative Com. Sheridan Hosp. Constrn. Bd. Adopted mem. Crow Indian Tribe. Mem. Nat. Assn. of Bank Women, Am. Legion Aux. (past unit pres., past dist. pres. Dept. of Wyo. (past state poppy chmn. and membership chmn.), C. of C. (past chmn. museum com.), VFW Aux., State Hist. Soc., Hist. and Museum Assn. of No. Wyo. and So. Mont. (pres.), P.T.A., Order Eastern Star (past matron, past grand chaplain, past grand marshal), Continental Confederation Adopted Indians, White Shrine of Jerusalem, Does (charter), Pythian Sisters (past chief), YWCA, YMCA (sustaining Century mem.), Daus. of the Nile (first queen Sahida Temple, Supreme Dep., 1951-52, 55-57), Social Order of Beauceant (past pres.), Internat. Order Job's Daus. (past grand guardian of Wyo., supreme dep. Nev., 1956-57, supreme jurisprudence com. 1956-59), Wyo. Fedn. Republican Women, Mont. Hist. Soc., Wyo. Beekeepers Assn., Community Concert Assn. (dir.), Order of Amaranth (charter), Sigma Tau Epsilon Pi, Phi Delta Sigma. Episcopalian. Clubs: Sheridan Garden, Sheridan Country, Bighorn Executive. Author: Handbook for Republican Party Workers, 1940, 44, 52, 56. Home: 334 W Burrows Sheridan WY 82801

REYNOLDS, GLADYS HOFER (MRS. ROBERT E. REYNOLDS), statistician; b. Freeman, S.D., May 13, 1936; d. Jacob M. and Elizabeth (Hofer) Hofer; B.A. cum laude, Yankton Coll., 1958; M.S., Va. Poly. Inst., 1960; Ph.D., Emory U., 1973; m. Robert E. Reynolds, Mar. 31, 1961; children—Robert Charles, Laurie Jo. Math. statistician Communicable Disease Center, Atlanta, 1960-63, chief exptl. design unit, 1963-65; asso. dept. biometry and statistics Emory U., Atlanta, 1965-67, NIH spl. research fellow, 1967-71; chief statistics research unit Bur. State Services Center for Disease Control, Atlanta, 1971—. Mem. Am. Statis. Assn. (chpt. sec. 1964-65, dist. rep. 1965-67), Biometrics Soc., N.Y. Acad. Sci., Sci. Research Soc. Am. Home: 2949 Hillbrook Way Decatur GA 30033 Office: Center for Disease Control 1600 Clifton Rd Atlanta GA 30333

REYNOLDS, HELEN LOUISE, editor; b. Washington, Aug. 27, 1925; d. John W. and Aurelia (Henlock) Reynolds; B.A., Dunbarton Coll., 1947; M.A., Am. U., 1972. Biochemist, NIH, Bethesda, Md., 1948-49; adminstrv. asst. Chgo. Apparatus Co., Washington, 1949-52; editorial asst. Am. Pharm. Assn., Washington, 1952-53; asso. editor Assn. Ofcl. Agrl. Chemists, Washington, 1953-60; tech. editor FDA, Washington, 1961—. Tchr. sci. writing U.S. Dept. Agr. Grad. Sch., 1962-64, FDA, 1965-67; editorial cons., 1958-60; tchr. sci. writing workshops, 1969-70. Recipient award of merit FDA, 1965. Fellow Assn. Ofcl. Analytical Chemists; mem. Am. Chem. Soc., A.A.A.S., Am. Inst. Chemists (treas. chpt. 1967), Soc. for Tech. Communication (sec. chpt. 1966-67), Fed. Editors Assn., Am. Soc. Information Sci., Council Biol. Editors. Club: Americana (Washington). Editor: Jour. Assn. Ofcl. Analytical Chemists, 1967—. Home: 4301 Columbia Pike Arlington VA 22204 Office: 200 C St SW Washington DC 20204

REYNOLDS, IRENE SHULL (MRS. KARL W. REYNOLDS), writer; b. Ft. Scott, Kan., Dec. 1, 1934; d. Burr Forest and Fern Emma (Strohm) Shull; B.S., McPherson Coll., 1957; postgrad. U. Kan., 1957-58; m. Karl W. Reynolds, July 21, 1957; children—Helen Karlene, Kevin Mark. Staff reporter Nevada (Ia.) Evening Jour., 1954-57; asst. dietitian U. Kan., Lawrence, 1958; tchr. Piper (Kan.) Rural High Sch., 1958-59; tchr. Bd. Edn., Lawrence, 1962-64; freelance writer articles for area publs., regional agrl. mags., fiction for religious publs., 1956—. Coordinator Douglas County Home Economists, 1959; vol. worker A.R.C., 1961-62; judge 4-H Fair, Douglas, Leavenworth, Franklin counties, 1963-68; leader 4-H Clubs, 1970—; county instr. 4-H Officers Tng. Sch., 1971-72. Mem. alumni bd. McPherson Coll., 1970-74; bd. dirs. Broken Arrow P.T.A. Mem. Women in Communications (local pres. 1972-73), Kan. Presswomen (dir.). Mem. Ch. of Brethren. Address: Route 2 Box 32 Lawrence KS 66044

REYNOLDS, JEAN EDWARDS, editor; b. Saginaw, Mich., Dec. 11, 1941; d. F. Perry and Katherine (Edwards) Reynolds; B.A., Wells Coll., 1963; M.A., City U. N.Y., 1967; m. Ernest A. Goldstein, Nov. 1, 1969 (div. May 1972). Sr. editor trade books Prentice-Hall, Inc., Englewood Cliffs, N.J., 1963-65, sr. editor and dir. children's books, 1965-69; sr. editor children's books McCall Pub. Co., N.Y.C., 1969-71; v.p., editorial dir. dir. Franklin Watts, Inc., N.Y.C., 1971—. Republican dist. leader 64th Assembly Dist., 1967-69; mem. Rep. State Com., 1968—. Mem. A.L.A., Child Study Assn., Women's Nat. Book Assn., Children's Book Council (dir. 1973—), Mensa. Home: Wallacks Dr Stamford CT 06902 Office: Franklin Watts Inc 730 Fifth Av New York City NY 10019

REYNOLDS, LESSIE PRATT MALLARD (MRS. CHRISTOPHER MACDONALD REYNOLDS), educator; b. Beulaville, N.C., Dec. 28, 1923; d. Alvin Raymond and Lessie Mae (Bostic) Mallard; A.B., U. N.C., 1953, M.A., 1957; Ph.D. (Horace Rackham grad. fellowship), U. Mich., 1969; m. Leslie Ralph Casey, Nov. 30, 1941 (div.); children—Mary (Mrs. Mary Casey Maltais), Michael; m. 2d, Christopher Macdonald Reynolds, Sept. 20, 1957. Film asst. U. N.C. Communication Center, Chapel Hill, 1955-56; staff mem. WUNC-TV, Chapel Hill, N.C., 1956-57; faculty Winthrop Coll., Rock Hill, S.C., 1957—, asso. prof. English, drama, affirmative action adminstr. 1973—. Free-lance theatre and film acting; free-lance theatre writing and directing. Second v.p., bd. mem. S.C. Council for Human Rights, 1973. Mem. League of Women Voters, Am. Assn. U. Women, Am. Assn. U. Profs., Womens Equity Action League, S.C. Employees Assn., Speech Communication Assn. (sec. mass communication div. 1973—), S.C. Council of Tchrs. of English (media com. 1972-73), Am. Theatre Assn., Southeastern Theatre Conf., South Atlantic Modern Lang. Assn., Phi Beta Kappa, Phi Kappa Phi, Zeta Phi Eta. Democrat. Home: 624 College Av Rock Hill SC 29730

REYNOLDS, LUCILE WILLIAMSON, former assn. exec.; b. Williamsport, Pa., Nov. 17, 1924; d. Richard Fortney and Grace Marie (Hollopeter) Williamson; student Dickinson Jr. Coll. (now Lycoming Coll.), 1942-43; m. Robert Edgar Reynolds, June 5, 1943; children—William, John, Judith (Mrs. Joseph McLain), Linda (Mrs. Russell Lowmiller). Officer local P.T.A.s, 1957-62; state chmn. program service Pa. P.T.A., 1962-64, state sec., 1964-66, v.p., 1966-68, pres., 1968-70; mem. nat. P.T.A. bd. mgrs., 1968-70, nat. v.p., 1973-75. Chmn. Lycoming County Health Council, 1968-71; sec. sex edn. for life in family Lycoming County Mental Health, 1970-71; mem. bd. Lycoming County Soc. for Mental Retardation, 1960-72; chmn. joint action com. P.T.A., Pa. Edn. Assn., Pa. Sch. Bds. Assn., 1969. Mem. Divine Providence Hosp. Aux. Hon. life mem. Nat., Pa. P.T.A.s; mem. Womens Club, Beta Sigma Phi. Home: 630 Lincoln Ave Williamsport PA 17701

REYNOLDS, MARIE ELIZABETH, ednl. adminstr.; b. Passaic, N.J., June 16, 1912; d. Patrick and Mary (Tracey) Reynolds; B.A. in Bus. Adminstrn., Syracuse U., 1935; M.A. in Guidance, N.Y. U., 1952, postgrad., 1952-67. With Passaic (N.J.) Pub. Libraries, 1929-30, U.S. Rubber Co., Passaic, 1930-31; tchr. bus. edn. Johnson City (N.Y.) High Sch., 1935-51; chmn. bus. edn. dept. Johnson City (N.Y.) Schs., 1951-59; pupil personnel services adminstr. Johnson City (N.Y.) Central Sch. Dist., 1958—. Mem. adv. Com. Broome Tech. Community Coll., 1968—. Bd. dirs. Broome County Social Planning Bd., 1969—, chmn. Family and Children's Soc. com.; pres. Broome County Com. Alcoholism, 1969-70; bd. dirs. Cath. Social Services Broome County, 1955-69, v.p. 1958-59, Sec. 1960-62; charter mem. Multiple Sclerosis Soc. Greater Broome County, 1965—, charter sec., 1964-66; exec. bd. Central N.Y. Sch. Study Council, 1971-75, Policy Council Broome County Head Start, 1971-74. Bd. dirs. Practical Nursing Sch., Binghamton (N.Y.) Pub. Schs., 1965—, sec., 1968—; bd. dirs. Broome County Youth Hostel for Retarded, Johnson City, 1974—. Named Nat. Bus. Tchr. of Year, Adminstrv. Mgmt. Soc., 1955. Mem. Nat. (charter), N.Y. State assns. pupil personnel adminstrs., N.Y. State Assn. Pupil Personnel Services Adminstrs. (sec. 1968, 69), Adminstrv. Mgmt. Soc. (internat. chmn. awards com. 1968-69), Triple Cities Adminstrv. Mgmt. Soc. (pres. 1961-62), Delta Kappa Gamma (chpt. pres. 1962-64), Delta Pi Epsilon. Clubs: Triple Cities Altrusa (charter mem., dir., v.p. 1972—), Catholic Women's (Binghamton, pres. 1954-55). Author: (with Emma Felter) Basic Clerical Practice, 1959; cons. A Career in the Modern Office, 1969, Basic Math Skills, 1972. Home: 360 Main St Johnson City NY 13790

REYNOLDS, MARTHA LOUISE, librarian; b. Indpls., Apr. 20, 1928; d. Richard Theodore and Gertrude (Ayers) Reynolds; A.B., Hanover Coll., 1950; M.S. in L.S., Ind. U., 1956. Br. asst. Indpls. Pub. Library, 1950-54; head adult services Vigo County Pub. Library, Terre Haute, Ind., 1955-63; asst. coordinator adult services Montgomery County Pub. Libraries, Bethesda, Md., 1963-65, asst. chief pub. services, 1965-67; dir. Frederick County Pub. Libraries, Frederick, Md., 1967—. Trainer library adult edn. project bur. studies in adult edn. Ind. U. and Purdue U., Bloomington, 1956-63; mem. adv. bd. Md. Materials Center, 1971—. Mem. Am. Assn. U. Women, Md. Assn. Pub. Library Adminstrs. (pres. 1970-71), Frederick Hist. Soc., Friends Nat. Ballet, A.L.A. (notable books council 1964-66, 74-76, chmn., 1965, bd. mem. staff organizations round table 1962-63, continuing edn. rep. reference and adult services div. 1972—), Ind. Library Assn. (chmn. in-service edn. com. 1957-59, mem. library certification com. 1959-61, editor Focus on Ind. Libraries 1961-63), Alpha Beta Alpha, Beta Phi Mu. Club: Frederick Woman's Civic. Home: 117 E 3d St Frederick MD 21701 Office: 520 N Market St Frederick MD 21701

REYNOLDS, MARY ANN VANDERZYL (MRS. HARRY EDWARD REYNOLDS), physician; b. Riverside, Cal., Sept. 10, 1934; d. John and Mary (Robinson) Vanderzyl; B.A., magna cum laude, Pomona Coll., 1956; M.D., Washington U., St. Louis, 1962; m. Harry Edward Reynolds, June 22, 1957; children—Katherine Ann, Ellen Marie. Intern, St. Lukes Hosp., St. Louis, 1962-63; research asst. to prof. and chmn. dept. pharmacology Washington U. Med. Sch., 1957-58; cons. med. outpatient dept. Washington U. div. St. Louis City Hosp., 1963-65; physician outpatient dept. Scenic Gen. Hosp., Modesto, Cal., 1967-72, Well Baby Clinic, Dept. Pub. Health, Stanislaus County, Cal., 1967-71; staff physician Emanuel Mental Health Center, Turlock, Cal., 1970—, Livingston (Cal.) Community Health Center, 1970-72. Med. cons. Bd. Edn., Turlock Elementary Sch. Dist. Program for Educationally Handicapped, 1969-70, Am. Cancer Soc., 1967-70; med. dir. Family Planning Clinic, Stanislaus County, Cal., 1969-70, bd. dirs., 1969—; bd. dirs. Salvation Army, Turlock, Cal., 1969—, med. cons., 1969—; lectr. veneral disease and sex edn. Stanislaus County Schs., 1967—. Mem. Stanislaus County Med. Soc., Cal. Med. Assn., Phi Beta Kappa. Home: 2665 Sierra Vista Turlock CA 95380 Office: 900 Delbon St Turlock CA 95380

REYNOLDS, MARY JANE SPENCER (MRS. ROBERT JACK REYNOLDS), occupational therapist; b. Cannonsburg, Pa., Feb. 15, 1932; d. Donald Agnew and Mary Anna (McKee) Spencer; B.A., Maryville Coll., 1953; B.S., Western Mich. U., 1956, postgrad., 1973; m. Robert Jack Reynolds, Dec. 30, 1957. Tchr. Chattanooga High Sch., 1953-54; occupational therapist VA. Hosp., Richmond, Va., 1956-57, Cerebral Palsy Clinic, Charleston, W. Va., 1958-64, W. Va. Rehab. Center, Institute, 1964—, instr. in counselor training program, 1965-70. Instr. Career Day, Charleston, W. Va., 1958—. Vol. bookkeeper Dunbar (W.Va.) Day Care Center, 1971—, Teen Canteen, Dunbar, W. Va., 1969-70. Tenn. Tuberculosis Assn. scholar, 1954-56. Mem. Am. Occupational Therapy Assn. (council on practice, 1967-73), W. Va. Occupational Therapy Assn. (v.p. 1972-73), Nat. Rehab. Assn., W. Va. Rehab. Assn. Presbyn. (deacon 1970-71, elder 1972—). Home: 2 Walnut Court Dunbar WV 25064 Office: W Va Rehab Center Institute WV 25112

REYNOLDS, MARY LOU, assn. exec.; b. Lamar, S.C., Sept. 25, 1917; d. William Baron and Ada (Spears) Reynolds; B.A., Columbia Coll., 1939; M.A., Scaritt Coll., 1943; A.N.R.C., Exec. Devel. Sch., 1961. Tchr., Chesterfield County, S.C., 1939-41; ch. social worker Meth. Ch., Hartshorne, Okla., 1943-44; social worker, field dir. Am. Nat. Red Cross, Southeastern states, 1945-54, exec. dir. Augusta chpt., 1954—. Bd. dirs. Richmond County Home Health Homemaker Agy. Mem. Nat. Assn. Social Workers (chpt. pres. 1956), Acad. Certified Social Workers, Ga. Conf. Social Welfare, Augusta Community Services Agys. Club. Methodist (mem. ofcl. bd.). Club: Pilot. Home: 2614 Springwood Ct Augusta GA 30901 Office: 811 12th St Augusta GA 30904

REYNOLDS, MARY TRACKETT (MRS. LLOYD G. REYNOLDS), polit. scientist; b. Milw., Jan. 11, 1914; d. James P. and Mary (Nachtwey) Trackett; B.A., U. Wis., 1935; M.A., 1935; postgrad. (Rebecca Green fellow) Radcliffe Coll., 1935-36; Ph.D. (U. fellow, Barnard fellow), Columbia, 1939; m. Lloyd G. Reynolds, June 12, 1937; children—Anne (Mrs. James F. Skinner), Priscilla (Mrs. Kermit Roosevelt, Jr.), Bruce. Research asst. Littauer Sch., Harvard, 1938-39; instr. Queens Coll., 1939-40, Hunter Coll., 1941-42, lectr., 1945-47; asso. in polit. sci. Johns Hopkins, 1942-43; lectr. Conn. Coll., 1947-48, asst. prof., 1948-50; asst. prof. U. Bridgeport, 1950-51; research asso. in econs. Yale, 1961-67; vis. lectr. in English, Yale, 1973—. Research asst. Pres.'s Com. Adminstrn. Mgmt., 1936; sr. economist Nat. Econ. Com., 1940; adminstrn. asst. Glenn L. Martin Aircraft Co., Balt., 1942-43; editorial asst. pub. adminstrn. com. Social Sci. Research Council, 1944-45; cons. Nat. Def. Adv. Commn., 1949, Nat. Municipal Assn., 1956, Orgn. Econ. Cooperation and Devel., Paris, 1964, U.S. State Dept.-AID 1965. Active Women's Civic League. Mem. Am. Polit. Sci. Assn., Dante Soc. Am., Am. Assn. U. Profs., Am. Soc. Pub. Adminstrn., League Women Voters, New Haven Hosp. Aux (bd. mem.), Phi Beta Kappa. Clubs: Lawn (New Haven); Appalachian Mountain. Author: Interdepartmental Committees in the National Administration, 1940; Joyce and Nora, 1964; Source Documents in Economic Development, 1966; Joyce's Debt to Dante, 1968; Two Essays on James Joyce, 1970; Joyce and Dante, 1974. Contbr. profl. jours. Home: 75 Old Hartford Turnpike Hamden CT 06517

REYNOLDS, MARYAN E., librarian; b. Mpls., Feb. 17, 1913; d. William Albert and Mable (Thyng) Reynolds; B.A., U. Minn., 1936; B.S., U. So. Cal., 1940. Circulation asst. Madera (Cal.) County Free Library, 1940-41; br. supr. Kern County Free Library, Bakersfield,

Cal., 1941-43; cons. Wash. State Library, Olympia, 1943-50, state librarian, 1951—; chief librarian Richland (Wash.) Pub. Library, 1950-51. Tchr. extension course U. Wash., 1944-46. Chmn. Interdeptl. Com. on Aging, 1963-64; dir. A.R.C., 1962—; sec. Gov.'s Commn. on Status of Women, 1963-71; gov.'s rep. on planning com. Wash. Conf. on Citizenship, 1963. Sec. bd. trustees. Citizens Conf. on Washington Cts. Mem. Capitol Hist. Soc. (exec. bd. 1963-66, pres. 1964-66), Am. Assn. U. Women (br. pres. 1962-64), A.L.A., Pacific N.W. (pres. 1969-71), Wash. State, Spl., Med. library assns., Wash. State Sch. Library Assn., Am. Soc. Pub. Adminstrs., Am. Assn. Adult Edn., Am. Assn. State Libraries (pres. 1965-66, exec. bd. 1964-67), Delta Kappa Gamma (hon.). Club: Soroptimist. Home: 3128 Villa Ct SE Lacey WA 98503 Office: Wash State Library Olympia WA 98504

REYNOLDS, MURIEL ELIZABETH, civic worker; b. Waterbury, Conn., June 23, 1903; d. Henry John and Susan (Goppelt) Reynolds; B.A., L.H.D., Wheaton Coll.; postgrad. N.Y.U. Grad. Sch. Bus., 1926-28. Tchr. social studies Bernardsville (N.J.) pub. schs., 1924-25; with Standard Oil Co., (N.J.), 1926-63, asst. to asst. sec., 1926-45, asst. sec. co., 1945-63, mgr. shareholder relations, 1948-63. Sec., bd. dirs. World Found., World Assn. Girl Scouts and Girl Guides, 1971—; nat. vol. Girl Scouts U.S.A., nat. bd. dirs., mem. exec. com., 1960-72, treas., 1963-72, mem. bus. and finance com., 1963—. Trustee Wheaton Coll., Norton, Mass., 1950—, Nat. Assembly Social Policy and Devel., Inc. Mem. Am. Assn. U. Women. Republican. Episcopalian. Clubs: Wheaton of N.J., Women's Nat. Republican. Home: 33 Duncan Hill Westfield NJ 07090

REYNOLDS, NANCY BRADFORD DUPONT (MRS. WILLIAM GLASGOW REYNOLDS), sculptor; b. Greenville, Del., Dec. 28, 1919; d. Eugene Eleuthere and Catherine Dulcinea (Moxham) duPont; student Goldey-Beacom Coll., Wilmington, Del., 1938; m. William Glasgow Reynolds, May 18, 1940; children—Kathrine Glasgow (Mrs. John Sturges, Jr.), William Bradford, Mary Parminter (Mrs. William Carter Bowles, Jr.), Cynthia duPont (Mrs. David Hillegas). Exhibited one man show Rehoboth (Del.) Art League, 1963; exhibited group shows Corcoran Gallery, Washington, 1943, Soc. Fine Arts, Wilmington, 1937, 38, 40, 41, 48, 50, 62, 65, N.A.D., N.Y.C., 1964, Pa. Mil. Coll., Chester, 1966, Del. Art Center, 1967; represented in permanent collections Wilmington Trust Co., E. I. duPont de Nemours & Co., Children's Home, Inc., Claymont, Del., Goldsbrough Bldg., Wilmington, Children's Bur., Wilmington, Stephenson Sci. Center, Nashville, Luterine Towers Bldg., Travelers Aid and Family Soc. Bldg., Wilmington, Wilmington. Guide, mem. research staff Henry Francis DuPont Winterthur Mus., 1955-63. Organizer vol. service Del. chpt. A.R.C., 1938-39; chmn. Com. for Revision Del. Child Adoption Law, 1950-52. Pres., bd. dirs. Children Bur. Del.; pres., trustee Childrens Home, Inc. Recipient Confrerie des Chevaliers du Tastevin Clos de Vougeot-Bourgogne France, 1960, Hort. award Garden Club Am., 1964. Mem. Pa. Hort. Soc., Wilmington Soc. Fine Arts, Brit. Embroidery Guild, English-Speaking Union, Mayflower Descs., Del. Hist. Soc., Colonial Dames, Am. Mus. in Britain, League Am. Pen Women, Nat. Trust For Hist. Preservation. Episcopalian. Clubs: Garden of Wilmington (past pres.), Garden of Am. (past asst. zone 4 chmn.), Vicmead Hunt, Greenville Country, Chevy Chase (Washington). Contbr. articles to profl. jours. Address: Foxwood Old Kennett Rd Greenville DE 19807

REYNOLDS, NAOMI FRANCES WARNECKE (MRS. WILLIAM D. REYNOLDS), musician; b. Clifton Hill, Mo.; d. Bruno Frederick and Louise (Galles) Warnecke; student Minn. U., 1917-18; m. William D. Reynolds, June 28, 1919 (dec. Nov. 1931); 1 son, George William. Co-owner, operator sta. KLZ, Denver, 1920-36; commentator Los Angeles Philharmonic Orch., 1938-45; radio chmn. Nat. Fedn. Music Clubs, 1937-51, visual chmn., 1951—; with Let's Talk Music, stas. KNX, KFI, KMPC, KCEA, Los Angeles, 1937-45; young artist auditions chmn. Sta. NFMC, 1959-63. Rec. sec. Nat. Assn. Am. Composers and Condrs., 1955—, Young Musicians Found., 1960-71, Music Guild, 1967—. Pub. relations chmn. Mayors Council Music and Art for Sr. Citizens, 1966—. Bd. dirs. So. Cal. Symphony Assn., 1960-62. Mem. Nat. Fedn. Music Clubs (chmn. nat. young artists' auditions), Sigma Alpha Iota (chpt. alumni past pres.). Home: 2130 Manning Av Los Angeles CA 90025

REYNOLDS, PEGGY (MARJORIE LOUISE) (MRS. GEORGE RICHARD REYNOLDS), publisher; b. Takoma Park, Md., Sept. 25, 1924; d. Lewis Henry and Minna (Abramson) Weiss; student U. Mo., 1941-42; B.A. in Polit. Sci., U. Mich., 1944; postgrad. George Washington U., 1946-47, U.S. Dept. Agr. Grad. Sch., 1963-64; m. George Richard Reynolds, July 31, 1954; 1 son, Michael Alan. Mgr., Aero Ins. Agy., Washington, 1947-57; columnist Washington Post, 1955-57; editor Mercer Island (Wash.) Reporter, 1967-68, pub., 1968—. Mem. Wash. Newspaper Pubs. Assn., Nat. Press Photographers Assn., Wash. Press Women. Home: 7727 SE 58th St Mercer Island WA 98040 Office: 2737 SE 77th St Mercer Island WA 98040

REYNOLDS, SARA SCHIEVER (MRS. JAMES HARRY REYNOLDS), physician; b. Butler, Pa., May 14, 1928; d. John Lewis and Gladys Kathryn (Kramerer) Schiever; B.S., Carnegie Inst. Tech., 1949; M.D., Med. Coll. Pa., 1953; m. James Harry Reynolds, June 24, 1952; children—James N., Ruth L., Grace R., John G., Carol E., Sara A. Intern, Bryn Mawr (Pa.) Hosp.; resident Norristown (Pa.) State Hosp.; gen. practice medicine, Wind Ridge, Pa., 1956-61, Knoxville, Pa., 1961-64; mem. staff Ariz. State Hosp., Phoenix, 1965-72; night coverage Maricopa County Health Dept., Phoenix, 1968-72; gen. practice medicine, Phoenix, 1972—. Mem. A.M.A., Christian Med. Soc., Am. Acad. Family Practice. Home: 2719 E Turney Av Phoenix AZ 85016

REYNOLDS, VALRAE, curator; b. San Francisco, Dec. 18, 1944; d. Ralph Stanley and Valberta May (Eversole) Reynolds; B.A., U. Cal. at Davis, 1966; M.A., N.Y. U., 1968, postgrad. (Ford Found. fellow), 1968-69; m. Richard Lee Huffman, Sept. 14, 1974. Curatorial asst. arms and armor dept. Met. Mus. Art, N.Y.C., 1968, Brundage collection, San Francisco, 1969; asst. curator Oriental collection Newark Mus., 1969-70, curator, 1970—. Mem. Asia Soc., Japan Soc., China Inst., N.Y.C., Tibet Soc. Bloomington. Contbr. articles to profl. publs. Home: 192 President St Brooklyn NY 11231 Office: 43 Washington St Newark NJ 07101

REYNOLDS, WYNETKA ANN KING (MRS. REX REYNOLDS, JR.), scientist; b. Coffeyville, Kan.; d. John E. and Glennie (Beanland) King; B.S., Kan. State Tchrs. Coll., 1958, M.S. (NSF fellow, hon. Woodrow Wilson fellow), 1958-62; Ph.D., U. Ia., 1962; m. Rex Reynolds, Jr., Sept. 13, 1958; children—Rachel Rebecca, Rex King. Asst. prof. biology Ball State U., 1962-65; asst. prof. anatomy U. Ill. Med. Center, Chgo., 1965-68, asso. prof., 1968-73, prof., 1973—. Recipient award Central Assn. Obstetrics and Gynecology, 1968, Outstanding Alumnus award Kan. State Tchrs. Coll., 1972. Mem. A.A.A.S., Am. Inst. Biol. Scis., Am. Soc. Zoologists, Nat. Assn. Biology Tchrs., Soc. Gynecol. Invest., Soc. Developmental Biology, Endocrine Soc., Am. Assn. Anatomists, Sigma Xi. Author: Key to Life, 1966; Structure and Function of the Cell, 1966; Mitosis and Meiosis, 1968; Heredity, 1970. Home: 322 Scottswood Rd Riverside IL 60546 Office: 1853 W Polk St Chicago IL 60612

RHETTA, HELEN LOWE, physician; b. Balt., Dec. 9, 1912; d. Barnett Milton and Georgia Clarissa (Brown) Rhetta; B.A., U. Mich., 1934; M.D., U. Mich., 1937, M.P.H. (USPHS fellow 1966-67), 1967. Intern Provident Hosp., Chgo., 1937-38, resident, 1938-39; attending physician Provident Hosp., Chgo., 1938-61, Chgo. Bd. Health, 1940-48, Cook County Bd. Health, 1951-67; practice medicine specializing in internal medicine, Chgo., 1940—; mem. staff Provident Hosp., Chgo.; clin. instr. dept. internal medicine U. Ill. at Chgo., 1948-61. Med. cons., regional program dir. Dept. Health, Edn. and Welfare, Chgo., 1968—. Recipient Superior Service award Dept. Health, Edn. and Welfare, 1971. Mem. A.M.A., Ill. Med. Assn., Chgo. Med. Soc., Chgo. Diabetes Assn., Am. Pub. Health Assn., Delta Sigma Theta. Home: 9404 S Martin Luther King Dr Chicago IL 60619 Office: 300 S Wacker Dr Chicago IL 60606

RHINE, LOUISA ELLA WECKESSER (MRS. JOSEPH BANKS RHINE), editor; b. Sanborn, N.Y., Nov. 9, 1891; d. Christian and Ella Elizabeth (Long) Weckesser; student Wooster Coll., 1914-17; B.S., U. Chgo., 1919, M.S., 1921, Ph.D., 1923; m. Joseph Banks Rhine, Apr. 8, 1920; children—Robert, Sara Louise Feather, Elizabeth, Rosemary (Mrs. Ian Fergusson). Research asst. Parapsychology Lab., Duke, 1948-65; with Inst. for Parapsychology Durham, N.C., 1965—, asst. editor Jour. Parapsychology, 1957—. Author: Hidden Channels of the Mind, 1961; Mind Over Matter, 1970; ESP in Life and Lab, 1967; Psi, What is it, 1975? Home: Route 3 Hillsborough NC 27278 Office: PO Box 6847 College Station Durham NC 27708

RHOADS, GERALDINE EMELINE, editor; b. Phila., Jan. 29, 1914; d. Lawrence Dry and Alice Fegley (Rice) Rhoads; A.B., Bryn Mawr Coll., 1935; unmarried. Publicity asst., Bryn Mawr (Pa.) Coll., 1935-37; asst. Internat. Students House, Phila., 1937-39; mng. editor The Woman mag., N.Y.C., 1939-42; editor Life Story mag., 1942-45; editor Today's Woman mag., N.Y.C., 1945-52, Today's Family mag., 1952-53; lectr. Columbia, 1954-56; asso. editor Readers Digest, 1954-55; producer NBC, 1955-56; asso. editor Ladies Home Jour., 1956-62, mng. editor, 1962-63; exec. editor McCall's mag., 1963-66; editor Woman's Day Mag., 1966—, v.p., 1972—. Dir. Green Giant Co., 1972—. Trustee Consumer Research Inst., 1971—. Mem. Fashion Group, Nat. Home Fashions League, Am. Soc. Mag. Editors (chmn. exec. com. 1971—), Washington Press Club (dir.). Home: 865 First Av New York City NY 10017 Office: 1515 Broadway New York City NY 10036

RHOADS, KATHRYN LYNN, pub. relations exec.; b. Shreveport, La., July 19, 1948; d. Paul Stewart and Jo Ann (Powell) Rhoads; B.A., Tex. Tech U., 1970; art courses Houston Community Coll., 1972. Asst. to pres. R.Z. Estes, Inc., advt. and pub. relations, Houston, 1971-72; publs. editor Tex. Inst. for Rehab. and Research, Houston, 1972; asst. dir. pub. relations and safety Am. Automobile Assn., Houston, 1972—. Mem. Women in Communications (sec. 1969-70), Sigma Delta Chi, Gamma Alpha Chi. Republican. Contbr. weekly travel column to various Tex. newspapers. Home: 4419 Meyerwood Houston TX 77035 Office: PO Box 1986 Houston TX 77001

RHOADES, BONNIE JEANNE, personnel exec.; b. Carbondale, Pa., Mar. 9, 1946; d. George Wallace and Elizabeth Mertie (Aylesworth) Rhoades; A.A., Keystone Jr. Coll., 1966; B.A. (grantee), Wilson Coll., 1968; M.A., U. Conn., 1969; m. Wayne Denis Bouchard, Jan. 15, 1972. Asst. registrar, student counselor U. Conn., Torrington, 1969-71; registrar Wilson Coll., Chambersburg, Pa., 1971-73; personnel specialist C.H. Masland & Sons, Carlisle, Pa., 1973—. Tchr. continuing edn. for adults U. Conn., 1971. Mem. Pennsylvanians for Women's Rights (coordinator legislative information center 1973). Democrat. Home: 6 Cumberland Dr Carlisle PA 17013 Office: 50 Spring Rd Carlisle PA 17013

RHODES, KATHLEEN, educator; b. London, Eng., Feb. 22, 1914 (came to U.S. 1946, naturalized, 1956); d. James Furness and Anne (Fletcher) Rhodes; tchrs. certificate, London U., 1935; M.S., Cornell U., 1947, Ph.D., 1950. Research asst. in Eng., 1935-36; tchr. secondary sch., 1936-37, Technol. Coll., 1937-41, Tng. Coll. in Eng., 1941-46; research asst. Cornell U., 1947-49; asso. N.Y. State Edn. Dept., 1949-53; chmn. home econs. dept. Douglass Coll., Rutgers U., 1953-56; asso. prof., prof. N.Y. State Coll. Human Ecology, Cornell U., Ithaca, 1956—, acting chmn. community service edn. dept., 1970-72; Fulbright lectr. U. Ghana, 1963-64, AID cons., 1964-65; spl. participant FAO/ECA/SIDA Seminar, Addis Abada, Ethiopia, 1972; cons. internat. programs Coll. Home Econs., U. Minn., 1969, FAO, Rome, 1973. Social Sci. Research Council grantee for African Studies, 1969-70. Mem. Am. Home Econs. Assn., Am. Ednl. Research Assn., Comparative and Internat. Edn. Soc., Phi Kappa Phi, Omicron Nu, Phi Upsilon Omicron, Pi Lambda Theta. Co-author: Your Life in the Family, 1965. Contbr. articles to profl. jours. Home: 206 Highgate Rd Ithaca NY 14850

RHODES, KATHLEEN HABLE, physician; b. Chippewa Falls, Wis., Jan. 23, 1937; d. Albert Peter and Felicitas Anne (Bruns) Hable; B.S., U. Wis., 1961, M.D., 1965. Intern, St. Elizabeth's Hosp., Boston, 1965-66; resident pediatrics, 1966-67; fellow pediatrics Mayo Clinic, Rochester, Minn., 1967-70, cons. pediatrics and infectious diseases 1971—; fellow infectious disease U. Minn., Mpls., 1970-71. Research fellow dept. neuropathology U. Wis., Madison, 1962-64. Recipient Westinghouse NSF award, 1955, outstanding achievement award Mayo Clinic, 1971. Mem. Am. Soc. Microbiology, Am. Acad. Pediatrics. Contbr. articles to profl. pubs. Home: 718 SW 5th St Rochester MN 55901 Office: 200 1st St SW Rochester MN 55901

RHODES, LUCILLE, prep. sch. dir.; b. Cleve., Dec. 19, 1921; d. Phillip Nathan and Rose (Werlin) Warshaw; m. Leo D. Rhodes, Dec. 19, 1957 (dec. May 1968); children—Anita (Mrs. Douglas M. Herron), Michelle; stepchildren—Janet (Mrs. James Lathan), John. Dir. personnel Fedn. Jewish Charities, Phila., 1948-57; nat. exec. dir. Pioneer Women, welfare service agy., N.Y.C., 1959-60; asst. dir. Robert Louis Stevenson Sch., ind. prep. sch. for spl. edn. adolescents, N.Y.C., 1961-68, dir., 1968—. Cons. spl. edn. Mem. Am. Assn. Sch. Adminstrs., Council for Exceptional Children, Assn. Tchrs. in Ind. Schs. Editor Stevenson Resource File, Notes from Stevenson. Home: 118 Riverside Dr New York City NY 10024 Office: 24 W 74th St New York City NY 10023

RHODES, MARY ELIZABETH FRECHTLING (MRS. IRWIN S. RHODES), editor; b. Madison, Ind., May 3, 1911; d. George William and Laura (Lory) Frechtling; student, Butler U., 1928-30; student Herron Art Sch., 1925-30; m. Irwin S. Rhodes, Dec. 12, 1941; children—Elana Susan, Irwin Lawrence. With Marx-Flarsheim Advt. Co., Cin., 1930-32; exec. sec. Perfect Mfg. Co., Cin., 1932-36; sales promotion, real estate mgmt. Am. Service Assos., Cin., 1936-40; asst. editor The Papers of John Marshall, U. Okla. Press, 1969, The Papers of Roger B. Taney, 1970—. Chmn. Cin. Fine Arts Dr., 1947-59, Cin. Summer Opera Womens Com., 1966-67; mem. adv. bd. Air Pollution Control League, 1958-62; adv. com. Cin. Juvenile Ct., 1960—; mem. exec. com. Am. Cancer Soc. Balls, 1966—; chmn., v.p. Women's Com. Cin. Symphony Orch., 1959-64; sponsor Irwin S. and Elizabeth F. Rhodes Legal History Collection, U. Okla. Mem. Soc. Ind. Pioneers, Cin., Ky., Md., Lancaster County (Pa.) hist. socs., D.A.R. Editor: C.A.R. Nat. Mag., 1966-67; asst. editor, research dir. The Papers of John Marshall, 1969, The Papers of Roger Brooke Taney. Home: 3815 Erie Av Cincinnati OH 45208

RHODES, NINA ROMAN FRIED, polit. worker, actress; b. Bklyn., Jan. 8, 1934; d. Jack and Claire (Crane) Fried; student Los Angeles Community Coll., 1962, Valley Jr. Coll., 1917; m. Michael Rhodes, June 4, 1961 (div.); children—Ross, Laura, Camila. Co-star Morningstar, NBC-TV, 1966-67; appeared in numerous TV shows including, Gunsmoke, NBC Movie of Week, Barnaby Jones, Toma. Tchr. asst. in dance, yoga exercise, and drama classes in community center for problem children, Los Angeles, 1968-72. Bd. dirs. Dem. Women's Forum, 1968-72, dir. of press, 1968; mem. Robert Kennedy Finance Com., 1968; del. Dem. Nat. Conv., 1968; mem. adv. bd. Assemblyman Howard Berman, 1972; mem. Cal. Dem. State Central Com., 1968—. Recipient Key Woman award Los Angeles Dem. party, 1970, 71. Jewish religion. Address: 4342 Nogales Dr Tarzana CA 91356

RHODES, VELMA MAY DAINES (MRS. HOWARD W. RHODES), lawyer; b. Firth, Ida., Sept. 4, 1940; d. Oliver J. and Lila M. (Barfuss) Daines; student Brigham Young U., 1958-59, Utah State U., 1959-60; LL.B., U. West Los Angeles, 1971; m. Howard W. Rhodes, Aug. 29, 1970; adopted children—Carolyn, Denise. Admitted to Cal. bar, 1971; trust adminstr. Security Nat. Bank, Century City br., 1969-70; practiced in Santa Monica, 1971—. Mem. Assistance League Santa Monica; active Blue Birds, Camp Fire Girls. Address: 463 24th St Santa Monica CA 90402

RHODES, WANDA MAE, educator; b. Hart, Tex., Feb. 9, 1930; d. Olen Lee and Nellie Maye (Reynolds) Rhodes; B.S., Bethany Nazarene Coll., 1952; M.S., Ore. State U., 1957; D. Phys. Edn., Ind. U., 1962. Prof., N.W. Nazarene Coll., Nampa, Ida., 1952-60; grad. asst. Ind. U., Bloomington, 1960-62; prof. phys. edn. Bethany Nazarene Coll., Okla., 1962—, dean of women, 1962-66. Treas. Okla. Bd. Women Ofcls., 1964—. Bd. mgmt. Westside YMCA, Bethany, Okla., 1965—; bd. dirs. Okla. City Tennis Assn., 1969-70. Mem. Okla. Assn. Health, Phys. Edn. and Recreation (past sec.-treas.), A.A.H.P.E.R., So. Assn. Coll. Women Phys. Edn., Oklahoma City Assn. (dir. 1970—), Phi Kappa Phi, Omicron Nu, Phi Lambda Theta. Mem. Nazarene Ch. Home: 1231 Chisholm Rd Oklahoma City OK 73127 Office: Bethany OK 73008

RHODUS, SALLY JEAN ENFIELD (MRS. DILLARD GROVER RHODUS), editor; b. Hutchinson, Kan., Oct. 28, 1947; d. Charlie Franklin and Katharine Buena Vista (Ebersole) Enfield; A.A., Hutchinson Community Jr. Coll., 1967; student Ft. Hays State Coll., 1967; B.S., Kan. State U., 1970; m. Dillard Grover Rhodus, Sept. 30, 1972. Teaching asst. editing Kan. State U., Manhattan, 1970; tchr. English and journalism Kingman (Kan.) Pub. Schs., 1970-71; feature writer and gen. news reporter Daily News of Johnson County, Olathe, Kan., 1971-73; feature writer, pub. relations asst. editor house organ ISC Industries, Inc., Kansas City, Mo., 1973—. Mem. Internat. Assn. Bus. Communicators, Kansas City Bus. Communicators. Home: Route 1 Excelsior Springs MO 64024 Office: 3430 Broadway PO Box 386 Kansas City MO 64141

RHUDE, BETH ESTHER, psychologist, clergyman; b. Quincy, Mass., July 1, 1935; d. Clarel P. and Mary E. (MacKenzie) Rhude; student Oberlin Coll., 1954-55; B.A. magna cum laude, Boston U., 1957; B.D., Harvard, 1960; Ed.D. (Pres.'s scholar), Columbia, 1967; postgrad. Union Theol. Sem., 1960, Mich. State U., 1968, N.Y. U., 1972—; m. Richard Morse Colgate. Ordained to ministry United Ch. of Christ, 1964; asst. chaplain Mt. Holyoke Coll., South Hadley, Mass., 1960-63; grad. fellow Danforth Found., St. Louis, 1963-64; chaplain, asst. prof. U. Seven Seas, Orange, Cal., 1964-65; campus minister Riverside Ch., N.Y.C., 1965-66; lectr. psychology, counselor Queensboro Community Coll., N.Y.C., 1966-67; dean of women, lectr. religion Dickinson Coll., Carlisle, Pa., 1967-68; psychotherapist in pvt. practice, N.Y.C., 1968—; adj. prof. N.Y.U., 1973—; family therapist Payne Whitney Clinic, 1973—. Asst. dir. Ecumenical Found. Higher Edn. and Religion, N.Y.C., 1968-71; lectr. N.Y. Theol. Sem., 1972. Billings scholar, 1954-57; Ford Travel grantee, 1962; Nat. Def. Edn. Act grantee, 1965, 67, 68; Danforth grantee, 1963; others. Mem. Nat. Assn. Coll. and Univ. Chaplains, Am. Psychol. Assn., Am. Assn. Women Deans and Counselors, Am. Assn. U. Profs., Am. Assn. U. Women, Am. Assn. Personnel and Guidance Counselors, Am. Assn. Marriage and Family Counselors, Inst. Practicing Psychotherapists, Ortho Psychiatry Assn., Am. Assn. for Higher Edn., Am. Acad. Psychotherapists, Phi Beta Kappa. Home: 501 W 123d St New York City NY 10027 Office: 315 Central Park W New York City NY 10025

RHYMER, MARY FRANCES, hist. mus. curator; b. Morris, Ill., Aug. 16, 1909; d. Kay Hiram and Caroline Lucille (Crewes) Murray; B.A., Ill. Wesleyan U., 1931; m. Paul Mills Rhymer, July 31, 1933 (dec. 1964); 1 son, Paul Parke. Interior designer, Chgo., 1949-52; curator prints and photographs Chgo. Hist. Soc., 1952—. Mem. Ill., Spl. libraries assns., Chgo. Chpt. Soc. Archtl. Historians. Episcopalian. Editor: The Small House Half-Way Up in the Next Block/Paul Rhymer's Vic and Sade, 1972. Address: 1366 N Dearborn Pkwy Chicago IL 60610

RHYNE, MARIE BRITT, physician, scientist; b. Lumberton, N.C., June 11, 1927; d. Luther Johnson and Beta (Elkins) Britt; B.S., Duke, 1946; M.D., Johns Hopkins, 1950, now postgrad. in epidemiology; 1 dau., Theresa Marie. Intern, sr. resident N.C. Bapt. Hosp., Winston-Salem, 1950-51, 52-53; house officer (intern) Johns Hopkins Hosp., Balt., 1951-52; fellow, chief resident U. Colo. Med. Center, Denver, 1953-55; practice pediatrics, Lumberton, 1955-57; fellow Allergy Found. Am. at Johns Hopkins, Duke, Charlotte Meml. Hosp., 1957-60; instr., asst. prof. pediatrics Johns Hopkins, Balt., 1960-68, dir. div. allergy, dept. pediatrics, 1960-68, spl. research fellow Nat. Center Health Services, Research and Devel., 1968-71, research asso. med. care and hosps., 1971-72. Fellow Am. Acad. Allergy, Am. Acad. Pediatrics, Royal Society Health; mem. Am. Thoracic Soc., A.M.A., Am. Pub. Health Assn., Royal Soc. Medicine (affiliate). Research and publs. in fields immunology, epidemiology, allergy, health services. Home: 127 Greenridge Rd Lutherville MD 21093 Office: Dept of Epidemiology Johns Hopkins U Sch Hygiene and Pub Health Baltimore MD

RICCA, ROCHELLE PEGGY SCUDERI, real estate broker; b. N.Y.C., Mar. 27; student N.Y. U., 1941-42, 43-44; m. Desiderio Ricca, June 30, 1935; 1 dau., Lois (Mrs. Theodore Wilson Markowski). Med. sec., N.Y.C., 1934-35; profl. mgmt. cons., N.Y.C., 1940-42; owner Realty & Exchange Co., Jamaica, N.Y., 1944—. Field cons., dir. instr. Profl. Guidance Inst., also Profl. Secretarial Inst., 1940-42. Vol. worker mental health Creedmore Project, Soroptimists, 1955-65; pres. Queens Opera Guild, 1962—; lectr. on safety of teenage drivers, 1955-57. Mem. county com. Women's Republican Club, Richmond Hill, 1942—; mem. Women's Nat. Rep. Club, 1968—; campaign chmn. for Nixon-Agnew, Rep. Bus. Women's Club Queens County, 1968, vice chmn., 1972—. Recipient Carol Lane award Soroptimists, 1955, 56, 57. Mem. Real Estate Brokers Queens County (dir. 1963—), Real Estate Women's Brokers Assn. (pres. 1966). Club: Soroptimist (pres. Kew Forest, N.Y. 1966). Address: 139-06 Pershing Crescent Briarwood Jamaica NY 11435

RICE, ANNABEL HESS (MRS. GLENN RICE), educator; b. Clovis, N.M., Mar. 22, 1912; d. Aaron Columbus and Sarah (Smith) Hess; B.A., Coll. of Ozarks, 1929; postgrad. (Scottish Rite grad. scholar 1960) La. State U., M.Ed., 1965; postgrad. (Ark. Congress P.T.A.'s grad. scholar) Miss. Coll., summer 1962; m. Glenn Rice, June 1, 1930; children—Ann Fontaine (Mrs. Donovan Webster Parker), Linda Celine (Mrs. Don Randolph Anderson), Rebecca Hess (Mrs. Bradley John Ilg). Tchr. bus. edn. pub. schs., Stamps, Ark., 1929-30, McGehee, Ark., 1940-45; legal sec. Brewer & Cracraft, attys., Helena, Ark., 1930-32; tchr. bus. edn. Dumas (Ark.) High Sch., 1932-34, guidance counselor, 1960—; sec. to pres. Stimson Lumber Trust, Dumas, 1934-36; asst. credit mgr. Gus Blass Co., Little Rock, 1936-38; tchr., guidance counselor Tillar (Ark.) High Sch., 1951-59. Charter mem. Ark. Gov.'s Adv. Council Edn., 1954-57; charter mem., mem. adv. council secondary edn. Ark. Dept. Edn., 1957; chmn. Desha County Com. Edn. Exceptional Children, 1960-62. Mem. Hwy. Garden Club, Walnut Lake County Club, Desha County Hosp. Aux.; mem. edn. unit Civil Def., Dumas; mem. Ark. Post council Girl Scouts U.S.A. Recipient Service award Girl Scouts U.S.A., 1958, 63. Mem. Ark. Assn. Student Councils Exec. Bd. (rec. sec. 1955—), Am. Personnel and Guidance Assn., Ark. Sch. Counselors Assn., Ark. Women Deans and Counselors Assn., N.E.A., Ark. Edn. Assn., Desha County Tchrs. Assn., Bus. and Profl. Women's Club, Am. Assn. U. Women. U.D.C., Phi Lambda Pi, Delta Kappa Gamma. Methodist (steward). Home: PO Box 2 Tillar AR 71670 Office: 315 S College St Dumas AR 71639

RICE, BEVERLY ANN (MRS. LARRY T. RICE), dept. store exec.; b. Evansville Ind., Feb. 2, 1934; d. Howard H. and Grace M. (Sawin) Boegaholtz; B.S., Ind. U., 1956; m. Larry T. Rice, Aug. 6, 1961. Asst. to fashion dir. L.S. Ayres & Co., Indpls., 1956-59, buyer, designer, 1959-65, fashion dir., 1965-66, div. mdse. mgr. better apparel, 1966-69, div. v.p., 1969-73, v.p., 1973—. Mem. N.Y. Fashion Group, 1965-72; sponsor better dress com. Asso. Merchandising Corp. Mem. Women's com. Ind. Symphony Soc. Mem. Women's C. of C., Ind. U. Alumni Assn., Indpls. Mus. Art, Alpha Omicron Pi, Beta Sigma Pi. Presbyn. Home: 4532 N Pennsylvania St Indianapolis IN 46205 Office: 1 W Washington St Indianapolis IN 46204

RICE, CLOVITA POWERS (MRS. CLARENCE RICE), educator, poet; b. Fayetteville, Ark., July 17, 1929; d. Elmer Herman and Mary Ola (Stotts) Powers; B.A., U. Ark., 1964; M.S., Ark. State U., 1965; m. Clarence Rice, Dec. 16, 1949; children—Joe David, Robbie Ann, Vicki Lee. Grad. asst. English, Ark. State U., Jonesboro, 1964-65; tchr. English and Spanish, Fuller High Sch., Little Rock, 1965-68, Mills High Sch., Little Rock, 1969—. Poetry cons. various local workshops. Recipient silver award for promoting poetry South and West, 1969; named Ark. Poet of Present, 1969. Mem. Poetry Soc. Am., Nat. League Am. Pen Women, South and West (dir.), Poets Roundtable Ark. Author: Blow Out the Sun, 1967; Red Balloons for the Major, 1969. Editor: Voices Internat., 1969—. Home: 6804 Cloverdale Dr Little Rock AR 72209

RICE, DOROTHY PECHMAN (MRS. JOHN DONALD), med. economist; b. Bkly., June 11, 1922; d. Gershon and Lena (Schiff) Pechman; student Bklyn. Coll., 1938-39; B.A., U. Wis., 1941; m. John Donald Rice, Apr. 3, 1943; children—Kenneth D., Donald B., Thomas H. With hosp. and med. facilities USPHS, Washington, 1960-61; med. econs. studies, Social Security Adminstrn., 1962-63, health econs. br. Community Health Service, USPHS, 1964-65; chief health ins. research br. Social Security Adminstrn., 1966-72, dep. asst. commr. for research and statistics, 1972—. Mem. U.S. Nat. com. Vital and Health Statistics; evaluation com. Nat. Center Health Statistics; Med. Care and Med. Econs. Adv. Com. Active PTA, 1955-60. Recipient Social Security Adminstrn. citation, 1968, Distinguished Service medal Dept. Health, Edn. and Welfare, 1974. Fellow Am. Pub. Health Assn.; mem. Inst. Medicine, Am. Econ. Assn., League Women Voters. Developer health ins. research program Social Securities Adminstrn. Contbr. articles to profl. jours. Home: 8410 Barron St Takoma Park MD 20012 Office: Office of Research and Statistics Social Security Adminstrn Dept Health Edn and Welfare 1875 Connecticut Av NW Room 1121 Washington DC 20009

RICE, EMILY MARIE (MRS. BERNARD RICE), lawyer; b. St. Louis, June 24, 1922; d. Herman and Freda S. (Cohn) Cronheim; A.B., Washington U., St. Louis, 1942, J.D., 1944; m. Bernard Rice, July 3, 1954; children—Ellen Sue, Nancy, Andrew, Henry, Rosemary. Admitted to Mo. Bar, 1944; appellate atty. Nat. Labor Relations Bd., Washington, 1944-47; staff counsel teamsters local, St. Louis, 1949-50; regional dir. Ams. for Democratic Action, St. Louis, 1950-52; asst. dir. Mayors Manpower Planning Office, St. Louis, 1970-71; dep. dir. Mayor's Council on Youth, 1973-74; exec. dir. Mo. State Council on the Arts, 1974—. Sec., Jewish Community Relations Council, 1965, Suicide Prevention, Inc., 1969, Am. Jewish Com. St. Louis, 1967; v.p. U. Mo. Extension Council, 1968-72. Bd. dirs. White House Conf. on Edn., St. Louis, 1968-74, St. Louis Mental Health Assn., 1950-65. Mem. Mo. Bar Assn., Nat. Council Jewish Women (v.p. 1959), Order of Coif, Phi Beta Kappa. Home: 7456 Parkdale St St Louis MO 63105 Office: 111 S Bemiston St Louis MO 63105

RICE, HELENE CALLAHAN (MRS. STANLEY ROHR RICE), club woman; b. N.Y.C., Feb. 6, 1914; d. Denis J. and Harriet (Donovan) Callahan; student Coll. of New Rochelle, 1934; student Am. Acad. Dramatic Art, 1935; m. Stanley Rohr Rice, July 23, 1936; children—Gloria (Mrs. John Paul Clark), Stanley Rohr, Diane (Mrs. George E. Davis). Goldwyn girl United Artists Studio, Hollywood, Cal., 1933-34. Pres., Stanley R. Rice Found. Mem. Greenwich Hosp. Aux.; nurse's aide Conn. Blood Bk. Program; dist. chmn., A.R.C., Greenwich; bd. dirs. St. Joseph's Hosp., Stamford, Conn. Mem. St. Elizabeth Guild, Greenwich Woman's Club, Internat. Platform Com. Mem. Womens Nat. Rep. Club. Recipient presdl. citation A.R.C., 1955. Clubs: University (Sarasota); Bird Key Yacht. Home: Brookside Dr Greenwich CT 06830 also 343 Bob White Way Sarasota FL 33579

RICE, JOAN ANN, journalist; b. Akron, O., Aug. 14, 1942; d. John Benjamin and Nancy Bertha (Zeig) Rice; B.A., Kent State U., 1964. Reporter Kent-Ravenna Record Courier newspaper, Kent, O., 1963-65, women's dept. editor, 1965-66; teen writer Akron (O.) Beacon Jour. newspaper, 1966-71, fashion writer, 1971—. Writer-broadcaster teen radio show sta. WAKR, Akron, 1966-69. Recipient Youth Service award YMCA, 1966, Fashion Board award J.C. Penney Co., 1968, Am. Legion Service citation, 1968. Mem. Ohio Newspaper Women's Assn. (awards 1969, 74), Ohio Press Women (awards 1968-70, 74), Kent State Journalism Alumni Assn., Women in Communications (pres. 1969-70, 70-71), Soc. Profl. Journalists, Sigma Delta Chi. Roman Catholic. Clubs: Hakko-Ryu Ju Jitsu Fedn., Akron Press. Home: 1101 Independence Av Apt 205 Akron OH 44310 Office: Akron Beacon Journal 44 E Exchange St Akron OH 44328

RICE, LOIS MARSHALL (MRS. JOHN SPENCE RICE), coll. adminstr.; b. Evansville, Wis., June 3; d. Ray A. and Vera Audrey (Dowse) Marshall; student U. Wis., 1938, 39-40, 46; m. John Spence Rice, July 28, 1940; 1 son, Jeffrey Marshall. Pub. relations dir. broadcast div. Bartell Media Corp., Milw., also N.Y.C., 1959-67; adviser edn. pub. relations WMVS/WMVT-TV, Milw., 1967-68; pub. relations dir. Milw. Art Center, 1968-71; dir. devel. Alverno Coll., Milw., 1971—. Adv. bd. HER/Milw. mag. Bd. dirs. Research Center for Women, Alverno Coll. Recipient award Nat. Broadcast Promotion Assn., 1967; Service award Alverno Coll., 1973. Mem. Am. Women Radio and TV (sec. 1967-68), League Women Voters, Florentine Opera Guild, Friends of Art, Milw. Ballet Guild, Laura Sherry League, Women in Communications (v.p. Milw. chpt. 1970-71). Democrat. Episcopalian (dir. Diocesan Women 1954-56). Home: 4031 N Bartlett Av Milwaukee WI 53211 Office: 3401 S 39th St Milwaukee WI 53215

RICE, MABEL MCCULLOUGH (MRS. CLINTON D. RICE), motor co. exec.; b. Lamoni, Ia., Jan. 8, 1904; d. Isaac and Bertha (Naylor) Bedell; B.Bus. Law, Blackstone Coll., Chgo., 1954-60; m. Guy Leroy McCullough, Aug. 2, 1921; 1 son, Gary; m. 2d. Clinton D. Rice, Aug. 13, 1948; 1 son, Clinton Thane. With McCullough Motor Co., Groundbirch, B.C., Can., 1936—, pres., 1948—, dir., 1936-72; officer Ringduck Corp., Mt. Ayr, Ia.; dir. Mount Ayr Developing Co. Bd. dirs. Ringgold County Hosp. Mem. Bus. and Profl. Women's Club. Republican. Methodist. Mem. Order of Eastern Star (worthy matron, 1928). Developer of land in Can. Address: 117 E Madison St Mount Ayr IA 50854 Office: Groundbirch BC Canada

RICE, MYRTLE GATES (MRS. JOHN C. RICE), educator, civic worker; b. Graham, N.C., Nov. 19, 1897; d. Gattis Tinsley and Margaret (Carson) Gates; student Guilford Coll., 1931-33; B.A., Catawba Coll., 1945; m. Arlen Wells Cockman, Dec. 26, 1915 (dec. Feb. 1960); children—Ruby Hazel (Mrs. Freeley Paul Smith), Bertha Venita (Mrs. Eddie F. Strock), Norman L., Arlen Wells. Tchr. pub. schs., Randolph County, N.C., 1934-41, Gaston County, N.C., 1943-45, Bunnell, Fla., 1945-61. Mem. Flagler County Sch. Bd., 1962—, vice chmn., 1967-68, chmn. bd., 1969—; bd. dirs. Fla. Sch. Bds. Assn., Inc., 1966—; sec. North Coastal div. Children's Home Soc. Fla., 1965. Mem. Nat. Retired Tchrs. Assn., Fla. Edn. Assn. Retired Tchrs., Delta Kappa Gamma (hon.). Home: Route 1 Box 152 St Augustine FL 32084 Office: Flager County Schs Bunnell FL 32010

RICE, NELLIE BARNES BALDWIN, ednl. adminstr.; b. Kenly, N.C., Apr. 14, 1912; d. William Orangie and Maggie Pauline (Barnes) Barnes; B.A., N.C. Coll., 1940, M.A., 1942; postgrad. Tchrs. Coll., Columbia, 1943-44, U. Chgo., 1950-52, State U. N.Y., 1956-62; m. Owen William Baldwin, Sept. 28, 1928 (dec.); 1 son, Owen William; m. 2d, Robert Edward Rice, Dec. 22, 1956 (dec.). Tchr., Durham (N.C.) City Schs., 1931-46; asst. prof., elementary tchr. tng. edn. Livingstone Coll., Salisbury, N.C., 1947-50; supr. schs. Wayne County, Goldsboro, N.C., 1950-53, Wilson (N.C.) City schs., 1951-56; supr. schs. Yonkers (N.Y.) pub. schs., 1957-61, prin. schs., 1961-70, prin., Martin Luther King Intermediate Sch., 1970—. Program dir. Tng. Sch. for Girls, Kinston, N.C., 1954-55. Pres. Women's Civic Club, Yonkers, 1962-64; mem. trustee com. Council for Arts in Westchester, 1967—; mem. human service com. Westchester Community Coll., 1969—; mem. Mayors Relations Com., Yonkers, 1963—. Bd. dirs. Nat. Urban League Westchester County, Getty Sq. Teen Center, Yonkers, Am. Cancer Soc., Yonkers. Recipient Jenkins Meml. award State Congress Parents and Tchrs. Assn., 1964; Delta Community Service award Delta Theta, 1971, Profl. award Westchester County Bus. and Profl. Womens' Clubs, 1963. Mem. Nat. Assn. Negro Bus. and Profl. Women's Club (Nat. Sojourner Truth award 1970), Nat. Council Women U.S., Westchester County Bus. and Profl. Women's Club (pres. 1967-71), Delta Sigma Theta. Clubs: Bridge (Yonkers); Garden (Yonkers, Wilson, N.C.). Home: 9 Hunt Av Yonkers NY 10710

RICH, ANNETTE LOUISE, educator; b. Uniontown, Pa., May 29, 1928; d. Clement and Rose (Barbar) Rich; B.Ed., Duquesne U., 1951; M.Ed., U. Pitts., 1953, Ph.D., 1960; postgrad. U. Cal., Los Angeles, summer 1964. Tchr. mentally retarded children Pitts. Pub. Schs., 1951-66; asso. prof. spl. edn. Millersville (Pa.) State Coll., 1966-68; dir. Central Pa. Spl. Edn. Resource Center, 1968—; instr. Shippensburg State Coll.; dir. Pa. Materials Center for Visually Handicapped. Vice pres. Columbus Sch. P.T.A., 1963-64, treas. 1964-66. Recipient Frick ednl. scholarship, 1953. Mem. N.E.A., Pa. Edn. Assn. (sec., pres. elect Pitts. br.), Council Exceptional Children (chpt. sec., pres. Pa. Fedn. 1973), Pa. Assn. Fed. Program Coordinators, Am. Assn. U. Profs., Assn. for Children with Learning Disabilities, U. Pitts. Doctoral Assn., Am. Assn. U. Women, Pi Lambda Theta. Author: Arithmetic Step-by-Step. Home: 1008 Eric Dr Harrisburg PA 17110 Office: 5601 N Front St Harrisburg PA 17110

RICH, ELIZABETH MARGARET ANN (MRS. WILLIAM NICOLO PROVENZANO), pub. relations exec.; b. N.Y.C.; d. Louis Anthony and Margaret Ann (Gilchrist) Rich; B.A., LL.B., St. John's U.; post-grad. Columbia; m. William Nicolo Provenzano, July 1, 1966. Reporter, editor Chgo. Tribune Press Service, N.Y.C., 1947-59; account exec. Rowland Co., pub. relations, N.Y.C., 1959-61; account exec. A.A. Schechter Assos., Inc., N.Y.C., 1961-62, v.p., 1967-73, sr. v.p., 1973—; account exec. Hill & Knowlton, Inc. pub. relations, N.Y.C., 1962-67. Lectr. journalism Dominican Coll. for Women, Blauvelt, N.Y., 1961. Mem. Am. Bar Assn., Nat. Assn. Women Lawyers. Club: Overseas Press (N.Y.C.). Contbr. to various mags. Home: 59 Kings Hwy Tappan NY 10983 Office: 551 Fifth Av New York City NY 10017

RICH, FRANCES L., sculptor; b. Spokane, Wash., Jan. 8, 1910; d. Charles H. and Irene (Luther) Rich; A.B., Smith Coll., 1931; student Cranbrook Acad. Art, Claremont Coll., Columbia, Boston Mus. Sch.; studied with sculptors Malvina Hoffman and Carl Milles, 1933-42. Monuments and reliefs include The Firestone St. Francis of Assisi, St. Margaret's Episcopal Ch., Palm Desert, Cal., 1970, also Mt. Hymettus St. Francis Pierce Coll., Athens, Greece, 1970, Madonna and Child, Holy Trinity Ch., Bremerton, Wash., 1969, Santa Barbara, The Milles St. Francis Millesgarden, Lidingo, Sweden, Mausoleum doors, fountains; portrait busts at Smith Coll., Army-Navy Nurse Monument in Arlington Nat. Cemetery, Washington; Bas Reliefs, Union Bldg. Purdue U., St. Cecilia's Ch., Stanwood, Wash., St. Peter's Episcopal Ch. at Redwood City, Cal.; bronze pelican in front of Pelican Bldg., U. of Cal. at Berkeley, 1958; bronze The Healer foyer David L. Reeves Meml. Library Cottage Hosp., Santa Barbara, 1973; marble bust Alice Stone Blackwell for Boston Pub. Library, 1960; ten foot bronze Madonna, Combermere, Ontario, Canada, 1960; six foot relief bronze Christ of the Sacred Heart St. Sebastian Ch., West Los Angeles; portrait bust Lotte Lehmann, Margaret Sanger, Diego Rivera, Lawrence Langher, Virgil Thompson, Katharine Hepburn, Frederick Sleight, Frederick Olsen, and numerous other portraits, fountains, small bronzes and silvers pvt. collections executed Rome, 1950—; one man show Santa Barbara Mus. Art, 1952, Cal. Palace of Legion of Honor, 1955; Palm Springs (Cal.) Desert Mus., 1969; exhibited group shows DeYoung Mus., 1952, Merrill Collection show, 1954, Botolph Soc. Liturgical show, Boston, 1954, Liturgical Arts show, Denver, 1955, Nat. Decorators show, San Francisco, 1956, Internat. Orchid Show Santa Barbara, 1958, First Nat. Biennale, Contemporary Religious Art, Seton Hall Coll., Greensburg, Pa., 1950, Nat. Liturgical Art Week Show at World's Fair, Seattle, 1962, Palm Springs Desert Mus., 1973, also others. Dir. pub. relations Smith Coll., 1947-50. Served from lt. (j.g.) to lt. comdr., USNR, 1942-46. Mem. Archtl. League N.Y., Amvets, Smith Coll. Alumnae Assn. Clubs: Cosmopolitan (N.Y.C.). Studio: Shumway Ranch nr Pinyon Crest PO Box 213 Palm Desert CA 92260

RICH, HELEN WALL (MRS. ARTHUR L. RICH), educator; b. Chester, S.C., May 4, 1912; d. George Addison and Georgia (Hardin) Wall; student Queen's Coll., 1930-32; B.S. summa cum laude, Catawba Coll., 1934; diploma in piano playing Juilliard Sch. Music, 1938; diplomas Christiansen Choral Sch., 1950, 51; m. Arthur Lowndes Rich, July 26, 1934; children—Arthur Lowndes, Ruth Anne. Instr. music Catawba Coll.; Salisbury, N.C., 1934-43; university organist Mercer U., Macon, Ga., 1944-50, asst. prof. music, 1950—; organ recitalist throughout S.E.; v.p. Tudor Apts., Inc., Atlanta, 1960-73; sec.-treas. Richelieu Apts., Inc., Macon, 1955-73. Mem. Federated Music Clubs (hon.; chmn. scholarship contest), Ga. Piano Tchrs. Guild Nat. Assn. Schs. Music (asso.), Am. Coll. and U. Concert Mgrs. Assn. (asso.), Cardinal Key Soc. Mercer U. (hon.), Delta Omicron. Club: Morning Music (Macon, dir.). Home: 369 Candler Dr Macon GA 31204

RICH, IRENE LUCILLE (MRS. WILLIAM EDWARD RICH), writer, editor; b. Buffalo, Dec. 13, 1932; d. Edward Joseph and Anna A. (Bevilacqua) Willett; B.A. (N.Y. Regents scholar), Rosary Hill Coll., 1954; M. Gen. Edn. (univ. grantee), U. Buffalo, 1959; postgrad. U. Montreal, Can., 1961; m. William Edward Rich, Mar. 12, 1966; children—Clifford Edward, Douglas Scott. Tchr. No. Tonawanda (N.Y.) Bd. Edn., 1954-55; pub. relations asst. J. Walter Thompson Co., N.Y.C., 1955-56; tchr. Buffalo Bd. Edn., 1956-58; pub. relations dir. Rosary Hill Coll., Buffalo, 1958-60; tchr., lang. cons. Diocese Buffalo, 1960-62; mag. editor Buffalo C. of C., 1962-65; publs. coordinator State U. N.Y., Buffalo, 1965-67; columnist Plainfield (N.J.) Courier-News, 1968-69; writer, editor, Basking Ridge, N.J., 1969—; consumer news editor Ind.-Press, Summit, N.J., 1974—. Instr., cons. Writers Workshop, Watchung Hills (N.J.) Adult Sch., 1970-73. Publicity coordinator N.J. Hemophilia Guild, 1970-72; resource personnel N.J. Women's Rights Task Force on Edn., 1973—; judge N.J. Humane Soc. essay contest, 1971. Mem. Women in Communications, Nardin Acad. Alumnae (publicity chmn. 1959-61), Words and Music (co-chmn. program com. 1971-72), Rosary Hill Alumnae Assn. (alumnae fund dir. 1958, mag. editor 1957-60), Nat. Council Coll. Publs. Advisers. Home and office: 80 Fairview Dr Basking Ridge NJ 07920

RICH, JENIFER GRACE (COLTMAN), psychiatrist; b. Farnborough, Hampshire, Eng., Aug. 2, 1939; d. Hugh Francis Lister and Enid Williamina (McAlester) Coltman; M.B., Ch.B., St. Andrews U., Fife, Scotland, 1964; m. David Malcolm Rich, Aug. 7, 1965; children—Charles David, Adrian Matthew. Intern, Ruchill Hosp., Glasgow, 1964-65, Law Hosp., Lanarkshire, 1965-66; resident psychiatry R.I. Med. Center, 1966-68, Medfield State Hosp., 1968-69; research tng. fellow Boston U., 1969-71; psychiatrist Rochester Mental Health Center, 1971—; asso. attending psychiatry Rochester Gen. Hosp.; clin. asst. prof. U. Rochester Sch. Medicine and Dentistry, 1972—. Diplomate Am. Bd. Psychiatry and Neurology. Home: 760 Eastbrooke Lane Rochester NY 14618 Office: 1425 Portland Av Rochester NY 14621

RICH, JUDITH, pub. relations exec.; b. Chgo., Apr. 14, 1938; d. Irwin M. and Sarah (Sandock) Rich; B.A., U. Ill., 1960. Staff writer, reporter Economist Newspapers, 1960-61; asst. dir. pub. relations, communications Council of Profit Sharing Industries, 1961-62; dir. advertising, pub. relations Chgo. Industrial Dist., 1962-63; account exec. Daniel J. Edelman Inc., 1963-67, account supr., 1967-70, v.p., 1970-73, sr. v.p., creative dir. Media div., 1973—. Recipient competition award Nat. Visual Communications Assn., 1971. Mem. Council Fgn. Relations, Pub. Relations Soc. Am., Publicity Club Chgo. (Golden Trumpet award 1964, 67, 70, 72). Office: Daniel J Edelman Inc 221 N LaSalle St Chicago IL 60601

RICH, LUCILLE C., broadcasting journalist; b. N.Y.C.; d. John G. and Ruth L. (Carter) Rich; B.A., Queens Coll., 1955; postgrad. Columbia, 1958, U. Madrid (Spain), 1962. City investigator N.Y.C. Dept. Hosps., 1956-61; field rep. N.Y. State Commn. for Human Rights, N.Y.C., 1962-68; corr. TV news sta. WCBS, N.Y.C., 1968—. Mem. pub. information com. Am. Cancer Soc., 1973—. Bd. dirs. The Beaux Arts Guild, Inc., pres., 1964-73; bd. mgrs. YMCA, 1966-68; bd. dirs. Manhattan adv. com. N.Y. Urban League. Recipient Achievement in Broadcasting award Ophelia DeVore Assos., 1969, Achievement in Broadcasting award Am. Parkinson Disease Assn., 1971, YMCA Black Achievers in Industry award, 1971. Office: 524 W 57th St New York City NY 10019

RICH, SUSAN ABBY, educator, speech therapist; b. Bklyn., Apr. 11, 1946; d. Milton and Jeanette (Merns) Rich; B.A., Bklyn. Coll., 1967. Speech improvement tchr. Bur. Speech Improvement, Bklyn., 1967-69; tchr. John Dewey High Sch., Bklyn., 1969-70; tchr. pub. speaking and drama South Shore High Sch., Bklyn., 1970—, instr. crafts adult edn. center, 1972—. Mem. United Fedn. Tchrs., Am. Theater Assn., N.Y.C. Speech Tchrs. Assn., N.Y. Civil Liberties Union. Office: 6565 Flatlands St Brooklyn NY 11236

RICH, VENITA BAE, talent scout; b. Chelsea, Ia., Feb. 24, 1906; d. Edward and Kate (Welch) Rich; student Normal Training Tchrs. Coll.; grad. Hinshaw Conservatory, Chgo., 1922. Tchr. rural schs., Ia., 1924, Chgo. Pub. Schs., 1925; appeared with Chautauquas in Middle West and East, 1926-27; developed marionette and art show performing in schs. throughout U.S., 1938-44; developed show for state and county fairs, 1950; talent scout Original Amateur Hour N.Y., 1952-70; performer monologues, character sketches numerous clubs and orgns. Author monologues, hist. pageants. Home: Rural Route Chelsea IA 52215

RICHARD, ADRIENNE GOODER (MRS. JAMES E. RICHARD), writer; b. Evanston, Ill., Oct. 31, 1921; d. Leslie MacDonald and Marguerite (Brown) Gooder; student U. Ariz., 1939-40, Northwestern U., 1941; A.B., U. Chgo., 1943; postgrad. U. Ia., 1948-50, Boston Coll., 1969-72; m. James E. Richard, Apr. 22, 1943; children—James, Daniel, Randall. Food editor Davenport (Ia.) Daily Times, 1947-48; producer, performer art edn. TV program for Davenport Municipal Art Gallery sta. WOC-TV, 1951-56; writer short stories, articles appearing in various publs., including Harper's, Boys' Life. Mem. League Women Voters, Authors Guild. Author: Pistol, 1969; The Accomplice, 1973; Wings, 1974. Home: 45 Chiltern Rd Weston MA 02193

RICHARD, CORINNE GENEVIEVE (MRS. ALBERT ARCHIBALD RICHARD), educator; b. Kansas City, Mo., Apr. 8, 1912; d. Eugene Ellsworth and Agnes Alma (Lueck) Cromwell; A.B., B.E., Washburn U.; M.E., U. Kan., 1961; m. Albert Archibald Richard, June 5, 1933. Tchr. Nemah, Jackson County schs., Kan., 1930-44; supt. pub. instrn. Jackson County, Halton, Kan., 1944-49, 1963-69; prin. Basehor Pub. Sch., Basehor, Kan., 1953-59, Holton (Kan.) Pub. Sch., 1949-52; counselor, supt. Netawaka (Kan.) Pub. Schs., 1959-63; prin. USD 338, Valley Falls, Kan., 1970-71, dir. spl. reading, 1971—; owner A-C Services, Holton, Kan., 1967—. Mem. Charles Kettering Fellows; mem. Holton Bus. Women (pres. 1948), N.E.A., Holton C. of C. (sec. 1967—, dir. 1967—), Delta Kappa

Gamma. Club: Pilot (pres. Holton 1969, gov. dist. 1971—). Address: Route 3 Box 167 Holton KS 66436

RICHARD, ST. CLAIR SMITH (MRS. GEORGE CHARLES RICHARD II), advt. exec.; b. Newton, Ia., Nov. 16, 1910; d. William Walter and Nelle Grace (Van Dusseldorp) Smith; student U. Ia., 1930, Barnard Coll., 1931; B.S., Columbia Sch. Journalism, 1933; m. George Charles Richard, II, Dec. 4, 1933; children—Thomas Lane, Randall St. Clair, Deborah Nell duChane. Mng. partner Halo House, Larchmont, N.Y., 1946—. Instr., Good Counsel Coll., White Plains, N.Y., 1961-64. Promotions asst. Westchester County Recreation Commn., 1960-61; asst. to mayor Mt. Vernon, N.Y., 1962-63; pub. relations dir. Westchester Library System, Mt. Vernon, 1966-71. Mem. pub. relations com. N.Y. State Recreation Soc., 1971—; mem. adv. bd. St. Paul's Eastchester, Mt. Vernon, 1971—; council adminstr. Larchmont Tng. Center, 1971. Press sec. vice-chmn. Republican State Com., 1964; pub. relations Westchester Democratic com., 1972—. Bd. dirs. UN Assn. U.S., Mt. Vernon chpt., Afro-Am. Cultural Found., White Plains; vice chmn. bd. Nat. Shrine/Bill of Rights. Named Outstanding Community Leader, 1971. Mem. Am. Assn. Improvement Boxing (chmn. publicity), Westchester County Assn., Westchester Park & Recreation Soc., Delta Gamma. Editor: Women in Public Service, 1964, Straight Talk, 1964, Women in the News, 1956-60, Men of the Pulpit, 1958-62, Scribblings, 1966-71, Newberry Award Newsletter, 1971-72, Westchester Ind. Herald, 1965-66. Home: 60 The Boulevard New Rochelle NY 10801 Office: Box 85 Larchmont NY 10539

RICHARDS, ANN (MRS. EDMOND JAMES ANGELO), actress, lectr.; b. Sydney, Australia (came to U.S., 1942); d. Mortimer Delaforce and Marion Bradshaw (Dive) Richards; student Stotts Coll., 1936-37, Studio Sch. of Drama, 1936-38; m. Edmond James Angelo, Feb. 4, 1949; children—Christopher E., Mark R., Juliet M. Appeared in lead role in various motion picture films, Cinesound Studio, Australia, 1937-42, Metro-Goldwyn Mayer, 1942-45, Hal Wallis-Paramount, 1945-47, R.K.O., 1947, Eagle-Lion Studios, 1947-48, Edmond Angelo Productions, 1953; pictures include An American Romance, Love Letters, The Searching Wind, Badman's Territory, Sorry, Wrong Number, Lost Honeymoon, Breakdown; v.p. Tchr. Remembrance Day Found., 1952—; internat. chmn. Apple of Gold Edn. awards, 1953—. Speaking and poetry reading in U.S. and Europe, 1970-71. Recipient meritorious service citation, Govs. of Great Britain, U.S., New Zealand, Australia, 1939-46; Star Pattern award, Inst. Profl. Direction, 1951. Mem. Nat. Profl. Speech Arts and Sciences Fraternity, Zeta Phi Eta (v.p. nat. council 1970—). Author: The Grieving Senses, poems, 1971. Home: 2131 Cedarhurst Dr Los Angeles CA 90027

RICHARDS, ARLENE KRAMER (MRS. ARNOLD DAVID RICHARDS), psychologist; b. N.Y.C., June 24, 1935; d. Emanuel and Edith (Burstein) K.; A.B., U. Chgo., 1953; M.A., Columbia, 1965, Ed.D., 1969; m. Arnold David Richards, Mar. 21, 1954; children—Stephan Louis, Rebecca Dawn, Tamar Beth. Research asso., project dir. Tchrs. Coll., Columbia, 1968-70; psychologist Northside Center for Child Devel., 1967-69; practice psychology, N.Y.C., 1971—; research dir. Center for Research and Edn. in Am. Liberties. Cons. White House Conf. on Children and Youth, 1971; lectr. N.H. Med. Soc. Conf. on Drug Abuse, 1971. Mem. Am. Psychol. Assn., Internat. Reading Assn., Nat. Council on Measurement and Edn. Author: Growing Pains: Uses of High School Conflict. Home: 305 Riverside Dr New York City NY 10025 Office: 40 E 89th St New York City NY 10025

RICHARDS, CARA E., educator; b. Bayonne, N.J.; d. Vere Stiles and Virginia (Tyler) Richards; A.B., Queens Coll., 1952; postgrad. Columbia, 1952-53; Ph.D., Cornell U., 1957; m. Henry F. Dobyns, Sept. 11, 1958 (div.); 1 son, York Henry. Mem. faculty Cornell U., Ithaca, N.Y., 1953-57, fellow Social Sci. Research Center, 1955-56, curatorial asst. in primitive art, White Art Mus., 1956-57, lectr., 1963-64, with Peace Corps, summer 1964, summers 65-67; resident Russell Sage Found., Ariz., 1958-59; field dir. Peruvian Family Life Study, Lima, Peru, 1960-61; profesora Escuela de Servicio Social del Peru, 1961, 62; asso. prof. Social Relations dept. Ithaca Coll., 1964-67; asso. prof. sociology Transylvania Coll., Lexington, Ky., 1967—, chmn. dept. econs., psychol. sociology, 1974—. With Peace Corps, various locations, area coordinator tng. program U. Wash., Seattle, 1963, Springfield (Mass.) Coll., 1963. Mem. Am. Anthropol. Assn. (dir. vis. lectr. program 1963—), Soc. Applied Anthropology, Am. Ethnol. Soc., Am. Mus. Natural History, Dewitt Hist. Soc. Tompkins County, Phi Beta Kappa. Author: Man in Perspective, 1972. Contbr. articles to profl. jours. Office: Transylvania College Lexington KY 40502

RICHARDS, CHRISTINE-LOUISE, artist, publishing co. exec.; b. Radnor, Pa., Jan. 11, 1910; d. Joseph Ernest and Catherine (Fletcher) Richards; student pvt. schs.; art schs. N.Y.C., Munich, Germany. One-man shows Stockbridge, Mass., 1947, 48, 52, 53, Oneonta, N.Y., 1960, 61; exhibited in group shows Stockbridge Art Assn., 1931-32; represented in collections, Cal., Mass., N.Y.; owner, founder, pres. Blue Star Music Pub. Co., Pittsfield, Mass., 1946—, now Morris, N.Y. Mem. Phila. Art Alliance, Am. Fedn. Musicians, Nightingale-Bamford Alumni Assn., Met. Mus. Art, Audubon Soc., Nat. Assn. Am. Composers and Condrs., Soc., Intercontinental Biog. Soc. Emergency Aid of Pa., Pa. Acad. Fine Arts, Internat. Platform Soc., others. Author: The Blue Star Fairy Book of Stories for Children; The Blue Star Fairy Book of More Stories for Children. Composer: (song) What Makes Me Dream of You, 1950, numerous others. Contbr. portrait to Artists U.S.A., 1970-71. Address: Blue Star Music PO Box 185 Morris NY 13808

RICHARDS, GLENORA, artist; b. New London, O., Feb. 18, 1909; d. Tracy Henry and Bertha (Huber) Case; student Cleve. Sch. Art, 1927-30; m. Walter DuBois Richards, June 20, 1931; children—Timothy, Henry Tracy. Exhibited Nat. Collection Fine Arts (Smithsonian Inst.), N.A.D., Portraits, Inc., N.Y.C., Phila. watercolor show with Pa. Soc. Miniature Painters (Phila. Mus. Art), Cal. Soc. Miniature Painters, Los Angeles, Royal Soc. Miniature Painters. Sculptors and Gravers, R.W.S. Galleries London, Eng., 1958, IBM Gallery Arts and Scis., N.Y.C., 1966; represented in permanent collection Phila. Mus. Arts, Smithsonian Instn. Recipient Levantia White Boardman Meml. medal Am. Soc. Miniature Painters, 1947; Pa. Soc. prize Pa. Soc. Miniature Painters, 1947; medal of honor miniature painting Nat. Assn. Women Artists, 1953, prize, 1962, 66; Elizabeth Muhlhoffer award Miniature Painters, Sculptors and Gravers Soc., 1956, 57, 61. Mem. Am. Soc. Miniature Painters, Nat. Assn. Women Artists, (Aileen O. Webb prize for watercolor 1971), Miniature Painters, Sculptors and Gravers Soc. Washington (hon. award for miniature portrait 1969), Miniature Art Soc. N.J. Home: 87 Oak St New Canaan CT 06840

RICHARDS, IRIS TERRY (MRS. FREDERICK FORREST RICHARDS), physician; b. Lynchburg, Va., Mar. 14, 1910; d. Hunter Hereford and Maude Kenny (Meredith) Terry; A.B., Hunter Coll., 1931; M.D., Howard U., 1935; m. Frederick Forrest Richards, July 6, 1936; children—Frederick F., Terry S., Iris M. Intern Harlem Hosp., N.Y.C., 1935-37; staff dr. Woman's House Detention, N.Y.C., 1937-38; practice medicine, Hempstead, N.Y., 1939—. Mem. Village Hempstead Drug Addiction Commission, 1971. Bd. dirs. Nassau Communities Health Services Found., 1969-72. Mem. N.Y., Nassau County med. socs., Nassau County Gen. Practitioners Assn., Alpha Kappa Alpha. Club: The Links Inc. Home: 146 Carolina Av Hempstead NY 11550 Office: 70 Grove St Hempstead NY 11550

RICHARDS, LACLAIRE LISSETTA JONES (MRS. GEORGE A. RICHARDS), social worker; b. Pine Bluff, Ark.; d. Artie William and Geraldine (Adams) Jones; B.A., Nat. Coll. Christian Workers, 1953; M.S.W., U. Kan., 1956; postgrad. Columbia, 1960; m. George Alvarez Richards, July 26, 1958; children—Leslie Rosario, Lia Mercedes. Psychiat. supervisory, teaching, adminstrv. and consultative duties Hastings State Hosp., Ingleside, Neb., 1956-60; supervisory, consultative and adminstrv. responsibilities for psychiat. and geriatric patients VA Hosp., Knoxville, Ia., 1960-74, field instr. for grad. students from U. Mo., equal employment opportunity counselor, 1969, com. chmn., 1969-70; social worker Mental Health Inst., Cherokee, Ia., 1974—. Mem. Knoxville Juvenile Adv. Com., 1963-65, 68-70, sec., 1965-66, chmn., 1966-68; sec. Urban Renewal Citizens' Adv. Com., Knoxville, 1966-68; mem. United Methodist Ch. Task Force Exptl. Styles Ministry and Leadership; counselor Knoxville Youth Line program; canvasser community fund drs., Knoxville, Fellow Royal Soc. Health; mem. Nat. Assn. Social Workers (co-chmn. Neb. chpt. profl. standards com. 1958-59), Acad. Certified Social Workers, Neb. Assn. Social Workers (chmn. 1958-59), Am. Assn. U. Women (sec. Hastings chpt. 1958-60). Methodist (Sunday sch. tchr. adult div.; mem. commn. on edn.; mem. Core com. for adult edn.). Home: 406 S Craig Dr Cherokee IA 51021 Office: Mental Health Inst Cherokee IA 51012

RICHARDS, LILLA DUNOVANT MCCUTCHEN (MRS. STANLEY I. RICHARDS), editor, civic worker; b. Washington, Apr. 17, 1939; d. James Malcolm and Emily (Dunovant) McCutchen; B.S., U. S.C., 1961; m. Stanley Irving Richards, July 24, 1965. Editor, econ. research publ. Office Mgmt. Services U.S. Dept. Agr., Washington, 1961-62, writer, staff editor Farm Index Mag., 1962-66, editor, asst. to chmn. Outlook and Situation Bd., 1966-68, supervisory editor econ. research publ., 1968-69. Mem. hospitality com. Custis-Lee Mansion, 1970—. Mem. Service League No. Va., 1962—, adv. com., 1970-71, corr. sec., 1971-72, bd. dirs., 1971-74, chmn. bldg. com., 1973-74; bd. dirs. S.C. State Soc., 1969-71; trustee No. Va. Fine Arts Assn., 1968-72, v.p., 1969-70, mem. adv. council, 1972-73; exec. com. Woodside Citizens Assn., 1973—; bd. dirs. Rocky Run Citizens Assn., 1973—, McLean Citizens Assn., 1973—; chmn. Joint Citizens Task Force McLean Planning Dist., 1974—. Recipient certificate merit U.S. Dept. Agr., 1963; certificate appreciation for vol. service Mrs. Pat Nixon, 1970. Mem. D.A.R. (treas. Alexander chpt. 1971-73; sr. pres. Abingdon Children Am. Revolution 1961-63, Nat. Rifle Assn. (life), S.C. Hist. Soc. Episcopalian. Club: Cotillion. Home: 8703 Brook Rd McLean VA 22101

RICHARDS, MARGARET PLUMMER (MRS. J.H. RICHARDS), journalist; b. Newton, Kan., Oct. 27, 1909; d. William Collins and Hattie Lee (Marshall) Plummer; A.B., U. Kan., 1931; m. J.H. Richards, Aug. 3, 1935; 1 son, Clinton H. Staff corr. U.P.I., Kansas City, Mo., 1931—. Recipient citation for achievement in journalism Kansas City chpt. Theta Sigma Phi, 1965. Mem. Women in Communications, Kappa Kappa Gamma, Delta Sigma Rho, Pi Kappa Delta. Methodist. Home: 1136 E 65th St Kansas City MO 64131 Office: 220 W 11th St Kansas City MO 64105

RICHARDS, MARGIE ANN GROSSKOPF (MRS. WILLIAM L. RICHARDS), lawyer; b. Union City, N.J., Apr. 4, 1939; d. John and Marie (Rothlein) Grosskopf; A.B., San Diego State Coll., 1965; J.D., U. San Diego, 1968; m. William L. Richards, Apr. 26, 1969. Law librarian Clark County Law Library, Las Vegas, 1968-69; admitted to Nev. bar, 1969, Supreme Ct. U.S., 1972; dep. dist. atty. Dist. Attys. Office, Las Vegas, 1969-71; dep. atty. gen. Atty. Gen. Office, Carson City, Nev., 1971—. Mem. Phi Alpha Theta, Phi Delta Delta. Home: 506 W Spear St Carson City NV 89701 Office: Supreme Ct Bldg Carson City NV 89701

RICHARDS, MOLLIE ANN YOUNG (MRS. RALPH HAYWARD RICHARDS), occupational therapist; b. Indpls., Oct. 23, 1944; d. Scott Leonard and Mollie Erlene (Simms) Young; B.S., Ind. U., 1967; m. Ralph Hayward Richards, May 11, 1967; 1 dau., Kimberly Leigh. Staff therapist St. Francis Gen. Hosp. and Rehab. Inst., Pitts., 1967-68; staff and asst. chief occupational therapist Glenn Dale Md. Hosp., 1968-70; instr. occupational therapy assts. program Community Coll. Balt., 1970-73; dir. occupational therapy St. John's Home, Rochester, N.Y., 1973-74; supr. activity therapy dept. alcohol and drug unit Western Mo. Mental Health Center, Kansas City, Mo., 1974—. Cons. to occupational therapy program James Lawrence Kernan Hosp., Balt., 1970-72. Mem. N.A.A.C.P., Arthritis Found., Am. Fedn. Tchrs., Am., Md. (v.p., membership chmn. 1971-73), Western Pa. (membership chmn. 1967-68) occupational therapy assns. Baptist. Home: 5604 W 79th St Prairie Village KS 66208 Office: 600 E 22d St Kansas City MO 64106

RICHARDS, RUTH FARNAN, educator, govt. ofcl.; b. Worcester, Mass., Apr. 5, 1917; d. Amedee Oliver and Ruth M. (Farnan) Richards; B.S., Worcester State Coll., 1938; M.A., Boston U., 1948; M.P.H., U. N.C., 1950. High sch. tchr., counselor, Framingham, Mass., 1938-48; officer naval intelligence USNR, Boston, Pearl Harbor, 1942-46; exchange tchr. Hutcheson's Girls Sch., Glasgow, Scotland, 1947-48; health educator Dist. Health Dept., Chapel Hill, N.C., 1950-51; health edn. cons. USPHS, Dept. Health, Edn. and Welfare with rank of health services dir. div. chronic diseases, Ore., Boston, Washington, regional health edn. cons., edn. officer Office of Dir. div. hosp. and med. facilities, Washington, 1951—, now dir. Consultation br. Div. Facilities Utilization; vis. prof. continuing edn. program U. N.C. Sch. Pub. Health; mem. Surg. Gen.'s Com. on Health Edn. in USPHS. Pres., permanent sec. Coll. Class Worcester State Coll., 1934—; leader Algonquin council Girl Scouts U.S.A., 1940s; co-chmn. class Sch. Pub. Health U. N.C., 1950—; mem. Civic League, Framingham, 1939-49; mem. edn. com. Arthritis Assn., N.Y.C., 1962-64. Recipient Commendation medal USPHS, 1969, Meritorious Service medal, 1973. Fellow Am. Pub. Health Assn., Soc. Pub. Health Edn. (com. chmn., past sec., v.p., bd. mem.); mem. Am. Hosp. Assn., Adult Edn. Assn., Am. Soc. Tng. and Devel., USPHS Com. Officers Assn., Federally Employed Womens Club, Kappa Delta Pi, Delta Kappa Gamma. Clubs: Framingham Womens, Framingham Catholic Womans. Home: 4322 Rosedale Av Bethesda MD 20014 Office: 5600 Fishers Lane Rockville MD 20852

RICHARDS, RUTH LOUISE, psychologist, educator; b. Lincoln, Neb., Apr. 3, 1944; d. Dexter Newell and Ruth Eleanor (Fulton) Richards; B.S. with honors in Physics, Stanford, 1965; M.A. in Edn., U. Cal. at Berkeley, 1969, Ph.D. in Edn., 1971. Tchr., English, Oakland (Cal.) Tech. Adult Sch., 1970-71; asst. prof. ednl. psychology Boston U., 1971—, dir. women's leadership project in adult edn., asst. prof. dept. childhood and curriculum edn., 1974—. NSF fellow, 1965-66. Mem. Am. Psychol. Assn., Am. Ednl. Research Assn., Am. Assn. Advancement Psychology, Am. Assn. U. Profs. Home: 295 Harvard St Cambridge MA 02139 Office: Boston Univ School of Education 765 Commonwealth Av Boston MA 02215

RICHARDS, RUTH (MARGARET), bacteriologist; b. Warren, Pa.; d. Alfred and Una (Thompson) Richards; B.S., U. Hawaii, 1945; postgrad. U. Ala., 1962-63, Duke, 1963, Cath. U. Am., 1965, U. Toronto, 1967; M.S., Wagner Coll., 1971. Night technician Queen's Hosp., Honolulu, 1941-45; bacteriologist Postgrad. Hosp. and Columbia U., N.Y.C., 1946; head technician Rip Van Winkle Clinic, Hudson, N.Y., 1947; serologist Blood Bank of Hawaii, Honolulu, 1947-51; bacteriologist Deaconess Hosp., Buffalo, 1952, Jackson Meml. Hosp., Miami, Fla., 1953-57; bacteriologist Municipal Lab., Jamestown, N.Y., 1957-71, N.Y. Hosp.-Cornell Med. Center Coll., N.Y.C., 1971—. Instr. med. tech. students Jamestown Community Coll. and Municipal Lab. Mem. Am. Soc. Clin. Pathologist Med. Technologists, Am. Soc. Microbiolgy, Am. Chem. Soc., Royal Soc. Health, Am. Pub. Health Assn., A.A.A.S., Nat. Registry Microbiologists, Am. Assn. U. Women. Home: 205 E 69th St New York City NY 10021

RICHARDSON, BETTY ALICE DUNCAN, ins. co. exec.; b. Millette, Okla., Aug. 22, 1925; d. Roscoe Patterson and Verna (Redding) Duncan; student Richmond Bus. Coll., 1944, El Centro Jr. Coll., 1968; m. Thomas L. Richardson, Sept. 5, 1947 (div. Dec. 1967); children—Rebecca R., Cynthia S., Nancy A. Various positions, 1943-48; sec. to dir. nursing Parkland Hosp., Dallas, 1948-49; sec. to regional mgr. Seaboard Finance Co., Dallas, 1958-59; with Allied Bankers Life Ins. Co., Dallas, 1959—, asst. treas., 1966—, sec., 1970—. Active Camp Fire Girls, 1957-65. Mem. Am. Bus. Women's Assn. (corr. sec. 1964-65, ways and means chmn. 1965-66, rec. sec. 1971-72, program chmn. 1972-73, treas. 1973-74), Bus. and Profl. Women Dallas. Democrat. Methodist (ch. sch. supt. 1966-67). Home: 10141 Casa View Av Dallas TX 75228 Office: Praetorian Bldg 1607 Main St Dallas TX 75201

RICHARDSON, BRENDA, mus. curator; b. Howell, Mich., July 15, 1942; d. Robert Burr and Helen Isabel (Wright) Richardson; B.A., U. Mich., 1964; M.A., U. Cal. at Berkeley, 1966. Exhibition asst. Univ. Art Mus., Berkeley, 1964-68, asst. curator, 1968-69, asso. curator, 1969-71, curator exhbn., 1971-72, asst. curatorial dir., 1972—. Distinguished Alumni lectr. U. Cal. at Berkeley, 1973. Democrat. Author: Hundertwasser, 1969; Free, 1970; William T. Wiley, 1971; Joseph Raffael: Water Paintings, 1973; Terry Fox, 1973; Joan Brown, 1974. Contbr. editor Arts Mag., 1970—. Contbr. articles to profl. jours. Home: 203 Yale Av Kensington CA 94708 Office: Univ Art Mus U of Cal Berkeley CA 94720

RICHARDSON, CAROLYN RAY CAMPBELL (MRS. WILLIAM NATHAN RICHARDSON), advt. cons., civic worker; b. Hopkinsville, Ky., Oct. 9, 1944; d. Weldon Ray and Flora Rosina (Blane) Campbell; B.A. in radio, tv, films, U. Ky., 1966; postgrad. Sch. Banking, U. Ky., 1972; m. William Nathan Richardson, Sept. 7, 1966. Moderator, producer Meet Gulf Park on WGCM radio, Gulfport, Miss., 1960-62; dir. children's program WBKY radio, 1962, prodn. dir., 1965-66, music dir., 1964-65; producer, moderator pub. service program WEPG radio, South Pittsburg, Tenn., 1967-69; sales mgr., spl. programs dir. WKDZ radio, Cadiz, Ky., 1966-67, bd. dirs., 1965—; pres. Communications Unltd., Cadiz, 1974—; dir. pub. relations and advt. Trigg County Farmers Bank, Cadiz, 1971—. Substitute tchr. Trigg County (Ky.) High Sch., 1970—. Chmn. A.R.C. Blood Program, Marion County, Tenn., 1968, publicity chmn. Trigg County chpt.; communications chmn. Marion County Friends of Library Bd., 1967-68; chmn. Trigg County (Ky.) Heart Fund, 1970-74; chmn. Trigg County Sesquicentennial Corp., 1970-71, Trigg County Library and Youth Center Bldg. Fund Drive, 1972, Trigg County Teen Center, 1971-72, Trigg County Bd. Edn., 1973-74; mem. Ky. Ednl. TV Adv. Council; mem. steering com. Christian County Area Vocational Edn. Center. Bd. dirs. Ky. Ednl. Med. Polit. Action Com. Named Bus. Woman of Year, 1974. Mem. Am. Med. Assn. Women's Aux. (past pres. Pennyrile), Ky. Women's Med. Aux. (chmn. pub. relations com., legislative com., del. 1971-73), Trigg County C. of C., Bus. and Profl. Women's Club, U. Ky. (v.p. Trigg County 1973-74, nat. membership com.), Gulf Park Coll. alumni assns., Nat. Assn. Bank Women, Bank Marketing Assn., Delta Delta Delta. Episcopalian. Home: 116 E Main St Cadiz KY 42211 Office: Trigg County Farmers Bank Cadiz KY 42211

RICHARDSON, CONSTANCE COLEMAN (MRS. EDGAR PRESTON RICHARDSON), artist; b. Indpls., Jan. 18, 1905; d. Christopher Bush and Juliet (Brown) Coleman; student Vassar Coll., 1923-25, Pa. Acad. Fine Arts, 1925-28; m. Edgar Preston Richardson, Sept. 15, 1931. One man shows Macbeth Gallery, N.Y.C., 1944, 46, 50, Wildenstein & Co., N.Y., 1955, Kennedy Galleries, N.Y., 1960, 63, 70; exhibited in group shows at Macbeth Galleries, Wildenstein & Co., Met. Mus. Art, Carnegie Inst., Corcoran Art Gallery, Whitney, Mus.; represented in permanent collections Pa. Acad., John Herron Art Inst., Indpls., Saginaw Mus. Grand Rapids Art Gallery, Detroit Inst. Arts, Art Mus. N.B. Inst., U. Del., Santa Barbara Mus., Columbus Gallery Fine Arts, Whitney Mus. Western Art, Joslyn Art Mus., Omaha, and others. Address: 285 Locust St Philadelphia PA 19106

RICHARDSON, DAISY ADELAIDE WATKINS (MRS. ROBERT WILLIAMS RICHARDSON, JR.), real estate developer; b. Swannanoa, N.C., Aug. 18, 1920; d. George Agustus and Kitty Sue (Wilson) Watkins; secretarial degree Asheville Bus. Coll., 1940; m. Robert Williams Richardson, Jr., Aug. 18, 1940; children—Catherine Gail (Mrs. Clark Gayle Crozer), Vicki Joan (Mrs. Peter Ashton Lyon), Robert Williams III. Real estate salesman Keystone Realty, Palm Beach, 1966-73, LeBaron Real Estate Corp., Palm Beach, 1973—; sec. Richardson Devel. Corp., Palm Beach, 1973—; v.p., sec. Nu-Lan Improvement Corp., Palm Beach, 1972—. Bd. dirs. Lake Dogwood Assos., Inc. Club: Sailfish (Palm Beach). Home: 111 Bradley Pl Palm Beach FL 33480 Office: Bradley House Arcade Palm Beach FL 33480

RICHARDSON, DEBORAH DUGGAN (MRS. JAMES MANNING RICHARDSON), psychologist; b. Miami, Fla., Sept. 29, 1948; d. William Richard and Doris Gertrude (Behling) Duggan; B.Ed., U. Fla., 1970, M.Ed., 1971; m. James Manning Richardson, Aug. 14, 1971. Sch. psychologist Palm Beach County Sch. Bd., West Palm Beach, Fla., 1971—. Mem. Nat. Assn. Sch. Psychologists, Palm Beach County Psychol. Assn., Am. Assn. Univ. Women. Home: 712 S 8th Av Lake Worth FL 33460 Office: North County Administration Center 1160 Av O Riviera Beach FL

RICHARDSON, DOROTHY MORRIS WILSON (MRS. VICTOR ETIENNE RICHARDSON), civic worker; b. Tripp, S.D., Apr. 24, 1901; d. Edwin Percy and Orpha Jane (Morris) Wilson; B.A. in Home Econs., Wash. State Coll., 1923, diploma, life diploma, 1926, postgrad. 1927, 54, 63; m. Victor Etienne Richardson, June 23, 1926; children—Shirley Yvonne (Mrs. Robert Lawrence Macumber), Marilyn Joyce (Mrs. M.R. Parrish). Tchr. pub. schs., Lind, Wash., 1923-24, Menlo, Wash., 1924-26, Episcopal Summer Sch., Lake Coeur d'Alene, Ida., 1927; with Fruit Growers Service Co., Monitor, Wash., 1931-64; communications chmn. Chelan County Homemakers Council, 1937-64. Chmn. March of Dimes, 1945, Chelan and Douglas Counties Hot Lunch Council, 1944, Monitor Community Chest Dr., 1944-45; bd. mem. Chelan County Extension Adv. Comm., 1950-53; charter mem. Wenatchee Valley YWCA, 1956—, rec. sec., 1958-61, bd. mem., sec., 1966—; mem. Wenatchee Ladies Mus., dir., 1954-56; charter mem., pres. Monitor P.T.A., 1933—; mem. Wenatchee United Good Neighbor Bd., 1964-71; charter mem., v.p., historian St. Anthony's Hosp. League; pres. Upper Wenatchee Valley council United Ch. Women, 1954-55; pres. Chelan County P.T.A. Council, 1944-45; chmn. Wash. State P.T.A., 1946; mem. citizens' adv. bd. Wenatchee Valley Community Coll., 1945-58, rec. sec., 1950-58; sec. Monitor Community Club, 1929-33, 59-62; founder, pres. Monitor Home Arts Club, 1930; charter mem. Chelan County Homemaker's Council, pres., 1931-33; pres. North Central Wash. Fedn. Women's Clubs, 1944-46, state chmn., 1946-48, state v.p., 1948; one of founders Wash. State Homemakers Council, sec., 1953-56; charter mem. Monitor Hosp. Guild, pres., 1936; patron Wenatchee Civic Ballet, Seattle Symphony, Wenatchee Valley Symphony League; Monitor rep. Wash. Dept. Civil Def.; mem. Chelan County Farm Labor Council, Wash. State Adv. Commn. Urban Renewal and Planning Grants-in-Aid Legislation; sponsor U. Wash. Forum Series; co-chmn. Helen Kingle Scholarship. Vice pres., chmn. Chelan County Republican Com.; pres. Monitor Rep. Women's Club. Bd. dirs. Emma P. Chadwick Nursing Home, 1954-60. Named one of 5 alumni for outstanding accomplishment Wash. State U., 1953, Outstanding Woman Grad. of Achievement Class of 1923, 1973. Mem. D.A.R. (chpt. regent 1963-65, state corr. sec. 1956-68, state bd. 1960-63; mem. state bicentennial com.; treas. state officers club, chmn. Indian Scholarship 1971-72), North Central Wash. Home Econs. Assn. (charter, pres. 1963), Daus. Colonial Wars (state council 1959-62), Nat. Soc. New Eng. Pioneer Women, Am. Assn. U. Women (charter, past pres., Wash. chmn. 1955-57), Daus. Am. Colonists (charter-regent 1958-61, state historian, state sec.), Nat., Monitor Wash. (life) ret. tchrs. assns.; Wash. State Tb Assn. (life), Daus. Union Vets. Civil War (pres. 1953-54, charter mem., past pres., club), League Women Voters, Nat. Home Demonstrations Council, Chelan County Pioneer Assn., Wash. State Music Clubs, Asso. Country Women World, P.T.A. (life), Internat. Platform Assn., Little Art Gallery, Zeta League-St. Anthony's Community Hosp., Allied Art Council North Central Wash., Wenatchee Panhellenic Assn. (historian 1955—), N. Central Wash. Heritage Com., Intercontinental Biog. Assn., Willis Carey Hist. Mus., Chelan County Old Timer's Assn. (mem. bd. 1971-72), Am. Assn. Ret. Persons, Douglas County Ret. Tchrs. Assn. (officer, chmn. 1966—), Phi Kappa Phi, Delta Kappa Gamma, Alpha Xi Delta (charter mem. pres.), Epsilon Sigma Omicron. Episcopalian (bishop's com.). Mem. Order Eastern Star (worthy matron, grand adah), Order White Shrine Jerusalem (worthy high priestess). Clubs: Wenatchee Women's (sec. 1962-64, treas., v.p.), Wash. State White Shrine (charter; v.p. 1956-58); Am. Home-Cashmere Women's (pres. 1929-31); Wenatchee Garden (charter; sec. 1929-31); Literary Tourist; Knife and Fork, Women of Rotary. Free-lance writer Wenatchee Daily World, 1923—. Home: Riverside Orchards E Richared Dr Monitor WA 98836

RICHARDSON, EILEEN BROAD, assn. editor; b. Sunderland, Ont., Can., May 18, 1914; d. John Thomas and Mariah Jane (Graham) Broad; B.A., United Coll., Winnipeg, Man., Can., 1933; m. Fred Richardson, Dec. 15, 1945; 1 dau., Joy. High sch. tchr., 1934-46; mng. dir. Dale Carnegie course in effective speaking and human relations, 1950-52; real estate broker, 1952-53; founder Internat. Assn. Master Penmen and Tchrs. of Handwriting, 1950, pres., 1960-62, editor Penmen's Newsletter, 1967—. Dir. Property Owners Assn. Trustee Ottawa Pub. Sch. Bd., 1959-70, Ottawa Bd. Edn., 1970-72. Mem. Heraldry Soc. Can., Mothercraft Soc. (dir. 1952-58). Home: 34 Broadway Av Ottawa KIS 2V6 ON Canada

RICHARDSON, HAZEL ADAMS, librarian; b. Chireno, Tex., Oct. 28, 1912; d. George Ernest and Mary (Barton) Adams; B.A., U. Tex., 1933, M.A., 1936; B.S. in L.S., La. State U., 1936; m. David Bonner Richardson, June 10, 1944 (div. May 1963); children—George Adams, William Darby. Childrens librarian Tyrrell Pub. Library, Beaumont, Tex., 1936-38, Detroit Pub. Libraries, 1938-42, 1944-45, asst. schs. dept., 1958-61; readers adv. Tex. A. and M. U., College Station, 1942-44; asst. adult circulation dept. Redwood City (Cal.) Pub. Library, 1946-48, childrens librarian, 1948-49; head librarian Bryan (Tex.) Pub. Library, 1961—. Columnist, Bryan Daily Eagle, 1961—. Mem. Tex. Bd. Library Examiners, Brazos County Hist. Survey Com. Mem. Am. Assn. U. Women, Bus. and Profl. Womens Club, D.A.R., Daus. Republic of Tex., Am., Tex. State library assns., Nat. League Am. Pen Women (br. pres. 1966-68), Poetry Soc., U.D.C. Democrat. Episcopalian. Clubs: Womans Civic League (pres. 1963), Womans, Briar Crest Country. Home: 800 S Ennis Bryan TX 77801 Office: 201 E 26th St Bryan TX 77801

RICHARDSON, JOSEPHINE ANTONETTE WAJERT, physician; b. New Castle, Pa., Feb. 22, 1926; d. John Charles and Gertrude (Krzyzan) Wajert; student Westminster Coll., New Wilmington, Pa., 1942-44; M.D., U. Buffalo, 1948. Intern Quincy (Mass.) City Hosp., 1948-49; gen. practice, Flint, Mich., 1950-58; gen. practice phys. medicine and rehab., Phila., 1961-69; asso. in medicine Jefferson Med. Coll., Phila., 1966-68, asst. prof., 1968-69; asso. med. dir. Inst. Phys. Medicine and Rehab., Louisville, 1970—; dir. dept. phys. medicine and rehab. Camden County Gen. Hosp., Lakeland, N.J., 1964-69, The Lankenau Hosp., Phila., 1968-69. Adj. asst. prof. medicine U. Louisville. Mem. A.M.A., Am. Acad. Phys. Medicine and Rehab., Am. Congress Rehab. Medicine, Am. Acad. Cerebral Palsy, Am., Ky. acads. family physicians, Am. Med. Womens Assn., Jefferson County Med. Soc., Ky. Med. Assn., Nat. Rehab. Assn., Pan Am. Med. Assn. Home: 501 Quail's Run Apt B-1 Louisville KY 40207 Office: 220 Abraham Flexner Way Louisville KY 40202

RICHARDSON, MABEL LOWE (MRS. HERBERT RANDALL RICHARDSON), state legislator; b. Randolph, N.H.; d. Thaddeus Sebisky and Frances Hines (Jenkins) Lowe; m. Herbert Randall Richardson, Feb. 15, 1917; children—Edwin H., Dwight B. Statewide recreational dir. crafts U. N.H., 1935-40; field sec. Gasoline Dealers Assn., N.H. and Vt., 1940-45; field rep. Independent Grocers Assn., 1945-60; mem. N.H. Ho. of Reps., 1947-48, 67—. Mem. N.H. Legislative Adminstrn. Leader 4-H Youth Extension Group; rep. Gen. Ct., 1947-48, 70-74; pres. Gorham P.T.A.; mem. Coos County Finance Com., 1967—; supr. Checklist-Randolph, 1971-75; mem. N.H. Gov.'s Council for Aged. Chmn. Coos County Republican Exec. Com. Mem. Am. Legion Aux. (past pres.). Conglist. Rebekah, Odd Fellow, Grange. Address: Randolph NH 03593*

RICHARDSON, MARIE SMITH (MRS. ELVA RICHARDSON), engring. co. librarian; b. Decaturville, Tenn., Sept. 2, 1924; d. Myron Cortell and Narcia (Ellison) Smith; student U. Tenn., 1943-46; B.S., U. Chattanooga, 1960; postgrad. So. Conn. State Coll., 1962; m. Elva Richardson, Oct. 18, 1946; children—Priscilla Ann (Mrs. Frederick M. Fuhrken), Stephen Fred. Dir. consumer research and testing Chicopee Mfg. Co., Milltown, N.J., 1956-57; chief librarian Combustion Engring., Inc., Chattanooga, 1957-60, chief librarian engring. research library, Windsor, Conn., 1961-63, departmental mgr. corporate library system, 1963—; tchr. pub. schs., Chattanooga, 1960-61. Cons. Dixie Mercerizing Co., Chattanooga, 1960, Bowaters So. Paper Corp., Calhoun, Tenn., 1960; John Cotton Dana lectr. La. State U., 1967. Mem. spl. adv. com. devel. and cooperation Conn. State Library. Mem. Tenn., Conn. Southeastern library assns., Spl. Libraries Assn. (pres. Conn. Valley chpt. 1966-67, cons. com. 1967-69, sec.-treas. engring. div. 1972—). Contbr. articles to profl. jours. Home: 1111 North St Suffield CT 06078 Office: 1000 Prospect Hill Rd Windsor CT 06095

RICHARDSON, MARTHA, nutrition analyst; b. Noble, La., Apr. 22, 1917; d. Alexander M. and Olive (Barlow) Richardson; A.B., U. Mo., 1938, Ph.D. 1953; M.S., Kan. State U., 1939. Dietitian William Newton Meml. Hosp., Winfield, Kan., 1940-42, Molly Stark Sanatorium, Canton, O., 1942-47; asst. dir. residence halls, instr. home econs. U. Mo., 1947-50, instr. home econs., 1951-53; head of foods and nutrition U. Utah, 1953-55; nutrition analyst Agrl. Research Service, Washington, 1955—. Named Distinguished Alumna, U. Mo., 1968. Fellow A.A.A.S.; mem. Am. Dietetic Assn., Am. Home Econs. Assn., Am. Med. Writers Assn., Am. Inst. Food Techologists, Am. Chem. Soc. Am. Assn. Cereal Chemists, Am. Forestry Assn., Am. Assn. U. Women, N.Y. Acad. Scis., Sigma Xi, Gamma Sigma Delta, Phi Upsilon Omicron, Sigma Delta Epsilon. Contbr. articles to profl. jours. Home: 7302 Yale Av College Park MD 20740 Office: Consumer and Food Econs Inst Agrl Research Service Hyattsville MD 20782

RICHARDSON, MARY ELIZABETH (MRS. HOWARD RICHARDSON), physician; b. Los Angeles, June 3, 1927; d. Edward G. and Eva (Kimbell) Dolch; B.A., U. Cal. at Los Angeles, 1949, M.S., 1952; M.D., Womans Med. Coll. Pa., 1956; m. Howard Lockhart Richardson, 1955. Rotating intern Providence Hosp., Seattle, 1956-57; resident in pathology U. Wash. and Affiliated Hosps., Seattle, 1957-61; spl. resident pathology Washington U. Sch. Medicine, St. Louis, 1961-62, trainee exptl. pathology, 1961-64; asst. pathologist Barnes and Affiliated Hosps., St. Louis, 1962-64; asst. prof. pathology U. Ark. Med. Center, Little Rock, 1964-67; cons. pathologist Maryvale Med. Center, Phoenix, 1967-68; research pathologist, chief electron microscopy Bur. Sci. FDA, Washington, 1968-70; research pathologist, chief electron microscopy Office of Pesticides, Environmental Protection Agy., Washington, 1970—. Diplomate Am. Bd. Pathology. Fellow Am. Soc. Clin. Pathologists; mem. Soc. Pharmacol. and Environmental Pathologists, N.Y. Acad. Scis., Internat. Acad. Pathologists, Electron Microscopy Soc. Am., La. Soc. Electron Microscopists, Am. Soc. Nephrology, A.M.A. Am. Med. Women's Assn., Sigma Xi. 2000 S Eads St Arlington VA 22202 Office: Registry Tissue Reaction to Drugs Armed Forces Inst Pathology Washington DC 20306

RICHARDSON, MARY MARGARET MILNER (MRS. JOHN LAWRENCE RICHARDSON), lawyer; b. Waco, Tex., May 14, 1943; d. James Wilbourne and Margaret (Wiebusch) Milner; A.B., Vassar Coll., 1965; J.D. with honors, George Washington U., 1968; m. John Lawrence Richardson, July 22, 1967. Summer intern Office Undersec. Army, Washington, 1963, USAF Cost Reduction Program, Washington, 1964; legal intern Equal Ednl. Opportunities Program, Office of Health, Edn. and Welfare, Washington, 1966; dir. research asst. Pres.'s Crime Commn., Washington, 1967; admitted to D.C., Va. bars, 1968; law clk. Judge Philip Nichols, Jr., U.S. Ct. of Claims, Washington, 1968-69; atty. Office Chief Counsel, Internal Revenue Service, U.S. Treasury Dept., Washington, 1969—. Research editor George Washington Law Rev., 1966-68; Docent Nat. Gallery Art, 1969-70, Alexandria Hist. Found., 1969. Mem. Jr. Friends YWCA. Mem. No. Va. Fine Arts Assn., Jr. League Washington, Va. State Bar, D.C. Bar Assn., Friends of D.C. Superior Ct. (pres. bd. 1973—) Friends of Stratford, Kappa Beta Pi. Clubs: City Tavern Assn.; Washington Vassar. Home: 501 Duke St Alexandria VA 22314 Office: 1111 Constitution Av Washington DC 20224

RICHARDSON, MAURINE ADAMS (MRS. EDWIN LELAND RICHARDSON), civic worker; b. Olla., La., Aug. 13, 1910; d. Lee Roy and Olive Bertha (Blake) Adams; student Lindenwood Coll., 1926-27; B.S., Asbury Coll., 1930; m. Edwin Leland Richardson, Dec. 31, 1932; 1 dau., Maurine (Mrs. Robert Lenard Modjeski). Tchr. biology and gen. sci. Columbia (La.) High Sch., 1930-32. Active A.R.C., 1941-55, March of Dimes, 1946-60, Muscular Dystrophy Soc., Baton Rouge Little Theater, Anglo-Am. Art Mus.; mem. Baton Rouge Mayor's Com. for Preservation and Restoration of Prince Murat House, 1967; mem. adv. bd. Baton Rouge YWCA; mem. ednl. com. La. Arts and Sci. Center, 1964-73; mem. Jr. League com. for La. Sch. for Blind, 1955-59. Recipient Certificate of Merit, Baton Rouge C. of C., 1950. Mem. Baton Rouge Charity Ball Assn. (dir. 1958-61), Baton Rouge Bar Assn. Aux., Opera Guild Baton Rouge (dir. 1948-64, sec. bd. 1948-52), Found. for Historic La., (dir. 1963-71, recipient spl. award 1966), Jr. League Baton Rouge, Woman's Soc. Christian Edn. Baton Rouge (mem. exec. bd. and sec. 1938-41), Our Lady of Lake Hosp. Aux., Mental Health Assn. Baton Rouge, Women's Club, D.A.R., Novel Book Club, Nat. Trust for Historic Preservation, Friends of Cabildo New Orleans, Delta Gamma. Home: 7815 Highland Rd Baton Rouge LA 70808

RICHARDSON, MILDRED TOURTILLOTT (MRS. HAROLD WELLINGTON RICHARDSON), psychologist; b. North Hampton, N.H., May 8, 1907; d. Herbert Shaw and Sarah Louise (Fife) Tourtillott; B.A., Bates Coll., 1930; M.A., U. Mich., 1948; Ed. Specialist, Butler U., 1961; Ph.D., Ind. U., 1965; m. Harold Wellington Richardson, June 25, 1932; children—Elizabeth (Mrs. E.B. Ruben), Constance (Mrs. J. Van Valer), Carol-Louise (Mrs. T. Eads). Tchr. math. Norwich (Conn.) Free Acad., Conn., 1930-32; war emergency tchr. sci., Port Huron, Mich., 1943-45; dir. psychol. services and guidance Franklin, (Ind.) Community Sch. Corp., 1956-64; sr. sch. psychologist Devereux Found., Devon, Pa., 1965—. Tchr. psychology of spl. edn. Pa. State U., 1966-68; cons. to pub. schs. on ednl. psychology, sch. psychology, pre-sch. edn. Diplomate Am. Bd. Profl. Psychology. Mem. Am. Psychol. Assn. (mem. div. 16 com. on profl. status 1972-73), Phi Kappa Phi. Baptist. Contbr. articles on spl. edn. to profl. jours. Home: 457 School Lane Strafford Wayne PA 19087 Office: Administrative Services Devereux Foundation Devon PA 19333

RICHARDSON, MYRTLE, abstracter, former judge; b. Jefferson County, O., July 2, 1907; d. Thomas and Blanche (Whitecotton) Heinselman; student Kansas State Tchrs. Coll., 1926; m. Harold E. Richardson, Mar. 4, 1929 (div.); dau., Nancy Lee (Mrs. Donald W. Ridgway). Tchr. pub. schs. Edwards County, Kan. 1924-28; reporter, advertiser Kinsley (Kan.) Graphic, 1928-35; editor, advt. mgr. So. Standard, McMinnville, Tenn., 1935-36; mgr. Kinsley Graphic, 1937-41; abstracter H. F. Thompson, Kinsley, 1943-54; editor Kinsley Mercury, 1954-57; abstracter, Kinsley, 1957—; probate judge, Kinsley, 1958-69; judge municipal ct. City of Kinsley, 1958-69. Bd. dirs. United Drive, 1947-57, Edwards County chpt. A.R.C., 1940-50; community and project leader 4-H Club, 1943-52; community and project leader Edwards County 4-H Who's Who Club, 1943-52; pres. P.T.A., 1940-44. Vice chmn. Edwards County Democratic Com. 1956—; pres. Edwards County Fedn. Dem. Women's Club, 1970-74. Mem. C. of C. (sec.-mgr. 1947-54), Edwards County Hist. Soc. (historian), S. Central Kan. Probate Judges Assn. (pres. 1966). Home: 120 N 2d St Kinsley KS 67547 Office: 218 W 8th St Kinsley KS 67547

RICHARDSON, RUTH ANN, librarian; b. Vinton, Ia., Dec. 30, 1923; d. Ashley Ryther and Elsie Elizabeth (Schmidt) Richardson; B.A., U. No. Ia., 1946; M.A., U. Wis., 1955. Tchr. Benton County (Ia.) Pub. Schs., 1942-43, Decorah (Ia.) High Sch., 1946-52, Harlandale High Sch., San Antonio, 1952-54; classifier Ia. State U. Library, 1955-56; head reference Cedar Rapids (Ia.) Pub. Library, 1956-60, head adult services, 1960—; vis. asst. prof. Fla. State U., 1959-60. Mem. A.L.A., Ia. Library Assn (pres. adult services sect. 1961), Ia. Adult Edn. Assn., Conn. Hist. Soc., New Eng. Hist. Geneal. Soc., Beta Phi Mu, Kappa Delta Pi. Presbyn. Home: 1400 2d Av SE Cedar Rapids IA 52403 Office: 428 3d Av SE Cedar Rapids IA 52401

RICHARDSON, SHIRLEY MAXINE (MRS. ARTHUR L. RICHARDSON), editor; b. Rising Sun, Ind., May 3, 1931; d. William Fenton and Mary (Phillips) Keith; grad. pub. high sch.; m. Arthur L. Richardson, Feb. 11, 1950; children—Mary Jane (Mrs. David M. Hamm), JoDee, Steven Lee. Editor, personnel mgr. Mayhill Publs., Knightstown, Ind., 1967—, editor Eastern Ind. Farmer, 1967—, Ind. Angus News, 1974—, editor The Banner, 1967-69, asso. editor Tri State Trader, 1968—. Mem. Am. Legion Aux., Home Econs. Club. Home: 366 E Carey St Knightstown IN 46148 Office: 27 N Jefferson St Knightstown IN 46148

RICHARDSON, SYLVIA ONESTI, physician; B. San Francisco, Sept. 12, 1920; d. Silvio J. and Johanna (Kristoffy) Onesti; B.A., Stanford, 1940; postgrad. U. Washington, 1940-41; M.A., Columbia U., 1942; M.D., McGill U., 1948; m. William R. Richardson, Sept. 8, 1951; children—William Charles, Christopher Lee. Intern Children's Meml. Hosp., Montreal, 1948-49; resident Children's Med. Center, Boston, 1949-50; instr. spl. edn. Columbia, 1942-43; supr. hearing handicapped New Rochelle pub. schs. 1942-43; clin. fellow in medicine Boston Children's Med. Center 1949-51, dir. speech clinic, 1950-52, asso. physician, 1951-52, research fellow in surgery, 1954-55; instr. speech dept. Boston U., 1950-52, San Diego State Coll., 1952-54; teaching fellow in medicine Harvard U., 1951-52; cons. dept. child health and maternal welfare State Mass., 1951-52; asst. clin. prof. pediatrics State U. N.Y., Downstate Med. Center, 1957-58; asst. prof. pediatrics and psychiatry, dir. child study center U. Okla. Sch. Medicine, 1958-65; asst. clin. prof. pediatrics U. Cin. Sch. Medicine, 1965-67; asso. prof., 1967—; cons. dept. child health and maternal welfare, Okla., 1957-65; spl. cons. Nat. Inst. Nervous Diseases and Blindness, 1960-62; spl. cons. on mental retardation Okla. State Dept. Public Welfare, 1963-65; cons. Bur. State Services USPHS, Bur. Edn. Handicapped, U.S. Office Edn. Mem. Okla. gov's com. White House Conf., 1960, White House Conf. on Children, 1970, Okla. citizen's com. Adequate Higher Edn., 1958-62. Named Okla. Woman of Year, 1964; recipient Internat. Learning Disabilities award for distinguished service, 1969, Okla. Pioneer award, 1970. Fellow Am. Speech and Hearing Assn. (mem. exec. council 1957-59; chmn. elect ho. of dels. 1964, chmn. 1965, pres. 1973), Royal Soc. Health; mem. A.M.A. Mass. Speech and Hearing Assn., (co-founder, pres. 1950-52, pres. elect. 1972), Am. Bd. Examiners in Speech Pathology and Audiology, Am. Assn. Cleft Palate Rehab., Am. Montessori Soc., Cin. Pediatric Soc., Assn. for Children with Learning Disabilities (profl. adv. bd. 1964—). Editorial bd. Acta Symbolica, Acad. Therapy, Human Devel. and Child Psychiatry. Children's House Mag. Home: 1032 Hatch St Cincinnati OH 45202 Office: Children's Pavilion 3300 Elland Av Cincinnati OH 45229

RICHARDSON, THELMA POWELL (MRS. THOMAS LEE RICHARDSON), librarian; b. Cuthbert, Ga., Aug. 1; d. Benjamin Joseph and Pearl Mattie (Alexander) Powell; A.B., W.Va. State Coll., 1940; B.L.S., Atlanta U., 1948; M.S. in Library Sci., Syracuse U., 1964; m. Thomas Lee Richardson, Feb. 16, 1954. Asst. librarian Lincoln U., Jefferson City, Mo., 1948-50; librarian Tyler Jr. Coll. br. at Tex. Coll., 1951-55; head librarian Alcorn A. and M. U., Lerman, Miss., 1955-57; librarian liberal arts, sci. and tech. Grambling (La.) Coll., 1960—. Active Girl Scouts Am. Mem. Beta Phi Mu, Zeta Phi Beta. Home: PO Box 258 Grambling LA 71245

RICHARDSON, WILDA, orgn. exec.; b. Seneca, S.C.; d. Silas Luther and Mary Alma (Kay) Richardson; student Agnes Scott Coll., also spl. courses various univs. Organizer, mgr. Welcome Car Service, Atlanta; ins., stocks, bonds salesman; exec. dir. Pilot Club Internat., Macon, Ga., 1939-71. Sec., D.F. Dickey, Inc., Macon. Mem. Freedom's Found. awards jury, 1951; mem. womens adv. com. President's Com. for Traffic Safety. Sec., Ga. Women's Democratic Club. Mem. Am. Soc. Assn. Execs., Nat. Council Women of U.S., Nat. Safety Council (womens' com.), Service Club Leadership Conf., Middle Ga. Hist. Soc. Club: Pilot Internat. (exec. dir. charitable and ednl. found.). Editor: Pilot Log, 1939-71. Address: 642 Orange St Macon GA 31201

RICHERT, MARLYS RUTH, educator; b. Wilmot, S.D.; d. Reuben C. and Elsie (Givney) Richert; B.S., Stout State U., 1935; M.S., U. Wis., 1957, Ph.D., 1961. Home econs. tchr., Mt. Hope, Wis., 1935-37; county extension home economist, Monroe, Wis., 1937-46, Waukesha, Wis., 1946-53; home econs. dist. leader U. Wis., Madison, 1953-59, prof. nat. extension center for advanced study, 1961-63, prof., state extension home econs. leader, 1963-66, prof. home econs. edn., state home econs. leader, dir. Center for Women and Family Living Edn., 1966—. Mem. county food rationing bd. Community Youth Council, 1943-45; chmn. County Nutrition Council, 1942-45. Recipient Meritorious award Wis. Extension Service, 1943, Distinguished Service award, 1966, Distinguished Service award Nat. Assn. Extension Home Economists, 1947, Distinguished Service award Stout State U. Alumni, 1967, W.K. Kellogg fellowships, 1957, 59-61. Mem. Adult Edn. Assn., Am. Council Consumer Interests, Assn. Land Instns. (mem. extension sub-com. on home econs. 1965-69), Am., Wis. home econs. assns., Phi Upsilon Omicron, Epsilon Sigma Phi. Club: Madison (Wis.) Civic. Home: 4805 Holiday Dr Madison WI 53711 Office: Univ Extension 610 Langdon St Madison WI 53706

RICHESIN, AILEEN KIMBROUGH (MRS. HENRY HUGH RICHESIN), city ofcl.; b. Loudon, Tenn., Oct. 31, 1911; d. Carl Henderson and Pearl (Hudson) Kimbrough; student Martha Washington Coll., 1929-30, U. Tenn., 1931-33; m. Henry Hugh Richesin, Oct. 28, 1932; 1 son, Don Henri. Owner, dir. Wee Wisdom kindergarten, Loudon, 1953—; city commr., Loudon, 1969-70, 71-72, 73-74, commr. civic affairs, 1969—; chmn. adv. com., Loudon, 1969—. Mem. Future Homemakers Am., Woman's Soc. Christian Service (pres. 1959-60), Tenn., East Tenn. hist. socs., D.A.R. (state rec. sec. 1954-56, state 2d vice regent 1956-59, dist. dir. 1952-54, 65-67, mem. state officers club), Daus. Am. Colonists (state librarian 1959-62, state 2d vice regent 1967-70, state chmn. nat. def. 1973—, mem. state officers club), Sons and Daus. Pilgrims (state elder 1964-67), Colonial Dames XVII Century (state registrar 1973—, Outstanding Mem. 1970). Democrat. Methodist. Home: 613 Mulberry St Loudon TN 37774 Office: City Hall Box 251 Loudon TN 37774

RICHEY, DOROTHY HILLIARD (MRS. NOYES RICHEY), writer, lectr., broadcaster; b. Norphlet, Ark.; d. Albert and Ruth (Germillion) Hilliard; B.A., U. S.W. La., 1946; postgrad. U. Okla.; m. Noyes Richey, Apr. 12, 1947; children—Noyes, Dorothy Ruth, Kenneth Albert, Jeanne Elizabeth, William Henry. Fashion coordinator, radio dir. Muller Co., Lake Charles, La., 1948-50; TV performer, Lake Charles, 1953-56, free-lance, Houston, Miami, Fla.; writer, fiction, non-fiction, network radio and TV, 1948—; lectr. 1953—; star daily radio show KLVI, Beaumont, Tex., 1967-72, now syndicated; v.p. BRB Film Prodns.; tchr. night classes Writing for TV, creative writing Lamar U., Beaumont, pres. Richey Internat.

Newspaper Service, Richey-Bosch Assos., Beaumont; editor weekly newspaper The Sentinel, 1973—. Mem. publicity com. Beaumont Symphony League, 1961-64, publicity scripts, Suicide Rescue, 1965-67, Beaumont Symphony Soc., 1967—. Recipient Golden Mike award, 1968. Mem. Am. Women in Radio and TV (chpt. v.p., pres., nat. dir. 1968-71), Women Broadcasters Am. (charter), Am. Assn. U. Women, Internat. Platform Assn., Nat. Acad. Television Arts and Scis., Internat. Radio and Television Soc., Women in Communications. Author: Battle Row, 1956; Road to San Jacinto, 1961; Marauders of the Sabine, 1964; (with Patricia Bosch) How to be Rich and Beautiful, 1968; The Early Morning Man, 1973; The Graftmaster, 1974; also syndicated Today's Woman in Today's World column, travel column Dorothy Richey's Travel Talk radio series. Contbr. articles to nat. mags. Office: PO Box 5201 Beaumont TX 77702

RICHEY, MARY ANNE REIMANN (MRS. WILLIAM K. RICHEY), judge; b. Shelbyville, Ind., Oct. 24, 1917; d. H. Wallace and Emma (Nading) Reimann; student Purdue U., 1937-40; J.D., U. Ariz., 1951; m. William K. Richey, Oct. 8, 1959; 1 dau., Anne Marie. Admitted to Ariz. bar, 1951; dep. county atty. Pima County, 1952-54; asst. U.S. atty., Dist. of Ariz., Tucson, 1954-59, U.S. atty., 1960; judge Superior Ct. of Pima County, Tucson, 1964—, asso. presiding judge, 1972—. Mem. Jud. Qualification Commn., 1970—, Criminal Code Revision Commn., 1973—, Gov.'s Commn. on Status of Women, 1971-73; co-chmn. Supreme Ct. Com. to Revise Civil Jury Instrns., 1971-73. Mem. adv. bd. Salvation Army, 1968—; pres. bd. dirs. YWCA, Tucson, 1968-69. Served with WASP, 1944-45. Mem. Am., Pima County bar assns., State Bar Ariz. Home: 2800 E River Rd Tucson AZ 85718 Office: Pima County Court House Tucson AZ 85701

RICHMAN, BEVERLY LINDA (MRS. LAWRENCE PRUTKIN), physician; b. N.Y.C., July 13, 1938; d. Alexander and Charlotte Dorothy (Yudell) Richman; A.B., U. Mich., 1960; M.D., N.Y. Med. Coll., 1964; m. Lawrence Prutkin, Nov. 28, 1970; 1 son, Brad. Intern Beth Israel Hosp., N.Y.C., 1964-65, resident, 1965-66; NIH hematology fellow N.Y. Med. Coll., 1967-68; asst. dir. blood bank Georgetown U. Hosp., 1969-70; also instr. medicine Georgetown U. Sch. Medicine; sr. staff physician Med. Services, Morris J. Bernstein Inst., Beth Israel Med. Center, also asst. attending hematologist Beth Israel Med. Center, N.Y.C., 1972—; clin. asso. in medicine Mt. Sinai Sch. Medicine, 1972—. Mem. Am. Assn. Blood Banks, N.Y. County Med. Soc., Med. Soc. State N.Y. Home: Fox Den Rd Mount Kisco NY 10549 Office: 307 2d Av New York City NY 10003

RICHMAN, EVELYN BEATRICE, audio vis. co. exec.; b. Mpls., Oct. 11, 1912; d. Mark and Gertrude (Weisburg) Braun; student Bryant Stratton Bus. Coll., 1934-35, Northwestern U., 1935; m. Paul Richman, Nov. 18, 1934 (dec. Jan. 1970); children—Melvyn, Gale (Mrs. Dennis Vales). Exec. sec. Jewish Community Center Niles Twp., Skokie, Ill., 1957-62; asst. to pres. Standard Projector & Equipment Co., Inc., Glenview, Ill., 1962-74, office mgr. credits and collections, 1964—. Recipient Outstanding journalistic Potential award, Writer's Digest, 1945. Mem. Edgewater B'Nai B'Rith (pres. 1947-48, editor Bull. 1948). Club: Edgewater Bowling League (pres. 1946-51). Home: 8801 Golf Rd Des Plaines IL 60016 Office: 3070 Lake Terrace St Glenview IL 60025

RICHMAN, GERTRUDE GROSS (MRS. BERNARD RICHMAN), civic worker; b. N.Y.C., May 16, 1908; d. Samuel and Sarah Yetta (Seltzer) Gross; B.S., Tchrs. Coll. Columbia, 1948, M.A., 1949; m. Bernard Richman, Apr. 5, 1930; children—David, Susan. Vol. worker Hackensack Hosp., 1948-70; mem. bd. dirs. YMHA, Bergen Co., N.J., pres. women's div., 1940-50; chmn. Leonia Friends of Bergen County Mental Health Consultation Center, 1959; founder, hon. pres. Bergen County Serv-A-Com., affiliated with women orgns. Div. Nat. Jewish Welfare Bd.; v.p. N.J. sect. Nat. Jewish Welfare Bd., 1964-71; hon. trustee women's group Bergen County Jewish Fedn. Community Services; vol. edn. chmn. Bergen County Office on Aging; Mem. Hackensack Bd. of Edn., 1946-51; mem. pub. relations com. Leonia Pub. Schs. 1957-58; N.J. del. White House Conf. on Aging, 1971. Trustee Mary McLeod Bethune Scholarship Fund; v.p. Bergen County nat. women's com. Brandeis U., 1966-67. Recipient citation Nat. Council Jewish Women and YWCA in Bergon County, 1962; citation Nat. Jewish Welfare Bd., 1964, Harry S. Feller award, N.J. Region, 1965. Mem. Kappa Delta Pi. Club: Woman's (scholarship bazaar chmn. 1958-60). Home: 355 Highwood Av Leonia NJ 07605

RICHMAN, JOAN, television producer; b. St. Louis, Apr. 10, 1939; d. Stanley M. and Barbara (Friedman) Richman; B.A., Wellesley Coll., 1961. Researcher, CBS News, N.Y.C., 1961-64, researcher spl. events unit, 1965-67, mgr. research for Republican and Democratic nat. convs., 1968, asso. producer news coverage, including funerals Martin Luther King and Robert Kennedy, flights of Apollo 7 and 8, 1968, primaries and nat. convs., 1972; producer CBS News, 1969-72, The Reasoner Report, ABC News, 1972—; broadcasts include flights of Apollo 9-16, funeral Dwight D. Eisenhower, Solar Eclipse, Opening Day at Expo '70, Pres. Nixon's 1970 European trip; asst. producer WNDT, N.Y.C., 1964-65. Recipient Television Acad. Award for CBS News space coverage, 1970-71, 71-72; Alumnae Achievement award Wellesley Coll., 1973. Mem. Wellesley Coll. Alumnae Assn. (pres. class of 1961, 1966-70). Home: 240 W 21st St New York City NY 10011 Office: 1926 Broadway New York City NY 10023

RICHMOND, HARRIET DIGGS, educator; b. Buffalo, Mar. 29, 1924; d. Harry Walker and Roberta Celeste (Diggs) Richmond; student Hiram Coll., 1941-42; B.Ed., U. Pa., 1945; certificate Phila. Sch. Occupational Therapy, 1946; postgrad. Seattle U., 1957; M.Ed., U. Puget Sound, 1967. Occupational therapist N.J. State Hosp., Trenton, 1946-48, Billings VA Hosp., Ft. Benjamin Harrison, Ind., 1948-49, Firland Sanitarium, Seattle, 1949-55; head occupational therapist Seattle Pub. Schs., 1955-64; instr. U. Puget Sound, Tacoma, Wash., 1964-67, asst. prof., 1967-72, asso. prof. occupational therapy, 1972—. Sec.-treas., trustee Westgate Green Homeowners Assn., 1972-73; mem. exec. bd. Tacoma br. Council on Aging, 1973-74; chmn. exec. bd. Tacoma Presbyn. Ednl. Parish. Mem. Am., Wash. (past v.p., sec., treas., now del.) occupational therapy assns., Council for Exceptional Children (past treas. King County chpt.), Am. Assn. Univ. Profs. Presbyn. (elder, chmn. bd. trustees 1974—). Home: 1372 Bel Air Rd Tacoma WA 98406

RICHMOND, JANICE DORIS SALTMAN (MRS. EDWARD STANLEY RICHMOND), social worker; b. Boston, Feb. 28, 1926; d. Harry Hyman and Lillian (Cohen) Saltman; B.S., Simmons Coll., 1946; M.S.W., U. Md., 1963; m. Edward Stanley Richmond, Nov. 26, 1950; children—Kenneth Arnold, Michele Dawn, Cheryl Ann. Field instr. U. Md., 1965-66; with welfare unit Sinai-Druid Comprehensive Pediatric Center, 1966-68, dist. supr. Western and Druid dists., 1968; caseworker protective services Balt. (Md.) City Dept. Social Services, 1961-64, chief div. day care, 1970-71, chief client rehab. through ednl. activities div., 1971-73, div. chief spl. projects, 1973—. Balt. adminstr. WIN II, 1973. Mem. Nat. Assn. Social Workers, Am. Pub. Welfare Assn., Md. State Conf. Social Welfare, Acad. Certified Social Workers. Mem. Order Eastern Star (chpt. matron 1960-61). Home: Apt 10 Stevenson Village Apts 12 Stonehenge Circle Pikesville MD 21208 Office: 312 E Oliver St Baltimore MD 21202

RICHMOND, LEE JOYCE BLANK (MRS. ALVIN RICHMOND), psychologist, educator; b. Balt., May 31, 1934; d. Alexander J. and Anne (Morganstern) Blank; B.S., Loyola Coll., Balt., 1961; M.Ed., Johns Hopkins, 1968; Ph.D., U. Md., 1972; m. Alvin Richmond, Aug. 9, 1953; children—Ruth Ellen, Stephen Arthur, Sharon Eve, Jessica Jane. Tchr. Balt. City Pub. Schs., 1959-60; free-lance writer, 1960-64; tchr. Seton High Sch., Balt., 1964-66; tchr., counselor Balt. City Pub. Schs., 1966-69; asst. prof. psychology, dir. continuing edn. for women Essex Community Coll., Balt., 1969-71; asso. prof. psychology Dundalk Community Coll., Balt., 1971—, chmn. div. social sci., 1971—; lectr. Johns Hopkins, 1972—. Mem. Md. Commn. on Status Women, 1970—, co-chmn. edn. com., 1971-72, chmn., 1973-74, chmn. ad hoc com. on child care, 1971—, exec. com., 1970—; mem. Md. 4-C Com., 1971—; mem. Baltimore County 4-C Com., 1971—. Mem. Am., Md. psychol. assns., Am. Personnel and Guidance Assn., Am. Assn. U. Profs., Am. Coll. Personnel Assn., Pi Lambda Theta, Phi Delta Gamma. Editor (with Eileen Weller) To Promote Good Will, 1964; cons. on film Workshop in Self-Discovery, 1972. Home: 8907 Greylock Rd Baltimore MD 21208

RICHMOND, PHYLLIS ALLEN, educator; b. Boston, Jan. 5, 1921; d. Charles Francis Hitchcock and Alberta (Currie) Allen; A.B., Western Res. U., 1942, M.S. in Library Sci., 1956; M.A., U. Pa., 1946, Ph.D., 1949; m. James Hugh Richmond, Sept. 24, 1949. Curator history Rochester Mus. Arts. and Scis., 1943-47; research asst. history of medicine Johns Hopkins, 1952; cataloger, supr. sci. libraries, information systems specialist U. Rochester Library, 1955-68; prof. library sci. Syracuse U., 1969, Case Western Res. U., 1970—. Predoctoral fellow Am. Council Learned Socs., 1947-48; Bennett fellow U. Pa., 1948-49. Mem. A.L.A., Am. Soc. Information Sci. (award of merit 1972), Spl. Libraries Assn., History of Sci. Soc., Am. Assn. History of Medicine, Classification Research Group, Am. Assn. Library Schs., Am. Assn. Variable Star Observers, Solar Flare Patrol, Phi Beta Kappa. Republican. Presbyn. Author: Americans and the Germ Theory of Disease, 1949; Index to Scientific Journal Title Abbreviations, 1964. Contbr. articles profl. jours. Home: 6628 Aintree Park Dr Mayfield Village OH 44143 Office: Baker Bldg Case Western Reserve University Cleveland OH 44106

RICHMOND, RUTH EDITH, archtl. and interior designer; b. Bklyn., Apr. 4, 1912; d. Louis and Dora (Markowitz) Silver; student Cooper Union, Pratt Inst. Art; children—Glenn, Roger. Former dress designer, owner Vogue Design Studio; radio personality WSUN, St. Petersburg, Fla.; corporate v.p., v.p. design Richmond Constrn. Corp., Sarasota, Fla. Mem. Fla. Gov.'s Com. on Status Women, 1973—; com. mem. Van Wezel Performing Arts, Sarasota, 1973—. Registered real estate broker, Fla. Mem. Fla. Residential Designers Assn., Inst. Practicing Designers (hon. London, Eng.), Women in Constrn., Women in Engring., Nat. Soc. Interior Designers. Home: Whittier Sarasota FL 33577 Office: 3500 S Tamiami Trail Sarasota FL 33579

RICHOUX, PATRICIA PLATT (MRS. HENRY J. RICHOUX), author; b. Omaha, Neb., Nov. 1, 1927; d. Howard Julius and Louise (Kinney) Platt; student Doane Coll., 1945-47; m. Henry J. Richoux, Aug. 8, 1947; children—Howard, David, John, Donna. Group leader, Cub Scouts, 1957-62, Campfire Girls, 1963-66. Mem. United Ch. Christ. Author: A Long Walk on a Short Dock, 1969; Follow the Leader, 1971; The Stardust Kid, 1973. Home: 6652 Richmond Av Richmond CA 94805

RICHTER, ANNE THORBECK (MRS. PAUL PHILIP RICHTER), polit. worker; b. Churches Ferry, N.D., June 15, 1911; d. George Henry and Synneva D. (Erie) Thorbeck; B.S., U. Minn., 1937; m. Paul Philip Richter, Dec. 28, 1940; children—Mary Ann, Paulette (Mrs. Don Genereux), Philip, Paul. 4-H agt. U. Minn. Extension Service, N.W. Minn., 1934-37, 39-40; home econs. tchr., Barnesville, Minn., 1937-38; home mgmt. supr. Farm Security Adminstrn., No. Minn., 1938-39, 40-42; spl. tchr., Wadena (Minn.) High Sch., 1966-69. Vol. cons. A.R.C. blood program, 1969—; sec., Recreation Bd., Wadena, Minn., 1946—; sec. Wadena (Minn.) Housing and Redevel. Authority, 1966—; mem. adv. bd. Fergus Falls Community Coll., 1972—; mem. regional adv. bd. A.R.C. Blood Program, St. Paul, 1965—. Sec., Wadena County Democratic-Farm-Labor party, 1951-55, chmn., 1955-65, 69-71, asso. chmn. 7th Congl. Dist., Minn., 1971-74; chmn. Minn. Vol. com. for re-election Gov. Wendell Anderson, 1974; nat. del. Dem. Nat. Conv., 1968, 72. Recipient Thanks Badge, Girl Scouts Am., 1952, Alumni Service award U. Minn., 1963, Alumni Recognition award State 4-H, 1964, Outstanding Community Service award Wadena C. of C., 1973, plaque appreciation Gov. Minn., 1974. Mem. Alumni Assn. U. Minn. Coll. Agr. for Home Econs. (pres. 1962). Roman Catholic. Home: 415 7th St SW Wadena MN 56482

RICHTER, BEATRICE H. OVERS (MRS. ELMER L. RICHTER SR.), real estate investor, civic worker; b. Buffalo, Aug. 12; d. Anthoney J. and Catherine E. (Novak) Schramka; student U. Buffalo, 1929, Cornell U., 1940, Stanford, 1963; m. Charles F. Overs, May 13, 1940 (dec. Aug. 1953); children—Ronald R., Charles F., Garold R.; m. 2d, Elmer L. Richter, Nov. 4, 1966. Officer, Internal Revenue Dept., Buffalo, 1936; adminstr. Eye & Throat Hosp., Buffalo, 1932; foreclosure officer Buffalo Savings Bank, 1928-31; asst. to county clk. San Bernardino (Cal.) Ct. House; supply officer Rome Air Depot, N.Y., 1942; social dir. Norton Air Force, San Bernardino, Cal., 1955; nursing dept. VA Hosp., Buffalo, 1946; asst. mgr. Sunnyside Country Club, Fresno, Cal., 1966; real estate investor, Fresno, Cal., 1960-66. Chmn. Tb Christmas Seals Drive, Madera, Cal., 1959, Cancer Drive, Madera, 1958, Mother's Polio March, Madera, 1957; instr. First Aid, A.R.C., 1949; mem. White House Conf. on Youth and Children, 1950; candidate City Council, Madera, Fresno Sch. Bd., 1964; mem. Fresno County Mental Health Adv. Bd.; mem. reception com. YWCA and People to People Aux.; chmn. prizes for Cancer League; vol. Fresno Community Hosp. Sec. Republican Central Com., 1958-59; insp. Fresno Election Bd. Mem. adv. bd. Sierra Hosp., 1965—. Mem. Fresno County Apts. Owners Assn., Infant of Prague Service Aux. (pres.), Fresno Community Theater Guild Bus. and Profl. Womens Club, Am. Legion Aux. (pres.), Pub. Relation Soc., Fresno Emblem Club, Womens Service Alliance Inc. of Community Hosp., Oakhurst, Fresno City and County (women's sect., membership award) chambers commerce, Cal. Congress Parents and Tchrs., Fresno Opera Guild, St. Agnes Hosp. Guild, Women's Symphony Ladies League, Waabis Internat., Fresno U. Booster Club, Palm Springs Owners Assn., City of Hope Aux. Home: 5011 N Van Ness Extension Fresno CA 93705

RICHTER, BELLA MIRIAM TELCHER, librarian; b. N.Y.C., Aug. 16, 1915; d. Jacob and Tillie (Friedman) Telcher; B.A., Hunter Coll., 1935; M.A., N.Y. U., 1936; M.L.S., Queens Coll., 1965; m. Harold Richter, June 9, 1940; children—William, Glenn. Pvt. sec. Powers Kaplan Berger, N.Y.C., 1936-38, Globe Shipping Co., N.Y.C., 1938-40; social investigator div. child welfare N.Y.C. Dept. Welfare, 1940-43; tchr., librarian Central Queens Sch., Jamaica, N.Y., 1950-55, N.Y.C. Pub. Schs., Flushing, N.Y., 1955-64; part-time librarian Queensborough Pub. Library, Jamaica, 1952-55; librarian in charge Marie Curie Jr. High Sch., Bayside, N.Y., 1964—. Mem. A.L.A., Beta Phi Mu. Home: 162-10 72d Av Flushing NY 11365 Office: 46-35 Oceania St Bayside NY 11361

RICHTER, ENITH BARBARA SCHNEIDER (MRS. ERVIN F. RICHTER), newspaper pub.; b. Cottonwood County, Minn., Mar. 12, 1913; d. Ambrose and Mathilda Wilhemena (Hageman) Schneider; student Sch. Nursing, U. Minn., 1931; m. Ervin F. Richter, July 26, 1932; 1 son, Gary. Partner (with husband) Comfrey (Minn.) Times, weekly newspaper, 1965—; owner, pub. (with husband) Jeffers (Minn.) Rev., 1970—. Bd. dirs. Community Chest, 1971-73. Mem. Christian Mothers Soc., Ladies Aid Guild, Ladies Guild (sec.-treas. 1945-47). Roman Catholic. Home: Comfrey MN 56019 Office: Comfrey Times Comfrey MN 56019

RICHTER, HARVENA, writer, educator; b. Reading, Pa., Mar. 13, 1919; d. Conrad and Harvena (Achenbach) Richter; B.A., U. N.M., 1938; M.A., N.Y. U., 1955, Ph.D., 1967. Advt. copywriter Saks Fifth Av., N.Y.C., 1942-43, Macy's, N.Y.C., 1943-46; copy chief Elizabeth Arden, N.Y.C., 1946-47; advt. dir. I. Miller, N.Y.C., 1947-48; feature writer N.Am. Newspaper Alliance, Women's Nat. News Service, European edit. N.Y. Herald Tribune and Christian Sci. Monitor, 1949-53; instr. English, N.Y. U., N.Y.C., 1953-66; asst. prof. English, U. N.M., Albuquerque, 1969—; writer fiction, poetry, articles, criticism, appearing in publs., including New Yorker, Sat. Eve. Post, Atlantic, Voices, Chelsea. Am. Assn. U. Women fellow, 1964-65, Yaddo writing fellow, 1962, 63, McDowell Colony fellow, 1965, 66, Wurlitzer Found. fellow, 1968, 73, 74. Mem. Authors Guild, Modern Lang. Assn., Kappa Kappa Gamma. Author: The Human Shore, 1959; Virginia Woolf: The Inward Voyage, 1970. Home: 11 Maple St Pine Grove PA 17963 Office: Dept English Humanities Bldg U NM Albuquerque NM 87131

RICHTER, MARY HELEN CARR (MRS. ROBERT FREDRICK RICHTER), occupational therapist; b. Eldorado, Kan., June 6, 1930; d. William Henry and Edith Jamie (Roberts) Carr; B.S., U. Kan., 1952; m. Robert Fredrick Richter, Oct. 19, 1952; children—Robert Scott, Craig Alan, Bradley Dean. Staff occupational therapist Cerebral Palsy Center, Kansas City, Mo., 1952-54; occupational therapist Pratt County Home-Health Service, Pratt, Kan., 1966-70; supr. Homemaker-Health Aide Service, Pratt, Kan., 1972—; occupational therapist, dir. Day Camp for Mentally Retarded, 1972, 73; occupational therapist, tchr-aide Chikaskia Area Tng. Sch., Pratt, Kan., 1972—. Mem. Am. Assn. U. Women, Am., Kan. occupational therapy assns., Pratt County Assn. Retarded Children, Pratt County Heart Assn. (sec. 1973—), Alpha Phi. Republican. Presbyn. Club: Book (Pratt). Home: 202 S New St Pratt KS 67124 Office: 421 Cherry St Pratt KS 67124

RICHTER, MELISSA LEWIS, educator, coll. dean; b. Mt. Vernon, N.Y., Jan. 31, 1920; d. Albert Munger and Althea (Erwin) Lewis; B.A., Sarah Lawrence Coll., 1947; M.A., Duke, 1951; Ph.D., U. Conn., 1959. Instr. physiology Vassar Coll., 1951-54, asst. prof., 1960-63; research asst. psychology Yale, 1954-55, 59-60; teaching asst. U. Conn., 1955-57; prof. biology Sarah Lawrence Coll., Bronxville, N.Y., 1963—, dean student and faculty services, 1969-70, dir. Center for Continuing Edn., dir. human genetics program, 1969—, dean grad. studies, 1970-73. USPHS research grantee, 1957-58, 60-68; NIH prin. investigator, program grantee, 1970—; Radcliffe Inst. fellow for ind. study, 1972-74; dir. women in higher edn. project Carnegie Corp., 1973—. Mem. A.A.A.S., Am. Soc. Human Genetics, Sigma Xi. Author: A Revolution in the Education of Women, 1972. Contbr. articles to profl. publs. Home: Sarah Lawrence College Bronxville NY 10708

RICHTER, ROBERTA BRANDENBURG (MRS. J. PAUL RICHTER), educator; b. Osborn, O., Dec. 29; d. Warren F. and Mary M. (Davis) Brandenburg; student Miami-Jacobs Coll., 1930, Wittenburg U., 1930-31, Coll. Music, U. Cin., 1931-32, U. Dayton, 1954, 64; B.S., Miami U., Oxford, O., 1958, M.Ed., 1959; postgrad. Wright State U., 1966-70, Ohio State U., 1969—; m. Jean Paul Richter, Oct. 6, 1934; 1 son, James Paul. Bus. mgr. T.D. Peffley, Inc., 1929-32; sec., prodn. mgr. Delco Products div. Gen. Motors, 1932-34; exec. sec. Meth. Union, 1932-38, League Women Voters, 1935-38, Elder & Johnston Dept. Store, 1938-40; adminstrv. asst. Ch. Fedn. Greater Dayton, O., 1946-50; audio-visual cons. schs., chs. Twyman Films, 1950-53; legal asst. Nadlin Law Offices, 1953-58; instr. stenotype, office practice Miami-Jacobs Coll., Dayton, 1952-59; tchr. stenotype, guidance counselor Stebbins High Sch., Dayton, 1958—; vocational guidance coordinator Mad River Planning Dist., Montgomery County, O., 1968—. Instr. workshop in stenotype Wright State U., Dayton, 1970, 72; 1st cellist youth div. Symphony Orch.; dir. Lang. Unlimited, Inc., Evanston, Ill. Supt., tchr., adviser youth div. Grace United Meth. Ch., Dayton, 1942—, sec. adminstrv. bd., 1940—, council on ministries, 1972—, past circle leader, laywoman chmn. Christian higher edn.; counselor Camp Miniwanca, Am. Youth Found., 1953-68. Mem. Am., Ohio, Miami Valley personnel and guidance assns., Ohio Bus. Tchrs. Assn., Am., Ohio sch. counselor assns., Nat., Ohio edn. assns., Nat. Vocational Guidance Assn., Dayton Area Bus. Soc. (v.p. 1969—), Delphian Soc. (past pres.), Pub. Speaker Bur., Council World Affairs, League Women Voters (past pres. and treas.), World Trade Club, Greater Dayton C. of C., Bus. and Profl. Women, Pi Omega Pi. Mem. Order Eastern Star. Club: Progressive Mothers (chmn. program Dayton 1969-70). Author numerous ednl. handbooks, pamphlets. Contbr. articles to profl. jours.; lectr. in field. Home: 3865 Seiber Av Dayton OH 45405

RICKARD, JUDITH MARIE, editor; b. Portland, Ore., Jan. 6, 1948; d. Emmett Glen and Erma Marie (Cole) Rickard; B.A., San Jose State Coll., 1970, M.S., 1974. Pubs. dir. Inst. for Bus. & Econ. Research, San Jose (Cal.) State Coll., 1970; editor, mgr. Lansford Pub. Co., Inc., San Jose, 1971—. Lectr., S.W. Tex. State U., San Marcos, 1973. Mem. Women in Communications, Am. Assn. Univ. Women, Sigma Delta Chi. Home: 1058 Bennett Way San Jose CA 95125 Office: PO Box 8711 San Jose CA 95155

RICKBEIL, CLARA EVELYN SHELLMAN (MRS. RAYMOND E. RICKBEIL), club woman; b. Gibson City, Ill.; d. Kilian and Anna Marie (Johnson) Shellman; grad. Brown's Bus. Coll., Champaign, Ill., 1922; student U. Ill., 1927-28; m. Raymond Earl Rickbeil, May 8, 1930. Office sec. Ford County Farm Bur. Gibson City, Ill., 1922-26; secretarial position Raymond E. Rickbeil, C.P.A., Springfield, Ill., 1928-61, Ernst & Ernst, Springfield, 1961-65. Mem. bd. King's Daus. Recipient award for work pub. accounting legislation Ill. Soc. C.P.A.'s, 1956. Mem. U. Ill. Alumni Assn., U. Ill. Pres.' Club, Am. Legion Aux. Republican. Presbyn. Mem. Order Eastern Star. Clubs: Woman's (reception com. 1962-63, social com. 1963-64, corr. sec. 1972—, dist. program chmn. dist. 21 1968-69, dist. corr. sec. 1969-72), Mariama (vice chmn. chpt. 5 1966-67, chmn. 1967-72), Amateur Musical, Zonta (treas. 1954-57, finance chmn. 1957-63, 64, service chmn., mem. service com. 1953-62). Home: 937 Feldkamp Av Springfield IL 62704

RICKEL, ANNETTE THERESE URSO (MRS. JOHN M. RICKEL), psychologist; b. Detroit, Apr. 6, 1941; d. Ralph Francis and Marguerite Catherine (Calcaterra) Urso; B.A., Mich. State U., 1963; M.A., U. Mich., 1965, Ph.D., 1972; m. John M. Rickel, Aug.

12, 1967. Tchr. kindergarten St. Clair Shores (Mich.) Pub. Schs., 1963-64, Grosse Pointe (Mich.) Pub. Schs., 1965-67; head tchr. nursery sch., instr. Merrill Palmer Inst., Detroit, 1967-69; psychologist The Northeast Guidance Center, Detroit, 1973—. Mem. faculty Wayne State U., 1972—, U. Mich., 1972—. Bd. dirs. Epilepsy Center Mich. Horace H. Rackham Research grantee, 1972. Mem. Am. Psychol. Assn., Soc. for Research in Child Devel., Jr. League of Detroit, Pi Beta Pi. Roman Catholic. Home: 68 Cloverly Rd Grosse Pointe MI 48236 Office: 17000 East Warren Detroit MI 48224

RICKER, DOROTHY VERNON KENNEDY (MRS. C. HAYDEN RICKER), columnist; b. Portland, Me.; d. J. Hartley and Sylvia May (Branscombe) Kennedy; ed. Boston U., spl. courses Tampa U.; m. C. Hayden Ricker (dec. Jan. 1971); 1 son, Huntley Norman. Writer nationally syndicated newspaper column for teen-agers and their parents, 1956—. Mem. Women in Communications. Home and studio: 2521 Watrous Av Tampa FL 33609

RICKERD, JOAN MILDRED POWERS, sci. writer; b. Ottawa, Ont., Can., Oct. 13, 1932; d. Lawrence John and Mildred Eva (Bennett) Powers; honor grad. Notre Dame Convent, Ottawa, 1950; grad. Nat. Bus. Coll., Ottawa, 1952; B.A., U. Toronto, 1961; m. Robert Campbell Rickerd, Sept. 29, 1966; 1 dau., Julie Anne. Pvt. sec. to pub. relations officer Nat. Research Council Can., 1952-58; asso. editor NRC Research News, 1962-69, also editor NRC Review, 1963-68; sci. writer Sci. Dimension, Ottawa, 1969—, acting editor, 1973-74, editor, 1974—. Press conf. moderator for wives of Apollo XI astronauts on Canadian visit, 1969. Mem. Canadian Sci. Writers Assn., Profl. Inst. Pub. Service Can., Media Club of Can., Assn. Bus. and Profl. Women, Delta Delta Delta. Club: Ottawa Hunt and Golf. Contbr. articles to profl. jours. Home: 594 Duff Crescent Rothwell Village Ottawa ON K1J 7C5 Canada Office: National Research Council of Canada Ottawa K1A OR6 ON Canada

RICKERS-OVSIANKINA, MARIA ARSENJEVNA, educator; b. Tschita, Russia, May 3, 1898; d. Arsenij V. and Olga (Rickers) Ovsiankina; student U. Berlin, 1922-26; Ph.D., U. Giessen (Germany), 1928. Came to U.S., 1931, naturalized, 1938. Tchr. U. Berlin (Germany), 1929-31; research asso. Worcester (Mass.) State Hosp., 1931-36; instr. to prof. Wheaton Coll., 1935-49; research asso. dept. social relations Harvard, Cambridge, Mass., 1947-48, Mass. Inst. Tech., Cambridge, 1947-48; prof., dir. grad. training in clin. psychology, dir. psychol. clinic U. Conn., Storrs, 1949-65; dir. training project para-profl. mental health workers, Berkeley, Cal., 1967—. Pres. Rorschach Inst., 1942-43. Recipient Grants Social Sci. Research Council, 1933-35, USPHS, 1956-58, 65-66. Fellow Am. Psychol. Assn.; mem. Orthopsychiat. Assn., Am. Assn. U. Profs., Cal. Psychol. Assn. Home: 1735 Highland Pl Berkeley CA 94709

RICKETSON, MARY CLAIRE KETT (MRS. LEONARD CHASE RICKETSON), lawyer; b. Somerville, Mass.; d. Thomas and Bridget T. (Kelly) Kett; student Calvin Coolidge Coll.; J.D., Portia Law Sch., 1937; m. Leonard Chase Ricketson, Nov. 30, 1940; children—Laura (Mrs. John Doherty), Stephanie (Mrs. Steven Mendelson), Leonard Paul. Admitted to Mass. bar, 1938, Fed. bar, 1962, U.S. Supreme Ct., 1970; became partner Drews & Kett, Boston, 1940, Jordan & Roddy, Boston, 1958-61, Jordan & Ricketson, Boston, 1962-67; individual practice law West Roxbury, 1967—. Founder, incorporator Warren Center for Emotionally Disturbed Children, 1961-72, pres., sec., 1972—, incorporator, mem. Parkway Concert Assos., Boston, 1963—; chmn. U.S. Selective Service Draft Bd., Boston, 1973-74; sec. Charles River Assn. for Retarded Children, 1973-74. Mem. Internat. Fedn. Women Lawyers, Mass. Assn. Women Lawyers (sec. 1971-72, treas. 1972-73, v.p. 1973-74). Address: 200 LaGrange St West Roxbury MA 02132

RICKETTS, DOROTHY ELIZABETH BRASWELL (MRS. WILLIAM AUGUSTUS RICKETTS), educator; b. Emporia, Va., Sept. 13, 1916; d. Thomas Hilliard and Lottie Beatrice (Coley) Braswell; B.A., Lynchburg Coll., 1953; M.Ed., Coll. William and Mary, 1962, postgrad., 1969, 70; postgrad. Union Theol. Sem., 1973—; m. William Augustus Ricketts; children—Ethleen (Mrs. R.D. Collins), William. Dir. music Brunswick Sch. Bd., Lawrenceville, Va., 1947-48, Rehoboth Sch. Bd., Rehoboth Beach, Del., 1943-44; organizer, dir. nursery-primary U.S. Army Base, Ft. Sherman, C.Z., 1949-50; tchr. Am. Dependent's Sch., Kobe, Japan, 1955-57; tchr. Warwick Sch. Bd., Hilton Village, Va., 1952-54; tchr. Newport News (Va.) schs., 1957-59; dist. mgr. Field Ednl. Enterprises, Newport Beach, 1959-60; dir. guidance Sussex (Va.) Schs., 1965-71, chmn. English dept., 1963-65; instr. counseling and guidance Coll. William and Mary, 1968-72; counselor, prof. psychology Richard Bland Coll., Petersburg, Va., 1971—. Deaconess Petersburg dist., Va. conf. United Meth. Ch., 1973—, mem. bd. Global Missions, N.Y.C., 1973—, mem. dist. council youth ministries, 1973—, sec. council of ministries, 1973-74. Bd. dirs. Teen Club, Rokko Heights, Japan, 1955-57, Petersburg (Va.) Tng. Sch. and Hosp., 1972—. Recipient Army Outstanding award in Community and edn., 1957; named Outstanding Educator, 1973. Mem. Am., Va. personnel and guidance assns., Am. Sch. Counselor Assn., Va. Edn. Assn., Am. Assn. U. Profs., Ret. Officers Assn., Kappa Delta Pi, Eta Tau. Democrat. Methodist. Mem. Order Eastern Star. Home: Route 3 Box 14 Emporia VA 23847 Office: Richard Bland Coll Petersburg VA 23803

RICKEY, AGNES BERTHA YOUNG (MRS. WALTER H. RICKEY), educator; b. Peabody, Mass., Mar. 2, 1912; d. James Edward and Eva Marie (Irons) R.; A.B., St. Joseph Coll., 1933; M.S., Barry Coll., Miami, Fla., 1956; postgrad. Cath. U. Am., summer 1938-39, 44-45, U. Miami, 1947-50, U. Notre Dame (NSF fellow), summer 1958, Cornell U. (Shell Merit fellow), summer 1960, Fla. State U., 1960-62; m. Walter H. Rickey, Nov. 24, 1949. Tchr. Immaculate Conception Acad., Washington, 1933-34, Cathedral Acad., Syracuse, N.Y., 1934-38, St. Joseph Coll., Emmitsburg, Md., 1938-41, U. Miami, Coral Gables, Fla., 1947-50, Miami (Fla.) Edison Sr. High Sch., 1950-58; supr. math. Dade County, Miami, 1958-71. Bd. dirs. Fla. Found. Future Scientists, 1960; mem. adv. bd. Sch. Math. Study Group, 1964-68, mem. editorial panel monograph project, 1965-68; mem. evaluation team Experienced Tchr. Fellowship Program, 1967. Mem. Fla. Assn. Math. Suprs., Math. Assn. Am., Cath. Tchrs. Guild (bd. dirs. 1965-72), Barry Coll. Alumni Assn. (v.p. 1966-67, pres. 1967-68), Delta Kappa Gamma (chapter v.p., program chmn. 1965-69, treas. 1970-72), Nat. Council Suprs. Math. (treas. 1969-72). Democrat. Roman Catholic. Author: (with E.A. Collins and J.L. Nanney) Experiencing Mathematics, 1968. Home: 13351 NW 1st Av Miami FL 33168

RICKEY, CAROL RONEMOUS (MRS. LARRY FLOYD RICKEY), counselor; b. Kansas City, Kan., Feb. 4, 1937; d. William T. and Albertha M. (Bibert) Ronemous; B.A., William Jewell Coll., 1959; M.A., Ind. U., 1963; m. Larry Floyd Rickey, June 27, 1964. Tchr. Kansas City (Mo.) Pub. Schs., 1959-61; asst. Ind. U. Residence Halls, 1961-63; dir. women's residence halls Ia. U., 1963-67; dean of women Coe Coll., Cedar Rapids, Ia., 1967-69, dean of students, 1969-71, dir. work/service and placement, 1971-72; human resource coordinator City of Cedar Rapids, 1972—. Mem. Cedar Rapids Human Rights Commn., 1971—. Bd. dirs. YWCA, Voluntary Action Center, Linn County Assn. Mental Health. Mem. Nat. Assn. Women Deans and Counselors, Pi Lambda Theta, Alpha Gamma Delta. Baptist. Home: Route 1 High Amana IA 52203

RICKEY, MOLLIE CHAPPELL, lawyer; b. St. Louis, July 16, 1908; d. William Chappell and Bonnie (Tarleton) Rickey; student Central Coll., Fayette, Mo., 1925-30; LL.B., Benton Coll. Law, 1934. With Southwestern Bell Telephone Co., St. Louis, 1930-73, comml. tng. supr., 1954-73; admitted to Mo. bar, 1937, since practiced in St. Louis. Mem. vol. bur. Health and Welfare Council St. Louis, 1959-62. Mem. city council City of Hazelwood (Mo.), 1971—, mayor pro tem, 1972-73. Chpt. bd. dirs. A.R.C., 1962-68, regional bd. dirs., 1962-68; bd. mgrs., v.p. Granada Condominium, Hazelwood, 1967—. Mem. Personnel Women Greater St. Louis (pres. 1954-55), Mo. Bar. Home: 8832 Santa Bella Dr Hazelwood MO 63042 Office: 100 N 12th St St Louis MO 63101

RICKING, MYRL, librarian; b. Cin., Aug. 2, 1918; d. Bernard John and Luella (Behler) Ricking; B.A., U. Cin., 1940. Sec. Bd. Edn., Cin., 1940-44; hosp. worker Am. Nat. Red Cross, 1945-46, asst. field dir., 1950-51; exec. sec.-personnel officer Yale U. Library, 1947-50; editor Field Enterprises, Chgo., 1951-53; personnel dir. Milw. Pub. Library, 1953-62; dir. office for recruitment A.L.A., Chgo., 1962-67; chief Manpower Utilization Office, Library of Congress, 1967—. Mem. Soc. for Personnel Adminstrn., A.L.A., D.C. Library Assn., Phi Beta Kappa. Home: 3133 Connecticut Av NW Washington DC 20008

RICKS, JOHNNIE SEARS (MRS. JAMES HUGH RICKS, SR.), nursing home adminstr., food center adminstr.; b. Glenwood, Ga., June 22, 1909; d. Johnny A. and Addie (Clark) Sears; R.N., U. Hosp., Augusta, Ga., 1931, postgrad., 1932-33; m. James Hugh Ricks, Sr., Sept. 13, 1932; children—Verona K. (Mrs. Robert Simmons) and James Hugh (twins). Operating room supr. Bartow (Fla.) Hosp., 1934-35, Claxton's Hosp., Dublin, Ga., 1935; operating room supr., hosp. adminstr. Treutlen County (Ga.) Hosp., 1954-73; adminstr. Treutlen Nursing Home, Soperton, Ga., 1970—. Vice pres., sec., half-owner Ricks' Red and White Food Center, Soperton, Ga., 1952—. Mem. Am. Acad. Med. Adminstrs., Bus. and Profl. Women's Club. Club: Garden (Soperton). Home: Belk St Soperton GA 30457 Office: PO Box 508 College St Soperton GA 30457

RICKS, MIRIAM GWINETTE, librarian; b. Elm City, N.C., Nov. 1, 1927; d. Wylie and Carrie Agatha (Parker) Ricks; B.A., Bennett Coll., 1948; diploma N.Y. Sch. Med. Dentistry, 1949; M.L.S., N.C. Central U., 1955; certificate advanced studies U. Denver, 1973; spl. courses N.C. A. and T. State U., N.C. State U., Hampton Inst., Queens Coll., U. N.C. Residence dir. Bennett Coll., 1949-51; librarian, girls counselor, English tchr. James E. Shepard High Sch., Zebulon, N.C., 1951-60; librarian Raleigh (N.C.) Pub. Schs., 1960-72; now asst. prof., dir. Early Childhood Library Specialist Program N.C. Central U.; vis. instr. library sci. Benedict Coll., summer 1966; vacation Bible sch. dir. Gen. Bapt. State Conv. N.C., summers 1944-48, 52-63. Nominee for Dist. 11 for Terry Sanford award, N.C. Assn. Educators, 1971; named tchr. of year, Raleigh Assn. Educators, 1971. Mem. N.C. Assn. Sch. Librarians, N.C. (chmn. dept. librarians 1960-61, 69-71), Raleigh (sec. 1963-70) tchrs. assn., N.C., Raleigh (sec.) assns. educators, Raleigh Assn. Classroom Tchrs. (sec.), N.C. Central U. Library Sci. Alumni Assn. (v.p.), N.C. Library Assn., A.L.A., Assn. Ednl. Communications land Tech., N.E.A. (life), Delta Sigma Theta. Baptist (young people's dir. Bapt. Tng. Union). Author: A Selective Study of African Writers of Today, 1964; Africa: Selected Resources for Library, 1964; Materials for Teaching Library Usage in Elementary Schools, 1962; Suggested Church Library Booklist, 1963; Chronological Listing of Outstanding Negroes with Contributions and Birthdate, 1965; A Study of Selected Learning Center Programs, Raleigh Public Schools, 1973. Home: PO Box 4 Elm City NC 27822

RIDDEL, MARILYN ANN (MRS. HAROLD RIDDEL), judge; b. Ashland, O., Aug. 22, 1932; d. Fred Leroy and Helen Adelaide (Mandeville) McClintock; student Bowling Green State U., 1949-51; B.A., La. State U., 1953; LL.B., U. Toledo, 1957, J.D., 1957; m. Harold Riddel, Apr. 30, 1960; children—Deborah Suzanne, Jeffrey Eugene. Admitted to Ohio Bar, 1957, Ariz. Bar, 1961; practiced law in Toledo, 1957-60, Phoenix, 1960-69; mem. firm Riddel & Riddel, 1960-69; trial ct. judge, Phoenix, 1969—. Mem. Am., Maricopa County, bar assns., State Bar of Ariz., Am. Judicature Soc., Law Soc. Ariz. State U., D.A.R., Bus. and Profl. Women, Legal Secs. Assn., Tavan P.T.A., Kappa Beta Pi, Delta Gamma (Cable award 1967), Republican. Presbyn. Mem. Soroptimists, Daughters of Nile. Home: 4519 E Cheery Lynn Rd Phoenix AZ 85018 Office: 125 W Washington St Phoenix AZ 85003

RIDDELL, MARY ELLEN, writer and poet; b. Rochester, N.Y., Dec. 20, 1897; d. John Blackwell and Jennie (Jordan) Riddell; student Pa. State U. Extension, Columbia. Exec. legal sec. Furst, McCormick Muir, Lynn & Reeder, Williamsport, Pa., 1931-62; registered rep. Waddell & Reed, Inc., 1968-71; registered rep., dir. Haven Securities Inc., 1971-74; sec. to head bond dept. Lycoming Trust Co., 1931; sec. to exec. v.p. Susquehanna Trust Co., 1928-30. Team capt. local fund drives United Fund, Heart Assn., A.R.C.; vol. worker Williamsport Hosp. Recipient Woman of Year award Susquehanna chpt. Am. Bus. Women's Assn., 1958, 1st prize for poetry Williamsport Community Arts Festival, 1961. Mem. Am. Bus. Women's Assn., D.A.R., Williamsport Hosp. Aux., Am. Legion Aux., Lycoming County Hist. Soc., Pa. Poetry Soc. Presbyn. Club: Creative Writers Forum. Author: (poetry) Thoughts in the Night, 1965. Contbr. poetry to anthologies and poetry jours. Home: 423-9 Sheoah Blvd Winter Springs FL 32707

RIDDER, JOYCE MARION, clin. psychologist; b. Livermore, Cal., Feb. 13, 1936; d. Louis Orville and Evelyn B. (Robb) Ridder; B.A., Brigham Young U., 1956; M.S., U. So. Cal., 1960, M.Ed., 1962, Ed.D., 1971; profl. diploma Los Angeles Center for Group Psychotherapy, 1971. Tchr. sci. Vina Danks Jr. High Sch., Ontario, Cal., 1956-60; tchr. Newton Jr. High Sch., La Puente, Cal., 1960-61; psychologist Pasadena (Cal.) Unified Sch. Dist., 1963-70; cons., counselor Cal. Pediatric Center, Los Angeles, 1969-71; dir. clinic mental health Cal. Hosp. Med. Center, 1971-74; dir. Footlighter's Child Guidance Clinic, Cal. Hosp. Med. Center, 1974—; pvt. practice marriage counseling, Pasadena, 1965-70; pvt. practice clin. psychology, Los Angeles, 1970—; psychol. field supr. Los Angeles City Coll., 1971—; chief psychologist, mem. faculty Los Angeles Center for Group Psychotherapy, 1971-74. Vol. worker Pasadena Mental Health Clinic, 1966-67; vol. cons. Ostomy Assn. Inland Empire, 1967-68. Mem. Am., Cal., Los Angeles County psychol. assns., A.A.A.S., Nat. Assn. Sch. Psychologists, Los Angeles Soc. Psychoanalytic Psychology, Sierra Club, Smithsonian Assos., Audubon Soc., Embroiderer's Guild Am., Beta Beta Beta, Pi Lambda Theta, Lambda Delta Sigma. Home: 538 S Oakland St Pasadena CA 91101 Office: 9201 Sunset Blvd Los Angeles CA 90069

RIDDLE, ALTHAE SPEAR IRELAND (MRS. NORMAN W. RIDDLE), artist; b. Burlington, N.C.; d. John Alfred and Inez (Spear) Ireland; student Guilford Bus. Coll., 1923-24, Elon Coll., 1933; m. Norman William Riddle, Aug. 11, 1931; 1 son, Norman William. Executed coats of arms, 1931—, owner bus., 1948-74; exhibited in numerous group shows in U.S. Co-chmn., flower show cons. Flower Show Schs., W.Va., 1963-67, master certificate as judge; past pres. Garden Lovers Club, Burlington, N.C., Cumberland Garden Club, Bluefield, W.Va., pest dir. Dist. 5, N.C. Garden Clubs (life mem.). Mem. D.A.R. (registrar chpt., 1962-68, regent John Chapman chpt., mem. house com. Nat. Soc., resolutions com. 1970-72), Bluefield Fine Arts Soc., Internat. Platform Assn., U.D.C. (pres. Bluefield 1965-68, pub. cook book 1967, v.p. W.Va. div. 1968-69, pres. Charles F. Fisher chpt. 1970-74), Elon Coll. Rose Soc., Nat. Soc. Magna Charta Dames, C. of C. (dir. women's div. 1974—), Alamance County Arts Assn., Soc. Ams. Royal Descent, Colonial Dames XVII Century, Delphian Lit. Soc. (pres. Bluefield), Nat. Geneal. Soc., Internat. Soc. Heraldry and Family Trees. Episcopalian (pres. women of ch. 1958-60, dir. altar guild 1961-68). Clubs: Bluefield Woman's (past sec.), Altrusa (dir. 1972-73, pres. 1974-75). Address: 1308 Sunset Dr Burlington NC 27215

RIDENHOWER, ELIZABETH MILLER, artist, educator; b. Brownwood, Tex., Sept. 24, 1930; d. Samuel Olin and Oran (Miller) Ridenhower; B.A., Baylor U., 1951; M.A., Columbia, 1959. Tchr. pub. schs., San Antonio 1951-55; art cons. Pub. Schs., Roslyn, N.Y., 1955-59; asst. asso. prof. art Trinity U., San Antonio, 1959—; represented in gov.'s residence Hemisfair 1968, San Antonio; exhibited in group shows at Columbia U. Galleries, Witte Meml. Mus., San Antonio, Houston Fine Arts Mus., Trinity U., La. Art Gallery, Houston, North Star Gallery, San Antonio, 2131 Gallery, Houston, Bright Shawl Gallery, San Antonio, Garden Gallery, San Antonio, Lester K. Henderson Galley, Monterrey, Cal., Dallas Mus. Invitational Show, 1972, Sol del Rio, San Antonio, Carlin Gallery, Ft. Worth; represented in pvt. collections. Named Camellia Award artist, 1968. Mem. San Antonio Art League (5th v.p. 1967), U.D.C., San Antonio Art League (dir. at large 1968, dir. 1974), San Antonio Symphony Soc. (women's com.). Baptist. Club: San Antonio Girls Cotillon. Home: 700 E Hildebrand St Apt #804 San Antonio TX 78212

RIDENOUR, NINA (MRS. M. ARNOLD BOLL), psychologist; b. Vincennes, Ind., Dec. 12, 1904; d. Horace Daniel and Ada (Allen) Ridenour; A.B. magna cum laude in psychology, Radcliffe Coll., 1926; A.M., Colo. Coll., 1930; postgrad. U. Chgo., 1935; Ph.D., N.Y. U., 1941; m. M. Arnold Boll, Aug. 26, 1941. Psychologist, Dennison Mfg. Co., Framingham, Mass., 1926-28, Bemis-Taylor Found. Child Guidance Clinic, Colorado Springs, Colo., 1928-31; chief psychologist Children's Center, Detroit, 1931-37; asst. exec. sec. N.Y. Com. Mental Hygiene of State Charities Aid Assn., 1937-47; exec. officer Internat. Com. Mental Hygiene, 1947-49; dir. edn. Nat. Assn. for Mental Health, N.Y.C., 1949-52; sec. Ittleson Family Found., 1952-67; ednl. cons. Mental Health Materials Center, 1953-68. Life fellow Am. Orthopsychiat. Assn. (sec. 1942-48); mem. Am. Psychol. Assn. (life), Phi Beta Kappa. Author: Mental Health in the U.S.; a Fifty-Year History, 1961; Mental Health Education: Principles in the Effective Use of Materials, 1969. Contbr. numerous articles to profl. jours. Home: 29 Mt Bolus Rd Chapel Hill NC 27514

RIDEOUT, ALICE CHALIFOUX (MRS. JOHN GORDON RIDEOUT), harpist; b. Birmingham, Ala., Jan. 22, 1908; d. Oliver Joseph and Alice (Halle) Chalifoux; B.Mus., Curtis Inst. Music, Phila.; m. John Gordon Rideout, Apr. 24, 1937; 1 dau., Alice Gordon (Mrs. John David Reilly). First harpist Cleve. Orch., 1931—; head harp dept. Cleve. Inst. Music, 1931—; instr. harp Oberlin Coll., 1971—; dir. Summer Harp Colony, Salzedo Sch., Camden, Me. Mem. Am. Harp Soc. Home: 115 South Lane Chagrin Falls OH 44022 Office: Severance Hall Cleveland OH 44106

RIDEOUT, ANNE CAROLYN HOLLOWAY (MRS. KENNETH VINAL RIDEOUT), univ. adminstr.; b. Murfreesboro, Tenn., Aug. 13, 1937; d. Eugene Cleveland and Carolyn Christobel (Cook) Holloway; B.S., Middle Tenn. State U., 1959; M.A., U. Conn., 1968; Ed.D., U. Mass., 1974; m. Kenneth Vinal Rideout, Jan. 13, 1973. Personnel and pub. relations with Eastover Resort, Lenox, Mass., 1959-60; tech. illustrator, field documentation unit Gen. Electric Co., 1961, publns. subcontracting, 1961-63, tech. editor, 1963-64; extension home economist U. Conn. Extension Service, 1964-70, coordinator spl. extension programs, asst. dir. extension programs, 1973-74; asst. dir. extension programs U. Mass. Extension Services, Amherst, 1974—. Sec. Conn. Council on Family, 1969-70; mem. state adv. assistance com. Conn. Commn. on Aging. Recipient Florence Hall award Nat. Assn. Extension Home Economists, 1967; scholarship award Women's aux. Hartford County Med. Soc., 1967; extension recognition and scholarship award Epsilon Sigma Phi, 1967; Ford Found. fellow, 1972; Am. Home Econs. Assn. Found. fellow, 1972. Mem. Am. (chmn. future devel. com. 1973—), Conn. (pres. 1970-72, counselor 1972-74) home econs. assns., Internat. Fedn. Home Econs., Conn.-R.I. Assn. Extension Home Economists (pres. 1967-69), Epsilon Sigma Phi, Kappa Omicron Phi, Pi Lambda Theta. Mem. Ch. of Christ. Clubs: Simsbury (Conn.) Junior Woman's; Hartford College (dir. 1972-74). Home: 7 Glenn Hollow Lane West Simsbury CT 06092 Office: Skinner Hall U Mass Amherst MA 01002

RIDER, BARBARA ABERNATHY BURNHAM (MRS. RICHARD T. RIDER), occupational therapist; b. Appleton, Wis., Dec. 9, 1931; d. John James and Dorothy Abernathy (von Berg) Burnham; student Lawrence Coll., 1950-51; B.S., U. Wis., 1954; postgrad. Washburn U., 1967-68; M.S. (Am. Occupational Therapy Assn. grantee), U. Kan., 1971; m. Richard T. Rider, Feb. 11, 1954; children—Deborah Allison, Sarah Elizabeth, Jill Suzanne. Dir. occupational therapy Madison (Wis.) Gen. Hosp., 1956; staff occupational therapist VA Hosp., Topeka, 1963-67; dir. occupational therapy Capper Found. for Crippled Children, Topeka, 1968-70; prof. occupational therapy U. Kan., Lawrence, 1971-73; chief occupational therapy VA Hosp., Topeka, 1973—. Cons. Shawnee County Infirmary, 1973. Mem. Am. Assn. U. Women, League Women Voters, Council Exceptional Children, Am. (chmn. publs. com. 1973-76), Kan. occupational therapy assns., Topeka Community Resources Council Inc., Nat. Fedn. Bus. and Profl. Women. Home: 1901 Damon Ct Topeka KS 66611 Office: Gage Blvd Topeka KS 66622

RIDGE, DAVY-JO STRIBLING, librarian; b. Anderson, S.C., Jan. 16, 1932; d. David Warren and Thelma Josephine (Braselton) Stribling; B.A., Queens Coll., 1954; M. Librarianship, Emory U., 1955; certificate in Med. Librarianship, Med. Library Assn., 1957; m. George Ross Ridge, June 9, 1956 (div. Dec. 1964). Instr. cataloging U. Ga. Libraries, 1955-56; head reference librarian DeKalb County Library System, Decatur, Ga., 1956-64; head, reference dept. U. S.C. Library, Columbia, 1965-72, asst. dir. libraries, 1973—. Patron, Friends of Emory U. Library, 1970—. Mem. A.L.A., Southeastern, S.C. (chmn. pub. relations com. 1972—) library assns., South Caroliniana Soc. (hon. life), Nat., Columbia (dir.) Audubon socs., Queens Coll. Alumnae Assn. (Spl. Recognition), Emory U. Alumni Assn. (Spl. Recognition), Sigma Mu, Alpha Kappa Gamma, Sigma Upsilon. Episcopalian. Clubs: Carolina Bird (S.C. and N.C.); Columbia Bird (pres. 1970) Palmetto Cat (sec. 1971-74) (Columbia). Editor: Rare Books in the McKissick Memorial Library of the University of South Carolina, 1966, A Checklist of Microforms in the University of South Carolina Libraries, 1971, Library Handbook, 1971. Contbr. articles to library jours. Home: 112 Carriage Hill Columbia SC 29206

RIDGE, EDITH NIELSON (MRS. R. HOWARD RIDGE), newspaper editor; b. Arthur, Utah, Dec. 22, 1912; d. John and Mary Elizabeth (Christensen) Nielson; ed. Henager's Bus. Coll., 1931, Pacific U., 1934; m. R. Howard Ridge, Dec. 18, 1937; children—Rebecca Mary (Mrs. Ronald Adams), Leslie (Mrs. Steven K. Nelson), Michele (Mrs. Steven M. Thiese). Owner, Copper Printing Co., Magna, Utah, 1934-72; pub.-editor Magna Times, 1934-37, editor, 1937-72; pub.-editor Garfield Leader, 1934-37, editor, 1937-45. Cons., Granite Sch. Dist. Adult Program, 1935-37; adviser to Magna Community Council, 1940-54. Republican dist. vice chmn., 1940-50; del. to Rep. State Convs., 1950-54. Mem. Utah Press Women (recipient prizes 1959-72), Nat. Fedn. Press Women (recipient first place weekly newspapers, 1965, 70), Utah Press Women (pres. 1969-70), Salt Lake County Women's Clubs (pres. 1940-42), Alpha Xi Delta (v.p. 1971-72). Lady Lion, Delphian. Home: 2212 Dallin St Salt Lake City UT 84109 Office: Magna Times 9124 W 2700 St S Magna UT 84044

RIDGEWAY, MARIAN ELIZABETH, educator; b. Kansas City, Mo., Sept. 20, 1913; d. William Jefferson and Esther L. (Crooks) Ridgeway; B.J., U. Mo., 1935, M.A., 1946; Ph.D., U. Ill., 1952. With Resettlement Adminstrn., Columbia, Mo., 1935-36, U.S. Farm Security Adminstrn., Indpls., 1936-40; jr. clerical examiner, jr. examiner adminstrv. U.S. Civil Service Commn., Washington, 1940-42, 42-44; survey quantifier Bur. Agr. Econs., U.S. Dept. Agr., 1942; instr. U. Mo., summers 1946-48, State Coll. Washington, 1946-47, U. Kan., 1947-49; lectr. So. Ill. U., Carbondale, 1952-53; asst. prof., 1953-56, asso. prof., 1956-70, prof., 1970-74, prof. emeritus. 1974—. Research cons. Commn. State Govt., Ill., 1966. Recipient Women's Centennial Honor award U. Mo., 1968. Mem. Am. Polit. Sci. Assn., D.A.R., Midwest Polit. Sci. Assn., League Women Voters (local past pres.), Nat. Municipal League, Dau. Am. Colonists, Am. Assn. U. Women (past asso. editor state bull.; treas.), Pi Sigma Alpha, Alpha Pi Zeta, Delta Phi Delta, Delta Kappa Gamma. Democrat. Mem. Christian Ch. Author: The Missouri Basin's Pick-Sloan Plan, 1955; Interstate Compacts: A Question of Federalism, 1971; also articles in field. Home: 1211 W Schwartz St Carbondale IL 62901

RIDGWAY, BRUNILDE MARIA SISMONDO (MRS. HENRY W. RIDGWAY, JR.), archaeologist, educator; b. Chieti, Italy, Nov. 14, 1929; d. Giuseppe G. and Maria (Lombardo) Sismondo; came to U.S., 1953, naturalized, 1963; Laurea (Dottore in Lettere Classiche), U. Messina (Italy), 1953; M.A., Bryn Mawr Coll., 1954, Ph.D., 1958; student Am. Sch. Classical Studies, Athens (Greece), 1955-57; m. Henry W. Ridgway, Jr., Sept. 6, 1958; children—Conrad W., Eric R., Kevin P., Christopher L. Faculty archaeology Bryn Mawr Coll., Pa., 1957-60, 61—, prof., 1970—; asst. prof., head dept. classics Hollins Coll., Va., 1960-61. Mem. Inst. Advanced Study Princeton, 1968. Grantee Am. Council Learned Socs., Phila. Philos. Soc., Nat. Endowment for Humanities Found.; Guggenheim fellow, 1974—. Mem. Archeol. Inst. Am. (life), German Archeol. Inst. (corr. mem. 1967), Internat. Soc. Classical Archaeology. Author: The Severe Style in Greek Sculpture, 1970; Classical Sculpture, Catalogue of Classical Collection, Museum of Art, Rhode Island School of Design, Providence, 1972. Contbr. articles to Am., French, German periodicals. Home: 225 N Roberts Rd Bryn Mawr PA 19010

RIDGWAY, EILEEN M., nurse, educator; b. Cherryvale, Kan., Apr. 5, 1921; d. John Joseph and Ellen (French) Ridgway; diploma Providence Hosp. Sch. Nursing, 1943; B.S. in Nursing Edn., St. Mary Coll., 1944; M.S. in Nursing Edn., St. Louis U., 1957; Ph.D., Cath. U. Am., 1963. Instr. nursing Providence Hosp. Sch. Nursing, Kansas City, 1944-46, 48-52; clin. instr. U. Kan. Med. Center, 1946-48, St. John's Hosp. Sch. Nursing, St. Louis, 1953-57; state supr. practical nurse edn. State Bd. Voc. Edn., Topeka, 1958-60; curriculum coordinator Seattle U. Sch. Nursing, 1963-68, dean, 1968—. Cons. curriculum improvement project Western Council on Higher Edn. for Nursing, 1966-68. Bd. dirs. Project CARITAS; bd. dirs., sec. Pope John Med.-Moral Research and Edn. Center. Mem. Am. Nurses Assn. (commn. on edn.), Am. Assn. Deans Coll. and U. Schs. Nursing, Wash. Council Deans and Dirs. Schs. Nursing (vice chmn.), Conf. Cath. Schs. Nursing (council mem. 1970—), Sigma Theta Tau. Home: 2323 43d Av E Seattle WA 98102 Office: 901 Broadway Seattle WA 98122

RIDICK, SISTER JOYCE, educator, psychotherapist; b. Worcester, Mass., Sept. 20, 1941; d. John Anthony and Anne Elizabeth (Bataitis) Ridick; B.A. magna cum laude, De Paul U., Chgo., 1969; Ph.D. in Clin. Psychology, U. Chgo., 1972. Joined Sisters of St. Casimir, 1959; tchr. St. Anthony's Sch., Cicero, Ill., 1962-65, St. Mary's Sch., Plano, Ill., 1965-66, Immaculate Conception Sch., Chgo., 1966-69, also, dir. religion, catechtics parish elementary sch., 1968-69; intern Psychosomatic and Psychiat. Inst. Michael Reese Hosp., Chgo., 1971-72; asst. prof. psychology and statistics Gregorian U., Rome, Italy, 1972—, also co-supr. clin. tng., 1973—, psychotherapist, 1971—. Cons. in formation program to Sisters of St. Casimir, 1973—. Nat. Inst. Mental Health grantee, 1971-72, USPHS grantee, 1970-71, U. Chgo. fellow, 1969-70. Mem. Am. Psychol. Assn., Insts. Religion and Health. Home: 2601 West Marquette Chicago IL 60629 Office: Pontifical Gregorian University Piazza della Pilotta 3 Rome 00187

RIDLEY, ESTHER JOANNE, biologist, educator; b. Pitts., Sept. 5; d. John Thomas and Maria Lee (Mullins) Ridley; B.A., Fisk U., 1945; M.S., U. Pitts., 1950; Ph.D. (NSF fellow), Okla. State U., 1967. Instr., grad. asst. U. Pitts., 1949-50; lab. technologist Med. Center, 1950-53, research asst., 1953-56, lab. supr., 1956-59; instr. biol. scis. Morgan State Coll., Balt., 1959-62, asst. prof., 1962-65, asso. prof., 1967-70, prof., 1970-71, chmn. dept. sci. edn., 1971—. Lectr. Okla. State U., Stillwater, 1966-67. Bd. dirs. Homewood Sch., Balt., 1973—. Mem. Am. Soc. Botany, Am. Soc. Plant Physiologists, A.A.A.S., N.Y. Acad. Scis., Md. Acad. Scis., Nat. Sci. Tchrs. Assn., E. African Wildlife Soc., Internat. Bot. Soc., Sigma Xi, Phi Sigma. Contbr. articles to profl. jours. Home: 4C Lemon Grove Ct Cockeysville MD 21030 Office: Morgan State College Hillen Rd Baltimore MD 21239

RIDLEY, JANICE LOUISE, mfr.; b. Wayne, Me., July 25, 1913; d. Janus A. and Minnie Ona (Knapp) Ridley; student Burdette Coll., 1934. Bank clk. Lynn Instn. Savs. (Mass.), 1935-42; draftsman, designer Boston Machine Works Co., Lynn, 1942-49, engr., 1949-58, personnel dir., purchasing agt., asst. to plant mgr., 1958-68, office mgr., asst. to pres., 1968-72, asst. to pres., 1972—. Mem. Soc. Women Engrs. (Boston sect. dir. 1962-66, treas. 1963-65). Home: 51 Ledge Rd Lynnfield MA 01940 Office: 7 Willow St Lynn MA 01903

RIDLEY, JEANNE ELIZABETH CLARE (MRS. CHRISTY RIDLEY), educator; b. Scranton, Pa., Aug. 8, 1925; d. Edward Walter and Margaret (Cary) Clare; B.A., U. Mich., 1947; M.A., Columbia, 1951; Ph.D., U. Mich., 1958; m. Christy Ridley, July 27, 1957. Research asst. Milbank Meml. Fund, N.Y.C., 1948-52; teaching fellow dept. sociology U. Mich., Ann Arbor, 1953-54, asst. study dir. Survey Research Center, 1954-55, research asst., dept. sociology, 1955-56; Ford Found. teaching intern Brown U., Providence, 1956-57; instr. dept. sociology and anthropology Vanderbilt U., Nashville, 1957-58, asst. prof., 1958-63; asso. prof. demography, population unit Grad. Sch. Pub. Health, asso. prof. sociology, dept. sociology U. Pitts., 1963-67; asso. prof. Sch. Pub. Health and Adminstrv. Medicine, dir. div. demography Internat. Inst. for Study of Human Reprodn., Columbia, N.Y.C., 1967-72; prof. sociology Georgetown U., Washington, 1972—. Mem. adv. panel Center for Population Research, NIH, 1968-71; mem. standing com. pub. health conf. on records and statistics Nat. Center for Health Statistics, 1972—. Mem. Am. Eugenics Soc. (dir. 1971-72), Population Assn. Am. (dir. 1971-74), Am. Social. Assn., Eastern Sociol. Soc., Am. Assn. U. Profs., Union Internationale Pour l'Etude Scientifique De La Population. Editor: (with M.C. Sheps) Public Health and Population Change: Current Research Issues, 1965; contbg. editor Social Biology, 1968-72; editorial cons. Demography, 1968—. Home: 4615 N Park Av Chevy Chase MD 20015 Office: Kennedy Institute Center for Population Research Georgetown U Washington DC 20007

RIECHEL, ROSEMARIE ADELE, librarian; b. Germany, Nov. 29, 1937; d. Carl and Maria Adele (Kohl) Riechel; came to U.S., 1938; B.A., Hunter Coll., 1959; M.S., Columbia, 1965. Gen. asst. Butler Library, Columbia, N.Y.C., 1961-65; librarian Queens Borough Pub. Library, Auburndale br., 1965-66, librarian lang. and lit. div. Central Library, 1966-67, asst. head pub. catalog, telephone reference div., 1967, acting head, 1967-68, head, 1968—. Mem. Am., N.Y. library assns., N.Y. Library Club, Queens Hist. Soc., Metropolitan Opera Guild. Home: 151-31 25th Av Whitestone NY 11357 Office: 89-11 Merrick Blvd Jamaica NY 11432

RIECKER, MARGARET ANN TOWSLEY (MRS. JOHN E. RIECKER), mem. Republican Nat. Com.; b. Ann Arbor, Mich., Nov. 9, 1933; d. Harry A. and Margaret (Dow) Towsley; B.A., Carleton Coll., 1954; postgrad. Mt. Holyoke Coll., 1955; m. John E. Riecker, July 30, 1955; children—John Towsley, Margaret Elizabeth. Vice chmn. Midland County Republican Com., Midland, Mich., 1962—, 10th Congl. Dist. (Mich.) Com., 1964—; spl. asst. for women's affairs Rep. state chmn. Mich., 1966—; 1st vice chmn. Mich. Rep. party, 1968—; Rep. nat. committeewoman from Mich., 1971—. Trustee Herbert H. & Grace A. Dow Found., 1962—, Harry A. and Margaret D. Towsley Found., 1961—. Mem. Midland Little Theatre Guild, 1958—; women's bd. trustees Northwood Inst., Midland, 1965—; mem. Midland Center for Arts, Midland Community Concerts. Mem. Midland Symphony Guild, Carleton Coll. Alumni Assn., Midland Art Assn. Clubs: Women's Study, Northwood Town and Campus (sec. 1967—), University of Michigan President's. Address: 3211 Valley Dr Midland MI 48640

RIEGELHAUPT, JOYCE FIRSTENBERG (MRS. EDWARD I. RIEGELHAUPT), educator; b. Bklyn., Aug. 26, 1936; d. Sol L. and Rosa E. (Miller) Firstenberg; B.A., Queens Coll., 1957; Ph.D. in Anthropology, Columbia, 1964; m. Edward I. Riegelhaupt, June 29, 1958. Asst. prof. anthropology Rutgers U., New Brunswick, N.J., 1963-66; asso. prof. anthropology Sarah Lawrence Coll., Bronxville, N.Y., 1966—. Cons., Assn. Aid to Crippled Children, 1965-67. Mem. Am. Anthrop. Assn. (co-chmn. ann. meetings 1971), Am. Ethnol. Soc. Contbr. articles to profl. jours. Research on peasant society and social change, econ. anthropology. Home: 98 Riverside Dr New York City NY 10024 Office: Sarah Lawrence Coll Bronxville NY 10708

RIEGER, BETTY JANE, advt. agy. exec.; b. Mexia, Tex., Sept. 25, 1927; d. Herman Thornton and Willie D. (Adams) Rieger; student U. Houston, 1945, 46, 47. Traffic mgr. radio sta. KTRH, Houston, 1950-55; space buyer McCann-Erickson, Houston, 1955-59; with Goodwin, Dannenbaum, Littlan & Wingfield, Houston, 1959—, prodn. mgr., 1960—. Presbyn. Home: 1241 Country Pl Houston TX 77024 Office: 2400 West Loop S Houston TX 77027

RIEGER, HELEN BREEDEN HEDRICK (MRS. WRAY MONTGOMERY RIEGER), mus. curator; b. Columbia, Mo., Oct. 13, 1903; d. Earle Raymond and Helen Breeden (Seidensticker) Hedrick; B.S., U. Mo., 1925; postgrad. Pomona Coll., 1926-27; m. Wray Montgomery Rieger, Sept. 15, 1927; children—Helen B. (Mrs. John Robert Anderson), Wray Montgomery. Substitute tchr., Chgo., 1927-28, Kirksville, Mo., 1941-57; curator E.M. Violette Mus., Kirksville, 1958—; archivist N.E. Mo. State U., Kirksville, 1966—. Bd. dirs. Sojourners Pub. Library, 1946-70. Mem. Alpha Gamma Delta. Baptist. Clubs: Sojourners, University Dames (pres. 1937) (Kirksville). Home: 516 S Halliburton Av Kirksville MO 63501

RIEKE, MARY NEILL WHITELAW (MRS. FORREST E. RIEKE), state legislator, civic worker; b. Oakesdale, Wash., Oct. 26, 1913; d. Henry Neill and Mary (Macklin) Whitelaw; B.S., Ore. State U., 1935; postgrad. Stanford, 1937-38; L.H.D. (hon.), Lewis and Clark Coll., 1971; m. Forrest E. Rieke, Dec. 25, 1940; children—Forrest Neill, John Whitelaw, Mary Macklin. Tchr., counselor Oakland (Ore.) High Sch. 1935-37; dean women, dir. residence Eastern Ore. Coll. Edn., LaGrande, 1938-41; mem. Ore. Ho. of Reps., 1970—. Mem. Portland Pub. Schs. Bd. Edn., 1958-70, chmn., 1961, 62, 65, 69; mem. exec. and legislative coms. Ore. Sch. Bds. Assn., 1963-68, pres., 1966-67; mem. Nat. Adv. Council, Edn. Professions Devel. Act, 1967-70, chmn., 1970-73; chmn. Ore. Council Econ. Edn., 1969—. Bd. dirs. Portland (Ore.) YWCA, 1947—, v.p., 1952-58; bd. dirs. Multnomah Co. Intermediate Edn. Dist., 1964-68, chmn., 1966-67. Named Portland Woman of Achievement, Ore. Jour., 1963; recipient Thom-McCann N.E.A. Nat. Sch. Bd. award for race and edn., 1966. Mem. League Women Voters (chmn. com. individual liberties 1953-54), Am. Assn. U. Women (state chmn. politics in pub. edn. 1967-68). Nat. Com. Support Pub. Schs., Ore. Council Econ. Edn., Mortar Board, Phi Kappa Phi, Pi Lambda Theta. Republican. Presbyn. Home: 5519 SW Menefee Dr Portland OR 97201

RIEKEHOF, LOTTIE LOUISE, educator; b. Lage, Germany; d. Henry and Laura (Warweg) Riekehof; came to U.S., 1923, naturalized, 1935; B.A., Central Bible Coll., 1951; M.A., N.Y. U., 1966, Ph.D., 1971. Dean women, asst. prof. Central Bible Coll., 1948-68; coordinator research in communication methods and interpreting Center Research Advance Tng. Deafness Rehab., N.Y. U., 1968-69, also dir. pastoral rehab. counselling deaf, 1969; dean women Gallaudet Coll., Washington, 1970-74, coordinator Interpreter Tng. program, 1974—. Cons. interpreting deaf people Dept. Health Edn. and Welfare, 1965—. Pres. Women's Aux. Central Bible Coll., 1964-65. Mem. Profl. Rehab. Workers Adult Deaf, Nat. Assn. Deaf, Nat. Assn. Deans Women, Delta Kappa Gamma. Author: The American Sign Language, 1961; Talk to the Deaf, 1963. Home: 6001 Arlington Blvd Falls Church VA 22044

RIEMER, BARBARA LYNN (MRS. DAVID I. RIEMER), lawyer; b. Blytheville, Ark., Jan. 24, 1937; d. William Russell and Dorothy Elizabeth (Dorris) Hemphill; B.A. in Anthropology, U. Mo., 1958; J.D., U. Cal. at Los Angeles, 1966; m. David I. Riemer; children—Alexandra, Jennifer. Admitted to Mass. bar, 1967; practice in Boston, 1967—; mem. firm Fine & Ambrogne, 1967-68, pvt. practice, 1968-73; spl. asst. dist. atty. Norfolk County, Dedham, Mass., 1973—. Bd. dirs. Dog Orphans, Inc., Wellesley, Mass., 1972—. Mem. Am., Mass., Boston bar assns., Mass. Assn. Women Lawyers, Delta Delta Delta. Home: 74 Westerly Rd Weston MA 02193 Office: 15 Court Sq Boston MA 02108

RIEMER, DELILAH (MRS. ABRAHAM DANIEL RUBENSTEIN), physician; b. Bklyn., Aug. 28, 1910; d. Moses Joseph and Sophia (Isacson) Riemer; B.S., Jackson Coll., 1931; M.D., Womans Med. Coll. Pa., 1936; fellowship Harvard, 1937-38; m. Abraham Daniel Rubenstein, Dec. 26, 1937; children—Joel Jay, David Harvey, Susan Sophia. Intern Univ. Hosp., Boston, 1937-38; jr. physician Boston Dispensary, 1937-47; physician in charge A.R.C. Blood Donor Center New Eng., Boston, 1942-45; ward physician VA Hosp., Bedford, Mass., 1948-53, chief phys. medicine and rehab. service, 1953-63; dir. John T. Berry Rehab. Center, Mass. Dept. Mental Health, North Reading, Mass., 1963—; asst. in psychiatry Tufts U., 1957-59, asst. in phys. medicine and rehab., 1959-63, instr. phys. medicine and rehab., 1963-66; asst. physician Boston Dispensary, 1958-66. Mem. task force on manpower and tng. Mass. Mental Retardation Project, 1965-66. Mem. A.M.A., Am. Psychiatric Assn., Am. Congress Rehabilitation Medicine, Mass. Med. Soc., New Eng. Soc. Phys. Medicine. Contbr. articles in field to profl. jours. Home: 164 Ward St Newton Center MA 02159 Office: Lowell Rd North Reading MA 01864

RIENOW, LEONA TRAIN (MRS. ROBERT RIENOW), author; b. Duluth, Minn.; d. George Lathrop and Mabel Almira (Pond) Train; B.A., U. Chgo.; M.A., U. Minn.; m. Robert Rienow, Apr. 8, 1931. Author: The Bewitched Caverns, 1948; The Dark Pool, 1949; The Year of the Last Eagle, 1970; co-author; (with husband) Of Snuff, Sin and the Senate, 1965; The Lonely Quest, 1966; Moment in the Sun: A Report on the Deteriorating Quality of the American Environment, 1967; To Rescue Earth: The Pathway to International Stewardship; The Creaking Gate: Immigration and the Environment, 1974; contbr. stories, articles to popular nat. mags. Mem. Nature Conservancy, Defenders of Wildlife, Humane Soc. U.S., Wilderness Soc., Save the Redwoods League, Hawk Mountain Sanctuary, Friends of the Earth, Desert Protective Council, Nat. Audubon Soc., Authors Guild, Sierra Club, Delta Zeta. Home: Hollyhock Hollow Farm RD Selkirk NY 12158

RIES, ESTELLE HELEN, author; b. Balt., Mar. 5, 1896; d. Elias Elkan and Helen (Hirshberg) Ries; student Barnard Coll., 1915-18; certified grapho-analytical psychologist Am. Inst. Grapho-Analysis, 1948; postgrad. Columbia, 1917-19. D. Litt., Academia Intergentilicia Americana, Washington, 1951; L.H.D., World U., 1973. Asso. editor Architect, N.Y.C., 1918-22; editor Longmans Green, N.Y.C., 1924; editor Better Homes, Detroit, 1924-28; mgr., dir. Writers Bur., N.Y.C., 1928-30; editor Personalized Publs., N.Y.C., 1930-33; dir. research Humaneering, N.Y.C., 1933-36. Trustee World U., Tucson, U. of Sci. and Philosophy, Swannanoa, Va. Mem. World Future Soc., Common Cause, Friends of Earth, Center for Study of Dem. Insts., Fedn. Am. Scientists, UN Assn. U.S.A., Citizens for Decent Lit., The Aetherius Soc., Rosicrucians. Author: Mother Wit—Highlights of Ingenuity, 1930; American Rugs, 1950; Elias E. Ries, Inventor, 1951; The Lonely Sex, 1962; Home Design for Modern Living, 1966; Artists and Artisans, 1968; Garden Hobbies, 1970; "Hot Line" to Idea Production, 1974; Human Engineering, 4 vols., 1940; Six Worlds are Yours, 6 vols., 1974. Contbr. articles on women's interests, historical, health and arts to nat. mags. Represented in Anthologies. Home: 533 W 112th St New York City NY 10025

RIESER, VIVIANNA ELIZABETH (MRS. ARTHUR J. RIESER), hosp. adminstr.; b. Las Cruces, N.M., Dec. 18, 1919; d. Martin Robert and Elizabeth Vivian (McClure) Smith; student N.M. State U., 1938-40, St. Lukes Sch. Nursing, 1940-43; R.N., N.M. U., 1959-60; m. Arthur J. Rieser, Feb. 4, 1947; 1 son, Arthur J. Head nurse St. Lukes Hosp., San Francisco, 1946-47, Santa Fe R.R. Hosp., Albuquerque, 1952-55; asst. charge nurse V.A. Hosp., Ft. Bayard, N.M., 1957-58; night supr. Presbyn. Hosp., Albuquerque, 1958-60; adminstr. E. Morgan County Hosp., Brush, Colo., 1960-70; adminstr. Chippewa Valley Area Hosp. and Nursing Home, Durand, Wis., 1970-74, Williams (Ariz.) Hosp., 1974—. Mem. adv. bd. for health edn. Morgan County Community Coll., Ft. Morgan, Colo., 1970; chmn. finance com. Morgan County Ambulance Service, 1965-68; mem. com. for emergency med. service, Durand, 1971—. Mem. Coll. Hosp. Adminstrs., Am. Fedn. Women's Clubs. Mem. Order Eastern Star. Home: 615 S 9th St Williams AZ 86046

RIESTERER, MARY ELLEN FISHER (MRS. RAPHAEL EARL RIESTERER), educator; b. Milw., Feb. 1, 1946; d. Norbert Clarence and Frances Elizabeth (O'Leary) Fisher; B.S. cum laude, Mt. Mary Coll., 1968; postgrad. U. Wis., 1969-70; m. Raphael Earl Riesterer, Apr. 18, 1970; 1 dau., Kimberly Marie. Occupational therapist I, staff therapist Milwaukee County Rehab. and Chronic Disease Hosp., Milw., 1969-71, occupational therapist II, staff therapist, 1971-72, acting occupational therapy supr., 1971-72, acting supr. student affiliates, 1971-72; instr. occupational therapy Mt. Mary Coll., Milw., 1973—. Mem. Am., Wis. (chmn. nominations com. Southeastern dist. 1973-74) occupational therapy assns., Pi Theta Epsilon, Delta Epsilon Sigma. Home: N 10 W27338 Rolling Ridge Dr Waukesha WI 53186

RIFE, JUDITH ANN, editor, publisher; b. Harrisburg, Pa., Mar. 2, 1946; d. Maurice Victor and Eva Pauline (Miller) Rife; student journalism Pa. State U., 1964-69. Continuity dir. sta. WPSX-TV University Park, Pa., 1965-66, sta. WRSC radio, State College, Pa., 1966; city editor, editor Daily Collegian, University Park, Pa., 1966-69; reporter, wire editor, Pa. Mirror, State College, 1969; propr., editor Centre Democrat, Bellefonte, Pa., 1970—. Instr. newspaper tng. programs for high sch. and coll. students, 1966—. Sec., Bellefonte Swimming Pool Authority, 1970—, Bellefonte Govt. Study Commn., 1973. Recipient Distinguished Service award Pa. Assn. Future Farmers Am., 1973. Mem. Women in Communications, Pa. Newspaper Pubs. Assn. (Keystone Press award 1973); Pa. Soc. Newspaper Editors, Bellefonte Area C. of C., Bellefonte Bus. and Profl. Woman's Club, Sigma Delta Chi. Home: 220 1/2 W High St Bellefonte PA 16823 Office: 140 W High St Bellefonte PA 16823

RIFF, LOUISE J.M., physician; b. Chgo., Apr. 21, 1938; d. Joseph Harold and Edna B. (Grimm) Riff; B.A., Millikin U., 1956; M.D., U. Ill. Coll. Medicine, 1964; 1 son, John. Intern U. Ill. Research and Ednl. Hosps., Chgo., 1964-65, resident medicine, 1965-67; fellow in infectious diseases USPHS, Chgo., 1967-70; research, edn. asso. medicine VA, Chgo., 1970-72; attending physician U. Ill. Hosp., Chgo., 1970—, West Side VA Hosp., Chgo., 1971—; mem. faculty U. Ill. Coll. Medicine, Chgo., 1970—, asst. prof. medicine 1971—. Recipient Physician's Recognition award A.M.A., 1969. Fellow A.C.P. (bd. regents); mem. Am. Soc. Microbiology, Am. Fedn. Clin. Research, A.A.A.S., Sigma Xi, Zeta Tau Alpha. Contbr. articles to sci. and med. jours. Office: Dept Medicine U Ill Hosp 840 S Wood St Chicago IL 60612

RIFFE, FREDORA GABLE, horse farmer; b. Green Twp., Ind., Dec. 11, 1900; d. Louis Clarence and Ella Erma (Starbuck) Gable; student DePauw U., 1919-20; B.S., Ball State U., 1929; m. Glenn Thomas Riffe, Mar. 8, 1935 (dec. 1968); 1 son, John Nelson. Tchr. bus. high schs. in Windfall, Summitville, Monticello, Cambridge City and Greentown, Ind., 1923-35; raiser standard bred horses, 1935—; owner, mgr. Glenn Riffe Farms, Windfall, 1968—. Mem. Ind. Farm Bur., Ind. Trotting and Pacing Horse Assn., U.S. Trotting Assn., United Methodist Women (sec.). Democrat. Mem. Order Eastern Star. Address: Rural Route 1 Windfall IN 46076

RIFFEE, JUDITH ANN MARTIN (MRS. WILLIAM HARVEY RIFFEE), pharmacist; b. Elkins, W.Va., July 31, 1944; d. Roscoe Russell and Freda Lucinda (Kerens) Martin; B.S., W.Va. U., 1967; m. William Harvey Riffee, June 17, 1967; 1 son, Evan Martin. Pharmacist, Chatkins Pharmacy, Hagerstown, Md., 1967; hosp. pharmacist U.S. Naval Hosp., Portsmouth, Va., 1967-70; pharmacist Maryview Hosp., Portsmouth, 1970; hosp. clin. pharmacist Ohio State U. Hosps., Columbus, 1970—, clin. instr. Coll. Pharmacy, Ohio State U., 1972—. 1st v.p. Lakeville Estates Garden Club, Virginia Beach, Va., 1969. Recipient Lilly Achievement award, 1967, Ethel J. Heath Scholarship Key, 1967. Kappa Psi scholar, 1966. Mem. Am. Pharm. Assn., Central Ohio Soc. Hosp. Pharmacists, Am. Orchid Soc., Lambda Kappa Sigma (past So. regional supr., grand treas., Midwestern regional supr. 1972-74), Rho Chi. Democrat. Lutheran. Club: Ohio State Pharmacy Wives. Home: 2206 Harwitch Rd Columbus OH 43221 Office: 410 W 10th Av Columbus OH 43210

RIFFLE, STELLA LEE MILLER (MRS. ROBERT ALLEN RIFFLE), educator; b. Webster Springs, W.Va., Jan. 3, 1932; d. Virgil Elvo and Lela Florence (Woods) Miller; B.A., Glenville State Coll., 1966; M.A., W.Va. U., 1972; m. Robert Allen Riffle, Aug. 14, 1949; children—Shelia Allen (Mrs. Gerald McFarland), Robert Allen, William Lloyd, Larry Thomas. Tchr. elementary sch. Webster County Schs., Webster Springs, W.Va., 1957-67, tchr. spl. edn. educable mentally retarded, 1968—. Sec., Economy Market, Inc., Cowen, W.Va., 1966—, Riffles, Inc., Webster Springs, 1973—. Mem. Council Exceptional Children, Alpha Delta Kappa. Baptist. Mem. Rebeccah Lodge. Home: Route 3 Box 83 Webster Springs WV 26288 Office: Point Mountain Rd Webster Springs WV 26288

RIFKIN, VIVETTE RAVEL, civic worker; b. El Paso, Tex., July 18, 1911; d. Erman and Taube Leah (Goodman) Ravel; grad. high sch.; m. Milton Rifkin, Feb. 8, 1935; children—Martyl (Mrs. Jerry Reinsdorf), Dovie (Mrs. Myron Horvitz), Jerelyn (Mrs. Paul Grundland), Jeremy. Founder, So. Suburban Hadassah, Chgo., 1948, pres. 1948—; founder, pres. Ednl. Tape Recordings for Blind, Chgo., 1966. Recipient Service to Mankind award S.W. Sertoma Club, 1969; certificate of recognition U. Mo. Coll. Edn., 1967; Victor Buttram Service award Ill. Fedn. Blind, 1972; Service award Cook County chpt. D.A.V., 1973. Home: 9906 S Campbell St Chicago IL 60642 Office: 10234 S Kedzie Av Evergreen Park IL 60642

RIFKIND, ARLEEN BRENNER, physician; b. N.Y.C., June 29, 1938; d. Michael C. and Regina (Gottlieb) Brenner; B.A., Bryn Mawr Coll., 1960; M.D., N.Y. U., 1964; m. Robert S. Rifkind, Dec. 24, 1961; children—Amy B., Nina L. Intern, Bellevue Hosp., N.Y.C., 1964-65, resident, 1965; clin. asso. Nat. Inst. Child Health and Human Devel. div. endocrinology Nat. Cancer Inst., 1965-68; physician to out-patient dept. N.Y. Hosp., N.Y.C., 1968-71; asst. prof. pediatrics, asst. prof. medicine Cornell U. Med. Coll., 1971—, asst. prof. pharmacology, 1973—; research asso., asst. resident physician Rockefeller U. Hosp., 1968-71; adj. asst. prof. Rockefeller U., 1971—; staff fellow NIH, Nat. Inst. Child Health and Human Devel., 1965-68. USPHS Spl. fellow, 1968-70, 1971-72; grantee Am. Cancer Soc., N.Y.C. Health Research Council, 1972—. Mem. Endocrine Soc., A.A.A.S., Assn. Women in Sci. Contbr. articles to tech. jours. Office: Cornell U Med Coll 1300 York Av New York City NY 10021

RIGBY, MARY ELIZABETH TROBAUGH (MRS. GRANT RIGBY), educator; b. Pontiac, Ill., Dec. 3, 1914; d. Henry Reno and Sarah Jessup (Pellett) Trobaugh; B.S., U. Wash., 1940; postgrad. San Francisco State U., Portland State U., 1961-72; m. Grant Rigby, Aug. 24, 1940; children—Grant Morris, Trova (Mrs. Gary M. Porter), Donald Bruce, John Michael. Tchr. multiple handicapped blind children Ore. Sch. for Blind, Salem, 1960—. Health, Edn. and Welfare grantee, 1964. Mem. Council Exceptional Children, Assn. for Edn. Visually Handicapped, Ore. Edn. Assn. Episcopalian (ch. sch. supt. 1949-53). Office: 700 Church St SE Salem OR 97310

RIGDON, ROSIE LEE BAGLEY (MRS. HARMON A. RIGDON), banker; b. Jacksonville, Fla.; d. Richard B. and Rose (Smith) Bagley; grad. Am. Inst. Banking, 1969; m. Harmon A. Rigdon, Mar. 14, 1941; children—Betty LaTrelle (Mrs. M.H. Studstill), Harmon Alvin, Donald B. Supt., mgr. transit dept. State Bank of Jacksonville, 1957-66, personnel officer, 1966-68, asst. cashier, 1968—, asst. v.p., 1969-72, v.p., 1972—, asst. operations officer, 1969—. Com. mem. Evans Scholarship Fund, 1969—. Mem. Nat. Assn. Bank Women (Fla. publicity chmn. 1969-70), Am. Bus. Women's Assn. (charter; pres. chpt. 1969-70), Fla. Bank Adminstrv. Inst. (dir. 1972-73). Baptist (mem. benevolent com. 1968-70, mem. finance com. 1968—). Home: 1301 Pinegrove Ct Jacksonville FL 32205 Office: 841 Miami Rd Jacksonville FL 32207

RIGGAN, JUDITH STUMPF, occupational therapist; b. St. Louis, Apr. 7, 1945; d. Alfred Fidelius and Evelyn Mary (Bursmeyer) Stumpf; student Webster Coll., 1963-65; B.S. in Occupational Therapy, Washington U., St. Louis, 1967; m. John Thompson Riggan, May 5, 1973. Commd. 2d lt. U.S. Army, 1967, advanced through grades to capt., 1969; student affiliate occupational therapy Letterman Gen. Hosp., San Francisco, 1967; staff occupational therapist Valley Forge Gen. Hosp., Phoenixville, Pa., 1968-70; chief occupational therapist Martin Army Hosp., Ft. Benning, Ga., 1970-73, dir. perceptual motor dysfunction program, 1973—. Cons. learning disabilities to sch. systems, 1971—. Mem. Am., Ga. occupational therapy assns., Chattaloochee Valley Assn. for Children Learning Disabilities. Home: 5242 Verdun Ct Columbus GA 31907 Office: Box 411 Martin Army Hosp Fort Benning GA 31905

RIGGENBACH, EMMA MAY MARTIN (MRS. JOSEPH AARON RIGGENBACH), civic worker; b. Monte Vista, Colo., Aug. 5, 1903; d. Edwin Woods and Christina (Mattson) Martin; student Colo. State Tchrs. Coll., 1921-22, Adams State Tchrs. Coll., 1956-57; m. Joseph Aaron Riggenbach, Jan. 22, 1921; children—Betty May (Mrs. James B. McEntyre), Shirley Jean (Mrs. Fred Quesenberry), Neil Martin. Tchr. South Fork (Colo.) Community Sch., 1920, Monte Vista (Colo.) Elementary Schs., 1923-36. Vice chmn. bd. dirs. Community Concert Assn., Monte Vista, 1955-59; bd. mem. area council Girl Scouts Am., Monte Vista, 1937-38, troop leader, 1937-39; rep. for youth, ofcl. bd. Colo. Synod Presbyn. Ch., 1950-51; social service vol. Spanish-Am. Community, 1967-69; mem. exec. council Southwest Colo. Library System, 1968-70. Vice pres. bd. trustees Monte Vista Pub. Library, 1960-64, pres. bd. trustees, 1965-70. Mem. San Luis Valley Hist. Soc. Colo. (charter mem.). Presbyn. (ch. sch. instr. 1948-58). Home: 248 Dunham St Monte Vista CO 81144

RIGGLE, MARGARET ANN, educator; b. Fostoria, O., Oct. 5, 1944; d. Chalmer Junior and Ruth Ida (Ramsey) Riggle; B.S. in Edn. (Freshman Student Theatre scholar), Bowling Green State U., 1966, M.A., 1969; postgrad. U. Toledo, 1967, Ohio No. U., 1968-73. Tchr., Toledo (O.) pub. schs., 1966, Washington Twp. Schs., Toledo, 1966-67; instr. speech Ohio No. U., Ada, 1968-73, dir. forensics, 1968-73; weather reporter news dept. WLIO-TV channel 35, Lima, O., 1974—. Speech cons. Ford Motor Co., Lima, O., 1969-71, The Vogues, Oil City, Pa., 1973; demonstrator Hoover, Inc., Lima, 1973; entertainer Caldwell Musical Prodns., Columbus, 1973; singer, dancer Children's Internat. Summer Villages, Inc., Ada, 1971—. Recipient Allegany Individual Events Coaches award, 1973, Forensic Coaches award So. Conn. State Coll., 1970; named Outstanding Cameo Actress, Lima Encore Theatre, 1972, Best Costume Designer, 1973. Mem. Am. Assn. Univ. Women (parliamentarian 1972-73), Ohio No. U. Liberal Arts Faculty (parliamentarian 1969-73), Northwestern Ohio Edn. Assn. (parliamentarian 1972), Speech Communications Assn., Am. Theatre Assn., Ohio Communications Assn., Ohio Forensic Assn., Alpha Delta Pi, Theta Alpha Phi, Pi Kappa Delta (sec., treas. 1972—). Methodist. Mem. Order Eastern Star. Home: 416 N Simon St Ada OH 45810

RIGGS, BELLE ROSE, realtor; b. Netcong, N.J.; d. George Francis and Elizabeth (McManus) Roche; student pub. schs.; m. Jetur R. Riggs, June 25, 1928 (div. Dec. 1951); children—Albert R., Bess Ann (Mrs. K. Carroll Kennedy), Virginia B. (Mrs. Irving Glickstein). Saleswoman, office mgr., sales mgr. with realtor, Orlando, Fla., 1950-56; pres. Riggs & Hausman, Inc., 1956-65; pres. Belle Riggs, Inc., Realtors, Orlando, 1965—. Mem. exec. bd. Orlando-Winter Park Bd. Realtors, 1957—, treas., 1969, 2d v.p., 1970, 1st v.p., 1971, pres., 1972. Mem. Nat. Assn. Realtors (gov. women's council 1964, 65, regional v.p. women's council 1966, 67), Fla. Assn. Realtors (pres. women's council 1963, woman of year 1963). Home: 1208 Chichester Av Orlando FL 32803 Office: 2122D E Colonial Dr Orlando FL 32803

RIGGS, KARYLENE JOY (MRS. MARION L. BOBB RIGGS), real estate co. exec.; b. San Francisco, Aug. 12, 1941; d. Karyll Francis and Joy Estelyn (Frazier) Betts; student Stockton Jr. Coll., 1959-61; 1 son, Scott Alan Smith; m. 2d, Marion L. Bob Riggs. Saleswoman, Crowl & Cyr Realtors, Stockton, Cal., 1964-70; owner, broker Riggs, Didier & Smith, Stockton, 1970—. Affiliate Miss San Joaquin County Pageant Assn. Named Salesman of Year, Stockton Bd. Realtors, 1969; recipient commendation Cal. Assembly, 1974. Mem. Cal. Real Estate Assn., Stockton Bd. Realtors (pres. 1973), Nat. Inst. Real Estate Brokers. Home: 6517 Shenandoah Pl Stockton CA 95207 Office: 5934 Pacific Av Stockton CA 95207

RIGGS, MYRTLE CRAVER (MRS. LARRY THOMAS RIGGS), motel exec.; b. Newberry, S.C., Mar. 28, 1920; d. William Everett and Myrtle (Ivey) Craver; student Converse Coll., 1936-37, Furman U., 1937-38, Coll. of Charleston, 1943-46; m. Richard Bradham, May 27, 1940 (dec.); 1 dau., Helen (Mrs. Robert Lindley Furnans); m. 2d, Larry Thomas Riggs, June 26, 1966. Owner, Mt. Vernon Motel, Charleston, S.C., 1950—; dir. Superior Motels, Inc., 1968—, v.p., 1969-70, pres., 1970-71. Chmn., St. Andrews Playground Commn., 1958-62; pres. St. Andrews Parish Exchange Aux., 1950-51, 70—, St. Andrews High Sch. P.T.A., 1956-58; life mem. S.C. P.T.A., v.p., chmn. Womens div. Greater Charleston Safety Council, 1969—; S.C. chmn. Am. Revolution Com. Bicentennial Gen. Fedn. Women's Clubs, 1972—; charter mem., pres. Trident chpt. Nat. Multiple Sclerosis, 1971-73. Sec., Democratic Club 4-St. Andrews Parish, 1950-62; mem. Pres.'s Club Dem. Party, 1964. Pres., bd. dirs. YWCA; bd. dirs. Florence Crittenton Home, St. Andrews Parish Community Center, Mental Health Assn., Citadel Edn. Found.; v.p., bd. dirs. Charleston chpt. Am. Cancer Soc.; chmn. women's crusade, bd. dirs. United Fund; trustee Progress Found. S.C. Fedn. Womens Clubs; bd. commrs. Oak Grove Orphanage, Charleston County Zoning Bd., 1971—; Steering Com. faculty Alumni Center Coll. Charleston. Named to Hospitality Mag. Hall of Fame, 1969; recipient Distinguished Service award Superior Motels, Inc., 1969, Mary Mildred Sullivan award Converse Coll. Alumni, 1970; named Charleston Woman of Year, 1958. Mem. Coll. of Charleston Alumni Assn. (past v.p., dir.), Charleston Fedn. Womens Clubs (So. dist. dir., past pres.), Charleston Trident C. of C., Chi Omega. Methodist (past pres. Wesleyan Service Guild). Home: 2826 Marshall Blvd Sullivans Island SC 29484 also 1265 Camerton St Charleston SC 29407 Office: Mt Vernon Motel Savannah Hwy Charleston SC 29407

RIGGS, VIRGINIA LOUISE HOLLOWAY (MRS. ARTHUR J. RIGGS), lectr., clubwoman; b. Conway, Ark.; d. Keith Leaming and Harriett (Bennett) Holloway; B.A., U. Ark.; m. Arthur J. Riggs, Oct. 15, 1942; children—Arthur James, Emily Adele (Mrs. John W. Freeman), Keith Holloway, George Bennett. Editor, Virginia's Kitchen. Park Cities N. Dallas News, 1955-60; lectr. cooking, related topics, 1955—, hist. topics, 1960—. Pres., LeBonnet Bleu Garden Club, 1966-68, Seneca Rev. Club, 1967-68, Dallas Browning Club, 1970-72, S'Amuser Club, 1966-67, Jr. Matheon Club, 1971-72. Zone chmn. Am. Cancer Soc., 1966-68; area capt. Carih, 1970. Mem. Kappa Kappa Gamma. Home: 4116 Amherst St Dallas TX 75225

RIGLER, RUTH LILLIAN, food co. exec.; b. Mpls., Mar. 27, 1911; d. Frank and Jeannette (Rosen) Rigler; B.S., U. Minn., 1933; M.S., Columbia, 1934; children—Rae (Mrs. Jon Brent), Terry. Instr., supr. Evanston (Ill.) Hosp., 1937-41; vis. nurse Keystone area, dept. infant and maternal welfare Chgo. Health Dept., 1943-45; with Adolph's, Ltd., Burbank, Cal., 1949—, dir. consumer edn., 1951—, v.p., 1961—, dir. Jeannette Frank Test Kitchens, 1951—. Recipient Marian L. Vanier scholarship in nursing, 1933. Mem. Am. Women in Radio and TV (chpt. v.p., trustee Nat. Edn. Found.), Am. Home Econs. Assn. (charter), Am. Marketing Assn., Elec. Women's Round Table, Internat. Platform Assn. Author: (pseudonym Jeannette Frank) The Modern Meat Cookbook, 1958, rev. edit., 1968. Home: 11837 Darlington St Apt 1 Los Angeles CA 90049 Office: 1800 W Magnolia Blvd Burbank CA 91503

RIGNEY, JANIS, bus. exec.; b. Los Angeles, Oct. 31, 1936; d. Fred L. Rigney and Gladys M. (Green) Rigney Sweatt; student Oklahoma City U., 1959-60. Asst. to pres. Doric Corp., Oklahoma City, 1963-69, sec., 1969—, v.p., 1971—. Mem. Am. Soc. Corporate Secs., Execs.' Secs., Inc. (pres. Oklahoma City chpt. 1969). Office: 3000 Liberty Tower Oklahoma City OK 73102

RIGNEY, KLEONA BROWN, physician; b. Phila., Aug. 14, 1922; d. Elbert Kleone and Elinor (Leaf) Brown; A.B., U. Pa., 1944, M.D., 1947; M.P.H., U. Cal., 1960; m. Raymond J. Corsini, Oct. 7, 1965; children by previous marriage—Michael John, Roberta Kay, Jonathan Leaf. Intern, Western Pa. Hosp., Pitts., 1947-48; resident internal medicine City Hosp., Akron, O., 1948-50, Permanente Hosp., Oakland, Cal., 1950-51; pvt. practice internal medicine, Berkeley, Cal., 1951-52; fellow chest diseases Highland Alameda County Hosp., Oakland, 1953-54; sch. and clinic physician, Berkeley and Oakland, 1952-57; asst. health officer Contra Costa County Health Dept., Martinez, Cal., 1957-65; chief chronic disease br. Hawaii Dept. Health, Honolulu, 1966—; asso. clin. prof. pub. health U. Hawaii. Chmn. Interagy. Council Smoking and Health, Hawaii, 1971; mem. Gov.'s Commn. on Aging, 1966—; Diplomate Am. Bd. Preventive Medicine. Fellow Am. Coll. Preventive Medicine; mem. A.M.A., Hawaii Med. Assn., Am. Pub. Health Assn. Home: 140 Niuiki Circle Honolulu HI 96821 Office: PO Box 3378 Honolulu HI 96801

RIGSBY, MARGUERITE LORENE SPIEGLE (MRS. GILBERT L. RIGSBY), librarian; b. Ensley, Ala.; d. Alonzo D. and Lena S. (Higgins) Spiegle; B.S., Auburn U., 1951; postgrad. Peabody Coll., 1965; m. Gilbert L. Rigsby, Apr. 25, 1934; children—Gilbert Lynn, Marguerite Lorene (Mrs. David Gerald Parsons), Charles Owen. Tchr., Cullman County (Ala.) Sch. System, 1931-44, sch. prin., 1944-51; tchr. Cullman City Sch. System, 1952-62; adminstr. Cullman County Pub. Library, 1962—. Participant, Ala. Writers Conclave, 1969. Bd. dirs. Music Concert Series, 1965-67. Mem. Ala. Library Assn. (chmn. publicity pub. libraries div. 1964-65, sec. div. 1967-68, v.p. pub. libraries div. 1971-72, pres. 1972-73), Cullman Fedn. Garden Clubs (civic project chmn. 1964-65), Ch. Women United (pres. 1967), Delta Kappa Gamma (pres. 1962-64), Alpha Beta Alpha. Mem. Christian Ch. (stewardess 1963-64, sec. bd. 1964-65, dir. youth groups 1947-54, choir dir. 1951-68). Club: Green Earth Garden (pres. 1963-64). Mem. editorial com. Cullman Centennial Book, 1972-73. Home: 212 12th St NE Cullman AL 35055 Office: 200 Clark St Cullman AL 35055

RIKE, PHYLLIS ILENE, orgn. exec.; b. Akron, O., Sept. 14, 1920; d. Leslie Chalmers and Mabel (Johnston) Rike; grad. Bliss Bus. Coll., Columbus, O., 1939. Clerical and secretarial work Lattimer-Stevens Co., Columbus, O., 1939-46; with Internat. Soc. Christian Endeavor, 1946—, editor The Christian Endeavor World, 1956—, asst. sec., 1957-60, adminstrv. sec., 1960—, dir. Outdoor Poster Program, 1957-67, sec. promotion and publicity, 1955-67, treas., clk., 1967—; exec. sec., clk. World's Christian Endeavor Union, 1967-72, 74—, treas., 1970—. Mem. Bus. and Profl. Women's Club (dir. Columbus), Ohio Fedn. Bus. and Profl. Women (treas.), Franklin County, Ohio Christian Endeavor unions. Presbyn. (elder, treas. Women's Assn.). Home: 2949 Sullivant Av Apt C Columbus OH 43204 Office: 1221 E Broad St PO Box 1110 Columbus OH 43216

RILEY, BRIDGET LOUISE BEAUCHAMP, artist; b. London, Eng., Apr. 25, 1931; d. John Fisher and Louise (Gladstone) Riley; student Goldsmiths Art Coll., London, 1949-52; Royal Coll. Art, London, 1952-55. Exhibited in one-woman shows in London, 1961, 63, 69, N.Y.C., 1965, 66, Los Angeles, 1965; touring one-man show Hanover, Berne, Switzerland, Dusseldorf, Germany, Turin, Italy, London, Eng., Prague, Czechoslovakia, 1970-71; group exhbns. in Eng., Am., Italy, France, Germany, Israel, Japan, Can.; represented in permanent collections Tate Gallery, Victoria and Albert Mus. (both London), Ferens Art Gallery, Hull, Eng., Manchester (Eng.) Art Gallery, Stuyvesant Found., Eng., Caluste Kulbenkian Found., Europe, Mus. Modern Art, N.Y.C., Pasadena (Cal.) Mus., Albright Knox, Buffalo., Art Gallery of Victoria. Recipient Internat. prize in painting 34th Venice Biennial, 1968. Address: Rowan Gallery 31A Bruton Place London W1 England

RILEY, CAROLYN HOPKINS, editor; b. Detroit, July 26, 1943; d. Harold Milton and Mary Elizabeth (Mackenzie) Hopkins; A.B., U. Mich., 1965; postgrad., Wayne State U., 1970-72; m. Robert E. Riley, Jan. 2, 1965 (div. Apr. 1967). With Gale Research Co., pubs., Detroit, 1965—, asst. editor, co-editor, editor Contemporary Authors, 1965-71, founding editor Contemporary Literary Criticism, 1971—. Editorial cons. various automated typesetting projects. Mem. A.A.A.S., Am. Civil Liberties Union. Author: (with Barbara Harte) Therefore Mord, 1967; book reviewer Best Sellers mag., 1969—. Home: 800 Ironwood Dr Rochester MI 48063 Office: 700 Book Bldg Detroit MI 48226

RILEY, CLARA MAE DEATHERAGE, educator, psychologist; b. Kilgore, Tex., July 27, 1931; d. Joseph Marion and Elsie (Richardson) Deatherage; A.A., Sacramento Jr. Coll., 1951; B.A., Pepperdine Coll., 1953, M.A., 1956; Ph.D., Fla. State U., 1963; m. Glyndon Daughtry Riley, July 6, 1952 (div.); children—Randall Glen, Rene Ellen. Counselor resident women Pepperdine Coll., 1953-54, asst. prof. child devel., family relations, 1963-66; tchr. Los Angeles City Schs., 1955-56; instr. dept. psychology Seattle Pacific Coll., 1956-60; profl. cons. family life edn. dept. Seattle City Schs., 1958-60; grad. asst. Fla. State U., 1960-63; marriage, family and child counselor, Santa Ana (Cal.) Inst. Therapeutic Psychology, 1965-67; mental health cons. Project Head Start, Los Angeles 1965-70; asst. prof. med. psychology dept. psychiatry and human behavior U. Cal. at Irvine, 1970—; vis. lectr., dept. home econs. and family life Cal. State Coll. at Long Beach, 1965-66. Camp dir. Tanda Lodge, Big Bear Lake, Cal., 1954-57, Camp Fire Girls, Bremerton, Wash., 1958; mem. pres.' council on curriculum devel. Compton Coll., 1966-70; mem. mental health adv. bd. Los Angeles Head Start. Mem. Am., Cal., Orange psychol. assns., Am., Cal. State home econs. assns., Soc. research in Child Devel., Am. Council Family Relations, Nat. Assn. for Edn. Young Children, Delta Sigma Theta. Democrat. Episcopalian. Author: Getting the Most out of College; A Guidebook, 1960; The Many Faces of Discipline, 1966; Head Start in Action, 1967; Riley Preschool Developmental Inventory, 1969. Office: 255 Thalia St Laguna Beach CA 92651

RILEY, EILEEN V., librarian; b. Hartford, Conn.; d. Jeremiah and Mary (Garvey) Riley; A.A., Boston U., 1952, B.A., 1954; M.S. in L.S., Columbia, 1959. Library intern Nat. Library of Medicine, Bethesda, Md., 1959-60, librarian cataloger, 1960-61, librarian acquisitions, 1961-71; chief tech. processes VA Central Office Library, Washington, 1971-73; chief acquisitions br. U.S. Dept. of Labor Library, Washington, 1973—. Mem. Med. Library Assn., Spl. Library Assn. Home: 6304 Haviland Dr Bethesda MD 20034 Office: US Dept of Labor Library Washington DC 20210

RILEY, JANET MARY, lawyer, educator; b. New Orleans, Sept. 20, 1915; d. John Nichols and Odile (Hymel) Riley; B.A. cum laude, Loyola U., 1936; B.S. in L.S., La. State U., 1940; J.D., Loyola U., 1952; fellow U. Va., 1959-60, LL.M., 1960. Tchr. Orleans Parish pub. schs., 1937-39; asst. circulation dept. New Orleans Pub. Library, 1940-41; asst. librarian Loyola U., 1941-43, law librarian, 1945-56, instr. law, 1952-55, asst. prof. law, 1956-61, asso. prof. law, 1961-71, prof. law, 1971—, chmn. univ. senate, 1970-72, bd. regents, 1970-72; librarian Camp Plauche, 1943-45, LaGarde Gen. Hosp., 1945; admitted to La. bar, 1953; admitted to U.S. Supreme Court bar, 1960. Mem. Orleans Parish Juvenile Ct. Adv. Com., 1971—; mem. steering and legislative coms. La. Gov.'s Task Force on Women and Credit. Mem. La. Supreme Ct.'s Committee to Draft Pattern Jury Instructions for Civil Trials, 1968-72. Bd. dirs. Community Relations Council Greater New Orleans, 1966—, 1st v.p., 1972—. Mem. La. (sec. sect. internat. comparative and mil. law 1955-58; mem. bar admissions adv. com. 1964-66, 67-68) Bar Assn., League Women Voters New Orleans, St. Thomas More Cath. Lawyers Assn., Council of La. State Law Inst. (reporter to draft revision La. community property laws 1972—), Am. Assn. U. Profs., Cardinal Key (faculty mem. 1966), Phi Kappa Phi, Phi Alpha Delta, Beta Phi Mu. Democrat. Roman Catholic. Club: St. Thomas More Law. Author: Louisiana Community Property; contbg. author Essays on the Civil Law of Obligations, 1969. Contbr. legal and library sci. profl. jours. Home: 3413 Vincennes Pl New Orleans LA 70125

RILEY, LOUISE ELISE, librarian; b. Roanoke, Ala., Dec. 12, 1912; d. James Andrew and Fannie Sarah (Johnson) Riley; B.S., Ala. State Tchrs. Coll., 1940; M.Ed., Atlanta U., 1949, M.S. in L.S., 1962; postgrad. Emory U., summer 1968. Tchr. Ala. Pub. Sch. System, 1932-50; tchr., librarian Randolph County Tng. Sch., Roanoke, 1950-61; asst. serials librarian Tuskegee (Ala.) Inst., 1961, asst. circulation librarian, 1962, supr. dept. libraries, 1963-66, serials librarian, 1966—. Life mem. Tuskegee Civic Assn.; mem. Ala. Council on Human Relations, sec., 1970—. Named Tchr. of Year, Randolph County Tchrs. Assn., 1958. Mem. Am. Civil Liberties Union, N.A.A.C.P., Ala., Southeastern (sec. coll. and spl. library div. 1970-71), Am. library assns., Am. Assn. U. Profs., Am. Assn. U.

Women, Beta Phi Mu, Sigma Gamma Rho. Home: PO Box 299 Tuskegee Institute AL 36088 Office: Hollis Burke Frissell Library Tuskegee Institute AL 36088

RILEY, VIRGINIA LEE, lawyer; b. Washington, June 17, 1923; A.A., Nat. U. Jr. Coll., 1945; LL.B., Nat. U., 1949; LL.M., George Washington U., 1956. Admitted to D.C. bar, 1949; sr. partner Pierson, Ball & Dowd, Washington. Mem. probate rules adv. com. Superior Ct., 1972-74. Bd. dirs., v.p. Potomac Area Council Camp Fire Girls. Mem. Am. (chmn. significant probate and trust decisions com. 1973-74), D.C. Unified (trustee client security fund), D.C. (chmn. D.C. affairs sect. 1971-72; dir. 1972-73) bar assns., Women's Bar Assn. of D.C., Kappa Beta Pi. Home: Kennedy Warren Washington DC 20008 Office: 1000 Ring Bldg Washington DC 20036

RIMMER, MARGRET KING MCDONALD (MRS. RAYMOND J. RIMMER), city ofcl.; b. Hitchcock, Okla.; d. William Cypert and Loretta (Truscott) King. Asso. in Music, Christian Coll., 1936; B.A., U. Mo., 1940; m. Robert W. McDonald, Sept. 16, 1940 (div. Sept. 1949); 1 son, Lance King; m. 2d, Raymond J. Rimmer, Aug. 15, 1956; step-children—Raymond J., Karen D. Dir. home econs. WBAP-TV, Ft. Worth, 1949-60, dir. publicity and promotion, 1953-60; owner fashion splty. shop, Fort Worth, 1960—; mem. Ft. Worth City Council, 1971—. Freelance radio, TV writer, 1960—; fashion coordinator style shows Am. Fashion Assn., 1963. Pres., Goodwill Aux., 1963-64; chmn. Met. div. Ft. Worth United Fund, 1960; mem. Gov.'s Commn. on Status of Women, 1970—. Bd. dirs. Casa Manana Musicals, Ft. Worth Soc. Crippled Children and Adults, Jr. Achievement, Goodwill Industries, Tex. Municipal League. Recipient Zenith TV Corp. award, 1953; named Female Newsmaker 1971, Ft. Worth Press Club. Mem. Am. Women in Radio and Television (area v.p. 1958-59), Tarrant County Med. Aux. (pres. 1969-70), Kappa Kappa Gamma, Women in Communications. Clubs: Colonial Country, Shady Oaks Country, Petroleum (Fort Worth). Contbr. column to Sunday newspaper. Home: 3209 Overton Park E Fort Worth TX 76109 Office: 1506 Pennsylvania St Fort Worth TX 76104

RING, CAROLYN MCLEAN, polit. party ofcl.; b. Mpls., Aug. 12, 1926; d. Milford Orville and Bessy (Martin) McLean; student U. Minn.; m. Ward Dashiell Ring, Dec. 27, 1947; children—Linda (Mrs. Gary Haugen), Peggy, Diane, Ward. Former chmn. Republican Party, Richfield, Minn., Hennepin County, Minn., 3d Congl. Dist.; former vice chmn. Minn. Rep. Party, now chmn. Mem. adv. council Richfield Sch. Bd., 1970-73; mem. Richfield Charter Commn., 1973—. Mem. Pi Beta Phi. Presbyn. Home: 6304 Russell Av S Richfield MN 55423 Office: 555 Wabasha Av St Paul MN 55102

RING, LUCILE WILEY (MRS. JOHN ROBERT RING), lawyer; b. nr. Kearney, Neb., Jan. 2, 1920; d. Myrtie Mercer and Alice (Cowell) Wiley; A.B., Kearney State Coll., 1944; J.D., Washington U., St. Louis, 1946; m. John Robert Ring, Mar. 28, 1948; children—John, James, Thomas. Admitted to Mo. bar, 1946; tchr. Nance County (Neb.) schs., 1937-41, Loup City, Neb., 1944; legal adviser, chief legal group U.S. Dept. Army, St. Louis, 1946-52; dir. Lawyers Reference Service, Bar Assn. St. Louis, 1960-70; staff law clk. U.S. Ct. Appeals, St. Louis, 1970-72; exec. dir. St. Louis Com. on Cts., 1972—, dir. St. Louis Criminal Cts. Improvement Project, 1972—. Legal adviser Mo. Anatomical Bd., 1965—. Vice pres. Webster Groves Council for Pub. Edn., 1958-59. Mem. Mo. Bar Assn., Mo. Assn. Women Lawyers (treas. 1959-60, pres. 1960-61), St. Louis Womens Law Soc. (treas. 1958-61, pres. 1961-62, 69-74), Washington U. Dental Faculty Wives (pres. 1972-74), Zonta. Editor: History of the St. Louis Bar, 1974. Home: 755 Catalpa Av Webster Groves MO 63119 Office: Civil Courts Bldg St Louis MO 63101

RINGLER, LENORE, educator, psychologist; b. N.Y.C., Feb. 8, 1928; d. Albert Haendel and Ida (Brafstein) Haendel; B.A., Bklyn. Coll., 1949; M.A., Queen's Coll., 1954; Ph.D., N.Y. U., 1965; m. Jerry Ringler, June 19, 1949; 1 son, Adam. Tchr., then reading specialist N.Y.C. Bd. Edn., 1949-65; mem. faculty N.Y. U., 1965—, prof., chairperson dept. ednl. psychology, 1974—; ednl. cons. test dept. Harcourt Brace Jovanovich. Grantee U.S. Office Edn., 1968-69. Mem. Am. Psychol. Assn., Am. Ednl. Research Assn., Internat. Reading Assn. (past pres. Manhattan council), Orton Soc., Pi Lambda Theta (Research fellow 1963-64), Kappa Delta Pi. Contbr. articles to publs., also tests. Home: 519 N Wyoming Av South Orange NJ 07079 Office: 933 Shimkin Hall New York Univ New York City NY 10003

RINGLER, NORMA MILLER (MRS. ALBERT RINGLER), educator; b. Cleve.; d. Alex and Dora (Snyder) Miller; B.A., Case Western Res. U., 1945, M.A., 1946, Ph.D. in Speech Pathology, 1973; m. Albert Ringler, Jan. 6, 1944; children—Ann Leslie, Kim Debra, Lisa Jean. Tchr. of deaf, Cleve., 1946-48; faculty Case Western Res. U., 1948-54, lectr., part-time 1954—; lang. cons. Cuyahoga County Retarded Children's Program div. Child Welfare, 1964-66; supr. students in tng. speech pathology Ohio U., Cleve. area, 1965—; asst. prof., dir. speech pathology, clin. dir. speech clinic Cleve. State U., 1971—. Sec., New Democratic Coalition, Cleve., 1968. Mem. ednl. com. Bellfaire-Residential Treatment Center for Emotionally Disturbed Children, Cleve., 1969—; co-chmn. Coalition To Support Human Services. Recipient Nat. League Women Voters award, 1963. Mem. Am., Ohio (constl. com. 1964) speech and hearing assns., Am. Assn. Mental Retardation, Learning Disabilities Assn., Cleve. Civil Liberties Union (chmn. dramatic arts 1965—), League Women Voters (state welfare com. 1969—, local v.p. 1964-68, local chmn. welfare 1968—, welfare chmn. Cuyahoga County 1972—). Home: 3721 Lytle Rd Shaker Heights OH 44122 Office: Cleveland State U Cleveland OH 44115

RINHART, MARION HUTCHINSON (MRS. FLOYD LINCOLN RINHART), author; b. Bradley Beach, N.J., Feb. 20, 1916; d. Harry Kelly and Bertha (Gifford) Hutchinson; grad. high sch.; m. Floyd Lincoln Rinhart, Mar. 3, 1935; children—Joan Carol (Mrs. Bernard Johnson), George Robert. Author, 1960—; cons. Ohio State U.; Am. pioneer photography, 1973—. Mem. Photog. Hist. Soc. N.Y., Daguerrean Soc. Author: American Daguerreian Art, 1967; American Miniature Case Art, 1969; America's Affluent Age, 1971. Contbr. editor: The New Daguerreian Journal. Address: Box 340 Route 3 Melbourne Beach FL 32951

RINK, PATRICIA JANE DONAHUE (MRS. VIRGIL WILLIAM RINK), educator; b. Moline, Ill.; d. John Dowey and Cena (Blackwell) Donahue; B.S., Northwestern U., 1943, M.A., 1967; postgrad. No. Ill. U., DeKalb, 1968-69; m. Virgil William Rink, May 25, 1946; children—Virgil William, Patrick Arthur, Kathleen Claire. Tchr., chmn. dept. speech Calvin Coolidge Jr. High Sch., Moline, Ill., 1943-44; tchr. English and speech Downers Grove (Ill.) High Sch., 1946-47; tchr. English, Washington Jr. High Sch., Naperville, Ill., 1960-65, chmn. dept., 1963-65; tchr. English and speech Naperville Community High Sch., 1965-66, 67—, mem. curriculum planning com. for English and speech, 1967-68. Tchr. English evening sch. Aurora (Ill.) Coll., 1967—, author English course under Project English, Nat. Council Tchrs. English, 1967; mem. Upstate Eight Workshop Planning Com., 1967-68. Staff aide A.R.C., 1946—; den mother Boy Scouts Am., 1959-60; troop chmn. Girl Scouts Am., 1964-66. Mem. N.E.A., Ill. Edn. Assn., Northwestern U. Alumni Assn., Speech Assn. Am., Nat. Council Tchrs. English, Am. Theatre Assn., Ill. Speech and Hearing Assn., Naperville Community High Sch. Tchrs. Assn., Internat. Platform Assn., Am. Assn. U. Women (drama study group chmn.), Chgo. Press Club, Omega Upsilon, Phi Rho, Alpha Xi Delta. Roman Catholic. Clubs: Garden of America (Naperville, Ill.), Benet Acad. Madonna (past publicity chmn.) (Lisle, Ill.). Author play dramatizing founding Am. Assn. U. Women, 1958. Home: 22 S Wright St Naperville IL 60540 Office: Aurora Av Naperville IL 60540

RINK, RITA MARIE PEDERSEN (MRS. RICHARD A. RINK), editor; b. Los Angeles, Apr. 29, 1946; d. John George and Mary Rita (Daly) Pedersen; B.A., San Jose State Coll., 1968; m. Richard A. Rink, 1972. Asst. women's editor, youth editor Fremont (Cal.) Daily Argus, 1968-72; staff Lord Elgin High Sch., Burlington, Ont., 1974—. Recipient Merit award Cal. Newspaper Pubs. Assn., 1970. Mem. Women in Communications, Sigma Delta Chi. Home: 5233 Banting Ct Burlington ON Canada

RINKEVICZ, ROSE MARY, securities co. exec.; b. Bklyn., Aug. 30, 1946; d. John and Anele (Kunzalauskas) Rinkevicz; student Hunter Coll., 1965-66. Credit adjuster United Mchts. and Mfrs., N.Y.C., 1964-65; with Merrill Lynch, Pierce, Fenner & Smith, Garden City, N.Y., 1966—, margin specialist, 1972—. Breeder standardbred race horses, 1967—. Mem. U.S. Trotting Assn., N.Y. and N.J. Standardbred Breeders Assn. Home: 209-10 41st Av Bayside NY 11361 Office: 1001 Franklin Av Garden City NY 11530

RINKOFF, BARBARA JEAN (MRS. HERBERT RINKOFF), author; b. N.Y.C., Jan. 25, 1923; d. John J. and Sophia B. (Frank) Rich; B.A., N.Y. U., 1943; m. Herbert Rinkoff, Dec. 17, 1944; children—Robert, Richard, June. Med. social worker Beekman Downtown Hosp., N.Y.C., 1943-47; author, Mt. Kisco, N.Y., 1964—. Instr. creative writing Mt. Kisco Elementary Sch., 1966, 67. Mem. curriculum council Bedford (N.Y.) Central Sch. Dist. 2, 1960-66. Recipient Book of Year award Child Study Assn., 1968, 69, 70, 72, Top Honor Book, Chgo. Exhbn., 1971, Graphic Arts award Printing Industries Am., 1971. Mem. Alpha Kappa Delta. Author numerous books, including: Elbert, The Mind Reader, 1967; Member of the Gang, 1968; Name: Johnny Pierce, 1969; The Pretzel Hero, 1970; A Guy Can Be Wrong, 1970; Rutherford T. Finds 21 B, 1970; The Watchers, 1972; Let's Go to a Jetport, 1973; Guess What Trees Do, 1974. Home and office: 25 Langland Dr Mount Kisco NY 10549

RINN, FAUNEIL JOYCE, educator; b. Boulder, Colo.; d. Michael McDonald and Fauneil (Hall) Rinn; B.A., U. Cin., 1946; M.S., Columbia, 1947; M.A., U. Chgo., 1954, Ph.D. (Brooks Inst. fellow), 1960. Clk., Nat. Conf. Christians and Jews, Cin., 1949; reporter, copy editor Watertown (N.Y.) Daily Times, 1947-49, 50-52; resident head woman's dormitory, U. Chgo., 1957-58, instr. social sci., 1959-60; editorial asst. Pub. Adminstrn. Clearing House, Chgo., 1953-56; asst. and asso. prof. polit. sci. San Jose State U., 1960-68, prof., 1969—, asso. dean Sch. Social Sci., 1973—. Mem. Am. Soc. Pub. Adminstrn., Am. Polit. Sci. Assn., Nat. Orgn. for Women. Home: 1447 McDaniel Av San Jose CA 95126

RINSCH, MARYANN ELIZABETH (MRS. CHARLES EMIL RINSCH), occupational therapist; b. Los Angeles, Aug. 8, 1939; d. Harry William and Thora Analine (Langlie) Hitchcock; B.A. in Occupational Therapy, U. Minn., 1961; m. Charles Emil Rinsch, June 18, 1964; children—Christopher, Daniel. Staff occupational therapist Hastings (Minn.) State Hosp., 1961-62; psychiat. occupational therapist U. Cal. Neuropsychiat. Inst., Los Angeles, 1962-64; staff therapist Los Angeles County Crippled Children's Services, 1964-66, sr. therapist, 1966-67, head therapist, 1967-68, research therapist U. So. Cal., Los Angeles, 1968-69; occupational therapist on sensory integrative therapy, Los Angeles, 1973—. Cons. Center for the Study of Sensory Integrative Dysfunction, 1971-73. Mem. Am., So. Cal. occupational therapy assns. Address: 19849 Greenbriar Dr Tarzana CA 91356

RINSLEY, JACQUELINE ANN (MRS. DONALD BRENDAN RINSLEY), hosp. adminstr.; b. Chgo., Apr. 5, 1933; d. John Lancelot and Margaret Elizabeth (Zeilinger) Louk; student Washington U., St. Louis, 1951-52; diploma in nursing St. Luke's Hosp. Sch. Nursing, 1955; m. Donald Brendan Rinsley, May 28, 1955. Psychiat. nurse Topeka State Hosp., 1955-56, sect. head nurse, 1955-56; gen. and pediatric nurse St. John's Hosp., Springfield, Mo., 1956-57, Burge Hosp., 1957-58; head pediatric nurse Stormont-Vail Hosp., Topeka, 1958-60; psychiat. nurse Kan. Neurol. Inst., Topeka, 1960-70, adminstr., 1970—. Mem. Am. Nurses Assn., Am. Assn. for Mental Deficiency, Nat. Rehab. Assn., Nat. Audubon Soc., Am. Mus. Nat. History, Smithsonian Assos., Common Cause, Zeta Tau Alpha. Democrat. Lutheran. Home: 3212 Eveningside Dr Topeka KS 66614 Office: Kansas Neurological Institute 3107 W 21st St Topeka KS 66604

RINZLER, MIRA CAROL HUTMAN, physician; b. Bucharest, Rumania, Nov. 17, 1927; d. Carol Chaim and Lucy Harry (Rosenstock) Hutman; M.D., U. Bucharest, 1952; m. Gabriel S. Rinzler, July 19, 1950; children—Julie, Andrew. Came to U.S., 1962, naturalized, 1967. Intern, White Plains (N.Y.) Hosp., 1962-63; resident N.Y.U., 1963-66; pvt. practice medicine, White Plains, N.Y., 1966; med. dir. dept. rehab. medicine St. Agnes Hosp., White Plains; asso. dir. div. phys. medicine and rehab. Grasslands Hosp., Valhalla, N.Y.; asst. clin. prof. N.Y. Med. Coll. Home: 11 Watch Hill Dr Greenwich CT 06830 Office: 41 E Post Rd White Plains NY 10621

RIORDAN, JOAN CHASE, govt. ofcl.; b. Fall River, Mass., Oct. 10, 1946; d. Donald Almy and Norma Harriet (Tripp) Chase; B.A. in Econs., Wellesley Coll., 1968. Mgmt. intern Gen. Services Adminstrn., San Francisco, 1968-70, tng. officer, 1970-71, coordinator of Fed. Information Centers, Washington, 1971—. Mem. Wellesley Alumnae (treas.). Home: 201 Eye St SW Apt 839 Washington DC 20024 Office: 18th and F Sts NW Washington DC 20405

RIPEPI, ANTOINETTE CATHERINE (MRS. ALAN THOMAS CRAMER), surgeon; b. Monongahela, Pa.; d. Angelo and Catherine (Quattrone) Ripepi; B.S., U. Pitts., 1957; M.D., Med. Coll. Pa., 1961; m. Alan Thomas Cramer, Aug. 1, 1968. Intern, U. Pa. Grad. Hosp., Phila., 1961-62; resident gen. surgery Jefferson Med. Coll., Phila., 1962-66; resident thoracic and cardiovascular surgery Baylor Coll. Medicine, Houston, 1966-67, now clin. instr. surgery; asso. surgeon Dr. DeBakey, 1968-69; practice medicine specializing in thoracic and cardiovascular surgery, Houston, 1969—; asso. surgeon Hermann Hosp., Houston. Recipient award of Achievement Am. Med. Woman's Assn., 1961. Hollander award of Leadership Med. Coll. Pa., 1961. Diplomate Am. Bd. Surgery, Bd. Thoracic Surgery. Fellow A.C.S.; mem. Am. Med. Womans Assn. (pres. br. 42, 1973-74), Tex. Med. Assn., Harris County Med. Soc., Houston Heart Assn., Alpha Omega Alpha. Home: 2630 Fairway Dr Sugar Land TX 77478 Office: 6436 Fannin St Houston TX 77025

RIPKA, G. ELIZABETH, mgmt. cons.; b. Phila., Apr. 18, 1924; d. Walter and Grace E. (Stevenson) Ripka; B.S., Temple U., 1946, M. Ed., 1948, Ed. D., 1963; m. Henry A. Homont, Sept. 6, 1949; 1 dau., Elizabeth Ann. Tchr. Ridley Township (Pa.) High Sch., 1946-47, West Chester (Pa.) High Sch., 1947-48; instr. Temple U., Phila., 1948-54; prof. bus. adminstrn. Harcum Coll., Bryn Mawr, Pa. 1954-57; asst. prof. econs. and bus. adminstrn. Beaver Coll., Glenside, Pa., 1957-65; dept. chmn. bus. and distributive edn. Drexel U., Phila., 1965-71; cons. Civil Service Commn. Phila., N.Y. and Atlanta regions, 1971—; cons. to several orgns.; dir., developer programs for unemployed. Sr. Asso. Danforth Found.; mem. World Affairs Council, 1971—. Dir. Valley Forge Rep. Women. Pres. bd. dirs. In Ho Oh Meml. Korea Center; treas. bd. dirs. Philadelphia House. Remington Rand fellow, 1958. Mem. Am. Vocational Assn., Am. Assn. U. Profs., Nat., Pa. bus. edn. assns., Am. Acad. Polit. and Social Sci., Eastern Bus. Tchrs. Assn., Am. Sci. Affilation, Delta Pi Epsilon, Phi Delta Gamma, Phi Gamma Nu. Author: Office Information and Skills Test, 1971; An Analysis of Shorthand Attrition and the Prediction of Success, 1972. Home: 2011 White Horse Rd Berwyn PA 19312

RIPP, JUDITH ELLEN SEELENFREUND (MRS. SEYMOUR LEICHMAN), editor; b. N.Y.C.; Sept. 10, 1940; d. Max and Gertrude (Roth) Seelenfreund; B.A., Cornell, 1961; m. Seymour Leichman, Oct. 25, 1970; 1 son, Samuel. Researcher, Colliers Ency., N.Y.C., 1961-63; asst. movie editor Parents Mag., N.Y.C., 1963-68, movie editor, 1968—. Home: 276 Riverside Dr New York City NY 10025 Office: Parents Mag 52 Vanderbilt Av New York City NY 10019

RIPPEL, FLORENCE LENA, educator; b. Phila., May 13, 1902; d. Henry O. and Amelia (Forderer) Rippel; B.S., U. Pa., 1927, M.A., 1930; postgrad. U. So. Cal., 1952-53, U. Cal. at Los Angeles, 1940-41. Tchr. elementary schs., Phila., 1922-26; tchr.-trainer Emlen Sch. of Practice and Demonstration, Phila., 1926-38; tchr. music Stetson Jr. High Sch., Phila., 1938-50, reading cons. 1950-52; reading cons. Rippel Sch. of Music, Phila., 1938-52, Lynwood (Cal.) Unified Sch. Dist., 1952—. Oboist, Phila. Women's Symphony, 1950-52; condr., organizer Moreno Valley Youth Orch., Riverside, Cal., 1960—. Social service worker St. Agnes Settlement House, Phila., 1949-52. Recipient Valley Forge Freedoms Found. Tchrs.' award, 1964; Harvard U. Secondary Distinguished Tchr. award, 1965; Spl. C. of C. Community Achievement award 1968, Spl. award and citation Moreno Valley Bd. Dirs., 1971. Hon. fellow Internat. Biog. Soc.; mem. N.E.A., Cal., Lynwood tchrs. assn., U. Pa. Alumni Assn., Cal. P.T.A. (life). Lutheran. Clubs: Matinee Musical (Phila.), Philadelphia Music. Home: 140 N Sunset Pl Monrovia CA 91016 Office: Lynwood Unified Sch Dist Lynwood CA 90262

RIPPEL, MABEL AMELIA, educator; b. Phila., Jan. 28, 1914; d. Henry O. and Amelia (Forderer) Rippel; B.S., U. Pa., 1935, M.A. in Psychology, 1937; postgrad. (fellow) Trinity Coll. Music, London, Eng., 1936-38; postgrad. U. So. Cal., 1954-55, U. Cal. at Los Angeles, 1940-41. Co-owner Rippel Sch. of Music, Phila., 1938-49; research asst. in psychology U. Pa., 1935-37; social worker St. Agnes Settlement House, Phila., 1936-48; tchr. Ramsey Mil. Sch., Santa Monica, Cal., 1950-51, Inglewood (Cal.) High Sch., 1951-52, Mountain View Sch. Dist., Bakersfield, Cal., 1952-53, Arcadia (Cal.) Sch. Dist., 1953-54; concert work and study 1954-55; music coordinator Midland Sch. Dist., Sunnymead, Cal., 1955—. Condr. Midland Sch. Dist. Bands and Choirs, 1955—; condr., organizer Moreno Valley Youth Orch., Riverside, Cal., 1960—. Recipient Spl. C. of C. Community Achievement award 1968, Spl. award and citation Moreno Valley Bd. Dirs., 1971. Hon. fellow Internat. Biog. Assn.; mem. Cal. Tchrs. Assn., Cal. P.T.A. (life). Lutheran (organist). Clubs: Psychology, Matinee Music, Music (Phila.). Home: 140 N Sunset Pl Monrovia CA 91016 Office: Midland Sch Dist Sunnymead CA 92388

RIPPLE, ELEANOR FENWICK (MRS. AMMON SYRIL RIPPLE), librarian; b. Leonardtown, Md., Feb. 2, 1938; d. Charles Edward and LaVerne (Miller) Fenwick; B.S., Towson State Coll., 1959; M.S., Fla. State U., 1963, advanced M.S., 1968; m. Ammon Syril Ripple, Jan. 2, 1971; children—Ammon Syril, Franklin Forsythe. Tchr. elementary sch. St. Mary's County Bd. Edn., Leonardtown, 1959-63, helping librarian, 1965-67, library supr., 1968—; librarian Baltimore County, Md., 1964-65. Title II-B Higher Edn. Act fellow, 1967-68. Mem. A.L.A. (life), Kappa Delta Pi, Beta Phi Mu. Home: PO Box 83 Clements MD 20624 Office: PO Box 343 Leonardtown MD 20650

RIPPY, FRANCES MARGUERITE MAYHEW (MRS. N. MERRILL RIPPY), educator; b. Ft. Worth, Sept. 16, 1929; d. Henry Grady and Marguerite Christine (O'Neill) Mayhew; B.A., Tex. Christian U., 1949; M.A., Vanderbilt U., 1951, Ph.D., 1957; postgrad. (Fulbright scholar), U. London, 1952-53; m. Noble Merrill Rippy, Aug. 29, 1955; children—Felix O'Neill, Conrad Mayhew, Marguerite Hailey. Instr., Tex. Christian U., 1953-55; instr. to asst. prof. Lamar State U., 1955-59; asst. prof. English, Ball State U., Muncie, Ind., 1959-64, asso. prof., 1964-68, prof., 1968—, coordinator English doctoral studies, 1966—, editor Ball State U. Forum, 1960—. Vis. asst. prof. Sam Houston State U., 1957; vis. lectr., prof. U. P.R., 1959, 60, 61. Recipient McClintock award, 1966. Danforth grantee, summer 1964, asso., 1965—; Ball State U. research grantee, 1960, 62, 70, 73. Mem. Modern Lang. Assn., Coll. English Assn., Johnson Soc. Midwest (sec. 1961-62), Am. Assn. U. Profs., Ind. Council Tchrs. English, Am. Soc. 18th Century Studies. Contbr. articles to profl. jours., chpt. to anthology. Home: 4417 W Jackson Muncie IN 47304

RIPY, SARA LOUISE, educator; b. Lawrenceburg, Ky., July 22, 1924; d. Robert and Flora Franklin (Witherspoon) R.; B.A., Randolph-Macon Woman's Coll., 1946; M.A., U. Ky., 1949, Ph.D., 1957. Instr. math. U. Ky., 1946-54, 56-57; instr. math. Randolph-Macon Womans Coll., Lynchburg, Va., 1954-56; instr. math. Vassar Coll., 1957-58; asst. prof. math. Agnes Scott Coll., Decatur, Ga., 1958-61, asso. prof., 1961-67, prof. math., 1967-70, prof., chmn. dept. math., 1970—; summer teaching NSF sponsored insts. at Morehead (Ky.) State U., 1960, Tex. Womans U., Denton, 1961-70. Mem. Am. Math. Soc., Math. Assn. Am., Phi Beta Kappa, Sigma Xi, Pi Mu Epsilon. Democrat. Mem. Disciples of Christ Ch. Home: 149 S McDonough St Decatur GA 30030

RISELEY, MARTHA SUZANNAH HEATER (MRS. CHARLES RISELEY), psychologist, educator; b. Middletown, O., Apr. 25, 1916; d. Elsor and Mary (Henderson) Heater; B.Ed., U. Toledo, 1943, M.A., 1958; student Columbia, summers 1943, 57; m. Lester Seiple, Aug. 27, 1944 (div. Feb. 1953); 1 son, L. Rolland III; m. 2d, Charles Riseley, July 30, 1960. Tchr. kindergarten Maumee Valley Country Day Sch., Maumee, O., 1942-44; dir. recreation Toledo Soc. for Crippled Children, 1950-51; tchr. trainable children Lott Day Sch., Toledo, 1951-57; psychologist, asst. dir. Sheltered Workshop Found., Lucas County, O., 1957-62; psychologist Lucas County Child Welfare Bd., Toledo, 1956-62; tchr. educable retarded, head dept. spl. edn. Maumee City Schs., 1962-69; practice clin. psychology, Maumee, O., 1969—; psychol. examiner, Toledo, 1956—; instr. spl. edn. Bowling Green State U., 1962—; instr. Owens Tech. Coll., 1973—; clin. psychologist Rehab. Center, Goodwill Industries of Toledo, 1967—, interim dir., 1967. Dir. camping activities for retarded girls and women, Camp Libbey, Defiance, O., summers 1951-62; group worker for retarded women Toledo YWCA, 1957-62; guest lectr. Ohio State U., 1957. Mem. Ohio Assn. Tchrs. Trainable Youth (pres. 1956-57), N.W. Ohio Rehab. Assn. (pres. 1961-62), Toledo Council for

Exceptional Children (pres. 1965), Nat. Assn. for Retarded Children, Ohio Assn. Tchrs. Slow Learners, Am. Assn. Mental Deficiency, Am. Psychol. Assn. (asso.), Assn. Psychologists in Marital Counseling, Psychologists in Pvt. Practice, N.W. Ohio Psychol. Assn. (sec.-treas. 1974—), Toledo Mus. Art, Compass Clubs, Inc. (pilot 1969-71), Samagama, Toledo Bar Assn. Aux., M.B.L.S., Greater Toledo Assn. for Mental Health (mem. bd.), N.E.A., Am. Assn. U. Women, Nat. Fedn. Bus. and Profl. Women (dist. sec. 1970-71, dist. legislative rep. 1972-74, chpt. pres. 1970-72), Zonta Internat. (pres. local chpt. 1973-74; mem. local bd.), Ohio Psychol. Assn., Bus. and Profl. Women's Club, P.E.O. (chpt. pres. 1950-51), Internat. Platform Assn., Toledo Council World Affairs, U.S. C. of C., Nat. Assn. Female Execs., Psychology and Law Assn. Baptist. Home: 322 River Rd Maumee OH 43537 Office: 338 Erie St Toledo OH 43624

RISEMAN, JACQUELINE SARAH, psychologist, educator; b. Boston, Mar. 14, 1938; d. Meyer and Edith (Levatinsky) Riseman; B.A., Wellesley Coll., 1959; M.A., Yeshiva U., 1964, Ph.D., 1972. Research asst. Rockefeller U., N.Y.C., 1965-67; sr. psychologist N.Y. Med. Coll., 1968-72; chief psychologist St. John's Episcopal Hosp., Bklyn., 1972—. Psychotherapist, N.Y.C., 1973—; adj. asst. prof. psychology Hunter Coll., N.Y.C., 1973—; cons. to N.Y. Assn. for Brain Injured Children, N.Y.C., 1972—, Inst. for Rational Mgmt., White Plains, N.Y., 1972—. Mem. Am. Psychol. Assn., Internat. Orgn. for Study Group Tensions, Aphasia Study Group. Home: 444 E 86th St New York City NY 10028 Office: 133 East 73rd St New York City NY 10021

RISH, DOROTHY MARGARETE, indsl. relations exec.; b. Alta., Can.; d. Charles and Ellen (Costley) Rish; came to U.S., 1917, naturalized, 1925; student Pacific Coll., 1932-33; R.N., St. Vincent's Sch. Nursing, 1937; grad. student U. Hawaii, 1948-50. Office and private duty nurse, 1937-41; with Del Monte Corp., Honolulu, 1941—, plant nurse, personnel asst., 1941-48, asst. to indsl. relations mgr., Honolulu, 1948-69, benefit plans adminstr., 1969-72, mgr. personnel services U.S. prodn., San Francisco, 1972—. Mem. Inter-Indsl. Workmens' Compensation Study Com., 1962-72, chmn., 1964-72; mem. adv. council State Adult Edn. Program, 1956-58; mem. State Labor & Industry Relations Appeal Bd., 1962-63. Mem. mgmt. com. State Commn. on Manpower and Full Employment, 1962-72; mem. mgmt. com. Fernhurst YWCA, 1966-72. Mem. Indsl. Nurses Assn., Am. Soc. Training and Devel. Club: Zonta (local dir.). Home: 1870 Jackson St San Francisco CA 94109

RITCHIE, ELISAVIETTA YURIEVNA ARTAMONOFF (MRS. LYELL HALE RITCHIE), author, educator, translator; b. Kansas City, Mo.; d. George Leonidovich and Jessie (Downing) Artamonoff; degre superieur, Sorbonne, Paris, 1951; student Cornell U., 1951-53; B.A., U. Cal. at Berkeley, 1954; m. Lyell Hale Ritchie, July 11, 1953; children—Lyell Kirk, Elspeth Cameron, Alexander George. Pub. relations asst. Bay Area Council & World Trade Center, San Francisco, 1956; publicity campaign Assemblyman John Busterud, San Francisco, 1956-58; translator French, Russian, various govt. agencies, pvt. business, 1960—; grad. teaching fellow lang. dept. Am. U., 1968-73; poet-in-residence Fairfax County and Washington Schs., 1972, 73; poetry readings at colls., libraries, schs., museums, on radio and TV. Recipient numerous prizes including Conrad Alken prize, Marion Reedy award Poetry Soc. Am., 1974. Author: Readings in French-Speaking World, 1969; Timbot, 1970; Tightening the Circle Over Eel Country, 1974; transl. The Twelve (Aleksandr Blok), 1968; contbr. numerous poems, stories, articles, revs., transls. pub. in various mags. and newspapers, including N.Y. Times, Washington Post, Paris Herald Tribune, Mass. Rev., Denver Post, Denver Quar., Chgo. Tribune, Epoch, New Republic, Christian Sci. Monitor, So. Poetry Rev., others; poems reprinted in The Diamond Anthology, New Generation Poetry, Adam Among the Television Trees, other anthologies. Home: 3207 Macomb St NW Washington DC 20008

RITCHIE, PATRICIA ANN, village ofcl.; b. Wheeling, W.Va., Nov. 23, 1933; d. Samuel and Helen (Vostatek) Greco; m. James Norman Ritchie, July 11, 1953; children—James Samuel, Michael John, Kenneth Lee. Distbn. clk. U.S. Post Office, Addison, Ill., 1964-69; village clk., Addison, 1969-71, village collector, 1971—. Sec., Addison Community Council, 1962-63; treas. Pleasant Homes Homeowners Assn., 1967-69; sec. Fullerton Sch. P.T.A., 1965; sec. Addison P.T.A. Council, 1966, v.p., 1967. Methodist (sec., ch. sch. tchr. 1962-67). Mem. United Meth. Women (treas., v.p. 1962-64, 66-69). Home: 425 Winthrop Av Addison IL 60101 Office: 130 Army Trail Rd Addison IL 60101

RITER, HENRIETTA WIND (MRS. WARREN CHARLES RITER), mus. exec.; b. Bklyn., Mar. 25, 1905; d. Adolph and Mary (Rosenstein) Wind; diploma Pratt Inst., 1927; postgrad. U. Toledo, 1930, 39; m. Warren Charles Riter, Aug. 6, 1928; 1 son, Warren Lee Talmadge. Free lance artist, cons., muralist, Toledo, Buffalo, Rochester; Tchr. art Amsterdam High Sch., 1927-28; tchr. comml. art Vocational Sch., Toledo, 1938-40; tchr. art Warsaw (N.Y.) High Sch., 1944-46; interior designer Henri Riter Assos., Rochester, 1947-60; exec. dir. Rensselaerville (N.Y.) Hist. Soc. Instr. color for interior decoration, adult edn. Rochester Bus. Inst. Mem. Rochester C. of C., Genesee Group Artists, Am. Iris Soc. (chmn. Capital Hudson Area, dir. Empire State). Presbyn. Clubs: Rochester Art; Clematis Garden (Rensselaerville). Author brochures, booklets, newsletter Rensselaerville Hist. Soc. Home: Methodist Hill Rd Rensselaerville NY 12147 Office: Box 8 Rensselaerville Hist Soc Rensselaerville NY 12147

RITHOLZ, SOPHIE, psychoanalyst; b. Zembrov, Russia; d. Juda and Ante (Kozak) Ritholz; brought to U.S., 1905, naturalized, 1910; B.S., Columbia U., 1941, M.A., 1942, postgrad., 1943-44; postgrad. Fordham U., 1942-43; D.Sc., Findlay Coll., 1963. Practice psychoanalysis and psychology, N.Y.C., 1945—. Psychol. cons. King Optical Co., Chgo. Mem. Am., N.Y. State psychol. assns., Acad. Religion and Mental Health, A.A.A.S., Am. Assn. U. Women, Columbia U. Alumni Assn. Author: Children's Behavior, 1959. Home: 52 Gramercy Park N New York City NY 10010

RITTENHOUSE, MIGNON (MRS. HORACE A. WOODMANSEE), writer; b. N.Y.C., Feb. 19, 1904; d. Rev. George and Catherine (Meiser) Rittenhouse; student Wheaton Coll., 1922-24; m. Horace Albro Woodmansee, Jan. 24, 1931; children—George H., Lois Kathleen (Mrs. Kellerman). Reporter, feature writer Bklyn. Eagle, 1924-36; columnist Morning Telegraph, 1926; contbr. articles N.Y. World, 1930, poetry Good Housekeeping, Today's Woman, poetry mags., 1953-57; free lance writer for mags., 1926—; editorial work Fawcett Publ., 1938-48. Author: The Amazing Nellie Bly, 1956, reprint, 1971; (operetta) The Magic Keys of Christopher Columbus, 1971; Seven Women Explorers, 1964, Cadmus edit., 1967. Mem. Author's League Am. Home: 39-25 202d St Bayside NY 11361

RITTER, LUCY ELIZABETH, business exec.; b. Shanghai, China, Sept. 10, 1910 (parents Am. citizens); d. Ovid Herbert and Lucy (Corker) Ritter; A.B., Stanford U., 1930, M.A., 1931. Research sec. Cal. Taxpayer's Assn., 1931-34; security analyst Cal. Western States Life Ins. Co., Sacramento, 1935-43, asst. treas., 1943-54, 2d v.p., asst. treas., mgr. securities dept., 1954-68, v.p. securities, 1968—. Bd. dirs. Sacramento Community Chest, 1953-56, Sacramento Children's Home, 1949-55; dir. nat. exec. bd. Stanford Alumni Assn., 1955-58; bd. govs. Mercy Hosps. Found., 1971—; trustee Sacramento Symphony Trust Fund Found. Mem. Cal. Gov.'s Retirement Bd., 1961-69; alternate del. Democratic Nat. Conv., 1956, 64; chmn. woman's Citizens for Kennedy, 3d congl. dist., 1960. Mem. Inst. Chartered Financial Analysts, Security Analysts of San Francisco, League Women Voters, Sacramento Opera Guild, Crocker Art Gallery Assn. Clubs: Del Paso Country, Sacramento; Metropolitan, San Francisco. Author: Lucy's Twentieth Century, 1974. Contbr. articles to profl. jours. Home: Capitol Towers 7th and O Sts Sacramento CA 95814 Office: 2020 L St Sacramento CA 95814

RITTER, PATRICIA SLAGLE (MRS. BILLIE EUGENE RITTER), assn. exec.; b. Greeneville, Tenn., Dec. 23, 1946; d. Albert William and Mildred Hazel (Bowlin) Slagle; B.S. magna cum laude, E. Tenn. State U., 1968; M.S., So. Ill. U., 1970; m. Billie Eugene Ritter, May 26, 1973. Phys. edn. tchr. Mathews (Va.) Sch. Dist., 1968-69; grad. asst. So. Ill. U., Carbondale, 1969; phys. edn. dir. Las Vegas YMCA, 1970—. State dir. Nev. Spl. Olympics, 1973-74. Mem. Nat. YMCA Phys. Edn. Soc., A.A.H.P.E.R., Assn. Profl. Dirs. YMCA, Alpha Lambda Delta. Home: 3601 E Wyoming St Las Vegas NV 89104 Office: Las Vegas YMCA Casino Center Blvd and Bonzana Rd Las Vegas NV 89101

RITTMAYER, JANE FOEHL (MRS. CALVIN CARL RITTMAYER), psychologist; b. Woodbury, N.J., Apr. 30, 1936; d. Willard Lindsey and Josephine (Moore) Foehl; B.A., Temple U., 1957, M.A., 1960; Ed.D., Rutgers U., 1968; m. Calvin Carl Rittmayer, June 19, 1954; children—Leslie, Mark, Christopher. Psychometrician dept. tests and measurements Temple U., 1956-57, Edward N. Hay & Assos., Phila., 1957-59; psychologist State Colony at New Lisbon, N.J., 1960; sch. psychologist, 1962—; pvt. practice psychology, 1967—; mem. cons. staff Mercer and Hamilton Hosp., Trenton, N.J., 1971—. Cons., Princeton Day Sch. for Exceptional Children, 1973-74. Mem. Am., N.J., Burlington, Camden County psychol. assns., N.J. Assn. Sch. Psychologists, Acad. Orthomolecular Psychiatry (asso.), Acad. Preventive Medicine (asso.). Author: The Origins of Emotional Disturbance, 1970. Home: 108 Avondale Av Haddonfield NJ 08033 Office: 110 Avondale Av Haddonfield NJ 08033

RITTMEISTER, RUTH, travel agy. exec.; b. Norway, Mar. 1, 1924; student U. Oslo (Norway), 1945-48; m. Henry Rittmeister, Sept. 1954 (div. 1963). Came to U.S., 1951, naturalized, 1958. Asso. Bob Burbank Travel Service, Los Angeles, 1951-54; with Internat. Travel Service, Honolulu, 1955—, v.p., 1972—. Coordinator internat. shows Kahala Hilton, Honolulu, 1967-74; free-lance writer articles for newspapers and mags., 1960-74. Vol. Am. Cancer Soc., Honolulu, 1972—; asso. mem. Friends of East-West Center, Straub Hosp. Women's Aux., 1972—; mem. Hawaii Council Nat. Council Crime and Delinquency, Honolulu, 1973—. Bd. dirs. English Speaking Union, Honolulu, 1973—. Mem. Am. Soc. Travel Agts. (chmn. press and publicity 1969—), Sales and Marketing Execs., Pacific Area Travel Assn. Club: Press (Honolulu). Home: Halekulani Hotel Honolulu HI 96815 Office: 2379 Kuhio Av Honolulu HI 96815

RITVO, LYNN LIEBERMAN (MRS. ROGER ALAN RITVO), univ. adminstr.; b. Canton, O., Apr. 18, 1946; d. George Bernard and Sylvia (Klein) Lieberman; B.S., Western Reserve U., 1967; M.Ed., Am. U., 1969; m. Roger Alan Ritvo, June 16, 1968; children—Roberta Andrea, Eric Steven. Tchr. Fairfax County (Va.) Pub. Schs., 1968-69, Oceanside (N.Y.) Pub. Schs., 1969-70; coordinator dormitories, resident dir., freshman faculty adviser, adviser to floor counselors, asst. to dean Case Western Res. U., Cleve., 1970—. Mem. Nat. Assn. Women Deans, Adminstrs. and Counselors (mem. coll. sect. com. 1974—), Flora Stone Mather Alumni Assn. Case Western Res. U. (dir., fund raising chmn. 1972-73), Psi Chi. Editor Floor Counselor's Manual, 1973-74. Home: 2874 Coleridge Rd Cleveland OH 44118 Office: Residence Office-Norton House 11443 Juniper Rd Cleveland OH 44106

RITZERT, MARION EUGENE (MRS. JOHN RITZERT), civic worker; b. Lincolnton, N.C., Apr. 3, 1903; d. Joseph Simpson and Annie May (Lipsey) Wise; student Columbia, summer, 1919, St. Mary's Jr. Coll., 1922, Asheville Normal, summer 1923, U. N.C., summer 1929; m. John Ritzert, Dec. 22, 1938 (dec. Mar. 1961). Tchr. mentally retarded, Lincolnton, N.C., 1923-25; tchr. grammar, Lincolnton, 1925-28; tchr. mentally retarded Dora Jones Sch., Chester, S.C., 1928-35, College St. Sch., 1935-38; Southeastern area rep. Nat. A.R.C., Atlanta, 1944-48, blood program rep., 1948-53, asst. dir. office of vols., 1953-59, rep., 1959-64, dir. vols., Ft. Bragg, N.C., 1965. Chmn. Lincoln County Hist. Commn., 1967—. Parliamentarian Republican Women's Club, Lincoln County, 1970-72. Mem. U.D.C. (v.p. 1971-74). Episcopalian. Club: Anna Jackson Book (Lincolnton). Home: 706 Dogwood Dr Lincolnton NC 28092

RIVERA, EDITH MARY IRVINE (MRS. PEDRO AMADO RIVERA), civic worker; b. N.Y.C., Oct. 13, 1880; d. James Elliot and Mary Coutts (Billups) Irvine; student Internat. Corr. Schs.; m. Pedro Amado Rivera, July 4, 1907; children—Mary C. (Mrs. Robert C. Paul), Pascual A. (dec.), Pedro N., James A. (dec.), Edith C. (Mrs. William S. McCrea). Copy editor P.R. Health Rev., 1929-31. World organizer W.C.T.U., 1932-65, pres. P.R. chpt. 1922-65; founder Woman's Civic Club, P.R., 1927, YWCA, P.R., 1940. Recipient numerous awards pub. service. Author: The Dry Blockade, 1950; Adventures for a Better World, 1968. Address: Cond Norte Plaza Apt 204 219 Rosario St Santurce PR

RIVERS, ALINE ALICE, univ. adminstr.; b. Windsor, Ont., Can., Apr. 20, 1932; d. Milton Augustus and Ann Belle (Washington) Adams; came to U.S., 1950, naturalized, 1956; B.A., Fisk U., 1954; M.A., Wayne State U., 1963; postgrad. U. Detroit, 1966, U. Mich., 1967-69; 1 son (by previous marriage), Alan Leslie. Tchr., Detroit pub. schs., 1956-65; reading diagnostician, 1965-66; counselor higher edn. opportunities com. Wayne State U., Detroit, 1966-68, directing counselor, 1968-70; dir. admissions Fisk U., Nashville, 1970—. Cons. Moten Consortium on Admissions and Financial Aid, 1971, 72, youth ednl. services tutorial project N.C. Fund, 1967, Youth Understanding Program, 1970. Pres., Tri City Pied Pipers, Detroit, 1964; chmn. Career Opportunities Workshop, Detroit, 1965; supr. Dept. Sch. Vols., Detroit pub. schs., 1965; bd. mgrs. Bordeau North YMCA. Recipient Focus award for Outstanding Community Service, WJR radio, Detroit, 1965; Mem. Nat. Assn. Coll. Admissions Counselors (chmn. employment assistance service com. 1970—), Am. Assn. Coll. Registrars and Admissions Officers (grantee 1972), Nat. Assn. Fgn. Students Affairs (grantee 1972), Nat. Assn. Coll. Deans, Registrars and Admissions Officers (chmn. membership com. 1973), Am. Assn. U. Women, Am. Personel and Guidance Assn., Phi Beta Kappa, Delta Sigma Theta. Club: Nashville Tots Thru Teens Mothers. Home: 2022 Jordan Dr Nashville TN 37218 Office: Admissions Office Fisk University Nashville TN 37203

RIVES, KATHLEEN LONG, physician; b. Mansfield, La., Dec. 12, 1926; d. Green and Kathleen (Long) Rives; B.A., Randolph-Macon Woman's Coll., 1947; M.A., U. Wis., 1949; M.D., Tulane U., 1959. Intern, N.Y. Hosp.-Cornell U. Med. Coll., 1959-60, resident internal medicine, 1960-62, fellow. endocrinology, 1962-64; physician to outpatients N.Y. Hosp.-Cornell U. Med. Coll., 1964-65, instr. medicine, 1964-65; asst. prof. medicine Tulane U. Sch. Medicine, 1965-70, asso. prof., 1970—; asst. vis. physician Charity Hosp. La., New Orleans, 1965-67, vis. physician, 1967—; cons. endocrinology USPHS Hosp., New Orleans, 1967—. Mem. Orleans Parish Med. Soc., Am. Fedn. Clin. Research, Musser-Burch Soc., Am. Thyroid Assn., Phi Beta Kappa, Alpha Omega Alpha, Theta Sigma Phi. Contbr. articles to profl. jours. Home: 4117 Danneel St New Orleans LA 70115 Office: 1430 Tulane Av New Orleans LA 70112

RIVES, TOBY MCDOWELL, univ. dean; b. Yantis, Tex., Sept. 3, 1928; d. Samuel Matthew and May (Bowie) McDowell; B.S., E. Tex. State U., 1968, M.Ed., 1969; m. Sam Carter Rives, June 2, 1946 (div. Dec. 1968); children—Kaye (Mrs. Mike Jacoby), John Ashton, Sam Carter, Mary Elizabeth. Exec. sec. Hopkins County C. of C., Sulphur Springs, Tex., 1966-67; dean of women S.W. Mo. State U., Springfield, 1969-71, Tex. A. and M. U., College Station, 1971—. Bd. dirs. Bluebonnet council Girl Scouts Am., 1973—, Brazos Valley Mental Health Center, 1973—. Mem. Am., Tex. personnel and guidance assns., Nat., Tex. (program chmn. 1973-74) assns. women deans, adminstrs. and counselors, Southwest, Tex. assns. student personnel adminstrs., Am., So. (mem. liaison com. 1973—) coll. personnel assns., Cap and Gown, Cwens, Alpha Lambda Delta, Phi Mu, Phi Delta Gamma. Episcopalian. Club: Brazos County A & M (dir. 1973—). Home: 3611 Holly St Bryan TX 77801 Office: Texas A and M Univ YMCA Bldg College Station TX 77843

RIVEST, MICHELINE, heating co. exec.; b. Montreal, Que., Can., June 6, 1941; d. Jacques Y. and Lorette (Chamberland) Rivest; grad. Paré Bus. Coll., Montreal, 1959. Sec. Standard Life Assurance Co., Montreal, 1959-62; with Canadian White Star Products Ltd., Montreal, 1962—, sec. to pres., 1964—, office supr., 1968—, sec., treas., 1972—. Mem. Montreal Bd. Trade, Nat. Secs. Assn. (chmn. secretaries week com. 1967, chmn. future secs. assn. 1968, librarian 1971-74, chmn. arrangements com. 1975 internat. conv.), Com. Canada, Que. Assn. Mentally Retarded. Office: 1240 Laurentien Blvd Montreal PQ H4R 1J8 Canada

RIVIELLA, CARMELLA GLORIA, banker; b. Niles, O., Nov. 4, 1908; d. Rocco and Maria Vincenza (Schiffito) Riviella; grad. high sch. With Union Savings and Trust Co., Warren, O., 1926-33; with Niles Bank Co., 1933—, mgr. foreign and safe deposit, 1947-69, asst. sec., 1969—, treas., 1972—. Vol. sec. Niles br. A.R.C., 1942-52; mem. Friends McKinley Meml. Library. Mem. Nat. Secs. Assn. (charter mem. Warren br. 1947), Niles Bus. and Profl. Women's Club. Roman Catholic (charter mem. Women's Guild 1947). Home: 420 N Cleveland Av Niles OH 44446 Office: 2 S Main St Niles OH 44446

RIVOIR, SARAH ELIZABETH STINER (MRS. WILLIAM H. RIVOIR, JR.), librarian; b. Harrisburg, Pa., Nov. 18, 1918; d. James and Daisy (Goodyear) Stiner; B.S., Temple U., 1940; M.S. in Library Sci., Drexel U., 1963; postgrad. Villanova U., 1971-72; m. William H. Rivoir, Jr., July 6, 1946; 1 son, William Henry III. Librarian, Upper Merion Jr. High Sch., King of Prussia, Pa., 1963; asso. prof., asst. librarian West Chester (Pa.) State Coll., 1964—. Mem. Am. Assn. U. Women (v.p. Valley Forge br. 1960-62), Am. Assn. U. Profs., Am., Pa. library assns., Pa. State Edn. Assn. (program chmn. local br. 1965-67), Tri-State Library Coll. Coop. (sec. 1973-74), D.A.R., Chester County Assn. Lawyers Wives (treas. 1971—). Home: 561 Bair Rd Berwyn PA 19312 Office: West Chester State Coll West Chester PA 19380

RIVOIR, YVONNE LETITIA, psychiat. social worker; b. South Bend, Ind., Feb. 3, 1929; d. Henry and Effie (Mossman) Rivoir; A.B., Boston U., 1951, M.S. in Social Service, 1957; certificate, Smith Coll. Sch. Social Work, 1964. With Mass. Dept. Pub. Welfare, 1951-56; with Bradley Hosp., Riverside, R.I., 1957-63, social work supr., 1960-63; with Family Service of Cin. (O.), 1964—, supr. social work students and staff, 1966-71, dir. No. Ky. dist. office, 1971—. Social work field instr. for Social Work Grad. Schs. at U. Conn., 1960-62, Simmons Coll., 1962-63, Smith Coll., 1966—. Mem. Nat. Assn. Social Workers, Acad. Certified Social Workers, Am. Orthopsychiatric Assn. Home: 6691 Iris Av Cincinnati OH 45213 Office: 615 Greenup St Covington KY 41011

RIZZO, MARY ANN FRANCES, internat. trade exec., former educator; b. Bryn Mawr, Pa., Jan. 11, 1942; d. Joseph Franklyn and Armella Louise (Grubenhoff) Rizzo; B.A. magna cum laude, Marymount-Manhattan Coll. (N.Y. State scholar), 1963; M.A. (fellow) Yale, 1965, Ph.D. (Lounsbury-Cross fellow), 1969. Instr. Romance langs., lit. Yale, New Haven, 1966-70; asst. prof. Finch Coll., N.Y.C., 1971-73; v.p. Joseph F. Rizzo Co., N.Y.C., 1969—. Mem. Am. Assn. Tchrs. of Italian, Women's Assn. of the Symphony, Modern Lang. Assn., Am.-Italy Soc. Republican. Roman Catholic (community council 1972-74). Clubs: Yale (N.Y.C.); Cercle Francais de Palm Beach (Fla.). Translator: From Time to Eternity, 1967. 923 Fifth Av New York City NY 10021 also Villa Serein 2170 Ibis Isle Rd Palm Beach FL 33480 Office: 350 Fifth Av New York City NY 10001

RIZZUTI, THERESA, polit. worker; b. Rome, N.Y., Nov. 9, 1918; d. Thomas and Angeline (Capponi) Rossi; student bus. and secretarial courses; m. Theresa Rossi, Dec. 26, 1942; children—Terry Philip, Patrice Gail (Mrs. Larry Barker), Thea Lynn, Chris Andrew. Employed various secretarial positions. Committeewoman, Republican Party 4th Congl. Dist. Okla., 1967-72; v.p. Central Okla. Rep. Women's Club, 1967-68, pres., 1968-69; v.p. 4th Dist. Rep. Women's Club, 1971-72; alternate del. Rep. Nat. Conv., 1968; parliamentarian Twin Lakes Rep. Women's Club, Carmichael, Cal., 1974—. Roman Catholic. Club: Newcomers. Home: 6915 Los Olivos Way Carmichael CA 95608

ROACH, HILDRED ELIZABETH, musician, educator; b. Charlotte, N.C., Mar. 14, 1937; d. Howard and Pearl (Caldwell) Roach; B.A., Fisk U., 1957; postgrad. Juilliard Sch. Music, 1958-59; M.M. (Lockwood scholard), Yale, 1962; postgrad. Oakland U., summer 1966, U. Ghana, summer 1969. Instr. Tuskegee (Ala.) Inst., 1957-60, Fayetteville (N.C.) State Coll., 1962-66; asst. prof. Howard U., 1966-67; asst. prof. Va. State Coll., Petersburg, 1967-68; asso. prof. Fed. City Coll., Washington, 1968—; tchr. pvt. piano lessons; lectr. Black music. John Hay Whitney scholar; Ford Found. scholar; Theodore Presser scholar; recipient Outstanding Young Woman award, 1973, Fisk Alumni award. Mem. Music Educators Assn., Afro-Am. Opportunities Music Assn., Yale, Fisk alumni assns., Phi Beta Kappa, Alpha Kappa Alpha. Author: Black American Music, 1973. Contbr. articles to profl. jours. Home: 10700 Cavalier Dr Silver Spring MD 20901 Office: Dept Music Fed City Coll 916 G St NW Washington DC 20001

ROACH, JEANNETTA COLE (MRS. GEORGE WASHINGTON ROACH), coll. librarian; b. Tougaloo, Miss., Jan. 10, 1939; d. Washington C. and Roxanna (Snowden) Cole; B.A., Tougaloo Coll., 1961; M.S. in Library Sci., Syracuse U., 1962; m. George Washington Roach, Jr., June 21, 1964; children—Donnell Washington, Georgetta Yvonne. Young adult librarian Enoch Pratt Free Library, Balt., 1962-63; cataloger U.S. Book Exchange Agy., Washington, 1963-64; cataloger Tougaloo Coll., 1967-68, acting head librarian, 1968-70, head librarian, 1970—. Recipient Library Adminstrs. Devel. award U.

Md., 1972; Jessie Smith Noyes Found. grantee, 1968. Mem. Am., Miss., Southeastern library assns., Internat. Platform Assn., Coop. Coll. Library Center, Alpha Kappa Alpha. Home: 615 Hickory Ridge Dr Jackson MS 39206 Office: L Zenobia Coleman Library Tougaloo MS 39174

ROACH, MARY ELLEN, educator; b. Easton, Kan., Sept. 15, 1921; d. John Morgan and Mary Jane (Mitchell) Roach; A.B., U. Kan., 1942; M.S., Ia. State U., 1948, Ph.D., Mich. State U., 1960. High sch. tchr., Kan., 1942-46; instr. U. Conn., 1948-53; asst. prof. U. R.I., 1953-54; instr. Mich. State U., 1957-59; asst. prof. U. Wis., 1960-63, asso. prof., 1963-68, prof., 1968—. Gen. Foods fellow, 1959-60. Mem. Am. (chmn. textiles and clothing sect. 1967-69), Wis. home econs. assns., Am., Midwest sociol. assns., Costume Soc., Am. Assn. U. Profs., Company Mil. Historians, Phi Beta Kappa, Omicron Pi Nu, Alpha Kappa Delta. Author: (with Joanne B. Eicher) The Visible Self: Perspectives on Dress, 1973. Editor: (with Joanne B. Eicher) Dress, Adornment, and the Social Order, 1965. Home: 406 N Segoe Rd Madison WI 53705 Office: 1270 Linden Dr Madison WI 53706

ROACH, MARY JEAN, univ. adminstr.; b. Loudonville, O., Sept. 14, 1938; d. Lester and Ruth Marian (Powell) Roach; B.S., Kent State U., 1960, M.Ed., 1965. Tchr. math., dean girls Loudonville High Sch., 1960-63; grad. counselor, resident counselor Kent (O.) State U., 1963-65; resident counselor Ohio Wesleyan U., Delaware, 1965-66, asst. dean women, 1966-69, asso. dean student devel., 1970-72, registrar, 1972—. Mem. Delaware Community Chorus, 1971-72. Mem. Am. Assn. Higher Edn., Am., Ohio assns. coll. registrars and admissions officers, Ohio Assn. Women Deans, Adminstrs. and Counselors (co-chmn. program com., chmn. membership, local arrangements coms.). Home: 175 Kensington Dr Delaware OH 43015

ROACH, NORA MAY STARNER (MRS. JAMES FRANCIS ROACH), hotel owner; b. Trinway, O., Aug. 11, 1917; d. John Edward and Carrie May (Messenger) Starner; student Royal Inn Hotel-Motel Sch., San Diego, 1970; 1 son (by previous marriage)—William M. Burch, Jr. (dec.); m. James Francis Roach, Dec. 4, 1940; 1 dau., Jayne (Mrs. Dennis Micheal Johnson). Co-owner, mgr. Zanesville Travelodge, 1963-67, New Royal Inns, Buffalo, Amarillo, Tex., 1970, Mesa, Phoenix, Flagstaff, Ariz., 1970-71, Indio, San Luis Obispo, Vallejo South, Cal., Clearwater, Jacksonville, Fla., 1971, Atlanta, 1972-74, Royal Inn-Airport Hotel, Hapeville, Ga., 1972—. Vice-pres. Bethesda Hosp. Guild, 1961-62; troup cons. Heart of Ohio council Girl Scouts U.S.A., 1953-55. Presbyn. Address: 301 Central Av at 175 Hapeville GA 30354

ROACH, SUSAN ELDER (MRS. ERIC T. ROACH), state ofcl.; b. Grand Rapids, Mich., Aug. 13, 1947; d. Stanley Trowbridge and Edith Mary (Bower) Elder; B.A., Mich. State U., 1969; m. Eric T. Roach, Mar. 20, 1969. Reporter-intern State Jour., Lansing, Mich., 1968-69; rep. U.S. Fidelity & Guaranty, Lansing, 1969-70; reporter, photographer, area editor Ingham County News, Mason, Mich., 1970-74; adminstrv. asst. Mich. Office Services to Aging, 1974—. Mem. Women in Communications (chpt. pres. 1973-74), Women's Polit. Caucus (dist. corr. sec. 1973), Mortar Bd., Panhellenic (pres. Greater Lansing 1973-74), Alpha Omicron Pi, Alpha Lambda Delta, Sigma Delta Chi. Home: 534 Bailey St East Lansing MI 48823 Office: 1026 E Michigan Av Lansing MI 48912

ROACHE, ESTHER WILSON (MRS. FRED W. ROACHE), civic worker; b. Osgood, Ind.; d. Clarence B. and Alice (Garrigues) Wilson; student Franklin Coll., 1915-16, Ind. U., 1919; m. Fred W. Roache, June 12, 1942 (dec. 1960). Asst. cashier Aurora (Ind.) State Bank, 1936-50, cashier, 1950-56; v.p. 1st Nat. Bank, Aurora, Ind., 1956-65, dir., 1956—. Treas., Dearborn County Social Council, 1962; mem. Gov. Commn. of the Arts, 1964-66. Exec. sec. Hillforest Hist. Found., 1956—; sec.-treas. Southeastern Ind. Recreational Council, 1963—; dir. Southeastern Ind. Recreational Council, 1964; dir. Tri State Air Com., 1970. Mem. Nat. Assn. Bank Women, D.A.R. (regent Col. Archibald Lochry chpt. 1969-71), Tri Kappa, Delta Delta Delta, Aurora Research Club (pres.). Home: 415 Manchester St Aurora IN 47001

ROBB, FRANCES STURMER (MRS. MELVIN L. ROBB), educator; b. Beatrice, Neb.; d. Hermann and Maria (MacKles) Sturmer; B.A., U. Omaha, 1949; M.A., U. Neb., 1955; m. Melvin L. Robb, Jan. 30, 1926 (dec. Oct. 1955); children—Owen Alexander, James Scott. Mem. Staff Fairchild Pubs., Omaha, 1950-54; tchr. U. Omaha, part-time, 1956-60, Western Ill. U., 1961-62, Macomb, Ill., 1962-67; now asst. prof. U. Wis. at Superior. Mem. Internat. Platform Assn., Am. Study Forum. Translator Theodor Storm's Poetry; contbr. articles to trade jours., poetry to anthologies. Home: 327 N 37th St Omaha NE 68131

ROBB, KAREN BROOKE, ednl. adminstr.; b. Kansas City, Kan., Oct. 12, 1939; d. James T. and Fenton (Smith) Robb; B.S., U. Kan., 1961; M.A., U. Colo., 1965. Classroom tchr., Littleton, Colo., 1961-64; grad. asst. U. Colo., Boulder, 1965; counselor, Robbinsdale, Minn., 1965-67; counselor U. Chgo. Lab. Schs., 1967-69, dir. guidance, 1969—. Instr. Grad. Sch. Edn. U. Chgo., 1970—. Mem. Am. Personnel and Guidance Assn., Am. Sch. Counselors Assn., Alpha Phi. Office: 1362 E 59th Chicago IL 60637

ROBBINS, EVELYN BERNICE WARD (MRS. ELBERT BRICE ROBBINS), automotive mfg. exec.; b. Commerce, Tex., May 29, 1923; d. Kelsey L. and Verdie (Standifer) Ward; student East Tex. State U., 1941-42, 49; m. Elbert Brice Robbins, Jan. 14, 1961 (dec. Apr. 1961). Office employee Lake Dick Farms, Inc. (Ark.), 1942; clk.-typist, storekeeper Pine Bluff (Ark.) Arsenal, 1942-45; partner Ward Body Co., Greenville, Tex., 1946-61, owner, 1961—; dist. dir. Pennyrich Internat., Dallas, 1968-69, regional dir., 1969; regional dir. Pennyrich Corp., 1970—. Civic chmn. Nat. Fedn. Ind. Business. Baptist. Home: 3302 Bonnielea St PO Box 443 Greenville TX 75401 Office: 4913 Hwy 66 W Greenville TX 75401

ROBBINS, LILLIAN CUKIER (MRS. EDWIN ROBBINS), psychologist, educator; b. Nancy, France, Sept. 6, 1933; d. Bernard and Cecile (Bleitrach) Cukier; B.A., City Coll. N.Y., 1954; M.A., U. Ill., 1956; Ph.D., N.Y.U., 1961; m. Edwin Robbins, Aug. 5, 1956; children—Hallie Jo, Russell Dana. Research asst. Community Service Div., City Coll. N.Y., 1952-54, Bur. Ednl. Research, Urbana, Ill., 1955-56, Research Center Human Relations, N.Y.U., 1956-58; Margaret Maltby fellow, Am. Assn. U. Women, N.Y.U., 1958-59; postdoctoral research fellow Nat. Inst. Mental Health, N.Y.U., 1960-62; research asst., research psychologist N.Y.U. Med. Center, 1962-67; asst. prof. psychology Hunter Coll., N.Y.C., 1967-70; asst. prof. edn. Coll. City N.Y., 1970-71; asso. prof. psychology Rutgers U., Newark, 1971—. Mem. Am., Eastern, N.Y. State psychol. assns., Soc. Research Child Devel., A.A.A.S., Assn. Psychol. Study Social Issues, Phi Beta Kappa. Contbr. articles in field to profl. jours. Home: 49 E 96th St New York City NY 10028

ROBBINS, LOUISE MARIE, anthropologist; b. Chgo., Oct. 24, 1928; d. Harry S. and Mary Gladys (Brand) Robbins; B.A., Ind. U., 1960, M.A., 1963, Ph.D., 1968. Instr. anthropology U. Neb. Sch. Dentistry and Arts and Scis., 1963-64; mem. faculty U. Ky., Lexington, 1964-67, asst. prof. anthropology, 1968-71; asst. prof., coordinator anthropology program Miss. State U., State College, 1971-73, asso. prof., 1973—, head anthropology dept., 1974—. Served with WAVES, 1950-56. Mem. Am. Assn. Phys. Anthropologists, Am. Anthrop. Assn., Am. Ethnol. Assn., Soc. Am. Archaeology, A.A.A.S., Am. Assn. U. Women, Nat. Geog. Soc., Human Biology Council, Bus. and Profl. Women, Sigma Xi. Home: 710 Cottonwood Dr Starkville MS 39759 Office: Dept Anthropology Miss State U State MS 39762

ROBBINS, MARY LOUISE, educator; b. St. Paul, Sept. 26, 1912; d. Orison Benjamin and Mary (Fiske) Robbins; B.A., Am. U., 1934; M.A., George Washington U., 1940; Ph.D., 1944; spl. tng. Harvard Med. Sch., 1949. Faculty George Washington U., 1944—, successively instr., asst. prof. bacteriology, 1944-52, asso. prof., 1952-59, prof. bacteriology, 1959-60, prof. microbiology 1960—, acting chmn. dept. microbiology, 1961-62; vis. scientist Naval Med. Research Unit No. 3. Cairo, Egypt, 1955, NIH, Tokyo, 1968; cons. bacteriology VA, Martinsburg, W.Va., 1955-64; vis. prof. Baghdad Med. Coll., Iraq, 1963, Kyushu U., Fukuoka, Japan, 1969. Mem. evaluation team Commn. Higher Edn. Middle States Assn. Colls. and Secondary Schs., 1973—; asso. mem. Com. on Internat. Exchange Persons. Chmn. bd. govs. Am. Univ. Alumni Assn., 1973-74. Recipient Alumni Recognition award, Am. U., 1966. USPHS spl. research fellowship, 1968-69. Diplomate Am. Bd. Microbiology, Fellow A.A.A.S., Am. Acad. Microbiology, Washington Acad. Scis. (pres. 1971-72), mem. Am. Assn. U. Profs., Am. Soc. Microbiology (pres. Washington br. 1960, chmn. com. on status of women microbiologists 1970—), Am. Assn. Immunologists, Grad. Women in Sci. (nat. pres. 1958, historian 1970—, meritorious service award 1972), Sigma Xi. Home: 825 New Hampshire Av NW Washington DC 20037 Office: 2300 I St NW Washington DC 20037

ROBBINS, MOLLIE JOAN, psychologist; b. San Diego, Nov. 9, 1932; d. Percy Whitehouse and Cordia Cecelia (Oliver) Robbins; R.N., San Diego County Gen. Hosp. Sch. Nursing, 1953; B.A., San Jose State Coll., 1965; M.A., Ohio State U., 1967, Ph.D. in Physiol. Psychology, 1969. Psychiat. nurse VA Psychiat. Hosp., Los Angeles, 1953-58, U.S. Naval hosps., U.S. and abroad, 1958-62, VA Psychiat. Hosp., Palo Alto, Cal., 1962-63, Agnew State Hosp., 1963-64; sch. psychologist Palm Beach County Bd. Edn., Palm Beach, Fla., 1969-70; cons. in exptl. psychology Montgomery County Pub. Schs., Md., 1970—; cons. in animal psychology, Wheaton, Md., 1972—. Served with Nurse Corps, USNR, 1958-62. Mem. Am., Midwestern, Md. psychol. assns., Md. Sch. Psychology Assn., Psi Chi, Alpha Kappa Delta, Phi Kappa Phi. Contbr. articles on exptl. and animal psychology to profl. jours. Home: 1508 Vivian Court Silver Spring MD 20902 Office: 11151 Georgia Av Suite 103 Wheaton MD 20902

ROBBINS, NAOMI BOGRAD (MRS. EDWARD LLOYD ROBBINS), statistician; b. Paterson, N.J., May 8, 1937; d. Samuel and Pauline (Klemes) Bograd; A.B., Bryn Mawr Coll., 1958; M.A., Cornell U., 1962; Ph.D., Columbia, 1971; m. Edward Lloyd Robbins, Mar. 3, 1962; children—Joyce Trina, Richard Alan. Mem. tech. staff Bell Telephone Labs., Whippany, N.J., 1960—. Mem. Inst. Math. Statistics, Am. Statis. Assn., Sigma Xi. Home: 11 Christine Ct Wayne NJ 07470 Office: Bell Telephone Labs Whippany NJ 07981

ROBBINS, PAULA ANN IVASKA, career counselor; b. Teaneck, N.J., Dec. 13, 1935; d. Paavo Waldemar Topias and Anna Maria Margareta (Snellman) Ivaska; m. Michael D. Robbins, 1956 (div. 1968); children—Jeffery Paul, Matthew Llewellyn. Med. research sec. Columbia U., N.Y.C., 1959-61, U. Rochester (N.Y.), 1961-62; dir. student employment Radcliffe Coll., Cambridge, Mass., 1962-64; dir. career counseling Trinity Coll., Hartford, Conn., 1970—. Chmn. Conn. Conf. on Econ. Conversion, 1971, Greater Hartford Consortium Career Counseling Center, 1973. Chmn. Concord (Mass.) Democratic Town Com., 1970; del. Mass. Dem. Conv., 1970. Mem. Assn. Advisers to Health Professions (sec. N.E. region 1972-74), N.E. Pre-Law Advisers (mem. exec. com. 1973-74), League Women Voters, Am. Civil Liberties Union. Club: Appalachian Mountain. Home: 158 Robin Rd West Hartford CT 06119 Office: Career Counseling Office Trinity Coll 300 Summit St Hartford CT 06106

ROBBINS, ROSEMARY ANN, psychologist; b. N.Y.C., July 15, 1945; d. Robert and Phyllis Mary (Norton) Robbins; A.B. cum laude, Wagner Coll., 1967; M.A. in Psychology, Temple U., 1970, Ph.D., 1973; m. Paul Boehringer, Aug. 25, 1968 (div. June 1973). Research asst. Wagner Coll., 1966-67; research asst. Narcotics Register Project N.Y. Dept. Health, N.Y.C., 1967; research asst. Temple unit Phila. State Hosp., 1970, clin. psychology intern, 1970-71; clin. psychology intern phys. medicine and rehab. Temple U. Hosp., 1971; clin. psychology intern Phila. Child Guidance Clinic, 1971-72; research asso. North Central Phila. Community Mental Health Center, 1972-73, sr. research psychologist, 1972-73; sr. clin. psychologist Camden County (N.J.) Psychiat. Hosp. and Community Mental Health Center, 1973—; mem. The Feminist Therapy Collective, Phila., 1972—. Mem. Am., Eastern psychol. assns., Assn. Women in Psychology, Women's Liberation Group. Contbr. articles to profl. jours. Home: 440 W Sedgwick St #108B Philadelphia PA 19119 Office: Camden County Psychiat Hosp Blackwood NJ 08012

ROBBINS, RUTH SCHNEIDER (MRS. LIONEL ROBBINS), civic worker; b. Bklyn., Sept. 24, 1920; d. Samuel and Ida (Stolarsky) Schneider; B.A., N.Y. U., 1940; m. Lionel Robbins, Sept. 24, 1940; children—Kathy, Paul Alan. Mem. Mamaroneck Human Rights Commn., 1965-66, Westchester Council Social Agys., 1968-72; discussion leader N.Y. U. Edn. in Extension Program on World Politics and Am. Democracy, 1961-65. Vice pres. bd. dirs. Nat. Com. Against Discrimination in Housing. Mem. League Women Voters N.Y. State (pres. 1971—), Phi Beta Kappa. Home: 555 Alda Rd Mamaroneck NY 10543 Office: 817 Broadway New York City NY 10003

ROBE, LUCY BARRY (MRS. ROBERT S. ROBE, JR.), author, journalist; b. Boston, Jan. 15, 1934; d. Herbert and Lucy Manning (Brown) Barry; B.A., Radcliffe Coll., 1955; postgrad. N.Y. U., 1962-63, 69, L.I. U., 1971-72; m. Robert S. Robe, Jr., Feb. 6, 1971; 1 dau., Parrish Cameron. Prodn. asst. various Broadway producers and writers, 1956-68, prodns. include Bells Are Ringing, 1958, How to Succeed, 1961, Generation, 1965; librarian Charisma Prodns., N.Y.C., 1968-70; reporter Oyster Bay (N.Y.) Guardian, 1972—. Lectr. for L.I. Council Alcoholism in schs., colls. Bd. dirs. North Nassau Mental Health Center. Mem. N.Y. County Republican Com., 1968-71. Author: Stagestruck Secretary, 1966. Contbr. articles to mags. Home: Box 82 Cold Spring Harbor NY 11724

ROBECK, MILDRED MARIE COEN (MRS. MARTIN J. ROBECK, JR.), educator; b. Walum, N.D., July 29, 1915; d. Archie B. Coen and Mary H. Coen Henninger; B.A., U. Wash., 1951, M.Ed., 1954, Ph.D., 1958; m. Martin J. Robeck, Jr., June 2, 1936; children—Martin Jay, Donna Jayne (Mrs. Henry D. Thompson), Bruce Wayne. Tchr. rural schs., Jackson County, Ill., 1940-42; munitions foreman Sherwin-Williams Paint Co., Crab Orchard, 1942-44; tchr. Day Care Center and Seattle Pub. Schs., 1945-51; demonstration tchr. Seward Demonstration Sch., Seattle, 1951-57; asst. prof. U. Cal., Santa Barbara, 1957-64; research cons., tchr. edn. cons. Cal. State Dept. Edn., 1964-67; prof. U. Ore. Coll. Edn., Eugene, 1967—. Cons. to govt. agys. Recipient Congl. award Air Age Edn., 50th Anniversary Powered Flight, 1953-54. Mem. A.A.A.S., Nat. Soc. Study Edn., Am. Ednl. Research Assn., Cal. Ednl. Assn., Internat. Reading Assn., Phi Beta Kappa, Pi Lambda Theta. Democrat. Conglist. Author: (with J. Wilson, W. Michael) Psychological Foundations of Learning and Teaching, 1969, 2d edit., 1974; Kindergarten Evaluation of Learning Potential (with J. Wilson), 1967; Psychology of Reading, 1973. Contbr. chpts. to books, articles to profl. publs. Home: 320 Ful Vue Dr Eugene OR 97405

ROBENS, ANNELIESE MANN (MRS. HOWARD HORST ROBENS), psychologist, ednl. adminstr.; b. Muhlhausen, Thuringen, Germany, Nov. 18, 1932; d. Carl and Meta Kathe (Selz) Mann; came to U.S., 1936; naturalized, 1946; B.A. (N.J. state scholar), Douglass Coll., 1953; M.Ed., Rutgers U., 1962, Ed.D., 1969; m. Howard Horst Robens, June 29, 1958; 1 dau., Melody. Sch. psychologist Warren Twp. Schs., N.J., 1966-68; sr. psychologist Met. Health Services Greater Vancouver (B.C., Can.), 1969-71; asst. prof. psychology dept. Fairleigh Dickinson U., Teaneck, N.J., 1971-74, dir. grad. program in sch. psychology, 1971-74; mem. faculty edn. U. B.C., 1974—. Mem. profl. adv. bd. Vancouver Assn. Children with Learning Disabilities, 1970-71. Mem. Am., N.J., B.C. Psychol. assns., N.J. Assn. Sch. Psychologists, Nat. Assn. Sch. Psychologists, Young Peoples League (pres. 1957-58). Home: 3150 E 58th Av #7 Vancouver BC Canada also 514 S East Av Clayton NJ 08312

ROBERDS, LOUISE FARHA (MRS. LOREN LEE ROBERDS), educator; b. Shamrock, Okla., July 23, 1918; d. Ellis L. and Mahaba (Barkett) Farha; A.B., Bristow Jr. Coll., 1936; B.S., Okla. A and M. Coll., 1938; M.S., Okla. State U., 1940, Ed.S., 1962; m. Loren Lee Roberds, Nov. 22, 1942; children—William Lance, Constance Lynne (Mrs. Roger C. Bradley), George Lane, Donna Louise, Angela Lee. Tchr. pub. schs., Guymon, Okla., 1938-39, Bristow, Okla., 1939-40, 45; librarian, dean girls Bristow Jr. High Sch., 1945-55; curriculum coordinator pub. schs., Bristow, 1955-62; dir. elementary edn. Phillips U., Enid, Okla., 1962—, supr. tchr. tng. program. Condr. workshops for tchrs. on coll. campuses throughout Okla., summers 1955—. Bd. dirs. Commn. on Instrn. Mem. N.E.A., Cimmarron Reading Council, Internat., Okla. (pres.) reading councils, Okla. Council Tchrs. English, Okla. Edn. Assn. (mem. com. instrn.), Nat. Council Tchrs. English, Nat. Council Social Studies, Assn. for Supervision and Curriculum Devel., Nat. Council Parents and Tchrs., Elementary-Kindergarten Nursery Edn., Kappa Kappa Iota, Delta Kappa Gamma, Kappa Delta Pi (sponsor Phillips U.). Home: 1805 E Maple St Enid OK 73701

ROBERSON, EILEEN MURPHY, coll. adminstr.; b. Boston, July 31, 1941; A.B., Boston U., 1964; M.S., Syracuse U., 1969; m. June 4, 1966. Intern grad. student personnel Syracuse (N.Y.) U., 1968-69; tng. specialist Bache & Co., N.Y.C., 1969; dir. student employment Simmons Coll., Boston, 1970—, dir. summer session, 1972—. Cons. on women in employment. Mem. Boston C. of C., Personnel Mgrs. Club (mem. exec. com. 1972-75), Eastern Coll. Personnel Officers, Nat. Assn. Women Deans, Adminstrs. and Counselors, Nat. Assn. Summer Sessions, Coll. and U. Personnel Assn., Nat. Orgn. Women (mem. nat. task force for credit). Home: 150 Clare Av Boston MA 02136 Office: Simmons College 300 The Fenway Boston MA 02115

ROBERSON, ELIZABETH WILLOUGHBY, marketing exec.; b. Phila., Dec. 15, 1927; d. Jason Theodore and Elizabeth (Sullivan) Roberson; student Columbia, 1947-52. Asst. field dir. Young & Rubicam, Inc., N.Y.C., 1947-52; eastern regional mgr. Crossley S-D Surveys, N.Y.C., 1953-56; sr. analyst Alderson Assos., N.Y.C., 1957-60; mgmt. cons. Diebold Group, Inc., N.Y.C., 1960-63; field dir. Market Facts, N.Y.C., 1964-68, Nat. Analysts, Inc., Phila., 1968; now field dir. Monroe Mendelsohn Research Co., N.Y.C. Mem. Market Research Assn. (Specification Writer's award 1966-67, MRA Pres.'s award 1972), Beta Sigma Phi. Home: 32-08 60th St Woodside NY 11377

ROBERSON, PATT FOSTER (MRS. MURRAY RALPH ROBERSON, JR.), editor, advt. cons.; b. Middletown, N.Y., Dec. 3, 1934; d. Gilbert Charles and Mildred Elizabeth (O'Neal) Foster; A.A., Canal Zone Jr. Coll., 1954; B.A., La. State U., 1957, M.A., 1973; m. Murray Ralph Roberson, Jr., May 10, 1963 (dec. July 1968). Asst. editor West Bank Highlights, C.Z., 1954-55; librarian La. State U., Baton Rouge, 1955-57, news editor Daily Reveille, 1956-57; photographer's and artist's model, 1955-57; free-lance sec. for architects and engrs., 1960-63; archtl. sec. Lionel H. Abshire & Assos., Baton Rouge, 1958-60, Murrell & Callari, Baton Rouge, 1960-63; exec. sec. A.I.A., 1960-63; ghost writer, 1960-63; editor Our Lady of Lake Hosp. Aux. Yearbook, Baton Rouge, 1962—; proofreader Franklin Press, Inc., Baton Rouge, 1973—. Editor Lake Echoes, house publ. Our Lady of Lake Hosp., 1963-64; bus. mgr. So. Rev., lit. quar., Baton Rouge, 1963-69; La. reporter Canal Record, quar. for Panama Canal Soc., 1967—; advt. mgr. Baton Rouge Little Theater, 1971—; editor, advt. mgr. Dinner Theater, Baton Rouge, 1973. Dist. supr. East Baton Rouge Parish Census, 1973; mem. City-Parish Plan of Govt. Study Com., Baton Rouge, 1973; pres. Our Lady of Lake Hosp. Aux., 1971-72; state dist. dir. La. Hosp. Com. Auxs., 1971-72. Recipient C.Z. Coll. Club scholarship, 1954; outstanding service trophy Women in Constrn., 1962. Mem. Women in Communications (chmn. Matrix Table 1971), Assn. for Edn. in Journalism, Nat. Orgn. Women (chpt. sec. 1971-72), Women in Constrn. (nat. historian 1961-62), La. State U. Journalism Sch. Alumni Assn. (sec.-treas. 1970—), La. State U. Alumni Fedn. (East Baton Rouge Parish rep. 1970—, La. retirement counselor to Panama C.Z. 1971—), Baton Rouge Sportsmen's League (sec. 1970-71), Hist. Bottle Assn. Baton Rouge. Author: Survey of Foreign, English-Language Literary Quarterlies Available for Exchange, 1965. Home: 4875 Maribel Dr Baton Rouge LA 70812

ROBERTS, AMELIA SEAWRIGHT (MRS. JAMES F. ROBERTS), educator; b. Sumter, S.C.; d. William and Lavinia (Barnes) Seawright; B.S., S.C. State Coll., 1946; M.A., Columbia, 1950; Ed.D., Okla. U., 1964; m. James F. Roberts, Mar. 9, 1946 (dec. Oct. 1967). Tchr. pub. schs., Horry County, 1940-43; substitute tchr. N.Y.C. Pub. Schs., 1946-47; tchr. Orangeburg (S.C.) City Schs., 1947-51; dir. elementary workshop S.C. State Coll., Orangeburg, summers 1949-52, asst. supr. of directed teaching, 1951-63, dir. Felton Lab. Sch., 1964-70, dean Sch. Edn., 1970—. State liaison rep. Am. Assn. Tchr. Edn.; adv. bd. S.C. Children's Bur.; chairperson Orangeburg Mental Health Bd.; mem. S.C. Com. on Children and Youth. Mem. So. Assn. Colls. and Schs. (mem. commn. on elementary schs.), Am. Assn. U. Profs., Am. Assn. Sch. Adminstrs., S.C. Edn. Assn., Nat. Lab. Sch. Adminstrs. Assn., Ladies Aux. V.F.W. (past pres.), Nat. Assn. Lab. Schs., Nat. Assn. Coll. Women (past pres.), Am. Assn. U. Women, Ch. Women United, Delta Sigma Theta (past pres.), Kappa Delta Pi. Baptist. Eagle. Mem. Order Eastern Star. Contbr. articles to profl. jours. Home: 2685 Old Cameron Rd Orangeburg SC 29115

ROBERTS, BETTY CANTRELL (MRS. KEITH D. SKELTON), lawyer, educator; b. Arkansas City, Kan., Feb. 5, 1923; d. David Murray and M. Pearl (Higgins) Cantrell; student Tex. Wesleyan Coll., 1941-42, Eastern Ore. Coll., 1955-56; B.S., Portland State Coll., 1958; M.S., U. Ore., 1962; J.D., Northwestern Sch. Law Lewis and Clark Coll., 1966; m. Keith D. Skelton, June 15, 1968; children—S. Dian Odell, John W. Rice, Jo R. Rice, Randall G. Rice. Tchr., dean girls

Reynolds High Sch., 1958-60, Centennial High Sch., 1960-62, David Douglas High Sch., 1962-66; admitted to Ore. bar, 1967; pvt. practice law, Portland, 1967—; instr. govt. and bus. law Mt. Hood Community Coll., 1967—. Mem. Lynch Sch. Dist. Bd., 1960-66. Mem. Ore. Ho. of Reps., 1965-69; mem. Ore. Senate, 1969—. Mem. League Women Voters, Bus. and Profl. Women, Urban League, Am. Civil Liberties Union, Ore. Bar Assn. Home: 319 SE Gilham St Portland OR 97215 Office: Boise Cascade Bldg Portland OR 97201

ROBERTS, BETTY KATHERINE WINKLER, editor; b. Ronceverte, W.Va., Aug. 29, 1926; d. James Louis and Adele L'Artigue Pinckney (Pettyjohn) Winkler; R.N., St. Luke's Hosp. Sch. Nursing, N.Y.C., 1947; student W.Va. U., 1948-50, U. N.C., 1950-51; B.A., U. Pitts., 1962; M.A., Marshall U., 1970; m. Charles Roberts, Dec. 4, 1954 (div. Nov. 1961); children—Holly Adele, Dean Scott. Staff nurse Monongalia Gen. Hosp., Morgantown, W.Va., part-time 1948-50; rehab. nurse Ohio State U. Hosp., Columbus, 1952-53; pub. health nurse Dept. Pub. Health, Columbus, 1953-54; tchr. English, Caroline County Sch. Bd., Bowling Green, Va., 1963-64; rehab. counselor W.Va. Dept. Vocational Rehab., Institute, 1964-67; tng. dir. New Careers program W.Va. Dept. Mental Health, Charleston, 1967-69; editor Nat. Rehab. Assn. Jour. Rehab., Washington, 1970—. Mem. Am. Newspaper Women's Assn., Advt. Club Met. Washington, Soc. Nat. Assn. Publs., Internat. Assn. Bus. Communicators, Express Assn., Assn. Humanistic Psychology. Club: Nat. Press. Home: 9504 Commons Dr Apt 102 Annandale VA 22003 Office: 1522 K St NW Washington DC 20005

ROBERTS, CARRIE BELLE HOOPER (MRS. DELMAR ROBERTS, SR.), social work adminstr.; b. Timpson, Tex., Apr. 15, 1905; d. Charles A. and Carrie Belle (Beazley) Hooper; B.A., So. Meth. U., 1928; postgrad. U. Tex., 1931—; M.S., U. So. Cal., 1936; m. Thomas George MacCarthy, Dec. 24 (dec. Aug. 1958); m. 2d, Delmar Roberts, Sr., June 6, 1962 (dec. Jan. 1963); 1 stepson, Delmar (dec.). Employed in social work, 1928—; supr. service to mil. A.R.C., 1941-62, supr. disaster-res., Las Cruces, N.M., 1962—, acting dir. service to mil., 1972; vol. program cons. State of N.M. Red Cross, Las Cruces, 1962—. Vol. tchr. social welfare, disaster tng., 1963—; bd. mem. local chpt. A.R.C., intermittently, 1963—; com. mem. research on ecology in So. N.M., N.M. State U. Mem. El Paso Museum and Community Theater, Farm Bur., Las Cruces Art Assn., Alpha Delta Pi. Republican. Episcopalian. Club: El Paso Woman's. Home: PO Box 446 Anthony NM 88021 Office: 1303 E Griggs Av Las Cruces NM 88001

ROBERTS, CELIA ANN, librarian; b. Bangor, Me., Feb. 6, 1935; d. William Lewis and Ruey Pearl (Logan) Roberts; A.A., U. Hartford, 1957, B.A., 1961; postgrad. So. Conn. State Coll., 1963—. With catalog, acquistion and circulation depts. U. Hartford Library, 1956-65; librarian Simsbury (Conn.) Free Library, 1965; reference librarian Simsbury Pub. Library, 1969—. Tchr. ballet classes, 1965-66; ballet mistress Ballet Soc. Conn., Inc., 1968-70; with corps de ballet Conn. Opera Assn., 1963-64; active in prodns. Simsbury Light Opera Assn., 1964, 69. Mem. A.L.A., Conn. Library Assn., Simsbury Hist. Soc., Ont. Geneal. Soc., Am. Assn. U. Women, Pro Dance, Conn. Soc. Genealogists, Dance Masters Am. Universalist. Office: 749 Hopmeadow St Simsbury CT 06070

ROBERTS, CLARA IRENE BROADWAY (MRS. PHILIP CAREY ROBERTS), civic worker; b. Pocahontas, Ark., Dec. 29, 1914; d. Rance Enmand and Olive (Alphin) Broadway; certificate Memphis Tech. Night Sch., 1954; licensed vocational nurse, Memphis Vocational Sch., 1956; m. Philip Carey Roberts, May 23, 1957 (dec. Feb. 1964); children by previous marriage—Clara Lee (Mrs. William David Burnside), Henrietta (Mrs. Wilbur Osburn Davis), Mildred Lucille (Mrs. Walter Eugene Dollahite). Co-owner, Lehman-Roberts Co., Inc., Memphis, 1964—. Sec., Recreation Services for Handicapped, Memphis, 1964-65, mem. exec. bd., 1965-67; treas. Lenna P. Hart circle King's Daus., 1961. Named Vol. of Year, Recreation Services for Handicapped, Inc., 1965, 66. Mem. Internat. Platform Assn. Home: 5452 N Suggs Dr Memphis TN 38117

ROBERTS, DOROTHY ELLIOTT (MRS. WALTER C. ROBERTS), educator; b. N.D., Oct. 16, 1908; d. Richard Corley and Catheryn Smith (Sprague) Elliott; B.A., U. Cal. at Los Angeles, 1930; M.A., U. So. Cal., 1938; Ph.D., U. Cal. at Berkeley, 1955; postgrad. U. Hawaii; m. Walter C. Roberts, Oct. 8, 1944; children—Madeleine M. (Mrs. K. W. Lee), Dixie Louise (Mrs. M. L. Hegg), Theodore T. Martin. Tchr., Los Angeles, 1941, Sierra Madre, Cal., 1941-44, Pasadena (Cal.) Jr. Coll., 1955-56; implements field edn. East-West Center, Honolulu, 1964—. Adminstrv. asst. to mgr. A.R.C., Honolulu, 1963-64. Mem. Am. Philos. Assn., Am. Assn. U. Women, Pi Delta Phi. Pi Epsilon Theta. Author: The International Programs of American Universities, 1965; Scholar's Guide to Japan, rev. edit., 1969; Scholar's Guide to Hong Kong, 1968; Scholar's Guide to the Republic of China, 1970; Primer to Philosophy, 1974. Home: 3379 Brittan Av San Carlos CA 94070

ROBERTS, DOROTHY F., educator; b. Jasper, Mo., Jan. 16, 1921; d. Ollie E. and Fay (Grim) Roberts; A.B., Park Coll., 1943; Ph.D., U. Chgo., 1956; LL.B., Columbia, 1960. Intern in State Dept., Nat. Inst. Pub. Affairs, Washington, 1943; adminstrv. asst. UNRRA, Washington, 1944-45, personnel officer, reports analyst, displaced persons operation, Germany, 1945-46; instr. dept. govt. and internat. relations U. Conn., 1951-56; individual law practice, Lamar, Mo., 1960-65; mem. faculty Davis and Elkins Coll., Elkins, W.Va., 1965-70, asso. prof. dept. history and polit. sci., 1965-70, prof., 1970—, chmn. dept. polit. sci., 1972—. Mem. steering com. Council for Children and Youth, Mo. Assn. Social Welfare, 1963-65, chmn. com. problems of juveniles, 1963-64. Mem. Mo. Bar (mem. exec. com. family laws com. 1964-65), Mo. Assn. Women Lawyers (pres. 1965), Am. Soc. Internat. Law, Am. Assn. U. Profs., Am., W.Va. (mem. exec. council 1967—, pres. 1969-70) polit. sci. assns., Internat. Studies Assn. Home: 113 Grandview Av Elkins WV 26241

ROBERTS, ELEANOR FLAVY GELINAS, electrologist; b. Chicopee, Mass., Sept. 8, 1918; d. Arthur Francis and Diane (Therrian) Gelinas; grad. Kree Inst. Electrolysis, N.Y.C., 1948; grad. Sch. Applied Hypnology, 1958; m. Wallace Earl Roberts, Oct. 10, 1936; 1 son, Wallace Arthur. Electrologist, 1948—; tchr. electrolysis, 1950—; commr. Bd. Registration Electrologists, 1958-66; established Eleanor F. Roberts Inst. Electrology, Boston, 1966, dean, 1966—. Lectr., writer electrology. Fellow Electrolysis Soc. Am. (citation, honor plaque); mem. Mass. Assn. Electrologists (past pres.), Am. Electrolysis Assn. (past. pres., honor plaque), Bus. and Profl. Women's Club (past dir.), Dale Carnegie Internat. (past pres. Duke U. br.). Roman Catholic. Club. Pioneer Valley Internat. (past pres.). Contbg. editor Nat. Jour. Electrolysis. Home: 151 Tremont St Boston MA 02111 Office: 59 Temple Pl Boston MA 02111

ROBERTS, ELEANOR J., home economist; b. Detroit; d. Richard and Hope (Webster) Roberts; B.S., Wayne State U., 1952. Asst. food editor Parents Mag., N.Y.C., 1953-54; home service counselor Mich. Consolidated Gas Co., Detroit, 1954-60, asst. dir. home service, 1961, dir. home service, Grand Rapids, 1962-70, mgr. consumer services, 1970—. Mem. Detroit Home Economists in Bus. (pres. 1959), Am., Mich. home econs. assns., Womens Advt. Club Grand Rapids (pres. 1964-65, sec. 1968-69), Am. Gas Assn., World Affairs Council (sec. 1972—), Alpha Gamma Delta, Central Mich. Home Economists in Bus. Clubs: Quota (dir. 1964-66, 71-73), Womens City. Home: 521 Fountain St NE Grand Rapids MI 49503 Office: 200 Monroe St Grand Rapids MI 49502

ROBERTS, ELLEN ANN, banker; b. Balt., May 29, 1926; d. Chandler P. and Ethel (Thomas) Roberts; B.A., Goucher Coll., 1948. With Downington Savs. & Loan Assn., 1948—, asst. sec., dir., mgr. assn., 1957-66, sec., mgr., 1966—, exec. v.p., 1973—. Mem. Chester County Planning Commn., 1969—. Organizer Young Republican Club of Chester County, 1952, asst. sec. Pa. state bd., 1957-58, nat. committeewoman, Pa., 1958-60, vice-chmn. 1960-62; alternate del. 9th congl. dist. Rep. Nat. Conv., 1956; vice chmn. Chester County Rep. Com., 1964—. Bd. dirs. Southeastern Pa. Transp. Authority, 1971—. Mem. Nat. Soc. Controllers and Financial Officers Savs. Instns., Pa. Savings and Loan League (treas. 1973—), Adminstrv. Mgmt. Soc., D.A.R., Bus. and Profl. Women's Club, Alumni Assn. Goucher Coll., Pi Beta Phi. Episcopalian. Home: 11 Park Lane Downingtown PA 19335 Office: 100 E Lancaster Av Downingtown PA 19335

ROBERTS, FRANCES CABANISS, educator; b. Gainesville, Ala., Dec. 19, 1916; d. Richard H. and Mary (Watson) Roberts; B.S., Livingston State U., 1937; M.A., U. Ala., 1940, Ph.D., 1956; postgrad. Vanderbilt U., 1949-50. Tchr. pub. schs., Huntsville, Ala., 1937-52; teaching fellow U. Ala., Huntsville, 1952-53, faculty, 1953—, prof. history, 1961—, chmn. dept., 1966-70. Bd. mem. Huntsville Civic Symphony, Twickenham Hist. Preservation Assn.; Ala. state dir. on exec. bd. So. Heritage Found., 1964-65; bd. mem. Burritt Mus., Huntsville; mem. Huntsville Historic Preservation Commn., 1972, Commn. Restoration Capitol Bdlg., 1973. Recipient Livingston State U. Alumni award, 1964; Ala. Historic Commn. award, 1969; N. Ala. Bar Assn. Liberty Bell award, 1970, Life Sharer's award Kiwanis, 1973. Mem. Ala. Ednl. Assn., Huntsville Hist. Soc. (exec. bd. 1950—), Ala. Council Social Studies (pres. 1947-48), Am., Ala. (pres. 1968-69, exec. bd. mem. 1951—), So., N. Ala. (exec. bd. 1956-64) hist. assns., Golden Key, Kappa Delta Pi, Phi Alpha Theta (Scholarship award 1973). Author: Shadows on the Wall, The Life and Works of Howard Weeden, 1962; Civics for Alabama Schools, 1968, rev., 1970. Home: 603 Randolph Av Huntsville AL 35801

ROBERTS, FRANCES V. TROUB (MRS. BERTRAM H. ROBERTS), educator; b. Hartford, Conn., July 15, 1924; d. Leonard Martin and Lonie (Morris) Troub; B.A., Vassar Coll., 1944; M.A., Yale, 1946; m. Bertram H. Roberts, Nov. 26, 1952 (dec. Aug. 1955); children—Margaret Hope, Priscilla Jane. Case aide Family Service Soc., Hartford, Conn., 1945, Union Settlement group worker, 1945; tchr. Rockwood Sch., N.Y.C., 1946-47, Brown Sch., Hartford, Conn., 1947-48, Am. Sch. for Deaf, Hartford, 1949-52, Quaker Lane Coop. Nursery Sch., West Hartford, Conn., 1955-57; edn. dir. Conn. Commn. on Alcoholism, Hartford, 1957-58; program asst. Conn. State Dept. Mental Health, Hartford, Conn., 1959-68, pub. information supr., 1968-70, chief mental health edn., 1970—. Lectr. Yale Sch. Epidemiology and Pub. Health, 1973—. Past bd. dirs. Am. Jewish Com., Jewish Family Service, Jewish Childrens Services Orgn., Service Bur. Womens Organizations, 1966-68, Am. Field Service, 1967—. Mem. Conn. Pub. Health Assn., Nat. Com. Mental Health Edn. (pres. 1972-74), Conn. Health League (sec.). Democrat. Jewish religion. Home: 124 N Main St West Hartford CT 06107 Office: 90 Washington St Hartford CT 06115

ROBERTS, GENEVA NICHOLS, banker; b. Jena, La., Aug. 16, 1918; d. William Thomas and Julia Azalia (White) Nichols; student Dodd Coll., 1931-33, Am. Inst. Banking, 1966-71; m. Willie Clifton Roberts, Nov. 1, 1940 (div. 1958); 1 dau. Linda Christine. Supr. teller operations Long Point Nat. Bank Houston, 1956-66; mgr. new accounts Internat. Bank, Houston, 1967-69; with Northwest Nat. Bank, Houston, 1969—, mgr. new accounts, also bus. devel., 1969—, asst. v.p., 1972—. Dir. Guardian Engring. Co., Inc. Mem. Nat. Assn. Bank Women, Am. Inst. Banking (conv. com. chmn. 1971, bd. govs. 1972-74, Outstanding Woman in Banking 1973), Bank Marketing Asso., Bus. and Profl. Women's Club. Club: The Bank Women's (past pres.) (Houston). Home: 6643 Edloe St Houston TX 77005 Office: 1716 Mangum St Houston TX 77018

ROBERTS, GERTRUD HERMINE KUENZEL (MRS. JOYCE O. ROBERTS), composer, concert harpsichordist; b. Hastings, Minn., Aug. 23, 1906; d. Adolph Gustav and Anna Marie (Kloetzer) Kuenzel; B.A., U. Minn., 1928; student Leipzig Conservatory Music, 1930-31; pvt. study piano Madame Julie Elbogen, Vienna, Austria, 1932-33; m. Joyce O. Roberts, June 4, 1934; children—Michael Stefen, Marcia Eveline. Tchr. piano dept. Summit Sch., St. Paul, 1931-32, 33-38; music tchr. pvt. studios, Bozeman, Mont., 1938-41, Washington, 1941-43, Honolulu, 1947—; ann. harpsichord concerts Honolulu Acad. Arts and various schs. and colls. of Hawaii, 1950—; premier 1st harpsichord compositions, St. Paul, 1936; appeared harpsichord concerts throughout U.S., including concert tours, 1964, 66—. Commd. to compose and record music for Honolulu Community Theatre, Honolulu Youth Theatre, drama dept. U. Hawaii. Founder, pres. Fritz Hart Found., also Jean Charlot Found. Mem. Nat. Guild Piano Tchrs., Nat. League Am. Pen Women, Nat. Assn. Am. Composers and Condrs., Nat. Soc. Arts and Letters (pres. 1971—), Honolulu Chamber Music Soc. (founder, patron), Honolulu Acad. Arts, Honolulu Piano Tchrs. Assn. (pres. 1970-72), Honolulu Community Theatre (hon. life), Am. Assn. U. Women, Alpha Gamma Delta, Sigma Alpha Iota. Composer: Chaconne (harpsichord), 1951; Triptych (harpsichord), 1961; Petite Suite (harpsichord), 1955; Hommage to Couperin (harpsichord), 1955; Passacaille (harpsichord), 1956; In a Secret Garden (voice and piano), 1954; Elegy (for piano or orchestra) for John F. Kennedy, 1965; Twelve Time Gardens (for piano); Das Kleine Buch der Bilder (harpsichord); Fantasie after Psalm 150, 1971; also numerous short children's pieces for harpsichord. Home: 4723 Moa St Honolulu HI 96816

ROBERTS, HASSELTINE NEAL, coll. librarian; b. Macon, Ga., Nov. 22; d. George Arthur and Sarah Belle (Roberts) Roberts; A.B., Wesleyan Coll., 1960; M.S., Fla. State U., 1964. Camp dir. Middle Ga. Girl Scout Council, Lizella, 1960-63; tchr. Dougherty County Bd. Edn., Albany, Ga., 1960-63; asst. librarian Wesleyan Coll., Macon, Ga., 1964-69, librarian, 1969—. Library cons. Internat. Safety Acad., 1970. Mem. Am., Southeastern, Ga. (fellow 1963-64) library assns., Quota Internat., Macon Quota Club (dir. 1967—), P.E.O. Sisterhood, Pi Gamma Mu, Delta Kappa Gamma. Presbyn. Contbr. book reviews to local newspaper. Home: 4521 Rivoli Dr Macon GA 31204 Office: Willet Library Wesleyan College Macon GA 31201

ROBERTS, HERMESE ESTELLE JOHNSON (MRS. EDWARD JAMES ROBERTS), sch. adminstr.; b. Panama, C.Z., Sept. 22, 1913; d. Jonathan Horatio and May (Callendar) Johnson; A.B., Hunter Coll., N.Y.C., 1934; A.M., Atlanta U., 1941; postgrad. Columbia, summer 1942, U. Chgo., 1947-53; D.Ed., Nova U., 1974; m. Edward James Roberts, Dec. 30, 1945; children—Hermese Edwina, Edward James. Tchr. Atlanta U. Lab. Sch., 1934-39; prin. Peach County Tng. Sch., Ft. Valley, Ga., 1939-45; dir. Reading Improvement Program So. U., Scotlandville, La., 1945-46; clinician U. Chgo. Reading Clinics, 1947-49; psychologist Chgo. Pub. Schs. Bur. Child Study, 1949-54; reading specialist Dartmouth ABC Project, 1964, Hanover, N.H.; prin. Mayo Sch., Chgo., 1961—. Dir. tchr. edn. workshops N.C. State Coll. at Durham, summer 1941, Bethune-Cookman Coll., Daytona Beach, Fla., summer 1943; Ft. Valley State Coll., 1944; instr. reading and lang. arts Roosevelt U., U. Chgo., Chgo. State Coll., summers 1946-60; dir. Summer Reading Lab. Chgo. Urban Youth Project of Gt. Cities Improvement Program, summer 1961. Mem. N.E.A., Internat., Chgo. Area reading assns., Elementary Prins. Assn. Mem. Christian Assembly Ch. Author: Usage Manual, Building Basic English, Set B: Phonic Series, 1967; The Third Ear, 1970; (with others) Dandy Dog Early Learning Program, 1966; Am. Book Co. READ Series: Each and All, Far and Away, Gold and Silver, 1971. Contbr. articles to profl. jours. Office: Mayo Sch 249 E 37th St Chicago IL 60653

ROBERTS, IDA M. LAFACE (MRS. JOHN PORTER ROBERTS), pub. relations ofcl.; b. Pitts., Oct. 8, 1942; d. Costa J. and Alma Rose (Cerar) LaFace; B.S., U. Fla., 1964; m. John Porter Roberts, 1970; 1 son, Samuel Randolph. With advt. dept. Howard Johnson's Inc. of Fla., Miami, 1962-64; pub. relations rep. Nat. Airlines Inc., Miami, Fla., 1965-73. Pub. relations United Fund, Dade County, Fla., 1966-70; dir., sec., pub. relations chmn. United Cerebral Palsy Assn., 1969— mem. nat. standing pub. relations exec. com., 1970—. Mem. Fla. Pub. Relations Assn., Women in Communications (mem. exec. bd. 1966—, treas. 1968-69, sec. 1969-70, v.p. 1970-71, pres. 1971—), Alpha Delta Phi Alumni Assn., U. Fla. Alumni Assn. Home: 600 NE 57th St Miami FL 33137

ROBERTS, KATHLEEN ELIZABETH, physician; b. Albion, Pa.,; d. James and Mable (Consedine) Stein; M.D., Syracuse U., 1949; m. Arden Roberts; children—Constance, Kathleen, William. Intern Syracuse; resident Cornell; fellow Cornell U., 1950-52; physiology asst. Sloan Kettering Inst., N.Y.C., 1952-57; pvt. practice medicine specializing in kidney disease, internal medicine, emphysema, arthritis, cardiovascular and renal disease, N.Y.C., 1957—. Mem. Am. Soc. Clin. Investigation, Am. Physiology Soc., Western Soc. Clin. Investigation, Harvey Soc., Sigma Xi. Author: Clinical Physiology, Electrolyte Changes in Surgery, 1961; Forgotten Organ. Home: Candor NY 13743 Office: 388 Front St Owego NY 13827

ROBERTS, LEILA-JANE BULLER SMITH (MRS. RUSSELL D. ROBERTS), librarian; b. Syracuse, N.Y., July 13, 1923; d. Reveley Herbert Buller and Ruth Gaylord (Mallory) Smith; A.B., Oberlin Coll., 1945; M.S., Simmons Coll., 1971; m. Russell David Roberts, Aug. 26, 1950; 1 dau., Jane Gaylord Burr. Tchr. English, Northfield (Mass.) Sch. for Girls, 1945-49; IBM programmer Boston Filter Co., 1949-51; tchr. Winchester (Mass.) High Sch., 1955-56; gen. profl. asst. Winchester Pub. Library, 1957-59, young adult librarian, head circulation, 1960-63, asst. head librarian, 1964-67, library dir., 1967—. Bus. mgr. Book Reviews Young Adult Coop. Book Review Group Mass., 1966-73. Mem. A.L.A., Greater Boston Pub. Library Adminstrs. (past pres.), New Eng. (past dir., pres. 1973-74), Mass. library assns., Round Table Librarians for Young Adults (past pres.), League of Women Voters. Conglist. Club: Quota (Winchester). Home: 17 Congress St Stoneham MA 02180 Office: 80 Washington St Winchester MA 01890

ROBERTS, MARJORIE KLAWITTER (MRS. ALAN SILVERMAN ROBERTS), psychologist; b. Cin., Dec. 3, 1938; d. George and Adelaide (Ackerman) Klawitter; B.S., N.Y. U., 1960, M.A., 1962; Ph.D., Catholic U., 1970; m. Alan Silverman Roberts, June 6, 1965; children—Michael Eric, Daniel Ian. Asst. dir. student center Douglas Coll., New Brunswick, N.J., 1962-63; tchr. elementary pub. schs., Falls Church, Va., 1963-64; instr. psychology Rosemont (Pa.) Coll., 1964-65, So. U. of New Orleans, 1967-68; pvt. practice family and marriage counseling, Los Angeles. Founder Mut. Amputee Aid Found., 1973. Mem. Am. Psychology Assn. Office: 10921 Wilshire Blvd Suite 1111 Los Angeles CA 90024

ROBERTS, MARY MARGARET, educator; b. Independence, Ia., Mar. 30, 1923; d. Thomas Robert and Bertha (Beal) Roberts; B.A., Luther Coll., 1944; M.A., Northwestern U., 1949; Ph.D., La. State U., 1959. Speech instr. high sch., Red Wing, Minn., 1944-46, Council Bluffs, Ia., 1946-49; asst. prof. Luther Coll., 1949-50; instr. Kan. State Coll., Pittsburg, 1950-54, asso. prof. speech 1961-65, prof. speech, dir. grad. studies in speech, 1965—; vis. instr. Appalachian State Tchrs. Coll., N.C. summer, 1955; editorial asst. Speech Assn. Am., 1954-55; grad. asst. La. State U., 1956-57; asso. dir. debate U. Pitts., 1957-60, dir. debate, asst. prof., 1960-61. Named Outstanding Kan. Coll. Speech Tchr. of Year, 1965; Distinguished Alumni award, 1966, Woman of Year in Edn. Pittsburg C. of C., 1973. Mem. Speech Communication Assn., Am. Forensic Assn., Kan. (v.p. 1952-54, pres. 1969-70), Pa., Central States (exec. com. mem.-at-large 1970-72) speech assns., Am. Assn. U. Women (v.p. Pittsburg br. 1965-67, pres. 1971-73, Kan. div. area rep. in edn. 1967-69), Delta Kappa Gamma (recipient Rho chpt. research award 1967). Editorial bd. The Speech Tchr., 1966-69, editor 1973—; editorial bd. The Kan. Speech Jour., 1964-68, editor-in-chief, 1966-68. Home: 212 E Belleville Pittsburg KS 66762 Office: Kansas State Coll of Pittsburg Pittsburg KS 66762

ROBERTS, MARY POLK, educator; b. Balt., Nov. 24, 1922; d. Brant Edward and Alberta (Pyle) Roberts; B.A., Goucher Coll., 1945; M.A., Loyola Coll., Balt., 1954. Instr. physiology Goucher Coll., 1948-50; tchr. chemistry, chmn. sci. dept. Towson (Md.) Sr. High Sch., 1950-63; adminstrv. asst., vice prin. Perry Hall Sr. High Sch., 1963-68; prin. Cockeysville High Sch., 1968—. Mem. Women's Internat. League Peace and Freedom, League Women Voters, D.A.R., Magna Carta Dames, Common Cause, Alpha Phi, Pi Lambda Theta. Episcopalian. Home: 907 Locustvale Rd Towson MD 21204

ROBERTS, NANCY CORRELL (MRS. BRUCE STUART ROBERTS), author; b. South Milwaukee, Wis.; d. Milton Lee and Maud (MacRae) Correll; student Centre Coll., 1942-44; B.A., U. N.C., 1947; postgrad. U. Miami (Fla.), 1947-48; m. Bruce Stuart Roberts, Feb. 27, 1957; children—Nancy Lee, David. Editor, Scottish Chief, Maxton N.C., 1953-57, owner, pub., 1955-57. Pres., Maxton Indsl. Devel. Corp., 1955-56. Town commr., Maxton, 1952-56; chmn. Democrats for Eisenhower, Lumberton, N.C., 1952. Presbyn. Club: Maxton (N.C.) Jr. Woman's (pres. 1952-53). Author: An Illustrated Guide to Ghosts in the Old North State, 1959; Ghosts of the Carolinas, 1962; David, 1968; Sense of Discovery: The Mountain, 1969; A Week in Robert's World, 1969; This Haunted Land: the South, 1970; Where Time Stood Still: A Portrait of Appalachia, 1970; The Governor, 1972; The Goodliest Land, North Carolina, 1973; You and Your Retarded Child, 1974; Ghosts and Specters, 1974. Contbr. articles to nat. mags. Home: 6701 Sunview Dr Charlotte NC 28210

ROBERTS, NAVADA CLOYTEEN (MRS. RAY EDWARD ROBERTS), lawyer; b. nr. England, Ark., Apr. 16, 1929; d. Elmer Cleveland and Marie C. (Tubb) Lyons; student Little Rock U., 1962-64; LL.B., Ark. Law Sch., 1967; m. Ray Edward Roberts, Dec. 2, 1945; children—Ray Edward, Marjorie (Mrs. Don R. Kesl), Jon Lynn. Bookkeeper Morris Gin Co., Keo, Ark., 1964-67; clk. to Ark. Supreme Ct. justice, 1967; admitted to Ark. bar, 1967, since practiced in England. Pres., England High Sch. Booster Band Club, 1972—. Sec. Lonoke County Democratic Party, 1968—. Mem. Am., Ark. (chmn. family law section 1972-73), bar assns., Am. Assn. Women Hwy. Safety Leaders (chmn. region I 1972—), Ark. Assn. Women Lawyers (pres. 1972), Central Ark. Estate Council, England C. of C. (sec. 1968-70). Club: England Country. Home: 209 Willow St England AR 72046 Office: 106 E Rordyce St England AR 72046

ROBERTS, RACHEL, actress; b. Llanelly, Wales; m. Rex Harrison, 1962. TV appearances include Jonathan North, Circus, Time, Sunday Out of Season, Shadow Squad; motion picture appearances include The Good Companions, The Weak and the Wicked, Valley of Song, Our Man in Havana, Saturday Night and Sunday Morning, Girl on Approval, This Sporting Life. Address: care Ethel Barrymore Theatre 243 W 47th St New York City NY 10036*

ROBERTS, RUTH LOVE (MRS. KEYTON F. ROBERTS), county ofcl.; b. Tulia, Tex., Sept. 8, 1906; d. Jim Ben and Mary Myrtle (Ward) Love; grad. high sch., Lovington, N.M.; m. Keyton F. Roberts, Jan. 23, 1928 (dec. Mar. 1957); 1 son, Harold Kelly. Telephone operator Lovington Telephone Exchange, 1925-27; dep. county clk. Lea County, Lovington, 1928-31, dep. county treas., 1936-45; dep. county clk. Otero County, Alamogordo, N.M., 1955-60, 65-68, county clk., 1961-64, 69-72, ret.; with Elliott & Waldron Abstract Co., Lovington, 1933-34, The Lovington Abstract Co., 1947-48. Mem. Otero County Democratic Women's Club. Hon. col. Gov. N.M.; hon. sec. state N.M. Mem. Nat. Assn. Bus. and Profl. Women, Nat., N.M. assns. county ofcls., Internat. Assn. Clks., Recorders, Election Ofcls., and Treasurers. Home: PO Box 916 Alamogordo NM 88310

ROBERTS, RUTH OLIVE, musician; b. Fryeburg, Me.; d. John Henry and Ellen (Deane) Roberts; A.B., Colby Coll.; pvt. study piano with Heinrich Gebhard, organ with John Hermann Loud; studied in Europe with Alfred Cortot, Switzerland and Zecchi, Austria, and others. Featured on several musical programs in London and Scotland during Coronation Season, 1953, Internat. Congress Organists, London, 1957, Am. Music Nat. Music Week, Nat. Fedn. Music Clubs; concert tour Europe, 1962; local musicales, 1968-71; concert engagements Am. and Europe, 1974. Mem. Am. Guild Organists, Am. Assn. U. Women, Leschetizky Assn., Inc., MacDowell Colony, Mus. Guild Boston, Assn. Am. Composers and Arrangers, Nat. Guild Pianoforte Tchrs., Am. Coll. Musicians, Nat. Fedn. Music Club, Victoria Soc. Me. (charter mem., pres. 1960-64), Portland Symphony Orch., Women's Com. Hon. mem. editorial bd. Music and Dance in New Eng. states. Home: 342 Main Saco ME 04072

ROBERTS, MRS. SAMUEL (HOPE ROBERTS), business exec.; b. Bklyn., Aug. 12, 1913; d. Emil Alexander and Lillie (Faber) Woerth; grad. pub. schs.; m. Samuel Roberts; 1 son, Glenn Allen. Sec. to advt. mgr. Nat. Bellas Hess, 1931-32; sec. to mgr. life ins. dept. Travelers Ins. Co., 1932-46; owner, operator Roberts Guest House, Reno, 1948-72; bus. mgr. K.D. Kelly Personnel, 1972—; asst. to pres. Scenic Tours, Inc., 1959-61. Chmn. local chpt. A.R.C., 1955-56; mem. adv. council Pacific area, 1956-59, nat. fund vice-chmn., 1959-60; supr. Reno Air Def. Filter Center, Washoe County, Nev., 1955-59; mem. Washoe County Civil Def. Council, 1955-61, Adv. Council State Vocational Tech. Edn., 1964—; chmn. Gov.'s Commn. on Status of Women, 1964. Bd. dirs. United Fund, 1971—; trustee Bus. and Profl. Women's Found., 1971-74. Recipient Air Def. Command awards 1955, 56; merit awards A.R.C., 1949, 53, 54; Bus. Woman of Month award Washoe County, 1954; Gov.'s Distinguished Nevadan citation, 1968; named 1 of 20 Outstanding Nev. Women of Century, 1974. Mem. Nev. Fedn. Bus. and Profl. Women's Clubs (dist. dir. 1955-56, pres. 1961-62), Nat. Assn. Parliamentarians, Women's Aux. Nev. Pharm. Assn. (pres. 1954-55), Bus. and Profl. Women's Club (Reno pres. 1954-55), Air Def. Command (hon. life), Nat. Fedn. Bus. and Profl. Women's Clubs (pres. 1968-69), Washoe Med. Center Women's League, Beta Sigma Phi. Mem. Order Eastern Star. Club: Reno Emblem. Home: 5026 Lakeridge Terrace E Reno NV 89502

ROBERTS, VERA MOWRY, educator; b. Pitts., Oct. 21, 1918; d. Joseph E. and Emma C. (Steinmann) Mowry; B.A., U. Pitts., 1938, M.A., 1945, Ph.D., 1951; m. Pernell E. Roberts, Jan. 5, 1951 (div. May 1960); 1 son, J. Christopher. Asst. prof. George Washington U., Washington, 1946-54; faculty Hunter Coll., N.Y.C., 1954—, asso. prof., 1965-68, prof., 1969—, chmn. dept. theatre and film, 1970—. Bd. dirs. Nuestro Teatro, N.Y.C., Periwinkle Prodns., N.Y.C. Served to lt. USNR, 1943-46. Fellow Am. Theatre Assn. (pres. 1973—); mem. Phi Delta Gamma (Nat. achievement award 1966). Presbyn. (elder 1960—, dir.). Author: On Stage: A History of Theatre, 1962; The Nature of Theatre, 1972. Home: 303 W 66th St New York City NY 10023

ROBERTS, VIRGINIA SWORD, bank exec.; b. Stonega, Va., Apr. 1, 1921; d. Olan Price and Mary Carelenous (Edens) Sword; elementary tchr.'s certificate Milligan Coll., 1942; grad. certificate Am. Inst. Banking, 1969; student Cannon Trust Sch., U. N.C. at Charlotte, 1970; grad. certificate Southeastern Trust Sch. and Campbell Coll., 1971; m. Ferris Ralph Roberts, Apr. 30, 1944 (div. 1958); 1 dau., Pamela R. Kellejian. Clk. Seaboard Airline Ry., Portsmouth, Va., 1943-47, Wallace Candy Co., Bklyn., 1948-49; dept. mgr. Manifold Supplies, Inc., Bklyn., 1950-51; bookkeeper Am. Nat. Bank, Portsmouth, Va., 1957-59, new accounts receptionist, 1959-61, supr., 1961-63, adminstrv. asst., 1963-66, asst. cashier, 1966-69, asst. v.p., 1969-71, trust officer, 1971—, also mem. pension and profit sharing coms., 1967—. Mem. women's com. Portsmouth Area United Fund, 1968-70. Recipient K. L. F. award Am. Inst. Banking Dist. (Tidewater chpt.), Mem. Nat. Assn. Bank Women (treas. Tidewater Va. group 1968-69, sec. 1969-70, vice chmn. 1970-71, chmn. 1971-72, adv. com. 1973-74), Am. Bus. Women's Assn. (program chmn. Portsmouth chpt. 1971-72), Portsmouth C. of C. (local legislative com. 1973-74, bldg. equipment com. 1974—). Mem. Christian Ch. (tchr. 1958-71; financial sec. 1968-71). Home: 2901 Bayview Blvd Portsmouth VA 23707 Office: 234 High St Portsmouth VA 23704

ROBERTSON, AMY, farm mgr.; b. Promise City, Ia., Aug. 28, 1897; d. Greenleaf Lincoln and Iona Robertson; B.A. in Music, Simpson Coll., 1921, H.H.D. (hon.), 1974; postgrad. Chgo. Musical Coll., 1935; M.A. in Music, De Paul U., 1935. Tchr., Audubon (Ia.) pub. sch., 1921-43; music supr. Smit Rob Craft Shop, Promise City, 1943-46; tchr. Wayne Community Sch., Corydon, Ia., 1950-51, Allerton Community Sch., 1951-52; now farm mgr. 1400 acres in Wayne and Appanoose counties. Chmn. Wayne County (Ia.) Hist. Soc., 1949—. Mem. Promise City town council, 1970—. Bd. dirs. Ia. Local Hist. Museum Assn., 1969—; trustee Simpson Coll., Indianola, Ia., 1950—; mem. bd. Wayne County Hosp., 1955—. Recipient Outstanding Citizens award Wayne County Jr. C. of C., 1974. Mem. Beta Sigma Phi (hon.). Home and office: Promise City IA 52583

ROBERTSON, BRENDA MARY TUBB (MRS. WILMOT WALDON ROBERTSON), Canadian govt. ofcl.; b. Sussex, N.B., Can., May 23, 1929; d. John James and Clara (Rothwell) Tubb; B.S. in Home Econs., Mt. Allison U.; L.H.D. (hon.), Mount Saint Vincent U., 1973; m. Wilmot Waldon Robertson, July 23, 1955; children—Douglas John, Leslie Rae, Tracy Beth. Formerly With Dept. Agr., (Can.) mem. N.B. Legislature from Albert County, 1967—; minister Youth and Social Services, 1970—. Pres. N.B. Womens Progressive Conservative Assn., 1968; mem. Coverdale Womens Progressive Conservative Assn. Mem. N.B. Home Econs. Assn. (provincial pres. 1952-53). Home: 821 Yale Av Riverview NB Canada Office: Box 6500 Centennial Bldg Fredericton NB Canada

ROBERTSON, DOROTHY SAGE (MRS. JAMES TAYLOR ROBERTSON), newspaperwoman; b. Englewood Cliffs, N.J.; d. Alfred Elwood and Edina (Person) Sage; m. James Taylor Robertson, Mar. 4, 1921; children—James Taylor II, Alfred Sage, John Alastair. Food editor, feature writer Richmond (Va.) Times-Dispatch, 1939—, columnist The Mixing Bowl, 1939—. Mem. adv. com. Nat. Food Editors' Conf., 1957; mem. consumer adv. com. Va. Dept. Agr., 1969-71; mem. Va. Council Health and Med. Care, 1946—. Writer food bulls. and films U.S. Q.M. Corps, Ft. Lee, Va., World War II. Mem. Pi Beta Phi. Episcopalian. Club: Richmond Woman's. Home: 3730 Brookside Rd Richmond VA 22523 Office: 333 E Grace St Richmond VA 23219

ROBERTSON, JUDITH YOUNG (MRS. CHARLES FRANCIS ROBERTSON), ednl. adminstr.; b. Mpls., Mar. 18, 1935; d. Eugene Cecil and Virginia Brunin (Cheyney) Young; certificate in fine art Atlanta Art Inst., 1956; B.F.A., Atlanta Sch. Art, 1970; m. Charles Francis Robertson, May 28, 1956; children—Frances Young, Julia Young, Charles Young. Cartographic draftsman U.S. Fish and Wildlife Service, Atlanta, 1956-57; sec. Atlanta Sch. Art, Atlanta, 1966, bus. mgr., 1972—, registrar, 1969—. Mem. Ga. Mineral Soc., Ga. Conservancy. Home: 1986 Westminster Way NE Atlanta GA 30307 Office: 1280 Peachtree St NE Atlanta GA 30309

ROBERTSON, LANA RUTH (MRS. VANNIE RALPH ROBERTSON), horse trainer; b. Sullivan, Ind., July 20, 1944; d. Everett Dwight and Violet June (Goodman) Bedwell; grad. high sch.; m. Vannie Ralph Robertson, Sept. 21, 1963; children—Scott Welker, Dustin Lee and Deanna Lynne (twins). Driver harness horses, 1960—; co-owner Robertson Stable, Carlisle, Ind., 1963—. Mem. U.S. Trotting Assn. Democrat. Methodist. Home: Route 2 Carlisle IN 47838

ROBERTSON, MARCIANA KATHLEEN, speech therapist; b. Denver, Aug. 27, 1945; d. Kenneth H. and Olive S. (Shields) Robertson; B.A., U. Denver, 1967; M.A., St. Joseph Coll., 1972; postgrad. audiology Boston U. Speech therapist Co-op. Hosps., Denver, 1967-68, Mansfield (Conn.) Tng. Center, 1968-69; pub. health speech and hearing therapist Conn. Dept. Pub. Health, Hartford, 1969-74. Mem. Am., Conn. assns. for mental deficiency, Am., Conn. speech and hearing assns., Conn. Assn. for Children with Perceptual Learning Handicaps. Home: PO Box 9111 South Denver Station Denver CO 80209 Office: 79 Elm St Hartford CT 06115

ROBERTSON, MARILYN COOPER (MRS. ALFRED W. ROBERTSON), television commentator; b. Victor, N.Y., July 12; d. Winfield Henry and Elzey (Carroll) Cooper; student Rollins Coll., 1921; m. William Layton Waterman, Feb. 14, 1925 (div. 1932); children—Douglas Arthur, Robert Hamilton; m. 2d, Alfred W. Robertson, Jan. 26, 1948 (dec. Jan. 1958). Soloist, Radio Sta. WGN, Chgo., 1931; staff soprano Saturday Night Nat. Barn Dance on Sta. WLS, NBC, Chgo., 1932-36, also soloist CBS; commentator CBS, N.Y.C., also Hollywood, Cal., 1938-40; originator news press show Hollywood News Club; capt. Hollywood Canteen Snack-Bar, 1942-45; commentator Channel 6, Meet Your Neighbor Pilot Show, Leisure World, Laguna Hills, Cal., 1970—. Mem. Santa Barbara Coral Casino, D.A.R., Internat. Platform Assn. Home: 2156-G Via Mariposa E Laguna Hills CA 92653 Office: Laguna Hills CA 92653

ROBERTSON, MARION DOANE (MRS. DONALD MACKENZIE ROBERTSON), author; b. Somerville, Mass., Oct. 30, 1910; d. Bertram and Nina (Smith) Doane; M. Liberal Arts, Mount Allison Ladies Coll., 1932; m. Donald MacKenzie Robertson, Aug. 9, 1944. Mem. Shelburne Hist. Soc. (sec. 1947). Author: Old Settlers' Remedies, 1961; Red Earth—Tales of the Micmacs, 1969; The Family of Donald McKay, 1970; Rock Drawings of the Mic Mac Indians, 1973; articles pub. in various newspapers, books, mags. Home: Shelburne NS Canada

ROBERTSON, MARY ELLA, ednl. adminstr., social worker; b. Lake Charles, La., Sept. 5, 1924; d. John and Mildred (Gardner) Robertson; B.A. summa cum laude, Xavier U., 1947; M.S.W., Atlanta U., 1949; advanced certificate in social work, Smith Coll., 1955; research fellow Adminstrv. Sci. Center, U. Pitts., 1959-60; D.Social Work, U. Pitts., 1962. Psychiat. social worker VA, Montrose, N.Y., 1949-53; supr. social services Family Service Assn., Ann Arber, Mich., 1953-54; asst. prof. Case Western Res. U. Sch. Social Work, Cleve., 1955-57; exec. dir. Cleve. Guidance Center, 1957-59; asst. dean, asso. prof. U. Pitts. Grad. Sch. Social Work, 1962-66; vis. prof., asst. dean curriculum devel. U. Wis., Milw., 1966-67; dean, prof. Howard U. Sch. Social Work, Washington, 1967-69; prof. Boston Coll. Grad. Sch. Social Work, Chestnut Hill, Mass., 1969-72; prof. social service Ind. U.-Purdue U. at Indpls., 1972-74; v.p. for community services at Gov.'s State U., Park Forest South, Ill., 1974—. Cons. social services various state and govt. agys. Mem. adminstrv. rev. panel child welfare policies Office of Children and Youth, Harrisburg, Pa., 1964-65; mem. com. on profl. edn. Comprehensive Mental Health Study Com. for Pa., 1964-66; mem. adv. com. to pres. Mt. Mercy Coll., Pitts., 1965-68; mem. adv. com. to sec. labor and industry Commonwealth of Pa., 1965-66. Bd. dirs. Human Life Found., Washington, Parents and Childrens Services Children's Mission, Boston. Named Pitts. Woman of Year Mayor's Com. on Pub. Service, 1965; Outstanding Alumna, Atlanta U. Sch. Social Work, 1969; Dau. Commonwealth of Pa. Mem. Nat. Assn. Social Workers, Council on Social Work Edn. (past chmn. nat. com. on admissions, mem. dean's adv. com., mem. Ho. of Dels. 1967-70), Pitts. Commn. Cath. Charities (del. assembly), Kappa Gamma Pi, Alpha Kappa Mu. Contbr. articles to profl. jours. Home: 3440 N Lake Shore Dr Apt G-10 Chicago IL 60657

ROBERTSON, MARY HELEN BASSETT (MRS. RAYMOND E. ROBERTSON), lawyer; b. Oak Park, Ill., Nov. 3, 1923; d. James J. and Isabelle S. Bassett; B.S., U. Chgo., 1945; J.D., Northwestern U., 1974; m. Raymond E. Robertson, May 25, 1946; children—Linda, James. Intern med. dept. Eastman Kodak Co., Rochester, N.Y., 1945-46; now asso. firm Hopkins, Sutter, Owen, Mulroy & Davis, Chgo. Pres. League Women Voters Hinsdale, 1957-59; bd. dirs. League Women Voters Ill., Chgo., 1959-63, v.p., 1963-67, pres. 1967-71. Mem. Ill. Commn. on Status Women, 1967, Ill. Com. for 1970 White House Conf. on Children and Youth; sec. Citizen's Com. for New Contstn. Bd. dirs. Ill. Com. Constl. Conv. Mem. U. Chgo. Alumni Assn., Phi Beta Kappa. Home: 3518 Madison St Oak Brook Hinsdale IL 60521 Office: 1 First Nat Plaza Chicago IL 60603

ROBERTSON, MARY PATRICIA (PEIRCE) (MRS. RICHARD E. ROBERTSON), librarian, educator; b. Key West, Fla., Jan. 10, 1942; d. Robert P. and Jemeile (Seamon) Peirce; B.S. magna cum laude (Centennial honor scholar), La. State U., 1963, M.S., 1964; M.Edn., Southeastern La. U., 1973; postgrad. Rutgers U., 1974—; m. Richard E. Robertson, June 15, 1969; 1 dau., Stephanie Dawn. Young adult librarian Enoch Pratt Free Library, Balt., 1964-65, adminstrv. asst., 1965-66; reference librarian Balt. Jr. Coll., 1966-67; library specialist and tchr. Ednl. Media Center, Covington, La., 1967-70; field librarian St. Tammany Parish Sch. Bd., Covington, 1967-70; librarian Southeast La. Hosp., Mandeville, 1970-73, coordinator adult edn., 1972-73; asst. prof. library and learning resources Bergen Community Coll., Paramus, N.J., 1973—. Tchr., cons. in reading, library work and spl. edn.; prodn. asso. CBS summer semester 1974. Mem. Am. Assn. U. Women (v.p.), Delta Kappa Gamma, Phi Kappa Phi, Mu Sigma Rho, Beta Phi Mu, Alpha Lambda Delta, Kappa Delta Pi, Tau Kappa Alpha. Home: 715 Lincoln Av Glen Rock NJ 07452 Office: Bergen Community College 400 Paramus Rd Paramus NJ 07652

ROBERTSON, MAY ROSE, librarian; b. Donaldsonville, La., May 17, 1924; d. Clarence J. and Rose (Juneau) Robertson; B.S., La. State U., 1943, B.S. in L.S., 1944, spl. student, 1944-46; student overseas program U. Md., 1960-61. Librarian La. State U. Library, 1944-46, U.S. Dept. Army, Bayreuth and Coburg, Germany, 1946-48, Ft. Riley (Kan.) Army Library, 1949, Mitchel AFB, N.Y., 1950-51, Hdqrs. 14th Air Force, Warner Robins, Ga., 1951-52, U.S. Dept. Army Library Program, Germany, 1952-62, Nat. Agrl. Library, Washington, 1962-65, F.D.A. Library, Arlington, Va., 1965-67, U.S. Dept. Transp. Library, Washington, 1967—. Mem. Spl. Libraries Assn., Am. Soc. Information Sci., Nat. Microfilm Assn., Library Automation, Research and Cons. Assn., Beta Phi Mu, Alpha Lambda Delta, Phi Kappa Phi, Kappa Delta Pi, Phi Sigma Iota. Democrat. Roman Catholic. Home: 3341 Ardley Ct Falls Church VA 22041 Office: Technical Processing Branch U S Dept of Transportation Library Washington DC 20590

ROBERTS-ROSE, MARION MARKELS, interior designer; b. Dneporpetrovsk, USSR (naturalized 1907); d. Ceasar and Elizabeth (Tull) Markels; student Am. Internat. Coll., 1919-20, N.Y Sch. Fine Applied Arts, 1921-22, 29; m. S. Ruben Roberts, Jan. 1, 1925 (dec. 1953); children—Jay Carleton, Margot Markels (Mrs. Ralph Cohen); m. 2d, Iver Rose, Mar. 23, 1956. Interior decorator Hampton House, 1937-45; owner Marion M. Roberts, decorating bus., Springfield, Mass., 1945—; lectr., tchr. interior decorating, painting, floral arrangements, 1937—. Mem. Springfield Fine Arts Com., 1973-75. Mem. Am. Inst. Decorators, Springfield Adult Edn., Springfield Symphony Orchestra Assn., Smithsonian Inst., George Walter Vincent Smith Mus., Springfield Library and Mus. Assn., Mus. Fine Arts, Modern Mus. Art. N.Y.C., Inst. Practising Designers, London Eng. (hon.), Literary Forum. Club: Crestview Country, Springfield Garden. Address: 210 Maple St Springfield MA 01105

ROBEY, DIANE MARGARET, co-owner drug store chain; b. Watsonville, Cal., Feb. 19, 1939; d. Paul Charles and Audrey Margaret (Newman) Robey; A.A., Monterey Peninsula Coll., 1959. Co-owner, Economy Drug Co., Watsonville, 1959—; v.p. Crown Leasing Corp., Watsonville, 1961—. Treas., Pajaro Valley Fedn. Republican Women, 1966-67, 71. Mem. Am. Philatelic Soc. Mem. Order Eastern Star. Presbyn. (deacon 1971-73). Home: 14-A Jefferson St Watsonville CA 95076 Office: PO Box 930 Watsonville CA 95076

ROBEY, KATHLEEN MORAN (MRS. RALPH WEST ROBEY), club woman; b. Boston, Aug. 9, 1909; d. John Joseph and Katherine (Berrigan) Moran; B.A., Trinity Coll., Washington, 1933; m. Ralph West Robey, Jan. 28, 1941. Actress appearing in Pride and Prejudice, Broadway, 1935, Tomorrow is a Holiday, road co., 1935, Death Takes a Holiday, road co., 1936, Left Turn, Broadway, 1936, Come Home to Roost, Boston, 1936; pub. relations N.Y. Fashion Industry, N.Y.C., 1938-43. Mem. Florence Crittenton Home and Hosp., Women's Aux. Salvation Army, Gray Lady, A.R.C.; mem. Seton Guild St. Ann's Infant Home. Mem. English-Speaking Union, Internat. Platform Assn. Republican. Roman Catholic. Clubs: Springdale Hall (Camden, S.C.); City Tavern, Cosmos (Washington), Woman's Republican. Home: 4000 Cathedral Av NW Washington DC 20016

ROBICHAUD, BERYL, pub. co. exec.; b. N.Y.C.; d. Walter and Marjorie (Huneke) Robichaud; B.A. cum laude, Mt. Holyoke Coll., 1940; M.A., Columbia, 1967; Ph.D., Rutgers U., 1971; m. Arthur B. Collins. Sec. edn. IBM Endicott, N.Y., 1940-42; mgr. contract termination system Sperry Gyroscope div. Sperry Rand Corp., Lake Success, N.Y., 1942-46; with McGraw-Hill, Inc., Hightstown, N.J., 1946—, systems mgr. accounting, 1946-50, gen. mgr. centralized services, 1950-57, asst. v.p. data processing, 1957-61, v.p., 1961-69, v.p. corporate mgmt. information services, 1969-71, sr. v.p., 1971—; asso. prof. grad. faculty Rutgers U., also research asso. Inst. Environmental Studies, 1971—. Dir. investment cos. Anchor Corp., Aetna Life & Casualty Co. Mem. N.J. State Planning Task Force, 1973—, mem. Gov.'s Adv. Council Future N.J., 1973; mem. Information Scis. Adv. Com. N.J. Dept. Higher Edn., 1973—; mem. Nat. Inst. Neurol. Diseases and Stroke, NIH, 1971—. Trustee Mt. Holyoke Coll. 1966—, Rider Coll., 1971—. Recipient Alumnae medal of honor Mt. Holyoke Coll. 1970. Mem. A.A.A.S., Ecol. Soc. Am., N.J. Acad. Sci., Data Processing Mgmt., Inst. Mgmt. Sci., Sigma Xi. Author: Scheduling, Planning, and Managing Office Space, 1958; Understanding Modern Business Data Processing, 1966; co-author: Vegetation of New Jersey: A Study in Landscape Diversity, 1973. Home: Fairway Dr Princeton NJ 08540 Office: McGraw-Hill Inc Princeton Rd Hightstown NJ 08520

ROBICHAUX, JOLYN HOWARD, ice cream co. exec.; b. Cairo, Ill., May 21, 1928; d. Edward C. and Margaret (Love) Howard; A.B., Chgo. State U., 1960; m. Joseph J. Robichaux, June 7, 1952 (dec. Apr. 1971); children—Sheila Veronica, Joseph Howard. Midwest rep. Betty Crocker home service dept. Gen. Mills Co., 1960-65; with Charles A. Davis & Assos., pub. relations, 1965-67; with Baldwin Ice Cream Co., Chgo., 1967—, pres., gen. mgr., 1971—; nutrition cons. Stste Dept. in Africa, 1956. Mem. Cook County (Ill.) Jury Commn., 1971-72. Recipient Community Service award Chgo. Jaycees, 1973; One of Ten Outstanding Black Bus. Persons award, Chgo. Blackbook, 1973. Roman Catholic. Club: Chgo. Women's Golf. Office: 4825 S Indiana Av Chicago IL 60615

ROBIE, KATHLEEN LYNCH (MRS. WILLIAM F. ROBIE), civic worker, state ofcl.; b. Knoxville, Tenn., May 27, 1919; d. Abel P. and Jessie (Seabolt) Lynch; m. William F. Robie, May 2, 1936; children—Eileen (Mrs. Norval R. Stephens), Nancy (Mrs. Martin George Hill), William F. Asst. statis. sect. chief U.S. Census Bur., Washington, 1940-41; sec. to powder expert Naval Powder Factory, Indian Head, Md., 1941-43, accountant, 1944-46; chief accountant Nat. Housing Agy., Potomac Heights, Md., 1943-44; sec. to chief So. lumber OPS, Washington, 1952-54; asst. to career devel. officer Bolling AFB, Washington, 1960-61; office mgr. regional office McCormick and Co., 1961-62. Chmn. high sch. services Md. Congress Parents and Tchrs., 1954-60, pres., 1960-63, sch. edn. chmn., 1963-66, hon. pres., 1973; nat. bd. mgrs. Nat. Congress Parents and Tchrs., 1960-67, mem. exec. com., 1962-63, nat. program service chmn., also hon. life mem.; judge Nat. Safety Patrol Lifesaving Medal, 1960-64; nat. publicity dir. Nat. Home Demonstration Council (now Nat. Homemakers Extension Council), 1958-61; past pres. Md. State Council Homemakers' Clubs, Charles County Homemakers' Clubs: pres. Prince George's County Extension Homemakers, 1971-73. Mem. Gov.'s Commn. Phys. Fitness, 1961-66, Gov.'s Com. to Keep Md. Beautiful, 1955-63; v.p. Md. Consumers Council, 1962-66; mem. Md. State Bd. Edn., 1963—, also mem. steering com. legislation and planning com. ann. edn. conf.; adv. com. adoption State Dept. Pub. Welfare, 1962-65; del. Md. Constl. Conv., 1966-68; mem. Pres.'s Ad Hoc Nat. Vol. Orgns.' Adv. Com. Consumer Interests; mem Nat. Citzens Com. Better Schs., Nat. Com. for Support Pub. Schs.; 1st v.p. Tb and Respiratory Disease Assn. So. Md., 1972—. Trustee State Tchrs. Coll., Towson, Md., State Tchrs. Coll., Frostburg, Md.,

Salisbury State Tchrs. Coll., Bowie State Coll., Coppin State Coll., Balt.; exec. dir. Prince George's County Assn. Mental Health; mem. Nat. Assn. Mental Health Staff Council; del. World Food Congress, 1964; dir.-at-large Nat. Assn. State Bds. Edn., 1966-67, v.p. N.E. area, 1969-71; vice chmn. Gov.'s Commn. on Malnutrition, 1969. Recipient Outstanding Leadership award U. Md., 1960; award Prince George's County Tchrs. Assn.; award Phi Delta Kappa, 1966. Mem. Asso. Country Women of World (del. internat. conf., 1953, 59, 65, 68, 71, 74), Country Women's Council, Tchrs. Edn. and Profl. Standards, Md. Tchrs. Assn., Delta Kappa Gamma (hon.). Home: Mt Carmel Woods Route 4 Box 4153 La Plata MD 20646

ROBIN, EVA EFFRON (MRS. EDWIN J. ROBIN), lawyer; b. Paterson, N.J.; d. William and Lena (Jeffe) Effron; LL.B., N.Y. U., 1920; m. Edwin J. Robin, Jan. 21, 1923; children—Richard, Jane (Mrs. Alfred W. deJonge). Admitted to N.Y. bar, 1921, Conn. bar, 1926; practice law, Stamford, Conn., 1926—. Moderator Stamford br. Gt. Books Found.; mem. Stamford Museum. Mem. Rep. Town Com., Stamford. Mem. Conn., Stamford bar assns., Am. Fedn. Art, Technion, Delta Phi Epsilon (co-founder). Mem. Hadassah. Address: 113 Old North Stamford Rd Stamford CT 06900

ROBINDER, CATHERINE MAE FITZPATRICK (MRS. WALLACE R. ROBINDER), mathematician; b. East Moline, Ill., July 24, 1922; d. Walter H. and Belva M. (Westerfield) Fitzpatrick; A.B. cum laude, Augustana Coll., 1956; M.S., U. Ia., 1961; m. Wallace R. Robinder, Nov. 5, 1966. Draftsman, Rock Island (Ill.) Arsenal, 1942-45, Swanson & Maiwald, Architects, Moline, Ill., 1946-47; mathematician Rock Island Arsenal, 1948—. Cons. field stress analysis. Recipient Rock Island Arsenal spl. award for published article, 1966, for outstanding analysis work, 1960, 69. Mem. Am. Math. Soc., Am. Assn. U. Women (br. treas. 1962-65), Illowa Gem and Mineral Soc., Sigma Xi. Baptist (chmn. music com. 1963—, financial sec. 1956-63, youth work com. 1954-71). Club: Blackhawk Gem and Mineral (v.p., program chmn. 1967, pres. 1972—). Home: 2115 25th Av Rock Island IL 61201 Office: Rock Island Arsenal Rock Island IL 61201

ROBINETTE, ADELLA ELEANOR THROOP HOLMAAS (MRS. JAY H. ROBINETTE), journalist; b. Detroit; d. William B. and Almira (McGregor) Throop; student occupational therapy Cass Tech. Sch., Detroit, 1924-27, Walter Reed Hosp., Army Med. Center, 1930-31; m. John Severin Holmaas, June 2, 1937 (dec. April 1968); 1 son, John William; m. 2d, Jay H. Robinette, Jan. 1, 1973. Clk., Detroit Edison Co., 1922-24; occupational therapist F.B. Leland Sanitorium, Ypsilanti, Mich., 1927-28, Vets. Hosp., Marion, Ind., 1928-30, U.S. Indian Hosps., Lapwai, Ida., 1931-34, Tacoma, 1934-38; news corr. Tacoma News Tribune, 1954-67; Gig Harbor reporter Radio Sta. KTNT, Tacoma, 1971—; N.W. regional editor Pen Woman mag., 1972—. Free-lance writer non-fiction for mags., 1959—. Pres., Peninsula Elementary P.T.A., 1953-54. Mem. Nat. League Am. Pen Women (pres. Tacoma br. 1968-70, state pres. 1970-72), Washington Occupational Therapy Assn., Dist. Assn. Gig Harbor Lady Mchts. (hon.), Peninsula Helmsmen, Daus. of Nile. Methodist. Mem. Order Eastern Star. Home: PO Box 381 Gig Harbor WA 98335

ROBINETTE, VIVIEN LUCILE BROOKER (MRS. JAMES F. ROBINETTE), author; b. Rogers, Tex.; d. William Theodore and Annie Emma (Smith) Brooker; student pub. schs.; m. James F. Robinette, Mar. 3, 1928. Author: We Moved to California, 1951; Down Catnip Trail, 1955; Orchestra of Storm, 1955; Mr. Tipps, 1956; Poems, 1956; Wind in the Night, 1964; (booklet) Three Famous Cats, 1969; Now In November, 1973; Four Paws, 1974; contbr. poems to mags. and anthologies. Mem. Cal. Fedn. Chaparral Poets. Home: 2021 Primrose Av South Pasadena CA 91030

ROBINS, LUCILLE MARIE (MRS. WILLIAM RANDOLPH ROBINS, JR.), civic worker, author; b. Buffalo, Dec. 4, 1912; d. Alfred Jacque and Bertha Christine (Schutt) LeCocq; B.S., Cornell U., 1934; m. William Randolph Robins, Jr., Nov. 6, 1937; children—William Randolph III, Alfred LeCocq. State dir. New Eyes for the Needy, Inc., 1966—; dir. Conservative Art Center, 1962-67. Chmn., committeewoman Republican Women Orgn., 1955-60. Mem. state bd. dirs. Nat. Assn. Prevention Blindness, 1964—. Mem. Kappa Delta (nat. bd. 1965-68), Oklahoma City Alumni Assn. (pres. 1962-64). Club: Garden (pres. 1967-68). Author: The Susannah Betsy Stories, 1969. Contbr. articles, stories mags. One man shows Okla. Art Gallery, Red Ridge Art Gallery. Home: 3109 Elmwood St Oklahoma City OK 73116

ROBINS, MARJORIE McCARTHY (MRS. GEORGE KENNETH ROBINS), civic worker; b. St. Louis, Oct. 4, 1914; d. Eugene Ross and Louise (Roblee) McCarthy; A.B., Vassar Coll., 1936; diploma St. Louis Sch. Occupational Therapy, 1940; m. George Kenneth Robins, Nov. 9, 1940; children—Carol (Mrs. Joseph A. Von Arx), G. Stephen, Barbara A. (Mrs. David Foorman). Mem. Mo. Library Commn., 1937-38; mem. bd. St. Louis Jr. League, 1945, 46, Occupational Therapy Workshop of St. Louis, 1941-46 (pres. 1945, 46); mem. bd. Ladue Chapel Nursery Sch., 1957-60, 61-64, pres. bd. 1963, 64; formerly regional chmn. United Fund; former mem. St. Louis Met. Youth Commn., St. Louis Health and Welfare Council; mem. bd. Internat. Inst. of St. Louis, 1966—, sec., 1968, 2d v.p., 1969, 70; mem. bd. Mental Health Assn. St. Louis, 1963-70, Washington U. Child Guidance and Evaluation Clinic, 1968—, Central Inst. for Deaf, 1970—; mem. bd. Met. St. Louis YWCA, 1954-63, 64—, pres. bd., 1960-63, co-chmn. YM-YW intercampus project, 1967-70; mem. nat. bd. YWCA, 1967—, nat. v.p., 1973—; vol. tchr. remedial reading clinic St. Louis City Schs., 1968-71. Trustee John Burroughs Sch., 1960-63, John Burroughs Found., 1965-70. Clubs: Vassar (sec. and pres. 1939-40), Wednesday (mem. bd. 1968-70) (St. Louis). Home: 45 Loren Woods St Louis MO 63124

ROBINS-MOWRY, DOROTHY, fgn. service officer; b. Bklyn., Sept. 21, 1921; d. William Albert and Emma J. (Koffre) Robins; B.A., Coll. Wooster, 1942, LL.D., 1966; M.A., Columbia, 1944; Ph.D., N.Y.U., 1960; m. David T. Mowry, Oct. 16, 1971. Dir. edn. Am. Assn. UN, 1944-52; program cons. Fgn. Policy Assn., N.Y.C., 1953-57, 63; asso. internat. relations Am. Assn. U. Women, Washington, 1957-62; fgn. service reserve officer USIA, 1963-70, fgn. service information officer, 1st. sec., 1970—; cultural programs officer Am. embassy, Tokyo, Japan, 1963-71; project mgr. Program Devel. on Polit. and Social Processes Am. Soc., 1974—; vis. research scholar Radcliffe Inst., 1971-72. Mem. exec. com., mem. edn. com. U.S. Com. for UN, 1957-63; exec. com. Women's Africa Com., 1960-63; chmn. Conf. Group of U.S. Orgns. on UN, 1963. Recipient Meritorious Honor award USIA, 1967. Am. Assn. U. Women Ednl. Found. grantee, 1971; Nat. Endowment for Humanities grantee, 1972. Mem. Am. Newspaper Women's Assn., Fgn. Corrs. Club Japan, Am. Polit. Sci. Assn., Am. Assn. U. Women, Assn. Phi Beta Kappa, Phi Alpha Theta, Phi Sigma Iota, Pi Sigma Alpha. Author: Evolving U.S. Policies Toward the Emerging Nations of Asia and Africa, 1961; UN in World Affairs, 1955; Experiment in Democracy, 1971. Home: 2737 Devonshire Place NW Washington DC 20008 Office: USIA Washington DC

ROBINSON, AGNES SOUTAR, educator; b. Chgo., Mar. 20, 1918; d. Forrest Glen and Roselle (Burns) Soutar; A.B. with honors, Cal. State U., San Francisco, 1949; M.A. in Sch. Adminstrn., Cal. State U. at Sacramento, 1952; Ed.D. in Ednl. Psychology, U. of the Pacific, 1957; div.; children—Harold H., Forrest G., Ross A. Tchr. primary pub. schs. Sacramento City Sch. Dist., Sacramento, 1949-51, speech therapist, 1951-54, sch. psychologist, dir. spl. edn., 1955-62; asst. to dep. supt. spl. programs, 1962-66, asst. supt. curriculum devel., 1966-68; asso. prof. edn. Cal. State U., Sacramento, 1968-71, prof. edn., 1971—, chmn. dept. ednl. adminstrn., 1973—. Cons., Peat, Marwick, Mitchell & Co., also sch. dists., ednl. agys. Vice chmn. Cal. Adv. Com. on Program and Cost Effectiveness, 1969-71; chmn. edn. com. Sacramento Community Commn. for Women, 1971-72; mem. Cal. adv. com. U.S. Commn. Civil Rights, 1974. Named Edn. Alumnus of the Year, U. Pacific, 1974. Mem. Am. Assn. Sch. Adminstrn., Am. Ednl. Research Assn., Am. Psychol. Assn., Assn. for Supervision and Curriculum Devel., Am. Assn. Univ. Women. Home: 925 Commons Dr Sacramento CA 95825 Office: California State Univ 6000 Jay St Sacramento CA 95819

ROBINSON, ALICE BIRMINGHAM (MRS. DAVID ROBINSON), educator; b. Manlius, N.Y., Sept. 29, 1924; d. Carl Prescott and Anna (Aungst) Birmingham; B.A., Wellesley Coll., 1946; M.A., Radcliffe Coll., 1947; Ph.D., Harvard, 1957; m. Charles G. Colburn, June 28, 1946 (div. Dec. 1965); children—Elizabeth Anne, Janet Patricia, Nancy Jean, Edward Goodspeed; m. 2d, David A. Robinson, June 7, 1968. Instr., Wellesley (Mass.) Coll., 1947-55, asst. prof., 1955-61, asso. prof., 1961-67, prof., 1967—, chmn. dept. history, 1968-71, 73-74. Mem. Am. Hist. Assn. Conf. on Brit. Studies. Home: 55 Denton Rd Wellesley MA 02181

ROBINSON, ALICE MERRITT, editor; b. Islip, N.Y., Dec. 4, 1920; d. William Beverly and Le Van (Cowell) Robinson; R.N., Duke, 1944; B.S., Cath. U. Am., 1948; M.S., Boston U., 1950. Psychiat. nurse coordinator George Washington U. Hosp., 1946-48; psychiat. nurse supr. VA Hosp., North Little Rock, Ark., 1948-49; teaching fellow Boston U., 1949-50; dir. nursing and nursing edn. Boston State Hosp., Dorchester, Mass., 1950-55; dir. nursing edn. Vt. State Hosp., Waterbury, 1956-63; editor Nursing Outlook, N.Y.C., 1963-71; sr. nursing editor RN Mag., Oradell, N.J., 1971—; cons. VA; lectr.; workshop and seminar leader; free lance writer; dir. East Harlem Nursing Council, Nurse's House, Inc. Chmn. Nat. Conf. Group Psychiat. Nursing, 1958-62. Mem. Am. Nurses Assn., Nat. League Nursing, Am. Heart Assn., Council Cardiovascular Nursing. Author: Working with the Mentally Ill, 1954; The Unbelonging, 1958; (with Mary E. Reres) Your Future in Careers in Nursing, 1972. Contbr. articles profl. jours. Home: 700 West End Av New York City NY 10025 Office: 496 Kinderkamack Rd Oradell NJ 07649

ROBINSON, ANNE DURRUM (MRS. HAROLD G. ROBINSON), state ofcl.; b. Hugo, Okla., May 14, 1913; d. William Landon and Effie Anne (Lear) Durrum; B.J., Tex. Women's U., 1935; M.A., U. Tex., 1960; m. Harold G. Robinson, June 6, 1945; 1 dau., Marye Lear. Staff writer NBC, Hollywood, Cal., 1945; continuity editor KTBC, Austin, 1942-44, KNOW Radio, Austin, 1946-49; KASE, hostess TV program Sta. KTBC-TV, Austin, 1955-56; editor Sta. KASE, Austin, 1959-61; hostess KLRN-TV, Austin, 1961-63, KHFI-TV, Austin, 1966-67; mng. editor jour., writer Travis County Med. Soc., Travis County Med. Soc. Blood Bank and Med. Exchange, Austin, 1961-63; free-lance writer, lectr., performer, tchr., 1968; copywriter, office mgr. David G. Benjamin, Inc., 1963-68; asst. dir. curriculum devel. Tex. Dept. Pub. Welfare, Austin, 1973—. Grantee research Women in Communications, Inc., 1959, 71, nat. one-act play prize Hermit Club, Cleve., 1947, 1948, three-act play prize Houston Little Theatre, 1947, song lyrics award Nat. Five Arts awards, 1947, numerous poetry prizes. Mem. Women in Communications (chpt. pres. 1952), Women's Symphony League, Internat. Platform Assn. Episcopalian. Home: 2309 Shoal Creek Blvd Austin TX 78705 Office: Fountain Park Plaza 3000 South Interregional Austin TX 78704

ROBINSON, ARNETHA THOMPSON (MRS. RICHARD PRICE ROBINSON), univ. dean; b. Lumberton, N.C., Sept. 22, 1923; d. Alexander Lee and Bessie Thompson; B.S., N.C. Central U., 1942; M.S., N.Y. U., 1951; postgrad. Columbia, 1952-54, E. Carolina U., 1965-67; m. Richard Price Robinson, June 26, 1947. Tchr. pub. schs., Fayetteville, Robeson County, 1942-70; asso. dean of students Fayetteville (N.C.) State U., 1970—. An organizer Fayetteville Youth Council, 1967-68; mem. evaluation team So. Assn. for Secondary Schs., Wilmington (N.C.) City Schs., 1967; mem. textbook commn. N.C. jr. and sr. high schs., 1963-64. Mem. Precinct 16 Voter Registration, 1961-67, sec., 1970-72. Named An Outstanding Educator of Am., 1973. Mem. Am. Assn. U. Women, N.C. Assn. Women Deans and Counselors (chmn. edn. div. 1970-73, 74-75), Links, Zeta Phi Beta. Mem. Daus. of Isis. Home: 1862 Broadell Dr Fayetteville NC 28301

ROBINSON, BARBARA VAN GAASBEEK (MRS. JOSEPH S. ROBINSON), social worker; b. Springfield, Mass., Sept. 7, 1915; d. Harold and Viola T. (Brown) Van Gaasbeek; A.B., Boston U., 1937; postgrad. N.Y. Sch. Social Work, 1944-48; M.S.W., U. Conn., 1961; postgrad. Smith Coll., 1968-69; m. Joseph S. Robinson, Nov. 27, 1957. Social caseworker Conn. Humane Soc., Hartford, 1938-49, dir. children's dept., 1949-59; sr. psychiat. social worker Undercliff Hosp., Conn. Dept. Mental Health, Meriden, 1961-63; social worker in charge Bristol office Family Service of Central Conn., 1963-66; chief psychiat. social worker Child Guidance Clinic for Central Conn., 1966—. Mem. Nat. Assn. Social Workers, Acad. Certified Social Workers, Assn. Child Guidance Clinics for Conn. (officer 1968-70), Conn. Soc. for Clin. Social Workers, Conn. Hist. Soc. Club: Soroptimist (pres. Meriden 1970-71, chmn. New Eng. regional com.). Home: 71 Southwood Rd Newington CT 06111 Office: 117 Lincoln St Meriden CT 06450

ROBINSON, DOROTHY BATTLE RANKIN (MRS. ROBERT HOUSTON ROBINSON), lawyer; b. Durham, N.C., Feb. 5, 1938; d. Robert Stanley and Dorothy (Newsom) Rankin; A.B., Duke U., 1959; LL.B., Yale, 1963; m. Robert Houston Robinson, June 12, 1970; 1 son, Robert Houston. Admitted to N.C. bar, 1963, Del. bar, 1971; atty. civil rights div. U.S. Dept. Justice, Washington, 1963-70; atty. Ho. of Reps., Dover, Del., 1971—. Mem. Gov.'s Council Women, 1972, Del. Family Ct. Revision Study Com., 1971; pres. Sussex County (Del.) Arts Council, 1972-73. Bd. dirs. Grand Opera House, 1973—. Recipient Atty. Gen.'s Sustained Superior Performance award, 1970. Mem. Phi Beta Kappa. Presbyn. Home: 112 N Bedford St Georgetown DE 19947 Office: Legislative Hall Dover DE 19901

ROBINSON, ELIZABETH ROSE PULLEY (MRS. FRANK ISAIAH ROBINSON, JR.), ednl. adminstr.; b. Longwood, N.C., Nov. 22, 1935; d. Edgar William and Gwendolyn E. (Bellamy) Pulley; A.A., Pineland Jr. Coll., 1953; B.S., East Carolina U., 1955, M.A., 1956; postgrad. (Nat. Def. Edn. Act scholar) N.C. State U., 1960-61, (tchrs. scholar) U. N.C., Chapel Hill, 1961-62; m. Frank Isaiah Robinson, Jr., Aug. 5, 1972. Tchr. English, Hobbton (N.C.) High Sch., 1956-71; dir. guidance Sampson County Bd. Edn., Clinton, N.C., 1971-73, reading specialist, 1973—. Mem. scholarship com. Lundy Found. Mem. N.E.A., N.C. Assn. Educators, Classroom Tchrs. Assn., Assn. Retarded Children, Alpha Delta Kappa (v.p. dist. VI, 1970-72). Baptist. Home: 206 Sampson St Clinton NC 28328 Office: 303-B E Rowan St Clinton NC 28328

ROBINSON, ELSA ELIZABETH (MRS. WILLIAM NELSON), psychologist; b. N.Y.C., Jan. 25, 1909; d. Elias P. and Marie (Friedland) R.; B.A., Barnard Coll., 1929; M.A., N.Y. U., 1934, Ph.D., 1937; m. William Nelson, July 13, 1930; children—Susan E. (Mrs. R. David Arkush), William A. Fellow, Judge Baker Found., Boston, 1929-30; faculty N.Y. U., 1930—, prof. psychology, 1968—, asst. dean, 1965—, dir. Washington Sq. Coll. Office Counseling Services, 1965—. Supervising editor psychology Crowell-Collier Ency., 1965-68. Fellow Am. Psychol. Assn.; mem. Eastern, N.Y. State psychol. assns., A.A.A.S., Soc. for Research in Child Devel., Phi Beta Kappa, Sigma Xi. Author: (with L.W. Crafts, T.C. Schneirla, R.W. Gilbert) Recent Experiments in Psychology, 1938, rev. edit., 1950; also articles on drug usage on coll. campuses. Home: 410 Riverside Dr New York City NY 10025

ROBINSON, ETHEL LOUISE, librarian; b. Cleve., Feb. 9, 1926; d. Edward Hunter and Louise Grace (Kroft) Robinson; B.S., Cleve. State U., 1948; M.L.S., Western Res. U., 1949, M.A., 1956. Asst. sci. and tech. dept. Cleve. Pub. Library, 1949-54, asst. order dept., 1954-64, asst. head gen. reference dept., 1964-68, head gen. reference dept., 1968-72, head main library, 1973—. Mem. A.L.A., Ohio Library Assn., Woman's Nat. Book Assn. Home: 9333 N Church Dr Parma Heights OH 44130 Office: 325 Superior Av Cleveland OH 44114

ROBINSON, EULA MAE HESTER, media center supr.; b. Rocky Mount, N.C., May 14, 1912; d. Thomas Henry and Netta Mae (Chamblee) Hester; student Mars Hill Coll., 1929-31; R.N., Ga. Bapt. Hosp. Sch. Nursing, 1934; spl. edn. courses U. N.C.; m. Mack H. Robinson, Nov. 26, 1936; children—Katheryn (Mrs. Robert K. Brotherton), Flora A. (Mrs. Wayne Garrett). Nurse, Mars Hill Coll., 1934-35, Dr. John Watkins, Asheville, N.C., 1935-39; nurse, dir. Red Bank Nursery Sch., Chattanooga, 1952-56; dir. Day Care Center, Laurinsburg, N.C., 1956-57; tchr., librarian Murdoch Center for Retarded, Butner, N.C., 1958—. Mem. N.C. Library Assn., N.C. Assn. for Retarded Children. Home: 2722 Newquay St Durham NC 27705 Office: Butner NC 27509

ROBINSON, EVELYN ROSE, educator; b. Boston, Mar. 15, 1909; d. Charles E. and Ellen Rose (Ritchie) Robinson; B.S., Boston U., 1950, Ed.M., 1951, Ed.D., 1962. Asst., Somerville (Mass.) Pub. Library, 1927-30; children's librarian Meml. Hall Library, Andover, Mass., 1940-53; sch. library supr., Andover, 1943-45; librarian Brockton (Mass.) High Sch., 1945-50; grad. asst. Boston U., 1950-51; sch. and pub. library cons. Mass. Dept. Edn., Boston, 1951-54; asst. prof. library sci. State U. Albany, N.Y., 1954-56; vis. asso. prof. U. Tenn., 1955; lectr. edn. Boston U. summer sch., 1956-59; lectr., instr. library sci. Queens Coll., Flushing, N.Y., 1956-59; vis. lectr. edn. Wheaton Coll., Norton, Mass., 1960-61; vis. instr. summer sch. edn. Clark U., Worcester, Mass., 1962; asso. prof., then prof. library sci. So. Conn. State Coll., New Haven, 1962-74, acting chmn. dept., 1967-68, dir. div. library sci., 1968-74. Mem. Com. on Evaluation Library Standards, 1958-59; mem. Red Cross Motor Corp., Andover, 1943-45. Mem. Nat. Council Tchrs. English (com. certification and preparation tchrs. English 1963-68), Canadian-Am. Women's Assn., Am., Mass., Conn. (v.p. pres. elect 1970-71, pres. 1971-72), New Eng. library assns., N.E.A., Am. Assn. Sch. Libraries (constn. com. 1965-69), Am. Ednl. Research Assn., Am. Assn. U. Women, New Eng. Sch. Library Assn. (com. library edn. 1965-68), Pi Lambda Theta. Editorial work Ginn & Co., Vanguard Press. Editor: Readings About Children's Literature, 1966. Home: 6455 La Jolla Blvd Apt 222 La Jolla CA 92037

ROBINSON, FAITH NABER (MRS. FRANK E. ROBINSON), librarian; b. Miltonvale, Kan., Sept. 27, 1920; d. Peter Gombert and Mary Orilla (Grise) Naber; A.A., Kendall Coll., Evanston, Ill., 1942; A.B., Otterbein Coll., 1944; postgrad. Hartford Sem., 1949-50; M. L.S., Ball State U., 1970; m. Frank E. Robinson, Sept. 5, 1943; children—Paul David, Mary (Mrs. Larry Howard), John Timothy, Faith (Mrs. David Gluckman), Frank Eric. Ednl. missionary Meth. Ch., Philippines, 1950-55; tchr. Mississinawa Valley Schs., Union City, O., 1957-60, librarian Ansonia (O.) High Sch., 1962-65, Wayne local schs., Waynesville, O., 1965-67, Middletown (O.) High Sch., 1967-69, Middletown Freshman Sch., 1969-70, Bluffton (O.) Pub. Library, 1970-71, H.H. Conrady Jr. High Sch., Hickory Hills, Ill., 1971—. Leader, Buckeye Trails council Girl Scouts U.S., 1955-56, Wapahani council, 1957-62. Mem. A.L.A., N.E.A., Am. Sch. Library Assn., Am. Assn. U. Women (recipient 3d prize short story, 1970), Methodist. Author 2 primers, also articles. Home: 14924 Riverside Dr Harvey IL 60426 Office: 97th and Roberts Rd Hickory Hills IL 60457

ROBINSON, FRANCES EDNA ALESANDER, ret. ednl. adminstr.; b. Council Bluffs, Ia.; d. Jay Harvey and Lulu (Smith) Alesander; B.A., La. Poly. Inst., 1939; postgrad. La. State U., 1946; M.A., U. So. Miss., 1955; m. John Harvey Robinson, Dec. 25, 1954 (div. Nov. 1955). Elementary tchr., Tallulah, La., 1925-39, high sch. tchr., 1939-42; dir. tng. 830 AFB, Memphis, 1942-46; elementary tchr. West Side Sch., Bastrop, La., 1946-54; supr. instrn. Madison Parish Schs., Tallulah, 1956-71. Partner, Alexander-Perry Real Estate Co., Bastrop, 1948—, Alexander Farm Account, Tallulah, 1945—. Pres., Madison Parish Mental Health Assn., 1965—, Madison chpt. Am. Cancer Soc., 1960-65. Mem. La. Tchrs. Assn., Assn. Supervision and Curriculum Devel., N.E.A., La. Sch. Suprs. Assn., 5th Dist. Suprs. Assn. (pres. 1960), Bus. and Profl. Women's Club, Am. Legion Aux. (pres. 1964), D.A.R. (vice regent 1970—), Colonial Dames Am., Delta Kappa Gamma (pres. 1957-58). Democrat. Methodist (tchr. young couples class 1960—, pres. Wesleyan service guild 1965-66). Mem. Order Eastern Star. Clubs: Federated Women's, Tallulah Book (pres. 1959-60). Home: 102 Cooper St Tallulah LA 71282

ROBINSON, GLADYS MABEL CHAMBERS (MRS. CARL TAPLEY ROBINSON), educator; b. New Orleans, Dec. 5, 1909; d. Oscar Louis and Susie Elizabeth (Lang) Chambers; A.B., Northwestern State Coll., 1929; M.S., U. Chgo., 1931, postgrad., 1947, 68; postgrad. Tulane U., 1932, Marine Biol. Lab., Woods Hole, Mass., 1938, U. Ill., 1955-57, Ill. Inst. Tech., 1964-65; m. Carl Tapley Robinson, Dec. 24, 1932. Asst. prof. biology Tougaloo (Miss.) Coll., 1931-41, U. Akron (O.), 1942-48; instr. George William Coll., Downers Grove, Ill., 1948-50, prof. biology, 1959—, dir. div. natural scis., 1965-73; instr. Cook County Sch. Nursing, Chgo., 1950-59. Recipient Golden Apple award for excellence in teaching, student body George Williams Coll., 1972. Ford Found. scholar, 1953, NSF scholar, 1964-65, 65, 68. Mem. Am. Assn. U. Profs., Bot. Soc. Am., Am. Soc. Microbiology, Am. Inst. Biol. Sci., Nat. Assn. Biology Tchrs., Assn. Midwest Coll. Biology Tchrs., Ill. Acad. Sci., Nature Conservancy, League for Nursing (chpt. dir. 1953-55), Phi Sigma, Sigma Delta Epsilon. Democrat. Baptist. Home: 7920 S Lafayette St Chicago IL 60620 Office: 555 31st St Downers Grove IL 60515

ROBINSON, GRUINE, govt. ofcl.; b. Petersburg, Va.; d. Samuel and Rachel (Aloof) Robinson; B.S., W.Va. U., 1948; M.P.H., Columbia, 1959. Reporter, editor A.P., Charleston, W.Va., 1944-46; editorial asst. McGraw-Hill Pub. Co., N.Y.C., 1948-51; editor A.P., Albuquerque, 1951-52, Sandia Corp., Albuquerque, 1952-56; dir. pub. information N.M. Dept. Health, Santa Fe, 1956-58; dir. Office of

Information and Tech. Publs., Div. Facilities Utilization USPHS, Dept. Health, Edn. and Welfare, Rockville, Md., 1959—. Exec. com., dir. N.M. Soc. for Crippled Children and Adults, 1957-58. Bd. dirs. Santa Fe County Tb Assn., 1957-58. Recipient Superior Service award Dept. Health, Edn. and Welfare, 1972. Mem. Am. Newspaper Womens Club, W.Va. U. Alumni Assn. (chpt. dir. 1967), Women in Communications. Home: 1311 Delaware Av SW Washington DC 20024 Office: 5600 Fishers Lane Rockville MD 20852

ROBINSON, HELEN MANSFIELD (MRS. FREDERICK W. JOBE), ret. educator, author; b. Athens, O., May 28, 1906; d. Merwin G. and Mabel Lynn (Butts) Mansfield; A.B., Ohio U., 1926; A.M., Ohio State U., 1927; Ph.D., U. Chgo., 1944; hon. doctorate Ill. Coll. Optometry, 1957; m. Frederick W. Jobe, Aug. 7, 1965. Dir. bur. spl. edn., asst. prof. Miami U., Oxford, O., 1928-31; supt., psychologist Orthogenic Sch., U. Chgo., 1931-43, instr. edn. U. Chgo., 1944-48, asst. prof., 1948-52, asso. prof., 1952-60, prof., 1960-61, Williams S. Gray Research prof. reading, 1960-68, emeritus prof., 1968—. Author Scott, Foresman & Co., Glenview, Ill., since 1960—. Recipient Apollo award Am. Optometric Assn., 1963, Citation of merit Internat. Reading Assn., 1969. Mem. Am. Ednl. Research Assn. (pres. Nat. conf. research in English 1960), Ill. Psychol. Assn., Internat. Reading Assn., Nat. Council Tchrs. English, Pi Lambda Theta. Author: Why Pupils Fail in Reading, 1946. Editor: Clinical Studies in Reading, Vol. I, 1949, Vol. II, 1953, Vol. III, 1968; Innovation and Change in Reading, 1969. Contbr. numerous articles on reading to profl. pubis. Address: 3710 Gulf of Mexico Dr Sarasota FL 33577

ROBINSON, JEANNE CROSSAN (MRS. HOWARD F. ROBINSON, JR.), pub. relations exec.; b. Oakland, Cal., Oct. 9, 1934; d. Edward Peter and Joan (Hall) Crossan; B.A., Stanford, 1956; grad. Harvard Radcliffe program in bus. adminstrn., 1957; m. Howard F. Robinson, Jr., June 7, 1958; 1 son, Scott Crossan. Market analyst Carters Ink Co., Boston, 1957; marketing research analyst W. P. Fuller & Co., San Francisco, 1957-62; econ. analyst State Dept. Employment, San Francisco, 1963-64; pub. relations dir. Jr. Center Art & Sci., Oakland, Cal., 1967-72; asso. Boyden Assos., Inc., San Francisco, 1973—. Radio-Television chmn. KQED auction, 1968-74. Pub. relations chmn. 1971, Harvard Bus. Sch. Western Regional Conf.; bd. regents Santa Clara U., 1973—. Mem. Harvard Bus. Sch. Club No. Cal. (publicity chmn. 1968-71, pres. 1972-74, Harvard Bus. Sch. Alumni recruiting rep. to Mills Coll.). Home: 126 Dudley Av Piedmont CA 94611

ROBINSON, LAURETTA DEBORAH, lawyer, bank exec.; b. Bayside, N.Y., Aug. 18, 1914; d. Henry and Lauretta (Fitz Gerald) Robinson; A.B., Cornell U., 1934, LL.B., 1944; student N.Y. Inst. Finance, 1959-60, Am. Inst. Banking, 1966-67; m. Albert A. Plentl, July 11, 1947 (div. 1957). Admitted to N.Y. bar, 1945; mem. legal staff Shearman & Sterling, attys., N.Y.C., 1944-53; account exec. Sterling Grace & Co., N.Y.C., 1959-61, Hardy & Co., 1961-65; with First Nat. City Bank, N.Y.C., 1965—, asst. trust officer, 1966-68, trust officer, 1968—. Bd. dirs. Girls Club N.Y., 1962—, v.p., 1964-67; bd. dir. Girls Clubs Am., 1964—, asst. treas., 1967-68; exec. com. Womens Aux. N.Y. Hosp., 1964—. Mem. N.Y. State Bar, Fed. Bar So. Dist. N.Y., Nat. Assn. Bank Women, English Speaking Union. Clubs: Cornell, Cosmopolitan. Home: 14 Sutton Pl S New York City NY 10022 Office: 399 Park Av New York City NY 10022

ROBINSON, LUCILE THURSTON (MRS. ROGER T. ROBINSON), educator; b. Stanford, Mont., June 13, 1916; d. H. Stanley and Alice C. (Carpenter) Thurston; B.A. in Journalism, Mont. State U., 1939, B.A. in Sociology, 1948; M.A., U. Redlands, 1956; Ph.D., Claremont Grad. Sch., 1970; m. Roger T. Robinson, Feb. 1, 1952; 1 dau., Susan (Mrs. Charles C. Couch). State supr. information service Mont. WPA, Butte, 1939-42; social worker San Bernardino (Cal.) County Welfare, 1948-50; elementary tchr. San Bernardino County Schs., 1950-62, demonstration tchr., 1962-66; research cons. Title I fed. projects Ont.-Montclair Sch. Dist., 1966-69, gen. cons., 1969—. Instr. elementary edn. U. Redlands (Cal.), 1962-72, U. Cal. at Riverside, 1970—, U. Cal. at Irvine, 1972. Early childhood edn. adv. bd. Chaffey Community Coll., 1973. Bd. dirs. U. Redlands Athenaeum, Redlands, 1970—, pres., 1973-74. Recipient hon. award for meritorious service U. Redlands, 1972. Mem. Nat. Soc. for Study Edn., Am. Soc. Child Devel., A.A.A.S., Assn. Cal. Sch. Adminstrs. (mem. exec. bd. region 7 1972-73), Am. Assn. U. Women, Internat., Cal. (chpt. pres. 1968-69) reading assns., Theta Sigma Phi, Pi Lambda Theta, Alpha Phi, Delta Kappa Gamma. Club: Zonta (pres. Ontario-Upland, Cal. 1973-74). Home: 603 S Buena Vista St Redlands CA 92373 Office: 950 West D St Ontario CA 91761

ROBINSON, MARGARET GLASGOW (MRS. GORDON THOMAS LA FLASH), physician, educator; b. Schenectady, Jan. 24, 1928; d. Lawrence Theodore and Ann (West) Robinson; student U. Tenn., 1946; M.D., U. Minn., 1956; m. Gordon Thomas La Flash, June 8, 1956. Intern pediatrics Kings County Hosp., Bklyn., 1956-57, resident pediatrics, 1957-59, fellow pediatric hematology, 1959-60; instr. pediatrics State U. N.Y., Downstate Med. Center, Bklyn., 1960-63, asst. prof., 1963-68, asso. prof. pediatrics, 1968-74; prof. pediatrics Med. Coll. Ohio, Toledo, 1974—; attending pediatrician State U. N.Y., Downstate Med. Center and Kings County Hosp., Bklyn., 1969-74; practice medicine, specializing in hematology, Bklyn., 1960-74; practice medicine specializing in hemotology, oncology, Toledo, 1974—; mem. staff L.I. Coll. Hosp. Guest lectr. pediatric depts. in N.Y.C., 1962-74, Newcastle-upon-Tyne U. Med. Sch., 1963. Mem. med. adv. bd. Bklyn. br. Sickle Cell Anemia Assn., 1970-74. Research grantee NIH, 1960—. Fellow Am. Acad. Pediatrics; mem. Am. Soc. Hematology, A.M.A., N.Y., Kings County med. assns., A.A.A.S., Soc. Study Blood, Am. Soc. Human Genetics, Am. Soc. Clin. Oncology, Assn. Am. Med. Colls. Home: 2448 Ragan Woods Dr Toledo OH 43614 Office: Med Coll Ohio Toledo OH 43614

ROBINSON, MARIE JOSEPHINE, educator; b. Monaca, Pa., Jan. 21, 1915; d. Harry and Marie Juliana Veronica (Schier) Robinson; B.Lit. Interpretation with honors, Emerson Coll., 1935; M.A. with honors, Mich. State U., 1944; Ph.D., Northwestern U., 1960. Tchr., play and contest dir. Lockport (N.Y.) Sr. High Sch., 1935-43; head speech and drama State Tchrs. Coll., Bemidji, Minn., 1944-45; instr. Syracuse (N.Y.) U., 1945-49; prof. speech Ill. Wesleyan U., Bloomington, 1950—, head speech dept., 1950—, dir. forensics, 1950—. Dir. community plays, Bloomington, 1960, 63; vis. lectr. S.D. State Coll., Brookings, 1969, 70, 71, Carthage Coll., Kenosha, Wis., 1966, 68, 70, Bowling Green (O.) State U., 1971. Recipient Distinguished Service award Dictionary Internat. Biography, 1971, 73, Community Leader Am. award, editorial bd. Community Leaders div. News Pub. Co., 1969; named Tchr. Year, Ill. Wesleyan U., 1966-67. Mem. Am. Theatre Assn., Am. Forensic Assn., Ill. Speech and Theatre Assn. (v.p. 1961-62, pres. 1962-63) Central States Speech Assn., Speech Communication Assn. (chmn. com. standards for interpretation 1972, 73), Am. Assn. Univ. Profs. (Ill. Wesleyan U. pres. 1963-65, 69-70), Internat. Platform Artists, Pi Kappa Delta (Ill. province lt. gov. 1972—), Theta Alpha Phi, Alpha Epsilon Rho, Phi Kappa Phi (Ill. Wesleyan U. pres. 1961-63) Alpha Lambda Delta. Contbr. articles to profl. jours. Home: 2205 Lamon Dr Bloomington IL 61701

ROBINSON, MARTHA STEWART (MRS. STEPHAN B. ROBINSON, JR.), lawyer, educator; b. Topeka, Mar. 2, 1914; d. Robert Bigger and Lenora (Stubbs) Stewart; A.B. cum laude, Washburn U., 1934, LL.B., 1940; LL.M., Stanford, 1953; m. Albrecht Marburg Yerkes, July 3, 1940 (dec. 1963); children—Robert Stewart, William Marburg; m. 2d, Stephan B. Robinson, Jr., July 17, 1971. Admitted to Kan. bar, 1940, Cal. bar, 1945; pvt. practice law, Los Angeles, 1946-55; instr. law Southwestern U. Sch. Law, Los Angeles, 1946-55; cons. Los Angeles Superior Ct. Com. on Standard Jury Instrns., 1957-64; prof. law Loyola U. Sch. Law, Los Angeles, 1965—. Judge pro tempore Los Angeles County Superior Ct., 1963; participant Inst. on Social Sci. Methods in Legal Edn., U. Denver, 1969; chmn. remedies sect. Am. Law Schs., 1973, 74. Mem. Am. (sect. legal edn.), Cal., Los Angeles County (legal ethics com.) bar assns., Women Lawyers Assn. (past pres.). Home: 625 Old Mill Rd Pasadena CA 91108 Office: Loyola U Law Sch 1440 W 9th St Los Angeles CA 90019

ROBINSON, MINA JEANINE (MRS. WILLIAM RONALD ROBINSON), scientist; b. St. Paul, Aug. 13, 1928; d. Ray Caldwell and Edna May (Gillespie) Shumway; student U. Cin., 1946-47; B.A., Ohio State U., 1952; M.S., U. Fla., 1972; m. William Ronald Robinson, June 10, 1952; children—Monica, Christopher, Teresa, Keenan. Instr. botany, electron microscopist U. Fla., Gainesville, 1968-72; electron microscopist, cytologist VA Hosp., Gainesville, 1973—. Mem. Bot. Soc. Am., Sigma Xi. Home: 2125 NW 7th Lane Gainesville FL 32601 Office: VA Hospital Gainesville FL 32601

ROBINSON, ORVETTA MURIEL, librarian; b. Easton, Ill., Aug. 19, 1921; d. Paul G. and Fay (Smith) Robinson; student Western Ill. State Tchrs. Coll., 1939-41, U. Ill. and Ill. State U., 1956-68. Tchr. Teheran Sch., Mason City, Ill., 1941-43; bus. sec. Charles C. Thomas, Pub., Springfield, Ill., 1943-45; bus. sec., mus. guide, proof-reader, librarian Ill. State Mus., Springfield, 1945-63, librarian, registrar, publs. editor, 1963—. Nominating com., Springfield YWCA, 1959-60, 65-66, 69-70, hospitality com., 1965-70; bd. dirs. Sangamon Conservation Council, 1963-68, 69-70, 72—, pres., 1965-66, sec., 1972—. Mem. Midwest Mus. Conf. (sec. 1955-58, adv. council 1958-59), Nat., Ill. (dir. 1971), Springfield (dir. 1960-71, pres. 1966-67, 69-70) Audubon socs., Ill. Library Assn., Nature Conservancy, Nat. Wildlife Fedn., Wilderness Soc., Abraham Lincoln Meml. Garden Assn. (dir. 1971—, sec. 1972—), Vachel Lindsay Assn. Home: 950 S Lincoln Av Springfield IL 62704 Office: Spring and Edward Sts Springfield IL 62706

ROBINSON, RAE FAITH, librarian; b. White Plains, N.Y., June 4, 1925; d. Raymond Vail and Susan Elizabeth (Van Wart) Robinson; A.B., Barnard Coll., 1948; M.S., Columbia, 1950. Sub-profl. librarian Barnard Coll., 1948-49; cataloger Hunter Coll., 1950-59, chief cataloger, asst. prof., 1960—. Mem. N. Broadway Citizens Assn., White Plains, N.Y., St. Agnes Hosp. Assn., White Plains. Mem. Am., N.Y. State, Westchester library assns., Am. Assn. U. Profs., N.Y. Tech. Services Librarians, Library Assn. City U. N.Y., N.Y. Library Club, Friends of Animals, Barnard, Middlebury Coll. alumnae assns., Barnard Club Westchester. Home: 68 Beech St Westminster Ridge White Plains NY 10604 Office: 695 Park Av New York City NY 10021

ROBINSON, RUTH ADELL, lawyer; b. Oklahoma City, July 11, 1924; d. C. Clyde and Minnie Frances (Wickmiller) Smith; student Ida. State U.; LL.B., George Washington U., 1947; m. Thomas B. Robinson, Dec. 23, 1944; children—Adell, Deborah, Sheryl. Admitted to D.C. bar, 1948, Colo. bar, 1966; atty. U.S. Dept. Labor, 1948; atty. U.S. Copyright Office, 1948; practiced in Denver, 1966—; now asso. firm Yegge Hall and Evans, Colo. co-chmn. Women Lawyers Centennial, 1969. Mem. Colo. Adv. Com. Jr. Colls., 1964; adv. com. mental health Emily Griffith Opportunity Sch., 1963; mem. Colo. Coordination Council Women's Orgns., 1959-61, Mayor Denver Citizen Budget Com., 1961-63; del. White House Conf. Children and Youth, 1960; pres. Slavens Sch. P.T.A., 1960-61; troop fund raising chmn. Girl Scouts U.S.; active numerous fund raising drives. Trustee spl. gifts Denver Symphony Guild, 1970-74, chmn. trustees, 1971-72. Mem. Am., Colo., Denver bar assns., Nat. Assn. Women Lawyers (chmn. regional states meeting 1968), Am. Assn. U. Women (dir. Colo. 1959-61, dir. Denver 1955-58, 59-61, legislative chmn. Colo. 1959-61), Kappa Beta Pi. Baptist. Club: So. Hills Gardeners (exec. bd. 1963-64). Home: 2775 E Dartmouth Av Denver CO 80210 Office: Yegge Hall & Evans 1340 Denver Club Bldg Denver CO 80202

ROBINSON, SALLY ANNE, clin. psychologist; b. Gassoway, W.Va., Aug. 13, 1923; d. Roland Robert and Malinda Bell (Hurt) Robinson; A.B., Marshall U., 1949, M.A., 1950; M.A., George Washington U., 1956, Ed.D., 1974. Tchr. pub. schs., W.Va. and Md., 1951-66; prof. Alliance Coll., Cambridge Springs, Pa., 1958-59; clin. psychologist D.C. Pub. Schs., Washington, 1966—. Served with WAVES, 1943-46. Mem. Alpha Sigma Tau. Baptist (mem. planning com.). Home: 2908 Belair Dr Bowie MD 20715 Office: Madison Adminstrn Bldg 10th and G St NW Washington DC 20009

ROBINSON, SALLY WINSTON, artist; b. Detroit, Nov. 2, 1924; d. Harry Lewis and Lydia (Kahn) Winston; B.A., Bennington Coll., 1947; student Cranbrook Acad. Art, 1949; grad. Sch. Social Work, Wayne U., 1948, M.A., 1972; M.F.A., Wayne State U., 1973; m. Eliot F. Robinson, June 28, 1949; children—Peter Eliot, Lydia Winston, Suzanne Finley, Sarah Mitchell. Psychol. tester Detroit Bd. Edn., 1944; pyschol. counselor and tester YMCA, N.Y.C., 1946; social caseworker Family Service, Pontiac, Mich., 1947; instr. printmaking Wayne State U., Detroit, 1973—. One person shows U. Mich., 1973, Wayne State U., 1974, Klein-Vogol Gallery, 1974; exhibited group shows Bennington Coll., Cranbrook Mus., Detroit Inst. Art, Detroit Artists Market, Soc. Women Painters, Soc. Arts and Crafts, Bloomfield Art Assn., Flint Left Bank Gallery, Balough Gallery, Detroit Soc. Women Painters, U. Mich., U. Ind., U. Wis., U. Pittsburg, Toledo Mus., Krannert Mus.; represented collections, Detroit, N.Y.C., Birmingham, Bloomfield Hills; tchr. children's art Detroit Inst. Art, 1949-50. Bd. dirs. Planned Parenthood, 1951-55, mem. exec. bd., 1963—; bd. dirs. P.T.A., 1956-60, Roeper City and Country Sch. Mem. Detroit Artists Market (dir. 1956—), Bennington Coll. Alumnae Assn. (regional co-chmn. 1954), Birmingham Soc. Women Painters (pres. 1974-75), Bloomfield Art Assn. (program co-chmn. 1956), Founders Soc. Detroit Inst. Art. Unitarian (mem. Council 1963—). Clubs: Village Women's, Democratic (Birmingham, Mich.); Women's City (co-ordinator art shows 1950) (Detroit). Home: 572 Linden Rd Birmingham MI 48009

ROBINSON, SARA KATHARINE MOORE (MRS. DONALD L. ROBINSON), lawyer; b. Chgo.; d. Herbert Jackson and Margaret Emma (Roberts) Moore; B.A., Beloit Coll., 1959; J.D., Columbus Sch. Law, Catholic U. of Am., 1965; m. Donald L. Robinson, Aug. 4, 1962; children—Marshall Jackson, Margaret Moore. Admitted to D.C. bar, 1966; state campaign sec. Wis. Humphrey for Pres. Com., Milw., 1959; exec. sec. Congressman Henry S. Reuss of Wis., Washington, 1960-65; legal asst. Congressman Henry S. Reuss, Wis., Washington, 1965-70, counsel, 1970—. Bus. mgr. St. Stephen's Ch. Enterprises, Inc., Washington, 1969-71. Vis. faculty mem. Civil Service Commn. Exec. Seminar Centers, Berkeley, Cal., Oak Ridge, Kings Point, N.Y. Bd. dirs. Washington Half-Way Home for Women, Inc., 1967—, Powerhouse, Inc., 1966-71. Mem. Kappa Beta Pi (chpt. dean 1967-69). Episcopalian (jr. warden 1968-69). Home: 1817 Kenyon St NW Washington DC 20010 Office: 2159 Rayburn House Office Bldg Washington DC 20515

ROBINSON, VALDA MOCK (MRS. CHASE ROBINSON), educator; b. Ft. Meade, Fla.; d. Byron Lloyd and Beulah (Simmons) Mock; B.S., Fla. State U., 1949, M.A., 1957; Ed.D., Columbia, 1966; m. Chase Robinson, June 7, 1959. Tchr., chmn. math. dept. Lakeland Jr. High Sch., Fla., 1950-55; counselor, chmn. math. dept. White Plains (N.Y.) High Sch., 1959-63; prof. counselor edn. Forham U., N.Y.C., 1965-70, chmn. div. psychology Sch. of Edn., 1970-72; prof. psychology Hillsborough Community Coll., Tampa, Fla., 1972—; cluster coordinator Hillsborough Cluster Nova U., 1973—. Cons., Bd. Examiners, N.Y.C., 1965-73. Mem. Am., N.Y. State personnel and guidance assns., Nat. Vocational Guidance Assn., Am. Ednl. Research Assn., Am. Psychol. Assn., Am. Sch. Counselors Assn. Home: Route 5 Box 138 Lutz FL 33549

ROBINSON, WAHNETA THERESA O'CONNOR (MRS. KENNETH DEWEY ROBINSON), museum curator; b. Adrian, Mich., Mar. 3, 1916; d. Harry Michael and Hazel Adeline (Underhill) O'Connor; B.A., Long Beach State Coll., 1960, M.A., 1962; postgrad. U. Cal. at Los Angeles, 1962-66; m. Kenneth Dewey Robinson, Aug. 16, 1946; 1 son, Keith David. Dress designer, owner Miss O'Connor's, Ft. Wayne, Ind., 1943-46; curator Long Beach (Cal.) Museum Art, 1966-74. Mem. Coll. Art Assn., Am. Assn. Museums, Am. Assn. U. Women, Art Historians So. Cal. Compiler: North American Landscape Painting, 1966; Seven Decades of Design, 1967; Alexander Calder's Gouaches, 1970; American Portraits-Old and New, 1971; William Gropper Paintings and Graphics, 1972; Hans Burkhardt Retrospective, 1972. Home: 103 Ravenna Dr Long Beach CA 90803

ROBISON, ANN GREEN (MRS. ADOLF ROBISON), textile co. exec.; b. N.Y.C., Nov. 19, 1904; d. Boris and Mary (Sugarmen) Green; B.A., U. Me., 1924; M.A., Columbia, 1936; grad. woman's inst. Jewish Theol. Sem. Am., 1959; m. Adolf Robison, Aug. 28, 1927; children—Peter Jordan, Michael Douglas. Tchr. French, Mattanawcook Acad., Lincoln, Me., 1924-25. New Rochelle, N.Y., 1925-38; v.p. Robison-Textile Co., 1941-59; v.p. Robison Industries, 1966—; treas. Robison-Anton Textile Co., Inc., 1959—; v.p. Dyerite Ltd., Grandmere, Can., 1964—; dir. Robison of Can., Ltd. Mem. adv. com. dept. Herbraic studies Rutgers State U. of N.J., chmn. spl. com. scholarships and grants. Accredited observer at UN in U.S. and France, 1947-52; lectr. U.S. Delegation in Italy, 1951. Mem. women's div. Am.-Israel Cultural Found., mem. program, interfaith and univ. coms; v.p. Robison Found., 1956—; mem. state com. Radio Free Europe; exec. com. Am. Israel Pub. Affairs Com., sec., 1973—; mem. bd., exec. com., chmn. program com. Tb-Respiratory Diseases Assn. Bergen and Passaic Counties, N.J.; mem. exec. com. Tb-Respiratory Diseases Assn. N.J.; mem. bd., co-chmn. Adult Center Jewish and Related Studies, YM-YWHA of Bergen County; mem. bd. Community Mus. of Bergen County; membership chmn. Am. Histadrut Cultural Exchange Inst.; nat. v.p. Nat. Jewish Community Relations Adv. Council, 1973—. Chmn. agenda com. plenary meeting, 1972; v.p. Jewish Fedn. for Community Services Bergen County. Mem. bd. Republican Women's Clubs of Bergen County, county rep. to state bd., 1967-68, chmn. internat. relations, 1969—; chmn. Bergen County Rep. Campaign Com. Recipient medal merit Fairleigh Dickinson U., 1966, Ann Robison House named in her honor 1964; Nat. citation Jewish Nat. Found., 1968; 1st Woman of Year, YM-YWHA, 1970; Brandeis award Zionist Orgn. Am., 1972; award Jewish War Vets., 1972. Mem. UN Assn., Am. Assn. U. Women (nat. com. on internat. relations, area program chmn., mem. bd. No. Valley br., 1st v.p. in charge program 1969-70, Ann Robison fellowship named in her honor 1968), Synagogue Council Am. (mem. UN com.), Nat. Council Jewish Woman (nat. dir., chmn. nat. internat. affairs 1968—, mem. bd. Mid-Atlantic dist., mem. numerous coms.), Internat. Council Jewish Women (U.S. rep. resolutions com., hospitality and pub. relations chmn. conv. 1969, chmn. resolutions com. 1969—, v.p. 1972—), Internat. Relations for Federated Woman's Clubs of N.J. (div. chmn.), Hadassah (life), Brandeis U. Womens Assn. (life), Internat. Program Assn., Phi Beta Kappa, Phi Kappa Phi. Club: Teaneck College (program chmn., mem. bd.). Author weekly column On the Go in the Jewish Standard, 1966—. Home: 554 S Forest Dr Teaneck NJ 07666 Office: 175 Bergen Blvd Fairview NJ 07022

ROBISON, SUE BESS JONES (MRS. JOHN CONRAD ROBISON), librarian; b. Manassas, Ga., Sept. 29, 1912; d. Daniel Elza and Annie Belle (Gilmore) Jones; A.A., Trevecca Coll., 1930; B.S., George Peabody Tchrs. Coll., 1932, M.A., 1933; M.L.S., Emory U., 1967; m. John Conrad Robison, June 25, 1946; children—Gilmore Conrad, John Stephen, Susan Daniel. Tchr., Anthony High Sch., Americus, Ga., 1933-37, Chamblee (Ga.) High Sch., 1937-41, E. Miss. Jr. Coll., Scooba, 1941-45, 46-50, Appalachian State Tchrs. Coll., Boone, N.C., 1945-46; librarian Lakeside High Sch., Atlanta, 1965—. Mem. Ga. Library Assn., Ga., DeKalb County assns. educators, P.T.A. Methodist. Home: 3018 Shenandoah Valley Rd N E Atlanta GA 30345 Office: 3801 Briarcliff Rd N E Atlanta GA 30345

ROBLIN, GLORIA LANDSMAN (MRS. DANIEL A. ROBLIN JR.), psychologist; b. N.Y.C., Apr. 29, 1925; d. Benjamin F. Landsman and Helen (Siegler) Lehman; B.A., Barnard Coll., 1945; M.A., Columbia, 1947; Ph.D., State U. N.Y. Buffalo, 1963; m. Daniel A. Roblin, Jr., May 22, 1949; children—Diane Siegler, Daniel Arthur III. Instr. psychology dept. U. Richmond (Va.), 1946-48, Columbia, N.Y.C., 1948-49, Med. Coll. State U. N.Y., Buffalo, 1963-65; research psychologist Research Found., State U. N.Y., Buffalo, 1963—, professorial lectr. Coll. Arts and Scis., 1965—, clin. asst. prof. psychiatry Med. Coll., 1966-72, clin. asso. prof., 1972—, ofcl. rep. Sch. Medicine to Center for Study Sex Edn. in Medicine U. Pa. Mem. Citizens Com. Intermunicipal Affairs. Bd. dirs. Psychiat. Clinic, Buffalo, 1956-62, pres., 1961-63, spl. cons., 1962—; bd. dirs. Nat. Council Jewish Women, 1954-60, chmn. social legislation, v.p., 1956-57; bd. dirs. Buffalo United Way, 1972, Canisius Coll. Council Religious Studies, 1969—. Mem. speakers bur. Erie County Republican Com., 1950—. Mem. Am. N.Y. State psychol. assns., Am. Assn. U. Profs., Psychol. Assn. Western N.Y., Sigma Xi. Clubs: Buffalo Athletic, Buffalo; Barnard of Western N.Y. (past pres.). Home: 50 Danbern Lane Williamsville NY 14221 Office: Dept Psychiatry Med Coll State U NY Buffalo 14214

ROBLING, MARIAN SPITZER (MRS. J. GERALD ROBLING), educator; b. Scranton, Pa.; d. Edward Joseph and Madelaine (Geiger) Spitzer; B.S., Marywood Coll.; M.A., Columbia, 1944; postgrad. Penn State U., 1948-50, U. Scranton, 1954-55; m. J. Gerald Robling, July 7, 1951. Sec., patent atty. Am. Cyanamid Research Lab., Stamford, Conn., 1946-48; instr. bus. edn. Laurel Coll., Meriden, Conn., 1941-42; tchr. Barrett High Sch., Cresco, Pa., 1942-44, Daniel Webster Sch., Scranton, Pa., 1950-60; counselor Scranton (Pa.) Sch. Dist., 1960-66, dir. elementary and secondary guidance, 1966—. Mem. bd. dirs. Lackawanna County Mental Health Assn., 1968—. Mem. Am. Personnel and Guidance Assn., Am. Sch. Counselors Assn., Assn. Counselor Edn. and Supervision, Assn. Measurement and Evaluation in Guidance, Pa. Sch. Counselors Assn. (dir. 1964-65,

68—), Northeastern Pa. Guidance and Personnel Assn. (pres. 1972—), Am. Assn. U. Women (br. pres. 1957-59), N.E.A., Pa. State Edn. Assn. (br. pres. 1963-65), C. of C., Kappa Delta Pi, Delta Pi Epsilon, Delta Kappa Gamma (pres. Mu chpt. 1972—). Club: Scranton Women Teachers. Home: 904 Woodlawn St Scranton PA 18509

ROBSON, EDNA BREENE, ins. co. ofcl.; b. Arkansas City, Kan., Mar. 8, 1929; d. John William and Pauline (Breene) Robson; grad. Arkansas City Jr. Coll., 1949; Ph.B., Marquette U., 1951; postgrad., Wichita State U., 1950, Dallas Coll. of So. Meth. U., 1958-59. Reporter, Arkansas City Daily Traveler, 1946-49; women's editor Cath. Herald Citizen, Milw., 1951-52; news editor Henryetta (Okla). Daily Free-Lance, 1953; women's editor Coffeyville (Kan.) Daily Jour., 1953-54; gen. news reporter Greenville (Tex.) Herald-Banner, 1955-57; news asst., staff writer Southwestern Bell Telephone Co., Dallas, St. Louis, 1957-62; pub. relations dir. Haggar Co., Dallas, 1962-64; editor Life News, Southwestern Life Ins. Co., Dallas, 1964-72, dir. field publs., 1972—. Bd. dirs. Camp Soroptimist for Crippled Children, 1970— (rec. sec. 1971-72). Recipient Katie award Dallas Press Club, 1967, Matrix award Dallas chpt. Theta Sigma Phi, 1968. Mem. Internat. Assn. Bus. Communicators (pres. Dallas chpt. 1968, named Editor of Year 1967). Home: 8175 Meadow Rd Dallas TX 75231 Office: PO Box 2699 Dallas TX 75221

ROBSON, MARGARET KATHRYN, assn. exec.; b. Coshocton, O.; d. Joseph Dean and Jean (Stockman) Robson; student pub. schs., Coshocton. Sec., sales mgr. Am. Art Works, Coshocton, 1926-30; supr. Babcock-Wilcox, Barberton, O., 1930-35; sec.-treas., dir. Monroe Letterhead Corp., Akron, O., 1935-50; asst. sec.-treas. Nat. Small Bus. Assn., Akron, O., Evanston, Ill., Washington, 1937-70, now hon. life trustee; program specialist Nat. Consumer Assistance Center Am. Assn. Ret. Persons and Nat. Ret. Tchrs. Assn., Washington, 1972-74. Mem. Nat. Consumer Product Safety Council; adviser U.S. Consumer Product Safety Commn. Sec. bd. dirs. YWCA, Akron, 1937-39; pres. Bus. Girls Council, 1932-34, Jr. Bus. League, 1930-38. Recipient Bus. Woman of Year award D.C. State Fed. Bus. and Profl. Women's Clubs, 1969. Mem. Washington Trade Assn. Execs., Bus. and Profl. Women's Club (treas. Potomac chpt. 1969-70). Episcopalian (vestry 1st woman). Author: Life of Letters, 1931. Editor (asso.): Pulling Together, 1957-58; Small Bus. Bull., 1958—. Home: 2725 29th St NW Washington DC 20008 Office: 1909 K St NW Washington DC 20036

ROBY, PAMELA ANN, educator; b. Milw., Nov. 17, 1942; d. Clark Dearborn and Marianna (Gilman) Roby; B.A. cum laude, Denver U., 1963; M.A., Syracuse U., 1966; Ph.D., N.Y. U., 1971. Asst. prof. dept. sociology, research asso. Center for Manpower Policy Studies, George Washington U., 1970-71; asst. prof. dept. sociology and Heller Sch. for Advanced Studies in Social Welfare, Brandeis U., Waltham, Mass., 1971-73; asso. prof. sociology and community studies, chmn. community studies U. Cal. at Santa Cruz, 1973—. Cons. U.S. Dept. Housing and Urban Devel., 1973—. Recipient research and travel grant Ford Found., 1971-73, research grant Russell Sage Found., 1973-74, faculty research grant, U. Cal., 1973-74. Mem. Nat. Acad. Scis. (com. on vocational edn. 1974—), Internat. Sociol. Assn. (mem. coordinating com., research div. on women), Eastern Sociol. Soc. (mem. exec. council 1973-74), Am. Council on Edn. (mem. commn. on women and higher edn. 1973—), Am. Sociol. Assn. (chmn. sec. on sex roles 1974—), Soc. for Study Social Problems (chmn. div. on poverty and human resources 1972-73), Nat. Orgn. Women (resource chmn. task force on labor 1973—), Alpha Kappa Delta, Phi Beta Kappa. Author: (with S.M. Miller) The Future of Inequality, 1970. Editor: Child Care—Who Cares? Foreign and Domestic Infant and Early Childhood Development Policies, 1973; The Poverty Establishment, 1974. Adv. editor Social Sci. Quar., 1973—, Sociol. Symposium, 1972—, Jour. Applied Behavioral Sci., 1972-73. Contbr. articles to profl. jours.

ROCCA, JOSEPHINE AUGUSTA, librarian; b. Iowa City, June 16, 1927; d. Peter Anthony and Mary Josephine (Pusateri) Rocca; B.A., U. Ia., 1950; B.S., U. Minn., 1953. Circulation asst. Iowa City Pub. Library, 1950-52; reference asst. Mead Pub. Library, Sheboygan, Wis., 1953-57, head reference librarian, 1957-63, head adult dept., 1963-67, coordinator adult services, 1967—. Mem. Wis. Council on Pub. Library Certificates and Standards, 1972-73. Bd. dirs. Sheboygan Human Rights Assn., 1974-75. Mem. Am., Wis. (chmn. pub. libraries div. 1971-72; named Librarian of Year 1969) library assns., U. Ia. Alumni Assn. (life), Bus. and Profl. Women, Civic Music Assn., Phi Beta Kappa. Democrat. Roman Catholic. Clubs: Altrusa, Camera (Sheboygan). Home: 3201 S 18th St Sheboygan WI 53081 Office: 808 N 8th St Sheboygan WI 53081

ROCERETO, LAVERNE RODGERS (MRS. RICHARD CLEMENT ROCERETO, SR.), educator; b. Pitts., June 21, 1932; d. Edward and Irene (Centanni) Rodgers; B.S. in Nursing, Duquesne U., 1955; M.Litt. in Nursing Edn. (Alpha Tau Delta scholar), U. Pitts., 1958, Ph.D. in Higher Edn. and Anthropology (USPHS grantee), 1972; m. Richard Clement Rocereto, Sept. 10, 1960; children—Richard Clement, Frances Marie, LaVerne Patricia. Clin. instr. Mercy Hosp., 1955-56; coordinator fundamentals nursing Montefiore Hosp., Pitts., 1956-58, asso. dir. nursing edn., 1958-60; med.-surg. instr. Mt. Mercy Coll., 1960-61; med.-surg. instr. U. Pitts., 1962-67, asst. prof. med.-surg. nursing, 1967-70, asst. prof. gen. nursing, 1970—. Cons. nursing technician groups. Active A.R.C., also various community fund raising drives; mem. alumni fund raising com. Duquesne U., Pitts., 1964—; pack com. Cub Scouts. Named Outstanding Young Woman of Am., Duquesne U., 1965, Distinguished Alumnus, U. Pitts., 1973. Mem. Am., Pa., (dist. pres. 1966—, adviser to bd. 1969—), nurses assns., Nat. League for Nursing (area pub. relations chmn. 1964-66), Pa. Nursing Educators (econ. sect. chmn. 1965-67), Coordinating Council Nursing Western Pa., Am. Assn. U. Profs., Hosp. Council Western Pa. (co-chmn. sensitivity com.), Alpha Tau Delta (nat. sec. 1964—, chpt. pres. 1962—), Sigma Theta Tau, Pi Lambda Theta. Club: University Catholic. Contbr. articles to nursing jours. Home: 5459 Stanton Av Pittsburgh PA 15206

ROCHE, DOROTHY MANCINI (MRS. RAYMOND JOSEPH ROCHE), librarian; b. N.Y.C., Dec. 24, 1912; d. Anthony T. and Maria Grazia (Pensiero) Mancini; A.B., Marywood Coll., 1933, M.A., 1939, postgrad., 1953, U. Scranton, 1959, 63, Montclair State U., 1960-63; m. Raymond Joseph Roche, Nov. 28, 1942; children—Raymond A., Marie (Mrs. Joseph Donovan). Librarian, Boys Club, Scranton, Pa., 1933-34; tchr. Old Forge (Pa.) High Sch., 1934-43, Shawnee (Okla.) High Sch., 1943-44; cataloger U. N.C., Chapel Hill, 1943, Cornell U., Ithaca, N.Y., 1945; tchr., librarian Jr. Sr. High Sch., Havre De Grace, Md., 1946-47; librarian Belleville (N.J.) High Sch., 1953—. Pres., P.T.A., Old Forge, 1950-51; v.p. Civic Club, Lyndhurst, N.J., 1966. Mem. N.E.A., Essex County, Belleville tchrs. assns., N.J. Sch. Media Assn., A.L.A. Home: 322 Kingsland Av Lyndhurst NJ 07071 Office: 100 Passaic Av Belleville NJ 07109

ROCHE, EVELYN FRANCES, govt. ofcl.; b. Fall River, Mass., Mar. 16, 1916; d. Frederick William and Elizabeth Frances (McMullen) Roche; diploma Thibodeau Coll., 1934. Asst. chief Mil. Property sect. C.E., War Dept., Washington, 1940-46; supervising sec. War Assets Adminstrn., San Francisco, 1946-47; sec. Office of Internat. Trade, Dept. Commerce, Washington, 1948-53; adminstrv. asst. program asst. and pvt. sec. to sec. of commerce ofcls., 1953-71, dir., exec. secretariat, 1971—. Recipient Meritorious Civilian award U.S. War Dept., 1946, Silver Medal U.S. Dept. Commerce, 1963, Suggestion award U.S. Dept. Commerce, 1965, Spl. Achievement award Dept. Commerce, 1974. Home: 12415 Keynote Lane Bowie MD 20715 Office: US Dept of Commerce Washington DC 20230

ROCHE, JUNE PATRICIA BROWNELL, fashion designer; b. New Bedford, Mass., Jan. 18, 1938; d. George H. and Freda (Robinson) Brownell; B.S., New Bedford Inst. Tech., 1960; m. David J. Roche, Oct. 7, 1961 (div.). Asst. textile designer dress fabrics Deering, Millikan, Inc., N.Y.C., 1960-65, textile designer sportswear fabrics, 1965-69, fashion dir., 1969—. Recipient Kappa Sigma Phi award, 1960, Design and Fashion award, 1960. Home: 196 Old King's Hwy N Darien CT 06820 Office: 1045 6th Av New York City NY 10018 also 39 W 54th St New York City NY 10019

ROCHE, MOLLY WEXLER, govt. ofcl.; b. Buffalo; d. Samuel and Ida (Loonsk) Wexler; student Am. U., 1948-51; m. Samuel B. Groner, Aug. 23, 1942 (div. Oct. 1961); children—Jonathan (dec.), Laurence; m. 2d, Morris Roche, July 28, 1963. Bus. analyst U.S. Govt., 1941-48; corp. sec., office mgr. Weinschel Engring. Co., Inc., Gaithersburg, Md., 1954-63; asst. facilities div. U.S. Coast and Geodetic Survey, Dept. Commerce, Washington, 1964-65; sr. mgmt. analyst Dept. Housing and Urban Devel., Washington, 1965—. Home: 413 Mansfield Rd Silver Spring MD 20910 Office: HUD Bldg 7th and D Sts SW Washington DC 20410

ROCHETTO, EVELYN MARIE, assn. exec.; b. Chgo.; d. Lucius J. and Clara M. (Jung) Young; Ph.B., Northwestern U., 1952; m. Paul A. Rochetto, June 9, 1937. Profl. musician, 1930-50; membership sec. Internat. Soc. Gen. Semantics, 1950-55, exec. sec., 1955—, dir., 1952—. Mem. Am. Assn. U. Women (pres. Chgo. br. 1956, 58, 64—, mem. bd. 1953—), Chgo. Story League (pres. 1970—), Am. Legion (mem. bd.), Friends Mentally Ill (pres. 1958—), Alpha Sigma Lambda (dir.). Club: Woman's University (pres. 1966—). Home: 901 W Margate Terrace Chicago IL 60640

ROCK, ELIZABETH JANE, chemist, educator; b. Plattsburgh, N.Y., Dec. 14, 1924; d. Herbert Joseph and Rose (Quinn) Rock; B.S., Coll. Mt. St. Vincent, 1946; M.A., Smith Coll., 1948; Ph.D., Pa. State U., 1951; postgrad. Oxford U., 1966-67. Research asso. Crystal Structure Lab., Pa. State U., 1951-52; instr. chemistry Vassar Coll., Poughkeepsie, 1952-55; asso. prof. U. Tenn., 1955-56, prof. textile chemistry, 1956-59, textile chemist Agr. Expt. Sta., 1955-59; lectr., 1959-61; asso. prof. chemistry Wellesley Coll., 1961-67, prof. chemistry, 1967—, chmn. dept., 1967-71, dir. Sci. Center, 1973—, Cohen prof. sci. as related to health, 1970—. Cons.; NSF fellow, vis. prof. Oxford U., 1966-67. Mem. Am. Chem. Soc., Sigma Xi, Phi Kappa Phi. Democrat. Roman Catholic. Home: 10 Fiske House Wellesley MA 02181

ROCK, LOUISE ESTHER HENDRICKS (MRS. JOHN M. ROCK), editor; b. Pitts., Mar. 13, 1928; d. William M. and Harriet (Cox) Hendricks; B.A., Westminster Coll., Pa., 1950; postgrad. Pitts.-Xenia Theol. Sem., 1950-51; m. John M. Rock, Sept. 1, 1951. Dir. Christian edn. Hebron U.P. Ch., Pitts., 1951-52, First U.P. Ch., Pitts., 1952-53; adult and family program dir. YMCA, Dearborn, Mich., 1955-56; children's librarian, Saginaw, Mich., 1956-58; librarian, Barrington, Ill., 1959-60; with editorial dept. David C. Cook Pub. Co., Elgin, Ill., 1960—, now primary editor, adminstrv. editor presch. publs. Childrens Sunday Sch. supt. Evang. Free Ch., 1960—, chmn. Women's Missionary Soc., 1965-67, chmn. ch. library com., 1970—. Editor: vol. I, Book of Life, 1962. Home: 414 E Lake Shore Dr Tower Lakes Estates Barrington IL 60010 Office: 850 N Grove Av Elgin IL 60120

ROCK, PHYLLIS ANN, ednl. adminstr.; b. Ripon, Wis., May 17, 1927; d. Byron J. and Florence (Graham) Rock; B.A., U. Wis., 1948, M.A., 1950. Staff aide Senator William Benton, Washington, 1951-53, Senator Hubert Humphrey, Washington, 1953-56; legislative asst. Senator Wayne Morse, Washington, 1956-68; profl. staff mem. Senate Com. on Labor and Pub. Welfare, Washington, 1968-70; v.p. for edn. and spl. audience Am. Forest Inst., Washington, 1970—. Mem. Am. Acad. Polit. and Social Sci. Democrat. Home: 3900 Watson Pl NW Washington DC 20016 Office: 1619 Massachusetts Av NW Washington DC 20036

ROCKAS, HELEN ROTOUS (MRS. CHRIS E. ROCKAS), pediatrician; b. Aberdeen, Wash., Nov. 6, 1933; d. Andrew Nick and Georgia (Zaniakou) Rotous; B.S., U. Wash., 1955, M.D., 1958; m. Chris E. Rockas, Apr. 16, 1961; children—Panagiota, Andreas. Intern Sacramento Med. Center, 1958-59; pediatric resident Valley Med. Center, Fresno, Cal., 1961-64; teaching staff, 1964—; practice medicine specializing in pediatrics, Fresno, 1964—; civilian med. officer McClellan AFB, Sacramento, 1959-61; mem. staffs Valley Children's Hosp., Fresno, chmn. guidance com., 1967-69; St. Agnes Hosp., Fresno, sec. pediatrics adv. com., 1964-66, Fresno Community Hosp., lectr. Am. Cancer Soc., 1968-71. Recipient outstanding service award, Am. Cancer Soc., 1969. Mem. Am., Cal. med. assns., Fresno County Med. Soc., Am. Assn. U. Women (chmn. fellowship com., 1970-71), Daughters of Penelope (pres. 1973-74, nat. chmn. Cooley's Anemia com.), Sigma Epsilon Sigma, Phi Sigma, Iota Sigma Pi. Greek Orthodox religion (Sunday sch. tchr. 1968-75; pres. youth assn. 1959-60). Home: 2555 W San Ramon Av Fresno CA 93705 Office: 735 W San Jose St Fresno CA 93704

ROCKEFELLER, BLANCHETTE HOOKER, orgn. exec.; b. N.Y.C., Oct. 2, 1909; d. Elon Huntington and Blanche (Ferry) Hooker; grad. Miss Chapin's Sch., 1927; A.B., Vassar Coll., 1931; m. John D. Rockefeller 3rd, Nov. 11, 1932; children—Sandra Ferry, John Davison IV, Hope Aldrich Spencer, Alida Davison. Trustee Mus. Modern Art, 1953—, pres., 1959-62, 72—, also mem. exhbns. com. Trustee Community Service Soc., 1933-57, vice chmn., 1952-57; trustee Brearley Sch., 1947-56; Vassar Coll., 1949-56; Juilliard Sch., 1972—; adv. com. Japan Found., 1972-75. Mem. Japan Soc., Asia Soc., Met. Opera Guild, Philharmonic Symphony Soc., Friends Asia House Gallery. Club: Cosmopolitan (N.Y.C.). Home: 1 Beekman Pl New York City NY 10022

ROCKEFELLER, MARGARETTA (HAPPY), wife of v.p. U.S.; m. Nelson Aldrich Rockefeller, May 1963; children—Nelson A., Mark F. Address: Vice Presdl Mansion Washington DC also Pocantico Hills Tarrytown NY 10591

ROCKEFELLER, MARY FRENCH (MRS. LAURANCE S. ROCKEFELLER), assn. ofcl.; b. N.Y.C., May 1, 1910; d. John and Mary Montague (Billings) French; grad. Rosemary Hall, 1927; student Vassar Coll., 1927-29, Art Students League N.Y.C., 1929-34; LL.D., Middlebury Coll., 1967; m. Laurance Spelman Rockefeller, Aug. 15, 1934; children—Laura (Mrs. Richard Chasin), Marion (Mrs. Warren T. Weber), Lucy (Mrs. Jeremy P. Waletzky), Laurance. Mem. nat. bd. YWCA, 1951-73, vice chmn. internat. div., 1955-64, chmn. Am. Centennial Observance and Celebration, 1956, chmn. World Service Council, 1958-64, chmn. world relations com., 1964-73, co-chmn. nat. convocation on racial justice, 1972, v.p., dir. N.Y. YWCA; trustee Whitney Mus. Am. Art; mem. council Found. for Child Devel.; mem. distbn. com. N.Y. Community Trust; bd. dirs. Community Fund, Inc.; chmn. centennial observance YWCA City N.Y., 1970; trustee Calvin Coolidge Meml. Found., Woodstock, Vt., Union Ch., Tarrytown, N.Y., Woodstock Hist. Soc.; hon. trustee Spelman Coll., Atlanta, 1970—. Mem. N.Y. Zool. Soc., Hort. Soc. N.Y., Am. Craftsmen Council, Met. Mus. Art, Mus. Modern Art, Philharmonic Symphony, Park Assn. N.Y.C. Clubs: Women's City, Cosmopolitan, Colony, Women's Nat. Republican (N.Y.C.). Home: 834 Fifth Av New York City NY 10021

ROCKLAGE, SISTER MARY NORMA, coll. adminstr.; b. St. Louis, July 18; d. Henry Bernard and Catherine Mary (Lohman) Rocklage; B.A., Marian Coll., 1962; M.A., also Ph.D. in Latin and Greek, 1965. Joined Franciscan Order, 1951; asso. prof. classical langs. Marian Coll., Indpls., 1965-69, asst. to dean acad. affairs, 1969-70, dean acad. affairs, dir. evening and summer div., 1970—. Pres., Ind. Classical Conf., 1971-72, Ind. Deans' Conf., 1972-73; sec., editor Newsletter for Indpls. Archdiocese, 1965-70. Mem. Am. Council on Edn. (fellow 1970-71), Am. Assn. Higher Edn., Ind. Bus. Women's Assn., Am. Conf. Acad. Deans, Nat. Catholic Edn. Assn. Home: 3200 Cold Spring Rd Indianapolis IN 46222

ROCKOFF, MAXINE LIEBERMAN (MRS. S. DAVID ROCKOFF), govt. ofcl.; b. Gary, Ind., July 15, 1938; d. Arnold Leo and Hilda (Kahan) Lieberman; student (Ford Found. Early Admissions scholar) Goucher Coll., 1954-56; B.S., George Washington U., 1958; M.A., U. Pa., 1960, Ph.D., 1964; m. S. David Rockoff, July 1, 1956; children—Lisa, Todd, Kevin. Programmer, U. Pa., 1958-61; mathematician Nat. Bur. Standards, 1961-64; reserach asso. U. Md. Inst. for Fluid Dynamics and Applied Math., 1964-65; research asso. Yale, 1965-68; asst. prof. Washington U., 1968-71; health scientist adminstr. Bur. Health Services Research, Rockville, Md., 1971—. Mem. Soc. for Indsl. and Applied Math. (mem. council), Am. Math. Soc., Math. Assn. Am., Assn. Computing Machinery, A.A.A.S., Phi Beta Kappa. Home: 11508 W Hill Dr Rockville MD 20852 Office: 5600 Fishers Lane Rockville MD 20852

ROCKWOOD, RUTH HUMISTON (MRS. GEORGE H. ROCKWOOD, JR.), educator; b. Chgo., Oct. 15, 1906; d. Charles Edward and Myrtle Isabelle (Wheeler) Humiston; A.B., Wellesley Coll., 1927; M.S., U. Ill., 1949; Ed.D., Ind. U., 1960; m. George H. Rockwood, Jr., Apr. 14, 1928; children—Charles E., Nancy R. (Mrs. Jack A. Haigh), Alice R. (Mrs. F. J. Bethke). Librarian, Chgo. Pub. Library System, 1927-29, Buxton Country Day Sch., Short Hills, N.J., 1937-39, U. Ill. Library and Library Sch., 1949-53; Fulbright lectr. library sci. Chulalongkorn U., Bangkok, Thailand, 1952-53; prof. Sch. Library Sci. Fla. State U., Tallahassee, 1953—. Prof. Ind. U. Library Sch., 1958-59; cons. Leon County (Fla.) Pub. Library, 1955-56. Mem. League Women Voters, Am. Assn. U. Profs., Am., Southeastern, Fla. (pres. 1963-64) library assns., Assn. Am. Library Schs., Beta Phi Mu. Club: Pilot (v.p. 1968-69) (Tallahassee) Contbr. articles to profl. jours. Home: 1503 Spruce Av Tallahassee FL 32303

ROCKWOOD, SUSAN WILLIAMS, microbiologist, educator; b. Cin., Nov. 26, 1924; d. Chester Dovall and Pearl (Williams) Rockwood; student U. Cin., 1942-44, M.S., 1958, Ph.D., 1962; B.A., Dension U., 1946. Chief technologist Bethesda Hosp., Cin., 1947-53; research bacteriologist R.A. Taft San. Engring. Center, Cin., 1953-56; fellow Cin. Gen. Hosp., 1958-59; instr. U. Cin., 1956-57; asst. prof. microbiology Miami U., Oxford, O., 1962-67, asso. prof., 1967-73, prof., 1973—, dir. med. tech. program, 1962—. Mem. Ohio bd. regents Adv. Com. on Higher Edn. Programs for Allied Med. Professions, 1970. Named Panhellenic Outstanding Adviser, 1964, 68, Miami U. Woman of Year, 1965; recipient Achievement award Kappa Kappa Kappa Alumnae, 1968. Mem. Am. Soc. Microbiology, Registry of Med. Technologists, Am., Soc. Clin. Pathologist, A.A.A.S., Allied Health Professions Assn., Ohio Acad. Sci., Sigma Xi, Phi Sigma, Kappa Kappa Gamma (nat. chmn. undergrad. scholarships 1964-70). Contbr. articles to profl. jours. Home: 614 Garrod Lane Oxford OH 45056

RODDY, ELLEN JAMES DUNIAS (MRS. H. LEIGHTON RODDY, JR.), home economist; b. Lubbock, Tex., Mar. 12, 1944; d. James Constantine and Kanella (Kallimani) Dunias; B.S., Tex. Tech. U., 1966; m. Harry Leighton Roddy, Jr., June 6, 1970. Cook, Glacier Nat. Park, Inc., Lake McDonald, Mont., 1965; comml. cookery specialist Tex. Electric Service Co., Fort Worth, 1966-72, home service supr., 1972-74, adminstrv. asst. to mgr. personnel planning, personnel dept., 1974, employment supr., 1974—. Mem. Am., Tex., Tarrant County home econs. assns., N.Tex. Home Economists in Bus. (sec. 1968-69), Fort Worth Restaurant Women's Aux. (corr. sec. 1969-70), Am. Assn. U. Women (4th v.p. 1969-71), Gamma Phi Beta (pres. 1970-71, art show chmn. 1971-72). Episcopalian. Home: 3008 Encino Dr Fort Worth TX 76116 Office: PO Box 970 Fort Worth TX 76101

RODDY, MARY CONSTANCE, dietitian; b. Johnstown, Pa., Jan. 1, 1919; d. Luther M. and Catherine (Conlin) Roddy; B.S., Carnegie Inst. Tech., 1940; M.S., Dexel Inst. Tech., 1952. Intern, Mass. Gen. Hosp., Boston, 1940-41; asst. dietitian St. Francis Hosp., Pitts., 1941-43; nutrition instr. Windber (Pa.) Hosp., 1943-44; therapeutic dietitian Presbyn. Hosp., Pitts., 1944-51; cons. dietitian Md. Dept. Health, Balt., 1953—. Mem. Am., Md. dietetic assns., Am., Md. home econs. assns., Am., Md. pub. health assns., Am. Hosp. Assn. Democrat. Roman Catholic. Home: 6865 Queen's Ferry Rd Baltimore MD 21239 Office: Md Dept Health 301 W Preston St Baltimore MD 21201

RODE, JANICE IRENE, educator; b. Chgo.; d. Fred E. and Florence (Blume) Rode; B.A., Cornell Coll., 1957; M.A., Northwestern U., 1960. Tchr., Oaklawn (Ill.) Hometown Elementary Sch. Dist., 1957-59; sch. counselor West Leyden High Sch., Northlake, Ill., 1960-66; dir. ednl. services Nat. Merit Scholarship Corp., Evanston, Ill., 1966—. Vol., water safety instr. A.R.C., Chgo., 1957—; mem. bd., faculty adviser Am. Field Service, 1963-66; mem. bd., sec. Parents' Club, 1965-66; mem. exec. com. Faculty Accreditation Com., 1966. Mem. Nat., Ill. assns. women deans and counselors, Nat. Assn. Secondary Sch. Prins., Ill. Personnel and Guidance Assn., Ill. Sch. Counselor Assn. 7654C N Sheridan Rd Chicago IL 60626 Office: 990 Grove St Evanston IL 60201

RODELL, MARIE FREID, literary agt.; b. N.Y.C.; d. Isadore and Elizabeth (Serber) Freid; B.A., Vassar Coll., 1932. Asst. to editor William Morrow & Co., N.Y.C.; fiction editor Modern Age Books, N.Y.C., head mystery dept. Dueli Sloan & Pearce, N.Y.C.; self-employed literary agt., N.Y.C., 1948—. Literary trustee, Rachel Carson, 1964; bd. dirs. Rachel Carson Trust for Living Environment, 1965; Mem. Soc. Authors Reps., Authors Guild. Author: 3 novels, 1 textbook, also articles, short stories. Office: 141 E 55th St New York City NY 10022

RODENBOUGH, JEANNETTE GREEN (MRS. CHARLES DYSON RODENBOUGH), author, city ofcl.; b. nr. Denver, Sept. 18, 1933; d. Philip Palmer and Juliette (Loving) Green; B.A. in Polit. Sci., Randolph-Macon Woman's Coll., 1955; M.A. in English, U. N.C., 1973; m. Charles Dyson Rodenbough, May 15, 1955;

children—Katherine Boone, Charles Dyson, John Ryan, Lucy Fitzpatrick. Instr. English Rockingham Community Coll., Wentworth, N.C., 1969-71; tchr. English Oak Ridge Acad., 1973; free-lance writer, 1960—. Pres. Madison Jr. Service League, 1965-66. Mem. Madison Bd. of Aldermen, 1973—. Bd. dirs. Rockingham County Fine Arts Festival, pres., 1973—. Recipient Best-in-Show award Fine Arts Festival, 1964, 73, 1st pl. Poetry award Wake Forest C. of C., 1972. Mem. Internat. Platform Assn., N.C. Poetry Soc., League of Women Voters. Democrat. Presbyn. Author: If I Were A Ghost, 1972; A History of Madison, 1968. Contbr. poetry and essays to various mags. Home: PO Box 46 Madison NC 27025

RODERICK, JESSIE ALICE, educator; b. Wilkes-Barre, Pa., June 6, 1934; d. Ariel Emlyn and Meta Henrietta (Lingertot) Roderick; B.A., Wilkes Coll., 1956; M.A., Columbia, 1957; Ed.D., Temple U., 1967. Tchr. Pennsbury Sch. System, Fallsington, Pa., 1957-58; instr. edn. Wilkes Coll., Wilkes-Barre, Pa., 1958-63; asst. prof. edn. Muhlenberg Coll., Allentown, Pa., 1965-67; asst. prof. edn. U. Md., College Park, 1967-70, asso. prof. early childhood, elementary edn., 1970—, research asso. nursery kindergarten, 1970-71, asso. dir. Center for Young Children, 1972—; cons. to pub. sch.; co-dir. Title IV projects Kent County, Md., 1968-69. Mem. Nat. Cathedral Choral Soc., Washington, 1967-73; edn. task force Lutheran Soc. Services Commn., Washington, 1968-69. Improvement of Teaching grantee, U. Md., 1970. Mem. Am. Assn. U. Profs. (sec.-treas. 1959-60), N.E.A., Nat. Council Tchrs. of English, Assn. of Tchr. Educators, Conf. on English Edn., Am. Ednl. Research Assn., Assn. for Supervision and Curriculum Devel., Am. Assn. U. Women, World Future Soc., World Council on Curriculum and Instruction, U.S. Nat. Com. for Early Childhood Edn., Kappa Delta Pi, Phi Delta Gamma. Club: Temple U Alumni (mem. bd. dirs. 1970) (Washington). Home: 3450 Toledo Terrace Hyattsville MD 20782 Office: U Md Coll of Edn College Park MD 20742

RODGERS, AVA DARCY, univ. adminstr.; b. Thomson, Ga.; d. Louis Franklin and Mary George (Darsey) Rodgers; B.S., Berry Coll., 1953; M.S., U. Ga., 1961; Ph.D., Fla. State U., 1967. Tchr. home econs. Lyerly (Ga.) High Sch., 1952-54; asst. home demonstration agt. U. Ga., Dalton, 1954-57, home demonstration agt., Ringgold, 1958-59, home furnishings specialist, Athens, 1960-67; asst. prof. Fla. State U., 1967-69; state leader extension home econs. U. Ark., Little Rock, 1969—. Adviser Ark. Extension Homemakers Council; mem. Nat. 4-H Consumer Edn. Com. Mem. Womens Com. on Pub. Affairs, 1970-71. Bd. dirs. Ark. Health Systems Found.; trustee Girls 4-H House, U. Ark., Fayetteville; mem. adv. bd. Ark. Women's Hwy. Safety Leaders. Recipient Distinguished Service Group award Dept. Agr., 1955. Mem. Nat. Assn. Extension Home Economists (mem. adv. council), Ark. Home Econs. Assn., Epsilon Sigma Phi, Phi Kappa Phi, Omicron Nu, Gamma Sigma Delta. Baptist. Clubs: Altrusa International, Farm and Ranch (Little Rock). Author: The Housing of Oglethorpe County, Georgia 1790-1860, 1971. Home: 62 Sherrill Heights Little Rock AR 72207 Office: Box 391 Little Rock AR 72203

RODGERS, DOROTHY FEINER (MRS. RICHARD RODGERS), sculptress, columnist; b. N.Y.C., May 4, 1909; d. Benjamin and May (Adelson) Feiner; diploma Horace Mann Sch., N.Y.C.; student Wellesley Coll., 1926-28; m. Richard Rodgers, May 5, 1930; children—Mrs. Henry Guettel, Mrs. Daniel Melnick. Pres. Repairs, Inc. N.Y.C., 1935-41; sculptress. Bd. dirs. N.Y. chpt. A.R.C., 1954-62; trustee at large Fedn. Jewish Philanthropies; mem. N.Y. State Council on Arts. Named Key Woman of Year, Fedn. Jewish Philanthropies, 1956. Press asso. mem. Am. Inst. Interior Designers. Club: Cosmopolitan (N.Y.C.). Inventor: Jonny Mop, Basic Try-On Dress Patterns. Author: My Favorite Things, 1964; The House in My Head, 1967; (with Mary Rodgers) A Word to the Wives, 1970, monthly column Of Two Minds, McCall's mag., 1971—, nat. syndicated radio program A Word to the Wives, 1971-72. Inventor: Turn and Learn Storybooks, 1972. Home: Fairfield CT 06430

RODGERS, ELLEN DAVIES (MRS. HILLMAN P. RODGERS), club woman, planter, author; b. Brunswick, Tenn., Nov. 13, 1903; d. Gillie M. and Frances Ina (Stewart) Davies; B.S., George Peabody Coll., 1924; M.A., Columbia, 1927; m. Hillman P. Rodgers, Dec. 21, 1932, foster-children—Sarah B. Gandy, Frances Gandy, Elba Gandy, Mary Gandy (Mrs. Burnell D. Hardee). Critic tchr. campus sch., Memphis State U., 1924-26, also prof. early childhood edn.; prof. elementary edn., Evansville (Ind.) Coll., summer, 1926; prin. Arlington High Sch., 1928-29, Lausanne Sch. Girls, 1953; state elementary supr. W. Tenn. 1938-40; mem. Shelby County Bd. Edn., 1961-65; dir. Tenn. Sch. Bds. Assn., 1963-65. First Shelby County (Tenn.) historian, 1965—. Organized Pleasant Hill Cemetery Assn., 1937, pres. 1937—. Del. Dem. Nat. Conv., 1956. Del. Tenn. Constl. Conv., 1953, 59. State exec. vice chmn. Woman's Adv. Council, Civil Def. Organized Zachariah Davies chpt. D.A.R. (organizing regent 1945-46, chpt. regent, 1946-48; state regent, 1956-59, hon. regent 1959, nat. vice chmn. Am. history month 1964-67). Named Woman of Year, Memphis Kiwanis Club, 1965; one of 10 women cited by Memphis Comml. Appeal, 1969. Mem. Tenn. Assn. Childhood Edn. (past pres.), Memphis and Shelby County Council Garden Clubs (past pres.), Memphis State U. Alumni Assn. (past pres.), Alumni Assn. Memphis St. U. (life), Daus. Am. Colonists, Children Am. Revolution (state and nat. promotor), Memphis Geneal. Soc., Hermitage Assn., Tenn. Hist. Soc. (v.p. W. Tenn. 1967), Tenn. Poetry Soc., So. Dames Am. (nat. parliamentarian 1965-67), Am. Assn. State and Local History, Nat. Congress P.T.A. (life), Nat. Council State Garden Clubs (life), Tenn. Fedn. Garden Clubs (life mem.; past pres.), YWCA, Internat. Platform Assn., Phi Mu (life mem.; pres. Memphis Kappa Lambda House Corp. 1960, treas. 1961, woman of year award 1966), Beta Sigma Phi (internat. hon. mem.). Episcopalian. Clubs: Brunswick Road Garden (organizing pres. 1965—); Quota (hon. mem.; past pres.) (Memphis); Nineteenth Century; Tenn. Woman's Press and Authors. Author (under name Ellen Davies-Rodgers): The Romance of the Episcopal Church in West Tennessee, 1964; The Holy Innocents, 1966; The Casket Case, 1970; Education, Then, Now and Yon, 1971; The Great Book, Calvary Protestant Episcopal Church 1832-1972, 1973. Contbr. numerous articles and items to mags. Home: Davies Plantation (Brunswick) Memphis TN 38134

RODGERS, FRANCES MARION, advt. firm exec.; b. Washington, May 9, 1918; d. Francis Marion and Evelyn Gertrude (Galloway) Rodgers; A.B., Duke, 1940. Copywriter, Brooke, Smith, French & Dorrance, Inc., Detroit, 1945-49, creative supr., 1949-56; copy and contact supr. VanSant, Dugdale & Co., Inc., Balt., 1956-61; account mgr., creative mgr. Griswold-Eshleman Co., Cleve., 1961—. Instr. Cleve. Advt. Club Advt. Sch., 1967—. Chmn. Cleve. Plan Com. for Truth and Good Taste in Advt., 1965-71. Mem. Nat. Sales Execs. Club, Cleve. Advt. Club, Central Ohio Indsl. Marketers. Home: 25812 Melibee Dr Westlake OH 44145 Office: 55 Public Square Cleveland OH 44113

RODGERS, JANET RUTH AHALT (MRS. TERRY C. RODGERS), educator; b. Hershey, Pa., June 15, 1935; d. Harold Alonzo and Margaret (Bittle) Ahalt; B.S., Wagner Coll., 1957; M.A., N.Y.U., 1964, Ph.D., 1971; m. Terry C. Rodgers, Feb. 17, 1962. Staff nurse N.Y. State Psychiat. Inst., 1957-59, head nurse, 1959-61; asst. dir. nursing Psychiat. Treatment Center, N.Y.C., 1961-62; mem. faculty Wagner Coll., S.I., 1964-68, asst. prof. nursing, 1966-68; coordinator psychiat. nursing Herbert H. Lehman Coll., U. City N.Y., 1971—, asst. prof., 1971-74, asso. prof., 1974—. Mem. Am. Nurses Assn., Council Nurse Researchers, Citizens Com. Children of N.Y., Council Advanced Practicioners in Psychiat.-Mental Health Nursing, Nat. League Nursing, Am. Assn. U. Profs., Pi Lambda Theta, Kappa Delta Pi, Sigma Theta Tau. Contbr. articles to profl. jours., chpts. to books. Home: 19 E 88th St New York City NY 10028 Office: Dept Nursing Herbert H Lehman Coll City Univ New York Bronx NY 10468

RODGERS, MARY (MRS. HENRY GUETTEL), composer; b. N.Y.C., Jan. 11, 1931; d. Richard and Dorothy (Feiner) Rodgers; student Wellesley Coll., 1948-51; m. Julian B. Beaty, Jr., 1951 (div. 1957); children—Richard Rodgers, Linda Mackay, Constance Peck; m. 2d Henry Guettel, Oct. 14, 1961; children—Adam, Alexander. Composer music, lyrics Some of My Best Friends Are Children, 1952, book and lyrics Three to Make Music, 1957, Mary Martin childrens' special, Easter NBC-TV, 1957, music, lyrics Davy Jones Locker, 1957; composer Once Upon a Mattress, opened Bdwy. 1959, Hot Spot, music, opened Broadway 1963, music Mad Show, New Theatre, 1966-67, Pinocchio for Bill Baird Marionettes, 1974; asst. to producer Philharmonic Young People's Concerts, CBS-TV, 1957—. Trustee Brearley Sch.; mem. council Dramatics Guild. Mem. A.S.C.A.P., Dramatists Guild. Author: The Rotten Book, 1969; Freaky Friday, 1972; (with Dorothy Rodgers) A Word to the Wives, 1970; A Billion for Boris, 1974; monthly column Of Two Minds, McCall's mag., 1972. Club: Cosmopolitan. Home: 115 Central Park West New York City NY 10023

RODGERS, NANCY MELISSE PAILING (MRS. CLARENCE W. RODGERS), librarian; b. Lincoln, Neb., Nov. 3, 1933; d. Aaron Edgar and Del Viola (Newkirk) Pailing; B.A., U. Neb., 1956; M.L.S., Rutgers U., 1962; m. Clarence W. Rodgers, June 13, 1955. Jr. librarian U. Neb. Libraries, Lincoln, 1956-60; librarian trainee Newark Pub. Library, 1960-62; librarian Fla. State U. Library, 1962-63; documents librarian Queensborough Pub. Library, 1963-66; head documents librarian Hofstra U. Library, Hempstead, N.Y., 1966—. Mem. Am. Assn. U. Profs., Am. N.Y. library assns., N.Y. Library Club, N.Y. Tech. Services Librarians, Nassau County Library Assn., Rutgers Sch. Library Service Alumni Assn., Phi Beta Kappa, Alpha Lambda Delta, Beta Phi Mu. Democrat. Methodist. Home: 485 Front St Hempstead NY 11550

RODGERS, ROSEMARY FLORENCE, physician; b. Cin., July 10, 1945; d. James Chester and Rosemary Virginia (Koenig) Rodgers; B.S., Northwestern U., 1967, M.D., 1969. Intern Evanston (Ill.) Hosp., 1969-70; resident internal medicine Northwestern U. Med. Sch., Chgo., 1970-74; fellow thoracic diseases Mayo Clinic, Rochester, Minn., 1974—. Mem. honors med. program Northwestern U., 1963-69. Diplomate Am. Bd. Internal Medicine. Mem. A.M.A., A.C.P. (asso.), Am. Thoracic Soc., Zeta Tau Alpha. Home: 2011 Viking Dr Apt 37 Rochester MN 55901 Office: Mayo Clinic Rochester MN 55901

RODKEY, ELIZABETH S., business exec.; b. nr. Hagerstown, Md.; d. Martin and Martha (Myers) Summers; B.C.S., Columbus U., 1947, M.C.S., 1948, postgrad. George Washington U., Am. U.; m. William Rodkey, Oct. 1942 (div. Oct. 1953). Govt. employee, 1940-50; chief accountant St. Agnes Hosp., Balt., 1950-55; C.P.A. on internat. staff Haskins and Sells, C.P.A.'s, 1956-59; dir. finance Nat. Fedn. Bus. and Profl. Women's Clubs, Inc., 1955-56; controller Nat. Fence Mfg. Co., Inc., Bladensburg, 1961-65; chief central accounting and purchasing office DAC, 1967—. Bd. dirs. St. Agnes Hosp., Balt. C.P.A., Md. Mem. Am. Soc. Women Accountants (chpt. pres. 1953), Am. Woman's Soc. C.P.A.'s, Md. Assn. C.P.A.'s, Nat. Assn. Accountants, Am. Accounting Assn., Soc. Advancement Mgmt. Mem. Christian Ch. Author articles in field. Home: PO Box 871 Columbia MD 21045 Office: Post Comptroller's Office Ft Meade MD 20755

RODMAN, ANNE JANET CLARK (MRS. PETER P. RODMAN), statistician; b. Balt., May 15, 1918; d. Admont Halsey and Janet Tucker (Howell) Clark; A.B., Bryn Mawr Coll., 1939; M.S., U. Rochester, 1941; postgrad., Johns Hopkins, 1939-40, 59-60; m. Peter P. Rodman, June 21, 1941; children—Janet Howell (Mrs. Donald Andrew Moller), Peter Stephens, Edith Billopp. Research asst. Johns Hopkins Dept. Pediatrics, Balt., 1966-68; asst. dept. biostatistics Johns Hopkins Sch. Hygiene & Pub. Health, Balt., 1960—; pub. health statistician Balt. Health Dept., 1961-64; biostatistician Md. Health Dept., 1964-65. Mem. Bryn Mawr Coll. Alumnae Assn. (1st v.p. 1961-64). Contbr. articles to profl. jours. Home: PO Box 548 Aberdeen MD 21001 Office: 615 N Wolfe St Baltimore MD 21205

RODMANN, DOROTHY ELLEN, orgn. exec.; b. Washington, Feb. 1, 1930; d. Michael Albert and Georgie Rebecca (Stant) Peters; B.A., George Washington U., 1954, postgrad., 1954-55; m. Horst Rodmann, June 7, 1958; children—Leslie Ann, Karen Lynn. Adminstr. asst. Am. Polit. Sci. Assn., Washington, 1954-58; personnel asst. N.E.A., Washington, 1959-69, personnel asso., sec.-treas. staff orgn., 1969-71, employment mgr., 1971-72; personnel mgr. Nat. League Cities-Conf. of Mayors, Washington, 1972—. Chmn. discipline com. P.T.A. Overlook Sch., 1971—. Mem. Placement Dirs. Assn., Washington Personnel Assn., Alpha Delta Pi. Club: Arminius Social (Washington). Home: 8395 Uxbridge Ct Springfield VA 22151 Office: 1620 Eye St NW Washington DC 20006

RODNEY, HELEN, librarian; b. Edmonton, Alta., Can., Feb. 4, 1924; d. John Craig and Annabelle (Ross) McGregor; B.A. with honors in English, U. Alta., 1949; B.L.S., U. Toronto, 1950; m. William Rodney, Sept. 2, 1950; children—Helen Catherine, John William McGregor. Gen. librarian Carleton U. Library, Ottawa, Ont., Can., 1952-53; reference librarian McPherson Library, U. Victoria (B.C., Can.), 1962-65, head reference div., 1965—, lectr., course coordinator div. continuing edn., 1970-73. Mem. B.C. Citizens' Conf. Libraries. Bd. dirs. lit. and lectures com., Community Arts Council, 1970-71. Served with Women's Royal Canadian Naval Service, 1945. Mem. Assn. B.C. Librarians (dir. 1965-68, pres. 1969-70), Canadian Library Assn. (information services sect. vice-chmn. 1957-68), Canadian Assn. Coll. and Univ. Libraries (pres. 1974-75), Canadian Assn. U. Tchrs. Inst. Victoria Librarians (pres. 1966-67), Delta Gamma. Editor: Creative Canada, Vol. 1, 1971, Vol. 2, 1972. Home: 308 Denison Rd Victoria BC V8S 4K3 Canada

RODRIGUEZ, ALMA IRIS, economist; b. San Juan, P.R., June 20, 1930; d. Bernardo and Justa (Ocasio) Rodriguez; B.A. magna cum laude, U. P.R., 1953; M.A., 1960; m. Eugenio Morales, Apr. 29, 1961 (div. Jan. 1963); 1 son, Eugenio B. Tchr. Dept. of Edn., Hato Rey, P.R., 1954-56; asst. economist Econ. Research Div., Legislative Reference Service, San Juan, P.R., 1956-57, economist, 1959-60; economist Econ. Research Div., Dept. of the Treasury, San Juan, 1961-62; economist, Econ. Devel. Adminstrn., Santurce, P.R., 1962-67; economist Econ. Research Dept., Santurce, 1967—; analysis studies Curet and Assos., Rio Piedras, P.R., 1967-68; statis. and research work Office of Investigation and Adminstrv. Service, Hato Rey, 1966-67. Bd. dirs. P.R. Devel. Bank Employees Assn. (pres. 1969-70); bd. dirs. Fomento Coop., 1971-74, mem. edn. com., spl. com. in charge of organization Coop. of Services. Mem. Am. Econ. Assn. Democrat. Roman Càtholic. Home: 180 San Lorenzo St Rio Piedras Heights Rio Piedras PR 00926 Office: PO Box 9183 Santurce PR 00908

RODRIGUEZ, JOSEFINA CARMEN HORTENSIA, physician; b. Santo Domingo, Dominican Republic, Mar. 16, 1929 (came to U.S., 1952, naturalized 1957); d. Raul Ernesto and Maria Carmela (Rodriguez) Rodriguez; B.S., Escuela Normal Salome Urena, 1946; M.D., U. de Santo Domingo, 1952. Intern, Lincoln Hosp., N.Y.C., 1953-54; resident internal medicine Cumberland Hosp., Bklyn., 1954-55, Med. Center, Jersey City, N.J., 1955-56, Met. Meml. Med. Center, N.Y.C., 1956-57; internist VA Hosp., Dublin, Ga., 1959-61; chief med. service McCook Meml. Hosp., Hartford, 1961-63; practice medicine specializing in internal medicine, Hartford, 1963—, Somers, Conn., 1966—; mem. staffs St. Francis, Hartford, Mt. Sinai Hosp., Hartford, Johnson Meml. Hosp., Stafford Springs. Fellow Am. Geriatrics Soc.; mem. A.M.A., Conn. State Med. Soc., Hartford County Med. Assn., Conn. Diabetes Assn. Office: Main St Somers CT 06071

RODRIGUEZ, PAULA PROVIDENCIA, educator; b. Lares, P.R., Aug. 26, 1933; d. Jose M. and Anna (Rodriguez) Rodriguez; student U. Barcelona (Spain), 1952-57; B.A., Inter-Am. U. P.R., 1960; M.A., Peabody Coll. for Tchrs., 1968, postgrad., 1970; m. Roberto A. Galva, June 6, 1955 (div. Nov. 1958); children—Roberto A., Ana Lorena. Chief chemist P.R. Organics, Arecibo, 1960-63; instr. biology Inter-Am. U., San German, 1963-68, asst. prof., 1968-72, asso. prof., 1972, dir. Arecibo regional coll., 1972—. Mem. evaluation team Middle States Coll. Assn.-Commn. Higher Edn., 1972-74. Asst. scoutmaster Boy Scouts Am., Arecibo, 1964-72; troop leader Girl Scouts U.S.A., 1970-72; treas. P.T.A. Colegio Capitan Correa en Arecibo, 1964-72. Recipient Commendation plaque Lions Club, Arecibo, 1973. Home: 50 Ave Dr Barbosa Arecibo PR 00612

RODRIGUEZ, VIOLA MARQUEZ (MRS. PEDRO RODRIGUEZ), physician; b. Havana, Cuba, Nov. 20, 1918 (came to U.S. 1965, naturalized 1974); d. Reinaldo Francisco and Mercedes Marta (Biscay) Marquez; M.D., U. Havana, 1944; m. Pedro A. Rodriguez, June 4, 1941; children—Rolando, Daniel. Intern Gen. Calixto Garcia U. Hosp., Havana, 1945-46, resident 1946-47; practice medicine specializing in internal medicine, pathology and research, Havana, 1945-60, Mexia, Tex., 1968-70, Lockhart, Tex., 1970—; mem. staffs Lockhart Hosp., Mexia Hosp.; asst. prof. bacteriology U. Havana Sch. Medicine, 1953-60, prof., 1946-60; dir. research dept. and med. dir. Laboratorio Reinaldo Marquez, Havana, 1950-60. Mem. Cuban Med. Assn. in Exile, A.M.A., Tex. Med. Assn., Nat. Fed. Bus. and Profl. Women's Club, Cuban Soc. Med. Pathologists (founder 1945). Contbr. articles to profl. jours. Home: 803 Vogel Dr Lockhart TX 78644 Office: 109 W San Antonio St Lockhart TX 78644

ROE, CATHERINE UPCHURCH (MRS. WILLIAM A. ROE), club woman; b. Galena, Kan., May 8, 1909; d. Syhon and Rosa Lee (Milligan) Upchurch; certificate Kan. State Tchrs. Coll., 1926-28; student Benedict's Coll., 1968-72; m. William A. Roe, Aug. 16, 1929; children—Laura (Mrs. Robert Bartlett), Frances (dec.), George, William Alfred. Pvt. tchr. piano and violin, Merriam and Galena, Kan., 1926-28, 44-48; tchr., Eudora, Kan., 1928-29; tchr. music and art, Eudora, 1929-30; job instrn. tng. Lake City Munitions Plant, Kansas City, Mo., 1942-43. Mem. Joint Health Bd., Atchison, Kan., 1960-70, Community Concert Bd., Atchison, 1950-74; mem. Atchison Hosp. Aux., 1957-74; dist. pres. P.T.A., 1957-58, mem. state bd., 1957-58; mem. Atchison Mayor's Bi-centennial Commn., 1974—. Pres. Women's County Republican Club, 1962, 63; vice chmn. Atchison County Reps., 1964-74. Bd. dirs. United Fund, 1959-69; pres. Atchison County Econ. Opportunity Bd., 1964-65. Mem. Kan. Fedn. Women's Clubs (state art chmn. 1961-64, dist. pres. 1963-64, state pres. 1973-74), Delta Sigma Epsilon. Methodist (mem. bd. 1955-67, pres. Women's Soc. Christian Service 1960-61). Club: Atchison Garden (pres. 1965-66). Home: 300 N 3d St Atchison KS 66002

ROE, DAPHNE ANDERSON (MRS. ALBERT S. ROE), physician; b. London, Eng., Jan. 4, 1923; d. Adrian and Lilian Marion (Adler) Anderson; M.B., B.S., U. London, 1946; M.D., 1950, M.R.C.P., 1948; m. Albert S. Roe, May 18, 1954; children—David, Laura, Adrian. Came to U.S., 1953, naturalized, 1958. Intern, Royal Free Hosp., London, 1946, A.M. Bird scholar in pathology, 1946-47; sr. house officer Bristol (Eng.) Gen. Hosp., 1948; registrar St. John's Hosp. for Diseases of Skin, 1948-52, 1st asst., 1952-53; registrar Royal Free Hosp., also Hosp. for Sick Children, London, 1948-52; research fellow Mass. Gen. Hosp., Boston, 1953-54; research asso. U. Pa., 1954-57; cons. dermatologist Wilmington (Del.) Hosps., 1959-61; mem. faculty Cornell U., Ithaca, N.Y., 1961—, cons. physician Univ. Health Services, 1961—, project dir. study health and nutrition in low income group women, 1971—, acting dean Grad. Sch. Nutrition, 1973-74; attending physician Tompkins County Hosp., Ithaca. Recipient Chesterfield medal in dermatology, 1950, Distinguished Service award N.Y. State Jour. Medicine, 1966. Fellow Royal Soc. Medicine; mem. A.M.A., Brit. Med. Assn., Am. Inst. Nutrition, A.A.A.S., Soc. Investigative Dermatology, Acad. Dermatology. Author: A Plague of Corn: The Social History of Pellagra, 1973. Home: 116 N Sunset Dr Ithaca NY 14850 Office: Div Nutritional Scis Cornell U Ithaca NY 14850

ROE, FAY DAPHNE CROSLIN (MRS. A. J. ROE, JR.), home economist; b. Powderly, Tex.; d. Claude B. and Hester (Lenoir) Croslin; B.S., Tex. Womans U., 1942; postgrad. Tex. A. and M. U., 1966-67; m. A. J. Roe, Jr., Feb. 3, 1946; children—Daphne Elayne (Mrs. James Everett Brown), A. J. III. Asst. dietitian coop. system Tex. Womans U., Denton, 1940-42; asst. home demonstration agt., Tyler, 1942-43; Civil Service cafeteria hostess, 1943-44; county extension agt. Robert Lee, Coke County (Tex.), 1944-46, 54-58, 61—. Substitute tchr., Silver Peak, 1958-61; dietary cons. Root Meml. Hosp., Valley Fair Lodge, Colorado City, Tex., 1969—, West Coke County Hosp., Robert Lee, Tex., 1968—. Recipient Distinguished Service award Nat. Extension Home Economists, 1971. Mem. Nat., Tex. home demonstration agt. assns., Coke County Hist. Soc., Nat., Tex. home econ. assns., Womens Soc. Christian Service, Epsilon Sigma Phi. Methodist (mem. family relations com.). Club: El Vallee Garden (com. mem. 1954—). Address: Box 126 Robert Lee TX 76945

ROE, INA LEA GALLAHER (MRS. DONALD ROE), educator; b. Wheat, Tenn., Nov. 25, 1930; d. William Ernest and Lucile Marie (Zimmerman) Gallaher; B.S., A.B., U. Tenn., 1952; M.S., Temple U., 1961; m. Donald Roe, Aug. 15, 1961. Office med. technologist, Knoxville, Tenn., 1952-58; med. technologist Meml. Hosp., Chattanooga, 1958-59; faculty Temple U., Phila., 1961—, prof., dept. med. tech., 1973—. Adviser Phila. Health Careers, 1965-68. Mem. Am. (Outstanding Technologist 1973), Pa. (pres. 1972-73) socs. med. tech., Acad. Clin. Lab. Physicians and Scientists, Assn. Schs. Allied Health Professions, Nat. Accrediting Agy. for Clin. Lab. Scis. Editor Am. Jour. Med. Tech., 1971—. Home: PO Box 382 Princeton NJ 08540 Office: 3307 N Broad St Philadelphia PA 19140

ROE, JANE ST. JOHN (MRS. BENSON B. ROE), civic worker; b. N.Y.C., July 1, 1920; d. Fordyce B. and Jane I. (Rignel) St. John; A.B., Vassar Coll., 1942; B.S., Columbia, 1944, R.N., 1945; m. Benson B. Roe, Jan. 20, 1945; children—David B., Virginia St. John. Staff nurse Columbia-Presbyn. Med. Center, N.Y.C., 1944-45; lab. technician, dept. bacteriology U. Pa., Phila., 1946, Harvard Med. Sch., Boston, 1947-48. Organizer, developer San Francisco Speech and Hearing Center, 1952-58; chmn. auction for ednl. TV, San Francisco, 1963; mem. San Francisco Comprehevsive Health Planning Council, 1965-74; v.p. San Francisco Homemaker Service, 1962-68. Bd. dirs. Planned Parenthood, 1964-75, v.p., 1970-72; bd. dirs. United Bay Area Crusade, 1969-73, v.p., 1970-71; bd. dirs. Bay Area Social Planning Council, 1965-75, sec., 1965-68; bd. dirs. Arthritis and Rheumatism Found., 1952-58, Speech and Hearing Center, 1952-58, Mental Health Found., 1966-68, Jr. League San Francisco, 1953-60, KQED Ednl. TV, 1958-71. Home: 1090 Chestnut St San Francisco CA 94109

ROEBLING, MARY G., banker; b. West Collingswood, N.J.; d. I.D., Jr. and Mary W. (Simon) Gindhart; Moorestown High Sch.; student bus. adminstrn., econs. and finance, U. Pa., econs. and finance N.Y. U.; hon. degrees, LL.D., Ithaca Coll., 1954; D.Sc., Muhlenberg Coll.; D.Sc. in Bus. Adminstrn., Bryant Coll.; Dr. Humanities Wilberforce U.; D.F.A., Rider Coll.; Dr. Comml. Sci., St. John's U.; m. Siegfried Roebling (dec.); children—Elizabeth (Mrs. David J. Hobin), Paul. Chmn. bd. Nat. State Bank. Econ. ambassador N.J.; dir. Companion Life Ins. Co., Tattersall Co.; civilian aide to sec. Army for N.J.; emeritus mem. Def. Dept. Com. Women in Armed Services; chmn. finance Invest-in-Am.; N.J. chmn. Hospitalized Vets. Service Musicians Emergency Fund; mem. N.J. Investment Council; adv. council 4th Dist. Naval Affairs; mem. citizens com. N.J. Cultural Center. Bd. govs. Del. Valley Council, Nat. Multiple Sclerosis Soc.; mem. adv. bd. Assn. U.S. Army; mem. exec. bd. Boy Scouts Am. Mem. 1971 Ann. Assay Commn. Comptroller, Trenton Parking Authority; hon. chmn., founder Donnelly Meml. Hosp. Women's Com. Mem. nat. bd. Med. Coll. Pa.; hon. chmn. Greater Trenton Symphony. Bd. dirs. Axe-Houghton Found. Recipient Geo. Washington Honor Medal Freedoms Found.; Distinguished Service award Marine Corps League; Humanitarian award N.J. Arthritis Found.; Outstanding Civilian Service medal Dept. Army; Pres.'s medal Assn. U.S. Army, others; decorated Royal Order Vasa, King Sweden, Order Star of Solidarity (Italy). Mem. N.J. Bankers Assn., Am. Acad. Polit. Sci. (mem. bd.), Am. Mus. Immigration (dir.), Bus. and Profl. Women's Club, Am. Legion Aux., N.J. Conf. Christians and Jews, Swedish Colonial Soc., League Women Voters, Am. Inst. Banking, Nat. Def. Transp. Assn. (life mem.), Internat. C. of C. (trustee U.S. council), Am. Bankers Assn., Soc. Mayflower Descs., Colonial Daus. 17th Century, Trenton C. of C., D.A.R., Geneal. Soc. Pa., Nat. Fedn. Music Clubs, Phila. Mus. Art, N.J. Firemen's Mut. Benevolent Assn. (hon. life). Clubs: Zonta, Trenton Country, Lake Placid, Sea View Country, Contemporary (Trenton); Overseas Press, 1925 F Street (Washington); Am. Newspaper Women's Club. Home: 777 W State St Trenton NJ 08618 Office: 28 W State St Trenton NJ 08605

ROECA, CONSTANCE KIVARI (MRS. SAMUEL FRANK ROECA), lawyer, educator; b. Denver, July 7, 1922; d. Arthur Matthew and Esther Wicks (Snyder) Kivari; A.B., U. So. Cal., 1943, LL.B., 1945; m. Samuel Frank Roeca, May 13, 1944; children—Richard, Arthur, Douglas, Russell, Jeffrey. Law clk. Betts, Ely & Loomis, Los Angeles, 1943-45; admitted to Cal. bar, 1945; practiced in Los Angeles, 1945—; asso. atty. Spray, Gould & Bowers 1966-71; prof. Southwestern U. Sch. Law, Los Angeles, 1971—; counsel firm Hillsinger & Costanzo, 1973—. Mem. Am., Los Angeles bar assns., Women's Lawyers Assn., Themis Soc., Phi Beta Kappa, Kappa Alpha Theta, Phi Delta Delta. Republican. Episcopalian. Office: 3345 Wilshire Blvd Los Angeles CA 90010

ROEDER, LUCILE FRANCES LANE, nursing educator; b. Corinth, N.C., May 22, 1915; d. Oscar Julius and Della Lane (Hughes) Lane; B.S. in Nursing, U. Md., 1960, M.S. in Maternal and Child Health Nursing, 1963; m. Charles Adam Roeder, Dec. 31, 1954; children—Lucile Frances, Sally (Mrs. Mark W. Dudderar), Charles Adam, Eric Michael. Asst. prof. nursing for children U. Md. Sch. Nursing, 1964-66, asst. prof. pub. health nursing, 1966-67; dir. nursing service and nursing edn. John F. Kennedy Inst., Johns Hopkins, 1967-71; asst. prof. maternal child nursing Atlantic Christian Coll., Wilson, N.C., 1972—. Grantee Nat. Inst. Mental Health, 1963-66. Mem. Women's Civic League Balt., Sigma Theta Tau, Phi Delta Gamma (past chpt. pres.). Lutheran (1st v.p. women's group 1970-71). Home: 5715 Falls Rd Baltimore MD 21209 Office: Dept Nursing Atlantic Christian Coll Wilson NC 27893

ROEDER, VIRGINIA LIBERTY VOIGT (MRS. MARVIN J. ROEDER), home economist; b. Tuttle, Okla., Feb. 6, 1927; d. Fred and Adda (Mitchell) Voigt; B.S., Okla. Coll. for Women, 1946; postgrad. U. Okla., summer 1946; M.Ed., Johns Hopkins, 1953, Ph.D. (Ford fellow, Johns Hopkins scholar, Florence Bamberger scholar), 1959; m. Marvin J. Roeder; children—Anne, James, Mary, Frederick. Grad. asst. U. Okla. Nursery Sch., 1946; tchr. home econs. Balt. Pub. Schs., 1946-47, 50-55, specialist in home econs, 1956-59, 60-61, supr. home econs. adult edn. program, 1959, vice prin. jr. and sr. high schs., 1960-63, prin. Herring Run Jr. High Sch., Balt., 1965-70; supr. home econs. Balt. Pub. Schs., 1970—. Lectr. sch. orgn. and adminstrn. Loyola Coll., Balt., summers 1963—; homemaking and food columnist Balt. Evening Sun, 1955—; star weekly TV program sta. WMAR-TV, Balt., 1953-54. Mem. adv. bd. St. Agnes Hosp. Sch. Nursing, Balt., 1958-62; mem. Balt. Mayor's Commn. for Phys. Fitness, 1961-62; mem. membership com. Md. Ednl. Television, 1964—. Mem. Am., Med. home econs. assns., Nat., Md. (pres. 1969-70) assns. secondary sch. prins., Pi Lambda Theta. Mem. P.E. Ch. Club: Johns Hopkins (Balt.). Author: Fun with Food, 1957; Fun with Seafood, 1960. Contbr. articles on edn. and food to profl. publs. Home: 5919 Meadowood Rd Baltimore MD 21212 Office: Balt Evening Sun Oliver and Eden Sts Baltimore MD 21218

ROEHM, MARYANNE EVANS (MRS. JOSEPH L. ROEHM), nursing educator; b. Terre Haute, Ind., Nov. 29, 1925; d. Herbert E. and Reba Fern (Lathrop) Evans; B.S. in Nursing, Ind. State U., 1953, M.S. in Edn., 1957; M.S. in Nursing Edn., Ind. U., 1965, Ed.D., 1966; m. Joseph L. Roehm, Aug. 10, 1947. Tchr., asst. dir. Union Hosp. Sch. Nursing, Terre Haute, 1946-55; tchr., asso. dir. St. Anthony Hosp. Sch. Nursing, Terre Haute, 1957-64; prof. nursing Ind. State U. Sch. Nursing, Terre Haute, 1966—, also dir. continuing nursing edn. Mem. Citizens Com. to Vigo County Home for Aged, 1966—; mem. adv. com. Vigo County Sch. Corp. Practical Nurse Program, 1967-71, adv. com. health occupations Ind. Vocational Tech. Coll., 1971—; mem. vocational adv. com. Vigo County Sch. Corp., 1967-71; nursing com. Ind. Regional Med. Program, 1968-73, area chmn.; mem. adv. com. Ind. Health Careers, 1968-71; chmn. nursing careers com. Dist. 3 Ind. State Nurses Assn., 1969—; chmn. Wabash Valley Health Careers Council, 1966-71; adv. com. Ind. Comprehensive Health Planning Council; co-chmn. manpower com. West Central Community Found., 1968—; del. Vigo County Comprehensive Health Planning Council, 1968—; regional chmn. sesquecentennial fund dr. Ind. U. Sch. Nursing, 1969-70, 72, 73; regional chmn. Statewide Planning Com. for Continuing Edn. in Nursing, also mem. exec. com. Mem. Assn. for Higher Edn., Am. Assn. U. Profs., Am., Ind. (platform com. 1971), Dist. nurses assns., Nat., Ind., West Central leagues for nursing, Ind. U., Ind. State U., Union Hosp. alumni assns., Kappa Delta Pi, Sigma Theta Tau, Pi Lambda Theta. Home: RR 22 Box 390-A Terre Haute IN 47802

ROELKER, NANCY LYMAN, historian, educator; b. Warwick, R.I., June 15, 1915; d. William Greene and Anne Rossiter (Koues) Roelker; A.B., Radcliffe Coll., 1936; Ph.D., Harvard, 1953. Tchr. history Winsor Sch., Boston, 1941-63; asst. prof. history Tufts U., Medford, Mass., 1963-66, asso. prof., 1966-69, prof., 1969-71; prof. European history Boston U., 1971—. Guggenheim fellow, 1965-66; Am. Philos. Soc. grantee, 1960, 70. Fellow Am. Acad. Arts and Scis.; mem. Am. Hist. Assn. (bd. editors 1971-76), Phi Beta Kappa. Author: The Paris of Henry of Navarre, 1958; Queen of Navarre: Jeanne d'Albret, 1528-1572, 1968; also articles. Home: 19 Ware St Cambridge MA 02138 Office: 226 Bay State Rd Boston MA 02215

ROELS, DOROTHY MARY (MRS. OSWALD ROELS), physician; b. Liverpool, Eng., June 28, 1925 (came to U.S. 1960, naturalized 1965); d. Harold Marland and Phyllis (Rhodes) Broadhurst; M.D., Liverpool Sch. of Medicine, 1949; Diploma of Tropical Medicine and Hygiene, Liverpool Sch. of Tropical Medicine, 1952; m. Oswald Roels, Sept. 16, 1950; 1 dau., Margaret Ann. Intern Liverpool Royal Infirmary, 1949, Sefton Gen. Hosp., Liverpool, 1950; resident 1950, Broadgreen Gen. Hosp., Liverpool; practice medicine practicing in gen. practice Eng., 1951-53; pub. health dr., Belgium, 1953-55; nutritional research, Belgian Congo, 1955-60; pub. health physician N.Y.C. Pub. Health Dept., 1961-68; now dir. ambulatory care and hosp. epidemiology St. Luke's Hosp., N.Y.C., 1968—, also asso. attending staff; adj. asst. prof. health adminstrn. Columbia Sch. Pub. Health, 1972—. Mem. Brit. Med. Assn., Royal Soc. Tropical Medicine, A.M.A., Am. Pub. Health Assn. Club: Nyack (N.Y.) Boat. Home: 292 Hardenburgh Av Demares NJ 07627 Office: St Luke's Hosp 440 W 114 St New York City NY 10025

ROEMER, ELIZABETH, astronomer; b. Oakland, Cal., Sept. 4, 1929; d. Richard Quirin and Elsie (Barlow) Roemer; B.A. with honors in Astronomy (Bertha Dolbeer scholar), U. Cal. at Berkeley, 1950, Ph.D. (Lick Obs. fellow), 1955. Teaching asst. U. Cal. at Berkeley, part time 1950-52, grad. research astronomer, 1955-56; tchr. adult class astronomy Oakland (Cal.) pub. schs., part time 1950-52; lab. technician U. Cal. Lick Observatory, Mt. Hamilton, 1954-55; research asso. U. Chgo. Yerkes Obs., Williams Bay, Wis., 1956; astronomer U.S. Naval Obs., Flagstaff, Ariz., 1957-66; asso. prof. dept. astronomy and Lunar and Planetary Lab., U. Ariz., Tucson, 1966-69, prof., 1969—. Participant program vis. profs. in astronomy Am. Astron. Soc., NSF, 1960—; Donohoe lectr., Astron. Soc. Pacific, 1962; mem. Panel Planetary Astronomy, Space Sci. Bd. Nat. Acad. Sci.-NRC, 1967-68; mem. NRC adv. com. on astronomy to Office Naval Research, 1969-70; NRC-NASA postdoctoral research asso. program, 1973—. Finalist Westinghouse Sci. Talent Search, 1946; recipient Dorothea Klumpke Roberts prize U. Cal., 1950, Mademoiselle Merit award, 1959, Benjamin Apthorp Gould prize U.S. Nat. Acad. Scis., 1971. Fellow A.A.A.S. (committeeman at large sect. D 1966-69, council rep. Am. Astron. Soc. 1972-73), Royal Astron. Soc. London; mem. Internat. Astron. Union (chmn. working group on orbits of periodic comets 1964—), No. Ariz. Soc. Sci. and Art, Am. Astron. Soc. (councilor 1967-70, vice-chmn. div. dynamical astronomy 1973, chmn. 1974), Astron. Soc. Pacific, Brit. Astron. Assn., Am. Geophys. Union, Phi Beta Kappa, Sigma Xi. Club: Sierra (San Francisco). Contbr. articles to sci. jours., encys. Office: Lunar and Planetary Lab U Ariz Tucson AZ 85721

ROEMER, LUCILE RUNNESTRAND, library dir.; b. Ft. Cobb, Okla., May 16, 1910; d. Erick George and Harriet (Meredith) Runnestrand; student Hamline U., St. Paul, 1926-28, U. Wis., 1928-29; B.A., U. Minn., 1930, B.L.S. cum laude, 1933; m. Claude Franklin Roemer, Sept. 4, 1937; children—John Meredith, Paul Crawford. Catalog librarian U. Minn. Library, Mpls., 1935-37; reference librarian, Watertown, S.D., 1933-35; high sch. tchr., librarian, 1944-45; catalog librarian library extension div. Minn. Dept. Edn., St. Paul, 1937-40; reference librarian U. Minn. Library, 1944-45; account exec. KDAL Radio, Duluth, Minn., 1960-61, radio sales mgr., 1962-63; dir. libraries City of Duluth, 1963—. Exec. dir. Nat. Library Week in Minn., 1966. Mem. Duluth Welfare Council Bd., 1962-65. Pres. League Women Voters, Duluth, 1953-55; mem. Duluth City Council, 1956-59; mem. Minn. League Women Voters Bd., 1959. Trustee Duluth Pub. Library Bd., 1959-63. Mem. Am., Minn. library assns., Bus. and Profl. Womens Club Duluth (past pres.), Delta Kappa Gamma (pres. Beta chpt. 1968-69). Home: 2152 Vermilion Rd Duluth MN 55803 Office: 101 W 2d St Duluth MN 55802

ROES, CAROL LASATER (MRS. HAROLD JOHN ROES), composer, lyricist; b. Pauls Valley, Okla.; d. Milas and Sarah (Waite) Lasater; student Oberlin Conservatory Music, 1925; A.B., Stanford, 1928; m. Harold John Roes, Feb. 12, 1938. Owner, Mele Loke Pub. Co., Honolulu, 1960—. Demonstrator Hawaiian songs at state univs., 1961—. Mem. Honolulu, Nat. socs. arts and letters, Hawaiian Profl. Songwriters Soc., Nat. League Am. Pen Women, Am. Soc. Composers, Authors and Pubs., Morning Music Club, Jr. League Hawaii. Composer: Children's Songs from Hawaii, 1972; 8 Children's Songs, 1960; Song Stories, 1960, Keiki Songs, 1966. Home: 988 Kealaolu Av Honolulu HI 96816 Office: PO Box 7142 Honolulu HI 96821

ROETMAN, LEE ANN, occupational therapist; b. Orange City, Ia., June 22, 1947; d. Edwin B. and Anna (Beyer) Roetman; student Central U. Ia., 1965-66, Ariz. State U., 1966-67; B.S. with distinction, U. Minn., 1970. Psychiatric occupational therapist Bethesda Hosp., Denver, 1971—. Mem. Am., Colo. Occupational Therapy assns. Home: 4295 E Mexico Av #707 Denver CO 80222 Office: 4400 E Iliff St Denver CO 80222

ROETTGER, DORYE, musician, author, lectr.; b. Utica, N.Y., Oct. 22, 1932; d. Albert Frank and Marion Emma (Farber) Rutger; student Ithaca Coll., 1949-51; Mus.B., U. Chgo. Extension, 1955; Ph.D., U. Eastern Fla., 1972; pvt. study music, dance, art. Profl. oboist, 1951—; appearances include Carnegie Hall, Town Hall, Aeolian Hall, N.Y.C., Music Center, Wilshire Ebell Theater, Bing Theatre, Los Angeles, numerous others, tours U.S., 1951—; vis. artist U. So. Cal., U. Cal. at Los Angeles, Immaculate Heart Coll., Cal. Inst. Tech., U. Nev., others, 1955—; creator over 1000 children's programs for schs., 1956—; producer ann. Chamber Music for Children Festival, 1968—; founder-dir. Festival Players of Cal., Los Angeles, 1958—; producer monthly concert series Nat. Pacifica Radio, 1971—; originator lectr. course Music and People: A Survey of World Cultures, 1973—. Vol., Los Angeles City Schs. Vol. Program, 1971—. Recipient commendation meritorious pub. service Cal. Assembly, 1968; certificate appreciation Los Angeles City Council, 1968; others; cited in Congl. Record, 1971. Mem. Nat. Fedn. Music Clubs (Western regional chmn. Music in schs. and colls. 1973—, state chmn. dept. edn. 1972—), Asso. Profl. Talent, Am. Fedn. Musicians, Internat. Platform Assn., Cal. Music Educators Assn., Nat. Assn. Music Therapy, Am. Musicological Soc. Christian Scientist. Mem. Order Eastern Star. Contbr. articles to profl. jours.; syndicated column Bridging the Culture Gap, 1971—. Address: Festival of Players Cal 3809 De Longpre Av Los Angeles CA 90027

ROFF, ROSELLA ZUBER (MRS. LOUIS F. ROFF), ednl. adminstr.; b. Lima, O., July 26, 1913; d. Jacob and Anna Viola (McClure) Zuber; diploma Bowling Green State U., 1933; B.S. in Edn., Ohio State U., 1939, M.A., 1955; m. Louis F. Roff, Dec. 28, 1952; 1 stepson, Franklyn Preston. Tchr., Shawnee Centralized Sch., Lima, 1933-43, prin., 1943-49; tchr. Highline Pub. Schs., Seattle, 1943-49, prin. elementary sch., 1949—. Mem.exec. bd. Big Bros. Highline; chmn. scholarship, edn. coms. Highline Area council P.T.A. Recipient Outstanding Service award Highline Area Council Parents, Students, Tchrs., 1973. Mem. Nat., Wash. (various coms.) edn. assns., Assn. Wash. Sch. Prins. (charter), Highline Sch. Prins. (charter), Highline-West Seattle Mental Health Assn. (co-organizer), Delta Kappa Gamma (steering com. for internat. conversation 1974, other coms., ofcl. positions). Home: 4410 S 148th St Seattle WA 98168 Office: 3702 S 168th St Seattle WA 98168

ROGALIN, WILMA CLARE SIVERTSEN (MRS. JOHN A. ROGALIN), airline exec., polit. worker; b. Mpls., Dec. 7, 1916; d. Ivar and Clare (Wilmes) Sivertsen; B.S., U. Minn., 1937; M.A., Columbia, 1944; m. John A. Rogalin, Apr. 24, 1962. Personnel mgr. Pan Am. World Airways, N.Y.C., 1942-73, now sr. mgr. women's opportunities. Mem. nat. laywomen's com. Nat. Council Chs. of Christ in U.S.A., 1952-55; chmn. employee contbns. Salvation Army, Queens, N.Y., 1961-62; mem. N.Y. State Women's Council, 1968—; mem. Def. Adv. Com. for Women in Services, chmn., 1974. Chmn. bd. dirs. N.Y. Young Women's Republican Club, 1947-48; pres. Young Women's Rep. Club N.Y.C., 1948-50; v.p. Assn. N.Y. State young Rep. Clubs, 1950-52; treas. Fedn. Women's Rep. Clubs N.Y. State, 1950-52, 1st v.p., 1952-54, pres., 1959-70; v.p. region 2 Nat. Fedn. Young Rep. Clubs, 1950-55; pres. N.Y.C. Rep. Bus. Women, 1953-55; asso. leader 9th Assembly Dist., N.Y. County Rep. Club, 1953-57, 58-59; vice chmn. N.Y. State Rep. Com., 1959-70; bd. dirs. Women's Nat. Rep. Club, 1959-65, 68-71; del., platform com. Rep. Nat. Conv., 1960, 64, 68. Bd. dirs. Queens YWCA, 1945-48, N.Y.C. Vis. Nurses, 1971—. Mem. N.Y. Personnel Mgmt. Assn., N.Y. Airlines Personnel Mgrs. Assn. (sec. 1958), U. Minn. Alumni of N.Y. (pres. 1953-54), Kappa Alpha Theta. Presbyn. Home: Cedar Hill Lane Pound Ridge NY 10576 Office: Pan Am Airways Pan Am Bldg New York City NY 10017

ROGALSKI, CAROL JEAN, psychologist; b. Chgo., Sept. 25, 1937; d. Casimir Joseph and Lillian Valentine (Wachowski) Rogalski; B.S., Loyola U., 1961; Ph.D., N.Y. U., 1968, certificate psychoanalysis-psychotherapy Center for Mental Health, 1973. Research asso. William Alanson White Psychoanalytic Inst., N.Y.C., 1963-66; intern Hillside Hosp., Queens, N.Y., 1966-68; asso. staff Postgrad. Center for Mental Health, N.Y.C., 1968-73; pvt. practice psychotherapy, N.Y.C., 1970-73, Portland, Ore., 1973—. Cons. Mt. Sinai Hosp., N.Y.C., 1970-73; instr. psychology John Jay Coll. of Criminal Justice, N.Y.C., 1971-73. Vol. ancient art dept. Bklyn Mus., YWCA, N.Y.C., Tel Gezer Archeol. Excavation Hebrew Union Coll., Israel. Recipient Ill. Psychiat. tng. and research project grant, 1959-61, USPHS grantee, 1961-62, Nat. Inst. Mental Health grantee, 1968-71. Mem. Am., Eastern psychol. assns., Pi Gamma Mu. Home: 4 Touchstone Apt 150 Lake Oswego OR 97034 Office: 2075 SW First Av Portland OR 97201

ROGERS, ADELE LANGSTON (MRS. WILLIAM P. ROGERS), univ. trustee; b. Haddon Heights, N.J., Aug. 15, 1911; d. Samuel MacDonald and Jessica (Wood) Langston; A.B., Cornell U., 1933, LL.B., 1936; postgrad. Stanford Law Sch., 1933-35; m. William P. Rogers, June 27, 1936; children—Dale (Mrs. Donald Jay Marshall), Anthony Wood, Jeffrey Langston, Douglas Langston. Trustee Cornell U., N.Y.C., 1959-74, mem. exec. com., 1966-74, trustee emerita, 1974—; trustee Gannett Newspaper Found., Meridian House Internat. Found. Recipient Presdl. Citizens medal, 1973. Mem. Mortar Bd. (pres. Washington chpt. 1964-65), Delta Delta Delta. Presbyn. Club: Chevy Chase (Md.). Home: 7007 Glenbrook Rd Bethesda MD 20014 also 870 UN Plaza 19F New York City NY 10017

ROGERS, MRS. ALICE BRADSHAW, public relations, advt. exec.; b. Dayton, Tex., Sept. 18, 1911; d. William Benjamin and Mannie Willis (Davis) Bradshaw; student U. Tex., 1927-29, U. Houston, 1953, 59; m. Evert A. Rogers, Aug. 17, 1934, (div. May 1950); children—Jane (Mrs. A. Russel Matthews), Elizabeth (Mrs. Wesley M. Bannister), Nancy Lynn (Mrs. Richard E. Stephanow). Sec., Henry L. Doherty, stocks and bonds, 1930-33, L. E. Norton Real Estate, 1933-34; sec. Fisk Electric Co., 1934-37; sec.-treas. Art Engraving Co., 1937-49, pres., 1949-50; pres. Advt. Arts Bldg. Corp., 1952-54, Houston Tradetypers, 1955-57, Goodwin-Dannenbaum Advt. Agy., 1957; dir., sec.-treas., pres. Art Engraving Co., Inc.; dir., pres. Advt. Arts Bldg. Corp.; v.p., dir., sec.-treas. Houston Advt. Club, Inc.; dir. 10th Dist. Advt. Fedn. Am., 1955—; pub. relations dir. Houston Youth Symphony, 1962—; bus. relations dir. Better Bus. Bur., Houston; community club awards dir. Houston Chronicle, 1963-65; now activities co-ordinator Houston Club, asso. editor, bus. mgr. The Houston Clubber. Adv. bd. Achievement Rewards Coll. Scientists Found.; dist. chmn. publicity bd. Girl Scouts of Am., 1946-50; mem. publicity com. United Fund, 1952-54; mem. Pin Oak Horse Show advt. program com., Houston Fat Stock Show advt. program com. Mem. C. of C., Advt. Fedn. Am., Houston Soc. Assn. Execs., Harris County Heritage Soc., Gamma Alpha Chi. Clubs: Advertising (sec.), Press (life) (Houston); Mothers (Zeta Tau Alpha). Home: 4723 Merwin Houston TX 77027 Office: Houston Club Houston Club Bldg Houston TX 77002

ROGERS, DIANE PATRICIA, ednl. adminstr.; b. Hamilton, Ont., Can., June 29, 1928; d. Harold Allin and Elspeth A. (McIlroy) Rogers; B.A. with honours, U. Toronto, 1950, M.A., (fellow), 1967. Program supt. Ont. Dept. Edn., Toronto, 1967—. Recipient J. Reginald Adams Gold medal, Victoria Coll., 1950. Mem. Canadian Inst. Internat. Affairs. Clubs: University Women's (Toronto); The Empire. Co-author: Inside World Politics, 1969; Dimensions of Man, 1972. Home: 45 Wynford Heights Crescent Apt 2205 Don Mills ON M3C1L3 Canada Office: 1152 Bay St Toronto ON Canada

ROGERS, ELIZABETH BANISTER, banker; b. Henderson, Ky., Nov. 24, 1911; d. Herman Buford and Emma Vera (Gunn) Banister; student Bowling Green Bus. U., 1929-31; m. Leonard Byron Rogers, June 20, 1932; 1 son, Leonard Byron. Asst. trust officer Farmers Bank & Trust Co., Princeton, Ky., 1941—, asst. cashier, 1943-51, sec. to bd. dirs., 1943—, cashier, 1951-68, v.p., 1968—. Treas., Princeton Rose and Garden Club Civic Beautification, 1960—. Mem. Princeton City Council, 1962-70. Mem. Nat. Assn. Bank Women (chmn. Ky. group 1969-70, membership chmn. So. region 1969-70), Princeton Bus. and Profl. Women's Club (past pres., woman of year 1969), Princeton C. of C. (treas. 1971—, dir.), Caldwell County Hosp. Aux., Caldwell County Homemakers. Mem. Christian Ch. (ofcl. bd.). Mem. Order Eastern Star. Club: Princeton Golf and Country. Home: 600 W Main St Princeton KY 42445 Office: Box 559 Princeton KY 42445

ROGERS, GENESIA LIU (MRS. ROBERT JORDAN ROGERS), psychiatrist; b. Peiping, China, Sept. 10, 1932; d. Su Jen and Jy-Shzow (Wey) Liu; M.D., Nat. Taiwan U., 1956; certificate in psychoanalysis and psychotherapy Postgrad. Center for Mental Health, N.Y.C., 1970; m. Robert Jordan Rogers, July 4, 1967; children—Leland Liu, Leif Liu. Came to U.S., 1957, naturalized, 1971. Intern Nat. Taiwan U. Hosp., Taipei, 1955-56, resident, 1956-57; resident Beekman Downtown Hosp., N.Y.C., 1957-58, U. Kan. Med. Center, 1958-59, Hillside Hosp., Queens, N.Y., 1959-61, Hudson River State Hosp., Poughkeepsie, N.Y., 1961-62, Grasslands Hosp., Valhalla, N.Y., 1962-63, Met. Hosp., N.Y.C., 1963-65; practice medicine specializing in psychiatry and psychoanalysis, N.Y.C., 1967—, Chappaqua, N.Y., 1971—; staff psychiatrist Essex County Guidance Center, East Orange, N.J., 1965-68; asso. staff Postgrad. Center for Mental Health, N.Y.C., 1965-70; clin. instr. Mt. Sinai Sch. Medicine, N.Y.C., 1971-73; asst. attending psychiatrist Beth Israel Med. Center, N.Y.C., 1971-73; child psychiatrist Mt. Kisco (N.Y.) Clinic, 1973-74; cons. psychiatrist BOCES, Yorktown Heights, N.Y., 1973—; attending psychiatrist Grasslands Hosp., 1973—, No. Westchester Hosp., Mt. Kisco, 1974—; dir. Lincolndale (N.Y.) Guidance Center, 1973—. Mem. Westchester Acad. Medicine, Am. N.Y. psychiat. assns., Am. Chinese Med. Assn. Address: 1266 Hardscrabble Rd Chappaqua NY 10514 Office: 255 W 88th St New York City NY 10024

ROGERS, GLADYS T. TULLOS (MRS. W.K. ROGERS), educator; b. Magee, Miss.; d. H.S. and Nan (Abernathy) Tullos; B.S., U. So. Miss., 1940; postgrad. San Diego State Coll., 1963-65; m. Wilburn K. Rogers, Dec. 22, 1941. News reporter soc. page Magee Currier, 1934-36; tchr. various schs., 1938-42; jr. high sch. tchr., Fallbrook, Cal., 1952-53, Oceanside, Cal., 1953; with Oceanside Union Sch. Dist., 1953—. Pupil personnel services, counselor Lincoln Jr. High Sch., Oceanside, 1963—. Writer, contbr. to news media and ednl. TV programs. Mem. standing rules com. San Diego County Service Center Council, 1971-72. Mem. Cal., San Diego personnel and guidance assns., Oceanside Elementary Tchrs. Assn. (pres. 1970-71, chmn. pub. relations 1972—), San Diego County Tchrs. Assn. (dir. North Coast area 1971—, curriculum and instrns. com. 1971-72), North San Diego County Guidance Assn., N.E.A., U. So. Miss. Alumni Assn. (chmn. 1970), Internat. Platform Assn., Delta Kappa Gamma (chpt. pres. 1968-70). 1826 Burroughs St Oceanside CA 92054

ROGERS, IDA ADRIAN (MRS. GEORGE P. ROGERS), educator; b. Calico Rock, Ark.; d. Alex and Edna (Cotheran) Adrain; B.A. in Art, Hendrix Coll., 1954; M.A., U. Ark., 1955; postgrad. Leyden U., 1960-61; grad. N. Am. Acad. Police Sci., 1974; m. John J. Rice, Apr. 1, 1926 (div. Jan. 1932); children—Sammie L., George J. (dec.), Sue; m. 2d, George P. Rogers, Feb. 26, 1943. Faculty, Little Rock U., 1957—, asst. prof. art and edn., 1958—, chmn. visual arts dept., 1957—. Portraits represented in pvt. collections; exhibited La Scala Gallery, Florence, Italy, 1971—, Aveta Gallery, Italy, 1973; archaeologist throughout Middle East, 1960-66. Tchr. arts, crafts North Rock Boys Club, 1942-72; art chmn. one-man shows Ark. Art Festival, 1962-63. Mem. bd. Centro stud. Escomb Internat., Rome, Italy. Recipient medal of merit Leonardo Di Vinci Acad., Rome, 1969, medal for distinguished service to arts and scis., 1972. Mem. Am. Artists League N.Y. (state chmn. Am. art week 1959-60), Nat. Hist. Soc. (charter), Nat., Ark. (art chmn. 1963) socs. arts and letters, Internat. Platform Assn., Poets Round Table Ark., Authors, Artists and Composers Ark. (art chmn. 1972), Am. League Pen Women (state chmn. 1969, art chmn. Ark. br. 1972), Internat. Assn. Investigators and Spl. Police, Delta Kappa Gamma. Contbg. author: L.Da Vinci in Quaderni Di Pocsia, 1970. Home: 2409 W 16th St North Little Rock AR 72114 Office: 33d and University Av Little Rock AR 72204

ROGERS, IRENE, librarian; b. Yonkers, N.Y., Oct. 12, 1932; d. Franklyn Harold and Mary Margaret (Nealy) Rogers; B.S. in Edn., New Paltz State Tchrs. Coll., 1954; M.L.S. (N.Y. State Tng. grantee), Columbia, 1959. Tchr., West Babylon (N.Y.) Sch. System, 1954-57, Yonkers (N.Y.) Sch. System, 1957-58; reference librarian Yonkers Pub. Library, 1959-67, adult services coordinator, 1967-73, asst. library dir., 1973—. Mem. Mayor's Adv. Com. Consumer Edn., Yonkers, 1970—; mem. Yonkers unit Am. Cancer Soc. West Library System grantee, 1966. Mem. Westchester, N.Y. library assns. Club: Soroptimist of Yonkers. Home: 41 Amackassin Terrace Yonkers NY 10703 Office: 70 S Broadway Yonkers NY 10701

ROGERS, JACQUELINE ARAPAKIS, physician; b. Akron, O., July 31, 1938; d. Peter Zacharias and Lillian Irene (Kosmetos) Arapakis; B.A., Case-Western Res. U., 1960, M.D., 1964; m. Robert Warren Rogers, Aug. 26, 1962 (div.); 1 dau., Kimberly Joy. Intern Univ. Hosps., Cleve., 1968-69, resident in psychiatry, 1969-71, fellow in child psychiatry, 1971-74; practice medicine specializing in child psychiatry, Cleve., 1974—; founder Parent Child Center. Mem. Am. Acad. Child Psychiatry, Mortar Bd., Beta Beta Beta. Home: 19411 Winslow Rd Shaker Heights OH 44122 Office: Parent Child Center Pkwy Med Center 3619 Park E Beachwood OH 44122

ROGERS, JUDITH, lawyer; b. Newark, N.J., Jan. 14, 1932; d. Meyer Miles and Florence Marks; B.S. in Bus. Adminstrn., U. Fla., 1952; J.D., Ind. U., 1961; m. Arthur Rogers, Aug. 4, 1951; children—Steven Bruce, Meryl Debra, Alison Gail. Admitted to Ark. bar, 1962; practiced in North Little Rock, 1962—; tchr. women and the law U. Ark., Little Rock, fall 1973. Mem. Atty. Gen. Ark. Consumer Protection Panel, 1969—; mem. Gov. Ark. Commn. Status Women, 1968—. Chmn. Pulaski County Cystic Fibrosis drive, 1969; chmn. bus. div. Little Rock United Fund drive, 1964. Mem. Ark. Democratic Central Com., 1966-70, 74—; nat. v.p. Young Dem. Clubs, 1968-70; del. Dem. Nat. Conv., 1968; exec bd. Pulaski County Dem. Com., 1970—; mem. exec. bd. Ark. Women's Polit. Caucus, 1973—, Ark. rep. nat. caucus, 1972—. Bd. dirs. Family Planning Bd. Pulaski County, Econ. Opportunity Agy. Pulaski County, Pulaski County Health and Welfare Council. Mem. Ark. Women Lawyers Assn., Ark. (past chmn. family law sect.), Am. bar assns., Bus. and Profl. Women's Club, Am. Assn. U. Women (lobbyist Ark. div. 1969), League Women Voters, Pulaski County Federated Women's Clubs (pres. 1970), Soroptomist Club (pres. 1968-69), Common Cause, A.C.L.U. (pres. Ark.), Beta Gamma Sigma. Unitarian. Author articles. Home: 3131 Lakeview Rd North Little Rock AR 72116 Office: 419 1/2 Main St North Little Rock AR 72119

ROGERS, JUDITH BALCOM, librarian, govt. ofcl.; b. Spencerport, N.Y.; d. Joseph Roy and Emma Starboard (Stoakes) Rogers; B.S. in L.S., Sci., State U. N.Y., 1937; M.L.S., Catholic Univ. Am., 1963. Librarian Bay Shore (N.Y.) Pub. Library, 1938-43; head catalog dept. U.S. Weather Bur., Washington, 1944-56; head catalog sect. Nat. Agrl. Library, Washington, 1957-70; asst. head editorial sect. Nat. Union Catalog, Library of Congress, 1970—. Mem. Am., Spl., D.C. library assns., Potomac Tech. Processing Librarians. Home: 4313 Knox Rd College Park MD 20740 Office: Library of Congress Washington DC 20540

ROGERS, KATE ELLEN, educator; b. Nashville, Dec. 13, 1920; d. Raymond Louis and Louise Adelaid (Gruver) Rogers; B.A., George Peabody Coll., 1946, M.A., 1947; Ed.D., Columbia U., 1956. Instr. Tex. Technol. Coll., Lubbock, 1947-53; co-owner, v.p. Design Today, Inc., Lubbock, 1951-54; prof., chmn. housing and interior design dept. Coll. Home Econs., U. Mo., 1954—. Served with WAVES, 1944-46. Recipient Faculty Alumni award, U. Mo., 1968. Mem. Interior Design Educators Council (pres. 1971-73, chmn. bd. 1973-75), Am. Inst. Interior Designers, Nat. Soc. Interior Designers, Am. Assn. of Housing Educators, Am. Home Econs. Assn., Soc. Archtl. Historians, Phi Lambda Theta, Kappa Delta Pi, Gamma Sigma Delta. Author: Modern House, U.S.A. 1962. Home: 1844 Cliff Dr Columbia MO 65201

ROGERS, KATHARINE MUNZER (MRS. KENNETH ROGERS), educator; b. N.Y.C., June 6, 1932; d. Martin and Jean Louise (Thompson) Munzer; B.A. summa cum laude, Barnard Coll., 1952; postgrad. (Fulbright scholar) Newnham Coll., 1952-53; Ph.D., Columbia, 1957; m. Kenneth Rogers, Aug. 4, 1956; children—Margaret, Christopher, Thomas. Instr. English Skidmore Coll., Saratoga Springs, N.Y., 1954-55; instr. English Cornell U., Ithaca, N.Y., 1955-57; instr. English Bklyn. Coll., 1958-64, asst. prof., 1965-70, asso. prof., 1971-73, prof., 1974—; mem. doctoral faculty City U. N.Y., 1972—. Mem. Nat. Orgn. for Women, Modern Lang. Assn., Phi Beta Kappa. Author: The Troublesome Helpmate, 1966, 68; William Wycherley, 1972. Contbr. to profl. jours. Home: Hoxie House Stevens Inst Tech Hoboken NJ 07030 Office: Dept of English Brooklyn Coll Brooklyn NY 11210

ROGERS, KATHLEEN VIRGINIA, ednl. adminstr.; b. West Point, N.Y., Apr. 6, 1916; d. James Edward and Mary (Quick) Rogers; B.A. (hon.) Notre Dame Coll. of Staten Island, 1937; M.A., Tchrs. Coll., 1941; postgrad. N.Y U. Sch. Edn., 1956. Tchr. home econs. elementary, jr. and sr. high schs., N.Y.C., 1944-53; tchr. home econs. Jersey City, 1940-42; tchr. home econs. and English, Hackensack, N.J., 1942-44; asst. dir. Bur. Home Econs., N.Y.C. Bd. of Edn., 1960-66, dir. 1966—; instr. Tchrs. Coll., Columbia U., N.Y.C., 1964-65; guest lectr. Hunter Coll., N.Y. U., 1965-72. Exec. bd. dirs. Nutrition Council of Greater N.Y., 1966-72; bd. trustees Notre Dame Coll. of S.I. alumnae, 1957-72. Mem. Nat. Council Adminstrv. Women in Edn. N.Y.C. (pres. 1964-66), N.Y. Acad. Pub. Edn. (sec. 1972—), Notre Dame Coll. S.I. Alumnae Assn. (pres. 1957-59), N.Y. State Home Econs. Southeastern Assn. (pres. 1964-65), N.Y.C. High Sch. Tchrs. Home Econs. Assn. (pres. 1955-57), Am. Vocational Assn., Am. Home Econs. Assn., Interagy. Council Home Econs. (chmn. prekindergarten -16, 1970-72, chmn. home econs. standing com. 1957-60), N.Y.C. Tchrs. Home Econs. Assn. (past pres.), Nat. Assn. City Suprs. Home Econs., N.Y.C. Exptl. Soc., The Fashion Group, The Rosarians, N.Y.C. Dirs. Council, Council Supervisory Assn., Internat. Platform Assn., Delta Kappa Gamma (chpt. v.p. 1970-72, pres. 1972—). Contbr. articles to jours. in field. Home: 20 W 45th St Bayonne NJ 07002 Office: 131 Livingston St Brooklyn NY 11201

ROGERS, LORENE LANE, biochemist; b. Prosper, Tex., Apr. 3, 1914; d. Mort M. and Jessie (Luster) Lane; B.A., N. Tex. State Coll., 1934; M.A., U. Tex., 1946, Ph.D., 1948; student Columbia, 1941-42; D.Sc. (hon.), Oakland U., 1972; m. Burl Gordon Rogers, Aug. 23, 1935 (dec. June 1941). Prof. chemistry Sam Houston State Coll., 1947-49; postdoctoral fellow U. Tex., 1949-50; research scientist Clayton Found. Biochemical Inst., U. Tex., 1950-64, exec. asst., 1951-57, asst. dir., 1957-64, prof. nutrition, 1962—, asst. dean grad. sch., 1964-65, asso. dean grad. sch., 1965-71, v.p., 1971—, mem. grad. record exam. bd., 1972—, vice chmn., 1973-74. Mem. Gov.'s Mental Health Planning Com. Bd. dirs. Austin (Tex.) chpt. Nat. Cystic Fibrosis Found. Recipient Teaching Excellence award U. Tex. Students Assn., 1963, Distinguished Alumnus award North Tex. State U., 1972. Fellow Am. Inst. Chemists; mem. Am. Inst. Nutrition, Am. Chem. Soc., A.A.A.S., Am. Soc. Human Genetics, Sigma Xi, Phi Kappa Phi, Iota Sigma Pi. Author numerous articles pub. in profl. jours. Research on hydantoin synthesis, intermediary metabolism, alcoholism, mental retardation and congenital malformations. Home: 4 Nob Hill Circle Austin TX 78746 Office: U Tex Austin TX 78712

ROGERS, MARGARET DWYER, pub. relations exec.; b. N.Y.C., July 21, 1922; d. Walter W. and Geraldine (McKeown) Dwyer; student Oberlin Coll., 1940-42; B.A., Mt. Holyoke Coll., 1944; M.S., Columbia, 1945; 1 son, Brian. Press rep. Met. Museum Art, N.Y.C., 1945-47; with Overlook Hosp., Summit, N.J., 1959—, dir. pub. relations, 1959—. Publicity chmn. New Eyes for Needy, Inc., Short Hills, N.J., 1954. Bd. dirs. Jr. League Oranges and Short Hills, 1958-59, chmn. pub. relations, 1958-59; adv. bd. YWCA, Summit, 1973-75. Recipient nat. award Pulse on Pub. Relations S.M. Edison Co./Colgate Palmolive, 1963, nat. award MacEachern competitions Am. Hosp. Assn., 1967, 74, Woman of Yr. award Summit Bus. and Profl. Women's Club, 1968. Mem. Am. Soc. Hosp. Pub. Relations Dirs., Acad. Hosp. Pub. Relations, N.J. Hosp. Assn., N.J. Hosp. Pub. Relations Assn. (pres. 1968-70). Conglist. (deaconess 1956-57). Club: Soroptimist (dir. 1973-76) (Summit, N.J.). Home: 27 The Crescent Short Hills NJ 07078 Office: Overlook Hosp Summit NJ 07901

ROGERS, MARGARET EM EAVES, ednl. adminstr.; b. Quitman, Miss., Nov. 12, 1913; d. Adie David and Margaret Mildred (White) Eaves; B.S., U. So. Miss., 1937; M.S., Miss. State U., 1970; m. Cecil Arthur Rogers, Aug. 28, 1937 (div. July 1946); children—Cecil Arthur, Lila Jean (Mrs. Charles K. Floyd, Jr.). Tchr. bus. edn. Meridian (Miss.) High Sch., 1948-51; admitted to Miss. bar, 1950; owner, mgr. Mid-South Bus. Coll., Meridian, 1951-62; counselor Meridian (Miss.) High Sch., 1962-65; vocational counselor, coordinator placement service Meridian Jr. Coll., 1965—. Mem. adv. bd. East Central chpt. Miss. Lung Assn., 1969—. Mem. Am., Miss. vocational assns., Miss. State Bar, Miss. Personnel and Guidance Assn., Assn. Miss. Jr. Coll. Counselors (sec. 1970—). Baptist. Home: 2612 19th St Meridian MS 39301

ROGERS, MARY-JANE REGINA (MRS. WILLIS N. ROGERS), librarian, educator; b. Pawtucket, R.I., Sept. 13, 1914; d. James L. and Amelia Marie (Barnes) Joels; A.B., Washington Square Coll., 1959; M.L.S., St. John's U., N.Y., 1961; m. Willis N. Rogers, July 4, 1952. Sec., U.S. Dept. Navy, Washington and Bklyn., 1938-55; asst. children's librarian then children's librarian Queens Borough Pub. Library, Jamaica, N.Y., 1961-64; librarian, tchr. Linden Jr. High Sch., St. Albans, N.Y., 1964-67, St. Andrew Sch., Orlando, Fla., 1968—. Mem. Am., Fla., Catholic Library assns., Central Fla. Civic Theater Acad., Internat. Platform Assn. Club: Navy Officers' Wives. Home: 1515 Campbell Av Orlando FL 32806 Office: 877 Hastings Dr Orlando FL 32808

ROGERS, SALLY CALVERT, psychologist, ednl. adminstr.; b. Balt., Jan. 13, 1921; d. Roger Atkinson and Emeline Agnew (Condict) Walke; B.A., Sweet Briar Coll., 1942; M.Ed., U. Pitts., 1965; m. John Cowden Rogers, May 21, 1942 (div. July 1971); children—Deborah (Mrs. Robert J. Grossman), Elizabeth, Philip. Indsl. therapy supr. Woodville State Hosp., Carnegie, Pa., 1963-67; supr. vocational adjustment services Ebensburg (Pa.) State Sch., 1969-73; unit supr., liaison tchr. counselor Lakeside Sch., Spring Valley, N.Y., 1973—. Tchr. remedial reading Pitts. Pub. Sch. System, 1967-68. Staff mem. Girl Scout Day Camp, McDonald, Pa., 1951-61; Girl Scout leader Penn's Woods Council, 1953-63. Bd. dirs. McDonald Free Library, chmn. 1949-68. Mem. Nat. Rehab. Assn., Am. Assn. Mental Deficiency. Republican. Episcopalian (dir. personnel Diocese Md. 1944-45). Club: Jr. Womens (pres. 1950-51). Home: Apt 24 440 Viola Rd Spring Valley NY 10977 Office: Lakeside School S Main St Spring Valley NY 10977

ROGERS, SHERRY ANNE HAMMOND (MRS. ROBERT HAMILTON ROGERS), physician; b. Syracuse, N.Y., Apr. 15, 1943; d. Rodney Wellington and Jayne (Marshall) Hammond; student State U. N.Y. Harpur Coll. (Regents scholar), 1961-63; B.A., Syracuse U., 1965; M.D., State U. N.Y. Upstate Med. Sch., 1969; m. Robert Hamilton Rogers, 1970. Intern, State U. N.Y. Med. Center, 1969-70; practice medicine, Auburn, N.Y., 1970; emergency room physician Community Gen. Hosp., Syracuse, 1971-72, now mem. teaching and attending staff; practice gen. medicine, Syracuse; v.p., dir. Robro Services Ltd. Nu Sigma Nu Scholar, 1965, NSF grantee, 1958, 72—. Diplomate Am. Bd. Family Practice. Asso. fellow Am. Coll. Allergists; mem. Onandaga County Med. Soc. Office: 2800 W Genesee St Syracuse NY 13204

ROGERS, THELMA THARP, mem. Republican Nat. Com.; b. Elkin, N.C., Mar. 4, 1904; d. Noah W. and Alice (Council) Tharp; ed. Winthrop Coll., Rock Hill; m. Louis G. Rogers, Oct. 14, 1924; children—Catherine (Mrs. Alexander C. Buchanan), Louise G. Active Rep. Party, 1940—; mem. N.C. Rep. Exec. Com., 1956—; mem. Rep. Nat. Com. for N.C., 1956—; mem. platform com. Rep. Nat. Conv., 1956, 60, 64, mem. reform com., 1967-68, mem. arrangements com., rules com., 1972; mem. exec. com. Rep. Nat. Com., 1972—. Del. White House Conf. on Aging, 1961, mem. nat. adv. com., 1959-61; asso. mem. Gov. N.C. Coordinating Com. Aging, 1959-61; mem. Gov.'s Com. Status Women, 1964. Methodist. Home: Route 3 Box 251 Charlotte NC 28210

ROGERSON, BETTIE FREEMAN (MRS. CUTHBERT H. ROGERSON), biostatistician, state ofcl.; b. Richmond, Va., June 25, 1907; d. Allen W. and Julia (Brown) Freeman; A.B. cum laude, Bryn Mawr Coll., 1929; Sc.D., Johns Hopkins Sch. Hygiene Pub. Health, 1934; m. Cuthbert H. Rogerson, Sept. 9, 1936; (dec. Feb. 1949); children—Allen Collingwood, Peter Freeman. Statistician dept. preventive medicine Dalhousie U., Halifax, N.S., Can., 1934, mental hygiene study Johns Hopkins, Balt., 1935-36, research project dept. psychol. medicine Guys Hosp., London, Eng., 1937; med. analyst, biostatistician, chief program evaluation, now asst. dir. Center for Health Statistics Md. Dept. Health and Mental Hygiene, Balt., 1949—. Fellow Am. Pub. Health Assn.; mem. Am. Assn. Vital Records and Pub. Health Statistics, Assn. Mgmt. in Pub. Health, Md. Pub. Health Assn., Delta Omega. Democrat. Episcopalian. Club: Johns Hopkins (Balt.). Contbr. articles on med. care to profl. publs. Home: 3803 Beech Av Baltimore MD 21211 Office: 301 W Preston St Baltimore MD 21201

ROGGE, RENA WOLCOTT (MRS. CARL FREDERICK ROGGE, JR.), librarian; b. Bklyn., Nov. 3, 1920; d. Ralph Stratton and Mona Florence (Shannon) Wolcott; student Tufts Coll., 1937-38; B.A. cum laude, Elmira Coll., 1941; certificate Katharine Gibbs Sch., 1942; M.L.S., Rutger's U., 1966, postgrad. 1967-68; postgrad. Montclair State Coll., 1965, Kean Coll. of N.J., 1966; M.A. in L.S., New Sch. for Social Research, 1972; m. Carl Frederick Rogge, Jr., Aug. 4, 1942; 1 son, Carl Frederick III. Sec. to asst. supt. sch. dist. South Orange and Maplewood, N.J., 1958-65; head reference librarian Cranford (N.J.) Pub. Library, 1966-68; reader's adviser Jersey City State Coll., 1968-69; reference librarian Nancy Thompson Library, Kean Coll. of N.J., Union, 1969-70, acquisitions librarian, 1970-72, head reference librarian, 1972—. Pres. adv. com. N.J. State Coll. Librarians, 1973—. Mem. Am. Soc. Indexers, Am., N.J. (inst. roundtable chmn. 1971) library assns., Kean Coll. N.J. Faculty Assn. (sec. 1972-73), Am. Assn. U. Profs., Am. Fedn. Tchrs. (council Kean Coll. N.J.). Club: Elmira Coll. (N.J.). Home: 27 Bodwell Terrace Millburn NJ 07041 Office: Library Kean College of NJ Union NJ 07083

ROGIER, CONSTANCE MARTHA, librarian; b. Chgo., Mar. 8, 1937; d. Clarence F. and Elizabeth (Grieshaber) Rogier; B.S., U. Wis., 1959; M.A., U. Ill., 1963; M.A. in L.S., Rosary Coll., 1970. Tchr., Anoakia Sch., Arcadia, Cal., 1961-62; asst. residence hall dir. No. Ill. U., DeKalb, 1962-64; tchr. Manlius (Ill.) Community Sch., 1964-66; research asso. Council of State Govts., Chgo., 1967-69; librarian, instr. U. Miami, Coral Gables, Fla., 1970—. Mem. Am. Polit. Sci. Assn. Author: Recent Constitutional Revision Activities, 1967-1968, 1969. Home: 9621 SW 77th Av Miami FL 33156

ROGUEMORE, LOIS EVELYN (MRS. JUDSON CARL ROGUEMORE), educator; b. Decatur, Ala., July 3, 1903; d. John Patrick and Lela Victoria (Johnson) Masterson; A.B. summa cum laude, N.M. Highlands U., 1940, M.A., 1944; m. Judson Carl Roguemore, May 31, 1923; children—Judson Carl, Mernice Ruth (Mrs. Philip Andrew Ross). Tchr., San Jon, N.M., 1920, Farmington (N.M.) City Schs., 1922-39, Las Vegas City Schs., 1940-59, El Paso (Tex.) City Schs., 1959—; faculty edn. dept. N.M. Highland U., 1939-55; florist Floralart Shop, Las Vegas, 1940-59. Precinct judge Republican Party. Named Poet of Year, J. Mark Press, 1973. Mem. Am. Assn. U. Women, Nat., Tex. (pres. Dist. 1) press women, El Paso Writers League (pres.), World, Tex.-N.M. poetry socs., Internat. Platform Assn., Sigma Sigma Sigma. Baptist. Mem. Order Eastern Star. Club: Manuscript. Contbr. poems to mags. Home: 1401 Randolph St El Paso TX 79902

ROGUS, FRANCES AGNES (MRS. HENRY JOSEPH ROGUS), horse trainer, owner; b. Chgo., Jan. 11, 1922; d. Albert and Agnes (Murzyn) Wojnicki; student Triton Coll., 1968, 74, Chgo. Conservatory of Music, 1950-52; m. Henry Joseph Rogus, June 6, 1942; children—Susan Barbara, William Henry, Nancy Rose (Mrs. John William Shields), Joseph Guy, Mary Jane Hope, Mark Andrew, Margot Ann. Code clk. Transp. Corp., Tracy, Cal., 1942-45; owner, tchr. ballet classes Sch. of Dance, Westchester, Ill., 1958; sec. to personnel dir. Alberto-Culver Co., Melrose Park, Ill., 1962; actress in Music Man, Temple Theatre, Westchester, 1961, Guys and Dolls, 1963, Pajama Game, 1964; sec. Oak Brook Sch. of Horsemanship, Oakbrook, Ill., 1967; owner harness horses, Westchester, 1964—, trainer harness horses, Chgo., 1968—, standardbred horse breeder, Harvard, Ill., 1968—. Bd. dirs. Divine Infant Guild, 1961-63. Mem. U.S. Trotting Assn., Ill. Harness Horseman's Assn. Club: Variety. Address: 1406 Gardner Rd Westchester IL 60153

ROGUSKA-KYTS, JADWIGA, physician; b. Warsaw, Poland, May 11, 1932; d. Jan and Jadwiga (Stokowska) Roguski; M.A., Poznan (Poland) U., 1954, M.D., 1958; m. Robert Kyts, June 11, 1960. Came to U.S., 1958, naturalized, 1965. Intern, Evanston (Ill.) Hosp., 1958-59; resident Passavant Meml. Hosp., Chgo., 1959-63, chief resident in internal medicine, 1963-64; NIH postdoctoral fellow Northwestern U., 1964-66; physician in charge dialysis unit Northwestern Meml. Hosp., Chgo., 1966-73, attending physician, 1972—, asst. chief div. medicine Passavant Pavilion, 1966—; attending physician Cook County Hosp., Chgo., 1968—, VA Research Hosp., Chgo., 1970—; asso. prof. Northwestern U. Med. Sch., 1974—; med. dir. circulation div. Time, Inc., 1969—. Fellow A.C.P.; mem. Am. Fedn. Clin. Research, A.A.A.S., Am. Heart Assn., Am. Soc. Nephrology. Home: 880 N Lake Shore Dr Chicago IL 60611 Office: 707 N Fairbanks Ct Chicago IL 60611

ROHDE, MARJORIE SHERRIFF, rehab. cons.; b. Detroit, July 8, 1927; d. Leslie Major and Edithia Lois (Wilde) Sherriff; student Brenau Coll., 1948-49, Hunter Coll., 1949-50, Stanford, 1950; B.A., San Jose (Cal.) State Coll., 1953; postgrad. U. So. Cal., 1957-59; Ed.M., Tchrs. Coll., Columbia, 1971; m. Max Spencer Rohde, June 22, 1946 (div. 1949; remarried Aug. 15, 1971; dec. May 1973). Asst. employment mgr. Helipot div. Beckman Instruments Co., Newport Beach, Cal., 1956-57; group worker Braille Inst. Am., Los Angeles, 1960-61; caseworker Bur. Pub. Assistance, Los Angeles, 1961-64; supr. Vacation Camp for Blind, N.Y., 1964; supr. Developmental Tng. Center, United Cerebral Palsy of N.Y.C., Inc., Bklyn., 1964-65; patient services coordinator Nat. Multiple Sclerosis Soc., N.Y. County chpt., 1966-68; research asso. Quaker Com. Social Rehab., N.Y.C., 1970—. Cons. for blind Nat. Council Jewish Women, Long Beach, Cal., 1961, Leadership Resources, Inc., 1968. Recreational vol. Santa Clara County Juvenile Delinquents Home, 1959; vol. Cal. Council of Blind, Inc., 1963; vol. instr. Crippled Children's Soc., Woodland Hills, Cal., 1951-60. Served to lt. (j.g.), Women's Res., USNR, 1953-56. Mem. Am. Nat. Rehab. Counseling Assn., Nat. Assn. Social Workers, Am. Psychol. Assn. Episcopalian. Home: 2 Horatio St New York City NY 10014 Office: 135 Christopher St New York City NY 10014

ROHLFS, RUTH ALEXANDRA, civic worker, religious orgn. exec.; b. Seattle, Nov. 28; d. Nels Anton and Emma Marie (Sundstrom) Swanberg; student U. Wash., 1926-28, 35, 36, Union Theol. Sem., 1938; m. Marcus Rohlfs, May 30, 1937 (dec. 1967); 1 son, Richard Marcus. Adminstrv. asst. YMCA, U. Wash., Seattle; dir. religious edn. First Bapt. Ch. Seattle; pres. Seattle Interdenominational Christian Youth Council; adviser Chinese Bapt. Coll. Students; pres. First Bapt. Women's Soc., mem. state bd., v.p. Nat. Bd. Bapt. Women, 1958-61; mem. Wash. Bapt. Com. Christian Higher Edn.; mem. Wash. World Mission campaign com.; mem. nat. Bapt. Evangelism div. com.; chmn. Social Orgns. Strategic Planning Bapt. Ch.; mem. nat. Am. Bapt. Conv. Gen. Council and Exec. Com., 1968-71, del. Nat. Council Chs. Assembly, 1968-71; v.p. Seattle Downtown Ecumenical Ministries; pres. Am. Bapt. Conv., 1971-72; mem. exec. com. Am. Bapt. Chs. USA, area Am. Bapt. Ordination Commn. Pres. Seattle YWCA, pres. nat. bus. and profl. council and assembly, mem. personnel com., mem. U. Wash. YWCA adv. bd., mem. numerous nat. coms., mem. nat. YWCA-YMCA liaison com.; chmn. div. recreation and informal edn. Seattle Council Social Agy.; mem. Seattle Peace Council, Seattle Inter-racial Council; pres. Seattle P.T.C. council, Seattle Expt. Internat. Living; mem. regional interviewing com. overseas tchrs. exchange Dept. Health, Edn., and Welfare; pres. Seabeck Conf. Grounds Bd. and Corp. Bd. dirs. Am. Bapt. Home Mission Socs., Seattle N.A.A.C.P., Am. Friends Service Com.; mem. adv. com. Japanese Internat. Christian U., Tokyo, Recipient Nat. U.S.O. award, Am. Bapt. Home Mission Soc. service award, award outstanding service internat. affairs Seattle Fedn. Women's Clubs, 1970. Author: History Turns a Page. Contbg. author Meditations for Women. Contbr. articles to mags. Address: 4303 54th St NE Seattle WA 98105

ROHMAN, LORRAINE LE MAR (MRS. CARL H. ROHMAN), writer, civic worker; b. Omaha; d. Harold Dihel and Luella (Petersen) Le Mar; A.A., Stephens Coll., 1946; B.A., Vassar Coll., 1948; postgrad. (Elizabeth Hubbard Skinner fellow) Columbia, Union Theol. Sem., 1948-49; m. Carl Henry Rohman, Dec. 29, 1952; children—Melanie, Carl Philip II, Stephen Le Mar, George Peter Dierks. Humanities tutor U. Omaha, 1950-52; free lance writer radio and tv scripts, children's plays, short stories, articles, 1951—; v.p. Marks, Inc., S.D., 1962—. Asso. del. Internat. Physiol. Conf., Copenhagen, Denmark, 1950; applied arts chmn. Jr. League, Omaha, 1951-52; mag. editor Jr. League, Lincoln, 1953-54, script chmn., 1954-55, corr. sec., 1962-63, project chmn., 1963-64, gallery docent chmn., 1964-65, spl. project chmn., 1966-67; docent Sheldon Gallery, 1964—; mem. music com. Gov.'s Council for Neb.'s Cultural Resources 1963-64; membership chmn. Brownville Hist. Soc., 1972—; treas. Altar Guild, St. Anne's Guild, 1972—. Bd. dirs. Jr. League, Lincoln, 1953-54, 62-67; pres. Brownville Fine Arts Assn., 1972—; trustee Neb. Art Assn., sec. bd., 1971—, v.p., 1973—. Republican precinct chmn., 1952, 60, 64; del. county and state convs., 1966, 72. Episcopalian (pres. women's council 1966-67, vestry 1972—). Club: Okoboji (Ia.) Yacht. Home: 1312 Fall Creek Rd Lincoln NE 68510

ROHN, MARY JANE TURLEY, advt. exec.; b. Norfolk, Va., Apr. 7, 1928; d. Robert Edgar and Lydia (Elmore) Turley; student Gulf Park Jr. Coll., 1946; B.A., U. Wis., 1948, M.A., 1949; m. Chester F. Rohn, Jr., Apr. 15, 1950 (div. Aug. 1960); 1 dau., Mary Lydia. Copywriter, Madison (Wis.) Advt. Agy., 1948-50, Baker Johnson & Dickinson, Milw., 1950-57; asst. set designer Miller Theatre (now Milw. Repertory Theatre), Milw., 1959; copy dir. William Eisner & Assos., Milw., 1959-63; creative dir. Page, Schwessinger Advt. Agy., Inc., Milw., 1963—. Guest lectr. U. Wis., 1965-73, Mt. Mary Coll., 1968, Wis. Broadcasters Seminar; guest panelist U. Marquette, 1962. Service chmn. Delta Delta Delta Milw. Alumnae, 1950-57; asst. dir. publicity, pub. relations Milw. County chpt. Nat. Found. March of Dimes, 1962-63; publicity chmn. Milw. County Leukemia Soc., 1963-64; youth publicity dir. Milw. County chpt. A.R.C., 1965-66; Wauwatosa comnl. chmn. United Fund, 1973; team solicitor Milw. County Community Chest, 1950-57, Milw. Music Hall, 1965; asst. service and profl. counsel Badger Home for Blind, Milw. Mem. Am. Women in Radio and Television (pres. Badger chpt. 1964-65), Milw. Advt. Club (columnist Torch mag. 1965-66, editor roster issue 1971, 72; hospitality chmn. 1966-67, bd. dirs. Brace Fund 1968—, graphic communications month com. 1968-69, named Advt. Woman of Yr. 1971, bd. dirs. 1970-72), Am. Advt. Fedn. (mem. publicity com. nat. conv. 1970), Milw. Women of Variety (pres. 1973-74), Am. Legion Aux. Advertising Women Milw. (ednl. chmn. 1963), Milw. Zool. Soc., Theta Sigma Phi, Gamma Alpha Chi (hon. life mem.). Presbyn. Home: 12500 Knoll Rd Elm Grove WI 53122 Office: Page Schwessinger Advt Agy 2433 N Mayfair Rd Milwaukee WI 53226

ROIDER, CATHERINE LEITER (MRS. KARL ANDREW ROIDER), educator; b. Rochester, N.Y., June 3, 1914; d. Leo Jacob and Susan (Baird) Leiter; B.A., U. Rochester, 1935; M.A., Bowling Green State U., 1963; m. Karl Andrew Roider, Aug. 19, 1939; children—Ruth Marian, Karl Andrew. Asst. to chmn. research photomicrography Eastman Kodak Co., Rochester, 1935-39; circulation librarian Vassar Coll., Poughkeepsie, N.Y., 1939-41; tchr. Mt. Vernon (N.Y.) pub. schs., 1954-55; math tchr. Ada (O.) High Sch., 1955-59; prof. math. Ohio No. U., Ada, 1959—. NSF grantee, 1959. Mem. Am. Assn. U. Profs., Math. Assn. Am., Nat. Council Tchrs. Math., Ohio Acad. Scis., Delta Zeta. Home: Rural Route 2 Box 11 Ada OH 45810 Office: Dept Mathematics Ohio Northern University Ada OH 45810

ROLF, CAROL LEE STONESIFER (MRS. ROBERT THOMAS ROLF), journalist; b. Fayetteville, Ark., Mar. 19, 1948; d. Leroy and Alwilda Mildred (Karnes) Stonesifer; B.J., U. Mo., 1970; m. Robert Thomas Rolf, June 28, 1969; 1 dau., Andrea Dawn. Reporter woman's dept. Ark. Gazette, Little Rock, 1970-73. Mem. Women in Communications. Home: 5512 McClellan Dr Little Rock AR 72209

ROLFSON, AUDREY ELAINE DAVIS (MRS. DALE ELGAR ROLFSON), coll. adminstr.; b. Lyle, Minn., Mar. 15, 1925; d. Ben F. and Doris Irene (Curley) Davis; student Austin Jr. Coll., 1944-45; m. Dale Elgar Rolfson, May 2, 1946; children—Sue (Mrs. Steven P. Johnson), Kirk Allen. Sec. to pres. Austin (Minn.) Jr. Coll., 1946-61; asst. registrar Austin State Jr. Coll., 1961-71; registrar Austin Community Coll., 1971—. Pres. YWCA Matrons, 1961. Mem. Coll. Personnel and Guidance Assn., Upper Midwest Assn. Collegiate Registrars and Admissions Officers, Austin Bus. and Profl. Women's Club (pres. 1971), Am. Legion Aux. (pres. 1970-72), Minn. Assn. Ednl. Secs. (pres. 1968). Club: Koinia (co-pres. 1969). Home: 810 22d St NW Austin MN 55912 Office: 1600 8th Av NW Austin MN 55912

ROLLINS, CHARLOTTE LOUISE (MRS. DAVID ALEXANDER ROLLINS), sch. adminstr.; b. Elm City, N.C., Feb. 6, 1922; d. Ben and Marie (McFadgen) Haynes; B.S., Fayetteville State Tchrs. Coll., 1942; M.Ed., N.Y. U., 1952; profl. diploma (Ford Found. fellow) Fordham U., 1969; m. David Alexander Rollins, Apr. 12, 1952; children—David Alexander, Leonard Earl. Tchr., Carteret County Elementary Sch., Beaufort, N.C., 1942-43, C.F. Pope High Sch., Burgaw, N.C., 1943-46; tchr., N.Y.C., 1946-64, acting asst. principal, 1964-68, sch. community liaison tchr., 1970-71, acting principal, 1972—. Recipient UN citation, 1958, Outstanding Elementary Tchr. Am. award Elementary Tchrs. Am., 1971, Essence of Black Womanhood in Edn. award, Pub. Sch. 79, 1971, certificate of Merit for Humanitarianism, Dictionary Black Am. Biography, 1970. Mem. N.Y. Soc. for Exptl. Study Edn., Fordham U. Sch. Adminstrs. Assn., Eastern Centre Poetry Soc. London. Home: 1370 St Nicholas Av New York City NY 10033 Office: PS 79 Manhattan 55 E 120 St New York City NY 10035

ROLLINS, DORIS ELIZABETH, social worker; b. Jennings, La., July 13, 1931; d. John Levi and Dallas (Wotten) Rollins; B.Mus. Edn., McNeese State Coll., 1953; M.S.W., La. State U., 1959. Tchr. vocal music Calcasieu and Rapides Parish Sch. Systems, La., 1953-57; psychiat. music therapist Central La. State Hosp., Pineville, summer 1955, instn. counsellor social service dept., summers 1956-57; instn. counsellor Evaluation Center Exceptional Children, New Orleans, summer 1958; chief psychiat. social worker White Male Service, Central La. State Hosp., Pineville, 1959-61; dir. social service dept. State Indsl. Sch. for Girls, Alexandria, La. 1961-64; med. social cons. La. Dept. Health, Handicapped Children Services, Lafayette, 1964—. Mem. profl. adv. com. Easter Seal Soc. La., 1970. Bd. dirs. S.W. La. Rehab. Center, 1971—. Mem. Acad. Certified Social Workers (charter), Nat. Assn. Social Workers (br. chmn. 1968-69), La. Pub. Health Assn., Acadian Citizen Band Assn. Baptist. Home: 156 S Orleans Dr Lafayette LA 70501 Office: PO Box 52114 Lafayette LA 70501

ROLLINS, HAZELLE HEDGES (MRS. JOHN WOODSON ROLLINS), toy mfg. co. exec.; b. Kansas City, Mo., Jan. 12, 1910; d. Ralph and Jessie Mildred (Hazelle) Hedges; B.F.A., U. Kan., 1932; postgrad. Kansas City Art Inst., 1933; m. John Woodson Rollins, Feb. 15, 1941; children—Nancy H. (Mrs. Eugene Krupa), John Woodson. Founder, pres. Hazelle, Inc., Kansas City, Mo., 1932—. Commr., Womans Kansas City Assn. for Internat. Relations and Trade, 1957—; founder Madelyn Brock Found.; mem. Naturalization Council of Kansas City. Founder, Bus. and Profl. Womens Republican Club Greater Kansas City, 1960. Trustee Kansas City Art Inst. Recipient Outstanding Kansas City Alumnae award Alpha Omicron Pi, 1963, Rose award, 1967; Outstanding Kansas City Bus. Woman award Mortar Bd. U. Kan., 1966; Bus. Woman of Year award Theta Sigma Phi, 1968; citation of merit for work as artist and designer Regional Conf. Nat. League Am. Pen Women, 1971, Pen Woman of Distinction, 1970; named One of Three Most Outstanding Bus. Women in Mo., U. Mo. Phi Chi Theta, 1969; One of Three Kansas City Women, 2d Dist. Mo. Fedn. Womens Clubs, 1971. Mem. Small Bus. Adminstrn. U.S.A. (chmn. Kansas City Dist. adv. council 1972-75). Author numerous puppet plays. Patentee in field. Home: 801 W 63d St Kansas City MO 64113 Office: 1224 Admiral Blvd Kansas City MO 64106

ROLLMAN-BRANCH, HILDA SHURMAN (MRS. MELVILLE C. BRANCH), psychiatrist; b. Essen, Germany; d. Max and Irma (Schiff) Schurmann; came to U.S., 1941, naturalized, 1949; B.S., Columbia, 1943; M.D., U. So. Cal., 1948; m. Melville C. Branch, Mar. 15, 1951; 1 dau. by previous marriage, Veronica Rollman (Mrs. Ben Kaufman). Intern Michael Reese Hosp., Chgo., 1947-48; resident VA Brentwood Hosp., Los Angeles, 1949-52; practice medicine specializing in psychiatry, also psychoanalysis, Los Angeles, 1952—; mem. staffs Westwood Hosp.; asso. clin. prof. U. Cal. Med. Sch., Los Angeles, 1966-73, clin. prof., 1974—; lectr. U. So. Cal. Law Sch., Los Angeles, 1966-70, asso. clin. prof. psychiatry in law, 1970—; sr. faculty Los Angeles Psychoanalytic Soc. Inst., 1963—, dir. extension div., 1963-66, tng. analyst, 1968—, supervising analyst, 1969—, asst. dir., 1973—. Diplomate Am. Bd. Psychiatry and Neurology. Fellow Am. Psychiat. Assn., Am. Psychoanalytic Assn. (bd. profl. standards); mem. A.M.A., A.A.A.S. Office: 9777 Wilshire Blvd Beverly Hills CA 90212

ROLLS, RUTH THORNE (MRS. MONROE LEE ROLLS), city ofcl.; b. N.Y.C., Apr. 13, 1914; d. Harry Henry and Johanna Matilda (Schott) Thorne; student Jamaica Tchrs. Tng., 1931-32, Hunter Coll., 1932-33; m. Monroe Lee Rolls, Jan. 18, 1950; children—Nancy (Mrs. Ray Reid), Joyce (Mrs. Roger Thmpson). Utility adminstr. Aransas Pass (Tex.) Ind. Sch. Dist., 1946-49; with city govt., Aransas Pass, 1950—, city sec., 1967—. Active Aransas Asso. Charities. Mem. C. of C., Nat. Assn. City Secs. Presbyn. Mem. Order Eastern Star. Home: 1374 Oak Park Dr Aransas Pass TX 78336 Office: City Hall PO Drawer X Aransas Pass TX 78336

ROLSTON, MARGARET ELIZABETH, realtor; b. Knox County, Mo., Mar. 10, 1910; d. Marvin and Beryl (Miller) Florea; B.S. in Music, North Mo. State Coll., 1932; m. Howard E. Rolston, Nov. 25, 1931 (dec.); children—Anna Sue Barlow, James M. Co-owner Rolston & Rolston Realtors, Kirksville, Mo., 1953—, also ins. agt. Organizer, 1st pres. state chpt. Womens Council, Mo. Real Estate Bd., 1957. Pres. Adair County Parents Assn., Washington Sch. P.T.A., 1947-48; organized Grey Lady Service, A.R.C., 1964, sec. Red Cross bd., 1951-62; mem. com. for Collegiate Nursing Program, North Mo. State Coll., 1972. Bd. dirs. Adair County Center Exceptional Children; mem. goverance com. Kirksville Coll. Osteopathic Medicine, 1972—. Mem. Kirksville (dir. 1973—) Mo. chambers commerce, Credit Bur., N.E. Central of Realtors (pres.), Nat. Bd. Realtors, Womens Council (past regional gov.), Omega Tau Rho. Republican. Mem. Christian Ch. Mem. El Kadir Jewels. Clubs: Sojourners, Kirksville Country. Home: 804 Shannon Lane Kirksville MO 63501 Office: 208 S Franklin St Kirksville MO 63501

ROMAIN, HARRIET, advt. agy. exec.; b. N.Y.C., Jan. 23, 1912; d. George and Elizabeth (Wolf) Romain; B.A., N.Y. U., 1933; divorced; 1 dau., Jessica Romain Weiss. Sculptor, operator Romain Studios, N.Y.C., 1937-40; from trainee to v.p., creative dir. Modern Merchandising Bur., N.Y.C., 1940-46; v.p. Friend, Sloane Advt. Inc., N.Y.C., 1946-52; pres., creative dir. Harriet Romain Advt. Inc., N.Y.C., 1952—. Painter, sculptor. Home: 20 Park Av New York City NY 10016

ROMAINE, MERTIE ELIZABETH PHILBROOK (MRS. LAWRENCE BOND ROMAINE), museum curator; b. Lynn, Mass., Jan. 23, 1893; d. George Alfred and Mertise Susan (Pray) Philbrook; student Simmons Coll., 1923-24, Harvard, 1926-27, Stonehill Coll., 1960; m. Lawrence Bond Romaine, June 25, 1966; 1 son (by previous marriage) Allan Alfred Witbeck. Chief librarian Middleborough Pub. Library, Middleboro, Mass., 1925-63; dir. Middleborough Hist. Mus., 1960-67, curator, 1967—. Trustee St. Luke's Hosp., Middleboro. Republican. Conglist. Author: History of the Central Congregational Church, 1847-1947, 1947; History of the Town of Middleboro, 1969. Home: Bedford St Middleboro MA 02346 Office: Middleborough Hist Assn Inc Jackson St Middleboro MA 02346

ROMAN, HOPE SEEGMAN, research exec.; b. Pitts., Dec. 15, 1927; d. Simon and Gladys (Debs) Seegman; B.A., U. Chgo., 1957; m. Robert M. Roman, Feb. 2, 1947 (div. Dec. 1953); 1 son, Cristofer A. Asst. dir. vol. services Topeka State Hosp., 1952-54; exec. sec. Temple Beth Sholom, Topeka, 1954-57; statis. mgr. Social Research, Inc., Chgo., 1957-61; marketing research supr. Container Corp. Am., Chgo., 1962-63; v.p., dir. research Post-Keyes-Gardner, Inc., Chgo., 1963-68; pres. Roman Assos., Ltd., Chgo., 1968-71; sr. research mgr. Joseph Schlitz Brewing Co., 1971-72; dir. market research div. U.S. Postal Service, Washington, 1972—. Mem. Am. Marketing Assn., Am. Statis. Assn., Am. Assn. Pub. Opinion Research, A.A.A.S., Assn. Consumer Research. Contbr. articles to profl. jours. Home: 2801 New Mexico Av NW Washington DC 20007 Office: Room 5945 475 L'Enfant Plaza Washington DC 20260

ROMANO, CHRISTINE DOROTHY PROVENZALE (MRS. CHARLES F. ROMANO), civic worker; b. Bklyn.; d. Leonardo and Concetta (Marino) Provencale; student Bklyn. Coll., 1956, Mitchell Coll., 1962; m. Charles F. Romano, Oct. 16, 1938; children—Charles, Katherine. Treas., Red Stack Towing Co., Bklyn., 1956-58, v.p., 1958, pres., 1958-61, dir., 1956-61; sec.-treas. New London Towing Co., Bklyn., 1956-58, v.p., 1958-61, dir., 1956-61; sec. A&R Towing Co. Ltd., Bklyn., 1969—. Sec., Bergen Beach Civic Assn., 1950-56, pres., 1956-62, dir., 1950-62; mem. Bklyn. Civic Council, 1956-62, dir., 1958-62; mem. 40th Sch. Dist. Sch. Bd., 1958-62, sec., 1959-62; chmn. A.R.C., 1956-63, vol. worker, Smoke Rise, N.J., 1964-66; vol. Heart Fund, Smoke Rise, 1964-66; chmn. Mothers March of Dimes, N.J. state rep., 1967-68; vice-chmn. No. N.J. chpt. Paterson Gen. Hosp. Aux., 1973—. Clubs: Women of Smoke Rise, Smoke Rise Garden. Home: 734 Ridge Rd Smoke Rise NJ 07405

ROMANO, CLARE CAMILLE (MRS. JOHN ROSS), artist; b. Palisade, N.J., Aug. 24, 1922; d. Antonio and Louise (Cafara) Romano; student Cooper Union Sch. Art, 1939-43, Ecole des Beaux Arts, Fontainebleau, France, 1949, Istituto Statale, Florence, Italy, 1959; m. John Ross, Nov. 30, 1943; children—Christopher, Timothy. Tchr. art New Sch., 1960—; asst. prof. Pratt Inst., 1964—, Manhattanville Coll., 1965-65, Pratt Graphic Center, 1963—; artist in residence USIA Exhbn., Ljubljana, Zagreb, Belgrade, Yugoslavia; one-man shows at Galleria Strozzina, Florence, Arwin Gallery, Detroit, Boston Mus. Fine Arts, Pa. State U., Ohio State U., Asso. Am. Artists Gallery, others; exhibited in group shows at Mus. Modern Art, Bklyn. Mus., Pa. Acad. Fine Art, Whitney Mus. Am. Art, Cin. Mus. Fine Art, Boston Mus., Met. Mus., Cal. Mus., The White House, others; represented in permanent collections, Mus. Modern Art, Whitney Mus. Am. Art, Met. Mus. Art, Bklyn. Mus. Library Congress, Tokyo Art Center, Phila. Mus. Art, many others. Fulbright grantee, 1958-59; Louis Comfort Tiffany grantee, 1952; recipient Bklyn. Mus. Purchase award, 1951, Audubon Artists awards, N.J. State Mus., Boston Printmakers, Library Congress Purchase award, 1966, citation for profl. achievement Cooper Union Sch. Art, 1966, others. Mem. Soc. Am. Graphic Artists, Phila. Print Club. Author: (with others) The Complete Printmaker. Contbr. articles to profl. jours. Home: 110 Davison Pl Englewood NJ 07631

ROMANO, EMILY FLORENCE (MRS. MICHAEL ROMANO), poet; b. Boonton, N.J., Dec. 28, 1924; d. Orlin S. and Jessie M. (Rhinesmith) Van Duyne; grad. high sch.; m. Michael Romano, May 28, 1942; children—Margaret (Mrs. Richard G. Smith III), Janice (Mrs. William Turner), Martha Jean, Carol Marie. Mem. N.J. Poetry Soc., Avalon Poets, World Poetry Soc., World Poetry Day Assn., Nat. Fedn. State Poetry Socs., Internat. Poetry Soc., Western World Haiku Soc. Contbr. poems to profl. mags., anthologies, popular mags. Home and office: 230 Madison St Boonton NJ 07005

ROMANOFF, ANASTASIA JULIA SAYENKO (MRS. ALEXIS LAWRENCE ROMANOFF), biologist; b. Warsaw, Poland; d. Jacob O. and Julia V. (Slauta) Sayenko; student Tomsk U. Med. Sch., Russia, 1920-23; B.Sc., Phila. Coll. Pharm. and Sci., 1927; M.Ed., Cornell U., 1954; postgrad. Mich. State U., 1962; m. Alexis Lawrence Romanoff, Sept. 1, 1928. Social worker Internat. Inst. YWCA, Phila., 1923-27; chemist, bacteriologist Reed and Carnrick, Jersey City, 1927-28; chemist Cornell U., 1931-34, lectr. Russian lang., 1944-45; translator USAAF, Fairfield, O., 1941-42; research asso. U. Md., 1946-48; research analyst Library of Congress, Washington, 1948-51; research asso. Mich. State U., 1960-62; collaborator in research Cornell U., Ithaca, N.Y., 1962—. Mem. bd. adult edn. adv. com. Ithaca City Sch. Dist., 1956—. Fellow A.A.A.S.; mem. Am. Chem. Soc., League Women Voters, Am. Assn. U. Women (internat. relations group), Internat. Platform Assn., Sigma Delta Epsilon. Clubs: Campus, Ithaca Woman's, Literature Department. Author: (with Alexis L. Romanoff) The Avian Egg, 1949, The Avian Embryo, 1960, Biochemistry of the Avian Embryo, 1967; Pathogenesis of the Avian Embryo, 1972. Contbr. various articles to profl. jours. Home: 700 Stewart Av Ithaca NY 14850

ROMANOWSKI, SONJA BILGER, social worker; b. Dallas, Nov. 23, 1940; d. Raymond Ernest and Elma Bettina (Bilger) Romanowski; B.A., H. Sophie Newcomb Coll., Tulane U., 1962; M.S.W., Tulane U., 1964. Social worker Hope Cottage-Children's Bur., Inc., Dallas, 1964-71, dir. intake, 1971-74, staff supr., 1974—; field instr. U. Tex. at Austin, 1968, 69, Arlington, Tex., 1969-71, Tex. Women's U., Denton, 1972. Mem. Nat. Assn. Social Workers (treas. local chpt. 1970-72; chmn. Whitney Young meml. scholarship com. 1971-72, sec. 1973-75), Acad. Certified Social Workers, Nat. Conf. Social Welfare, Tex. Assn. Services to Children (sec. North Tex. chpt. 1972-73), Dallas Mus. Fine Arts, Delta Zeta. Home: 5904 Sandhurst Lane No 147 Dallas TX 75206 Office: 2301 Welborn St Dallas TX 75219

ROMANSKI, JOYCE MARIE CULKIN (MRS. ANDREW H. ROMANSKI), bank exec.; b. Bklyn., July 15, 1936; d. Harold Joseph and Mildred (Mills) Culkin; grad. Speedwriting Inst., 1957; student Life Underwriters Assn., 1958, N.Y. U., 1963-64; m. Andrew H. Romanski, Sept. 17, 1966. With Manhattan Savs. Bank, N.Y.C., 1956—, exec. sec. real estate and mortgage dept., 1961-64; exec. asst. exec. offices, 1964-66, asst. sec. securities, 1966-70, dep. sec., presdl. asst., 1970-72, dep. sec.-asst. to the chmn. bd., 1972—. Mem. Savs. Bank Women N.Y., Dix Hills (sec. 1967—), L.I. horse owners assns. Lutheran. Office: Manhattan Savs Bank 385 Madison Av New York City NY 10017

ROMENESKO, REBECCA ROBINSON (MRS. THOMAS DONET ROMENESKO), ednl. adminstr.; b. Morgantown, W. Va., July 30, 1947; d. Dexter Parks and Lenora Pebble (Tinnell) Robinson;

B.S. in Social Work (Rena Angell scholar), U. Wis., 1969; M.S. in Student Personnel, 1971; postgrad. So. Ill. U., 1969-70; m. Thomas Donet Romenesko, Dec. 28, 1968; 1 dau., Sarah Jane. Grad. asst. dean students office So. Ill. U., Carbondale, 1969-70; head resident U. Wis., La Crosse, 1970-72; asst. dean student affairs Okla. State U., Stillwater, 1972—. Mem. Am. Personnel and Guidance Assn., Coll. Student Personnel Assn., Nat. Assn. Women Deans, Adminstrs. and Counselors, Delta Zeta (treas. coll. chpt. 1967, chmn. standards local chpt. 1968, parliamentarian local chpt. 1968, dir. coll. chpt. 1970-72). Home: 1107 E 4th St Stillwater OK 74074 Office: 372 Student Union Oklahoma State University Stillwater OK 74074

ROMERO, PATRICIA LYNN STEVENS, educator; b. Wichita, Kan., Dec. 8, 1948; d. Merle Dale and Cleta Edna (Smith) Stevens; B.A. in Edn., Wichita State U., 1970; M.A. in Speech Communications, U. N.M., 1971; m. James Daniel Romero, Dec. 30, 1971. Instr. U. N.M., Albuquerque, 1972, acad. and spl. admissions adviser, 1972-73; instr. U. Albuquerque, 1972—. Mem. Speech Communication Assn., Am. Assn. U. Profs., N.M. Communication Assn. (sec. 1972-74), Alpha Phi, Zeta Phi Eta. Home: 6405 Louise Pl NE Albuquerque NM 87109

ROMIGH, LINDA LEE, educator; b. New Brighton, Pa., Oct. 1, 1948; d. H. H. and Grace E. (Niffenegger) Romigh; B.A., U. South Fla., 1970. Tchr. speech, debate, drama and English, Edgewater High Sch., Orlando, Fla., 1970—; instr. Fla. Forensic High Sch. Speech Work Shop, U. South Fla., 1972, dir., 1973, dir. high sch. plays. Named Outstanding Tchr. Year Kiwanians, 1974. Mem. Speech Assn. Am. (high sch. rep. legislative council 1974—), Orange County Tchrs. Speech and Drama (chmn. exec. council 1973-74), Fla. Forensics Exec. Council (rep. dist. III, 1973-74). Home: 2435 E Jersey Av Orlando FL 32806

ROMINE, MARY BAILEY, lawyer; b. Dewar, Okla., Dec. 15, 1929; d. Charles Eugene and Barbara Roberta (Martin) Bailey; A.A., William Woods Coll. Women, 1948; B.A., East Central State Coll., 1951; J.D., U. Okla., 1964; m. R.K. Romine, June 3, 1951 (div. Oct. 1962); children—Christopher Kenneth, Jeffrey Lee. Admitted to Okla. bar, 1964, practiced in Okmulgee, 1964—; partner Bailey & Romine 1964-67, Bailey, Ash & Romine, 1971—; county judge, Okmulgee County, Okla., 1967-69, asso. dist. judge, 1969-71; city atty., Okmulgee, 1971—; dir. Citizens Nat. Bank, Okmulgee, Okla. Bd. dirs. Creek Nation Assn. Children with Learning Disabilities. Coll. Juvenile Ct. Judges, grantee, 1968. Mem. Am., Okla., Okmulgee County bar assns., Kappa Beta Pi. Democrat. Episcopalian. Home: 1421 E 9th St Okmulgee OK 74447 Office: PO Box 159 Okmulgee OK 74447

ROMM, ETHEL GRODZINS, interior designer; b. Lowell, Mass., Mar. 3, 1925; d. David M. and Taube (Bialoblotka) Grodzins; ed. pub. schs.; m. A.N. Romm, July 10, 1954; children—David, Daniel, Joseph. Project supr. USAAF, 1942-45, Assn. Engrs., Agawam, Mass., 1946-54; newspaper columnist Springfield (Mass.) Union, Danbury (Conn.) News-Times, New Bedford (Mass.) Standard Times, 1956—; home editor Middletown (N.Y.) Times Herald-Record, 1957—; lectr. interior design at colls., 1960—, free-lance writer, 1967—. Recipient Dorothy Dawe cup for reportage in interior design Times Herald-Record, 1956, 58, 60. Author: Open Conspiracy, 1970; Throw Out Wednesday, 1973; also articles. Home: 17 Highland Av Middletown NY 10940 Office: Times Herald Record Middletown NY 10940

ROMNEY, LENORE LAFOUNT (MRS. GEORGE WILCKEN ROMNEY), civic worker; b. Logan, Utah; d. Harold Arundel and Alma (Robison) Lafount; A.B., George Washington U., 1929; postgrad. (Performance award) Am. Lab. Sch. Theatre, N.Y.C., 1930; L.H.D., Hillsdale (Mich.) Coll., 1964, Gwynedd-Mercy Coll., 1971; LL.D., Central Mich. U., Mt. Pleasant, 1966; Hum. D., Hope Coll., 1967, Eastern Mich. U., 1969, Detroit Coll. Bus., 1970; m. George Wilcken Romney, July 2, 1931; children—Lynn (Mrs. Loren G. Keenan), Jane (Mrs. Bruce H. Robinson), George Scott, Willard Mitt. Poetry reader NBC radio show Poetical Hitchhiker, Washington, 1933-34; commentator WJR radio sta. program Point of View, 1974—; active Detroit Symphony Orch. Women's Assn., Project Hope, YWCA; hon. co-chmn. Muscular Dystrophy Assn., 1963; mem. spl. com. Am. Mothers Com., 1965—; mem. nat. adv. bd. Am. Field Services, 1958-70; vice chmn. exec. com. Nat. Center for Voluntary Action, 1972—; co-chmn. Nat. Women's Polit. Caucus, 1972; chmn. Brotherhood Commitment, Nat. Conf. Christians and Jews, 1970; mem. nat. adv. council U. Utah, 1970—; mem. adv. com. Thomas Jefferson Research Center. Republican candidate for U.S. Senate from Mich., 1970. Bd. dirs. Jr. Group Goodwill Industries, Detroit Mus. Art Founders Soc., United Community Services, Citizens for Mich. Com., Mich. Child Guidance Study, co-chmn. bd. Met. Opera Season, Detroit, 1961, chmn., 1962. Recipient citation Mich. State U., 1964, citation Mich. Fedn. Music Clubs, 1964, Ad Club of Year award, 1964, Orgn. through Tng. award Hadassah Women's Zionist Orgn. Am., 1964, Silver medallion Nat. Conf. Christians and Jews, 1967, citation Mich. Assn. Future Homemakers, 1965, Woman of Year award Brigham Young U., 1969, citation Bus. and Profl. Women, 1968, citation Internat. Platform Assn., 1967, citation Glendale Coll., 1969, Dr. George Derry award Marygrove Coll., 1965, William Booth award Salvation Army, 1974, others; named ch. woman of the year Religious Heritage Am., 1972. Mem. Greater Lansing chpt. UN Assn. (hon.), Detroit chpt. Ikebana Internat., Hist. Soc. Mich. Mem. Ch. of Jesus Christ of Latter-day Saints (mem. Relief Soc. 1942—, tchr. theology and lit. 1943-62, Sunday sch. 1974—), Am. Assn. U. Women. Contbr. chpt. to Joy of Being a Woman, 1972. Contbr. articles to Look, Ladies Home Jour., Cosmopolitan. Home: 1830 East Valley Rd Bloomfield Hills MI 48013

ROMODA, RUTH WHITNALL (MRS. JOSEPH JOHN ROMODA), librarian; b. Syracuse, N.Y., May 19, 1910; d. Willis Benedict and Mame Lamoureux) Whitnall; B.S., Syracuse U., 1932, M.S., 1969; m. Joseph John Romoda, Aug. 18, 1941; children—Thomas Halsey, Alan Joseph. Sec., Syracuse U. Sch. Edn., Syracuse, N.Y. 1930-41; asst. librarian State U. N.Y. Agr.-Tech. Coll., Canton, N.Y., 1966-70, head librarian, 1970—. Sec. bd. trustees Canton Free Library, 1959—. Mem. N.Y. Library Assn., North Country Reference and Research Resources Council, Kappa Alpha Theta, Delta Kappa Gamma. Universalist. Home: 47 Judson St Canton NY 13617 Office: State U NY Ag-Tech Coll Canton NY 13617

ROMOSER, RUTH AMELIA MIELKE (MRS. EDWARD LOUIS ROMOSER), artist; b. Balt., Apr. 26, 1916; d. Charles James and Clothilda (Schaar) Mielke; grad. Balt. Art Inst., 1944; student Robert Motherwell Workshop, 1962, Xavier Corbero Workship, 1965, Joseph Ruffo Workshop, 1971; m. Edward Louis Romoser, Mar. 13, 1937; children—Eric, Deborah (Mrs. William Young). One man shows Miami (Fla.) Museum Modern Art, Nat. Design Center N.Y., Mirell and Rogue Gallery; exhibited art in group shows at Ringling Southeast Nat. Art Show, Sarasota, Fla., Four Arts Plaza Nat. Show, Palm Beach, Fla., Hortt Meml. Regional, Ft. Lauderdale, Fla., Nat. Design Center, N.Y.C.; represented in permanent collections at Miami Mus. Modern Art, Miami, Lowe Mus., Miami, Miami Herald, Nat. Cardiac Hosp., Miami. Pres. Blue Dome Art Fellowship, 1973-74. Recipient Eighth Hortt Meml. award Fort Lauderdale Mus. Art, 1966. Mem. Miami Art Center, Lowe Mus., Fla. Artist Group, Inc. Address: 8025 SW 64th St Miami FL 33143

ROMWEBER, MARGARET TOLL, librarian; b. Highstown, N.J., Apr. 11, 1918; d. Gustav William and Sara (Toll) Romweber; student Bucknell U., 1936-38; B.S., Simmons Coll., 1940; M.S., Syracuse U., 1957; postgrad. State U. N.Y. at Geneseo, 1965. Librarian Albert Wisner Meml. Library, Warwick, N.Y., 1940-42; children's librarian, asst. librarian Rocky River (O.) Pub. Library, 1942-45; asst. br. librarian Buffalo Pub. Library, 1945-46; librarian Ten Broeck Acad. and Franklinville (N.Y.) Central Sch., 1946—. Life mem. N.Y. State Congress Parents and Tchrs. Mem. A.L.A., N.E.A., N.Y. Library Assn. (pres. sch. libraries sect. 1953), Cattaraugus County Tchrs. Assn. (pres. dist. 1 1959-60), N.Y. State Tchrs. Assn., Delta Kappa Gamma, Pi Lambda Sigma, Beta Phi Mu. Home: 6 2d Av Franklinville NY 14737 Office: 31 N Main St Franklinville NY 14737

RONA, ELIZABETH, geochemist; b. Budapest, Hungary; d. Samuel and Ida (Mahler) Rona; Ph.D., U. Budapest, 1916. Asst. prof. biochemistry U. Budapest; research asst. Kaiser Wilhelm Inst., Berlin-Dalem, Germany, 1926; research asst. Berlin Dahlem, Inst. de Radium, Lab. Curie, Paris, France, 1927; research fellow Inst. Radium and Nuclear Study, Vienna, Austria, 1927-38; with Trinity Coll., 1941-47; asso. prof., Washington, 1947-50; research scientist Argonne Nat. Lab., Chgo., 1950; sr. research scientist Oak Ridge Inst. Nuclear Studies, 1950-65; sr. research scientist Inst. Marine Scis., U. Miami (Fla.), 1965-72. Mem. Am. Chem. Soc., Am. Inst. Physics, A.A.A.S. Home: 115 Nasson Lane Oak Ridge TN 37830

RONA DACSO, MAGDA, pathologist; b. Osjek, Yugoslavia, Jan. 8, 1910; d. Dezso and Margit (Hentz) Rona; M.D., Royal U. Budapest (Hungary), 1934; m. Michael M. Dacso, June 6, 1936; 1 son, Clifford Clark. Came to U.S., 1940, naturalized, 1945. Pathologist, Sydenham Hosp., N.Y.C., 1950-53, Morrisania Hosp., N.Y.C., 1953-65; asso. pathologist Queens Hosp. Center, Jamaica, L.I., 1965—. Asst. clin. prof. Albert Einstein Coll. Medicine, N.Y.C., 1958—, State U. N.Y. at Stony Brook, 1971—. Fellow Coll. Am. Pathologists, Am. Soc. Clin. Pathologists. Home: 56 Middle Neck Rd Roslyn NY 11576 Office: Queens Hosp Center 164th St Jamaica Long Island NY 11432

RONEY, CANDACE BELL, editor; b. Evanston, Ill., Aug. 3, 1948; d. Jerome Bonaparte and Frances Fredrica (VanWart) Bell; A.A., Santa Rosa Jr. Coll., 1968; B.A. with distinction (dean's scholar), San Jose State U., 1970; m. Gerard Francis Roney, June 3, 1972. Asst. activities adviser Santa Rosa (Cal.) Jr. Coll., 1970-71; asst. editor Cal. Sch. Employees Assn., San Jose, Cal., 1971—. Named Woman of Year, Santa Rosa Jr. Coll., 1968. Mem. Women in Communications (v.p. Pal Alto chpt. 1973), Assn. Employees of Cal. Sch. Employees Assn. (pres. 1973), Sigma Delta Chi. Home: 2727 Midtown Ct Palo Alto CA 94303 Office: 2350 Paragon Dr San Jose CA 95131

RONK, SALLY STEWART, economist, govt. ofcl.; b. Newtonville, Mass., Aug. 28, 1912; d. Gilbert H. and Elizabeth (Barnard) Stewart; A.B., Smith Coll., 1934; M.B.A., N.Y. U., 1948, Ph.D., 1965; m. Alfred J. Ronk, June 30, 1939 (div. Apr. 1946); children—Susan B. Gossen, Stewart Von Houten. Jr. economist Fed. Deposit Ins. Corp., Washington, 1935-40, asso. economist, 1940-44; with Bankers Trust Co., N.Y.C., 1945-71, econ. analyst, 1945-60, asst. economist, 1960-64, asso. economist, 1964-68, v.p., 1968-71; v.p., chief economist Drexel Burnham & Co., Inc. (formerly Drexel Firestone), N.Y.C., 1971-74; financial economist Office Sec. Treasury, Washington, 1974—. Fellow Nat. Assn. Bus. Economists; mem. Am. Econ. Assn., Am. Finance Assn. (dir. 1973—), Money Marketeers (gov. 1963-69, sec. 1972—, treas. 1973-74, v.p. 1974—), Met. Econ. Assn. N.Y.C. (pres. 1967-68), Social Sci. Research Council (com. on econ. stability 1971—), Securities Industries Assn. (com. on municipal securities 1971-73), Am. Statis Assn. (council, past chmn. ann. forecasting conf., mem. com. on women in statistics, program chmn. ann. meeting 1973), Downtown Economist Luncheon Group (chmn. 1961-62), Alumnae Assn. Smith Coll. (finance com. 1964-69, treas. 1969-71, chmn. finance com. 1972—). Club: Women's Bond (exec. bd. 1958-60, program chmn. 1964-65, gov. 1972—). Contbr. articles to profl. publs. Home: 824 New Hampshire Av NW Washington DC 20037 Office: Treasury Dept 15th and Pennsylvania Av NW Washington DC 20220

RONQUILLO, MARIA CONSOLACION ROSALES, biologist; b. Manila, P.I., Jan. 1, 1927; d. Hiplolito and Paz (Hernandez) Rosales; B.S., U. Philippines, 1950; M.S., U. Ill., 1965, Ph.D., 1968; m. John Ronquillo, Dec. 9, 1950 (div.); children—Carlos, David. Came to U.S., 1963. Asst. prof. U. of East, Philippines, 1951-63; teaching asst. U. Ill. at Urbana, 1963-65, research asst., 1965-68, research asso., developmental biologist, 1968-73; research asso. biologist, clin. prof. biology, U. N.M., Albuquerque, 1973—. Am. Inst. Biol. Scis. grantee, 1968. Mem. Am. Inst. Biol. Scis., Entomol. Soc. Am., Soc. Developmental Biology, Tissue Culture Assn., Sigma Xi, Phi Sigma. Establishment of primary culture of mosquito cells, 1969-71, cultivation of malarial parasites in vitro. Office: Dept Biology U NM Albuquerque NM 87131

RONSHEIM, SALLY BOBER (MRS. JULIAN RONSHEIM), educator; b. N.Y.C.; d. Hymen and Fanny (Newman) Bober; B.A., Bklyn. Coll., City U., 1940; M.S., L.I. U., 1962; certificate U. London, 1964; Ph.D., N.Y.U., 1967; m. Julian Ronsheim, 1940; children—Nancy, Jane (Mrs. Eugene Ring), Carol (Mrs. Philip Fox). Asst. dir. Grad. Library Sch., L.I. U., 1960-62, asso. prof. English, C.W. Post Center, Greenvale, N.Y., 1967—; tchr. English, librarian Herricks High Sch., New Hyde Park, N.Y., 1962-67. Mem. com. to evaluate Eric Documents, Conf. English Educators, 1968—. Trustee Nassau Reference Library, J.F. Kennedy Cultural Center, N.Y. State English Educators. Dept. Health, Edn. and Welfare grantee to study Internat. Schs. in Western Europe, 1964; research grantee L.I. U. Center, 1971—, C.W. Post L.I. U. research grantee, 1972. Mem. Am. Assn. U. Profs. (pres. C.W. Post chpt. 1972-73), L.I. Tchrs. English, Kappa Delta Pi. Author: New York Portrait: A Literary Look at the Empire State, 1965; Grammatical Terminology: A Combined Traditional and Modern Linguistic Glossary, 1972. Home: 39 Windsor Rd Great Neck NY 11021 Office: C W Post Center Greenvale NY 11548

ROONEY, JUDITH J. WOODRUM (MRS. WILLIAM HENRY ROONEY), real estate broker; b. Newton County, Mo., Aug. 6, 1919; d. Lee and Tony (Hamilton) Woodrum; student Mo. State Coll., 1937-38; m. William Henry Rooney, May 18, 1940; children—Patricia (Mrs. Frank Stelwagon), Judith L. Fraser, Colleen (Mrs. Kent Heaps), Michael, Timothy. Realtor Sidney S. Lippow Co., Martinez, Cal., 1961—, sales mgr., 1964—. Past pres. Cal. 23d Agrl. Dist. Sec.-treas. Martinez Democratic Club, 1964—; mem. Dem. State com., 1971—. Mem. Contra Costa Bd. Realtors, Cal. Assn. of Realtors, Nat. Assn. of Real Estate Bds., Martinez Area C. of C. (dir.), P.T.A. (life). Roman Catholic. Home: 1127 Grand View Av Martinez CA 94553 Office: 611 Las Juntas St Martinez CA 94553

ROONEY, RUTH MARION, graphic designer; b. Chgo., Oct. 6; d. George William and Nanette Isabel (Madigan) Rooney; ed. Denver Acad. Art, Art Inst. Chgo. Art dir., designer Bielefeld Studios, Inc., Chgo., 1939-59; owner, dir. Ruth Rooney Graphic Design, Chgo., 1959—; designer, illustrator children's books, library sets, Ency. Brit. True to Life Series. Mem. Artists Guild Chgo., Art Inst. Chgo. (life), Chgo. Book Clinic, Children's Reading Round Table. Club: Women's Advertising of Chicago. Office: 307 N Michigan Av Chicago IL 60601

ROOT, NINA J., librarian; b. N.Y.C., Dec. 22, 1934; d. Jacob J. and Fannie G. (Slivinsky) Root; B.A., Hunter Coll., 1955; M.S. in Library Sci., Pratt Inst., 1958; postgrad. City U. N.Y., 1965-66. Reference and serials librarian Albert Einstein Coll. Medicine Library, Bronx, N.Y., 1958-59; asst. chief librarian Am. Cancer Soc., N.Y.C., 1959-62; chief librarian Am. Inst. Aeros. and Astronautics, N.Y.C., 1962-64; head reference and library services sci. and tech. div. Library of Congress, Washington, 1964-66; mgmt. cons. Nelson Assos., Inc., N.Y.C., 1966-70; head librarian Am. Mus. Natural History, N.Y.C., 1970—. Cons. library planning and free lance mgmt., 1970—. Mem. Vols. of the Shelter, N.Y.C., 1967—. Recipient Meritorious Service award Library of Congress, 1965. Mem. A.L.A., Spl. Libraries Assn. (sec. documentation group N.Y. chpt. 1972-73, 2d v.p. N.Y. chpt. 1975—), treas. sci. and tech. div. N.Y. chpt. 1975—), A.A.A.S., Am. Sci. Information Sci., Archons of Colophon, Library Automation Research and Cons. Orgn. Author reports in field. Home: 325 E 57th St New York City NY 10022 Office: Library of American Museum of Natural History Central Park W at 79th New York City NY 10024

ROPES, MARIAN W. (MRS. ANDREW B. FIELDING), physician; b. Salem, Mass., Dec. 1, 1903; d. Reuben W. and Grace (Tuttle) Ropes; A.B., Smith Coll., 1924, D.Sc., 1965; M.S., Mass. Inst. Tech., 1926; M.D., Johns Hopkins, 1931; m. Andrew B. Fielding, June 12, 1948. Intern, Johns Hopkins Hosp., Balt., 1931-32; resident Mass. Gen. Hosp., Boston, 1932-34; practice medicine, specializing in internal medicine, Boston, 1933—; mem. staff Mass. Gen. Hosp.; asso. clin. prof. medicine Harvard, 1962-70; cons. Chelsea Naval Hosp. Diplomate Am. Bd. Internal Medicine. Master A.C.P.; mem. Am. Rheumatism Assn. (pres. 1963-64), Am. Soc. Clin. Investigation, New Eng. Rheumatism Soc. (pres. 1952-53). Home: 12 Lawrence St Winchester MA 01890 Office: Mass Gen Hosp Boston MA 02114

RORABAUGH, MILDRED ELAINE, psychologist, educator; b. Westmoreland County, Pa., Jan. 31, 1920; d. Mortimer and Alice (Irvin) Rorabaugh; student Women's Med. Coll. Pa., 1942; B.S., Pa. State U., 1951, M.S., 1952. Caseworker, Family and Children's Service, Lancaster, Pa., 1951-52; psychologist Lancaster Cleft Palate Clinic, 1952-55; tchr. handicapped State Hosp. for Crippled Children, Elizabethtown, Pa., 1955-56; county sch. psychologist, supr. spl. edn. classes County Bd. Sch. Dirs., Clearfield, Pa., 1956-71; supr.-psychologist Central Intermediate Bd. Sch. Dirs., Philipsburg, Pa., 1971—. Instr. Pa. State U., 1960-67. Mem. state governing bd., chpt. sec. and v.p. Council for Exceptional Children, 1964-70. Trustee Clearfield County 4-H Devel. Fund. Mem. Am., Pa. psychol. assns., Clearfield County Sch. Adminstrs. (past pres.), Nat., Pa. fedns. bus. and profl. women's clubs, Clearfield Bus. and Profl. Women's Club (past pres.), Am. Assn. U. Women, Clearfield County Hist. Soc., Pa. State Alumni Assn., Iota Sigma Pi. Presbyn. Home: 13 Pauline Dr W Clearfield PA 16830 Office: Central Intermediate Unit Radio Park Philipsburg PA 16866

ROREX, MARY EVELYN, architect; b. Panhandle, Tex., Dec. 29, 1931; d. Joe and Lydia (Lill) Rorex; student West Tex. State Coll., 1949-50; B. Arch., Tex. Tech. Coll., 1955. Draftsman, designer Tex. Tech. Coll. Campus Landscape Architect, 1953-55, Parks and Recreation Dept. Lubbock, Tex., 1953-55; with Atcheson, Atkinson and Cartwright, architects and engrs., Lubbock, 1955-72, asso. mem. firm, 1966-72; partner Atcheson, Atkinson, Cartwright & Rorex, architects, and engrs., Lubbock, 1972—. Mem. A.I.A. (Outstanding Grad. Student award, Panhandle chpt. 1955, corporate treas. 1970). Lubbock Cultural Affairs Council (dir. 1970-73), Alpha Chi. Democrat. Methodist. Designs include Swisher Meml. Hosp., Tulia, Tex., Big Spring (Tex.) High Sch. Home: Route 1 Box 610 Lubbock TX 79401 Office: 1214 14th St Lubbock TX 79401

RORKE, LUCY BALIAN (MRS. ROBERT RADCLIFFE RORKE), neuropathologist; b. St. Paul, June 22, 1929; d. Aram Haji and Karzouhy (Ousdigian) Balian; B.A., U. Minn., 1951, M.A., 1952, B.S., 1955, M.D., 1957; m. Robert Radcliffe Rorke, June 4, 1960. Intern Phila. Gen. Hosp., 1957-58, resident anatomical pathology and neuropathology, 1958-62, asst. neuropathologist, 1962-67, chief pediatric pathologist, 1967-68, chief neuropathologist, 1968-69, chmn. dept. anatomical pathology and chief neuropathologist, 1969—; practice medicine specializing in neuropathology, Phila., 1962—; neuropathologist Children's Hosp. Phila., 1965—. Cons. neuropathologist Wyeth Research Labs., Radnor, Pa., 1961—, Wistar Inst. for Anatomy and Biology, Phila., 1967—; asso. prof. pathology U. Pa. Sch. Medicine, Phila., 1970-73, prof., 1973—. NIH fellow in Neuropathology, 1961-62, NIH grantee for study of neonatal brain, 1963-68. Diplomate Am. Bd. Pathology in Anatomic Pathology and Neuropathology. Fellow Coll. Am. Pathologists, N.J. Soc. Pathologists; mem. Phila. Gen. Hosp. Med. Staff (pres. 1973—), Phila. Neurol. Soc. (v.p. 1971-72, editor Transactions 1973), Am. Assn. Neuropathologists, Am. Neurol. Assn., Am. Acad. Neurology, A.M.A., Burlington County Med. Soc., Phila. Coll. Physicians, Sigma Xi. Author: Myelinization of the Brain in the Newborn, 1969. Contbr. articles to profl. jours. Home: 120 Chestnut St Moorestown NJ 08057 Office: Phila Gen Hosp Philadelphia PA 19104

RORRO, CELESTE MARY, ednl. adminstr.; b. Trenton, N.J.; d. Michael and Filomena (Guglielmelli) Rorro; A.B., Douglass Coll., 1949; M.S. in Edn., U. Pa., 1964; postgrad. Rutgers, The State U., 1949-50, Temple U., 1949-51, Glassboro State Coll., 1958, Trenton State Coll., 1965, Rider Coll. Tchr. various schs., N.J., 1951-63; counselor, coll. counselor Trenton (N.J.) High Sch., 1963-67; asso. dir. admissions, dir. financial aid Mercer County Community Coll., Trenton, 1967-68, dir. admissions, 1968-70; dir. student personnel services Lawrence Twp. Schs., 1970-73, asst. prin. in charge instruction, 1973—. Mem. adv. commn. Mercer County (N.J.) Community Coll. Recipient Carnegie grant, 1955, Albert B. Kahn Found. scholarship, 1963-64. Mem. Am. Assn. U. Women, N.E.A., Nat. Assn. Secondary Sch. Prins., Assn. Tchr. Educators, N.J. Edn. Assn., N.J. Assn. Tchr. Educators (exec. bd., editor publ.), U. Pa. Alumni Club, Bus. and Profl. Women's Club, Delta Kappa Gamma, Sigma Delta Pi. Clubs: Trenton College, Zonta (Trenton). Home: 295 Hamilton Av Trenton NJ 08609

RORSCHACH, CAROL ANN, geophys. exploration co. exec.; b. Coffeyville, Kan., May 17, 1940; d. Gerald Stewart and Naomi Oree (Riggs) Rorschach; B.A., U. Tulsa, 1966. Jr. tech. writer, Seismograph Service Corp., Tulsa, 1962-64, tech. writer, 1964-65, head of tech. publ. dept., 1965-68, mgr. pub. relations, advt. and tech. writing, 1968—. Vol. A.R.C., 1957-66; active Girl Scouts Am., 1947-65; adv. Jr. Achievement, 1969-71. Mem. Am. Mgmt. Assn., Assn. Indsl. Advertisers, Pub. Relations Soc. Am., Seismograph Service Corp. Fed. Credit Union (pres. 1970-72), Chi Omega (treas. and sec. 1957-61), Phi Gamma Kappa. Home: 1407 S Richmond Tulsa OK 74112 Office: 6200 E 41st St Tulsa OK 74145

ROSALES, GENEVIEVE MARIE, psychiat. social work cons.; b. Corpus Christi, Tex.; d. Indalecio Ramon and Susan Yvonne (ChRalle) Rosales; B.S., Columbia, 1942, postgrad., 1948; M.S., Fordham U., 1948. With Tex. Dept. Pub. Welfare, 1936-41; med. social worker Goldwater Meml. Hosp., Welfare Island, N.Y., 1942-43; psychiat. social worker Inst. for Crippled and Disabled, N.Y.C., 1948; family caseworker Family Service, Cath. Charities N.Y., Bronx, N.Y., 1948-50; supr. East Harlem Family Service Agy., N.Y.C., 1950-53; psychiat. social worker Cath. Charities Guidance Inst., White Plains, N.Y., 1953-54; clinic supr. Cath. Charities Guidance Inst., Peekskill, N.Y., 1954-61; chief psychiat. social worker, clinic adminstr. Variety Children's Hosp., Miami, Fla., 1962-67; dir. social service Children and Youth Project 636 Dade County Dept. Pub. Health, Miami, Fla., 1967-69; individual practice as therapist. Cons. Dade Family Therapy Center, Inc., Miami. Served from 2d lt. to 1st lt. U.S. Army Nurse Corps, 1943-45. Mem. Acad. Certified Social Workers, Nat. Assn. Social Workers (charter), Am. Group Psychotherapy Assn. Inc., Mental Health Assn. Dade County Inc., Fla. Pub. Health Assn. Inc. Home: 1110 SW 99th Pl Miami FL 33144 Office: 1110 SW 99th Pl Miami FL 33144

ROSE, BEATRICE KARTUS (MRS. LEONARD B. ROSE), physician; b. N.Y.C.; d. Samuel J. and Lena D. (Ziskind) Kartus; B.A., George Washington U., 1943, M.D., 1946; m. Leonard B. Rose, Jan. 11, 1948; children—Susan G., Jeffrey S. Rotating intern Gallinger Municipal Hosp. (name changed to D.C. Gen. Hosp.), Washington, 1946-47, resident internal medicine, 1947-48; staff physician internal medicine VA Hosp., Perry Point, Md., 1948-51, Albany, N.Y., 1953-55, Portland, Ore., 1956-58; practice medicine specializing in internal medicine, Portland, 1960—; clin. instr. U. Ore. Med. Sch., Portland, 1959-63. Mem. Ore. Bd. Health, 1967—, lab. adv. com., 1967—, v.p., 1970—; mem. Ore. Health Manpower Council, 1967—, chmn., 1970—; mem. Comprehensive Health Planning Authority of Ore., 1971. Bd. dirs. Family Counseling Service, 1968—, chmn. profl. services com., 1970—, mem. homemaker services com., 1968—. Recipient service award Multnomah County Med. Soc., 1967; Named Woman of Accomplishment, Ore. Jour., 1967, Dr.-Citizen of Year, Ore. Med. Assn., 1971. Mem. Multnomal County Med. Soc. (trustee 1969—), Ore. Med. Assn. (chmn. veneral disease edn. subcom. 1971), A.M.A. Home: 4831 SW Humphrey Park Crest Portland OR 97221 Office: 2311 NW Northrup Portland OR 97210

ROSE, BEATRICE SCHROEDER (MRS. WILLIAM H. ROSE), harpist, educator; b. Ridgewood, N.J., Nov. 15, 1922; d. Henry William and Ida (LeHovey) Schroeder; student Inst. Mus. Art, 1940-41; studied with Lucile Lawrene and Carlos Salzedo; student (scholar) Mannes Coll. Music, 1942-44; m. William Harrison Rose, Apr. 10, 1954; 1 son, Daniel. Concert and radio debut N.Y. Worlds's Fair, 1939; soloist, Damrosch Music Appreciation Hour Broadcast, 1940, for Duke Windsor's Save the Children Fund Gov. House, Nassau, Bahamas, 1941; asso. harpist Radio City Music Hall Orch., N.Y.C., 1944-50; various radio and solo performances N.Y. area, 1944-51; concert artist, Italy, 1952, U.S., Canada, 1953; prin. harpist Houston Symphony, 1953—; harp instr. U. Houston, 1953—; mem. Contemporary Music Soc., soloist, 1959, 60; soloist Houston Chamber Orch., 1969; founder, dir. Houston Harp Ensemble. Recipient 1st prize Fed. Music Clubs Contest, 1936; winner N.Y. Hour of Music award, 1945. Mem. Am. Harp Soc. (charter), Phi Beta. Author (with Grace Follet) Outline of Six-Year Harp Course for Elementary, Jr. and Sr. High School, 1966. Music pub.: Enchanted Harp, 1955; also recs. for Houston Symphony, Stokowski, Everest and Capitol records. Home: 1315 Friarcreek Lane Houston TX 77055 Office: care of Houston Symphony Jones Hall Houston TX 77002

ROSE, ELINOR KIESS (MRS. DANA ROSE), writer; b. Edon, O.; d. David Theodore and Bertha Laura (Twichell) Kiess; A.B., Hillsdale Coll., 1933; m. Dana Rose, Dec. 25, 1935 (dec. Dec. 1968); children—Stuart, Douglas, Bruce. Light verse writer for Allied Features Syndicate, 1952—; writer of prose/poetry pub. in mags. including Readers Digest, Good Housekeeping, Christian Herald, Sat. Eve. Post, Quote, Wall St. Jour., McCall's. Judge in scholastic writing awards, 1957—. Trustee Hillsdale Coll., 1970—. Recipient Nat. Achievement award Kappa Kappa Gamma, 1968; Achievement award Hillsdale Coll., 1955; Writer of Year award Detroit Women Writers, 1959. Mem. Detroit Press Club, Women in Communications, Detroit Women Writers. Author: Relax, Chum, 1954; Sugar and Spice, 1959; Rhyme and Reason, 1967. Home and office: 25560 Dundee Rd Royal Oak MI 48070

ROSE, GEORGIA ROCKEFELLER (MRS. J. HARDEN ROSE), philanthropist; b. Greenwich, Conn., Oct. 11, 1933; d. James Stillman and Nancy Campbell Sherlock (Carnegie) Rockefeller; B.A., Vassar Coll., 1955; m. J. Harden Rose, June 29, 1957; children—James Stillman Rockefeller, Andrew Carnegie, Georgia Rockefeller. Mem. N.Y. Philharmonic Ladies Bd., 1965—. Trustee Foxcroft Sch.; bd. dirs. Amateur Needlework of Today, Inc. Home: 155 E 70th St New York City NY 10021

ROSE, HARRIETT GRACE (MRS. STANLEY IRWIN ROSE), educator; b. Shelbyville, Ky., Sept. 13, 1920; d. Isadore J. and Hilda (Rosenthal) Abraham; student Brenau Coll., 1937-38; B.S. in Music, U. Ky., 1941, M.A. in Counseling and Guidance, 1962, Ph.D., 1964; m. Stanley I. Rose, June 27, 1943; children—Richard Norvin, David Andrew, Tchr. pub. schs., Maysville, Ky., 1941-43; editor USAAF, Dayton, O., 1943-45; dir. religious edn. Temple Adath Israel, Lexington, Ky., 1954-60; counselor U. Ky., 1961-63, acting dir. counseling service, 1963-65, dir. Counseling and Testing Center, 1965—, asso. prof. psychology, 1970—. Mem. Am., Ky., Central Ky. (pres. 1972) psychol. assns., Am. Personnel and Guidance Assn., So., Am. (editor monographs 1971—) coll. personnel assns., Kappa Delta Pi, Psi Chi. Contbr. articles to profl. jours. Home: 712 Beechmont Rd Lexington KY 40502

ROSE, IVAH ELIZABETH (MRS. CHARLES LOVELL ROSE), educator; b. Romeo, Mich., Aug. 5, 1905; d. Herbert E. and Anna M. (Dryer) Livermore; tchrs. certificate in speech and English, Eastern Mich. U., 1925; m. Charles Lovell Rose, July 17, 1928; children—David, Charles. Pub. sch. tchr., Evart, Mich., 1925-27, St. Clair Shores, Mich., 1927-28; mem. Mich. Library Bd., 1965—; chmn., 1970-74, mem. council post-secondary edn. Mich. Dept. Edn., 1973—. Bd. dirs. Girlstown Found., 1964-68, treas., 1964-66. Mem. Gen. (clean environment chmn. 1968-70), Mich. (pres. 1966-68), Northwestern Dist. (pres. 1935-36) fedns. women's clubs. Methodist. Mem. Order Eastern Star (past matron). Club: Evart Woman's (pres. 1944-46, 69-70). Author: Evart 100 Years, 1972. Home: 408 N Main St Evart MI 49631

ROSE, JEAN BAKER (MRS. GILBERT WHITE ROSE), assn. exec.; b. Rochester, N.Y., June 7, 1920; d. Harold Wallace and Ethel (Froass) Baker; student Elmira Coll., 1939-40; m. Gilbert White Rose, Dec. 17, 1943; children—Merilee R. (Mrs. Lynn R. Davis), Peter M., Katherine W. (Mrs. George F. Williams). Treas., exec. dir. Cat Fancier's Assn., Inc., Red Bank, N.J., 1958—; treas., dir. Robert H. Winn Found. Cat Research. Mem. Solid Color of East Club (dir.), Garden State Cat Club of N.J. Home: 103 Cloverdale Circle New Shrewsbury NJ 07724 Office: 11 Globe Ct Red Bank NJ 07701

ROSE, JERLENE (MRS. WILLIAM FOREST ROSE), newspaper editor; b. Stanton, Ky., Sept. 2, 1942; d. Morgan Lyle and Hoyt Wynona (Bush) Bellamy; student Eastern Ky. U., 1961-62; m. William Forest Rose, Aug. 20, 1961; 1 dau., Leigh Michele. Tchr.'s aide Head Start program Powell County Bd. Edn., 1965; typist, proof reader Clay City (Ky.) Times, 1965, reporter, 1966, editor, bus. mgr., 1968—; bus. mgr. Menifee Jour., Frenchburg, Ky., 1972—. Mem. adv. com. Powell County Pub. Library Bd., 1972-73. Recipient 1st place journalism award Ky. Press Assn., 1971, 72, 1st place award in painting Powell County Fair Exhibit, 1973. Mem. Nat. Assn. Press Women (rec. sec. 1973—, charter), Ky. Press Assn., Nat. Newspaper Assn., Ky. Weekly Newspaper Assn., Red River Hist. Mus. Soc. (charter mem., treas.). Democrat. Mem. Christian Ch. Club: Powell County Art (pres. 1974—). Home: PO Box 2 Old Forge Rd Clay City KY 40312 Office: PO Box 218 7th Av Clay City KY 40312

ROSE, KATHERINE CAST (MRS. HORACE CHAPMAN ROSE), civic worker; b. Akron, O.; d. John Frederick and Amy (Motz) Cast; A.B., Wellesley Coll., 1929; m. Horace Chapman Rose, Oct. 1, 1938; 1 son, Jonathan Chapman. Actress, Cleve. Play House, Chautauqua Repertory Co., 1919-36; trustee Goodrich Social Settlement, 1936-43, Jr. League Cleve., Nat. Cathedral Assn., Washington, 1948-56, 59-65, Children's Theatre of Washington, 1947-49, Cleve. Internat. Youth Leaders, Cleve. Playhouse; chmn. stage com. Washington Stage Door Canteen, 1943-46; chmn. box com. Nat. Symphony Orch., 1947-48; mem. adv. council Nat. Inst. Mental Health, 1956-59; co-chmn. Ohio Citizens for Eisenhower, 1952, 56; vice chmn. women's div. Nat. Citizens for Eisenhower's Congl. Com., 1954; mem. adv. council Nat. Accident Prevention Bur., 1959-63; chmn. Blueprint for Life, Cleve., 1963. Republican. Episcopalian. Clubs: Intown (Cleve.); Sulgrave (Washington). Home: 12407 Fairhill Rd Cleveland OH 44120 also 2701 31st St NW Washington DC 20008

ROSE, LILLIAN LERNER (MRS. JULIAN BARNET BOOKSTAVER), recreational service adminstr.; b. N.Y.C., May 4, 1916; d. Louis and Yetta (Swiger) Lerner; A.B., N.Y. U., 1939, M.A., 1967; m. Jules N. Rose, Feb. 24, 1940 (dec. July 1955); children—Elicia May (Mrs. Seymour Faitell), Andrew David, Elliot Ian; m. 2d, Julian Barnet Bookstaver, Oct. 9, 1969. Pres., Camp Allegro, Pittsfield, Mass., 1946—; exec. dir. Allegro Sch., Pittsfield, Mass., 1958—; dir. Lerner-Rose-Lerner Corp., Pittsfield. Mem. fund com. Nat. Found. Infantile Paralysis, 1948-52, Orgn. for Rehab. Tng., N.Y.C., 1946—; executrix Louis Lerner philanthropic scholarship fund N.Y. U., N.Y.C., 1953, Jules N. Rose scholarship fund Manhattan Sch. Music, 1962. Mem. Am. Camp Assn., Assn. Pvt. Camps (govs. 1962), Western Mass. Camp Dirs. Group, New Eng. Camp Group. Home: 371 Audubon Rd Englewood NJ 07631 Office: Camp Allegro Pittsfield MA 01201

ROSE, MARY CARMAN, educator; b. Mpls., Feb. 23, 1916; d. Charles M. and Lulu (Gassmann) Carman; B.A., U. Minn., 1937, M.A., 1939; Ph.D., Johns Hopkins, 1949; m. Alexander G. Rose, Dec. 12, 1942; children—David (dec.), John M. Asst. prof. philosophy George Washington U., 1949-53; asso. prof. philosophy, 1956-61, now prof., chmn. dept. philosophy Goucher Coll., 1956—; lectr. philosophy religion. Mem. Am. Philos. Assn., Am. Aesthetics Soc., Metaphys. Soc., Am. Cath. Philos. Assn., Soc. Sci. Study Religion, So. Soc. for Philosophy and Psychology, So. Soc. for Philosophy Religion, Brit. Soc. for Aesthetics, Charles Peirce Soc., Am. Assn. U. Profs., Phi Beta Kappa. Roman Catholic. Clubs: Washington Philosophy, Johns Hopkins. Contbr. articles to profl. jours. Home: 402 E Gittings Av Baltimore MD 21212 Office: Goucher Coll Towson MD 21204

ROSE, MARY JOY, educator; b. Cin., Mar. 14, 1935; d. Clarence Jacob and Mary (Andrews) Rose; B.S. in Edn., Ohio State U., 1959, M.A., 1967, M.A., 1972. Tchr. journalism and English, Mentor (O.) Shore Jr. High Sch., 1959-60, Pleasant View High Sch., Grove City, O., 1960-69, Westerville (O.) High Sch., 1969—. Mem. Ohio Tchr. Edn. and Profl. Standards Commn. Mem. Nat., Ohio (sec. women's caucus 1973), Central Ohio (mem. exec. com. 1972-73), Westerville (pres. 1972-73) edn. assns., Franklin County Council Edn. Assns. (pres. 1972—), Ohio Assn. Classroom Tchrs. (mem. resolutions com. 1972—), Women in Communications (sec. Columbus, O. chpt. 1973—), Nat. Sch. Pub. Relations Assn., Nat. Women's Polit. Caucus, Nat. Orgn. Women, Ohio State U. Alumni Assn., Minerva Park (O.) Women's Club, Kappa Tau Alpha, Phi Delta Kappa. Home: 2945 Berry Lane Columbus OH 43229 Office: 303 S Otterbein Av Westerville OH 43081

ROSE, NANCY ANN, author; b. Chamberlain, S.D., May 6, 1934; d. Milton Leroy and Helen Dorothy (Matson) Mortensen; grad. high sch.; m. Robert J. Rose, Sept. 13, 1952; children—Randy, Julie (Mrs. Richard J. Drew), Kenton, Bruce, Stewart, Melissa, Philip. Author four childrens books, 1970-71. Program dir. Wis. Penal Instns.; chmn. Instl. Program for Writing; dir. Scripters Manuscript Group. Recipient 1st place short story div. Ind. U., 1971, hon. mention nat. poetry contests Nat. Fedn. State Poetry Socs., 1971. Mem. Wis. Regional Writers Assn. (dir., 1st place juvenile book awards Jade Ring Awards 1967, 73), Wis. Fellowship of Poets (dir., 2d place Trophy Poem Contest 1973, 1st place Trophy Poem Contest 1974). Roman Catholic. Address: 215 Oak Hill Dr Green Bay WI 54301

ROSE, NATASHA RICHMAN (MRS. JAMES M. ROSE), lawyer; b. N.Y.C., Sept. 22, 1945; d. Samuel M. and Sandra Hope (Rubin) Richman; B.A., Brandeis U., 1966; J.D., Boston Coll., 1969; postgrad. N.Y. U., 1974—; m. James M. Rose, Aug. 13, 1966; children—Robert, Eve. Admitted to Mass. bar, 1970, N.Y. bar, 1972; staff atty. Nat. Consumer Law Center, Brighton, Mass., 1969; staff atty. Cambridge (Mass.) Inst., 1970; mem. firm Rose & Rose, Scarsdale, N.Y., 1970—. Teaching asst. urban law workshop Boston Coll. Law Sch., 1969-70; asso. dir. Am. Assembly in Black Econ. Devel., Boston, 1970. Mem. N.Y. State, Mass. bar assns., Westchester Civil Liberties Union. Hadassah (v.p. White Plains 1972-73). Address: 10 Ridgecrest E Scarsdale NY 10583

ROSE, ROSLYN (MRS. FRANKLIN BLOU), artist; b. Irvington, N.J., May 28, 1929; d. Mark and Anne Sarah (Green) Rose; student Rutgers U., 1949-51, New Sch., 1966, Pratt Center for Contemporary Printmakers, 1967; m. Franklin Blou, Nov. 26, 1950; 1 son, Mark Gordon. One-man shows at Newark Mus., Lozowick Art Center, Millburn, N.J., Kean Coll., Caldwell (N.J.) Coll.; exhibited in group shows at Seattle Mus., Portland Mus., Wadsworth Atheneum, Hartford, Conn., Montclair (N.J.) Mus., Audubon Artists, N.Y.C., Palazzio Vecchio, Florence, Italy, other; prints included in various traveling exhbns.; represented in permanent collections at N.J. State Mus., Trenton, Upsala Coll., Rosenberg Library, Galveston, Tex., McAllen (Tex.) Internat. Mus., Bennett Coll., Millbrook, N.Y., Contemporary Art of N.J., others; instr. printmaking Newark Mus., Summit (N.J.) Art Center, Art Gallery of Maplewood-South Orange (N.J.); commd. edits. graphics N.Y. Graphic Soc. Ltd., Nabis Fine Arts Inc. Recipient awards including Best-in-show Summit Art Center, 1969, Mary Karasick prize Nat. Assn. Women Artists, N.Y.C., 1969, Best-in-Show award Livingston Art Assn., 1971, graphic award Rochester Internat. Religious Exhibit, 1970, Westchester (N.Y.) Art Soc., 1973, Painters and Sculptors Soc. N.J., 1971. Mem. Nat. Assn. Women Artists, Artists Equity (mem. exec. bd. 1971—), Print Club Phila. Home: 457 Baldwin Rd Maplewood NJ 07040 Office: Atelier 3 Maplewood NJ 07040

ROSE, WILLIE PERRY (MRS. EDWIN A. ROSE), educator; b. West Blocton, Ala.; d. William Walter and Alice (Woods) Perry; A.B., Samford U., 1937; M.A., U. Ala., 1958; postgrad. Columbia; m. Edwin A. Rose, Sept. 17, 1930 (dec. 1960); children—Ann Rose Humphreys (Mrs. Robert L. Humphreys), Edwin A. Tchr. pub. schs., Birmingham, Ala., 1937-57, supr. speech arts, 1957—, dir. poetry festival. Ednl. chmn. Women's Com. of 100, Birmingham Centennial Year, 1972; mem. Ala. High Sch. Fine Arts Com., 1972—, Birmingham Hist. Commn., 1972—, Pres.'s Com. on Employment Handicapped, 1972—. Bd. dirs. Birmingham Civic Opera, Birmingham Civic Ballet, Children's Theatre; bd. dirs., v.p. edn. Birmingham Festival Arts, Silver Bowl award, 1971; mem. exec. bd. Freedom Ednl. Found., Birmingham. Recipient Freedoms Found. Valley Forge award, 1964; Merit certificate A.R.C., 1938; named Samford U. Alumna of Year, 1972. Mem. Ala. Speech Assn. (sec.-treas. 1958-62), Birmingham Women Symphony League, Birmingham Art Mus., Women's C. of C., D.A.R. (chmn. Ala. Sesquicentennial library and lit. com. region III), Altrusa Internat. (bd. dirs., 1st v.p., Altrusan of Year 1971), Delta Kappa Gamma (v.p. 1966-67, pres. 1968-72), Kappa Delta Pi, Kappa Delta Epsilon (pres. 1966-67). Participant ednl. tv programs. Home: 2643 B Park Lane Ct E Birmingham AL 35223

ROSECRANCE, WINIFRED LEROY SMITH (MRS. RALPH CLAYTON ROSECRANCE), civic worker; b. Somerset, Mich.; d. LeRoy Torrence and Bessie (Sickley) Smith; student Hillsdale (Mich.) Coll., 1914-16; m. Ralph Clayton Rosecrance, Sept. 11, 1920; children—Robert Bruce, Marjorie (Mrs. Peter Scott). Bd. dirs. YWCA, Rockford, Ill., 1920-23, 57-63, Rockford Day Nursery, 1961-64; bd. dirs. women commrs. Hillsdale Coll., 1951—; mem. Rosecrance Home Aux. of Rosecrance Meml. Home for Boys, Rockford. Recipient awards for vol. work A.R.C., 1945, Rockford Meml. Hosp., 1957. Mem. Jr. League Rockford, Kappa Kappa Gamma. Conglist. Clubs: Rockford Woman's, Rockford Country, Republican Women's. Home: 2216 Clinton Pl Rockford IL 61103

ROSELL, ANTOINETTE FRASER (MRS. EARL LEONARD ROSELL JR.), state senator, dean of girls; b. Princeton, Ill., Sept. 18, 1926; d. Robert Berkeley and Rosebel (Walter) Fraser; B.A. in Psychology, Mont. State U., 1948; diploma U. Oslo (Norway), 1951; M.A. in Student Personnel Adminstrn., Columbia, 1952; m. Earl Leonard Rosell, Jr., Mar. 29, 1957; 1 dau., Rene Fraser. Dean of girls Missoula County (Mont.) High Sch., 1950-51; dir. student activities Eastern Mont. Coll. Edn., Billings, 1954-56; mem. Mont. House of Reps., 1957-58, 61-64, Mont. Senate, 1967—; girls counselor Youth Guidance Council, Billings 1958-59, 61—; dean of girls Billings Sr. High Sch.; now guidance counselor Lincoln Jr. High Sch., Billings; partner ET Ranch, Billings, 1959—; dir. R. B. Fraser, Inc., Fraser Land and Livestock Co. (Billings). Chmn. Billings Symphony Women's Com., 1957-58; pink lady Deaconess Hosp.; sec. Billings Arts Assn., 1957-58; vice chmn. Mont. Commn. on Exec. Reorgn., vice chmn. subcom. on sch. laws; mem. adv. com. on disadvantaged to state supt. schs. Sec. Mont. Young Republicans 1954-56, nat. committeewoman, 1957-59; sec. Yellowstone County Young Reps., 1957-58. Bd. dirs. YWCA, Billings. Named Mont. Woman of Year, 1967. Mem. Nat. Order Women Legislators, N.E.A., Mont. Inst. Arts, League Women Voters, Am. Legion Aux., Am. Assn. U. Women, Mont. Personnel and Guidance Assn., Bus. and Profl. Women's Club (1st v.p. Billings 1957-58, named one of the three women of Year 1957), D.A.R., Billings C. of C., Nat. Legislative Conf. (mem. intergovtl. relations com., exec. com. 1972-74, legislative tng. com. 1972-74), Mont. Legislative Council (vice chmn.), Daus. of the Nile, Kappa Delta Pi, Kappa Alpha Theta, Delta Kappa Gamma. Republican. Presbyn. Club: Zonta. Home: 4200 Rimrock Rd Billings MT 59102

ROSEMAN, GLORIA SAMUELSON (MRS. BENJAMIN M. ROSEMAN), librarian; b. N.Y.C., June 17, 1920; d. Sidney Edgar and Dorothy A. (Soskin) Samuelson; B.A., Antioch Coll., 1941; M.S. in Library Sci., Villanova U., 1963; m. Benjamin M. Roseman, June 15, 1946; children—Merilynn (Mrs. Michael Brodherson). Office mgr. Nat. Found. Infantile Paralysis, Phila., 1944-46; librarian, media specialist Wanamaker Jr. High Sch., Phila., 1959-66; supr. Phila. Sch. Libraries, 1966—. Rec. sec. Allens Lane Art Center, Phila., 1955-60. Mem. Am. Assn. Sch. Librarians, Am. Library Assn., Assn. Phila. Sch. Librarians, Phila. Assn. Sch. Adminstrs. Mem. B'nai B'rith Women Educators. Office: 21st and Pkwy Philadelphia PA 19103

ROSEN, ANDREA PENKOWER (MRS. DAVID A. ROSEN), psychologist, state ofcl.; b. N.Y.C., Apr. 19, 1939; d. Murry S. and Lillian Harriet (Stavisky) Penkower; B.A., Barnard Coll., 1960; M.A., Columbia, 1962, Ph.D., 1970; m. David A. Rosen, June 25, 1961; children—Alexis Michael, Amanda Brooke, Avery Brendan. Instr. Columbia, N.Y.C., 1969-70; sr. research scientist N.Y. State Dept. Mental Hygiene, N.Y.C., 1970—. Nat. Inst. Mental Health fellow, 1965-67. Mem. Am., N.Y. State, Eastern psychol. assns., Council of Research Scientist of N.Y. State Dept. Mental Hygiene, Am. Mizrachi Women, Sigma Xi. Mem. Hadassah. Home: 110 Riverside Dr New York City NY 10024 Office: 75 Morton St New York City NY 10014

ROSEN, BEATRICE MARKS (MRS. JULIUS ROSEN), statistician; b. N.Y.C., July 11, 1925; d. Henry and Sonia (Routman) Marks; B.S., Queens Coll., 1947; postgrad. U. N.C., 1963, 64, Am. U., 1964-65; m. Julius Rosen, Feb. 27, 1949; children—Jeffrey, Barbara, Michael. Mathematician, U.S. Naval Obs., Washington, 1947-49; statistician U.S. Bur. of Census, Suitland, Md., 1949-52, biometry br. Nat. Inst. Mental Health, Rockville, Md., 1958—. Fellow Am. Pub. Health Assn.; mem. Am. Statis. Assn., Soc. Epidemiologic Research, League Women Voters (unit chmn. 1957, 58). Contbr. articles on mental health to profl. jours. and books. Home: 11702 College View Dr Wheaton MD 20902 Office: 5600 Fishers Lane Rockville MD 20852

ROSEN, EDITH PRESS (MRS. BERNARD ROSEN), social work adminstr.; b. Bklyn., July 28, 1919; d. Abraham and Sima (Berkowitz) Press; B.A., Bklyn. Coll., 1939; M.S.W., N.Y. U., 1963; m. Bernard Rosen, Apr. 23, 1956. Elementary tchr., Waterford Twp., Albany, N.Y., 1941-42; adminstrv. asst., exec. sec. Internat. Resistance Co., Phila., 1942-46; dir. personnel Mogar Home Products, Inc., N.Y.C., 1946-49; with Bklyn. Bur. Community Service, 1951—, dir. dept. rehab. services, 1967—. Mem. steering com. Council Teaching Agys., N.Y. U. Grad. Sch. Social Work, 1970. Recipient Greater N.Y. Fund Community Service award, 1961, 66. Mem. Nat. Assn. Social Workers, Nat. Conf. Social Welfare, Nat. Rehab. Assn., N.Y. State Fedn. Workers for Blind, Inc., N.Y. U. Alumni Assn. (dir. Grad. Sch. Social Work 1963—). Club: Personnel (N.Y., mem. exec. com. 1958-60). Home: 101-13 Flatlands Av Brooklyn NY 11236 Office: 285 Schermerhorn St Brooklyn NY 11217

ROSEN, ESTHER YOVITS (MRS. MYOR ROSEN), painter; b. Schenectady, June 3, 1916; d. Albert and Goldie (Goldsmith) Yovits; student N.Y. Sch. Fine and Indsl. Art, 1923-25; m. Myor Rosen, May 25, 1941; children—Linda, David. Exhibited one-woman shows at Arthur Wakeling Gallery, Woodridge, N.J., 1962, Newark (Del.) Art

Gallery, 1969, Lord and Taylor, Paramus, N.J., 1969, Golden Caravan, Paramus, 1971, Albert Einstein Coll. Medicine, N.Y.C., 1972; exhibited in group shows, 1938—, including Pa. Acad. Fine Arts Ann., 1938, Nat. Acad. Ann., N.Y.C., 1938, Am. Fedn. Arts Traveling exhbn., 1938-39, numerous Modern Artist Guild exhbns., N.J., 1961—. Tchr., lectr. Teaneck (N.J.) pub. schs., 1953-71; tchr. cultural enrichment program for disadvantaged children, Hackensack, N.J., 1972; tchr. YM-YWHA of Bergen County, Hackensack, 1965—. Recipient best painting award Prentice Hall, 1963. Mem. Modern Artists Guild (pres. 1969-70), N.J. Cultural Council, Nat. Assn. Women Artists. Address: 243 Cherry Lane Teaneck NJ 07666

ROSEN, IDA, librarian; b. Rome, N.Y., Nov. 26, 1922; d. Jacob and Sima (Lifschitz) Rosen; B.A., N.Y. State Tchrs. Coll., 1943, M.A., 1944; B.M., Eastman Sch. Music, 1947; M.A., Cornell U., 1952, Ph.D., 1961; M.S., Columbia U., 1960. Tchr. social studies Rome Jr. High Sch., 1944-45; piano tchr. Bartram Sch., Jacksonville, Fla., 1947-49; librarian Buffalo and Erie County Library, Buffalo, 1962-64; librarian music and art div. Milw. Pub. Library, 1964-65; head phonograph record librarian music dept. Princeton U. (N.J.), 1965—. Mem. Music Library Assn., Am., Internat. musicological socs., Assn. for Recorded Sound Collections (chmn. edn. and standards com. 1967-71, chmn. com. on qualifications sound archivists 1971—), Internat. Assn. of Music Libraries, Internat. Assn. Sound Archives. Author: The Treatment of Dissonance in the Motets of Josquin Desprez, 1961. Contbr. to profl. jours. Home: 120 Prospect Av Princeton NJ 08540

ROSEN, MARY KATZ (MRS. DAVID ROSEN), violinist, condr., educator; b. Chgo., 1918; d. Meyer and Annie (Abrams) Katz; student Columbia Sch. Music, 1932, Boguslawski Coll. Music, 1936-40, Chgo. Conservatory Music, 1940-42; m. David Rosen, Mar. 10, 1946; children—Jordan, Eden. Debut as violinist, 1928, began teaching, 1931; became head violin dept. Ravinia Conservatory, 1937; became mem. faculty Chgo. Conservatory, 1941, Boguslawski Coll., 1942; mem. faculty De Paul U. Sch. Music, 1967—; string intern Sch. Dist. 68, Skokie, Ill.; condr. Met. Youth Symphony Orch.; toured U.S. as violinist on stage and radio, also U.S.O., until 1946; founder, condr. Congregation Kehilath Israel Symphony, 1958-61, Southlawn Meth. Ch. Symphony, 1961-62, Chgo. Young Judaea Symphony, 1960—, Skokie Valley Youth Symphony, 1971-72; now also violinist City Symphony Orch. Chgo., Joseffer String Quartet, Silver Strings Quartet; sec. City Symphony Orch. Chgo., 1965; music dir. Camp Yehudah, Watervilet, Mich., 1962; first violinist Rosen String Quartet; instr. violin, instr. youth string orch. De Paul U. Vol. worker various civic and philanthropic causes; mem. P.T.A.; organized Women Musicians, publicity chmn., 1964-65. Recipient Victory award for boosting sale U.S. bonds, 1945; plaque for devoted service Young Judaea Symphony Orch., 1965. Mem. Chgo. Fedn. Musicians, Hadassah (hon. life), Am. String Tchrs. Assn. (treas. Ill. unit). Home: 7157 N Laramie Av Skokie IL 60076 Office: De Paul U Sch Music 25 E Jackson Blvd Chicago IL 60604

ROSEN, MILDRED PAFUNDI (MRS. N. HILTON ROSEN), state ofcl., lawyer; b. Bklyn., Nov. 26, 1929; d. Michael and Rose (Sabina) Pafundi; B.B.A., St. John's U., 1954, LL.B., 1957; m. N. Hilton Rosen, Mar. 15, 1963; 1 dau., Sharon. Asst. to pub. relations dir. Harriet Hubbard Ayer, Lever Bros., 1947-49; market analyst, researcher make-up and layout N.Y. Herald Tribune, 1949-58; admitted to N.Y. bar, 1958; practiced in N.Y.C., 1958—; asst. atty. gen. State N.Y., 1959-64; law asst. to surrogate Kings County, acting chief adoption dept. Surrogates Ct., 1964-66; councilwoman-at-large from Bklyn. N.Y.C. Council, 1966-69; commr. N.Y. State Labor Relations Bd., 1970—. Mem. Bklyn. Heights Jr. Com. South Bklyn. Neighborhood House; mem. Vol. Park Slope Civic Council, 1957-64; leader St. Francis Xavier council Girl Scouts U.S.A., 1957-60; adv. bd. Labor Mgmt. Relations Inst., Pace Coll. Pres., Young Republicans Bklyn., 1959; alternate del. Rep. Nat. Conv., 1964, 68; bd. govs. Kings County Rep. Club. Mem. Bklyn. Womens Bar Assn. (bd. govs.), Bklyn. Heights Assn. (bd. govs.), Phi Delta Delta. Roman Catholic. Home: 242 Henry St Brooklyn NY 11201 Office: 2 World Trade New York City NY 10047

ROSEN, RUTH CHIER (MRS. RICHARD ROSEN), publishing co. exec., author; b. Mpls., June 13, 1925; d. Maurice Charles and Esther (Bentson) Chier; B.A. cum laude, Smith Coll., 1947; m. Richard Rosen, Sept. 13, 1947; children—Richard A., Roger C. Co-founder, v.p. Richards Rosen Assos., N.Y.C., 1950—; co-founder, treas. Richards Rosen Press, N.Y.C., 1960—; treas. Lester Richards Assos.; sec.-treas. Richards Rosen Realty Company, 1959. Dir., founder Creative Recipe Inst., N.Y.C., 1959—. Author: The Epicurean Guide, 1950; A Guide, to Pink Elephants, Vol. 1, 1950, Vol. 2, 1958; The Big Spread, 1952; The Chef's Tour, 1952; Cyrano de Casserole, 1953; From Nets to You, 1953; A Tomato Well Dressed, 1953; Wendy's Kitchen Debut, 1953; The Terrace Chef, 1954; Thank You, Mr. Columbus, 1954; Wick and Lick, 1954; Wurst You Were Here, 1954; The Ancestral Recipes of Shen Mei Lon, 1955; Tooth Sweet, 1955; Pop Monsieur-Champagne Cook Book, 1956; Just Between Us, 1957; Pardon My Foie Gras, 1957; Stirring Saucery, 1957; Have Cook Book Will Marry, 1958; His, 1958; Restaurant-Tour, 1958; Freeze 'n Easy, 1959; Having A Ball, 1959; State Fair, 1959; Dig That Dish, 1960; Spicemanship, 1960; Cooking With Spirit, 1961; Nippon These, 1961; After Dark, 1962; Masquerade, 1962; Three Crowns, 1966; Entertainingly Yours, 1967; Instantly Delicious, 1967; Fondue is Beautiful, 1970; Vita Party Book, 1972. Home: 137 E 19th St New York City NY 10003 Office: 29 E 21st St New York City NY 10010

ROSEN, WILMA SYLVIA FRIEDMAN (MRS. ROBERT H. ROSEN), psychiatrist; b. Phila.; d. Philip and Minnie (Kaplan) Friedman; B.A., Temple U., 1954; M.D., 1958, postgrad. 1959-62; postgrad. Boston Psychoanalytic Inst., 1966-72; m. Robert H. Rosen, July 14, 1961; children—Allyson, Elizabeth. Intern Albert Einstein Med. Center, Phila., 1958-59; resident Temple U. Med. Center, Phila., 1959-62, psychiat. cons. Student Health Center, instr. psychiatry Med. Sch., 1962-66, VISTA tng. program, 1966; mem. staff Wilmington Child Guidance Center, 1962-64; mem. staff Pa. Inst., 1965-66; practice medicine specializing in psychiatry, Providence, 1966—; supr. psychotherapy R.I. Med. Center, 1968-69; active staff Butler Hosp., Providence, 1968—, sec.-treas. staff assn., 1970-73, v.p., 1973—; clin. asst. prof. div. Med. Sci., Brown U.; cons. student health R.I. Sch. Design. Diplomate Am. Bd. Psychiatry and Neurology. Mem. Am. Psychiat. Assn. (membership com. R.I. br. 1969—, continuing edn. com. 1972). Address: 319 Wayland Av Providence RI 02906

ROSENBAUM, BARBARA MOORE (MRS. CARL ELWOOD ROSENBAUM), lawyer; b. Franklin County, Ky., Dec. 2, 1921; d. Hugh Robert and Nellie McAfee (Richardson) Moore; student Georgetown Coll., 1938-39; J.D., U. Ky., 1943; m. Carl Elwood Rosenbaum, Apr. 15, 1945; children—Robert Leslie, Joseph Larue. Admitted to Ky. bar, 1942; atty. Commonwealth of Ky. Dept. Revenue, 1943-44; adjudication and authorization officer VA, Lexington, 1944-46; asso. Elwood Rosenbaum, Atty., Lexington, 1953-68, Rosenbaum & Smith, Lexington, 1968—. Treas. U. Ky. United Campus Ministry Bd., Inc., 1970—. Mem. Ky., Fayette County bar assns. Club: Altrusa (pres. Lexington 1973-74, dist. sec. 1971-73). Home: 1940 Alexandria Dr Lexington KY 40504 Office: Lexington Bldg Lexington KY 40507

ROSENBAUM, SYLVIA PORTUGAL (MRS. MURRAY ROSENBAUM), poet; b. Bklyn., Aug. 16, 1928; d. Jack and Ida Olga (Kanover) Portugal; student City Coll. N.Y., 1946; m. Murray Rosenbaum, Mar. 19, 1961; 1 son, Robert Jay. Artist Birnbaum & Co., N.Y.C., 1952-58; sec. Consol. Ins. Co., N.Y.C., 1959-61; poetry included in Bitterroot, New Dawn Publs., United Poets, Am. Poet, Am. Voice, Am. Poetry League, Best Poets 20th Century, others, 1968—. Recipient 1st prize Nat. Fedn. State Poetry Socs., Inc., 1973; 2d. Prize Am. Poets Fellowship Soc., 1973. Mem. Internat. Poetry Soc., Pa. Poetry Soc., Inc., Poets Study Club Terre Haute. Address: 10 Heritage Ct Valley Stream NY 11581

ROSENBERG, CATHRINE FRITZI RAWICH (MRS. HOWARD IRVING ROSENBERG), creativity educator; b. Chgo., Nov. 5, 1926; d. Jack David and Edna (Pressman) Rawich; R.N., Mt. Sinai Hosp. Sch. Nursing, Chgo., 1947; B.A., Loretto Heights U., 1972; M.A. in Communication, U. Colo., 1974; m. Howard Irving Rosenberg, Mar. 29, 1953; children—Paul, David, Hyla. Various nursing positions, 1947-69; dir. nurses Children's Asthma Research Inst. Hosp., Denver, 1955-58; actress, improvisational theatre The Works, Denver, 1969-70; facilitator, cons., creativity workshops Evergreen Inst., Gestalt Inst., Neighborhood Youth Corps, also pvt. groups, Denver, 1971-73; facilitator, instr. adventure in arts Roger Williams Coll., Bristol, R.I., 1973. Co-chmn., treas. Values Conf., Denver, 1964. Mem. local county com. Democratic party, 1959-74. Mem. Am.-Psycho-Drama Assn., Actors Equity. Jewish religion. Home: 330 Lafayette St Denver CO 80218

ROSENBERG, FLORENCE PESSAH (MRS. MAURO ROSENBERG), lawyer; b. Bklyn., Jan. 8, 1922; d. Morris N. and Fannie (Cantor) Pessah; LL.B., St. John's U., 1946; student Coll. City N.Y., 1939-41; m. Mauro Rosenberg, Sept. 29, 1946; children—Richard C., Sheryl R., Barry C. Admitted to N.Y. bar, 1946, Cal. bar, 1961; mem. firm Goodman, Hirschberg & King, 1969; atty. Legal Aid, Los Angeles, 1969; pvt. practice law, Encino, Cal., 1970—. Tchr. sex discrimination Mid Valley Coll. Law, 1974. Active San Fernando Valley chpt. Nat. Orgn. for Women. Mem. Am., N.Y., San Fernando, Los Angeles Bar assns., Nat. Council Jewish Women, Orgn. Rehab. and Tng. Mem. Ind. Order Foresters. Home: 16220 Meadow Ridge Rd Encino CA 91316

ROSENBERG, LUCILLE MYRNA (MRS. WILLIAM SAMUEL ROSENBERG), librarian; b. Cleve., Jan. 13, 1912; d. Sol and Helen (Goldsmith) Lieberman; technician certificate U.S. Navy Hosp. Corp. and Lab.; m. William Samuel Rosenberg, May 19, 1946; 1 dau., Susan Esther. Librarian pub. library, Youngstown, O., 1930-43; lab. technician Lincoln, Neb., 1945-63; librarian Lincoln Gen. Hosp. Sch. of Nursing, 1963—. Mem. aux. bd. Lincoln Gen. Hosp. 1961-69, chmn. Pinkie and Candy Striper, 1963-69. Served with WAVES, 1943-45. Mem. Nat., Neb. leagues for nursing, Am. Legion. Jewish religion (mem. Nat. Sisterhood). Home: 2505 Marilynn Av Lincoln NE 68502 Office: 2440 St Mary's Av Lincoln NE 68502

ROSENBERG, MARLENE, labor union adminstr.; b. N.Y.C., Apr. 20, 1946; d. Joseph and Irene (Turkin) Rosenberg; B.A., Bklyn. Coll., 1967; M.L.S., Rutgers U., 1968. Pres., local 1482 Bklyn. Library Guild. Am. Fedn. State, County and Municipal Employees, AFL-CIO, N.Y.C., 1970—; sr. librarian Bklyn. Pub. Library, N.Y.C., 1968—. Democrat. Home: 222 Lenox Rd Brooklyn NY 11226 Office: 140 Park Pl New York City NY 10007

ROSENBERG, SHIRLEY SIROTA (MRS. JEROME DAVID ROSENBERG), editor, writer; b. N.Y.C., June 30, 1925; d. Charles and Donia (Rudoy) Sirota; B.A., Bklyn. Coll., 1946; m. Jerome David Rosenberg, Aug. 24, 1947; children—Hindy, Jonathan. Mag. editor weekly newspapers, Bklyn., Washington, 1946-49, 50-56; free-lance writer articles, books, pubs., reports for nat. mags., newspapers, govt. agys., other, since 1958—; Washington corr. Parents' mag., 1965-70; editor Smithsonian Instn., 1972—. Mem. Soc. Mag. Writers. Author: The First Oil Rush, 1967; How Children Grow, 1972. Editor Alcohol and Health, 1971, Population Dynamics Quar., 1972—. Contbr. numerous articles to newspapers, mags. Home: 6805 Pyle Rd Bethesda MD 20034

ROSENBERGER, ELISABETH PATRICIA MCGEE (MRS. HAROLD MARTIN ROSENBERGER), art center adminstr.; b. Walsenburg, Colo., July 18, 1922; d. Walter E. and Leah Eunice (Allan) McGee; student U. Ida., 1969, Walla Walla Community Coll., 1970, 71; m. Harold Martin Rosenberger, Jan. 1, 1942; 1 son, Garry Allan. Med. sec. Drs. Robert and Charles Foster, Clarkston, Wash., 1942-43; PBX and desk clk. Lewis Clark Hotel, Lewiston, Ida., 1945-46; hostess Los Angeles Welcome Wagon, 1952; interim exec. dir. YWCA, Lewistown, Ida., 1952-53; med. sec. Dr. George Thompson, 1953-57; chmn. bd., vol. exec. dir. Valley Art Center, Inc., Clarkston, Wash., 1968—. Chmn. Am. Cancer Soc. Asotin County, Wash., 1954-56; nat. del. Clarkston Sch. Dist. Adv. Com., 1970-75. Bd. dirs. YWCA, 1952-68, Civic Arts, Inc., Valley Art Center. Mem. Nat. Fedn. Flower and Garden Clubs, Beta Sigma Phi. Republican. Seventh Day Adventist (deaconess 1973-75). Club: Pioneer Garden (Clarkston). Home: 1131 15th St Clarkston WA 99403 Office: 842 6th St Clarkston WA 99403

ROSENBLATT, ALICE A., artist, educator; b. N.Y.C.; B.S., Columbia, 1934, diploma for supr. fine arts, 1934, M.A., 1938; B.S. (S.A.), Pratt Summer Sch., 1924; Grand Central Sch. Art; studied with Arthur Woefle, Henry B. Snell, Eliot O'Hara, George Bridgman, Robert Brackman, Prof. Martin. Tchr. elementary sch. N.Y.; drawing, painting and art history, Jr. High Sch., No. 55; fine arts, sr. high schs. including Monroe, George Washington, Morris and Theodore Roosevelt; methods of teaching fine arts, Fordham U.; classroom methods, F. A. Sacred Heart Convent; chmn. Sch. Art League program of Bronx Group; stage settings, Theodore Roosevelt High Sch.; conducted clubs for gifted children in toycraft, puppetry, cartooning, leather tooling, woodcarving, painting, clay modeling, arts and crafts, posters, executed mural Children at Play, Jr. High Sch., 55; five leather tooled volumes, James Monroe High Sch.; painted in Cuenca, Seville and Granada, Spain; St. Cere, Paris, Carcassone and Concarneau, France; Fez and Algiers, Africa; Cuernavaca, 1930; Taxco and Xachimilco, Mexico, 1935; exhibited at Grand Central Art Gallery, 1930, Barbizon Plaza Gallery, 1930, Pa. Acad., 1936, Ind. Soc. Artists, 1932, pvt. gallery 775 Beck St., 1937-38; pvt. gallery Tybee place, Tuckahoe, N.Y., 1939—. Awarded 1st prize water color Westchester Co. Fair and Flower Show, 1949; prizes from Hudson River Mus., and Women's Clubs. Mem. Yonkers Mount Vernon (bd. dir. 1955-56) art assns., Westchester Arts and Crafts Guild, High Sch. Tchrs. Assn. (sch. del.), Sch. Art League, Am. Fedn. Arts, N.E.A. (invited to preside at Art Section, Conv. 1938), Bronx Boro-Wide Assn. Tchrs., N.Y. Exptl. Soc. Tooled 9 leather covered illuminated testimonials and a scroll of greeting from the schools of U.S. to those of Brazil, June 1944; made initial plan for modern house which is listed in guidebook by Mus. Modern Art; Decorations for Luncheons; Designed contemporary furniture. Exhibited at Hudson Valley Art Assn., 1951-52, Fla. So. Coll., 1952, 1st Int. Exhbn. Address: Tybee Pl Mohegan Heights Yonkers NY 10710

ROSENBLATT, JOAN ELIOT RAUP (MRS. DAVID ROSENBLATT), mathematician; b. N.Y.C., Apr. 15, 1926; d. Robert Bruce and Clara (Eliot) Raup; A.B., Barnard Coll., 1946, postgrad. (Rice fellow), 1946-47; postgrad. (Gen. Edn. Bd. fellow), U. N.C., 1948-50, Ph.D., 1956; m. David Rosenblatt, June 10, 1950. Intern. Nat. Inst. Pub. Affairs, Washington, 1946-47; statis. analyst U.S. Bur. Budget, 1947-48; research asst. U. N.C., 1953-54; mathematician Nat. Bur. Standards, Washington, 1955—, asst. chief statis. engring. lab., 1963-68, chief, 1969—. Chmn. com. on women in sci. Joint Bd. on Sci. Edn., Washington, 1963-64. Recipient Silver medal U.S. Dept. Commerce, 1969; Fed. Woman's award, 1971. Fellow A.A.A.S., Am. Statis. Assn. (program chmn. 1974, chmn. sect. phys. and engring. scis. 1975), Washington Acad. Scis. (award achievement math. 1965), Inst. Math. Statistics (past program sec.); mem. Soc. Indsl. and Applied Math. (asso. editor Jour.), Am. Math. Soc., Royal Statis. Soc. (London), Internat. Assn. Statistics in Phys. Scis., Internat. Assn. Survey Statisticians, Va. Acad. Sci., Philos. Soc. Washington, Am. Assn. U. Women, Phi Beta Kappa, Sigma Xi. Editorial Bd. Communications in Statistics. Home: 2939 Van Ness St NW Washington DC 20008 Office: Nat Bur Standards Washington DC 20234

ROSENBLATT, KATHERINE PHILIPSBORN, educator; b. Chgo., Apr. 26, 1922; d. Herbert F. and Ruth (Cohn) Philipsborn; B.A., Mills Coll., 1944; M.Ed. (State of Fla. fellow), U. Miami, 1968; postgrad. Union Grad. Sch., Yellow Springs, O., 1974; children—Susan Lee, Harold Lee, John Lee, Elizabeth Lee. Case worker Dept. Pub. Welfare, Balt., 1945-46; classroom tchr. Sunlard Tng. Center, Opa Locka, Fla., 1968-69, demonstration tchr. BKR project, 1969-71, coordinator community services BKR project, 1970-73, treas., coordinator community services BKR ednl. projects, Ft. Lauderdale, Fla., 1972—; acting supt. Sunland Center, Miami Fla., 1974—. Cons. on multiply handicapped children/parent relations to state and pvt. agys., 1971—; chmn. Dade County Community Com. on Developmental Handicaps and Retardation, 1973-74; guest lectr., speaker various ednl. instns. and profl. groups. Bd. dirs. Winnetka (Ill.) Pub. Sch. Nursery, 1955-60, pres., 1959-60. Co-grantee Dept. Health, Edn. and Welfare, 1969-73. Mem. Am. Assn. Mental Deficiency, Council for Exceptional Children, Epsilon Tau Lambda, Kappa Delta Pi, Dade County League Women Voters (dir. 1961-62, pres. 1962-64). Home: 4501 Monserrat St Coral Gables FL 33146 Office: 20000 NW 47th Av Opa Locka FL 33054

ROSENBLITH, JUDY FRANCIS (MRS. WALTER A. ROSENBLITH), psychologist, educator; b. Salt Lake City, Mar. 20, 1921; d. John Edward and Mary Louise (Slack) Francis; student Occidental Coll., 1938-40; A.B., U. Cal. at Los Angeles, 1942; M.A., Radcliffe Coll., 1950, Ph.D., 1958; m. Walter A. Rosenblith, Sept. 27, 1941; children—Sandra Yvonne, Ronald Francis. Teaching fellow Harvard, Cambridge, Mass., 1948-50, 53-56, instr., research asst. Grad. Sch. Edn., 1956-57, lectr. 1963-64, asso. in. psychology, Med. Sch., Boston, 1961-64, clin. asso., 1964-67; asst. prof. psychology Simmons Coll., Boston, 1951-52; asst. prof. psychology Brown U., Providence, 1957-61, asst. mem., asso. mem. Inst. of Life Scis., 1963-71, mem., 1971—; asso. prof. psychology Wheaton Coll., Norton, Mass., 1965-68, prof. 1968—, Meneely prof., 1972-74; New Eng. supr. Nat. Opinion Research Center, 1953-57; vis. colleague Dept. of Psychology, U. Hawaii, 1970-71. NIH grantee, 1958-64, 61-70; McDermott Found. grantee, 1970-71; Grant Found. grantee, 1971—. Fellow Am. Psychol. Assn.; mem. Eastern, New Eng., Mass. (dir. 1967-70) psychol. assns., Nat. Council Measurement in Edn., Brookline Mental Health Assn. (dir., profl. adv. bd. 1958-67), Soc. for Research in Child Devel. (sec. 1965-69), Sigma Xi. Sr. editor: The Causes of Behavior, 1962, rev., 1966, 72. Contbr. articles to profl. jours. Home: 164 Mason Terrace Brookline MA 02146 Office: Wheaton College Psychology Dept Norton MA 02766

ROSENBLUM, LOUISE BLACKSTONE, health co. exec.; b. Chgo., Jan. 1, 1925; d. Abraham Jacob and Sonya (Cherches) Blackstone; B.S., U. Ill., 1947; postgrad. U. Cal. at Los Angeles, 1969, U. So. Cal., 1972, Cal. State U. at Northridge, 1973; children—Karen, Lauren (Mrs. Bradley Sievers). Asst. adminstr. Extended Care Facilities, Los Angeles, 1967-68; project coordinator Cal. Med. Centers, Los Angeles, 1968-70; adminstr. Extended Care Facilities, Los Angeles, 1968-72; exec. v.p. Nat. Prepaid Health Plan, Inc., Los Angeles, 1972-74, also dir. Mem. Am. Pub. Health Assn., Am. Coll. Nursing Home Adminstrs., Am. So. Cal. occupational therapy assns., Hadassah (past pres.). Home: 1314 N Fuller St No 105 Los Angeles CA 90046

ROSENBLUM, SADIE SKOLETSKY (MRS. JOSEPH ROSENBLUM), artist; b. Russia, Feb. 12, 1899; d. Aaron and Ida (Sharfman) Skoletsky; came to U.S., 1906, naturalized, 1921; student New Sch. Social Research, N.Y. U., 1920-21; m. Joseph Rosenblum, Sept. 18, 1921; children—Bruce, Arthur, Beatrice (Mrs. Leanord Larsen). One man shows Roko Gallery, N.Y.C., 1960, 65, Mus. Arts, Ft. Lauderdale, Fla., 1962-65, 327 Gallery, Albany, N.Y., 1962, Art Gallery, Ft. Lauderdale, 1963, Joe and Emily Lowe Art Gallery, 1964, Little Gallery, Phila., 1965, Chas. Mann Gallery, 1967, Columbus (Ga.) Mus. Arts and Crafts, 1971, 72; exhibited in group shows Norton Gallery, Palm Beach, Fla., 1950, Corcoran Inst., Washington, 1954, Cleve. Mus. Fine Arts, 1954, Riverside Mus., N.Y.C., 1954, Columbia Mus., S.C., 1954, High Mus., Atlanta, 1954, San Francisco Mus., 1954, Graham Gallery, N.Y.C., 1954, Rudolph Galleries, Woodstock, N.Y., Coral Gables, Fla., 1958—, Four Arts, Palm Beach, 1958, art U.S.A., N.Y.C. 1958, Mus. Modern Art-N.Y.C. Lending Library, 1960, Joe and Emily Lowe Art Gallery, 1967; now with the Gallery, Ft. Lauderdale, Gallery 99, Miami Beach, Fla., London Gallery, Montreal, Que., Can.; represented in permanent collections Phila. Mus., Brandeis U. Mus., Waltham, Mass., Joe and Emily Lowe Art Gallery, Coral Gables, Mus. Arts, Ft. Lauderdale, Peabody Mus., Nashville, Norton Gallery, Palm Beach, Columbus Mus. Leader adult groups Brandeis U., 1963; dir. groups U. Miami, 1964. Tchr. art, art appreciation to underpriviledged children, 1964-66; state chmn. N.Y. Temple Youth, 1941-42; mem. bd. Am. Jewish Com., 1965-67, edn. com., 1967-68; mem. bd. Friends Lowe Gallery U. Miami, 1965—; asso. mem. adv. bd. Peabody Mus., 1962-65. Mem. Woodstock Art Assn., Artists Equity. Address: 5750 Collins Av Miami Beach FL 33140

ROSENFELD, BARBARA RAE, psychiatrist; b. Chgo.; d. Joseph and Anne (Valstein) Rosenfeld; M.D., Woman's Med. Coll., 1965. Social worker Contra Costa (Cal.) County Social Service, 1955-61; intern Beth Israel Hosp., N.Y.C., 1965-66; resident in psychiatry N.Y. State Psychiat. Inst., N.Y.C., 1966-69, sr. research psychiatrist, 1969-72, supr. group therapy, 1972—; dir. group and family therapy Mt. Sinai Hosp. Service, Elmhurst, N.Y., 1970—; asst. attending psychiatrist Columbia Presbyn. Hosp., N.Y.C., 1969—; instr. Columbia, 1970—. Diplomate Am. Bd. Psychiatry and Neurology. Mem. Am. Psychiat. Assn. (Councilor N.Y. County dist. br.), Assn. for Social Psychiatry. Office: 200 East End Av New York City NY 10028

ROSENFELD, REBA, educator; b. Balt.; d. Max and R. Clara (Shorr) Rosenfeld; student Goucher Coll., Johns Hopkins, 1954-56, 61; B.F.A., Md. Inst. Coll. Art, 1956; M.Ed. in Guidance and Personnel, U. Md., 1962; postgrad. Johns Hopkins, summer 1965,

66-67. Social worker Dept. Pub. Welfare, Balt., 1944-45, A.R.C., 1945-46; tchr. pub. schs., Balt., 1946-54, 56-59, counselor, 1959—. Former med. field agt. SSS. Mem. Am., Md. personnel and guidance assns., Am. Sch. Counselors Assn., Nat. Vocational Guidance Assn., Md. Tchrs. Assn., Pub. Sch. Tchrs. Assn. Home: 3422 Barry Paul Rd Randallstown MD 21133

ROSENFIELD, LEONORA COHEN (MRS. HARRY N. ROSENFIELD), educator, author; b. N.Y.C., Feb. 14, 1909; d. Morris R. and Mary (Ryshpan) Cohen; Diplome superieur d'etudes de civilisation francaise, Sorbonne, Paris, France, 1929; B.A. cum laude, Smith Coll., 1930; M.A., Columbia, 1931, Ph.D., 1940; m. Harry N. Rosenfield, June 25, 1936; 1 dau., Marianne J. (Mrs. David J. Smigelskis). Instr., Smith Coll., Northampton, Mass., 1934-35, Bklyn. Coll., 1936-46; asst. prof. U. Md., College Park, 1947-59, asso. prof., 1959-66, prof., 1966—; asst. prof. Grad. Sch., U.S. Dept. Agr., Washington, 1948-49. Research investigator U.S. Senate War Investigating Com., 1945-46; reader Bollingen Series, N.Y.C., 1946-47. Faculty Study fellow Am. Council Learned Socs., 1951-52. Mem. Am. Assn. Tchrs. French, Modern Lang. Assn., Am. Philos. Assn., History Sci. Soc., Am. Assn. U. Profs., Am. Soc. 18th Century Studies, Soc. francaise des Etudes du 18e Siecle, Phi Beta Kappa (treas. Md. chpt. 1964-66), Sigma Delta Tau (hon.). Author: From Beast-Machine to Man-Machine, Animal Soul in French Letters, From Descartes to La Mettrie, 1941, rev. edit., 1968; Portrait of a Philosopher, Morris R. Cohen in Life and Letters, 1962; also chpts. in books. Editor: Pardies, Discours de la Connoissance des Bestes, 1972. Translator: Discovering Plato (Alexandre Koyre) 1945. Contbr. to Internat. Ency. Social Scis., 1968, Critical Bibliography French Lit., vol. 3, 1961; also articles to profl. jours. Home: 3749 Chesapeake St NW Washington DC 20016 Office: Dept French and Italian U Md College Park MD 20740

ROSENFIELD, PATRICIA BYRNE, educator; b. Boston, June 6, 1925; d. Charles Edward and Patricia Magdalene (McDermott) Byrne; A.S. with distinction, Newton Jr. Coll., 1967; B.S. in English Edn., Boston U. Sch. Edn., 1972; children—Peter, Robert. Dir. Learning Lab., Newton (Mass.) Jr. Coll., 1967-69; adminstrv. asst. Harvard Grad. Sch. Edn., 1970, asst. to dir. Harvard-Newton summer program, 1971-72; tchr. English Wellesley (Mass.) Sr. High Sch., 1972—. Recipient Mary F. Lindsley award N.Y. Poetry Forum, 1968. Mem. Nat. Council Tchrs. English, Mass. Council Tchrs. English, N.E.A., N.Y. Poetry Forum. Club: New England Poetry (Boston). Author: Cat in the Mirror, 1970. Home: 42 Wessex Rd Newton Centre MA 02159 Office: 50 Rice St Wellesley MA 02181

ROSENFIELD, ROSLYNE EISENBERG, lawyer; b. Bklyn., Feb. 15, 1926; d. Samuel and Minnie (Barkin) Eisenberg; B.S. magna cum laude, U. Conn., 1946, J.D., 1971; m. Robert Rosenfield, June 22, 1947 (dec. 1970); children—Stephen, Samuel, Matthew, David. Admitted to Conn. bar, since practiced in Hartford; atty. Phoenix Mut. Life Ins. Co., Hartford, 1971—, asst. counsel, 1973—. Mem. Am., Conn., Hartford bar assns., Greater Hartford C. of C., Am. Jewish Congress. Home: 50 Lincoln Av West Hartford CT 06117 Office: 1 American Row Hartford CT 06115

ROSENGREN, CAMILLE DUANE (MRS. FRANK DUANE ROSENGREN), research cons.; b. San Antonio, Sept. 26, 1926; d. Emmett Thomas and Camille Georgette (Lodovic) Sweeney; B.A., Incarnate Word Coll., 1948; M.S., Our Lady of the Lake Coll., 1951; m. Frank Duane Rosengren, Jan. 13, 1951; 1 dau., Emily (Mrs. Stephen Ferry). Script reader for various N.Y. prodn. firms, 1954-58; reference librarian, cataloger Met. Mus. of Art, N.Y.C., 1959-61; circulation and reference librarian San Antonio Coll., 1964-67; registrar, librarian Inst. of Texan Cultures, San Antonio, 1967-70; freelance research cons. on history and fine arts, San Antonio, 1970—; sec., treas. Rosengren's Bookshop, Inc., San Antonio, 1970—. Mem. Citizens for a Better Environment, San Antonio, 1971-74; mem. San Antonio Symphony Soc., 1964-72. Mem. women's com. Bexar County Dem. Women, 1963-74; del. Bexar County Dem. Conv., 1964-65. Bd. dir. San Antonio Conservation Soc., 1964-68, v.p. pub. relations 1966-68. Mem. A.L.A., Am. Assn. U. Profs., Am. Civil Liberties Union. Home and office: 801 Garraty Rd San Antonio TX 78209

ROSENHEIM, MARGARET KEENEY (MRS. EDWARD W. ROSENHEIM, JR.), lawyer, educator; b. Grand Rapids, Mich., Sept. 5, 1926; d. Morton and Nancy (Billings) Keeney; student Wellesley Coll., 1943-45; J.D., U. Chgo., 1949; m. Edward W. Rosenheim, Jr., June 20, 1947; children—Daniel, James, Andrew. Admitted to Ill. bar, 1949; mem. faculty U. Chgo. Sch. Social Service Adminstrn., 1950—, asso. prof., 1961-66, prof., 1966—; vis. prof. Law Sch., U. Wash., 1965. Acad. visitor London Sch. Econs., 1973. Cons. Pres.'s Commn. Law Enforcement and Adminstrn. Justice, 1966, Nat. Adv. Commn. Criminal Justice Standards and Goals. Ford Found. fellow, 1967-68. Mem. Am., Chgo. bar assns. Editor, contbr. to Justice for the Child, 1962. Contbr. articles and book revs. to profl. publs. Address: 5805 Dorchester Av Chicago IL 60637

ROSENKRANTZ, GAYLE NIN (MRS. DAVID E. ROSENKRANTZ), lawyer; b. Bogota, Colombia, July 24, 1932; d. Thorvald Joaquin and Teresa de Jesus (Castillo) Nin; student Stanford, 1949-52; B.S., U. San Francisco, 1960, J.D., 1964; m. David E. Rosenkrantz, Oct. 5, 1951; children—Bruce, Lisa, Karen, Eric, Valerie. Admitted to Cal. bar, 1965; clk. Cal. Ct. Appeal, San Francisco, 1964-65; with Bacigalupi, Elkus, Salinger & Rosenberg, San Francisco, 1965-73; mem. firm Matzger, Melnick, & Rosenkrantz, San Francisco, 1973—. Mem. San Francisco Lawyers Com. for Urban Affairs, 1972-73. Bd. dirs. Stepping Stone. Mem. Bar Assn. San Francisco (dir.), Barristers Club San Francisco (sec. 1967-68). Home: 990 Randolph St San Francisco CA 94132 Office: 300 Montgomery St San Francisco CA 94104

ROSENQUEST, BARBARA UNGERLEIDER (MRS. DONALD ROSENQUEST), bus. exec.; b. Phila., June 20, 1927; d. Harry Eduarde and Marian (Rice) U.; B.A., Smith Coll., 1949; postgrad. Columbia, U., 1951, U. Cal. at Los Angeles, 1967—; m. Donald Rosenquest, Apr. 19, 1952; children—Nils Christopher, Elin Jordis. Asso. producer DuMont TV, N.Y.C., 1950-52; dir. TV-motion picture dept. Mary Webb Davis, Inc., Los Angeles, 1955-57; v.p. Robert S. Howell Assos., Los Angeles, 1962; commentator, fashion dir. Kay Windsor, Inc., Los Angeles, 1957—; asso. merchandising editor Harper's Bazaar, Los Angeles, 1962—; exec. v.p. The FMH Co., Studio City, Cal., 1966-72, pres., 1972—; costume designer, 1969—. Cons. fashion coordination, pub. relations, 1966—; lectr. U. Cal. at Los Angeles. Exec. bd. Assn. Retail Mgmt. Information Systems. Mem. Assistance League So. Cal., 1953—. Mem. Am. Women in Radio-TV, Los Angeles C. of C. (dir.), Fashion Group, Smith Coll. Alumnae Assn., Smith Coll. Club So. Cal. (past pres.). Republican. Address: 3525 Berry Dr Studio City CA 91604

ROSENSTEIN, GERTRUDE L., television exec.; b. N.Y.C.; d. Harry and Bertha (Zins) Rosenstein; A.B., Barnard Coll. Exec. asst. to George Balanchine and Lincoln Kirstein, N.Y.C. Ballet, N.Y.C., 1950-52; coordinator Drama Workshop Project, Barnard Coll., N.Y.C., 1953; asso. dir. NBC, N.Y.C., 1954-64; asso. dir. NBC-TV Opera Theatre, 1954-57, prodns. include: Amahl and The Night Visitors, The Magic Flute; dir. (1st woman dir. on NBC staff) NBC, N.Y.C., 1964-65; ind. TV dir., 1965—. Prodn. asso. Am. Shakespeare Festival, Stratford, Conn., 1957; prodn. asso. with Gian Carlo Menotti, Festival of Two Worlds, Spoleto, Italy, 1964. Organized (with Francis T.P. Plimpton) Deferred Giving Program, Barnard Coll., 1969—. Bd. dirs. Asso. Alumnae Barnard Coll., 1967-70. Mem. Dirs. Guild Am. (Eastern regional bd. 1965), Nat. Acad. TV Arts and Scis. Club: Cosmopolitan (N.Y.C.). Home: 14 Sutton Pl S New York City NY 10022

ROSENTHAL, BEATRICE HOLT (MRS. JOSEPH S. ROSENTHAL), mem. Dem. Nat. Com.; b. Bklyn., June 7, 1900; d. Hamilton and Alexina (Smith) Holt; student Columbia Tchrs. Coll., 1917-18; m. Joseph H. Chadbourne (div. 1948); children—William Holt, Joseph H., Grace (Mrs. Johnson); m. 2d, Joseph S. Rosenthal, 1950. Past pres. Democratic Federated Clubs Conn.; chmn. Dem. party Waterford; mem. Dem. Nat. Adv. Com. in Polit. Orgn., 20th Senatorial Dist. Dem. Central Com.; mem. Dem. Nat. Com. for Conn., 1958—, also mem. exec. bd.; chmn. women's activities Chester Bowles for Congress campaign, 1958; del. Dem. Nat. Conv., 1960, 68, mem. nat. credentials and site coms., 1968; mem. Conn. Revision Party Rules Commn.; mem. Dem. Town Com., Waterford. Mem. Conn. Commn. Tourism and Conservation, Conn. Personnel Appeals Bd., Conn. Hist. Commn. Trustee, sec. Mystic Oral Sch. for Deaf; trustee Lesley Coll., Eugene O'Neil Theater Performing Arts, Roseland Park, Waterford Pub. Library, Hearing and Speech New London County; pres. aux. bd. Norwich State Hosp.; corporator Lawrence Meml. Hosp.; chmn. bd. Goodspeed Opera House; exec. bd. Humane Soc. U.S. Named woman of year Niantic (Conn.) News, 1960; recipient award Nat. Sclerosis Soc. Mem. Antiquarian and Landmarks Soc. Conn. (state pres. 1965—), Fedn. Dem. Women, Colonial Dames. Home: Jordan Village Waterford CT 06385

ROSENTHAL, DOROTHY W., corporate exec.; d. Samuel Lewis and Mollie (Friedman) Weiner; B.S., U. Pitts., 1942; m. Bernard Raphael Rosenthal, Sept. 26, 1943 (dec. Feb. 1955); children—Marc Stephen, Helen (Mrs. Robert Tonetti). Classification analyst def. transp. Office Emergency MGT, Washington, 1942-43; recruiting rep. U.S. Civil Service Commn., Pitts., 1943-44; with Airway Industries, Inc., West Pittsburg, Pa., 1955—, personnel dir., 1957-64, asst. treas., 1960-69, v.p. personnel and corporate relations, 1964—, corp. sec., 1970—, dir., 1958—. Pres. New Castle (Pa.) council P.T.A., 1956-57; mem. Lawrence County Com. for Employment of Handicapped, 1957-70; founding mem., officer Lawrence County Mental Health Assn. Mem. sch. bd., New Castle, 1960-65. Bd. dirs. New Castle Area Schs., 1960-65, United Fund Lawrence County, 1968-72. Mem. Nat. Council Jewish Women (life mem., local pres. 1951-55), Pa. Congress Parents and Tchrs. (hon. life), League Women Voters. Jewish religion (bd. dirs. temple). Office: Airway Industries Inc West Pittsburg PA 16160

ROSENTHAL, ELAINE POSNER (MRS. ROBERT J. ROSENTHAL), librarian; b. Troy, N.Y., Apr. 2, 1921; d. Samuel and Dorothy (Weinstein) Posner; A.B., George Washington U., 1960; M.S. in L.S., Cath. U. Am., 1962; m. Robert J. Rosenthal, Feb. 8, 1943. Asst. chief reference services U.S. Dept. Interior Library, Washington, 1962-65, chief reference services, 1965-68, chief Information Services, 1968-73; librarian Nat. Ret. Tchrs. Assn. and Am. Assn. Ret. Persons, Washington, 1973—. Docent Nat. Gallery Art, Washington, 1959-61. Trustee George Washington U. Friends of Library; mem. library bd. Martin Luther King Pub. Library, Washington. Mem. D.C. Library Assn. (chmn. nominating com. 1967-68), Spl. Libraries Assn. (chpt. v.p. 1967-68, mem. nat. membership com.), Cath. U. Am. Sch. Library Sci. Alumni (sec. 1964—), Phi Beta Kappa, Beta Phi Mu (chpt. chmn. nominating com. 1967-68, chpt. pres. 1970-71). Home: 4000 Massachusetts Av NW Washington DC 20016 Office: 1909 K St NW Washington DC 20006

ROSENTHAL, GLORIA MARIE (MRS. ALFRED MAX ROSENTHAL), artist; b. Bklyn., May 24, 1928; d. Herbert E. and Palomel (Savarese) Dreifus; student U. Cin., 1951; m. Alfred Max Rosenthal, Dec. 3, 1950; children—Diane (Mrs. Jeffrey Whatley), Jayne, Alice. Exhibited in one woman show at Saratoga Performing Art Center, 1970; exhibited in numerous group shows throughout U.S.; represented in permanent collections at Sperry Gyroscope Co., Bankers Trust Co.; owner, operator, v.p. Rocky Neck Art Colony, Gloucester, Mass. Vice pres. Syosset Players, 1960, pres., 1961. Recipient awards Garvies Point Mus., 1967, Bklyn. Mus., 1969-71, Hecksher Mus., 1969, Washington Sq. Art Exhibit, 1969-71, Nat. Assn. Women Artists, 1971, Audubon Artists, Nat. Acad., 1970, Silver medal Am. Vets. Soc., 1972. Mem. Nat. Assn. Women Artists. Home: 43 Miller Blvd Syosset NY 11791 Office: 77 Rocky Neck Av East Gloucester MA 01930

ROSENTHAL, JANE, editor, writer; b. Kansas City, Mo.; d. William Alfred and Mabelle (Waggoner) Rosenthal; certificate in fine arts and art history Kansas City (Mo.) Art Inst., 1938. Instr., docent jr. edn. dept. W.R. Nelson Gallery Art, Kansas City, Mo., 1938-46, asst. Friends of Art, 1946-49, exec. sec., coordinator membership activities, lectr., 1949-68; mng. editor Bon Voyage mag., Kansas City, 1968-73; travel editor Bon Appetit mag., 1974—. Samuel H. Kress Found. Travel grantee, 1967. Mem. Soc. Am. Travel Writers. Episcopalian. Home: 5623 Suwanee Rd Shawnee-Mission KS 66205 Office: 4700 Belleview St Kansas City MO 64112

ROSENTHAL, JOYCE ELAINE, lawyer; b. Detroit, Mar. 30, 1944; d. Marvin James and Madolyn (Lefkovits) Rosenthal; B.A., U. Mich., 1965; J.D., Wayne State U., 1969. Research law clk. Greyhound Food Mgmt., Inc., Detroit, summers 1968-69, corporate atty., 1974—; admitted to Mich. bar, 1969; staff atty. Kelly Services, Inc., Southfield, Mich., 1969-74. Campaign mgr. County Commr. candidate, 1972; vice chmn. Troy Republican Womens Club, 1972-73; precinct del., 1972—; mem. exec. bd. Oakland County Young Republicans, 1973; treas. Mich. Fedn. Young Reps., 1973; treas. state legislator campaign, 1974; mem. Oakland County Rep. Com., 1973. Recipient Am. Jurisprudence award for labor law, 1969, Sales award Jr. Achievement, Curved bar Girl Scouts Am. Mem. Am., Mich., Detroit bar assns., U. Mich. Alumni Assn., Law Study Soc., Phi Alpha Delta. Home: 2329 Golfview Dr Troy MI 48084 Office: 2301 W Lafayette Blvd Detroit MI 48216

ROSENTHAL, LENORE, librarian; b. Bklyn., Aug. 21, 1924; d. Abraham and Rebecca (Sheier) Doniger; B.A., Bklyn. Coll., 1963; M.L.S., Pratt Inst., 1966; m. Edward Rosenthal, Aug. 12, 1943; children—Ruth Mullen, Michael, Beth. Trainee Bklyn. Pub. Library, 1963-66, librarian, 1966-67, sr. librarian, 1967-72, supervising librarian, 1972—; active Creative Dramatics Workshops for Children, 1973—. Del. for Bklyn. Library Guild AFL-CIO, local 1482, exec. bd., 1973-74. Mem. Bklyn. Library Council (corr. sec. 1968, rec. sec. 1969-72, 1st v.p. 1972, rec. sec. 1973), Phi Beta Kappa, Alpha Sigma Lambda, Beta Phi Mu. Home: 2023 E 18th St Brooklyn NY 11229 Office: Grand Army Plaza Brooklyn NY 11238

ROSENTHAL, SANDRA BRENER (MRS. STANFORD HAYEM ROSENTHAL), educator; b. New Orleans, Sept. 27, 1936; d. Sol and Rose (Feldman) Brener; B.A., Newcomb Coll., 1964; M.A. (Woodrow Wilson fellow 1964-65), Tulane U., 1965, Ph.D. (Woodrow Wilson dissertation fellow 1966-67), 1967; m. Stanford Hayem Rosenthal, Nov. 20, 1954; children—Stephen Rene, Leslie. Asst. prof. philosophy Dominican Coll., New Orleans, 1967-69; asso. prof. philosophy Loyola U., New Orleans, 1969-73, prof., 1973—. Summer research grantee, 1970. Mem. Am. Assn. U. Women, Am. Assn. U. Profs., Am. Philos. Soc., So. Soc. Philosophy and Psychology, Southwestern Philos. Soc., Phi Beta Kappa. Jewish religion. Contbr. to profl. jours. Home: 5817 Chestnut St New Orleans LA 70115

ROSENTHAL, SYLVIA WEISMAN (MRS. JOSEPH ROSENTHAL), civic leader; b. Gulfport, Miss.; d. Joseph and Elisa (Berliner) Weisman; grad. Murphy High Sch., Mobile, Ala., 1927; student Telegraph Sch., Rome, Ga., 1929; m. Joseph Rosenthal, June 29, 1936 (dec. Nov. 1966); children—Alice (Mrs. Malcolm Brachman), Michael Jay, Judith Susan (Mrs. Steven Winter). Tchr. pub. relations; also conv. sec., mgr. brs. Western Union at Mobile, Miami Beach, Fla., Coral Gables, Fla., Washington, 1929-36; chief communications dept. U.S. Resettlement Div., Washington, 1935-36; v.p. Ellenville Lumber Co. (N.Y.), 1962-68; tchr. beaded flowers S.S. Rotterdam and S.S. Statendam, 1970—; asso. Asta Travel Sch., 1970, Saltaire Travel Agy., 1970—. Vice pres. So. Young Judea, 1934; conv. chmn. Jamaica (L.I., N.Y.) A.R.C., 1947; v.p. fund raising Kew Gardens (N.Y.) Hadassah, 1954-56; chmn. women's div. Queens (N.Y.) Fedn. Jewish Philanthropies, 1966-68, chmn. bd., 1969-70; chmn. advance gifts Hillcrest (N.Y.) United Jewish Appeal, 1968; vol. tchr. crafts local charities; sponsor Internat. Synagogue, 1968, also past chmn. Lincoln Center (N.Y.C.); active Garment Center Congregation and Sisterhood, elected brother congregation, 1937, trustee, 1968—, pres. sisterhood, 1942-46, hon. pres., 1946—, benefit theatre party chmn., 1950-70; past mem. bd. Jamaica Jewish Center, past pres. Sisterhood, founder vol. catering dept.; past mem. bd. Fedn. Jewish Women's Orgns.; former mem. youth activities bd. Hillcrest Jewish Center and Sisterhood; mem. Forest Hills Council Jewish Women, Hias, Brandeis, Hillcrest Hadassahs; founding pres. Henley Sch. Parents Assn.; founder (with others) chair Hebrew culture N.Y.U. Pres. Myer and Joseph Rosenthal Meml. Found; mem. women's bd. Queens Coll. Speech and Hearing Center; mem. Found. for Ileitus and Colitis; mem. bd. Greater Flushing YM-YWHA, chmn. swimming pool devel. com., 1969-73. Recipient Citizen of Week award, Mobile, 1934, This is Your Life Award Garment Center Congregation and Sisterhood, 1958, Woman of Year award Fedn. Jewish Women's Orgns., 1961. Mem. Women's Cross County Golf Assn., Women's Met. Golf Assn., Technion (Haifa, Israel), Internat. Platform Assn. Democrat. Mem. B'nai B'rith. Clubs: N.Y. University, Fresh Meadow Country (former chmn. youth activities, ladies' tournament; La Costa Country. Address: 70-20 108th St Forest Hills NY 11375 also Rancho La Costa CA 92008

ROSHONG, DEE ANN DANIELS, educator; b. Kansas City, Mo., Nov. 22, 1936; d. Vernon Edmund and Doradell (Kellogg) Daniels; B.Mus.Ed., U. Kan., 1958; M.A. in counseling and guidance, Stanford U., 1960; postgrad. Fresno State U., U. Cal.; m. Richard Lee Roshong, Aug. 27, 1960 (div.). Counselor, psychometrist Fresno City Coll., 1961-65; counselor, instr. psychology Chabot Coll., Hayward, Cal., 1965—; writer, coordinator I, a Woman symposium, 1974; writer, coordinator Feeling Free to be You and Me symposium, 1975; mem. cast Eve and Co. TV prodn. Mem. Assn. Humanistic Psychologists, Western Psychol. Assn., Nat. Assn. Women Deans and Counselors, Alpha Phi. Home: 808 Cornet Dr Foster City CA 94404 Office: 25555 Hesperian Blvd Hayward CA 94545

ROSMAN, BERNICE L., psychologist, health service adminstr.; b. N.Y.C., Aug. 14, 1932; d. Jack and Mary (Croll) Lieberman; B.A., Hunter Coll., 1953; M.S., Yale, 1958, Ph.D., 1962; m. Abraham Rosman, 1951 (div. 1970); children—Daniel, Lewis. Psychologist Hudson River State Hosp., Poughkeepsie, N.Y., 1959-60; research psychologist Fels Research Inst., Yellow Springs, O., 1960-61; research asso. Yale Med. Sch., 1961-63; research psychologist Wiltwyck Sch., N.Y.C., 1962-65; research psychologist William Alanson White Inst., N.Y.C., 1967-72; dir. research Phila. Child Guidance Clinic, Phila., 1972—. Mem. Am., Eastern psychol. assns., Am. Orthopsychiat. Assn., Phi Beta Kappa. Author: (with others) Families of the Slums, 1967. Office: #2 Children's Center 34th St and Civic Center Blvd Philadelphia PA 19104

ROSMOND, BABETTE (MRS. HENRY STONE), author, mag. editor; b. N.Y.C., Nov. 4; m. Henry Stone, Apr. 2, 1944; children—James Martin, Eugene Robert. Editor, 2 Street & Smith Mags., N.Y.C., 1941-48, Today's Family, N.Y.C., 1952-54; fiction editor Better Living, N.Y.C., 1953-55, Seventeen mag., N.Y.C., 1957—. Cons. editor for various publs., 1948-52; numerous appearances various TV programs, 1973—. Lit. adviser Iona Coll. Writers Ann. Conf. Author: The Dewy, Dewy Eyes, 1946; A Party for Grown-Ups, 1948; Lucy, or, The Delaware Dialogues, 1952; The Children, 1956; The Lawyers, 1962; (with Henry Morgan) Shut Up, He Explained (Ring Lardner Selection), 1962; Robert Benchley: His Life and Good Times, 1970; The Invisible Worm, 1972. Editor: Seventeen Book of Short Stories, 1958; Seventeen from Seventeen, 1967; Today's Stories from 17, 1971. Contbr. short stories and articles to New Yorker, Vogue, McCalls, Punch, Ladies Home Jour., Mademoiselle, Ellery Queen, Good Food and others. Home: 22 E 36th St New York City NY 10016 Office: 320 Park Av New York City NY 10022

ROSS, BARBARA JUNE, journalist, editor; b. Cloquet, Minn., June 27, 1947; d. Howard Eugene and Irene Elna (Granvick) Ross; B.A., U. Minn., 1969. Reporter, feature writer Owatonna (Minn.) People's Press, 1969-70, news editor, 1970—. Adviser Marian High Sch. newspaper and yearbook, 1970—. Mem. Owatonna Am. Field Service Com., 1973—; publicity chmn. Owatonna and Marian High Schs., 1973—. Steele County Republican precinct chairwoman, 1970-72; mem. Steele County Dem. Farmer Labor exec. com., 1972—. Recipient State First Place award Minn. Newspaper Assn., 1973, State 2d Place photo award Minn. Asso. Press, 1973. Mem. Women in Communications, Minn. Press Women. Lutheran. Club: Little Theatre of Owatonna. Home: 419 20th St Cloquet MN 55720

ROSS, BEATRICE BROOK (MRS. ALEXANDER ROSS), artist; b. N.Y.C.; d. Alexander and Ray (Tennenbaum) Brook; student Hunter Coll., 1941-42, Coll. City N.Y., 1943-44, Bklyn. Mus. Art Sch., 1960-61, 64-65; m. Alexander Ross, Dec. 23, 1945; children—Robert Alan, Kenneth Jay, Sefani Lynn. Operator, Bea Ross-Jean Rosenthal Gallery, Jericho, N.Y., 1962-64; exhibited one-man shows R.A.A. Gallery, N.Y.C., Gillary Gallery, Jericho, 1971-72, 73-74; exhibited in group shows Gallery Dix, Gillery Gallery, Nat. Acad. Galleries, Hecksher Mus., Hofstra U., Audubon Artists, Suffolk Mus., Fordham U., Bklyn. Coll., Silvermine Guild, 1969, 71, Lever House, N.Y.C., 1970, UN Plaza, 1970, Park Av. Synagogue, N.Y.C., 1970, Nat. Arts Club, 1971, Suffolk Mus., 1971, C.W. Post Coll., 1972, Bryant Library, 1973; represented in permanent collections and many pvt. colls.; founder Jericho and Mid Island Art League and Sch., 1957-63; guest artist Etobecoke (Ont., Can.) Bd. Edn., 1971-72. Recipient 1st prize Jericho Art League, 1958-61; Locust Valley Ann. award, 1967, 1st prize, 70; Benjamin Altman award N.A.D., 1968; 2d prize Hecksher Mus., 1970. Mem.

Profl. Artists Guild (v.p. admissions). Home: 19 Briar Lane Jericho NY 11753 Studio: 807 Middleneck Rd Great Neck NY

ROSS, CAROL JOY, writer; b. Chestnut Hill, Mass., Feb. 15, 1936; d. H. John and Kathryn Harrel (Perkins) Ross; B.A., U. Miami, 1957. Writer, Miami News, Miami, Fla., 1955-57, News Bur. Bahamas Devel. Bd., Nassau, 1957-59; dir., mgr. Office Research Inst., Miami, 1959-71; free-lance writer, photographer, Miami, 1969—. Mem. Women in Communications, Audubon Soc. Christian Scientist. Contbr. articles to newspapers, mags. Home and office: 408 Valencia Apt 4 Coral Gables FL 33134

ROSS, CHARLOTTE PACK, suicidologist; b. Oklahoma City, Oct. 21, 1932; d. Joseph and Rose Pearl (Traibich) Pack; student U. Okla., 1949-52; m. Roland S. Ross, May 6, 1951 (div. July 1964); children—Beverly Jo, Sandra Gail. Exec. dir. Suicide Prevention Center of San Mateo County, San Mateo, Cal., 1966—. Chmn. spl. programs in suicide prevention U. Cal. Sch. of Medicine, San Francisco, 1970—. Dir. spl. edn. demonstration programs, 1962-63; mem. youth task force Comprehensive Health Planning Council, 1968-69; pres. Mental Health Aux. of San Mateo County, 1964-65. Bd. dirs., v.p. Belmont Hills Neuropsychiat. Hosp. Adolescent Found., 1965-66. Nat. Inst. Mental Health grantee, 1969-70. Mem. Am. Assn. Suicidology (sec. 1972-74), Internat., Bay Area (founder, 1st. chmn. 1967-69) assns. for suicide prevention. Author: Standards for Suicide Prevention and Crisis Intervention Centers, 1974. Home: 1254 Edinburgh St San Mateo CA 94402 Office: 220 W 20th Av San Mateo CA 94403

ROSS, DIANA, singer, entertainer; b. Detroit; d. Fred Earl and Ernestine Ross; grad. high sch. Lead singer Diana Ross and the Supremes; now soloist; star motion picture Lady Sings the Blues, 1972. Recipient citation Vice Pres. Humphrey for efforts on behalf Pres. Johnson's Youth Opportunity Program; citation Mrs. Martin Luther King and Rev. Abernathy for contbn. to So. Christian Leadership Conf. cause; awards Billboard, Cash Box and Record World as worlds outstanding signer; named Female Entertainer Yr., N.A.A.C.P., 1970; Grammy award as Top Female Singer Yr.; London Musical Express Poll winner as Top Female Singer in World; nominee Acad. award for best actress, 1972. Office: 6464 Sunset Blvd Los Angeles CA 90028

ROSS, DORIS G., civic worker; b. Thompsonville, Conn., Mar. 15, 1919; d. Philip A. and Eva (Saffir) Sisitzky; student Barnard Coll., Max Reinhardt Drama Workshop, N.Y. U. Radio Workshop; m. Lewis H. Ross, Jan. 4, 1942; children—Phyllis, Allyne. Dir. New Eng. Zionist Youth Com., 1943-45; dir. theatre arts Manchester Inst. Arts and Scis., 1947-48; pres. Manchester Girls Club, 1950-51, dir. 1949-53, 54-58, 59-69; bd. dirs. Girls Clubs Am., 1954—, mem. exec. com., 1955—, chmn. nat. adv. bd., 1955-57, v.p., 1956-57, pres., 1957-59, first acting chmn. past pres. com., 1974, chmn. silver jubilee com., 1969-70, mem. devel. com., 1969—; mem. exec. com. Girls Clubs N.Y., 1970-73, bd. dirs., 1970—, co-chmn. long-range planning com., 1970-71; 1st pres. Theatre Art Players, Temple Emanuel, N.Y.C., 1970-71; chmn. 15th ann. conf. Girls Clubs Am., 1960; dir. Manchester Settlement Assn., 1951-54, Manchester Vis. Nurses Assn., 1955-61; del. Nat. Soc. Welfare Assembly, 1957-59, White House Conf. on Children and Youth, 1960, voting del. nat. council state coms., 1960, mem. N.H. state exec. com., 1960, N.H. state sub-com. on Leisure Time Activites chmn., 1960. mem. Pres.'s Citizens Adv. Com. on Fitness of Am. Youth, 1958-60; mem. exec. com. Gov.'s Com. on Children and Youth, 1961-63; gov.'s rep. to Pres.'s Conf. on Youth Fitness, 1962; pres. Manchester Garden Club, 1963-64; dir. Opera League New Hampshire, Inc., 1964-69. Mem. League of Women Voters. Hadassah (pres. Manchester chpt. 1943-44, dir. Manchester chpt. 1942-49, New Eng. regional v.p. 1944-46). Address: 985 Fifth Av New York City NY 10021

ROSS, DOROTHY ROBINSON (MRS. F. WARD ROSS), educator; b. Ludington, Mich., Jan. 31, 1908; d. George Cooper and Winifred (Walker) Robinson; B.S., Mich. State U., 1928, M.A., 1950; m. F. Ward Ross, Sept. 27, 1930 (dec. Sept. 1948). Chemist, Ruggles & Rademaker Salt Co., Manistee, Mich., 1928-30; counselor, asso. prof. counseling Mich. State U. Counseling Center, East Lansing, 1949-70, prof., 1971—. Mem. Am., Mich. personnel and guidance assns., Am., Mich. coll. personnel assns., Nat. Vocational Guidance Assn., Lansing Area Personnel and Guidance Assn., Mortar Bd., Alpha Phi, Kappa Delta Pi, Tau Sigma, Pi Kappa Delta. Contbr. articles to profl. jours. Home: 230 Ridge Rd East Lansing MI 48823

ROSS, EDITH WILFSON (MRS. NATHANIEL ROSS), psychologist; b. N.Y.C., Feb. 24, 1913; d. Joseph and Ruth (Levy) Friedmann; B.A. magna cum laude, Columbia, 1954; Ph.D., Tchrs. Coll., Columbia, 1967; grad. Washington Sq. Inst. Mental Health, 1967; m. Maurice L. Handler, Aug. 14, 1932 (div.); children—Greta (Mrs. Allen Newman), Louise (Mrs. Bruce Cody); m. 2d, Nathaniel Ross, Sept. 7, 1963. Intern, Inst. Rehab., N.Y.C., 1958-59, Dept. Phys. Medicine and Rehab., Goldwater Meml. Hosp., N.Y.C., 1961-62; psychologist Asso. Therapists, White Plains, N.Y., part time 1961-62; staff psychologist to sr. psychologist N.Y. U. Med. Center, N.Y.C., 1962-67; individual practice clin. psychology, 1961—. Mem. Am. Psychol. Assn., Phi Beta Kappa. Home: 830 Park Av New York City NY 10021 Office: 123 E 7th St New York City NY 10021

ROSS, EDNA GENEVIEVE REED (MRS. ANDREW WILSON ROSS), polit. worker; b. Wheeling, W.Va., Mar. 2, 1916; d. Eugene Edwin and Estella May (McConnaughy) Reed; student U. Ariz., 1963-67; m. Andrew Wilson Ross, June 30, 1934; children—Kenneth Reed, Ellen Penelope (Mrs. H. Lewis Kruse), Carolyn Jennifer (Mrs. William R. Donges). Bus. mgr., choir mother Tucson Boys Chorus, 1949-51; dist. mgr. 1970 Census Dept. Commerce, Bur. Census, Congl. Dist. 2, Tucson, 1970. Adviser Robert A. Taft Inst. Govt., 1972—; dir., sec. Tucson Trunk and Tusk, 1967-72. Sec., vice-chmn., 3d vice-chmn. Pima County Republican Com., 1963-73; state registration chmn. Ariz. State Rep. Exec. Com., 1971—; del., sec. credentials com. Rep. Nat. Conv., 1968. Recipient Art Wales Citizenship award Pima County Republicans, 1970. Mem. Ariz. Profl. Engrs. Aux., Episcopalian. Club: University Ariz. Faculty Wives (sec. 1947-73) Suburban Women's (v.p. 1962-65) (Tucson). Home: 3117 E 29th St Tucson AZ 85713

ROSS, EILA ISABEL HOPPER (MRS. JOHN R. ROSS), med. artist; b. Hamilton, Ont., Can., Nov. 5, 1913; d. David Alexander and Marie C. (Houston) Hopper; student Wentworth Art Sch., 1934; Asso., Ont. Coll. Art, 1937; postgrad. Johns Hopkins Med. Art Sch., 1939; m. John Robert Ross, Mar. 8, 1941; children—Gordon David, John Donaldson, Eila Marian. Asst. med. artist U. Toronto, 1940-48; med. artist visual edn. dept. Sick Children's Hosp., Toronto, 1960-67; dir. med. art dept. Sunnybrook Hosp., 1967—. Asso. prof. art applied to medicine U. Toronto, 1963—. Mem. Assn. Med. Illustrators, Canadian Acad. Med. Illustrators (pres. 1970-73), Faculty Club U. Toronto, Imperial Order Daus. of Empire (regent 1965-67). Mem. United Ch. of Can. Clubs: Toronto Ladies Golf, Toronto Granite. Home: 3 Bluejay Pl Don Mills Toronto ON Canada Office: Sunnybrook Hospital Bayview Av Toronto ON Canada

ROSS, ELISABETH KUBLER (MRS. EMANUEL ROBERT ROSS), psychiatrist; b. Zurich, Switzerland, July 8, 1926; d. Ernst and Emmy (Villiger) Kubler; M.D., U. Zurich, 1957; hon. degrees Albany Med. Sch., 1974, Notre Dame U., 1974; m. Emanuel Robert Ross, Feb. 7, 1958; children—Kenneth Lawrence, Barbara Lee. Intern Glen Cove, N.Y., 1958-59; resident Manhattan State Hosp., also Montefiore Hosp., N.Y.C., 1959-62; instr. psychiatry Psychopathic Hosp., Denver, 1962-63, U. Colo. Med. Center, Denver, 1963-65; asst. prof. psychiatry U. Chgo., 1965-70; chief consultation and liaison service La Rabida Children's Hosp., Chgo., 1969-70; cons. Lighthouse for Blind, Peace Corps; med. dir. South Cook Co. Mental Health and Family Services, Chgo. Heights, Ill., 1970-73. Mem. adv. and editorial bd. Thanatology Found., Columbia U., N.Y.C. Mem. Acad. Religion and Health (mem. bd. Chgo. chpt.), Am. Psychiat. Assn., Am. Psychosomatic Soc., Soc. for Psychophysiol. Research, A.A.A.S. Author: Questions and Answers On Death and Dying, 1969. Contbr. articles to profl. jours. Home: 1825 Sylvan Ct Flossmoor IL 60422

ROSS, ELLA VIRGINIA, univ. dean; b. Buffalo; d. Elmer Ampudia and Susan (Turner) Ross; B.S., East Tenn. State Coll., 1928; A.M., Duke, 1936; Ed.M. Harvard, 1945. Tchr. high sch., Johnson City, Tenn., 1922-32; prin. elementary sch., Johnson City, 1932-37; dean women, dir. student personnel service East Tenn. State U., Johnson City, 1940-62, dean students, 1962—. Dir., Johnson City Foundry & Machine Works, Inc.; magistrate Washington County (Tenn.) Ct., 1969. Mem. Tenn. Gov.'s Commn. on Status of Women, 1972, Tenn. Bd. Regents, 1972. Mem. 3d Army Adv. Com., 1943, Tenn. Constn. Conv., 1953; vice chmn. Johnson City Preaching Mission, 1970, chmn., 1972. Dir. Appalachian Heart Fund, Johnson City chpt. A.R.C. Named hon. citizen of Bogota, Colombia, 1962, Santiago, Chile, 1962, St. Petersburg, Fla., 1962; named Ky. col., 1966; recipient Washington County and Tenn. Bar assn. Liberty Bell awards, 1965, Valley Forge Freedom Found. award, 1968. Mem. Am., So. coll. personnel assns., Nat. Assn. Deans Women (chmn. S.E. region 1953-55), N.E.A. (dept. deans women), Tenn. Edn. Assn., Johnson City C. of C., Am. Assn. U Women (1st v.p. Tenn. 1966—), Nat. Fedn. Bus. and Profl. Women, League Women Voters, D.A.R., Colonial Dames 17th Century (v.p. Tenn. div.), Kappa Delta Pi, Pi Lambda Theta, Phi Kappa Phi. Republican. Baptist. Contbr. articles to profl. jours. Home: 708 E Unaka St Johnson City TN 37601

ROSS, ESSYE BUCH (MRS. LEONARD ROSS), lawyer; b. N.Y.C., Nov. 9, 1920; d. Samuel Montgomery and Rebecca (Harris) Buch; B.A., Hunter Coll., 1940; J.D., N.Y. U., 1945; m. Leonard Ross, June 3, 1943; children—Richard K., Robert S. Admitted to N.Y. bar, 1946, U.S. Supreme Ct. bar, 1966; mem. firm Ross & Ross, Hempstead, N.Y., 1951—. Law guardian Family Ct. Nassau County, 1964-70; adv. counsel Nat. Orgn. for Women, L.I., 1969-74; alternate rep. of Internat. Fedn. Women Lawyers to UN, 1970. Organizer, chmn. com. to aid in bldg. of Hofstra U. Law Sch., 1970; v.p. Central Nassau unit Am. Cancer Soc., 1968-69. Recipient Woman of Yr. award Bus. and Profl. Women's Club Nassau County, 1972. Mem. Am., Nassau County bar assns., Nat. Assn. Women Lawyers, Internat. Fedn. Women Lawyers (regional chmn. Mid-East br. 1970-73), Nassau-Suffolk Women's Bar Assn. (pres. 1965-66), Bus. and Profl. Women's Club Nassau County, East Meadow C. of C. (dir. 1968-74). Home: 510 Poplar Lane East Meadow NY 11554 Office: 91 N Franklin St Hempstead NY 11550

ROSS, EUNICE LATSHAW (MRS. JOHN A. ROSS), judge; b. Bellvue, Pa., Oct. 13, 1923; d. Richard Kelly and Eunice Maxine (Weidner) Latshaw; B.S., U. Pitts., 1945, LL.B., 1951; m. John A. Ross, May 29, 1943; 1 dau., Geraldine (Mrs. Peter Reed Hanchak). Admitted to Pa. bar, 1952; law clk. Ct. Common Pleas Alleghany County, Pitts., 1952-54, Orphans' Ct. Allegheny County, Pitts., 1954-60; pvt. practice law, Pitts., 1954-60; mem. firm Wilde & Ross, Pitts., 1965-67; dir. Family Ct. Allegheny County, 1970-72; judge Ct. Common Pleas Allegheny County, 1972—. Adj. prof. law U. Pitts. Sch. Law, 1967—. Mem. Allegheny Conf. Gov.'s Justice Commn., 1972—. Democratic committeewoman 3d Dist., 14th Ward, City of Pitts., 1972, ward vice chmn. Dem. com., 1972. Adv. bd. Pitts. YWCA, Animal Friends; exec. bd. U. Pitts. Law Sch., 1965-73. Recipient Distinguished Alumna award U. Pitts., 1973. Mem. Pitts. History and Landmarks Found., Western Pa. Conservancy, Pitts. Zool. Soc., Group Against Smog and Pollution, Bus. and Profl. Women, Order of Coif, Psi Chi Eta, Sigma Kappa Phi. Club: Monday Luncheon (Pitts.). Home: 1204 Denniston Av Pittsburgh PA 15217 Office: City County Bldg Pittsburgh PA 15219

ROSS, HARRIET ELIZABETH DOWNS, museum exec.; b. Sioux City, Ia., June 16, 1913; d. Newton L. and Johanna (Baisch) Downs; student U. S.D., 1932-33, Horner's Fine Arts Sch., Kansas City, 1933-34; m. James Holloway Ross, Oct. 6, 1934; 1 son, Philip Alan. Dir. pub. relations Oklahoma City Symphony Orch., 1955-58, asst. mgr., 1958-60; free-lance publicist, Oklahoma City, 1960-61; adminstrv. coordinator, neurocardiology research center Okla. U. Med. Center, Oklahoma City, 1961-68; dir. pub. relations Okla. Sci. and Arts Found., Oklahoma City, 1968-70, exec. dir., 1970—. Exec. mgr. Oklahoma City Chamber Music Series, 1958—. Bd. dirs. Oklahoma City Ballet Soc., Oklahoma City Arts Council. Named Woman of Yr., Theta Sigma Phi. Mem. Women in Communications, Pi Beta Phi. Episcopalian. Home: 6428 NW Grand Blvd Oklahoma City OK 73116 Office: Oklahoma Sci and Arts Found 3000 Pershing Blvd Fair Park Oklahoma City OK 73107

ROSS, JACQUELENE PATTON (MRS. DAVID GILBERT FLAUM), journalist; b. Ashland, Ky., Nov. 4, 1946; d. Herbert Claude and Rebecca Frances (Patton) Ross; student U. Ga., 1964-65; B.J., U. Ky., 1968; postgrad. Central Conn. State Coll., 1973—; m. David Gilbert Flaum, Oct. 14, 1972. Clk. Louisville Courier-Jour., Lexington, Ky., 1968; radio-TV news writer A.P., Hartford, Conn., 1968; youth page editor The Hartford Courant, 1968-70, reporter, 1970—. Sec. U. Ky. Young Republicans, 1966; chmn. reelection campaign of U.S. senator of Ky., U. Ky., 1966. Mem. Women in Communications (pres. Conn. chpt. 1972—), Sigma Delta Chi. Address: 1175 Farmington Bristol CT 06010

ROSS, JAYNE FREEMAN (MRS. GEORGE MATSUDA), broadcasting exec.; b. Cranford, N.J., Feb. 29, 1932; d. Floyd W. and Elsie (Krautman) Freeman; grad. pvt. schs.; m. George Matsuda, Mar. 8, 1969. Exec. dir. Netherland Am. Found., N.Y.C., 1957-66; editor Farm Vacation Guide, N.Y.C., 1966; mgr. awards ABC, N.Y.C., 1967-73; dir. spl. projects, children's programming CBS, N.Y.C., 1973-74; mgr. editorial services investor relations, 1974—. Named Ambassadress of Internat. Brotherhood, Dutch Govt., 1963. Mem. Am. Women in Radio and TV (chpt. pres. 1973). Home: 55 E 11th St New York City NY 20003 Office: CBS 51 W 52d St New York City NY 10019

ROSS, LAURA MARIE (MRS. MAX LEROY ROSS), real estate co. exec.; b. Fonda, Ia., Jan. 22, 1921; d. Earl Malalou and Laura Nell (Van Hoosier) Heflin; student pub. sch., Chgo.; m. Max LeRoy Ross, Apr. 22, 1957; children—Jeanette (Mrs. Tom Badagliacco), Eugene A. Pawlik. Singer, Chgo., 1943-52; cosmetics buyer for drug stores, Cal., 1952-62; real estate salesperson Moore Realty, Fullerton, Cal., 1962-66; broker Tom Key Realty, Fullerton, 1962-66, mgr., 1966-70; owner Red Carpet Realtors, Fullerton, 1970—; pres. and v.p. Four Links Investments Inc., Fullerton, 1970—. Named Top Realtor, North Orange County Bd. Realtors, 1972. Mem. N. Orange County Bd. Realtors (dir. 1973—), Fullerton C. of C. Democrat. Roman Catholic. Home: 5236 Los Altos Dr Yorba Linda CA 92686 Office: 3246 E Yorba Linda Blvd Fullerton CA 92631

ROSS, LEABELLE I. (MRS. CHARLES R. ROSS), psychiatrist; b. Lorain, O., Feb. 11, 1905; d. Charles E. and Harriet (Dobbie) Isaac; A.B., Western Res. U., 1927, M.D., 1930; m. Charles R. Ross, Sept. 23, 1941; children—Charles R., John Edwin. Surg. intern Lakeside Hosp., Cleve., 1931-32; resident obstetrics and gynecology Ia. State U. Hosp., 1932-33; resident obstetrics and surgery N.Y. Infirmary, N.Y.C., 1933-34; pvt. practice, Cleve., 1935-40; staff physician Cleve. State Hosp., 1938-42; dir. student health Bowling Green (O.) State U., 1942-45; psychiatrist Bur. Juvenile Research, Columbus, O., 1946-47; psychiat. cons., 1948-51; psychiatrist Mental Hygiene Clinic, Columbus VA, 1951-55; dir. med. services Juvenile Diagnostic Center, 1955-59, acting supt., 1958, 61-62, dir. psychiat. services, 1959-62, clin. dir., 1962-70. Mem. Am., Ohio psychiat. assns., Am. Group Psychotherapy Assn., Tri-State Group Psychotherapy Soc., Neuropsychiat. Assn. Central Ohio, Assn. Physicians Div. Mental Hygiene and Correction (pres. 1963-64), Alpha Sigma Rho, Nu Sigma Phi. Club: Soroptimist. Home: 2708 Welsford Rd Columbus OH 43221

ROSS, LORRAINE WILCOX (MRS. MALCOLM ALEXANDER ROSS), real estate broker, pub. relations exec.; b. nr. Watford City, N.D., July 9, 1919; d. Eugene Howard and Inga Gunvalda (Jaeger) Wilcox; grad. Seattle Secretarial Sch., 1939; m. Earl Marion Meyer, Oct. 22, 1939 (div. Mar. 1951); children—Kathleen Adele, Richard Lee, Kristy Ilona; m. 2d, Malcolm Alexander Ross, Mar. 12, 1951; 1 son, Malcolm Alexander. Bookkeeper Seattle Wholesale Grocery, 1939; sec., bookkeeper Rayonier, Inc., Port Angeles, Wash., 1951-54, Olds Oil Depot, Lynwood, 1954; saleswoman, display advt. Port Angeles Evening News, 1957-59; editor Clallam County Shopping News, Port Angeles, 1961; owner Publicity by Lorraine, Port Angeles, 1960—; pub. Port Angeles This Week, tourist guide, 1960—. Real estate saleswoman, Port Angeles, 1963— now real estate broker owner Lorraine Ross, Realtor; employed with Strait of Juan de Fuca Realty. Organizing sec. Olympic Peninsula Ind. Woodworkers Union, 1954; organizing publicist Wash. Timber Utilization Assn., 1960; publicity coordinator Port Angeles Centennial, 1962. Mem. Port Angeles City Council, 1969—; Republican committeewoman Clallam County, 1961—; sec. Clallam County Rep. Central Com., 1956-58; pres. Clallam County Rep. Club, 1960; Republican presidential (chpt. treas. Women's Council, v.p.). Mem. D.A.R. Episcopalian. Author: (with John McCallum) Port Angeles, U.S.A., 1961. Home: 418 E Front St Port Angeles WA 98362 Office: Suite 2 Aggie's Motel 1st and Albert Sts Port Angeles WA 98362

ROSS, LUCILE M. JONES (MRS. EUGENE M. ROSS), ret. social worker; b. Rockland, Wis.; d. Richard A. and Alice (Jones) Jones; B.A., Taylor U., 1933; M.A., U. Cin., 1936; postgrad. Rutgers U., 1967, 69, U. Utah, 1968, U. Chgo., 1966, Ind. U., 1959-61; m. Eugene M. Ross, Dec. 25, 1938; 1 son, Paul E. Social worker Unemployment Relief Commn., Cin., 1934-37; field staff mem. Ind. Dept. Pub. Welfare, Indpls., 1937-42; social worker Family Service Assn., Indpls., 1942-45, Community Service Council, Indpls., 1945-46; psychiat. social worker Ind. Div. Alcoholism, Indpls., 1961-69; adminstr. Central State Hosp. Alcoholism Clinic, Indpls., 1969-72. Mem. Nat. Assn. Social Workers, Acad. Certified Social Workers, Alpha Delta Omega. Home: 4946 W 15th St Indianapolis IN 46224 Office: 3000 W Washington St Indianapolis IN 46222

ROSS, MARY COWELL (MRS. JOHN O. ROSS), lawyer; b. Oklahoma City, Okla., Oct. 1, 1910; d. Sears F. and Elizabeth (Van Zwaluwenburg) Riepma; A.B., Vassar Coll., 1932; LL.B., Memphis State U., 1938; LL.D., U. Neb., 1973; m. Richard N. Cowell, Mar. 1, 1946 (dec. Jan. 1953); m. 2d, John O. Ross, Mar. 31, 1962 (dec. June 1966). Admitted to Tenn. bar, 1938, D.C. bar, 1944, N.Y. bar, 1947; atty. U.S. Govt., Washington, 1940-44; pvt. practice Cromelin & Townsend, Washington, 1944-46. Royall, Koegel & Rogers and predecessors, N.Y.C., 1946-61; individual practice law, 1961—. Treas., dir. 39 E. 79th St. Corp., 1966-73. Mem. adv. com. N.Y. Commn. on Estates, 1965-67. Bd. dirs. Silver Cross Day Nursery, N.Y.C., 1963-70, Cunningham Dance Found., 1969-72; trustee U. Neb. Found., 1966—, bd. dirs., 1974—; hon. trustee Neb. Art Assn. Mem. Am., D.C. bar assns., N.Y. Women's Bar Assn. (pres. 1955-57, dir. 1957-63, adv. council 1963—), Bar Assn. City N.Y. (mem. surrogate cts. com. 1961-65, library com. 1965—, com. on profl. responsibility), Nat. Assn. Women Lawyers (assembly del. 1962-64, 73-74, UN observer 1965-67, v.p. 1967, chmn. 1971 ann. conv., distinguished service award 1973), Vassar Coll. Alumnae Assn., Phi Delta Delta, Delta Gamma. Clubs: Metropolitan, Regency, Vassar (N.Y.C.). Address: 2 E 61st St New York City NY 10021

ROSS, MARY ELLEN, recreation exec.; b. McKean County, Pa., Sept. 11, 1933; d. Alan Francis and Agnes Elizabeth (Benson) Ross; B.S., Slippery Rock State Coll., 1959; M.Ed., Pa. State U., 1971. Tchr. health and phys. edn. Coudersport (Pa.) Area Schs., 1959-64; office clk. United Natural Gas Co., Kane, 1953-54; dir. camping Easter Seal Soc. N.J., Bloomfield, 1967—. Cons. camping, recreation. 4-H leader. Mem. Am. Camping Assn. (N.J. pres. 1974—), Nat. Parks and Recreation Assn. Home: 311 Reynolds Terrace Orange NJ 07050 Office: 9 Terminal Rd PO Box 1937 New Brunswick NJ 08902

ROSS, MARY HARVEY (MRS. ROBERT DONALD ROSS), insect geneticist; b. Albany, N.Y., Apr. 1, 1925; d. Roy Newman and Myrtle Adele (King) Harvey; B.A., Cornell U., 1945, M.A., 1947, Ph.D., 1950; m. Robert Donald Ross, Dec. 20, 1947; children—Mary Jane, Robert Douglas, Nancy Lee. Grad. asst. Cornell U., 1947-50; biologist Oak Ridge Nat. Lab., 1950-51; instr. dept. entomology Va. Poly. Inst. and State U., Blacksburg, 1959-70, asst. prof., 1970-74, asso. prof., 1974—; co-investigator USPHS grants, 1969-71; prin. investigator NSF grants, 1971-73, mem. organizing com. genetics sect. XV Internat. Congress Entomology, 1976. Office Naval Research grantee, 1974. Mem. Entomol. Soc. Am., Va. Acad. Sci., Am. Genetic Assn., Phi Beta Kappa, Sigma Xi, Phi Kappa Phi. Contbr. to profl. jours. Home: 614 Airport Rd Blacksburg VA 24060

ROSS, RAMONA LYNN, journalist; b. Laurel, Miss., Aug. 22, 1948; d. Marius Dave and Alliene Rita (Keyes) Ross; B.A. in Journalism (Robert Ewing Journalism scholar), La. State U., 1970. Staff writer Palm Beach Times, West Palm Beach, Fla., 1970-73; spl. assignment writer Daytona Beach (Fla.) News Jour., 1973; staff writer Marietta (Ga.) Daily Jour., 1973—, Palm Beach Post, West Palm Beach, 1974—. Recipient William R. Hearst award, 1969. Mem. Kappa Alpha Theta, Theta Sigma Phi, Alpha Lambda Delta. Roman Catholic. Home: 1208 NE 13th Av Fort Lauderdale FL 33304 Office: 2751 S Dixie Hwy West Palm Beach FL 33405

ROSS, ROBERTA ALICE WARREN (MRS. HUBERT LLOYD ROSS), author; b. Baird, Tex., Feb. 28, 1911; d. Robert Marion and Alice Eudora (Morris) Warren; B.S., Abilene Christian Coll., 1938, M.Ed., 1957; hon. certificate Eugene Field Soc. Writers, 1930; m. Hubert Lloyd Ross, Apr. 4, 1930; childreDwight Mayes, Robert Ross, Kitsy (Mrs. Merle Pounds), Danny. Tchr. pub. schs., Tex., to 1974;

author material Scott Ednl. Div., Minn.-Visual Aids for Young Americans, Baird, 1959—, Vanguard Visuals, Dallas, 1969—, Perceptual Devel. Lab., Big Spring, Tex., 1972—. Co-owner Visual Aids for Young Ams. Big Spring, 1972—; instr. arts and crafts, 1970-73. Recipient gold medals, Freedoms Found., 1965, 67, 72, scholarship, 1967. Mem. Mid-Cities Poetry Soc. (councillor 1970-73), Internat. Reading Assn., Tex. Assn. Improvement Assn., Tex. State Tchrs., Poetry Soc. Tex., Internat. Reading Assn. Author: Wings of Thought, 1930. Author portfolios and ednl. material. Address: 1815 Benton St Big Spring TX 79720

ROSS, SANDRA ANN, educator; b. Kenosha, Wis., Apr. 22, 1938; d. W. DeVere and Mary Francis Stein (Davin) Johnson; diploma Racine-Kenosha Tchrs. Coll., 1958; B.S. in Edn., Wis. State U., 1964; M.S., U. Wis., 1969; postgrad. N.M. State U., 1970—. Tchr. Consol. Dist. No. 1, Racine-Kenosha, Wis., 1958-63, Kenosha (Wis.) Unified Sch. Dist. No. 1, 1964-69; tchr., edn. diagnostician Alamogordo (N.M.) Center for Exceptional Students, 1969—. Profl. Tng. grantee, U. Wis., 1966. Mem. Council for Exceptional Children (pres. Otero County chpt. 1973), Am. Assn. Mental Deficiency, N.M., Alamagordo classroom tchrs. assns., N.E.A., N.M., Alamogordo edn. assns., Epsilon Sigma Alpha. Mem. Order of Amaranth. Club: Junior Woman's of Alamogordo. Home: 2702 Highland Dr Alamogordo NM 88310 Office: 301 Texas St Alamogordo NM 88310

ROSS, VIRGINIA LOUISE, librarian; b. Covina, Cal., Aug. 31, 1915; d. Verne Ralph and Isabel (Bumgarner) Ross; B.A., Stanford, 1937; M.A., Yale, 1939; librarianship certificate U. Cal., 1941. Asst. reference librarian U. Cal. at Davis, 1941-42; librarian U.S. Naval Tng. Sta., Farragut, Ida., 1942-44; hosp. librarian U.S. Naval Hosp., Bethesda, Md., 1944-46; librarian 7th Inf. Div. USAF, Seoul, Korea, 1946-48, Oakland (Cal.) Pub. Library, 1948-50; supr. br. librarian San Mateo County (Cal.) Library, 1950-52, asst. county librarian, 1952-54, county librarian, 1954—; mem. faculty Coll. San Mateo Evening Coll., 1968-71. Bd. dirs. United Cerebral Palsy Assn. San Mateo County, 1970—. Mem. Cal. Library Assn. (pres. 1965), U. Cal. Library Sch. Alumni Assn. (pres. 1964), Cal. Congress Parents and Tchrs. (adv. council state bd. mgrs. 1964-66), A.L.A., Am. Assn. U. Women, Am. Soc. Pub. Adminstrn., Pub. Library Execs. Central Cal., Women's Nat. Book Assn., San Mateo County Hist. Soc. (dir.), San Mateo County Suprs. Assn. Club: Soroptimist (Redwood City). Home: 3648 Jefferson Av Redwood City CA 94062 Office: 25 Tower Rd Belmont CA 94002

ROSSE, ALLIANORA E., artist; b. Clarkstown, N.Y.; d. Herman and Sophia Helena (Luyt) Rosse; student Art Acad. of The Hague (Netherlands), 1942-46; m. Don Munson, Nov. 22, 1968. Staff illustrator Flower Grower (later Home Garden) mag., N.Y.C., 1953-69; illustrator Ladies' Home Jour., Life Mag., Woman's Day, House Beautiful, exhibited Garden Symposium, Williamsburg, Va., Anheuser Busch Visitors' Gallery, Tampa, Fla. Mem. Garden Writer's Assn. Am., Soc. Illustrators, Embroiderer's Guild, Am. Hort. Soc. Author: (with Kathryn Murray) The Best Day for Every Little Girl; author (with Don Munson) and illustrator The Paper Book, Flower Embroidery. Illustrator: The Complete Book of Chrysanthemums; A Treasury of American Gardening; Contemporary Perennials; The Amaryllis Manual; A Sense of Seasons; Wild Flowers to Know and Grow; The Chrysanthemum Book; The New York Times Guide to House Plants; House Plants; The Iris Book; Time-Life Ency. of Gardening, 7 vols., Flowering Shrubs and Small Trees; Book on Vegetables. Home: Haverhill NH 03765

ROSSE, MARYVONNE, sculptor; b. Palo Alto, Cal., Mar. 4, 1917; d. Herman and Sophia Helena (Luyt) Rosse; diploma cum laude Acad. Fine Arts, The Hague, Netherlands, 1937. Instr. art King-Coit Sch., N.Y.C., 1947-48; instr. sculpture Rockland Found., Nyack, N.Y., 1948; one-man show Pen's Brush Gallery, 1971; exhibited art in group shows at Nat. Acad., Nat. Arts Club, Salmagundi Club, Pulchri Studio, Holland, Mich.; represented in permanent collections at Holland, Mich. Recipient Pen and Brush Solo Exhbn. award, 1971; Gold Medal for sculpture Catharine Loriland Wolfe Art Club, 1972, Anna Hyatt Huntington Horse Head trophy, 1973. Fellow Nat. Sculpture Soc.; mem. Burr Artists (2d. v.p. 1973-74), Pen and Brush Club (chmn. sculpture 1970-74). Clubs: Catherine Lorillard Wolfe Art (dir. 1969-74) (N.Y.C.); Soroptimist (pres. 1974-75). Address: 431 Buena Vista Rd New City NY 10956

ROSSELOTT, BERNICE BOYD (MRS. HERMAN J. ROSSELOTT), banker; b. Mt. Orab, O., Feb. 6, 1898; d. Edward E. and Heater (Day) Boyd; student Wilmington Coll., 1921, Miami U., Oxford, O., 1919; m. Herman J. Rosselott, May 20, 1926; 1 dau., Mary Lou (Mrs. David W. Steritz). Tchr. Mt. Orab pub. schs., 1924-32; v.p., dir. The Farmers Exchange Bank, Lynchburg, O., 1945—; dir. First Nat. Bank, Sardinia, O., 1950—. Mem. Ohio Bankers, Am. Bankers Assn., Ohio Women Bankers Assn. (pres.). Mem. Order Eastern Star. Home: 333 S Main St Lynchburg OH 45142 Office: Farmers Exchange Bank 104 N Main St Lynchburg OH 45142

ROSSMAN, BETTY JEAN (MRS. EUGENE CHARLES ROSSMAN), real estate broker; b. Elgin, Ill., Apr. 6, 1931; d. Leon Alfred and Anna Willamina (Reuter) Anderson; grad. Real Estate Inst., 1972; m. Eugene Charles Rossman, Apr. 3, 1954; children—Darice Ann, Dawn Marie. Purchasing agt. Aetna Plywood & Veneer Co., Chgo., 1950-55; real estate broker, Crystal Lake, Ill., 1965—; tchr. knitting adult edn. classes, 1964-65; tchr. real estate course McHenry County Coll., 1970—; pres., dir. Gateway Assos., Inc., realtors. Sec.-treas. McHenry County Bd. Realtors, 1969-70, pres., 1971, dir., 1973—. Sec., dir. from Cary, McHenry County Ednl. Found.; mem. adv. com. McHenry County Coll. Recipient Family Living Queen award Jr. Womans Club, 1966, certificate of appreciation Pres. Nixon, 1971. Mem. Nat., Ill. assns. real estate bds. Mem. United Ch. of Christ. Club: Fox Valley Jr. Womans (Cary). Home: 305 Crest Dr Cary IL 60013 Office: 6111 Route 14 Crystal Lake IL 60014

ROSSMAN, MARY HELEN (HONTS) (MRS. JOSEPH E. ROSSMAN, JR.), counselor; b. Bklyn., Sept. 30, 1944; d. Emory Ralph and Helen Marie (Elder) Honts; B.A. in Econs., Tex. Tech. U., 1965; postgrad. No. Ill. U., 1965-67; M.S. in Counseling Psychology, Ia. State U., 1970; m. Joseph E. Rossman, Jr., Dec. 19, 1967; 1 dau., Janet Michelle. Family counselor Ia. Dept. of Social Services, Des Moines, 1968-69; grad. asst. in teaching and research Student Counseling Center, Ia. State U., Ames, 1969-70; staff psychologist Fulton County Tng. Center for Retarded, Atlanta, 1970-71; counselor Ga. Inst. Tech., Atlanta, 1971-73; counselor DeKalb Coll., Clarkston, Ga., 1973—, also mem. adj. faculty, 1971. Mem. pub. affairs com. YWCA, Atlanta, 1973—. Mem. Am. Psychol. Assn., Ga. Coll. Personnel Assn. Ga. Assn. Women Deans, Adminstrs. and Counselors, League Women Voters, Psi Chi, Omicron Delta Epsilon, Pi Sigma Alpha. Club: Garden (pres. 1973-74). Home: 4136 Indian Manor Dr Stone Mountain GA 30083 Office: Counseling Office DeKalb College Clarkstone GA 30021

ROSS-VENNING, LAURA, physician; b. Charlotte, N.C., July 29, 1913; d. Otho Bescent and Lucy (Harris) Ross; A.B., U. N.C., 1934, M.P.H., 1958; M.D., U. Pa., 1938; m. William Lucas Venning, June 13, 1941 (div. July 1958); children—Charles, Virginia (Mrs. Fred DeVenny), Margery, William. Intern Duke, 1938-39, resident pediatrics, 1939-40; resident pediatrics Children's Hosp., Cin., 1940-41; practice medicine specializing in pediatrics, Charlotte, part time, 1941-57; dir. child health services, Charlotte, 1958—, dir. Developmental Evaluation Clinic, 1960-73. Pres., P.T.A., Charlotte, 1952-54; chmn. health N.C. Congress Parents and Tchrs., 1951-55; mem. mental health adv. bd. N.C. Family Life Council, 1955-62. Bd. dirs. Mental Retardation Planning Council. Named Woman of Year in Medicine and Health, Charlotte Mchts. Assn., 1967. Diplomate Am. Bd. Pediatrics. Fellow Am. Pub. Health Assn.; mem. Am., N.C., Charlotte pediatric assns., N.C. Pub. Health Assn. Club: Country (Charlotte). Home: 1620 Queens Rd Charlotte NC 28203 Office: 1200 Blythe Dr Charlotte NC 28203

ROST, KIM ELLEN JOHNSON (MRS. DUANE F. ROST), sch. psychologist; b. Council Bluffs, Ia., Aug. 3, 1943; d. Earl A. and Jean J. (Jenkins) Johnson; B.S., Ia. State U., 1964, M.S., 1966; m. Duane F. Rost, Jan. 16, 1965; 1 dau., Kelley Jean. Sch. psychologist, Boone County, Ia., 1966-71; psychologist, Vocational Edn. Project, Mahoning Bd. Edn., Youngstown, O., 1971-72, sch. psychologist, 1972—; instr. Ia. State U., summer 1970. Mem. Nat., Kent-Akron area assns. sch. psychologists, Council Exceptional Children, Ohio Sch. Psychologists Assn., Mensa. Presbyn. Club: Sports Car of America (Mahoning Valley region). Home: 85 Hilltop Blvd Canfield OH 44406 Office: Mahoning County Bd Edn 21 W Boardman St Youngstown OH 44503

ROSTAS, EDITH SEBESTYEN (MRS. STEVEN M. ROSTAS), educator; b. Lugos, Hungary, Jan. 25, 1908; d. Paul Leopold and Ella Elvira (Sternlicht) Sebestyen; A.B., Gymnase de la Ville de Lausanne, Switzerland, 1926; diploma U. Vienna, 1929; M.S., Mass. State Coll., 1941; m. Steven M. Rostas, May 16, 1934. Came to U.S., 1939, naturalized, 1946. Tchr. French and German Bement Sch., Deerfield, Mass., 1941-43; instr. French Mt. Holyoke Coll., South Hadley, Mass., 1943-46, prof. French, 1946-73, emeritus, 1973—; instr. French Smith Coll., Northampton, Mass., 1946-48. Ford Found. grantee for research in teaching langs. East Africa, spring and summer 1966. Home: 466 S Pleasant St Amherst MA 01002 Office: Mt Holyoke Coll South Hadley MA 01075

ROSTOW, EDNA GREENBERG (MRS. EUGENE V. ROSTOW), welfare adminstr., psychotherapist; b. Waterbury, Conn.; d. Isaac and Anna (Berman) Greenberg; B.A., Smith Coll., 1934; M.S.W., U. Conn., 1963; postgrad. London Sch. Econs., 1959; m. Eugene V. Rostow, 1933; children—Victor, Jessica (Mrs. Dana Stevens), Nicholas. Research asst. Student Mental Hygiene div. and Inst. Human Relations, Yale, 1935-36, research asso., 1936-41, research asso., exec. asst. to dir. spl. project on mil. manpower study U.S. Office Sci. Research and Devel., 1941-49, cons. psychiatry Student Mental Hygiene div., 1950-66, asst. to pres. on co-edn. Yale, 1966; practice psychotherapy; cons. Dir. of Office Health Affairs, Office Econ. Opportunity, Washington, 1966-67, chief health manpower devel., 1967-69, cons., 1969-70; cons. student affairs com. Am. Assn. Med. Colls., 1969-70, Centre for Study Adolescence, London, Eng., 1970-71, Isis Centre, Oxford, Eng., 1970-71; cons. psychiatry div. student mental hygiene, dept. univ. health Yale, 1971—. Trustee, U.S. Grant Found., New Haven; dir. Phoenix Theatre Inc., N.Y.C. Clubs: Cosmopolitan (N.Y.C.); New Haven Lawn; University Women's (London). Co-Author: Mental Health in College, 1942; contbg. author: The Urban Condition, 1963; In the Prescence of This Continent: American Themes and Ideas, 1971; The Woman in America, 1965. Contbr. monographs and articles in field to profl. jours. Home: 208 Saint Ronan St New Haven CT 06511

ROSWELL, MAY M. (MRS. CHARLES ALFRED ROSWELL), educator; b. Dublin, Ireland; d. Patrick F. and Mary (Kelly) MacGinnis; B.A., U. Dublin, 1936; M.A., U. Md., 1957, Ph.D., 1961; m. Charles Alfred Roswell, Oct. 10, 1940; children—Charles, David, Anne, John, Rosemary, Joan. Fgn. lang. dept. U. Md., 1955—, asso. prof. fgn. langs. Baltimore County br., 1966—, chmn. modern lang. dept., 1971—. Sec., Julius Hoffman Meml. Fund, 1970—. Mem. Am. Assn. U. Profs., Am. Assn. Tchrs. French, Am. Assn. Tchrs. German (pres. Md. br. 1966-69), Balt. Goethe Soc. (v.p. 1971-72), Phi Kappa Phi. Home: 6145 Montgomery Rd Elkridge MD 21227 Office: U Md Baltimore County 5401 Wilkins Av Baltimore MD 21228

ROTCHSTEIN, JANICE ANN, pub. relations co. exec.; b. Coronado, Cal., Sept. 2, 1944; d. Morris and Elizabeth Margaret (Wolke) Rotchstein; B.A., San Diego State U., 1966; M.S. in Journalism, Northwestern U., 1967. Asst. account exec. The Alexander Co., N.Y.C., 1967-68, media dir., 1967-68; media dir. Pierce Promotions, N.Y.C., 1968-70, v.p., 1970-72; creative dir. Peter Martin Assos., Inc., N.Y.C., 1972—. Dir., producer, broadcaster KFMB-AM, San Diego, 1964-66, KEBS-FM, 1962-66. Mem. Internat. Platform Assn., Quill and Scroll, Mortar Bd., Theta Sigma Phi, Alpha Epsilon Rho. Republican. Roman Catholic. Club: St. Bartholomew Community. Home: 339 E 57th St New York City NY 10022 Office: 141 E 63rd St New York City NY 10021

ROTERS, RAMONA MORGAN, librarian; b. Port Washington, N.Y., Mar. 21, 1916; d. Arthur Cecil and Hazel Olga (von Fleidner) Morgan; B.A. in Painting, Syracuse U., 1938, M.L.S., 1969; student Art Students League N.Y., 1938; m. Carl George Roters, Mar. 21, 1941; children—Tania (Mrs. William R. Farrell), Carlene (Mrs. David Gordon), David Morgan. Color asst. Norcross Greeting Co., 1939; profl. portrait painter, 1938—; tchr. Everson Museum, Syracuse, N.Y., 1947-62; mem. staff Syracuse U. Library, 1958—, slide curator, 1965—. Grantee Library Fund, 1965; recipient Popular award Everson Mus., 1947-49. Mem. Syracuse Asso. Artists, Art Research Libraries Internat. Soc. N.Am., Phi Beta Mu. Home: 100 Ostrom Av Syracuse NY 13210 Office: 205A Bird Library Syracuse Univ Syracuse NY 13210 also Box 1547 Jackson Hole WY 83001

ROTH, CLARE HANSCHMAN (MRS. HAROLD C. ROTH), C.S. practitioner; b. Neillsville, Wis.; d. William and Madonna (Baumann) Hanschman; student Howard Sch. Music, 1913-16; m. Charles Schumaker, Dec. 11, 1916; (dec. May 1951); m. 2d, Harold C. Roth, Sept., 1967. First reader 1st Ch. of Christ Scientist, Superior, Wis., 1925-28; mem. The First Ch. of Christ Scientist, Boston; C.S. practitioner, 1928—. Pres., gen. mgr. Roosevelt Heating Co., Superior, 1962—. Mem. Internat. Platform Assn. Author: Biblical Historians, 1972. Home: 1708 N 21st St Superior WI 54880

ROTH, SISTER E. SUE, social work adminstr.; b. Cleve.; d. Walter H. and Adele M. (Schlueter) Roth; Ph.B., Mt. Mary Coll., 1944; M.A. in Social Work, U. Minn., 1949. Supr. case work Mpls. Soc. for Blind, 1946-48, Luth. Children's Bur., Phila., 1950-52; registrar Luth. Deaconess Sch. Ch. Workers, 1952-58, dir. clin. tng., 1952-58; cons. Services to Blind and Partially Sighted with Luth. Synod Eastern Pa. Bd. Social Ministry, Phila., 1958-67, with Luth. Synod Southeastern Pa., Com. on Social Ministry, Phila., 1967-70; dir. social service Center for Blind, Phila., 1970—. Guest lectr. Scheie Eye Inst., Phila., 1972. Mem. tech. adv. com. Nat. Aid to Visually Handicapped, 1966-72. Diaconate Luth. Ch. Am. Recipient Madonna medal for profl. achievement Mt. Mary Coll., Milw., 1966; Community Service award Pa. Acad. Ophthalmology and Otolaryngology, 1970. Mem. Acad. Certified Social Workers, Nat. Assn. Social Workers, Nat. Assn. Workers for Blind, Luth. Social Welfare Conf. Am. Home: 1810 Rittenhouse Sq Philadelphia PA 19103 Office: 36th and Lancaster Av Philadelphia PA 19104

ROTH, JANE KELLOND RICHARDS (MRS. WILLIAM V. ROTH, JR.), lawyer; b. Phila., June 16, 1935; d. Robert Henry and Harriett (Kellond) Richards; B.A., Smith Coll., 1956; LL.B. cum laude, Harvard, 1965; m. William V. Roth, Jr., Oct. 9, 1965; children—William V. III, Katharine Kellond. Sec., Fgn. Service, U.S. Dept. of State, Tehran, Iran, 1957-59, Salisbury, S. Rhodesia, 1959-60, Brazzaville, Republic of Congo, 1960-62; admitted to Del. bar, 1965, since practiced in Wilmington, 1965—; mem. firm Richards, Layton, Finger, 1965—. Pres. Del. chpt. Arthritis Found., 1972—. Mem. rules com. Family Ct. Active Young Republicans New Castle County, 1964-65. Bd. dirs. Boys Home of Del., Wilmington, 1969-71. Mem. Am., Del. bar assns. Home: Old Kennett Rd Wilmington DE 19807 Office: Dupont Bldg Wilmington DE 19801

ROTH, JUNE DORIS SPIEWAK (MRS. FREDERICK ROTH), author; b. Haverstraw, N.Y., Feb. 16,, 1926; d. Harry I. and Ida (Glazer) Spiewak; student Pa. State U., 1942-44; grad. Tobe-Coburn Sch. for Fashion Careers, 1945; m. Frederick Roth, July 7, 1945; children—Nancy, Robert. Vice pres. evening group Teaneck (N.J.) br. Nat. Council Jewish Women, 1954, pres., 1955, v.p. day group, 1956. Mem. Authors League Am., Tobe-Coburn Alumni Assn., Internat. Platform Assn., Town and Gown Soc. Fairleigh-Dickinson U., Soc. Mag. Writers. Author: The Freeze and Please Homefreezer Cookbook, 1963; The Rich and Delicious Low-Calorie Figure Slimming Cookbook, 1964; Thousand Calorie Cookbook, 1967; How to Use Sugar to Lose Weight, 1969; Fast and Fancy Cookbook, 1969; How to Cook like a Jewish Mother, 1969; The Take Good Care of My Son Cookbook for Brides, 1969; The Indoor/Outdoor Barbecue Book, 1970; The Pick of the Pantry Cookbook, 1970; Let's Have a Brunch Cookbook, 1971; Edith Bunker's All in the Family Cookbook, 1972; The On-Your-Own Cookbook, 1972; Healthier Jewish Cookery; The Unsaturated Fat Way, 1972; Elegant Desserts, 1973; Old-Fashioned Candy making. 1974. Address: 1057 Oakland Ct Teaneck NJ 07666

ROTH, LUCY TARBELL, educator, rancher; b. Colorado Springs, Colo., Aug. 22, 1902; d. Winfield Scott and Grace Elizabeth (Butler) Tarbell; certificate Denver U., 1924; postgrad. U. Mexico, 1953; m. Charles B. Roth, July 1, 1924; children—Patricia (Mrs. J.E. Coulter), Meri (Mrs. Merlyn Wheeler). Prin., tchr. Ralston Sch., Arvada, Colo., 1947-48; rancher, breeder of Arabian horses, 1936—. Active March of Dimes, A.R.C., Community Chest Drives; girl scout leader, 1967-68; pres. Salvation Army Rehab. Aux., 1969-70; pres. Friends of Library, Arvada, 1972. Republican councilwoman in Denver, 1934, 35. Mem. Photog. Soc. Am., D.A.R., Pikes Peak Cowbell Assn., Pi Beta Phi. Clubs: Arvada Garden (pres. 1950, 65-66, 69-70), Woman's (pres. 1951). Home: 7995 Alkire St Arvada CO 80002

ROTH, RITA WOODS (MRS. JOSEPH ROBERT ROTH), banker; b. Phila.; d. Peter James and Blanche Elizabeth (Ryan) Woods; courses Am. Inst. Banking; m. Joseph Robert Roth, Sept. 21, 1944. Various positions with U.S. Govt., Washington, 1937-54; with First Park Bank, Pinellas Park, Fla., 1958—, asst. cashier, 1960-64, asst. v.p., 1964-73, v.p. customer relations also consumer financial adviser, 1973—, also corp. sec. Mem. St. Petersburg Civic Opera Guild, 1965—; bd. dirs. Christmas Toy Shop, 1960—, pres., 1964-65; bd. dirs. United Fund of. Pinellas County, 1965—, chmn. residential div., 1972—, corporate sec., mem. exec. com., 1973-74, mem. Pinellas Park steering com., 1960-65; chmn. Pinellas Park March of Dimes, 1968; chmn. Pinellas Park and Seminole area Bid by Phone Auction, WEDU ednl. TV. Coordinator women's activities, campaign treas. Pinellas County Democratic candidates for local, county, state offices, U.S. Congress, Pres. U.S. Named Woman of Achievement, Seminole Ridge Bus. and Profl. Women's Club, 1965; King Boss, St. Petersburg Credit Women's Club, 1965; Outstanding Citizen of Pinellas County, 1965; Outstanding Citizen Pinellas Park Jaycees, 1966. Mem. Nat. Assn. Bank Women (treas. Gulf Central group 1965-66), vice chmn. 1966-67, chmn. 1967-68, chmn. Fla. group 1968-69, Am. Inst. Banking (bd. govs. 1960—), Greater Pinellas Park (2d v.p. 1965-66, dir. 1961—), Pinellas Park (chmn. com. for revision city's occupational ordnance 1964-65) chambers commerce, Internat. Platform Assn., Fla. Suncoast Opera Assn. (speakers bur.). Democrat. Clubs: Yacht, Bath. Home: 5940 49th Av N St Petersburg FL 33709 Office: 5100 Park Blvd Pinellas Park FL 33565

ROTH, SALLY SAUNDERS (MRS. ROBERT ALLEN ROTH), pediatrician; b. Cleve., Feb. 4, 1943; d. Henry Frank and Marjorie Jane (Marx) Saunders; A.B., Smith Coll., 1964; M.D., Case Western Res. U., 1968; m. Robert Allen Roth, Jan. 7, 1968; children—Julie, Daniel. Intern in pediatrics Yale New Haven Hosp., 1968-69, resident in pediatrics, 1969-70; fellow in pediatrics U. Fla., Gainsville, 1970-71; instr. U. Fla., 1971-73; staff NIH, Bethesda, Md., 1973-74; Cons. Montgomery County (Md.) Health Dept., 1974—. Mem. Fla., Alachua County med. socs. Home: 4902 Brookeway Dr Sumner MD 20016 Office: 12701 Twinbrook Pkwy Rockville MD 20852

ROTHBERG, JUNE SIMMONDS (MRS. JACOB ROTHBERG), univ. dean; b. Phila., Sept. 4, 1923; d. David and Rose (Protzel) Simmonds; diploma in nursing Lenox Hill Hosp., 1944; B.S., N.Y.U., 1950, M.A., 1959, Ph.D. (NIH fellow), 1965; m. Jacob Rothberg, Sept. 7, 1952; children—Robert, Alan. USPHS traineeship, N.Y. U., 1957-59; sr. pub. health nurse, Bklyn. Vis. Nurse Assn., 1951-53; prin. investigator in nursing, homestead study project Goldwater Hosp. and N.Y.U., 1959-61; instr. N.Y. U., 1964-65, asst. prof., 1965-68, asso. prof., 1968-69; dean, prof. nursing Adelphi U., Garden City, N.J., 1969—; project dir. grad. program rehab. nursing, N.Y.U., 1964-69; cons. to various ednl. and service instns. Bd. dirs. Nurses for Polit. Action, Inc., 1971—; bd. visitors Duke Med. Center, 1970-74. Mem. Nat. League for Nursing (mem. exec. com. council of baccalaureate and higher degree programs 1969-73), Am. Nurses Assn. (mem. joint liaison com. 1970-72), Comm. on Accreditation of Rehab. Facilities, Am. Congress Rehab. Medicine (3d v.p. 1973—), Am. Assn. Colls. Nursing (pres. 1974-76), Kappa Delta Pi, Sigma Theta Tau, Pi Lambda Theta. Contbr. articles in field to profl. jours. Home: 305 Elm St West Hempstead NY 11552 Office: Adelphi University School of Nursing Garden City NJ 11530

ROTHENBERG, BARBARA ANN BROSS (MRS. STEPHEN ROTHENBERG), psychologist; b. Yonkers, N.Y., June 1, 1940; d. Samuel and Fannie (Stelzer) Bross; B.S., Carnegie-Mellon U., 1962; Ph.D. (Nat. Inst. Mental Health fellow), Cornell U., 1967; m. Stephen Rothenberg, June 21, 1964; 1 son, Bret. Intern psychology U. Wash. Sch. Medicine, Seattle, 1964-66; research psychologist Ednl. Testing Service, Princeton, N.J., 1966-68; child clin. psychologist Children's Health Council, Palo Alto, Cal., 1968-73, program chief child rearing edn. and counseling program, 1973—. Lectr. child psychology Rutgers U., New Brunswick, N.J., 1967-68. Organizer, Portola Valley Mothers of Young Children, 1972. U.S. Office Edn. Research grantee, 1969-70. Mem. Am. Psychol. Assn., Soc. Research in Child Devel. Contbr. articles to profl. jours. Home: 117 Pinon Dr Portola Valley CA 94025 Office: 700 Willow Rd Palo Alto CA 94304

ROTHENBERG, ELAINE RUTH (MRS. HERMAN H. ROTHENBERG), univ. dean; b. N.Y.C., Feb. 25, 1921; d. Hyman and Rose (Blumberg) Zipes; B.A. magna cum laude (univ. scholar), Queens Coll., 1941; M.S. in Social Work, Smith Coll., 1943; m. Herman H. Rothenberg, Sept. 26, 1943; children—Joel Barry, Richard Saul. Caseworker, Dept. Pub. Welfare, Bartow, Fla., 1943-45, Family Service Soc., Richmond, Va., 1947-48; psychiat. caseworker Meml. Guidance Clinic, Richmond, 1949-51, casework supr., 1951-60, dir., 1960—. Asst. prof. Va. Commonwealth U., Richmond, 1960-66, prof., asso. dean sch. social work, 1967-72, dean, 1972—; cons. to grad. schs. social work, since 1967—. Mem. Comprehensive Health Planning Council, Richmond, 1973—; mem. Commn. on Accreditation, Council on Social Work Edn.; chmn. Task Force on Social Services, Task Force on Educationally Disadvantaged. Bd. dirs. Richmond Urban League. Named Social Worker of Year, Va. chpt. Nat. Assn. Social Work, 1965. Mem. Nat. Assn. Social Work (dir. 1969—, nat. treas. 1971—, dir. Central Va. chpt. 1958—), Council on Social Work Edn. Contbr. articles to profl. jours. Home: 6107 Bremo Av Richmond VA 23226 Office: 326 N Harrison St Richmond VA 23284

ROTHFIELD, NAOMI FOX (MRS. LAWRENCE ROTHFIELD), physician, educator; b. Bklyn., Apr. 5, 1929; d. Morris and Violet (Bloomgarden) Fox; B.A., Bard Coll., 1950; M.D., N.Y. U., 1955; m. Lawrence Rothfield, Sept. 18, 1953; children—Susan, Lawrence, John, Jane. Intern, Lenox Hill Hosp., N.Y.C., 1955-56; practice medicine, specializing in rheumatology, N.Y.C., 1963-68; Hartford, Conn., 1968—; asst. prof. Sch. of Medicine, N.Y. U., 1962-68; asso. prof. Sch. Medicine, U. Conn., Farmington, 1968-73, prof., 1973—, head arthritis sect., 1971—; mem. staff U. Conn. Hosps., Hartford and Farmington; cons. Hartford Hosp., St. Francis Hosp., Newington VA Hosp. Bd. dirs. Arthritis Found., 1971-72. Recipient clin. scholarship Arthritis Found., 1963-68. Mem. Am. Soc. Immunologists, Am. Soc. for Clin. Investigation, Am. Rheumatism Assn. Contbr. articles to various publs. Home: 130 Mountain Rd West Hartford CT 06105 Office: Conn School Medicine Farmington CT 06107

ROTHFUS, HELEN TEFFT (MRS. ROBERT RANDLE ROTHFUS), physician; b. Rochester, N.Y., Aug. 19, 1917; d. Ola Minor and Jeanette Isabelle (McCuaig) Tefft; A.B., U. Rochester, 1939; M.D., George Washington U., 1943; m. Robert Randle Rothfus, May 30, 1942; children—Elizabeth (Mrs. David C. Lenz), Ann (Mrs. George J. Hoyer, Jr.), William. Intern, Rochester Gen. Hosp., 1943-44; resident physician Iola Sanatorium, Rochester, 1944-48; Tb cons. C.H. Marcy State Hosp., Pitts., 1949-53; clinician Allegheny County Health Dept., Pitts., 1953-71; chief, Tb control, 1971—. Mem. A.M.A., Pa. Med. Assn., Allegheny County Med. Soc., Am., Pa. thoracic socs., Women's Med. Soc. Pitts. Home: 81 Seneca Dr Pittsburgh PA 15228 Office: 2851 Bedford Av Pittsburgh PA 15219

ROTHKOPF, CAROL ZEMAN (MRS. ERNST ROTHKOPF), author, editor; b. N.Y.C., Sept. 16, 1929; d. Frederic David and Madeleine Edythe (Arnold) Zeman; B.A., Goucher Coll., 1951; M.A., Columbia, 1952; m. Ernst Zacharias Rothkopf, Aug. 28, 1952; children—David, Paul, Marissa. Author: Tolstoy, 1968; Jean Henri Dunant, 1969; The Red Cross: A First Book, 1971; Yugoslavia: A First Book, 1971; East Europe: A First Book, 1972; The Opening of the Suez Canal, 1972; Czechoslovakia: A First Book, 1973; Austria: A First Book, 1975; others. Editor: Our Wonderful World, 1953-56; sr. editor The New Book of Knowledge, 1961-65, Lands and Peoples, 1968-71; developmental editor Gen. Learning Press, 1972—. Home: 16 Rotary Lane Summit NJ 07901

ROTHLISBERGER, HAZEL MARIE, educator; b. Elgin, Ia., May 10, 1911; d. Charles and Lulu Ann (Kerr) Rothlisberger; B.A., Ia. State Tchrs. Coll., 1938; M.A., U. Wis., 1950; postgrad. U. Colo., summers 1951-52, 54, 56, Ia. State Coll., summer 1960. Tchr. math., prin. Owasa (Ia.) High Sch., 1941-43; prof., head dept. math. U. Dubuque (Ia.), 1943—. NSF fellow, summers 1958-60. Mem. Nat. Council Tchrs. Math., Ia. Acad. Sci., Math. Assn. Am., P.E.O., Kappa Delta Pi. Delta Kappa Gamma. Home: 1245 S Grandview St Dubuque IA 52001 Office: U Dubuque Dubuque IA 52001

ROTHMAN, CAROL ANN (MRS. HERBERT ROTHMAN), anesthesiologist; b. Nanticoke, Pa., Sept. 27, 1940; d. William Thomas and Helen Jane (Krushinski) Milchenski; B.A., Boston U., 1962, M.D., 1966; m. Herbert Rothman, Sept. 22, 1968. Intern, St. Vincent's Hosp., N.Y.C., 1966-67, med. resident, 1967-68, anesthesia resident, 1968-70; practice medicine, specializing in anesthesiology, N.Y.C., 1970—; attending anesthesiologist N.Y.C. Hosp., 1970-72; dir. anesthesia Gracie Sq. Hosp., N.Y.C., 1973—. Diplomate Am. Bd. Anesthesiology. Fellow Am. Coll. Anesthesiologists; mem. A.M.A., N.Y. Med. Soc. Home: 1385 York Av New York City NY 10021 Office: 1385 York Av New York City NY 10021

ROTHMAN, ESTHER POMERANZ, educator-psychologist; b. N.Y.C.; d. Max and Annie (Reiner) Pomeranz; B.A., Hunter Coll., 1942; M.A., Columbia, 1946; M.A., Coll. City N.Y., 1951; Ph.D., N.Y.U., 1957; m. Arthur Rothman, Apr. 13, 1946; 1 dau., Amy. Tchr., N.Y.C. schs., 1942-49, Bellevue Psychiat. Hosp., N.Y.C., 1949-55, tchr.-therapist, 1957-58; psychologist Univ. Hosp., 1956-57; research supr. Shield of David, 1958-62; prin. Livingston Sch. for Girls, 1959—; staff psychologist Girls Service League, 1959-62; guest lectr. Queens Coll., N.Y.U., Hunter Coll.; adj. prof. Fordham U., 1973-74. Cons., Center for Urban Edn., 1967-71; project dir. Crisis Intervention by Use of Telephone Therapy, 1972—. Recipient Am. Educators Medal award Freedoms Found. Valley Forge; elected to Hunter Coll. Hall of Fame. Fellow Am. Orthopsychiat. Assn.; mem. Am., N.Y. State psychol. assns., Council Exceptional Children (chpt. pres.), Pi Lambda Theta, Kappa Delta Pi. Author: (with Pearl Berkowitz) Disturbed Child, 1958; Buttons: Projective Test of Personality, 1963; (with Pearl Berkowitz), Education for Disturbed Children in N.Y.C., 1966; Angel Inside Went Sour, 1971; Troubled Teachers, 1974. Contbr. numerous articles to profl. jours. Home: 200 E 16th St New York City NY 10003 Office: 29 King St New York City NY 10014

ROTHSCHILD, VIVIAN AUERBACH (MRS. WALTER S. ROTHSCHILD), TV and film producer; b. Jersey City; d. Michael and Gertrude (Schreiber) Leib; m. Walter S. Rothschild, Jan. 29, 1950; 1 son, Richard Leib. Fashion and promotion dir. Aronoff, Richling & Fein, N.Y.C., 1949-51; fashion, publicity dir. Richard Englander Co., Dallas, N.Y.C., 1951-53; owner, adv., fashion dir. Enton, Ltd., Englewood, N.J., 1953-56; advt., promotion and fashion dir. Regal Knitwear, N.Y.C., 1957-63; fashion, mdse. dir. Poise Mag., N.Y.C., 1963-64; advt., promotion, fashion dir., v.p. Regal Knitwear, N.Y.C., 1964-69; retail promotion dir. McCall's Mag., N.Y.C., 1969-70; pres. Vivian Auerbach Assos., N.Y.C., 1970—. Teen-age fashion cons., dept. stores throughout U.S., various press and TV panels. P.T.A., Teaneck, N.J., 1962—; v.p. Women's Am. ORT, 1956-57; program chmn. Englewood chpt. United Jewish Appeal, 1960, program co-chmn., Tenafly, 1965-66; publicity worker Los Angeles Sanitorium, 1958-60; spl. events Am. Cancer Soc., 1962; writer, spl. events Assn. for Mentally Retarded. Mem. Advt. Women N.Y., Alliance of Three Arts (v.p. 1970—), Fashion Group N.Y. (mem. children's com. 1966, chmn. career course 1970-71). Democrat. Contbr. articles to popular mags., newspapers. Home: 626 Sunderland Rd Teaneck NJ 07666 Office: 9 E 19th St New York City NY 10017

ROTHSTEIN, BARBARA JACOBS (MRS. TED L. ROTHSTEIN), lawyer; b. Bklyn., Feb. 3, 1939; d. Solomon and Pauline (Fabricant) Jacobs; B.A., Cornell, 1960; LL.B., Harvard, 1966; m. Ted L. Rothstein, Dec. 29, 1969. Admitted to Mass. bar, 1966, Wash. bar, 1969; asso. Widett & Kruger, Boston, 1966-69; asst. atty. gen. State of Wash. Consumer Protection Div., Seattle, 1970—. Alternate del. Wash. State Presdl. Dem. Conv., 1972. Bd. dirs. Seattle Mental Health Inst., 1970—, treas., 1970-71; bd. advisers Family House, 1969-71; bd. dirs. Seattle Treatment Center, 1970—, v.p., 1971-72. Mem. Am., Wash. State, Mass., Seattle-King County (trustee young lawyers sect. 1971—, chmn. ct. reform com. 1971-72) bar assns., Phi Beta Kappa, Phi Kappa Phi, Phi Sigma Sigma. Home: 714 39th Av Seattle WA 98122 Office: Dexter Horton Bldg Seattle WA 98104

ROTHSTEIN, RUTH M. (MRS. DAVID ROTHSTEIN), hosp. adminstr.; m. David Rothstein; children—Martha, Jonathan. Past dir. personnel dept., Jackson Park Hosp., Chgo., adminstrv. asst. until 1966; chief admitting officer Mt. Sinai Hosp. Med. Center, Chgo., 1966-70, adminstr., 1970-72, exec. dir., 1972-74, v.p., exec. dir., 1974—. Address: Mt Sinai Hosp Med Center 2750 W 15th Pl Chicago IL 60608

ROTMAN, ELEANOR LEA (MRS. BERTRAM T. ROTMAN), psychologist; b. N.Y.C., Apr. 7, 1938; d. Isidore and Dora (Lapchinsky) Katz; B.S., Hofstra U., 1959; M.S., L.I. U., 1962; postgrad. U. Ottawa, 1962-63, Newark State Coll., 1966-68, Paterson State Coll., 1968-69, Montclair State Coll., 1969-71; m. Bertram T. Rotman, June 12, 1960; 1 son, Scott. Psychologist, Alcoholism and Drug Addiction Clinic, Ottawa, Ont., Can., 1961-64; psychologist Met. State Hosp., Waltham, Mass., 1964-66; cons. psychologist to pvt. and pub. schs., 1969—. Licensed dog show judge Am. Kennel Club. Mem. Paterson Gen. Hosp. Women's Aux., 1972—. Bd. dirs. P.T.A., Wayne, N.J. Mem. Am., N.J. psychol. assns., Nat., N.J. assns. sch. psychologists, Women's Am. Orgn. for Rehab. Tng., Psi Chi. Club: Watchung Mount Poodle (pres. 1972—), K-9 Obedience Training (sec. 1967-73). Home and office: 701 Valley Rd Wayne NJ 07470

ROTTMANN, BETTY COOK (MRS. LEROY F. ROTTMANN), univ. ofcl.; b. Longton, Kan., Oct. 9, 1922; d. J. Fred and Ora Mae (Allen) Cook; A.A., Central Wesleyan Coll., 1940; B.J. (Benjamin Franklin scholar), U. Mo., 1958, postgrad., 1963—; postgrad. U. Denver, 1968, 69, 70; m. Leroy F. Rottmann, Apr. 4, 1942; children—Larry, Tina. Asst. librarian U.S. Spl. Services, Ft. Campbell, Ky., 1944-45; asst. librarian Columbia (Mo.) Pub. Library, 1945-48; substitute tchr., Mo., 1948-56; reporter, columnist Ste. Genevieve Herald, 1956-57; women's columnist Mo. Ruralist and Kan. Farmer, 1957-58; corr. Fairchild Publs., 1960-62; newswriter, information specialist U. Mo.-Columbia Office Pub. Information, 1968—. Co-founder Mo. Women's Polit. Caucus, 1972, Mo. Equal Rights Coalition, 1973; Exec. sec. A.R.C., Ste. Genevieve, Mo., 1950; mem. Columbia Community Congress, 1970-72; mem. bldg. bd. Nora Stewart Nursery, 1966—. Research grantee Women in Communications, 1965. Mem. Am. Assn. U. Women (media topic chmn. 1973-75), Women in Communications (Award df Excellence, Columbia chpt. 1961, chpt. pres. 1961), Am. Coll. Pub. Relations Assn., Mo. Press Women (pres. 1966), Mo. Writers Guild, Sigma Delta Chi, Kappa Tau Alpha. Home: 1200 Coats St Columbia MO 65201

ROTUNDO, FRANCES JOAN, youth orgn. adminstr., personnel psychologist; b. N.Y.C., July 2, 1938; d. Louis and Margaret (Santo) Rotundo; B.S. in Indsl. Psychology, Le Moyne Coll., 1961; M.A. in Personnel Psychology, Columbia, 1968, now postgrad. Personnel asst. Career's Inc., N.Y.C., 1961-64; personnel mgr. Internat. Latex Co., N.Y.C., 1965, Kenyon & Eckhardt Advt. Agy., N.Y.C., 1965-67; dir. personnel adminstrn. Camp Fire Girls, Inc., N.Y.C., 1967—. Cons. to N.Y.C. Council on the Environment. Mem. Pres.'s Com. on Employment of the Handicapped. Mem. Am. Psychol. Assn., Personnel Mgmt. Assn., Am. Soc. for Tng. and Devel., Altrusa Internat. Republican. Toastmistress. Home: 160 88th St New York City NY 10028 Office: 1740 Broadway New York City NY 10019

ROUDYBUSH, ALEXANDRA BROWN (MRS. FRANKLIN ROUDYBUSH), author; b. Hyères, Côte d'Azur, France, Mar. 14, 1911 (parents Am. citizens); d. Constantine and Ethel (Wheeler) Brown; B.A., London Sch. Econs., 1930; m. Franklin Roudybush, May 22, 1941. Corr., London Evening Standard, Washington, 1931; sec. to Drew Pearson, 1932; asst. Agence Havas, 1935; research news analyst Time mag., N.Y.C., 1936; sec. to chief news dept. CBS, 1936; White House corr. MBS, 1940; asst. to sect. head Nat. Acad. Scis., Washington, 1957-60; adminstr., sec. firm Dewey, Ballantine, Bushby, Palmer & Wood, attys., Paris, 1965—. Mem. Writers Guild U.S.A. Author: Before the Ball was Over, 1965; Death of a Moral Person, 1967; A Capital Crime, 1969; The House of the Cat, 1970; A Sybaritic Death, 1972; Gastronomic Murder, 1973; Suddenly in Paris, 1975. Home: 15 Av du President Wilson Paris 16e France Office: 45 Av George V Paris 8e France

ROUGAGNAC, GERALDINE CORAL RUSSELL (MRS. WARD ROUGAGNAC), service agy. exec.; b. Rogersville, Pa., Aug. 25, 1912; d. Robert Paul and Margaret (Eagon) Russell; B.S. in Bus. Adminstrn. with high honors, U. Pitts., 1945; M.S., U. Houston, 1954; m. Ward Rougagnac, Aug. 11, 1950. With Houston Lighthouse for Blind, 1950—, exec. dir., 1950—; dir. Royal-Maid, Hazelhurst, Miss. Mem. tech. adv. com. housing Mayor's Model Cities Program, Houston, 1969—. Bd. dirs. Houston Lighthouse Found. Recipient Distinguished Citizen award, 1968; named Battlesteins Memo Set Woman of Year, Goodwill Industries, 1965. Mem. Am. Assn. Workers for Blind, Nat. Industries for Blind (exec. com. bd. dirs., recipient R.B. Irwin award 1973), Nat. Accreditation Council for Agys. Serving Blind People, Nat. Rehab. Assn., Houston C. of C. (mem. ednl. com. 1966—), Beta Gamma Sigma. Home: 10023 Briar Rose St Houston TX 77042 Office: 3530 W Dallas St Houston TX 77019

ROUGIER, JANET ROSE, educator; b. Osseo, Minn., Feb. 4, 1911; d. Peter and Clementine Valentine (Chastek) Rougier; B.S., U. Minn., 1931; M.S., U. Alaska, 1961. Tchr. math., Latin, physics, Osseo, 1932-39; tchr. jr. high math., Hastings, Minn., 1939-42; tchr. radio mechanics USAF, 1942-43; with aero. test lab. Mpls. Honeywell Co., 1943-45; tchr. secondary math., Mpls., 1945-46; tchr., head dept. math. Anchorage High Sch., 1946—; faculty U. Alaska Night Sch., 1965. Chmn. Greater Anchorage Area Secondary Math Curriculum com., 1968-69. Sponsor, Future Tchrs. Am., 1951-59, Cath. Youth Orgn., 1959-68. Shell Merit fellow Stanford, 1957, NSF scholar, 1958, 60, Acad. Year scholar Wesleyan U., Middletown, Conn., 1963-64, NSF scholar U. Okla., summer 1963. Mem. N.E.A., Alaska (past pres.), Anchorage (sec.) edn. assns., Nat. Council Tchrs. Math., Math. Assn. Am., Mu Alpha Theta. Co-editor: Alaska Teacher, 1958-61. Home: 1463 W 25th St Anchorage AK 99503 Office: 1700 W Hillcrest Dr Anchorage AK 99503

ROULET, ANN EDELEN (MRS. NORMAN LAWRENCE ROULET), ednl. adminstr.; b. St. Joseph, Mo., Mar. 7, 1933; d. Cloyd Chambers and Mary Ann (McDonald) Edelen; B.Ed. magna cum laude, Toledo U., 1954; M.A., Case Western Res. U., 1960, Ph.A., 1971; m. Norman Lawrence Roulet, Jr., June 26, 1954; children—Laura, Norman Lawrence III. Tchr. English, Eddystone High Sch., Eddystone, Pa., 1954-56, West Philadelphia High Sch., Phila., 1956-58; lectr. English, Case Western Res. U., Cleve., 1958-63; prof. English, Cleve. Inst. Art, 1963—, dean of students, 1972—. Adviser, discussion leader Women's Com. for Continuing Edn., 1969—; mem. jr. council Cleve. Museum Art, 1972—, trustee Print Club, 1970; mem. women's com. Cleve. Inst. Art, 1960—. Mem. Am. Assn. U. Profs., Contemporary Art Soc. Cleve., New Orgn. for Visual Arts (trustee 1972—). Club: University Print (Cleve.). Home: 17400 Shaker Blvd Shaker Heights OH 44120 Office: Cleveland Inst Art Cleveland OH 44106

ROUND, BETTYE HAMMONS (MRS. THORNTON EDGERLY ROUND), realtor; b. Barberville, Fla.; d. Benjamin Abner and Alice Adella (Ward) Hammons; grad. high sch.; student various courses in real estate, decorating, bus. mgmt.; m. Thornton Edgerly Round, July 27, 1961; 1 dau., Alice Adair Gilbert (Mrs. Darrell D. Brown). Free-lance interior designer, Coral Gables, Miami, Fla., 1935-39; agt., Independence Life Ins. Co., Orlando, Fla., 1950-51; broker Homestead Devel. Co., 1952-56; owner real estate broker firm Bettye H. Gilbert, 1956-61, Betty H. Round Realtor, 1961—; owner, Windsor Manor, Inc., Orlando, 1961—; co-owner Lee's Inn, Highlands, N.C., 1961-69. Mem. Vis. Nurses Assn., 1962—; mem. Orlando Day Nursery, 1964-72; mem. women's com. Fla. Symphony Orch., 1964-71. Mem. Orlando Winter Park Bd. Realtors (sec. 1958, pres. women's council 1959-60), Fla. Bd. Realtors (corr. sec. 1958). Democrat. Episcopalian. Clubs: Sorosis, Dubsdread Country, Orlando Country (Orlando). Home: 722 Alameda Dr Orlando FL 32804 Office: 1216 Edgewater Dr Suite II Orlando FL 32801

ROUNER, EVELYN IRENE, educator; b. Iowa City, Ia., Apr. 2, 1921; d. Jacob Frank and Emma Mae (Reber) Rouner; B.A., U. Ia., 1945; M.S., U. Ill., 1951, Ed.D., 1959; postgrad. Brigham Young U., summer 1962, Colo. State U., summer 1971. Tchr., Jr. High Sch., tchr., prin. Amana High Sch., 1945-50; chmn. vocational div. Hesston Community Coll., 1951-57; nursery sch. tchr., research asst., fellow U. Ill., 1957-59; prof. family and child Central Mich. U., Mt. Pleasant, 1959—, chmn. dept., 1967-70, with Project Head Start Tng. Program, 1965-67; postdoctoral fellow U. N.C. at Greensboro, 1974. Lectr. family life edn., child devel. Pres. Mich. Council on Family Relations, 1967-71; co-chmn. Gov. Romney's Task Force on Family, 1965-69; cons. Mt. Pleasant Nursery Sch.-Day Care Programs. Nat. chmn. AHEA/NCFR Family Life Conf., 1971. Recipient Central Mich. U. Student Thank You award, 1965, Mich. Council Family Relations Ann. award, 1970, Outstanding Woman Prof. award Asso. Women Students 1972; named Outstanding Tchr. Educator, 1971. Mem. Mich. Assn. Higher Edn., N.E.A., Mich. Edn. Assn., Am., Mich. home econs. assns., Nat., Mich. councils on family relations, Nat. Assn. Edn. Young Children, Delta Kappa Gamma, Kappa Delta Pi, Phi Kappa Phi, Kappa Omicron Phi. Contbr. articles profl. jours. Home: 2435 East Dr Mount Pleasant MI 48858

ROUNTREE, LOUISE MARIE, librarian; b. Barnwell, S.C.; d. Clarence C. and Mary M. (Patterson) Rountree; A.B., Morris Coll., 1941; B.L.S., Atlanta U., 1950; M.S. in Library Sci., Syracuse U., 1956; postgrad. Columbia, 1962. Tchr., librarian Bethlehem High Sch., Barnwell, 1943-45; tchr. Estill (S.C.) High Sch., 1945-48, Allendale (S.C.) High Sch., 1948-51; asst. librarian Livingstone Coll., Salisbury, N.C., 1951-68, asst. prof. library sci., 1958-71, acting librarian, 1969-70, head librarian, 1970—. Mem. Rowan Historic Properties Commn. Bd., 1973. Bd. dirs. Rowan Citizens for Better Libraries, sec., 1971. Recipient Jennie Smallwood Price award Womens Assembly, 1970. Mem. Am. Assn. Univ. Women (dir.), A.L.A., N.C., Rowan, Southeastern library assns. Baptist (mem. sr. choir 1970—). Home: 1301 W Horah Salisbury NC 28144 Office: 801 W Monroe Salisbury NC 28144

ROUNTREE, PATRICIA ANN, assn. exec.; b. Rochester, N.Y., Apr. 2, 1942; d. Robert James and Myrtle Margaret (Cuthbertson) Rountree; A.A., Cazenovia Coll., 1961; B.A., Parsons Coll., 1965. Elementary tchr. Wayland (N.Y.) Central Sch., 1965-67; field dir. Seven Lakes council Girl Scouts U.S., Geneva, N.Y., 1967-73, program dir. Palm Glades council, Lake Worth, Fla., 1973—. Mem. Assn. Girl Scout Profl. Workers, Alpha Omicron Pi. Presbyn. Home: 4844 NW 24th Ct Apt 106 Lauderdale Lakes FL 33313 Office: 2728 Lake Worth Rd Lake Worth FL 33460

ROUSCULP, MARY ELIZABETH, broadcasting exec.; b. Columbus, O., July 9, 1927; d. Oakley Ernest and Edith (Childs) Wiseman; B.A., Ohio State U., 1950; m. Robert Allen Rousculp, Oct. 14, 1950 (div. Oct. 1967); children—Catherine Ann, John Philip, Eric Robert. Broadcaster WBNS Radio, Columbus, 1949-50; continuity writer WCOL-Radio, 1950-51; English newscaster Hashemite Kingdom of Jordan Broadcasting, Amman, Jordan, 1960; music dir. WOSU-Radio, Columbus, 1966—. Mem. Theta Sigma Phi. Home: 464 Selby Blvd S Worthington OH 43085 Office: 2400 Olentangy River Rd Columbus OH 43210

ROUSE, BEULAH JANE (MRS. PHILIP MILTON ROUSE), hosp. adminstr.; b. Port Arthur, Tex., July 4, 1922; d. Robert Emmett and Lou Victor (Tunis) Lynch; grad. Port Arthur Bus. Coll., 1942; m. Philip Milton Rouse, Feb. 19, 1943; children—Robert Wilson, John Philip, Phyllis Anne, Linda Jane. Sec., Gulf Oil Corp., Port Arthur, 1942-47; office mgr. Bill Swanson Plumbing, Bellaire, Tex., 1959-63, Swanson Mech. Contractors, 1959-63; adminstr. Youens Meml. Hosp., Weimar, Tex., 1967—. Mem. Area Health Commn., Houston, 1972—. Mem. Tex. Hosp. Assn., Tex. Assn. Hosp. Accountants, Am. Acad. Med. Adminstrs., Weimar C. of C. (v.p. 1972-73). Club: Weimar Woman's. Home: PO Box 621 Weimar TX 78962 Office: 104 N East St Weimar TX 78962

ROUSE, BOBBYE MURIEL, physician, educator; b. Ft. Worth, Feb. 3, 1928; d. Warren Harvey and Anna Bess (Wilkins) R.; B.S. magna cum laude, Abilene Christian Coll., 1947; M.D., U. Tex., Dallas, 1959. Chemist, Gulf Oil Corp., Ft. Worth, 1947-55; intern, resident pediatrics St. Pauls Hosp., Dallas, 1959-61; resident, chief resident pediatrics U. Tex. Med. Br., Galveston, 1961-63, fellow child devel., 1963-65, asst. prof. pediatrics, 1965—, coordinator mental retardation facilities, 1967—; cons. Project Head Start, 1966-69, Office Econ. Opportunity; mem. profl. adv. bd. Galveston County Mental Health-Mental Retardation Center, 1967-68, Galveston Independent Sch. Dist., 1970—. Mem. exec. bd. Island Assn. for Retarded Children, 1964-70. Diplomate Am. Bd. Pediatrics. Mem. Am. Acad. Pediatrics, So. Soc. for Pediatric Research, Am. Assn. Mental Deficiency, Galveston County Med. Soc., Sigma Xi. Contbr. articles profl. jours. Office: U Tex Medical Branch Galveston TX 77550

ROUSE, SUE THOMPSON, educator; b. Ulman, Mo., Aug. 28, 1920; d. Clyde Waldo and Retta (Darr) Thompson; A.B., Harris Tchrs. Coll., 1942; M.A., U. N.C., 1950; Ed.D. (fellow), George Peabody Coll. for Tchrs., 1963; m. Linwood I. Rouse, Aug. 29, 1945

(div. May, 1962). Dir., Shaw Playground, St. Louis, summers 1937-41; tchr. elementary schs., Normandy, Mo., 1942-43, Ayden, N.C., 1947-48, Winterville, N.C., 1948-49, Greenville, N.C., 1950-57; tchr. educable mental retardates Greenville Jr. High Sch., 1957-59; asst. prof. Coll. Edn., U. S.C. at Columbia, 1961-66, asso. prof., 1966-74, prof., 1974—. Ednl. cons. S.C. Gov.'s Legislative Com. on Mental Health and Mental Retardation, 1970—, S.C. Dept. Corrections, 1967—; S.C. chmn. Found. for Exceptional Children, 1972—. Mem. S.C. Commn. on Ministry Christian Ch., 1972—. Served to lt. (j.g.), Women's Res., USCGR, 1943-46. Fellow Am. Assn. on Mental Deficiency; mem. N.E.A. (life), Council for Exceptional Children (S.C. mem. to internat. bd. govs. 1963-68, pres. Central S.C. chpt. 1968-69), Am. Assn. U. Profs., S.C. Mental Health Assn., S.C. Edn. Assn., S.C. Psychol. Assn., Fedn. Delta Kappa Gamma. Contbr. articles to profl. jours. Home: 1115 Glen Oaks Rd Columbia SC 29210

ROUSE, VIRGINIA ARIAIL (MRS. LEGRAND ROUSE), ret. educator, civic worker; b. Rock Hill, S.C., Mar. 29, 1906; d. William Hamilton and Nancy Elizabeth Ozella (Daniel) Ariail; student Converse Coll., 1923-24; Mus.B. (Theodore Presser Co. mus. scholar 1924-26), Columbia (S.C.) Coll., 1927, diploma in voice, 1927; postgrad. Wofford Coll., summers 1930-46, 47; M.Ed., U. S.C., 1949; m. LeGrand Rouse, Feb. 7, 1930 (dec. June 1972); children—LeGrand Ariail, Virginia Gail (Mrs. Edwin C. Klebau), Sharon Lynne. Asst. voice tchr. Columbia (S.C.) Coll., 1926-27; primary tchr. Spartanburg (S.C.) city schs., 1927-32; soprano soloist Episcopal Ch. of the Advent, Spartanburg, 1927-28, Central Meth. Ch., 1928-32; pub. sch. music and intermediate grade tchr. Roebuck (S.C.) schs., 1946-53; pub. sch. music and lang. arts tchr. Clifton (S.C.) Elementary Sch., 1953—; pvt. tchr. voice and piano, 1939—. Mem. Spartanburg Little Theatre; sec. Spartanburg Philharmonic, 1947-48, rating chmn., 1950-52, chmn. scholarship com., counsellor Jr. Philharmonic, 1966-68, chmn. publs., 1968-70; mem. Marie Chiles Jr. Music Club, 1947-48, Monday Afternoon Jr. Music Club, 1953-54; canvasser Columbia (S.C.) Loyalty Fund, 1969; active Salvation Army, Community Chest, A.R.C., March of Dimes, Crippled Children, Tb Assn., Epworth Orphanage, Boy's Town, Cancer Fund, others. Mem. Spartanburg County Council. Recipient Brunson medal in Speech Florence, S.C., 1923; Lachicotte medal in music excellence Columbia Coll., 1927. Mem. Am. Assn. U. Women (S.C. 1st v.p. 1954-56, S.C. dir. 1953-56, Spartanburg br. legislative chmn., 1950-51, pres. 1951-53, membership chmn. 1955-57, chmn. social and econ. issues 1959-60, historian 1963-65), N.E.A., P.T.A., Nat. Soc. Colonial Dames XVII Century (chpt. charter pres. 1963-65, 3d v.p. 1965-69, chmn. by-laws 1965-71, chmn. publicity and press relations 1965-69; parliamentarian 1967-71, chmn. music 1967-71), Spartanburg County Hist. Assn., S.C. Soc. Colonial Dames XVII Century (state music chmn. 1967-69, mem. state exec. bd. 1969-71, state historian), United Daughters Confederacy (chpt. music chmn. 1963-65), S.C., Spartanburg County edn. assns., Women's Soc. Christian Service (charter mem), S.C. Fedn. Music Clubs (no. dist. dir. 1949-50, gen. chmn. state conv. 1938-39, state publicity chmn. 1947-51), S.C. Fedn. Women's Clubs (dir. 1952-53, youth conservation chmn. 1952-53), Past President's Music Assembly (local v.p. 1946-47), Civic Music Assn., Columbia Coll. (key rep. 1957—, chpt. pres. 1961), Converse Coll., U. S.C. alumni assns., Columbia Coll. Alumnae Assn. (sec. 1960-62), Nat. Ret. Tchrs. Assn., Beta Omicron Delta. Democrat. Methodist. Clubs: Monday Afternoon Music (publicity chmn. 1939, 52, pres. 1939-41), Jubal Music, Art (publicity chmn. 1955-56), Metropolitan Dinner, Woman's (youth conservation and edn. chmn. 1949-54, music chmn. 1955-56, pres. 1947-48 (Spartanburg). Author several poems. Home: 619 Norwood St Spartanburg SC 29302

ROUSEK, SISTER MARIE, librarian; b. East Orange, N.J., July 12, 1925; d. Charles Elmer and Bertha Marie (Everett) Rousek; A.B., Coll. St. Elizabeth, 1947; A.M., Seton Hall U., 1955; M.L.S., St. John's U., 1958. Joined Sisters of Charity, 1947; tchr. English Bayley-Ellard High Sch., Madison, N.J., 1949-55, St. Michael High Sch., Union City, N.J., 1955-56; asst. librarian Coll. St. Elizabeth, Convent Station., N.J., 1956-63; librarian, 1963—. Mem. Am., N.J., Cath. library assns., Asso. Libraries of Morris County, Met. Cath. Coll. Librarians (mem. exec. com. 1970—), Kappa Gamma Pi. Address: Mahoney Library Coll of St Elizabeth Convent Station NJ 07961

ROUSSEAU, LOUSENE GWENDOLYNNE (MRS. EDMUND DE SCHWEINITZ BRUNNER), author; b. Madison, Wis., July 14, 1895; d. Louis A. and Selina Eva (Douville) Rousseau; B.A., U. Wis., 1916, M.A., 1923; m. Henry J. Fry, Dec. 1930 (dec. Aug. 1941); m. Edmund de Schweinitz Brunner, Nov. 1948 (dec. Dec. 1973). Prof. speech Western Mich. U., Kalamazoo, 1916-25; fellow in speech U. Wis., 1926-27; sec., Nat. Assn. Tchrs. Speech, 1924-25; editor speech and home econs. textbooks coll. dept. Harper & Row Pubs., N.Y.C., 1927-62. Mem. Gamma Phi Beta. Author: Effective Speech, 1931, revised edit., 1936; Connecticut Cookbook, 1942; New Connecticut Cookbook, 1947; Casserole Magic, 1953; Magic with Leftovers, 1955; Casserole Treasury, 1964; New Casserole Treasury, 1972. Home: 10 High Ridge Rd Wilton CT 06897

ROUSSMAN, VICTORIA IRENE, univ. adminstr.; b. Miami, Fla., Jan. 31, 1947; d. Harold and Jeannette Elaine (Faber) Roussman; B.A., U. South Fla., 1969; M.A., U. Ia., 1971. Grad. asst. U. Ia., 1969-71, asst. program adviser, 1969-71; program dir. Central Fla. Jewish Community Center, Orlando, 1971-72; dir. student activities, dir. student center Wilmington (O.) Coll., 1972—. Block book coordinator Ohio unit Nat. Entertainment Conf., 1973-74. Travel grantee Am. Zionist Youth Found., 1970. Mem. Nat. Assn. Women Deans, Adminstrs. and Counselors, Nat. Assn. Student Personnel Adminstrs., Assn. Coll. Unions-Internat., Am. Assn. U. Women. Home: 536 Orange Av Apt 10 Altamonte Springs FL 32701

ROWDEN, MARJORIE COLE (MRS. PAUL D. ROWDEN), ednl. adminstr.; b. Atlanta, Apr. 4, 1924; d. Byron H. and Alma (Kelly) Cole; B.A., Agnes Scott Coll., 1945; M.R.E., New Orleans Bapt. Theol. Sem., 1962; m. Paul D. Rowden, June 8, 1946; children—Rebecca (Mrs. Robert C. Walker), Robin, Richard, Paige. Missionary, So. Bapt. Fgn. Mission Bd., Israel, 1951-59; dir. pub. relations, asst. prof. religion William Carey Coll., Hattiesburg, Miss., 1962—. Publicity dir. United Givers Fund, 1966, Cancer Drive, 1968; sec. Hattiesburg Civic Arts Council, 1972-73. Named Outstanding Alumnae, New Orleans Bapt. Sem., 1973, Mother of Year, Hattiesburg, 1973. Mem. Bapt. Assn. for Profs. of Religion, Alpha Delta Kappa, Pi Tau Chi. Baptist (mem. youth outreach commission 1968-72). Author: Three Davids, 1963; The Flying Dragon, 1969; also articles. Home: 615 Woodbine Lane Hattiesburg MS 39401

ROWE, CAROLIN BOEHM (MRS. THEODORE SPURLING ROWE), rubber co. exec.; b. Ceylon, O., May 19, 1900; d. Conrad and Kathryn (Ackerman) Boehm; student Akron U., 1932-33, Kent State U., 1941; m. Theodore Spurling Rowe, June 30, 1931; children—Julie (Mrs. Scott Thomas Schueneman). Vice pres. and dir. Hamilton Kent Mfg. Co., Kent, O., 1945—; dir. Flexlock Corp., Kent, 1945—, Hamilton Kent of Can., Toronto, 1957—, Freeport Rubber Co. (Bahamas), 1960—. Co-founder Kent Girl Scout Assn., 1935, pres. 1935-37; mem. Women's Assn. Robinson Mem. Hosp. Mem. Thenus Soc. (pres. 1968), Dulin Art Gallery, Cuyahoga Falls Art Center, Sarasota Art Assn., Delta Zeta Alumnae Assn. (past pres.). Clubs: Women's City (Akron, O.); Twin Lakes Country (Kent, O.). Home: 1613 Woodway Rd Kent OH 44240 Office: 2144 E Main St Kent OH 44240

ROWE, DORIS EVELYN WILSON (MRS. JOHN H. ROWE), pediatrician; b. Spokane, Wash., June 2, 1926; d. Paul G. and Florence H. (Butler) Wilson; B.S., Wash. State U., 1948; M.D., Washington U., St. Louis, 1952; m. John H. Rowe, June 8, 1950; children—Stuart, Chip, Patricia, Scot, Kel. Intern, USPHS Hosp., Chgo., 1952-53; resident Henrietta Eggleston Hosp., Memphis, 1953-54; pediatrician So. Cal. Permanente Med. Group, Harbor City, 1954—; mem. staff Kaiser Found. Hosp., Harbor City. Mem. So. Bay, Los Angeles County pediatric socs. Home: 2609 Via Segunda St Palos Verdes Estates CA 90274 Office: 1050 Pacific Coast Hwy Harbor City CA 90710

ROWE, JO ANN (MRS. PRENTISS ELDON ROWE), columnist, radio news reporter; b. Colorado Springs, May 9, 1924; d. Carl Ransom and Zoe Ella (Smith) Osborn; student Colo. Coll., 1943-47, Tulsa U., 1947-49, Colo. U., 1973-74; m. Prentiss Eldon Rowe, Aug. 7, 1947; children—Carl Osborn, Prentiss Tomblin, Melanie Ann, David Lee. Womens dir. sta. KVOR-CBS, Colorado Springs, Colo., 1951-56, sta. KKTV, Colorado Springs, 1958-68, sta. KRDO-ABC AM-TV, Colorado Springs, 1957-64; pub. affairs dir. sta. KSSS, Ridder Publs., Colorado Springs, 1964—; columnist Colorado Springs Free Press, 1963-65, Times publ., 1972—. Bd. dirs. Nat. Council on Alcoholism, Civil Def. Authority. Mem. Am. Women in Radio and TV, Colorado Springs Press Assn., Am. Assn. U. Women, Foremost Women in Communication. Published: The Party Line Cookbook, 1963; The Best of Party Line, 1968. Home: 1009 Parkview Blvd Colorado Springs CO 80906 Office: 3939 E San Miguel Colorado Springs CO 80901

ROWE, JUDITH LYNN CORDSEN, occupational therapist; b. Lake Charles, La., Aug. 22, 1940; d. Frederick Casper and Mary Jane (Jernigan) Cordsen; B.S. with honors, U. Puget Sound, 1962; m. Ronald Kenneth Rowe, Sept. 15, 1962; children—Kent Michael, Scott Benson. Staff therapist H.T. Buckner Rehab. Center, 1963-64; co-dir. occupational therapy U. Ore. Med. Sch., 1965; cons. establishment of stroke unit Good Samaritan Hosp., 1969; pvt. practice occupational therapy, cons., 1966-71; staff therapist Holladay Center for Physically Handicapped Children of Portland (Ore.) Pub. Sch. Dist., 1971—. Chmn. Western Internat. Conf. for Occupational Therapy and Physical Therapy, 1968. Mem. Am., Ore. occupational therapy assns., Occupational Therapy Assn. Ore. (pres. 1966-68), Pi Beta Phi. Home: 7120 S W Gable Pkwy Portland OR 97225 Office: 2600 S E 71st St Portland OR 97206

ROWELL, MARGARET KENNY (MRS. GORDON ALLEN ROWELL), librarian; b. Fall River, Mass., June 11, 1906; d. Bernard Francis and Catherine (Connell) Kenny; A.B., Brown U., 1927; M.Ed., Boston U., 1932; B.S. in L.S. with high honors, Columbia, 1937; m. Gordon Allen Rowell, Nov. 20, 1948; 1 dau., Mary (Mrs. Georges Emile Mony). Tchr. English, librarian St. Regis Falls (N.Y.) High Sch., 1929-31; tchr. English, librarian Central Square (N.Y.) High Sch., 1933-36; cataloger Hunter Coll. Library, N.Y.C., 1937-42; chief catalog librarian Bklyn. Coll. Library, 1942-64; librarian-in-charge Grad. Sch. Library, City U. N.Y., 1965—. Mem. Spl. Libraries Assn., Am. Soc. Information Sci., N.Y. Tech. Service Librarians, Beta Phi Mu. Club: New York Library, Brown University, Pembroke (N.Y.C.). Editor library catalogs. Home: 67-38 108th St Forest Hills NY 11375 Office: 33 W 42d St New York City NY 10036

ROWELL, ZOULA ORENA FERYALL (MRS. CLINTON H. ROWELL), civic worker; b. Hudson, N.H., July 31, 1902; d. Fred Alex and Angeline (Salvail) Feryall; student Nashua Bus. Coll., 1920-21, N.H. Coll., 1959-60; m. Clinton H. Rowell, Sept. 18, 1923; children—Clifton H., Maizelle Louise (dec.), Fred Winston. Exec. sec. A.R.C., Nashua, N.H., 1919-24; supr. registry of deeds indexing project Hillsborough County, 1935-39; exec. asst. to supr. U.S. Forest Service, Nashua, 1939-40; personnel supr., base hosp. exec. asst. to comdg. officer base hosp. Grenier Field, Manchester, N.H., 1941-50; exec. sec. State Bd. Architects and Engrs., State of N.H., Concord, 1951-54; office mgr. Rowell & Miller, Inc., elec. contractors, Hudson, 1954-64, dir., 1954-56. Mem. Hudson Civil Def. Com., 1955-57; dist. dir. Girl Scouts, Hudson, 1950-54; chmn. or clk. Recreation Commn. Town of Hudson, 1945-72; Hudson chmn. A.R.C. drive, 1940, Cancer drive, 1950-60, Heart Fund drive, 1971, Dollars for Scholars, 1972-74; mem. Com. for Celebration of 300th Anniversary of Founding of Hudson, 1973; vol. worker St. Joseph Hosp. Aux., Nashua, 1960-68; Hudson chmn. St. Joseph Hosp. Bldg. Fund, 1967. Recipient Thanks Badge, Girl Scouts U.S.A., 1951; commendation Hudson Women's Club, 1960, N.H. Assn. of Blind, 1966; Citizen of Yr. award Hudson C. of C., 1973. Mem. N.H. Fedn. Women's Clubs (dir. 1958—), Cath. Daus. Am. (grand regent 1966-67, trustee 1967-70), St. John's Cath. Women's Guild (pres. 1949-50), Hudson Hist. and Cultural Soc. (dir. 1966-72). Clubs: Hudson Fortnightly Woman's (pres. 1957-59, 72-73), Hudson County Extension Service (pres. 1935-40), Hudson Sr. Citizens' Club (v.p. 1974-75). Home: 164 Webster St Hudson NH 03051 Office: 154 Webster St Hudson NH 03051

ROWEN, RUTH HALLE (MRS. SEYMOUR M. ROWEN), musicologist; b. N.Y.C., Apr. 5, 1918; d. Louis and Ethel (Fried) Halle; B.A., Barnard Coll., 1939; M.A., Columbia, 1941, Ph.D., 1948; m. Seymour M. Rowen, Oct. 13, 1940; children—Mary Helen (Mrs. David Obelkevich), Louis Halle. Mgt. ednl. dept. Carl Fischer, Inc., N.Y.C., 1954-63; asso. prof. musicology Coll. City N.Y., 1967-72, prof., 1972—; mem. doctoral faculty in musicology City U. N.Y., 1967—. Mem. A.S.C.A.P., Am. Musicological Soc., Music Library Assn., Coll. Music Soc., Nat. Fedn. Music Clubs (nat. musicianship chmn. 1962—, nat. young artist auditions com. 1964—), Phi Beta Kappa. Author: Early Chamber Music, 1948; (with Adele T. Katz) Hearing—Gateway to Music, 1959; (with William Simon) Jolly Come Sing and Play, 1956. Home: 115 Central Park W New York City NY 10023

ROWLAND, BETTY A., orgn. exec.; b. Phila., Mar. 7, 1930; d. Robert A. and Zora (Whitehead) Rowland; B.S., Tex. Christian U., 1952; M.S.W., Tulane U., 1957. Health and edn. dir. Ft. Worth YWCA, 1950-52; dist. adv. Circle T Girl Scout Council, Ft. Worth, 1952-55, asst. exec. dir., 1959-63; dist. adv. council Girl Scouts of Am., New Orleans, 1957-59; exec. dir. Lone Star Council, Girl Scouts of Am., Austin, Tex., 1963—. Mem. Assn. Girl Scout Profl. Workers. Home: 7409 Shadow Hill Apt 109 Austin TX 78731 Office: 1305 W 34th St Austin TX 78705

ROWLAND, E(DITH) ALDREA JOHNSON, librarian; b. Virginia, Minn., Oct. 18, 1911; d. Emil Aldren and Mary Helga (Forsberg) Johnson; A.B. with honors, Bradley U., 1933; B.S. in L.S., U. Ill., 1940, M.S. (Am. Assn. U. Women scholar), 1960; postgrad. Del Mar Coll., Tex. Coll. Arts and Industries, Simpson Coll., U. Wis. at Milw., Ill. State U.; m. John W. Ranstead, Aug. 24, 1943 (div. 1952); m. W. Hugh Rowland, June 18, 1954 (div. 1955). Cataloger, asst. librarian Peoria (Ill.) Pub. Library, 1933-39, 54-56, Bradley U., 1940-42, 56-59, U.S. Naval Air Tng. Sta., Corpus Christi, Tex., 1942-46, Del Mar Coll., 1946-50, 53-54; librarian Robstown (Tex.) High Sch., 1950-54, Simpson Coll., 1960-64, U. Wis. at Milw., 1964-67, Ill. Central Coll., East Peoria, 1967—; book reviewer. Mem. A.L.A., Ill. Library Assn., Ill. Valley Librarians Assn., Am. Assn. U. Women, YWCA, Lakeview Center Arts and Scis., Sweet Adelines, Inc. Republican. Christian Scientist. Home: 1310 N Glenwood Av Peoria IL 61606 Office: PO Box 2400 East Peoria IL 61611

ROWLAND, SISTER M. JOYCE, coll. pres.; b. Mpls., Oct. 31, 1922; d. John F. and Olivia (Joyce) Rowland; B.A., Coll. St. Teresa, 1949; M.A., U. Minn., 1953; Ph.D., St. Louis U., 1962. Instr. Catholic jr. and sr. high schs., Diocese of Winona, Minn., 1944-53; instr. dept. edn. Coll. St. Teresa, Winona, 1953-56; directress of postulants Sisters of St. Francis, Rochester, Minn., 1953-57; asst. dept. philosophy St. Louis U., 1960-61; asst. prof., chmn. dept. religion and philosophy Coll. St. Teresa, 1962-66; asst. to chaplain Newman Center, Winona State Coll., 1963-66; initiator Upward Bound program, dir. Coll. St. Teresa, 1965-66, v.p., dean, 1967-69, pres., 1969—; Ford fellow Atlanta U., 1966-67. Mem. Winona County Assn. for Retarded Children, 1968—. Bd. dirs. Nat. Council Ind. Colls. and Univs., 1973-75, Community Devel. Corp., Southeastern Minn. Citizens Action Council, 1972-74. Mem. Am. Assn. U. Women, Am. Assn. Higher Edn., Minn. Edn. Assn., Nat. Council Adminstr. Women in Edn., Assn. Minn. Colls. (pres. 1971-72), Nat. Cath. Edn. Assn. (exec. com. coll. and univ. dept. 1973-74), Nat. Indian Edn. Assn., Am. Assn. Univ. Adminstrs. Home: Coll Saint Teresa Winona MN 55987

ROWLAND, PATSY DEAN, educator; b. Simsboro, La., Mar. 6, 1926; d. Talmage and Dora Mae Durrett; ed. Northwestern State Coll. (La.), East Tenn. State U.; B.A., M.A.; m. Oct. 6, 1946; children—Malissa, Roger, Shell. Tchr. elementary schs.; now tchr. Andrew Jackson Sch., Kingsport, Tenn., and organizer Sch. Children's Mus. Mem. Sullivan County Am. Bicentennial Com. Mem. N.E.A., Tenn., East Tenn., Kingsport edn. assns., Alpha Delta Kappa. Home: 580 Bays View Rd Kingsport TN 37660 Office: Andrew Jackson School Jackson St Kingsport TN 37660

ROWLEY, ELIZABETH VANCE (MRS. DAVID ALLEN), advt. exec.; b. Bellingham, Wash., Aug. 13, 1927; d. Edward Daniel and Esther Lucile (Wright) Whalen. Student U. Wash., 1945-46; m. David Allen Rowley, Aug. 4, 1956. Media dir. Cole & Weber, Inc., Seattle, Wash., 1955-68, Ricks-Ehrig, Inc., Seattle, 1968—; owner Media Monitor Service, Seattle, Portland, Ore. and Spokane, Wash., 1971—. Club: Seattle Yacht. Home: 2831 W Elmore Pl Seattle WA 98199 Office: 1810 Plaza 600 Seattle WA 98101

ROWLEY, KATHLEEN ALICIA, editor; b. Collingdale, Pa., Feb. 8, 1925; d. Bart J. and Virginia F. (Burk) Rowley; student Harvard, summers 1949, 50; B.A. in Polit. Sci., Bryn Mawr Coll., 1951; M.A., Yale, 1954; postgrad., 1955-56; postgrad. U. Brussels (Belgium), 1954-55. Intern pub. adminstrn., Fulbright scholar Internat. Inst. Adminstrv. Scis., Brussels, 1954-55; tng. rep. Strawbridge & Clothier, Phila., 1958-60; instr. polit. sci. Vassar Coll., Poughkeepsie, N.Y., 1957-58; acting instr. govt. Coll. William and Mary, Williamsburg, Va.; reporter Phila. Inquirer, 1944-45; reporter Courier-Post, Camden, N.J., 1960-69, consumer writer, 1970-72, spl. features editor, 1972-74, asst. news feature editor, 1974—. Served with USNR, 1945-46. Recipient pub. service award Sigma Delta Chi, 1968. Mem. N.J. Daily Newspaper Women (pres. 1974—, 1st place award for series 1964, best in series 1969, 1st place fashion 1972, named Woman of Year 1972, dir. 1967-72, 73-74), Phila. Press Assn. (Gold Typewriter award 1964, 70). Phila. Press Assn. (sec. 1966-73), Nat. Editorial Assn. (1st prize for feature series 1964), N.J. Press Assn. (2d place award for series on poverty 1966). Club: Zonta (dir. Camden 1974—). Home: 715 Clifton Av Collingdale PA 19023 Office: Courier-Post Camden NJ 08101

ROXAS, SAVINA AMICO D'AGNESSA (MRS. RICHARD A. ROXAS), educator, writer; b. N.Y.C., Nov. 3, 1916; d. Peter Mario and Rosa (Muscillo) D'Agnessa; B.A., Duquesne U., 1957; M.L.S., Carnegie Inst. Tech., 1960; Ph.D., U. Pitts., 1970; m. Richard A. Roxas, Sept. 2, 1939; children—Dianne (Mrs. Ross K. Lindsey), Rita. Reference librarian Carnegie Inst. Tech., Pitts., 1960-61; cataloger Duquesne U., Pitts., 1961-63, instr., 1962-64; teaching fellow U. Pitts., 1964-65, instr., 1965-70; prof. library information sci. Clarion (Pa.) State Coll., 1970-72; writer, cons., 1972—. Chmn. parochial schs. Women's Assn. Pitts. Symphony, 1960—; area chmn. Am. Cancer Soc., 1962-63, United Fund, 1973. Mem. Am., Pa. library assns., Spl. Libraries Assn., Am. Assn. U. Profs., Pitts. Bibliog. Soc., Psi Chi, Sigma Tau Delta, Beta Phi Mu. Author: Library Education in Italy: an Historical Survey, 1869-70, 1971. Contbr. to Ency. of Library and Information Sciences. Address: 265 Sleepy Hollow Rd Pittsburgh PA 15216

ROY, ELSIJANE TRIMBLE (MRS. JAMES M. ROY), lawyer; b. Lonoke, Ark., Apr. 2, 1916; d. Thomas Clark and Elsie Jane (Walls) Trimble; J.D., U. Ark., 1939; m. James M. Roy, Nov. 23, 1943; 1 son, James Morrison. Admitted to Ark. bar, 1939; mem. firm Reid, Evrard & Roy, Blytheville, Ark., 1947-54, Roy & Roy, Blytheville, 1954-63; atty. Ark. Revenue Dept., Little Rock, 1939-64; law clk. Ark. Supreme Ct., Little Rock, 1963-65; judge Pulaski County Circuit Ct., Little Rock, 1966; asst. atty. gen. State of Ark. Little Rock, 1967; sr. law clk. U.S. Dist. Ct., Little Rock and Ft. Smith, 1968-73. Mem. med. adv. com. U. Ark. Med. Center, 1952-54; mem. chmn. com. Ark. Constnl. Commn., 1967-68. Committeewoman Democratic party 16th Jud. Dist., 1940-42; vice-chmn. Ark. Dem. State Com., 1946-48. Mem. Nat. Assn. Women Lawyers, Ark. Bar Assn., Am. Assn. U. Women, Little Rock Women Lawyers (pres. 1939, 42), U. Ark. Alumni Assn. (dir. 1946-48), Ark. Women Lawyers (pres. 1940-1941), Mortar Bd., P.E.O., Chi Omega. Home: El Conquistador Apts 5900 Kinkead Apt #110 Fort Smith AR 72901 Office: Box 1623 Fort Smith AR 72901

ROY, GABRIELLE (MRS. MARCEL CARBOTTE), writer; b. St. Boniface, Man., Can.; d. Leon and Melina (Landry) Roy; student Institut Collegial St. Joseph, St. Boniface, Normal Sch., Winnipeg, Man.; m. Marcel Carbotte, Aug. 30, 1947. Tchr. pub. schs., St. Boniface; free-lance writer for Canadian papers and mags., Montreal, Que., 1939—. Recipient Prixfemina, 1947; Gov. Gen. award; Prix Duvernay; Medaille de L'Academie Francaise; companion Order of Can. Mem. Royal Soc. Can. Author: (novels) The Tin Flute, 1947; Where Nests the Water Hen, 1951; The Cashier; Street of Riches; The Hidden Mountain; The Road Past Altamont, 1966; Windflower, 1970. Address: 135 W Grande Allee Apt 302 Quebec Canada

ROY, JOYCE ELIZABETH ENSLIN (MRS. HAROLD E. ROY), educator; b. N.Y.C., Apr. 28, 1923; d. Eugene and Elizabeth Enslin; student Duke, 1941-43; B.S. in Early Childhood Edn., Tchrs. Coll., Columbia, 1945; M.A. in Spl. Edn. (Elks scholar), Cal. State U., 1967; m. Harold E. Roy, Oct. 4, 1946; children—Glenn E., Barbara Anne and Suzanne Elizabeth (twins). Tchr. elementary schs., 1945—, including Byron Thompson Orthopedic Sch., El Monte, Cal.; instr. LaVerne (Cal.) Coll., 1968-70, Pepperdine U., Los Angeles, 1970—. Tchr. parents handicapped children Tri-Community Adult Sch., Covina, Cal., 1967-70; adviser, lectr. Hope House for Multiple Handicapped Children; condr. art insts. for tchrs. of physically handicapped. Mem. Cal. Assn. for Neurologically Handicapped Children (dir., lectr.), Cal. Assn. Profs. Spl. Edn., Am. Assn. U. Women, N.E.A., Cal. Tchrs. Assn., Allied Artists Glendora, Acad. Parapsychology and Medicine, Kappa Delta Pi (regional alumni dir. 1967-69). Republican. Mem. P.E. Ch. Contbr. articles to local newspapers. Home: 18853 E Sierra Madre Av Glendora CA 91740 Office: Pepperdine University 8035 S Vermont Av Los Angeles CA 90044

ROYE, JOSEPHINE ELIZABETH SHULTZ (MRS. BENJAMIN FRANKLIN ROYE), librarian; b. Washingtonboro, Pa., Sept. 21, 1914; d. John Jacob and Elizabeth (Shertzer) Shultz; B.S., Millersville State Coll., 1958; M.S., Drexel U., 1964; postgrad. Cath. U. Am.; m. Benjamin Franklin Roye, Mar. 2, 1940; children—Madeline (Mrs. Max Zung), Charles Richard. Librarian, Eastern High Sch., Wrightsville, Pa., 1958-63, Columbia (Pa.) High Sch., 1963-66; acquisitions librarian Pa. State U., Middletown, 1967-69; reference librarian Lancaster (Pa.) Pub. Library, 1969; reference librarian York Coll. of Pa., 1969—. Library cons. Antiques News, 1970—. Neighborhood chmn. Girl Scouts U.S.A., Columbia, Pa., 1954-55; mem. Lancaster County council Girl Scouts U.S.A., 1955-58. Mem. A.L.A., Lancaster County Library Assn., Am. Assn. U. Women, Am. Assn. U. Profs., Mennonite Hist. Soc., D.A.R. (chmn. geneal. research 1970—). Contbr. articles to publs. Home: 27 S 6th St Columbia PA 17512 Office: 321 Country Club Rd York PA 17405

ROYER, MARY NEUHAUSER, educator; b. Goshen, Ind., Dec. 26, 1907; d. Isaiah W. and Christina M. (Neuhauser) Royer; B.A., Goshen Coll., 1930; M.A., George Peabody U., 1931; Ph.D., Ohio State U., 1950; postgrad. U. Chgo., 1936, Columbia, 1943, U. Minn., 1955, U. Akron, 1956, Claremont Grad. Sch., 1964. Tchr. elementary schs., Orrville, O., 1931-33; tchr., dir. Goshen Coll. Lab. Kindergarten, 1934-36; prof. edn. Goshen Coll., 1933—; primary curriculum writer, editor Mennonite Pub. House, Scottdale, Pa., 1937-50, nursery curriculum cons., 1950—; grad. asst. dept. edn. Ohio State U., 1947-48. Mem. N.E.A., Assn. for Supervision and Curriculum Devel., Assn. for Childhood Edn., Assn. Tchr. Educators, Nat. Council Tchrs. English, Mennonite Hist. Soc. Author: Stories about God's Friends, 1948. Contbr. articles to ch. periodicals. Home: 1804 S 12th St Goshen IN 46526 Office: Goshen College Goshen IN 46526

ROZAN, DOROTHY NATALEE CAMIN, social worker; b. Detroit, Oct. 9, 1911; d. David Samuel and Minnie (Oppenhiem) Camin; student Lasell Jr. Coll., 1928-30; B.A., Mich. State U., 1938, M.S.W., 1958; m. Josef S. Rozan, Oct. 6, 1931 (dec. Dec. 1965); children—Dale (Mrs. Melvin Applebaum), Gerry Michael). Caseworker A.R.C., 1944-45; caseworker Lansing (Mich.) Family Service Agy., 1958-63, supr. Grad Sch. Social Work Students, 1963-67, exec. dir., 1967-68; psychiat. social worker Community Mental Health Center, St. Lawrence Hosp., Lansing, 1969—. Med. social work cons. Vis. Nurses Assn., Lansing, 1963-68. Pres. Ingham County Med. Aux., 1951; mem. Gov's. Conf. on Children and Youth, 1950-51; chmn. family and children's services Community Service Council, 1948-52. Bd. dirs. Planned Parenthood Assn., United Community Chest, Council on Alcoholism. Recipient award Radar Air Warning Service, 1942, awards A.R.C., 1940-43. Mem. Nat. Assn. Social Workers, Acad. Certified Social Workers, Coll. Women's Vol. Service (pres. 1950), Mich. Assn. Emotionally Disturbed Children. Author: (with Anne DeRose) Blueprint . . . A Volunteer Program, 1973. Contbr. articles, short stories to nat. publs. Home: 1271 Mulberry Lane East Lansing MI 48823 Office: St Lawrence Hosp Community Mental Health Center Oakland Av Lansing MI 48914

RUBEN, NOREEN ANN BADRY (MRS. GUENTER RUDI RUBEN), librarian; b. Galahad, Alta., Can., Mar. 29, 1948; d. Joseph Adolph and Helen (Lenhart) Badry; B.S., Notre Dame U., Nelson, B.C., 1969; m. Guenter Rudi Ruben, Nov. 24, 1973. Dir. med. records dept. Edmonton (Alta.) Gen. Hosp., also instr. extension div. No. Alta. Inst. Tech., Edmonton, 1969—. Cons. med. record sci. No. and So. Alta. insts. tech., N.W.T. Hosp. Assn. Recipient Provincial Govt. grant, 1967-69, Citizenship award Nelson, B.C., 1969. Mem. Canadian Assn. Med. Record Librarians (pres.), Med. Record Assn. Alta. (pres. 1971-72). Home: 31 St Vital Av St Albert AB Canada Office: 11111 Jasper Av Edmonton AB Canada

RUBENS, GLORYA RUTH (MRS. JEROME RUBENS), acad. therapist; b. Chgo., Mar. 19, 1929; d. Samuel Joseph and Fritzi (Kaufman) Somberg; student U. Ill., 1946-48; B.A. in Edn., Roosevelt U., 1950; postgrad. No. Ill. U., 1968-69; M.A. in Spl. Edn., Northeastern Ill. U., 1971; m. Jerome Rubens, May 30, 1950; children—Tom, Joy, Diane, Peggy. Tchr., Chgo. pub. schs., 1949-51, Glencoe, Winnetka, Highland Park, Ill., 1955-56; tchr., counselor emotionally disturbed New Trier East High Sch., Winnetka, 1969-71, Spl. Edn. Dist. Lake County (Ill.), Gurnee, 1971—. Mem. Clergy and Laymen Concerned, Council on Fgn. Relations, Internat. Visitors Assn., Common Cause, Am. Civil Liberties Union, Am. Orthopsychiat. Assn., Council on Exceptional Children, Fund for Perceptually Handicapped, Am. Council U. Women. Home: 476 Oakdale St Glencoe IL 60022 Office: Barrington High School 615 Main St Barrington IL 60010

RUBERT, FLORENCE (MRS. PAUL A. ROSSI), author, editor, pub.; b. N.Y.C.; d. Harlem George and Florence (Cadugan) Rubert; student Elydia Shipman's Sch. Journalism, 1934-35; m. John S. Graves, Jr., June 25, 1939 (div. Aug. 1952); children—John Samuel III, Gerald Beekman, Stephen Rubert; m. 2d, John E. Wray, July, 1959 (div. Aug. 1966); m. 3d, Paul A. Rossi, Oct. 29, 1969. Founder, editor, pub. Rubert Publs., Fayetteville, Ark. 1963—, Bella Vista Press, Fayetteville, 1964—; established Asso. Arts Services, 1968. Lectr. poetry, creativity, writing. Edn. chmn. Am. Cancer Soc., Fayetteville, United Ch. Women; founder-pres. Bella Vista Fine Arts Center, 1963-67. Bd. dirs. Ark. Arts Festival, 1966-71; sec. bd. dirs. South and West, Inc., 1962-64. Recipient numerous prizes, awards for poetry. Fellow Internat. Inst. Arts and Letters (life); mem. Nat. Hist. Soc., Acad. Am. Poets, Authors Composers and Artists Soc., Poetry Soc. Ga., Poetry Soc. Tenn., Poets Roundtable Ark., Ariz. State Poetry Soc., Poetry Soc. Tex., Ozark Writers and Artists Guild (pres. 1967-71), World Poetry Soc., Nat. League Am. Pen Women, Ark. Writers Conf., United Poets Laureate Internat., Soc. Southwestern Authors (dir. 1973—), Nat. Fedn. State Poetry Socs. Inc. (2d vice chancellor 1966-67, 4th v.p. 1968-69, editor Strophes), also member of Sigma Alpha Iota, Sigma Omicron Alumnae. Episcopalian. Author: Spring Tide, 1963. Editor numerous books, anthologies. Home: 814 W Chula Vista Rd Tucson AZ 85704

RUBERT, SHIRLEY LANEY, physician; b. Little Falls, N.Y., Mar. 7, 1927; d. Charles A. and Geraldine A. (Gilman) Rubert; B.A., Cornell U., 1948; M.D., Woman's Med. Coll. Pa., 1952. Intern, asst. resident, resident, instr. internal medicine State U. N.Y. Upstate Med. Center, Syracuse, 1952-57, resident to chief resident psychiatry, 1957-60, instr. psychiatry, 1960-61, asst. prof., 1961-68, clin. asst. prof., 1968-70, clin. asso. prof., 1970-72, asso. prof., 1972—; practice medicine, specializing in psychiatry, 1968—; unit chief Hutchings Psychiat. Center, Syracuse, 1972—. Diplomate Am. Bd. Psychiatry and Neurology. Democrat. Home: Rose Hill Rd RD 1 Marietta NY 13110 Office: 415 State Tower Bldg Syracuse NY 13202

RUBIN, AUGUSTA, musicologist; b. N.Y.C., July 1, 1904; d. Samuel and Ray (Whitestone) Katz; B.S., Juilliard Sch. Music, 1942; M.A., Columbia U., 1943; artist diploma as pianist, 1922; diploma of theory and composition Inst. Mus. Art Conservatory, 1940; m. Samuel Rubin, Mar. 21, 1921; children—Isaiah A., Gabriel K., Matonah A. Tchr. theory and composition Inst. Mus. Art, 1923-26, and privately, 1926-43; dir. Rubin Bros. Holding Co. Mem. Met. Opera Guild, Music Library Assn., Am. Mus. Soc., Renaissance Soc. Am. (founding mem.). Author: J.S. Bach, The Contemporary Composer, 1974. Home: 62 E 80th St New York City NY 10021 Office: care Rubin Bros Holding Co 375 Fifth Av New York City NY 10021

RUBIN, BLANCHE AUDREY, social worker; b. N.Y.C.; d. Alfred Bennett and Beatrice (Schan) Rubin; B.S., N.Y. U.; M.S.W., Columbia; postgrad. U. Pitts., Yale. Caseworker, Family Service Allegheny County, Pitts.; asst. dir. Jewish Family Service, Hartford, Conn.; chief psychiat. social worker Bklyn. Child Guidance Center, N.Y.C.; psychiat. social worker Bellevue Psychiat. Hosp., N.Y.C.; unit supt. Service to Mil. Families A.R.C. Greater N.Y., case supr., asst. dir., dir., 1963-73; dir. govt.-funded programs Harriman-Met. div. A.R.C., 1973—. Cons. A.R.C. neighboring chpts., 1965—; mem. Selective Service Bd., Queens, N.Y.; pres., Hebron Yeshivah Jr. League. Mem. Acad. Certified Social Workers, Scroll. Mem. B'nai B'rith. Club: Quota Internat. (pres. N.Y.C. 1973). Address: 41-10 Bowne St Flushing NY 11355 Office: 150 Amsterdam Av New York City NY 10023

RUBIN, DOROTHY WEIMAN (MRS. JACOB S. RUBIN), clubwoman; b. Detroit, July 19, 1913; d. Hyman and Sarah (Franklin) Weiman; B.S., Wayne State U., 1936, M.Ed., 1952; m. Jacob S. Rubin, Mar. 19, 1967. Tchr. pub. schs., Detroit, 1937-67. Served with A.R.C., ETO, 1944-45; treas. Detroit local Am. Overseas Assn., 1947-48; nat. treas. Women's Overseas Service League, 1951-52; pres. Assn. Univ. Women, Crookston, Minn., 1968-69; mem. exec. bd. Am. Assn. U. Women, 1970-72; sec. Hadassah, Alexandria, La., 1972—. Jewish religion (pres. Temple Sisterhood 1974). Home: 5024 Jackson St Alexandria LA 71301

RUBIN, JOAN ALLEMAN (MRS. ROBERT RUBIN), editor; b. Hanover, Pa., Oct. 1, 1931; d. Richard B. and Kathrine (Eckert) Alleman; B.A., William and Mary Coll., 1953; m. Robert Rubin, July 30, 1955; children—Thomas, Andrew. Asso. editor Mademoiselle mag., N.Y.C., 1953-60; free-lance mag. writer, 1960-65; editor-in-chief Playbill Mag., N.Y.C., 1965—. Home: 172 Sullivan St New York City NY 10012 Office: 485 Lexington Av New York City NY 10021

RUBIN, LAURA CONSTANCE GUINNUP (MRS. HOWARD SAUL RUBIN, JR.), pub. relations exec.; b. Franklin, Ind., July 5, 1947; d. James Edward and Nell Alford (Finlay) Guinnup; B.A., Purdue U., 1969; postgrad. U. Mo., 1969; m. Howard Saul Rubin, Jr., June 12, 1971. Grad. asst. U. Mo., Columbia, summer 1969; women's staff writer Jour.-Courier newspaper, Lafayette, Ind., 1969-71; freelance writer Noble-Dury & Assos., pub. relations, Nashville, 1971; editorial asst. for alumni publs. Vanderbilt U., Nashville, 1971-73; promotions dir. Haines & Co., Inc., pubs., North Canton, O., 1974—. Mem. League Women Voters, Women in Communications, Chi Omega, Psi Iota Xi. Republican. Episcopalian. Home: 1302 McGregor Av NW Canton OH 44703 Office: 8050 Freedom Av NW North Canton OH 44720

RUBIN, ROBERTA GAIL (MRS. WALTER D'ULL), physician; b. Bklyn., Apr. 2, 1934; d. Victor and Pearl (Berger) Rubin; student Cornell U., 1951-54; M.D., State U. N.Y. Downstate Med. Center, 1958; m. Walter D'Ull, Nov. 1, 1964; children—Leon Jesse, Victoria Roslyn. Intern, Jewish Hosp., Bklyn., 1958-59; resident N.Y. U.-Bellevue Med. Center, 1959-63; spl. fellow Inst. Neurol. Diseases and Blindness, N.Y. State Psychiat. Inst., N.Y.C., 1963-64; asst. pathologist Maimonides Hosp. Center, Bklyn., 1964-67; asso. pathologist Bronx-Lebanon Hosp. Center, Bronx, 1967-68; pathologist Chilton Meml. Hosp., Pompton Plains, N.J., 1968—; dir. Pathologists' Med. Lab., Wayne, N.J., 1973—; clin. instr. pathology State U. N.Y. Downstate Med. Center, Bklyn., 1964-67; clin. instr. pathology Albert Einstein Coll., Bronx, 1967-68. Diplomate Am. Bd. Pathology. Fellow Am. Soc. Clin. Pathologists, Coll. Am. Pathologists; mem. N.J. Soc. Pathologists, N.Y. Pathol. Soc., A.M.A., Am. Med. Women's Assn., N.J. Med. Assn., Passaic County Med. Soc. Home: 168 Midland Av Montclair NJ 07042 Office: 97 W Parkway Pompton Plains NJ 07444 also 1777 Hamburg Turnpike Wayne NJ 07470

RUBIN, ROSALYN AARON, psychologist, educator; b. Mpls., Sept. 29, 1933; d. Meyer and Mary (Resnick) Aaron; B.A. magna cum laude, U. Minn., 1954, B.S., 1955, M.A., 1957, Ph.D., 1961; m. Edmond H. Rubin, Dec. 18, 1960; children—Ellen Judith, Beth Joanne. Sch. psychologist, research coordinator Robbinsdale (Minn.) Pub. Schs., 1960-63; asst. prof. psychology Macalester Coll., St. Paul, 1964-66; research asso. ednl. psychology and spl. edn. U. Minn., Mpls., 1966—, interim dir. research and devel. Center in Edn. Handicapped Children, 1971, asso. prof. ednl. psychology and spl. edn., 1971—, project dir. Ednl. and Behavioral Sequelae of Prenatal and Perinatal Conditions, 1971—. Ednl. and psychol. cons. local pub. and pvt. schs., 1963-68. Mem. Am. Ednl. Research Assn., Am. Psychol. Assn., Council for Exceptional Children. Contbr. articles profl. jours. Home: 681 Woodlawn Av St Paul MN 55116 Office: Pattee Hall U Minn Minneapolis MN 55455

RUBIN, SUSAN SMITH, museum ofcl.; b. St. Petersburg, Fla., Sept. 8, 1943; d. George Theo and Lorraine Adair (Olsen) Smith; B.A. in Sociology, U. Ariz., 1965; postgrad. Okla. State U.; m. Robert H. Rubin, Sept. 4, 1965; children—Mark, Barry, Karen. Distributive edn. tchr.-coordinator Guthrie (Okla.) High Sch., 1967; service rep. Southwestern Bell Telephone Co., 1968-71; asso. dir. Okla. State U. Mus., 1971—. County sec. Cancer Crusade, 1971-73; vol. caseworker County Dept. Social Services, 1968-71. Bd. dirs. Stillwater United Fund, 1973—; mem. Sheerar Community Center Mus. Trust. Carnegie Found. grantee, India, 1963-64. Mem. Okla. Mus. Assn. (curriculum and profl. standards com.), Rotary Anns (pres. Stillwater 1971-72), Tau Beta Sigma, Phi Gamma Mu, Delta Pi Epsilon. Home: 901 W Eskridge St Stillwater OK 74074

RUBINOWITZ, ARTHUREA BROWN (MRS. STANLEY HENRY RUBINOWITZ), educator; b. nr. Mobile, Ala.; d. Arthur Isom and Beatrice (Knight) Brown; student Livingston (Ala.) Coll., 1934-36, Hardin-Simmons U., Tex., 1941-42; B.A., Am. U., 1958, M.A., 1960, Ed.D., 1966; m. Stanley Henry Rubinowitz, Aug. 6, 1943; children—Arthur Lee, Ben Brown. Tchr. schs., Ala., Tex., Va., Germany, 1935-60; prin. Fairfax Pub. Schs., Va., 1961-68; asst. adminstr., dir. instrn. K-12, Fairfax County Pub. Schs., 1968-70, area sch. supt., 1971—; professorial lectr. Am. U., 1964—, U. Va., 1967—. Cons. Title III Edn. Center, Ft. Belvoir, Va. Mem. Nat., Va., Fairfax County (personnel policy and salary coms.) edn. assns., Nat. Council on Measurement Edn., Assn. of Supervision and Curriculum Devel., Nat., Va., Fairfax County (pres. 1967-68) elementary prins. assns., Am. Edn. Research Assn. (participant 1967 pre-session), Assn. for Childhood Edn. Internat., Dept. Elementary Sch. Prins., Delta Kappa Gamma, Alpha Delta Kappa. Author articles in field. Home: 6115 Clearbrook Dr Springfield VA 22150

RUBINTON, PHYLLIS NEWMAN (MRS. NOEL RUBINTON), librarian; b. Bklyn., Mar. 24, 1927; d. Simon and Lillian Leata (Levy) Newman; B.A., Wellesley Coll., 1949; M.L.S., Pratt Inst., 1967; m. Noel Rubinton, June 19, 1949; children—Sarah Beth, Noel. Asst. librarian N.Y. Psychiat. Inst., 1967-69; librarian N.Y. Psychoanalytic Inst., N.Y.C., 1970—. Mem. Am. Library Assn., Spl. Libraries Assn., Med. Library Assn., Regional Med. Library Assn. (mem. continuing edn. com. 1972—), Beta Phi Mu. Club: Wellesley (pres. Bklyn. 1960-61, program chmn. N.Y.C. 1963-65) (N.Y.C.). Editorial bd. Vital Notes on Med. Periodicals, 1970—; co-editor Psychoanalytic Libraries Newsletter, 1972—. Home: 505 E 79th St New York City NY 10021 Office: 247 E 82d St New York City NY 10028

RUBIS, LORRAINE JOYCE, surgeon; b. Mpls., Aug. 23, 1943; d. Lawrence Martin and Ann (Bakos) Rubis; B.A., U. Minn., 1964, M.D., 1968. Intern, Cleve. Met. Gen. Hosp., 1968-69; resident surgery Case Western Res. U., Cleve., 1969-73; resident cardiovascular surgery Hosp. for Sick Children, Toronto, Ont., Can., 1973—. Mem. Phi Beta Kappa, Alpha Chi Omega. Home: 191 St George St Toronto ON M5R 2M6 Canada

RUCK, CHRISTINE MAE HETTMANNSPERGER (MRS. WILLIAM LEWIS RUCK), constrn. co. exec.; b. Charlotte, Mich., Oct. 3, 1917; d. Adam P.H. and Marie Ione (Davis) Hettmannsperger; student Western State Coll.; m. William Lewis Ruck, Nov. 29, 1934; children—Princess (Mrs. Donald Greenawalt), Charles Adam, Lillie Marie (Mrs. Juan Curtis), William Lewis II. Office mgr. Ruck Constrn. Co., Inc., 1960-69, v.p., sec., treas., after 1969. Mem. Ariz. Desert Museum, Tucson Art Center, Tucson Festival Soc. Commr., Housing Adv. and Appeals Bd. Tucson. Mem. Nat. Aero. Assn., Internat. Assn. Turtle, Trunk and Tusk, Fraternal Order of Police, 99s (local sec. 1969-70), League Women Voters. Club: Sertoma (Tucson, Ariz.). Died Nov. 15, 1973. Home: 2202 Rainbow Ridge Tucson AZ 85705

RUCKER, HELEN BORNSTEIN (MRS. B. WALLACE RUCKER), author; b. Seattle; d. Maurice and Julia (Gyle) Sello; grad. Nat. Park Coll., 1923; student Cornish Sch. Allied Arts, 1934-35, 46-47, 55-56, U. Wash.; m. B. Wallace Rucker, Jan. 30, 1932; children—B. Wallace, Stephen Morley. Unit chmn. A.R.C., 1940-45; trustee, membership chmn., sec., corrs. sec., chmn. programs spastic children Seattle Jr. Programs, 1941-56; trustee Cornish Sch. Allied Arts, 1935-38, Friends Seattle Pub. Library, 1957-60, Franklin Guild Children's Orthopedic Hosp., 1972-73; chmn. N.W. Authors Bookshelf, Seattle Pub. Library, 1964-66; mem. Jewish Am. history project U. Wash. Libraries, 1969-70. Mem. Nat. League Am. Pen Women (Seattle trustee 1964-66), Seattle Free-Lance Writers, N.W. Internat. Writers Conf., Pioneer Assn. State Wash., Phi Delta Nu. Club: Soroptimist (Seattle; co-chmn. student loan fund 1968-69). Author: Cargo of Brides, 1956, 69; The Wolf Tree, 1960; also short stories. Editor: The Bull., Friends Seattle Pub. Library, 1958-60. Home: 1620 43d Av E Seattle WA 98112

RUCKER, JUANITA JANE, educator; b. Crothersville, Ind., Nov. 5, 1910; d. Shiveral Garfield and Lutie Pearl (Deputy) Rucker; B.A., DePauw U., 1932; M.A., Northwestern U., 1939; M.A., Mich. State U., 1959. Tchr. New Castle (Ind.) Sr. High Sch., 1933-43; asst. club dir. A.R.C., London, club dir., Paris, 1943-46; tech. officer Am. Mil. Govt. Intelligence, Berlin, Germany, 1946-47; tchr. Chrysler High Sch., New Castle, Ind., 1947-71, chmn. speech dept., 1949-71; asso. prof. Center for Radio-TV, Ball State U., Muncie, 1971—. Recipient Valley Forge Freedom Found. award, 1960, New Castle Civic award Bus. and Profl. Women, 1963. Mem. Speech Assn. Am., Central States, Ind. (pres. 1960-62), speech assns., Nat. Assn. Ednl. Broadcasters, N.E.A., Nat. Council Tchr. English, Delta Kappa Gamma, Kappa Kappa Kappa (province officer 1952-56), Delta Delta Delta. Methodist. Mem. Order Eastern Star. Home: 920 Lincoln Av New Castle IN 47362 Office: Center for Radio-TV Ball State U Muncie IN 47306

RUCKER, MOLLY PATRICIA, lawyer; b. Paducah, KV., Aug. 4, 1941; d. Jack Morton and Edna Earl (Moneymaker) Rucker; student U. Miss., 1959-61, Memphis State U., 1961-62; B.S., U. Ky., 1965; J.D., Ind. U., Indpls., 1970. Accountant, Ky. Dept. Hwys., Frankfort, 1963-65, Inland Container Corp., Indpls., 1965-66; asst. controller Methodist Hosp., Indpls., 1966-67; auditor Def. Contract Audit Agy., Ft. Harrison, Ind., 1967-69; placement officer Ind. U. Law Sch., Indpls., 1969; sr. legislative analyst Ind. Legislative Council, Indpls., 1969-71; admitted to Ind. bar, 1970; pvt. practice, Indpls., 1971—. Lectr. environmental course Marian Coll., 1971. Lobbyist, Equal Rights Amendment, 1973; mem. Marion County Democratic Finance Com., 1973, Hoosiers for Equal Rights Amendment, 1973. Mem. Am. (del.), Ind., Indpls., Student (dir., treas.) bar assns., Womens Polit. Caucus, Bus. and Profl. Women. Baptist. Home: 5722 Radnor Rd Indianapolis IN 46226 Office: 2951 E 38th St Indianapolis IN 46218

RUDD, VELVA E., botanist; b. Fargo, N.D., Sept. 6, 1910; d. Harald M. and Magdelin (Schatz) Rudd; B.S., N.D. Agrl. Coll., 1931, M.S., 1932; postgrad. U. Cin., 1932-33, 37-38, U. Minn., 1933-34; Ph.D., George Washington U., 1953. Supr. sci. courses N.D. Supervised Studies, Fargo, 1935-37; sci. aid Dept. Agr., Washington, 1938-42, personnel classification officer, 1942-43; agrl. program officer Inst. Interam. Affairs, Venezuela, 1943-45; agrl. program analyst UNRRA, Washington, 1945-48; asst. curator botany dept. Nat. Mus., Smithsonian Instn., 1948-51, asso. curator, 1951-66, curator, 1966-73, research asso., 1973—; sr. research fellow, dept. biology Cal. State U., Northridge, 1973—. Instr. botany George Washington U., Washington, 1948-49, 57. Fellow A.A.A.S.; mem. Internat. Assn. Plant Taxonomists, Am. Soc. Plant Taxonomists, Soc. Bot. Mexico, Ecol. Soc. Am., Sigma Xi, Sigma Delta Epsilon. Research on leguminosae. Home: 7307 Newcastle Av Reseda CA 91335 Office: Dept Biology Cal State U Northridge CA 91324

RUDDICK, PATSY RUTH, librarian; b. Arma, Kan., Dec. 16, 1932; d. Joseph Clarence and Eva (Alumbaugh) Ruddick; A.A., Labette County Community Jr. Coll., 1952; B.S., Kan. State Coll., 1954; M.A., U. Denver, 1963; postgrad. U. Houston, Temple U., Ft. Hays Kan. State Coll. Tchr. English, Garden City (Kan.) Jr. High Sch., 1954-63; dir. library services Garden City (Kan.) Community Jr. Coll., 1963—. Faculty, Kan. State Tchrs. Coll., Emporia, 1965. Edn. chmn. Finney County unit Am. Cancer Soc., 1972-74. Mem. N.E.A., Nat. Faculty Assn., Am., Kan. library assns., Finney County Women's C. of C., Finney County Hist. Soc., City Library Assn., Delta Kappa Gamma. Methodist. Home: 628 W Olive St Garden City KS 67846 Office: 801 Campus Dr Box 977 Garden City KS 67846

RUDEN, VIOLET HOWARD (MRS. CHARLES VAN KIRK RUDEN), Christian Sci. tchr., practitioner; b. Dallas; d. Millard Fillmore and Henrietta Frederika (Kurth) Howard; B.J., U. Tex., 1931; C.S.B., Mass. Metaphys. Coll., 1946; m. Charles Van Kirk Ruden, Nov. 24, 1932. Radio continuity writer Home Mgmt. Club broadcast Sta. WHO, Des Moines, 1934; joined First Ch. of Christ Scientist, Boston, 1929; C.S. practitioner, Des Moines, 1934—; C.S. minister WAC, Ft. Des Moines, 1942-45; 1st reader 2d Ch. of Christ Scientist, Des Moines, 1952, Sunday sch. tchr., 1934—; instr. primary class in Christian Sci., 1947—. Trustee Asher Student Found. Drake U., Des Moines, 1973. Mem. Women in Communications, Mortar Bd., Orchesis, Cap and Gown. Republican. Club: Des Moines Women's. Home: 5808 Walnut Hill Dr Des Moines IA 50312 Office: 322 Shops Bldg Des Moines IA 50309

RUDER, DORIS EDITH, educator; b. Cleve., Mar. 23, 1926; d. Fredrick and Edith Catherine (Lampus) Ruder; B.S., Cleve. State U., 1949; M.A., Western Res. U. (now Case Western Res. U.), 1953. Elementary tchr. Cleve. Emergency Day Care Centers, 1944-46, Merrick House Nursery, Cleve., 1946-49, Benjamin Franklin Sch., Cleve., 1949-50, Nathaniel Hawthorne Sch., Cleve., 1950-51, Artemus Ward Sch., Cleve., 1951-56, William Rainey Harper Sch., Cleve., 1956-68, Tom L. Johnson Sch., Cleve., 1970—. Garden tchr., supr. Cleve. Sch., 1960-63; selector, writer and evaluator for Once Upon a Time, Sta. WBOE Kindergarten series, Cleve., 1966-67, writer, co-producer Here We Go Round the World series, 1969-73. Cons. Cleve. Kindergarten, 1969-70, mem. curriculum com., 1970-72. Recipient Master Tchr. award for excellence Martha Holden Jennings Found., 1968. Martha Holden Jennings Found. scholar 1966. Mem. Assn. Childhood Edn. Internat. (pres. Cleve. br. 1968-72, chmn. Internat. affairs com. Ohio state 1971). Cleve. Tchrs. Union, Cleve. State and Western Res. Alumni Groups, Delta Kappa Gamma (pres. Rho chpt. 1966-68). Conglist. (hon. deaconess 1966, dir., compiler for chs. 100th anniversary book 1959, chmn. ch. council, ch. moderator 1972-73). Home: 8306 Bauerdale Dr Parma OH 44129

RUDIN, CLAIRE L(ENORE) (MRS. LEO RUDIN), librarian; b. N.Y.C., Dec. 12, 1929; d. Joseph and Bertha (Zeeman); B.A. cum laude, Hunter Coll., 1951; M.L.S., Queens Coll., 1967; m. Leo Rudin, July 15, 1951; children—Joel, Laura. Sch. librarian N.Y.C. Bd. Edn., 1965-67; research librarian The Edn. Council, Mineola, N.Y., 1967-68; coordinator library services, Nassau Bd. Coop. Ednl. Services, Jericho, N.Y., 1968-71; coordinator Media Center, New Rochelle, N.Y., 1971-73; library media specialist P.S. 174, Bronx, N.Y., 1973—; vis. lectr. Ball State U., Muncie, Ind., 1971, Queens Coll., N.Y.C., 1971; cons. Nassau County (N.Y.) sch. dists., 1968-71; instr. Summer Insts., Nassau County Elementary Secondary Edn. Act. Regional Center, 1969-70. Active local and civic orgns. Mem. A.L.A., N.Y. Library Assn., Assn. Ednl. Communications and Tech., N.Y. State Ednl. Communications Assn., Phi Beta Kappa. Designer Mobile Instructional Media Center. Author: Media in Educating the Disadvantaged; Impact on Achievement, 1968; Teams for Advancing Teacher Training, 1969; Books for Multi-ethnic Studies, 1969; How Schools Can Fight the VD Menace, 1973; Communications and Language, 1973. Home: 15-78 Bell Blvd Bayside NY 11360 Office: 456 White Plains Rd Bronx NY 10473

RUDINSKAS, JOANNE ZEROLIS, health orgn. exec.; b. Mobile, Oct. 25, 1941; s. John and Hazel T. (Bartlett) Zerolis; A.B. in Sociology, U. Cal. at Berkeley, 1963; M.S.W., U. Wash., 1966; m. Algis Rudinskas. Psychiat. social worker Agnews State Hosp., San Jose, Cal., 1966-69; chief social worker, supr. psychiat. day treatment program San Jose Hosp., 1969-72; dep. dir. San Jose Community Mental Health Center, 1972—; cons. Child Care Centers San Jose; guest lectr. Stanford, 1973, San Jose State U., 1973. Bd. dirs. Pathways Drug Abuse Soc., 1972-74; Golden Gate Group Psychotherapy Soc., 1972—. Menninger Found. grantee, 1966; recipient Achievement award Bank Am., 1959. Provisional teaching mem. Internat. Transactional Analysis Assn.; mem. Am. Dance Therapy Assn., Am. Hosp. Assn., Golden Gate Group Psychotherapy Soc., Hosp. Social Work Dirs. Soc., Am. Assn. U. Women, Am. Assn. Mental Deficiency, Sierra Club. Democrat. Contbr. articles, revs. in field. Home: 655 S Fair Oaks Av B-301 Sunnyvale CA 94086 Office: 105 N 14th St San Jose CA 95112

RUDKO, DORIS JOAN EBENER (MRS. LIONEL RUDKO), dancer, choreographer, educator; b. Milw., Oct. 18, 1919; d. Joseph and Catherine B. (Froehlig) Ebener; B.S., U. Wis., 1943; pvt. studio study, N.Y.C., 1947; m. Lionel Rudko, Nov. 17, 1947; 1 dau., Lisa. With dance dept. High Sch. of Performing Arts, N.Y.C., 1947-54, acting chmn., 1950-54; asst. to Louis Horst, Conn. Coll. Summer Sch. of Dance, Neighborhood Playhouse Sch. of Theatre, 1955-63; mem. composition faculty Conn. Coll. and Long Beach Summer Sch. of Dance; mem. dance faculty Juilliard Sch., N.Y.C., 1969—; mem. dance faculty Sch. Edn., N.Y. U., 1973—; artistic dir. N.Y. Improvisation Ensemble; performed in Broadway musicals Shooting Star, On The Town, Concert Stage. Bd. dirs. Contemporary Dance Prodns., Inc. Asso. editor: Dance Observer. Mem. editorial adv. bd. Dance Scope. Home: 277 Upper Mountain Av Upper Montclair NJ 07043 Office: Juilliard Sch Lincoln Center New York City NY

RUDMAN, FRANCES ZIMMERMAN (MRS. JACK RUDMAN), pub. co. exec.; b. N.Y.C., June 26, 1912; d. Isadore and Dora (Deutsch) Zimmerman; m. Jack Rudman, Jan. 30, 1943; children—Gerald J., Stephanie R. (Mrs. William K. Joseph), Michael P. Vice pres., treas., sec., dir. Coll. Pub. Corp., Bklyn., 1954-66; v.p., sec., dir. Nat. Learning Corp., Bklyn., 1967—, v.p., treas., dir. subsidiaries Delaney Books Inc., Frank Merriwell Inc., 1967—. Mem. Assn. Am. Publishers. Home: 20 Johnstone Rd Great Neck NY 11021 Office: Nat Learning Corp 20 DuPont St Plainview NY 11803

RUDOLPH, MARGARET STILES (MRS. ALBERT L. RUDOLPH), banker; b. Genoa, Ill., June 18, 1909; d. Asahel A. and Jennie L. (Sowers) Stiles; grad. high sch.; m. Albert L. Rudolph, Sept. 16, 1937. Stenographer, Genoa State Bank, 1930-50, asst. cashier, 1950-62, cashier, 1962—, v.p., 1971—. Mem. Am. Safe Deposit Assn. (exec. com. 1969-72, asst. sec. 1972-74), Ill. Safe Deposit Assn. (pres. Rockford group 1964-66), DeKalb County Bankers Fedn. (pres. 1957-58). Methodist. Mem. Order Eastern Star. Home: 445 S Genoa St Genoa IL 60135 Office: 327 W Main St Genoa IL 60135

RUDOLPH, MARY JANE BROWN, librarian; b. Chgo., Sept. 5, 1931; d. Walter Xystus and Helen Elizabeth (Simpson) Brown; Ph.B., U. Chgo., 1949; M.Ed., Chgo. Tchrs. Coll., 1961. High sch. librarian U. Chgo. Lab Sch., 1952-53; librarian Kennedy-King Coll., City Colls. Chgo., 1954—. Fifth ward sec. Ind. Voters Ill., 1964-65. Bd. dirs. Ill. Regional Library Council, 1972—. Mem. U. Chgo. Grad. Library Sch. Alumni Assn., Cook County Coll. Tchrs. Union (sec. 1970-73, v.p. 1973—). Democrat. Club: Chicago Library. Home: 1428 E 54th St Chicago IL 60615 Office: 6800 S Wentworth St Chicago IL 60621

RUDOLPH, NANCY KALLMAN (MRS. ALAN G. RUDOLPH), photographer; b. N.Y.C., Dec. 26, 1923; d. Morris and Eva (Cohn) Kallman; student Cedar Crest Coll., 1941-42, Artist's Workshop, 1945-46, Art Student's League, 1946-48; m. Alan G. Rudolph, Nov. 27, 1951; children—John, Lucy. Free-lance photographer, 1954—; photographs have been pub. in Nat. Parent Tchrs. mag., Vineyard Gazette, N.Y. Times Mag., Annuarium Societatus Iesu, Cosmopolitan, Archtl. Forum, Childhood & Adolescence, Harpers mag., Tuesday, others; exhibited photographs at Met. Museum Art, Parents Mag. Gallery; tchr. Elizabeth Irwin High Sch., N.Y.C., 1968—. Recreation cons. Riverton, Henrietta, N.Y., 1970, Small Playground Renovation Com., N.Y.C., 1972. Bd. dirs. Citizens Com. for Children of N.Y.C., 1970—. Mem. Soc. Photographers in Communications (dir. 1973-74), Am. Soc. Mag. Photographers. Author, photographer: Workyards-Playgrounds Planned for Adventure, 1974. Photographer: New Lives, New Neighborhoods, 1964; Play and Playgrounds, 1970. Home: 35 W 11th St New York City NY 10011

RUDOLPH, RHONA SAX (MRS. ABRAHAM M. RUDOLPH), physician; b. Johannesburg, South Africa, Dec. 6, 1924; m. Abraham M. Rudolph, Nov. 2, 1949; children—Linda, Colin, Jeffrey. Intern, Coronation Hosp., Johannesburg, 1948-49, resident, 1949-50; instr. pediatrics Albert Einstein Coll. Medicine, N.Y.C., 1960-66; staff physician Golden Gate Regional Center, San Francisco, 1968-71; med. dir., 1971—; asst. clin. prof. pediatrics U. Cal. Med. Center, San Francisco, 1969—; pediatric cons. Asso. Students Child Care Centers, U. Cal. at Berkeley, 1971-72. Mem. com. on child care Berkeley City Council, 1971-72; mem. task force on women Berkeley Bd. Edn., 1972-73. Home: 1506 Willard St San Francisco CA 94117 Office: 346 9th St San Francisco CA 94103

RUDOLPH, SUSANNE HOEBER, educator; b. Mannheim, Germany, Apr. 3, 1930; d. Johannes U. and Elfriede (Fischer) Hoeber; A.B., Sarah Lawrence Coll., 1951; M.A., Radcliffe Coll., 1953, Ph.D. in Polit. Sci., 1955; m. Lloyd I. Rudolph, July 19, 1952; children—Jenny W., Amelia C., Matthew C. Instr., lectr. govt., history and gen. edn. Harvard, 1957-64; asso. prof. polit. and social scis. U. Chgo., 1964-71, prof., 1972—, master social scis. Collegiate div., exec. sec. Com. on So. Asian Studies, 1972—. Cons. Am. Council Learned Socs. Mem. overseers vis. coms. to Grad. Sch. Arts and Scis., Gen. Edn. Program, Harvard. Ford Found. fgn. area tng. fellow, India, 1956-57; sr. fellow Fulbright program, India, 1962-63; faculty fellow Am. Inst. Indian Studies, India, 1966-67; Guggenheim fellow, 1970-71; Fulbright-Hays fellow, 1970-71; NSF grantee, 1973-74. Mem. Am. Polit. Sci. Assn. (v.p. 1973-74), Assn. Asian Studies (dir.), Am. Soc. Pub. Adminstr. Author: (with Lloyd I. Rudolph) The Modernity of Tradition: Political Development in India, 1967; Education and Politics in India, 1972; also articles. Asst. editor jour. Asian Studies, 1963-64. Home: 4943 Woodlawn Av Chicago IL 60615

RUELLAN, ANDREE, artist; b. N.Y.C., Apr. 6, 1905; d. Andre and Louise (Lambert) Ruellan; student Art Students League, 1920-22; art schs. France and Italy; m. John W. Taylor, May 28, 1929. One-man shows Paris, France, 1925, Weyhe Galleries, N.Y.C., 1928, 31, Maynard Walker Galleries, 1937, 40, Kraushaar Galleries, 1945, 52, 56, 63, Phila. Art Alliance, 1955, S.I. Mus., 1958, Drawings and Gouaches, Newcomb Coll., Tulane U., 1959, Lehigh U., 1965; nat. exhbns. include Pa. Acad., Detroit Mus., Mus. City N.Y., Carnegie Inst., Whitney Mus., Art Inst. Chgo., Corcoran Gallery, Internat. Expn., San Francisco, Artists for Victory Exhbn., N.Y.C., and other exhbns.; group shows in Woodstock Artists Assn., Kraushaar Gallery, Columbia (S.C.) Mus., Sarasota Artist Assn., Heckscher Mus., N.Y.C., 1972; retrospective exhbn. Storm King Art Center, 1966; executed murals in Emporia, Va., Lawrenceville, Ga.; represented in collections of Met. Mus., Whitney Mus. Am. Art (N.Y.C.), Phila. Mus., Library of Congress, Ency. Brit., Art Inst., Zanesville, U., Butler Inst. Art, Pa. Acad. Fine Arts, Storm King Art Center, Lehigh U., Columbia (S.C.) Mus. Art, Bethlehem (Pa.) City Center, U. Fla. Gallery, Gainesville, numerous pvt. collections; instr. Pa. State U., summer 1957. Awarded 3d prize for painting Charleston, Worcester Mus. Biennial, Jan. 1938; 1,000 grant in Arts, Am. Acad. Inst. Arts and Letters, 1945; Pennell medal, Pa. Acad., 1945, Medal of Honor and purchase Pepsi-Cola Paintings of the Year, 1948; Dawson Meml. medal, Pa. Acad., 1950; Purchase award N.Y. State Fair, 1951; J. S. Guggenheim fellowship, 1950-51; Drawing award, Ball State Tchrs. Coll., 1958. Mem. Woodstock Artists Assn., Art Students League (life mem.), Phila. Watercolor Soc. Home: Shady NY 12479 Office: care Kraushaar Galleries 1055 Madison Av New York City NY 10028

RUETH, MARION URSULA, librarian; b. Washington; d. George A. and Belle (Skinner) Rueth; student Ursuline Coll., Santa Rosa, Cal., Georgetown Visitation Convent, Trinity Coll.; M. Mus., Cath. U. Am., 1946; M.A. in Library Sci., Fla. State U., 1962. Dir. Silver Studio Music, Silver Spring, Md., 1944-50; library asst. St. Petersburg (Fla.) Pub. Library, 1953-58; music specialist and cataloger Fla. State U. Library, Tallahassee, 1958-62; asst. head acquisitions McKeldin Library, U. Md., 1962-66; head librarian Hood Coll., Frederick, Md., 1966—. Mem. Am., Md. music library assns., Beta Phi Mu, Pi Kappa Lambda. Roman Catholic. Author: The Tallahassee Years of Ernst von Dohnanyi, 1962. Home: Willowbrook Old Middletown Rd Jefferson MD 21755 Office: Hood Coll Frederick MD 21701

RUETHER, ROSEMARY RADFORD (MRS. HERMAN J. RUETHER), theologian; b. St. Paul, Nov. 2, 1936; d. Robert Amstrong and Rebecca Cresap (Ord) Radford; B.A., Scripps Coll., 1958; M.A., Claremont Grad. Sch., 1960, Ph.D., 1965; m. Herman J. Ruether, Aug. 31, 1957; children—Rebecca, David, Mimi. Faculty Howard U. Washington, 1966—. Lectr. Princeton Theol. Sem., 1971, 73; prof. Roman Cath. studies Harvard, Cambridge, Mass., 1972-73; lectr. Yale Div. Sch., 1973-74. Kent fellow, 1962-65; Danforth fellow, 1960-61. Mem. Soc. for Religion in Higher Edn., Am. Theol. Assn., Soc. Arts, Religion and Culture. Author: The Church Against Itself, 1967; Communion Is Life Together, 1968; Gregory Nazianzus, Rhetor and Philosopher, 1969; The Radical Kingdom, 1970; Liberation Theology, 1972; Religion and Sexism: Images of Women in the Judeo-Christian Tradition, 1974. Contbg. editor Christianity and Crisis, The Ecumenist. Contbr. articles to profl. jours. Home: 1438 Montagne St NW Washington DC 20011

RUFFO, VINNIE CATALANO (MRS. PAUL D. RUFFO), author, tchr.; b. Rome, N.Y., Sept. 22, 1928; d. Dominiche and Marian (Barbieri) Calalano; A.B., San Jose State U., 1953; m. Paul D. Ruffo, July 19, 1953; children—Paul, Joe, Laurie. Former tchr. Jefferson Elementary Sch., Santa Clare, Cal.; now tchr. creative writing Met. Adult Edn. Program, San Jose, Cal. Served with WAVES. Mem. Nat. League Am. Pen Women. Contbr. stories and articles to various mags. Author: Behind Barbed Wire; Trapped in Death Valley; To The New World With Christopher Columbus; The Devil Wore an Orchid. Address: 16601 McAbee Rd San Jose CA 95120

RUGGLES, NANCY DUNLAP (MRS. RICHARD RUGGLES), economist; b. Providence, June 29, 1922; d. Charles H. and Doris (Bishop) Dunlap; A.B., Pembroke Coll., 1943; Ph.D., Radcliffe Coll., 1949; m. Richard Ruggles, June 1, 1946; children—Ann Patricia, Catherine Joan, John Steven. Econ. analyst Treasury Dept., Div. Tax Research, 1944-46; cons. on nat. accounts ECA, 1950-53; econ. affairs officer UN. Dept. Econ. Affairs, 1957-59, cons. Spl. Fund., 1961; research asso. Yale Econ. Growth Center, 1961-66; sr. research staff Nat. Bur. Econ. Research, New Haven, 1966—. Mem. Internat. Assn. for Research in Income and Wealth (sec. 1962—), Econometric Soc. (treas. 1955-70). Author: (with Richard Ruggles) Design of Economic Accounts, 1970, National Income Accounts and Income Analysis, 1956. Home: 88 Prospect St New Haven CT 06511 Office: Box 2020 Yale Sta New Haven CT 06520

RUGH, KAREN ANN (MRS. MICHAEL CRAIG RUGH), editor; b. Pitts., Mar. 5, 1943; d. Willard D. and Mary Belle (Campbell) Zimmerman; B.A., Pa. State U., 1965; m. Michael Craig Rugh, Apr. 3, 1965. Asst. home econs. editor coop. extension service, The Pa. State U., University Park, Pa., 1967—. TV producer Farm, Home, and Garden, Pa. Pub. TV network, also selected comml. stas. Home: 424 E Irvin Av State College PA 16801 Office: 401 Agrl Adminstrn Bldg Pa State U University Park PA 16802

RUHANEN, PEARL WRIGHT (MRS. ARTHUR U. RUHANEN), real estate agt.; b. Richford, Vt., Feb. 11, 1920; d. Llewellyn Edward and Lucia Sarah (Derby) Wright; student Burlington Bus. Coll., 1941, Gavilan Coll., 1970; m. Arthur U. Ruhanen, Nov. 27, 1943; children—Sandra (Mrs. Robert Freeman), Patricia (Mrs. William Schrupp), Kimberly. Sec. to mgr. Gas. & Electric Co., Burlington, Vt., 1941; sec. U.S. Govt., Dept. Engring. and Factory Inspection, Washington, 1942; sec. to patent atty., Washington, 1944; sec. real estate firm, Los Altos, Cal., 1960-63; with firm Hank Seward Realty, Gilroy, Cal., 1963-70; broker Ruhanen Realty, Gilroy, 1970—. Sec., World Aviation Conf., Chgo., 1943. Sec., Heart Fund, Gilroy, 1969; campaign vol. Model Childrens Home Soc., Gilroy, 1964; chmn. Gilroy United Fund, 1973. Mem. Womens Council (mem. ethic com. 1970), Gilroy C. of C., Tri County Apt. Assn., Gilroy Theatre Angels. Baptist. Home: 11370 Watsonville Rd Gilroy CA 95020 Office: 620 1st St Gilroy CA 95020

RUHLE, BARBARA ELEANOR, educator; b. Chgo., Dec. 24, 1934; d. Stanley Chester and Hazel Mabel (Ruhle) Novak; B.A., Willamette U., 1956; postgrad. San Jose State Coll., 1956-57; M.S., Ore. Coll. Edn., 1973. Tchr. English, dir. drama McNary High Sch., Salem, Ore., 1969—. Actress Pentacle Theatre, Salem, Ore., 1953-73, dir., 1959-61; actress, Orlando (Fla.) Players Little Theatre, 1962-63. Mem. Nat. Council Tchrs. English, Ore. Theatre Tchrs. Am. Home: 4904 5th Pl NE Salem OR 97303 Office: 505 Sandy Dr NE Salem OR 97303

RUHLY, VELMA SUE (MRS. KING RUHLY), sch. prin.; b. Fulton, Ky., Jan. 19, 1918; d. A. Boaz and Ola (Hopkins) Meacham; B.A. in Edn., Wayne State U., 1957, M.Ed., 1962, Ph.D., 1970; m. King Ruhly, Feb. 12, 1940; children—Patricia (Mrs. Joseph Halasz), James, John, Robert. Tchr. pub. schs., Birmingham, Mich., 1968-69, psychologist, 1969-70; prin. Franklin (Mich.) Elementary Sch., 1970—. Oakland County Court Govt. grantee, 1968. Mem. Am., Mich. psychol. assns., Mich. Assn. Elementary Prins., Soc. for Research in Child Devel., Mich. Assn. of Learning Disabilities, Wayne State Alumni Assn., Delta Gamma Chi. Home: 17395 Locherbie Birmingham MI 48009 Office: 32220 Franklin Franklin MI 48025

RUIZ, BRUNILDA, prima ballerina; b. Rincon, P.R., June 1, 1936; d. Eusebio and Maria (Perez) Ruiz; grad. Performing Arts High Sch., N.Y.C.; m. Paul Sutherland, Oct. 27, 1968; 1 dau., Mhari Theresa. Prima Ballerina Robert Joffrey Ballet, N.Y.C., 1955-64, N.Y.C. Center Opera Co., 1957-59, Harkness Ballet, 1964-67, 69-70; guest soloist Ballets de San Juna, P.R., 1966; joined City Center Joffrey Ballet, 1968. Home: 53 Harrison Av Waldwick NJ 07463 Office: 4 E 75th St New York City NY 10022

RUIZ, ROSEMARY, journalist; b. Panama City, Panama, Mar. 21, 1943; d. Camilo Raphael and Rosemary (Guidry) Ruiz; B.S., Loyola U. of South, New Orleans, 1964. Staff writer Loyola U. Pub. Relations, 1964-66, asst. dir. pub. relations, 1967; advt. copywriter Godchaux's Dept. Store, 1967-68; prodn. asst., editorial writer WDSU-TV News, 1968-71; columnist, reporter New Orleans States-Item, 1971—. Actress. Mem. Women in Communications, Screen Actors Guild, Am. Fedn. TV and Radio Artists. Home: 521 Dauphine St New Orleans LA 70112 Office: 3800 Howard Av New Orleans LA 70140

RUIZ-DE-CONDE, JUSTINA, educator; b. Madrid, Spain, Nov. 30, 1909; Lic. en Derecho, U. Cent. de Madrid, 1931; postgrad. U. Paris, 1939, (Faculty fellow) Wellesley Coll., 1943-44; Ph.D., Radcliffe Coll., 1945; m. 1934. Prof. French, Inst. Natl. de Segunda Ensenanza de Valdepenas (Spain), 1933-34, Salmeron, Barcelona, Spain, 1936-38; tchr. Spanish, Abbot Acad., Mass., 1939-41; instr. Spanish Wellesley (Mass.) Coll., 1941-46, asst. prof. 1946-49, asso. prof., 1948-58, prof., 1958—, chmn. dept., 1946-52, 54-58, 61-62, 64-65, 67-68, 69-70. Mem. Modern Lang. Assn., Am. Assn. Tchrs. Spanish and Portuguese, Hispanic Soc. (corr.). Author: El amor y el matrimonio secreto en los libros de caballerias, 1948; Antonio Machado y Guiomar, 1964; El cantino americano de Jorge Guillen, 1973. Research on romance of chivalry, contemporary Spanish poetry. Address: Dept of Spanish Wellesley College Wellesley MA 02181

RULE, IVA DAINTY, ret. educator; b. Hico, W.Va., Oct. 10, 1907; d. Henry Oliver and Lizzie (Arnold) Rule; A.B., Marshall Coll., 1934; M.A., W.Va. U., 1941. Tchr., Victor, W.Va., 1928-31, 34-36; tchr. elementary sch., Lansing, W.Va., 1931-34; tchr. Ansted (W.Va.) Jr. High Sch., 1936-71. Chmn. Fayette County Heart Fund Drive, 1968—; leader 4-H Club, 1937-70. Mem. Fayette County Hist. Soc. (pres. 1971-72). Fayette County 4-H Leaders Assn. (pres. 1948-50, 68-69), Delta Kappa Gamma. Baptist (sec.-treas. 1937—). Home: Hico WV 25854

RULE, JANE, author; b. Plainfield, N.J., Mar. 28, 1931; d. Arthur Richards and Carlotta Jane (Hink) Rule; B.A., Mills Coll., 1952. Asst. dir. Internat. House, U. B.C., 1958-59, lectr. English, 1959-70. Can. Council grantee, 1969-70, 70-71. Mem. Phi Beta Kappa. Author: Desert of the Heart, 1965; This Is Not For You, 1970; Against the Season, 1971; (short stories) Theme for Diverse Instruments, 1974. Home: Rural Route 1 Galiano BC V0N 1P0 Canada

RULE, MARY EMMA (MRS. DOYLE RULE), editor; b. Marquez, Tex., Jan. 11, 1924; d. John H. and Eula M. (Lanier) Winn; student Houston Bus. Coll., 1940; m. Doyle Rule, Apr. 14, 1943; children—Doyle, Kay (Mrs. Joe Johnson). Sec.-bookkeeper W.D. Haden Co., Houston, 1948-62; 1st dep. McIntosh County Treas.'s Office, Eufaula, Okla., 1965-70; mng. editor Indian Jour., 1970—. Bd. dirs. Eufaula City Hosp., 1972—. Named Career Woman of Year, Eufaula, 1972. Mem. Eufaula Bus. and Prof. Women (pres. 1966-67, treas. 1965-66, rec. sec. 1964-65, dist. dir. 1968-69), Eufaula C. of C. (dir. 1970—), Am. Legion Aux. (Eufaula pres. 1968—, spl. events chmn. 1970—). Democrat. Baptist. Home: PO Box 289 110 Janeway Dr Eufaula OK 74432 Office: PO Box 689 Eufaula OR 74432

RULE, VETA FRANKLIN TURNER (MRS. EDGAR WRIGHT RULE, JR.), writer, civic worker; b. Montgomery, Ala.; d. William Prescott and Lucy Houston (Reynolds) Turner; student U. Denver, 1927-31; m. Edgar Wright Rule, Jr., May 18, 1932; children—Lucie (Mrs. Gordon Lee Kidd, Jr.), James Randolph. Free lance writer, 1927—; pres. Denver Press Council, 1968—; writer, promoter original steering com. for Channel 6, Denver Ednl. TV, 1951-53; publicity dir. Colo. br. Am. Ch. Union, 1963-65; mem. Denver Civic Theater; mem. pub. relations staff, Presbyn. Hosp. Aux., 1951-55. Mem. Nat. League Am. Pen Women (pres. Denver br. 1956-58), Poetry Soc. Colo. (pres. 1969-70, asst. in compilation Golden Anniversary anthology), Nat. Assn. Parliamentarians, Denver Press Council (hon.), Alpha Gamma Delta. Episcopalian. Contbr. articles to profl. jours. Home: 2467 S Milwaukee St Denver CO 80210

RULIFFSON, ROBERTA JONES, psychotherapist; b. Arlington, Mass., Apr. 18, 1932; d. Ernest E. and Edna (Penniman) Jones; A.B., Drew U., 1956; M.S.W., Smith Coll., 1962; postgrad. Inst. for

Psychoanalytic Training and Research, 1967—. Caseworker N.J. Bur. Children's Services, 1957-59, supr., 1959-61, supr. staff devel., 1962-63; psychiat. social work supr. Guidance Clinic, Cath. Welfare Bur., Trenton, N.J., 1963-65, acting chief psychiat. social worker, 1965-67, chief psychiat. social worker, adminstvr. asst., 1967-71, dir. child therapy, 1971-73, clin. dir., 1973—; pvt. practice psychotherapy, Lawrenceville, N.J., 1967—. Cons. Family Service Assn., Princeton, N.J. 1968; mem. profl. adv. com. Mercer County Mental Health Bd., 1966. Mem. Nat. Assn. Social Workers, Acad. Certified Social Workers, A.A.A.S. Home: 26 George St Lawrenceville NJ 08648 Office: 39 N Clinton Av Trenton NJ 08609 also 25 George St Lawrenceville NJ 08648

RUMAGE, NANCY SIMMS (MRS. JOSEPH PAUL RUMAGE), psychologist; b. Chgo., Aug. 15, 1927; d. William Augustus and Sarah (Price) Simms; B.S., Northwestern U., 1948; M.A., U. Neb., 1951; postgrad. Tulane U., 1951-52; m. Joseph Paul Rumage, June 15, 1955; children—Sarah Agnes, Joseph Paul, William Simms. Research asst. Tulane U., Urban Life Research Inst., 1951-52, chief psychologist, children's unit Tulane U. Med. Sch., 1952-56; psychologist Jefferson Parish Sch. Bd., Gretna, La., 1953-63; gen. practice psychology, New Orleans, 1956—; chief psychologist New Orleans Regional Mental Health Center, 1965-68; psychologist Ednl. Research and Treatment Center, 1968—; v.p. Terry Cay Co., Ltd., Nassau, Bahamas, treas. Mem. bd. Orleans Neighborhood Centers, 1963-65; mem. Jefferson Parish Social Welfare Planning Council, 1965-66. Mem. Am., La. psychol. assns., Midwestern 4 Assn., Southwestern Assn., Soc. Child Devel., Psi Chi. Home: 1754 Robert E Lee Blvd New Orleans LA 70122 Office: 3619 Prytania St New Orleans LA 70115

RUMFORD, BEATRIX TYSON, museum ofcl.; b. Balt., June 16, 1939; d. Lewis and Rose (Clymer) Rumford; B.A., Wellesley Coll., 1962; M.A., State U. N.Y. Oneonta, 1965. Art research editor D.C. Heath & Co., Boston, 1962-64; research asso. Chgo. Hist. Soc., 1965-67; curator, dept. collections Colonial Williamsburg (Va.), 1967-71; asso. dir. Abby Aldrich Rockefeller Folk Art Collection, Williamsburg, 1971-73, dir., 1973—. Cons. Bermuda Nat. Trust, 1973; mem. accession com. Exec. Mansion, Richmond. Contbr. to Antiques mag., 1969—. Home: Tayloe House Williamsburg VA 23185 Office: Abby Aldrich Rockefeller Folk Art Collection Drawer C S England St Williamsburg VA 23185

RUMP, RONNIE BETH, coll. adminstr.; b. Fremont, Neb., Mar. 6, 1947; d. Richard Bryant and Margaret Louise (Neff) Rump; B.A. cum laude, Midland Lutheran Coll., 1969; postgrad. U. Neb., 1970. Account exec. J. Lipsey & Assos., Omaha, 1969-70; dir. pub. relations Coll. St. Mary, Omaha, 1970—. Mem. Am. Coll. Pub. Relations Assn., Omaha Press Club, Pub. Relations Soc. Am. Home: 7108 S 86th St Omaha NE 68128 Office: 1901 S 72nd St Omaha NE 68124

RUNBECK, JUNET EILEEN, educator; b. Portland, Ore., June 1, 1914; d. Albin Eric and Jennie Victoria (Neil) Runbeck; A.A., Pacific Luth. U., 1935; B.A., Coll. Puget Sound, 1939; M.A., Stanford, 1957; Ed.D., No. Colo. U., 1961. Tchr., Issaquah, Wash., 1935-45, Tacoma, 1945-52; asso. prof. edn. Pacific Luth. U., Tacoma, 1952-62; prof. edn., chmn. dept. edn. Bethel Coll., St. Paul, 1962—. Cons. tchr. edn., Ethiopia, 1970-71. Wash. State Delta Kappa Gamma scholar, 1960. Mem. Nat., Minn. edn. assns., Am. Assn. U. Women, Assn. for Student Teaching, Minn. Assn. Colls. Tchr. Edn., Nat. Soc. for Study of Edn., Internat. Reading Assn., Delta Kappa Gamma, Pi Lambda Theta. Baptist. Home: 1526 Arona St St Paul MN 55108

RUNDEN, CHARITY EVA WILLIAMS (MRS. JOHN PAUL RUNDEN), educator; b. Lake City, Minn., Oct. 1, 1910; d. Harley Albert and Edith (Burchard) Williams; A.B., Ball State U., 1933, M.A., 1940; M.S. in Pub. Health (USPHS fellow), U. N.C., 1944; Ph.D., Ind. U., 1951; m. John Paul Runden, Aug. 23, 1944; children—John Paul, Ingrid Eve. Tchr. high schs., Ind., 1937-43; health educator, N.C. and Ind., 1944-46; faculty Ind. U., 1950-52, U. Ky., 1952-54; instr. Western Ill. U., Macomb, 1954-57, acting dean grad. div., 1957-59; asst. prof. psychology and edn. Montclair State Coll., Upper Montclair, N.J., 1959-63, dean of women, 1963-65, asso. chmn. grad. studies, 1965-67, prof. psychology and edn., 1966—, exec. dir. Ednl. Found. for Human Sexuality, 1967—. Fellow Am. Pub. Health Assn.; mem. Modern Lang. Assn., N.J. Health Edn. Council, N.J. Assn. Health, Phys. Edn. and Recreation, Nat. Council on Family Relations, Am. Assn. Sex Educators and Counselors, Sex Information and Ednl. Council U.S. (asso.). Author: Twentieth Century Educators, 1965; Selected Readings in Sex Education, 1968. Contbr. articles to profl. jours. Home: Glen Rock Rd Little Falls NJ 07424 Office: Montclair State College Valley and Normal Avs Upper Montclair NJ 07043

RUNDLE, MARJORIE ARNOLD, educator; b. Eaton, O., Jan. 21, 1916; d. William Allen and Emma Margaret (Neidhart) Arnold; A.B., Miami U., Oxford, O., 1936, B.S. in Edn., 1937, M.A., 1940; Ph.D., U. Cin., 1956; m. James Urvin Rundle, June 5, 1946; children—Marcia, Margaret. Tchr. English and French, Mt. Healthy (O.) High Sch., 1937-43; Taft teaching fellow U. Cin., 1944-46; instr. Park Coll., Parkville, Mo., 1947-48; lectr. Wagner Coll., S.I., N.Y., 1956, asst. prof., 1964-66, asso. prof., 1967; prof. English, Franklin Pierce Coll., Rindge, N.H., 1968-70; prof. Greater Hartford (Conn.) Community Coll., 1970—. Bd. mem. S.I. Citizens' Planning Com., 1957-64; sec. Jr. Mus. Guild, S.I., 1960-62, br. chmn., 1958-60; Voters, pres. Greater Middletown (Conn.) area, 1971-73. Mem. S.I. League Women Voters (former br. chmn.), Alpha Omicron Pi (alumnae adviser Wagner Coll. 1965-67). Unitarian. Home: 3 Summer St Portland CT 06480 Office: Greater Hartford Community Coll Hartford CT 06480

RUNKLE, JUDITH ANN, educator; b. Dallas, Wis., Dec. 12, 1941; d. Gaylord Raymond and Ardis (Shellito) Runkle; B.S., Wis. State Coll., 1963; M.S., Ill. State U., 1964; Ph.D., U. Minn., 1972. Instr., dir. forensics, speech dept. U. Wis., Whitewater, 1965-68; grad. teaching asst. U. Minn., Mpls., 1968-71; asst. prof., dir. communication U. Wis., Superior, 1971-73; asst. prof. speech-communications dept. U. Del., Newark, 1973—. Mem. com. to coordinate and promote interscholastic debate in Del. high schs. Del. Secondary Edn. and Related Programs Div. Mem. Am. Forensics Assn., Central States, Tri-State speech assn., Speech-Communications Assn., Pi Kappa Delta, Kappa Delta Pi. Lutheran. Home: 260 Elkton Rd Apt A8 Newark DE 19711

RUNYON, ALICE LOUISE MINNERLY (MRS. JAMES G. RUNYON), restoration research, educator, musician; b. North Tarrytown, N.Y., June 12, 1902; d. Percy Charles and Phernettie Elizabeth (Miller) Minnerly; grad. New Paltz State Normal Sch., 1921; B.S., N.Y. U., 1943, M.A., 1947; grad. Guilmant Organ Sch., 1940; m. James Garfield Runyon, June 30, 1928 (dec. 1955). Tchr. pub. sch., 1921-46; asst. dir. Philipse Castle restoration, 1943-47; head research for restoration Sunnyside, Washington Irving's home, 1945-47; asso. dir. Philipse Castle and Sunnyside, 1947-51, Sleepy Hollow Restorations, Inc., 1951-55, corp. sec., trustee, 1951-55; dir. Specialized Research, 1956—. Curator Horace Greeley Mus., 1958-68; genealogist Dutch Colonial of Del., 1967-71. Organist and choir master Christ Evang. and Ref. Ch., N.Y.C., 1942-52; lectr. Sec., v.p. U.S.O., the Tarrytowns, World War II. Mem. Am. Guild Organists, Hist. Soc. Tarrytowns (dir., sec.), Sons and Daus. Pilgrims (organizing pres. past nat. officers club, 1st dep. gov. gen., N.Y. State gov., dep. gov., treas., sec., nat. bd. mem.), Am. Hist. Soc., Patriotic Women Am., Daus. Am. Colonists, Colonial Daus. 17th Century, D.A.R. (chmn. Jr. Am. Citizens registrar), Daus. Founders and Patriots Am. (N.Y. pres., v.p., nat. councillor, nat. chmn. hist. edn., nat. corr. sec.), Daus. Colonial Wars (pres. N.Y. State, nat. historian, mem. nat. exec. bd., rec. sec., 2d v.p. Nat. Officers Club), Ams. Armorial Ancestry (nat. councillor, nat. pres., nat. treas., nat. registrar, genealogist), Manuscript Soc., Soc. Holland Dames, Ames. Royal Descent (past nat. councillor), Colonial Dames Am., Huguenot Soc. Am. (nat. registrar, mem. council), Descs. Knights of Garter, Women's Nat. Republican Club, Am. Friends Lafayette Daus. Union 1861-1865, Order of Washington, Order Three Crusades, Descs. William the Conqueror, N.Y. State Hist. Assn. (organizer 1st jr. chpt.), Westchester County, Chappaqua (trustee), Somers (hon.) hist. socs., Kappa Delta Pi. Contbr. articles in field. Historian village of N. Tarrytown, N.Y.; past archivist Order of Crown of Charlemagne in Am. Home: 483 Munroe Av North Tarrytown NY 10591 Office: Specialized Research PO Box 187 North Tarrytown NY 10591

RUNYON, JEAN HAMILTON (MRS. S. MERCER RUNYON, JR.), advt.-pub. relations exec.; b. Concordia, Kan., Mar. 6, 1927; d. Brutus Kerr and Rowena (Thornburg) Hamilton; A.A., U. Cal. at Berkeley, 1949; m. S. Mercer Runyon, Jr., Nov. 4, 1947 (dec. Nov. 1970); children—Stephen Hamilton, Elizabeth Mary. Pres. Runyon & Assos., 1956-63, Runyon & Craig, 1963-68; chmn. bd. Dannenfelser, Runyon, Craig, Inc., 1968—. Bd. dirs. Crocker Art Gallery, Salvation Army, Children's Home, Goodwill Industries. Mem. chmns. adv. com. Democratic party, 1968-70. Recipient Merit Plaque, City of Hope and United Crusade and Symphony League, 1971; named Pub. Relations Man of Year, Pub. Relations Round Table 1964. Mem. Pub. Relations Soc. Am., Pub. Relations Roundtable, Kappa Alpha Theta. Home: 122 Tivoli Way Sacramento CA 95819 Office: 1616 Jay St Sacramento CA 95814

RUNYON, RUTH ANN JORDAN (MRS. C. RUNYON), physician; b. nr. Richmond, Ind., Oct. 12, 1928; d. Willard T. and Esther (Fouts) Jordan; A.B., Ind. U., 1950; M.D., Coll. Physicians and Surgeons, Columbia U., 1957; m. Robert C. Runyon, Sept. 4, 1954; children—Diane M., Linda J. Intern. St. Luke's Hosp., N.Y.C., 1957-58, intern, asst. resident in medicine, 1958-59; physician clinic Met. Life Ins. Co., N.Y.C., 1960-62; physician med. clinic Standard Oil Co. of N.J., N.Y.C., 1962; physician in med. dept. Mass. Inst. Tech., 1963-72; asst. med. dir. New Eng. Mut. Life Ins. Co., Boston, 1972-74; fellow in internal medicine Mass. Gen. Hosp., Boston, 1974-75; physician med. clinic New Eng. Mut. Life Ins. Co., Boston, 1963-66; therapeutic dietitian Meth. Hosp., Indpls., 1951-53, Presbyn. Hosp., N.Y.C., part-time, 1954-57. Active Brownies. Mem. Ind. Dietetic Assn. (past pub. relations chmn.), A.M.A., Norfolk County Med. Soc., Mass. Med. Soc., Alpha Chi Omega. Clubs: Boston Skating, Annisquam Yacht. Home: 105 Rockwood St Brookline MA 02146

RUOTSALA, GEORGIANNA JEANNE CALLIES (MRS. SULO KALERVO RUOTSALA), librarian; b. Oshkosh, Wis., May 3, 1920; d. Karl Theodore and Florence (Simpson) Callies; B.S., Wis. State Coll., 1942; B.S. in L.S., U. Wis., 1945; m. Sulo Kalervo Ruotsala, May 4, 1946; children—Michael Gregory, Matthew Karl. Tchr., Columbus Twp. High Sch., Macmillan, Mich., 1942-43, Consol. High Sch., Norway, Ia., 1943-44; asst. librarian Detroit Pub. Library, 1945-46; tchr., librarian Rock (Mich.) High Sch., 1959-61; base librarian K.I. Sawyer AFB, Mich., 1961—. Mem. A.L.A., Mich. Library Assn., Am. Legion Aux., U. Wis. Alumni Assn., Wis. State U.-Oshkosh Alumni Assn., Phi Beta Sigma. Home: Route 1 Box 50 Rock MI 49880 Office: FL 4515 KI Sawyer AFB MI 49843

RUPP, ALICE CAROLYN, librarian; b. Waterville, O., Oct. 1, 1917; d. Herman Utz and Phillippine M. (Beil) Rupp; B.A., Bowling Green State U., 1939; M.S., Western Res. U., 1940. Asst. Toledo-Lucas County Pub. Library, 1940-58, 59-60, head art-music-sports dept., 1960—; 1st asst. art-music-drama dept. Flint (Mich.) Pub. Library, 1958-59. Mem. Toledo Museum Art. Trustee Citizens for Metro Parks, 1972—. Mem. Ohio Library Assn., Toledo Naturalists Assn. Unitarian. Home: 2645 Whiteway St Toledo OH 43606 Office: 325 Michigan St Toledo OH 43624

RUPPERT, GRETCHEN ANN BROWN (MRS. GERALD PETER RUPPERT), bridge tchr.; b. Davenport, Ia., May 22, 1919; d. George Steven and Leona (Bock) Flinchbaugh; grad. med. tech. Mpls. Inst. Med. Tech. and Radiology, 1936; m. Gerald Peter Ruppert, Jan. 3, 1937; children—Michelle (Mrs. Jerry Vest), Patricia (Mrs. Fred Van Winkle, Jr.), James, Melody Arlidge, Marcie. V.p. Sunland Oil Co., Artesia, N.M., 1949—; artist in resident Mattatuck Museum, Waterbury, Conn., 1969-71, museum staff, 1971-73; bridge tchr. Wallingford (Conn.), Cheshire (Conn.), Wolcott (Conn.) recreational depts., 1972—, New Eng. Tennis Camp, Cheshire, Conn., 1972—74; duplicate dir. Wolcott (Conn.), Cheshire (Conn.) bridge clubs, 1972. Art judge local area women's clubs, 1970; art judge, state level Women's Club Show, 1971, 73; organizer duplicate bridge club for sr. citizens, Wallingford, 1973. Mem. Am. Bridge Tchrs. Assn. (nat sec. 1967), Cape Cod Art and Craft Assn., Waterbury Arts Assn., Internat. Bridge Press Assn. Home: 190 Mixville Rd Cheshire CT 06410 Office: 70 Bank St Waterbury CT 06702

RUPRECHT, MARY MARGARET WYANT, word processor, mgmt. cons.; b. O'Neill, Neb., Oct. 20, 1934; d. Charles Ellsworth and Mary Loretto (Cuddy) Wyant; student Coll. St. Benedict, 1952-54; certificate, Am. Inst. Banking, 1970; m. Gregory Earl Ruprecht, Sept. 24, 1955; children—Mary Debra, Sharie Marie. Dist. clk. U.S. Soil Conservation, Aitkin, Minn., 1956-68; comml. loan sec. No. City Nat. Bank, Duluth, Minn., 1965-71; office mgr. Fryberger, Buchanan Law Firm, Duluth, 1971-72; pvt. practice word processing and mgmt. consulting, Duluth, 1972—; tchr. Am. Inst. Banking. Finance dir. 8th Congl. Dist. Dem.-Farm Labor Party, 1972-73. Mem. Internat. Word Processing Assn. (chmn. 1974-75), Am. Inst. Banking (nat. chmn. women's com. 1970-71), Adminstrv. Mgmt. Soc., Bus. and Profl. Women's Assn., Internat. Platform Assn. Contbr. articles to profl. jours. Home: 140 W Myrtle St Duluth MN 55811

RUSCH, MEDRA HALL (MRS. HERMAN WILLIAM RUSCH), home economist; b. Bozeman, Mont.; d. John Alexander and Anne Louise (Ivy) Hall; B.S., Mont. State Coll., 1918, postgrad. summers 1952, 54, 59; postgrad. summers U. Ore., 1922, U. Cal. at Berkeley, 1924; m. Herman William Rusch, May 31, 1931. Home economist, Manhattan, Mont., 1918-19; home economist, social dir., Ft. Benton, Mont., 1919-20; tchr., supr. home econs., Bozeman Jr. High Sch., 1920-27; home economist, supr. Jr. A.R.C., Sioux Falls, S.D., 1927-31; instr. adult night sch., Bozeman, Sioux Falls, 1925-31; supr. dept. Bozeman City Library, 1959—. Founding mem. Mont. Inst. Arts; mem. Shuttle Craft Guild. Recipient scholarship Am. Child Health, 1924. Mem. Am. Pub. Health Assn., Phi Upsilon Omicron. Presbyn. Mem. Order Eastern Star, Daus. of Nile, White Shrine Jerusalem. Home: 509 S 5th Av Bozeman MT 59715 Office: 35 N Zozeman Av Bozeman MT 59715

RUSH, ELIZABETH ANN, physician; b. Fairfield, Ill., July 9, 1935; d. Cassius Edgar and Lucy Pauline (Roy) Rush; student U. Cin., 1953-54, U. Fla., 1954-56; M.D., U. Miami, 1960. Intern, Tampa (Fla.) Gen. Hosp., 1960-61; gen. practice medicine, Bonita Springs, Fla., 1961-64; trainee in clin. investigation Oak Ridge Inst. Nuclear Studies, 1964-65; asst. resident in medicine U. Tenn., Memphis, 1965-66, USPHS fellow in metabolism, 1966-68; fellow Leukemia Soc. Am., U. Tenn. Meml. Research Center, Knoxville, 1968-69, staff physician hosp., 1969—; asso. prof. U. Tenn. Meml. Research Center Hosp., 1972—. Mem. Sigma Xi, Alpha Omicron Pi, Alpha Omega Alpha. Home: 615 Lookout Ct Knoxville TN 37920 Office: Alcoa Hwy Knoxville TN 37920

RUSH, JULIA ANN HALLORAN (MRS. RICHARD HENRY RUSH), artist; b. St. Louis, Oct. 25, 1927; d. E. R. and Flavia Hadley (Griffin) Halloran; student Washington U., St. Louis, 1947-47; B.A., George Washington U., 1949; m. Richard H. Rush, Aug. 15, 1956; 1 dau., Sallie Haywood. One-man shows at Fort Amador Officers Club, Panama Canal Zone, El Panama Hotel, Panama, George Washington U., Statler Hotel, Roosevelt Hotel, Washington, Newspaper Womens Club, Washington, Waukegan (Ill.) Library, Epworth Heights Hotel, Ludington, Mich.; exhibited in group shows at Panama Art League, Corcoran Gallery; represented in permanent collections at U. Panama; also pvt. collections; model John Robert Powers Agy., 1950; sec.-treas., dir. N. Am. Acceptance Corp., 1956-58; v.p. Rush and Halloran, Inc., 1957-58, partner, 1954-57. Recipient First Prize (Panama) Newspaper Women's Club, 1953, First Prize Panama Art League, 1953. Mem. D.A.R., Nat. League Am. Penwomen, Florence Crittenton Circle (rec. sec. 1968-69), Kappa Kappa Gamma. Club: Washington. Illustrator: Antiques As An Investment (author Richard H. Rush), 1968. Home: Box 62 Glenville Greenwich CT 06830 also Villa Palladio at Piombino Dese Italy

RUSH, SHARON JUANITA (MRS. HERBERT G. RUSH), marriage and family counselor; b. Anadarko, Okla., Sept. 11, 1938; d. Robert Thomas and Ruth Jewell (Morris) Robinson; student U. Okla., 1956-57; B.S., N.Tex. State U., 1969, M.S., 1970; m. Herbert G. Rush, Nov. 20, 1971; children from previous marriage—Paula Koehn, David Koehn. Psychologist, Midland (Tex.) Community Center, 1969-71; counselor Tarrant County Jr. Coll., Ft. Worth, 1971; founder Family Therapy Assos., Ft. Worth, 1971—. Tchr. psychology Midland Jr. Coll., 1969—; human relations trainer Ft. Worth chpt. Amigos de las Americas, 1974—; cons. Ft. Worth Neuropsychiat. Center; lectr. psychology women in scuba diving. Mem. Am., Tex. (a founder), Tarrant County (a founder, past sec.) assns. marriage and family counselors, Am. (asso.), Tarrant County psychol. assns., Nat. Orgn. Women (asst. instr. scuba diving), Profl. Assn. Scuba Diving. Home: 6457 Hilldale Rd Fort Worth TX 76116 Office: 1320 Lake St Fort Worth TX 76102

RUSHTON, MARY FAY HOPKINS (MRS. LONNIE CONNON RUSHTON), educator; b. Dallas; d. John Raymond and Viola (Shultz) Hopkins; B.A., U. Tex., 1940; M.A. in Counseling Psychology, Tex. A. and I. U., 1964; m. Lonnie Connon Rushton, Oct. 20, 1935; children—Mary Ann (Mrs. Joe A. Hoppe), Nancy Martha (Mrs. Jere P. Parrish). Curator anthropology mus. U. Tex., 1940-42; tchr. pub. schs., Mercedes, Tex., 1954-72, vocational adjustment coordinator Mercedes Schs., 1964-72; psychologist, counselor Rio Grande Habitation Ind. Sch. Dist., Edinburg, Tex., 1972—. Registrar council Girl Scout, Am., 1948-53; mem. Nat. Safety Council, 1955-64; pres. bd. dirs. Mercedes Pub. Library. Mem. Am. Assn. Mental Deficiency, Tex. Psychol. Assn., Am. Assn. Sch. Psychologists, Council for Exceptional Children, Colonial Dames of 17th Century, Nat. Soc. Magna Carta Dames, D.A.R., Am. Assn. U. Women, Tex. State Tchrs. Assn., Am. Anthrop. Assn., Phi Theta Kappa. Club: Garden (pres. 1949-50). Home: Box 687 Mission TX 78572

RUSKAMP, JUDITH SARA, editor; b. Chgo., June 2, 1946; d. John Arthur and Mildred Sara (Schneider) Ruskamp; B.A., U. Chgo., 1969; postgrad. Loyola U., Chgo., 1969-70. Asso. editor Chgo. Rev., 1966-69, fiction editor, 1969-70, editor, 1970-72, editorial adviser, 1972—. Co-dir. The Speakers Series Midwest Lecture Circuit, 1969-70. Mem. D.A.R. Home: 8345 S Kostner St Chicago IL 60652 Office: 5757 S Drexel Av Chicago IL 60637

RUSS, JOANNA, sci. fiction writer, educator; b. Bronx, N.Y., Feb. 22, 1937; d. Evarett and Bertha (Zinner) Russ; B.A. with distinction and high honors, Cornell U., 1957; M.F.A., Yale, 1960. Instr. English, Cornell U., 1967-70, asst. prof., 1970-72; asst. prof. English, Harpur Coll. State U. N.Y., 1972—. Author: Picnic on Paradise, 1968; And Chaos Died, 1970. Contbr. short stores to profl. jours. Office: Dept English Harpur Coll State U NY Binghamton NY 13901

RUSSELL, AGNESS REED (MRS. JESSE S. RUSSELL), educator, psychologist; b. Seymour, Tex., Mar. 7, 1914; d. Kirby Smith and Nora (Richeson) Reed; B.A., McMurry Coll., 1937; M.Ed., Tex. Tech. U., 1952, postgrad., 1955-56; postgrad. U. Tex., 1955, N. Tex. State U., 1950-51; m. Jesse S. Russell, Mar. 7, 1936 (dec. Jan. 1969). Prin., Lake Creek Sch., Baylor County, Tex., 1933-35; tchr. Foard City (Tex.) High Sch., 1935-37, Vernon (Tex.) Pub. Schs., 1937-55; guidance dir. Wilbarger County Schs., Vernon, 1956-65, Vernon Pub. Schs., 1965—. Mem. Tex. State Tchrs. Assn., Tex. Classroom Tchrs. Assn., Am. Assn. U. Women, N.E.A., Am., Tex. personnel and guidance assns., Delta Kappa Gamma. Presbyn. Home: 3115 Martindale St Vernon TX 76384

RUSSELL, ATTIE YVONNE WERNER, physician; b. Washington; d. George and Kathleen (Milliner) Werner; B.S., Am. U., 1944; M.S., U. Ia., 1948, Ph.D., 1952; M.D., U. Chgo., 1958; m. Rex Hillier, Apr. 19, 1954 (dec. June 1954); m. 2d, Henry John Russell, Jan. 9, 1960 (div. Aug. 1971); children—Richard George, Margaret Jane. USPHS fellow Med. Research Council, London, Eng., 1952-54; intern Phila. Gen. Hosp., 1958-59; resident pediatrics Albert Einstein Coll. Medicine, Bronx Municipal Med. Center, 1959-60; fellow pediatric cardiology Albert Einstein Coll. Medicine, 1960-61; resident pediatrics Del. Hosp., Wilmington, 1962; dir. crippled children's services Del. Bd. Health, 1963-67, dir. maternal, child and crippled children's services, 1967-68; clin. asso. prof. pediatrics Women's Med. Coll. Pa., 1966-68; asst. dean for community affairs, asso. prof. pediatrics U. Cin. Coll. Medicine, 1968-71; cons. pediatrics, attending pediatrician in community medicine Cin. Children's Hosp., 1969-71; cons. pediatrics Cin. Convalescent Hosp. for Children, 1970-71; clin. asso. prof. pediatrics Med. Coll. Pa., 1971—; dir. Bur. Community Health Services, Div. Pub. Health, Del. Dept. Health and Social Services, 1971-73, dep. dir. div., 1972-74; dir. med. instns. County Santa Clara, Santa Clara Valley Med. Center, San Jose, Cal., 1974—; clin. prof. pediatrics Stanford, 1974—; mem. exec. bd. Child Diagnostic and Devel. Center of Del., 1964-68; mem. exec. com. Coordinating Council for Handicapped Child of Del., 1964-68; mem. med. adv. bd. Del. Assn. for Retarded Children, 1963-68; mem. com. for Jefferson Presch. for emotionally disturbed children Del. Mental Health Assn., 1965-68; mem. bd. Cin. Child Health Assn., 1969-71. Diplomate Am. Bd. Pediatrics. Fellow Am. Acad. Pediatrics, Am. Pub. Health Assn. (sec. maternal and child health sect.); mem. Am. Physiol. Soc., A.M.A., Assn. State Maternal and Child Health and Crippled Children's Dirs. (sec.-treas. 1966-68), Cal. Med. Assn.,

Santa Clara County Med. Soc., Sigma Xi, Alpha Omega Alpha. Home: 102 Vista del Prado Los Gatos CA 95030 Office: Santa Clara Valley Med Center 751 S Bascom Av San Jose CA 95128

RUSSELL, BARBARA LEE EDMONDS (MRS. ROBERT R. RUSSELL), physician; b. Kansas City, Mo., Jan. 9, 1922; d. Gilbert H. and M. Louise (Young) Edmonds; A.B., U. Kan., 1943, M.A., 1944, Ph.D., 1948, M.D., 1950; m. Robert R. Russell, Aug. 13, 1943; children—John Malcolm, James Andrew, Robert Edmond Bruce. Intern, St. Margaret's Hosp., Kansas City, 1950-51; resident in pediatrics U. Mo., Columbia, 1967-68; practice medicine specializing in pediatrics, Rolla, Mo., 1951—; chief staff Phelps County Hosp., 1970-72; Rolla preceptor U. Mo. Sch. Medicine, 1965—, now clin. instr. pediatrics; med. dir. Regional Diagnostic Center for Mental Retardation, Rolla, 1968—. Mem. Rolla Community Orch., 1964—. Diplomate Am. Bd. Pediatrics. Mem. Am. Acad. Pediatrics, Am. Assn. U. Women, A.M.A., Mo. State Assn. (soc. sec. 1966-68), Mid-Mo. Med. Soc. (pres. 1973), Am. Acad. Gen. Practice, Am. Med. Women's Assn., Am. Soc. Microbiology, League Women Voters, Sigma Xi, Alpha Omega Alpha. Home: Box 766 Rolla MO 65401 Office: 11th and Bishop Sts Rolla MO 65401

RUSSELL, BONNEY BEATRICE LINSLEY (MRS. MAX W. RUSSELL), social worker; b. nr. Hays, Mont., June 14, 1919; d. Clarence H. and Maud (Miller) Linsley; B.A. U. Cal. at Los Angeles, 1940; M.S.W., So. Cal., 1955; m. Max W. Russell, May 29, 1941. Elementary tchr. Pasadena (Cal.) city schs., 1948-50; child welfare worker, div. child welfare services Bur. Pub. Assistance Los Angeles County, 1952-60, supervising child welfare worker, El Monte, 1961-64, head child welfare worker, Los Angeles, 1964-67; dep. dist. dir. family and children's services Dept. Pub. Social Service Los Angeles County, 1967-72, dep. regional services adminstr. Bur. Social Service, 1972—. Mem. Nat. Assn. Social Workers (charter; mem. local council family and children's services), Acad. Certified Social Workers (charter), U. Cal. at Los Angeles Westwood Club Alumni Assn. Democrat. Presbyn. (Christian edn. com. 1966). Mem. Order Eastern Star (worthy matron 1965). Home: 1814 Alisal St West Covina CA 91790 Office: 1124 E Garvey St West Covina CA 91790

RUSSELL, DOROTHY MAY, social work adminstr.; b. Pitts., Aug. 31, 1910; d. Herbert A. and May (Lighthall) Russell; B.A., Chatham Coll., 1932; M.S., U. Pitts., 1935; M.S.W., Carnegie Mellon U., 1946. Grad. asst. U. Pitts., 1933-34; caseworker Allegheny County Bd. Assistance, 1933-42; caseworker Family and Children Service, Pitts., 1942-51, supr., 1951-52; dir. social service Zoar Home, Allison Park, Pa., 1952-65, Columbia Hosp., Pitts., 1965—. With Office Econ. Opportunity, Wilkinsburg, Pa., 1968—; coordinator United Presbyn. Home for Children, Mars, Pa., 1965—. Cons., Oakmont (Pa.) Residence. Mem. Nat. Assn. Social Workers, Child Welfare League Am., Am. Hosp. Assn., Am. Soc. Hosp. Dirs. Social Service, Pitts. Zool. Soc., Allegheny County Hosp. Council. Phi Sigma. Presbyn. (hon. mem. bd. christian edn. 1960—, pres. christian edn. council 1950-60). Home: 11203 Frankstown Rd Pittsburgh PA 15235 Office: Columbia Hosp Penn and West Sts Pittsburgh PA 15221

RUSSELL, ELSIE WELLS (MRS. JOHN P. RUSSELL), nutritionist; b. Farina, Ill., Sept. 16, 1901; d. Oscar Clarke and Ines (Fitz-Randolph) Wells; dietitians diploma Battle Creek Coll., 1921; B.S., U. Cal. at Berkeley, 1944; M.P.H., U. Mich., 1948; m. John Paul Russell, Dec. 24, 1926 (dec. Mar. 1941); 1 son, John Randolph. Intern Walter Reed Gen. Hosp., Washington, 1922, dietitian in charge of woman's ward, 1923-24; chief dietitian John D. Archbold Meml. Hosp., Thomasville, Ga., 1925 indsl. nutrition cons. Ninth Service Command, San Francisco Bay Area, 1944-46; nutrition cons. Oakland (Cal.) City Health Dept., 1946-47; dir. nutrition div. Los Angeles City Health Dept., 1948-64; supr. and coordinator Los Angeles City and County Dist. Nutrition Services, 1964-71; nutrition cons., 1971—. Consumer cons. Fed. FDA, 1952—. Bd. dirs. Meals for Millions Found., 1948—, exec. com., sec., 1972—; membership chmn. So. Cal. com. WHO; mem. bd. Planned Parenthood Assn. Los Angeles. Recipient Fed. Civil Def. Pub. Service award AEC Nev. Test Site, 1955. Fellow Am. Pub. Health Assn.; mem. Internat. Union Nutritional Scis., Royal Soc. Health Eng., Inst. Food Technologists, Nat. Soc. Magna Charta Dames, Daus. Founders and Patriots Am., Nat. Soc. U.S. Daus. 1812, Soc. Colonial Govs., Cal. Dietetic Assn. (pres. 1956-57), Greater Los Angeles Nutrition Council (pres. 1955-56), Am. (chmn. social welfare and pub. health 1953-55), Cal. (counselor 1957—, home safety chmn. Los Angeles dist.) home econs. assns. Cal. Huguenot Soc. (membership chmn.), D.A.R., Dau. Am. Colonists, Colonial Dames XVII Century, C. of C. Nat. Soc. Women Descs. Ancient and Honorable Arty. Co. (pres. 1972—), Colonial Dames Am., Daus. Colonial Wars, Plantagenet Soc. Home: 825 S Hobart Blvd Los Angeles CA 90005 (summer) Cornelian Bay Lake Tahoe CA 95730

RUSSELL, ESTHER FORBES, journalist; b. New Haven, Mar. 5, 1919; d. William Abner and Esther Harrison (Eliot) Forbes; B.A. cum laude, Smith Coll., 1940; m. William LaRoche Russell, June 7, 1952; 1 son, Hollis Forbes. Freelance aviation writer, 1943—; editorial researcher Bell Aircraft Corp., Niagara Falls, N.Y., 1943; asst. dir. women's publicity Republican Nat. Com., 1944; contbg. editor U.S. Air Services, Washington, 1944-56; asso. editor Payload mag., N.Y.C., 1947-52; mgr. speakers' bur. Smith Coll. 75th Anniversary Fund, N.Y.C., 1946-47; reporter, columnist Southampton Press, newspaper chain, 1966—; contbr. L.I. Press, 1970—; reporter WRIV, Riverhead, N.Y., 1971—. Publicity chmn. Jr. League City N.Y., 1944-46; founder Southampton Twp. Preservation Soc., 1966, sec., 1966-74, pres., 1974—. Bd. dirs. Com. for A New County, 1967—, mem. exec. com., 1967—; bd. dirs. Hampton Bays Civic Assn., 1966-72, v.p., 1970-72. Mem. Aviation/Space Writers Assn., Phi Beta Kappa. Episcopalian. Clubs: Quogue (N.Y.) Beach; Quogue (N.Y.) Field; Shinnecock Yacht (Quogue, N.Y.). Home: 11 White Lane Hampton Bays NY 11946

RUSSELL, ETHEL ELAINE JOHNSON, brands co. exec.; b. Westfield, Wis.; d. Samuel C. and Anna (Long) Johnson; B.S., U. Wis., 1941; m. R. Pled Russell, June 18, 1935 (div. Dec. 1959); children—Ralph P., Kent H. Head home econs. Midwest Research Inst., Kansas City, Mo., 1950-57; v.p., treas. Niven-Russell Research, Inc., Kansas City, Mo., 1957-69; dir. consumer research Interstate Brands Corp., Kansas City, Mo., 1970—; dir. Faultess Starch Co. Mem. Internat., Am., Mo. home econs. assns., Nat. Home Economists in Bus., Research Soc. Am., Kansas City Home Economists in Bus., Women's C. of C. (mem. consumer edn. com. 1970). Home: 4712 Roanoke Pkwy Kansas City MO 64112 Office: 12 E Armour St Kansas City MO 64111

RUSSELL, FAY LAVERNE FORTENBERRY (MRS. GEORGE PERRY RUSSELL), nurse educator; b. Columbia, Miss., Nov. 27, 1927; d. Henry Reese and Willie (Conerly) Fortenberry; diploma Bapt. Meml. Hosp. Sch. Nursing, 1949; B.S., U. Tenn., 1962; M.Nursing, Emory U., 1966; postgrad. U. Wash., summers 1972, 73; m. George Perry Russell, Nov. 20, 1950; children—Patricia LaStarr (Mrs. John R. Dolan, Jr.), Perry Lamont Faulkner. Staff nurse Bapt. Meml. Hosp., Memphis, 1949-53, head nurse, 1953-55, supr., 1955-59, instr. nursing, 1962-65, asst. dir. Sch. Nursing, 1966-67; asso. prof., chief nursing U. Tenn. Child Devel. Center, Memphis, 1967—. Mem. Am., Tenn. nurses assns., Am., Southeastern (chmn. nursing div. 1973-74) assns. mental deficiency, Sigma Theta Tau. Mem. Order Eastern Star. Author: (with M. Haynes) A Nursing Study of Day Care for Mentally Retarded Children, 1971. Editor: The Identification and Management of Selected Developmental Disabilities, 1973. Home: 23 S Evergreen St Memphis TN 38104 Office: 711 Jefferson St Memphis TN 38105

RUSSELL, HELEN DIANE, mus. ofcl.; b. Kansas City, Mo., Apr. 8, 1936; d. Harry Fay and Georgia (Canfield) Russell; B.A., Vassar Coll., 1958; postgrad. (Woodrow Wilson Nat. fellow 1958-59), Radcliffe Grad. Sch., 1958-60; Ph.D. (fellow 1961-63), Johns Hopkins, 1970. Research asst. Smithsonian Inst. Traveling Exhbn. Service, Washington, 1960-61; curator Nat. Gallery of Art, Washington, 1965-70, asst. curator graphic arts, 1970—. Profl. lectr. dept. art Am. U., Washington, 1966-72. Recipient Samuel H. Kress Found. fellowship, 1973; Alumnae fellowship, Vassar Coll., 1959-60. Mem. Coll. Art Assn. Am., Washington Print Club, Washington Women Art Profls. Contbr. articles and rev. to various publs. Home: 3406 Annandale Rd Falls Church VA 22042 Office: Nat Gallery of Art Washington DC 20565

RUSSELL, HELEN LOUISE, coll. dean; b. Champaign, Ill., Mar. 20, 1914; d. Fred A. and Myra (Parker) Russell; A.B., U. Ill., 1935, Ph.D., 1944; M.S., Wellesley Coll., 1937. Instr. phys. edn. Wellesley Coll., 1937-39, U. Wis., 1939-42; asst. prof. phys. edn. Smith Coll., Northampton, Mass., 1944-47, asso. prof., asst. dir. dept., 1947-54, prof., acting warden, 1954-56, dean of students, 1956—. Trustee The People's Inst., Northampton, Mass., 1956—. Mem. Colonial Dames Am., Nat. Assn. Women's Deans, Mortar Bd., Torch, Phi Beta Kappa, Phi Kappa Phi, Kappa Alpha Theta, Alpha Lambda Delta, Kappa Delta Pi. Conglist. Author articles athletic jours. Home: 115 Elm St Northampton MA 01060

RUSSELL, HELEN ROSS (MRS. ROBERT STANLEY RUSSELL), author; b. Myerstown, Pa., Feb. 21, 1915; d. George Smith and Helen Louise (Boyd) Ross; teaching certificate West Chester State Coll., 1934; B.A., Lebanon Valley Coll., 1943, D.H.L., 1973; M.A., Cornell, 1947, Ph.D., 1949; m. Robert Stanley Russell, Sept. 24, 1960. Tchr. pub. sch., Jackson Twp., Lebanon County, Pa., 1934-35, Bethel Twp. Sch., Berks County, 1935-42; tchr. Lebanon (Pa.) City Schs., 1942-46; grad. asst. Cornell U., 1947-49; prof. biology Fitchburg (Mass.) Coll., 1952-56, chmn. sci. dept., 1952-56, dean of studies, 1956-66. Dir. nature inst. Gay Valley Camp, Brevard, N.C., summers 1951, 52; cons. Wave Hill Center for Environmental Studies, Bronx, N.Y., 1967-70; sci. cons. Manhattan Country Sch., N.Y.C., 1970—. Fellow A.A.A.S.; mem. Am. Nature Study Soc. (pres. elect 1973), United Meth. Women (pres. 1970-73). Author: City Critters, 1969; True Book of Buds, 1970; Of Springtime Tree Seeds, 1973; Clarion the Killdeer, 1970; Winter Search Party, 1971; Winter: A Field Trip Guide, 1972; Soil..., 1972; Small Worlds..., 1972; Water..., 1973; Earth The Great Recycler, 1973; Ten Minute Field Trips, 1973; Foraging for Dinner, 1974. Contbr. to publs. in field. Address: 44 College Dr Jersey City NJ 07305

RUSSELL, IRENE ELIZABETH HOOGE (MRS. THOMAS J. RUSSELL), banker; b. Syracuse, N.Y.; d. Ferd M. and Anna M. (Gravius) Hooge; student Am. Inst. Banking, 1928-33, Am. Mgmt. Assn., 1969; m. Thomas J. Russell, Dec. 7, 1946. Sec. First Trust and Deposit Co., Syracuse, N.Y., 1928-56, asst. mgr. credit dept., 1956-63, mgr. credit dept., 1963-68, asst. sec., 1968-72, asst. v.p., 1972—, sec. officer's loan com., 1968—. Hon. mem. Am. Inst. Banking (chmn. women's com. 1932-33), mem. Nat. Assn. Bank Women, Syracuse Assn. Credit Men, First Trust Club (sec. 1932-33). Home: 106 DeWolfe Rd Syracuse NY 13224 Office: 201 S Warren St Syracuse NY 13201

RUSSELL, JEAN BUCK (MRS. JAMES W. RUSSELL), govt. ofcl.; b. Atlanta, Sept. 3, 1926; d. Edgar Allen and Jessie Lee (Casey) Buck; student U. Ga., 1944-47; m. James W. Russell, June 29, 1949; children—Nancy Jean, Alicia Eileen. Pub. information officer U.S. Armed Services Forces Depot, Conley, Ga., 1944-45; with Atlanta Constitution, 1945-46; polit. and feature reporter Internat. News Service, Atlanta, 1946-49, columnist, feature writer Miami bur., 1949; free-lance pub. relations writer, 1949-70; dir. communications Dade County, Dept. Housing and Urban Devel., Miami, 1972—. Mem. Women in Communications. Methodist. Home: 4800 SW 64th Ct Miami FL 33155 Office: Dade County Housing and Urban Development PO Box 250 Riverside Station Miami FL 33135

RUSSELL, JUDITH LYNN, coll. dean; b. Anamosa, Ia., June 26, 1938; d. Glen A. and Wilma M. (Hanna) Russell; B.A. cum laude, U. Ia., 1960; M.A., Syracuse U., 1962. Asst. dean of women Ripon (Wis.) Coll., 1962-65; dean of women Wagner Coll., S.I., N.Y., 1965-67; asst. dean of students Ohio State U., Columbus, 1967-71; dean of students Colo. Women's Coll., Denver, 1971—. Mem. Denver office adv. panel Coll. Entrance Exam. Bd., 1973—. Mem. Nat. Assn. Women Deans, Adminstrs. and Counselors (chmn. bylaws revision com. 1971-72), Colo.-Wyo. Assn. Women Adminstrs. and Counselors (chmn. coll. and univ. sect. 1973-74), Nat. Assn. Student Personnel Adminstrs., Mountain-Plains Deans, Mortar Bd., Alpha Lambda Delta, Pi Lambda Theta. Home: 6923 Montview Blvd Denver CO 80207 Office: Colo Women's Coll Montview Blvd and Quebec Denver CO 80220

RUSSELL, LAO COOK (MRS. WALTER RUSSELL), philosopher, author, educator; b. Ivinghoe, Buckinghamshire, Eng., Nov. 6; d. Alfred William and Florence (Hills) Cook; naturalized, 1947; ed. pvt. tutors; m. Walter Russell, July 29, 1948. Founder Walter Russell Found. (now known as U. of Sci. and Philosophy), 1948, mng. dir., 1948—, pres., 1949—; lectr. numerous cities in U.S., 1947—; founded Shrine of Beauty at Swannanoa Palace, nr. Waynesboro, Va., 1948. Founder Man-Woman Equalization League, 1955, Internat. Age of Character, Arts and Cultural Centers, 1966, Internat. Age of Character Clubs, 1966. Mem. Internat. Platform Assn. Author: God Will Work With You But Not For You, 1955 (named one of 6 best book of year N.Y. Herald-Tribune, 1955); An Eternal Message of Light and Love, 1964; My Love I Extend to You, 1966; Love-A Scientific and Living Philosophy of Love and Sex, 1966; Why You Cannot Die-The Continuity of Life, Reincarnation Explained, 1972; (with Walter Russell) One Year Home Study Course in Universal Law, Natural Science and Living Philosophy, 1950, Atomic Suicide, 1957; The World Crisis—Its Explanation and Solution, 1958; The One-World Purpose—A Plan to Dissolve War by a Power More Mighty than War, 1960. Executed 5-foot statue (with husband) The Christ of the Blue Ridge, 1948, also colossal model, 1950. Address: Swannanoa Palace Waynesboro VA 22980

RUSSELL, LOIS ROBERTA LANGLEY (MRS. ARMAND RUSSELL), musician; b. Upland, Cal., Feb. 21, 1932; d. Robert William and Velma (Clark) Langley; student U. Wash., 1950-52; m. Armand Russell, Aug. 22, 1953; children—Sherrilyn Ann, Sheldon Lee. First percussionist Seattle Symphony Orch., 1948-55, Fargo-Moorhead (N.D.) Symphony, 1958-61, Honolulu Symphony Orch., 1961—; instr. percussion U. Hawaii, 1961—. Mem. Percussive Arts Soc., Nat. Assn. Rudimental Drummers, Sigma Alpha Iota (patroness). Performs in chamber music recitals works for percussion by modern composers of Asian and Western countries. Home: 3296 Huelani Dr Honolulu HI 96822

RUSSELL, MADELEINE HAAS, museum trustee; b. San Francisco, Apr. 2, 1915; d. Charles William and Fannie Marie (Stern) Haas; B.A. magna cum laude, Smith Coll., 1937; children—Alice Cornelia, Charles Phillips, Christine Haas. Dir. Dept. of State Reception Center, San Francisco, 1962-69. Mem. Nat. Democratic Com. from Cal. Trustee San Francisco Mus. Art, World Affairs Council No. Cal., War Meml. Opera House, Brandeis U.; bd. dirs. San Francisco Planning and Urban Renewal Assn.; bd. govs. San Francisco Symphony Assn. Mem. Phi Beta Kappa. Home: 3778 Washington St San Francisco CA 94118

RUSSELL, MARIAN ADDIE KETTLE (MRS. HARRY EDGAR RUSSELL), civic worker; b. LeRoy, N.Y., June 30, 1908; d. William Richard and Addie Mae (Burkhart) Kettle; B.A., U. Rochester, 1930; postgrad. Geneseo State Tchrs. Coll., 1934, Albany State Coll., 1935; M.A. in Psychology, Columbia, 1941; m. Harry Edgar Russell, Aug. 12, 1950 (dec. Dec. 1966); 1 son, William Harrison. Tchr. rural sch., Little Canada, N.Y., 1931-32, Prin. Linwood, N.Y., 1932-34, LeRoy High Sch. (N.Y.), 1934-66. Chmn., Youth Recreation, 1943—; founder LeRoy Girl Scout council, 1933; chmn. Central Western zone classical lang. sect. N.Y. State, 3 years; mem. LeRoy Park Commn., 1968—; chmn. Genesee County Bicentennial Commn. Named LeRoyan of Year, 1972. Mem. LeRoy Hist. Soc. (founding 1940, sec. 1963—), N.Y., Nat., LeRoy geneal. and hist. socs., Delta Kappa Gamma (a founder Geneseo County 1964, treas. 1964—). Mem. Order Eastern Star, Rebeckah. Contbr. hist. articles to profl. jours. Home: 26 Lincoln Av LeRoy NY 14482

RUSSELL, MARY ELSA, editor; b. Springfield, Mass.; d. Patrick William and Mary (Flanagan) Russell; B.A., Mt. Holyoke Coll.; M.A., Columbia U. English tchr. Windsor (Conn.) High Sch., Danbury (Conn.) High Sch., N.Y.C. High Sch. of Sci.; scriptwriter NBC, N.Y.; contbg. editor Reader's Digest, Pleasantville, N.Y.; staff mem. Writers Conf. Georgetown U., Cape Cod Writers Conf. Mem. Overseas Press Club, Womens Nat. Book Assn., Vols. of the Shelters, Women in Communications. Club: Mt. Holyoke of N.Y. Home: Prospect Tower 45 Tudor City Pl New York City NY 10017

RUSSELL, MATTIE UNDERWOOD, librarian; b. Randolph, Miss., May 14, 1915; d. William Vance and Mattie Pearl (Underwood) Russell; B.A., U. Miss., 1937, M.A., 1940; Ph.D., Duke, 1956. Tchr. social studies Center High Sch., Blue Springs, 1937-40, Union (Miss.) High Sch., 1940-41, Carthage (Miss.) High Sch., 1941-43; asst. prof. history Mars Hill (N.C.) Coll., 1943-46; asst. curator manuscripts Perkins Library, Duke U., Durham, N.C., 1948-52, curator manuscripts, 1952—; vis. asso. prof. library sci. U. N.C., Chapel Hill, spring semester, 1969—. Mem. Am. Assn. for State and Local History, Am. Assn. U. Profs., Am. Assn. U. Women, Am., So. (mem. program com. 1971-72) hist. assns., Am., N.C., Durham County library assns., Hist. Soc. N.C. (v.p. 1965), Manuscript Soc., Oral History Assn., Soc. Am. Archivists, N.C. Lit. and Hist. Assn., Soc. Archivists (British). Contbr. to Dictionary of North Carolina Biography, also articles to profl. jours. Home: 2209 Woodrow St Durham NC 27705 Office: 344 Perkins Library Duke U Durham NC 27706

RUSSELL, NELLIE MARVEL BROTHERTON (MRS. ALBERT HALL RUSSELL), radio-TV broadcaster; b. Joplin, Mo., May 19, 1912; d. Walter and Lottie (Anderson) Brotherton; grad. high sch.; m. Albert Hall Russell, Nov. 1, 1935; children—Susan (Mrs. James Monroe), William, Mary Elizabeth Wilson. Hostess Marvel Russell Show, KWTX Radio, Waco, Tex., 1953—; women's editor Better Living show, KWTX-TV, Waco, 1955—. Pres. City P.T.A. Council, 1953, 54. Bd. dirs. Camp Fire Girls, 1956-58. Mem. Book Traders Study Club. Home: 1509 Northcrest Dr Waco TX 76710 Office: KWTX Waco TX 76710

RUSSELL, OLGA WESTER (MRS. HENRY G. RUSSELL), educator; b. Hartford, Conn., June 20, 1913; d. Thomas Nielsen and Olga S.K. (Iversen) Wester; Diplome d'Etudes Francaises, U. Poitiers, 1932; Diplome de Civilisation, U. Paris, Sorbonne, 1933; A.B., Conn. Coll., New London, 1934; A.M., U. Cal. at Berkeley, 1939; A.M., Harvard, 1944, Ph.D., 1957; m. Henry G. Russell, Mar. 8, 1938; 1 dau., Olga Louise (Mrs. Donald L. Maxwell). Asst. in French, U. Cal. at Berkeley, 1939; instr. Cambridge Jr. Coll., 1943-44, Wheaton Coll., Mass., 1944-46, Tufts U., 1946-48, 51-52; asst. prof. Chatham Coll., Pitts., 1956-61; tchr. WQED, Ednl. TV, Pitts., 1956-60; asst. prof. U. South Fla., Tampa, 1961-63; prof., chmn. dept. fgn. langs. Longwood Coll., Farmville, Va., 1963-65; asso. prof. Eastern Ill. U., 1965-66; prof. U. Me. at Orono, 1966—. Fellow Radcliffe Coll., 1955. Mem. Modern Lang. Assn. Am., Am. Assn. U. Profs., Phi Beta Kappa. Conglist. Author: Etude historique et critique des Burgraves de Victor Hugo, 1962. Office: Little Hall U Me Orono ME 04473

RUSSELL, PHEBE GALE (MRS. FRANK M. RUSSELL), broadcasting exec.; b. N.Y.C., Dec. 23, 1910; d. George H. and Marian (Hyde) Gale; grad. high sch.; m. Frank M. Russell, Sept. 25, 1940; children—Gale, Morgan N. Publicity dir. NBC, Washington, 1929-39; v.p. radio sta. WICO, Salisbury, Md., 1958-62; pres. Ellensburg Television Cable Corp., Washington, 1961-68, PGR Enterprises, Inc., 1962-71; owner TV Cable Cos. Appalachia, Norton, Big Stone Gap, Va., 1962—; dir. Delmarva Broadcasting Co., 1958-62. Mem. women's bd. George Washington U. Hosp. Mem. D.A.R., Mayflower Soc., Huguenot Soc., D.C. Women's Golf Assn. Clubs: Kenwood Garden (pres. 1963-64), Congressional Country (Washington). Address: 5101 River Rd Washington DC 20016

RUSSELL, ROSANNE PEARL, ednl. adminstr.; b. Meadville, Pa., Jan. 9, 1939; d. Charles E. and Catherine E. (Pratt) Russell; B.A., Cin. Bible Sem., 1960; M.Ed., U. Cin., 1965. Tchr., Conneaut Valley Elementary Sch., Conneautville, Pa., 1962-64; exec. dir. YWCA, Meadville, 1964-72; registrar Cin. Bible Sem., 1972—. Mem. Meadville (Pa.) Juvenile Delinquency Com., 1965-68, Youth-Smoking and Health Council, Meadville, 1965-71; sec. Youth Employment Service, Meadville, 1968-72. Bd. dirs. Crawford County (Pa.) Community Council, 1965-72, treas., 1965-67. Mem. Ohio Assn. Collegiate Registrars and Admission Officers. Home: 549 Howell Av Cincinnati OH 45220 Office: 2700 Glenway Av Cincinnati OH 45204

RUSSELL, RUTH LOIS STELLING (MRS. CAMP WELLS RUSSELL), educator; b. San Diego, July 22, 1928; d. Henry George and Nina May (Newman) Stelling; B.A. in Microbiology, U. Cal., Los Angeles, 1952, Ph.D. in Microbiology, 1963; m. Camp Wells Russell, Jan. 28, 1954; 1 son, Brian Camp. Teaching asst. microbiology dept. U. Cal., Los Angeles, 1952-56; instr. biology Occidental Coll., Los Angeles, 1956-57; pre-doctoral fellow Nat. Tb Assn., 1957-59; research microbiology VA Hosp., San Fernando, Cal., 1959-62, Olive View (Cal.) Hosp., 1962-63; asst. prof. microbiology Cal. State U., Long Beach, 1963-67, asso. prof. microbiology, 1967-72, prof., 1972—, acting dean grad. studies, 1972-73, dir. environmental studies, 1974—. Cons. pathology dept. Meml. Hosp. Long Beach. Bd. dirs. Long Beach Tb and Health Assn., 1967—. Mem. A.A.A.S., Am. Soc. Microbiology, Am. Mus. Nat. History, Cal. Acad. Sci., Am., So.

Cal. pub. health assns., Am., Cal. tissue culture assns., Sigma Xi. Home: 1316 Josie Av Long Beach CA 90815

RUSSELL, SANDRA LORELEI, city ofcl.; b. Flushing, N.Y., Mar. 3, 1936; d. Walter James and Dorothy Allen (Dunderdale) Russell; B.A., Hofstra Coll., 1957; postgrad. N.Y.U., 1957-58, Cooper Union Art Sch., 1960-64. Musician, singer clubs, N.Y., 1950-60; exhibited in group shows at Cooper Union Art Sch., N.Y.C., St. Marks Ch., N.Y.C., Washington Square Outdoor Art Show, N.Y.C.; evaluator, admissions office N.Y.U. Sch. Edn., 1957-58; asso. to literary agt., N.Y.C., 1958; editor Horse Show Mag., Am. Horse Shows Assn., 1958-59; asso. editor Modern Plastics Ency., N.Y.C., 1959-60; promotion and pub. relations, N.Y. Conv. and Visitors Bur., 1960; trainer harness racehorses Roosevelt and Yonkers raceways, & Goshen, N.Y., 1961-63; sr. copy editor New Book of Knowledge, Grolier, Inc., 1964-67; sr. copy editor Am. Heritage Pub. Co., Inc., N.Y.C., 1967-69; graphics designer, writer dept. pub. affairs N.Y.C. Econ. Devel. Adminstrn., 1970—; freelance graphics designer, photographer, writer, editor, cons., 1964—; corp. sec. N.Y. Inst. Ocean Resources, Inc., 1973-74. Sec. Mayor's Oceanographic Adv. Com., 1971—. Pres., Phoenix Reform Democratic Club, 1969-70, v.p., 1969, rec. sec., 1968-69, treas., 1970-71, exec. com., 1968, 71-73; Democratic county committeeman, 1969—; alternate del. Dist. Jud. Conv., 1970, 71, 72. Mem. Cooper Sq. Community Devel. Com. and Businessmen's Assn., Am. Civil Liberties Union, Nat. Wildlife Fedn., Hall of Fame of the Trotter, South Street Seaport Mus., U.S. Trotting Assn., N.Y. Inst. Ocean Resources (sec. 1973—), Soc. for Animal Rights, Defenders of Wildlife, Humane Soc. U.S., Nichiren Shoshu Acad. Home: 332 E 9th St New York City NY 10003 Office: 225 Broadway New York City NY 10007

RUSSELL, SUSAN WHITTINGTON, lawyer; b. Balt., Apr. 17, 1945; d. Thomas Edgie and Dorothy Irenus (Baier) Russell; B.A., Conn. Coll., 1967; J.D., Boston U., 1970. Admitted to Md. bar, 1970; practiced law in Balt., 1971—; mem. firm Sauerwein, Boyd & Decker, Balt., 1971—. Dep. gen. counsel Md. State Tchrs. Assn., Balt., 1973—. Mem. 3d Dist. Citizen's Com., Balt., 1973—. Mem. Am., Md., Balt. City (exec. com. Young Lawyers' sect. 1973-74), Women's bar assns. Club: Baltimore Country. Home: 308 E Lake Av Baltimore MD 21212 Office: 9 W Mulberry St Baltimore MD 21201

RUSSELLO, LUCILLE DAVOLIO, lawyer; b. N.Y.C.; d. Robert and Mary (Stirnweiss) Davolio; B.A., Seton Hall U., 1960, LL.B., J.D., 1963; married; 1 son, Mark M. Admitted to N.J. bar, 1964; practice in North Arlington, 1964—; trial atty. Henry Habick, Esq., East Orange, N.J., 1965-67; pub. defender, Bergen County, N.J., 1969-72. Founder, 1st pres. Queen of Peace Parents Assn., North Arlington, 1965-66; del. Seton Hall Fedn., 1961-66. Pres. North Arlington Womens Democratic Club, 1965-67; candidate for Surrogate of Bergen County, 1967; mem. exec. com. Bergen County Dem. Womens Club, 1970—. Trustee Bergen County Vocational, Tech. Schs., Hackensack, N.J.; mem. adv. bd. Seton Hall U. Recipient Woman of Achievement award Bus. and Profl. Womens Club, 1971. Mem. Am., N.J., Bergen County (trustee) bar assns., Kappa Beta Pi. Address: 158 Ridge Rd North Arlington NJ 07032

RUSSFIELD, AGNES SANXAY BURT (MRS. LEWIS L. RUSSFIELD), pathologist; b. Portland, Ore., Jan. 9, 1917; d. Francis Sidney and Margaret Taylor (Browning) Burt; B.A., Reed Coll., 1935; M.A., U. Cal. at Los Angeles, 1937; Ph.D., U. Chgo., 1943; M.D., Cornell U., 1949; m. Lewis L. Russfield, June 18, 1954. Intern, Mass. Gen. Hosp., Boston, 1949-50, resident, 1950-51, asst. pathologist, 1951-58; research asso. Bio Research Cons., Inc., Cambridge, Mass., 1958-60; asso. pathology Children's Hosp. Med. Center, Boston, 1961-67; resident to asst. pathologist Boston City Hosp., 1968-71; sr. research asso. Bio-Research Cons., Inc., Cambridge, 1972—; asso. clin. prof. pathology Harvard Med. Sch., 1965-67, lectr. pathology, 1967; asso. prof. pathology Tufts Med. Sch., 1968-71; cooperating scientist Worcester Found. for Exptl. Biology, Shrewsbury, Mass., 1965-72. Served to lt. (j.g.) USNR, 1943-45. Mem. Am. Assn. Pathologists-Bacteriologists, Am. Assn. Exptl. Pathology, Internat. Acad. Pathology, Endocrine Soc., Am. Assn. Cancer Research, A.M.A. Home: 34A Park St Brookline MA 02146 Office: 9 Commercial Av Cambridge MA 02141

RUSSO, HELEN TERESA, psychologist; b. Cin., July 30, 1939; d. Frank and Lucy (Pellegrino) Russo; B.A. magna cum laude, Xavier U., 1963, M.Ed., 1965. Clk.-typist Franciscan Mission Union, Cin., 1957-59; tchr. St. Francis Seraph, Cin., 1959-65, Reading (O.) Middle Sch., 1965-68; psychologist Hamilton County Bd. Edn., Cin., 1968—. Mem. exec. com. Cin. Mental Health Assn., 1970—; co-chmn. Com. for Childhood Mental Health, 1971—. Mem. Xavier U. Alumnae Assn. (v.p. 1970-72, exec. bd. 1972—, gen. chmn. alumnae living endowment fund 1972-73). Roman Catholic (mem. exec. com., dir. St. Anthony Nat. Shrine Soc. 1968—). Home: 4129 Kirby Av Cincinnati OH 45223 Office: 325 E Central Pkwy Cincinnati OH 45202

RUSSO, JANIS ARLENE, pub. relations ofcl.; b. Burbank, Cal., Nov. 16, 1947; d. James Joseph and Louise Agnes (Giamela) Russo; B.A., Cal. State U., Northridge, 1969. Editor, writer S.W. Regional Lab., Los Alamitos, Cal., 1969-70; pub. relations specialist Security Pacific Bank, Los Angeles, 1971-73; account exec. Cline, Fast & Senning Pub. Relations, Los Angeles, 1973-74; pub. relations rep. Met. Water Dist. So. Cal., Los Angeles, 1974—. Recipient 1st place award for investigative article in coll. publ. Cal. Intercollegiate Press Assn., 1970. Mem. Los Angeles Jr. C. of C., Women in Communications.

RUSSO, JOAN PHYLLIS EARNST (MRS. DONALD JOSEPH RUSSO), instrument co. exec.; b. Buffalo, May 4, 1928; d. Philip John and Katherine Charolette (Schmidt) Earnst; student Jean Summers Bus. Coll., 1945-46, Millard Fillmore div. U. Buffalo, 1948-50; m. Donald Joseph Russo, July 22, 1950; 1 dau., Pamela Joan (Mrs. Clifford Stage). Exec. sec. product devel. and engring. Columbus McKinnon Corp., Tonawanda, N.Y., 1959-64; exec. sec. Curry, McLaughlin & Len, Inc. (name now Microwave Systems, Inc.), East Syracuse, N.Y., 1964-66, treas., 1966-73, sec.-treas., 1973—. Mem., sec. Mayor's Adv. Council, Tonawanda, N.Y., 1960-64. Mem. Onondaga Nature Soc., Eastwood Bus. and Profl. Women's (pres. 1970-71), N.Y. State Fedn. Bus. and Profl. Women's Clubs (nominating com. chmn. 1971-72, pub. relations chmn. 1973-74), Syracuse C. of C., Nat. Fedn. Bus. and Profl. Women's Clubs, Inc. Clubs: World Trade (Syracuse, N.Y.); Eastwood. Home: 4150 Birchwood Dr S Liverpool NY 13088 Office: 1 Adler Dr East Syracuse NY 13057

RUSSO, KAREN SORLIE, lawyer; b. Grand Forks, N.D., Oct. 2, 1943; d. George Esterly and Elphie (Langen) Sorlie; B.A., U. N.D., 1963, postgrad., 1963-66; postgrad. Nat. U. Mexico, 1963-64; J.D., U. San Francisco, 1967; m. Salvatore B. Russo, Nov. 8, 1969; 1 son, Peter Sorlie. Fashion model, 1961-64; state chmn. N.D. Coll. Republications, 1962; mem. N.D. exec. com. Republican Party, 1962; v.p. nat. Regional Young Republicans, 1963; research dir. Cal. Rep. Party, 1968; admitted to N.D. bar, 1968, Cal. bar, 1968; adminstrv. asst. to Sen. George Deukmejian, Cal., 1968-70; legal affairs analyst Cal. Office Econ. Opportunity, 1970; dep. atty. gen. for criminal appeals State of Cal., Sacramento, 1970—. Appellate justice McGeorge Sch. Law for moot ct. work; judge Cal. Hwy. Patrol moot ct. Mem. Am. Trial Lawyers Assn., Alpha Phi. Mem. Order Rainbow Girls. Club: Sacramento Ski. Author: California Fact Book, 1968; Budding Portia, 1975. Home: 3042 Kadema St Sacramento CA 95825 Office: 555 Capitol Mall Sacramento CA 95814

RUSSU, JO ANN (MRS. JULIUS L. RUSSU), lawyer; b. Harrisburg, Ill., Mar. 22, 1934; d. Claude C. and Gladys Lillian (Little) Bowen; student Blackburn Coll., 1952-54; A.B., Wayne State U., 1957; J.D., Detroit Coll. Law, 1964; m. Julius L. Russu, Mar. 28, 1959; 1 dau., Julia Lee. Admitted to Mich. Bar, 1964; practiced in Birmingham, 1964-71, 73; mem. firm McTigue, Connelly, Kramer & McTigue, Sterling Heights, Mich., 1971-73, Kennedy & Hannick, Warren, Mich., 1973—. Dir. So. Oakland Co. Chmn. Law Revision Com.; active Girl Scouts Am. Mem. Mich., So. Oakland County, Oakland County, Macomb County Bar assns., Kappa Beta Pi (vice dean 1960-61), Delta Zeta. Club: On the Hill Rochester.

RUST, MATA ANN METZ (MRS. JAMES LEE RUST), educator; b. Boonville, Ind., Oct. 8, 1944; d. Paul Jacob and Elizabeth Carolyn (Watson) Metz; B.S., Ind. State U., 1967; M.S., So. Ill. U., 1969. Teaching asst. So. Ill. U., Carbondale, 1967-69; elementary tchr. Klamath County Schs., Klamath Falls, Ore., 1969-72; instr. Ore. Inst. Tech., Klamath Falls, 1972—. Speech therapy cons. for stroke patients Washburn Manor Presbyn. Hosp., Klamath Falls, 1970—. Mem. Speech Communication Assn., Delta Sigma Rho, Zeta Tau Alpha, Tau Kappa Alpha. Presbyn. Home: Box 60B Harriman Route Klamath Falls OR 97601

RUST, VELMA IRENE MILLER (MRS. RONALD STUART RUST), govt. ofcl.; b. Edmonton, Alta., Can., May 22, 1914; d. Cecil Johnstone and Lillie (Runions) Miller; B.Sc., U. Alta., 1934, tchrs. diploma, 1935, B.Ed., 1944, M.Ed., 1947; Ph.D., U. Ill., 1959; m. Ronald Stuart Rust, Apr. 9, 1955. Tchr., 1936-42, 43-44; insp. Inspection Bd. U.K. and Can., Montreal, 1942-43; mem. staff, faculty U. Alta., 1944-56, asst. prof. edn., 1955-56; grad. asst. U. Ill., 1956-59; researcher in directorate of personnel planning RCAF Hdqrs., 1960-62; chief staff tng., inspection services Dept. Nat. Def., Ottawa, 1962-65; statistician Aviation Statistics, Fed. Govt., 1965-67; supr. math. research and analysis Can. Dept. Nat. Health and Welfare, Ottawa, 1967—. Mem. Canadian Edn. Assn. Profl. Inst., Nat. Council Tchrs. Math., Canadian Math. Congress, Am. Statis. Assn., Math. Assn. Am., Am. Soc. Quality Control, Canadian, Am. econs. assns., U. Alta. Alumni Assn. (br. sec. 1967-68, br. v.p. 1968-69, pres. 1969-70), Kappa Delta Pi. Mem. United Ch. of Can. (mem. session 1966—). Clubs: University Women's (Ottawa), Ottawa Women's Canadian. Home: 811 Adams Av Ottawa K1G 2Y1 ON Canada Office: Brooke Claxton Bldg Tunney's Pasture Ottawa K1A OK9 ON Canada

RUSTEBAKKE, ANN CECILIA REDDAN, newspaper editor; b. Little Rock, May 9, 1928; d. John Gordon and Emma Parthenia (Williams) Reddan; B.A. with honors (Younkers scholar), Grinnell Coll., 1949; M.A. (Frank Ross Chambers fellow), Columbia, 1950; postgrad. U. N.M., intermittently, 1960—; m. Albert R. Rustebakke, Aug. 1, 1949 (div. July 1972); children—Leif, Siri. Program dir. YWCA, Phila., 1950-51, Bklyn., 1951-53; with tng. dept. Abraham & Straus Dept. Store, Bklyn., 1953-57; editor Sandoval County Times-Independent, Bernalillo, N.M., 1971—. Treas., dir. Plaza del Pueblo Corp. Community cons. Mexican-Am. counselor edn. program Tex. Tech. U., summers, 1969, 70. Chmn. Bernalillo Sch. Dist. Study Com., 1969-71, chmn. bond issue campaigns, 1964-68; mem. regional adv. group N.M. Regional Med. Program, 1973—; chmn. urban-rural planning com. Sandoval County Goals, Mid Rio Grande Council Govts., 1970-71. Bd. dirs., N.M. Multiple Sclerosis Soc., 1961; chmn. bd. Placitas Library Trustees, 1967—. Sec. Dem. Precinct 5, Placitas, N.M., 1969-73. Mem. Am. Assn. U. Women, N.M. Press Assn., N.M. Designer-Craftsmen, League Women Voters (county pres. 1967), Albuquerque Press Club, Phi Beta Kappa. Unitarian. Home: PO Box 585 Placitas NM 87043 also PO Box 37 Jemez Springs NM 87025 Office: PO Box 68 Sandoval County Courthouse Bernalillo NM 87004

RUTENBER, CLEMINETTE DOWNING (MRS. RALPH DUDLEY RUTENBER, JR.), educator; b. Augusta, Ga., Oct. 17, 1908; d. George Edward and Clemmie Nette (Gunn) Downing; A.B., Agnes Scott Coll., 1930; m. Ralph Dudley Rutenber, Jr., Dec. 29, 1932; children—Anne (Mrs. Roger L. Clifton), John Downing. Tchr. Grant Park Elementary Sch., Atlanta, 1930-32; asso. head MacDuffie Sch. for Girls, Springfield, Mass., 1941-72. Active Belchertown (Mass.) State Sch. Friends Assn., 1968—. Bd. dirs. Children's Study Home, Springfield, 1956-70; trustee, sec., asst. treas. MacDuffie Sch. for Girls, Springfield, 1941-72, hon. trustee, 1972—; corporator Springfield Hosp. Med. Center, 1944—, Wesson Meml. Hosp., Springfield, 1946—, Girls' Club, Springfield, 1948-50. Recipient (with husband) citation for services to young people Bd. of Springfield Coll., 1972. Mem. Headmistresses' Assn. East, Am. Assn. U. Women, Cum Laude Soc. Clubs: Women's (dir. 1964-66, corr. sec. 1964-66) (Springfield); College (dir. 1943-46, corr. sec. 1943-46) Century, Colony (Springfield). Home: 334 Maple St Springfield MA 01105

RUTGERS, KATHARINE PHILLIPS (MRS. FREDERIK LODEWIJK RUTGERS), dancer; b. Butler, Pa., Sept. 2, 1910; d. Thomas Wharton and Alma (Sherman) Phillips; diploma Briarcliff Coll., 1928; student L'Hermiage, Versailles, France, 1929-30; pupil ballet Vera Trefilova, Paris, Carl Raimund, Vienna, Varga Troyanoff, Budapest; pupil modern dance with Iris Barbura, Bucharest Ballet, Vincenzo Celli, N.Y.C., Igor Schwezoff, N.Y.C., Jean Yazvinsky, N.Y.C.; m. Frederik Lodewijk Rutgers, Feb. 2, 1942; children—Alma (Mrs. Dimitri Bulazel), Corinne (Mrs. David Fitelson). Performed dance concerts Bucharest, 1937-40, U.S., 1941—; repertoire includes religious, patriotic, dramatic, poetical dances; dance therapist St. Barnabas Hosp., N.Y.C., 1965-70. Chmn. ethnol. dance dept. Bruce Museum Assos., Greenwich, Conn., 1970—. Bd. dirs. Bruce Museum. Recipient citation for promoting culture with dance programs Nat. Fedn. Music Clubs, 1973. Mem. Conn. Fedn. Music Clubs (chmn. dance dept. 1965-66), Nat. League Am. Pen Women (local v.p. 1973-74), Alliance Francaise, Colonial Dames Am., D.A.R., Internat. Platform Assn. Clubs: York (N.Y.C.), Indian Harbor (Greenwich, Conn.). Author numerous pamphlets on the dance, also verses for choreographies. Home: La Cova Pecks Land Rd Greenwich CT 06830 Studio: 211 W 58th St New York City NY 10023

RUTH, BARBARA SNYDER, govt. economist; b. Harrisburg, Pa., Nov. 8, 1931; d. Edgar Clinton and Kathryn (Myers) Snyder; A.B., Vassar Coll., 1953; M.S., Columbia, 1954, student, 1954-55, 56-57, student Dickenson Coll., 1950, Pa. State U., 1951; children—Michele Carletta, Michael Charles, Steven Edward. Instr. econs. Hood Coll., Frederick, Md., 1955-56, Elizabethtown Coll., Pa., 1966-71; economist Pa. Senate Majority Staff, 1971—. Pres., Friends Colonial Park Library, 1967-70; mem. League Women Voters, 1964—; mem. Gov.'s Adv. Council on Library Devel., 1971—. Mem. Pa. Democratic State Com., 1968—; mem. Dem. Exec. Com. Dauphin County, 1964—; pres. Dem. Womens Club Dauphin County, 1973-74; v.p. Pa. Fedn. Dem. Women, 1973—. Chmn. Dauphin County Library Adv. Council, 1970-71. Bd. dirs. Pa. Mental Health, Inc., 1969—; trustee Harrisburg Pub. Library, 1970—. Ford Found. fellow, 1956-57. Mem. Am. Assn. U. Women, Beta Gamma Sigma. Lutheran. Club: Colonial Country. Home: 1141 Green Tree Rd Harrisburg PA 17112

RUTHENBERG, ARLENE AMELIA, librarian; b. Lime Springs, Ia., May 1, 1917; d. Herman A. and Frieda W. (Simdorn) Ruthenberg; B.A., Ia. State Tchrs. Coll., 1953, postgrad., summers 1957-63; M.Ed. in Library Sci., Wayne State U., 1967. Tchr. jr. high sch. English, Marshalltown, Mason City and Cedar Falls, Ia., 1937-59; prin. Gladbrook (Ia.) Elementary Sch., 1942-43; librarian, tchr. English, Anson Jr. High, Marshalltown, 1944-54; tchr. English, Roosevelt Jr. High Sch., Mason City, 1954-57; librarian Peet Jr. High Sch., Cedar Falls, 1957-68; librarian youth collection U. No. Ia., Cedar Falls, 1968—, instr. library sci., 1969-70, summers, 1967-70. Mem. Ia. Library Assn., Ia. Assn. Sch. Librarians, Internat. Assn. Librarians, Ia. Higher Edn. Assn., N.E.A., Am. Assn. U. Profs., Am. Assn. U. Women, Alpha Delta Kappa (chpt. pres. 1963-64, state sec. 1964-66). Methodist. Contbr. book revs. to Sch. Library Jour. Office: U Northern Iowa Cedar Falls IA 50613

RUTHERFORD, M. LOUISE, lawyer; b. Phila.; d. Frederick A. and Louise C. (Hess) Schuman; B.A. cum laude, U. Pa. 1926, A.M. cum laude, 1930, Ph.D., 1936; J.D., Temple U. Law Sch., 1921; m. John B. Rutherford, July 21, 1920. Admitted to Pa. bar, 1920; in practice of law, Phila., 1920—; dep. atty. gen. Commonwealth of Pa., 1939-55; spl. counsel to atty. gen. Dept. Justice, Commonwealth of Pa., 1963—. Mem. Gov.'s Com. to Study Adminstrn. of Pub. Assistance in Various States, 1943; mem. Conf. of Govs., Hershey, 1944, White House Conf., June 1944, White House Conf. on Children and Youth, 1950. Del. 6th Conf. Internat. Bar Assn., Oslo, XII Conf. Internat. Fedn. U. Women, Paris, 47th Conf. Internat. Law Assn., Yugoslavia; del. Am. Bar Assn., Internat. Bar Assn., Salzburg, 1960. Mem. Pa. Rep. Com., past chmn. profl. and bus. women's com. Recipient Woman of Year award Harrisburg Quota Club, 1946; Outstanding Profl. Woman award Phila. Bus. and Profl. Woman's Club, 1947. Mem. Internat. Bar Assn. (patron), Am. Bar Assn., Am. Judicature Soc., Am. Soc. Internat. Law, Phila. Bar Assn. (del. to Am. Bar Assn. Ho. of Dels. 1946, 1948), Fgn. Policy Assn. (v.p.) Harrisburg, Pa., Pa. Bar Assn. (chmn. admissions com., asst. sec. criminal law sect., del. to Inter-Am. Bar Assn., Lima, Peru, 1947), Pa. Council Rep. Women (mem. legislative com.), Cresheim Valley Council of Republican Women (pres.), Nat. Fedn. Rep. Women (gen. counsel), Grad. Alumni Assn. U. Pa. (pres.), Am. Polit. Sci. Assn., Pa. Polit. Sci. Assn. (pres.), Phila. County League of Women Voters, Phi Beta Kappa, Pi Gamma Mu, Phi Delta Delta. Republican. Presbyn. Clubs: Quota (Harrisburg, Pa.) (pres.); Quota Internat. (chmn. com. on legislative and pub. affairs); Phila. Fedn. Women's Clubs and allied orgn. (former chmn. polit. sci. com.), New Century (v.p.). Author: The Influence of the A.B.A. on Public Opinion and Legislation; contbr. many articles to social and legal pubs. Home: Mayfair House Philadelphia PA 19144 Office: 1411 Walnut St Philadelphia PA 19102

RUTLEDGE, MARY LOUISE (MRS. WILLIAM E. MCGREGOR), physician; b. Florence, S.C., Jan. 10, 1916; d. Robert Kennedy and Mary Louise (Scarborough) Rutledge; B.S., Furman U., 1937, M.A., 1939; M.D., Temple U., 1947; m. William E. McGregor, Nov. 15, 1952; children—William E., Ann Rutledge. Tchr. sci. Parker Dist., Greenville, S.C., 1937-39; med. technologist Charlotte (N.C.) Meml. Hosp., 1940-42; rotating intern Hosp. U. Pa., 1948-49, jr. resident, 1949-50; jr. resident Duke Hosp., Durham, N.C., 1950-51; practice medicine, specializing in pediatrics, Charlotte, 1951—. Diplomate Am. Bd. Pediatrics. Fellow Am. Acad. Pediatrics. Home: 1729 Queens Rd Charlotte NC 28207 Office: 211 Greenwich Rd Charlotte NC 28211

RUTLEDGE, PHYLLIS J. (MRS. RALPH RUTLEDGE), state legislator; b. Charleston, W.Va., Mar. 11, 1932; d. Roger C. and Inez (Snodgrass) Lewis; ed. pub. schs., ins. tng.; m. Ralph Rutledge, Sept. 1, 1951; children—Jeannie, Jimmy. Mem. W. Va. Ho. of Dels., 1968—; vice chmn. Industry and Labor Com. Mem. intergovt. relations com., nat. legislative conf. Democrat Issue Task Force, 1972—; W. Va. chmn. Dem. Telethon II, 1973. Bd. dirs. Kanawha County Mental Health Assn.; mem. Stonewall Jackson Sponsors Club and P.T.A. Co-chmn. Dollars for Democrats drive Kanawha County, 1968; mem. Kanawha County Democratic Woman's Club, South Charleston Democratic Women's Club, Kanawha County Dem. Exec. Com. (past sec.). Mem. Am. Bus. Women's Assn. (treas.), Consumer Assn. W. Va. Baptist. Address: 1332 Frame St Charleston WV 25302*

RUTTIGER, KATHERINE JENNINGS FORD, psychologist; b. Metuchen, N.J., Mar. 11, 1902; d. Benjamin Dorset and Bettie Jennings (Smith) Ford; A.B., Douglass Coll., 1923; student N.Y. Sch. Social Work, 1937-38; M.S., Rutgers U., 1944, Ph.D., 1960; m. Henry Charles Ruttiger, Apr. 2, 1925; children—Joan Parke (Mrs. Robert Boyd Gordon), Peter Ford. Research asso. dept. sociology Rutgers U., New Brunswick, N.J., 1948-55; researcher N.J. Bd. Control, 1956-57; clin. psychologist N.J. State Diagnostic Center, Menlo Park, 1960-69, prin. psychologist, 1969—, dir. dept., 1971—; individual practice clin. psychology. Mem. Am., N.J. psychol. assns., Am. Soc. Clin. Hypnosis, Phi Beta Kappa. Episcopalian. Contbr. articles to profl. jours. Home: 48 Linden Av Metuchen NJ 08840 Office: New Jersey State Diagnostic Center Menlo Park Edison NJ 08837

RUYFFELAERE, DIANNE ANDREE, coll. dean; b. Nuremburg, Germany, Dec. 30, 1948 (parents Am. citizens); d. Raymond Francis and Hannah (Ashby) Ruyffelaere; B.A., Grinnell Coll., 1970; M.A., Claremont Grad. Sch., 1974. Recreational counselor, tchr. YWCA, Bangkok, Thailand, 1969; elementary tchr. Internat. Sch., Bangkok, 1971; specimen collector, coral reef animals Bang Sagn (Thailand) U., 1970; asst. dean of students, resident adviser Carleton Coll., Northfield, Minn., 1971-73; asst. dean of students Grinnell (Ia.) Coll., 1973-74, asso. dean students, 1974—. Counselor Free Clinic, La Puente, Cal., 1970-71; small group Co-leader Nat. Center for Exploration of Human Potential, 1971. Mem. Nat. Assn. Student Personnel Adminstrs., Nat. Assn. Women Deans, Adminstrs. and Counselors (workshop discussion leader nat. conv. 1973), Minn. Personnel and Guidance Assn., Audubon Soc., Sierra Club. Home: 1405 1/2 Park St Grinnell IA 50112 Office: Office of Dean of Student Affairs Grinnell College Grinnell IA 50112

RUYS, CONSTANCE, educator; b. Maassluis, The Netherlands, Jan. 30, 1922; d. Jan Daniel and Woutrina Johanna (Lambrechtsen) Ruys; brought to U.S., 1927, naturalized, 1943; student San Francisco State Coll., 1940-41, Pasadena Playhouse Sch. Theatre, 1941-43; B.A., U. Cal. at Berkeley, 1947; M.S., U. Cal. at Los Angeles, 1951; postgrad. U. Leiden, Netherlands, 1952-53, Columbia, 1953-54; Ph.D., Stanford, 1956. Stage mgr. Small Co., Hollywood, 1943; tech. dir. Theatre U. Cal. Extension, Berkeley, 1946-48; teaching asst. Stanford, 1954-56; faculty San Jose State Coll., 1957, Cedar Crest Coll., Allentown, Pa., 1957-62; prof., chmn. dept. theatre Wesleyan Coll., Macon, Ga., 1962—. Mem. Am., Brit. socs. for theatre research, Am. Theatre Assn., Am. Assn. U. Profs., Malone Soc., Phi Kappa Phi, Alpha Psi Omega. Club: Macon Altrusa. Address: Wesleyan Coll Macon GA 31201

RYAN, ADA E. BIFFAR, physician; b. N.Y.C., Mar. 22, 1922; d. Harry Melchoir and Catherine Agnes (Lanigan) Biffar; B.S., U. Ala., 1943; M.D., N.Y. Med. Coll., 1947; m. Edward Anderson Ryan, July 24, 1948; children—Louise (Mrs. Brendon Buschi), Mary Ann, Edward Anderson, Thomas, Catherine, Joseph. Intern Queens Gen. Hosp., 1947-48; gen. practice medicine, Levittown, N.Y., 1948-69; emergency room physician Flushing (N.Y.) Hosp. Med. Center, 1969—; also founder drug identification unit; mem. med. dept. Samaratin Halfway Soc., 1969—. Pres. N.Y. State Physicians and Nurses Against Abortion. Mem. exec. bd. Flushing Drug Alert Com., Flushing Drug Abuse Council; hon. physician local troop Boy Scouts Am. Recipient Woman of Achievement award Bus. and Profl. Women's Club of Greater Flushing, 1973; Woman of Yr. award V.F.W. Aux., 1973. Mem. Am. Coll. Emergency Physicians, N.Y., Queens County med. socs., N.Y. Med. Coll., Queens Gen. alumni assns. Roman Catholic (mem. council). Home: 30-23 148th St Flushing NY 11354

RYAN, AILEEN BARLOW, city ofcl.; b. Bronx, N.Y.C.; d. Patrick F. and Anna B. (Farrelly) Barlow; B.S., Hunter Coll., 1935; m. E. Gerard Ryan, Sept. 4, 1938; children—Gerald, Alanna, Francis X. Dir. edn. Mus. N.Y.C., 1934-50; tchr. elementary schs., N.Y.C., 1957—; assemblywoman 11th assembly dist., Bronx County, 1958-65; councilman at large Bronx N.Y.C. Council, 1966—. Vice pres. Siwanoy Dem. Club, 1954—. Mem. Misericordia Women's Hosp. Aux.; bd. advisors Bronx Community Coll.; bd. dirs. Bronx Multiple Sclerosis, Bronx chpt. A.R.C. Recipient Humanitarian award B'nai B'rith, 1961; plaques from numerous orgns. Mem. Bus. and Profl. Woman's Club (bd. dirs.), N.Y. League Women Voters, Nat. Council Negro Women, N.A.A.C.P. Home: 2051 St Raymonds Av Bronx NY 10462 Office: Council City NY City Hall New York City NY 10007

RYAN, CLARA ETHEL SZEBENYI (MRS. FRANK M. RYAN), editor; b. Budapest, Hungary, Apr. 17, 1908; d. Joseph and Rose Marie (Klein) Szebenyei; came to U.S., 1920, naturalized, 1927; student pvt. schs.; m. Frank M. Ryan, Aug. 24, 1939; children—Sheila, Nancy. Translator Hungarian articles, plays, 1945-55; writer, editor publs. Am. Inst. Mgmt., N.Y.C., 1956-71; editor Bur. Bus. Practice div. Prentice-Hall, N.Y.C., 1972—. Freelance writer articles on bus. mgmt., 1974—. Home: 242 E 38th St New York City NY 10016

RYAN, CLARE ELLEN, librarian; b. Springfield, Mass., June 17, 1927; d. John T. and Helen M. (Rougier) Ryan; A.B., Coll. of Our Lady of Elms, Chicopee, Mass., 1949; M.L.S., Carnegie Inst. Tech., 1954. Cataloger, Enoch Pratt Free Library, Balt., 1954-56; head, tech. services dept. Racine (Wis.) Pub. Library, 1956-60, Arlington County (Va.) Library, 1960-61; head catalog dept. Carnegie Library, Pitts., 1961-68; head tech. services div. N.H. State Library, Concord, 1968—. Mem. Dewey Decimal Editorial Policy Com., 1970—. Home: 203 Loudon Rd Bldg 1 Concord NH 03301 Office: 20 Park St Concord NH 03301

RYAN, DORIS ANN, banker; b. Three Rivers, Que., Can., Dec. 23, 1926; d. Joseph Arthur and Daisy (Cunningham) Fish; grad. pub. schs.; m. John Marshall Ryan, Nov. 6, 1950. With The State Nat. Bank of El Paso (Tex.), 1950—, asst. trust officer, 1967-70, trust officer, 1970—. Mem. El Paso Estate Planning Council, El Paso Council Exec. Women, Nat. Assn. Bank Women. Republican. Episcopalian. Club: Soroptimist Club of El Paso. Home: 9909 Fenway Dr El Paso TX 79925 Office: 1 State Nat Plaza El Paso TX 79901

RYAN, G. JACQUELINE, public relations co. exec.; b. Meadville, Pa.; d. John Anthony and Helen (Corrigan) Ryan; A.A. Traphagen Sch. Fashion; B.A., Coll. William and Mary; B.A., Green Mountain Coll. Retail exec. Hahne & Co., Newark, 1957-58, tng. exec., 1958; asst. to fashion coordinator Charm Mag., N.Y.C., 1959; fashion editor Parents' Mag., N.Y.C., 1959-63; asso. editor trade div. McCalls Corp., N.Y.C., 1963-64; account exec. Darcy McManus Interpole, N.Y.C., 1964-68; pub. relations dir. Streisand, Zuch & Freedman, N.Y.C., 1968-71; pub. relations exec. J. Walter Thompson, N.Y.C., 1971—. Lectr. in fashion Pratt Inst., N.Y.C., 1968—, Foam Fashion Forum, N.Y.C., 1970; fashion adviser Traphagen Sch. Fashion, N.Y.C., 1970; cons. Nat. Inst. Drycleaning, Silver Springs, Md., 1970—. Named Am.'s Foremost Woman in Communications, Am.'s Speakers Platform, 1970. Mem. Advt. Women N.Y., Am. Women in Radio and TV. Home: 69 Cedar Grove Pkwy Cedar Grove NJ 07009

RYAN, HELEN BYERLY (MRS. JOSEPH ANTHONY RYAN), lawyer; b. Waterloo, Ia., June 15, 1915; d. Claude Michael and Gertrude May (Fenstermaker) Byerly; B.A., U. Ia., 1937, J.D., 1939; m. Joseph Anthony Ryan, Mar. 10, 1964; children—Joseph Anthony, Matthew M.B. Admitted to Ia. bar, 1939, N.Y. bar, 1944, Hawaii bar, 1965; practiced in Syracuse, N.Y., 1940-64, Honolulu, 1965—; partner Ryan & Ryan, 1965—. Dist. price atty. OPA, 1942-46; 1st asst. dist. atty. Onondaga County, Syracuse, 1961-64. Mem. Oahu Commn. on Status of Women, 1971—. Mem. exec. com. Democratic County Com., Onondaga County, 1959-64. Past pres. Syracuse YWCA. Mem. Manoa Kai Bus. and Profl. Women (past pres.), Zonta, Nat. Orgn. Women. Home: 4005 Blackpoint St Honolulu HI 96816 Office: 1136 Union Mall Honolulu HI 96813

RYAN, IRENE (MRS. JOHN RYAN), state ofcl.; b. Boston, Sept. 10, 1909; d. Leonard and Esther (Irvine) Laukki; B.S. in Geol. Engring. with mining option, N.M. Sch. Mines, 1940; postgrad. Alaska Meth. U., 1967-69; m. John Ryan, Feb. 1938; children—Marcella (Mrs. Patrick L. Sharrock), Patricia (Mrs. Thomas Wright). Asst. airways engr. CAA, 1941-44; self-employed cons. engr., Anchorage, Alaska, 1944-46, 47-70; expediter Birch-Johnson-Lytle Constrn. Co., 1946-47; commr. Alaska Dept. Econ. Devel., Juneau, 1970-74; sec.-treas. Ryan Devel. Co., Inc., 1951-56; sec.-treas., dir. Oil Well Service Co., Inc., 1958-61. Mem. Alaskan Territorial Ho. of Reps., 1955-58, Alaska State Senate, 1959-60; chmn. South Central Democratic Dist. Com., 1956-58. Mem. A.A.A.S., Am. Soc. C.E., Soc. Women Engrs., Am. Inst. Mining and Metall. Engrs., Arctic Inst., Nat. Assn. Geol. Tchrs. Clubs: Anchorage Democratic (pres.), Anchorage Democratic Womens (pres.). Author: Alaska as a Potential Petroleum Producer, 1948; The Geology of the Houston, Alaska Area, 1953; So You Are Thinking About Alaska, 1958; Rampart Project, 1963; The Good Friday Earthquake, 1964. Contbr. articles in field. Home: Box 84 SRA Anchorage AK 99501 Office: Pouch EE Juneau AK 99801

RYAN, SISTER KARA, coll. adminstr.; b. St. Louis, Aug. 23, 1935; d. Francis Joseph and Ruth Marie (Zell) Ryan; B.S., Notre Dame Coll., St. Louis, 1957; M.A., La. State U., 1964; M.S., Loyola U., New Orleans, 1965; postgrad. Computer Systems Inst., 1970. Joined Sch. Sisters of Notre Dame, 1955; Tchr., Redemptorist High Sch., New Orleans, 1957-65, Redemptorist Sr. High Sch., Baton Rouge, 1965-66; asso. prof. Notre Dame Coll., St. Louis, 1966-72, dean students, 1972—. Computer programmer, systems analyst Corp. Sch. Sisters Notre Dame, St. Louis, 1970—. AEC grantee, 1967, 68. Mem. Nat. Council Tchrs. Math., Math. Club St. Louis. Author: Computer Supplemented Course in Probability and Statistics, 1970. Contbr. articles to profl. jours. Office: 320 E Ripa St St Louis MO 63125

RYAN, LINA LEE LEWIS (MRS. KEN W. RYAN), pub. relations exec.; b. St. Louis, Dec. 8, 1920; d. William Lloyd and Lina Allen (Tuttle) Lewis; B.S., Okla. State U., 1941; m. Ken W. Ryan, June 7, 1941; children—Jay Patrick, David Lloyd. Secretarial position Sinclair Oil Co., Tulsa, 1941-48; traffic dir. WJTV TV, Jackson, Miss., 1955-57; with KOTV, Tulsa, 1958-66; prodn. mgr. White Advt. Agy., Tulsa, 1967-68; dir. pub. relations St. John's Hosp., Tulsa, 1969—. Recipient certificate of merit Tulsa Power Squadron, 1968, 69, 70. Mem. Am. Women in Radio and Television (Tulsa pres. 1962-63, pres. Okla., 1962-63, vice chmn. nat. conv. 1964, program chmn. S.W. conf. 1967), Okla. (pres. pub. relations soc. 1973-74), Tulsa (pres. pub. relations sect. 1970-71) hosp. councils, Tulsa Press Club, Advt. Club Tulsa, Tulsa Advt. Fedn. (dir. 1968). Office: St John's Hosp 1923 S Utica St Tulsa OK 74104

RYAN, L(ORETTA) DOLORES, librarian; b. Cleve., July 8, 1913; d. Miles Francis and Lola Loretta (Wagner) Ryan; B.S., Western Res. U., 1935, B.S. in Library Sci., 1943; postgrad. Kent State U., 1946-49, Cleve. State U., 1968-69, 72-73. State rep. Nat. Child Labor Com., Cleve., 1935-37; library asst. Cleve. Pub. Library, 1937-46; librarian Glenville High Sch., Cleve., 1943-46, Cleve. Trade Sch., 1946-58, Max S. Hayes Sch., Cleve., 1958-62; head reference librarian Cleve. State U., 1962-65, undergrad. librarian, 1966-68, coll. librarian, 1968-72, head pub. services Cleve. State U., 1972—. Library cons. Nat. Radio Sch., Cleve., 1960-61; instr. Cuyahoga Community Coll., Cleve., 1965-66; instr. Grad. Sch. Library Sci., U. Ill., summer 1969. Mem. adv. com. Cuyahoga Community Coll., Cleve., 1965—. Mem. exec. com. Cuyahoga County Rep. Party, 1935-36. Recipient McKinley Gavel award C. of C., Canton, O., 1936, award Cleve. Downtown Kiwanis, 1959. Mem. Am. Library Assn. (sec. history div. 1967-68), Spl. Libraries Assn. (chpt. pres. 1964-65), Tri-State Assn. Coll. Librarians (treas. 1971-72), Women's Nat. Book Assn., Am. Assn. U. Women, Theta Phi Omega. Home: 11811 Lake Av Lakewood OH 44107 Office: Euclid Av and East 24 Cleveland OH 44115

RYAN, LORRAINE SCHNEIDER, mus. dir.; b. Lindenhurst, N.Y., Mar. 21, 1920; d. John William and Johanna (Roeske) Schneider; B.A., Hofstra U., 1941, M.S. in Edn., 1946; m. Charles C. Pebler, Aug. 15, 1948 (dec.); children—Charles Dean, Wendy L.; m. 2d, Harold A. Ryan, Dec. 27, 1971. Tchr. social studies Lindenhurst High Sch., 1942-50, 54-56; sec. Neptune Marine Service, 1961-70; dir. Old Village Hall Mus., Lindenhurst, 1970—, guide, 1958—. Trustee Lindenhurst Meml. Library, 1957-65; active Lindenhurst Centennial, 1970, Lindenhurst Golden Jubilee of Incorporation, 1973. Mem. Soc. for Preservation of L.I. Antiquities, Lindenhurst Hist. Soc. (pres. 1960-61), Kappa Omicron. Mem. Order Eastern Star. Home: 687 Adams Av Lindenhurst NY 11757 Office: PO Box 296 215 S Wellwood Av Lindenhurst NY 11757

RYAN, MALPHA MARYN MCGEE (MRS. MARTIN S. RYAN), business exec.; b. nr. Waxahachie, Tex., Aug. 22, 1912; d. Joseph L. and Flossie (Overton) McGee; student McBrides Bus. Coll., 1930-32; m. Martin Stanley Ryan, May 8, 1932; children—Jacqueline Patricia (Mrs. Hermann William Ashlaw). Cotillion dir. Armed Forces in U.S. for Fred Astaire Studios, N.Y.C., 1956-57; exec. sec. Richmond (Va.) chpt. Am. Inst. Banking, 1957-71, exec. dir., 1971—; instr. teen-age cotillion clubs, Rocky Mount, N.C., 1949-52, social etiquette and dancing pub. schs., Rocky Mount, 1949-52. Dance instr. Ft. Lee and Def. Gen. Supply Center, Va., 1958—. Co-founder, bd. dirs. Children's Mus., Rocky Mount, 1950-52; adv. com. banking and financial mgmt. J. Sargeant Reynolds Community Coll., Richmond, Va., 1974—. Recipient Mil. citation for aiding and counseling dependents of service personnel U.S. Army, (Chgo.), 1945-46. Mem. Mace and Gavel, Cross Keys, Nat. Assn. Parliamentarians, KLF Soc. Am. Inst. Banking. Clubs: Officers Wives (past pres.), Rocky Mount Women's (chmn. art dept.), Soroptimist; Parliamentary Law (Richmond). Home: PO Box 114 Richmond VA 23201 Office: 501 Heritage Bldg Richmond VA 23219

RYAN, MARILYN CAMERON, occupational therapist; b. Columbus, O., July 10, 1935; d. Don Stuart and Jane Elizabeth (Rodgers) Cameron; B.S. in Occupational Therapy, Ohio State U., 1959; student Ohio Wesleyan U., 1953-56; m. Finley L. Ryan, Jr., July 1, 1961; children—Finley Lee, Jane Elizabeth. Work evaulation and tng. dir. Goodwill Industries of Central Ohio, Columbus, 1959-62, 63-64; cons., activities program dir. Sunridge Convalescent Center, Columbus, 1964-65; occupational therapy asst. tng. program dir. Columbus Bd. Edn., 1967-74; occupational therapist Franklin County Soc. Crippled Children, 1974—. Dir. Jandon, Inc. Del., Franklin County Republican Conv., 1974. Bd. dirs. N.W. Worthington Civic Assn., 1974. Mem. Am. (council on edn.), Ohio (dir.) occupational therapy assns., Mid Ohio Health Planning Assn., Central Ohio Adult Edn. Assn., P.E.O. (sec. 1971-73), Zeta Tau Alpha (dir.), Order Eastern Star. Conglist. Home: 6715 Schreiner St E Worthington OH 43085

RYAN, MARY CATHERINE CROWLEY, trust officer; b. Chgo., May 3, 1939; d. Joseph B. and Mabel F. (O'Brien) Crowley; B.A., Rosary Coll., 1961; student Villa des Fougeres, U. Fribourg (Switzerland), 1959-60; postgrad. DePaul Law Sch., 1961-62; m. Allan Charles Ryan, III, Feb. 10, 1968. With Continental Ill. Nat. Bank and Trust Co. Chgo., 1964—, trust officer, 1970—. Home: 2912 N Commonwealth St Chicago IL 60657 Office: 231 S LaSalle St Chicago IL 60690

RYAN, MARY HOFFMANN, ret. religious educator; b. Mansfield, O., Aug. 17, 1903; d. Irving Singleton and Ethleen May (Carter) Hoffmann; student Hastings Coll., 1920-21, Oberlin Coll., 1921-22; B.S. in Edn., Ohio State U., 1924; postgrad. Schauffler Coll., 1945, 48; M.A. in Edn. and Guidance Counseling, Western Res. U., 1960; M.R.E., Oberlin Grad. Sch. Theology, 1966; m. Norman Arden Ryan, Aug. 17, 1925; children—Frances (Mrs. Harold H. Millward), Katherine (Mrs. Robert McWilliams), Irving Andrew, John Douglas. Substitute tchr., tutor Cleve. Pub. Schs., 1948-51; tchr. Juvenile Detention Home, Cleve., 1951-52; tchr., dir. recreation House Correction for Women, Cleve., 1952-59; tchr. literacy classes Cleve. Bd. Edn., asst. minister Dunham Christian Ch., Cleve., 1957-60; dir. Christian edn. Olmsted Community Ch., Olmstead Falls, O., 1960-65; ordained to ministry Christian Ch., 1966; asst. to minister Euclid Av. Congl. Ch. United Ch. Christ, Cleve., 1966-67; minister Christian edn. Trinity Congl. Ch. United Ch. Christ, Pepper Pike, O., 1968-70, Calvary Presbyn. Ch., Cleve., 1971-74. Dir. children's programs Camp Farthest Out, 1947—. Trustee Laymen's Retreat Project at Shadybrook House, Mentor, O. Mem. Internat. Assn. Women Ministers (trustee, treas. 1970—), Pilot Internat. (chaplain Cleve. chpt. 1969—, dist. 10 1970-71). Home: 1464 W 101st St Cleveland OH 44102

RYAN, MARY PATRICIA, educator; b. Chgo., Feb. 27, 1926; d. Richard Martin and Mary Josephine (Hyde) Ryan; Nursing diploma Charity Hosp., Cleve., 1947; B.S. in Nursing, St. Louis U., 1952; M.S. in Nursing, Boston U., 1960, M.A. in Psychology, 1965, Ph.D. in Psychology, 1971. Staff nurse VA Hosp., Dayton, O., 1947-48, Cleve., 1948; office nurse, Cleve., 1948-50; instr. Charity Hosp., Cleve., 1952-54, De Paul Hosp., St. Louis, 1954-56, St. Louis U., 1956-57, Boston U., 1959-61; staff nurse, instr. State Mental Hosp., Copenhagen, Denmark, 1961-63; asso. prof. Ohio State U., Columbus, 1970-73; asso. prof. Loyola U., Chgo., 1973—. Nursing cons. VA Hosp., Chillicothe, O., 1971-73, VA hosps., Battle Creek, Mich., Downey, Ill., 1974—. Trustee Children's Mental Health Center, Columbus, O., 1972-73. Mem. Am. Nurses Assn., Council of Nurse Researchers, Am. Assn. Mental Deficiency, Am. Pub. Health Assn., Sigma Theta Tau, Psi Chi. Office: Loyola U 6525 N Sheridan Rd Chicago IL 60626

RYCHECK, JAYNE BOGUS (MRS. R. RICHARD RYCHECK), ret. ednl. adminstr.; b. Schenectady; d. Peter and Sylvia (Cywinski) Bogus; M.A., N.Y. U., 1953; B.S., State U. N.Y., Albany, 1941; postgrad. Syracuse U., 1957-66; m. R. Richard Rycheck, July 26, 1942. Tchr. various schs., 1935-43; elementary sch. tchr. Schenectady (N.Y.) City Schs., 1943-51, leadership intern, 1951-52, elementary sch. prin., 1952-61, dir. spl. edn., 1961-72. Instr. Russell Sage Coll., 1955-58, State U. N.Y., Omeonta, 1956; cons. bur. handicapped children N.Y. Edn. Dept., 1966—, mem. commrs. and hoc coms., 1964—, State Planning Com. Insts. for In-Service Edn., 1964-67; rep. to Community Welfare Council Schenectady County, 1961—; adv. council N.Y. State Joint Legislative Com. Mental and Phys. Handicap, 1970-72. Recipient Humanitarian service awards United Cerebral Palsy Schenectady County, 1966, 67, Capital dist. Assn. for Brain-Injured Children, 1967; Meritorious Alumni award State U. N.Y. Coll. at Oneonta, 1972; Capitol Dist. Speech and Hearing award, 1972; Distinguished Service award N.Y. Fedn. chpts. Council for Exceptional Children, 1972; Joseph P. Kennedy, Jr. Found. award for outstanding activity for the mentally retarded, 1972. Mem. N.Y. State (sec. 1967-68), Nat. Councils Adminstrs. Spl. Edn., Assn. Childhood Edn. (state sec. 1952-55, state exec. bd. 1951-59), Council Exceptional Children (mem. chpt. regional and state bds. 1966—, state regional dir. 1966-68, state adv. bd. 1966-72, chpt. sec. 1962-65, v.p. 1968-69, state pres. 1970), Schenectady County Assn. Childhood Edn. (treas. and v.p. 1952), Am. Assn. Mental Deficiency, N.Y. State Assn. Brain-Injured Children (state adv. bd. 1963-67, dist. adv. bd. 1966—), Nat. Soc. Autistic Children, Assn. Retarded Children (adv. bd.), Gifted Children Soc. (adv. com.), Schenectady C. of C. (edn. com.), Schenectady County Ret. Tchrs. Assn. (v.p. 1973, pres. 1974), Am. Assn. Ret. People (program com. chpt. 1973), N.Y. Assn. Elementary Prins. (hon. life), Delta Kappa Gamma. Contbr. articles to publs. Home: 1537 Kingston Av Schenectady NY 12308

RYD, BEVERLY JEAN, librarian; b. Boston, Aug. 3, 1935; d. Eric Albert and Vinita (Blake) Ryd; B.S., Simmons Coll., 1957; M.S., Columbia, 1959. Law librarian Conn. Gen. Ins. Corp., Hartford, 1957-58; reference librarian Grad. Sch. Bus. and Pub. Adminstrn., Cornell U., Ithaca, N.Y., 1959-64; asst. cataloger Fed. Res. Bank N.Y., N.Y.C., 1964-65; librarian First Boston Corp., N.Y.C., 1965—. Mem. Spl. Libraries Assn. (chmn. bus. and finance group N.Y. chpt. 1969-70), Simmons Coll. Alumnae Assn. Club: New York Library. Home: 345 E 52d St New York City NY 10022 Office: 20 Exchange Place New York City NY 10005

RYDELL, WENDY WILNER (MRS. CHESTER RYDELL), writer; b. Perth Amboy, N.J., Sept. 12, 1927; d. Abraham and Sadie (Gottesman) Wilner; B.A., Ohio State U., 1947; M.A., Mexico City Coll., 1949; m. Chester Rydell, Apr. 6, 1952; children—Susan, David. Reporter Newark Evening News, Newark, 1947-48; copywriter various N.Y.C. dept. stores, 1953-56; free-lance writer children's stories pub. New Directions Edn., other publs. Trustee Commack (N.Y.) Pub. Library, 1969-73, v.p., 1972, 73. Recipient service award Union Free Sch. Dist. 10, Commack, N.Y., 1970, citizenship award Commack Dem. Club, 1971. Mem. Women in Communications, Chi Delta Phi, Alpha Lambda Delta. Author: Baseball, 1971; Football, 1971; Basketball, 1972; others. Writer ednl. filmstrips Eye-Gate House, AVNA, Inc., others. Home: 51 Wintercress Lane East Northport NY 11731

RYDER, SHAUNEILLE PERRY (MRS. DONALD P. RYDER), theatre dir.; b. Chgo.; d. Graham Turner and Pearl (Gantt) Perry; B.A., Howard U., 1950; M.F.A., Goodman Theatre, Art Inst. Chgo., 1952; Fulbright fellow, Royal Acad. Dramatic Art, London Acad. Dramatic Art, 1954-55; m. Donald P. Ryder, Aug. 24, 1958; children—Lorraine, Natalie. Instr., A. & T. Coll., Greensboro, N.C., 1953-54; instr. Dillard U., New Orleans, 1954-55; lectr. Hunter Coll., N.Y.C., 1960; tchr., dir. plays Fieldston Sch., 1960-65; lectr. City Coll., N.Y.C., 1969-70; asst. prof. Manhattan Community Coll., N.Y.C., 1970—; writer Chgo. Daily Defender, tchr. Goodman Theatre, 1956-58; dir. plays Black Girl, Off Broadway and touring co., 1971, Sty of the Blind Pig, N.Y. and touring co., 1972, Internat. tour, Munich, 1972, Rosalie Pritchett, 1970, Jaminma, 1972, Moon on a Rainbow Shawl, 1973, Ladies-in-Waiting, 1973, numerous others, also radio pilot scripts. Recipient Broadcast Media award for TV script A Holiday Celebration, Zebra Assos., N.Y., 1970, 2d prize Ebony Mag. Essay Contest, 1959. Mem. exec. bd. Soc. Stage Dirs. and Choreographers; mem. Actors Equity Assn., Screen Actors Guild, A.F.T.R.A. Author: (TV scripts) Our Street, 1973. Address: New Federal Theatre 204 E 3d St New York City NY 10009

RYGIEL, WANDA JADWIGA WESOLEK (MRS. WITOLD RYGIEL), physician, educator; b. Poznan, Poland, May 18, 1923; d. Kazimir and Heddy (Michel) Wesolek; M.D., Med. Sch. Frankfurt/Main (Germany), 1950; m. Witold Rygiel, June 5, 1965. Intern, Ottawa (Ont., Can.) Civic Hosp., 1951-52, resident, 1952-53; resident Montreal (Que., Can.) Children's Hosp., 1953-57; practice medicine, specializing in pediatrics and pediatric cardiology, Montreal, 1957-67, Hamilton, Ont., 1968—; mem. staff Montreal Children's Hosp., 1958-67, Hamilton Gen. Hosp., 1969—; lectr. McGill U., Montreal, 1962-67; asst. prof. McMaster U., Hamilton, 1968-72, asso. prof., 1972—. Cons Dr. Rygiel's Home for Children, Hamilton, 1968—. Phillip's Research grantee 1962-63. Contbr. articles to profl. jours. Home: 560 Crane Crescent Watertown ON Canada Office: Hamilton General Hosp Hamilton ON Canada

RYLE, ANNE LIBBY, educator; b. Washington, Apr. 13, 1930; d. John Hermiston and Violet Kelway (Bamber) Libby; A.B., Smith Coll., 1951; Ed.M., Harvard, 1953, Ed.D., 1966; m. Walter Harrington Ryle, Nov. 28, 1958. Asst. buyer Garfinckel's, Washington, 1952-54; elementary tchr. Washington, 1954-56, 57-58, USAF Dependent Sch., Upper Heyford, Eng., 1956-57, Durham, N.C., 1960-62; teaching fellow, supr. student tchrs. Grad. Sch. Edn., Harvard, 1962-66; instr. sci. and math. edn. Simmons Coll., Boston, 1964-66; editor lang. arts Sci. Research Assos., IBM, Chgo., 1966-69; reading author D.C. Heath Raytheon, Lexington, Mass., 1969—; dir. Edco Reading and Learning Center, Boston, 1971—, Ednl. Research Corp., 1972—. Milton Fund grantee, 1964-66; Title III Discretionary Fund grantee, 1971—. Mem. Internat. Reading Assn., Am. Ednl. Research Assn., League Women Voters (unit chmn. 1965-66, mem. voters service com. 1970-71). Mem. Ch. of Covenant (trustee 1971—, elder 1973—, pres. women's assn. 1970—). Clubs: Woman's City Club (Boston). Author: (with John Steuber) Growing with Composition, 1969; (with Phyllis Barnes and others) A Manual of Diagnostic Tests and Activities, Reading K-3, 1972; (with Judith Mencusi and others) A Manual of Diagnostic Tests and Activities, Reading 4-6, 1973. Home: 770 Boylston St Boston MA 02199 Office: 186 Hampshire St Cambridge MA 02139

RYLE, DORIS JEAN (MRS. HOWARD RUSSELL RYLE), fashion designer for dolls; b. Rising Sun, Ind., Dec. 18, 1920; d. Stanley Harris and Della Pearl (North) Stegmiller; student Miller Sch. Bus., 1942, Lifetime Career Schs., 1967, Famous Artists Sch., 1973; m. Howard Russell Ryle, Mar. 14, 1946; children—Stanley Bruce, Russell Gene. Sec., bookkeeper Shillito's Co., Cin., 1941-43, Brown Tool & Mfg. Co., Rising Sun, 1943-44; key punch operator Ind. Internal Revenue Service, Indpls., 1944, Stokley Van Camp, Indpls., 1946; owner Ryle Doll Hosp., Rising Sun, 1965—. Active Boy Scouts Am., 1957-60. Mem. Magic Valley Fine Arts Assn. (v.p. 1973), Ohio County Hist. Soc. (sec. 1970—), Bus. & Profl. Women (v.p. 1967-69, pres. 1970-72), Rising Sun P.T.A. (v.p. 1960, pres. 1961). Methodist. Home and office: Route 2 Rising Sun IN 47040

RYMER, GRACE MCNUTT, floral design cons.; b. Knoxville, Tenn., Nov. 20, 1915; d. George Edgar and Daisy (Fox) McNutt; student Brailey Music Studio, U. Tenn., 1930-35, Tenn. Wesleyan Art Dept., 1942-45, Chadek Conservatory, U. Chattanooga, 1942-46, N.Y. Sch. Interior Design, 1965, Ohara Sch. Floral Design (Tokyo), 1965, Rob Thomas Abstract Design, 1966; m. Marvin Joseph Rymer, Oct. 29, 1947 (dec. Sept. 1968); children—Edwin Frank, Christopher Joseph. Free-lance floral designer, cons., 1950—; exhibited Internat. Flower Show, N.Y., 1957-70; assisted in decorations for Pres. Nixon's Inaugural Balls, Rose Bowl Parade, 1965, Miss Am. Pageant, 1962-63, Everette Conklin Design team, 1957—; lectr. in U.S., Can., 1970, Japan, 1973, Lisbon, Portugal, 1973. Pres., Am. Cancer Soc., 1969-70. Bd. dirs. Bradley County Nursing Home, Tenn. Cancer Soc. Recipient Silver trophy Nat. Flower Show, Washington, 1958, Purple award Federated Garden Club, 1959, Silver trophy Internat. Flower Show, 1962-70, 1st award Nat. Orchid Growers, 1966, Sylvia award Expose, Balt., 1967. Mem. Am. Act Florists (nat. bd. 1972—), Cleveland Garden Club (pres. 1971-72), 3d Dist Garden Club (dir. 1957-58, 71-72). Author: Art of Floral Design, 1963. Home: 1755 N Ocoee St Cleveland TN 37311

RYSANEK, LEONIE, soprano; b. Vienna, Austria, Nov. 14, 1928; d. Peter and Josefine (Hoeberth) Rysanek; student Vienna Conservatory, 1947-49; m. Rudolf Grossmann, Aug. 26, 1950; m. 2d, Ernst-Ludwig Gausmann, Dec. 23, 1969. Singing engagements Innsbruck, 1949-50, Saarbruecken, 1950-52, Munich State Opera, 1952-54, also Vienna, Berlin, Stuttgart, London, Paris, Milan, Rome, Naples; appeared Sieglinde, Bayreuth, 1951, Senta, San Francisco, 1956, Lady Macbeth, Met. Opera, N.Y.C., 1959; now appears with Met. Opera, also Vienna, Berlin, Bayreuth; recordings RCA Victor, Deutsche Grammaphon, London Records, EMI. Recipient Chappel gold medal of singing, London, 1956; Silver Rose, Vienna Philharmonic, 1956. Home: Altebeuern ueber Rosenheim Federal Republic of Germany

RYSDALE, ANNE NICHOLAS, architect; b. Detroit, Sept. 3, 1920; d. William Stuart and Barbara (Preston) Nicholas; B.F.A., U. Ariz., 1940; 1 dau., Valerie Anne. Engring. officer Naval Air Sta., Seattle, 1943—; practice architecture, Tucson, 1949—; mem. firm Rysdale Assos., Architects, 1949—; cons. architect, Gila County; dir. Am. Bank of Commerce, Phoenix. Sustaining mem. Jr. League, Tucson, 1941—, bd. dirs., 1952-60. Recipient Home Builders Assn. award, 1955, Gregson award Am. Registry Architects, 1964; mem. A.I.A., Soc. Am. Registered Architects (founder), Delta Gamma. Club: Tucson Country. Prin. works include, boarding schs. and dormitories at Dennehotso and Seba Dalkai, Navajo Reservations, Ariz., Oxford Plaza Regional Center, Tucson, Highland Park, Berkshire Village, comml. med. complex, Glenfair Mall, Phoenix, Sierra Vista (Ariz.) Center, Babbitts Store, Page, Ariz., 2 Woolco Centers, Tucson, Smitty's Shopping Center, Phoenix. Home: 119 S Irving St Tucson AZ 85716 Office: 20 N Tucson Blvd Tucson AZ 85716

SA, NAOMI FAY (MRS. JOHN EFTIS), theatre dir.; b. Bklyn., May 18, 1933; d. Abraham and Evelyn (Litsky) Brown; B.A. in Music, Bklyn. Coll., 1957; m. John Eftis, June 28, 1958; children—Victoria, Paul. Tchr., pub. schs. N.Y.C., 1958-59, Prince Georges County, Md., 1960-61, Washington, 1961—; founder, producer, dir. Back Alley Theatre, Inc., Washington, 1967—. Community vol. Glenwood Community Center, Bklyn., 1955-56, Arlington Dept. Recreation, 1962-63, Washington CORE, 1963-65; dir. Operation Turn On, Washington, 1972—. Recipient Emmy awards prodn. Johnnas, 1972; Nat. Endowment for Arts grantee, D.C. Arts Commn. grantee, Stern Found. grantee, Cafritz Found. grantee, Strong Found. grantee, Meyer Found. grantee; recipient Mid-Atlantic Am. Theatre Alliance award 1973. Composer: The End of the Rainbow, 1967; Sir Percival and the Hydra, 1968; The Genie's Daughter, 1970; Teatro Doble, 1973; El Chivo Egoista, El Grillo y las Hormigas, 1974. Home: 1715 S Kent St Arlington VA 22202 Office: 1365 Kennedy St NW Washington DC 20011

SAARINEN, YVETTE, editor; b. Portland, Ore., Nov. 23, 1947; d. Ted and Mimi Marian (Fleming) Saarinen; B.A., Portland State U., 1972. Spanish translator, corr. Richard Abel & Co., Portland, 1970-71; tchr. English Liminganm Kansanopisto, Liminka, Finland, 1971-72; reporter Tigard (Ore.) Times, 1973, family living editor, 1973—. Mem. Citizens Park Com., Tualatin, Ore., 1972, Tigard's Jr. Miss Selection Com., 1973. Mem. Women In Communications. Democrat. Club: Tualatin Booster (pres. 1972-73). Home: 7880 SW Nyberg Tualatin OR 97062 Office: 12271 SW Main Tigard OR 97223

SABATHIE, CHARLOTTE KELLER, interior and indsl. designer; b. N.Y.C.; d. Harry and Lena (Malina) Keller; student City Coll. N.Y.; m. Joseph N. Sabathie, Mar. 17, 1947 (div. Oct. 1955); 1 son, Steven. With Dorothy Draper & Co., Inc., N.Y.C., 1954-71, sec., 1960-62, treas., 1962-66, exec. v.p., 1966-71; pres. Charlotte Sabathie Design Assos., Inc., N.Y.C., 1971—. Mem. Nat. Home Fashions League, Am. Fedn. Arts, Am. Craftsman Council. Participant in designing Westbury Hotel, Toronto, Ont., Can., Westbury Hotel, N.Y.C., Westbury Hotel, London, Eng., Westbury Hotel, Brussels, Belgium, Berskhire Hotel, N.Y.C., Internat. Hotel, John F. Kennedy Airport, N.Y.C., Westbury Hotel, San Francisco, Greenbrier Hotel, White Sulphur Springs, W.Va., Sheraton-Waikiki, Hawaii, Dromoland Castle, County Clare, Ireland, Limerick (Ireland) Inn, Clare Inn, County Clare, Shannon Internat. Hotel, Middle Bay Country Club, Oceanside, N.Y., Lincoln Sq. Moton Inn, N.Y.C., Engrs. Club, Phila., Crofton, (Md.) Country, Baiting Hollow Country Club, Riverhead, N.Y., Rolling Hills Country Club, Wilton, Conn.; designer charity balls for Project Hope, Damon Runyan Cancer Fund, Polish Mut. Assistance, J.O.B. Home: 200 E 84th St New York City NY 10028 Office: 250 E 63d St New York City NY 10021

SABINE, CORNELIA MANLEY (MRS. PAUL E. SABINE), psychologist; b. Elgin, Ill.; d. Joseph Morris and Mary Elizabeth (Glennan) Manley; student, Radcliffe Coll., 1944-45; A.B. magna cum laude, Colo. Coll., 1949, M.A., 1950; Ednl. Specialist in Guidance and Counseling, Stanford U., 1954; m. Paul E. Sabine, Apr. 16, 1938 (dec. Dec. 1958). Clin. psychologist Pikes Peak Family Counseling and Mental Health Center, Colorado Springs, Colo., 1960-70; pvt. practice as clin. psychologist, Colorado Springs, 1970—. Faculty, U. Colo., Colorado Springs, 1968-69. Fellow Am. Orthopsychiatric Assn.; mem. Nat. Vocational Guidance Assn., Nat. Assn. Disability Examiners, Am., Colo. psychol. assns., Women Psychologists of Colo., El Paso County Psychol. Soc. (co-founder), League of Women Voters. Club: Altrusa (Colorado Springs). Home: 20 W Espanola St Colorado Springs CO 80907 Office: 228 N Cascade Av Colorado Springs CO 80903

SABO, PAT IRENE PATTERSON (MRS. LOUIS A SABO), editor; b. Hunter, Ark., Jan. 2, 1931; d. Cecil and Edna (Crutchfield) Patterson; student U. Miss., 1946-47; m. Louis A. Sabo, Aug. 21, 1949; 1 dau., Lynn Michelle. Editorial staff Times Herald, Washington, 1947-48, Ark. Gazette, Little Rock, 1948-49; womans editor Mesa (Ariz.) Tribune, 1958-69; staff reporter Ariz. Republic, Phoenix, 1969-73, Phoenix Gazette, 1973—; adviser Mesa Indoor Sports, 1960—, Mesa C. of C., 1964. Asst. to Altrusa Clubs Mature Womans Clinic, 1965-66. Bd. dirs. Mesa Assn. for Retarded Children, Maricopa County chpt. Am. Cancer Soc. Recipient numerous writing awards Ariz. Press Women, 1958-68; Service award Ariz. Cosmetologist Assn., 1961; Ernie Pyle newspaper award and spl. citation Nat. V.F.W. Aux., 1967; named Woman of Achievement Ariz. Press Women, 1961. Ark. Traveler. Mem. Nat., Ariz. (dist. program chmn., past dist. v.p.) assns. press women. Presbyn. Home: 1010 W 4th Pl Mesa AZ 85201 Office: 120 E Van Buren St Phoenix AZ 85001

SABOL, LOUISE CAROL JUSTIN (MRS. JOHN ROBERT SABOL), ophthalmologist; b. Pottsville, Pa., Nov. 16, 1933; d. Peter Alfred and Alma Mae (Bachman) Justin; B.S., Pa. State U., 1955; M.D., Woman's Med. Coll. Pa., 1959; m. John Robert Sabol, Aug. 16, 1958; children—Jennifer Lane, Carolyn Louise. Intern, Geisinger Med. Center, Danville, Pa., 1959-60, resident, 1960-63; practice medicine, specializing in ophthalmology, Danville, 1970—; mem. staff Geisinger Med. Center, asso. dept. ophthalmology, 1970—. Diplomate Am. Bd. Ophthalmology and Otolaryngology. Mem. A.M.A., Pa. State, Montour County med. assns., Pa. Acad. Ophthalmology, Kappa Kappa Gamma. Mem. Ch. of Christ. Home: Ravine Rd Williamsport PA 17701 Office: Geisinger Med Center Danville PA 17821

SABREY, SHEILA ANN, educator; b. Chgo., Dec. 4, 1940; d. John D. and Margaret Elizabeth (O'Grady) Sabrey; B.A., Mary Manse Coll., 1961; M.A., Bowling Green State U., 1963. Social worker, Hamilton County Welfare, Cin., 1964-70; adoption worker Child Family Service, Toledo, 1970-72; instr. theatre U. Toledo, 1972—. Exec. com. Toledo Repetoire Theatre, 1972—; vocal cons. Toledo Dem. party, 1973—; faculty adviser Students Internat. Meditation Soc., 1972—; acting mem. Colo. Shakespeare Festival, 1973-74. Mem. Interdenominational Com. to Serve Unmarried Parents, 1970-73. Named one of 10 outstanding young women in Toledo by Womens Service Orgn.-Mercy Guild, 1972. Club: Phythian Castle (dir., 1972-73). Home: 1525 W Bancroft St Toledo OH 43606 Office: Dept Theatre Univ Toledo Toledo OH 43606

SABSHIN, EDITH, physician; b. N.Y.C., Dec. 10, 1923; d. Benjamin and Ida (Moses) Goldfarb; B.S., Bklyn. Coll., 1944; M.S. in Physics, Yale, 1945; M.D., U. Chgo., 1951; m. Melvin Sabshin, June 12, 1955; 1 son, James. Intern, Michael Reese Hosp., Chgo., 1951-52, resident in psychiatry, 1952-53, attending psychiatrist, 1969—; resident in psychiatry U. Chgo., 1953-54, U. Ill., 1954-55; practice medicine, specializing in psychiatry and psychoanalysis, Chgo., 1955—; tng. and supervising analyst Chgo. Inst. Psychoanalysis; professorial lectr. U. Chgo., 1968—. Fellow Am. Psychiat. Assn.; mem. Am. Psychoanalytic Assn., Ill. Psychiat. Soc., Chgo. Psychoanalytic Soc., Chgo. Med. Soc. Home: 850 N DeWitt Pl Chicago IL 60611 Office: 180 N Michigan Av Chicago IL 60601

SACHS, ALICE, editor; b. Kansas City, Mo.; d. Charles and Flora (Well) Sachs; B.A., Wellesley Coll.; Certificat d'Etudes Francais, The Sorbonne. Editor Lenox Hill Press, Crown Pubs., N.Y.C., 1937—. Mem. sub-com. edn. and past chmn. housing Borough Pres.'s Community Planning Bd., 1963-73; co-chmn. Com. Joint Use 94th St. Armory for Pub. Sch. and Middle-Income Housing, 1964-65; mem. Com. Fair Apportionment, 1963—, Com. Proportional Representation, 1960—; mem. benefit com. Wiltwyck Sch., 1958—; commr. N.Y. Bd. Elections, 1973—. Bd. dirs. Freedom Residence Fund. Democratic dist. leader 66th assembly dist. Manhattan, 1953—; mem. exec. com. Lexington Dem. Club, 1950—; mem. N.Y. New Dem. Coalition; mem. platform com. N.Y. Dem. State Com., 1964; chmn. human relations com. N.Y. Dem. County Com., 1962-63; Dem. and Liberal candidate N.Y. State Assembly, 1956, 58, 60, N.Y. State Senate, 1962. Mem. Ams. Dem. Action (vice chmn. nat. bd.), Lenox Hill Neighborhood Assn., League Women Voters, Citizens Union, Am. Civil Liberties Union, Urban League, N.A.A.C.P., Phi Beta Kappa. Mem. B'nai B'rith. Club: Women's City (municipal affairs com.). Home: 140 E 63d St New York City NY 10021 Office: 419 Park Av S New York City NY 10016

SACHS, BERNICE COHEN (MRS. ALLAN ELI SACHS), physician; b. Passaic, N.J., Sept. 16, 1918; d. Joseph and Rose (Mirelson) Cohen; B.S. with distinction, U. Mich., 1939, M.D. cum laude, 1942; m. Allan Eli Sachs, Dec. 21, 1941; children—Lee William, Robin Beth. Intern, Michael Reese Hosp., Chgo., 1942-43; resident Inst. for Psychosomatic and Psychiat. Research and Tng., Chgo., 1945-49; practice medicine specializing in psychiatry and psychosomatic medicine, Seattle, 1949—; mem. staffs Michael Reese Hosp., 1942-49, Group Health Hosp., Seattle, 1949—; cons. Chgo. Bd. Pub. Health Bd. dirs. Health and Welfare Council, Seattle, Seattle-King County Safety Council. Mem. Gov.'s Com. on Youth Employment. Mem. nat. women's com. Brandeis U. Named Woman of Achievement, Theta Sigma Phi, 1965. Fellow Acad. Psychosomatic Medicine (credentials com., councillor 1974—), Am. Geriatrics Soc. (founding); mem. Am., Wash., King County (media relations com., mental health com.) med. assns., Am. Psychosomatic Soc., Am. Med. Women's Assn. (pres.; sponsor Bernice C. Sachs Jr. Br. U. Wash., Med. Woman of Year 1966), Med. Women's Internat. Assn., Pan-Am. Med. Women's Alliance (v.p. U.S.A.), Am. Psychiat. Assn., Intercollegiate Assn. Internat. Platform Assn., Women Students (nat. resource personnel bd.), Wash. Acad. Clin. Hypnosis (pres.), Nat. Forensic League, Past Presidents' Assembly (trustee), Am. Soc. Clin. Hypnosis (treas. 1974), Soc. Clin. and Exptl. Hypnosis, Am. Assn. U. Women Am. Assn., Council Med. Adminstrs., Group Psychotherapy, Puget Sound Group Psychotherapy Assn., Nat. Council Jewish Women, A.A.A.S., Mortar Board, Phi Beta Kappa, Alpha Omega Alpha, Phi Kappa Phi, Iota Sigma Pi, Alpha Lambda Delta. Mem. Hadassah (Myrtle Wreath award 1967), B'nai B'rith Women. Clubs: Women's University; Soroptimist; Glendale Country. Contbr. articles to med. jours. Home: 13 El Dorado Beach Club Dr Mercer Island WA 98040 Office: 200 15th Av E Seattle WA 98112

SACHS, LISBETH JOSEPHINE (MRS. BERNARD H. STERN), psychiatrist; b. Grandenz, Germany; d. Sally and Johanna (Leiser) Samulon; B.S., U. Wurzburg, 1930; M.D., U. Berlin, 1934; M.D., U. Berne, 1938; m. 2d, Bernard Herbert Stern. Intern, Berlin (Germany) Jewish Hosp., 1935-36, resident 1936-38; resident in pathology Lincoln Hosp., Bronx, N.Y.C., 1941-42, Queens Gen. Hosp., N.Y.C., 1942-44; asst. pathologist Greenpoint Hosp., 1944-46; resident psychiatrist Hillside Hosp., 1952-54; pvt. practice, N.Y.C., 1951—; resident psychiatrist Kings County Hosp. Center, 1954-55, chief psychiatrist Children's and Adolescent Services and Child Guidance Clinic, 1955-58; attending psychiatrist Gracie Sq. Hosp., N.Y.C., 1962—; asso. attending psychiatrist Flower, Fifth hosps., 1966—, Brookdale Hosp. Med. Center; cons. psychiatrist Jewish Bd. Guardians, Madeleine Borg Child Guidance Inst., 1962-63; asst. prof. psychiatry State U. N.Y. Downstate Med. Center, 1957-66, N.Y. Sch. Psychiatry, N.Y.C., 1958-60; asso. clin. prof. N.Y. Med. Coll., 1966—, N.Y. U. Med. Center. Mem. profl. adv. com. Childville, Inc. Qualified psychiatrist, State N.Y. Recipient grant State U. Research Found., 1958-68. Mem. A.M.A., Research Soc. N.Y. State Med. Center, N.Y. Council Child Psychiatry, A.A.A.S., Internat. Platform Assn., Bklyn. Assn. Mental Health, Kings County Med. Soc., N.Y. Path. Soc., Am., Bklyn. psychiat. assns., Am. Orthopsychiat. Assn., Royal Soc. Health, Am. Soc. Adolescent Psychiatry, Am. Acad. Child Psychiatry, N.Y. Acad. Scis., A.A.A.S., Hadassah. Author articles in med. jours., books in field. Address: 10 Plaza St Brooklyn NY 11238 also 750 Kappork St Riverdale NY 10463

SACHS, MARILYN STICKLE (MRS. MORRIS SACHS), author; b. N.Y.C., Dec. 18, 1927; d. Samuel and Anna Lois (Smith) Stickle; A.B., Hunter Coll., 1949; M.S., Columbia U., 1953; m. Morris Sachs, Jan. 26, 1947; children—Anne, Paul. Children's librarian Bklyn. Pub. Library, 1949-60, San Francisco Pub. Library, 1961-67; writer of childrens books, 1964—. Book reviewer N.Y. Times, 1971—. Mem. Am. Civil Liberties Union, Sierra Club. Democrat. Jewish religion. Author: Amy Moves In, 1964; Laura's Luck, 1965; Amy and Laura, 1966; Veronica Ganz, 1968; Peter and Veronica, 1969; Marv, 1970; The Bears House, 1971; The Truth About Mary Rose, 1973; A Pocketfull of Seeds, 1973. Home: 733 31st Av San Francisco CA 94121

SACHS, ROSE BRUSSELL, dentist; b. Aberdeen, S.D., July 25, 1914; d. Ben and Jennie (Levine) Brussell; student No. Coll. (S.D.), 1932-34; D.D.S., Northwestern U., 1938; m. Arthur Sachs, Jan. 25, 1942 (dec. 1967); children—Bruce, Stuart. Dentist pub. schs., St. Paul, 1938-41, Vista Del Mar children's foster Home, Los Angeles, 1957-59, Jewish Home for Aged, Los Angeles, 1956-57; program rep. continuing edn. in dentistry U. Cal. at Los Angeles extension, 1970-72; pub. relations lectr. U. Cal. at Los Angeles Dental Sch., chmn. recruiting program for female students to dentistry, 1972-74. Pres. Canfield Av. P.T.A., Los Angeles, 1955-56; pres. Los Angeles chpt. women's com. Brandeis U., Waltham, Mass., 1959-60. Founder med. library Inst. Cancer and Blood Research, Beverly Hills, Cal., 1967. Home: 9309 Cresta Dr Los Angeles CA 90035 Office: Dental Extension U Cal Los Angeles CA 90024

SACHSE, JANICE HARRIET RUBENSTEIN (MRS. VICTOR A. SACHSE, JR.), artist; b. New Orleans, May 6, 1908; d. Isaac Harry and Madeleine (Phillips) Rubenstein; student art La. State U., 1927-29; Newcomb Coll., 1928, Corcoran Gallery Art Sch., 1939; m. Victor A. Sachse, Jr., Jan. 2, 1929; children—Victor Alphonse III, Harry Rubenstein. One-man shows at La. State U. Union Gallery Invitational, 331 Galleries, New Orleans, others; now mem. B.R. Gallery, Inc.; exhibited in group shows at La Boetie, N.Y.C., N.Y. World's Fair, 1965, Berlin, Germany Volkfest, Joslyn Art Mus., Omaha, New Orleans Mus. Art, Witherspoon Gallery, U.N.C., others. Represented in permanent collections at La. State U., Alexandria, La. State Art Commn., Baton Rouge, So. Bell Telephone Co., Birmingham, Ala., others. Co-organizer Baton Rouge Gallery, Inc., 1964; judge art groups, 1964-72. Bd. dirs. Vols. Am. Recipient Purchase award Bi-Centennial Art Exhbn., 1974. Mem. La. Council Performing Arts, La. Craft Council, Am. Fedn. Art. Mem. B'nai B'rith. Club: Baton Rouge Country. Home and studio: 370 S Lakeshore St Baton Rouge LA 70808

SACK, LOIS CLAIRE (MRS. BERNHARD A. SACK II), pub. relations exec.; b. New Rochelle, N.Y., June 5, 1941; d. Joseph Arvid and Florence (Selin) Arvidson; A.A., Centenary Coll., 1961; postgrad. St. Josephs Coll., 1965-68, Temple U., 1968-72; m. Bernhard A. Sack II, June 23, 1962; 1 dau., Jody Lynn. Copywriter, Sears Roebuck & Co., Phila., 1965, N.W. Ayer & Son, Inc., Phila., 1966; account exec. Ramsdel, Bright & Nathans, Phila., 1967-71, Lewis & Gilman, Inc., Phila., 1971—. Presbyn. Home: 170 Clubhouse Rd King of Prussia PA 19406 Office: 1700 Market St Philadelphia PA 19103

SACKLER, MARIETTA LUTZE (MRS. ARTHUR MITCHELL SACKLER), psychotherapist, psychoanalyst; b. San Francisco, Mar. 17, 1919; d. Felix and Frederika C. (Durkes) Lutze; M.D. with honors, U. Berlin, Germany, 1943; m. Arthur Mitchell Sackler, 1949; children—Arthur Felix, Denise Marica. Intern, Rockaway (L.I., N.Y.) Beach Hosp., 1946-47, Queens Gen. Hosp., Queens Village, N.Y., 1948-49; psychiatrist Creedmore State Hosp., Queens Village, 1953-54; coordinator videotape dept. of family therapy dept. Postgrad. Center Mental Health, N.Y.C., 1964—, asso. dir. family therapy dept., 1974—; pvt. practice individual and family therapy, N.Y.C., 1974—; owner, chmn. bd. Kade, Inc., pharm. firm, Berlin and Konstanz, Germany, 1949—. Mem. internat. task force to assess future needs world med. health manpower WHO. Mem. adv. council dept. art history and archaeology Columbia U., N.Y.C., 1971; trustee Mus. of Am. Indians, N.Y.C., 1973—. Life fellow Met. Mus. Art, N.Y.C.; mem. Internat. Assn. Social Psychiatry (sec.-gen. 1972), A.M.A., Am. Group Psychotherapy Soc., World Fedn. Mental Health. Address: 860 United Nations Plaza New York City NY 10017

SACKS, SUSAN TAISCH (MRS. IRVING SACKS), statistician; b. Detroit, June 1, 1943; d. Nathan and Lillian (Sherman) Taisch; A.B., U. Mich., 1965; M.S., U. Cal. at Los Angeles, 1967; postgrad. U. Cal. at Berkeley, 1971—; m. Irving Sacks, Jan. 7, 1968. Statistician, Abbott Labs., North Chicago, Ill., 1967-69, U. So. Cal. Critical Care Unit, Los Angeles, 1969-70, Cancer Epidemiology Research Project, U. Cal. at Berkeley, 1970—. Tchr. statistics to radiologists VA Hosp., Los Angeles, 1969-70. Mem. Am. Statis. Assn., Biometric Soc., Soc. for Epidemiologic Research, Phi Beta Kappa, Phi Kappa Phi. Home: 4758 17th St San Francisco CA 94117 Office: 2120 Berkeley Way Berkeley CA 94704

SADDAM, ALMA MONTANO, nutritionist; b. Manila, Philippines, Feb. 6, 1938; d. Tomas Abrina and Jesusa Juan (Montano) Saddam; B.S. in Home Econs., U. Philippines, 1957; M.S., Ohio State U., 1960. Came to U.S., 1958. Adminstrv. dietitian Yale Med. Center, 1960-61; instr. Coll. Home Econs., U. Philippines, 1961-63; sr. dietitian Univ. Hosp., Ohio State U., 1964-68, extension nutritionist Ohio Coop. Extension Service, 1969—. Asst. sec., sect. chmn. Dietetic Assn. Philippines, 1961-63. Mem. Am., Ohio (co-chmn. sect. 1973-74), Columbus (sect. co-chmn. 1971-72) dietetic assns., Franklin County Home Econs. Assn. (sec. 1971-72). Address: 1787 Neil Av Columbus OH 43210

SADDLEMYER, ELEANOR ANN, educator; b. Prince Albert, Sask., Can., Nov. 28, 1932; d. Orrin Angus and Elsie Sarah (Ellis) Saddlemyer; student Humboldt Collegiate Inst., 1946-50; B.A., U. Sask., 1953; M.A, Queen's U., Kingston, Ont., Can., 1956; Ph.D., Bedford Coll. U. London, 1961. Mem. faculty U. Victoria (B.C., Can.), 1960-71, asso. prof. English, 1965-68, prof., 1968-71; prof. Victoria Coll. U. Toronto, 1971—, dir. Grad. Centre for Study Drama, 1972—. Mem. com. Anglo-Irish manuscripts Royal Irish Acad., 1969. Bd. govs. Theatre Canada, 1971, Theatre Plus Toronto, 1973, Imperial Order Daus. Empire War Meml. II scholar, 1957; Canada Council scholar, 1958, 59; Guggenheim fellow, 1965; Canada Council

Research fellow, 1968. Mem. Internat. Assn. Study Angl.-Irish Lit. (founding, chmn. 1973—), Soc. Authors, Soc. Theatre Research, G.B. Shaw Soc., Canadian Assn. U. Tchrs., Assn. Canadian U. Tchrs. English, Canadian Assn. Irish Studies. Author: (with Robin Skelton) The World of W.B. Yeats, 1965; In Defense of Lady Gregory, Playwright, 1966; The Plays of J.M. Synge: Books One and Two, 1968; J.M. Synge: Plays, 1969; The Plays of Lady Gregory in four volumes, 1970; Letters to Molly: J.M. Synge to Maire O'Neill, 1971; Letters from Synge to W.B. Yeats and Lady Gregory, 1971. Editorial bd. Yeats Studies, 1970, Irish Univ. Rev., 1970, Jour. Irish Lit., 1971, Modern Drama, 1972, English Studies in Can., 1973, Canadian Theatre Rev., 1973. Contbr. to profl. jours. Office: Dept English Victoria Coll U Toronto Toronto 5 ON Canada

SADLER, ELVA ELIZABETH, editor; b. Birmingham, Ala., Feb. 22, 1905; d. James Reed and Mary Christine (Craig) Sadler; B.A., Howard Coll., 1927; M.A., U. Ala., 1941; postgrad. U. N.C., 1929, U. Bonn, 1955, U. Mexico, 1961. Tchr. pub. schs., O'Hatchee, Ala., 1927-28, Birmingham, Ala., 1928-43; instr. Ward-Belmont Coll., 1943-44; asst. prof. English No. Mont. Coll., 1947-48; editor Abingdon-Cokesbury Press, Nashville, 1944-47, fgn. service officer USIA, Japan, 1950, Thailand, 1950-51, Philippines, 1951-53, Germany, 1953-58, Washington, 1958-62, El Salvador, Peru, 1962, Costa Rica, Haiti, Dominican Republic, Bolivia, Brazil, 1963, Washington, 1964; editor USIA English Teaching Forum, 1965—, also writer; English teaching cons., 1961—. Bd. dirs. Parkfairfax Citizens Assn., 1968—, treas., 1968-71. Mem. Nat. Council Tchrs. English, N.E.A., Delta Zeta. Presbyn. Club: Parkfairfax Garden (pres. 1969-70). Author articles New Eng. Quarterly, Link, Chaplain, Pacific Stars and Stripes, also English teaching books. Home: 3114 Wellington Rd Alexandria VA 22302 Office: 1750 Pennsylvania Av NW Washington DC 20547

SADLER, NAN CARTER (MRS. ROBERT ALEXANDER SADLER 3D), horse breeder and trainer; b. Passaic, N.J., Mar. 8, 1941; d. Creed Fulton and Mary Virginia (Monteiro) Carter; student Converse Coll., 1958-60, U. Tex., 1960-61; m. Robert Alexander Sadler 3d, Dec. 31, 1959; 1 son, Creed Carter. Riding instr. Swain Sch., Allentown, Pa., 1963-69, Cedar Crest Coll., Allentown, 1968-69; v.p. Car-Nan-Sa Farms, Inc., Allentown, 1965-66, pres., 1967—, also dir.; partner Nanco Corp., Allentown, 1971—. Organizer, chmn. jr. women's com. Allentown Symphony, 1965-66; ball chmn. Allentown Symphony Assn., 1967-68; den mother Cub Scouts, 1968-69, 70—, coach, 1970—; v.p. Swain Sch. P.T.A., 1966-67, pres., 1968-71; active fund drives various organized charities, 1961-67; mem. Allentown Art Mus. Bd. dirs. Arthritis and Rheumatism Soc. Lehigh Valley, 1973—, pres. aux., 1973—, v.p. vols., 1973—. Named Rider of Year, Northeastern Pa. Horse Show Assn., 1966, Outstanding Rider in Open Jumper Div., 1967. Mem. Soc. Arts Allentown (charter mem., hostess chmn. for artists 1963), Lehigh County Hist. Guild (charter mem.), Pa. Jumper Assn. (adviser 1971—), Pa. Horse Breeders Assn., Am. Horse Show Assn., Penn-Jersey Horse Assn., D.A.R. (dir. 1968-69, chmn. jr. div. 1971—). Lutheran. Clubs: Lehigh Country, Junior Woman's, Three Oaks Riding and Hunt (sec.-treas. 1963-69, v.p. 1970-72, pres. 1973—, dir. 1963—) (Allentown). Home: 471 S Cedarbrook Rd Allentown PA 18104 Office: 4337 Hamilton Blvd Allentown PA 18104

SADLER, RUTH ELLEN, journalist; b. Phila., Apr. 20, 1950; d. Alvin and Frances (Lubar) Sadler; grad. Baldwin Sch., Bryn Mawr, Pa., 1968; B.A. cum laude, Syracuse U., 1972. Gen. assignment reporter Buffalo Evening News, 1972; sports writer Watertown (N.Y.) Daily Times, 1972-73; asst. sports editor Titusville (Fla.) Star-Advocate, 1973-74; sports writer Port Huron (Mich.) Times-Herald, 1974—. Mem. Am. Assn. U. Women, Sigma Delta Chi, Zeta Tau Alpha. Home: 1720 Military St Apt 12 Port Huron MI 48060

SADOVNIKOFF, MARY DEQUEDVILLE BRIGGS (MRS. VSEVOLOD SADOVNIKOFF), concert pianist; b. St. Paul, July 4, 1926; d. John DeQuedville and Marjorie Scott (Winslow) Briggs; A.B., Radcliffe Coll., 1949; M.F.A., Brandeis U., 1955; m. Vsevolod Sadovnikoff, June 21, 1952; children—Nicholas, Gregory, Laura. Tchr., The Masters Sch., Dobbs Ferry, N.Y., 1951-52; teaching fellow Brandeis U., 1954-56; tchr., Lincoln Sch., Providence, 1959-66; instr. applied music program Brown U., 1971; solo recitals at Carnegie Recital Hall, N.Y.C., 1968, Town Hall, 1970; solo and chamber music concerts throughout R.I., Gardner Mus., Boston, Hamline U., St. Paul, other colls. and univs.; founding mem. Providence Chamber Players, 1968—, Providence New Music Ensemble, 1970—. Co-founder, co-dir. Mus. Concert Series, R.I. Sch. Design Mus., Providence, 1968—. Frank Huntington Beebe fellow, 1949, asso. fellow Radcliffe Inst., 1964-66. Mem. Musicians Union, Music Tchrs. Nat. Assn., R.I. Music Tchrs. Assn. Address: 21 John St Providence RI 02906

SADOWSKA, KRYSTYNA KOPCZYNSKA (MRS. STEFAN SIWINSKI), artist, designer, sculptor; b. Lublin, Poland; d. Wladyslaw and Kzzimiera (Szelagowska) Kopczynski; ed. Acad. Fine Arts, Warsaw, Poland, 1933-37, Central Sch. Arts and Crafts, London, Eng., 1940-44, Grande Chaumiere, Paris, France, 1939-40; m. Konrad Sadowski, July 2, 1939 (dec. Mar. 1960); m. 2d, Stefan Siwinski, May 15, 1963. Came to Can., 1949, naturalized, 1954. Lectr. design Ontario (Can.) Coll. Art, Toronto, 1953-59; exhibited in one-man shows paintings St. George Gallery, London, 1946, paintings, tapestries, ceramics, Gallery Ministry Edn., Rio de Janiero, Brazil, 1947, Inter-Americana Cultural Centre, Curitiba, Brazil, 1948, Consulate of Can., N.Y.C., 1964, also Toronto, Montreal, Vancouver, London, Windsor, Ottawa, Halifax (all Can.); exhibited in group shows and internat. exhbns. tapestry Paris (gold medal), 1937, Helsinki, Finland, 1937, N.Y.C., 1939, Rio de Janeiro (silver medal), 1947, Greensboro, N.C., 1949 (2d prize), 50, 51, Ottawa, 1957, Lausanne, Switzerland, 1962, ceramics Toronto and Montreal, 1957, Syracuse, N.Y. (Drakenfeld prize), 1958; also exhibited Warsaw, Poland, 1957, Brussels Exposition (Belgium), 1958, Salzburg, Austria, 1964; executed sculptures, altars, textile murals for schs., churches, parks, univs., comml. bldgs. Can., Brazil, U.S. Recipient Grand award and 1st prize tapestry 1st Exhbn. Can. Weaving, London, Ont., 1953. Mem. internat. (London), Polish (Warsaw) artists assns., Ont. Soc. Artists, Hampstead Artists Council, London, Central Inst. Arts and Design, London, Arts, and Crafts Exhbn. Soc., London, Sindicato dos Artistas Plasticos de Sao Paulo (Brazil). Home: 561 Spadina Rd Toronto 10 ON Canada Office: 86 Parliament St Toronto 2 ON Canada*

SADTLER, BARBARA ANN KOLTES (MRS. DAVID ROTH SADTLER), advt. exec.; b. Hutchinson, Kan., Mar. 1, 1940; d. Edwin Michael and Rose (Meyers) Koltes; B.A., U. Minn., 1961; m. David Roth Sadtler, Aug. 24, 1963 (div. June 1974). With fashion dept. Dayton's in Mpls., 1956-61; fgn. affairs analyst Dept. of Def., Washington, 1961-63; fashion coordinator Jordan Marsh, Boston, 1963-65; fashion editor, columnist Staten Island Advance, Newhouse Publs., Inc., 1965-72, fashion editor Newhouse Nat. Wire Service; v.p. advt. and creative services Leslie Fay, Inc., N.Y.C., 1972—. Bd. dirs. Jr. Guild of S.I., 1967, Young Republicans of Washington, 1961-63. Mem. Am. Assn. U. Women, Fashion Group, Inc. (regional com.), Delta Gamma. Home: Putnam Green 33D Greenwich CT 06830 Office: 1400 Broadway New York City NY 10018

SAENZ, NANCY ELIZABETH KING (MRS. MICHAEL SAENZ), civic worker; b. Greenville, Tex., Jan. 28, 1930; d. Henry M. and Vallie (Wheatley) King; A.B. with honors, Tex. Christian U., 1950, B.S. magna cum laude, 1952; postgrad. Hartford Sem. Found., 1952-53; Escuele de Idiomas, 1953; Lexington Theol. Sem., 1953; m. Michael Saenz, July 28, 1950; children—Michael King, Cynthia Elizabeth. Missionary, United Christian Missionary Soc., Indpls., serving in P.R., 1954-65; bd. dirs. Adminstrv. Bd. Christian Chs., P.R., 1950-65; counsellor and tchr. State Christian Youth Fellowship Conf., P.R., 1954-57; chmn. dept. Christian edn. Christian Chs., P.R., 1962-64, sec., 1959-61, state dir., 1963; dept. Christian edn. P.R. Council Chs., 1959-64, sec., 1959-60; sec. and counsellor State Christian Women Fellowship of Christian Chs., P.R., 1955-57, 59-63, dist. chmn., 1968—. Sec., Disciples of Christ Acad. P.T.A., Bayamon, P.R., 1962-63; mem. state com. Home for Aged, United Ch. Women, P.R., 1963; womens com. Ind. State Symphony Soc., 1967—; womens com. Internat. Christian U. Japan, 1962-64, 65—, pres. Indpls. chpt. 1967-68; mem. vocational-tech. adv. council Laredo Ind. Sch. Dist., 1971—; dist. cons., mem. adminstrv. com. Christian Women's Fellowship in Tex., 1971-74. Bd. dirs. Greater Indpls. Fedn. Chs., 1970-71; bd. dirs. Planned Parenthood Assn. Webb County, 1972-74, v.p., 1973-74; bd. dirs. Civic Ballet Laredo, 1972—; mem. Mercy Hosp. Aux. Mem. Irvington Union of Clubs (exec. bd. 1966—, 2d v.p. 1968-70), Young Mothers Club Irvington (v.p. 1965, pres. 1967), Marion County Guardian Home Guild (pres. 1968-70), Art Assn. Indpls., Art League, Civic Music Laredo, Irvington, Am. Assn. U. Women, Laredo Pan Am. Roundtable, Alpha Chi, Phi Sigma Iota. Mem. Christian Ch. (dist. exec. bd. 1971—). Clubs: Rotary Anns, Women's College (R.P.); Irvington Womens; Laredo Tuesday Music and Literature (pres. 1973-74), Women's City. Author: Winds of Change, 1968. Home: P-34 Fort McIntosh Laredo TX 78040

SAFA, HELEN MARGARET ICKEN (MRS. MANOUCHEHR SAFA-ISFAHANI), educator; b. Bklyn., Dec. 4, 1930; d. Gustav F. and Erna S. (Keune) Icken; B.A., Cornell U., 1952; M.A., Columbia, 1958; Ph.D. in Social Anthropology, 1962; m. Manouchehr Safa-Isfahani, Dec. 23, 1962; 1 dau., Mitra; stepchildren—Kaveh, Arya. Cons. research office N.Y. State Div. Housing, 1956-57, Urban Renewal and Housing Adminstrn., Commonwealth of P.R., 1959-60; sr. research asso. Youth Devel. Center, Syracuse (N.Y.) U., 1962-67; asso. prof. anthropology Livingston Coll., Rutgers U., New Brunswick, N.J., 1967-72, prof. anthropology and urban studies, 1972—, asso. dir. Latin Am. Inst., 1970-73, dir., 1973—. Cons. to Cinva, Bogota, Colombia, 1961—, joint urban program Exec. Council Episcopal Ch., 1966-67; asso. Columbia U. seminar on devel. pre-indsl. areas, Latin Am. seminar. Recipient grants U. P.R., 1957-59, Nat. Insts. Mental Health, 1960-61, 1963, 69-70, U.S. Office Edn., 1966-67; Research Council of Rutgers U., 1971, 73. Fellow Am. Anthrop. Assn., Am. Ethnol. Soc., Soc. Applied Anthropology, Latin Am. Studies Assn. (exec. council 1973—), Internat. Congress Americanists; mem. Am. Civil Liberties Union, N.Y. Acad. Sci., Phi Beta Kappa. Home: 42 Gloucester Ct East Brunswick NJ 08816 Office: Div Urban Studies Livingston College Rutgers U New Brunswick NJ 08903

SAFRAN, CLAIRE, writer, editor; b. N.Y.C., Mar. 18, 1930; d. Simon and Flora (Rand) Safran; B.A. in English cum laude, Bklyn. Coll., 1951; m. John Milton Williams, June 8, 1958; 1 son, Scott Edward. News editor Photo Dealer mag., 1951-53; asso. editor TV Radio Mirror, 1954-58; mng. editor Photoplay mag., 1958-61; editor TV Radio Mirror, 1961-65, IN mag., 1965-66; asso. editor Family Weekly, 1967-68; editor Coronet, 1968-71; freelance contbr. to nat. mags., 1972—; contbg. editor Redbook mag., 1974—. Mem. Soc. Mag. Writers. Home: 361 E 50th St New York City NY 10022

SAFT, VIRGINIA WITHERS COLEBECK (MRS. JAMES SAFT), physician; b. Greensboro, Ala., Feb. 8, 1928; d. Edward L. and Mary Winn (Withers) Colebeck; B.S., Newcomb Coll., 1949; student Yale Med. Sch., 1949-51; M.D., U. Chgo., 1953; grad. Chgo. Inst. Psychoanalysis, 1972; m. James H. Saft, July 7, 1951; children—Elizabeth W., James. Intern, Ill. Research and Edn. Hosp., Chgo., 1953-54; resident, Psychosomatic and Psychiat. Hosp., Michael Reese Hosp., Chgo., 1954-57; pvt. practice psychiatry, Chgo., 1957—. Mem. A.M.A., Am. Psychiat. Assn., Am. Psychoanalytic Soc. Home: 49 E Cedar St Chicago IL 60611

SAGER, RUTH, geneticist, educator; b. Chgo.; B.S., U. Chgo., 1938; M.S., Rutgers U., 1944; Ph.D., Columbia, 1948. Merck fellow NRC Rockefeller Inst. Med. Research, 1948-50, staff mem., 1950-54; research scientist Columbia, 1955-65; prof. biology City U., Hunter Coll., N.Y.C., 1966—; non resident fellow Inst. Animal Genetics, U. Edinburgh (Scotland), 1962. Mem. Internat., Am. socs. cell biology, Genetic Soc. Am., Soc. Am. Naturalists, Phi Beta Kappa, Sigma Xi. Author: (with F. J. Ryan) Cell Heredity, 1961. Contbr. articles to profl. jours. Pioneered research in cytoplasmic heredity. Address: 405 W 118th St New York City NY 10027

SAGISI, VIVIEN RANJO BATOYON (MRS. GLOCRITO G. SAGISI), obstetrician and gynecologist; b. Manila, P.I., Oct. 20, 1942; d. Teodoro Udaundo and Estrela Orque (Ranjo) Batoyon; M.D., U. Philippines, 1965; m. Glocrito G. Sagisi, Aug. 21, 1969; 1 son, Patrick Carlos. Intern, Greater Balt. Med. Center, 1966-67; resident St. Joseph's Hosp., Balt., 1967-70; obstetrician-gynecologist Cath. Med. Center, Agana, Guam, 1970—, Guam Polyclinic, 1973—; mem. staff, spl. cons. Guam Meml. Hosp. Com. chmn. for med. profls. Guam chpt. A.R.C., 1972—. Bd. dirs. Guam unit Am. Cancer Soc., 1973—. Mem. Guam Med. Soc. (exec. sec. 1970—). Address: PO Box AX Agana GU 96910

SAGON, PATRICIA ANN, editor; b. Washington, Dec. 18, 1949; d. Philip Herbert and Martha (Silverstein) Sagon; B.S., Northwestern U., 1971, M.S., 1972; Intern, office of Senator Kennedy, 1968; press sec. to congl. candidate, Md., 1970; with Washington bur. Cox Newspapers, 1970; guest editor Mademoiselle mag., N.Y.C., 1971; editor Pres.'s Commn. on Financial Structure and Regulation, Washington, 1971; editor Securities Regulation and Law Report, Washington, 1972-74; staff reporter Boston bur. Wall Street Jour., 1974—. Mem. Women in Communications, Sigma Delta Chi. Home: 65 East India Row Boston MA 02110 Office: 10 Post Office Square Boston MA 02110

SAGONE, ANITA MAE, pathologist; b. Pitts., May 15, 1939; d. Arthur Lawrence and Gertrude Ellen (Evans) Sagone; B.S., U. Pitts., 1961, M.D., 1965. Intern, U. Health Center Hosps., Pitts., 1965-66, resident in pathology, 1966-69; asst. pathologist Montefiore Hosp., Pitts., 1969—; clin. instr. U. Pitts. Sch. Medicine, 1970-72, asst. prof. pathology, 1972—. Mem. Am. Soc. Clin. Pathology, Coll. Am. Pathologists, Pitts. Pathology Soc. Home: 5435 5th Av Pittsburgh PA 15232 Office: 3459 5th Av Pittsburgh PA 15213

SAHAKIAN, MABEL MARIE LEWIS (MRS. WILLIAM S. SAHAKIAN), educator; b. West Newton, Pa., Mar. 2, 1921; d. Paul Tyson and Blanch Theresa (d'Happart) Lewis; student W.Va. U., 1939-40; A.B., Gordon Coll., 1944; S.T.B. (Hester Ann Beebe fellow 1947), Boston U., 1947, postgrad., 1947-49; D.Sc., Curry Coll., 1957; m. William S. Sahakian, Mar. 27, 1945; children—James William, Richard Lewis, Barbara Jacquelyn, Paula Leslie. Ordained to ministry Conglist. Ch., 1953; asso. pastor Riverdale Congl. Ch., Dedham, Mass., 1953-55, pastor, 1967-68; asso. pastor First Congl. Ch., Chelsea, Mass., 1956-58, Ch. of Christ, Bedford, Mass., 1958-60; lectr. philosophy, speech Northeastern U., Boston, 1960-72, sr. lectr., 1972—, counseling service, 1963—. Interim minister E. Congl. Ch., Milton, Mass., 1966-67, S. Congl. Ch., Braintree, Mass., 1968-69, 1st Congl. Ch., Norwood, Mass., 1972-73. Chmn. drive Am. Cancer Soc., Dedham, Mass., 1964-65. Mem. Am. Philos. Assn., D.A.R. (regent 1964-67), Mass. Children Am. Revolution (sr. state chaplain 1967-69), Met. Boston Ministerial Assn., Boston Authors Club, Boston Bus. and Profl. Women, Alpha Phi. Author: (with William S. Sahakian) Realms of Philosophy, 1965; Ideas of the Great Philosophers, 1966; Rousseau As Educator, 1974; John Locke, 1974. Home: 135 Booth Rd Dedham MA 02026

SAHAR, MARIANNE MOEHLENBECK (MRS. ANTHONY SAHAR), physician; b. Bielefeld, West Germany, Feb. 24, 1942 (came to U.S. 1968, naturalized 1972); d. Kurt and Dorothea (Huebner) Moehlenbeck; Physikum, Heidelberg U., West Germany, 1963; M.D. cum laude, Heidelberg Ruprecht Karl U., 1966; m. Anthony I. Sahar, Nov. 24, 1967; children—Christoph, Annette. Intern, Monmouth Med. Center, Long Branch, N.J., 1968-69; now mem. staff; gen. practice medicine, 1969—; mem. staff Riverside Hosp., Red Bank, N.J.; sch. physician Red Bank Cath. High Sch., 1969-72. Diplomate Am. Bd. Family Practice. Mem. Am. Med. Women's Assn. Inc. Address: 552 Westwood Av Long Branch NJ 07740

SAIFER, PHYLLIS LYNNE TROMMER (MRS. MARK GARY PIERCE SAIFER), allergist; b. Phila., May 19, 1940; d. Philip R. and Evelyn N. (Milgram) Trommer; student Wellesley Coll., 1957-58; B.A., U. Pa., 1961; M.D., U. Cal. at San Francisco, 1966; M.P.H., U. Cal. at Berkeley, 1971; m. Mark Gary Pierce Saifer, Jan. 28, 1961; children—Scott David, Alandria Gail. Intern, Mt. Zion Hosp., 1966-67, resident in pediatrics, 1967-68, 71-72; child health physician Erie County Health Dept., 1968-69; practice medicine specializing in family medicine Lackawanna (N.Y.) Community Health Center, 1969-70, specializing in pediatric and adult allergy, San Francisco, 1970—. Childbirth edn. tchr. Assn. Psychoprophylaxis in Obstetrics, 1963—. Recipient NIH fellowship, 1970-72. Mem. Am. Coll. Allergy, Assn. Psychoprophylaxis in Childbirth, Berkeley Coalition. Home: 1428 Arch St Berkeley CA 94708 Office: 2211 Post St San Francisco CA 94115

SAIKI, PATRICIA (MRS. STANLEY MITSUO SAIKI), state legislator; b. Hilo, Hawaii, May 28, 1930; d. Kazuo and Shizue (Inoue) Fukuda; B.S., U. Hawaii; m. Stanley Mitsuo Saiki, June 19, 1954; children—Stanley Mitsuo, Sandra S., Margaret C., Stuart K., Laura H. Tchr., Dept. Edn. Hawaii, 1959-66; research asst. to state senator, 1966-68; mem. Hawaii Ho. of Reps., 1968—. Dir. Amfac, Inc. Mem. Pres.'s Adv. Council on Status of Women, 1969—; commr. Western Interstate Commn. on Higher Edn.; fellow Eagleton Inst., Rutgers U., 1970. Mem. Kaopiolani Hosp. Aux. Sec. Hawaiian Republican Com., 1964-66, vice chmn., 1966-68; del. Hawaii Constl. Conv., 1968; alternate del. Rep. Nat. Conv., 1968; mem. Fedn. Republican Women. Bd. dirs. Aloha council Boy Scouts Am.; trustee Hawaii Pacific Coll. Mem. Nat. Soc. State Legislators (bd. govs. 1972—). Episcopalian. Address: 784 Elepaio St Honolulu HI 96816*

SAIKOWSKI, CHARLOTTE, journalist; b. Chgo.; d. Frank and Antoinette (Warsowicz) Saikowski; B.A., Principia Coll., 1947; M.A., Columbia, 1952. Instr. English, U. Warsaw (Poland), 1947-49; asst. editor The Current Digest of the Soviet Press, N.Y.C., 1952-62, also acting editor, 1960-61; with The Christian Sci. Monitor, Boston, 1962—, fgn. corr., 1967—, now Moscow Bur. chief. Recipient USIA pub. service award, 1959. Christian Scientist. Editor: (with Leo Gruliow) Current Soviet Policies IV: The Documentary Record of the 22d Congress of the Communist Party of the Soviet Union, 1962. Home: 1 Norway St Boston MA 02115 Office: 12-24 Sadovo Samotechnaya Moscow USSR*

ST. CYR, CAROL RUTH, educator; b. Meriden, Conn., Dec. 25, 1924; d. Donald J. and Margaret (Horan) St. Cyr; B.S., Willimantic State Coll., 1946; M.A., Trinity Coll., 1949; Ph.D., U. Mich., 1955. Elementary tchr., Meriden, 1946-53; research asst. U. Mich., Ann Arbor, 1953-55; asst. prof. George Washington U., Washington, 1955-60, asso. prof., 1960- 64, prof. edn., 1964—. Mem. Nat. Aerospace Edn. Assn. (dir. 1957—, pres. 1972—), Am. Assn. U. Women, Am. Assn. U. Profs., Assn. for Supervision and Curriculum Devel., A.A.A.S., Pi Lambda Theta. Home: 1701 N Kent St Arlington VA 22209 Office: George Washington University School of Education 2201 G St Washington DC 20006

SAINT DENIS, BARBARA LOUISE DION, artist; b. Muskegon, Mich., Sept. 8, 1928; d. Halley Joseph and Helen Sophia (Johnson) Dion; grad. high sch.; m. Richard Breen Saint Denis, Sept. 20, 1947 (div. 1969); children—Peggy (Mrs. James F. Witham), Michele (Mrs. Joseph Hecksel), Richard L. Advt. mgr. Muskegon Grocery Wholesale Co. Co-op. (Mich.), 1953-56; dir. Grand Haven (Mich.) Art Center, 1957-60; account exec. Indsl. Advt. Agy., Muskegon, 1960-63; owner Saint Denis Fine Arts Studios, Muskegon, 1963—; exhibited one-woman shows Grand Haven Art Center, 1960, Battle Creek (Mich.) Civic Art Center, 1969, Chgo. Uptown Savs. & Loan, 1967, Grand Haven Civic Center, 1968, Americana Hotel, N.Y.C., 1967, Jenny Wren Art Gallery, Pentwater, Mich., 1971; groups shows Hackley Art Gallery, Muskegon, 1962-66, Grand Rapids Art Museum, 1965, 67-69; represented in permanent collections Mus. Contemporary Crafts, N.Y.C., 1963. Chmn. Seaway Art Festival, 1961-62, Am. Art Week, 1965, Muskegon Cultural Series, 1964-66; mem. bldg. com. St. Francis de Sales Ch., Muskegon, Mich., 1965-67; mem. Liturgical Art Commn., Diocese Grand Rapids, Mich., 1969. Recipient Major Art award Hackley Art Gallery, 1965. Mem. Mich. Acad. Arts, Sci. and Letters, N.A.A.C.P. Roman Catholic. Home: 2108 LeTart Av Muskegon MI 49441 Office: 2005 Lakeshore Dr Muskegon MI 49441

SAINTE-MARIE, BUFFY, singer, composer; b. Piapot Reserve, Craven, Sask., Can., Feb. 20, 1941; adopted dau. Albert C. and Winifred (Kenrick) Sainte-M.; B.A. in Philosophy, U. Mass., 1962; m. Dewain Kamaikalani Bugbee, Sept. 16, 1967. Appearances at Saladin, Gaslight, Village Gate, Troubedour, also various coffeehouse theatres; concert appearances at Carnegie Hall, 1965, Royal Albert Hall, London, Eng., 1965, N.Y. Philharmonic, 1967, Queen Elizabeth Theatre, Vancouver, Can., 1967, Newport Folk Festival, 1965, 67, Helsinki (Finland) Music Festival, 1967; pres. Gypsy Boy Music Inc.; rec. artist for Vanguard Rec. Soc. Adviser Upward Bound. Recipient Billboard award, 1965. Mem. A.F.T.R.A., Am. Fedn. Musicians. Roman Catholic. Compositions include: Its My Way, 1964, Many a Mile, 1965, Little Wheel Spin and Spin, 1966, Fire and Fleet and Candlelight, 1967, Welcome, Welcome Immigrants, 1967. Home: Summit Hill Harrison ME 04040 Office: care Chartoff Winkler 101 W 55th St New York City NY 10019*

ST. GEORGE, BETTY LOUISE (MRS. WILFRED CLARENCE ST. GEORGE), owner bookstore; b. San Pedro, Cal., May 15, 1926; d. Martin Leonard and Ethyl Joesphine (Sherer) Mayer; B.S., U. So. Cal., 1947; postgrad. Albert Ludwig U., Freiburg, Germany, 1960; m. Wilfred Clarence St. George, Sept. 11, 1953; children—Virginia Lee, Martin Glenn. Tchr. elementary grades Los Angeles City Schs., 1947-53, Dept. Army, Tokyo, Japan, 1950-52; owner St George's Book Shop, Paso Robles, Cal., 1966—. Del. Internat. Conf. Am. Women's Activities in Europe, Bershtesgaden, Germany, 1957, 58. Mem. Cal. Atty. Gen.'s Vol. Adv. Council, 1972-74; pres. Los Ninos chpt. Childrens Home Soc. Cal., 1971, v.p. Santa Lucia council, 1972—. Regional v.p. Cal. Central div. Fedn. Republican Women, 1966, 67, 68, 2d v.p., 1969-71, bd. dirs., 1974-75; chmn. campaign Lt. Gov. Robert Finch, 1966, Pres. Nixon, 1968; chmn. San Luis Obispo County campaign Cal. treas. Ivy Baker Priest, 1970. trustee, Paso Robles Union Elementary Sch. Dist., 1967-71; trustee Paso Robles Joint Union High Sch. Dist., 1967-71, pres. bd. trustees, 1969, 71; bd. dirs. Community Concert Assn., pres., 1968-69; bd. dirs. San Luis Obispo County Am. Cancer Soc. 1962-69, chmn. fund dr. for Paso Robles, 1968-69. Mem. Am. Assn. U. Women (v.p. 1964), Am. Booksellers Assn., C. of C., Zeta Tau Alpha. Home: 647 Bolen Dr Paso Robles CA 93446 Office: 619 12th St Paso Robles CA 93446

ST. HILAIRE, T(HERESE) FOREST (MRS. LORENZO L. ST. HILAIRE), clin. psychologist; b. Detroit, Mar. 11, 1926; d. John George and Olga Marie (Lippert) Forest; A.B., Marygrove Coll., 1947; M.A., Cath. U., 1950; postgrad. George Washington U., 1953-54; m. Lorenzo Louis St. Hilaire, June 24, 1950; children—John Forest, Camille Mary, Colette. Coordinator, staff psychologist D.C. Sec. Crippled Children, Washington, 1947-68; parent cons. Lighthouse for The Blind, 1968—; parent cons. Mich. State Normal Coll., 1950-55; cons. psychologist Montgomery County (Md.) Bd. Edn., 1952—, Barker Adoption Found., Bethesda, Md., 1955-59, Arlington County Dept. Welfare, 1960—, Leary Sch., Annandale, Va., 1967—; dir. spl. edn. workshop Cath. U., 1953-56; clin. psychologist Arlington (Va.) Cooperative Sch. Handicapped Children, 1954-64; mem. planning com. sch. health Nat. Health Council; dir. Mary Mount Jr. Coll. Non-directive group psychotherapy classes, 1958—; mem. bd. dirs. St. Anthony Child Counseling Clinic; chmn. com. cerebral palsy Health, Welfare and Edn. Council, Prince George and Montgomery Counties. Mem. Va. Commn. Outstanding Women, 1972. Bd. dirs. United Cerebral Palsy No. Va., Fairfax Opportunities Unltd. Mem. Marygrove Alumna Assn., Cath. Family Movement, Assn. Retarded Children, Nat. Conf. Cath. Women, Nat. Conf. Exceptional Children. Club: Lake Barcroft Women's. Home: 3518 Duff Dr Falls Church VA 22041

SAINT JAMES, SUSAN, actress; b. Los Angeles, Aug. 14, 1946; d. Charles Daniel and Constance (Geiger) Miller; grad. Acad. Sacred Heart, Lake Forest, Ill., 1963. TV appearances on Fame is the Name of the Game, 1967-68, The Name of the Game, 1968—, MacMillan and Wife, 1971-72. Recipient Emmy award, 1969. Home: 2128 N Beverly Glen Blvd Universal City CA 91604 Office: Universal City Studio Universal City CA 91604*

ST. JOHN, OLIVE ELEANOR (MRS. CARTER B. ST. JOHN), educator; b. Terre Haute, Ind., Jan. 19, 1914; d. Victor Hugo and Lavina (Welch) Forsythe; B.S., Ind. State U., 1935; M.A., N.Y. U., 1952, Ph.D., 1960; m. Carter B. St. John, Jan. 29, 1965. Health Edn. sec. YWCA, Terre Haute, Ind., 1935-38; tchr. phys. edn., biology Thornton Jr. High Sch., Terre Haute, 1938-41; supr. phys. edn. Lab. Sch. Ind. State U., Terre Haute, 1941-45, prof. phys. edn., 1945—, chmn. women's phys. edn. dept., 1962—. Mem. Am., Ind. assns. health, phys. edn. and recreation, Nat., Midwest assns. phys. edn. coll. women, Am. Assn. Univ. Profs., Am. Assn. Univ. Women, Ind. Tchrs. Assn., Delta Psi Kappa, Delta Kappa Gamma. Home: 119 Arcadia Dr Terre Haute IN 47803

ST. JOHN, TERRY MARGARET (MRS. TERRY MCKENZIE ST. JOHN), journalist; b. Pensacola, Fla., Oct. 31, 1934; d. Wilfred Manning and Eula Gene (Watson) McKenzie; B.J., U. Tex., 1956; m. Terry McKenzie St. John, Aug. 24, 1968. Editorial asst. Gulf Pub. Co., Houston, 1956-58; asso. editor, publ. Transcontinental Gas Pipe Line Corp., Houston, 1958-69; free lance writer, pub. relations, 1969—; editor Racquets, 1974—. Mem. Women in Communications (pres. 1962-63, 72-73), S.E. Tex. Indsl. Editors (v.p. 1963-65). Mem. United Ch. of Christ. (sec. 1968). Address: 2312 West Main Houston TX 77006

ST. JOHN, WYLLY FOLK, journalist, author; b. nr. Ehrhardt, S.C., Oct. 20, 1908; d. William Obed and Annie Claire (Mattox) Folk; A.B. in Journalism summa cum laude, U. Ga., 1930; m. Thomas F. St. John, Jan. 1, 1930; 1 dau., Anne (Mrs. Neil D. Pratt). Staff writer Atlanta Jour. and Constn. mag., 1941—; free lance writer. Bd. dirs. Sr. Citizens Council, Walton County, Ga. Named Ga. Author of Year, 1968; Ga. Author of Yr. in Fiction, 1973; nominated for juvenile Edgar award Mystery Writers Am. 1972-73. Mem. Authors Guild, Atlanta Press Club, Mystery Writers Am., Phi Beta Kappa, Phi Kappa Phi, Theta Sigma Phi (Brenda award for outstanding contbn. to journalism 1970). Clubs: Atlanta Plot, Social Circle Garden. Author: The Secrets of Hidden Creek, 1966; The Secrets Of The Pirate Inn, 1967; The Mystery Of The Gingerbread House, 1968; The Christmas Tree Mystery, 1969; The Mystery Of The Other Girl, 1971; The Ghost Next Door, 1971; Uncle Robert's Secret, 1972; The Secret of the Seven Crows, 1973. Contbr. stories, articles to numerous mags. Home: 198 Dogwood Av Social Circle GA 30279 Office: 72 Marietta St Atlanta GA 30302

ST. JOHNS, ADELA ROGERS, author; b. Los Angeles, May 20, 1894; d. Earl and Harriet (Greene) Rogers; grad. Hollywood (Cal.) High Sch., 1910; m. William Ivan St. Johns, Dec. 24, 1914; children—William Ivan II (dec.), Elaine, McCullah, Richard Rogers. Newspaper reporter, feature writer San Francisco Examiner, 1913, Los Angeles Herald, 1914-18, Chgo. Am., 1928, N.Y. Am., 1929, Internat. News Service, 1925-54; covered Hauptmann trial and Lindbergh kidnapping; first woman sports writer; mem. faculty Grad. Sch. Journalism, U. Cal. at Los Angeles, 1950-52; lectr. Stephens Coll., Stanford, U. Pa., Loyola U., others. Bd. dirs. Meals for Millions, Women's C. of C. Los Angeles, WAIFS. Author: A Free Soul, 1924; Single Standard, 1925; How to Write a Short Story, 1952; Affirmative Prayer in Action, 1955; Final Verdict, 1962; Tell No Man, 1966; The Honeycomb, 1970; also short stories, serials Sat. Eve. Post, Good Housekeeping, McCall's, Ladies Home Jour., Cosmopolitan, Am. Weekly, This Week, Red Book, Readers Digest, London Daily Express and Evening Standard. Home: 106 Malibu Colony Malibu CA 90265

SAKAJIAN, ROSEMARY, writer; b. Franklin, Mass., Mar. 2, 1912; d. Hagop and Hartoon (Dallagian) Sakajian; ed. pub. schs. Writer of stories, articles and poems pub. in various mags., U.S. and Canada, 1950—. Mem. Nat. League of Am. Pen Women, Nat. Writers Club. Home and office: 261 Christopher Dr San Francisco CA 94131

SAKUMA, MABEL YOSHIKANE (MRS. JOHN M. SAKUMA), home economist; b. Honolulu, Aug. 24, 1934; d. Shigeichi and Hisano (Fujiwara) Yoshikane; B.S., U. Hawaii, 1956; m. John M. Sakuma, Feb. 14, 1959; children—Joy M., Shari S. Extension home economist U. Hawaii, 1956-59, extension home economist 4-H youth coordinator, Wailuku, Maui, Hawaii, 1965—. Mem. Hawaii 4-H Adv. Council; mem. Maui Children and Youth Com., 1972—; mem. Maui Mental Health Assn., 1971—; del. 4-H Leaders Forum, Washington, 1965. Recipient Distinguished Service award Nat. Assn. Extension Home Economists, 1973. Hawaii Home Economists scholar, 1969. Mem. Nat. Home Econs. Assn. (conv. del. 1971), Hawaii Home Economists in Extension (v.p. 1968), Nat. 4-H Agts. Assn., Epsilon Sigma Phi. Club: Maui Woman's (rec. sec. 1970-71, corr. sec. 1972). Home: 611 Pio Dr Wailuku HI 96793

SALAMONE, BARBARA MARIE (MRS. ALBERT A. PINEDA), physician; b. Newark Sept. 19, 1935; d. Joseph Vincent and Angela (Anania) Salamone; B.S., Coll. St. Elizabeth, 1955; M.D., U. Rome, 1960; m. Albert A. Pineda, Oct. 19, 1963; children—Stephen, Mark. Intern, St. Joseph's Hosp., Paterson, N.J., 1961-62; resident pediatrics N.Y. Med. Coll., 1962-64; practice medicine, specializing in pediatrics, Clifton, N.J., 1965—; with Project Head Start, Paterson, 1965, Child Health Centers, 1966-67; sch. physician, Clifton, N.J., 1969-71; med. cons. Project Follow Thru, Paterson, 1969—; pediatric ednl. coordinator St. Joseph's Hosp., Paterson, 1965—, dir. pediatric outpatient dept., 1970. Mem. Am., N.J. women's med. Assns., N.J., Passaic County med. socs. Home: 45 Pearl Brook Dr Clifton NJ 07013

SALANITRO, ANGELA SIBILIA (MRS. FRANK J. BELLIZZI), physician; b. Bloomfield, N.J., Nov. 7, 1934; d. Alfred Alfio and Amelia Adrianna (Sibilia) Salanitro; A.B., Barnard Coll., 1956; M.D., Coll. Medicine and Dentistry N.J., 1960; m. Frank J. Bellizzi, May 29, 1965; children—Frank John, Angela Teresa. Intern, Jersey City Med. Center, 1960-61, resident in pediatrics, 1961-63; fellow pediatric allergy N.Y. Med. Center, Bellevue, 1963-65, St. Vincent's Hosp., N.Y.C., 1965-66; practice medicine, specializing in pediatric allergy, Upper Montclair, N.J., 1964—; asst. attending physician pediatric allergy Roosevelt Hosp., N.Y.C., 1969—; asso. attending physician Mountainside Hosp., Montclair, N.J., 1965—; clin. instr. pediatrics N.Y. Med. Sch., Bellevue, 1964-66, Coll. Medicine and Dentistry N.J., 1966—. Regional med. cons. Children's Asthma Research Inst. Hosp., Denver, 1970—. Mem. A.M.A., Am. Med. Women's Assn., Am. Acad. Allergy, Coll. Medicine and Dentistry N.J. Alumni Assn., N.Y., N.J. allergy socs., Asso. Physicians Montclair and Vicinity, Essex County Med. Soc. Republican. Roman Catholic. Office: 4 Duryea Rd Upper Montclair NJ 07043

SALAZAR, LAURA ALICE GARDNER (MRS. HUGO SALAZAR), educator; b. Gilbert, Minn., Feb. 22, 1935; d. Lloyd William and Isabel Mary (Aldrich) Gardner; B.S., Wis. State U., 1957; M.A., Kent State U., 1960; m. Hugo Salazar, June 12, 1962; children—Anthony, Catherine. High sch. tchr. Barron, Wis., 1957-58, Lake Orion, Mich., 1960-64; asst. prof. theatre arts Grand Valley State Coll., Allendale, Mich., 1966—, chmn. theatre dept., 1969-71. Partner Theatrical Pattern Service, 1974—; co-artistic dir. The Pattern Players. Pres. Council Performing Arts for Children, Grand Rapids, Mich., 1973. Bd. dirs. Grand Valley Friends of Arts, 1967—, Grand Rapids Arts Council, 1971—. Mem. Am., Childrens theatre assns., Puppeteers Am., Assn. Internat. du Theatre pour l'Enfance et Jeunesse, Alpha Psi Omega. Author: The Best Clown (childrens play), 1961; The People of the Sacred Monkey (childrens play), 1973. Home: 0-1937 Luce Route 5 Grand Rapids MI 49504 Office: College Landing Grand Valley State College Allendale MI 49401

SALBERG, ANNE SCHOLBERG (MRS. RICHARD LETFORD SALBERG), librarian; b. Haddonfield, N.J., Jan. 2, 1940; d. Harold Milton and Yarmila Ann (Meuller) Scholberg; student U. Colo., 1958-60; m. Richard Letford Salberg, June 4, 1960; children—Suzanne, Katherine. Librarian, Glenn A. Jones M.D. Meml. Library, Johnstown, Colo., 1966—, head librarian, 1966—. Mem. parents adv. bd. Johnstown Bilingual Edn. Program. Mem. Colo. Library Assn., High Plains Library System, P.E.O. (chpt. v.p. 1973—). Clubs: Johnstown Women's, Estrellita. Home: 1111 N Park Av Johnstown CO 80534 Office: Glenn A Jones MD Meml Library Idaho and Jay Sts Johnstown CO 80534

SALEMBIER, OLIVE LYNN, packaging and materials handling engr.; b. San Francisco, Sept. 3, 1915; d. William John and Mary (Linn) Lynn; grad. comml. tchr., U. Victoria (B.C., Can.), 1934; postgrad. in engring. U. Cal. at Los Angeles, 1954-55, Mass. Inst. Tech., 1953, N.Y. U., 1955, Purdue U., 1958. Comml. tchr. Victoria High Sch., 1934-36; newspaper and radio writer, 1936-39; pub. relations Republic Studios, North Hollywood, Cal., 1939-43; owner Bus. Service, Los Angeles, 1943-50; pres., chief engr. Specification Packaging Engring. Corp., Los Angeles, 1950-60, Specialized Packaging Engring. Co., Phoenix, 1960-67; cons. engr. in packaging, transp., materials handling and logistics, Phoenix, 1967-72; packaging engr. Honeywell Information Systems, Phoenix, 1972—. Mem. staff U. Cal. Los Angeles Engring. Extension Div., 1958-61; v.p. Ariz. chpt. Nat. Def. Transp. Assn., 1964-66; seminar chmn. Ariz. State U., Packaging and Materials Handling, 1968-72; chmn. confs. on women in engring. Engring. Found., 1971-72. Recipient citations for mil. packaging tng. program U.S. Navy, 1956, 59; nat. award winner corrugated packaging design, 1961, mil. packaging, 1964. Fellow Soc. Packaging and Handling Engrs. (nat. dir. 1958, 64, 72, chmn. certification exam. com. 1971—); mem. Soc. Women Engrs. (sr. life mem.; nat. pres. 1970-72), Ariz. World Trade Assn. (charter), Nat. Inst. Packaging, Handling and Logistics Engrs., Pi Beta Epsilon. Home: 13231 98th Av Sun City AZ 85351 Office: PO Box 621 Sun City AZ 85351

SALINAS, MARTHA RUIZ (MRS. JOE DAMASO SALINAS), food products co. exec.; b. Kingsville, Tex., Oct. 19, 1937; d. Abel Ruiz and Dora Alvarez Ruiz; B.A. in Art, Our Lady of the Lake Coll., 1961; postgrad. Tex. A. and I. U., 1961-63; m. Joe Damaso Salinas, Dec. 27, 1965; children—Martha Loreen, Linda Jo, Michael Joseph. Librarian Gregory-Portland High Sch., Gregory, Tex., 1962-65, Foy H. Moody High Sch., Corpus Christi, Tex., 1967-69, Richard King High Sch., Corpus Christi, 1969-70; owner Ruiz Tortilla Factory, Corpus Christi, 1970—. Mem. Corpus Christi C. of C. Home: 717 Bradshaw Corpus Christi TX 78412 Office: 422 14th St Corpus Christi TX 78401

SALISBURY, CAROLYN SCOTT, pediatrician; b. Chgo., May 27, 1914; d. William Conyne and Dorothy Drummond (Scott) Salisbury; student Ypsilanti State Tchrs Coll., 1932-35; B.S., U. Mich., 1936; M.S., M.D., Northwestern U., 1946. Phys. edn. tchr. pub. schs., Owosso, Mich., 1936-42; intern Cook County Hosp., Chgo., 1946-48; resident Harper Hosp., Detroit, 1948-49, Children's Meml. Hosp., Chgo., 1949-50; practice medicine specializing in pediatrics, Detroit, 1950-59, Oak Park, Mich., 1959—; mem. staffs William Beaumont, Mount Carmel Mercy, Children's hosps.; pediatrician William Booth Meml. Hosp., 1952-70. Mem. A.M.A., Am. Women's Med. Soc., Detroit Pediatric Soc., Mich. Med. Soc., Alpha Omega Alpha. Home: 367 Westchester St Birmingham MI 48009 Office: 21580 Greenfield St Oak Park MI 48237

SALKIN, NANCY MAZUR (MRS. HERBERT SALKIN), advt. and pub. relations cons.; b. N.Y.C., May 11, 1930; d. Paul Myer and Adolphia (Katzsky) Mazur; A.B. magna cum laude, Smith Coll, 1951; postgrad. Radcliff Coll., 1951-52; m. Herbert Salkin, Nov. 27, 1957; children—Jeffrey, Jennifer. Presentation writer, researcher ABC, N.Y.C., 1952-57; dir. color information, spl. asst. to pres. NBC, N.Y.C., 1957-67; dir. advt. and promotion, spl. asst. to mgr. Teleprompter Cable TV, N.Y.C., 1967-73; pres. Nancy Salkin, Ltd., N.Y.C., 1973—. Bd. dirs. Hall of Sci. City of N.Y. Mem. Phi Beta Kappa. Republican. Home: 360 E 69th St New York City NY 10021 Office: 1370 Av of Americas New York City NY 10019

SALKIND, THEDA MOSS (MRS. WILLIAM SALKIND), social worker; b. N.Y.C., July 10, 1917; d. Bernhard and Beatrice (Greenberg) Moss; A.B., N.Y. U., 1937; M.A., U. Minn., 1941; m. William Salkind, Apr. 27, 1964; children—Phyllis, Louis. Caseworker Children's Protective Assn., Washington, 1941-47; caseworker Jewish Child Care Assn. of N.Y., N.Y.C., 1948-53, supr., 1953-61; psychiat. social worker Westchester Children's Assn., Guidance Center, White Plains, N.Y., 1961-63; unit supr. Children's Village, Dobbs Ferry, N.Y., 1963-65; field instr. family service div. Community Service Soc., N.Y.C., 1965-67; case supr. Jewish Hosp. and Med. Center, Bklyn., 1967-74, asst. dir. social service dept., 1974—. Mem. Nat. Assn. Social Workers, Am. Orthopsychiat. Assn., League Women Voters, Am. Civil Liberties Union, Arden Heights Jewish Center. Home: 61 Forest Green Staten Island NY 10312 Office: Jewish Hospital and Medical Center of Brooklyn 555 Prospect Pl Brooklyn NY 11238

SALLES, VIRGINIA HAZEL FRAGO (MRS. EDWARD GASPAR SALLES), real estate broker; b. Merced, Cal., Dec. 13, 1925; d. Frank Joaquin and Marian Martha (Silva) Frago; certificate in real estate Merced Coll., 1971; m. Edward Gaspar Salles, Apr. 27, 1946; children—Lawrence, Linda, Geri, Betty. Teller Bank of Am., Atwater, Cal., 1943-47; receptionist Ed Salles Realty, Atwater, Cal., 1960-74, real estate broker, 1966—. Vice pres. Base Community Council, Atwater, Cal., 1974—. Recipient Realtor of Year award, Merced County Bd. Realtors, 1969. Club: Merced (Cal.) Emblem (chmn. trustees 1973-74). Home: 1829 2d St Atwater CA 95301 Office: 1299 5th St Atwater CA 95301

SALLIE, MARJOIRIE WHITCOMB, educator; b. Foxboro, Mass., Aug. 18, 1906; d. Lewis Curtis and Laura Maude (Emery) Sallie; A.B. magna cum laude, Pembroke Coll. in Brown U., 1927; M.A., Smith Coll., 1938. With Northampton Sch. for Girls, 1934-38; asst. prin. Ashley Hall, 1938-50; headmistress Brownmoor Sch., 1954-57, St. Paul's Sch., Walla Walla, 1958-60, Bloomfield Country Day Sch., Bloomfield Hills, Mich., 1961—. Chmn. bd. trustees Adirondack-So. Sch.; trustee Oakland Country Day Sch. Mem. Nat. Assn. Prins. Schs. for Girls, Ind. Schs. Assn. Central States, Am. Assn. U. Women, Phi Beta Kappa, Sigma Xi. Republican. Episcopalian. Clubs: Altrusa (bd. dirs.), Village Woman's. Home: 747 Colonial Ct Birmingham MI 48009 Office: 1050 E Square Lake Rd Bloomfield Hills MI 48013

SALMON, MARGARET BELAIS (MRS. DOUGLAS A. SALMON), dietitian; b. N.Y.C.; d. Arnold and Hortense (Levy) Belais; B.S., U. Cal. at Berkeley, 1941; certificate hosp. dietetics Duke U., 1943; M.S., profl. diploma, Columbia, 1964, 67, postgrad., 1968; m. Douglas A. Salmon, Oct. 19, 1945; children—Robert, Betty Lynn, Donald Richard. Mem. vitamin research staff, dept. biochemistry, dietitian Duke, 1942-43; therapeutic dietitian Columbia-Presbyn. Med. Center, N.Y.C., 1942-45, research dietitian, 1957-66; mem. staff vitamin research dept. food technology U. Cal. at Berkeley, 1945; therapeutic dietitian St. Luke's Hosp., N.Y.C., 1966-70; chief therapeutic dietitian Bronx-Lebanon Hosp., 1970-72, St. Joseph's Hosp., Paterson, N.J., 1972—. Lectr. extension div. Rutgers U. Hackensack, N.J., 1964—, chronic diseases div. N.J. Dept. Health, 1965—, Montclair State Coll., Passaic Country Community Coll., Radio Sta. WFDU, nutrition cons. prenatal program A.R.C., Hackensack, 1958—; cons. dietitian physicians, hosps. and nursing homes. Leader Girl Scouts, Harrington Park, N.J., 1962-65; hostess Am. Field Service, Harrington Park, 1960—. Mary Swartz Rose scholar, 1961. Mem. Am. N.J., No. N.J. (pres. 1966-68) dietetic assns., Kappa Delta Pi, Pi Lambda Theta, Omicron Nu. Unitarian. Author: Food Facts for Teenagers, 1965; contbr. chpt. to the Young Female: A Study in Career Guidance, 1974. Editor: Enjoying Your Restricted Diet, 1972. Home: 435 Lynn St Harrington Park NJ 07640 Office: St Joseph's Hosp and Med Center 703 Main St Paterson NJ 07503

SALMON, MARY WALLACE MACFARLANE, anesthesiologist; b. Cumbernauld, Scotland, Sept. 30, 1933; d. Walter and Marion Routledge (Pollock) Macfarlane; M.B., Ch.B., Glasgow U., 1957; m. George Salmon, Jan. 31, 1963; children—Marion, Fiona. Came to U.S., 1959, naturalized, 1973. Intern, Stirling (Scotland) Royal Infirmary; resident anesthesia Columbia Presbyn. Hosp., N.Y.C., 1960-63; attending anesthesiologist N.Y. Eye and Ear Infirmary, N.Y.C., 1964—. Home: 400 Central Park West Apt 15R New York City NY 10025 Office: 237 1st Av New York City NY 10025

SALMON, WILMA H., social worker; b. Corbin, Ky., Nov. 8, 1922; d. David M. and Edna (Warren) Salmon; B.A., U. Ky., 1943; M.S.W., Tulane U., 1951. Caseworker A.R.C., New Orleans, 1943-47; caseworker, supr. Bd. Pub. Welfare, Washington, 1947-49; caseworker, supr. Dept. Pub. Welfare, State La., Orleans Parish Childrens Div., New Orleans, 1949-63, social analyst, parish pub. assistance supr. Orleans Parish Pub. Assistance Div., 1963-71; dir. Orleans Parish Dept. Pub. Welfare, 1971-73; cons. day care div. family services State of La., Baton Rouge, 1973—. Field work instr. Tulane U., 1950-58, La. State U., 1951-57; mem. La. Health Planning Adv. Council, 1972. Mem. Vieux Carre Property Owners and Assos.; bd. dirs., mem. exec. com., sec. New Orleans Area Health Planning Council, v.p., 1973—; bd. dirs. St. Marks Community Center. Mem. Am., Nat. (dir. 1968) assns. social workers, Am. Pub. Welfare Assn., La. Conf. Social Welfare (dir. 1960—), Internat., La. (dir. 1960—) confs. social work, Acad. Certified Social Workers, Tulane U. Sch. Social Work Alumni Assn. (2d v.p. 1961), Nat. Council on Aging (regional conf. com. 1972), Child Welfare League Am., Common Cause, Goals to Grow, League Women Voters, Phi Beta Kappa. Home: 923 Dumaine St New Orleans LA 70116 Office: PO Box 44065 Baton Rouge LA 70804

SALOM, ROSA LORRAINE (MRS. DANULFO ODUWALDO), airline co. exec.; b. Havana, Cuba, June 17, 1942; d. Felicito and Hilda Esther (Orihuela) Hernandez; came to U.S., 1961, naturalized, 1968; B.S. in Math., U. Miami, 1964, M.S. in Indsl. Engring., 1973; m. Danulfo Oduwaldo, Dec. 27, 1963; children—Eric, Alexis, Lorraine. Programmer Inst. Marine Scis., U. Miami, Fla., 1967-70, mgr. computing center, 1970-73; sci. programmer Eastern Airlines, Miami, 1973—. Tchr. dept. indsl. engring. U. Miami, 1968-69; tchr. electronic data processing dept. South Dade Jr. Coll., Miami, Fla., 1969. Treas. S. Fla. council Cub Scouts Am., 1973. Bd. dirs. Kendall Point Homeowners Assn., 1972. Mem. Nat. Profl. Geog. Frat. (treas. 1962-63). Republican. Roman Catholic. Clubs: Everglades Archery, Eastern Archery. Home: 8420 SW 87 Terrace Miami FL 33143 Office: Eastern Airlines Miami FL 33148

SALOME, SISTER ROSALINE, religious order adminstr.; b. Atlanta, May 17, 1927; d. Dave A. And Rosa (Kaliphy) Salome; A.B., Fontbonne Coll., 1946; M.A., St. Louis U., 1958; postgrad. Marquette U., 1961, 62, Coll. St. Thomas, 1963; Ph.D. (Univ. fellow), Emory U., 1968. Tchr. English Mt. St. Joseph Acad., Augusta, Ga., 1951-54, St.

Pius X High Sch., Atlanta, 1955-60; instr. Coll. St. Catherine, St. Paul, 1960-61; instr. Fontbonne Coll., St. Louis, 1961-65, asst. prof., 1965-68, asst. prof. English, 1968-70, asso. prof. English, 1970-71; adminstr., personnel cons. Sisters of St. Joseph in Ga., Ala., Tex., Okla., 1971—. Bd. trustees St. Joseph Hosp., Augusta, 1970—. Am. Council Learned Soc. grantee, Eng., 1970. Mem. Nat. Council of Tchrs. of English, Mo. Council of Tchrs. of English, Modern Lang. Assn., Am. Assn. U. Profs., Kappa Gamma Pi, Delta Epsilon Sigma. Home: 1413 S 10th St St Louis MO 63104 Office: 6400 Minnesota Av St Louis MO 63111

SALSANO, EILEEN AGNES, banker; b. Elizabeth, N.J., June 8, 1931; d. Martin August and Margaret Patricia (Roche) Danielson; grad. Am. Inst. Banking, 1957-70; m. Henry James Salsano, June 16, 1947; children—Sharon (Mrs. Emil Peterson), Kathryn (Mrs. John P.F. Slingerland), Henry James. Clk., Union County Trust Co., Elizabeth, 1957-63; supr. 1st Bank Colonia (N.J.), 1963, asst. treas., 1964-66, asst. v.p., 1966-69, v.p., 1969-74; v.p., treas. Springfield State Bank, 1974—. Adviser finance Colonia 1st Aid Aquad Aux., 1969-72; chmn. Mother's March of Dimes, 1969; mem. P.T.A. Sch. 17, St. John Vienney's, 1970-72. Treas. Elizabeth Downtown Democratic Club, 1965. Mem. Am. Inst. Banking (bd. govs. 1968-72, bank relations officer 1971-72, chpt. 2d v.p. 1972-73, 1st v.p. 1973-74, pres. Middlesex-Somerset-Union chpt. 1974—, chmn. So. adv. council), N.J. Bankers Assn. (edn. com.), Nat. Assn. Bank Women, Safe Deposit Assn. N.J., Woodbridge Twp. Bus. and Profl. Women's Club (treas. 1968-69, 1st v.p. 1973-74). Home: 88 Berdine Ct Colonia NJ 07067

SALTARELLI, CORA GENTILE (MRS. GERALD C. SALTARELLI), educator; b. Buffalo, Apr. 5, 1916; d. Zachary M. and Betty (Petschke) Gentile; B.A. in Biology, U. Buffalo, 1959; Ph.D. in Biology, State U. N.Y., 1964; m. Gerald C. Saltarelli, Dec. 2, 1938; children—Peter Paul, Gerald Gentile. Asst. to med. dir. E. I. DuPont, Tonawanda, N.Y., 1939-42; instr. biology, U. Buffalo, 1959-60; asst. prof. engring., head dept. bioengring. Sch. Engring. State U. N.Y., Buffalo, 1964-68, asso. prof. Grad. Sch. Biology, 1968—; dir. life scis. engring. lab., asso. cancer research scientist Roswell Park Meml. Inst., 1968—; research prof. Niagra U., Canisius Coll., 1968—; prof. Rosary Hill Coll., 1969—. Mem. adv. bd. Rehab. Med. and Engring. Lab. of Buffalo, 1971-72. Pres., Psychiat. Clinic, Buffalo, 1965-66, also dir. Trustee United Way Buffalo and Erie County, 1969—, Alfred U., Western N.Y. Library Resources Council; adv. bd., acad. com. Villa Maria Coll., Buffalo; bd. mgrs., mem. planning com. Buffalo Mus. Sci. mem. gen. research support adv. com. NIH, 1974—. Mem. Am. Assn. U. Women (dir.), Am. Soc. Clin. Pathologists, Bot. Soc. Am., Mycol. Soc. Am., Am. Inst. Biol. Scis., A.A.A.S. Research in physiology and genetics pathogenic yeasts, tumor cells. Home: 316 Brantwood Rd Snyder NY 14226 Office: Roswell Park Inst 666 Elm St Buffalo NY 14203

SALTER, DOROTHY COOPER, librarian; b. Greenfield, Ind., May 20, 1919; d. De Witt Clinton and Vera (Southwick) Cooper; A.B., De Pauw U., 1941; B.S. in L.S., Carnegie-Inst. Tech., 1942; m. Eugene L. Salter, Feb. 19, 1949 (dec.); children—Michael, Patricia. Children's librarian Bklyn. Pub. Library, 1942-46, Milw. Pub. Library, 1949-53; head Central Children's Room, Enoch Pratt Free Library, Balt., 1946-49, children's librarian, adminstrv. asst., 1961—. Corr. sec. Milw. chpt. Nat. Paraplegia Assn., 1958-60. Mem. Md. Library Assn. (membership chmn. 1948), Alpha Chi Omega. Republican. Episcopalian. Home: 14 W Cold Spring Lane Apt 711 Baltimore MD 21210 Office: 5910 Harford Rd Baltimore MD 21214

SALTER, MARGARET MILLER, educator; b. Pitts., Jan. 5, 1919; d. Malcolm Edward and Eva Elizabeth (Putnam) Miller; B.A., U. Tenn., 1941; M.A., U. Tenn., 1942; m. John Matthew Salter, Nov. 3, 1946; 1 son, Jeremy Malcolm. Air traffic controller C.A.A., LaGuardia Field, N.Y.C., 1943-46; asst. prof. fine arts Monmouth Coll., 1968-73; tchr. English, speech and drama The Ranney Sch., New Shrewsbury, N.J., 1973-74; adj. faculty speech Kean Coll., Union, N.J., 1974—. Recipient Pauline Capell Walker prize, U. Tenn., 1941. Mem. Internat. Platform Assn., Speech Communication Assn., Eastern Communication Assn. Presbyn. Home: 217 Bath Av Long Branch NJ 07740 Office: English Dept Kean Coll Union NJ 07083

SALTER, MAUD (MRS. LESLIE E. SALTER), music educator, composer; b. Galena, Kan., Oct. 13, 1899; d. Gideon Pitt and Ethel (Goodner) Carroll; A.A., Stephens Coll., 1917, B.M., 1918; Mus.B., U. Okla., 1922; postgrad. Am. Conservatory Music, 1951-53; m. Leslie Earnest Salter, Mar. 7, 1925; children—Edwin Carroll, Robert Earnest. Composed series of piano pieces for beginners known as Story Solos including Little Horny Horn, Seven Stars, Mistress Mouse, Tall Grass Green, Fishing Is My Dream, Susy Waves, Galoshes, and Tecolote, 1951-52. Mem. D.A.R., Am. Coll. Musicians, Nat., State mus. tchrs. assns., Fedn. Music Clubs, Guild Piano Tchrs., Ill. Fedn. Music Clubs (dist. chmn. jr. and sr. composers 1956—), Mu Phi Epsilon. Mem. Order Eastern Star. Home: 716 Park Dr Flossmoor IL 60422

SALTER, NORMA S. BRISTOW (MRS. CLARENCE L. SALTER), educator; b. Wetumpka, Ala., Feb. 10, 1898; d. Daniel James and Martha (Davison) Smith; B.S., George Peabody Coll. Tchrs., 1925; M.A., Columbia, 1929; grad. study Syracuse U., Union Theol. Sem.; m. John Thomas Bristow, Apr. 28, 1936 (dec. 1958); 1 dau., Martha Davison (Mrs. Henry Theodore Hoffmann); m. 2d, Clarence L. Salter, Dec. 15, 1960. Tchr., prin. Montgomery County Schs., 1917-24; supr. rural schs. Covington County, Ala., 1925-27; state supr. elementary edn. Alt. Dept. Edn., 1928-36; supr. instr. Montgomery City and County Schs., 1937-60; summer sch. faculties, various summers univs. in Ala., Miss., Fla. State chmn. rural health Ala. Women's Aux. Ala. Med. Soc., 1st v.p., 1967—; pres. Women's Aux. Talladega County Med. Soc., 1963-64; circle leader Woman's Missionary Soc., 1967-69. Recipient Algernon Sidney Sullivan award Peabody Coll., 1929; nat. achievement award Delta Kappa Gamma, 1936; named woman of year Bullock County, 1951; alumnus of year Troy State Tchrs. Coll., 1955. Mem. D.A.R. (chpt. treas. 1968—, chpt. regent 1973-75), Argus Lit. Club (1st v.p.), Ret. Tchrs. Assn. Talladega County (sec.-treas.), Ala. Edn. Assn. (past pres.), edn. assns., Delta Kappa Gamma (nat. pres. 1933-36, state exec. sec. 1939-60, state expansion chmn. 1963-69). Baptist (dir. Woman's Missionary Union 1969-72). Address: 410 East St Talladega AL 35160

SALTONSTALL, ELIZABETH, artist; b. Chestnut Hill, Mass., July 26, 1900; d. Endicott Peabody and Elizabeth Baldwin (Dupee) Saltonstall; diploma Boston Museum Sch., 1925; pvt. study painting with Andre Lhote, Paris, lithography with Stow Wengenroth, landscape with Frank Swift Chase. Tchr. art dept. Winsor Sch., Boston, 1923, 24, 27, 28; tchr. art Milton (Mass.) Acad., 1928-65; exhibited group shows Nat. Assn. Women Artists, Carnegie Inst., Bklyn. Mus., Audubon Artists; lithographs in permanent collections Library of Congress, Mus. Fine Arts, Boston, Boston Pub. Library, Yale Art Gallery, Bixler Mus. of Colby Coll. Home: 231 Chestnut Hill Rd Chestnut Hill MA 02167

SALTZMAN, DOROTHY JEANNE (MRS. IRVING J. SALTZMAN), psychologist; b. N.Y.C., Feb. 18, 1926; d. William and Ethel Ruth (Osserman) Coleman; B.A., Hunter Coll., 1946; M.A., Johns Hopkins, 1948; m. Irving J. Saltzman, June 6, 1948; children—Linda (Mrs. William Anderson), Nancy, Robert, Andrew. Lectr. dept. psychology and dept. ednl. psychology Ind. U., Bloomington, intermittently, 1949-68, psychometrist, guidance counselor, staff psychologist Speech and Hearing Center, 1968—. Mem. Am. Psychol. Assn., Soc. for Research in Child Devel., Sigma Xi, Phi Beta Kappa. Home: 1302 Longwood Dr Bloomington IN 47401 Office: Speech and Hearing Center Ind U Bloomington IN 47401

SALTZMAN, HELEN GURWITT (MRS. HENRY SALTZMAN), advt. and pub. relations exec.; b. Bklyn., June 24, 1925; d. David and Dorothy Sara (Garey) Gurwitt; B.S., N.Y. U., 1946, postgrad., 1946-48; m. Henry Saltzman, Feb. 5, 1972. Advt. dir. Martins Fashion Specialists, 1955-69; advt. and sales promotion dir. Howlands, New Eng. Div., 1969-70; pub. relations dir., asst. advt. mgr. Westons Shoppers Cities, Inc., N.Y.C., 1973—; promotion cons., N.Y.C., 1970—. Mem. Advt. Women N.Y., Inc. (life), Bklyn. C. of C. (mem. pub. relations and meetings coms. 1962-69), Pi Alpha Tau. Mem. B'nai B'rith Women. Editor: N.Y. Young Democratic Club Newspapers, 1952-54, Ad Libber, 1949-50.

SALVATORE, MARGARET ANN, virologist, epidemiologist; b. Phila., Mar. 10, 1935; d. Arthur A. and Marian (Young) Salvatore; grad. Villa Victoria Acad., 1952; B.A., Seton Hill Coll., 1956; postgrad. Seton Hall U., 1956-58. Research asst. in virology Merck, Sharp & Dohme Research Labs., Merck Inst. for Therapeutic Research, West Point, Pa., 1958-62; research asst. dept. pediatrics Hastings Found. Infectious Disease Lab., U. So. Cal., Los Angeles, 1962-66, research asso. med. sch. faculty, 1966—, research analyst Los Angeles Med. Center, 1970-71, chief research analyst health care planning and evaluation, 1971—. Mem. Am. Soc. Microbiology, Am. Pub. Health Assn., A.A.A.S. Democrat. Roman Catholic. Contbr. articles to profl. jours. Research in respiratory illness in infants and children, health care delivery. Home: 420 Rees St Playa Del Rey CA 90291 Office: 1200 N State St Los Angeles CA 90033

SALVINO, SHARON KAY, coll. ofcl.; b. Kansas City, Mo., Dec. 29, 1947; d. George and Katharine (Bambic) Salvino; B.S. in Home Econs. and Journalism, Kan. State U., 1969. With Southland News, Englewood, Colo., 1969; asst. editor University Park News, Inc., Denver, 1969-70; information rep. Arapahoe Community Coll., Littleton, Colo., 1970—. Mem. Women in Communications, Inc. (pres. Denver profl. chpt. 1972-73, treas. 1971-72), Denver Woman's Press Club, Kappa Delta. Club: Denver Dow Dames Stock. Office: 5900 S Santa Fe Dr Littleton CO 80120

SALWEN, JEANETTE JO ORNSTEIN (MRS. LEONARD B. SALWEN), artist; b. N.Y.C., May 1, 1920; d. Aaron Noah and Clara (Yoshpa) Ornstein; B.A. cum laude, Bklyn. Coll., 1942; M.A. (scholar), Oberlin Coll., 1943; m. Leonard B. Salwen, Aug. 2, 1945; children—Richard, Walter. Asst. art dir. Am. Crayon Co., N.Y.C., 1943-48; painting and design instr. Westchester County Workshop, 1947-52; design instr. Craft Students League, N.Y.C., 1951-53; design instr., adult edn. Queens Coll., N.Y.C., 1952-53; instr. painting Bridgeport (Conn.) Community Center, 1969—; free-lance furniture designer, 1960-70; designer Christmas cards Designers & Illustrators, 1946, Fayette Press, 1947. Exhibited paintings in shows at Ligoa Duncan, N.Y.C., Raymond Duncan, Paris, France, George W. Smith Mus., Springfield, Mass., Palazzo Vecchio, Florence, Italy. Recipient scholarship Art Students League, 1932-42, Prix de Paris award Ligoa Duncan Gallery, N.Y.C., 1964, Fund Prize and J. Genius award Pen and Brush Club, N.Y.C., 1973. Mem. Nat. Assn. Am. Women Artists, Women in Arts, Westport-Weston Arts Council. Artist: Children's Book A-Z, 1945. Home: 4 Hawthorne Lane Westport CT 06880

SALZMAN, NANCY SMITH, city ofcl.; b. San Luis Obispo, Cal., May 29, 1932; d. Walter Olney and Effie Lorraine (Jenkins) Smith; B.A., Whittier Coll., 1954; J.D., U. Pacific, 1969; m. Ed Salzman, Dec. 19, 1957; children—Mary Ruth, Jane, Peter. Elementary sch. tchr., Sacramento and Orinda, Cal., 1959; admitted to Cal. bar, 1969; dep. city atty., Sacramento, 1970-74; legal counsel Cal. Employment Dept., 1974—. Mem. League Women Voters (dir. Sacramento 1965, mem. speakers bur. 1965-72). Home: 2915 25th St Sacramento CA 95818 Office: 812 10th St Sacramento CA 95814

SALZMANN, RUTH ELIZABETH, ins. exec.; b. Highland, Wis., Jan. 24, 1919; d. Elmer H. and Margaret (Doll) Salzmann; Ph.B., U. Wis., 1940. Asso. actuary Hardware Mut. Casualty Co., Stevens Point, Wis., 1940-59; asso. actuary Ins. Co. N.Am., Phila., 1959-64, sec. underwriting, 1967; group actuary Life Ins. Co. N. Am., Phila., 1964-67; v.p., actuary Sentry Ins., Stevens Point, 1968—. Fellow Casualty Actuarial Soc.; mem. Am. Acad. Actuaries, Internat. Actuarial Assn., Midwest Actuarial Forum (pres. 1972). Contbr. articles to profl. publs. Home: 1400 6th Av Stevens Point WI 54481 Office: 1421 Strongs Av Stevens Point WI 54481

SAMARAS, MARY STENNING, ednl. cons.; b. Detroit, June 19, 1928; d. Walter Jeffrey and Laura Eugenia (Karas) Stenning; B.A., Wayne State U., 1949, M.A., 1952; Ed.D., U. So. Cal., 1974; m. William T. Jones, 1949 (div. 1961); children—William T., Daniel Victor; m. 2d, Thomas T. Samaras, June 23, 1962. Speech therapist, tchr., Mich. and Cal., 1951-70; dir. Claremont (Cal.) Speech and Reading Lab., 1965-70. Mem. Am. Assn. Mental Deficiency, Cal. Speech and Hearing Assn., Council for Exceptional Children, Nat. Soc. for Autistic Children, Internat. Reading Assn. Research on cooperation among profoundly retarded children and adults. Address: 705 W Arrow Hwy Claremont CA 91711

SAMBORSKY, MERCEDES CASADO, lawyer; b. Bronx, N.Y., Dec. 28, 1929; d. Ramon Perez and Sarah Marie (Shulman) Casado; B.Mus. Edn., Syracuse U., 1952; J.D., U. Md., 1969; postgrad. San Diego State U., 1964, Coll. City N.Y., 1949-50; m. Andrew Milton, July 1, 1949; children—JoAnne, Sara Marie, Ramon, Barbara. Tchr. choral and instrumental music Baldwinsville (N.Y.) Jr. and Sr. High Sch., 1952-53; elementary music supr. Penn Yan (N.Y.) Central Sch. System, 1953-54; dir. choir Evang. and Ref. Ch., La Mesa, Cal., 1962-63; admitted to Md. bar, 1969, since practiced in Jeppatowne; admitted to U.S. Supreme Ct. bar, 1973. Former bd. dirs., v.p. P.T.A.; pres. Edgewood Booster's Assn., 1968. Mem. Am., Harford County, Women's bar assns., Md. Trial Lawyers Assn., Jeppatowne Women's Club. Democrat. Home and office: 309 Garnett Rd Jeppatowne MD 21085

SAMET, DEE-DEE, lawyer; b. Greensboro, N.C., Sept. 18, 1942; d. Theodore and Charlotte Mae (Solins) Samet; student U. N.C., 1957, U. S.C., 1958; B.A., U. Ariz., 1962, J.D., 1963. Admitted to Ariz. bar, 1964; with State Compensation Fund, Tucson, 1964-74; with firm Johnson, Hayes & Dowdell, Tucson, 1974—. Mem. State Bar Ariz. Home: 6616 Calle Padre Felipe Tucson AZ 85712 Office: 250 N Church St Tucson AZ 85701

SAMFORD, DORIS EVELYN, educator, librarian; b. Johnstonville, Ill., Sept. 3, 1923; d. Leonard Francis and Mable Lucinda (Pedicord) Samford; diploma Eastern Ill. State Tchrs. Coll., 1942; student U. Wis., 1946-47, U. Colo., 1950-52; B.A., U. Denver, 1953, M.A., 1960; m. John N. Post, Apr. 14, 1946 (div. June 1948). Tchr. rural schs., Wayne County, Ill., 1942-43, Arapahoe County, Colo., 1947-48; sec. to provost marshall U.S. Civil Service, Okinawa, 1949-50; tchr. Coll. View Sch., Arapahoe County, 1951-52; tchr.-librarian Teller Sch., Denver, Valverde Sch., Denver, 1953—. Sec., Denver Sci. Com., 1955-62; chmn. Denver Elementary Library Study Com., 1962-70. Served to sgt. WAC, 1943-45. Decorated SWPA ribbon with 1 bronze battle star, Philippine Liberation ribbon with 1 bronze battle star. Mem. Denver Classroom Tchrs. Assn. (rep. 1955-56), Colo., Nat. edn. assns., Denver Tchrs. Club (rep. 1964—), Am. Legion, Women's Overseas League, Colo. Authors League, Nat. WAC Vets. Assn. Republican. Episcopalian. Author: Ruffles and Drums, 1967. Contbr. poems to Denver Post, Hence mag. Home: 4960 W Oregon Pl Denver CO 80219

SAMMONS, FRANCES ELIZABETH, banker; b. Conyers, Ga., May 23, 1924; d. William Andrew and Helen Marell (Johnson) Sammons; certificate comml. banking Am. Inst. Banking, 1951; grad. Sch. Mortgage Banking Northwestern U., 1965; B.B.A. in Finance, Ga. State U., 1974. Sec. Coca-Cola Co., Atlanta, 1941-46; with Fulton Nat. Bank Atlanta, 1946—, asst. v.p., 1962-71, v.p., 1971—. Mem. Atlanta Women's C. of C., Am. Inst. Banking, Nat. Assn. Bank Women, Am. Soc. Women Accountants, Alpha Iota Delta, Mortar Bd. Baptist. Club: Kingwood Country (Clayton, Ga.). Home: 2862 Blackwood Rd Decatur GA 30033 Office: 55 Marietta St NW Atlanta GA 30303

SAMMONS, MARGARETTE ALYCE (MRS. KEITH K. SAMMONS), pub. relations exec.; b. Albany, Ore., Oct. 22, 1940; d. James Lewis and Lily Emily (Wellington) Blackburn; B.S., Ore. State U., 1962; postgrad. U. Cal. at Berkeley, 1974—; m. Keith K. Sammons, Oct. 14, 1966; 1 dau., Paige Blackburn. With Singer Bus. Machines, San Leandro, Cal., 1964-74, publicity mgr., 1970-74. Home: 4328 Circle Av Castro Valley CA 94546

SAMPLE, A. DOROTHY, metals co. exec.; b. Youngstown, O.; d. Harry W. and Miriam (Williams) Sample; grad. Spencerian Coll., 1927-28, Cleve. Coll., 1937-39. Sec., Apex Paper Box Co., Cleve., 1928-32, Corrigan McKinney Steel Co., 1932-34; with Riester & Thesmacher Co., Cleve., 1934—, bookkeeper, 1934-40, chief accountant, 1940-56, asst. sec., 1956-65, dir., treas., 1965—; dir., sec.-treas. The R and T Co., 1956-72, Erie Artisan Corp., 1966-72. Mem. Cleve. Credit Women's Club (pres. 1956-57), Cleve. Assn. Credit Mgmt., Am. Soc. Women Accountants, Women in Constrn. Industry. Baptist. Clubs: Zonta, Women's City (Cleve.), White Shrine Jerusalem. Home: 3363 Warrensville Center Rd Shaker Heights OH 44122 Office: 1526 W 25th St Cleveland OH 44113

SAMPLES, MERNA ANNETTE SMITH (MRS. JAMES SAMPLES), educator; b. Lignite, N.D., Sept. 18, 1915; d. Gordon and Marion (Armstrong) Smith; B.S., Syracuse U., 1936; M.A., N.Y.U., 1952, Ed.D., 1966; m. James Samples, Jan. 18, 1941 (dec. Jan. 1948); children—James Haskell (dec.), John Henry. Tchr. home econs. Corning (N.Y.) Free Acad., 1936-40, Antwerp (N.Y.) High Sch., 1948-50, Voorheesville (N.Y.) Central Sch., 1950-52; tchr. educator home econs. Oneonta State Coll., 1952-56; tchr. educator home econs., asso. prof. Rutgers U., 1956-57, asso. prof., acting chmn. home econs. dept., 1957-58, prof., chmn. dept. home econs., 1959-67; chmn. dept. home econs. Cal. State U., Long Beach, 1967—. Exec. bd. YWCA, New Brunswick, N.J., 1963-67. Recipient Founders Day award N.Y.U., 1966; named an Outstanding Educator Am., 1972. Mem. Am. Home Econs. Assn., Am. Vocational Assn., N.E.A., Phi Kappa Phi, Kappa Delta Pi, Omicron Nu. Co-author secondary textbook. Home: 3328 Druid Lane Los Alamitos CA 90720 Office: Cal State U Long Beach CA 90801

SAMPSON, DOROTHY VERMELLE, lawyer, social worker; b. Sumter, S.C., Aug. 4, 1920; d. William B. and Bessie Vermelle (Moore) Sampson; B.S. in Edn., Hampton Inst., 1941; M.S.W., Atlanta U., 1952; J.D., N.C. Central U., 1963. Tchr. Durham (N.C.) pub. schs., 1950-52; social worker Ill. Pub. Aid Commn., Chgo.; social worker VA Hosp., Tomah, Wis., 1955-56; admitted to S.C. bar, 1964, U.S. Supreme Ct. bar, 1967; practiced in Sumter; partner firm Sampson & Sampson, Sumter. Mem. S.C. Pub. Welfare Services, Columbia, S.C. Candidate for S.C. Senate, 1968; mem. Sumter Black Caucus. Bd. dirs. YMCA, Sumter. Recipient United Fund award, 1968. Mem. Am. Bar Assn., N.A.A.C.P. Democrat. Club: Progressive Federated. Address: 39 S Washington St Sumter SC 29150

SAMPSON, MYRTLE BOYKIN, educator; b. Parkersburg, N.C., Mar. 30, 1929; d. Thomas Jefferson Lee and Mallie (Farrior) Boykin; B.S., N.C. Central U., 1951, M.S. in L.S., 1952; M.A., U. Mich., 1957; M.Ed. in Guidance and Counseling, U. N.C., 1972, Ph.D., 1974; m. Robert Russell Sampson, Dec. 21, 1958; 1 son, Frank Ricardo. Tchr., librarian Dunbar High Sch., Mooresville, N.C., 1952-54; librarian N.W. Jr. High Sch., Charlotte, N.C., 1954-61, Atkins High Sch., Winston-Salem, N.C., 1961-62; asst. prof. psychology Bennett Coll., Greensboro, N.C., 1962-72; asst. prof. psychology and guidance A. and T. State U., Greensboro, 1972—. Supr. community mental health paraprofls., psychiat. hosps., nursing homes, day care centers, alcoholic rehab. centers. Named woman of year, Old North State Pharm. Soc. Aux. Mem. Am., N.C. personnel and guidance assns., N.C., Southeastern psychol. assns., N.C., Greensboro mental health assns., Greensboro Assn. Retarded Children, N.C., Nat. socs. autistic children, Am. Assn. U. Profs., Holidays, Inc., Epicureans, Inc. Beta Kappa Chi, Alpha Kappa Alpha. Home: Rt 10 Box 633 B Lake Haven Greensboro NC 27406

SAMPSON, PATSY HALLOCK, educator, psychologist; b. Picher, Okla., July 9, 1932; d. Daniel W. and Gladys (Whitehead) Hallock; B.A., U. Okla., 1961; Ph.D., Cornell U., 1966; m. Samuel F. Sampson, 1961 (div.); children—Catherine, Jacquelyn, Rebecca. Postdoctoral fellow Cornell U., Ithaca, N.Y., 1965-66; asst. prof. sociology State U. N.Y. at Binghamton, 1966-67; asst. prof. psychology Wellesley (Mass.) Coll., 1967-70, dir. child study center, 1969-70; asst. social psychologist McLean Hosp., Belmont, Mass., 1968-70; prof., chmn. dept. Cal. State Coll., Bakersfield, 1970—. Mem. Am. Psychol. Assn., Phi Beta Kappa, Sigma Xi. Address: Cal State Coll 9001 Stockdale Hwy Bakersfield CA 93309

SAMSOVA, GALINA MARTINOVNA, ballet dancer; b. Stalingrad, U.S.S.R., Mar. 17, 1937; d. Martin Archipovich and Yevdokia Grigorievna (Yerankevich) Samsov; diploma Ballet Sch., Kiev, U.S.S.R., 1956; m. Andre Prkovsky, Apr. 11, 1972. Soloist, Kiev Opera House, 1956-60; prima ballerina Nat. Ballet Can., 1961-63, London (Eng.) Festival Ballet, 1964-73; founder, dir., prima ballerina New London Ballet, 1973—. Recipient Gold medal for best dancer 1st Internat. Festival, Paris, France, 1963, Gold medals Madrid (Spain) festivals, 1965, 1967. Home: 102A Castlenau St London SW 13 England Office: 406 Harrow Rd London W9 England

SAMUELS, GERTRUDE, author, editor; b. Manchester, Eng. (parents Am. citizens); d. Sam and Sarah (Benjamin) Samuels; student George Washington U., 1935-37, Busch Conservatory Music, Chgo., 1933; 1 son, Paul Oppenheimer. With N.Y. Post, 1937-41, Newsweek mag., 1942, Time mag., 1943; mem. staff N.Y. Times, 1943—, staff writer, photographer, 1943-72, editor mag. staff, 1972—. Cons. UNICEF, 1948—; vol. tchr. journalism Harlem's Haryou, 1970-71. Recipient Page One award N.Y. Newspaper Guild, 1959, 65, George Polk award L.I. U., 1955, citation for refugee coverage Overseas Press Club, 1956, publisher's award for articles on juvenile delinquency N.Y. Times, 1959. Mem. Authors Guild, Dramatists Guild, Drama Desk, Newspaper Guild, UN Corrs. Assn., Actors Studio. Author: (fiction) The People Vs. Baby, 1965; Run, Shelley, Run!, 1974; (non-fiction) B-G: Fighter of Goliaths, the Story of Ben-Gurion, 1961, The Secret of Gonen, 1969; (plays) The Corrupters, 1969, Judah, the Maccabee And Me, 1970, Thank You, Mr. President, 1970, The Assignment, 1973. Contbr. stories and articles to newspapers and mags. Home: 75 Central Park W New York City NY 10023 Office: NY Times 229 W 43d St New York City NY 10036

SAMUELSON, MARY LOU JAGGER (MRS. JAMES A. SAMUELSON), author; b. Massillon, O., Mar. 6, 1928; d. George Nicholas and Rhoda A. (Meyer) Bollinger; student Kent State U., 1945-47, Ohio State U., 1947-49; m. James A. Samuelson, Feb. 15, 1958; 1 dau., Linda Diane. Woman's editor San Gabriel Valley Daily Tribune, 1955-62; co-pub. Covina Valley Newspapers, Inc., Covina, Cal., 1962—. Mem. bd. San Gabriel Valley YWCA. Mem. Internat. Platform Assn. Club: Soroptimist. Home: 315 S Grand Av West Covina CA 91791 Office: 128 E College St Covina CA 91722

SANASAC, LOIS HESTER HATCH (MRS. ORRIE J. SANASAC), club woman; b. Eau Claire, Wis., July 18, 1917; d. Clinton Louis and Hester (Fear) Hatch; student pub. schs.; m. Orrie J. Sanasac, Apr. 25, 1936. Vice pres. Oak Park Dairy, Inc., Eau Claire, 1940. Mem. League Women Voters (state treas. 1964-66, state dir. 1966-68), Wis. Fedn. Womens Clubs (2d v.p. 1968-70, 1st v.p. 1970-72, pres. 1972-74), Am. Guild Organists (chpt. treas. 1964), Mehara Shrine Aux. (v.p. 1967), D.A.R. (regent Chippewa Valley chpt. 1963-65), Sigma Alpha Iota. Mem. United Ch. of Christ. Clubs: Eau Claire League (pres. 1961-64), Eau Claire Womans (pres. 1967-68). Home: 3209 Rudolph Rd Eau Claire WI 54701

SANBONMATSU, JOAN MEREDITH LOVERIDGE (MRS. AKIRA SANBONMATSU), educator; b. Hartford, Conn., July 5, 1938; d. Gilbert Thomas and Rosabel (Nowry) Loveridge; B.A., U. Vt., 1960; M.A., Ohio U., 1963; Ph.D. Pa. State U., 1971; m. Akira Sanbonmatsu, Aug. 29, 1964; children—James Michael, Kevin Yosh. Appeared on WCAX Radio-TV and WRUV, 1956-60; served with A.R.C. in Far East, appeared on AFKN, 1960-61; grad. asst. in speech Ohio U. and for WOUB, 1962-63; asst. prof. speech State U. Coll., Brockport, N.Y., 1963-66, 1968-70, Rochester Inst. Tech., 1971; instr. Pa. State U., 1966-67; instr. English as fgn. lang. Internat. Soc. of State U. N.Y. at Brockport, 1971-72; adj. asso. prof. speech Monroe Community Coll., Rochester, N.Y., 1972—; lectr., participant various workshops and symposia in field. Dir. Ecumenical Coffee House-The Crypt, Brockport, 1967; mem. Race Relations Interest Group, 1968. Recipient letter of commendation for work in Korea with A.R.C., 1961. Grantee Pa. State U., 1970. Mem. Speech Communication Assn. Am., Eastern States, N.Y. State speech assns., Ednl. Childbirth Assn., Women's Polit. Caucus, Nat. Orgn. Woman (co-chairperson employment com.), Women's Caucus State U. N.Y., Faculty Women's Assn. (co-chairperson scholarship com. 1972-73). Contbr. poems to Remember Me, 1963; One Golden Day, 1964. Home: 14 Beverly Dr Brockport NY 14420

SANBORN, SISTER HARRIET, educator; b. Sault Ste. Marie, Mich., June 30, 1905; d. William Henry and Catherine Harriet (Kuemin) Sanborn; B.S., Wayne State U., 1936; A.M., Cath. U. Am., 1945; Ph.D., U. Mich., 1958. Joined Sisters of St. Dominic, 1937; tchr. Detroit Pub. Schs., 1925-36; tchr. Am., English lit. St. Joseph High Sch., Muskegon, Mich., 1939-49, St. Joseph Sch., Bay City, Mich., 1949-55; faculty Aquinas Coll., Grand Rapids, Mich., 1957—, prof., 1967—, dir. Upward Bound program 1966-68. Mem. Grand Rapids Council for Civic Responsibility, 1965-66; chmn. Jewish-Catholic Dialogue, 1965. Mem. Mich. Psychologists, Nat. Coll. Edn. Assn., Nat. Council Tchrs. English, Nat. Soc. Secondary Edn., Pi Lambda Theta. Home: 1607 Robinson Rd SE Grand Rapids MI 49506

SANCHEZ, BARBARA DOLORES, recreation therapist; b. Jamaica, N.Y., Apr. 10, 1940; d. Joseph H. and Mildred Claire (Jobstl) Sanchez; B.A. in Recreation Edn., Cal. State U., San Francisco, 1963; M.A. in Edn., Cal. State U. at Los Angeles, 1973. Recreation therapist Pacific State Hosp., Pomona, Cal., 1963-69, Mental Retardation Center, Neuropsychiat. Inst., U. Cal., Los Angeles, 1969—. Cons., tng. coordinator local colls., univs., 1969—. Mem. program forum steering com. Nat. Parks and Recreation Assn., Western Region, 1974—. Mem. Nat. Therapeutic Recreation Soc., Cal. Parks and Recreation Soc., Am. Assn. Mental Deficiency, Council for Exceptional Children. Home: 10122 Palms Blvd Los Angeles CA 90034 Office: Mental Retardation Center Neuropsychiat Inst U Cal Los Angeles CA 90024

SANDAGE, IRMA ELLEN VON DER PORTEN, social worker; b. Hamburg, Germany, Apr. 4, 1921; d. Paul Maximillian and Dora (Ruebner) Von der Porten; came to U.S., 1936; naturalized, 1944; A.B., Miami U., Oxford, O., 1945, M.A., 1948; M.S.W., Ohio State U., 1961; m. Curtis N. Sandage, Oct. 1941 (div. Aug. 1959); children—Dennis Dean, Carol Lynn (Mrs. Timothy Smith), Martha Anne (Mrs. Gregory Bell). Instr., Miami U., 1948-50; caseworker Dept. Pub. welfare, Butler County, O., 1957-59; social worker Family Service, Hamilton, O., 1961-62; med. social worker VA Hosp., Cin., 1962-63; supr. Family Service, Hamilton, 1963-65, Richmond, Ind., 1965-67; clinic br. dir. Mental Health Clinic, Middletown, O., 1967-71; exec. dir. Family Service of Butler County, Inc., 1971—. Cons., Headstart, Pastoral Counseling Service, Juvenile Ct., Welfare Dept., 1973, Friends in Action, Hamilton, 1973—. Bd. dirs. Planned Parenthood, 1968-69. Mem. Am. Contract Bridge League, Met. Opera Guild, Common Cause, Germerican Friendship Soc., Butler County Social Service Assn. Club: Executive of Butler County. Home: 208 W Chestnut St Oxford OH 45056 Office: 111 Buckeye St Hamilton OH 45011

SANDBERG, ANNA SOPHIA, educator; b. Muskegon, Mich., Oct. 11, 1923; d. Karl John and Sigrid Christine (Karlson) S.; R.N., B.A., U. Mich., 1952, M.A., 1955; postgrad. U. Wis., 1955-57, Ind. U., 1959-60, U. Ia., 1965-66. Nurse, U. Mich. Med. Center, Ann Arbor, 1945-55; faculty Frostburg State Coll., Frostburg, Md., 1958-59, La. State U., Baton Rouge, 1960-61, Ohio State U., Columbus, 1962-63, U. Okla., Norman, 1963-64, U. S.D., Vermillion, 1964-65. Home: 32520 Florence St Garden City MI 48135

SANDBERG, BARBARA BAER (MRS. ARTHUR LOEB KATZ), educator; b. McAllen, Tex., Dec. 19, 1934; d. Dean Morgan and Katherine Louise (Hurlbert) Baer; B.S., Ind. U., 1959; M.A., Columbia, 1963, Ed.D., 1974; m. Arthur Loeb Katz, Aug. 23, 1968. Drama tchr., children's theatre dir. Ann Arbor (Mich.) Bd. Edn. and Recreation, 1958-62; speech and theatre faculty William Paterson Coll., Wayne, N.J., 1963—, asst. prof. theatre and speech; instr. drama in child devel. Tchrs. Coll. Columbia, 1970—. Drama cons. Tital III, Wayne Pub. Schs., 1968-71; drama evaluator Project Moppet, Title III, Woodbridge, N.J., 1971—; screening judge Am. Coll. Theatre Festival. Mem. Am. Theatre Assn. (regional gov. children's theatre conf. 1970-72 regional dir. 1971-72, nat. bd. 1971-72), Children's Theatre Assn. (nat. bd. 1970-72, adminstrv. asst. to pres. 1973—), Theta Alpha Phi, Delta Gamma. Home: 164 French Hill Rd Wayne NJ 07470 Office: William Paterson Coll Wayne NJ 07470

SANDBERG, BARBARA JO (MRS. ROBERT CHARLES SANDBERG), educator, interior designer; b. Indpls., Aug. 6, 1939; d. Robert Brown and Mary (Rankin) Canatsey; B.A., Butler U., 1961; M.A., U. Minn., 1964; postgrad. U. Hawaii (tour Asia), 1967, U. Cal. at Los Angeles, 1967—; m. Robert Charles Sandberg; 1 son, Robert Charles. Teaching asst. U. Minn., St. Paul, 1961-63; asst. prof. interior design Eastern Mich. U., Ypsilanti, 1963-65, Univ. Center for Adult Edn., U. Mich., Wayne State U., Eastern Mich. U., Ann Arbor, 1964-65; asst. prof. housing, interior design Cal. State Coll. Los Angeles, 1965-70; owner Barbara Sandberg Interiors, Pasadena, Cal., 1971—. Cons. interior design, 1965—; speaker various profl. groups, 1968—. Mem. New Pasadena Art Mus., Am. (Cal. del to conv. 1968), Cal. (exec. com.), Los Angeles Dist. home econ. assns., Coll. Tchrs. Clothing, Textiles and Related Art, Nat. Soc. Interior Designers, Nat. Home Fashions League, Am. Assn. Housing Educators, Am. Assn. U. Women, Am. Assn. U. Profs., Assn. Cal. State Coll. Profs., Nat. Trust for Historic Preservation U.S., Mortar Bd., Omicron Nu, Phi Upsilon Omicron, Pi Lambda Theta, Kappa Kappa Gamma. Club: Southwestern University Law School Students Wives. Address: 972 E California Blvd Pasadena CA 91106

SANDBURG, HELGA, author; b. Maywood, Ill.; d. Carl and Lillian (Steichen) Sandburg; student Mich. State Coll., 1935-36; m. George Crile, Jr., Nov. 9, 1963; children—John Carl Steichen, Karlen Paula Steichen (by previous marriage). Dairy goat breeder, 1944-51; personal sec. to father, 1944-51; sec. manuscripts div., and keeper of collections Library of Congress, Washington, 1952-56; adminstrv. asst. for papers of Woodrow Wilson, Woodrow Wilson Found., N.Y.C., 1958-59; lectr. W. Colston Leigh Lecture Bur., Inc., N.Y.C., 1960-64, bur. cultural and ednl. affairs Dept. State, 1961; ind. lectr., 1964—. Mem. council Save the Dunes, Finnish Am. Soc. and Svenska Institutet grantee, 1961; recipient prize for best short story Va. Quar. Rev., 1959, 2d prize Borestone Mountain Poetry award, 1962, also others. Mem. Authors Guild, Poetry Soc. Am., Am. Milk Goat Record Assn., Am.-Scandinavian Found., Poetry Soc. Am., Am. Luxembourg Soc. Club: Nat. Nubian. Author: (novels) The Wheel of Earth, 1958; Measure My Love, 1959; The Owl's Roost, 1962; The Wizard's Child, 1967; (non-fiction) Sweet Music: A Book of Family Reminiscence and Song, 1963; (with George Crile, Jr.) Above and Below, 1969; (poetry) The Unicorns, 1965; To A New Husband, 1970; (young adult novels) Blueberry, 1963; Gingerbread, 1964; (children's books) Joel and The Wild Goose, 1963; Bo and The Old Donkey, 1965; Anna and The Baby Buzzard, 1970; also contbr. short stories, poems and articles to popular mags. including New Yorker, Saturday Rev., McCalls, Sat. Eve. Post, Harpers, Good Housekeeping, also translations. Address: 2060 Kent Rd Cleveland OH 44106

SANDEEN, MARY REED (MRS. RUSSELL G. SANDEEN), educator; b. Ernest, Pa., Dec. 22, 1903; d. William and Sarah (Anderson) Reed; B.S., Ind. U., 1930; M.A., Columbia, 1952; m. Russell G. Sandeen, June 30, 1945. Tchr., Indiana County (Pa.) Schs., 1922-28, Bradford Area Schs., McKean County, Pa., 1930-69, Smethport area schs., 1969-70. Treas., McKean County Sch. Employees Credit Union, 1942-70, Bradford Twp. Sch. Employees Service League, 1956-58. Mem. Pa., Nat. edn. assns., Elementary Prins. Assn., Am. Assn. U. Women (area rep. in edn.), Delta Kappa Gamma (state treas. 1953-55, state budget and finance chmn. 1955-67, conv. treas. 1960, 62). Methodist. Mem. Order Eastern Star. Address: 205 Congress St Bradford PA 16701

SANDEMAN, SONJA ELINOR (MRS. HAROLD M. MALKIN), lawyer; b. San Francisco, Nov. 25, 1938; d. William Charles and Georgia Barbara (Jones) Sandeman; B.A., Coll. Notre Dame, 1960; J.D., Hastings Coll. Law, 1964; m. Harold M. Malkin, Dec. 30, 1972; 1 dau., Dinal Elba. Admitted to Cal. bar, 1966; since practiced in San Francisco. Mem. San Francisco Bar Assn., Cal. Attys. for Criminal Justice Nat. Council Jewish Women (legislative chmn. San Francisco sect. 1974-75). Club: Commonwealth. Home: 1570 University Av Palo Alto CA 94301 Office: 656 Post St Suite 1 San Francisco CA 94109

SANDER, ELLEN, journalist; b. N.Y.C., Jan. 7, 1944; d. Eitel and Faye Sander; ed. Hunter Coll. 1 son, Marin Paul. Freelance journalist; critic Saturday Rev.; contbr. criticism Sunday N.Y. Times, articles Village Voice, Rolling Stone, Vogue, MLLE, Cavalier. Author: Trips: Rock Life in the Sixties, 1973. Home: PO Box 9 Bolinas CA 94924 Office: care Rhoda A Weyr William Morris Agy New York City NY

SANDERLIN, EVA MAY SLOVER (MRS. ALLEN CLEVELAND SANDERLIN), educator, librarian; b. Leakey, Tex., Oct. 18, 1924; d. Leo Lloyd and Annie May (Holmes) Slover; B.S., Mary Hardin-Baylor Coll., 1945; M.Ed., Our Lady of Lake Coll., 1966; m. Allen Cleveland Sanderlin, May 14, 1947; children—Judith Peggy (Mrs. Richard Beloat), Ted Allen, Claudia Ann. Elementary tchr. Knippa (Tex.) Ind. Sch. Dist., 1959-66, kindergarten tchr., librarian, 1966—. Treas. Knippa P.T.A., 1965-66; v.p. Knippa Community Builders, 1970—. Mem. Tex. Tchrs. Assn. (county pres. 1968-69), Tex. Assn. Ednl. Tech., Women in Communications, Am. Legion Aux. (post pres. 1968). Republican. Methodist. Home: Box 245 Knippa TX 78870 Office: Knippa Ind Sch Dist Knippa TX 78870

SANDERS, DOREEN MARION (MRS. RICHARD SANDERS), journalist, editor; b. Portland, Ore., Jan. 17, 1921; d. Herbert Jesse and Doris Marion (Glazbrook) McKenzie; came to Can., 1921; B.A. with honors in Journalism, U. Western Ont., Can., 1961; m. Richard Sanders, Mar. 19, 1947; children—Peter, Brook. Reporter, columnist The Vancouver (B.C., Can.) Daily Province, 1941-47; spl. corr. The Financial Post, Toronto, Ont., 1961-63; editor, pub., Bus. Quar., U. Western Ont., London, 1963—, editor Western Mgmt., 1973—, also tchr. sch. bus. Dir. Canadian Bus. Press. Free lance writer, 1949—; tchr. Mem. Editors Assn. Can. Clubs: London Hunt, University Club. Home: 1231 Richmond St London ON Canada Office: School of Business University of Western Ontario London ON Canada

SANDERS, FAYE BEVELEY (MRS. JOHN HOLLIS MARTIN), lawyer; b. nr. Brooklet, Ga., Feb. 6, 1934; d. Carroll Eugene and Addie Louise (Prosser) Sanders; student Ga. So. Coll., 1952-54, Woodrow Wilson Coll. Law, 1955-56; m. John Hollis Martin, Feb. 26, 1960; children—Janna, Jenny Lynn. Admitted to Ga. bar, 1956; practiced in Statesboro, Ga., 1956—; mem. firm Anderson and Sanders, 1956—. Mem. Ga., Bulloch County (sec.-treas. 1966—), Ogeechee bar assns., Ga. Assn. Women Lawyers (v.p. 1959-60), Statesboro Bus. and Profl. Womens Club, Statesboro-Bulloch County C. of C., Zeta Tau Alpha. Home: 106 Chelsea Circle Statesboro GA 30458 Office: 8 Siebald St Statesboro GA 30458

SANDERS, LUIDA ELIZABETH, health cons.; b. Rhinelander, Wis., Apr. 21, 1917; d. Charles A. and Ida Irene (Clermont) Sanders; B.A., U. Wis., 1949, M.A., 1960; M.P.H., U. Cal. at Berkeley, 1964. Rural sch. tchr., Wis., 1939-43; elementary tchr. Dudgeon Sch., Madison, Wis., 1949-50; editor Wis. Bd. Health, 1950-56, dir. div. health edn., 1956-66; health cons. Wis. Dept. Pub. Instruction, Madison, 1966—, dir. Drug Edn. Project, 1970—. Treas., Wis. Equal Rights Coalition, 1973—. Served with WAC, 1943-46. Mem. Am., Wis. (pres. 1966-67, 69-70) pub. health assns., Nat. Orgn. for Women, Women In Communications, Wis. Assn. Health, Phys. Edn. and Recreation, Am. Sch. Health Assn., Internat. Union for Health Edn., Phi Beta Kappa. Methodist (lay speaker 1964—). Home: 614 Welch Av Madison WI 53704 Office: 126 Langdon St Madison WI 53704

SANDERS, MARY ELIZABETH (MRS. EDMOND J. PERRY), physician; b. Worthington, Ind., June 18, 1917; d. Ben H. and Gail (Williams) Sanders; B.A., DePauw U., 1939; M.B., Northwestern U., 1943, M.D., 1943; m. Edmond J. Perry, Sept. 14, 1946; children—Sarah Elizabeth, Martha Gail. Intern, Cook County Hosp., Chgo., 1943, resident, 1944-47; practice medicine, specializing in internal medicine, Redfield, S.D., 1947—; mem. staff Community Meml. Hosp., Dakota Midland Hosp., St. Luke's Hosp.; cons. Redfield State Sch. and Home; preceptor U. S.D. Med. Sch., 1951—. Chmn. Gt. Plains Regional Heart Com., 1971-72. Bd. dirs. S.D. Heart Assn., 1966-72, Am. Heart Assn., 1970-72. Diplomate Am. Bd. Internal Medicine. Mem. A.M.A., S.D. Med. Assn. (commn. on allied orgns. 1966—), Aberdeen Dist. Med. Soc. (pres. 1971), Am., S.D. (pres. 1972—) socs. internal medicine, P.E.O. Methodist. Home: Redfield SD 57469 Office: Med Arts Redfield SD 57469 also Vogele Medical Clinic 1200 S Main St Aberdeen SD 57401

SANDERS, RITA DIANE OLSON (MRS. RICHARD M. SANDERS), advt. agy. exec.; b. Fargo, N.D., Mar. 15, 1948; d. H. Rex. and Selma Louise (Gronvold) Olson; B.S., U. N.D., 1970; m. Richard M. Sanders, Aug. 30, 1968. Continuity dir. KTHI-TV, Grand Forks, N.D., 1969; communications cons. Grand Forks Pub. Sch. Dist., 1969-70; women's and pub. affairs dir. KILO Radio, Grand Forks, 1970-71; dir. pub. relations health agency, Ia., 1971-72; copy dir. Advt. Communications, Inc., Davenport, Ia., 1972-73; copy and media dir. Corp. Advt. div. Norm Ulrich Studios, Oak Park, Ill., 1973-74; copywriter Hudson Mfg., Chgo., 1974—. Free-lance work in pub. relations, advt., community relations. Bd. dirs. Miss. Valley Heart Assn., 1971-72. Recipient Outstanding Dir. award Ia. Heart Assn., award Girl Scouts Am., Keep Am. Beautiful. Mem. Women in Communications, Delta Delta Delta, Delta Sigma Kappa, Theta Sigma Phi. Home: 65 Redstart Rd Naperville IL 60540

SANDERS, SYLVIA NICOARA, lawyer; b. Detroit, Jan. 15, 1931; d. John and Draga (Bugarin) Nicoara; A.B. in Sociology, U. Mich., 1952; LL.B., Detroit Coll. Law, 1958; m. Willard E. Sanders, Mar. 15, 1952 (div. Aug. 1957); 1 son, Brandon Michael. Admitted to Mich. bar, 1958, practiced in Detroit, 1959-60, Gaylord, 1960—; pres., chmn. bd., gen. mgr. Otsego County Abstract Co., Gaylord, 1971—; atty. VA, 1960-63, Farmers Home Adminstrn., 1961-69; examining atty. Saginaw Savs. & Loan Assn. (Mich.), 1972—. Mem. Democratic State Central Com., 1973—. Mem. State Bar Mich., Mich. Land Title Assn. (chmn. com. on constn. and bylaws 1972—). Home: 880 North Dr Gaylord MI 49735 Office: 120 E Main St Gaylord MI 49735

SANDERSON, JANET GOETZE (MRS. WILLIAM JOSEPH SANDERSON), journalist; b. Portland, Ore., Nov. 23, 1942; d. Gerhard and Eva May (Bonar) Goetze; B.A. (Jackson Found. scholar), U. Ore., 1964, postgrad., 1966-68; m. William Joseph Sanderson, Sept. 13, 1970. Asst. to spl. editorial adviser Look mag., N.Y.C., 1964-65; A.P. reporter, Los Angeles and Louisville, 1965-66; grad. asst. U. Ore., 1966-67; reporter Eugene (Ore.) Register-Guard, 1967-68; copy editor The Oregonian, Portland, 1968-70, staff writer, 1970—. Mem. Women in Communications, Sigma Delta Chi. Home: 2719 NE 19th Av Portland OR 97212 Office: 1320 SW Broadway Portland OR 97201

SANDERSON, SARAH ELIZABETH POLICE (MRS. RICHARD A. SANDERSON), educator; b. Fairmont, W.Va., Jan. 17, 1932; d. Louis and Sarah (Spatafore) Police; A.B. in Edn., Fairmont State Coll., 1953; M.A., Bowling Green State U., 1955; Ph.D., U. So. Cal., 1965; m. Richard A. Sanderson, Jan. 26, 1956; children—S. Laurie, Linda Rose. Instr. Alliance (O.) High Sch., 1953-54; teaching asst. Bowling Green (O.) State U., 1954-55, U. So. Cal., 1955-56, 57-58; asst. prof., mgr. campus radio sta. Georgetown (Ky.) Coll., 1956-57; instr. Los Angeles City Coll., 1957-58; instr. Los Angeles Harbor Coll., 1959-61; prin. Lahore (West Pakistan) Sch., 1961-62; asst. prof. dept. speech-communication U. Hawaii, Honolulu, 1963-68; vis. lectr. faculty of humanities Chiengmai (Thailand) U., 1968-69; vis. fellow Ohio State U., Columbus, 1969-70; asst. prof. dept. speech-communication U. Hawaii, Honolulu, 1970-72, asso. prof. dept. communication, 1972—. Vol. program dir. Hawaii Camp Fire Girls, 1972. Mem. Hawaiian Malacological Assn. (v.p. 1966-67), Speech Communication Assn., Pacific Speech Assn. (chmn. bd. publs. 1966-68), Internat. Soc. Gen. Semantics, Western Speech Assn., Pacific Assn. Communication Tech., Manoa Film Council, Asian Mass Communication Research and Information Centre. Editor: Pacific Speech Quar., 1966-68. Contbr. articles to publs. Home: 4502 Sierra Dr Honolulu HI 96816

SANDERSON, SHIRLEY JOWERS (MRS. RAY L. SANDERSON), banker; b. Monroe, La., July 13, 1940; d. Frank and Viola (Gibson) Jowers; grad. high sch.; m. Ray L. Sanderson, Aug. 14, 1959; 1 son, Ray L. With Central Bank, Monroe, La., 1959—, head teller, 1967-68, main office supr., 1968-69, new account officer, 1969-72, asst. mgr., 1972-73, br. mgr., 1973—. Vice pres. Central United Found., Monroe, 1968-72. Mem. Nat. Assn. Banking Women. Club: Pilot. Home: 907 Dean Chapel Rd West Monroe LA 71291 Office: PO Box 4928 Monroe LA 71201

SANDFORD, HELEN REGINE, educator, composer; b. Zanesville, O., Jan. 11, 1907; d. William Emanuel and Eva Regine (Phillips) Sandford; student Knox Conservatory, Galesburg, Ill., 1925-26; Mus.B., Am. Conservatory Music, Chgo., 1929, Mus.M., 1932, Mus.B. in Piano, 1935; pupil Robert Casadesus, Nadia Boulanger, 1948. Prof. theory and piano Am. Conservatory Music, Chgo., 1929—. Mem. Phi Beta. Composer: String Quartet in C Minor, 1950 (performed at Am. Conservatory Artist Faculty Program 1969); Mexican Travelogue Suite for Orch. (performed by Am. Conservatory Symphony Orch. 1972), numerous others. Home: 5120 S Harper Av Chicago IL 60615 Office: 410 S Michigan Av Chicago IL 60605

SANDLER, BERNICE (MRS. JERROLD SANDLER), assn. exec.; b. N.Y.C., Mar. 3, 1928; d. Abraham Hyman and Ivy (Ernst) Resnick; B.A. cum laude, Bklyn. Coll., 1948; M.A., Coll. City N.Y., 1950; Ed.D., U. Md., 1969; LL.D., Bloomfield Coll., N.J., 1973; m. Jerrold Sandler, May 25, 1952; children—Deborah Jo, Emily Maud. Research fellow Coll. City N.Y., 1951-52; lectr., instr. faculty research asst. U. Md., 1964-69; instr. Mt. Vernon Coll., Washington, 1968-69; ednl. specialist U.S. Ho. of Reps. Spl. Subcom. on Edn., 1970; dep. dir. Women's Action Program, Dept. Health, Edn. and Welfare, Washington, 1971; dir. Project on Status and Edn. Women, Assn. Am. Colls., Washington, 1971—. Mem. adv. com. econ. role women Pres.'s

Council Econ. Advisers, 1973—. Bd. dirs. Women United, Washington Opportunities for Women, The Spokeswoman, Women's Rights Law Reporter, Women's History Research Center, Center for Women's Policy Studies, Inst. for Ednl. Leadership. Named Woman of Year Intercollegiate Assn. Women Students, 1974. Mem. Am. Psychol. Assn., Am. Personnel and Guidance Assn., Women's Equity Action League (dir., chairperson action com. for contract compliance 1969-71). Contbr. numerous articles in field of women's rights. Office: 1818 R St NW Washington DC 20009

SANDLER, LOUISE BERNSTEIN (MRS. MILTON SANDLER), psychologist; b. Bklyn., N.Y., Mar. 28, 1926; d. Aaron and Edna (Korowitz) Bernstein; B.A., Bklyn. Coll., 1946, M.A., 1953; Ph.D. (Dept. Health, Edn. and Welfare fellow), Bryn Mawr Coll., 1964; m. Milton Sandler, July 5, 1953; children—Lynda (Mrs. Hugh Melnick), Richard. Clin. prof. mental health scis. Hahnemann Med. Coll. and Hosp., Phila., 1964-72; prin. scientist Franklin Inst. Research Labs., Phila., 1972—. Project dir. demonstration program Dept. Health Edn. and Welfare, 1971—. Contbr. articles to profl. jours. Home: 609 Ashbourne Rd Elkins Park PA 19117 Office: Franklin Inst Research Labs Benjamin Franklin Pkwy Philadelphia PA 19103

SANDLER, MARION OSHER (MRS. HERBERT M. SANDLER), savs. and loan exec.; b. Biddeford, Me., Oct. 17, 1930; d. Samuel and Leah (Lowe) Osher; B.A., Wellesley Coll., 1952; grad. Harvard-Radcliffe Grad. Program in Bus. Adminstrn., 1953; M.B.A., N.Y. U., 1958; m. Herbert M. Sandler, Mar. 26, 1961. Asst. buyer Bloomingdales Dept. Store, N.Y.C., 1953-55; security analyst Dominick & Dominick, N.Y.C., 1955-61; sr. financial analyst Oppenheimer & Co., N.Y.C., 1961-63; sr. v.p., sec., dir. Golden West Savs. & Loan Assn., Oakland, 1963—, Golden West Financial Corp., Oakland, Cal., 1963—. Mem. campaign policy com. United Bay Area Crusade, 1973; vice pres. Jr. Center Art and Sci., 1969-70, trustee, 1968-70; mem. adv. council Sch. Bus., U. Cal., 1973. Recipient thesis prize Money Marketeers, 1958. Mem. Nat. Honor Soc., Phi Beta Kappa, Beta Gamma Sigma. Club: Harvard Bus. Sch. of No. Cal. (dir. 1968). Office: 1970 Broadway Oakland CA 94612

SANDLIN, DOROTHY, musician; b. Glen Rose, Tex., June 5, 1919; d. Walter A. and Margaret (Parks) Sandlin; Mus.B., U. San Antonio, 1938; postgrad. American Conservatory of Music, Chgo., 1938-39; m. Murray Sands Marvin, 1970. Guest soloist Detroit Symphony, N.Y. Philharmonic Symphony, 1941-51; star in leading operetta companies, Dallas, Los Angeles, San Francisco, St. Louis, N.Y.C., 1941-57, productions of Bittersweet, Bloomer Girl, The Merry Widow, The Great Waltz, The King and I; Cosi Fan Tutti; Los Angeles Opera Co., 1961, Street Scene, N.Y.C., 1959-60; Fidelio, Santa Barbara, Cal., 1961, The Marriage of Figaro, Los Angeles Opera Co., 1962, Salome, Beverly Hills Symphony, 1962, Tristan and Isolde, 1963; The Merry Widow, 1967, revival The King and I; World Premiere, Psalm of Faith (J. Wagner), 1962. Mem. women's com. Los Angeles Philharmonic Orch.; mem. membership com. Hollywood Bowl Assn.; adv. bd. Beverly Hills Symphony Assn.; mem. So. Cal. Symphony Assn. Established Dorothy Sandlin Found., 1969; patron Los Angeles Mus. Art; founder, asso. Los Angeles Music Center; founder, mem. Huntington Hartford Theatre. Mem. Am. Acad. Achievement (dir. 1971-74). Club: Los Angeles (dir. 1974-75). Home: 1103 Bel Air Place Los Angeles CA 90024

SANDOVAL, ALICIA CATHERINE, television performer, producer; b. Glendale, Cal., May 2, 1943; d. Crescent Dominguez and Lucy (Sauceda) Sandoval; student Immaculate Heart Coll., 1961-64; B.A., U. Cal. at Los Angeles, 1966; M.S., U. So. Cal., 1969-71. Tchr. high sch. English, Los Angeles Unified City Sch. Dist., 1969-71; instr. English Cal. State U. at Northridge, summer 1969; field dir. Chicano studies dept. United Tchrs. Los Angeles, 1970-71; documentary researcher, prodn. asst. Chicano Heritage series KNBC Studios; moderator, co-producer Let's Rap, daily pub. affairs program Metromedia, Inc., Channel 91, also community services coordinator. Mem. Cal. Democratic Central Com. Bd. dirs. Girl Scouts U.S.A., 1971-72. Poytner fellow in modern journalism Yale, 1973. Mem. Los Angeles Jr. C. of C., League Women Voters, Am. Civil Liberties Union, Catholic Alumni Assn., A.F.T.R.A. Writer weekly column Los Angeles Free Press. Home: 5209 N Babcock Av North Hollywood CA 91607 Office: 5746 W Sunset Blvd Hollywood CA 90028

SANDOVAL-DEHOYOS, ANGELINA ANDREA, comml. artist; b. Nueva Rosita, Mexico, Jan. 24, 1926; d. Estenio and Maria (DeHoyos) Sandoval; came to U.S., 1927; grad. comml. artist Fox. Tech. Sch., 1943; student San Antonio Coll., 1944, Fine Arts Inst., 1946. Free-lance comml. artist, fashion illustrator, designer for various local firms, 1950—; owner, operator Craft Studio, San Antonio, 1950-53; co-owner Sombrero Rec. Co., San Antonio, 1957-59. Instr. arts and crafts Nat. Rehab. Assn., 1950-53; gen. sec. Latin Artists Enterprises, San Antonio, 1955-58; hon. rep. Accademic Internat. Leonardo Da Vinci, Centro Studi E Scambi Internazionali, Rome, Italy, 1968—; mem. bd. translators World Poetry Soc. Intercontinental, India, 1970—. Recipient Distinguished Service citation World Poetry Soc., 1970, 71; bronze medal of honor Leonardo Da Vinci Accademia, Rome, 1967, silver medal of honor, 1968, Diploma Di Benemerenza, 1969. Fellow Internat. Poetry Soc.; mem. Nat. Writers Club, Composers and Vocalists Tex. (sec. San Antonio 1954-57). Contbr. poems, transls. to nat., internat. mags., coll. jours., newspaper, anthologies. Home: 4946 Luz Av San Antonio TX 78237

SANDOW, LYN ANDERSON, editor; b. Boston, June 19, 1937; d. George Amos and Gertrude (Brassard) Anderson; B.A., U. Conn., 1959; postgrad. So. Conn. State Coll., 1959-61. Tchr. pub. schs., Shelton, Conn., 1959-61; project supr. Resources Devel. Corp., East Lansing, Mich., 1961-67; sr. editor Grolier Ednl. Corp., N.Y.C., 1967—. Tng. cons., free-lance writer. Active worker Dem. Party. Mem. Nat. Soc. for Programmed Instrn., Internat. Reading Assn., Soc. for Study of Edn., Assn. for Childhood Edn. Internat., Am. Civil Liberties Union, Common Cause. Home: 17 Suburban Av Cos Cob CT 06807 Office: Grolier Ednl Corp 845 3d Av New York City NY 10022

SANDS, ADELE GOODWYN GRIFFIN (MRS. JAMES SANDS), educator; b. Swarthmore, Pa., June 25, 1920; d. Frank Hastings and Priscilla (Goodwyn) Griffin; A.B. cum laude, Vassar Coll., 1941; M.A., Villanova U., 1970; m. William Logan MacCoy, Jr., Dec. 28, 1942 (dec. June 1944); 1 dau., Marguerite L. (Mrs. James Pinckney Borden); m. 2d, James Sands, Jan. 18, 1947; children—Priscilla G. (Mrs. Robert Ernest Watson III), James, William Franklin, Elizabeth Keating, Adele Griffin, Geoffrey Keating. Tchr. English, Agnes Irwin Sch., 1941-43; head middle sch. Agnes Irwin Sch., Rosemont, Pa., 1964-67, asso. headmistress, 1967—. With Red Cross Valley Forge Gen. Hosp., 1950-62. Mem. bd. dirs. Country Day Sch. Sacred Heart, Sleighton Farms Schs. Mem. Headmistresses Assn. of East, Pa. Assn. Women Deans and Counselors, Nat. Assn. Prins. Girls Schs. Home: Sunnyside Wawa PA 19063 Office: Ithan Av Rosemont PA 19010

SANDS, EDITH SYLVIA ABELOFF (MRS. ABRAHAM M. SANDS), educator, author; b. Bklyn.; d. Louis and Jennie (Goldstein) Abeloff; B.A., Adelphi Coll., 1932; M.B.A., Baruch Sch. Bus. Adminstrn., City Coll. N.Y., 1956; Ph.D., N.Y.U., 1961; m. Abraham M. Sands, June 5, 1932; children—Stephanie Lou (Mrs. Fersko), John Eliot. Asst. prof. L.I. U., Bklyn., 1961-65, asso. prof., 1965-69, prof., 1969—, chmn. bus. finance dept., 1961-72. Corr. sec. Welfare Council Bklyn Cancer Com., 1956-58; mem. council Friends of Adelphi Coll. Library, 1955-60; pres. Foster Care Aux., 1959-61. Bd. dirs. Nat. Council Jewish Women, 1935-38, community com. Bklyn. Mus., 1950-52; women's aux. Prospect Hts. Hosp., 1954-56, Bklyn. Eye and Ear Hosp., 1950-53; mem. asso. bd. Jewish Child Care Assn., 1959-61. Recipient Outstanding Educators of Am. award, 1971. Mem. Am. Assn. U. Women, Am. Econ. Assn., Econ. History Assn., Am. Finance Assn., Acad. Mgmt., A.I.M., Soc. Advancement Mgmt., Am. Mgmt. Assn., Am. Assn. U. Profs., City Coll. Alumni Assn. (recipient Achievement award 1968), N.Y.U. Alumni Assn., Adelphi Coll. Alumnae Assn. (chpt. pres. 1957-59), Nat. Assn. Bus. Economists, Beta Gamma Sigma (pres. N.Y.C. alumni 1966-69, chmn. bd., nat. exec. com. 1972—), N.Y. Soc. Security Analysts, Nat. Economists Club, Phi Sigma Sigma. Clubs: Women's City, City College, Princeton U. (N.Y.). Author: How to Select Executive Personnel, 1963. Editor: The Tape, 1966-71. Home: 874 Carroll St Brooklyn NY 11215 Office: Long Island U Brooklyn NY 11201

SANDS, NANETTE ELISABETH LISSAUER MURNAN (MRS. ROBERT JAMES SANDS), lawyer; b. Haarlem, Netherlands, Feb. 8, 1915; d. Eduard A. and Antoinette (van Dantzig) Lissauer; Doctoranda juris, Leyden (Netherlands) U., 1938; M. Comparative Law, George Washington U., 1951; m. Robert James Sands, Aug. 18, 1964; 1 son by previous marriage, Robert Jackson Murnan. Admitted to gen. practice of law before Dist. Ct. Rotterdam (Netherlands), 1938; admitted to D.C. bar, 1952; law librarian, instr. Sch. Law, U. Mo., Kansas City, 1946-49; asst. counsellor, legal dept. IMF, also atty. Internat. Bank for Reconstrn. and Devel., Washington, 1949-53; head legal dept. N.Y. br. Algemene Bank Nederland N.V., N.Y.C., 1953—; sec., dir. Netherlands Trading Co. (Can.), Ltd., Netherlands Trading Soc. East, Inc., A.B.N. Corp. Mem. Am. Bar Assn., Nat. Assn. Women Lawyers, Am. Arbitration Assn. (panel mem.), Kappa Beta Pi. Presbyn. Home: 25 Robin Hood Rd Suffern NY 10901 Office: 84 William St New York City NY 10038

SANDS, ROSALIND MINTZ (MRS. LOUIS S. SANDS), social worker; b. N.Y.C., July 30, 1915; d. Samuel and Dora (Bader) Mintz; B.A., Bklyn. Coll., 1935; M.S., Columbia Sch. Social Work, 1948; m. Louis S. Sands, May 30, 1942; 1 son, Jonathan Bader. Dir. group programs N. Shore Child Guidance Center, Manhasset, N.Y., 1968—; cons. psychiat. social work N. Shore Hosp., Manhasset, 1971—. Fellow Am. Orthopsychiat. Assn.; mem. Acad. Certified Social Workers. Contbr. articles to profl. jours. Home: 170 Park Row New York City NY 10038 Office: North Shore Child Guidance Center 1495 N Blvd Manhasset NY 11030

SANDSTROM, ALICE WILHELMINA, accountant; b. Seattle, Jan. 6, 1914; d. Andrew William and Agatha Mathilda (Sundius) Sandstrom; B.A., U. Wash., 1934. Office mgr. Star Machinery Co., Seattle, 1935-43, Howe & Co., Seattle, 1943-46; practice as C.P.A., Seattle, 1945—; controller Children's Orthopedic Hosp. and Med. Center, Seattle, 1948—. Lectr., U. Wash., Seattle, 1957-72. C.P.A., Wash. Fellow Hosp. Financial Mgmt. Assn. (charter, state pres. 1956-57, nat. treas. 1963-65, Robert H. Reeves merit award 1970), Wash. State Hosp. Assn. (treas. 1956-70), Am. Soc. Women Accountants (pres. Seattle 1946-48), Am. Soc. Women C.P.A.'s. Club: Women's University (Seattle). Home: 5725 NE 77th St Seattle WA 98115 Office: 4800 Sand Point Way NE Seattle WA 98105

SANDY, CATHERINE ELLEN, librarian; b. Italy, May 29, 1908; d. Felice Antonio and Guglielma Elena Santaniello; student Rosary Coll., 1933-34, U. Florence, Italy, 1951; B.S., Columbia, 1953. Librarian, Port Washington (N.Y.) Pub. Library, 1926-73. Mem. Bicentennial Commn., Port Washington. Bd. dirs. Adult Edn. Program, Port Washington, Art Adv. Council, Port Washington Pub. Library, Port Washington Community Concerts Assn.; trustee, charter mem. Cow Neck Peninsula Hist. Soc. Recipient Alumni medal Columbia, 1970. Mem. Am., N.Y., N.C. library assns., U.N. Assn., Gen. Studies Alumni Assn. Columbia (dir.). Roman Catholic. Editor: Cow Neck Peninsula Hist. Jour. Home: 35 Davis Rd Port Washington NY 11050

SANDY, JUDY MARGARET THORNHILL, securities co. adminstr.; b. Jamaica, N.Y., Feb. 9, 1942; d. Laurence Ballantyne and Margaret Virginia (Mayfield) Thornhill; B.A., U. Conn., 1963; married. Stewardess United Airlines, Newark, 1963; accounting supr. Service Rev., Inc., Skokie, Ill., 1963-65; supr. N.Y. Telephone, N.Y.C., 1965-67; asst. v.p. William D. Witter, Inc., N.Y.C., 1967-71; asst. v.p. Mitchum, Jones, Templeton, Los Angeles, 1971—. Sec.-treas. Transactions Research Assn., N.Y.C., 1968—. Mem. Am. Horse Shows Assn., Internat. Arabian Horse Assn., Amateur Horsemen's Assn. (treas. 1967-68), Arabian Horse Assn. San Fernando Valley, Financial Analysts Fedn., Wilderness Soc., Arabian Horse Assn. So. Cal. Home: 1827 San Pasqual St Pasadena CA 91107 Office: 555 S Flower St Los Angeles CA 90071

SANDY, MARY ANN ELIZABETH, state ofcl., biostatistician; b. Highland, N.Y., Dec. 11, 1936; d. Herman and Anna Elizabeth (Palazzo) Sandy; B.A. in Math., Coll. of St. Rose, Albany, N.Y., 1958; M.S. in Biostatistics, Columbia, 1961, postgrad. (Health, Edn. and Welfare fellow), 1961. Biostatistician N.Y. State Dept. Health, Albany, 1959-62, sr. statistician N.Y. State Dept. Taxation and Finance, 1962-64; asso. biostatistician N.Y. State Dept. Mental Hygiene, 1967; asso. statistician, asso. research analyst N.Y. State Drug Abuse Control Commn., Albany, 1967—. Mem. Am. Pub. Health Assn., Am. Statis. Assn. Roman Catholic. Home: 105 Beverwyck Dr Guilderland NY 12084 Office: NY State Drug Abuse Control Commn Executive Park S Albany NY 12203

SANECKI, SISTER MARY MIRANDA, hosp. adminstr.; b. Chgo., Sept. 9, 1917; d. Joseph and Sophie (Misiak) Sanecki; B.S., DePaul U., 1961; M.H.A. cum laude, St. Louis U., 1963. Nurse anesthetist St. Mary's Hosp., Centralia, Ill., 1953-55, operating room supr., 1955-60, adminstr., 1963—; joined Felician Sisters, Chgo. province, 1939. Vice pres. Marion County Mental Health Assn., Centralia, Ill., 1966. Mem. adv. bd. Kaskaskia Jr. Coll., 1968—; mem. bd. dirs. Central Comprehensive Mental Health Center, 1965—. Mem. Am. Coll. Hosp. Adminstrn., Am. Assn. Nurse Anesthetists, Ill. Hosp. Assn. Address: 400 N Pleasant Av Centralia IL 62801

SANFORD, ANN LAWRENCE (MRS. FILLMORE H. SANFORD), assn. exec.; b. Boston, Sept. 28, 1917; d. Charles Freeman and Bertha Gertrude (Perry) Snow; A.B cum laude, Radcliffe Coll., 1938; m. Fillmore H. Sanford, June 29, 1940; children—Sarah Ann (Mrs. Lane Conn), Margaret Taylor, Thomas Ryland, Mary Lawrence (Mrs. Mary Lawrence George), John Steven and David Lawrence (twins), Robert Perry. Dir. girls activities Dorchester (Mass.) House, 1939-40; asst. to editor Contemporary Psychology, Austin, Tex., 1961-68; managing editor publs. Psychonomic Soc., Austin, 1968—. Mem. Women In Communications, League of Women Voters. Club: Austin Lake Estates Recreation (sec. 1973-74). Home: Rural Route 8 Box 418 A Austin TX 78703 Office: Publications Office The Psychonomic Society 1108 W 34th St Austin TX 78705

SANFORD, DOROTHY ZERZAN (MRS. FLOYD I. SANFORD), educator; b. Portland, Ore., Nov. 20, 1924; d. Charles Joseph and Margaret (Mahony) Zerzan; A.B., Willamette U., 1946; M.A., U. Ore., 1948; Ph.D., St. Louis U., 1950; student McGeorge Sch. Law, 1950-51, Nacional U. Mexico, summer 1946; m. Floyd I. Sanford, June 30, 1950; children—Mary Victoria, Veronica, Virginia, Thomas, Judith, Theresa, Timothy, Katie. With Montgomery Ward Co., Fireman's Fund Ins. Co., 1951-52; grad. asst. U. Ore., Eugene, 1946-47; instr. St. Louis U., 1947-50; prof. econs. Coll. Notre Dame, Belmont, Cal., 1954—, chmn. dept. bus. adminstrn.-econs., 1974—. Commr., exec. com. Econ. Opportunity Commn., San Mateo County, Cal., 1968-71; dir., exec. com. Bay Area Social Planning, 1964—; cons. Cal. Dept. Edn., Mini-Corp., 1972, Catholic Social Services, 1974—. Mem. Am., Western econ. assns., Am. Marketing Assn., Assn. Cal. Consumers, Assn. Social Economists (exec. bd. 1969-72). Home: 1222 Dore Av San Mateo CA 94401 Office: Coll Notre Dame Belmont CA 94002

SANG, ELSIE OLIN (MRS. PHILIP DAVID SANG), hist. documents exhibitor; b. Chgo., Feb. 5, 1906; d. Louis Benjamin and Ida Kalman (Klein) Olin; Litt.D., Lincoln Coll., 1969; Litt.D., Rosary Coll., 1970; D.F.A., North Central Coll., 1972; m. Philip David Sang, Aug. 21, 1923; children—Robert H., Donald G. Co-producer Ann. Philanthropic European Antiques Show at Oak Park Temple, 1963—; exhibited hist. documents and rare manuscripts on human freedom and Am. history at Rutgers U., So. Ill. U., U. Ill., Champaign-Urbana, U. Hawaii, Brandeis U., Knox Coll., Galesburg, Ill., Lincoln U. (Pa.), Newberry Library, Chgo., Ill. State Hist. Library, Springfield, Jewish Theol. Sem., N.Y.C., Chgo. Hist. Soc., No. Ill. U., Rosary Coll., River Forest, Ill., Ga. State Archives, Atlanta, McCormick Place, Chgo., Ill. Inst. Tech., Lincoln (Ill.) Coll., U. Ky., State U. Ia., North Central Coll., Naperville, Ill., Music Center, Los Angeles, U. Wyo.; co-sponsor Olin-Sang Am. Civilization Center, Brandeis U., Olin-Sang Pavilion, Mt. Sinai Hosp., Chgo., Olin-Sang Hall and Presidential Mus., Lincoln Coll., Olin-Sang Library, Hebrew Union Coll. Bibl. and Archaeol. Sch., Jerusalem, Olin-Sang Camp (Union of Am. Hebrew Congregations), Oconomowoc, Wis., Olin-Sang chair in Leukemia Research, Weizmann Inst. Sci., Rehovot, Israel; co-sponsor Excellence in Teaching ann. awards at various univs. and colls. Bd. dirs. Alliance Francaise; trustee Lincoln Coll., 1955-62, Rosary Coll. Recipient Distinguished Service award Lincoln Coll., 1962; co-recipient Nat. Joshua Ben Gamala Gold Medal award for outstanding contbn. to religious and secular edn., 1967. Fellow U. Ky., 1968. Mem. Ill. Hist. Soc. (v.p.). Club: Standard (Chgo.). Home: 1025 N Lathrop Av River Forest IL 60305

SANGER, JOAN OYAAS (MRS. FRANK DE WOLFE SANGER), editor; b. Eau Claire, Wis., Aug. 3, 1924; d. John and Martha M. (Arnsdorf) Oyaas; B.A. (with honors), U. Wis., 1946; M.A., N.Y. U., 1970; m. Frank de Wolfe Sanger, Mar. 18, 1961. Feature writer Eau Claire (Wis.) Leader Telegram, 1944-46; activities editor Rhinelander (Wis.) Daily News, 1946-49; asst. dir. sch.-coll. activities, St. Paul chpt. A.R.C., 1950-53; prodn. editor Frat. Press, St. Paul, 1953-57; editor Personal Efficiency, dir. publs. LaSalle Extension U., Chgo., 1957-59; asso. editor Nat. Assn. Social Workers, N.Y.C., 1960-61; mng. editor Phys. Therapy N.Y.C., 1962-69; free lance writer, copy editor Nursing Research, N.Y.C., 1971—. Cons. Hospitalized Vets. Writing Project, 1963-72, nat. chmn., 1972—. Treas. Community Chest, Douglaston, N.Y., 1973—; mem. Douglaston (N.Y.) Civic Assn., sec. 1965-69. Mem. Am. Studies Assn., N.Y. Assn. Indsl. Communicators, U. Wis. Alumni Club of N.Y. (dir. 1966—, pres. 1970-72), Wis. Alumni Assn. (Spark Plug award 1972, dir. 1972—), Women in Communications, Kappa Delta. Home: 73 Poplar St Douglaston NY 11363 Office: 10 Columbus Circle New York City NY 10019

SANGER, MARGARET ANNE JONES (MRS. CURT SANGER), librarian; b. Salem, O., June 15, 1924; d. Alford and Nina J. (Brent) Jones; A.B., Western Reserve U., 1945, B.L.S., 1946, postgrad., 1949-51; m. Curt Sanger, May 16, 1953; children—Bruce Marshall, Brent Michael, Kenneth Bateson. Librarian, Holmes County (O.) Pub. Library, 1946-48, Akron (O.) Pub. Library, 1948-52, Pub. Library Cin. and Hamilton County, 1952—; head Reader's Bur., Cin., 1962—; editor Guide Post, Cin., 1963—. Tchr. book selection Miami U. Norwood Extension Center, 1964-65. Mem. Ohio Library Assn. Mem. Order Eastern Star. Contbr. articles to profl. jours. Home: 7819 Pinemeadow Lane Cincinnati OH 45224 Office: 800 Vine St Cincinnati OH 45202

SANGSTER, PAOLA, advt. exec.; b. Urbana, Ill., July 22, 1939; d. Cesare and Verna Bertha (Daily) Gianturco; B.A., Stanford, 1961; postgrad. U. So. Cal., 1971; 1 son, Scott. Pub. relations dir. Joseph Magnin, San Francisco, 1962-67; pub. relations dir., account exec. Hall & Levine Advt. Agy., Los Angeles, 1968-73, v.p., 1973—. Mem. Women in Communications, Fashion Group, Los Angeles County Museums Art Mus. Council, Stanford Bay Area Alumni. Home: 8775 Wonderland Av Los Angeles CA 90046 Office: 2727 W 6th St Los Angeles CA 90057

SANICKY, MARILYN KATHERINE, chemist; b. Cleve., Sept. 17, 1932; d. Louis J. and Ann (Chorney) Sanicky; student Fenn Coll., 1951-53. Electroplating chemist R. O. Hull Co., Cleve., 1953-54; chief chemist service and nickel research INCAR, INC. div. Am. Smelting & Refining Co., Cleve., 1954-67, corporate sec., 1955-61, asst. tech. dir., 1964-67; tech. dir. Electrochems., Inc., 1967-72; supr. nickel service R.O. Hull Co., Cleve., 1972—. Mem. women's sports adv. com. Cleve. Recreation Dept., 1961-63; mem. women's sports adv. com. C.Y.O. Mem. Am. Electroplaters Soc., Amateur. Athletic Union of U.S. (Lake Erie dist. chmn. girls age group track 1959-70, U.S. chmn. girls age group track and field 1959-65), Cleve. Phys. Edn. Assn. (asso.), Cleve. Bd. Women Ofcls. (treas. 1964-69, chmn. 1969-71). Patentee bright nickel plating. Home: 10233 Barr Rd Brecksville OH 44141 Office: 3203 W 71st St Cleveland OH 44102

SANK, DIANE (MRS. I. LESTER FIRSCHEIN), research scientist, educator; b. N.Y.C., Dec. 22, 1927; d. Max and Fannie (Leitman) Sank; B.S., L.I. U., 1949; M.S., U. Ill., 1951; Ph.D., Columbia, 1963; m. I. Lester Firschein, Nov. 2, 1950; children—Brian Douglas Sank, Dean Evan Sank, Gayle Dawn Sank. Sr. research sci. N.Y. State Psychiat. Inst., N.Y.C., 1952-67; research asso. Columbia U., 1953-67; asso. prof. Hunter Coll., N.Y.C., 1967-68; asso. prof. sociology/anthropology City Coll., N.Y., 1968-69, prof., 1971—, chmn. dept. anthropology, 1969-72; chief investigator Research Center Rockland State Hosp., Orangeburg, N.Y., 1967—; lectr. Columbia, 1967—. Asso., Columbia U. Seminar on Genetics and the Evolution of Man, 1957-74. Fellow Am. Anthrop. Assn., A.A.A.S.; mem. Soc. for Study of Human Biology, Internat. Conf. on Dermatoglyphics, Am. Assn. Phys. Anthropologists, Behavior Genetics Assn., Soc. for the Study of Evolution, Am. Soc. Human Genetics, Soc. Med. Anthropology, Council Anthropology and Edn. Research in mental illness, mental retardation, deafness, normal human behavior. Contbr. articles in field to profl. jours. Home: 173 Charlotte Pl Englewood Cliffs NJ 07632 Office: City Coll New York

City NY 10031 also Research Center Rockland State Hosp Orangeburg NY 10962

SANKARY, WANDA YOUNG KAZMAREK (MRS. MORRIS SANKARY), lawyer; b. Scranton, N.D., Dec. 22, 1919; d. Michael and Katherine (Busch) Kazmarek; LL.B., U. So. Cal., 1950; m. Morris Sankary, Aug. 31, 1952; children—Timothy, Ronald. Admitted to Cal. bar, 1951; practiced in Los Angeles, 1951-52, San Diego, 1952—; mem. firm Sankary & Sankary, 1952—. Mem. Cal. Assembly, 1954-55. Mem. State Bar Cal., San Diego Bar Assn. Democrat. Roman Catholic. Home: 4919 Cresita Dr San Diego CA 92115 Office: 110 West C St San Diego CA 92101

SANKEY, HARRIET ELLEN, jour. editor; b. Terre Haute, Ind., Sept. 5, 1915; d. James Madison and Mary Samuel (Hill) Sankey; B.A., Western Coll., 1936; postgrad. Northwestern U., 1944-46. Desk editor Am. Bus. Mag., The Dartnell Corp., Chgo., 1938-42; asso. editor Sci. Research Assos., Chgo., 1942-46; mng. editor Jour. of The Am. Dietetic Assn., Chgo., 1946—. Clubs: Chgo. Color Camera, Chgo. Shell. Office: 430 N Michigan Av Chicago IL 60611

SANNER, FERN ALICE RUSTEBERG (MRS. LOUIS ANTHONY SANNER), anesthesiologist; b. Chgo., Sept. 8, 1921; d. August and Anna (Kemper) Rusteberg; B.S., Central YMCA Coll., 1945; M.D., U. Ill., 1948; m. Louis Anthony Sanner, Feb. 18, 1949; children—Lorraine, Louis, John, Joseph. Intern, Cook County Hosp., Chgo., 1948-50; resident U. Ill. Research Hosp., 1950-51; practice medicine, specializing in anesthesiology, Chgo., 1952—; chmn. dept. anesthesia Franklin Blvd. Community Hosp., Chgo., 1956—, Central Community Hosp., Chgo., 1972—; prof. Loyola U. Sch. Dentistry, Maywood, 1968—, instr. Sch. Medicine, 1971—; prof. Ill. Coll. Podiatric Medicine, Chgo., 1970—. Mem. Am., Ill. socs. anesthesiologists, Chgo. Anesthesiologists Soc., A.M.A., Ill., Chgo. med. socs., Alpha Omega Alpha. Home: 6139 N Tripp St Chicago IL 60646 Office: 3240 W Franklin Blvd Chicago IL 60624

SAN SOUCIE, PATRICIA MOLM, artist; b. Mpls., Nov. 4, 1931; d. Ralph and Evangeline (Nusbaum) Molm; B.S. in Applied Arts, U. Wis., 1953; m. Robert Louis San Soucie, Sept. 5, 1953; children—Richard Peter, Marc David, Mary Frances. Exhibited Wis. Painters and Sculptors, Milw., 1953, Mem.'s Gallery, Albright-Knox, Buffalo, 1961-64, St. Louis Artists Guild, 1963-71, St. Louis City Art Mus., 1963, Watercolor U.S.A. Ann., 1965-73, Cal. Nat. Watercolor Soc., Los Angeles, 1966-73, Am. Water Color Soc., N.Y.C., 1972, Nat. Assn. Women Artists, 1972-73; one man shows, Mo. and N.J., 1966, 67, 69, 70, 71, 73. Juror, Nat. Scholastic Art Awards, N.Y.C., 1972-73. Recipient state show awards, N.Y., Mo. and N.J., 1961—, prize and medal of honor for watercolor Nat. Assn. Women Artists, 1972, Watercolor U.S.A. Purchase award, 1973. Mem. St. Louis Artists Guild, Cal. Nat., Garden State watercolor socs., Nat. Assn. Women Artists. Address: 35 Cayuga Way Short Hills NJ 07078

SANTIESTEVAN, STINA ELLEN (MRS. HENRY SANTIESTEVAN), political assn. editor; b. Los Angeles, Jan. 10, 1921; d. Carl Emil and Lily Ethel (Hardwick) Sternlov; B.A., Occidental Coll., 1942; m. Henry Santiestevan, June 3, 1942; children—Stina Marie (Mrs. Stuart Trager), Signe Serena, Carl Rique. Information specialist U.S. Govt., Washington, 1945-46; dir. edn. and research Greater Los Angeles CIO Council, 1949-51; editor, publicity dir. D.C. Citizens for Better Pub. Edn., Washington, 1964-65; dir. pub. relations Ams. for Democratic Action, Washington, 1966-67, editor ADA World, 1967—. Free lance polit. campaign assignments, Los Angeles, 1952-58; vol. worker, Detroit, 1958-64. Ford Found grantee, 1954. Mem. Mich. Bot. Soc. Democrat. Club: Sierra (San Francisco). Contbr. articles to profl. publs. Home: 2716 Colt Run Rd Oakton VA 22124 Office: 1424 16th St NW Washington DC 20036

SANTMYER, HELEN HOOVEN, author; b. Cin., Nov. 25, 1895; d. Joseph Wright and Bertha (Hooven) Santmyer; B.A., Wellesley Coll., 1918; Litt.B., Oxford U., 1927. Sec. to mag. editor Charles Scribner's & Sons, N.Y.C., 1920-22; asst. to head of English lit. dept. Wellesley (Mass.) Coll., 1922-24; dean of women, head English dept. Cedarville (O.) Coll., 1937-53; asst. reference dept. Dayton (O.) Pub. Library, 1953-60. Author: Herbs and Apples, 1925; The Fierce Dispute, 1929; Ohio Town, 1964. Home: 113 W 3rd St Xenia OH 45385

SANTORO, ELISSA JEANNE, surgeon; b. Newark, Oct. 18, 1938; d. James Joseph and Jean Margaret (Cannella) Santoro; A.B., Coll. St. Elizabeth, N.J., 1960; M.D., Woman's Med. Coll. Pa., 1965. Intern, Hosp. Women's Med. Coll. Pa., 1965-66, surg. resident, 1966-67; sr., chief surg. resident St. Vincent's Hosp. and Med. Center, N.Y.C., 1968-70; NIH fellow cancer tng. N.Y. Med. Coll., N.Y.C., 1970-71, instr. surgery, asso. clin. investigator central oncology group, 1970—; asst. vis. surgeon, chief chemotherapy service Met. Hosp. Center, 1970-72; asst. attending surgeon Flower and Fifth Av. Hosps., N.Y.C., 1970-71; clin. asst. prof. surgery Coll. Medicine and Dentistry N.J., Newark, 1973—; mem. courtesy staff in surgery and oncology St. Barnabas Med. Center; asso. attending in surgery and oncology Irvington Gen. Hosp. Recipient Surgery award Am. Italian Women Achievement, 1972. Am. Cancer Soc. fellow, 1968-69. Diplomate Am. Bd. Surgery. Mem. A.M.A. (Physician Recognition award 1969), Assn. Am. Med. Colls., Med. Soc. N.J., Essex County Med. Soc., Am., N.J. med. women's assns., Surg. Soc. N.Y. Med. Coll., Acad. Medicine N.J., N.Y. Cancer Programs Assn., Inc., Am. Assn. Cancer Edn. Contbr. articles to profl. jours. Assn. for Acad. Surgery. Home: 987 Sanford Av Irvington NJ 07111 Office: 987 Sanford Av Irvington NJ 07111

SANZ, ELAINE BOUGHNER (MRS. ROBERT BOISSON SANZ), educator; b. Catonsville, Md., Oct. 4, 1914; d. Arthur Gray and Marie (Terry) Boughner; A.B. in English and Drama, Brenau Coll., 1936; m. Robert Boisson Sanz, Sept. 30, 1939; children—Elaine, Robert Louis. Passenger rep. B. & O. R.R., Washington, 1935-39; v.p., tchr. English, cons. on progressive methods Sanz Sch. Langs., Washington, 1939—, collaborator Sanz system teaching langs. Spanish, 1940, English, 1942, French, 1950. State dir. radio and TV, Children Am. Revolution, Washington, 1959-61; chmn. books and records Salvation Army Aux. Guild, Washington, 1963—, pres., 1967-68. Mem. Md. Hist. Soc., D.A.R., Zeta Phi Eta, Delta Zeta. Democrat. Roman Catholic. Clubs: Internat., Congressional Country (Washington); Capital Speakers (pres. 1966-67, 70). Collaborator: (with Robert B. Sanz) Espanol con Sanz, 1973, English With Sanz, 1973. Home: Apt 722 The Colonnade 2801 New Mexico Av NW Washington DC 20007 Office: 1404 New York Av NW Washington DC 20007

SANZONE, JEAN FAY (MRS. ANTHONY JOSEPH SANZONE), sch. adminstr.; b. Cleveland Heights, O., Mar. 13, 1926; d. James Samuel and Alice Madeleine (Deveres) Fowls; A.A., St. Petersburg Jr. Coll., 1946; Ed.B., Fla. State U., 1948, Ph.D., 1968; Ed.M., U. Miami, 1957; m. Anthony Joseph Sanzone, Nov. 19, 1950; children—Patricia Ann, Nancy Jean. Tchr. exceptional child edn. Dade County, Fla., 1956-62; tchr. varying exceptionalities Pinellas Sch. System, Nina Harris Sch., St. Petersburg, Fla., 1962-64; prin. St. Petersburg Exceptional Child Center, 1964-65; coordinator exceptional child edn. Pinellas County Sch. System, Clearwater, Fla., 1965-70, cons. specific learning disabilities, 1970; prin. Gulf Beaches Sch., St. Petersburg, Fla., 1970—. Mem. Fla. Gov.'s Com. on Employment Handicapped, 1962-65. Bd. dirs. St. Petersburg Speech and Hearing Clinic, 1962-72. Mem. Nat. Assn. for Elementary Sch. Prins., Am. Assn. Mental Deficiency, Pinellas Assn. for Retarded Children (past sec., v.p.), Council for Exceptional Children (state pres. 1964-65), Assn. for Supervision and Curriculum Devel., Kappa Delta Pi, Delta Kappa Gamma, Sigma Delta Pi. Contbr. articles to profl. jours. Home: 6801 17th St S St Petersburg FL 33712 Office: 8600 Boca Ciega Dr St Petersburg Beach FL 33706

SAPERSTEIN, ESTHER, state senator; b. Chgo.; ed. Northwestern U.; widow; children—Sidney, Natalie. Mem. Ill. Ho. of Reps., 1956-66; mem. Ill. Senate, 1966—. Mem. Mayor's Com. on Human Relations, Chgo., Mayor's Juvenile Welfare Com., Chgo.; former pres. Chgo. Region P.T.A.; chmn. Ill. Commn. on Status Women, Ill. Com. on Mental Health and Mental Retardation; former sec. Juvenile Protective Assn.; mem. Citizens. Adv. Council of Met. Chgo., Citizens Com. for Day Care Centers, White House Conf. on Children, 1970, Com. on Emotionally Distrubed Children, Senate-Pub. Aid adv. com., Com. on Profl. and Para-profl. relations. Mem. State Democratic Mental Health Task Force. Bd. dirs. Jewish Community Center of Rogers Park (Ill.), Little City, Chgo. Sch. for Retarded Children, Drs. Gen. Hosp. Recipient Freedom award Roosevelt U., 1973; Merit award Ill. Psychol. Assn., 1973; Merit award Ill. Adult Edn. Assn., 1972; Woman of Year award Women's Aux. Jewish War Vets., 1968; Spl. recognition Ill. Assn. Chaplains, 1973; Spl. award for improving care for retarded of Ill., Ill. Assn. Mentally Retarded, 1973. Mem. League of Women Voters, Am. Soc. Pub. Adminstrn., Am., Ill. (merit award 1967) pub. health assns., Delta Kappa Gamma (hon., Woman of Year award 1970). Democrat. Jewish Religion. Office: 1316 Arthur St Chicago IL 60626

SAPERSTEIN, ROSE BALLINE, dermatologist; b. Chgo., July 2, 1918; d. Jacob Harry and Anina (Cohen) Balline; B.S., U. Ill., 1940, M.D., 1943; m. Jerome Louis Saperstein, Mar. 12, 1944; children—Judith (Mrs. Braun), Harry Bart. Intern Los Angeles County Ge. Hosp., 1943; resident Bellevue Hosp., N.Y.C., 1944-46; asst. to Dr. Marion B. Sulzberger, N.Y.C., 1947; pvt. practice dermatology, Los Angeles, 1948—; mem. staff Cedars-Sinai Med. Center, chief dermatology div. medicine, 1971—. Life mem. P.T.A., 1962—; clinic dermatologist P.T.A. Health Center, Los Angeles, 1955-72. Mem. Los Angeles County Med. Women's Assn. (pres. 1971, 72), Met. Dermatol. Soc. Los Angeles (pres. 1962), Soc. Investigative Dermatology. Contbr. articles to profl. jours. Patentee Brasivol soap for acne. Home: 5619 Park Oak Pl Los Angeles CA 90068 Office: 3916 Wilshire Blvd Los Angeles CA 90010

SAPINSLEY, LILA MANFIELD, state legislator; b. Chgo., Sept. 9, 1922; d. Jacob and Doris (Silverman) Manfield; B.A., Wellesley Coll., 1944; D. Pub. Service, U. R.I., 1971; Ph.D., R.I. Coll., 1973; m. John M. Sapinsley, Dec. 23, 1942; children—Jill Sapinsley Mooney, Carol Sapinsley Rubenstein, Joan, Patricia. Mem. R.I. senate, 1972—, minority leader, 1974—. Mem. Gov.'s Commn. on Women, R.I.; commr. Edn. Commn. of States. Vice pres. bd. trustees Butler Hosp.; trustee R.I. State Colls., 1965-70, chmn., 1967-70; trustee U. R.I., R.I. Coll. Found.; bd. dirs. Miriam Hosp., Hamilton House, Trinity Repertory Co., Lincoln Sch. Recipient Alumnae Achievement award Wellesley Coll., 1974. Republican. Jewish religion. Home: 25 Cooke St Providence RI 02906

SAPP, PHYLLIS WOODRUFF (MRS. J. D. SAPP), author, lectr., real estate co. exec.; b. Oklahoma City, Oct. 21, 1908; d. John A. and Maude (Laws) Woodruff; student Oklahoma City U., 1926-27; B.A., Okla. U., 1930; m. J. D. Sapp, June 5, 1930; children—Kathryn (Mrs. Karl Malthaner), John Davis, Phillip Woodruff. Organizer, dir. Oklahoma City's first children's theatre, 1930-35; dir. Okla. City Theatre Guild, 1940-42; jr. high sch. tchr. drama Oklahoma City pub. schs., 1946-49; writer curriculum materials Women's Missionary Union of So. Bapt. Conv., 1969—; real estate broker; co-dir. J.D. Sapp Sch. Real Estate, 1972—. Recipient $4,000 first prize Zondervan's Christian Fiction Contest, 1957. Mem. Nat. League Am. Pen Women (br. v.p. 1963, pres. 1968-70, treas. 1973—, 4th nat. v.p. 1970-72, chmn. nat. letters bd. 1972-74, nat. chaplain 1974—), Internat. Platform Assn., Okla. Heritage Assn. (sustaining), Mortar Bd., Alpha Phi (distinguished alumnae award of honor 1972), Pi Kappa Delta. Baptist (writer Jr. Pupil and Jr. Tchr. for So. Bapt.Sun. Sch. Bd. 1952-71). Author: Accidental Hero (3-act play), 1949; The Ice Cutter, 1948; Whisper Out of the Dust, 1951; For Such a Time, 1954; The Long Bridge, 1957; God of All the Earth, 1960; Gifts from God, 1962; Small Giant, 1957; Life at Its Best, 1963; Living for Jesus, 1961; Working Together in Our Church, 1963; Lighthouse on the Corner, 1964; Creative Teaching in the Church School, 1967; Children of Men, 1968; Fifty Nine Programs For Pre-Teens, 1969; Teaching Guide for Youth Sunday School Work, 1970; Jeff the Baptist, 1972; Real Estate Workbook, 1972. Address: 7100 S Kentucky Av Oklahoma City OK 73159

SARA, DOROTHY, graphologist, author; b. Bklyn.; d. Isaac and Rose (Lupitinsky) Chatcuff; student pub. schs. Graphologist, 1934—; editor-in-chief Cadillac Pub. Co., N.Y.C., 1946-50; asso. editor Ziff-Davis Pub. Co., Chgo., 1950-51. Mem. faculty Henry George Sch. Social Sci., N.Y.C., 1951—. Mem. Womens Nat. Book Assn., Mensa, Advt. Club N.Y. Author: Personality and Penmanship, 1969; Handwriting Analysis for the Millions, 1967; Sewing Made Easy, 1950; Home Nursing Care, 1965; American Family Garden Book, 1954; American Family Baby Book, 1955; numerous others. Home: 10 Park Av New York City NY 10016

SARBEY, IRENE SCHWARTZ (MRS. JACK SARBEY), educator; b. Akron, O., Dec. 20, 1922; d. Charles E. and Rae N. (Nobil) Schwartz; B.S., Northwestern U., 1944, M.S., 1944; postgrad. U. Akron, summers 1961-63; m. Jack Sarbey, May 8, 1947; children—Edward H., Janet R. Reporter, copy editor Akron Beacon Jour., 1945-47, cons. on journalistic errors, 1958; dir. writer's workshop, Akron, 1957-60; tchr. secondary sch., Bath, O., 1961-65; faculty Kent State U., Kent, O., 1965—, prof. journalism, since 1966—. Mem. liaison com. Nat. Conf. Editorial Writers-Assn. for Edn. in Journalism, 1971-72. Mem. governance com. Kent State U., 1972—. Recipient awards Ohio Press Women, 1969, 70, nat. outstanding adviser award Women in Communications, 1971. Mem. Am. Assn. U. Profs., Assn. for Edn. in Journalism, Nat. Conf. Editorial Writers, Women in Communications, Akron-Canton-Kent Northwestern U. Alumni Assn. (sec. 1970—). Editor Kent State U Summer News and Coll. Quar., 1965-71. Home: 1865 Brookfield Dr Akron OH 44313 Office: 118 Taylor Hall Kent State U Kent OH 44242

SARDO, ARLENE ANN, sch. adminstr.; b. Cortland, N.Y., Aug. 18, 1937; d. Silvio Anthony and Rose (Gabriel) Sardo; B.S., N.Y. State U., 1958, postgrad., 1968; M.A., Tchrs. Coll., Columbia, 1963. Tchr., Ramapo Central Sch. Dist. #2, Spring Valley, N.Y., 1958-64, reading specialist, 1965-67; tchr. Cheshire (Conn.) Dept. Edn., 1967-68; elementary curriculum supr. Baldwinsville (N.Y.) Acad. and Central Schs., 1968—. Cons., Perceptual Motor Devel. Program, 1970-72. Mem. Friends in Service Here, Baldwinsville, 1972—. Mem. Internat., N.Y. State, Oswego (treas. 1971-72, dir. 1973—) reading assns., N.E.A., Nat. Soc. for the Study of Edn., N.Y. State Assn. for Supervision and Curriculum Devel. Home: F-98 Cedar Court Baldwinsville NY 13027 Office: Baldwinsville Central School District Office Baldwinsville NY 13027

SARGENT, EILEEN SEVERSON, ednl. adminstr.; b. Deerfield, Wis., Oct. 8, 1922; d. Martin Arthur and Lillian Myrtle (Vaage) Severson; B.S., State Coll., Whitewater, Wis., 1950; M.S., U. Wis., Madison, 1955, Ph.D., 1971; certificate advanced studies Syracuse U., 1969; m. Merle E. Sargent, Dec. 17, 1962. Tchr. rural sch., 1942-46; teaching prin. Dousman St. Graded Sch., Dousman, Wis., 1946-49; tchr. high sch., Madison, 1949-55; curriculum coordinator, reading cons. Nicolet High Sch., Milw., 1955-72; instr. Syracuse U., 1964, Marquette U., 1969; extension instr. U. Wis., Milw., 1966-69; asst. prof. Marquette U., 1972—, dir. reading and learning abilities center, 1972—. Ford fellow, 1955. Mem. Nat. (life), Wis. edn. assns., Am. Soc. Curriculum Devel., Nat. Council Tchrs. English, Internat. (conv. exhibit mgr. 1954—, past dir.), Wis. (past pres.) reading assns., Milw. Area Reading Council, Order Easter Star, Daus. of Nile, Delta Kappa Gamma, Pi Lambda Theta (life mem.; past pres. Wis.), Phi Beta Kappa. Author: How to Read a Book, 1970; The Newspaper As A Teaching Tool; also articles in field. Home: 1100 W Wells St Apt 1007 Milwaukee WI 53233 Office: 502 N 15th St Milwaukee WI 53233

SARGENT, JESSIE FAY (MRS. FRANCIS W. SARGENT), author, civic worker; b. Wellesley, Mass.; student Milton Acad., 1925-31, Masters Sch., Dobbs Ferry, N.Y., 1931-32; grad. pub. high sch., 1933; m. Francis W. Sargent; children—Fay (Mrs. James W. McLane), Jessie (Mrs. Brian Flynn), F(rancis) Williams. Founder, pres. Better Housing, Inc. (name changed to Assn. for Better Living, Inc.), Boston, 1967-71, chmn. bd., 1971-72, chmn. emeritus, 1972—; founder, pres. Doric Dames vol. guides for State House tours, 1969—; hon. chmn. Mass. Antioquia (Colombia) Project, 1971—; Gov.'s rep. Mass. Partners of Americas Survey Team to Antioquia, 1971; dir. Nat. Assn. Partners of the Americas, 1973—; mem. Mass. Partners of the Americas, 1972—; bellringer chmn. fund drive Mass. Mental Health Assn., 1969—; chmn. ladies com. WHO meeting, Boston, 1969, mem. WHO, 1971; mem. adv. bd., speakers bur. Dept. Community Affairs, 1970—; mem. task force on handicapped children Edn. Commn. of the States, 1971, vice chmn., 1973; founder, dir. Mass. Children's Lobby, 1972, dir. Nat. Com. for Children's Lobby, 1972—; co-hostess New Eng. Conf. Nat. Birth Defects, Boston, 1971; mem. Conf. Human Rights and Soviet Jewry, 1971, 72; hon. big sister chmn. Big Sister Assn. Boston, 1971; mem. Greater Boston council Camp Fire Girls, 1970-71; hon. chmn. Mothers March Mass., 1969, 70, 71, mem. Nat. Found. March of Dimes, 1969—; hon. chmn. Archives of Am. Art N.E. Bd., 1971-72, mem., 1972—; chmn. Vols. for the Commonwealth, 1972—; state chmn. Nat. Vol. Action Com. in Mass., 1971—; mem. state adv. bd. Commonwealth Service Corps, 1971-72; mem. adv. com. poverty OEO, 1971-72; sponsor youth vol. program Lyman Sch., Westboro, 1971; instituted greeting card project for rehab. Boston State Hosp., 1971—; chmn. Nat. Governors' Wifes Conf. sect. on Early Childhood Devel., 1973; co-chmn. Gov.'s Conf. on Mental Retardation, 1973-74; mem. Mental Retardation Survey Team, Neb., 1973, Sweden, 1973; chmn. bd. dirs. Mental Health Job Placement Project, 1973—; chmn. Am. Cancer Soc. Met. Boston, 1974; co-chmn. Gov.'s Commn. on Citizen Participation, 1972-73; mem. Gov.'s Commn. on Status of Women; mem. Cardinal Medeiros' Com. on Drugs, 1972—; chmn. Trial and Error, 1974, V-Day-'74 Vol. Fair, 1974, Conf. on Mentally Disabled, 1974. Bd. dirs. Mass. 4-H Found., Inc., 1969—, Center House Found., Boston, 1969—. Decorated Order of San Carlos (Colombia); recipient Service award Mass. Council of Crime and Corrections, 1973; Woman of Year award Greater Boston Assn. for Retarded Citizens, 1973; Jessie Sargent Humanitarian Service award Mass. Assn. Private Residential Facilities for Mentally Retarded, 1974; Distinguished Service award Reach Out, Inc., 1974. Mem. Mass. Mental Health Assn., Women Concerned with Criminal Justice. Author: The Governor's Wife, A View from Within, 1973; Kids of Colombia, 1974; also numerous articles in human service field. Home: Governor's Residence Farm St Dover MA 02030

SARKAR, NELLIE NOLIDO, pathologist; b. Hinigaran, Philippines, Mar. 12, 1932; d. Simeon Neuda and Expectacion Villa (Mondragon) Nolido; M.D., Far Eastern U., 1957; m. Sushil C. Sarkar, July 4, 1964 (dec. June 1969). Came to Can., 1964, naturalized, 1969. Intern Lincoln Hosp., N.Y.C., 1959-60, resident, 1960-61; resident Beth Israel Med. Center, N.Y.C., 1961-62, Mt. Carmel Hosp., Detroit, 1962-64; practice medicine specializing in pathology, Halifax, N.S., Can., 1965—; pathologist Pathology Inst., Halifax, 1965—. Lectr. pathology Dalhousie U., Halifax, 1971—. Mem. Fedn. Med. Women Can., Canadian Med. Assn., N.S. Med. Soc., Dalhousie Faculty Assn. Home: 5908 Pine Hill Dr Halifax NS Canada Office: 5788 University Av Halifax NS Canada

SARLAT, GLADYS, pub. relations exec.; b. Elizabeth, N.J., July 22, 1923; d. Max and Dora (Levin) Sarlat; B.S., U. Wash., 1946; student N.Y.U., 1942-43, Columbia, 1947. Asst., Kay Sullivan Assos., N.Y.C., 1949-50; fashion dir. Warsaw & Co., N.Y.C., 1950-54; asst. fashion coordinator Emporium Dept. Store, San Francisco, 1955-56; asst. prodn. mgr. Cunningham & Walsh Advt., San Francisco, 1958-59; v.p., pub. relations dir. Harwood Advt. Inc., Tucson and Phoenix, 1959-68; v.p., dir. Waller & Sarlat Advt., Inc., Tucson, 1968-69; pres. Gladys Sarlat Pub. Relations, Inc., Tucson, 1970—. Pub. relations campaign fund raising Coll. Medicine, U. Ariz., 1964. Bd. dirs. Marshall Home for Men. Named Woman of Year for Bus., Ariz. Daily Star, 1963. Mem. Fashion Group N.Y., Tucson Press Club (sec. bd. dirs. 1967), Pub. Relations Soc. Am., Alpha Epsilon Phi. Club: Old Pueblo (Tucson). Home: 3239 E 3d St Tucson AZ 85716 Office: 180 W Broadway La Placita Village Tucson AZ 85701

SARNOFF, LILI-CHARLOTTE DREYFUS (MRS. STANLEY J. SARNOFF), artist, business exec.; b. Frankfurt, Germany, Jan. 9, 1916; d. Willy and Martha (Koch von Hirsch) Dreyfus; grad. Reimann Art Sch. (Germany), 1934, U. Berlin, 1935; student U. Florence (Italy), 1936-37; m. Stanley Jay Sarnoff, Sept. 11, 1948; children—Daniela Martha, Robert B.L. Came to U.S., 1941, naturalized, 1944. Research asst. Harvard Sch. Pub. Health, 1948-54; research asso. cardiac physiology Nat. Heart Inst., Bethesda, Md., 1954-59; pres. Rodana Research Corp., Bethesda, 1958-61; v.p. Catrix Corp., Bethesda, 1958-61; inventor FloLite light sculptures under name Lolo Sarnoff, 1968; exhibited in one man show Agra Coll., Washington, 1969, Corning Glass Center Mus., Corning, N.Y., 1970, Gallery Two, Woodstock, Va., 1970, Gallery Marc, Washington, 1971, Hood Coll., Frederick, Md., 1972, Internat. Art Mart, Basel, Switzerland, 1972; represented in collections Corning Glass Center Mus., R. and M. von Hirsch Collection, Basel, Switzerland, David Lloyd Kreeger Collection, Washington, Kennedy Center, Washington, Nat. Acad. Sci., U.S. embassy New Delhi, others. Trustee Nat. Ballet; bd. dirs. Fgn. Student Service Council, Washington Performing Arts Soc. Mem. Women's Com. Corcoran Gallery of Art. Club: City Tavern (Washington). Democrat. Co-inventor electrophrenic respirator; inventor flowmeter. Home: 7507 Hampden Lane Bethesda MD 20014 also Barnard VA 05031

SAROFF, MARIE IQBAL JABBAR (MRS. JACK SAROFF), physician; b. Hyderabad, India, Apr. 16, 1928 (came to U.S. 1955, naturalized 1960); d. Syed Abdul and Kitty (Guha) Jabbar; M.B.B.S.,

Christian Med. Coll., Vellore, South India, 1952; M.D., U. Buffalo, 1964; m. Jack Saroff, Sept. 22, 1956; children—David, Rahel Kitty. Intern, Ottawa (Ont., Can.) Gen. Hosp., 1954-55; resident, Children's Meml. Hosp., Kansas City, Mo., 1955-57; asst. dir. out patient dept., pediatric dept., Salt Lake City, 1958-59; fellow child devel. program Children's Hosp., Buffalo, 1959-61; pub. health physician, Buffalo, 1961-66; asst. dir. Neuromuscular Clinic, Cin., 1967-72; sch. physician Sch. for Retarded and Assn. for Retarded Children, Buffalo, 1972—; practice medicine specializing in pediatrics and developmental medicine, Buffalo, 1959-66, Cin., 1967-72; mem. staff Children's Hosp., Cin., Gen. Hosp., Cin.; staff physician Ambulatory Pediatric Clinic, Meyer Meml. Hosp., Buffalo, 1972—. Bd. dirs. Camp Livingston. Fellow Am. Acad. Pediatrics; mem. League Women Voters, Am. Med. Women's Assn. Home: 501 Woodland Dr Buffalo NY 14223

SARRATT, MARY JANE SANFORD (MRS. CLAUDE H. SARRATT), lawyer; b. Charleston, S.C., Mar. 14, 1920; d. Andrew George and Georgia Etta (Toops) Sanford; A.B., Winthrop Coll., 1941; J.D., Am. Univ., 1951; m. Claude H. Sarratt, July 1, 1943; 1 dau., Mary Georgia (Mrs. John Jay Myers). Admitted to D.C. bar, 1952, Md. bar, 1959, U.S. Supreme Ct. bar, 1971; practiced in Balt., 1959-63; atty. Social Security Adminstrn., Balt., 1965—. Served with USNR, 1942-44. Home: 7014 York Rd Baltimore MD 21212 Office: Social Security Administration 6401 Security Blvd Baltimore MD 21235

SARRAUTE, NATHALIE, writer; b. Ivanovo, Russia, July 18, 1902; d. Ilya and Pauline (Chatounowski) Tcherniak; ed. Lycee Fenelon, U. Paris, U. Oxford; m. Raymond Sarraute, July 28, 1925; children—Claude, Anne, Dominique. Author: Tropisms, 1939; Portrait of a Man Unknown, 1948; Martereau, 1953; The Age of Suspicion, 1956; The Planetarium, 1959; The Golden Fruits, 1963 (Internat. Prize of Lit. 1964); Silence and the Lie, 1967; Between Life and Death, 1968; Isma, 1970; Do You Hear Them?, 1972; It Is Beautiful, 1974. Address: 12 Avenue Pierre 1 de Serbie Paris France

SARTIN, BEULAH (MRS. JOSEPH ARTHUR SARTIN), county ofcl., bus. exec.; b. Clinton, Mo., Nov. 20, 1906; d. William H. and Anabel (Jones) Riead; student pub. schs.; m. Joseph Arthur Sartin, Dec. 27, 1929 (dec.); 1 dau., Dixie (Mrs. Donald O. Batschelett). Tchr. pub. schs., Henry County, Mo., 1924-32; owner, operator Sartin Bookkeeping & Tax Service, Clinton, Mo., 1935—; ofcl. weather observer, 1938-44; owner Comml. Loan & Credit Co. Pub. adminstr. Henry County, Mo., 1963—. Chmn. Henry County Easter Seal Campaign, 1962—. Mem. Ind. Accountants Soc. Mo., Jefferson Club Henry County, Nat. Soc. Pub. Accountants, Clinton C. of C. (dir.), Women's Fedn. of Democratic Clubs (dist. treas.). Baptist. Mem. Order Eastern Star. Club: Business and Professional Women's (pres.). Home: 112 E Tebo St Clinton MO 64735 Office: 209 S Washington St Clinton MO 64735

SASAK, MARIANNE IRENE, educator; b. Cleve., Oct. 2, 1950; d. Arpad Joseph and Helen Irene (Kiraly) Sasak; B.S., Bowling Green State U., 1972. Tchr. English, speech and drama North Olmsted (O.) Jr. High Sch., 1972—. Vol. worker Fairview Gen. Hosp., Cleve. Mem. Ohio, North Olmsted edn. assns., N.E. Ohio Tchrs. Assn. Mem. Hungarian Ref. Ch. of Am. Home: 25072 Carey Lane North Olmsted OH 44070 Office: North Olmsted Jr High Sch North Olmsted OH 44070

SASLOW, JULIA AMY IPCAR (MRS. GEORGE SASLOW), counseling psychologist; b. Bklyn., Oct. 21, 1906; d. Aaron Louis and Rose (Leichtman) Ipcar; B.A., Hunter Coll., 1926; M.Ed., Ore. State U., 1963; Ph.D., U. Ore., 1971; m. George Saslow, July 28, 1928; children—Michael George, Rondi, Steven, Marguerite. Counselor, instr., div. continuing edn. Counseling Center, Portland (Ore.) State U. 1963-66, counselor, instr. 1966-68, counselor, asst. prof. Counseling Center, 1968-74; psychologist VA Hosp., Sepulveda, Cal., 1974—. Mem. Am., Ore. personnel and guidance assns., Am., Northwest coll. personnel assns., Pi Lambda Theta. Home: 02403 SW Greenwood Rd Portland OR 97219

SASNETT, MARTENA TENNEY (MRS. J. RANDOPH SASNETT), author; b. Patchoque, L.I., N.Y., May 2, 1908; d. Henry Allen and Grace (Kelley) Tenney; grad. Bradford Coll., 1925, Acad. Speech Arts, 1927; student George Washington U., 1927-28, Paris, France, 1928-29; m. J. Randolph Sasnett, Sept. 23, 1943. Monodramatist, 1931-47; fgn. student admissions officer U. So. Cal., 1947-52; guest of Scandinavian Ministries of Edn. to study ednl. exchange, 1957. Recipient citation from Boston U. for work in internat. edn., 1958. Mem. Nat. Assn. Fgn. Student Affairs, Am. Assn. Collegiate Registrars and Admissions Officers. Author: Personalities, 1947; Educational Systems of the World, 1952; A Guide to the Admission and Placement of Foreign Students, 1957; Educational Systems of Africa, 1966; Graduate Study in the United States, 1966; Financial Planning for study in the United States: A Guide for Students from other Countries, 1967; Interpretations for Use in the Evaluation of Foreign Secondary Academic Credentials, 1971; co-author The Country Index, 1971. Editor: Fgn. Students Look at the U.S., 1960. Home: 2829 Miradero Dr Santa Barbara CA 93105

SASSER, DOROTHY PILLEY (MRS. JOHN T. SASSER), educator; b. Pantego, N.C., Aug. 15, 1926; d. Leonard R. and Mattie (Winfield) Pilley; B.S. in Secretarial Adminstrn., Woman's Coll. U. N.C., 1947; postgrad. U. Tenn., 1952; m. John T. Sasser, Dec. 30, 1951; children—Sandra, Sabrina. Co-owner, dir. Myrtle Beach (S.C.) Bus. Coll., 1952; owner Quality Mimeograph Shop, Whiteville, N.C., 1953—; tchr. pub. schs., Clarkton, N.C., 1953-57; tchr. Hallsboro (N.C.) Sch., 1957-59, Elizabethtown (N.C.) Sch., 1959, Alexander Graham Jr. High Sch., Fayetteville, N.C., 1960; chmn. bus. edn. dept. Terry Sanford Sr. High Sch., Fayetteville, 1961—. Mem. N.C. Edn. Assn., Bus. and Profl. Woman (corr. sec. 1958), Nat., So., N.C. bus. edn. assns., Delta Kappa Gamma. Democrat. Presbyn. Clubs: Evening Garden (sec. 1957-58), Executives, Merrymakers (Elizabethtown). Home: 906 Emeline Av Fayetteville NC 28303 Office: Fort Bragg Rd Fayetteville NC 28303

SASSOWER, DORIS LIPSON (MRS. GEORGE SASSOWER), lawyer; b. N.Y.C., Sept. 25, 1932; d. Abraham and Rose (Weitz) Lipson; B.A. summa cum laude, Bklyn. Coll., 1954; LL.B. cum laude (Florence Allen scholar), N.Y. U., 1955, J.D., 1968; m. George Sassower, Aug. 24, 1952; children—Elena Ruth, Carey Adina, Lizbeth Avery. Admitted to N.Y. bar, 1955, U.S. Supreme Ct. bar, 1961, U.S. Ct. Claims, 1961, U.S. Ct. Mil. Appeal, 1961, U.S. Customs Ct., 1969; partner firm Sassower & Sassower, N.Y.C., 1955—; law asst. chief justice Ct. of Appeals N.J., 1955-56. Co-organizer Nat. Conf. Profl. and Academic Women, 1970; founder, spl. cons. Profl. Women's Caucus, 1970; founder Profls. Organized for Women's Equal Rights, 1970; co-chmn. Nat. Conf. Lawyers and Social Workers. Bd. dirs. Inst. on Women's Wrongs, Internat. Inst. Women Studies. Named N.Y. Outstanding Young Woman of Year, Outstanding Young Women Am., 1968; recipient Distinguished Alumna award Bklyn. Coll., 1973. Mem. Internat., Am. (mem. steering com. of women's rights com. sect. on individual rights and responsibilities), N.Y. State (jud. selection com. 1972), N.Y. Women's (pres. 1968-69), Westchester (family law com.) bar assns., Bklyn. Coll. Alumni Assn. (pres. Lawyers Group 1963-65, spl. citation distinguished service 1965, bd. dirs. 1965-69), Am. Judicature Soc., Exec. Women (adv. bd., dir.), N.Y. U. Law Alumni Assn. (dir.), Assn. Bar City N.Y. (com. on sex and law, chmn. sub-com. on women in legal profession, sub-com. matrimonial law reform), Am. Arbitration Assn. (mem. nat. panel arbitrators), Am. Acad. Matrimonial Lawyers, N.Y. State Trial Lawyers Assn., Nat. Assn. Women Lawyers (ofcl. observer to UN 1969-70), Consular Law Soc., Nat. Council Women, Women United for UN, Women Equity Action League, Phi Beta Kappa (N.Y. alumnae chpt., pres. 1970-71), Iota Tau Tau. Contbr. articles profl. jours. Home: 30 Mildred Pkwy New Rochelle NY 10804 Office: Pan Am Bldg 200 Park Av New York City NY 10017

SATHER, VERLIE MELICENT, educator; b. Houston, Minn., May 21, 1908; d. Joseph Alfred and Amanda Mathilda (Stenberg) Sather; diploma Winona State Coll., 1926, B.S., 1942; M.A., U. Minn., 1952; postgrad. Cornell U., 1956, U. Chgo., 1962, St. Cloud State, 1963, U. Fla., 1965-66. Elementary tchr. Minn. pub. schs., Dover, 1927, Zumbro Falls, 1927-28, Caledonia, 1928-38, Blue Earth, 1938-42, Winona, 1942-56; exchange tchr. London, Eng., 1948-49; elementary reading cons. Winona, 1956-59; asst. prof. edn. Winona State Coll., 1959-74. Vol. nurses aide A.R.C., Winona, 1943-48. Named Soroptimist Woman of the Year, Winona, 1958. Mem. Internat., Minn. (pres. 1969-71) reading assns., Southeastern Minn. Reading Council (pres. 1962-63), Minn. Acad. of Reading, N.E.A., Minn. Edn. Assn., Interfaculty Assn., Assn. for Childhood Edn. (pres. 1952-54), Am. Assn. U. Women, Winona Bus. and Profl. Womens Club (pres. 1954-56), Winona Mental Health Assn., Delta Kappa Gamma (pres. 1972-74), Sons of Norway. Club: Minn. Exchange Tchrs. Home: 68 E Sarnia St Winona MN 55987

SATINOVER, TERRY KLIEMAN, lawyer; b. Chgo., Apr. 25, 1936; d. Charles D. and Mary (Klieman) Satinover; student Shimer Coll., 1952-54; B.A. cum laude, U. Chgo., 1955, J.D. magna cum laude (Weymouth Kirkland scholar), 1958; m. Richard Rees Fager, June 15, 1958 (div. June 1970); children—Sharon, Ruth, Elizabeth, Michael. Admitted to Ill. bar, 1970; practice in Chicago, 1971—; asso. Pope, Ballard, Shepard & Fowle, Chgo., 1971—. Bd. dirs. Charles Satinover Fund. Mem. Am., Ill., Chgo. (sec. exec. and real taxation subcoms. of real property com. 1972-73, mem. exec. subcom. 1973-74, co-chmn. newsletter) bar assns., Order of Coif, Phi Beta Kappa. Home: 5125 S Cornell St Chicago IL 60615 Office: 69 W Washington St Suite 3200 Chicago IL 60602

SATMARY, HELEN JOANNE (MRS. PETER CHARLES SATMARY), realtor; b. Washington, Oct. 22, 1932; d. Earl Clyde and Lena Marie (Polvinale) Coppock; student Am. U., 1952, George Washington U., 1955-56, Grad. Realtors Inst., 1971-72, Fairfield U., 1969; m. Peter Charles Satmary, Oct. 5, 1957; children—Pamela, Stephen, Mark, Karen, Vincent. Sec., Commerce Dept., analytical asst. Dept. Agr., Washington, 1952-57; sales mgr. Fairfield County Real Estate (Conn.), 1966-68; owner, realtor Joanne Satmary Real Estate, Fairfield, 1969—. Vol., Providence Hosp., Washington, 1951-57. Mem. Fairfield Bd. Realtors (edn. chmn. 1971, chmn. grievance com. 1973, chmn. round table 1973, dir. 1974—), Nat. Assn. Real Estate Bds., Bridgeport Bd. Realtors, Nat. Assn. Farm and Land Brokers, Conn. Assn. Real Estate Bds., Nat. Inst. Real Estate Brokers. Home: 14 Morning Glory Dr Easton CT 06612 Office: 2069 Black Rock Turnpike Fairfield CT 06430

SATTEN, NORMA FRANCES (MRS. JOSEPH SATTEN), health planner; b. Bklyn., Nov. 7, 1922; d. Herman and Belle (Lubart) Goldstein; B.A. magna cum laude, Bklyn. Coll., 1943; M. City Planning, Mass. Inst. Tech., 1945; m. Joseph Satten, June 17, 1945; children—Neal Richard, Deborah Lee, Sara Lynn. Research asso. Urban Renewal Project, The Menninger Found., Topeka, 1963-65; planner State Planning Div., Topeka, 1966-68; dir. Kan. Comprehensive Health Planning Program, Kan. Bd. of Health, Topeka, 1968-71; asso. dir. Bay Area Comprehensive Health Planning Council, San Francisco, 1971-72; exec. dir. Alameda County Comprehensive Health Planning Council, Oakland, Cal., 1972—. Mem. steering com. Topeka Inst. of Urban Affairs, Washburn U., 1966-71; mem. regional adv. com. Sch. of Health, U. Okla. Med. Center, 1969-71. Mem. Am. Inst. Planners (chpt. sec. 1959-60), Am. Soc. Planning Ofcls., Am. Pub. Health Assn. (vice chmn. community health planning sect. 1973-74), Am. Acad. Comprehensive Health Planning (sec. 1970-71 recipient achievement award 1971), League of Women Voters (pres. 1961-63, sec. state bd. 1963-64). Home: 2370 Broadway San Francisco CA 94115 Office: 499 5th St Oakland CA 94607

SATTER, RUTH LYTTLE (MRS. ROBERT SATTER), plant physiologist; b. N.Y.C., Mar. 8, 1923; d. George and Lilian (Siegel) Lyttle; A.B., Barnard Coll., 1944; Ph.D., U. Conn., 1968; m. Robert Satter, Nov. 27, 1946; children—Richard, Mimi, Shoshana, Jane. Fellow, biology dept. Yale U., New Haven, 1968-72, research asso. biology dept., 1972—. Mem. Am. Soc. Plant Physiologists, Am. Bot. Soc., Am. Inst. Biol. Scis., A.A.A.S., Sigma Xi. Contbr. articles to profl. jours. Home: 75 Brookside Rd Newington CT 06111 Office: 912 Kline Biology Tower Yale U New Haven CT 06520

SATTERFIELD, DONNA OLSEN (MRS. JOHN CREIGHTON SATTERFIELD, JR.), psychologist; b. Wis., Nov. 25, 1933; d. Marvin N. and Marjorie M. (Wolfe) Olsen; B.A., Swarthmore Coll., 1956; Ph.D., U. Ariz., 1966; m. John Creighton Satterfield, Jr., Jan. 3, 1964. Community mental health psychologist Mental Health Services Los Angeles County Dept. Health Services, 1967—; clin. asso. dept. psychiatry U. So. Cal. Med. Sch., 1971—, research asso. dept. continuing edn., 1970-72: clin. asso. prof. Grad. Sch. Psychology Fuller Theol. Sem., 1972-73; cons. Cal. Sch. Profl. Psychology, Los Angeles, 1972-73; instr. Sch. Continuing Edn., Pepperdine U., 1972—. Treas., Psychol. Center Los Angeles, 1973-74. Mem. Am., Western, Cal. (vice chmn. div. 4) psychol. assns., Los Angeles County Psychol. Assn., Psychologists in Pub. Service Los Angeles County (rep. to bd. dirs. Psychol. Center 1972—). Office: 12148 Victory Blvd North Hollywood CA 91606

SATTLEY, HELEN ROWLAND, sch. adminstr.; b. St. Paul; d. Robert Carlos and Minnie (Rowland) Sattley; B.A., Northwestern U., 1933, M.A. in Psychology, 1934; B.S. in Library Sci., Western Res. U., 1936. Librarian Haven Sch., Evanston, Ill., 1936-44; asst. prof. Library Sch., Columbia U., N.Y.C., 1947-50; asso. prof. Library Sch., Western Res. U., Cleve., 1950-53; dir. sch. libraries Bd. Edn. N.Y.C., 1953—. Mem. various adv. coms. N.Y. State Dept. Edn., 1953—; cons. children's books on India to Asia Soc., 1965; cons. Asia Found., Taiwan and Japan, 1966; cons. H.W. Wilson Co., N.Y.C., 1969-71; mem. nat. adv. com. Automated Instructional Materials System project Los Angeles pub. schs., 1969—. Mem. English Speaking Union, Common Cause, Delmetsch Found. Recipient Librarians award Dodd, Mead Co., 1958, Child Study award, 1958. Mem. Am. (chmn. Newbery-Caldecott awards com. 1963-64; pres. children's services divs. 1964-65), N.Y. library assns., N.Y. Library Club (mem. bd. dirs. 1957-60; chmn. scholarship com. 1960-61), Authors Guild, Am. Assn. Sch. Librarians, Woman's Nat. Book Assn., L.I. Hist. Soc., Council Suprs and Adminstrs. N.Y.C. Author: Young Barbarians, 1947; Shadow Across the Campus, 1957; Day the Empire State Went Visiting, 1958; Annie, 1961. Editor: Children's Books about Foreign Countries, 1949; cons. editor Have you Seen a Comet?, 1971. Contbr. profl. jours. Home: 433 W 21st St New York City NY 10011 Office: 110 Livingston St Brooklyn NY 11201

SAUCIER, WILHEMINE EVELYN (MRS. DAVID OWEN SAUCIER), recreational equipment mfg. co. exec.; b. Mankato, Minn., July 31, 1935; d. Durant Alfred and Dorothy Evelyn (Black) LaBrie; student U. Minn., 1962-65; m. Richard Holzinger, 1954 (div. 1963); children—Stephen, Renee, Todd, John; m. 2d David Owen Saucier, Apr. 11, 1970. With Mpls. Honeywell Co., 1953, Pillsbury Co., 1955, Gen. Mills, Inc., 1956, U.S. Air Conditioning Co., 1957, Corrick & Dietrich, Mpls., 1958; with urban planning firm Nason, Wehrman, Knight and Chapman, Mpls., 1962; with Medtronic, Inc., Mpls., 1965-72, v.p., 1973—. Mem. Pub. Relations Soc. Am., Assn. Advancement Med. Instrumentation, Minn., Am. water ski assns., Am. Mgmt. Soc. Club: Towers (dir.) (Mpls.). Home: 4647 Ellerdale Rd Minnetonka MN 55343 Office: 12985 Pioneer Trail Minneapolis MN 55343

SAUER, DOROTHY CATHERINE (MRS. CLIFFORD W. GARDNER), lawyer; b. Dubuque, Ia., Mar. 14, 1926; d. Clarence Joseph and Rose Margaret (Casutt) Sauer; student Clarke Coll., 1943-44; m. Clifford W. Gardner, May 7, 1957 (dec. Dec. 1958); 1 son, Clifford W. Admitted to Ia. bar, 1952, since practiced in Dubuque. Pres. Dubuque County Young Republican Club, 1953-54. Bd. dirs. Dubuque Safety Council, 1954—, Dubuque County Tb Assn., 1954-56, Dubuque County Conservation Soc., 1953-56. Mem. Am., Ia., Minn., Dubuque County, Ramsey County bar assns., Nat. Assn. Women Lawyers, Dubuque Bus. and Profl. Women's Club (pres. 1953). Home: Route 1 Peosta IA 52068 Office: 405 Fischer Bldg Dubuque IA 52001

SAUER, MARIE FRANCES, journalist; b. Elizabeth, N.J., Dec. 16, 1908; d. Alfred F. and Lucy (Blatz) Sauer; B.S., Sch. Journalism, Columbia, 1935. Sunday editor The Washington Post, 1936-42, women's editor, 1946-69. Served from lt. (j.g.) to lt. USNR, 1942-45. Mem. Columbia U. Alumni Assn., Friends of the Kennedy Center, Friends of Music at Tanglewood, Soc. Four Arts, English Speaking Union, Women in Communications, Smithsonian Assos., Common Cause. Clubs: Washington Press (pres. 1952-53), Am. Newspaper Women's. Home: 437 Chilean Av Palm Beach FL 33480 also 520 Westfield Av Elizabeth NJ 07208

SAUERTEIG, SUSAN ARLINE, marketing exec.; b. N.Y.C., Sept. 12, 1941; d. Harry C. and Ida June (Lansky) Sauerteig; B.A., Cornell U., 1963. Promotion asst. WCBS-TV, N.Y.C., 1963-64; asst. to pres. Humanities Press, N.Y.C., 1964-66; promotion and advt. mgr. jr. book div. McGraw-Hill Book Co., N.Y.C., 1966-70; dir. marketing services Franklin Watts Inc., N.Y.C., 1970—. Mem. Pub.'s Library Promotion Group, Pub.'s Ad Club, Children's Book Council, A.L.A. Home: 225 E 70th St New York City NY 10021 Office: 730 Fifth Av New York City NY 10019

SAUL, ANNE MARIE (MRS. CECIL R. FOISTER), journalist; b. Beaconsfield, England, June 8, 1944 (came to U.S. 1952, naturalized 1967); d. John Edward and Mildred Mary (Forde) Saul; student Lynchburg Coll., 1962-64; B.S., U. Fla., 1966; m. Cecil R. Foister, Mar. 16, 1968; 1 son, Quentin. Edn. writer, reporter Pensacola (Fla.) News Journal, 1966-68; reporter Orlando (Fla.) Sentinel, 1969; edn. writer, reporter Today, newspaper, Cocoa, Fla., 1969-74, asst. editorial page editor, 1974—. Co winner Frank Tripp Meml. award Gannett Newspapers, 1971; 1st pl. award spot news reporting Nat. Council Advancement Edn. Writing, 1972; Fla. Sch. Bell award, 1973. Mem. Nat. Assn. Edn. Writers. Democrat. Home: 3418 Phillip Lane Cocoa FL 32922 Office: Today 308 Forrest Av Cocoa FL 32922

SAUL, MARION JEAN, media specialist; b. East Greenville, Pa., Mar. 30, 1926; d. John Eugene and Carrie Elizabeth (Treichler) Graber; B.S. in Edn., Kutztown (Pa.) State Coll., 1947; m. Carlton Joseph Saul, July 5, 1950. Asst. librarian Muhlenberg Coll., Allentown, Pa., 1947-53; media specialist Parkland Sr. High Sch., Orefield, Pa., 1953—. Mem. Am., Pa. (chmn. children's young people's and sch. librarians div. 1973-74) library assns., Pa. Sch. Librarians Assn. (membership chmn. 1965—), Am. Assn. Supervision and Curriculum Devel. (panel mem.), Pa. Learning Resources Assn., N.E.A., Pa. Ednl. Assn., Greater Lehigh Valley Library Council, Soroptimists. Home: 38 S 14th St Allentown PA 18102 Office: Orefield PA 18069

SAULNIER, LEDA M., educator; b. Sully, Que., Can., July 6, 1918; d. Napoleon and Vitaline (Gauthier) Saulnier; M.A. in English, Montreal U., 1958; M.A. in Theology, Providence Coll., 1962; Specialist certificate Tchr. Edn. (fellow 1967-68), So. Ill. U., 1968; Ed.D. in Human Relations, U. Mass., 1972. Tchr. English pvt. high schs., Montreal, 1940-55, Manchester, N.H., 1955-64; prin. St. Anthony High Sch., New Bedford, Mass., 1964-65; prof. English, Notre Dame Coll., Manchester, 1965-67; curriculum coordinator Manchester Schs., 1967-68; curriculum coordinator New Hartford Schs., 1972, group facilitator, 1969-73; prof. continuing edn. U. Mass., 1973; prof. psychology Adult Edn. Center, St. Petersburg (Fla.) Jr. Coll., 1974—. Mem., prof. psychology Fla. Humanistic Inst., 1975—. Author: (with Teresa Simard) Personal Growth and Interpersonal Relations, 1973. Home: 1001 Ulmerton Rd Apt 291 Largo FL 33540

SAULS, DIANE ANITA DAHL (MRS. ROGER W. SAULS), physician; b. Chippewa Falls, Wis., Apr. 29, 1932; d. Ralph B. and Alice (Kennedy) Dahl; B.S., U. Wis., 1953, M.D., 1956; m. Roger W. Sauls, Aug. 25, 1957; children—Emily Anne, Wayne Gordon. Intern Charles T. Miller Hosp. St. Paul, 1956-57; gen. practice medicine, Mahtomedi, Minn., 1957-62; physcian No. Colony and Tng. Sch., Chippewa Falls, 1963—. Bd. dirs. Chippewa County (Wis.) Mental Health Clinic, Chippewa Falls, 1964-70, chmn. recruitment com.; exec. bd. sec. St. Joseph Hosp., Chippewa Falls, 1968-72; pres. Chippewa County Blood Bank, 1971-73; mem. Chippewa County Welfare Adv. Bd., chmn., 1972—; profl. edn. chmn. Chippewa unit Am. Cancer Soc., 1971-73; med. adviser Indian Waters council Girl Scouts U.S. Mem. A.M.A., Am. Acad. Gen. Practice, Am. Assn. U. Women (study group leader 1968-69), Wis., Chippewa County (pres. 1969-70) med. socs. Lutheran (sec. ch. council 1970-73). Home: 707 W Haven Rd Chippewa Falls WI 51729 Office: Box 340 Chippewa Falls WI 51729

SAUNDERS, BEATRICE NAIR (MRS. DERO AMES SAUNDERS), editor, assn. exec.; b. New Britain, Conn., Dec. 26, 1915; d. Frank and Sophie (Adler) Nair; B.A., Smith Coll., 1936; m. Dero Ames Saunders, May 23, 1936; children—David Nair, Richard Ames. Tchr. pub. schs., New Britain, 1936; editorial asst. Cordon Co., N.Y.C., 1937-39, Family Welfare Assn. Am., N.Y.C., 1939-42; supr. editorial div. publs. div. A.R.C., Washington, 1943-46; free-lance editor various publs. N.Y.C., 1946-50; editor-in-chief, publs. dept. Girl Scouts U.S.A., N.Y.C., 1950-55; dir. publs. dept., editor Social Work, Nat. Assn. Social Workers, N.Y.C., 1955—. Vol., A.R.C., Freeport, L.I., 1946-47, Child Care Center, Freeport, 1946-47; chmn. parents assn. Downtown Community Sch., 1948-50; chmn. 22d-21st St. Community Council, 1954-58, 62-63; chmn. com. on existing housing Chelsea Community Council, 1957-60; vice chmn. Chelsea Com. for Neighborhood Devel., 1960-63, chmn., 1963-65. Club:

Advertising. Home: 446 W 22d St New York City NY 10011 Office: Nat Assn Social Workers 2 Park Av New York City NY 10016

SAUNDERS, BETTY HUEY (MRS. AULUS WARD SAUNDERS), writer; b. St. Louis, July 11, 1909; d. Leslie and Kathryn Artimissia (Hyer) Huey; A.A., Stephens Coll., 1929; B.J., U. Mo., 1931; m. Aulus Ward Saunders, June 12, 1931; children—Alan Ward, Susan Beth (Mrs. William Harry Cook). Staff writer, corr., columnist, advt. salesman News-Champion, St. Louis County, Mo., 1937; playwright, one-act plays and radio plays, 1930—; free-lance writer with works pub. in newspapers and mags., including Reader's Digest, New Yorker, St. Louis Post-Dispatch, Wall St. Jour., People, numerous others. Pub. relations chmn., playwright, v.p. Oswego (N.Y.) Players, 1941-69; cons. pub. relations to N.Y. community theatres, 1949-69; lit. critic Nat. Writers Club, 1964—; playwrighting cons. Oswego (N.Y.) Chancel Theatre Group, 1973—. Formerly mem. exec. bd., chmn. pub. relations Oswego County chpt. A.R.C., also Community Chest. Recipient Poetry and short story writing prizes Nat. Writers Club Contests, 1959, 64; prize N.Y. State Drummond One-Act Playwrighting Contest, 1956. Mem. Bus. and Profl. Women's Club. Conglist. Editor The Grail, weekly religious mag., 1928-30. Editor-agt.-collaborator (with Dan Saunders) non-fiction books on Alaska. Address: 165 E 3d St Oswego NY 13126

SAUNDERS, ELISE MCABEE (MRS. J. EVERITT SAUNDERS), materials engr.; b. N.Y.C., July 28, 1920; d. Daniel H. and Ruth (Edgecombe) McAbee; student Alfred U., 1936-38; B.S. in Chem. Engring., U. W.Va., 1942; m. J. Everitt Saunders, June 30, 1973. Metallurgist, Wright Aero. Corp., Cin., 1942-45; chemist Kolmar Labs., Elenville, N.Y., 1946-47; test supr. Casein Co. Am., Bainbridge, N.Y., 1947-48; chemist Polah's Frutal Works, Middletown, N.Y., 1948-49; materials engr. Picatinny Arsenal, Dover, N.J., 1950—. Recipient Research and Devel. Achievement award Dept. Army, 1965, Research and Devel. Achievement award Picatinny Arsenal, 1964, 65. Mem. Sci. Research Soc. Am., Am. Soc. for Testing and Materials, Internat. Platform Assn., Soc. Rheology, A.A.A.S. Club: Lake Mohawk Country. Home: Box 110 RD 3 Wharton NJ 07885 Office: Picatinny Arsenal Dover NJ 07801

SAUNDERS, MARJORIE INEZ, univ. ofcl.; b. Dallas, Apr. 25, 1916; d. Claude Whitfield and Cordelia (Croxdale) S.; LL.B., Jefferson U., Dallas, 1934; student So. Meth. U., 1943-44; grad. Dallas Acad. Speech and Drama, 1946. Admitted to Tex. bar, 1934; practiced law, Dallas, 1935-45; with Baylor U. Med. Center, Dallas, 1945—, dir. pub. relations, 1952—. Mem. vol. service adv. com. Council Social Agys. Dallas, 1958-69; mem. pub. relations com. Dallas unit Am. Cancer Soc., 1962-68. Recipient Silver Anvil award. Mem. Am. Assn. Blood Banks (originator, sec. 1947-57, mem. legal and ins. com. 1953, com. on constn. and by-laws 1953, nat. clearinghouse com. 1953, subcom. for adminstrv. manual 1955, chmn. pub. relations com. 1955-57, John Elliott award 1957), Tex. Assn. Blood Banks (organizer, sec. 1949-57, mem. clearinghouse com. 1954-58, publs. com. 1954, constn. and by-laws com. 1955-58, editorial and publs. com. 1955-58, liaison com. to Tex. Hosp. Assn. 1955-57), Baptist Pub. Relations Assn. (membership v.p. So. Bapt. Conv. 1956-58, 73-74, pres. Tex. chpt. 1957-58, mem. program com. 1959), Bapt. Pub. Relations Assn. Tex. (program v.p. 1961, program chmn. 1962, chmn. com. on constn. and by-laws 1962-63, editor newsletter 1963, sec.-treas. 1969-70), So. Bapt. Pub. Relations Assn. (program v.p. 1969-70), Bapt. Pub. Relations Assn. (membership v.p. 1973-74), Nat. Assn. Women Lawyers, Nat. Religious Pub. Relations Council (gov., awards com. 1970), Am. Soc. Hosp. Pub. Relations Dirs. (charter, dir. 1967-73, pres. 1970-71), Am. Hosp. Assn. (com. on aux. community relations information programs 1964, intra-deptl. com. on pub. information 1964), Dallas Hosp. Council (chmn. pub. relations com. 1954-56, 62, 65-66, 72-73), Dallas Bar Assn. Author numerous publs. in field. Address: 6208 Malcolm Dr Dallas TX 75214

SAUNDERS, RUBIE AGNES, editor; b. N.Y.C., Jan. 31, 1929; d. Walter St. Clair and Rubie Gwendolyn (Ford) Saunders; B.A., Hunter Coll. City U. N.Y., 1950. Editorial sec. Parents Mag. Enterprises, Inc., N.Y.C., 1950-51, editorial asst., 1951-53, asst. editor, 1953-54, mng. editor, 1955-60, editor, 1960-67, editorial dir., 1967—. Bd. dirs. Assn. Neighbors and Friends Hunter Coll. Named to Hunter Coll. Hall Fame, 1972. Author: Calling All Girls Party Book, 1966; Marilyn Morgan, R.N., 1969; Marilyn Morgan's Triumph, 1970; Concise Guide to Baby Sitting, 1972; Concise Guide to Smart Shopping and Consumerism, 1973; others. Home: 26 Glenwood Av New Rochelle NY 10801 Office: 52 Vanderbilt Av New York City NY 10017

SAUNDERS, SALLY LOVE, poet; b. Bryn Mawr, Pa., Jan. 15, 1940; d. Lawrence and Dorothy (Love) Saunders; student Sophia U., Tokyo, Japan, 1963, U. Pa., Columbia; B.S., George Williams Coll., 1965. Poet, 1946—, poems pub. in periodicals including Times Lit. Supplement, N.Y. Times, Christian Sci. Monitor; social group worker U.S. Govt. War on Poverty, 1966—. Group worker Margaret Fuller Settlement House, 1959-61, U. Settlement House, 1961-63; social group worker Good Shepherd, Navajo Mission, 1963; poetry therapist Pa. Inst., Phila., Haverford State Inst. Mem. Acad. Am. Poets, Nat. Pen Women Club, Am. Poetry League, Nat. Fedn. State Poetry Soc., Poetry Soc. N.H., Pa. Poetry Soc., Poetry Therapy Assn. Am. Clubs: Nat. Writers', Pen and Brush. Home: 802 Lombard St Philadelphia PA 19147

SAUSEDO, ANN ELIZABETH, librarian; b. Douglas, Ariz., Nov. 19, 1929; d. Eugene Ephraim and Bertha Evelyn (Kimpton) Bertram; ed. Cal. schs.; m. Richard Edward Sausedo, July 22, 1952 (div. 1966); 1 dau., Robin Marie. Asst. librarian Stockton (Cal.) Record, 1948-51, head librarian, 1955-67; librarian Washington Star News, 1967—; stewardess Cal. Central Airlines, 1951. Mem. Spl. Libraries Assn., Am. Bus. Women's Assn. Address: 225 Virginia Av SE Washington DC 20003

SAUVAGEOT, LUDEL BODEN (MRS. J. PAUL SAUVAGEOT), hosp. exec.; b. New Marshfield, O., Feb. 8, 1906; d. James H. and Cleo (Withers) Boden; A.B., Ohio U., 1927; m. J. Paul Sauvageot, Dec. 24, 1931; children—Jean Andre, Jules. Dir. pub. relations Akron (O.) Gen. Hosp., 1946-57, dir. pub. relations, 1967—; exec. sec. Internat. Council Indsl. Editors, Akron, 1957-60. Guest lectr. Ohio U., Athens, 1955-69; contbg. editor MD's Wife, jour. of Am. Med. Aux., 1966-70, editor, 1970—. Bd. dirs. United Fund, Cancer Soc., Summit County, O., Goodwill Industries, 1950-62, Akron Area council, Girl Scouts U.S.A., 1960-61, 69-71; adv. bd. Hawthornden State Hosp. Recipient Malcolm T. MacEachern plaque for outstanding pub. relations program Hosp. Mgmt. Mag., 1954, 55, 56, Bronze plaque for contbn. to indsl. editing House Mag. Inst., 1958; named Woman of Achievement, Akron Beacon Jour., 1969. Mem. Pub. Relations Soc. Am. (sec. Akron chpt. 1972, 73), Ohio Med. Assn. Aux. (pres., 1967-68), Women's Aux. A.M.A. (dir. 1968-71), Ohio Hosp. Assn. (pub. relations com., Distinguished Service award 1973), Women in Communications (pres. 1971-73), Delta Kappa Gamma (hon.). Club: Akron Press (sec. 1972—). Editor: MD's Wife, 1970—. Home: 2443 Ridgewood Rd Akron OH 44313 Office: 400 Wabash Av Akron OH 44307

SAUVIGNE, CECILE DEVENISH (MRS. GEORGE E. SAUVIGNE), television exec.; b. Asheville, N.C., Oct. 4, 1921; d. Cecil Francis and Allye Berry (Campbell) Devenish; student Asheville-Biltmore Jr. Coll., 1938-39; certificate U. N.C., 1940; m. George E. Sauvigne, Oct. 12, 1946; children—Diana (Mrs. Arthur Donly Chase), Patricia (Mrs. Larry Barnett), George Alan, Cecile, John Doherty. Office mgr. Asheville (N.C.) Willys Co., 1940-41; pvt. sec. to officer in charge constrn., U.S. Naval Air Sta., Jacksonville, Fla., 1941-44; pvt. exec. sec., office mgr. Santa Fe R.R., Dallas, 1945-46; account exec., air personality WENK Radio, Union City, Tenn., 1964-67; women's dir. WGBS Radio, Miami, Fla., 1968-72; banquet cons. David William Hotel, Coral Gables, Fla., 1972; pub. service dir., pub. relations dir. WTVJ-TV Channel 4, Miami, 1972—. Mem. communications com. A.R.C., Miami, 1972—; mem. Pres.'s Com. on Total Employment, Miami, 1973—; mem. Citizens Fire Prevention Com., 1973, Banquet Mgrs. Guild, 1973. Bd. dirs. Dade County div. Arthritis Found., v.p. in charge publicity; bd. dirs. Heart Assn. Greater Miami, 1970—, chmn. assn. luncheon, 1970. Mem. Am. Women in Radio and TV, Women in Communications, Council for Continuing Edn. Women, Coral Gables (mem. city beautiful com. 1973—), Miami (mem. mass transp. com. 1973—) chambers commerce. Episcopalian (pres. ch. women 1968-69). Home: 6065 Rolling Rd Dr Miami FL 33156 Office: 316 N Miami Av Miami FL 33128

SAVAGE, EDITH CHANDLER JONES (MRS. PHILLIP H. SAVAGE), educator, writer, lectr.; b. Lovell, Wyo., Apr. 25, 1920; d. Archie Israel and Edith (Neff) Jones; B.S. in Edn., U. Mo., 1942; M.S. in Edn., Tex. Coll. Arts and Industries, 1954; Ed.D., U. Colo., 1960; m. Phillip H. Savage, Apr. 27, 1943; children—Phillip H., Leslie Anne (Mrs. Francis William Redmon), Alan Lowell. Tchr. rural schs. Mo., 1936-42; music specialist, Corpus Christi, Tex., 1942-44; prin. Sch. for Mil. Dependents, Saipan, P.I., 1947-52; tchr. classroom music Corpus Christi Schs., 1952-54; music specialist Guantanamo Bay, Cuba, 1954-57; Denver Schs., 1957-60; prof. music edn. San Diego State Coll., 1960—. Cons. music curricula various sch. dists.; clinician choral festivals. Recipient Distinguished Teaching award, 1969-70. Mem. Music Educators Nat. Conf. (nat. chmn. student memberships 1972-74), San Diego County Music Educators Assn. (pres.), Cal. Music Educators Assn., Coll. Music Soc., Sigma Alpha Iota. Author: (with Lyman C. Hurd III) First Experiences in Music, 1966; (with Josephine D. Cunningham) Exploring the Fine Arts, 1966; (with A. Oren Gould) Teaching Children to Sing, 1972; (with Mary Val Marsh and Carroll Rinehart) The Spectrum of Music, 1974. Contbr. articles to profl. publs. Home: 4691 59th St San Diego CA 92115

SAVAGE, GLADIOLA HAIRSTON (MRS. GEORGE HENRY SAVAGE), educator; b. Pittsylvania County, Va., July 9, 1940; d. Benjamin Franklin and Essie (Walton) Hairston; B.S., Va. State Coll., 1963; postgrad., Morgan State Coll., 1966; Ed.M., Coppin State Coll., 1971, postgrad., 1971—; m. George Henry Savage, Dec. 23, 1965. Phys. edn. tchr. Balt. City Pub. Sch., Hampstead Hill Jr. High, 1963-65; elementary tchr. Anne Arundel County Pub. Sch., Friendship, Md., 1965-67; elementary spl. edn. tchr. Anne Arundel County Pub. Sch., Marley Glen Sch., Glen Burnie, Md., 1967—, adminstrv. intern, 1971—. Mem. Nat., Md. tchrs. assns., Tchrs. Assn. of Anne Arundel County (alternate del. 1971-72), Agrl. Stabilization and Conservation Service. Baptist (chmn. deaconess bd. 1969—). Faculty editor P.T.A. Newsletter, 1972—. Home: 1005 Wicklow Rd Baltimore MD 21229 Office: Marley Glen Sch Scott Av Glen Burnie MD 21061

SAVAGE, GRETCHEN SUSAN (MRS. TERRY R. SAVAGE), cons. library and information systems; b. Seattle, Jan. 15, 1934; d. Lester Walter and Gretchen Marian (Percy) Wood; A.B., U. Cal. at Los Angeles, 1955; m. Terry R. Savage, Sept. 26, 1964; children—Terry C., Christopher W., Richard T. Tchr., Franklin Sch., Santa Monica, Cal., 1955-57; head librarian and library supr. McDonnell Douglas, missiles and space systems engr., Santa Monica, 1957-63; mgr. publ. systems Documentation, Inc., Bethesda, Md., 1963-64; cons. information systems design and devel., Washington and Santa Barbara, Cal., 1964—; librarian Goleta (Cal.) Union Schs., 1970-73. Mem. Am. Soc. Information Sci., Spl. Libraries Assn., Cal. Assn. Sch. Librarians, Am. Chem. Soc., Am. Assn. Univ. Women, Phi Beta Kappa, Pi Lambda Theta, Delta Phi Upsilon, Alpha Phi. Contbr. articles on information systems to profl. publs. Address: 30000 Cachan Pl Palos Verdes Peninsula CA 90274

SAVAGE, MARGARET AVIS (MRS. ISAAC DOUGLAS SAVAGE), ret. nurse, civic worker; b. Flint, Mich., Dec. 2, 1909; d. Walter Ralph and Myrtle (Gould) Conquest; grad. Genesee County Normal Sch., 1931; R.N., Hurley Hosp. Sch. Nursing, Flint, 1935; B.S. in Pub. Health Nursing, U. Mich., 1959, postgrad., 1960—; M.Ed., Eastern Mich. U., 1966; m. Isaac Douglas Savage, Sept. 6, 1936 (dec.); children—David Douglas, Thomas Michael. Clk., Grand Blanc (Mich.) Agrl. High Sch., 1924-28; operator Mich. Bell Telephone Co., Flint, 1928-30; clk. Grand Blanc P.O., 1930-31; operating room staff nurse Hurley Hosp., 1935-36; operating room and emergency room nurse, 1944-45; sch. nurse Flint Pub. Schs., 1936-40; staff nurse Flint Health Dept., 1940-44; relief nurse obstetrics St. Joseph Hosp., 1945-50, head nurse, operating room and emergency service, 1953-54, clin., surg. supr., 1955-57; instr. mothercraft classes Genesee County Clara Elizabeth Fund for Maternal and Child Health, Flint, 1950-51, 60-61; staff nurse U. Mich. Hosp., Ann Arbor, 1950-51; obstetric nurse Goodrich (Mich.) Gen. Hosp., 1952-53; sch. nurse, counselor Beecher Jr. High Sch. and Elementary Schs., Flint, 1958-59; tchr. mentally handicapped children Flint Community Schs., 1960-61; nurse counselor McKinley Jr. High and Elementary Sch., Flint, 1961-71. Instr. first aid, home nursing A.R.C., Flint, 1942-44, blood bank nurse, 1937-54; chmn. community nursing com. Fenton (Mich.) Community Council, 1946-51; tchr. cultural refinement in relief soc.; sec. Sunday sessions Relief Soc.; dir. presch. storyhour Otter Lake, Mich.; rec. sec. Lapeer County Gen. Hosp. Aux., co-dir. Marathon Unit. Recipient award for outstanding community service Fenton Community Council, 1946; Mich. Pub. Health fellow, 1958-59. Mem. Am., Mich. (sec. pub. health nursing sect. 1957-60, chmn. sch. nurse br. 1967—), Flint Dist. (treas. 1936-38, chmn. 1966-68), nurses assns., Nat., Mich. (regional co-chmn. health, phys. edn. and recreation group 1963), Flint (mem. personnel and pub. relations com. 1968—) edn. assns., Mich. Sch. Nurses Assn., Mich., Flint (chmn. nominating com. 1960-61) councils for exceptional children, Mich. Sch. Health Assn., U. Mich. Alumni Assn., Flint Goodwill Aux. Women's Soc. Christian Service, Flint Genealogy Soc., Ret. Genesee County Sch. Employees Soc., Lakeville Area United Ch. Women, Otter Lake Lit. Club (pres. 1974). Mem. Ch. Jesus Christ Latter Day Saints (mem. choir). Mem. Order Eastern Star. Home: 9474 E Lake Road Otisville MI 48463

SAVAGE, MARY ELIZABETH, educator; b. Yonkers, N.Y., June 4, 1920; d. Claude and Mary Josephine (Tunston) Savage; B.S., N.Y. U., 1942, M.A., 1946; Ph.D. magna cum laude, Fordham U., 1956; postgrad. St. John's U., St. Michael's Coll. Tchr. math. Ridgefield (N.J.) Jr. High Sch., 1942-49, Longfellow Jr. High Sch., Yonkers, 1949-56; teacher Eastchester (N.Y.) Sch. Dist., 1956—, coordinator math. program, K-12, 1968—. Guest lectr. Good Council Coll., White Plains, N.Y., 1968; faculty U. Hartford (Conn.), 1968-69, New Rochelle (N.Y.) Coll., 1973-74. Troop leader Girl Scouts Am., 1940-50; active fund raising campaigns Mt. Vernon (N.Y.) Hosp. Mem. N.E.A., N.Y. State, Westchester County, Eastchester tchrs. assns., Westchester Suprs. Assn., Kappa Delta Pi. Home: 114 Middleton Place Bronxville NY 10708 Office: Eastchester Sch Dist Stewart Place Eastchester NY 10707

SAVAGE, MILDRED (MRS. BERNARD L. SAVAGE), author; b. New London, Conn.; d. Ezekiel and Sadie (Fabricant) Spitz; B.A., Wellesley Coll.; spl. student Yale Law Sch., 1971-72; m. Bernard L. Savage; children—Susan Jean, Michael Donald. Lectr. writer's confs. Pa. State Tchrs. Coll., 1960, Pa. State U., 1961; adj. asso. prof. law John Jay Coll., N.Y.C., 1970-71. Recipient Edgar Allan Poe award, 1970. Author: Parrish, 1958 (made into movie 1960); In Vivo, 1964; A Great Fall, 1970. Address: 235 Harland Rd Norwich CT 06360

SAVAGE, VICTORIA ANNE HANSON (MRS. ROBERT BRUCE SAVAGE), artist; b. Spokane, Wash.; d. John Martin and Cecilia (Anderson) Hanson; B.A., Wash. State U., 1932; m. Robert Bruce Savage, June 23, 1934; children—Kathleen (Mrs. L. Wayne Wilson), John Savage. Exhibited in one man shows at Charles & Emma Frye Art Mus., Seattle, 1964, 74, Kinorn Gallery, Seattle, 1961, Artists' Sales Gallery, Seattle, 1961—, Llub's Gallery, Edmonds, Wash., 1963, 67, Freemanson Gallery, Issaquah, Wash., 1962, 63, 64, 66, 67, 68, 69, 70, 71, 72, White Whale Gallery of Gig Harbor, 1969, Burien (Wash.) Art Gallery, 1972, Sidney Galleries, Port Orchard, Wash., 1972, Little Gallery, Seattle, 1961—, McKenzie Galleries, Belleview, Wash., 1973, Cascade Gallery, 1974; exhibited in group shows including at Am. Water Color Soc. N.Y.C., 1966, Watercolor U.S.A., Springfield, Mo., 1964, Nat. Oil Exhbns., Miss., 1965, Smithsonian Instn., Washington, 1966, Tulsa Exhbn. Am. Pen Women, 1962, Seattle Art Mus., N.W. Watercolor Exhbn., other group shows in schs., libraries, banks, hosps. throughout U.S. and Europe; represented in permanent collections of schs. banks, hosps., museums, also pvt. collections; lectr. on northwest art; art tchr. pvt. studio, Seattle. Recipient Owl award Nat. League Am. Penwomen, 1962, 65, Craftsmen Press Purchase award, 1967, Seattle First Nat. Bank Purchase award, 1966; awards Renton Art Festival, 1968, 71, 73, Frye Mus., 1972, Woman Painters Wash., 1967, 70, 72, 74; others. Trustee Music and Art Found., Seattle. Mem. Seattle Co-Arts. (pres. 1962-63), Women Painters Wash. (pres. 1965-67), Artists Equity (chpt. pres. 1968-73), Progressive Animal Welfare Soc., Northwest Watercolor Soc. (pres. 1974—), Classical Music Supporters, Alpha Omicron Pi. Address: 20309 8th Av NW Seattle WA 98177

SAVATE, ROSE DELL (MRS. SIDNEY A. SAVATE), lawyer; b. N.Y.C., Feb. 18, 1925; d. Herman and Ray (Isreal) Rosenzweig; student San Fernando Valley State Coll., 1960-63; B.A., U. San Francisco, 1967, J.D., 1967; m. Bernard Dell, Oct. 6, 1945 (dec. Apr. 1972); children—Marla (Mrs. Loren Silver), Carol; m. 2d, Sidney A. Savate, Nov. 10, 1972. Admitted to Cal. bar, 1968; dep. city atty. City of Los Angeles, 1968—. Group therapist East Valley Clinic for drug abuse, 1971—. Mem. Am., Los Angeles bar assns., San Fernando Criminal Bar, Los Angeles Women Lawyers (gov. 1968-74). Home: 14710 Valerio St Van Nuys CA 91405 Office: 205 N Broadway Los Angeles CA 90012

SAVICH, ELIZABETH SLJIVICH (MRS. PETER SAVICH), physician; b. Belgrade, Yugoslavia, June 17, 1937; d. R. Branko and Radojka (Pesich) Sljivich; M.D., U. Belgrade, 1962; m. Peter Savich, Apr. 4, 1959; children—Alexander, Helen, Natalie. Came to U.S., 1962, naturalized, 1969. Intern, Springfield (Mass.) Med. Center, 1967-68, resident in gen. pediatrics, 1968-70; fellow in neonatology Wesson Women's Hosp., Springfield, 1971-72, physician spl. care unit neonates, 1972—; practice medicine specializing in pediatrics, 1972—. Recipient Physician's Recognition award for continuing med. edn. A.M.A., 1970. Home: 214 Captain Rd Longmeadow MA 01106 Office: 264 Summer Av Springfield MA 01105

SAVITT, BEVERLY BLOCH, lawyer; b. Pitts., May 12, 1926; d. Gustave J. and Molly D. (Labowitz) Bloch; B.S., Carnegie Inst. Tech., 1946; J.D., U. Cal. at Berkeley, 1967; children—Charles, Susan. Tchr., social worker pub. schs., Pitts., 1946-48; tchr. elementary sch., Montgomery County, Md., 1948-50; admitted to Cal. bar, 1967; practice law, San Rafael, Cal., 1968—; partner Diamond & Baty, San Rafael, 1969-70, Diamond & Savitt, 1971-73, Diamond, Savitt, Mellini & Lannon, Inc., 1973—. 1st v.p. League Women Voters, Park Forest, Ill., 1955-56, mem. juvenile justice study com. So. Marin County, 1968-69; pres. Park Forest Coop. Nursery Sch., 1955-57; chmn. Park Forest Non-partisan Com., 1956; commr. Marin County Juvenile Justice Commn., 1972—. Mem. City Council, Park Forest, 1961-65; Democratic committee woman Rich Twp., Ill., 1956-61. Bd. dirs. Marin Council Civic Affairs, San Rafael, 1968—. Home: 9 Fern Av Belvedere CA 94920 Office: 828 Mission Av San Rafael CA 94901

SAVOY, CHYRL LENORE, artist, educator; b. New Orleans, May 23, 1944; d. Frank Peter and Bobby Adrienne (Rawls) Savoy; B.A., La. State U., 1966; postgrad. Accademia di Belli Arti, Florence, Italy, 1966-67; M.F.A., Wayne State U., 1970. One-man show New Orleans Mus. Art, 1972; exhibited numerous group shows including Detroit Artists Market, 1970, 58th Exhbn. Mich. Artists, Detroit, 1971, Artists' Biennial Exhbn. from Southeast and Tex., Delgado Mus., New Orleans, La. Art Commns. Galleries, Baton Rouge, La., 1971, Ark. Art Center, Little Rock, 1971, Delmar Coll., Corpus Christi Tex., 1973, Mint Mus. Art, Charlotte, N.C., 1973, Old State Capitol, Baton Rouge, 1974, R.S. Barnwell Meml. Garden and Art Center, Shreveport, La., 1973; important works include sculpture of St. John the Baptist, Our Lady Star of the Sea Ch., Cameron, La., sculpture Our Lady Queen of All Saints Ch., Ville Platte, La., design of chapel Our Lady of the Bayous Convent, Abbeville, La. Tchr. art St. Martin's sch., Detroit, 1969-70; grad. asst. Wayne State U., Detroit, 1970; asst. prof. fine arts La. State U., Shreveport, 1973—. Recipient Samuel Wiener Sculpture award, 1973. Home: 1009 Poinciana Av Mamou LA 70554 Office: 8515 Youree Drive Shreveport LA 71105

SAVOY, MARGARET CECELIA BURNS (MRS. JAMES EDWARD SAVOY, SR.), former hosp. adminstr.; b. RoseLynn, Alta., Can., Oct. 2, 1914; d. James Sinon and Beatrice Edna (Gray) Burns; came to U.S., 1941, naturalized, 1948; diploma Holy Cross Hosp., 1937; m. James Edward Savoy, Sr., Feb. 28, 1948; children—Stanley Francis, James Edward. Gen. duty nurse Ore. State Tb Hosp., Salem, 1941-43; nurse outpatient dept. No. Permanente Hosp., Vancouver, Wash., 1943-46; pvt. duty nurse, 1946-50; gen. duty nurse Salem Meml. Hosp., 1950-57, night supr., 1957-60; adminstr. Salem Convalescent Center, 1960-63; supr. Fairview Hosp. and Tng. Center, Salem, 1966-73. Mem. Cath. Daus. Am. (regent 1964-66). Home: 4915 Swegle Rd NE Salem OR 97301

SAWATSKI, DOROTHY ELIZABETH LUSK (MRS. CARL E. SAWATSKI), educator, mezzo soprano; b. Little Rock; d. John Thomas and Nettie (Barley) Lusk; B.S. in Voice, Tex. Women's U., 1947; m. Carl E. Sawatski, Dec. 31, 1950; children—John Paul, Charles David. Opera singer N.Y.C., including Times Hall, Town Hall, Oratorios; concertized throughout Southwest with various symphony orchs.; owner Studio of Voice, Little Rock, 1948-51; prof. voice Little Rock U. (now U. Ark. at Little Rock), 1961—. Soloist Temple B'nai Israel, 1948—, Christ Episcopal Ch., 1948—. Mem. Nat. Assn. Tchrs. Singing, Nat. Assn. Arts and Letters, Music Tchrs.

Nat. Assn., Mus. Coterie, P.E.O., Delta Kappa Gamma, Sigma Alpha Iota, Phi Mu, Alpha Psi Omega. Home: 3 Van Lee Dr Little Rock AR 72205

SAWHILL, ISABEL VAN DEVANTER (MRS. JOHN C. SAWHILL), educator; b. Washington, Apr. 2, 1937; d. Winslow B. and Isabel (Earling) Van Devanter; student Wellesley Coll., 1955-58; B.A., N.Y. U., 1962, Ph.D. (Ford Found fellow), 1968; m. John C. Sawhill, Sept. 13, 1958; 1 son, James Winslow. Instr., Howard U., Washington, 1968; cons. U.S. Dept. Health, Edn. and Welfare, also U.S. Office of Mgmt. and Budget, Washington, 1968-69; lectr. Goucher Coll., Balt., 1969-70, asst. prof. econs., 1970-73, chmn. econs. dept., 1971-73; sr. research asso. Urban Inst., 1973—. Mem. Am. Econ. Assn., nat. Economists Club. Home: 3403 O St NW Washington DC 20007 Office: Urban Inst 2100 M St NW Washington DC 20036

SAWIN, NANCY CHURCHMAN, educator; b. Wilmington, Del., June 21, 1917; d. Sanford W. and Ellen (Quigley) Sawin; B.A., Principia Coll., 1938; M.A., U. Del., 1940; D.Ed., U. Pa., 1962. With Sanford Sch., Hockessin, Del., 1938-74, dean girls, 1945-62, head sch., 1962-74; profl. artist. Chmn., Del. State Sci. Fair com., 1962; mem. com. Jr. Sci. and Humanities Symposium, 1962—; mem. English, lang. arts adv. com. State Del., 1965-68; sec., dir. Recreation, Promotion and Service, Inc., 1963—; chmn. Gov.'s Council for Women, 1970-73. Dir. Del. Safety Council, 1964—; pres. trustees Goldey-Becom Coll. Mem. Headmistress Assn. East, Cape May County Art League, Middle Atlantic States Assn. Colls. and Secondary Schs. (pres.), Commn. for Secondary Schs., Red Clay Creek Valley Assn., U.S. Field Hockey Assn. (past pres.), Internat. Fedn. Women's Hockey Assns. (past pres.), Del. Field Hockey Assn. (past pres.), Delta Kappa Gamma (past pres.), Pi Lambda Theta. Republican. Presbyn. (elder). Club: Quota (v.p. Wilmington 1966-71, pres. 1971-73). Editor: The Eagle, 1961-62. Address: Sanford Sch Hockessin DE 19707

SAWYER, CORINNE HOLT (MRS. HUGH A. SAWYER, JR.), educator; b. Chisholm, Minn., Mar. 4, 1924; d. Grover Justine and Grace Margaret (Leland) Holt; B.A. summa cum laude, U. Minn., 1945, M.A., 1947; Ph.D., U. Birmingham (Eng.), 1954; postgrad. U. Fla., 1951; m. Hugh A. Sawyer, Jr., Aug. 28, 1965. Asst. instr. U. Minn., Mpls., 1946-47; asst. prof. U. Miami (Fla.), 1947-50; instr. U. Md. Overseas, Eng., 1954-58; asst. prof., coordinator closed circuit TV, East Carolina U., Greenville, N.C., 1958-66; asso. prof. English, Clemson (S.C.) U., 1966—, chmn. univ. honors program, 1973—. Women's editor, continuity dir. WNCT-TV, Greenville, N.C., 1963-65. Pres. Clemson U. Faculty Senate, 1971-72; sec. Clemson Arts Council, 1973. Mem. South Atlantic Modern Lang. Assn., Renaissance Soc., Malone Soc., Nat. Collegiate Players, Phi Beta Kappa, Alpha Omicron Pi, Zeta Phi Eta, Phi Kappa Phi. Home: 105 Hunnicutt Lane Clemson SC 29631

SAWYER, DESSIE LEWIS (MRS. U. D. SAWYER), mem. Dem. Nat. Com.; b. Tex.; d. R. R. and Mary Elizabeth (Coventon) Lewis; student pub. schs., Brownfield, Tex.; m. Uyless Devoe Sawyer; children—Fern (Mrs. Scharbauer Eidson) Myrl (Mrs. Jeff Good). Democratic state vice chmn., 1948-52, nat. committeewoman, 1952—. Apptd. chmn. Old Lincoln County Commn., staff Gov. N.M., 1936—. Chmn. Red Cross, March Dimes campaigns, North Lea County. Home: Crossroads NM 88114*

SAWYER, EVE LYNN FREEMAN (MRS. JORDAN ENOCH SAWYER), journalist; b. Pine Bluff, Ark., Apr. 5, 1922; d. Edmond Wroe and Elizabeth Evelyn (Councill) Freeman; B.A., U. Ark., 1942; m. Jordan Enoch Sawyer, Nov. 7, 1942; children—Jordan Freeman, Janie (Mrs. Wayne David Marty), Jan (Mrs. Thomas Hugo Stephens). Fashion editor San Antonio Light, 1957-64; society columnist Express-News, San Antonio, 1967—. Recipient award for best feature story in San Antonio newspaper Sigma Delta Chi, 1961, citation Men's Fashion Industry, 1961. Mem. Am. Soc. Indsl. Editors, Mortar Bd., Women in Communications (Headliner award 1973), Chi Omega. Club: San Antonio Media. Home: 1715 Merriford Rd San Antonio TX 78209 Office: Av E and 3d St San Antonio TX 78297

SAWYER, HELEN ALTON, painter; b. Washington; d. Wells Moses and Kathleen Alton (Bailey) S.; student Master's Sch., Dobbs Ferry, 1914-18; studied art with Johansen and Hawthorne; m. Jerry Farnsworth, Aug. 26, 1925. Painter, artist in oil and water color, lithographer. Exhibited at principal galleries and museums of U.S. Represented permanent collections museums, IBM collection. Recipient numerous awards and honors. Mem. N.A.D., Nat. Arts Club, Provincetown, Yonkers, Sarasota art assns., Audubon Artists, Fla. Artists Group (pres. 1953-55), Nat. Assn. Women Artists, Inc. Contbr. of articles and verse to jours. Has painted in U.S., Spain, France, Mexico. Home: 3482 Flamingo St Sarasota FL 33581

SAWYER, KATHERINE H. (MRS. CHARLES BALDWIN SAWYER), librarian; b. Cleve., July 11, 1908; d. Willard and Martha (Beaumont) Hirsh; A.B., Smith Coll., 1930; M.S. in Library Sci., Western Res. U., 1956; m. Charles Baldwin Sawyer, Aug. 19, 1933; children—Samuel Prentiss, Charles Brush, William Beaumont. With Cleve. Pub. Library, profl. librarian hosps., instns. dept., 1956-61; med. librarian St. Luke's Hosp., Pittsfield, Mass., 1965-66; library cons. Ministry of Health, Guyana, S.Am., 1966-68; curator Sophia Smith Collection, Smith Coll., 1970-71; parish librarian St. Paul's Episcopal Ch., Cleveland Heights, O., 1971—, mem. vestry, 1974—. Library chmn. exec. com. Garden Center of Greater Cleve., 1959-65; chmn. Friends of Western Res. Hist. Library, 1972—. Bd. mgrs. Episcopal Ch. Home, 1954-64, pres., 1961-64, trustee, 1965—; bd. govs. Western Res. U., 1957-66, bd. visitors Sch. Library Sci., 1958-68, 69—; trustee Friends of Cleve. Pub. Library, 1962-67. Mem. Am., Ohio library assns., Western Res. Hist. Soc., Archeol. Inst., Spl. Libraries Assn., Nat. League Am. Pen Women. Clubs: Union, Kirtland Country. Co-author (talking books for blind) Gardening for Blind Persons, 1962; Beauty, Glamour and Style, 1963. Home: 17485 Shelburne Rd Cleveland OH 44118

SAWYER, MARGARET DOLAN (MRS. ROBERT BRUCE SAWYER), realtor, civic worker; b. Chgo., Aug. 17, 1933; d. Earl Jeremiah and Maybelle (Knox) Dolan; B.A., U. Colo., 1955; m. Robert Bruce Sawyer, Sept. 4, 1954; children—Margaret Elizabeth, Robert Bruce, Patrick Dolan, John Knox, Mary Regina, Joseph McAndrew, Michael McLean. Tchr. pub. schs., Adams City, Colo., 1955-56, St. Mary Euphrasia, Denver, 1956; tv comml. talent, weather girl KBTV, Denver, 1957-62; staff Billings and Co. Real Estate, 1973—. Various activities Jr. League Denver, 1962-73; puppetry chmn., pre-sch. hearing testing, Children's Theater; admissions, fund raising educationally handicapped, placement; radio-TV publicity for Met. Opera auditions; mem. speakers bur. Denver Olympic Com. 1969-72. Mem. Crestmoor Community Assn., Internat. Platform Assn., Denver Bd. Realtors, Alpha Phi, P.E.O. Roman Catholic. Republican. Clubs: Medical Wives, Arlberg Ski, Ladies of Rotary (pres. 1969-70), Denver Athletic, Hoolualea Dance. Home: 700 Franklin St Denver CO 80218 Office: Billings and Co Real Estate 3711 Cherry Creek N Dr Denver CO 80209

SAWYIER, FAY HORTON (MRS. CALVIN SAWYIER), educator; b. Chgo., Feb. 16, 1924; d. Horace Babcock and Phyllis (Fay) Horton; B.A., U. Chgo., 1944, Ph.D., 1964; m. Calvin Sawyier, Apr. 3, 1943; children—Terry (Mrs. Albert Straus), Michael, David, Stephen. Prof., Ill. Inst. Tech., 1964-71; lectr. Sch. Social Service Adminstrn., U. Chgo., 1971—; high sch. guest lectr., 1968—. Trustee Shipley Sch., Bryn Mawr, Woodlawn Hosp. Recipient Alumni citation as Best Tchr. Ill. Inst. Tech., 1971. Mem. U. Chgo. Alumni Assn. (past pres.), Am. Civil Liberties Union, N.A.A.C.P., Inst. Psychoanalysis, Phi Beta Kappa. Home: 1360 E 56th St Chicago IL 60637

SAXBE, ARDATH LOUISE KLEINHANS (MRS. WILLIAM B. SAXBE), wife of former atty. gen. U.S.; b. Toledo, June 19, 1917; d. Charles L. and Mata (Gennings) Kleinhaus; B.S., Ohio State U., 1939; m. William B. Saxbe, Sept. 14, 1940; children—William Bart Jr., Juliet (Mrs. Lopeman), Charles R. Mem. churchwomen's bd. Episcopal Diocese So. Ohio; mem. Senate Ladies Red Cross. Republican. Club: Congressional (dir. art show 1970). Address: 560 N St SW Washington DC 20024

SAXON, CLAIRE LYN (MRS. VERNON PARKER SAXON, JR.), photographer, pub. relations; b. Buffalo, Dec. 6, 1944; d. Clair Lincoln and Dorothy Louise (Wullenweber) Newton; B.S., Syracuse U., 1966; m. Vernon Parker Saxon, Jr., Oct. 23, 1971; children—Jennifer Lind, Vernon Jeffrey. Passenger service rep. Am. Airlines, Buffalo, 1967, 69, Los Angeles, 1967-68. Dir. March of Dimes Mothers March, Wichita Falls, Tex., 1973. Bd. dirs. March of Dimes, 1972-73. Served with WAF, 1969-72. Mem. Women In Communications. Editor: The Sheppardess Mag., 1972-73. Home: 6971 Locustview Dayton OH 45424

SAXTON, CARLYN KAISER (MRS. ANDREW ELLIOTT SAXTON), camp dir.; b. Washington, Oct. 24, 1933; d. Edgar Fosburgh and Sue (Mead) Kaiser; student Bryn Mawr Coll., 1952-54; m. Andrew Elliott Saxton, June 17, 1973; children by previous marriage—Kathy, Richard, David, Shelley, Kim, Robin, Anne-Marie, Andy, Mead. Counselor Four Winds Camp, Deer Harbor, Wash., 1952-54, dir., 1968—, mem. found. bd., 1970—; dir. Four Winds-Westward Ho Camps, Deer Harbor, 1968—. Bd. dirs. Children's Hosp., East Bay, Cal., 1965-68; trustee Totem Girl Scout Council, Seattle, 1970—. Mem. Am. Camping Assn., San Francisco Opera Assn. (dir. 1966-69). Clubs: Berkeley Yacht, Royal Vancouver Yacht. Home: 3637 Angus Dr Vancouver BC V6S 4H4 Canada Office: Box 90 Deer Harbor WA 98443

SAXTON, EVELYN JUNE, librarian; b. Joplin, Mo., Sept. 9, 1930; d. Chester Earl and Gladys (Dall) Saxton; student U. Colo., 1949-51, U. Denver, 1963. Broiler raiser, Yuma, Colo., 1951-59; librarian Yuma Pub. Library, 1960—. Mem. Am., Colo. library assns. Home: Rural Route 1 Box 89 Yuma CO 80759 Office: 114 W 3rd Av Yuma CO 80759

SAXTON, MARYELLEN (MRS. JERRY J. SAXTON), real estate broker; b. Gratiot County, Mich., Oct. 14, 1930; d. Harry Lee and Ethel Ellen (Hazen) Bushre; grad. high sch.; m. Lloyd Clifton Clark, Oct. 29, 1949; children—Kay Ellen, Connie, Toni Sue; m. 2d, Jerry J. Saxton, Dec. 3, 1966; stepchildren—Rosemary (Mrs. Michael Leydorf), Jimmy Lee, Mark Alan, Max James, Carol B. Insp., Fed. Mogul Corp., St. Johns, Mich., 1952-68; real estate saleswoman Harper & Young, Inc., Harrison, Mich., 1969-70; co-owner Jerry Saxton, Realtor, Harrison, Mich., 1970—. Asst. instr. fundamentals of real estate for adult edn. classes Harrison High Sch., 1970-71; sec. Fed. Mogul Employee's Credit Union, 1962-66, pres., 1966-68. Pres., P.T.A., 1965. Mem. Clare County Bd. Realtors (sec. 1970-73), Harrison C. of C. (sec. 1972-73), Harrison C. of C. Aux. (pres. 1972-73). Mem. Christian Ch. Mem. Order of Eastern Star. Home: 320 Hillcrest Av Harrison MI 48625 Office: 152 S First St Harrison MI 48625

SAY, MARLYS MORTENSEN, ednl. adminstr.; b. Yankton, S.D., Mar. 11, 1924; d. Melvin A. and Edythe (Fargo) Mortensen; B.A., U. Colo., 1949, M.Ed., 1953; m. John Theodore Say, June 21, 1951; children—Mary Louise, James Kenneth, John Melvin, Margaret Ann. Tchr. Huron, S.D., 1946-49, Lamar, Colo., 1950-52; Rock Springs, Wyo., 1952-55; supt. schs. Madison County, Norfolk, Neb., 1963—. Mem. N.E.A. (life), Am. Assn. U. Women (pres. Norfolk br. 1963-65), Neb. Elementary Prins. Assn. Nat. Assn. Women Deans and Counselors, Neb. Edn. Assn., Neb., N.E. Neb. (pres.) county supts. assns., Am., Neb. assns. sch. adminstrs., Nat. Council Adminstrv. Women in Edn., Madison County Edn. Assn., Neb. Council Ednl. TV, Am. Assn. Sch. Bus. Ofcls., Delta Kappa Gamma, Kappa Delta Pi. Republican. Methodist. Home: 4805 S 13th St Norfolk NE 68701 Office: Madison NE 68748

SAYERS, OPAL MARIE KIMBALL (MRS. ROBERT DELL SAYERS), bus. exec.; b. Jacksonville, Fla., Aug. 13, 1940; d. George Sharpe and Thelma (Huckaby) Kimball; student pub. schs.; m. Robert Dell Sayers, Oct. 3, 1958; children—Sheila Marie, Treca Marie. Bookkeeper Perry (Fla.) News-Herald, 1959-60, sales rep., 1968-70; treas. Aluminum Fabricated Products, Inc., 1968—; mgr. Perry-Taylor County C. of C., 1961-65; treas. C. St. Enterprises, Inc., 1973—. Taylor County rep., Tallahassee Democrat newspaper, 1961-64. Sec. Taylor County's Ann. Pine Tree Festival, 1961-66; sec. Fla.'s Forest Festival, 1966-67, mem. steering com., 1972—. Democrat. Nazarene. Clubs: Perry Junior Woman's (chmn. conservation natural resources, past pres.), Perry Woman's (1st v.p. 1972—). Address: 200 Pace Dr Perry FL 32347 Office: PO Box 1107 Perry FL 32347

SAYLER, MAURINE FAULKNER BERGLAND (MRS. JAMES NORVEL SAYLER), book store owner; b. Fort Scott, Kan., Jan. 19, 1914; d. Erwin Phyllitus and Minnie Mae (Munday) Faulkner; B.S., Kan. State Coll., 1934, M.S., 1942; m. Bert E. Bergland, May 4, 1935 (dec. Sept. 1963); 1 son, Bert Eugene; m. 2d, James Norvel Sayler, Apr. 8, 1966. Asst. prof. Fort Hays (Kan.) State Coll., 1939-45, 49-50; mgr., owner, pres. Campus Book Store, Inc., Hays, Kan., 1936—; owner Bygones Mail Order Antique Bus., Maryville, Mo., 1966-68; pres. Walburn Grocery, Inc., 1966-68; freelance writer, 1949-63. Active Girl Scouts Am., A.R.C., United Fund, Arts Council, Library Bd., U.S.O. Trustee Maryville Pub. Library. Mem. League Women Voters, Nodaway Arts Council, Kan. Authors Club, Nat. Writers Club, Delta Zeta. Republican. Methodist (pres. women's orgn. 1951—). Mem. Order Eastern Star. Club: Fort Hays Alumni (v.p. 1954-55) (Hays). Home: 3 Elm Square Maryville MO 64468

SCAFURI, ALLISON LOWELL (MRS. H.E. SCAFURI), lawyer; b. Detroit, Nov. 18, 1929; d. Alphonse Lowell and Georgia Virginia (Kutak) Scafuri; A.B., U. Mich., 1951, J.D., 1954; postgrad. Fletcher Sch. Law, 1954-55; m. H.E. Scafuri, Dec. 23, 1959; 1 son, Alan Lowell. Admitted to Mich. bar, 1954, U.S. Supreme Ct., 1966; mem. firm McClintock, Fulton, Donovan & Waterman, Detroit, 1955-58; pvt. practice law, Detroit, 1958—. Pres., Modena Research Corp., Detroit, 1972—; adj. prof. internat. law Thomas Cooley Law Sch., Lansing, Mich., 1973—. Counsel, Mich. Senate Com. to Investigate Adminstrv. Practices Hwy. Dept., 1959-61. Mem. White House Conf. on Internat. Cooperation, 1965—. Recipient Certificate of honor Air Force Assn., 1971. Mem. Internat. Humanitarian Law Assn. (dir. gen. 1971—), State Bar Mich. (co-founder space law com. 1959, chmn. 1963—, founder, 1st chmn. sci. and tech. com. 1973—), Am., Detroit bar assns., Am. Soc. Internat. Law, Am. Arbitration Assn. (mem. panel of arbitrators 1964—), Am. Inst. Aeros. and Astronautics, Air Force Assn., Zeta Psi, Phi Alpha Delta. Club: University (Detroit). Author: Working Principles of the Wankel Rotary Engine, 1973. Contbr. articles to profl. jours. Home: 13123 Elgin Huntington Woods MI 48070 Office: 116 International Plaza 23300 Greenfield Detroit MI 48237

SCALAMANDRE, FLORA ADRIANA (MRS. FRANCO SCALAMANDRE), fabric designer; b. N.Y.C., May 21, 1907; d. Gino Claudio and Maria (Poletti) Baranzelli; B.A., Parsons Sch. Design, 1926; m. Franco Scalamandre, Nov. 14, 1929; children—Gino, Adriana (Mrs. Edwin Bitter). Estimator for artificial stonework Baranzelli Cast Stone Co., N.Y.C., 1926-29; designer Scalamandre Silks, Inc., Long Island City. N.Y., 1929—, sec.-sales, 1929—. Bd. dirs. Italian Welfare League. Recipient award for wallpaper Am. Inst. Inerior Designers, 1967. Mem. Manhasset Art Assn. Republican. Roman Catholic. Club: North Hills Country (Manhasset, N.Y.). Designer all reprodn. work for fabrics used in Monticello, Mount Vernon, White House, Bowne House, Gardiner Mus., Tryon Palace. Home: 1776 Heritage Way Plandome Manor NY 11030 Office: 37-24 24th St Long Island City NY 11101

SCALES, GRETCHEN ATTANASIO, artist; b. N.Y.C., Aug. 16, 1900; d. John Battista and Ida (Treptow) Attanasio; grad. Pratt Inst. Sch. Fine and Applied Arts, 1922; student Lynchburg Fine Arts Center, 1955-65; m. Baxter Boyd Scales, June 30, 1923; 1 son, John Baxter. Free-lance fashion artist, Hempstead, N.Y., 1939-43; advt. mgr. Franklin Shops, Inc. Hempstead, 1943-47; free-lance artist, Lynchburg, Va., 1947-51; advt. mgr. Guggenheimer's Dept. Store, Lynchburg, 1951-55, Patterson Drug Co., Inc., Lynchburg, 1955-63; exhibited one-man shows Lynchburg Little Theater, 1959, U. Theater, Charlottesville, Va., 1967, Boonsboro Theatre, Lynchburg, 1969; exhibited group shows Lynchburg Fine Arts Center, 1955-65, Little Theater, 1962, First Southside Fine Arts Exhibit, Danville, Va., 1965, U. Va. Newcomb Hall, 1967; represented in permanent collections. Recipient 2d pl. awards Va. Fedn. Women's Clubs Art Competition, Roanoke, 1960, Arlington, 1961; hon. mention U. Va. Newcomb Hall, 1967. Mem. Lynchburg Art Club (program chmn. 1955-57), Nat. League Am. Pen Women (2d pl. award Va. art competition 1963, corr. sec. Lynchburg br. 1964-66, membership chmn. 1964-66, 70-72, pres. 1966-68, corr. sec. 1970-72, rec. sec. 1972-74), Lynchburg Fine Arts Center, Va. Mus. Art, Lynchburg Hist. Soc. Home: 705 Riverside Dr Lynchburg VA 24503

SCALES, MARGARET BERON (MRS. A. STARK WOLKOFF), pathologist; b. N.Y.C., Apr. 5, 1925; d. Nicholas and Margaret (Hess) Beron; A.B., Barnard Coll., 1946; M.A., Columbia, 1947, Ph.D., 1955; M.D., U. N.C., 1960; m. A. Stark Wolkoff, June 1, 1956. Instr., Conn. Coll. for Women, New London, 1952-53; asst. prof. U. Louisville, 1954-56; intern U. N.C. at Chapel Hill, 1960-61, resident, 1961-64; research fellow pathology, 1963-64, instr., 1964-65; asst. clin. prof. U. Kan. Med. Sch., Kansas City, 1965—; pathologist Bapt. Meml. Hosp., Kansas City, Mo., 1965—. Dir, Smith, Ost, Scales Med. Lbas., Inc., Kansas City, Mo. Cons. Midwest Research Inst., Kansas City, Mo., 1969—; tech. adviser Kansas City Community Blood Bank, 1965—. Trustee Laura Elizabeth Scales Meml. Found. Diplomate Am. Bd. Pathology. Fellow Am. Soc. Clin. Pathologists; mem. Am. (Mo. rep. 1969—), Mo. (pres. 1969-70) assns. blood banks, Coll. Am. Pathologists, Internat. Acad. Pathology, Am. Soc. Cytology, Sigma Xi. Club: Saddle and Sirloin (Kansas City, Kan.). Home: 6532 Belinder St Shawnee Mission KS 66208 Office: 6601 Rockhill Rd Kansas City MO 64131

SCAMPINI, LOIS JEAN, lawyer; b. San Mateo, Cal., Nov. 10, 1929; d. Herman Paul and Josephine Louise (Pinzi) Scampini; A.B. magna cum laude, Dominican Coll. San Rafael, 1950; J.D., U. San Francisco, 1958. Tchr. jr. high sch. South San Francisco, 1951-55, high sch., 1955-59; admitted to Cal. bar, 1959, Fed. Ct. bar, 1959, U.S. Supreme Ct. bar, 1962; dep. dist. atty. civil div. San Mateo County, Redwood City, Cal., 1959-67; mem. firm Goth, Dennis & Aaron, Redwood City, 1967—. Tchr. adult edn. South San Francisco Unified Sch. Dist., 1972—; lectr. preventive law for layman Coll. San Mateo, 1970, forensic psychiatry McAuley Neuropsychiat. Inst. St. Mary's Hosp., San Francisco, 1966, 67; mem. profl. adv. com. San Francisco Suicide Prevention Center, 1968; tchr. real estate and family law San Mateo Community Coll. Dist. Bd. dirs. San Mateo County Council on Alcoholism, 1965-66. Teaching fellow Dominican Coll., 1950-51. Mem. Cal. State Bar, San Mateo County Bar Assn. (pres. 1970), San Mateo Bench-Bar-Press Com., Trial Lawyers Assn., U. San Francisco Alumni Assn. (bd. govs. 1968-69). Democrat. Roman Catholic. Mem. Sons of Italy. Home: 126 Elm St San Mateo CA 94401 Office: 1000 Marshall St Redwood City CA 94063

SCANLAN, MARTHA THERESA, physician; b. Decatur, Ill., 1891; d. John Patrick and Martha (Kitchen) Scanlan; B.A., U. Cal. at Berkeley, 1921; M.D., Columbia, 1924; m. Charles A. Green, Oct. 22, 1928 (dec.); children—Patricia (Mrs. Robert Means Prioleau), Constance (Mrs. George Raymond). Intern, Meml. Hosp., Worcester, Mass., 1924; resident Bellevue Hosp., N.Y.C., 1926-28; practice medicine, N.Y.C., 1928—; asst. attending Fifth Av Hosp., 1930-40; asst. attending N.Y. Hosp., N.Y. Infirmary. Rep., Internat. Womens Med. Assn. to UNICEF, 1954—. Served with A.R.C., 1918. Fellow A.C.P.; mem. A.M.A., N.Y. State (citation for 50 years practice 1974), N.Y. County (econs. com.) med. socs., N.Y. State (Woman of Year award 1968, past pres.), N.Y.C. (exec. com.) womens med. socs., Sorosis Soc. Republican. Home: 34 Gramercy Park New York City NY 10003 Office: 133 E 58th St New York City NY 10022

SCANLON, DOROTHY THERESE, educator; b. Bridgeport, Conn., Oct. 7, 1928; d. George F. and Mazie (Reardon) Scanlon; A.B., U. Pa., 1948, M.A., 1949; M.A., Boston Coll., 1953, Ph.D., 1956; postdoctoral scholar Harvard, 1962-64, 72. Tchr. history and Latin Marycliff Acad., Winchester, Mass., 1950-52; tchr. history Girls Latin Sch., Boston, 1952-57; prof. State Coll. at Boston, 1957—. Mem. Am. Assn. U. Profs., Am. Assn. U. Women, Pan-Am. Soc., Latin Am. Studies Assn., Am. Hist. Assn., Orgn. Am. Historians, Am. Studies Assn., Am. Assn. History of Medicine, Phi Alpha Theta, Delta Kappa Gamma. Author: Instructor's Manual to Accompany Lewis Hanke, Latin America: A Historical Reader, 1974. Home: 140 Thornton Rd Chestnut Hill MA 02167 Office: 625 Huntington Av Boston MA 02115

SCANLON, JANE CRONIN (MRS. JOSEPH C. SCANLON), educator; b. N.Y.C., July 17, 1922; d. John Timothy and Janet Smiley (Murphy) Cronin; B.S., Wayne State U., 1943; M.A., U. Mich., 1945, Ph.D. (Office of Naval Research fellow), 1949; m. Joseph C. Scanlon, Mar. 5, 1953; children—Justin, Mary, Emer, Edmund. Math. Air Force Cambridge (Mass.) Research Center, 1951-54; instr. math. Wheaton Coll., Norton, Mass., 1954-55; asst. prof. math. Poly. Inst. of Bklyn., 1957-58, asso. prof. 1958-60, prof. math. 1960-65; prof. math. Rutgers U., New Brunswick, N.J., 1965—. Cons. Gen. Precision Corp., 1963-66, Naval Research Lab., 1967—. U. Mich. fellow, 1950-51, Rutgers U. Research Council fellow, 1968-69, 72-73; U.S. Army Research Office grantee, 1960—. Mem. Am. Math. Soc.,

Soc. for Indsl. and Applied Math. Author: Fixed Points and Topological Degree in Nonlinear Analysis, 1964; Advanced Calculus, 1967. Contbr. articles to profl. jours. Home: 110 Valentine St Highland Park NJ 08904 Office: Dept. Mathematics Rutgers University New Brunswick NJ 08903

SCANLON, ROSEMARY MACLELLAN, research economist; b. N.S., Can., Dec. 25, 1939; d. Donald Angus and Mary Agnes (MacDonald) MacLellan; B.A., St. Francis Xavier U., N.S., 1959; M.A. in Econs., U. N.B., 1960; postgrad. N.Y. U., 1971-72; m. Michael Scanlon, Apr. 24, 1965; children—Sean, Jennifer. Came to U.S., 1960, naturalized, 1972. Instr. econs. Coll. William and Mary, Williamsburg, Va., 1960-63; asst. prof. econs. Old Dominion U., Norfolk, Va., 1963-65; staff econ. analyst planning and devel. dept. Port Authority N.Y. and N.J., N.Y.C., 1969—. Chmn., N.Y.C. Labor Market Adv. Council, 1972-73. Active P.T.A. Imperial Order Daus. Empire scholar, 1955-59; Ford Found. scholar, 1959-60. Mem. Am. Statis. Assn., Soc. Govt. Economists (chmn. regional econs. session ann. meeting 1973). Author publs. in field. Home: 27 Pierrepont St Brooklyn NY 11201 Office: One World Trade Center New York City NY 10048

SCARBERRY, ALMA SIOUX (MRS. THEODORE A. KLEIN), pub. relations exec.; b. Carter County, Ky., June 24, 1899; d. George Washington and Caledonia Lee (Patrick) Scarberry; student New Bethlehem Bus. Coll., 1917; m. Theodore A. Klein, Aug. 30, 1930; 1 son, Theodore A. Reporter Elmira (N.Y.) Advertiser, 1919; columnist King Features, 1920-21; reporter N.Y. Am., 1922; singer Shubert's Mikado, 1924, Irving Berlin's Music Box Revue, 1922-23; feature writer N.Y. Graphic, 1924-25; reporter N.Y. Mirror, 1925-26, Pitts. Sun-Telegraph, 1926-28; columnist, serial writer Central Press Assn., 1928-30, Bell Syndicate, 1930-40; columnist Washington Herald Times, 1937-38; with writing dept. Mut.-Don Lee Network, Hollywood, Cal., 1944-45; dir. radio bur. N.Y. Nat. War Fund, 1946-47; pub. relations dir. Columbus (O.) Plastics, 1959-65; pub. relations dir. Job Preparation Center, Austin, Tex., 1969—. Served with U.S. Navy, 1917-18. Mem. Am. Fedn. Women's Clubs, Am. Fedn. Music Clubs, Nat. League Am. Pen Women, Women in Communications. Democrat. Episcopalian. Author 21 novels, including Make Up, The Flat Tire, High Hat, Dimpled Racketeer, Flighty, Puppy Love, Thou Shalt Not Love. Contbr. columns to newspapers. Home: 1312 Pasadena Dr Austin TX 78757

SCARBOROUGH, MARION ELSIE NICHOLS (MRS. MAT SCARBOROUGH), nutritionist, educator; b. Enosburg Falls, Vt., July 26, 1915; d. George Leonard and Clara (Woodward) Nichols; Asso. Sci., Green Mountain Jr. Coll., 1935; B.S., Kan. State U., 1937; certificate dietetics Worcester Meml. Hosp., 1938; M.P.H., Harvard, 1947; postgrad. U. Fla., 1967; m. Mat Scarborough, Aug. 30, 1950 (dec. Mar. 1960); 1 dau., Mary Anne. Teaching and adminstrv. dietitian Newton Wellesley Hosp., Newton, Mass., 1938-41, chief dietitian, 1941-43; chief nutritionist diabetes sect. USPHS, 1947-50; regional nutritionist Fla. Bd. Health, Jacksonville, 1950-52; owner Happy Acres Ranch, kindergarten and day camp, Jacksonville, 1953—. Teaching dietitian St. Vincent's Hosp., Jacksonville, part-time, 1956-58, Brewster Meth. Hosp., Jacksonville, part-time, 1955-62. Mem. day care adv. bd. Fla. Div. Family Services, Jacksonville, 1969, 70; mem. adv. bd. Child Care Services, Fla. Jr. Coll., Jacksonville, mem. sub-com. Task Force on Child and Youth Care in Jacksonville, 1969; mem. day care study com. Community Planning Council of Jacksonville, 1969-71; mem. service area adv. com. for home econs. edn. Fla. Jr. Coll., 1971—; mem. adv. com. for home econs. career edn. Duval County Sch. Bd., 1972—; mem. Community Coordinated Child Care Program of Jacksonville, 1971—; mem. adv. bd. Parent Child Center of Jacksonville, 1970—; mem. Fla. Adv. Council on Early Childhood Devel. Served to 1st lt. AUS, 1943-45; commd. officer USPHS, 1947-50. Fellow Am. Pub. Health Assn.; mem. Am., Fla., Jacksonville dietetic assns., Fla. Assn. on Children Under Six (area chmn. 1964-66, rec. sec. 1966-68, pres. 1968-70), N. Fla. Assn. on Children Under Six (Jacksonville treas. 1964-68), Am. Camping Assn., Am. Assn. U. Women, Jacksonville Area C. of C., Duval Children's Nursery Assn. (charter; pres. 1956, 57, 64), Duval County Kindergarten Council (treas. 1966-68). Episcopalian. Address: 7117 Crane Av Jacksonville FL 32216

SCARBROUGH, LINDA CLAIRE (MRS. HIRAM KNOTT), publisher; b. Austin, Tex., May 10, 1944; d. Donald Lee and Clara May (Stearns) Scarbrough; B.A., George Washington U., 1966; postgrad. in history N.Y. U.; m. Hiram Knott, Nov. 1969. Sci. writer New York Daily News, 1966-69; editor Butner-Creedmoor News, Creedmoor, N.C., 1969-70; reporter Raleigh (N.C.) News and Observer, 1970-71; advt., speech writer, position papers for candidate N.C. Ho. of Reps., Durham, 1972; free lance writer on environment and medicine, N.Y.C., 1972—; pub. Granger (Tex.) News, 1965—. Recipient 1st pl. awards for column writing and spl. series, 2d pl. award for spot news writing N.C. Press Assn. competition for weekly newspapers and newspapermen, 1971. Address: 32 Gramercy Park S New York City NY 10003

SCARF, MAGGIE (MARGARET) KLEIN (MRS. HERBERT ELI SCARF), author; b. Phila., May 13, 1932; d. Benjamin and Helen (Rotbin) Klein; student, Temple U., Stanford U., So. Conn. State Coll., Yale; m. Herbert Eli Scarf, June 28, 1953; children—Martha, Elizabeth, Susan. Sci. article writer N.Y. Times Mag., 1968—; reviewer N.Y. Times Book Review, 1970—. Club: New Haven Lawn. Author: Meet Benjamin Franklin, 1968; Antarctica: Exploring the Frozen Continent, 1970. Home and office: Blake Rd Hamden CT 06517

SCARLETT, DOROTHY GLADYS FERRELL (MRS. FLOYD MACK SCARLETT), mus. dir.; b. Faxon, Okla., Mar. 7, 1909; d. Fred Chunning and Elizabeth Mozell (Walls) Ferrell; student Okla. Coll. For Women, 1927-28, Okla. State Tchrs. Coll., 1928-29, Kan. State U., 1961-72; m. Floyd Mack Scarlett, Aug. 31, 1929; 1 dau., Sandra Jean (Mrs. David Louis Beem). Bookkeeper, Scarlett's, Goltry, Okla., 1937-40; timekeeper, Boeing Airplane Co., Wichita, Kan., 1942-43; bookkeeper, Scarlett's, 1945-53; dir. Downtown Art Gallery, Harper, Kan., 1970—. Active Girl Scouts Am. Mem. Harper Art Assn., Inc. (pres. 1961, 70), Harper City Hist. Soc. (sec. 1963), Harper County Hist. Soc. (sec. 1964), Bus. and Profl. Women's Club. Democrat. Methodist. Mem. Order Eastern Star. Clubs: Twentieth Century, Study and Social (pres. 1948), City Council of Clubs (pres. 1949), County Council of Clubs (pres. 1950) (Harper). Home: PO Box 275 Harper KS 67058 Office: 105 W Main St Harper KS 67058

SCATES, ALICE YEOMANS, govt. ofcl.; b. Pitts., Jan. 21, 1915; d. William E. and Georgiana L. (Lloyd) Yeomans; B.S., State Tchrs. Coll., Glassboro, N.J., 1936; M.Ed., Duke, 1949; Ed.D., George Washington U., 1963. Elementary Sch. tchr. Haddon Heights, N.J., 1937-43; civilian personnel officer Sedalia Army Airfield, Mo., Greenville Army Air Field, S.C., 1944-46; tng. officer VA Center, Dayton, O., 1947-48; research asso., dir. Am. Council on Edn. Staff for Office Naval Research Projects, 1949-53; asst. dir. Nat. Home Study Council, 1954; editor, research asst. Office of Edn., U.S. Dept. Health, Edn. and Welfare, 1955, research analyst and coordinator Coop. Research Program, 1956-64, program planning officer Occupational Research Program, 1965-66, dir. basic research br. secondary edn., 1967-69, program planning and evaluation officer Nat. Center Ednl. Research and Devel., 1969-71, Office of Planning, Budgeting and Evaluation, 1971—. Served to capt. AUS, 1943-46. Fellow A.A.A.S.; mem. Am. Sociol. Assn., Am. Anthrop. Assn., Am. Acad. Polit. and Social Sci., Am. Ednl. Research Assn. Adult Edn. Assn., Kappa Delta Pi, Phi Delta Gamma. Author research reports, articles in field. Home: 560 N St SW Washington DC 20024 Office: Office of Planning Budgeting and Evaluation US Office Edn Washington DC 20202

SCATES, DORIS SUMMERS (MRS. CARLYS P. SCATES), educator; b. Martin, Tenn., Mar. 30, 1935; d. Floyd Mitchell and Lillie Edith (Stafford) Summers; B.A., Mich. State U., 1957; M.S., U. Tenn., 1961; m. Carlys P. Scates, June 3, 1956; children—Craig Summers, Dawn Carlyn. Instr. bus. adminstrn. U. Tenn., Martin, 1957-59; instr. bus. U. Louisville, 1959-60; tchr. Louisville Pub. Schs., 1960-63; asst. prof. bus., asst. to bus. dept. head Miami-Dade Jr. Coll., Miami, Fla., 1963-68; asst. prof. bus. data processing, dir. computer center Lambuth Coll., Jackson, Tenn., 1968—. Mem. Am. Assn. U. Profs., Data Processing Mgmt. Assn., Assn. for Computing Machinery, W. Tenn. Edn. Assn. Republican. Baptist. Home: 180 Channing Way Jackson TN 38301

SCHAAR, JACQUELINE KAY COUCH (MRS. ROBERT L. SCHAAR), pub. relations exec.; b. San Diego, Apr. 2, 1933; d. Edwin Newton and Nina Mae (Sweetwood) Couch; grad. pub. schs., 1951; m. Robert L. Schaar, May 11, 1962; children—Robert, Denise. Exec. sec. various firms, 1951-57; asst. to community relations dir. Convair-Astronautics, San Diego, 1957-59; advt., pub. relations exec. Frederick C. Whitney & Assos., San Diego, 1959-62, J. Jessop & Sons, 1962-64; regional dir. pub. relations United Way, Arcadia, Cal., 1964-73; dir. pub. relations Orange County United Way, 1973—. Mem. Assistance League of Arcadia (asso.), Pasadena C. of C. (pub. relations com. 1965—), Pub. Relations Soc. of Am. (chmn. attendance com., mem. community service com.), Orange County Press Club. Home: 29432 Troon St Laguna Niguel CA 92677 Office: 72 Montreal S PO Box 5854 Orange CA 92667

SCHABER, LILLY SEVALL, violinist, educator; b. St. Charles, Ill., Sept. 16, 1911; d. Otto and Kerstin (Bengtson) Sevall; student Am. Conservatory Music, 1928-31, Wheaton Coll., 1930-33; B.M., Am. Conservatory Music, 1962; m. Robert James Schaber, Aug. 13, 1938; children—Lynn Alice, Robert Sevall. Orch. dir. Bethlehem Luth. Ch., St. Charles, Ill., 1930-35; concert violinist, No. Ill., also organist, 1932-35; dir. music Bethlehem Luth. Ch., 1933-35; tchr. instrumental music, orch. dir. Mt. St. Mary's Acad., St. Charles, Ill., 1930-33; pianist Sevall Sisters Trio, 1935-52; tchr. violin and viola, 1930—, Am. Conservatory of Music, Chgo., 1962—; asst. concertmaster West Suburban Symphony, 1954-68; concertmaster Symphony Woods Orch., 1954—. Recipient Paganini gold medal, Am. Conservatory of Music, 1931. Mem. Chgo. Fedn. Musicians, Am. String Tchrs. Assn., Soc. Am. Musicians, Organized Women Musicians. Club: Western Springs (Ill.) Music. Office: 410 S Michigan Av Chicago IL 60605

SCHACHT, LEATRICE STYRT (MRS. MERVYN SCHACHT), psychologist; b. Chgo., Sept. 29, 1923; d. Hyman A. and Sophie (Workenoff) Styrt; B.S., Columbia, 1946; M.A., Kan. U., 1949; m. Mervyn Schacht, Feb. 11, 1951; children—Walter, Paul, Jennie, Susan. Clin. psychologist Winter VA Hosp., Topeka, 1946-48; individual practice psychology, Scarsdale, New Rochelle, N.Y., 1949—; adj. asst. prof. spl. edn. Coll. at New Rochelle (N.Y.). Asso. psychologist Postgrad. Center for Psychotherapy, N.Y.C., 1948-53; cons. psychologist Alcoholics Treatment Center, 1949-53, High Point Hosp., Portchester, N.Y., 1952—; cons. Beechmont Nursery Sch., New Rochelle, 1956-62. Chmn. bd. Westchester Center for Psychol. Edn., White Plains, N.Y., 1969—, chmn. edn. com., 1962-69. Fellow Am. Orthopsychiat. Soc.; mem. Am., N.Y. State del. 1969-73, chmn. awards com., Westchester County (pres. 1971-73, chmn. edn. com. 1962-69, mem. com. liaison with allied professions) psychol. assns., Soc. Projective Techniques. Address: 3 Oakway Scarsdale NY 10583

SCHACHT, MARYANN SCHEFTELL (MRS. HERMAN DAVID SCHACHT), lawyer; b. Milw., Feb. 26, 1938; d. Bernard Harry and Hazel Wilma (Wolff) Scheftell; B.S., Marquette U., 1959; J.D., U. Wis., 1964; m. Herman David Schacht, June 20, 1964; children—Stephanie Katherine, David Bernard. Admitted to Wis. bar, 1964; apprentice atty. Milw. Legal Aid Soc., 1962-63; mem. firm Schacht & Schacht, Fox Lake and Beaver Dam, Wis., 1964—; Dodge County (Wis.) Pub. Defender, 1973—; asst. city atty. of Beaver Dam and Fox Lake, Wis., 1972—. Mem. Selective Service Bd., Dodge County, 1971—; lectr. law and related matters. Chmn. Fox Lake Bldg. Program, 1970—; vol. legal services Wis. Prison, Dodge County; mem. Dodge County Mental Health Adv. Bd., 1973; parents adv. bd. Washington Grade Sch., Beaver Dam, 1974. Alderman City of Fox Lake, 1966-69; worker coms. Gov. and Democratic Party in Wis., 1972; mem. Wis. Law Enforcement Standards Bd., 1974—. Dodge County rep. Marquette U., 1972. Mem. Am., Wis., Dodge County (legal aid com. 1974) bar assns., Marquette U. Alumni Assn. Home: 1209 Homestead Rd Beaver Dam WI 53916 Office: 300 Spring St Fox Lake WI 53933

SCHACHTEL, BARBARA HARRIET (MRS. HYMAN JUDAH SCHACHTEL), psychologist; b. Rochester, N.Y., May 27, 1921; s. Lester and Ethel (Neiman) Levin; student Wellesley Coll., 1939-41; B.S., U. Houston, 1951, M.A., 1967; m. Hyman Judah Schachtel, Oct. 15, 1941; children—Bernard, Ann Mollie. Psychol. testing Center for Developmental Pediatrics, Tex. Childrens Hosp., Houston, 1967—; faculty dept. pediatrics Baylor Coll. Medicine, 1967—. Mem. Houston Welfare Bd. of United Fund, 1967-69. Bd. dirs. Houston and Harris County Mental Health Assn., 1963-69, v.p., 1968; bd. dirs. Vocational Guidance Service, 1965-69; bd. mgrs. Harris County Hosp. Dist., 1970—, vice chmn. bd., 1973. Mem. Am., Tex., Southwestern, Houston (chmn. psychol. assos. com.) psychol. assns., Houston Wellesley Club (pres. 1968-70), Sisterhood Temple Beth Israel. Home: 2527 Glen Haven St Houston TX 77025 Office: 6621 Fannin St Houston TX 77025

SCHACHTER, JUDITH ANN SPECTOR (MRS. JOSEPH SCHACHTER), psychiatrist; b. Bklyn., June 12, 1928; d. Herman and Pauline (Goldstein) Spector; B.A., Radcliffe Coll., 1949; M.D., N.Y. U., 1953; certificate in psychoanalytic medicine Columbia, 1960; certificate in psychoanalysis of children and adolescents U. Pitts., 1973; m. Joseph Schachter, June 12, 1949; children—Rachel Susan, Beth Ann, Daniel Eben. Intern pediatric service Bellevue Hosp., N.Y.C., 1953-54; resident psychiat. div., 1954-55, N.Y. State Psychiat. Inst. and Hosp., N.Y.C., 1955-57; practice medicine specializing in psychiatry, N.Y.C., 1957-68, Pitts., 1968—; asst. attending psychiatrist Vanderbilt Clinic, N.Y.C., 1957-68; tng. and supervising analyst Columbia Psychoanalytic Clinic for Tng. and Research, 1966-68; asso. admitting psychoanalyst, 1967-68; mem. faculty Coll. Phys. and Surg., Columbia, 1960-68, asso. in psychiatry, 1967-68; tng. and supervising analyst Pitts. Psychanalytic Inst., 1970—; clin. asst. prof. Sch. Medicine U. Pitts., 1970—. Recipient Spl. Merit award Assn. Psychoanalytic Medicine, 1967. Mem. Am. Psychiat. Assn., Am. Psychoanalytic Assn., Columbia Psychoanalytic Clinic Alumni Assn. (v.p. 1966-68), Pitts. Neuropsychiatric Soc., Pitts. Psychoanalytic Soc. (sec. 1971—, v.p. 1973-74). Home: 5400 Darlington Rd Pittsburgh PA 15217

SCHACHTER, MERI, psychiatrist; b. Elizabeth, N.J., Mar. 20, 1939; d. Milton I. and Elsa (Meyrson) Schachter; B.A., Adelphi Coll., 1961; postgrad. Columbia, 1962-65; M.D., N.Y. Med. Coll., 1969. Intern, Beth Israel Med. Center, N.Y.C., 1969-70; resident psychiatry Roosevelt Hosp., N.Y.C., 1970-71, N.Y. State Psychiat. Inst., N.Y.C., 1971, Mt. Sinai Hosp., N.Y.C., 1971-73; attending psychiatrist Barnert Meml. Hosp., Paterson, N.J., 1973—. Mem. Am. Psychiat. Assn. Home: 203 W 86th St New York City NY 10024 Office: 12-04 Saddle River Rd Fair Lawn NJ 07410

SCHAEF, ANNE WILSON, psychologist; b. Siloam Springs, Ark., Mar. 22, 1934; d. Virgil E. and Manilla M. (Longan) Willey; A.B., Washington U., St. Louis, 1956, postgrad., 1957-64; m. Robert F.A. Schaef, Dec. 24, 1968 (div. May 1974); children—Beth Anne, Rodney Walter. Clin. intern Bellevue Hosp., N.Y.C., 1960-61; sch. psychologist, White Plains, N.Y., 1961-64; supervising psychologist Youth Center, Alton (Ill.) State Hosp., 1966-68; community psychol. cons. Ill. Dept. Mental Health, 1966-68; pvt. practice, Denver, 1968—. Cons. in feminist therapy, 1969—; cons. on psychology of women to U. Cal. Neuropsychiat. Inst., Los Angeles, Denver Gen. Hosp., Her Majesty's Royal Commn. on the Status of Women in Can., 1971—; co-founder Women's Inst. Alternative Psychotherapy, Denver, 1974, Black Trainer Program for Nat. Tng. Labs., St. Louis, 1968-70. Nat. Inst. Mental Health fellow, 1957, Danforth Grad. fellow, 1956. Mem. Am. Psychol. Assn., Assn. for Humanistic Psychology, Assn. for Transpersonal Psychology, Assn. Women Psychologists, Research Found. for Psychol. Synthesis. Mem. Soc. of Friends. Author: (with Patricia Budd Kepler) Women in the New Creation. Home: 301 Hawthorn Boulder CO 80302 Office: 1633 Vine Denver CO 80206

SCHAEFER, ANNE MARIE GAMBARDELLA (MRS. WILLIAM J. SCHAEFER), social worker; b. Amsterdam, N.Y., Aug. 21, 1922; d. Vincent and Nancy (Salamack) Gambardella; student Larson Jr. Coll., 1941-42; B.A. in Sociology, U. Buffalo, 1947, M.S.W., 1956; m. William J. Schaefer, Aug. 11, 1957; children—Susan, Judith. Caseworker, Erie County Dept. Social Welfare, 1947-53; social worker Cath. Charities Buffalo, 1953-55; psychiatric social worker Dept. Mental Hygiene-Children's Clinic, 1956-57, Buffalo State Hosp., 1958-60; caseworker, Kenmore Community Service, Kenmore, N.Y., 1960-62; supr. Family and Children's Service Niagara Falls, 1962-71, exec. dir., 1971—. Mem. jr. bd. E.J. Meyer Meml. Hosp. Mem. Ladies Charity, 1969—; mem. St. Edmunds Ladies Guild, 1967—. Mem. Nat. Assn. Social Workers, Family Service Assn. Am. (summer inst. com.), Acad. Certified Social Workers, Social Workers Club, Chi Omega Nat. Sorority Alumnae Assn. (sec. 1947—). Zonta Internat. Home: 7 Willowgrove Ct Tonawanda NY 14150 Office: 826 Chilton Av Niagara Falls NY 14301

SCHAEFER, JACQUELINE THIBAULT (MRS. ARTHUR M. SCHAEFER), educator; b. Caen, France, Apr. 5, 1930; d. Emile Gustave and Denise (Feuillet) Thibault; Licence ès Lettres, Université de Caen, 1952, D.E.S., 1953; Agrégation de l'Université, Sorbonne, 1962; m. Arthur M. Schaefer, June 30, 1960; 1 son, Mark Thibault. Prof. French and comparative lit. U. Edinburg (Scotland), 1954-55, Middlebury (Vt.) Coll., 1956-59, Mt. Allison U., N.B., Can., 1959-60, Carleton Coll., Northfield, Minn., 1962-67, U. of the South, Sewanee, Tenn., 1967—. Fgn. service prof. dept. cultural relations State Dept. Fgn. Affairs, French Govt., 1956—. Recipient Fulbright award, 1956, Nat. Found. Arts and Humanities award, 1967. Mem. Société des Professeurs Français en Amérique, Société des Anglicistes de l'Enseignement Supérieur, Modern Langs. Assn., Société des Agrégés, Modern Humanities Research Assn., Am. Assn. U. Women. Home: Florida Av Sewanee TN 37375

SCHAEFER, JOAN CLARK METCALF, ednl. adminstr.; b. Mt. Vernon, O.; d. James Henry and Edna (Clark) Metcalf; B.S., Miami U., Oxford, O., 1943, M.A., 1955; postgrad. Toledo U., 1953-55. Music supr. No. Ohio Schs., 1943-46; dean women Carnegie Mellon U., Pitts., 1953-55, U. So. Cal., Los Angeles, 1956—. Prof. counseling, guidance U.S. Dept. Health, Edn. and Welfare Summer Program Abroad, Weissbaden, Germany, 1962. Bd. dirs. YWCA at U. So. Cal. Mem. Cal. Assn. Women Counselors and Vice-Prins., Nat. Assn. Student Personnel Adminstrn., Am. Personnel and Guidance Assn., Nat. Assn. Womens Deans and Counselors, Trojan League U. So. Cal., Nat. Assn. Personnel Adminstrs., Town and Gown Assn., P.E.O., Mortar Bd., Phi Beta Kappa (hon.), Phi Kappa Phi, Delta Zeta, Mu Phi Epsilon. Home: 6205 Temple Hill Dr Hollywood CA 90068 Office: U So Cal Univ Park Student Union Bldg Los Angeles CA 90007

SCHAEFER, KATHLEEN MARIE (MRS. DORTH OTIS SPURLOCK), physician; b. Piapot, Sask., Can., Oct. 27, 1921; d. Leo Hobson and Marie Gertrude (Palmer) Sanderson; came to U.S., 1941 naturalized, 1947; B.A., Walla Walla Coll., 1942; M.D., Loma Linda U., 1946; m. Dorth Otis Spurlock, Mar. 19, 1969; children—Christine Schaefer, Sandra Schaefer. Intern, Detroit Receiving Hosp., 1945-46; resident White Meml. Hosp., Los Angeles, 1947-49, Children's Hosp., Los Angeles, 1949-53; mem. faculty, clin. anesthesiologist Loma Linda U., Los Angeles, 1954-64; anesthesiologist Glendale (Cal.) Adventist Hosp., 1964—; mem. staff Behrens Meml. Hosp., Glendale. Mem. Am., Cal., Los Angeles County med. assns., Am. Soc. Anesthesiology. Home: 1580 Riviera Dr Pasadena CA 91107 Office: 1451 E Chevy Chase St Glendale CA 91206

SCHAEFER, MARY MAGDALINE, editor; b. Ocean City, Md., Oct. 3, 1913; d. Joseph and Anna Mary (Ruez) Schaefer; A.B., Trinity Coll. D.C., 1935; postgrad. Cath. U., summer 1935, nights, 1938-39. Sec., Nat. Conf. Cath. Charities, Washington, 1937-39, U.S. Senator J.A. Danaher, Washington, 1939-41, Nat. Cath. Community Service, U.S.O., Washington, 1941-43; tech. editor War Dept., Washington, 1943-46; tech. writer, Naval Ordnance Lab., Silver Spring, Md., 1946-51; sci. staff asst. Naval Research Lab., Washington, 1951-53; tech. editor Vitro Labs., Silver Spring, 1953-60; sr. tech. editor Applied Physics Lab. Johns Hopkins U., Silver Spring, Md., 1960—. Tchr., Trinity Coll. Prep. Sch., Ilchester, Md., 1935-36; U.S. del. Internat. Council for Tech. Communication, 1973—. Vice pres. Montgomery Hills Citizen Assn., Silver Spring, 1957-58. Recipient award for distinguished tech. communication Soc. Tech. Writers and Pubs., 1970. Asso. fellow Soc. Tech. Communication (dir. 1967-68, pres. 1970-71); mem. Am. Assn. Univ. Women, A.A.A.S., Govt. Information Orgn., Trinity Coll. Alumnae Assn. (pres. D.C. chpt. 1948-49). Democrat. Roman Catholic. Home: 1951 Seminary Rd Silver Spring MD 20910 Office: Applied Physics Lab Johns Hopkins U 8621 Georgia Av Silver Spring MD 20910

SCHAEFFER, ANNABELLE VINCOW (MRS. ROBERT SCHAEFFER), pediatrician; b. N.Y.C., Sept. 17, 1929; d. Samuel and Minnie (Kurtzman) Vincow; B.A., Bklyn. Coll., 1950; M.D., State U. N.Y. at Bklyn., 1956; m. Robert Schaeffer, June 30, 1957; children—Steven, Susan. Rotating intern Maimonides Hosp., N.Y.C., 1956-57; fellow pediatrics, asst. in pediatrics N.Y. Hosp.-Cornell U., N.Y.C., 1958-59; asst. resident pediatrics Bellevue Hosp., N.Y.C.,

1959-60; chief pediatrics, Pima County Hosp., Tucson, 1961-62; asst. dir. pediatrics, out-patient dept. Kings County Hosp., Bklyn., 1962-63, pediatrician in charge premature and full term nurseries, 1963-64; asso. attending pediatrician Montefiore Morrisania Affiliation, Bronx, N.Y., 1968—; clin. asst. prof. pediatrics Albert Einstein Coll. Medicine, Bronx, 1968—. Home: 14 Walden Rd Tarrytown NY 10592 Office: Morrisania Hosp 168th St and Gerard Av Bronx NY 10452

SCHAEVITZ, STELLA ARONOW (MRS. HERMAN SCHAEVITZ), engring. co. exec.; b. Phila., Jan. 4, 1916; d. Harry and Fanny (Patkin) Aronow; B.S., Temple U., 1936, M.S. in Sociology, 1938; m. Herman Schaevitz, June 29, 1938; children—Howard Allen, Phyllis (Mrs. Terry Howard). Tchr. Camden (N.J.) schs., 1938-41; with Schaevitz Engring., Pennsauken, N.J., 1955—, corp. sec., 1960—. Organizer, pres. Citizens Com. Edn., Haddon Twp., N.J., 1950-55; mem. Bd. Edn., Haddon Twp., 1955-58; trustee Camden County Mental Health Assn., 1960, v.p., 1968-71, pres., 1971-73; mem. state bd. Mental Health Assn., 1973—. Mem. League Women Voters, Camden County Israel Bonds Orgn. (div. chmn. 1963). Jewish religion. Office: Route 130 and Union Av Pennsauken NJ 08110

SCHAFER, ALICE PAULINE, artist; b. Albany, N.Y., Feb. 11, 1899; d. Henry and Emma (Gersbach) Schafer; grad. cum laude Albany Sch. Fine Arts, 1919. One-woman shows Albany Inst. History and Art, 1957, Print Club Albany, 1962, So. Vt. Art Center, 1972; exhibited in group shows Print Club Albany, 1940—, Soc. Am. Graphic Artists, U.S., 1947—, Eng., 1955, Japan, 1967, Nat. Assn. Women Artists, U.S., 1952—, Europe, 1956, 57, India, 1966, Acad. Artists Assn., Springfield, Mass., 1953—; represented in permanent collections Met. Mus. Art, N.Y.C., N.Y. Pub. Library, Butler Inst. Am. Art, Youngstown, O., So. Vt. Art Center, Manchester, Boston Pub. Library, U. S.C., Hunt Library, Carnegie-Mellon U. Recipient Grumbacker award of merit Fla. Internat. Art Exhbn., 1952, other awards. Mem. Pen and Brush Club (Alice Standish Buel prize 1965), Am. Artists Profl. League (Gold medal 1966), Print Club Albany (pres.; recipient John Taylor Arms Meml. Purchase prize 1968), So. Vt. Artists, Nat. Assn. Women Artists, Nat. Arts Club, Old Bergen Art Guild, Catharine Lorillard Wolfe Art Club, Salmagundi Club. Address: 33 Hawthorne Av Albany NY 12203

SCHAFER, ALICE TURNER (MRS. RICHARD DONALD SCHAFER), educator; b. Richmond, Va., June 18, 1915; d. John H. and Cleon (Dermott) Turner; B.A., U. Richmond, 1936, D.Sc., 1964; S.M., U. Chgo., 1940, Ph.D. (fellow), 1942; m. Richard Donald Schafer, Sept. 8, 1942; children—John Dickerson, Richard Stone. Tchr., Glen Allan (Va.) High Sch., 1936-39; instr. math. Conn. Coll., New London, 1942-44, asst. prof., 1954-57, asso. prof., 1957-61, prof., 1961-62; prof. math. Wellesley Coll., 1962—, Helen Day Gould prof. math., 1969—; instr. U. Mich., Ann Arbor, 1945-46; lectr. Douglass Coll., New Brunswick, N.J., 1946-48; asst. prof. Swarthmore (Pa.) Coll., 1948-51; Drexel Inst. Tchr., Phila., 1951-53. Mathematician, Johns Hopkins Applied Physics Lab., Silver Spring, Md., 1945; NSF Sci. Faculty fellow Inst. for Advanced Study, Princeton, N.J., 1958-59. Mem. Am. Math. Soc., Math. Assn. Am., Am. Assn. U. Profs., Assn. Women in Math. (pres. 1973—), Phi Beta Kappa, Sigma Xi, Sigma Delta Epsilon. Contbr. articles to math. jours. Office: Wellesley College Wellesley MA 02181

SCHAFER, NOVELLA ANN, physician; b. Columbus, Neb., Aug. 4, 1931; d. Leander Herman and Novella (O'Rourke) Schafer; B.A., Marycrest Coll., 1953; M.D., Creighton U., 1957. Intern, St. Mary's Hosp., Rochester, N.Y., 1957-58; resident internal medicine Christ Hosp., Cin., 1958-59, fellow infectious disease, 1959-61; practice medicine, specializing in internal medicine, Rockford, Ill., 1961—. Mem. A.M.A., Winnebago County, Ill. State med. socs., Am. Acad. Gen. Practice. Asst. editor No. Ill. Jour. Home: 1620 Benton St Rockford IL 61107 Office: 1345 Charles St Rockford IL 61108

SCHAFFER, GLORIA WALINSKY, state ofcl.; b. New London, Conn., Oct. 3, 1930; d. Arthur and Charlotte (Reiner) Walinsky; ed. Sarah Lawrence Coll. Mem. Conn. Senate, 1959-71; sec. state State of Conn., Hartford, 1971—. Bd. dirs. Greater New Haven Arts Council, New Haven Coll., Foster Sch. and New Haven Community Council, Urban League, Conn. Hosp. Planning Commn., Order Women Legislators. Recipient Nat. Merit award Council Crime and Delinquency; award Nat. Cystic Fibrosis Soc., Conn. Assn. Hearing Impaired Children, Conn. Assn. Vocational instrs.; citation Jewish War Vets. Home: Tumblebrook Rd Woodbridge CT 06525 Office: State Capitol Hartford CT 06103

SCHAFFER, ROSE NUSSBAUM (MRS. JACOB SCHAFFER), artist; b. Newark; b. Adolph and Carrie (Kolber) Nussbaum; student N.Y. U., 1919-20, Art Students League, 1931-34, Pratt Graphic Center, 1958; pvt. study with Bernard Karfiol, Morris Davidson, Sol Wilson, Antonio Frasconi, Seong Moy; m. Jacob Schaffer, June 4, 1923; children—Judith (Mrs. Leonard Howard), Ruth Ann. Exhibited various one-man shows N.Y.C.; exhibited group shows Nat. Acad., Audubon Artists, Nat. Assn. Women Artists, ACA Gallery, N.Y.C., Barzansky Galleries, N.Y.C., Argent Gallery, N.Y.C., Library of Congress, Washington, Smithsonian Instn., Washington, Montclair Museum, Newark Museum, Jersey City Mus., Delgado Mus., New Orleans, Boston Mus., Wichita Mus., Bklyn. Mus., Rochester Meml. Gallery, Conn. Acad., Cape Cod Gallery, Provincetown Gallery, Albany Print Club, Henry Clews Found., Napoule, France, Casino Municipal, Cannes, France; represented in permanent collections Smithsonian Instn., Montclair (N.J.) Mus., Tenn. Fine Arts Center, Nashville, Art Assn. Richmond (Ind.), Mus. Fine Arts, Norfolk, Va., Rutgers Coll. Mus., Springfield (Mass.) Art Mus., Newark and West Orange (N.J.) Library, Daus. of Israel Pleasant Valley Home, West Orange, Burpee Art Mus., Rockford, Ill., others. Vice pres. Newark sect. Nat. Council Jewish Women, 1945; founder Essex unit Nat. Assn. Retarded Children, 1948; founder, sec. Occupational Center Essex County, 1950-69; founder Curative Workshop (now N.J. Rehab. Bur.), Newark, 1923. Recipient Ida Wells Stroud award Am. Artists Profl. League, 1951, award Painters and Sculptors Soc. N.J., 1956, Ross Gallery, 1932, Art Center of Oranges, 1947, Terry Nat., 1935, Short Hills at Mall, 1969, Seton Hall U., 1956, New Haven Paint and Print Club, 1958, South Orange-Maplewood Gallery, 1958, L. Bamberger & Co., 1960, purchase award Art for Overlook Hosp., 1961, 62. Mem. Am. Fedn. Arts, Art Students League, Nat. Assn. Women Artists, Internat. Platform Assn., Artists Equity, United Order True Sisters (pres. 1931). Address: Rossmoor 119A Old Nassau Rd Jamesburg NJ 08831

SCHAFFNER, DOROTHY WEBER (MRS. MURRAY M. SCHAFFNER), educator; b. N.Y.C.; d. Louis and Anna (Greenberg) Weber; B.A. cum laude, Bklyn. Coll., 1935, M.A., 1957; m. Murray M. Schaffner, Apr. 4, 1936; 1 dau., Amy (Mrs. Lewis Kargman). Tchr., Pub. Sch. 91, Bklyn., 1946-56; guidance counselor various schs., N.Y.C., 1946-52; resource cons. Bd. Edn. of N.Y.C., 1962-63; supr. guidance counselors City of N.Y., 1962—. Script writer, cons., participant TV guidance program, 1961; moderator radio program Growing Up, 1961, Looking Ahead, 1961. Mem. Am., N.Y. personnel and guidance assns., Bklyn. Coll. Alumni Assn., Guidance Suprs. Assn., Bklyn. Coll. Guidance Assn. (editor Newsletter 1957-60; historian 1960-62), Kappa Delta Pi. Contbg. author, illustrator: How To Help Your Child with Spelling, 1956. Author, illustrator: Happy Bunny, series for children, 1959. Illustrator: Education for the Growing Family, 1959. Asst. editor Guidance News (N.Y.C. Bd. Edn.), 1961. Co-author: Helping Children Grow-A Job for Parents and Teachers; Marching Ahead to Career; Counselor's Guidebook; Elementary School Guidance Manual. Home: 2515 Av I Brooklyn NY 11210 Office: 2 Linden Blvd Brooklyn NY 11226

SCHALE, FLORENCE CLAIRE, educator; b. Chgo., Nov. 3, 1928; d. Anton and Florence Francis (Chodera) Sachtschale; B.S., Northwestern U., 1951, M.A., 1952; Ph.D., U. Chgo., 1964. Instr. personnel services, U. Wis., 1952-55; dir. reading improvement services Northwestern U., Chgo., 1955—. Tchr. elementary grade Chgo. Pub. Sch. System, 1960-61; writer, instr. series Rapid Reading, CBS-TV, 1970-71; reading cons. to sch. systems, govt. agys., business and industry. Chmn. bd., pres. Found. for Reinforced Reading, Ltd., 1967—, mem. Nat. Task Force for Ind. Living, Am. Found. Blind, 1970—. Mem. Internat. Reading Assn. (Chgo. area rep. 1967-70), Am. Ednl. Reading Assn., Nat. Reading Conf., Inter House Assn. U. Chgo., Internat. Council for the Improvement of Reading Instrn. (founder and hon. bd. mem. Milw. chpt. 1953-55), Am. Assn. U. Women, Eta Sigma Phi, Delta Zeta. Author: Reinforced Reading Manual, TV series, 1970-71, Rapid Reading Program, 1973. Contbr. articles to Ency. Brit., 1970 edit., also to profl. jours. Patentee in field. Address: 1700 E 56th St Chicago IL 60637

SCHALK, ALLACE CARROLL, coll. adminstr.; b. N.Y.C., Apr. 12, 1909; d. John William and Lillian (Graves) Carroll; student Smith Coll., 1928-29, Columbia, nights 1930; div.; children—Chandler (dec.), Erica Dudley (Mrs. Richard A. Burleson). Actress with Milton Aborn's Gilbert and Sullivan Co., N.Y.C., 1931-32, Children's Players, N.Y.C., 1932-34, summer stock, 1931-35; appearances in Peace on Earth, 1934, Small Miracle, 1935, Hamlet, 1936; exec. sec. dept. preventive medicine U. Vt., 1954-63; mem. staff Champlain Coll., Burlington, Vt., 1964—, asst. to pres. for research and devel., 1970—; condr. ballroom dancing classes, 1950—. Mem. Vt. Council Arts, Coll. Advancement Assn. Vt. Co-editor, contbr.: History of Champlain College, 1974. Home: RD 1 Cheese Factory Rd South Burlington VT 05401 Office: Box 670 Champlain Coll Burlington VT 05401

SCHALLIG, DOROTHY WALSH, physician; b. Los Angeles, Feb. 17, 1903; d. George Francis and Anna Mabel (Turner) Walsh; A.B., U. Cal. at Berkeley, 1924; M.D., U. Cal. at San Francisco, 1928; m. W.H.C. Schallig, 1928; m. 2d. Charles V. Cowan, May 16, 1952. Intern, St. Lukes Hosp., San Francisco, 1927-28; resident St. Mary's Hosp., San Francisco, Sacramento County Hosp.; practice medicine, specializing in treatment of arthritis, Sacramento, 1929—; mem. sr. staffs Sutter Gen. Hosp., Sutter Meml. Hosp. (both Sacramento); research in arthritis treatment Eli Lilly Co., 1934-40. Mem. Endocrine Soc., N.Y. Acad. Sci., A.M.A., Cal. Med. Assn., Sacramento County Med. Soc., Pub. Health League. Home: 1218 Teneight Way Sacramento CA 95818 Office: Suite 5 St Lukes Medical Bldg 2600 Capital Av Sacramento CA 95814

SCHALOW, GERTRUDE ELINORE, librarian; b. Fond du Lac, Wis., Dec. 9, 1925; d. Berthold Erich and Lina Katherine (Keopka) Schalow; student Colo. Woman's Coll., 1943-44; B.S. in Chemistry, U. Denver, 1946, M.S. in Math., 1948, M.S. in L.S., 1951. Instr. sci. Colo. Woman's Coll., Denver, 1948-50; cataloger, sr. catalog reviser, sr. subject reviser librarian U.S. Naval Ordnance Test Sta., China Lake, Cal., 1951-52; sr. subject indexer, cataloger tech. reports, librarian U.S. Bur. Reclamation, Denver, 1962—. Denver area regional rep. Task Force on Recruitment Fed. Librarians, Fed. Library Com., 1968-74. Recipient Meritorius Service certificate Bur. Reclamation, 1964. Mem. Spl. Libraries Assn. (pres. Colo. chpt. 1963-64), U. Denver Grad. Sch. Librarianship Alumni Assn. (treas. Rocky Mountain chpt. 1972-74). Mem. United Ch. of Christ. Club: Altrusa (corr. sec. 1974-75). Home: 2584 S Gaylord St Denver CO 80210 Office: PO Box 25007 Denver Federal Center Denver CO 80225

SCHAMUS, CLARITA GERSHOWITZ, lawyer; b. Cleve., June 23, 1930; d. Max and Esther (Anker) Gershowitz; A.A., Pierce Jr. Coll., 1965; B.A., U. San Fernando Valley, 1968, J.D., 1970; m. Julian John Schamus, Mar. 14, 1954 (div. June 1974); children—David Paul, James Allan, Lisa Anne. Admitted to Cal. bar, 1970; individual practice law, Van Nuys, 1970-72; dep. dist. atty. County of Los Angeles, Juvenile div., Pasadena, 1972—. Legislative chmn. P.T.A., 1969; cons. women's rights seminars, 1972-73; v.p. Fair Housing Council San Fernando Valley, 1972-73; mem. professions and finance com. City of Hope, Duarte, 1972—. Home: 11934 Riverside Dr Apt 107 North Hollywood CA 91607 Office: 300 E Walnut St Pasadena CA 91101

SCHANBACHER, NANCY JO MCINTYRE (MRS. RICHARD E. SCHANBACHER), pub. relations exec.; b. Hannibal, Mo., Aug. 24, 1934; d. Charles Wesley and Georgia Belle (Donaldson) McIntyre; A.A., Cottey Jr. Coll., 1954; B.J., U. Mo., 1956; m. Richard E. Schanbacher, Oct. 9, 1960; children—Andrew Willmann, Anne Marie. News reporter, editor United Press Internat., Dallas, 1956-58; reporter-editor womans page Decatur (Ill.) Herald and Review, 1958-60; free lance writing and pub. relations, Maryland Heights, Mo., 1960—. Coordinator annual historic preservations tour of St. Louis Landmarks, 1972—. Vice pres. Sci. Museum, St. Louis, 1973—. P.E.O. scholar, 1952-54; U. Mo. Journalism Sch. scholar, 1955-56. Mem. Women In Communications (membership chmn. 1973—), P.E.O., Gamma Phi Beta. Presbyn. Home and office: 1437 Glenmeade Maryland Heights MO 63043

SCHANDORFF, ESTHER MAY DECH (MRS. MARVIN E. SCHANDORFF), librarian; b. Modoc, Ind., Aug. 9, 1923; d. George L. and May (Whillans) Dech; A.B., Pasadena Coll., 1951; M.S. in L.S., U. So. Cal., 1954; m. Marvin E. Schandorff, June 18, 1946 (dec.); children—Sina May (Mrs. Wesley Allan Thomas), Marvin Eugene. Cataloguer, Pasadena Coll. Library, 1954-67, acting librarian, 1967-68, coll. librarian, 1968-73; coll. librarian Point Loma Coll. Ryan Library, 1973—. Served with USNR, 1944-46. Mem. Cal. Library Assn., Christian Library Assn. (pres. 1973-74), Am., Western (v.p.) theol. library assns., Cal. Book Club., Beta Phi Mu. Republican. Mem. Ch. of the Nazarene. Home: 4930 Del Mar San Diego CA 92107 Office: 3900 Lomaland Dr San Diego CA 92106

SCHANTZ, BETTY BAIRD (MRS. RODERICK A. HILSINGER), univ. dean; b. Lock Haven, Pa., Oct. 13, 1929; d. Alfred Everett and Nellie May (Munro) Baird; B.S. magna cum laude, Lock Haven State Coll., 1959; M.Ed., Pa. State U., 1960, Ed.D., 1963; m. Troy Melvin Schantz, Apr. 15, 1961 (dec. Nov. 1965): children—Cynthia K., Randall E., Laurie Sue; m. 2d, Roderick A. Hilsinger, Jan. 8, 1971. Grad. research asst. Reading Clinic, Pa. State U., 1959-60; grad. teaching asst., dir. student teaching Penn Hill Sch. Dist., Pitts., 1960; tchr. Lancaster (Pa.) Gen. Hosp., 1965-67; faculty Millersville (Pa.) State Coll., 1965-67, Franklin and Marshall Coll., Lancaster, 1965-67, Harrisburg (Pa.) Center for Univ. Teaching, 1965-67, Albright Coll., Reading, Pa., 1965-66; instr. Temple U., Phila., 1961-63, asst. prof., 1963-66, asso. prof., 1966-69, prof., 1967—, asst. dean univ.-sch. relations, 1970—. Mem. steering com. Council Gt. Cities Schs., 1970—. Bd. dirs. Urban Edn. Inst., 1968-72; adv. bd. 12th and Oxford Corp., 1967-72. Recipient grant Office Econ. Opportunity, 1971-72, Kettering Found., 1971, Woman of Yr. award Temple U. Faculty, 1972, Distinguished Tchr. Edn. award for Portal Sch. concept Nat. Assn. Tchr. Educators, 1972. Mem. Am. Assn. Colls. for Tchr. Edn. (instnl. rep. 1971-72), Am. Assn. U. Profs., Am. Ednl. Research Assn., Assn. for Productive Teaching, Assn. for Tchrs. Educators, N.E.A., Pa. Assn. Tchr. Educators (regional v.p. 1969-70), Pa. Edn. Assn., Kappa Delta Pi. Mem. Order Eastern Star. Home: 421 E Gowen St Philadelphia PA 19119 Office: 249 Ritter Broad and Montgomery Philadelphia PA 19119

SCHAPIRO, ELLEN EARDLEY (MRS. HAROLD A. SCHAPIRO), psychiatrist; b. Oakland, Cal., Jan. 25, 1937; d. George Gillespie and Katherine (Cole) Eardley; A.B., U. Cal. at Berkeley, 1959; M.D., U. Cal. at San Francisco, 1963; m. Harold Andrew Schapiro, July 26, 1966. Intern, St. Elizabeth Hosp., Washington, 1963-64; resident Georgetown U. Hosp., Washington, 1965-68; pvt. practice medicine specializing in psychiatry, Los Angeles, 1968-71, Santa Monica, Cal., 1971—; staff psychiatrist Community Mental Health Center, St. John's Hosp., Santa Monica, 1968—; asst. clin. prof. Med. Sch. U. Cal. at Los Angeles, 1969-72. Mem. A.M.A., Cal. Med. Assn., So. Cal., Am. psychiat. assns. Club: Sierra. Home: 1126 Tellem Dr Pacific Palisades CA 90272 Office: 270 26th St Santa Monica CA 90402

SCHAPIRO, RUTH GOLDMAN (MRS. DONALD SCHAPIRO), lawyer; b. N.Y.C., Oct. 31, 1926; d. Louis Albert and Sarah (Shapiro) Goldman; A.B., Wellesley Coll., 1947; LL.B., Columbia, 1950; m. Donald Schapiro, June 29, 1952; children—Jane Goldman, Robert Andrew. Admitted to N.Y. bar, 1950; asst. to reporters Am. Law Inst. Fed. Income Tax Statute, N.Y.C., 1950-51; asso., then mem. Proskauer Rose Goetz & Mendelsohn, 1955—. Mem. Am., N.Y. State (chmn. com. partners and partnerships tax sect. 1974—) bar assns., Assn. Bar City N.Y. (taxation com. 1974—), N.Y. County Lawyers Assn., Am. Judicature Soc. Jewish religion. Club: N.Y. Wellesley (N.Y.C.). Notes editor Columbia Law Rev., 1949-50. Contbr. articles to legal jours. Home: 1035 Fifth Av New York City NY 10028 Office: 300 Park Av New York City NY 10022

SCHARDING, GERTRUDE LOUISE, press relations exec.; b. N.Y.C., June 8, 1913; d. Francis Aloysius and Emma Veronica (Heege) Seidler; B.S., N.Y. U., 1950; m. Raymond F. Scharding, 1932 (dec.). Asst. mgr. press relations pub. relations dept. Union Carbide Corp., N.Y.C., 1958—. Home: 120 E 37th St New York City NY 10016 Office: 270 Park Av New York City NY 10017

SCHARF, SUZANNE MADDOX, pub. relations exec.; b. Beaumont, Tex., Nov. 2, 1948; d. William Autrey and Evelyn Harrell (Dunnam) Maddox; A.B., Marshall U., 1970; postgrad. Coll. Grad. Studies, 1972—; m. Martin Howard Scharf. Reporter, photographer Kanawha Valley Leader, Nitro, W.Va., summer 1969; coordinator of pub. information Kanawha County Bd. Edn., Charleston, W.Va., 1970-73; media specialist Putnam County Bd. Edn., Winfield, W.Va., 1973—. Charter mem. Citizens Recycling Council, Charleston, sec. 1971—; Active Girl Scouts U.S.A., Campfire Girls; mem. Nat. Alliance Businessmen JOBS program, Charleston, 1973, The United Fund, Charleston, 1970. Recipient state pub. awards, W.Va. Press Women, 1972, 73, nat. pub. award, Fed. Press Women, 1972, publ. awards, Nation's Schs. Mag., 1972-73. Mem. W.Va. Communicators (newsletter editor 1971-72), W.Va. Press Women (sec. 1974), Women in Communications (charter mem., pres. chpt. 1969-70), Beta Sigma Phi (v.p. 1971-72, rec. sec. 1972-73). Club: Advertising (bd. dirs. 1972-74) (Charleston, W.Va.). Home: Apt 15 5094 Washington St W Charleston WV 25312 Office: Putnam County Bd Edn Winfield WV 25213

SCHARFF, CONSTANCE KRAMER (MRS. HARRY SCHARFF), artist; b. N.Y.C., Nov. 27, 1903; d. Charles and Rebecca (Blankfort) Kramer; grad. Normal Sch., Bklyn., 1925; study art Bklyn. Mus., 1944-45; m. Harry Scharff, Aug. 29, 1928; 1 son, Matthew Daniel. Exhibited one-man shows Furman U., Greenville, S.C., Lenox (Mass.) Library, Bodley Gallery, N.Y.C., Greenville Mus., others; exhibited in group shows Library of Congress, 1954, 55, 63, Smithsonian Instn., 1960, Bklyn. Mus., 1955, 66, Silvermine Guild, 1960, 61, 64, 65, Inst. of Jamaica (W.I.), 1964, also S.Am., Mex., Japan, India, Can., France; represented in permanent collections Bklyn. Mus., Norfolk Mus., Israel Mus., Phila. Mus., Furman U., Columbia U., N.Y.C., N.Y. Pub. Library, Boston Pub. Library, Inst. of Jamaica (W.I.), various businesses. Recipient awards and medals in various media. Mem. Nat. Soc. Painters in Casein and Acryllic (rec. sec. 1967—), Am. Soc. Contemporary Arts (rec. sec. 1973—), Soc. Am. Graphic Artists, Audubon Artists, N.Y. Soc. Women Artists, Nat. Assn. Women Artists (chmn. print jury 1973—). Club: Manhattan Beach Garden (Bklyn.). Address: 115 Jaffrey St Brooklyn NY 11235

SCHATZ, ANNE ELIZABETH, educator; b. Edgeley, N.D., Nov. 23, 1932; d. Carl and Mary Magdalena (Blake) Larson; B.S., N.D. State U., 1954; M.S., U. N.D., 1967, vocational certification, 1972; m. Arlen Elroy Schatz, Sept. 16, 1957 (div. 1966); children—David A., Kevin P., Steven A. Tchr. phys. edn. and home econs., jr. and sr. high sch., Bismarck, N.D., 1956-61; bus. instr. Capital Comml. Coll., Bismarck, 1962-66; bus. edn. instr. Bemidji (Minn.) State Coll., 1967-68; bus. and office edn. instr., writer multimedia instructional materials Mt. San Jacinto Coll., San Jacinto, Cal., 1968—. Workshop leader and cons. Program with Developing Institutions, Am. Assn. Jr. Colls., 1970-72; speaker Cal. Bus. Edn. Assn., 1969-72; workshop leader Cal. Community Colls., 1969. Mem. Nat., Western, Cal. bus. edn. assns., Classroom Educators in Bus. and Office Edn., Faculty Assn. Cal. Community Colls., Am. Vocational Assn., Delta Pi Epsilon, Delta Kappa Gamma. Republican. Contbr. articles to profl. jours. Home: 26300 Scot Lane Hemet CA 92343 Office: Mt San Jacinto Coll San Jacinto CA 92380

SCHATZ, CECIL RUSKAY (MRS. ARTHUR H. SCHATZ), social worker, civic worker; b. Far Rockaway, N.Y., Jan. 9, 1923; d. Cecil Benjamin and Sophie (Liebovitz) Ruskay; A.B., Cornell U., 1943; M.S. in Social Work, Columbia, 1945; m. Arthur H. Schatz, Feb. 11, 1945; children—Ellen L., Robert F., Daniel N. Placement worker specializing in handicapped children Children's Services Conn., Hartford, 1946-51, 62-71. Mem. nat. bd., life mem. women's div. Am. Soc. Technion, N.Y.C., 1961—; life mem. women's div. Brandeis U., Waltham, Mass., 1960—; life mem. Hadassah, 1961—, Mt. Sinai Hosp. Assn., Hartford, 1970—; bd. dirs. Hartford div. Nat. Council Jewish Women, 1958—, v.p., 1966-68, pres., 1968-71; mem. bd. Beth El Temple Sisterhood, 1964—; chmn. Artists in Residence Scholarship Program, 1969-73; co-chmn. Beth El Art Show, Hartford, 1964-66; mem. Jewish Theol. Sem.; counselor Sr. Citizens Jobs Bank, West Hartford, 1973—; bd. dirs. Hartford Women's Aux. Brandeis U., 1968—, Hartford Jewish Community Center, 1974—. Am. Mem. Am. Assn. Social Workers. Clubs: Cliffside Country (Simsbury, Conn.); Bloomfield (Conn.) Indoor Tennis. Author: Placement of Handicapped Children, 1945. Donor, Celia Pessin Scholarship Technion, Haifa, Israel, 1962. Home: 33 Juniper Rd Bloomfield CT 06002

SCHAUER, ANNE HOLIDAY (MRS. ROLAND EZRA SCHAUER), govt. ofcl.; b. Balt., May 24, 1939; d. Thomas I. and Delta T. (Moore) Edwards; B.A., Grinnell Coll., 1960; M.S., U. Minn., 1962; m. Roland Ezra Schauer, Dec. 22, 1962; children—Caroline, Stephen. With Sci. Information Exchange, Washington, 1963; with NSF, Washington, 1963—, asst. program dir. for developmental biology, 1963—. Carolyn Crosby fellow, 1961-62. Mem. A.A.A.S., Bot. Soc. Am., Soc. for Developmental Biology. Home: 5129 Macomb St NW Washington DC 20016 Office: 1800 G St NW Washington DC 20550

SCHAUER, CATHARINE MAUD (MRS. IRWIN JAY SCHAUER), writer, b. Woodbury, N.J., Sept. 24, 1945; d. Jack and Anna Ruth (Felipe) Guberman; A.B., Dade Jr. Coll., 1965; B.Ed., U. Miami, 1967; postgrad. Mercer U., 1970; m. Irwin Jay Schauer, July 4, 1968; children—Cheryl Anne, Marc Cawin. Tchr., Palm Springs Jr. High Sch., Miami, Fla., 1967-68, Lanier High Sch., Macon, Ga., 1968; coordinator pub. information, newspaper adviser Macon Jr. Coll. (Ga.), 1969; free lance writer, 1970—; editor Killian Hill Manor's Community Newspaper, Lilburn, Ga., 1970-72. Recipient First Place award in feature and news writing Fla. Jr. Coll. Press Assn., 1965. Democrat. Home and office: 2301 Galley Ct Woodbridge VA 22191

SCHAULER, EILEEN (MRS. IRWIN CHARONE), soprano; b. Millburn, N.J., July 1, 1928; d. Vincent A. and Marion (Farley) Schauler; diploma, postgrad. diploma Juilliard Sch. Music; m. Irwin Charone, Nov. 14, 1954; 1 son, Jeffrey. First profl. appearance Chautauqua Opera Assn., then Papermill Playhouse, Millburn; soloist with Robert Shaw at Carnegie Hall at age seventeen; played feature roles at St. Louis Municipal Opera, Lambertville Music Circus, Kansas City Starlight Theater; Broadway debut in title role My Darlin' Aida, 1952; appeared in major opera prodns. singing leading roles Albuquerque Symphony, St. Paul Civic Opera, Central City Opera Festival, N.Y.C. Center, Chgo. Theatre of Air, Atlanta Theatre Under Stars, Pocono Playhouse, Cleve. Musicarnival, Hyannis, Mass., Pitts. Symphony, Ft. Worth Opera, Canadian Opera Co., others; more recent appearances include: Marfa in The Tsar's Bride, N.Y. Philharmonic, Marschallin in Rosenkavalier (excerpts), Met. Opera Lewisohn Stadium Concert, Renata in Am. premiere of The Flaming Angel, also Tosca, La Boheme, Der Rosenkavalier; N.Y. City Opera; two world premiers The Servant of Two Masters, also Nine Rivers From Jordan. Home: New York City NY 10019 Office: care Ludwig Lustig 111 W 57th St New York City NY 10019

SCHAUS, EMELIA CHRISTINA, lawyer; b. Provemont, Mich., Sept. 2, 1891; d. Simon B. and Frieda (Erdt) Schaub; J.D., Detroit Coll. Law, 1924; LL.M., U. Detroit, 1926. Admitted to Mich. bar, 1924; individual practice law, Detroit, 1924-37, Leelanau, Mich., 1937—; pros. atty. Leelanau County, 1937-49; pub. adminstr. Wayne County, 1934. Mem. Women Lawyers Mich., Leelanau Hist. Soc. (pres. 1972-73). Republican. Roman Catholic. Home and office: 1212 Manitou Trail W Lake Leelanau MI 49653

SCHECHTER, DOROTHY LOUISE, lawyer; b. Oklahoma City, July 28, 1934; d. Ernst Onne and Louise Gertrude (Schaale) Buenting; B.S. in Law, U. So. Cal., 1962, LL.B., 1964; m. Thomas Lisle Schechter, Mar. 14, 1954. Admitted to Cal. bar, 1965, U.S. Supreme Ct. bar, 1969; law clk. County of Ventura (Cal.), 1964-65, dep. dist. atty., 1965-66, asst. county counsel, 1966-70, acting chief asst. county counsel, 1970-71, chief asst. county counsel, 1971-73, county counsel, 1973—. Mem. Cal., Ventura County bar assns., Dist. Attys.-County Counsels Assn. Cal., Nat. Orgn. Legal Problems of Edn., Tri-Counties Govt. Attys. Assn., Women Attys. Assn. Home: 1120 N Signal St Ojai CA 93023 Office: 501 Poli St Ventura CA 93001

SCHECHTMAN, BEVERLY BETH, lawyer; b. Jersey City, Dec. 4, 1946; d. Bernard Joseph and Ruth (Steinfeld) Schechtman; student Boston U., 1963-65; B.S., Monmouth Coll., 1968; J.D., Seton Hall U., 1971. Admitted to N.J. bar, 1971; atty. Dept. of Army, Phila., 1972—. Mem. Am., N.J., Fed. bar assns., Fed. Bus. Assn., Nat. Orgn. for Women, Phi Alpha Delta. Home: 1131 Jeffrey Av Wanamassa NJ 07712 Office: 225 S 18th St Philadelphia PA 19103

SCHECKTER, STELLA JOSEPHINE, librarian; b. Phila., Nov. 30, 1926; d. Isaar Jerome and Rose (Levin) Scheckter; A.B., Temple U., 1948; M.L.S., Drexel U., 1952. Continuations asst. acquisitions dept. Temple U. Library, 1949-52; jr. asst. reference dept. Hartford (Conn.) Pub. Library, 1952-53; asst. br. librarian, 1953-54; asst. lit. and lang. dept. Enoch Pratt Free Library, Balt., 1954-56, asst. bus. and econ. dept., 1956-58; head reference and loan div. N.H. State Library, Concord, 1958—. Mem. Concord Bicentennial Com., 1965, Concord Arts Council, 1966-68, Citizens Com. for a Broad Based Tax, 1966-67. Recipient best set design award community theatre div., New England Theatre Conf., 1968. Mem. Am. (state membership chmn. 1964-69), New England (chmn. bibliography com. 1971—) library assns., N.H. Library Council (pub. relations com. 1971—), N.H. Hist. Soc. Clubs: Woman's College (dir. 1965-67), Concord Community Players (dir. 1965-67), Concord Music (bd. dirs. 1967-69), Concord Artists. Home: 53 School St Concord NH 03301 Office: 20 Park St Concord NH 03301

SCHEERER, WYNELLE MIMS (MRS. T. ANTHONY HART), educator; b. Baxley, Ga., Sept. 6, 1932; d. John and Jeanette (Lasket) Mims; B.S. in Nursing, Fla. A. and M. U., 1956; M.S. in Nursing Edn., Ind. U., 1960, postgrad., 1967; postgrad. Centres Universitaires (France), summer 1970; Ed.D., Ind. U., 1973; m. F. Joseph Scheerer, Apr. 21, 1958 (dec. July 1965); m. 2d, T. Anthony Hart, Oct. 17, 1970. Staff nurse Fla. A. and M. U., 1956-57, instr., 1960-61; staff nurse Fremont Hosp., Yuba City, Cal., 1959; asst. dir. nursing service Mercy Hosp., Denver, 1962; asso. dir. nursing edn. Yorkton Union Hosp., Sask., 1962-65; asst. prof. nursing edn. Mont. State U., Billings, 1965-71; asst. prof. U. Wis., Oshkosh, 1971-73; asso. prof. Ball State U., Muncie, Ind., 1973—. Vis. asst. prof. U. Ghana, Africa, 1970. Served to lt., Nurses Corp, USAF, 1957-59. Mem. Am., Mont. (dist. rec. sec. 1967—) nurses assns., Am. Assn. U. Profs., Am. Assn. Higher Edn., Internat. Platform Assn., Alpha Kappa Alpha. Home: PO Box 2134 Muncie IN 47902

SCHEETZ, SISTER MARY JOELLEN, coll. pres.; b. Lafayette, Ind., May 20, 1926; d. Joseph Albert and Ellen Isabelle (Fitzgerald) Scheetz; A.B., St. Francis Coll., 1956; M.A., U. Notre Dame, 1964; Ph.D., U. Mich., 1970. Tchr., English, Bishop Luers High Sch., Fort Wayne, Ind., 1965-67; acad. dean St. Francis Coll., Fort Wayne, 1967-68, pres., 1970—. Bd. dirs. Catholic Social Service, Fort Wayne, 1972—. Mem. Am. Assn. Higher Edn., Delta Epsilon Sigma. Address: 2701 Spring St Fort Wayne IN 46808

SCHEFELBEIN, BARBARA ELLEN, coll. adminstr.; b. Peoria, Ill., Oct. 28, 1926; d. Herman Frederick and Sara Eunice (Miller) Schefelbein; B.S., Bradley U., 1948, M.A., 1967. Med. technologist Meth. Hosp., Peoria, Ill., 1950-57; chmn. technician Caterpillar Tractor Co., Peoria, 1957-65, personnel research analyst, 1965-67, tchr. human relations, 1968-69; counselor Ill. Central Coll., East Peoria, 1967-68, registrar, 1968-73, asst. prof. psychology, 1973—. Bd. dirs. Blind Peoples Center, Peoria, 1955-57, Ill. Valley Mental Health Assn., 1971—. Mem. Am. Ill. (pres. 1973) assns. collegiate registrars, Jr. League Peoria, Pi Lambda Theta. Home: 6213 St Mary's Rd Peoria IL 61614 Office: Box 2400 East Peoria IL 61611

SCHEFF, BETTY-JANE (MRS. BENSON H. SCHEFF), social scientist; b. Bklyn., Apr. 23, 1932; d. Nat J. and Mabel N. (Bernstein) Weiss; student Oberlin Coll., 1949-51; B.S. cum laude, Columbia, 1953; M.Ed., Boston U., 1966; m. Benson H. Scheff, May 30, 1953; children—Andrew Jon, James Lloyd, Brian Cyril, Ann-Mara. Dir., Watertown (Mass.) Children's Theater, 1956-69; sr. research asst. McLean Hosp., Belmont, Mass., 1969-73, research cons., 1973—; staff psychologist Elliot Day Center, Concord, Mass., 1973—. Cons. in creative activities, Boston area, 1956-70. Pres. Watertown P.T.A., 1967-68; pres. Beth-El Nursery Sch., Belmont, 1960-62. Bd. dirs. Cambridge Jewish Community Center; trustee Fayerweather St. Sch., Cambridge, Mass., 1969-70. Mem. Am. Ednl. Theater Assn., Dance Circle of Boston (treas. 1963-64), League Women Voters (dir. Watertown 1960-71), Pi Lambda Theta. Jewish religion (mem. religious sch. com. 1970—). Home: Concord Rd Lincoln MA 01773 Office: Elliot Day Center Concord MA 01742

SCHEIBLA, SHIRLEY HOBBS (MRS. LOUIS COLLINS SCHEIBLA, JR.), editor; b. Newport News, Va., Sept. 29, 1919; d. Wage Hampton and Maude Celestine (Bean) Hobbs; student Coll. William and Mary, 1938-39; B.A., U. N.C., 1941; m. Louis Collins Scheibla, Jr., Sept. 12, 1941; 1 son, Louis Collins III. Staff corr. Wall St. Jour., Washington, 1943-48; Washington corr. Richmond (Va.) News Leader & Newport News Daily Press, 1949-53; Washington editor Barron's mag., 1958—. Lectr., Adminstrv. Law Judges Conf., Nat. Security Indsl. Assn. Mem. Am. Newspapers Women's Club (financial sec. 1960-61, corr. sec. 1950-51), Washington Press Club, Chi Delta Phi. Author: Poverty Is Where the Money Is, 1968. Home and office: 6630 Tansey Dr Falls Church VA 22042

SCHEIBLE, SISTER MARIE CLARE, hosp. adminstr.; b. Rochester, N.Y., June 27, 1924; d. Anthony Leo and Florence Aurelia (Servatius) Scheible; student St. Marys Hosp. Sch. Nursing, 1942-43; R.N., St. Johns Hosp. Sch. Nursing, 1952; B.S. in Nursing, St. Louis U., 1954; M.B.A., Xavier U., 1965. Factory worker Stromberg Carlson Co., Rochester, 1943-44; receptionist E.E. Bausch & Son, Rochester, 1944-47; joined Hosp. Sisters of Third Order of St. Francis, 1947; staff nurse, asst. head nurse St. Johns Hosp., Springfield, Ill., 1952-53, clin. instr. Sch. Nursing, 1954-63; adminstrv. resident St. Josephs Hosp., Syracuse, N.Y., 1964-65, St. Lukes Hosp. Campbell County, Ft. Thomas, Ky., 1965; asst. coordinator hosp. services St. Mary's Hosp., Streator, Ill., 1965-67, asst. adminstr., 1967-68; exec. v.p. St. Josephs Hosp., Highland, Ill., 1968—. Sec., treas., bd. dirs. Home Health Services, Highland, 1973-74. Mem. Bd. Health City of Highland, 1969—; mem. governing bd. St. Elizabeth Hosp., Granite City, Ill., 1972—; mem. community adv. com. sch. nursing div. So. Ill. U., Edwardsville, Ill., 1969—. Mem. Am. Coll. Hosp. Adminstrs., Am., Ill. (region pres. 1973-74), Cath., Ill. Cath. hosp. assns., Southwestern Ill. Hosp. Planning Council (sec. 1972), Highland Right to Life, Xavier U. Alumni Assn., C. of C. Home: 1635 Main St Highland IL 62249 Office: 1515 Main St Highland IL 62249

SCHEIBNER, RUTH MARTIN (MRS. LAWRENCE F. SCHEIBNER, JR.), educator, psychologist; b. Phila., Aug. 24, 1921; d. James Frederick and Rebecca Bamford (Carmen) Martin; A.B., Temple U., 1960, M.A., 1962, Ph.D., 1969; m. Lawrence Frederick Scheibner, Jr., May 27, 1950; 1 dau., Judith (Mrs. John Joseph Massaro). Psychology intern VA Hosp., Coatesville, Pa., 1961-62, VA Hosp., Phila., 1962-63; instr., counseling psychologist, acad. adviser Temple U., 1963-69; sch. psychologist, Marlton, N.J., 1966-67; lectr. Thomas Jefferson U., 1968-69; asst. prof. Phila. Coll. Pharmacy and Sci., 1968-70, asso. prof., 1971—. Individual practice psychotherapy, 1968—; counsellor family relations com. Phila. Soc. Friends, 1969—. Bd. dirs. Phila. br. human engring. lab. Johnson O'Connor Research Found., 1954-56. Recipient award for excellence in psychology Psi Chi, 1962. Mem. Am., Eastern, Pa. psychol. assns., Am. Assn. U. Profs., A.A.A.S., Phila. Soc. Clin. Psychologists, Kappa Epsilon. Home: Orchard Dr MR #2 Ambler PA 19002 Office: Phila Coll of Pharmacy and Sci 43d St and Woodland Av Philadelphia PA 19104

SCHEIN, LORRAINE SANDRA (MRS. AARON MEYER SCHEIN), librarian; b. Bklyn., Jan. 29, 1933; d. Abraham Isaac and Belle (Siegel) Charnoff; B.A., Adelphi U., 1954; M.S., N.Y. U., 1959; postgrad. Bklyn. Coll., 1956-59; M.S. in L.S., C.W. Post Coll., 1967; m. Aaron Meyer Schein, June 5, 1960; children—Adam Michael, Rachel Jennifer. Teaching fellow N.Y. U., 1954-56; lit. chemist Scientific Design Co., Inc., N.Y.C., 1956-60; patent liaison Leesona-Moos Corp., Gt. Neck, 1960-66; librarian Grumman Aerospace Corp., Beth-Page, 1966-67; head librarian L.I. Center Library, Poly. Inst. N.Y., Farmingdale, 1970—. Mem. A.A.A.S., Am. Chem. Soc., Assn. for Computing Machinery, Spl. Libraries Assn., Am. Soc. Information Scis., Nassau County Library Assn., Phi Sigma Sigma, Delta Tau Alpha, Delta Phi Alpha, Gamma Sigma Epsilon. Hadassah. Home: 17 Admiral Lane Hicksville NY 11801 Office: Route 110 Farmingdale NY 11745

SCHEINBLUM, RUTH MIRIAM BLOOM (MRS. FREDERICK SCHEINBLUM), educator; b. Norwood, N.J.; d. David and Kate (Rosen) Bloom; student U. Chgo., 1935-37, N.Y. U., 1937-39; B.S., Columbia, 1964, M.A., 1965; m. Kalman Levitan, Mar. 9, 1939 (div. May 1950); children—Robert P., Richard A., Robin Elaine; m. 2d, Frederick Scheinblum, Aug. 2, 1950; children—Ralph F., Randi Lynn. Tchr. Lotte Kaliski Sch., Englewood, N.J. 1959-65, dir. Kaliski Schs., 1967—; founder, pres., dir. Camp Randi, Milford, N.J., 1961—; with Bd. of Edn., Fort Lee, N.J., 1965-67; dir. Hill Crest (N.J.) Nursery Camp, 1959-61. Mem. Pi Lambda Theta, Kappa Delta Pi. Home: 161 Van Nostrand Av Englewood NJ 07631 Office: 127 W 79th St New York City NY 10024

SCHEINER, ELLEN, physician; b. Bklyn., Jan. 27, 1932; d. Morris and Pauline (Harber) Scheiner; A.B cum laude, Bklyn. Coll., 1952; M.D., U. Lausanne, 1960. Intern, Kings County Hosp., Bklyn., 1960-61; resident N.Y. Infirmary, 1961-62; resident Meml. Hosp., N.Y.C., 1962-64, sr. pub. health trainee, 1964-66, asst. attending medicine, clin. physiology and renal service, 1970—, cons. med. audit, 1973—; asso. clinician Sloan-Kettering Inst., N.Y.C., 1970—; asst. prof. medicine Cornell U. Med. Coll., N.Y.C., 1970—; co-dir. biomed. data sect. div. med. systems Meml. Sloan-Kettering Cancer Center, N.Y.C., 1974—. Ellse L'Esperance fellow, 1962-63. Diplomate Am. Bd. Internal Medicine. Mem. A.C.P., N.Y. Acad. Scis., A.A.A.S., N.Y. Nephrology Soc., Thanatology Soc. (profl. adv. bd.). Home: 345 E 68th St New York City NY 10021 Office: 1275 York Av New York City NY 10021

SCHELL, EILEEN (MRS. ALLAN CARTER SCHELL), market research co. exec.; b. Chgo., July 1, 1934; d. Paul Roscoe and Madeline Eulalia (Mooney) Conaghan; B.A. with distinction, Stanford, 1956; postgrad. (Fulbright scholar), Internat. Tng. Centre for Aerial Survey, Delft, Netherlands, 1956-57; M.A., Boston U., 1959, Ph.D., 1964; m. Allan Carter Schell, May 23, 1957; children—Alice Rosalind, Cynthia Anne. Owner, market research cons. Eileen Schell—Market Research, Winchester, Mass., 1964—; dir. United Mortgage Co., Gulf Me. Lobster Corp. Lectr. bus. Harvard, 1971—. Bd. dirs. A Better Chance, Winchester, 1973—, program chmn., 1973. Mem. Am. Marketing Assn., Assn. Am. Geographers, Urban Land Inst., Real Estate Brokers Assn. Club: Jubilee Yacht (Beverly, Mass.). Home and office: 19 Wedgemere Av Winchester MA 01890

SCHELLBERG, RUTH MILDRED, educator; b. Omaha, July 22, 1912; d. Otto Emil and Clara Elizabeth (Schmitz) Schellberg; B.S., U. Neb., 1934; M.A., N.Y. U., 1937, Ph.D., 1951. Tchr., Nebraska City (Neb.) Pub. Schs., 1934-36; instr. U. Minn., 1937-38; asst. prof. Macalester Coll., 1938-46; asst. prof. Mankato (Minn.) State Coll., 1946-48, prof. phys. edn., 1952—; asso. prof. U. Neb., 1949-52. Canoe guide Superior Quetico Wilderness Area, 1941—; camp dir. Camp Sealth, Wash., 1946-49. Bd. dirs. Mankato United Fund; bd. dirs. Mankato council Camp Fire Girls, 1952—, Nat. council, 1970—. Recipient Gulick award Camp Fire Girls, 1962. Mem. A.A.H.P.E.R. (archivist 1972—), Minn. Assn. Health, Phys. Edn. and Recreation (pres. 1960, Lou Kellar award 1973), Central Assn. Phys. Edn. Coll. Women (pres. 1969-71). Contbr. articles to camping, canoeing and skiing to popular mags. Home: 50 Skyline Dr Mankato MN 56001

SCHELLENBERG, HELENE GLADYS CHAMBERS (MRS. CARL E. SCHELLENBERG), author; b. Saskatoon, Sask., Can.; d. Stanley W. and Lillian (Lancaster) Chambers; B.A., San Diego State Coll., 1938; m. Carl E. Schellenberg, Feb. 25, 1938 (dec.); 1 son, Carl S. Tchr. adult edn., lectr. Mem. Cal. Writers Club. Author: Sons of The Ocean, 1963; Beth Adams, Private Duty Nurse, 1964; Nurse's Journey, 1967; Breath of Life, 1970; Nurse in Research, 1974. Address: 2593 Vallejo St Santa Rosa CA 95405

SCHEMBERGER, RUTH MARIE, sch. ofcl.; b. Regent, N.D., Nov. 3, 1919; d. John Henry and Fredericka Anna (Pertner) Monke; grad. high sch.; m. Phillip Schemberger, Dec. 14, 1940; 1 dau., Dianne (Mrs. James Peter Andrew Beneteau). With Citizens State Bank New England (N.D.), 1960-73, asst. cashier, 1969-73, security officer, 1970-73; treas. New England Pub. Sch. Dist. 9, 1971-72, 74—. Lutheran. Home: New England ND 58647

SCHEMMEL, JANET ELEANOR (MRS. DOUGLAS SCHAUER), physician; b. Beaver Dam, Wis., Oct. 6, 1928; d. Harold Carl and Edith Luise (Rettig) Schemmel; A.B., U. Colo., 1949, M.D., 1954; m. Douglas Schauer, Aug. 26, 1961; 1 dau., Joann Luise. Intern, Denver Gen. Hosp., 1954-55; resident St. Joseph Hosp., Denver, 1955-56; resident U. Colo., 1956-57, asso. prof. medicine, 1969—; clin. instr. St. Joseph's Hosp., Denver, 1961-73, chief medicine, 1973-75; practice medicine, specializing in endocrinology, Denver, 1961—; chief endocrine clinic VA Hosp., Denver, 1973—. Mem. Gov.'s Med. Adv. Bd., 1973-75. USPHS fellow in metabolism, 1957-59. Fellow A.C.P.; mem. A.M.A., Colo. (del.), Denver (del.) med. socs., Am. Soc. Internal Medicine, Colo. Soc. Internal Medicine (past sec.), Colo. Diabetic Assn. (past pres.), Am. Diabetic Assn. (vice chmn. camp com. 1971-73), Endocrine Soc. Author papers on metabolism and endocrinology. Home: 34 Albion Denver CO 80220 Office: 2045 Franklin Denver CO 80205

SCHENCK, JANET D. (MRS. MARTIN A. SCHENCK), ednl. adminstr.; b. Evanston, Ill.; d. Henry E. C. and Mary (Williams) Daniels; grad. St. Mary's Sch., Garden City, L.I., N.Y., N.Y. Sch. Social Work, Am. Inst. Applied Music, N.Y.C.; spl. courses Columbia; studied with Harold Bauer, Paris; M.A. (hon.), Rutgers U., 1946; Mus.D. (hon.), Lafayette Coll., 1948; m. Martin A. Schenck, Aug. 1916 (dec.). Founder, dir., trustee, head piano dept. Manhattan Sch. Music, N.Y.C., 1917-56, trustee, trustees rep. to adminstrn., dir. emeritus, 1956—; mem. adv. bd. Juilliard Mus. Found., 1924-25, lectr. summer sch., 1939; lectr. N.Y. Sch. Social Work, 1931-33. Mem. Municipal Art Com. of One Hundred, N.Y.C., 1934; mem. adv. bd., mem. examining com. adjustment service Fed. Music Project, 1934; pres. Nat. Guild Community Music Schs., 1934-41. Bd. dirs. Rachmaninoff Fund, 1944-46; adv. bd. High Sch. Performing Arts, 1949—. Recipient Handel medallion City of N.Y., 1968; Presdl. citation Nat. Fedn. Music Clubs; citation Assn. Am. Composers and Condrs., 1970. Mem. Nat. Assn. Schs. Music (v.p. 1947-49, mem. publicity com. 1950). Author: Music, Youth and Opportunity; Adventure in Music—A Reminiscence, 1961; also articles in Progressive Edn. and other mags. Home: 1165 Park Av New York City NY 10028 Office: Manhattan Sch Music 120 Claremont Av New York City NY 10027

SCHENCK, NORMA ELAINE (MRS. ARTHUR H. SCHENCK), sch. adminstr.; b. South Connellsville, Pa., Oct. 14, 1926; d. Gloster Dale and Etta L. (Hall) Hepler; B.S., Ind. U., 1949, M.S., 1963; postgrad. Ind. State U., 1973; m. Arthur H. Schenck, July 21, 1951; children—Lynn L., Kenneth Arthur. Sec. to chief recruitment sec. VA, Washington, 1946-47; tchr. bus. edn., St. Joseph County, Ind., 1949-50, Lakeville, Ind., 1950-53, Washington High Sch., South Bend, Ind., 1959-65; chmn. bus. edn. dept. Co-op. Office Edn., coordinator Jackson High Sch., South Bend, 1965-70; coordinator bus. edn. South Bend Community Sch. Corp., 1970—. Project dir. Career Guidance Inst., South Bend, 1973-74; tchr. Am. Inst. Banking, South Bend, 1972-73, Ind. U., South Bend, 1972-74. Mem. Nat. Suprs. Bus. Edn., Nat., Ind. bus. edn. assns., Am. Assn. U. Women (br. pres. 1964-66), Am. Soc. Tng. and Devel. (2d v.p. Michiana chpt. 1973-74), Am. Soc. Personnel Adminstrn. (pres. Michiana chpt. 1973-74), Am., Ind. (Merit award, 1973), vocational assns., Delta Kappa Gamma. Home. 1354 E Huffman Dr South Bend IN 46614 Office: 635 South Main St South Bend IN 46623

SCHENK, FAYE L. ZEICHIK (MRS. MAX SCHENK), club woman; b. Des Moines, Aug. 17, 1909; d. Naphtali H. and Rebecca (Rotkow) Zeichik; B.A., Drake U., 1930, M.A., 1932, L.H.D., 1974; m. Max Schenk, Sept. 3, 1933; children—Mina (Mrs. Herbert B. Hechtman), Raphael I. Chmn. Youth Aliyah-Hadassah, N.Y.C., 1960-64, sec., 1957-61, v.p., 1961-64, treas., 1964-68, nat. pres., 1968-72; del. 30th Ann. Conf. World Youth Aliyah, Jerusalem, 1965. Del., Zionist Gen. Council, mem. presidium, 1972—; mem. Conf. of Presidents Major Am. Jewish Orgn., 1968—; del. to Brussels Conf. on Soviet Jewry, 1971; v.p. World Confedn. of Gen. Zionists; U.S. del. to World Zionist Conf., 1964, 68, 72; chmn. exec. com. Am. Zionist Fedn., 1972—. Bd. govs. Hebrew U., Jerusalem. Mem. Univ. Womens Orgn., Phi Mu Gamma. Home: 115 Central Park W New York City NY 10023 Office: 65 E 52d St New York City NY 10022

SCHENKER, TILLIE ABRAMSON, librarian; b. Baton Rouge, Nov. 12, 1910; d. Abraham and Mathilde (Mendelsohn) Abramson; B.S., La. State U., 1930, B.S. in L.S., 1934; m. Michael Max Schenker, Mar. 31, 1940. Field worker, circulation dept. La. State Library, 1934-39; asst. librarian East Baton Rouge (La.) Parish Library, 1939-46, librarian, 1947—. Sec. bd. dirs. Community Services Council, 1957-63; bd. dirs. Baton Rouge Guidance Center, 1962-63; mem. bd. Family Counseling Service, 1957-60; mem. bd. Baton Rouge Area Tb Assn., 1960-68, sec., 1964-66; dir. bd. La. Tb and Respiratory Assn., 1968-69. Mem. Am., La. (pres. 1962-63) library assns. Democrat. Jewish religion. Club: Library (Baton Rouge). Home: 220 Steele Blvd Baton Rouge LA 70806 Office: 700 Laurel St Baton Rouge LA 70802

SCHERER, FLORA ELLA (MRS. HOWARD R. LIMBACHER), psychiatrist; b. New Philadelphia, O., Oct. 3, 1901; d. Frederick and Frances Emma (Stoeckline) Scherer; B.S., Coll. of Wooster, 1925; M.A., Ohio State U., 1928; M.D., Ohio State U., 1937; m. Howard R. Limbacher, Mar. 20, 1935. Tchr. elementary sch., New Philadelphia, 1922-23; tchr. high sch., Jacksonville, Fla., 1925-26, Port Washington, O., 1926-27; prof. biology dept. Alfred (N.Y.) U., 1928-30; grad. asst. physiology Ohio State U., Columbus, 1930-32; intern Akron (O.) Peoples Hosp., 1937-38; resident psychiatry Hardings Sanitarium, Worthington, O., 1938-41; practice medicine, specializing in psychiatry, Westerville, O., 1941-43; coll. physician Otterbein Coll., Westerville, O., 1941-43; psychiatrist Kalamazoo State Hosp., 1943-67; psychiat. examiner Probate Ct., Kalamazoo, 1967—. Active Kalamazoo Art League, Kalamazoo Symphony Soc.; lectr. on gardening. Mem. A.M.A., Mich. Med. Soc., Kalamazoo Acad. Medicine, Sigma Delta Epsilon, Kappa Delta. Clubs: Altrusa (sec. Kalamazoo 1950), Kalamazoo Garden. Address: 3628 Bronson Blvd Kalamazoo MI 49008

SCHERF, MARGARET, writer, state legislator; b. Fairmont, W.Va., Apr. 1, 1908; d. Charles Henry and Miriam (Fisher) Scherf; student Antioch Coll., Yellow Springs, O., 3 yrs.; m. Perry E. Beebe, Dec. 9, 1965. Reader, sec. to editor Robert M. McBride & Co., N.Y.C., 1928-29; worked on leader's mag. Camp Fire Girls, 1932-34; sec. and copy writer Wise Book Co., N.Y., 1934-39; writer, 1939—; sec. to a naval comdr., Bklyn., 1942-44; mem. Mont. Ho. of Reps., 1965—. Author: (detective novels) The Corpse Grows a Beard, 1940; The Case of the Kippered Corpse, 1941; They Came to Kill, 1942; The Owl in the Cellar, 1945; Always Murder a Friend, 1948; Murder Makes Me Nervous, 1948; Gilbert's Last Toothache, 1949; The Gun in Daniel Webster's Bust, 1949; The Curious Custard Pie, 1950; The Green Plaid Pants, 1951; The Elk and the Evidence, 1952; Dead: Senate Office Building, 1953; Glass on the Stairs, 1954; The Cautious Overshoes, 1956; Judicial Body, 1957; Never Turn Your Back, 1958; (novel) Wedding Train, 1960; The Diplomat and the Gold Piano, 1963; The Mystery of the Velvet Box, 1963; The Corpse in the Flannel Nightgown, 1965; The Mystery of the Shaky Staircase, 1965; The Mystery of the Empty Trunk, 1966; The Banker's Bones, 1967; The Beautiful Birthday Cake, 1971; To Cache a Millionaire, 1972; If You Want a Murder Well Done, 1974. Home: 737 1st Av W Kalispell MT 59901

SCHERGER, MOZELLE SPAINHOUR (MRS. GEORGE RICHARD SCHERGER), librarian; b. Forsyth County, N.C., Dec. 17, 1916; d. Earnest Sidney and Mertie Blanche (Hauser) Spainhour; B.S., Appalachian State Tchrs. Coll., Boone, N.C., 1937; B.S. in L.S., U. N.C., 1943; m. George Richard Scherger, Feb. 23, 1946; children—Teresa Ann (Mrs. Richard Martin), George Richard, Joseph John, Daniel M. Tchr. English and French, sch. librarian Cramerton (N.C.) High Sch., 1937-42; librarian Laurinburg-Maxton AFB, 1943, Piedmont Jr. High Sch., 1944, Pope Field AFB, 1945-46, Charlotte (N.C.) Coll., 1957-64; documents and serials librarian U. N.C. at Charlotte, 1965-69, asst. reference librarian, 1969—. Mem. Am. Assn. U. Profs. Home: 701 St Julien St Charlotte NC 28205

SCHERICH, ESTHER ANNE, educator; b. New Haven, Dec. 15, 1943; d. Millard and Esther (Petersen) Scherich; B.A., Ore. State U., 1966; M.A., U. Ore., 1970, D.Arts, 1973, postgrad. 1973—. Sec. dept. English, U. Ore., Eugene, 1966-69; research asst., 1969-70, teaching fellow English, 1970—. Mem. Women in Communications, Modern Lang. Assn. Am., Am. Assn. U. Profs., Am. Soc. for Eighteenth Century Studies, Kappa Delta. Republican. Presbyn. Home: 821 N Washington Wheaton IL 60187 Office: Dept English U Ore Eugene OR 97403

SCHERMERHORN, SANDRA LEIGH, lawyer; b. Easton, Pa., July 7, 1944; d. George Lewis and Martha Claire (Cunningham) Schermerhorn; B.A., Beaver Coll., 1966; J.D., U. Mo., 1969. Admitted to Mo. bar, 1970; law clk. to U.S. dist. judge Western Dist. Mo., Kansas City, 1970-73; mem. firm Spencer, Fane, Britt & Browne, Kansas City, 1973—. Mem. Am., Kansas City bar assns., Mo. Bar, Trial Lawyers Assn., Kappa Beta Pi. Home: 12914 Beacon St Grandview MO 64030 Office: 1000 Power and Light Bldg Kansas City MO 64105

SCHERR, LOIS HELEN BROWN, lawyer, found. exec.; b. Rockville Centre, N.Y., Apr. 1, 1927; d. Irving and Sadie Jeannette (Berlinger) Brown; A.B., U. Mich., 1948, J.D., 1950; m. Merle Sundrell Scherr, Mar. 9, 1952; children—Sara Jeannette, Carol Anne, Robin Diane, Martha Barrie. Law clk., Roosevelt, N.Y., 1950-52; admitted to N.Y. bar, 1951, W.Va. bar, 1953; exec. sec. Legal Aid Soc., Charleston, W.Va., 1952-53; practice law, Charleston, 1953—; exec. dir. Allergy Rehab. Found., Inc., Charleston, 1971—. Instr. polit. sci. dept. Morris Harvey Coll., 1972-73. Chmn. health econs. com. Regional Health Planning Council, 1973—. Trustee, sec. Allergy Rehab. Found., Inc., 1965-71. Mem. W.Va., Kanawha County bar assns., Nat. Assn. Women Lawyers, Charleston Estate Planning Council, Am. Coll. Allergists Womens Aux. (parliamentarian 1964-73), Kanawha Med. Soc. Womens Aux., Nat. Council Jewish Women, Quota (pres. Charleston 1965-66, parliamentarian 1973—). Jewish religion. Home: 1204 Colonial Way Charleston WV 25314 Office: Atlas Bldg Charleston WV 25301

SCHERZER, DORIS ANNA BROWN (MRS. THEODORE SCHERZER), violinist; b. Parma, O.; d. Fred Irving and Ruth (Juengling) Brown; grad. cum laude, Baldwin-Wallace Coll., 1937; m. Theodore Scherzer, June 25, 1938; 1 dau., Carol. Played in ann. Bach Festival at Baldwin-Wallace Coll., 1930-38, concertmistress Coll. Orch., 1936-37; violinist Cleve. Philharmonic Orch., 1937-46; concertmistress, asst. conductor Columbus Orchestral Soc., 1955-60; 1st violinist Columbus Symphony Orch., 1956-68; on tour Am. Community Symphony Orch., Europe, summer 1968; pvt. violin tchr. Partner, Scherzers Bakery, Columbus. Mem. Music Educators Nat. Conf., Am. String Tchrs. Assn. Mu Phi Epsilon, Delta Kappa Gamma. Home: 396 Mimring Rd Columbus OH 43202 Office: 31 E Long St Columbus OH 43215

SCHETLIN, ELEANOR M., univ. adminstr.; b. N.Y.C., July 15, 1920; d. Henry Frank and Elsie (Chew) Schetlin; B.A., Hunter Coll., 1940; M.A., Tchrs. Coll., Columbia, 1942, D.Edn., 1967. Playground dir. Dept. of Parks, N.Y.C., 1940-42; librarian Met. Hosp. Sch. Nursing, N.Y.C., 1943-44, dir. recreation, 1944-48, dir. recreation and guidance, 1948-59; coordinator student activities State U. N.Y., Plattsburgh, 1959-63, asst. dean students, 1963-64; asst. prof., coordinator student personnel services City U. N.Y., Hunter Coll., 1967-68; asst. dir. student personnel Columbia U., Coll. Pharm. Scis., N.Y.C., 1968-69, dir. student personnel, 1969-71; asso. dean for students, health scis. center State U. N.Y. at Stony Brook, 1971-73, asst. v.p. student services, 1973—. Mem. So. N.Y. League Nursing (dir. 1954-56, 64-66), Student Nurse Assn. N.Y. State (adviser 1955-59), N.Y. State League Nursing, N.E.A., Am. Assn. Higher Edn., Am. Personnel and Guidance Assn., Nat. Assn. Women Deans, Adminstrs. and Counselors, Am. Coll. Personnel Assn. Contbr. articles to profl. jours. Home: 20 Barberry Lane Sea Cliff NY 11579 Office: Health Scis Center State U Stony Brook NY 11790

SCHEUREN, CHARLOTTE PORTER BAYLISS, civic worker; b. Melrose, Mass., May 8, 1936; Clayton and Violet (Porter) Bayliss; B.A., Western Md. Coll., 1959; m. Clarence William Scheuren, June 14, 1958 (div. 1971); 1 dau., Page Porter. With Reader's Digest, Pleasantville, N.Y., 1954-56; tchr. English, Collegeville (Pa.) High Sch., 1959. Flag chmn. Gen. David Forman chpt. D.A.R., Trenton, N.J., 1962-65, 68-70, jr. membership chmn., 1961-62, publicity chmn., 1965-68, program chmn., 1968-70, 2d vice regent, 1965-68, 1st vice regent, 1968-70, page N.J. State confs., 1960—, personal page state regents, 1961-70, pres. gen., 1965-68, state jr. membership chmn., 1965-68, state page chmn., 1968-71, state mag. chmn., 1971-74, page Nat. Continental Congresses, 1961-68, chief lobby pages, 1962, 64, 65, personal page to pres. gen., 1965-68, page marshal, 1964-65, nat. vice chmn. page com., 1968—, nat. vice chmn. jr. membership, 1965-68, speakers staff, 1971—, nat. def. chmn. Valley Forge (Pa.) chpt., 1962-65, Christmas hostess, program chmn., 1964-65, vice chmn. ann. jr. tea, 1964; escort for Princess Christina of Sweden on tour of Trenton, 1965; vol. worker Trent House Assn., 1966—, bd. dirs., 1970; cart chmn. Helene Fuld Hosp. Aux., Trenton, 1967—. Mem. Republican Women of Pa. Mem. Union League, Gen. (past pres., dir.), Montgomery County (past county rec. sec.) fedns. women's clubs, Freedoms Found. at Valley Forge women's com.), Valley Forge Hist. Soc., Nat. Assn. Parliamentarians, Americans for Patriotism (nat. jr. chmn. nat. insignia com.), Colonial Daus. 17th Century (jr. chmn. Pa. chpt.), New Eng. Women, Daus. of Founders and Patriots, Daus. Colonial Wars (N.J. rec. sec. 1968-71), Sons and Daus. of Pilgrims, Daus. Ancient and Hon. Arty. Co., Daus. Am. Colonists, Internat. Platform Assn., Questers, Germantown Hist. Assn., Am. Assn. U. Women, Phila. Art Mus., Eastern Amateur Ski Assn. Jr. League (edn. sec., arts com.). Baptist. Clubs: Collegeville Women's, Aronimink Golf (Newton Square, Pa.). Home: Apt A5 222 Sullivan Way Trenton NJ 08628

SCHIAVINA, LAURA MARGARET, ins. co. exec., artist; b. Springfield, Mass., Nov. 27, 1917; d. Joseph A. and Egidia (Bernini) Schiavina; student Traphagen Sch. of Fashion, 1944-46, U. R.I., 1967, Cornell U., 1968, Art Students League, 1973-74. With Eastern States Farmers Exchange, Springfield, 1935-44; with Marsh & McLennan, 1944—, adminstrv. asst., 1971—; exhibited in one-man shows at Little Gallery, Barbizon Hotel, N.Y.C., 1968, Galerie Internat., N.Y.C., 1969; exhibited in group shows at Westfield (Mass.) Coll., 1968, Nat. Acad., N.Y.C, 1969; Lever House, N.Y.C., 1973, 74, also various exhbns. with Wall St. Art Assn., Nat. Art. League and Jackson Heights Art Club; represented in pvt. collections. Recipient numerous prizes, awards. Mem. Wall St. Art Assn. (v.p. 1972—), Am. Artist Profl. League, Nat. Art League. Club: Jackson Heights Art (pres. 1970-71), Salmagundi (N.Y.C.). Home 35-25 78th St Jackson Heights NY 11372 Office: 1221 Av of the Americas New York City NY 10021

SCHIEFERSTEIN, GRACE ANNA, librarian; b. Glen Moore, N.J., Dec. 28, 1915; d. William and Carolina (Braun) Schieferstein; A.B., Albright Coll., 1938; postgrad. State Tchrs. Coll., California, Pa., 1939-40; M.S., Syracuse U., 1956. Asst. children's librarian Reading (Pa.) Pub. Library, 1943-49, br. librarian, 1949-55, head circulation, 1956-67, dir. adult services, 1967—. Mem. Am., Pa. library assns., Beta Phi Mu. Republican. Lutheran. Home: 1907 Bernville Rd Reading PA 19601 Office: Reading Pub Library 5th and Franklin Sts Reading PA 19602

SCHIFF, DOROTHY, publisher; b. N.Y.C., Mar. 11, 1903; d. Mortimer L. and Adele A. (Neustadt) Schiff; student Brearley Sch., N.Y.C., 1912-20, Bryn Mawr Coll., 1920-21; m. Richard B. W. Hall, Oct. 17, 1923; children—Mortimer W., Adele T.; m. 2d, George Backer, Oct. 21, 1932; 1 dau., Sarah Ann; m. 3d, Theodore Olin Thackrey, July 29, 1943; m. 4th, Rudolf Sonneborn, 1953. Pres., pub. N.Y. Post, 1942—. Mem. Ellis Island Investigating Com., 1934; bd. dirs. Henry St. Settlement, Mt. Sinai Hosp., 1934-38, Woman's Trade Union League of N.Y., to 1939, N.Y.C. Bd. Child Welfare, 1937-39. Decorated Legion of Honor (France). Democrat. Address: NY Post 210 South St New York City NY 10002

SCHIFF, E. JEAN, educator, artist; b. Keokuk, Ia., Oct. 20, 1929; d. Eli and Miriam (Rossman) Brody; student Chgo. Art Inst., 1949-52, Washburn U., 1957-60, U. Kan., 1961-63, Coll. San Mateo, 1963-64; B.F.A., U. Denver, 1966; M.F.A. (Grad. fellow), U. Colo., 1970; m. Samuel B. Schiff, Nov. 23, 1950 (div. May 1971); children—Ellen Janet, Robin Merrill. Instr., Jr. Sch. Art, Mulvane Art Center, Washburn U., Topeka, 1957-61; instr. art U. Colo., Denver, 1970; art instr. Met. State Coll., Denver, 1970-71, asst. prof., 1971—; instr. art Colo. Womens Coll., Denver, 1970-71, Community Coll. Denver, 1971; tchr. childrens art classes Jewish Community Center, Denver, 1970. Exhibited in one-woman shows Met. State Coll., Denver, 1971, Creighton U., Omaha, 1971, Friends of Contemporary Art, Denver, 1973, William Kastan Gallery, Denver, 1973, Berry Coll., Ga., 1974; Stanislaus State Coll., Turlock, Cal.; exhibited in group shows U. N.D., Joslyn Mus., N.A.D., Houston Mus. Fine Art, Dublin Gallery Art, Knoxville, Tenn., Nelson Atkins Mus., Kansas City, Mo., San Francisco Mus. Art, Denver Art Mus., Okla. Art Center, Am. Acad. Arts and Letters, N.Y.C.; represented in permanent collections at U. Colo., Denver U., Wichita (Kan.) Art Assn., Bucknell U., Lewisburg, Pa., Mulvane Art Center, St. Paul Art Center, Francis McCray Gallery Western N.M., Silver City, Stanislaus State Coll., Brena Gallery, Denver, Kastan Gallery, also pvt. collections. Juror, Nat. Graphic Arts and Drawing Exhbn., Wichita Art Assn., 1969. Upward bound adviser Met. State Coll., 1972-73; mem. Denver Art Mus., 1969—. Recipient numerous awards, honors. Mem. Coll. Art Assn., Friends of Contemporary Art. Jewish religion. Home: 945 S Downing Denver CO 80209 Office: Met State Coll 250 W 14th Av Denver CO 80214

SCHIFTER, MARGARET HOYT, edn. adminstr.; b. N.Y.C., June 25, 1931; d. J. King and Jean (Ware) Hoyt; B.A., Sarah Lawrence Coll., 1953; children—Lisa, Timothy W. Asst. dir. admissions Sarah Lawrence Coll., Bronxville, N.Y., 1953-56, dir. ann. giving, 1966-67, dir. devel., 1972—; dir. devel. and pub. relations Hampton Day Sch., L.I., N.Y., 1967-68; v.p. Catalyst, Inc., N.Y.C., 1968-72. Mem. parent com. Brearley Sch., N.Y.C., 1970-72. Pres. Alumnae Assn., Sarah Lawrence Coll., 1959-65; bd. trustees, 1957-60, 1965-66; bd. dirs. Catalyst, N.Y.C., 1972—. Author: (with Felice Schwartz) How to Go to Work When Your Husband's Against It, Your Children Aren't Old Enough, and There's Nothing You Can Do Anyhow, 1971. Home: 139 E 94th St New York City NY 10028 Office: Sarah Lawrence Coll Bronxville NY 10708

SCHILDE, BARBARA DELILAH, home economist; b. Baton Rouge, La., Aug. 21, 1933; d. Alvin and Delilah Young (Hobgood) Schilde; B.S., La. Tech. U., 1955; M.S., La. State U., 1963, postgrad. 1967, 68, 69. Asst. home demonstration agt. La. Coop Extension, Pointe Coupea Parish, 1955-56; asst. and asso. home demonstration agt. Ascension Parish, 1956-58; home demonstration agt. St. Charles Parish, 1958-70, asso. specialist, Baton Rouge, 1970—. Mem. March of Dimes Antique Show (displayed dolls 1970-71). Mem. Am., La. home econs assns., Nat., La. assns. extension home economists (Distinguished Service award 1970), St. Charles Hosp. Aux., Nat. Assn. Miniature Enthusiasts, Gamma Sigma Delta, Sigma Kappa, Epsilon Sigma Phi. Mem. Order of Eastern Star (worthy matron 1966). Clubs: Pilot (Baton Rouge); River Road Garden (Hahnville, La.); United Fedn. of Doll Clubs, Inc.; Woman's Faculty La. State U. Home: 1913 Glenmore Ave Baton Rouge LA 70808 Office: Louisiana State University Knapp Hall Baton Rouge LA 70803

SCHILLER, AMELIA MARGARETE, educator; b. Bklyn.; d. Gustav and Maria (Schleif) Schiller; B.A., Queens Coll., 1951, M.A., 1953; postgrad. N.Y. U., 1961, City U., 1963. Tchr., Grover Cleveland High Sch., Ridgewood, N.Y., 1951-52; tchr. Jr. High Sch. 125, N.Y.C., 1952-58, ednl. and vocational counselor, 1958-66, asst. to prin., 1966—, now asst. prin. Woodside (N.Y.) Jr. High Sch. Gen. Electric Guidance fellow, 1960. Mem. Am. Personnel and Guidance Assns., Nat. Vocational Guidance Assn., Nat. Assn. Women Deans and Counselors, Assn. Asst. Prins., N.Y. State Guidance and Personnel Assn., Kappa Delta Pi, Pi Lambda Theta. Home: 89-10 Rutledge Av Glendale NY 11227 Office: 46-02 47th Av Woodside NY 11377

SCHILLER, ANNE MARIE (MRS. JOHN D. SCHILLER), broadcasting co. exec.; b. San Antonio, Dec. 8, 1947; d. John and Olivia Hagy; student San Antonio Coll., 1966-68; B.J., U. Tex., 1970; m. John D. Schiller, Oct. 23, 1971. Copy, pub. service dir. radio sta. KTSA, San Antonio, 1970—. Office: PO Box 18128 San Antonio TX 78218

SCHILLER, RUTH PHYLLIS, physician; b. Phila., Jan. 21, 1941; d. Albert Harris and Laura (Weiser) Schiller; A.B., Temple U., 1962; M.D., Woman's Med. Coll., 1966. Intern, Albert Einstein Med. Center, Phila., 1966-67; resident St. Christopher's Hosp. for Children, Phila., 1967-69; practice medicine, specializing in pediatrics, Sellersville, Pa., 1969—; mem. teaching staff Temple Med. Sch., St. Christopher's Hosp., Phila., 1969—; mem. staff Grand View Hosp., Sellersville, Pa. Fellow Am. Acad. Pediatrics. Home: 104 W Broad St Souderton PA 18969 Office: Lawn Av Profl Bldg Sellersville PA 18964

SCHILLING, KATHERINE LEE TRACY (MRS. CLARENCE R. SCHILLING), educator; b. Mitchell, S.D., May 31, 1925; d. Ernest Benjamin and Mary Alice (Courier) Tracy; B.A., Dakota Wesleyan U., 1947; M.A., U. S.D., 1957; postgrad. U. Wyo., U. Neb., Kearney State Coll.; m. Clarence R. Schilling, Oct. 14, 1951; 1 dau., Keigh Leigh. Tchr. elementary and secondary schs., also colls., S.D. and Neb.; now with specially funded project for disadvantaged children Winnebago Indian reservation, Neb. Mem. staff S.D. Girls' State, 1950-51; mem. S.D. Gov.'s Com. on Library, Neb. Gov.'s Com. on Right to Read. Recipient Outstanding Tchr. award S.D. High Sch. Speech Tchrs., 1966. Mem. N.E.A., Neb., Thurston County (pres.) edn. assns., Winnebago Tchrs. Assn., Delta Kappa Gamma. Mem. Order Eastern Star. Club: Internat. Toastmistress (internat. dir. 1963-65, Mitchell Toastmistress of Year 1959). Contbr. articles to profl. jours., also poetry. Home: 39 S Harmon Dr Box 578 Mitchell SD 57301 also Hotel Fuller Walthill NE 68067 Office: Winnebago Public Sch Winnebago NE 68071

SCHILTZ, JUANITA D., real estate exec.; b. Dallas, July 7, 1927; d. Edward Henry and Daisy (Taliaferro) Schiltz; student Hockaday Jr. Coll., 1945-46, Sophie Newcomb Coll., 1946; B.S., So. Meth. U., 1947; M.S., Boston U., 1958. Instr. journalism So. Meth. U., Dallas, 1947; mng. editor Ins. Graphic, Dallas, 1947-51; commd. pvt. 1st class U.S. Air Force, 1951, advanced through grades to maj., 1967, retired, 1972; information officer, 1951-72; advt. dir., salesman Tom Pico, Inc., real estate, Kailua, Hawaii, 1973; broker Velva Bergevin, Ltd., Honolulu, 1974—. Mem. pub. relations com. Girl Scouts of Pacific, 1970—, Aloha council Boy Scouts Am., 1969—. Mem. Women in Communications, Honolulu Press Club, Honolulu Bd. Realtors, Air Force Assn., Tau Mu Epsilon. Mem. Order Eastern Star. Home: 1290 Ulunahele St Kailua HI 96734 Office: 572 Kailua Rd Kailua HI 96734

SCHIMPF, MARGARET FITZGERALD (MRS. WILLIAM PAUL SCHIMPF), ednl. adminstr.; b. N.Y.C., Sept. 11, 1946; d. Donald Francis and Mary Margaret (Brooks) Fitzgerald; B.A., Coll. New Rochelle, 1968; m. William Paul Schimpf, June 12, 1971. Adminstrv. asst. to v.p. for univ. relations Fairfield (Conn.) U., 1968-70; dir. coll. relations Coll. New Rochelle (N.Y.), 1970-74; staff asst. pub. relations So. New Eng. Telephone Co., New Haven, 1974—. Recipient Certificate Achievement awards Printing Industries Met. N.Y., 1973. Mem. Am., Westchester colls. pub. relations assns., Westchester County Assn. Home: 80 Dogwood Dr Easton CT 06425 Office: 227 Church St New Haven CT 06506

SCHINAGL, MARY SONORA, educator; b. Phila., June 18, 1914; d. Joseph S. and Mary (Sonora) Schinagl; student Phila. Conservatory Music, 1940-45; B.A., Chestnut Hill Coll., 1941; M.A., U. Pa., 1946; M.Ed., Temple U., 1960; Ph.D., U. Pa., 1962. Jr. civil engr. Naval Air Material Center, Phila., 1942-45; price economist OPS, Phila., 1951-52; mgmt. analyst Frankford Arsenal, Phila., 1952-56; tchr. Rancocas Valley Regional High Sch., 1956-58; counselor Souderton Area Joint High Sch., 1959-60; asst. dean women West Chester (Pa.) State Coll., 1959-60; guidance dir. Overbrook Regional High Sch., Lindenwold, N.J., 1960-62; faculty Monmouth Coll., W. Long Branch, N.J., 1962—, prof. polit. sci. and bus. adminstrn., 1967—. Recipient NSF award, 1965. Mem. Internat. Personnel Mgmt. Assn., Am. Mgmt. Assn. Author: History of Efficiency Ratings, 1966. Contbr. articles to profl. jours. Home: 1409 Webb St Asbury Park NJ 07712 Office: Monmouth College West Long Branch NJ 07764

SCHINDELAR, KATHRYN ANNE, lawyer; b. Camden, N.J., Sept. 2, 1941; d. Francis Joseph and Jeanne Edna (Best) Schindelar; B.A. in Russian Studies and History, Syracuse U., 1964; J.D., Detroit Coll. Law, 1968. Admitted to Mich. bar, 1969, N.J. bar, 1971; practiced in Oakland County, Mich., 1969—. Spl. adviser on equal rights amendment Mich. Ho. of Reps. Judiciary Com. Mem. Mich. State Bar, Oakland County, South Oakland, N.J. bar assns. Home: 8263 Tipisco Trail Tipisco Lake MI Office: 207 Pontiac Mall Bldg Pontiac MI 48053

SCHIPPER, EDITH WATSON (MRS. GERRIT SCHIPPER), educator; b. Fenchow, Shansl, China, Nov. 4 1909 (parents Am. citizens); d. Percy Theodore and Clara (French) Watson; B.A., Carleton Coll., 1931; M.A., Radcliffe Coll., 1934, Ph.D., 1937; m. Gerrit Schipper, June 17, 1937; 1 dau., Margaret (Mrs. Tom Reed). Instr. philosophy Elmira (N.Y.) Coll., 1936-37, Carleton Coll., Northfield, Minn., 1934-35; instr. Uniao Cultural Brasil-Estados Unid, Sao Paulo, Brazil, 1944-46; asst. prof. philosophy U. Miami, Coral Gables, Fla., 1947-53, asso. prof., 1953-65, prof., 1965—. Mem. Fla. Philos. Assns. (pres. 1966-67) Am. Soc. Aesthetics, So. Soc. Philosophy and Psychology, Phi Beta Kappa. Author: First Course in Modern Logic, 1960; Forms in Plato's Later Dialogues, 1965. Home: 5785 Blue Rd Miami FL 33155 Office: Dept Philosophy U Miami Coral Gables FL 33124

SCHIRMER, HARRIET CROCKER JACKSON (MRS. DONALD KENNETH SCHIRMER), physician; b. Mineola, N.Y., Sept. 25, 1926; d. Myron Robinson and Mildred (Wicker) Jackson; A.B., U. Mich., 1946; M.D., N.Y. U., 1950; m. Donald Kenneth Schirmer, Oct. 1, 1961; 1 son, Jack Myron. Intern Meadowbrook Hosp., Hempstead, N.Y., 1950-52; resident U. Colo. Med. Center, Denver, 1952-54; med. officer in charge pub. health service Alaska

Native Hosp., Bethel, 1954-57; dir. eye, ear, nose, throat research project Alaska Dept. Health, 1957-59; practice medicine Bethel, 1959-65; Livonia, N.Y., 1965-70; coroner Livingston County, 1967-70; now pres. staff Wrangell (Alaska) Gen. Hosp. Chmn. Livingston County (N.Y.) Pub. Health Adv. Com., 1967-69; pres. Livingston County Bd. Health, 1969-70. Mayor, Bethel, Alaska, 1960-62. Diplomate Am. Bd. Family Practice. Mem. Am. Acad. Gen. Practice (chpt. pres. 1968), A.M.A., Alaska State Med. Assn., Aerospace Med. Assn. Presbyn. Address: Box 773 Wrangell AK 99929

SCHISGALL, JANE KUSHNER, educator; b. Washington, Nov. 21, 1934; d. David Howard and Yvonne (Levy) Kushner; A.B., Smith Coll., 1956; M.A., N.Y. U., 1959; m. Richard M. Schisgall, June 7, 1957; children—Laura, Lesley, David. Tchr., Riverdale (N.Y.) Country Sch., 1957-59, Garden City (N.Y.) pub. schs., 1959-61; drama specialist Boys Clubs N.Y.C., 1961-62, Detroit Recreation Dept., 1964-66, YMCA, Beth, Md., also Jewish Community Center, Rockville, Md., also Rockville Recreation Dept., 1966-70, Mark Twain Sch., Rockville, 1970—. Instr. drama Montgomery Coll., Rockville, 1969-70; cons. drama George Washington U., 1970-72; instr. inservice course Montgomery County Pub. Schs., 1970-73. Vice pres. Adventure Theatre, Bethesda, Md., 1968-69. Bd. dirs. North Chevy Chase Elementary Sch., 1968-71. Recipient fellowship Smith Coll., 1956-57. Mem. Am. Theatre Assn., Children's Theatre Assn., Secondary Sch. Theatre Assn. Home: 8814 Brierly Rd Chevy Chase MD 20015 Office: Mark Twain Sch 1551 Avery Rd Rockville MD 20015

SCHLAPFER, JOAN FRANCES, univ. ofcl.; b. Trenton, N.J., Nov. 15, 1947; d. Morris Leroy and Florence (Rowe) Schlapfer; Asso. Sci., Endicott Jr. Coll., 1968; B.S., Boston U., 1970; M.Ed. in Coll. Counseling, Northeastern U., 1972. Grad. adminstrv. asst. Programmed Learning Center, Northeastern U., Boston, 1970-72; counselor with rank instr. Stonehill Coll., North Easton, Mass., 1972-73; asst. dean students U. Cal. at Berkeley, 1973—, asst. dir. student activities, 1973—. Student tchr. Kundalini Yoga and meditation, 1974—. Mem. Am. Personnel and Guidance Assn., Nat. Assn. for Women Deans, Adminstrs. and Counselors, Cal. Assn. Women Adminstrs. and Counselors. Home: Guru Ram Das Ashram 2200 Roosevelt Av Berkeley CA 94703 Office: 201 Sproul Hall U of Cal at Berkeley Berkeley CA 94720

SCHLAYER, MARY ELIZABETH, mgmt. cons.; b. Harrisburg, Pa., Apr. 1, 1915; d. Charles Edward and Mary (Kennedy) Schlayer; B.S., Carnegie Inst. Tech., 1938; postgrad. Pa. State Coll., summers 1938-39; M.A., U. Hawaii, 1946; Ed.D., U. Fla., 1951; m. Carlos M. Cardeza (USN ret.), Aug. 20, 1951. Asst. state coordinator Pa. Area Colls., 1946-49; vis. lectr. bus. adminstrn. State Tchrs. Coll., Shippensburg, Pa., 1947; asst. dir. post high sch. edn. survey Pa. Legislature, 1948; mgmt. cons., 1951—; field dir. The Delphian Soc., 1954-56, regional dir., 1957—; adv. dir. Liberty Bank, Houston, 1972—. Chmn. Interested Citizens Com., Sanibel Is., Fla., 1968-69. Bd. dirs. Houston-Harris County Tb Assn., gen. chmn. women's div. Tb drive, 1964; bd. dirs. Nat. Cystic Fibrosis Found.; exec. com. Houston Youth Council; chmn. Joske's Consumer Adv. Bd., 1972-74. Publicity chmn. home econs. scholarship fund U. Houston, also mem. library adv. com., chmn. financial adv. bd. women, 1972—; chmn. boosters def. adv. com. Women in Services; mem. pub. relations council St. Joseph's Hosp., Houston; mem. adv. vis. com. bd. trustees Carnegie-Mellon U.; mem. bd. woman's pavilion Hemis Fair, 1968. Served as lt. comdr. USNR, 1942-56; rep. to comdt. on spl. recruiting problems since World War II; commd. two Fast Attack Transports, U.S. Naval Base Green Cove Springs, Fla., 1951. Recipient Outstanding Alumni award Carnegie-Mellon U., 1969; named Houston Profl. Woman of Yr., 1965. Mem. Am. Legion, U. Fla. Alumni Assn., Carnegie Tech. Alumni Assn. (pres.), Tex. Fedn. Women's Clubs (dist program chmn., dir. local dist., state chmn. Americanism dept.), Res. Officers Assn. (treas. 1952-53), Alpha Chi Alpha, Kappa Delta Pi. Author: Principles of Organization and Administration of Institutions of Higher Learning; Excerpts from Lady Get Organized, 1968. Author: (tapes) For Women Only: How to Feather Your Nest in Real Estate, How to Prepare to be a Widow; also articles on principles mgmt. and human relations in mags.; lectr. in field. Editor: The Tex. Clubwoman, 1962-64. Home: PO Box 6746 Houston TX 77005 also 1718 Jewel Box Dr Sanibel Island FL 33957

SCHLEGEL, DOROTHY MILDRED BADDERS (MRS. MARVIN W. SCHLEGEL), educator; b. Harford County, Md., July 18, 1910; d. John Joseph and Lucy Alice (Davis) Badders; B.A., Dickinson Coll., 1932; M.A., Coll. William and Mary, 1948; Ph.D. U. N.C., 1954; postgrad. U. Vienna, 1954, Sorbonne, 1955, U. Frankfurt, 1954-55, 62; m. Marvin W. Schlegel, Apr. 9, 1941. Tchr. English, Hannah Penn Jr. High Sch., York, Pa., 1932-34; tchr. English, French, Latin, William Penn Sr. High Sch., York, 1934-47; instr. English, St. Helena Extension, Coll. William and Mary, 1948; asst. prof. English and comparative lit. Longwood Coll., Farmville, Va., 1953-57, asso. prof., 1957-63, prof., 1963-66, chmn. freshman English, 1964-66; prof. English, Norfolk State Coll., 1966—. Mem. Internat. Comparative Lit. Assn., Freies Deutches Hochstift, Modern Lang. Assn., South Atlantic Modern Lang. Assn., Coll. English Assn., N.C.-Va. Coll. English Assn., Nat. Council Tchrs. English, Va. Assn. Tchrs. English, Am. Assn. U. Profs., Va. Council on Human Relations, D.A.R., Mayflower Soc., Cabell Soc. (pres. 1969-72), Phi Beta Kappa, Sigma Alpha Iota. Episcopalian. Author: Shaftesbury and the French Deists, 1956; Writing from Research, 1964; also articles. Home: 476 Linkhorn Dr Virginia Beach VA 23451 Office: Norfolk State Coll Norfolk VA 23504

SCHLENK, VIOLET MARIE, stock brokerage co. exec.; b. Milltown, N.J., Aug. 19, 1910; d. Jacob W. and Barbara E. (Baier) Schlenk; student various corr. courses. With Harris, Upham & Co., Inc., mem. N.Y. Stock Exchange, New Brunswick, N.J., 1932—, asst. office mgr., 1965. Club: Zonta. Home: 64 Riva Av Milltown NJ 08850 Office: 700 Park Av Plainfield NJ 07060

SCHLESINGER, PATRICIA CAROL (MRS. HARLAN MILTON SCHLESINGER), city ofcl.; b. Buffalo, Oct. 3, 1932; d. John and Ann Marie (Ostrowski) Kielich; grad. in police supervision Erie Community Coll., 1972; m. Harlan Milton Schlesinger, June 22, 1950; children—James, Joel, John. With Buffalo Police Dept., 1969—, sgt. narcotics task force, 1971-74; dir. Erie County Sheriff's Trg. Acad., 1974—. Recipient Boy Scout award for outstanding service to youth, 1972. Mem. Internat. Assn. Women Police, Judges and Police Exec. Conf., N.Y. State Sheriffs Assn., Orchard Park C. of C. Clubs: Erie, Badge and Shield, Springeville (N.Y.) Country. Author: Scream, 1972. Home: 55 Jolls Lane Orchard Park NY 14127 Office: 10 Delaware Av Buffalo NY 14202

SCHLOSSER, ISABELLA JONES, librarian; b. Pitts., Oct. 1, 1912; d. James Alton and Estella Sibonic (Oxley) Jones; A.B., Syracuse U., 1933, B.S. in L.S., 1936; M.S. in L.S., Drexel U., 1969; m. Galen Henry Schlosser, June 18, 1938; children—Barbara (Mrs. Louis Vincent Rivera), Neil, Carol (Mrs. Daniel Vincent Scully). Tchr., librarian Truxton (N.Y.) High Sch., 1933-34; tchr. Elizabethtown (Pa.) High Sch., 1934-36, Temple U. High Sch., Phila., 1936-38; tchr., librarian Springside Sch., Phila., 1956—. Home: 4101 Gypsy Lane Philadelphia PA 19144 Office: 8000 Cherokee St Philadelphia PA 19118

SCHLOTFELDT, ROZELLA MAY, educator; b. DeWitt, Ia., June 29, 1914; d. John W. and Clara C. (Doering) Schlotfeldt; B.S., State U. Ia., 1935; M.S., U. Chgo., 1947, Ph.D., 1956; D.Sc. honoris causa, George Washington U., 1972. Staff nurse State U. Ia., VA Hosp., 1935-39; instr., supr. maternity nursing State U. Ia., 1939-44; asst. prof. U. Colo. Sch. Nursing, 1947-48; asst., then asso. prof. Wayne State U. Coll. Nursing, 1948-55, prof., asso. dean Coll. Nursing, 1957-60; prof., dean Frances Payne Bolton Sch. Nursing, Western Res. U., 1960-72, prof., 1972—; cons. Walter Reed Army Inst. Nursing Research. Spl. cons. Surgeon Gen.'s Adv. Group on Nursing, 1961-63; mem. nursing research study sect. USPHS, 1962-66; mem. adv. council on nursing U.S. VA, 1965-69, chmn., 1966-69; mem. Nat. League for Nursing-USPHS Com. on Nursing Edn. Facilities, 1962-64; com. on health goals Cleve. Health Council, 1961-66; Cleve. Citizens Com. on Nursing Edn. Resources, 1962-64; adv. com. div. nursing W. K. Kellogg Found., 1959-57; rev. panel Nursing Research, 1963—; mem. supply and edn, panel Health Manpower Commn., 1966-67; Rev. Com. Nurse Tng. Act, 1967-68; bd. visitors Med. Center Duke U., 1968-70; mem. Ohio Bd. Nursing Edn. and Nurse Registration, 1968-72, v.p., 1970-71, pres., 1971-72; mem. Nat. Center for Health Services Research Tng. Com., 1970-71; mem. Health Planning and Devel. Commn., Cleve. Welfare Fedn., 1969-72; mem. def. adv. com. on women in services Dept. of Def., 1972—; mem. adv. council Nat. Center Health Services Research and Evaluation, 1971—; mem. Study Com. on Pharmacy, 1973—. Served to 1st lt. Nurse Corps, AVS, 1944-46. Recipient Distinguished Service award U. Ia., 1973. Mem. Am. (chmn. commn. on nursing edn. 1966—, chmn. 1967-70), Ohio (chmn. com. on legislation 1964-67) nurses assns., Inst. of Medicine (mem. council 1971—), Nat. Acad. Scis., Sigma Theta Tau (nat. v.p. 1948-50), Pi Lambda Theta. Contbr. numerous articles to profl. jours. Editorial bd. Nursing Forum. Home: 1111 Carver Rd Cleveland Heights OH 44118 Office: 2121 Abington Rd Cleveland OH 44106

SCHLUTER, NANCY HURD, polit. ofcl.; b. Buffalo, Jan. 1, 1929; d. Laurance Lankler and Nancy (Albright) Hurd; student Smith Coll., 1946-49, U. Buffalo, 1951-52; m. William E. Schluter, July 3, 1950; children—William E., Nancy, Sally, Peter, Stephen, Philip. Vice chmn. Mercer County Optional Study Commn., 1973-74, Republican municipal chmn., 1965-73; mem. bd., officer N.J. Fedn. Rep. Women, 1961—; mem. N.J. Rep. State Com., 1965—; N.J. chmn. Women for Nixon, 1968. Recipient award for efforts for Soviet Jewry, Jewish War Vets., 1972. Presbyn. Club: Wilmurt Lake (Hoffmeister, N.Y.). Home: 205 S Main St Pennington NJ 08534 Office: 176 W State St Trenton NJ 08608

SCHMALZRIED, DARLENE MARIE, journalist; b. Evanston, Ill., Aug. 7, 1948; d. Marvin Eugene and Jean (Landino) Schmalzried; B.S. in Journalism, Northwestern U., 1970, M.S. in Journalism, 1971. Washington corr. Shreveport Jour., Washington, 1971-73, capital corr. Shreveport Jour., Baton Rouge, 1973-74; asst. editor White House News Summary, Washington, 1974—. Mem. Common Cause. Mem. White House, Capital corrs. assns. Democrat. Roman Catholic. Home: 1517 Corcoran St NW Washington DC 20009 Office: Room 127 Executive Office Bldg Washington DC 20500

SCHMEING, MARY KAY DODD (MRS. RICHARD H. SCHMEING), educator; b. Lexington, Ky., Sept. 15, 1939; d. William Joseph and Anita (Keller) Dodd; A.B., Thomas More Coll., 1963; M.Ed., Xavier U. (Cin.), 1967; m. Richard H. Schmeing, Feb. 1, 1964. Service worker Ky. Dept. Pub. Assistance, Covington, 1963-65; guidance counselor, tchr. Seton High Sch., Cin., 1965-68; supr. family dept. and staff tng. and devel. Catholic Charities, Cin., 1968—; instr. English, Thomas More Coll., Ft. Mitchell, Ky., 1967—. Administered civil service tests potential city employees City of Covington, Ky., 1964-69. Mem. Am. Personnel and Guidance Assn., Social Service Assn. Cin., Am. Assn. U. Profs., No. Ky. Heritage League. Internat. Catholic Alumni Assn. (editor newspaper 1964-67).

SCHMELZER, LOLA MAE (MRS. MILTON JAMES SCHMELZER), retail automobile co. exec.; b. Beecher, Ill., Dec. 25, 1924; d. Elmer Henry and Della (Hartman) Tatge; grad. high sch.; m. Milton James Schmelzer, Sept. 11, 1948; 1 dau., Carol. Bookkeeper, Weber-Costello Co., Chicago Heights, Ill., 1942-47; accountant Larry Faul Oldsmobile, Inc., Harvey, Ill., 1948-51; office mgr., accountant Harry Smith Oldsmobile, Harvey, 1951-63; sec., treas., office mgr. Watson Oldsmobile, Inc., Harvey, 1963—, also dir., trustee Profit Sharing Plan. Mem. Glenwood (Ill.) Firemen's Aux., 1956-61. Recipient 15 Year Service award Oldsmobile Bus. Mgmt. Club, 1973, 1st Pl. Nat. award for State of Ill. Eight and Forty Press Book, 1967. Mem. Am. Legion Aux. (pres. 1957-58, 61-62), Eight and Forty (pres. 1964-65), Oldsmobile Bus. Mgmt. Home: 155 Country Club Rd Chicago Heights IL 60411 Office: 369 E 147th St Harvey IL 60426

SCHMERTZ, MILDRED FLOYD, editor; b. Pitts., Mar. 29, 1925; d. Robert Watson and Mildred Patricia (Floyd) Schmertz; B.Arch., Carnegie Mellon U., 1947; M.F.A., Yale U., 1957. Archtl. designer John Schurko, Architect, Pitts., 1947-55; asso. editor Archtl. Record, N.Y.C., 1957-65, sr. editor, 1965—. Bd. mgrs. Jr. League, City of N.Y., 1964-65. Mem. A.I.A., Archtl. League N.Y. Club: Yale (N.Y.C.). Editor: Open Space for People, 1972; Campus Design, 1973. Home: 505 E 79th St New York City NY 10021 Office: 1221 Av of Americas New York City NY 10020

SCHMIDEBERG, MELITTA RENE, psychiatrist; b. Czechoslovakia; d. Arthur S. and Melanie (Reizes) Klein; M.D., U. Berlin, 1933. Physician London (Eng.) Clinic Psycho-Analysis, 1933-47; Psychiatrist Inst. Sci. Treatment Delinquency, 1933-49; prof. psychiatry Adelphi Coll., L.I., N.Y., 1949-51; co-founder, dir. clin. services Assn. Psychiat. Treatment Offenders, N.Y.C., internat. pres., 1961—; mem. adv. bd. Bd. Corrections, N.Y.C., 1958-61. Fellow Royal Coll. Psychiatry, Am. Psychiat. Assn. (corr.). Author: Children in Need, 1949. Editor-in-chief: Internat. Jour. Offender Therapy and Comparative Criminology, 1957—. Contbr. numerous articles to profl. jours. Address: 199 Gloucester Pl 6BV London NW 1 England also 620 Madison Av West Hempstead NY 11552

SCHMIDT, CATHERINE ELIZABETH (MRS. J. THOMAS SCHMIDT), city ofcl.; b. Chgo., June 2, 1934; d. Osa Leonard and Dorothy Alice (McComas) Clark; B.A., Ia. Wesleyan Coll., 1956; m. J. Thomas Schmidt, Apr. 18, 1959. Sec., Am. Inst. Baking, Chgo., 1956-58; asst. finance dir. City of Park Ridge, Ill., 1958-63, finance dir., 1963—. Adviser to Spl. Legislative Study Com. on Revising Accounting and Auditing Laws. Mem. Municipal Finance Officers (sec.-treas. Chgo. Met. chpt. 1965, pres. Ill. chpt. 1969), Pi Beta Phi. Home: 500 S Emerson St Mount Prospect IL 60056 Office: 505 Park Pl Park Ridge IL 60068

SCHMIDT, DIANN COOKE (MRS. FOLKERT ALLEN SCHMIDT V), electric lighting co. exec.; b. Detroit, Aug. 30, 1926; d. Irving Deming and Hazel (Baldwin) Cooke; m. Folkert Allen Schmidt V, Aug. 26, 1961. Free-lance model, 1944-49; clerical positions RCA, 1949-52; asst. clerk ct., City Shaker Heights, O., 1952-56; hostess Gen. Electric Lighting Inst., Nela Park, Cleve., 1956-69, specialist program and conf. scheduling, 1969—. Episcopalian (mem. altar guild 1955—). Home: 4240 Giles Rd Chagrin Falls OH 44022 Office: Nela Park Cleveland OH 44112

SCHMIDT, ESTHER IRENE SMITH, educator; b. Van Meter, Ia., Apr. 19, 1918; d. Ryman Jackson and Meriam (Baur) Smith; B.S., Ia. State U., 1941; m. Wilbur C. Schmidt, Sept. 7, 1946; children—Susan Lynn, Carl Ryman, Vicki Jane. With home service Union Electric Co., St. Louis, 1941-45; asst. dir. test kitchens Aluminum Cooking Utensil Co., New Kensington, Pa., 1945-46; extension adviser U. Ill., Urbana, 1956—, asst. state leader co-op. extension, 1969-70. Home economist Internat. Harvester, 1950-52. Mem. Am., Ill. home econs. assns., Nat. Assn. Extension Home Economists (Florence Hall award 1965, Distinguished Service award, 1967), Ill. Home Advisers Assn. (1st v.p. 1967-69), Gamma Sigma Delta, Epsilon Sigma Phi. Club: Altrusa (sec. 1960-62, 1st v.p., program coordinator 1969-71, pres. 1971-72). Home: 3309 S 4th St Springfield IL 62703 Office: 2449 N 31st St Springfield IL 62702

SCHMIDT, GWENDOLYN LOUISE BOYD (MRS. KENNETH D. SCHMIDT), anesthesiologist; b. Houston, Apr. 22, 1943; d. David Milton and Louise (Van Deventer) Boyd; student U. Colo., 1961-64; M.D., U. Ill., 1968; m. Kenneth D. Schmidt, Sept. 10, 1966. Intern medicine U. Ill. Hosps., 1968-69, resident anesthesiology, 1969-71; practice medicine specializing in anesthesiology, 1972—; mem. staff U. Ill. Hosps.; asst. prof. U. Ill. Coll. Medicine, Chgo., 1972—. Mem. Chgo. Beautiful Com., 1970—; mem. Landmarks Preservation Council, 1971—. Mem. A.M.A., Am., Ill. socs. anesthesiologists, Ill. State, Chgo. med. socs., Alpha Omega Alpha. Home: 820 S Bishop St Chicago IL 60607 Office: U Ill Hosps Chicago IL 60612

SCHMIDT, LORRAINE MARIE HERTELL BECKER (MRS. ALBERT EDWARD SCHMIDT), psychologist; b. Tomahawk, Wis., Sept. 18, 1920; d. Oscar James and Leona Marie (Behrens) Hertell; diploma Lincoln County Normal, 1938-40; B.E., Central State Tchrs. Coll., 1947; M.S., U. Wis., 1963; m. Raymond John Becker, May 29, 1947 (dec. Sept. 1969); m. 2d, Albert Edward Schmidt, May 26, 1973; stepchildren—Sharon (Mrs. Larry R. Hopper), Martin E., Denise (Mrs. Denise Frank). Elementary tchr. Lincoln County, Wis., 1940-42, Gillett, Wis., 1942-45; spl. tng. tchr. of soldiers Ft. Sheridan, Ill., 1945; elementary tchr. Merrill (Wis.) Pub. Schs., 1945-67; teaching prin. Washington Sch., 1962-67, sch. psychologist, 1967—. State fund raising chmn. Eagles Aux., Merrill, Wis., 1963-64, 69-70. Mem. Nat., Wis., Central Wis., Merrill edn. assns., Nat., Wis., Lincoln County assns. for retarded children, Council for Exceptional Children (membership chmn. 1971—), Assn. for Edn. Exceptional Children (pres. 1970-71), Central Wis. (sec.-treas. 1972—), Wis. (mem. state membership review com. 1972-73) sch. psychologists assns., Elementary Prins. Assn. (pres. Merrill area 1965-66), Wis. Fedn. Exceptional Children (sec. adv. council 1971-72), Eagles Aux. (chpt. pres. 1957-59, state trustee 1960-62, state treas. 1971—), Sweet Adelines. Mem. United Ch. of Christ. Editor Merrill Eagles Newsletter, 1969—. Home: 1304 E 8th St Merrill WI 54452 Office: 1111 N Sales St Merrill WI 54452

SCHMIDT, MARTHA R(OWLETT), librarian; b. Washington, Dec. 10, 1907; d. Alfred F. W. and Cornelia May (Jones) Schmidt; A.B., U. Mich., 1930, A.B.L.S., 1937. Mem. catalog dept. gen. library U. Mich., 1928-31; asst. librarian George Washington U., 1931-32; classification dept. gen. library U. Mich., 1932-35; librarian Rep. Nat. Com., 1937-51; on leave as expert cons. with U.S. Army in Vienna, 1947, gave course in Am. library techniques to Austrians employed at U.S. Information Centers; librarian Radio Free Europe, Munich, 1951-58; dir. library Dowling Coll. (formerly Adelphi Suffolk Coll.), Oakdale, N.Y., 1959—. Mem. Am., D.C., N.Y. library assns., Spl. Libraries Assn. (chmn. nat. social sci. group, 1940-42, chmn. D.C. employment com. 1941-44, chmn. bus. group 1945-47), Am. Assn. U. Women (mem. nominating com., reorgn. Wash. br. 1949, mem. internat. relations com. 1937-39, Islip area world problems rep. 1962-64, Islip area edn. rep. 1964-65, legislative officer 1966-67), Am. Assn. U. Profs. Republican. Unitarian (trustee, editor Newsletter, 1960-63). Club: Zonta. Author articles in field. Home: 311 Vanderbilt Blvd Oakdale NY 11769

SCHMIDT, SISTER MARY THECLA, coll. pres.; b. Pitts., June 26, 1911; d. Henry Kloman and Mabel Marian (Grine) Schmidt; B.A., Seton Hill Coll., 1932; M.A., U. Pitts., 1934; Ph.D., Yale, 1943. Mem. Sisters of Charity of Seton Hill, 1934—; asst. prof. Seton Hill Coll., Greensburg, Pa., 1943-48, asso. prof., 1949-56, prof., 1957—, exec. v.p., 1957-70, pres., 1970—. Mem. edn. com. U.S. Cath. Conf., Washington, 1968-72; mem. edn. com. Westmoreland Hosp., Greensburg, 1963-72. Mem. Central Westmoreland C.of C. (bd. dirs. 1969-73), Modern Lang. Assn. (life), Assn. Am. U. Women. Club: Greensburg College. Editor: Supplication of Soules (Thomas More), 1950. Address: Seton Hill College Greensburg PA 15601

SCHMIDT, MELBA IRENE (MRS. MARQUIS RIGHTMIRE SCHMIDT), drug. co. exec.; b. Grand Junction, Colo., Jan. 14, 1908; d. Claud DeNel and Gertrude Beatrice (Cartmel) Smith; student U. Cal., Los Angeles, 1926-27; grad. pianoforte pedagogy, New England Conservatory of Music, 1930; m. Marquis Rightmire Schmidt, Aug. 2, 1932; children—Mark Ronald, Ralph Normand, Beatrice Jane (Mrs. Jerry Roberson). Pvt. tchr. piano and musical readings, Grand Junction, 1930-40; tchr. harmony and music theory Mesa Jr. Coll., Grand Junction, 1943; dir. publicity and pub. relations C.D. Smith Co., drug and sundries wholesalers, Grand Junction, 1951-73, v.p., dir., 1970-73; partner Smith Assos., real estate and investments, 1948—; dir. Hy Grade Labs., Inc., cosmetics mfr., Sterling Co., real estate; v.p., dir. Smith Chem. Co., indsl. and agrl. chems. distributor. Gen. chmn., an organizer Mesa County Community Concert Assn., 1944-60. Bd. dirs. Grand Junction Art Center, 1951-54. Mem. Music Assos., of Aspen (regional dir. 1962-66), Nat. Fedn. Music Clubs (chmn. Aspen music sch. scholar 1964—), Colo. Fedn. Music Clubs (pres. 1962-64, state bd. mem. 1959—), P.E.O., Pi Kappa Lambda, Alpha Chi Omega. Republican. Presbyn. Club: Wednesday Music (pres. 1952-55). Home: 536 N 7th St Grand Junction CO 81501 Office: PO Box 756 Grand Junction CO 81501

SCHMIDT, MITTIE JANE SLOAN (MRS. ARTHUR ROBERT SCHMIDT), designer; b. St. Louis, Mar. 22, 1922; d. Cary Ray and Edith L. (Lane) Sloan; B.Arch., Washington U., St. Louis, 1944; m. Arthur Robert Schmidt, Dec. 11, 1945; children—Arthur Gary, Mittie Lane, Robert Warren. Display mgr. Scruggs Vandervoort & Barney, St. Louis, 1944-45; designer exhibits Mus. Sci. and Natural History, St. Louis, 1967—. Active Girl Scouts and Cub Scouts, 1952-60; del. McCall Congress Better Living, Washington, 1957, moderator, 1959. Mem. A.I.A. Designer: Nature Interpretive Center, Babler Park, Chesterfield, Mo., Egyptian, Mineral and Atmosphere Halls Mus. Sci., St. Louis. Home: 68 Frederick Lane Glendale MO 63122 Office: 2 Oak Knoll Park St Louis MO 63105

SCHMIDT, SISTER MONICA MARIE, ednl. adminstr.; b. Linton, N.D., Dec. 25, 1938; d. George G. and Mildred (King) Schmidt; B.A., Maryhurst Coll., 1957; M.Ed., Seattle U., 1963; Ph.D., U. Ill., 1970. Elementary tchr., Portland, Ore., elementary tchr., 1957-60; Spokane, Wash., 1960-63, elementary sch. supr., 1963-65; instr. Ft. Wright Coll., Spokane, 1965-67, pres., 1970-74; asst. supt. pub. instrn. for profl. services, Olympia, Wash., 1974—. Lectr. Gwelo, Rhodesia and Africa, 1970; cons. Wash. State Office of Edn., 1973; psychol. clin. worker Chanute AFB, 1969-70. Mem. citizens com. Eastern Wash. State Hosp., Spokane, 1971—. Bd. dirs. UN Assn., 1971—, Expo 74, 1974—. Recipient Tchr. of Year award Catholic Diocese of Spokane, 1963. Mem. Nat. Edn. Honor Soc., Wash. Personnel and Guidance Assn., Am. Psychol. Assn., Am. Council Higher Edn., Assn. Wash. Bus., Assn. Am. Colleges, Wash. Friends Higher Edn., Ind. Colls. Wash., Kappa Delta Pi. Club: Soroptimist (Spokane). Home: Route 7 Box 621 Olympia WA 98504 Office: W 4000 Randolph Rd Spokane WA 99204

SCHMIDT, ROSE MARIE, ednl. adminstr.; b. Detroit, July 22, 1924; d. Kurt George and Martha Mary (Kurzynsky) S.; B.S., Wayne State U., 1942, M.Ed., 1948, Ed.D., 1964. Tchr., Detroit Pub. Schs., 1945-53, elementary sch. adminstr., 1953-61, personnel adminstr., 1961—. Mem. Am. Assn. Sch. Adminstr., Am. (sec. 1971, dir. 1974), Mich. (sec.-treas. 1970—) assns. sch. personnel adminstrs., Wayne State U. (2d v.p. 1971), Wayne State U. Coll. Edn. (dir. 1968-71) alumni assns., Alpha Sigma Tau (nat. chmn. 1950—). Home: 5106 Harvard Rd Detroit MI 48224 Office: 5057 Woodward St Detroit MI 48202

SCHMIDT, RUTH VEDDER (MRS. GEORGE E. SCHMIDT), village ofcl.; b. Catskill, N.Y., Feb. 26, 1913; d. Henry Martin and Mary Florence (Blakelock) Vedder; grad. Moran-Spencer Bus. Sch., 1932; m. George E. Schmidt, Sept. 21, 1935; children—George Lawrence, Mark Vedder (dec.). Sec. to ins. adjuster, then office mgr. J. Richard Miller, Inc., Kingston, N.Y., 1931-35, 45-60; sec. Agrl. Conservation Dept., Catskill, N.Y., 1939-42; sec. Imperial Lifeboat Co., Athens, N.Y., 1943-45; village clk.-treas. collector Village of Catskill, N.Y., 1960—. Sch. tax collector, treas. Catskill (N.Y.) Sch. Dist. #10, 1947-61; treas. Ladies Aux. Leeds Hose Co. #1, 1960-70, treas., 1972—. Financial sec. Womens Rep. Club, 1956-58. Mem. N.Y. Assn. City and Village Clks., N.Y. Soc. Municipal Finance Officers, Town and Country Bus. and Profl. Womens Club (pres. 1966-68), D.A.R. (vice regent 1968-74, regent 1974—). Mem. Dutch Ref. Ch. Clubs: Woman's (pres. 1961-62, treas. 1963—) (Leeds, N.Y.); Capital Dist. Mineral (treas. 1972—) (Albany, N.Y.). Home: Pine Cliff Dr Leeds NY 12451 Office: 422 Main St Catskill NY 12414

SCHMIDT, VICTORIA, educator; b. St. Louis, July 19, 1908; d. Gottfried and Christina Anna (Juenger) Schmidt; A.B., Harris Tchrs. Coll., 1929; M.A., Columbia, 1930; postgrad. Wigman Sch. of Dance, Dresden, Germany, 1935, U. Wis., 1940, St. Louis U., 1949, Washington U., 1949-51; Ed.D., U. Colo., 1952. Tchr. phys. edn. Beaumont High Sch., St. Louis, 1928-29, Fanning Elementary Sch., 1930-31, Soldan High Sch., 1931-32, Shaw Elementary Sch., 1932-39; tchr. English and phys. edn. Southwest High Sch., 1939-40; tchr. phys. edn. Roosevelt High Sch., 1940-46; asst. prof. phys. edn. Harris Tchrs. Coll., St. Louis, 1946-49, asso. prof., 1949-59, prof., 1959—. Lectr. reading U. Coll., Washington, U., 1951-70, phys. edn. St. Louis U., summer 1952. Mem. leadership council YWCA, 1971—. Mem. A.A.H.P.E.R. (central dist. dance chmn., nat. dance vice chmn. 1948), Mo. State Tchrs. Assn., Internat. Platform Assn., Common Cause. Home: 3667 Lierman Av St Louis MO 63116 Office: Harris Tchrs Coll 3026 Laclede Av St Louis MO 63103

SCHMIDT, VICTORIA DABROWSKI, public relations co. exec.; b. East Orange, N.J.; d. Eugene and Emily (Gocek) Dabrowski; A.B. in English, Douglass Coll., New Brunswick, N.J., 1942; m. Ralph Schmidt, June 20, 1943; 1 dau., Lisa. Publicity and sales promotion L. Bamberger & Co., Newark, N.J., 1948-50; fashion editor Woman's Day mag., 1950-53; pub. relations, fashion coordinator Owens Corning Fiberglass Co., N.Y.C., 1953-57; account exec. Roy Bernard Co., N.Y.C., 1957-58; exec. v.p., owner Communications Council Inc., Bernardsville, N.J., 1958—; cons. Bernardsville Bd. Edn., 1965—. Chmn. Mayor Bernardsville Youth Com., 1972-74, Bernardsville Shade Tree Commn., 1970—; mem. cultural com. Greater Newark C. of C., 1968-69. Bd. dirs. Somerset Hills YMCA, 1970—, Somerset Hills Community Chest, 1970—. Mem. World Trade Assn., Fedn. Republican Women, Nat. Soc. Interior Designers, Nat. Home Fashions League, Fashion Group, League Women Voters, Bus. and Profl. Women's Club, Newark Museum, Douglass Coll. Alumnae Assn. (pres. 1966). Home: PO Box 768 Post Kennel Rd Bernardsville NJ 07924 Office: PO Box 2000 115 Morristown Rd Bernardsville NJ 07924

SCHMIDT-NIELSEN, BODIL MIMI (MRS. ROGER G. CHAGNON), physiologist; b. Copenhagen, Denmark, Nov. 3, 1918; d. August and Marie (Jorgensen) Krogh; D.D.S., U. Copenhagen, 1941, D.Odont., 1946, Ph.D., 1955; m. Knut Schmidt-Nielsen, Sept. 20, 1939 (div. Feb. 1966); children—Astrid (Mrs. John McHugh), Bent, Bodil; m. 2d, Roger G. Chagnon, Oct. 1968. Came to U.S., 1946, naturalized, 1952. Faculty, Duke, 1952-64; prof. biology Case Western Res. U., Cleve., 1964-71, chmn. dept., 1970-71; trustee Mt. Desert Island Biol. Lab., resident investigator, 1971—. Mem. tng. grant com. NIGMS, 1967-71. Trustee, Coll. of Atlantic, Bar Harbor, Me., 1973—. Recipient Career award NIH, 1962. John Simon Guggenheim Meml. fellow, 1952-53; Bowditch lectr. 1958. Fellow N.Y. Acad. Scis., Am. Acad. Arts and Scis., A.A.A.S.; mem. Am. Physiol. Soc. (council 1971—, pres. elect 1974—), Soc. Exptl. Biology and Medicine. Research, publs. on biochemistry of saliva, water metabolism of desert animals, comparative kidney physiology, comparatory physiology of excretory organs. Home: Salisbury Cove ME 04672

SCHMITT, EDITH ANNA, educator; b. N.Y.C., Jan. 14, 1920; d. Phillip C. and A. Dorothy (Nitshke) Schmitt; grad. Ann May Sch. of Nursing, Jersey Shore Med. Center, 1938-41; B.S., U. Pa., 1943, M.S., 1948; Ed.D., N.Y.U., 1963; certificate nurse practitioner U. Rochester, 1974. Tchr. sci. and asst. prin. Sch. Nursing, Jersey Shore Med. Center, Neptune, N.J., 1943-46; asst. prin. Sch. Nursing, Cooper Hosp., Camden, N.J., 1946-50; asst. prof. Wagner Coll. Sch. Nursing, S.I., N.Y., 1950-56, asso. prof., 1956-62, prof., 1962—, chmn. dept. nursing, 1969—; vis. prof. summer session Sch. Nursing, Gustavus Adolphus Coll., St. Peter, 1967. Mem. Am. Nurses Assn., Nat. League for Nursing, Am. Assn. U. Profs., Sigma Theta Tau. Contbr. articles to profl. jours. Home: 610 Victory Blvd Staten Island NY 10301

SCHMITT, SISTER LILIAN, coll. adminstr.; b. Kenosha, Wis., Feb. 13, 1904; d. Peter and Barbara (Jana) Schmitt; student Viterbo Coll., 1922-26; student U. Wis., 1925, 27, 34; B.A., Gonzaga U., 1931; M.A., Marquette U., 1948; postgrad. Loras Coll., 1933-35, Cath. U. Am., 1935, St. Louis U., 1936; Jr. high sch. tchr., 1925-31; secondary tchr., 1931-67; prin. sr. high schs., Superior, Wis., 1955-56, West Point, Ia., 1956-62, Spokane, 1962-64; acad. dean Mt. Senario Coll., Ladysmith, Wis., 1967-69; dir. placement services Viterbo Coll., LaCrosse, Wis., 1969—, instr. history, summers 1950, 53-56. Recipient Merit award Ground Observers Corps, 1954. Mem. Wis. Career Planning and Placement Assn. (mem. nominating com. 1973-74, treas. 1973—), Wis. Assn. Sch. Personnel Adminstrs. (asso.), Coll. Placement Council, Midwest Coll. Placement Assn., Assn. for Sch., Coll. and Univ. Staffing, Great Lakes Asst. for Sch., Coll. and Univ. Staffing, Pi Kappa Delta. Home: 815 S 9th St LaCrosse WI 54601 Office: Viterbo College 9th and Winnegago St LaCrosse WI 54601

SCHMITT, NATALIE CROHN, educator; b. Chgo., Aug. 10, 1936; d. Nathan N. and Lera Christina (Amlingmeyer) Crohn; B.A., U. Chgo., 1958, M.A., 1961; Ph.D., Stanford, 1968. Dir., Looking Glass Theatre, Providence, 1963-65; asst. prof. dept. speech and theatre U. Ill., Chgo., 1968-72, asso. prof., 1972—. Asso. editor Ednl. Theatre Jour. Contbr. articles to profl. jours.

SCHNACK, GAYLE HEMINGWAY JEPSON (MRS. HAROLD CLIFFORD SCHNACK), corp. exec.; b. Mpls., Aug. 14, 1926; d. Jasper Jay and Ursula (Hemingway) Jepson; student U. Hawaii, 1946; m. Harold Clifford Schnack, Mar. 22, 1947; children—Jerrald Jay, Georgina, Roberta, Michael Clifford. Skater Shipstead & Johnson Ice Follies, 1944-46; v.p. Harcliff Corp., Honolulu, 1964—, Schnack Indsl. Corp., Honolulu, 1969—; v.p. Nutmeg Corp., Cedar Corp.; ltd. partner Koa Corp.; dir. Bus. Efficiency Sales & Service Inc. Mem. Beta Sigma Phi (chpt. pres. 1955-56, pres. city council 1956-57). Home: 4261 Panini Loop Honolulu HI 96816 Office: PO Box 3077 Honolulu HI 96802

SCHNALL, EDITH LEA (MRS. HERBERT SCHNALL), educator; b. N.Y.C., Apr. 11, 1922; d. Irving and Sadie (Raab) Spitzer; A.B., Hunter Coll., 1942; A.M., Columbia, 1947, Ph.D., 1967; m. Herbert Schnall, Aug. 21, 1949; children—Neil David, Carolyn Beth. Clin. pathologist Roosevelt Hosp., N.Y.C., 1942-44; instr. Adelphi Coll., Garden City, N.Y., 1944-46; asst. med. mycologist Columbia Coll. Phys. and Surg., N.Y.C., 1946-47, 49-50; instr. Bklyn. Coll., 1947; faculty Sarah Lawrence Coll., N.Y.C., 1947-48; lectr. Hunter Coll., N.Y.C., 1947-67; adj. asso. prof. Lehman Coll., City U. N.Y., 1968; asst. prof. Queensborough Community Coll., City U. N.Y., 1967, asso. prof. microbiology, 1968—; vis. prof. Coll. Physicians and Surgeons, Columbia U., N.Y.C., 1974. Advanced biology examiner, U. London, 1970—. Mem. Alley Restoration Com., N.Y.C., 1971—; mem. legislative adv. com. Assembly of the State of N.Y., 1972. Mem. Community Planning Bd. #11, Queens, N.Y., 1974-75. Pub. dir. of the bd. dirs. Inst. for Continuing Dental Edn. of the Eleventh Dist. of the Dental Soc. of the State of N.Y. and Am. Dental Assn., 1973—. Research fellow NIH, 1948-49; Faculty Research fellow, grantee-in-aid Research Found. of State U. N.Y., 1968-70; Faculty Research grant Research Found. City U. N.Y., 1971-74. Mem. Internat. Soc. for Human and Animal Mycology, A.A.A.S., Am. Soc. for Microbiology, Med. Mycology Soc. of N.Y. (sec.-treas. 1967-68, v.p. 1968-69, pres. 1969-70), Bot. Soc. Am., Med. Mycology Soc. Americas, Mycology Soc. Am., N.Y. Acad. Scis., Sigma Xi, Phi Sigma. Clubs: Torrey Botanical (N.Y. State); Queensborough Community Coll. Womens (pres. 1971-73) (N.Y.C.). Editor Newsletter of Med. Mycology Soc. N.Y., 1969—; founder, editor Female Perspective newsletter of Queensborough Community Coll. Womens Club, 1971-73. Home: 214-06 29th Av Bayside NY 11360

SCHNALL, MAXINE MIRIAM SWARTTZ (MRS. NATHAN SCHNALL), author; b. Phila., Sept. 7, 1934; d. Isadore Richard and Clare (Salzmann) Swarttz; B.S., U. Pa., 1956; postgrad. Temple U. Sch. Law, 1959; m. Nathan Schnall, Mar. 31, 1957; children—Ilene, Rona. Co-founder Wives-Self Help. Mem. Rowland Park Civic Assn. (sec. 1960—), Phi Delta Epsilon. Mem. B'nai B'rith. Author: My Husband, the Doctor, 1966; The Broadbelters, 1970. Creator TV series The New Woman, 1971. Home: 527 Davis Rd Cheltenham PA 19012

SCHNAUFER, LOUISE, pediatric surgeon; b. Balt., June 12, 1925; d. William Stanley and Emma Louise (Otto) Schnaufer; A.B., Wellesley Coll., 1947; M.D., Woman's Med. Coll. Pa., 1951. Intern, Union Meml. Hosp., Balt., 1951-52, resident, 1952-56; resident Children's Hosp., Phila., 1957-58, pediatric surgeon, 1971—; practice medicine specializing in pediatric surgery, Balt., 1958-71, Phila., 1971—; asst. prof. pediatric surgery Johns Hopkins, 1966-71, U. Pa., 1971—. Diplomate Am. Bd. Surgery. Mem. A.C.S., Am. Acad. Pediatrics, Am. Pediatric Surg. Assn., Brit. Assn. Pediatric Surgery. Home: 3901 Conshohocken Av Philadelphia PA 19131 Office: Childrens Hosp Pa 1 Children's Center Philadelphia PA 19104

SCHNEEBERGER, MARY LOUISE LOVE, film producer; b. Honolulu; d. William Alfred and Edith (Moore) Love; student U. Hawaii, 1924-25, U. Cal. at Berkeley, 1925-26, Paris br. Parson's Sch. Fine and Applied Art, 1926-27, 28-29; student piano with Isidor Philipe, Nadia Boulanger, Paris; m. Philip Schneeberger, Oct. 13, 1933 (dec.); 1 dau., Paula Sara (Mrs. John Thomas Brooke). Creator Versymphony, correlating work Carmel poets and Cal. composers; producer films Poet at Lobos, From the Tower, A Child's Garden of Verses, Within a Painted Grove, From the Tower; concert pianist. Founder Monterey County Symphony Guild; active Jr. League. Bd. dirs. Carmel Bach Festival, 1965-66, v.p., 1967-68; bd. dirs. Monterey County Symphony Assn., Carmel Music Soc., 1959-61, Chamber Music Soc. Monterey Peninsula, 1965-68; nat. adv. bd. Friends of Photography, 1969-72; women's bd. Northwood Inst. Republican. Club: Carmel Valley Golf and Country. Address: PO Box 161 Carmel CA 93921

SCHNEIDER, BEKKI JO (MRS. DUDLEY SAUNDERS), childrens theatre exec.; b. Louisville, Nov. 14, 1946; d. Joseph Cletus and Rogerlene Marie (Hicks) Schneider; student, U. Louisville, 1964-65; B.A., U. Ky., 1970; m. Dudley Saunders, Nov. 10, 1972; 1 stepson, Dudley. Artistic dir. Lexington (Ky.) Childrens Theatre, drama tchr. Lexington Sch., 1968-70; mng. dir. Louisville Childrens Theatre, 1970—. Creative dramatics adviser to various schs., Louisville, 1970—. Artistic mem. Louisville Fund, 1970—; mem. Foreign Study League, 1968—. Mem. Young Dem. Club, 1968—. Bd. dirs. Youth Performing Arts Center, Louisville, 1972—. Recipient Troupers award Louisville Childrens Theatre, 1964. Mem. Am., Southeastern, Ky. (v.p. 1972-73, pres. 1973-74) theatre assns. Author: Hansel and Gretel, 1973. Home: Rural Route 2 Box 241 Anchorage KY 40223 Office: 830 S 4th St Louisville KY 40203

SCHNEIDER, EVELYN RUTH, librarian; b. Chgo., Feb. 20, 1929; d. George Walter and Evelyn Charl (Burr) Schneider; B.Sc. in Edn., St. John Coll., 1954; M.S. in Library Sci. (scholar), Case Western Res. U., 1969; specialist in arts Western Mich. U., 1974. Tchr. elementary and secondary schs., 1948-69; faculty U. Akron (O.), 1972—; library supr. Diocese Cleve., 1969—. Recipient Freedom Found. Educator award, 1964. Mem. Am., Ohio, Catholic library assns., Ohio Assn. Sch. Librarians, council Library Tech., Beta Phi Mu. Author: New Ways in Numbers, 1964. Home: 1230 West Market St Akron OH 44313 Office: 1375 West Exchange St Akron OH 44313

SCHNEIDER, GAIL MARGO (MRS. EDWARD A. SCHNEIDER), zoologist; b. Chgo., Nov. 26, 1941; d. Raymond A. And Lee G. (Solon) Jacobson; student North Central Coll., Naperville, Ill., 1960—; m. Edward A. Schneider, Mar. 5, 1965; children—Katherine Marie, Erik George. Keeper, Children's Zoo, Chgo. Zool. Park, Brookfield, Ill., 1960-69, supt., 1969—. Fellow Am. Assn. Zool. Parks and Aquariums; mem. Am. Mus. Natural History (asso.), Ill. Game and Pet Breeders Assn., Am. Scotch Highland Breeders Assn., Am. Soc. Mammalogists, Colo. Humane Soc., Chgo. Zool. Soc. Clubs: Great Pyrenees of America (Menomonee Falls, Wis.); Akita of America (Hermosa Beach, Cal.). Author: Children's Zoos, Organization and Operation, 1970. Designer heated display and exhibit barn Children's Zoo. Office: 8400 Golf Rd Brookfield IL 60513

SCHNEIDER, JO ANNE FEDERMAN (MRS. NORMAN SCHNEIDER), artist; b. Lima, O., Dec. 4, 1919; d. Joseph and Laura (Office) Federman; B.F.A., Syracuse U., 1941; m. Norman Schneider, May 15, 1941; children—Melanie, Lois (Mrs. Ellis Oppenheim). One-man shows Frank Rehn Gallery, N.Y.C., Benson Gallery, Bridgehampton, L.I., N.Y.; exhibited group shows Whitney Mus., Pa. Acad., Corcoran Gallery, Washington, Butler Inst. Fine Arts, Youngstown, O.; represented in permanent collections St. Lawrence U., Colby Coll. Recipient prize Audubon Artists, 1972, Nat. Assn. Women Artists, 1965, 68, 71. Mem. Women in Arts, Audubon Artists, Nat. Assn. Women Artists. Home: 35 E 75th St New York City NY 10021

SCHNEIDER, SISTER LORITA, coll. adminstr.; b. St. Louis.; d. George and Anne (Jebani) Schneider; A.B., Loyola U. South, New Orleans, 1931; M.Ed., St. Louis U., 1947, M.Ed. in Guidance and Counselling, 1964; postgrad. Stout Coll., 1932-34, Marquette U., 1935-36. Tchr. English, Latin and Spanish in Miss., Ark., La., Tex., Ill., Mo., 1923-64; prin., Sacred Heart High Sch., Morrilton, Ark., 1949-55, Cath. High Sch., Tyler, Tex., 1958-60, St. Peter's High Sch., Jefferson City, Mo., 1948-49; vice prin. Acad. Notre Dame, Belleville, Ill., 1962-64, dir. guidance, 1964-73; dir. coll. placement Notre Dame Coll., St. Louis, 1973—. Cons. in planning and equipping Cath. High Sch., Tyler, Tex., new convent Sacred Heart High Sch., Morrilton, Ark. Community supr. Diocese Little Rock, 1949-55; sec. Belleville Diocesan Guidance Council, 1967-68, pres., 1969-72; treas. Belleville Diocesan Prins. Assn., 1963-64; mem. Nat. Cath. Guidance Conf., 1963-67. Recipient citation A.R.C., 1946; citation, Propeller Club U.S., 1957; trophy as Newspaper Adviser of Yr., So. Ill. Sch. Press Assn., 1967. Mem. Am. Personnel and Guidance Assn., Am. Sch. Counselors Assn., Ill. Personnel and Guidance Assn., Ill. Sch. Counselors Assn., Am. Measurement and Evaluation in Guidance, St. Louis Guidance Personnel Assn., Midwest Coll. Placement Assn., Quill and Scroll Assn. (life). Home: 320 E Ripa Av St Louis MO 63125

SCHNEIDER, LOUISE WARNER (MRS. HAROLD O. SCHNEIDER), educator; b. Geneva, Neb., June 21, 1912; d. Leonard H. and Flora (Nunns) Warner; B.A., Lindenwood Coll., 1933; postgrad. (Houteling fellow), U. Chgo., 1937; M.A., Western Res. U., 1945; m. Harold O. Schneider, Jan. 7, 1939; 1 son, Dan W. Case worker Nebraska County, county welfare dir. Albion and Boone County, Neb., 1936; social worker Kalamazoo Pub. Schs., 1938; social worker Ore. Dept. State, Salem, 1964-68; case worker, then dir. social service Ore. Girls Tng. Sch., Salem, 1964-68; supr. social service Head Start Program, Omaha Pub. Schs., 1968-69; prof. Grad. Sch. Social Work, U. Neb., Lincoln, 1969-73; staff tng. officer Lancaster County Welfare, Lincoln, Neb., 1973—. Civil def. dir. Am. Med. Aux., Salem, 1956-64. Chmn. womens aux. Meml. Hosp., Salem, 1949; pres. YWCA, Salem, 1951-53; pres. United Church Women, Salem, 1960-62. Mem. Woman of Year Ct., Salem, 1959. Fed. Emergency Relief Agy. grantee, 1934-35. Mem. Nat., Neb. (sec. 1973—) assns. social work, Acad. Certified Social Workers, Soroptimist, Delta Delta Delta. Democrat. Conglist. Home: 512 Mulder Dr Lincoln NE 68510 Office: 2200 St Marys Av Lincoln NE 68502

SCHNEIDER, SALLY LORRAINE, physician; b. Friend, Neb., Sept. 22, 1943; d. Lloyd William and Mary Ellen (Lewellen) Schneider; B.S., with distinction, U. Neb., 1965, M.D., 1968. Intern, Cook County Hosp., Chgo., 1968-69; resident obstetrics and gynecology U. Neb. Hosp., Omaha, 1969-72; with Olmsted Med. Group P.A., Rochester, Minn., 1972—. Jr. fellow Am. Coll. Obstetricians and Gynecologists; mem. Nat. Assn. Residents and Interns, Alpha Lambda Delta, Delta Phi Alpha, Phi Beta Kappa. Home: 8112 Arbor St Omaha NE 68124 Office: Olmsted Medical Group PA Rochester MN 55901

SCHNEIDER, VALERIE LOIS, educator; b. Chgo., Feb. 12, 1941; d. Ralph Joseph and Gertrude Blanche (Gaffron) Schneider; B.A., Carroll Coll., 1963; M.A., U. Wis., 1966; Ph.D., U. Fla., 1969. Tchr. English and history Montello (Wis.) High Sch., 1963-64; dir. forensics and drama Montello High Sch., 1963-64; instr. speech U. Fla., Gainesville, 1966-68, asst. prof. speech, 1969-70; asst. prof. speech Edinboro (Pa.) State Coll., 1970-71; asso. prof. speech East Tenn. State U., Johnson City, 1971—. Chmn. Am. Assn. U. Women Mass Media Study Group Com., Johnson City, 1973-74. Recipient Creative Writing award Va. Highlands Arts Festival, 1973. Mem. Speech Communication Assn. (Tenn. rep. to states adv. council), So., Tenn. speech communication assns., Am. Assn. U. Women (v.p. chpt. 1964-66), Tenn. Intercollegiate Forensics Assn., Bus. and Profl. Women's Club, Internat. Platform Assn., Delta Sigma Rho, Tau Kappa Alpha. Presbyn. Contbr. articles on speech to profl. jours. Home: C-5 Greenwood Apts 1409 Colony Park Rd Johnson City TN 37601

SCHNEPF, DOROTHY JEAN (MRS. JACK SCHNEPF), psychologist; b. Decatur, Ind., Jan. 31, 1926; d. Carl Ivan and Edna Katherine (Kabisch) Hammond; student Ind. U., 1944-45; A.B., St. Francis Coll., 1960, M.S., 1963, postgrad., 1964-70; m. Jack Schnepf, Nov. 19, 1947; children—Thomas, Michael, Ann (Mrs. D. Gosser). Tchr. Decatur High Sch., 1960-67, counselor, 1964-67; guidance counselor Bluffton (Ind.) High Sch., 1967-70; psychometrist East Allen County Sch., New Haven, Ind., 1970—; psychologist, Decatur, 1967—; lectr. St. Francis Coll. Mem. Nat. Assn. Sch. Psychologists, Ind. Psychol. Assn. Home: 226 Oakridge Decatur IN 46733 Office: 15209 US 30 East New Haven IN 46774

SCHNITZER, ARLENE DIRECTOR, art gallery exec.; b. Salem, Ore., Jan. 10, 1929; d. Simon M. and Helen (Holtzman) Director; student U. Wash., 1947-48, Portland Art Mus. Sch., 1959-61; m. Harold J. Schnitzer, Sept. 11, 1949; 1 son, Jordan Director. Owner, dir. Fountain Gallery, Portland, Ore., 1961—; ind. TV producer with Mut. Enterprises, Inc., 1969—; producer, interviewer ednl. TV program, 1972—; dir. Harsh Investment Corp., Portland. Art cons. U.S. Steel Corp., Pitts., 1971-72, U.S. Nat. Bank Ore., 1st Nat. Bank Ore., Bank of Cal., Portland, others. Founder, Fountain Village Assn., 1962; mem. gov.'s task force and adv. com. Ore. Hwy. Commn.; active Portland Chamber Orch., Portland Civic Theater, Parry Center for Disturbed Children, Ore. Symphony Assn. Mem. Portland Art Assn. (past trustee, asso. chmn. gen. fund), Albina Art Assn. (charter), Contemporary Crafts Assn. (past trustee). Jewish religion. Home: 2121 SW 16th Av Portland OR 97201 Office: 115 SW 4th Av Portland OR 97204

SCHNURMANN, ERIKA, librarian; b. Paterson, N.J.; d. Karl and Martha (Buegen) Schnurmann; A.B., Pembroke Coll., 1937; postgrad. Simmons Coll., 1938; M.L.S., Columbia, 1947. Head pub. relations and order dept. Paterson (N.J.) Pub. Library, 1940-65; dir. Hawthorne (N.J.) Pub. Library, 1966-68; librarian-cons. Wayne (N.J.), Pub. Library, 1960-64, West Paterson Pub. Library, 1961-62, Nursing Edn. Library, Paterson Gen. Hosp., 1963-69; dir. Little Falls (N.J.) Pub. Library, 1968-69; dir. Kearny (N.J.) Pub. Library, 1969—. Asso. book reviewer Paterson Morning Call, 1955-57. Past chmn. Women's Civic

Council; sec., program chmn. Council Service Clubs, 1960-62; mem. Kearny Safety Council; active various civic affairs; sec. Hudson County Am. Revolution Bicentennial Com., 1973—. Mem. Am. Assn. U. Women (v.p.), N.J. Press Women's Club, Nat. League Am. Pen Women (pres.), N.J. Library Assn. (chmn. book auction 1955, 57, treas. 1956-57), Bergen-Passaic County (past pres.), Hudson County (pres. 72-74) library clubs, North Jersey Libraries Round Table (past chmn.), Library Pub. Relations Council of N.Y. (exec. bd., 1963-69), West Hudson C. of C., Passaic County Health, Edn. and Welfare Assn. (past pres.). Contbr. articles profl. jours. and newspapers. Editor: N.J. Library Assn. Newsletter, 1955-56. Home: 335 Sylvan St Rutherford NJ 07070 Office: Pub Library 318 Kearny Av Kearny NJ 07032

SCHNURPEL, HELEN MAMIE PERSELL (MRS. HANS KARL SCHNURPEL), realtor; b. Omaha, Aug. 25, 1902; d. John Alva and Mamie Ethel (Davis) Persell; student U. Neb., 1930; certificate in real estate, U. Cal. at Los Angeles, 1959; m. Hans Karl Schnurpel, May 10, 1937. Co-owner Lynwood (Cal.) Realty Co. 1945—, Real Estate Sch. So. Cal., Lynwood, 1951—. Mem. Compton-Lynwood Bd. Realtors (sec.-treas. 1966-67, dir.; pres. 1970), Internat. Platform Assn. Republican. Club: Lynwood Womens. Home: 11627 Warren Av Lynwood CA 90262 Office: 11228 Atlantic Av Lynwood CA 90262

SCHOALS, DOROTHY ISABELLE TURNER (MRS. WILLIAM M. SCHOALS), hosp. controller; b. Corunna, Mich., Dec. 15, 1915; d. Harry Ellsworth and Maude Myra (Rose) Turner; grad. with high honors Owosso Bus. Inst., 1935; m. William Miles Schoals, Oct. 30, 1937; 1 dau., Adella Anna (Mrs. Ronald Dimon Lyon). Cashier, bookkeeper Owosso-Flint Bus. Lines, Inc., Owosso, Mich., 1935-36; asst. cashier Union State Bank of Laingsburg (Mich.), 1936-44, 53-59; bookkeeper Laingsburg Press, 1946-56; controller Clinton Meml. Hosp., St. Johns, Mich., 1959—, acting adminstr., 1971-72. Sec. Clinton County Assn. for Retarded Children, St. Johns, 1961-65; sec. Laingsburg com. Christ Bank into Christmas Com., 1955. Mem. Hosp. Financial Mgmt. Assn. (chpt. dir. 1968-70, pres. 1971-72, mem. adv. council 1972—, mem. coordinating council of Mich. chpts. 1972-74, William C. Follmer Merit award 1972, Francis E. Williams Achievement award Central Mich. chpt. 1973). Home: 10422 S Krepps Rd De Witt MI 48820 Office: 805 S Oakland St St Johns MI 48879

SCHOBER, DOROTHY FLORENCE, educator; b. Green Bay, Wis., Sept. 19, 1910; d. Max William and Addie (Stone) Schober; B.A., U. Wis., 1932; M.P.H., Yale, 1948. Visitor, dist. supr., dist. dir. Fla. Welfare Bd., Jacksonville, 1932-37; dir. Pub. Welfare Dept., Green Bay, Wis., 1937-42; cons. Div. Pub. Assistance, State Dept. Pub. Welfare, Madison, Wis., 1942-44; counselor USPHS, 1944-45; health edn. cons. Council Social Agys., New Haven, 1946-49; heart work cons. State Com. on Tb and Pub. Health, N.Y., 1949-52; program cons., exec. asst. Am. Heart Assn., 1952-64, asst. dir. affiliate relations and services, 1964-65, asst. dir. dept. councils and internat. program, 1965-70, asso. dir., 1970-73, asso. dir. div. sci. affairs, chief sci. councils, 1973—. Recipient Gold Heart Bracelet in appreciation 10 year service Staff Conf. Heart Assn., 1962. Fellow Am. Pub. Health Assn.; mem. Nat. Assn. Social Workers, Phi Kappa Phi, Alpha Kappa Delta. Home: 4 Park Av New York City NY 10016 Office: 44 E 23d St New York City NY 10010

SCHOCH, JACQUELINE LOUISE, educator; b. DuBois, Pa., July 17, 1929; d. Horace Gordon and Cora (Wineberg) Schoch; B.Sc. in Health and Phys. Edn., Pa. State U., 1951, M.Edn. in Counseling and Psychology, 1960, D.Ed. in Counseling and Psychology, 1965. Tchr. girls' phys. edn. Jr.-Sr. High Sch., Ford City, Pa., 1951-52; tchr. girl's phys. edn., acad. U.S. history DuBois Area Sr. High Sch., 1952-53, girls' guidance counselor, 1956-65; dir. guidance DuBois Area Sch. Dist., 1965-67, dir. instrn., 1967-70; asst. dir. for resident instruction DuBois campus Pa. State U., 1970—. Instr. polit. action courses local C. of C., 1963; instr. adult swimming classes local YMCA, 1953-55; instr. continuing edn. program Pa. State U., 1967-70, also asst. prof. edn., 1970—. Cons. Appalachia project, W.Va., 1967-68; mem. evaluating teams for evaluating secondary schs. Middle States Evaluation Com., 1960-62. Bd. dirs. DuBois area United Fund, co-chmn. fund raising campaign, 1967-68, 2d v.p., 1970—; dir. DuBois council Girl Scouts, 1954-56. Mem. Assn. for Higher Edn., Nat. Rehab. Assn., Assn. for Supervision and Curriculum Devel., Am. Assn. U. Women, Bus. and Profl. Women, Iota Alpha Delta, Delta Kappa Gamma, Pi Lambda Theta. Home: 908 S Brady St DuBois PA 15801 Office: DuBois Campus Pa State U DuBois PA 15801

SCHOELZEL, ELAINE PATRICIA, physician; b. Denver, Dec. 24, 1926; d. Charles William and Lona (Balay) Schoelzel; B.F.A., U. Colo., 1949; M.D., 1958. Intern Hermann Hosp., Houston, 1958-59; resident pediatrics Colo. Med. Center, Denver, 1959-60, Baylor Med. Sch. Residency Program Houston, 1960-61; fellow in allergy U. Tex. Southwestern Med. Sch., Dallas, 1961-62; practice medicine specializing in allergy, Irving, Tex., 1962—; mem. staff Irving Community Hosp., 1964—, sec. staff, 1966-67; clin. asst. prof. pediatrics U. Tex. Southwestern Med. Sch., 1969—. Diplomate in pediatric allergy, Am. Acad. Pediatrics. Fellow Am. Coll. Allergists, Am. Acad. Allergy; mem. A.M.A., Delta Gamma. Methodist (mem. commn. social concerns 1965-66). Club: Soroptomist (Irving, corr. sec. 1968). Home: 3812 W Pioneer St Irving TX 75061 Office: 2101 MacArthur Blvd Irving TX 75061

SCHOEN, JOANNE A., obstetrician, gynecologist; b. Cleve., Mar. 29, 1935; d. Frank J. and Mathilda (Verheyen) Schoen; B.A. (grantee), Case Western Res. U., 1959; M.D. (Joseph Collins scholar), U. Ottawa, 1965. Research technician U. Hosp. Cleve., 1959-61, staff, 1970—; intern, St. Luke's Hosp., Cleve., 1965-66, resident obstetrics-gynecology, 1966-70; practice medicine specializing in obstetrics and gynecology, Cleve., 1970—; mem. staff Hillcrest Hosp., Mayfield Heights, O.; mem. staff, tchr. obstetrics-gynecology Case Western Res. U., U. Hosps. Cleve., 1970—. Diplomate Am. Bd. Obstetrics and Gynecology. Fellow Am. Coll. Obstetrics and Gynecology; mem. A.M.A. (life, Physicians Recognition award 1970-73), Cleve. Soc. Obstetrics and Gynecology, Cleve. Acad. Medicine, Central Assn. Obstetrics and Gynecology, Ohio Med. Soc. Home: 5154 Graham Dr Lynhurst OH 44124 Office: 20620 N Park Blvd Shaker Heights OH 44112

SCHOEN, REM, bus. exec.; b. N.Y.C.; d. Harry L. and Rita (Connors) Schoen; B.S., Trinity Coll., Burlington, Vt., 1951. Registered rep. Bache & Co., N.Y.C., 1956-61; instl. sales Gruntal & Co., 1961-65; v.p., partner, dir. instl. sales Pressman, Frohlich & Frost, Inc., N.Y.C., 1965-74; v.p. Philips, Appel & Walden, Inc., 1974—; mem. N.Y. Stock Exchange; financial adviser to banks in Paris, Milan, Geneva. Vol., Lighthouse, N.Y. Assn. for Blind. Author: Childhood Poems, 1972. Home: 225 E 70th St New York City NY 10021 Office: 111 Broadway New York City NY 10006

SCHOENBERG, BARBARA A. ZUCKERMAN (MRS. LAWRENCE SCHOENBERG), social worker; b. Bklyn., Aug. 3, 1931; d. Max and Mollie (Blazer) Zuckerman; B.A., Bklyn. Coll., 1953; M.S.W., Boston U., 1955; m. Lawrence Schoenberg, June 24, 1956; children—Douglas, Eric, Julie. Sch. social worker Rochester (N.Y.) Bd. Edn., 1955-56; psychiat. social worker Jewish Bd. Guardians, N.Y.C., 1956-59; psychiat. social worker Youth and Family Counseling, Westfield, N.J., 1963-70, Jewish Family Service of Eastern Union County, 1970—. Mem. Acad. Certified Social Workers, League Women Voters (dir. 1962-64). Home: 248 Hollyglen Lane Berkeley Heights NJ 07922 Office: 150 Westfield Av Elizabeth NJ 07083

SCHOENBERGER, MARALYN MORTON (MRS. WALTER SMITH SCHOENBERGER), govt. ofcl.; b. Pitts., Oct. 1, 1929; d. Stanley Francis and Eleanor Birdetta (Hill) Morton; student (George Dean Merchandising scholar), Gimbel Bros., 1947-48; spl. student U. Me., 1967-68; m. Walter Smith Schoenberger, Feb. 2, 1952; 1 dau., Karen. Bookkeeper, Mellon Nat. Bank & Trust Co., Pitts., 1948-50; receptionist Harbison Walker Refractories, Pitts., 1950-53; library asst. Fletcher Sch. Law and Diplomacy, Medford, Mass., 1953-56; administrv. asst. registrar's office U. Me., Orono, 1961-64; v.p. Health Council Me., Inc., Orono, 1971—. Adviser to Am. Legion Boy's State, 1968—; mem. Orono Environment and Conservation Commn., 1970—. Mem. bd. voters registration, Orono, 1966-68; Democratic State committeeperson, 1968—; mem. Gov.'s Com. Children and Youth, 1969-73, chmn., 1973-75; chairperson Orono Democratic Town Com., 1971-72; mem. credentials com. Dem. Nat. Conv., 1972. Mem. League Women Voters, Nat. Council State Coms. for Children and Youth (dir.). Home and office: 25 College Heights Orono ME 04473

SCHOENBROD, MARY HARDEN (MRS. BARRY STEPHEN SCHOENBROD), security analyst; b. Chgo., Aug. 28, 1941; d. Aubrey Colwell and Alicia Jane (Augusty) Harden; B.S.H.E., (Alumni scholar, Mortar Bd. grad. fellow), Purdue U., 1963; M.B.A., U. Chgo., 1965; m. Barry Stephen Schoenbrod, Dec. 28, 1968. Portfolio analyst Shields & Co., N.Y.C., 1966-67; security analyst Duff, Anderson & Clark, Chgo., 1967-70, Continental Bank, Chgo., 1970-73, Allstate Ins. Co., Northbrook, Ill., 1973—. Mem. Investment Analysts Soc. Chgo., Chgo. Council on Fgn. Relations. Home: 4554 Lawn Ave Western Springs IL 60558 Office: Allstate Plaza Northbrook IL 60302

SCHOENFELD, ELIZABETH STROBEL (MRS. JAMES STANLEY SCHOENFELD), journalist, author; b. Astoria, L.I., Apr. 12, 1932; d. Joseph and Gysbertje (Slieker) Strobel; B.S. in Journalism, U. Utah, 1969; m. James Stanley Schoenfeld, June 5, 1951; children—Mark, Jamie Elizabeth, Marilee Elizabeth. Editor manuscripts Bookcraft, Inc., Salt Lake City, 1960-69; editor Soroptimist Publ., Salt Lake City, 1964-69; feature writer women's dept. Deseret News, Salt Lake City, 1969-72, city desk feature writer, 1972—. Stringer for Utah for Nat. Enquirer, Lantana, Fla. Local vice chmn. Republican party, 1969-71. Recipient Feature Story award Deseret News, 1970, 71; In Appreciation award Elk Club, 1973. Mem. Am. Pen Women, Utah League of Utah Writers, Utah Hist. Soc., Literary Art Guild. Mem. Ch. of Jesus Christ of Latter-day Saints (mem. bd. Val Verda Young Women's MIA, 1959-61, pres. 1961-64; coordinator Jr. Sunday Sch., Booneville Ward 1969-71). Author: Please Tell Me, 1966; Thoughts for an LDS Mother, 1967; Thoughts for LDS Youth, 1968; Latter-day Laughs, 1963; More Latter-day Laughs, 1965; co-author: (games) Progress, 1957; Seek, 1958; Mormon Baseball, 1959; Bible Baseball, 1960; Exaltation, 1960; Golden Questions, 1965. Home: 1575 Yalecrest Av Salt Lake City UT 84105 Office: 34 East First South Salt Lake City UT 84110

SCHOENFELDER, ELIZABETH MARGARET (MRS. GEORGE A. SCHOENFELDER), librarian; b. Amana, Ia., July 9, 1915; d. George John and Henrietta (Roemig) Erzinger; B.A., summa cum laude, U. Ia., 1956; M.A., Rutgers U., 1958; m. George A. Schoenfelder, Sept. 30, 1940; children—Jeanette (Mrs. William Hemphill), Georgia (Mrs. Charles Geiger). With Cedar Rapids (Ia.) Pub. Library, 1958—, reference specialist, 1963—. Mem. Phi Beta Kappa, Alpha Lambda Delta. Club: Zonta (Cedar Rapids). Home: Rural Route Amana IA 52203 Office: 3rd Av at 5th St Cedar Rapids IA 52401

SCHOENRICH, EDYTH HULL, pub. health adminstr.; b. Cleve., Sept. 9, 1919; d. Edwin John and Maud (Kelly) Hull; A.B., Duke, 1941, postgrad., 1941-42; M.D., U. Chgo., 1947; M.P.H., Johns Hopkins, 1971; m. Carlos Schoenrich, Aug. 9, 1942; children—Lola, Olaf. Intern, Johns Hopkins Hosp., Balt., 1948-49, resident, 1949-52, asst. prof. Sch. Medicine, 1966—, asso. dept. epidemology Sch. Hygiene and Pub. Health, 1970—, asso. dept. pub. health adminstrn., 1971—; acting chief dept. chronic and community medicine Balt. City Hosp., 1965-66; dir. Bur. Chronic Diseases, Md. Dept. Health, Balt., 1966-71; dir. adminstrn. for services to chronically ill and aging Md. Dept. Health and Mental Hygiene, 1971—. Com. mem. Md. Regional Med. Program, 1966—; mem. com. health, med. services Md. Commn. on Aging, 1966-68; mem. coms. Am. Heart Assn., 1965-68; mem. med. adv. com. Md. Kidney Found., 1969—; mem. adv. bd. Sinai Home Care Program, 1969—. Bd. dirs. Md. Hosp. Edn. and Research Found., Md Tb. and Respiratory Disease Assn., Met. Sr. Citizens Center. Diplomate Am. Bd. Internal Medicine, Am. Bd. Preventive Medicine. Fellow A.C.P.; mem. Assn. State and Territorial Chronic Diseases Program Dirs. (mem. exec. com.), Am. Hosp. Assn. (chmn. governing council on chronic disease, rehab. hosps. 1971), A.M.A., Med. and Chirurgical Faculty Md., Balt. Med. Soc., Gerontol. Soc., Johns Hopkins Med. and Surg. Assn., Md. Conf. on Social Concern, Am., Md. pub. health assns., Nat., Md. rehab. assns. Home: 1402 Boyce Av Baltimore MD 21204 Office: 301 W Preston St Baltimore MD 21201

SCHOESSOW, MATHILDE M(ARTHE), librarian, educator, musician; b. Milw., Feb. 7, 1900; d. August A.F. and Amalia Victoria (Stock) Schoessow; diploma Wis. Conservatory of Music, 1919; U. Chgo., 1937-39; M.A., U. Wis.-Madison, 1951. Tchr. piano Wis. Conservatory of Music, Milw., 1919-71, tchr. organ, 1940-71; librarian U. Wis.-Milw., 1940-70, asst. prof. library skills, 1956-70; cataloger of rare books Concordia Coll., Milw., 1970—, asst. prof., 1974—; head librarian Wisconsin Coll.-Conservatory, Milw., 1971—. Mem. Am. Guild of Organists (dean Milw. chpt. 1951-53), Wis. Library Assn., Milw. Music Tchrs. Assn., U. Wis. Ret. Tchrs. Assn., Milw. Symphony Women's League, Wis. Coll.-Conservatory League, U. Wis.-Milw. Women's League, Music Library Assn., Am. Assn. U. Profs., Mac Dowell Club (accompanist 1940—), Wis. Conservatory of Music Alumni Assn. (pres. 1949-50). Lutheran (organist, choir dir. 1943—). Home: 4812 West Washington Blvd Milwaukee WI 53208 Office: 1584 North Prospect Av Milwaukee WI 53202 also 3201 W Highland Blvd Milwaukee WI 53208

SCHOICKET, SALLY ESTHER GUNSBERG (MRS. DANIEL P. SCHOICKET), psychologist; b. N.Y.C., Mar. 22, 1932; d. Morris and Anna (Sussman) Gunsberg; B.S., N.Y. U., 1953; M.S., Columbia, 1955, Ed.D., 1968; m. Daniel P. Schoicket, June 26, 1955; children—Saundra, Julian. Pvt. practice psychoanalytic psychotherapy and marriage counseling, East Brunswick, N.J., 1963—. Mem. Am. Psychol. Assn., Am. Assn. Marriage and Family Counseling, Acad. Certified Social Workers, Am. Acad. Psychotherapists. Office: 67 W Prospect St East Brunswick NJ 08816

SCHOLNICK, ELLIN KOFSKY (MRS. MYRON I. SCHOLNICK), educator; b. Bklyn., July 10, 1936; d. Irving and Celia (Greenberg) Kofsky; A.B., Vassar Coll., 1958; Ph.D., U. Rochester, 1963; m. Myron I. Scholnick, Mar. 21, 1965. Instr. med. psychology, pediatrics Johns Hopkins U. Sch. Medicine, 1963-67, asst. prof. med. psychology, 1967; mem. faculty U. Md., College Park, 1967—, asso. prof. dept. psychology, 1969-73, prof., 1973—. Asso. editor Child Devel., 1974—; cons. editor Developmental Psychology, 1973—. Mem. Am., Eastern psychol. assns., Soc. Research in Child Devel., A.A.A.S., N.Y. Acad. Scis., Phi Beta Kappa, Sigma Xi. Contbr. articles to publs. Home: 10147 Pasture Gate Lane Columbia MD 21044 Office: Dept Psychology U Md College Park MD 20742

SCHOLZ, CATHERINE HAMMERSLEY, artist; b. N.Y.C., June 1, 1915; d. Frederick and Mary (Hammersley) Scholz; grad. (scholar) N.Y. Sch. Fine and Applied Art, 1935. Free-lance fashion illustrator Harpers Bazaar, McCalls, Lentheric, Mademoiselle, 1935—, House Beautiful, Good Housekeeping, Ladies Home Jour., Seagrams, Am. Druggist, packaging for Richard Hudnut, William R. Warner, 1940—, Pantene, 1965-66. Mem. Women's Nat. Book Assn., Berkshire Garden Center. Republican. Episcopalian. Illustrator over 25 books, 1949—, including: Understanding Why, 1951, Its Fun to Cook, 1952, Christmas in Song and Story, 1953, Before I Go To Sleep, 1953, Sewing Is Fun, 1958, Ballet for You, 1959, Lords of the Blue Pacific, 1962, Shari Lewis Book of Fairy Tales, 1961, Adventure at Riverton Zoo, 1966, Play A Part, 1970; Instant Macrame, 1971; Instant Money from Your Crafts, 1972; The Instant Art of Needlepoint, 1972; also textbooks, readers. Address: 39-24 215 Pl Bayside NY 11361

SCHONHOLTZ, JOAN SONDRA HIRSCH (MRS. GEORGE J. SCHONHOLTZ), civic worker; b. N.Y.C., Sept. 8, 1933; d. Joseph G. and Mildred (Klebanoff) Hirsch; student Vassar Coll., 1950-52; B.A., Barnard Coll., 1954; postgrad. Am. U., 1963; m. George J. Schonholtz, Aug. 21, 1951; children—Margot Beth, Steven Robert, Barbara Ellen. With Meml. Hosp., N.Y.C., 1954. Pres. Fort Benning (Ga.) Med. Wives, 1962-63; sec. Montgomery County (Md.) Women's Med. Aux., 1968; sec. Service Guild of Washington, 1969-70; bd. dirs., 1968—; mem. Washington adv. council on deaf-blind children, 1972—; bd. dirs. Pilot Sch. for Blind Multiply Handicapped Children, Washington, 1968—; spl. gifts chmn. Cancer Soc., Montgomery County, Md., 1968, 69. Recipient Outstanding Service award Service Guild of Washington, 1969. Republican. Jewish religion. Clubs: Vassar, Barnard. Home: 11310 Old Club Rd Rockville MD 20852

SCHOOLEY, DOLORES HARTER, artist mgr.; b. Nora Springs, Ia., May 2, 1905; d. Amil A. and Elizabeth (Sefert) Zemke; B.E., B.A., U. Colo., 1927; M.A., Northwestern U., 1931; m. Leslie J. Harter, June 5, 1934 (dec. 1963); m. 2d, Charles Earl Schooley, Apr. 1, 1966. Tchr. high sch. Consol. Schs., Johnstown, Colo., 1927-28, Byers, Colo., 1928-29, Clayton, Mo., 1931-34; theatrical makeup, 1937—; instr. theatrical makeup, dramatic clubs, N.J. Theatre League; lectr., demonstrator theatrical makeup, dramatic and women's clubs, high schs., N.J. and N.Y. area, 1937-53; dir., entertainer mil. posts First Army, 1951-53; dir. mil. project Phi Beta, 1951-61, nat. officer, mem. nat. council, 1956-61, cons. radio broadcast series WNYC, 1962-65; dir. community relations Wingspread Summer Theatre, Colon, Mich., 1955; co-chmn. Valley Shore Community Concerts, Conn., 1958-61; artist mgr., 1959—; chmn. benefit ball Sharon Hosp., 1970; founder, pres. Berkshire Hills Music and Dance Assn., 1970—. Trustee Sharon Creative Arts Found., 1970-73; hon. trustee Bar Harbor Festival, 1968—. Mem. Alpha Omicron Pi, Phi Beta. Conglist. Clubs: Montclair Dramatic (chmn. makeup, instr. makeup); Rehearsal (program chmn.); Women's (dir. plays, chmn. drama dept.) (Glen Ridge, N.J.); Sharon Women's, Sharon Country (Conn.). Address: Wingspread Sharon CT 06069

SCHOONMAKER, MEYRESSA HUGHES (MRS. DONALD O. SCHOONMAKER), lawyer; b. Guilford County, N.C., Jan. 7, 1940; d. Lee A. and Mildred (Bumgarner) Hughes; B.A. cum laude (John Hankins scholar), Wake Forest U., 1962, J.D., 1968; postgrad. Free U. Berlin, W. Germany, 1960-61, Rutgers State U., 1962-63; m. Donald O. Schoonmaker, Sept. 2, 1962; children—Kirsten Lee, Trevor Owen. Admitted to N.C. bar, 1968; asso. Westmoreland, Sawyer & Schoonmaker, Winston-Salem, N.C., 1968-71, partner, 1971-72; pvt. law practice, Winston-Salem, 1973—. Instr. Salem Coll., Winston-Salem, 1965-66. Mem. Forsyth County Alcoholism Bd., 1973—; trustee Forsyth County Legal Aid Soc., 1969—. Named N.C. Most Outstanding Young Woman of Year, 1972. Mem. Am., N.C., Forsyth County bar assns., Phi Beta Kappa. Home: 2090 Royal Dr Winston-Salem NC 27106 Office: 1008 Brookstown Av Winston-Salem NC 27101

SCHOONOVER, BARBARA ANN, county ofcl.; b. Fort Scott, Kan., May 26, 1934; d. Orville Henry and Marie Teresa (Schahuber) Lantis; grad. high sch.; m. Cloyd C. Schoonover, Jr., May 1, 1954; 1 son, Frank Wayne. Sec., Western Ins. Co., Fort Scott, Kan., 1952-56; dep. clk. Bourbon County, Fort Scott, 1957-66, assessor, 1966—. Mem. Kansas County Assessor Assn. (sec.-treas. 1970-71). Democrat. Home: RR 1 Box 141 Fort Scott KS 66701 Office: 210 S National St Fort Scott KS 66701

SCHOONOVER, SARAH MOREHART (MRS. DONALD JOHN SCHOONOVER), psychologist, health service adminstr.; b. Syracuse, N.Y., Mar. 27, 1925; d. Grover Cleveland and Clara Caroline (Keesecker) Morehart; A.B., Syracuse U., 1946, A.M., 1949; Ph.D., U. Mich., 1953; m. Donald John Schoonover, Aug. 19, 1950; children—John Morehart, Charles Philip, Suzanne Rebecca. Personnel trainee Sears, Roebuck & Co., Syracuse, 1946-48; asst. psychometrican U. Mich. Elementary Sch., Ann Arbor, 1948-49, chief psychometrican, 1949-51; supr. employee testing program GTE Sylvania Electric Products, Inc., Ottawa, O., 1951-52; staff psychologist Northwest Guidance Center, Inc., Lima, O., 1958-62, chief psychologist, 1962-63, psychologist dir., 1969-71; psychologist dir. Hancock County Mental Health Clinic, Findlay, O., 1963-69; psychologist Putnam County Schs., Ottawa, 1969-70; clinic dir. Putnam County Mental Health Clinic, Inc., Ottawa, 1970—. Mem. Am., Ohio, Northwest Ohio psychol. assns., Mich. Alumni Assn., Alumni Assn. of Syracuse U., Psi Chi, Alpha Kappa Delta, Theta Beta Phi, Pi Lambda Theta, Phi Kappa Phi, Alpha Chi Omega. Club: Tawa Bridge. Home: 550 North Thomas St Ottawa OH 45875 Office: 122 1/2 North Oak St Ottawa OH 45875

SCHOONOVER, THELMA IRENE, psychologist, educator; b. Columbus, O.; d. Harry O. and Nellie M. (Patrick) Schoonover; B.S., Ohio State U., 1927, M.A., 1948, Ph.D., 1955. Supr. Ohio schs., 1927-33; psychologist, categorical aid programs Ohio, 1933-44; dir. counseling and guidance Franklin U., Columbus, 1944-47; psychologist Upper Arlington Schs., Columbus, 1947-50; chief psychologist Akron (O.) Bd. of Edn., 1950-54; prof. psychology U. Akron, 1950-54; prof., dept. psychology Capital U., Columbus, 1954-72, chmn. dept., 1962-72, prof. emeritus, 1972—; pvt. practice, 1972—; Ohio State U., 1957—. Psychol. cons. Municipal Civil Service Commn., Columbus, 1960-70, commr., 1972—, pres., 1974—; vis. prof. Miami U., Ore. State Coll., 1955-60. Mem. Womens State Com. for Health, Edn. Welfare, 1953-69, vice chmn., 1960-66; mem. Franklin County Mental Health Assn., 1957—; mem. Gov.'s Task

Force Mental Health, 1969-72. Mem. Am., Ohio (bd. examiners 1964-68, chmn. membership com. 1960-72, chmn. legislation com. 1972-73) psychol. assns., Nat. Council Measurement in Edn., Am. Assn. U. Profs., Am. Assn. U. Women, Ohio State U. Alumni Assn., Psi Chi, Pi Lambda Theta (sec. 1959-60), Delta Kappa Gamma, Phi Delta Gamma (pres., nat. council 1957-58). Clubs: Saturday Music; Business and Professional Women's, Clintonville Woman's. Co-author: Horrocks and Schoonover, Measurement For Teachers, 1968. Contbr. articles in field to profl. jours. Home: 355 Clinton Heights Av Columbus OH 43202 Office: 683 E Broad St Columbus OH 43215

SCHOPPE, ELIZABETH WENTWORTH, pub. relations exec.; b. Malden, Mass., June 2, 1915; d. Hillard Coffin and Nell Hartwell (Wentworth) Schoppe; ed. privately. Reporter, Bangor (Me.) Daily Comml., 1939-43; reporter, feature writer Boston Herald Am., 1943-47; pub. relations dir. Unitarian Service Com., Boston, 1947-52, Mass. Easter Seal Soc. for Crippled Children and Adults, Boston, 1953—. Mem. Pub. Relations Soc. Am., Advt. Club Boston. Home: 9 Hawthorne Place Boston MA 02114 Office: 14 Somerset St Boston MA 02108

SCHOPPER, BARBARA, lawyer; b. Kansas City, Mo., Aug. 11, 1922; d. Arthur Franklin and Berenice Anna (Metsker) Schopper; student Nat. Park Jr. Coll., 1939-40, U. Kansas City, 1940, U. Mo., 1941-42, 42-43; J.D., U. Ariz., 1945. Admitted to Mo. bar, 1945, Ariz. bar, 1947; with firm Stinson, Mag, Thomson, McEvers & Fizzell, Kansas City, Mo., 1945; practice law, Phoenix, 1947-52; law clk. Justice Levi Udall, Supreme Court of Ariz., Phoenix, 1947; policy specialist Social Security Adminstrn., Balt., 1959-64, Kansas City, Mo., 1950-52, 64-72; practice law, Kansas City, Mo., 1956-59, 64-73; trust asst. City Nat. Bank, Kansas City, Mo., 1953-56; dist. counsel Equal Employment Opportunity Commn., Kansas City, Mo., 1973—. Mem. Friends of Art Inst., Kansas City, Mo., 1953-59; mem. women's com. Philharmonic Orch., Kansas City, Mo., 1953-59; mem. Women's Anti-Crime Crusade, 1971—; v.p. Recs. for the Blind Assn., 1969—. Bd. dirs. Maricopa Council Girl Scouts, Phoenix, 1947-50, Kansas City Council Girl Scouts, 1953-57, Childrens Convalescent Center, 1953-57; trustee Soroptimist Welfare Fund, 1969-73. Mem. Mo. Bar, State Bar Ariz., Kansas City Women's C. of C., Am. Legion Aux., Chi Omega, Phi Theta Kappa. Club: Soroptimist (Kansas City, Mo.). Home: 7734 Mercier Kansas City MO 64114 Office: 911 Walnut Kansas City MO 64106

SCHOR, MARY ANN MCCARTHY (MRS. WARREN SCHOR), pub. relations exec.; b. Washington; d. Jeremiah John and Ann (Horstkamp) McCarthy; student George Washington U., 1958-62; m. Warren Schor, May 2, 1964; 1 dau., Elizabeth Ann. Pub. relations, various accounts, Washington, 1962-66; dir. pub. relations program Met. Police Dept., Washington, 1966-69; pub. information specialist pub. relations D.C. Dept. Pub. Health, Washington, 1969-70, Met. Police Dept., Washington, 1970—. Mem. pub. relations adv. com. D.C. Tb and Respiratory Disease Assn., 1969—. Mem. Am. Newspaper Womens Club, Advt. Club Washington, Cosmopolitan Bus. and Profl. Women's Club. Home: 6206 Wedgewood Rd Bethesda MD 20034

SCHORR, THELMA MERMELSTEIN (MRS. NORMAN A. SCHORR), editor; b. New Haven, Dec. 15, 1924; d. Simon Emanuel and Rebecca (Katz) Mermelstein; diploma Bellevue Hosp. Sch. Nursing, 1945; B.S., Columbia, 1951; m. Norman A. Schorr, Mar. 6, 1955; children—Susan Rebecca, Marjorie Jane, Elizabeth Laura. Head nurse Med. Pavilion, Bellevue Hosp., N.Y.C., 1945-50; asst. editor Am. Jour. Nursing, N.Y.C., 1950-53, asso. editor, 1953-61, sr. editor, 1961-71, editor, 1971—. Mem. West Side Narcotics Com., 1961-63. Mem. New York County Democratic Com., 1959-62. Mem. Am. Nurses Assn., Nat. League Nursing, Am. Civil Liberties Union, Am. Hosp. Assn., Am. Soc. Bus. Press Editors, Am. Soc. Mag. Editors, Sigma Delta Chi, Phi Kappa Lambda. Club: Deadline. Home: 32 E 64th St New York City NY 10021 Office: 10 Columbus Circle New York City NY 10019

SCHOSHEIM, PEARL ESTELLE (MRS. ARNOLD M. SCHOSHEIM), ednl. adminstr.; b. Bklyn., Aug. 3, 1922; d. George Bernard and Tillie (Levy) Sugarman; B.A., N.Y. U., 1942; M.A., Columbia, 1943; m. Arnold M. Schosheim, Dec. 22, 1946; children—John Paul, Peter Mark. Tchr. English Rhodes Prep. Sch., N.Y.C., 1943-45; tchr. speech improvement N.Y.C. Bd. of Edn., 1945-66; lectr. speech edn. Queen's Coll., Flushing, N.Y., 1966-68; acting supr. Speech Improvement and Coordinator Title I, Non-pub. Sch. Speech Program, N.Y.C., 1970; supr. Speech Improvement Tchrs., N.Y.C. Bd. of Edn., 1970—. Mem. Community Chest Drive Com., 1960-65. Mem. N.Y. State, L.I. speech and hearing assns., N.Y. State, Eastern States speech assns., Speech Communication Assn., Council for Exceptional Children (hospitality chmn. 1974), Am. Jewish Congress, Alpha Epsilon Phi. Mem. Hadassah. Home: 250 Clent Rd Great Neck NY 11021 Office: 110 Livingston St Brooklyn NY 11201

SCHOTT, BARBARAJO WOERNER (MRS. JOSEPH LAWRENCE SCHOTT), newspaper pub.; b. San Antonio, Nov. 18, 1939; d. Martin Rudolph and Lillie Erna (Lipke) Woerner; grad. high sch.; m. Joseph Lawrence Schott, June 17, 1956; children—Robert Joseph, Kathryn Anne. Copy writer advt. dept. Rucker-Rosenstock Dept. Store, Petersburg, Va., 1956-58; established (with husband) Medina Valley & County News Bull., Castroville, Tex., 1958, mng. editor, advt. mgr., 1958-68, editor, pub., 1968—. Recipient 2d place award news features Tex. Press Assn. State Contest, 1965, 3d place award news pictures, 1966, 3d place award news features, 1968; 2d place award, news writing, 1970, 3d place award appearance, 1972, 3d place award news writing, 1972; Anson Jones award Tex. Med. Assn., 1970, 72; R.S. Reynolds award for religious coverage Gen. Council Presbyn. Ch. U.S., 1971; Tex. Sch. Bell citation for sch. news Tex. Tchrs. Assn., 1971; Golden Press award Am. Legion Aux., 1972. Mem. Tex. Press Assn., Castroville C. of C. Home: 121 Karm St PO Box D Castroville TX 78009 Office: 405 Paris St Box D Castroville TX 78009

SCHOTT, MARYLEE KING (MRS. EUGENE E. SCHOTT), ednl. adminstr; b. Woden, Tex., Aug. 7, 1921; d. James Ed and Mae (Morton) King; B.A., Stephen E. Austin State U., 1940; m. Eugene E. Schott, Sept. 12, 1964. Tchr. Hudson Ind. Sch. Dist., Lufkin, Tex., 1940-42, French High Sch., Beaumont, Tex., 1942-44; sec. Airline Motor Coaches, Nacogdoches, Tex., 1944-47; office mgr., corporate sec., asst. treas. Bennett-Clark Co. Inc., Nacogdoches, 1947-71; adminstrv. sec. Sch. Liberal Arts, Stephen F. Austin State U., Nacogdoches, 1971—. Tchr. secretarial subjects Nacogdoches Bus. Coll., 1946-50. Precinct election judge Dem. primary, Nacogdoches County, 1958—. Named Sec. of the Year Nacogdoches and Lufkin, Nat. Secs. Assn., 1958. Mem. Nat. Secs. Assn. (pres. 1964), Daus. Republic of Tex., Beta Sigma Phi, Xi Gamma Tau. Clubs: Altrusa; Nacogdoches (pres. 1971-72, dir. 1972—). Home: 112 Wortham Dr Box 882 Nacogdoches TX 75961

SCHOWENGERDT, MARY REBECCA, lawyer; b. Ottawa, Kan., June 26, 1930; d. Theodore Louis and Winston Herndon (Easley) Schowengerdt; B.A. with honors, Ottawa U., 1952; J.D. cum laude, Washburn U., 1957. Tchr. Conway Springs (Kan.) pub. schs., 1952-54; clk. Probate Ct. of Shawnee County, Topeka, 1954-57; admitted to practice Kan. bar, 1957, U.S. Supreme Ct., 1972; asso. Stumbo & Irwin, Topeka, 1957-61; partner Stumbo & Irwin, Topeka, 1961-66, Irwin, Irwin & Schowengerdt, Topeka, 1966—. Instr. bus. law Clark's Bus. Coll., Topeka, 1964-65. Trustee Kan. Multiple Sclerosis Soc., Wesley Found., Topeka, Meth. Home for Ages, Sheltered Living, Inc., Shawnee County Mental Health Assn. Named Woman of Yr. Topeka chpt. Am. Bus. Women's Assn., 1963. Mem. Am., Topeka bar assns., Bar Assn. Kan. Home: 1259 High Av Topeka KS 66604 Office: 1520 First Nat Bank Tower Topeka KS 66603

SCHRADER, DOROTHY VIRGINIA, educator; b. Boston, Jan. 2, 1921; d. William Otto and Mary Ann (Ryan) Schrader; B.S., Mass. State Coll. at Bridgewater, 1942; M.A., Boston Coll., 1946; Ph.D., U. Wis., 1961. Instr. math. Coll. St. Teresa, Winona, Minn., 1946-52; asst. prof. Dominican Coll., Racine, Wis., 1952-61; asso. prof. So. Conn. State Coll., New Haven, 1961-64, prof., 1964—, also chmn. dept. Mem. Math. Assn. Am., History of Sci. Soc., A.A.A.S., Sigma Xi. Home: 7 Valley Brook Rd Branford CT 06405 Office: Dept Math Southern Conn State College New Haven CT 06515

SCHRAGER, GLORIA OGUR (MRS. ALVIN SCHRAGER), physician; b. N.Y.C., July 11, 1924; d. Ellis M. and Edith L. (Levine) Ogur; B.A., Bklyn. Coll., 1945; M.D., Woman's Med. Coll. Pa., 1948; m. Alvin Schrager, May 25, 1952; children—Lewis Karl, Ralph Matthew. Intern, Met. Hosp., N.Y.C., 1948-49, resident pediatrics, 1949-51; pediatric fellow N.Y. Hosp.-Cornell Med. Center, 1951-52; asst. med. dir. N.Y. Regional Blood Program, A.R.C., 1952-53; practiced medicine specializing in pediatrics, Westfield, N.J., 1953-72; staff Overlook Hosp., Summit, N.J., chief dept. pediatrics, 1970-72, dir. edn. in pediatrics, 1972—; cons. pediatrician Children's Specialized Hosp., Mountainside, N.J., 1965—. Diplomate Am. Bd. Pediatrics. Fellow Am. Acad. Pediatrics; mem. A.M.A., A.A.A.S. Contbr. articles to profl. jours. Address: 1020 Summit Av Westfield NJ 07090

SCHRAM, GLORIA VERDA, retail trade co. exec.; b. Calgary, Alta., Can., Aug. 5, 1941; d. Albert Bruce and Claire Marie (Schaal) Schram; student Palomar Jr. Coll., 1960-61. Store mgr. Alma's Fashions Co., Vista, Cal., 1956-63; asst. dept. head Sax Fifth Av., Chgo, 1963-64, dept. mgr., Los Angeles, 1964, dept. head, Palm Springs, Cal., 1965-66; buyer trainee J.C. Penney Co., Inc., Los Angeles, 1966-67, asst. and buyer, 1968—. Home: 608 Manhattan Av Manhattan Beach CA 90266 Office: 110 East 9th St Suite 800A Los Angeles CA 90015

SCHREER, ARLENE LINDA (ARLENE ALEN), scenic designer; b. Bklyn., Aug. 5, 1947; d. William and Helen C. (Schlacter) Schreer; student Carnegie Inst. Tech., 1965-66; B.Theater Arts, Pasadena Playhouse Coll. Theatre Arts, 1968. Scenic artist Pasadena (Cal.) Playhouse, 1969; tech. dir., designer City Los Angeles Cultural Arts Center, 1968-69; staff artist Aquarius Theatre, Hollywood Cal., 1969-71; tech. dir., scenic and lighting designer Children of Queen's Revels Repetory Theatre, 1971-73; art dir. Gemini II Prodns., Los Angeles, 1971-74; scenic artist NBC-TV, Hollywood, 1972-73, art dir., 1973—; art dir. ABC-TV, Hollywood, 1973—. Scenic artist, asso. art dir. play Oh! Calcutta!, Los Angeles, 1969; scenic artist Hair prodns., Los Angeles, Las Vegas, 1969, Toronto, Boston, 1970; art dir. films Balloon Man, 1969, The Yellow Sea, 1970. N.Y. Phoenix Sch. Design fellow, 1964. Mem. Internat. Alliance Theatrical Stage Employees, Scenic Artists Local 816, Soc. Motion Picture and Television Art Dirs., U.S. Inst. Theatre Tech., Am. Theatre Assn. Home: 3930 Kentucky Dr Hollywood CA 90068 Office: 7429 Sunset Blvd Hollywood CA 90046

SCHREIBER, BERNICE NEICE, journalist; b. Miami, Jan. 18, 1943; d. Irvin Maurice and Ann F. (Yane) Schreiber; B.A., U. Miami, 1967, M.A., 1974; A.A., Miami-Dade Community Coll. Music and art critic Times-Guide Pub. Co., 1968-71; art history instr. U. Miami, 1968-69; gen. assignment writer Miami Herald Newspaper, 1968; free-lance photo journalist, Miami, 1971—. 2d v.p. Archie Stone Found., 1971—. Press sec. Young Democratic Clubs Fla., 1967-68. Recipient Grad. Fellowship, U. Miami, 1967, Bradford Art Scholarship, 1966, Presidental award for outstanding Service to Dem. Party, 1966. Mem. Am. Med. Writers Assn., Internat. Platform Assn., Nat. Press Photographer's Assn., Women in Communications, Inc., Fla. Women's Press Club, Hist. Assn. S. Fla., Sigma Delta Chi. Club: South Fla. Shell (Miami). Home: 2823 SW 36th Av Miami FL 33133

SCHREIBER, EILEEN SHER, artist; b. Denver, May 5, 1925; d. Michael Herschel and Sarah Deborah (Tannenbaum) Sher; student U. Utah, 1942-45, N.Y. U. extension, 1966-68, also pvt. art study; m. Jonas Schreiber, Mar. 27, 1945; children—Jeffrey, Barbara, Michael. Exhibited Morris Mus. Arts and Scis., Morristown, N.J., 1965-73, N.J. State Mus., 1969, Lever House, N.Y.C., 1971, Paramus (N.J.) Mus., 1973, Am. Water Color Soc., Audubon Artists, N.A.D. Gallery, N.Y.C., Pallazzo Vecchio Florence (Italy); represented in permanent collections Morris Mus., Seton Hall U., Bloomfield (N.J.) Coll., Lanza Industries, N.J., Morris County State Coll., Broad Nat. Bank, Newark, others. Recipient awards N.J. Watercolor Soc., 1969, 72, Nat. Assn. Women Artists, 1970; 1st award in watercolor Hunterdon Art Center, 1972; numerous others. Mem. Nat. Assn. Women Artists (chmn. watercolor jury), N.J. Artists Equity, Nat. Painter and Sculptors Assn., Hunterdon Art Center. Home: 236 S Valley Rd West Orange NJ 07052 Office: care Lillian Kornbluth Gallery 7-21 Fair Lawn Av Fair Lawn NJ 07410

SCHREIBER, FLORA RHETA, theatre arts and speech specialist, author, educator; b. N.Y.C., Apr. 24, 1918; d. William and Esther (Aaronson) Schreiber; B.S., Columbia, 1938, M.A., 1939; certificate Central Sch. Speech Tng. and Dramatic Art, U. London, 1937, N.Y. U. Radio Workshop, 1942. Instr., speech and dramatic art dept. Bklyn. Coll., 1944-46; creator-producer Bklyn. Coll. Radio Forum on WNYC, N.Y.C., 1944-46; drama critic Players mag., 1941-46; instr. Exeter Coll., U. Southwest, Eng., 1937; asst. prof. speech and dramatic arts dept. Adelphi Coll., Garden City, L.I., 1947-53, dir. radio-TV div. Center Creative Arts, 1948-51; lectr. New Sch. Social Research, U. City N.Y., 1952—, now asso. prof. English and speech, dir. publs., asst. to pres. John Jay Coll. Criminal Justice. Cornelia Otis Skinner scholar, 1937. Mem. Am. Assn. U. Women, Am. Assn. U. Profs., Speech Assn. Am., ANTA, Speech Assn. Eastern States, Soc. Mag. Writers (sec. 1963), Authors League Am. Author: Wm. Schuman (biography), 1954; Your Child's Speech, 1956; Jobs With a Future in Law Enforcement, 1970; also short stories, plays, opera libreti and art songs. Contbr. nat. mags. including Cosmopolitan, Reader's Digest, Good Housekeeping, The Freeman, Redbook, Mademoiselle, Am. Mercury, N.Y. Times, Quar. of Film, Radio, and Television, Family Weekly, Today's Health, Woman's Day, others; formerly monthly columnist Sci. Digest. Producer radio forum on Community Theater for NBC, 1949; other radio and TV appearances. Home: 32 Gramercy Park S New York City NY 10003

SCHREYER, GRETA LOBL, artist; b. Vienna, Austria; d. Sigmund and Irene (Kohn) Lobl; M.Degree, Jewelers Guild, Vienna; student Art Students League, N.Y.C.; m. Oscar Schreyer; children—Leslie John, Linda Joyce. One-woman shows in N.Y.C., 1956, Washington, 1960, LaSalle Coll., Phila., 1966, Sienna Heights Coll., Adrian, Mich., 1966, St. Olaf Coll., Northfield, Minn., 1966, La Boetie, N.Y.C., 1970, Roko Gallery, N.Y.C., 1972; exhibited in group shows at Art Center, New Sch. for Social Research, N.Y.C., 1960, 63, 65, Provincetown (Mass.) Art Assn., 1961, Mus. Fine Arts, Springfield, Mass., 1965, Donnell Library, N.Y., 1965, Mus. Arts and Sci., Norfolk, Va., 1965, Knickerbocker Artists, N.Y.C., 1971, La Boetie, 1966-69, Roko Gallery, 1967-72; represented in permanent collections Mus. Arts and Sci., Norfolk, Jersey City State Coll., Strang Clinic, N.Y.C., Syracuse U. Library, Pasadena Art Mus., New Sch. Social Research, Mus. Haaretz, Tel Aviv, Israel, others; also represented in numerous pvt. collections. Guest lectr. various schs. and groups. Mem. Artists Equity. Home: 4 Pine Terrace Highland NY 12528 Studio: 54 W 74th St New York City NY 10023

SCHRIDER, SYLVIA LUANN, assn. exec.; b. Thornville, O., May 29, 1938; d. Bert and Vera Alice (Milbaugh) Schrider; B.S., Ohio State U., 1960; postgrad. U. N.M., 1968. Phys. edn. tchr. No. Local Sch. Dist., Thornville, O., 1960-63, Truth or Consequences (N.M.) Municipal Schs., 1963-64, 65-69, Estancia (N.M.) Schs., N.M., 1964-65; tchr. LaPorte (Ind.) Community Schs., 1969-70; field adviser, camp dir. East Lake Porter Counties, Girl Scouts U.S.A., Gary, Ind., 1971—. Recipient Appreciation Service award Girl Scouts of Cleve., 1962. Mem. Ohio State U. Alumni Assn. Roman Catholic (instr. confrat. Christian doctrine). Home: 121 S Jackson St Crown Point IN 46307 Office: 3725 Broadway Gary IN 46409

SCHROCK, ALTA ELIZABETH, educator; b. Grantsville, Md., Apr. 3, 1911; d. Alvin C. and Amelia (Miller) Schrock; B.A., Waynesburg Coll., 1937; M.A., Kent State U., 1939; Ph.D., U. Pitts., 1944; H.H.D., Waynesburg Coll., 1972. Instr. biology Bluffton (O.) Coll., 1940, U. Pitts., Erie, 1943; asst. prof. biology Am. U., Washington, 1944-46; asso. prof. biology Goshen (Ind.) Coll., 1946-58; prof. biology Frostburg (Md.) State Coll., 1960—. Exec. dir. Springs Hist. Soc., 1957—, curator Springs Mus., 1958—; chmn. Springs Folk Festival, 1958-64; exec. sec. Penn Alps, Inc., 1958—; pres. Council of Alleghenies, 1961-67, exec. sec., 1968—; exec. sec. The Highland Assn., 1963—. Recipient awards Ohio Acad. Sci., Pa. Acad. Sci. Republican. Mennonite. Author: (with Olen L. Miller) The Joel B. Miller Story, 1960. Editor: The Casselman Chronicle, 1961—, Jour. of Alleghenies, 1963—. Home: Little Crossings Grantsville MD 21536 Office: Frostburg State Coll Frostburg MD 21532

SCHROEDER, ANITA GAYLE, statistician; b. Wichita, Kan., Mar. 23, 1944; d. Christie Louis and Maurine Jeannette (Essex) Schroeder; B.S., Baker U., 1966; M.S., Kan. State U., 1968; Ph.D., Ore. State U., 1972. Dir. emergency med. services Evaluation sect. Ark. Health Systems Found., Little Rock, 1973—; asst. prof. biometry div. U. Ark. Med. Center, Little Rock, 1972—. Statis. cons. Ark. div. Am. Cancer Soc.; spl. cons. Ark. Consumer Research. Nat. Def. Edn. Act fellow, 1966-69; Am. Assn. U. Women fellow, 1971-72. Mem. Am., Central Ark. (sec.-treas.) statis. assns., Biometric Soc., Population Assn. Am., Caucus for Women in Statistics, Nat. Wildlife Fedn., Wilderness Soc., Nat. Orgn. Women, Ozark Soc., Sierra Club, Alpha Delta Sigma, Sigma Xi. Author articles in field. Home: 6004 Kenwood St Little Rock AR 72207 Office: Southland Plaza Little Rock AR 72205

SCHROEDER, ANNA MARIA, educator; b. Windsor, Ont., Can., Sept. 16, 1931; d. Leonard George and Maria Sophia (Lembke) Schroeder; came to U.S., 1950, naturalized, 1959; B.S., Concordia Tchrs. Coll., 1953; M.A., U. Mich., 1966, postgrad., 1973—. Tchr. elementary sch., 1953-60; tchr. emotionally disturbed children, 1960-66; lectr. State U. N.Y. at Albany, 1967-69; asso. in spl. projects N.Y. State Edn. Dept., 1969-70; exec. dir. Albany County chpt. Assn. for Retarded Children, 1970-72; asst. prof. State U. N.Y. at New Paltz, 1972—; adj. prof. Russell Sage Coll., Albany. Ednl. cons. Edmark Assos.; cons. spl. edn. N.Y. State Edn. Dept. Sec. bd. trustees Oak Hill Sch., Scotia, N.Y. Mem. Council for Exceptional Children (chpt. pres. 1968, 72), Council for Children with Behavioral Disorders, Pi Lambda Theta, Phi Kappa Phi. Fellow Am. Orthopsychiat. Assn. Lutheran. Home: 2708 Glenbrige St Ann Arbor MI 48104 Office: State Univ Coll New Paltz NY 12561

SCHROEDER, GLORIA IMOGENE, constrn. co. exec.; b. Glenwood, Minn., June 27, 1929; d. Clayton Leland and Alma Josephine (Roll) Kirkwold; grad. high sch.; m. Robert Richard Schroeder, Nov. 15, 1947; children—Linda Lu (Mrs. Edward Arthur Sievert), Loren Robert. Sec., Acme Constrn. Co., 1957-62; sec.-treas. Robert R. Schroeder Constrn., Inc., 1962—, Glenwood Bridge, Inc., 1970—. Mem. Glenwood Mrs. Jaycees (charter mem., sec. 1953). Address: Long Beach Glenwood MN 56334

SCHROEDER, LEILA OBIER (MRS. MARTIN CHARLES SCHROEDER), educator; b. Plaquemine, La., July 11, 1925; d. William Prentiss and Daisy Larinia (Mays) Obier; B.A., Tulane U., 1946; M.S.W., La. State U., 1953, J.D., 1965; postgrad. Yale, 1968; m. Martin Charle Schroeder, Sept. 19, 1969; 1 son by previous marriage—James Michael Cutshaw. Dir., Evangeline Area Guidance Center, La. State Dept. Hosps., Lafayette, 1955-57, dir. Soc. Service Dept. E., 1957-60, psychiat. social work cons., 1960-61; research asst. La. State U., Baton Rouge, 1965-68, asst. prof., 1968-73, asso. prof. bus. law, 1973—. Bd. dirs. Greater Baton Rouge Council on Alcoholism, 1969-72. Recipient La. State U. Found. Research grant, 1970-71. Mem. Am., La., Baton Rouge bar assns., Nat. Assn. Social Workers, Acad. Certified Social Workers, Alpha Delta Pi, Phi Kappa Phi. Episcopalian. Home: 4336 Oxford Av Baton Rouge LA 70808

SCHROEDER, MARY, author; b. Sale, Cheshire, Eng., May 13, 1903; d. William Lawrence and Katherine (Farquer) Schroeder; M.A., Girton Coll., Cambridge, Eng., 1925; postgrad. Columbia Sch. Journalism, N.Y.U., 1933-35. Secondary sch. tchr. Badminton Sch., Bristol, 1927-33, County Sch., Bishop-Auckland, 1940-42; reporter Leeds Mercury & Yorkshire Post, 1935-40; lectr. Southlands Coll. Edn., 1942-49, Alnwick Coll. Edn., 1951-68. Mem. English Speaking Union. Author: Look at the Past, 1950; Man's Forward March, 1956; Family Tree, 1960; My Horse Says, 1963; The Story Teller, 1968; The Hunted Prince, 1969; Hey, Robin, Hide!, 1974. Home: 65 Grantchester Meadows Cambridge England

SCHROEDER, PATRICIA SCOTT (MRS. JAMES WHITE SCHROEDER), congresswoman, educator, lawyer; b. Portland, Ore., July 30, 1940; d. Lee Combs and Bernice (Scott) Scott; B.A., magna cum laude, U. Minn., 1961; J.D., Harvard, 1964; m. James White Schroeder, Aug. 18, 1962; children—Scott William, Jamie Christine. Admitted to Colo. bar, 1964; field atty. NLRB, Denver, 1964-66; pvt. practice law, Denver, 1966—; mem. faculty U. Colo., Denver, 1969—, Community Coll., Denver, 1969-70, Regis Coll., Denver, 1970—; mem. 93d Congress from 1st dist. Colo. Dir. Century Casualty Co., Denver. Bd. dirs. Jefferson County Human Relations Council, 1966—, Denver Young Dems., 1968—; Dem. Precinct Committee Woman, 1968—; Dem. candidate for U.S. Ho. of Reps., 1972. Mem. Denver Bar Assn., League Women Voters (unit leader 1967-68), Internat. House, Fair Housing Center. Conglist. Home: 1440 High St Denver CO 80218 Office: 1313 Longworth House Office Bldg Washington DC 20515

SCHROLL, SISTER AGNES CLAIRE, educator; b. Greenleaf, Kan., Jan. 30, 1910; d. Albert J. and Margaret M. (Hoover) Schroll; A.B., Mount St. Scholastica Coll., 1933; M.A., Cath. U. Am., 1940, Ph.D., 1944. Joined Benedictine Sisters, 1929; instr. sociology Mount St. Scholastica Coll., 1943-45, asso. prof., 1945-48, prof. 1948—, also pres.; vis. prof. Cath. U. Am., summers 1955-58. Mem. Am., Cath., Rural sociol. soc., Am. Polit. Sci. Assn., Conf. Cath. Charities, Am. Acad. Polit. and Social Sci., Nat. Probation Assn., Am. Benedictine Acad. (sec. social sci. sect. 1953), Pi Gamma Mu. Author articles religious periodicals. Home: Mount St Scholastica Coll Atchison KS 66002

SCHROM, HERTA MARIA, pediatrician; b. Altmunster, Austria, July 4, 1921 (came to U.S. 1957, naturalized 1963); d. Franz M. and Grete M. (Heuberger) Schrom; A.B., Franklin Coll., 1939; M.D., U. Innsbruck (Austria), 1946. Intern, Allgemeines Krankenhaus, Linz, Austria, 1946-49; pediatric resident Sauglingshelm Riesenhof, Linz, 1949-50, med. dir, 1953-56; resident Kinderklinik Glanzing, Vienna, 1950-53; pediatric resident, fellow Woman's Med. Coll. Pa., 1957-59; pediatric resident St. Christopher's Hosp. for Children, Phila., 1959-60, mem. staff, 1960-66, instr., 1960-66; practice medicine specializing in pediatrics, Phila., 1966-72; asst. prof. pediatrics Med. Coll. Pa., Phila., until 1972; asso. prof. Sch. Medicine, So. Ill. U., Springfield, 1972—. Diplomate Am. Bd. Pediatrics. Home: 1415 Cherry Rd Springfield IL 62704

SCHUBACH, DEANE FORD, educator; b. Bluefield, W.Va.; d. Lawrence Elbert and Helen Haller (Ewald) Ford; B.A., U. Va., 1957; M.S. (grad. fellow 1957-58), Boston U., 1959; Ed.D., Highland U., 1975; m. Harry Frederick Schubach, Apr. 2, 1960; children—Holland Ford, Franz Josef. Asst. to placement dir. Mary Washington Coll., U. Va., 1954-57; asst. to pres. Intercontinental Services Ltd., N.Y.C., 1958-59; staff mem. U.S. Congress, 1960-61; office mgr., pub. relations asst. Nat. Counsel Assos., Washington, 1961; pub. relations asst. A.A.A.S., 1961-62; tchr. schs., Troy, N.Y., 1963-66; exec. sec. Virgin Islands Govs. Conf., 1967-68; pub. relations dir. Comprehensive Health Planning, Virgin Islands, 1968-69; mem. faculty Coll. Virgin Islands, St. Thomas, 1969—, asst. prof. communication and speech, 1971—; faculty Ann. Creative Problem Solving Inst., State U. N.Y. Coll. at Buffalo. Pres. St. Thomas Mental Health Assn., 1972-73; co-founder, v.p. St. Thomas Pub. Information Assn., 1968; mem. Citizens for Drug Edn., 1969—. Mem. Am. Assn. U. Profs. (chpt. pres. 1973-74), Speech Communications Assn., Internat. Soc. Gen. Semantics, Inst. Gen. Semantics, Creative Edn. Found., League Women Voters. Home: Box 3565 St Thomas VI 00801

SCHUBB, SHIRLEY LENORE REICH, realtor; b. Oakland, Cal., Jan. 20, 1927; d. Harold and Eleanor (Moskowitz) Reich; student U. Cal. at Berkeley, 1944-47, Diablo Valley Coll., 1965—; m. Elliott Schubb, Feb. 16, 1947 (div. Feb. 1966); children—David, Thomas, Deborah. Real estate saleswoman Bob Magrath, Realtor, Lafayette, 1964, Hillside Realty, Lafayette, 1965-67, John M. Grubb Co., Orinda, 1968-71; realtor Better Homes Realty, Lafayette, 1972—; treas. Bethola Corp., Lafayette, 1972—. Mem. Cal. Real Estate Assn., Contra Costa Bd. Realtors (mem. various coms.), Women's Am. O.R.T., Lafayette C. of C. Jewish religion. Republican. Home: 1051 Larch Av Moraga CA 94556 Office: 1014 Oak Hill Rd Lafayette CA 94549

SCHUCK, CECILIA, educator; b. Louisville; d. John Henry and Ella (Adams) Schuck; A.B., Ind. State U., 1922; M.S., U. Minn., 1923; Ph.D., U. Chgo., 1934. Asst. prof. nutrition Fla. State U., Tallahassee, 1930-33; asst. prof. nutrition Purdue U., Lafayette, Ind., 1936-41, asso. prof., 1941-46, prof., 1946-58; prof. nutrition S.D. State U., Brookings, 1958-65; prof. No. Ill. U., DeKalb, 1965-66; prof. nutrition Alcorn A. and M. Coll., Lorman, Miss., 1966—; cons. research project Tenn. State U., 1972. Recipient Distinguished Alumni award, Ind. State U., 1960; named Outstanding Educator Am., 1970. Mem. Am. Chem. Soc., Am. Pub. Health Assn., A.A.A.S., Am. Dietetic Assn., Am., Internat. home econ. assns., Sigma Xi, Iota Sigma Pi, Kappa Mu Sigma. Research in field nutrition. Contbr. articles to profl. jours. Home: 314 Sherman St Joliet IL 60433

SCHUCK, MARJORIE BRACKENRIDGE MASSEY (MRS. FRANZ SCHUCK), publisher, editor; b. Winchester, Va., Oct. 9, 1921; d. Carl Frederick and Margaret Harriet (Parmele) Massey; student U. Minn., 1941-43, New Sch., N.Y.C., 1948, N.Y. U., 1952, 54-55; m. Ernest George Metcalfe, Dec. 2, 1943 (div. Oct. 1949); m. 2d, Franz Schuck, Nov. 11, 1953 (dec. Jan. 1958). Mem. editorial bd. St. Petersburg Poetry Assn., 1967-68; co-editor, pub. Poetry Venture Mag., St. Petersburg, Fla., 1968-69, editor, pub., 1969—; pub., editor poetry anthologies, 1972—; founder, owner, pres. Valkyrie Press, Inc., 1972—; cons. designs and formats, trade publs. and ann. reports, lit. books and pamphlets, 1973—; lectr. in field. Judge poetry and speech contests Gulf Beach Women's Club, 1970, Fine Arts Festival dist. 14. Am. Fedn. Women's Clubs, 1970, South and West, Inc., 1972, The Sunstone Rev., 1973, Internat. Toastmistress Clubs, 1974. Corr.-rec. sec. Women's Aux. Hosp. for Spl. Surgery, N.Y.C., 1947-59; active St. Petersburg Mus. Fine Arts (charter), St. Petersburg Sister City Com., St. Petersburg Arts Center Assn. Bd. dirs., pub. relations chmn. Soc. for Prevention Cruelty to Animals, 1968-71. Mem. Acad. Am. Poets, Fla. Suncoast Writers' Confs. Assn. (v.p., lectr. 1973—), Internat. Platform Assn., Com. Small Mag. Editors and Pubs., Coordinating Council Lit. Mags., St. Petersburg C. of C., Friends of Library of St. Petersburg, Pi Beta Phi. Democrat. Episcopalian. Author: Speeches and Writings for Cause of Freedom, 1973. Contbr. poetry to profl. jours. Home: 8245 26th Av N St Petersburg FL 33710 Office: 2135 1st Av S St Petersburg FL 33712

SCHUCK, VICTORIA, educator; b. Oklahoma City, Mar. 16, 1909; d. Anthony B. and Anna (Priebe) Schuck; A.B. with great distinction, Stanford, 1930, M.A., 1931, Ph.D., 1937. Fellow, Stanford, 1931-33, teaching asst., 1934-35, acting instr., 1935-36, instr., 1936-37; asst. prof. Fla. State Coll. for Women, 1937-40; asst. prof. Mt. Holyoke Coll., South Hadley, Mass., 1940-44, asso. prof., 1944-50, prof. polit. sci., 1950—; prin. program analyst OPA, Washington, 1942-44; vis. lectr. Smith Coll., 1948-49; vis. prof. Stanford, summer 1952; guest scholar Brookings Instn., 1967, 68. Regional editor Ency. Brit., 1958-61. Mem. Secretariat, UN Conf., San Francisco, 1945; mem. Mass. Commn. on Interstate Cooperation, 1957-60; mem. Mass. adv. com. to U.S. Commn. on Civil Rights, 1962—; mem. Berkshire Community Coll. Planning Com., 1964-68, Greenfield Community Coll. Planning Com., 1965-67, mem. Planning Bd., South Hadley, 1959-67, chmn. bd., 1961-67; mem. Pres.'s Commn. on Registration and Voting Participation, 1963. Trustee U. Mass., 1958-65, mem. bldg. authority, 1960-68. Haynes Found. grantee, 1951-52; Asia Soc. S.E. Asia Devel. Group grantee, 1971-72. Mem. Am. Soc. for Pub. Adminstrn., Am. Assn. U. Profs. (pres. Mt. Holyoke 1962-64), Am. Assn. U. Women (state pres. 1946-50, dir. 1965-69), New Eng. (pres. 1950-51), Am. (sec. 1959-60, v.p. 1970-71), Northeastern (v.p. 1971-72), Internat., Northeastern (pres. 1972-73) polit. sci. assns., Am. Assn. Polit. Cons., Mortar Bd., Chi Omega, Phi Beta Kappa. Club: Cosmopolitan (N.Y.C.). Contbr. articles in field to profl. jours. Home: 15 Jewett Lane South Hadley MA 01075

SCHUCMAN, HELEN COHN (MRS. LOUIS SCHUCMAN), psychologist, educator; b. N.Y.C.; d. Sigmund and Rosa (Black) Cohn; B.A., N.Y. U., 1936, M.A., 1953, Ph.D., 1957. Asso. research scientist N.Y. U., 1958-59; chief research psychologist child devel. program Columbia Coll. Physicians and Surgeons, 1959-68, asst. prof. med. psychology, 1962—, asso. prof. med. psychology, 1971—; chief psychologist Neurol. Inst., Columbia-Presbyn. Med. Center, 1963—; research cons. Inst. Retarded Children of Shield of David, 1958—, Study Program in Human Ecology, Cornell U. Med. Coll., 1961—. Fellow Internat. Council Psychologists, Am. Assn. Mental Deficiency; mem. A.A.A.S., N.Y. State, Am. psychol. assns., Psychometric Soc., Psi Chi, Pi Lambda Theta, Kappa Delta Pi. Author publs. in field. Home: 200 E 16th St New York City NY 10003 Office: 622 W 168th St New York City NY 10032

SCHUDER, VERNON MARIE CLEVELAND (MRS. RAYMOND SCHUDER), ret. educator; b. Riverside, Tex., July 20, 1916; d. Aubrey Peoples and Effie Myrtle (Koehl) Cleveland; B.A., Sam Houston U., 1939, postgrad., 1940-66; postgrad. Baylor U., 1950, Colo. State U., 1955, Eastern N.M. U., 1967; m. Bill Fitzgerald, May 28, 1938 (dec. 1963); 1 son, Bill III; m. 2d, Raymond Schuder, Dec. 24, 1965. Band dir., high schs. in Fredonia, Tex., 1935-36, Montgomery, Tex., 1936-37, Livingston, Tex., 1937-38, Warren, Tex., 1938-39, Van Horn, Tex., 1939-40, Coldspring, Tex., 1940-41, Lovelady, Tex., 1941-42, 49-52, Trinity, Tex., 1942-49, 57-64, Willis, Tex., 1952-57, Eden, Tex., 1964-66, Ft. Sumner, N.M., 1966-68, Bloomfield, N.M., 1968-71. Chmn. Walker County Hist. Commn., 1971—. Mem. C. of C. (mem. tourism com. 1972—), V.F.W. Aux. (dist. chaplain 1972, musician 1973), D.A.R., Delta Kappa Gamma, Sigma Tau Delta, Kappa Delta Pi. Methodist. Home: Box 14 Riverside TX 77367

SCHUELEIN, MARIANNE IDA (MRS. RALPH M. KRAUSE), physician; b. Stuttgart, Germany, Apr. 16, 1934; d. Curt C. and Gertrude (Weil) Schuelein; came to U.S., 1938, naturalized, 1944; A.B., Wellesley Coll., 1955; M.D., N.Y. U., 1959; m. Ralph M. Krause, June 26, 1960; children—Peter Carl, Steven Charles. Intern pediatrics Yale, 1959-60; resident in pediatrics Michael Reese Hosp., Chgo., 1960-62; fellow neurology D.C. Children's Hosp., 1962-63; resident neurology Georgetown U., Washington, 1963-66; asst. prof. pediatrics and neurology, 1967—. Mem. adv. bd. Muscular Dystrophy Assn., Washington, 1969—; cons. D.C. Soc. Crippled Children, NIH, Arlington County Mental Retardation Clinic. Fellow Am. Acad. Pediatrics, Am. Acad. Neurology, Am. Acad. Cerebral Palsy; mem. D.C. Med. Soc., Women's Med. Assn. D.C. (pres.), Child Neurology Soc. Home: 3208 44th St NW Washington DC 20016 Office: 3800 Reservoir Rd NW Washington DC 20007

SCHUELKE, GERTRUDE LUISE, ret. educator; b. Hammond, Ind., Aug. 12, 1908; d. Paul Arthur and Alma Wilhelmina (Teichman) Schuelke; A.B., Ind. U., 1930, M.A., 1933; postgrad. German Summer Sch., Middlebury Coll., 1939, 41; Ph.D., Stanford, 1950. Acting instr. Ind. U., 1930-32; field worker Family Service Bur., 1932-33; tchr. German high sch., Hammond, 1933-43, 46-47; successively acting instr., instr., asst. prof., asso. prof., prof. Germanic philology Stanford (Cal.), 1948-73, asso. exec. head dept. modern European langs., 1958-68; ret., 1973. Served from ensign to lt. (j.g.), USNR, 1943-45. Ford Found. fellow, 1951-52. Republican. Lutheran. Home: 994 Parma Way Los Altos CA 94022

SCHUERCH, MARGARET PRATT (MRS. CONRAD SCHUERCH), anesthesiologist; b. N.Y.C., Aug. 9, 1923; d. Edward Dana and Merle Marion (Fares) Pratt; M.D., U. Man., 1945; diploma Anesthesia (Am. Nat. Research Council fellow), McGill U., 1949; m. Conrad Schuerch, June 26, 1948; children—Barbara, Conrad, William, Peter. Intern, Winnipeg (Man.) Gen. Hosp., 1944-45, Winnipeg Children's Hosp., 1945-46; resident McGill U., 1946-49; practice medicine, specializing in anesthesiology, Syracuse, N.Y., 1957—; mem. staffs Twin Elms Hosp., St. Joseph's Hosp., Community-Gen. Hosp., State U. N.Y. Upstate Med. Center. Bd. dirs. Syracuse Girls Club, 1971—, Am. Youth Hostels, 1970—. Served to capt. M.C., Royal Canadian Women's Army Corps, 1943-46. Licentiate Med. Council Can. Diplomate Am. Bd. Anesthesiologists. Home and office: 125 Concord Pl Syracuse NY 13210

SCHUETTE, SISTER DOROTHY, hosp. adminstr.; b. Hamilton, O., Sept. 5, 1942; d. Louis Joseph and Elizabeth (Taphorn) Schuette; B.S., Our Lady of Cincinnati Coll., 1965; M.B.A., Xavier U., 1971. Dietetic intern Good Samaritan Hosp., Cin., 1966; dietitian Mt. Mary Hosp., Hazard, Ky., 1966-67, Estill County Hosp., Irvine, Ky., 1967-71, St. Joseph Hosp. and Manor, Florence, Colo., 1967-69, Madonna Manor, Covington, Ky., 1967-71; resident hosp. adminstrn. Mercy Hosp., Watertown, N.Y., 1970-71; adminstr. St. Joseph Hosp., Florence, Colo., 1971—, mem. bd. dirs., 1971—. Mem. San Isabel Area Health Planning Council, 1971—, Fremont County Profl. Adv. Com., 1971—, Fremont County Head Start Health Adv. Bd., 1971—, Sangre de Cristo Health Careers Council, 1972—. Mem. Am. Dietetic Assn., Am. Hosp. Assn., Colo. Hosp. Assn., Colo. Conf. Cath. Health Services (pres. 1973-74). Home: 410 E 2d St Florence CO 81226 Office: 600 W 3d St Florence CO 81226

SCHUILING, ERNA IRENE MEYER (MRS. WALTER C. SCHUILING), polit. orgn. exec.; b. Frazee, Minn., Jan. 25, 1919; d. Herman F.W. and Rika (Krenz) Meyer; B.S., Bemidji State Coll., 1940; postgrad. U. Ill., 1943-44, Macalester Coll., 1946, U. Cal. at Riverside, 1960-64; m. Walter C. Schuiling, Aug. 28, 1941; 1 son, William T. Tchr. high schs., Barnum, Minn., 1940-41, Bemidji, Minn., 1942-43, Champaign, Ill., 1943-45, St. Paul, 1946-51, San Bernardino, Cal., 1951-58; youth dir. A.R.C., San Bernardino, 1962-66; exec. dir. Inland Adolescent Clinic, San Bernardino, 1966-71. Mem. Cal. Task Force for Integrated Edn., 1969—; mem. Inland Counties Comprehensive Health Planning Council, 1971—; mem. Regional Plan Assn. So. Cal., 1968-72; chmn. San Bernardino County Regional Parks Commn., 1969—; pres. League Women Voters Cal., 1970-73; mem. Urban League, 1969—, N.A.A.C.P., 1969—; mem. San Bernardino Local Agy. Formation Commn.; mem. Equal Ednl. Opportunity Adv. Commn. to Cal. Bd. Edn., also chmn. com. for integrated edn. Bd. dirs. Cal. Center for Research and Edn. in Govt., Inland Adolescent Clinic, San Bernardino County chpt. A.R.C. Mem. Nat. Recreation and Parks Assn., San Bernardino County Mus. Assn. Home: 3577 Lugo Av San Bernardino CA 92404

SCHULER, ANNE KATHERINE, utility co. exec.; b. Rochester, N.Y., Nov. 10, 1921; d. William Robert and Katharine (Christof) Schuler; B.A. cum laude, U. Tex., 1954, postgrad., 1954-57. Editor Herald-Bull., Burley, Ida., 1946-47; staff reporter, sch. editor Dallas Morning News, 1947-49; with Bur. Bus. Research, U. Tex., Austin, Tex., 1954-58; with Lone Star Gas Co., Dallas, 1958—, writer, 1958-70, coordinator, 1970-71, mgr., 1971—; dir. Lone Star Employees Fed. Credit Union. Served with WAC, 1943-45, 50-51. Mem. Bus. and Profl. Women's Club (treas. Dallas 1974—), Internat. Assn. Bus. Communicators, Women in Communications, North Dallas C. of C., Women for Change. Home: 8222 Park Lane Apt 114 Dallas TX 75231 Office: 301 S Harwood St Dallas TX 75201

SCHULER, BARBARA ROTH (MRS. ROBERT ALLEN SCHULER), newspaper co. exec.; b. Tucson, Mar. 27, 1948; d. Bernie and Suzanne (Kwass) Roth; B.A., U. Ariz., 1970; m. Robert Allen Schuler, Aug. 24, 1968; 1 dau., Kiva Cecilia. Staff writer Ariz. Daily Star, Tucson, 1970-72, asst. women's editor, 1972-73, lifestyle editor, 1973—. Bd. dirs. Tucson Civic Ballet, 1972-73. Mem. Ariz. Press Women, Women in Communications (pres. 1971-72, treas. 1972—), Jr. League of Tucson, Mortar Bd., Phi Beta Kappa, Kappa Tau Alpha. Home: 210 E Burrows St Tucson AZ 85704 Office: PO Box 26807 Tucson AZ 85726

SCHULMAN, EVELINE DOLIN (MRS. SOL SCHULMAN), psychologist, educator; b. N.Y.C.; d. George and Fannie (Simon) Dolin; B.S., Coll. City N.Y., 1939, postgrad., 1940-42; M.Ed., U. Md., 1954, Ed.D., 1957; postgrad. Am. U., 1947, State U. Ia., 1939; m. Sol Schulman, June 3, 1941; children—Mark H., Ken S. Tchr., Childrens Colony, N.Y.C., 1941-42; registrar, tchr. Rockwood Nursery Sch., N.Y.C., 1942-43; asst. dir. settlement house Juanita Kaufman Nye Council House, Washington, 1943-44; dir., tchr. Greenway Coop. Nursery Sch., Washington, 1947-48, Fairfax Coop. Nursery Sch., Washington, 1948-50, Community Nursery Sch., Silver Spring, Md., 1952-54; grad. asst. U. Md., College Park, 1954-55; psychol. cons. Prince George County Council Kindergartens and Nursery Schs., 1955-57; lectr. Am. U., Washington, 1957; instr. psychology Community Coll,. Balt., 1958-62, chmn, psychology dept., 1962-72, prof. psychology, 1964-73; lectr. U. Md., College Park, 1967-68, 69-71; prof. community mental health Morgan State Coll., 1971—. Cons. nursery schs., dir. mental health Tech. curriculum Community Coll., Balt., 1967-73; adminstr. evaluation design community programs for developmentally disabled Md. Mental Health Retardation Adminstrn., 1974—; pvt. practice counseling and cons. Mem. citizen's adv. bd. Clifton T. Perkins Hosp. Mem. Am., D.C., Md. Eastern psychol. assns., Am. Assn. U. Profs., Am. Jr. Coll. Assn., Am. Assn. Mental Deficiency, Md. Assn. Jr. Coll. Psychologists (pres. 1967-69), Am. Personnel and Guidance Assn., Assn. Schs. of Allied Health Professions. Author: Intervention in Human Services, 1974. Contbr. to profl. publs. Home: 1103 Caddington Av Silver Spring MD 20901 Office: 301 W Preston St Baltimore MD 21201

SCHULMAN, GRACE JAN, poet, editor; b. N.Y.C.; d. Bernard and Marcella (Freiberger) Waldman; B.S., Am. U.; M.A., N.Y. U., 1960, Ph.D., 1971. Poetry editor The Nation, N.Y.C., 1972—; asst. prof. Baruch Coll., City U. N.Y.; poetry dir. Poetry Center YM-YMHA. Recipient Andiron award N.Y. U., 1971. Yaddo fellow, MacDowell Colony fellow, Karolyi Found. fellow, Vence, France, 1973. Mem. Poetry Soc. Am., Grad. English Assn. N.Y. U. Editor: Ezra Pound: A Collection of Criticism, 1974. Contbr. poems and articles to profl. publs. Home: 1 University Pl New York City NY 10003 Office: 333 6th Av New York City NY 10014

SCHULMAN, ROSALIND SADOFF (MRS. SIDNEY SCHULMAN), economist, educator; b. N.Y.C., June 9, 1914; d. Louis and Masha (Palley) Sadoff; A.B., Smith Coll., 1934; M.A., Columbia, 1938; Ph.D., U. Pa., 1964; m. Sidney Schulman, May 8, 1943. Nat. research dir. Indsl. Union Marine & Shipbldg. Workers Am., AFL-CIO, Camden, N.J., 1943-64; econ. cons. Joint State Govt. Commn., Gen. Assembly Commonwealth Pa., 1964-69; prof. econs. Drexel U., Phila., 1965—. Cons. to Sch. Dist. Phila., Consumer affairs div., 1969, Smith, Kline & French, 1968-69, human relations com. Bethlehen Steel Co., 1968-69. Mem. adv. com. Econ. Edn. Nat. Council Invest-in-America, 1966—; mem. adv. com. to Bur. Labor Statistics and subcoms., 1943-64; statis. adv. com. to Div. Statis. Standards, Bur. Budget, 1963-64; mem. Pa. Gov.'s Com. on Tax Reform, 1972, Gov.'s Energy Council, 1974—. Mem. Am. Econ. Assn., Am. Statis. Assn., Indsl. Relations Research Assn. (founding mem., steering com. Phila. chpt. 1960-61), Am. Assn. U. Women, Am. Assn. U. Profs. Internat. Cybernetic Assn., Regional Sci. Research Assn. Author: Economics of Consumption for a Changing Society, 1972; Communication and Feedback in the Technology of Consumption and a General Theory of Adapting Behavior, 1973. Home: 2401 Pennsylvania Av Philadelphia PA 19130 Office: Drexel U 11-507A Philadelphia PA 19104

SCHULTE, MARGARET MURRAY (MRS. EUGENE JAMES SCHULTE), cosmetic co. exec.; b. Grand Forks, N.D., Aug. 12, 1917; d. Martin William and Margaret Elizabeth (Murphy) Murray; B.A., U. N.D., 1940; M.A., Ariz. State U., 1964; m. Eugene James Schulte, June 30, 1941; children—Paul, Philip, Stephen, Margaret, Thomas, Gene. English, comml. tchr. Miles City (Mont.) High Sch., 1959-63; instr. English Ariz. State U., Tempe, 1964-69; owner Vivian Woodward Cosmetics, Tempe, Ariz., 1970—. Blood recruitment chmn. Red Cross, Miles City, Mont., 1960-62; pres. Barn Theatre Group, Miles City, 1960, dir. 1959-61; pres. Holy Rosary Hosp. Guild, Miles City, 1959-61. Mem. Nat. Council Tchrs. English, Am. Assn. U. Women, Modern Lang. Assn., Rocky Mountain Lang. Assn., Renaissance Soc., Coll. English Tchrs., Small Bus. Mgmt., Alpha Phi. Club: Faculty Womens (pres. 1968-69) (Tempe). Home and office: 999 E Baseline Rd Tempe AZ 85283

SCHULTE, MARIE ELLEN JACOBSON (MRS. JOHN WILLIAM SCHULTE), coll. bookstore ofcl.; b. Blackfoot, Ida., Sept. 3, 1912; d. Martin Eugene and Ella Marie (Burns) Jacobson; student Utah State Coll., 1932-33, U. Ariz., 1949-50; m. John William Schulte, Feb. 3, 1938; 1 son, John Larry. Bookkeeper, Bank of Ariz., Prescott, 1944-46; with Employment Security Commn., Casper, Wyo., 1955; bookkeeper Wyo. Nat. Bank, Casper, 1956; office mgr. YMCA, Casper, 1957; mgr. Casper Coll. Bookstore, 1958—. Mem. Nat. Assn. Coll. Stores Mgmt. (participant seminar 1969-70), Rocky Mountain Skyline Bookstore Assn. Democrat. Roman Catholic. Home: 142 N Iowa Casper WY 82601

SCHULTZ, EDNA MURIEL (MRS. CHARLES SERVIS SCHULTZ), author; b. Ellettsville, Ind., Mar. 5, 1912; d. Emerson Ellsworth and Anna Margaret (Hinshaw) Moore; grad. high sch.; m. Charles Servis Schultz, Mar. 9, 1931; children—Charles David, Nancy (Mrs. Raymond E. Morningstar), Janice (Mrs. Thomas K. Dalbo), Christine (Mrs. Darwin D. Overholt), Kathleen (dec.). Feature writer Am. Mission for Opening Closed Chs. Challenge Mag., Buffalo; typist Chevrolet Co., Buffalo, 1943-44; feature writer Lancaster Enterprise and Depew Herald, Depew, N.Y., 1963-72, poet, poetry column; radio broadcaster WDCX-FM, Buffalo, 1963—. Baptist. Club: Christian Womens (Buffalo). Author: They Said Kathy was Retarded, 1963; Mother and Daughter Banquet Ideas. Home: 113 Zurbrick Rd Depew NY 14043

SCHULTZ, EILEEN HEDY, artist; b. N.Y.C.; d. Harry A. and Hedy (Morchel); grad. design Sch. Visual Arts, 1957; postgrad. Columbia, 1958-59, Art Students' League, 1960-61, Acad. des Beaux Arts, Paris, France, 1957. Comml. artist C.A. Parshall Studios, N.Y.C., 1957-58; art dir. Paradise of Pacific Mag., Honolulu, 1958-59; art dir. Good Housekeeping mag., N.Y.C., 1959—. Judge N.Y. Art Dirs. Club ann. exhbn. Advt., Editorial and TV Art and Design, 1963, 65, 67, 69; cons. graphic cons. Yonkers ambassador good will, Netherlands, 1955; tutor underprivileged children Divine Providence Temporary Shelter, N.Y.C., 1967-68; mem. Foster Parents' Plan, 1966—. Recipient 1st prize advt. design Sch. Visual Arts, 1957; design awards Gilbert Paper Co., N.Y.C., 1960—, Advt. Sales Promotion Mag., 1969; Grand award, Merit award Soc. Publ. Designers Ann. Poster Competition, 1970; Design award Art Dirs. Club Los Angeles, 1970. Mem. N.Y. Art Dirs. Club (design award 1957, dir.), Nat. Soc. Art Dirs., Soc. Illustrators. Office: 959 8th Av New York City NY 10019

SCHULTZ, ELEANOR NINMAN (MRS. WALDO R. SCHULTZ), fashion editor; b. Peoria, Ill., July 6, 1919; d. Leonard Theodore and Annie (Smith) Ninman; student Okla. Coll. for Women, 1937-40, Okla. A. & M. U., 1940-42; m. Waldo R. Schultz, Sept. 7, 1946 (dec. June 1957); children—Thomas John, Patricia Ann, Paul Richard. Feature writer to various Okla. newspapers, 1937-42; artist Hallmark Greeting Co., Kansas City, Mo., 1943-45; free lance greeting card artist, 1946-51; editor Brooks newspapers, Apache Junction, Ariz., 1961-63; Saturday editor, home furnishings and garden editor Phoenix Gazette, 1963-68; with Ariz. Republic, Phoenix, 1968—, fashion editor, 1970—. Recipient Nat. Press Women award, 1968, ann. award Ariz. Press Club, 1974; Fashion writing award Penney-Mo. Newspapers, 1974. Mem. Ariz. Press Women (dist. pres., editor bull.), Nat. Fedn. Press Women, Women in Communications (treas.), Sigma Delta Chi. Home: 716 S Lewis St Mesa AZ 85202 Office: Box 1950 120 E Van Buren Phoenix AZ 85001

SCHULTZ, ESTELLE BERNSTEIN (MRS. MAXWELL SCHULTZ), paper co. exec.; b. N.Y.C., Nov. 6, 1914; d. Mark and Helen (Kaas) Bernstein; student Juilliard Sch. Music, 1931-33, N.Y. U., 1964; m. Maxwell Schultz, June 6, 1933; children—Philip, Arlene Huntington, Eva Lynn Liberman. Pvt. tchr. piano and art, Scarsdale, N.Y., 1935-65; sec. Mountain Paper Products Corp., N.Y.C., 1962—. Recipient many prizes in art. Mem. White Plains Art Assn. Clubs: Woman's (Scarsdale); Pen and Brush (N.Y.C.). Home: 29 Brite Av Scarsdale NY 10583 Office: 50 Rockefeller Plaza New York City NY 10020

SCHULTZ, GWENDOLYN M., writer; b. Milw.; d. Herbert A.F. and Aurelia (Nickel) Schultz; M.A., U. Wis., 1950. Asso. prof. geography U. Wis., Madison. Writer Wis. Geol. and Natural History Survey, 1969—. Mem. Internat. Assn. Quaternary Research, Internat. Glaciol. Soc., Arctic Inst. N. Am., Assn. Am. Geographers, A.A.A.S., Am. Assn. U. Profs., Am. Quaternary Assn., Geol. Soc. Am., Wis. Archaeol Soc., Authors Guild, Council for Wis. Writers, Nat. Writers Club. Author: Glaciers and the Ice Age, 1963; The Blue Valentine, 1965; Crest Colorprint World Atlas, 1966; Ice Age Lost, 1974. Contbr. articles to jours. and mags. Home: 111 W Wilson St Madison WI 53703 also 115 W Saveland Av Milwaukee WI 53207

SCHULTZ, HELEN ELIZABETH, business exec.; b. Quincy, Ill., Dec. 21, 1930; d. Homer A. and Charlotte (Pollock) Schultz; B.A., Culver-Stockton Coll., 1951; postgrad. Gem City Bus. Coll., 1954. Tchr. high sch., Cantril, Ia., 1951-52, Campbell, Mo., 1952-53; personnel records clk. Ill. Bell Telephone Co., Peoria, 1954-57; sec. P.F. Goodrich, Indpls., 1957-73; sec., treas. Liberty Fund, Inc., Indpls., 1960-74, dir., 1967—, exec. dir., 1970-74, pres., chief exec. officer, 1974—; sec. Central Shares, Inc., Indpls., 1960-74, dir., 1961—, treas., 1965-73, pres., 1974—; sec. Engrs., Inc., Indpls., 1961-69, treas., 1965-69; sec., treas. Thirty-Five Twenty, Inc., Indpls., 1965-74, dir., 1965—, exec. dir., 1970-74, pres., 1974—; sec. Ind. Telephone Corp., Seymour, Ind., 1965-73, treas., 1965—, dir., 1971—, pres., 1973—; dir. Pub. Telephone Corp., Greensburg, Ind., 1968—, v.p., 1973—; sec. Patoka Coal Co., Indpls., 1961-69, treas., 1965-69; dir. Winchester (Ind.) Found., 1971—, vice-chmn., 1973—. Mem. Mont Pelerin Soc. Methodist. Home: 5707 Brockton Dr Apt 312 Indianapolis IN 46220 Office: 3520 Washington Blvd Indianapolis IN 46205

SCHULTZ, JEAN EUNICE (MRS. GRANVILLE EUGENE JUDD), psychiatrist; b. Grantwood, N.J., Jan. 12, 1929; d. Otto Frederick and Wilhelmine Caroline (Wendt) Schultz; B.S., Bates Coll., 1950; M.D., Womans Med. Coll. Pa., 1956; M.P.H., Columbia, 1960, M.S., 1966; m. Granville Eugene Judd, May 23, 1959; children—Kim, Kathleen Ann, Corey. Intern, asst. commr. Nassau County Health Dept., N.Y.C., 1960-63; resident in psychiatry and community psychiatry Columbia Presbyn. Med. Center, 1963-66; chief community psychiatry North Shore Hosp., Manhasset, N.Y., 1967-73; asst. dir. dept. psychiatry North Shore Univ. Hosp., Manhasset, 1973—; asst. attending psychiatrist Roosevelt Hosp., N.Y.C., 1967-70; asst. clin. prof. psychiatry Cornell Med. Coll., 1970—; cons. psychiatrist Northeast Nassau Psychiat. Hosp., 1971—. Diplomate Am. Bd. Psychiatry and Neurology. Fellow Am. Psychiat. Assn.; mem. N.Y. State, Nassau County med. socs., Nassau Neuropsychiat. Assn. Home: 2 Addison Lane Greenvale NY 11548 Office: North Shore Hospital Manhasset NY 11030

SCHULTZ, MARY KATHERINE, pub. relations and advt. exec.; b. St. Paul, Feb. 13, 1943; d. Arnold M. and Burdette Catherine (Sheehan) Niemeyer; B.A. in Journalism, U. Minn., 1965; m. Frederick William Schultz, Dec. 27, 1972. Editor co. publs. Hoerner Waldorf Corp., St. Paul, 1965-66; product publicist 3M Corp., St. Paul, 1967-69, publicist various divs., 1969-71, sr. publicist comml. tape div., 1971-73, supr. div. pub. relations services, 1973-74, advt. supr. consumer products div., 1974—. Past mem. Minn. Women's Adv. Council. Mem. Pub. Relations Soc. Am. (asso.), Kappa Kappa Gamma, Kappa Tau Alpha. Home: Apt 315 167 N McKnight Rd St Paul MN 55119 Office: 3M Co 220-8E 3M Center St Paul MN 55133

SCHULZ, MILDRED VALETTE MABERRY (MRS. RALPH E. SCHULZ), librarian; b. Monmouth, Ill.; d. J. Frank and Evelyn Nellie (Patch) Maberry; B.A., Augustana Coll., 1930; postgrad. Columbia Sch. L.S., 1944-45; m. Ralph E. Schulz, May 3, 1946 (dec. Nov. 1957). Head history dept. East Moline (Ill.) Elementary Schs.; head librarian Pub. Library, East Moline, 1945-64; reference librarian Ill. State Hist. Library, Springfield, 1964-70, head librarian, 1970—. Exec. dir. Nat. Library Week, Ill., 1960. Bd. dirs., chmn. Rock Island County chpt. Am. Cancer Soc., 1959-61. Recipient citations Nat. Library Week, 1960, C. of C. East Moline, 1961, 62. Mem. Am. (chmn. conf. program com. history sect. 1968, exec. com. history sect. 1969-72), Ill. (sec. 1968-69) library assns., Am. Assn. U. Women (pres. Rock Island-Moline chpt. 1959-61), Am. Bus. Women's Assn. (Capital City chpt. Woman of Year 1964). Methodist. Club: Women's (chmn. community improvement East Moline 1963). Home: 725 S 4th St Springfield IL 62703 Office: Old State Capitol Springfield IL 62706

SCHULZE, ELAINE MARY PATIN (MRS. HERMAN J. SCHULZE), social worker; b. Breaux Bridge, La.; d. John J. and Birdie (Dupuis) Patin; B.A., Southwestern La. Inst., 1939; certificate in social work La. State U., 1940; M.S., Simmons Coll., 1947; m. Herman J. Schulze, Apr. 30, 1949; children—Elaine, Herman, Gretchen, Diane, Richard, Rudolph. Caseworker St. Landry Dept. Pub. Welfare, Opelousas, La., 1941-42; caseworker asst. field dir. and asst. dir. S.E. Area Hosp. Service A.R.C., Atlanta, 1942-46, disaster caseworker, 1946, 47-48; med. social cons. La. State Dept. Health, New Orleans, 1948-49; clin. social worker Tulane U. Cardiac Work Evaluation Unit, New Orleans, 1960-62; chief social worker Delgado Vocational Rehab. Center, New Orleans, 1962-69; dir. social service dept. Touro Infirmary, New Orleans, 1969-70; chief med. social worker Rehab. Inst. New Orleans Charity Hosp., 1971—. Mem. Acad. Certified Social Workers, Nat. Assn. Social Workers, Nat. Rehab. Assn., La. Pub. Health Assn. Home: 7830 Freret St New Orleans LA 70118 Office: 1532 Tulane Av New Orleans LA 70140

SCHULZE, THEODORA ECONOMOU (MRS. RICHARD SCHULZE), music dir.; b. Hammond, Ind., Sept. 19, 1930; d. Xenophon and Emily (Mueller) Economou; pvt. study music with Alfred Barthel, Kenneth Gekeler; student Chgo. Civic Orch. Sch., 1948; m. Richard Schulze, Apr. 16, 1950; 1 son, Otto Theodore. Solo oboe Am. Conservatory Symphony Orch., Chgo., 1948-51; asso. dir. Chgo. Soc. Ancient Instruments, 1951-53; with The Telemann Soc., Inc., N.Y.C., 1953—, dir. soc. sch., 1953—, asso. music dir. soc., 1955—, asso. condr., solo oboe, solo recorder soc. orch., 1955—, condr. chorus, 1955—, also bd. dirs.; rec. artist Vox, Nonesuch, Amphion, and Counterpoint-Esoteric Records; faculty Wolfe Conservatory, Larchmont, N.Y., 1955-58, Met. Music Sch., N.Y., 1960-63; chmn. Nat. Com. to Preserve Felsengarten, 1973—. Active radio program prodn. for Council for Homeopathic Research and Edn., 1963. Author: Complete Guide to Playing the Recorder, 1959, We Begin, Music Note Reading and Fundamentals of Music Notation, 1970; co-author: Elements of Musical Style: Slurs, 1962. Editor: Joseph Sellner: 180 Studies for the Development of Uniform Velocity and Muscular Control, 1962. Office: 15 1/2 Independence Ct Concord MA 01742

SCHULZE, TONI WITHINGTON, real estate, photog. co. exec.; b. Honolulu, Feb. 21, 1943; d. Leonard and Grace Gaylord (Smith) Withington; B.S. in Journalism, Northwestern U., 1965; m. Richard P. Schulze, Jr., Dec. 12, 1970; 1 son, Justin More. Polit. reporter Honolulu Star-Bull., 1965-70; planning cons., salesman RLT Realty, Kamuela, Hawaii, 1970—; pres. Pleasant Co., Inc., Kamuela, 1973—. Coordinator, U.S. Senate campaign of Cecil Heftel, Honolulu, 1970; instr. real estate law U. Hawaii, 1969-72; freelance photographer, writer. Camp dir. Juneau-Douglas (Alaska) council Girl Scouts, 1965; mem. Mayor's Water Safety Adv. Com., 1967-70; water safety instr. A.R.C., 1964-72; mem. Hawaii Conservation Council, 1969-73, Gov.'s Commn. on Year 2000, 1971-72. Washington Journalism Center fellow, 1968. Recipient outstanding reporter award Windward C. of C., 1968. Mem. Women in Communications (past officer), Honolulu Press Club (past officer), John Howard Assn., Alpha Gamma Delta. Home: PO Box 795 Kamuela HI 96743

SCHUMAN, FRANCES PRINCE (MRS. WILLIAM SCHUMAN), civic worker; b. N.Y.C., June 12, 1913; d. Leonard and Gertrude E. (Rheinhauer) Prince; B.A., Barnard Coll., 1933; m. William Schuman, Mar. 27, 1936; children—Anthony William, Andrea (Mrs. Donald D. Weiss). Spl. counselor Vocational Counseling for Handicapped, Vocational Adv. Service, N.Y.C., 1935-49. Founding mem. Cerebral Palsy Assn. So. Westchester, dir. 1951-55, mem. exec. com. 1951-55; mem. Urban League Westchester, dir. 1955-58, mem. exec. bd. 1955-58; v.p. Vol. Bur. Westchester, 1958-61; pres. New Rochelle (N.Y.) Vol. Bur., 1959-63; initiated New Rochelle Camperships Fund, 1960, New Rochelle Community Christmas Giving Program, 1960; mem. exec. com. Vocational Adv. Service, N.Y.C., 1963-70; founder, chmn. Friends Channel 13, N.Y.C., 1966-72, hon. chmn., 1972—; founder, chmn. Nat. Friends Pub. Broadcasting, 1970—. Bd. dirs. Riverdale Country Sch., N.Y.C., 1949-63; pres. bd. dirs. City Center Acting Co., 1973—. Clubs: Women's City N.Y. (dir. 1964-66), Cosmopolitan Club. Home: Richmond Hill Rd Greenwich CT 06830

SCHUMAN, MARY ELLEN, extension agt.; b. Columbia City, Ind., Jan. 18, 1935; d. Homer Earl and Dorothy Charlotte (Kanable) Schuman; B.S., Purdue U., 1957; M.S., Colo. State U., 1968. Merchandising trainee Morehouse Fashion Dept. Store, Columbus, O., 1957-58; home demonstration agt. Purdue U., Portland, Ind., 1958-62, New Castle, Ind., 1962-67, area extension agt. youth, 1969-73; extension agt. youth, Marion County (Ind.), Indpls., 1973—. Mem. Ind. Youth Council, 1971. Mem. Nat. Assn. Extension Home Economists (Distinguished Service award 1972), Am., Ind. home econs. assns., Ind. Extension Agts. Assn., Ind. Extension Home Economists (pres. 1967), Nat. Assn. 4-H Agts. (Distinguished Service award 1972), Purdue Alumni Assn., Epsilon Sigma Phi. Club: Altrusa (Indpls.). Home: Apt B1 7115 Cider Mill Circle Indianapolis IN 46226 Office: 421 City-County Bldg Indianapolis IN 46204

SCHUMER, FLORENCE COOPER (MRS. LEO SCHUMER), psychologist; b. N.Y.C.; d. William and Bessie (Goodman) Cooper; B.A., Bklyn. Coll., 1945; M.A., Yale, 1946, Ph.D., 1949; m. Leo Schumer, Mar. 28, 1946; 1 son, Robert Adam. Clin. psychologist, dept. psychiatry Yale, 1946-48; psychol. counselor Prudential Ins. Co., Counseling Center, Newark, 1948-49; research asso. N.Y.U., Research Center for Human Relations, N.Y.C., 1949-50; sr. psychologist N.Y.U., Testing and Advisement Center, N.Y.C., 1949-53; operator Parent-Child Workshops, N.Y.U., 1953-54; sr. clin. psychologist Cornell U. Med. Coll., Adult Counseling Center, N.Y.C., 1953-56; research asso. Dr. David M. Levy, N.Y.C., 1956-61; sr. research scientist Columbia U., Research Found. Mental Health, N.Y.C., 1956-65; sr. research asso. Wiltwyck Sch. for Boys, Family Research Unit, N.Y.C., 1964-66; sr. research scientist N.Y.U., Inst. Developmental Studies, N.Y.C., 1967-72; individual practice psychodiagnostics and psychotherapy, N.Y.C., 1949—. Instr. Bklyn. Coll., summer 1945, New Haven Coll. Phys. Therapy, 1947-48, Hunter Coll., summer 1948; asst. prof. N.Y.U., 1949-53; clin. cons. Pride of Judea Childrens Home, 1956-60; adj. asst. prof. Barnard Coll., 1956-60, adj. asso. prof., 1965-66. Fellow Am. Psychol. Assn.; mem. N.Y. State, Eastern psychol. assns., N.Y.C. Soc. Clin Psychologists, Soc. Psychol. Study Social Issues, A.A.A.S. Author: (with J. Zubin & L. Eron) An Experimental Approach to Projective Techniques, 1965; (with S. Minuchin, others) Families of the Slums: An Exploration of their Structure and Treatment, 1967; (with C. Deutsch) Brain-damaged Children: A Modality-Oriented Exploration of Performance, 1970. Home: 1040 Park Av New York City NY 10028

SCHUPBACH, HAZEL LESTER (MRS. LLOYD C. SCHUPBACH), librarian; b. Ashland, Ky., Oct. 21, 1912; d. Conn L. and Carrie M. (Webb) Lester; A.B., Ky. Christian Coll., 1938; postgrad. Butler U., 1942-44; m. Lloyd C. Schupbach, June 1, 1944; 1 son, Frederick Alan. Circulation librarian Butler U., Indpls., 1944-46; librarian Ky. Christian Coll., Grayson, 1946-57; bibliographer acquisitions dept. U. Cal. at Riverside, 1957-62, interlibrary loans librarian, 1963—. Tchr. missions dept. Ky. Christian Coll., Grayson, 1955-57. Home: 2674 Sepulveda San Bernardino CA 92404 Office: University of California Riverside CA 92507

SCHURCH, MARTHA ANNE, social work adminstr.; b. Barneveld, Wis.; d. Ernest and Martha (Maag) Schurch; B.A., U. Wis., 1938; certificate in social work U. Minn., 1939; M.S. in Social Work, Columbia, 1950. Caseworker Grant County (Wis.) Dept. Welfare, 1939-42; children's worker Green County (Wis.) Dept. Welfare, 1942-43; with Nat. A.R.C., 1943-46, field dir., 1945-46; social worker VA, Milw., 1946-47; with Wis. Dept. Health and Social Services, Madison, 1950—, agy. service supr. div. family services, 1950—. Mem. Nat. Assn. Social Workers (chpt. sec. 1969—), Am. Pub. Welfare Assn., Nat. Conf. Social Welfare, Wis. Welfare Council, Wis. Pub. Welfare Assn., League Women Voters, Nature Conservancy. Home: 309 Orchard Dr Madison WI 53705 Office: 1 W Wilson St Madison WI 53702

SCHURRER, AUGUSTA LOUISE, educator; b. N.Y.C., Oct. 11, 1925; d. Karl and Louise (Kainz) Schurrer; A.B., Hunter Coll., 1945; M.A., U. Wis., 1947, Ph.D., 1952. Mem. faculty dept. math. U. No. Ia., Cedar Falls, 1950—, asso. prof., 1958-64, prof., 1964—. NSF faculty fellow U. Mich., 1957-58. Mem. Am. Math. Soc., Math. Assn. Am., Nat. Council Tchrs. Math., Am. Assn. U. Profs., Am. Assn. U. Women, Phi Beta Kappa, Sigma Xi, Pi Mu Epsilon, Kappa Mu Epsilon, Sigma Pi Sigma. Home: 1224 W 20th St Cedar Falls IA 50613

SCHUSLER, MARIAN LUCILLE MARTIN (MRS. HERBERT HENRY SCHUSLER), educator; b. Woodcliff, N.J., Oct. 14, 1926; d. Theodore and Marian (Rover) Martin; B.S., Bucknell U., 1946; M.Litt., U. Pitts., 1950, Ph.D., 1964; m. Herbert Henry Schusler, Mar. 3, 1955; 1 dau., Dawn Lucille. Tchr., Reno Sr. High Sch., 1953-55; analytical statistician Census Bur., Washington, 1951-52, Navy Dept., Washington, 1952-53; tchr., chmn. dept. math. Wilkinsburg (Pa.) Sr. High Sch., 1955-66; lectr. U. Pitts., 1964-66; asso. prof. math. Slippery Rock State Coll., Pa., 1966-70; tchr. Shady Side Acad., Fox Chapel, Pa., 1970—. Mem. Am. Host Program, Vols. Internat. Tech. Assistance; vol. Children's Hosp., Pitts. Recipient NSF award, summer 1961. Mem. Am. Assn. U. Profs., Am. Ednl. Research Assn., Pi Mu Epsilon, Kappa Delta Epsilon. Presbyn. Club: South Butler Women's. Contbr. articles to profl. jours. Home: RD 1 Box 325 Saxonburg PA 16056 Office: Shady Side Academy Fox Chapel PA 15238

SCHUSTER, CARLOTTA LIEF (MRS. DAVID ISREAL SCHUSTER), physician; b. N.Y.C., Sept. 16, 1936; d. Victor Filler and Nina Lincoln (Rayevsky) Lief; B.A., Barnard Coll., 1957; M.D., N.Y. U., 1964; m. David Isreal Schuster, Sept. 2, 1962; 1 dau., Amanda. Intern, Lenox Hill Hosp., N.Y.C., 1964-65; resident, dept. psychiatry St. Luke's Hosp. Center, N.Y.C., 1965-68, chief resident, 1967-68; instr. N.Y. Med. Coll., N.Y.C., 1969-72; asst. attending physician Met. Hosp., 1969-72; sr. staff psychiatrist Silver Hill Found., New Canaan, Conn., 1972—, preceptor psychiatry St. Luke's Hosp., 1969—. Fellow U. Pa., 1968-69. Diplomate Am. Bd. Psychiatry and Neurology. Mem. Am. Psychiat. Assn., Fairfield County Med. Soc. Home: 64 Musket Ridge Rd Wilton CT 06897

SCHUSTER, E(ULA) ELAINE, lawyer; b. Oklahoma City, June 8, 1936; d. John Otto and Eula Delone (Campbell) Schuster; B.A., Sweet Briar Coll., 1958; M.A., U. Okla., 1962, J.D., 1968. Instr. econs. Southeastern State Coll., Durant, Okla., 1961-65; admitted to Okla. bar, 1968; mem. firm Whitten and Whitten, 1969-72; asst. dist. atty. Oklahoma County, Oklahoma City, 1972—. Bd. dirs., sec. Kidney Found. Okla-So. Kan., Inc., 1969—. Mem. Am., Okla. bar assns., Am. Assn. U. Women (rep. ednl. found. 1972-74), Kappa Beta Pi (grand registrar 1971-73). Mem. Christian Ch. Home: 1224 NW 33d St Oklahoma City OK 73118 Office: Office Dist Atty Oklahoma County Court House Oklahoma City OK 73102

SCHUSTER, NANCY CAROLINE (MRS. ROBERT KAY SCHUSTER), lawyer; b. Cleve., June 28, 1932; d. Arthur and Mildred Sara (Sampliner) Wise; B.S., U. Wis., 1954; J.D. cum laude, (grantee), Cleve. Marshall Law Sch., 1968; postgrad. Northwestern U., 1970; m. Robert Kay Schuster, Jan. 30, 1954; children—Kenneth Robert, Lyanne Kay, Stuart Carl, Richard Wise. Admitted to Ohio bar, 1968; with Legal Aid Soc., Cleve., 1966-72; asst. U.S. atty. No. dist. Ohio, U.S. Dept. Justice, Cleve., 1972—. Organizer, 1st pres. Am. Field Service, Parma, O., 1962; organizer, v.p. Greater Cleve. Sch. Bd. Assn., 1967-69; area chmn. WVIZ Auction Com., Cleve., 1970-71; mem. task force on youth and delinquency Cleve. Fedn. for Community Planning, 1972-74, chmn. ad hoc com. community schs., 1973-74; mem. task force on crime and delinquency Nat. Assn. Social Workers, Cleve., 1972; mem. Parma Bd. Edn., 1962—, pres., 1968-70. Organizer, trustee S.W. Community Music Assn., 1966-67; trustee Cleve. Area Council for the Arts. Recipient Claude E. Clarke award Legal Aid Soc. Cleve., 1971; Regional for legal writing A.S.C.A.P., 1967. Mem. Ohio (criminal justice com. 1973), Cleve. (co-chmn. juvenile ct. com. 1972, mem. editorial com. 1973) bar assns. Home: 10498 Lake Av Cleveland OH 44102 Office: US Courthouse Cleveland OH 44114

SCHUSTER, SARAH ELIZABETH FLETCHER PLATT (MRS. FRANK P. SCHUSTER), art gallery exec.; b. El Paso, Tex., Sept. 12, 1929; d. Frank Barron and Mildred (Sullivan) Fletcher; A.B., Vassar Coll., 1950; postgrad., U. Tex., 1973; m. Frank P. Schuster, May 17, 1972; children by previous marriage—Susan (Mrs. H. Peterson Redman), Anne C. Platt, Jack Fletcher Platt. Owner, dir. Two-Twenty-Two Gallery, El Paso, Tex., 1963—. Founding mem. Valuor's Consortium, Houston, 1973; designer, partner Lacita Needlepoint Design, El Paso, 1969-73. Mem. El Paso Mus. Art, 1963—, Womens Dept. El Paso Symphony, 1961—; v.p. El Paso Sun Carnival Assn., 1961. Mem. Appraisers Assn. Am., Jr. League of El Paso. Episcopalian. Author: (with Frank P. Schuster) The Status Game, 1973. Home: 6109 Pinehurst St El Paso TX 79912 Office: 6006 N Mesa El Paso TX 79902

SCHUTTE, EILEEN PAULINE, educator; b. Sigel, Ill., Mar. 17, 1925; d. Harry Peter and Eva Leah (Bigler) Schutte; B.S., Eastern Ill. U., 1947; M.Ed., U. Ill., 1953; Ed.D., No. Ill. U., 1967. Tchr. high sch., Byron, Ill., 1947-51, Bradley-Bourbonnais High Sch., Bradley, Ill., 1951-52, Antioch (Ill.) High Sch., 1952-55; chmn. dept., tchr. Elmwood Park (Ill.) High Sch., 1955-67; tchr. secretarial and vocational courses Eastern Ill. U., Charleston, 1967-69; coordinator, tchr. bus. Coop. Office Edn., Mayfair Coll., Chgo., 1969—. Supr. student tchrs. Chgo. State U., 1971—. Mem. Nat., North Central (v.p. 1959-60), Ill. (pres. 1972-73), Chgo. area bus. edn. assns., Ill. Edn. Assn., N.E.A. (life), Am. (life), Ill. vocational assns., Delta Pi Epsilon, Pi Omega Pi, Kappa Delta Pi. Home: 9815 Schiller Blvd Franklin Park IL 60131

SCHUTZ, ESTELLE SHAPIRO (MRS. IRVING SCHUTZ), artist; b. N.Y.C., Oct. 10, 1907; d. Benjamin and Bertha (Sirota) Shapiro; grad. Cooper Union, 1929; m. Irving Schutz, June 30, 1929; children—Phyllis (Mrs. Mark I. Halpern), Jill (Mrs. Manus Pinkwater). Exhibited one-man shows Kan. State U., Western Mich. Coll., Baldwin-Wallace Coll., Fla. State U., Hofstra Coll.; exhibited group shows Bklyn. Mus., Pa. Acad. Fine Arts, Nat. Arts Club of N.Y., Boston Mus., Jersey City Mus. Art, Phila. Print Club, Silvermine Guild, Pratt Graphic Miniature Traveling Shows, Soc. Am. Graphic Artists Exchange show U.S. and Japan, Audubon Artists Ann., numerous regional shows; represented in permanent collections Bklyn. Mus., Phila. Mus. Art, McAllen (Tex.) Mus., also pvt. collections; pvt. tchr. painting and printmaking. Recipient awards, including Nat. Arts Club N.Y., 1964, Jersey City Mus. Art, 1965, 67, Hofstra Coll., 1965, John Taylor Arms purchase award Audubon Ann., 1957, Silvermine Ann., 1972, Nat. Assn. Women Artists, 1973, Nassau County Cultural Devel./Bankers Trust award, 1972, also numerous regional awards. Mem. Nat. Assn. Women Artists, Soc. Am. Graphic Artists, Silvermine Guild. Club: Kings Point (N.Y.) Garden (pres. 1955-65). Home: 19 Gilbert Rd Great Neck NY 11024

SCHUTZ, NANCIE JEANNE, advt. exec.; b. Mpls.; d. Earl Leon and Ida Helena (Mellum) Schutz; student, Wells Coll., 1951-52; B.A., U. Minn., 1955. Writer, Knox-Reeves Advt., N.Y.C., 1955-61, Kenyon & Eckhardt Advt., N.Y.C., 1961-63; group head Ogilvy &

Mather, N.Y.C., 1963-68; with Dancer Fitzgerald Sample Inc., N.Y.C., 1968—, v.p., 1969—. Mem. Phi Beta Kappa, Kappa Tau Alpha, Theta Sigma Phi, Pi Beta Phi. Republican. Lutheran. Home: 435 E 57th St New York City NY 10022 Office: 347 Madison Av New York City NY 10017

SCHUTZE, GERTRUDE, library and information specialist; b. N.Y.C.; d. John and Ann Marie (Kastner) Schutze; B.S., Hunter Coll., 1939; M.L.S., Columbia, 1949. Research librarian Pa. Salt Mfg. Co., Phila., 1940-46; tech. librarian Bristol-Myers Co., Hillside, N.J., 1946-53; mgr. information services Grace Chem. Research & Devel. Co., N.Y.C., 1953-59; mgr. library and information services Standard & Poor's Corp., N.Y.C., 1959-60; chief librarian Union Carbide Research Inst., Eastview, N.Y., 1960-63; cons., library and information specialist, Woodhaven, 1963-68; mgr. information services Ayerst Labs., N.Y.C., 1968—. Mem. Am. Soc. Information Sci., Am. Chem. Soc., Med. Library Assn., Spl. Libraries Assn. Author: Bibliography of Guides to the Scientific-Technical-Medical Literature, 1958, supplements, 1963-67; Documentation Source Book, 1965; The Social Sciences, Bibliography of Guides to the Literature, 1968, supplement, 1974; Information and Library Science Source Book, 1972. Editor: Documentation Digest, 1949-59. Contbr. articles to profl. jour. Home: 7620 86th Av Woodhaven NY 11421 Office: 685 3d Av New York City NY 10017

SCHWAB, BECKI (REBECCA) MARIE, realtor; b. Ellwood City, Pa., Aug. 18, 1930; d. Ralph Joseph and Mary (Ferresse) Salerno; student San Diego City Coll., 1948-49, San Diego State Coll., 1950-51; m. Milton David Schwab, June 16, 1952; children—Mary Elizabeth, John David. Owner, broker Schwab Realty Co., La Mesa, Cal., 1967—. Mem. Nat. Assn. Realtors, Nat. Inst. Real Estate Brokers, Cal. Real Estate Assn. (dir. 1973—), La Mesa Bd. Realtors (dir. 1971-72, exec. v.p. 1973, pres. 1974, certificate for outstanding service 1967, realtor of year award 1973), San Diego County Council Realtors. Home: 8009 Forrestal Rd San Diego CA 92120 Office: 9083 Dallas St La Mesa CA 92041

SCHWAB, LOIS OPPER (MRS. KENDALL DREISBACH SCHWAB), educator; b. Lincoln, Neb., Jan. 26, 1925; d. Raymond Theodore and Lena Dorothea (Schroeder) Opper; student Westmar Coll., 1942-43; B.S., U. Neb., 1946, M.A., 1947, Ed.D., 1966; m. Kendall Dreisbach Schwab, Aug. 6, 1949; children—Ronald Opper, Brian Edward, Kendra Joan. Am. Home Econs. Assn.-Rehab. Services Adminstrn. traineeship U. Neb., 1964-66, instr., 1947-53, asso. prof. home econs., dir. programs for home economists in rehab., 1966—. Co-dir. Easter Seal Found. research grant, 1970-71; cons. to home economists in rehab. U. Ala., 1971, N.D. State U., 1972. Mem. Neb. Gov's. Com. on Employment Handicapped, 1969—, Lincoln Mayor's Com. on Employment Handicapped, 1967—; mem. com. on community programs Am. Heart Assn., 1972—; mem. exec. com. Neb. Heart Assn., 1968—; mem. nat. task force on ind. living Am. Found. Blind, 1972—. Chmn. bd. dirs. Lincoln Heart Assn., 1967; trustee Neb. Wesleyan U., 1971—. Mem. Am., Neb. psychol. assns., Neb. (exec. com. 1968—) home econ. assns., Nat., Neb. (mem. exec. com. 1967-72) rehab. assns., Mortar Bd., Phi Upsilon Omicron, Omicron Nu. Methodist. Home: 6721 Everett St Lincoln NE 68506

SCHWAB, MARILYN, psychiatrist; b. N.Y.C., Feb. 14, 1929; d. Robert L. and Helen (Perlmutter) Schwab; B.A., N.Y. U., 1949; M.B., Chgo. Med. Sch., 1953, M.D., 1954. Intern, Kings County Hosp., N.Y.C., 1953-54, resident gen. psychiatry, 1954-56; practice psychiatry, N.Y.C., 1958—; psychiat. coordinator Brookwood Child Care, Bklyn., 1958—; vis. asso. staff psychiatrist Hillside Hosp., N.Y.C., 1969—; asso. attending North Shore Hosp., Manhasset, N.Y., 1969—; clin. instr. State U. N.Y., Bklyn., 1958-64; lectr., dept. edn., cons. ednl. clinic City U. N.Y., Bklyn. Coll., 1958-68; clin. instr. dept. psychiatry Cornell U., N.Y.C., 1971—. Diplomate Nat. Bd. Med. Examiners, Am. Bd. Psychiatry and Neurology. Fellow Am. Orthopsychiat. Assn., Am. Geriatrics Soc.; mem. A.M.A., N.Y. Council on Child Psychiatry, Soc. Adolescent Psychiatry, Nassau Psychiat. Assn. Home: 16 Dunster Rd Great Neck NY 11021 Office: 25 Canterbury Rd Great Neck NY 11021

SCHWAB, MILDRED ANN, city ofcl.; b. Portland, Ore., Jan. 9, 1917; d. Gustav and Frances (Zell) Schwab; LL.B., J.D., Northwestern Sch. Law Lewis and Clark Coll., 1939. Admitted to Ore. bar, 1939; practiced in Portland. Mem. Portland Planning Commn., 1970-72, vice chmn., 1971, chmn., 1972; City Portland commr. pub. affairs, 1973—. Mem. Am., Multonomah bar assns., Ore. State Bar, Am. Judicature Soc. Home: 4666 NW Woodside Portland OR 97210 Office: 414 City Hall Portland OR 97204

SCHWAGER, ALICE M., author; b. Peoria, Ill., Feb. 7, 1924; d. Phillip Otto and Mary Anna (Rothlisberger) Goetze; student U. Wash., 1949, Sacramento State Coll., 1971; B.S., Bradley U., 1974; m. Conrad E. Schwager, Sept. 2, 1945; 1 son, William Frederick. Sec. to supt. recreation, Peoria, 1945-48; sec. to personnel supr. Boeing Airplane Co., Seattle, 1948-50; v.p. United Spraying, Inc., St. Louis, 1951-56; now free lance writer. Asst. dir. Motor Corps, A.R.C., St. Louis, 1951-54. Bd. muses Peoria Lakeview Center for Arts and Scis. Mem. Sigma Delta Chi, Phi Beta Psi. Presbyn. Club: Illinois Valley Antique Auto. Contbr. articles to local and nat. publs. Home: 4503 N Knoxville Av Peoria IL 61614

SCHWAGER, EDITH COHEN (MRS. EMANUEL SCHWAGER), editor; b. Trenton, N.J., Dec. 16, 1916; d. Michael and Clara (Panitch) Cohen; m. Emanuel Schwager, May 13, 1950; children—Michael J., Karen S. Exec. editor Hahnemann Med. Coll. and Hosp., Phila., 1966—, adminstrv. dir. Alcoholism Clinic, 1967-71. Mem. membership com. Central Br. YMCA. Mem. Am. Med. Writers Assn. (pres. Delaware Valley chpt., mem. nat. bd.). Home: 4404 Sherwood Rd Philadelphia PA 19131 Office: 230 N Broad St Philadelphia PA 19102

SCHWAGER, GLORIA DEVORE (MRS. HENRY R. SCHWAGER), TV broadcaster; b. Ft. Worth, Oct. 15, 1920; d. Fred E. and Olive (Green) DeVore; student El Capital Coll. of the Theatre, 1937; drama degree, U. Cal. at Los Angeles, 1942; m. Henry R. Schwager, Jan. 22, 1957; 1 son, Mark C. Rochester. With KGNC, Amarillo, Tex., 1945-47, KRLD-TV, Dallas, 1948-50, KFDM-TV, Beaumont, Tex., 1955-60, WBRZ-TV, Baton Rouge, 1961-69; with WLOX-TV, Biloxi, Miss., 1970—, producer, host Potpourri; weathercaster, 1955—. Served with WAF, 1942-45. Mem. Women In Communications. Club: Altrusa (pres. Baton Rouge 1967-68). Home: c/o Rowntowner Inn Biloxi MS 39351 Office: Box 4596 WLOX-TV Biloxi MS 39531

SCHWANER, ANNIE MAE GINN (MRS. NELSON MARSHALL SCHWANER), state legislator; b. Carnesville, Ga., Apr. 24, 1912; d. Charles Holman and Mary Elizabeth (Terrell) Ginn; m. Nelson Marshall Schwaner (dec. 1967); children—Gordon Wesley, Audrey Mae, Susan Anne, Marsha Mae, Nelson Marshall II. Sec., Tubize Corp., Hopewell, Va., 1934-35; former reporter Hopewell News; former columnist Progress Index, Petersburg, Va.; mem. N.H. Ho. of Reps., 1963—, mem. municipal and county govt. com., 1963, constl. conv., 1964, resources, recreation, and devel. com. Mem. State Security Task Force, also Price Stblzn. Bd., 1964—; founder, 1st pres. Plaistow (N.H.) Civic Orgn., 1959-60; chmn. vols. Greater Haverhill (Mass.) chpt. A.R.C., 1954-57, nat. del., 1955, exec. bd., 1954-57; com. chmn. P.T.A. council, Worcester, 1947-48; exec. bd. Sea Coast Regional Plan, 1965-67; v.p. Seacoast Regional Devel. Assn.; mem. Diocesan Sch. Bd., 1965-71; chmn. various fund-raising drs.; mem. nat. fund raising and adv. bd. Am. Heart Assn.; mem. Rockingham County Selective System Draft Bd. Pres., Plaistow Women's Republican Club, 1964-66. Bd. dirs. N.H. Heart Assn., state heart fund chmn., 1973. Recipient Bronze medal N.H. Heart Assn, 1959, certificate of merit Am. Mothers Com., 1960, certificate of honor N.H. D.A.V., 1965. Mem. Cath. Daus. Am., Cath. Women's Guild (past pres.), Am. Judicature Soc., N.H. Council on World Affairs, N.H. Council for Better Schs., Nat. Order Women Legislators (state pres. 1973). Roman Catholic (ch. adv. bd.). Home: Elm St Plaistow NH 03865

SCHWANKE, BEULAH POYNTER, univ. adminstr.; b. North Liberty, Ind., May 7, 1916; d. Harvey B. and Anna Marie (Sheaks) Poynter; R.N., Michael Reese Hosp. Sch. Nursing, 1938; B.S., Bethel Coll., 1961; A.M., U. Notre Dame, 1966; m. Frank Richard Schwanke, Feb. 10, 1940 (dec.); children—Frank Richard, Ronald Leigh, Nancy Gay. Registered nurse Michael Reese Hosp., Chgo., 1939-44; coll. nurse, tchr. health edn. and first aid Bethel Coll., 1961-65; adminstrv. asst., dean student services Ind. U., South Bend, 1966-69, registrar, 1969—. Mem. Am. Assn. U. Women, Am. Assn. Higher Edn., Am. Assn. Collegiate Registrars and Admissions Officers, Michael Reese Hosp. Alumni Assn. (life). Lutheran. Club: Altrusa (rec. sec. South Bend 1973-74). Home: 61594 Elderberry Lane South Bend IN 46614

SCHWANKE, JENNIFER JILL BROWN (MRS. DONALD LEE SCHWANKE), occupational therapist; b. Roswell, N.M., Dec. 12, 1944; d. Blanchard Welton and Frances Louise (Read) Brown; B.S., Tex. Woman's U., 1968; m. Donald Lee Schwanke, Aug. 7, 1971; 1 dau., Jennie Lou. Occupational therapist Laredo (Tex.) Rehab. Center, 1967-68, El Paso (Tex.) Rehab. Center, 1969-70; occupational therapist, supr., asst. instr. occupational therapy U. Tex. Med. Br., Galveston, 1971; occupational therapist, dir. day treatment services El Paso (Tex.) Center Mental Health and Mental Retardation, 1971—. Named Handicapped Employee of Year, El Paso C. of C., 1970. Mem. Am. Occupational Therapy Assn., El Paso Assn. Occupational and Phys. Therapists (sec.-treas. 1969-70). Home: Big Springs PO Lecompton KS 66050 Office: 501/9 Centerville 89 Augsburg Germany

SCHWANS, BERNARDINE MARY, newspaper editor; b. Mitchell, S.D., Mar. 11, 1942; d. Lawrence Michael and Marie Elizabeth (Schroeder) Schroeder; student U. S.D., 1960-63; m. Daniel Schwans, Sept. 28, 1963; children—Troy, Jay, Roxanne. Sec. Shanard Ins. Agy., Bridgewater, S.D., 1966-68; mem. staff Bridgewater Tribune, weekly, 1968—, asst. editor, 1968—. Sec., treas. McCook County Soc. Crippled Children and Adults, 1968—. Mem. Nat. Catholic Soc. Foresters (officer local chpt.), Pi Beta Phi. Republican. Club: McCook County Country (Salem, S.D.). Home: 320 N Hill St Salem SD 57058 Office: Bridgewater SD 57319

SCHWANTZ, MOLLIE MILLIKEN, educator; b. Washington, Nov. 26, 1925; d. John Barnes and Juliette Dandridge (King) Milliken; B.S., U. Cal. at Los Angeles, 1948; postgrad. U. So. Cal., Occidental Coll., 1950, Whittier Coll., 1962-64, U. Cal. at Irvine, 1965; m. June 20, 1947 (div. July 1971); children—Suzan, Juliette, Christine. Tchr., El Centro, Cal., 1950-61, Lowell Joint Sch. Dist., Whittier, Cal., 1961—. Miller math. tchr. State Cal., 1971-72; instr. Pepperdine Coll., 1971, U. Cal., Riverside, 1972. 2d v.p. Parents Without Partners, 1972-74. Recipient Cal. Tchr. of Year award Parents for Better Edn., 1963. Mem. Nat., Cal. tchrs. assns., Nat., Cal. assn. math. tchrs. Episcopalian. Home: 2512 Monterey Pl Fullerton CA 92633 Office: 950 Briercliff St La Habra CA 90631

SCHWARTZ, ANNE EARLE (MRS. HAROLD A. SCHWARTZ), mental health-rehabilitation specialist; b. Balt., Sept. 2, 1943; d. Walter C. and Julia (Feddeman) Moses; B.S., U. Colo., 1965; M.A., U. N.M., 1967; m. Harold A. Schwartz, Feb. 15, 1969. Undergrad. resident adv. U. Colo., Boulder, 1963-65; grad. counselor U. N.M., Albuquerque, 1965-66; counselor, psychometrician Packard Bell Electronics, Albuquerque Job Corps Center for Women, 1966-67; vocational counselor Horizon House, Psychiat. Rehab. Agy., Phila., 1967-68; dir. community placement Norristown (Pa.) State Hosp., 1968-72, dir. vocational adjustment services, 1972—. Pres. Shopmates, Inc. Bd. dirs. Pa. Assn. Rehab. Facilities, Montgomery County Mental Retardation Center. Mem. Am. Personnel and Guidance Assn., Am. Rehab. Counselors Assn., Nat. Vocational Guidance Assn., Alpha Gamma Delta. Episcopalian. Club: Soroptimist. Home: White Hall 1763 W Main St Norristown PA 19401 Office: Norristown State Hosp Norristown PA 19401

SCHWARTZ, BARBARA WILNER, lawyer; b. Newark, Mar. 1, 1941; d. Louis and Ann (Shoolman) Wilner; B.A. summa cum laude, U. Buffalo, 1962; LL.B. magna cum laude, Columbia, 1965; m. Victor Elliot Schwartz, July 8, 1964. Admitted to N.Y. bar, 1965, Ohio bar, 1973; asso. firm Rosenman Colin Kaye Petschek Freund & Emil, N.Y.C., 1965-67; asso. firm Dinsmore, Shohl, Coates & Deupree, Cin., 1967-73, partner, 1974—. Cons., Legal Research Group, Inc., Charlottesville, Va., 1970; lectr. in field. Recipient Charles Bathgate Beck prize, 1963, Jane Marks Murphy prize, 1964; Sixth Circuit scholar, 1963-65; James Kent scholar, 1963; Harlan Fiske Stone scholar, 1964-65. Mem. Assn. Bar City N.Y., Cin. (sec. taxation sect.), Am. bar assns., Cin. Estate Planning Council, Phi Beta Kappa. Editor: Columbia Law Rev., 1964-65; Banks and Banking, vols. 4 and 8. Contbr. profl. jours. Home: The Cloisters 1052 Hatch St Cincinnati OH 45202 Office: 511 Walnut St Cincinnati OH 45202

SCHWARTZ, MRS. CHARLES (BERTIE GRAD SCHWARTZ), lawyer, club woman; b. N.Y.C., Sept. 16, 1901; d. Samuel and Lottie (Prager) Grad; LL.B., N.Y.U., 1926; m. Charles Schwartz, June 20, 1926; children—Stuart G., Louise (Mrs. David Horowitz), Ernest Saul. Admitted to N.Y. bar, 1946. Nat. chmn. books and publs. Nat. Women's League of United Synagogue Am., 1950—; nat. v.p. Am. Mothers Com., 1950—; v.p. Sisterhood of B'nai Jeshurun, 1948—, co-chmn. Torah Fund. Active Hadassah, 1929—, v.p. and membership chmn. N.Y. chpt., 1946-62, chmn. books N.Y. chpt., 1946—. Bd. dirs. Woman's Press Club of N.Y.C., Nat. Jewish Book Council Am. of Nat. Jewish Welfare Bd., 1966—, mem. exec. bd. Mem. Am. Jewish Hist. Soc., N.Y. County Lawyers Assn., Women's Div. Soc. for Advancement Judaism, Am. Jewish Congress (mem. bd. nat. commn. Jewish affairs). Author: (with husband) Faith Through Reason, 1946. Editorial bd. Outlook mag., 1955—. Home: 146 Central Park West New York City NY 10023 also Lake Placid NY 12946 Office: 48 E 74th St New York City NY 10021

SCHWARTZ, DIANNE PAULINE DRUCKER (MRS. HOWARD SCHWARTZ), pub. relations exec.; b. Chgo.; d. Adolph and Faye (Beezy) Drucker; B.S., Northwestern U., 1957; m. Howard Schwartz, Sept. 7, 1959. Reporter Skokie (Ill.) News, 1957-58; asso. editor indsl. mag. Telephony, 1958-62; with Michael Reese Hosp. and Med. Center, Chgo., 1962—, asst. dir. community relations, 1966-72, dir. pub. relations, 1972—. Mem. Internat. Council Indsl. Editors (nat. v.p. 1969-70), Indsl. Editors Assn. Chgo. (pres. 1968), Women in Communications (chmn. ladies of press 1966-67). Home: 7141 N Kedzie Av Chicago IL 60645 Office: 2929 S Ellis St Chicago IL 60616

SCHWARTZ, ELIZABETH, ednl. adminstr.; b. Sharon, Wis.; d. Christian and Barbara (Straka) Schwartz; Ph.B. cum laude, U. Chgo., 1927; M.S., Northwestern U., 1931. Tchr., Lombard (Ill.) Pub. Schs., 1924-27, Gary (Ind.) Pub. Schs., 1927-29; asst. in publicity office Chgo. YWCA, 1929-30; tchr. Oak Park (Ill.) Pub. Schs., 1936-46; spl. publicity worker Office of Pres., U. Chgo., 1932-33; tchr. Sacramento City Unified Sch. Dist., 1946-66, program asst. lang. arts curriculum devel. services, 1966-68; chmn. English dept. Kennedy Sr. High Sch., Sacramento, 1969-71. Founder, dir. Oak Park (Ill.) Children's Theater, 1936-45. Mem. Sacramento City Tchrs. Assn., Nat. Audubon Soc., P.T.A. (hon. life), Cal. Writers' Club, Delta Kappa Gamma. Author: (with others) Three O'Clock Courage, Four Corners of the Sky. Editor: Chi State News, 1959—.

SCHWARTZ, ESTHER KRETZMAN (MRS. JACOB SAMUEL SCHWARTZ), club woman; b. N.Y.C., Sept. 13, 1893; d. Isaac and Freida (Greenberg) Kretzman; ed. pub. schs., Ft. Wayne and Wabash, Ind.; m. Jacob Samuel Schwartz, June 4, 1917; children—Isaac Ralph, Leah Sarah. Bd. dirs. Ft. Wayne Jewish Fedn.; 1st v.p. Ft. Wayne chpt. Council Jewish Women, 1930; charter mem. Aux. Jewish War Vets., pres., 1961-62; v.p. Ind. dept. Jewish War Vets., 1948; legislative chmn. northeastern dist. Garden Clubs of Ind., 1957; parliamentarian Ft. Wayne Council Garden Clubs, 1953-54, pres., 1955. Trustee, parliamentarian Orthodox Jewish Cemetery Assn., Ft. Wayne, 1960-62. Recipient nat. award for pub. relations Jewish War Vets. Aux. U.S., 1961. Mem. Zionist Orgn. Am., Allen County, Ft. Wayne hist. socs., Internat. Platform Assn., Hadassah (charter), Council Ft. Wayne Garden Clubs (past pres.), B'nai B'rith Women, Fort Wayne Community Concerts. Mem. Amaranth (charter mem.). Clubs: Rose Garden (pres. 1950-51) (Fort Wayne); Toastmistress (named Woman of Influence, Gt. Lakes region 1969). Home: 1255 Sunset Dr Fort Wayne IN 46807

SCHWARTZ, HELEN FRENCH (MRS. HARRY MARVIN SCHWARTZ), librarian; b. Scranton, Pa., Nov. 29, 1924; d. Myron Everett and Dorothy Lillian (Jones) French; B.A. magna cum laude, Waynesburg Coll., 1948; postgrad. (Stipend scholar), Pa. State U., 1949-50; M.L.S., Drexel U., 1968; postgrad. Millersville State Coll., 1972; m. Harry Marvin Schwartz, Mar. 23, 1952; children—Myron Eliot, Judith Rose. Instr. English, Waynesburg (Pa.) Coll., 1948-49; mgr. bookstore Rutgers U., Camden, N.J., 1950-52; library asst. Farrell Sch., Phila., 1966-67; librarian Conwell Middle Magnet Sch., Phila., 1967-68; cataloger Free Library of Phila., 1968-71, asst. head central children's dept., 1971-72; librarian Frederick Douglass Instructional Materials Center, Phila., 1972—. Library Resource person for Child Advocacy Program, Frederick Douglass Sch., 1973-74. Mem. Am., Pa. library assns., Assn. for Ednl. and Communications Tech., Pa. Sch. Librarians Assn., Assn. Phila. Sch. Librarians, Library Pub. Relations Assn. Greater Phila., Booksellers Assn., Beta Phi Mu, Phi Alpha Theta. Democrat. Jewish religion. Home: 1458 Higbee St Philadelphia PA 19149 Office: 22nd and Norris St Philadelphia PA 19121

SCHWARTZ, HELENE ENID, lawyer; b. N.Y.C., Oct. 25, 1941; d. Melvin C. and Ethel (Weisenthal) Schwartz; A.B. magna cum laude, Brown U., 1962; LL.B., Columbia, 1965. Admitted to N.Y. bar, 1965, The U.S. Dist. Cts. for the So. and Eastern Dists. of N.Y., 1967, the U.S. Cts. of Appeal for the Second Circuit, 1967, Seventh Circuit, 1970, U.S. Supreme Ct., 1971; pvt. practice law, N.Y.C., 1965—. Faculty Rutgers Law Sch., Camden, N.J., 1972—. Bd. dirs. Center for Constl. Rights, N.Y.C., 1973—. Mem. Phi Beta Kappa. Author: (Kinoy, Peterson) Conspiracy on Appeal: Appellate Brief on Behalf of the Chicago Eight, 1971; Demythologizing the Historic Role of the Grand Jury, 1972.

SCHWARTZ, HILDA G., judge; b. N.Y.C.; d. Solomon and Anna Leah (Rubin) Ginsburg; B.S., Washington Sq. Coll. of N.Y. U.; LL.B., N.Y. U., 1929; m. Herman N. Schwartz, Feb. 21, 1930; 1 son, John Michael. Admitted to N.Y. bar, 1930; pvt. practice law, 1930-46; sec., bur. head, trial commr. Bd. Estimate, 1946-51; city magistrate, N.Y.C., 1951-58; treas., head dept. finance City of N.Y., 1958-62, dir. finance, 1962-65; judge N.Y.C. Civil Ct., 1965-71; justice N.Y. State Supreme Ct., 1972—. Chmn. law com. Bd. Magistrates, 1953-58; chmn. home term panel judges, 1954-56; judge Adolescent Ct., 1952-58; mem. welfare adv. bd. N.Y. Jr. League, 1953-56; bd. mgrs. Greenwich House, 1946-48; bd. dirs. Washington Sq. Outdoor Art Exhibit, 1950-58; bd. dirs. Washington Sq. Coll. Pres., Women's Nat. Democratic Club, 1942-44; v.p. Young Dem. Club, 1935-37. Mem. N.Y. Women's Bar Assn. (past pres.), Nat. Assn. Women Lawyers (past v.p.), Assn. Bar City N.Y., N.Y. County Lawyers Assn., Am., N.Y. State bar assns. Home: 43 Fifth Av New York City NY 10003 Office: 60 Centre St New York City NY 10007

SCHWARTZ, JUDY IRIS, educator; b. N.Y.C.; d. Samuel and Fay (Stein) Schwartz; B.A., Hunter Coll., 1961, M.S., 1965; Ph.D., N.Y. U., 1970. Early childhood tchr. Hewlett-Woodmere (N.Y.) Sch. Dist., 1961-66; teaching fellow N.Y. U., 1967-68, instr., summer 1968; instr. early childhood edn. Queens Coll., City U. N.Y., Flushing, 1969-70, asst. prof., 1970—. Mem. Am. Ednl. Research Assn., Assn. Childhood Edn. Internat., Nat. Assn. Edn. Young Children, Nat. Soc. Study Edn., Internat. Reading Assn., Nat. Council Tchrs. Edn., U.S. Commn. for Early Childhood Edn. Home: 175-20 Wexford Terrace Jamaica NY 11432 Office: Queens Coll Dept Edn Flushing NY 11367

SCHWARTZ, KAREN BARBARA, Journalist; b. L.I., N.Y., Feb. 21, 1951; d. Stanley Charles and Shirley Esther (Spar) Schwartz; B.A., Am. U., 1972. Washington corr. Donrey Media Group, Washington, 1972—. Mem. White House Corrs. Assn., D.C. Sociol. Assn., Congl. Press Galleries, Sigma Delta Chi. Home: 940 25th St Washington DC 20037

SCHWARTZ, LITA LINZER (MRS. MELVIN JAY SCHWARTZ), educator; b. N.Y.C., Jan. 14, 1930; d. Aaron Jerome and Dorothy Claire (Linzer) Linzer; A.B., Vassar Coll., 1950; M.Ed., Temple U., 1956; Ph.D., Bryn Mawr Coll., 1964; m. Melvin Jay Schwartz, June 18, 1950; children—Arthur Lee, Joshua David, Frederic Seth. Psychologist, Psychol. Service Center, Phila., 1957-61; faculty Pa. State U., Ogontz campus, Abington, 1961—, asso. prof. ednl. psychology, 1971—. Recipient Humanitarian award N.Y. Philanthropic League, 1973. Fellow Pa. Psychol. Assn.; mem. Am. Psychol. Assn., Phila. Soc. Clin. Psychologists (mem. exec. bd. 1968-72, newsletter editor 1971-73). Jewish religion (mem. congregation sch. com. 1960—, chmn. 1970-72). Author: American Education: A Problem-centered Approach, 1969, rev. edit., 1974; Educational Psychology: Focus on the Learner, 1972. Home: 411 Lodges Lane Elkins Park PA 19117 Office: Pa State U Abington PA 19001

SCHWARTZ, LOIS SIEGEL (MRS. JAMES A. SCHWARTZ), lawyer; b. Bklyn., June 10, 1939; d. Irving and Lillian (Rakusin) Siegel; B.A. (scholar 1956-60), Barnard Coll., 1960; J.D. (Honors fellow 1962-63), N.Y. U., 1963; m. James A. Schwartz, May 14, 1972. Admitted to N.Y. State bar, 1964, D.C. bar, 1966, U.S. Ct. Appeals bar, 1966, U.S. Supreme Ct. bar, 1967; atty. adviser, broadcast bur. FCC, Washington, 1963-65; asso. mem. firm Haley, Bader & Potts, Washington, 1965-70, partner, 1970-73; individual practice law, Washington, 1973—. Mem. Am. Civil Liberties Union, 1971—. Samuel Rubin fellow, 1961-62; N.Y. State Regents scholar and fellow, 1956-61. Mem. Am., FCC bar assns., Am. Women in Radio and TV. Democrat. Jewish religion. Club: Women's Nat. Dem. Home: 13007 Middlevale Lane Silver Spring MD 20906 Office: 2011 Eye St NW Washington DC 20036

SCHWARTZ, MILDRED, psychologist; b. N.Y.C., Nov. 23, 1931; d. Herman and Sadie (Pressler) Myerson; B.A., Hunter Coll., 1952; M.A., Coll. City N.Y., 1954; Ph.D., N.Y. U., 1969; postgrad. William A. White Inst., 1970-74; m. Irving Schwartz, Oct. 28, 1961; children—Emily, Paul. Dir. group therapy Westchester Mental Health Bd., White Plains, N.Y., 1956-60; tchr., supr. psychotherapy L.I. Consultation Center, N.Y.C., 1958-71; tchr., dir. treatment service, supr., bd. dirs. Inst. Contemporary Psychotherapy, 1971-74; pvt. practice psychotherapy, N.Y.C., 1958—. Mem. Am., N.Y. State psychol. assns., N.Y. Soc. Clin. Psychologists (dir. 1956-58), Assn. Psychoanalytic Psychologists, Phi Beta Kappa, Psi Chi. Home: 275 Central Park West New York City NY 10024 Office: 1 W 91st St New York City NY 10024

SCHWARTZ, NEENA BETTY, physiologist; b. Balt., Dec. 10, 1926; d. Paul H. and Pauline (Shulman) Schwartz; A.B. with honors, Goucher Coll., 1948; M.S., Northwestern U., 1950, Ph.D., 1955. Asst. prof. physiology U. Ill., 1953-56, prof., 1961-72; dir. biol. labs. Michael Reese Hosp., Chgo., 1956-61; asst. dean U. Ill. Coll. Medicine, 1968-70; prof. physiology Coll. Medicine Northwestern U., Chgo., 1970—, prof., chmn. dept. biology, Evanston, 1974—; cons. USPHS, NIH., Ford Found.; Gregory Pincus Meml. lectr. Laurentian Hormone Conf., 1968. USPHS research grantee, 1956-74. Mem. Endocrine Soc. (v.p. 1971-72), Assn. Women in Sci. (pres. 1972-73), Soc. Study Reprodn., Biomed. Engring. Soc., Am. Physiol. Assn., Phi Beta Kappa. Contbr. articles to profl. jours., chpts. to books. Research in reproductive physiology. Home: 1215 Chancellor St Evanston IL 60211

SCHWARTZ, PAULA BEER (MRS. LAZAR M. SCHWARTZ), pediatrician; b. Cimpulung, Rumania, Jan. 18, 1926; d. Jacob and Leah (Fuhrer) Beer; M.D., U. Cluj, Rumania, 1951; m. Lazar M. Schwartz, July 12, 1946; 1 dau., Riry (Mrs. Elias Muhlrad). Came to U.S., 1966, naturalized, 1971. Specialist pediatrician State Hosp. Suceava, Rumania, 1951-61, Kupath-Cholim Sick-Fund, Tel-Aviv, Israel, 1962-66; intern Bronx-Lebanon Hosp. Center, Bronx, N.Y., 1966, resident in pediatrics, 1967-68; adj. attending pediatrician Bronx-Lebanon Hosp., Bronx, N.Y., 1969-73; pediatrician Mae Laufer Clinic, Bronx, 1974—; asst. attending pediatrician Holy Name Hosp., Teaneck, N.J., 1974—. Diplomate Am. Bd. Pediatrics. Mem. Bergen County Med. Soc. Address: 1257 Kensington Rd Teaneck NJ 07666

SCHWARTZ, VICTORIA ELIZABETH, writer; b. Sharon, Wis.; d. Christian and Barbara (Straka) Schwartz; B.S., Northwestern U., 1924. Asst. editor Nat. Real Estate Jour., 1925-28; exec. dir. Chgo. Art Theatre, 1928-31; social sec., 1931-42; with Office Indian Affairs, 1942-46; security examiner U.S. Treasury Dept., 1947-62. Mem. Am. Assn. U. Women, Woman's Forum, Sacramento Regional Arts Council, Theta Sigma Phi. Clubs: Cal. Writers, Tuesday. Author juvenile stories; co-author daily syndicated column Folks at Home, 1944-47. Home: 1901 9th Av Sacramento CA 95818

SCHWARZE, ESTELLA GERALDINE, social work adminstr.; b. New Orleans; d. William J. and Mary (Reynolds) Schwarze; B.S. in Social Sci., Loyola U., New Orleans, 1957, postgrad., 1958-59, 61-62; M.S.W., Tulane U., 1962. With Asso. Cath. Charities, 1946-59; exec. dir. Assn. for Retarded Children, 1956-57; with social service dept. Charity Hosp. of La., New Orleans, 1958—, supr., 1965—. Field work instr. Atlanta U. Grad. Sch. Social Work, 1967—; lectr. community medicine La. State U. Sch. Medicine, Tulane U. Sch. Medicine. Cons. social work to Treme Neighborhood Improvement Assn. Organizer Project Aquarius; del. White House Conf. on Children and Youth, 1970, White House Conf. on Aging, 1971; founder Irish Channel Action Found., New Orleans, 1964, charter mem.; organizer Parent's Inst., New Orleans, 1962; coordinator symposium Socialization of the Am. So. TeenAger, 1973. Adv. bd. health consumer edn. program Urban League. Mem. Nat. Assn. Social Workers (social worker of year S.E. La. chpt. 1965), La. Consumers League, Mercy Acad. Alumnae (pres. 1956-58), Am. Pub. Health Assn., League Women Voters. Democrat. Home: 915 Jefferson Av New Orleans LA 70115 Office: Social Service Dept Charity Hosp of La 1542 Tulane Av New Orleans LA 70130

SCHWARZKOPF, ELISABETH, soprano; b. Jarotschin, Posen, Poland; d. Friedrich and Elizabeth (Frohlich) Schwarzkopf; student pvt. schs., Hochschule fur Musik, Berlin; pupil Maria Ivogun; m. Walter Legge. Debut, Stadtische Opera, Berlin, Staatsoper, Vienna, 1946-48, Convent Garden, London, 1948-50; Am. opera debut, San Francisco, 1955; with La Scala, Milan, 1949—; appeared festivals, Salzburg, Bayreuth, others; concert singer specializing in German art songs, classical oratorio; prin. roles include Marschallin, Fiordiligi, Contessa Almaviva, Donna Elvira Mimi, Liu, Pamina, others. Recipient Lilli Lehmann medal, Salzburg; first Orfeo D'Oro Mantvua. Address: care Musical Adviser Establishment Vaduz Liechtenstein

SCHWARZSCHILD, BETTINA (MRS. ARTHUR SCHWARZSCHILD), writer; b. Ludwigshafen, Germany, June 14, 1925; d. Feiwel and Sima (Sipper) Freireich; came to U.S., 1938, naturalized, 1946; student Bklyn. Coll., 1942-45; m. Arthur Schwarzschild, Jan. 30, 1949; children—Michael, Jane. Author: The Not-Right House, 1968. Home: 83-15 98th St Woodhaven NY 11421 Office: 59-05 94th St Elmhurst NY 11373

SCHWEBEL, RENATA MANASSE (MRS. JACK P. SCHWEBEL), sculptor; b. Zwickau, Germany, Mar. 6, 1930; d. George and Anne Marie (Simon) Manasse; brought to U.S., 1940, naturalized, 1946; B.A., Antioch Coll., 1953; M.F.A., Columbia, 1961; m. Jack P. Schwebel, May 10, 1955; children—Judi, Barbara, Diane. Cartographer, Ecostat, Inc., Ridgewood, N.J., 1949; display artist Silvestri, Inc., Chgo., 1950-51; asst. Mazzolini Art Found., 1952; student asst. art dept. Antioch Coll., Yellow Springs, O., 1952-53; exhibited one man shows Columbia; exhibited group shows Wadsworth Atheneum, Hudson River Mus., New Britain Mus. Am. Art, Stamford Mus., Silvermine Guild, Bergen County Mus., Audubon Artists Ann., others; represented in permanent collections Columbia. Bd. dirs. Antioch Coll. Assn., 1971—. Recipient Purchase award Columbia U., 1961; awards Westchester Art Soc., 1969—. Mem. Nat. Assn. Women Artists, Conn. Acad. Fine Arts, Westchester Art Soc., New Rochelle Art Assn. Home: 36 Silver Birch Dr New Rochelle NY 10804 Studio: 170 Webster Av New Rochelle NY 10801

SCHWEIG, CHARLOTTE GLASS (MRS. HARRISON G. SCHWEIG), realtor; b. Phila., Oct. 11, 1913; d. Max and Tillie (Lock) Glass; B.F.A., U. Pa., 1935; m. Harrison G. Schweig, Feb. 5, 1938. Pvt. practice as realtor, Jenkintown, Pa., 1954-74, Phila., 1974—; pres. Hideaway Hills, Inc., Horsham, Pa., 1959-68, Hideaway Haven, Inc., Doylestown, Pa., 1963-66; v.p. Schweig and Genghini, Inc., Builders and Land Developers, Elkins Park, Pa., 1959-68; partner George E. Schweig & Son, 1965—. Former mem. Glee Club of U. Pa. Mem. East Montgomery County Bd. Realtors, Pa. Realtors Assn., Nat. Assn. Real Estate Bds., Gen. Alumni Soc. U. Pa. (life), U. Pa. Alumnae Club Phila. (charter), Alpha Epsilon Phi (life mem. Theta chpt.). Address: Rittenhouse Plaza 1901 Walnut St Philadelphia PA 19103

SCHWEINHAUT, MARGARET C., state senator; b. Washington; ed. George Washington U., Nat. U. Law Sch.; LL.D., St. Joseph Coll. Mem. Md. Ho. of Dels., 1955-61; mem. Md. Senate, 1961-63, 67—, chmn. exec. nominations com. Chmn. Md. Commn. on Problems of the Aging. Bd. dirs. Nat. Council of Aging. Recipient Certificate of Merit, Nat. Council of Sr. Citizens. Mem. Internat. Gerontological Soc., Montgomery Retarded Children's Assn. Address: 3601 Saul Rd Kensington MD 20795

SCHWEITZER, CLARA ELIZABETH (MRS. EMIL P. SCHWEITZER), museum ofcl.; b. Waterbury, Conn., Nov. 25, 1900; d. John and Elizabeth (Swanson) Johnson; grad. high sch.; m. Emil P. Schweitzer, June 12, 1922. Bookkeeper, sec. Edward J. Burns Realty Co., 1917-30; vol. worker womens div. YMCA, 1930-39; food rationing clk. Ration Office, 1939-42; exec. sec. Torrington Community Chest, 1943-59; treas., asst. curator Goshen (Conn.) Hist. Soc., 1965—. Treas., Cornwall-Goshen Pub. Health Nursing Assn., 1966-69; sec.-treas. Goshen Homemakers, 1966—. Conglist. (trustee). Club: Goshen Garden (treas. 1962-66). Home: RFD North St Goshen CT 06756

SCHWEITZER, GERTRUDE, artist; b. N.Y.C. One-woman shows Montclair (N.J.) Art Mus., Washington Water Color Club, Cayuga Mus. History and Art, Auburn, N.Y., Potsdam Gallery Art, Currier Gallery of Art, Manchester, N.H., Bevier Gallery, Rochester (N.Y.) Inst. Tech., Erie (Pa.) Pub. Mus., Cortland Library, N.Y.C., Norton Gallery and Sch. Art, West Palm Beach, Fla., Galerie Charpentier, Paris, France (1st Am. one-man show), Hanover Gallery, London, Eng., Worth Av. Gallery, Palm Beach, Fla., Galleria Al Cavallino, Venice, Italy, Galleria Il Naviglio, Milan, Italy, Galleria L'Obelisco, Rome, Italy, High Mus., Atlanta, Witte Meml. Mus., San Antonio, Phila. Art Alliance, Hokin Gallery, Palm Beach, Fla., Pratt Manhattan Center, N.Y.C., New Britain (Conn.) Mus. Am. Art, many others; exhibited in Washington, Chgo., Phila., Denver, Sarasota, Fla., N.Y.C., Los Angeles, Bklyn., Minn., Ill., Santa Fe, Newark; represented in permanent collections Bklyn. Mus., Toledo Mus., Hackley Art Gallery (Muskegon, Mich.), Davenport (Ia.) Municipal Gallery, Canajoharie (N.Y.) Library and Art Gallery, Norton Gallery and Sch. of Art, W. Palm Beach, Witte Meml. Mus San Antonio, Mus. Modern Art, Paris, Albi Mus., France, Rochester (N.Y.) Meml. Art Gallery, Met. Mus. Art, N.Y.C., Whitney Am. Art, N.Y.C., Walker Art Mus. Bowdoin Coll., Brunswick, Me., Atlanta Art Assn. Galleries, Montclair (N.J.) Art Mus., Chgo. Art Inst., N.A.D., others; also numerous pvt. collections, U.S., Eng., France. Served as chmn. arts and skills corps, N.Y. chpt. A.R.C., Ft. Jay Regional Hosp., Governor's Island, N.Y., World War II. Recipient Am. Water Color Soc. medal; Am. Artists Profl. League medal for water color, State of N.J., Pauline Wick award (oil); Phila. Water Color prize, Pa. Acad. of Fine Arts; First prize Norton Gallery of Art, West Palm Beach, Fla.; First prize Soc. Four Arts; oil and watercolor awards; Grand Nat. Exhbn., Miami, Fla.; 1st prize, best woman painter N.J. State Exhbn.; N.Y. State award Am. Artists Profl. League, Nat. Arts Club; First prize Am. Artists Profl. League, Seton Hall U.; First Grumbacher Purchase award Audubon 17th Am. Exhbn., N.Y.C.; others. Mem. Am. Water Color Soc., Nat. Acad., Audubon Soc., N.J. Water Color and Sculpture Soc. Home: Colts Neck NJ 07722 also Palm Beach FL 33480

SCHWEITZER, MARY-ELIOT SMITH (MRS. ROBERT SCHWEITZER, JR.), civic worker, social service worker; b. San Jose, Cal., July 7, 1927; d. Julius Avery and Elise (Peyton) Smith; A.A., Marymount Coll., 1948; m. Robert Schweitzer, Jr., Sept. 18, 1952; children—Mary-Eliot, James-Peyton, Mary-Neale. Sec., Teen-age Jr's, Stanford Convalescent Home, Palo Alto, Cal., 1944-45; receptionist, driver A.R.C., Palo Alto, 1947-51; mem. Jr. League, San Francisco, 1950-54; mem. Jr. League, N.Y.C., 1956-58; mem. Jr. League, Mpls., 1963—, bd. dirs., 1966-67. Leader, Girl Scouts of Am., Mpls., 1966-69; mem. Citizens Com. for Pub. Edn., Mpls., 1968—, Citizens League, Mpls., 1968—; docent Mpls. Inst. Arts, 1965-66, Hennepin County Hist. Soc., 1965-66; pres. Douglas Elementary Sch. P.T.A., 1968-70; v.p. West High Sch. P.T.A., 1970-71, pres., 1971-73. Bd. dirs. Womens UN Rally, 1966-72; bd. dirs. Assos. James Ford Bell Library, 1968—, pres., 1972—; bd. dirs. Friends Mpls. Inst. Arts, 1968-73, Mpls. Council P.T.A.'s, 1969—, Minn. World Affairs Center, 1969—, UN Assn. of Minn., 1970—; adv. bd. Childrens Theatre Co., Mpls., 1969-72, house mgr., 1971-72; vice chmn. Hennepin Lowry Council, 1972—; chmn. bd. Jr. League Thrift Shop, 1966-67. Named Beautiful Activist, 1973. Mem. D.A.R., Eugenia Washington Chpt., Mpls. Soc. Fine Arts, Womens Assn. Minn. Symphony Orch., Mpls. League Catholic Women, League Women Voters, English Speaking Union, Univ. Hosps. Vol. Assn., West Dist. Schs. Assn. (vice-chmn. 1972—), Peyton Soc. Va. Republican. Home: 1925 Dupont Av S Minneapolis MN 55403

SCHWENCK, HELEN WIXCEY, educator; b. Salt Lake City, Oct. 9, 1901; d. William Thomas and Mary Artimecia (Bouton) Wixcey; A.B., U. Utah, 1927; diploma Cours de Civilisation Francaise, Sorbonne, 1925; student numerous summer lang. courses, U. Mexico City, U. Madrid, U. Paris; m. Julius Rae Schwenck, July 31, 1927; children—Dale Mary (Mrs. John Ele), Carolyn Rae (Mrs. H.D. Yorston). Instr. Spanish, U. Utah, 1922-24, supr. student tchrs. French and Spanish, Univ. Tng. Center, 1924-27; tchr. English settlement house, Paris, 1924-25; personnel and safety work McClellan (Ark.) AFB, 1942-43; elementary sch. tchr. San Juan (Cal.) Unified Sch. Dist., 1943-63; tchr. English and reading to dyslectic students, also fgn. born wives of USAF officers, 1967—. Pres. Fgn. Students Assn., Sorbonne, 1924-25. Research grantee U. Utah, 1923; John R. Park fellow, 1924-25; Cal. State Dept. Edn. grantee San Francisco State Coll., 1953. Mem. World Affairs Council, Sigma Kappa Phi, Phi Kappa Phi. Club: Faculty Wives Sacramento City Coll. (past pres.). Compilor monograph. Address: 8735 Fallbrook Way Sacramento CA 95826

SCHWEPPE, VERA CLEVELAND, city ofcl.; b. Hale, Mo., Sept. 25, 1900; d. Arlie E. and Julia Emory (Otey) Cleveland; student Chillicothe Bus. Coll., 1917-18, LaSalle U., 1924; m. John T. Schweppe, Aug. 29, 1922 (dec.); children—John K., Barbara Ann (Mrs. Alfred C. Hanes). Sec. to D.R. Beckstrom, lawyer, Tribune, Kan., 1918-22; sec. to D.V. Schwartz, sch. supt., Ft. Scott, Kan., 1949-53; city clk. Fort Scott, 1953—. Mem. Internat. Inst. Municipal Clks., City Clks. Assn. Kan., Kan. Municipal Clks. (chmn. membership 1971-74). Mem. Order Eastern Star, Order White Shrine Jerusalem. Home: 508 S Main St Fort Scott KS 66701 Office: 1 E 3d St Fort Scott KS 66701

SCHWIER, ANN STRANQUIST (MRS. J.F. SCHWIER), educator; b. St. Louis, Jan. 11, 1924; d. E.A. and Katherine (Hemp) Stranquist; B.S. summa cum laude, St. Louis U., 1944, M.A., 1949, Ph.D., 1952; m. J.F. Schwier, June 2, 1948; 1 son, Charles. With, Bee Angell & Assos., St. Louis, 1945-49; instr. St. Louis U., 1947-50, lectr., 1950-60; statistician, market researcher Inland Research Co., St. Louis, 1953-60; faculty So. Ill. U., Edwardsville, 1960—, prof. econs., 1972—. Mem. Am. Statis. Assn. (pres. St. Louis chpt. 1970-71), Am. Marketing Assn. (pres. St. Louis chpt. 1956-57), Am., Mo. Valley econ. assns. Home: 18 N Taylor St St Louis MO 63108 Office: Box 51 Southern Illinois University Edwardsville IL 62025

SCHWINKENDORF, LAURA MAE, mfg. co. exec.; b. Valparaiso, Ind., June 17, 1938; d. Howard Richard and Elizabeth Rose (Toth) Schwinkendorf; high sch. grad. Bookkeeper, First Nat. Bank, Valparaiso, Ind., 1956-60; with Am. Nat. Bank, Chgo., 1961-66; with Sterling Products Co., Inc., Chgo., 1966—, sec., treas. 1970—. Lutheran. Home: 2088 Whippoorwill Portage IN 46368 Office: 121 N Jefferson St Chicago IL 60606

SCIALABBA, ELMERINDA CACCAVO (MRS. DOMINICK ANTHONY SCIALABBA), pediatrician; b. Bklyn., July 12, 1933; d. Nicholas James and Gilda (De Mare) Caccavo; B.S., St. John's U., 1955; M.D., Woman's Med. Coll. Pa., 1959; m. Dominick Anthony Scialabba, Apr. 29, 1961; children—Fred Anthony, Damian Angelo, Marion Alexia. Rotating intern Kings County Hosp. Center, Bklyn., 1959-60, vis. physician in pediatrics, 1963-64; asst. resident pediatrics L.I. Coll. Hosp., N.Y.C., 1960, chief resident pediatrics, 1961; chief resident Coney Island Hosp., N.Y.C., 1962-63; practice medicine specializing in pediatrics, Bklyn., 1961-64, Plainfield, N.J., 1964-66; practice pediatric neurology, mental retardation and developmental disorders, Plainfield, 1966—; staff physician Woodbridge (N.J.) State Sch., 1965-66, med. dir., 1966-68; clin. instr. pediatrics N.J. Coll. Medicine and Dentistry, Newark, 1966—; staff dept. pediatrics Muhlenberg Hosp., Plainfield, 1964-66, courtesy staff, 1966—; cons. child devel. and pediatric neurology Union County (N.J.) Cerebral Palsy League. Fellow Am. Acad. Pediatrics; mem. A.M.A., N.J., Union County med. socs., Am. Assn. Mental Deficiency, Am. Med. Woman's Assn., Plainfield Area Med. Assn., Alumnae Assn. Woman's Med. Coll. Roman Catholic. Office: 963 Park Av Plainfield NJ 07060

SCIONTI, ISABEL LAUGHLIN, concert pianist, tchr.; b. Premont, Tex.; d. Charles Martin and Martha Louise (Haley) Laughlin; Mus.B., Baylor U., 1932, Mus.D. (hon.), 1945; Mus.M., Chgo. Musical Coll., 1934; m. William R. Hicks, Dec. 17, 1955 (dec.); m. 2d, Silvio Scionti (dec.). Debut as concert pianist Rome, Italy, 1937, Carnegie Hall, N.Y.C., 1938; presented two piano concerts Europe, Mexico, Hawaii and U.S., 1937-47; presented first all Bach piano recital Town Hall, N.Y.C., 1941; piano tchr. Isabel Scionti Piano Studio, Denton, Tex., 1942—. State chmn. collegiate artists competition, sponsored by Nat. Music Tchrs. Assn., 1969-76. Mem. Tex. Music Tchrs. Assn. (dir. 1968-72, Tchr. of Year award 1974), Sigma Alpha Iota (hon. life mem.). Home: 1111 Emerson Lane Denton TX 76201

SCOBEY, JOAN MOISSEIFF (MRS. RAPHAEL G. SCOBEY), author; b. N.Y.C., May 19, 1927; d. Siegfried and Frieda (Loewe) Moisseiff; B.A., Smith Coll., 1948; m. Raphael G. Scobey, May 3, 1953; children—David, Richard. Asst. editor Modern Plastics, N.Y.C., 1949-52. Trustee Scarsdale (N.Y.) Adult Sch. Mem. League Women Voters Scarsdale (dir. 1967-72), Soc. Mag. Writers. Author: (with L.P. McGrath) Creative Careers for Women, 1968, What Is a Mother, 1968, What Is a Father, 1969, What Is a Brother, 1970, What Is a Sister, 1970, What Is a Grandmother, 1971, What Is a Grandfather, 1971, Do-It-All Yourself Needlepoint, 1971, Celebrity Needlepoint, 1972; Needlepoint From Start to Finish, 1972; Rugmaking From Start to Finish, 1972; (with N. Myers) Gifts From the Kitchen, 1973, Rugs and Wall Hangings, 1974. Address: 9 Lenox Pl Scarsdale NY 10583

SCOCCA, MARY ANGELA FERRANTE, pre-cast concrete co. exec.; b. Bernardsville, N.J., July 16, 1909; d. Vincent and Anna (Diana) Ferrante; m. Joseph Scocca, June 13, 1926 (dec. July 1966); children—Peter Joseph, James F., Gertrude (Mrs. Frank L. Petrozzo). Vice-pres. Scocca Bros., contractors, 1948—, Central Pre Con Products, Millington, N.J., 1960—; owner, mgr. clothing store, 1938-60; partner Bernardsville Diner (N.J.), 1958-72. Police matron, 1958-73. Mem. Bus. and Profl. Women Am. Roman Catholic. Home: 36 Olcott Av Bernardsville NJ 07924 Office: Whitebridge Rd Millington NJ 07946

SCOFIELD, NANETTE EISLER (MRS. MILTON N. SCOFIELD), vocational counselor, writer; b. N.Y.C.; d. Nathan Anthony and Miriam (Wallach) Eisler; B.A., Barnard Coll., 1939; student Smith Coll., 1935-38, Tchrs. Coll., Columbia, 1962; m. Milton N. Scofield, Sept. 5, 1945; children—Elizabeth M., Anthony L. Project mgr. Commerce and Industry Assn., N.Y.C., 1969—. Mem. bd. dirs. Family Inst., 1963, Fedn. Employment and Guidance Service, 1964, Scarsdale Adult Sch. Adv. Com., 1968. Mem. Nat. Vocational Guidance Assn., Am. Personnel and Guidance Assn. Author: So You Want to Go Back to Work, 1968; articles pub. in jours. and mags., including Seventeen, N.Y. Times mag., N.Y. mag., others. Nat. cons. Commn. on Occupational Status of Women, 1969. Home: 58 Garden Rd Scarsdale NY 10583

SCOFIELD, SUNSHINE COLE (MRS. JAMES LAMONTE SCOFIELD), TV broadcaster; b. San Angelo, Tex.; d. Cullen Charles and Minnie Lee Alice (Taylor) Cole; m. James LaMonte Scofield, Jan. 29, 1955; 1 son, David Gregory Lane. Dir. Community Club Awards, producer, hostess Sunny Scofield Show, KBAK-TV, Bakersfield, Cal., 1961-67; producer, hostess Sunny Today Show, KERO-TV, Bakersfield, 1967-72; producer, moderator Sunny Today Show, Warner Cable, Bakersfield, 1973—. Pres. YWCA, Bakersfield, 1969-70; mem. TV adv. com. Regional Occupation Center of Kern, 1970—; dir. auxiliaries San Joaquin dist. Children's Home Soc., 1973—. Bd. dirs. Teen Challenge, Bakersfield, 1969—. Recipient Golden Mike award Am. Women in Radio and TV, 1968; Spl. award Cal. Fedn. Women's Club, 1968, 69; Bernice Harrell Chipman Woman of Year award Jr. Woman's Club, 1971. Mem. Nat., Cal. press women, Nat. Acad. TV Arts and Sci., Am. Women in Radio and TV (western v.p. 1971-73), Kern County Colton Wives (hon.), P.E.O., League Women Voters (pres. 1950-52), Symphony Assos. (pres. 1964-65), Delta Kappa Gamma (hon.), Beta Sigma Phi. Republican. Presbyn. (pres. women's assn. 1962-63). Club: Womans of Bakersfield (pres. 1959-60). Home: 1612 Hillside Dr Bakersfield CA 93306 Office: 703 Truxtun Av Bakersfield CA 93301

SCOGGINS, (MILDRED) ANNE GLENN (MRS. JAMES WILBURN SCOGGINS III), educator, home economist; b. Athens, Ga., Dec. 5, 1941; d. Willis Anderson and Mildred (Floyd) Glenn; student W. Ga. Coll., 1959-61; B.S. in Home Econs., U. Ga., 1962; m. James Wilburn Scoggins III, Apr. 4, 1964. Franklin County home demonstration agt. Coop. Extension Service, U. Ga., Carnesville, 1962-63, Haralson County extension home economist, Buchanan, 1963—, chmn., 1973—. Sch. lunch cons. Haralson County Schs., 1966—; hostess weekly radio program WWCC, 1963—. Mem. Ga. (dist. dir., v.p. state exec. bd. 1967—, pres. 1973—), Nat. (Distinguished Service award 1973) assns. extension home economist, Am., Ga. home econs. assns., U. Ga., U. Ga. Coll. Agr. alumni socs., Haralson County Farm Bur., Phi Kappa Phi, Phi Upsilon Omicron, Gamma Sigma Delta. Baptist. Contbr. weekly column to various newspapers, 1963—. Home: 224 Tallapoosa St Bremen GA 30110 Office: PO Box 10 Buchanan GA 30113

SCOGGINS, SARAH HAMRIC, retail stores propr.; b. Griffin, Ga., Oct. 20, 1912; d. M.J. and Sarah (Autry) Hamric; student Wesleyan Conservatory of Music, 1929-30, Athens Bus. Coll., 1930; m. James Wilburn Scoggins, Jr., June 11, 1933; children—James Wilburn III, Alice Elizabeth (Mrs. John V. Holland). Pvt. sec., 1930-33; legal sec. Erwin & Nix, Athens, Ga., 1933-39; asst. in operation Scoggins 5 & 10 also Scoggins Furniture, Bowdon, Ga., 1949-68, owner, operator, 1968—. Pres., Bowdon Elementary P.T.A., 1953-54. Baptist. Club: Sprig 'n Dig Garden (charter mem., 1st pres.). Home: Bowdon GA 30108 Office: College St Bowdon GA 30108

SCOGLAND, THESTA KENNEDY (MRS. JOHN C. SCOGLAND), club woman, civic worker; b. Rayne, La., Aug. 26, 1907; d. Gustavus Adolphus and Effie (McClendon) Kennedy; B.A., U. Colo., 1927, postgrad. 1927-29; m. John C. Scogland, June 6, 1929 (dec. May 1968); children—John Kennedy, Helen Quentina. Membership chmn. Boulder (Colo.) Woman's Club, 1937-39, corr. sec., edn. chmn. 1949-52, youth conservation chmn., 1952-55, 3d v.p., program chmn., 1956-57, 2d v.p., 1957-59, 1st v.p., 1959-61, pres., 1961-62, parliamentarian, publicity chmn., 1969—; 1st v.p., No. dist. 1964-66; pres., internat. affairs chmn. Colo. Fedn. Women's Clubs, 1966-68, editor, mag., 1968—, parliamentarian No. dist., 1968-72, conv. mgr., 1966; radio chmn. Arapahoe chpt. D.A.R., Boulder, 1948-50, corr. sec. 1940-42, rec. sec., 1950-54, 2d v.p., 1st v.p., regent, 1954-60, mgr. Colo. soc. conv., 1960, conv. treas., 1964; sr. pres. Children Am. Revolution, Boulder, 1943-44, sr. rec. sec. Colo. soc., 1955-56, sr. conservation chmn., 1959-60, bylaws chmn., 1960-61, parliamentarian, 1961; active Boulder council Camp Fire Girls, 1948-60; active Community Chest Fund Drives, A.R.C. Fund Drives, Mother's March, Muscular Dystrophy Fund Drives, Boulder; residential chmn. Am. Cancer Soc. Neighbor-to-Neighbor Drive, Boulder, 1956-57; mem. Community Hosp. Aux., Boulder; hospitality chmn. Boulder High Sch. P.T.A., 1956-57, pres., 1957-58, pres. Boulder County council, 1953-54, tchr. edn. grant chmn., 1956-57, publicity chmn., 1955-56; membership chmn. Colo. Congress Parents and Tchrs., 1952-53, v.p. dist. 2, 1954-56, publicity chmn., 1956-58, 3d v.p., 1958-59, 1st v.p. 1959-60. Mem. Am. Assn. U. Women (social chmn. Boulder 1951-53, pres. 1954-56, parliamentarian 1971-73, treas. Colo. div. 1959-63, fellowships chmn. 1962-67), Women's Soc. Christian Service (circle devotions chmn. 1961-62, sec. student activities 1962-64, treas. 1964-68, pres. 1968-69, parliamentarian 1968-73), Nat. Assn. Parliamentarians (treas. Boulder unit 1963-65, 69-71, auditor 1965-67, pres. 1967-69, treas. Colo. 1970-72), Colonial Dames 17th Century (parliamentarian Colo. 1971—; 1st v.p. Boulder chpt. 1973—), Soc. Magna Charta Dames, Colonial Order Crown. Methodist (treas. ch. sch. 1953-68). Mem. Order Eastern Star (rec. sec. Rayne, La. 1931, 32, conductress 1934). Home: 704 Mapleton Av Boulder CO 80302

SCOLLANTE, ELIZABETH LU, electronic mfg. co. exec.; b. Long Branch, N.J., Dec. 28, 1940; d. Domonic Andrea and Katherine Elizabeth (Acerra) Scollante; accounting degree Internat. Accountants Soc. Clk. to head cashier Atlantic & Pacific Tea Co., 1958-62; clk. typist U.S. Army, Ft. Monmouth, N.J., 1961-62; cost clk. Electronic Assos., Inc., West Long Branch, N.J., 1962-67; controller Electronic Measurements, Inc., Neptune, N.J., 1967—. Mem. Ladies Aux. V.F.W. (treas. Brighton Meml. post 1960-62, sec. 1966-68). Home: 449 Brighton Av Long Branch NJ 07740 Office: 405 Essex Rd Neptune NJ 07753

SCORE, GERTRUDE ARLENE (MRS. WILLIAM SMITHEAL), lawyer; b. Denver; d. Ingwald and Stella (Berglund) Score; J.D., Denver U., 1970; m. William Smitheal, Nov. 18, 1969; children—Shelley Williams, Edna. Admitted to Colo. bar; practiced law, Denver, 1962-73. Mem. Order of Eastern Star. Home: 2501 Taxco Rd Fort Worth TX 76111 Office: 327 S Bannock St Denver CO 80209

SCOTT, (ALICE) ADELAIDE LEHMANN (MRS. JAMES DOUGLAS SCOTT), bank exec.; b. Kinston, N.C., Aug. 25, 1929; d. Franklin Patrick and Emma (Jones) Lehmann; grad. Carolina Sch. Banking, 1959; grad. certificate Am. Inst. Banking, 1961; m. James Douglas Scott, May 21, 1950. With Peoples Bank & Trust Co., Rocky Mount, N.C., 1946—, asst. cashier, 1961-67, asst. v.p., 1967—. Tchr. principles bank operations Rocky Mount chpt. Am. Inst. Banking, 1966-68. Mem. bd. YWCA, 1961—; chmn. Rocky Mount Area Cystic Fibrosis Found., 1969—; mem. budget com. United Fund, 1971. Named Altrusan of Year, 1964, 71. Mem. Am. Inst. Banking (pres. 1957-58), N.C. Bankers Assn. (group chmn. 1966-67, mem. Women's com. 1971-72), Bank Adminstrn. Inst. (mem. bd. 1969-70), Nat. Assn. Bank Woman (chmn. N.C. group 1971-72, regional edn. and tng. chmn. 1970-71, chmn. regional membership com. 1973—), N.C. (dir., mem. state nominating com. 1963), Wilson-Rocky Mount (Outstanding Service award 1962-63, sec. 1962-64, Bowler of Year 1969), Rocky Mount (pres. 1969-71) woman's bowling assns. Methodist. Clubs: Altrusa (pres. 1966-67), Rocky Mount Lady Bowlers (organizer, 1st pres. 1963). Home: 2823 Winstead Rd Rocky Mount NC 27801 Office: 1818 Sunset Av Western Sts Rocky Mount NC 27801

SCOTT, BARBARA ANN LOW, newspaper pub.; b. Toronto, Ont., Can., Aug. 10, 1939; d. William St. Clair Ferguson and Marie Violet (Reay) Low; student Cantab Coll., 1956-57, Banff Sch. Fine Arts, 1955-57; children—Danielle Suzanne, David Elton. Sec., Diocesan Bd. Religious Edn., Inc. Synod Anglican Ch. Can., 1958-63; pub., Ft. Erie (Ont.) Times-Review, 1971—; pres. Epic Printing Ltd., 1971—. Publicity dir. Ft. Erie Progressive Conservative Assn., 1971—. Bd. dirs. YMCA. Presbyn. Office: Box 70 240 Jarvis St Fort Erie ON L2A 5M6 Canada

SCOTT, BARBARA JEAN, landscape engr., educator; b. Lamar, Colo., Nov. 11, 1932; d. Merrill Lockler and Ruth Elizabeth (Brown) Scott; student U. Denver, 1950-51; B.S., U. Wyo., 1959, M.S. in Civil Engring., 1973. Computer, Wyo. Hwy. Dept., Cheyenne, 1951-53, jr. draftsman, 1953-54, jr. testing technician, 1954, testing technician, 1955-58, materials engr., 1958-65, landscape engr., 1965-68; city planner City of Cheyenne, 1968-69; environmental devel. engr. Tex. Hwy. Dept., 1970-71; instr. comprehensive planning U. Wyo. Coll. Engring., Laramie, 1971—. Mem. Wyo. Hwy. Bowling Assn., Wyo. State Hwy. Employees Assn. (v.p. 1961), Am. Concrete Inst., Am. Soc. C.E. (asst. to pres. 1964-66), Am. Soc. Testing and Materials, Wyo. Engring. Soc., Nat., Wyo. (sec. 1967—) socs. profl. engrs., Assn. Asphalt Paving Technologists, Am. Acad. Polit. and Social Scis., Am. Judicature Soc., Am. Inst. Planners, Met. Assn. Urban Designers and Environmental Planners, Pi Beta Phi. Presbyn. Home: Route 3 Box 71-A Sealy TX 77474 Office: U Wyo Coll Engring Sch Civil and Archtl Engring Laramie WY 87020

SCOTT, BERNICE SCHNEIDER, educator; b. N.Y.C.; d. Julius and Anna Schneider; B.A., Hunter Coll., 1942; M.Ed., U. Pitts., 1958; Ed.D., Columbia, 1967; postgrad. U. Fla., 1967, U. London, 1960; m. children—Stephen Allen, Fredric Joseph, Penny Jane. Tchr. Oakmont (Pa.) Pub. Schs., 1957-58; tchr. English, pub. schs., Pitts., 1958-62, guidance counselor, 1962-65; asst. prof. edn. Jacksonville U. (Fla.), 1966; dir. research and program evaluation Duval County Schs., Jacksonville, 1966-70, dir. curriculum planning and design, 1970-72; dir. evening programs U. Fla., Gainesville, 1972—; adj. prof. edn. Fla. A. and M. U., Tallahassee, 1967-72; adj. prof. edn., coordinator Ed.D. program Nova U., Ft. Lauderdale, Fla., 1971—. Cons., State Depts. Edn., Miss., S.C., Fla. Mem. Am., Fla. ednl. research assns., Am. Personnel and Guidance Assn., Assn. Supervision and Curriculum Devel., Kappa Delta Pi, Pi Lambda Theta. Home: 405-C NW 39th Rd Gainesville FL 32607

SCOTT, CATHERINE DOROTHY, librarian; b. Washington, June 21, 1927; d. Leroy Sterns and Agnes Frances (Meade) Scott; A.B., Cath. U. Am., 1950, M.S. in L.S., 1955. Asst. librarian Export-Import Bank Washington, 1950-55; asst. librarian Nat. Assn. Home Builders, Washington, 1955-62; tech. librarian Bellcomm, Inc., Washington, 1962-72; librarian Nat. Air and Space Mus., Smithsonian Instn., Washington, 1972—. Mem. Nat. Commn. Libraries and Information Sci., 1971—, vice chmn., 1971-72. Republican nat. committeewoman, 1956-57, dir. Young Rep. Club, Washington, 1952-58, 1st v.p., 1958-59; del. Young Rep. Nat. Conv., 1955, 57; v.p. Eisenhower-Nixon Club, 1956; chmn. Coll. Fedn. Young Reps., 1957, vice chmn. Eisenhower Inaugural Com., 1957, co-chmn. program com. Eisenhower Inaugural Ball, 1957; dir. League Rep. Women, Washington, 1956-72; mem. Washington Rep. Com., 1959-68, vice chmn., 1960-68; v.p. Nixon-Lodge Club, 1960; Washington precinct campaign coordinator, 1960, 64; del. Rep. Nat. Conv., 1964, 68, sec. platform com., 1964; co-chmn. Goldwater-Miller campaign, D.C., 1964; exec. sec. Women for Nixon-Agnew Nat. Adv. Council, 1968; 1st v.p. Everett McKinley Dirksen Rep. Forum, 1969-72. Bd. visitors Cath. U. Am., 1974—. Mem. Spl. Libraries Assn. (pres. Washington chpt. 1971-72, 1st v.p. 1970-71, corr. sec. 1966-67, sec. aerospace div. 1968-69), Am. Soc. for Information Sci. (pub. chmn. conf. 1972), Internat. Fedn. Library Assns. (pub. chmn. conf. 1974). Roman Catholic. Home: 700 7th St SW Washington DC 20024 Office: Nat Air and Space Mus Smithsonian Instn Washington DC 20560

SCOTT, DONNA JEAN, savs. and loan exec.; b. Shadyside, O., Oct. 9, 1928; d. Beauford Therion and Wilma Elizabeth (Book) Scott; grad. high sch. With Woodsfield (O.) Savs. & Loan Co., 1953—, mgr., 1961—. Mem. central com. Democratic Party, 1960—. Bd. dirs. Monroe County chpt. A.R.C., 1959-62. Mem. Ohio Savs. and Loan League (dist. v.p. 1971-72, pres. 1972-73), Switzerland C. of C., Monroe Bus. and Profl. Women's Club (past v.p.). Methodist (ch. treas. 1965-70). Home: 109 Hillcrest Dr Woodsfield OH 43793 Office: 105 W Court St Woodsfield OH 43793

SCOTT, DOROTHY MARGOT HAMILTON (MRS. WALTER SCOTT, JR.), ret. research co. exec.; b. Kansas City, Mo., May 20, 1908; d. Frank Carl and Augusta Matilda (Swisher) Hamilton; student, Kansas City Jr. Coll., 1925-26; m. Walter Scott, Jr., Sept. 20, 1930; 1 dau., Judith Ann (Mrs. Robert William LeVeau). Market research interviewer Elmo Roper & Assos., N.Y.C., 1946-47, W. coast supr., 1947-57; with Field Research Corp., 1957-73, field dir., Los Angeles, 1957-73, ret., 1973. Pres., Research Hosp. Aux., Kansas City, Mo., 1944; gen. U.S. War Bond Drives, Kansas City, Mo., 1943-44; chmn. Ways and Means Com., Nat. Charity League, Los Angeles, 1949. Mem. Am. Marketing Assn., Market Research Trade Assn. (chmn. ethics com. 1969, mem. conf. com. 1969). Home: 1032 San Marino Dr Lake San Marcos CA 92069

SCOTT, ELIZABETH L., educator; b. Fort Sill, Okla., Nov. 23, 1917; d. Richard C. and Elizabeth (Waterman) Scott; B.A., U. Cal. at Berkeley, 1939, Ph.D., 1949. Various research, fellowships U. Cal. at Berkeley, 1939-49, instr., 1949-51, asst. prof., 1951-57, asso. prof., 1957-62, prof. statistics, 1962—, chmn. dept. statistics, 1968-73, asst. dean Coll. Letters and Sci., 1965-67. Mem. Inst. Math. Statistics, Am. Astron. Soc., Astron. Soc. Pacific, Biometric Soc., Internat. Astron. Union, Internat. Assn. Statistics in Phys. Sci. (sci. sec. 1960-72), Royal Statis. Soc., Internat. Statis. Inst., A.A.A.S. (chmn. sect. univ. statistics 1971-72). Research in math. statistics and applications. Home: 34 Tunnel Rd Berkeley CA 94705

SCOTT, ETHEL MARION, ret. nursing adminstr.; b. Galt, Ont., Can., Jan. 1, 1909; d. William Alexander and Ethel Elizabeth (Graham) Scott; ed. Elgin Acad., Morayshire, Scotland, 1929. Trainee as nurse Scotland and Eng., 1929-41; served with Royal Army Nursing Service, 1941-46, 48-53, assignments include Fayid, Egypt, 1948, 50, Khartoum, Sudan, 1949, Benghazi, Libya, 1952, Desna, Libya, 1952, Glasgow, Scotland, 1953; nurse Norman M. Home, Johannesburg, South Africa, 1946-47, Anglo Am. Hosp., Chingola, No. Rhodesia, 1947-48; office supr., tchr. anatomy and physiology McKellar Hosp., Ft. William, Ont., 1953-55; dir. nursing Gen. Hosp., Smith Falls, Ont., 1955-57; supt. Mayo (Yukon Terr.) Hosp., 1957-61; dir. nursing Gen. Hosp., Port Alberni, B.C., 1963-65; dir. nursing with Great War Meml. Hosp. of Perth (Ont.) Dist., 1966—. Mem. Registered Nurse Assn. Ont. Home: 16 Wilson St Perth ON Canada

SCOTT, GWENDOLYN DAWN, educator; b. Hamiota, Man., Can., Apr. 2, 1921; d. William and Florence (McBride) Scott; came to U.S., 1923, naturalized, 1945; B.S. in Edn., Bowling Green State U., 1942; M.A., Ohio State U., 1948; Ed.D., Western Res. U., 1963. Tchr. various schs., 1942-48; instr. Muskingum Coll., 1948-49; asst. prof. U. Akron (O.), 1949-55; mem. faculty Kent (O.) State U., 1955—, prof. allied health scis., 1969—. Recipient Meritorious award Ohio Assn. Health Phys. Edn. and Recreation, 1968. Mem. Am., Midwest (dir. 1971-72), Ohio (historian 1968—, v.p. gen. div. 1969-70, dir., pres. 1971-72) assns. health, phys. edn. and recreation, Nat., Midwest (mem. health edn. com. 1953-55, 57-59) assns. phys. edn. coll. women, Ohio Coll. Assn. (mem. women's phys. edn. sect. exec. com. 1952-54, 59-61, 63-64), Am. Sch. Health Assn., Soc. Pub. Health Educators, Am. Assn. U. Profs. (chmn. com. W 1972), Assn. Supervision and Curriculum Devel., Delta Psi Kappa (asso.). Lutheran. Home: 1647 Overlook Dr Twin Lakes Kent OH 44240

SCOTT, GWENDOLYN L. MORRIS (MRS. GLEN T. SCOTT), physician; b. Akron O., May 25, 1924; d. Alfred C. and Charlotte (Armstrong) Lutz; student U. Akron, 1942-44; B.S., Ohio State U., 1946; M.D., U. Cin., 1950; m. Joseph Vincent Morris, June 6, 1949 (div. Apr. 1968); m. 2d, Glen T. Scott. Intern Grant Hosp., Chgo., 1950-51; resident internal medicine U. Chgo., 1951-53; trainee cardiac lab. U. Cin., 1953-55; practice medicine specializing in internal medicine, cardiology, Cin., 1955-67; resident in neuropsychiatry Rollman's Psychiat. Inst., Cin., resident psychiatry, 1967-69, chief resident, 1969-70, dir. outpatient dept., 1970-71; staff psychiatrist Anclote Manor Hosp., Tarpon Springs, Fla., 1971—; mem. staff Bethesda, Holmes, Deaconess, Christ, Good Samaritan hosps.; clinician Cardiac Clinic, Cin. Gen. Hosp., 1953-67; instr. U. Cin., 1953-67. Fellow Am. Geriatrics Soc., Internat. Coll. Angiology; mem. Am., Ohio State, Cin. heart assns., Ballistocardiographic Research Soc., Cin. Rheumatism Soc., Am. Psychiat. Assn., Planned Parenthood Fedn., Cin. Soc. Internal Medicine, Cin. Acad. Medicine, Fla., Pinellas County, Ohio State med. assns., Am. Med. Women's Assn., Fla. Psychiat. Soc., Cin. Med. Women's Club, Kappa Kappa Gamma, Sigma Xi, Chi Delta Phi, Alpha Delta Epsilon. Baptist. Home: 2290 Demaret Dr Dunedin FL 33528 Office: Anclote Manor Hosp Tarpon Springs FL 33589

SCOTT, IRENE FEAGIN, judge; b. Union Springs, Ala., Oct. 6, 1912; d. Arthur H. and Irene (Peach) Feagin; A.B., U. Ala., 1932, LL.B., 1936; LL.M., Cath. U. Am., 1939; m. Thomas Jefferson Scott, Dec. 27, 1939; children—Thomas Jefferson, Irene (Mrs. Franklin L. Carroll III). Law librarian U. Ala. Law Sch., 1932-34; admitted to Ala. bar, 1936; atty. Office Chief Counsel, Internal Revenue Service, 1937-50, mem. excess profits tax council, 1950-52, spl. asst. to head of appeals div. Office of Chief Counsel, 1952-59, staff asst. to chief counsel, 1959-60; judge U.S. Tax Ct., 1960—. Mem. Fed., Am., D.C. (hon.) bar assns., Nat. Assn. Women Lawyers, Ala. Bar, Am. Judicature Soc., Kappa Delta, Kappa Beta Pi. Methodist. Club: Nat. Lawyers (Washington). Home: 4815 25th Road N Arlington VA 22207 Office: US Tax Ct Box 70 Washington DC 20044

SCOTT, IRENE (MRS. JOHN SCOTT), club woman; b. Longmont, Colo., May 28, 1908; d. Walter and Grace (Kistler) Stewart; student Colo. State Coll., 1936-37, 44, Greeley State Tchrs. Coll., 1945, Denver U., 1951; m. John Scott, Apr. 24, 1926; children—Grace Lily (Mrs. Jack Hathaway), John Walter, Irene Susan (Mrs. F. C. Konzal). Tchr. elementary sch., Weld County, Colo., 1925-27, Yuma County, Colo., 1943-47; tchr. floral design Loretto Heights Coll., 1960-61; tchr. floral design, landscaping, horticulture Adult Edn. Div., Englewood, Colo., 1960—. Lectr. demonstrator floral design and related fields. Leader 4-H Clubs, 1950-62; state dir. Judges Council, 1960-61; state chmn. High Sch. Gardeners, 1960-62. Recipient many awards in horticulture. Mem. Colo. Assn. Pub. Adult Edn., Ladies Aux. Patriarch Militant, Am., Denver rose socs., Nat. Chrysanthemum Soc., Aril Soc., Herb Soc. Am., Council Colo. Federated Garden Clubs, Sunshine Seeders Federated Garden Club, Garden Writers Assn. Am., Nat. Fedn. Press Women, Colo. Press Women, Green Thumb, St. Joseph's Guild, Blue Spruce, Internat. Platform Assn., D.C. Bar Assn. (hon.). Clubs: Cosmopolitan, Floral Benders Corsage. Nationally Accredited Amateur Flower Show Judge. Contbr. numerous articles to profl. jours., mags. Home: 4550 S Galapago St Englewood CO 80110

SCOTT, ISABEL ROBERTSON (MRS. FREDERICK J. SCOTT), plastics co. exec.; b. Scranton, Pa., July 18, 1909; d. John Law and Retta (Church) Robertson; student Sweet Briar Coll., 1929, Cornell U., 1930-31; m. Frederick J. Scott, Oct. 28, 1933; children—Susan (Mrs. Donald Featherman), Isabel M. (Mrs. Randolph H. Norton), Gregory D. Corporate exec., dir. Scott Plastic Co., Sarasota, Fla., 1958—. Mem. D.A.R., Jr. League, Brandeis U. Nat. Women's Com., Kappa Alpha Theta. Presbyn. Home: 1321 Magellan Dr Sarasota FL 33580 Office: PO Box 2958 Sarasota FL 33578

SCOTT, JACQUELINE DORIS FREDELL, ednl. adminstr.; b. Reed City, Mich., Jan. 12, 1948; d. Duane Ellsworth and Doris Elvera (Remus) Fredell; B.S. in Elementary Edn., Ind. State U., 1970, M.Ed. in Counseling, 1973; m. Thomas Wilson Scott, Aug., 22, 1969 (div.); 1 dau., Katherine Keely. Asst. residence hall dir. Ind. State U., Terre Haute, 1970-71, residence hall dir., 1971-74; dir. resident life Grand Valley State Colls., Allendale, Mich., 1974—. Mem. Am. Personnel and Guidance Assn., Nat. Vocational Guidance Assn., Nat. Assn. Women Deans, Adminstrs. and Counselors, Nat. Assn. Student Personnel Adminstrs., Assn. Coll. and Univ. Housing Officers. Delta Gamma. Home: 18278 Swiss Dr Apt C Spring Lake MI 49456 Office: 325 Manitou Hall Grand Valley State Colls Allendale MI 49401

SCOTT, KATHLEEN MORRIS (MRS. THOMAS E. PILLA), pediatrician; b. Swarthmore, Pa., Dec. 1, 1927; d. Walter James and Sylvia J. (Morris) Scott; student Carleton Coll., 1945-46; B.A., Swarthmore Coll., 1949; M.D., U. Pa., 1953; m. Thomas E. Pilla, Dec. 18, 1954; children—Timothy, Constance, Kathleen, Janet. Intern, Abington (Pa.) Meml. Hosp., 1953-54, pediatric resident, 1954-55, pediatric staff, 1955—; asso. dir. Youth Health Clinic at Aldersgate, Willow Grove, Pa., 1972—. Med. cons. Jenkintown Day Nursery, 1964—; child health conf. clinician Bucks County Health Dept., Doylestown, Pa. 1957—; clinician Vis. Nurse Assn. Eastern Montgomery County, 1954-55, 64—; clinician Pa. Dept. Health, 1973—. Mem. Am. Acad. Pediatrics, Phila. Pediatric Soc. Home: 3530 Buck Rd Huntingdon Valley PA 19006

SCOTT, LIZABETH VIRGINIA, actress; b. Scranton, Pa.; d. John and Mary (Pennock) Matso; ed. Marywood Sem., Marywood Coll., Alviene Sch. Theatre. Actress numerous films, including You Came Along, 1947, The Strange Love of Martha Ivers, Dead Reckoning, Desert Fury, Variety Girl, I Walk Alone, Pitfall, Two of a Kind, Scared Stiff, Bad for Each Other, Silver Lode, Loving You, Pulp, also numerous TV films. Office: 170 S Beverly Dr Beverly Hills CA 90212

SCOTT, LOUISE BINDER, educator, author; b. Hamburg, Ia.; d. Stephen A. and Emma Constance (Binder) Scott; B.Lit. Interpretation, Emerson Coll., 1933; Ed.M., Boston U., 1939. Guidance dir. speech, East Haven, Conn., 1936-43; tchr. dept. speech Ventura Jr. Coll., 1943-46; cons. speech and hearing San Marino (Cal.) Elementary Schs., 1946-54; asso. prof. speech Cal. State Coll., 1956-69. Mem. Nat. Assn. Edn. Young Children, Writers Guild So. Cal., Zeta Phi Eta. Author: Talking Time, 1951, rev., 1966; Singing Fun, 1961; Time for Phonics, 1963; Learning Time: Language Experience for Young Children, 1968; My First Writing Book, 1968, Learning about our Language Filmstrips, 1968; Words and Sounds Filmstrips, 1972; Tell-Again Story Cards, 1968; Workers in Our Neighborhood, 1968; Stories For Listening, 1970; Learning Language Skills, 1972; others. Home: 14851 Jeffrey Rd Irvine CA 92705

SCOTT, LOUISE TINSLEY (MRS. ROBERT CLAUDE SCOTT, JR.), ednl. adminstr.; b. Greenville, S.C., Aug. 10, 1925; d. Jerry William and Alice Lee (Smith) Tinsley; B.A., Furman U., 1946, M.A., 1966; Ph.D., U. S.C., 1974; m. Robert Claude Scott, Jr., Oct. 5, 1946; children—Ronald Charles, Susan Scott Jones. Tchr., Parker High Sch., Greenville, 1946-47, Pendleton (S.C.) Elementary Sch., 1954-59, Central Elementary Sch., Laurens, S.C., 1959-66; dir. reading services Darlington (S.C.) Area Schs., 1966-67; dir. lang. arts curriculum Florence (S.C.) Pub. Schs., 1967—. Cons. sch. dists. in N.C. and S.C. Mem. N.E.A., Internat. Reading Assn., Delta Kappa Gamma. Author: (with others) Contemporary English, 1973. Contbr. articles profl. publs. Home: 1430 Fairfax Rd Florence SC 29501 Office: 109 W Pine St Florence SC 29501

SCOTT, MARGARET ANN, social worker; b. Waco, Tex., Aug. 20, 1929; d. Curtis Kelton and Adele (Pritchett) Scott; B.S. in Home Econs., Tex. Christian U., 1950; M.S. in Social Work, U. Tex., Austin, 1960. With Tex. Dept. Pub. Welfare, Ft. Worth, 1951—, regional dir. child welfare div., 1965-69, program dir. social services, 1969—. Sec. S.W. Regional Conf., Child Welfare League Am., 1970; mem. adv. com. child care program Tarrant County Jr. Coll., 1968—; mem. profl. adv. com. homemaker program Family Service Assn., 1968-71; del. Nat. Conf. Day Care Services, Washington, 1965; mem. Catholic Charities commn. Diocese of Fort Worth, 1967; mem. nat. day care licensing task force Office of Child Devel., Health, Edn. and Welfare, 1971-72. Recipient Herculean award Tarrant County Community Council, 1972. Mem. Acad. Certified Social Workers, Am. Pub. Welfare Assn., Nat. Assn. Social Workers (charter mem.), Tex. Assn. Edn. Young Children Inc. (bd. mem.), Nat., Fort Worth assns. edn. young children, So. Assn. Children Under Six, Tex. Christian U. Women Execs. (2d v.p.), Alpha Chi. Democrat. Roman Catholic.

Home: 2307 W Magnolia St Fort Worth TX 76110 Office: 711 W 7th St Fort Worth TX 76102

SCOTT, MARGARET BRODIE, educator; b. Dundee, Scotland, Mar. 31, 1924; d. John McGill and Ann (Brodie) Scott; immigrated to Can., 1924; B.A., U. Toronto, 1942; B.L.S., 1957. Tchr., Kitchener (Ont.)-Waterloo Collegiate Sch., 1943-45; tchr.-librarian R.H. King Collegiate Sch., Scarborough, Ont., 1945-61; mem. faculty U. Toronto, 1961—, prof. sch. librarianship Faculty Edn., 1961—, chmn. dept., 1970—. Mem. Canadian (council 1971-74), Am. library assns., Canadian Sch. Library Assn. (chmn. 1970-71), Internat. Assn. Sch. Librarianship (dir. 1971-74). Co-author: Cataloguing for School Libraries, 2d edit., 1973. Editor: Selection Aids for Canadian School Libraries, 1972. Home: 26 Lynndale Rd Scarborough ON M1N 1C1 Canada Office: 371 Bloor St W Toronto ON M5S ZRT Canada

SCOTT, MARIAN DALE (MRS. F. R. SCOTT), artist; b. Montreal, Que., Can., June 26, 1906; d. Robert John and Marian (Barclay) Dale; student Art Assn. Montreal, 1918-20, The Study, 1920-23, Ecole des Beaux Arts, 1923-24, Slade Sch. Art, London, Eng., 1925-26; m. F. R. Scott, Jan. 30, 1928; 1 son, Peter Dale. Painting instr. pvt. sch. Montreal Mus. Fine Arts, 1948-52; one-man shows Queen's U., Kingston, 1948, Dominion Gallery, Montreal, 1954, 56, 58, Laing Gallery, Toronto, Ont., Can., 1961, Galerie Camille Hebert, Montreal, 1964, Galerie Libre, Montreal, 1967, Galerie d'Atelier, Renee de Sieur Quebec, Que., 1970; exhibited in group shows at Montreal Mus., 1947-60, Art Gallery Ont., 1953, Hart House, Toronto, 1953; executed murals Med. Bldg. McGill U., Montreal Gen. Hosp.; paintings on tour U.S., Australia, New Zealand; represented in Biennial of Sao Paulo (Brazil), 1951-53, paintings Dept. External Affairs, Ottawa, Can.; represented in permanent collections Nat. Gallery Can., Musée d' Art Contemporain Montreal, also various art galleries, museums. Recipient First prize Canadian Group Painters, 1966, Purchase prize Thomas More Inst., 1967, Baxter Purchase award Ont. Soc. Artists, 1969. Mem. Royal Canadian Acad. Arts. Address: 451 Clarke Av Montreal 217 PQ Canada

SCOTT, MARIAN HUNTINGTON CHASE (MRS. HUGH SCOTT), wife of U.S. senator; b. Wilkes-Barre, Pa.; d. Luther William and Augusta Dana (Coolbaugh) Chase; student Phila. Coll. Art, 1917-18; m. Hugh D. Scott (U.S. senator from Pa.); 1 dau., Marian Lee Concannon. Active various fund-raising drives; mem. Senate Ladies unit A.R.C., v.p., 1972—; mem. women's aux. Chestnut Hill Hosp. Mem. nat. bd. Med. Coll. Pa.; mem. bd. Woodmere Art Gallery, Phila. Mem. D.A.R., Colonial Dames, Smithsonian Assos. Clubs: Republican Congressional Wives (pres. 1965-67); Congressional; International Neighbors. Home: 44 Hillcrest Av Chestnut Hill PA 19118 also: 3014 Woodland Dr Washington DC 20008

SCOTT, NORMA LINN (MRS. JOHN MITCHELL SCOTT), ret. educator; b. Wharton, Tex., Oct. 13, 1894; d. John Edward and Elizabeth Frances (Bolton) Linn; student Hollins Coll., 1913-14; B.S. in Edn., U. Tex., 1943, M.A., 1949; m. John Mitchell Scott, July 22, 1914; children—John Linn, Norma Elizabeth (Mrs. John R. Johnson), Lawrence Evans, Virginia Randolph (Mrs. N.B. Dismukes), Patricia Ruth (Mrs. Louis Meade Burton). Tchr. history, govt. and English in high schs., Tex., 1918-65, formerly with McCallum High Sch., Austin; asst. dept. govt. U. Tex., 1946-49; prin. Mullin (Tex.) High Sch., 1925-33, Buffalo (Tex.) High Sch., 1945-47. Rep. Austin Pub. Sch. System on panel A.A.A.S., Atlantic City, 1959. Leon County chmn. Jr. Red Cross, 1943-47; chmn. Buffalo (Tex.) chpt. A.R.C., 1945-46; active Infantile Paralysis, War Bond, United Fund, Community Chest drives; mem. Austin and Travis County Community Council; mem. Austin com. solicitation for State Home for Ret. Tchrs., at Waco, Tex.; chmn. on membership, pres. Austin br. YWCA, 1970—, now pres.; mem. Tex. Hist. Found.; mem. Tex. State Hist. Survey Com., Travis County Hist. Commn.; mem. Bicentennial Hist. Preservation and Publ. com., 1973-74; mem. Internat. Good Neighbor Council, 1971-74; vol. worker Old Bakery Mus., Austin. Kellogg Found. scholar U. Tex., 1944. Mem. Am. Assn. U. Women (mem. county council, chmn. nomination com., del. county council Austin br., pres. Austin br. 1962-64), Austin Classroom Tchrs. Assn. (v.p. and program chmn. 1956-57, pres. 1958-60), Heritage Soc., U.D.C. (state legislative chmn. 1954-55, chmn. Norma Linn Scott scholarship to high sch. grad., v.p. Tex. div., state pres. 1968-70, pres. chpt. 1970-74), Am. Acad. Polit. and Social Scis., Tex. Tchrs. Assn. (pres. English sect. dist. X 1956—, mem. Ho. of Dels., 1956—), Austin Ret. Tchrs., Tex. Geneal. Soc., Daus. Republic of Tex., Delta Kappa Gamma (pres. local chpt.), Alpha Epsilon, Gamma Psi. Baptist (tchr. Sunday sch.). Clubs: Austin Woman's, Forty Acres of University of Tex. Home: 3001 Beverly Rd Austin TX 78703

SCOTT, RUTH ELAINE (MRS. BRODY), copywriter; b. Schenectady, Oct. 8, 1923; d. Frederick William and Esther Bella (Schaffer) Silberkraus; B.A. with honors, Pa. State U., 1943; div.; 1 son, Jonathan Scott Brody. Account exec. Staples Smith, Inc., display firm, N.Y.C., 1947-49; fashion publicity dir. Abraham & Straus, Bklyn., 1951-53; with Rockmore Agy., N.Y.C., 1961-64, Rumrill Hoyt, N.Y.C., 1964-67; with Grey Advt., N.Y.C., 1968—, creative supr., 1973—, v.p., 1972—. Served to lt. Women's Res., USCG, 1943-47. Recipient Andy awards, 1969, 72, Clio award for heroin hot line campaign, 1973, Advt. Age ann. advt. award, 1973. Mem. Fashion Group. Home: 405 E 54th St New York City NY 10022 Office: 777 3d Av New York City NY 10017

SCOTT, VALERIE WEEKS (MRS. JEFFREY J. SCOTT), lawyer; b. Kansas City, Mo., Nov. 3, 1939; d. William Henry and Elizabeth (Kelley) Weeks; B.S., Northwestern U., 1960; LL.B., Yale, 1964; m. Jeffrey J. Scott, June 9, 1962; children—Matthew Henry, Emily Louise. Research asst. Library of Congress, Washington, 1960-61; admitted to Mont. bar, 1964, Neb. bar, 1972; asso. Sandall, Moses & Cavan, Billings, Mont., 1964-67; mem. firm Scot, Scott & Baugh, Billings, 1967-72; clk. Mont. Supreme Ct., Helena, 1971; practice law, Omaha, 1972-73; atty. law dept. U.P. R.R., Omaha, 1973—. Justice of peace, Yellowstone County, Billings, 1969-70. Co-chmn. Mont. Gov.'s Commn. on Status Women, 1969-72; mem. Omaha Commn. on Status Women, 1973—; adv. bd. Salvation Army, 1966-72. Bd. dirs. Omaha Girls Club, Inc., 1973—. Mem. Nat. Assn. Women Lawyers, Am., Neb., Omaha bar assns., Omaha Jr. League. Home: 908 Hillcrest Dr Omaha NE 68132 Office: 1416 Dodge St Omaha NE 68102

SCOTT, VIRGINIA BRYAN (MRS. GERALD SIDNEY SCOTT), coll. dean; b. Canton, Miss., Oct. 9, 1929; d. George Newton and Theta (P'Pool) Bryan; student Kan. State U., 1947-48; B.S., U. So. Miss., 1950; postgrad. Millsaps Coll., 1953; M.E., Miss. Coll., 1956; m. Gerald Sidney Scott, Feb. 1, 1957; children—Randall Lee, Kathryn Ann, Gerald Sidney. Tchr. pub. schs. Miss., 1952-58, 64-70; instr. elementary edn. William Carey Coll., Hattiesburg, Miss., 1970-71, acting dean women, instr. elementary edn., 1971—. Active Retarded Children's Assn., various community drives. Mem. Nat., Forrest County assns. retarded children, Miss. Edn. Assn., Miss. Assn. Higher Edn., Miss. Assn. Women Deans and Counselors, Kappa Kappa Gamma. Baptist. Home: 404 5th Av Hattiesburg MS 39401

SCRIABINE, HELENE A., educator; b. Russia, Feb. 13, 1906; d. Aleksander and Nadeshda (Posnanskaja) Gorstkine; came to U.S., 1950, naturalized, 1955; A.M., U. Leningrad, 1941; Ph.D. (fellow), U. Syracuse, 1962; 1 son, Alex. Faculty, U. Iowa, Iowa City, 1960—, prof. Russian lang. and lit., 1966—. Author: Les Faux Dieux, 1963; V. Blockade, 1964; Short Stories, 1964; Siege and Survival, 1971; Leningrader Tagebuch, 1972; Siege and Survival, 1973; Short Stories, 1974. Home: 28 W Park Rd Iowa City IA 52240

SCRITCHFIELD, MARYELLE DODDS (MRS. ARLYNN DUANE SCRITCHFIELD), educator; b. Oak Park, Ill., July 5, 1919; d. Eugene Haddock and Ruth Blackstone (Thompson) Dodds; student Park Coll., 1937-39; B.S., U. Ill., 1941; postgrad. U. Mich., 1942; No. Ill. State Tchrs. Coll., 1943; certificate Phila. Sch. Occupational Therapy, 1945; postgrad. Ohio State U., 1948-50; M.A., U. So. Cal., 1951; m. Arlynn Duane Scritchfield, Aug. 10, 1968. Tchr. 5th and 6th grades Lincoln Park Elementary Sch., Rockford, Ill., 1941-43; tchr. biology Rochelle (Ill.) High Sch., 1943-44; occupational therapist U.S. Army, 1945-48; instr. occupational therapy Ohio State U., 1948-50; occupational therapist U.S. Army, 1951-68; asso. prof. occupational therapy Coll. St. Catherine, St. Paul, 1969—. Served with AUS, 1951-68. Decorated Legion of Merit. Players of the Flower fellow, 1950. Fellow Am. Occupational Therapy Assn. (treas. 1967-69); mem. World Fedn. Occupational Therapists, Am. Occupational Therapy Found. (treas. 1969), Minn. Occupational Therapy Assn. Presbyn. Home: 1276 E Cope Av St Paul MN 55109 Office: 2004 Randolph Av St Paul MN 55105

SCRUGGS, MARY MARGUERITE, coll. dean; b. Lawton, Okla., June 15, 1920; d. Palmer Gordon and Marguerite Anthony (Bohan) Scruggs; student Cameron State Agrl. Coll., 1937-39; B.S., Okla. State U., 1941, M.S., 1946; Ph.D., Ia. State U., 1959. Tchr. vocational home econs. pub. schs., Cloud Chief, Okla., 1941-42, Calumet, Okla., 1942-46; dist. supr. home econs. edn. Okla. Dept. Pub. Instrn., Oklahoma City, 1946-47, asst. state supr., 1947-52; nat. adviser Future Homemakers Am., Washington, 1952-56; asst. prof. home econs. edn. Ia. State U., Ames, 1958-60, prof., 1960-73, head home econs. edn., 1960-66, asst. dean Coll. Home Econs., 1966-71, asso. dean, asso. dir. Home Econs. Research Inst., 1971-73, asst. dir. Agr. and Home Econs. Expt. Sta., 1972-73; asso. dean div. home econs., prof. home econs. edn. Okla. State U., Stillwater, 1973—. Chmn. Ia. Gov.'s Commn. Status of Women, 1963-68. Trustee Ia. State U. Research Found., 1970-73, v.p., 1972-73. Ellen H. Richards fellow, 1957-58. Mem. Am. Home Econs. Assn. (coordinator status women 1968-72), Okla. Home Econs. Assn., Am. Vocational Assn., Internat. Fedn. Home Econs., Am. Vocational Edn. Research Assn. (sec. 1967-69), Am. Edn. Research Assn., Am. Assn. Higher Edn., Soc. Profs. Edn., Nat. Assn. Tchr. Educators in Home Econs., Am. Assn. U. Women, Phi Kappa Phi, Omicron Nu, Phi Upsilon Omicron, Delta Kappa Gamma. Democrat. Roman Catholic. Home: 2805 N Husband Stillwater OK 74074

SCRUGGS, ROSEMARY JANE (MRS. NORMAN MADISON SCRUGGS), librarian; b. Culver, Ind. Aug. 14, 1919; d. Frank Harrison and Ethel Huldah (Wiseman) Taber; grad. high sch.; m. Norman Madison Scruggs, Aug. 29, 1937; children—Norma Janeen (Mrs. Mitchell Barry Resnick), Phillip David. With Culver (Ind.) Pub. Library, 1944—, head librarian, 1958—. Mem. Ind. Library Assn. Small Library Div. Methodist. Mem. Order Eastern Star. Club: Culver City. Home: 311 S Main St Culver IN 46511 Office: N Main St Culver IN 46511

SCULL, FLORENCE DOUGHTY, author; b. Somers Point, N.J., June 16, 1905; d. James English and Ada Bell (Doughty) Scull; B.S., Columbia U., 1931, M.A., 1934; postgrad. U. Cal. at Berkeley, Rutgers U. Elementary tchr., Linwood, N.J., 1924-28, Somers Point, 1928-30; supt. schs., Somers Point, N.J., 1934-46; prin. Lincoln Elementary Sch., New Brunswick, N.J., 1946-64. Pres., Atlantic County Hist. Soc., Somers Point, 1971-72. Pres. bd. trustees Somers Point Free Pub. Library, 1968-73. Named N.J. Ret. Tchr. of Year, Nat. Ret. Tchrs. Assn., 1972. Mem. Nat., N.J. ret. tchrs. assns., Nat. Edn. Assn., Am. Assn. U. Women, N.J. P.T.A., Atlantic City Art Center, D.A.R., Pa., N.J. hist. socs. Author: Bear Teeth for Courage, 1964; John Dickinson Sounds the Alarm, 1972. Home: 41 E Meyran Av Somers Point NJ 08244

SCULLIN, DOROTHY DODWORTH (MRS. RICHARD J. SCULLIN, JR.), artist, author; b. Pitts., Jan. 22, 1929; d. James Russell and Dorothy (Thompson) Dodworth; student Winchester-Thurston Sch., 1947; A.B., Chatham Coll., 1951; B.F.A., R.I. Sch. Design, 1952; postgrad. Boston U., 1955; m. Richard J. Scullin, Jr., Nov. 16, 1957; children—Laura, Charlotte, Richard III. Asst. children's librarian Boston Pub. Library, 1953-55, Arlington, Mass. Town Library, 1955-57; illustrator books, mags., newspapers; author children's books and articles for newspapers; portrait commissions of children; paintings exhibited Assn. Artists Pitts., Carnegie Museum, 1951, 54, 56, Boston Pub. Library, 1956, One Hundred Friends of Art, Latrobe, Pa., 1956, Soc. Graphic Artists, Pitts., 1956, No. Shore Art Assn., 1958, 59, Berkshire Art Assn., 1964-73, Embroiderer's Guild, N.Y.C., 1970; one-woman shows Robbins Library, Arlington, Mass., 1956, McCullough Mansion, Bennington, Vt., 1972, North Adams State Coll., 1972. Cons., tchr. creative writing and puppetry in elementary schs.; vol. docent Clark Art Inst.; lectr. writing and illustrating children's books; tchr. adult and children's art classes. Mem. Puppeteers Am., The Embroiderer's Guild, Berkshire Art Assn., Jr. League Boston, Christmas Brook Figure Skating Club. Episcopalian. Author-illustrator: A Dangerous Day for Mrs. Doodlepunk, 1954; Mrs. Doddlepunk Trades Work, 1957; Look Out, Mrs. Doodlepunk, 1961. Home: Stone Hill Rd Williamstown MA 01267

SCULLY, MARGARET GUILD (MRS. JOHN C. SCULLY), health services adminstr.; b. Cambridge, Mass., Dec. 28, 1909; d. Thacher Howland and Lois (Greene) Guild; B.A., U. Ill., 1930; m. John C. Scully, June 4, 1932; 1 son, John Dennis. Advt. copywriter Marshall Field & Co., Chgo., 1943-45, feature writer Chgo. Tribune, 1945-52; dir. pub. relations Grant Hosp., Chgo., 1953-58; chief. publs. and pub. relations Am. Assn. Med. Record Librarians, Chgo., 1958-62; dir. pub. relations Ill. Masonic Med. Center, Chgo., 1964—. Bd. mgrs. Service Club Chgo., 1960-71. Mem. Am. Soc. Hosp. Pub. Relations Dirs., Acad. Hosp. Pub. Relations (dir. 1973-74), Kappa Alpha Theta. Conglist. Home: 457 Oakdale St Chicago IL 60657 Office: Illinois Masonic Medical Center 836 W Wellington Av Chicago IL 60657

SCUPI, AMY ROSS, lawyer; b. N.Y.C., Aug. 19, 1936; d. Arthur Ross and Ruth L. (Rosenthal) Loeserman; B.A. magna cum laude, Coll. City N.Y., 1956; J.D., U. Chgo., 1959; m. Richard John Scupi, June 22, 1956 (div. Nov. 1967); 1 dau., Simone. Admitted to D.C. bar, 1960; asso. Galland, Kharasch, Calkins & Brown, Washington, 1960-67, partner, 1967—. Mem. D.C. Bar (gov. 1972—), Phi Beta Kappa. Home: 3830 Windom Pl NW Washington DC 20016 Office: 1054 31st St NW Washington DC 20016

SCURRAH, LORE STERN (MRS. MARK B. SCURRAH), state ofcl.; b. Bielefeld, Germany, Aug. 26, 1928; d. Herbert and Helen (Pieck) Stern; student Hunter Coll., 1946-48; B.A. summa cum laude, State U. N.Y. at Albany, 1960; M.L.S., 1962, postgrad., 1968-73; m. Mark B. Scurrah, Mar. 6, 1973; children (by previous marriage)—Robert E. Howard, Richard K. Howard. Sch. librarian Jefferson Sch., Schenectady, 1960-66; asso., bur. sch. libraries N.Y. State Edn. Dept., Albany, 1966-69, chief bur. sch. libraries, 1969—. State adminstr. Elementary and Secondary Edn. Act Title II, 1969—, Nat. Def. Edn. Act. Title III, 1969—; cons. U.S. Office Edn.; cons. state edn. dept. Md., 1972, Wyo., 1972; cons. Syracuse U., 1972-74, WMHT TV series Dateline: America, 1965-66. Mem. Am., N.Y. library assns., N.Y. Ednl. Communications Assn., Assn. Ednl. Communications and Tech. Contbr. articles to profl. jours. Home: Rural Route 205A Berne NY 12023 Office: State Edn Dept Albany NY 12234

SEABROOKS, NETTIE HARRIS (MRS. FRANKLYN E. SEABROOKS), librarian; b. Mt. Clemens, Mich. Feb. 22, 1934; d. Ivan Joseph and Katherine Marshall (Davis) Harris; B.S., Marygrove Coll., 1955; M.L.S., U. Mich., 1957; m. Franklyn E. Seabrooks, Aug. 23, 1958; children—Victoria Diane, Franklyn E. II. Reference asst. Detroit Pub. Library Tech. Dept., 1956-58; asst. circulation librarian, instr. Tenn. State U., 1958-62; library asst. pub. relations staff Gen. Motors Corp., Detroit, 1962-67, librarian, 1967-72, mgr. Detroit library, 1972—. Mem. Spl. Libraries Assn., Delta Sigma Theta. Home: 19480 Cumberland Way Detroit MI 48203 Office: 3044 W Grand Blvd Detroit MI 48202

SEAGLE, GLADYS INEZ, educator; b. nr. Lincolnton, N.C., Jan. 17, 1919; d. Thomas Clyde and Nettie (Lutz) Seagle; A.B., Lenoir Rhyne Coll., 1939; M.R.E., N.Y. Theol. Sem., 1946; Ph.D., N.Y. U., 1963; postgrad. Scarritt Bible Coll., 1942, Chgo. Luth. Sem., 1958, U. Ore., 1963; postgrad. Union Theol. Sem., 1957, M.Div., 1973. Prof. Lenoir Rhyne Coll., Lincolnton, N.C., 1947-61, chmn. dept. sociology, 1967—; vis. asso. prof. N.Y. U., 1961-63, vis. prof., summer 1967; head dept. Newberry (S.C.) Coll., 1964; head dept. Capital U., Columbus, O., 1964-67; prof. World Campus Afloat, spring semesters 1971-72, chaplain, prof., spring 1973, pres. faculty, 1973-74. Mem. sub-com. Ohio Govs. Com. on Status Women and Vocational Rehab., 1966-67; chmn. social relations com. United Ch. Women, Columbus, O., 1966; mem. religious edn. com. YWCA, Columbus, 1966; dir. pilot project Bd. Coll. Edn., Luth. Ch. Am., 1966; insp. Job Corps OEO, 1967; editor, writer Nat. Assn. Fgn. Students Adv., N.Y.C., 1963. Named Most Distinguished Prof. Aboard World Campus Afloat, 1969; vis. scholar Ohio Acad. Sci., 1965-67; NSF grantee, summer 1963. Mem. Am. Sociol. Soc., Am. Anthrop. Soc., A.A.A.S., Am. Assn. U. Profs., Ohio Valley Sociol. Soc., Am. Acad. Polit. and Social Sci., Soc. for Sci. Study Religion, Zonta Internat., Pi Lambda Theta, Internat. Speakers' Platform, Alpha Kappa Delta. Contbr. articles to profl. jours. and ch. mags. Home: 312 S Rhyne St Lincolnton NC 28092

SEAMAN, EDNA LIZBETH, broadcasting co. exec.; b. Spartanburg, S.C., Nov. 26, d. Joseph and Amelia (Latuf) Seaman; student Furman U., 1955-56, U. S.C., 1957-58. Sec. in charge officers pay sect. Donaldson AFB, Greenville, S.C., 1942-45; sec. to v.p. Dunean Mills, div. J. P. Stevens & Co., Inc., Greenville, S.C., 1945-55; promotion and pub. relations dir. WFBC-TV, 1955-68; adminstrv. asst. Multimedia Broadcasting Co., Greenville, 1969—. Woman's chmn. St. Francis Community Hosp. Fund Drive, 1968; judge, Western N.C. Community Devel. Program, 1965, 67, 68, Greer Peach Festival, 1962, 63, N.C. Apple Festival, Hendersonville, N.C., 1964, 65, 66, 69, 70, 71. So. area trustee Am. Women in Radio and TV Ednl. Found., 1973-75; bd. dirs., publicity chmn. Greenville Little Theatre; bd. dirs. Greenville Symphony Assn., Friends of Library. Recipient Certificate of Appreciation, C. of C., 1971. Mem. Am. Women in Radio and Television (pres. Palmetto chpt. 1965-66). Greater Greenville C. of C. (pres. women's div. 1967). Roman Catholic (sec. parish council 1972-73, vice-chmn. 1973-74). Home: 111 Batesview Dr Greenville SC 29607 Office: Box 788 Greenville SC 29602

SEAMAN, LILA ROSE, real estate broker; b. Louisville, Dec. 25, 1912; d. Kiaser George and Rebecca (Trad) Waheed; student Coll. of Sequois, 1971; m. Jay G. Seaman, Oct. 8, 1932; children—Salle (Mrs. Jim Soladay), Jay, Keith. Owner, broker Seaman Realty, fruit broker, owner L. Seaman, both Visalia, Cal. Mem. Visalia C. of C. Republican. Clubs: Emblem; Visalia Country. Home: 1742 Manor Dr Visalia CA 93277 Office: 1109 Mooney Blvd Visalia CA 93277

SEARCY, CLAYTIE ODESSA ROSS (MRS. DETROIT SEARCY), found. exec.; b. Pittsburg, Tex.; d. Clifton and Mary (Neil) Ross; B.S., Bishop Coll., 1955; M.A., U. Tex., 1956; postgrad. So. Meth. U., 1964-65, E. Tex. State U., 1965; m. Detroit Searcy; 1 foster son, Anderson Hugh. Adminstrv. asst. boys work dept. Moorland br. YMCA, 1945-48; tchr. art Dallas Ind. Sch. Dist., 1956-60; instr. art Bishop Coll. Extension Sch., Dallas, 1956-58, instr. edn. Bishop Coll., 1961-66, freshman counselor, 1961-63; founder Searcy Youth Found., Dallas, 1966, dir., 1966—, also pres. found., dir. Early Childhood Center. Mem. Gov.'s Com. on Human Relations. Del., Fifth World Youth Conf., Toronto, Ont., Can., 1958; vol., sponsor Dallas Soc. Negro Blind, 1947-50; chmn. re-location fund raising campaign women's div. Bishop Coll., 1956-61. Recipient Woman of Year award Florence Brooks Lit. Soc., Ft. Worth, 1967; Membership Leader award Negro C. of C., Dallas, 1954; Service award Bishop Coll. Women's Council, 1965; Ch. Service award Good St. Bapt. Ch., Dallas, 1965; Citizenship award KGKO, 1965; Hats-Off award Dallas Council Republican Women, 1967; Trail Blazer award, 1971. Mem. N.A.A.C.P., South Oak Cliff Bus. and Profl. Womens Club (pres.), Young Women Christian Assn., Bishop Coll. Alumni Assn. (nat. pres.), Nat. Council Negro Women, Internat. Platform Assn., Alpha Kappa Alpha, Alpha Kappa Mu. Home: 2642 Plaza Blvd Dallas TX 75241 Office: 6042 Highland Hills Dr Dallas TX 75241

SEARIGHT, MARY DELL (MRS. PAUL JAMES SEARIGHT), educator; b. Cordell, Okla., Jan. 14, 1918; d. John Quitman and Grace Jewel (Giles) Williams; diploma St. Francis Hosp. Sch. Nursing, 1940; B.S. with honors, U. Cal. at Berkeley, 1960, M.S., U. Cal. at San Francisco, 1961; m. Paul James Searight, June 12, 1953; children—Gregory Newton, Sara Ann. Clin. nursing in various hosps., clinics, industries, drs. offices, 1940-59; instr. nursing Merritt Coll., Oakland, Cal., 1961-66; lectr. U. Cal. at San Francisco Sch. Nursing, 1966-68; nursing cons. regional med. programs, lectr. U. Minn., Mpls., 1968-71; prof. nursing, chmn. dept. Cal. State Coll., Sonoma, 1971—, mem. acad. senate, 1972—. Cons. Bur. Health Resources Devel., San Francisco, 1973—. Mem. chancellor's liaison com. nursing edn. Cal. State U. and Colls. Office of Chancellor, Los Angeles, 1973—; chmn. Sonoma County Health Facilities Planning Com., Santa Rosa, Cal., 1970-72; mem. planning com. Sonoma Health Services/Edn. Activities, Santa Rosa, 1972—. Mem. exec. com., bd. dirs. Sonoma County Comprehensive Health Planning Com., 1970-72. Mem. Nat. League for Nursing, Am. Assn. U. Women, Am., Cal. nurses assns., Sigma Theta Tau. Author: Your Career in Nursing, 1970. Contbr. articles to profl. jours. Home: 50 Fairlie Dr Santa Rosa CA 95401 Office: 1801 E Cotati Av Rohnert Park CA 94928

SEARIGHT, PATRICIA ADELAIDE, radio, TV cons., assn. exec.; b. Rochester, N.Y.; d. William Hammond and Irma (Winters) Searight; B.A., Ohio State U. Program dir. radio sta. WTOP, Washington, 1952-63, gen. mgr. information, 1964; radio and TV cons., 1964—; producer, dir. many radio and TV programs; spl. fgn. news corr. French Govt., 1956; v.p. Micro Beads, Inc., 1955-59; sec., dir. Dennis-Inches, Corp., 1955-59; exec. dir. Am. Women in Radio and Television, 1969-74. Mem. Am. Women in Radio and Television (program chmn.; corr. sec.; mem. bd. Washington chpt.; pres. 1958-60, nat. membership chmn. 1962-63, nat. chmn. Industry Information Digest 1963-64, Mid-Eastern v.p. 1964-66), Soc. Am. Travel Writers (treas. 1957-58, v.p. 1958-59), Nat. Acad. TV Arts and Scis., Kappa Kappa Gamma (Achievement award). Episcopalian. Clubs: Soroptimist, Women's Advertising (2d v.p. Washington 1958-59, pres. 1959-60), Washington Press. Home: The Colonnade 2801 New Mexico Av NW Washington DC 20007

SEARLES, ANNA HAWLEY, educator; b. Norwich, Vt., Sept. 8, 1898; d. Fred Woodman and Helen Jay (Batchelder) Hawley; student Damrosch Inst. Mus. Art, N.Y.C., 1914-15 Columbia; student State U. Ia., 1920-21, 22-24, James Millikin U., 1929-30; m. Herbert Leon Searles, June 15, 1918; 1 son, Herbert Hawley. Asst. to student pastor and counsellor Presbyn. students State U. Ia., 1918-25; Ia. state sec. for young people Presbyn. Ch., Iowa City, 1924; instr. dept. Romance langs. U. Ia., 1922-23, substitute tchr. character edn., storytelling, lit. critic and research asso. Inst. Character Research, 1925-30; chmn. staff Inst. Character Research, Sch. Philosophy, U. So. Cal., 1930-37, dir. lit. project, 1937-43, acting dir. Inst. Character Research, 1943-46, dir. 1946—, acad. coordinator Navy Coll. Tng. program, 1943-57; vis. instr. Whittier Coll., 1936-37. Bd. dirs. Palmer Found., Texarkana, Tex., Ark. Mem. Los Angeles World Affairs Council, Los Angeles County Mus. Assn., Friends of Huntington Library, Philol. Assn. Pacific Coast, Cal. Tchrs. Assn., Modern Lang. Assn. Am., Nat. Council Tchrs. English, So. Cal. Council Tchrs. English Am. Philol. Assn., A.L.A., Internat. Reading Assn., Los Angeles Community Concert Assn., Nat. Soc. New Eng. Women Los Angeles Colony (pres. 1961-62), Nat. Soc. Daus. Colonial Wars, Delta Kappa Gamma (chpt. v.p. 1947-49). Episcopalian. Clubs: Faculty Women's (pres. 1941-42), The Town and Gown, Faculty Wives. Lectr. spl. groups. Author: A Guide to Literature for Character Training (with Starbuck and others), 1928, A Guide to Books for Character, 1930; The Searles Readers; Living Through Reading Series; Fun To Be Alive, 1950; Time to Live, 1951; Living All Your Life, 1951; The Manner and The Means, 1951; The Reason and the Rhyme, 1952; The Teacher and the Tools, 1952. Editor: The Wonder Road series; Familiar Haunts; Enchanted Paths; Far Horizons (with Starbuck and others), 1930. Author and co-editor: Living Through Biography series: The High Trail; Actions Speak; Real Persons; Teacher's Manual, 1936; Lives That Guide, 1939; Look to This Day, selected writings of Edwin Diller Starbuck, 1945. Contbr. to The Personalist. Home: 10381 Glenbarr Av Los Angeles CA 90064

SEARLES, ANNA MAE HOWARD (MRS. ISAAC ADAMS SEARLES), educator, civic worker; b. Osage Nation Indian Terr., Okla., Nov. 22, 1906; d. Frank David and Clara (Bowman) Howard; A.A., Odessa (Tex.) Coll., 1961; B.A., U. Ark., 1964; M.Ed., 1970; postgrad. (Herman L. Donovan fellow), U. Ky., 1972—; m. Isaac Adams Searles, May 26, 1933; 1 dau., Mary Ann Rogers (Mrs. Herman Lloyd Hoppe). Compiler news, broadcaster sta. KJBC, 1950-60; corr. Tulsa Daily World, 1961-64; tchr. Rogers (Ark.) High Sch., 1964-72; tchr. adult class rapid reading, 1965—; tchr. adult edn. Learning Center Benton County (Ark.), Bentonville, 1973-74. Sec. Tulsa Safety Council, 1935-37; leader, bd. dirs. Kilgore, Tex. Girl Scouts, 1941-44, leader, Midland, Tex., 1944-52, counselor, 1950-61; exec. sec. Midland Community Chest, 1955-60; gray lady Midland A.R.C., 1958-59; organizer Midland YMCA, Salvation Army; dir. women's div. Savings Bond Program, Midland; mem. citizens com. Rogers (Ark.) Hough Meml. Library, women's aux. Rogers Meml. Hosp.; sec. Beaver Lake Literacy Council, Rogers, 1973. Bds. dirs. Globe Theatre, Odessa, Tex., Midland Community Theatre, Tri-County Foster Home, Guadalupe, Midland youth centers, DeZavala Day Nursery, P.T.A. Recipient Thanks badge Midland Girl Scout Assn., 1948. Mem. N.E.A. (del. conv. 1965), P.T.A. (life), Future Homemakers Am. (life), Delta Kappa Gamma. Episcopalian. Clubs: Altrusa (pres.), Apple Spur Community (both Rogers). Home: Route 2 Rogers AR 72756 Office: 610 SW A St Bentonville AR 72712

SEARLES, CLARA KALHOEFER, social worker, educator; b. Hanover, Kan.; d. Fred W. and Marguerite (Segebade) Kalhoefer; B.S., Colo. State Tchrs. Coll., 1933; R.N., Johns Hopkins Hosp., 1938; postgrad. social work Washington U., St. Louis, 1950-52; M.A., No. Ill. U., 1959; m. Wade T. Searles, June 29, 1946 (dec. Jan. 1962). Tchr. Elementary Consol. Schs., Otis, Colo., 1930-32; tchr. social studies Jr. High Sch., Sterling, Colo., 1933-35; pub. health nurse, dir. field services Denver Tb. Soc., 1938-43; cons. Nursing Homes and Central Services for Chronically Ill, Chgo., 1946-50, 52-56; sch. social worker Downer Grove Consol. Schs., 1956—; tchr. psychology So. High Sch., 1964-71; dir. pvt. agy. for counseling Searles Center, Downers Grove, Ill., 1965—. Chmn. Mayor's Com. for Mental Health, 1960-66; mem. DuPage County Mental Health Clinic Bd., 1956-65 v.p., publicity chmn. Sch. Bd. Caucus; 1964—; chmn. Downers Grove Sch. Bd. Caucus, 1969-70. Mem. Nat. Com. for Senator Margaret Chase Smith for Pres., 1964. Served to capt., Nurse Corps, WAC, 1943-46. Mem. Am. Assn. U. Women, Nat. League Nurses (life), Ill., Nat. welfare assns., N.E.A. (life), D.A.V. (life), Internat. Platform Assn., Royal Soc. Health London, Johns Hopkins Alumni (life), Acad. Certified Social Workers (hon.), Acad. Polit. Sci., Acad. Polit. and Social Scis., Am. Orthopsychiat. Assn., Am. Assn. U. Women, No. Ill. U. Alumni, Downer's Grove Bus. and Profl. Women's Club (pres. 1963-65), Smithsonian Instn. (asso.), Pi Lambda Theta (charter, life), Theta Sigma Upsilon. Presbyn. Mem. Order Eastern Star. Club: Booster. Home: 5228 Cornell Av Downers Grove IL 60515 Office: 911-913 Burlington Downers Grove IL 60515

SEARLS, EILEEN HAUGHEY, librarian, educator; b. Madison, Wis., Apr. 27, 1925; d. Edward M. and Anna Mary (Haughey) Searls; B.A., U. Wis., 1948, J.D., 1950, M.S., 1951. Admitted to Wis. bar, 1950; cataloger Law Library, Yale, New Haven, 1951-52; law librarian St. Louis U., 1952—; instr., 1952-53, asst. prof. legal research and writing, 1953-56, asso. prof., 1956-62, prof., 1962—. Mem. Am., Cath. library assns., Am. Assn. Law Libraries, Wis. Bar Assn. Home: 4946 Buckingham Ct St Louis MO 63108 Office: 3700 Lindell Blvd St Louis MO 63108

SEARS, CHRISTINE GRAVES (MRS. JOSEPH VERNON SEARS), librarian; b. Chandler, Okla., Nov. 7, 1913; d. Chester Arthur and Lula (Miller) Graves; B.S., U. Kan., 1936, postgrad., 1973; B.L.S., U. Ill., 1940, postgrad., 1969; M.A., U. Mo. at Kansas City, 1962; L.S. (Nat. Def. Edn. Art fellow), Okla. State U., 1967; m. Joseph Vernon Sears, Nov. 16, 1940; children—Karen Patricia (Mrs. George E. Vertreese), Michele Sue (Mrs. Vaughn E. Jones), Joseph Vernon, Deborah Christine (Mrs. Roderick J. Harrison). Head librarian N.E. br. Kansas City (Kan.) Pub. Library, 1936-40; librarian Northeast Jr. High Sch., 1952-53; librarian Sumner High Sch., Kansas City, 1953-73, sponsor Lit. Explorers Club, 1965-73; librarian F.L. Schlagle High Sch., Kansas City, Kan., 1973—, also Sponsor History Club. Sponsor Sumner High Sch. br. Future Tchrs. of Am., 1955-65, state sponsor, 1960-61. Mem. Wyandotte County (Kan.) Library Bd., 1973-75. Mem. Kan. State Tchrs. Assn., Kan. Assn. Sch. Librarians, Nat., Kansas City edn. assns., Alpha Kappa Alpha. Clubs: Pierian Study, L'Espirit (Kansas City). Home: 737 Parallel Av Kansas City KS 66101 Office: 2214 N 59th St Kansas City KS 66104

SEARS, CHRISTINE SEWARD, physician, marriage counsellor; b. N.Y.C., Nov. 17, 1902; d. John Perry and Edith de Charms (Hibbard) Seward B.A., Mt. Holyoke Coll., 1925; M.D., Coll. Phys. and Surg. Columbia, 1929; m. Laurence M. Sears, Dec. 31, 1930 (dec. Feb. 1958); children—Peter S., John Holt; m. 2d, Allen C. Blaisdell, Jan. 30, 1960 (dec. Sept. 1973). Intern, Nyack (N.Y.) Hosp., 1929, Bellevue Hosp., N.Y.C., 1930; med. dir. Planned Parenthood Clinic, Columbus, O., 1939-45; gen. practice medicine, Delaware, O., 1939-45; parent cons. Children's Hosp. of the East Bay, Oakland, Cal., 1947-53; family and marriage counselling therapist, Berkeley, San Leandro and Oakland, 1953—; instr. gynecology Med. Sch. Ohio State U., Columbus, 1943-45. Home: 1606 La Vereda Berkeley CA 94709

SEARS, DOROTHY WINGETT, civic worker; b. Salem, Mass., Oct. 30, 1923; d. Charles Marshall and Dorothy Maude (Wingett) Sears; Asso. in Sci., Colby Jr. Coll., 1944; B.S., 1945; postgrad. Mary Hitchcock Sch. Med. Tech., 1945. Lab. technologist Laconia (N.H.) Hosp., 1945-46; lab., EKG and x-ray technologist Smith Coll. Infirmary, Northhampton, Mass., 1946-48; technologist, pvt. lab., Providence, 1948-50; chief technologist, biochemistry Mary Fletcher Hosp., Burlington, Vt., 1950-53, research technologist biochemistry, 1953; chief technologist, hematology research lab. Dartmouth Med. Sch., Hanover, N.H., 1958-61, diagnostic radioisotope lab. Mary Hitchcock Meml. Hosp., Hanover, 1961-69. Mem. Lyme (N.H.) Bicentennial Com., 1958-61, mem. budget com., 1972—. Mem. Nat. Wildlife Fedn., Nat. Geographic Soc., Am. Heritage Soc., N.H. Hist. Soc., Grafton County Humane Soc., Early Am. Soc. Club: Utility (Lyme, N.H.). Home: 22 N Thetford Rd Lyme NH 03768

SEARS, MARSHA ANN BAXTER (MRS. KELLEY DEAN SEARS), radio service for blind ofcl.; b. Herington, Kan., Mar. 29, 1946; d. Walter Russell and Leota Marie (Koegeboehn) Baxter; B.S., U. Kan., 1969, postgrad.; m. Kelley Dean Sears, May 30, 1970. Occupational therapist Mar Vista Med. Treatment Unit, Crippled Children's Services, Los Angeles, 1969-70; activities dir., occupational therapist Orchard Park Convalescent Center, Tacoma, Wash., 1970-71; asst. dir. Audio-Reader, U. Kan., Lawrence, 1972—. Mem. Am. Occupational Therapy Assn., Alpha Delta Pi, Kappa Tau Alpha. Lutheran. Home: 1619 NE Clubhouse Dr North Kansas City MO 64116 Office: Broadcast Hall U Kan Lawrence KS 66045

SEARS, ORETTA DIANORA (MRS. DONALD A. SEARS), lawyer; b. Carrara, Italy, Feb. 1, 1928; d. Angelo Count and Andreinna Countess (Baratta) Ferri; came to U.S., 1946, naturalized, 1948; B.A. summa cum laude, Upsala Coll., 1960; J.D., U. Cal. at Los Angeles, 1963; m. Donald Albert Sears, Jan. 6, 1964. Admitted Cal. bar, 1963, U.S. Supreme Ct. bar, 1966; trial atty. lands div. Dept. Justice, Washington, 1963-66; lectr. English and law Ahmadu Bello U., Nigeria, 1966-67; practice law, Oakland, Cal., 1967; dep. dist. atty. head writs and appeals sect. Dist. Atty's Office, Orange County (Cal.), 1968—. Lectr. AID program for Vietnam students Cal. State U., Fullerton, 1968. Mem. Cal. Atty. Gen.'s Commn. Obscenity. Recipient Distinguished Student award Upsala Coll., 1960. Mem. Cal. State Bar, Coll. English Assn., Am., Fed. (chmn. com. natural resources 1966-67), Orange County bar assns. Clubs: National Lawyer's (Washington); Lotos (N.Y.C.). Mem. U. Cal. Los Angeles Law Rev., 1961-63; editorial bd. Orange County Bar Jour., 1974—. Contbr. articles to profl. pubs. Home: 1448 Sunny Crest Dr Fullerton CA 92632 also 9 Via Delle Mantellate Florence Italy Office: 700 W 8th St PO Box 808 Santa Ana CA 92708

SEARS, VICTORIA CONASON (MRS. SAM WADE SEARS), physician; b. N.Y.C., Nov. 3, 1929; d. Emil G. and Celia (Rubin) Conason; B.A., N.Y.U., 1950; M.D., U. Geneva, 1958; postgrad. N.Y. Sch. Psychiatry, 1964; m. Sam Wade Sears, Feb. 13, 1954; 1 son, John Andrew. Intern, St. Johns Episcopal Hosp., Bklyn., 1958-59; resident, sr. psychiatrist Creedmoor State Hosp., Queens, N.Y., 1961-64; practice medicine specializing in psychiatry, 1961—; staff psychiatrist Nassau County Family Ct. Mental Health Clinic, 1964-66; dir. treatment Nassau County Drug Abuse and Addiction Program, 1966-73; med. dir. Mental Health Clinic Long Beach (N.Y.) Meml. Hosp., 1973—; attending psychiatrist Meadowbrook Hosp., East Meadow, N.Y., 1966—; psychiatrist North Shore Hosp., 1964-67, cons. dept. psychiatry, 1972—; adj. asso. prof. speech and hearing Adelphi Coll., 1966-67; clin. asst. prof. psychiatry Cornell Med. Coll., 1972—. Mem. A.M.A., Am. Psychiat. Assn., A.A.A.S. Home: 17 Kings Pl Great Neck NY 11024 Office: Long Beach Meml Hosp Long Beach NY 11561

SEASHORE, MARGRETTA REED (MRS. JOHN H. SEASHORE), physician; b. Red Bank, N.J., June 20, 1939; d. Robert Clark and Lillie Ann (Heaviland) Reed; A.B., Swarthmore Coll., 1961; M.D., Yale, 1965; m. John H. Seashore, Dec. 26, 1964; children—Robert Harold, Carl John. Intern Yale Sch. Medicine, 1965-66, resident, 1966-68, postdoctoral fellow, metabolism and genetics, Yale, 1968-70, asst. clin. prof. human genetics and pediatrics, 1973—; attending physician, metabolism and genetics, U. Hosp., Jacksonville, Fla. 1970-71; asst. prof. pediatrics U. Fla., Gainesville, 1971-73, charge metabolic screening program, dept. pediatrics, 1971-73; attending physician Hope Hope Haven Children's Hosp., Jacksonville, 1970-73, Yale-New Haven Hosp., 1973—. Fellow Am. Acad. Pediatrics; mem. Am. Soc. Human Genetics, So. Soc. Pediatric Research, Fla. Pediatric Soc. Contbr. articles profl. pubs. Home: Anthony Ct Bethany CT 06525

SEAVER, BLANCHE EBERT (MRS. FRANK ROGER SEAVER), composer, civic worker; b. Chgo., Sept. 15, 1891; d. Theodore and Anna Mathilde (Mathisen) Ebert; grad. Chgo. Mus. Coll., 1911; L.H.D., U. So. Cal., 1966; D.F.A., Pepperdine U., 1969; LL.D., Pomona Coll., 1970; D.B.A., Woodbury Coll., 1970; D. Humanities, Okla. Christian Coll., 1972; Dr. Pub. Service, Mac Murray Coll., 1973; m. Frank Roger Seaver, Sept. 16, 1916. Piano tchr., accompanist coach Hull House, Chgo., 1909-12, Los Angeles, 1912-16; chmn. Seaver Inst.; hon. chmn. Hydril Co., Los Angeles. Active Los Angeles Symphony Assn. (trustee 1949-51, adv. bd. 1951-55), Nine O'Clock Players, Las Madrinas (dir. 1941-44), Womens' Com. Symphony Salons (program chmn. 1956-60), Symphony Orch. (chmn. sponsoring patronesses 1951), Hollywood Bowl Patronesses Com. (founding mem.). Mem. adv. bd. St. Elizabeth Day Nursery, Los Angeles, Social Service Aux., St. Anne's Hosp. Guild, Los Angeles; bd. dirs. St. John's Hosp. Guild, Los Angeles Orphanage Guild, St. Vincent's Hosp. Aux., Los Angeles, St. Joseph's Hosp. Guild. Trustee U. So. Cal., Pomona Coll., Freedoms Found. at Valley Forge, Pepperdine U. Decorated Grand Cross Dame Knightly Order St. Brigitte; named Woman of Year, Los Angeles Times, 1963; recipient Jane Addams award. Rockford Coll. (Jane Addams Coll), 1963; distinguished citizenship award Nat. Soc. S.A.R., 1965; award Freedom Club, 1966; bd. trustees award Pepperdine Alumni Assn., 1968; Am. Patriot award Americanism Ednl. League, 1971; honor certificate award Freedoms Found. at Valley Forge, 1971; John Wayne Golden Circle of Cal. award, 1970; Merit award Rep. Party of Los Angeles County, 1970; award of excellence Christian Freedom Found., 1971; Distinguished Patriot award Religious Heritage Am., 1973, others. Mem. Symphony Opera Patroness Com. (chmn. sponsoring opera patronesses 1951). Conglist (trustee), Composer: Calling Me Back To You, 1921, Just For Today, 1926, If God Sent Me You, 1927, The Flower, 1928, Stay With Me, O Lord, 1931, Alone With Thee, 1932, No Llores yo Volveri, 1934, Morrow Rock, 1937, Remember Me, 1946, Close at Thy Feet, My Lord, others. A spl. arrangement of Battle Hymn of the Republic, Phila. Symphony Orch., 1919. Home: 20 Chester Pl Los Angeles CA 90007

SEAY, HELEN PICKERING, banker; b. Clarksville, Tenn., Jan. 23, 1924; d. George Roscoe and Geneva Annie (Nichols) Pickering; grad. high sch.; m. William Malcolm Seay, Jan. 26, 1944; 1 son, William Michael. With 1st Nat. Bank Clarksville, 1951—, trust officer, 1971—, v.p., 1972—. Bd. dirs. A.R.C., Clarksville-Montgomery County, 1970. Mem. Bus. and Profl. Women's Club Clarksville (pres. 1969; Woman of Achievement, 1972), Nat. Assn. Bank Women. Mem. Ch. of Christ. Club: Altrusa. Home: 129 Lookout Dr Clarksville TN 37040 Office: 1st Nat Bank Franklin St Clarksville TN 37040

SEAY, PEGGY CASEY (MRS. WILLIAM ROBERT SEAY), real estate broker; b. Atlanta, Aug. 24, 1928; d. John and Gussie Garrison (Brown) Casey; R.N., Ga. Bapt. Hosp., U. Ga., 1950; student Smith-Hughes, 1961; license Ga. Inst. Real Estate, 1967; m. William Robert Seay, Sept. 2, 1950 children—William Robert, Camilla Elizabeth. Head nurse St. Joseph's Infirmary, Atlanta, 1952; supr. obstetrics nursery Ga. Bapt. Hosp., Atlanta, 1958-62; indsl. nurse Rich's Dept. Store, Atlanta, 1964-67; sales agt. Bullard Realty Co., Atlanta, 1962-67; real estate broker Seay Realty Co., Fayetteville and Clayton County, Ga., 1967—. Chmn., Fayette County Heart Fund Drive, 1968-69, Am. Cancer Soc., County Fund Drive, 1970. Bd. dirs. Fayette County Cancer Soc., 1969—, chmn. bd., 1972, pres., 1971. Recipient award as outstanding vol. Am. Cancer Soc., 1970, Realtor of the Year Fayette County Bd. Realtors, 1972. Mem. Nat. Assn. Real Estate Brokers (mem. met. Atlanta women's council 1970—, pres. 1972—, mem. ednl. com. 1972), Fayette County Bd. Realtors (founder 1969, charter pres. 1969-70, dir. 1969—), Ga. Assn. Realtors (chmn. Make America Better com. 1972), Fayette County Mchts. Assn., Ga. Nurses Assn., Ga. Retail Assn., Atlanta, Fayette County real estate bds., Women's Soc. Christian Service (pres. 1969-70), Fayette County Bus. and Profl. Women's Club (charter sec. 1970). Clubs: Fayette County Garden (founder 1968, pres. 1969) (Fayetteville); Flat Creek Country Club (Peachtree City, Ga.). Methodist. Home: 130 Walker Av Fayetteville GA 30214 Office: 520 N Glynn St Fayetteville GA 30214

SEBASTIAN, CAROL ANN (MRS. MERLE W. SEBASTIAN), editor, publisher; b. Grand Rapids, Mich., Jan. 2, 1940; d. Robert David and Neva Irene (Vanderlip) McWhinney; student Mich. State U., 1958-61; m. Merle W. Sebastian, Oct. 1, 1970; children—Lisa Lee, Stacy and Tracy (twins). Asst. editor, bookkeeper Lowell (Mich.) Ledger, 1955-68, editor, pub., 1971—; asst. purchasing agt. Attwood Corp., 1968-70; receptionist, bookkeeper No. Equipment Co., 1970. Bd. dirs. Lowell Showboat Corp. Mem. Lowell Women of Moose (publicity chmn.). Home: 606 Grindle Dr Lowell MI 49331 Office: 105 N Broadway Lowell MI 49331

SEBBAS, MILDRED WICKS (MRS. ARTHUR C. SEBBAS), hosp. adminstr.; b. Paris, N.Y., June 30, 1910; d. Harry Staples and Emily Eliza (Arnold) Wicks; R.N., Utica Meml. Hosp., 1931; m. Arthur C. Sebbas, June 11, 1938; 1 son, LeRoy Arnold. Pvt. duty nurse, N.Y., also Nev., 1931-37, 38-42; surgery nurse Pershing Gen. Hosp., Lovelock, Nev., 1942-54, hosp. adminstr. since 1954—. Co-chmn. Alcoholics Anonymous and Drug Abuse Council, Lovelock, 1973—. Trustee Nev. Hosp., 1971—. Mem. Am., Western, Nev. (pres. 1961-62) hosp. assns., Beta Sigma Phi. Republican. Methodist (lay leader 1969—). Club: Soroptimist (Lovelock). Home: 1420 Central Lovelock NV 89419 Office: 6th Av and County Rd Lovelock NV 89419

SEBENTHALL, ELIZABETH ROBERTA, author; b. Eau Claire, Wis., Jan. 6, 1917; d. Robert Graham and Laura Rose (Cote) Sebenthall. Recipient Nat. Endowment for the Arts award, 1970. Author numerous novels including: If the Shroud Fits, 1969; The Cold Ones, 1972; The Bronze Claws, 1972; (poetry) Acquainted with a Chance of Bobcats, 1969. Home: 104 Thompson St Mount Horeb WI 53572

SEBERT, SHIRLEY MAE (MRS. RICHARD F. SEBERT), mus. ofcl.; b. Purcell, Okla., Nov. 26, 1934; d. Orin A. and Vena Leonore (Lokey) Johnston; student Okla. State U., 1952-53, U. Okla., 1953, Draughn's Sch. Bus., 1957; m. Richard F. Sebert, Sept. 25, 1954; children—Richard Alan, Cynthia Ann. Sec. to br. mgr. Motors Ins. Corp. div. Gen. Motors, Oklahoma City, 1955-59; med. asst. Dr. William L. Savage, Oklahoma City, 1962-64; with Cowboy Hall of Fame, Oklahoma City, 1966—, adminstrv. asst. 1970—. Democrat. Baptist. Home: Rural Route 3 Box 193M Edmond OK 73034 Office: 1700 NE 63rd St Oklahoma City OK 73034

SEBEST, EDWINA, psychologist, health service adminstr.; b. McKeesport, Pa., May 19, 1941; d. Edward and Irene (Havanchak) Sebest; B.A., Carlow Coll., 1963; M.A., De Paul U., 1966; Ph.D., U. Pitts., 1973. Instr. psychology Carlow Coll., Pitts., 1964-65; asst. chief of testing Psychol. Services of Pitts., 1965-66; psychometrist Pitts. Psychol. Counseling Center, 1966-70; sch. psychologist Allegheny County (Pa.) Intermediate unit, 1967—; chief of assessment services, chief psychologist South Hills Child Guidance Center, Pitts., 1970—. Instr. psychology Pa. State U. at McKeesport, 1972—; psychol. cons. and evaluator for sch. dists. in South Hills area, 1973—. Mem. Am., Pa. psychol. assns., Pi Gamma Mu. Home: 3615 Ashland Dr Bethel Park PA 15102 Office: South Hills Child Guidance Center 300 Mt Lebanon Blvd Pittsburgh PA 15234

SECH, EITHEL F. PARTLOW (MRS. CHARLES EDWARD SECH), psychiat. social worker; b. Sleeper, Mo.; d. Laud Allen and Rosa Jane (Bowman) Partlow; student S.W. State Coll., 1939-40; B.A., U. Mo., 1945; M.S.W., U. Mich., 1957; m. Charles Edward Sech, Jan. 18, 1957. Social worker Lucas County Child Welfare Bd., Toledo, 1946-57, U. Mich. Med. Center, Neuropsychiat. Inst., Ann Arbor, 1957-64, Mental Health Clinic, U. Mich. at Ann Arbor, 1964—, social work supr., 1965-71, chief psychiat. social worker, 1971—, coordinator services for women, 1971-72. Mem. Nat. Assn. Social Workers, Acad. Certified Social Workers, Alpha Kappa Delta, Phi Kappa Phi, Beta Sigma Phi. Lutheran. Home: 5993 Winans Lake Rd Brighton MI 48116 Office: 207 Fletcher St Ann Arbor MI 48104

SECHRIST, ELIZABETH HOUGH, librarian, author; b. Media, Pa., Aug. 31, 1903; d. Willard Graham and Mary (Parker) Hough; grad. Media High Sch., 1922; student U. Pitts. (night sch.), 1923-25, Carnegie Library Sch. of Carnegie Inst. of Tech., 1923-24; m. Walter Levere Sechrist, Oct. 6, 1930. Asst. children's librarian, Carnegie Library, Pitts., 1924-25, children's librarian, 1937-39; head children's dept., Bethlehem (Pa.) Pub. Library, 1925-31; free lance editorial work juvenile publs., Phila., 1931—. Mem. Am. Folklore Soc. Author: Christmas Everywhere, 1931, rev., 1936, 62; A Little Book of Hallowe'en, 1934; Rufie Had A Monkey, 1939; Red Letter Days, 1940, rev., 1965; Once in the First Times, 1949, rev., 1969; (with Janette Woolsey) New Plays for Red Letter Days, 1953; It's Time to

Give a Play, 1955; It's Time for Thanksgiving, 1957; It's Time for Christmas, 1959; It's Time for Easter, 1961; It's Time for Brotherhood, 1962, 73; It's Time for Story Hour, 1964; Terribly Strange Tales, 1967. Editor: Thirteen Ghostly Yarns, 1932, rev. 1942, 63; Pirates and Pigeons, 1933; Marry Meet Again, 1941; Heigh-Ho For Halloween!, 1948. Editor: One Thousand Poems for Children, 1946; Poems for Red Letter Days, 1951. Contbr. to mags. Contbg. editor World Book Ency. and Britannica Jr. Ency. Home: 337 W State St Media PA 19063

SECOR, FRANCES VERNOR GUILLE (MRS. WALTER TODD SECOR), educator; b. Atlanta, Mar. 1, 1908; d. B. Frank and Margaret Davis (Baker) Guille; student Muskingum Coll., 1926-27; B.A., Coll. of Wooster, 1930; M.A., Western Res. U., 1936; postgrad. Middlebury Lang. Sch., summers 1934, 38, Ohio State U., summer 1940; Docteur de l'Universite, U. Paris, 1949; m. Walter Todd Secor, Dec. 23, 1973. Tchr., Fairview High Sch., Cleve., 1930-37; tchr. French, Coll. of Wooster, O., 1937—, prof., 1955—, chmn. dept. French, 1969-72, acting dean women, 1944-46; instr. math. and geopolitics Naval Flight Prep. Sch., 1943-44; tchr. Central Mich. Coll., summer 1950, Western Res. U., summer 1955; dir. Wooster-in-Paris Summer Program, 1951-59, Crossroads-Africa group to Senegal, summer 1960, Corr. Bur. for Students of French, 1953—. Recipient Research grants Gt. Lakes Coll. Assn., 1967, 68; decorated chevalier des Palmes Academiques; French Govt. scholar, 1947-49, Vis. scholar Radcliffe Coll., 1961-62. Mem. Am. Assn. Tchrs. French (past pres. Ohio chpt.), Modern Lang. Assn., Am. Assn. U. Women (past pres. local chpt.), Midwest, Ohio modern lang. assns., Am. Council on Teaching Fgn. Langs., Assn. Depts. Fgn. Lang., Phi Beta Kappa, Phi Sigma Iota, Delta Sigma Rho. Presbyn. Author: Francois-Victor Hugo et son Oeuvre, 1950; (with Bonthius, Davis, Drushal and Spencer) Independent Study Programs in the U.S., 1957. Editor: Le Journal d'Adele Hugo, Vol. I, 1968, Vol. II, 1971. Asso. editor Wooster Alumni Mag., 1941-44. Home: 504 Burg St Granville OH 43023

SECOR, JOHANNA (MRS. ELIAS SECOR), artist; b. Stamford, Conn.; d. Nicholas and Mary (Korychuck) Matrofil; B.F.A., Pratt Inst., 1941; postgrad. Silvermine Coll., 1956, 60; m. Elias Secor, Feb. 26, 1944; 1 son, Michael Reid. Exhibited in one-man shows including Ahda Artzt Gallery, N.Y.C., 1967, John Wanamaker Gallery, N.Y.C., Cochrane Gallery, Darien, Conn., 1966, Couterier Gallery, Stamford, 1965, Iona Coll., New Rochelle, N.Y. 1969, John Wanamacher, N.Y.C., 1969, Bruce Mus., Greenwich, Conn., 1970, Greenville (N.C.) Art Mus., 1972; exhibited in group shows Galleria de Arte, Lisbon, Portugal, 1968, Modern Masters Gallery, N.Y.C., 1968, Sakal Lehn Galleries, New Rochelle, Denver, 1968, John Wanamaker Galleries, N.Y.C., 1968, Gallery on Wheels, Paramus, N.J., 1967, Nat. Acad. Galleries, N.Y.C., 1968, Dept. Interior Art Gallery, Washington, 1968, Stamford Mus., 1968, Ezry Gallery, Jerusalem, Israel, 1969, Venise Cadre, Casablanca, Morocco, 1969, Salt Lake Palace Civic Center, Salt Lake City, 1969, Bruce Mus., Greenwich, Conn., 1969, Sergez Rubenstein Gallery, Denver, 1969. Recipient awards art shows, Darien, Norwalk, Bridgeport, Conn., 1965-68, Conn. State Art Show, Nat. League Am. Pen Women, 1970. Mem. Nat. Assn. Women Artists, Nat. League Am. Pen Women (art chmn. pioneer group 1969), Greenwich, Old Greenwich art socs. Address: Prince's Pine Rd Norwalk CT 06850

SECREST, DAISY HOWERTON (MRS. RAYMOND M. SECREST), ret. home economist; b. Red Oak, Va., May 9, 1911; d. Samuel Lewis and Nannie Louis (Murray) Howerton; elementary certificate Ferrum (Va.) Tng. Sch., 1928-29; normal profl. certificate Radford Coll., 1930, B.S., 1940; postgrad. Va. Poly. Inst., 1940, U. Ark., 1950, Ohio State U., 1963-65, U. Colo., 1965, U. Ariz., 1971; m. Raymond M. Secrest, Dec. 1, 1968. Prin. mission sch., Patrick County, Va., 1930-32; elementary sch. tchr., Charlotte County, 1933-34, prin., 1934-39; county home demonstration agt., Va., 1940-59; dietitian C. & O. Ry. Hosp., Clifton Forge, Va., 1959-61; county extension agt., Carroll County, O., 1961-69, Noble County, O., 1969-71; instr. emeritus co-op. extension service Ohio State U., 1971—; now tchr. elementary sch. Charlotte County. Recipient wall plaques Carroll County Dairy Assn., Carroll County Fair Assn., 1969, scholarships Farm Found., 1965-71, Nat. Recognition for outstanding services Extension Service, 1969; named Hon. Chpt. Farmer, Carrolton High Sch. Future Farmers Am., 1969, Hon. Citizen Carroll County, 1969. Mem. Nat. (dist. pres. 1951), Va. home econs. assn., Nat., Ohio extension agts assns., Epsilon Sigma Pi (certificate 25 years service 1967). Methodist (tchr. Sunday schs. 1934-46). Home: 310 W Sycamore St Chase City VA 23924

SECREST, JUNE MERYLE, journalist; b. Bath, Somerset, Eng.; d. Albert Edward and Olive Edith May (Love) Doman; certificate London Higher Sch., 1948; m. David Waight Secrest, Sept. 12, 1953 (div.); children—Cary, Martin, Gillian Anne. Came to U.S., 1953, naturalized, 1957. Reporter, Hamilton (Ont.) News, 1949-50, 51-53, Bristol (Eng.) Evening Post, 1950-51; food editor Columbus (O.) Citizen, 1954-56; reporter Washington Post, 1965—, asst. editor Style sect., 1972-74, food prodn. editor, 1974—. Author: Between Me and Life, 1974. Contbr. articles to mags. Home: 3511 Turner Lane Chevy Chase MD 20015 Office: 1150 15th St NW Washington DC 20005

SECREST, VIVIAN VIRGINIA (MRS. ROBERT MADISON SECREST), univ. librarian; b. Hartford, Ind., May 8, 1917; d. Ora Albert and Cora Belle (Thornburgh) Smith; B.S. in Edn., Ball State U., 1943; M.L.S., Tex. Woman's U., 1960; postgrad. U. Ill., 1970; m. Robert Madison Secrest, Aug. 1, 1940; children—David Lance, Keren Ann (Mrs. Robert Wych). Tchr., Gov. I.P. Gray High Sch., Portland, Ind., 1944-45; tchr. pub. schs., Denver, 1957-58; catalog librarian Washington U., St. Louis, 1961-68, head cataloging div., 1968-70, dir. art and architecture library, 1970—, faculty basic cataloging Sch. Continuing Edn., 1968—, advanced cataloging, 1971—. Mem. A.L.A., Coll. Art Assn. Am., Art Library Soc. N.Am., Asian Art Soc. Club: Greater St. Louis Library. Home: 5000 Foxdale Dr St Louis MO 63128

SEE, CAROLYN PENELOPE, journalist, educator; b. Pasadena, Cal., Jan. 13, 1934; d. George Newton and Kate Louise (Sullivan) Laws; B.A., Cal. State Coll. at Los Angeles, 1957; M.A., U. Cal. at Los Angeles, 1959, Ph.D., 1963; children—Lisa Lénine, Clara Elizabeth Marya Sturak. Freelance journalist, mags. and newspapers; asst. prof. English, Loyola U., Los Angeles, 1970—. Mabel Wilson Richards fellow, 1968-69; Woodrow Wilson teaching fellow, 1967-68. Author: The Rest is Done With Mirrors, 1970; Blue Money, 1973. Home: PO Box 107 Topanga CA 90290 Office: 7101 W 80th St Los Angeles CA 90045

SEEBACH, LYDIA MARIE, internist; b. Red Wing, Minn., Nov. 9, 1920; d. John Henry and Marie (Gluesen) Seebach; B.S., U. Minn., 1942, M.B., 1943, M.D., 1944, M.S. in medicine, 1951; m. Keith Edward Wentz, Oct. 16, 1959; children—Brooke Marie, Scott Seebach. Intern Kings County Hosp., Bklyn., 1944; resident Mayo Clinic, Rochester, Minn., 1945-51; practice medicine specializing in internal medicine, Oakland, Cal., 1952-60, San Francisco, 1960—; mem. staff Pacific Med. Center, St. Francis, Childrens, St. Marys, St. Joseph, St. Lukes hosps., San Francisco; head arthritis clinic St. Mary's Hosp., 1968-72. Mem. Mayor's Com. on Status of Women, 1971—. Exec. bd. med. and sci. com. Arthritis Found., 1967-72. Diplomate Am. Bd. Internal Medicine. Fellow A.C.P.; mem. Bay Area and San Francisco Women Physicians (pres. 1968-70), A.M.A. (recipient Recognition award 1969), Cal., San Francisco med. assns., Am. Rheumatism Assn., Am., Cal. socs. internal medicine, Iota Sigma Pi. Soroptimist. Contbr. to profl. jours. Home: 2813 Scott St San Francisco CA 94123 Office: 450 Sutter St San Francisco CA 94108

SEEDOR, MARIE MARCIA, nursing educator; b. Frackville, Pa.; d. Wasyl and Anna (Socker) Seedor; B.S. in Nursing, Villanova U., 1953; M.S. in Edn., U. Pa., 1958; Ed.D., Tchrs. Coll., Columbia, 1962. Instr., Presbyn. Hosp. Sch. Nursing, Phila., 1953-56, U. Md. Sch. Nursing, Balt., 1958-59, instr. Tchrs. Coll., Columbia, N.Y.C., 1962-63, research asso., 1963-66, asso. prof. nursing edn., 1966—. Cons. programmed instrn. nursing, Pan Am. Health Orgn., Am. Hosp. Assn. Mem. Am. Nurses Assn., Nat. League Nursing, Pi Lambda Theta, Sigma Theta Tau, Kappa Delta Pi. Author: Introduction to Asepsis, 1962; Programmed Instruction for Nursing, 1963; Aids to Diagnosis, 1963; Therapy with Oxygen, 1964; Aids to Nursing Judgment, a programmed unit, 1972; Physical Assessment, 1974. Home: 820 Meredith Dr Wesley Manor Media PA 19063 Office: 400 W 119th St New York City NY 10027

SEEFRIED, IRMGARD MARIA THERESIA, opera and concert singer; b. Koengetried, Bavaria; d. Henrich and Marie (Scharpf) Seefried; student coll., conservatory, Augsburg; m. Wolfgang Schneiderhan; children—Barbara Maria, Monica Maria. First engagement Aachen under von Karajan; Kammersaengerin at Vienna State Opera; concert tours all over world; also appeared Met. Opera. N.Y.C., Covent Garden Opera, London, La Scala, Milan, also festivals at Salzburg, Lucerne, Edinburgh, Ann. Recipient various Mozart medals, Lilly Lehmann medal, Golden Cross for culture and sci.; Officer's Cross of Royal Danish Danebrog medal., Cross of the Order of Merit 1st class (Germany). Hon. mem. Boston Symphony Orch., Vienna Philharmonic Orch. Address: care Vienna State Opera Vienna Austria

SEELBACH, LINDA ZUMETA (MRS. CHRISTOPHER REA SEELBACH), pub. relations exec.; b. Dallas; d. Julio and Madge Weaver (Burton) Zumeta; B.A., Gettysburg Coll., 1962; certificate with honor U. Barcelona, 1960; postgrad. N.Y. U., 1962-65; m. Christopher Rea Seelbach, June 7, 1969. Supr. publicity Mut. of N.Y., N.Y.C., 1962-71; mgr. presentations Am. Stock Exchange, Inc., N.Y.C., 1971-72; mgr. creative services Securities Industry Automation Corp., N.Y.C., 1972-73; adminstr. pub. relations services Times Mirror Co., Los Angeles, 1973—. Mem. Pub. Relations Soc. Am., D.A.R., Pi Delta Epsilon, Chi Omega. Home: 401 E 74th St Apt 12D New York City NY 10021 Office: Times Mirror Sq Los Angeles CA 90053

SEELER, RUTH ANDREA, physician; b. N.Y.C., June 13, 1936; d. Thomas Darlington and Olivia (Patten) Seeler; B.A. cum laude, U. Vt., 1959, M.D., 1962. Intern, resident Bronx Municipal Hosp., 1962-65; practice medicine specializing in pediatrics and hematology, Chgo., 1965—; pediatric hematology fellow U. Ill.; 1965-67; asso. prof. pediatrics Abraham Lincoln Sch. Medicine, U. Ill.; chmn. div. pediatric hematology, Cook County Childrens Hosp., Chgo., 1967—. Diplomate Am. Bd. Pediatrics. Fellow Am. Acad. Pediatrics; mem. Midwest Soc. Pediatric Research, Am. Soc. Hematology, Phi Beta Kappa, Gamma Phi Beta. Contbr. articles to profl. jours. Home: 2431 N Orchard Chicago IL 60614 Office: Cook County Children's Hosp 700 S Wood St Chicago IL 60612

SEELY, ELIZABETH CAVEN, librarian; b. Poughkeepsie, N.Y.; d. Alexander and M.E. (Scoville) Caven; A.B., Vassar Coll.; B.S. in L.S., Columbia; m. William E. Seely. Reference librarian Tompkins Sq. br. N.Y. Pub. Library, then librarian Westchester County (N.Y.) Union Catalog; librarian Sarah Lawrence Coll. Library, 1965-74, librarian emeritus, 1974—. Mem. Am., N.Y. State (dir. coll. and univ. libraries sect. 1968-70), Westchester County (past pres. editor bull.) library assns., Assn. Coll. and Research Libraries. Home: 137 Cedar Lane Bronxville NY 10708

SEELYE, BARBARA JANE, educator; b. Peoria, Ill., Nov. 29, 1930; d. John Arvel and Mayme (Dwyer) Seelye; B.S., Eureka Coll., Ill., 1952; postgrad. Western Ill. State U., Bradley U., Washington U., St. Louis; M.A., U. Denver, 1955, Ph.D., 1966. Tchr., Delavan Unit High Sch., Ill., 1952-55; exec. asst. U. Denver Children's Speech Clinic, 1955-56; tchr. Forman Unit High Sch., Manito, Ill., 1956-57; speech pathologist, instr. Sch. Medicine, Washington U., St. Louis, 1957-59, speech pathologist instr., div. child psychiatry, 1959; instr. speech, asso. dir. speech clinic St. Louis U., 1959-61, instr., dir. speech clinic, 1961-63, asst. prof. speech, dir. speech and hearing clinics, 1963-66, asso. prof. speech, dir. speech and hearing clinics, 1966-74, chmn. dept. communication disorders, 1968-74, profl., 1972-74, asst. to pres. for community relations, 1973-74; dean Coll. Profl. Studies, No. Ill. U., DeKalb, 1974—. Cons. in communications depts. nursing and psychology Jefferson Barracks VA Hosp., Cardinal Ritter Inst. Active Girl Scouts Am.; mem. adv. bd. Projects, Inc., St. Louis, 1962—, St. Louis Speech and Hearing Center. Recipient Matrix award Theta Sigma Phi, 1968, Civic and Cultural award Ladies Aux. U.S. Navy, Marine Corps Fleet Res., 1968; Downtown St. Louis Edn. award 1969. Mem. Nat., Ill. edn. assns., Speech and Hearing Assn. Greater St. Louis, Am., Mo. speech and hearing assns., Washington U. Child Study Group, Central States Speech Assn., Internat. Platform Assn., Am. Council Edn. Internship Acad. Adminstrn., Met. Council on Developmental Disabilites (chmn. steering com.), Sigma Alpha Eta. Contbr. articles to profl. jours. Home: 506 N 1st St DeKalb IL 60115 Office: No Ill U DeKalb IL 60115

SEELYE, MARGARET ANN RAMBO (MRS. CARROLL E. SEELYE), educator; b. Monaca, Pa., May 9, 1909; s. William A. and Sarah Rose (Bell) Rambo; A.B., Greenville Coll., 1938; M.A., N.Y. U., 1953; postgrad. U. Chgo., 1968-74; m. Carroll E. Seelye, Mar. 22, 1957; children—Carolyn (Mrs. William R. MacElroy), Tedd F. Founder, dir. Sch. Nursing, Roberts Wesleyan Coll., Rochester, N.Y., 1950-57; coordinator nursing edn. Dept. Registration and Edn., State of Ill., Chgo., 1959-67; dir. dept. baccalaureate nursing Olivet Nazarene Coll., Kankakee, Ill., 1968-74; now cons. nursing edn. Council mem. Deans and Dirs. Baccalaureate and Higher Degree Programs, 1968—; mem. Comprehensive Health Planning Council Will, Grundy and Kankakee County, 1973-74. Mem. Nat. Soc. for Study Edn., Am., Ill. (mem. bd. Chgo. dist. dir. 1964-66) nurses assns., Nat. League for Nursing, Pi Lambda Theta. Home: Bonnie Oaks PO Box 37 Bourbonnais IL 60914 Office: Nursing Edn Dept Olivet Nazarene Coll Kankakee IL 60901

SEEMAN, MARY VIOLETTE (MRS. PHILIP SEEMAN), psychiatrist; b. Lodz, Poland, Mar. 24, 1935; d. Alexander and Sonia (Brzezinska) Szwarc; diploma lit. Sorbonne U., Paris, 1956; B.A., McGill U., 1955, M.D., 1960; m. Philip Seeman, June 30, 1959; children—Marc, Bob, Neil. Intern, Harper Hosp., Detroit, 1960-61; resident psychiatry Manhattan State Hosp., N.Y.C., 1961-64, research scientist, 1964-66; research scientist Fulbourn Hosp., Cambridge, Gt. Britain, 1966-67; practice medicine specializing in psychiatry, Toronto, Ont., Can., 1967—; mem. staff Toronto Western Hosp., 1967—; asst. prof. psychiatry U. Toronto, 1972—. Fellow Royal Coll. Physicians and Surgeons; mem. Canadian, Ont. med. assns., Canadian, Ont. psychiat. assns. Office: 25 Leonard Av Toronto ON Canada

SEFERI, MANIA MARIE-LOUISE, social scientist, educator; b. Athens, Greece, Nov. 7, 1945; d. Constantine D. and Roubini M. (Georgouli) Seferis; came to U.S., 1967, naturalized, 1971; A.A., Briarcliff Coll., 1964; B.A., Pierce Coll., Athens, 1966; M.A., U. Colo., 1969, Ph.D., 1970. Research asst. Athenean Inst. of Anthropos, Athens, 1964-67; data analyst Inst. for Research in Communication, Athens, 1966-67; social psychol. cons. Thymio Papayannis & Assos., Architects, Planners, Engrs., Athens, 1966-67; researcher, bd. mem. Environment Planning Center, Athens, 1966-67; teaching asst. Pierce Coll., Athens, 1967; research asst. U. Colo., Boulder, 1967-68, teaching asst., 1968-69; teaching asst. U. Colo. Denver Center, 1969-70; social sci. cons. Denver Design Center, 1969-70; advisor, project dir. Environment Inc., Denver, 1969-70; asst. prof. city planning Harvard, Cambridge, Mass., 1970—, dir. urban field service, 1970—. Program dir. tng. in community work Peace Corps, Denver, 1969-70. Mem. Am. Inst. Planners (vice chmn. edn. com. 1970-71), Citizens Housing and Planning Assn. (dir. 1971—), Urban Planning Aid (dir. 1970—). Contbr. articles to profl. jours. Home: 22 Centre St Watertown MA 02172 Office: 7 Marshal St Boston MA 02108

SEGAL, ARLENE ESTA (MRS. RICHARD T. LOGAN), physician; b. N.Y.C., Nov. 12, 1937; d. Moe and Fanny (Schlussel) Segal; A.B., Duke U., 1958; M.D., Albert Einstein Coll. Medicine, 1962; m. Richard T. Logan, Aug. 14, 1969. Intern Bronx (N.Y.) Municipal Hosp. Center, 1962-63, resident, 1963-66; instr. dept. radiology Albert Einstein Coll. Medicine, Bronx, 1966-68, asst. prof., 1968-71, clin. asst. prof., 1971—; practice medicine specializing in radiology, Rye, N.Y., 1971—. Mem. Soc. Pediatric Radiology, Phi Beta Kappa, Alpha Epsilon Phi, Alpha Omega Alpha. Home: 35 Englewood Av Nanuet NY 10954 Office: 175 Purchase St Rye NY 10580

SEGAL, DEBORAH WEBBER, sportswear co. exec.; b. Boston, Oct. 30, 1945; d. Jacob and Sylvia (Webber) Segal; B.S. in Polit. Sci., Boston U., 1968; M.Ed. in Vocational Rehab. Adminstrn. (scholarship), Northeastern U., Boston, 1970. Tchr. Franklin Sch., Brockton, Mass., 1968-69; originator Soborarium Clinic, Salvation Army, Boston, 1969-70; job psychologist Mass. Div. Employment Security, 1970-71; pres., dir. D&H Sportswears, Inc., Boston, 1971—. Social coordinator Canterbury House, Boston State Hosp., 1967. Sec. Milton (Mass.) Young Republicans, 1965; mem. Mass. Council Young Reps., 1966—; pres. Boston U. Polit. Club, 1967; mem. town platform com., Sharon, Mass., 1973. Bd. dirs. Teenagers Against Polio, 1963. Mem. Intra-Univ. Drama Club, Gamma Sigma Sigma (social chmn. 1968). Clubs: Junior Fortnightly, Boston Univ. Downtown Alumni (Boston). Home: 52 Pleasant St Sharon MA 02067 Office: 23 Beach St Boston MA 02111

SEGAL, ELEANOR SUSAN (MRS. CHARLES RAY SIX), physician; b. Chgo., Dec. 18, 1942; d. Harry R. and Mae Charlotte (Beck) Segal; M.D., U. Mich., 1966; m. Charles Ray Six, Dec. 5, 1970. Intern, Kaiser Found. Hosp., San Francisco, 1966-67, clinic physician, Bellflower, Cal., 1967; gen. physician Union Health Service, Chgo., 1968-70; practice gen. medicine specializing in family care Ill. Masonic Family Health Care Center, Chgo., 1970-72; physician Multiple Risk Factor Intervention Trial, Northwestern U., instr. dept. community health and preventive medicine; mem. staff Ill. Masonic Hosp.; clin. asso. dept. family practice Abraham Lincoln Sch. Medicine, U. Ill.; courtesy staff Louis A. Weiss Hosp. Bd. dirs. Lakeview Learning Center, Chgo. Recipient merit scholarship U. Mich. Med. Sch., 1962-66. Mem. Am., Ill. acads. family practice, Am. Med. Women's Assn., Alpha Epsilon Iota. Mem. Jewish religion. Club: Green Acres Country (Northbrook, Ill.). Home: 3535 W Ardmore Av Chicago IL 60659 Office: Suite 1421 122 S Michigan Av Chicago IL 60603

SEGO, ARLENE FRONTROTH (MRS. MICHAEL A. SEGO), educator; b. Cleve., Mar. 13, 1938; d. Henry John and Hazel Elizabeth (Kunkle) Frontroth; B.S., Indiana U. of Pa., 1959; M.Natural Scis., Ariz. State U., 1962; m. Michael A. Sego, July 4, 1974. Tchr., West High Sch., Cleve., 1959-61, head dept. math., 1962-66; asst. prof. math. Cuyahoga Community County, Parma, O., 1966-69, asso. prof., 1969-72, prof., 1972—, also head dept., faculty marshall, 1972. Program coordinator, dir. adult programs West High, Cleve., 1966-67, coordinator Head Start Program, 1966. Leader, Girl Scouts U.S.A., Cleve., 1962-64. Shell Merit fellow, 1965; Marth Holden Jennings scholar, 1963-64. Mem. Greater Cleve. (pres. 1966-67), Ohio, Nat. councils tchrs. math., Math. Assn. Am., Am. Assn. U. Profs., Ohio Assn. Community Jr. Colls. (sec. 1969-70), Assn. Women in Math., Am. Assn. U. Women, Alpha Sigma Alpha, Delta Kappa Gamma. Club: Zonta. Home: 938 Penny's Dr Brunswick OH 44212 Office: 7300 York Rd Parma OH 44130

SEGRE, ANN WHITE (MRS. ALFREDO SEGRE), filmstrip producer; b. N.Y.C.; d. David and Regina (Kolber) White; m. Alfredo Segre, Aug. 24, 1950. Pub. relations dir. J.B. Williams Co., N.Y.C., 1949-55; editor Jour. of Lifetime Living, Miami, Fla., 1955-60; pres. Ann Segre Assos., N.Y.C., 1961-69; pres. Audio-Visual Sch. Service, N.Y.C., 1969—. Editorial/promotion cons. Nat. Council on Illegitimacy, Am. Assn. Ret. Persons, Nat. Assn. Residents and Interns, others; columnist Scholastic mag. Author: four children's books; collaborator six books on food and nutrition. Office: 155 W 72d St New York City NY 10023

SEGURA, PEARL MARY, librarian, educator; b. Lafayette, La., June 12, 1909; d. Joseph Sidney and Celestine (Gutierrez) Segura; B.A., U. Southwestern La., 1930, postgrad., summer 1932, 42-43, 46-48, 51-52; B.S. in L.S., La. State U., 1941; postgrad summers Tulane U., 1931, Columbia, 1939, U. Ill., 1948, U. Houston, 1954. Tchr., librarian Indian Bayou (La.) High Sch., 1930-31; tchr. Maurice (La.) High Sch., 1931-33, tchr., librarian, 1933-41; asst. circulation librarian Stephens Meml. Library U. Southwestern La., Lafayette, 1941-44, acting reference librarian, 1944-46, reference librarian, 1946-62, librarian Jefferson Caffery La. room Dupre Library, 1962—, asso. prof. library sci., 1953—. Mem. Bicentennial Com., Lafayette. Mem. Am., Southwestern, La. library assns., Assn. Coll. and Reference Libraries, Spl. Libraries Assn., Am. Assn. U. Women, Nat. Trust for Historic Preservation, La., Attakapas hist. assns., La. Geneal. and Hist. Soc., La. Folklore Soc., La. Tchrs. Assn., Met. Opera Guild, Lafayette Community Concerts Assn., Lafayette Little Theatre, Lafayette Art Assn., Am. Camellia Soc., Am. Assn. for State and Local History, La. State U., U. Southwestern La. alumni assns., D.A.R. (1st chpt. vice regent 1968-71, state chmn. U.S.A. bicentennial com. 1967-71, chpt. chmn. 1968—), Attakapas Hist. Assn., U.D.C., Cath. Daus. Am., St. Ann's Guild, Am. Iris Soc., S.W. La. Poetry Soc., France Amerique de la Louisiane Acadienne, Phi Kappa Phi (pub. relations officer USL chpt. 1958—), Beta Phi Mu, Delta Kappa Gamma (pres. Alpha chpt. 1947-49), Kappa Kappa Iota (state handbook chmn. 1960-61, pres. Lambda conclave 1957-60). Democrat. Roman Catholic. Author: Acadians in Fact and Fiction: A Classified Bibliography, 1955. Contbr. articles to profl. jours. Home: 140 S Magnolia St Lafayette LA 70501

SEIBEL, MARION IRMA, state legislator; b. Fond du Lac, Wis., Jan. 31, 1922; d. Simon Albert and Irma Willemena (Spielberg) Arthur; grad. Fond du Lac High Sch. Bus. Sch., 1940; m. John Parshall Seibel, Sept. 11, 1943; children—Susan (Mrs. Douglass C. Day), John Henry III, Richard James. With OPA, 1941-43; campaign coordinator Del. Congl. Campaign, 1964; mgr. 2d dist. Republican Hdqrs., Wilmington, Del., 1965-68; mem. Del. Ho. of Reps. from 26th Dist., 1968—. Mem. regional com. consumer protection Council State Govts.; del. White House Conf. on Children and Youth, 1970. Republican committeewoman, 1957-70; pres. Rep. Woman's Club, Newark, Del., 1962. Bd. dirs. Del. Adolescent Program. Mem. League Women Voters. Methodist. Home: 20 Knickerbocker Dr Newark DE 19711 Office: Legislative Hall Dover DE 19901

SEIBERT, ISABELLE L. PRING (PSEUDONYM DENI), author; b. St. Louis, June 12, 1922; d. George Harry and Isabelle (McAdie) Pring; student U. Ill., 1939-41; B.A. cum laude, Washington U., St. Louis, 1943; postgrad. U. San Marcos, 1944; M.A., U. Del., 1965; m. Russell Jacob Seibert, Dec. 26, 1942; children—Michael, Donna, Lisa. Pres. Ruden, Kennett Square, Pa., 1962—; free lance writer of articles on travel, gardens, history and sci. appearing in N.Y. Times Garden Page, 1970—, Christian Sci. Monitor, Travel Mag., The Rotarian and House Beautiful. Bd. dirs. Health and Welfare Council of Chester County, Pa., 1964-68, Kennett Community Symphony Orchestra, 1967-70. Recipient Weymms Found. fellowship, 1965. Mem. Nat. League Am. Pen Women (pres. br. 1968-70, state pres. 1970-72), Pi Beta Phi. Home and office: Longwood Kennett Square PA 19348

SEIBERT, JANICE BOONE (MRS. GEORGE H. SEIBERT, JR.), lawyer; b. Mount Hope, W.Va., Dec. 8, 1915; student Averett Coll., 1932-34; A.B., W.Va. U., 1936, LL.B., 1938; m. George H. Seibert, Jr., July 18, 1939; children—Nancy Sue (Mrs. Carlyle D. Farnsworth), James E., Sally Ann. Admitted to W.Va. bar, 1938, practiced in Wheeling, 1942-43, 52—. Bd. dirs. Vis. Nurses Assn., 1963-66, 73—, pres. 1966. Mem. Nat. Assn. Women Lawyers, Am. Judicature Soc., Am., W.Va., Ohio County (mem. exec. com. 1969-71) bar assns., Pi Beta Phi. Presbyn. Club: Wheeling Woman's. Home: 1684 National Rd Wheeling WV 26003 Office: First National Bank Bldg Wheeling WV 26003

SEIBERT, LUCILLE CARTER (MRS. JOE EDDIE SEIBERT), univ. dean; b. Halls, Tenn., Nov. 2, 1939; d. William and Luella (Hudson) Carter; A.B in English, Tenn. State U., 1961, M.Ed., 1966, postgrad., 1968-71; m. Joe Eddie Seibert, Nov. 22, 1962; children—Michael, Ronald. Tchr. English Mt. Pisgah High Sch., Memphis, 1961-64, Wharton Jr. High Sch., Nashville, 1965, Pearl High Sch., Nashville, 1966-70; Madison High Sch., Nashville, 1970-71, guidance counselor, 1971-72; dean of women, Tenn. State U., Nashville, 1972—. Mem. Gov.'s Commn. for the Status of Women for State of Tenn. Mem. Nat., Tenn. edn. assns., Nat., Tenn. assns. of women deans, adminstrs. and counselors, Tenn., So. (mem. grad. liaison com. 1973-74) coll. personnel assns., Tenn., Middle Tenn. personnel and guidance assns., Morning Star Missionary Soc. (asst. sec. 1971-72), Alpha Kappa Alpha. Baptist. Asso. editor Pilgrim Progress. Home: 3816 Dunbar Dr Nashville TN 37207 Office: 3500 Centennial Blvd Nashville TN 37203

SEIBERT, SISTER MARY ANGELICE, educator; b. Louisville, Jan. 16, 1922; d. William Karl and Cathedrine A. (Schmidt) Seibert; B.S. summa cum laude, Ursuline Coll., 1947; M.S., Institutum Divi Thomae, 1950, Ph.D., 1952; Damon Runyon postdoctoral fellow St. Louis U., 1953-54. Tchr. Cath. elementary schs., Louisville, 1942-47; instr. chemistry and biology Ursuline Coll., Louisville, 1950, chmn. div. natural scis., 1952-65, dir. coll. relations and devel., 1960-62, acting pres., 1964-65, pres., 1965-68; Fulbright-Hays vis. lectr. U. Coll., Galway, Ireland, 1968-69; vis. prof. biochemistry Smith Coll., 1969-70; prof. chemistry, chmn.-div. allied med. scis. Jefferson Community Coll., Louisville, 1970—. Mem. Ky. Acad. Sci., Am. Chem. Soc., Ky. Sci. Tchrs. Assn. A.A.A.S., Ky. Chemistry Tchrs. Assn., Sigma Xi. Address: 3105 Lexington Rd Louisville KY 40206

SEIDE, MARILYN SUE (MRS. RAY SEIDE), psychologist; b. Bklyn., Dec. 25, 1930; d. Louis and Hannah Rose (Bistrong) Bernstein; B.A., Bennington Coll., 1952; M.A., New Sch. for Social Research, 1973; m. Ray Seide, Nov. 20, 1960; children—Jared David, Liam Evan. With Jewish Bd. of Guardians, N.Y.C., 1961-65; asst. for psychol. services Coney Island Mental Health Services, Bklyn., 1965-67; adminstrv. coordinator, researcher, children's mental health service Lincoln Hosp., Bronx, N.Y., 1967-70, with research and evaluation unit, dept. psychiatry, 1970-73; research asso., office children's services Office Ct. Adminstrn. State of N.Y., N.Y.C., 1973—. Mem. Am. Orthopsychiat. Assn. Home: 54 W 82nd St New York City NY 10024 Office: Office of Childrens Services 270 Broadway New York City NY 10007

SEIDEL, GLADYS LOUISE, civic worker; b. Henderson, Ky., Jan. 26, 1931; d. James H. and Hattie (Wood) Burns; student Evansville U., 1951-55; m. Allen J. Seidel, Oct. 15, 1949; children—Linda Kay, Allen Jett, Mary Louise. Owner, mgr. Seidels Garden Center, 1957-67; foreman Zeidler Floral Co., Evansville, Ind., 1967-69; pres. Henderson Altrusa Club, 1969—; v.p. Henderson County High Band Boosters, 1969-71, chmn. uniforms, 1967-70, chmn. benefit concers, shows and dinners, 1965—; vol. care for sick. Recipient certificate of appreciation Mayor of Henderson, 1973. Home: 1224 S Main St Henderson KY 42420

SEIDEL, JOAN BROUDE (MRS. ARNOLD SEIDEL), stock broker; b. Chgo., Aug. 16, 1933; d. Ned and Betty (Treiger) Broude; student Hunter Coll., 1950-51; B.A., U. Cal. at Los Angeles, 1954, postgrad., 1955; postgrad. N.Y. Inst. Finance, 1969; m. Arnold Seidel, Aug. 18, 1957; children—David M., Craig H. Tchr., counselor Los Angeles Unified Sch. Dist., 1955-59; tchr. Beverly Hills (Cal.) Unified Sch. Dist., 1968-70; stock broker Morton Seidel & Co., Inc., Los Angeles, 1970—, v.p., dir., 1974—. Mem. Los Angeles Mayor's Council for Internat. Visitors, 1968; Cal. Gov.'s appointee as ofcl. hostess for Luxembourg, 1966; mem. Citizen's Com. for Tax Over-ride, Beverly Hills, 1967-68; exec. com. Music Center Opera Assn., Los Angeles, 1968; pres. Vista Sch. P.T.A., Beverly Hills, 1967-69; mem. KCET, Ednl. TV, Los Angeles, 1969; v.p. Am. Field Service, Beverly Hills, 1968. Campaign chmn. Jack Paul Bd. Edn. Election, 1971. Recipient certificate of appreciation Beverly Hills Sch. Dist., 1968. Mem. Financial Analyst Soc., Assistance League of So. Cal., Opera Assos. (pres. 1968-69), Cal. Chamber Soc., League Women Voters, Friends of Library, Los Angeles C. of C., Phi Sigma Alpha. Club: Athletic (Los Angeles). Home: 419 S Camden Dr Beverly Hills CA 90212 Office: 458 S Spring St Los Angeles CA 90013

SEIDEN, ESTHER, educator; b. Ropczyce, Poland, Mar. 3, 1908; d. Menahem Mendel and Taube (Nussbaum) Seiden; Mag Phil., Stefan Batory U., Wilno, Poland, 1931; Ph.D., U. Cal. at Berkeley, 1949. Came to U.S., 1947, naturalized, 1956. Lectr., U. Cal. at Berkeley, 1949-50; asst. prof. statistics U. Buffalo (N.Y.), 1950-52; cons. UN Statis. Office, 1952; research asso. U. Chgo., 1952-54, asst. prof., 1953-54; asst. prof. Howard U., Washington, 1954-55; asst. prof. Northwestern U., Evanston, Ill., 1955-58, 59-61; lectr. Indian Statis. Edn. Center, also cons. Indian Statis. Inst., Calcutta, 1958-59; asso. prof. statistics Mich. State U., East Lansing, 1961-65, prof., 1966—; Fulbright vis. prof. U. Istanbul (Turkey), 1965-66; exchange scientist, USSR-U.S. Acad. Sci., Inst. Scis. at Novosibirsk, 1967. Fellow Inst. Math. Statistics; mem. Am. Math. Soc., Math. Assn. Am., London Math. Assn., Canadian Math. Soc., Sigma Xi. Home: 308 Michigan Av East Lansing MI 48823

SEIDL, CATHERINE CARLISLE (MRS. ALFRED L. SEIDL), therapist; b. Milw., Oct. 29, 1924; d. Colin Campbell and Frances Ellen (Wink) Carlisle; diploma in Occupational Therapy, Milw.-Downer Coll., 1947, B.S., 1946; m. Alfred L. Seidl, Mar. 3, 1951; children—Stephen, Mark, Charles, Ellen. Occupational therapist Cuyahoga County Nursing Home, Cleve., 1947-48, Wood (Wis.) VA Hosp., 1948-52, Milw. Jewish Convalescent Hosp., 1963-64, Hollywood (Fla.) Hills Nursing Home, 1964-73, Hollywood Meml. Hosp., 1965-67; dir. occupational therapy dept. Hollywood Pavilion, 1973—. Instr., Fla. Nursing Home Activity Dirs. Tng. Program, 1973. Vol., St. Coletta Day Sch. for Retarded Children, 1956-57; instr. Annunciation Confrat. Christian Doctrine, 1969—. Mem. Am., Fla. occupational therapy assns., St. Sebastian Christian Mothers (ways and means chmn. 1960-62). Home: 3301 SW 40th Av Hollywood FL 33023 Office: 1201 N 37th Av Hollywood FL 33021

SEIDL, JEAN ELAINE (MRS. RICHARD H. HAMILTON), physician; b. N.Y.C., Sept. 26, 1927; d. Frank Norbert and Jennie (Vavra) Seidl; B.A., Barnard Coll., 1946; M.D., N.Y. U., 1950; m. Richard H. Hamilton, Oct. 31, 1957; children—Elizabeth, Minard, Gordon. Intern Bellevue Hosp., N.Y.C., 1952-54, resident internal medicine, 1954-57; fellow in endocrinology N.Y. U. Coll. Medicine, 1957-58; practice medicine specializing in internal medicine, N.Y.C., 1958-63; asst. univ. physician N.Y. U. Student Health Service, Washington Square, N.Y., 1960-72; asst. prof. clin. medicine N.Y. U. Hosp. and Coll. Medicine, N.Y.C., 1958—. Diplomate Am. Bd. Internal Medicine. Mem. A.M.A., N.Y. State, New York County (mem. pub. health com. 1964—) med. socs. Presbyn. Home: 63 E 66th St New York City NY 10021 Office: 35 E 35th St New York City NY 10016

SEIDMAN, RUTH KERTZER (MRS. AARON SEIDMAN), librarian; b. St. Catherines, Ont., Can., May 29, 1938; d. Morris Norman and Julia (Hoffman) Kertzer; A.B., Pembroke Coll., 1960; M.A., Harvard, 1963; M.S., Case Western Res. U., 1968; m. Aaron Seidman, Sept. 7, 1958; children—Daniel Isaac, Joshua Jacob. Research asst. Assn. for Internat. Research, Inc., Cambridge, Mass., 1963-64; librarian Russian Research Center, Harvard, 1964-65; freelance worker library and research fields, 1965-68; librarian Region I, U.S. Environmental Protection Agy., 1970—. Mem. Fed. Library Com., 1974—. Mem. Spl. Libraries Assn., Phi Beta Kappa, Beta Phi Mu. Home: 22 Atherton Rd Brookline MA 02146

SEIFFERT, FAYE E., educator, civic worker; b. Litchfield, Minn., Mar. 10, 1936; d. Henry Ernest and Evelyn J. (Hawkinson) Seiffert; B.S. in Music Edn., Olivet Nazarene Coll., 1959; postgrad. U. N.M., U. Minn., U. Albuquerque; 1 son, Todd Michael. Vocal chmn. Wichert (Ill.) Elementary Sch., 1959-61, New London (Minn.) High Sch., 1961-62, Albuquerque Indian Schs., 1962-64; choral instr. Albuquerque Pub. Schs., 1967—; producer, narrator Albuquerque Pub. Schs. TV Music Program, 1973; choral dir. numerous chs., 1958-62; pvt. voice and piano tchr., 1959—; mezzo-soprano performer in numerous opera, oratorio and light opera prodns. Mem. prodn. staff Albuquerque Symphony, 1973-74, Albuquerque Little Theater, 1973—; mem. prodn. staff Albuquerque Civic Light Opera Assn., 1969—, make-up chmn., 1973-74, pub. relations chmn., 1973-74; accompanist Albuquerque Civic Chorus, 1961-65; active Nat. Diabetic Assn., N.M. Kidney Found., Women's Assn. for Albuquerque Symphony Orch., Albuquerque Civic Light Opera Assn.'s Amigos Bd., Albuquerque Red Cross, United Fund. Recipient Outstanding Tchr. award, 1968, 71, 73. Mem. N.E.A., Albuquerque Classroom Tchrs. Assn., Albuquerque Fedn. Tchrs., Theatre Guild, Inc., N.M. Opera Guild, Nat. Educators Music Commn., League Women Voters. Republican. Home: 5513 El Encanto NE Albuquerque NM 87110 Office: 4500 Comanche NE Albuquerque NM 87110

SEIJO, DEZAYAS ESTHER (MRS. HECTOR ZAYAS CHARDON), nutritionist; b. Arecibo, P.R.; d. Sergio and Celia (Tizol) Seijo; B.S., U. P.R., 1935; M.S., U. Chgo., 1938, Ph.D., 1944; m. Hector Zayas Chardon, July 3, 1948; children—Hector F. (dec.), Francisco, Luis Jose. Asst. dir. Home Demonstration, Extension Service, 1943-51; dir. Bur. Nutrition and Dietetics, P.R. Dept. Health, 1951-57; asso. prof. nutrition U. P.R., 1957-66; prof., 1966—, dir. Sch. Home Econs.; dir. Tng. Center Applied Nutrition Program in Latin Am., 1964. Pres. Govs. of P.R. Commn. Devel. Isolated Areas, 1959—; spl. nutrition cons. WHO/Pan Am. Health Orgn., 1965—; coordinator Gov. of P.R. Juvenile Delinquency Programs, 1964. Dir. Family Relationship Assn., 1962—, Coop. Met., 1953-57, 61—; sec. Dept. Health Credit Union, 1951-57; bd. dirs. U. P.R. Mem. P.R. Pub. Health Assn. (pres. 1955), Am., P.R. (pres. 1951), dietetic assns., P.R. Home Econ. Assn. (pres. 1953), P.R. Nutrition Com. (pres. 1945, 51), Alpha Delta Kappa. Author numerous articles profl. jours. Home: Vesta 831 Rio Piedras PR 00923

SEIPLE, COLETTE MORGAN, lawyer, assn. exec.; b. San Francisco, July 28, 1935; d. Thomas Ralph and Althea (Ball) Morgan; A.B. in Polit. Sci., U. Cal. at Berkeley, 1959; J.S.D., U. San Francisco, 1964; m. Jack B. Seiple, Jr., Aug. 17, 1969; 1 dau., Dorthea Anne. Admitted to Cal. bar, 1965; personal sec. to Patricia Nixon, Washington, 1960; employment mgr. H.C. Capwell Co., Oakland, Cal., 1961-62; practice law, Orinda and Walnut Creek, Cal., 1964-71; asst. to vice chancellor U. Cal. at Berkeley, 1971-72; exec. dir. U. Cal. Alumni Assn., 1972—. Del. nat. conf. women in economy Ladies Home Jour., 1972. Pres., Family Service Guild of Oakland, 1967-68, Oakland Repertory Theatre, 1969, Orinda C. of C., 1968-69, Jr. Aux. Goodwill Industries, 1971-72. Bd. dirs. Univ. YWCA, 1966-68, Contra Costa County Mental Health Assn., 1966-67, Home Health Counseling Service, 1966-67, United Bay Area Crusade, 1968, Oakland Symphony Guild, 1967-68; trustee Cal. Alumni Found. Recipient Rosalie Stern award U. Cal., 1969. U.S. Office Edn. fellow, 1972. Mem. Am. Bar Assn., Cal. State Bar, Cal. Trial Lawyers Assn., Mt. Diablo Bar Assn. (dir. 1968-70), Queens Bench, Alpha Delta Pi. Club: Little Jim (San Francisco). Home: 1 Montrose Rd Berkeley CA 94707 Office: Alumni House U Cal Berkeley CA 94720

SEITSIVE, LILLIAN PAULA (MRS. ROBERT EPSTEIN), physician; b. N.Y.C., May 19, 1906; d. Benjamin and Ida Seitsive; B.S., N.Y. U., 1926; M.D., Woman's Med. Coll. Pa., 1931; m. Morris Rood, June 16, 1934 (dec. Apr. 1960); children—Robert Paul, Madeline (Mrs. Elliott Taft); m. 2d, Robert Epstein, Feb. 1, 1969. Intern Coney Island Hosp., Bklyn., 1931-33; resident Riverdale Hosp., Bklyn., 1933-34; practice gen. medicine, Bklyn., 1934-53, Los Angeles, 1954—; mem. active staff Northridge Hosp., trustee, mem. exec. bd., 1965—. Hon. v.p. Bklyn. League Child Welfare; founder Music Center, Los Angeles; patron U. Judaism. Named Woman of Year Valley Beth Shalom, 1974. Fellow Acad. Psychosomatic Medicine, Acad. Geriatrics, Am. Acad. Family Physicians; mem. Am. Med. Women's Soc., Med. Women's Internat. Assn., Pan Am. Med. Women's Assn., World Med. Assn., A.M.A., Cal. Acad. Gen. Practice, Hadassah. Jewish religion (bd. govs. temple). Office: 8833 Reseda Blvd Northridge CA 91324

SEKLA, LAILA HABIB (MRS. FAHMY FARAG), physician; b. Cairo, Egypt, Aug. 23, 1931; d. Habib Selim and Isis Tewfick (Habib) Sekla; M.B. B.Ch., U. Alexandria (Egypt), 1957, D.T.M. and H., 1959, D.M., 1960; Ph.D., London Sch. Hygiene and Tropical Medicine, 1968; m. Fahmy Farag, May 29, 1972. Intern, Univ. Hosp., Alexandria, 1957-58, resident, 1958-60, clinician, 1960-64; mem. faculty medicine dept. parasitology and tropical medicine, demonstrator London Sch. Hygiene, 1964-68; research fellow Man. (Can.) Provincial Pub. Health Labs., Winnipeg, 1968—, assa dir. Mem. Canadian Med. Assn., Canadian Pub. Health Assn., Canadian Internat. Health and Tropical Medicine, Canadian Med. Microbiologists, Royal Soc. Tropical Medicine, Am. Assn. Tropical Medicine. Home: 65 Guelph St Winnipeg MB R3M 3A5 Canada Office: 770 Bannatyne St Winnipeg MB R3E 0W3 Canada

SELBY, CECILY CANNAN (MRS. HENRY M. SELBY), assn. exec.; b. London, Eng., Feb. 4, 1927; d. Keith and Catherine Anne Cannan; A.B. cum laude, Radcliffe Coll., 1946; Ph.D. in Phys. Biology, Mass. Inst. Tech., 1950; m. Henry M. Selby, Aug. 11, 1951; children—Norman, William, Russell. Teaching asst. in biology Mass. Inst. Tech., 1948-49; adminstrv. head virus study sect. Sloan-Kettering Inst., 1949-50, asst. mem. of Inst., 1950-55; research asso. Sloan-Kettering div. Cornell U. Med. Coll., 1953-55, also instr. microscopic anatomy, 1955-57; tchr. sci. Lenox Sch., N.Y.C., 1957-59, headmistress, 1959-72; nat. exec. dir. Girl Scouts U.S.A., N.Y.C., 1972—. Dir. Avon Products, Inc., RCA, NBC. Mem. adv. bd. Yorkville Youth Council. Pres., Headmistresses of East, 1970-71; dir. Nat. Assn. Ind. Schs., 1969-72; founder, chmn. N.Y. Ind. Schs. Opportunity Project, 1968-72; trustee N.Y. State Assn. Ind. Schs., 1966-72, Bklyn. Law Sch. Mem. Cum Laude Soc. (past chpt. pres., dist. regent), Sigma Xi. Clubs: Cosmopolitan (N.Y.C.); Westhampton Country (gov. 1969-73). Adv. editor Parents' mag.; mem. adv. com. Ladies Home Jour. Contbr. articles to profl. jours., chpt. to book. Office: 830 3d Av New York City NY 10022

SELBY, HAZEL DORIS BROWN, lawyer; b. Hampton Beach, N.H., Oct. 13, 1898; d. Frederick H. and M. Elizabeth (Brown) Brown; LL.B., Portia Law Sch., 1941; m. Oliver F. Selby, Oct. 9, 1919 (div. Oct. 1947); 1 son, Oliver Franklin. Admitted to Mass. bar, 1945; U.S. Dist. Ct., 1947, U.S. Supreme Ct. bar, 1950; clk. city treas. office, Haverhill, Mass., 1915-17; civilian sec.-specialist USAC, Washington, 1917-19; asso. law firm Wells and Hale, Haverhill, Mass., 1919-23, Hale, Sanderson, Byrnes and Morton, Boston, 1927—, office mgr., 1939—. Active A.R.C., U.S.O., World War II. Recipient service award Nat. Assn. Women Lawyers. Mem. Am., Mass.; Boston, Norfolk County, Quincy bar assns., Nat. (treas. 1949-57), Mass. assns. women lawyers, Bus. and Profl. Women's Club, Am. Legion Aux., Phi Delta Delta. Republican. Conglist. Home: 8 Merrymount Av Wollaston MA 02170 Office: 10 Post Office Sq Boston MA 02109

SELBY, MARJORIE LOUISE, county ofcl.; b. San Antonio, Feb. 11, 1913; d. Meyer Louis and Beatrice Bertha (Goodman) Collat; student U. Cal. at Berkeley, 1930-32; m. James Franklin Selby, Aug. 11, 1934 (dec. Jan. 1966); children—Sharon (Mrs. Francis Darsey Jr.), Robert, James Franklin. With Selby-Collat Co., Oakland, Cal., 1932-51; asst. county auditor Shawnee County, Topeka, 1959-66, county auditor, 1966-73, county financial adminstr., 1973—. Mem. Democratic Action Com., 1966—. Bd. dirs. Topeka Civic Theatre, 1967—, Shawnee County Employees Credit Union, 1966—; hon. chmn. James F. Selby Meml. Fund, 1966—; pres. elect Shawnee County Mental Health Assn., 1973—. Mem. Am. Bus. Women's Assn., Nat. Finance Officers' Assn. Home: 2920 Gage St Topeka KS 66614 Office: 200 E 7th St Topeka KS 66603

SELDEN, ELLEN JACOBI, artist; b. Cin., Mar. 30, 1921; d. Lester E. and Helen (Rothschild) Jacobi; A.B., Wilson Coll., 1943; m. Walter Selden, Aug. 12, 1944 (div. 1949); children—Peter W. (dec.), William Lester. Exhibited in one-man show Crespi Gallery, 1963, Berkshire Playhouse, Stockbridge, 1949, Compass Gallery, Nantucket, 1969, Pocker & Son, 1970, Main St. Gallery, Nantucket, 1971, 72; one man sculpture show Roko, 1967; exhibited in group shows Kenneth Taylor Gallery, Nantucket, 1950, 68—, Contemporary Arts Gallery, N.Y.C., 1949, 54, 61, 62, Art U.S.A., 1958, Positano Art Workshop, Italy, Ahda Ardst Gallery, N.Y.C., 1960, Allied Artists Am. 1959, Nat. Assn. Women Artists, 1960—, Bertuch Gallery, N.Y.C., 1962, Roko Gallery, 1966, Lobster Pot Gallery, 1968, Munson Gallery, Nantucket, Compass Gallery, Allied Artists, Audubon Artists, Winetraub Gallery, Emil Walters, Lever House; represented in permanent collections Galleria Schneider, Rome, Italy, Butler Art Inst., Wilson Coll., Dartmouth, Venice Artists Workshop; also pvt. collections; pvt. tchr. art, 1958—. Vol. occupational therapy art tchr. Montefiore Hosp., 1959-62; vol. Mt. Sinai Hosp., 1950-55; ambulance driver, A.R.C., 1942-44; chmn. art com. Montefiore Hosp., 1962—; mem. com. for Positano Art Workshop. Recipient prize Nat. Assn. Women Artists, 1970, Amelia Peabody award, 1973. Mem. Nantucket Artists Assn. (dir. 1972—). Home: 1185 Park Av New York City NY 10028

SELDON, MARY E. BYERS (MRS. NICHOLAS N. SELDON), educator; b. Ch'angch'un, China, Aug. 28, 1921; d. George and Helen (Kessler) Byers; student Judson Coll., 1939-41, Southwestern U., 1941-42; A.B., Ind. U., 1942, M.A., 1945, Ph.D., 1959; m. Nicholas N. Seldon, June 17, 1950; children—Henry Lee, Nicholas Alan, Mary Alexandra. Instr. history Judson Coll., Marion, Ala., 1943-44; instr. history Ind. U., Indpls., 1949-63, asst. prof., 1963-66, asso. prof., 1966-73, prof., 1973—. Mem. Am. Hist. Assn. Home: 6563 N Ferguson St Indianapolis IN 46220 Office: 925 W Michigan St Indianapolis IN 46202

SELDOWITZ, ESTELLE, govt. ofcl.; b. N.Y.C., Feb. 6, 1923; d. Samuel and Ida (Arluck) Seldowitz; B.S., Am. U., 1953. Internat. economist U.S. Dept. Commerce, Washington, 1952-61; med. economist USPHS, 1961-66; pub. health analyst, Children's Bur. Dept. Health, Edn. and Welfare, 1966-67, dep. dir. policy and standards div., med. services administrn., 1968—. Mem. U.S. delegation 4th round Tariff Negotiations, Geneva, Switzerland, 1956. Mem. Am. Econ. Assn., Soc. Govt. Economists. Contbr. articles to profl. publs. Home: 2800 Quebec St NW Washington DC 20008 Office: Dept Health Edn and Welfare Washington DC 20201

SELIGSOHN, NANCY, artist; b. N.Y.C., Mar. 26, 1929; d. Samuel and Stella (Winter) Seligsohn; student R.I. State Coll., summer 1947, U. Ia., 1947-49, Columbia, summer 1949, N.Y. U., 1949-50, Art Students League, 1950-52, Beaux Art Sch., Paris, France, 1950, also pvt. study. Asso. art dir. Chem. Week, McGraw Hill Co., N.Y.C., 1952-53; art dir. pattern promotions McCall's, N.Y.C., 1954-56; free-lance illustrator, designer, painter, tchr., 1956—, including This Is Goggle, 1955; Let's Go to a Bakery, 1956; Pippi Longstocking, 1959; Pippi Goes Aboard, 1960; Mechido, Aziza and Ahmed, 1969. Guest lectr. Grace Avenue Sch., Gt. Neck, N.Y., 1961, U. Miami (Fla.), 1965, Birch Sch., Merrick, N.Y., 1966, Flower Hill Sch., Huntington, N.Y., 1972; pvt. tchr. art, also tchr. Lenox Hill Neighborhood House, N.Y.C., 1970—; one-woman show, N.Y.C.,

1974; exhibited in group shows Ligoa Duncan Gallery, N.Y.C., 1956, at Nat. Arts Club, N.Y.C., 1960, Greenes Gallery, N.Y.C., 1961, Viscaya Art Exhbn., Miami, 1965, Nat. Council Jewish Women Exhbn., 1970; represented in permanent collections Loring Gallery, N.Y.C., Tenafly Gallery, N.Y.C., Steffans Gallery, N.Y.C., Picture House, N.Y.C., also in pvt. collections. Mem. Graphic Artists Guild, Children's Book Council, Friends of Central Park. Address: 145 E 15th St New York City NY 10003

SELLAND, MABELLE MAASEN (MRS. HAROLD V. SELLAND), assn. exec.; b. Chgo., Mar. 7, 1926; d. Sam and Frances (Casey) Maasen; B.A., Fresno State Coll., 1950; M.A., Cal. State U., 1971; m. Harold V. Selland, June 17, 1951; children—Julie, Eric, Bethany. Social worker Fresno County (Cal.) Welfare Dept., 1951, Ore. Dept. Social Welfare, Albany, 1951-53, Fresno County (Cal.) Dept. Social Welfare, 1953-55; teaching asst. Fresno (Cal.) State Coll., 1969; adminstr. Fresno County Hist. Soc., 1973—. Instr. U. Cal. at Santa Cruz Extension, 1973. Pres. People to People, Fresno, 1962-64; chmn. Fresno-Maulmein Sister City Com., 1962-66. Recipient awards for meritorious achievement in Town Affiliation Program, Nat. League of Cities, 1964, 66. Mem. Assn. Asian Studies, Phi Kappa Phi. Home: 1483 E Portals Fresno CA 93710 Office: 7160 W Kearney Fresno CA 93706

SELLE, MARY ETTA S. BROOKES (MRS. WILBUR A. SELLE), educator; b. Bellefonte, Pa.; d. William J. and Velta (Williams) Brookes; B.A., U. So. Cal., 1937, M.A., 1938, Ph.D., 1960; student U. Hawaii, 1949-50, U. Cal. at Los Angeles, 1966-67; m. Wilbur A. Selle, Dec. 30, 1964. Tchr., San Bernardino (Cal.) High Sch., 1938-40; tchr. fgn. lang., head dept. El Monte (Cal.) Union High Sch., 1940-56; asso. dean students Cal. State Poly. Coll. at San Luis Obispo, 1956-61; dean of women Cal. State Poly. U. at Pomona, 1961—. Mem. Am., Cal. State, Western psychol. assns., Nat. Assn. Women Deans and Counselors, Cal. Assn. Women Adminstrs. and Counselors, Cal. State Marriage Counseling Assn., Am. Personnel and Guidance Assn., Am. Coll. Personnel Assn., Phi Mu. Mem. Order Eastern Star. Home: 4545 Perham Rd Corona del Mar CA 92625 Office: 3801 W Temple St Pomona CA 91768

SELLECK, CATHERINE JEAN YOUNG (MRS. WILLIAM ROBERT SELLECK), systems co. exec.; b. Los Angeles, Oct. 2, 1933; d. John Parke and Florence (Hensel) Young; B.A. in Econs., Occidental Coll., 1955; m. William Robert Selleck, Sept. 8, 1957. With IBM Corp., Los Angeles, 1955—, systems service rep., 1955-56, instr. computers, 1957-61, systems engr., 1961-63, systems engring. mgr., 1963-67, design and installation mgr. Western region, 1968, field services mgr., 1969-71, br. mgr., 1972-73, mgr. market support, Mpls. area, 1974—. Recipient Achievement award Soroptimist Club Los Angeles, 1968. Mem. Asso. Women Execs. (pres. 1969-70), Friends Occidental Coll., Zeta Tau Zeta. Home: 6931 Mark Terrace Circle Edina MN 55435 Office: 7900 Xerxes Av Bloomington MN 55434

SELLERS, PATRICIA BAILY, lawyer; b. Oklahoma City, Sept. 23, 1937; d. Louis Elmer and Wanda Lorraine (Patrick) Baily; student U. Okla., 1953-56; LL.B., Oklahoma City U., 1969; children—David Morris Dunlap, Michael Stephen Dunlap. Admitted to Okla. bar, 1969; mem. firms Chiaf & Holmes, Oklahoma City, 1968-69, Rinehart, Cooper & Stewart, Oklahoma City, 1969-70, Sellers & Sellers, Oklahoma City, 1971-73; asst. city atty., Oklahoma City, 1973-74; atty. Sellers & Sellers, Sapulpa, Okla., 1974—. Mem. women's com. Oklahoma City Symphony, 1959-71; mem. Lyric Theatre Guild, 1965-71, Tulsa Opera Chorus, 1972-73. Mem. Am. Bus. Women's Assn., Am., Okla., Creek County (v.p. 1973) bar assns., Okla. Trial Lawyers Assn., L.E.G.A.L., Canterbury Choral Soc., Alpha Delta Pi, Iota Tau Tau. Republican. Episcopalian. Clubs: Women's Gridiron, Junior Hospitality (Oklahoma City). Home: 11004 Redbud Lane Oklahoma City OK 73120 Office: Municipal Bldg 200 N Walker Oklahoma City OK 73102

SELLS, MARGALEE ANN, psychologist; b. Admire, Kan., Mar. 15, 1928; d. Roy Sylvester Sells and Edna Juanita (Hembree) Ryan; A.A., No. Okla. Coll., 1947; B.Mus. Edn., Phillips U., Enid, Okla., 1950; M.S., Kan. State Tchrs. Coll., 1959; edn. specialist in Sch. Psychology, 1970. Band and music dir., Kan., Colo., 1950-57; counselor Hastings (Neb.) Jr. High Sch., 1958-65, Robinson (Kan.) Jr. High, 1966-69; sch. psychologist Brown County Spl. Edn. Coop., Horton, Kan., 1970—. Cons., Kanza Mental Health Clinic, Hiawatha, Kan., 1967-70. Mem. N.E.A., Kan., Brown County edn. assns., Nat. (charter), Kan. (exec. com. 1972) assns. sch. psychologists, Am. Assn. Learning Disabilities, Kan. Assn. Children with Learning Disabilities, Nat., Kan., Brown County (chmn. screening com.) assns. retarded children, Nat., Kan., Brown County (pres. 1973-74), assns. mental health. Mem. Ch. of Nazarene. Home: Box 216 Robinson KS 66532 Office: Brown County Spl Edn Coop 1st and Kickapoo St Hiawatha KS 66434

SELSAM, MILICENT ELLIS (MRS. HOWARD SELSAM), author; b. Bklyn.; d. Israel and Ida (Abrams) Ellis; B.A., Bklyn. Coll., 1932; M.A., Columbia, 1934; m. Howard Selsam, Sept. 1, 1936; 1 son, Robert. Recipient Eva L. Gordon award, Am. Nature Study Soc., 1964; Four-Leaf Clover award Lucky Book Club, 1973. Mem. Am. Nature Study Soc., Authors Guild. Author, editor numerous books, including editor Stars, Mosquitoes and Crocodiles, The American Travels of Alexander von Humboldt (Gold Medal award Boys Club Am. 1962), 1962; Lets Get Turtles, 1965; (with J. Bronowski) Biography of an Atom, 1965 (Thomas A. Edison award 1965); Animals as Parents, 1965; Benny's Animals and How He Put Them In Order (Boys Club Am. jr. book award), 1966; How to be a Nature Detective, 1966; When An Animal Grows, 1966; Bug That Laid the Golden Eggs, 1967; How Animals Tell Time, 1967; Milkweed, 1967; Questions and Answers About Ants, 1967; Maple Tree, 1968; The Tiger, 1969; Peanut, 1969; Hidden Animals, 1969; The Tomato and Other Fruit Vegetables, 1970; Egg to Chick, 1970; The Carrot and Other Root Vegetables, 1971; Vegetables from Stems and Leaves, 1972; More Potatoes, 1972; How Puppies Grow, 1972; Is This a Baby Dinosaur, 1972; A First Look at Leaves, 1972; A First Look at Fish, 1972; A First Look at Mammals, 1973; The Apple and Other Fruits, 1973; Questions and Answers about Horses, 1973; A First Look at Birds, 1974; Bulbs, Corms and Such, 1974. Juvenile Sci. editor Walker & Co. Pubs. Home: 100 W 94th St New York City NY 10025 Office: 720 Fifth Ave New York City NY 10019

SELTZ, BERNICE SILVERSTEIN (MRS. SAMUEL SELTZ), social worker; b. Cin., May 22, 1915; d. Herman and Anna (Bloch) Silverstein; B.A., U. Cin., 1935, certificate in pub. welfare adminstrn., 1937; student Columbia, 1946; m. Samuel Seltz, Oct. 1, 1948. Case worker Aid to Dependent Children, Cin., 1935-37, 42, United Jewish Social Agys., Cin., 1937-40; employment counselor Nat. Youth Adminstrn., Cin., 1942-43; parent cons. Emergency Child Care Program, Cin., 1943-44; cons. Lanham Day Care Center Program, Cin., 1945; vocational counselor Cin. Pub. Schs., 1945-47; exec. sec. Family-Child Welfare Div., Council Social Agys., Cin., 1947-55; asst. exec. sec. Community Health and Welfare Council, Cin., 1955-69; exec. sec. Family Life Fedn. Community Health and Welfare Council, Cin., 1955-65; exec. sec. Ohio Com. for 1970 White Ho. Conf. on Children and Youth, Cin., 1969—. Mem. adv. com. Hamilton County Welfare Dept., 1967-70, planning coordinator, 1971—. Bd. dirs. Ohio Citizens Council, 1963-69. Mem. Nat. Assn. Social Workers, Acad. Certified Social Workers. Contbr. articles to profl. jours. Home: 5300 Hamilton Av Cincinnati OH 45224 Office: 628 Sycamore St Cincinnati OH 45202

SELTZER, RUTH JOAQUIN, ret. banker; b. Fremont, Neb., June 18, 1909; d. William Stephan and May Luella (Harber) Seltzer; grad. Sch. Banking of South, La. State U., 1962. With First Nat. Bank, Paducah, Ky., 1927-31; with Peoples First Nat. Bank & Trust Co., Paducah, 1931-74, v.p. 1957-74. Adv. council mem. project VIII, Paducah Bd. Edn., 1971-72, adv. council mem. distributive edn., 1971. Mem. Urban Renewal Bd., 1965-68; chmn. Citizens Adv. Com., 1967; co-chmn. Paducah Summer Festival, 1967-69, gen. chmn. 1970-71; mem. Paducah Mayor's Commm. Cable TV, 1973. Bd. dirs. McCracken County chpt. A.R.C., 1958-63, 69-74, vice chmn. 1968—, mem. Eastern area adv. council, 1969-72, mem. nat. conv. planning com., 1969—; bd. dirs., sec. Met. Community Council, 1967-71; mem. Paducah-McCracken County Riverport Authority, 1972-74. Recipient Spearhead award C. of C., 1971; named Woman of the Year Bus. and Profl. Women's Club, 1972. Mem. Nat. Assn. Bank Women (Ky. state chmn. 1960-61, regional vice chmn. 1964-65), Ch. Women United (organized night group, pres. 1965-66). Mem. Christian Ch. (deaconess 1955-57, 69—). Home: 2712 Washington St Paducah KY 42001

SELTZER, VIVIAN, child psychologist, marriage counselor; b. Mpls., May 27, 1931; d. Aaron and Hannah (Chazanow) Center; B.A. summa cum laude, U. Minn., 1951; M.S.W., U. Pa., 1953; postgrad. Bryn Mawr Coll., 1964-66, 72—; m. William Seltzer, Aug. 30, 1953; children—Jonathan, Francesca, Aeryn. Caseworker Sleighton Farm Sch. for Girls, Phila., 1951-53, Children's Aid Soc. Phila., 1954-55; family counselor Jewish Family and Children's Service, Miami, Fla., 1956-60, Jewish Family Service, Phila., 1965-68; partner Marriage and Family Therapy Assos., child guidance and marital counselling, Jenkintown, Pa., 1970—. Adv. council Foster Home Services, Health and Welfare Council, Phila., 1973-74; lectr. family life edn., 1965—. Cons. Green Tree Sch. Emotionally Disturbed Children, Phila., 1970—; mem. commn. on Jewish Edn., Phila., 1973—; bd. overseers Gratz Coll., Phila., 1971—, chmn. sch. observation and practice div. community services, 1973—, chmn. subcom. accreditation, 1973—; admissions com. Reconstructionist Coll., 1973—. Fellow Soc. Clin. Social Work; mem. Nat. Assn. Social Workers (mem. div. practice and knowledge 1968-69; chmn. family and childrens council 1968-70, chmn. nominating com. family and childrens council 1969-70, chmn. research com. increased participation community users health and welfare services 1969-70), Acad. Certified Social Workers, Internat. Transactional Analysis Assn., Am. Assn. Marriage and Family Counsellors (clin. mem.), Nat. Council Family Relations, Pa. Psychol. Assn., Otto Rank Soc., Jean Piaget Soc., Phi Beta Kappa. Home: 1042 Pheasant Rd Rydal PA 19046 Office: 179 Washington Lane Jenkintown PA 19046

SELVIG, JETTIE COLEEN PIERCE (MRS. ROLF STANLEY SELVIG, SR.), lawyer; b. Bee Branch, Ark., Dec. 16, 1932; d. Jefferson Davis and Ruba (Bivens) Pierce; LL.B., Ark. Law Sch., 1954; postgrad. San Francisco Law Sch., 1960, Lincoln U., 1961; m. Rolf Stanley Selvig, Jan. 27, 1962; children—Rolf S., Erik K., John L. Admitted to Ark. bar, 1953, Cal. bar, 1961, U.S. Supreme Ct. bar, 1969; mem. staff Ark. Atty. Gen., 1952-54; legal sec., San Francisco, 1958-61; asso. firm Belli, Ashe, Ellison & Choulos, San Francisco, 1961—. Named Countess of Pulaski by County Judge of Pulaski County, Ark. Mem. Nat. Assn. Women Lawyers (nat. treas. 1965-67, nat. pres. 1969-70), Cal. Applicant's Atty.'s Assn., Queen's Bench (dir. 1972, v.p. 1974), Ark. Assn. Women Lawyers, Am., Cal. San Francisco bar assns., Am., Cal. trial lawyers assns., Lawyers Club San Francisco, Judicature Soc., Women's Equity Action League (treas. Cal. div. 1971-72, pres. 1973). Club: Commonwealth of Cal. Home: 469 Molino Av Mill Valley CA 94941 Office: 722 Montgomery St San Francisco CA 94111

SEMANS, CATHERINE WICHERN BERG (MRS. FRANK MERRICK SEMANS), educator; b. Marletta, O., Nov. 27, 1908; d. Phillip Theobald and Ida F. (Wichern) Berg; A.B., Ohio State U., 1929; M.A., 1933; postgrad. Western Res. U., 1947-48, Ohio U., 1953-58; m. Frank Merrick Semans, Sept. 6, 1928; children—Ruth Merrick (Mrs. Irving W. Wood), Patricia Berg (Mrs. Louis M. Meier, Jr.). Asso. prof. psychology Youngstown (O.) U., 1936-44, dean women, 1942-44; with Family Service Soc., Youngstown, 1945-46; mem. faculty Hiram Coll., 1946-47; psychologist Woodside Hosp., Youngstown, 1947-48, St. Joseph Mercy Hosp., Sioux City, Ia., 1949-52; psychologist Athens (O.) State Hosp., 1952-62, Southeastern Ohio Guidance Center, Athens, 1962-63; mem. faculty Ohio U., Athens, 1963—, lectr., asst. chmn. psychology, 1963-73, asst. chmn. dept., 1967-71, chmn. emerita, 1973—. Mem. Am., Midwestern, Ohio, Southeastern Ohio psychol. assns., Unitarian Fellowship of Athens, Am. Civil Liberties Union, Common Cause, Audubon Soc., Wilderness Soc., Psi Chi. Home: 1 Patton St Athens OH 45701

SEMEL, RITA ROHER, religious assn. ofcl.; b. N.Y.C., Nov. 15, 1921; d. Harry and Henrietta (Silverstein) Roher; B.A., Barnard Coll., 1941; m. Max Semel, Sept. 26, 1942; children—Elisabeth, Jane (dec.). Reporter, San Francisco Chronicle, 1944-45; asst. editor Jewish Bull., San Francisco, 1945-47; publicity dir. Jewish Welfare Fund, San Francisco, 1947-48; free lance publicity, pub. relations, San Francisco, 1947-64; coordinator San Francisco Conf. Religion, Race and Social Concerns, 1964—; asso. dir. San Francisco Jewish Community Relations Council, 1968—, bd. dirs., Jewish Community Center, 1964-68; pres. Family Service Agy., San Francisco, 1974—. Bd. dirs. Am. Jewish Congress, No. Cal., 1964—, Family Service Agy. San Francisco, 1972—. Recipient Stephen S. Wise award Am. Jewish Congress, 1970, Honor certificate City and County San Francisco, 1970. Mem. League Women Voters. Jewish religion. Home: 928 Castro St San Francisco CA 94114 Office: San Francisco Conf Religion Race and Social Concerns 583 Market St San Francisco CA 94105

SEMMONS, MARTHA BETTY, lawyer; b. Cin., July 12, 1916; d. Herman and Florence (Stein) Semmons; B.A., U. Cin., 1936, LL.B., 1939. With Farm Security Adminstrn., U.S. Dept. Agr., 1942-44; admitted to Ohio bar, 1939; with Paxton & Seasongood, Cin., 1944—, partner, 1967—. Mem. Cin., Ohio bar assns. Home: 2444 Madison Rd Cincinnati OH 45208 Office: Central Trust Tower Cincinnati OH 45202

SEMROW, ELLEN HARTLEV, research inst. exec.; b. Chgo.; d. Louis and Julie Frederika (Pedersen) Hartlev; B.S., Ia. State U., 1941; 1 son, Harry Herbert. Home economist soya div. Glidden Co., 1943-44; asst. dir. Hotpoint, Inc., 1948-50; dir. home econs. Nat. Assn. Margarine Mfrs., 1950-51; dir. nutrition and edn. and consumer services depts. Am. Inst. Baking, Chgo., 1951-73, pres., 1973—. Recipient Distinguished Service award Coll. Home Econs., Ia. State U., 1971. Mem. Am. Home Econs. Assn., Home Economists in Bus. (chmn. Chgo. chpt. 1952-53), Chgo. Nutrition Assn., Phi Kappa Phi, Omicron Nu, Iota Sigma Pi. Club: Zonta (Chgo.). Home: 4937 Montana St Chicago IL 60639 Office: 400 E Ontario St Chicago IL 60611

SENDERS, VIRGINIA LOFTUS (MRS. JOHN W. SENDERS), psychologist, educator; b. N.Y.C., Apr. 21, 1923 d. Frank R. and Ruth A. (Russell) Loftus; A.B. magna cum laude, Mt. Holyoke Coll., 1943; A.M., Radcliffe Coll., 1945, Ph.D., 1947; m. John W. Senders, June 30, 1945; children—Warren Russell, Stefan John. Instr. psychology Wellesley (Mass.) Coll., 1947-50; asso. prof. psychology, also dir. aviation psychology lab. Antioch Coll., Yellow Springs, O., 1950-56; lectr. psychology U. Minn., 1957-62, co-ordinator and co-dir. women's continuing edn. program, 1960-62; asso. dir. New Eng. Bd. Higher Edn., 1963-66; prof. psychology Simmons Coll., Boston, also dir. career planning and counseling center, 1966-68; fellow in psychology McLean Hosp., Belmont, Mass., and Brandeis U., Waltham, Mass., 1968-70; prof. psychology Mass. State Coll., Framingham, 1970—; vis. prof. psychology U. Toronto (Ont., Can.), 1973-74. Mem. edn. com. Pres. Commn. Status of Women, 1962-64; cons., lectr. groups women's edn. Recipient Woman of Conscience award Nat. Council Women of U.S., N.Y.C., 1965. Mem. Am., New Eng., Eastern, Mass. psychol. assns., Psychonomic Soc., Am. Assn. U. Profs., Mt. Holyoke Alumnae Assn. Author: Measurement and Statistics, 1958. Contbr. articles to profl. jours. Home: Conant Rd RFD Lincoln MA 01773 Office: Framingham State Coll Framingham Center MA 01701

SENEGAL, PHYLLIS JEAN (MRS. CHARLES SENEGAL), assn. exec., lawyer; b. Cleve., Apr. 28, 1930; d. John Benson and Mildred Geraldine (Hoffman) Howell; student Western Res. U., 1950-52; LL.B. Cleve. Marshall Law Sch., 1966; m. Charles Senegal, June 26, 1968; children—Gregg Spencer, Gary Spencer, Guy Spencer. Admitted to Ind. bar, 1967; asso. F. Lawrence Anderson, Gary, Ind., 1967-68; asst. city atty., Gary, 1967-68, city atty., 1968-69; dir. Legal Aid Soc., Gary, 1969—. Mem. Nat., Am., Ind., Gary bar assns., Am. Trial Lawyers Assn., Am. Assn. U. Women, N.A.A.C.P., League Women Voters, Urban League Gary. Home: 454 McKinley St Gary IN 46404 Office: 31 E 5th Av Gary IN 46402

SENGENBERGER, KATHLEEN JANE (MRS. DAVID GORDON SENGENBERGER), TV producer; b. Portland, Ore., June 13, 1942; d. Howard Emmett and Jane (Lowe) Nealond; B.A., U. Ore., 1964; m. David Gordon Sengenberger, Nov. 1, 1969. Production asst. J. Walter Thompson Co., N.Y.C., 1964-66; traffic coordinator D'Arcy, Inc., San Francisco, 1967; TV producer KATU-TV, Portland, Ore., 1967-71; TV film producer and writer U. Ore. Med. Sch., Portland, 1971—. Instr. advt. Mt. Hood Community Coll., Gresham, Ore., 1972, mem. TV adv. bd. 1972-73. Bd. dir. Am. Cancer Soc., 1969-71; trustee Nat. Psoriasis Found. Mem. Women in Communications (gen. chmn. nat. conv. 1973), P.E.O. (recording sec. 1969-71), Delta Delta Delta, Gamma Alpha Chi. Clubs: Altrusa (recording sec. Portland 1971); Metro Women's (membership chmn. Portland 1973—). Home: 12935 NE Stanton Portland OR 97230

SENGSTACKE, MYRTLE E., former pub. co. exec., civic worker; ed. Los Angeles Sch. Law and Bus. Adminstrn.; m. John H. Sengstacke, July 8, 1939; children—John H., Robert A., Lewis W. Former exec. sec. bd. dirs. Robert S. Abbott Pub. Co., Chgo., now exec. v.p. bd. Mem. Ill. Adoption Information Service, Women's div. Crusade of Mercy, Chgo. Women's div. United Negro Coll. Fund; treas. Defender Charities; mem. Friends Provident Hosp.; mem. City assos. Women's Bd. Art Inst. Chgo.; founding mem. Women's Scholarship Assn. Roosevelt U.; mem. Chgo. Sch. Arch. Found., Chgo. Lyric Opera Guild, Mus. Contemporary Art, YWCA Women's Recognition Com. Bd. dirs. Chgo. council Girl Scouts U.S.A. Mem. Friends Chgo. Pub. Library, Girl Friends, Inc., Northeasterners, Chgo. Council Fgn. Relations, TV sta. WTTW, Nat. Council Negro Women, Am. Assn. Media Women. Mem. Women in Rotary. Address: 601 E 32nd St Chicago IL 60616

SENNETT, BETH ANNE (MRS. JORDAN AVERY SENNETT), occupational therapist; b. Milw., Mar. 2, 1947; d. Nathan and Catherine (Flox) Wahlberg; B.S., Tufts U., 1969; m. Jordan Avery Sennett, July 14, 1969; 1 son, Ethan David. Staff occupational therapist Mass. Gen. Hosp., Boston, 1969-70; dir. occupational therapy in rehab. services Middlesex County Hosp., Waltham, Mass., 1970-71; dir. occupational therapy spinal cord injury unit, dir. students VA Hosp., Cleve., 1971-73. Mem. Fed. VA Women's Speaker Bd., 1971-72. Mem. Am. Occupational Therapy Assn., Archaeological Assn. Am., House Officers Wives Assn. Home: Iroquois Apts 111 Old Hickory Blvd Nashville TN 37221

SENS, LEE ANNA, occupational therapist; b. Mobile, Ala., July 30, 1940; d. Charles Anthony and Mary Nell (Alford) Sens; student, Belhaven Coll., 1958-60; B.A., Samford U., 1962; advanced degree occupational therapy, Tex. Womans U., 1966, M.A., 1970. Jr. teenage program dir. YWCA, Jacksonville, Fla., 1962-63; supr. occupational therapy, male service, Central La. State Hosp., Pineville, 1966-67; chief, occupational therapy, 1967-68; chief, occupational therapy dept. VA Hosp., Shreveport, La., 1969; cons. occupational therapy Northeast La. U., Monroe, 1969-70, curriculum dir., asst. prof. occupational therapy, 1970-74, asso. prof., 1974—. Mem. Northeast La. Regional Health Planning Council, Monroe, 1970—, mem. rehab. com. 1972—; merit badge counselor Boy Scouts Am., Monroe, La., 1972-73. Rehab. Services Adminstrn. Dept. Health, Edn. and Welfare grantee, 1970. Mem. Am., La. occupational therapy assns., Kappa Pi, Pi Theta Epsilon. Home: 1203 Filhiol Monroe LA 71201

SENSENBRENNER, JUDITH ANN LAUBSCHER (MRS. LYLE LEE SENSENBRENNER), physician; b. Lock Haven, Pa., Feb. 27, 1941; d. Bruce Edward Laubscher and Norma Katherine (Quigg) Laubscher Winter; B.S., Bucknell U., 1963; M.D., Johns Hopkins, 1967; m. Lyle Lee Sensenbrenner, July 2, 1966; children—John Theodore, Eric Bruce. Intern, pediatrics Balt. City Hosp., 1968-69; fellow med. genetics Johns Hopkins Hosp., Balt., 1970-72, asst. in medicine, out-patient dept., 1972—. Mem. Balt. Symphony Orch. Chorus. Mem. Phi Beta Kappa, Alpha Lambda Delta, Phi Sigma, Alpha Sigma Alpha. Democrat. Roman Catholic. Home: Evna Rd Box 245 Parkton MD 21120

SENSENICH, ILA JEANNE, magistrate; b. Pitts., Mar. 6, 1939; d. Louis E. and Evelyn M. (Harbourt) Sensenich; B.A., Westminster Coll., 1961; J.D., Dickinson Sch. Law, 1964. Admitted to Pa. bar, 1964; asso. Stewart, Belden, Sensenich & Herrington, Greensburg, Pa., 1964-70; first asst. pub. defender Westmoreland County, Pitts., 1970-71; U.S. magistrate Western Dist. Pa., Pitts., 1971—. Lectr. legal topics U. Pitts., 1967, 70, Seton Hill Coll., 1970, Westmoreland Community Coll., 1972. Mem. Friends of Mus., Westmoreland County Mus. Art, Pitts., 1965—. Bd. dirs., legal adviser Westmoreland Community Concerts, Inc., 1966-71. Mem. Am., Pa. (sec. young lawyers sect. 1968), Westmoreland County, Alleghany County bar assns., Jud. Conf. Third Jud. Circuit U.S. Club: Pittsburgh Ski. Home: 415 Bigham St Apt 36 Pittsburgh PA 15211 Office: US Post Office and Courthouse Pittsburgh PA 15219

SENTNER, MARY STEELE (MRS. DAVID SENTNER), writer; b. Mount Olive, N.C.; d. William Calvin and Kate (Southerland) Steele; student Peace Coll., Raleigh, N.C., 1917-19; B.Lit. Columbia Sch. Journalism; 1 dau., Joyce (Mrs. Raymond Glennon Daly, Jr.). Reporter, Goldsboro News-Argus, N.C., 1920-23; writer King Features, N.Y.C., 1923-25; fashion writer N.Y. Evening World, 1925;

book reviewer 20th Century Fox, London, Eng., 1935-37; Washington rep. Good Housekeeping mag., 1956—; owner research bur., Washington, 1953-56. Mem. Am. Newspaper Women's Club. Presbyn. Author: Hollywood Comet, 1937. Address: 2601 Woodley Pl NW Washington DC 20008

SENZ, MARSHA ROBERTS (MRS. HERBERT SENZ), editor; b. N.Y.C., June 1, 1937; d. Samuel A. and Sarah (Alpern) Roberts; student Cornell U., 1955-57; B.A., Douglass Coll., 1959; m. Herbert Senz, July 14, 1957; children—Lisa, Michael. Editor, pub. Somerset Spectator (N.J.), 1969—. Recipient Distinguished Service award Jr. C. of C., 1971. Mem. League Women Voters (pres. 1967-69), N.J. Press Assn., Franklin Twp. C. of C. Home: 16 Kingsbridge Rd Somerset NJ 08873 Office: 900 Hamilton St Somerset NJ 08873

SERGIO, LISA, broadcaster, journalist, lectr.; b. Florence, Italy, Mar. 17, 1905; d. Agostino and Margaret (Fitzgerald) S.; ed. privately; L.H.D., Keuka Coll., 1963; LL.D., St. Mary's Coll., Notre Dame, Ind., 1966, Valparaiso U., 1970. Came to U.S., 1937, naturalized, 1944. Asst. editor, then editor Italian Mail, Florence, 1922-27; free-lance writer, 1928-30; exec. sec., bibliographer Assn. Mediterranean studies, Rome, Italy, 1930-32; initiator first fgn. lang. radio service, Rome, 1932-37; moderator radio programs, commentator NBC, N.Y.C., 1937-39, ABC, N.Y.C., 1940-47; lectr., condr. European tours, 1947-50; lectr., New Eng. area, 1950-55; editor Worldaround Press, Woodstock, Vt., 1955-58; lectr., commentator Frontiers of Faith series NBC-TV, New Nations of Africa, ABC-TV, 1959-60; Danforth vis. lectr. Assn. Am. Colls., 1960-71; condr. weekly broadcast Prayers through the Ages, 1962—. Bd. mgrs. Broadcasting and Film Commn. Nat. Council Chs.; mem. coms. Pres.'s Commn. Internat. Cooperation Year; bd. dirs. Vt. Council World Affairs; trustee Lena Madesin Phillips Fund Internat. Fedn. Bus. and Profl. Women, Helen Dwight Reid Edn. Found., Washington Community Sch. Music. Decorated Chevalier Legion of Honor (France); recipient Am. Women's Assn. award, Billboard award, N.J. Press Women's award. Author: Prayers of a Woman, 1965; I am My Beloved—The Life of Anita Garibaldi, 1969; A Measure Filled, 1972. Contbr. numerous articles to mags. and jours. Address: care Richard Fulton Inc 200 W 57th St New York City NY 10019

SERIGHT, HELEN ELIZABETH VICKROY (MRS. MARION ROSS SERIGHT), mus. curator; b. Woodward, Ia., Feb. 2, 1902; d. Edward Walter and Jennie Maud (Clark) Vickroy; grad. high sch.; m. Marion Ross Seright, June 8, 1921; children—Edward, Cecil, Orval, Naomi (Mrs. Robert R. Rucker), Merle. Clk., Anthony's Dry Goods Store, Fort Benton, Mont., 1942-45, Agr. Stblzn. Conservation, 1946, Price Rite Grocery, Fort Benton, 1961-67; curator Ft. Benton Mus., 1969—; farmer Montague, Mont., 1928-61. Tchr. first aid and med. self help A.R.C., 1942—; adv. officer Fort Benton Theta Rho Girl Club, 1952-72. Mem. V.F.W. Aux. Mem. Rebekah Lodge. Home: 616 Franklin St Fort Benton MT 59442 Office: 1801 Front St Fort Benton MT 59442

SERNAK, SANDRA RITA, lawyer; b. Scranton, Pa., May 4, 1943; d. Paul and Helene Kathryn (Gydosh) Sernak; B.A., Pa. State U., 1964; postgrad. Universite de Strasbourg, France, 1964; J.D., Villanova U., 1967. Admitted to Pa. bar, 1968; practiced in Scranton, Pa., 1968—; mem. firm Gelb, Notarianni & Mullaney, 1968-74; Dolphin, Notarianni, Solfanelli & Sernak, 1974—, asst. solicitor City of Scranton, 1970-74. Mem. Pa., Lackawanna County, Luzerne County bar assns., Pa. Trial Lawyers Assn., Young Musicians Soc. Scranton-Wilkes-Barre (pres.), Phi Sigma Iota. Home: 302 Cherry St Duryea PA 18642 Office: Suite 900 Mears Bldg Scranton PA 18503

SERRA, CATHERINE GILDA (MRS. CHARLES MACHATA), pediatrician; b. Larchmont, N.Y., Apr. 28, 1928; d. Frank G. and Gilda Adelina (Ubriaco) Serra; B.S. magna cum laude, Coll. New Rochelle, 1946; M.D., N.Y. Med. Coll., 1950; m. Charles Machata, Jan. 21, 1962; 1 son, Christopher David. Intern, Morrisania City Hosp., Bronx, N.Y., 1950-51; resident Flower and Fifth Av. Hosp., N.Y.C., 1951-53; practice medicine, specializing in pediatrics, New Rochelle, 1951-61; coordinator house staff teaching, pediatric out-patient dept. Met. Hosp., N.Y.C., 1953-71; vis. pediatrician New Rochelle Hosp., 1953—; med. supr. New Rochelle Sch. System, 1961—; asst. clin. prof. pediatrics N.Y. Med. Coll., N.Y.C., 1953-69, asso. clin. prof., 1969—. Diplomate Am. Bd. Pediatrics. Fellow Am. Acad. Pediatrics; mem. New Rochelle Med. Soc. Home: 3 Shore Rd Rye NY 10580 Office: 515 North Av New Rochelle NY 10580

SERSTOCK, DORIS SHAY, bacteriologist, civic worker; b. Mitchell, S.D., June 13, 1926; d. Elmer Howard and Hattie (Christopher) Shay; B.A., Augustana Coll., 1947; postgrad. U. Minn., 1966-67, Duke, summer, 1969, Communicable Disease Center, Atlanta, 1972; m. Ellsworth I. Serstock, Aug. 30, 1952; children—Barbara Anne, Robert Ellsworth, Mark Douglas. Bacteriologist, Civil Service, S.D., Colo., Mo., 1947-52; research bacteriologist U. Minn., 1952-53; clin. bacteriologist Dr. Lufkin's Lab., 1954-55; chief technologist St. Paul Blood Bank of A.R.C., 1959-65; microbiologist in charge mycology lab VA Hosp., Mpls., 1968—; instr. Coll. Med. Scis., U. Minn., 1970—. Mem. Richfield Planning Commn., 1965-71, sec., 1968-71. Mem. Am., Minn. assns. blood banks, Internat. Platform Assn., Minn. Planning Assn. Republican. Lutheran. Clubs: Richfield Women's Garden (pres. 1959), Wild Flower Garden (chmn. 1961). Author articles in field. Home: 7201 Portland Av Richfield MN 55423 Office: VA Hosp Minneapolis MN 55417

SESNO, ALICE HEALY, educator; b. N.Y.C.; d. Harold J. and Alice (Shine) Healy; B.A., Coll. Mt. St. Vincent, 1955; M.S., Fordham U., 1956, Ph.D., 1968; m. Frank Sesno, Apr. 12, 1973. Tchr. elementary sch., N.Y.C., 1955-60; guidance counselor Bur. Ednl. and Vocational Guidance, N.Y.C., 1961-67; asso. Bur. of Guidance, Con. on Elementary Sch. Guidance, N.Y. State Edn. Dept., Albany, after 1968; dir. Ill. Project for Law Focused Edn., Chgo.; coordinator regional projects Nat. Center Law Focused Edn.; adj. asst. prof. Fordham U., N.Y.C., 1966-68; cons. in pupil services to Office Los Angeles County Supt. Schs., Downey, Cal., 1974—; lectr. in field. Asso. bd. dirs. St. Peter's Hosp., Albany. Mem. Am. (exec. bd.), N.Y. State, Fordham U., Capital Dist. (pres. elect) personnel and guidance assns., Am. Psychol. Assn. Author: Third Year Report of Pilot Projects in Elementary Guidance in N.Y. State, 1969. Contbr. articles to profl. jours. Home: 6568 Beachview Dr Palos Verdes CA 90274 Office: 9300 E Imperial Hwy Downey CA 90242

SETHNESS, MARY GERARDINE (MRS. CHARLES H. SETHNESS, JR.), food coloring mfg. co. exec.; b. New Orleans, Nov. 1, 1917; d. Daniel P. and Theresa (Murphy) Buckley; student Soule Coll., 1934-36; m. Charles H. Sethness, Jr., Feb. 12, 1938; children—Mary (Mrs. Joseph C. Arnold), Chalres B., Daniel B., Henry B. With Sethness Products Co., Chgo., 1955—, treas., 1960—, also dir. Mem. woman's bd. U.S.O., Grant Hosp.; regent Lincoln Acad. Ill. Bd. dirs. North Av. Day Nursery, Travelers Aid Soc.; nat. bd. U.S.O.; Club: Woman's Athletic (Chgo.). Home: 1500 Lake Shore Dr Chicago IL 60610 Office: 444 Lake Shore Dr Chicago IL 60611

SETLIFF, MARGARET HOLDEN (MRS. JAMES A. SETLIFF), librarian; b. Providence, May 28, 1922; d. Robert Emmett and Ada (Jackson) Holden; student R.I. Coll. Edn., 1939-42; B.S., Wayne U., 1943, M.A., 1945; B.L., U. Chgo., 1948; m. James A. Setliff, Dec. 22, 1965. Instr. English, Wayne U., 1945-46; asst. reference and catalogue librarian Joint Reference Library, Chgo., 1948-53; research librarian legislative reference bur. U. Hawaii, 1953-58, asst. researcher, 1958-62; law librarian Hawaii Supreme Ct., 1962-65, 67—; dir. Hawaii State Library Service, 1965-66. Bd. dirs. Legal Aid Soc. Hawaii, 1968—. Mem. Am., Hawaii (pres. 1958-59) library assns., Am. Soc. Pub. Adminstrn. (sec. Honolulu 1955-59), League Women Voters, Friends of Library Hawaii, Am. Assn. Law Libraries. N.A.A.C.P., Hawaii Hist. Soc., Am. Civil Liberties Union Hawaii (pres. 1965-66). Unitarian. Home: 3032 Alencastre Pl Honolulu HI 96816 Office: PO Box 779 Honolulu HI 96808

SETLIFF, MYRA LOIS, editor; b. Plainview, Tex., Oct. 25, 1948; d. Hubert Ezra and Dessie Dale (Morrison) Setliff; B.A., Tex. Tech. U., 1971. Gen. news-TV sect. editor Lubbock (Tex.) Avalanche-Jour., 1971—. Mem. Women in Communications, Inc. (v.p. Lubbock chpt. 1973-74, pres. 1974—). Mem. Ch. of Christ. Home: 1515-A Paris Av Lubbock TX 79401 Office: 710 Av J Lubbock TX 79408

SETO, JANE MEI-CHUN WONG, physician; b. China, May 15, 1927; d. Jee Kwan and Shee (Li) Wong; M.D., Kwang-Hwa Med. Coll., China, 1951; postgrad. Queen's U., Ireland, 1952-57, Tulane U., 1961-63; m. Yeb Jo Seto, Feb. 14, 1958; children—Samuel, Susanna. Intern, Regina (Sask.) Grey Nun's Hosp., 1957-58; resident Providence Hosp., Seattle, 1958-59; physician U. Wash. Health Center, 1959-61, Austin (Tex.) State Sch., 1961-62; research asst. M.D. Anderson Hosp., U. Tex., 1964-66; serologist State Bd. Health, New Orleans, 1967-69; instr. medicine Tulane U., 1969-70, research asso. electrosci. and biophysics research group, 1969—. Active Beverly Hill Civic Club (Metairie, La.). Fellow Royal Soc. Health; mem. A.M.A., Am. Pub. Health Assn., Am. Women in Medicine. Contbr. articles to profl. jours. Home: 4824 Purdue St Metairie LA 70003 Office: Tulane University New Orleans LA 70118

SETON, CYNTHIA PROPPER (MRS. PAUL H. SETON), author; b. N.Y.C., Oct. 11, 1926; d. Karl and Charlotte (Janssen) Propper; B.A., Smith Coll., 1948; m. Paul H. Seton, June 19, 1949; children—Anthony Mitchell, Julia Meredith, Margaret Propper, Jennifer Richardson, Nora Janssen. Columnist, Berkshire Eagle, Pittsfield, Mass., 1956-69, Washington Post, 1959-60. Democrat. Author: I Think Rome is Burning, 1962; A Special and Curious Blessing, 1968; The Mother of the Graduate, 1970; The Sea Change of Angela Lewes, 1971; The Half-Sisters, 1974. Contbr. articles to Redbook, McCall's, Atlantic. Address: 34 Harrison Av Northampton MA 01060

SETTLE, LOUISE SMYTH, civic worker; b. Honaker, Va., Sept. 13, 1915; d. Blythe Deems and Mary Douglas (Howard) Smyth; student Concord Coll., 1958, Marshall U., 1959, Va. Poly. Inst. and State U., 1969-70; m. Charles Robert Settle, Jan. 8, 1939. Active A.R.C. Precinct chmn. Democratic party, 1970-72; mem. county Democratic Com., 1970-73; mem. Pulaski (Va.) Planning Commn., 1968-71, vice-chmn., 1971—; vice chmn. Dem. Women's Nominating Com., 1974. Recipient Community Service award S.W. Times, 1969. Mem. D.A.R. Methodist (coordinator community service groups 1973-74, chmn. ecumenical affairs). Clubs: Woman's Pulaski County, Garden, Book Rev. (Pulaski). Home: 2221 Pleasant Hill Dr Pulaski VA 24301

SETTLEMIRE, SHARRON, educator; b. Jonesboro, Ark., Dec. 27, 1946; d. C.L. and Morene (Wilson) Settlemire; student Ark. State U., 1965-68; B.S., So. State Coll., 1970; M.S., Henderson State Coll., 1971; postgrad. U. So. Miss., 1972. Grad. teaching asst. Henderson State Coll., 1970-71; instr. phys. edn. Centenary Coll., 1971-74; swimming instr., playground dir. YMCA, 1960-65. Mem. Am., La. assns. H., P.E. and R., Am. Assn. U. Women, U.S. Lawn Tennis Assn., Zeta Tau Alpha (adviser). Asst. editor of Ark. State Univ. Directory, 1967-68. Home: 1302 Georgia St Shreveport LA 71104

SEUFERT, GLADYS HENRIETTA BENDER (MRS. FRANCIS ARTHUR SEUFERT), mus. ofcl.; b. Clearfield, Ia., Jan. 2, 1912; d. Richard Leslie and Rachel (Chandler) Bender; elementary edn. certificate U. No. Ia., 1931; R.N., U. Neb., 1935; m. Francis Arthur Seufert, Sept. 29, 1939; 1 son, Francis Arthur, Jr. Sec. The Dalles (Ore.) Mus. Commn., 1967—. Chmn. women's lectrs. Div. Continuing Edn., 1967-74; vol. photographer Ore. Hist. Soc., Portland, 1956-74. Vol. Republican Central Com., Wasco County, Ore., 1969-74. Mem. Am. Assn. U. Women (treas. 1968-72). Home: 913 Laughlin St The Dalles OR 97058 Office: Ft Dalles Mus 16th St and Garrison St The Dalles OR 97058

SEVERANCE, KATHLEEN THOMAS, educator; b. Pineville, La., Aug. 25, 1945; d. William Eleria and Estella Lorraine (Page) Thomas; B.A., Northwestern State Coll., 1970; M.A., Northwestern State U., La., 1971, postgrad., 1971—; m. Robert Norman Severance, Sept. 22, 1963; 1 son, William Charles. With Travelers Ins. Co., Omaha, 1963-65, Mut. of Omaha, 1965-67; grad. asst. Northwestern State U., Natchitoches, La., 1970-71; dir. ednl. developmental labs. Red River Parish Sch. Systems, Coushatta, La., 1971-73. Mem. Am., La. folklore socs., Galactic Assn. (pres. 1967—), Red River Jaynes, V.F.W. Aux., Sigma Tau Delta, Alpha Lambda Delta, Phi Kappa Phi, Beta Sigma Phi. Author newspaper column Folks Say. Contbr. articles on folk medicine to profl. jours. Home: Rural Route 5 Box 128A Coushatta LA 71019

SEVY, BARBARA FLORENCE (MRS. ROGER WARREN SEVY), librarian; b. Montpelier, Vt., June 4, 1926; d. Cecil Burns and Florence Delima (Barber) Snetsinger; B.S., U. Vt., 1947; M.S., Drexel U., 1955; m. Roger Warren Sevy, Aug. 16, 1948; children—Pamela Jane, Jonathan Carl. Librarian, Commn. on Financing of Hosp. Care, Chgo., 1951-54; cataloging librarian Am. Philos. Soc., Phila., 1954-57; asst. librarian Phila. Museum Art, 1965-67, librarian, 1968—. Mem. A.L.A., Spl. Libraries Assn. (sec.-treas. museum div. 1967-68), Phila. Art Alliance, Abington Library Soc. (dir.), Beta Phi Mu (pres. chpt. 1970-72). Home: 242 Mather Rd Jenkintown PA 19046 Office: 26th St and Benjamin Franklin Pkwy Philadelphia PA 19101

SEVY, RUTH, educator; b. Garden City, Mo., Aug. 6, 1912; d. Thomas Perry and Clara E. (Clark) Sevy; B.S. in Edn., Central Mo. State Coll., 1935; M.A. in Health, Phys. Edn. and Recreation, Colo. State Coll., 1947; postgrad. Am. U., 1944; fellow in recreation Colo. State Coll., Greeley, 1950-54. Instr. health and phys. edn., Glasgow, Mo., 1938-41, Nevada, Mo., 1941-44, Portales, N.M., 1946-50; asst. prof., head div. health, phys. edn. and recreation, Hays, Kan., 1950-53; asst. dir. recreation U. No. Colo., Greeley, 1953-54; asso. prof. health, phys. edn. and recreation Ft. Hays State Coll., Hays, Kan., 1954-61; asso. prof. health, phys. edn. and recreation, head women's dept. U. S.D., Vermillion, 1961-67; asso. prof. health and phys. edn. U. No. Ia., Cedar Falls, 1967—. Sec., Constrn. Corp., summer 1936. Jr. case worker, social welfare worker, Mo., 1935-38. Girl Scout counselor Camp Metamora, Detroit, 1939-55; program dir. in recreation Am. Nat. Red Cross, overseas, 1944-47; chmn. soccer div. Girls and Women's Sports, 1956-60; chmn. Western Kan. Bd. Women Ofcls., 1954-61; sec. Greeley Recreation Bd., 1953-54; chmn. Officiating services area S.D., 1962-67; soccer coordinator div. Girls and Women's Sports, 1962-63; girl scout dir. Nevada (Mo.) Girl Scouting, 1942-43, also mem. bd.; mem. State of Ia. Com. for Phys. Edn. for Mentally Retarded, 1971—. Recipient awards of honor, Am. Nat. Red Cross and 20th Div. Air Force. Fellow Am. Sch. Health Assn.; mem. Kan. (v.p. 1957-58, pres. 1959-60), Central Dist. (v.p. phys. edn. 1961-62, v.p. health 1969-71), S.D. (pres. 1966) assns. for health, phys. edn. and recreation, A.A.H.P.E.R. (dir. student services S.D. 1959-60, recipient Honor award 1971), Nat. Mentally Retarded Assn., Central Dist. Assn. for Coll. Women (mem. bd.), Royal Neighbors Am., Phi Lambda Theta. Methodist (mem. ch. bd.). Editor: Guide-Soccer-Speedball, 1956-58; editor, contbr. articles to Soccer Speedball Guide, 1960-62. Home: 2019 White Way Cedar Falls IA 50613

SEWELL, ELIZABETH (MRS. ANTHONY C. SIRIGNANO), educator, author; b. Coonoor, India, Mar. 9, 1919; d. Robert B. Seymour and Dorothy (Dean) Sewell; B.A. in Modern Langs., Cambridge U. (Eng.), 1942, M.A., 1945, Ph.D., 1949; D.Litt. (hon.), St. Peter's Coll., 1962, Fordham U., 1968; m. Anthony C. Sirignano, Jan. 2, 1971. Vis. lectr. English, Vassar Coll., 1951-52; vis. prof. English, Fordham U., 1954-55, 58-59, Bennett Coll., Greensboro, N.C., 1960-61, Tougaloo Coll., 1963-64; prof. English, chmn. Bensalem Coll., Fordham U., 1967-69; prof. English, Hunter Coll., 1971-74; Joe Rosenthal prof. humanities U. N.C., Greensboro, 1974—. Trustee Goddard Coll., Plainfield, Vt., 1973—. Howald fellow, 1949-50, Sr. Simon research fellow, 1955-57. Mem. Am. Assn. U. Profs., P.E.N. Internat., Lewis Carroll Soc. N. Am. Author: The Structure of Poetry, 1951; The Dividing of Time, 1951; Paul Valery: The Mind in the Mirror, 1952; The Field of Nonsense, 1952; The Singular Hope, 1955; The Orphic Voice, 1960; Now Bless Thyself, 1963; Poems, 1947-61, 1963; The Human Metaphor, 1964; Signs and Cities, 1968. Home: 3913 Dogwood Dr Greensboro NC 27410 Office: care Harold Ober Associates Inc 40 E 49th St New York City NY 10017

SEWELL, MARGARET HIX, librarian; b. Birmingham, Ala., July 16, 1901; d. William Tarplay and Cora Jane (Coggins) Hix; student Agnes Scott Coll., 1919, Randolph Macon Woman's Coll., 1919-21; B.A., Fla. State U., 1949, M.A. in L.S., 1952; m. Robert O. Sewell, July 18, 1936; children—Jane (Mrs. Thomas L. Harling, Jr.), Robert O., Mary Lucile (Mrs. Walter W. Collins). Tchr. sci. Pinellas County (Fla.) Sch. System, 1926-39, librarian, 1939-68; adminstr. Govt. Library for the Elderly, St. Petersburg, Fla., 1968—; vis. prof. Fla. State U., summers 1953-57, extension tchr., 1956-57; vis. prof. U. Ala., 1958-67. Mem. St. Petersburg Art Mus., Stuart Soc. Mem. Fla. (past pres. sch. and children's sect., past sec.), Pinellas County (past pres.) library assns., Alpha Delta Pi, Alpha Beta Alpha, Beta Phi Mu. Contbr. articles to profl. jours. Home: 6919 7th Av N St Petersburg FL 33710 Office: St Petersburg Housing Authority Library 305 9th St St Petersburg FL 33705

SEWELL, MARGARET ROWE (MRS. JOHN EDWARD TAYLOR SEWELL), hosp. cons.; b. Holtville, Cal., Apr. 2, 1920; d. Robert P. and Mildred Frances (Smith) Rowe; student Santa Barbara State Coll., 1937-39; A.B., U. Cal. at Los Angeles, 1941; m. John Edward Taylor Sewell, July 13, 1946; children—Michelle (Mrs. William Mims), John Edward Taylor, Patricia (Mrs. Richard Lewis), Susan (Mrs. Gary Copeland), Mary, Estelle. Tchr. elementary secondary schs., Cal., Hawaii, 1942-47; tchr. Camarillo State Hosp., 1949-59, Orange County Schs., 1959-61; tchr. Fairview State Hosp., Costa Mesa, Cal., 1961-63, supr. acad. instrn., sch. prin., 1963-71, cons. Office Program Rev., 1971—. Grantee, Mental Retardation Seminar, 1969, Mgmt. Devel. Inst., 1971. Mem. Am. Assn. Mental Deficiency, Council Exceptional Children, Pi Lambda Theta. Office: 2501 Harbor Blvd Costa Mesa CA 92626

SEWELL, WINIFRED, pharm. librarian; b. Newport, Wash., Aug. 12, 1917; d. Harold Arthur and Grace (Vickerman) Sewell; B.A., State Coll. Wash., Pullman, 1938; B.S. in L.S., Columbia, 1940 Asst., Columbia U. Library, 1938-42; asst. librarian Wellcome Research Labs., Tuckahoe, N.Y., 1942-43, librarian, 1943-46; librarian Squibb Inst. Med. Research, 1946-61; subject heading specialist Index Medicus, Nat. Library Medicine, Bethesda, 1961-62, dep. chief Bibliog. Services Div., 1962-65, head of drug lit. program, 1965-70; editor Unlisted Drugs, 1949-59, 62-64, asso. editor, 1959-61; instr. pharm. lit. and librarianship Columbia, summer 1959; adj. lectr. U. Md. Sch. Librarianship & Information Services, 1969—, coordinator drug information services Health Scis. Library, 1970—. Mem. Internat. Fedn. Pharmacy Commn. Pharm. Abstracts, 1958-61; mem. com. on modern methods of handling chem. information Nat. Acad. Scis.-NRC, 1964-67. Mem. A.L.A., Drug Information Assn. (pres. 1970-71), Am. Soc. Information Sci., Med. Library Assn., Spl. Libraries Assn. (chmn. pharm. sect., sci-tech. div. 1952-53, treas. N.Y. chpt. 1944-47, pres. 1960-61). Author: Reader in Medical Librarianship, 1973. Home: 6513 76th Pl Cabin John MD 20731

SEXTON, ANNE HARVEY, poet; b. Newton, Mass., Nov. 9, 1928; d. Ralph Churchill and Mary Gray (Staples) Harvey; student Garland Jr. Coll., 1947-48, (scholar) Radcliffe Inst. for Ind. Study, 1961-63; m. Alfred M. Sexton II, Aug. 16, 1948 (div. 1974); children—Linda, Joyce. Fashion model, Boston, 1950-51; now gives poetry readings in East and at colls. throughout U.S.; lectr. creative writing Boston U., 1969-72, prof., 1972—; Crawshaw Chair of Lit., Colgate U., 1972; Robert Frost fellow Breadloaf Writers Conf., 1959; recipient Audience Poetry prize, 1958-59; Levinson prize for 7 poems in Poetry mag., 1962; Guggenheim award, 1969-70. Author: To Bedlam and Part Way Back, 1960; All My Pretty Ones, 1962; Live or Die (Pulitzer prize in poetry 1967); Love Poems, 1969; Transformations, 1971; Book of Folly, 1972; The Death Notebooks, 1974. Contbg. author The Partisan Review Anthology; The Hudson Review Anthology (Fredrick Morgan), 1962; New World Writing, Vol. XVI, 1960; also poetry in mags. Home: 14 Black Oak Rd Weston MA 02193

SEXTON, RUBY LAYSON (MRS. MASON SEXTON), journalist; b. Henderson, Ky., Oct. 1, 1927; d. Cyrus Steele and Ruby Lee (Sandefur) Layson; A.B. summa cum laude, Wesleyan Coll., Macon, Ga., 1949; M.A., Ind. U., 1952; postgrad U. Cal. at Los Angeles, N.Y. U., Cal. State Coll.; m. Mason Sexton, Nov. 22, 1952; children—Randall John, Pamela Jo. Reporter, Harlan (Ky.) Daily Enterprise, intermittently, 1945-50; corr., feature writer Macon News, 1947-49; free-lance writer mag. articles and news features, 1950-65; prof. journalism and English, Woodbury Coll., Los Angeles, 1966-67; reporter Post-Advocate, Alhambra, Cal., 1968-69, feature writer, 1969-70, asst. city editor, 1970-71, city editor, 1971; staff writer, asst. bur. chief Copley News Service, Los Angeles, 1971-72, bur. chief, 1972—. Recipient Ring of Truth award Copley Newspapers, 1968, 71, 72; Citation of Honor, D.A.V., 1970; Journalism award Los Angeles County Employees Assn., 1973. Mem. Soc. Profl. Journalists, Sigma Delta Chi. Democrat. Unitarian (religious edn. dir. 1961-62). Ind. Order Foresters. Clubs: Greater Los Angeles Press Club So. Cal. Home: 2009 Hanscom Dr South Pasadena CA 91030 Office: 500 W Temple St Los Angeles CA 90012

SEYBOLD, MARY ANICE, educator; b. Baylis, Ill. Jan. 29, 1908; d. John Ellsworth and Mary (Wade) Seybold; A.B., Ill. Coll., 1929; M.A., U. Ill., 1931, Ph.D. in Math., 1947. Tchr. high schs., Chandlerville, Ill., 1929-30, Monticello, Ill., 1931-42, Freeport, Ill., 1942-43; instr. Ill. Coll., Jacksonville, 1943-44; asst. U. Ill., Urbana, 1944-46; asst. prof. math. N. Central Coll., Naperville, Ill., 1946-48, prof., 1948-69, prof. on leave, 1969—, head math. dept., 1946-69, pioneer internship program, 1960-61. Evaluator summer insts. NSF, Ohio, N.C., Kan., Ia., 1957, fellow Summer Computing Inst., U. Okla., Norman, 1959, spl. lectr. Summer Inst., Normal (Ill.) U., 1960, Conf. Undergrad. Research math., Carleton Coll., summer 1961. Mem. Math. Assn. Am. (pres. Ill. sect. 1962-63), Ill. Council Tchrs. Math. (mem. exec. bd. 1956-59), Ill. Com. Strengthening of Teaching Math. (founder 1953), Phi Beta Kappa, Sigma Delta Epsilon, Phi Delta Sigma, Pi Mu Epsilon. Home: 1036 Grove St Jacksonville IL 62650

SEYLAR, MARGARET MELCHIOR (MRS. ROBERT PARKER SEYLAR), educator; b. Bethlehem, Pa., Oct. 17, 1908; d. Charles Cassat and Mary May (Leidich) Melchior; B.S., Kutztown State Coll., 1940; M.A., Lehigh U., 1945; m. Robert Parker Seylar, Aug. 22, 1934. Tchr. pub. schs., Bucks County, Pa., 1927-49; elementary supr. pub. schs., Blooming Glen, Pa., 1949-55; supervising prin. Deep Run Valley Joint Schs., Blooming Glen, Pa., 1955-65; vis. lectr. Lehigh U., Bethlehem, Pa., 1966-70, prof. dept. elementary edn., 1970—, dir. intern teaching program, 1972—. Lectr., cons., part time writer Pa. Dept. Pub. Instrn., 1950—, chmn., editor Self Evaluation of the Elementary Sch., 1971-72. Pres. Bucks County chpt. A.R.C., 1955-56; chmn. schs. div. Bucks County Community Chest, 1960; chmn. exec. bd. Prison Adv. Commn., 1967—. Recipient award Delta Kappa Gamma, 1949, outstanding leadership award Pa. Dept. Pub. Instrn., 1963, award Pa. Sch. Librarians, 1968, Margaret M. Seylar Elementary Sch., Bucks County, Pa. named in her honor, 1966. Author: Mary Elizabeth and Mr. Lincoln, 1959. Home: Route 1 Riegelsville PA 18077

SEYMOUR, BARBARA JEAN JACOBSON (MRS. DOUGLAS SEYMOUR), govt. adminstr.; b. Chgo., Feb. 7, 1930; d. Louis C. and Amelia (Potasch) Jacobson; Ph.B., U. Chgo., 1948, M.A. with honors, 1962; m. Calvin Steimetz, July 16, 1950 (div. Sept. 1955); children—Kim Louis Colin, Leif Mardan; m. 2d, Douglas Seymour, Sept. 15, 1963. With Ore. Pub. Welfare Div., 1950-51, 54-60, 62-71, supr. manuals and informational services, 1969-71; information dir. Ore. Dept. Environmental Quality, Portland, 1971—. Lectr. social work Portland State U., 1972—. Vol. caseworker Salem (Ore.) Family Counseling Service, 1969—; play dir. Pentacle Theater, Salem, 1963-69; discussion leader Great Books, 1954—; founder, dir. First Friday, 1970-73. Mem. Ore. Social Welfare Assn., Joint Legislative Council Social Welfare (vice chmn. 1967-71), Am. Pub. Welfare Assn. (sect. chmn. div. adminstrn. 1969-71, Western regional membership chmn. 1969-70, dir. 1969-70), Ore. Environmental Council, Portland C. of C. (cultural affairs task force 1973—), Planned Parenthood Assn. Ore. Democrat. Jewish religion. Home: 1234 Heather Lane SE Salem OR 97302 Office: 1234 SW Morrison St Portland OR 97205

SEYMOUR, ELIZABETH ANNE, therapist; b. Madison, Wis., Apr. 13, 1935; d. Francis Okerson and Evelyn Bertha (Day) Seymour; B.S., U. Wis., 1957; 1 son, David Francis. Staff therapist, student clin. supr. VA Hosp., Long Beach, Cal., 1957-64; staff therapist Woodruff Gables Hosp., Bellflower, Cal., 1961-62, El Cerritos County Hosp., Long Beach, Cal., 1965-66; with Central Wis. Colony & Tng. Sch., Madison, 1966—, chief phys. therapist, 1970—. Mem. Am. Phys. Therapy Assn., Am. Assn. for Mental Deficiency, Parents Without Partners. Lutheran. Home: 4430 Northview Dr Madison WI 53704 Office: 317 Knutson Dr Madison WI 53704

SEYMOUR, JUDITH ANN, psychologist; b. Danville, Ill., June 7, 1943; d. William Peter and Margaret Esther (Bolton) Seymour; B.S., Fla. State U., 1965, M.S. (Nat. Def. Edn. Act fellow), 1968. Psychologist, acting dir. psychology Sunland Tng. Center, Marianna, Fla., 1967-69; psychologist Jackson County Guidance Clinic, Marianna, 1969—. State rep. Chipola Services Assn., 1972-73, pres., 1974. Bd. dirs. Easter Seal Soc. Crippled Children and Adults Gulf Coast. Mem. Am. Assn. Mental Deficiency, Am. Psychol. Assn. Presbyn. Club: Pilot (Marianna Compass Club chmn. 1972, Outreach div. chmn. 1974). Home: Route Box 588 Marianna FL 32446 Office: 903 4th St Marianna FL 32446

SEYMOUR, RACHEL, civic worker; b. Phila., Mar. 28, 1937; d. W. Curtis and Nellie-Lee (Holt) Bok; student Sweet Briar Coll., 1955-57, U. Pa., 1957-59, 60-61, 73—; m. James Nelson Kise, Dec. 20, 1958 (div. 1974); children—Jefferson Bok, Charles Curtis. Dir. Elfreth's Alley Assn., 1962-65, sec., 1963-64, 64-65. Bd. dirs. Am. Found., bd. dirs., pres. Community Sch. Phila., Inc., 1971—; trustee Phila. award; mem. Indian com. Phila., 1971—. Mem. Soc. Friends. Democrat. Home: 220 Locust Street Philadelphia PA 19106

SEYMOUR, STEPHANIE KULP (MRS. R. THOMAS SEYMOUR), lawyer; b. Battle Creek, Mich., Oct. 16, 1940; d. Francis Bruce and Frances Cecelia (Bria) Kulp; B.A. magna cum laude (Ford Found. grantee), Smith Coll., 1962; J.D., Harvard, 1965; m. R. Thomas Seymour, June 10, 1972; 1 dau., Sara Callas; children by previous marriage—Anderson G., Bria Kulp. Admitted to Okla. bar, 1965; pvt. practice law in Boston, 1965-66, Tulsa, 1966-67, 71—, Houston, 1967-69; mem. firms Goodwin, Procter & Hoar, Boston, 1965-66, Lupardus, Holliman & Huffman, Tulsa, 1966-67, Baker, Botts, Shepherd & Coates, Houston, 1968-69, Doerner, Stuart, Saunders, Tulsa, 1971—. Mem. women's task force Tulsa Community Relations Commn., 1973—. Mem. Okla. Bar Assn. (asso. bar examiner), Phi Beta Kappa. Home: 2637 S St Louis St Tulsa OK 74114 Office: 1200 Atlas Life Bldg Tulsa OK 74103

SHABLESKY, MARTHA PONTIUS (MRS. PETER PAUL SHABLESKY), real estate investment co. exec.; b. Orrville, O., June 29, 1918; d. Howard Taggart and Nova (Mead) Pontius; B.S., Miami U., Oxford, O., 1940; m. Peter Paul Shablesky, Nov. 1, 1947; Exec.dir. Temple Israel, Dayton, O., 1953-58; accountant-adminstr. Anchor Rubber Co., Dayton, 1958-63; controller-gen. mgr. Jos. Patterson & Assos., Dayton, 1963-73; sec., asst. treas., dir. Drake Investment, Inc., Drake Investment, Inc. of Ind., Fair Plaza, Inc., Barlo, Inc., Haa-Guar, Inc., Augusta Plaza, Inc., Skyway Plaza, Inc., Anderson Southdale, Inc., Frontenac Apts., Inc., Sherwood Apts., Inc.; mgr. Gen. Apts. Co. Asst. treas. Montgomery County chpt. Nat. Arthritis Found., 1970-71. Mem. Internat. Council Shopping Centers, Alpha Omicron Pi. Presbyn. Home: 3660 Briar Pl Dayton OH 45405 Office: 1959 Riverside Dr Dayton OH 45405

SHAEFFER, MARGARET WHITING MURRY, mus. dir.; b. Warren, Ariz.; d. Alexander and Marguerite (Whiting) Murry; B.A. with distinction, U. Ariz., 1932, M.A., 1937; postgrad. U. So. Cal., 1934, 35, U. Okla., 1959-60, U. N.W. Fla., 1971; m. James Ball Shaeffer, Apr. 7, 1939 (div. Dec. 1972); children—James Murry, Sarra Rugee, Peter Wallace. Art supr. English, Flagstaff (Ariz.) Schs., 1933; tchr. art Phoenix Union High Sch., 1934-42; curator Kinishba Mus., Ft. Apache, Ariz., 1948-51; craft specialist So. Plains Indians Mus., Anadarko, Okla., 1955-56; tchr. English, Moore and Norman (Okla.) High Schs., 1960-61; asst. dir. Stuhr Mus., Prairie Pioneer, Grand Island, Neb., 1962-70, curator outdoor mus., 1965-70; curator Ecol. Mus., Environmental Sensitivity Project, Pensacola, Fla., 1970-71; edn. curator Jefferson County Hist. Soc., Watertown, N.Y., 1971-72, dir. mus., 1972—. Cons. N.Y. State Council on Arts, 1972; mem. art com. Neb. Arts Council, 1963-67. Exec. chmn. Child Care Center, Parris Island, S.C., 1951-52; v.p. Jr. Assembly, Norman, 1959. Mem. Am. Assn. Museums, Am. Assn. U. Women, N.E. Mus. Conf. Democrat. Episcopalian. Clubs: North Country Bird, College Women's (chmn. antiques sect. 1973-74) (Watertown). Asst. editor Plains Anthropologist, 1959-63. Home: 129 Mullin St Watertown NY 13601 Office: 228 Washington St Watertown NY 13601

SHAFER, ANNE WHALEN (MRS. ROBERT SHAFER), civic worker; b. Memphis, Aug. 22, 1923; d. Paul Solomony and Marguerite (Bonelli) Whalen; grad. U. Tenn. Jr. Coll., Martin, 1947; student Memphis Acad. Art, Southwestern Coll.; m. Robert Weldon Shafer, June 5, 1948; 1 son, Robert Jr. With U.S. Army Supply Depot, Memphis, 1942-45, Chgo. & So. Airlines, 1947-50, Wilson Packing Co., 1952; speaker Grooming a City Tenn. Fedn. Garden Clubs, Memphis, 1966, Community Beautification Nat. Recreation and Parks Assn. Congress, Miami Beach, Fla., 1967; panel speaker Cath.-Jewish Dialogue YWCA Brotherhood program. Mem. West Tenn. Council Cath. Women; sec. Citizens Assn. Memphis and Shelby County, 1962-63; pres. Cath. Human Relations Council, 1971-72; pres. Memphis Alliance of Community Orgns., 1972-73; chmn. Memphis City Beautiful Commn., 1964-66; del. Tenn. Constl. Conv., 1965; sec. Memphis and Shelby County Mental Health Clinic; project dir., asst. coordinator Memphis Panel of Am. Women, 1973—; mem. Women's Polit. Caucus, Vol. Women's Roundtable. Recipient Woman Doer award Nat. Democratic Com., 1966. Mem. Cath. Bus. Women's League, UN Assn., League Women Voters, Fgn. Policy Assn., Ch. Women United (Cath. rep., 1969—), Tenn. Fedn. Dem. Women, Nat. Assn. Vols. Venezuela, Panel Am. Women. Clubs: Sprig and Twig Garden; Colonial Acres Civic; Sigma Phi Epsilon Wives and Mothers. Address: 4963 Essexshire Av Memphis TN 38117

SHAFER, CAROLYN TREVORROW, assn. exec.; b. Tom's Creek, Va., May 23, 1935; d. Bane Dickenson and Ruth (Trevorrow) Shafer; B.S. in Edn., Otterbein Coll., 1957. Tchr. Madison (O.) Meml. High Sch., 1957-61; home service rep. East Ohio Gas Co., Warren, 1961-63; program dir. Dairy Council Mich., Flint, 1963-67, Lansing, 1967-72, exec. dir., Detroit, 1972—. Bd. dirs. Flint chpt. Am. Heart Assn., 1964-67. Mem. Am., Mich. home econ. assns., Central Mich. Home Economists in Bus. Assn. (pres. 1970-71), Am. Pub. Health Assn., Am. Assn. U. Women. Club: Altrusa. Office: Dairy Council of Michigan 704 New Center Bldg Detroit MI 48202 Home: Bloomfield Hills MI 48013

SHAFER, CEILIA ANN MCCALLISTER (MRS. JACK ALVIN SHAFER), mus. curator; b. San Bernardino, Cal., June 9, 1946; d. Harold Othel and Leora Margaret (Poteet) McCallister; B.A., Okla. State U., 1970; m. Jack Alvin Shafer, July 14, 1967; children—Kelli, Kristen (dec.). Curator collections Okla. Territorial Mus., Okla. Hist. Soc., Guthrie, 1972—. Substitute tchr. Guthrie Pub. Schs., 1969, Guthrie Job Corps Center, 1970. Sponsor, Teen-Age Republicans, Guthrie, 1970. Okla. Coll. Liberal Arts grantee, 1972. Mem. Am. Assn. State and Local History, Okla. Museums Assn., Okla. Hist. Soc., Mountain-Plains Mus. Conf., Alpha Delta Pi. Republican. Baptist. Home: PO Box 245 Mulhall OK 73063 Office: 402 E Oklahoma St Guthrie OK 73044

SHAFER, NANCY LOUISE, social worker; b. Jamestown, N.Y., Oct. 3, 1930; d. Morris V. and Minnie Alice (Rashley) Phillips; student Alfred U., 1948-50, Jamestown Community Coll., 1950-51, Bowling Green State U., 1951-53; m. Theodore J. Shafer, June 12, 1954; children—James, Thomas, Joseph, Michael, Mary Timothy. Caseworker, Lucas County (O.) Aid to Dependent Children, 1953-55; social worker Mt. Vernon (O.) State Inst., 1963-72, release implementation planning coordinator, 1972—. Committeewoman, Cub Scouts, 1970-71, Boy Scouts, 1971-73, Little League Aux.; treas. Babe Ruth League Aux. Bd. dirs. Knox County Assn. for Retarded Children. Mem. Am. Assn. for Mental Deficiency, Ohio Civil Service Employees Assn., V.F.W. Aux. (past treas.). Roman Catholic (parish council rep. 1973—). Home: 8 Emmett Dr Mount Vernon OH 43050 Office: Box 762 Mount Vernon OH 43050

SHAFER, WILMA CLARE, educator; b. Evansville, Ind., Apr. 6, 1916; d. Alfred Bruce and Lillian (Collins) Cox; student Ind. U., 1934-36; B.A., U. Evansville, 1951; M.A., Ind. U., 1958, Ed.D., 1962; m. Ivan John Shafer, Dec. 22, 1940; children—John Allan, David Bruce (dec.). Tchr. pub. schs., Daviess County, Ind., 1936-42, 44-46, Dubois County, Ind., 1943-44, Vanderburgh County, Ind., 1947-60; mem. faculty U. Evansville, 1960—, prof. edn., 1967—, dir. elementary edn., 1970—. Mem. council Ind. Adv. Council Tchr. Certifacation and Licensing, 1960-63, 71-72; dir. Head Start Orientation, 1967, project dir., supplementary tng., 1971—. Mem. Am. Bus. Women's Assn. (pres. 1955-56), Ind. Tchr. Educator's Conf. (chmn. steering com. 1971-72), D.A.R. (chaplain 1970-71, v.p. 1973-74), Am. Assn. U. Women (state pres. 1971-73), Ind. Assn. Childhood Edn. (pres. 1960-62), Ind. Assn. Tchr. Edn. (pres. 1968-69), League Women Voters, Daus. of Nile, Phi Kappa Phi, Pi Lambda Theta (nat. pres. 1973—), Delta Kappa Gamma, Phi Mu, Beta Sigma Phi. Mem. Order Eastern Star. Clubs: Women's Rotary, Altrusa Internat. Home: 2621 Oak Hill Rd Evansville IN 47711

SHAFFER, DOROTHY ANNE, educator; b. Boston, Apr. 13, 1916; d. Ned Welch and Anne Welch; B.S. in Edn., Mass. State Coll., Framingham, 1963; M.A. in Counselling, Ariz. State U., 1966, Ph.D. in Secondary Edn., 1973; m. Ralph Weldon Shaffer, Dec. 21, 1942; children—Virginia A. (Mrs. Gary P. Fields), Robert E., Richard G., Patricia E. Speech and hearing clinician pub. schs., Ariz., 1961-68; instr. freshman English for adults Maricopa County Community Coll., Phoenix, 1970—; mem. faculty Ariz. State U., 1970—; cons. non-verbal communciation, 1970—. Mem. Ariz. Assn. Deans Women, Delta Kappa Gamma. Author: Communication: Sound and Silence and the Grade Teacher, 1965; The Sound of Speech, 1966; also programmed cassette series in non-verbal communication. Contbr. articles to profl. jours. Editor Ariz. Speech and Hearing Jour., 1966. Home: 8426 N Central Av Phoenix AZ 85020 Office: Top of the Towers 4750 N Central Av Phoenix AZ 85012

SHAFFER, JOANNE FRANCES (MRS. RICHARD HENRY SHAFFER), advt. co. exec.; b. Elizabeth, N.J., July 15, 1939; d. Michael D. and Dorothy M. (Leiner) Colaneri; grad. Newark Secretarial Sch., 1958; m. Richard Henry Shaffer, Feb. 20, 1960; children—Joanne Elizabeth, Tiffney Ann. Sec. to pres. Choice-Vend Corp., Hartford, Conn., 1958-60; sec. to pres. Black-Russell-Morris, Newark, N.J., 1966-68; account exec. Collaterial Marketing Services, Inc., Union, N.J., 1968-70; with Advt. Material Services, Inc., Union, 1970—, pres., 1973—. Leader, Girl Scouts Am., Cranford, N.J. Mem. Assn. Indsl. Advt. Home: 720 Lincoln Av Cranford NJ 07016 Office: 931 Lehigh Av Union NJ 07083

SHAFFER, MARGARET ESTHER THOMPSON, research co. exec.; b. Cumberland, Md., Mar. 28, 1938; d. Robert Finley and Elizabeth (Brengle) Thompson; B.Mus., U. Rochester, 1960; M.S. (USPHS fellow), U. So. Ill., 1964; m. Michael Edward Shaffer, Feb. 20, 1960; children—Ian Montgomery, Marc Christopher. Dir. planning research Century Research Corp., Arlington, Va., 1964-66; asst. mgr. human factors group Tracor, Inc., Rockville, Md., 1966-69; v.p. Urban Scis., Bethesda, Md., 1969-70; pres. Urban Studies Assos., Potomac, Md., 1970—. Mem. Am. Inst. Planners, Transp. Research Bd., Am. Psychol. Assn., Internat. Ergonomics Assn. Address: 8815 Quiet Stream Ct Potomac MD 20854

SHAFFER, WILMA LOIS HATFIELD (MRS. BRUCE H. SHAFFER), editor, author; b. Warrensburg, Ill., 1916; d. Jasper and Ethel (Thomas) Hatfield; student U. Neb., 1953-54; asso. degree U. Cin., 1965, B.S., 1970; m. Bruce H. Shaffer, July 5, 1934; children—Janice Jeanne (Mrs. Charles H. Smith), Lawrence Bruce, Roger Alan. Author devotional material, stories for children Standard Pub., Cin., 1957—, editor, 1963—; editor Christian Mother, Cin., 1963—. Speaker, workshop leader Christian edn., various colls., 1964—. Past pres. Criterion Club; den mother Cub Scouts, 1948-50; band mother, 1947-52, active P.T.A., 1948-52. Registrar for voters, 1950-52. Mem. Nat. League Am. Pen Women, Cin. Women's Press Club (corr. sec. 1962-63, treas. 1972-74), Internat. Platform Assn., Phi Kappa Epsilon. Republican. Mem. Ch. Christ (Sunday sch. tchr. 1934—). Mem. Order Eastern Star. Author: Serenity of the Soul, 1961; Church Women at Work, 1961; A Psalm for Every Mood, 1964; Psalms and Programs for Women, 1964; Nursery Rhyme Bible Stories, 1969; Proverbs and Programs for Women, 1972; Lullaby Memories, 1974. Contbr. articles to Christian edn. mags. Home: 9984 Lake Park Dr Cincinnati OH 45231 Office: 8121 Hamilton Av Cincinnati OH 45231

SHAFFRON, JENNIFER JANET, newspaper co. exec.; b. Welch, W.Va., Mar. 27, 1947; d. Andrew and Evelyn Trent (Walker) Shaffron; B.S.J., W.Va. U., 1969. Staff reporter Pitts. Cath. Newspaper, 1969-70; asst. city editor Rep.-Delta, Buckhannon, W.Va., 1970-71; staff reporter The Enterprise, Lexington Park, Md., 1971-73, mng. editor, 1973—. Bd. dirs. St. Mary's County Citizens Scholarship Found. Recipient Golden Quill award Western Pa. Sigma Delta Chi, Theta Sigma Phi, 1970. Mem. Women In Communications, St. Mary's County Journalists Assn. (v.p. 1972—), W.Va. U. Alumni Assn. Democrat. Methodist. Home: Box 258 California MD 20619 Office: Box 218 Lexington Park MD 20653

SHAHINIAN, SIROON PASHALIAN, ednl. adminstr.; b. N.Y.C., June 28, 1926; d. Leon and Margret (Mardirosian) Pashalian; B.A. in Math., Hunter Coll., 1946; M.A., N.Y. U., 1949, Ph.D. in Indsl. Psychology, 1972; m. Zareh Shahinian, Dec. 5, 1960; 1 son, John Zareh. Research asso. Fordham U., N.Y.C., 1951-53; research specialist Community Service Soc., N.Y.C., 1955-58; asst. personnel mgr. N.W. Moody Corp., N.Y.C., 1958-59; staff asso. Herrold Assos., N.Y.C., 1959-60; research psychologist N.Y. State Dept. Mental Hygiene, Queens Village, N.Y., 1961-68; research asso. Hillside Hosp., Glen Oaks, N.Y., 1965-69; asst. to dir. profl. exam. service Am. Pub. Health Assn., 1970; placement counselor Alpha Employment Agy., Great Neck, N.Y., 1971-72; adminstrv. asst. N.Y. State Psychol. Assn., N.Y.C., 1972; tchr. placement counselor York Coll., City U. N.Y., Jamaica, 1972—. Lectr. in psychology Queens Coll., N.Y.C., 1951-55. Sec., also dir. Armenian Welfare Assn., N.Y.C., 1968-72. Bd. dirs., also exec. dir. Hye Bardez Nursery Sch., Bayside, N.Y., 1968-69, 71—. Office of Naval Research grantee, 1951-53; NIMH grantee, 1965-69. Mem. Am., Eastern, N.Y. State Psychol. assns., Psychometric Soc., Gerontological Soc., Met. N.Y. Assn. of Applied Psychologists, Psi Chi. Contbr. articles to profl. jours. Home: 36-33 169th St Flushing NY 11358 Office: York College City U NY 150-14 Jamaica Av Jamaica NY 11432

SHAKIN, GRACE MARIAN, librarian; b. Chgo., Feb. 21, 1918; d. Samuel B. and Kathryn Margaret (Hart) Shakin; B.E., No. Ill. U., 1938; B.S. in L.S., Carnegie Inst. Tech., 1948; M.A., Columbia, 1948. Tchr. Maywood (Ill.) pub. schs., 1938-47; librarian, elementary sch., Oak Ridge, Tenn., 1948-49; campus sch. librarian Oneonta (N.Y.) State Tchrs. Coll., 1949-51; librarian Gt. Neck (N.Y.) pub. schs., 1951—. Lakeville Elementary Sch., 1951—. Instr. Grad. Sch. Library Sci., St. John's U., Jamaica, N.Y., summers, 1953-65. Mem. Internat. Reading Assn., N.E.A., A.L.A. (mem.-at-large Newbery-Caldecott awards com. 1970, chmn. mag. evaluation com. children's service div. 1960-61), N.Y. State Tchrs. Assn., Delta Kappa Gamma, Beta Phi Mu, Kappa Delta Pi. Home: 94 Old Mill Rd Great Neck NY 11023

SHALALA, DONNA EDNA, educator; b. Cleve., Feb. 14, 1942; d. James Abraham and Edna (Smith) Shalala; A.B., Western Coll., 1962; M.S.Sc., Syracuse U., 1968, Ph.D., 1970. Peace Corps vol., Iran, 1962-64; asst. to dir. met. studies program Syracuse (N.Y.) U., 1965-69, instr. asst. to dean Maxwell Grad. Sch., 1969-70; asst. prof. dept. polit. sci. Bernard M. Baruch Coll., City U. N.Y., 1970-72; asso. prof. politics and edn. Tchrs. Coll., Columbia, 1972—. Asst. to chmn. com. on local govt. N.Y. State Constl. Conv., 1967. Vice chmn. New Dem. Coalition of N.Y. State, 1970-72. Trustee Western Coll., Oxford, O.; bd. dirs. N.Y. Citizens Union. Recipient Ohio Newspaper Women's scholarship, 1958, trustee scholarship Western Coll., 1958-62, Carnegie fellowship, 1966-68; Spencer fellow Nat. Acad. Edn., 1972—. Mem. Am., N.Y. polit. sci. assns. Author: Neighborhood Governance, 1971; The City and the Constitution, 1972; The Property Tax and the Voters, 1973; The Decentralization Approach, 1974. Home: 201 E 21st St New York City NY 10010

SHALON, RAHEL (MRS. URIEL SHALON), educator; b. Sieradz, Poland, Apr. 15, 1904; d. Hanoch and Tova Gitel (Lifszyc) Znamirowski; B.Sc., Technion, Israel Inst. Tech., 1930, C.E., 1931, M.Sc., 1957; m. Uriel Shalon, Aug. 19, 1929. Faculty, Israel Inst. Tech., 1931—, asst. prof., 1946-52, asso. prof., 1952-57, prof., 1957—, head bldg. research sta., 1952-72, dean Sch. Grad. Studies, 1959-62, v.p. for research, 1963-65, sr. v.p. for acad. affairs, 1965-66, chmn. Grad. Studies in Bldg. Scis. and Constrn. Mgmt., 1967-71. Mem. governing body Internat. Union Testing and Research Labs. for Materials and Structures, 1954—, pres., 1960-61, chmn. research group concrete and reinforced concrete in hot countries, 1961—; mem. research group corrosion reinforcement; mem. exec. com. Internat. Council Bldg. Research, 1962-68. Mem. Israel Council for Higher Edn., 1961-71, Israel Council Engring. and Architecture, 1961—. Trustee Israel Found.; bd. govs. U. Beer-Sheba; bd. dirs. Israel Bldg. Centre. Served to maj. Israel Def. Army, 1948-49. Ford Found. grantee, 1960, 66. Mem. Assn. Engrs. and Architects of Israel, Am. Concrete Inst. Club: Soroptimist Internat. (pres. European Fedn. 1974—). Author: Cement and Concrete 1939; Cementitious Materials, 1964. Editor: In the Field of Building, 1954—. Contbr. articles to profl. jours. Home: 30 Vitkin St Haifa 34755 Israel Office: Technion Haifa Israel

SHALUCHA, BARBARA, educator; b. Springfield, Vt., Dec. 9, 1915; d. Joseph Wasil and Sophie (Buda) Shalucha; Ph.B., U. Vt., 1937, M.S., 1938; Ph.D., Ohio State U., 1947; postdoctoral U. London, 1954. Grad. research fellow Vt. Exptl. Sta., Burlington, 1937-38; Dow research asst. Conn. Coll. Women, New London, 1938-42, instr. botany, 1942-43; grad. research fellow Ohio Agr. Exptl. Sta., Wooster, 1943-45; asst. curator Pub. Instr., Bklyn. Botanic Garden, 1945-47; instr. botany Ind. U., Bloomington, 1947-52, asst. prof., 1952-70, asso. prof., 1970—. Adviser, Washington Youth Garden Council, 1963—; vis. prof. Cornell U., 1970-71, Royal Botanic Garden, Kew, Eng., 1971; v.p. Nat. Civic Garden Centers, 1973—; cons. numerous garden centers. Bd. dirs., co-founder Bloomington Youth Garden Center. Mem. Bot. Soc. Am., Am. Soc. Hort. Sci., Ind. Acad. Sci., Nat. Sci. Tchrs. Assn., Am. Nature Study Soc., Nature Conservancy, Am. Hort. Soc., Hort. Edn. Assn. (Eng.), Nat. Audubon Soc., Sigma Xi, Delta Kappa Gamma, Pi Alpha Xi, Sigma Delta Epsilon, Am. Assn. U. Women. Methodist. Clubs: Bloomington Garden, University, Womens Faculty (pres. 1966-67). Contbr. articles to profl. jours. Author: Horticulture in General Education, 1966. Home: 1603 E 3d St Bloomington IN 47401

SHAMBURGER, (ALICE) PAGE, author; b. Aberdeen, N.C.; d. Frank Dudley and Alice (Page) Shamburger; grad. St. Mary's Sch. and Jr. Coll., 1945, Marjorie Webster Coll., 1947. Roving editor Am. Aviation Mag., 1949-51; script writer Radio Sta. WHUC, 1951-53; Eastern editor Cross Country News, 1954-67; contbg. editor Air Progress, 1966-74; mem. Woman's Adv. Com. on Aviation, 1964-68; mem. aviation div. N.C. Emergency Transp. Task Force, 1966-67; cons. N.C. Vet. Research Found.; adviser Nat. Inter-collegiate Flying Assn., 1970—. Sec. Mid-South Horse Show Assn.; asst. sec. Moore County Hounds; mem. N.C. Aviation Edn. Council. Recipient commendations N.C. Gov., USAF Tactical Command, 1966; Lady Hay-Drummond-Hay trophy, 1971; Doris Mullen Meml. scholar, 1969. Mem. Aviation/Space Writers Assn., 99s-Internat. Orgn. Licensed Woman Pilots (gov. S.E. sect. 1969-71, curator Ninety-Nines Mus 1969), Aircraft Owners and Pilots Assn., Univ. Aviation Assn. (dir.), Nat. Aero. Assn., Carolina Aero Club, Nat. Pilots Assn., Air Force Hist. Found., Air Force Assn., Am. Aviation Hist. Soc., Wingfoot Lighter-than-air Soc., Antique Airplane Assn., Am. Assn. Jr. Colls. (adv. com. aviation guidelines), Exptl. Aircraft Assn., Southeastern Aviation Trades Assn. Democrat. Methodist. Author: Tracks Across The Sky, 1964; Classic Monoplanes, 1966; co-author: Command the Horizon, 1968; Aces and Planes, World War I, 1968; Summon the Stars, 1970; The Curtiss Hawks, 1972. Contbr. articles to profl. publs. Address: 500 Carolina St Aberdeen NC 28315

SHAMES, CONSTANCE (MRS. A. ALLEN BLOCK), physician, educator; b. Omaha, Oct. 9, 1933; d. Frank Aaron and Anne (Small) Shames; B.A., Hunter Coll., 1955; M.A., Coll. City N.Y.; M.D., State U. N.Y., 1963; m. A. Allen Block, Sept. 17, 1967; children—Sharon Ruth, Marla Anne. Intern St. Lukes's Hosp., N.Y.C., 1963-64; resident Flower Fifth Av. Hosp., N.Y.C., 1964-67; practice medicine specializing in internal medicine, N.Y.C., 1967-70; asso. dir. Med. Clinics at Met. Hosp., N.Y.C., 1969-71; asst. prof. medicine N.Y. Med. Coll., N.Y.C., 1970-71; clin. asst. prof. State U. N.Y. Downstate Med. Center, Bklyn., 1971—; dir. Med. Clinics Kings County Hosp., Bklyn., 1973—. Recipient Physicians Recognition award A.M.A., 1970-73. Diplomate Nat. Bd. Med. Examiners. Fellow Royal Soc. Health; mem. Am. Psychol. Assn., A.M.A., Phi Beta Kappa, Psi Chi. Home: 1655 Flatbush Av A 1406 Brooklyn NY 11210 Office: Kings County Hospital OPD 451 Clarkson Av Brooklyn NY 11203

SHANAHAN, ELWILL MATTSON (MRS. PAUL R. SHANAHAN), state ofcl.; b. Salina, Kan., Sept. 22, 1912; d. August G. and Adine (Peterson) Mattson; R.N., Swedish Covenant Hosp., Chgo.; m. Paul R. Shanahan, Oct. 13, 1951 (dec. Apr. 1966). Sec. of state Kan., Topeka, 1966—. Republican. Home: 1320 W 27th St Topeka KS 66611 Office: State Capitol Bldg Topeka KS 66612

SHANAS, ETHEL (MRS. LESTER J. PERLMAN), educator; b. Chgo., Sept. 6, 1914; d. Alex and Rebecca (Rich) Shanas; A.B., U. Chgo., 1935, M.A., 1937, Ph.D., 1949; m. Lester J. Perlman, May 17, 1940; 1 son, Michael S. Research asso., instr. U. Chgo., 1947-52; sr. research analyst Office Redevel. Coordinator, Chgo., 1952-53; lectr. social sci. U. Ill., 1954-56; research asso., asso. prof. U. Chgo., 1956-65; prof. sociology U. Ill. at Chgo. Circle, 1965—. Chmn., Research Com. for White House Conf. on Aging, State of Ill., 1960, mem. tech. com., 1971. Fellow Am. Sociol. Assn., Gerontol. Soc. (sec. 1963-69, pres. 1974); mem. Internat. Assn. Gerontology (sec. Am. br. 1964-72, governing body 1973—), Ill. Sociol. Assn. (pres. 1971-72). Author: Recreation and Delinquency, 1942; The Health of Older People: A Social Survey, 1962; (with G. F. Streib) Social Structure and the Family: Generational Relations, 1965; (with P. Townsend, D. Wedderburn, H. Friis, P. Milhoj, J. Stehouwer) Old People in Three Industrial Societies, 1968; (with J. Madge) Methodological Problems in Studies in Aging, 1968. Home: 609 Sheridan Rd Evanston IL 60202 Office: U Ill at Chicago Circle Chicago IL 60680

SHANE, CORINNE (MRS. NATHAN SHANE), pub. relations exec., broker; b. N.Y.C.; d. Samuel and Hanna (Greenberg) Saltzman; B.A. in Econs., Hunter Coll.; m. Nathan Shane, Nov. 18, 1962; children—Scott Andrew, Cari Meredith. Editorial asst. Parents Mag., N.Y.C.; asst. account exec. Edward Gottlieb & Assos., N.Y.C.; account exec. Theodore R. Sills Co., N.Y.C.; group supr., v.p. Harshe-Rothman & Druck, Inc., N.Y.C.; now pres. Terminal Adv. Services, Inc., N.Y.C. Specialist ins. and mutual funds for women. Mem. Parents League N.Y., Westport Tennis Assn., N.Y. Turn Verein. Office: 61 W 23 St New York City NY 10010

SHANE, RITA (MRS. DANIEL F. TRITTER), singer; b. N.Y.C.; d. Julius J. and Rebecca (Milner) Shane; B.A., Barnard; student voice under Beverley Peck Johnson, Santa Fe Opera Apprentice Program, 1962-63, Hunter Coll. Opera Theater, 1962-64, Juilliard Opera Theater, 1965; m. Daniel F. Tritter; 1 son, Michael Shane. Made debut as Olympia, Chattanooga Opera, 1964; appeared in N.Y.C. Opera, Chgo. Lyric Opera, Santa Fe Opera, San Diego Opera, St. Louis Opera Festival, Chautauqua Opera, Lake George Opera, North Shore Opera, Ky. Opera, New Orleans Opera Lincoln Center Mozart Festival, Aspen Festival, La Scala, Milan, Munich Festival, Geneva Opera, Netherlands Opera, Bavarian State Opera, Vienna State Opera, Vienna Festival, Santa Cecilia, Rome, Salzburg Festival, also various U.S. orchs., recitals; debut Met. Opera, 1973; recorded with RCA Victor, Columbia Records, Louisville Premiere Recs. Martha Baird Rockefeller Fund grantee, 1964; Walter Matheus Sullivan Found. grantee, 1965. Mem. Am. Guild Mus. Artists. Club: Knickerbocker Dachshund (N.Y.C.). Address: care Herbert Breslin 119 W 57th St New York City NY 10019

SHANEYFELT, SHIRLEY NADENE FEARN, artist, educator; b. Hastings, Neb.; d. Oris C. and Calla (Wary) Fearn; student Hastings Coll., Corcoran Sch. Art, George Washington U., 1972; pvt. study with Andrea Di Zerega, Laura Douglas, Joseph Pielage, Yolande Mayhall; m. Lyndal L. Shaneyfelt, June 16, 1940; 1 son, Terry Leroy. One-man shows at Lee Galleries, Alexandria, Va., 1961, FBI, Washington, 1965—, Heron House Gallery, Reston, Va., 1966, Galleries, Art League No. Va., 1967, others; exhibited in group-shows at Smithsonian Instn., Washington, 1952, 57, Georgetown U., Washington, 1963, Old Towne Gallery, Alexandria, 1965, Washington Gallery Art, 1965, U. Va., Charlottesville, 1965, Hadassah Invitational Shows, Alexandria, Va., 1967-74, Alexandria br. Pen Women Group Show, Gallery on Mall, 1969, Gilliam Show, Art League, Alexandria, 1972, Cottage Tour Art, Rehoboth Beach, Del., 1972, Corcoran Sch. Art, 1972, others; represented in permanent collections Gen. Testing Labs., Alexandria, Crestwood Elementary Sch., Springfield, Va., Atlantic Research Corp., Alexandria; also pvt. collections. Recipient 1st prize Springfield Contemporary Show, 1956; 4th prize No. Va. Art League, 1959, 2d, 3d prizes, 1959; 1st prize (2), 2d prize Women's Club of Va., 1959; 1st prize Art League Marshall Show, 1961; 1st prize Art League, 1963, 3d prize, 1963; 3d prize Picasso Show, Hecht's, Washington, 1963; 1st prize Galleries, Art League, 1967; Artist of Year award No. Va. Cotillion, 1973. Mem. Nat. League Am. Pen Women (1st v.p. 1964-65), Art League No. Va. (2d v.p. 1962-63; gallery hanging chmn. 1967), Am. Art League, Shane Painters (dir. 1962—). Clubs: Women's Belle-Haven (art chmn. Alexandria 1963-65). Address: 6125 Vernon Terrace Alexandria VA 22307

SHANK, DOROTHY ROTH, writer, editor, radio broadcaster; b. Turbotville, Pa., Aug. 18, 1907; d. William H. and Bessie L. (Lotz) Roth; B.A., Brown U., 1929; m. Lawrence S. Shank, June 24, 1937. Instr. English and history jr. high sch., Malvern, Pa., 1931-37; coach dramatics Footlighters Wayne, Pa. and Niagara Falls Little Theatre; radio broadcaster WHLD, Niagara Falls, 1944-45; copywriter for radio broadcast advt. Adam Meldrum Anderson's (dept. store), Buffalo, 1945-57, personnel dir. and tng. for 5 br. stores, 1957—; fashion editor women's news feature writer Niagara Falls Gazette, 1957-59; radio commentator as Amanda, WEBR, Buffalo, 1945-57; broadcaster, woman's dir., sta. WJJL, 1959—. Pub. relations dir. Niagara Falls Winter Festival, 1968-70. Chmn. bd. dirs. Niagara County Vol. Action Com., 1966-68, 1st v.p., 1971—; mem. exec. bd. Niagara County Cancer Soc., 1970—; bd. dirs., exec. com., vice chmn. Niagara Falls Youth Bd.; exec. bd. Niagara County Kidney Found., 1972—. Named Nat. Outstanding Woman in Communications, 1969-70; Woman of Yr., Niagara Council of Women's Assns., 1971. Recipient award Am. Cancer Soc., 1969. Mem. Am. Women in Radio and TV (past pres. Western N.Y.), Bus. and Profl. Women's Club (dir., pres. Niagara Falls chpt., 1963-65, 70-71), Nat. Screen Guild Council, Buffalo Advt. Women, Albright Art Gallery, Am. Pen Women (bd. mem. Western N.Y.), Assn. Profl. Women Writers (past pres.) Nat. League Am. Pen Women (radio chmn. Western N.Y. br. 1966-67, 1st v.p. 1968-70, pres. 1970-72), Niagara Falls C. of C. (dir. women's com. 1963-65, chmn. women's div. 1965-67), Internat. Platform Assn. Lutheran. Club: Coll. (bd. dirs. 1959-61) (Niagara Falls); Zonta (bd. mem.; pres. 1966-68). Home: 205 59th St Niagara Falls NY 14304 Office: 1224 Main St Niagara Falls NY 14301

SHANK, MARGARETHE ERDAHL (MRS. OLIVER REYNOLDS SHANK), educator, author; b. Turtle Lake, N.D., July 21, 1910; d. Bertinus N. and Gyda (Jaastad) Erdahl; B.A., U. Ariz., 1932; postgrad. U. Cal., 1938; M.A., Ariz. State U., 1959; m. Oliver Reynolds Shank, July 10, 1935; 1 son, Stephen Henry. Tchr. English, Chandler (Ariz.) High Sch., 1932-35, Sweetwater High Sch. Dist., Chula Vista, Cal., 1940-42, Washington High Sch., Phoenix, 1958, 59; faculty Phoenix Coll., 1959-65; faculty Glendale (Ariz.) Community Coll., 1966—, prof. English, 1970—. Mem. Am. Assn. U. Profs., Author's Guild, Alpha Delta Kappa. Republican. Lutheran. Author: The Coffee Train, 1953; Call Back The Years, 1966. Contbr. articles, short stories to various publs. Home: 9860 N 29th Pl Phoenix AZ 85028 Office: Glendale Coll Glendale AZ 85301

SHANK, MARY ELLEN, assn. exec.; b. Saint John, Kan., Dec. 24, 1935; d. Harry Judah and Cora Helen (Long) Waters; teaching certificate McPherson Coll., 1956; m. Robert Henry Shank, Mar. 17, 1957; children—Theryne Kay, Kevyn Ray. Sec. to dean women McPherson Coll. (Kan.), 1955-56; tchr. Johnson (Kan.) Grade Sch., 1956-58; co-owner, co-mgr. wheat and livestock farm, Saint John, 1957—; state pres. Kan. Fedn. Women's Democratic Clubs, 1971—. Mem. Gov.'s Commn. on Status of Women, 1968—. Vice chmn. Stafford County Central Dem. Com., 1964-68, chmn., 1968—. Mem. D.A.R. Mem. Ch. of Brethren. Clubs: Junior Golden Circle, St. John Saddle, Women's Kansas Day, Kansas Woodrow Wilson. Home and Office: Route 2 Box 126 Saint John KS 67576

SHANK, ORELIA W. HIGH, health services adminstr., ret. educator; b. Zebulon, N.C., May 12, 1915; d. Windric Clarence and Ada Blanche (Cox) High; student Hampton Inst., 1936-38; A.B., N.C. State Coll., 1942; certificate Chgo. Tchrs. Coll., 1960; postgrad. Columbia U., 1953-60; M.A. in Teaching, Northeastern Ill. U., 1968; m. Grady O'Neal Shank, May 5, 1945. Riveter, Eastern Aircraft Corp., Tarrytown, N.Y., 1942-45; tchr. Laurinburg (N.C.) Inst., 1945; clk. City Tax Office, Los Angeles, 1948-50; bd. clk. SSS, Chgo., 1951-52; tchr. Chgo. Bd. Edn., 1952-73; clk. med. records Greenburgh Neighborhood Health Center, White Plains, N.Y., 1973—; also tchr. adult edn., White Plains. Mem. Chgo. Tchrs. Union, Speech Assn. Am., Phi Delta Kappa, Zeta Phi Beta (recipient Finer Womanhood award 1968). Author: Who Am I?, 1975. Home: 2 Hayes St Elmsford NY 10523 Office: 330 Tarrytown Rd White Plains NY 10607

SHANKMAN, FLORENCE VOGEL, educator; b. Norwalk, Conn., July 16, 1912; d. Morris and Betty (Jacobson) Vogel; student Danbury State Coll., 1930; B.S., Tchrs. Coll., Columbia, 1934, M.A., 1936; M.A., N.Y.U., 1955, Ed.D., 1959; m. Louis Shankman, Aug. 29, 1937 (dec. 1952); children—Martin, Robert S., Susan E. Pub. sch. tchr., Norwalk, Conn., 1930-37, 53-59; tchr. fgn. born and high sch. equivalency courses, Norwalk, 1939-47, New Rochelle, N.Y., 1950-51, Wilton, Conn., 1952-53; instr. N.Y.U. Sch. Edn., also N.Y.U. Reading Inst., 1955-59; supr. instrn. N.Y.U. Reading Inst., N.Y.C., 1959-62; asso. prof. edn. U. So. Cal., summer 1962; asst. prof. edn. U. Bridgeport (Conn.), 1962-65, asso. prof. edn. Keene (N.H.) State Coll., 1965-67; asso. prof. Temple U. Coll. Edn., Phila., 1967-72, prof. curriculum and instrn., 1972—; guest prof. State U. Colo., Greeley, 1967; vis. prof. U. Colo., Greeley, summer 1969; reading cons., author, 1955—. Mem. Acad. Reading Experts to assist N.Y.C. Bd. Edn., 1961—; mem. N.H. Ednl. Policies Commn., 1966—; del. World Congress of Reading, Sydney, Australia, 1970, Buenos Aires, Argentina, 1972. First aid instr. A.R.C.; active Conn. Mental Health Assn., Tb and Health Assn., Crippled Children's Assn. drives; mem. women's com. Norwalk Symphony Orch. Exec. bd. Danbury State Coll. Mem. Nat. Soc. for Study Edn., N.E.A., Conn. Edn. Assn., Am. Assn. U. Profs., Am. Assn. U. Women, Am. Psychol. Assn., Elementary Prins. Assn., Assn. Supervision Curriculum Devel., Nat. Council Tchrs. English, Internat. Reading Assn., New Edn. Fellowship, Am. Assn. Sch. Adminstrs., Assn. Childhood Edn. Internat. (life), Nat. Council Jewish Women (pres. 1938), Am. Ednl. Research Assn., Assn. Student Teaching, Nat. Council Social Studies (exec. bd. dirs. New Edn. fellowship N.Y. chpt.), Coll. Reading Assn., Piaget Soc., Pa. Edn. Assn., N.Y. U. Faculty Club and Alumni Assn., Internat. Platform Assn., U. Bridgeport, Newcomers Faculty Club (sec.-treas. 1963—, Kappa Delta Pi (life mem.), also Pi Lambda Theta (life). Club: Women's Press of New York City; Temple U. Faculty Women's (sec.-treas. 1973-74). Author: (with Robert Kranyik) How To Teach Study Skills, 1963; Successful Practices in Remedial Reading, 1963; How to Teach Reference and Research Skills, 1964; Readings About Reading Instruction, 1968; Research Studies in Reading, Vol. I, II, 1969; Readings in the Language Arts, 3 vols., 1969; Reading Success for Young Children, 1970; Reading for Inner City Children, 1970; Methods of Teaching Reading, 1970; Specialized Methods of Teaching Reading, 1970; Teaching Reading and Language to Inner-City Children, 1971; Teaching Techniques With Phonics, Linguistics and Games, 1971; Games and Activities to Reinforce Reading Skills, 2d edit., 1973; Crossword Puzzles for Phonics, 1972; film We Discover the Encyclopedia, 1971; also revs. Contbr. to profl. mags. Home: 32 West Av South Norwalk CT 06854 also Columbia Av Philadelphia PA 19122 Office: Temple U Coll Edn Philadelphia PA 19122

SHANKS, ANN ZANE KUSHNER (MRS. ROBERT HORTON SHANKS), photographer, writer; b. N.Y.C.; d. Louis and Sadye (Rosenthal) Kushner; ed. Carnegie Inst. Tech., Columbia; m. Ira Zane (dec.); children—Jennifer, Anthony; m. 2d, Robert Horton Shanks, Sept. 25, 1959; 1 son, John. Photographer, filmmaker, writer for numerous mags., newspapers including Life, Time, Esquire, Fortune, N.Y. Times, Redbook, Cosmopolitan; spl. assignments include Redevel. and Housing Authority, Newark, Norfolk, N.Y.C., Newark Bus., Queens Borough libraries, others; producer Women on the Move, NBC-TV; script editor CBS, also dir. nat. TV script competition for coll. students; asso. producer World Video, Inc.; producer, dir. Central Park (movie short, U.S. entry Edinburgh Film Festival; Cine Golden Eagle, Cambodia Film Festival award), 1969; producer, dir. Denmark . . . A Loving Embrace (Cine Golden Eagle 1973), Tivoli (movie short, San Francisco Film Festival award, Am. Film Festival award), 1972, TV series American Life Style (silver and gold medal awards Internat. TV and Film Festival N.Y.); exhibited photographs Mus. Modern Art, Mus. City N.Y., Met. Mus. Art, Caravan Gallery, Parents Mag. Tchr., moderator spl. symposiums Mus. Modern Art, Ednl. Alliance (N.Y.C.). Recipient 4 awards, internat. competitions, also named one of 6 young talents in Am., Photography Mag., award U.S. Camera Ann., 3 awards for photography Nat. Housing Yearbook; named New Talent in Photography, Art in Am. Mag., 1959. Mem. Am. Soc. Mag. Photographers (bd. govs.), Overseas Press Club Am. (chmn. 1970 photog. awards). Author: The Name's the Game (photographs and text), 1961; New Jewish Ency. (photographs), 1966; Adolescent Development (photographs), 1967. Writer, photographer: (juvenile) Garbage and Stuff. Home: 201B E 82d St New York City NY 10028

SHANNON, ILA WEESE WHITE, educator; b. Monticello, Ark., Apr. 22, 1912; d. John Wesley and Charity Elizabeth (Ragland) White; student Northwestern U., Evanston, Ill., 1929-31, U. Fayetteville (Ark.), 1931-32; B.S. in Speech, Northwestern U., 1935; m. Harry Lee Shannon, Jr., Dec. 26, 1938; children—Harry Lee III, John White. Tchr., Fairview Sch., Camden, Ark., 1932-33, 36-39, Star City (Ark.) High Sch., 1951-57, Ark. A. and M. Coll., Monticello, 1965-70, U. Ark. at Monticello, 1971—. Life mem., past sec. P.T.A. Recipient Commendation service to arts; Shannon Creative Dramatics award given in her honor, 1974—. Mem. D.A.R. (regent Col. David Love chpt. 1972-73), Drew County Hist. Soc. (life), Wesleyan Service Guild (past pres., life mem.), Am. Assn. U. Women (life), Ark. Speech Assn., Ark. Edn. Assn. Zeta Phi Eta, Chi Omega. Methodist (Sunday sch. tchr.). Home: Star City AR 71667 Office: University of Arkansas Monticello AR 71655

SHANNON, MARGARET RITA, educator; b. Cambridge, Mass., May 20, 1915; d. James J. and Catherine M. (McDonough) Shannon; B.S., Mass. State Coll., 1936; M.Ed., Harvard, 1947, Ed.D., 1959. Tchr. pub. schs., Cambridge, 1936-51; asst. prof. Mass. State Coll., Lowell, 1951-59, asso. prof. 1959-65, prof., 1965—, chmn. dept. edn., 1969-74; dean Sch. Edn. U. Lowell, 1974—; sometimes lectr. Mem. Internat. Reading Assn. (cons. nat. conf.), Am. Ednl. Research Assn., Nat. Council Tchrs. English (com. on linguistics and reading), Am. Assn. U. Profs., Am. Assn. U. Women, Delta Kappa Gamma, Pi Lambda Theta (chpt. pres. 1958-61). Author textbooks. Contbr. articles to profl. jours. Home: 374 Park Av Arlington MA 02174 Office: Sch Edn U Lowell St Lowell MA 01854

SHANOFF, CAROLYN SEIGEL (MRS. BARRY S. SHANOFF), editor; b. Bklyn., Apr. 13, 1947; d. Kalman Arthur and Lillian (Turetsky) Seigel; B.A., U. Vt., 1967; student Inst. for Am. U., Aix-en-Provence, France, 1965-66; M.S. in Journalism, Northwestern U., 1968; m. Barry S. Shanoff, Feb. 14, 1970; 1 son, Daniel Aaron. Harris Found. fellow, ednl. intern WTTW, Channel 11, Chgo., 1968-69; account exec. Herbert H. Rozoff Assos., Chgo., 1969-70; supr. editorial services Quaker Oats Co., Chgo., 1970-71; press and community relations asso. Continental Ill. Nat. Bank, Chgo., 1971-72; free lance press relations and editing Student Am. Med. Assn., also Morton B. Stone & Asso. Pub. Relations, 1973—. Mem. Nat. Orgn. for Women, Women In Communications, Common Cause, Chgo. Ednl. TV Assn. Jewish religion. Editorial cons. The New Physician, 1973—. Home: 513 W Aldine Av Chicago IL 60657

SHAPERO, ESTHER BAILEY GELLER (MRS. HAROLD SHAPERO), artist; b. Boston, Oct. 26, 1921; d. Harry and Fannie (Geller) Geller; diploma Sch. Boston Mus. Fine Arts, 1943; m. Harold Shapero, Sept. 21, 1945; 1 dau., Hannah. One-man shows Boris Mirski Gallery, 1945, 49, 52, 61, Addison Gallery Am. Art, 1945, Children's Art Center, Boston, 1946, 53, Marion (Mass.) Art Center, 1965, Decenter Gallery, Copenhagen, Denmark, 1969, St. Mark's Sch., Mass., 1969, Regis Coll., 1970, Am. Acad. Gallery, Rome, Italy, Newton (Mass.) Free Library, 1973; exhibited in group shows including San Francisco Mus. Art, Va. Mus. Fine Arts, Worcester Art Mus., Chgo. Art Inst., U. Ill., De Cordova and Dana Mus., Lincoln, Mass., Brandeis U., U. Miami, Boston Art Festivals; represented in permanent collections Boston Mus. Fine Arts, Addison Gallery Am. Art, Brandeis U., also pvt. collections. Tchr. Boston Mus. Sch., 1943, private art classes, 1944, 52, Boris Mirski Art Sch., 1947, 48, Natick Art Assn., 1955, 61. Cabot fellow, 1949. Address: 9 Russell Circle Natick MA 01760

SHAPIRO, BARBARA LINDA, educator; b. N.Y.C., June 17, 1941; d. Charles Wright and Olga Ethel (Soderstrom) Pedersen; B.A. summa cum laude, William Smith Coll., 1963; M.A., Harvard, 1964, Ph.D., 1973; m. Daniel W. Shapiro, June 27, 1965; 1 son, Benjamin. Instr. English, U. Denver, 1967-69; adj. instr. English, Dartmouth, 1972-73; asst. prof. English, Colo. State U., Ft. Collins, 1973—. Mem. Modern Lang. Assn., Am. Civil Liberties Union, Phi Beta Kappa. Home: 2917 Calle Princesa Juana Santa Fe NM 87501

SHAPIRO, BETTY KRONMAN (MRS. MICHAEL SHAPIRO), civic worker; b. Washington; d. Nathan and Mollie (Bogorad) Kronman; student Cornell U., George Washington U.; m. Michael Shapiro, July 5, 1936. Sec., Langley Jr. High Sch., Washington, 1924-28; office mgr., sec. to gen. counsel Washington office Hebrew Immigrant Aid Soc., 1929-43. Pres., B'nai B'rith Women Dist. 5, Eastern Seaboard region, 1955-56; chmn. pub. affairs com. B'nai B'rith Women, 1965-68, 2d v.p., 1st v.p., mem. exec. bd., 1957, internat. pres., 1968-71, chmn. internat. affairs, 1971—, mem. exec. com. Anti-Defamation League; mem. adv. bd. vol. services D.C. Gen. Hosp., 1952—; mem. exec. com. Jewish Community Council Greater Washington, 1953-69, 71—, sec., 1957-61, also chmn. com. on Soviet Jewry; mem. exec. com. United Jewish Appeal Greater Washington, 1955-57, Am.-Israel Pub. Affairs Com., 1968—; mem. exec. com. womens div. Washington Conf. Christians and Jews, 1963-67; chmn. Washington ad hoc com. Conf. Nat. Jewish Women's Orgns.; mem. steering com. Internat. Visitors Information Services, 1969. Mem. Women's Nat. Democratic Club, 1969—. Mem. League Women Voters, Capital Area chpt. UN Assn.-U.S.A. Home: 6946 33d St NW Washington DC 20015 Office: 1640 Rhode Island Av NW Washington DC 20036

SHAPIRO, CAROL SADIE, plastic surgeon; b. Pitts., Sept. 24, 1939; d. Leo I. and Charlotte H. (Heller) Shapiro; B.S., U. Pitts., 1961; M.D. Woman's Med. Coll. Pa., 1965; m. Donald E. Morgan, May 1974. Intern, Phila. Gen. Hosp., 1965-66; resident gen. surgery Georgetown U. Hosp., Washington, 1966-69, resident plastic surgery, 1969-71, post tng. fellow, 1971-72; practice medicine specializing in plastic surgery Dumfries (Va.) Med. Center, 1972—; mem. staff Potomac Hosp., Woodbridge, Va., Prince William Hosp., Manassas, Va., Commonwealth Hosp., Fairfax, Va.; clin. instr. Georgetown U. Sch. Medicine, 1972—. Vol. team physician Garfield High Sch. Football Team, 1971—. Home: 6120 Shiplett Blvd Burke VA 22015 Office: Dumfries Med Center Dumfries VA 22026

SHAPIRO, DEBORAH PHYLLIS MUND (MRS. ISAIAH LEON SHAPIRO), occupational therapist; b. N.Y.C., May 2, 1932; d. Benjamin and Anna (Lichtenstein) Mund; B.S., N.Y. U., 1955; m. Isaiah Leon Shapiro, Dec. 16, 1962; 1 son, Nathan Barry. Staff therapist Kingsbrook Hosp., Bklyn., 1955-56; mem. staff Meadowbrook Hosp., East Meadow, N.Y., 1956-59; chief Crippled Children's Clinic, Bridgeport, Conn., 1959-61, Kingsbrook Hosp., Bklyn., 1962-65; sr., Pilgrim State Hosp. West Brentwood, N.Y., 1967-70, head, 1970-73, chief, 1973—. Mem. Am., N.Y., L.I. occupational therapy assns. Jewish religion. Home: 115 Bowling Lane Deer Park NY 11729 Office: Pilgrim State Hosp West Brentwood NY 11717

SHAPIRO, DEE MANDELL (MRS. STANLEY SHAPIRO), artist; b. Bklyn.; d. Charles I. and Irene (Watner) Mandell; B.A., Queens Coll., 1958, M.S., 1960; postgrad. U. Mexico, 1956, Bklyn. Mus. Art Sch., 1962-65; m. Stanley Shapiro, Jan. 2, 1960; children—Adam Marc, Nina Lisbeth. Tchr., Creedmoor State Hosp., 1958-61, N.Y.C. Pub. Schs., 1961-65, Great Neck (N.Y.) Pub. Schs., 1967; art tchr. Queens Children's Hosp., 1968-71; coordinator Central Hall Artists' Gallery, Port Washington, N.Y., 1973—. Lectr. Nassau County Council Arts, 1973—. Recipient Anonymous award Nat. Assn. Women Artists, 1973. Award of Excellence, Huntington Twp. Art League Heckscher Mus., 1973. Mem. Women in the Arts, Nat. Assn. Women Artists.

SHAPIRO, DENA MECKLER (MRS. BARRY ALAN SHAPIRO), occupational therapist; b. Cleve., May 17, 1946; d. Sam and Esther Ida (Faigen) Meckler; student Cuyahoga Community Coll., 1964-65; B.S., Ohio State U., 1969; m. Barry Alan Shapiro, June 9, 1968. Occupational therapy technician Mt. Sinai Hosp., Cleve., 1967, Westwood Psychiat. Hosp., Los Angeles, 1967; staff Rancho Los Amigos Hosp., Downey, Cal., 1969-71; acting sr. staff occupational therapist, 1971-72; occupational therapy cons. Greater Los Angeles Orthopedic Group 1973—; dir. occupational therapy, White Meml. Med. Center Rehab. Center, Los Angeles, 1974—; cons. Donald Hager, Inc., 1974—. Vice Pres., sec. Budget Analysis Systems, Inc., Los Angeles, 1973—. Mem. Am., So. Cal. occupational therapy assns., So. Cal. Schs. Council, Am. Rheumatism Assn., Cal. Assn. Physically Handicapped. Home: 2653 Corning Av Los Angeles CA 90034 Office: White Meml Med Center Rehab Center 1720 Brooklyn Av Los Angeles CA 90033

SHAPIRO, EDITH TENNENBAUM (MRS. HARRIS SHAPIRO), physician; b. Zloczow, Poland, Feb. 7, 1935; d. Samuel Lipa and Elisabeth (Horowitz) Tennebaum; B.A., Barnard Coll., 1956; M.D., N.Y.U., 1961; m. Harris Shapiro, Sept. 11, 1955; children—Diana Lynn, Mark Leon. Came to U.S., 1946, naturalized, 1952. Intern, Hackensack (N.J.) Hosp., 1961-62; resident N.Y. Med. Coll., N.Y.C., 1962-65, Nat. Inst. Mental Health career tchr., 1966-68, dir. residency tng. program psychiatry, 1965-70, dir. residency tng. program for physician mothers, 1965-70, instr., 1964-67, asst. prof. psychiatry, 1968—; practice medicine, specializing in psychiatry, Englewood, N.J., 1968—; asso. attending psychiatrist Beth Israel Hosp., N.Y.C., 1970-72; asso. in psychiatry Mt. Sinai Sch. Medicine, 1970-72; clin. asso. prof. psychiatry N.J. Coll. Medicine and Dentistry at Newark, 1972—; mem. staff Hackensack Hosp.; dir. in-patient service psychiatry, acting clin. dir. psychiatry Martland Hosp.-N.J. Med. Sch. and Community Mental Health Center, 1973. Diplomate Am. Bd. Psychiatry and Neurology. Mem. Am. Psychiat. Assn., A.M.A., Womens Med. Assn., Bergen County Med. Soc., Am. Jewish Congress. Hadassah. Home: 211 Davison Pl Englewood NJ 07631 Office: 211 Davison Pl Englewood NJ 07631

SHAPIRO, MARY FRANCES (MRS. KIEVE L. SHAPIRO), lawyer; b. Akron, O., Jan. 20, 1937; d. Francis William and Marian Estelle (Fetter) Spicer; B.A., Heidelberg Coll., 1958; M.A., U. Chgo., 1960; J.D., U. Akron, 1965; m. Kieve L. Shapiro, Oct. 8, 1960. Psychiat. social worker Summit County Receiving Hosp., Cuyahoga Falls, O., 1960-65; admitted to Ohio bar, 1965; mem. firm Spicer & Shapiro, Akron, 1965—. Psychiat. social worker Kieve L. Shapiro, M.D., Akron, O., 1962-73. Mem. Nat. Council Juvenile Court Judges, Nat. Assn. Social Workers, Am. Judicature Soc., Am., Ohio, Akron bar assns., Am. Assn. U. Women. Home: 663 Polk Av Akron OH 44314 Office: 974 Kenmore Blvd Akron OH 44314

SHAPIRO, PHYLLIS (MRS. ABRAHAM SHAPIRO), hotel adminstr.; b. Montreal, Que., Can., Mar. 12, 1922; d. Isadore and Sadie (Novack) Hochmitz; student Sullivan Bus. Coll., Montreal, 1939-41; m. Abraham Shapiro, Aug. 22, 1961. Asst. mgr. Nat. Food Store Ltd., Montreal, 1942-45; office comptroller Dixon Watch Importing Co., 1945-48, adminstr. Bernard Schaeffer & Sons, importing agy., 1948-51; exec. sec. William Rosenberg, architect, 1951-57; exec. sec. Eugene Meth Assos., financier, 1957-61; adminstr., conv. mgr. Twin City Motel, Brewer, Me., 1968—; v.p. Bangor House Motor Hotel (Me.), 1973—. Mem. Jewish religion. Mem. B'nai Brith, Hadassah. Home: 58 Broadway Bangor ME 04401 Office: 453 Wilson St Brewer ME 04412

SHAPIRO, SANDRA BERNSTEIN (MRS. EDWIN SHAPIRO), artist; b. Bklyn., Jan. 21, 1934; d. Harry and Ethel Bernstein; B.S., Sarah Lawrence Coll., 1955; m. Edwin Shapiro, Sept. 20, 1957; children—James, Sarah. Textile designer M. Lowenston & Co., 1955-56, John Wolfe Co., 1956-57; tchr. elementary sch., 1957-58; one-woman show Briarcliff Coll., Katonah Gallery, St. Peter's Lutheran Ch., N.Y.C. Mem. Art Lending Service, Katonah Gallery, Hudson River Mus. Recipient Medal of Honor, Nat. Assn. Women Artists, 1973. Mem. Silverming Guild.

SHAPIRO, SYLVIA CELIA, lawyer; b. Boston, Sept. 26, 1913; d. Isadore Rubin and Mollie (Fishman) Cohen; J.D. cum laude, Boston U., 1935; m. Robert Shapiro, July 6, 1935; children—Roberta (Mrs. Marc E. Saperstein), Richard N. Admitted to Mass. bar, 1935; pvt. practice law, 1935-39; atty. Boston Housing Authority, 1939-42, Boston Ordnance Dist., 1942; practice law, Boston, 1970—; asso. firm Foley, Hoag & Eliot, Boston, 1972—. Former bd. dirs. Beth Israel Hosp. Women's Aux., Women's Div. Am. Jewish Congress, Parents Assn. Cambridge Sch., others; former chmn. Brookline women's div. Combined Jewish Philanthropies. Served as capt. WAC, 1942-45. Mem. Mass., Boston bar assns., Mass. Assn. Women Lawyers. Asso. editor Boston U. Law Rev. Home: 155 Seaver St Brookline MA 02146

SHARMAT, MARJORIE EVELYN WEINMAN (MRS. MITCHELL BRENNER SHARMAT), author; b. Portland, Me., Nov. 12, 1928; d. Nathan and Anna (Richardson) Weinman; student Lasell Jr. Coll., 1946-47; grad. Westbrook Jr. Coll., 1948; m. Mitchell Brenner Sharmat, Feb. 24, 1957; children—Craig Lynden, Andrew Richard. Mem. circulation staff U. Library, Yale, 1951-54, Yale Law Library, 1954-55; writer advt. copy, 1949—, greeting card verse, 1957—. Vol. worker Am. Heart Assn., Am. Cancer Soc., 1958-67; mem. Friends of Irvington Library. Republican. Jewish religion. Author: Rex, 1967; Goodnight, Andrew Goodnight, Craig, 1969; Gladys Told Me to Meet Her Here, 1970; A Hot Thirsty Day, 1971; 51 Sycamore Lane, 1971; Getting Something on Maggie Marmelstein, 1971; A Visit with Rosalind, 1972; Nate the Great, 1972; Sophie and Gussie, 1973; Morris Brookside, A Dog, 1973; Nate the Great Goes Undercover, 1974; Morris Brookside is Missing, 1974; I Want Mama, 1974; I'm Not Oscar's Friend Any More, 1975. Home: 51 Sycamore Lane Irvington-on-Hudson NY 10533

SHAROFF, GWENDOLYN IDELL ANDERSON, educator; b. Houston, July 16, 1940; d. Leroy Lawrence and Harriett Idell (Galbreath) Anderson; B.A., Baylor U., 1962, M.A., 1963; postgrad. U. So. Cal.; m. Michael Sharoff, June 20, 1970. Tchr., Victoria (Tex.) High Sch., 1963-64; dir. Galveston (Tex.) Teen-Children's Theatre, 1964-66; asst. prof. speech and drama, dir. theatre Culver-Stockton Coll., Canton, Mo., 1966-69; instr. speech and drama, costumer Bradley U., Peoria, Ill., 1969-70; prodn. supr. studio co. Acad. Dramatic Art, Oakland U., Rochester, Mich., 1970-71; instr. theatre Fullerton (Cal.) Jr. Coll., 1971-72, Cypress Coll., 1972-73, Cal. State Coll., San Bernardino, 1972-73; asst. prof. communications Chapman Coll., Orange, Cal., 1973—. Mem. Speech Assn. Am., Am. Nat. Theatre and Acad., Am. Theatre Assn., So. Cal. Ednl. Theatre Assn., Alpha Lambda Delta, Alpha Chi, Tau Beta Sigma, Alpha Psi Omega, Pi Alpha Lambda (parliamentarian, historian), Theta Alpha Phi, Mu Phi Epsilon. Contbr. book revs. to profl. jours. Home: 2032 Victoria Dr Fullerton CA 92631 Office: Chapman Coll 333 N Glassell St Orange CA 92666

SHARP, JEAN HARRIET SMITH (MRS. JACK K. SHARP), surgeon, physician; b. Alameda, Cal., Sept. 30, 1923; d. Kenneth Clyde and Anne (Kelsey) Smith; B.S., U. Cal. at Berkeley, 1944, Ph.N., 1947; M.D., Johannes Guttenberg U., Mainz, Germany, 1961; m. Jack Kenton Sharp, May 28, 1949; children—David Kelsey, Kathleen Lee. Pub. health nursing dept. staff, San Francisco, 1946-47, Berkeley, 1947-48, Alameda, 1951-52, Hayward, Cal., 1955-56, intern Amersham, Buckinghamshire, Eng., 1961-62, Herrick Meml. Hosp., Berkeley, 1963; pvt. practice pediatrics London, Eng., 1961; pvt. practice specializing in surgery, obstetrics-gynecology-pediatrics, Alameda, 1962—; now with South Shore Med. Group; mem. staff Alameda City Hosp., Herrick Meml. Hosp., Berkeley, Oakland Hosp., Children's Hosp. East Bay, St. Rose Hosp., Hayward, San Leandro (Cal.) Meml. Hosp. Home: 2034 Santa Clara St Alameda CA 94501 Office: 512 Westline Dr Alameda CA 94501

SHARP, LINDA NELL, communications co. exec.; b. Clayton, N.M., Feb. 17, 1947; d. Frank and Ada Francis (Bell) Sharp; student N.M. Inst. Mining and Tech., 1965-67; B.S., Ore. State U., 1969; m. Paul V. Spillar. News corr. KOAT-TV, Albuquerque, 1966-67; teaching asst. indsl. publs. Ore. State U., Corvallis, 1969; acting dir. pub. relations St. Vincent Hosp. and Med. Center, Portland, Ore., 1969-71; editor, mem. pub. relations staff Am. Tel. and Tel. Long Lines, San Francisco, 1971-73; prin. Sharp Communications, San Francisco, 1973—. Pub. relations cons. Mayor Alioto's com. on Status of Women Mayor's Forum, San Francisco, 1973. Recipient awards Internat. Assn. Bus. Communicators, 1973, Bay Area Soc. Indsl. Communicators, 1973, Ore. Assn. Editors and Communicators, 1970, Ore. Press Women, 1972. Mem. Internat. Assn. Bus. Communicators, Nat. Fedn. Press Women (chpt. co-founder), Women In Communications, Pi Mu Epsilon. Home and office: 80 Rosenkranz San Francisco CA 94110

SHARP, MARIANNE CLARK, religious orgn. ofcl.; b. Salt Lake City, Oct. 28, 1901; d. Joshua Reuben and Luacine Annetta (Savage) Clark; B.A. with high honors, U. Utah, 1924; D. Humanities, Brigham Young U., 1974; m. Ivor Sharp, June 15, 1927; children—Luacine (Mrs. Cecil E. Lloyd), Louise (Mrs. James C. Davis, Jr.), Annetta (Mrs. Morris L. Mower). Teaching fellow in Latin U. Utah, 1924, instr., 1925; mem. gen. bd. Relief Soc. Ch. of Jesus Christ of Latter-Day Saints, 1940-74, mem. gen. presidency, first counselor, 1945-74. Bd. govs. Latter-Day Saints Hosp., Salt Lake City. Del. tricentennial meeting Internat. Council Women, Washington, 1963, Montreal. Mem. Gamma Phi, Phi Kappa Phi. Mem. Ch. Jesus Christ of Latter-Day Saints (stake positions). Republican. Clubs: Fine Arts, Bookwomen. Author: (with others) A Centenary of Relief Society, 1942. Editor: A History of Relief Society, Relief Society Magazine, 1945-70. Home: 66 D St Salt Lake City UT 84103 Office: 76 N Main St Salt Lake City UT 84111

SHARP, MARTHA PEARMAN, music educator; b. Clay City, Ind.; d. Thomas and Gertrude (Beck) Pearman; B.S., Ind. State Tchrs. Coll., 1939; Mus.M., Northwestern U., 1943; postgrad. Ind. U., 1950; Ed.D. in Music Edn., U. Ill., 1964; m. Riley M. Sharp, May 16, 1974. Music supr. West Terre Haute Schs., 1940-42; tchr. vocal music and English, Milford (Ill.) Twp. Sch., 1943-46; music supr. Washington (Ind.) Schs., 1946-50; faculty Ind. State U., Terre Haute, 1950-74, prof. music, 1964-74. Clinician, Western Ky. State Music Tchrs., 1964, Elkhart (Ind.) Music Tchrs. 1964, Mpls. Music Educators, 1968, 69, Michigan City, 1968, 5 workshops for Ind. Dept. Edn., 1970; coordinator pub. sch. music project Vigo County Sch. Corp.-Ind. State U., 1967-68; supr. weekly gen. music classes for jr. high schs., 1968; resource cons. for program in gen. music, 1967-68; music dir. Community Theatre, 1958, 59. Mem. bd. Terre Haute Symphony, 1959-62. Mem. Music Educators Nat. Conf. (sec., clinician for elementary com. North Central div. 1965), Ind. (chmn. research com. 1965), Indpls. music educators assns., Kokomo Elementary Music Educators, Pi Kappa Lambda, Delta Kappa Gamma (chpt. v.p. 1967), Sigma Alpha Iota, Delta Gamma. Democrat. Presbyn. Author: (with Bonney, Miller) The Understanding of Music, 1966; General Music in the Elementary School, 1971; also jr. high sch. texts, numerous articles. Home: 1012 Main Elwood IN 46036

SHARP, RUTH COLLINS (MRS. CHARLES S. SHARP), civic worker; b. Dallas; d. Carr P. and Ruth (Woodall) Collins; B.A., So. Meth. U., 1948; m. Charles S. Sharp, June 21, 1947; children—Sally, Stanton, Susan. Pres., Jr. League, 1961-62, ofcl. hostess Internat. Conf. in Dallas, 1961; pres. Vis. Nurse Assn., 1956-58; pres. Dallas Day Nursery Assn., 1964-66; pres. Dallas Woman's Club, 1967-69. Sec. bd. dirs. YWCA, 1961-62; mem. bd. KERA Ednl. TV; bd. dirs. Grand Jury Assn., Salvation Army, Dallas; trustee So. Meth. U. 1968—, Hockaday Sch., 1974—. Recipient Zonta award as Dallas Woman of the Year, 1965, Golden Plate award Am. Acad. Achievement for Community Service, 1965; named Woman of Achievement, So. Meth. U. Alumni Assn., 1967; Arete award for community Service, 1969. Methodist. Home: 5227 Meaders Lane Dallas TX 75229

SHARP, SUSIE MARSHALL, judge; b. Rocky Mount, N.C., July 7, 1907; d. James Merritt and Annie (Blackwell) Sharp; LL.B., U. N.C., 1929; LL.D., Woman's Coll., U. N.C., 1950, Queens Coll., 1962, Elon Coll., 1963; L.H.D., Pfeiffer Coll., 1960; LL.D., Wake Forest Coll., 1965, Catawba Coll., 1970, U. N.C., 1970. Admitted to N.C. bar, 1928; gen. law practice with father Sharp & Sharp, Attys., 1929-49; city atty. Reidsville, N.C., 1939-49; spl. judge Superior Ct. of N.C., 1949-62; asso. justice Supreme Ct. of N.C., 1962—. Mem. Am. Law Inst., Am., N.C. bar assns., Order of Valkyries, Order of Coif, Phi Beta Kappa. Delta Kappa Gamma. Democrat. Methodist. Clubs: Soroptimist (hon.); Altrusa (hon.). Home: 629 Lindsey St Raleigh NC 27601 Office: Justice Bldg Raleigh NC 27601

SHARPE, MARY WILLIE CHANDLER (MRS. WILL HENRY SHARPE), assn. exec.; b. Lambertville, Ark., June 2, 1912; d. Walter Louis and Viola Rebecca (Mangrum) Chandler; student U. Ill., 1940, U. Chgo., 1944, Chgo. Bapt. Inst., 1952-56, Moody Bible Inst., 1956, student Adminstrn. George Williams Coll., 1966; m. Will Henry Sharpe, Jan. 16, 1942; children—Walter, Deborah Lynn. Tchr. adult remedial edn., Joliet, Ill., 1938-42; nursery sch. dir. State of Ill., 1943-45; dir. christian edn. Mount Olive Bapt. Ch., Joliet, 1951-63; sec., dental asst. Dr. L.H. Holman, Joliet, 1962-63; women and girls dir. YMCA, Joliet, Ill., 1963-69, acting exec. dir., 1970—. Sec. Will County (Ill.) Unit Am. Cancer Soc., 1968-72, treas., 1972—; chmn. community service div. Joliet (Ill.) Community Relations Commn., 1973—; mem. Joliet (Ill.) Police Adv. Com., 1972—; instr. Will County (Ill.) Council of Chs., 1953-62, dean Lebanon Dist., 1960-64, pres., 1968-70. Bd. dirs. Family Counseling Agy., Joliet, 1968—; mem. adv. com. Joliet Jr. Coll., 1972—. Recipient Outstanding Christian Service award Masons, 1963. Mem. Ill. State Bapt. Congress (instr. 1946—). Baptist (youth dir. Lebanon Bapt. Congress 1972—, conf. leader Am. Bapt. conv. 1964). Home: 207 Edward St Joliet IL 60436 Office: 472 S Joliet St Joliet IL 60436

SHARPE, RUTH COLLIER (MRS. RICHARD SHARPE), writer; b. Gladstone, Mich., Aug. 6, 1897; d. Parrie Oliver and Harriet (McGannon) Collier; student pub. schs., Portland, Ore.; m. Richard Sharpe, Sept. 9, 1940. Recipient The Olcott Found. award for The Song of the Paramahamsa, 1940; 1st prize for Am. Poets and Songwriters Valiant House, pubs., 1949, other poetry awards. Mem. Pen and Brush, Internat. Platform Assn. Mem. Christian Ch. Author: Tristram of Lyonesse (novel), 1949; The Song of the Paramahamsa (vol. poems), 1940; Important American Poets and Songwriters of 1948, 1949; When Falcon from the Wrist (vol. poems), 1949; The Poetry Digest Anthology, 1950; Poets on Parade, 1939; The Mid-Century Anthology of Prose & Poetry, 1950. Home: El Morya 956 West Point Rd Lake Oswego OR 97034

SHARPLES, SISTER MARIAN, educator; b. Long Beach, Cal., Feb. 23, 1920; d. Rufus and Maud (Wilcox) Sharples; B.A., Immaculate Heart Coll., 1942; M.A., U. So. Cal., 1951, Ph.D., 1957. Tchr. elementary schs., Los Angeles, 1939-43, secondary schs., Los Angeles, 1943-49; instr. Immaculate Heart Coll., Los Angeles, 1949-51, asso. prof. English, 1952-65, prof., chmn. dept. English, 1965—. Mem. Nat. Council Tchrs. English, Modern Lang. Assn. Home: 1832 N Garfield Pl Los Angeles CA 90028

SHARPLESS, JEAN SLEIGHT (MRS. RICHARD KENNEDY SHARPLESS), realtor; b. Los Angeles, Feb. 4, 1921; d. C. William and Mary Irene (Frick) Sleight; jr. certificate U. Cal. at Los Angeles, 1940; grad. Levitan Bus. Sch., 1942; certificate Kinji Kanazawa Sch. Real Estate, 1972; student U. Hawaii, 1973; m. Richard Kennedy Sharpless, July 23, 1948; children—Kendall Deborah, Richard Kennedy, Lincoln Kennedy. Sec. labor div. Red Cross War Fund, Phila., 1942; stenographer Selective Service Appeals Bd., Phila., 1942-43; sec., Fidelity-Phila. Trust Co., 1945-46, trust dept. Bank Am. Nat. Trusts' Savs. Assn., Los Angeles, 1946-48; clk.-stenographer constrn. br., engr. div. U.S. Army, Fort Shafter, Honolulu, 1967-68; sec. Greenleigh Assos., Inc., N.Y.C., 1969; sec.-librarian Hawaiian Hist. Soc., Honolulu, 1969-72; realtor asso. Velva Bergevin, Ltd., Honolulu, 1972—, sec., 1973—. Asst. sec. State Central Com. Democratic party Hawaii, 1960-62, mem. state central com., 1960-64. Mem. Common Cause, Honolulu Acad. Arts, Hawaii Legal Aux., U. Cal. at Los Angeles Alumni, Pi Beta Phi. Episcopalian. Clubs: Uluniu Swimming (Laie, Hawaii); Outrigger Canoe (Honolulu). Home: Hilton Lagoon Apt 16-A 2003 Kalia Rd Honolulu HI 96815 Office: 2222 Kalakaua Av Suite 1215 Honolulu HI 96815

SHATTO, GLORIA MCDERMITH (MRS. ROBERT J. SHATTO), economist, educator; b. Houston, Oct. 11, 1931; d. Ken E. and Gertrude (Osborne) McDermith; B.A., Rice U., 1954, Ph.D., 1966; m. Robert J. Shatto, Mar. 19, 1953; children—David Paul, Donald Patrick. Market research Humble Oil & Refining Co., Houston, 1954-55; tchr. pub. sch. Canal Zone, 1955-56; tchr. Houston Independent Sch. Dist., 1956-60; asst. prof. econs. U. Houston, 1965-69, asso. prof., 1969-72; prof. econs., asso. dean Coll. Indsl. Mgmt., Ga. Inst. Tech., Atlanta, 1973—. Mem. Tex. Gov.'s Commn. on Status of Women, 1970-72. Mem. Am. Econ. Assn., Am. Finance Assn., So. Econ. Assn., Am. Assn. U. Profs., Am. Assn. U. Women (area rep. 1967-68, Tex. chmn. legis. program 1970-71, mem. internat. fellowships and awards com. 1970—, chmn. 1974—), Phi Beta Kappa, Phi Kappa Phi, Omicron Delta Epsilon. Contbr. articles in field to profl. jours. Editor: Employment of the Middle-Aged, 1972. Address: College of Industrial Management Ga Inst of Technology Atlanta GA 30332

SHATTUCK, CATHIE ANN, lawyer; b. Salt Lake City, July 18, 1945; d. Robert Ashley and Lillian Francis (Culp) Shattuck; B.A., U. Neb., 1967, J.D., 1970. Vice pres. Shattuck Farms, Inc., Hastings, Neb., 1966-69, pres., 1969-70; admitted to Neb. bar, 1970, Colo. bar, 1971; atty., asst. project dir. Colo. Civil Rights Commn., Denver, 1971-73; trial atty. Equal Employment Opportunity Commn., Denver, 1973—; trainer, speaker in field. Patron Denver Art Mus. Mem. Am., Neb., Colo., Denver bar assns., Am. Judicature Soc., Nat. Assn. Women Lawyers, Alpha Xi Delta, Delta Sigma Rho, Tau Kappa Alpha (pres. 1966-67), Pi Sigma Alpha (v.p. 1966-67). Home: 2481 Briarwood Dr Boulder CO 80303 Office: 1531 Stout St Denver CO 80202

SHAW, BEA, advt. exec.; b. Dallas; d. Charles B. and Estelle (Goldstein) Shaw; student U. Tex.; m. Sam Passman (div.); 1 son, Donald Shaw; m. 2d, Bruce Hayes (div.). Hostess, Bea Shaw's Charm Sch., Sta. WFAA-TV, Dallas, 1952-57, Panorama Pacific, Sta. KNXT-TV, Hollywood, Cal., 1963; news reporter Sta. KFWB, Hollywood, Cal., 1959-61, KABC-TV, 1961-62; exec. producer Bea Shaw Prodns.; writer, producer radio and TV commls., 1963—. Recipient numerous internat. broadcasting awards, 1963—; citation Los Angeles Advt. Women, 1971, 74; 25 awards Advt. Assn. West, 1965—; 17 Lulu awards, 1965—; 7 RAB awards, 1966-70; 4 Don Belding award, 1966—; So. Cal. Broadcasting award, 1968; Broadcasting award Nat. Retail Mchts. Assn., 1973; Canadian Broadcasting award, 1970; Am. Advt. Fedn. Western States citation, 1974; named Los Angeles Advt. Woman of Year, 1974. Mem. Internat. Platform Assn., Los Angeles Advt. Women, Nat. Acad. TV Arts and Scis., Hollywood Radio and TV Soc., Actors Equity Assn., A.F.T.R.A., Screen Actors Guild. Clubs: Dallas Woman's, Lakewood Country (Dallas); Advt. of Los Angeles. Home: 10527 Sarah St North

Hollywood CA 91602 Office: 5330 Laurel Canyon Blvd North Hollywood CA 91607

SHAW, CATHERINE FRASER, educator; b. Boston, Feb. 28, 1924; d. Stephen S. and Catherine (Fraser) Shaw; B.S., Boston U.-Sargent Coll., 1945; M.S., Smith Coll., 1946. Instr. phys. tng. for women U. Tex., Austin, 1946-48; asst. prof. phys. edn. U. Me., Orono, 1948-54; asso. prof., then prof., head dept. phys. edn. Lake Erie Coll., Painesville, O., 1954—. Instr., trainer water safety A.R.C., 1954—. Mem. A.A.H.P.E.R., Nat. Assn. Phys. Edn. for Coll. Women, Am. Assn. U. Profs., Cleve. Bd. Women Ofcls., Ohio Coll. Assn., Phi Kappa Phi. Home: 55 Wood St Painesville OH 44077

SHAW, DAISY K. (MRS. FREDERICK SHAW), ednl. administr.; b. N.Y.C., Sept. 26, 1913; d. Littman and Lena (Kaplan) Katz; B.A., Hunter Coll., 1933; M.A., N.Y. U., 1955; postgrad. Columbia U., 1933-35, 44, Cornell U., 1940, 61, Hunter Coll., 1950-52; m. Frederick Shaw, Nov. 21, 1940; children—Richard, Ellen. Tchr. French, N.Y.C. High Schs., 1935-43; tchr.-in charge L.I. City Evening High Sch., 1944-47; gen. asst. in charge guidance Washington Irving Evening High Sch., N.Y.C., 1950-58, coordinator citywide evening guidance center, 1951-62, asst. prin. high sch., 1958-62; asst. prin. Simon Baruch Jr. High Sch., N.Y.C., 1955-58; dir. Bur. Ednl. and Vocational Guidance of N.Y.C. Schs., 1962—. Adj. asst. prof. dept. guidance and counseling Hunter Coll., 1964-71. Recipient Bourse Bargy traveling fellowship to France, 1936, Ford Found. fellowship, 1954-55; elected to Hunter Coll. Hall of Fame, 1972. Mem. Assn. Adminstrv. Women in Edn., N.Y. Acad. Pub. Edn., Am., N.Y. State, N.Y.C. (pres. 1973-74) personnel and guidance assns., Assn. Counselor Edn. and Supervision, Nat. Vocational Guidance Assn., Am. Sch. Counselors Assn., Council of Dirs. N.Y.C. Bd. Edn., Large City Dirs. Guidance (pres. 1969-70), Phi Beta Kappa. Club: Women's City. Contbr. articles to encys., textbook, profl. jours. Home: 41 Henry St Brooklyn NY 11201

SHAW, ELIZABETH HARRIET (MRS. ELLSWORTH SHAW), editor; b. Mpls., Sept. 7, 1919; d. Albert Lawrence and Edna Ruth (Raymond) Lewis; B.A., U. Ariz., 1941, M.A., 1967; m. Ellsworth Shaw, May 27, 1943; children—Victoria, Franklin, Rebecca, Thomas, John, Mary. Women's editor Ariz. Daily Star, Tucson, 1942-43, 44-49, fine arts editor, reviewer, 1944-49; free-lance writer, editor, 1949-59; asso. editor, editorial coordinator U. Ariz. Press, Tucson, 1959—; exec. sec. 20th Century Chamber Theater Performing Arts, 1974—. Com. mem. Tucson Music Coop., 1974—. Mem. Soc. Southwestern Authors (v.p., dir. 1972), Cultural Exchange Council (dir. 1974). Home: 3602 E Flower St Tucson AZ 85716 Office: Box 3398 College Station Tucson AZ 85722

SHAW, ELIZABETH ORR (MRS. DONALD HARDY SHAW), lawyer, state senator; b. Monona, Ia., Oct. 2, 1923; d. Harold Topliff and Hazel (Kean) Orr; A.B., Drake U., 1945; postgrad. pub. adminstrn. U. Minn., 1945-46; J.D., U. Ia., 1948; m. Donald Hardy Shaw, Aug. 16, 1946; children—Elizabeth Ann, Andrew Hardy, Anthony Orr. Admitted to Ill. bar, 1949, Ia. bar, 1956; atty. Legal Aid Soc. Chgo., 1949; asso. firm Lord, Bissell and Brook, Chgo., 1950-51; practiced in Arlington Heights, Ill., 1952-56; partner firm Wood and Shaw, Davenport, Ia., 1968-72; mem. Ia. Ho. of Reps., 1967-72, Ia. Senate, 1973—; chmn. constl. amendments reapportionment com., 1971—. Mem. League Women Voters, P.E.O., Am. Bus. Women's Assn., Order of Coif, Phi Beta Kappa, Kappa Kappa Gamma. Republican. Conglist. Clubs: Davenport Country, Davenport, Outing, Federated Women's, Pilot Internat. (Davenport). Home: 29 Hillcrest Av Davenport IA 52803 Office: Ia State Capitol Des Moines IA 52819

SHAW, GRACE GOODFRIEND (MRS. HERBERT FRANKLIN SHAW), editor; b. N.Y.C., Dec. 27, 1920; d. Henry Bernheim and Jane Elizabeth (Stone) Goodfriend; student Bennington Coll., 1938-39, Fordham U., 1970—; m. Herbert Franklin Shaw, Dec. 7, 1943; 1 son, Brandon Hibbs. Reporter, Port Chester (N.Y.) Daily Item, 1942-45; editorial coordinator World Scope Ency., N.Y.C., 1946-50; asso. editor Clarence L Barnhart, Inc., Bronxville, N.Y., 1950; free-lance writer for reference books, 1951-61; sr. editor, coll. dept. Bobbs-Merrill, N.Y.C., 1961-62, mng., editor, 1963-65; editing supr. World Pub Co., N.Y.C., 1965-68, mng. editor, 1968-69, sr. editor, 1969; mng. editor Peter H. Wyden Co., N.Y.C., 1969-70; asso. editor Dial Press, N.Y.C., 1971-72, sr. editor, 1972; sr. editor David McKay Co., N.Y.C., 1972—; gen. editor Ams. All series Garrard Press, 1970. Home: 85 Lee Rd Scarsdale NY 10583 Office: 750 3d Av New York City NY 10017

SHAW, KARYLL NOREEN, ednl. adminstr.; b. Flint, Mich., Nov. 13, 1947; d. Charles Frank and E. Noreen (Tippett) Shaw; B.A., Mich. State U., 1970, M.A., 1972. Head adviser student affairs Mich. State U., East Lansing, 1971, hall dir., 1971-73; dir. housing U. Md., College Park, 1973—. Mem. Am. Coll. Personnel Adminstrs., Nat. Assn. Women Deans, Adminstrs. and Counselors. Home: 8655 Greenbelt Rd No 201 Greenbelt MD 20770 Office: 108 Garrett Univ of Maryland College Park MD 20740

SHAW, KATHERINE ALCID, anesthesiologist; b. Cuyapo, N. Ecija, Philippines; d. David D'Silva and Josefa Hernandez (Alcid) Shaw; A.A., U. Santo Tomas, Manila, Philippines, 1958-60, M.D., 1965. Came to U.S., 1965. Intern, Bristol (Conn.) Hosp., 1965-66; resident St. Francis Hosp., Hartford, Conn., 1966-70; fellow Mass. Gen. Hosp., Boston, 1970—, instr. anesthesia, 1971—; instr. anesthesia Harvard Med. Sch., Boston, 1971—. Diplomate Am. Bd. Anesthesiology. Fellow Am. Coll. Anesthesiologists; mem. Am., Mass. socs. anesthesiologists. Home: 6 Ridgecrest Lane Bristol CT 06010 Office: Dept Anesthesia Mass Gen Hosp Boston MA

SHAW, MARGERY WAYNE SCHLAMP, physician, lawyer, educator; b. Evansville, Ind., Feb. 15, 1923; d. Arthur George and Louise (Meyer) Schlamp; student Hanover Coll., 1940-41; A.B. magna cum laude, U. Ala., 1945; M.A., Columbia, 1946; postgrad. Cornell U., 1947-48; M.D., U. Mich., 1957; J.D., U. Houston, 1973; m. Charles Raymond Shaw, May 31, 1942 (div. Nov. 1972); 1 dau., Barbara Rae (Mrs. Frederic L. Ferri). Intern, St. Joseph Mercy Hosp., Ann Arbor, Mich., 1957-58; practice medicine, specializing in human genetics, Ann Arbor, 1958-67, Houston, 1967—; instr. dept. human genetics Med. Sch. U. Mich., 1958-61, asst. prof., 1961-66, asso. prof., 1966-67; asso. prof. dept. biology Grad. Sch. Biomedical Scis. U. Tex., Houston, 1967-69, prof., 1969—, dir. Med. Genetics Center, 1971—. Mem. genetics study sect. NIH, Bethesda, Md., 1966-70, mem. genetics tng. com. 1970—, chromosome studies astronauts NASA, 1970-71; mem. med. adv. bd. Nat. Genetics Found., 1972—, research adv. bd. Planned Parenthood Houston, 1972—. First aid instr. A.R.C., 1962-67; unit chmn. United Fund, 1966. Recipient Billings Silver medal A.M.A., 1966; Achievement award Am. Assn. U. Women, 1970-71. Mem. Am. Soc. Human Genetics (past sec., dir.), Genetics Soc. Am. (sec. 1971-73), Tissue Culture Assn. (trustee 1970-72), Environmental Mutagen Soc. (council), Am. Soc. Cell Biology, Phi Beta Kappa, Alpha Omega Alpha. Asso. editor: Am. Jour. Human Genetics, 1962-68; editorial bd. In Vitro. Cons. editor: Cytogenetics, 1962—. Contbr. articles to profl. jours. Home: 3614 Montrose Blvd Houston TX 77006 Office: MD Anderson Hosp and Tumor Inst Houston TX 77025

SHAW, MARJORIE MONROE (MRS. EVERETT LESLIE SHAW), ednl. adminstr.; b. N. Reading, Mass., Sept. 15, 1920; d. Lawrence Clifford and Lillian Maud (Giles) Monroe; B.E., Salem State Coll., 1938, M.S., 1965; M.S., Boston U., 1960; m. Everett Leslie Shaw, Dec. 28, 1940 (dec.); children—Carol (Mrs. James H. Furneaux), Richard Allen. Elementary sch. tchr., North Reading, Mass., 1938-40, 56-58, Middleton, Mass., 1949-56; tchr. spl. edn., sch. psychologist, North Reading, 1958-66; dir. spl. edn., acting prin., spl. edn. collaborative, Mass., 1966-69; dir. Spl. Edn. Edn. Mut., North Reading, Mass., 1969—, N. Reading (Mass.) Jr. High Sch., 1974—. Mem. Mass. Tchrs. Assn. (pres. 1952, 62-64), Bus. and Profl. Women's Club (pres. 1967-69). Republican. Mem. Order Eastern Star. Home: 75 Dale St Methuen MA 01844 Office: Junior High School Sherman Rd North Reading MA 01864

SHAW, RAY, photographer, writer, sculptor; b. Lithuania, June 5; came to U.S., naturalized, 1943; d. David and Lillian (Levinson) Shaw; student N.Y. U., Northwestern U.; m. Eugene Rappoport, Nov. 12, 1946 (dec. May 1968); children—Lee, Faith. Sculptor, specializing in modeling of hands, subjects include Albert Einstein, Franklin D. Roosevelt, Jack Dempsey, Joe Louis, Archbishop Fulton Sheen, Helen Hayes, Clara Booth Luce, others; now photo journalist for UNICEF, IBM Corp., World Bank, Macmillan & Co., others. Mem. Woman's Press Club N.Y., Overseas Press Club, Artists Equity. Author: The Nutcracker, 1970; Catnips, 1970; Lateef, Kashmiri Child, 1970; New York for Children, 1972; Candle Art, 1973; Washington for Children, 1974; How To Get Those Great Overseas Jobs, 1974. Address: 255 W 90th St New York City NY 10024

SHAW, RETA, actress; b. South Paris, Me.; d. Howard W. and Edna M. (Easson) Shaw; ed. Leland Powers Sch. Theatre, Boston, 1933; div.; 1 dau., Kathryn Forester. Stage appearances include Pajama Game, Picnic; TV appearances include Red Skelton Show, I Spy, The Ghost and Mrs. Muir; appeared in films including Mary Poppins, Pollyanna; tchr. Bishop-Lee Sch., Boston. Mem. Screen Actors Guild, A.F.T.R.A. (bd. dirs., sec. credit union), Cal. P.T.A. (hon. life), Zeta Phi Eta. Home: 12403 Addison St North Hollywood CA 91607*

SHAW, THELMA SKAGGS, social welfare vol.; b. Romont, W.Va., July 20, 1901; d. Edward Wallace and Lydna Goodridge (Spinks) Skaggs; A.B., W.Va. U., 1922; LL.D., W.Va. Wesleyan Coll., 1972; m. Victor Shaw, July 24, 1928 (dec. 1928). Tchr. pub. schs., W.Va., Fla., Del., 1922-27; social welfare vol., speaker, 1932—; mem. Nat. Conf. Social Welfare 1938—, pres. 1960-61; v.p., sec. Family Service Assn. Am., 1958-60; sec. Nat. Social Welfare Assembly, 1958-60; mem. bd. Nat. Travellers Aid Internat. Social Service Am., 1958—; mem. vis. com. Sch. Nursing, W.Va.; mem. W.Va. Planning Commn. for Nursing, Inc.; mem. by-laws com. Nat. League Nursing; U.S. com. for UNICEF; adv. council W.Va. Council Crime and Delinquency; nat. adv. council Nurse Tng. USPHS; nat. citizens coms. United Way; mem. adv. com. Fairmont State Coll., mem. Gov.'s Adv. Com. on Mental Health. Trustee W.Va. Wesleyan Coll. Recipient Red Feather award United Community Funds and Councils Am., 1954; also awards Family Service Assn. Am., W.Va. Welfare Conf., others. Mem. Assn. Jr. Leagues Am. (nat. v.p. 1940-41), Am. Assn. U. Women, Bus. and Profl. Womens Club, Alpha Xi Delta, Beta Sigma Phi (hon. internat. mem.). Club: Soroptimist. Home: 425 Morgantown Av Fairmont WV 26554 Office: Deveny Bldg Fairmont WV 26554

SHAWL, JANICE HAYS (MRS. WILLIAM FRANK SHAWL), librarian; b. Spokane, Wash., Jan. 7, 1932; d. Glen G. and Mary Katherine (Kolbeck) Hays; B.A., U. Mont., 1953; M.L.S., U. Wash., 1958; postgrad. Eastern Washington State Coll., 1951-52, U. Cal. at Los Angeles (Kellog Jr. Coll. Leadership Program fellow) 1967; m. William Frank Shawl, Aug. 4, 1951. Tchr., librarian Highline Pub. Schs., Seattle, 1955-58; sr. librarian Seattle Pub. Library, 1958-62; instr. English, Highline Coll., Seattle, 1961-63; catalog librarian Bellevue (Wash.) Pub. Schs., 1963-67; librarian U. Cal. at Los Angeles Research Library, 1966-67; vis. lectr. U. Wash., 1967, 71; head catalog dept. U. Cal. at Irvine, 1968-70, lectr. 1969; asst. prof., reference librarian Chapman Coll., Orange, Cal., 1971—. Mem. Newport Harbor Art Mus., Orange County Philharmonic Soc. Mem. A.L.A., Orange County Library Assn., So. Cal. Tech. Processes Group, Am. Assn. U. Profs., Am. Civil Liberties Union, League of Women Voters, Nat. Orgn. Women, Kappa Alpha Theta. Home: 5772 Southall Terrace Irvine CA 92664 Office: Library Chapman College Orange CA 92666

SHAWVER, LEONA MARY HERING (MRS. ROBERT W. SHAWVER), savs. and loan exec.; b. Cin., May 5, 1921; d. Charles D. and Alice W. (Lenton) Hering; student U. Cin., 1938-40; B.A., Coll. Wooster, 1942; m. Robert W. Shawver, Nov. 25, 1948; children—Robert Wellington, William G., Margaret L. Bookkeeper, Comm. Nat. Bank, Tiffin, O., 1942-44; sec. to supt. Tiffin Pub. Schs., 1944-46; nat. exec. sec. Alpha Omicron Pi, 1946-51; asst. treas. Oxford (O.) Savs. Assn., 1964-66, treas., 1966-69, sec.-treas., mng. officer, 1970-74, exec. v.p., 1974—. Bd. dirs., sec. Oxford Community Improvement Corp. Treas. P.T.A., 1969; active McCullough-Hyde Hosp. Woman's Aux. Mem. Alpha Omicron Pi. Republican. Episcopalian (parish treas. 1964-68). Club: Country (dir., treas. 1971-72) (Oxford). Home: 316 E Vine St Oxford OH 45056 Office: 29 W High St Oxford OH 45056

SHAY, JANET C. YEAGER (MRS. HOWELL LEWIS SHAY, JR.), pub. relations exec.; b. Phila., July 20, 1935; d. H. Osborne and Marie Clare (Shanfelter) Yeager; grad. Charles Morris Price Sch. Advt. and Journalism, 1954; student U. Pa., 1955-58, evening 65-66; m. Howell Lewis Shay, Jr., July 5, 1969. Pub. relations mgr. Certain-Teed Products Corp., Valley Forge, Pa., 1958-61; pub. relations dir. St. Christopher's Hosp. for Children, Phila., 1962-64; asst. to publisher, news and feature reporter Jamestown (N.Y.) Sun. 1961; v.p., dir. Ernest William Greenfield, Inc., Phila., 1964-71; mem. pub. relations staff N.W. Ayer & Son, Phila., 1972-74; now pub. relations cons. Eisenhower Exhange Fellowships, Phila., 1965—. State pub. relations chmn., nat. pub. relations task force United Citizens for Nixon-Agnew, 1968. Mem. D.A.R. (nat. vice chmn. jr. com. 1958-61; state jr. dir. 1967-70, chpt. sec. 1967-70), Internat. Platform Assn. (world affairs council 1968—), Am. (past nat. com. chmn.), Phila. pub. relations assns., Phila. Club Advt. Women (1st pl. pub. relations awards 1967, 68). Home: Box 172 Rose Valley PA 19065

SHAYEVITZ, MYRA LEE BAKER (MRS. BERTON ROBERT SHAYEVITZ), physician; b. Holyoke, Mass., Aug. 27, 1934; d. Harry Abraham and Rose (Saltman) B.; B.A., Barnard Coll., Columbia U., 1956; postgrad. Tufts U. Coll. Medicine, 1955-57; M.D., N.Y. U., 1959; m. Berton Robert Shayevitz, Jan. 24, 1957; children—Jessie Rebecca, Adam Jason. Intern VA Hosp., Dallas, Southwestern Med. Sch., 1959-60, resident in medicine, 1960-61; chief resident internal medicine, chief resident pulmonary physiology lab. Springfield (Mass.) Hosp., 1961-63; practice medicine specializing internal medicine, chest diseases, Holyoke, 1963—; asso. attending staff Holyoke Hosp., organizer pulmonary function lab., 1965—, planned parenthood clinic, 1967—, rehab. program for chronic pulmonary diseases, 1970—; dir. Holyoke Assos. in Internal Medicine, Inc. cons. in pulmonary disease VA Hosp., Florence, Mass., 1967-73, chief pulmonary clinic, 1973—. Diplomate Am. Bd. Internal Medicine. Fellow Am. Thoracic Soc., Am. Coll. Chest Physicians; mem. A.C.P. (asso.), Internat. Platform Assn., Hadassah, Sisterhood Sons of Zion, Hampden Dist. Med. Soc., Mass. Med. Soc. Home: 119A S Hampton Rd Holyoke MA 01040 Office: Holyoke Regional Med Bldg 10 Hospital Dr Holyoke MA 01040

SHEA, DOROTHY P. (MRS. HAROLD SHEA), state senator; b. Montpelier, Vt., Dec. 6, 1902; grad. high sch.; m. Harold Shea; children—two sons, three daus. Mem. Vt. Ho. of Reps., 1959-65; mem. Vt. Senate, 1966—. Mem. Washington County (Vt.) Farm Bur., womens aux. Heaton Hosp. Mem. Woman's Club, St. Vincent de Paul Soc., Emblem Club. Republican. Roman Catholic. Address: Hackamore Rd Montpelier VT 05602*

SHEA, ISABELLE CATHERINE O'BRIEN (MRS. JAMES A. SHEA), found. ofcl.; b. Hydeville, Vt.; d. William R. and Mary Jane (Keenan) O'Brien; grad. spl. courses Castleton State Coll., N.Y.U., Am. Inst. Banking. Conn. Coll., Hillyer Coll.; m. James A. Shea, June 9, 1925 (dec. Feb. 1955). Head bookkeeper G. M. Williams Co., New London, Conn., 1931-33; with Bur. Internal Revenue, Hartford, 1934-46, supr. audit div., 1946; mgr. tax dept. Phoenix State Bank & Trust Co., Hartford, 1946-58; co-executor estate, tax cons., 1958-60; co-trustee George A. and Grace L. Long Found., Tucson, 1959—. Patroness, mem. Tucson Art Center, 1967—; mem. So. Ariz. Heart Assn., Tucson, 1966—, Cancer Soc., Tucson, 1966—, Father Flanagans Boys Town, Omaha, 1950—. Mem. Alumni Castleton State Coll., Common Cause, Catalina Foothills Assn. Democrat. Roman Catholic. Clubs: Elks Aux., City (Hartford, hon. mem.), Avon Country (Conn., hon. mem.) Home: 5601 N Camino Real Tucson AZ 85718

SHEAR, DAPHFINE LUNDY (MRS. WARREN DAVID SHEAR), Democratic nat. committeewoman; b. Davis, Okla., May 15, 1919; d. Benjamin Frank and Eula Mae (Boyles) Lundy; student So. Meth. U., 1938, Dallas Little Theatre Sch., 1939, St. Louis Little Theatre, 1940; m. Warren David Shear, Aug. 29, 1940; children—Ken, Sue, Lynn, Sloane, David. Dir. Pryor (Okla.) Daily Times, Milford Argosy Corp. Co-chmn. 6th Congl. Dist. Dem. Party, 1962-64; mem. platform com. Dem. Nat. Conv., 1964, 68. mem. Dem. Nat. Com., 1964—; originator First Dem. workshop U. Okla., 1965. Home: 2918 Pine Ridge St Oklahoma City OK 73120

SHEARER, MINERVA ZENDT (MRS. GLENN CHARLES SHEARER), former indsl. corp. exec.; b. Juniata County, Pa., Sept. 4, 1914; d. Howard Millet and Sylvia Elizabeth (Lauver) Zendt; B.S., Juniata Coll., 1941; m. Glenn Charles Shearer, Nov. 21, 1942; 1 dau., Zenda K. (Mrs. George C. Brackbill). Elementary tchr. Juniata County, Pa., 1933-62; sec. Shearer Bros. Lumber Co., East Waterford, Pa., 1942-71, partner, 1960-71; dir. E. Waterford Community Industrial Corp., 1960-73, treas., 1960-73. Trustee Juniata County Library Bd., 1968-74, sec. bd. 1970-73; trustee central Pa. Dist. Library, 1972-73. Mem. Literary Guild of Port Royal. Republican. Presbyn. (trustee 1971-74). Mem. White Shrine Jerusalem. Home: Box 245 Port Royal PA 17082

SHEARER, MOIRA (MOIRA SHEARER KING), actress, ballerina; b. Dunfermline, Scotland, Jan. 17, 1926; d. Harold Charles and Margret Crawford Reid (Shearer) King; studied dancing in No. Rhodesia, later with Madame Nicholas Legat, Ninette de Valois; m. Ludovic Kennery, 1950; children—Ailsa Margaret, Rachel Katharine, Fiona Jane, Alastair Charles Conerly. Made debut with Internat. Ballet, 1941; joined Sadler's Wells, 1942, on tour Am., 1949, 50; ballet roles include Les Sylphides, Sleeping Beauty, Giselle, Symphonic Variation, Coppelia, Swan Lake; appeared in motion picture Red Shoes, 1947, others include Tales of Hoffman, 1950, Story of Three Loves 1952, The Man Who Loved Redheads, 1954; stage roles include Titania in Midsummer Night's Dream, 1954 (with Old Vic Touring Co.); I Am a Camera, 1955. Office: MCA 139 Picadilly London W1 England

SHEARER, RUTH EASTER MANSBERGER (MRS. RICHARD E. SHEARER), educator; b. Turtle Creek, Pa., Apr. 3, 1920; d. Arlie Roland and Mary Mildred (Smith) Mansberger; B.A. summa cum laude, Western Md. Coll., 1941; M.Ed., U. Pitts., 1943; Ed.D. (Benedum scholar), Tchrs. Coll., Columbia, 1963; m. Richard E. Shearer, June 16, 1944; children—Patricia (Mrs. Richard F. Wilson), Suzanne (Mrs. Terry Lynn Jones), Richard Judson. Tchr. jr. high sch. Weirton, W.Va., 1941-42, sr. high sch., 1942-44, Rumson (N.J.) Country Day Sch., 1944-46; dean women Alderson Broaddus Coll., Philippi, W.Va., 1951-56, prof. edn., 1956—, supr. student internships in pub. schs., 1956—. Danforth fellow Colo. Coll., 1963, Stephens Coll., 1965. Mem. Am. Assn. U. Women, Assn. Higher Edn., N.E.A., Am. Assn. U. Profs., Am. Personnel and Guidance Assn., Am. Assn. Colls for Tchr. Edn., P.E.O., Delta Kappa Gamma, Pi Lambda Theta, Kappa Delta Pi. Republican. Baptist. Club: College. Contbr. articles to jours. Home: Broaddus Knolls Philippi WV 26416

SHEARIN, ROBERTA BROOKS (MRS. WILLIAM GASTON SHEARIN), librarian; b. Washington, Oct. 2, 1924; d. Ulysses Simpson and Marzette I. (Tate) Brooks; student Spelman Coll., 1940-42; A.B. cum laude, Johnson C. Smith U., 1944; B.S. in Library Sci., Atlanta U., 1945; m. William Gaston Shearin, July 21, 1947; children—Moneta Marzette (Mrs. Dennis W. Howland), William Gaston. Asst. librarian Talladega Coll., Ala., 1945-47; library asst. Army Library Pentagon, 1952-54, reference librarian, 1955-66, acting chief periodicals, 1967-70, chief periodicals, 1970—. Editor Tots and Teens, Inc. Recipient Sustained Superior Performance award Dept. Army, 1963, Outstanding Performance award Dept. Army, 1971. Mem. A.L.A., Nat. Council of Negro Women, N.A.A.C.P., Delta Sigma Theta. Home: 1461 Monroe NW Washington DC 20010 Office: The Army Library Room 1A522 The Pentagon Washington DC 20310

SHEARMAN, CAROLINE WOOD, hosp. dietitian; b. Woburn, Mass., Feb. 5, 1927; d. Arthur Henry and Martha Lillian (Stackpole) Shearman; B.S., Simmons Coll., 1948. Therapeutic dietitian Mary Hitchcock Meml. Hosp., Hanover, N.H., 1949—, nutrition instr. Sch. Nursing, 1968—. Mem. Am. Dietetic Assn., N.H., Hanover hist. socs., Granite States Simmons Coll. Alumni Assn. (v.p. 1972-73). Conglist. Author: Diets are for People, 1963. Home: 4 Sargent Hanover NH 03755 Office: Mary Hitchcock Memorial Hosp Sch of Nursing Hanover NH 03755

SHECTER, PEARL S., artist; b. N.Y.C., Dec. 10, 1910; d. Daniel and Annie (Mantel) Schechter; B.F.A., Hunter Coll., 1934; M.F.A., Columbia, 1938; certificate New Bauhaus Sch. Design, 1947, Hans Hofmann Sch. Painting, 1951; student (scholar) Archipenke Sch. Art, N.Y.C., 1950, La Grande Chaumière, Paris, 1959; postgrad. Harvard, summers 1962-63. Exhibited Walker Art Mus., Mus. Modern Art, Lehigh U., other instns.; represented in collections N.Y. U., John F. Kennedy Library; artist Newton-Harvard Creative Art Center, 1963; art lectr. Head Start program, 1966, N.Y. U., 1957-68; art dir. Elisabeth Irvin High Sch., N.Y.C., 1973—. Recipient Gold medal Pationate Scholastico, Lucca, Italy, 1963. Mem. Artists N.Y. (pres.), Artists Equity N.Y., Expts. in Art and Tech. Home: 60 E 9th St New York City NY 10003

SHEEHAN, ANGELA MARGARET, educator; b. Mt. Pulaski, Ill., Oct. 12, 1948; d. Edward Benedict and Nellie Myrtle (Fishburn) Sheehan; B.A. in Speech and English, Ill. State U., 1970, M.S. in Speech Communication, 1971. Mem. staff Alumni Information and Research Ill. State U., Normal, 1968-70, grad. teaching speech communication, 1970-71; tchr. lang. arts and speech West Lincoln (Ill.) elementary sch., 1971—. NSF counselor Ill. State U., 1973-74. Mem. Nat., Ill. edn. assns., Am. Bus. Women's Assn. (pres.), Speech Communications Assn., Ill. Speech and Theatre Assn., Nat. Thespian Soc., D.A.R. Home: Rural Route 1 Mount Pulaski IL 62548 Office: Rural Route 1 Lincoln Elementary School Lincoln IL 62656

SHEEHAN, MARGARET FILSON (MRS. WILLIAM E. SHEEHAN), govt. ofcl.; b. N.Y.C.; d. John McKee and Sarah (Hiscock) Filson; grad. St. Luke's Hosp. Sch. Nursing, N.Y.C., 1935 A.B., Skidmore Coll., 1939; M.A., Columbia, 1942; m. William E. Sheehan, May 26, 1956. Staff nurse, St. Luke's Hosp., N.Y.C., 1935, instr. nursing arts, 1939-41; part time infirmary staff nurse Skidmore Coll., Saratoga Springs, N.Y., 1935-39; staff nurse Henry St. Vis. Nurse Service, N.Y.C. summer, 1942; instr. nursing arts U. Minn., 1942-46, dir. nursing service, asso. prof., 1946-53; instr. Tchrs. Coll., Columbia, summer 1945; cons. VA, Washington, 1948; research asso. U. Pitts. Sch. Nursing, 1953-54; dir. nursing service, asst. prof. U. Chgo. Hosps. and Clinics, 1954-65; nurse cons. Div. Nursing, USPHS, Dept. Health, Edn., and Welfare, Washington, 1965—, also chief instl. nursing br. Vice pres. Chgo. Council Community Nursing, 1963-64. Exec. com., med. div. Chgo. Welfare Council, 1954-60; mem. expert adv. com. USPHS, 1956-60. Mem. Am. Nurses Assn. (dir.), Am. Nurses Found., Nat. League Nursing, Sigma Theta Tau. Co-author: Nursing Arts (with Mildred L. Montag), 1948. Home: 10401 Grosvenor Pl Rockville MD 20852 Office: 9000 Rockville Pike Bethesda MD 20014

SHEEHAN, PATRICIA ANN QUEENAN (MRS. DANIEL M. SHEEHAN), economist, state ofcl.; b. Newark; d. Michael and Sarah (McAfee) Queenan; A.B., Trinity Coll., 1955; postgrad. Rutgers U.; LL.D., St. Elizabeth's Coll., 1974; m. Daniel M. Sheehan, June 22, 1957 (dec. Dec. 1961); children—Elizabeth, Daniel, Michael. Jr. economist Air Transport Assn., Personnel Relations Conf., Washington, 1955-57; research asst. Ednl. Testing Service, Princeton, N.J., 1957-58; compensation analyst Johnson & Johnson, New Brunswick, 1963-74; mayor of New Brunswick, 1967-74; commr. Dept. Community Affairs, State of N.J., Trenton, 1974—. Mem. Middlesex County Lay Adv. Bd. Catholic Welfare Bur. Diocese of Trenton; v.p. St. Peter's Hosp. Aux., 1966-68; nat. rec. sec. Trinity Coll. Alumnae Assn., 1967-69, v.p., 1971—; mem. N.J. State Tax Policy Commn., 1970; chmn. Hackensack Meadowlands Commn., 1974—. Mem. state policy com. Democratic party N.J., 1970-74; mem. N.J. Dem. State committeewoman, 1968-74. Mem. Am. Assn. U. Women (hon.), Pi Gamma Mu. Home: 5 Llewellyn Pl New Brunswick NJ 08902 Office: 363 W State St Trenton NJ 08625

SHEEHAN, SUSAN (MRS. NEIL SHEEHAN), writer; b. Vienna, Austria, Aug. 24, 1937; d. Charles and Kitty C. (Herrmann) Sachsel; came to U.S., 1941, naturalized, 1946; B.A. (Durant scholar), Wellesley Coll., 1958; m. Neil Sheehan, Mar. 30, 1965; children—Maria Gregory, Catherine Fair. Editorial researcher Esquire-Coronet, N.Y.C., 1959-60; free-lance writer, N.Y.C., 1960-62; staff writer New Yorker mag., N.Y.C., 1962—. Mem. Phi Beta Kappa. Author: Ten Vietnamese, 1967. Contbr. articles to various mags. including N.Y. Times Sunday Mag., Harper's, Atlantic, New Republic, McCall's, Holiday. Home: 4505 Klingle St NW Washington DC 20016 Office: New Yorker Mag 25 W 43d St New York City NY 10036

SHEEHY, MARIE ANN PAVELKA (MRS. VINCENT THOMAS SHEEHY), govt. ofcl.; b. Kyjov, Czechoslovakia, Apr. 1, 1920; d. Joseph Louis and Marie (Navratil) Pavelka; came to U.S., 1924, naturalized, 1930; student Bryant and Stratton Bus. Coll., Chgo., 1938; m. Vincent Thomas Sheehy, May 13, 1941; 1 dau., Marie W. (Mrs. Thomas M. Lisi). Sec., Ingersoll-Rand Machinery Co., Chgo., 1939-40; sec. Internat. Boundary Commn. U.S. and Can., Dept. State, Washington, 1940—, adminstrv. asst., 1956-63, adminstrv. officer 1963—. Asst. financial drives Trinity Coll. Alumni, Washington, 1968. Roman Catholic. Home: 2205 Beechwood Rd Lewisdale-Adelphi MD 20783 Office: GAO Bldg 441 G St NW Washington DC 20548

SHEERIN, MARY THEREZON, psychologist, educator; b. Jackson Heights, N.Y., Sept. 28, 1927; d. Harold Gerard and Anastasia Geraldine (McHugh) Sheerin; A.B., Regis Coll., 1957; A.M., Catholic U. Am., 1962. Instr., Sch. System, Archdiocese Boston, 1948-59; asst. prof. psychology Regis Coll., Weston, Mass., 1960—. NSF participant Psychology for Coll. Tchrs., U. Mich., summers 1966-67; dir. Summer Inst., Psychology for Secondary Sch. Tchrs. supported by NSF, 1973. Nat. Inst. Mental Health research grantee, 1963. Mem. Am. Psychol. Assn., Psychologists Interested in Religious Issues, Insts. Religion and Health, Sigma Xi. Home: 235 Wellesley St Weston MA 02193

SHEETS, ELVA DARAH, author; b. Huntington County, Ind., May 24, 1898; d. James and Lottie Jane (Bailey) Summers; grad. Bradley U., 1919; m. Nov. 17, 1921; children—M. Cosette, Sumner B. Collector, exhibitor Nature Colorama, creations of nature, primarily seashells and other ocean life. Mem. Smithsonian Assos., Am. Analocological Union, Internat. Oceanographic Found., Am. Mus. Natural History, Am. Malacologists. Methodist. Club: Womens (Huntington, Ind.). Author: The Fascinating World of the Sea, 1974. Home: Rural Route #4 Huntington IN 46750

SHEETZ, ANN KINDIG (MRS. LOREN DEAN SHEETZ), editor; b. Silver Lake, Ind., Oct. 8, 1934; d. Foster Leon and Margaret Louise (Hammerel) Kindig; student Ind. U., 1952-53, Manchester Coll., 1965; m. Loren D. Sheetz, June 28, 1953; children—Todd Kevin, Douglas Brian. News and feature editor Akron (Ind.) News, 1962-68; editor Mentone (Ind.) News, 1964-68; editor Akron/Mentone News, 1968—. Recipient writing awards Hoosier Press Assn., 1968-69, Womans Press Club Ind., 1970-74. Mem. Womans Press Club Ind. (corr. sec.), Nat. Fedn. Press Women (nat. writing award 1970), Hoosier Press Assn., Fulton County Hist. Soc. Republican. Methodist. Home: Rural Route 2 Akron IN 46910 Office: Box 427 Mentone IN 46539

SHEFFER, PATRICIA ELLEN (MRS. FRANK HALE SHEFFER), psychologist; b. Worcester, Mass., Nov. 3, 1926; d. Carroll Wilson and Mary Bessie (Tuttle) Gorman; B.A., Carleton Coll., 1948; M.S., San Jose State U., 1966; m. Frank Hale Sheffer, Sept. 11, 1948; children—Steven Hale, James Timothy. Tchr., Minot, N.D., 1951-53, Ft. Collins, Colo., 1957-59; trainee sch. psychologist, Saratoga, Cal., 1966-67; sch. psychologist, Morgan Hill, Cal., 1967—, also marriage and family counselor; pvt. practice Whole Person Inst., 1973—; cons. Bridge Child-Family Clinic, Chamberlain Day Treatment Center (both Morgan Hill). Mem. Cal. Assn. Sch. Psychologists (rep. in learning disabilities to Cal. Dept. Edn. 1970-74), Am., Bay Area psychol. assns., Humanistic Psychol. Assn., Internat. Transactional Analysis Assn. (clin. mem.), Bay Area Psychologists Sorority. Address: 19911 Fig Tree Ct Cupertino CA 95014

SHEFFIELD, DOROTHY JOHNSON (MRS. CLINTON A. SHEFFIELD, JR.), civic worker, educator; b. Mpls., Apr. 1, 1925; d. Ernest William and Madeline (Jones) Johnson; B.S. with honors, St. Cloud State Coll., 1947; M.A., Eastern Ill. U., 1968; m. Clinton Anson Sheffield, Jr., Aug. 25, 1951; children—Clinton Anson, III, Phillip Richard. Tchr. high schs., Motley and Royalton, Minn., 1947-49; tchr. elementary schs., Duluth, Minn. and Ft. Lee, N.J., 1950-52; tchr., dir. pvt. kindergarten, Dickinson, N.D., 1957-71; tchr. health and safety A.R.C.; den mother Boy Scouts Am., Mo. Valley council, 1960-68, den leader coach, 1968—, dist. den mother tng., 1968-71. Condr. weekly crafts program St. Lukes Home for Aged, 1954-65; established The Anchorage (pvt. sch. for trainable mentally retarded children), 1965-66. Mem. D.A.R. (regent N.D. Soc. 1970-72), Am. Assn. U. Women (pres. Dickinson br. 1958-60), Kappa Delta Pi. Episcopalian (chmn. ch. women 1958, deanery chmn. 1959, Sunday sch. tchr. and supt. 1952-66). Rebekah (noble grand 1972). Home: 1059 W 6th St Dickinson ND 58601

SHEFFIELD, HELEN MAURINE PETERSON, librarian; b. Cardston, Alta., Can., Sept. 29, 1912 (parents Am. citizens); d. John and Jessie Ellen (Lofgreen) Peterson; student U. Utah, 1930-32; B.S., Brigham Young U., 1936; postgrad., U. Utah, 1952-54; m. Wayne Kinnett Sheffield, June 28, 1936; children—Kay Sheffield Murray, Anne Sheffield Courtney, Paul Wayne. Tchr. elementary sch., Kaysville, Utah, 1934-36, Farmington, Utah, 1952-53; sch. librarian Central Davis Jr. High Sch., Layton, Utah, 1954-63; librarian Davis High Sch., Layton, 1963-65; sch. library cons. Davis County, Utah, 1965—. Mem. evaluative coms. for sch. media centers, Utah Bd. of Edn. Vice pres. P.T.A., Kaysville; chmn. youth activities Kaysville Civic Assn. Historian Davis County Democratic Central Com., 1971-73; mem. Women's State Legislative Council, Utah, 1971—; mem. Gov.'s Conf. on Libraries, Planning Com., 1971. Mem. Am. Assn. U. Women (past pres.), Utah Library Assn., Utah Ednl. Media Assn., Utah Assn. Supervision Curriculum Devel., Delta Kappa Gamma (past pres.). Clubs: Shatanka (past pres.), Athena (past pres.). Home: 242 West 1st South Kaysville UT 84037 Office: 45 East State St Farmington UT 84025

SHELBY, ANNETTE NEVIN (MRS. RICHARD CRAIG SHELBY), educator; b. Kinston, Ala., Jan. 22, 1939; d. Edwin Claude and Gladys (Price) Nevin; B.A., U. Ala., 1960, M.A., 1962; Ph.D., La. State U., 1973; m. Richard Craig Shelby, June 11, 1960; children—Richard Craig, Claude Nevin. Instr. speech U. Ala., 1962-63, asst. to dir. of debate, 1963-64, instr. speech, 1970-73, asst. prof., 1973—. Fund raising chmn. Jr. Welfare Assn., 1971-72; mem. Tuscaloosa Arts and Humanities Council, Tuscaloosa County Preservation Soc. Mem. Speech Communication Assn. Am., So. Speech Communication Assn., Ala. Speech Assn., Tuscaloosa County Bar Assn. Aux. (pres. 1971-72), Phi Beta Kappa, Tau Kappa Alpha, Alpha Lambda Delta, Zeta Phi Eta, Chi Delta Phi, Phi Kappa Phi, Delta Delta Delta. Presbyn. Democrat. Clubs: Pickwick Study, Merrimakers and Gaities Mardi Gras. Home: 66 High Forest Tuscaloosa AL 35401 Office: PO Box 1965 University AL 35486

SHELBY, MARTHA JANICE, educator; b. Austin, Tex., Mar. 26, 1920; d. Lemuel Evart and Mabel Clair (Wright) Shelby; B.A. magna cum laude, U. Tex., 1942, Ph.D. (Nat. Def. scholar), 1971; M.A., Sul Ross State Coll., 1947. Ednl. adminstr. Meth. Mission Schs., India, 1949-53; faculty Huston-Tillotson Coll., Austin, Tex., 1963-64, 67—, asso. prof. social scis., 1970-74, prof., 1974—; prof., head history dept. Butimba Coll., Mwanza, Tanzania, E. Africa, 1964-66. Served with WAC, 1942-45. Recipient Ford Found. grant, 1963-64. Mem. Am. Acad. Polit. and Social Scis., Am. Assn. U. Profs., Women In Communications, Sierra Club, Phi Beta Kappa, Kappa Tau Alpha, Phi Kappa Phi, Audubon Soc. Democrat. Methodist. Contbr. articles in field to profl. jours. Home: PO Box 1261 Austin TX 78767

SHELDEN, MIRIAM ALDRIDGE, univ. dean; b. Washington, N.Y., Sept. 30, 1912; d. Obed Wheeler and Marita Rushmore (Vail) Shelden; B.S., Russell Sage Coll., Troy, N.Y., 1933; A.M., N.Y.U., 1938, Ph.D., 1958; O.D., Gymnastic Peoples Coll., Ollerup, Denmark, 1933. Asst. dir. phys. edn. for women Berea (Ky.) Coll., 1933-38; instr. Woman's Coll., U. N.C., Greensboro, 1938-42; dean of women U. Ill., Urbana, 1947-72, dean student personnel, asso. prof. higher edn., asso. chancellor for affirmative action, 1972—, on leave, 1974—. Formerly cons. to women Job Corps Centers; mem. Gov.'s Commn. on Status Women. Mem. Champaign County bd. Ill. Children's Home and Aid. Served from ensign to lt. comdr. Women's Res., USNR, 1942-47; promoted to comdr. USNR; planned the establishment of Waves on primary naval air stations within U.S.A., later established program for Waves in Hawaii. Awarded Commendation Ribbon; recipient Doris Crockett Alumnae medal for distinguished service Russell Sage Coll., 1963. Mem. Am. Coll. Personnel Assn. (mem. at large, exec. council), Nat. (past pres.), Ill. assns. women deans and counselors, Am. Assn. U. Women, Aircraft Owners and Pilots Assn., Mortar Bd., Alpha Lambda Delta (nat. sec., historian). Address: 1516 S Lakeside Dr Lake Worth FL 33460

SHELDON, BEATRICE EVERETT (MRS. ANSON H. SHELDON), polit. worker; b. Gunn, Miss., May 16, 1915; d. John Broadus and Pency Ann (Wooley) Everett; R.N., Dr. Willis Walley Sch. Nursing, Jackson, Miss., 1937; m. Anson H. Sheldon, Feb. 5, 1939; children—Patricia Ann (Mrs. Harry C. Strauss), Anson H., Lawson. Nurse, Kings Daus. Hosp., Canton, Miss., 1937, Greenville, Miss., 1937, Helena (Ark.) Hosp., 1938-39; sec.-treas. Machinery Inc., 1966—; County com. Miss. Republican Party, 1944-60; alternate del. to Rep. State Conv., 1948, 52, 56, 60. Trustee South Washington County Hosp., Hollandle, Miss. Mem. Miss. Registered Nurse Assn. Episcopalian. Club: Longwood Community Culture. Home: Keystone Plantation Avon MS 38723

SHELDON, ELEANOR HARRIET BERNERT, research council exec., sociologist; b. Hartford, Conn., Mar. 19, 1920; d. Morris G. and Fannie (Myers) Bernert; A.A., Colby Jr. Coll., 1940; A.B., U. N.C., 1942; Ph.D. (William Rainey Harper fellow), U. Chgo., 1949; m. James Sheldon, Mar. 19, 1950 (div. Jan. 1960); children—James, John Anthony. Asst. demographer Office Population Research, Washington, 1942-43; social scientist U.S. Dept. Agr., Washington, 1943-45; asso. dir. Chgo. Community Inventory, U. Chgo., 1947-50; social scientist Social Sci. Research Council, N.Y.C., 1950-51, UN, N.Y.C., 1950-52; asso. research sociologist, lectr. U. Cal. Sch. Nursing, Los Angeles, 1957-61; sociologist, exec. asso. Russell Sage Found., N.Y.C., 1961-72; pres. Social Sci. Research Council, 1972—; dir. Equitable Life Assurance of U.S., dir. 1st Nat. City Corp. & Bank, RAND Corp. Vis. prof. sociology Columbia U., N.Y.C., 1970, U. Cal. at Santa Barbara, 1971. Cons. to depts. of govt. Bd. dirs. Moblzn. for Youth, N.Y.C., 1965-71, UN Research Inst. for Social Devel., 1973—. Recipient research grant Social Sci. Research Council, 1953-55. Mem. Am. Sociol. Assn., Eastern Sociol. Soc., Population Assn. Am. (bd. dirs.), A.A.A.S., Am. Assn. Pub. Opinion Research, Am. Statis. Assn. (vice chmn. social statistics 1969), Internat. Union Sci. Study of Population, Sociol. Research Assn. (pres. 1971), Council on Fgn. Relations. Author: (with L. Wirth) Chicago Community Fact Book, 1949; America's Children, 1958; (with R. Glazier) Pupils and Schools in New York City, 1965; (with Wilbert E. Moore) Indicators of Social Change; Concepts and Measurements, 1968. Editor: Family Economic Behavior, 1973. Home: 174 E 74th St New York City NY 10021 Office: Social Science Research Council 605 3d Av New York City NY 10016

SHELDON, GEORGIANA HORTENSE, govt. ofcl.; b. Lawrenceville, Pa., Dec. 2, 1923; d. William Franklin and Georgiana (Root) Sheldon; B.A., Keuka Coll., 1945; M.S., Cornell U., 1949. Dir. admissions Stetson U. Coll. Law, 1954-56; exec. asst. Republican Nat. Com., 1956-61; exec. sec. to Hon. Rogers Morton of Md., 1962-69; dep. dir. Office Civil Def., Dept. Army, Washington, 1969-72; now dep. dir. Def. Civil Preparedness Agy., Washington. Recipient Alumni award for profl. advancement Keuka Coll., 1966. Republican. Presbyn. Home: 1200 N Nash St Arlington VA 22209 Office: Dept Def The Pentagon Washington DC 20310

SHELDON, MARY MARGUERITE WOLF (MRS. DANA M. SHELDON), psychiatrist; b. Pitts., Feb. 20, 1932; d. Frederick Enyeart and Clarice Maud (Bechhold) Wolf; A.B., Western Res. U., 1953, M.D., 1957; m. Dana M. Sheldon, Feb. 2, 1963; children—Susan, Barbara, Hilary. Intern, U. Hosps., Cleve., 1957-58, resident internal medicine, 1958-60; resident psychiatry Inst. Pa. Hosp., Phila., 1960-63; fellow Harvard, 1963-65, asst. psychiatrist, 1965-68, asso. psychiatrist, 1968-72, psychiatrist, 1972—. Candidate, Boston Psychoanalytic Inst. and Soc., 1965—. Diplomate Am. Bd. Psychiatry and Neurology, Nat. Bd. Med. Examiners. Mem. Am. Psychiat. Assn. Home: Grasshopper Lane Lincoln MA 01773 Office: 75 Mt Auburn St Cambridge MA 02138

SHELL, HELEN HUFF, educator; b. Vincennes, Ind., Nov. 26, 1900; d. William H. and Caroline (Willmore) Shell; student Butler U., 1920-22; Ph.D., U. Chgo., 1925; M.A., Northwestern U., 1940. Office supr. Hart, Schaffner & Marx, Chgo., 1924-30; personnel supr. Bauer and Black, 1930-38; vocational dir. Katharine Gibbs Sch., 1940-43; supr. employee relations Wright Aero. Corp., Paterson, N.J., 1943-47; partner Bing-Cronin Personnel Service, N.Y.C., 1949-54; instr. City Coll. N.Y. 1951-66, dept. supr. 1959-66; instr. New Sch. for Social Research, 1954-60; asst. adminstr., counselor Vocational Adv. Service, N.Y.C., 1958-66. Pres., Horizon House for Sr. Citizens La Jolla, 1968-70; v.p., bd. dirs. Protective Services for Sr. Adults, 1968—. Bd. dirs. Horizons, Inc. Mem. Am., N.Y.C. personnel and guidance assn., Internat. Assn. Personnel Women, U.S. Adult Edn. Assn., Nat. Vocational Guidance Assn., White Sands President's Assn. (pres. 1967-69, v.p. 1969-71), Kappa Kappa Gamma. Episcopalian. Club: Cosmopolitan (N.Y.C.). Research in field. Home: The White Sands 7450 Olivetas Av La Jolla CA 92037

SHELL, MARY KATHERINE JAYNESS HOSKING (MRS. JOSEPH C. SHELL), newspaper columnist; b. Bakersfield, Cal., Feb. 9, 1927; d. Walter Charles and Mary Ellen (Young) Jaynes; student Bakersfield Coll., 1946-48; m. Richard Hosking, Aug. 21, 1948 (div. 1968); children—Geoffrey Richard, Timothy William, Meredith Katherine; m. 2d, Joseph C. Shell, Jan. 8, 1970. Mem. editorial staff Bakersfield Californian, 1944-45; mem. editorial staff Bakersfield News Bull., 1965-68, mng. editor, 1969; polit. columnist Capitol News Service and Bakersfield Californian, 1971—. Founding pres. Bakersfield Jr. Woman's Club, 1954-55. Mem. Kern County Republican Central Com., 1956-60; founder, state sec. United Reps. Cal., 1963; mem. Cal. delegation Rep. Nat. Conv., 1964. Mem. Cal. Press Women, Kern Press Club (founder 1967). Home: 2928 21st St Bakersfield CA 93301 also 2701 Azalea Rd Sacramento CA 95825 Office: State Capitol Sacramento CA 95814

SHELLENBERGER, MADALINE HAGAN (MRS. ORVILLE C. SHELLENBERGER), constrn. co. exec.; b. Marietta, Okla., Sept. 18, 1908; d. William Leroy and Lela Ann (Mann) Hagan; student Greenville Bus. Sch., 1943; m. Orville C. Shellenberger, Jan. 18, 1924; children—Orvillyn Joyce (Mrs. Roger W. Palmer), Billy Frank. Co-owner, sec.-treas., dir. Shellenberger, Inc., Sherman, Tex., 1957—, Texoma Equipment Co., Sherman, 1961—. Mem. tech.-occupational adv. com. Grayson County Coll., 1973-74. Mem. Bus. and Profl. Women's Club (1st v.p. 1954—). Democrat. Presbyn. Mem. Order Eastern Star. Club: Soroptimist (sec. Sherman 1954-74). Home: 2720 W Houston Hwy 82 W Sherman TX 75090 Office: PO Box 880 Hwy 75 N Sherman TX 75090

SHELLEY, FLORENCE DUBROFF, editor, ednl. cons.; b. Balt., Jan. 21, 1921; d. Nathan and Charlotte (Weisman) Dubroff; A.B., Barnard Coll., 1940; M.S., Columbia, 1941; m. Edwin Freeman Shelley, Aug. 29, 1941; children—Carolyn Shelley (Mrs. Phillip LeBel), William Edson. Editor-writer J. Walter Thompson Co., N.Y.C., 1941-46; freelance editor, writer, 1946—. Editorial, ednl. program cons. N.Y. State Citizens Com. for Pub. Schs., Nat. Center for Citizens in Edn., 1965-68; editorial and ednl. cons., dir. E.F. Shelley & Co., Inc., N.Y.C., 1967—; pub. Edn.-Tng. Market Report, 1970-73; cons. Nat. Commn. on Resources for Youth, 1971—, Nat. Program for Ednl. Leadership, 1973—; pub. affairs cons. Nat. Com. for Citizens in Edn., 1973—; resource cons. N.Y. State Dept. Edn., 1967. Pres., New Rochelle (N.Y.) Council P.T.A.'s, 1964-66, Barnard Coll. Class of 1940, 1965-70; co-chmn. program com. Catholic Judeo Conf., Iona Coll., 1966; chmn. edn. com. City Mgr.'s Conf. on Human Relations; mem. Nat. Com. for Support Pub. Schs., Mayor's Adv. Com. on Youth and Employment; adv. bd. New Rochelle Community Action Program. Hon. trustee Wildcliff Youth Mus. Mem. Am. Ednl. Research Assn., Am. Acad. Polit. Sci., Nat. Soc. Study Edn. Club: Women's City. Contbr. articles to mags. Home: 339 Oxford Rd New Rochelle NY 10804 Office: 415 Madison Av New York City NY 10017

SHELLEY, JEAN LOUISE, educator; b. Freeland, Md., Feb. 16, 1925; d. Harry G. and Elva (Hampsher) Shelley; B.S., Madison Coll., 1949; M.Ed., U. Va., 1965; fellowship Boston U., 1967; postgrad. Loyola Coll., U. Md. Tchr. girls phys. edn. Milford Mill Sr. High Sch., Baltimore County, Md., 1949-64; guidance counselor Overlea Sr. High Sch., Baltimore County, 1965-72; dir. guidance Parkville Sr. High Sch., Baltimore County, 1972—. Camp counselor, camp dir., 1949-55. Recipient Alumni Attainment award Sparks High Sch., 1945. Mem. Md. Personnel and Guidance Assn. (treas. 1970-71, Outstanding Individual award 1973), Baltimore County Womens Coaches Assn. (hon.), N.E.A., Md. Sch. Counselors Assn. (v.p. 1971-72), Md. State Tchrs. Assn., Tchrs. Assn. Balt. County, Madison Coll. Alumni Assn. (dir. 1958-70, pres. 1962-64), Baltimore County Counselors Assn. (pres. 1971-72), Alpha Sigma Alpha. Lutheran. Home: 105F Versailles Circle Baltimore MD 21204

SHELLEY, SALLY SWING (MRS. JAMES M. SHELLEY), internat. ofcl.; b. Kent, Eng., Aug. 3, 1924; d. Raymond Gram and Betty (Gram) Swing; A.B., Smith Coll., 1945; M.F.A., Columbia, 1971; m. Marcello Spaccarelli, Feb. 12, 1950 (div. July 1954); 1 son, Sidney S.; m. James M. Shelley, Nov. 26, 1960. Feature writer Boston Globe, 1944-46; fgn. corr. U.P.I., 1946-50; radio news editor U.S. Army Field Service for Japan, 1950-52, Voice of Am., N.Y.C., 1952; exec. sec., mgr. Am. Soc. Indsl. Designers, N.Y.C., 1952-57; chief information officer UNESCO, N.Y. Office, 1957-72; chief edn. information programmes Office Pub. Information, UN, N.Y.C., 1973—. Trustee Robert Flaherty Found., Brattleboro, Vt., 1960-70, William Alanson White Inst. Psychiatry, Psychoanalysis and Psychology, N.Y.C., 1965-68. Assn. World Lang., 1959-63. Home:

510 E 23d St New York City NY 10010 Office: Room 1045B United Nations New York City NY 10017

SHELLEY, SUSANNE MARIE LANGER (MRS. ROBERT E. SHELLEY), educator; b. Vienna, Austria, Feb. 2, 1928; d. Joseph and Paula (Grunbaum) Langer; came to U.S., 1946, naturalized, 1948; B.A., Cal. State U., 1961, M.A., 1963; m. Robert E. Shelley, July 21, 1946; children—Frances (Mrs. Michael MacCallum), Mark Robert. Tchr., Hiram Johnson High Sch., Sacramento, 1961-65; lectr. math. Cal. State U. 1961-68, Sacramento City Coll., 1965—. Mem. Nat. Council Tchrs. Math., Math. Assn. Am., Pi Mu Epsilon. Author: (with Vivian Groza) Modern Elementary Algebra, 1969, Modern Intermediate Algebra, 2d edit., 1974, Precalculus Mathematics, 1972; (with Crowdis and Wheeler) Calculus, 1972, Finite Mathematics, 2d edit., 1974. Home: 28 Shoreline Circle Sacramento CA 95831

SHELLY, ALICE ELIZABETH, archtl. specifications writer; b. Roseville, O., Jan. 1, 1936; d. Lewis Amos and Lois Elizabeth (Wilcox) Shelly; A.B. in Psychology, Baldwin-Wallace Coll., Berea, O., 1958. Personnel asst. Standard Oil Co. Ohio, Cleve., 1958-60, patent sec., 1960-62; secretarial, gen. officer work Manpower, Inc., Honolulu, 1962-64; tech. asst. Lemmon, Freeth, Haines, Jones & Farrell, Honolulu, 1964-65, specifications writer, 1965-73; chief specifications writer Haines, Jones, Farrell, White & Gima, 1973—; pres. Diamond Head Surf Corp., 1972—, also dir. Lectr. constrn. specifications, U. Hawaii. Vice chmn. Oahu Young Republicans, 1964-65, nat. commiteewoman, 1965-67, dir. teen-agers, Hawaii, 1965, chmn. membership Hawaii, 1965; precinct pres. Hawaii Rep. Party, 1964, dist. sec., 1965, chmn. Honolulu County com., 1968-69, county committeewoman 16th dist., 1967-68. Named Outstanding Young Rep., Oahu Young Reps., 1964, Hawaii Young Reps., 1964; recipient Bronze Hard Chargers award Young Rep. Nat. Fedn., 1968, Outstanding Service award Honolulu Bus. and Profl. Club, 1967. Mem. Constrn. Specifications Inst. (pres. Honolulu chpt. 1971-72, edn. chmn. 1972—, region 11 conf. program chmn. 1974, certificate appreciation region 11 1973), Bus. and Profl. Club (v.p. chpt. 1965-67), Delta Zeta (Honolulu alumni chpt. pres. 1962-64, 72-73). Home: 3824 Leahi Av Honolulu HI 96815 Office: 190 S King St Suite 300 Honolulu HI 96813

SHELTON, BESSIE ELIZABETH, educator; b. Lynchburg, Va.; d. Robert and Bessie Ann (Plenty) Shelton; B.A. (scholar), W.Va. State Coll., 1958; student Northwestern U., 1953-55, Ind. U., 1956; M.S., State U. N.Y., 1960. Young adult librarian Bklyn. Pub. Library, 1960-62; asst. head central reference div. Queens Borough Pub. Library, Jamaica, N.Y., 1962-65; instructional media specialist Lynchburg (Va.) Bd. Edn., 1966—. Guest singer radio sta. WLVA, 1966—, WLVA-TV Christmas concerts, 1966—; cons. music and market research. Mem. YWCA, Lynchburg, 1966—, Fine Arts Center, Lynchburg, 1966—. Mem. Nat., Va., Lynchburg edn. assns., Va. State Dept. Sch. Librarians, Internat. Entertainers Guild, Music City Songwriters Assn., Vocal Artists Am., Internat. Clover Poetry Assn., Intercontinental Biog. Assn., World Mail Dealers Assn., North Am. Mailers Exchange, Pi Delta Phi, Sigma Delta Pi. Contbr. poems to various publs. Democrat. Baptist. Clubs: National Travel, Gulf Travel. Home: 1800 Bedford Av Apt 12 Lynchburg VA 24504

SHELTON, RUTH BETTY (MRS. ROBERT DUANE SHELTON), educator; b. Waukegan, Ill., Mar. 18, 1936; d. Edward Max and Dorothy Margaret (Swanson) Klein; B.A., Cornell Coll., 1960; M.S., Tex. Woman's U., 1961, Ph.D. (Cotton Research, teaching fellowships), 1963; m. Robert Duane Shelton, Nov. 30, 1963; 1 son, Duane Edward. Asst. prof. Sam Houston U., Huntsville, Tex., 1963-66, U. Houston, 1966-68; asso. prof. Tex. Tech. U., Lubbock, 1969-70, U. Louisville, 1971-73, 74—; asso. prof. textile tech. Spalding Coll., Louisville, 1973-74. Mem. Internat. Fedn. Home Economics, Am. Assn. Textile Chemists and Colorists, Am. Home Econs. Assn., Phi Upsilon Omicron. Home: 1006 Old Cannons Louisville KY 40207

SHEMANSKI, FRANCES, writer; b. Arena, N.Y., Jan. 9, 1925; d. John and Helen Mary (Goleneski) Shemanski; B.A., Hunter Coll., 1947. Religion, edn. and travel and resort editor N.Y. Jour.-Am., 1949-66; travel writer Lufthansa German Airlines, 1967-69; contbg. editor Travel Agt. Mag., 1969—. Mem. Soc. Am. Travel Writers (dir. 1964-66), N.Y. Travel Writers Assn. (v.p. 1971-73), Women in Communications (v.p. 1967-68), N.Y. Newspaper Women's Club. Home: 2312 Wickham Av Bronx NY 10469

SHEN, MARGARET C.Y. WU, cytogenetist; b. Soochow, China, May 5, 1915; d. Ming Sih and Jim Ying (Shen) Wu; B.S., Soochow (China) U., 1937; M.S., U. Neb., 1958; m. Eugene Y.F. Shen, Jan. 2, 1940; children—Grace (Mrs. Ta-chen Lo), Albert C.K., Alice (Mrs. Charles Cha). Came to U.S., 1963, naturalized, 1974. Tchr. Bapt. Union High Sch., Shanghai, China, 1938-40; asst. instr. Sino-French Coll. of Pharmacy, Shanghai, 1940-45; instr. Soochow (China) U., 1946-48; dean of sch. Wei-Ling High Sch., Soochow, 1948-49; asst. prof. Taiwan Christian Coll., Chungli, 1955-56; asso. prof. Provincial Chung-Hsing U., Taichung, Taiwan, 1958-63; research scientist asso. Academia Sinica, Taipei, 1958-63, U. Tex. at Austin, 1964—. Research grantee Nat. Council on Sci. Devel. in Taiwan, 1959-63. Mem. Bot. Soc. Am., Genetics Soc. Am., Beta Beta Beta. Contbr. articles to profl. jours. Home: 2903 Stardust Dr Austin TX 78757 Office: U Tex Austin TX 78712

SHEN, MARY EUYANG (MRS. CHANG-JUI SHEN), broadcasting exec.; b. Chgo., Apr. 4, 1924; d. Herbert and Pauline (Chiang) Euyang; certificate Grad. Sch. Journalism, Columbia, 1944; B.A., Wesleyan Coll., 1946; m. Chang-Jui Shen, Apr. 3, 1970; 1 son, Paul Loh. Adminstrv. asst. Am. aid program in China, China Relief Mission, 1948-50; writer, spl. events officer Chinese Br., Voice Am., 1951-59; chief Asian feed service Voice Am., Washington, 1959-74; press officer Fgn. Press Center USIA, 1974—. Recipient Meritorious Service award USIA, 1962, Quality Service award USIA, 1966, Alumni Spl. Achievement Citation award Wesleyan Coll., 1972. Mem. Am. Women in Radio and TV. Home: 7 Peter Cooper Rd Apt 9F New York City NY 10010 Office: 866 2d Av New York City NY 10017

SHENKER, LILLIAN ROSE KOPLAR (MRS. MORRIS A. SHENKER), lawyer; b. St. Louis, May 8, 1913; d. Sam and Jeannette (Grollnek) Koplar; B.S., B.A., Washington U., St. Louis, 1934, LL.B., 1939; m. Morris A. Shenker, Dec. 23, 1939; children—Morris Arthur, Patricia Ann. Admitted to Mo. bar, 1939; provisional judge St. Louis Municipal Ct., 1949, St. Louis Ct. Criminal Correction, 1949-53; pres. Park Plaza Drug Co., St. Louis, 1935-68, sec., 1968—; v.p. 220 TV Inc., St. Louis, 1953—; sec. Hotel Mgmt. Co., St. Louis, 1964—; pres. Murrieta Hot Springs Corp. (Cal.), 1972—. Chmn. ann. Inst. Human Rights, St. Louis, 1951-54; vice chmn. St. Louis Council Human Relations, 1950-53, chmn., 1953; chmn. Jewish Welfare Dr., 1957; co-chmn. St. Louis Bd. State Israel Bonds, 1960-65, nat. bd. dirs., 1963—; mem. citizens adv. com. St. Louis Juvenile Ct., 1962-63; mem. Mo. adv. com. U.S. Commn. on Civil Rights, 1965-67; mem. Nat. Small Bus. Adv. Council, 1965-67. Chmn. Bus. and Profl. Women Mo. for Johnson-Humphrey, 1964; mem. adv. bd. Dismas Clark Found., 1960—; bd. dirs. Jewish Fedn. women's div., 1950—, pres. bd., 1955-57, life mem., 1965—; bd. dirs. Am.-Israel Cultural Found., Am. Friends Hebrew U., Jerusalem; bd. dirs. St. Vincent's Hosp. Aux., chmn. ann. Christmas prelude 1971-72. Mem. Mo. Bar Assn., Am. Assn. U. Women, Mo. Assn. Social Welfare, Adult Edn. Council Greater St. Louis, League Women Voters, Nat. Council Jewish Women, Hadassah, Mo. Hist. Soc. Jewish religion (trustee temple 1965-68). Club: Westwood Country. Home: 1230 Topping Rd St Louis MO 63131 Office: 408 Olive St St Louis MO 63102 also Murrieta Resort Hotel Country Club Spa Murrieta CA 92362

SHENNAN, EDITH MURIEL, coll. dean; b. Chgo., Dec. 10, 1930; d. Alexander Gordon and Agnes Ruby (Sinclair) Shennan; B.A., MacMurray Coll., 1952; M.Ed., U. Ill., 1953. Head resident DePauw U., Greencastle, Ind., 1953-60; asst. dean women Kent (O.) State U., 1960-65, U. Denver, 1965-66; dean women West Liberty (W.Va.) State Coll., 1966—. Mem. arts and crafts com. Oglebay Inst., 1970—; actress Brookehills Playhouse, Summer Stock Theatre Prodns., 1971—. Mem. Nat. (mem. commn. on profl. ethics 1972-74, chmn. 1974—), Ohio assns. women deans, adminstrs. and counselors, W.Va. Assn. Student Personnel Adminstrs., Alpha Phi. Clubs. Federated Womens, Faculty (pres. 1968-69) (West Liberty). Home: 120 Faculty Dr West Liberty WV 26074

SHEPARD, ELAINE ELIZABETH, writer; b. Olney, Ill.; d. Thomas J. and Bernice E. (Shadle) Shepard; m. Terry D. Hunt, Apr. 16, 1938; m. 2d, George F. Hartman, Oct. 1, 1943 (div. June 1958). Film and theater actress, Hollywood, N.Y.C., also Europe, 1939-50; cover girl John Robert Powers, 1939-43; under contract to RKO and Metro-Goldwyn-Mayer, 1940-45; covered nat. polit. convs. for Stas. WTTG-TV and WINS Chgo., 1952, Chgo., 1956, polit. reporter for NANA and WINS, Chgo. and Los Angeles, 1960; reporter Congo rebellion for N.Am. Newspaper Alliance and N.Y. Mirror, 1960-61; corr. covering Pres. Eisenhower's Middle East, Far East and S.Am. tour, 1959-60; Vietnam corr. MBS, 1965-66; guest commentator for Voice of Am.; contbr. feature articles to various mags., including McCall's, Pageant, Better Homes and Gardens, Parade, N.Y. News Sunday Mag., 1953—; columnist, contbg. editor Twin Circle mag. Nat. Catholic Press, 1969-74. Has been granted pvt. interviews with Khrushchev, Castro, Tito, Chou En-lai, Nasser, Shah of Iran, King Hussein, King Faisel, Duvailer, Lumumba, Chiang-Kai-Shek, Nehru, Menzies, John F. Kennedy, Richard M. Nixon, others; mem. White House Press Corps accompanying Pres. Nixon to Austria, Iran, Poland, Moscow, 1972. Mem. Screen Actors Guild, A.F.T.R.A., Actors Equity. Club: Overseas Press (N.Y.C.). Author: Forgive Us Our Press Passes, 1962; The Doom Pussy, 1967. Home: 12 E 62d St New York City NY 10021

SHEPARD, KATHARINE, art mus. curator; b. Bristol, Conn.; d. Charles Norman and Marguerite (Dunbar) Shepard; B.A., Bryn Mawr Coll., 1928, M.A., 1929, Ph.D., 1936; student Am. Sch. Classical Studies, Athens, Greece, 1930-31. Pvt. tutoring, research, N.Y.C., 1936-41; mus. aide Nat. Gallery Art, Washington, 1941-43, asst. registrar, 1943-55, asst. curator graphic arts, 1955—; lectr. grad. sch. dept. art Catholic U. Am., 1960-69. Mem. Am. Assn. Museums, Archaeol. Inst. Am. (sec. Washington chpt.), Print Council Am. Episcopalian. Home: 1260 21st NW Washington DC 20036 Office: Nat Gallery of Art Washington DC 20565

SHEPARD, LORAINE V., educator; b. Algoma, Wis., Sept. 27, 1914; d. Thomas Lee and Ella Johanna (Hubert) Shepard; B.A., Western Wash. Coll., 1939; M.Ed., Mills Coll., 1942; Ph.D., U. Mich., 1954. Tchr. pub. schs., Randal, Wash., 1934-35, Longview, Wash., 1935-40, 41-42; exec. sec. Casa Pan-Americana, Mills Coll., Oakland, summer 1942; statistician Bur. Ednl. Reference & Research, U. Mich., Ann Arbor, 1945, teaching asst., Sch. Edn., 1945; asst. prof. Eastern Mich. Coll. Edn., summer 1945; asso. prof. So. Ore. Coll., summer 1953; asso. prof. Western Wash. Coll., winter 1959; asst. prof. ednl. psychology Mich. State U., East Lansing, 1945-54, asso. prof. 54-61, prof. ednl. psychology and coordinator honors in edn., 1961-67, prof. Center for Experiential Edn., adj. mem. psychology dept. Antioch Coll., Yellow Springs, O., 1967—. Pres. Mich. Council for UNESCO, 1956-57. Bd. dirs. Yellow Springs Community Children's Center, 1970-73, v.p., 1972. Mem. Am. Assn. U. Profs., Menninger Found., Am. Civil Liberties Union, Common Cause, Phi Kappa Phi, Pi Lambda Theta. Home: 1332 Shawnee Dr Yellow Springs OH 45387

SHEPARD, M. JOAN, tv exec.; b. Erie, Pa., Aug. 10, 1929; d. Samuel Henry and Margaret (Dunham) Shepard; B.S., Syracuse U., 1951, M.S., 1960. Producer, dir., lectr. Bklyn. Coll. TV Center, 1965-67; coordinator, asso. producer Pub. Broadcast Lab., Ford Found., N.Y.C., 1967-69; N.Y.C. grand dir. Viviane Woodard Cosmetics, 1969—; profl. make-up artist, dir. N.Y. area field tng. acads. Writer, dir. producer series What's New for Nat. Ednl. TV. Mem. Vols. of Shelters, Inc., N.Y.C., 1964—. Named Outstanding Woman Grad. in TV, Syracuse U., 1963. Mem. Dirs. Guild Am., Nat. Acad. TV Arts and Scis., Nat. Assn. Ednl. Broadcasters, Alpha Gamma Delta, Alpha Epsilon Rho. Baptist. Home: 210 E 73d St New York City NY 10021

SHEPARD, MARIETTA (DANIELS) (MRS. JAMES JOSEPH SHEPARD, JR.), library adminstr., govt. ofcl.; b. Mt. Washington, Mo., Jan. 24, 1913; d. James Howard and Ettie May (Graham) Daniels; A.A., Kansas City (Mo.) Jr. Coll., 1931; A.B., U. Kan., 1933; B.S. in L.S., Columbia, 1943; M.A., Washington U., St. Louis, 1945; m. James Joseph Shepard, Jr., Feb. 29, 1964. Order asst. Kansas City (Mo.) Pub. Library, 1934-38; chief of circulation Washington U. Library, St. Louis, 1938-43; library dir. and prof. sch. library service Juan D. Arosemena Normal Sch., Santiago, Panama, 1943-46; instr. library sci. Universidad Central, Quito, Ecuador, summer, 1944; spl. asst. to librarian of Congress, 1946-48; asso. librarian Columbus Meml. Library Orgn. Am. States, Washington, 1948-68, chief library and archives devel. program, Washington, 1956—. Tchr. library sci. Nat. U. of Panama, summers 1949, 50, U.S. Dept. Agr. Grad. Sch., 1950-52; cons. reorgn. of library of Sociedad Economica de Amigos del Pais, Havana, 1948; cons. on librarian's examinations Phila. Civil Service Commn., 1953-54; chmn. Internat. Exec. Council, Inter-Am. Library Sch., Medellin, Colombia, 1956-63; exec. sec. seminars on the acquistion of Latin Am. Library Materials, Washington, 1956-73. Chmn. Books for the People Fund, Inc., Washington, 1961—. Mem. Am. (exec. bd. 1956, 57-60, 69-74, letter librarian award 1954), D.C. (pres. 1957-58) library assns., Latin Am. Studies Assn., Soc. of Woman Geographers, Pan Am. Liaison of Women's Orgns., Altrusa, Beta Phi Mu. Episcopalian. Author: La Infraestructura Bibliotecologica de Sistemas Nacionales de Informacion, 1972. Contbr. articles on libraries and books in the Americas to profl. publs. Home: 3025 Ontario Rd NW Washington DC 20009 Office: Organization of the American States 1735 Eye St NW Washington DC

SHEPARD, MURIEL IRWIN (MRS. VIRGIL E. SHEPARD), civic worker; b. Lake View, Ia., May 13, 1911; d. Orie Franklin and Elizabeth Reed (Fulcher) Irwin; B.Sch. Music, Morningside Coll., 1932; postgrad. U. Wash., 1935; M.A., U. Ia., 1937; m. Virgil E. Shepard, June 16, 1937; children—Gene W., James I. Tchr., Wall Lake (Ia.) Pub. Schs., 1932-35; asst. in music U. Ia., 1936-37; tchr. Clarksville (Ia.) pub. schs. 1952-54, Greene (Ia.) pub. schs., 1954-56. Mem. Butler County (Ia.) Bd. Edn., 1939-62, Allison (Ia.) Pub. Sch. Bd., 1943-46; mem. Ia. Bd. Pub. Instrn., 1962—, v.p., 1970-71, pres., 1972—; mem. Ia. Extension Adv. Com., 1966-68. Trustee Allison Pub. Library. Mem. Pi Lambda Theta. Republican. Mem. United Ch. of Christ. Mem. Order Eastern Star. Club: Women's (Allison). Address: 620 Pine St Allison IA 50602

SHEPHERD, ADA WATSON, ret. county ofcl.; b. Los Angeles, May 6, 1908; d. Thomas and Alice Lyle (Battersby) Watson; student Sch. Citizenship and Pub. Affairs, Syracuse U.; m. Stuart G. Shepherd, Dec. 22, 1972. Budget clk. City of Berkeley (Cal.); research asst. Rochester Bur. Municipal Research; financial cons. Pub. Adminstrn. Service, Chgo.; spl. cons. Monroe County, N.Y., establishing office of county auditor and installing system for budgetary control; dep. controller of Monroe County, 1936-49, in charge of all phases of budget work under county mgr. form of govt., exec. sec. to county mgr. and dir, budget, 1950-60, budget dir., 1960; dep. dir. county social welfare adminstrn., former dep. dir. Social Services-adminstrn., ret., 1969; cons. Mem. Municipal Finance Officers Assn., League Women Voters, Am. Assn. U. Women, Bus. and Profl. Women's Club, Am. Soc. Pub. Adminstrn., Am. Pub. Welfare Assn., West Marin C. of C. Clubs: Western Woman's (San Francisco). Author: Section I—Survey of the Government of Monroe County. Home: 13795 Hwy 9 Boulder Creek CA 95006

SHEPHERD, BUNNY WEST (MRS. LYNN H. SHEPHERD), craftsman, photographer; b. Kanawha, Ia., May 11, 1911; d. Lloyd Dring and Marcia May (Rankin) Petheram; ed. high sch., jr. coll., Pasadena, Cal.; m. Lynn Holmes Shepherd, May 22, 1961. With advt. sales dept. Pasadena Star News, 1940-49; owner Bunny's Portrait Studio, Pasadena, 1950—. Tchr. photography West Coast Sch. of Brooks Inst., Santa Barbara, Cal., Acad. Photographic Arts, North Hollywood; lectr. to numerous photography orgns.; chmn. Regional Photographers Conv., 1971. Mem. Profl. Photographers of West (dir., v.p., other offices; recipient Pres.'s award 1972), Profl. Photographers Am. (Cal. rep. to bd., chmn. regional Western states conv. 1976). Mem. Ch. Religious Sci. (Sunday Sch. dir. and tchr.). Home: 1712 Veranada Altadena CA 91001 Office: 1763 E Colorado St Pasadena CA 91106

SHEPHERD, FLORENCE MILDRED, missionary, educator; b. Corbin, Ky., Jan. 12, 1916; d. William Warden and Florence Mildred (Swartz) Shepherd; B.A., Union Coll., Barbourville, Ky., 1937; postgrad. Asbury Theol. Sem., Wilmore, Ky., 1937; M.A., U. Ky., 1939; postgrad. Kennedy Sch. Missions Hartford Theol. Sem., 1939; Ph.D., George Peabody Coll. Tchrs., 1949; student Inst. Bibl. Theology Lincoln Coll., Oxford (Eng.) U., 1958; L.H.D., Union Coll., 1966. Tchr. French Union Coll., summers 1935-37; tchr. English Mountain Settlement Sch., Linefork, Ky., 1937-38; missionary, India, 1940; mgr. Parker Br. Sch., Moradabad, India, 1941-42; tchr. edn. George Peabody Coll. for Tchrs., 1948; tchr. English, librarian Lal Bagh Girls' High Sch., Lucknow, India, 1950; prin. Lal Bagh Girls' Intermediate Coll., Lucknow, 1950-52; mgr., prin. Howard Plested Girls' High Sch., Meerut, India, 1952; mgr. Howard Plested Girls' Intermediate Coll., Meerut, 1957-66, also mgr. Methodist Elementary Sch., Meerut, 1959-66; instr. English Sue Bennett Coll., London, Ky., 1968—, chmn. communications div., 1971—, fgn. student adviser, 1972—, chmn. religious life com., 1973—. Tchr. english Grad. Sch. Union Coll. part time, 1974—. Sec. woman's conf. North India Conf. Meth. Ch. in South Asia, 1943-45, chmn. schs. com. Delhi conf., 1955-56, Agra conf., 1957-58, chmn. music com. Centenary Forward Movement, 1956—. Bd. govs. Isabella Thoburn Coll., Lucknow, 1950-66, Moradabad Meth. Girls' Intermediate Coll., 1958-65, Bareilly Meth. Girls' Intermediate Coll., 1958-65, Lal Bagh Girls Intermediate Coll., 1950-52. Recipient Distinguished Alumni Achievement award Union Coll., 1954. Mem. Nat. Council English Tchrs., So. Lang. Assn., South Atlantic Modern Lang. Assn., Internat. Platform Assn., Internat. Assn. Women Ministers, Ky. Hist. Soc., Smithsonian Assos., Univ. Women's Assn. Lucknow, Ky. Assn. Jr. Colls., United Meth. Women, Iota Sigma Nu, Kappa Delta Pi. Author: John Wesley, 1956. Contbr. to English Written Usage in Selected High Schools in India and America, 1951. Address: 113 Ashbury Dr Wilmore KY 40390

SHEPHERD, LORETTA DALE THURESON (MRS. FRANK COPELAND SHEPHERD), health service exec.; b. San Jose, Cal., Oct. 14, 1930; d. Victor Henry and Violet Irene (Miller) Thureson; B.A., San Jose State U., 1952; m. Frank Copeland Shepherd, June 6, 1953; children—Sharon Lynn, Robert Frank. Dir. occupational therapy Tre Monte Found., Los Gatos, Cal., 1953-54, San Jose Rehab. Center, 1954-57; adminstr. Lori Shepherd & Assos., Saratoga, Cal., 1967—. Cons. convalescent hosps., physicians; speaker occupational therapy San Jose State Coll., 1971. Pres. Argonaut Sch. P.T.A., Saratoga, 1963, Redwood Sch., 1967; leader Girl Scouts Am., Saratoga, 1963-67. Bd. dirs. Valle Monte League, 1966-73, Adult and Child Guidance Clinic, 1968—. Mem. Am., No. Cal. occupational therapy assns., Alliance Franceis (pres. 1969; bd. dirs. 1966-73), Montalvo Assn., Eastfield League Saratoga (co-founder 1965), Delta Gamma (pres. 1955), Delta Gamma (pres. house corp. 1957). Home: 19743 Glen Brae Dr Saratoga CA 95070

SHEPHERD, MARGARET ANN, occupational therapist; b. Danville, Va., Mar. 25, 1929; d. Henry Clayton and Alice (Ewell) Johnson; A.A., Old Dominion U., 1949; B.S. (Am. Occupational Therapy Assn. fellow), Richmond Profl. Inst., Va. Commonwealth U., 1953; m. Leonard Ray Shepherd, Nov. 20, 1954; children—Susan Rae, Steven Joseph, David Edward, Thomas Giles. Occupational therapist Vanderbilt U., 1953-54, Med. Coll. Va., Richmond, 1954, 68—, Tidewater Cerebral Palsy Center, Norfolk, Va., 1955. Cons., Tidewater Multiple Sclerosis Soc., 1956. Pres., Bristol (Tenn.) Jaycettes, 1963; adult leader Commonwealth council Girl Scouts Am., 1965-71. Mem. Am., Va. occupational therapy assns., Sigma Epsilon Phi. Methodist. Club: Garden Cedar Valley (Bristol). Home: 2627 Thurloe Dr Richmond VA 23235 Office: Med Coll VA 1200 Broad St Richmond VA 23298

SHEPHERD, VIVIAN DAVIS (MRS. JAMES RENICK SHEPHERD), orgn. exec.; b. Weir, Kan., Dec. 30, 1904; d. Fred Carl and Gertrude (Hallam) Davis; B.S., Central Mo. U., 1929; M.A., U. Mo., 1954; postgrad. Mo. U., 1944, Washington U., 1945; m. James Renick Shepherd, Oct. 27, 1923; 1 dau., Mrs. Emma Ladd S. Johnson. Elementary tchr. Mo. schs., 1922, 23, 26; pub. relations, office mgr. Postal Telegraph Co., Kansas City, Mo., 1929-34; counselor Mo. Div. Vocational Rehab., Kansas City, Mo., 1942-47; exec. dir. Rehab. Inst., Kansas City, Mo., 1947—. Cons. Rehab. Survey and Project for Disabled, Kansas City, Mo., 1958, Comprehensive Survey of Needs and Services in Kansas City (Mo.), 1970-71, others. Mem. Mayor's Com., Kansas City, Mo., 1971—, Met. Council for Devel. Disabilities, Kansas City, Mo., 1972—, Gov.'s Com. on Employment of Handicapped, Kansas City, Mo., 1960-74; chief of staff United Way Campaign, Kansas City, Mo., 1958-72. Recipient Citation for Service to Handicapped, Assn. Rehab. Facilities, 1958, Distinguished Alumni award Alumni Assn. U. Mo., 1959, Meritorious Service award Nat. Rehab. Assn., 1973, Commendation for Service to Others, Pres. Nixon, 1973, others. Mem. Nat. Rehab. Assn. (bd. mem. 1956-62, pres. 1957-58), Assn. Rehab. Facilities (bd. mem., v.p. 1960-63), Inst. on Workshop Standards (chmn. 1959-65), Women's C. of C. (bd. dirs. 1955-57). Methodist. Club: Soroptimist (bd. mem., v.p. Kansas City,

Mo. 1964-67). Home: 311 Brush Creek Blvd Kansas City MO 64112 Office: Rehab Inst 3011 Baltimore Av Kansas City MO 64108

SHEPHERD-LOOK, DEE LORIS (MRS. LAUNIS ALLEN LOOK), psychologist, educator; b. Peoria, Ill., Dec. 24, 1943; d. Dee Edgar and Dolores Elaine (Hollister) Shepherd; B.A. cum laude, Immaculate Heart Coll., 1965; Ph.D. (USPHS fellow), U. Cal. at Los Angeles, 1972; m. Launis Allen Look, Sept. 4, 1971; 1 son, Launis Allen. Cons. to Parent Co-op., nursery schs. in the Los Angeles area, 1968—; asso. prof. psychology Cal. State U. at Northridge, 1970—; psychologist Psychol. Service Assos., Westwood, Cal., 1971-73; supr. trainees Los Angeles Free Clinics, 1973—. Guest lectr. ednl. and parent groups in Los Angeles area, 1970—. Bd. advisers Los Angeles Valley Coll. Research fellow Yale, 1968. Mem. Am., Western psychol. assns., Soc. for Psychol. Study of Social Issues, Western Assn. Women Psychologists (applied program dir. 1974). Democrat. Roman Catholic. Contbr. research articles on child devel., psychotherapy and learning in the retarded to profl. jours. Home: 614 East Acacia Av Glendale CA 91205 Office: 18111 Nordoff Blvd Northridge CA 91234

SHEPPARD, ELEANOR COYLE PARKER (MRS. THOMAS E. SHEPPARD), state ofcl.; b. Pelham, Ga., July 24, 1907; d. John William and Irwin (Baggs) Parker; student Limestone Coll., 1924-27; m. Thomas E. Sheppard, Feb. 23, 1928; children—Edith Logan (Mrs. Matthew Nelson Ott, Jr.), Sara Irwin (Mrs. Robert Earl Dunnington). Mem. Va. Ho. of Dels., 1968—, chmn. edn. com., 1974—. Dir. Nat. Lab. for Higher Edn., 1972—. Mem. Richmond Regional Planning and Econ. Devel. Commn., 1960-62, Richmond City Planning Commn., 1964-66; mem. Nat. Com. Uniform Traffic Laws and Ordinances, 1963—; mem. adv. com. Surgeon Gen. on air pollution, 1963-66; mem. Gov.'s Commn. Status Women, 1965-66; mem. def. adv. com. Women in Services, 1968-71; Va. commr. Edn. Commn. States, 1974—; mem. Va. Adv. Legislative Council grants-in-aid to localities, 1966-67, Commn. to Study Establishment State U. Richmond Met. Area, 1966-67. Pres., Ginter Park P.T.A., 1949-51, Richmond Fedn., 1951-53; chmn. adv. com. practical nurse edn., 1966-68; mem. adv. bd. Inst. Bus. and Community Devel. U. Richmond, 1965—; mem. adv. council Project Head Start and Early Childhood Edn., 1966-68, chmn., 1966-67; mem. Council Mental Health Services, 1964-68; mem., v.p. Richmond area Community Council. Mem. Richmond Library Bd., 1960-62; mem. Richmond City Council, 1954-67, vice mayor 1960-62, mayor, 1962-64. Bd. dirs. YWCA, U.S.O., Commonwealth council Girl Scouts U.S., Sr. Center, Richmond Internat. Council, Maymont Found., Central Va. Ednl. TV. Recipient Richmond First Club Good Govt. award, 1964, Gold Feather award Richmond Jr. C. of C., 1968. Mem. Soroptimist (pres. 1969-70, 73-74), Bus. and Profl. Woman's Club (Woman of Achievement award 1968), Kappa Delta Epsilon (hon.) Alpha Delta Kappa (hon.). Democrat. Baptist. Clubs: Ginter Park Woman's, 2300, Colony (Richmond). Home: 1601 Princeton Rd Richmond VA 23227 Office: 808 8th St Office Bldg Richmond VA 23219

SHEPPARD, JOCELYN FORTIER, educator; b. Woonsocket, R.I., Nov. 9, 1941; d. Conrad U. and Marie-Jeanne (Dube) Fortier; A.B., Coll. New Rochelle, 1962; M.A. summa cum laude, Universite Laval, Que., Can., 1963; postgrad. Providence Coll., 1963-65, U. Cal. at Berkeley, 1967-69, U. Cal. at Los Angeles, 1968, U. Cal. at San Diego, 1970-71. Faculty modern fgn. lang. dept. R.I. Coll., 1963-66; faculty evening div. modern fgn. lang. dept. San Jose City Coll., 1966-67; head French program Buchser High Sch., 1966-68; prof., head French dept. Southwestern Coll., Chula Vista, Cal., 1969—. Vol. pediatrics Bellevue Hosp., N.Y.C., 1960, U. Cal. at Los Angeles Med. Center, 1968, U. Hosp., San Diego, 1973. Recipient award in French, Laval U., 1962. Mem. Am. Assn. U. Profs., Modern Lang. Assn., Faculty Assn. Cal. Community Colls., San Diego Opera Assn.

SHEPPARD, POSY (MRS. JOHN WADE SHEPPARD), vol. social worker; b. New Haven, Aug. 23, 1916; d. John Day and Rose Marie (Herrick) Jackson; student pub., pvt. schs.; student Vassar Coll., 1938; m. John W. Sheppard, May 16, 1936; children—(Mrs. Allan Gray Rodgers), Gail (Mrs. J. Truman Bidwell, Jr.), Lynn (Mrs. William M. Manger), John W. Vol. field cons. for Conn. A.R.C., 1955-61, nat. bd. govs., 1960-66, vice chmn. bd. govs., 1962-66; rep. League Red Cross Socs. to UN, 1957—; rep. Am. Nat. Red Cross to com. internat. social welfare Nat. Social Welfare Assembly, 1957-62; chmn. NGO Com. UNICEF, 1962-64, 71-73; social welfare com. White House Conf. Internat. Coop. Year.; chmn. exec. com. NGO/OPI Conf., UN, 1963-65; pres. conf. ECOSOC, 1966-69. Mem. Nat. Soc. Colonial Dames, Jr. League Greenwich (vice chmn.), Nat. Inst. Social Scis., Am. Soc. Polit. and Social Sci., Internat. Platform Assn., Soc. Internat. Devel. Home: 535 Lake Av Greenwich CT 06830

SHEPS, ELAINE RUDNICK, lawyer; b. N.Y.C., Sept. 3, 1924; d. Leon J. and Sylvia (Levine) Rudnick; A.B., Bklyn. Coll., 1945; M.A., Columbia U., 1947; J.D., N.Y. Law Sch., 1967; children—Caren, Cynthia. Music instr. Bard Coll., Annandale, N.Y., 1944, Columbia U., 1946; admitted to N.Y. bar, 1968; mem. firm Rudnick & Sheps, N.Y.C., 1968—. Cons. Citizens Com. for Children, 1973. Bd. dirs. Symphony of New World, 1971-72, Adoptive Parents Com., 1969—. Mem. Internat., Am. (chmn. coms. on adoption and pub. information 1972-73), N.Y. (chmn. com. on juvenile justice 1971-72) bar assns., N.Y. Women's Bar Assn., Internat. Assn. Women Lawyers, Brit. Soc. Forensic Scis., Nat. Assn. Women Lawyers. Editorial bd. Behavior, Law and Remedies, 1973—. Office: 160 Broadway New York City NY 10038

SHER, JOANNA HOLLENBERG (MRS. NORMAN SHER), neuropathologist; b. Winnipeg, Man., Can., May 23, 1933 (came to U.S. 1949, naturalized 1958); d. Joseph and Dorothy Moya (Osovsky) Hollenberg; A.B., U. Chgo., 1952; M.D., 1956; m. Norman Sher, Dec. 28, 1955; children—Jonathan, Katherine Amy. Intern, Kings County Hosp. Center, Bklyn., 1956-57; resident and fellow in pathology, Kings County Hosp. Center and State U.N.Y. Downstate Med. Center, 1957-58, 60-62; spl. fellow, neuropathology 1962-64, asst. pathologist, 1965-70, neuropathologist, 1970—; asso. prof. pathology, State U.N.Y. Downstate Med. Center, Bklyn., 1970—. Cons. in pathology and neuropathology, Mountainside Hosp., N.J., 1965—, Maimonides Hosp., 1973—, Brookdale Hosp., 1974—. Mem. Am. Assn. Neuropathologists, Phi Beta Kappa, Alpha Omega Alpha. Contbr. articles in field to profl. jours. Home: 2347 E 63rd St Brooklyn NY 11234 Office: Kings County Hospital Center Brooklyn NY 11203

SHERBELL, RHODA, sculptor; b. Bklyn.; d. Alexander and Syd (Steinberg) Sherbell; student Art Students League, 1950-53, Bklyn. Mus. Art Sch., 1959-61; also pvt. study art; m. Mervin Honig, Apr. 28, 1956; 1 dau., Susan. Exhibited one-man shows Country Art Gallery, Locust Valley, N.Y., Bklyn. Mus. Art Sch., Adelphia Coll., A.C.A. Galleries, N.Y.C., 1967, Capricorn Galleries, Rehn gallery, Washington, 1968, Gallery Modern Art, N.Y.C., 1969; one-man retrospective at N.Y. Cultural Center, 1970; two-man shows at Bklyn. Mus., Country Art Gallery, Rehn Gallery; exhibited group shows Downtown Gallery, N.Y.C., Maynard Walker Gallery, N.Y.C., F. A. R. Gallery, N.Y.C., Provincetown Art Assn., Detroit Inst. Art, Pa. Acad. Fine Arts, Bklyn. and L.I. Artists Show, Old Westbury Gardens Small Sculpture Show, Audubon Artists, N.A.D., Allied Artists, Heckscher Mus., Nat. Mus. Sport, others; represented permanent collections at Colby Coll. Mus., Oklahoma City Mus., Smithsonian Inst., Baseball Hall of Fame, Nassau Community Coll., also pvt. collections; TV Shows ABC, 1968; important works include Walking Ballerina, Adolescent Girl, The Sunday Hat, Standing Woman, Seated Ballerina; portraits Casey Stengel, Yogi Berra, Marguerite and William Zorach. Recipient Am. Acad. Arts, Letters and Nat. Inst. Arts and Letters grant, 1960; Louis Comfort Tiffany Found. grant, 1962; Alfred G. B. Steel Meml. award Pa. Acad. Fine Arts, 1963-64; Ford Found. purchase award. Mem. N.Y. Soc. Woman Artists, Allied Artists Soc. Home: 64 Jane Ct Westbury NY 11590

SHERER, PAMELA DARLENE, coll. adminstr.; b. Kenosha, Wis., July 7, 1949; d. Earl Leroy and Esther Annette (Jefferson) Sherer; B.A., Carthage Coll., 1971; mem. World Campus Afloat Semester Abroad of Chapman Coll., 1968, 71; M.S., So. Ill. U., 1973. Resident counselor World Campus Afloat of Chapman Coll., 1971; with internat. student services So. Ill. U., 1971-72, head resident and counselor, 1972-73; asst. dean students Quincy (Ill.) Coll., 1973—. Mem. Ill. Council Youth, 1966-72, adult advisor, 1972—; mem. Ill. com. White House Conf. Children and Youth, 1970; Ill. del. White House Conf. Children, 1970. Mem. Nat. Assn. Student Personnel Adminstrs., Nat. Assn. Women Deans and Counselors. Home: 2005 Elm St Quincy IL 62301

SHERIDAN, HARRIET SUSAN WALTZER (MRS. E. P. SHERIDAN), educator; b. N.Y.C., July 21, 1925; d. Ben and Mildred (Wolff) Waltzer; A.B. (Helen Gray Cone fellow 1945-46), Hunter Coll., 1944; M.A. (Trustee fellow 1944-45, Marjorie Hope Nicholson fellow 1945-46), Smith Coll., 1945; Ph.D. (U. fellow 1946-47), Yale, 1950; m. E. P. Sheridan, June 30, 1950; children—Alison, Ruth. Instr. English, Hunter Coll., 1947-49; from asst. prof. to asso. prof. English and edn. Carleton Coll., Northfield, Minn., 1953-67, prof., 1967—, chmn. faculty, 1971-73, chmn. dept. English, 1973—, Andrew W. Mellon prof. humanities, 1974—. Field reader curriculum improvement program U.S. Office Edn., 1963—; tchr. NDEA Inst. in English, summer 1965, dir., summer 1966; coordinator McKnight Edn. Found. English Awards; mem. Gov.'s Adv. Council on Minn. Right to Read Program, 1972—. Recipient Louis W. and Maud Hill Family Found. research grant to improve methods of instrn. in secondary sch. teaching of English, 1962—. Mem. Nat. Council Tchrs. English (Minn. chmn. achievement awards program 1962-65), Minn. Council Tchrs. English (mem. liaison com. to State Bd. Edn. 1969—), Assn. Minn. English Dept. Chairmen (chmn. 1973—), Internat. Reading Assn., Orton Soc., Modern Lang. Assn., Am. Assn. U. Profs., Phi Beta Kappa (pres. Carleton chpt. 1968-69). Author: Structure and Style: An Analytical Approach to Prose Writing, 1966. Editor Minn. English Jour. Home: 501 E 2d St Northfield MN 55057

SHERIDAN, JANET BRYANT SAWYER (MRS. JOSEPH L. SHERIDAN), assn. exec.; b. Wakefield, Mass., Aug. 23, 1924; d. John Bryant and Elinor (Clark) Sawyer; A.A., Green Mountain Coll., 1943; occupational therapist Tufts U. Boston Sch. Occupational Therapy, 1945; m. Joseph L. Sheridan, June 4, 1949; children—Anne, Kathryn. Staff occupational therapist Goldwater Meml. Hosp., N.Y.C., 1945-46; designer Rahnee Design Group, Woburn, Mass., 1946-47; mem. occupational therapy staff St. Elizabeth's Hosp., Washington, 1947-50; costume designer N.E. Opera Theater, 1946-47; dir. information services Am. Occupational Therapy Assn., Rockville, Md., 1972—. Cons. period costumes U.S. Park Service, 1971-73; directory spl. services Textile Mus., Washington, 1958-70. Mem. League Women Voters (mem. bd. D.C. 1935-58). Unitarian (mem. bd. 1964-67). Democrat. Home: 3740 Oliver St NW Washington DC 20015 Office: 6000 Executive Blvd Rockville MD 20852

SHERIDAN, MARGARET GERTRUDE (MRS. LAURENCE W. SHERIDAN), soprano, educator; b. Buffalo, Oct. 3, 1908; d. Frederick Henry and Margaret Anna (Frischholz) Hanne; B.A., U. Buffalo, 1929, M.A., 1932; postgrad. Juilliard Opera Sch., 1939-40; B.S. in Singing, Juilliard Inst. Mus. Art, 1941, postgrad., 1941-42; B.S. in L.S., Coll. St. Catherine, 1956; m. Laurence W. Sheridan, June 30, 1937; 1 dau., Christine Margaret. Tchr. English, Buffalo pub. high schs., 1929-38; pvt. tchr. singing, 1940—; tchr. singing Prep. Center, Juilliard Inst., 1942; asst. to pres., tchr. oral communications Am. U., 1943-44; sometime vocal instr. Chevy Chase Jr. Coll., U. Minn., St. Catherine Coll., U. Buffalo; tchr. English, Penn Hall, 1955-56; librarian J. Frank Faust Jr. High Sch., Chambersburg, Pa., 1956-60; instr. English and L.S., Pa. State U., 1960-63, asst. prof., 1963-73, asso. prof., 1973-74, chmn. curriculum com. for Asso. Degree English at all Commonwealth campuses, 1970-74; soprano soloist Merriam Park Presbyn. Ch., St. Paul, 1947-55, Central Presbyn. Ch., Chambersburg, Pa., 1956-60; soprano profl. quartet Trinity United Ch. of Christ, 1960—; founder, mem. profl. vocal quartet of women, 1971—; co-sponsor, dir. Music-Makers series concerts, 1972—; appeared on TV series Girl Talk, ABC, 1965, several appearances WTAJ, 1972—; concert soloist appeared in Yonkers, N.Y.C., Buffalo, St. Paul, Mpls., Washington elsewhere; pioneered music therapy Walter Reed Hosp., 1943-45. Exhibited sculpture Washington County Mus., Hagerstown, Md., Ivyside Gallery, Altoona, Pa. Pres., Logandale Park Assn., 1965; historian Blair County Arts Found., 1965—. Bd. dirs. Blair County Symphony Orch., 1966—, program commentator, 1971—. Recipient 3d prize poetry Central Pa. Writers Contest, 1973. Grantee Inst. for Arts and Humanistic Studies, Pa. State U. Mem. Nat. Assn. Tchrs. Singing (past lt. gov. for So. Pa. and W. Md.), A.L.A., Pa. Library Assn., Central Pa. Writers Guild (charter, editor-in-chief The Rambler 1972, pres. 1974), Am. Assn. U. Women (v.p. Franklin County 1957-59, v.p. Blair County 1969-71, pres. 1971-73), Blair County Educators Assn. (sec. treas. 1967—), Chambersburg Edn. Assn. (pres. 1958-60, 1st v.p. 1960-61), N.E.A. (life), Pa. Council Tchrs. English, Pa. State Edn. Assn. (life), Mu Phi Epsilon. Mem. United Ch. of Christ (deaconess 1970-72). Author: Blair County Culture, 1967; also news column Ink Blobs from A Singing Pen; articles. Editor: Altoona Campus Faculty Gazette, 1964-65, 69-70, The Rambler, 1972. Profl. music critic, reviewer The Altoona Mirror, 1963—. Pub. speaker, lecture-recitalist. Home: RD 4 Box 843 Altoona PA 16601

SHERIDAN, MARION CAMPBELL, educator, editor; b. New Haven; d. Richard Moylan and Fannie (Campbell) Sheridan; B.S., Columbia U.; M.A., Yale, 1928, Ph.D., 1934. Head English dept. Hillhouse High Sch., 1930-61; dir. New Haven summer session able secondary students, 1961-62; co-author Sr. English Activities, Book 3, and workbook, Am. Book Co., 1939; sr. editor Macmillan English Series, Grades 9-12, co-author Grade 10, 1955-67; chmn. com. on step writing tests and essay tests, coop. test div. Ednl. Testing Service, 1956; examiner Coll. Entrance Exam. Bd., 1937-46; mem. Conn. service council steering com. WNHC-TV, Channel 8, 1964-71, WTNH, Channel 8, 1971—. Mem. citizens adv. com. edn. New Haven; mem. citizens com. court reorgn., Conn., 1957; exec. bd. Conn. Council Edn., 1956-58. Non-voting del. Conf. Internat. Fedn. U. Women, Paris, 1956, Helsinki, 1959, alternate voting del., Australia, 1965, mem. fellowships panel experts, 1966—; chmn. Sch. and Coll. Conf. English, 1944-46, archivist, 1962—. Recipient gold key Columbia Scholastic Press Assn., 1949; citation outstanding contbns. teaching English secondary sch., Nat. Council Tchrs. English, 1958; Yale U. Distinguished Tchr. award, 1962; award Ednl. Press Am., 1972. Mem. Internat. Fedn. U. Women, English-Speaking Union, New Haven Colony Hist. Soc. (life), Nat. Council Tchrs. English (chmn. com. cooperate with Teaching Film Custodians 1949-65; pres. nat. council 1949, mem. commn. English curriculum 1945-61, chmn. Conn. 1962-63 achievement awards program, dir. grant from Teaching Film Custodians 1963-65), Columbia Scholastic Press Advisers Assn. (life mem.), New Eng. Assn. Tchrs. English (life mem.; pres. 1935, 52), Am. Assn. U. Women (pres. Conn. div. 1954-58, 1st v.p. 1953, chmn. nat. nominating com. 1958-59, mem. 1956-57, 64-65; state historian 1958-62, state chmn. fellowships programs 1962-66, nat. com. study nominating procedures 1963-65, pres. New Haven br. 1963-65, state chmn. pub. information 1966-70). Author: (with others) The Motion Picture and the Teaching of English, 1965. Editor: (text edition) The Human Comedy (Saroyan). Contbr. profl. jours. Home: Lake Shore 1057 Whitney Av Hamden CT 06517

SHERIDAN, SISTER MARY FLORIANNE, nursing sch. adminstr.; b. Hymera, Ind., Dec. 27, 1908; d. William Sherman and Della May (Bledsoe) Sheridan; R.N., St. Anthony Hosp. Sch. Nursing, Terre Haute, Ind., 1938; certificate in primary edn. Ind. State Tchrs. Coll., 1928, B.S., 1941; postgrad. DePaul U., 1948-49, M.S., 1954; postgrad St. Louis U., summers 1953, 54. Elementary tchr. Terre Haute, Ind., 1929-35; nursing arts instr. St. Anthony Hosp. Sch. Nursing, Terre Haute, 1939-42; clin. instr. med., surg. nursing St. Francis Sch. Nursing, Evanston, Ill., 1942-44; joined Order of St. Francis, 1944; dir. nursing, dir. Sch. Nursing, St. Margaret Hosp., Hammond, Ind., 1946-58; dir. Sch. Nursing, St. Elizabeth Hosp., Lafayette, Ind., 1958—. Mem. adv. bd. Am. Security Council. Bd. dirs. Vis. Nursing Service Lafayette; trustee St. Francis Coll., Fort Wayne, Ind., 1957—. Mem. Am., Ind. nurses assns., Nat., Ind. (v.p. 1957-60) leagues nursing, Ind. Conf. Cath. Schs. Nursing (pres.), Nat. Council Cath. Nurses, Cath. Audio-Visual Edn. Assn., Ind. Cath. Nurses, Cath. Audio-Visual Edn. Assn., Med. Library Assn., Ind. Cath. Hosp. Assn. (pres. 1965-66), Smithsonian Assos. Home: St Francis Convent Mount Alverno Mishawaka IN 46544 Office: 1508 Tippecanoe St Lafayette IN 47904

SHERIDAN, SONIA LANDY (MRS. JAMES EDWARD SHERIDAN), artist; b. Newark, O., Apr. 10, 1925; d. Avrom Mendel and Goldie (Hanon) Landy; A.B., Hunter Coll., 1945; student Columbia, 1946-48; M.F.A., Cal. Coll. Arts and Crafts, 1961; m. James Edward Sheridan, Sept. 27, 1947; 1 son, Jamy. Instr. Cal. Coll. Arts and Crafts, 1960-61; asso. prof. Sch. Art Inst. of Chgo., 1961—; artist-in-residence, con. 3M Color Center, St. Paul, 1970; one-man show Rosenberg Gallery, Chgo., 1967; exhibited in group shows at Boston Mus. Fine Arts, Pa., Conn. acads. fine arts, N.Y. Soc. Am. Graphic Artists, Software Show at Jewish Mus., Smithsonian Inst., Washington, travelling Midwest Invitational, Walker Art Center, 1973-74, Friends of Photography show, Carmel, Cal., 1973—, others; internat. photog. exhbn. Hampstead Artists Council Ltd., London, 1972-73; established Generative Systems dept. Art Inst. Chgo., 1970. Guggenheim fellow, 1973-74; Nat. Endowment for Arts Workshop fellow, 1974—. Mem. Am. Assn. U. Profs. Editor, pub.: 80 Prints '70. Home: 718 Noyes St Evanston IL 60201 Office: Art Inst Chgo Michigan at Adams Chicago IL 60603

SHERIF, CAROLYN WOOD, educator; b. Loogootee, Ind., June 26, 1922; d. Lawrence Anselm and Bonny (Williams) Wood; B.S., Purdue U., 1943; M.A., State U. Ia., 1944; Ph.D. in Psychology, U. Tex., 1961; m. Muzafer Sherif, Dec. 29, 1945; children—Sue, Joan, Ann. Grad. asst. psychology U. Ia., 1943-44; asst. to research dir. Audience Research, Inc., Princeton, N.J., 1944-45; asst. Princeton, 1945-47; research, free-lance writer, Norman, Okla., 1949-58; research asso. Inst. Group Relations U. Okla., Norman, 1959-65, asso. prof. sociology, 1963-65; cons. asst. prof. U. Okla. Med. Sch., 1963-65; vis. lectr. Pa. State U., 1962, asso. prof. psychology, 1965-66, asso. prof., 1966-69, prof., 1970—; vis. prof. psychology and sociology Cornell U., 1969-70. Fellow Am. Psychol. Assn.; mem. Am. Sociol. Assn., Am. Assn. U. Women, A.A.A.S., Sigma Xi, Mortar Bd., Theta Alpha Phi, Alpha Lambda Delta, Pi Beta Phi. Author: (with M. Sherif) Groups in Harmony and Tension, 1953, An Outline of Social Psychology, 1956, Problems of Youth: Transition to Adulthood in a Changing World, 1965, Attitude, Ego-Involvement and Change, 1967, Interdisciplinary Relationships in the Social Sciences, 1969, Social Psychology, 1969; (with M. Sherif, O.J. Harvey, B.J. White, W.R. Hood) Intergroup Conflict and Cooperation, 1961; (with M. Sherif and R. Nebergall) Attitude and Attitude Change, 1965; Instructor's Manual for Social Psychology, 1969; Orientation in Social Psychology, 1975. Contbr. numerous articles to profl. jours. Home: 507 Shannon Lane State College PA 16801 Office: 515 Moore St Pa State U University Park PA 16802

SHERIN, CAROLYN RICHARDS, clin. psychologist; b. Effingham, Ill., Oct. 8, 1937; d. Virgil Long and Mearle (Young) Richards; B.A., U. Fla., 1959; M.S., U. Miami, 1961, Ph.D. (Nat. Def. Edn. Act. fellow), 1966. Clin. psychologist Duke U. Med. Center, Durham, N.C., 1963-64; clin. psychologist Jackson Meml. Hosp., Miami, Fla., 1965—, also asst. dir. forensic service, 1973—. Instr. psychiatry U. Miami Sch. Medicine, 1966-72, clin. asst. prof. psychiatry, 1972—. Mem. Am., Fla., Dade County psychol. assns., Am. Assn. Correctional Psychologists, Mayan Studies Inst., Miami Mineral. and Lapidary Guild, Phi Beta Kappa, Phi Kappa Phi, Alpha Omicron Pi. Office: The Institute Jackson Memorial Hospital 1700 NW 10 Av Miami FL 33136

SHERMAN, AUDREY ESTELLE CUTLER (MRS. ROBERT CLARKE SHERMAN), purchasing exec.; b. Avon, Ill., Sept. 11, 1923; d. Lloyd Merle and Ruth (Alexander) Cutler; student Brown's Bus. Coll., 1942; m. Robert Clarke Sherman, May 21, 1971; children—Marcus Edgar Howerter, James Joseph Howerter. With Briggs div. Celotex Corp., Abingdon, Ill., 1942—, pvt. sec. to plant mgr., 1942-65, purchasing agt., 1965—. Gray lady A.R.C., 1944-45; co-chmn. United Fund, Orange Twp., Ill., 1966-67; mem. Abingdon High Sch. Citizens Adv. Com. Vocational Edn., 1973-74. Recipient highest achievement award Dale Carnegie Course, 1969. Mem. Nat. Secs. Assn. (pres. and toastmistress Galesburg chpt. 1957-58), Parents Without Partners (edn. chmn. Galesburg chpt. 1969-70), Nat., Tri-City assns. purchasing mgmt. Conglist. (Sunday Sch. supt. 1966-67). Home: 501 N Pennsylvania Av Abingdon IL 61410 Office: 801 N Main St Abingdon IL 61410

SHERMAN, CLAUDIA GAIL, orgn. exec.; b. Omaha, Apr. 14, 1947; d. Irvin Joseph and Martha (Zusman) Harris; B.J., U. Mo., 1969; m. Marc Richard Sherman, Feb. 28, 1971. Community relations asst. United Community Services, Omaha, 1969-73, community relations asso., 1973-74; membership registrar Jewish Community Center of Omaha, 1974—. Mem. Neb. Assn. Bus. Communicators (sec. exec. com. 1972), Pub. Relations Soc. Am., Women in Communications, Sigma Delta Tau (1st v.p. 1967-68), Omaha Press Club, Nat. Honor Soc. Home: 12118 Shirley St Omaha NE 68144 Office: 333 S 132d St Omaha NE 68102

SHERMAN, EDNA SCHULTZ (MRS. ROY V. SHERMAN), civic worker; b. Muscatine, Ia., July 27, 1907; d. George John and Helen (Pope) Schultz; student U. Ia., 1927, U. Ky., 1928-29; B.A. with distinction, U. Akron, 1962; postgrad. Stanford, 1970, U. Cal., 1971;

m. Roy V. Sherman, Sept. 6, 1927; children—John Roger, Julia (Mrs. Stanley G. Payne), Patricia (Mrs. Walter L. Popper). Library asst., Muscatine, Ia., 1925-27, Akron, O., 1930-31; supr. employment counseling War Manpower Commn., Akron, 1942-46; partner Sherman Realtors, Akron, 1951-67. Vocational counselor Akron Area Heart Assn., 1960-67; mem. Com. on Complete Revision Akron City Charter, 1965-67; mem. women's com. U. Akron, 1948—; active Girl Scouts U.S.A. Mem. Am. Assn. U. Women, Am. Assn. Ret. Persons (publicity chmn. Palo Alto chpt. 1973), Cal. Writers, Akron League Women Voters (pres. 1942-43), Akron and Summit County Fedn. Women's Clubs, U. Akron Faculty Wives (pres. 1949-50), Phi Sigma Alpha, Pi Sigma Alpha. Contbr. articles to various mags., jours. Home: 840 Warren Way Palo Alto CA 94303

SHERMAN, INGRID KUGELMANN, educator, poet; b. Cologne, Germany, June 25, 1919; d. Abraham and Gertrude (Schloss) Kugelmann; D. Naturopathy, D. Osteopathy, Ango-Am. Inst. Drugless Therapy, Eng., 1961; D. Naturopathy (hon.), Coll. Natural Therapeutics, Ceylon, 1969; D.Poetry Therapy, Internat. U. India, 1970; D.D., Universal Life Ch., 1970; D.Liberal Arts, Gt. China Arts Coll., 1970; D.Litt., World Acad. Langs. and Lit., Brazil, 1973; Ph.D., Acad. Philosophy, Brazil, 1973; D.Psychology, World U., Brazil, 1974; D.World Lit., U. Lincoln, Brazil, 1974; m. Morris Sherman, May 22, 1943; 1 son, Robert Arnold. Founder, tchr., counselor Peace of Mind Studio, Yonkers, N.Y., 1960—; tchr. high schs. Yonkers Bd. Edn., 1963—; lectr. Cumberland Hosp., Bklyn., 1962, Lambert Castle, Paterson, N.J., 1964, Hotel Astor, N.Y.C., 1966, hotels in Catskill Mountains, N.Y., World U., Washington, 1970, Brandeis U., 1970; writer Voice of Truth, Cin., 1962-67, Pet Mag., Chgo., 1965—, Health and Longevity, Ceylon, 1969—, Sr. Citizen, 1969; made TV appearance, 1965, radio appearances, 1967-73. First woman poetry therapist in State N.Y.; communications cons. World-Wide Assn. for Anomalous Sci. Phenomena, 1973. Founder, Westchester Philco-Cultural Soc., Yonkers, N.Y. Recipient prizes for poetry; named Lady of Grace and Devotion, Royal Order of Piast (Poland), 1970; golden laurel wreath United Poets Laureate Internat., Philippines, 1967. Mem. Acad. Internat. Leon da Vinci (Italy; corr. mem., hon. rep.), Armed Forces Writers League (poetry cons.), Soc. Psychology Internat. (poetry editor jour.), Acad. Am. Poets (co-founder), Poetry Soc. London (life), Internat Clover Poetry Soc. (life), A.S.C.A.P., Assn. Social Psychology Washington (dist. dir.), Am. Poetry League, World Poetry Soc. (India), Poetry Soc. Australia, Am. Bell Assn., Internat. Platform Assn., Internat. Soc. Naturopathic physicians, United Poets Laureate Internat. Philippines, Westchester Philo-Cultural Soc., Brit. Guild Drugless Practitioners; Nat. Fedn. Health, Robert Louis Stevenson Soc. N.Y., Natural Food Assn., ESP Research Assn., Vols. Am. Assn., Internat. Songwriters Club, Internat. Naturopathic Assn. Author numerous poems including poetry booklets Thoughts For You, 1960; For Your Reading Pleasure, 1965; Face to Face With Nature, 1965, Ripples of Wisdom, 1966; Poems That Speak on Love, 1966; Gems From Above, 1966; Radiations Self-Help, 1967; Philosophical Tidbits, 1967; Prayer Poems that Heal, 1967; Strange Patterns, 1967; As I Recall It, 1970; (book) National Remedies for Better Health, 1970; others. Contbr. poems to newspapers, mags., anthologies, paperbacks, 1971—. Recorded music and lyrics of own compositions. Home: 102 Courter Av Yonkers NY 10705

SHERMAN, JEANNETTE ULLMAN (MRS. SAMUEL A. SHERMAN), bus. exec., club woman; b. West Haven, Conn., Feb. 22, 1910; d. Maurice A. and Yetta (Kraft) Ullman; student Emerson Coll., 1928-20, Syracuse U., 1929-30; m. Samuel A. Sherman, Oct. 20, 1929; children—Arnold Kraft, Jonathon Fredric, Richard Bruce. Co-owner Carroll Drug Co., Rutland, Vt., 1935—; dir. Sherman Shopping Services. Mem. Adv. Com. on Vt. Community Affairs. Pres. Green Mountain Theatre Assos., 1958-60; mem. citizens Adv. Council Aging. Trustee Vt. Epilepsy Assn., 1972—, mem. com. on information and edn., 1973—; bd. dirs. Vt. Natural Resources Council. Mem. Vt. Fedn. Womens Clubs (1st v.p. 1970-72, pres. 1972-74, dir. publicity 1974—). Rutland League Women Voters, Rutland Hosp. Aux. Clubs: Rutland Womans, Castleton Woman's (pres. 1970-72). Home: 3 Hill Pond Rd Rutland VT 05701 Office: 21-29 Center St Rutland VT 05701

SHERMAN, JOAN BETTI, lawyer; b. N.Y.C., Aug. 11, 1939; d. Nathan and Anne Dorothy (Kushner) Sherman; B.A. with honors, Washington Square Coll., N.Y. U., 1961; J.D., Rutgers U., 1964. Admitted to N.J. bar, 1964; research asst., then trial atty. Lamb, Hutchinson, Thompson & Chappell, Jersey City, 1964-68; trial atty. firm John W. Taylor, East Orange, N.J., 1968—. Instr. skills and methods courses, trial clinics, 1965—. Mem. Am., N.J. bar assns. Home: 33D Rustic Ridge Little Falls NJ 07424 Office: 240 S Harrison St East Orange NJ 07019

SHERMAN, JUDY WERBA, lawyer; b. Los Angeles, Oct. 30, 1942; d. Jack and Eva Leah (Klapp) Werba; B.A., U. Cal. at Berkeley, 1964; postgrad. Loyola U., Los Angeles, 1964-66; J.D., U. West Los Angeles, 1968; m. M. Ronald Sherman, July 11, 1965. Admitted to Cal. bar, 1969; staff atty. San Fernando Valley Neighborhood Legal Services, 1969-70; vol. atty. Freda Mohr Center, 1970-72; part time research atty. Joseph Shalant, Los Angeles, 1971-72; part time staff atty. Jaffe & Orliss, Los Angeles, 1973. Mem. Am., Los Angeles County, Beverly Hills bar assns. Home: 1136 Tellem Dr Pacific Palisades CA 90272

SHERMAN, JUNE MARIE ROACH, vol. service coordinator; b. White Pigeon, Mich.; d. Arthur William and Eva May (Clark) Roach; student Wayne U., 1931, Western Mich. U., 1953-54, 60-63, Mich. U., 1962; children—Nola M. (Mrs. William Benson), V. Clayton. Occupational and recreational therapist Kalamazoo State Hosp., 1947-49, coordinator vol. services, 1949—. Founding mem., sec., Citizens Assn. for Kalamazoo State Hosp., Inc., 1959—, Kalamazoo State Hosp. Guild, 1969; chmn. com. on aging Kalamazoo County Council Chs., 1961-66; chmn. Friendly Visitors Com., 1966-68, active Kalamazoo Civic Players. Bd. dirs. Sr. Services, Inc. Recipient citation Citizen's Assn. Kalamazoo State Hosp., 1970. Fellow Am. Assn. Vol. Service Coordinators; mem. Nat. Assn. Recreational Therapists (charter), World Fedn. Mental Health, Bus. and Profl. Womens Club (chmn. civic participation com. 1967-68), Zonta Internat. (chmn. service com. Kalamazoo), Internat. Platform Assn., Mich. Soc. Mental Health, Mich. Health and Welfare League, Assn. for Retarded Children, Assn. for Emotionally Disturbed Children, Council Human Relations, Mich. Mental Health Soc. (chpt. pres. 1968-70). Home: 2019 Douglas Av Kalamazoo MI 49007

SHERMAN, MARY LOUISE WRIGHT (MRS. JAMES A. SHERMAN), univ. ofcl.; b. Bellefonte, Pa., July 20, 1940; d. Calvert Charles and Luretta (Bagby) Wright; B.A., Scripps Coll., 1962; B.A., U. Wash., 1963-64; m. James A. Sherman, Mar. 24, 1962; children—Jill Anne, Cristopher James. Bus. mgr. Jour. Applied Behavior Analysis, Dept. Human Devel., U. Kan., Lawrence, 1968—. Dir. Lawrence Planned Parenthood Clinic, 1966-68. Mem. Centennial Sch. P.T.A. Bd., Lawrence, 1971-74. Treas., bd. dirs. Lawrence Reclamation Center, 1973-74. Mem. Soc. for Exptl. Analysis of Behavior (hon.). Club: Daffodil (treas. Lawrence 1973). Home: 1734 Illinois St Lawrence KS 66044 Office: Dept of Human Devel Univ Kansas Lawrence KS 66044

SHERMAN, NANCY MARGARET (MRS. JEROME G. SHERMAN), judge; b. Chgo., Nov. 13, 1925; d. David and Esther Buttrick (Brimblecom) Bush; Ph.B., U. Chgo., 1945, J.D., 1948; m. Jerome G. Sherman, June 11, 1948. Admitted to Ill. bar, 1949; appellate atty. Nat. Labor Relations Bd., Washington, 1950-58, legal asst., 1958-59, appellate atty., 1959-64, supervisory appellate atty., 1964-72, adminstrv. law judge, 1972—. Mem. Fed. Bar Assn., Fed. Adminstrv. Law Judges Conf., Womens Bar Assn. Ill. Home: 2427 Chain Bridge Rd NW Washington DC 20016 Office: Nat Labor Relations Bd 1717 Pennsylvania Av NW Washington DC 20570

SHERMAN, RUTH GOLDSMITH (MRS. MARTIN SHERMAN), psychologist; b. N.Y.C., Sept. 3, 1921; d. William Benjamin and Estelle (Lipset) Goldsmith; B.A., Douglass Coll. Rutgers U., 1942; M.A., U. Hawaii, 1964; m. Martin Sherman, Sept. 25, 1943; children—Laurel Deborah, Susan Leslie (Mrs. Seizen Jeffrey Bonk). Statistician, Squibb's Pharms., N.J., 1943-45; research asst. psychology dept. U. Hawaii, 1960-64; counseling psychologist Counseling and Testing Center, 1964—; counseling psychologist Center for Psychol. Services, Tng. and Research, Honolulu, 1968—, also v.p. Instr. race relations and leadership U.S. Army; cons. Hawaiian Telephone, Honolulu Police Dept., Pan Am., Savs. and Loan Inst., others. Mem. pub. relations com. Mental Health Assn. Hawaii. U. Hawaii grantee, 1969; McInerny Found. grantee, 1972. Mem. Am., Hawaii (sec. 1971-72, rep. at large, 1972-73) psychol. assns. Contbr. articles to profl. lit. Home: 1121 Koloa Honolulu HI 96816 Office: 2327 Dole Honolulu HI 96822

SHERMAN, SARA JO, writer, broadcaster; b. Monterey, Tenn.; d. Everett B. and Lula (Sehon) Berry; student Tenn. Coll. for Women, Ward-Belmont Sch. 1 son, Johnny B. Formerly dir. theatrical prodns., Wayne P. Sewell Producing Co., Atlanta; civil service USAF; columnist Evening Chronicle, North Attleboro, Mass.; broadcaster radio sta. WRIB, Providence; women's dir., broadcaster WARA, Attleboro, Mass.; radio reporter, broadcaster Monitor NBC, N.Y.C., Voice of Am., Armed Forces Radio (Broadcasting) Europe; broadcaster WSM radio and television, Nashville; women's editor, fashion and social editor Nashville Mag.; spl. events reporter, writer-editor, NBC-TV News Syndicate; feature fashion writer Sunday Gleaner, also Evening Star, Jamaica; fashion columnist Holiday Inn Mag.; broadcaster RJR, Jamaica; dir. pub. relations Holiday Hills Resort, Crossville, Tenn. First newswoman from U.S. to visit US-USSR Border at Bad Kissingen, Germany, Recipient Golden Mike award, 1960. Hon. mem. 14th Armored Cavalry Div. U.S. Army, Bad Kissinger. Methodist. Home: Mountain Manor Monterey TN 38574

SHERMAN, WINNIE BORNE (MRS. LEE DANIEL SHERMAN), artist, educator; b. N.Y.C., Nov. 10, 1902; d. Max and Lena (Fischman) Bornstein; student Columbia Tchrs. Coll., 1920-22; B.F.A., Cooper Union Inst., 1924; student Art Students League 1922-29, N.A.D., 1920-21; m. Lee Daniel Sherman, Oct. 4, 1925 (dec. Apr. 1970); children—Marjorie Ann (Mrs. Henry Cahn), Robert Lee, Paul Jay, Frances Lucille (Mrs. Kenneth Goodenday). Tchr. fine arts, high schs., N.Y.C., 1925; art dir. Beaupre Sch. Music and Art, Lenox, Mass., summers 1946-48; fine arts tchr., extension div. Coll. City N.Y., 1960-65; watercolor tchr. Inst. for Ret. Profls., New Sch., N.Y.C., 1966—; exhibited one-man shows New Rochelle Pub. Library, Burr Gallery, New Sch., Westchester County Center, Archtl. League N.Y.; exhibited group shows Vendome Gallery, Grand Central Art Galleries, Newton Gallery, Ligoa Duncan Gallery, Burr Gallery, N.A.D., others; represented in permanent collections at Seton Hall U. Library, IBM, Thomas Watson Coll., Grumbacher Artists Palette Collection, pvt. collections, Recipient Am. Artist Mag. Watercolor award, 1953; Graphic award, Westchester Arts and Crafts Guild, 1954; others. Fellow Royal Soc. Arts and Letters (London) (life); mem. Art Students League (life), Internat. Platform Soc., Nat. Soc. Arts and Letters (corr. sec. 1964-66, pres. Empire State chpt. 1968-70, nat. art chmn. 1966-68, v.p. 1970-72, membership chmn. 1972—), Nat. League Am. Pen Women (v.p. N.Y. br. 1968-72), Am. Watercolor Soc., Artists Equity, Am. Artists Profl. League (juror of awards 1970), Kappa Pi. Clubs: Catherine Lorillard Wolfe Art (pres. 1968-71), Nat. Arts (past social chmn.). Home: 500 E 77th St Apt 934 New York City NY 10021

SHERR, LYNN BETH, journalist; b. Phila., Mar. 4, 1942; d. Louis and Shirley (Rosenfeld) Sherr; B.A., Wellesley Coll., 1963. Writer, editorial asst. Conde Nast Publs., N.Y.C., 1963-65; news writer, feature writer A.P., N.Y.C., 1965-72; reporter, corr. WCBS-TV News, N.Y.C., 1972-74. Winner Mademoiselle mag. Guest Editor Contest, 1962, four Blue Ribbon awards Ednl. Film Library Assn., 1966-69. Author: (with Jurate Kazickas) The Liberated Woman's Appointment Calendar, 1971-75. Contbr. numerous articles to mags., jours. Home: 140 West End Av New York City NY 10023

SHERRILL, SARAH BARKER, editor; b. Boston, Sept. 1, 1935; d. Gibbs Wynkoop and May (Gould) Sherrill; B.A., Smith Coll., 1957. Sec., Houghton Mifflin Co., Boston, 1957-58; sec., mng. editor Atlantic Monthly Press, Boston, 1958-64; asst. editor G.P. Putman's Sons, N.Y.C., 1964-65; asst. editor Shorewood Press, N.Y.C., 1965-66; asst. editor Pub. Interest, N.Y.C., 1966-67; asst. editor Antiques Mag., N.Y.C., 1967—. Mem. N.Y. Rug Soc. Hajji Baba Club, Phi Beta Kappa. Office: 551 Fifth Av New York City NY 10017

SHERWOOD, DEBBIE, writer; b. Tulsa; d. John Thornton and Ardis Ruth (Nott) Beasley; student N.Y. U, 1965-67, New Sch. for Social Research, 1968—. Former actress, model; appeared in films Can Can, Spartacus, The Hustler; guest appearances on TV shows including The Many Loves of Dobie Gillis, Ozzie and Harriet, Twilight Zone; writer articles appearing in various mags. including TV Guide. Lectr. to convs., woman's clubs, other orgns., throughout U.S. Mem. Screen Actors Guild, Authors Guild, Arthors League Am. Author: A Redhead in Red Square, 1969; How to Become a Model, Step by Step, 1971; Your First Job—How to Get it and How to Keep it, 1971; On Your Own: A Girl's Guide to Independence, 1971; The World of Daytime TV Drama, 1972; The Story of a Happy Witch, 1973; Your Unborn Child, 1973. Address: 14 Christopher St New York City NY 10014

SHERWOOD, SYLVIA R., gerontologist; b. N.Y.C., Jan. 13, 1925; d. Harry and Molly Lutzker; B.A., Hunter Coll., 1946; M.A., N.Y. U., 1950; Ph.D., 1955; m. Clarence C. Sherwood, June 22, 1951; children—Laurie Rohde, Steven Rohde. Research asst., div. research, dept. sociology Grad. Sch. Arts and Sci., N.Y. U., 1950-55, conductor statistics lab., 1950; research asso. with Dr. Max Wolff, community cons., N.Y.C., 1955; research cons. N.Y. State Commn. Against Discrimination, 1956; research asso. instr. Hofstra Coll., Hempstead, N.Y., 1958-60, research asso., bur. bus. and community research, 1959-60; research cons. L.I. Bus. Research Assos., Hempstead, 1960-63; instr. Tufts U., Medford, Mass., 1958-65, dir. Nat. Inst. Mental Health sub-contract from Vt. Youth Study, Goddard Coll., 1965; dir. social gerontological research Hebrew Rehab. Center for Aged, Roslindale, Mass., 1965—. Mem. faculty Bklyn. Coll., 1951-56, Adelphi Coll., Garden City, N.Y., 1956-58, C. W. Post Coll., Greenvale, N.Y., 1960-63; cons. Plainview (N.Y.) High Sch. System, 1958. Mem. adult com. for South Hempstead Youth Activites, 1957-62; mem. adult crime and juvenile delinquency task force for mental health planning for Mass., Med. Found., Inc.; participant 7th Internat. Congress Gerontology Vienna, Austria, 1966. Recipient Post-Doctoral Founders Day award N.Y. U., 1956. Mem. Gerontol. Soc. (ad hoc social welfare sect.), Alpha Kappa Delta. Contbg. author: Ethnic Relations in the United States (M. C. Donagh, E. S. Richards), 1953; The Unusual Child, 1962. Asso. editor The Geronotologist, Geriatric Opinion. Contbr. papers to profl. jours. Home: 483 Boylston St Brookline MA 02146 Office: 1200 Centre St Boston (Roslindale) MA 02131

SHEWEY, LANA LEE, physician, educator; b. Groveland, Fla., Mar. 9, 1941; d. James Edwin and Eva Lee (Morgan) Shewey; student Emory U., 1959-60; B.A., Winthrop Coll., 1962; M.D., Med. Coll. Ga., 1966. Intern, Tulane U. Med Sch., Charity Hosp., New Orleans, 1966-67, resident in medicine, 1967-70, cardiology fellow, 1970-72, instr. medicine, 1966-72, asst. prof. medicine, 1972—, staff teaching physician, supervisory physician Charity Hosp., 1970—, dir. phys. diagnosis course Tulane U., 1972—; med. staff cons. Lallie Kemp Charity Hosp. Staff cardiologist Handicapped Crippled Children's Program, New Orleans, Alexandria, La. Recipient Physician's Recognition award A.M.A., 1969, 72. Guggenheim fellow, 1972. Diplomate Am. Bd. Internal Medicine. Mem. A.C.P., Am. Soc. Internal Medicine, La. Heart Assn. (cardiopulmonary resuscitation com.), Musser-Burch Med. Soc., Alpha Omega Alpha. Home: 1218 Soniat St New Orleans LA 70115

SHEWEY, NANCY MAE, coll. adminstr.; b. Buena Vista, Va., Nov. 19, 1925; d. John Fortner and Ola Beatrice (Higginbotham) Shewey; B.S., Madison Coll., 1946. Sec. to pres. So. Sem. Jr. Coll., Buena Vista, 1946-65, dir. admissions, 1965—. Mem. Va. Assn. Collegiate Registrars and Admissions Officers, Madison Coll. Alumni Assn., Pi Omega Pi, Alpha Sigma Tau, Beta Sigma Phi. Methodist. Club: Junior Woman's (pres. Buena Vista, 1954-56). Home: 1966 Walnut Av Buena Vista VA 24416

SHIDELER, SHIRLEY ANN WILLIAMS, lawyer; b. Mishawaka, Ind., July 9, 1930; d. William Harmon and Lois Wilma (Koch) Williams; LL.B., Ind. U., 1964 1 dau., Gail (Mrs. David Souders). Legal sec. Barnes, Hickam, Pantzer & Boyd, Indpls., 1953-63; admitted to Ind. bar, 1964; practiced in Indpls., 1964—; asso. firm Barnes, Hickam, Pantzer, & Boyd, 1963-70, partner, 1971—. Active fund drives Indpls. Symphony, 1968—, Indpls. Mus. Art, 1969—. Bd. dirs. bus. unit gals Indpls. Mus. Art. Mem. Am., Ind., Indpls. (bd. mgrs. 1968-70, 72, v.p. charge affairs 1972) bar assns., Estate Planning Council. Club: Woman's Rotary (pres. 1969-71, dir. 1968—) (Indpls.). Home: 5150 Hawthorne Dr Indianapolis IN 46226 Office: 1313 Merchants Bank Bldg Indianapolis IN 46204

SHIELDS, CAROLE ANN, advt. agy. exec.; b. Bronx, N.Y., May 7, 1935; d. Andrew James and Dorothy Patricia (Schrader) Shields; B.A., State U. N.Y., 1953-57. Research dir. L.I. Bus. Review, Syosset, N.Y., 1964-70, Creative Contacts, Syosset, N.Y., 1970-71; media dir. Garber & Philipson, Inc., Carle Place, N.Y., 1971—. Mem. League of Mercy Hosp., L.I., N.Y. Democrat. Roman Catholic. Club: Long Island Advertising. Home: 36 Low Lane Levittown NY 11758 Office: 1 Old Country Rd Carle Place NY 11514

SHIELDS, ELEANORE LORETTA MCHALE (MRS. JOHN DANIEL SHIELDS), librarian; b. Phila., Mar. 8, 1917; d. James and Margaret (Madgey) McHale; B.A., Immaculata Coll., 1938; postgrad. Bloomsburg State Coll., 1944, Pa. State U., 1945; M.L.S., Marywood Coll., 1973; m. John Daniel Shields, Nov. 25, 1943; children—James (dec.), Eleanore Anne, Mary Jacqueline, John. Tchr. Our Lady Lourdes Regional High Sch., jointure Mt. Carmel and Shamokin, Pa., 1958-65; tchr. English, social sci. Mt. Carmel Area Sch. Dist., 1938-48, 66-71, librarian, 1971—. Mem. Mt. Carmel Woman's Club, 1948—, pres., 1952-53; mem. Harrisburg Diocesan Council Cath. Women, 1957—, pres., 1962-64; grand regent Cath. Daus. Am., Mt. Carmel, 1959-62, Pa. dist. dep., 1964-66, 72—; nat. pres. Nat. Council Cath. Women, 1966-68; co-pres. 3d World Congress, Apostolate of Laity, Rome, Italy, 1967. Recipient citation Am. Cancer Soc., 1964. Mem. Am. Assn. U. Women, N.E.A., Pa. Edn. Assn., Villa Maria Alumnae, Immaculata Coll. Alumnae. Home: 5 Front St Strong PA 17851

SHIELDS, LESLIE CHEVANNES, ednl. adminstr.; b. Jamaica, N.Y., May 17, 1950; d. Waddell Pierce and Sylvia Lorraine (Chevannes) Shields; B.A., Howard U., 1972, M.Ed., 1973. Tchr. Action Program Howard U., Washington, 1971-72, grad. asst. dept. student housing, 1972-73, adminstrv. counselor Upward Bound Program, 1973, asst. dir., 1973—. Mem. D.C. Consolidation of Ednl. Services, sec., 1973. Bd. Trustees scholar, 1970. Mem. Am. Personnel and Guidance Assn., Am. Assn. for Higher Edn., Nat. Assn. Student Personnel Adminstrs., Nat. Assn. Women Deans, Counselors and Adminstrs., Assn. Non White Concerns in Personnel and Guidance, Am. Coll. Personnel Assn. Home: 201 I St SW Washington DC 20024

SHIELDS, LORA MANGUM, educator; b. Choctaw, Okla., Mar. 13, 1912; d. William Lee and Ethel (Talbott) Shields; B.S., U. N.M., 1940, M.S. in Biology, 1942; Ph.D. in Botany, U. Ia., 1947; m. Clarence L. Mangum, Oct. 19, 1931; 1 son, William K. Pub. sch. tchr., N.M., 1931-43; grad. asst. dept. botany, U. Ia., 1943-47; with dept. biology N.M. Highlands U., Las Vegas, 1947—, successively instr., asst. prof., asso. prof., 1947-51, prof. biology, 1951—, chmn. biology dept., 1951-71, dir. allied health program and environmental health div., 1971—. Dir. N.M. div. Am. Cancer Soc., 1950—, mem. exec. com., 1955-58. Recipient research grants NSF, AEC, NIH, Sigma Xi (total more than, 50,000); Scientist of Year award N.M., 1965. Mem. A.A.A.S. (div. pres. 1959-60), N.M. Acad. Sci. (pres.), Ecol. Soc. Am. (v.p. 1962), Phi Kappa Phi, Sigma Sigma Sigma. Contbr. numerous articles to profl. jours. Office: Dept Biology NM Highlands U Las Vegas NM 87701

SHIH, VIVIAN EAN (MRS. PAUL C.K. LU), pediatrician; b. Nanking, China, Dec. 27, 1934; (came to U.S., 1958); d. Fu-Chang and Shang-lan (Chang) Shih; M.D., Nat. Taiwan U., 1958; m. Paul C.K. Lu, Sept. 11, 1965; children—David T.K., Mark C.K. Intern Edgewater Hosp., Chgo., 1959; pediatric resident Phila. Gen. Hosp., 1960-62; fellow in neurology Children's Hosp. Phila., 1962-65; clin. and research fellow in neurology Harvard Med. Sch., Mass. Gen. Hosp., 1965-67; in charge Amino Acid Disorder Lab., Joseph P. Kennedy Jr. Meml. Labs. and Inborn Errors of Metabolism Clinic, Mass. Gen. Hosp., Boston, 1967—, asst. in neurology, 1968—; instr. Harvard Med. Sch., 1967-70, asst. prof. neurology, 1970—, asso. Center for Human Genetics, 1971—; cons. Mass. metabolic disorder program Mass. Dept. Pub. Health, 1967—. Recipient acad. award in sci. Fedn. Overseas Chinese Assns., 1970. Mem. Soc. Pediatric Research, A.A.A.S., Am. Assn. Fgn. Med. Grads., Mass. Med. Soc. Address: Mass General Hospital Fruit St Boston MA 02114

SHIMER, DOROTHY BLAIR (MRS. WILLIAM A. SHIMER), educator; b. Hackensack, N.J., Apr. 24, 1911; d. Myers and Sarah (Jackson) Blair; A.B., Skidmore Coll., 1932, A.M., Middlebury Coll., 1945; postgrad. Columbia, 1942-43, Syracuse U., 1946, U. Hawaii, 1954, Oxford (Eng.) U., 1961; m. William A. Shimer, June 21, 1947. Asst. exec. sec. United Chpts. Phi Beta Kappa, N.Y.C., 1932-44, asst. editor Key Reporter, 1937-40, editor, 1940-44, circulation and prodn.

mgr. Am. Scholar, N.Y.C., 1941-44; dir. pub. relations Colby Jr. Coll., New London, N.H., 1944-45; dir pub. relations Marietta (O.) Coll., 1945-47, dean women, 1946-47; travel throughout Europe, 1949-50; co-dir. Hawaii chpt. also Asia-Pacific div. World Brotherhood, Honolulu, 1951-60, editor Brotherhood, 1955-60; research and organizational work, 13 Asian countries, 1956-58; faculty Maunaolu Coll., Paia, Maui, Hawaii, 1960-68, asso. prof. lit., 1963-68; lectr. world lit. U. Hawaii, 1969-70; instr. world and oriental lit., 1970-72, asst. prof., 1972—. Mem. Hawaii Commn. on Status Women, 1970—. Trustee Skidmore Coll., 1943-46, asso. trustee, 1946—. Mem. Am. Assn. U. Women (pres. Hawaii div. 1966-70, v.p. from S. Pacific region 1971—), Modern Lang. Assn. Am. Nat. Council Tchrs. English, Asia Soc. Contbr. articles to ednl., gen. and ch. publs. Mem. United Ch. of Christ (v.p. Hawaii conf. 1968-70, pres. 1970-71). Editor: Mentor Book of Modern Asian Literature, 1969; Voices of Modern Asia: An Anthology of 20th Century Asian Literature, 1973; Bhabani Bhattacharya, 1974. Address: 45-090L Namoku St Kaneohe HI 96744

SHIMM, CYNIA BROWN (MRS. MELVIN GERALD SHIMM), psychiatrist; b. N.Y.C., June 29, 1926; d. Harry and Rosslyn (Koffler) Brown; A.B., Cornell U., 1945; M.D., Yale, 1950; m. Melvin Gerald Shimm, Aug. 15, 1948; children—David Stuart, Jonathan Evan. Intern pathology Montefiore Hosp., N.Y.C., 1950-51; intern 1st Columbia med. div. Bellevue Hosp., N.Y.C., 1951-52; resident pathology Duke Med. Center, Durham, N.C., 1957, resident psychiatry, 1965-68; candidate U. N.C.-Duke Psychoanalytic Inst., Meml. Hosp., Chapel Hill, N.C., 1967—, asst. instr., 1971—; asst. clin. prof. psychiatry Duke Med. Center, 1974, lectr. Law Sch., 1974—; practice medicine, specializing in psychiatry, Durham, 1968—; courtesy staff Watts Hosp. Diplomate Am. Bd. Psychiatry and Neurology. Mem. Am. Psychiat. Assn., N.C. Neuropsychiat. Assn., Am. Psychoanalytic Assn. (asso.), Durham-Orange County Med. Soc., Phi Beta Kappa. Home: 2429 Wrightwood Av Durham NC 27705 Office: 923 Broad St Durham NC 27705

SHIMMON, CAROLYN LOUISE TANDLER (MRS. MALEK SHIMMON), hotel exec.; b. Chgo., Jan. 12, 1932; d. Richard Nelson and Ida (Winslow) Tandler; student Md. Coll., Russell Sage Coll., 1953; Katherine Gibbs Sch., N.Y.C., 1954; m. Malek Shimmon, Mar. 16, 1958; 1 dau., Marion Elizabeth. Sec., mortage analyst Bowery Savs. Bank, N.Y.C., 1953-54; exec. sec. Bankers Trust Co., N.Y.C., 1955-56, Fed. Res. Bank, San Francisco, 1957-58; mgr., treas. Smugglers' Notch Inn, Inc., Jeffersonville, Vt., 1959—. Pres., Women's Vt. Fire Fighters Assn., 1960; mem. Lamoille County Devel. Assn.; chmn. Red Cross drive, Eastern Lamoille County, 1964. Mem. exec. com. Republican Women, 1960-61; mem. Vt. Women's div. Republicans. Mem. vol. staff Mary Fletcher Hosp., Burlington, Vt. Mem. Smugglers' Notch Assn. (pres. 1961), Madonna Area Assn. (treas.-sec. 1964-65), Jeffersonville Women's Fellowship. Clubs: Crescendo (v.p. Jeffersonville 1963-64); Federation of Women's (del. for Vt. 1964). Address: Smugglers' Notch Inn Jeffersonville VT 05464*

SHINDEL, DOROTHY LOUISE (MRS. ALFRED CHARLES LABOCCETTA), pediatrician; b. York, Pa., May 18, 1916; d. William Henry and Mamie (Hake) Shindel; B.S., Ursinus Coll., 1935; M.D., Temple U., 1939; M. Pub. Health, U. Pa., 1944; m. Alfred Charles LaBoccetta, May 22, 1947; children—Carol Anne, Susan. Intern, Harrisburg (Pa.) Hosp., 1939-40; resident pediatrics St. Christophers Hosp. for Children, Phila., 1940-41, Pa. Hosp., Phila., 1941-42; resident Phila. Hosp. for Contagious Diseases, 1942-45; practice pediatrics, Phila., 1945—; mem. staff Hosp. Med. Coll. Pa., Phila., also asst. prof. pediatrics Hosp. of Med. Coll. Pa.; clin. affiliate dept. medicine Children's Hosp. Phila. Trustee Harcum Jr. Coll. Home: 3421 W School House Lane Philadelphia PA 19144 Office: 5501 Greene St Philadelphia PA 19144

SHINDLER, ANNE WOSKOFF, educator; b. Smithland, Ia., July 29, 1919; d. John and Rose (Eirinberg) Woskoff; student U. Ia., 1936-38; B.B.A., U. Minn., 1940; M.S., Ariz. State U., 1959; postgrad. Stanford, U. So. Cal., Phoenix Coll., IBM Edn. Center; m. George Shindler, July 30, 1942; children—Joan Rae, Susan Jean. Sec. to adminstrv. asst. Cohen Wholesale Grocer, Sioux City, Ia., 1941-42; sec. to dist. price dir. OPA, Sioux City, 1942-43, sec. to dist. rent dir., 1943-45, sec. to information dept., 1945-46; co-owner George's Market, Akron, 1946-53; part-time office mgr. credit dept., bookkeeper Miracle Mdse. Mart, Phoenix, 1953-58; grad. asst. instr. Ariz. State U., 1959-59; instr. bus. dept. Phoenix Coll., 1959—. Mem. Hillel Adv. Council Ariz. State U. Mem. N.E.A., Ariz. Edn. Assn., Nat., Ariz., Western bus. edn. assns., Am. Vocational Assn., Delta Pi Epsilon, Kappa Delta Nu, Sigma Delta Tau. Home: 5208 N 17th St Phoenix AZ 85016 Office: 1202 W Thomas Rd Phoenix AZ 85013

SHINE, CAROLYN RICHARD, museum ofcl.; b. Cin., Sept. 26, 1918; d. Bartholomew Jennings and Florence Louise (Farbach) Shine; B.A. cum laude, Bryn Mawr Coll., 1939; various courses U. Cin. and Art Acad. Cin., 1939-43. Employed in various positions, 1943-53; exec. sec. Contemporary Arts Center, Cin., 1953-58; registrar Cin. Art Museum, 1958—, asst. gen. curator, 1973—. Mem. McDowell Soc. Clubs: Cincinnati Woman's Art, College. Home: 250 Greendale St Cincinnati OH 45220 Office: Cincinnati Art Museum Cincinnati OH 45202

SHINE, FRANCES LOUISE, author, educator; b. Worcester, Mass., Jan. 8, 1927; d. Henry Joseph and Margaret Louise (Finegan) Shine; B.A., Radcliffe Coll., 1948; M.A., Cornell U., 1952. Tchr. sch., Montreal, Que., Can., 1953-54, Gloucester, Mass., 1954-56, tchr. pub. schs., Framingham, Mass., 1956—, tchr. Juniper Hill Sch., 1959—. Sec., trustees office Boston Pub. Library, 1948-50; sec. to interdepartmental com. on lit. Cornell U., 1951-52. Recipient prize in short story category Nat. Fine Arts award competitions, 1952. Author: The Life-Adjustment of Harry Blake, 1968; Johnny Noon, 1973. Contbr. fiction and poetry to publs., including Grecourt Rev., N.Y. Times, Cath. World, The Writer. Home: 17 Clark St Framingham MA 01701

SHINE, MARY TONISSEN (MRS. JAMES M. SHINE), advt. agy. exec.; b. Jacksonville, Fla., Apr. 16, 1926; d. Otto John and Anna Ruth (Simms) Tonissen; student Salem Coll. for Women, 1944-45; grad. Greenleaf Bus. Sch., 1946; m. James Munnerlyn Shine, Mar. 12, 1955; children—James Munnerlyn, Wallace Tonissen. Sec., Morris Plan Bank, Jacksonville, Fla., 1945-46, Riverside Bank of Jacksonville, 1947, Northwestern Bank of Henderson County (N.C.), 1947-48, Fla. Nat. Bank Jacksonville, 1948-50; office mgr., sales service Harry E. Cummings Radio/TV Rep., Jacksonville, 1950-62; with radio sta. WJAX, Jacksonville, 1963-64; media dir. William Cook Advt., Inc., Jacksonville, 1966—. Pres. parents group Morning Star Sch. for Exceptional Children, 1973-74. Mem. Jacksonville Advt. Fedn. (dir., treas. 1974-75). Democrat. Episcopalian. Home: Box 223-C Switzerland Route Green Cove Springs FL 32043 Office: 1700 Am Heritage Bldg Jacksonville FL 32202

SHINEY, MARGARET LOUISE, physician; b. Hays, Kan., Nov. 27, 1926; d. Edward W. and Harriet Pearl (Dague) Shiney; A.B cum laude, Bryn Mawr Coll., 1948; M.D., U. Kan., 1954. Intern, St. Francis Hosp., Wichita, Kan., 1954-55; gen. practice medicine, Wichita, 1955-59; splty. tng. Dayton (O.) VA Hosp., U. Pa. Grad. Sch. Medicine, Phila., Denver Gen. Hosp., 1960-62; staff physician dept. internal medicine Meml. Hosp., Topeka, 1962-68, chief dept. medicine, 1968—, mem. exec. com. staff, 1968—. Mem. A.M.A., Am. Med. Women's Assn., Kan., Shawnee County med. socs., Bryn Mawr Coll. Alumnae Assn. Home: 1617 W 26th St Topeka KS 66611 Office: 417 E 6th St Topeka KS 66607

SHIPP, KATHRYN GROVE, ret. research chemist; b. Annandale, Pa., Apr. 4, 1904; d. Leon Vance and Frances (Conner) Grove; B.A. magna cum laude, Mills. Coll., Oakland, Cal., 1925, LL.D., 1967; Ph.D., Yale, 1930; D.Sci., Hood Coll. 1967; D.Sc., D'Youville Coll., Buffalo, 1967; m. Joseph Harrel Shipp, June 18, 1932 (div. Mar. 1957); children—Frances Elizabeth (Mrs. John T. Urban), Sarah Jane (Mrs. Thomas Bollinger Cox), Howard Grove, Richard Sterling. Asst. instr. Vassar Coll., Poughkeepsie, N.Y., 1925-27, Yale, 1927-29; NRC fellow Oxford U., Eng., 1930-31; research chemist U.S. Naval Ordnance Lab., Silver Spring, Md., 1957-70. Mem. Am. Chem. Soc., Phi Beta Kappa, Sigma Xi. Contbr. articles to profl. jours. Home: 17 Janet Way Tiburon CA 94920

SHIPP, MAURINE SARAH HARSTON (MRS. LEVI ARNOLD SHIPP), realtor; b. Holiday, Mo., Mar. 6, 1913; d. Paul Edward and Sarah Isabel (Mitchell) Harston; grad. Ill. Bus. Coll., 1945; student real estate Springfield Jr. Coll., 1962; student law LaSalle Extension U., 1959-62; m. Levi Arnold Shipp, Jan. 30, 1941; children—Jerome Reynolds, Patricia (Mrs. Rodney W. England). With Ill. Dept. Agr., Springfield, 1941-65, supr. livestock industry Brucellosis sect.; saleswoman Morgan-Hamilton Real Estate Co., Springfield, 1962-64; owner, mgr. Shipp Real Estate Agy., Springfield, 1965—. Prin. appraiser urban renewal Dept. Housing and Urban Devel., 1971-72. Bd. dirs. Springfield Travelers Aid, 1971—. Mem. Springfield Bd. Realtors, Nat., Ill. assns. real estate bds., N.A.A.C.P., Urban League, Iota Phi Lambda. Episcopalian. Mem. Order Eastern Star. Club: Bridge. Home: 31 Bellerive Rd Springfield IL 62704 Office: 1115 E Ash St Springfield IL 62703

SHIPPEY, ORRLINE ELLIS (MRS. WOODROW W. SHIPPEY), librarian; b. Italy, Tex.; d. Forest Pierce and Mary Ella (Orr) Ellis; B.A., Trinity U., 1936; B.L.S., Tex. Women's U., 1938; postgrad. George Peabody Coll., summer 1941; m. Woodrow W. Shippey, Oct. 21, 1945. Librarian pub. schs., Jefferson, Tex., 1936-39, White Oak Pub. Schs., Longview, Tex., 1939-58; cataloger Enging. Library, Tex. A. and M. Coll., College Station, summer 1942; dir. Nicholson Meml. Pub. Library, Longview, Tex., 1958—. Mem. Am. Assn. U. Women, A.L.A., Tex. Library Assn. (chmn sch. div. 1944-45, chmn. children's div. 1950-51, chmn. dist. IV 1967-68), Methodist. Author articles profl. jours. Home: PO Box 1311 Longview TX 75601 Office: 400 S Green St Longview TX 75601

SHIRE, SISTER MARY LOUISE, educator, psychologist; b. N.Y.C.; d. John and Elizabeth Shire; B.S., St. John's Coll., Toledo; M.A., U. Notre Dame; Ph.D. (scholar 1942-45), Fordham U.; postgrad. Cath. U. Am. Former tchr., prin., supr. in elementary schs., English tchr. in secondary schs.; coll. prof., 1933—, head edn. dept. and psychology dept., dir. tchr. tng., prof. spl. edn. Active child guidance services Toledo Catholic Charities, 1956-66, Mary Mense Reading Center, 1950—; lectr. drug use and abuse in family life edn. Toledo Pub. Schs., 1970-73. Mem. Am. Psychol. Assn., Assn. for Children with Learning Disabilities, Internat. Reading Assn., Internat. Council for Exceptional Children. Home: 2413 Collingwood Toledo OH 43620 Office: 2413 Collingwood St Toledo OH 43620

SHIRK, EVELYN URBAN, educator; b. Flushing, N.Y., Sept. 12, 1918; d. Urban Amos and Mary Jane (Welchans) Shirk; B.A. cum laude, Wilson Coll., 1940; M.A., Columbia, 1942, Ph.D., 1949; m. Justus Buchler, Feb. 20, 1943; 1 dau., Katherine Urban. Instr. philosophy Bklyn. Coll., 1942-48; mem. faculty Hofstra Coll., Hempstead, N.Y., 1949—, asso. prof., 1953-63, prof., 1963—. Mem. Am. Philos. Assn., Am. Assn. U. Profs., Am. Assn. U. Women, Ethical Culture Soc. L.I., Phi Beta Kappa. Author: Readings in Philosophy, 1946; Adventurous Idealism: The Philosophy of Alfred Lloyd, 1952; The Ethical Dimension, 1965; In Pursuit of Awareness, 1967. Home: 3 Homestead Av Garden City NY 11530 Office: Dept Philosophy Hofstra U Hempstead NY 11550

SHIRLEY, BETTY ELAINE, advt. exec.; b. Tampa, Fla.; d. Lyman William and Betty Idell (Bridges) Shirley; B.A., Fla. State U., 1948; M.A., N.Y. U., 1951. Prodn. asst. Broadway plays, N.Y.C., 1952-56; personal sec., prodn. asst. Miss Katharine Cornell, N.Y.C., 1956-62; casting dir. Doyle, Dane, & Bernbach Advt., N.Y.C., 1962-64, Papert, Koening & Lois Advt., N.Y.C., 1964-65, NBC The Doctors, N.Y.C., 1965-66, McCaffrey & McCall Advt., New York City, 1966—. Mem. Zeta Phi Eta, Delta Delta Delta. Home: Walker's Hollow Alpine NJ 07620 Office: 575 Lexington Av New York City NY 10022

SHIRLEY, FRANCES ANN, educator; b. Altoona, Pa., June 11, 1931; d. Stanley Wallace and Frances Wren (Swengle) Shirley; A.B., Bryn Mawr Coll., 1953, M.A., 1954, Ph.D., 1960; postgrad. Johns Hopkins, 1954-56, U. Birmingham (Eng.), 1959. Instr., McCoy Coll., Johns Hopkins U., Balt., 1955-56; instr., Wheaton Coll., Norton, Mass., 1960-63, asst. prof., 1963-67, asst. dean, 1964, asso. prof., 1968-73, prof. English, 1973—, chmn. dept., 1973. Mem. Norton (Mass.) Hist. Commn., 1970-72. Recipient Fellowship, Johns Hopkins U., 1954-55; Spl. European Study Grant, Bryn Mawr Coll., 1959. Mem. Am. Assn. U. Profs. (chpt. pres. 1971), Modern Lang. Assn., Shakespeare Assn., Am., British scs. theatre research, Norton Hist. Soc. (sec. 1969—). Club: Penn (London, Eng.). Author: Shakespeare's Use of Off-Stage Sound, 1963. Editor: Devil's Law-Case (John Webster), 1972. Home: Cedar St Ant Hills Hollidaysburg PA 16648 Office: Wheaton Coll Norton MA 02766

SHIRLEY, JOAN FLORISELLE KNIGHT (MRS. RICHARD CLAYTON SHIRLEY), newspaper owner; b. Gettysburg, S.D., July 13, 1931; d. Claude Elvin and Clara (Graf) Knight; student U. Mont., 1949-50; m. Richard Clayton Shirley, Nov. 3, 1950; children—Steven Douglas, Robert Richard, Katherine Joyce, Keith Allen. Reporter, Daily Ravalli Republican, 1947-50; owner, Hot Springs (Mont.) Sentinel, 1950-60, Tobacco Valley News, Eureka, Mont., 1960—. Tchr. community art classes Hot Springs, Eureka, 1958—. Chmn. Tobacco Valley Improvement Assn. Bd. Arts, 1970—. Trustee Lincoln County Free Library. Recipient Ann. Community Service award Tobacco Valley Improvement Assn., 1972, awards Mont. State Press Assn., 1970, 71, Lincoln County Fair Bd. Our Fair Lady award, 1970. Mem. Tobacco Valley Art Club, Mont. Inst. Arts. Democrat. Baptist. Club: Study (Eureka). Address: PO Box 627 Eureka MT 59917

SHIRLEY, PATRICIA BATTLE (MRS. MAURICE E. SHIRLEY), psychiat. social worker; b. Mobile, Ala. May 29, 1939; d. Charles T. and Lucile (Finley) Battle; student Talladega Coll., 1957-59; A.B., U. Mo. 1962; M.S.W., Atlanta U., 1964; m. Maurice E. Shirley, Aug. 1, 1964; children—Maureen Patrice, Karole Leana. Childrens probation officer Milw. County Childrens Ct. Center, 1964-67; psychiat. social worker Day Hosp. Pilot Project, Milw. County Mental Health Center, 1967-69, psychiat. social work supr., 1969—. Field work instr. U. Wis.-Milw.; mem. Judge's Delinquency Criteria Study Com., 1967; mem. Luth. Social Action Com., 1968; mem. Mayor's Beautification Com., 1967-69; mem. task force on disadvantaged Wis. Assn. Mental Health, 1972. Mem. adv. bd. Cedarcrest Girls Residence, 1969-72, St. Vincent's Group Home, 1972; bd. dirs. Greater Milw. YWCA, 1972-74. Mem. Nat. Assn. Social Workers, Acad. Certified Social Workers. Home: 9239 N Broadmoor Rd Bayside WI 53217 Office: 9191 W Watertown Plank Rd Wauwatosa WI 53226

SHIRLEY, VIRGINIA LEE, media buying exec.; b. Kankakee, Ill., Mar. 24, 1936; d. Glenn Lee and Virginia Helen (Ritter) Shirley. Mgr. media dept. Don Kemper Co. Inc., Chgo., 1951-69; v.p., mgr. SMY, Inc., Chgo., 1969—. Home: 1350 N Lake Shore Dr Chicago IL 60610 Office: 360 N Michigan Av Chicago IL 60601

SHISSLER, BARBARA JOHNSON (MRS. LEWIS H. NOSANOW), gallery dir.; b. Roanoke, Va.; d. Willis Morton and Kathryne Sabin (Bradford) Johnson; A.B., Smith Coll., 1951; postgrad. Sorbonne, Paris, Ecole du Louvre, 1951-52; M.A., Case Western Reserve, 1957; postgrad. U. Minn.; m. John L. Shissler, Jr., July 28, 1951; children—John III, Ada Holly; m. 2d, Lewis H. Nosanow, Oct. 15, 1973. Asst. mng. editor Jour. Aesthetics and Art Criticism, Cleve. Mus. Art, 1957-62; editor Mpls. Inst. Arts, 1963-72; dir. U. Minn. Gallery, 1972—. Author of TV scripts on art. Mem. Nat. Trust, Am. Soc. for Aesthetics, Coll. Arts Assn. Author: Sports and Games in Art, 1966; The Worker in Art, 1970; The New Testament in Art, 1970. Contbr. articles in field to profl. jours. Home: 2801 France Av S Minneapolis MN 55416 Office: 110 Northrop U Minn MN 55455

SHIVER, NELTA ROYAL (MRS. FRED MANNING SHIVER), shoe store exec.; b. Arabi, Ga., Aug. 9, 1925; d. Nixon Monroe and Tulalah (Ritchie) Royal; grad. high sch.; m. Fred Manning Shiver, Dec. 26, 1943 (dec.); children—Ronald Fred, Marsha Lynn. With SR&J Corp., Columbus, Ga., 1947—, chmn. bd., 1968—; owner Sam Neil's Shoes, Columbus, 1947—. Baptist. Club: Beautification Garden (Columbus). Home: 5752 Roaring Branch Rd Columbus GA 31906 Office: 1250 Broad St Columbus GA 31902

SHKLAR, JUDITH NISSE (MRS. GERALD SHKLAR), educator, author; b. Riga, Latvia, Sept. 24, 1928; d. Aaron and Agnes (Berner) Nisse; B.A., McGill U., 1949, M.A., 1950; Ph.D., Radcliffe Coll., 1955; m. Gerald Shklar, June 16, 1948; children—David, Michael, Ruth. Came to U.S., 1950, naturalized, 1955. Instr. Harvard, 1956—, asst. prof., 1959—, lectr. govt., 1963-72, prof., 1972—. Guggenheim fellow, 1960. Author: After Utopia, 1957; Legalism, 1964; Men and Citizens, 1969. Home: 33 Clinton Rd Brookline MA 02146 Office: Widener Library Harvard U Cambridge MA 02138

SHNIDER, DARLENE ANNE, youth and camp dir.; b. Washington, June 4, 1944; d. Sol and Esther Rose (Sherman) Shnider; B.S., U. Md., 1966; M.A., U. Ia., 1972. Supr. teenage activities Jewish Community Center, Balt., 1966-68, supr. health and physical edn., 1968-71, day camp dir., 1966-70; youth dir. and Camp Shalom dir. Jewish Community Center, Nashville, 1972—. Instr. Red Cross First Aid and Water Safety, 1970—; cardiopulmonary instr. Am. Heart Assn., 1971—; mem. nat. health and phys. edn. com. Jewish Welfare Bd., 1969-71; mem. cardiopulmonary resuscitation com. Middle Tenn. Heart Assn., 1972; mem. Mayor's Council for Youth Opportunity, 1972—. Mem. Nat. Recreation and Parks Assn., Am. (pub. relations chmn. Md. sect., 1970-71), Tenn. Valley Sect. camping assns. Jewish religion. Office: 3500 W End Av Nashville TN 37205

SHOCKLEY, ANN ALLEN, librarian; b. Louisville, June 21, 1927; d. Henry and Bessie (Lucas) Allen; B.A., Fisk U., 1948; M.S. in Library Sci., Case Western Res. U., 1959; div.; children—William Leslie, Tamara Ann. Asst. librarian Del. State Coll., Dover, 1959-60; asst. librarian U. Md., Eastern Shore, 1960-66, asso. librarian, 1966-69; spl. collections librarian Fisk U., Nashville, 1969-70, asso. librarian, head spl. collections, 1970—, asso. prof. library sci., dir. Black oral history program, 1970—. Recipient short story award Am. Assn. U. Women, 1962. Mem. Assn. Study Afro-Am. Life and History, Am. Assn. U. Profs., Am., Tenn. library assns., Soc. Am. Archivists, Oral History Assn. Author: (with Sue P. Chandler) Living Black American Authors, 1973; Loving Her, 1974. Mem. editorial bd. Blackomedia. Home: 1809 Morena St Nashville TN 37208

SHODELL, MARGARET JOAN (MRS. BENJAMIN SHODELL), psychologist; b. N.Y.C., Aug. 23, 1919; d. Samuel and Celia (Reiner) Moskowitz; B.A., Hunter Coll., 1939; M.A., Bklyn. Coll., 1953; Ph.D., Yeshiva U., 1966; m. Benjamin Shodell, July 28, 1939; children—Michael, Carole (Mrs. George Frankfurter). Tchr. pub. schs., N.Y.C., 1946-56; pvt. practice as therapist, Great Neck, N.Y., 1956-58; clin. dir. Nassau Center for Emotionally Disturbed Children, Woodbury, N.Y., 1958—. Asso. prof. dept. edn. C.W. Post Coll., Greenvale, N.Y., 1968-70; lectr. Hofstra U., Hempstead, N.Y., 1970-72. Mem. Fire Island (N.Y.) Sch. Bd., 1971—. Fellow Am. Ortopsychiat. Assn.; mem. Am. Psychol. Assn. Home: Box 232 Ocean Beach NY 11770 Office: 72 S Woods Rd Woodbury NY 11797

SHOECRAFT, CORA E., social worker; b. LaPorte, Ind.; d. Ezra C. and Helen (Baldwin) Shoecraft; A.B., U. Mich., 1935, M.A., 1936. Family caseworker Family Service, Allentown, Pa., 1936-38; supr. research project Childrens Center Childrens Fund of Mich., Detroit, 1938-48; supr. child guidance, sr. social worker Wayne County Child Guidance, Detroit, 1948-57; dir. Huron Valley Child Guidance Clinic, Ypsilanti, Mich., 1957-73; coordinator Children's Services Washtenaw County Community Mental Health Center, 1973—. Coordinating cons. Washtenaw County Mental Health Center, 1968—. Fellow Am. Orthopsychiat. Assn.; mem. Nat. Assn. Social Workers, Acad. Certified Social Workers. Home: 2605 Washtenaw St Ann Arbor MI 48104

SHOEMAKE, LORRAINE SMITH (MRS. J.B. SHOEMAKE), city ofcl.; b. Gueydan, La., May 7, 1923; d. Harry and Ophelia (Foreman) (dec.) Smith; student Spencer Bus. Coll., 1951-52, U. Southwestern La., 1964-65; m. J.B. Shoemake, Sept. 22, 1949; children—Cheryl (Mrs. A.B. Raphael, Jr.), Kathy (Mrs. Byron C. Cermillion III). Exec. sec. to mayor City Lafayette, La., 1952-56, Superior Oil Co., Lafayette, 1956-67; owner, operator Oil City Employment Service, Lafayette, 1967-69; exec. sec. Owen Oil Co., Lafayette, 1969-72; city clk. City Lafayette, La., 1972—. Counselor Oil City Employment Service, Lafayette, La., 1967-69, cons., 1967-69, dir., 1967-69. Vol. Lukemia Drive, Lafayette, La., Muscular Dystrophy, Lafayette, Arthritis Drive, Lafayette, 1970-73. Methodist. Home: 1111 W St Mary Blvd Lafayette LA 70501 Office: 733 Jefferson St Lafayette LA 70501

SHOEMAKER, HELEN E. MARTIN ACHOR, educator; b. Houston, Mar. 24, 1915; d. Earl L. and Blanche L. (Williams) Martin; A.B., Anderson (Ind.) Coll., 1960; m. Harold E. Achor, Oct. 11, 1935; children—Diane (Mrs. Robert Johnston), Lana (Mrs. Winston Dean); m. 2d, Robert N. Shoemaker, May 19, 1972. Resident dir. Anderson Coll., 1967-69, dir. alumni services, 1969-72; legislative counsel Ind. Colls. and Univ. Ind., 1970-72; spl. asst. Center Pub. Service, Anderson, 1973—. Sec.-treas. Ind. State Library and Hist. Bldg. Expansion Commn., 1973—. Mem. com. region VII, Girl Scouts U.S.,

1958-66. Mem. Ind. Ho. of Reps. from Madison County, 1968-70; v.p. Ind. Fedn. Women's Republican Clubs, 1945-46; treas. Nat. Fedn. Women's Rep. Clubs, 1947-51; Rep. precinct vice chmn. Madison County, 1946-68, vice chmn., Anderson, 1967-68. Bd. dirs. Urban League Madison County, 1969—, Madison County League Women Voters, 1973—. Hon. mem. Anderson Symphony Orch. Guild; mem. Anderson Council Women, Anderson Fine Arts Center. Mem. Ch. of God. Home: 707 Dresser Dr Anderson IN 46011

SHOEMAKER, LOIS MEIER (MRS. M. B. SHOEMAKER), former educator, author; b. Ipava, Ill., Oct. 20, 1899; d. W. H. D. and Elizabeth (Campbell) Meier; A.B., Wellesley Coll., 1921; M.A., Columbia Tchrs. Coll., 1924, Ph.D., 1930; Wellesley scholar, Am.-German exchange fellow, U. Frankfurt am Main Germany, 1927-28; m. M. B. Shoemaker, Aug. 26, 1931; children—Robert M., William E., Mary E., Alice C. High sch. tchr. Framingham, Mass., 1921-23, White Plains, N.Y., 1924-26; prof. sci. N.J. State Tchrs. Coll., 1929-59. Fellow A.A.A.S.; mem. Nat. Geog. Soc., Nat. Assn. Research in Sci. Teaching, Kappa Delta Pi. Republican. Methodist. Club: Trenton Naturalist. Author: (with W. H. D. Meier) Essentials of Biology, 1943; (with Meister and Keirstead) Wonderworld of Science, 1943. Contbr. to N.J. State Mus. Bulls. on wildlife. Home: 515 Ewingville Rd Trenton NJ 08638

SHONNARD, CHRISTY FOX (MRS. LUDLOW SHONNARD, JR.), journalist; b. Rochester, N.Y.; d. James Franklin and Marjorie (Mossman) Fox; grad. Marlborough Sch. Girls, Los Angeles; B.A., U. So. Cal.; m. Ludlow Shonnard, Jr.; children—Ludlow Shonnard III, Christy Susan. Reporter-corr. Los Angeles Times, soc. editor, columnist 1953—; performer, radio writer Christy Fox show, KNX, CBS, Los Angeles; numerous guest appearances as mistress of ceremonies on TV spls., Los Angeles. Trustee, Webb Sch., Claremont, Cal., 1968—; mem. Jr. Philharmonic, Pasadena Guild Childrens Hosp., Art Alliance of Pasadena Art Mus. Bd. dirs. Trojan League, Mem. Nine O'Clock Players, Women in Communications, Pi Beta Phi. Club: Valley Hunt (Pasadena). Home: 1151 Arden Rd Pasadena CA 91106 Office: Los Angeles Times Los Angeles CA 90053

SHONT, ESTHER MAY, trust co. exec.; b. N.Y.C., Nov. 23, 1916; d. Levon Sarkis and Lillian Katherine (Blume) Shont; B.A., Hunter Coll., 1937; M.B.A., N.Y.U., 1949, postgrad. Sch. Law, 1951-53; postgrad. N.Y. Law Sch., 1950-51; certificate Bank Adminstrn. Inst., Sch. of Banking U. Wis., 1963-65. With Bankers Trust Co., N.Y.C. 1943—, dep. auditor 1965-68, v.p. securities operations, 1969—, group head, computer systems devel. dept., 1971-73, planning and marketing U.S. banking dept., 1973—. Mem. Bank Adminstrn. Inst. (nat. trust commn. 1968-69, nominating com. 1972, chmn. by laws com. N.Y.C. chpt. 1971—, dist. dir. 1972—), Nat. Assn. Banking Women. Home: 135 Willow St Brooklyn NY 11201 Office: 280 Park Av New York City NY 10017

SHONTZ, PATRICIA O'DONNELL (MRS. PETER M. SHONTZ, JR.), economist, educator; b. Milw., Oct. 1, 1933; d. James Joseph and Erma (Graap) O'Donnell; B.S. summa cum laude, U. Detroit, 1955, M.B.A., 1956; Ph.D., Wayne State U., 1963; m. Peter M. Shontz, Jr., Feb. 29, 1964; 1 dau., Deborah Jane. Instr., dept. econs. U. Detroit, 1955-60; grad. asso. Wayne State U., 1960-63; asst. prof. econs. U. Windsor, Can., 1963-66; adj. prof. econs. U. Mich., Dearborn, 1966-67; economist, editorial writer, columnist Detroit News, 1966-73; syndicated columnist Universal Press Syndicate, N.Y., 1970-73; prof. bus. adminstrn., dir. publs. Grad. Sch. Bus. Adminstrn., U. Mich., Ann Arbor, 1973—. Partner, dir. econ. research R.A. Helling & Assos., Detroit, 1965-68; dir. Detroit Edison Co., Mfrs. Nat. Bank Detroit, Jacobson Stores, Inc., Blue Shield Mich., Parke-Davis & Co.; cons. U.S. Treasury. Recipient G.M. Loeb award, nation's best financial column, 1970. Mem. Am., Canadian econ. assns., Am. Statis. Assn., Nat., Detroit (sec. 1966-67) assns. bus. economists, Detroit Bd. Commerce, Detroit Econ. Council (chmn.), Inst. Econ. Edn. (trustee), Sigma Sigma Sigma, Beta Gamma Sigma (chpt. sec. 1955-60). Home: 806 Bishop Rd Grosse Pointe Park MI 48230 Office: Grad School Business Adminstrn Univ of Mich Ann Arbor MI 48104

SHOOK, ANN JONES (MRS. GENE E. SHOOK, SR.), lawyer; b. Canton, O.; d. William M. and Lura (Pontius) Jones; A.B., Wittenberg Coll., 1947; LL.B., William McKinley Law Sch., 1955; m. Gene E. Shook, Sr., Nov. 30, 1956; children—Scott, William, Gene. Cost accountant Hoover Co., North Canton, O., 1947-51; with uniform dependents act sect. Stark County Prosecutor's Office, Canton, 1951-53; office claims adjusters Travelers Ins. Co., Canton, 1953-56; admitted to Ohio bar, 1956; with firm Rhyne & Rhyne (formerly Rhyne, Mullin, Connor & Rhyne), Washington, 1956-57; practice real estate law Shook & Shook, Toledo, 1958-62; practice probate and real estate law Shook & Shook, North Olmsted, O., 1962—. Cons., Community Com. for Youth, North Olmsted, 1966—. Sec., North Olmsted Community Council, 1964—; area chmn. United Appeal, 1963; rec. sec. constrn. com. Regional Planning Commn. in Stark County, Canton, 1956; chmn. scholarship com. North Olmsted Jr. Women Community Service Com., 1964-65; publs. chmn. North Olmsted Sci. Fair, 1967-68; ways and means chmn. P.T.A., 1968; active Chestnut P.T.A., North Olmsted. Mem. Ohio, Toledo, Stark County, Cleve. bar assns., League Women Voters (v.p. Toledo 1960-62), Kappa Delta. Address: 5130 Devon Dr North Olmsted OH 44070

SHOOK, BARBARA RHINES (MRS. JACK RICHARD SHOOK), editor; b. Mankato, Minn., Mar. 15, 1948; d. Harvey Carter and Joyce Ruth (Davis) Rhines; B.A., U. Houston, 1971; m. Jack Richard Shook, Oct. 10, 1969. Editorial asst. Houston Natural Gas Corp., 1971-72, editor, 1972—. Recipient 1st place award Tex. Gulf Coast Journalism Assembly, 1971. Mem. Internat. Assns. Bus. Communicators, Women in Communications (chpt. sec. 1972-74), Harris County Women's Polit. Caucus, Sigma Delta Chi (dir. 1972—). Home: 13634 Greenway Rd Sugar Land TX 77478 Office: PO Box 1188 Houston TX 77001

SHOOP, MARY ANN, occupational therapist; b. Youngstown, O., Oct. 1, 1939; d. James Beswick and Katherine (Schumacher) Shoop; B.Sc. in Bus. Adminstrn., Ohio State U., 1961, B.Sc. in Occupational Therapy, 1966. Sect. dir., campaign div. Salvation Army, N.Y.C., 1961-62; staff occupational therapist Ohio State U. Hosps., Columbus, 1966-68; dir. student and inservice edn., adjunctive therapy dept. program coordinator Day Treatment Program, Harding Hosp., Worthington, O., 1968—. Clin. instr. occupational therapy div. Ohio State U.; extramural faculty Columbus Bd. Edn. Occupational Therapy Assts. Program. Mem. North Central Area Planning Com., intermediate facility subcom. Franklin County Mental Health and Retardation Bd., 1973. Mem. Am. (pres. 1966—), Ohio (trustee 1970-72, chmn. Columbus dist. 1970-72, treas. elect. 1975) occupational therapy assns., Nat. Orgn. Women, Gamma Alpha Chi (pres. 1960-61), Phi Mu (v.p. 1960-61). Democrat. Roman Catholic. Home: 515 Riverview Dr Columbus OH 43202

SHORE, CLOVER VIRGINIA PETERS (MRS. DAVID PRESTON SHORE), artist; b. Durango, Tex., Aug. 1, 1906; d. William Allen and Virginia (McCreary) Peters; student Toby Bus. Coll.; m. David Preston Shore, Dec. 27, 1927; children—Shirley Clover (Mrs. Lloyd Smith Parker), David Preston II. Art tchr. Fort Worth pub. high schs., 1944-46; asst. prof. art Tex. Christian U., Fort Worth, 1946-48; mem. faculty Arlington State Coll., 1957, 60, 61, 62; chmn. art Met. Abilene Christian Coll., Ft. Worth, 1968—. Exhibited one-man shows Collin Art Gallery, Fort Worth, 1958, Hellum's Gallery, Fort Worth, 1953, 57, Denton (Tex.) Gallery, 1959, Studio Gallery, Waco, Tex., 1960; exhibited in group shows including Tex. Fedn. Womens Clubs, Austin, Abilene (Tex.) Mus. Art, Forth Worth Art Center, Dallas Mus. Art, Jackson (Miss.) Mus. Art, Birmingham (Ala.) Mus. Art, Smithsonian Instn. Annex Gallery, Washington, Butler Art Inst., Youngstown, O., Del Gado Mus. Art, New Orleans, Tex. Fine Arts Assn. Exhbn., Austin; traveling exhbns. Tex. Fine Arts Assn. Austin, 1960-61, 62-63, Nat. League Am. Pen Women Cultural Exchange Art Exhibit, 1966; represented in permanent collections. Recipient First Place in Graphics, Abilene Mus. Art, 1952, Blanche McVeigh award Fort Worth Art Center, 1964. Mem. Fort Worth Art Assn., Tex. Fine Arts Assn., Nat. League Am. Pen Women (pres. br. 1964-66, 68-70, Tex. pres. 1968-70, South Central regional chmn. 1971-72, nat. resolutions chmn. 1972—). Tex. State Tchrs. Assn. (life), Delta Zeta (State council pres. dist. 4, 1968, Fort Worth alumnae pres. 1966-68), Kappa Pi. Clubs: Fort Worth Womans, Texas Christian University Faculty Women's. Home: 2200 Glenco Terrace Fort Worth TX 76110

SHORR, MIRIAM KRONFELDT (MRS. ELI YALE SHORR), artist; b. N.Y.C.; d. A.L. and Carrie (Grossberger) Kronfeldt; student Hunter Coll.; m. Eli Yale Shorr, May 10, 1931. Exhibited one-man shows R.I. U., 1966, Rutgers U., 1967, U. Me., 1967, Brandeis U., 1967, Norfolk Mus. Art, 1971; group shows Audubon Anns., 1948, 50, 53, 66, Nat. Soc. Painters in Casein, 1958, 60-65, 70, Jewish Tercentenary Exhibit, Riverside Mus., 1954; and traveling shows throughout U.S., Contemporary Gallery, City Center Gallery, N.Y.C., 1955, 56; represented in pvt. and permanent collections. Recipient Nat. Assn. Women Artists First prize drawing, 1962; Mem. Artists Equity Assn. (dir. 1958-64), Nat. Assn. Women Artists (Newcastle award 1961, 65, dir. 1970-72), Contemporary Artists Bklyn. Home: 650 Ocean Av Brooklyn NY 11226 Studio: 10 E 23d St New York City NY 10010

SHORT, LUCILLE DOUGHTON (MRS. EDWARD PRESTON SHORT), educator, poet, lectr.; b. Bryan, O., July 23, 1903; d. F.L. and Lamenta Campbell (Bayes) Doughton; A.B., Ohio Wesleyan U., 1926; A.M., Boston U., 1927, B.S. in Edn., 1943; postgrad. Tex. Womans U., 1958, U. Chgo., 1962; m. Edward Preston Short, June 26, 1952. Instr. English and speech, Kenton, O., 1929-39, Vt. Coll., 1944-46, Margaret Hall Sch. for Girls, Versailles, Ky., 1946-49, Radford Sch. for Girls, El Paso, Tex., 1949-50, Midway Jr. Coll., Lexington, Ky., summer 1947, St. Marys-on-the-Mountain Sch., Sewanee, Tenn., 1950-54, Germantown Sch., Memphis, 1954-68. Hostess radio program, Montpelier, Vt., 1944-45; writer Guidelines for fgn. lang. teaching Tchrs. of Shelby County, Tenn., 1959. Mem. Internat. (London), World (Madres, India), Tenn. (pres. 1965-66, program dir.) poetry socs., Nat. League Am. Pen Women (membership com. br. 1974-76), Am. Assn. U. Women, Latin Tchrs. in West Tenn. (pres.), Am. Assn. Tchrs. Spanish and Portuguese (life), Liga Panamericana, Am. Classical Assn., Speech Assn., English Assn., New York Browning Soc., Acad. Am. Poets, Athenaeum Lit. Club, Alpha Delta Kappa (life). Episcopalian. Club: Tenn. Woman's Press and Authors (chaplain 1974-76). Contbr. poems to profl. publs. Home: 207 S Marne St Memphis TN 38111

SHOTWELL, SALLY STUART, coll. counselor; b. Lincoln, Neb., July 11, 1943; d. Gordon Stuart and Leah Jane (Carlsen) Shotwell; B.A., U. Denver, 1965; postgrad. Ariz. State U., 1966-67; M.A., Claremont Grad. Sch., 1970. Tchr. Pomona (Cal.) Unified Sch. Dist., 1967-69; grad. resident Pomona Coll., 1970-71; financial aid counselor Scripps Coll., Claremont, Cal., 1971-74; work-study coordinator San Francisco State U., 1974—. Mem. Nat., Cal., Western assns. student financial aid adminstrs. Democrat. Home: 610 Clipper #17 San Francisco CA 94114

SHOWALTER, RONDA KERR (MRS. GRAHAM CLAYTON SHOWALTER), health edn. cons.; b. Lima, O., Oct. 2, 1942; d. John Russell and Arnita Ruth (Baier) Kerr; B.S. in Edn., Capital U., 1964; M.S. in Health Sci., Ind. U., 1968; postgrad. Bucknell U., 1973; m. Graham Clayton Showalter, Aug. 23, 1969. Tchr. phys. edn. Spencerville (O.) High Sch., 1964-65; instr. health and phys. edn. Ohio Northern U., 1965-68; asst. prof. health edn. Pa. State U., University Park, 1968-72. Cons. to Houghton-Mifflin Pub. Co., Boston, 1973; health edn. cons. in sex edn. for continuing edn. Pa. State U., Wilkes-Barre, Dubois, Allentown, King of Prussia Campuses, 1972—. Vol. for United Fund, 1972-74, Heart Fund, 1972-74; mem. Lewisburg Council on the Arts, 1971—. Mem. Young Republican Club of Union County, Pa. Trustee Pa. Community Services. Mem. Am. Sch. Health Assn., Am. Assn. U. Women (publicity chmn. Susquehanna br. 1973—), League of Women Voters. Presbyn. Author: (with Brice Corder) It's Your Life, 1970, Health Science and College Life, 1972. Address: 36 South 3d St Lewisburg PA 17837

SHOWERS, LORENA IVADELL WILLIAMS (MRS. ROYDON P. SHOWERS), labor union exec.; b. nr. Boone, Ia., Feb. 12, 1904; d. Abner and Ida (Richardson) Williams; student pub. schs., Boone; m. Roydon P. Showers, June 16, 1924; children—Dorothy Marilyn, Donald Roydon, Edward LeRoy. Tchr. pub. schs., 1922-24; sec.-treas. Local 878, Hotel and Restaurant Employees, Anchorage, 1951-71, pres., 1971—; sec.-treas. Alaska Fedn. Labor, 1956-66, sec.-treas. emeritus, 1966—; sec.-treas. Alaska Alliance Hotel and Restaurant Employees and Bartenders, Anchorage, 1956-70. Mem. Alaska Employment Security Adv. Council, 1959-69; columnist Alaska Cope Reporter, 1960-70. Mem. adv. bd. Providence Hosp., 1958-60; Alaska labor rep. White House Conf. Children and Youth, 1960, White House Conf. Aging, 1971; chmn. Gov.'s Adv. Com. on Aging, 1972—; del. 3d Internat. Conf. Social Gerontology, Dubrovnik, Yugoslavia, 1972, 4th Internat. Conf., Oslo, Norway, 1973. Mem. Older Persons Action Group, Anchorage, Am. Assn. Ret. Persons. Democrat. Baptist. Club: Zonta (Anchorage). Home: PO Box 1978 Anchorage AK 99510

SHRADER, DOROTHY HECKMANN, editor; b. Hermann, Mo., Dec. 3, 1913; d. Edward and Alice Sophie (Bock) Heckmann; B.J., U. Mo., 1935, B.S. in Edn., 1947; m. William Duncan Shrader, June 8, 1935; children—John, David, Margaret (Mrs. George Dudley Ford). Tchr., Pearsall, Tex., 1943-44, U. Mo. Lab. Sch., Columbia, 1945-46, Linden, Midway schs., Columbia, 1947-50; prin. Willson Spl. Edn. Sch., Ames, Ia., 1952-54; founder, tchr. Beloit Sch. for Emotionally Disturbed, Ames, 1956-59; dir. pub. relations City of Ames, 1960-65; tchr. bi-nat. center Alianza, Montevideo, Uruguay, 1966-68; editor, pub., owner Bull. Bd., Ames, 1951-75. Mem. Ames City P.T.A. Council, 1951-54, pres., 1952-53. Mem. Ames (Ia.) City Planning Commn., 1970-75, vice chmn., 1973-75. Bd. dirs. Camp Fire Girls, 1953-55, Central Ia. Mental Health Center, 1961-63. Mem. Women in Communications (Matrix award 1965, pres. profl. chpt. 1969-70), Nat. (mem. exec. bd.), Ia. (1st Pl. Writing awards 1964-66, 70-72, 74, v.p. 1973-74, pres. 1974-75) press women, Octagon, Actor's, Ames Internat. Festival Assn., Amateur Ia. Artists, Phi Mu. Democrat. Mem. Ch. of Christ Congregational. Clubs: Faculty Woman's Iowa State Univ. (Ames). Home: 222 Parkridge Circle Ames IA 50010 Office: PO Box 1186 Ia State U Sta Ames IA 50010

SHRAGER, JOANN FRANCES (JOANNA SEATON), performing artist; b. N.Y.C., Mar. 15, 1949; d. John and Emily (Snyder) Shrager; A.B., Cornell U., 1971. Artistic dir., founder, actress Major's Inn Elizabethan Dinner Theatre, Gilbertsville, N.Y., 1971—; organizer Her Majesties Jewel, Dallas, 1974. Am. the Beautiful Fund grantee, 1973. Clubs: Cornell Folk Dance, Cornell Glee, Cornell Savoyards, Octagon Dramatics (Ithaca, N.Y.). Home: Box 1 Gilbertsville NY 13776

SHREEVES, EVELYN ROBERTSON (MRS. CHARLES SHREEVES), librarian; b. Portsmouth, Va., Dec. 13, 1911; d. Joseph Henry and Zanaida (Liggan) Robertson; B.A., Coll. William and Mary, 1934; m. Charles Bidgner Shreeves, July 10, 1937; children—Margaret (Mrs. A. Garland Moseley), Charles Edward. Librarian, Waynesboro (Va.) High Sch., 1934-36, Petersburg High Sch., 1936-37, County Warwick (Va.), 1951-52, City Warwick, 1952-58, City Newport News, 1958-69; librarian sch. bd. City Newport News, 1969—; tchr. pvt. sch., Newport News, 1943-45. Mem. Am. Assn. U. Women, Va. Library Assn., N.E.A., Kappa Delta Pi, Delta Kappa Gamma. Home: 24 Holly Dr Newport News VA 23601

SHREVE, BLANCHE (MRS. CHARLES UPTON SHREVE III), educator; b. Butte, Mont., Jan. 28, 1916; d. Bancroft and Georgia (Sarchet) Gore; B.E., U. Cal. at Los Angeles, 1939; M.B.A., Wayne State U., 1963; m. Charles Upton Shreve, Apr. 18, 1946; children—C. Upton IV, Elizabeth Gore, Georgia Sarchet. Formerly tchr. pub. schs., Los Angeles; tchr. pub. schs., Detroit, 1959—. Mem. Ancient and Hon. Art. Co. (state pres. 1959-60), D.A.R. (dir. Louisa St. Clair chpt. 1954-58), Katharine Gibbs Alumnae Assn., Phi Chi Theta, Kappa Kappa Gamma. Research on better means to teach arithmetic and math. Home: 1040 Iroquois Av Detroit MI 48214

SHRIVER, DOROTHY ANN, city ofcl.; b. Haskell, Tex., Apr. 6, 1939; d. J.N. and Golda Mae (Bouldin) Gibbs; student Odessa Coll., 1966—; m. William B. Shriver, Jr., Mar. 4, 1960; children—Robert Wade, Eric Todd, Amber Lynn. Counselor, Lena Pope Children's Home, Ft. Worth, Tex., 1957-60; saleswoman Mary Kay Cosmetics, Dallas, 1968-70; councilwoman City of Lake Worth (Tex.), 1972—; saleswoman H.W. Lisby Real Estate, Ft. Worth, 1973—. Chmn., Com. to Establish Sub-Courthouse, 1972-73; co-chmn. Lake Worth Park Com., Bur. Outdoor Recreation, 1972—; mem. legislation com. Tex. Municipal League, 1972—; mem. Ft. Worth System Customer Council, 1972, N.W. Hwy. Com., 1973—, Mechem Field Joint Airport Zoning Bd., 1973—. Devotional chmn. presch. P.T.A. 1971-72. Mem. Lena Pope Home Alumni (sec. 1972—). Baptist (Sunday sch. tchr., 1960-73, nursery coordinator 1966-67, co-chmn. prayer league 1972-73, bus. coordinator 1972-73, outreach dir. 1973—). Home: 4012 Lakewood Dr Lake Worth TX 76135 Office: 3126 E Rosedale Fort Worth TX 76105

SHRIVER, EUNICE MARY KENNEDY (MRS. ROBERT SARGENT SHRIVER, JR.), civic worker; b. Brookline, Mass.; d. Joseph P. and Rose (Fitzgerald) Kennedy; student Manhattanville Coll. of Sacred Heart, L.H.D., 1963; B.S. in Sociology, Stanford, 1943; Litt.D., U. Santa Clara, 1962; L.H.D., D'Youville Coll., 1962; LL.D., Regis Coll., 1963; m. Robert Sargent Shriver, Jr., May 23, 1953; children—Robert Sargent III, Maria Owings, Timothy Perry, Mark, Anthony. With spl. war problems div. U.S. State Dept., Washington, 1943-45; adviser on prevention and control juvenile delinquency Dept. Justice, Washington, 1947-48; social worker Fed. Penitentiary for Women, Alderson, W.Va., 1950; exec. v.p. Joseph P. Kennedy, Jr. Found., 1956—, pres. Spl. Olympics, 1968—; social worker House of Good Shepherd, Chgo., also Juvenile Ct., Chgo., 1951-54; regional chmn. women's div. Community Fund-Red Cross Joint Appeal, Chgo., 1958; cons. to Pres. John F. Kennedy's Panel on Mental Retardation, 1961. Active worker in congl. and presdl. campaigns of John F. Kennedy, 1948-60; co-chmn. women's com. Democratic Nat. Conv., Chgo., 1956. Recipient (with husband) Philip Murray-William Green award, 1966, Albert Lasker Pub. Service award in health, 1966. Home: Timberlawn Edson Lane Rockville MD 20852

SHRIVER, JOYCE ELIZABETH, educator, neuroanatomist; b. Quincy, Ill., Sept. 14, 1937; d. Victor Henry and Alma (Henerhoff) Shriver; B.A. magna cum laude, William Jewell Coll., 1959; Ph.D., U. Kan., 1965. Teaching asst. anatomy U. Kan., 1959-61, predoctoral fellow neuroanatomy NIH, 1961-63; research asst. anatomy U. Kan. Med. Center, 1963-64; postdoctoral fellow neuroanatomy Nat. Inst. Neurol. Diseases and Blindness, dept. anatomy Columbia Coll. Physicians and Surgeons, N.Y.C., 1964-68, asst. prof. anatomy Mt. Sinai Sch. Medicine, N.Y.C., 1968-71, asso. prof. anatomy, 1971—; mem. doctoral faculty Mt. Sinai Grad. Sch. Biol. Scis. of City U. N.Y., 1971—. Recipient 1st ann. City U. N.Y. award excellence in teaching, 1973. Mem. Am. Assn. Anatomists, Am. Soc. Zoologists, Internat. Primatological Soc., N.Y. Acad. Scis., Soc. for Neurosci., A.A.A.S., Am. Acad. Polit. and Social Sci., Sigma Xi. Home: 711 West End Av New York City NY 10025

SHRIVER, MARCIA ANN (MRS. CHARLES WILLIAM SHRIVER), metal products co. exec.; b. Lima, O., Apr. 7, 1921; d. Ralph Berman and Lillian Francis (Botkin) Gould; grad. pub. high sch., 1939; m. Charles William Shriver, June 18, 1939; children—Melinda Sharon, James Charles. Co-propr. Superior Plating Co., Columbus, O., 1945—, sec. treas., since 1945—, also dir. Mem. nat. adv. bd. Am. Security Council. Mem. Am. Electroplaters Soc., Nat. Assn. Metal Finishers, Nat. Bus. and Profl. Women Assn., Nat. Assn. for Female Execs., Early Am. Soc. Mem. Order Eastern Star (past matron). Clubs: Brookside Country, Two Square Dance. Home: 8891 Brock Rd Plain City OH 43064 Office: 915 N 20th St Columbus OH 43219

SHRUM, ADA ELIZABETH, city councillor; b. Upshur County, Tex., Dec. 30, 1920; d. William Archie and Eura Ethel (LaRue) Dacus; student East Tex. Baptist Coll., 1941-42; Asso. in Bus. Edn., Baylor U., 1945; student Tex. Women's U., 1955, Austin Coll., 1962, bus. law and real estate Grayson County Jr. Coll., 1971-72; m. Bailey Everett Shrum, June 16, 1946; children—Rebecca Sue May (Mrs. Roy Louis May), Linda Beth (Mrs. John W. Duncan III), David Vincent. Tchr., cons. sewing classes, 1955-59; owner retail sewing machine bus., 1953-59; asst. mgr. Grayson Hotel, Sherman, Tex., 1959-62; exec. sec. to mgr. sales and distbn. services Johnson & Johnson, 1962-67, exec. sec. to dir. mfg., 1967-71, pub. plant newspaper, adminstr. financial aid to edn. and suggestion program, 1971-73; mem. Sherman City Council, 1971-73, council rep. to Texoma Regional Planning Commn., 1971-73. Active coms. and drives United Fund, Heart Fund, Salvation Army, Muscular Dystrophy. Mem. Bus. and Profl. Women's Clubs (past officer Sherman, dist. legislation chmn., named woman of year 1972, Torch award 1971), Soroptimist Club Ams. (charter mem., past local officer, dist. sec. 1966-68, dist. dir. 1968-70, regional nominating chmn. 1964-66, 72-74), Am. Bus. Women's Club (charter), Toastmistress Club (past local officer). Baptist (Sunday sch. tchr.). Home: 1131 West College St Sherman TX 75090

SHUFF, LILY (MRS. MARTIN SHIR), artist, wood engraver; b. N.Y.C.; A.B., Hunter Coll.; student Art Students League, Bklyn. Acad. Fine Arts, N.Y. Sch. Social Research, Columbia; m. Dr. Martin

Shir, May 12, 1950; children—Lewitt, Lawrence. One-man shows Argent Gallery, N.Y.C., 1947, 56, Van Dieman Lilenfeld Gallery, N.Y.C., 1948, 52, Giraudeau Gallery, Paris, 1951, Utica (N.Y.) Library Gallery, Cortland (N.Y.) Gallery, Mercersburg (Pa.) Acad., Thiel Coll., Greenville, Pa., Freemont (Mich.) Found., St. Vincent's Coll., Latrobe, Pa., 1960, State Coll., Conn., Purdue U., Ind., McPherson Coll., Kan., Regar Mus., Ala., Fairleigh Dickinson Coll., 1961, East Side Gallery, Erie (Pa.) Public Mus., Pack Meml. Mus., Asheville, N.C., State U. N.Y., U. N.D., Wesleyan U., S.D., Ore. Coll., East Side Gallery, N.Y., also others; exhibited in group shows at N.A.D., Whitney, Riverside, Bklyn., Jersey City museums, Nat. Print Show Library of Congress, Portland Mus. Arts, Nat. Sarasota Smithsonian Instn., others, also in France, Belgium, Holland, Switzerland, Can., Greece, Japan, Latin Am., India, South America; represented in permanent collections Bat Yam Mus., Israel, Pakistan Consulate, James Fenimore Cooper High Sch., Robert Mueller, Paris, Mme. Germaine Richier, Paris, Yale, Ga. Mus. Art, Am. Fedn. Art, Library of Congress, Monsieur Rene de Solier, Paris, Bezalel Nat. Mus., Jerusalem, Norfolk Mus., Met. Mus., Neville Mus., Purdue U., Regar Mus., Dakota Wesleyan U., State U.N.Y., Baylor U., Mayville State Coll., St. Vincent Coll., Central Okla. Mus., Butler Mus. Am. Art, City Coll. N.Y., McPherson Coll., U. N.D., Met. Mus., N.Y.C., Rosenberg Library, Galveston, Tex., Erie (Pa.) Mus., many pvt. collections. Recipient prize oil Bklyn. Soc. Artists, 53, 56; N.J. Painters and Sculptors Soc., 1956, 68, 69, 70, oil, 1960; wood block print Conn. Acad. Fine Art, 1956, 1st prize oil, Caravan Gallery, 1957, print, Nat. Assn. Women Artists, 1959, Casein, 1958; Casein prize, Argent Gallery, 1958, Riverside Mus. Print, 1959, National Soc. Painters in Casein, 1963, 65; Bklyn. Soc. Artists prize oil, 1960; Gold medal of honor Jersey City Mus., 1962; prize Nat. Soc. Casein Painters, 1966, 67; prize in oil Knickerbocker Artists, 1966; prize in oil Am. Soc. Contemporary Artists, 1966, 67, 68, 70; Nat. Assn. Women Artists prize, 1969, 70, 71, and others. Mem. Bklyn. Soc. Artists (dir., oil jury), N.Y. Soc. Woman Artists (dir., treas.), Nat. Assn. Woman Artists (dir., chmn. membership jury, oil jury, mem. adv. bd.), Nat. Soc. Casein Painters (sec.), Nat. Casein Soc. (oil jury), Artists Equity (mem. adv. bd.), Mus. Modern Art, Silvermine Guild Artists, Soc. Wash. Printmakers, Conn. Acad. Fine Arts, N.J. Painters and Sculptors Soc. (mem. jury selection), Audubon Artists Assn., Hunterdon County Art Center, Am. Soc. Contemporary Artists, Am. Color Print Soc., Physicians Wives League Greater N.Y. Club: Woman Pays. Contbr. to Art Collector's Almanac. Address: 465 West End Av New York City NY 10024

SHUGART, GRACE SEVERANCE (MRS. HAROLD W. SHUGART), educator; b. Palouse, Wash., Feb. 26, 1910; d. George and Ethel (Espy) Severance; B.S., Wash. State U., 1931; M.S., Ia. State U., 1938; m. Harold W. Shugart, June 11, 1939. Dietetic intern U. Minn., 1932; dietitian No. Pacific Ry. Hosp., Glendive, Mont., 1932-34; food dir. Cooperative Dormitories, Ia. State U., 1934-39; instr. instn. mgmt. Ia. State U., 1945-50; coordinator residence hall food service, asst. prof. instnl. mgmt. Kan. State U., 1951-57, asso. prof., head instnl. mgmt. dept., 1957-62, prof., head instnl. mgmt. dept., 1962—. Mem. Manhattan C. of C., Am. Home Econs. Assn., Inst. Food Technologists, Nat. Restaurant Assn., Am. Mgmt. Assn., Am. Sch. Food Service Assn., Soc. for Advancement Food Service Research, Am. Dietetic Assn. (pres. 1968-69), Women in Communications, Phi Kappa Phi, Omicron Nu, Kappa Kappa Gamma. Author: (with others) Food for Fifty, 1961, 5th edit., 1971. Home: 1514 Givens Dr Manhattan KS 66502

SHUHANY, ELIZABETH ANNA, educator; b. Chelmsford, Mass., Apr. 9, 1925; d. Andrew Michael and Anna (Klatka) Shuhany; A.B., Boston U., 1947, A.M., 1949, Ph.D., 1959. Faculty, Boston U., 1947-64, asst. math. dept., part-time instr., 1947-52, instr. math., 1952-56, asst. prof., 1956-62, asso. prof., 1962-64; prof. math., chmn. dept. Regis Coll., Weston, Mass., 1964—. Mem. Am. Statis. Assn. (mem. council 1970-71), Math. Assn. Am., Am. Assn. U. Profs., Phi Beta Kappa (chpt. treas. 1961-64), Sigma Xi. Home: 24 Tippling Rock Rd Sudbury MA 01776 Office: Wellesley St Weston MA 02193

SHULER, ALEXANDERINA VIGH (MRS. LYNN WILLIAM SHULER), editor; b. Passaic, N.J., Oct. 13, 1943; d. Alexander and Margaret (Duzs) Vigh; B.S., Seton Hall U., 1965; postgrad. Alfred U., 1965-66; m. Lynn William Shuler, June 14, 1969. High sch. tchr., Saddle Brook, N.J., 1964-65; copywriter, asst. editor McGraw Hill, Inc., N.Y.C., 1966-68; editor Front Lines, AID, Washington, 1968—; editor, writer, layout designer News Dispatch, 1966-68, free lance writer. Recipient Meritorious Honor award U.S. Govt., 1970, Blue Pencil awards Fed. Editors Assn., 1969, 71, 72, 73, Soc. Tech. Communication award, 1973. Home: 2328 Freetown Ct Reston VA 22091 Office: 4955 Office Pub Affairs AID Washington DC 20523

SHULL, CLAIRE (MRS. LEO SHULL), editor; b. N.Y.C., Oct. 26, 1925; d. Barnet and Fannie (Florea) Klar; student Am. Acad. Dramatic Arts, 1943; m. Leo Shull, Aug. 8, 1948; children—Lee (Mrs. Ken Tannenbaum), David. Actress, entertaining at USO camp shows, 1945-46; appeared in Broadway prodns., road tours Junior Miss, 1944, The Front Page, 1945, Tenting Tonight, 1946; editor Summer Theatre Directory, Show Bus. Publs., N.Y.C., 1955—, editor asso. pub., 1957—; founder Claire/Casting, TV comml. casting and prodn. co., 1973. Mem. Actors Equity Assn., Drama Desk. Mem. Hadassah. Home: 420 E 72d St New York City NY 10021 Office: 136 W 44th St New York City NY 10036

SHULMAN, ALIX KATES, author; b. Cleve., Aug. 17, 1932; d. Samuel Simon and Dorothy (Davis) Kates; B.A., Western Res. U., 1953; postgrad. Columbia, 1953-54, N.Y. U., 1960-61; m. Martin Shulman, June 19, 1959; children—Theodore, Polly. Author: Bosley on the Number Line, 1970; To The Barricades: The Anarchist Life of Emma Goldman, 1971; Awake or Asleep, 1971; Red Emma Speaks, 1972; Finders Keepers, 1972; Memoirs of an Ex-Prom Queen, 1972; contbr. articles to Aphra, MS, Women: A Jour. of Liberation, Up From Under, Atlantic Monthly, Evergreen Rev., N.Y. Mag., Redbook, Cosmopolitan, Works in Progress. Mem. Nat. Orgn. Women, 1968, Redstockings, 1969-71, N.Y. Radical Feminists, 1971-72, Feminists on Children's Media, 1970-72. Mem. Assn. for Women in Psychology. Office: c/o Ellen Levine Curtis Brown Ltd 60 E 56th St New York City NY 10022

SHULMAN, CORINNE SALTZMAN (MRS. ADLEY M. SHULMAN), lawyer; b. Mpls., Apr. 12, 1931; d. Albert and Esther (Korsh) Saltzman; A.A., U. Cal. at Los Angeles, 1950, B.A. with highest honors, 1952, J.D., 1956; m. Adley M. Shulman, June 22, 1952; children—Gail Denise, Susan Linda, Nancy Ann, Barton Alan. Admitted to Cal. bar, 1957; partner firm Shulman & Shulman, Beverly Hills, Cal., 1958—. Mem. adv. bd. Anti-Defamation League, 1964—; mem. panel arbitrators Am. Arbitration Assn. 1972—. Co-recipient First Ann. Human Relations award Los Angeles City Human Relations Bur., 1970. Mem. State Bar Cal., Los Angeles, Beverly Hills bar assns., Am. Judicature Soc., Los Angeles Trial Lawyers Assn., League Women Voters. Home: 1244 2d St Manhattan Beach CA 90266 Office: 485 S Robertson Blvd Beverly Hills CA 90211

SHULMAN, YONA LEE NELSON (MRS. HERBERT BYRON SHULMAN), educator; b. Norwich, Conn., Jan. 14, 1946; d. Zev K. and Florence (Strum) Nelson; student (H. Greenberg scholar), Hebrew U. Jerusalem, 1964-65; B.Hebrew Edn., Hebrew Coll., 1966; B.A., Brandeis U., 1967; M.Sc., London Sch. Econs. and Polit. Sci., 1970; m. Herbert Byron Shulman, June 16, 1973. Research asst. Joint Center for Urban Studies, Harvard and Mass. Inst. Tech., 1969, Research Center for Mental Health, N.Y. U., 1971; lectr. psychology women New Sch. Social Research, N.Y.C., 1972-73; vis. lectr. Yale, 1972-73; instr. psychology City U. N.Y., 1971—. Calhoun Coll. (Yale) fellow, 1972-73. Mem. Assn. Women in Psychology (head speaker's bur. 1972—), Women's Com. Profl. Concerns (exec. bd. 1972-73), Am. Psychol. Assn., N.Y. Acad. Scis. Home: 1801 John F Kennedy Blvd Philadelphia PA 19103 Office: Dept Environmental Psychology Grad Center 33 W 42d St New York City NY 10036

SHULSTAD, MARIANA ROCA (MRS. RONALD CRAIG SHULSTAD), lawyer, govt. ofcl.; b. Washington, July 1, 1940; d. Paul McLennen and Elizabeth Anne (Yeager) Roca; student Mills Coll., 1957-58; B.S., Ariz. State U., 1962; J.D., U. Colo., 1966; m. Ronald Craig Shulstad, June 29, 1968; 1 dau., Sara Chae. Admitted to Colo. bar, 1966, Ariz. bar, 1966, D.C. bar, 1970, U.S. Supreme Ct. bar, 1969; law clk. to chief justice Colo. Supreme Ct., Denver, 1966-67; asso. Lewis & Roca, Phoenix, 1967-68; atty. office of solicitor U.S. Dept. Interior, Washington, 1968-70, Mpls.-St. Paul, 1970—; instr. Guadalupe area project, St. Paul, Minn., 1972-73. Mem. Chanhassen (Minn.) City Planning Commn., 1974—, Chanhassen City Human Rights Commn., 1973-74, Chanhassen Housing Study Task Force, 1973-74; co-chmn. Chanhassen Bicentennial Commn., 1974—. Bd. dirs. League Minn. Human Rights Commns., 1973—. Mem. Fed. (Twin Cities chpt. sec. 1972-73), Am., Ariz., Washington bar assns., Jr. League Mpls., Mills Coll. Alumnae Assn., Minn. Arboretum Soc., Minn. Civil Liberties Union, Children's Home Soc. Minn., Kappa Beta Pi, Phi Alpha Delta. Editor: The Bill of Rights, 1963. Home: 8031 Cheyenne Av Chanhassen MN 55317 Office: 686 Federal Bldg Ft Snelling Twin Cities MN 55111

SHULTERBRANDT, ELDRA LAURA MONSANTO (MRS. LOUIS SHULTERBRANDT), psychologist, govt. ofcl.; b. St. Thomas, V.I., Dec. 22, 1913; d. Wilfred and Daisy (Hendricks) Monsanto; A.B., Spelman Coll., 1936; M.A., Columbia, 1940; Ed.M., Harvard, 1945; postgrad. U. Denmark at Copenhagen and Aarhus, 1958-59; m. Louis Shulterbrandt, Jan. 24, 1942; 1 dau., Michele Saranne. Tchr., guidance counselor Charlotte Amalie High Sch., St. Thomas, 1936-48, asst. prin., 1936-48; asso. prof. psychology N.Y. U., 1950; dir. Mental Health Services, V.I., 1949—; co-founder Caribbean Fedn. Mental Health. Chmn., V.I. Bd. Edn., 1961-68; exec. sec. V.I. Gov.'s Commn. Human Services, 1964-69; mem. V.I. Law Enforcement Commn., 1968—, V.I. Pub. TV System, 1968—; V.I. rep. Caribbean Folk Festival, 1953; mem. steering com. Edn. Commn. of States, 1967—. Bd. dirs. V.I. Ballet Theatre; trustee, co-founder Coll. of V.I.; trustee Antilles Sch. Recipient award for 30 years service to V.I. govt., 1966; named St. Thomas Woman of Year, Bus. and Profl. Women's Clubs, 1967. Mem. Nat. Assn. Mental Health Program Dirs., World Edn. Mental Health, St. Thomas Soc. Friends of Denmark (pres. 1969-70), Internat. Assn. Women Psychologists, Am. Pub. Health Assn. Contbg. author: Frontiers in General Hospital Psychiatry, 1961. Editor: Children of the Caribbean, 1959. Home: 33-34 Droningens Gade St Thomas VI 00801 Office: VI Dept Health Div Mental Health St Thomas VI 00801

SHULTZ, AUDREY FLITCH (MRS. BENNIE SHULTZ), lawyer; b. Ponca City, Okla., Oct. 31, 1896; d. Sylvester and Dollie (Mehaffey) Flitch; B.A., U. Okla., 1917, M.A., 1918, J.D., 1967; m. Bennie Shultz, Apr. 12, 1917; children—Evalee (Mrs. Edward Samuel Homan), Ruth (Mrs. Harry Eugene Stanley), Marie (Mrs. Lewis F. Hatch), Bennie. Lab. asst. zoology, medic embryology and household bacteriology U. Okla., Norman, 1914-17; sci. tchr. Norman High Sch., 1918; real estate salesman, Norman, 1963-65; admitted to Okla. bar, 1968; pvt. law practice, Norman, 1968-73. Mem. adv. bd. Norman Am. Exchange Bank, 1970-72. Chmn. Norman (Okla.) March of Dimes, 1938; mem. Norman (Okla.) Improvement Council, 1970-73. Mem. Norman (Okla.) Sch. Bd., 1938-42. Audrey Flitch Schultz Ednl. Found. fellowship honor award given by Am. Assn. U. Women, 1964; recipient 50 Year Service award, also Law Sch. Merit award U. Okla., 1967. Mem. Am., Okla. bar assns., 10th Circuit U.S. Court Appeals Assn., Am. Assn. U. Women, U. Okla. Alumni Assn., League of Women Voters, Mortar Bd., Phi Beta Kappa, Kappa Beta Pi. Presbyn. (elder 1967-70, trustee 1973—). Mem. Order of Eastern Star. Home: 412 W Main St Norman OK 73069

SHUMATE, CARRIE MAE SPIVEY (MRS. CLIFFORD THEADORE SHUMATE), textile mfg. co. exec.; b. Irvine, Ky., Nov. 22, 1913; d. Isaac and Sarah Ellen (Rose) Spivey; grad. Paris Bus. Sch., 1933; m. Clifford Theadore Shumate, Dec. 23, 1933; children—Clifford Wayne, Rose Carol (Mrs. James T. Myers). Foreladу, Hansley Mills Inc., Paris, Ky., 1942-47; with Blue Grass Industries, Inc., Carlisle, Ky., 1947—, supr., 1948-50, corporate dir., 1948—, product mgr., 1950-52, gen. mgr., 1952-64, dir. mfg., corporate sec., 1964—. Recipient Decade of Service award City of Carlisle, 1957, Community Service award Carlisle-Nicholas County C. of C., 1960, Industry Appreciation award, 1965. Mem. Ky., Bourbon, Nicholas, Harrison, Montgomery, Mason county chambers commerce. Mem. Christian Ch. Mem. Order Eastern Star (chpt. worthy matron 1972-73). Club: Business and Professional Women's (Paris). Home: Route 1 WindSton Farm Carlisle KY 40311 Office: Hwy 36 Carlisle KY 40311

SHUMATE, MARION LOUISE GUILFORD (MRS. D.J. SHUMATE), accountant; b. Three Rivers, Tex., Oct. 12, 1922; d. William Robert and Mary Lorraine (Harris) Guilford; grad. high sch.; m. D.J. Shumate, Sept. 22, 1951; children—Lorraine (Mrs. Henry E. Toerck), Linda (Mrs. Joe A. Crawford). Teller-bookkeeper First State Bank, Three Rivers, 1942-44; office mgr. House Auto & Tractor, Three Rivers, 1949-66, D.J. Shumate, distbr. Gulf Oil Co., Three Rivers, 1966—; city alderman Three Rivers, 1972—. Methodist (sec. adminstrv. bd. 1969-72). Home: Hill St Three Rivers TX 78071 Office: PO Box 220 Three Rivers TX 78071

SHUMWAY, HETTIE LAKIN (MRS. FRANK RITTER SHUMWAY), civic worker; b. Cornish, N.H., Sept. 1, 1903; d. Herbert Conrad and Helen W. (Beaman) Lakin; ed. pvt. schs., Md.; m. Frank Ritter Shumway, Sept. 8, 1930; children—Mary Ellen (Mrs. Preston Arms Gaylord, Jr.), Frank Ritter, Charles Lakin. Served as vol. various orgns., N.Y.C., Westchester County, Rochester, until 1935; vol. Strong Meml. Hosp., Rochester, 1935—, chmn. vol. services; mem. Mayor's Women's Com on Registration for Civilian Def. Vol. Office, 1941-42; chmn. Civil Def. Vol. Office of Rochester War Council, World War II, Korean War; charter mem. Monroe County Bd. Health, 1958-66, pres., 1966—; incorporator East House Corp., 1966, also v.p., pres., 1968—; hon. chmn. Project HOPE, 1966—; mem. nat. adv. bd. Nat. Tech. Inst. Deaf, 1967—. Charter mem. Susan B. Anthony Republican Club, 1949—; mem. 8th Dist. Republican Com., Brighton, 1957-66, mem. Monroe County Rep. Com., 1960-66. Bd. dirs. Health Assn. Rochester and Monroe County, 1937—, Jr. League Rochester, Inc., 1939—, Dept. Vols. Council of Social Agys., 1939-50, Council of Social Agys., 1946-48, Rochester Sch. for Deaf, 1941—, YWCA, 1944-47, Mental Health Chpt., 1949—, N.Y. State Assn. Mental Health, 1956-65, Monroe County chpt. Assn. for Help of Retarded Children, 1957-59, Genesee Valley Heart Assn., 1964-68, Monroe County Assn. Hearing Impaired, 1973; charter mem. Women's Council Rochester Inst. Tech.; trustee Rochester Inst. Tech. Co-recipient (with F. R. Shumway) Civic award Rochester Rotary Club, 1967, Asso's. medal U. Rochester, 1968, Rotary Citizen of Year award 1973, others. Mem. Mental Health Center Bd. (ad hoc com. mental health council on psychiat. services in gen. hosps. 1963), Rosemary Twig of Rochester Gen. Hosp. Club: Chatterbox. Address: 375 Ambassador Dr Rochester NY 14610

SHUMWAY, MARY LOUISE, educator, writer; b. Portage, Wis., Aug. 21, 1926; d. Oliver Arden and Margaret Martha (Tolleth) Shumway; A.B., U. Chgo., 1957; M.A., San Francisco State Coll., 1965; Ph.D., U. Denver, 1971. Editorial asst. acad. jours. U. Chgo., 1954-56, 58-59; instr. English and anthropology George Williams Coll., Chgo., 1957; dean women, coordinator undergrad. studies, instr. English and social scis. San Francisco Art Inst., 1960-64; prof. English, U. Wis. at Stevens Point, 1965—. Hattie M. Strong Found. grantee, 1957-58, 64-65; recipient Acad. Am. Poets prize 1965, 69. Robert Frost fellow poetry Bread Loaf, 1969; MacDowell fellow, 1973-74. Fellow Soc. Arts, Religion and Culture (asso.); mem. Am. Assn. U. Profs., Assn. U. Wis. Faculties. Author: Song of the Archer and Other Poems, 1964; Headlands, 1972. Contbr. to Arts in Society, Commonweal, Christian Scholar, Cimarron Rev., Denver Quar. and others. Home: PO Box 232 Plover WI 54467 Office: Dept English U Wis Stevens Point WI 54481

SHUTE, ALBERTA VAN HORN (MRS. DONALD SHUTE), editor; b. East Boothbay, Me., Nov. 18, 1906; d. Simeon B. and Julia (Dodge) Van Horn; student Colby Coll., 1925-26, Gorham State Coll., 1931-32; B.A., U. Me., 1970; m. Donald Shute, Feb. 12, 1943; children—Leon, Sarah, Daniel. Tchr. elementary sch., Boothbay, Me., 1926-30; librarian Manchester (Me.) Consol. Sch., 1961-68; columnist Daily Kennebec Jour., Augusta, Me., 1949-58; editor Star in the East, WCTU State Paper, Portland, Me., 1960—. Mem. Alpha Delta Pi. Methodist. Author: Year and a Day Along Bond Brook, 1954; Year and a Day in the Park, 1956; Or Ever the Silver Cord, 1957; Year and a Day from my Kitchen Window, 1965; Year and A Day on the Farm, 1972. Home: RFD 5 Augusta ME 04330

SIBLEY, ANTOINETTE, ballerina; b. Bromley, Kent, Eng., Feb. 27, 1939; d. Edward George and Winifred M. (Smith) Sibley; student Royal Ballet Sch., 1949-56; m. Michael Somes, July 22, 1964 (div. 1974); m. 2d Panton Corbett, July, 1974. Performed leading roles in ballets Swan Lake, Sleeping Beauty, Giselle, Coppelia, Cinderella, The Nutcracker, La Fille Mal Gardee, Romeo and Juliet, Harlequin in April, Les Rendezvous, Jabez and the Devil (created role of Mary), La Fete Etrange, the Rakes Progress, Hamlet, Ballet Imperial, Two Pigeons, La Bayadere, Symphonic Variations, Scenes de Ballet, Lilac Garden, Daphnis and Chloe, The Dream (created Titania); leading solo roles in Laurentia, Good Humoured Ladies, Blue Bird pas de deux in Sleeping Beauty, Peasant pas de deux in Giselle, Aristocrat in Mam'zelle Angot, Facade, Song of the Earth, Monotones, Jazz Calendar (created Friday's Child), Enigma Variations (created Dorabella), Thais, Triad (created The Girl), Pavane, Manon (created leading role). Decorated comdr. Brit. Empire. Address: Royal Opera House London WC 2 England

SIBLEY, GRETCHEN, educator; b. Los Angeles, May 14, 1914; d. Richard Earle and Alda (Shuttleworth) Sibley; B.A., Pasadena Coll., 1943; M.A., U. So. Cal., 1947; postgrad. Otis Art Inst., U. Cal. at Los Angeles, U. So. Cal. Sci. tchr. Garvey Jr. High Sch., 1943-46; mus. edn. specialist in sci. Natural History Mus., Los Angeles, 1946—. Lectr. in biology Pepperdine Coll., 1954-69; script writer ednl. films Internat. Ednl. Films, 1964—, also ednl. marketing and research, Q-Ed Prodns. Fellow So. Cal. Acad. Scis.; mem. A.A.A.S., Soc. Woman Geographers, Sigma Xi, Sigma Delta Epsilon, Phi Delta Gamma, Delta Kappa Gamma, Phi Sigma, Phi Lambda Theta. Author: La Brea Story, 1967; also numerous articles. Research on micropaleontology La Brea Pleistocene deposits, pleistocene paleopathology. Home: 7310 W 90th St Los Angeles CA 90045 Office: 900 Exposition Blvd Los Angeles CA 90007

SICA, CAROL, educator; b. Bklyn., Sept. 12, 1941; d. Carmine and Millie (Bua) Sica; B.A. in Theatre, Hofstra U., 1963; M.F.A., Yale, 1966. Profl. actress appearing at Court Theatre, Woodstock Theatre, Orleans Arena Theatre, Off-Broadway showcases; resident artistic dir. Meadowbrook Repertory Theatre, Hempstead, N.Y., 1968-69; faculty theatre Hofstra U., Hempstead, 1967—, asst. prof. Hofstra U., 1974—; asst. prof. Purdue U., 1973-74; dir. USO Tour Far East Command, 1965; radio and TV comml. work. Mem. Actor's Equity, Am. Theatre Assn., Am. Assn. U. Profs., A.F.T.R.A., Women's Polit. Caucus N.Y., Nat. Orgn. Women, Am. Assn. U. Women, Orgn. Women Profls. Hofstra U., Hofstra Alumni Theatre, Phi Beta, Alpha Psi Omega. Club: Hofstra Faculty Women's. Home: 408 Moriches Rd St James NY 11780 Office: Drama Dept Hofstra U Hempstead NY 11550

SICKAFUS, RUTH FIELDS (MRS. CHARLES R. SICKAFUS), mus. adminstr.; b. Grayson, Ky., Sept. 7, 1925; d. Austin and Stella (May) Fields; A.B. magna cum laude, Morehead State U., 1946; m. Charles R. Sickafus, Aug. 21, 1946. Asst. to dean Morehead State U., Ky., 1946-48; sec. to gen. traffic mgr., Mountain States Tel. & Tel. Co., Denver, 1948-51; adminstrv. sec. to exec. v.p. Pa. Tire Mfg. Co., Mansfield, O., 1951-56; music programming WGMS and WMAL-FM, Washington, 1960-68; exec. dir. People-to-People Music Com., Inc., Washington, 1960—; asst. dir. Nat. Opera Inst., 1971—. Mem. com. on internat. music relations and music UNESCO. Bd. dirs. People-to-People, Inc., Kansas City, Mo., 1967—, Nat. Oratoria Soc., Washington, 1962-65. Mem. Nat. Music Council, Sigma Alpha Iota. Presbyn. Home: 712 Auburn Av Takoma Park MD 20012 Office: John F Kennedy Center Washington DC 20566

SICKELS, DOROTHY JUDD (MRS. ROBERT SICKELS), editor; b. New Haven, Jan. 24, 1904; d. Charles Hubbard and Ella (LeCompte) Judd; student U. Chgo., 1920-22; B.A., Vassar Coll., 1924; m. Robert Sickels, Aug. 29, 1927; children—Jane (Mrs. Martin Jorgensen), Robert Judd. Editor, U. Chgo. Press., 1924-25, Macmillan Co., N.Y.C., 1925-27; univ. editor Syracuse U., 1953-59, dir. publs. Utica Coll., 1961-67; univ. editor Colgate U., Hamilton, N.Y., 1968-69; publs. editor Policy Inst., Syracuse U. Research Corp., N.Y., 1969-72; freelance editor, 1972—. Cons., Bowling Green U., 1967. Episcopalian. Author: Eskimos, Hunters of the Arctic, 1940; Indians, Hunters of the Plains, 1940; Travel by Land, 1940; Travel by Water, 1940; Travel by Air, 1940; Riding the Air, 1943. Home: 13 John St Hamilton NY 13346

SICKINGER, SELMA BRECHER (MRS. ROBERT SICKINGER), theater adminstr.; b. Phila., Nov. 29, 1932; d. Harry and Rose (Mankin) Brecher; student Tyler Art Sch., Temple U., 1952; m. Robert Sickinger, Aug. 31, 1955; children—Denise, Robin, Robert. Prodn. and costume asst. Circle in the City, Phila., 1954; costume designer, tchr., asst. dir. Phila. Civic Theater, 1955-56; dir., costume designer, drama coach, head drama edn. Children's Theater, Hull House Theater, Chgo., 1963—, head prodn., 1964—. Club: Arts (Chgo.). Home: 503 Aldine Chicago IL 60657 Office: 3213 N Broadway Chicago IL 60657

SICOTTE, GRACE DARLENE DEMENT (MRS. ALBERT EDWARD SICOTTE), assn. exec.; b. Livingston, Mont., Nov. 17, 1922; d. Randolf and Dollie Mae Butler (Clauson) Dement; student U. Portland, 1973; m. Albert Edward Sicotte, Jan. 24, 1939; children—Joseph Edward, Nancy Darlene (Mrs. Frank Cassidy), Charles David. Reporter Butte (Mont.) Credit, 1953; asst. mgr. Nat. Loan Co., Butte, 1954; credit mgr. Phil Judd Sporting Goods Store, Butte, 1954-61; sec. Operating Engrs. Union #378, Butte, 1961-67; credit mgr., office personnel Buttreys Dept. Store, Butte, 1968-69; dir. of spa, YMCA, Butte, 1969—. Fitness Finders instr., Butte, 1972-74; phys. fitness examiner; Red Cross and emergency med. tech. Mem. Nat. Secs. Assn. (pres. 1969-71, Sec. of Year 1971), Bus. and Profl. Women's Club (corr. sec. 1971-72), Christian Womens Assn. Elk. Home: 1937 Florida St Butte MT 59701 Office: YMCA 405 W Park St Butte MT 59701

SIDAMON-ERISTOFF, ANNE PHIPPS (MRS. CONSTANTINE SIDAMON-ERISTOFF), museum ofcl.; b. Sept. 12, 1932; d. Howard and Harriet Dyer (Price) Phipps; B.A., Bryn Mawr Coll., 1954; m. Constantine Sidamon-Eristoff, 1957; children—Elizabeth, Simon, Andrew. Asst. librarian Conservation Found., 1954-55; v.p. Am. Mus. Natural History, N.Y.C., 1974—, also trustee, chmn. exhbn. com., mem. Women's com., Vol. com. Bd. dirs. St. Bernard's Sch., The Conservation Found., Highland Falls (N.Y.) Pub. Library. Mem. Hudson River Environmental Soc. (dir.). Address: American Museum of Natural History 79th St and Central Park West New York City NY 10024

SIDENER, VICTORIA IRENE TUNSTALL, mus. curator; b. Santa Rosa, Cal., Oct. 13, 1931; d. Morgan Clay and Dorothy Winifred (Lacey) Tunstall; grad. high sch.; m. Gene Harold Sidener, May 10, 1968; children—John, Barbara, Victoria. Supr. traffic div. Municipal Ct., San Bernardino, Cal., 1961-63; clk. Superior Ct., San Bernardino, 1963-69; curator, Jackson Hole Hist. Mus., Jackson, Wyo., 1970—. Active P.T.A., Boy Scouts Am., Girl Scouts Am. Mem. Pink Garter Plaza Merchants Assn. (pres. 1973-74). Mem. Order Eastern Star. Club: Soroptimist (publicity chmn. 1973-74, dir. 1974-75). Home: PO Box 1821 Jackson WY 83001

SIDERITS, MARY ANNE TERESA, psychologist, educator; b. Milw., Mar. 28, 1936; d. Edward Louis and Anna (Gmoser) Siderits; A.B. summa cum laude, Marquette U., 1957; A.M., U. Mich., 1958, Ph.D., 1966. Intern psychology service, dept. pediatrics, U. Mich., 1959-60; asst. in psychology Children's Psychiat. Hosp., Ann Arbor, Mich., 1960-61; instr. Marquette U., Milw., 1961-66, asst. prof. psychology, 1966—, clin. psychologist, 1961—, asso. dir. Center for Psychol. Services, 1970—. Individual practice clin. psychology, Milw., 1967—. Mem. Am., Wis. (corr. sec. 1972-73, corr. sec.-treas. 1973-74), Milwaukee County (treas. 1968-70, pres. 1971-72) psychol. assns., Am. Assn. U. Profs. (chpt. sec. 1964-65, 66-67, pres. 1973—), Delta Zeta. Home: 9324 W Keefe Av Milwaukee WI 53222 Office: 617 N 13th St Milwaukee WI 53233

SIDES, PATRICIA ANN, producer; b. Pendayia, Cyprus; d. Claude Emerson and Dorothy (Smith) S.; B.A., Pomona Coll.; postgrad. Stanford, Universita Di Firenze, Italy. Researcher ABC TV, N.Y.C., 1962-64, asso. producer, 1964-68, producer-writer, 1970—; asso. producer/writer John H. Secondari Prodns., N.Y.C., 1968-70; formerly journalist, San Francisco Chronicle; formerly publicity dir. Council Student Travel, N.Y.C. Mem. Americans for Democratic Action, Am. Civil Liberties Union, Writers Guild Am., Am. Women in Radio and Television, Nat. Orgn. for Women. Home: 53 E 67th St New York City NY 10021

SIDHU, NANCY CHADWICK DAYTON (MRS. VICTOR S. SIDHU), educator; b. Evanston, Ill., Sept. 2, 1941; d. Ward Winchell and Elizabeth Kendall (Larcom) Dayton; student Smith Coll., 1959-61, Northwestern U., 1961-62; B.A., U. Ill., 1963, M.S. (Univ. fellow 1965), 1965, Ph.D. (NDEA Title IV fellow 1965-68), 1971; m. Victor S. Sidhu, 1962; 1 dau., Mary Chadwick. Mem. faculty Northeastern Ill. U., Chgo., 1968—, asst. prof. econs., 1968-73, asso. prof. econs., 1973—. Vice pres., chief economist, dir. RMI Corp., Winnetka, Ill., 1970—. Recipient Dissertation award Nat. Tax Assn., 1971. Mem. Am. Econs. Assn., Am. Statis. Assn., Nat. Tax Assn., Econometric Soc. Contbr. articles to profl. jours. Home: 580 Vernon Av Glencoe IL 60022 Office: Northeastern Ill U 5500 N St Louis Av Chicago IL 60625

SIDNEY, ARLENE MISKIN JASSENOFF, personnel exec.; b. Phila., Apr. 9, 1936; d. Herman and Sonia (Packer) Jassenoff; student June McAdams Modeling and Finishing Sch., 1951-52, Camden County Coll., 1973; children—Barry M. Miskin, Steven R. Miskin. Asst. personnel mgr. Ultronics Systems, Mt. Laurel, N.J., 1963-66; owner, Sidney-Evans Personnel Assos., Cherry Hill, N.J., 1966-71; personnel dir. Elkins-Sinn, Inc., Cherry Hill, 1971—. Active United Fund. Bd. dirs. Vets. Job Opportunity Fair, 1971. Mem. Nat. (dir. 1966-71), N.J. State employment assns., South Jersey Mfrs. Assn., South Jersey Mfrs. Assn. Personnel Group. Home: 117 Watergate Condominiums Maple Shade NJ 08052 Office: 2 Esterbrook Lane Cherry Hill NJ 08002

SIEBERT, EVELYN MARIE KANNEL (MRS. VIRGIL J. SIEBERT), librarian; b. Akron, O., Aug. 7, 1916; d. Emmet Franklyn and Julia Veronica (McGuigan) Kannel; B.A., Akron State U., 1939; M.L.S., Western Res. U., 1940; m. Virgil J. Siebert, Sept. 8, 1939; children—John, Thomas, Keith and Craig (twins). Children's librarian Cleve. Pub. Library, 1940-43, sch. librarian curriculum center, 1941-42; sch. librarian Lakewood (O.) Pub. Library, 1961-62, Vermilion (O.) pub. schs., 1962-72; librarian head Vermilion Pub. Library, 1973—. Mem. Am., Ohio library assns., Ohio Sch. Librarians Assn. Club: College of Vermilion. Home: 5331 Portage Dr Vermilion OH 44089 Office: 5680 Liberty Av Vermilion OH 44089

SIEBERT, MARILYN ANNE, editor; b. Dayton, O., Aug. 12, 1936; d. Richard W. and Marie Agnes (Schoening) Siebert; B.A., U. Minn., 1959. Advt. copywriter Gamble-Skogmo, Inc., Mpls., 1959-61; editor, pub. Mpls. Athletic Club Gopher Mag., Mpls., 1961—. Home: 2438 Grand Av S Minneapolis MN 55405 Office: 615 2d Av S Minneapolis MN 55402

SIEBERT, MURIEL, securities analyst; b. Cleve.; d. Irwin J. and Margaret (Roseman) Siebert; student Western Res. U., 1946-50. Security analyst Bache & Co., 1954-57; analyst Utilities & Industries Mgmt. Corp., 1958, Shields & Co., 1959-60; partner Stearns & Co., 1961, Finkle & Co., 1962-65, Brimberg & Co., N.Y.C., 1965-67; pres. Muriel Siebert & Co., Inc., mems. N.Y. Stock Exchange, 1969—; individual mem. N.Y. Stock Exchange, 1968—. Asso. in mgmt. Simmons Coll. Mem. N.Y. Soc. Security Analysts, Money Marketeers N.Y.U. (gov.), Airline Analysts Soc., Sales Execs. Club (v.p., dir.). Clubs: Wings (dir.), Westchester Country, El Morrocco. Home: 60 Sutton Pl S New York City NY 10022 Office: 280 Park Av New York City NY 10017

SIEBERT, WENDY LOEBBAKA, data processor; b. Chgo., Dec. 14, 1942; d. Harold J. and Beatrice M. (Jebavy) Loebbaka; student, Ill. Inst. Tech., 1960-62; student, Bradley U., 1963-65. Programmer, Western Electric Corp., Chgo., 1965-67; system analyst Westinghouse Electric, Chgo., 1969-71; systems analyst Midas Internat. Corp., Chgo., 1971—. Mem. Data Processing Mgmt. Assn. (v.p. 1973—). Office: 3949 S Keeler Chicago IL 60632

SIEGEL, ALBERTA ENGVALL (MRS. SIDNEY SIEGEL), research psychologist, educator; b. Pasadena, Cal., Feb. 24, 1931; d. Albert and Portia (Powers) Engvall; B.A., Stanford, 1951, M.A., 1954, Ph.D., 1955; m. Sidney Siegel, July 31, 1954 (dec. 1961). Mem. faculty Pa. State U., 1955-61; fellow Center Advanced Study Behavioral Scis., 1961-63; faculty Stanford U., 1963—, prof. psychology in psychiatry, 1969—. Cons., mem. growth and devel. research and tng. com., Nat. Inst. Child Health and Human Devel., 1972—; cons., Nat. Inst. Mental Health, also mem. com. research scientist tng. 1965-69; mem. sci. adv. com. on TV and social behavior U.S. Surgeon Gen., 1969-72; mem. com. on child devel. and early edn. Ednl. Testing Service, Princeton, N.J., 1973—; mem. adv. com. on ethical and human value implications of sci. and tech. NSF, 1973—. Fellow Am. Psychol. Assn. (pres. div. developmental psychology 1973), Center Advanced Study Behavioral Scis.; mem. Soc. Research Child Devel., Phi Beta Kappa, Sigma Xi. Democrat. Club: Stanford University Faculty (pres. 1973-74). Editor: Child Development, 1964-68. Home: 1850 Willow Rd Palo Alto CA 94304 Office: Dept Psychiatry Sch Medicine Stanford U Stanford CA 94305

SIEGEL, BETTY LENTZ (MRS. JOEL HERBERT SIEGEL), educator; b. Cumberland, Ky., Jan. 24, 1931; d. Carl Nickolas and Vera (Hogg) Lentz; A.A., Cumberland Jr. Coll., 1950; B.A., Wake Forest Coll., 1952; M.Ed., U. N.C., 1953; Ph.D., Fla. State U., 1961; postgrad. Ind. U., 1964-66; m. Joel Herbert Siegel, June 6, 1965; children—David Jonathan, Michael Jeremy. Instr. psychology A.L. Brown High Sch., Kannapolis, N.C., 1953-56; asso. prof. psychology and edn. Lenoir Rhyne Coll., Hickory, N.C., 1956-64; vis. prof. edn. Ind. U., Bloomington, 1964-66; prof. psychol. founds. U. Fla., Gainesville, 1967—, dean acad. affairs, 1972—; individual practice child psychology, Bloomington, Ind., 1966-67. Cons. in edn., 1967—. Co-dir. Noyes Found. Fellowship Grant for Humanistic Processes in Edn., 1971-74. Recipient teaching award Standard Oil Co., 1969. Mem. Inst. Devel. of Human Resources, Center for Humanistic Edn., Am. Psychol. Assn., Assn. Supervision and Curriculum Devel., Am. Ednl. Research Assn., Soc. Research Child Devel., Pi Lambda Theta. Author: (with others) Problem Situations in Teaching, 1971. Home: 2280 NW 21st St Gainesville FL 32601

SIEGEL, CAROLE ETHEL (MRS. BERTRAM SIEGEL), mathematician; b. N.Y.C., Sept. 29, 1936; d. David and Helen (Mayer) Schore; M.S., N.Y. U., 1959, Ph.D., 1963; m. Bertram Siegel, Aug. 18, 1957; children—David, Sharon. Research asst. Courant Inst. Math. Sci., N.Y. U., 1959-63, univ. research scientist, 1963-64; research mathematician Rockland Research Center, Orangeburg, N.Y., 1965—. Prin. investigator Nat. Inst. Mental Health Evaluation Contract, 1973 adj. asst. prof. N.Y. U., 1965-68, 69; adj. prof. Fairleigh Dickinson U., Teaneck, N.J., 1968. Mem. Inst. Math. Statistics, Assn. Women Math., Phi Beta Kappa, Pi Mu Epsilon. Contbr. articles to profl. jours. Home: 1304 Colonial Ct Mamaroneck NY 10543 Office: Rockland Research Center Orangeburg NY 10962

SIEGEL, DORIS, author; b. N.Y.C.; d. Russell E. and Cora G. (Davis) Taylor; B.A., U. Cal. at Los Angeles; m. William E. Siegel, Dec. 31, 1932; 1 son, Richard Taylor. Author (under pen name Susan Wells) Murder Is Not Enough, Footsteps in the Air, Death Is My Name, The Witches Pond; (under own name) How Still My Love, 1957. Docent Los Angeles County Mus. Art; women's com. So. Cal. Symphony Assn.; costume council Los Angeles County Mus. Art; mem. dean's council Coll. Fine Arts U. Cal. at Los Angeles; trustee U. Cal. at Los Angeles Found. Mem. Colonial Order Crown, Nat. Soc. Magna Charta Dames, Colonial Dames 17th Century (past chpt. pres.; nat. chmn. def. programs 1969-72), Los Angeles World Affairs Council, Friends Huntington Library, Sovereign Colonial Soc. Ams. Royal Descent, Le Salon Francais, Cal. Writers Guild, Los Angeles County Mus. Alliance, Alumni Assn. U. Cal. Los Angeles, Friends Flintridge Library, Affiliated U. Cal. Los Angeles, Las Hermanas Guild Childrens Hosp. Soc., Chi Omega, Chi Delta Phi. Clubs: Bel-Air; Founders (U. Cal. at Los Angeles); Los Angeles Country. Home: 1520 San Remo Dr Pacific Palisades CA 90272

SIEGEL, MARGOT MARJORIE (MRS. HAROLD SIEGEL), pub. relations exec.; b. St. Paul, Apr. 2, 1923; d. William and Jeanne (Braunschweig) Auerbacher; B.A., U. Minn., 1944; m. Harold Siegel, Oct. 26, 1956; children—William Joseph, Sandra Marguerite. Editor, corr. Fairchild Publs., N.Y.C., also Europe, 1946-60; pub. relations dir. Walker Art Center, Mpls., 1962-66; free lance book reviewer, travel writer Mpls. Star and Tribune, 1969-72; partner Siegel-Hogan Enterprise, Mpls., 1970—. Mem. Mpls. Fashion Group (dir. 1967-68), Women in Communications, Pub. Relations Soc. Am., U. Minn. Alumni Assn. (dir.), Overseas Press Club Am., Minn. Press Club. Author: Look Forward to a Career: Fashion, 1970. Home: 25 Park Lane Minneapolis MN 55416 Office: 920 Nicollet Mall Minneapolis MN 55402

SIEGEL, SHIRLEY ADELSON (MRS. ELWOOD SIEGEL), lawyer; b. N.Y.C., July 3, 1918; d. Henry and Rose (Zagor) Adelson; B.A., Barnard Coll., 1937; student fellow London Sch. Econs., 1937-38; LL.B., Yale, 1941; m. Elwood Siegel, Sept. 22, 1946; children—Eric David, Ann Barbara. Admitted to N.Y. bar, 1942, Cal. bar, 1947, U.S. Supreme Ct., 1963; asso. firm Proskauer, Rose, Goetz & Mendelsohn, 1941-45, 51-52, Tannenbaum, Steinberg & Shearer, 1948-50, Rosenman Goldmark, Colin & Kaye, 1954-59; asst. atty. gen. State N.Y. charge Civil Rights Bur., 1959-66; legal cons. Park, Recreation and Open Space Project of N.J., N.Y., Conn. met. region, 1958-59; instr. city and regional planning dept. Mass. Inst. Tech., 1961-62; asst. adminstr., gen. counsel N.Y.C. Housing and Devel. Adminstrn., 1966-72; gen. counsel N.Y.C. Housing Devel. Corp., 1972-73; asst. atty. gen. N.Y. State Appeals div., 1973—; lectr. law Columbia U., 1971. Exec. dir. Citizens Housing & Planning Council N.Y., 1945; asso. counsel, commn. law and social action Am. Jewish Congress, 1946; exec. dir. Los Angeles Citizens Housing Council, 1946-48; cons. housing and city planning sect. UN, 1953; asso. counsel Temporary Commn. on Cts., N.Y. State, 1953; mem. housing adv. council and Manhattan Council, N.Y. State Commn. Against Discrimination 1956-59; mem. Community Planning Bd. Number 7, N.Y.C.; mem. exec. com. Am. Jewish Com., Los Angeles, 1949-50, N.Y.C., 1967—; mem. bd. dirs. and housing chmn. Cal. Fedn. Civic Unity, 1949-50, Los Angeles County Conf. Community Relations, 1948-50. Bd. dirs. Community Action for Legal Services, 1973. Named Woman of Year, Mademoiselle Mag., 1947. Mem. Am. Civil Liberties Union (dir. N.Y.C., 1943-46), Assn. Bar City N.Y. (chmn. housing and urban devel. com. 1974—), N.Y. County Lawyers' Assn., Regional Plan Assn., League Women Voters, Am., Cal. bar assns., League Women Voters Los Angeles (legislative chmn. 1948-49), Women's City Club N.Y., Barnard Coll. Alumnae Assn. (dir. 1965-68), Yale Law Sch. Assn. (exec. com.), Phi Beta Kappa. Democrat. Author: Better Housing for Everyone, 1954; (with other) Toward City Conservation, 1959; The Law of Open Space, 1960; also law rev. articles. Editor: Yale Law Jour., 1939-41. Home: 317 W 89th St New York City NY 10024 Office: 2 World Trade Center New York City NY 10047

SIEGFRIEDT, SARAJANE, journalist; b. Rapid City, S.D., Apr. 20, 1949; d. Edgar Frederick and Joan (Eames) Siegfriedt; B.S., Northwestern U., 1971; postgrad. Center Photog. Studies, Louisville, 1971. Staff writer Cooper & Golin, Inc., Chgo., 1971-72; copy editor Sphere The Betty Crocker Mag., Chgo., 1972-73; pub. relations writer Playboy Enterprises, Inc., Chgo., 1973-74; pub. relations writer CNA/Ins., Chgo., 1974—. Mem. Women in Communications, Northwestern U. Young Alumni Council (pub. relations chmn. 1971-72), Sierra Club, Phi Beta Phi. Clubs: Lake Shore Ski (dir., mng. editor 1973-74, ski master 1974-75) (Chgo.); Winnetka Yacht Thistle Fleet; Canyon; Cycle Paths. Home: 444 W Belmont Av Chicago IL 60657 Office: CNA Plaza Chicago IL 60685

SIEGLER, CAROL ANN (MRS. GEROLD SIEGLER), mfg. co. exec.; b. Chgo., May 7, 1937; d. Jack M. and Fannie (Plonsky) Zuckerberg; B.S., U. Ill., 1958; m. Gerold Siegler, Dec. 16, 1962; children—Joel Phillip, Jennifer Ellen. Counselor, trainer Lynn Davis Employment Service, Inc., Chgo., 1958-66; partner, sec., treas. J. Phillip Industries, Inc., Chgo., 1969—. Office: 5707 Northwest Hwy Chicago IL 60646

SIEH, NANCY MANNERS (MRS. FRANK OSBORNE SIEH), lawyer; b. N.Y.C., Jan. 14, 1947; d. George and Nancy T. (Marasa) Manners; B.A., U. Cal. at Santa Barbara, 1968; J.D., U. Cal. at Davis, 1971; m. Frank Osborne Sieh, June 3, 1972. Admitted to Cal. bar, 1972; partner Everhart & Sieh, Oxnard, Cal. Mem. State Bar Cal., Ventura County Bar Assn., Phi Beta Kappa, Phi Sigma Alpha. Home: 349 Agnus Dr Ventura CA 93003 Office: 501 Poli St Ventura CA 93003

SIEMS, CHRISTA MARTHA, steel co. exec.; b. Uelzen, Germany, June 18, 1934; d. Erich and Else (Lilje) Siems; ed. schs. in Germany. Came to U.S., 1963, naturalized, 1970. Apprentice, Schuhhaus Hoeber, Uelzen, 1950-54; trainee Schuh Schulze, Bueckeburg, Germany, 1954-55; buyer Carl Deckert Co., Goslar/Harz, Germany, 1955-58, Eng., 58-60; sec. Hammer Dental Depot, Goettingen, Germany, 1960-61, Farbwerke Hoechst AG, Hoechst, Germany, 1961-63; with Oetiker, Inc., Livingston, N.J., 1963—, treas., 1969—, also dir.; dir. Oetiker Ltd., Downsview, Ont., Can. Mem. Nat. Right to Work, Animal Protection Inst. Home: 121 River Rd East Hanover NJ 07936 Office: 71 Okner Pkwy Livingston NJ 07039

SIEMS, MARGARET VANCE, physician; b. Fort Valley, Ga., Jan. 16, 1922; d. Charles Sewell and Helen (Floyd) Vance; B.S., U. Ga., 1942; M.D., Med. Coll. Ga., 1945; m. Lawrence Littig Siems, Aug. 1, 1953; children—Margaret Ann, Mark. Intern, St. Louis City Hosp., 1945-46; resident Cin. Gen. Hosp., 1946-47, Alexandria (Va.) Hosp., 1949-50; fellow internal medicine Univ. Hosp., Iowa City, Ia., 1950-51, instr. internal medicine, 1953-54; practice medicine specializing in internal medicine, San Diego, Cal., 1954-60; med. cons. San Diego Community Mental Health Services, 1970—. Diplomate Am. Bd. Internal Medicine. Mem. Phi Beta Kappa. Roman Catholic. Home: 8021 LaJolla Scenic Dr La Jolla CA 92037 Office: 345 W Dickinson St San Diego CA 92103

SIEVING, SHERRI LYNNE, television exec.; b. St. Louis, Dec. 16, 1942; d. Frederick Ralph and Dorothy Francis (Winkler) Sieving; B.J., U. Mo., 1964, postgrad., 1964-67. Dir., news producer, traffic mgr. TV sta. KOMU-TV, Columbia, Mo., 1963-67; woman's program mgr. radio sta. KFRU, 1964-67; asst. advt. and sales promotion mgr. WBZ-TV, Boston, 1967-69; advt. and sales promotion mgr. WJZ-TV, Balt., 1969-73; account exec. KDKA-TV, Pitts., 1973—; Instr. radio and TV prodn. U. Mo., 1964-66. Mem. Broadcast Promotion Assn. Home: 1060 Pennsbury Blvd N Pittsburgh PA 15205 Office: KDKA-TV One Gateway Center Pittsburgh PA 15222

SIGEL, FREDERICA EVAN (MRS. EFREM JOEL SIGEL), pub. co. exec.; b. Boston, May 21, 1945; d. Leon and Emma Ruth (Alper) Evan; B.A. in English, U. Mich., 1967; M.A. in English, Tufts U., 1971; m. Efrem Joel Sigel, June 7, 1968. Editorial asst. Beacon Press, Boston, 1967-68; writer, editor Arthur Fommer, Inc., N.Y.C., 1968-69; mng. editor Bartholomew House, N.Y.C., 1970-71; head promotion dept. Lenox Hill Pub., N.Y.C., 1971—. Author: Arthur Frommer's European Almanac, 1969. Home: 126 Franklin Av New Rochelle NY 10805 Office: Lenox Hill Pub 235 E 44th St New York City NY 10017

SIGMAN, BERNICE, pediatrician; b. Balt., June 11, 1936; d. Edward Isaac and Anna Frieda (Green) Sigman; student U. Va., 1956; M.D., U. Md., 1960; M.S., U. Wash., 1967. Intern U. Md., Balt., 1960-61, resident dept. pediatrics, 1961-63, chief resident dept. pediatrics, 1963-64, now mem. staff; fellow med. genetics U. Wash., Seattle, 1964-66; cons. Children's Orthopedic Hosp., Seattle, 1964-66; asst. prof. pediatrics U. Md. Sch. Medicine, Balt., 1966—, asst. dean student affairs, 1971—; practice medicine specializing in pediatrics, Balt., 1966—; mem. staff Kernan's Hosp., Balt., Union Meml. Hosp., Balt. Diplomate Am. Bd. Pediatrics. Home: 1111 Park Av Baltimore MD 21201 Office: U Md Sch Medicine Baltimore MD 21201

SIGNOR, ESTEL LUANN TERRILL, mag. editor, journalist; b. Los Angeles, Oct. 21, 1925; d. Elmer L. and Stella L. (Schellenger) Terrill; student pub., pvt. schs.; m. Robert Signor, Sept. 22, 1945 (div. Sept. 1959); children—John R., Carol Ann. Writer (under name Ann Terrill) articles for nat. travel, religious, hist. mags. including The Freeman, Together, Signs of the Times, Dodge News, Nat. Motorist, Guideposts; mag. editor The Register, Santa Ana, Cal., 1960—, finance editor, 1960-63. Cons., lectr. various local groups. Co-founder Orange County chpt. women's div. Freedoms Found. at Valley Forge, 1967, v.p. ednl. affairs, 1967-70, 1st v.p. 1971-72; active various cultural groups including Orange County Symphony Assn., Orange County Cultural Arts Assn. Active Los Angeles County Rep. party; mem. Orange County Rep. Women. Recipient awards Cal. Press Women, 1971, Pacific Area Travel Assn., 1972; Nat. Honor certificate Freedoms Found. at Valley Forge, 1974. Mem. Cal. Press Women, Cal. Writers Guild. Office: The Register Box 11626 Santa Ana CA 92711

SIGNORET, SIMONE (SIMONE-HENRIETTE-CHARLOTTE KAMINKER), actress; b. Wiesbaden, Germany, Mar. 25, 1921; d. Andre and Georgette (Signoret) Kaminker; ed. schs. in Paris; m. Yves Allegret, 1947 (div.); 1 dau., Catherine; m. 2d, Yves Montand, June 15, 1950. Tutor, English and Latin, Paris; typist for newspaper Le Nouveau Temps; appeared in motion picture Des Demons d'i'Aube, 1946, other roles in Dedee d'Anvers, La Ronde, 1950, Therese Raguin, 1953, La mort en ce jardin, Diabolique, 1955, Les Sorcieres de Salem (with husband in play version Paris stage, 1954), 1958, Room at the Top, 1958; TV acting debut in Don't You Remember, Gen. Electric Theater, 1960. Recipient Prix Suzanne Blanchetti for performance in Macadam, 1946, Prix feminin du Cinema, 1952, Grand Prix d'Interpretation feminine de l'Academla du Cinema, 1953; Brit. Film Acad. award for performance as queen of Apaches in Casque d'Dr, 1951; Best Actress award Brit. Film Acad. and Cannes Film Festival, 1959; prize as best fgn. actress German Film Critics, 1959; Acad. Award for best actress of 1959. Home: 15 Place Dauphine Paris ler France

SIGOLOFF, VIOLET PAULINE BRUCE (MRS. SAMUEL SIGOLOFF), artist; b. Huntington, W.Va.; d. Rufus Otho and Rachel (Witt) Bruce; student Huntington Coll., Trinity U., 1964-65; studied with portrait artist David Philip Wilson, 1963-64; m. Samuel Sigoloff, Oct. 20, 1945; children—Bruce Myron, Nelson Witt. Owner, Wonderland Gallery, 1966—, Sigoloff Fine Art Gallery, San Antonio, 1972—; exhibited one-man shows St. Mary's U., 1966, Southwestern Fine Arts Inst., U. Tex., 1967, HemisFair, 1968, Trinity U., 1968; exhibited in groups shows at River Art, 1964-68, San Antonio Art League, 1964-70; represented in pvt. collections. Chmn. edn. for family living P.T.A., 1962, v.p., 1964-65; art judge Hallmark Contest, 1969. Recipient 1st Pl. award in miniatures Composers Authors and Artists Am. Nat. Exhibit, N.Y.C., 1965; named San Antonio's Outstanding Woman in Art, San Antonio Express and San Antonio Evening News, 1967. Mem. Tex. Fine Art Assn., San Antonio Art League, San Antonio River Art Group. Clubs: Acacia (pres. 1961, 64), Zonta (San Antonio). Home: 8410 Tiffany Dr San Antonio TX 78230 Office: Sigoloff Gallery San Anthony Hotel San Antonio TX 78205

SIKKEMA, MILDRED, social work educator; b. Garden Plain, Ill.; d. J. W. and Elizabeth (Van den Berg) Sikkema; B.S., U. Chgo., 1937, Ph.D., 1964; M.S.S., Smith Coll., 1939. Social worker Child Guidance Clinic, Wilkes Barre, Pa., 1939-40; supr. Children's Aid Soc., Phila., 1940-44; supr. social service dept. Queen's Hosp., Honolulu, 1944-45; asst. dir. Pupil Personnel dept. Hawaii Territorial Dept. Pub. Instrn., 1945-47; exec. sec. Nat. Assn. Sch. Social Workers, N.Y.C., 1947-51; supr., cons. Balt. City Schs., 1951-52; prof. social work U. Hawaii, Honolulu, 1952-54; cons. ednl. standards Council on Social Work Edn., N.Y.C., 1954-68; prof. Sch. Social Work, U. Hawaii, Honolulu, 1968—; instr. Queen's Hosp. Sch. Nursing, Honolulu, 1944-45. Mem. Nat. Assn. Social Workers, Nat. Conf. Social Welfare, Internat. Conf. Social Work, Am. Pub. Welfare Assn. Author: Report of a Study of School Social Work Practice in Twelve Communities, 1953. Editor: Field Learning and Teaching: Explorations in Graduate Social Work Education, 1968. Home: 326 Halaki St Honolulu HI 96821

SIKKEMA, STELLA HAZEN (MRS. JOHN SIKKEMA), physician; b. Rudyard, Mich., Dec. 1, 1913; d. Sibley Orrin and Sadie Belle (Pennington) Hazen; B.S., Mich. State Coll., 1936; M.D., U. Mich., 1941; m. John Sikkema, Sept. 11, 1938; children—Bruce Hazen, Carol Louise. Rotating intern Wis. Gen. Hosp., Madison, 1941-42, resident internal medicine, 1942-45, instr. internal medicine, 1945-46; staff physician U. Colo. student health service, Boulder, 1946-50; staff internist univ. health service U. Minn., Mpls., 1950—. Diplomate Am. Bd. Internal Medicine. Fellow A.C.P.; mem. Minn., Mpls. socs. internal medicine, Minn. Heart Assn., Twin Cities Diabetes Assn., Alpha Epsilon Iota. Home: 3941 40 Av S Minneapolis MN 55406 Office: Univ Health Service U Minn Minneapolis MN 55455

SIKORSKI, HELEN FRANCES, physician; b. Cheektowaga, N.Y., Mar. 1, 1926; d. Frank Joseph and Helen Mary (Szymanski) Sikorski; student U. Buffalo, 1944-46, M.D., 1950; div.; children—Mary Ann, Camille Hemlock. Intern, Deaconess Hosp., Buffalo, 1950-51, resident, 1951-52; gen. practice medicine, Buffalo, 1952-55, West Seneca, N.Y., 1955—; mem. active staff Mercy Hosp., Buffalo; teaching preceptorship U. Buffalo Med. Sch., 1970—. Named Woman of Year, Nat. Med. and Dental Assn., 1968. Fellow Am. Acad. Family Physicians; mem. Nat. Med. and Dental Assn. (pres. 1968), Multiple Sclerosis Assn. (adv. 1968-72), Western N.Y. Heart Assn., Erie County Gen. Practitioners (membership com. 1967-68), A.M.A. (Physicians recognition award 1972), N.Y. State, Erie County med. socs., Am. Acad. Gen. Practice, Women's Med. Soc. N.Y., Med. Arts. Soc., Profl. Businessmen's Assn. Home: 65 Boynton Av Buffalo NY 14206

SILAGI, SELMA, research scientist, educator; b. Montreal, Que., Can., Sept. 5, 1916; d. Israel Jacob and Anna (Dorinson) Epstein; B.A. magna cum laude, Hunter Coll., 1936; M.A., Columbia, 1938, Ph.D. (USPHS fellow), 1961; m. Robert Silagi, Nov. 26, 1936; children—Daniel, Laura (Mrs. Michael Weinraub). Tchr. biology N.Y.C. Pub. Schs., 1938-43, 46-50, 52-56; lectr. Queens Coll., 1956-59; research asso. Rockefeller U., 1962-65; asst. prof. Cornell U. Med. Sch., 1965-70, asso. prof. genetics in obstetrics and gynecology, 1970-74, prof., 1974—. Pres., Queensview Summer Playsch., Inc., 1950-52. USPHS pre and postdoctoral fellow, 1959-62; Am. Cancer Soc., Damon Runyon Meml. Fund, NIH grantee. Mem. Hunter Coll. Hall of Fame. Mem. Am. Soc. Cell Biology, Genetics Soc. Am., Soc. Developmental Biology, Harvey Soc., A.A.A.S., Phi Beta Kappa, Sigma Xi. Contbr. articles to profl. jours. Home: 21-36 33d Rd Long Island City NY 11106 Office: Cornell U Med Center 1300 York Av New York City NY 10021

SILBERBERG, INGA (MRS. HERBERT M. SINAKIN), dermatologist; b. Kassel, Germany, Sept. 16, 1934 (came to U.S. 1938, naturalized 1944); d. Willi and Erna (Rosenbaum) Silberberg; B.A., Hunter Coll., 1955; M.D. (Jonas Salk scholar), State U. N.Y. Coll. Medicine at Bklyn., 1959; M.S. in Dermatology, N.Y. U., 1965; m. Herbert Morris Sinakin, Feb. 16, 1969; 1 son, William Elias. Intern Kings County Hosp. Center, Bklyn., 1959-60; resident N.Y. U. Postgrad. Med. Sch., N.Y.C., 1960-61, Bellevue Hosp., N.Y.C., 1961-62; fellow dept. pathology and dermatology N.Y. U. Med. Center, N.Y.C., USPHS research fellow, 1962-65; fellow dept. dermatology Wayne State U. Coll. Medicine, Detroit, 1965-66; practice medicine specializing in dermatology, N.Y.C., 1966-69, Jersey City, 1969—; asst. vis. physician dermatology service Bellevue Hosp. Center, 1963—; asst. dermatology service Univ. Hosp., N.Y.C., 1964—; instr. dept. dermatology N.Y. U., 1963-65, clin. asst. prof. dermatology, 1965-66, asst. prof., 1966, clin. asso. prof., 1971—. Recipient Henry Silver award Dermatologic Soc. Greater N.Y., 1962, 65. NIH grantee to study transepidermal absorption of mercury, 1968-71. Diplomate Am. Bd. Dermatology. Mem. Am. Fedn. Clin. Research, N.Y. Soc. Electron Microscopy, Electron Microscopy Soc. Am., Soc. Investigative Dermatology. Office: 2954 Kennedy Blvd Jersey City NJ 07306 also 566 1st Av New York City NY 10016

SILBERMAN, ARLENE PROPPER (MRS. CHARLES E. SILBERMAN), writer; b. N.Y.C., Apr. 30, 1929; d. Irving A. and Clarice (Rainess) Propper; B.A., Barnard Coll., 1949; M.A., Tchrs. Coll. Columbia; m. Charles E. Silberman, Sept. 12, 1948; children—David, Ricky, Jeff, Steve. Tchr., Riverdale Country Sch., N.Y.C., 1949-50, Baldwin (N.Y.) Pub. Schs., 1955-60; free-lance writer Readers Digest, Good Housekeeping, Ladies Home Jour., Redbook, Pageant, Women's Day, others, 1963—; chief research Carnegie Study of Edn. of Educators, N.Y.C., 1966-68, Study Law and Justice, Mt. Vernon, N.Y., 1972—. Cons. to various publs. schs., 1970—. Mem. Soc. Mag. Writers, Phi Beta Kappa. Home: 110 Stuyvesant Plaza Mount Vernon NY 10552 Office: 30 Park Av Mount Vernon NY 10550

SILBERSTEIN, MURIEL ROSOFF, educator; b. Bklyn.; d. Samuel and Mara (Elly) Rosoff; B.F.A., Carnegie Inst. Tech., 1944; m. Richard M. Silberstein, May 20, 1944; children—Wendy Alexandra, Jeffrey Scott, Charles Henry. Asst. tech. dir. Pitts. Playhouse, 1944-46; display artist interior display Gimbel's Dept. Store, Pitts., 1946-47; contract artist program drawings Phila. Symphony Children's Concerts, 1949; mem. staff, instr. children's art Inst. Modern Art, Mus. Modern Art, N.Y.C., 1963-73; art instr. Internat. Playgroups Art Workshops, Inc., 1970-73, art instr., cons. Met. Mus. Art, 1972-73; mem. staff Napeague Inst. Art, 1973—. Executed murals, other decorating projects, Mt. Sinai Hosp., Phila. Psychiat. Hosp., 1949-51; group exhbn. Keersage Group, Southhampton Coll., L.I., 1965; one woman show Panora's Gallery, N.Y.C., 1972. Art cons. S.I. Mental Health Soc. Family Holiday Fair, 1961—; chmn. art edn. Art Rental Gallery, S.I., N.Y. Mus. Arts and Scis., 1961-62; art cons. Head Start Sch., 1966—; art edn. cons. S.I. Community Coll.; program cons. Community Environments; instr. art S.I. Community Coll.; mem. N.Y.C. Art Commn., 1970—; mem. visual arts adv. com. to N.Y.C. Cultural Council. Founding mem. S.I. Children's Theater Assn., 1960—; vol. S.I. Mental Health Assn., 1952—; leader Borough of Richmond council Girl Scouts U.S.A., 1960-65; mem. Woman's Aux. to Richmond County Med. Soc., 1954—; mem. vis. com. to community programs Met. Mus. Art, 1971, co-chmn., 1972; mem. visual arts adv. com. N.Y.C. Cultural Council, 1972—; trustee, chmn. vis. com. 20th Century Art dept. Met. Mus. Art. Bd. dirs. Martin Luther King Heritage House, Napeague Inst. Art; Children's Museum, N.Y.C.; trustee Met. Mus. Art; bd. dirs. S.I. Council on Arts, 1972—, visual arts com., 1972—. Recipient Woman of Achievement award S.I. Advance, 1967; Achievement award Lambda Kappa Mu, 1972. Mem. Keersarge Painter's Group, Mortar Bd., Alpha Kappa Psi. Jewish religion. Clubs: Concordia (Pitts.); Richmond County Country (S.I.). Home: 427 E 74th St New York City NY 10021

SILBOWITZ, FREDA (MRS. MURRAY HERTZ), judge; b. N.Y.C., July 16, 1915; d. Benjamin and Yetta (Sklar) Silbowitz; B.A., Hunter Coll., 1935; LL.B., Columbia, 1938; m. Murray Hertz, July 3, 1950. Admitted to N.Y. bar, 1938; practiced in N.Y.C., 1938—; judge Civil Ct. City N.Y., 1973—. Mem. Internat. Women's Bar Assn., Nat. Assn. Women Lawyers, N.Y. Women's Bar Assn. (pres. 1963-64), N.Y. State Assn. Trial Lawyers, N.Y. County Lawyers Assn., Assn. Bar City N.Y., Phi Beta Kappa. Home: 1409 Albermarle Rd Brooklyn NY 11226 Office: 32 Broadway St New York City NY 10004

SILLERY, ROSEMARIE MADELEINE BEITZER (MRS. HAROLD G. SILLERY), home economist; b. N.Y.C., Mar. 29, 1935; d. William J. and Frances (Staniow) Beitzer; B.S., Seton Hill Coll., 1957; postgrad. N.Y. U., Los Angeles State Coll., Long Beach Coll., San Francisco Coll., Sonoma State Coll.; m. Harold G. Sillery, Mar. 11, 1960. Home econs. tchr. Los Angeles City Schs., 1957-58; recreation dir. U.S. Army Spl. Services, Germany, 1958-60; dir. home econs. La. Gas Service Co., Metarie, 1960-61; tchr. home econs. Whitter (Cal.) Schs., 1961-62; dir. Ankara (Turkey) USAF Recreation Center, 1963-64; fashion stylist Simplicity Patterns, N.Y.C., 1964-65; tchr. home econs. San Rafael (Cal.) City Schs., 1965-66; nutrition edn. cons. Dairy Council Cal., San Francisco, 1966-69; supr. ednl. services Del Monte Corp., San Francisco, 1969—. Recipient Gold Leaf award excellence creating nutrition edn. materials, 1973. Mem. San Francisco Home Economists in Bus. (sec. 1968-69, consumer interests chmn. 1969-70, chmn. elect 1971-72, group chmn. 1971-72), Soc. for Nutrition Edn. (program com.), Cal. Home Econs. Assn. (v.p. 1973-75), San Francisco Food Service Execs. Assn. (pres. 1974-75), Kappa Omicron Phi. Home: 8 Fairview Ct San Anselmo CA 94960 Office: 215 Fremont St San Francisco CA 94119

SILLIMAN, JANET MARIE ENGLISH (MRS. JOHN PARKS SILLIMAN), univ. adminstr.; b. St. Cloud, Minn., Dec. 9, 1944; d. Arthur John and Viola Marie (Gohman) English; B.S., Coll. St. Catherine, 1967; m. John Parks Silliman, July 10, 1971. Admissions counselor Coll. St. Catherine, St. Paul, 1967-70; dir. career counseling and placement Hamline U., St. Paul, 1970—. Mem. Mayors Manpower Planning Commn., 1972—. Mem. Assn. Sch., Coll. and Univ. Staffing, Midwest Coll. Placement Assn. (assemblyman 1973—), Assn. Minn. Recruiters and Placement Dirs. (pres. 1972-73), Assn. Minn. Post-Secondary Ednl. Instns. (mem. exec. bd. 1972—), Minn. Instl. Tchr. Placement Assn. (mem. exec. bd. 1972—), Minn. Assn. Sch. Personnel Adminstrs. (liaison rep. 1973-75), Coll. St. Catherine Alumni Assn. (dir. 1968-69). Home: 694 Iona Lane St Paul MN 55113

SILLS, BEVERLY (BELLE SILVERMAN) (MRS. PETER B. GREENOUGH), coloratura soprano; b. Bklyn., 1929; grad. pub. schs.; student voice Estelle Leibling, piano Paolo Gallico, stagecraft Desire Defrere; hon. doctorates N.Y. U., New Eng. Conservatory, Temple U.; m. Peter B. Greenough, 1956; stepchildren—Lindley, Nancy, Diana; children—Meredith, Peter B. Radio debut as Bubbles Silverman on Uncle Bob's Rainbow House, 1931; appeared on Maj. Bowes Capitol Family Hour, 1934-41, Our Gal Sunday; toured with Shubert Tours, Charles Wagner Opera Co., 1950, 51; debut with N.Y.C. Opera Co., 1955—, as Rosalinda in Die Fledermaus; debut San Francisco Opera, 1953, La Scala, Milan, 1969, Royal Opera, Covent Garden, London, 1971; recital debut, Paris, 1971; appeared throughout U.S., Europe, S.Am., including Vienna State Opera, Teatro Fenise, Venice, Teatro Colon, Buenos Aires, N.Y. State Theatre, 1967, Boston Symphony, Tanglewood Festival, 1968, 69, Robin Hood Dell, Phila., 1969; star roles in Handel's Julius Caesar, Manon, La Traviata, Tales of Hoffman, Lucia di Lammermoor, Roberto Deveraux, Anna Bolena, Maria Stuarda. Office: care Mgmt Ludwig Lustig 111 W 57th St New York City NY 10019

SILLS, MRS. KENNETH CHARLES MORTON (EDITH LANSING KOON SILLS), club woman; b. Hancock, Md., Dec. 3, 1888; d. Rev. J. C. and Nancy Moore (Williams) Koon; student Hannah More Acad., Reisterstown, Md.; A.B., Wellesley Coll., 1911; postgrad. Columbia, 1917-18; L.H.D., Bowdoin Coll., 1952; m. Kenneth Charles Morton Sills (pres. Bowdoin Coll., 1918-52), Nov. 21, 1918 (dec. 1954). Tchr. Greek, English, Portland (Me.) High Sch., 1912-16; tchr. Latin, Lenox Sch. of Finch Coll., N.Y.C., 1916-18. Active A.R.C., U.S.O., Brunswick, Me., World War II; past mem. State Me. Adv. Com. Nat. Commn. Civil Rights; past diocesan pres., past mem. nat. bd. Woman's Aux., Episcopal Ch.; mem. com. ch. unity and ecumenical relations Ch. Women United; mem. com. Sr. Citizens Portland, Model City Devel. Program, Portland; past pres. Nat. Soc. Colonial Dames of Am.; resident in Me., past nat. corr. sec.; past pres. Western Me. Wellesley Club; past mem. bd. Portland YWCA, Me. br. Am. Assn. U. Women; mem. bd. First Radio Parish Am., Portland, Friendship, Inc.; incorporator, mem. bd. Greater Portland Landmarks for Preservation; past pres. Portland Women's Coll. Club, Victoria Soc. Me. Women; past pres. Me. br. English Speaking Union; mem. Me. adv. com. Job Corps Tng. Center for Girls, Roland Spring, Me. Trustee Waynflete Sch. for Girls, Portland, Me.; mem. bd. St. Mary's-in-the-Mountains Sch. for Girls (N.H.). Mem.-at-large assembly Me. Council Chs. Recipient Woman of Achievement award Women's Coll. Club, Portland, Me., 1956; Deborah Morton award Westbrook Jr. Coll., 1961; Edith Lansing Koon Sills Lectureship fund Soc. Bowdoin Women, 1961; Nat. Honor Roll, Nat. Soc. Colonial Dames, 1967; girls' scholarship for coll. study named in her honor by Portland Women's Coll. Club, 1971. Home: 134 Vaughan St Portland ME 04102

SILLS, RUTH CURTIS FRANK (MRS. H. DONALD SILLS), civic worker; b. N.Y.C.; d. Charles Stuart and Catherine (Curtis) Frank; m. H. Donald Sills; 1 son, Charles Frank. Chmn. bd., mem. exec. com. Internat. Debutante Ball; mem. N.Y. adv. com. World Council Christian Edn., 1965-67; vice chmn. N.Y. com. Easter Seal Soc. for Crippled Children, 1965-68; chmn. Arthur Rubinstein Concert, Carnegie Hall for Collegiate Sch., 1965; chmn. Pan Am. Fiesta, 1964, Spring Festival of Fragrance, 1965-68; pres. bd. Kidney Found. of N.Y., 1964-65; v.p. Muscular Dystrophy Assn.; chmn. spl. events N.Y. Heart Fund. Trustee Met. chpt. Nat. Hemophelia Found.; bd. dirs. Walderman Med. Research Found., Pearl S. Buck Found., People for the UN. Mem. Womens Service League (past pres.). Presbyn. Club: York. Author: Sweet Bitter Charity. Home: 3 E 69th St New York City NY 10021

SILTON, HANNAH LORA KLEIN (MRS. HAROLD LEWIS SILTON), vinyl mfg. co. exec.; b. Kaiserslautern, Germany, Aug. 19, 1924; d. Erich E. and Bertha (Zeiger) Klein; B.A., Mundelein Coll., 1950; M.A. (scholar), Loyola U., 1952; m. Harold Lewis Silton, July 26, 1952; children—Randall Scott, Dori Ann. Came to U.S., 1936, naturalized, 1942. With time-study dept. Bell and Howell Co., Lincolnwood, Ill., 1942-45; with Erell Mfg. Co., Chgo., 1947—, v.p., 1953-67, pres., gen. mgr., 1967—. Mem. Splty. Advt. Assn. Internat., Splty. Advt. Assn. Chgo. (dir. 1972-75), Chgo. Assn. Commerce and Industry (mem. govtl. affairs com. 1972—), Mundelein Coll., Loyola U. alumni assns. Office: 1243 S Wabash Av Chicago IL 60605

SILVA, MARCIA PAULA (MRS. GERALD RAYMOND SILVA), town ofcl.; b. Providence, Apr. 26, 1943; d. Matthew Paul and Hazel (Rostron) Romano; grad. East Providence Sr. High Sch., 1961; m. Gerald Raymond Silva, July 15, 1961; 1 dau., Gina Lynn. Exec. sec. R.I. Council Community Services, Providence, 1961-64; exec. sec. Office of Mental Retardation State of R.I., Providence, 1964-66; town clk. Rehoboth, Mass., 1967—. Vol. Camp Fire leader, 1964-66, 72-73. Treas. Rehoboth Republican Town Com., 1971—; pres. Rehoboth Police Wives Guild, 1972-73. Recipient Nat. Camp Fire award, 1964. Mem. Mass. Town Clks. Assn., New Eng. Assn. Town Clks., Town Clks. Assn. of Bristol, Plymouth and Norfolk Counties, Internat. Inst. Municipal Clks. Home: RFD 5 Pine Rehoboth MA 02769 Office: Town Office Bldg Rehoboth MA 02769

SILVA, RUTH CARIDAD, educator; b. Lincoln, Neb.; d. Ignatius Dominic and Beatrice (Davis) Silva; A.B., U. Mich., 1943, A.M., 1943, Ph.D., 1948. Instr., Wheaton Coll., Norton, Mass., 1946-48; mem. faculty Pa. State U. at University Park, 1948—, prof. polit. sci., 1959—. Fulbright prof. polit. sci. Cairo (Egypt) U., 1952-53; vis. prof. Hunter Coll., N.Y.C., 1958, Johns Hopkins, 1965; spl. cons. U.S. Dept. Justice, 1957, N.Y. State Constn. Commn., 1959-60, Pa. State Constn. Commn., 1967-68. Mem. Pres.'s Commn. Post Secondary Edn., 1972-73. Mem. Am. Polit. Sci. Assn. (past sec., chmn. com. status of women in profession 1972-73, v.p. 1972-73), Acad. Polit. Sci., Am. Assn. U. Profs. (chmn. com. relation of govt. to higher edn., 1964-68), Nat. Municipal League, Phi Kappa Phi, Chi Omega. Republican. Roman Catholic. Clubs: University, U. Mich. Presidents (Ann Arbor). Author: Presidential Succession, 1951; Legislative Apportionment in New York, 1960; Rum, Religion and Votes; 1928 Re-examined, 1962. Contbr. articles in field to profl. jours. Home: 1000 Plaza Dr State College PA 16801 Office: Burrowes Bldg University Park PA 16802

SILVER, BETTY WINSTON WALES (MRS. CHARLES HINTON SILVER), assn. exec., editor; b. Edenton, N.C., May 2, 1923; d. Charles Paddock and Duncan (Winston) Wales; grad. St. Mary's Jr. Coll., 1941, Drake Secretarial Sch., 1942; m. Charles Hinton Silver, Dec. 18, 1943; children—Charles Hinton, Winston Sprague, John Wales. Clk., N.C. State Senate Com., 1949, 51, 53; real estate broker, Raleigh, N.C., 1956-61; exec. dir. N.C. chpt. Am. Inst. Architects, also editor N.C. Architect, Raleigh, 1961—. Charter mem., sec. Wake Environment, Inc., 1972. Mem. Wake County Planning Bd., 1973—. Mem. Jr. League of Raleigh, Wake County Com. Colonial Dames, Carolinas Soc. Assn. Execs. (pres. 1968-69), Wake County Hist. Soc. (charter mem., chmn. tour com. 1967, sec. 1967-68, v.p. 1973-74, pres. 1974—), Wake County Soc. Prevention Cruelty to Animals (organizer), Daus. Revolution (chpt. treas. 1970-73), A.I.A. (hon.). Episcopalian. Home: Midway Plantation Route 5 Raleigh NC 27604 Office: 115 W Morgan St Raleigh NC 27601

SILVER, ETHEL MARIE, polit. party ofcl.; b. Hemet, Cal., June 25, 1926; d. George Andrew and Myrtle Josephine (Johnson) Gruber; student Riverside (Cal.) City Coll., 1945-47; R.N., Los Angeles County Gen. Hosp., 1947; m. Harrison Edward Silver, Apr. 17, 1948; children—Jeffrey, Jennifer. Pres. Riverside County Republican Women, 1966; mem. Cal. Rep. Central Com., also Riverside County Rep. Central Com., 1968—; campaign mgr. numerous campaigns. Past pres. Riverside County Med. Assn. Aux.; mem. Riverside Press Council, 1972—, Atty. Gen. Cal. Environmental Task Force. Bd. dirs. World Affairs Inland So. Cal. Mem. Jr. League, Opera Guild. Address: 5741 Grand Av Riverside CA 92504

SILVER, EVELYN BLOTNER, lawyer; b. N.Y.C., Nov. 14, 1914; d. Joseph B. and Bertha (Sugarman) Blotner; student Temple U., 1931-33, Columbia, 1933-35; LL.B., Bklyn. Sch., 1936; postgrad. Parker Sch. Comparative Law, Columbia, 1967; m. Harold J. Silver, Nov. 22, 1936 (dec. Oct. 1961); children—Andrew Jeffrey, Patricia Merle. Admitted to N.Y. bar, 1938, also various fed. cts.; individual practice law, N.Y.C., 1938—; gen. counsel Intercontinental Mfg. Co., Garland, Tex., 1948-55; treas., pres. Municipal Securities Co., Dallas, 1955; gen. counsel Banque de Credit Internation, Geneva, Switzerland, 1959-61; partner Dickstein, Shapiro, Silver & Galligan, N.Y.C., 1962—. Dir. Garden City Trust Co., Newton, Mass.; pres. E.J. Scannel, Inc., Somerville, Mass., 1963—; exec.-atty., internat. Counsel Nat. Patent Devel. Corp., N.Y.C., 1971; dir. Hydron Europe, Inc., Paris, France. Chmn. com. on traffic and shipping, adv. com. on coop. edn. Community Coll. City N.Y., 1967; sponsor N.Y. Shakespeare Festival, 1965—; patron N.Y. Infirmary, 1963—, Nat. Kidney Found., 1963—; mem. Met. Opera Guild, 1963. Trustee Worcester Found., Assumption Coll., Harlyn Found.; bd. dirs. Boston Council Internat. visitors. Brandeis U. fellow. Mem. Am. Bar Assn. (sect. internat. and comparative law), Internat. Fedn. Women Lawyers (econ. commn. Geneva, Switzerland), Am. Soc. for Internat. Law, Nat. Assn. Women Lawyers, Queens County Women's Bar Assn., UN Assn., N.Y. Trial Lawyers, Comml. Law League (chmn. world trade, commerce com.), Women's League for Histradut Scholarships. Home: 24 Central Park South New York City NY 10019 also Whipsuppenicke 333 Howard St Northboro MA 01532 Office: 375 Park Av New York City NY 10022

SILVER, IDA OSTREICH (MRS. BERNARD EURIC SILVER), ednl. adminstr.; b. N.Y.C., May 26, 1911; d. Jacob and Anna (Leventhal) Ostreich; A.B., Adelphi Coll., 1931; M.A., Bklyn. Coll., 1955; m. Bernard Euric Silver, Nov. 21, 1931; children—Stephen Euric, Naomi Ruth (Mrs. David S. Neft). Tchr., counselor, dean, high schs., N.Y.C. Bd. Edn., 1938-55; asst. prin. Wingate High Sch., N.Y.C., 1955-65; coordinator funded-program for handicapped children N.Y.C. Bd. Edn., N.Y.C., 1965—; instr. Bklyn. Coll., 1960-62. Field supr. Bklyn. Coll. Guidance Program, 1963-64. Coordinator, N.Y.C. Adv. Com. Federally Funded Programs for Handicapped Children, 1967—. Mem. Am., N.Y. State personnel and guidance assns., N.Y. State Assn. Deans and Guidance Personnel,

N.Y.C. Assn. High Sch. Guidance Personnel (pres. 1962-64). Home: 45 W 10th St New York City NY 10011

SILVER, NETTIE WENGROVER (MRS. LEWIS SILVER), artist, educator; b. Bklyn., Dec. 19, 1922; d. Jacob and Lena (Karon) Wengrover; B.A., Bklyn. Coll., 1940; M.A., Columbia, 1941; certificate in adminstrn. and supervision Queens Coll., 1972; postgrad. St. John's U., 1973; m. Lewis Silver, June 24, 1943; children—Judy, Roberta. With drafting dept. U.S. Navy, N.Y.C., 1941-43; with Bd. Edn., N.Y.C., 1944-52, 64—, adviser-tchr., 1953—. Vice pres., editor newspaper P.T.A., Pub. Sch. 90, N.Y.C., 1954-56; mem. parent com. Girl Scouts, 1950-55. Recipient Regents scholarship, 1936-40; Leopold-Schepp Found. scholarship to Columbia U., 1940-41. Mem. Am. Watercolor Assn. (asso.), Nat. Soc. for Study Edn., English Tchrs. Assn., Art Students League (life). Jewish religion (pres. sisterhood 1965-68). Illustrator: From Earth to Moon (Jules Verne), 1958. Exhibited art at City Center, 1963-65.

SILVER, RUTH STANLIE SMITH (MRS. HAROLD F. SILVER), civic worker; b. Salt Lake City, Nov. 1, 1930; d. Joseph F. and Ruth (Pingree) Smith; B.S., U. Utah, 1952; M.A., U. Hawaii, 1955; m. Harold F. Silver, Sept. 16, 1964. Missionary, Ch. of Jesus Christ of Latter-day Saints, 1955-56; grad. asst. speech dept. U. Hawaii, Honolulu, 1952-54; instr. dept. speech Ch. Coll. Hawaii, Lale, Oahu, 1957-60; instr. dept. speech Brigham Young U., Provo, Utah, 1960-62, 63-64; instr. dept. speech Colo. Womens Coll., Denver, 1966. Mem. Sec.'s Com. on Automated Personal Data Systems for U.S. Dept. Health, Edn. and Welfare, 1972-73. Treas., Hilltop Area unit Denver Symphony Guild, 1969-73, sec. exec. bd., 1969-71, asst. sec., 1971-73, membership chmn., 1972-73, mem. young artists' competition com. 1972-73, pres. elect, 1973-74, pres., 1974-75; sec. Colo. Women's Coll. Library Assos., 1968-70, pres., 1970-72, membership v.p., 1972-74; mem. bd. Denver Lyric Opera, 1967-70, guild dir., 1968-69, asst. sec. guild, 1971-72; dir. Denver Civic Ballet, 1967—; mem. Colo. chpt. Embroiderers Guild Am., Children's Hosp. Aux., Denver Civic Ballet Guild, Central City Opera Guild. Mem. Nat. Soc. Gen. Semantics, Nat., Colo. assns. parliamentarians, Denver U. Faculty Women, Denver U. Womens Library Assn. Mem. Ch. of Jesus Christ of Latter-day Saints. Club: Jane Herrick Literary (pres. 1967-68, treas. 1972-73). Home: 315 Clermont St Denver CO 80220

SILVERBERG, DORIS POMERANCE (MRS. HERBERT I. SILVERBERG), psychiatrist; b. Bklyn., Aug. 29, 1931; d. William and Ruth (Landsberg) Pomerance; B.A., Smith Coll., 1952; M.D., Johns Hopkins, 1956; postgrad. N.Y. Sch. Psychiatry, 1963-65; m. Herbert I. Silverberg, Mar. 31, 1957; children—Jamie Lynn, John Eric, Susan Ellen. Intern, Kings County Hosp., Bklyn., 1956-57; resident Kings Park (N.Y.) State Hosp., 1958-59, 63-65; practice medicine specializing in psychiatry, Smithtown, N.Y., 1965—; instr. psychiatry State U.N.Y. at Stonybrook, 1971—; psychiat. cons. St. John's Smithtown Hosp., 1966—, Smithtown Gen. Hosp., 1965—. Mem. Am. Psychiat. Assn. (sec. Suffolk County br. 1965-67), Phi Beta Kappa. Home: 24 Pinoak Lane St St James NY 11780 Office: 100 Lawrence Ave Smithtown NY 11787

SILVERMAN, CHARLOTTE, physician; b. N.Y.C., May 21, 1913; d. Harry and Gussie (Goldman) Silverman; B.A., Bklyn. Coll., 1933; M.D., Woman's Med. Coll. Pa., 1938; M.P.H., Johns Hopkins Sch. Hygiene and Pub. Health, 1942, Dr.P.H., 1948. Intern, Beekman Hosp., N.Y.C., 1939-40; field analyst Children's Bur., 1942-43; Tb control div. USPHS, 1943-45, sr. surgeon, inactive Res., 1954—; asst. dir. Bur. Tb, Balt. City Health Dept., 1946-49, dir., 1950-56; chief div. epidemiology Md. State Dept. Health, 1956-59, chief Office Planning and Research, 1959-62; cons. mental health in pub. health Nat. Inst. Mental Health, Bethesda, Md., 1962-65, asst. chief social phychiatry sect., 1965-66, chief epidemiologic studies br., 1966-67; chief population studies program Nat. Center for Radiol. Health, Rockville, Md., 1968-70, dep. chief, div. biol. effects, 1971—; lectr. preventive medicine Johns Hopkins Sch. Medicine, 1947-52; lectr. epidemiology Johns Hopkins Sch. Hygiene and Pub. Health, 1950-52, 54-56, asst. prof. epidemiology, 1956-63, lectr. chronic diseases and epidemiology, 1966—. Diplomate Am. Bd. Preventive Medicine. Fellow Am. Pub. Health Assn., Am. Coll. Preventive Medicine; mem. Am. Psychiat. Assn., N.Y. Acad. Scis., A.A.A.S. Club: Johns Hopkins. Author: The Epidemiology of Depression, 1968. Contbr. articles in field to profl. jours. Home: 4977 Battery Lane Bethesda MD 20014 Office: 5600 Fishers Lane Rockville MD 20852

SILVERS, ABIGAIL ADAMS (MRS. WILLYS KENT SILVERS), physician; b. Boston, Jan. 31, 1934; d. Weston Woollard and Mildred Culver (Boyd) Adams; student Baldwin Sch., Bryn Mawr, Pa., 1940-52; A.B., Mt. Holyoke Coll., 1956; M.D., U. Pa., 1961; m. Willys Kent Silvers, Sept. 29, 1956; children—Deborah, Willys Kent. Intern, Bryn Mawr Hosp., 1961-62, resident, 1962-64, asst. to dir. med. edn., 1965-70, physician to outpatient clinic service of hematology and oncology, 1965—; fellow hematology Hosp. U. Pa., 1964-65; practice medicine specializing in internal medicine, Bryn Mawr, 1965—; mem. Bryn Mawr Med. Specialists, Ltd., 1970—. Diplomate Am. Bd. Internal Medicine with subsplty. in oncology. Mem. Am. Soc. Internal Medicine, Am. Med. Women's Assn., Alpha Omega Alpha. Home: 210 Mill Creek Rd Ardmore PA 19003 Office: 933 Haverford Rd Bryn Mawr PA 19010

SILVERS, ELNORE HARRIETT, realtor; b. Waterloo, Ia., May 13, 1909; d. Lucien West and Orrie Ray (Hoxie) Fleming; grad. high sch.; m. Carl V. Silvers, Mar. 1, 1926; children—Carl V. Real estate broker, Monterey, Cal., 1947—; appraiser Alameda County (Cal.), 1966—. Active A.R.C. Mem. Cal. Grandmothers Club (past state sec., past local pres.). Address: 925 Portola Dr Monterey CA 93940

SILVERSTEIN, ELIZABETH BLUME, lawyer; b. Newark, Nov. 2, 1892; s. Selig and Goldie R. (Aranowitz) Blume; LL.B., N.J. Law Sch. (now Rutgers U.), 1911; m. Max Silverstein, Aug. 23, 1934 (dec.); 1 son, Nathan Royce. Admitted to N.J. bar, 1913, U.S. Supreme Ct. bar, 1921; practiced in Newark, 1913—. Mem. legal adv. bd., Essex County, N.J., 19—; mem. exec. bd. Am. Jewish Congress, 1932-37; mem. World Jewish Congress, 1936. Del. Republican Nat. Conv., 1932. Mem. Am. Judicature Soc., Fed., Am., N.J. State, Essex County bar assns., Mem. Order Brith Abraham. Office: 62 Osborne Terrace Newark NJ 07108

SILVESTRI, BARBARA FRANCIS (MRS. ALGERD MONSTAVICIUS), ophthalmologist; b. Chgo., Apr. 13, 1939; d. Humbert and Sophie (Wencel) Silvestri; M.D., U. Ill., 1964; m. Algerd Monstavicius, Dec. 29, 1964. Intern, Cook County Hosp., Chgo., 1964; resident ophthalmic surgery U. Ia., Iowa City, 1966-67, Pacific Med. Center, San Francisco, 1967-69; practice ophthalmology, San Francisco, 1969—; mem. staff St. Mary's Pacific Med. Center, St. Francis Hosp.; glaucoma cons., teaching service, dept. ophthalmology Pacific Med. Center, San Francisco, 1969—. Fellow A.C.S.; mem. A.M.A., Am. Acad. Ophthalmology and Otolaryngology, Cal. Med. Assn., Am. Med. Women's Assn., Cal. Women's Physician Club. Republican. Roman Catholic. Clubs: Metropolitan, Lithuanian Republican, Olympic (San Francisco). Home: 43 Topaz St San Francisco CA 94131 Office: 450 Sutter St San Francisco CA 94108

SILVEY, BILLIE WESLEY (MRS. FRANK EDWARD SILVEY), pub. co. exec.; b. Sacramento, Cal., Sept. 21, 1942; d. Cecil LaRoe and Clara June (Huxford) Wesley; student West Tex. State U., 1961-62, Abilene Christian Coll., 1963-65; B.A. cum laude, Pepperdine U., 1967, postgrad., 1968-73; m. Frank Edward Silvey, Aug. 25, 1963; children—Kathryn Dale, Robert LaRoe. Publicity asst. Abilene (Tex.) Christian Coll., 1963-64, editor Optimist newspaper, 1964-65; acting news editor Christian Chronicle, Abilene, 1965; pub. information asst. Pepperdine U., Los Angeles, 1965-69; acting publicity dir. Lubbock (Tex.) Christian Coll., 1967; asst. editor 20th Century Christian Pub. Co., Los Angeles, 1970—. Instr. Lighthouse Youth Program, 1968-69. Mem. Asso. Women for Pepperdine (rec. sec. 1972-73, pres. 1974-75), Childbirth Edn. Assn. (No. Va. newsletter editor 1969-70), Women in Communications. Mem. Ch. of Christ. Author: In the Beginning, 1974; (with M. Norvel Young) How to Keep Fit and Growing, 1974. Editor: Patterns for Living (Irene Y. Mattox), 1971. Address: 1236 W 79th St Los Angeles CA 90044

SILVING, HELEN (MRS. PAUL K. RYU), educator; b. Krakow, Poland; d. Szaje and Salome (Bauminger) Silberpfennig; Dr. Polit. Sci., U. Vienna (Austria), J.U.D., 1936; LL.B., Columbia, 1944; m. Paul K. Ryu, Jan. 3, 1957. Came to U.S., 1939, naturalized, 1944. Research asst. to prof. Hans Kelsen, Harvard, 1939-42; admitted to N.Y. bar, 1944; practiced in N.Y.C., 1944-45; atty. adviser U.S. Dept. Justice, Office Alien Property, Munich, Germany and Washington, 1948-53; research asso. Harvard Law Sch., Cambridge, 1954-56; vis. prof. law U. P.R., Rio Piedras, 1956-57, prof. law, 1957—; vis. lectr. Yale Law Sch., 1958-59. Adviser Legislative Penal Reform Commn. of Commonwealth of P.R. and Commonwealth Dept. Justice, 1959-66. Recipient Spl. Presdl. citation Am. Soc. Criminology and Criminal Justice, 1971. Mem. Am. Bar Assn. Author: Essays on Criminal Procedure, 1964; Constituent Elements of Crime, 1967; Essays on Mental Incapacity and Criminal Conduct, 1967; Sources of Law, 1968, Criminal Justice 2 vols., 1971. Home: Condominio Darlington No 601 Rio Piedras PR 00925 Office: U PR Law Sch Rio Piedras PR 00931

SIMARD-BROWN, TERESA MADELINE, ednl. adminstr.; b. Nashua, N.H., Nov. 27, 1920; d. Michael J. and Rose M. (Emery) Simard; B.A., Notre Dame Coll., 1956; M.A., St. Michael's Coll., 1964; Ed.D., U. Mass., 1972; m. May 25, 1974. Tchr., St. Anthony High Sch., New Bedford, Mass., 1940-49, Holy Rosary High Sch., Rochester, N.H., 1949-56, Notre Dame Coll., Manchester, 1956-57, St. Louis High Sch., Nashua, 1957-64; prin. St. Anthony High Sch., Manchester, 1964-67; counselor, prof. psychology Northwestern Conn. Community Coll., Winsted, 1968-71, dir. counseling services, 1971-73; prof. psychology Adult Edn. Center, St. Petersburg, Fla., 1974—. Recipient Scholarship U. Havana, 1958. Mem. Am. Assn. U. Profs., Nat., Conn. assns. women deans, adminstrs. and counselors, Eastern Assn. Coll. Deans and Advisers Students, New Eng. Jr. Coll. Student Personnel Assn. (rec. sec. 1970-72). Author: Personal Growth and Interpersonal Relations, 1973. Home: 1001 Ulmerton Rd #60 Largo FL 33540

SIMENDINGER, MARGARET RING (MRS. WILLIAM HENRY SIMENDINGER), author; b. Elizabeth, N.J., Sept. 12, 1911; d. Frederick Garthwaite and Grace Ellis (Higbie) Ring; student Sorbonne U., Paris, France, 1930-31; m. William Henry Simendinger, Aug. 7, 1931; children—William Henry, Richard Frederick. Reporter, Newark Sunday Call, 1941-45, Newark News, 1945-53; free-lance writer short stories and novelettes nat. mags. and British mags., Charlotte, N.C., 1954—. Mem. Charlotte Writers Club, Charlotte Civinettes (pres. 1961-63), Theta Sigma Phi. Episcopalian. Author: (with Myron B. Harkavy) Childbirth, 1962. Home: 1001 Scalybark Rd Charlotte NC 28209

SIMKINS, ALICE CYNTHIA, mus. curator; b. Dallas, May 13, 1946; d. William Stewart and Elsie (Nicholson) Simkins; B.F.A., Newcomb Coll., Tulane U., 1968; postgrad. U. Tex., 1968—. Asst. curator McNay Art Inst., San Antonio, Tex., 1970-73, registrar, 1970—, curator, 1973—. Mem. Coll. Art Assn. Office: 6000 N New Braunfels St San Antonio TX 78209

SIMKINS, BEATRICE RACHEL HEMINGWAY (MRS. CHESTER ELDREDGE SIMKINS), state ofcl.; b. Boston, Mar. 4, 1906; d. William A. and Rachel (Johns) Hemingway; student Boston Clerical Sch., 1925-27, Boston U., 1947-50; m. Chester Eldredge Simkins, Nov. 26, 1925; children—Chester Eldredge, Jean Audrey (Mrs. Clifford Wallace). Probation clk. Roxbury Dist. Ct., 1950-52; sec. gov. Mass., Boston, 1952-56; ins. examiner div. ins. Commonwealth of Mass., 1956-68, dept. commn. ins., 1968—. Sec. bd. dirs. Mass. Republican Com., 1961-68; Rep. state committeewoman, 6th Suffolk Dist., Boston 1955-68. Pres. Boston br. Women's Aux. to Nat. Alliance of Postal and Fed. Employees, 1943-53, nat. sec., 1953-57, nat. financial sec.-treas., 1957-65, nat. pres., 1965—; bd. dirs. Freedom House, Boston, 1960. Named Woman of Yr., Delta Omicron Zeta chpt. Zeta Phi Beta, 1963. Mem. N.A.A.C.P., Urban League Boston, Zeta Amicae of Boston (past pres.). Episcopalian. Mem. Order Eastern Star (past grand matron). Club: Wisteria Charity Bridge (treas. 1952—). Home: 49 Crawford St Dorchester MA 02121 Office: 100 Cambridge St Boston MA 02202

SIMLEY, EVELYNE CLAUDER, cosmotologist; b. Wiota, Wis.; d. Nim and Rhodnelda (Stewart) Johnson; student pub. schs.; m. Earle Clauder, Oct. 1936 (div. 1953); 1 son, John Charles; m. 2d, I. T. Simley. Clerical researcher Wis. Advt. Co., Madison, 1918-21; beautician 1921; owner Square Salon, 1923-28; traveled as cons., instr. and saleswoman Gibbs & Co., Chgo., also Realistic Co. Cin., 1929-33; mgr. beauty salons for Saligman & Latz, N.Y., Manchester's Dept. Store, Madison, Sophis & Co., N.Y., Schuster's Dept. Store, Milw., 1934-36; own shop, Madison, 1937-60; sec.-treas., part-owner John Charles Salons, Inc., 1960—, treas., part-owner John Charles Master Hair Designs, Ltd., 1962—. Mem. Wis. Hairdressers and Cosmetologists Assn., Madison Art Center, Wis. Union at U. Wis., Internat. Platform Assn., Madison Civic Music Assn., Madison Art Assn. First royal matron local ct. Order of Amaranth (dep. Supreme royal matron 1967-68), Order Easter Star, 1951-52, grand royal matron, Wis., 1958-59, grand lectr. Wis., 1962—, internat. dep. supreme royal matron, 1963, alternate del. to Supreme Council Order of Amaranth, 1964, handmaiden at Shrine 6, 1954, star point Monoma chpt. 5, 1964, supreme page, 1964, dep. supreme royal matron, 1965-66; worthy guide White Shrine Jerusalem, 1965-66; worthy chaplain White Shrine 1967-68, noble prophetess White Shrine 1968-69, worthy high priestess 1969-70, dep. supreme royal matron Amaranth Supreme Council 1972. Clubs: Maple Bluff Country; Zonta (past pres.). Home: 902 Farwell Dr Madison WI 53704 Office: 14 E Mifflin Madison WI 53703

SIMMEL, MARIANNE LENORE, psychologist, educator; b. Jena, Germany, Jan. 3, 1923; d. Hans E. and Else R. (Rapp) Simmel; A.B., Smith Coll., 1943; M.A., Harvard, 1945, Ph.D., 1949. Intern psychology Worcester (Mass.) State Hosp., 1943; research asst. Tufts Coll. Med. Sch., Neurol. Lab., Boston Dispensary, 1943-45; instr. psychology Cambridge Jr. Coll., 1945-46, Hofstra Coll., Hempstead, L.I., N.Y., 1946-48; vis. lectr. dept. psychology Wellesley Coll., 1948-49, med. psychology Dept. Psychiatry, Duke U. Med. Sch., Durham, N.C., 1958-59; instr. dept. psychiatry Coll. Medicine, U. Ill., 1950-52, asst. prof., 1952-57, clin. asso. prof., 1957-58; psychophysiologist, head psychol. lab. Ill. State Psychopathic Inst., 1952-58, asst. dir., 1952-55; became research asso. dept. psychology Brandeis U., Waltham, Mass., 1959, now prof. psychology; USPHS Spl. Research fellow Mass. Gen. Hosp., Boston, 1959—. Diplomate in clin. psychology Am. Bd. Examiners Profl. Psychology. Fellow Am. Psychol. Assn.; mem. Eastern Psychol. Assn., Am. Assn. U. Profs., Phi Beta Kappa, Sigma Xi. Author articles in field. Office: Brandeis U Dept Psychology Waltham MA 02154

SIMMONDS, SOFIA (MRS. JOSEPH S. FRUTON), educator, biochemist; b. N.Y.C., July 31, 1917; d. Lionel J. and Clara (Gottfried) Simmonds; B.A., Barnard Coll., 1938; Ph.D., Cornell U., 1942; m. Joseph S. Fruton, Jan. 29, 1936. Research asso. dept. biochemistry Cornell U. Med. Coll., 1942-45; research asst., instr. botany and microbiology Yale, 1946-49, asst. prof., 1949-50, asst. prof. biochemistry, 1950-54, asso. prof. biochemistry, 1954-69, asso. prof. molecular biophysics and biochemistry, 1969—, dir. undergrad. studies in molecular biophysics and biochemistry, 1974—, fellow Helen Hadley Hall, 1961-72; fellow Calhoun Coll., 1971—. Mem. Am. Chem. Soc. (Garvan medal 1968), Am. Soc. Biol. Chemists, Sigma Xi. Author: (with J.S. Fruton) General Biochemistry, 1953, rev. edit., 1958. Editorial bd. Jour. Biol. Chemistry, 1959-64. Home: 123 York St Apt 19A New Haven CT 06511

SIMMONS, ETHEL LORETTA, editor; b. Detroit, Mar. 15, 1933; d. John and Elizabeth Florieanna (Kotulis) Smilick; B.A. in Journalism, Wayne State U., 1954. Club editor Highland Parker, Highland Park, Mich., 1952-54; asso. editor Guest (now Key) Mag., also Skyliner Mag., Detroit, 1954-56; publicity dir. WJBK-TV, Detroit, 1956-57; staff writer Pictorial Living, Detroit Times, 1956-60; arts editor, feature editor, news editor Eccentric, Birmingham, Mich., 1962-72, asst. mng. editor, 1972-74, mng. editor news operations The Observer and Eccentric, 1974—. Recipient hon. mention awards for features Mich. Press Assn., 1964, 68. Mem. Women in Communications, Bloomfield Art Assn., Soc. Profl. Journalists, Arts Council Triangle of Birmingham-Bloomfield-Troy (dir. 1972-73), Nomads (publicity dir. 1970-71), Delta Gamma Chi. Home: 2182 Dorchester St Troy MI 48084 Office: 1225 Bowers St Birmingham MI 48012

SIMMONS, HELEN HOLM (MRS. CLIFFORD L. SIMMONS), lawyer; b. Omaha, Apr. 23, 1922; d. Sophus Ingemann and Rasmine Kristine (Hansen-Holm) Jensen; B.A., U. Neb., 1943; M.A., Creighton U., 1955, J.D., 1971; m. Clifford L. Simmons, Feb. 8, 1948; children—Gregory Clifford, Douglas Jeffrey, Gary Warren. Tchr. Omaha and Douglas County Sch. Bds., 1952-56; admitted to Ia. bar, 1971, Neb. bar, 1971; pvt. practice of law, Omaha, 1971-72; atty. U.S. Corps of Engrs., Omaha, 1972—. Fed. women's program rep. C.E., Omaha, 1972—, equal employment upward mobility counselor, 1972—. Mem. Am., Neb., Ia., Omaha bar assns., Am. Assn. U. Women, Neb. Writers Guild, Neb. Assn. Trial Lawyers, Am. Legion Aux. Contbr. articles and short stories to profl. jours. and newspapers. Home: 2588 Whitmore St Omaha NE 68112 Office: US Post Office and Court House 210 N 17th St Omaha NE 68102

SIMMONS, HELEN IRENE WESTERLUND (MRS. SHIRLEY ERNEST SIMMONS), coll. adminstr.; b. Iowa Falls, Ia., May 12, 1918; d. Oscar Eugene and Elva May (Davis) Westerlund; B.A. summa cum laude, Sioux Falls Coll., 1939; m. Shirley Ernest Simmons, July 19, 1942; children—Charles Ernest, Jane (Mrs. Dennis Kruit), Diane (Mrs. Johnny Nelson). High sch. English, music tchr., White, S.D., 1939-51; county supt. schs., Brookings County, S.D., 1952-55; asst. registrar Dakota State Coll., Madison, S.D., 1955-70, registrar, 1970—. Cons. unit ver. registrar's office Dakota Wesleyan U., 1972-73. Contralto soloist Community Chorus, 1960—. Mem. Am. Assn. U. Women, P.E.O., Delta Kappa Gamma. Republican. Methodist. Mem. Rebekah Lodge. Home: 420 NE 6th St Madison SD 57042

SIMMONS, JEAN ELIZABETH MARGARET (MRS. GLEN R. SIMMONS), educator; b. Cleve., Jan. 20, 1914; d. Frank Charles and Sarah Anne (Johnston) Saurwein; B.A., Western Res. U., 1933; Ph.D. (Stieglitz fellow 1935-37), U. Chgo., 1938; m. Glen R. Simmons, Nov. 14, 1935; children—Sally Anne, (Frank) Charles, James Fraser. Faculty, Barat Coll., Lake Forest, Ill., 1938-58, prof., chmn. dept. chemistry, 1948-58; faculty Upsala Coll., East Orange, N.J., 1959—, prof., 1963—, chmn. dept. chemistry, 1965-71, 74, chmn. sci. curriculum study, Lutheran Ch. Am. grantee, 1965-68, chmn. div. natural scis. and maths., 1965-69, asst. to pres., 1968-73. Coordinator basic scis. Evang. Hosp. Sch. Nursing, Chgo., 1943-46; lectr. sci. topics. Troop leader Girl Scouts U.S.A., Wheaton, Ill., 1952-58, neighborhood chmn., 1956-57, dist. chmn. Dupage County, 1958; chmn. U. Chgo. Alumni Fund Dr., Wheaton, 1957, 58, Princeton, N.J., 1964, 65; mem. nursing adv. com. East Orange (N.J.) Gen. Hosp., 1963-73; v.p. Virginia Gildersleeve Ednl. Fund. Recipient Lindback Found. award for distinguished teaching, 1964. Fellow, Am. Inst. Chemists, A.A.A.S. (council 1969-71); mem. Am. Chem. Soc., Am. Assn. U. Women (br. treas. 1960-62, chmn. sci. topic 1963—, state v.p. program 1964, nat. sci. topic implementation chmn. 1965, 66, state dir. 1967-68, 71-72, state pres. 1968-70), Internat. Fedn. U. Women (alternate del. for U.S. at conf. 1968, del. conf. 1974), Am. Assn. U. Profs. (charter, past chpt. pres.), Phi Beta Kappa (pres. alumni assn. 1973-74), Sigma Xi, Sigma Delta Epsilon (nat. pres. 1970-71, dir. 1972—). Episcopalian. Contbr. articles to publs. in field.Home: 40 Balsam Lane Princeton NJ 08540 Office: Kenbrook Upsala Coll East Orange NJ 07019

SIMMONS, MARY WILLIAMS (MRS. JOE LOUIS SIMMONS), univ. adminstr.; b. Tuskegee, Ala., Feb. 26, 1945; d. George and Mary (Chappell) Williams; B.S., Tuskegee Inst., 1967, M.Ed., 1969; postgrad. Lincoln U., 1972, U. Mo., 1973; m. Joe Louis Simmons, Sept. 2, 1972. Counselor, Lincoln U., Jefferson City, Mo., 1969-70, dean women, 1970-73, dir. housing, 1973—, asso. dean students, 1974—. Named Outstanding Educator, 1974. Mem. Nat. Assn. Personnel Workers, Nat. Assn. Student Personnel Adminstrs., Mo. Assn. Social Welfare, Alpha Kappa Alpha. Baptist. Club: Quettes (v.p. Jefferson City 1973). Home: 712 Adams St Jefferson City MO 65101

SIMMONS, MURIEL HELEN, (MRS. WILLIAM JAMES SIMMONS), educator; b. Ehrhardt, S.C., Apr. 12, 1913; d. Richard C. and Annie (Smith) Jones; student Coll. City N.Y., 1939-40; B.S., Tenn. State U., 1957, M.S., 1959; Edn. Specialist, George Peabody Coll., 1967; m. William James Simmons, July 19, 1936; children—Richard C. (dec.), William James, Roxane Muriel (Mrs. Emmett Morton Stewart). IBM tech., psychology dept. Tenn. State U., Nashville, 1960-63, asst. prof. edn., 1963—, acad. student counselor, 1972—. Mem. Nat. Soc. for Study Edn., Kappa Delta Pi, Zeta Chi, Alpha Kappa Mu, Alpha Kappa Alpha, Alpha Delta Omega. Democrat. Presbyn. Home: 304-22nd Av N Nashville TN 37203

SIMMONS, NEVAH HOWELL (MRS. CLARENCE LEE SIMMONS), newspaperwoman; b. nr. Pana, Ill., May 7, 1904; d. Charles Ottis and Essie Jane (Cruce) Howell; student pub. schs.; m. Clarence Lee Simmons, July 26, 1924 (dec. Dec. 1965); 1 son, Wilber Dean. Reporter, Pana Daily Record, 1923, Canton (Ill.) Daily

Register, 1923-25; supr. Postal Telegraph Co., Peoria, Ill., 1942-43; reporter Peoria Jour. Star, Inc., 1943—, garden editor, columnist, 1957—. Mem. Garden Writers Assn. Am., Am. Hemerocallis Soc., Photog. Soc. Am. Democrat. Presbyn. Clubs: Peoria (Ill.) Color Camera; Photocrafters Camera (Rock Island, Ill.). Home: 6807 N Mount Hawley Rd Peoria IL 61614 Office: 1 News Plaza Peoria IL 61601

SIMMONS, PHYLLIS M. BRATHWAITE (MRS. MAJOR SIMMONS), social worker; b. N.Y.C., May 23, 1927; d. Delbert and Maxine (Sargeant) Brathwaite; B.A., Hunter Coll., 1951; M.S.W., Adelphi U., 1965; m. Major Simmons, Feb. 9, 1946; children—Pamela, Sharon. Social caseworker N.Y.C. Dept. Social Services, 1953-60, supr. 1, 1960-65, case supr., 1966-67, sr. case supr., tng. specialist, 1967-68, dir. tng. Bur. Pub. Assistance, 1968-69, asst. to commr., dir. office of tng., since 1969-71; asst. adminstr., dir. Office Staff Devel. and Tng., Human Resources Adminstrn., N.Y.C., 1971-73, asst. dep. adminstr., asst. commr. Office Community Services, 1973—; caseworker Community Service Soc., N.Y.C., 1963-64; social worker Long Beach, L.I. Sch. Dist., 1964-65; social worker clin. team Bur. Child Guidance, N.Y.C. Bd. Edn., 1966-67. Pvt. tchr. supervisory social service staff Union Orgn., 1966-68; mem. U.S. team U.S.-U.K. Exchange Project on Social Services, 1973. Mem. Roosevelt Civic Assn., 1960-63; group worker Youth Services Project, Family Services Assn., Freeport, L.I., 1963-65; co-chmn. devel. and presentation of Negro History project, Glen Cove (L.I.) Community Center, 1967; chmn. community adv. bd. Comprehensive Community Mental Health Center Nassau County Med. Center, East Meadow, N.Y., 1973—. Bd. dirs., v.p. Roosevelt Community Mental Health Center, 1972—. Nat. Assn. Social Workers, Council Social Work Edn., Bur. Child Guidance (mem. bd. end. 1966), Acad. Certified Social Workers, N.A.A.C.P., Mental Health Assn. Nassau County, Inter-Agy. Tng. Officer's Council, Am. Pub. Welfare Assn., Delta Sigma Theta. Democrat. Episcopalian. Club: Women's City. Home: 3 Stevens St Roosevelt NY 11575 Office: NYC Dept Social Services Human Resources Administration 250 Church St New York City NY 10013

SIMMONS, SANDRA LEAH, journalist; b. Macon, Ga., Aug. 21, 1949; d. John Thomas and Eunice Carolyn (Cash) Simmons; student Norman Coll., 1967-69, Baylor U., 1969-71. News writer Baylor U. Office News and Information, Waco, Tex., 1969-71; asst. editor home missions mag. Bapt. Home Mission Bd., Atlanta, 1971-73; news reporter Columbus (Ga.) Enquirer, 1973—. Mem. Women in Communications, Nat. Orgn. Women, Sigma Delta Chi. Home: 1018 18th St Columbus GA 31901 Office: 17 12th St Columbus GA 31901

SIMMONS, SYLVIA H. (MRS. HANS H. NEUMANN), writer; b. N.Y.C.; B.A. cum laude, Bklyn. Coll., 1940; M.A. in English Lit., Columbia, 1941; m. Hans H. Neumann, 1963. Staff asst., clubmobile group head A.R.C., Italy, 1942-45; copywriter Grey Advt. Agy., N.Y.C., 1950-52, promotion copy chief, 1952-54; creative dir. Amos Parrish Co. Advt. Agy., N.Y.C., 1955; asso. creative dir., dir. direct mail and contests McCann-Erickson, Inc., advt., N.Y.C., 1955-60; spl. projects group Young & Rubicam Inc., N.Y.C., 1960-62, v.p., asst. to pres., 1962-68, v.p., asst. to chmn., 1968-71. Decorated Medal of Freedom, 1945, Purple Heart, 1944; recipient award for outstanding profl. contbn. to advancement better sales promotion, various awards for best indsl. film of year from bus. groups. Mem. Author's Guild, Advt. Women N.Y., Copy Club N.Y., Direct Mail Advt. Assn., Sales Promotion Execs. Club, Internat. Platform Assn., Sigma Tau Delta. Author: Successful Contests and How to Create Them; The Creative Approach to Premiums; New Speakers Handbook: How to be the Life of the Podium, 1972. Author: (with Hans H. Neumann) The Straight Story on V.D., 1973. Contbr. numerous articles to bus. and consumer publs. Home: 74 Old Belden Hill Rd Wilton CT 06897

SIMMONS, SYLVIA JEANNE QUARLES (MRS. HERBERT G. SIMMONS, JR.), coll. adminstr.; b. Boston, May 8, 1935; d. Lorenzo Christopher and Margaret Mary (Thomas) Quarles; B.A., Manhattanville Coll., 1957; M.Ed., Boston Coll., 1962; m. Herbert G. Simmons, Jr., Oct. 26, 1957; children—Stephen, Alison, Lisa. Montessori tchr. Charles River Park Nursery Sch., Boston, 1965-66; registrar Boston Coll. Sch. Mgmt., Chestnut Hill, Mass., 1966-70; dir. financial aid Radcliffe Coll., Cambridge, Mass., 1970-75, asso. dean admissions, 1972-75, asso. dean admissions, financial aid and women's edn., 1975—. Cons. Mass. Bd. Higher Edn., 1973—. Bd. dirs. Rivers Country Day Sch., Weston, Mass., Simon's Rock Coll., Great Barrington, Mass., Wayland (Mass.) Fair Housing, Cambridge Mental Health Assn.; alumnae bd. dirs. Manhattanville Coll. Mem. adv. com. Upward Bound, Chestnut Hill Boston Coll., 1972—, Camp Chimvey Corners, Becket, Mass., 1971—. Named One of Ten Outstanding Young Leaders, Boston Jr. C. of C., 1971. Mem. Women in Politics, Nat. (exec. council 1973—), Eastern (1st v.p. 1973) assns. financial aid officers, Links, (pres. local chpt. 1967-69), Jack and Jill Am. (pres. Newton chpt. 1972-74, Delta Sigma Theta. Club: Manhattanville (pres. Boston 1966-68). Home: 3 Dean Rd Wayland MA 01778 Office: 10 Garden St Cambridge MA 02138

SIMMONS, VIRGINIA MAY BARBER (MRS. HARYL C. SIMMONS), clin. psychologist; b. Kissimmee, Fla., Apr. 11, 1913; d. William Isaac and May Belle (Patterson) Barber; B.S. in Math., Fla. State U., 1934; postgrad. Duke, 1936; M.A., State U. Ia., 1937, Ph.D., 1939; m. Haryl C. Simmons, Feb. 8, 1942; 1 son, William Haryl. Dir. child study service Davenport (Ia.) Schs., 1939-41; chief psychologist Ia. Div. Child Welfare, 1941-42; personnel mgr. Simmons Engring. Co., Davenport, 1943-45; sec.-treas., pres. Gopher Grinders, Inc., Anoka, Minn., 1949-68; cons. to Minn. sch. dist., 1956-68; pvt. practice clin. psychology, 1954-68; research psychologist Gateway Sch., Orlando, Fla., 1968-70; pvt. practice, Orlando, 1970—. Mem. Am., Fla., Southeastern psychol. assns., Am. Soc. Clin. Hypnosis, Central Fla. Assn. Profl. Psychologists, Am. Assn. U. Women, League Women Voters (pres. 1950-51), Phi Beta Kappa, Sigma Xi, Phi Kappa Phi. Republican. Presbyn. Home: 11 Glendale Dr Kissimmee FL 32741 Office: 2111 E Michigan Av Orlando FL 32806

SIMMONS-MARTIN, AUDREY ANN, educator; b. Sioux Falls, S.D.; d. Frank U. and Teresa (Coleman) Simmons; student Fontbonne Coll., 1937-39; B.S., Washington U., St. Louis, 1941, M.S., 1945, Ed.D., 1963; m. James A. Martin. Tchr. Gallaudet Day Sch. for Deaf, St. Louis, 1941-42, Central Inst. for the Deaf, Washington U., St. Louis, 1942-49, lectr. tchr. edn. program, 1949-56, lectr., 1956-64, dir. aural Rehab. dept., 1949-73, dir. partially-deaf and primary div., 1959-73, dir. early edn., 1968—, asst. prof., 1964-67, asso. prof., 1967-71, prof. edn. of the deaf, 1971—; prof. U. Mich., summers 1949-51, Los Angeles State Coll., summer 1954, U. Minn., summers 1955-57, Northwestern U., summer 1958, U. Hawaii, 1971; participant numerous seminars and workshops; field reader Dept. Health, Edn. and Welfare, 1968—. Bd. dirs. YWCA, St. Louis, 1970-72. Named St. Louis Outstanding Woman in Edn., 1968, St. Louis Woman of Achievement, 1970. Fellow Am. Speech and Hearing Assn.; mem. Alexander Graham Bell Assn. (mem. gov. bd. 1962-70, adv. bd. 1970), Am. Assn. Women Adminstrs., A.A.A.S., Soc. Research Child Devel., Mo. Speech and Hearing Assn. Greater St. Louis (pres. 1965-66), Am. Instrs. Deaf, Nat. Assn. Edn. Young Children, Internat. Council of Exceptional Children, Central Inst. Deaf Alumni (hon.), Beta Sigma Phi (internat. hon. mem.), Delta Kappa Gamma. Club: Zonta (pres. 1966-67, area dir. 1968-69). Contbr. articles to profl. jours. Home: 6036 Highfield St St Louis MO 63109 Office: 818 S Euclid St St Louis MO 63110

SIMMS, UCA FRANCES (MRS. DICK RAPER), anesthesiologist; b. Oklahoma City, Apr. 13, 1918; d. Jacob D'Bord and Ruby Irene (Perry) Simms; A.B., Washington U., St. Louis, 1939; M.D., Tulane U., 1943; m. Dick Raper, Sept. 28, 1947; children—Judy (Mrs. John Hensley), Suzie (Mrs. Frank Robinson), Tricia (Mrs. Chris Grant). Intern, Jefferson Davis Hosp., Houston, 1943-44; resident Colo. Gen. Hosp., Denver, 1949-50; practice medicine, specializing in anesthesiology, Tulsa, 1944-49, Denver, 1949-66, Saginaw, Mich., 1966-70, Midland, Tex., 1970—; mem. staff Midland Meml. Hosp. Pres., Uca Frances Simms M.D. Asso., Midland, 1970—. Diplomate Am. Bd. Anesthesiologists. Mem. A.M.A., Am. Soc. Anesthesiologists, Tex., Okla., Colo., Mich., Miss. med. socs. Home: 3107 Shell St Midland TX 79701 Office: Midland Meml Hosp Midland TX 79701

SIMON, ANNE W., author. Formerly TV editor The Nation, McCalls. Author: Stepchild in the Family, 1964; The New Years: A New Middle Age, 1968; No Island is an Island: The Ordeal of Martha's Vineyard, 1973. Home: 1 W 81st St New York City NY 10024

SIMON, CHARLOTTE BLAUSTEIN (MRS. MARVIN SIMON), hosp. adminstr.; b. Bayonne, N.J.; d. John and Dora (Grodberg) Blaustein; B.A., Syracuse U., 1938; grad. N.Y. Sch. Social Work, 1941, Sch. Pub. Health and Hosp. Adminstrn., Columbia, 1962; m. Marvin Simon, Dec. 24, 1939; children—John, Richard, Barbara. Caseworker dept. pub. welfare, Bayonne, 1943-47; dir. social service Jewish Family Service, Bayonne, 1947-52, pres., 1948-51; dir. social service Hebrew Home and Hosp. N.J., Jersey City, 1952-62, exec. dir., 1962-65, exec. v.p., 1965—. Trustee, cons. Nat. Parkinson Found., N.Y.C., 1964—. Pres., Council Social Agys., Bayonne, 1948-51; v.p. Community Council, Bayonne, 1947-52; chmn. regional com. Aging-Council Jewish Fedns. and Welfare Fund, 1947-49; Bayonne mayor's rep. White Ho. Conf. on Aging, 1961; mem. Gov.'s Study Commn. on State Aid Care Indigent, 1966—, participant various symposia. Recipient Merit award Hebrew Home and Hosp. N.J., 1962; Merit and Phi Sigma Sigma, 1964. Fellow Nat. Gerontological Soc., Am. Coll. Hosp. Adminstrs., Am. Pub. Health Assn., Royal Soc. Health London; mem. N.J. Assn. Homes for Aged (dir.), Am. Hosp. Assn., Nat. Geriatric Soc., Nat. Conf. Jewish Communal Service, Nat. Council Jewish Women (sect. pres. 1940-42), Psi Chi. Home: 70 W 31st St Bayonne NJ 07002 Office: 198 Stevens Av Jersey City NJ 07305

SIMON, DORIS ELIZABETH SELLS (MRS. ARTHUR GOODMAN SIMON), librarian; b. Cairo, Ill.; d. Edward Upson and Carrie Lee (Kindred) Sells; student U. Ill., U. Louisville, 1967, U. Ky., 1971; m. Arthur Goodman Simon, Oct. 16, 1932; children—Doris (Mrs. Boyce Clayton), Arthur David, Martha Goodman. Librarian, head circulation dept. Puducah (Ky.) Library, 1950-68, acting dir., 1968, head reference, pub. affairs depts., 1968—. Recipient Public Servant award Paducah Jaycees, 1973; named Duchess of Paducah by Mayor, Ky. Col. Mem. Am., Ky. (scholarship com. 1970-72) library assns., Bus. and Profl. Women's Club, (exec. bd. 1970-72), Jackson Purchase Hist. Soc., Filson Club. Episcopalian. Mem. Order Eastern Star. Editor: Centennial Celebration of Grace Episcopal Church, 1973. Home: Madison Apts 7th and Madison St Paducah KY 42001 Office: 555 Washington St Paducah KY 42001

SIMON, DOROTHEA JONES, C.S. practitioner; b. Rayville, La.; d. Claude Charles and Ada (Ellis) Jones; certificate home econs. St. Mary's Sch., Raleigh, N.C., 1924; m. George Manning Simon, Jan. 2, 1927; 1 son, George Manning. Joined Christian Sci. Ch.; C.S. practitioner, Baton Rouge, 1947—. Mem. Com. Arsenal Mus., 1960; life mem. Baton Rouge Found. Hist. La., Inc., Y.W.C.O. Chmn. trustees Christian Sci. Orgn., La. State U., 1961—. Mem. Colonial Dames Am., Nat. Trust for Historic Preservation, D.A.R., Delta Delta Delta. Club: Woman's. Home: 2995 Reymond Av Baton Rouge LA 70808

SIMON, DOROTHY MARTIN, chemist; b. Harwood, Mo., Sept. 18, 1919; d. Robert William and Laudell (Flynn) Martin; A.B., S.W. Mo. State Coll., 1940; Ph.D., U. Ill., 1945; Sc.D. (hon.), Worcester Poly. Inst., 1971; m. Sidney L. Simon, Dec. 6, 1946. Grad. teaching asst. U. Ill., 1941-45; research chemist rayon div. E.I. Du Pont de Nemours & Co., Inc., Buffalo, 1945-47; chemist Oak Ridge Nat. Lab., 1947; asso. chemist Argonne Nat. Lab., Chgo., 1948-49; aero. research scientist, group leader NACA, Cleve., 1949-53, asst. br. chief chemistry br., 1954-55, group leader combustion fundamentals Magnolia Petroleum, Dallas, 1955-56; prin. scientist, tech. asst. to pres. research and advanced devel. div. Avco Corp., 1956-62, dir. corporate research Def. and Indsl. products group, 1962-68, v.p., 1964-68, v.p., dir. corporate research, 1968—. Marie Curie lectr. State U. Pa., 1962. Mem. NSF panel sci. and tech., 1973. Trustee Worcester Poly. Inst.; mem. vis. com. sponsored research Mass. Inst. Tech. Recipient Rockefeller Pub. Service award Cambridge U., Eng., 1953-54; Outstanding Alumnus award S.W. Mo. State Coll., 1957; Outstanding Profl. Woman award Bus. and Profl. Women's Club N.Y., 1966; Fellow Am. Inst. Chemists; mem. Am. Chem. Soc., Internat. Combustion Inst., Am. Inst. Aeros. and Astronautics, Soc. Woman Engrs. (Achievement award 1966), Sigma Xi. Contbr. articles to profl. jours. Home: 69 Londonderry Dr Greenwich CT 06830 Office: 1275 King St Greenwich CT 06830

SIMON, HAZEL TIPPET JONES (MRS. THEODORE CHARLES SIMON), counselor; b. Chgo., July 7, 1905; d. Thomas M. and Ethel (Tippet) Jones; teaching certificate Chgo. Normal Coll., 1925; B.A., Roosevelt U., 1956, M.A., 1962; M.Ed., Chgo. State Coll., 1964, postgrad., 1964; m. Theodore Charles Simon, Aug. 27, 1927; children—Patricia Jean (Mrs. Robert Orr Mosher), Theta Joanne (Mrs. Ronald D. Osucha). With adult edn. evening div. home econs. Chgo. Bd. Edn., 1925-35, elementary tchr. home econs., 1927-32, lunchroom mgr., supr. high sch., 1932-39, tchr. high sch., 1939-64, counselor high sch., 1964-66, supr. vocational edn., 1966-67; asso. prof. edn. Roosevelt U., Chgo., 1967-68. Leader family finance Planned Parenthood, 1954-55; vol. counselor Contact, 1970—; pres. Vols. for Geriatric Services, Little Rock, 1969; vol. counselor Adult Edn. Center, El Mirage, Ariz.; vol. Gold Lady, Sun Valley Lodge, Sun City, Ariz. Mem. Bus. and Profl. Women's Circle (pres. 1950), Am. Personnel and Guidance Assn., Am. Home Econs. Assn., Nat. Counsel Family Relations, Am. Assn. Ret. People, Delta Kappa Gamma (chpt. pres. 1966-68). Methodist. Home: 10018 Oak Ridge Dr Sun City AZ 85351

SIMON, IRIS (MRS. EUGENE PROTTER SIMON), artist; b. N.Y.C., Dec. 23, 1926; d. Nathan Abraham and Anna Zelda (Gittelson) Horowitz; B.A., Smith Coll., 1947; m. Eugene Protter Simon, Aug. 15, 1947; children—Daniel, Althea, Clea. Exhibited one-man shows at Hofstra U., 1964, Gallery Beyond Blue Door, Merrick, N.Y., 1966, Valley Nat. Bank, Westbury, N.Y., 1970; exhibited in numerous group shows, including Honolulu Acad. Art, 1959, Hecksher Mus., Huntington, N.Y., 1964, 66, 68, Nat. Arts Club, N.Y.C., 1970, 71, Nat. Acad. Galleries, N.Y.C., 1971-73; represented in permanent collections at Free Library, Phila., Roosevelt Raceway, Westbury, Tanglewood Preserve, Rockville Center, N.Y., East Meadow (N.Y.) Pub. Library, Jonas Salk Jr. High Sch., Levittown, N.Y. Recipient numerous prizes, including Medal in Graphics, Hofstra Coll., 1963; Purchase prize graphics Roosevelt Raceway, 1964; first prize watercolor Nassau County Art Socs., 1970. Mem. Nat. Assn. Women Artists (co-chmn. travelling painting exhbn. 1972—), L.I. Artists Alliance. Jewish religion. Home: 850 Richmond Rd East Meadow NY 11554 Office: 1740 Front St East Meadow NY 11554

SIMON, LORENA COTTS, music tchr., composer, poet; b. Sherman, Tex., Jan. 16, 1897; d. George Godfrey and Willie (Jones) Cotts; student Am. Conservatory, summer 1938, Juilliard Music Sch., summer 1939; diploma Sherwood Music Sch., 1941; Dr. Lit. Leadership, Internat. Acad. Leadership, Quezon City, Philippines; L.H.D., No. Pontificial Acad., Malmo, Sweden, 1969; Mus.D. (hon.), St. Olav's Acad., Sweden, 1969; m. Samuel C. Simon, Nov. 6, 1918 (dec.). Tchr. violin, piano, theory and harmony, Port Arthur, Tex., 1919—. Organizer, dir. Schubert's Violin Choir, Port Arthur, 1919-55. Named Poet Laureate of Tex. 1961; Poet Laureate of Magnolia Dist., 1962-64; Poet Laureate of Port Arthur, 1962—; recipient gold plaque Tex. Fedn. Women's Club, 1962, spl. award 1st place in poetry and music Tex. heritage dept., 1963; medal of merit and diploma of merit Centro Studi Scambi Internat., Rome, Italy, 1965; Gold medal award, and hon. poet laureate-musician United Poets Laureate Internat., 1966; Greatness and Leadership award U. Manila, 1967; Silver medal, Gold medal, Diploma Centro Studi E. Scambi—Internazionali, 1967; Gold Laurel Wreath, Gold medal, Karte of Award, 1966; named to International Poets' Hall of Fame, 1969, named most outstanding woman internationally, Congress of Doctors, Quezon City, Philippines, 1969. Mem. Nat., Tex. press women's assns., Nat. Council Cath. Women, Nat. Guild Piano Tchrs. (charter mem.; adjudicator), Am. Coll. Musicians (adjudicator), Internat. Guild Library, Am. Poetry League, Poets Soc. Tex. (critic judge), Am. Poets Fellowship Soc. Corp., UN Assn. U.S.A., Alpha Delta Kappa. Clubs: Writers' (pres. 1963-64), Symphony. Author: The Golden Kay, 1958; From My Heart (1st place award Ann. Poetry Writers Contest of Tex. Press Women's Assn. 1961), 1959; Children's Story Hour (1st place award Nat. Fedn. Press Women's Ann. Writers' Contest 1962), 1960. Songs pub. include: Live Expectantly, 1962, In Search for Growth, 1963, Freedom's Light, 1963, What Can I Do for Jesus, 1963, I Was a Star, I Was a Lamb, I Was a Donkey; organ piece Mediation, 1967. Chmn. spl. editorial com. World Poets Laureate Anthology, 1969-70. Donor funds for constrn. of four churches in Africa. Home: 411 Fifth Av Port Arthur TX 77640

SIMON, MARTHA EVANS (MRS. BERNARD RAY SIMON), auditor; b. Owensboro, Ky., Mar. 3, 1944; d. Ezra and Gola Martha (Howard) Evans; student Georgetown Coll., 1963; m. Bernard Ray Simon, Mar. 1, 1964; children—Carolyn Raye, Mary Cathleen, Bernard Ray. Bookkeeper, Central Bank & Trust, Owensboro, Ky., 1965-66; teller Central Bank & Trust, Owensboro, 1966-67; with First Security Bank, Island, Ky., 1969—, audit supr., 1970—. Baptist. Home: 7th St Calhoun KY 42327 Office: 1st and Main Sts Island KY 42350

SIMON, RENEE BLATT (MRS. HARRY J. SIMON), city ofcl.; b. Bklyn., Mar. 25, 1928; d. Irving and Fanny (Miller) Blatt; B.A., Adelphi U., 1947; M.S. (Swift fellow, Cal. Pub. Health fellow), Stanford, 1948; M.L.S., U. Cal. at Los Angeles, 1966; m. Harry J. Simon, Mar. 22, 1949; children—Joel, Amy, Matthew. Chief med. librarian Long Beach (Cal.) Community Hosp., 1966-72; mem. Long Beach City Council, 1972—. Free-lance writer, 1958—; chmn. Long Beach Mayor's Task Force on City Planning, 1970-72; mem. Long Beach Mayor's Charter Revision Com., 1961-63. Bd. dirs. Los Angeles County Comprehensive Health Planning Com. Recipient Torch of Liberty award, 1972. Mem. League Women Voters, Long Beach C. of C., Beta Phi Mu. Home: 545 Orlena Av Long Beach CA 90814 Office: 205 W Broadway Long Beach CA 90802

SIMON, RITA JAMES (MRS. JULIAN SIMON), educator; b. Bklyn., Nov. 26, 1931; d. Abraham and Irene (Waldman) Mintz; B.A., U. Wis., 1952; postgrad. Cornell U., 1952-54; Ph.D., U. Chgo., 1957; m. Julian Simon, June 25, 1961; children—David Meyer, Judith Debs, Daniel Hillel. Research asso. U. Chgo., Law Sch., 1957-61, asst. prof. sociology dept., 1959-61; research asso. Columbia Sch. Social Work, 1961-63; prof. sociology dept. Inst. Communications Research U. Ill., Urbana, 1963—, head dept., 1968-70. Guggenheim fellow, 1966-67; Ford Found. fellow, 1970-71. Mem. Am. Sociol. Assn. (nat. council), Soc. for Study Social Problems. Jewish religion. Author: The American Jury: The Plea of Insanity, 1966; As We Saw the Thirties, 1967; The Sociology of Law, 1968; (with Jeffrey O'Connell) Payment for Pain and Suffering-Who Wants What, When and Why? Home: 1105 S Busey St Urbana IL 61801

SIMON, SHIRLEY SCHWARTZ (MRS. EDGAR H. SIMON), author; b. Cleve., Mar. 21, 1921; d. Bernard H. and Sylvia (Silverman) Schwartz; student Western Res. U., 1938-40; B.A., Goddard Coll., 1973; m. Edgar H. Simon, Mar. 1, 1942; children—Allen Harold, Ruth Esther. Tchr. juvenile writing div. gen. studies Western Res. U., Cleve., 1965-68, Shaker Heights (O.) Adult Edn. Program, Cleve., 1968-70, John Carroll U., 1969—; instr. creative writing extended learning program Ohio U., 1972—; tchr. Children's lit. Glen Oak Sch., Gates Mills, O., 1973—; speaker Cleve. Book Fair, 1963-68, Dayton (O.) Book Fair, 1965. Mem. Women's Nat. Book Assn., Authors Guild. Author: Molly's Cottage, 1959; Molly and the Rooftop Mystery, 1961; Cousins at Camm Corners, 1963; Best Friend, 1964, paperback edit., 1968; Libby's Stepfamily, 1966. Contbr. stories, serials and plays to Jack and Jill, Child Life, The Writer, and other nat. juvenile and tchrs. publs. Home: 3630 Cedarbrook Rd Cleveland OH 44118

SIMON, VIVIEN JEAN, found. exec.; b. Chgo., May 19, 1939; B.J., U. Tex., 1961; postgrad. U. Houston, 1971-74; 1 son, Robert James. Pub. relations, advt. asst. Tex. Med. Assn., Austin, 1962-64; adminstrv. dir. Houston chpt. Tex. Soc. C.P.A.'s, 1964-70; adminstr. assos. program Coll. of Bus. Adminstrn., U. Houston, 1970-72; exec. dir. Houston Found. for Accounting Edn., 1972—. Mem. Women In Communications (pres. 1970, nat. chmn. ann. meeting 1972), Pub. Relations Soc. Am. (accredited). Lutheran. Home: 6118 Fairdale #30 Houston TX 77027 Office: 3130 SW Freeway Houston TX 77006

SIMONDS, MARY ELIZABETH MINARD (MRS. STUART SWIFT SIMONDS), ret. educator; b. Westminster, Vt., Mar. 27, 1910; d. Seymour Henry and Elizabeth Frances (Frazer) Minard; diploma Vt. Acad., 1927; diploma Springfield Kindergarten-Primary Normal Sch., 1929; student Columbia Tchrs. Coll., 1937, Springfield Coll., 1943, U. Conn., 1944-45, U. Vt., 1949-50, 71, Ore. Coll. Edn. (Nat. Def. Edn. Act fellow), 1967; m. Stuart Swift Simonds, Aug. 21, 1941. Asst. mng. dir. Springfield Girls Club, Mass., 1929-30; tchr. rural schs. Vt., 1931-38; dir. pvt. kindergarten, Saxtons River, Vt., 1939-41; tchr. kindergarten Israel Putnam Sch., Putnam, Conn., 1942-45, Brattleboro (Vt.) Pub. Schs., 1945-73. Chmn. kindergarten study com. New Eng. Sch. Devel. Council, 1953-58; steering com. New Eng. Kindergarten Ann. Conf., 1960—. Instigator and chmn. Westminster Devel. Com., 1953-63; chmn. Airport Planning Com. of

Windham Regional Planning and Devel. Commn., 1967—; chmn. analysis com. Westminster Planning and Devel. Commn., 1970—. Pres. Vt. Fedn. Republican Women, 1961-63, vice-chmn., 1973—. Trustee Westminster Pub. Funds, 1956-62; treas. Vt. Acad. Alumni Fund, 1940—. Active state, county and local Republican Party. Mem. Vt. Soc. Colonial Dames (pres. 1970—), Vt. Assn. Childhood Edn. (pres. 1950-55), Windham-Southeast Edn. Assn. (pres. 1971-72), Vt. Geneal. Soc. (charter). Episcopalian. Order Eastern Star (past matron). Club: Brattleboro Woman's (Vt.). Author: History of Westminster, 1941. Home: Route 3 Westminster West Putney VT 05346 Office: Pleasant St Saxtons River VT 05154

SIMONS, BARBARA BROOKS, ency. editor; b. Rockford, Ill., Dec. 4, 1934; d. Ralph Raymond and Ruth Laura (Freed) Brooks; B.S. in Journalism, Northwestern U., 1955; div. 1 dau., Elizabeth. Subeditor, Ency. Britannica, 1957-60; staff editor Sci. Research Assos., Chgo., 1960-64; editor Systems for Education, Chgo., 1964-68; free lance editor-writer, Chgo., 1965-71; mng. editor Contemporary Publishers (Times-Mirror), Chgo., 1971—, also mng. editor Volume Library, 1971—. Mem. Women in Communications, Alpha Omicron Pi. Author: (with Richard Whittingham) The Earth and the Stars, 1968; (with Richard Whittingham) Holidays and Entertainments, 1968. Home: 511 W Aldine Av Chicago IL 60657 Office: 154 E Erie St Chicago IL 60611

SIMONS, JEANNE REIDY (MRS. JOSEPH B. SIMONS), educator; b. Rock Island, Ill., Feb. 3, 1929; d. John Cyril and Evelyn (Peterson) Reidy; B.A., Marycrest Coll., 1951, M.A., 1963; Ph.D., U. Notre Dame, 1969; m. Joseph B. Simons, May 22, 1969. Tchr., Ottumwa (Ia.) Heights Coll., 1953-66; instr. humanities U. Notre Dame, 1968-69; tchr. philosophy Santa Rosa (Cal.) Community Coll., 1969—. Counselor, Sonoma County Mental Health Services, 1970—, co-dir. group dynamics workshops, 1967—. Mem. Am. Philos. Assn. Author: (with Joseph B. Simons) The Risk of Loving, 1968; (with Joseph B. Simons) Wisdom's Child: Exploring Adult Immaturity, 1969; (with Joseph B. Simons) The Risk of Freedom, 1970; (with Joseph B. Simons) The Human Art of Counseling, 1971. Home: 1333 W Steele Lane Santa Rosa CA 95401

SIMONS, LOUISE BEDELL (MRS. MANLEY HALE SIMONS, JR.), artist; b. Jacksonville, Fla., July 31, 1912; d. George Chester and Louise (Gale) Bedell; student Auburn U., 1930—; m. Manley Hale Simons, Jr., Oct. 7, 1931; 1 dau., Louise Gale (Mrs. Spottswood Blair Burwell). Exhibited one-woman shows, Norfolk, Va., Georgetown, D.C.; exhibited in group shows at Fine Arts div. Smithsonian Instn., Arts Club, Washington; Norfolk Art Mus., Down East Gallery, Glen Echo, Md., Art Mus., Charleston, S.C.; Nat. Miniature Show, N.J.; represented in permanent collections; v.p. Miniature Painters, Sculptors & Gravers Soc., Washington, 1968-72, pres., 1972-73. Vol., House of Mercy, Washington, 1967-70. Recipient 1st prize in watercolor Mems. Show, Arts Club Washington, 1968; 3d pl. Am. Art League Show, 1964, hon. mention, 1972; hon. mention Nat. Miniature Show, Washington, 1971; others. Mem. Arts Club Washington, Am. Art League, Chi Omega. Republican. Episcopalian. Address: 5506 Cromwell Dr Bethesda MD 20016

SIMONS, NETTY ROTHENBERG (MRS. LEON GEORGE SIMONS), composer; b. N.Y.C., Oct. 26, 1913; d. Charles and Cecelia (Tandick) Rothenberg; student N.Y. U. Sch. Fine Arts, 1931-33, 34-37, (scholarship) Juilliard Grad. Sch. Music, 1933-34; m. Leon George Simons, Dec. 27, 1936; children—Ellen Ann, Thomas Manuel. Tchr., Third St. Music Sch. Settlement, N.Y.C., 1928-33; pvt. music tchr., piano, theory, counterpoint and composition, 1928-56; producer, scriptwriter radio broadcasts Am. Composers Alliance, WNYC, N.Y.C., 1966-71; scriptwriter series contemporary music stas. WUOM-WVGR, U. Mich., 1971; producer, coordinator Composers Concerts, Carnegie Recital Hall, 1960, 61. Music chmn. bd. dirs. Rockland Found., Nyack, N.Y., 1959-61. Recipient rec. pub. award Ford Found., 1971. Mem. Am. Music Center, Am. Composers Alliance (bd. govs. 1972-74), Broadcast Music, Inc. Composer music for soloists, chamber groups, chorus, orch., dance and opera; works performed U.S., Europe, Japan, Australia; also recs. Home: 303 E 57th St New York City NY 10022

SIMONS, VIVIAN YEVETTA (MRS. CHARLES MCLYLE SIMONS), educator; b. Meridian, La., Dec. 18, 1913; d. Silas Cooper and Adeline Rebecca (Lutz) Carroll; B.A., Baylor U., 1935; postgrad. U. Chgo., 1945-47, Northwestern U., 1947-48, U. Houston, 1967-69; M.A., Lamar U., 1963, postgrad., 1971-72; m. Charles McLyle Simons, Feb. 21, 1948; children—Diana Lynne (dec.), Janet Carroll. Tchr. Southland Ind. Sch. Dist., Beaumont, Tex., 1935-36; tchr. South Park Ind. Sch. Dist., Beaumont, Tex., 1936-42, 58-66, 69-71, TV master tchr., 1966-69, ombudsman, 1971-73, editor South Park Highlights, 1971—, fed. grant project dir., 1973—; purchasing agt. M.W. Kellogg Co., Chgo., 1942-48; tchr. Beaumont (Tex.) Ind. Sch. Dist., 1951-53. Cons. Nystrom Co., 1961-65, Lamar Area Sch. Study Council, 1960-63, Tex. Assn. for Improvement of Reading, 1967-69. Mem. N.E.A., Tex. State Tchrs. Assn., S. Park Adminstrv. Council, Tex. Joint English Com. (gen. chmn. 1969-70), Altrusa Internat., Eta Nu, Delta Kappa Gamma. Baptist. Home: 3939 North St Beaumont TX 77706 Office: 1025 Woodrow St Beaumont TX 77705

SIMONSON, JOY ROSENHEIM (MRS. RICHARD C. SIMONSON), govt. ofcl., civic worker; b. N.Y.C.; d. Sidney T. and Rosalie (Spiegel) Rosenheim; B.A. magna cum laude, Bryn Mawr Coll., 1940; postgrad. Am. U., 1941; m. Richard C. Simonson, Nov. 3, 1945; 3 children. Research aid House Com. Interstate Migration, Washington, 1941; labor market analyst War Manpower Commn., Washington, 1942-44; statistician UNRRA, Yugoslavia, 1944-45; personnel control officer U.S. Forces ETO, Frankfurt, Germany, 1945-48. Vice-chmn. Washington Action for Youth, 1963-65; mem. Citizens Council D.C., 1963-64, Pub. Health Adv. Council, 1959-64; chmn. Alcoholic Beverage Control Bd., Washington, 1964-72; exec. dir. D.C. Manpower Adv. Com., 1972—. Mem. Adv. Com. Women Sec. Labor, Washington, 1973—, D.C. Adv. Council on Vocational Edn., 1974—. Vice pres. League Women Voters D.C., 1955-61, pres., 1961-63; mem. D.C. Commn. Status of Women, 1966—; pres. Interstate Assn. Commns. on Status Women, 1972—. Ky. col., 1965. Democrat. Home: 2929 University Terrace NW Washington DC 20016 Office: 1100 Vermont Av NW Washington DC 20005

SIMPSON, MRS. DONALD J., mountaineer, club woman; b. Paola, Kan., Nov. 2, 1906; d. Charles T. and Carrie (Carpenter) Wheeler; B.S. in Speech, Northwestern U., 1929; m. Donald J. Simpson, July 6, 1931; children—John Douglas, Marcia Lynne. Mem. bd. Ill. Opera Guild, Chgo. Drama League. Recipient nat. award Am. Assn. State and Local History. Mem. Am., Swiss Ladies Alpine clubs, Evanston Hist. Soc. (mem. bd. guild; trustee, curator costumes), Orchesis, Delta Delta Delta, Zeta Phi Eta (nat. distinguished service award). Conglist. Clubs: Alpine of Canada (Calgary, Alta.); Chicago Mountaineering; Evanston Drama. Mountains scaled include Matterhorn, 1951, 55, 59, Mont Blanc, 1954-69, Dent De Geant, 1953, Dom, 1953, Obergabelhorn, 1957, Piz Palu, 1957, Jungfrau, 1954 (all Alps), Mt. Sir Donald, 1952, Mt. Victoria, 1952, Mt. Huber, 1956 (all Can.), Grand Teton, 1958 (U.S.), Dent Blanche, 1962, Kilimanjaro, 1964, 66. Home: 2733 Lincoln St Evanston IL 60201

SIMPSON, ELIZABETH LÉONIE, educator; b. Pasadena, Cal.; d. George Gaylord and Anne (Roe) Simpson; B.A., U. Mich., 1951, M.A., 1953; Ph.D., U. Cal. at Berkeley, 1970; postdoctoral study U. So. Cal., 1971-72; children—Martha Korwin-Pawlowski, Bethany Korwin-Pawlowski, Garth Simpson. Research asso. Center for the Study of Instrn., San Francisco, 1963-68; acting instr. U. Cal. at Berkeley, 1969-70; asst. prof. edn. U. So. Cal., University Park, 1970-72, asso. dir. Center for Internat. Edn., 1970-72, adj. asso. prof., 1972-74; vis. asso. prof. social ecology U. Cal. at Irvine, 1974—. Cons. U.S. Office Edn., Nat. Inst. Edn., Nat. Endowment Humanities, Ford Found. Recipient Distinguished Research award Pi Lambda Theta, 1970. Mem. Soc. Psychol. Study of Social Issues, Am. Polit. Sci. Assn., Am. Ednl. Research Assn., Am. Psychol. Assn., Assn. Humanistic Psychology, Pi Lambda Theta. Author: Democracy's Stepchildren: A Study of Need and Belief, 1971; Tramontane, 1968; (with others) The Social Sciences: Concepts and Values, 1970-72; River Run Deep, River Run Strong: Confluence in Humanistic Education, 1974; The American Revolutionary Experience, 1776—, 1974. Contbr. poems and short stories to lit. jours., and articles to profl. jours. Home: 850 2d St Santa Monica CA 90403 Office: Program in Social Ecology U Cal at Irvine Irvine CA 92664

SIMPSON, ELLEN, physician; b. Avalon, Wis., Aug. 9, 1917; d. Robert Henry and Emily Ann (Moore) Simpson; B.S., U. Cal. at San Francisco, 1941, M.D., 1949. Intern pediatrics U. Cal. at San Francisco, 1949-50, 51-53, USPHS fellow in cardiology, 1953-54, instr. pediatrics, 1954-57, asst. prof., 1957-67, staff cardiovascular research inst., 1958—; resident pediatrics Children's Med. Center, Boston, 1950-51; chief pediatrics St. Lukes Hosp., San Francisco, 1969-71. Asst. dir. Children's Diabetic Camp; cons. cardiology San Francisco Dept. Pub. Health; med. service Children's Med. Relief, Saigon, Vietnam, 1972, 73. Bd. dirs. Diabetic Youth Found., Gov.'s San Francisco Heart Assn. Mem. Am., Cal. med. assns., Am. Camping Assn. (dir. No. Cal. sect.), San Francisco Med. Soc., Am., San Francisco heart assns. Home: 1651 8th Av San Francisco CA 94122

SIMPSON, GWEN HOLLY (MRS. ALBERT MILLER SIMPSON), educator; b. Mpls., Jan. 14, 1915; d. Alexander Curt Von and Kathlyn Madge (MacDonald) Holly; B.A., Coll. of St. Catherine, St. Paul, 1934; postgrad. Goodman Sch. of Theatre, Chgo., 1934, U. Minn., 1948-57, Southampton (Eng.) U., 1967-69; M.A., Occidental Coll., 1960; advanced study Oxford completion Ph.D., U. London, 1971; m. Albert Miller Simpson, Feb. 6, 1935 (dec. Dec. 1943); 1 dau., Pamela Algwen. Head theatre arts, asst. dean Marywood Little Theatre, Marywood Sch. for Girls, Anaheim, Cal., 1947-56; dir. theatre dept. San Diego Coll. for Women, 1956-58; tchr. Pasadena (Cal.) City Schs., 1958—, dir. theater arts, 1958-68. Tchr. adult edn., Arcadia, Cal., 1954-56; guest instr. Southampton U., 1967-68; instr. modern drama and Shakespeare, Internat. U., 1971-72. Mem. Cal. Republican Central Com., 1968-72, mem. fine arts com., 1970-72; mem. Los Angeles County Rep. Loyalty Club. Chmn., Coll. of St. Catherine Los Angeles County Alumnae, 1940-52. Recipient Community Service award United Crusade, 1966, Flynn Found. award, 1953, 54, five nat. awards in performing arts Nat. Thespian Soc. Mem. Nat. Thespian Soc. (state dir. 1964-69), Friends Huntington Library, Am. Theatre Assn., Profl. Educators Group Cal., Nat. Assn. Profl. Educators (founder), Profl. Educators Pasadena (charter pres.), Am. Inst. Foreign Study (area sec. 1967-69), Internat. Platform Assn., Nat. Collegiate Players (hon.). Roman Catholic. Author: An Approach to Children's Theatre, Dramatics, 1968; Assignments in Drama Text, 1970; (plays) The Bridal Path, 1952, Low I Kneel, 1952, A Time for Love, 1956. Office: Box 8431 San Marino CA 91108

SIMPSON, JOANNE GEROULD (MRS. ROBERT H. SIMPSON), meteorologist; b. Boston, Mar. 23, 1923; d. Russell and Virginia (Vaughan) Gerould; B.S., U. Chgo., 1943, M.S., 1945, Ph.D., 1949; m. W.V.R. Malkus, 1948 (div. 1964); children—David, Steven, Karen; m. 2d, Robert H. Simpson, Jan. 6, 1965. Asst. prof. physics, meteorology Ill. Inst. Tech., Chgo., 1945-51; meteorologist Woods Hole (Mass.) Oceanographic Instn., 1951-61; prof. meteorology U. Cal. at Los Angeles, 1961-65; dir. Exptl. Meteorology Lab. Nat. Oceanic and Atmospheric Adminstrn., Coral Gables, Fla., 1965-73; adj. prof. atmospheric scis. U. Miami, Coral Gables, 1967-73; prof. environmental scis. U. Va., Charlottesville, 1973—. Mem. Fla. Gov.'s Environmental Coordination Council, 1971—. Guggenheim fellow, 1954. Recipient Meisinger award, 1962; Dept. Commerce gold medal, 1972. Fellow Am. Meteorol. Soc., Royal Meteorol. Soc. (Britain). Author: (with Herbert Riehl) Cloud Structure and Distributions Over the Tropical Pacific Ocean, 1964. Home: Route 743 Charlottesville VA Office: Brooks Mus Dept Environmental Scis U Va Charlottesville VA 22904

SIMPSON, LOUISE LEDYARD GARDINIER (MRS. GEORGE G. SIMPSON), journalist; b. Laurel, Miss., Mar. 17, 1914; d. Dewey Francis and Anice Ledyard (Halsell) Gardinier; grad. high sch.; m. George G. Simpson, May 27, 1937. Soc. editor Laurel (Miss.) Daily Leader, 1932-38; asso. women's editor Laurel Leader-Call, 1961-69, women's editor, 1969—; reporter Clarion Ledger, Jackson, Miss., 1958—. Bd. dirs. Laurel YWCA, 1969—. Recipient first place awards Miss. Press Women's Contest, 1965, 69, 70, 71, 73, 2d place award 1969; award Council Garden Clubs, 1973. Mem. Miss. Press Women, Nat. Press Women, Beta Sigma Phi (hon.). Episcopalian (pres. churchwomen 1946-48). Clubs: Argus, Park Place Garden (Laurel). Home: 843 6th Av Laurel MS 39440 Office: 130 Beacon St Laurel MS 39440

SIMPSON, LUBERTA STREATER (MRS. LUTHER G. SIMPSON), Christian Sci. practitioner; b. West Point, Miss.; d. Thomas and Mamie (Boatman) Streater; student Justice Bus. Coll., N.Y.C., 1932-33; m. Clem O. Williams, Jan. 1, 1924 (div. Mar. 1942); children—Clem O., Clarence R.; m. 2d, Luther G. Simpson, Apr. 16, 1943. Christian Sci. practitioner, 1961—. Sunday sch. tchr. Missionary Bapt. Ch., West Point, 1922-23, pres. Young People's Union, 1922-23; mem. 1st Ch. Christ Scientist, Boston, 1944—; supt. 39th Ch. Christ Scientist, Los Angeles, 1957, sec. Sunday Sch., 1947-50, 1st reader, 1953-54, clk., 1955-59, chmn. bd. dirs., 1952—, clk., librarian, 1964—, 2d reader, 1963—; librarian Christian Sci. Reading Room, Los Angeles, 1953, supt. Sunday Sch., chmn. ch.'s lecture com. Address: 2021 7th Av Los Angeles CA 90018

SIMPSON, MADELINE LOUISA, educator; b. Norfolk, Va., June 22, 1923; d. David Edward and Zenobia Eleanor (Ross) Simpson; student Va. Union U., Norfolk div. jr. coll., 1940-42; B.A., Fisk U., 1944; M.S., Boston U., 1951; M.A., New Sch. Social Research, 1967. Dean of women Va. Theol. Sem. and Coll., 1945-46; with Norfolk County Dept. Pub. Welfare, 1946-51; with dept. social service Harlem Hosp., 1951-53, Dept. Social Service, Hosp. Joint Diseases, 1953-55; founder, dir. L'Institut du Bien-Etre Social, Port-au-Prince, Haiti, 1959-61; with Speedwell Service for Children, N.Y.C., 1964-68, Salvation Army Foster Home Service, 1968-69; mem. faculty Del. State Coll., 1969-71, Salisbury State Coll., 1971-72; asso. prof. psychology Cheyney State Coll. (Pa.), 1972—. Adj. instr. Montclair State Coll., Jersey City State Coll., Wesley Coll. Mem. Am. Assn. U. Profs., Am. Psychol. Assn. (asso.), Delta Sigma Theta. Home: 91 Schuyler Rd Goldsboro MD 21636

SIMPSON, MILDRED JEAN (MRS. RICHARD H. SIMPSON), librarian; b. Bethlehem, Pa., Mar. 15, 1939; d. Norman Oscar and Meda Elizabeth (Young) Weierbach; student Bucknell U., 1957-59; B.A., U. Del., 1960; M.S. in L.S., U. So. Cal., 1962; m. Richard H. Simpson, June 13, 1959; children—Richard Evan, Andrew Henry. Asst. circulation librarian U. So. Cal., Los Angeles, 1962-64; asst. librarian Acad. Motion Picture Arts and Scis., Los Angeles, 1964-68, chief librarian, 1968—. Mem. graphic arts council Los Angeles County Mus. Art, 1968—. Mem. No. Ariz. Soc. Sci. and Art, A.L.A., Spl. Libraries Assn., Soc. Cal. Archivists, Soc. Am. Archivists, Alpha Chi Omega, Beta Phi Mu. Editorial adv. bd. Am. Film Inst. Catalog, 1968—. Home: 3122 Butler Av Los Angeles CA 90066 Office: 9038 Melrose Av Los Angeles CA 90069

SIMPSON, MINNIE ELIZABETH MILLER (MRS. KNOWLTON SIMPSON), artist, art instr.; b. Linden, Tex., Jan. 31, 1903; d. Buford and Evie (Simmons) Miller; pvt. studies Frederic Taubes; m. Knowlton Simpson, July 11, 1925. One-man shows Centennial Mus., Corpus Christi, 1953, YWCA, Corpus Christi, 1954, Waco, 1956, Loredo, 1958, others; exhibited in group shows Smithsonian Inst., 1954-56, Internat. Platform Assn., Washington, 1965; art instr. Recipient silver trophy for distinguished community service, Corpus Christi. Mem. Corpus Christi Art Found. (pres. 1953-54), Corpus Christi Fine Art Colony (pres. 1953-54), South Tex. Traditional Art Assn. (pres. 1961—), Corpus Christi Art Guild (chmn. 1951-54), Nat. League Am. Pen Women, Internat. Platform Assn., Council Am. Artists Socs. N.Y.C., Centro e Scambi Internazionali Rome Italy (hon. rep. bd.). Address: 722 Drexel Dr Corpus Christi TX 78412

SIMPSON, PEGGY ANN, journalist; b. San Antonio, Dec. 26, 1938; d. Robert H. and Mazie (Houston) Simpson; B.A., North Tex. State U., 1957-60, postgrad., 1960. News editor, Hondo, Tex., 1960-62; reporter, Associated Press, Dallas, 1962-68, Washington, 1968-73, house gen. staff, 1973—; lectr. U. Fla. Sch. Communications. Guest lectr. Sears Journalism Intern program, 1970-73. Pres., Uplift House Community Center, Inc., 1972—, v.p., 1973-74. State committeeman Young Democrats, 1958-60. Mem. Women in Communications, Journalists Profl. Equality, Sigma Delta Chi. Methodist (rep. to bd. 1970-72). Club: Washington Press (1st v.p. 1973-74). Home: 1711 Massachusetts Av No 728 Washington DC 20036 Office: House Press Gallery Capitol Washington DC 20005

SIMPSON, REBECCA MAY (MRS. JOHN ANDERSON SIMPSON), lawyer; b. Massillon, O., July 8, 1892; d. Jefferson and Gwendolyn (Davis) Packer; m. John Anderson Simpson, June 11, 1914; children—John P., Esther (Mrs. William J. Peck). Admitted to Ill. bar, 1926; mem. firm Simpson & Simpson, Aurora, Ill., 1945—. Mem. Kane County Bar Assn. Democrat. Baptist. Home: PO Box 205 Batavia IL 60510 Office: 105 E Galena Blvd Aurora IL 60504

SIMPSON, RITA ADAMS (MRS. JOSEPH BRADFORD SIMPSON, JR.), county ofcl.; b. Charlotte, N.C., Jan. 14, 1928; d. Leary Warren and Will O'Mae (Gettys) Adams; student Agnes Scott Coll., 1945-47; A.B., U. N.C., 1949; m. Joseph Bradford Simpson, Jr., June 3, 1951 (div. Apr. 1968); children—Cynthia Adams, Joseph Bradford III, John Avery. Reporter, The Charlotte Observer, 1949-51; dir. alumnae affairs Queens Coll., Charlotte, 1964-68; religion editor The Charlotte News, 1968-72; editor Quest, 1972-73; pub. service and information officer, Mecklenburg County, N.C., 1973—. Chmn. pub. information com. Arlington (Va.) chpt. A.R.C., 1951-52. Bd. dirs., chmn. season ticket campaign Charlotte Symphony Orch., 1957-58; bd. dirs. Presbyn. Hosp. Aux. Mem. Agnes Scott Alumnae (chpt. pres. 1956-57), D.A.R., Women in Communications, Alpha Delta Pi. Home: 2221 Westminster Pl Charlotte NC 28207 Office: County Office Bldg 720 E 4th St Charlotte NC 28202

SIMPSON, SHIRLEY ROSE, physician; b. Pierce, Fla., Dec. 25, 1933; d. William Nathaniel and Rose Pearl (Taylor) Simpson; B.S., Fla. State U., 1955; M.D., U. Fla., 1965. Tchr. phys. edn. N.E. High Sch., St. Petersburg, Fla., 1955-57, Meadow Lawn Jr. High Sch., St. Petersburg, 1957-59; intern, Lakeland (Fla.) Gen. Hosp., 1965-66; resident Jacksonville (Fla.) Hosps. Ednl. Program-Duval Med. Center, including Bapt. Hosp., Hope Hosp. and St. Vincent Hosp., 1966-67; practice medicine specializing in gen. medicine and pediatrics, Port St. Joe, Fla., 1967—; mem. staffs Municipal Hosp., Port St. Joe; med. adviser Gulf County (Fla.) Mental Health Clinic, 1972-73. Bd. dir. Am. Cancer Soc., Fla. div., 1972-73, pres. Gulf County sect., 1973. Mem. Franklin-Gulf County Med. Soc. (sec. 1967-70). Home: Simmons Bayou Port St Joe FL 32456 Office: 324 Long Av Port St Joe FL 32452

SIMPSON, VALERIE JEAN TAYLOR (MRS. DONALD SIMPSON), mus. ofcl.; b. St. John, N.B., Can., Nov. 12, 1936; d. Joseph Hazen and Marjorie Abigail (Jones) Taylor; student U. N.B. at St. John, 1969; m. Donald Simpson, Mar. 3, 1959; children—Wade Donald, Kelly Jean, Tracey Dawn. Stenographer, Fed. Govt., St. John, 1955-59; clk. typist N.B. Mus., St. John, 1968, curatorial asst. history dept., 1969, registrar, 1970—. Founder, St. John Heritage Trust, 1971, rec., corr. sec., 1972, 1st v.p., 1973. Mem. Canadian Mus. Assn., St. John Conservation Council (dir. 1971), N.B. Hist. Soc. (exec. council 1969-72). Author: Fort Ste. Marie, 1969. Home: 52 Candlewood Lane Saint John NB Canada Office: 277 Douglas Av Saint John NB Canada

SIMPSON, VICTORIA MAGALINE, home economist; b. Fernandina Beach, Fla., Sept. 19, 1923; d. Leroy and Catherine D.E. (Wilson) Simpson; B.S., Fla. A. and M. U., 1945; postgrad. summers Mich. State U., 1947, Prairie View A. and M. U., 1950. Tchr. home econs., Marion County, Fla., 1945-47, Fla. A. and M. U., Tallahassee, 1947-49; extension home econs. agt., Columbia County, Fla., 1949-50, Dade County, Miami, Fla., 1950—. Adv. com. Booker T. Washington Community Sch., Miami, 1971—; active Dade County Assn. Retarded Children, Greater Miami, Urban League, Dade County Youth Fair, Dade County 4-H Youth Found., Dade County YMCA, Carver br. Recipient Distinguished Service award Nat. Assn. Extension Home Economists, 1961, Booker T. Washington Community Sch. Assn., award for 4-H work, service awards Dade County Cooperative Extension Service, Dade County Youth Fair. Mem. Am. Home Econs. Assn., Nat., Fla. assns. extension home econs. agts., Epsilon Sigma Phi, Alpha Kappa Mu, Delta Sigma Theta (Community service award). Home: 13840 Monroe St Miami FL 33158 Office: 2690 NW 7th Av Miami FL 33127

SIMPSON, (ZELMA) ALENE (MRS. EUGENE L. SIMPSON), librarian; b. Bristow, Okla., Nov. 2, 1923; d. Robert E. and Zelma (Wolfe) Tidrow; B.S., Central State U., Edmond, Okla., 1948, also postgrad.; m. Eugene L. Simpson, Dec. 26, 1945 (dec. Apr. 1967); 1 son, Lantz Eugene. Tchr. Okla. County Schs., 1948-65; with Okla Hist. Soc. Library, Oklahoma City, 1965—, head librarian, 1965—. Lectr. on local history, beginning genealogy. Sec.-treas. Broncho Basketball Boosters, Central State U., Edmond, Okla., 1967—. Mem. Okla. Geneal. Soc. (chmn. 1967-69; 1st v.p. 1970-71, acquisitions chmn. 1971-72, pres. 1972-73), Am., Okla. library assns., Eastern Okla., Cimarron Valley hist. socs., Pontotoc County Hist. and Geneal. Soc., State Hist. Soc. Mo. Home: 33 E 9th St Edmond OK 73034 Office: Historical Bldg Oklahoma City OK 73105

SIMS, LYNN C. LEARNED (MRS. JAMES MARION SIMS), artist; b. Los Angeles, Dec. 26, 1937; d. Richard Hall and Kathryn (Klitten) Learned; student U. So. Cal., 1955-57; m. James Marion Sims, Jan. 8, 1957; children—James Marion, John Morgan, Richard Michael. Tchr. Creative Arts Planning Group, N.J., 1968, Mendocino (Cal.) Art Center, 1969—; one-man shows at Franklin Lakes Gallery; exhibited in group shows at Tucson Art Center, Am. House, N.Y.C., N.J. Cultural Council, Egg and Eye Gallery, L.A.; Fairtree Gallery, N.Y.C., Cal. Design Xi, Pasadena Art Mus.; represented in pvt. collections. Dir. Mendocino Art Center Gallery, 1969. Chmn. Los Madrinas Debutantes of Los Angeles Children's Hosp., 1955, mem. Peninsula com., 1957—; Participating mem. Los Angeles Center for Internat. Visitors, 1965-67; chmn. coordinating com., instr. art Office Econ. Opportunity, Upward Bound Program, Marymount Coll., 1967. Recipient award for valor Girl Scouts Am., 1950. Mem. Am. Craftsmen's Council, Palos Verdes Art Assn. (co-dir. art festival 1966), Pi Beta Phi. Home and studio: PO Box 66 Mendocino CA 95460

SIMS, PATSY, journalist; b. Beaumont, Tex., Feb. 14, 1938; d. Robert Ray and Edna (Shanks) Sims; B.A., Tulane U., 1960; m. Lawrence G. Hountha, Nov. 25, 1960 (div. 1970). Women's sect. reporter States-Item, New Orleans, 1958-60, news side reporter, 1962-63, asst. womens editor, 1963-69, womens editor, 1969-71, spl. assignment writer, 1972-73; staff women's dept. San Francisco Chronicle, 1971, acting women's editor, 1971, staff people's sect., 1971-72; feature writer Phila. Inquirer, 1973—; pub. relations information La. Bd. Health, 1960-62. Recipient Catherine O'Brien award, 1964, First prizes New Orleans Press Club, 1964, 66, 68-70, 72; Headliner of Year award New Orleans chpt. Theta Sigma Phi, 1971; first place best investigative reporting La.-Miss. Asso. Press award. Mem. New Orleans Press Club, La. Press Women's Assn., Women in Communications. Home: 725 Walnut St 3A Philadelphia PA 19106 Office: 400 N Broad St Philadelphia PA 19101

SIMS, RUTH LEISERSON (MRS. ALBERT G. SIMS), state ofcl.; b. Rochester, N.Y., Mar. 4, 1920; d. William M. and Emily Nash (Bodman) Leiserson; B.A., Oberlin Coll., 1940; m. Albert G. Sims, Aug. 30, 1941; children—Christopher Albert, William James, Marjorie (Mrs. Scott Lawrence), Jennifer Emily. Pres., League Women Voters, Greenwich, Conn., 1962-64, state pres. Conn., 1967-71, dir. election systems survey project League Women Voters U.S.-Nat. Municipal League, 1971-72, dir.; action chmn. nat. orgn., 1972—, trustee edn. fund, 1972—; vice chmn. Conn. Compensation Commn., 1971-73, chmn., 1973—. Dir. So. New Eng. Telephone Co.; incorporator First Women's Bank and Trust Co. Conn., 1974—. Pres., Greenwich High Sch. P.T.A., 1958-59; mem. Conn. Gov.'s Conf. on Human Rights and Opportunities, 1967, Citizens Conf. on Conn. Gen. Assembly, 1968—; chmn. adv. com. Greenwich Bd. Edn., 1972-73. Mem. Greenwich Representative Town Meeting, 1967-69. Bd. dirs. Citizens Conf. on State Legislatures, 1974—; trustee Oberlin Coll., 1975—, Overseas Edn. Fund, 1973—. Mem. Oberlin Coll. Alumni Assn. (dir.). Unitarian-Universalist (past clk., trustee). Home: 50 Hidden Brook Rd Riverside CT 06878

SIMUNICH, MARY ELIZABETH HEDRICK (MRS. WILLIAM A. SIMUNICH), pub. relations exec.; b. Chgo.; d. Tubman Keene and Mary (McCamish) Hedrick; student Phoenix Coll., 1967-69, Met. Bus. Coll., 1938-40; m. William A. Simunich, Dec. 6, 1941. Exec. sec. sales mgr. KPHO radio, 1950-53; exec. sec. mgr. KPHO-TV, 1953-54; account exec. Tom Rippey & Assos., 1955-56; pub. relations dir. Phoenix Symphony, 1956-62; co-founder, v.p. Paul J. Hughes Pub. Relations, Inc., 1960-65; owner Mary Simunich Pub. Relations, Phoenix, 1966—. Pub. relations dir. Walter O. Boswell Meml. Hosp., Sun City, Ariz., 1969—. Bd. dirs. Anytown, Ariz. Named Phoenix Advt. Woman of Year, Phoenix Jr. Advt. Club, 1962; recipient award Blue Cross, 1963; 1st Pl. award Am. Press Women, 1966. Mem. Internat. Assn. Bus. Communicators (pres. Ariz. chpt. 1970-71, dir.), Pub. Relations Soc. Am., Am. Soc. Hosp. Pub. Relations (dir.), Nat., Ariz. press women, Bus. and Profl. Women's Club. Club: Phoenix Press. Home: 4133 N 34th Pl Phoenix AZ 85018 Office: PO Box 15178 Phoenix AZ 85018

SINCLAIR, EDNA MARGARET ROSS, book reviewer, dramatist; b. Bloomington, Ill.; d. Oscar Fredrick and Delia (Johnson) Ross; student Ill. Wesleyan U., 1942, Bradley U., 1944; m. Duane C. Sinclair, Nov. 21, 1943; children—Gary Lee, Stephen Ross. Book rev. appearances maj. cities U.S., 1950—, Rantoul (Ill.) High Sch. assemblies, 1959-60; guest speaker Dist. Rally Meth. Young Adults, Kankakee, Ill., 1963; guest speaker Lions Club of Saybrook, 1963. Pres., Colfax (Ill.) P.T.A., 1960; chmn. Park Project, Colfax, 1958; pres. Library Bd. Colfax, 1953—; mem. Brokaw Hosp. Service League, 1961—. Named Career Woman of Year, Bus. and Profl. Women, 1972. Mem. Internat. Platform Assn. (luncheon chmn., hostess, sec. 1966—), Am. Legion Aux. (unit Americanism chmn. local post), Women's Div. Assn. Commerce Bloomington-Normal, Ill. Fedn. Women's Club (div. chmn. lit. and drama div.), Beta Sigma Phi, Alpha Gamma Delta. Methodist (supt. primary dept., past pres. Wesleaders group). Mem. Order Eastern Star (past worthy matron). Clubs: Colfax Woman's (past pres.), Women's (McClean County pres.), Zonta Bloomington-Normal (past pres. Normal, Ill.). Home: 302 Cooper St Colfax IL 61728 Office: 106 S Grove St Colfax IL 61728

SINCLAIR, ORRIETTE COINER (MRS. JAMES A. SINCLAIR), Republican nat. committeewoman for Ida.; b. Twin Falls, Ida., Sept. 17, 1921; d. Walter A. and Marietta Hunsberger (Detweiler) Coiner; student U. Utah, 1939-40; B.S., U. Ida., 1943; m. James A. Sinclair, Apr. 21, 1946; children—Rose Ann (Mrs. John Astorquia), Judy (Mrs. James Imlay), Jan (Mrs. Brent Johanson). Walt. With Bur. Entomology, 1944; dep. clk. Dist. Ct., 1945; with E.W. McRoberts Securities, 1946. Past pres. high sch. P.T.A. Pres., Young Womens Republican Club, 1954-63; mem. Ida. Rep. Com., 1966-70, vice chmn., 1966; Rep. nat. committeewoman for Ida., 1971—. Mem. Am. Legion Aux., P.E.O., Kappa Kappa Gamma. Toastmistress (pres. Twin Falls). Home: PO Box 249 Twin Falls ID 83301

SINCO, EDELMIRA D MADRAGON (MRS. LEANDRO G. SINCO), coll. dean; b. Madila, Philippines, June 16, 1935; d. Jose M. and Esperanza M. (Portilla) MaDragon; came to U.S., 1968; B.S., U. Philippines, 1956, M.Ed., 1964; Ph.D., Mich. State U., 1968; m. Leandro G. Sinco, Apr. 4, 1957; children—Victor Vicente, Luis Leandro. Counselor, prof. Found. U., Dumaguete City, Philippines, 1961-64, head grad. sch. edn., 1961-64, head student affairs, 1961-64; internat. programs specialist Mich. State U., East Lansing, 1968-69; dean of women St. Martin's Coll., Olympia, Wash., 1970-71, fgn. student adviser, 1970—, dean of students, 1971—. Recipient Fulbright-Hays grant, 1964-66. Mem. Am. Personnel and Guidance Assn., Am. Coll. Personnel Assn., Am. Assn. U. Women, Nat. Assn. Women Deans, Adminstrs. and Counselors, Nat. Assn. Fgn. Student Affairs, Zonta Internat., Phi Kappa Phi, Pi Gamma Mu, Delta Kappa Gamma. Home: 5445 Donnelly Dr SE Olympia WA 98501

SINES, VONDA JEAN, advt. copywriter; b. Findlay, O., Nov. 30, 1947; d. Harold Lawrence and Lucille Evelyn (Marquart) Sines; B.S. in Journalism, Northwestern U., 1970. Reporter, feature writer Republican-Courier Newspaper, Findlay, summers, 1969, 70; asst. extension dept. journalism, U. Wis., Madison, 1970-71; editor Am. Soc. Agronomy, Madison, 1971-73; editor, publicist World Council Credit Unions, Madison, 1973-74; retail advt. copywriter Montgomery Ward & Co., Chgo., 1974—. Marathon Oil Co. grantee, 1966-70, Scripps-Howard grantee, 1969, 70. Mem. Women in Communications, Madison Press Club, Zeta Tau Alpha. Democrat. Episcopalian. Home: 832 W Buckingham Pl Chicago IL 60657 Office: 619 W Chicago Av Chicago IL 60606

SINGER, CATHERINE FAULKNER, ednl. adminstr.; b. Barbourville, Ky., Aug. 2, 1913; d. James Edward and Eulah Mae (Swearingen) Faulkner; B.A. summa cum laude, Union Coll., Barbourville, Ky., 1932; postgrad. U. Chgo., 1932; m. Wilson H. Singer, June 12, 1937 (div.); children—Donald Winston, Marcia Catherine. Sec. to pres. Union Coll., Barbourville, Ky., 1933-35, dir. admissions and dir. student work, 1935-37, alumni sec., 1961-70, dir. alumni affairs, 1970—, sec. com. on publs. and communications, 1965—. Bd. dirs. Daniel Boone Festival, 1967-69. Recipient Distinguished Service award Union Coll., 1969. Mem. Alumni Assn. Union Coll. (exec. sec. 1961—), Am. Alumni Council, Woman's Soc. Christian Service, Wesleyan Service Guild, Ministers' Wives' Retreat (leader 1958-59), Iota Sigma Nu (historian 1963—), Beta Chi Alpha, Gamma Beta Phi (faculty adviser 1966—). Methodist (tchr. adult class 1952-60). Clubs. Union College Woman's (pres. 1969-70), General Federation Women's. Editor: Union College Alumnus, 1961—. Home: 501 N Main St Barbourville KY 40906

SINGER, ESTHER FORMAN (MRS. SIDNEY SINGER), artist; b. N.Y.C., Oct. 14; d. Maurice and Sarah (Shaller) Forman; R.N., Albert Einstein Hosp., Phila., 1944; B.A., N.Y.U., 1957; postgrad. Fairleigh Dickinson U., Madison, N.J., 1960-63, New Sch. Social Research, 1965-71; m. Sidney Singer, Oct. 29, 1950; children—Keith Arlen, Maurene Forman. Exhibited in one man shows Papermill Playhouse Galleries, 1965, Bambergers Dept. Store, 1965, Gallery 9-Chatham, 1967, Seton Hall U., 1969, Centenary Coll., Hackettstown, N.J., 1970, Bloomfield Coll., 1970, County Coll. of Morris, 1971, Mus. Modern Art, Paris, France, 1973, Gallery 52, 1973, N.J. State Mus., 1973, one-man show tour, 1973-75; exhibited numerous group shows throughout U.S.; represented in permanent collections at Finch Mus. Contemporary Art, N.Y.C., Newark Mus., Hudson River Mus., Yonkers, N.Y., N.J. State Mus., Trenton, Seton Hall U. Mus. Collection, N.Y. Hosp. Collection, others; art critic Am. Artist mag., Worrall Publs.; tchr. elementary sch. art class Recreation Center South Orange; guest lectr. B'nai B'rith, Deborah; guest panelist Channel 7 TV, 1967-68, radio, 1968-69. Judge local and regional art shows. Served as 1st lt. Army Nurse Corps, 1944-46. Mem. Artists Equity N.J., Artists Equity N.Y., Art Exhbns. Council, Old Bergen Art Guild, Painters and Sculptors Soc. N.J., Am. Vets. Soc. Artists, Miniature Art Soc. N.J. Address: 70 Glenview Rd South Orange NJ 07079

SINGER, JANE SHERROD, editor; b. Wichita Falls, Tex., May 26, 1917; d. St. Claire and Nina (Bean) Sherrod; B.Ed., U. Cal. at Los Angeles, 1938, M.A., 1954; m. Kurt D. Singer, Jan. 21, 1955; children—Marian B., Ken W. Demonstration tchr. elementary edn., U. Cal. at Berkeley, 1940-45; supr. elementary edn., Piedmont, Cal., 1942-45; instr. edn. San Francisco State Coll., 1946-49, Whittier Coll., 1951; cons. edn. John C. Winston Co., 1946-54; mng. editor BP Singer Features, Anaheim, Cal., 1955—, now v.p., editor-in-chief; fgn. corr. Singapore Straits Times, Manila Woman's Weekly, Ceylon Observer and others. Active worker A.R.C., USO. Author: (with Kurt Singer) Spies for Democracy, 1960, Great Adventures of the Sea, 1961, Ho-I-Man and His Friends, 1962; True Adventures in Crime, 1962; Hollywood Star Cook Book, 1960; Albert Schweitzer, Medical Missionary; The Life of Ernest Hemingway; The Danny Kaye Story, Ghost Book, all 1963; Folk Tales from the South Pacific, 1966; Folktales From Mexico, 1968; What You Should Know About Yourself, 1970; Hollywood Star Cookbook, 1971; Test Yourself, 1972; co-author: Lyndon Baines Johnson, Man of Reason, 1964; Folk Tales from Mexico, 1969; Psychological Test Book, 1969; also articles for newspapers, teenage mags., syndicated column Pathways to Success. Office: 3164 W Tyler Av Anaheim CA 92801

SINGER, JUNE, psychologist; b. Cleve., Oct. 23, 1918; d. Jonas E. and Regine V. (Jaulusz) Kurlander; A.B., Ohio State U., 1939; M.A., Northwestern U., 1959, Ph.D., 1968; diploma in analytical psychology C. G. Jung Inst., 1964; m. Richard E. Singer Oct. 23, 1939 (dec. Feb. 1965); 1 dau. Judith (Mrs. Michael Sharp) (dec.). Writer Sci. Research Assos., Chgo., 1959-60; psychologist Virginia Frank Child Devel. Center, Chgo., 1964-66; individual practice psychology, Chgo. 1964—; lectr. Jungian psychology U. Chgo., 1970. Tng. analyst N.Y. Assn. Analytical Psychologists, 1969—. Trustee, C.G. Jung Found. of N.Y. Mem. Analytical Psychology Club Chgo. (founder 1965), Am. Psychol. Assn., Internat. Assn. Analytical Psychologists. Author: The Unholy Bible: A Psychological Study of William Blake, 1970; Boundaries of the Soul: The Practice of Jung's Psychology, 1972. Contbr. poems, articles and book revs. to jours. Home and office: 3200 Lake Shore Dr Chicago IL 60657

SINGER, MARCIA B., educator; b. N.Y.C., Apr. 11, 1923; d. Meyer and Sadie (Brosterman) Bosniaki B.A., N.Y. U., 1943, M.A. in Edn., 1959; profl. diploma in guidance and counseling, Columbia Tchrs. Coll., 1971; m. Jules Singer, June 12, 1943; children—Barbara (Mrs. Theodore Kozlof), Nancy, Michael. Tchr. salesmanship for women, Port Washington and New Hyde Park, N.Y., 1959-60; tchr. course for women returning to labor market, Rockville Center (N.Y.) and Dewanaka Sch. Dist., 1963-65, White Plains (N.Y.) Center and Nassau County, auspices, N.Y. U., 1963-65; counselor Manpower Devel. and Tng., 1965-67; guidance counselor Port Washington Sr. High Sch., 1967-68; asst. dean students N.Y. Inst. Tech., Old Westbury, N.Y., 1968—; vocational counselor for mature women, also pvt. practice and lectr. in field. Mem. adv. bd. Vol. Services Bur. Westchester County, New Sch. Social Research. Named Greek Faculty Woman of Year, Greek Soc., N.Y. Inst. Tech. Mem. Nat. Assn. Women Deans, Adminstrs. and Counselors, Am., L.I. personnel and guidance assns., Nat. County Bus. and Profl. Women's Assn., Eta Mu Phi, Alpha Phi Epsilon. Author courses in field. Home: 65 Green Leaf Hill Great Neck NY 11023 Office: NY Inst Tech Old Westbury NY 11568

SINGER, MARTHA JANE HOUX (MRS. LAWRENCE A. SINGER), writer; b. Warrensburg, Mo., Feb. 7, 1942; d. James Robert and Doris Lorraine (Smith) Houx; B.J., U. Mo., 1963; m. Lawrence A. Singer, July 23, 1967; children—Robert Alan, Michael Stuart. Advt. copywriter Sears Roebuck Co., Chgo., 1963-66; account exec. Pub. Relations Bd. Chgo., 1966; asst. to exec. dir. Chgo. Maternity Center, 1966-67; staff writer Santa Monica (Cal.) Evening Outlook Newspaper, 1969; free lance writer, pub. relations firms and newspapers, Los Angeles and Santa Monica, Cal., 1970—. Dem. precinct worker Ind. Voters of Ill., 1966-67. Mem. Women In Communications (v.p. events 1973-74), Nat. Orgn. for Women, ADS, U. Mo. Alumni Assn. Home: 2311 Greenfield Av Los Angeles CA 90064

SINGER, PHYLLIS JEAN (MRS. JOHN DONALD SINGER), journalist; b. Boone, Ia., Nov. 1, 1927; d. Jesse Jean and Florence Lucile (Ostrand) Wheeler; B.A., MacMurray Coll., 1949; m. John Donald Singer, July 15, 1949; children—Pamela (Mrs. Ronald A. Lambert), Julie. Sports editor, city reporter Boone (Ia.) News Republican, 1945-46, 47-48, 50-51; daily columnist Waterloo (Ia.) Daily Courier, 1952—, women's editor, 1952-74, asso. editor, 1974—. Frequent pub. speaker social and civic orgns. Mem. adv. council environmental edn. Fed. Edn. Commn., 1971-73. Mem. Internat. Platform Assn., Am. Pen Women and Press Women, Waterloo C. of C. (bd. dirs. 1971—). Home: 320 Lillian Lane Waterloo IA 50701 Office: Box 540 Waterloo IA 50704

SINGER, RITA, govt. ofcl.; b. Toronto, Ont., Can., July 23, 1915; d. Harry and Hilda (Brody) Singer; A.B., U. Mich., 1935; LL.B., 1938; m. Fred Brandeis, Jan. 15, 1943. Admitted to Mich. bar, 1938, Cal. bar, 1957; atty. Gen. Counsel's Office U.S. Dept. Agr., Washington, 1942-44; mem. staff U.S. Dept. Interior, 1944—, asst. regional solicitor, Sacramento, 1970—. Mem. Sacramento Fed. Women's Program Council (pres. 1973), Fed. Bar Assn. (v.p. 1971-74), Nat. Fedn. Fed. Employees (pres. Sacramento chpt. 1968-70), Am. Civil Liberties Union (pres. Sacramento chpt. 1967), League Women Voters (dir. Sacramento League 1957-63). Home: 5732 Coda Lane Carmichael CA 95608 Office: 2800 Cottage Way Sacramento CA 95825

SINGER, SARAH BETH (MRS. LEON EUGENE SINGER), poet; b. N.Y.C., July 4, 1915; d. Samuel and Rose (Dunetz) White; B.A., N.Y. U., 1934; postgrad. New Sch. for Social Research, 1961-63; m. Leon Eugene Singer, Nov. 23, 1938; children—Jack, Rachel. Tchr. poetry couses Hillside Hosp., Queens, N.Y., 1965—. Recipient Stephen Vincent Benet awards Poet Lore quar. 1968, 71; James Joyce award Poetry Soc. Am., 1972, Consuelo Ford Meml. award, 1973. Mem. Nat. League of Am. Penwomen (poetry chmn. 1957—), Poetry Soc. Am. Author: Magic Casements (Poems), 1957; After the Beginning, 1974. Contbr. poems to various mags. Home: 38 Stephan Marc Lane New Hyde Park NY 11040

SINGER-MAGDOFF, LAURA JOAN SILVER (MRS. SAMUEL MAGDOFF), psychotherapist; b. N.Y.C., Mar. 21, 1917; d. Max David and Minnie (Stabsky) Silver; student N.Y. U., 1936-38, U. Minn., 1938-39; B.S., M.A., Columbia, 1946, Ed.D., 1961; m. Edward I. Plotkin, 1938 (dec. 1945); 1 dau., JoAnn Melanie; m. 2d, Arthur I. Singer, 1948 (div. 1962); m. 3d, Samuel Magdoff, Dec. 23, 1963. Nursery, elementary sch. tchr., dir., Bronxville, N.Y., 1943-45; tchr. Cherry Lawn Sch., Darien, Conn., 1943-44, Columbia Grammar Sch., 1951-53; ednl. dir. N.Y. Childrens Colony, 1953-54; psychotherapist, marital, family counselor Community Guidance Service, N.Y.C., 1958—; pvt. practice, 1958—; pres. Save a Marriage, Inc., Interpersonal Networks, Inc. Lectr., Tchrs. Coll. Columbia, 1961-70, adj. asso. prof., 1970-73; faculty fellow Inst. for Practicing Psychotherapists, N.Y.C., 1964—, Met. Inst. Psychoanalytic Studies; faculty Nat. Acad. Profl. Psychologists, New Sch. Social Research, cons. parent edn. State Edn. Dept., YMCA. Adv. bd. League Parent Edn.; adv. council, bd. dirs. Community Sex Information. Bd. dirs. Sex Information and Edn. Council U.S. Fellow Am. Assn. Marriage Counselors (pres. N.Y. div., nat. pres. 1972); mem. N.Y. Soc. Clin. Psychologists (past editor Newsletter, mem. exec. bd.), Am. Psychol. Assn., Assn. for Applied Psychoanalysis, Nat. Council Family Relations. Psychology editor Coronet mag., 1972-73. Address: 41 Central Park W New York City NY 10023

SINGLETON, MARY LITTLEJOHN, state legislator, restaurant exec.; b. Jacksonville, Fla., Sept. 20, 1926; d. Harry C. and Laura (Crowd) Littlejohn; student Hampton Inst., 1943-44; B.S., Fla. A. and M. U., 1949; m. Isadore Singleton, June 20, 1955 (dec. Feb. 1964); children—Carol (Mrs. Charles Scott), Isadore. Tchr. high sch., Duval County, Fla., 1950-55; owner, mgr. Singleton's Superior Bar-B-Que Stores, Jacksonville, 1955—; mem. Jacksonville City Council, 1967-72, v.p., 1967-68; mem. Fla. Ho. of Reps., 1972—, mem. edn., natural resources; health and rehab. services com. Mem. Local Govt. Study Commn., 1966; charter mem. Better Govt. for Duval County, 1967; sec. Jacksonville Housing Bd. Adjustments and Appeals, 1964-67; mem. Sheriff's Interagy. Council, 1971-72; hostess Progress Report, Sta. WOBS, 1967-71; faculty local and state govt. Edward Waters Coll., 1971, dir. devel. fund, 1971-72. Mem. exec. bd., sec. Duval Democratic Club, Jacksonville, 1967-72; 1st v.p. Profl. Women's Dem. Club Duval County, 1968; del. Dem. Nat. Conv., 1968; mem. Electoral Coll., 1968; mem. adv. com. of host Com. for Dem. Nat. Conv., 1972; mem. charter commn. Nat. Dem. party, 1972—. Bd. dirs. Planned Parenthood, Prevention Suicide Service Center, Mental Health Assn., U.S.O. Council, Community Planning Council, North Fla. U. Adv. Council, Meth. Hosp., Jacksonville Exptl. Health Delivery System, Inc., Nat. Council Christians and Jews, Catholic Charities Bur., Jacksonville Urban League, Eartha M. White Nursing Home, Cancer Soc., others; chmn. Child Care Program; mem. sch. bd. Bishop Kenny Catholic High Sch.; dir. devel. Edward Waters Coll., 1971-72. Recipient numerous awards including Meritorious award Fla. A. and M. U., 1967, Fla. Meml. Coll., 1968, Jacksonville br. N.A.A.C.P., 1968, Jacksonville C. of C., 1971, Community Planning Council, 1971. Mem. Black Legislators Assn., Orgn. Women Legislators, Dem. Women in Action, N.A.A.C.P., Zeta Phi Beta. Roman Catholic (ch. council 1972—). Home: 1353 W 33d St Jacksonville FL 32209 Office: 5521 Norwood Av Jacksonville FL 32208 also Suite 232 House Office Bldg Tallahassee FL 32304

SINK, ALVA GORDON (MRS. CHARLES A. SINK), clubwoman; b. Rose Twp., Mich.; d. Nathaniel J. and Ella M. (Highfield) Gordon; student Eastern Mich. U., summers 1914, 18; A.B., U. Mich., 1923; m. Charles A. Sink, June 18, 1923 (dec.). Tchr. pub. schs., Rose Center, Mich., 1914-17, Hickory Ridge, Mich., 1917-18, Holly, Mich., 1918-19, Canfield Pvt. Sch., Ann Arbor, Mich., 1919-22. Mem. Women's Republic Club, Ann Arbor. Dir. Washtenaw County chpt. A.R.C., 1943-48, 53-59, in charge First Aid and Accident Prevention, 1941-61; pres. Mich. House and Senate Club, 1929-30, U. Mich. Alumnae Club, 1931-33, Sara Browne Smith Group Alumnae Club, 1957-59, Women's Soc. Congl. Ch., 1946-48; regent Sarah Caswell Angell chpt. D.A.R., 1955-57. Recipient Red Cross citation, 1959, Alumnae Council award U. Mich., 1971; Alva Gordon Sink Group of U. Mich. Alumnae named in her honor. Mem. Hist. Soc. Mich., Alumni Assn. U. Mich., French Huguenots, Am. Assn. U. Women, Ann Arbor Art Assn., P.E.O., Clubs: Art Study, Garden, Faculty Women, Presidents of University of Mich. Home: 1325 Olivia Av Ann Arbor MI 48104

SINKFORD, JEANNE CRAIG (MRS. STANLEY SINKFORD), dental educator; b. Washington; d. Richard E. and Geneva (Jefferson) Craig; B.S., Howard U., 1953, D.D.S., 1958; M.S., Northwestern U., 1962, Ph.D., 1963; m. Stanley Sinkford, Dec. 8, 1951; children—Dianne Sylvia, Janet Lynn, Stanley McClellan III. Instr., Howard U. Coll. Dentistry, Washington, 1958-60, head dept. prosthodontics, 1964—, research coordinator, 1966—, asso. dean, 1967—; clin. instr. Northwestern U. Dental Sch., Chgo., 1963-64; attending staff Freedmen's Hosp., Washington, 1964—; cons. VA Hosp., Washington, 1965—, St. Elizabeth's Hosp., 1969—. Mem. nat. adv. council Nat. Insts. for Dental Research; mem. Nat. Bd. Dental Examiners; cons. FDA; mem. adv. panel Tuskegee Syphilis Study

Dept. Health, Edn. and Welfare, 1972-73. Mem. Civic League, North Portal Estates. Trustee Inst. Grad. Dentists, 1973—. Recipient Alumni Achievement award Northwestern U., 1970; Distinguished Alumnus award Howard U. Alumni Fedn., 1971. Louise C. Ball fellow, 1960-63. Mem. Am. Coll. Dentists, A.A.A.S., Am. Dental Assn., Am. Prosthodontic Soc., D.C. Dental Soc., Internat. Assn. Dental Research, Assn. Am. Women Dentists, D.C. Council Adminstrv. Women in Edn., Am. Assn. U. Profs., Am. Assn. Dental Schs., Phi Beta Kappa, Sigma Xi, Omicron Kappa Upsilon. Home: 1765 Verbena St NW Washington DC 20012

SINKHORN, MARY ALASKA THOMPSON (MRS. CLARENCE W. SINKHORN), newspaper editor; b. Greensburg, Ind., May 5, 1929; d. Charles F. and Mary Baen (Wright) Thompson; student U. Ore., 1949-51; m. Clarence W. Sinkhorn, July 21, 1952; children—Paul, Scott, Sarah, Suzanne. Editor, Springfield (Ore.) News, 1947-50; free lance feature writer, 1953-66; contbr. to Brit. mags., Bedford, Eng., 1963-66; editor 12 Southwest Messenger Newspapers, Cook County, 1968—. Dir. pub. relations Village of Midlothian (Ill.), 1970—. Served with WAF, 1951-53. Mem. Ill. Press Assn., Vets. Press Assn., Midlothian C. of C., D.A.R., V.F.W., Epsilon Sigma Alpha. Republican. Episcopalian. Home: 4217 W 149th Pl Midlothian IL 60445 Office: 3840 W 147th St Midlothian IL 60445

SINNEN, JEANNE, pub. co. editor; b. St. Paul, July 25, 1926; d. Frank William and Myrtle Elinda (Fredericksen) Sinnen; B.A., U. Minn., 1948, M.A., 1949. Editorial asst. U. Minn. Press, Mpls., 1949-53, editor, 1953-57, sr. editor, 1957—. Mem. Am. Studies Assn., Am. Civil Liberties Union, Phi Beta Kappa. Democrat. Lutheran. Home: 967 Wakefield Av St Paul MN 55106 Office: 2037 University SE Minneapolis MN 55455

SINTON, NELL WALTER, artist; b. San Francisco, June 4, 1910; d. John I. and Florence (Schwartz) Walter; student Katherine D. Burke Sch., 1918-28, San Francisco Art Inst., 1938-39; m. Stanley H. Sinton, Jr., June 15, 1930 (div. 1971); children—Margot (Mrs. Perry Biestman), Joan (Mrs. Bruce Dodd), John W., Wendy W. Exhibited one man shows: Palace Legion House San Francisco, 1949, Santa Barbara Mus., 1950, Bolles Gallery, San Francisco, N.Y.C., 1957, San Francisco Mus., 1957, 63, 70, Quay Gallery, 1966-69; exhibited group shows Met. Mus., N.Y.C., 1952, Oakland Mus., Vancouver Mus., 1958, Denver Mus., 1958-60, Am. Acad. Arts, N.Y.C., 1967, Am. Fedn. Arts, 1956, 63, Stanford Research Inst., 1958, Los Angeles County Mus., 1961, U. Cal. at Berkeley Art Mus., 1972, others; traveling shows, 1948—; represented permanent collection Quay Gallery, San Francisco, numerous others. Artist mem. faculty mem. bd. trustees San Francisco Art Inst., 1966-73. Mem. San Francisco Art Commn., 1958-63. Recipient various prizes in local exhbns. Home: 1020 Francisco San Francisco CA 94109*

SINZ, MARION MADELEINE, occupational therapist; b. San Jose, Cal., Mar. 20, 1929; d. Louis Albert and Madeleine (Baird) Sinz; B.A., U. Cal., San Jose, 1950; M.A., Columbia, 1963. Staff therapist Langley Porter, U. Cal. Hosp., San Francisco, 1951-52, Hosp. for Joint Disease, N.Y.C., 1952-54, Bellevue Hosp., N.Y.C., 1954-56; dir. psychol. occupational therapy St. Luke Hosp., N.Y.C., 1956-59; dir. occupational therapy Jewish Home and Hosp., N.Y.C., 1959—. Faculty, Frederic D. Zeman Center for Instrn., 1965—, French and Polyclinic Med. Sch. and Health Center, 1970-72; cons. in field. Mem. Am. Occupational Therapy Assn., World Fedn. Occupational Therapists, Gerentological Soc. Home: 850 Amsterdam Av New York City NY 10025 Office: 120 W 106th St New York City NY 10025

SIPORIN, RAE LEE, univ. ofcl.; b. Detroit, Apr. 12, 1940; d. Morris and Zelda (Brown) Siporin; B.A., Wayne State U., 1962; M.A., U. Cal. at Los Angeles, 1964, Ph.D., 1968. Asst. prof. English, U. Pitts., 1968—, asst. dean Coll. Arts and Scis., 1970-72, exec. asst. to vice chancellor planning and budget, 1973—; Am. Council Edn. adminstrv. acad. intern, asst. to pres. Ohio State U., 1972-73; cons. in field. Emma Wilson Richards fellow, 1967-68; Distinguished scholar U. Cal. at Los Angeles, 1968. Mem. Linguistic Soc. Am., Am. Dialect Soc., Am. Assn. Higher Edn., Phi Beta Kappa. Democrat. Author: Women and Education: The Conference as Catalyst, 1972. Editor: Female Studies V, 1972. Dir., initiator nat. conf. Women and Edn.: A Feminist Perspective, 1971. Home: 5616 Elmer St Pittsburgh PA 15232 Office: 1817 Cathedral St Univ Pitts Pittsburgh PA 15260

SIRRIDGE, MARJORIE SPURRIER, physician; b. Kingman, Kan., Oct. 6, 1921; d. Frank R. and Fannie (Watson) Spurrier; B.S., Kan. State U., 1942; M.D., Kan. U., 1944; m. William Thomas Sirridge, Oct. 28, 1944; children—Mary Jeanette, Stephen Thomas, Patrick Michael, Christopher Frank. Intern, Charity Hosp. La., New Orleans; fellow Cleve. Clinic; pvt. practice medicine specializing in hematology, Kansas City, Kans., 1955-71; mem. faculty Kan. U. Sch. Medicine, 1955-71, asst. clin. prof. medicine, 1964-71; docent, prof. U. Mo.-Kansas City Sch. Medicine, 1971—; cons. Wadsworth VA Hosp., 1955-69. Bd. dirs. Community Blood Bank, 1958-61, mem. corp. bd., 1958-72; bd. dirs. Wyandotte County Guidance Center, 1964-66. Recipient Matrix Honor award, 1963; Soroptomist award, 1969. Mem. A.M.A., Wyandotte County, Jackson County med. socs., S.W. Clin. Soc., Am. Soc. Hematology, Mortar Bd., Phi Kappa Phi, Alpha Omega Alpha, Kappa Kappa Gamma. Author: Laboratory Evaluation of Hemostasis, 1967, 2d edit., 1974. Home: 8201 Rosewood Lane Shawnee Mission KS 66208 Office: 2220 Holmes St Kansas City MO 64108

SISK, DOROTHY DENNING (MRS. JAMES HAROLD SISK), educator; b. Nashville, July 26, 1936; d. Roy Link and Vera Pauline (Martin) Denning; B.S., Mt. Union Coll., 1958; M.A., U. Cal. at Long Beach, 1960; Ed.D., U. Cal. at Los Angeles, 1966; m. James Harold Sisk, Apr. 10, 1959; 1 son, Jeffrey Neal. Tchr. Garden Grove, Cal., 1958-64; teaching asst. U. Cal. at Los Angeles, 1965; gifted child cons., Inglewood, Cal., 1966; asst. dir. tchr. tng. gifted child edn. and early childhood disadvantaged, U. So. Fla., Tampa, 1966-68, dir. tchr. tng. gifted edn., 1968-73, chmn. Human Effectiveness dept., 1974—. Cons. in gifted edn. for state depts. of edn. Fla., La., N.C., S.C., Conn., also Brazil, 1968—; edn. cons. Media Inc., 1968-74. Mem. Model Cities adv. bd., 1968—. Bd. dirs. Horizion Sch., Miami, Hillsborough County Assn. for Gifted Edn. Recipient Internat. Speakers award, 1972, Outstanding Gifted Educator award, 1972, Outstanding Spl. Educator award U. So. Fla., 1972. Mem. Council for Exceptional Children (mem. research council), Nat. (dir.), Fla. (pres. 1974) assns. for gifted, Am. Ednl. Research Assn., Pi Lambda Theta, Delta Kappa Gamma (v.p. 1973, pres. 1974-75), Alpha Xi Delta. Democrat. Methodist. Contbr. articles in field to profl. jours. Home: 53 Adalia St Tampa FL 33606 Office: Univ of So Fla Tampa FL 33606

SISLEY, NINA MAE (MRS. GEORGE W. FISCHER), physician; b. Jacksonville, Fla., Aug. 19, 1924; d. Leonard Percy and Verna (Martin) Sisley; B.A., Tex. Women's U., 1944; M.D., U. Tex., 1950; M.P.H., U. Mich., 1963; m. George W. Fischer, May 16, 1962. Intern, Detroit Receiving Hosp., 1950-51; resident gen. practice St. Mary's Infirmary, Galveston, Tex., 1951-52; practice medicine, Galveston, 1952-57, Hereford, 1957-58, Borger, 1958-59; dir. med. services San Antonio Health Dept., 1960-63, acting dir., 1963-64; dir. community health services Corpus Christi-Nueces County Health Dept., 1964-67; dep. dir. pub. health region 10, dir. region Tb control Tex. Dept. Health, Corpus Christi, 1967-73; dir. Chronic Illness Control div. Houston Dept. Health, 1973—. Chmn., Coastal Bend Council of Govt. Health Services Com., 1972-73. Diplomate Am. Bd. Preventive Medicine. Mem. A.M.A., Tex., Harris County med. assns., Am., Tex. assns. pub. health physicians, Am., Tex. (chmn. health officers sect. 1970-71) pub. health assns., Am. Coll. Preventive Medicine, Am., Tex. thoracic socs., San Jacinto Lung Assn. (dir.). Home: 7819 Bellerive Houston TX 77036 Office: 1115 N Mac Gregor St Houston TX 77025

SISON, MEHELINDA BELMONTE GABORNE (MRS. RAFAEL ACOSTA SISON), social worker; b. Philippines, June 4, 1936; d. Gregorio D. and Maria (Belmonte) Gaborne; B.A. (Coll. scholar, Univ. scholar), U. Philippines, 1955; M.S.W., U. Minn., 1962; m. Rafael Acosta Sison, July 26, 1957; children—Rafaelito, Maria Regina, Teresa Grace, Sylvia Paz, John Thaddeus, Robert Horatio, Keith Gregory. Vol. social worker Operation Brotherhood Vietnam, Saigon, 1955-56, sr. social worker, Vientiane, Laos, 1957-58; research asst. U. Minn. Sch. Social Work, Mpls., 1958-60; social service supr. to students, staff and group worker Spring Grove State Hosp., Balt., 1960-65, VISTA coordinator, asst. to dir. for staff devel. and tng. social service dept., 1965-67; dean, lectr. Grad. Sch. Social Work Asian Social Inst., Philippines, 1967-69; coordinator mental Health program Spring Grove State Hosp., Balt., 1969-72, dir. edn., tng. and manpower devel., social service dept., 1972-73; coordinating dir. Hosp. Center-wide edn. services Spring Grove Hosp. Center, 1973—; lectr. sch. social service Cath. U. Am., 1974—. Sec. bd. dirs. Asian Devel. Bank Women's Club, 1968. Mem. Philippine Council Social Work Edn., Nat., U.S. assns. social workers, Acad. Certified Social Workers, Nat. Conf. Social Welfare, Internat. Conf. Social Welfare, Council on Social Work Edn. Home: 421 Westside Blvd Baltimore MD 21228 Office: Spring Grove Hosp Center Baltimore MD 21228

SITARZ, ANNELIESE LOTTE, physician; b. Medellin, Colombia, Aug. 31, 1928; d. Hans and Elisabeth (Noll) Sitarz; came to U.S. 1935, naturalized 1946; B.A. cum laude, Bryn Mawr Coll., 1950; M.D., Columbia, 1954. Intern, Children's Med. Center, Boston, 1954-55; resident Babies Hosp., N.Y.C., 1955-57, vis. fellow, 1957-59, asst. pediatrician, 1959-64, asst. attending pediatrician, 1964-74, asso. attending pediatrician, 1974—; asst. pediatrics Coll. Phys. and Surg. Columbia, N.Y.C., 1957-62, instr. pediatrics, 1962-64, asso. in pediatrics, 1964-68, asst. prof., 1968-74, asso. prof. clin. pediatrics, 1974—; cons. Harlem Hosp., 1967-72. Advanced clin. fellow Am. Cancer Soc., 1962-65; NIH grantee, 1967. Mem. Am. Soc. Hematology, N.Y. Acad. Sci., Am. Assn. Cancer Research, Am. Acad. Pediatrics, Internat. Soc. Hematology, The Harvey Soc. Contbr. articles to profl. pubs. Office: Babies Hospital Broadway and 167th St New York City NY 10032

SITLER, LYDIA ARLENE, educator, social worker; b. Kingman, Alta., Can., May 14, 1919; d. Jeremiah and Hannah (Buschert) Sitler; came to U.S., 1939, naturalized, 1956; B.A., Goshen Coll., 1944; M.A., Columbia, 1960; Ed.D., Ind. U., 1968; M.S.W., U. Ky., 1972. With Mennonite Central Com., 1944-56, Canadian hdqrs. sec., Kitchener, Ont., 1944, European sec., London, Eng. and Basel, Switzerland, Akron, Pa., pub. relations rep., Reedley, Cal., pub. relations rep., bus. mgr. La. Junta (Colo.) Mennonite Sch. Nursing, 1951-53, dir. women's and children's activities, Akron, 1953-54, pub. relations rep. Prairie View Hosp., Newton, Kan., 1956; dir. Christian Children's Fund, South Korea, 1954-55; exec. sec. Friends Pusan Children's Charity Hosp., Washington, 1957-59; dean of women Manchester Coll., 1962-65; asso. prof. social sci. Eastern Mennonite Coll., Harrisonburg, Va., 1969-71; asso. prof. social work Millersville (Pa.) State Coll., 1972-74; asso. prof. Sch. Social Work, Meml. U. Nfld., St. John's, 1974—. Mem. Am. Assn. U. Women, Canadian Assn. East Asian Studies, Council Social Work Edn., Nat. Assn. Social Workers. Contbr. articles to profl. jours. Office: Sch Social Work Meml U Newfoundland St John's NF A1C 5S7 Canada

SITLEY, DOROTHEA WIELLAND, pub. relations exec.; b. West Collingswood, N.J., Mar. 15; children—Ralph L., Gloria. Dir. consumer relations Gimbels, Phila., 1947—. Bd. dirs. Emergency Aid of Pa., Rep. Women of Pa., Phila. area UNICEF; commonwealth com. of Women's Med. Coll.; mem. bd. women mgrs. Am. Oncologic Hosp.; Phila. County chmn. women's activities U.S. Savs. Bonds, 1953—; sec. women's com. Hero Scholarship Fund; active Phila. March Dimes; mem. women's aux. Pa. Hosp., com. of 1926 for Strawberry Mansion; mem. Phila. women's com. Phila. Orch., Phila. Flag Day Assn. Recipient awards for vol. work from A.R.C., 1946, U.S. Treasury Dept., 1946; named Sweetest Woman of Year, Chestnut St. Bus. Men's Assn., 1952; Phila. Motion Picture Preview Group award, 1956; Hero Scholarship Fund citation, 1957; named Dsitinguished Dau. of Pa., 1958; award Ort Women, 1965, Phila. Fedn. Women's Clubs; Phila. Friendship Fete Fame award, 1969; others. Mem. Am. Pub. Relations Assn. (nat. dir. 1953-60, nat. sec. 1953-55, Phila. dir. 1953-60), Ams. for Coop. Enterprise System (dir. Phila. 1955—), Phila. Fashion Group (dir. 1950—), Nat. Retail Mchts. Assn. (pub. relations com.), Pub. Relations Soc. Am., World Affairs Council, Acad. Natural Scis. Phila., Am. Cancer Soc., Am. Heart Assn., Am. Theatre Soc., Bus. and Profl. Women's Club Phila. (Nat. Bus. Women's Week award 1953), Colonial Phila. Hist. Soc., Fairmount Park Art Assn., Friends Central Sch. Alumnae Assn., Nat. Council Women, Nat. Home Fashions League, Nat. Trust Historic Preservation in U.S., Pa. Acad. Fine Arts, Pa. Hort. Soc., Phila. Club Advt. Women, Phila. Mus. Art Zool. Soc. Phila., YWCA. Club: Cosmopolitan (Phila.). Home: Parkway House 2201 Pennsylvania Av Philadelphia PA 19130 Office: care Gimbels 9th and Market Sts Philadelphia PA 19105

SITTEL, MRS. RALPH A., clubwoman. Corr. sec. Ore. Fedn. Women's Clubs, 1966-68, 1st. v.p. 6th dist., 1966-68, 1st. state v.p., 1968-70, pres., 1970-72, chmn. Returnee div., 1972-74; pres. Metzger Women's Club, 1952-56, pres. parliamentary unit, 1961-62; pres. Zenith Women's Club, 1961-64. Mem. nat. adv. com. vol. service VA. Home: 10560 SW 72d Av Portland OR 97223

SITTERLY, ADA MARTHA, educator; b. Spring Valley, Ill., June 16, 1899; d. John Clifford and Elizabeth (Nelson) Sitterly; student U. Wis., 1919-20; A.B., Rockford Coll., 1921. Registrar, Harris Sch., Chgo., 1928-45, sec., treas., 1938-65, dir., 1945-53, trustee, 1938-65. Sec., Western Sand & Gravel Co., Spring Valley, 1940—. Pres., Rockford Coll. Club, Chgo., 1941-43; mem. women's aux. United Charities, Chgo., 1953—, sec., 1956, v.p., 1961, pres., 1964—, v.p. sr. bd., 1972-73, mem. woman's bd. Chgo. Hearing Soc., 1954—, sec., 1955-56, chmn. bd., 1959-61; mem. Women's Coll. Bd. Chgo., 1940-48. Hon. trustee Harris Sch., Chgo., hon. chmn. devel. co. Named First Lady of Day, Radio Sta. WAIT, Chgo., 1972. Clubs: Saddle and Cycle (Chgo.); Dunham Woods Riding (Wayne). Home: 2440 Lake View Av Chicago IL 60614

SITTON, MARGARET ANN WILSON, ednl. adminstr.; b. Wellington, Tex., Nov. 8, 1928; d. J.D. and Peggy (Hill) Wilson; B.S., North Tex. State U., 1949; M.E., Southwest Tex. State Coll., 1953; Ed.D., Tex. Tech. U., 1965; div.; 1 dau., Peggy L. Tchr. home econs., Hubbard, San Marcos, Austin and Amarillo, Tex., 1949-53; part-time instr. dept. home econs. edn. Tex. Technol. U., Lubbock, 1962-65, asst. prof. home econs. edn., 1965-66, asso. prof. home econs. edn., asst. dean Coll. Home Econs., 1966-69, prof. home econs. edn., asst. dean, 1969-72; prof. home econs. edn., dean Sch. Home Econs., Fla. State U., Tallahassee, 1972—. Recipient Grant-In-Aid Sears-Roebuck, 1966-68; Social and Rehab. Service grant Dept. Health Edn. and Welfare, 1971-72. Mem. Am. Assn. Higher Edn., Am. Home Econs. Assn., Am. Vocational Assn., Am. Ednl. Research Assn., Assn. Adminstrs. Home Econs., Phi Upsilon Omicron, Alpha Chi. Home: 2836 Shamrock S Tallahassee FL 32303

SIVERSEN, ANNETTE K., social ins. adminstr.; b. Glen Cove, N.Y., Jan. 7, 1934; d. Andrew and Garda (Kyllo) Siversen; B.S., N.D. State U., 1955. Claims rep. trainee Social Security Adminstrn., Minot, N.D., 1955-56, claims rep., Bremerton, Wash., 1956-58, claims authorizer, San Francisco, 1958-62, tech. asst., 1962-66, claims sect. supr., San Francisco, 1966-67, dist. mgr., Walla Walla, Wash., 1967-68, sr. staff asst., San Francisco, 1968-70, data processing procedures coordinator, San Francisco and Seattle, 1970-71, staff asso., Seattle, 1971-73, asst. regional rep., Seattle, 1973—. Bd. dirs. Social Security Fed. Credit Union, 1961-67. Mem. Pacific N.W. Personnel Mgrs. Assn. (sec. 1968), Bus. and Profl. Womens Club, Zonta (treas. 1968), Alpha Gamma Delta, Phi Kappa Phi. Republican. Lutheran. Home: 14318 NE 7th Pl Bellevue WA 98007 Office: 1321 2d Av Seattle WA 98101

SIVULICH, ALICE BILEWICZ (MRS. STEPHEN SIVULICH), ednl. adminstr.; b. Pitts., June 7, 1943; d. John James and Elsie (Peters) Bilewicz; B.A., U. Pitts., 1965, M.Ed., 1966; m. Stephen Sivulich, Sept. 1, 1968. Tchr. South Hills High Sch., Pitts., 1966-67; asst. dean women U. Pitts., 1967-68; tchr. Hyre Jr. High Sch. and South High Sch., Akron, O., 1968-69; dir. off-campus affairs, frat. affairs Kent State (O.) U., 1969-72; asst. dean students LaFayette Coll., Easton, Pa., 1972—. Mem. Nat. Assn. Women Deans and Counselors, Nat. Assn. Student Personnel Adminstrs., Ukranian Orthodox League U.S.A. (nat. first v.p. 1972—), Alpha Delta Pi, Pi Lambda Theta. Home: 465 College Station Easton PA 18042

SIZEMORE, MARGARET DAVIDSON, univ. ofcl.; b. Birmingham, Ala.; d. Julius Weston and Ruth (Lee) Davidson; A.B., Samford U., 1928, M.A., 1930; normal degree U. Paris, 1929; postgrad. Western Res. U., U. Ala., Sorbonne, Paris ; m. James Middleton Sizemore, June 19, 1937;children—James Middleton, Ruth Lee. Asso. prof. modern langs. Howard Coll., 1947-58, dean women, 1950-70; asst. to pres. Samford U., 1970—. Mem. Ala. Constn. Commn., 1969—, Tannehill Furnace and Foundry Commn., 1969—, U.S. Dept. Def. Adv. Com. Women in Service. Chmn. speakers' bur. Birmingham Civic Opera Bd., 1959-60; mem. adv. bd. Birmingham Mus. Art; mem. woman's com. Birmingham Symphony; bd. dirs. Ala. Pops Orch.; chmn. Birmingham Festival of Arts, 1960-61, hon. chmn., 1962, sec., 1962-63; bd. visitors Monterrey Tech (Mex.); bd. Lighthouse Lectrs.; pres. Freedom Ednl. Found.; dir. Am. Scholars Library Ala. Lives; mem. Gov.'s Com. Status Women; pres. Women's Com. 100 Greater Birmingham; sec. Jefferson County Hist. Commn.; mem. adv. bd. Ala. Hist. Commn.; mem. Ala. Commn. on Ethics and Morals, 1971—; mem. Ala. Gov.'s Com. for Employment of Handicapped; chmn. Ala. Commn. on Women, 1972—. Bd. dirs. Jefferson County-Shelby Lung Assn., 1970-73. Cited ami de France, City Paris, 1951; scroll from Archbishop of Canterbury, Eng., 1951; ofcl. guest City of Birmingham, Eng., 1953; Woman of Achievement in Edn. citation, 1956; Birmingham Woman of Year, 1962; recipient Freedoms Found. Valley Forge award, 1963; Vigilant Patriot award, 1963; Ala. Merit Mother, 1964; award for civic service Birmingham Jr. C. of C., 1965. Fellow Royal Soc. Arts; mem. Nat. (membership chmn. Ala.), Ala. (sec. 1951-53) assns. women deans, Nat. League Am. Penwomen (pres. Birmingham br. 1966-68, state pres. 1973-75), Antiquarian Soc. (pres. 1960-61), Nat. Soc. Arts and Letters, Ala., Birmingham, Arlington (pres. 1970), Forney (v.p.) hist. socs., English Speaking Union, Presidents and Deans Am. Colls., Brit. Am. Soc. Am., Ala. Guidance Assn. (pres. 1955-57), Am. Assn. U. Women, Ala. Writers Conclave (pres. 1962-63), Daus. Colonial Wars, Daus. Barons of Runnemede, D.A.R., Daus. Am. Colonists (state regent 1964-67), Soc. Lees Va., U.D.C., Internat. Platform Assn., Alpha Delta Pi. Clubs: Bibliophiles, New Era, Concordia, Faculty Wives (hon.); Altrusa (pres. Birmingham 1955-56); Overseas (pres.), Scottish Clan (Chattan). Co-author: The Amazing Marriage of Marie Eustis and Josef Hofmann, 1965; author hist. sketches. Home: 3084 Sterling Rd Birmingham AL 35213

SIZEMORE, PATRICIA ANNE HAMLIN (MRS. THOMAS C. SIZEMORE), newspaper owner; b. Middlesboro, Ky., Dec. 24, 1941; d. Charlie Lewis and Myrtle (Shupe) Hamlin; student Tampa U., 1964; m. Thomas C. Sizemore, Apr. 16, 1963; children—Pamela Lynne, Timothy Curtis. Owner, pub. The People's Jour., Booneville, Ky., 1965—. Judge, dir. beauty pageant, Lexington, Ky., 1970. Pres., founder Democratic Women's Club, 1968, Young Dem. Club, 1968. Mem. V.F.W. Aux., Nat., Ky. Weekly newspaper assns. Baptist. Club: Homemakers (Booneville). Address: PO Box 278 Booneville KY 41314

SKAFTE, MARJORIE DORIS WESTEGARD (MRS. LLOYD A. SKAFTE), mag. editor, pub.; b. Ossee, Wis., Aug. 1, 1921; d. Nels E. and Rena B. (Severson) Westegard; student St. Olaf Coll., 1939-41, U. Minn. at Duluth, 1965-66; m. Lloyd A. Skafte, Feb. 14, 1942; children—Merilee (Mrs. James Main), Patricia, Linwood, Robert. Editorial asst. Ojibway Press (became publs. div. Harcourt Brace Jovanovich Publs., Inc., 1971), Duluth, Minn., 1964-67, mng. editor, 1967-68, editor, 1968—, pub. editor The Hearing Instruments, 1971—. Sec. Hearing Aid Industry Conf., 1971-74, Better Hearing Inst., 1973-74; active Girl Scouts Am., Duluth, 1952-57, Boy Scouts Am., Duluth, 1959-61. Mem. Order Eastern Star. Club: Soroptimist (Duluth). Home: 2403 Somerset Av Duluth MN 55803 Office: 1 E First St Duluth MN 55802

SKAGGS, SHIRLEY TINSTMAN, psychologist; b. Hardin County, Ky., May 28, 1935; d. Wayne Gatton and Zelma Belle (Bush) Overall; B.S., Oklahoma City U., 1966; M.S., U. Okla., 1969, Ph.D. in Clin. Psychology, 1970; m. Robert M. Tinstman, June 6, 1953 (div. Nov. 1972); children—Robert O., Torre R., Tracy D.; m. 2d, Edward W. Skaggs, Nov. 22, 1973. Psychol. evaluation applicants VISTA (Vols. in Service to America), Norman, Okla., summer 1967; staff psychologist Austin (Tex.) State Hosp., 1969-71, chief psychologist, 1971—; individual practice psychol. counseling, Austin, 1970—; cons. Mary Lee Sch. Spl. Edn., Austin, 1970-71. Mem. Model Cities div. Sr. Citizens Adv. Bd., 1972. Tex. Dept. Mental Health and Mental Retardation tng. grantee, 1971-72. Mem. Am., Tex. (pub. relations co-chairperson 1974), psychol. assns. Home: 3932 Balcones Dr Austin TX 78731 Office: 3910 Medical Parkway 255 Austin TX 78756

SKAIFE, AUDREY MAE, psychologist, educator; b. Regina, Sask., Can., July 1, 1921; d. Wilfrid and Edith (Manifold) Skaife; student U. Man., 1939-40; B.A., U. Sask., 1943; M.A., U. Ore., 1963, Ph.D., 1966; student San Jose State Coll., 1959-61. Sec. Brit. Air Commn., Washington, 1943-45; pub. stenographer, Washington, 1945-46; asst. to credit mgr. Wilcox & Follett Pub. Co., Chgo., 1946-48; adminstrv. Sec. No. Engraving & Mfg. Co., Edwin Shields Hewitt & Assos., Pure Foods, Inc., Simoniz Co., 1949-53; sec. to head Med. Audio-Visual Inst., Assn. Am. Med. Colls., Evanston, Ill., later film librarian, then adminstrv. asst. and acting head inst., 1953-59; asso. prof. dept. psychology U. Wis.-Oshkosh, 1966—. Mem. Am., Midwestern psychol. assns., Nat. Orgn. Women, Internat. Soc. History Behavioral and Social Scis., Psi Chi. Home: 516 Algoma Blvd Oshkosh WI 54901

SKALLERUP, NANCY MCGHEE BAXTER (MRS. WALTER THORWALD SKALLERUP, JR.), civic worker; b. Cleve.; d. Charles McGhee and Marcella (Andrews) Baxter; B.A., Smith Coll., 1946; postgrad. Western Res. U., 1947; m. Walter Thorwald Skallerup, Jr., Dec. 16, 1950; children—Paula, Walter Thorwald III, Andrew McGhee (dec.), Nancy White. Tchr. English, Madeira Sch., 1946-49; mem. research staff CIA, 1949-50. Mem. Fairfax County Condemnation Commn., 1968; v.p. Hillcrest Children's Center, Washington, 1953-54, 67; v.p. nat. capital area YWCA, 1966-68, pres., 1969-72, dir. YWCA/USA, 1973—; chmn. founds. devel. council Smith Coll., 1972—. Mem. Madeira Sch. Alumnae Assn. (dir., pres. bd. 1965-71). Club: Smith College (chmn. scholarship com. 1963) (Washington). Home: 1155 Crest Lane McLean VA 22101

SKANES, ROSEMARY STELLA WREN (MRS. EDGAR R. SKANES), town ofcl.; b. Thorndike, Me., Oct. 29, 1926; d. William Prescott and Mary Martha (Crocker) Wren; grad. high sch.; m. Edgar Reginald Skanes. Bookkeeper Town of Skowhegan (Me.), 1960-63, dep. tax collector, registrar of voters, 1961-63, dep. treas., 1963-66, dep. town clk., 1963-66, excise tax collector, 1971, town treas., 1966—, town clk., 1966—, chmn. bd. voters registration, 1971-73. Mem. Me. Somerset County Municipal Assn. (treas. 1971), Internat. Inst. Municipal Clks., Me. Somerset Clks. Assn. (pres. 1972-74), New Eng. Assn. of City and Town Clks. (mem. resolution com. 1973—, pres. 1974), Me. Town and City Clks. Assn. (mem. legislative com. 1969—), Me. Municipal Assn., Me. Municipal Tax Collectors and Treas. Assn. Baptist. Mem. Order Eastern Star, Rebekah. Home: 74 E Maple St Skowhegan ME 04976 Office: Municipal Bldg Box 6 Water St Skowhegan ME 04976

SKATOFF, MARY MARGARET (MRS. LEONARD LEO SKATOFF), realtor; b. Boston, Apr. 16, 1921; d. Walter Joseph and Teresa (Morgan) Smith; student Mass. Real Estate Inst., 1967-70; m. Leonard Leo Skatoff, Sept. 29, 1940; children—Mary Jane (Mrs. Thomas J. MacKay, Lenore (Mrs. R. Timothy Stone), Leonard Leo. Founder, Hatherly Realty, Inc., Rockland, Mass., 1962, pres., 1962—; builder, designer Colonial Homes, 1973. Dir. Greater Brockton Multiple Listing Service, Inc.; sec. Rockland Indsl. Devel. Commn., 1970-71, chmn. 1971-72. Recipient spl. commendation Nat. Conf. Christians and Jews, 1965. Mem. Greater Brockton Bd. Realtors (dir. 1970-72), Rockland C. of C., Mass. Assn. Real Estate Bd. (edn. com. 1972-73), Nat. Assn. Real Estate Bd. (Nat. Inst. Real Estate Brokers), Nat. Fedn. Ind. Bus. Roman Catholic. Home: 275 Beech St Rockland MA 02370 Office: 437 Webster St Rockland MA 02370

SKEEL, DOROTHY JUNE, educator; b. Erie, Pa.; d. Kenneth Selby and Cora Minnie (Gidner) Skeel; B.S., Edinboro State Coll.; M.Ed., Pa. State U., 1961, Ed.D., 1966. Asst. prof. Kutztown (Pa.) State Coll., 1961-64; asso. instr. Pa. State U., University Park, 1964-66; asso. prof. edn. Ind. U., Bloomington, 1966—. Vis. prof. U. Nev., summer 1968, U. Wash., summer 1969; ednl cons. W.H. Sadlier, Inc., N.Y.C., 1969—. Vol., U. Wash. Hosp., 1968-69. U. Wash. fellow, 1968-69. Mem. Nat. Council Social Studies, Ind. Council Social Studies (dir. 1971—), Nat. Soc. Study Edn., Delta Kappa Gamma, Pi Lambda Theta, Pi Gamma Mu. Author: The Challenge of Teaching Social Studies in the Elementary School, 1970; Children of the Street: Teaching in the Inner City, 1971; The Process of Curriculum Change, 1971; The Challenge of Teaching Social Studies in the Elementary School: A Book of Readings, 1972. Home: 1600 E Hillside Dr 32 Bloomington IN 47401

SKEEN, EVELYN DELANEY (MRS. RICHARD B. SKEEN), pub. relations exec.; b. Lecompte, La., Nov. 8, 1918; d. John M. and Fannie (Burroughs) Delaney; B.A., La. State U., 1939; m. Richard B. Skeen, June 8, 1940; 1 dau., Mrs. Sally Searle. Commentator, interview show KALB-Radio, Alexandria, La., 1939-40; reporter Chronicle, Middleburg, Va., 1956-60; women's editor Let's See mag., Milw., 1958-61; account exec. Zigman-Joseph & Assos. (now Zigman, Joseph, Skeen), Milw., 1961-63, dir. women's dept., 1963-66, v.p. 1966-72, sr. v.p. 1972-74, exec. v.p., partner, 1974—, dir. dept. specialized programs, 1973—. Recipient 8th Dist. award Am. Fedn. Advt., 1966; Outstanding Service award Am. Distributive Edn. Clubs, 1968. Mem. Internat. Platform Assn., Pub. Relations Soc. Am., Theta Sigma Phi. Home: 205 Green Bay Rd Thiensville WI 53092 Office: 700 N Water St Milwaukee WI 53202

SKEEN, KARIN TROEDSSON, lawyer; b. Orange, N.J., Apr. 16, 1943; d. Bror Siqurd and Kathryn (Pohlman) Troedsson; student, U. Minn., 1961-62; B.S., U. Wis., 1965; J.D., Hastings Coll. Law, 1968; m. John Kenneth Skeen, June 18, 1966 (div. 1974). Admitted to Cal. bar, 1969; atty. Goth, Dennis & Aaron, Redwood City, Cal., 1969; atty. Regional Counsel's Office, Internal Revenue Service, San Francisco, 1969—, tchr. enforcement atty. tng., chief counsel's office, Washington, 1972-73. Mem. State Bar Cal. (del. conv. 1973, 74), Fed. (formal procs. com. 1974), San Francisco (vice-chmn. legal ethics com. 1973—, chmn. legal ethics com. 1974, co-chmn. minority hiring com. 1972-73, mem. other coms.) bar assns., Sierra Club, San Francisco Zool. Soc., U. Wis., Hastings Coll. Law alumni assns., Kappa Alpha Theta. Republican. Presbyn. Home: 2157 Jackson St Apt 5 San Francisco CA 94115 Office: 447 Sutter St San Francisco CA 94108

SKEGGS, HELEN R., microbiologist; b. Schuylkill Haven, Pa., Mar. 9, 1918; d. Hugh Todd and Mary (Standiford) Ryan; B.A., U. Wis., 1939; m. Paul L. Skeggs, Oct. 23, 1943. Med. technician Ohio Valley Gen. Hosp., Wheeling, W.Va., 1940-41, Meml. Hosp., Milford, Del., 1941, Women's Homeopathic Hosp., Phila., 1941-42; chemist Houdry Process Labs., Marcus Hook, Pa., 1942-43; research asst. pharmacology Sharp & Dohme, Glenolden, Pa., 1943-45, research asso. microbiol. chemistry, 1945-53, research asso. microbiol. chemistry, West Point, Pa., 1953-56, research asso. pharmacological chemistry, 1956-65, sr. research biologist clin. pathology, 1965-73, research fellow safety assessment, 1973—. Fellow A.A.A.S.; mem. Am. Soc. Microbiology, Med. Tech. Registry, Am. Soc. Clin. Pathologists, Am. Soc. Indsl. Microbiology, Am. Inst. Biol. Scis., N.Y. Acad. Sci., Am. Inst. Nutrition, Sigma Xi, Sigma Delta Epsilon (nat. pres. 1968-69, dir. 1971—). Contbr. numerous articles on microbial nutrition, microbiol. assay to sci. jours. Home: 505 Cricket Av Ardsley PA 19038 Office: Merck Sharp & Dohme Research Labs West Point PA 19486

SKELTON, DOROTHY GENEVA SIMMONS (MRS. JOHN WILLIAM SKELTON), educator; b. Woodland, Cal.; d. Jack Elijah and Helen Anna (Siebe) Simmons; B.A., U. Cal., 1940, M.A., 1943; m. John William Skelton, July 16, 1941. Sr. research analyst War Dept., Gen. Staff, M.I. Div. G-2, Pentagon, Washington, 1944-45; vol. researcher, monuments, fine arts and archives sect. Restitution Br., Office Mil. Govt. for Hesse, Wiesbaden, German, 1947-48; vol. art tchr. German children in Bad Nauheim, Germany, 1947-48; art educator, lectr. Dayton (O.) Art Inst., 1955; art educator Lincoln Sch., Dayton, 1956-60; art, art edn. instr. U. Va. Sch. Continuing Edn., Charlottesville, Va., 1962—; researcher genealogy, exhibited in group shows, Cal., Colo., Ohio, Washington and Va. Represented in permanent collections Madison Hall, Charlottesville, Madison Center, Madison, Va. Mem. Nat. League Am. Pen Women, Am. Assn. U. Women, Am. Assn. Museums, Coll. Art Assn. Am., Inst. for Study of Art in Edn., Dayton Soc. Painters and Sculptors, Nat. Soc. Arts and Letters (life), Va. Mus. Fine Arts, Cal. Alumni Assn., Air Force Officers Wives Club. Republican. Methodist. Clubs: Army Navy Country; Lake of the Woods (Va.) Golf and Country. Chief collaborator: John Skelton of Georgia, 1969. Address: Lotos Lakes Brightwood VA 22715

SKELTON, ROBERTA ANNE, banker; b. Chgo., June 8, 1931; d. Arthur and Edythe Alice (George) Skelton; B.A., Carleton Coll., 1953. With Continental Ill. Nat. Bank, Chgo., 1953—, asst. cashier, 1967-71, 2d v.p., 1971-73, v.p., 1973—. Mem. Am. Assn. U. Women, Nat. Assn. Bank Women, Phi Beta Kappa. Home: 710 W Dempster St Mount Prospect IL 60056 Office: 231 S LaSalle St Chicago IL 60693

SKERLY, NADA JOSEPHINE, journalist; b. Cleve., May 1, 1934; d. Joseph and Jennie (Primc) Skerly; B.A., Mt. Holyoke Coll., 1956. Guide, U.S. State Dept., Brussels (Belgium) World Expn., 1958; various pub. relations positions including Lion Packaging Co., N.Y.C., Dudley Anderson Yutzy, N.Y.C., Inst. Internat. Edn., N.Y.C., 1959-64; asso. dir. TV and radio programming N.Y. Worlds Fair, 1964; corr. U.P.I., Vienna, Austria, 1968, Time-Life News Service, Vienna, Austria, 1965-68; TV personality WLW-TV, Cin., 1968-69; reporter, columnist Cin. Post Times-Star, 1969-71; reporter, columnist "Life Over 60" Newsday, Garden City, N.Y., 1972—. Alicia Patterson Found. fellow Newsday, 1971-72. Recipient Nat. Headliners Club award, 1972. Mem. A.F.T.R.A. Home: 225 E 324th St Willowick OH 44094 Office: Newsday 500 Stewart Av Garden City NY 11530

SKETCHLEY, MILLIE WHITE, banker; b. Greenville, Ala., Dec. 23, 1930; d. Clifton and Victoria (Hughes) Hughes; student Pacific Coast Sch. Banking, Seattle, 1971—; m. Fred J. Sketchley, June 24, 1971. With Security Pacific Nat. Bank, Long Beach, Cal., 1953—, asst. mgr., 1963-69, mgr., 1969—. Lectr., U. So. Cal., 1972. Mem. Mayor's Citizens Adv. Com., Long Beach, 1971—. Mem. Am. Inst. Banking (pres. 1970-71), Credit Women's Breakfast Club (v.p. 1965), Naples Islands Bus. Assn. (v.p.), Belmont Shore Bus. Assn. Soroptimist. Poetry included in Anthology of Contemporary Authors, 1948. Home: 436 Bellflower Blvd Long Beach CA 90814 Office: 5850 Naples Plaza Long Beach CA 90803

SKEWES, EDYTHE HARRIET (MRS. W. CHARLES SKEWES), assn. exec.; b. Butte, Mont., June 15, 1920; d. Emil John and Edith Harriet (Hutchison) Budreck; grad. high sch.; m. William Charles Skewes, Sept. 18, 1948. Supr. directory dept. Mountain Bell Telephone Co., Butte, 1941-64; exec. sec. Butte chpt. A.R.C., 1967-68; exec. dir. United Givers Silver Bow County, Butte, 1972—. Mem. Ladies' Aux. V.F.W., Butte Bus. and Profl. Women. Mem. Order Eastern Star. Clubs: Soroptimist, Pioneers (Butte). Home: 2054 Robert Av Butte MT 59701 Office: 107 E Granite St Butte MT 59701

SKIBINE, MARJORIE LOUISE TALLCHIEF (MRS. GEORGE SKIBINE), ballerina; b. Denver; d. Alexander and Ruth (Porter) Tallchief; ballet tng. with Bronislava Nijinska, David Lichine. Became soloist Am. Ballet Theater while in 'teens; became ballerina Grand Ballet du Marquid de Cuevas, at age 19; later 1st American to become premiere danseuse etoile Paris Opera, 1st American to star at Bolshoi Theater, Moscow; now artistic dir. Dallas Civic Ballet Soc. Decorated chevalier du Nisham Iftikar for artistic achievement (Tunisia). Home: 7250 Kenny Lane Dallas TX 75230

SKIDMORE, SHERRY LOU, clin. psychologist, educator; b. Delta, Colo., Jan. 21, 1944; d. Gerald Ernest and Ruby Evelyn (Engelstad) Skidmore; student Walla Walla Coll., 1962-65; B.A., Columbia Union Coll., 1967; M.A., Pepperdine U., 1968; postgrad. U.S. Internat. U., 1970—. Juvenile ct. worker Los Angeles County, Los Angeles, 1967-69; staff psychologist San Bernardino County, San Bernardino, Cal., 1969-72; clin. psychologist Riverside (Cal.) County Mental Health, 1972—. Instr. psychology Chapman Coll., Orange, Cal., 1969—, San Bernardino Valley Coll., 1969, Loma Linda U., Riverside, 1969, Pepperdine U., Los Angeles, 1970—. Mem. Am., Western, Cal. State psychol. assns. Home: 4803-A Jackson St Riverside CA 92503 Office: Riverside County Mental Health Dept Riverside CA 92503

SKINNER, HELEN ELIZABETH LUCAS (MRS. JOHN SKINNER), automobile agy. exec.; b. Jersey City, Sept. 22, 1916; d. Frank and Mary (Derenko) Lucas; B.S. magna cum laude (scholar), Syracuse U., 1941; M.Ednl. Guidance and Counseling, Fla. Atlantic U., 1971-72; m. John Borst Skinner, Aug. 26, 1942; children—John H., Mary Louise, Elizabeth (Mrs. Robert Morrison), William. Tchr. bus. edn. Middleburgh (N.Y.) Central Sch., 1941-42; sec. Dept. Navy, Pensacola, N.Y., 1942-45; bus. mgr. Skinner Chevrolet, Middleburgh, 1946—. Ind. ins. broker Middleburgh, 1953—; tchr. Pine Crest Prep. Sch., Ft. Lauderdale, N.Y., 1961-62; treas. Putnam Motors, Oneonta, N.Y., 1968-72. Mem. Dist. Federated Womens Clubs of N.Y. State (sec. 1954-56), Elks Aux. (treas. 1965-66), Beta Gamma Sigma, Pi Lambda Theta. Clubs: Twentieth Century (pres. Middleburgh 1956-57), Cooperative (pres. Middleburgh 1954-56). Home: 206 River St Middleburgh NY 12122

SKINNER, MIRANDA MAE (MRS. CECIL WILLIAM SKINNER), antique co. exec.; b. Osage City, Kan., Jan. 5, 1916; d. John William and Mary Bertha (Peterson) Campbell; student Stricklers Coll. Bus., 1934-35, U. Cal. at La Jolla, 1971-72; m. Cecil William Skinner, Oct. 6, 1943; children—William David, Chris Alan. Med. sec. Security Benefit Hosp., Topeka, 1936-43; owner Miranda's Melange, Lemon Grove, Cal., 1970—. Exhibitor, collection 18th Century English Pottery and Porcelain, San Diego, 1969. Mem. Nat. Trust for Historic Preservation, Smithsonian Instn., Fine Arts Soc. San Diego, Buten Mus. of Wedgwood. Club: British Social (San Diego). Home and office: 7144 Mt Vernon Lemon Grove CA 92045

SKOG, HAZEL JOHNSON, accountant; b. Mpls., Apr. 12, 1903; d. John A. and Clara C. (Anderson) Johnson; B.C.S., Kinman Bus. U., 1933; m. Carl E. Skog, June 14, 1941 (dec. Apr. 1947). Accountant, office mgr. Keystone Frame & Mfg. Co., 1929-44; pvt. practice pub. accounting Spokane, 1944—. Mem. Gov.'s Com. Employment Handicapped, 1974. Chmn. Spokane Service Clubs Youth in Service Lunch, 1971, 72, co-chmn., 1973; v.p. Spotlight on Youth Month Assn., 1972-73, pres., 1974. Bd. dirs. Spokane County Assn. for Mentally Retarded Children, treas., 1973; bd. dirs. Prevocational Tng. Center for Mentally Retarded, treas. 1970-72, 73—, sec. 1972-73. C.P.A., Wash. Mem. Am. Inst. C.P.A.'s, Wash. Soc. C.P.A., (sec.-treas. Spokane 1943-51, v.p. 1951-52, pres. 1952-53, chpt. rep. state bd. 1954, chmn. state by-laws com. 1965-73, state sec. 1973—), Am. Women's Soc. C.P.A.'s (nat. pres. 1944-45), Women's Missionary Soc. Augustana Lutheran Ch. (treas. Columbia conf. Northwestern states 1949-54, pres. 1954-59), Augustana Luth. Ch. Women (nat. treas. 1958-63), Am. Soc. Women Accountants (organizer, pres. Spokane 1938), Internat. Platform Assn. Club: Soroptimist (pres. 1969-70, treas. 1972-74) (Spokane). Address: 3118 E 15th Av Spokane WA 99203

SKOG, SUE OLDHAM, realtor; b. Mt. Sterling, Ky., Apr. 18, 1927; d. Abner B. and Gwendolyn (Goodridge) Oldham; student Ward Belmont Coll., 1944-45, Centre Coll., 1945; m. William B. Cheney, Jr., Dec. 22, 1945; children—William B. III, Camilla Sue, Ann Oldham; m. 2d, Reidar M. Skog, Nov. 8, 1968. Owner, operator White Caps Apts., Deerfield Beach, Fla., 1962-70; saleswoman Dennis & Barnes, Realtors, Montgomery, Ala., 1959-61, saleswoman, appraisal asst., Melbourne, Fla., 1961-62; broker, saleswoman, appraisal asst., Delray Beach, Fla., 1962-63; realtor, Deerfield Beach, 1963—. Treas., Horseless Carriage Corp., 1970; adv. com. Deerfield Beach State Bank, 1972. Precinct committeewoman Democratic Party, 1964-66. Mem. Nat. Assn. Real Estate Bds., Nat. Inst. Farm and Land Brokers, Pompano Beach, Deerfield Beach bds. realtors, Soroptimists (pres. 1968). Home: 287 SE 8th Terrace Deerfield Beach FL 33441 Office: 977 SE 10th St Deerfield Beach FL 33441

SKOMP, NANCY ANN KRIEG (MRS. JOHN KRAMER SKOMP), judge; b. Logan, O., Apr. 8, 1929; d. Leland I. and Hazel Mae (Rosser) Krieg; B.S. in Bus. Adminstrn., Ohio State U., 1950, J.D., 1952; m. John Kramer Skomp, Oct. 6, 1954 (div. 1972); children—Anna, Krieg, Karl, Casey. Admitted to Ariz. bar, 1974; pvt. practice law, Nelsonville, O., 1952-54, 57-61; research analyst Ct. of Appeals, Phoenix, 1965-72; commr. Maricopa County Superior Ct., Phoenix, 1972—. City solicitor Nelsonville, 1958-60. Bd. dirs. Alexander Sch. for Retarded, Phoenix, 1973—. Mem. Ariz., Maricopa County bar assns., Pi Beta Phi, Kappa Beta Pi. Club: Soroptimist (Phoenix). Home: 7630 N 3d Av Phoenix AZ 85021 Office: 1918 N 16th St Phoenix AZ 85006

SKONBERG, MADELON BAENZIGER (MRS. JOSEPH E. SKONBERG), educator; b. Chgo., Sept. 8, 1906; d. Rudolph Solomon and Olga Mathilde (Schiska) Baenziger; student Bush Conservatory, 1927-28, Ill. State Normal U., 1932, Chgo. Mus. Coll., 1935-37, North Park Coll., 1940-42, Tchrs. Coll., 1957-58; Mus.B. in Piano, Mus.B. in Theory, Cosmopolitan Sch. Music; postgrad. Northwestern Sch. Music Grad. Sch. 1963—; m. Joseph Emil Skonberg, Apr. 20, 1935; children—Kristin, Karen. Music reviewer Mus. Leader, Chgo., 1950-67; adjudicator Nat. Guild Piano Tchrs., Austin, Tex., 1955—; tchr. piano, organ Cosmopolitan Sch. Music, Chgo., 1956-62. Mem. Art Inst. Chgo., Soc. Am. Musicians, Nat. League Am. Pen Women, Nat., Ill. State music tchrs. assns., Nat. Fedn. Music Clubs, Nat. Soc. Sci. Study Edn., Nat. Fedn. Women Clubs, Mu Phi Epsilon. Club: Women's Literary. Home: 2601 W Sunnyside Av Chicago IL 60625

SKOOG, ANNE CATHERINE, librarian; b. Rochester, Pa., Jan. 21, 1917; d. Carl Albert and Catherine Gertrude (Elm) Skoog; B.S., Carnegie Inst. Inst. Tech., 1939, B.S. in L.S., 1940. Cataloger, Westminster Coll. Library, New Wilmington, Pa., 1940-44; asst. bus. br. Carnegie Library, Pitts., 1944-46; social relations br. librarian Carnegie Inst. Tech., 1946-50, asst. cataloger, 1950-66; asso. cataloger Carnegie-Mellon U., 1966—, also fine and rare books librarian; curator Archetype Press, 1973—. Mem. Am., Pa. (editor bull. 1957-60) library assns., Tri-State Assn. Coll. and Research Libraries, Bibliog. Soc. Am., Pitts. Bibliophiles, Pitts. Drama League, Hist. Soc. Western Pa., Pitts. History and Landmarks Found., Nat. Fedn. Bus. and Profl. Women's Clubs (pres. Oakland club 1966-68), Phi Kappa Phi (chpt. jour. corr.). Methodist. Contbr. articles to publs. Home: 506 5th Av Apt 206 Pittsburgh PA 15232

SKORKA, DARLENE LILLIAN MCDONALD HINER (MRS. DON TIMOTHY SKORKA), clin. psychologist; b. Downey, Cal., June 4, 1942; d. Winfred Asa and Rose Muriel (Gabriel) McDonald; B.S. in Psychology, U. Ida., 1964; Ph.D., U. Houston, 1971; m. Don Timothy Skorka, Nov. 25, 1972. Social worker Stanislaus County Welfare Dept., Modesto, Cal., 1964-66; psychology intern So. Cal. Permanente Med. Group, Los Angeles, 1969-70, clin. psychologist, 1974—; staff psychologist VA Hosp., Houston, 1971-74, asst. dir., 1972. Clin. asst. prof. U. Houston, Baylor Coll. of Medicine. Mem. Citizen for Animal Protection. Mem. Am., Houston psychol. assns., Phi Beta Kappa, Phi Kappa Phi, Psi Chi. Home: 1126 Bloomwood Rd San Pedro CA 90732 Office: So Cal Permanente Med Group 1515 N Vermont Los Angeles CA 90027

SKORODIN, ELAINE (MRS. SHERWOOD E. FOHRMAN), violinist; b. Milw., Aug. 28, 1936; d. Abram M. and Anne (Einsfeld) Skorodin; B.M., Chgo. Mus. Coll., Roosevelt U., 1957, Mus.M., 1959; m. Sherwood E. Fohrman, July 21, 1959; children—Richard Hartley, John Kennedy. Profl. concert violinist, Chgo., 1946; tours maj. music centers, 1957—, including N.Y.C., 1957, London, 1963, Vienna, 1963, Berlin, 1964, Stockholm, 1963; violin soloist White House recital, 1963; European concert tours, 1963-72; guest U.S. embassy on tour Japan, 1965, Churchill Meml. concert Blenheim Palace, 1972; recital Iranian embassy, Washington, 1971. Recipient Oliver Ditson award, Farwell award Paganini Internat. Violin competition, 1961; 1st prize Friday Morning Music Club, 1955, Soc. Am. Musicians, 1957, Nat. Fedn. Music Clubs competition, 1963; Myrtle Wreath Achievement award, 1969; Roosevelt U. Alumni award, 1970. Home: 888 Oak Dr Glencoe IL 60022 Office: Wilfrid Van Wyck 235/241 Regent St London W1 A2JT England

SKOUSEN, JUDY KAY, lawyer; b. Mesa, Ariz., Feb. 7, 1947; d. K.K. and Elisabeth Ann (Griffith) Skousen; student Brigham Young U., 1965-66; B.S., Ariz. State U., 1968, J.D., 1971; student U. Guadalajara (Mexico), 1967. Admitted to Ariz. bar, 1971, Cal. bar, 1972, Colo. bar, 1973; asst. county atty. Yuma County, Ariz., 1971-72; practice law, Phoenix, 1973; asso. Dwight K. Shellman Jr. & Asso., Aspen, Colo., 1973—. Mem. Nat. Orgn. for Women, Pitkin County, Yuma County bar assns., Women Lawyers Assn. Home: PO Box 654 Cave Creek AR 85331 Office: Wheeler Opera House PO Box G-3 Aspen CO 81611

SKUBIC, VERA, educator; b. Chgo., Apr. 8, 1918; d. Albin H. and Sophie M. (Roth) Skubic; B.S., U. Ill., 1940; M.A., U. Cal. at Los Angeles, 1947; Ph.D., U. So. Cal., 1954. Tchr. phys edn. Wayzata (Minn.) Pub. Schs., 1940-42, Faulkner Sch., Chgo., 1942-45; faculty Morningside Coll., Sioux City, Ia., 1945-46, La. State U., 1947-50; grad. teaching asst. U. Cal. at Los Angeles, 1946-47; prof. phys. edn. U. Cal. at Santa Barbara, 1951—, chmn. women's dept. phys. edn., 1958-63. Mem. Cal. Com. on Fitness Research, 1956-59. Fellow Am. Coll. Sports Medicine, A.A.H.P.E.R. (asso. editor Research Quar., com. formulate sports skills tests); mem. A.A.A.S., Am. Assn. Health and Phys. Edn. (research council), N.E.A., Nat. Assn. Phys. Edn. for Coll. Women (research com. exec. bd. 1958-61), Western Soc. Phys. Edn. (exec. bd. 1957-61), Am. Acad. Phys. Edn., Cal. Assn. Phys. Edn. (chmn. publs. com.), Cal. Assn. Health, Phys. Edn. and Recreation, Women's Nat. Ofcl.'s Rating Com. (nat. exec. com. 1954-58), Human Factors Soc., Delta Psi Kappa (nat. scholarship com.). Contbr. articles to prof jours. Home: 6885 Del Playa Dr Goleta CA 93017 Office: U Cal Santa Barbara CA 93106

SKYPEK, DORA HELEN (MRS. CHARLES SKYPEK), educator; b. Noma, Fla., Sept. 18, 1915; d. Frederick Hiram and Vitano (Ward) Baggott; B.A., Fla. State U., 1937; M.A. (fellow), Emory U., 1961; Ph.D. (NSF fellow), U. Wis., 1966; m. Charles Skypek, Feb. 12, 1944; children—Genevieve, Michael Charles. Tchr. math. Bay County High Sch., Fla., 1937-41, Leesburg (Fla.) High Sch., 1941-42, Leon County (Fla.) High Sch., 1942-44, St. Johns Country Day Sch., Fla., 1954-58;

asst. prof. math. and edn. Emory U., Atlanta, 1963-69, asso. prof., 1969—, dir. U.S. Office of Edn. Insts., summers 1966, 67, 68, acad. year 1968-69. Cons., Ga. State Dept. Edn. Math. Curriculum Guide, 1969-71. Mem. Nat. Council Tchrs. Math., Math. Assn. Am., Ga. Council Tchrs. Math. (dir. 1973-75), Pi Mu Epsilon, Kappa Delta Epsilon (regional dir. 1966-69). Democrat. Methodist. Editorial panel The Arithmetic Tchr., 1974—. Contbr. articles to jours. in field. Home: 2120 Trailmark Dr Decatur GA 30033 Office: Emory University Atlanta GA 30322

SKYPEK, GENEVIEVE, psychologist; b. Panama City, Fla., May 27, 1945; d. Charles Stanley and Dora Helen (Baggott) Skypek; B.A., Tulane U., 1966; M.A., U. Fla., 1969, Ph.D., 1971. Clin. intern William S. Hall Psychiat. Inst., Columbia, S.C., 1970-71; coordinator walk-in centers Columbia Drug Abuse Edn. Project, 1971-73; asst. dir. methadone maintenance treatment program Columbia Drug Response Operation, 1973, dir. outpatient services, 1973—; instr. bus. psychology Preston Coll., Columbia, 1972-73; individual practice psychotherapist and tng. cons., Columbia; faculty S.E. Inst., Chapel Hill, N.C. Chmn., Symposium on Community Based Drug Intervention, 1971; mem. First Internat. Congress on Drug Edn., Montreux, Switzerland, 1973. Mem. Am. (div. humanistic psychology), Southeastern psychol. assns., Internat. Transactional Analysis Assn., Alpha Omicron Pi. Home: 600 Arcadia Lakes Dr E Columbia SC 29206 Office: 304 Kittrell Center 2711 Middleburg Dr Columbia SC 29204

SLABAUGH, SHARON LYNN (MRS. FREDERICK MARCH SLABAUGH), research co. exec.; b. Detroit, Feb. 21, 1944; d. John Edward and Dorothy Sarah (Miley) Grumbley; A.A., Pasadena City Coll., 1963; B.S., U. So. Cal., 1965; m. Frederick March Slabaugh, July 12, 1968; 1 son, Jeffrey March. Asst. buyer Nash & Co., Pasadena, Cal., 1960-64; research analyst, asst. project dir. Security Pacific Bank, Los Angeles, 1964-68; corporate officer Parker Research Corp., South Pasadena, Cal., 1968—. Mem. Am. Marketing Assn. (chpt. sec. 1964-66). Home: 2014 Camden Pkwy South Pasadena CA 91030 Office: 715 Fremont South Pasadena CA 91030

SLACK, FLORENCE KANTOR (MRS. MELVIN F. SLACK), educator; b. N.Y.C.; d. Philip and May (Kreiness) Kantor; B.A., Hunter Coll., 1960, M.S., 1962; postgrad. City Coll. Grad. Sch. Econs., 1962-64; M.A. in Psychology, New Sch. for Social Research, 1972; m. Melvin F. Slack, Sept. 5, 1942; 1 dau., Brenda. With FHA, San Diego, 1943-45; tchr. Drake Bus. Sch., N.Y.C., 1961-62, N.Y.C. Bd. Edn., 1963—. Fellow Internat. Biog. Assn.; mem. Kappa Delta Pi, Delta Pi Epsilon (chpt. newsletter editor Highlights 1963-67). Address: 9 Farrand Dr Parsippany NJ 07054

SLACK, FRANCES EDNA (MRS. WILLIAM HENRY SLACK), museum adminstr.; b. Youngstown, O., May 17, 1920; d. Thomas Henry and Alpha Meda (Bair) Nees; student, Bliss Coll., 1937-39; student Ohio State U., 1939-41, Franklin U., 1943; m. William Henry Slack, Apr. 3, 1939; children—Susan Kathryn (Mrs. Charles Harrison Horn), William Trenton, Robert John, Nancy Patricia. Chief clk. div. Purchasing and Printing, State of Ohio, Columbus, 1939-42; sec. Adj. Gen.'s. Office, 1943-46; asst. William H. Slack Funeral Home, Sunbury, O., 1949-61; with Lake County Hist. Soc., Mentor, O., 1974—, museum adminstr., hist. researcher, 1965—. Mem. dist. bd. Girl Scouts Am., Mentor, 1966-69. Mem. Western Res. Hist. Soc. (geneal. adv. com. 1969-74), Lake County Hist. Soc., Ohio, Lake County, Geauga County, Wayne County, Morrow County geneal. socs. Republican. Methodist. Mem. Order Eastern Star. Home: 7318 Maple St Mentor OH 44060 Office: 8095 Mentor Av Mentor OH 44060

SLACK, JANIS CHARLENE HELTON (MRS. ROBERT WILLIAM SLACK), broadcasting exec.; b. Dayton, O., Aug. 26, 1942; d. Roland and Eula Mae (Seals) Helton; student U. Fla., 1960-62; student U. Dayton, 1966-67; m. Robert William Slack, May 18, 1961; 1 son, Barry Regan. Prodn. mgr. Trend Pub., Tampa, Fla., 1962-65; asst. radio TV advt. mgr. Rike's Dept. Store, Dayton, O., 1965-67; asst. promotion publicity mgr. WLWD, Dayton, 1967—. Mem. Women in Communications, Am. Women in Radio and TV. Home: 7325 Far Hills Av Dayton OH 45459 Office: 4590 Avco Dr Dayton OH 45401

SLACK, KATIE FRANK, ednl. adminstr.; b. Tishmingo, Okla., Apr. 16, 1924; d. William Bebee and Marion Eliza (Naylor) Slack; B.A., So. Meth. U., 1946; M.Ed., N. Tex. State U., 1956. Tchr., Hot Springs (Ark.) Pub. Schs., 1946-47, Wichita Falls (Tex.) Pub. Schs., 1947-51, Greenville (Tex.) Pub. Schs., 1951-55, Shady Brook (Tex.) Schs., 1957-59; asst. prof. psychology, dean women Southeastern State Coll., Durant, Okla., 1959—. Mem. Am. Assn. U. Women, D.A.R., Nat. Assn. Women Deans and Counselors, P.E.O., Delta Kappa Gamma, Gamma Phi Beta, Beta Kappa Gamma, Psi Chi, Kappa Delta Pi. Methodist. Home: 1224 N 5th St Durant OK 74701

SLACK, MARY KNOX PULLIAM (MRS. RICHARD JOHN SLACK), librarian; b. San Angelo, Tex., Oct. 1, 1912; d. Mark Bell and Mary Knox (Powell) Pulliam; student So. Meth. U., 1929-30; B.J., U. Mo., 1933; postgrad. Shorter Coll., 1968; M. Librarianship, Emory U., 1970; m. Richard John Slack, Aug. 19, 1935; children—Ann Knox (Mrs. Richard R. Lorelle), Mary Susan (Mrs. Robert Wycliffe Cheatham, Jr.). Corr., Dallas Jour., 1934-35; copywriter Robert E. Martin Co., Atlanta, 1943-44; serials librarian Shorter Coll., Rome, Ga., 1968-70, reference, serials librarian, 1970-72, asst. prof. ednl. media, 1971-72; founder, head bus. library Tri-County Regional Library, Rome, 1972-74; med. librarian N.W. Ga. Regional Hosp., 1974—. Founder, Floyd Hosp. Sch. Nursing Library, Rome, 1968, cons., 1968—. Vol., A.R.C., 1957-67. Mem. Am. (regional audiovisual rev. com. Booklist 1970-73), Southeastern, Ga. (2d v.p. 1973—) library assns., Am. Assn. Higher Edn., Ga. Assn. Educators, N.E.A., Med. Library Assn., Spl. Libraries Assn., D.A.R., Gamma Alpha Chi, Delta Gamma. Democrat. Episcopalian. Home: 600 Redmond Rd Apt B-2 Rome GA 30161 Office: 606 W 1st Av Rome GA 30161

SLACK, WINIFRED SOPP, accountant, bldg. constrn. co. exec.; b. Erie, Pa., July 27, 1920; d. Henry and Lynette Catherine (Weber) Sopp; B.S. magna cum laude in Bus. Adminstrn., U. Pitts., 1972; m. Frederick M. Slack, May 3, 1941; children—Judith L. Slack Steinberg, William D. Accountant Schaefer Equipment Co., Pitts., 1940-48; individual practice accounting, Pitts., 1954-68; accountant, Pitts., 1954-68; treas. Campbell-Ellsworth, Inc., Pitts., 1968—, dir., 1970—, sec., 1972—. Girl Scout leader Pitts. council, 1940-43. C.P.A., Pa. Mem. Am., Pa. (state adv. com. mems. in industry) insts. C.P.A.'s, Zonta Internat., Phi Chi Theta (Gold medal writing award 1970). Editorial bd. Iris mag., 1971—. Home: 101 Cedar Dr McMurray PA 15317 Office: 1143 Cochran Mill Rd Pittsburgh PA 15236

SLAGLE, LAVERNA EILEEN WIRE (MRS. ERVIN L. SLAGLE), steel co. exec.; b. York, Pa., Jan. 12, 1923; d. Harry W. and Susan C. (Myers) Wire; grad. high sch.; m. Ervin L. Slagle, Nov. 27, 1942. With Wm. Christensen Co., Inc., York, 1942—, asst. treas., 1963-67, treas., 1967-73, sec.-treas., dir., 1973—. Mem. York Area C. of C. Clubs: Soroptomist, Out Door Country (York). Home: 1600 Altland Av York PA 17404 Office: 400 S Sherman St York PA 17405

SLATE, JOAN MCGUCKEN (MRS. SHERWOOD SLATE), found. exec.; b. Milw., Feb. 24, 1932; d. John Joseph and Harriett Helen (Todes) McGucken; student Marquette U. Coll. Journalism, 1950-51; B.S. in Journalism, U. Wis. at Madison, 1954; m. Sherwood Slate, Nov. 10, 1968. Advt. mgr. Hill's Dept. Store, Madison, Wis., 1954, Milw., 1954-55; adminstrv. asst. pub. relations Med. Soc. Milw. County, 1955-61, pub. relations mgr., 1955-68; pub. relations dir. Deaconess Hosp., Milw., 1969, dist. coordinator Wis. Arthritis Found., Madison, 1970—. Mem. Wis. gov.'s Task Force on Mental Health and Mental Retardation, 1964; mem. pub. Informational Task Force Gov.'s Commn. on Edn., 1969. Mem. Pub. Relations Soc. Am. (dir. Madison chpt. 1971—, treas. 1971-73, pres. 1974—), Milw. Advt. Club (pres. 1963-64, dir. 1964-66), Am. Assn. U. Women, Women in Communications (pres. Milw. Profl. chpt. 1960-61). Home: 505 N Midvale Blvd Madison WI 53705 Office: 1245 E Washington Av Madison WI 53703

SLATER, BERNICE GARSON (MRS. MANNING SLATER), broadcasting exec.; b. New Haven, Apr. 29, 1924; d. Samuel and Ida (Nemoroff) Garson; student U. Cal. at Berkeley, 1949-50, Sacramento State Coll., 1964-69; grad. Advanced Mgmt. Program, Harvard, 1968; m. Manning Slater, Aug. 8, 1953; children—Gary, Richard. Mgr. Rand's, dress shop, Bridgeport, 1944-47; operations mgr. G & G, appliance co., New Haven, 1947-51; designer kitchens Louis Garson, 1951-53; treas. Hercules Broadcasting Co., Sacramento, 1960-65, v.p., 1965—, dir., 1965—. Democrat. Home: 3330 American River Dr Sacramento CA 95825 Office: PO Box 6347 Sacramento CA 95860

SLATER, ELEANOR FRANCES, former state senator, state ofcl.; b. Jersey City, Oct. 16, 1908; d. Francis P. and Eleanor (Krieg) Boland; grad. Montclair State Coll., 1929; m. William Richard Slater, Oct. 15, 1934; children—William Richard, Thomas Francis. Mem. Warwick (R.I.) Sch. Com., 1954-58; mem. R.I. Ho. of Reps., 2d dist., Warwick, R.I., 1958-66; mem. R.I. Senate, dist. 18, 1967-68; adminstr. on aging Dept. Community Affairs, now coordinator R.I. Div. Aging; mem. R.I. Commn. to Study Needs Higher Edn., 1956-58, Pres., Kennedy's Spl. Com. on Youth Employment; mem. Blue Cross/Blue Shield Dental Bd.; exec. bd. mem. R.I. Health Planning Council; mem. R.I. Action Plan Task Force; exec. bd. Nat. State Units Aging; mem. Gov.'s Task Force on Med. Care Costs; New Eng. rep. planning White House Conf., Post White House Conf., 1971; mem. adv. council Title IV-A State Instl. Library Services. Vice chmn. Democratic State Com. R.I.; alternate del. Dem. Nat. Conv., 1956; del. Dem. Nat. Conv., 1960, 64, 68. Chmn. adv. commn. task force New Eng. Gerontology Center, New Eng. Center Continuing Edn.; mem. gerontology com. U. R.I. Club: Exeter Country. Home: 14 Church Lane North Kingstown RI 02852

SLATER, HELENE FORD SOUTHERN, pub. relations exec.; b. Phila.; d. William Bette and Henrietta Harriet (Ford) Southern; B.A., New Sch. for Social Research, 1955, M.A., 1959; postgrad. Yeshiva U., Coll. City N.Y., Fordham U., Temple U., Howard U.; m. Chester E. Slater, June 22, 1955 (div. Dec. 1968). Reporter, columnist, feature writer various newspapers, 1940—; pres. Southern-Slater Enterprises, pub. relations, N.Y.C., 1955—; supr. bur. attendance Bd. Edn. City N.Y., 1970—. Pub. relations officer Shirley Chisholm Community Action Corp., 1972—. Recipient Outstanding Community Person award Radio Sta. WWRL, 1965, Achievement award Lambda Kappa Mu, 1971, Citation of Merit, 1973, Outstanding Soror of Year, 1967. Mem. Nat. Assn. Media Women (nat. pub. relations dir. 1973—, charter mem.), Nat. Assn. Coll. Women, Lambda Kappa Mu. Club: Howard University Alumni (v.p. 1973—) (N.Y.C.). Editor: The Acorn, Lambda Kappa Mu Sorority Ann. House Organ, 1960-65, The Media Woman, Nat. Assn. Media Women Ann. House Organ, 1966-67. Home: 360 W 22d St New York City NY 10011 Office: 360 W 22d St New York City NY 10011

SLATER, LUCILLE FLORENCE, librarian; b. Junction City, Ark., June 7, 1904; d. William Thomas and Florence Elizabeth (Wallace) Slater; B.S., North Tex. State U., 1947; M.A. in L.S., George Peabody Coll., 1952. Tchr. El Dorado (Ark.) Pub. Schs., 1923-45; librarian Union County Library, El Dorado, 1945-58, Barton Library, El Dorado, 1958—. Mem. Ark. (pres. 1957), Southwestern (treas. 1957-58) library assns., Bus. and Profl. Women's Club (past sec.), League Women Voters, Delta Kappa Gamma. Baptist. Club: Self Culture (El Dorado). Home: 104 Merle St El Dorado AR 71730 Office: 200 E 5th St El Dorado AR 71730

SLATTERY, MARGARET BARBARA LANG (MRS. GERARD R. SLATTERY), civic worker; b. Kitchener, Ont., Can.; d. George C.H. and Eleanor (Foley) Lang; Litt.D., U. Detroit, 1952; m. Frank Couzens, Oct. 19, 1922 (dec. 1950); children—Frank, Eleanor (Mrs. Edward C. Roney, Jr.), James II, Mary Elizabeth, Barbara (Mrs. Leo J. Brennan, Jr.), Homer J. (dec.), George Lang; m. 2d, Gerard R. Slattery, Dec. 29, 1955; 1 step-dau., Patricia (Mrs. Peter Quall). Mem. Hist. Commn. Detroit, 1966; past v.p. United Community Services. Bd. dirs. United Found., Southeastern Mich. chpt. A.R.C., Detroit Area Hosp. Council, Med. Center Corp.; chmn. bd. trustees Childrens Hosp. Mich., 1956-73, life trustee. Mem. Founders Soc. Detroit Mus. Art, Detroit Hist. Soc., League Catholic Women (past pres.). Roman Catholic. Clubs: Country Detroit, Detroit Athletic; Grosse Pointe Yacht (Mich.). Home: 95 Lake Shore Rd Grosse Pointe MI 48236

SLATTERY, SISTER MARGARET PATRICE, coll. pres.; b. St. Louis, June 19, 1926; d. Patrick Joseph and Margaret Mary (Harris) Slattery; B.A., Incarnate Word Coll., 1952; M.A., Marquette U., 1955; Ph.D., Cath. U., 1966. Faculty, Incarnate Word Coll., San Antonio, Tex., 1952—, instr., asst. prof. English, 1952-66, asso. prof. English, 1967-72, prof., 1972—, chmn. dept. English, 1966-69, acad. dean, 1969-72, pres., 1972—. Newspaper Fund fellow Wall St. Jour., 1961. Mem. Modern Lang. Assn., Nat. Council Tchrs. English, Am. Assn. Higher Edn. Home: 4301 Broadway San Antonio TX 78209

SLATTERY, MARY MICHEL, health service exec.; b. Breckenridge, Minn., Nov. 19, 1938; d. James Michael and Bridget Anges (Fogarty) Slattery; B.S., Coll. of St. Catherine, St. Paul, 1960; M.S., U. Wis., 1969; Kellogg fellow, U. Ill., 1972-73. Counselor, Sch. Edn., coordinator occupational therapy clin. teaching Med. Sch., U. Wis., Madison, 1965-68; trainer VISTA, 1969-70; asst. prof., supr. med./surg. services U. Ill., Chgo., 1969, 70-72; tng. dir. Nat. Drug Abuse Tng. Center, Chgo., 1972—. Democratic precinct capt., 1968—. Mem. Nat. Council for Internat. Health (steering com.), Am. (chmn. Nat. Conf. 1973), Wis. (pres. 1966) occupational therapy assns., Chgo. Council Fgn. Relations. Home: 2034 N Sheffield Av Chicago IL 60614 Office: 3310 Peterson St Chicago IL 60645

SLAUGHTER, BERNICE, psychologist; b. Jeffersonville, Ind., Nov. 29, 1920; d. Strother Frye and Irene Arbella (Marshall) Slaughter; B.S., Ind. State Tchrs. Coll., 1944; M.A., U. Minn., 1951. Elementary tchr., Jeffersonville, 1943-54, Flint, Mich., 1954-67; tchr. academically talented, 1957-60. Girl Scout leader, 1945-52; sec. Council Chs., 1951-54. Mem. Nat. Assn. Sch. Psychologists, Nat., Mich. edn. assns., United Tchrs. Flint, Alpha Kappa Alpha, Delta Kappa Gamma. Baptist. Home: 2057 Chelan St Flint MI 48503 Office: 2941 Raskob St Flint MI 48504

SLAUGHTER, BETTY JO ZACHARY, civic worker; b. Ft. Smith, Ark., Aug. 1, 1925; d. J. Mack and Lola (Hall) Zachary; student Tex. Woman's U., 1942-45, U. Mexico, summer 1944, Tex. Christian U., 1945; m. George Morgan Slaughter III, Jan. 11, 1945 (div. Nov. 1960); children—George Morgan IV, Cynthia Ann, J. Mack, Robert Hill. Charter pres. Roswell (N.M.) Assistance League, 1949; mem. Jr. League, 1954—; leader's asst. Camp Fire Girls, 1961-62; mem. women's com. William Edrington Scott Theatre; mem. mothers com. Trinity Valley Sch., 1963-65; active Wyckoff Assn. in Am., Ft. Worth Opera Guild, Ft. Worth Community Theatre, A.R.C. drive, Jewel Charity Ball. Mem. Nat. Fedn. Republican Women, Met. Federated Rep. Women's Club of Tarrant County. Mem. D.A.R., P.E.O. Mem. Christian Ch. Home: 4312 Bellaire Dr S Fort Worth TX 76109

SLAUGHTER, CONSTANCE IONA, lawyer; b. Jackson, Miss., June 18, 1946; d. Willie Lee and Olivia (Kelley) Slaughter; B.S. cum laude, Tougaloo Coll., 1967; diploma Harvard, 1966; J.D. (Ford Found. fellow, Herbert Lehman fellow), U. Miss., 1970. Admitted to Miss. bar, 1970; law clk. Michael Trister, N. Miss. Rural Legal Services, Oxford, 1968-70; staff att. Lawyers' Com. for Civil Rights Under Law, Jackson, Miss., 1970-72; pvt. practice law, Forest, Miss. and Jackson, 1972—; exec. dir. So. Legal Rights Assn., Forest, Miss., 1972—. Instr. constitutional law, polit. and legal analysis Tougaloo (Miss.) Coll., 1970-72. Campaign mgr. Mayor Benny Thompson, Bolton, Miss., 1973. Bd. dirs. N. Miss. Rural Legal Services, Jackson, 1970—, Community Legal Services, Oxford, 1970—. Recipient Elks Civil Libertian award, 1971; named Woman of the Year, Greyhound Corp., YWCA and Jackson Advocate, 1972. Mem. Nat. Women's Alliance (dir. 1973—), Am. Civil Liberties Union (dir. Miss. 1972—), Am. Bar Assn., Nat. Assn. Criminal Def. Lawyers, Nat. Bar Assn., Miss. State Bar, Am. Judicature Soc., Miss. Trial Lawyers Assn., Hind County Bar Assn., Nat. Lawyers Guild, Magnolia Bar Assn., Nat. Conf. Black Lawyers, Nat. Council Negro Women, Nat. Assn. Women Lawyers, Black Am. Law Students Assn. (adviser 1970-73), So. Legal Action Movement, N.A.A.C.P., Delta Sigma Theta. Roman Catholic. Home: 1118 Pecan Blvd Jackson MS 39209 Office: 568 Jones St Forest MS 39074

SLAUGHTER, MARIA TORREGROSA, lawyer; b. Agnadilla, P.R., Sept. 2, 1918; d. Angel and Monserrate (Guevara) Torregrosa; B.A., U. P.R., 1940, LL.B., 1943; m. H. Leon Slaughter, Mar. 30, 1963; 1 son, Leon; children by previous marriage—Luisita Lopez, Angeles (Mrs. Guillermo Villeda), Amaury Lopez, Carmen (Mrs. Bryan Lewis), Sara (Mrs. Rick Lawrence), Olga Lopez; stepchildren—Jerry Slaughter, Anna Jo Wyatt. Admitted to P.R. bar, 1945, Tex. bar, 1967; sec.-atty. Superior Ct., San Juan, P.R., 1945-48; atty. div. legislation P.R. Dept. Justice, 1951-53, registrar of property Caguas sect., 1953-63; dir. Community Action Program, Sweetwater, Tex., 1968-69; planning dir. Community Action Program Taylor County, Tex., 1970-71; dir. Project LAW (Legal Action Workshop), Abilene, Tex., 1971-73; practice law, Cleveland, Tex., 1973—. Commr., Pub. Housing Authority, Abilene, 1971-73. Mem. Nat. Assn. Women Lawyers, State Bar Tex., P.R. Bar Assn., Cleveland C. of C. Address: 703 Rickey St Cleveland TX 77327

SLAUGHTER, MARY VERNIS WESLEY (MRS. GRADY FRANK SLAUGHTER), librarian; b. Wrightsville, Ga., June 15, 1937; d. Walter William and Mary Bell (Kemp) Wesley; B.S., Paine Coll., 1961; M.L.S., Atlanta U., 1971; m. Grady Frank Slaughter, Nov. 11, 1973. Tchr. elementary sch., Johnson County (Ga.) Bd. Edn., 1961-63, tchr. librarian, 1963-65, tchr. librarian high sch. grade, 1965-66; librarian Dock Kemp Sch., Wrightsville, 1966-70; librarian Wrightsville Elementary Sch., 1970—. Active Girl Scouts Am.; adviser Christian Youth Fellowship, 1961—. Mem. Johnson County Assn. Educators (pres. 1967-69), A.L.A., Ga., nat. edn. assns. Democrat. Methodist.

SLAVENS, SHIRLEY ANN (MRS. DONALD SLAVENS), precision machine co. exec.; b. Bend, Ore., May 19, 1927; d. Harris Gordon and Winifred Beatrice (Webb) Meagher; student Northwestern Sch. Commerce, Ore., 1946; m. Donald Slavens, Oct. 7, 1946; children—Denise Ann (Mrs. Richard Landreth), William Donald. Sec., Santiseptic Co., cosmetics, Portland, Ore., 1946; with purchasing dept. Compton (Cal.) Jr. Coll., 1948-50; sec.-treas. S & S Industries, Paramount, Cal., 1962—. Pres., P.T.A., LaMirada, Cal., 1963-64. Mem. Alpha Iota. Club: Ebell (rec. sec. Fullerton, Cal. 1971-72, 2d v.p. 1973-74, 1st v.p. 1974—, dean fedn. extension). Home: 3020 Terraza Pl Fullerton CA 92635 Office: 7322 E Madison St Paramount CA 90723

SLAVIK, JULIE CONSTANCE BRES (MRS. JURAJ LUDEVIT JAN SLAVIK), orgn. exec.; b. Wallace, Ida., July 8, 1936; d. Allen Vincent and Frances (Jordan) Bres; B.A., Vassar Coll., 1958; m. Juraj Ludevit Jan Slavik, May 13, 1961; children—Juraj Michal Daniel II, William Nicholas Allen. Adminstrv. asst. Govt. Affairs Inst., 1959-61; sec. to gen. counsel Textile Mfrs. Inst., 1962-65; office mgr. Jr. League Washington, 1965—. Mem. jr. guild Davis Meml. Goodwill Industries, Washington, 1965-70; corr. sec. Washington Antiques Show, 1972; sec. Parents Assn. St. Patrick's Episcopal Day Sch., 1971-72; chmn. ball Washington chpt. Czechoslovak Nat. Council, 1965, mem. ball exec. com., 1971. Bd. dirs. St. Stephen's Community Center, 1964-69, pres., 1966-67, sec., 1967-69; trustee St. Patrick's Epis. Day Sch., 1973—, exec. com. capital fund dr., 1973—. Episcopalian (aux. vestry 1971-73, mem. calling com. for new rector, mem. music, finance fund raising, organ, worship coms., choir, vestrywoman). Home: 5264 Loughboro Rd NW Washington DC 20016 Office: 3039 M St NW Washington DC 20007

SLAVIN, SABINA SPRAGUE (MRS. WALTER SLAVIN), chemist; b. Derby, Conn., Mar. 30, 1941; d. George Ricker and Agnes Sabina (Donohue) Sprague; B.A., Coll. New Rochelle, 1962; m. Walter Slavin, Nov. 22, 1965. Chemist, Perkin Elmer Corp., Norwalk, Conn., 1962—. Sec., Ridgefield (Conn.) Democratic Club, 1971-73, pres., 1973—. Recipient assistantships Ill. Inst. Tech., Chgo., 1962, Rutgers U., 1962. Mem. Am. Chem. Soc., Am. Assn. Clin. Chemists, Soc. Applied Spectroscopy (treas. 1964-74, candidate pres.-elect 1974). Editor: Atomic Absorption Newsletter, 1967—, Clin. Chemistry Newsletter (name now Lab. Medicine Newsletter), 1969—. Patentee in field. Home: 128 W Mountain Rd Ridgefield CT 06877 Office: Perkin Elmer Corp 750 Main Av Norwalk CT 06856

SLAVOV, EUGENIA MARGARET (MRS. ASSEN IVANOV SLAVOV), educator; b. Reims, France, Feb. 18, 1925; d. Michael Alexander and Elisabeth Vladimir (Maximovitch) Hintze; LL.D., U. Rome, Italy, 1954; certificate U. Paris, 1964, U. Del., 1965, 69; m. Assen Ivanov Slavov, Sept. 9, 1951. Came to U.S., 1956, naturalized, 1962. Accountant, corr. Sperrwaffenarsenal, Linz-Ebelsberg, Austria, 1944-45; interpreter, Hdqrs. Allied Command, Linz, Austria, 1945; tchr. Latin, Russian, Spanish, French, Tower Hill Sch., Wilmington, Del., 1957-64; faculty U. Del., Newark, 1964—, asst. prof. Russian, German, French and Italian, 1965—. Mem. Am.-Swiss Soc., Am. Contract Bridge League, Wilmington Friends Italian Culture, Am. Assn. Tchrs. German Am. Assn. Tchrs. Slavic and East European Langs., Alliance Francaise, Delta Phi Alpha. Home: Fiske Lane Newark DE 19711

SLAYBAUGH, JANET LOUISE, social worker; b. Gettysburg, Pa., Oct. 29, 1942; d. Robert Paul and Ruth Bell (Cook) Slaybaugh; student, Florence State Coll. 1960-61; B.S., U. Ala., 1963, postgrad., 1971-72; postgrad. Northwestern State U., 1964-65; M.S.W., La. State U., 1967; postgrad. Tulane U., 1968-69. Instn. counselor Leesville (La.) State Sch., 1964-66, clin. social worker, 1967—. Mem. Nat. Assn. Social Workers, Am. Assn. Mental Deficiency, Acad. Certified Social Workers, La. Conf. Social Welfare, La. Mental Health Assn. Lutheran. Clubs: Piolet, Toastmistress (Leesville). Address: 150 Riverside Mall Room 711 Baton Rouge LA 70804

SLEEMAN, MARY (MRS. JOHN PAUL SLEEMAN), librarian; b. Cleve., June 28, 1928; d. John and Mary Lillian (Jakub) Gerba; B.S., Kent State U., 1965; m. John Paul Sleeman, Apr. 27, 1946; children—Sandra (Mrs. Walter Swyrydenko), Robert, Gary, Linda. Supervising librarian elementary schs. Nordonia Hills Bd. Edn., Northfield, O., 1965—; children's librarian Twinsburg (O.) Pub. Library, 1965-66. Mem. A.L.A., Ohio Sch. Librarians Assn., N.E.A., Summit County Librarians Assn., North Eastern Ohio Tchrs. Assn. Methodist. Home: 18171 Logan Dr Walton Hills OH 44146 Office: 115 Ledge Rd Northfield OH 44067

SLEEPER, ELEANOR RUSSELL (MRS. DONALD CAMPBELL SLEEPER), real estate exec.; b. Little Rock, Feb. 6, 1922; d. Everett Adams and Lena (Faisst) Ham; B.S. in Home Econs., Memphis State U., 1943; m. William Chapman Chilton, June 22, 1944 (dec. Sept. 1946); m. 2d, James K. Russell, Mar. 18, 1952 (dec. Mar. 1970); children—Branch J., Kirk Everett, Lydia Martha, Scott Ham; m. 3d, Donald Campbell Sleeper, Sept. 23, 1973. With U. Cal. Med. Sch., San Francisco, 1947-48; army hostess, program dir. Army Spl. Services, Japan, 1948-49; real estate salesman, Oakland-Orinda area (Cal.), 1950-52; owner Eleanor Russell Realtor, Orinda, Cal., 1969—. Mem. Am. Assn. Univ. Women, World Affairs Council No. Cal., Diablo Home Exons., Orinda C. of C. Republican. Mem. Community Ch. Club: Commonwealth. Home: 129 Sleepy Hollow Lane Orinda CA 94563 Office: 16 Orinda Way Orinda CA 94563

SLEET, CAMMIE LEE KENT (MRS. JAMES TURNER SLEET), coll. adminstr.; b. Itta Bena, Miss., Sept. 25, 1927; d. Phillip Henry and Carrie Lee (Butler) Kent; B.S., Lewis Bus. Coll., 1948; B.A., Wayne State U., 1963, M.A., 1972; m. James Turner Sleet, Nov. 11, 1951; 1 son, Craig Collins. Social research supr. aged study U. Mich., Ann Arbor, 1964-65, research field supr. travel survey, 1965-67; registrar, dir. admissions, fgn. students adviser Mich. Luth. Coll. (name changed to Shaw Coll. 1972), Detroit, 1968-73; asst. dir. admissions U. Mich.-Dearborn, 1973—; Participant W. African Higher Edn. Workshop, 1973. Am. Assn. Collegiate Registrars and Admissions Officers, Nat. Assn. Fgn. Student Affairs edn. grantee, summer 1973. Mem. Nat. Assn. for Fgn. Student Affairs, Am. Assn. Collegiate Registrars and Admissions Officers. Home: 19590 Roselawn Detroit MI 48221 Office: 4901 Evergreen St Dearborn MI 48128

SLEETER, ALENE MAE, speech and hearing therapist; b. Herrin, Ill., May 1, 1922; d. Lee Ford and Margaret M. (Miller) Griffiths; B.Ed., So. Ill. U., Carbondale, 1943; M.S., Ind. State U., 1951; m. Hescal R. Sleeter, July 2, 1946; children—Marlene and Darlene (twins). Tchr. high schs., Ill., 1943-47; speech and hearing therapist Peoria (Ill.) Pub. Schs., 1947-48, Vigo County Sch. Corp., Terre Haute, Ind., 1949—; supervising tchr. speech and hearing therapy Ind. State U., 1951—. Active local Heart Assn., Arthrithis Found., Nat. Myasthenia Gravis Found. Mem. Am., Ind. speech and hearing assns., Vigo County, Ind. tchrs. assns., N.E.A. (life), Alexander Graham Bell Assn., Exceptional Children Assn., Speech Communications Assn., Sigma Tau Delta, Delta Kappa Gamma. Contbr. articles to profl. jours. Address: 3218 S 7th St Terre Haute IN 47802

SLEIGHT, JESSIE ADELE, editor; b. Stony Brook, L.I., N.Y.; d. Charles Mills and Adella Abigail (Bayles) Sleight; student pub. schs.; pvt. study piano, organ. Staff mem. Mus. Am., asst to A. Walter Kramer, 1920-21; asst. to editor George Matthew Adams Service, N.Y.C., newspaper syndicate, 1922-34, editor, 1935-64; exec. editor Washington Star Syndicate, 1965-67; organist St. James Episcopal Ch., St. James, L.I., 1942-55. Mem. Authors League Am., English-Speaking Union. Episcopalian. Club: Woman Pays. Home: PO Box 73 Stony Brook NY 11790

SLEIGHT, VIRGINIA MAE, lawyer; b. Queensbury, N.Y., Mar. 10, 1932; d. Henry Jay and Helen Adelaide (Bennett) Sleight; B.A., Russell Sage Coll., 1962. Bookkeeper, office mgr. Sleight Transit Mix Concrete, Glens Falls, N.Y., 1948-54; hearing reporter, clk. of ct. Warren County Children's Ct., Glens Falls, 1954-62; clk. Warren County Family Ct., Queensbury, N.Y., 1962-71; admitted to N.Y. bar, 1964; law asst. to judge Warren County Ct., Lake George, 1971—. Mem. Am., N.Y. State, Warren County bar assns., Bus. and Profl. Women (pres. 1973—), Am. Assn. U. Women (corr. Adirondack br. sec. 1965-69, mem. state legislative com. 1972—), Nat. Assn. Legal Secs. Presbyn. Home: 123 Aviaion Rd Glens Falls NY 12801 Office: Municipal Center Lake George NY 12845

SLENCZYNSKA, RUTH (MRS. JAMES RICHARD KERR), pianist; b. Sacramento, Jan. 15, 1925; d. Josef and Dorothy (Goldstein) Slenczynska; studied with Egon Petri, Artur Schnabel, Alfred Cortot, Sergei Rachmaninoff, Nadia Boulanger; student U. Cal., 1941-44; m. James Richard Kerr, Aug. 1967. First recital, Mills. Coll., Oakland, Cal., 1929, German debut, Berlin, 1932, N.Y. debut, Town Hall, 1933; performed with many major orchs.; broadcast recital BBC, 1956, also Radio Diffusion, Paris; numerous Decca Gold Label recordings; soloist transcontinental tour Arthur Fielder and Boston Pops Orch., tour S.Am., 1958, 60, Europe, 1953, 54, 55, Far and Near East, 1965, 66, Africa, S.Am., 1963; appeared on radio and TV programs, including NBC Home Show, Monitor, Night Beat, Breakfast Club; master classes in piano repertoire U. R.I., Kingston, 1962—; now artist in residence, prof. piano So. Ill. U., Edwardsville; Artist of Year, Baldwin Piano Co. Recipient Nat. Tchr. Recognition award M.T.N.A., 1972. Fellow Internat. Inst. Arts and Letters; mem. Tower and Flame Soc., Delta Omicron. Author: (with W. Louis Biancolli) Forbidden Childhood, 1957; (with Ann Lingg) Music at Your Fingertips, 1960. Contbr. articles to profl. publs. Home: 1270 Fifth Av New York City NY 10029 also 14 Brookside Ct Edwardsville IL 62025

SLIDER, DORLA DEAN WEEKS (MRS. JAMES HAROLD SLIDER), artist; b. Tampa, Fla., Sept. 9, 1929; d. Samuel Manning and Ida C. (Heller) Weeks; student Walter Emerson Baum, 1940-48, Famous Artists Schs., 1960-63; m. James Harold Slider, July 8, 1951; 1 dau., Cindi Darnel. Exhibited one-man shows Gallery 252, Phila., Wanamaker's Phila., Wilmington-Centerville Gallery, Del., Hazelton Art League, Camp Hill Acad., Harrisburg, Pa., Pa. Clubhouse Gallery, Media; Chadds Ford (Pa.) Gallery, Janet Fleischer Gallery, Phila., Quadrangle Gallery, Dallas; exhibited in group shows Allied Artists Am., Nat. Acad. N.Y., Catherine Lorillard Wolf Art Club, Nat. Acad. N.Y., Am. Water Color Soc., Audubon Artists, N.Y.C., Allentown (Pa.) Art Mus., Pa. Acad. Fine Arts, Phila., Comml. Mus. Phila., Franklin and Marshall Coll., William Penn Mus., Harrisburg, Pa., Phila. Art Mus., Brandywine Arts Festival, Wilmington, Del., Motorola Regional, Allentown, Pa., Nat. League Am. Pen Women at Salt Palace, Salt Lake City, Knickerbocker Artists, N.Y.C., others; represented in permanent collections Wilkie Buick, Phila., State Farm Ins., Pottstown, Pa., Vincent Schs., Phoenixville, Pa., Plymouth Meeting Mall Mchts. Assn., Philco Corp., Lansdale, Pa., DuPont Corp., Wilmington, Del., Wilmington Trust Co., Pa. Mil. Coll., Chester, Hartford (Conn.) Ins. Group Washington Sch., Norristown, Pa., Marietta (O.) Coll. Recipient art awards including Winsor and Newton award, Gold medal for watercolor Catherine Lorillard Wolf Art Club, Nat. Acad. N.Y., 1970, 71, C.L. Wolf award watercolor, 1973, six Gold medals Perkiomen Valley Art Center, Schwenksville, Pa., 1965, 66, 67 (2), 68, 69; Silver medal Buxmont Regional, Souderton, Pa.; Jr. C. of C. Silver medal Lansdale (Pa.) Art League, 1966; Lansdale (Pa.) Art Club Silver medal for Watercolor, 1969; Grand prizes Stone Harbor (N.J.) C. of C., 1967, 70, 71; Grumbacher award for Watercolor Woodmere Art Gallery, Phila., 1970; Award of Excellence, Mainstreams '71 Internat., Marietta, O.; Anco Wood Found. award Nat. Soc. Painters in Casein and Acrylic Nat. Acad. N.Y., 1973. Mem. Phila. Watercolor Club, Am. Watercolor Soc. (Herb Olsen award 1972), Nat. League Am. Pen Women, Woodmere Art Gallery, Chester County Art Assn., Pottstown Area Artists Guild, Nat. Forum Profl. Artists Equity, Chadds Ford Gallery, Little Gallery Phila. Address: 1387 Kutz Dr Pottstown PA 19464

SLIFER, ROSEJEANNE, autograph, manuscript, map dealer; b. Paris, France; d. Oscar Keran and Cesarie (Figuiera) Slifer; student Marquette U., 1926-27; spl. classes Syracuse U., 1928. Pianist, Binghamton Symphony, 1928-29; piano tchr. Binghamton Inst. Mus. Art, 1927-29; compiler directory R. R. Bowker Co., 1932; with B. Altman & Co., N.Y.C., 1933-67, buyer books, rare books, old maps, autograph letters, also picture and print gallery, 1936-67; dealer, cons. in autographs, manuscripts, antique maps, N.Y.C., 1967—. Mem. Am. Geog. Soc., Manuscript Soc., Antiquarian Booksellers Assn. Am., N.Y. Hist. Soc., Soc. History Discovery. Author: (with Louise Crittenden) Giant Quiz Book, 1938, Second Giant Quiz Book, 1939, Quizmakers' Giant Quiz Book, 1942; (with Virginia French) Army-Navy Guide, 1942. Specialist in early cartography, manuscripts and autograph material. Home: 30 Park Av New York City NY 10016 Office: 30 Park Av New York City NY 10016

SLINGSBY, PHYLLIS LAVERNE (MRS. PERK A. SLINGSBY), journalist; b. Bakersfield, Cal., Oct. 12, 1917; d. Marion Lee and Stella Grace (Hughes) Crum; grad. high sch.; m. Perk A. Slingsby, Aug. 20, 1938; 1 dau., Sandra Lu (Mrs. Gerald Wayne Johnson). Women's editor Contra Costa Times Green Sheet, Walnut Creek, Cal., 1949-73. Charter mem. Walnut Creek Hist. Soc. Mem. Order Eastern Star, Order of White Shrine of Jerusalem (charter, past worthy high priestess). Clubs: Soroptimist (pres. 1961), Walnut Creek Professional and Business Women's (pres. 1965), East Bay Women's Press (pres. 1969). Home: 10 Walaka Rd Kikei Maui HI 96753

SLITER, DOROTHY BROWNING MURRAY (MRS. ERNEST DANIEL SLITER), poet; b. Kingston, Ont., Can., Mar. 25, 1905; d. David Browning and Lottie Mae (Maxwell) Murray; student Queen's U., 1926-27; m. Ernest Daniel Sliter, Jan. 10, 1927. Recipient award for poetry Canadian Poetry mag., 1938, award Abbey Dawn, poets festival, 1937, 52. Mem. Canadian Authors Assn. Author: The Friendly Village (prose), 1967. Author: High Wind, 1944; Father Lucas and Other Poems, 1971. Home: Box 53 Verona ON Canada

SLITER, WALLY BERNADETTE (MRS. LESTER AUSTIN SLITER), nursing adminstr.; b. Chgo., Oct. 12, 1910; d. Alois Joseph and Wally (Osterkorn) Kremsreiter; R.N., Marquette U., 1932; Bach. Nursing, U. Fla., 1961; m. Lester Austin Sliter, Jan. 13, 1933; children—Gerald, Wally Anne, Betsy, Rosemary (Mrs. Don McFall), William, Lester Austin, John Michael, Karl. Gen. nursing Walter Reed Gen. Hosp., Washington, 1932-38; gen. staff, supr. Columbia Hosp., Washington, 1938-40; supr. Doctor's Hosp., Washington, 1940-42; office nurse, Washington, 1949-50; supr. Tampa (Fla.) Gen. Hosp., 1954-61, dir. nursing service, 1961-66; dir. nursing service Meml. Hosp., Colorado Springs, Colo., 1966—. Pres. Health Assn. Pikes Peak Region, Inc., 1972-74. Bd. dirs. United Fund, 1970—, Vis. Nurse Assn., 1971—, Chronic Chest Disease, 1970—; chmn. lay adv. bd. Beth El Sch. Nursing, 1971—. Named Tampa Woman of Year, Pres.'s Roundtable, 1965. Mem. Am. Hosp. Assn., Colo. Hosp. Assn., Nat. League Nursing, Am. Soc. Nursing Service Adminstrs., Marquette U. Alumni Assn. Club: Altrusa (pres. Tampa 1964-65, pres. Colorado Springs 1970-72). Home: 6885 Duke Dr Colorado Springs CO 80907 Office: 1400 E Boulder St Colorado Springs CO 80909

SLOAN, GRACE MCCALMONT, state ofcl.; b. Dayton, Pa.; d. Charles Plumer and Minnie Boals (Elwinger) McCalmont; student pub. schs.; m. John E. Sloan (dec.); children—Mary Kathryn (Mrs. George Meyer), Jacqueline (Mrs. Donald Ketner). Treas., State of Pa., 1961-65, 69—, auditor gen., 1965-69. Treas. Gen. State Authority, State Pub. Sch. Bldg. Authority, Pa. Transp. Assistance Authority, Pa. Higher Edn. Facilities Authority, State Hwy. and Bridge Authority; mem. Pa. State Roadside Council. Co-founder, Clarion (Pa.) unit Nat. Found. Infantile Paralysis, 1935; mem. Def. Adv. Com. on Women in Services, 1966-69. Active Democratic Party, 1926—; mem. Pa. Dem. Com., 1944-60, Pa. Dem. Exec. Com., 1950-56, Pa. Dem. Policy Com., 1957-71, Pa. Dem. Nomination Recommendation Com., 1971—; pres. Pa. Fedn. Dem. Women, 1956-60; mem. Dem. Women's Club, Clarion, Pa., del. Dem. Nat. Conv., 1952, 56, 60, 64, 68; Dem. candidate for Congress 23d Dist. Pa., 1956. Mem. Nat. Assn. Auditors, Comptrollers and Treasurers (v.p.), Bus. and Profl. Women's Club Harrisburg, Nat. Woman's Party, Am. Legion Aux., Clarion County Hist. Soc. Presbyn. Club: Civic (Clarion). Home: 1104 Main St Clarion PA Office: Treasury Dept Finance Bldg Harrisburg PA 17120

SLOAN, ROSE MARY, educator; b. Youngstown, O., Apr. 28, 1938; d. William Bingham and Idalene (Davis) Sloan; B.D. in Edn., Youngstown State U., 1961, M.S., 1971; NDEA summer student, Kent State U., 1965; Ph.D. candidate, Ohio State U., 1973. Accountant, Lordstown (O.) Depot, 1961-62; tchr. elementary and secondary schs., Cleve., 1962-69; tchr. secondary sch., counselor, Youngstown, 1969-71; dean women Wilberforce U., 1971-73; cons. ednl. programming, mem. human relations team Ohio State U., Columbus, 1973—, also mem. adv. com. devel. edn. Moderator Panel Am. Women, 1969—; membership chmn. N.A.A.C.P., Youngstown and Cleve., 1965-69; exec. dir. South Side Happening House, 1969-71. Trustee Columbus Area Civil Rights Commn. Mem. Am. Personnel and Guidance Assn., Am. Assn. U. Women, Nat. Assn. Student Personnel Adminstrs., Nat. Assn. Women Deans and Counselors (program com.), Am. Assn. Higher Edn., Nat. Assn. Personnel Workers, Nat. Orgn. Women, Nat. Council Negro Women, Women's Polit. Caucus Franklin County, Young Profls. Assn. Negro Women, Jr. Civic League, Delta Sigma Theta (v.p. 1968—). Home: 125 W Dodridge St Columbus OH 43202

SLOAN, RUTH CHANTLER, librarian; b. Attleboro, Mass., Mar. 28, 1926; d. Samuel Wilson and Margaret Eleanor (Whalley) Chantler; A.B., Case Western Res. U., 1946; M.L.S., Rutgers U., 1968; m. Walter F. Sloan, May 4, 1946; children—Bruce W., Richard D., Catherine W., Philip E., Marion E. Librarian, Sch. of the Holy Child, Suffern, N.Y., 1968-70, Waldrick (N.J.) High Sch., 1970—. Chmn. service unit Ridgewood (N.J.) Salvation Army, 1956—; pres. Benjamin Franklin Home and Sch. Assn., 1959-61; mem. alumni adv. com. Case Western Res. U., 1973—. Mem. Nat., N.J., Bergen County edn. assns., N.J., Bergen County sch. library assns. Clubs: Woman's, College (v.p. 1968-70) (Ridgewood). Home: 328 Graydon Terrace Ridgewood NJ 07450 Office: Waldwick High Sch Waldwick NJ 07456

SLOANE, CECILIA CZAJA, psychologist; b. Adams, Mass., Jan. 2, 1930; d. John Frank and Sophie Ann (Janas) Czaja; B.S. in Chemistry, cum laude, Fordham U., 1961; M.S. in Psychology, Catholic U. Am., 1970; m. Joseph Sloane, June 27, 1971. Elementary sch. tchr. Archdiocese N.Y., 1953-59; secondary sch. tchr. Our Lady of Angels Acad., Enfield, Conn., 1960-65, vice prin., 1964-65; psychologist Howard County (Md.) pub. schs., 1968-75. Mem. adv. council Howard County Mental Health Com., 1970-73. NSF grantee, 1961-62, 62-63; study scholar Cath. U. Am., 1967-68. Mem. Nat. Assn. Sch. Psychologists, Md. Sch. Psychologists Assn. (membership chmn. 1972-73, county rep. 1969-71), Psi Chi. Home: 4461 Orchid Blvd Cape Coral FL

SLOANE, JANELLE ALEXANDER (MRS. EDWARD M. SLOANE), physician; b. Marshall, Tex., May 4, 1929; d. George P. and Fannye (Pierce) Alexander; student Tex. State Coll. for Women, 1946-47, U. Tex. at Austin, 1947-49; B.S., Lamar State Coll. Tech., 1956; M.D., U. Tex. at Galveston, 1961; m. Edward M. Sloane, July 2, 1948; children—Berengaria, Javonne, Martha, Marsha. Rotating intern U. Tex., Galveston, 1961-62, resident pathology, 1962-66, asst. prof. pathology, 1966-71; surg. pathologist John Sealy Hosp., Galveston, 1966-71; pathologist Deaconess Hosp., Oklahoma City, 1971—; asst. prof. pathology Okla. U. Sch. Medicine, 1971—. Mem. A.M.A., Am. Soc. Clin. Pathologists, So., Okla., Oklahoma County med. assns., Sigma Xi (asso.), Mu Delta. Home: 6404 Brentford Pl Oklahoma City OK 73132 Office: Deaconess Hosp Oklahoma City OK 73112

SLOANE, PATRICIA HERMINE, artist; b. N.Y.C., Nov. 21, 1934; d. David and Marian (Frauenthal) Sloane; student (scholar 1949) Dayton Art Inst., 1947-49; B.F.A. (scholar 1953, 54), R.I. Sch. Design, 1955; student (scholar) Ohio U. Grad. Coll., 1955-56, (scholar) N.A.D., 1956-58; M.A., Hunter Coll., 1968; Ph.D., N.Y.U., 1972; pvt. study with Hans Hoffman, Provincetown, summer 1954. Exhibited in one-man shows at Camino Gallery, 1962, Brata Gallery, 1963, U. R.I., 1968, Grand Central Moderns Art Gallery, 1968, Fordham U., 1968, Amerika-Haus, Vienna, 1970; two-man shows at Camino Gallery, N.Y.C., 1962; exhibited in group shows Corcoran Gallery, Providence Art Club, R.I. Artists' Ann., Beryl Lush Gallery, Provincetown, Dayton Art Inst., Ohio U., Camino Gallery, Terrain Gallery, Morris Gallery, N.A.D., Village Art Center, Brata Gallery, Osgood Gallery, Alan Stone Gallery, Silvermine Guild, others; represented in lending collection Mus. Modern Art; represented in pub. collections at Andrew Dickson White Mus., Cornell U., Notre Dame U., others; also pvt. collections. Free-lance or cons. book design, layout, graphic and typographical design, 1960-66; tchr. Scarsdale Studio Workshop, 1965, N.Y.U., 1966, Mercer County Community Coll., 1966-68, U. R.I., summer 1967, Kingsborough Community Coll., 1968, New Sch. for Social Research, 1971—; prof. City U. N.Y., 1969—. Lyra Brown Nickerson scholar, 1952; Scholastic Mags. scholar, 1957; N.Y. State Regents scholarships, 1967-68, 69-70. Mem. Coll. Art Assn., New Art Assn., Am. Soc. Aesthetics. Author: Colour: Basic Principles and New Directions, 1968. Contbr. articles to profl. mags. and jours. Address: 79 Mercer St New York City NY 10012

SLOBODZIAN, EVELYN MAE BIRDSALL, educator; b. Hammonton, N.J., Mar. 2, 1915; d. Ralph N. and Pearl (Thurston) Birdsall; B.S., Glassboro State Coll., 1940, M.S., 1958; postgrad. Newark and Trenton State Coll., 1960-61; Ed.D., Temple U., 1968; m. Alex S. Slobodzian, Apr. 21, 1940 (dec. 1944); 1 dau., Stephanie Ann (Mrs. Gregory B. Woolf). Tchr., Hammonton Pub. Schs., 1935-43, Monroe Twp. (N.J.) Pub. Schs., 1950-61; asso. prof. edn. Glassboro (N.J.) State Coll., 1961-70, prof. reading, 1970—, chmn. reading dept., 1970—, dir. Community Reading Clinic, 1961-64, Campus Sch. Reading Clinic, 1964-67. Cons. Curriculum Devel. Council, Temple U. Reading Inst., Gloucester County Abilities Center; cons., speaker South Jersey Schs., N.J. Reading Tchrs. Inst., Internat. Reading Tchrs. Convs. Mem. Nat., N.J., Gloucester County edn. assns., Internat. Reading Assn., South Jersey, Glassboro reading councils, N.J. Reading Tchrs. Assn. (editorial com. 1965-68, pres. 1968-69, dir. 1969-73), N.J. State Coll. Faculty Assn. Contbr. articles to profl. jours. Home: 23 Kent Rd Williamstown NJ 08094

SLOCUM, HESTER ALBERTA BEAUCHAMP (MRS. JOHN WILLIS SLOCUM), librarian; b. Corning, Kan., Oct. 4, 1909; d. Edward Edgerton and Lona (Butler) Beauchamp; B.A., Baker U., 1932; postgrad. U. Mo., 1940-41, Ariz. State U., 1964-66; M.S., La. State U., 1967; m. John Willis Slocum, Oct. 4, 1943. Instr. accounting Baker U., Baldwin, Kan., 1932-33; engaged in banking, ins., real estate businesses, 1933-55; with Scottsdale (Ariz) Pub. Library, 1955-66, acting dir., 1966; adminstrv. asst., head tech. services dept., New Orleans Pub. Library, 1967-70, asst. city librarian, 1970—. Named Woman of Year, Bus. and Profl. Women's Club, Scottsdale, 1956. Mem. Am., Southwestern (chmn. pubs. com. 1970-74), La. (chmn. pub. library standards study com. 1973-75, conv. chmn. 1970-71, pub. library statistic study com. chmn. 1970-72) library assns., Greater New Orleans Library Club, Alumni Assn. La. State U. Library Sch., UN Assn. Greater New Orleans (La. chmn., dir.), League Women Voters, Phi Kappa Phi, Beta Phi Mu, Alpha Chi Omega. Presbyn. Home: 7209 Martin Dr New Orleans LA 70126 Office: 219 Loyola Av New Orleans LA 70140

SLOMINSKI, ALFREDA W. (MRS. RICHARD SLOMINSKI), city ofcl.; b. North Tonawanda, N.Y., Jan. 11, 1929; d. Stanley and Teresa G. (Suchocki) Wilczek; B.A., U. Buffalo, 1950; J.D., U. Buffalo, 1952; m. Richard A. Slominski, Nov. 14, 1953; children—Barbara Anne, Mary Margaret. Admitted to N.Y. bar, 1954; practice law, Buffalo; mem. Bd. Edn. Buffalo, 1962-67; councilman at-large Buffalo, 1968—. Bd. dirs. Greater Buffalo Republican Club. Recipient Appreciation award for service to edn. Beltline Bailey Broadway Homeowner's League; named Woman of Year Greater Buffalo Autobody Guild, 1968. Mem. Bus. and Profl. Womens Club Buffalo (dir. 1971-72, chmn. legislation 1969-72). Roman Catholic. Home: 48 Thatcher Blvd Buffalo NY 14215 Office: City Hall Buffalo NY 14202

SLONAKER, ETHEL MAE (MRS. PAUL JEREMIAH SLONAKER), librarian; b. Andreas, Pa., Dec. 2, 1916; d. Harry Daniel and Annie Priscilla (Steiner) Houtz; B.A., Lebanon Valley Coll., 1938; postgrad. United Theol. Sem., 1942, Western Md. Coll., 1958-59; M.S. in L.S., U. N.C., 1967; m. Paul Jeremiah Slonaker, Mar. 17, 1939; children—Linda (Mrs. Edgar W. Conrad), Jerry Paul, Noel Gerard, David Lowell. Tchr. English and French high sch., Berkeley Springs, W.Va., 1959-60; librarian Shenandoah Coll. and Conservatory, Winchester, Va., 1960-69; asst. head reference and circulation Va. State Library, Richmond, 1969—. Mem. Am. Assn. U. Women, Southeastern, Va. library assns., Phi Alpha Epsilon, Beta Phi Mu. United Methodist. Home: 4816 Finlay St Richmond VA 23231 Office: 12th and Capitol Sts Richmond VA 23219

SLOSHBERG, LEAH PHYFER (MRS. WILLARD SLOSHBERG), museum exec.; b. New Albany, Miss., Feb. 21, 1937; d. Sisco Knox and Mary Rachel (Sandlin) Phyfer; B.F.A., Miss. State Coll., 1959; M.A. (Woodrow Wilson fellow), Tulane U., 1961; m. Willard Sloshberg, Dec. 8, 1961; 1 son, Simeon. Arts curator N.J. State Mus., Trenton, 1968-69, asst. dir., 1969-71, dir., 1971—. Home: Box 494 RFD 2 Stockton NJ 08559 Office: New Jersey State Museum Trenton NJ 08625

SLOTTER, CAROLE LOUISE BEECH (MRS. GILBERT FRYLING SLOTTER), coll. adminstr.; b. Portland, Ore., Sept. 18, 1935; d. Oscar Grant and Ruth Mae (Eitleman) Beech; B.A., U. Ore., 1957; M.S., Shippensburg State Coll., 1974; m. Gilbert Fryling Slotter, Mar. 23, 1958; children—Kathryn Mari, Patricia Lynn. News editor Cottage Grove (Ore.) Sentinel, 1956; editorial asst. TV Info, Portland, Ore., 1957; corr. Lancaster (Pa.) Newspapers, 1965-69; reporter Lancaster New Era, 1967; pub. information officer Millersville (Pa.) State Coll., 1967-69, dir. pub. relations and coll. publs., 1969—. Bd. dirs. United Campus Ministry, Millersville State Coll., 1970—, sec., 1971—. Recipient publ. leadership award Am. Coll. Pub. Relations Assn., 1971, student media service award Millersville State Coll., 1973. Mem. Am. Coll. Pub. Relations Assn., Pub. Relations Assn. Pa. State Colls. and Univs. (sec. 1970—), Women in Communications, Lancaster League Women Voters (2d v.p. 1964-66), Am. Assn. U. Women, Lancaster Urban League. Lutheran (mem. commn. on higher edn. Central Pa. Synod). Home: 67 W Charlotte St Millersville PA 17551

SLOVITER, DOLORES KORMAN, lawyer; b. Phila., Sept. 5, 1932; d. David and Tillie (Raevsky) Korman; B.A., Temple U., 1953; LL.B., U. Pa., 1956; m. Dr. Henry A. Sloviter, 1969. Asso. editor U. Pa. Law Review, 1954-55; legal trainee law dept. City of Phila., summer 1955; note editor U. Pa. Law Review, 1955-56; admitted to Pa. bar, 1956; practiced in Phila., 1956—; mem. firm Dilworth, Paxson, Kalish, Kohn & Levy, 1956-69, Harold E. Kohn, P.A., 1969-72; asso. prof. law Temple U., Phila., 1972-74, prof., 1974—; vis. asso. prof. U. Pa. Law Sch., 1974. Mem. law and social action com. Am. Jewish Congress, 1966—. Treas. Central Phila. Reform Democrats, 1965-67. Mem. Phila. Bar Assn., Am. Bar Assn., Order of Coif (mem. exec. com. chpt. 1964-67, v.p. 1973—), Phi Alpha Theta, Pi Gamma Mu. Home: 2215 Panama St Philadelphia PA 19103 Office: 1715 N Broad St Philadelphia PA 19122

SLOYAN, SISTER MARY STEPHANIE, coll. pres.; b. N.Y.C., Apr. 18, 1918; d. Jerome J. and Marie V. (Kelley) Sloyan; B.A., Georgian Ct. Coll., Lakewood, N.J., 1945; M.A., Cath. U. Am., 1949, Ph.D. in Math., 1952. Asst. prof. Georgian Ct. Coll., 1952-56, asso. prof., 1956-59, prof. math., 1959—, pres., 1968—. Mem. Am. Math. Soc., Math. Assn. Am., Am. Assn. U. Women, Sigma Xi. Address: Georgian Court Coll Lakewood NJ 08701

SLUIZER, SHIRLEY ADELE, city ofcl.; b. Detroit, June 15, 1925; d. Dan M. and Minnie (Fisher) Silverblatt; B.S., Ohio State U., 1948; postgrad. Northeastern Ill. State Coll., 1964-65; children—Susan, Eric, Howard. With Wilmette (Ill.) Recreation Dept., 1966—, leisure arts coordinator, 1972—. Mem. U.S. Inst. Tech. Theatre, Am., Ill., Childrens theatre assns., Nat., Ill. park and recreation assns., Am. Community Theatre Assn. Office: 7th and Laurel Wilmette IL 60091

SLYKHOUSE, GLORIA BURSEY (MRS. ROGER ALLEN SLYKHOUSE), editor, pub.; b. Tupper Lake, N.Y., Oct. 30, 1934; d. Jack J. and Ada C. (DeGraff) Bursey; B.A., Lindenwood Coll., 1955; m. Roger Allen Slykhouse, Apr. 6, 1957; children—Roger Allen, Gary Bursey, Holly Jane. Asst. editor Mich. Travelor, 1966; asst. account exec. Aves Advt., Grand Rapids, Mich., 1967-68; owner, editor Glory Etc., Grand Rapids, Mich., 1970—; editor Interstate mag.; pub. relations Trans American; partner Genie Services, 1973—. Pub. information chmn. Kent County Cancer Unit, 1968-72, bd. dirs., 1968—. Recipient award United Fund Service, 1972, Pub. Edn. award Cancer Slide Show, 1973. Mem. Bus. and Profl. Women. Republican. Club: Womens City. Home: 2221 W Leonard St Grand Rapids MI 49504 Office: 1260 Leonard St NW Grand Rapids MI 49504

SMAARDYK, ELLEN LOUISE CARLSON, librarian; b. Ft. Wayne, Ind., May 8, 1920; d. Carl Edward and Josephine (Zitka) Carlson; B.A., Hanover Coll., 1942; M.A.L.S., Rosary Coll., 1964; postgrad. other colls. and univs.; m. Abraham Smaardyk, Aug. 7, 1943; children—John, Nancy, Jane, James. Librarian, Cook County (Ill.) Sch. Dist. 102, 1964—; mem. library tech. asst. adv. com. Coll. of DuPage, 1967-69; mem. Lyons Twp. Multi-Media Coop., 1966—, chmn., 1968-72. Mem. N.E.A., A.L.A., Ill. Library Assn., Edn. Assn. Dist. 102 (pres. 1970-72), Am., Ill. assns. sch. libraries, Chgo. Suburban Audio Visual Roundtable, Assn. Supervision and Curriculum Devel., Ill. Audio Visual Assn., Beta Phi Mu. Unitarian. Home: 257 Middaugh St Clarendon Hills IL 60514

SMALL, ALICE JEAN, artist; b. Sandpoint, Ida., Dec. 18, 1918; d. Edward Hayes and Alice (McNeel) Small; B.A., U. Wash., 1939, M.F.A., 1943; postgrad. U. Cal. at Berkeley, 1944; student Cranbrook Acad. Fine Arts, Chgo. Inst. Design. Ala. Poly. Inst., Ecole de Beaux Art, Paris, France, U. Tokyo (Japan); pupil Fernand Leger, Paris; Prof. Watercolor U. Wash., 1941-43, U. W. Va., 1947-48; chmn. art dept. U. Tampa (Fla.), 1949-51; regional crafts dir. U.S. Army, Far East, Japan, 1951-54; with USIS, Mexico, 1958-65; mem. research staff for creative projects Ft. Ord (Cal.) adult edn. Program, 1971—; one-woman shows Seattle Art Mus., Henry Gallery Art, U. Wash., Ringling Mus., Sarasota, Fla., Sarasota Art Assn., 1974 Riverside Gallery, N.Y.C., Am. Cultural Center, Tokyo, Japan, U.S. Army Exhbn., Europe, Los Institutos Culturales de Relaciones Mexicano Norteamericano, Cal. Centennial, 1974; exhibited in numerous one-woman shows throughout U.S., Europe, Mexico, Japan; represented in numerous pvt. and mus. collections throughout world. TV lectr. U.S., also Mexico. Recipient 1st prize in watercolor Fla. State Fair, 1950, named Outstanding Woman of Achievement U. Wash., 1950. Mem. Nat. Assn. Women Artists, N.W. Soc. Printmakers, N.W. Water Color Soc., Nat. League Am. Pen Women (Outstanding Achievement award 1966), Internat. Platform Soc., Am. Assn. U. Women, Chi Omega. Author, photographer, illustrator numerous travel articles; illustrator essays My Around the World Sketchbook, Oriental Sketchbook, Mexican Sketchbook. Contbr. articles Christian Sci. Monitor, European Publs. Home: Box 376 Pebble Beach CA 93953 Studio: Casa Alicia Piedra Barrenada Ajijic Jalisco Mexico

SMALL, ELISABETH CHAN (MRS. DONALD MACFARLAND SMALL), psychiatrist; b. Peking, China, July 11, 1934; d. Stanley Hong and Lily Luella (Lum) Chan; B.A., U. Cal. at Los Angeles, 1955, M.D., 1960; m. Donald MacFarland Small, July 8, 1957; children—Geoffrey Brooks, Philip Willard Stanley. Intern, Newton (Mass.) Wellesley Hosp., 1960-61; asst. dir. venereal diseases Mass. Dept. Pub. Health, Boston, 1961-63; jr. asst. physician dept. dermatology and syphilology Boston Dispensary and Boston City Hosp., 1961-63; fellow psychiatry Boston State Hosp., 1965-66; resident psychiatry Tufts New Eng. Center Hosp., Boston, 1966-69; teaching fellow psychiatry Tufts U. Sch. Medicine, 1969-70, instr. psychiatry, 1970-73, asst. clin. prof. psychiatry, 1973—; practice medicine specializing in psychiatry, Newton Highlands, Mass., 1968—. Joseiah Macy fellow Radcliffe Inst., 1967-70. Mem. Am. Psychiat. Assn., Mass. Med. Soc. Address: 17 Norman Rd Newton Highlands MA 02161

SMALL, JOYCE GRAHAM (MRS. IVER FRANCIS SMALL), physician, educator; b. Edmonton, Alta., Can.; d. John Earl and Rachel (Redmond) Graham; B.A. with very great distinction, U. Sask., 1951; M.D., U. Man., 1956; M.S., U. Mich., 1959; m. Iver Francis Small, May 26, 1954; children—Michael, Jeffrey, Douglas, Mona. Came to U.S., 1956, naturalized, 1962. Intern, Winnipeg (Man.) Gen. Hosp., 1955-56; resident psychiatry Ypsilanti (Mich.) State Hosp., 1956-59; instr. psychiatry Neuropsychiat. Inst., U. Mich., 1959-60; instr. psychiatry U. Ore. Med. Sch., 1960-61, asst. prof., 1961-62, research asso. dept. neurology, 1960-62; asst. prof. psychiatry Washington U. Sch. Medicine, St. Louis, 1962-65; clin. dir. Malcolm Bliss Mental Health Center, St. Louis, 1962-65; asso. prof. psychiatry Ind. U. Sch. Medicine, Indpls., 1965-69, prof. psychiatry, 1969—; clin. dir. research and labs. Larue D. Carter Meml. Hosp., Indpls., 1965—. Diplomate Am. Bd. Neurology and Psychiatry. Fellow Am. Psychiat. Assn.; mem. Am. EEG Soc. (bd. qualifications 1963), Soc. Biol. Psychiatry, Soc. Psychophysiol. Research, Ind. Neuropsychiat. Assn., Soc. for Neurosci., A.A.A.S., N.Y. Acad. Sci. Central, Eastern EEG assns. Home: 4300 Glencairn Lane Indianapolis IN 46226 Office: 1315 W 10th St Indianapolis IN 46202

SMALL, MARGARET LORING, sch. adminstr.; b. Pownal, Me., Oct. 27, 1914; d. Roy M. and Florence H. (Hodsdon) Loring; B.S., Gorham State Coll., 1957; postgrad. U. Me.; m. Harold P. Small, July 12, 1940. Rural sch. tchr., North Yarmouth, Me., 1935-40; spl. edn. tchr. Berman Sch. Pineland Center, Pownal, 1953-65; prin. Berman Sch. at Pineland Center, Pownal, 1965—. Mem. Am. Assn. Mental Deficiency, Council Exceptional Children, Me. Assn. Spl. Edn., Me. Tchrs. Assn., Me. State Employees Assn. Mem. Order Eastern Star. Home: 261 Main St Cumberland Center ME 04021 Office: Box C Pownal ME 04069

SMALL, SYLVIA SCHERTZER (MRS. ALBERT H. SMALL), economist; b. N.Y.C., June 13, 1921; d. Samuel S. and Mena (Coopersmith) Schertzer; B.A., Bklyn. Coll., 1942; postgrad. Am. U., 1943-45; m. Albert H. Small, Aug. 16, 1942; 1 son, Jeffrey Read. Economist, OPA, Washington, 1942-47, chief economist leather sect., 1945-47; free-lance economist R & S Research and Statistics Assos., Washington, 1954-59; editor, research White House Conf. on Children, 1959-60; researcher, writer weekly newsletter on nat. accounts Bur. Labor Statistics, 1961-66; sr. economist, 1966—; lectr. Asia and Africa. Co-founder Bannockburn Swimming Pool Assn., Bethesda, 1955. Bd. dirs. Clara Barton Sch. P.T.A., Montgomery County, Md., 1956-58. Recipient Presdl. letter of commendation. Mem. Am. Econ. Assn., Nat. Economists Club, Bannockburn Civic Assn., Montgomery County Community Arts Assn. Jewish religion. Club: Bannockburn Community (Bethesda). Author: Social and Economic Conditions of Negroes in the U.S., 1969, 70; Black Americans: A Decade of Occupational Change, 1972. Contbg. author: Changes in Urban America, 1968. Contbr. articles and bulls to profl. pubs. Home: 7119 Braeburn Pl Bethesda MD 20034 Office: Bureau Labor Statistics Washington DC 20212

SMALLENBURG, CAROL JANE THORNTON (MRS. HARRY WALTER SMALLENBURG), educator; b. Santa Barbara, Cal.; d. Virgil Orville and Margaret Ann (Thompson) Thornton; A.B., Stanford, 1935, Ed.D., 1948; postgrad. Mills Coll., U. Chgo., Columbia, U. Hawaii, U. Cal. at Los Angeles; m. Harry Walter Smallenburg, Aug. 23, 1940; children—Harry Russell, John Lynden, Carol Anne, Robert Thompson. Tchr. Portola Jr.-Sr. High Sch., 1938, Burbank (Cal.) High Sch., 1939; tchr., counselor Gompers Jr. High Sch. and Reed Jr. High Sch., Los Angeles, 1939-50; mem. faculty Cal. State U. at Los Angeles, 1950—, prof. edn., 1967—; now also tchr. European Grad. Program U. So. Cal. Bd. dirs. Mints Ednl. Assistance Fund, 1963—; mem. Burbank Human Relations Council, 1963-68; chmn. edn. com. Community Relations Conf. So. Cal., 1969-71. Named Woman of Year Assn. Women Students, Cal. State U. at Los Angeles, 1956. Mem. Am. Assn. U. Women (br. chmn. scholarship com. 1967-68), So. Cal. Social Sci. Assn. (pres. 1968—), Cal. Assn. Supervision Curriculum Devel. (sect. pres. 1962-63), Cal. Tchrs. Assn., Nat., Cal. (v.p. So. region 1969-71, citation 1972) councils social studies, Assn. Supervision Curriculum Devel. (mem. commn. evaluation 1960-62), Coll. U. Faculties Assn., Am. Assn. U. Profs., Pi Lambda Theta (chpt. sponsor, adviser 1956-72, citation 1972), Delta Kappa Gamma. Contbr. articles to mags. Home: 849 S Sunset Canyon Dr Burbank CA 91501 Office: 5151 State University Dr Cal State U Los Angeles CA 90032 also Edn Center FPO New York City NY 09540

SMALLEY, MARGUERITE VIOLA (MRS. JAMES A. SMALLEY), stock broker; b. New Market, Ohio, July 11, 1906; d. John Lynn and Bertha Olivia (Rexroth) Eyler; student Western Tchrs. Coll., 1925; m. James A. Smalley, Aug. 24, 1930. Sportswear buyer Fashion Shop, Ann Arbor, Mich., 1945-50; postmistress, Whitmore Lake, Mich., 1950-56; broker H. Cleon Johnson Co., securities firm, Galesburg, Ill., 1957—. Tchr. arts and crafts, 1940—; tchr. investment seminars, 1968—. Sec. exec. com. bd. dirs., coordinator blood bank A.R.C., 1940-50; sec. bd. dirs., Humane Soc., Washtenaw County, Mich., 1940-45. Mem. Bus. and Profl. Women's Clubs. Mem. Order Eastern Star, White Shrine. Club: Altrusa (pres. 1971-72) (Monmouth, Ill.). Home: 726 E Broadway Monmouth IL 61462 Office: 1346 N Prairie St Galesburg IL 61401

SMALTZ, CARROLL ANNE SPELKE (MRS. DONALD C. SMALTZ), pub. relations exec.; b. Stamford, Conn., Jan. 31, 1940; d. Harold Strauss and Constance Mary (Carroll) Spelke; Asso. Bus. Adminstrn., Lasell Jr. Coll., 1959; student Chatham Coll., 1959-60; B.A., Cal. State, 1971; m. Donald C. Smaltz, Sept. 14, 1959; children—Connie Carroll, Carrie Sue, Jennifer Delene. With Fran Hynds Pub. Relations, Los Angeles, 1972; pub. relations coordinator Huntington Library, Art Gallery and Bot. Gardens, San Marino, Cal., 1972-74; partner Barr/Smaltz Pub. Relations, South Pasadena, Cal., 1974—. Mem. Cal. Coalition for Equal Rights Amendment, Los Angeles, 1972—. Mem. Women in Communications, Pub. Interest Radio and TV Ednl. Soc. Club: Publicity (Los Angeles). Home: 1906 Alpha Av South Pasadena CA 91030 Office: 1906 Alpha Av South Pasadena CA 91030

SMART, DOROTHY CAROLINE, social worker; b. Osborn, Mo.; d. Allen A. and Caroline (Totzke) Smart; student U. Mo., 1929-30; A.B., U. Kan., 1937, M.S.W., 1950; postgrad. U. Chgo., 1963, 65. Advt. copy writer Emery Bird Thayer, Kansas City, Mo., 1937-38; case worker Dept. Pub. Welfare, Kansas City, 1938-44, Jackson County chpt. A.R.C., Kansas City, 1944-49; disaster rep. Am. Nat. Red Cross, St. Louis, 1950-59, home service rep. area office, 1959-65, regional dir. service mil. families, 1965-70, asst. area dir. service to mil. families, 1970—. Mem. Nat. Assn. Social Workers, Acad. Certified Social Workers, Nat. Conf. Social Welfare, Women in Communications. Club: Pilot (Internat.). Home: 4475 W Pine St St Louis MO 63108 Office: 10139 Corporate Sq St Louis MO 63132

SMART, IRENE BALOGH, lawyer, former state legislator; b. Cleve., Mar. 24, 1921; d. John and Elizabeth (Szaszak) Balogh; B.S., Wittenberg U., 1942; student Harvard Med. Sch., 1943; LL.B., William McKinley Sch., 1955; m. Charles Eugene Smart, May 17, 1945; children—Charles Eugene II, Mary Smart Radebaugh, Jennifer Lynn. Phys. therapist Cleve. Clinic, 1943-44; asst. supr. phys. therapy John Hopkins Hosp., Balt., 1944-45; phys. therapist Sunbeam Sch. for Crippled Children, Cleve., 1945-46; head phys. therapy Mercy Hosp., Canton, O., 1946-47; admitted to Ohio bar, 1956; mem. firm Smart & Smart, Canton, 1956—; mem. Ohio Ho. of Reps., 1973-75. Mem. urban devel. commn. City of Canton, O., 1957-58; council-at-large City of Canton, O., 1959-72. Mem. Stark County (O.) Central Com. Democratic party; mem. Federated Dem. Women of Ohio, Dem. Womens Club. Trustee United Cerebral Palsy Assn., 1966—, v.p., 1972—; trustee Ohio War Orphans Scholarship Bd., 1973—. Recipient Alumni award Wittenberg U., 1973; Mayors Citation for outstanding performance in urban renewal, 1972; Citations, Canton City Council, 1972; Conservation award Am. Sportsman Club, 1974. Mem. Ohio Bar Assn., Am. Univ. Womens Assn., C. of C., Delta Zeta. Presbyn. Mem. Order Eastern Star. Home: 3807 Third St NW Canton OH 44708 Office: 430 Citizens Bldg Canton OH 44702 also Ohio Ho Reps Columbus OH

SMART, MARGARET CATHERINE (MRS. HAMISH MATHESON SMART), physician, anesthesiologist; b. Invergordon, Scotland, Aug. 7, 1928; d. Vincent Lindsay and Christina (Boyd) Lee; L.R.C.P., Edinburgh U. Med. Sch., 1951, L.R.C.S., 1951; L.R.F.P. and S., Glasgow U., 1951, L.M.C.C., 1956; m. Hamish Matheson Smart, Aug. 20, 1952; children—Susan Irene, Mhairi, Norma, Joanne. Interne, Inverness, Scotland, 1951-52; pvt. practice medicine specializing in family practice, Scotland, 1952-53, Hotel Dieu Hosp., Sherbrooke, Que., Can., 1957-58; anesthestist and family practice, Sherbrooke, 1958—; mem. staff Sherbrooke Hosp., 1954—. Mem. Can. Med. Assn., Can. Coll. Family Practitioners. Presbyn. Home: 604 Quebec St Sherbrooke PQ J1H 3M2 Canada Office: 461 Argyle St Sherbrooke PQ Canada

SMART, MARY-LEIGH CALL (MRS. J. SCOTT SMART), farm operator; b. Springfield, Ill., Feb. 27, 1917; d. S(amuel) Leigh and Mary (Bradish) Call; jr. coll. diploma Monticello Coll., 1934; student Oxford U., 1935; B.A., Wellesley Coll., 1937; M.A., Columbia, 1939, postgrad., 1940-41; postgrad. N.Y. U., 1940-41; painting student with Bernard Karfiol, 1937-38; m. J. Scott Smart, Sept. 11, 1951 (dec. 1960). Dir. mgmt. Central Ill. Grain Farms, Logan County, Ill., 1939—; art collector, patron, publicist, 1954—; program dir. sec. bd. Barn Gallery Assos., Inc., Ogunquit, Me., 1958-69, pres., 1969-70, hon. dir., 1970—; owner Lowtrek Kennel, Ogunquit, 1957-73, Cove Studio Art Gallery, Ogunquit, 1961-68. Mem. acquisition com. DeCordova Mus., Lincoln, Mass., 1966—. Mem. chancellor's council U. Tex., 1972—. Chmn. Outdoor-Display Bd. Perkins Cove Assn., Ogunquit, 1972. Bd. dirs. Ogunquit C. of C., 1966, treas. 1966-67, hon. life mem., 1968—; bd. overseers Strawbery Banke, Inc., Portsmouth, N.H., 1971—, 3d vice-chmn., 1972-73, 2d vice-chmn., 1973-74; bd. advisers Paul Creative Arts Center U. N.H., 1973—. Served to lt. jg WAVES, 1942-45. Mem. Am. Fedn. Arts, Am. Assn. Museums, Friends of Rose Art Mus. Brandeis U., Mus. Modern Art, Springfield Art Assn., Solomon R. Guggenheim Mus., Whitney Mus. Am. Art, Portland Soc. Art, Fogg Art Mus., Jr. League of Springfield, Inst. Contemporary Art Boston (corporator). Republican. Episcopalian. Club: Western Maine Wellesley. Editor: Hamilton Easter Field Art Found. Collection Catalog, 1966; originator, dir. show, compiler of catalog Art: Ogunquit, 1967. Address: Surf Point York ME 03909

SMART, MOLLIE STEVENS (MRS. RUSSELL COOK SMART), educator; b. Chatham, Ont., Can., Apr. 11, 1916; d. Stanley Starr and Mildred (MacLean) Stevens; B.A., U. Toronto, 1936; M.A., U. Mich., 1942; Ph.D., U. Delhi (India), 1970; m. Russell Cook Smart, Aug. 9, 1939; children—Susan (Mrs. John Charles Smith), Ellen, Laura (Mrs. Craig M. Szwed). Came to U.S., 1936, naturalized, 1942. Mem. psychology dept. Merrill-Palmer Inst., Detroit, 1937-41; clin. psychologist Consultation Bur., Detroit, 1941-42; lectr. part-time, dept. child devel. and family relationships Cornell U., Ithaca, 1945-50; prof. child devel. and family relations U. R.I., Kingston, 1953-73, adj. prof., 1973—. Fullbright research prof. Child Guidance Clinic, Coll. Nursing, U. Delhi, India, 1966-67, Massey U., New Zealand, 1971-72; vis. prof. family studies U. Guelph (Ont., Can.), 1974-75; co-dir. Wis. U. Year-ins India program, India, 1967-68; cons. Office Econ. Opportunity. Fellow Soc. for Research in Child Devel.; mem. Am. Home Econs. Assn., Nat. Council on Family Relations, Nat. Assn. for Edn. Young Children, Am., New Eng., R.I. psychol. assns., Phi Kappa Phi. Author: (with L. Schulz) Understanding Your Baby, 1941; (with R. Smart) It's A Wise Parent, 1944, Babe In a House, 1950, Living in Families, Living and Learning With Children, 1966, Children: Development and Relationships, 2d edit., 1972, Readings in Child Development and Relationships, 1972, Infants: Development and Relationships, 1973, Preschool Children Development and Relationships, 1973, School-age Children: Development and Relationships, 1973, Adolescents: Development and Relationships, 1973. Co-editor: Ency. for Mothers (Parents' Inst.). Contbr. articles to profl. jours. Home: 10 Bayberry Rd Kingston RI 02881

SMART, SARA MCALPIN PYLE (MRS. PAUL H. SMART), educator; b. Morristown, N.J., July 27, 1891; d. James Tolman and Francis Adelaide (McAlpin) Pyle; student Child Edn. Found., N.Y.C., 1916-17; m. Paul Hurlburt Smart, May 10, 1917; children—Paul Gordon, Hilary Hurlburt. Founder, dir. The Children's Home Sch., N.Y.C., 1921; founder, dir. Daycroft Sch., Greenwich, Conn., 1928-42, pres. 1942-58, pres. emeritus 1958—, also mem. bd. trustees. Mem. Women's Nat. Republican Club. Christian Scientist. Home: 138 Goodwives River Rd Darien CT 06820

SMEAL, RUTH DUGAN, librarian; b. Milton, Pa., Aug. 16, 1917; d. Raymond Brady and Ellen Josephine (Young) Dugan; B.S. in Edn., Bloomsburg (Pa.) State Coll., 1939; M.S. in L.S., Marywood Coll., Scranton, Pa., 1960; m. Albert Wayne Smeal, June 17, 1944; children—Albert Wayne, Beryl (Mrs. Stephen J. Kubik, Jr.), Kay Anne (Mrs. D. Kerry Klinefelter), Joan (Mrs. Dale S. Patterson). Tchr., Shickshinny (Pa.) Sch. Dist., 1941-44; high sch. librarian Millville Area (Pa.) Joint Sch. Dist., 1955-64, circulation librarian, 1964-69; librarian juvenile collection Harvey A. Andruss Library, Bloomsburg State Coll., 1969—. Mem. Am., Pa. library assns., Assn. Pa. State Coll. and Univ. Faculties, Pa. Assn. Higher Edn., Kappa Delta Pi, Gamma Theta Upsilon. Republican. Presbyn. Mem. Order Eastern Star. Home: 740 Market St Bloomsburg PA 17815

SMEATON, JOY AUTHIER (MRS. ROBERT W. SMEATON), health service adminstr., occupational therapist; b. Washington, July 4, 1918; d. George Francis and Nancy Russell (Dunnigan) Authier; B.S. in Occupational Therapy, Milw. Downer Coll., 1940; m. Robert W. Smeaton, June 14, 1941; children—Robert, Amy (Mrs. David Hendrickson, Glenn, Carol (Mrs. Allen Hambrecht), Kathleen, George. Occupational therapist Milwaukee County, Wis., 1941-42, Shorehaven, Wis. Lutheran Homes, Inc., Oconomowoc, 1962-64; dir. occupational therapy Summit Hosp., Oconomowoc, 1965-73, Westmoreland Manor, Waukesha, Wis., 1973—. Cons. River Hills

West Nursing Home, Wis., 1970—. 4-H leader Oconomowoc, 1970. Mem. Am. Occupational Therapy Assn. Home: 3159 N Golden Rd Oconomowoc WI 53066 Office: 1810 Kensington Dr Waukesha WI 53186

SMELCER, ETHEL MITCHELL (MRS. FRED SMELCER), savs. and loan exec.; b. nr. Greeneville, Tenn., Sept. 15, 1931; d. Rome and Glenna (Prather) Mitchell; grad. Greeneville Bus. Coll., 1951; standard diploma Am. Savs. and Loan Inst., 1970; m. Fred Smelcer, June 28, 1958. Bookkeeper, Interstate Supply Co., Inc., Greeneville, Tenn., 1951-55, Interstate Vending Co., Inc., 1955-60; office mgr. Fed. Savs. and Loan Assn., Greeneville, 1960—. Mem. Am. Savs. and Loan Inst. (chpt. pres. 1969-70), Internat. Accountants Soc., Tenn. Savs. and Loan League (sec.-treas. staff leadership conf. 1969). Home: Route 1 Greeneville TN 37743 Office: Summer at Irish Sts Greeneville TN 37743

SMELKINSON, MARSHA ELLEN, pub. relations ofcl.; b. Balt., Dec. 29, 1948; d. Isidore I. and Florence Lynn (Ruben) Smelkinson; B.S. in journalism magna cum laude, Syracuse U., 1970. Advt. copywriter Rouse Co., Columbia, Md., 1970-71; free lance writer, 1971—; asso. publicist, editor AAU News, publs. coordinator Amateur Athletic Union U.S., Indpls., 1971-73, dir. pub. relations, 1973; dir. pub. relations and advt. Palmetto Dunes Resort, Inc., Hilton Head Island, S.C., 1973—. Mem. Women in Communications, Inc. Jewish religion. Author: Amateur Athlete 1971; Amateur Athlete 1972; Amateur Athlete 1973. Home: Palmetto Dunes 551 Hilton Head Island SC 29928 Office: PO Box 5628 Hilton Head Island SC 29928

SMELLEY, CAROL BARCLAY LINDSAY (MRS. FRANCIS AARON SMELLEY), govt. ofcl.; b. Atlanta, Oct. 17, 1922; d. John Samuel and Florence Gertrude (Hand) Lindsay; student U. Ala., 1952; m. Francis Aaron Smelley, June 30, 1948; children—Dorothy Ann Echols (Mrs. Richard Raymond), Susan Grace. With Dept. Health, Edn. and Welfare, Social Security Adminstrn., Tuscaloosa, Ala., 1946—, claims rep., 1947-55, field rep., 1955—. Neighborhood chmn. Tombigbee council Girl Scouts Am., 1959-62. Mem. Tuscaloosa County Preservation Soc. (trustee 1969—, rec. sec. 1970—), Birmingham Geneal. Soc. Methodist. Clubs: Altrusa (dir. 1968-73, 1st v.p. 1970-71, pres. 1971-72), Tuscaloosa Country, Woodland Hills Garden (pres. 1965-66) Woodland Hills Swim (Tuscaloosa). Home: 171 Woodland Hills Tuscaloosa AL 35409 Office: 1118 Greensboro Av Tuscaloosa AL 35401

SMELSER, RUTH EVLIN CUNNIFF, anthropologist, educator; b. Trinidad, Colo., Nov. 20, 1926; d. Luke Joseph and Laura Estelle (Reid) Cunniff; B.A. cum laude, U. Colo., 1966, M.A. in Anthropology, 1969, postgrad., 1969—; m. Peter Smelser, Aug. 26, 1948; children—Peggy Ann, Daniel Crispin. Tchr. anthropology U. Colo., 1968-70, research asst. Bella Bella prehistory project B.C., 1969-70; research asso. Inst. Behavioral Sci., Boulder, Colo., 1971-72; asst. prof. anthropology Evangel Coll., Springfield, Mo., 1973-74. Former treas. March. of Dimes; active Christmas and Easter seal drives. Former Bd. dirs. Boulder Art Assn., Vetsville Nursery, Boulder Standards Credit Union. Mem. Soc. Am. Archaeology, Am. Anthrop. Assn., A.A.A.S., Soc. Am. Ethnology, Colo., Mo. archaeol. socs. Home: Star Route Bruner MO 65620

SMELTZER, JUDY SIMPER SHEETS (MRS. GLENN KEITH SMELTZER), newspaper editor; b. Elkhart, Ind., Feb. 19, 1937; s. Lowell Lamar and Donna Belle (Simper) Sheets; grad. high sch.; m. Glenn Keith Smeltzer, Sept. 25, 1955; children—James Lamar, Jill Louise. Corr. Elkhart Truth, 1967-68; editor, photographer, writer Wakarusa (Ind.) Tribune, 1969—. Leader Girl Scouts, Wakarusa, 1958-69; pres. Parent Tchr. Orgn., Wakarusa, 1968-69; mem. Wakarusa Ambulance Service, 1973, Wa-Nee Drug Council, 1971-73, Northwood Home Econs. Adv. Commn., 1970-72. Mem. Ind. Dem. Editorial Assn., C. of C. (sec. 1969). Home: Route 1 Box 70 Wakarusa IN 46573 Office: Wakarusa Tribune Wakarusa IN 46573

SMILEY, VIRGINIA E(VELYN), librarian; b. nr. Union City, Ind., Nov. 11, 1924; d. Noah F. and Lucy L. (Cultice) Smiley; student Ind. U., 1942-47, George Peabody Coll., 1949; A.B., Ind. U., 1947, M.A., 1954. Librarian sch. library, Winchester, Ind., 1947-48, Valparaiso, Ind., 1948-50, San Diego, Cal., 1950-55; U.S. Army spl. services librarian, Germany, 1955-57, 59-61; librarian Gen. Motors Inst., Flint, Mich., 1958, Cin. Pub. Library, 1962-65; librarian Ohio State U., Columbus, 1965—. Mem. Am., Ohio library assns. Home: 2611 Charing Rd Columbus OH 43221 Office: 65 S Oval St Columbus OH 43210

SMIRL, JODY GUTHRIE (MRS. DAN W. SMIRL), legislator; b. Mobile, Ala., Aug. 30, 1935; d. Raymond Booth and Emmajeanne (Cole) Guthrie; secretarial sci. certificate Auburn U., 1957; m. Dan W. Smirl, Dec. 17, 1955; children—Thomas Booth, Daniel Marvin. Legal sec. McCorvey, Turner, Rogers, Mobile, 1953-54; mem. Ho. of Dels., W.Va. Legislature, 1966—. Active YWCA, P.T.A. Vice pres. Republican Women Huntington, 1965-66, pres., 1972-73. Bd. dirs. GOP Youth Tng. Camp; adv. bd. Green Acres Center for Retarded Children; youth mgmt. bd. YMCA. Recipient award for outstanding service to youth Bd. Dirs. GOP Youth Tng. Camp, 1970; awards for distinguished community service Huntington Jaycee's, 1966, 67; outstanding service award W. Va. Fedn. Blind, 1973; named Most Outstanding Jr., Jr. Dept. Woman's Club Huntington, 1969. Mem. Am. Assn. Comprehensive Health Planning, Region II Health Planning Assn., League Women Voters, Isaac Walton League, W.Va. Consumers Assn., Nat. Order Women Legislators, Alpha Gamma Delta Alumnae, Beta Sigma Phi (council sponsor 1971—). Home: 507 Forest Rd Huntington WV 25705 Office: State Capitol Charleston WV 25305

SMITH, ADELINE MERCER, librarian; b. Saratoga Springs, N.Y., May 28, 1915; d. Thomas Elwood and Hazel Belle (Farrington) Mercer; B.S. in L.S., N.Y. State Coll. Tchrs., Albany, 1937; M.S. in L.S., State U. N.Y. at Albany, 1968; m. Jack Monroe Smith, Mar. 3, 1946; 1 son, Jeffrey Monroe. Designer, sampling supr. Van Raalte Co., Saratoga Springs, 1939-63; jr.-sr. high sch. librarian Hoosic Valley Central Sch., Schaghticoke, N.Y., 1964—; guest lectr. Sch. Library and Information Sci., State U. N.Y. at Albany, 1972—. Mem. A.L.A., Am. Assn. Sch. Librarians, N.Y. State United Tchrs., Eastern N.Y. Sch. Library Media Assn., Am. Assn. U. Women, N.E.A., Beta Phi Mu. Baptist. Contbr. articles to profl. jours. Home: RD 1 Lake Lonely Rd Saratoga Springs NY 12866 Office: Hoosic Valley Central High Sch Schaghticoke NY 12154

SMITH, AGNES LORRAINE, health and beauty aids co. exec.; b. Brookhaven, Pa., July 21, 1927; d. George John and Agnes Blossom (Rennie) Keil; grad. high sch.; m. Marvin Lester Smith, Mar. 27, 1946; children—Doris (Mrs. Wiley Marshall Woolard), Marvin Lester. With Smith Bros. Grocery, Washington, N.C., 1951—, sec.-treas., 1971—; with Giant Discount, Inc., Washington, 1964—, sec.-treas., 1971—. Sec.-treas. vols. Beaufort County Hosp., Washington, 1970-71; sec.-treas. Washington Band Parents, 1964-66. Mem. Washington Women's Club. Methodist. Home: 342 E 15th St Washington NC 27889 Office: PO Box 1236 Washington NC 27889

SMITH, AGNES O'BRIEN (MRS. CLIFFORD L. SMITH), judge; b. San Francisco; d. Matthew S. and Agnes M. (Griffen) O'Brien; A.B., San Francisco State Coll., 1934; LL.B., U. San Francisco, 1941; m. Clifford L. Smith, May 25, 1946; 1 son, J. Philip. Admitted to Cal. bar, 1941; practiced in San Francisco, 1942-52; dep. city atty., 1952-70; judge Municipal Ct., San Francisco, 1971—. Tchr. pub. schs., San Francisco. Mem. Status of Womens Com., San Francisco, Def. Adv. Com. Women in Service. Bd. dirs. Easter Seal Campaign, Muscular Dystrophy, Nat. Council Christians and Jews; bd. govs. U. San Francisco. Mem. San Francisco Bar Assn. (dir.), Native Daus. of Golden West, Navy League (dir.), Queen's Bench, Nat. Assn. Women Lawyers. Home: 2088 15th Av San Francisco CA 94114 Office: 850 Bryant St San Francisco CA 94103

SMITH, AGNES RUST (MRS. PAUL JAMES SMITH), rancher; b. San Angelo, Tex., Nov. 12, 1905; d. John Yellott and Agnes (Bustin) Rust; student St. Mary's Coll., Dallas, 1923-24, U. Tex.-Austin, 1924; m. Robert Easley Gordon, Mar. 13, 1925 (dec.); 1 dau., Jean (Mrs. Charles D. Rainey); m. 2d, Paul James Smith, Dec. 10, 1969. Owner-operator 3R Ranch, raisers Angus cattle, Rambouillet and Columbia sheep and Angora goats, San Angelo, 1933—. Organizer indigent med. care, 1941; mem. Ft. Concho Restoration Found. Mem. Nat. Wool Growers Assn., Am. Cattlemen's Assn., Am. Soc. Range Mgmt., Tex. Sheep and Goat Raisers Assn., Tex. Angus Assn., Colonial Dames Am., Ams. Royal Descent, Descs. King William I, Colonial Order Crown, Order Washington, Am. Heritage Soc., Dames Ct. Honor, Mil. and Hospitaller Order St. Lazarus Jerusalem, numerous other geneal. socs., Nat. Travel Club, San Angelo Cotillion (charter), Pi Beta Phi. Episcopalian. Clubs: San Angelo Country, Garden (pres. 1940), 20th Century, River, Executive (San Angelo). Address: 1102 Algerita Dr San Angelo TX 76901

SMITH, ALICE LORRAINE, physician; b. Trinity, Tex.; d. Frederick Adair and Alice (Mansell) Smith; B.A. summa cum laude, U. Tex., 1940; M.D., Southwestern Med. Sch., 1946. Teaching fellow U. Tex. Southwestern Med. Sch., Dallas, 1947-50, asst. prof., 1950-54, asso. prof. pathology, 1962—; resident pathology Parkland Hosp., 1948-50; asst. pathologist Baylor U. Hosp., Dallas, 1954-55, asst. prof. pathology, Houston, 1955-56, asso. prof., 1956-57; pathologist, chief dept. cytology and electron microscopy Wadley Research Inst. and Blood Bank, Dallas, 1957-61; dir. div. diagnostic cytology and Sch. Cytotech. of Dallas County Hosp. dist., 1962—. Project dir. USPHS Cervical Cancer Screening Project, 1962-71. Bd. dirs. Am. Cancer Soc. Fellow A.C.P., Am. Soc. Clin. Pathologists, Coll. Am. Pathologists; mem. Tex., North Tex. socs. pathologists, A.M.A., Dallas County Med. Soc., Dallas So. Clin. Soc., Internat. Acad. Pathology, Am. Assn. Blood Banks, Mortar Bd., Phi Beta Kappa. Author: Microbiology and Pathology, 10th edit.; Principles of Microbiology, 7th edit.; Microbiology Laboratory Manual and Workbook, 3d edit. Home: 3326 Blackburn St Dallas TX 75204 Office: 5323 Harry Hines Blvd Dallas TX 75235

SMITH, ALLENA COLLINS (MRS. M.A. SMITH, JR.), bank exec.; b. Montgomery, O., Oct. 7, 1909; d. Henry T. and Susan M. (Allen) Collins; B.B.A. magna cum laude, Tex. A. and I. U., 1931, M.S., 1951; m. M.A. Smith, Jr., Dec. 23, 1933 (dec. Apr. 1967); 1 dau., Susan (Mrs. Milton Solon Kimball). With State Bank of Kingsville (Tex.), 1931—, cashier, 1955-68, v.p., 1963-74, exec. v.p., 1974—, also dir. Mem. Tex. Assn. Ins. Agts., Assn. Pub. Accountants, Colonial Dames XVII Century (pres. 1970-72), D.A.R. (state auditor 1963-64), Am. Assn. U. Women, Alpha Chi, Zeta Tau Alpha. Presbyn. Club: Kingsville Womans, Zonta. Home: 407 University Blvd Kingsville TX 78363 Office: 300 E King St Kingsville TX 78363

SMITH, AMELIA HALL, musician, opera dir.; b. Oklahoma City; d. Charles Jordan and Marie Helen (Ferris) Hall; grad. Drew Sem. for Young Women, Carmel, N.Y., 1930; summer student Woman's Coll., Greensboro, N.C., Juilliard Sch. Music, N.Y.C.; certificate Am. Guild of Organists, 1954; postgrad. seminar (scholar) Manhattan Sch. Music, 1970; m. Willard Cardwell, Nov. 18, 1936, (div. Nov. 1954); children—Marie Lorraine (Mrs. James Albert Harrill, Jr.), Christine Amelia (Mrs. Ray D. Dodge); m. 2d, Harry Logan Smith, Jr., Aug. 19, 1956. Profl. accompanist, 1925—; soprano soloist, 1934—, appeared with Piedmont Festival Orch., 1943-49; Jacksonville (Fla.) Symphony Orch., 1957, others, appeared as Marie Bartered Bride, 1941; founder, leading soprano Music Theatre Repertory Group, 1947-52; founder, dir. Opera Workshop, Jacksonville U. Coll. Music, 1956-61, Jacksonville Opera Guild, Inc., 1967; founder mng. dir. Opera Repertory Group (TV and touring opera co.), 1961, also pres.; music columnist N.C. and Fla. newspapers; pianist Jacksonville Symphony Orch., 1963-67. Tchr., Greensboro Coll., Bennett Coll., Greensboro, N.C., U. N.C., Opera Inst., Jacksonville U., Edward Waters Coll., Jacksonville; organist, choirmaster San Jose Episcopal Ch., Jacksonville. Active Arts Festival Jacksonville Council of Arts, 1958—, music chmn., 1958-59; dean Am. Guild Organists, Jacksonville, 1958-61, chmn. Southeastern regional conv., 1963; mem. Jacksonville Bicentennial Commn., 1973—. Mem. Jacksonville Friday Musicale (life), Music Tchrs. Assn. Jacksonville, Am. Guild of Organists, Jacksonville Council of the Arts, Nat. Assn. Tchrs. Singing, Nat. Assn. Am. Composers and Condrs., Central Opera Service, Am. Guild Mus. Artists, Musicians Assn. Jacksonville. Episcopalian (mem. music commn. Diocese of Fla. 1966-67). Club: Altrusa (pres. 1967-68) (Jacksonville, Fla.). Home and studio: 4227 Peachtree Circle E Jacksonville FL 32207 Office: San Jose Episcopal Church 7423 San Jose Blvd Jacksonville FL 32217

SMITH, ANGELA PENNA, univ. adminstr.; b. Beaumont, Tex., Feb. 17, 1945; d. Joseph Anthony and Anita Marie (Messina) Penna; B.A. in Journalism, N. Tex. State U., 1967; m. Charles L. Smith, Jr., June 12, 1971. Teaching asst. in journalism N. Tex. State U., 1965-67; reporter Daily Oklahoman, Oklahoma City, 1966; writer Dallas and Capitol bur. A.P., Austin, 1967-69; information officer S.W. Ednl. Devel. Lab., Austin, 1969-74; dir. information services and publications St. Edwards U., Austin, 1974—. Corr. sec. Young Democrats Club, 1967; vol. worker Dem. Party. Recipient scholarships Dallas and Oklahoma City press clubs. Mem. Women in Communications (pres. 1966-67), Council for Edn. Devel. and Research (contbg. editor 1972—), Soc. for Tech. Communicators, Tex. Tchrs. Assn., Alpha Lambda Delta. Episcopalian. Author: (with others) Handbook for Parent-School-Community Involvement, 1971, Instructor's Manual for New Careers Program, 1972; also articles. Editor: Promising School Practices for Mexican American Children, 1971; Keys to the Elementary School Environment, 1971. Office: 3001 S Congress Austin TX 78704

SMITH, ANNA BEATRICE PICKETTE (MRS. AARON ANTHONY SMITH), social worker; b. Meadville, Miss., Feb. 14, 1937; d. Monroe and Rosie (Bishop) Pickett; B.A., San Jose State Coll., 1959; M.S.W., Howard U., 1964; m. Aaron Anthony Smith, June 17, 1964; children—Angela Kathryn, Amy Khristen. Caseworker family and children's div. Santa Clara County Welfare Dept., San Jose, Cal., 1960-62, home study social worker bur. adoptions, 1964-69; homemaker supr. Homemaker Service Santa Clara County, Inc., 1969-70, homemaker supr., 1969-70; social worker Santa Clara Unified Sch. Dist. Children's Centers, 1972-73; social worker Bur. Children's Services, Santa Clara County Dept. Social Services, 1973—. Vol., Children's Home Soc. Cal., 1970-72; mem. adv. com. Creative Learner Inc. Presch., San Jose, 1972; mem. Community Coordinated Child Devel. Council Santa Clara County, 1972, Black Caucus Santa Clara Valley; mem. parent adv. com. Laurelwood Elementary Sch., 1972-74, pres. Laurelwood Home and Sch. Club, 1974—. Recipient Am. Legion Sch. award, 1951. Mem. Am. Assn. U. Women, Acad. Certified Social Workers, Nat. Council Negro Women, Torch and Laurel Girls Honor Soc., Methodist. Home: 2854 Pinecrest Ct San Jose CA 95121

SMITH, ANNA GREENE, educator; b. Lebanon, Tenn., Oct. 19, 1912; d. Denis Burton and Annie Mae (Smith) Smith; B.A., Cumberland U., 1934; M.A., George Peabody Coll. for Tchrs., 1936; Ph.D., U. N.C., 1949; postgrad. Columbia, 1942, 44, U. Cal. at Berkeley, 1949. Tchr. history, Trousdale County, Tenn., 1934-36; instr. econs., sociology La. Tech. U., 1936-42; teaching fellow, asst. research inst. U. N.C., 1943-46; asst. prof. econs., sociology Meredith Coll., 1946-48; asso. prof. econs., sociology Agnes Scott Coll., Decatur, Ga., 1948—; vis. prof. sociology U. N.C., summers 1947-49, Emory U., summers 1954, 61, Oglethorpe U., summer 1960, Chapman Coll. World Campus Afloat, 1971, Emory U., 1971-72. Atlanta ednl. dir. Am. Assn. U. Women Scholarship Program, 1962-64. Active A.R.C., Family Service. Recipient Carnegie award for research, 1949. Danforth Found. grantee, 1959, Gen. Ednl. Bd. grantee, 1950, Am. Assn. U. Women nat. fellow, 1970-71. Mem. Am., So. sociol. socs., So. Econ. Soc., Am. Assn. U. Women, Am. Assn. U. Profs., Alpha Kappa Delta, Pi Gamma Mu. Home: 600 Webster Dr Decatur GA 30033

SMITH, ANNA HESTER, librarian, museum dir.; b. London, Eng., Apr. 30, 1912; d. Johannes Jacobus and Mabel Florence (Hardy) Smith; M.A., U. Stellenbosch, 1933. Mem. staff Stellenbosch U. Library, 1934-38; mem. staff Johannesburg (South Africa) Pub. Library, 1938—, city librarian, 1960—; dir. Africana Mus., Johannesburg, 1960—; part-time lectr. librarianship U. Witwatersand, 1958—. Fellow S. African Library Assn.; mem. S. African Museums Assn., S. African Acad., Transvaal Automobile Club. Author: Pictorial Atlas of the History of South Africa, 1949; Pictorial History of Johannesburg, 1956; Claudius Water-Colours in the Africana Museum, 1952; The Spread of South African printing, 1971; Johannesburg Street Names, 1971. Home: 103 Montevideo 9th St Killarney Johannesburg South Africa Office: Pub Library Market Sq Johannesburg South Africa

SMITH, ANNABEL CLIFT (MRS. ARDELL M. SMITH), hosp. adminstr.; b. nr. Sioux City, Ia., Oct. 11, 1920; d. Charles O. and Emily (Lockwood) Clift; student U. Minn., 1972-73; m. Ardell M. Smith, Oct. 25, 1939; children—Nancy (Mrs. Marvin Steffes), William C., Bonnie (Mrs. Vernon Ames), Barbara E., Judith. Med. asst. J.L. Garred, M.D., Whiting, Ia., 1962-63, W.C. Meredith, M.D., Drayton, N.D., 1964-69; med. records clk. United Hosp., Grad Forks, N.D., 1969; adminstr. Drayton Community Hosp., 1970-74; resident adminstr. Mpls. Med. Center, Inc., at Dawson (Minn.) Hosp. and Johnson Meml. Hosp., Dawson, 1974—. Bd. dirs. Drayton Vol. Ambulance Assn. Mem. Order Eastern Star. Home: 1057 Pine St Dawson MN 56232 Office: Mpls Med Center Inc 2545 Chicago Av Minneapolis MN 55404

SMITH, ANNE PEARSE, clergywoman; b. Grand Rapids, Mich., Sept. 16, 1908; d. Edward and Bessie (Hogadone) Pearse; B.D., Hartford Sem. Found., 1936; m. Alvin L. Smith, Jan. 27, 1946. Mem. profl. staff Muskegon YWCA, 1927-30; dir. Christian edn., Muskegon, Mich., 1930-32; ordained to ministry Congl. Ch. (now United Ch. Christ), 1937; recreational tng. technician, Mich., 1938-42; minister in Tacoma, 1953-56, Cheboygan, Mich., 1936-38, Seattle, 1956-62, Milw., 1962-65, Portland, Ore., 1965—; vice moderator Ore. conf. 1973-74; mem. nat. Bd. Homeland Ministries. Served as lt. USNR, 1942-46. Mem. Nat. Assn. Women Ministers, Nat. Grange, Zonta (dir. chpt.). Home: 1645 SW Filmont Av Portland OR 97225 Office: 1126 SW Park Av Portland OR 97205

SMITH, ANNIS PEARL BLUM (MRS. JESSE D. SMITH), city ofcl.; b. Basco, Wis., May 12, 1925; d. Edward and Anna (Blumer) Blum; grad. Madison Bus. Coll., 1944; m. Jesse D. Smith, Dec. 18, 1944; children—Gregory D., Gayle Diane. Sec. to gen. agt. N.Y. Life Ins. Co., Madison, Wis., 1944-46; sec., bookkeeper State Mut. Assurance Co., Kansas City, Mo., 1946-48; sec., bookkeeper, City of Colby (Kan.), 1961-66, city clk., 1966—. Mem. adv. com. Colby Community Jr. Coll., 1970—. Recipient City service award League Kan. Municipalities, 1971. Mem. Am. Legion Aux., Epsilon Sigma Alpha. Presbyn. Club: Music (sec. 1963-66) (Colby). Home: 875 S Lincoln St Colby KS 67701 Office: 585 N Franklin St Colby KS 67701

SMITH, ARMIDA BEDOYA (MRS. JOSEPH SMITH), realtor; b. Caborca, Mexico, Dec. 10, 1900; d. Filiberto and Juana (Rivera) Bedoya; tchr.'s degree, Normal Tchrs. Coll., Hermosilla, Mexico, 1932; m. Joseph Smith, Aug. 20, 1933; children—Joan (Mrs. Harold Spector), Clara (Mrs. Louis Maltone). Came to U.S., 1930, naturalized, 1936. Prin. high schs., Pitiquito, Mexico, 1928-29, Nogales (Mexico) High Sch., 1930-31, Hermosilla, 1931-32; owner, operator Armida B. Smith Realty Co., Waikiki, Honolulu, 1958—. Mem. Honolulu Symphony Soc., 1971—. Mem. Honolulu Realty Bd. (gov. 1958—), Nat. Assn. Real Estate Bds. (state pres. women's council 1962-63, recipient medal Omega Tua Rho 1962), Bus. and Profl. Women Honolulu (pres. 1967-68). Democrat. Roman Catholic. Home: 141 Poloke Pl Honolulu HI 96822 Office: 190 S King St Honolulu HI 96813

SMITH, BARBARA JEAN, librarian; b. Windsor, Ont., Can., Apr. 23, 1929; d. Frank Alfred Richard and Helen Victoria (Suddaby) Smith; B.A. with honors, U. Toronto, 1952, B.L.S., 1953, M.Ed., 1969. Children's librarian Brantford (Ont.) Pub. Library, 1954-55, Oshawa (Ont.) Pub. Library, 1956; chief librarian Port Credit (Ont.) Pub. Library, 1957-58; supr. children's services Provincial Library Service, Ont. Govt., Toronto, 1959-63; dir. elementary sch. libraries Ont. Dept. Edn., 1964-67; prof. sch. library and information sci. U. Western Ont., 1968-69; coordinator learning resources Peel County Bd. Edn., Mississauga, Ont., 1969—. Bd. dirs. Canadian Edn. Showplace, chmn. resource centre com. 1971—. Mem. Canadian, Ont., Am. library assns., Children's Recreational Reading Council, Ont. Ednl. Assn. (co-chmn. budget com., Canadian Sch. Media Standards). Home: 10 Lamport Av Toronto ON M4W 1S6 Canada Office: 90 Dundas St W Mississauga ON Canada

SMITH, BARBARA JEAN NICHOLS (MRS. JAMES M. SMITH), coll. adminstr.; b. Mobile, Ala., May 3, 1946; d. Clauzell and Margaret (Miller) Nichols; B.A., Mobile Coll., 1968; m. James M. Smith, June 1, 1968. Records officer Mobile (Ala.) Coll., 1968-72, registrar, 1972—. Mem. Am. Assn. U. Women (dir. 1972—, community chmn. 1973, 2d v.p. 1974—), Ala. Assn. Collegiate Registrars and Admissions Officers. Baptist. Home: 4254 Halls Mill Rd Mobile AL 36609

SMITH, BERT(HA)(MAE) KRUGER (MRS. SIDNEY S. SMITH), found. exec.; b. Wichita Falls, Tex., Nov. 18, 1915; d. Sam and Fania (Feldman) Kruger; B.J., U. Mo., 1936; M.A., U. Tex., 1949; m. Sidney S. Smith, Jan. 19, 1936; children—Sheldon Stuart, Jared

Burt (dec.), Sarann (Mrs. Jon Campbell Huke). Asso. pub. Coleman (Tex.) Democrat-Voice, 1950-51; asso. editor Jr. Coll. Jour., 1952-55; exec. asso. Hogg Found. for Mental Health, Austin, 1952—. Mem. citizens adv. com. Travis County Juvenile Ct., 1963-66; mem. research utilization com. Gov.'s Com. on Aging, 1973—; mem. spl. edn. adv. com. Austin Ind. Sch. Dist., 1969—; mem. Tex. Edn. Agy. Continuing Adv. Com. for Spl. Edn., 1973—; chmn. profl. information com. Tex. Assn. Children with Learning Disabilities; mem. Tex. Commn. Orgns. for Handicapped; mem. vol. council Austin State Sch., 1962—; mem. med. profl. adv. and evaluation bd. United Cerebral Palsy of Tex., 1962. Bd. dirs. Austin Council on Alcoholism, 1962-69, pres., 1965; bd. dirs. Human Opportunities Corp., 1967-70, chmn. community involvement project, 1968-70. Recipient Outstanding Career Woman award Austin-Am.-Statesman, 1966, Nat. Headliner award Theta Sigma Phi, 1966, Golden Key award Tex. Assn. for Children with Learning Disabilities State Conv., 1970, certificate of merit Assn. for Children with Learning Disabilities, San Antonio, 1973. Mem. Author's Guild, Women in Communications, Nat. Assn. for Sci. Writers, Delta Kappa Gamma (hon.). Jewish religion. Mem. Hadassah, B'nai B'rith Women. Author: No Language But A Cry, 1964; Your Non-Learning Child: His World of Upside Down, 1968; A Teaspoon of Honey, 1970; Insights for Uptights, 1973; Aging in America, 1973. Contbr. articles to profl. jours. Home: PO Box 9116 Northwest Station Austin TX 78766 Office: Hogg Found for Mental Health PO Box 7998 U T Station Austin TX 78712

SMITH, BETTE COLLEEN WHITTAKER, librarian; b. Columbia, Mo., Mar. 24, 1928; d. William Harold and Emma Matilda (Faulkner) Whittaker; student Utica (N.Y.) Coll., 1963-64, Mohawk Valley Community Coll., 1969-70, 72-73; m. James Abbuhl Smith, Aug. 3, 1946; children—Karen Lynne (Mrs. Jonathan Mix), Linda Kay (Mrs. Peter Opromolla). Library asst. Rome Air Devel. Center, Griffiss AFB, N.Y., 1956-62, librarian phys. scis. and engring., 1962—, chief documents library, 1975—. Sec.-treas. aux. Rome Murphy and Meml. Hosp., 1972. Recipient Incentive award Rome Air Devel. Center, 1958. Mem. Rome Home Demonstration Club (pres. 1967). Home: RD 4 Pennystreet Rd Rome NY 13440 Office: Documents Library TILD RADC Griffiss AFB NY 13441

SMITH, BETTIE MAE, educator; b. Knoxville, Tenn., Apr. 26, 1914; d. William Henry and Mattie (Bailey) Snow; B.S., Tenn. A. and I. U., Nashville, 1949; M.A. in Health and Phys. Edn., N.Y.C., 1951, Ed.D. in Adminstrn. and Health, 1962; m. David L. Smith, Mar. 5, 1933. Tchr., coach schs. in Ga., 1931-50; instr. tng. in dept. sch. food service program Ga. Dept. Edn., 1950-58; prin., girls varsity coach Stephens Sch., Calhoun, Ga., 1951; prin. Harrison High Sch., West Point, Ga., 1969; instr. religious edn. Twin Cities extension Am. Theol. Sem., Nashville, 1967; prof. phys. edn., health and recreation Stillman Coll., Tuscaloosa, Ala., 1971—; instr. health edn. N.Y. U., summers 1958-62; asso. prof. Fla. A. and M. U., summers 1970, 71. Mem. Ga. com. White House Conf. Youth, 1955. Named Woman of Year, Women New Hope, Dalton, Ga., 1963. Mem. Nat., Ga. edn. assns., Nat. Assn. Secondary Sch. Prins., Ga. Council Secondary Sch. Prins., Am., Ala. assns. health, phys. edn. and recreation, Am. Sch. Food Assn., Am. Sch. Health Assn., Schoolmasters Club Ga., Alpha Kappa Mu, Alpha Kappa Alpha. Baptist (minister music). Mem. Order Eastern Star. Co-author nutrition guide. Office: Phys Edn Dept Stillman Coll Tuscaloosa AL 35401

SMITH, BETTY DENNY, civic worker, fashion showroom dir.; b. Centralia, Ill., Nov. 12, 1932; d. Otto and Ferne Elizabeth (Beier) Hasenfuss; student U. Ill., 1950-52, Los Angeles City Coll., 1953-57, U. Cal. at Los Angeles, 1965; m. Peter S. Smith, Dec. 5, 1964; children—Carla Kip, Bruce Kimball. Free-lance fashion coordinator, Los Angeles and N.Y.C., 1953-58; instr. fashion Rita LeRoy Internat. Studios, 1959-60; mgr. Mo Nadler Fashions, Los Angeles, 1961-64; showroom dir. Jean of Cal. Fashions, Los Angeles, 1966—; staff writer Valley Citizen News, 1963; free-lance polit. book reviewer community newspapers, 1961-62. Dir. Pet Assistance Found., 1969—; founder, pres., dir. Vol. Services to Animals of Los Angeles, 1972—; mem. County Com. to Discuss Animals in Research, 1973-74; mem. blue ribbon com. on animal control Los Angeles County, 1973-74; ind. legislative advocate for humane causes, 1969—. Mem. exec. com. Republican State Central Com., 1971-72; mem. Cal. Rep. Central Com., 1964-72; mem. Rep. Los Angeles County Central Com., 1964-70, mem. exec. com., 1966-70; chmn. 29th Congl. Central Com., 1969-70; sec. 28th Senatorial Central Com., 1967-68, 45th Assembly Dist. Central Com., 1965-66; mem. speakers bur. George Murphy for U.S. Senate, 1970; campaign mgr. Los Angeles County for Spencer Williams for Atty. Gen., 1966. Mem. Lawyers Wives San Gabriel Valley (dir. 1971-74, pres. 1972-73), Mannequins Assn. (dir. 1967-68), Internat. Platform Assn., Delta Gamma, Pi Phi Theta. Club: San Gabriel Valley Country (San Gabriel). Home: 1766 Bluffhill Dr Monterey Park CA 91754

SMITH, BETTYE L. SEBREE, bus. coll. exec.; b. Owensmouth, Cal., Feb. 25, 1926; d. Roy Albert and Thelma Hattie (Alexander) Sebree; student Brigham Young U., 1944-45, Links Sch. of Bus., Boise, Ida., 1946, Nampa (Ida.) Bus. Coll. 1956; B.A., Alaska Meth. U., 1972; m. George R. Motschman, Feb. 26, 1948 (div. June 1959); children—Jerye Lou, Marie Louise; m. 2d, Leroy I. Smith, Mar. 13, 1961 (div. 1968). Office mgr. Intermountain Surg. Supply Co., Boise, 1945-48; sec., payroll, cost accountant Morrison-Knudsen Co., Fairbanks, Alaska, Boise, 1948-52; payroll, cost accountant Lytle, Green, Birch Contractors, Fairbanks, 1952-54; owner Fairbanks Secretarial Sch., 1957-58, Anchorage Secretarial Sch., 1958-59; pres. Alaska Bus. Coll., Inc., Anchorage, 1959—; owner City Employment Center, Anchorage, 1962-68; pres. Arctic Tech. Industries, 1972—; partner B.E.E. Enterprises; asso. Manpower, Inc., 1969-72, Anchorage. Franchise holder Western Girl, Inc., 1962-68, Speedwriting Shorthand, 1957—, Nancy Taylor Finishing Sch., 1960—, Weaver Sch. of Real Estate 1959-72, I.T.T.-National Data Processing, 1968—, Taylor Airline Careers; 1968—, Taylor Hotel-Motel Tng., 1971— (all Anchorage). Bd. dirs. Community YMCA. Mem. Anchorage C. of C., Anchorage Businessmens Assn., Nat. Secs. Assn. (chpt. v.p. 1962, seminar chmn. 1961, 67, 73), Credit Women Internat., Internat. Platform Assn., U.S. Ski Assn. Methodist. Clubs: Zonta; Captain Cook Health. Office: 328 E 4th Av Anchorage AK 99501

SMITH, BEVERLY BUSH (MRS. ROBERT PAUL SMITH, JR.), writer; b. Omaha, Oct. 16, 1927; d. Martin William and Zoe Marguerite (Fries) Bush; student Knox Coll., 1945-47; B.A. magna cum laude, U. Omaha, 1949; m. Robert Paul Smith, Jr., Dec. 29, 1956; children—David Bush, Bryan Gedge. Advt. copywriter Radio Sta. KBON, Omaha, 1949-52, Radio Sta. KOIL, Omaha, 1952-53, Bozell & Jacobs, Chgo., 1953-55, R. Jack Scott, Chgo., 1955-56, Malcolm Howard, Chgo., 1957-58; free-lance writer articles for various mags., including House Beautiful, Redbook, Better Homes & Gardens, Today's Health, Parents', Woman's Day, also Chgo. Tribune, Los Angeles Times. Mem. exec. bd. La Leche League Internat., Franklin Park, Ill., 1960-63; preview chmn. women's bd. Orange County Philharmonic Soc., Newport Beach, Cal., 1973-74. Home: 1949 Port Trinity Pl Newport Beach CA 92660

SMITH, BEVERLY JEAN BISHOP (MRS. JACK A. SMITH), home economist; b. Wichita, Kan., Apr. 18, 1937; d. Adelbert E. and Anna (Winter) Bishop; B.A., Friends U., 1959; M.S., Kan. State U., 1971; m. Jack A. Smith, July 17, 1965. Tchr. home econs. and speech Rozel (Kan.) High Sch., 1959-61; extension home economist Kan. Coop. Extension, Jewell County, Mankato, Kan., 1961-64, Saline County, Salina, Kan., 1964—. Bd. dirs. Community Action Program Saline County. Mem. Nat., Kan. (dir.) home econs. assns., Nat., Kan. (pres. 1968, coordinating com. 1967-70) assns. extension home economists, Bus. and Profl. Womens Assn. (sec. 1967, 2d v.p. 1969-71), Kan. Council Women, Omicron Nu. Home: 502 Aullwood Rd Salina KS 67401 Office: 300 W Ash Salina KS 67401

SMITH, BEVERLY JEAN TANEY, occupational therapist; b. Snyder, Neb., July 6, 1934; d. Willis Calvin and Ella Marie (Legband) Taney; B.S., U. Kan., 1956; M.A., Tex. Woman's U., 1973; m. Charles Thomas Smith, Dec. 22, 1962 (div. 1966); 1 dau., Victoria Marie. Joined USNR, 1955, advanced through grades to lt., 1959, discharged, 1963; staff therapist Nat. Naval Med. Center, Bethesda, Md., 1956-59, dir. occupational therapy, 1959-61; staff therapist U.S. Naval Hosp., San Diego, 1961-63; staff therapist Timberlawn Psychiat. Hosp., Dallas, 1965, VA Hosp., Coatesville, Pa., 1966-67; dir. occupational therapy Presbyn. Hosp. of Dallas, 1968; dir. occupational and recreational therapy Beverly Hills Psychiat. Sanitarium, 1968; dir. occupational therapy Presbyn. Village, also Cliff Towers Nursing Home, Dallas, 1969-70; staff Woodlawn Hosp., Dallas County, 1970-71; dir. occupational therapy Elmwood Hosp., Ft. Worth, 1973—. Dept. Health, Edn. and Welfare grantee. Mem. Am., Tex. occupational therapy assns., Beta Sigma Phi. Lutheran. Home: 6514 Glendora Av Dallas TX 75230 Office: Elmwood Hosp 2805 Kimbo Rd Fort Worth TX 76111

SMITH, BIRDEAN BOILEAU (MRS. ELLSON F. SMITH), civic worker; b. Pomona, Cal., Sept. 11, 1916; d. John Frederick and Pearl (May) Boileau; B.A., Pomona Coll., 1937; m. Ellson Franklin Smith, June 29, 1938; children—Raymond Frederick, Susan Elizabeth. Mem. council Camp Fire Girls, 1949-55, pres. council, 1953-55, mem. nat. bd., 1956-65, pres., 1963-65, vice chmn. Region V, 1955-56, v.p. nat. council, 1961-63, pres., 1963-65; mem. Pomona Valley Community Hosp. Aux., 1945—, Foothill Philharmonic Com., 1958—; mem. alumni council Pomona Coll., 1963-72, v.p., 1968—; pres. Assistance League Pomona Valley, 1946, Kingsley-Emerson Sch. P.T.A., 1955-56. Bd. dirs. Pomona Welfare League. Recipient Gulick award Camp Fire Girls, 1954. Mem. P.E.O. (pres. Pomona chpt. 1956-58), Pomona Coll. Alumni Assn. (pres.). Conglist. Clubs: Shakespeare, Ebell (Pomona). Home: 1155 Loma Vista St Pomona CA 91766

SMITH, BONNETTA MAE, sch. psychologist; b. Loma Linda, Cal., Feb. 28, 1928; d. Elmer and Tressa Mae (Burg) Cornell; B.A. in Edn. with distinction, Ariz. State U., 1967, M.A., 1968; postgrad. U. So. Cal., 1973—; divorced; children—Calvin Duane, Robley Douglason, David Jay, Melissa Mae. Sec. Boeing Aircraft Co., Seattle, 1951-58; flight instr. Ft. Lewis (Wash.) Flying Club, 1958-60; tchr. Gloria Felix Sch., Caracas, Venezuela, 1963-65; psychologist Gomper's Rehab. Center, Phoenix, 1968-69; psychometrist Dixie Sch. Dist., San Rafael, Cal., 1969; sch. psychologist San Francisco Unified Sch. Dist., 1969—, adminstrv. asst. guidance service centers, 1971-73; summer tchr., 1970, 71; psychologist Emergency Evaluation Center, 1973-74; psychologist-coordinator basic skills project Youth Guidance Center, San Francisco, 1974—; cons. in field, conductor workshops. Mem. Nat. Assn. Sch. Psychologists, Cal. Assn. Sch. Psychologists/Psychometrists, San Francisco Personnel and Guidance Assn., Cal. Marriage-Child Counselor Assn., Cal. Assn. Neurologically Handicapped Children, Pi Lambda Theta, Kappa Delta Pi. Democrat. Episcopalian. Home: 112 Jefferson Dr Belverdere-Tiburon CA 94920 Office: Youth Guidance Center 375 Woodside St San Francisco CA 94127

SMITH, CAROL CROSSWELL, (MRS. GILBERT W. SMITH), lawyer; b. Buffalo, Dec. 21, 1925; d. Albert L.L. and Helen (McDowell) McCormick; student Radcliffe Coll.; LL.B. cum laude, U. Buffalo, 1947; postgrad. Columbia, 1960, Harvard; 1961; m. William J. Crosswell (dec. 1947); m. 2d, Gilbert Wheatland Smith, Feb. 2, 1952; children—Carol, Linda. Admitted to N.Y. bar, 1948, Washington bar, 1953, Fla. bar, 1967; mem. legal staff UN, 1948-52; mem. U.S. Govt. Psychol. Strategy Bd., 1952-53; U.S. del. Inter Am. Council Jurists, Santiago, Chile, 1960; practiced in N.Y.C., 1952—; mem. firm Weiden and Crosswell, 1950-66. Mem. Fla. Marine Commn., 1968—. Bd. dirs. Jr. League, Millard Fillmore Hosp., Buffalo, Save the Children Fedn., Gebbie Found., Radcliffe Inst. Advanced Studies; gov. Nova Law Center, Ft. Lauderdale, Fla., 1974—. Mem. Soc. Women Geographers, Fellows of Harvard. Clubs: Indian Harbor Yacht (Greenwich, Conn.); Buffalo Country; N.Y. Skating; Beach, Sail Fish (Palm Beach, Fla.); Royal Canadian Yacht (Toronto, Ont.). Author: Protection of International Personnel, 1956; Financing Foreign Investment, 1962; International Business Techniques, 1962. Home: 1204 N Ocean Blvd Palm Beach FL 33480

SMITH, CAROLYN ANN, horse trainer; b. Laconia, N.H., Feb. 23, 1951; d. Norman Draper and Grace Ann (Cousins) Smith; A.A. with honors U. N.H., 1971. Second trainer Tisbert Stables, Foxboro, Mass., 1971—; standardbred yearling buyer Jewel Stables, Vernon, N.Y., 1972—. Mem. U.S. Trotting Assn., Am. Morgan Horse Soc., U.S. Pony Trotting Assn., Standardbred Breeders and Owners Assn. N.H., Harness Pony of Am. Assn. Home: 243 Gilford Av Laconia NH 03246

SMITH, CAROLYN B. NELSON, counselor; b. Oakland, Neb., June 29, 1930; d. Joseph E. and Bertha C. (Bippes) Nelson; B.A., Neb. Wesleyan U., 1951; M.A., U. Houston, 1967, Ed.D., 1972; m. Dwight E. Smith, Aug. 23, 1950; children—Mark, Cara. Acad. counselor, premed. adviser U. Houston Coll. Arts and Scis., 1972-74, asst. prof. speech, 1972—, dir. Office Acad. Information Services, 1974—, chairperson premed. com., premed. adviser, 1974—. Bd. dirs. Sch. of the Woods. U. Houston fellow, 1965-72, Faculty Devel. grantee, 1973. Mem. Am. Psychol. Assn., Speech Communication Assn., Assn. Higher Edn., Am. Personnel and Guidance Assn., Coll. Personnel Assn. Contbr. articles to profl. jours. Home: 1721 Ronson St Houston TX 77055

SMITH, CATHERINE COLLIER, educator, writer; b. Geneva, Ill., Aug. 8, 1929; d. Frederick Charles and Evalyn France (Nesbitt) Collier; A.B. cum laude, U. Miami, 1950; m. Rufus E. Smith, Jr., Dec. 8, 1951; 1 dau., Patricia Diane. Elementary tchr. Dade County Pub. Schs., Coral Gables, Fla., 1952-54, 65-70, tchr. homebound, 1970—. Author: Parakeets and Peach Pies, 1970; also juvenile stories. Mem. Nat. League Am. Pen Women, Beaux Arts Club, Mortar Bd., Delta Kappa Gamma, Delta Zeta. Home: 7521 SW 53d Pl Miami FL 33143 Office: 47 Zamora St Coral Gables FL 33146

SMITH, CATHERINE WOOD RICHARD (MRS. CHARLES WILLOUGHBY SMITH), physician; b. nr. Winchester, Va., Aug. 2, 1912; d. James Edgar and Annie E. (Lockhart) Richard; student. Va. Intermont Coll., 1932-34; A.B., George Washington U., 1938, M.D., 1941; m. Charles Willoughby Smith, June 17, 1939; children—Charles Michael, Patrick Richard, Daniel Willoughby. Intern, Garfield Meml. Hosp., Washington, 1941-42; with USPHS, Va. and Ga., 1942; health officer, dept. maternal and child health Va. Health Dept., Richmond, 1943-44; dir. dept. maternal and child health Ga. Health Dept., Columbus, 1944-45; resident anesthesiologist Johnston Meml. Hosp., Abingdon, Va., 1948-50; mem. teaching staff Sch. Nursing 1950-58; practice medicine specializing in obstetrics, Abingdon, 1950-64; resident gen. and child psychiatry N.Y. Med. Coll.-Met. Hosp., N.Y.C., 1964-68; practice medicine specializing in psychosomatic medicine, counseling, psychiatry, Abingdon, 1968—; dir. Smyth County (Va.) Mental Health Clinic, Marion, Va., 1968-73; med. adv. bd. Va. League Planned Parenthood, 1950—. Bd. dirs. Va. Highlands Festival of Arts and Crafts, 1957-59. Mem. Am. Med. Women's Assn. (br. pres. 1959-60), Am. Assn. U. Women (br. pres.), S.W. Va., Va., Washington County (pres. 1960-61) med. socs., A.M.A., Internat. Fedn. U. Women, Smith Reed Russell Med. Honor Soc. Democrat. Presbyn. Club: Booklovers (pres. 1957-59). Home and Office: 488 Walden Rd Abingdon VA 24210

SMITH, CHARLIE MAE, librarian; b. Rosenberg, Tex., May 5; d. Robert and Charline (Dyer) Brown; B.S. with great distinction, Prairie View A. and M. U., 1954; M.L.S., Tex. Woman's U., Denton, 1972; m. Charles Eldon Smith, Jr., Nov. 20, 1967. Librarian Dunbar Elementary Sch., Dallas, 1950-64; asst. reference librarian Bishop Coll., 1962; librarian H.S. Thompson Elementary Sch., 1965-66, Oliver Wendell Holmes Jr. High Sch., Dallas, 1966—. Sec.-treas. Pier 7A div. Pirate's Pier, Inc., Dallas, 1972—. Active local YWCA, PTA. Mem. instrn. com. bull. The Library in the Sch., Dallas Ind. Sch. Dist., 1965. Mem. Am., Tex., Dallas County (chmn. nominating com. 1973), Dallas Sch. library assns., N.E.A., Tex. State Tchrs. Assn., Classroom Tchrs. Dallas, Nat. Council Negro Women, Alpha Phi Mu, Delta Sigma Theta (chpt. corr. sec. 1964, financial sec. 1965). Baptist. Author: Selected Bibliography of Developments in Black Literature, 1972. Home: 1004 E Pentagon Pkwy Dallas TX 75216 Office: 2001 E Kiest Blvd Dallas TX 75216

SMITH, CHARLOTTE GROESBEECK (MRS. EVERETT HENSEL SMITH), lawyer; b. San Antonio, July 23, 1918; d. George and Charlotte Henry (Groesbeeck) Boeck; student, San Antonio Jr. Coll., 1934-36; B.A., U. Tex., 1940, J.D., 1940; m. Everett Hensel Smith, Dec. 25, 1944; children—Charlotte Frances (Mrs. James Darrell Carr), Catherine Lucile (Mrs. Harold Eugene Dayton, Jr.). Admitted to Tex. bar, 1940; asso. Kelly & Looney, Edinburg, Tex., 1941-44; tchr., Panama C.Z., also San Antonio, 1961-63, 65-67; mem. firm Smith & Smith, Kingsland, Tex., 1967—. Vice pres. Lackland P.T.A., San Antonio, 1965-66. Mem. Nat. Assn. Women Lawyers, Am. Judicature Soc., State Bar Tex., Bus. and Profl. Womens Club (past local pres.), Mortar Bd., Bertram C. of C., Phi Mu (past pres.), Phi Theta Kappa, Pi Lambda Theta, Kappa Beta Pi (past dist. pres.). Methodist. Mem. Order Eastern Star (past matron 1972-73 sect. visitation chmn. Tex. chpt.). Clubs: Keesler AFB Womens (pres. Biloxi, Miss. 1951-52); Pen Chat (Burnet, Tex.); Kingsland (Tex.) Culture. Home: PO Box 96 Buchanan Dam TX 78609 Office: PO Box 446 Kingsland TX 78639

SMITH, CHERYLE CURTIS, engr.; b. LaPorte, Ind., Dec. 8. 1924; d. Ethelred and Marvel Ann (Stevens) Curtis; B.A. in Math., Ind. U., 1947, M.S. in Physics, 1949; m. Robert T. Smith, Jr., June 24, 1950. Teaching asst. Ind. U., 1946-49; asst. detail engr. Allison div. Gen. Motors Corp., Speedway, Ind., 1949-50; research physicist S.W. Research Inst., San Antonio, 1950-51; chief math. analysis sect. Air Force Spl. Weapons Center, Kirtland AFB, N.M., 1952-53; supr. aero.-math. analysis N.Am. Aviation, Columbus, O., 1953-55; operations research analyst Air Force Systems Command, Wright-Patterson AFB, O., 1956-66; staff engr. TRW Systems Group, Redondo Beach, Cal., 1966—. Recipient Meritorious civilian service award USAF, 1964, Presdl. citation operations research, 1964. Mem. Operations Research Soc. Am., Beach Cities Symphony Orch. Contbr. numerous articles to profl. jours. Office: TRW Systems Group 1 Space Park Redondo Beach CA 90266

SMITH, CHLOETHIEL WOODARD, architect; b. Peoria, Ill., Feb. 2, 1910; d. Oliver Ernest and Coy Blanche (Johnson) Woodard; B-Arch. with honors, U. Ore., 1932; M.Arch., Washington U., 1933; m. Bromley Keables Smith, Apr. 5, 1940; children—Bromley Keables, Susanne Woodard. Various drafting positions, Portland, Ore., Seattle, 1920-32, drafting and design, N.Y.C., 1933-36; chief research and planning FHA, Washington, 1936-39; asso., pvt. practice architecture, Washington, 1939-40; city planning exhibit, drafting, Montreal, Can., 1940-41; prof. architecture U. San Andres, cons. Servico Cooperativo de Salud Publica, La Paz, Bolivia, 1942-45; prin. Chloethiel Woodard Smith & Assos., Washington, 1945—; prin. works include Am. Embassy Chancery and Residence, Asuncion, Paraguay, Chestnut Lodge, Rockville, Md., Capitol Park, Washington, store and exec. offices Harcourt, Brace & World, Inc., N.Y.C., master plan for Washington Channel Waterfront, E Street Expressway, Washington, numerous pvt. residences, also urban renewal plans. Jury mem. house awards A.I.A., Nat. Assn. Home Builders; design rev. panel Boston Redevel. Agy.; participated exhibits City for Living, Montreal, Can., 1940, German Bldg. Expn., Hanover, 1951; mem. architects adv. com. Nat. Capital Downtown Com., Inc.; mem. President's adv. council on Pennsylvania Av., 1963; mem. Nat. Commn. on Urban Problems, Commn. Fine Arts, Washington. Trustee Fred L. Lavanburg Found. Recipient Award of Merit, A.I.A., 1960, award for architecture Capitol Park Apts., Washington; John Simon Guggenheim Meml. Found. fellow, 1944. Fellow A.I.A. (chmn. 1965 Pan-Am. Congress com.); mem. Am. Inst. Planners, Am. Planning and Civic Assn., Com. of 100 on Fed. City, Washington Bldg. Congress, Washington Planning and Housing Assn., Columbia Hist. Soc. Washington, Met. Washington Bd. Trade, Alpha Omicron Pi. Home: 2328 Massachusetts Av NW Washington DC 20008 Office: 1056 Thomas Jefferson St NW Washington DC 20007*

SMITH, CHRISTINE, educator; b. Picayune, Miss.; d. Jesse Deloach and Addie (Stewart) Smith; A.B., Miss. State Coll. Women, 1938. Tchr. English, Moss Point, Miss., 1938-41, Biloxi, Miss., 1941-42; instr. electronic prins. dept. Kessler AFB, Biloxi, 1942-47, instr., supr. airborne electronics dept., 1947-50, instr. tng. dept., 1950-54, tng. specialist electronic prins. dept., 1955-61, tng. specialist closed circuit tv br., 1961-70, tng. specialist communications and electronics, 1970—. Recipient Outstanding Career Woman award Keesler AFB, 1973. Mem. Armed Forces Communications Electronics Assn. (Lady of Month 1967, sec. Gulf Coast chpt. 1960-67), P.E.O. (sec., treas. 1964-66), Nat. Assn. Edn. Broadcasters, Div. Audio-Visual Instrn. Episcopalian. Club: Altrusa (pres. Biloxi 1970-72). Home: Chateaux Apts Biloxi MS 39531 Office: TV Operations Br Keesler AFB MS 39534

SMITH, CLAIRE ALMA (MRS. LEON MASON SMITH), govt. ofcl.; b. Lawrence, Mass., Apr. 6, 1922; d. Joseph Elphege and Alma (Gervais) Gravel; student Am. U., 1948-50; George Washington U., 1961-62, 66-67; m. L(eon) Mason Smith, Jan. 3, 1948 (dec.). With U.S. Postal Service, Washington, 1947—, internat. tng. officer, 1968—. Sec., treas. Smith Bros. Electronics, Inc., Annapolis, Md., 1952-56. Mem. Colonial Players, Inc., Annapolis, 1964—. Bd. dirs. Annapolis Summer Garden Theatre. Mem. Soc. Fed. Linguists (recording sec. 1966-67). Democrat. Baptist. Club: Severn Town (pres. Annapolis 1955-56, mem. exec. bd. 1956-69). Home: Rural

Route 3 Box 224 Edgewater MD 21037 Office: US Postal Service Office International Postal Affairs 475 L'Enfant Plaza West SW Washington DC 20260

SMITH, CLARA LOITMAN (MRS. JOSEPH SMITH), physician; b. Boston, Aug. 31, 1900; d. Morris and Fannie (Castleman) Loitman; M.D., Tufts U., 1923; m. Joseph Smith, Aug. 14, 1932 (dec. Sept. 1966); children—Ruth (Mrs. Lewis Battist), Deborah (Mrs. Gerald D. Weintraub), Charles, David. Intern, Mass. U. Hosp., Boston, 1923-24; resident Boston Floating Hosp., 1924, 26; resident pediatrician Willard P. Hosp., 1926-27; practice medicine specializing in pediatrics, Providence, 1933—; mem. pediatric staff R.I., Miriam, Providence Lying-In hosps., Providence; pediatrician Providence Health Centers, 1966—; physician R.I. Coll., 1954-70. Bd. dirs. R.I. Tb. and Health Assn., 1964—, Family and Child Assn., Providence, 1966—. Named Rhode Island Merit Mother, R.I. Mother's Assn., 1968. Address: 281 Olney St Providence RI 02906

SMITH, DIANE MARGARET, reporter; b. Harvard, Ill., Dec. 6, 1942; d. Amos Harley and Helen L. (Mihelich) Smith; student Lake Forest Coll., 1961-62; B.A. with honors in Mass Communications, U. Wis., 1972. Comml. copywriter and prodn. asst. WTMJ-TV, Milw., 1972-73; anchorperson and gen. assignment reporter WJIM-TV, Lansing, Mich., 1973—. Free lance comml. copywriter; lectr., 1973—; union steward Assn. Broadcast Employees and Technicians. Mem. Nat. Orgn. for Women, Mich. Women's Polit. Caucus, Women in Communications, Phi Kappa Phi. Producer film Rape, 1974. Home: 936 N Fairview St Lansing MI 48912 Office: WJIM-TV 2820 E Saginaw St Lansing MI 48904

SMITH, DOLLILEE DAVIS, author, real estate broker; b. Sandia, Tex.; b. Walter Clifton and Edna (Reece) Davis; student Central City Comml. Coll., Waco, Tex.; m. Mack Douglas Smith; 1 son, C. Douglas. Owner a'Nardo's Perfumes; real estate loan broker, Dallas. Past state chmn. Am. Mothers Com. Past poet laureate Tex. Mem. Internat. Platform Assn., Cumtux Soc. (hon.), Delta Kappa Gamma (hon.). Mem. Order Eastern Star. Author: Today Is Mine; Santa's Magic Eye; Dear Santa; Especially For You; Satin and Sandpaper. Composer: Wake and Pray; No Funeral For My Soul. Address: 9504 Ash Creek Dr Dallas TX 75228

SMITH, DONNA MARIE, advt. agy. exec.; b. Wichita, Kan., July 10, 1946; d. J. Gordon and Juanita Maxine (Crum) Smith; B.S., U. Ore., 1968. Receptionist, copywriter media buyer KERG Radio, Eugene, Ore., 1968; copywriter, media buyer Reynolds & Assos., Eugene, 1969; copy chief, media dir. Advt. Services, Eugene, 1970-74; owner, partner Adlib Advt. Agy., Ltd., Eugene, 1974—. Recipient Sparkplug award Ore. Advt. Fedn., 1973. Mem. Am., Ore. (sec. 1972-73), advt. fedns., Am. Bus. Women, Theta Sigma Phi, Zeta Tau Alpha. Mem. Christian Ch. Mem. Order Eastern Star, Daughters Nile. Club: Advertising (award banquet chmn. Eugene 1971—). Home: 290 Woodlane Dr Springfield OR 97471 Office: 1200 High St Eugene OR 97401

SMITH, DOROTHY ALDEN, book designer; b. Atlantic City, N.J., June 1, 1918; d. Paul Ray and Mary Agnes (McCloskey) Smith; student Sch. Profl. Art, N.Y.C., 1936-38; grad. N.Y. Sch. Fine and Applied Art, 1939; student Bryn Mawr Coll., summer 1942, Spring Garden Coll., 1970-71. Asst. advt. dir. Theodore Presser Music Pubs., Phila., 1940-41; photogrammetric engr. Dept. Interior, Washington, 1941-42; designer Lotz Photoengraving Co., Phila., 1942-43; art dir. Westminster Press, Phila., 1943—. Lectr., Phila. Mus. Sch. Art, 1967-68, Moore Sch. Design, Phila., 1967-68, Hussian Sch. Art, 1968-69, Religious Books Pubs. Council, 1968; graphics cons. Episcopal Ch., 1968; graphics designer Young Republican Club Phila., 1951-53, Tredyffrin Twp. Library, 1968-69. Bd. dirs. Phila. Book Clinic. Recipient Art Dirs. Club medal, 1950, Bronze medal award Freedoms Found., 1958. Mem. Phila. Art Alliance, Mainline Aux. Soc. Prevention Cruelty to Animals. Clubs: Phoenixville (Pa.) Country; Martins Dam (Wayne, Pa.); Peale (Phila.). Home: 608 Weadley Rd Strafford Wayne PA 19087 Office: 929 Witherspoon Bldg Philadelphia PA 19107

SMITH, DOROTHY CAROLINE, librarian; b. Shawmut, Ala., Jan. 3, 1924; d. L. Cooper and Dorothy (Ector) Smith; A.B., Randolph-Macon Woman's Coll., 1944; M.A., U. S.C., 1947; B.S. in L.S., U. N.C., 1951. Instr. history dept. Columbia (S.C.) Coll., 1945-46; head printed materials div. S.C. Library, U. S.C., Columbia, 1946-48; head reference dept. Richland County (S.C.) Pub. Library, Columbia, 1949-50, adult services librarian, 1961-63; reference asst. Pub. Library of Charlotte and Mecklenburg County (N.C.), Charlotte, 1951; librarian Horry County (S.C.) Meml. Library, Conway, 1952-57; field cons. S.C. State Library Bd., Columbia, 1957-61; sr. library supr. library devel. div., N.Y. State Edn. Dept., Albany, 1963-67, asso. pub. library services div., 1967—. Instr. Winthrop Coll., Rock Hill, S.C., summer 1954. Mem. Am., N.Y. (state rep. to Personnel Adminstrn. Com. 1964—) library assns., Phi Beta Kappa. Episcopalian. Home: 2135 McClellan St Schenectady NY 12309 Office: Div Library Devel New York State Edn Dept 99 Washington Av Albany NY 12210

SMITH, DOROTHY ELIZABETH, ret. mus. curator; b. Colorado Springs, Colo., Sept. 14, 1900; d. Frederic Russell and Margaret (Greenwood) Smith; B.A., Wellesley Coll., 1924; M.A., Colo. Coll., 1935. Tchr. pub. sch. system, Colorado Springs, Colo., 1925-34, Hillsdale Sch., Cin., 1934; mus. dir. Pioneers' Mus., Colorado Springs, 1938-70; chmn. bd. trustees Pioneers' Mus. Fund, Inc., 1970—. Mem. D.A.R. (regent 1946-48), El Paso County Pioneers Assn. (pres. 1969—), Descs. Covered Wagon Pioneers (hon.). Conglist. Author: (with others) Henry McAllister, Colorado Pioneer, 1972. Home: 1131 N Custer Av Colorado Springs CO 80903

SMITH, DOROTHY JANET (MRS. JAMES ROY MARTIN), librarian; b. Newark, Sept. 15, 1943; d. Wendell Vandervort and Virginia Stella (Anderson) Smith; A.B., Oberlin Coll., 1965; M.L.S., Rutgers U., 1967; m. James Roy Martin, May 25, 1974. Library trainee Nutley (N.J.) Pub. Library, 1965-66; profl. library asst. Boston Pub. Library, 1967-69, adults librarian, 1969-72, br. librarian, 1972—. Club: Sierra. Home: 10 Spring Rd Arlington MA 02174 Office: Mattapan branch Boston Pub Library 10 Hazelton St Mattapan MA 02126

SMITH, DOROTHY LASSETER (MRS. WILLIAM SPENCER SMITH), educator; b. Rochelle, Ga., Sept. 5, 1910; d. Zadoc Wilder and Ava Alye (Sutton) Lasseter; A.B., Tift Coll., 1930; postgrad. U. Ga., 1934-35, So. Ga. Coll., 1954; m. William Spencer Smith, Mar. 15, 1935; children—Dorothy (Mrs. Paul Perry Fidler), Diana (Mrs. Robert Sparks Highsmith). Sec., Fed. Mut. Ins. Co., Atlanta, 1930, 35; tchr., Douglas, Ga., 1953-64; tchr. Underwood Hills Elementary Sch., Atlanta, 1968—. Founder Community Concert Series, Douglas, 1948, Safety Council, Douglas, 1952; organizer, dir. Douglas Girl Scouts, 1949; leader Girl Scouts, Atlanta; chmn. Coffee County chpt. A.R.C., 1950, 51, 52; dir. Polio Drive, Douglas, 1950, 51, 52, Red Cross Drive, 1950, 51, 52; pres. P.T.A., Douglas, 1952. Mem. Fulton County Tchrs. Assn. (rep. to Ga. Educators 1962). Baptist (dir. jr. dept. Sunday Sch. 1950-52). Home: 1051 Frazier St Apt E2 Roswell GA 30075 Office: 335 Colewood Way Atlanta GA 30328

SMITH, DOROTHY OTTINGER (MRS. JAMES EMORY SMITH), jewelry designer; b. Indpls., May 22, 1922; d. Albert Ellsworth and Leona Aurelia (Waller) Ottinger; student Herron Art Sch. of Purdue U. and Ind. U., 1941-42; m. James Emory Smith, June 25, 1943; children—Michael Ottinger, Sarah Anne, Theodore Arnold, Lisa Marie. Comml. artist William H. Block Co., Indpls., 1942-43, H.P. Wasson Co., 1943-44; dir. Riverside (Cal.) Art Center, 1963-64; jewelry designer, Riverside, 1970—. Adviser Riverside chpt. Freedom's Found. of Valley Forge; co-chmn. Fund Raising Com., Riverside Art Center and Mus., 1966-67; mem. Riverside City Hall art selection panel Nat. Endowment Arts. Mem. mayor's Com. on Civic Beauty, mayor's Com. on Sister City Sendai, 1965-66. Bd. dirs. Children's League of Riverside Community Hosp., 1952-53; bd. dirs. Crippled Children's Soc. of Riverside, spl. events chmn., 1952-53; bd. dirs. Jr. League of Riverside, rec. sec., 1960-61; bd. dirs. Nat. Charity League, pres. Riverside chpt., 1965-66. Mem. Riverside Art Assn. (pres. 1961-63, 1st v.p. 1964-65, 67-68, trustee 1959-70), Art Alliance of Riverside Art Center and Museum (founder 1964, pres. 1969-70). Address: 3979 Chapman Place Riverside CA 92506

SMITH, EDITH ANN HENDRIX (MRS. CHARLES WILBURN SMITH), banker; b. DeQueen, Ark., Sept. 8, 1932; d. Carl Edward and Lilla (Sullivan) Hendrix; B.S.E., U. Ark., 1953, M.A., 1955; m. Charles Wilburn Smith, Oct. 6, 1964; 1 dau., Margaret Ann. Tchr. pub. schs., Odessa, Tex., 1953-54, jr. high sch., Caddo Parish, Shreveport, La., 1955-56; bookkeeper, teller Horatio State Bank, Horatio, Ark., 1956-62, cashier, 1962-69, v.p., 1969—, also dir.; partner Horatio Ins. Agy., 1967—. Chmn., Heart Fund, Cancer, Cystic Fibrosis, Mothers March drives; organizer Horatio Indsl. Devel. Corp. Recipient Ark. Community Devel. award Ark. State C. of C., 1973. Mem. Horatio C. of C. (sec.), D.A.R., Kappa Kappa Gamma, Kappa Delta Pi, Lambda Tau. Baptist. Home: PO Box 42 Horatio AR 71842 Office: PO Box 347 Horatio AR 71842

SMITH, EDNA CASCIOLI (MRS. STEVEN GEORGE SMITH), ednl. adminstr.; b. Sayre, Pa., Dec. 31, 1947; d. Tobias Salvador Joseph and Edna Earl (Hearn) Cascioli; student Wake Forest U., 1966-67; B.A., East Carolina U., 1970, M.A. in Psychology, 1973; m. Steven George Smith, Aug. 18, 1972. Recreation dir. Grifton, N.C., 1969; residence hall adminstr., East Carolina U., Greenville, N.C., 1970-73, residence counselor, 1973-74; mem. psychology faculty, dir. counseling, dean student services St. Joseph Coll., Bennington, Vt., 1974—. Active Tuberculosis Assn., 1969-70. Mem. Nat., N.C. assns. women deans and counselors, N.C. Personnel and Guidance Assn., Psi Chi. Democrat. Presbyn. Home: PO Box 402 Bennington VT 05201

SMITH, ELEANOR TOUHEY, librarian; b. Portland, Ore., Jan. 4, 1910; d. Thomas and Sarah (Ford) Touhey; B.A., U. Ore., 1930; certificate Los Angeles Library Sch., 1932; M.S., Columbia, 1952; m. S. Stephenson Smith, June 11, 1949 (dec. 1961). Gen. asst., readers adviser Library Assn., Portland, 1932-43; book columnist Portland Oregonian, 1937-45; head librarian Vanport (Ore.) Pub. Library, 1943-45; asst. librarian Santa Monica (Cal.) Pub. Library, 1945-49; head extension Ferguson Library, Stamford, Conn., 1949-51; personnel dir. Bklyn. Pub. Library, 1953-55, coordinator adult services, 1955-67; regional adminstr. fed. library grants Library Services Program, U.S. Office Edn., 1967—; instr. Sch. Library Service U. So. Cal., 1947; reviewer Library Jour., 1954—; asst. prof. Sch. Librarianship U. Wash., summer, 1964; TV, radio, newspaper book reviewer. Pres. Library Pub. Relations Council, 1957-58; mem. bd. N.Y. Booksellers League, 1958-74, pres., 1966-68; bd. N.Y. Adult Edn. Council, 1961-70; bd. mem. Women's Nat. Book Assn. 1961-74, pres. N.Y. chpt., 1963-64, nat. sec., 1964-68. Recipient Friends award Bklyn. Pub. Library, 1961. Mem. Am. (mem. various coms., pres. adult services div. 1964-65), N.Y. State (pres. adult services sect. 1958-59; pres. 1969-70), Cath. library assns., N.Y. Library Club (pres. 1957-58), Columbia Sch. Library Service Alumnae (pres. 1962-63), Am. Soc. for Psychical Research, Phi Beta Kappa. Democrat. Roman Catholic. Editor: Pacific N.W. Library Assn. Quar., 1943. Author: Psychic People, 1968. Contbr. to profl. publs. Home: 96 Fifth Av New York City NY 10011 Office: Room 3950 26 Federal Plaza New York City NY 10007

SMITH, ELENOR RUTH HARSCH (MRS. IVAN GERHOLD SMITH), mfg. co. exec.; b. N.Y.C., Apr. 12, 1928; d. Hermann Joseph and Elsa Julia (Reser) Harsch; B.A., Wagner Coll., 1950; m. Ivan Gerhold Smith, May 22, 1962; children by previous marriage—Suzanne Oschmann, Chris Oschmann. With Hago Products, Mountainside, N.J., 1950—, v.p., 1965—. Trustee Girls Collegiate Sch., Claremont, Cal., 1972—. Mem. Am. Assn. U. Women, United Women So. Cal. (pres. 1972-73), Alpha Omicron Pi. Home: 1239 El Paraiso Dr Pomona CA 91768 Office: 1120 Globe Av Mountainside NJ 07092

SMITH, ELIZABETH HAMMOND WEST, writer, editor; b. Crewe, Va.; d. Henry Clay and Bessie Boggs (Jones) Smith; A.B. in Journalism, W.Va. U., 1939. Asst. editor Courier-Record, Blackstone, Va., 1936-39; established, directed So. States Coop. News Service, 1939-46; editorial asst. Southside Pub. Co., Petersburg, Va., 1946-48; writer many feature stories for state and nat. publs. Richmond and Norfolk, Va. Sunday newspapers, 1940-53; mng. editor The Star and Lamp of Pi Kappa Phi, Richmond, 1951-61; mng. editor nat. mag. U.D.C., Richmond, 1969-74. Pub. information dir. Va. Heart Assn., Richmond, 1956-63; Va. publicity dir. Woodrow Wilson Centennial Birthplace Restoration Fund, Staunton, Va., 1956-58; publicity dir. Christchurch (Va.) Sch. Fund Raising Campaign, 1961; dir. pub. relations Va. Thanksgiving Festival, Richmond, 1967-68; exec. dir., promotion dir. joint com. fund raising Diocesan Homes, Episcopal Diocese Va., Richmond, 1963-68. Mem. women's planning com. Japan Internat. Christian U. Found. Mem. Jamestowne Soc., Soc. Descs. Hon. Henry Fox and His Wife Anne West, D.A.R., Va. Hist. Soc., Bus. and Profl. Women's Club, Richmond. Methodist (life mem. Woman's Soc. Christian Service). Editor: The Family of Coghill Continued (by Will H. Coghill), 1956; The "Elect Ladies" of Centenary Methodist Church, Richmond, Virginia (Edith Denny White), 1964. Address: 2512 Monument Av Richmond VA 23220

SMITH, ELIZABETH STERLING (MRS. W. BRYCE SMITH), civic worker; b. N.Y.C.; d. Theodore Anton and Pauline (Green) Sterling; B.A., Cornell U., 1952; postgrad. Northwestern U., 1952; m. W. Bryce Smith, June 28, 1968; 1 dau., Elizabeth Sterling. Social sec. to Perl Mesta, 1953-54, Vivian Beaumont Allen, 1952-53; dir. 345 E. 52d St. Corp., 1968-69, N.Y. Coop., 1968-69. Vol. tchr. retarded children, Palm Beach, Fla., 1954-56; sponsor Internat. Debutante Ball, 1963-68, Soldiers, Sailors and Airman's Club, 1955-60, UN rep. Young Women's Republican Club, 1954-57; program chmn. Newcomers Club of New Canaan, 1971-72, pres., 1972-73. Mem. Soc. Four Arts, Outdoor Cleanliness Assn., Round Table. Club: Everglades (Palm Beach). Home: Indian Waters Dr New Canaan CT 06840 also Vassar Rd Poughkeepsie NY

SMITH, ELLA, theatrical dir., author, educator; b. Danbury, Conn., Sept. 28, 1933; d. George and Ella (Orser) Smith; B.S., Danbury State Coll., 1955; M.F.A., Yale, 1961; student Yale Shakespeare Inst., 1958, Martha Graham Sch. Contemporary Dance, 1962. Dir., asst. prof. theatre and film R.I. Coll., 1964-71; dir., asst. prof. dramatic arts U. Conn., 1971-72; artistic dir. Emerson Coll. Center for Performing Arts, Deertrees Theatre, Me., 1967; guest dir. Cedar Crest (Pa.) Coll., 1973; cons. 8th N.Y. Film Festival, 1971; actress Drama Quartet, U. Conn., TV and Off-Broadway prodns. John Brown's Body, indsl. film Everybody Knows Brooklyn, WLAD Workshop, Conn., Redding (Conn.) Players, Bklyn. Heights Players, Contemporary Drama Center, N.Y.C.; choreographer, dancer Masque of Oberon, Columbia U.; prodn. asst. Theatre East, Nutmeg Playhouse, Conn. Mem. Am. Theatre Assn., Yale Drama Alumni Assn., Nat. Honor Soc. Author, designer: Starring Miss Barbara Stanwyck, 1974. Author: Introduction to A World of Movies, 1974. Address: Box 366 Beverly Hills CA 90213

SMITH, ELLEN SUE, psychologist; b. Bklyn., Nov. 11, 1945; d. Solomon Charles and Evelyn (Zeluck) Smith; B.A., Simmons Coll., 1967; M.Ed., Columbia, 1970. Tchr., Newton (Mass.) Pub. Schs., 1967-68; research asso. Harvard Center for Community Health and Med. Care, Boston, 1970-71; staff psychologist Kennedy Meml. Hosp. for Children, Boston, 1971—. Mem. organizing com. Area 4 Office for Children, 1973-74, bd. dirs., 1974—. Bd. dirs. Allston Brighton Community Family Center, 1973-74. Rehab. Services Adminstrn. trainee, 1968-70. Home: 872 Massachusetts Av #308 Cambridge MA 02139 Office: 30 Warren St Brighton MA 02135

SMITH, ELLEN YEO, psychologist; b. Clay Center, Kan., Dec. 11, 1922; d. Leo Grant and Ethel (Ball) Yeo; B.S., Kan. State U., 1943, M.A., 1949; m. Robert Baldwin Smith, June 28, 1944; children—Alexa Ruth, Kelli Ellen. Tchr. schs. in Kan. and Wis., 1945-47; psychometrist Kan. State U., 1947-49, U. Ia., 1954-55; instr. psychology Carthage (Ill.) Coll., 1950-52; mgr. Travel Unlimited, Manhattan, Kan., 1952-54; psychologist Burlington (Ia.) pub. schs., 1955-58, Des Moines County Mental Health Clinic, Burlington, 1959; guidance counselor New Berlin (Wis.) pub. schs., 1961-68, dist. psychologist, 1968—; pvt. practice, Waukesha, Wis., 1969—; guest lectr. learning disabilities U. Wis. at Oshkosh, 1969—; cons., conductor workshops in field. Mem. exec. bd. Waukesha County Mental Health Assn., 1962-64; mem. Waukesha County Task Force Mental Health Needs, 1973. Mem. Ia. Acad. Sci., Am. Psychol. Assn. Nat. Assn. Sch. Psychologists, Orton Soc., Am. Council Learning Disabilities, Internat. Inst. Suburban Sch. Psychologists Assn., Waukesha County Counseling Cons., Delta Kappa Gamma. Address: 510 McCall St Waukesha WI 53186

SMITH, ETHEL CLOSSON, soprano, educator; b. Germantown, Pa., Dec. 8, 1921; d. Harry Framer and Mary (Closson) Smith; student Westminster Choir Coll., Princeton, N.J., 1939-41; B. Mus. Edn., Wheaton (Ill.) Coll., 1943; M.Mus. Edn., Temple U., 1945; postgrad. N.Y. Theol. Sem., 1946-47, Juilliard Sch. Music, summer 1948, Princeton Theol. Sem., 1950-51, Union Theol. Sem., N.Y.C., 1951-52; Mus.D., Ind. U., 1968; student Mozarteum, Salzburg, Austria, 1969, U. Florence (Italy), 1969, Goethe Inst. (Prien am Chiemsee, Germany). Soprano soloist various chs., N.Y., Pa., 1946-59; appeared in various concerts and recitals various cities, 1946—, including Radio City Music Hall, 1949, Silver Bay, N.Y., 1951, Chautauqua, N.Y., 1955, Ind. U. opera performances, 1960; worked with Presbyn. students Westminster Found., Temple U., Pa., 1950-51; dir. ch. choir and Christian edn. 3d Presbyn. Ch., Chester, Pa., 1953-54; mem. faculty Summer Tng. Inst. Presbyn. Ch., Wooster, O., summers 1953, 54; asst. prof. music Eastern Bapt. Coll. and Sem., Phila., 1955-59; asst. prof. music, dean of women Eastern Bapt. Sem., 1955-59; asso. prof. music Ind. State U., Terre Haute, 1962-71, prof. music, 1971—. Asso. mem. Nat. Council Met. Opera, Central Opera Service; mem. Nat. Assn. Tchrs. Singing (pres. Ind. chpt. 1965-66, mem. nat. com. sci. research of voice, 1968-69, lt. gov. Ind. 1970-72), Internat. Assn. for Research in Singing, Am. Assn. U. Profs., Am. Assn. U. Women, Bus. and Profl. Women, Music Tchrs. Nat. Assn., Ind. Music Tchrs. Assn., Ind. U. Alumni Assn. (exec. council), Pi Kappa Lambda, Sigma Alpha Iota. Home: 130 Jackson Blvd Terre Haute IN 47803

SMITH, ETHEL LILLIE KNOTT (MRS. BUDD ELMON SMITH), librarian; b. nr. Oxford, N.C., July 21, 1915; d. Fielding and Lillie (Overton) Knott; student Queens Coll., 1933-34; A.B., Meredith Coll., 1937; B.L.S., U. N.C., 1942; M.A., Appalachian State Tchrs. Coll., 1955; postgrad. U. Chgo.; m. Budd Elmon Smith, Dec. 28, 1943; children—James Fielding, William Budd. Tchr., Guilford (N.C.) Coll. High Sch., 1937-38, Roanoke Rapids (N.C.) High Sch., 1938-42; librarian Gastonia (N.C.) High Sch., 1942-43, U.S. Army, Camp Butler, N.C., 1943-44, Cornell Library Assn. Library, 1944-45; instr. Wake Forest Coll., 1946-51; librarian Oxford City Schs., 1952-53; instr. Wingate (N.C.) Coll., 1953-55, librarian, 1955—. Exec. sec. N.C. Nat. Library Week, 1963. Sec., Wingate P.T.A., 1957-58, Woman's Missionary Union, 1958-60, Union County Planning Bd., 1964—; mem. com. Self-Study Baptist Colls. N.C., 1964-65. Named Union County Woman of Yr., 1969. Mem. Am. Assn. U. Women (pres. N.C. div.), Am., Southeastern, N.C. (past chmn. Jr. Coll. sect., chmn. coll. and univ. sect.) library assns., Nat. Council Tchrs. English, Modern Lang. Assn., Delta Kappa Gamma. Democrat. Baptist. Clubs: Woman's Garden. Contbr. articles to profl. jours. Home: Route 2 Box 121 A Benson NC 27504

SMITH, ETHEL MAE STACKHOUSE (MRS. GEORGE ROBERT SMITH), surgeon; b. Jennings, La., Mar. 20, 1936; d. Claude Earl and Ama Lee (Fears) Stackhouse; B.S., La. State U., 1957, M.D., 1961; M.S. in Surgery, U. Minn., 1967; m. George Robert Smith, Sept. 11, 1962; children—Michael Kevin, Margaret Elizabeth. Intern, Confederate Meml. Med. Center, Shreveport, La., 1961-62; resident surgery Mayo Clinic, Mayo Grad. Sch. Medicine, Rochester, Minn., 1962-67; practice gen. surgery, Lafayette, La., 1968—; vis. staff Lafayette Charity Hosp.; active surg. staff Lafayette Gen., Our Lady of Lourdes hosps., Lafayette. Mem. Jr. League Lafayette. Bd. dirs. Lafayette Juvenile and Young Adult Program. Diplomate Am. Bd. Surgery. Fellow A.C.S.; mem. Southeastern Surg. Congress, La., Lafayette Parish med. socs., La Surg. Soc., Mayo Alumni Assn., Am. Trauma Soc., Priestley Soc., Mortar Bd., Alpha Lambda Delta, Mu Sigma Rho, Phi Kappa Phi. Republican. Methodist. Home: 210 Broadmoor Blvd Lafayette LA 70501 Office: 1432 S College Rd Lafayette LA 70501

SMITH, ETHELEE RAY (MRS. DENNIS HAROLD SMITH), anesthesiologist; b. Kansas City, Mo., Nov. 26, 1931; d. Johnie Nelson and Ethel Benola (Sudduth) Ray; A.B., U. Mo., 1952, B.S. in Medicine, 1954; M.D., Washington U., St. Louis, 1956; m. Dennis Harold Smith, Nov. 20, 1960; children—Margaret Ellen, Ethel Anne, Dennis H. Nelson, Antonia Marie. Intern, U. Kan. Med. Center, Kansas City, 1956-57, resident internal medicine, 1957-58, resident anesthesiology, 1958-60, instr. surgery, 1960; practice medicine, specializing in anesthesiology, Cleve., 1961—; mem. staff Cleve. Clinic, 1961—. Mem. Am., Ohio, Cleve. socs. anesthesiologists, Am., Ohio, Cleve. med. assns., Phi Beta Kappa, Alpha Omega Alpha. Home: 2490 Kenilworth Rd Cleveland Heights OH 44106 Office: 9500 Euclid Av Cleveland OH 44106

SMITH, EUNICE CLARK (MRS. CHARD POWERS SMITH), educator; b. Flushing, N.Y., Oct. 29, 1912; d. Paul Franklin and Alice (Schiedt) Clark; A.B. magna cum laude, Radcliffe Coll., 1934; M.A., U. Wis., 1935, Ph.D. in French, 1945; postgrad. Institut de Touraine, Tours, France, 1936, Harvard, 1937, Middlebury Coll., 1942; m.

Chard Powers Smith, Oct. 18, 1957. Tchr. high sch. French and German, Morris, Ill., 1935-39; instr. French, Spanish, Lawrence Coll., 1941-43; teaching asst. French, Bryn Mawr Coll., 1944-46; asst. prof. French, Spanish, Beloit Coll., 1947-49; prof. French, dean Milw.-Downer Coll., 1949-52; prof. French, chmn. dept. Romance langs. Skidmore Coll., 1952-58; asso. prof. French, State U. N.Y. at Albany, 1958-66; directrice des cours du premier cycle Williams Coll., 1966—. Vol. relief worker Am. Friends Service Com., Paris, 1946-47. Mem. Am. Assn. U. Women (holder various br. offices), Am. Assn. U. Profs. (chpt. v.p., chmn. com. W), Modern Lang. Assn., Am. Assn. Tchrs. French (past chpt. pres.), Alliance Francaise, Phi Sigma Iota. Mem. Soc. of Friends. Author (with John Savacool) Voix du Siecle, 1960, Voix du Siecle 2, 1966. Home: Arlington VT 05250 Office: Williams Coll Williamstown MA 01267

SMITH, EUNICE YOUNG (MRS. STUYVESANT C. SMITH), illustrator, author; b. LaSalle, Ill., June 10, 1902; d. Arthur Merriman and Katherine (Whitmarsh) Young; student Rosary Coll., 1920, Lakeview Comml. Art Sch., 1921, Ind. U., 1935-36, Acad. Fine Arts Chgo., 1945; m. Stuyvesant Chatteris Smith, June 17, 1927; children—Stuyvesant Chadwick, Sharon Katherine (Mrs. Herbert Kane). Oil paintings, etchings exhibited in univs., libraries and museums throughout U.S. Illustrator: The Children's Treasury, 1947; Merry Songs, 1949; Merry Christmas Book, 1948; Come and Hear, 1952; Fun for Chris, 1956. Author, illustrator: The Jennifer Wish, 1949; Moppet, 1950; The Jennifer Gift, 1950; The Jennifer Prize, 1951; Denny's Story, 1952; Jennifer is Eleven, 1952; Sam's Big Worry, 1953; Jennifer Dances, 1954; The House with the Secret Room, 1956; The Little Red Drum, Le Petit Tambour Rouge, Where From, 1961; Where To, Tillie Turtle, 1964; High Heels For Jennifer, 1964; Shoon, Wild Pony of the Moors, 1965; To Each A Season, 1965; the Knowing One, 1967. Illustrator film strips Soc. Visual Edn., 1961—; contbr. to Humpty Dumpty mag., Ency. Brit.'s Lang. Arts Reading Program. Recipient award for best juvenile Ind. U., 1965. Mem. Authors League Am., Am. Assn. U. Women, Children's Reading Round Table Chgo., Artists Equity, Old Bergen Art Guild, South Bend Art Center. Address: 15026 Dragoon Trail Mishawaka IN 46544

SMITH, EVA BLANCHE, sch. psychologist; b. Rosendale, Wis., Apr. 10, 1914; d. Frank and Anna Augusta (Konow) Smith; B.S., U. Wis. at Oshkosh, 1955, M.S. at Madison, 1965, postgrad. at Milw., 1967-68, U. Colo. at Greely, Nicolet Coll. Tchr. Fremont Sch., Rosendale, 1933-37, Rosendale State Grade Sch., 1937-46, Dodd Sch., Rosendale, 1957-59; principal Alice Callen Elementary Sch., Ripon, Wis., 1949-61; tchr. Oshkosh Pub. Schs., 1961-67; sch. psychologist Cooperative Ednl. Service Agency No. 13, Waupun, Wis., 1967—. Mem. Wis. Sch. Psychologists Assn., Nat. Assn. Sch. Psychologists, Delta Kappa Gamma, Phi Beta Sigma. Republican. Rebekah Pilgrim. Home: LaFayette St Rosendale WI 59474 Office: 908 W Main St Waupun WI 53963

SMITH, FERN MAY, physician; b. East Palermo, N.Y., June 14, 1892; d. Jerome Victor and Ida May (Pickard) Smith; B.S., Syracuse U., 1917; postgrad. Phila. Coll. Osteopathy, 1924-26; D. O., Los Angeles Coll. Osteopathy, 1928; M.D., Cal. Coll. Medicine, 1962; m. Niles H. Steenbergh, Mar. 29, 1919 (div. Feb. 1934); 1 dau., June (Mrs. George Hoyt). High sch. tchr., Berlin, N.Y., 1917-20, 23-25; intern osteo. unit Los Angeles County Gen. Hosp., 1929-30; gen. practice medicine, Huntington Park, Cal., 1932—; mem. staff Los Angeles County-U. So. Cal. Med. Center, 1932—. Home: 2551 Hope St Huntington Park CA 90255 Office: 6308 Pacific Blvd Huntington Park CA 90255

SMITH, FRANCES C., author, editor; b. Washington, Kan., Sept. 6, 1904; d. Henry D. and Marjorie (Whittet) Smith; B.A., U. Kan., 1926; M.A., Columbia, 1936. Tchr., Washington (Kan.) High Sch., 1927-30; staff mem. Columbia, 1931-42; mem. editorial staff Boys' Life mag. Boy Scouts Am., New Brunswick, N.J., 1943-54, asso. editor, 1954-66, now contbg. editor; free-lance writer, 1940—. Trustee Cranbury Pub. Library; bd. dirs. Cranbury Housing Assos. Mem. Soc. Am. Travel Writers, Western Writers Am., Sierra Club. Democrat. Presbyn. Club: Appalachian Mountain (exec. com. N.Y. chpt. 1964). Author: First Book of Conservation, 1954, rev. edit., 1972; Find a Career in Conservation, 1959; First Book of Water, 1960; The World of the Arctic, 1960; Find a Career in Education, 1960; The First Book of Mountains, 1964; Men At Work in Alaska, 1967; First Book of Swamps and Marshes, 1968. Contbr. articles to mags. Address: PO Box 5422 Santa Fe NM 87501

SMITH, FRANCES SNYDER, librarian; b. Niota, Tenn., Feb. 10, 1912; d. Robert H. and Sophia Elizabeth (Brock) Snyder; student Mars Hill Coll., 1931; B.A. in L.S., Our Lady of Lake Coll., San Antonio, 1962; m. Voyle V. Smith, May 25, 1933; children—Sandra (Mrs. James T. Matthews), Voyle Gilbert. Tchr., McMinn County (Tenn.) Schs., 1931-33; library asst. San Antonio Pub. Library, 1957-59, head circulation dept., 1959-61, librarian for bus., sci. and tech., 1961-68, head art, music and films dept., 1968—. Mem. women's com. San Antonio Symphony Soc. Mem. A.L.A., Southwestern, Tex., Bexar library assns., Am. Guild Organists, San Antonio Art League, San Antonio Mus. Assn., Art Libraries Soc. N.Am., D.A.R., Coppini Acad. Fine Art (hon. life), San Antonio River Art Group (hon.). Contbr. articles to profl jours. Home: 2358 W Gramercy St San Antonio TX 78201 Office: 203 S St Mary's St San Antonio TX 78205

SMITH, GAY BEALE, educator, costume designer; b. Fayetteville, N.C., Jan. 24, 1943; d. Richard L. and Loretta E. (Bell) Beale; B.F.A., U. Okla., 1963; M.F.A., So. Meth. U., 1970; m. Williams Ward Smith, June 22, 1963; children—Steven Todd, Catherine Tracy. Costume designer Okla. Civic Ballet, Oklahoma City, 1963-64; tchr. advt. Dallas Coll., 1965; costume designer Theatre III, Dallas, 1965; advt. artist, indsl. designer Freeman, design and display, Dallas, 1967-69; instr. dept. dramatic arts U. Conn. at Storrs, 1970—; artistic dir. Woodstock Playhouse. Gen. Mills scholar, 1960-62. Mem. Am. Theater Assn., Southeastern Theatre Conf. Costume designer play Things Went Badly in Westphalia (Martin Sherman's), Storrs, Conn., 1971, Tommy—A Rock Opera (E. Wolas, D. Heilweil, J. Rojo), Hartford, Conn., 1971, also Going Away (Tom Dulac), Leave of Absence (Stephen Foreman). Home: 44 Hanks Hill Rd Storrs CT 06268 Office: Box 127 U Conn Storrs CT 06268

SMITH, GEORGIA MAXINE ATKINS (MRS. VASCO ALBERT SMITH, JR.), civic worker; b. Memphis, Oct. 31, 1929; d. Joseph P. and Georgia (Rounds) Atkins; A.B., Spelman Coll., 1949; M.A., Middlebury Coll., 1950; m. Vasco Albert Smith, Jr., Sept. 19, 1953; 1 son, Vasco Albert III. Instr. French, Prairie View A. and M. U., 1950-52, Fla. A. and M. U., 1952-53; asst. prof. French, English, LeMoyne Coll., 1955-56; with N.A.A.C.P., Memphis, 1962—, bd. dirs., 1957—, membership chmn., 1958-61, exec. sec., 1962—; mem. Memphis Sch. Bd., 1971—; coordinator Memphis Freedom Movement, 1960-61; dir. Memphis Voter Registration drive, 1963. Bd. dirs. Voter Edn. Project. Recipient Thalheimer award with others Memphis br. N.A.A.C.P., Nat. orgn., Ann. Merit award Memphis br., 1961; Outstanding Citizen award Frontiers Internat., 1970; Distinguished Citizen award Mallory Knights, 1970; plaque Saturday Luncheon Club, 1971; named Woman of Year in Civil Rights YWCA, 1964; named Woman of Action Alpha Kappa Alpha, 1969, plaque outstanding service, 1972; Achievement award Omega Psi Phi, 1961, Outstanding Citizen of Year, 1969; plaque meritorious service Kappa Alpha Psi; Black History Week plaque; numerous others. Home: 1208 E Parkway S Memphis TN 38114 Office: 588 Vance Av Memphis TN 38126

SMITH, GRACE ELIZABETH (MRS. LEONARD V. SMITH), real estate broker; b. Kenosha, Wis., July 30, 1908; d. Edward Nicholas and Clara Belle (Russell) Werve; grad. high sch.; m. Ralph G. Barnes, Feb. 26, 1927 (dec. 1940); children—William J., Diane (Mrs. Gilbert A. Hall), Deborah (Mrs. Norman A. Wickert); m. 2d, Leonard V. Smith, Oct. 28, 1950. Owner, mgr. Grace Barnes Studio, Kenosha, also Racine, Wis., 1936-62; v.p., pub. relations dir. Leonard V. Smith, Inc., Kenosha, 1963-65; owner, real estate broker Old Town Realty, Los Gatos, Cal., 1967—. Pres., mgr. Taxpapers Orgn., Kenosha, 1962-65; membership com. Shrine Aux. for Crippled Children, Kenosha, 1960-65; fund raising chmn. Wis. Heart Assn., 1959-63. Vice chmn. Kenosha County Reps., 1961-63. Mem. Nat. Assn. Real Estate Brokers, Los Gatos (sec., treas. 1971), Saratoga bds. realtors, San Jose Real Estate Bd., Bus. and Profl. Womans Club. Club: Emblem (Los Gatos). Home: 17260 Clara St Los Gatos CA 95030 Office: 233 N Santa Cruz Av Los Gatos CA 95030

SMITH, GRACE HERITAGE (MRS. ERNEST CHARLES SMITH), lawyer; b. Mickleton, N.J., Mar. 26, 1908; d. Howard John and Martha Batten (Kircher) Heritage; A.B., Swarthmore Coll., 1929; J.D., U. Pa., 1932; m. Ernest Charles Smith, Oct. 29, 1932; 1 son, Robert Heritage. Admitted to N.J. bar, 1934; mem. firm French, Richards & Bradley, Camden, N.J., 1939-50, Richards, Capehart, Smith & Wood, Camden, 1950-56; pvt. practice of law, Wenonah, N.J., 1956—. Bd. dirs. Vis. Nurse Assn. of Gloucester County, 1957—, pres. 1970-73; trustee Mullica Hill (N.J.) Friends Sch. Mem. Am., Camden bar assns. Clubs: Gloucester County Nature, Gloucester County Camera (Wenonah, N.J.). Home and office: 5 S Glassboro Rd Wenonah NJ 08090

SMITH, GRETCHEN HART (MRS. SIDNEY WEBER SMITH), club woman; b. Omaha, July 14, 1902; d. George W. and Martha J. (Vogt) Hart; violin student, 1916-27; student U. Omaha, 1921-26; m. Sidney Weber Smith, Mar. 9, 1927. Bd. dirs. Ida. Fedn. Garden Clubs, 1953—, rec. sec. 1955-57, pres., 1957-59, state chmn. flower show schs., 1961, state historian, 1963—; pres. Magic Valley Iris Soc., So. Ida., 1963-64; life mem., dir. Nat. Council State Garden Clubs, 1957-59, 61-63, amateur accredited judge flower shows, 1960; Pacific region chmn. Blue Star Meml. Hwys., 1965-67, 69—; pres. Twin Falls (Ida.) Garden Club, 1957-58, 65-67, 67-68; state chmn. Symposium Advanced Flower Show Sch., 1966, 69, 72; master flower show judge, 1969; accredited judge Am. Iris Soc., 1947—, regional v.p. 1948-50, 72—; regional dir. Am. Hemerocallis Soc., 1952-54, charter mem., 1946—; life accredited flower show judge, 1968; critic Nat. Council Landscape Design, 1968; mem. nominating com. Nat. Council State Garden Clubs, 1967-69, area chmn. calendar com., 1969—, dist. chmn. environmental conservation com., 1970, Pacific regional dir., 1973-75. Mem. Am. Hort. Soc., Am. Rose Soc., Am. Primrose Soc. (accredited judge 1959), Am. Daffodil Soc. (accredited judge), African Violet Soc. Am. (life, accredited judge 1961), Leaf and Petal Club (pres.), Nat. Fedn. Music Clubs (life), Nat. Tulip Soc., Nat. Chrysanthemum Soc., Am. Dahlia Soc., Twin Falls Music Club (pres. 1970). Republican. Episcopalian. Address: Route 2 Twin Falls ID 83301

SMITH, HAZEL LAMBERT (MRS. CLOUD SMITH), civic worker; b. Rulo, Neb., Mar. 12, 1901; d. Elmer R. and B. Belle (Kermoade) Lambert; student U. Neb., 1921-22, Colo. State Coll., 1946; m. Cloud Smith, Aug. 12, 1928. Coordinator adult distributive edn. Lincoln (Neb.) Pub. Schs., 1942-66; promotion, pub. relations Roberts Skyline Dairy, 1968-70; owner-mgr. Newcomer Hostess Service, 1968—. Mem. region II Mayor's Com. on Crime, 1968—; chmn. Mayor's Com. on Internat. Friendship, 1968—; mem. Symphony Guild, 1966—, Lincoln Community Playhouse Bd. Guild, 1968—, Lincoln Artists Guild, 1965-70, Gov.'s Commn. on Status of Women, 1964-70, Lincoln Community Chest, 1969—; life mem., bd. YWCA 1956-62. Bd. dirs., mem. bd. Community Concerts, 1969-70; bd. dirs. Govt. Research Inst., Lincoln Vol. Bur. Mem. Lincoln GOP Club, 1956-70; alternate Republican Nat. Conv., 1956; state Rep. pub. relations, 1958-64. Co-organizer, Lincoln Interclub Council, 1946, pres. 1965. Recipient Missouri Valley Conf. award, 1964. Mem. C. of C. (pres. women's div. 1945-46), Am. (treas.), Neb. (awards 1942, 71) vocational assns., Neb. Art Assn., Ret. Tchrs. Assn. Altrusa Internat. (state organizer 1968, 70; mem. bd. 1969-70), P.E.O., Alpha Delta Pi, Gamma Alpha Chi. Home: 2202 Washington Lincoln NE 68502

SMITH, HELEN BREKKE (MRS. REGINALD A.A. SMITH), civic worker, ret. educator; b. Ballard, Wash., Mar. 7, 1907; d. Lars Olesen and Kristianne Marie (Fosnes) Brekke; A.B., Whitman Coll., 1927; student summers McGill U. French Sch., 1931, U. Cal., 1936, U. Wash., 1932, 37, 49, Mills Coll., 1943; m. Reginald A.A. Smith, Dec. 18, 1949; children—Jean (Mrs. Michael A. Thornsbury), Dale Reginald Ian. Tchr. high schs., Roslyn, Wash., 1927-29, Grangeville, Ida., 1929-30, Longview, Wash., 1930-46, 47-49; mem. faculty Ruston Acad., Havana, Cuba, 1946-47; substitute tchr. Cowlitz County, Wash., 1950-70. Pres. Evergreen area council Girl Scout U.S.A., 1948-50, Longview Garden Club, 1955-56, Badoura Club of Daus. of Nile, 1964-65; chmn. Cowlitz County Jr. chpt. A.R.C., 1954-58, S.W. Wash. Anti-Litter Com., 1969-72; sec. Cowlitz-Wahkiakum Tb Assn., 1968-71; chmn. fgn. relations Longview Aux. Am. Legion, 1957-74; adv. council S.W. Wash. Lung Assn., 1973-74. Vice pres. Cowlitz County Republican Women, 1969-74. Mem. S.W. Wash. bd. Children's Home Soc. Wash., 1956-61; trustee Longview Pub. Library, 1960-70; bd. dirs. Cowlitz County United Fund, 1958-61. Recipient Longview Distinguished Service award '23 Club, 1968, 100-hour award for vol. work VA Hosp., Vancouver, Wash. Mem. Am. Assn. U. Women (pres. Cowlitz County br. 1942-43; grant named for her by Cowlitz County br. 1970), Delta Kappa Gamma (pres. Chi chpt. 1966-68). Club: Longview Woman's (trustee 1969-71, conservation chmn. 1972-74). Home: 1521 22d Av Longview WA 98632

SMITH, HELEN CATHARINE, author; b. Chgo., June 7, 1903; d. J. A.; B.A., U. Cal. at Los Angeles, 1926; postgrad. U. Wis., 1954-56; M.Sc., Christian Coll., 1962, Ph.D., 1965, Psy.D., 1966; Ph.D. (hon.) Free U., hon. doctorate Gt. China Arts Coll., 1969, St. Olav's Acad., Sweden, 1969, Internat. Acad. Soverign Order Alfred Gt., Eng., 1969; J.D., Ohio Christian Coll., 1969; m. H. C. Smith, June 7, 1932; children—Glen Dean, DeEtta Ellen (Mrs. Gerald L. Amdahl), George Dale. Tchr. 2d grade Maple Lawn Sch., Clinton, Wis.; legal sec., Janesville, Wis., Office of City Atty. Evansville, Wis., 1933—; v.p., dir. Blue Moon poetry mag., 1952-57. Recipient 1st pl. award for article Herdman Meml. Competition Brit. Press, 1957; John Francis Sims Meml. award for poetry, 1955; award of honor UN Day, Philippines, 1967; laurel wreath, gold medal Pres. Philippines, 1967; certificate recognition Nat. Poetry Day Com., 1972; named Hon. Poet Laureate (Am.-Visayan), 1967. Fellow Intercontinental Biog. Assn.; mem. Am. Assn. U. Women (awards poetry, short stories 1972), Wis. Regional Writers Assn. (sec. 1949-55, 61—, hon. life dir., leadership citation 1956, Jade Ring winner for short story 1957), Nat. League Am. Pen Women, Am. Poetry League, Wis. Fellowship Poets, Wis. Acad. Scis. Arts and Letters, Brit. Press Assn., United Poets Laureate Internat. (Karta award), Council for Wis. Writers (life), Centro Studie Scambi Internazionali Roma (medal of honor 1966-67, internat. exec. bd.), Wis. Edn. Assn., Wis. Regional Artists, state Hist. Soc. Wis., Accademia Internazionale Leonardo Da Vinci (Rome, Gold medallion 1972), Accademia Internazionale Di Pontzen, Am. Lit. Assn. (life), World Poetry Soc. (hon. life), UN Assn., Phi Beta Kappa (sustaining), Alpha Psi Omega, Sigma Iota Xi. Author: Laughing Child, books I, II, III, 1945, 46, 47; Off the Record, 1949; From the Countryside, 1952; Stars in My Eyes, 1954; Wind-Falls, 1955; Chiaroscura, 1964; But Not Yet, 1973; You Can't Cry All the Time, 1974. Editor: Evansville Anthology of Verse, 1952, No. Spring, anthology, 1956; Chiaroscura, 1964. Contbr. articles, stories to numerous mags., newspapers, anthologies. Home: 409 Lincoln St Evansville WI 53536 Office: 14 W Main St Evansville WI 53536

SMITH, HELEN LOUISE, educator, med. technologist, bacteriologist; b. Berea, Ky., Sept. 15, 1930; d. Jeff Frank and Martha (Dean) Smith; student Christian Coll., 1947-48; B.S. in Med. Tech. with high distinction, U. Ky., 1951; M.Ed., U. Cin., 1973. Bacteriologist, supervising med. tech. Owensboro (Ky.) Daviess County Hosp., 1951-61; hosp. bacteriologist Cin. Gen. Hosp., 1961-67, med. tech. ednl. coordinator, after 1967, now program dir. Sch. Med. Tech. U. Cin. Med. Center; instr. lab. medicine U. Cin. Coll. Medicine. Recipient Am. Legion Citizenship medal; named Ky. col. Mem. Am., Ohio, Dist. 8 socs. med. tech., Soc. Med. Technologists (dist. pres.-elect 1969-70), Am. Soc. Microbiologists, South Central Assn. Clin. Microbiologists, U. Ky. Alumnae Assn., Am. Assn. U. Women, Phi Beta Kappa, Phi Theta Kappa. Republican. Baptist (deaconess 1967-70). Clubs: Pilot (pres. Cin. 1966-67), University Cincinnati Woman's. Home: 7240 Reading Rd Cincinnati OH 45237 Office: 234 Goodman Av Cincinnati OH 45229

SMITH, HENRIETTA TAMAR, educator; b. Huntsville, Ala., Dec. 9, 1925; d. Clifton Conway and Inez (Townsend) Smith; B.A., U. Cin., 1946, M.A., 1948; Ph.D., Radcliffe Coll, 1953. Instr. psychology Allen U., Columbia, S.C., 1947-49, 53-54; instr. Vassar Coll., Poughkeepsie, N.Y., 1954-59, asst. prof., 1959-63, asso. prof., 1963-68, prof. psychology, 1968—. Mem. Am., Eastern psychol. assns., Soc. Research in Child Devel., Am. Assn. U. Profs., A.A.A.S., N.Y. Acad. Scis. Home: 6 Vassar Lake Dr Poughkeepsie NY 12601

SMITH, INNES ADAMS COMER (MRS. EDWARD SAMUEL SMITH), civic worker; b. Birmingham, Ala., May 10, 1920; d. Robert Thornton and May (Adams) Comer; student Birmingham So. Coll., 1937-38; A.B., Randolph-Macon Womans Coll., 1940; m. Edward Samuel Smith, May 5, 1942; children—Edward Samuel, Innes Comer (Mrs. George C. Cameron). Proof clk. First Nat. Bank, 1940-41; proof trainer Birmingham Trust Nat. Bank, 1941-43; censor U.S. Postal Censorship, 1943; receptionist Textron, Inc., 1943-44; teller Union Trust Co., 1961-62; new accounts clk. Chevy Chase br. Nat. Bank Washington, 1962-64; exec. v.p., dir. Logical Products, Inc., Balt., 1968—. Active vol. work hosps., Birmingham, Washington and Balt., various fund drives; leader Cub Scouts, Boy Scouts Am., 1952-55. Mem. Jr. League Washington (finance bd. 1956-57; dir. 1957-58), Jr. League Balt., Nat. Soc. Colonial Dames Am. in Md., Nat. Soc. Daus. Barons of Runnymede, Descs. of Lords of Md. Manors, Order of Crown in Am., Nat. Soc. Daus. Am. Revolution, Kappa Delta. Democrat. Episcopalian. Clubs: Homesteaders Garden, Colonial Dames (Washington). Home: 101 Longwood Rd Baltimore MD 21210 Office: PO Box 5654 Baltimore MD 21210

SMITH, IOLA RAGINS (MRS. JAMES ALEXANDER SMITH), ednl. psychologist; b. Phila.; d. Edward and Callie (Watkins) Ragins; B.A., Pa. State U., 1956; M.A., Am. U., 1960; Ph.D., Cath. U. Am., 1966; m. James Alexander Smith, Sept. 1, 1956; children—Staci Gabrielle, Shanon Gervaise. Lectr., Cath. U. Am., 1963-67; asso. prof. edn. Morgan State Coll., Balt., 1966-69, prof. edn., 1969—, acting chmn. dept., 1972—. Lectr., Howard U., 1969—; cons., evaluation in-service tchr. workshop on desegregation Washington Pub. Schs., 1967; cons. workshop on sch. desegregation U. Md., 1967; cons. spl. planning Inst. for Center on Urban Studies, Morgan State Coll., 1968, Calvert County (Md.) Pub. Schs., 1969. Recipient Distinguished Tchr. of Year award Morgan State Coll., 1969. Mem. League Women's Voters, Citizens' Planning and Housing Assn., Delta Sigma Theta, Pi Lambda Theta, Pi Gamma Mu, Phi Sigma Iota. Co-editor: Educational Psychology and Teaching, 1968—. Contbr. articles to profl. publs. Home: 11216 Green Dragon Ct Hobbits Glen Columbia MD 21043 Office: Morgan State Coll Coldspring Lane and Hillen Rd Baltimore MD 21212

SMITH, JANE HARDESTER (MRS. GEORGE L. SMITH), city ofcl.; b. Balt., Nov. 28, 1905; d. Harry G. and Amy M. (Hamilton) Hardester; student Taylor Bus. Sch., 1926; m. George L. Smith, June 11, 1937; 1 dau., Amanda L. Sec., N.Y. Shipbuilding Co., Camden, N.J., 1926-28, Warner Co., Phila., 1928-42; adminstr. Borough of Lititz, Pa., 1960—. Home: 449 S Broad St Lititz PA 17543 Office: 7 S Broad St Lititz PA 17543

SMITH, JANICE M(INERVA), educator; b. Osco, Ill., Oct. 13, 1906; d. Jared Heber and Minnie May (Hadley) S.; A.B., U. Ill., 1930, M.S., 1932, Ph.D., 1937. Research asst. U. Ill., 1932-34, 36-37, prof. nutrition, 1944—, acting head dept. home econs., 1949-50, head, 1950-71; asst. and asso. prof. human nutrition research Pa. State Coll., 1937-43; nutritionist War Food Adminstrn., U.S. Dept. Agr., Washington, 1943-44. Mem. Nat. Adv. Commn. on Food and Fiber, 1965-67. Fellow A.A.A.S.; mem. Am. Home Econs. Assn., Am. Dietetic Assn., Am. Inst. Nutrition, N.Y. Acad. Scis., Phi Beta Kappa, Sigma Xi, Phi Kappa Phi, Omicron Nu, Phi Upsilon Omicron, Sigma Delta Epsilon, Iota Sigma Pi, Phi Sigma. Home: 1112 S Pine St Champaign IL 61820 Office: Bevier Hall U Ill Urbana IL 61801

SMITH, JEAN CAROL BECHTOLD (MRS. BARRY F. SMITH), physician; b. Laurel, Md., Oct. 25, 1930; d. Charles A. and Jennie (Johannesen) Bechtold; B.S., U. Md., 1952, M.D., 1954. Intern Queens Gen. Hosp., N.Y.C., 1954-55; resident ophthalmology N.Y.U., Bellevue Med. Center, N.Y.C., 1955-59; practice medicine specializing in ophthalmology, N.Y.C., 1962—; dir. Pediatric Eye Clinic, Bellevue Hosp., N.Y.C., 1966—; asst. clin. prof. ophthalmology, N.Y.U., 1968—; cons. ophthalmologist Dept. Health, N.Y.C., 1962—, Vacation Camp for Blind, N.Y.C. Diplomate Am. Bd. Ophthalmology. Mem. A.M.A., N.Y. County Med. Soc., Am. Acad. Ophthalmology and Otolaryngology. Home: 175 E 62d St New York City NY 10021 Office: 521 Park Av New York City NY 10021

SMITH, JEAN CHANDLER, librarian; b. Phila., Apr. 13, 1918; d. Chandler White and Philena P. (Cheetham) S.; A.B., Bryn Mawr Coll., 1939; M.S., Yale, 1953. Circulation, reference librarian D.C. Pub. Library, 1939-43; translator U.S. Office Censorship, Panama, C.Z., 1943-44; librarian Kaneohe (Hawaii) Naval Air Sta., 1944-46; reference asst., asst. reference librarian, research asst. Yale Library, 1947-58; reference librarian in biol. scis., acting chief acquisitions sect. NIH Library, Bethesda, 1959-63; chief reference services dept. library Dept. Interior, Washington, 1963-65; asst. dir. libraries Smithsonian Instn., 1965-68, spl. asst. to dir. libraries, 1968-72, asst. dir. libraries for bur. services, 1972—. Guest investigator Osborn Meml. Lab.,

Yale, 1953-57. Mem. Spl. Libraries Assn. (treas. D.C. chpt. 1966—, nat. sec.-treas. natural resources div., 2d v.p. Washington chpt.), Conn. Acad. Arts and Scis., Am. Soc. Limnology and Oceanography, Bibliog. Soc. Am., Am. Soc. Information Scis. Home: 3601 Connecticut Av NW Washington DC 20008 Office: Smithsonian Instn Washington DC 20560

SMITH, JEAN HARCOURT, psychologist; b. Milroy, Ind., Sept. 3, 1921; d. James Roy and Ila Mildred (Hite) Harcourt; B.S., Ball State U., 1943, M.A., 1952; postgrad., Whittier Coll., 1962-64, Los Angeles State U., 1962, U. Cal. at Los Angeles, 1964-67, Pepperdine Coll., 1966-67, U. So. Cal., 1968-70; m. Robert Leroy Smith, Oct. 4, 1942 (dec. Jan. 1974); 1 son, Robert Stephen. Tchr., Harrison Twp., Ind., 1943-44, Yorktown (Ind.) High Sch., 1944-45, Muncie (Ind.) City Schs., 1951-60, East Whittier (Cal.) Sch. Dist., 1961-67; psychometrist Ocean View Sch. Dist., Cal., 1967-68; psychologist Orange Unified Sch. Dist., Cal., 1968—. Individual practice pvt. and family counseling, psycho-diagnostic testing, 1971—. Mem. Laguna Beach Festival of Arts, Laguna Beach Moulton Playhouse. Bd. dirs. Thompson Clinic for Ednl. Therapy, Newport Beach, Cal., Eastern Los Angeles County Coordinating Council. Mem. Nat., Cal. assns. sch. psychologists, Cal. Assn. Sch. Psychologists and Psychometrists, Am., Cal., Orange County psychol. assns., Orange County Assn. Ednl. Psychologists, Council for Exceptional Children, Cal. Marriage, Family and Child Counseling, Nat. Alliance Family Life, Harbor Clin. and Exptl. Hypnosis Soc., Am. Assn. Marriage and Family Counselors, Laguna Beach Hist. Soc., Beta Sigma Pi, Pi Lambda Theta, Sigma Kappa. Mem. Order Eastern Star. Home: 3125 Alta Laguna Blvd Laguna Beach CA 92651 Office: 17341 Irvine Blvd Suite 205 Tustin CA 92680

SMITH, JEAN WEBB (MRS. WILLIAM FRENCH SMITH), civic worker; b. Los Angeles; d. James Ellwood and Violet (Hughes) Webb; B.A. summa cum laude, Stanford, 1940; m. George William Vaughan, Mar. 14, 1942 (dec. Sept. 1963); children—George William, Merry; m. 2d, William French Smith, Nov. 6, 1964. Mem. Nat. Council Vol. Service (ACTION), 1973—, vice chmn., 1974. Bd. dirs. vol. bur. Mental Health Devel. Commn. Los Angeles, 1966-69; bd. dirs., mem. exec. com. Los Angeles chpt. A.R.C., 1965—; mem. Cal. Arts Commn., 1971—, vice chmn., 1973—; bd. dirs. The Founders, Music Center, Los Angeles, costume council Los Angeles County Mus. Art, 1971-73, United Way, Inc., 1973—; trustee Cal. Hist. Soc., 1970-71, Hosp. Good Samaritan, 1973—. Named Woman of the Year for Community Service, Los Angeles Times, 1958. Mem. Jr. League of Los Angeles (pres. 1954-55), Assn. Jr. Leagues of Am. (dir. Region XII, 1956-58, pres. 1958-60), Phi Beta Kappa, Kappa Kappa Gamma. Home: 1256 Oak Grove Av San Marino CA 91108

SMITH, JEANETTE MARIE (MRS. KENNETH L. SMITH), state ofcl.; b. nr. Peoria, Ill., Aug. 13, 1930; d. Alfred George and Marie G. (Gangloff) Rohman; grad. Metamora High Sch., 1948; m. Kenneth L. Smith, June 4, 1949; children—Susan K., Cathleen D., Carol L. Mem. office staff Hart Carter Mfg. Co., Peoria, Ill., 1948-49; office clk. Ill. Dept. Conservation, Metamora, 1963—. Bd. dirs. Salvation Army, Metamora, chmn., 1971—. Mem. Woodford County Hist. Soc., Woodford County Old Settlers Assn., St. Marys Altar and Rosary Soc., Am. Legion Aux. Home: 303 N Hanover Metamora IL 61548 Office: 113 E Partridge Metamora IL 61548

SMITH, JOAN, occupational therapist; b. Bklyn., Feb. 9, 1944; d. Max and Bella (Nussbaum) Smith; B.A. cum laude, Bklyn. Coll., 1965; B.R.E. summa cum laude Yeshiva U., 1965; certificate occupational therapy Columbia, 1967; M.A., N.Y. U., 1973. Staff occupational therapist, dept. rehab. medicine Downstate Med. Center, Bklyn., 1967-71, acting supr. occupational therapy, 1969; chief occupational therapy Bklyn. VA Hosp., 1971—. Recipient N.Y. State Regents scholarship, 1961. Mem. Am., N.Y. State (vice chmn. Met. N.Y. dist. 1969-71) occupational therapy assns., World Fedn. Occupational Therapy. Office: 800 Poly Pl Brooklyn NY 11209

SMITH, JOSEPHINE ANN GIADONE (MRS. ROBERT MCDONALD SMITH), automobile dealer exec.; b. Pueblo, Colo., Oct. 5, 1931; d. Carl P. and Pauline M. (Plutt) Giadone; student Midwest Bus. Coll., 1948-49; m. Robert McDonald Smith, Dec. 29, 1956; children—Patty (Mrs. Larry E. Minkler), Carl Robert, Tina Marie. Service sec. Colo. Motor Car Co., 1949-51, deal clk., 1951-54, bookkeeper, 1954-56, asst. office mgr., 1954-56; bookkeeper Hurd Pontiac, Pueblo, 1962-65, sec., office mgr., 1965—; office mgr. L.J. Pontiac Motor Co., 1971—. Sec.-treas. South Pine Dr. Water Assn., 1973. Precinct chairwoman Beulah Democratic Com., 1970—. Mem. Beulah C. of C. (dir. 1970-72), Pontiac Honor Accountants. Clubs: Citizens Radio (sec. 1970-71) (Pueblo); Junior Rifle (dir. 1969-72), Senior Rifle (Beulah, Colo.). Home: Route 1 Box 77A Beulah CO 81023 Office: 222 W 7th St Pueblo CO 81003

SMITH, JUDITH BEATRICE LEON (MRS. SCOTT MURRAY SMITH), occupational therapist; b. Austin, Tex., Mar. 6, 1929; d. Harry Joshua and Ernestine (Franklin) Leon; B.S. in Child Devel., U. Tex., 1949; B.S. in Occupational Therapy, Tex. State Coll. for Women, 1951; M.Ed., Our Lady of Lake Coll., 1967; m. Scott Murray Smith, Dec. 27, 1963; children (of previous marriage)—Paul Marvin Garner, David Leon Garner. Nursery sch. tchr. Dallas Day Nurseries, 1949-50; occupational therapist supr. VA Hosp., Tuscaloosa, Ala., 1952-54, Tb sect. VA Center, Temple, Tex., 1954-55; occupational therapist children's unit Norman (Okla.) State Hosp., 1955-56; psychiat. occupational therapy supr. VA Hosp., Oklahoma City, 1956-57; occupational therapist Austin (Tex.) State Hosp., 1957-58, Austin Cerebral Center, 1958-59; tchr. Centro Colombo Americana, Manizales, Colombia, 1959-61; dir. rehab. therapy Confederate Home, Austin, 1961-63; occupational therapy dir. San Antonio State Hosp., 1963-66; spl. edn. tchr. Harlandale Ind. Sch. Dist., San Antonio, 1967-69; vocational adjustment coordinator Stinson Vocational High Sch., San Antonio, 1969-70; spl. edn. counsel Cluster 4 Pupil Appraisal Center, San Antonio, 1970-72, asso. sch. psychologist, 1972—. Cons. occupational therapy Mission Rd. Found., San Antonio, 1972-74. Am. Occupational Therapy Assn. grantee, 1966. Mem. Am., Tex. (publicity chmn. south central dist. 1964-66) occupational therapy assns., Council Adminstrs. Spl. Edn. No. 4 (treas. 1973-74), Tex. State Tchrs. Assn., Harlandale Adminstrs. Assn., Assn. for Children with Learning Disabilities (sec. San Antonio br. 1974, 3d v.p. 1974—), Council for Exceptional Children, Half-Way House Aux. Home: 1440 Greer San Antonio TX 78210 Office: 902 March Av San Antonio TX 78214

SMITH, JULETTA MARY MATHERN (MRS. WARREN FREDRICK SMITH), banker; b. Kintyre, N.D., Apr. 16, 1934; d. Ludwig and Katherina (Welder) Mathern; grad. high sch.; m. Warren Fredrick Smith, Apr. 27, 1957; 1 dau., Catherine Onalee. With First Nat. Bank of Aberdeen (S.D.), 1952-56, Internal Revenue Service, U.S. Treasury Dept., 1957; stenographic supr. dist. office Internat. Harvester Co., Aberdeen, 1957-61; advt. sec. Dakota Farmer mag., Aberdeen, 1961-63; gen. clk. Bur. Indian Affairs, U.S. Dept. of Interior, Aberdeen, 1963-69; v.p., dir. First State Bank of Sharon (N.D.), 1969—. Past sec. St. Ann's Soc. Cath. Daus., Aberdeen. Recipient Superior Performance award U.S. Dept. of Interior, 1969. Mem. Sharon Hist. Soc., Epsilon Sigma Alpha (past pres.). Clubs: Esquire, Sharon Hill 'N Dale, Trionion Commercial (sec. 1951-52), Extension. Home: PO Box 66 Sharon ND 58227 Office: First State Bank of Sharon Sharon ND 58277

SMITH, JULIA BOWER (MRS. ROBERT BARR SMITH), lawyer; b. Anderson, Ind., June 5, 1930; d. James Arthur and Mary Magdalene (Risser) Bower; student DePauw U., 1947-48; A.B., W.Va. U., 1951, LL.B., 1953; m. Robert Barr Smith, Dec. 20, 1952; children—Leslie, Natalie, Melanie. Admitted to W.Va. bar, 1954; practice law, Grantsville, W.Va., 1954-62; trial atty. Fed. Power Commn., Washington, 1962-64; regional counsel Small Bus. Adminstrn., Washington, 1964-70, atty. central office, 1970—. Commr. in chancery W.Va. 5th Jud. Dist., 1955-62. Republican candidate W.Va. legislature, 1956. Mem. W.Va. State Bar (grievance com. 1960-62), W.Va. State Soc. D.C., Delta Gamma. Episcopalian. Home: 3017 Sylvan Dr Falls Church VA 22042 Office: 1441 L St NW Washington DC 20416

SMITH, JULIETTE SUMMERVILLE (MRS. GREGORY ROBERT SMITH), coll. librarian; b. Jacksonville, Ala., Nov. 28, 1940; d. James Theodore and Rosa (Ogletree) Summerville; B.S., Ala. State U., 1961; postgrad. U. Minn., 1966-67; M.S., Atlanta U., 1967; m. Gregory Robert Smith, Feb. 6, 1967. Tchr., librarian Boteler High Sch., Holt, Ala., 1961-66; librarian Talladega (Ala.) Coll., 1967—. Mem. adv. bd. Co-op. Coll. Library Center, Atlanta, 1970—, mem. common selection system 1972—. NSF fellow, 1966-67. Recipient Student Senate award of excellence in teaching Talladega Coll., 1973. Mem. Am., Ala. library assns., Alpha Kappa Mu, Delta Sigma Theta. Home: 812 W Battle St Talladega AL 35160

SMITH, KAREN LYNNE (MRS. DAVID L. SMITH), sch. dir.; b. Milw., Dec. 27, 1943; d. Hugo Arthur and Ruby (Tiegs) Rosseisen; B.S., U. Wis. at Milw., 1967; postgrad. U. Va., 1968; m. David Lee Smith, Sept. 3, 1966; 1 son, Stephen Scott. Youth worker, Luth. Ch. Am., Phila., 1962, 63; dir. Muriel Humphrey Sch., Woodbridge, Va., 1967—; exec. dir. Eastern Prince William Assn. for Retarded Children, Woodbridge, 1968—. Dir. Adult Activity Center, admissions and policy bds. No. Va. Tng. Center, Fairfax, 1972—; mem. adv. com. spl. edn. Prince William County Sch. Bd., 1972-73; mem. Prince William County Drug Council, 1971; mem. spl. ministry to handicapped bd. Va. Council Chs., 1972—. Recipient Outstanding Young Educator award Woodbridge Jr. C. of C., 1972, Civitan award, 1972. Mem. Am. Assn. Mental Deficiency. Lutheran. Home: 13010 Colby Dr Woodbridge VA 22191 Office: PO Box 52 Woodbridge VA 22191

SMITH, KATHERINE ANNE DILLON (MRS. LEROY F. SMITH), artist, craftsman; b. Drummond, Mont., July 5, 1914; d. John B. and Mary C. (Morris) Dillon; student Archie Bray Found., Helena, Mont., 1957-58, U. Mont., 1962-63, Famous Artists Sch., Westport, Conn., 1964-65; pvt. study with Harriet Tidball, Polly Yori, 1959-65; m. LeRoy F. Smith, May 30, 1945; children—John T. Harrington, Rodney, Nancy Katherine (Mrs. Steven J. Greytak). One-man shows in Butte, Missoula, Gt. Falls; exhibited pottery, sculpture, weaving, and water colors in shows at Henry Gallery, Seattle, Russell Gallery, Gt. Falls, Mont., Senate Chambers, Washington, Nat. Art Roundup, Las Vegas, Balt. Mus. Fine Arts, Contemporary Crafts Mus., Portland, Ore., Mus. Comtemporary Crafts, N.Y.C.; represented in permanent collections Mont. Inst. Arts, State Hist. Mus., Helena. Co-founder, chmn. bd. Hilltop Gallery, Butte, Mont., 1960-62; state chmn. fine arts Mont. Inst. Arts, 1964-65, state chmn. crafts 1964-65; vol. tchr. crafts to tchrs. of handicapped children, Missoula, 1962-63; chmn. visual arts for festival City of Missoula, 1972; dir. coordinator Missoula Festival Arts, 1972-73. Pres. Missoula Area Arts Council, 1973. Bd. dirs. Mont. Inst. Arts. Recipient Kahrouba award N.W. Craftsman Show, 1958; Nat. Merit award Mus. Contemporary Crafts, 1966. Mem. Am. Craftsman Council (state rep. 1964-65). Home: 2121 39th St Missoula MT 59801 also 10420 Pineaire Dr Sun City AZ 85351

SMITH, KATHERINE SCHMITTOU (MRS. JOHN CLEMONS SMITH), assn. exec.; b. Memphis; d. Suall and Iva Lou (Spears) Schmittou; ed. Memphis State U., 1937-41; m. John Clemons Smith, Aug. 10, 1949. Mem. staff Ariz. Republic, Phoenix, 1955-57; exec. sec., mgr. Ariz. Newspapers Assn., Phoenix, 1957—. Named Advt. Woman of Yr., Phoenix Advt. Club, 1970. Mem. Internat. Newspaper Promotion Assn., Am. Soc. Assn. Execs., Newspaper Assn. Mgrs. (pres. 1973-74), Phoenix Advt. Club, Ariz. Soc. Assn. Execs., Ariz. Press Women, Women in Communications (pres. Phoenix chpt. 1964-66). Phoenix Press Club. Office: 3443 N Central Av Suite 611 Phoenix AZ 85012

SMITH, KATHLEEN, psychiatrist; b. Fayetteville, Ark., Oct. 9, 1922; d. Carl Anton and Maryann (Henderson) Smith; B.S., U. Ark., 1944; M.D., Washington U., St. Louis, 1949. Intern, St. Louis City Hosp., 1949-50; resident psychiatry Barnes, McMillan, Malcolm Bliss Psychiat. hosps., St. Louis, 1950-53; practice medicine specializing in psychiatry, St. Louis, 1953—; mem. staff Malcolm Bliss Mental Health Center, supt., 1964—; prof. psychiatry Washington U. Sch. Medicine, St. Louis, 1972—. USPHS research fellow in psychiatry, dept. neuropsychiatry Washington U., St. Louis, 1952-53. Mem. Am., Eastern Mo. psychiat. assns., Am. Assn. Suicidology, A.M.A., A.A.A.S., Am. Schizophrenic Found. Contbr. articles to profl. jours. Home: 1161 S McKnight St Richmond Heights MO 63017 Office: 1420 Grattan St St Louis MO 63004

SMITH, KATHLEEN LOMAX BLAND (MRS. JAMES WESLEY SMITH), editor; b. Orange, Tex., July 9, 1925; d. David Clarence and Kathleen (Lomax) Bland; B.A., U. Tex., 1945; M.J., Columbia, 1946; m. James Wesley Smith, Sept. 20, 1947; children—Michael Bland, Christopher John, Philip David. Copywriter radio sta. KTBC, Austin, summers 1943-44; reporter The Houston Post, 1946-52; news editor The Pasadena (Tex.) Citizen, 1961; instr. English, San Jacinto (Tex.) Jr. Coll., 1962-63; instr. journalism San Jacinto Coll., 1963-64, head journalism dept., 1964-67, head div. publs., 1967-72; asst. prof. journalism Point Park Coll., Pitts., 1972-73; editor PPG Products, PPG Industries, Pitts., 1973—. Mem. Mortar Bd., Phi Beta Kappa, Alpha Lambda Delta, Theta Sigma Phi, Pi Delta Phi, Chi Omega. Home: 836 Florida Av Pittsburgh PA 15228 Office: Pub Relations PPG Industries One Gateway Center Pittsburgh PA 15222

SMITH, LAURA IRENE IVORY (MRS. GORDON HEDDERLY SMITH), missionary, author; b. Dalrymple, Ont., Can., Sept. 28, 1902; d. George Washington and Agnes (Plewes) Ivory; diploma Toronto Bible Coll., 1923; student Moody Bible Inst., 1924-25; m. Gordon Hedderly Smith, June 12, 1928; children—Douglas Hedderly, Leslie Gordon, Stanley Earl. Came to U.S., 1923, naturalized, 1966. Missionary to Indochina (now Cambodia and Vietnam), Christian and Missionary Alliance, N.Y.C., 1928-55, World-Wide Evangelization Crusade, Ft. Washington, Pa., 1958-67, United World Mission, St. Petersburg, Fla., 1968—. Author, illustrator: Mawal, Jungle Boy, 1944; E-Mil, A Raday Boy, 1945; Light in the Jungle, 1945; Gongs in the Night, 1944; Farther into the Night, 1954; Victory in Viet Nam, 1964. Home: United World Mission Box 8000 St Petersburg FL 33738

SMITH, LAURA KIMBALL, educator; b. Palo Alto, Cal., Oct. 19, 1923; d. William Sheperd and Ruth Aileen (Brown) Smith; B.A., San Jose State Coll., 1945; postgrad. Stanford, 1945-46; Ph.D., Baylor U. Coll. of Medicine, 1967. Staff phys. therapist Los Angeles County Hosps., 1946-47, N.Y. State Rehab. Hosp., West Haverstraw, 1948; instr. phys. therapy Stanford (Cal.), 1949-52; dir. phys. therapy Tex. Inst. Rehab. and Research, Houston, 1959-67; clin. instr. Baylor U. Coll. of Medicine, Houston, 1957-62; asso. prof. phys. therapy Tex. Woman's Univ., Houston, 1965—. Mem. health professions adv. com. Houston Community Coll.; mem. med. adv. com. Cerebral Palsy Treatment Center. Nat. Found. Research fellow, 1961-64, NIH fellow, 1965. Fellow A.A.A.S.; mem. Am. Phys. Therapy Assn. (v.p. research sect. 1965-67, sec. edn. sect. 1969-73), Sigma Xi. Contbr. to Treatment of Acute Poliomyelitis, 1954; Correlation of Physiology and Therapeutic Exercise, 1956; Motor Integration, 1962. Contbr. articles on phys. therapy to profl. jours. Home: 10045 Lazy Oaks Dr Houston TX 77055 Office: 1130 MD Anderson Blvd Houston TX 77025

SMITH, LOIS LYNETTE (MRS. DONALD WILLIAM SMITH), newspaper editor; b. Bon Ami, La., Aug. 5, 1919; d. Samuel Martin and Annie Laura (Phifer) Sexton; student Agnes Scott Coll., 1936-38; m. Donald William Smith, July 6, 1943; children—Samuel Martin, Beatrice Annette, Louisa Lucille. Free lance writer Charlotte (N.C.) Observer, 1939-69, Gastonia (N.C.) Gazette, 1939-70, Gaston Citizen, 1956-58; editor Bessemer City (N.C.) Record, 1959—. Leader, Girl Scouts U.S.A., Bessemer, 1940-42; chmn., dir. Christmas Parade, Bessemer, 1964. Named N.C. Handicapped Worker of Year, N.C. Gov.'s Com. Hire the Handicapped, 1967. Mem. N.C. Press Assn., N.C. Press Women, D.A.R. Presbyn. (pres. women of ch. 1955-56, historian, 1962—). Club: Bessemer City Womans (pres. 1957-58). Address: 211 W Washington Av Bessemer City NC 28016

SMITH, LOUISE KOHL, artist; b. Jersey City, Sept. 5, 1922; d. Henry and Lavenia B. (Yale) Kohl; grad. Finch Jr. Coll., 1942; m. Arthur William Nelson, Aug. 26, 1944 (div. Aug. 1951); 1 dau., Lavenia Yale (Mrs. Guy Bentley Meeker, Sr.); m. 2d, Lloyd Victor Smith, Feb. 14, 1953 (div. Dec. 1960); 1 dau., Lucinda Rockwood; One man shows at Stead Air Force Library, Reno, 1963, Washoe Med. Center, 1963, 64, Colonial Title & Loan, Reno, 1964, Continental Restaurant, Reno, 1964-65, 68; exhibited in two-man show at Reno Art Gallery, 1963; group shows include Dade County Ann. Jr. Art Show, West Palm Beach, Fla., 1937, Chautauqua (N.Y.) Art Gallery, 1961, 62, 63, Sonora Regional Art Show, 1963, 20th Century Club, Reno, 1963, Nev. Mus., Carson City, 1963. Active Girl Scouts U.S.A., 1942-44, founder troops, 1962-64; Red Cross nurse's aid, 1951-64; active A.R.C., Cancer Fund, United Fund, St. Mary's Hosp. Guild, Washoe Med. Center Women's League, Civil Def.; state dir. Women's Activities, 1960-64; chmn. Washoe Med Center Women's League Ann. Tombola, 1957-59, league pres., 1961-62; state chmn. Nat. Cathedral Sch. for Girls, 1972-73. founder Henry Kohl Meml. Chapel Washoe Med. Center, 1964. Recipient 2d award Dade County Art Show, 1937, 2d award 20th Century Club, Reno, 1963. Mem. Nat. League Am. Pen Woman Nat. Soc. Arts and Letters (life), Nat. Cathedral Assn. (Nev. regional chmn.), Chautauqua Art Assn., Pacific Internat. Trap Assn. (life), Nat. Skeet Shooting Assn. (life), Amateur Trapshooting Assn. (life)., Nat. Assn. Underwater Instrs. Republican. Episcopalian. Club: Phoenix Emblem. Address: 91 Mountain Shadows West Scottsdale AZ 85252

SMITH, LOUISE MCEWEN (MRS. HERMAN H. SMITH), lumber co. exec.; b. Asheville, N.C., Oct. 24, 1907; d. Wooster Baird and Caroline (Nickols) McEwen; student Randolph-Macon Woman's Coll., 1926-28; m. Herman H. Smith, Oct. 24, 1928; children—Linda McEwen, Randolph H. Vice pres. McEwen Lumber Co., High Point, N.C., 1959—, pilot, 1960—. Capt., Civil Air Patrol, 1942—; charter mem. Women's Adv. Com. on Aviation, 1964-67. Mem. Ninety-Nines (pres. 1961-63), Jr. League High Point, Whirley-Girls, Alpha Delta Pi. Methodist. Home: 421 Edgedale St High Point NC 27262 Office: 1601 English St High Point NC 27261

SMITH, LUCILLE SAAD, govt. ofcl., club woman; b. Pikeville, Ky., Aug. 13, 1917; d. Jasper I. and Clara (Sword) Saad; student Pikeville Coll., 1934-35; m. Chester Woodrow Smith, July 9, 1938; 1 son, Gregory Clinton. Dep. county ct. clk., Pike County, Ky., 1935-49; tax commr. Pike County, 1950-61, 65-67; postmaster, Pikeville, Ky., 1967—; condr. daily news radio program, 1964—. Pres. Woman's Club, 1959-61, Bus. and Profl. Women's Club, 1943-45, Xi chpt. Beta Sigma Phi, 1947-48; 62-63; dist. dir. Ky. Fedn. Women's Clubs; hon. mem. Kiwanis Club; sec.-treas. Ky. Tax Commrs. Assn., 1958-61, 66-67; mem. exec. bd. Pikeville C. of C., 1959—; sec. Pike County chpt. Nat. Found., 1948—; pres. P.T.A., 1964-67, chmn. March Dimes, 1943-45. Named Outstanding Clubwoman of Year, 1965, Girl of Year, 1964. Presbyn. Home: Peach Orchard Pikeville KY 41501 Office: Post office S Mayo Trail Pikeville KY 41501

SMITH, LULA MARGARET (MRS. CHILTON WAYNE SMITH), assn. exec.; b. Clovis, N.M., Oct. 3, 1919; d. Warren Wade and Berniece Irene (Barrett) Coplen; student Benson Sch. Commerce, 1939; m. Chilton Wayne Smith, Mar. 20, 1941; 1 son, Chilton Warren. Chmn. bd. A.R.C., Portales, N.M. Mem. United Daus. Confederacy (pres. N.M. chpt.), Daus. Colonial Wars (pres. N.M. chpt.), Federated Woman's Club (past pres.), Federated Garden Clubs (past pres.), Beta Sigma Phi (sec.). Mem. Christian Ch. Home: 905 W 17th St Portales NM 88130

SMITH, M. ESTELLIE (MRS. CHARLES A. BISHOP), anthropologist; b. Buffalo, Dec. 1, 1935; d. O. Roy and Marietta (Perry) Smith; B.A., U. Buffalo, 1962; M.A., State U. N.Y., 1964, Ph.D., 1967; m. Charles A. Bishop, Sept. 16, 1968. Asst. prof. anthropology Fla. State U., Tallahassee, 1966-69, Eastern N.M. U., Portales, N.M., 1969-70; asso. prof. anthropology State U. N.Y.-Brockport, Brockport, N.Y., 1970—. Fellow Am. Anthrop. Assn., Royal Anthrop. Inst., Soc. for Applied Anthropology; mem. So. Anthrop. Soc., Am. Ethnol. Soc., Soc. Am. Archeology, Linguistic Soc. Am., Internat. Congress Americanists, Sigma Xi, Phi Beta Kappa. Editor: Studies in Linguistics: Papers in Honor of George L. Trager, 1972; book rev. editor Urban Anthropology, Studies in European Society. Home: 51 E Main St Ontario NY 14519

SMITH, MADALYN SYLVIA, sec., librarian; b. Burlington, Vt., July 28, 1921; d. Albert Frederick and Mabel Mae (Swinyer) Smith; B.A., Heidelberg Coll., Tiffin, O., 1950; A.A.S., Rochester (N.Y.) Inst. Tech., 1958; M.L.S., Case-Western Res. U., 1962. Librarian, Eastman Kodak Co., Rochester, 1941-61; acquisitions librarian State U. N.Y. at Geneseo, 1963-68; cataloger Colgate-Rochester Div. Sch., 1968-69; tech. process librarian Community Coll. Finger Lakes, Canadaigua, N.Y., 1969-71; librarian Holy Angels Sch., Rochester, 1973-74; sec. B. Forman Co., Rochester, 1974—. N.Y. State Dept. Ednl. Advancement scholar, 1961-62. Mem. Am. Soc. Information Services, Am. Mus. Natural History, Civic Music Assn. Home: 1028 Winston Rd N Rochester NY 14609 Office: Midtown Plaza Rochester NY 14604

SMITH, MAGGIE, actress; b. Dec. 28, 1934; d. Nathaniel and Margaret Little (Hutton) Smith; ed. Oxford Playhouse Sch.; m. Robert Stephens, 1967; children—Christopher, Toby. Major roles in

Twelfth Night, 1952, New Faces, 1956, Share My Lettuce, 1957, The Stepmother, 1958, The Double Dealer, 1959; with Old Vic Co., 1959-60, roles in As You Like It, Richard II, The Merry Wives of Windsor, What Every Woman Knows; major roles in Rhinoceros, 1960, Strip the Willow, 1960, The Rehearsal, 1961, Mary, Mary, 1963, The Country Wife, 1969; Nat. Theatre Co. prodns. The Recruiting Officer, 1964, Othello, 1964, The Master Builder, 1964, Hay Fever, 1964, Much Ado About Nothing, 1965, Miss Julie, 1965, A Bond Honoured, 1966, Three Sisters, Beaux Stratagem, Hedda Gabler, 1970; other stage appearances include Design for Living, 1971, Private Lives, 1972; film roles include The VIP's, 1963, The Pumpkin Eater, 1964, Young Cassidy, 1965, Othello, 1966, The Honey Pot, 1967, Hot Millions, 1968, The Prime of Miss Jean Brodie, 1968, Oh! What a Lovely War, 1968, Love and Pain and the Whole Damn Thing, 1971, Travels With My Aunt, 1972; Television appearances in Merchant of Venice (BBC), 1971, The Millionairess (BBC), 1972. Recipient Actress of the Year award Variety Club of Great Britain, 1963, 1968; Drama award London Eve. Standard, 1962, 70; Oscar award Am. Acad. Motion Picture Arts and Scis., 1969; Los Angeles Critic award, 1970; decorated comdr. Brit. Empire. Address: care Fraser and Dunlop 91 Regent St London W 1 England

SMITH, MARGARET CHASE, former U.S. senator; b. Skowhegan, Me., Dec. 14, 1897; d. George Emery and Carrie (Murray) Chase; student Skowhegan High Sch., 1912-16; m. Clyde H. Smith, May 14, 1930 (dec. 1940). Began as tchr. Skowhegan, Me., 1916; office exec. Independent Reporter, 1919-28, Daniel E. Cummings Co., 1928-30; treas. New Eng. Process Co., Skowhegan, 1928-30; became mem. 76th Congress, 2d Me. Dist., 1940; mem. 77th to 80th Congresses, 2d Me. Dist., 1941-49. senator from Me., 1949-73. Republican. Home: Norridgewock Av Skowhegan ME 04976

SMITH, MARGARET LOUISE, rehab. center exec.; b. Fond Du Lac, Wis., Nov. 27, 1931; d. Frank Richard and Myrtle Martha (Mauer) Smith; B.S. cum laude, Mt. Mary Coll., 1953. Dir. profl. services Crossroads Rehab. Center, Indpls., 1955-66; dir. occupational therapy dept. Buffalo Childrens Hosp. and Rehab. Center, 1966-67; instr. State U. N.Y. at Buffalo, 1966-67; dir. patient services Easter Seal Goodwill Industries Rehab. Center, New Haven, 1967-74; asso. adminstr. Ga. Warm Springs Found. Hosp., 1974—. Vis. lectr. Va. Commonwealth U., U. Fla., Boston U.; cons. U. Conn., Wheeling (W.Va.) Easter Seal Soc. Mem. Am. (past del. bd. mem., sec. Ho. of Dels.), Conn. occupational therapy assns., Conn. Coalition Independent Health Professions (sec.), Rehab. Council Greater New Haven (pres.), Nat. Rehab. Assn., Delta Epsilon Sigma. Home: Ga Warm Springs Found Warm Springs GA 31830

SMITH, MARGARET PHYLLIS, editor; b. Plymouth, Pa., Aug. 24, 1925; d. Harold Dewitt and Mae E. (Bittenbender) Smith; student Wilkes Coll., 1943-44; A.B. magna cum laude, Bucknell U., 1946, A.M., 1947; postgrad. U. Pa., summers 1951-54. Instr. English, Bucknell U., Lewisburg, 1947-52, asst. prof., 1952-55; personnel asst. RCA Labs., Princeton, N.J., 1955-58, staff writer pub. affairs, 1958—, mem. editorial staff Radiations mag., 1955-70, asso. editor, 1970—, editor DSRC Newsletter, 1969—. Pa. State Senatorial scholar, 1943-46, Alpha Lambda Delta scholar, 1946. Mem. Am. Assn. U. Women, Phi Beta Kappa, Kappa Delta Epsilon, Sigma Delta Pi, Sigma Tau Delta. Episcopalian. Home: 276 Nassau St Princeton NJ 08540 Office: RCA Labs David Sarnoff Research Center Princeton NJ 08540

SMITH, MARGERY WEYRAUCH (MRS. HARRY GARRY), physician; b. Port Washington, N.Y., Jan. 23, 1926; d. Frank B. and Margery (Weyrauch) Smith; A.B., Syracuse U., 1946, M.D., 1950; m. Harry Gerry, Nov. 28, 1953; children—Charles, Franklin, Johanna, David (dec.), Elizabeth. Intern, Albany Med. Center, 1950, resident, 1953; instr. pediatrics Albany Med. Coll., 1952-53; practice medicine specializing in family practice, East Berne, N.Y., 1956—; sch. physician, Clarksville, N.Y., 1957—, Berne Knox Central Sch., 1959—; dep. mental health officer Albany County, 1969—; med. dir. Guilderland Center Nursing Home, 1973—. Mem. Berne Narcotic Guidance Council, 1970, Altamont Narcotic Guidance Council, 1971; bd. dirs. Albany Plan for Med. Care, Inc., 1973—. Diplomate Am. Bd. Family Practice. Mem. Am., N.Y. (mem. commn. on legislation 1971-73, mem. commn. on membership and credentials 1971-73, del. 1971—), Albany County (sec.-treas. 1970-73, pres. 1974—) acads. family physicians, A.M.A., N.Y. State, Albany County (bd. censors 1971-72) med. socs., Albany County Farm Bur., East Berne Vol. Fire Co. Aux., St. Bernadette Altar Rosary Soc. (pres. 1967-68). Address: RD 1 Hillcrest Farm East Berne NY 12059

SMITH, MARGUERITE BEATRICE GORTON (MRS. CARTHEL HILL SMITH), bus. exec.; b. Waterloo, Ia., Nov. 9, 1908; d. Edward and Ida (Gushard) Gorton; student U. Ia., 1935-36, George Peabody Coll., 1936, U. Ky., 1955; m. Carthel Hill Smith, Oct. 16, 1937; 1 son, Edward Whitfield. Partner C.H. Smith Motor Co., Prestonburg, Ky., 1944-50; partner, buyer Chevy Chase Hardware, Lexington, Ky., 1952-56; v.p., treas., mgr. Lexington Outboard Marine, Inc., Ky., 1957-74, pres., treas., 1974—. Mem. Marine Dealers Assn. Bus. and Profl. Women's Club, Am. Soc. Women Accountants, Siniwak. Presbyn. Club: Zonta (charter; pres. 1964-66) (Lexington). Home: 370 Andover Dr Lexington KY 40502 Office: 175 New Circle Rd NE Lexington KY 40505

SMITH, MARIAN ADAMS (MRS. JULIUS CLARENCE SMITH III), civic worker; b. Winston-Salem, N.C., June 6, 1928; d. Roger Lee and Blanche Evelyn (Brann) Adams; B.F.A., U. N.C., 1951; m. Julius Clarence Smith III, June 21, 1951; children—Stephen Manly, Thomas Julius, Marian Keith. Art supr. Raleigh (N.C.) Pub. Schs., 1951; art tchr. Greensboro (N.C.) Pub. Schs., 1952-55. Pres., Southeastern Theatre Conf., 1970-71, chmn. children's theatre div., 1964-66, chmn. endowment fund, 1969—; pres. N.C. Theatre conf., 1970-71; regional dir. Am. Coll. Theatre Festival, 1971-73; v.p. Pixie Theatre for Young People, Greensboro, 1962—; chmn. adv. com. of theatre U. N.C. at Greensboro, 1962—; chmn. children's theatre Jr. League of Greensboro, 1962-63, chmn. TV, 1964-65; v.p. Jr. League sustainers, 1970-71. Bd. govs. Nat. Children's Theatre Conf., 1967-69. Mem. Am. Theatre Assn. (dir. 1972), Southeastern Theatre Conf. (adminstrv. dir. 1973—), Children's Theatre Assn. (chmn. bi-centennial festival 1973—), Greensboro Women's Investment Club (pres. 1965-66). Club: Greensboro Study (pres. 1964-65). Home: 310 Irving Pl Greensboro NC 27408

SMITH, MARILU CRAFTON (MRS. A. EDWARD SMITH), mem. Republican Nat. Com.; b. Dublin, Ga., Dec. 15, 1913; d. John Claxton and Mattie Julia (Adkins) Crafton; grad. Kalgler Bus. Coll., Macon, Ga., 1931; m. A. Edward Smith, Mar. 5, 1931 (dec. 1962); children—Marilyn Crafton and Edwina Crafton (twins). Mem. Republican Party, 1945—; chmn. 3d Dist. Ga. Draft Goldwater Campaign, 1964, also Goldwater campaign chmn.; mem. Muscogee Rep. Women, 1954—, mem. exec. com., 1962; mem. Ga. Fedn. Rep. Women, 1954—, Nat. Fedn. Rep. Women, 1954—, mem. 3d Dist. Ga. Rep. Com., 1963; mem. Rep. Nat. Com. for Ga., 1964—. Mem. adv. bd. Muscogee County Juvenile Ct., 1963—; an organizer Columbus (Ga.) Lawyer's Aux., 1959, pres., 1960-61; pres. Columbus Area Tb Assn., 1961-63, mem. bd. dirs., exec. com., 1961-66; bd. dirs., exec. com., patient services com. Ga. Tb Assn., 1961—; mem. Ga. Litter Bug Com., 1963—; chmn. publicity com. Columbus Symphony Orch., 1962-64; pub. relations and publicity dir. local Girl Scouts Am., 1956-60, interim dir., World War II; mem. exec. com., publicity dir. Community Counseling Center, 1966—; vol. Gray Lady, A.R.C., World War I mem. adv. council Southeastern area A.R.C., 1966; mem. Ga. Bd. Edn., 1970—. Named Woman of Year in Columbus, 1962. Methodist. Clubs: Wynnton Study, Pinetree Garden, Columbus Country (Columbus). Address: 801 Peachtree Dr Columbus GA 31906

SMITH, MARILYNN KNOWLTON, librarian; b. Indpls., May 1, 1915; d. Lynn Orlando and Hazel Mary (Vliet) Knowlton; B.A., Butler U., 1936; M.A., U. Colo., 1951; M.S., Columbia, 1964; m. David Lane Smith, Dec. 3, 1955 (dec. Nov. 1960). Council exec. Girl Scouts Am., Richmond, Ind., 1937-39, Ft. Wayne, Ind., 1939-41, Salt Lake City, 1942-43; various stenographic and clerical positions, 1943-49, 52-59, 61-62; librarian trainee Gen. Theol. Sem., N.Y.C., 1962-64; cataloger Library, State U. N.Y. at Stony Brook, 1964-66; reference librarian U.S. Mil. Acad., West Point, N.Y., 1966-72, asst. librarian pub. services div., 1972—. Served with WAC, 1944-46. Mem. Am., N.Y. library assns., Spl. Libraries Assn., N.Y. Tech. Services Librarians, Phi Kappa Phi, Kappa Delta Pi, Pi Gamma Mu, Phi Alpha Theta. Episcopalian. Home: Pine Terrace Highland Falls NY 10928 Office: US Mil Acad Library West Point NY 10996

SMITH, MARIWYN FAITH MCCLAIN (MRS. GEORGE ADRAIN SMITH, JR.), newspaper editor; b. Morgantown, W.Va., Apr. 17, 1937; d. Russell Kenneth and Christine Faith (Reynolds) McClain; B.S., Davis and Elkins Coll., 1959; m. George Adrain Smith, Jr., June 4, 1960; children—Kenneth Edward, Barbara Lynne, Faith Anne. Elementary tchr. Harrison County, W.Va., 1959-60; tchr. Greene County, N.Y., 1960-61; type setter Preston County News, Terra Alta, W.Va., 1967-71; with Parsons (W.Va.) Advocate, 1971—, editor, 1971—. Dir. McClain Printing Co., 1971. Presbyn. Author: ". . . and live forever", 1974. Home: 134 Pennsylvania Av Parsons WV 26287 Office: 212 Main St Parsons WV 26287

SMITH, MARJORIE KATHERINE, physician; b. Miles City, Mont., Apr. 14, 1902; d. Henry Charles and Katherine (Wilson) Smith; A.B., Smith Coll., 1924; M.D., Tufts U., 1930; M.P.H., Mass. Inst. Tech., 1943; postgrad. U. N.C., 1943, N.Y. U., 1947. Intern, resident Medfield (Mass.) State Hosp., 1930-34; resident Boston Floating Hosp., 1934-35, Univ. Hosp., N.Y.C., 1952; physician Miss. State Coll. for Women, 1937-40; dir. Mont. Crippled Children Service, Helena, 1941-43; sch. physician, Longview, Wash., 1943-49; rural pediatrician Ore. State Bd. Health, summers 1945, 46, 48; chief med. officer Internat. Refugee Children's Village, Germany, 1949-50; sch. physician, Flint, Mich., 1950-51, Mt. Vernon, N.Y., 1952-53, N.Y.C. Health Dept., 1954-58; ships physician Floating Hosp., N.Y.C., summers 1952-54, 56, 57, 63-65; asst. vis. physician pediatric service Bellevue Hosp., 1963—; physician at Hunter Coll., 1963-71; clin. instr. pediatrics N.Y. U. Med. Center, 1964—; physician Judson Health Center, N.Y.C., 1954-58, 62—; instr. maternal, child health Hunter Coll., 1956-58; med. dir. Ky. Commn. Handicapped Children, Louisville, 1958-62; specialist in charge tng. Bur. Sch. Health, N.Y.C. Health Dept., 1962—; asst. attending N.Y. Infirmary-Adolescent Nutrition Clinic, 1967-72; preceptress nursing asso. program Cornell U. Mem. gov.'s planning com. White House Conf., Ky. del., 1960; mem. Ky. Gov.'s Com. for Youth, 1961-62, WMO, 1970—; mem. Food and Nutrition Council Greater N.Y. 1971—. Named Ky. col., 1962. Fellow Am. Sch. Health Assn.; mem. Am., N.Y., Am. Women's med. assns., Am., N.Y. State, N.Y.C. pub. health assns., N.Y. Med. Soc., P.E.O. Clubs: Appalachian Mountain. Home: 360 W 22d St New York City NY 10011 Office: Bur Sch Health 125 Worth St New York City NY 10013

SMITH, MARTHA MOORE, owner pub. relations and talent agy.; b. Cin., Jan. 15, 1921; d. Edward Staples and Susie Elizabeth (Thum) Smith; student Va. Intermont Coll., 1939-41; B.A., U. Cin., 1943; M.A., Fletcher Sch. Law and Diplomacy, 1947. With CIA, Washington, 1947-49; pub. relations dir. Cin. Symphony Orchestra, 1949-51; cultural fund raiser, booking agt., pub. relations dir. Nat. Concert Artists Corp., N.Y.C., 1953-58; owner Martha Moore Smith Enterprises, N.Y.C., 1958—. Exec. sec. Nat. Assn. Tchrs. of Singing, N.Y.C., 1969-71; press rep. Saratoga (N.Y.) Performing Arts Center, 1968-71; nat. press rep. Saint Paul Opera, N.Y.C., 1971-73; press rep. Manhattan Sch. Music, N.Y.C., 1971-74; personal mgr. Eleanor Steber, Met. Opera, N.Y.C., 1951-53, 72—. Served with WAVES, 1943-45. Mem. Alpha Gamma Delta. Presbyn. Editor: Selective Segregation (Edward S. Smith), 1950. Home and office: 2109 Broadway New York City NY 10023

SMITH, MARY ALICE, educator; b. Conestoga, Pa., Feb. 29, 1920; d. Martin W. and Agnes M. (Groff) Smith; B.S., Millersville State Coll., Pa., 1942; M.A., Columbia, 1947; Ed.D., Pa. State U., 1958. Tchr. elementary Schs., Lancaster County, 1942-48, tchr. spl. edn. for mentally retarded, 1948-53; coll. tchr., supv. kindergarten Lock Haven State Coll., 1953-63, dir. spl. edn., 1963-73, chmn. dept. specialized studies, 1974—. Bd. dirs. Child Welfare Assn., 1965—; bd. dirs. pub. relations chmn. Community Service Assn., 1966—; bd. dirs. Crafts, Inc., 1967—, Enterprises for Handicapped. Mem. Nat., Pa. edn. assns., Am. Assn. for Mental Deficiency, Pa. (mem. bd.), Nat. Assns. for Retarded Children, Council for Exceptional Children, Assn. for Childhood Edn. Internat., Pi Lambda Theta. Home: Conestoga PA 17615 Office: Lock Haven PA 17745

SMITH, MARY ANN HARVEY, nutritionist, educator; b. Camden, Ark., Jan. 29, 1940; d. Doyle B. and Sarah (Wilson) Harvey; B.S. in Edn., Henderson State Coll., 1960; M.S., U. Tenn., 1962, Ph.D., 1965; m. Garland Thomas Smith, July 10, 1971. Instr., U. Ala., 1962-65; asst. prof. Middle Tenn. State U., 1965-67; asso. prof., chief of nutrition, child devel. center med. units U. Tenn., Memphis, 1967—, adj. asso. prof. dept. nutrition Coll. Home Econs., Knoxville, 1967—. Adj. asso. prof. U. Ark., 1971—. Mem. Am. (nat. com. profl. registration), Tenn., Memphis Dist. dietetic assns., Tenn., Memphis Area nutrition councils, Sigma Xi, Kappa Delta Pi. Mem. Ch. of Christ. Editor: Feeding the Handicapped Child, 1971. Home: 4958 Shady Grove Memphis TN 38117 Office: 711 Jefferson St Memphis TN 38105

SMITH, MARY CLAY BENTON (MRS. THOR MERRITT SMITH), journalist; b. Madill, Okla., Aug. 19, 1903; d. John Wiley and Mary Jane (Scobee) Benton; student U. Cal. at Los Angeles, 1924-25; B.S., U. Ore., 1928; m. Thor Merritt Smith, Apr. 17, 1930; children—Deanne (Mrs. Jay McMurren), Suzanne (Mrs. Richard P. Mueller), Marianne (Mrs. Henry Hudson Hubbard III). Reporter, News-Pilot, San Pedro, Cal., 1921-24, News Bur., U. Ore., 1925-28; editor jr. page Press-Telegram, Long Beach, Cal., 1928-32; acting corr., chief bur. A.P., Reno, 1943-45; A.P. accredited corr. to signing of Japanese Peace Treaty, San Francisco, 1951; spl. corr. Life and N.Y. Mirror, 1944-45; travel scout researcher Sunset, Menlo Park, Cal., 1945-51; report editor Nowland & Co., Greenwich, Conn., 1957-59; sr. exec. publicity Macy's, San Francisco, 1951-52; contbg. editor Pacific Travel News, San Francisco, 1962-73; free lance writer, 1973—. Instr. journalism and English, U. Nev., 1942-43. State publicity co-chmn. A.R.C., Reno, 1942-45; publicity dir. San Francisco Protestant Orphanage, 1950. Bd. dirs. Pa. YMCA, 1952. Mem. Am. Assn. U. Women (dir. 1961-62), Theta Sigma Phi, Alpha Chi Omega. Republican. Episcopalian. Author: Sunset Travel Books: Hong Kong, 1964; (with Mimi Bell) Japan, 1964; (with Mary Ellen Fox) Australia, 1964, New Zealand, 1964; Islands of the South Pacific 1966; Taiwan, 1966; Southeast Asia, 1968. Address: 74 La Cumbre Circle Santa Barbara CA 93105

SMITH, MARY ELINOR, univ. dean; b. Louisville, Dec. 18, 1913; d. Harry Robert and Susan (Corrigan) Smith; A.B., Catherine Spalding Coll., 1935; M.A., Cath. U. Am., 1950. Tchr. math. pub. schs., Jefferson County, Ky., 1935-36, Louisville, 1936-44; social worker Louisville, Jefferson County Children's Home, 1946-48; grad. asst. Cath. U. Am., Washington, 1948-50; lectr., 1952-60, dean women, 1952-69, asso. dean students, 1969—; dean women Quincy Coll., 1950-52; lectr. Ursuline Coll., 1953. Hosp. staff aide A.R.C., Pearl Harbor Naval Hosp., 1944-45. Mem. Internat. Fedn. Cath. Alumnae (vice-gov. Ky. 1938-42, vice regent D.C. 1956), Am. Personnel and Guidance Assn., Am. Psychol. Assn., Nat., Regional (pres. 1966-68) assns. women deans and counselors, Am. Assn. U. Women, Am. Coll. Personnel Assn., Sigma Alpha Iota (patron), Theta Phi Alpha (hon.). Home: 917 Varnum St NE Washington DC 20017

SMITH, MARY ELIZABETH, chemist; b. N.Y.C., Mar. 15, 1928; d. Charles Albert and Mabel (Hanson) Smith; B.S., Roosevelt U., 1954. Research chemist Olin Matheson Chem. Corp., New Haven, 1954-55; editorial asst. nuclear data Nat. Acad. Scis., Washington, 1955-57; chief chemist of Fairfax County (Va.), 1957-74; lab. supr. VerSar, Inc., Springfield, Va., 1974—. Cons. water pollution control. Mem. Am. Chem. Soc., Am. Phys. Soc., A.A.A.S., Am. Water Works Assn., Am. Mgmt. Assn., Water Pollution Control Fedn., English Speaking Union. Home: 4326 Adrienne Dr Alexandria VA 22309 Office: 6621 Electronic Dr Springfield VA 22151

SMITH, MARY ELIZABETH BOYER (MRS. JOSEPH EARL SMITH), univ. dean; b. Homestead, Pa., Nov. 24, 1911; d. John Franklin Hicks and Sarah (Price) Boyer; A.B., Hiram Coll., 1939; M.A., Ohio State U., 1947; m. Joseph Earl Smith, Nov. 22, 1939. Tchr., Mecca Pub. Schs., Trumbull County, O., 1932-36; alumni sec. Hiram Coll., 1936-39; admissions counselor, instr. biology Youngstown (O.) Coll., 1939-43; tchr. Hayes Jr. High Sch. and Youngstown Pub. Schs., 1943; asst. registrar, recorder Youngstown (O.) U., 1944-66, head dept. health and phys. edn., asst. prof. marriage psychology, 1947-57, registrar, 1966-71, asst. dean admissions and records, 1971-73, dir. career planning and placement, 1973—. Bd. dirs. YWCA, Youngstown, chmn. personnel com. 1946-52, 53-56; pres. Family Life Edn. Council, Youngstown, 1949-51, treas., 1970-72. Recipient Hiram Coll. Alumni Achievement award, 1970. Mem. Am. Assn. U. Women (edn. com. 1965—, v.p. 1972), Wimodaughsis (pres. 1968-69), N.E.A., A.A.P.H.E.R., Gamma Sigma, Delta Kappa Gamma, Sigma Alpha Iota (chpt. patroness 1956—), Phi Kappa Phi, Sigma Sigma Sigma (faculty sponsor 1957—). Republican. Mem. Christian Ch. Club: Altrusa (pres. 1959-60 Youngstown). Home: Route 1 Box 242 North Jackson OH 44451 Office: 410 Wick Av Youngstown OH 44503

SMITH, MARY JEAN (MRS. WILLIAM K. SMITH), journalist; b. LaCrosse, Wis., Jan. 6, 1933; d. George Daniel and Clara Weilep (Ballhorn) Scott; B.S. in Edn., Wis. State U., LaCrosse, 1954; m. William K. Smith, Oct. 14, 1961; children—David Hugh, Julie Kay. Tchr. pub. schs., Coolidge, Ariz., 1955-57, Eau Claire, Wis., 1958-61, Mauston, Wis., 1963-64, Mineral Point, Wis., 1970-73; co-pub. Mineral Point Democrat Tribune, 1964—. Organizer first Winter Carnival, 1967. Mem. United Ch. of Christ. Home: 130 Pine St Mineral Point WI 53565 Office: Box 262 Mineral Point WI 53565

SMITH, MARY JORDAN (MRS. ROBERT L. SMITH), personnel exec.; b. Jackson, Miss., Aug. 12, 1938; d. Charlie Franklin and Henrine (Brown) Jordan; A.B., Tougaloo Coll., 1960; M.B.A., Miss. Coll., 1972; m. Robert L. Smith, Dec. 19, 1959; children—Xavier Yvette, Robert L., Deirdre LaShaunn, Gigi Alisha. Sec., Tougaloo (Miss.) Coll., 1964-65, dir. personnel, 1967-72; checker Vegas Village Shopping Center, Las Vegas, Nev., 1965; reservation agt. Western Airlines, Inc., Las Vegas, 1965-67; personnel asst. Miss. Research and Devel. Center, Jackson, 1972—. Tchr., Jackson Pub. Sch. System, 1960-63; cons. to pres. Mary Holmes Coll., West Point, Miss., 1972—. Mem. Delta Sigma Theta. Baptist. Home: 3295 Albermarle Rd Jackson MS 39213 Office: PO Box 2470 Jackson MS 39205

SMITH, MARY KATHRYN, club woman; b. Frederick, Md., Mar. 29, 1908; d. John Algar and Nellie Blanche (Gaver) Heard; grad. high sch.; m. Ralph Owen Smith, Jan. 6, 1934 (dec. May 1968); children—Nancy (Mrs. James W.E. Vittetoe, Jr.), Blanche (Mrs. Blanche Koogle). Md. vice regent D.A.R., 1970-73, regent, 1973—. Home: 207 Kemble Rd Baltimore MD 21218

SMITH, MAUREEN BERNADETTE (MRS. JOHN ANTHONY SMITH), psychologist; b. N.Y.C., Aug. 13, 1945; d. Francis Edward and Evelyn Marion (Feeley) Foley; B.A., Hunter Coll., 1967, M.S., 1969; M.A., Columbia, 1971, Ph.D., 1973; m. John Anthony Smith, Aug. 28, 1966; 1 son, Kenneth Justin. Elementary sch. tchr. N.Y.C. Bd. Edn., 1967-68; research asst. Center for Urban Edn., N.Y.C., 1969; sch. psychologist Franklin Lakes (N.J.) Bd. Edn., 1972-73; clin. asso. psychology dept. Columbia, N.Y.C., 1973-74; sch. psychologist Ramsey (N.J.) Bd. Edn., 1974-75. Pearl Waisblatt grantee, 1969, Nat. Inst. Mental Health grantee, 1969-70. Recipient Office Edn. award, 1971-72. Mem. Am. Psychol. Assn., Phi Beta Kappa, Psi Chi, Kappa Delta Pi. Home: 47 W Clarkstown Rd New York City NY 10956

SMITH, MILDRED LOIS JACKSON, ret. social worker; b. Hot Springs, Ark.; d. John Warren and Eliza (Christian) Jackson; student Crane Jr. Coll., 1932-33, George Williams Coll., 1933-34., A.B., U. Ill., 1937; M.A., U. Chgo., 1947; m. Charles E. Hambrick, Feb. 19, 1938 (div. Jan. 1962); 1 dau., Carol Elizabeth (Mrs. Melvin McConico); m. Javan Smith, Sept. 21, 1962 (div. Aug. 1969). Sr. social worker Chgo. Welfare Dept., 1937-39, sr. child placement worker, 1939-42, supervising caseworker, 1942-49; caseworker Cook County Dept. Welfare, Chgo., 1951-52; child welfare services caseworker Sacramento County Bur. Adoptions, 1952-53; adoptions caseworker Los Angeles County Welfare Dept., 1953-54; caseworker VA, Los Angeles, 1954; day care licensing worker Cal. State Dept. Social Welfare, 1954-58, day care licensing supr., 1958-64, adult services rep., 1964-66, state hosp. coordinator, 1966-68, social service rev. officer, 1968-72; social service cons. Robincroft Home, Pasadena, Cal., 1968-74. Mem. Acad. Certified Social Workers, Nat. Conf. Social Welfare, Alpha Kappa Alpha. Methodist. Home: 227 W Las Flores Dr Altadena CA 91001

SMITH, MILDRED (MRS. HOMER LESTER SMITH), artist; b. nr. Ripley, O., Jan. 18, 1910; d. Samuel Emery and Elhel (Evans) Sears; grad. high sch.; m. Homer Lester Smith, Nov. 8, 1927; (dec. June 1970); children—Jauneth (Mrs. Joseph Calim), Lonny Berle, Linda (Mrs. Edward G. Womacks). Dressmaker, 1924-40; mgr. Fed. Dining Room, Georgetown, O., 1947-54; bookkeeper, Home Oil Co., Georgetown, 1955-65; one-woman shows Russellville, O., 1966, Brown County Fair, 1967-73, Presbyn. Ch., Ripley, O., 1973, Lake Waynoka, 1973; exhibited in group shows in Cin. area; murals in Brown County Gen. Hosp., Georgetown, Sardinia, O., Mt. Orab, O.,

Goshen, O., Sebring, O., Decatur, O., Ripley, Danville, Cal.; pvt. art instr., 1968—; custom framer, 1970—. Pres., P.T.A., 1933-35, 41-42; vol. Brown County Gen. Hosp., 1970—. Mem. Bus. and Profl. Womens Club (sec. 1950-54), Brown County Hist. Club (treas. 1970-71, pres. 1972-73). Mem. Ch. of Christ. Club: Senior Citizens. Home: 114 State St Georgetown OH 45121

SMITH, MILTREN LEWIS HARDWICK (MRS. ALPHONSO SMITH, JR.), univ. adminstr.; b. Kansas City, Mo., July 3, 1927; d. Luther Martin and Vivian Camille (Doneray) Lewis; B.S., Tuskegee Inst., 1953, M.S. in Edn., 1968; postgrad. (Esso Found. fellow) Harvard, 1972; m. Alphonso Thriston Smith, Jr., Dec. 21, 1972. Dir. ednl. center Tuskegee (Ala.) Inst. Community Edn. Program, 1965-68, YMCA, YWCA, 1968-69; dean women Cheyney (Pa.) State Coll., 1969-70; dean women Central State U., Wilberforce, O., 1970—, adminstr. student activities, 1973—, instr. awareness series, 1973—, chmn. student concerns com., 1970-71. Mem. Nat., Pa. assns. women deans and counselors. Home: PO Box 232 Wilberforce OH 45384 Office: Wilberforce University Wilberforce OH 45384

SMITH, MINERVA JANE (MRS. DONALD HARRY SMITH), editor; b. Whitney Point, N.Y., Feb. 15, 1937; d. Lee Edwin and Mabel Rosemond (Hoadley) Watrous; grad. high sch.; m. Donald Harry Smith, June 2, 1957. With Windsor (N.Y.) Standard Press, 1955—, editor, mng. editor, 1967—. Democrat. Methodist. Club: Triple B Home Demonstration (pres. 1962-66, 72-74) (East Windsor, N.Y.). Home: Rural Route 1 Box 161 Nineveh NY 13813 Office: 14 Main St Windsor NY 13865

SMITH, MOVANE MADELINE (MRS. DENNIS JEROME SMITH), educator; b. nr. Comfrey, Minn., Aug. 9, 1937; d. William Frederick and Madeline Loretta (McPhee) Juhnke; B.S., U. Minn., 1959; M.S., Old Dominion U., 1974; m. Dennis Jerome Smith, July 28, 1962; 1 son, Jay Patrick. Tchr. English and speech Montgomery (Minn.) Ind. Sch. Dist., 1959-62; tchr. English, Churchland High Sch., Norfolk County, Va., 1962-68; chmn. English dept. Western Branch High Sch., Chesapeake, Va., 1968—. Mem. Nat., Va., Chesapeake edn. assns., Nat. Council Tchrs. English, Conf. Secondary Sch. English Dept. Chmn., Speech Communication Assn., Va. Assn. Tchrs. English (v.p. Dist. I), Delta Kappa Gamma. Roman Catholic. Home: 4620 Avocet Ct Portsmouth VA 23703 Office: 4222 Terry Dr Chesapeake VA 23321

SMITH, MURIEL FOREMAN (MRS. MALCOLM N. SMITH), civic worker; b. Chgo., Nov. 9, 1921; d. Edwin G., Jr. and Helen (Friedman) Foreman; ed. Colby Jr. Coll., 1939-40, Lake Forest Coll., 1941; m. Malcolm N. Smith, Feb. 14, 1943; 1 dau., Louise K. Vice-chmn. budget rev. com. Chgo. Community Fund, 1965-67. Mem. bds. St. Marylebone Housing Assn., London, Eng., 1952-56, Nat. Council Household Employment (U.S.), 1967—; mem. George Williams Coll. Assos. (sec. 1967-68), mem. women's bd. U. Chgo., 1968—. Nat. bd. dirs. YWCA; bd. dirs., exec. v.p. YWCA Met. Chgo., 1961— pres. bd. dirs., 1971-73; bd. dirs. Lyric Opera Chgo., Leadership Council for Met. Communities, World Council YWCA; bd. dirs., exec. com. Council for Community Services Chgo., Erikson Inst. Early Edn.; exec. com., bd. dirs. Hull Ho. Assn., Chgo., 1965—, pres. bd. trustees, 1968-71; bd. dirs. Herrick House Assn., 1957-62, treas., 1959-60, v.p., 1961-62. Recipient Jane Addams medal, 1971-73. Mem. Women's Western Golf Assn. (dir. 1971-73), Arts Club Chgo. Home: 309 Maple Av Highland Park IL 60035

SMITH, MYRNA MILDRED (MRS. DAVEY STIRMAN SMITH), journalist; b. Tipton, Okla., July 7, 1916; d. Jinks Denny and Carrie Mae (Myers) McCorcle; grad. high sch.; m. Davey Stirman Smith, Oct. 16, 1934; children—Kara Ann (Mrs. Robert Frank Scott), Larry Mac, Don Paul. With Tipton (Okla.) Tribune, 1934-38; feature and spl. assignments writer Wichita Falls (Tex.) Record News-Times, 1948-55; asst. editor Christian Chronicle, ch. publ., Abiline, 1955-57; woman's editor Vernon (Tex.) Record, 1957-59; news and feature writer Plainview (Tex.) Herald, 1959-63, woman's editor, 1963—, writer Potpourri column, Sunday edit., 1970—. Mem. D.A.R., Plainview C. of C. Mem. Ch. of Christ. Club: Plainview Women's (mem.-at-large). Home: 103 Southwest 8th St Plainview TX 79072 Office: 801 Broadway Plainview TX 79072

SMITH, NADINE RENO (MRS. POTTER LEWIS SMITH), civic leader; b. Chgo., Mar. 17, 1898; d. Harry Spencer Lindley and Margaret A. (McGrath) Reno; student parochial schs., Chgo., pvt. study music, piano, voice, 1916-20; m. Potter Smith, Aug. 1, 1921 (div. Feb. 1939); children—Renault (Mrs. William Kenneth Witsiepe), Balfe (Mrs. Ralph E. Peterson) (dec.). Mgr., The Card Bar, Evanston, Ill., 1953-56; sales exec. Stork Styles, Evanston, 1956-66; sales Wieboldt's, Evanston; with W. T. Grant Co., Wilmington, Del., 1960-61. Past treas. Lighthouse for the Blind; vol. worker Travelers Aid Soc. Mem. Jr. League of Evanston, Chgo. Drama League (past v.p.), D.A.R. Episcopalian. Republican. Club: Garden (Barrington, Ill.). Home: 1615 Hinman Evanston IL 60201

SMITH, NANCY BISHOP (MRS. ERIC CRAIG SMITH), audiologist; b. Phila., Sept. 20, 1944; d. Edward Harry and Frances Elizabeth (Irons) Bishop; B.A., Am. U., 1966; M.A., Temple U., 1969; m. Eric Craig Smith, Feb. 10, 1973. Instr. audiology, dept. otolaryngology Temple U. Sch. Medicine, Phila., 1969-73; audiologist Princeton (N.J.) Med. Center, 1973—; cons. audiologist Episcopal Hosp., Phila., 1969-72, Elwyn (Pa.) Inst., 1969-73. Mem. Internat. Soc. Audiology, Pa. Speech and Hearing Assn., Am. Speech and Hearing Assn., Acoustical Soc. Am. Home: 1609 Iredell Dr Raleigh NC 27608

SMITH, NETTIE DELLENE, educator; b. Waldo, O., Oct. 19, 1924; d. Walter F. and Marie (Curren) Smith; B.S., Ohio State U., 1946; M.A., N.Y. U., 1953, Ed.D., 1964. Recreation dir.-tchr. Community Center, Steubenville, O., 1946-47; instr. phys. edn. Notre Dame Coll., South Euclid, O., 1947-48; tchr. Palmer (Alaska) Ind. Schs., 1949-51, Woodrow Wilson High Sch., Youngstown, O., 1952-55; prof., chmn. dept. phys. edn. Kean Coll. N.J. (formerly Newark State Coll.), Union, N.J., 1956—. Cons. Matawan Schs., 1969. Mem. N.E.A., Am. Assn. U. Profs., Nat. Found. Health, Phys. Edn. and Recreation, Coll. Sports Medicine, Nat., Eastern assns. phys. edn. for coll. women, N.J. Edn. Assn., Am. (parliamentarian Eastern dist. 1972-73, by laws com. 1973—), N.J. (pres. 1968-69, Past Pres. award 1969, Honor award 1972) assns. health, phys. edn. and recreation, N.J. State Coll. Faculty Assn., Am. Assn. Higher Edn., Am. Assn. Elementary-Kindergarten Nursery Educators, Delta Kappa Gamma. Home: 101 Fern Rd East Brunswick NJ 08816 Office: Morris Av Union NJ 07083

SMITH, NILA BANTON, educator; b. Altona, Mich.; d. George Addison and Ella (Banton) Smith; B.A. summa cum laude, U. Chgo., 1928; M.A., Columbia, 1929, Ph.D., 1932. Tchr., supr. reading Detroit Pub. Schs., 1928-33; head dept. edn. Greensboro (N.C.) Coll., 1933-34; dean Whittier (Cal.) Coll. Sch. Edn., 1934-37; asso. prof. edn. Ind. U., 1937-39; prof. edn. U. So. Cal., 1939-49; prof. edn., dir. Reading Inst., N.Y. U., 1949-36; Distinguished Service prof. edn. Glassboro (N.J.) State Coll., 1963-68; Distinguished prof. edn. U. So. Cal., Los Angeles, 1968—. Lectr. reading Instrn., U.S., Eng., France, Australia, 1960, 71-72. Mem. Nat. Soc. for Study Edn., N.E.A., Assn. for Childhood Edn. Internat., Internat. Reading Assn. (citation merit 1964, pres. 1963-64), Nat. Conf. Research English, Nat. Council Tchrs. English, Phi Beta Kappa, Pi Lambda Theta, Kappa Delta Pi, Delta Kappa Gamma (state pres.), Delta Phi Upsilon (hon.). Author: Learning to Read, basic series, 1940; Read Faster and Get More from Your Reading, 1958; Be a Better Reader, high sch. series, 1970-71; The Best in Children's Literature, 1962; Reading Instruction for Today's Children, 1965; American Reading Instruction, 1965; Foundations of Reading, elementary series, 1968. Contbr. numerous articles to profl. jours. Home: 800 W 1st St Los Angeles CA 90012

SMITH, NORA, psychiatrist; b. Fulda, Germany; d. Max and Bella (Nussbaum) Smith; came to U.S., naturalized, 1944; B.S., Bklyn. Coll., 1956; M.D., State U. N.Y. Downstate Med. Center, 1960. Intern, Maimonides Hosp., Bklyn., 1960-61; resident psychiatry Kings County Hosp., Bklyn., 1961-64; fellow child psychiatry S.I. Mental Health Center, N.Y., 1964-66, fellow community psychiatry, 1966-67, research psychiatrist, 1967-69, dir. infant evaluation service, 1969—, adminstrv. dir., 1970-73, asso. dir. clin. services, 1973—; practice medicine specializing in psychiatry, Bklyn., 1964—; attending in psychiatry St. Vincents Med. Center of Richmond; clin. asst. prof. psychiatry Cornell U. Med. Coll., 1969—. Diplomate in Psychiatry and Child Psychiatry Am. Bd. Psychiatry and Neurology. Mem. Am. Psychiat. Assn., N.Y. Council on Child Psychiatry, Med. Soc. County Kings, N.Y. Soc. for Clin. Psychiatry. Office: 657 Castleton Av Staten Island NY 10301 Office: 380 E 18th St Brooklyn NY 11226

SMITH, NORMA ELLEN (MRS. CLAUDE P. SMITH), coll. adminstr.; b. Wayne County, Miss., July 14, 1937; d. Norman Lee and Selma Ellen (Mills) Tyner; student Truett McConnell Coll., 1969-70; m. Claude P. Smith, Apr. 15, 1965. Bus. mgr. Truett McConnell Coll., Cleveland, Ga., 1969-72, treas., 1972-73, sec., treas., asst. to pres., 1973—. Address: Truett McConnell Coll Cleveland GA 30528

SMITH, NORMA LOUISE, educator; b. Hutchinson, Kan., Dec. 29, 1934; d. Roscoe Fred and Alta Adele (Wilson) Smith; B.A., B.S., Tex. Woman's U., Denton, 1956; M.A. in English, U. Va., 1959. Tchr. English, Hockaday Sch., Dallas, 1959-60; tchr. English, admissions sec. St. Catherine's Sch., Richmond, Va., 1960-64; asst. dir. admissions Goucher Coll., Balt., 1964-67; dir. admissions Randolph-Macon Woman's Coll., Lynchburg, Va., 1967-70; acad. dean, tchr. English, St. Agnes Sch., Alexandria, Va., 1970—. Mem. Nat. Assn. Prins. Sch. Girls, Nat. Assn. Women Deans, Adminstrs. and Counselors (chpt. treas. 1972-76). Democrat. Episcopalian. Home: 2920 S Buchanan St Arlington VA 22206 Office: St Agnes Sch Jefferson Park Alexandria VA 22302

SMITH, OLIVE IRENE PERRY (MRS. WILLIAM SMITH), realtor; b. nr. Shelbyville, Ill., Dec. 13; d. Joseph Luther and Pearl (Bushart) Perry; grad. Sparks Coll., 1928; student Milligan U., 1929, Northwestern U., 1934-36, U. Cal. at Los Angeles, 1959-60; m. William Smith, May 11, 1942. Hosp. librarian, registrar Chgo. State Hosp., Cook County, 1929-40; dep. assessor, San Diego County, Cal., 1951-52; real estate broker O. I. Smith, Hemet, Cal., 1953—. Local rep. Nat. Inst. Real Estate Bds. Active Southland Water Com., 1960-68. Mem. adv. bd. San Jacinto (Cal.) Jr. Coll., 1967-68. Mem. Nat. Inst. Real Estate Brokers, Nat. Traders, Comml., and Investment Brokers Div. (pres. 1961), Hemet-San Jacinto Bd. Realtors (sec. 1960), Cal. Real Estate Assn. (regional v.p. 1964-65), Riverside Art Assn. Republican. Club: Soroptimist (San Jacinto-Hemet, Cal.). Home: 10381 N Lynn Circle Mira Loma CA 91752 Office: PO Box 331 Hemet CA 92343

SMITH, PATRICIA, editor; b. Spokane, Wash., Sept. 8, 1933; d. Thomas Millard and Dora Olive (Brittain) Smith; B.A. in History, Whitman Coll., 1955. Women's page editor Spokane (Wash.) Valley Herald, Opportunity, Wash., 1955—. Com. mem. Spokane chpt., A.R.C., 1971—. Bd. dirs. Spokane Jr. Symphony, sec., 1973-74. Recipient Inland Empire Press award Theta Sigma Phi, 1962, Wash. Newspaper Pubs. Assn. Women's Page awards, 1963, 64. Mem. Women in Communications (pres. Spokane chpt. 1972-73), Spokane Advt. and Sales Assn., Alpha Chi Omega. Presbyn. (elder 1959-62). Club: Spokane Press. Home: East 10726 Riverside Opportunity WA 99206 Office: Box 14027 Opportunity WA 99214

SMITH, PATRICIA ALICE, educator; b. Dallas, Nov. 26, 1934; d. James Douglas and Willie Maye (Forrester) Dabney; B.A., So. Methodist U., 1957, M.A., 1959; M.S. (Univ. fellow 1959-60), U. Ill., 1960; m. David Alan Smith, Nov. 10, 1961. Librarian, Nat. Lab. Medicine, Bethesda, 1960-63; with FAA, 1963-69, adminstrv. librarian, 1967-69; chief div. field services, acting chief div. lending Nat. Agrl. Library, Beltsville, Md., 1969-70; spl. asst. to asso. commr. Bur. Libraries and Learning Resources, U.S. Office Edn., Washington, 1970-73; policy asso. policy analysis service Am. Council Edn., 1973—. Mem. D.C. Library Assn., Phi Beta Kappa, Phi Alpha Theta, Beta Phi Mu. Home: 206 G St SW Washington DC 20024 Office: 1 DuPont Circle Washington DC 20036

SMITH, PATRICIA ANN, polit. party worker; b. Johnstown, Pa., Aug. 5, 1929; d. Delbert Hill and Neila Amanda (Nelson) Pape; student Northwestern U., 1946-48; m. Francis Anthony Smith, Sept. 2, 1949; children—Thomas Anthony, David Michel. Precinct committeewoman Republican party, 1960-70; chmn. Sheridan County (Wyo.) Republican Central Com., 1969-72; program chmn., v.p. Wyo. Fedn. Rep. Women, 1969-71, pres., 1973—; del. Nat. Conv. Rep. Women, 1971, 73; alternate del. Rep. Nat. Conv., 1972. Mem. Alpha Xi Delta. Episcopalian. Home: Route 1 Box 3 Sheridan WY 82801

SMITH, PATRICIA ANN CAIN (MRS. OLIN W. SMITH), educator; b. Mpls., Oct. 28, 1917; d. J. Ingram and Jennie (Anderson) Cain; B.A., U. Neb., 1938; postgrad. Bryn Mawr Coll., 1939-40; Ph.D., Cornell U., 1942; m. Olin W. Smith, Mar. 18, 1942. Personnel intern Aetna Life & Affiliated Cos., Hartford Conn., 1942-44; dir. psychol. div. Kurt Salmon Assos., Washington, 1944-49; lectr. Wells Coll., Ithaca Coll., 1948-49; faculty Cornell U., Ithaca, N.Y., 1949-66; prof. psychology Bowling Green (O.) U., 1966—. Supervising cons. Cain-Smith Assos., Ithaca, Bowling Green, 1949—. Mem. Am. (rep. to council 1967-70, mem. exec. com. div. indsl. psychology 1964-70), Ohio, Midwestern, Eastern psychol. assns., Am. Statis. Assn., Psychonomics Soc., Psychometric Soc. Author: (with T.A. Ryan) Principles of Industrial Psychology, 1954; (with L.M. Kendall, C.L. Hulin) Measurement of Satisfaction in Work and Retirement: A Strategy for the Study of Attitudes, 1969. Contbr. articles to profl. jours. Home: 505 Donbar Dr Bowling Green OH 43402

SMITH, PATRICIA FRANCES, librarian; b. N.Y.C., Sept. 15, 1935; d. Edward Charles and Jane Elizabeth (Burke) Smith; B.A., Coll. New Rochelle, 1957; M.S., Columbia, 1959. Jr. librarian New Rochelle (N.Y.) Pub. Library, 1959-61, sr. bookmobile librarian, 1961-63; librarian N.Y. Pub. Library, N.Y.C., 1963-65, ser. librarian, 1965-69, supervising br. librarian, 1969—. Mem. A.L.A. (mem. TV com. young adult services div. 1971-73), Alumni Assn. Sch. Library Service, Columbia, Alumnae Assn. Coll. New Rochelle. Club: Woman's (New Rochelle). Home: 2 Errol Place New Rochelle NY 10804 Office: 280 W 231st St Bronx NY 10463

SMITH, PATRICIA JOAN LINDEN (MRS. PAYTON SMITH), editor; b. Tonasket, Wash., Oct. 22, 1939; d. William Eugene and Harriet Marie (Hudnall) Linden; B.A., Wash. State U., 1960, M.A., 1961; m. Payton Smith, Dec. 28, 1963; 1 dau., Elizabeth Joann. Asst. editor Modern Lang. Quar. and Pacific N.W. Quar., Seattle, 1961-63; editor U. of Wash. Press, Settle, 1963—. Founder ann. meeting western univ. presses; western corr. Scholarly Pub., 1970-72. Bd. dirs. Seattle Youth Tennis Found. Mem. Western History Assn., Phi Beta Kappa, Kappa Kappa Gamma. Home: 5535 NE 55th St Seattle WA 98105 Office: University of Washington Press Seattle WA 98105

SMITH, PATRICIA SCHERF, pub. relations exec.; b. Canton, S.D., Oct. 30, 1930; d. Earl Roy and Laura Ruth (Swenson) Scherf; B.A., Cornell Coll., Mt. Vernon, Ia., 1952; m. Carlton Smith, Aug. 29, 1965. Reporter, Marshalltown (Ia.) Times-Republican, 1952-54; pub. relations asst. Rock River Conf., Meth. Ch., Chgo., 1954-55; news release editor A.M.A., Chgo., 1955-59; press relations specialist Am. Hosp. Assn., Chgo., 1959-63; dir. pub. relations Am. Acad. Pediatrics, Evanston, Ill., 1963-65; dir. publs. div. Am. Found. for Blind, N.Y.C., 1965-68, dir. dept. information, 1968—. Mem. Nat. Assn. Sci. Writers, Pub. Relations Soc. Am., Women Execs. in Pub. Relations, Am. Assn. Workers for Blind, Mortar Bd., Phi Beta Kappa. Independent. Methodist. Exec. editor New Outlook for the Blind. Home: 441 Pacific St Brooklyn NY 11217 Office: 15 W 16th St New York City NY 10011

SMITH, PEGGY HOUSE (MRS. MICHAEL MCKENZIE SMITH III), journalist; b. Uniontown, Pa., Nov. 20, 1948; d. Thomas Issac and Martha (Oleksik) House; student, Pa. State U., 1966-68; B.A., Duquesne U., 1970; m. Michael McKenzie Smith III, Sept. 25, 1971. With work study program, legal div. VA, Pitts., 1968-70; desk asst., copywriter WTAE-TV, Pitts., 1970-71; advt. asst. Spenley Newspapers, Homestead, Pa., 1973; women's editor Dardanell Publs., Inc., Monroeville, Pa., 1974—. Home: 623 Whitney Av Pittsburgh PA 15221

SMITH, PHYLLIS CALLAHAN (MRS. JOHNNY H. SMITH), social worker; b. Balt., July 7, 1942; d. Leon Jasper and Juanita Virginia (Hines) Callahan; A.B., Morgan State Coll., 1963; postgrad. U. Md., 1968, Coppin State Coll., 1973; m. Johnny H. Smith, Sept. 23, 1966; children—Erik Dwayne (dec.), Terri Lynn. Counselor, for mentally retarded Children's Center, Forest Haven, Laurel, Md., 1964-70, social service rep., 1970—. Bd. dirs. Mt. Washington Assn., 1973. Mem. Am. Assn. Mental Deficiency, Council Exceptional Children, Regional Assn. Deaf and Blind. Home: 5802 Merrville Av Baltimore MD 21215 Office: Children's Center Forest Haven Laurel MD 20810

SMITH, PHYLLIS KOERNER (MRS. CARROLL JAY SMITH), securities dealer; b. Providence, Sept. 22, 1927; d. Frank Little and Mabel Irene (Koerner) Downer; student U. Cal. at Los Angeles, 1962-63; bus. edn. degree Johnson and Wales Bus. Coll., 1943, basic law completion certificate, 1944; m. Carroll Jay Smith, Apr. 10, 1948. Purchasing agt. navy tng. films Dept. Navy, Washington, 1948-51, dep. disbursing officer, Point Mugu, Cal., 1951-57; chief disbursing operations C.E., Honolulu, 1957-59; accountant Hughes Aircraft Co., Fullerton, Cal., 1959-60, indsl. recreation adminstr., 1960—; v.p., treas. Smith Technivest, Inc., Hacienda Heights, Cal., 1969—. Mem. facilities and organizational com. Orange County Servicemen's Center, Anaheim, 1968-70. Recipient Superior Performance award Dept. Navy, 1954, C.E., 1958. Mem. Nat. Indsl. Recreation Assn. (program chmn. regional conf. 1971, conf. co-chmn. 1973), Nat. Notary Assn. Club: Altrusa (local pres. 1968-70, 72-73, dist. information chmn. 1971-73, dist. 1st vice gov. 1973—). Address: 2448 Amelgado Dr Hacienda Heights CA 91745

SMITH, PRISCILLA ROBINSON, educator; b. Barre, Vt., Apr. 10, 1919; d. Carl Franklin and Helen (Benson) Robinson; A.B., John B. Stetson U., 1941; M.Ed., Nat. Coll. Edn., Ill., 1955; Ed.D., U. Denver, 1963; postgrad. U. Vt., U. N.H., Columbia, U. Miami, Northwestern U. 1 dau., Suzanne (Mrs. Jack Robin Ziegler). Tchr. elementary schs., Dade County, Fla., 1941-55; faculty Eastern Mont. Coll. Edn., Billings, 1955-59, 61-66, asso. prof. edn., 1963-66; grad. asst. U. Denver, 1959-61; prof. curriculum Western State Coll., Gunnison, Colo., 1966-68; faculty Cal. State Coll. Stanislaus, Turlock, Cal., 1968—, dir. grad. studies, 1971—, dir. edn. master's program, 1974—, prof., 1974—, dir. student tchr. placement, 1974—, Elementary edn. cons. Colo., Cal. schs.; mem. Evaluation Team Modesto and Merced (Cal.), 1968—. Asst. dir. Assn. for Mentally Retarded Children, Billings, 1957-66. Recipient Civitan award, 1965. Contbr. articles to publs. Home: 224 S Western Av Waterford CA 95386 Office: Cal State Coll Stanislaus Turlock CA 95380

SMITH, REA T. WATERS (MRS. SHIRLEY D. SMITH), assn. exec.; b. Jamestown, N.Y., Apr. 13, 1918; d. F. Coy and Rena L. (Schultz) Waters; student Allegheny Coll., 1937, Jamestown Bus. Coll., 1938; m. Shirley D. Smith, Nov. 24, 1945. Asst. sec., time study accountant Am. Aviation Co., Jamestown, 1941-45; account exec., pub. relations counselor, partner Shirley D. Smith & Assos., Memphis, 1947-57; asst. to exec. dir. Pub. Relations Soc. Am., N.Y.C., 1957-70, v.p. adminstrn., 1971—. TV performer, producer, Memphis, 1949-52. Asst. sec. Found. for Pub. Relations Research and Edn. Mem. Nat. Pen Women Soc., Women Execs. in Pub. Relations (treas. 1971-73), Quota Internat. Home: 4 Peter Cooper Rd New York City NY 10010 Office: 845 3d Av New York City NY 10022

SMITH, REBECCA LOU, librarian; b. Murfreesboro, Tenn., Nov. 26, 1927; d. William Hoyt and Mary Pearl (Marlin) Smith; B.A., David Lipscomb Coll., 1949; M.A., George Peabody Coll. Tchrs., 1952. Tchr., Franklin (Ky.) Simpson Jr. High Sch., 1949-51; bibliographer Ohio State U., 1952-55; circulation librarian David Lipscomb Coll., 1955-59; asst. reference librarian Middle Tenn. State U., Murfreesboro, 1969—; substitute summer librarian, 1958-69. Mem. Am., Southeastern, Tenn., Mid-State library assns. Democrat. Mem. Ch. of Christ. Home: 1910 Lebanon Rd Murfreesboro TN 37130

SMITH, RITA IRENE, journalist; b. Olean, N.Y., Dec. 9, 1923; d. Christopher F. and Dorothy (Considine) Smith; B.A. magna cum laude, D'Youville Coll., Buffalo, 1944. Staff reporter Buffalo Courier Express, 1944-65, asst. womens editor, 1965-67, womens editor, 1967—. Travel lectr. mens and womens clubs, community groups, schs., chs. Recipient Page One writing awards Buffalo Newspaper Guild, 1960-68. Home: 2 Osgood Av West Seneca NY 14224 Office: 795 Main St Buffalo NY 14240

SMITH, ROSE MARIE, educator; b. Oklahoma City, Mar. 12, 1927; d. Lawrence F. and Effie M. (McDaniel) Smith; B.A. in Speech, Okla. Coll. Women, 1949; M.A. in Theatre, U. Mich., 1952; Ph.D. in Speech Communication, U. So. Cal., 1974. Tchr. high schs. in N.M. and Okla., 1949-58; mem. faculty Okla. Coll. Women, 1958-65, No.Ill. U., 1965-67; mem. faculty Ariz. State U., Tempe, 1967—, asst. prof. speech and theatre, 1967—, faculty Career Opportunity Program for Indian Students, summer 1969; active Okla. Recreation Dept., summers 1947-52, Twilight Time Musical Theatre, Oklahoma City, summers 1956-58, Project Upward Bound, DeKalb, Ill., summers 1966-67. Bd. dirs. Okemah Day Care Center, Tempe, 1970, 75, Okla.

Shakespeare Studies Found., 1952-75. Fellow Inst. Shakespearean Studies, Stratford-on-Avon, Eng., 1964; named Tchr. of Year, Okla. Coll. Women, 1961. Mem. Speech Communication Assn., Western, Speech Communication Assn., Internat. Communication Assn., Ariz. Speech and Drama Assn. (v.p.), Okla. Speech Assn. (past exec. sec., v.p.), Zeta Phi Eta. Mem. Christian Ch. (chmn. bd. elders). Home: 2201 W Carson Dr Tempe AZ 85282

SMITH, RUBIE EUDORA, ret. educator; b. nr. Marshall County, Ky.; d. George W. and Lillian (Smith) Smith; A.B., Murray State U., 1933; H.H.D., 1974; M.A., George Peabody Coll. for Tchrs., 1939. Tchr. elementary schs., Marshall County and Benton, Ky., 1933-39; supervising tchr. Univ. Sch., Murray, Ky., 1939-45; asst. prof. edn. Murray State U., 1945-57, asso. prof., 1958-64, prof. edn., 1964—, chmn. elementary edn. dept., 1966-74; asso. prof. edn. George Peabody Coll. for Tchrs., 1957-58; faculty U. Ky. Bur. Sch. Service, 1945, Pa. State U., summer 1950, Woman's Coll. N.C., 1954. Life mem. P.T.A.; del. White House Conf. on Children, 1970. Recipient Scroll of Ky. Elementary Prins. Assn., 1954, Distinguished prof. award Murray State U. Alumni Assn., 1973; named Ky. col. Mem. Nat., Ky., 1st Dist. (past pres.) edn. assns., Ky. Assn. Childhood Edn. (past pres.), Assn. for Childhood Edn. Internat., Assn. for Supervision and Curriculum Devel., Nat. Sci. Tchrs. Assn., Peabody, Murray State U. alumni assns., Murray U. Womans Soc. (founder, past pres.), Nat. Council Tchrs. English, Dept. Elementary Sch. Prins., Nat. Council Social Studies, Kappa Delta Pi (past chpt. pres., counselor), Delta Kappa Gamma (past pres.). Democrat. Methodist. Club: Murray Womans (past pres. Delta dept.). Contbr. articles to profl. jours. Home: 1308 Olive Blvd Murray KY 42071

SMITH, RUBY LUCILLE, librarian; b. Nobob, Ky., Sept. 19, 1917; d. James Ira and Myrtie Olive (Crabtree) Jones; A.B., Western Ky. State Tchrs. Coll., 1943, M.A., 1966; m. Kenneth Cornelius Smith, Dec. 25, 1946; children—Kenneth Cornelius, Corma Ann. Tchr. rural schs., Barren County, Ky., 1941-42; tchr. secondary sch. English, librarian Temple Hill Consol. Sch., Glasgow, Ky., 1943-49, 49-51, 53-56, sch. librarian, 1956—. Sec. Barren County Cancer Soc., 1968-70, Barren County Fair Bd., 1969-70; leader 4-H Club, 1957-72, mem. council Barren County. Trustee Mary Wood Weldon Meml. Library, 1964—; trustee Barren County Pub. Library, 1969—, sec., 1969—. Mem. N.E.A. (life), Ky. Edn. Assn., Ky. Assn. Sch. Librarians (sec. 1970-71), 3d Dist. Library Assn. (pres. 1963, 66), Barren County Edn. Assn. (pres. 1960-62), Ky. Audio Visual Assn., Barren County Republican Women's Club, Monroe Assn. Woman's Missionary Union (dir. 1968-72), Monroe Assn. Baptists (library dir. 1972—). Home: Route 1 Box 38 Summer Shade KY 42166 Office: Route 4 Box 210 Glasgow KY 42141

SMITH, RUTH IDA, librarian; b. Gowanda, N.Y., Aug. 9, 1911; d. Eber LeRoy and Ruth Edna (Bull) Russell; B.A., Allegheny Coll., Meadville, Pa., 1933; B.L.S., U. Wis., 1939; m. John Amasa Smith, July 26, 1941; 1 son, James Russell. Elementary tchr., prin., East Otto, N.Y., 1944; children's librarian Monroe (Wis.) Pub. Library, 1939-41; elementary sch. librarian Jamestown (N.Y.) pub. schs., 1955-72; founder, adminstr. mus. Indian and pioneer artifacts. Mem. N.Y. State Ret. Tchrs. Assn., Chautaugua County Hist. Soc., Iroquois Seneca Archaeol. and Hist. Soc., Chautaque Archaeol. Soc., Grange. Methodist (treas. 1965-69). Clubs: Country Life, Camera (Chautauqua, N.Y.). Address: RD 1 Cassadaga NY 14718

SMITH, RUTH KRAATZ (MRS. DONALD T. SMITH), banker; b. Maywood, N.J., Dec. 21, 1932; d. Rudolph Paul and Gertrude Augusta (Mitschele) Kraatz; grad. Katharine Gibbs Sch., N.Y.C., 1951; certificate Am. Inst. Banking, 1967, Grad. Sch. Banking of South, La. State U., 1971; m. Donald T. Smith, June 23, 1951; 1 dau., Donna Jean. With 1st Nat. Bank of Merritt Island (Fla.), 1962—, sr. v.p., 1973—. Mem. Am. Inst. Banking, Merritt Island C. of C., Bank Adminstrn. Inst. Lutheran. Club: Merritt Island Women's. Home: 1135 N Tropical Trail Merritt Island FL 32952 Office: 15 E Merritt Island Causeway Merritt Island FL 32952

SMITH, RUTH LILLIAN SCHLUCHTER (MRS. T. GUILFORD SMITH), librarian; b. Detroit, Oct. 18, 1917; d. Clayton John and Gertrude Katherine (Kastler) Schluchter; A.B., Wayne U., 1939; A.B. in L.S., U. Mich., 1942; m. T(homas) Guilford Smith, Sept. 28,1948; 1 son, Pemberton III. Jr. librarian Detroit Pub. Library, 1942-43; research asst. Moore Sch. Elec. Engring., Phila., 1946-47; reference librarian Inst. for Def. Analyses, Arlington, Va., 1961-64, chief reader services, 1964-65, chief open library, 1965-67, head librarian, 1967—. Served with WAVES, 1943-46. Mem. Spl. Libraries Assn., Am. Soc. for Information Sci., Ch. and Synagogue Library Assn. (pres. 1967-68). Author: Publicity for a Church Library, 1966; Workshop Planning, 1972. Home: 5304 Glenwood Rd Bethesda MD 20014 Office: 400 Army Navy Dr Arlington VA 22202

SMITH, RUTH NEWBURN (MRS. CARLETON D. SMITH), writer; b. Cleve., Dec. 26, 1907; d. Theodore Walter and Florence (Payne) Newburn; spl. student Sorbonne, Paris, France, 1927-28; B.A., George Washington U., 1929; m. Robert Weir Sedam, Feb. 28, 1931 (dec. July 1957); children—Robert Gordon (dec. July 1958), William Turner; m. 2d, Carleton D. Smith, Apr. 29, 1959; 1 stepson, Carleton Craig. Copywriter, Woodward & Lothrop, Washington, 1929-31; columnist Bronxville (N.Y.) Reporter, 1941-43; copywriter Ellington & Co., advt., N.Y.C., 1947-49; editor Baby Talk mag., N.Y.C., 1949-52; free-lance writer articles pub. various mags. including Better Homes & Gardens, Charm, Family Circle, McCall's, Pageant, Parents', Today's Woman, 1952—; writer booklets, publicity Beechnut Packing Co., 1952-54; writer pamphlets, publicity Glass Container Mfrs. Inst., N.Y.C., 1954-59; writer ads. TV, booklets Heinz Baby Foods, 1956-64. Mem. women's bd. George Washington U. Hosp., 1961—. Mem. Pi Beta Phi, Delta Sigma Rho. Episcopalian. Club: Sulgrave (Washington). Home: Indies West 2200 Gulf Shore Blvd Naples FL 33940

SMITH, SANDI (SANDRA) YVONNE SHORT (MRS. HOWARD L. SMITH), broadcaster; b. Mobile, Ala., Dec. 11, 1941; grad. high sch., 1960; m. Howard L. Smith, Jan. 4, 1969; children—John Edward, Daniel Eric, Howard Leland. Sec. to auditor Mchts. Nat. Bank of Mobile, 1959-61; owner secretarial shop, Mobile, 1968-69; sec. to dir. news dept. WALA TV, Mobile, 1967-68; office mgr., program dir., bookkeeper, WLPR Stereo FM, 1969-70, hostess Encore program, 1970—; operations mgr. Mobile Broadcast Service, Inc., 1970—. Home: Rt 1 Box 181-C Mobile AL 36605 Office: 758 St Michael St Mobile AL 36602

SMITH, SANDRA JEAN, journalist; b. Great Lakes, Ill., July 6, 1949; d. Dennis Murray and Olga (Grosheff) Smith; B.S. in Journalism (Ill. State scholar), Northwestern U., 1971. Family life editor, staff writer Daily News of Camarillo, Cal., 1971—. Mem. Camarillo Bicentennial Com. Recipient Gold L, Nat. Honor Soc. Mem. Am. Assn. U. Women, Camarillo Bus. and Profl. Womens Club, Women in Communications, Inc., Sigma Delta Chi. Republican. Presbyn. Club: Camarillo Art. Home: 200 S Glenn Dr Camarillo CA 93010 Office: 99 S Glenn Dr Camarillo CA 93010

SMITH, SARAH ANNA LITTLE (MRS. KENNETH SOLOMON SMITH), aerospace co. exec.; b. Upland, Pa., Oct. 22, 1920; d. William Francis and Luella Elizabeth (Jones) Little; student Sleepers Coll., 1942-43, City Coll. N.Y., 1946-48; m. Kenneth Solomon Smith, Sept. 17, 1961; children—Ruth (Mrs. Roy Tabron, Jr.), Kathryn (Mrs. Robert G. Clarke, Jr.), Charles E. Minor, Jr. Specialist urban affairs and community relations Gen. Electric Co., Phila., 1959—. Active Phila. Urban League, Heritage House. Recipient Chapel of Four Chaplains award, One in a Thousand award Gen. Electric Co., 1968. Mem. Nat. Assn. Market Developers (nat. sec. 1969-72), Nat. Alliance Businessmen (adv. com. youth motivation task force 1966-72), Am. Found. Negro Affairs, Phila. Guidance Assn. Author: (booklet) A Look into the Future. Home: 315 Yale Av Broomall PA 19008 Office: PO Box 8555 Philadelphia PA 19101

SMITH, SELMA MOIDEL, lawyer; b. Warren, O., Apr. 3, 1919; d. Louis and Mary (Oyer) Moidel; student Los Angeles City Coll., 1936-37, U. Cal., 1937-39, U. So. Cal., 1939-41; LL.B., Pacific Coast University, 1942; 1 son, Mark Lee. Admitted to practice before the California bar, 1943, U.S. dist. ct., 1943, United States Supreme Court, 1958; gen. practice of law; mem. Moidel, Moidel, Moidel & Smith. Field dir. civilian adv. com. WAC, 1943. Mem. nat. bd. Woman's Med. Coll. Pa., 1953—. Decorated La Order del Merito Juan Pablo Duarte (Dominican Republic). Mem. Am., Cal. (servicemen's legal com.), Los Angeles (psychopathic ct. com.) bar assns., Mexico-American Lawyers Club, National Association of Women Lawyers (chmn. com. unauthorized practice of law, social commn. UN, regional dir. western states, Hawaii, 1949-50, mem. judicial adminstrn. com. 1960, nat. chmn. world peace through law com. 1966-67), League of Americas (dir.), Inter-Am. Bar Assn., So. Cal. Women Lawyers Assn., (pres. 1947, 48), Women Lawyers Assn. (chairman Law Day committee 1966), State Bar Conference Committee, Council Bar Associations Los Angeles County (charter sec. 1950), Cal. Bus. Women's Council (dir. 1951), Los Angeles Bus. Women's Council (pres. 1952), Cal. President's Council (1st v.p.), Iota Tau Tau (dean Los Angeles, supreme treas. 1959-62). Club: Los Angeles Lawyers (pub. defenders com.). Home: 15730 Woodvale Rd Encino CA 91316 Office: 408 S Spring St Los Angeles CA 90013

SMITH, SHIRLEY, state ofcl.; b. N.Y.C., Dec. 4, 1931; d. Walter Carl and Hazell Dell (Kendrick) Subke; B.A., U. Cal. at Berkeley, 1952; postgrad. U. Tex., 1953-54, U. Cal. Sch. Law, 1954-55; LL.B., U. Pa., 1956; m. M.E. Bitterman, Oct. 1, 1952 (div. 1964); children—Joan, Ann; m. 2d, Albert F. Smith, Jr., Aug. 2, 1967. Admitted to Pa. bar, 1956, N.Y. bar, 1964, Cal. bar, 1968, Hawaii bar, 1971; law clk. to U.S. Dist. Ct. judge for Eastern Dist. of Pa., 1956-57; asst. city solicitor for City of Phila., 1957-58, dep. city solicitor, 1959-60; asso. firm Schnader, Harrison, Segal and Lewis, Phila., 1960-64; asso. firm Nixon, Mudge, Rose, Guthrie and Alexander, N.Y.C., 1964-67; dir. of litigation for Western Center on Law and Poverty, U. So. Cal., Los Angeles 1967; house counsel Commonwealth United Corp., Beverley Hills, Cal., 1967; litigation specialist Fendler and Fendler, Beverley Hills, 1968-70; dep. atty. gen. for state of Hawaii, Honolulu, 1970—. Mem. State Bar of Cal., Bar Assn. of Hawaii, Am. Civil Liberties Union, N.Y. Bar, Pa. Bar., D.A.R., Phi Beta Kappa, Sigma Kappa. Episcopalian. Home: 34 White Sands Place Kailua HI 96734 Office: Office of the Attorney General State Capitol Honolulu HI 96813

SMITH, STELLA JUNE (MRS. HAROLD SMITH, JR.), store owner; b. Granada, Colo., Aug. 13, 1908; d. Frans Oscar and Nannie (Smeltz) Johnson; grad. high sch.; m. Willis Jay Allison, Oct. 14, 1930 (dec. Dec. 1940); 1 dau., Norma June (Mrs. Russell Lee Ausmus); m. 2d, Harold Smith, Jr., Feb. 24, 1966. Clk., Two Buttes (Colo.) Grocery Market, 1952-54, owner, 1954—. Sec., Two Buttes Water, 1942-70; clk., Two Buttes, 1940—. Mem. Rebekah Lodge. Home and office: Two Buttes CO 81084

SMITH, SUSAN J., co-owner art gallery; b. Topeka, Kan., Dec. 1, 1942; d. Thomas Francis and Lucille Frances (Daniel) Smith; student Washington U., St. Louis, 1960; student Kansas City Jr. Coll., 1961-62; B.F.A., Kansas City Art Inst., 1966; postgrad. U. Cal. at Davis, 1966; m. Charles Martin Harrison, Oct. 31, 1966 (div. Jan. 1974). Partner, East of the Sun, retail book and folk arts store, San Francisco, 1967-73; partner, curator West of the Moon, Am. Indian and other arts gallery, San Francisco, 1971—; exhibited shows William Rockhill Nelson Gallery Art, Kansas City, Mo., 1972, M.H. de Young Mus., San Francisco, 1972. Office: 3464 Sacramento St San Francisco CA 94118

SMITH, SUSY, author; b. Washington; d. Merton M. and Elizabeth (Hardegen) Smith; student U. Tex., 1930-33, U. Ariz., 1934. Newspaper reporter, Oakland, Md., Daytona Beach, Fla., 1945-54; columnist Salt Lake Tribune, Salt Lake City, 1955. Parapsychology Found. grantee, 1958-65. Pres., Survival Research Found. Mem. Soc. for Psychical Research, Am. Soc. for Psychical Research, Assn. for Humanistic Psychology, Spiritual Frontiers Fellowship, Acad. Parapsychology and Medicine, Authors Guild, Pen Women, Soc. Southwestern Authors, Chi Omega. Author: ESP, 1962; The Mediumship of Mrs. Leonard, 1963; World of the Strange, 1963; The Enigma of Out-of-Body Travel, 1965; ESP for the Millions, 1965; A Supernatural Primer for the Millions, 1966; Haunted Houses for the Millions, 1967; Reincarnation for the Millions, 1967; More ESP for the Millions, 1967; Prominent American Ghosts, 1967; Out of Body Experiences for the Millions, 1968; Adventures in the Supernormal, 1968; Ghosts Around the House, 1970; Today's Witches, 1970; Widespread Psychic Wonders, 1970; Susy Smith's Supernatural World, 1971; Confessions of a Psychic, 1971; ESP and You, 1972; How to Develop Your ESP, 1972; She Spoke to the Dead, 1972; ESP and Hypnosis, 1973; Life is Forever, 1974. Editor: Human Personality and its Survival of Bodily Death (F.W.H. Myers), 1961. Address: 101 W River Rd Tucson AZ 85704

SMITH, TERRY HAMMOND (MRS. TERRY B. SMITH), journalist; b. Wilmington, N.C., Mar. 22, 1950; d. William Franklin and Elizabeth Williams (Bland) Hammond; student U. N.C., 1968-72; postgrad., 1971-72; m. Terry B. Smith, Apr. 17, 1971. Staff writer Star-News Newspapers, Wilmington, 1968-69; news editor News of Orange County, Hillsborough, N.C., 1972-74; gen. assignment reporter Raleigh (N.C.) Times, 1974—. Recipient Newswriting award N.C. Press Women, 1973. Mem. N.C. Press Women, N.C. Press Assn. Home: PO Box 32 Cary NC 27511 Office: PO Box 647 Hillsborough NC 27278

SMITH, VALENE LUCY (MRS. EDWIN CHESTEEN GOLAY), educator; b. Spokane, Wash., Feb. 14, 1926; d. Ernest Frank and Lucy (Blachy) Smith; B.A., U. Cal. at Los Angeles, 1946, M.A., 1950; Ph.D., U. Utah, 1966; m. Edwin Chesteen Golay, June 7, 1970. Faculty Los Angeles City Coll., 1947-66, prof. earth sci., until 1966; Fulbright lectr. U. Peshawar, Pakistan, 1953-54; prof. anthropology Cal. State U., Chico, 1967—. Cons. Office Econ. Opportunity project Headstart, Alaska, 1965. Recipient Dept. Indian Affairs and No. Devel. Research grant, 1969. Mem. Soc. Woman Geographers (chmn. So. Cal. group 1962-66), Cal. State Colls. and Univs. Club: Soroptimist (Chico, Cal.). Author: East of Shannon, West of Moscow, 1965. Cons., dir. film Three Stone Blades, 1971. Home: 2956 Cohasset Rd Chico CA 95926

SMITH, VERENA GASSER, lawyer; b. Berne, Switzerland, Apr. 17, 1928; d. Edward and Frieda (Steiner) Gasser; came to U.S., 1949, naturalized, 1962; B.S., U. Cin., 1964; J.D., Salm P. Chase Coll., 1968. Admitted to Ohio bar, 1968, Ky. bar, 1974; asso. firm Frost & Jacobs, Cin., 1968—. Mem. Am., Ohio, Cin. bar assns., Cin. Lawyers Club (sec. 1974—). Home: 231 Riverside Dr Covington KY 41011 Office: DuBois Tower Cincinnati OH 45202

SMITH, VIRGINIA LOUISE BISSELL (MRS. MELVIN EUGENE SMITH), educator; b. Marcellus, Mich., Apr, 14, 1921; d. Santford and Bessie Mabel (Manier) Bissell; student Montmorency County Normal Sch., 1940, Central Mich. U., 1941; B.S., Eastern Mich. U., 1957, M.A., 1964; m. Melvin Eugene Smith, Nov. 24, 1943;1 son, Ronald Eugene. Elementary tchr., rural schs., Calhoun, Clare and Genesee counties, Mich., 1941-45, 48-53; tchr. city schs., Davison, Mich., 1955-65, speech therapist, 1965-68, dir. spl. edn., 1968—. Mem. Mich. Pub. Sch. Employees Retirement Bd., 1968-74. Chmn. Republican com., Davison Twp. and City of Davison, 1968. Mem. Mich. Speech and Hearing Assn., Council Exceptional Children, Assn. Retarded Children, Mich., Nat. assns. children with learning disabilities, Mich. Assn. Emotionally Disturbed Children, Delta Kappa Gamma (charter). Home: 318 North Dr Davison MI 48423 Office: 615 E Clark St Davison MI 48423

SMITH, WILMINA ROWLAND, ret. religious worker; b. Augusta, Ga., Mar. 17, 1908; d. William Maltbie and Susan Alexander (Myers) Rowland; B.S., Wilson Coll., 1929, L.H.D., 1957; M.A., Yale, 1937; B.D., Union Theol. Sem., 1941. Tchr. Presbyn. Ch., Taichow, Kiangsu, China, 1930-33; traveling sec., later hdqrs. sec. Student Vol. Movement, N.Y.C., 1933-36; dir. religious activities Woman's Coll. U. N.C., Greensboro, 1938-40; exec. sec. World Student Service Fund, N.Y.C., 1941-45; asst. gen. sec. World Student Relief, Geneva, Switzerland, 1945-47; asso. sec. World Council Christian Edn., N.Y.C., 1949-54; dir. council promotion and publs. United Ch. Women of Nat. Council Chs. of Christ in U.S.A., N.Y.C., 1954-55; administrv. asst. to dir., prof. religion The Merrill-Palmer Sch., Detroit, 1955-57; asso. minister Indian Hill Ch., Cin., 1957-60; dir. edn. loans and scholarships Bd. Christian Edn. United Presbyn. Ch. U.S.A., Phila., 1960-73. Recipient Order of the White Lion, first class, Czechoslovakia, 1947. Fellow Soc. for Religion in Higher Edn.; mem. Am. Assn. U. Women, Am. Assn. for UN, League Women Voters. Democrat. Presbyn. Address: PO Box 10441 St Petersburg FL 33733

SMITH, WINIFRED JANE, educator; b. Clarksburg, W.Va., Jan. 12, 1919; d. James Howell and Geraldine Winifred (Stager) Smith; B.S. in Edn., Kent (O.) State U., 1941, M.A., 1952. Tchr. high schs. in Ohio, Cal. and Ariz., 1941-56; librarian Akron (O.) Pub. Library, 1956-59; tchr. English, Coronado High Sch., Scottsdale, Ariz., 1961—; librarian (Mesa) Community Coll., 1967-68. Mem. Scottsdale Citizens STEP Com., 1969-70. Mem. N.E.A., A.L.A., Alpha Delta Kappa (chpt. rec. sec. 1969-70). Home: 8455 E Orange Blossom Lane Scottsdale AZ 85253 Office: 2501 N 74th St Scottsdale AZ 85257

SMITHBURG, MARY MCANLIS, lawyer; b. Fort Wayne, Ind., Dec. 1, 1919; d. Chauncey Ruthven and Helen (Harper) McAnlis; student Coll. Wooster, 1937-38; A.B., U. Ill., 1941; J.D., DePaul U., 1952; m. Donald Winston Smithburg, Feb. 10, 1942; children—Donald Rowan, Laura. Examiner adminstrv. and mgmt. placement sect. U.S. Civil Service Commn., 1942-44; placement officer U.S. War Relocation Authority, 1944-46; ins. and property officer Chgo. Dept. Welfare, 1953-56; admitted to Ill. bar, 1952, Ala. bar, 1969; atty. Legal Aid Bur., Chgo., 1956-60; staff asst. Nat. Legal Aid and Defender Assn., Chgo., 1960-63; atty. Legal Aid Bur. Mandel Clinic, 1963-67. Vice chmn. Madison County (Ala.) Democratic Women, 1971-72. Mem. Am. Bar Assn., Women's Bar Assn. Ill., Ala. State Bar, D.A.R., Albuquerque Symphony Women's Assn., Phi Beta Kappa, Delta Gamma, Kappa Beta Pi, Phi Kappa Phi. Episcopalian. Club: Univ. Women's (Huntsville, Ala.). Contbr. to Lawyers Ency. Home: 2413 Ada Pl NE Albuquerque NM 87106

SMITHSON, ELLEN CONLEY, educator; b. Buffalo, Jan. 8, 1946; d. Richard Patrick and Pauline Patricia (Dell'Omo) Conley; B.S., Slippery Rock (Pa.) State Coll., 1967; M.Ed., U. Pitts., 1968; M.S. in Edn., State Univ. Coll. at Buffalo, 1973; postgrad. State U. N.Y. at Buffalo, 1973—; m. John Kenneth Smithson, Apr. 27, 1968. Grad. asst. U. Pitts., 1967-68; instr. phys. edn. State Univ. Coll. at Buffalo, 1968-70; instr. Canisius Coll., Buffalo, 1970-72, asst. prof. phys. edn., 1972—, coordinator Women's Athletics Assn., 1974—. Mem. Western N.Y. Coll. Personnel Assn. (adv. bd.), Delta Psi Kappa, Kappa Delta Pi. Home: 55 Woodbine Av West Seneca NY 14224 Office: 1833 Main St Buffalo NY 14208

SMITHSON, SUZANNE KAY, therapist; b. Mpls., Jan. 15, 1944; d. Edward Argyle and Katherine (Davis) Smithson; A.A., St. Petersberg Jr. Coll., 1964; B.S., U. Fla., 1966. Staff occupational therapist Spain Rehab. Center, U. Ala., Birmingham, 1966-68; perceptual-motor therapist, supr. Vanguard Sch., Ft. Lauderdale, Fla., 1969—. Mem. Am. Occupational Therapy Assn. Eckankar. Home: 709 SE 15th St Fort Lauderdale FL 33316 Office: 1801 S Andrews Av Fort Lauderdale FL 33316

SMOCK, MARTHA FLORENCE (MRS. CARL FRANCIS SMOCK), mag. editor; b. Kansas City, Mo., Nov. 3, 1913; d. James Vincent and Maybelle Frances (Snell) McNamara; student Kansas City Jr. Coll.; m. Carl Francis Smock, Jan. 25, 1935; children—Stephanie (Mrs. John Thomas), Katherine (Mrs. Andrew Wales). With Unity Sch. of Christianity, Unity Village, Mo., 1933—, editor Daily Word, non-sectarian devotional mag., 1944—. Author: Meet It With Faith, 1966; Halfway Up The Mountain, 1971. Home: 6408 High Dr Shawnee Mission KS 66208 Office: Unity Village MO 64063

SMOLKER, ROSEMARY GILMARTIN (MRS. ROBERT E. SMOLKER), editor; b. Phila., July 30, 1925; d. William J. and Rebecca Dolores (O'Donnell) Gilmartin; B.A., Bryn Mawr Coll., 1947; M.S., Yale, 1951; postgrad. U. Chgo., 1950-54; m. Robert E. Smolker, Mar. 18, 1950; children—David, Michael, Rachel. Instr. natural scis. Mich. State U. East Lansing, 1955-57; instr. biology State U. N.Y. at Stony Brook, 1964-65, mng. editor, gen. bus. mgr. Quar. Rev. Biology, 1965—. Mem. League Women Voters (dir. 1962-65), Council Biology Editors, Sigma Xi. Home: Box 889 Mt Grey Rd Setauket NY 11733 Office: Quarterly Review of Biology State University of NY at Stony Brook Stony Brook NY 11790

SMOOT, LUCILLE D. HEIN (MRS. CHARLES EFFINGER SMOOT), govt. ofcl.; b. West Pittston, Pa., July 25, 1920; d. John Jonas and Elizabeth Boam (Coffee) Hein; student Am. U., 1940-45, Cornell U., 1969; m. Gerald Arthur Butler, Oct. 7, 1942 (div. July 1946); 1 son, Gerald Allan; m. 2d, Charles Effinger Smoot, Sept. 9, 1961. With Personnel Div., Internal Revenue Service, Washington, 1942—, successively asst. clerk, sr. clerk. personnel technician, personnel officer, 1942-59, employee relations specialist, 1959-66, labor mgmt. and employee relations specialist, 1967-70, program leader for employee relations, 1970-72, chief conduct and appeals sect. 1972-74, spl. adviser labor relations, 1974—. Vice pres. Young Peoples League, 1946-48; chmn. Information Bur., Community Chest, 1948-50. Mem. Soc. Personnel Adminstrn. Republican. Presbyn.

Club: Government Girl. Home: 2006 Columbia Rd Washington DC 20009 Office: Treasury Dept Washington DC 20224

SMOTHERS, BETTYE JEAN (MRS. THOMAS G. SMOTHERS), ednl. adminstr.; b. Memphis, May, 1934; d. Robert C. and Lois K. (Griffith) Turner; B.S., Union U., 1955; M.A., Western Ky. U., 1963; m. Thomas G. Smothers, June 6, 1954; 1 dau., Cynthia. Tchr. Jefferson County schs., Louisville, 1957-62; tchr. Finneytown (O.) High Sch., 1964-66; adminstr. Alderson-Broaddus Coll., Philippi, W.Va., 1966-70; adminstr. Palm Beach (Fla.) Atlantic Coll., 1970—. Mem. Am. Assn. Univ. Women (v.p. 1968-70). Clubs: College (v.p. 1969-70), All Seasons Garden (pres. 1968-70). Home: 532 Bayberry Lake Park FL 33403 Office: 1101 S Olive West Palm Beach FL 33401

SMOTHERS, DORIS M. WEST (MRS. JOHN W. SMOTHERS), social worker; b. Chgo.; B.A., Roosevelt U., 1953; M.A., U. Chgo., 1963; m. John W. Smothers, Oct. 2, 1946 (dec. Oct. 1968); 1 son, John W. Jr. Caseworker pub. assistance div. Cook County Dept. Pub. Aid, Chgo., 1953-58, caseworker children's div., 1959-65; caseworker Juvenile Protective Assn., Chgo., 1965-67; dist. supr. child and family services, North Suburban Homemaker Service, Evanston, Ill., 1967-71; social worker Chgo. Bd. Edn., 1971—. Mem. Nat. Assn. Social Workers, Nat. Conf. Welfare, Acad. Certified Social Workers, Ill. Welfare Assn., Chgo. Council for Exceptional Children, Nat. Assn. Black Social Workers, N.A.A.C.P., Urban League, Alumni Assn. Roosevelt U., Alumni Assn. U. Chgo. Home: 351 Washington Av Glencoe IL 60022 Office: 5025 N Laramie Av Chicago IL 60630

SMUTNY, JOAN PRISCILLA (MRS. HERBERT PAUL SMUTNY), educator; b. Chgo.; d. Eugene and Mabel (Lind) Franklin; B.S., M.A., Northwestern U.; m. Herbert Paul Smutny; 1 dau., Cheryl Ann. Tchr., New Trier High Sch., Winnetka, Ill.; faculty, founder, dir. Nat. High Sch. Inst., Northwestern U. Sch. Edn., Evanston, Ill.; faculty, founder dir. high sch. workshop in critical thinking and edn., chmn. dept. communications Nat. Coll. Edn., Evanston, 1967—, founder, dir. Woman Power Through Edn. Seminars, 1969, dir. Center for Continuing Edn., 1974—, dir. Workshop in Elementary Edn. for Gifted Students, 1974—, dir. Thinking for Action in Career Edn. Project, 1974—; co-dir., instr. Critical Thinking Seminar, Ill. Family Services, 1972. Writer ednl. filmstrips in lang. arts and lit. Soc. for Visual Edn., 1960—; mem. speakers bur. Council Fgn. Relations, 1968—; mem. adv. com. Edn. Professions Devel. Act, U.S. Office Edn., 1969, dir. Right to Read Office Workshop in Critical Reading, 1973; writer, cons. Radiant Ednl. Corp., 1969-71; cons. A.L.A., 1969—. Mem. Nat. Soc. Arts and Letters, Am. Assn. U. Profs., Mortar Bd., Pi Lambda Theta, Phi Delta Kappa. Editor, contbr. Maturity in Teaching, 1962. Writer ednl. filmstrips The Brother's Grimm, 1960, How the West Was Won, 1960, Mutiny on the Bounty, 1960, Dr. Zhivago, 1964, Space Odessey 2001, 1969; Talking Picture Story Study Prints in Poetry; author, cons. filmstrip series Christmas Around the World. Home: 633 Forest St Wilmette IL 60091 Office: 2840 Sheridan Rd Evanston IL 60201

SMUTZ, DOROTHY DRING, pianist, music educator; b. Kansas City, Mo.; d. Johnson and Emma L. (Mack) Dring; studied with Walter Goff, Sterling, Colo., Dr. Ernest R. Kroeger, St. Louis, E. Robert Schmitz, Paul Badura-Skoda; postgrad. Kroeger Sch. Music, 1926-28; m. Harold Turk Smutz, Oct. 27, 1930; 1 son, Robert Allen. Radio, TV appearances, also concerts, recitals; soloist St. Louis Philharmonic, St. Louis Little Symphony, St. Louis Symphony orchestras; harpsichordist St. Louis Bach Soc., 1940-44; piano, clavichord, seminars for tchrs., 1946—; debut Town Hall, N.Y.C., 1949; guest artist, forum leader Okla. Music Tchrs. Assn., 1950; lecture recital Mo. Music Tchrs. Assn.; mem. faculty, adjudicator Nat. Guild Piano Tchrs.; lectr., guest artist various assns. convs.; dir. tchrs. clinic and workshop So. Ill. U., 1963; guest artist, condr. workshop Coll. William and Mary, 1973; piano faculty St. Louis Conservatory Music, 1974—; adjudicator state and dist. piano auditions sponsored by Music Tchrs. Nat. Assn. Mem. Nat. (recipient Recognition award 1971), Mo. (exec. bd.) music tchrs. assns., Am. Piano Tchrs. Assn., St. Louis Piano Tchrs. Round Table, Mu Phi Epsilon (past pres. St. Louis alumnae). Presbyn. Home: 619 Hollywood Pl Webster Groves MO 63119

SMYTH, MARY ELLEN, medical supply co. exec.; b. Lander, Wyo., July 2, 1935; d. Fred and Mary (Kosanovich) Savage; B.A. with honors, U. Wyo., 1956, M.A., 1960; m. W. Patrick Smyth, June 20, 1964; children—Timothy Murphy and Kevin Anthony (twins). Tchr. secondary schs. in Colo., 1956-59; instr. U. Wyo., 1959-60, 63-64; instr. speech Pa. State U., 1960-63; tchr. high sch. in Ill., 1964-70; bus. mgr. Orthopaedics Corp., Oak Park, Ill., 1973—. Summer theatre stock appearances, 1959-70; TV show hostess, 1962; speech cons., 1974—. Mem. Ill. Com. on Media. Vice pres. aux. MacNeal Hosp., 1973-74; program dir. aux. Oak Park Hosp., 1973-74. Mem. Speech Communication Assn., Ill. Speech Assn., Chgo. Council Fgn. Relations, Common Cause, Am. Assn. U. Women (dir. Ill. div., pres. Riverside br. 1972-74, del. nat. conv. 1973), Phi Beta Kappa, Pi Beta Phi (pres. Chgo. West Suburban chpt. 1973-74), Phi Kappa Phi, Kappa Delta Pi, Theta Alpha Phi. Contbr. articles to publs. Address: 7600 Augusta St River Forest IL 60305

SMYTH, MARY VIRGINIA MCINTIRE (MRS. JAMES MARVIN SMYTH), govt. ofcl.; b. Ardmore, Okla.; d. Hugh and Natalie (Kocher) McIntire; A.A., William Woods Coll., 1938; B.A., U. Okla., 1940; M. Social Sci., Smith Coll., 1947; m. James Marvin Smyth, Dec. 3, 1956. Child welfare worker, dir. Day Care Program, Sunbeam Home, Oklahoma City, 1941-44; social worker Service to Mil. Hosps., A.R.C., 1945-49, field dir. mil. and navy hosps., Midwestern area, 1951-54, asst. dir. services to mil. and vets. hosps., Southeastern Area Hdqrs., Atlanta, 1955-57; psychiat. social worker Mental Hygiene Clinic, Oklahoma City, 1950; chief geriatric unit, mental health div., Ga. Dept. Pub. Health, Atlanta, 1957-59; regional rep. on aging, adminstr. on aging, Dept. Health, Edn. and Welfare, Atlanta, 1960-67, regional commr. social and rehab. service, 1967—. Mem. Met. Atlanta Red Cross Com. on Nursing, 1962-65; mem. study com. on establishing a sch. of social work Ga. Bd. Regents, 1963. Adv. mem. bd. trustees Presbyn. Homes, Atlanta, 1961—; mem. adv. com. Sch. Social Work, U. Ga., 1966—. Recipient Cocharan Citizenship award William Woods Coll., 1938, Citation for Outstanding Service, Am. Assn. Ret. Persons, 1967, Ga. Gerontology Soc., 1967, Ga. Conf. Social Welfare, Regional Dirs. award Dept. Health, Edn. and Welfare, 1966, Dept. Health, Edn. and Welfare Superior Service award, 1968, Dept. Health, Edn. and Welfare Distinguished Service award, 1970. Mem. Ga. Gerontology Soc. (pres. 1961), Ga. Conf. Social Welfare (pres. 1961-63), Am. Pub. Welfare Assn. (mem. com. aging 1965-66), Nat. Commn. for Social Workers Careers, Nat. Assn. Social Workers (mem. nat. nominating com. 1967-68), Am. Soc. Pub. Adminstrs., Nat. Rehab. Assn., Nat. Council Aging, Atlanta Fed. Exec. Bd. Presbyn. Clubs: Leafmore Hills Civic (sec. 1957-65) (Decatur, Ga.) Leafmore Hills Garden (sec. 1958-60) (Decatur). Home: 2315 Leafmore Dr Decatur GA 30033 Office: 50 7th St NE Atlanta GA 30323

SMYTH, RUTH BROWN, educator; b. Norwalk, O., Mar. 3, 1903; d. Ralph Whittlesey and Carlene (Kubach) Brown; A.B., Oberlin Coll., 1927, M.A., 1928; postgrad. Purdue U., 1955-56; m. Bertram James Smyth, Aug. 24, 1929 (dec. Nov. 1946); children—Ruth Elizabeth (Mrs. William Solis), James Ralph. Prof., Cedarville Coll., 1927-28; instr. math. Oberlin Coll., 1930-46; asso. prof. Coll. Wooster (O.), 1954-70, prof., 1970—; prof. math. Miles Coll., 1966-67. Mem. Ohio Acad. Sci. (lectr. 1962), Am. Assn. U. Profs., Am. Math. Assn. Presbyn. Mem. Order Easter Star. Author: (with Melcher P. Fobes) Calculus with Analytic Geometry, 1963. Home: 706 Northwestern Av Wooster OH 44691

SMYTHE, ANNE PARKER, banker; b. Goshen, N.Y., June 27, 1932; d. Edwin Ridgeway and Kathryne (Batchelder) Smythe; student Wood Secretarial Sch., 1950-51. Supr. bookkeeping dept. Union Nat. Bank & Trust Co., Mt. Holly, N.J., 1958-60, asst. trust officer, 1962-69, trust officer, head trust dept., 1969-70; trust officer S.Jersey Nat. Bank, Mt. Holly, 1970—. Assn. mem. Childrens Home of Burlington County. Mem. D.A.R., Met. Opera Guild, Nat. Assn. Bank Women, Internat. Platform Assn., Early Am. Soc., Humane Soc. of U.S. and N.J., Mt. Holly Hist. Soc. Episcopalian. Club: Soroptimist of Burlington County (pres. 1965-68). Home: 41 Union St Mount Holly NJ 08060 Office: S Jersey Nat Bank Union Nat Office Mount Holly NJ 08060

SMYTHE, BETTY BRIGGLE (MRS. GEORGE C. SMYTHE), educator; b. Fredericktown, O., Apr. 4, 1922; d. Edgar Frank and Cora (Ewers) Briggle; B.S., Muskingum Coll., 1943; M.S., Ohio State U., 1956, Ph.D., 1967; m. George C. Smythe, July 23, 1960. Research asst. Am. Gas Assn., Cleve., 1943-44; tchr. econs. Fredericktown High Sch., 1944-55; asst. prof. home econs. Ohio Wesleyan U., Delaware, 1956-70, asso. prof., 1970-72, prof., 1972—, chmn. dept. home econs., 1971-72, chmn. dept. human devel. and family studies, 1973—. Mem. Am., Ohio (exec. council) home econs. assns., Am., Ohio (chmn. membership com.) pub. health assns., A.A.A.S., Ohio Acad. Sci., Ohio Nutrition Com. (rep.; chmn. 1968—), Nat. Coordinating Com. for Coll. and U. Tchrs. of Food and Nutrition (past sec.), Am. Assn. U. Women, Omicron Nu, Phi Upsilon Omicron, Delta Kappa Gamma. Home: 10 Hillside Dr Delaware OH 43015

SMYTHE, MABEL M. (MRS. HUGH H. SMYTHE), assn. exec.; b. Montgomery, Ala., Apr. 3, 1918; d. Harry S. and Josephine (Dibble) Murphy; student Spelman Coll., 1933-36; A.B., Mt. Holyoke Coll., 1937; M.A., Northwestern U., 1940; Ph.D. (Nat. fellow, Harriet Remington Laird fellow, Julius Rosenwald fellow), U. Wis., 1942; postgrad. N.Y. U., 1949; m. Hugh H. Smythe, July 26, 1939; 1 dau., Karen Pamela. Tchr., Fort Valley Normal and Indsl. Inst., 1937-39; asst. prof., asso. prof., acting head dept. econs., bus. adminstrn. Lincoln (Mo.) U., 1942-45; prof. econs. Tenn. Agrl. and Indsl. U., 1945-46; lectr. econs. Bklyn. Coll., 1946-47; vis. prof. econs. Shiga U., Japan, 1951-53; dep. dir. non-legal research N.A.A.C.P. Legal Def. and Ednl. Fund, 1953; core tchr. New Lincoln Sch., N.Y.C., 1954-59, coordinator secondary edn., 1959-69; dir. research and publs. Phelps-Stokes Fund, N.Y.C., 1970—, v.p., 1972—. Lectr. econs. Coll. City N.Y., 1959-60; asso. prof. Queens Coll., Flushing, N.Y., summer 1962; cons. Carnegie Corp., AID, 1964-66, Urban Coalition, 1968—, Ency. Brit. Ednl. Corp., 1969—; scholar-in-residence U.S. Commn. Civil Rights, 1973-74. Mem. U.S. Adv. Commn. on Edn. Exchange, 1961-62, on Internat. Ednl. and Cultural Affairs, 1962-65, del. UNESCO Gen. Conf. Paris, 1964; mem. U.S. Nat. Commn. UNESCO, 1965-70; mem. adv. council African affairs U.S. Dept. State, 1962-69; cons. mem. adv. com. Operation Crossroads Africa, 1958-65; mem. pub. affairs com. Nat. YWCA, 1959-65, mem. nat. resources com., 1963-65; mem. Women's Africa Com., 1959-64; mem., incorporator Com. Assessing Progress of Edn. 1964-69; mem. panel bd. examiners N.Y. State Civil Service Commn., 1960-65; mem. Com. on Research Devel. Internat. Instns., 1965—, Internat. Cooperation Year Com., 1965; mem. adv. com. Nat. Assessment Ednl. Progress, 1969—; mem. exec. com. L.A.W.S. div. Atlantic Found. Bd. dirs. African-Am. Inst., 1964-65, N.Y. Center Internat. Visitors, Internat. Schs. Services (vice chmn. bd. 1970-71), Nat. Corp. for Housing Partnerships; trustee Cottonwood Found., Conn. Coll., Hampshire Coll. (vice chmn.), Mt. Holyoke Coll. Fellow African Studies Assn.; mem. Nat. Council Women U.S., Am. Acad. Polit. and Social Sci., Acad. World Econs., Am., Met. econ. assns., Am. Assn. U. Profs., Am. Soc. African Culture, Pub. Edn. Assn. (coordinating com.), N.Y. Urban League (chmn. edn. com.), Nat. Assn. African-Am. Edn. Clubs: Cosmopolitan, Mt. Holyoke. Author: (with Alan B. Howes) Intensive English Conversation, 2 vols., 1953, 54; (with Hugh H. Smythe) The New Nigerian Elite, 1960. Editor: (with Edgar Bley) Curriculum For Understanding, 1965; American Negro Reference Book, 1974. Home: Parmalee Hill Rd Newtown CT 06470 Office: Phelps-Stokes Fund 10 E 87th St New York City NY 10028

SMYTHE, SHEILA MARY, ins. exec.; b. N.Y.C., Nov. 1, 1932; d. Patrick John and Mary Catherine (Gonley) Smythe; student Manhattanville Coll., 1951; B.A., Creighton U., 1952; M.S., Columbia, 1956; L.H.D. (hon.), Manhattanville Coll., 1974. Research analyst Nat. Blue Cross Assn., N.Y.C. and Chgo., 1957-59, research asso., 1959-62, asst. dir. research and planning, 1962-63; exec. asso. Blue Cross Greater N.Y., N.Y.C., 1963-72, v.p., 1972-74, asst. to pres., 1973-74, sr. v.p. Blue Cross and Blue Shield of Greater N.Y., N.Y.C., 1974—. Fellow Royal Soc. Health; mem. Am. Hosp. Assn., Am. Pub. Health Assn., Am. Statis. Assn., A.A.A.S., Am. Assn. Risk and Ins., Operations Research Assn., Manhattanville Coll. Alumnae Assn. (dir. 1957-63). Home: 235 E 73d St New York City NY 10021 Office: 622 3d Av New York City NY 10017

SNAPP, ELIZABETH, librarian; b. Lubbock, Tex., Mar. 31, 1937; d. William James and Louise (Lanham) Mitchell; B.A. magna cum laude, N. Tex. State U., Denton, 1968, M.L.S., 1969; m. Harry Franklin Snapp, June 1, 1956. Asst. to archivist Archive of New Orleans Jazz, Tulane U., 1960-63; catalog librarian Tex. Woman's U., Denton, 1969-71, head acquisitions dept., 1971-74, coordinator readers services, 1974—. Co-sponsor Irish Lecture Series, Denton, 1968, 70, 73. Sec. Denton County Democratic Caucus, 1970. Mem. Am., Southwestern, Tex. library assns., Am. Assn. U. Women (legislative br. chmn. 1973-74), So. Conf. Brit. Studies, Am. Assn. U. Profs., Tex. Assn. Coll. Tchrs. (sec.-treas. Tex. Woman's U. chpt. 1974-75), Woman's Shakespeare Club (pres. 1967-69), Beta Phi Mu, Alpha Chi, Alpha Lambda Sigma (pres. 1970-71), Pi Delta Phi. Episcopalian (directress altar guild 1966-68, 73—). Asst. editor Tex. Academe, 1973—; book reviewer Library Resources and Tech. Services, 1973—. Contbr. articles to profl. jours. Home: 612 Grove St Denton TX 76201

SNEAD, KATHRYN WIESENFELD (MRS. JOHN L. S. SNEAD, JR.), warehouse co. exec., civic worker; b. Jacksonville, Fla., July 9, 1922; d. Reginald S. and Amelia (Kennelly) Wiesenfeld; ed. St. Paul's, Jacksonville; m. John L.S. Snead, Jr., Mar. 6, 1953; children—Paul Alexander, Corby Elizabeth. Partner, v.p. Wiesenfeld Warehouse Co., Jacksonville, 1966—. Mem. women's bd. Henrotin Hosp., Chgo., Chgo. br. Am. Cancer Soc., Mem. Chgo. Drama League, Peninsula Vols., Art Inst. Chgo. Clubs: Lake Shore, Union League (Chgo.); Menlo Country (Redwood City, Cal.); Ponte Vedra (Fla.), Ponte Vedra Women's; Menlo Circus. Home: 717 Ponte Vedra Blvd Ponte Vedra Beach FL 32080 Office: 33d St PO Box 1133 Jacksonville FL 33201

SNEDDEN, MARY JANE HEFFNER (MRS. HOMER GRANGER SNEDDEN), govt. ofcl.; b. McKeesport, Pa., Mar. 14, 1917; d. Samuel Harrison and Meda (Calhoun) Heffner; secretarial student Douglas Bus. Coll., McKeesport, Pa., 1936-37; student Duquesne U., 1942; m. Homer Granger Snedden, Nov. 6, 1943. Sec., legal dept. Westinghouse Air Brake Co., Wilmerding, Pa., 1940-44. Leader Brownie Scouts, Fayetteville, N.C., 1947-48. Pres. East McKeesport Recreation Bd., 1968—; majority inspector, dist. 1, East McKeesport Election Bd., 1966-69; councilwoman Borough of East McKeesport, 1972—, chmn. finance, 1972—; mem. Rep. Com., Dist. 1, East McKeesport, 1971—. Bd. dirs. Pre-Sch. for Exceptional Children Greater McKeesport Area, 1966—; trustee Allegheny Acad., 1969-74. Recipient Gov.'s award for outstanding contbn. to traffic safety Commonwealth of Pa., 1968-73. Mem. Pa. Huguenot Soc., D.A.R. (chpt. regent 1966-68, state vice chmn. U.S.A. Bicentennial com. 1971-74, state chmn. Am. history month 1974—), Internat. Platform Assn. Presbyn. Mem. Order Eastern Star (past matron). Club: Ligonier (Pa.) Country. Home: 722 Broadway East McKeesport PA 15035

SNEED, GENEVA BELL (MRS. LUTHER J. SNEED), union ofcl.; b. nr. Knoxville, Tenn., Oct. 10, 1920; d. Westly W. and Louie V. (Stallings) Fox; student U. Tenn., 1952-53; m. Luther J. Sneed, May 15, 1936; children—Mackie A., Larry K., Linda K. (Mrs. Wendell Helton), Martha Lou (Mrs. Everette Mashburn). Office mgr. Western Union, Sevierville, Tenn., 1936-45; operator Pub. Shirt Corp., Knoxville, 1946-49; head grievance ofcl. Local 90, AFL-CIO, Knoxville, 1948-50; pres. Knoxville CIO Council, 1951-53; dir. Women's Activities div., AFL-CIO Area Council, 1953-55; staff rep. Amalgamated Clothing Workers Am., Knoxville, 1952-69, asst. mgr. Southeastern clothing regional bd., 1969—, sec.-treas. Southeastern Clothing Bd. Realty Corp., 1969—; v.p. Tenn. State Labor Council, 1959—. Co-chmn. women's div. Estes Kefauver campaign, 1956; v.p. Tenn. AFL-CIO Com. on Polit. Edn., 1959—; exec. 2d v.p. Tenn. State Labor Council AFL-CIO, 1971—. Mem. Southeastern Clothing Regional Bd. (sec.-treas.), local P.T.A. Democrat. Methodist. Home: Route 1 Love Addition Sevierville TN 37862 Office: 1124 N Broadway Knoxville TN 37917

SNEED, MARIE ELEANOR WILKEY (MRS. JOHN SNEED, JR.), educator; b. Dahlgren, Ill., June 12, 1915; d. Charles N. and Hazel (Miller) Wilkey; student U. Ill., 1933-35; B.S., Northwestern U., 1937; postgrad. Wayne State U., 1954-60, U. Mich., 1967; m. John Sneed, Jr., Sept. 18, 1937; children—Suzanne (Mrs. Geoffrey B. Newton), John Corwin. Tchr. English, drama, creative writing Berkley (Mich.) Sch. Dist., 1952—. Mem. Mich. Statewide Tchr. Edn. Preparation, 1968-72, (regional sec. 1969-70). Mem. N.E.A., Mich., Berkley (pres. 1961-62) edn. assns., Oakland Tchr. Edn. Council (exec. bd. 1973—), Student Tchr. Planning Com. Berkley (chmn. 1971-72), Phi Alpha Chi, Pi Lambda Theta, Alpha Delta Kappa, Alpha Omicron Pi. Home: 21 Norwich Rd Pleasant Ridge MI 48069 Office: 14450 Manhattan St Oak Park MI 48237

SNEED, NANCY KAY (MRS. EDGAR M. SNEED, JR.), journalist; b. Columbus, O., Jan. 15, 1947; d. Nicholas and Betty Jane (Briggs) Popa; B.A., Ohio State U., 1969, M.A., 1970; m. Edgar Morris Sneed, Jr., Nov. 7, 1970; 1 dau., Mary Elisa. Sports stringer, Columbus Dispatch, summer 1968; asso. Nicholas Popa & Assos., pub. relations and advt., Columbus, summers 1968-70, cons., 1970—; corr., Golf World mag., 1972-73, contbg. editor, 1973—. Cons., Nat. Collegiate Athletic Assn. Golf Championship, 1970. Home: 2114 Chardon Rd Columbus OH 43220

SNEED, RUBY BLAKE, realtor; b. Chgo., July 20, 1918; d. Sanders and Lola Belle (Fitzpatrick) Ray; grad. Kennedy-King Coll., 1938; student U. Chgo., 1955-57, Drake U., 1959-60, LaSalle U., 1965-67; m. David A. Blake, Sept. 25, 1958 (dec. Jan. 1970); 1 dau., Lola Belle (Mrs. Lola Belle Campbell); m. 2d, Herbert Ray Sneed, Aug. 1972. Supr. finance and statistics dept. Dept. Pub. Welfare Cook County, Western dist. office, 1943-58; owner, operator Equal Opportunity Housing Center-S. Ray & Blake Realty Co., Harvey, Ill., 1967—; mgr. Ebenezer-Primm Towers Homes for Sr. Citizens, Evanston, Ill. Owner L&R Lettershop, Harvey, Ill., 1967-69. Mem. Harvey League Women Voters, 1969—; housing chmn. South Suburban N.A.A.C.P., 1969—; mem. Harvey Area Leadership Resource Forum, 1970—; office mgr. Women in Community Services, Springfield, Ill., 1964-66; mem. various human relations coms. Mem. real estate exam. com. Ill. Dept. Registration and Edn., 1973—. Chmn. bd. dirs. Found. for Freedom and Democracy in Community Life, Evanston, Ill., 1971—; trustee Ill. Freedom Residence Com., 1965—; bd. dirs. Ill. Human Rights Commn., 1964-66. Recipient citations Women in Community Service, 1965, Leadership Council Met. Open Communities, 1973. Mem. Evanston-North Shore, S. Suburban, Ill., Nat., Homewood-Flossmor bds. realtors, Dearborn Real Estate Bd. (legis. chmn., 1971—), Nat., Ill. (legislative rep.) assns. realtors, Equal Opportunity Brokers Assn. Mem. A.M.E. Ch. Home: 1001 Emerson St Evanston IL 60201 Office: 108 W 154th St Harvey IL 60426 also 1932 Maple Evanston IL 60201

SNELL, C. JANE (MRS. JOHN D. SNELL), educator; b. Wabash County, Ind., Mar. 5, 1942; d. Hayden Roscoe and Mary Gladys (Knowlton) Renz; B.S. cum laude, Manchester Coll., 1964; M.S., St. Francis Coll., 1967; Ph.D., Ind. U., 1971; m. John D. Snell, June 5, 1971; children—Steven John, Matthew Howard. Elementary sch. tchr., Ft. Wayne, Ind., 1964-68; teaching asst. Ind. U., Bloomington, 1968-70, asst. dir. Eric/Crier, 1968-70; asst. prof. Meml. U., St. John's Nfld., Can., 1970-71; remedial reading tchr. Cortland (N.Y.) Pub. Schs., 1971-73; asst. prof. edn. State U. N.Y., Cortland, 1973—. Cons., Nat. Reading Center, 1971; cons., mem. bd. advisers Vol. Tutors, Cortland, 1972—. Mem. Internat. Reading Assn., Nat. Soc. for Study Edn., Nat. Council Tchrs. English, Nat., Am. edn. assns., Pi Lambda Theta. Methodist. Home: 66 Floral St Cortland NY 13045

SNELL, FAYE LUGINBYHL (MRS. VERNON BRIGHT SNELL), educator; b. Chickasha, Okla.; d. Fred Myers and Minnie (Kilgore) Luginbyhl; B.A., Okla. Coll. Liberal Arts, 1924; postgrad. U. Okla., 1932; m. Vernon Bright Snell, June 4, 1925; 1 dau., Connie Jane Smith. Tchr., English, journalism Anadarko (Okla.) High Sch., 1924-25; tchr. English, Cushing (Okla.) High Sch., 1925-26, Capitol Hill Jr. High Sch., Oklahoma City, 1927-33; tchr. social studies Taft Jr. High Sch., Oklahoma City, 1954-69, head social studies dept., 1957—. Profl. adv. bd. Living Textbook, 1965-67. Recipient certificate of recognition Oklahoma City Bd. Edn., 1963. Mem. Nat. (Okla. profl. relations rep. 1965-68), Okla. (sec. 1956-57), Oklahoma City (pres. 1961-62) councils social studies tchrs., N.E.A., Okla. Edn. Assn. (life), Okla. Classroom Tchrs. Assn., Internat. Soc. Women Educators, Alumnae Assn. Okla. Coll. Liberal Arts, Okla. Art League (exec. bd.), U.D.C., Delta Kappa Gamma. Democrat. Baptist (past pres. women's mission union). Clubs: McDowell Allied Arts (pres. 1945-47, exec. bd.), Ladies Music (exec. bd.), Sorosis (sec. 1972, v.p. 1973-74). Home: 3329 Goodger Dr Oklahoma City OK 73112

SNELL, RENEE (MRS. LORNE CAMPBELL SNELL), librarian; b. London, Eng., June 19, 1918; d. James Wagland and Irene Marguerite (Marshall) Evans; ed. pub. schs.; m. Lorne Campbell Snell, May 27, 1944; children—Anne (Mrs. Arthur A. Healey), Wanda (Mrs. James L. Saunders), Yvonne (Mrs. Lawrence Powell), Jeanne

(Mrs. David C. Rideout). Came to Can., 1945, naturalized, 1945. Library asst. Deptford and Finsbury Pub. Libraries, London, 1934-41; br. librarian Coulsdon and Purley Pub. Libraries (Eng.), 1941-44; first librarian Elliot Lake, Ont., Can., 1958-62; first librarian, Labrador City, Nfld., Can., 1963-66; sch. librarian Labrador City Schs., 1964-70, librarian elementary grades, 1970—. Active Girl Guides, Eng. and Can., 1929-66; mem. Royal Commn. on Labrador, 1972-74; active various civic orgns. Vice pres. Labrador City Library Bd., 1966-67. Mem. Canadian, Nfld., Atlantic Provinces library assns., Nfld. Tchrs. Assn. Home: 624 Caribou Crescent Labrador City NF A2V 1P7 Canada Office: AP Low Elementary Sch Bartlett Dr Labrador City NF A2V 1G6 Canada

SNELLING, MARJORIE GAHRING (MRS. WALTER OTHEMAN SNELLING), patent atty., business exec.; b. Waterford Twp., Pa., May 5, 1901; d. John William and Lena Mary (Klemmer) Gahring; student pub. schs., pvt. tutoring; m. Walter Otheman Snelling, May 5, 1919, (dec. Sept. 1965); children—William A., Robert F. (dec.), Constance C. (Mrs. Charles T. Noonan), Richard A., Charles D., Thomas E., Priscilla C., Walter P.; 1 adopted dau., Marilyn (Mrs. Richard Wells). Admitted to practice U.S. Patent Office, 1934; research dept. Trojan Powder Co., 1919-54; mem. firm Snelling & Snelling, 1934—. Co-owner, dir. Mohr Orchards, 1960—. Active Girl Scouts U.S.A., Boy Scouts Am., YWCA; pres. Swain Sch. P.T.A., 1950-53; mem. Gov.'s Conf. on Air Pollution, 1967. Bd. dirs., treas. Family and Childrens Service Lehigh County. Mem. World Affairs Council Phila., Am. Acad. Polit. and Social Sci., Allentown Art Mus., League Women Voters, Altrusa Internat. (dir. Allentown, internat. relations dist. chmn. 1968-70, dist. sec. 1970-72, internat. Lehigh Valley community council), Fedn. Women's Clubs (state div. chmn.), Women's Club Allentown (dir. 1972—, pres. 1968-70), Met. Mus. Art, Allentown Art Mus., Allentown Community Concert Assn., Allentown Symphony. Republican. Club: Sierra. Address: 1509 Linden St Allentown PA 18102

SNIBBE, HOMA MAHMOUDI (MRS. JOHN R. SNIBBE), psychologist, educator; b. Tehran, Iran, Apr. 24, 1944; d. Jalil and Badri (Behnam) Mahmoudi; came to U.S., 1959; B.A., Utah State U., 1962; M.A., U. Utah, 1968, Ph.D., 1970; m. John R. Snibbe, Aug. 30, 1969; 1 son, Jason Cameron. Tng. officer Peace Corps, 1963-68; dir. police selection research dept. personnel Los Angeles County, 1970-73; asst. prof. psychiatry Sch. Medicine U. Cal. at Los Angeles, 1973—, dir. research Drug Treatment Center; founder, dir. Transcultural Communication and Tng. Center. Cons. Hughes Aircraft Co., 1974. Mem. Am. Psychol. Assn., Psychologists in Pub. Service, Psi Chi. Mem. Baha'i Assembly. Author: (with J.R. Snibbe) The Urban Policeman in Transition: A Psychological and Sociological Review, 1973. Contbr. numerous articles on psychol. research to profl. jours. Home: 909 Stonehill Lane Los Angeles CA 90049

SNIDER, FAYE L. LEVINSKY (MRS. MARVIN SNIDER), social worker; b. Portland, Me., Apr. 29, 1932; d. Jacob N. and Goldie R. (Romanow) Levinsky; student Simmons Coll., 1950-52; A.B., Wayne State U., 1954; M.S.W., U. Mich., 1956; student Merrill-Palmer Inst., 1953-54; m. Marvin Snider, June 13, 1954; children—Craig, Beth. Psychiat. caseworker Ypsilanti (Mich.) State Hosp., 1956; clin. caseworker VA Hosp., Ann Arbor, Mich., 1956-58; family caseworker Family Service Assn., Boston, 1958-60, summers 1964, 66; tchr. Modern Living and Family Relationships, Adult Edn. Div., Brookline, Mass., 1963-66; research social worker Harvard Sch. Pub. Health, Boston, 1967; instr. family and social welfare Northeastern U., Boston, 1968-69; program dir. Widow-to Widow Program, Lab. Community Psychiatry, Harvard Med. Sch., Boston, 1969-71; exec. dir. Newton-Wellesley-Weston Multi-Service Center, Newton, Mass., 1971-72; clin. coordinator Liberty St. Assos., Newton, 1972—; family individual and couple therapist and cons., 1972—; staff cons. Freeport, Inc., Newton, 1973—; lectr. Boston U., 1969. Mem. Newton Youth Commn. Adv. Bd., 1973—. Mem. Nat. Assn. Social Workers. Jewish religion. Home: 33 Oak Vale Rd Waban MA 02168 Office: 73 Union St Newton Centre MA 02168

SNIDER, IRIS G. (MRS. JAMES FERGUS SLOWEY III), physician; b. Enid, Okla., May 23, 1943; d. Raymond Leland and Irene (Jett) Snider; B.S., U. Tenn., 1965, M.D., 1967; m. James Fergus Slowey III, June 21, 1968; children—James IV, Joseph Leland. Intern, St. Joseph Hosp., Memphis, 1968-69; resident pediatrics City of Memphis Hosp., 1969-70, U. Tenn. Meml. Research Center and Hosp., Knoxville, 1970-71; plant physician Oak Ridge Gaseous Diffusion Plant div. Union Carbide Corp., 1971-72; staff pediatrician, chief emergency room Oceanside (Cal.) Community Hosp., 1973—; courtesy staff pediatrics U. Tenn. Meml. Hosp., Knoxville. Mem. A.M.A., Tenn. Med. Assn., Blount County Med. Soc. Republican. Presbyn. Home: 126 Dolphin Dr Oceanside CA 92054 Office: 1100 5th St Oceanside CA 92054

SNIDER, NANCY RUTH, editor; b. Louisville, Mar. 29, 1937; d. Hiram and Ruth (Saam) Snider; student Purdue U., 1955-57; B.S., Ia. State U., 1962, M.S., 1970; Recipe editor Gen. Foods Corp., White Plains, N.Y., 1962-63; asst. food editor McCall's mag., N.Y.C., 1963-65; home economist Pillsbury Co., Mpls., 1966-68; food and nutrition editor Instns. Vol. Feeding Mag., Chgo., 1969—. Partner, Small Bus. Communications, Chgo., 1973—. Mem. Nat. Press Club, Inst. Food Technologists (councilor 1971-74), Am. Home Econ. Assn., Home Economists in Bus., Women in Communications, Soc. for Nutrition Edn. Author: The Professional Chef's Soy Protein Recipe Ideas, 1971. Office: care Institutions/VFM 5 S Wabash Av Chicago IL 60603

SNITOW, VIRGINIA LEVITT (MRS. CHARLES SNITOW), educator, civic worker; b. N.Y.C.; d. Louis L. and Tania (Rosenberg) Levitt; B.A., Hunter Coll., 1931; postgrad. Columbia, 1931-32; m. Charles Snitow, Nov. 2, 1935; children—Ann, Alan. Tchr. English, N.Y.C. High Schs., 1932-45. Vice pres. U.S. World Trade Fair, N.Y.C., 1957-66; v.p. Encounter Films, Inc., 1970—; chmn. nat. exec. bd. women's div. Am. Jewish Congress, N.Y.C., 1962-65, nat. pres., 1965-71, co-chmn. governing council, 1971—; organizer dir. ednl. forums, 1949-62; rep. Non-Govtl. Orgn. UN, 1960-62; chmn. leadership conf. Nat. Jewish Women's Orgn., 1970—. Del. Democratic nat. convs., 1968, 72. Mem. Pan Pacific and S.E. Asia Womens Assn., League Women Voters, Nat. Womens Party. Contbr. articles to profl. jours. Home: 81 Walworth Av Scarsdale NY 10583 Office: 331 Madison Av New York City NY 10017

SNODDERLY, MARY LOUISE DAVIS, librarian; b. Polk County, Ore., Feb. 1, 1925; d. Charles Benjamin Franklin and Grace Lucille (Cassady) Davis; B.S., E. Tenn. State U., 1946; M.S., U. Tenn., 1962; m. Charles Hugh Snodderly, May 19, 1949; 1 son, Lynn Jerome. Tchr., basketball coach pub. schs., Tenn., 1948-50; tchr., librarian Maury High Sch., Dandridge, Tenn., 1951-54; librarian Rush Strong High Sch., Strawberry Plains, Tenn., 1954-62; cataloger central officer Knoxville (Tenn.) City Schs., 1962-67; reference and periodicals librarian Carson Newman Coll., Jefferson City, Tenn., 1967—. Commr., Jefferson County (Tenn.) Schs., 1974—. Mem. Am., Tenn., E. Tenn., Southwestern library assns., Nat., East Tenn. edn. assns., Farm Bur., Am., Tenn. sch. bds. assns., Phi Lambda Theta. Republican. Baptist. Mem. Order Eastern Star. Club: Carson Newman Coll. Faculty Women's. Home: Route 3 Box 1965 Strawberry Plains TN 37871 Office: Carson Newman Coll Jefferson City TN 37760

SNODGRASS, KATHRYN MARIE, lawyer; b. Richmond, Cal., Aug. 18, 1943; d. Marion Myers and Marie Louise (Quillin) Snodgrass; A.A., Contra Costa Coll., 1963; A.B., San Francisco State Coll., 1965; J.D., Hastings Coll., 1968. Admitted to Cal. bar, 1968, since practiced in Richmond and Martinez. Dept. dist. atty. Contra Costa County, Cal., 1968—. Office: 100 37th St Richmond CA also PO Box 670 Martinez CA 94553

SNOW, ALICE BIGLEY, clergywoman; b. Winchester, Mass., Nov. 15, 1911; d. George and Thenora (Mitton) Bigley; B.A., Smith Coll., 1932; M. Div., Andover Newton Theol. Sch., 1934; m. Arthur Joseph Snow, June 7, 1934; children—George A., John R. Ordained to ministry United Ch. of Christ, 1934; asst. minister Payson Park Ch., Belmont, Mass., 1932-35; minister Kensington (N.H.) Congl. Ch., 1935-37; acting asst. minister Plymouth Congl. Ch., Mpls., 1943-44; interim minister 2d Congl. Ch., Beloit, Wis., 1966; minister Chirst Congl. Ch., Clintonville, Wis., 1966-73, Ch. of Red Rocks, Sedona, Ariz., 1973—. Dir. N.H. Congl. Conf., 1937-39; mem. bd. World Ministries United Ch. of Christ, 1969-75, vice moderator Wis. Conf., 1972, moderator, 1973. Hon. chmn. Wis. Gov.'s Conf. on Home and Family, 1970. Bd. dirs. YMCA, Mpls., 1944-45, Beloit, 1959-62, 64-66. Named Wis. Mother of Year, Am. Mother's Com., 1970. Mem. Internat. Assn. Women Ministers (v.p. 1971-72), Am. Assn. U. Women, P.E.O., Order Eastern Star, Phi Beta Kappa. Home: 112 Redstone Dr Sedona AZ 86336 Office: Church of Red Rocks Hwy 179 Sedona AZ 86336

SNOW, JEANYSE REITH (MRS. HAROLD A. SNOW), lawyer; b. Seattle, Mar. 28, 1945; d. Floyd Harrison and Laura May (Ihander) Reith; student Sweet Briar Coll., 1965-66; B.A., U. Ore., 1967; J.D., Willamette U., 1970; m. Harold A. Snow, Sept. 1, 1967. Clk., Supreme Ct. Ore., summer 1969; admitted to Ore. bar, 1970; legal counsel Columbia Region Assn. Govts., Portland, Ore., 1970; asso. Macdonald, Dean, McCallister & Snow, Astoria, 1971—. Bd. dirs. counsel Clatsop Youth Devel. Assn. Mem. Am., Ore., Clatsop County (sec. 1972) bar assns. Home: Route 1 Box 399 Warrenton OR 97146 Office: PO Box 508 Astoria OR 97103

SNOW, MARY RUTH BALLARD (MRS. PHILIP J. CORR), artist; b. Logan, Utah; d. Melvin Joseph and Martha (Jones) Ballard; A.B., U. Utah, 1929; student Art Students League, Los Angeles Mus. Art, Corcoran Gallery Art, Phillips Gallery; m. Ralph Dale Snow, Aug. 18, 1934 (dec. July 1955); 1 son, Peter Ballard; m. 2d, Philip Joseph Corr, July 28, 1956. Exhibited one-man shows Washington Gallery Art, Panoras Gallery, N.Y.C., 1965, Lighthouse Gallery, Tequesta, Fla., 1970, 73, Studio II Gallery, Tequesta, 1972; exhibited in group shows Corcoran Gallery, Washington, Smithsonian Instn., Va. Mus. Fine Arts, Phillips Gallery, N.A.D., Los Angeles Art Mus., Bremer Gallery, Berlin, Germany, Arts Club Washington, Washington Water Club, U.S. Depts. State and Interior, George Washington U., Am. U., Washington, Norfolk (Va.) Mus. Art, Contemporary Gallery, Palm Beach, Fla., Norton Gallery, West Palm Beach, Lighthouse Gallery, others; represented in permanent collections Massillon (O.) Mus., Lighthouse Gallery, Jeane Dixon's Children to Children Collection, Washington. Chmn., Soc. Washington. Artists exhibit for benefit Kennedy Cultural Center; chmn. Lighthouse Gallery Beaux Arts Ball, 1974. Mem. Adv. Bd. Edn. Arlington, Va., 1952; chmn. Appearance Bd., Tequesta, 1973—. Recipient Grumbacher Watercolor award, 1966. Mem. Nat. Assn. Women Artists (out-of-town rep. for Washington), Soc. Washington Artists (past pres.-1st woman elected to this office, 1st prize 1952, 3d prize 1952, hon. mention 1950), Artists Guild Washington (sec. 1957, pres. 1958-59), Washington Watercolor Club, Artists Equity, Am. Fedn. Arts, Artists Guild Palm Beach Art Inst., Artists Guild Norton Gallery (sec. 1973—), Chi Delta Phi, Chi Omega. Club: Rotary Wives. Home: 291 River Dr Tequesta FL 33458

SNOW, PHYLLIS ROBERTA, univ. adminstr.; b. Phila., Aug. 26, 1912; d. Lawrence C. and Mattie (McArthur) S.; B.A., U. Utah, 1934; M.S., Cornell U., 1953, Ph.D., 1956. Caseworker, Fed. Emergency Relief Adminstrn., Salt Lake City, 1934-35; tchr. Midvale (Utah) Jr. High Sch., 1935-39, Salt Lake City Sch. System, 1939-43; dir. home service dept. Mountain Fuel Supply Co., Salt Lake City, 1943-52; teaching asst. Cornell U., Ithaca, N.Y., 1953-54, research asst., 1954-56, asst. prof., food and nutrition, 1956-59, asso. prof., 1959-61; dean Coll. Family Life, Utah State U., Logan, 1961—. Mem. Inst. Food Tech., Am. Home Econs. Assn., Omicron Nu, Phi Kappa Phi, Phi Upsilon Omicron. Contbr. to home econs. publs. Home: 250 N 6th E Logan UT 84321 Office: Utah State U Logan UT 84322

SNOWDAY, JANE MORIN COLLINS, dept. store advt. exec.; b. Pitts., Jan. 20, 1925; d. John M. and Dorothea (Wilson) Morin; student U. Pitts., 1943-44, Inst. Design, Chgo., 1945-46, New Sch. for Social Research, 1947-48; m. Robert Michael Snowday, Aug. 21, 1968; children (by previous marriage)—Christopher Charles, Catherine Victoria. Asst. dir. Outlines Gallery-Library-Theatre, Pitts., 1944-47; copywriter W.T. Grant Co., N.Y.C., 1947-50, Kaufmann's Dept. Store, Pitts., 1951-56, R.H. Macy Co., N.Y.C., 1957-58; copy chief J.C. Penney Co., N.Y.C., 1959-60, McCann-Erickson, advt. agy., N.Y.C., 1960-61; home furnishings editor Arcinco Pub., Passaic, N.J., 1961-65; with J. Walter Thompson Co., N.Y.C., 1965-73, asso. creative supr., 1970, v.p., 1971-73; advt. mgr. mail order div. Lane Bryant, N.Y.C., 1973—. Mem. N.Y. County Dem. Com., 1969-71. Mem. nat. adv. bd. Profl. Children's Sch., N.Y.C., 1972—. Recipient Dorothy Dawe award Nat. Home Furnishings Assn., 1969. Mem. Soho Artists Assn. Home: 133 Wooster St New York City NY 10012

SNOWDEN, DOROTHY PARR, librarian, editor; b. Waco, Tex., July 27, 1927; d. William Lindsay and Lula Ann (Cooper) Parr; grad. magna cum laude Flat River (Mo.) Jr. Coll., 1958; B.S. in L.S., East Tex. State U., 1964, M.S. in L.S., M.S. in Edn., 1965; m. Claude Joseph Snowden, Aug. 14, 1944; children—Claudia, Gloria (Mrs. Gail Chandler), Tricia (Mrs. Richard A. Glasco, Jr.). Head reference dept. S.W. Tex. State U., San Marcos, 1965-71; reviewer adult books The Booklist, A.L.A., Chgo., 1971-73, asst. editor, adult books editor, 1973, asso. editor mag., 1974—. Cons., Project Upward Bound, 1967-69; univ. tchr. ednl. research, library orientation, 1965-72. Mem. Am. Civil Liberties Union, N.A.A.C.P., A.L.A., Am. Assn. U. Profs., Nat. Council Social Studies, Soc. Psychol. Study Social Issues, Assn. Supervision and Curriculum Devel., Common Cause, Chgo. Council Fgn. Relations, Art Inst. Chgo., Mus. Contemporary Art, Kappa Delta Pi. Home: PO Box 11145 Chicago IL 60611 Office: 50 E Huron St Chicago IL 60611

SNYDER, ADELAIDE R. SNYDER (MRS. JOSEPH G. SNYDER), univ. adminstr.; b. Rochester, N.Y., Nov. 9, 1925; d. Isadore Samuel and Cecelia (Richardson) Snyder; B.A., Kent State U., 1944, M.A., 1950; m. Joseph G. Snyder, Dec. 23, 1943; children—Richard R., Florence. Instr., Youngstown (O.) U., 1947-56; producer, hostess WFMJ-TV, Youngstown, 1955-59; redevel. dir., relocation dir. Fed. Urban Renewal Project, Youngstown, 1957-60; dir. admissions and publs. Miami (Fla.)-Dade Jr. Coll., 1960-62; dir. univ. relations Fla. Atlantic U., Boca Raton, 1962—. Cons. pub. relations, 1960—. Chmn., Mahoning County (O.) White Ho. Conf. on Edn., 1956-57; mem. Youngstown Mayor's Com. on Human Relations, 1956-60. Mem. Am. Coll. Pub. Relations Assn. (S.E. dist. dir. elect 1973), Women in Communications, Phi Beta Kappa, Phi Kappa Delta, Cardinal Key. Home: 1334 SW 14th St Boca Raton FL 33432 Office: Fla Atlantic U Boca Raton FL 33432

SNYDER, ALZORA ELLEN PAVEY (MRS. ALBERT DONALD SNYDER), museum ofcl.; b. Enid, Okla., Sept. 30, 1912; d. Harold Blaine and Rose Griffith (Shafer) Pavey; A.A., Hollister Jr. Coll., 1931; student U. Cal. at Berkeley, 1933; m. Albert Donald Snyder, Sept. 2, 1933; children—Donald Robert, Carl Eugene, Shirley Irene (Mrs. Windsor Merritt Buzza). Taxi driver Pavey Taxi Co., Watsonville, Cal., 1939-44; tchr., adminstr., dir. City of Watsonville Child Care Center, 1942-44; chmn. home econs. dept. Santa Cruz County Fair, Watsonville, 1951—; archivist, curator W.H. Volck Mus., Watsonville, 1962-74. Mem. Hist. Landmark Adv. Commn. for Santa Cruz County, 1968—. Commr. 5th supervisorial dist. Santa Cruz County Parks and Recreation Commn., 1973—. Bd. dirs. Pajaro Valley Community Council. Recipient community service statuette Girl Scouts, 1963, blue ribbon plaque Western Fairs Assn., 1973; named Woman of Year, Watsonville C. of C., 1974. Mem. Santa Cruz County Soc. for Hist. Preservation (sec. 1968-73), U. Cal. Alumni Assn. (life). Home: 79 Hill Av Watsonville CA 95076 Office: 261 E Beach St Watsonville CA 95076

SNYDER, ARDIS BESSIE MCCONNEL (MRS. GERALD A. SNYDER), ednl. cons.; b. Caldwell, Ida., Sept. 11, 1918; d. Walter Hall and Bessie L. (Vinson) McConnel; student Coll. Ida., 1936-38, B.A., 1956, M.A., 1963; tchrs. certificate Ida. Standard, 1938; m. Gerald A. Snyder, July 11, 1948 (dec. 1953); 1 dau., Susan Marie (Mrs. L.G. Rinebold). Tchr. rural schs., 1938; tchr. Caldwell Sch. System, 1939-49; intermediate tchr., music instr., 1953-56; music instr., vice-prin., 1956-59; prin. Washington Elementary Sch. Prin., Caldwell, 1959-67; dir. migrant edn., Caldwell, 1966-67; cons. migrant edn. Ida. Dept. Edn., Boise, 1967—. Active A.R.C. Mem. P.T.A. (life), Nat., Ida. edn. assns., Nat. Dept. Elementary Sch. Prins., Assn. Supervision Curriculum Devel., P.E.O., Delta Kappa Gamma. Presbyn. Mem. Order Eastern Star. (past matron). Guardian Council Order Jobs Daus., Bethel 8, 1965—. Club: Boise Soroptimist. Home: 1611 Joyce Boise ID 83706 Office: Len Jordan State Office Bldg Boise ID 83720

SNYDER, EDNA MAE, supply co. exec.; b. Joliet, Ill., May 4, 1923; d. Joseph Samuel and Agnes Mary (Santoski) Snyder; diploma, tchrs. certificate Joliet Jr. Coll., 1943; B.S., U. Ill., 1948. Employment interviewer Dodge Plant, Chgo., 1943-45; advt. and sales promotion mgr. Ames Supply Co., Downers Grove, Ill., 1948—. Mem. Lockport Bus. and Profl. Women's Club (historian, 1972-73), Will County Farm Bur. Roman Catholic. Home: Rural Route 1 Box 55 Lockport IL 60441 Office: 2537 Curtiss St Downers Grove IL 60515

SNYDER, ELAYNE PHYLLIS, business exec., writer; b. Atlantic City, N.J., Mar. 2, 1931; d. Samuel and Bella (Lewis) Snyder; B.A., U. Miami, 1952. Women's dir. Sta. WOND, 1952-53; co-owner Et Cetera Advt. Service, 1953-54; asst. account exec. Reed Advt., Inc., 1954-56; administrv. asst. Kenyon & Eckhardt, Inc., 1956-59; adminstrv. asst. Colgate-Palmolive Co., 1959-69; research dir. Young Group, Inc., N.Y.C., 1969-73; pres. Feminist Invention Group, Inc., 1973—. Mem. Assn. Advt. Men and Women, U. Miami Alumni Assn. (sec. N.Y. 1955-59, exec. com. 1959-62; co-editor Met. Miamian Quar. Newsletter 1960-62), Nat. Orgn. for Women (chairperson N.Y. chpt. 1972, pres. 1974), Manhattan, Nat. women's polit. caucuses, Delta Phi Epsilon (editor-in-chief Triad nat. mag. 1956-62). Clubs: Wednesday Writers (co-founder, pres. 1961, 64); Nat. Writers (chpt. 2d v.p.). Author: (play) A Little Piece of Earth, 1968; (poetry) Prairie Schooner. Address: 333 E 49th St New York City NY 10017 also 203 N Harvard Av Ventnor NJ 08406

SNYDER, ELISE WECHSLER, physician; b. N.Y.C., May 4, 1934; d. Harry L. and Dora (Burg) Wechsler; B.S., Queens Coll., 1954; M.D., Columbia U., 1958; m. Arthur I. Snyder, Nov. 10, 1957 (div. Aug. 1965); children—Margaret I., Katherine V.; m. 2d, Victor H. Rosen, Dec. 17, 1965 (dec. Feb. 1973). Intern, Bronx Municipal Hosp. Center, N.Y.C., 1958-59, resident, 1959-62; practice medicine specializing in psychiatry, N.Y.C., 1962-72, Deep River, Conn., 1972—. mem. staff Bronx Municipal, Kings County hosps.; instr. psychiatry Albert Einstein Coll. Medicine, 1959-62, Columbia U., 1964-66; asst. prof. psychiatry State U. N.Y., 1966-72, Yale, 1972—. Mem. Am. Psychiat. Assn., N.Y. Acad. Scis., Fedn. Am. Scientists. Address: Cedar Swamp Rd Deep River CT 06417

SNYDER, ELOISE COLLEEN, educator; b. Hazleton, Pa.; d. Michael J. and Mildred (Snyder) Bartos; B.A., Lycoming Coll., 1952; M.A., Pa. State U., 1953, Ph.D., 1956. Asso. prof. sociology So. Ill. U., 1956-67; prof. sociology U.S.C., 1967-68; prof. sociology Columbia (S.C.) Coll., 1968-71, Pa. State U., State College, 1970—. Recipient Gerontology fellowship U. Cal., 1959. Author: (with Herman Lantz) Marriage: An Examination of the Man Woman Relationship, 1962, rev. edit., 1969; Teacher's Manual for Marriage, 1962, rev. edit., 1969. Contbr. articles to profl. jours. Home: 621 E Irvin Av State College PA 16801

SNYDER, EVELYN MARIE, editor; b. Princeville, Ill., Dec. 8, 1920; d. Benjamin Le Roy and Hazel Marie (Young) Snyder; student Brown's Bus. Coll., 1956, Ill. Central Coll., 1974. Operator Gen. Telephone Co., Princeville, Ill., 1955-56; reporter, gen. office asst. editor Princeville Telephone, 1959-69, editor, 1969—. Co-chmn. Cancer Crusade, Princeville Twp., 1973; sec. Princeville Migrant Council, 1972-73; chmn. Harvest Festival, Peoria, Ill., 1973—. Tax collector Princeville Twp., 1969—. Mem. Ill. Twp. Ofcls. United Methodist. Home: 724 West Main Princeville IL 61559 Office: 126 N Walnut Princeville IL 61559

SNYDER, GLADYS REID (MRS. HUGH ALFRED SNYDER), pension cons.; b. Preston, Ida., Apr. 12, 1918; d. Royal Shields and Marcia Esther (Porter) Reid; student Utah State U., 1935-38, Life Office Mgmt. Assn. courses, 1963-64, various securities courses; m. Hugh Alfred Snyder, Feb. 6, 1938; children—Sharon (Mrs. David Earl Kamerath), Clyde Reid, Barbara (Mrs. John Phillip Colton), Ronald Hugh, Steven Wayne, Kenneth Clair. Sec., Walter C. Green & Assocs., cons. actuaries, Salt Lake City, 1960-65; cons., office mgr. Income Trust Plan Assos., 1965—; prin., chmn., pres. Income Investment Plans, Inc., 1968-73. Active as officer PTA various times. Voting dist. chmn. Salt Lake City Republican Com., 1969-73. Mem. Nat. Assn. Securities Dealers. Mem. Ch. of Jesus Christ of Latter-day Saints (active youth group orgn. 1952-71). Lady Lion. Club: Kappa Kappa Gamma Mother's. Home: 2790 E 3000 South Salt Lake City UT 84109 Office: 1088 S 1100 E Salt Lake City UT 84101

SNYDER, JANE PETERS (MRS. ARTHUR LELAND SNYDER), pub. relations exec.; b. Manassas, Va., July 23, 1925; d. James Walker and Alma Dorothy (Cross) Peters; student George Washington U., 1943-45, Columbia U. Sch. Pub. Health, 1962; m. Arthur Leland Snyder, June 7, 1944; children—Susan Leland, James Peters. Reporter, Montgomery County (Md.) Sentinel, 1952-54, Chatham (N.J.) Courier, 1956-59, Morris County (N.J.) Daily Record, 1959-61; pub. relations asst. East Orange (N.J.) Gen. Hosp.,

1962-64, United Hosp. Newark, 1964-65; dir. community relations Georgetown U. Hosp., Washington, 1966-68; dir. pub. relations Hosp. Council and Met. Regional Med. Program, Washington, 1968-70, Washington Hosp. Center, Washington, 1970—. Lectr. George Washington U. Sch. Health Care Adminstrn., 1973. Mem. Am. Soc. Hosp. Pub. Relations (dir. 1973—), Acad. Hosp. Pub. Relations (treas. 1973) (MacEachern awards 1963, 72, 73). Home: 5235 Elliott Rd Washington DC 20016 Office: 110 Irving St NW Washington DC 20010

SNYDER, JEAN MACLEAN (MRS. JOEL MARTIN SNYDER), writer; b. Chgo., Jan. 26, 1942; d. Norman Fitzroy and Jessie (Burns) Maclean; B.A., U. Chgo., 1963; m. Joel Martin Snyder, Sept. 4, 1964; 1 son, Jacob Samuel. Research asso. A.M.A., Chgo., 1963-68; home safety specialist Dept. Pub. Information, Nat. Safety Council, Chgo., 1968-70; dir. pub. relations Planned Parenthood Assn., Chgo., 1970; editor Ill. Consumer Action, 1970-71, free lance writer, 1970—. Mem. Maroon Key. Club: Esoteric Women's (pres. 1961-62). Contbr. articles to McCall's, Today's Health, Chgo. Guide, others. Home: 5627 S Dorchester Av Chicago IL 60637

SNYDER, JESSIE EDITH, librarian; b. Lucerne, Mo., Sept. 17, 1910; d. William H. and Sarah Della (Ricketts) Bruce; B.S., N.E. Mo. State Coll., 1970; m. Murl C. Snyder, May 17, 1933; children—Wanda (Mrs. O. Duane Whitney), Duane, Ronald. Tchr. rural schs., Putnam County, Mo., 1928-33; librarian Putnam County Pub. Library, Unionville, Mo., 1966—. Mem. Mo. Library Assn., Putnam County Hist. Soc. (past pres.), Grand River Library Conf. (past pres.), United Meth. Women, P.E.O., Bus. and Profl. Women's Club. Republican. Methodist. Republican. Club: Women's Extension (Lucerne, Mo.). Home: 315 N 19th St Unionville MO 63565 Office: 1618 Main St Unionville MO 63565

SNYDER, JOAN, painter; b. New Brunswick, N.J., Apr. 16, 1940; d. Leon D. and Edythe E. (Cohen) Snyder; A.B. in Sociology, Douglass Coll., 1962; M.F.A. in Painting, Rutgers U., 1966; m. Laurence Fink, Oct. 12, 1969. Exhibited in one-man shows at Paley & Lowe, Inc., N.Y.C., 1971, 72, 73, Parker 470, Boston, 1972, Michael Walls Gallery, San Francisco, 1971; exhibited in group shows at Whitney Mus. Am. Art, N.Y.C., 1972, 73; instr. painting Princeton, 1973; vis. lectr. Yale, 1974. Paintings reproduced in Time mag., 1972, Art Forum, 1971. Home: 105 Mulberry St New York City NY 10013

SNYDER, LESLIE CROCKER (MRS. FREDRIC E. SNYDER), lawyer; b. N.Y.C., Mar. 8, 1942; d. Lester G. and Billie (Danziger) Crocker; A.B., Radcliffe Coll., 1962; certificate Harvard-Radcliffe Program Bus. Adminstrn., 1963; J.D., Western Res. U., 1966; m. Fredric E. Snyder, May 17, 1968. Admitted to Ohio bar, 1966, N.Y. bar, 1967; practiced in N.Y.C., 1966-68; asst. Dist. Atty., N.Y.C., 1968—. Mem. Am., N.Y., Ohio bar assns., Nat. Assn. Women Lawyers. Clubs: Harvard Business School, Radcliffe, Harvard. Home: 122 E 76th St New York City NY 10021 Office: 155 Leonard St New York City NY 10013

SNYDER, LYNNE RENAY MINKIN, lawyer; b. Omaha, Sept. 11, 1944; d. Sam and Nellie (Edel) Minkin; student U. Cal. at Los Angeles, 1962-65; A.B., U. Cal. at Berkeley, 1966; J.D., Hastings Coll. Law, U. Cal., 1969; m. Mark Alan Snyder, June 20, 1965; 1 dau., Mahala Rachel. Admitted to Cal. bar, 1970; staff atty. Contra Costa Legal Services, Richmond, Cal., 1970-73, U. Santa Clara Law Clinic, 1974—; practice law, San Jose, Cal., 1973—. Legal adviser, cons. community groups, new bus. enterprises; lectr. to schs., tchr., supr. law students and paraprofls.; lectr. dept. polit. sci. Cal. State U., San Jose. Alumni scholar U. Cal. at Los Angeles, 1962-63. Mem. Nat. Legal Aid and Defenders Assn., Am. Civil Liberties Union, State Bar Cal., Bar Assn. Santa Clara, San Mateo County, Am. Assn. U. Women, Nat. Orgn. Women, Hastings Coll. Alumni Assn., Pi Sigma Alpha. Democrat. Jewish religion. Office: 12 S 1st St San Jose CA 95113

SNYDER, MARGARET MARY LEARY (MRS. GUY SNYDER), found. exec.; b. Pittsfield, Mass.; d. John Joseph and Lola (Winchell) Leary; R.N., St. Luke's Hosp., Pittsfield, 1934; student Leland Stanford U., 1944; m. Guy Snyder, Oct. 18, 1944 (dec. 1966). Pvt. duty nursing, 1934-43; phys. therapist Richmond Field Hosp., Kaiser Shipbldg. Co., Richmond, Cal., 1944-45; head phys. therapy dept. Children's Hosp. Home, Utica, N.Y., 1945-47, Moses Taylor Hosp., Scranton, Pa., 1947-48, emergency polio Santa Clara County Hosp., San Jose, Cal., 1948; head. phys. therapy dept. Bishop and Swenson Orthopedic Clinic, Phoenix, 1949-51; exec. dir. Cerebral Palsy Found., Beaumont, Tex., 1951—. Mem. Tex. Crippled Children Soc., Tex. Welfare Assn., Am. Phys. Therapy Assn. Home: 3660 Bryan Dr Beaumont TX 77707 Office: 855 S 8th St Beaumont TX 77701

SNYDER, MARY ALICE DEXHEIMER (MRS. GUY MAXWELL SNYDER), photo processing co. exec.; b. Sedalia, Mo., Mar. 22, 1921; d. Harry Melvin and Hazel Inez (Gorrell) Dexheimer; bus. adminstrn. Central Bus. Coll., Sedalia, 1939-41; m. Guy Maxwell Snyder, Dec. 31, 1952; children—Giana Marie, Aric Nelson. Sec., office mgr. Inter-State Studio (named changed to Inter-State Processing Co., Inc. 1951), Sedalia, 1941-43, plant mgr., 1943-52, personnel mgr., exec. v.p., 1952—, exec. v.p., personnel mgr. several sales subsidiaries, 1967—. Pres. Horace Mann Elementary P.T.A., Sedalia, 1965-66, Smith-Cotton High Sch. P.T.A., Sedalia, 1972-73; an organizer Parent-Tchr.-Student Assn., Smith-Cotton High Sch., 1972; pres. Sedalia City P.T.A. Council, 1969-72; rep. to Mo. P.T.A. Convs., 1963-71. Mem. Am. Bus. Women, Christian Bus. and Profl. Women's Club. Baptist (sec. Sunday sch. 1964—). Home: Route 2 Sedalia MO 65301 Office: 601 W 16th St Sedalia MO 65301

SNYDER, MARYANN MAZUREK (MRS. WILLIAM GEORGE SNYDER), statistician; b. Phila., Mar. 31, 1940; d. Stanley Leonard and Pauline Sophia (Czarnik) Mazurek; B.S., Ursinus Coll., 1962; M.S., Villanova U., 1966; m. William George Snyder, June 3, 1967. Statistician, Smith Kline & French Labs., pharmaceuticals, Phila., 1962-64, sr. statistician, 1964—. Mem. Am. Statis. Assn. Home: 3249 Byberry Rd Philadelphia PA 19154 Office: 1500 Spring Garden St Philadelphia PA 19101

SNYDER, MARY-JANE RYAN, family planning, population communications cons.; b. Chgo., July 25, 1916; d. Edward Groves and Florence Margaret (James) Ryan; B.S. in Journalism, U. Ill., 1938; m. Clark Quin Snyder, May 27, 1939 (dec.); children—Lindsay (Mrs. James Cantoni), Nadine, Kevan, Courtnay. Asst. editor St. Luke's News, 1938-40; advt. dir. Multicolor Sales Co., 1940-55; partner Med. Writers & Researchers, 1957-59; prin. Mary-jane R. Snyder-Writing For You, communications consultants, 1955-63; dir. pub. relations Planned Parenthood Assn., Chgo. area, 1959-70; prin. Mary-jane R. Snyder, Population/Family Planning Communications, Wilmette, Ill., 1970—. Lectr. population and family planning; instr. communications sect., summer workshops Community and Family Study Center, U. Chgo., 1962-72. Mem. Ill. Gov.'s Commn. on Status Women, 1965-69; mem. information and edn. com. Planned Parenthood/World Population. Bd. dirs. Zero Population Growth, Ill. Family Planning Council, N. Shore Youth Health Service, Gates House, Wilmette. Recipient Cody Baker award, 1963, 65, 66, 73; Mem. Welfare Pub. Relations Forum, Am. Med. Writers, Nat. Orgn. for Women (charter), Women in Communications, (Distinguished Service award 1973, nat. v.p. 1965-70). Episcopalian (vestryman 1971—). Address: 1012 Ashland Av Wilmette IL 60091

SNYDER, PEGGY POPE, child psychologist; b. Elizabeth, N.J., Jan. 27, 1933; d. Ira Stanley and Regina Elizabeth (McLaughlin) Pope; B.S. in Edn., Seton Hall U., Orange, N.J., 1961; M. Teaching Sci., Catholic U., 1970, Ph.D. candidate, 1971—; m. Robert Thomas Snyder, Nov. 3, 1972. Elementary sch. tchr. in N.J., 1962; dir. Ridgefield Park (N.J.) Child Study Center, 1964-65; psychotherapist Wiltwyck Sch., N.Y.C., 1965-66; psychologist Prince George's County (Md.) pub. schs., 1966—; individual practice ednl./psychol. diagnosis, 1966—; cons. in field. Mem. Am., Md., D.C. psychol. assns., Nat. Assn. Sch. Psychologists (del. Md. 1973—), Md. Sch. Psychologists Assn. (pres. 1974-75). Contbr. articles to profl. jours. Home: 210 Vierling Dr Silver Spring MD 20904 Office: 4913 Tilden Rd Bladensburg MD 20710

SNYDER, PHYLLIS REISS (MRS. OLIVER SNYDER), social worker; b. Bklyn., Feb. 25, 1929; d. Bernard Reiss and Rosy (Winters) Reiss Haveson; B.A. summa cum laude, Barnard Coll., 1950; postgrad. (Fulbright scholar), Universite de Lyon, France, 1950-51; M.S., Columbia Sch. Social Work, 1957; m. Stanley Mellon, June 15, 1948 (div. 1956); m. 2d, Oliver Snyder, Feb. 28, 1958; stepchildren—Kezia, Pamela. Caseworker, N.Y. State Tng. Sch. for Girls, Hudson, 1959-60, supr. casework, 1960-62, dir. community services, 1962-64; dir. community services Berkshire Farm Center and Services for Youth, Canaan, N.Y., 1964—. Fellow Am. Orthopsychiat. Assn. (com. on law and mental health 1966-69, chmn. nominating com. 1972, ex-officio 1973, task force on concepts of adequacy treatment children in trouble 1972—); mem. Nat. Assn. Social Workers (sec., com. on corrections N.Y.C. chpt. 1969-74), Acad. Certified Social Workers, Nat. Council on Crime and Delinquency, N.Y. State Assn. Child Care Agys. (chmn. social service com. 1972-74, com. on profl. issues 1974—). Home: Washington Rd Carmel NY 10512 Office: 200 Park Av S New York City NY 10003

SNYDER, REBECCA, clin. psychologist; b. Portland, Me., Nov. 6, 1915; d. Louis and Ida (Reif) Snyder; B.A., Goucher Coll., Balt., 1936; M.Sc., Johns Hopkins, 1938; Ph.D., U. Kan., 1956; postgrad. psychoanalysis and psychotherapy, N.Y. U., 1961-68. Research biochemist Johns Hopkins, 1936-38; asst. research technician biochemistry Johns Hopkins Hosp., 1938-40; research fellow biochem. research schizophrenia St. Elizabeth's Hosp., Washington, 1940-43; biochem. cancer research NIH, 1946-48; clin. psychologist VA Hosp., East Orange, N.J., 1956—; pvt. practice psychotherapy and psychodiagnosis, East Orange, 1961—; clin. instr. psychiatry N.J. Coll. Medicine and Dentistry, 1967—; psychotherapist Low Cost Clinic Essex County, N.J., 1957-64. Served as officer WAVES, 1943-46. Diplomate clin. psychology Am. Bd. Profl. Psychology. Mem. Am., Estern, N.J. psychol. assns., World Fedn. Mental Health. Contbr. articles, chpt. in book. Address: 250 Prospect St East Orange NJ 07017

SNYDER, RUTH EVELYN (MRS. ROBERT STANTON SHERMAN), radiologist; b. Canadian, Tex., May 21, 1911; d. Edward Henry and Nona Agnes (Alexander) Snyder; B.A., Park Coll., 1932; M.D., U. Tex., 1936; m. Robert Stanton Sherman, Oct. 16, 1942; children—Robert Snyder, Roger Holmes, Ruth Ann. Intern, N.Y. Infirmary, 1936-37, fellow Strang Clinic, 1937-38, cons. radiologist, 1953—; clin. fellow radiation therapy Meml. Cancer Center, N.Y.C., 1939-41, asst. roentgenologist, 1942-45, 51-52, asso. roentgenologist, 1952—; grad. asst. N.Y.C. Hosp., 1941-43, asst. radiologist, 1943-44; asso. roentgenologist, 1944-47; practice medicine specializing in radiology, N.Y.C., 1951—; clin. asst. prof. radiology Cornell U. Diplomate Am. Bd. Radiology. Mem. Am. Coll. Radiology, A.M.A., N.Y., New York County med. socs., N.Y. Roetgen. Soc., James Ewing Soc., Alpha Omega Alpha, Sigma Pi Sigma. Republican. Episcopalian. Contbr. articles to profl. jours. Home: 222 E 68th St New York City NY 10021 Office: 222 E 68th St New York City NY 10021

SNYDERMAN, SELMA ELEANORE (MRS. JOSEPH SCHEIN), physician; b. Phila., July 22, 1916; d. Harry S. and Rose (Koss) Snyderman; A.B., U. Pa., 1936, M.D., 1940; m. Joseph Schein, Aug. 4, 1939; children—Roland Milo Hyatt, Oliver Douglas. Intern, Einstein Med. Center, Phila., 1940-42; resident Bellevue Hosp., N.Y.C., 1944-45; practice medicine specializing in pediatrics, N.Y.C., 1946—; asst. physician Bellevue Hosp., N.Y.C., 1946-49, asso., 1949-58, vis. physician, 1958—; asst. physician Univ. Hosp., 1949-56, asso. physician, 1956-60, attending physician, 1960—; instr. pediatrics N.Y. U. Med. Sch., 1941-49, asst. prof., 1950-56, asso. prof., 1957-67, prof., 1967—; dir. Metabolic Disease Center, N.Y. U. Med. Center, 1966—; career scientist Health Research Council N.Y.C., 1961—. Diplomate Am. Bd. Pediatrics, Am. Bd. Nutrition. Mem. Soc. Pediatric Research, Am. Pediatric Soc., Am. Inst. Nutrition, Am. Soc. Clin. Nutrition, Phi Beta Kappa. Contbr. articles to profl. pubs. Home: 300 Central Park W New York City NY 10024 Office: 550 1st Av New York City NY 10016

SOARES, LOUISE MARIE, educator; b. Plymouth, Mass., June 2, 1933; d. Frank Louis and Dorothy Marie (Ferrell) Gavoni; B.Music, Boston U., 1954, M.Edn., 1956; Ed.D., U. Ill., 1962; m. Anthony Thomas Soares, Aug. 15, 1954; children—Donna Marie, Steven. Instrn. supr. Bancroft Sch., Worcester, Mass., 1954-56; asst. dir. residence, instr. Eastern Ill. U., Charleston, 1956-59; instr. ednl. psychology U. Ill., Champaign, 1959-62; lecturing prof. Boston Coll., Chestnut Hill, Mass., 1962-65; prof. psychology and ednl. research U. Bridgeport (Conn.), 1965—. Cons. dir. research pub. schs., Bridgeport, Conn., 1967-70; dir. Children's Theatre, Worcester, Mass., 1954-56; adminstr. pub. recreation, Charleston, Ill., 1957-58; vis. lectr. U. Ill., summers 1965, 66. Bd. dirs. Mental Health Facility, Bridgeport, 1967-70. Recipient research grant U.S. Rehab. Agy., 1967-68, U. Bridgeport, 1969-70, 71-72, 73-74. Mem. Am., Eastern psychol. assns., Am., Northeastern ednl. research assns., Internat. Soc. Psychology, Interam. Soc. Psychology, Nat. Soc. Study Edn., A.A.A.S., Am. Soc. Coll. Tchrs. Edn., Kappa Delta Pi. Roman Catholic. Editor: A Sourcebook in Educational Psychology, 1968. Contbr. profl. jours. Home: 111 Teeter Rock Trumbull CT 06611 Office: Dept Psychology U Bridgeport Bridgeport CT 06602

SOBEL, EDNA H., pediatric endocrinologist; b. N.Y.C., Nov. 2, 1918; d. Samuel P. and Frances B. (Selkin) Sobel; B.A. with high honors, U. Wis., 1939, M.A. in Zoology, 1940; M.D. cum laude, Boston U., 1943. Intern, Montefiore Hosp., N.Y.C., 1944; fellow Mass Gen. Hosp. Harvard Med. Sch., Boston, 1944-50; research and teaching, specializing in pediatrics and endocrinology, Cin., 1950-53, Boston, 1953-56, N.Y.C., 1956—; asst. prof. pediatrics Albert Einstein Coll. of Medicine, Bronx, N.Y., 1956-60, asso. prof. pediatrics, 1960-68, prof. 1968—; asso. vis. pediatrician Bronx Municipal Hosp. Center, 1956-60, asso. vis. pediatrician, 1960-68, vis. pediatrician, 1968—. Commonwealth Fund of N.Y. fellow, 1963-64; NIH grantee, 1957-72. Fellow N.Y. Acad. Medicine; mem. Am., Bronx pediatric socs., Soc. for Pediatric Research (v.p. 1963-64), A.A.A.S., Am. Fedn. for Clin. Research, Endocrine Soc., Sigma Xi. Home: 1 Garrett Pl Bronxville NY 10708 Office: Albert Einstein College of Medicine Bronx NY 10461

SOBEL, SUZANNE BARBARA, psychologist; b. Bklyn., May 2, 1943; d. Albert E. and Jeannette (Schneider) Sobel; student Clark U., 1960-62; B.A., Adelphi U., 1964, M.A., 1966; Ph.D., U. Tenn., 1971. Research asst. Albert Einstein Coll. Medicine, Bronx, N.Y., 1966-67; instr. U. Tenn. Extension Sch., Knoxville, 1969; jr. clin. psychologist Oak Ridge Mental Health Center, 1969-70; psychology intern La. State U. Med. Center, New Orleans, 1970-71; psychologist Orleans Parish Sch. Bd., 1971-72; clin. psychologist Irish Channel Crisis Center for Children, 1972-73; asst. prof. Dillard U., New Orleans, 1972-73; clin. psychologist Children's Center, Laurel, Md., 1973—. Counselor, Health Emergency Aid Dispensary, New Orleans, 1970-72, bd. dirs., 1971; counselor Boarding House, New Orleans, 1972; cons. to bd. dirs. Coffee House, First United Presbyn. Ch., Oak Ridge, 1970. Nat. Inst. Mental Health trainee in clin. psychology, 1968-70. Mem. Am., D.C. (community affairs com.), Md. (pub. information com.), Southeastern psychol. assns., Am. Personnel and Guidance Assn., Council for Advancement Psychol. Professions and Scis. (gov., pub. policy research com.), Assn. for Humanistic Psychology, UN Assn. of U.S.A., Psi Chi. Home: 308 2d St SE Washington DC 20003 Office: DC Childrens Center Laurel MD 20810

SOBRINO, JOSEPHINE, educator; b. San Antonio, Aug. 1, 1915; d. Fausto and Maria (Gutierrez de la Vega) Sobrino; A.B., Incarnate World Coll., 1936; diploma (U.S. State Dept. grantee), U. Mexico, 1945; M.A., U. Tex. 1946; Ed.D., U. Houston, 1960; postgrad. U. Valladolid, 1953, (Instituto Spanish cultural grantee) U. Madrid, 1954. Chmn. dept. modern langs. Tex. Southmost Coll., Brownsville, 1942-59; chmn. dept. Spanish, U. Houston, 1959-73, dir. profl. edn. U. Houston at Clear Lake City, 1973—, univ. research grantee, 1968. Cons. Spanish, Modern Lang. Assn., 1963-65, Tex. Edn. Agy., 1960-63; del. conv. Internat. Fedn. U. Women, Paris, 1956. Mem. bd. Brownsville Library Assn., 1954-59, Charro Days, Brownsville, 1949-59, Mercy Hosp. Nursing Sch., Brownsville, 1955-59. Nat. Conf. Christians and Jews grantee, 1954. Repipient Magnificate Medal award Mundelein Coll., Chgo., 1962; Spanish Consulate Gen. award, 1962; Matrix award Theta Sigma Phi, 1965. Mem. Internat. Fedn. Cath. Alumnae (state sec. 1940), Am. Assn. U. Women (Brownsville pres. 1954-56, state conv. chmn. 1958), Tex. Fgn. Lang. Assn. (pres. 1954-56, 67-68, dir., award 1974), Houston Council Tchrs. Fgn. Langs. (pres. 1962-63), Alliance Francaise (mem. bd. Houston 1964—). Author: Influence of Continuing Cultural Patterns Reflected by Pertinent Folklore of Selected Indian Tribes on the Education in Mexico, 1960; The Bilingual Child, 1961; (with Bourne, Silman) Repaso de Espanol-Lateoria y la practica, 1971; (with Silman, Vergara) Repaso de espanol: Lo esencial, 1972. Contbr. articles to profl. jours. Home: 1022 Willowdale Seabrook TX 77586

SOCHET, MARY MARGARET ALLEN (MRS. MARVIN JOSEPH SOCHET), psychotherapist, educator; b. Plattsburgh, N.Y., Feb. 10, 1938; d. Edwin Elisha and Mary Elizabeth (Thompson) Allen; B.S., State U. Coll. at Plattsburgh, 1958; M.A., N.Y. U., 1961, Ph.D., 1963; m. Marvin Joseph Sochet, Mar. 13, 1963; children—Melorra, David. Tchr. kindergarten L.I. pub. schs., 1958-62, N.Y.C., 1962-64; prof. early childhood edn., child devel. and psychology Bklyn. Coll., 1964-66, 68-71; program director and acting exec. dir. Newark Pre-Sch. Council, 1965-66; psychotherapist Community Guidance Service, N.Y.C., 1966-74. Lectr. and editorial cons. to pub. cos. in early childhood edn. field; cons. and trainer for various Head Start and Tchr. Aid Tng. Programs, 1966-71. Founder Community Loft, N.Y.C., 1971; participant in devel. Children's Free Sch., N.Y.C., 1969-74. Recipient Founders Day award N.Y. U., 1963. Mem. Am. Psychol. Assn., Soc. Psychol. Study Social Issues, Kappa Delta Pi. Contbr. articles on social psychology and edn. to profl. jours. Address: 380 Riverside Dr New York City NY 10025

SOCKOLOSKY, JANET MARTHA SEIBERT (MRS. JAMES MICHAEL SOCKOLOSKY), artist; b. Detroit, July 5, 1945; d. Warren Lovelace and Rose Jean (Agee) Seibert; B.S., U. Mich., 1967, M.A., 1968; m. James Michael Sockolosky, June 13, 1970; 1 dau., Karen Jean. Artist, ednl. TV channel 56, Detroit Bd. Edn., summer 1966; jr. preparator Children's Mus., Detroit Bd. Edn., 1968-73, engaged in art work and type specifying for African culture series portfolios 1969—. Mem. Willistead Art Gallery, Windsor, Afro-Am. Museum, Detroit. Mem. U. Mich. Alumni Assn., Wayne U. Alumni Assn. Presbyn. Home: 16218 Braile St Detroit MI 48219 Office: Children's Museum 67 E Kirby St Detroit MI 48202

SODERBERG, MARGARET ANN, educator; b. Pontiac, Mich., Oct. 30, 1932; d. Henry G. and Annie (Callaghan) Soderberg; B.A., Marygrove Coll., 1954; M.S. in L.S., Cath. U., 1957; M.A., Wayne State U., 1960; Ph.D., Washington U., St. Louis, 1963. Asst. to editor Cath. Periodical Index, Washington, 1954-56; young adult librarian Detroit Pub. Library, 1956-59; acting head ref. dept. Hamtramck (Mich.) Pub. Library, 1959-60; legislative intern Office Senator Philip Hart, Washington, 1960; asst. prof. Eastern Ill. U., Charleston, 1962-68, asso. prof. polit. sci., 1968-72, prof., 1972—. Bd. dirs. Internat. Center Found. Charleston, 1967-68, Amnesty Internat., 1967. Mem. Ind. Voters Ill., Ams. for Dem. Action, League Women Voters (chmn. fgn. policy 1966-68), Internat., Am., Midwest polit. sci. assns., Midwest Assn. for Latin Am. Studies, Soc. Internat. Devel., Am. Assn. U. Profs. (chpt. sec.-treas. 1964-65), African, Latin Am. studies assns., Am. Civil Liberties Union, World Assn. World Federalists. Home: 2315 University Dr Charleston IL 61920

SOENTGEN, MARY LOUISE, physician; b. Tarentum, Pa., Oct. 9, 1930; d. Henry Lawrence and Catherine G. (Brown) Soentgen; B.A., Seton Hill Coll., 1951; M.A. in Bacteriology (Teaching fellow), U. Pitts., 1952; M.D. (USPHS fellow), Woman's Med. Coll. Pa., 1956; postgrad. Laval (Que., Can.) U., 1950, U. Kan. Med. Center, 1960, U. Colo. Med. Sch., 1962, Med. Sch. U. Wis., 1968. Intern hosp. Woman's Med. Coll., Phila., 1956-57; preceptorship obstetrics, gynecology Miner's Meml. Hosp., Beckley, W.Va., 1957-59, resident in pediatrics, 1959-61; practice medicine specializing in pediatrics, Virginia, Minn., 1961-64; staff pediatrician Virginia (Minn.) Municipal Hosp., 1961-64, Eveleth-Fitzgerald (Minn.) Community Hosp., 1961-64; cons. pediatrics Cook (Minn.) Municipal Hosp., 1961-64; instr. pediatrics Jefferson Med. Coll., Phila., 1964-65, asso. clin. pediatrics, 1966-67, asst. prof. clin., 1967-68, asst. prof., 1968-70, asso. prof. pediatrics, 1970—, asst. prof. obstetrics and gynecology, 1968-71, asso. prof. obstetrics and gynecology, 1971—; dir. newborn nurseries, 1965—; asst. attending pediatrics Jefferson Med. Coll. Hosp., 1964-67, attending pediatrics, 1967—. Lectr. hosps., med. centers, med. colls. and profl. orgns. in U.S. Named Outstanding Young Woman of Am., Woman's Med. Coll. Pa., Phila., 1967; recipient Commonwealth award Med. Coll. Pa., 1972. Diplomate Am. Bd. Pediatrics, Nat. Bd. Med. Examiners. Fellow Am. Acad. Pediatrics; mem. Am., Internat. med. woman's assns., Am. Assn. U. Women, Philadelphia County Med. Soc., Phila. Pediatric Soc., Am. Soc. Bacteriologists, Am. Fedn. Clin. Research; Royal Soc. Health. Contbr. articles to profl. jours. Home: 910 Meetinghouse Rd Jenkintown PA 19046

SOFFER, MARJORIE SUE, information specialist; b. St. Louis, Sept. 9, 1950; d. Harry Leon and Helen (Evraiff) Soffer; student N.E. Mo. State Coll., 1970, Va. Intermont Coll., 1970-71; A.A., Penn Valley Coll., Kansas City, Mo., 1972; journalist degree Def.

Information Sch., 1973. Pvt. 2d class U.S. Army, 1973-74, pvt. 1st class, 1974—; information specialist Safeguard Office, Pentagon, Washington, 1973-74, Dept. Def. Lang. Inst., Washington, 1974—. Active theatre groups. Mem. Phi Theta Kappa. Democrat. Jewish religion. Home: Box 738 Bldg 402 Fort Myer Arlington VA 22211 Office: Pub Information Office Def Lang Inst Washington Naval Sta Washington DC 20390

SOFILLAS, GRACE SOPHIE JOANOU (MRS. WILLIAM C. SOFILLAS), journalist; b. Wheeling, W.Va., Oct. 29, 1932; d. John Frank and Gazel (Klochan) Joanou; B.S., W.Va. U., 1955; m. William C. Sofillas, Sept. 2, 1962; 1 son, Constandino William. Women's editor Intelligencer, Wheeling, 1957-62; comml. writer Sta. WLAN, Lancaster, Pa., 1963; women's editor Intelligencer Jour., Lancaster, 1963-73, reporter-columnist, 1973—; co-owner Dino's Market, Lancaster, 1966-72. Recipient State Journalism award W.Va. Press Assn., 1960. Mem. Am. Legion Aux., Alpha Delta Pi. Mem. Hellenic Orthodox Ch. of North and S.Am. Home: 1300 Maple Av Lancaster PA 17603 Office: 8 W King St Lancaster PA 17604

SOKOL, ESTHER LEAH ROBERTS (MRS. HERBERT Z. SOKOL), pianist, assn. exec.; b. Boston, Feb. 25, 1932; d. Louis Perry and Eva (Sherman) Roberts Perry; Mus.B., Boston U., 1952; M.A., Harvard Sch. Edn., 1953; Wooley Scholar in Music, Paris Conservatoire, 1953-54; postgrad. Cleve. Inst. Music, 1956-57, Paris Conservatoire and Walter Gieseking Masterclass, Graham-Eckes School, Palm Beach, Fla., 1957-58; m. Herbert Z. Sokol, Sept. 8, 1953 (dec. 1967); children—Bruce David, Todd Sherman, Cynthia Jeannette. Made concert debut, Miami, Fla., 1955; dir. community edn. Jewish Fedn. Palm Beach County, West Palm Beach, Fla., 1975—. Winner Young Artists Competition, Miami Music Club, 1955. Home: 243 Rutland Blvd West Palm Beach FL 33405 Office: 502 Citizens Bldg West Palm Beach FL 33401

SOKOLOFF, ALICE HUNT (MRS. BORIS SOKOLOFF), author; b. Bedford, N.Y., June 3, 1912; d. James Ramsay and Alice St. John (Nolan) Hunt; student Spence Sch., N.Y.C., Miss Porter's Sch., Farmington, Conn., 1927-28, Radcliffe Coll., 1932-33; m. Boris Sokoloff, Oct. 24, 1946; 1 son, Kiril. Writer weekly classical record rev. Ledger, Lakeland, Fla. and Patent Trader, Mount Kisco, N.Y., 1961-69. Mem. Author's Guild, Mystery Writers Am., Southeastern Composers League. Club: Cosmopolitan (N.Y.C.). Author: Cosima Wagner-Extraordinary Daughter of Franz Liszt, 1969; Kate Chase for the Defense, 1971; Hadley: The First Mrs. Hemingway, 1973. Contbr. articles to Pageant, Ellery Queen Mystery Mag., Saturday Review. Address: Mt Holly Rd Katonah NY 10536

SOLANDER, HELEN BERKEY SHANK (MRS. CARL K. SOLANDER), civic worker; b. Goshen, Ind., June 25, 1920; d. Wilbert Elgin and Elva (Berkey) Shank; student Ind. U., 1938-39; R.N., Grant Hosp. Sch. Nursing, Chgo., 1941; m. Carl K. Solander, Mar. 27, 1941; children—Carl Lewis, Alan Robert, Helen Carole. Region capt. Seeing Eye, Chgo., 1955-56; mem. benefit exec. com. United Charities, Chgo., 1956-60; Cookie chmn. Girl Scouts U.S.A. Drive; Chgo., 1957; vice chmn. Latin Sch. Parent Council, Chgo., 1958-59, co-chmn. book fair, 1959-60; regional co-chmn. woman's div. drive Crusade of Mercy, Chgo., 1957, 60, regional chmn., 1958, v.p., 1959; treas. Bargains United. Bd., Chgo., 1960, pres., 1961-62; gen. regional chmn. Chgo. People to People Book Drive, 1961; mem. woman's bd. Grant Hosp. Nominee Almoner award, 1961; bldg. chmn. Chgo. Heart Assn. Mem. Chgo. Council Fgn. Relations, Chgo. Hist. Soc., English-Speaking Union. Republican. Presbyn. Home: 2350 Lincoln Park W Chicago IL 60614

SOLBERG, MARGARET JANE OLSEN (MRS. ARCHIE NORMAN SOLBERG), civic worker; b. Mpls., May 20, 1913; d. Nels Robert and Viola (Leber) Olsen; B.S., N.D. State U., 1934; m. Archie Norman Solberg, Sept. 12, 1934; children—Norman Robert, James Joseph, Mary Anne, Marilyn Jean, Eric Archie, Elizabeth Jane. Formerly vol. worker fund drives various local charitable orgns.; mem. P.T.A., 1945—, P.T.A. Council, 1951-53; organizer social dancing classes for jr. high sch. students, 1952; leader, bd. mem. Girl Scouts, 1952-64; leader Cub Scouts, 1950-53, 62-65; developer and tchr. knitting and stichery courses Toledo Bd. Edn., 1966-69; mem. India Assn., 1965—, adviser to Indian women in Toledo, 1965—; mem. Pan-Pacific S.E. Asian Women's Assn., 1967—, mem. nat. bd., 1968—, chpt. pres. 1970, del. internat. conf., 1968; mem. preventive edn. com. Toledo Area Program on Drug Abuse, 1972; asst. to coordinator for Toledo area fund raising Relief for Bangladesh, 1972; treas. Toledo area com. for UNICEF, 1972-73. Mem. Republican County Central Com., 1968—. Recipient citation for service Lucas County Republican Party, 1969. Mem. Mortar Bd., Kappa Delta (chpt. pres. 1933-34), Phi Kappa Phi. Conglist. Clubs: University Women's (chmn. host family program for fgn. students 1968—)(Toledo). Home: 3215 Kylemore Rd Toledo OH 43606

SOLBERG, MARY MELINDA, editor; b. Sioux Falls, S.D., Oct. 9, 1947; d. Richard William and June Joanne (Nelson) Solberg; B.A., Swarthmore Coll., 1968; postgrad. U. Heidelberg (Germany), 1968-69. Book editor Stein & Day Pubs., N.Y.C., 1969—. Lutheran. Home: 700 Minneford Av City Island NY 10464 Office: Scarborough House Briarcliff Manor NY 10510

SOLBERG, NELLIE FLORENCE COAD, educator, artist; b. Sault Ste. Marie, Mich.; d. Sanford and Mary (McDonald) Coad; B.A., Minot State Tchrs. Coll., 1930; M.A., N.D. State U., 1963; postgrad. Wash. State U., 1960, Wyo. U., 1964, St. Cloud (Minn.) Coll., 1971; m. Ingvald Solberg, Aug. 24, 1930; children—Jeanne Elaine (Mrs. Clarence Unruh), Walter Eugene, Kay Louise (Mrs. Arthur Link). Tchr., Bismarck (N.D.) Elementary Schs., 1954-63, art dir. high sch., 1963-72; art instr. Bismarck Jr. Coll., 1964-67; exhibited one-man shows Minot State Coll., 1963, Dickinson State Coll., 1964, Jamestown Coll., 1964, U. N.D., Valley City State Coll., Bismarck Jr. Coll., 1963, 65, 68, 69, N.D. State U., 1970, 74, Linha Gallery, Minot, N.D., 1972, Bank of N.D., 1972-74; exhibited group shows Gov. John Davis Mansion, 1960, Concordia Coll., Moorhead, Minn., 1965, N.D. Capitol, 1968, 69, Gov. William Guy Mansion, 1971, Internat. Peace Gardens, 1969; mem. Indian Culture Found., 1964—; dir. N.D. Petroleum Art Show, 1962, 64, Statewide Religious Arts Festival, Bismarck, 1970—; dir. State Treas.'s Gallery, N.D. State Capitol, Bismarck, 1973—; co-dir. Indian Art Show, Nat. Congress Am. Indians, Bismarck, 1963. Mem. religious arts com. Conf. Chs., 1973. Recipient 3d pl. graphics Five State Show, Pierre, S.D., 1968; Purchase award S.D. Arts Council, 1968. Mem. Bismarck (charter, Honor award 1960, pres. 1963-64, 71-72), Jamestown art assns., Linha Gallery (Minot), Nat. League Am. Pen Women (pres. N.D. 1964-66, pres. Medora br. 1972—), Mpls. Soc. Fine Arts, Am. Crafts Council, Am. Assn. U. Women, P.E.O. (chpt. pres. 1967-69), Order Eastern Star, Republican Wives Club, Republican Women 1st Ladies Club, Sigma Sigma Sigma. Presbyn. Home: 925 N 6th St Bismarck ND 58501 Studio: 1021 N 6th St Bismarck ND 58501

SOLEM, HELEN MARIE SALLER, accountant; b. nr. Parnell, Ia., Dec. 2, 1922; d. George F. and Florence Eulalia (Cain) Saller; student Portland State Coll., 1949-53; m. Robert H. Solem, Aug. 1, 1943 (div. 1957); children—Evanne, Vance. IBM machine accountant Tektronix, Inc., Beaverton, Ore., 1956-63; pub. accountant Peat, Marwick, Mitchell C.P.A.'s, and John A. Fought, C.P.A., Portland, Ore., 1963-68; accountant, controller Portland Art Assn., 1968-72; adminstr. Portland Pub. Schs., 1972—. C.P.A., Ore. Mem. League Women Voters (unit com. head 1966-72, pub. relations 1962-63), Am. Soc. Women Accountants (bull. editor 1968). Contbr. articles to profl. jours. Address: 666 E Main St Hillsboro OR 97123

SOLIDAY, MAUREEN HARTER (MRS. DONALD M. SOLIDAY), civic worker; b. Sioux City, Ia., Nov. 15, 1925; d. Charles Melvin and Mary (Hassenger) Harter; student State U. Ia., 1943-44, Morningside Coll., 1946-48; m. Donald M. Soliday, June 17, 1948; children—Jeffrey P., Karen, Melissa, Heidi, Amanda, Jay B., Joel P., Rebecca, Sarah, Jon A., Jeremy B., Joshua L., Jason M. Mem. West Des Moines and Polk County One Vote Com., 1952-56; chmn. fund drive Mercy Hosp., 1955-56; pub. relations chmn. Catholic Women's League 1958-62; active Amateur Athletic Union, 1958—, asst. dir. Ia. spl. olympics com., 1969-71, state dir., 1972—, mem. nat. adv. com., 1969—; nat. chmn. Jr. Olympic Luge Com., 1972—, mem. adv. bd. Ia. Assn. Swim Clubs, 1966—, treas., 1970—; founding mem. Stillwell Jr. High Sch. P.T.A., West Des Moines, Ia., 1960—. Mem. Polk County Democratic Central Com., 1969—, Polk County Dem. Women's Club, 1957—; candidate for a Ho. of Reps., 1968. Bd. dirs. Polk County chpt. Easter Seal Drive, 1961-62, Polk County Soc. Crippled Children and Adults, 1961-66; bd. dirs., sec. Concerned Christians Assn., Des Moines, 1967-68; bd. dirs. Polk County Human Rights Com., 1969-70. Roman Catholic. Home and office: 1133 16th St West Des Moines IA 50265

SOLIMAN, PATRICIA KATHLEEN BREHAUT (MRS. ANWAR EL SAYED I. SOLIMAN), editor; b. New Rochelle, N.Y., Oct. 11, 1937; d. Ernest Henry and Winnifred (Gatehouse) Brehaut; B.A., Tufts U., 1959; M.A., Stanford, 1962; m. Anwar el Sayed I. Soliman, Sept. 26, 1964. Editorial asst. Harper & Row, Pubs., Inc., 1962-65; asso. editor Coward McCann & Geoghegan, Pubs., Inc., N.Y.C. 1965-68, sr. editor, 1968-71, exec. editor, 1971-72, exec. editor, v.p., 1972—. Woodrow Wilson fellow, 1959. Mem. Phi Beta Kappa. Home: 245 W 4th St New York City NY 10014 Office: 200 Madison Av New York City NY 10016

SOLINGER, JANET LOUISE WEILAND, ednl. adminstr.; b. Cin.; d. Fred and Dorothy (Gross) Weiland; B.A., U. Cin.; M.A., N.Y. U.; children—Dorothy, Regina, Martha. Asst. to pres. Hebrew Union Coll.-Jewish Inst. Religion, Cin., 1957-60; adminstr. Jewish Mus., N.Y., 1961-65; asst. to pres. Finch Coll., N.Y.C., 1966; dir. pub. information and spl. events N.Y. U. Sch. Continuing Edn., 1966-72; dir. resident asso. program Smithsonian Instn., Washington, 1972—. Chmn. publs., pub. information Nat. U. Extension Assn., 1971-73. Mem. art adv. com. Child Study Assn.; chmn. arts com. Manhattan IHB. Bd. dirs. Citizens for Artists' Housing. Mem. Assn. Coll. and U. Concert Mgrs., Am. Assn. Museums, Adult Edn. Assn. (publ. com.), Women's Democratic Club (arts and humanities com.), Phi Beta Kappa. Home: 2801 New Mexico Av NW Washington DC 20007 Office: Smithsonian Instn Washington DC 20560

SOLIT, ADELE PISKULICK, advt. exec.; b. St. Louis, July 13, 1925; d. William and Estelle C. (Kamer) Piskulick; B.S., Harris Tchrs. Coll., 1945; postgrad. Columbia, 1945-46, Washington U., St. Louis, 1952-54; m. Samuel Solit, May 20, 1945; 1 dau., Luann Estelle (Mrs. L.R. Povich). With Premier Clothing Co., 1945-52, W.T. Thompson Co., 1952-56; corporate sec., mgr. F.B. Chamberlain Co., 1956-61; corp. sec., dir.-controller, media dir. Clayton-Davis & Assos., Inc., St. Louis, 1961-66, sec., treas., dir.-controller, media dir., 1966-71, exec. v.p., 1971—; sec.-treas., dir. Design Corp. Am., Clayton-Davis Pub. Relations, Celebrities Unltd., Inc. Mem. Womens Advt. Club, Nat. Assn. Credit Mgmt., Am. Women in Radio and Television, St. Louis Assn. Credit Mgmt. (dir. 1973—), Adminstrv. Mgmt. Assn., Am. Assn. Bus. Mgmt., Credit Women St. Louis (pres. 1973-74), C. of C., Better Bus. Bur. Mem. and Ref. Ch. Mem. Evang. Order Eastern Star (past matron, dist. dep. grand), Order Rainbow Girls (past chmn. bd.). Home: 8650 Otto Westway Sunset Hills MO 63127 Office: 408 Olive St St Louis MO 63102

SOLLERS-RIEDEL, HELEN, entomologist, govt. ofcl.; b. Balt., Sept. 29, 1911; d. William and Helen (Day) Sollers; B.S., James Ormond Wilson Tchrs. Coll., 1934; m. F. Atherton Riedel, May 11, 1962 (dec.) With U.S. Bur. Entomology and Plant Quarantine, Washington, 1937-53, sci. aide div. insect pest survey, 1937-42, jr. entomologist div. insects affecting man and animals, 1942-47, asst. entomologist, 1947-53; entomologist Plant Protection div. Agrl. Res. Service, Washington, 1953-71; med. entomologist, NIH grantee, 1971—. Hon. fellow Indian Soc. for Malaria and Other Communicable Diseases; fellow Royal Soc. Tropical Medicine and Hygiene; mem. Insecticide Soc. Washington, Entomol. Soc. Am., Entomol. Soc. Washington (custodian 1950-52, rec. sec. 1958-60, pres. 1969), Ga. Entomol. Soc., Fla. Anti-Mosquito Assn., Entomol. Soc. Can., Am. Soc. Tropical Medicine and Hygiene, Tropical Medicine Soc. Washington (dir. exec. com. 1961-64), Am. Mosquito Control Assn. (dir. S.E. Central region 1962-64), Am. Soc. Parasitologists, Australian Entomol. Soc., Entomol. Soc. Egypt. Asso. editor Mosquito News. Contbr. articles profl. jours. Home: 1218 Floral St NW Washington DC 20012 Office: PO Box 19009 Washington DC 20036

SOLLIE, VIOLET JOHNSON (MRS. ALLEN N. SOLLIE), lawyer; b. Mpls., Jan. 18, 1907; d. Claus August and Priscilla (Jones) Johnson; B.A. magna cum laude, Hamline U., 1928; M.A., U. Minn., 1929; LL.B., cum laude, William Mitchell Coll. Law, 1957; m. Allen N. Sollie, Feb. 11, 1944. Statistician, Minn. Tax Dept., 1933-39; asso. statistician govts. div. Census Bur., Washington, 1942-43; investigator Minn. Dept. Labor and Industry, 1943-51; analyst, exec. asst. region 1 Wage Stabilization Bd., Mpls., 1951-53, Mpls. Labor Rev., 1953-57; admitted to Minn. bar, 1957; pvt. practice law, Mpls., 1958-72, Mound, 1973—. Mem. Minn. High Sch. Student Lawyer Council, 1973. Bd. dirs. Legal Assistance Minn., 1972-73, Sch. Social Devel., Mpls., 1960-61. Mem. Hennepin County (sec. referral service 1963-67, gov. council 1963-67), Minn., Am. bar assns., Nat. Assn. Women Lawyers, Phi Delta Delta. Author: (with Roy G. Blakey) State Income Taxes, 1942. Home: 2855 Cambridge Lane Mound MN 55364

SOLOMON, ELINOR HARRIS (MRS. RICHARD A. SOLOMON), financial economist; b. Brookline, Mass., Feb. 26, 1923; d. Ralph and Linna (Ehrenfried) Harris; A.B., Mt. Holyoke Coll., 1944; M.A., Radcliffe Coll., 1945, Ph.D., 1948; m. Richard A. Solomon, Mar. 30, 1957; children—Joan Lynn, Robert Harris, Thomas Herbert. Research asst. Boston Fed. Res. Bank, 1944-47; financial economist bd. govs. Fed. Res. System Divs. Research, Statistics and Internat. Finance, Washington, 1949-56; internat. economist Bur. Far Eastern Affairs, Dept. State, 1956-58; pvt. econ. cons., 1958—; cons. U.S. Dept. Justice, 1961-62, 66—, sr. financial economist, 1969—. Lectr., Am. U., Washington, 1964-66, professorial lectr., 1966-67. Mem. Phi Beta Kappa. Clubs: Radcliffe, Mount Holyoke (Washington). Contbr. articles to profl. jours. Address: 6805 Delaware St Chevy Chase MD 20015

SOLOMON, GAIL ELLEN (MRS. HARVEY L. HECHT), physician, educator; b. Bklyn., May 26, 1938; d. Samuel and Estelle (Suffin) Solomon; A.B., Smith Coll., 1958; M.D., Albert Einstein Coll. Medicine, 1962; m. Harvey L. Hecht, Oct. 28, 1962; children—Daniel Hayes, Jonathan Lewis, Elizabeth Merrie. Intern, Bronx Municipal Hosp., 1962-63, resident pediatrics, 1963-64; resident pediatrics N.Y. Hosp. and Cornell U. Med. Center, 1964-65; NIH fellow pediatric neurology Neurol. Inst., Columbia Presbyn. Med. Center, 1965-68, NIH fellow clin. neurophysiology and EEG, 1968-69; asst. prof. pedicatrics and neurology Cornell U. Med. Center, N.Y.C. dir. EEG lab., 1969—; asst. attending neurology, pediatrics N.Y. Hosp., N.Y.C., 1969—; practice medicine specializing in pediatric neurology, N.Y.C., 1963; mem. staffs N.Y. Hosp., Cornell Med. Center, N.Y.C. Fellow Am. Acad. Pediatrics; mem. A.M.A., N.Y. County Med. Soc., Am. Acad. Neurology, Am. Women's Med. Assn., Eastern EEG Soc., Am. Epilepsy Soc. Home: 50 Brewster Rd Scarsdale NY 10583 Office: NY Hosp and Cornell Med Center 525 E 68th St New York City NY 10021

SOLOMON, GOODY LOVE (MRS. THEODORE A. BRAUN), author, editor, cons.; b. N.Y.C., June 1, 1929; d. Frank A. and Anna (Caplan) Solomon; B.A. cum laude, Bklyn. Coll., 1950; M.A. summa cum laude, N.Y. U., 1955; m. Theodore A. Braun, July 1, 1953. With Commentary Mag., N.Y.C., 1950-55; asst. editor Stores Mag., Nat. Retail Mchts. Assn., N.Y.C., 1955-61; free lance writer N.Y.C., Washington, 1961-71; instr. George Washington U., 1966—. Cons. Office Spl. Asst. to Pres. on Consumer Affairs, Washington, 1966—; editor U.S. Consumer, 1970—; exec. editor Office Consumer Services, Dept. Health, Edn. and Welfare, 1972—; consumer edn. dir. N.Y. State Consumer Protection Bd., 1973; moderator TV show The Knowing Consumer, 1973. Mem. Women's Democratic Club Washington, 1969—. Mem. League Women Voters, Bus. and Profl. Women's Club, Am. Newspaper Women's Club, N.Y. U. Alumni Fedn., Nat. Fedn. Press Women, Am. Women in Radio and TV. Author: The Radical Consumers Handbook, 1972. Contbr. to Barron's Weekly, Changing Times, Redbook, Ladies Home Jour., others. Address: 1712 Taylor St NW Washington DC 20011

SOLOMON, LYDIA SIMIU (MRS. MARCEL SOLOMON), pathologist; b. Bucharest, Romania, Mar. 5, 1929; d. Bernard and Sofia (Finkelstein) Simiu; M.D., Med. Sch. Bucharest, Romania, 1953. Came to U.S., 1963, naturalized, 1969; m. Marcel Solomon, Dec. 18, 1948; 1 son, Paul. Intern, White Plains Hosp. (N.Y.), 1963-66; resident Kings County Hosp., Bklyn., 1966, Montefiore Hosp., Bronx, N.Y., 1966-68; asso. pathologist Bronx Lebanon Hosp., 1969—; instr. pathology Albert Einstein Coll. Medicine, 1970—. Diplomate Am. Bd. Pathology. Mem. A.M.A., Bronx County Med. Soc. Home: 357 N Broadway Yonkers NY 10701 Office: Grand Concourse and Mount Eden Pkwy Bronx NY 10457

SOLOMON, MARGARET CLAIRE, educator; b. Enid, Okla., Nov. 27, 1918; d. David Hamilton Moore and Ida Candace (Morrison) Boyle; B.A., U. Hawaii, 1960; M.A. (Woodrow Wilson fellow), U. Cal. at Berkeley, 1961; Ph.D., Claremont Grad. Sch., 1967; m. Marland Robert Solomon, Dec. 8, 1938 (div. Dec. 1952); children—Stephen Lewis, Stuart Grant. Instr. English, U. Hawaii, Honolulu, 1961-64, asst. prof., 1966-69; asso. prof., 1969-73, prof., 1973—. Instr. English, LaVerne (Cal.) Coll., 1965. Mem. Modern Lang. Assn., Am. Assn. U. Profs., James Joyce Found. Author: Eternal Geomater: The Sexual Universe of Finnegans Wake, 1969. Home: 212 Hawaii Loa St Honolulu HI 96821 Office: Dept English U of Hawaii Honolulu HI 96822

SOLOMON, RUTH FREEMAN (MRS. JOSEPH SOLOMON), author; b. Kiev, Russia, Apr. 21, 1908; d. Harry and Jenny (Packard) Freeman; came to U.S., 1911, naturalized, 1932; A.B., Syracuse U., 1929; postgrad. U. Vienna, 1930; m. Joseph C. Solomon, Mar. 21, 1930; children—George Freeman, Daniel Freeman. Mem. Adv. Com. to 6th Army, 1973-74. Bd. dirs. Paramount Theatre Performing Arts, San Francisco Opera Guild. Mem. Phi Beta Kappa, Delta Sigma Phi, Phi Sigma Phi. Club: Commonwealth (San Francisco). Author: The Candlestick and the Cross, 1967; The Eagle and the Dove, 1971; The Ultimate Triumph, 1974. Home: 34 25th Av San Francisco CA 94121

SOLOMON, SUSAN GOLDBERG (MRS. ROBERT SAMUEL SOLOMON), museum ofcl.; b. Perth Amboy, N.J., July 4, 1943; d. Nathan and Rita Elaine (Levine) Goldberg; B.A., Skidmore Coll., 1965; M.A., U. Pa., 1969; m. Robert Samuel Solomon, Dec. 29, 1966; 1 son, Jonathan. Asst. curator Richard L. Feigen & Co., N.Y.C., 1969-70; curator painting and sculpture Newark Museum, 1970-73, dir. spl. projects, 1973—; founder N.J. Art Index, 1972. Mem. Am. Assn. Museums, Nat. Trust for Historic Preservation, Victorian Soc. Home: 47 Hardy Dr Princeton NJ 08540 Office: 43-49 Washington St Newark NJ 07101

SOLOMON, VITA PETROSKY (MRS. CHARLES M. SOLOMON), artist; b. Phila., Dec. 16, 1916; d. Harry and Rose (Bobrow) Petrosky; diploma Moore Inst. Art, 1937; B.F.A., Tyler Sch. Fine Arts of Temple U., 1958, B.S. in Edn., 1958, M.F.A., 1960; m. Charles M. Solomon, Apr. 8, 1941; children—Robert Charles, Henry Andrew, Jon David. One-artist shows Phila. Art Alliance, 1953, 54, 58, Red Door Gallery, 1959, 1960, 1961, Newman Gallery, 1964; tchr. art and art history Cheltenham High Sch.; tchr. art and English, Elkins Park Jr. High Sch.; exhibited group shows United Soc. Artists, London, Pa. Acad. Fine Art, Phila. Art Mus., Detroit Inst. Art, Butler Inst. Art, Silvermine Guild (Conn.), N.A.D., Am. Water Color Soc., Audubon Soc., Royal Acad. Arts, London, Silvermine Guild Conn., Paris Salon, Woodmere Art Gallery, Phila. Art Alliance, Royal Inst. London, Nat. Arts Club (N.Y.), Met. Mus. Art, others; represented in permanent collections Nat. Portrait Gallery, others, including portraits on commn. J.F. Lewis traveling fellow, Europe by Moore Inst., 1937; recipient Gross Meml. award Silvermine Guild. 1958; Chandler prize Allied Artists Am., 1960; prizes Moore Inst., 1957, 60, 61; purchase prize Temple U., 1959, (2) 1960, painting prize, 1966; Burdine meml. prize Woodmere Gallery, 1964; painting prize Wharton Art Center, 1964; Lowell Painting Prize C. L. Wolfe Club, Nat. Arts Club, 1966; Painting prize Silver medal Paris Salon, 1966; award Phila. Watercolor Club, 1973; Benedictine Art award, 1972; Blumenthal prize Cheltenham Art Centre, 1973. Mem. Am. Watercolor Soc., Cheltenham Twp. Art Centre, Art Alliance, Artists Equipty, Phila. Art Tchrs. Assn., Nat., Pa., Cheltenham tchrs. assns., Phila. Water Color Club, Allied Artists Am. Address: 112 Glenview Av Wyncote PA 19095

SOLOMONS, HOPE COWEN (MRS. GERALD SOLOMONS), psychologist; b. Providence, Sept. 20, 1932; d. Morris Louis and Anna Emma (Wunsch) Cowen; student Pembroke Coll., 1949-50, Harvard, summer 1951; student Boston U., summer 1952, Ed.D., 1957; B.A. (Alice Friend Newton scholar), Clark U., 1952; A.M., Wellesley Coll., 1954; m. Gerald Solomons, June 12, 1955; children—Nan Martha, Mary Lorna. Individual practice psychology, Providence, 1952-62; instr., asst. prof. R.I. Sch. Design, 1956-60; asst. prof. R.I. Coll., 1960-62; research asso. U. Ia., Iowa City, 1962-63, asso. prof., 1967—; sch. psychologist, Iowa City, 1963-67; cons. psychologist Community Workshops R.I., 1959. Mem. Am., Ia. (exec. council 1969-70, treas. 1970-72, chmn. ways and means 1972—) psychol. assns., Council for Exceptional Children, Am. Assn. U. Profs., Ia.-Yucatan Partners of

Americas, Partners Rehab. and Edn. Program, Ia. Wellesley Club (pres. 1974—), Pan Am. Club, Sigma Xi, Pi Lambda Theta. Contbr. articles to profl. jours. Home: 319 Mullin Av Iowa City IA 52240 Office: Coll Nursing U Ia Iowa City IA 52242

SOLOOK, BARBARA A. STRYKER (MRS. MICHAEL J. SOLOOK), social worker; b. Bound Brook, N.J., Feb. 22, 1928; d. Gysbert O. and Beatrice (Porter) Stryker; B.A., Keuka Coll., 1950; M.S., Columbia, 1953; m. Michael J. Solook, June 11, 1966; 1 dau., Nancy Ann. Staff psychiat. social worker Union County Psychiat. Clinic, Plainfield, N.J., 1953-56, 57-60, dir. psychiat. social work, 1960—; psychiat. social worker Rochester (N.Y.) Guidance Center, 1956-57; pvt. practice social work, 1970—. Cons. Union County Commn. Sch., Westfield, N.J., 1971—. Co-chmn. Bound Brook Bi-Centennial Celebration, 1974—. Fellow Am. Orthopsychiat. Assn.; mem. Am. Assn. U. Women (1st v.p. br. 1968-70, pres. br. 1970-72), Am. Assn. Psychiat. Services for Children, Nat. Assn. Social Workers, Zonta. Office: 18 E Union Av Bound Brook NJ 08805

SOLOWAY, VICTORIA, physician; b. N.Y.C., Apr. 23, 1910; d. Morris and Katie (Fetlow) Soloway; B.A., Hunter Coll., 1929; M.D., N.Y. U., 1933; M.P.H., Columbia, 1955; children—Edward P. Friedman, Daniel J. Friedman. Intern, Morrisania Hosp., N.Y.C., 1933-35, resident pediatrics, 1935, Willard Parker Hosp., 1936; practice medicine specializing in pediatrics, N.Y.C., 1936-42; pub. health physician, N.Y.C., 1954—; mem. staff N.Y. U. Med. Center, N.Y.C., clin. instr. Sch. Medicine, 1968—. Fellow Am. Pub. Health Assn.; mem. N.Y.C. Pub. Health Physicians' Assn. (v.p. 1970-73), N.Y.C. Pub. Health Assn., Am. Med. Women's Assn., P.E.O., Phi Beta Kappa. Home: 453 E 14th St New York City NY 10009 Office: 125 Worth St New York City NY 10013

SOLTESZ, KATHRYN MARIA, librarian; b. Cluj, Romania, Nov. 30, 1910; d. Alexander and Kathryn (Surek) Soltesz; B.A., Lyceum Domnita Ileana, Sibiu, Romania, 1932; M.A., U. Cluj, 1938, Coll. Carmen Sylva, Cluj, 1939, U. Szeged (Hungary), 1945; M.S. in L.S., Case Western Res. U., 1960. Came to U.S., 1957, naturalized, 1963. Educator in Romania, 1938-44, Hungary, 1944-48, 54-56, 57; library asst. Ohio State U., Columbus, 1957-60; asst. catalog librarian Cornell U., 1960-62; sr. serials cataloger U. Cin., 1962-63; asst. coll. librarian, acting head State U. N.Y. at Fredonia, 1963-66, asso. librarian Internat. Library, Oyster Bay, N.Y., 1966-68; asst. prof., head catalog sect. York Coll. Library City U. N.Y., 1968—. Life fellow Intercontinental Biog. Assn.; mem. Am. Assn. U. Profs., Library Assn. City U. N.Y., UN Assn. U.S.A. Home: 3 Glen Keith Rd Glen Cove NY 11542 Office: 150-14 Jamaica Av Jamaica NY 11432

SOLTZ, JUDITH ELAINE, lawyer; b. Boston, July 5, 1946; d. Joseph Benjamin and Beatrice (Belis) Soltz; B.A. cum laude, Barnard Coll., 1968; J.D. cum laude, Boston Coll., 1971; m. Jeffrey L. Marx, Mar. 30, 1974. Admitted to Mass. bar, 1971; staff atty., Brookline (Mass.) Rent Control Bd., 1971-72; partner firm Kopelman & Soltz, Boston, 1973—. Mem. legal com. Jewish Community Council, Boston, 1973—. Mem. Town Meeting, Brookline, 1973. Mem. Am., Mass., Boston bar assns., Mass. Women Lawyers, Order Coif. Home: 20 Radcliffe Rd Allston MA 02134 Office: 10 Post Office Sq Boston MA 02109

SOLYST, DOROTHY DEHMER (MRS. GARY GENE SOLYST), occupational therapist; b. Mpls., Oct. 26, 1942; d. Oscar Carl and Magdalen Elisabeth (Diem) Dehmer; student St. Cloud State Coll., 1960-62, U. Minn., 1962-63; B.S., Coll. St. Catherine, 1964; postgrad. U. Wis., 1968-69, N.Y. U., 1967, 70; m. Gary Gene Solyst, Apr. 12, 1969. Staff occupational therapist, student supr. Woodrow Wilson Rehab. Center, Fishersville, Va., 1964-67; staff therapist Central Wis. Colony, Madison, 1967-68; occupational therapy supr. Fairfax County Health Dept., Fairfax, Va., 1969-71; chief occupational therapist Phys. Therapy Service, Alexandria, Va., 1971—. Lectr. rehab. techniques U. Va., 1973—. Rehab. Services Adminstrn. grantee, 1967, 69, 71. Mem. Nat. Rehab. Assn., Nat., D.C. occupational therapy assns. Roman Catholic. Home: 828 S 31st St Arlington VA 22202 Office: 1510 Collingwood Rd Alexandria VA 22308

SOMAN, SHIRLEY CAMPER ISENBERG (MRS. ROBERT O. SOMAN), author; b. Boston, Mar. 7, 1922; d. David and Fannie (Apteker) Isenberg; B.A., U. Wis., 1945; M.S.S., Smith Coll., 1946; m. Frederic R. Camper, Oct. 12, 1945 (div. 1961); children—Frederic Douglas, Frances Ann; m. 2d, Robert O. Soman, Nov. 10, 1962. Asso. editor My Baby Mag. and Shaw's Market News, 1952-53; sch. social worker Bur. Child Guidance, N.Y.C. Bd. Edn., 1956-57; family life cons., editor, pub. information cons. Family Service Assn. Am., 1957-64; v.p. Asso. Film Consultants and Mercury News Film, 1967-72. Cons., lectr. social agys. and community groups, 1960—; chmn. nat. symposium on child advocacy, 1974. Mem. Authors League Am. (chmn. program adv. com. 1972-73), Nat. Assn. Sci. Writers, Soc. Mag. Writers (chmn. non-fiction writers' workshop 1975), Acad. Certified Social Workers, Nat. Assn. Social Workers, Oral History Assn., Nat. Council Family Relations, Nat. Acad. Television Arts and Scis., Nat. Orgn. Women, Am. Hist. Assn., Am. Pub. Welfare Assn., Am. Med. Writers Assn., Writers Guild East, N.Y. State Certified Social Workers. Author: How to Get Along With Your Child, 1962; Let's Stop Destroying our Children, 1974. Editor: Forging Tools for Mental Health (Jewish Bd. Guardians), 1955; editor Family Service Highlights-Jour., 1957-61. Home: 40 W 77th St New York City NY 10024

SOMERS, CATHERINE LYON (MRS. HOWARD B. SOMERS), civic worker; b. Portland, Ore., Nov. 16, 1919; d. Chester A. and Catherine (Moritz) Lyon; B.A., Lewis and Clark Coll., 1941; postgrad. Oberlin Coll., 1941; m. Howard B. Somers, Dec. 31, 1943; children—Linda, JoAnne, Carol, Debra. Teenage dir. YWCA, Fresno, Cal., 1941-43, Spokane, Wash., 1943-44; camp dir. YWCA, also Meth. youth camps, Cal. and Ore., 1942-45. Mem. nat. bd. dirs. YWCA, 1964-68; Ore. rep. YWCA World Service Council, 1962—; bd. dirs. YWCA, Portland, 1945-48, 1956-58, 1964-70—, pres., 1958; bd. dirs. Tri-County United Good Neighbors, 1961-64, exec. com., 1963-64, chmn. neighborhoods div. fund-raising campaign, 1961, residential coordinator Washington County, 1970—; bd. dirs. Alameda P.T.A., Portland, 1960-64, pres., 1964; mem. bd. Grant High P.T.A., 1966; pres. Tigard area Ore. State U. Mothers Club, 1973; pres. Ore. Older Girls Conf., 1940, adv. bd., 1948-63, asst. dir., 1956-63, exec. dir., 1968—; mem. Portland Family Counseling Service, 1962—, Citizens Sch. Com., Portland, 1961, 1963; mem. Ore. council U.S.O., 1959—, mem. nat. council, 1967-69; state coordinator OPT-Ore.: Population Target, 1971-72; mem. local arrangements com. nat. assembly Women's Soc. Christian Service, Portland, 1966; mem. program com. Western Jurisdictional Conf., Methodist Ch., 1964; mem. Ore. Meth. Family Life Com., 1960-63; mem. Ore. Conf. Bd. Deaconesses, Meth. Ch., 1947-50; mem. youth com. Portland Council Chs., 1961-62, chmn. women's com. fund-raising campaign, 1963; mem. Columbia Region Assn. Govts., 1970—; sr. adviser Portland Area council Epsilon Sigma Alpha, 1969—. Pres., Alameda Republican Club, Portland, 1966-67. Mem. bd. overseers Lewis and Clark Coll., Portland; bd. dirs. Wesley Found., Portland State U., exec. com., 1965—; bd. dirs. Portland Jr. Symphony, 1971-72; exec. bd. dirs., explorer tng. chmn. Columbia-Pacific council Boy Scouts Am., 1973—. Named Outstanding Sr. Woman, Lewis and Clark Coll., 1941, recipient Distinguished Alumni Achievement award, 1967; Portland Woman of Year, Portland Women's Forum and C. of C., 1959; One of Portland's Ten Women of Accomplishment, Ore. Daily Jour., 1964; Tigard Lay Educator of Yr. award Tigard (Ore.) Edn. Assn., 1972. Mem. Portland Jaycettes (pres. 1953), Am. Heritage Assn. Mem. Mystic Order of Rose, Ore. Ch. Women United. Clubs: Multnomah Athletic (Portland); Mt. Hood Golf and Country (Wemme, Ore.); Metro Womens. Contbr. articles, fiction to nat. mags. Panelist-moderator Challenge of Books, Multnomah County Library Assn., KGW-TV, Portland, 1961-64. Pub. speaker to service clubs, high sch. assemblies, ch. tng. confs. throughout Pacific N.W., 1945—. Home: 12585 SW Bull Mountain Rd Portland OR 97223

SOMERS, JEAN ELIZABETH, univ. adminstr.; b. Chgo., May 12, 1936; d. Paul Peter and Helen J. (Sullivan) Somers; B.A., Rosary Coll., 1958. Soc. editor News-Gazette, Champaign, Ill., 1958-63; editor U. Ill., Champaign, 1963-70, adminstrv. asst. personnel adminstrn., 1970—. Chmn. pub. relations Mercy Hosp. Women's Aux., Urbana, 1973; mem. alumni bd. Rosary Coll., River Forest, Ill., 1969-71. Bd. dirs. Green Meadows council Girl Scouts U.S.A., 1968-71, mem. pub. relations com., 1973; bd. dirs. U. Ill. Employees Credit Union. Mem. Nat. League Am. Pen Women, Women in Communications (sec.-treas. 1973, adv. com.), Coll. and Univ. Personnel Assn. (editor 1973), Cath. Women (chmn. pub. relations Danville deanery). Club: Altrusa (Champaign-Urbana). Home: 311 W University Av Champaign IL 61820

SOMERS, MARY LOUISE, educator, social worker; b. Zanesville, O., Dec. 17, 1915; d. Charles Henry and Clara M. (Stitt) Somers; B.A., Muskingum Coll., 1937; M.S., Case Western Reserve U., 1943, D. Social Work, 1957; L.H.D., Muskingum Coll., 1962. Tchr. pub. schs., Zanesville, O., 1937-41; exec. dir. Toledo Council, Girl Scouts of U.S.A., 1943-45; faculty field instr. Sch. Social Work, U. Pitts., 1945-49; asst. prof. Sch. Social Work, U. So. Cal., Los Angeles, 1949-53; asso. prof. Sch. Applied Social Scis., Case Western Reserve U., Cleve., 1957-58; prof. social work Sch. Social Service Adminstrn., U. Chgo., 1958—. Mem. Am. Assn. U. Profs., Council Social Work Edn., Nat. Soc. Study Edn., Nat. Assn. Social Workers, Acad. Certified Social Workers, Internat. Conf. Social Welfare, Nat. Conf. Social Welfare, UN Assn. Am., Am. Civil Liberties Union, Sigma Alpha Iota, Delta Kappa Gamma. Club: Sierra. Home: 6019 Ingleside Av Chicago IL 60637 Office: 969 E 60th St Chicago IL 60637

SOMMER, ANNEMARIE, physician; b. Konigsberg, Germany, Jan. 1, 1932; d. Heinrich and Maria Magdelena (Kruppa) Sommer; B.A., Wittenberg U., 1960; M.D., Ohio State U., 1964. Came to U.S., 1955, naturalized 1961. Intern, Grant Hosp., Columbus, O., 1964-65; resident pediatrics Children's Hosp., Columbus, 1965-67, pediatrician, 1967—, also instr. pediatrics; instr. pediatrics Ohio State U., Columbus, 1967-70, asst. prof. pediatrics, 1970—. Fellow genetics NIH, 1968-70. Mem. Am. Med. Women's Assn., Alpha Omega Alpha. Home: 7530 Bellaire Av Dublin OH 43017 Office: Childrens Hosp Columbus OH 43205

SOMMER, LAURA JANE WELLENS, stock broker; b. N.Y.C., Apr. 6, 1948; d. Philip L. and Portia (Pomerantz) Wellens; student Columbia, 1965. Stockbroker, Bache & Co., N.Y.C., 1968-70, E.F. Hutton & Co., Inc., N.Y.C., 1970—. Active Republican Club, 1973—. Recipient Silver Merit award E.F. Hutton, 1972. Mem. Women's Stockbroker Assn. Home: 405 E 63d St New York City NY 10021 Office: 280 Park Av New York City NY 10017

SOMMER, MARY BROWN JEFFERY (MRS. ALAN R. SOMMER), business exec.; b. Ashland, Wis., Jan. 31, 1936; d. Stanley C. and Fannie (Brown) Jeffery; B.S. in Bus. Adminstrn., U. Buffalo, 1956; m. Alan R. Sommer. With Phillips, Wertman & Co., Pub. Accountants, Buffalo, 1956-62, partner, 1960-62; adminstrv. asst. tax div. trust dept. Marine Midland Bank Western, 1962-64, accounting officer comptroller's dept., 1964-68, asst. v.p. profit planning & budgetary control dept., 1968-71; asst. v.p. accounting policy Marine Midland Banks, Inc., 1971-74, v.p. accounting policy, 1974; v.p., treas. Marine Midland Leasing Corp., 1974—. C.P.A., N.Y. Mem. Am. Women's (past nat. dir., past nat. pres., nat. v.p.), N.Y. socs. C.P.A.'S, Am. Soc. Women Accountants (past pres. Buffalo chpt.), Nat. Assn. Banking Women, Nat. Assn. Accountants, Am. Inst. C.P.A.'s, Am. Inst. Banking, Beta Gamma Sigma. Club: Zonta Internat. Home: 114 Amberwood Dr Grand Island NY 14072 Office: One Marine Midland Center Buffalo NY 14203

SOMMERBURG, MIRIAM, sculptor, painter; b. Hamburg, Germany; d. David and Nanny (Munk) Cahn; student Richard Luksch, Friedrich Adler (Bauhaus) (Stadtliche Kunstschule, Hamburg, Germany); m. Rudolf Sommerburg, Feb. 10, 1927 (dec.); children—Sascha, Dimitri, Sonia (Mrs. Nathan Rabin), David P., Gioconda (Mrs. Howard L. Richards). Came to U.S., 1946, naturalized, 1951. One man shows Village Art Center, 1950-58, Creative Gallery, 1951, Harry Saltpeter Gallery, 1953, Kaufman Gallery, 1954-63, Karl Schurz Found. Phila., 1955, Almus Gallery, 1959, Am. Union Hebrew Congregations, 1965; exhibited in group shows Syracuse Mus. (N.Y.), Boston Art Mus., Pa. Acad. Phila., Isaac Delgado Mus. (New Orleans), Bklyn. Mus., Whitney Mus. (N.Y.C.), Burlington Galleries (London), Berlin Acad. Fine Arts, Palazzo Vecchia, Florence, Italy, 1972, Pompeiian Pavilon, Naples, 1972, Palace of Fine Arts, Mexico City, 1972, Lever House, N.Y.C., Union Carbide, N.Y.C., 1972, La Napule, Musee de Cognac, Cannes, 1966, ann. U.S. Mus. Traveling Exhbns., 1972—, numerous others, also exhibited in India, France, Mex., Scotland, Brazil, Argentina, others; represented in permanent collections Met. Mus. N.Y.C., Norfolk (Va.) Mus., Springfield (Mo.) Mus., Fla. So. Coll., Butler Inst. Am. Art, numerous pvt. collections. Recipient Creative Sculpture medal Audubon Artists, 1966; silver medal Knickerbocker Artists, 1954; 1st prize Creative Gallery, 1951; Silvermine Guild Artists award, 1959, numerous others. Fellow Internat. Biog. Assn. (life); mem. Nat. Assn. Women Artists, Audubon Artists, Am. Soc. Contemporary Artists, Print Council of Am., Fedn. Am. Art, Artists Equity Assn. N.Y. Address: care Westbeth-Artists Housing 463 West St New York City NY 10014

SOMMERMAN, KATHRYN MARTHA, ret. entomologist; b. New Haven, Jan. 11, 1915; d. George Van Name and Anna Hilda Agusta (Sperling) Sommerman; B.S., U. Conn., 1937; M.S., U. Ill., 1941, Ph.D., 1945. Instr., Wells Coll., Aurora, N.Y., 1945-46; asst. prof. Eastern Ill. State Coll., Charleston, 1946; entomologist Army Med. Center, Washington, 1946-51, U.S. Dept. Agr., Army Contract Project, Washington, 1951-53; ind. researcher on psocoptera, Orlando, Fla., 1953-55; collaborator U.S. Nat. Mus., 1953-58; research entomologist Arctic Health Research Center, Anchorage, 1955-67, College, Alaska, 1967-73. Postdoctoral Research fellow U. Ill., 1949; recipient Exceptional Civilian Service award U.S. Dept. Army, 1950; Sustained Superior Performance award Dept. Health, Edn. and Welfare, 1960. Mem. Am. Inst. Biol. Sci., Am. Mosquito Control Assn., Ecol. Soc. Am., Entomol. Soc. Am. (sect. A sec. 1955), Soc. for Study Evolution, Wilderness Soc., Entomol. Soc. Washington, Sigma Xi, Phi Sigma, Sigma Delta Epsilon. Home: 11 Laydon Av North Haven CT 06473

SOMMERVILLE, MARGARET JEAN, physician; b. Columbus, Neb., Feb. 21, 1925; d. Edward Gustav and Emma (Luers) Loseke; student Wartburg Coll., 1942-45; B.A., State U. Ia., 1947, M.D., 1951; m. James Julian Sommerville, Nov. 6, 1954; children—Jean, Ann, Margaret. Intern, King's County Hosp., Bklyn., 1951-53; pvt. practice, Strawberry Point and Des Moines, 1953-55; practice medicine, White Plains, Tuckahoe, Port Chester N.Y., 1956-59, Atlanta, 1959—. Diplomate Nat. Bd. Med. Examiners. Mem. Fulton County Med. Assn., P.E.O., Nu Sigma Phi. Lutheran. Home: 3269 Laramie Dr NW Atlanta GA 30339 Office: 90 W Wieuca Rd NE Atlanta GA 30342

SOMMERVILLE, MARIE-THERESE GRANDJEAN, educator; b. France; d. Louis A. and Marie-Louise (Morel) Grandjean; Licence en Droit, U. Paris, 1941; Diplome, Ecole Libre des Science Politiques, 1941; Licence es Lettres, Sorbonne, 1943; divorced. Came to U.S., 1946, naturalized, 1950. Instr. French, George Washington U., Washington, 1946-49; from asst. prof. to asso. prof. French, Lang. div. Naval Intelligence Sch., Washington, 1949-62; chmn. dept. French, Def. Lang. Inst., Washington, 1962-65; prof. French, Sweet Briar Coll. (Va.), 1965—. Recipient Prix de la Ville de Paris, 1940, 43. Mem. Am. Assn. U. Women, Am. Assn. Tchrs. of French, Am. Assn. U. Profs., Alumni Assn. Sch. Polit. Sci. Paris. Address: Sweet Briar Coll Sweet Briar VA 24595

SOMMERVILLE, REBA FRANCES (MRS. OLLEN SOMMERVILLE), ednl. adminstr.; b. Ft. Worth, Tex., Sept. 17, 1926; d. William Francis and Reba Ellen (Helm) Mercer; B.S., Tex. Wesleyan Coll., 1950, M.Ed., 1960; postgrad. North Tex. State U., 1964, 65, Tex. Christian U., 1966; m. Ollen Sommerville, Apr. 5, 1950; children—Ollen Francis, Leland Duane, Reba Janee. Tchr. sci., math. Arlington (Tex.) pub. schs., 1958-61, counselor jr. high schs., 1961-64, elementary sch. counselor, 1964-71, coordinator of elementary sch. counselors, 1971—. Chmn. Profl. Adv. Com. Easter Seal Soc. of Tarrant County, Tex., 1967-69. Mem. Am., Tex., North Central Tex. (pres. 1972-73, dir. 1973-74) personnel and guidance assns., Tex. Assn. Counselor Educators-Suprs. (chmn. resolution com. 1973-74), Tex. State Tchrs. Assn. (bldg. rep. 1973-74), Tex. Sch. Counselors Assn. (pres. elect 1974-75, Am. Assn. Counselor Educators-Suprs., Council of Exceptional Children, Mental Health Assn. (mem. planning com. 1972-74), Mental Health Assn. of Tarrant County (dir. 1974), P.T.A. (life), Delta Kappa Gamma. Mem. Assembly of God Ch. (Sunday sch. tchr. 1945—). Home: 1008 Ravenwood Arlington TX 76013 Office: 1203 Pioneer Parkway Arlington TX 76013

SONDEREGGER, THEO BROWN (MRS. PAUL ERNEST SONDEREGGER), psychologist, educator; b. Birmingham, Ala., May 31, 1925; d. Ernest Theodore and Vera (Sillox) Brown; B.S. cum laude with distinction in Chemistry, Fla. State U., 1946; M.A. in Chemistry, U. Neb., 1949, M.A. in Psychology, 1960, Ph.D., (USPHS grantee, Nat. Inst. Mental Health fellow) 1965; m. Paul Ernest Sonderegger, Dec. 21, 1947; children—Richard Paul, Diane Carol, Douglas Robert. Clin. psychologist Neb. Psychiat. Inst., Omaha, 1964—; instr. med. psychology U. Neb. at Omaha, 1965-68, asst. prof., 1968-71, asso. prof. psychology, 1971—, asso. prof. psychiatry Med. Sch., 1972—; asst. prof. psychology Neb. Wesleyan U., Lincoln, 1965-73. Mem. Neb. Bd. Examiners in Psychology, 1970. Mem. Am., Midwestern, Neb. (pres. 1972-73) psychol. assns., Psychonomic Assn., Internat. Soc. Devel. Psychobiology, Soc. Neuroscis., Phi Beta Kappa, Sigma Xi, Sigma Delta Epsilon, Phi Kappa Phi, Psi Chi, Iota Sigma Pi, Alpha Gamma Delta, Gamma Sigma Epsilon (pres. 1945). Contbr. articles to profl. jours. Home: 1710 S 58th St Lincoln NE 68506

SONDERGAARD, GALE, actress; b. Litchfield, Minn.; A.B., U. Minn.; m. Herbert Biberman. Appeared on stage in Strange Interlude, Red Rust, others; appeared in motion pictures Anthony Adverse, Maid of Salem, Seventh Heaven, Cat and the Canary, The Life of Emile Zola, The Blue Bird, The Strange Death of Adolph Hitler, Mark of Zorro, Never Say Die, The Letter, The Spider Woman, The Spider Woman Strikes Back, The Climax, The Invisible Man's Revenge, Gypsy Wildcat, Christmas Holiday, Anna and the King of Siam, Road to Rio, Pirates of Monterrey, East Side, West Side, Juarez, others. Recipient Acad. award as best actress in supporting role in Anthony Adverse, 1936; Outstanding Achievement award U. Minn., 1968; nominated Acad. award best actress supporting role Anna and the King of Siam, 1946. Address: care Shiffrin Agy 941 N La Cienega Blvd Los Angeles CA 90069*

SONENSHINE, SHEILA PRELL (MRS. YGAL SONENSHINE), lawyer; b. Butte, Mont., July 9, 1945; d. Milton G. and DeVora (Zion) Prell; student Brandeis U., 1963-64; B.S., U. Cal. at Los Angeles, 1967; J.D., Loyola U., Los Angeles, 1970; postgrad. U. So. Cal., 1971; m. Ygal Sonenshine, June 18, 1967; children—Jacob, Daniel. Law clk., Mattel Toy Co., Hawthorne, Cal., 1969-70; admitted to Cal. bar, 1970; individual practice law, Newport Beach, 1971-72; partner Sonenshine & Armstrong, Newport Beach, 1972—; dir. Raygal Design Assos., Inc., Costa Mesa, Cal. Mem. faculty Irvine (Cal.) Sch. Law, 1973-74. Mem. Orange County Jewish Fedn. Council, 1972—; legal lectr. Nat. Orgn. Women, 1973—; co-chmn. atty. div. United Jewish Appeal Orange County, 1972-74; mem. atty. adv. com. Senator Cranston, 1972-73. Mem. Brandeis U. Women, Orange County Bar Assn. Women's rights sect. 1973-74, Advocates, Town Hall Los Angeles, Los Angeles Assn. Women Attys., Phi Alpha Delta. Democrat. Home: 1338 Santiago St Newport Beach CA 92660 Office: 500 Newport Center Dr Suite 545 Newport Beach CA 92660

SONG, AGNES YOUNG-OK (MRS. RALPH HEUGN-SIK SONG), psychologist; b. Pusan, Korea, July 28, 1937; d. Keyoon and Kosoon (Kim) Bae; student Younsei U., Korea, 1956-57; B.A., Coll. of St. Francis, Joliet, Ill., 1960; M.A., Cath. U. Am., 1962, Ph.D. (Soroptimist Found. fellow), 1965; m. Ralph Heug-Sik Song, July 28, 1968; children—Lisa, Sandra, Thomas. Came to U.S., 1957, naturalized, 1972. Mem. psychology dept. Rosewood State Hosp., Owings Mills, Md., 1964-68; tchr. Johns Hopkins, 1968; sch. psychologist Co-op Ednl. Service Agy., Burlington, Wis., 1968-71; mem. psychology dept. So. Wis. Colony and Tng. Sch., Union Grove, Wis., 1971—. Guest speaker U. Wis., Parkside, Kenosha, 1972. Nat. Inst. Mental Health Pub. Health research grantee, 1967. Mem. Am., Wis. psychol. assns., Am. Assn. Mental Deficiency, Wis. Sch. Psychology Assn. Home: 309 South Oakland Av Burlington WI 53105 Office: So Wis Colony and Tng School Union Grove WI

SONNE, ANN VIERHUS (MRS. ROSCOE NEWBOLD SONNE, JR.), pub. relations exec.; b. San Diego, Sept. 7, 1931; d. Albert Victor and Elizabeth (Blakeslee) Vierhus; student U. Mexico, 1951; B.A., U. So. Cal., 1953; m. Roscoe Newbold Sonne, Jr., July 2, 1955; children—Elizabeth, Margaret, Christian, James. Reporter, Los Angeles Times, 1953-56, soc. editor, 1964-67; free lance writer, Los Angeles, 1956-60; publicist Los Angeles Turf Club, Santa Anita, Arcadia, Cal., 1960-63; publicist, pub. relations cons., Los Angeles, 1967—; dir. pub. relations Albert C. Martin & Assos. Bd. dirs. Cal. Pediatric Center, treas. bd., 1972; bd. dirs. Childrens Bur. of Los Angeles, 1967-73; treas. U. So. Cal. Journalism Alumni Bd., 1965—. Mem. Women in Communications, Kappa Alpha Theta. Home: 1425

Laurel St South Pasadena CA 91030 Office: Union Bank Sq 445 S Figueroa St Los Angeles CA 90060

SONNEMANN, NELL BATTLE BOOKER, artist, educator; b. Chapel Hill, N.C., Aug. 19, 1918; d. John Manning and Nell (Battle) Booker; A.B., U. N.C., 1938, M.A., 1940; postgrad. Art Students' League, N.Y.C., 1940-42, N.Y. Coll. Ceramics, Alfred, 1954-55; M.F.A., Cath. U. Am., 1959; m. Ulrich Sonnemann, Aug. 9, 1948 (div.). Exhibited one man shows U. N.C., Chapel Hill, 1970, Chapel Hill Art Gallery, 1970, Community Ch., Chapel Hill, 1971, St. Bernard's Ch., Saranac Lake, N.Y., 1972, U. of South, Sewanee, Tenn., 1972, George Thomas Hunt Gallery, Chattanooga, 1972; exhibited in group shows Asso. Contemporary Artists, N.Y.C., 1942, N.C. State Ann. Art Exhbns., 1943—, Corcoran Art Gallery Ann., 1957, Norfolk (Va.) Mus. Arts and Scis., 1966, Fisk U., 1967, 72, George Washington U., 1971, Lock Haven Art Center, Orlando, Fla., 1971, St. Petersburg (Fla.) Mus., 1972, Guild for Religious Architecture, 1971, 72, 73, Art Barn, Washington, 1972, Athenaeum Mus., Alexandria, Va., 1973, Corning Mus., N.Y., 1973; numerous art exhibits, 1961—; nat. touring wall-hanging exhbn., 1968-69, 69-70; illustrator World Pub. Co. instr. div. art Cath. U. Am., Washington, 1959-64, asst. prof., 1964-74, asso. prof., 1974—. Lectr. liturgical art civic, ednl., religious groups, 1961—; participant seminar in popular culture Smithsonian Instn., 1969-70, 4th internat. symposium, 1970; staff and spl. research Royal Coll. Art, London, Eng., 1973. Recipient award for wall-hanging Guild for Religious Architecture, 1970; Nat. Community Arts Program Competition award Dept. Housing and Urban Devel., 1974. Mem. Phi Beta Kappa, Pi Beta Phi, Alpha Kappa Gamma. Roman Catholic. Home: 4807 Cumberland Av Chevy Chase MD 20015 Office: Dept Art Cath U Am Washington DC 20017

SONNICHSEN, SHIRLEY COTTON (MRS. JOHN WILLIAM SONNICHSEN), real estate and ins. broker; b. New Haven, Oct. 20, 1934; d. Mortimer Euclid and Martha Ruth (Swirsky) Cotton; grad. high sch.; m. John William Sonnichsen, June 29, 1965. Ins. Agency, New Haven, 1952-62; owner Sonnichsen Ins. Agy., Madison, Conn., 1963—; sec., treas. J.W. Sonnichsen, Inc., also Buck Hill Assos., Inc., Madison, 1967—. Charter mem., past v.p., Women's Republican Club Madison. Mem. Madison C. of C., Kenilworth Kennel Club, Shoreline Bd. Realtors (dir., 1969-71), Nat., Conn. assns. realtors, Nat., Shoreline (charter mem.) bus. and profl. women. Clubs: Kenilworth Kennel, Women's of Madison (sec. 1966-68, treas. 1969-71). Address: 153 Wildwood Av Madison CT 06443

SONNTAG, IDA MAY, educator; b. Toledo, Sept. 23, 1935; d. Fred and Ida (Mayr) Sonntag; B.Edn., U. Toledo, 1957, M.Ed., 1957, postgrad., 1957-73. Tchr. pub. schs. Maumee, O., 1957-66, 69—; chmn. audiovisual dept. U. Toledo, 1967, instr., 1969. Mem. Internat. Platform Assn., Ohio Edn. Assn. (life), Toledo Reading Assn., Toledo Area Math. Council, Phi Kappa Phi, Kappa Delta Pi. Author: Community Resources in Science Education, 1968; Prehistoric Ohio, 1970. Home: 5101 Norwich St Toledo OH 43615 Office: 716 Askin St Maumee OH 43537

SONOWSKI, BARBARA ANNE (MRS. A. RONALD SORVINO), physician; b. Newark, Dec. 7, 1932; d. Walter Aloysius and Lucy Matilda (Kleinowski) Sonowski; A.B., Coll. of St. Elizabeth, Convent, N.J., 1954; M.D., State U. N.Y., 1958; m. A. Ronald Sorvino, June 14, 1958; children—Noel Regina, Ronald Ford, Heidi Jan, Damian Walter, Kerry Lucia, Krista Celia. Intern medicine Kings County Hosp., Bklyn., 1958; resident pediatrics St. Michael's Med. Center, Newark, 1963-65; asst. med. dir. Hoffman LaRoche, Nutley, N.J., 1965-74; practice medicine, specializing in pediatrics, Newark, 1974—; asst. attending physician, cons. pediatric cardiology St. Michael's Med. Center, Newark, 1965—. Mem. A.M.A., N.J. Acad. Medicine, Am. Med. Women's Assn. Address: 484 Old Short Hills Rd Short Hills NJ 07078

SOO, BETTY SHUI MUI, pediatrician; b. Honolulu, Apr. 27, 1933; d. Young Ken and Kam Chew (Ching) Soo; B.A., U. Hawaii, 1955; B.S., U. N.D., 1957; M.D., U. Kan., 1959. Intern, resident Sacramento County Hosp., 1959-61; resident pediatrics Highland Alameda County Hosp., Oakland, Cal., 1961-62, Kauikeolani Children's Hosp., 1962-63; practice medicine specializing in pediatrics, Honolulu, 1963—; mem. staff Kauikeolani Children's, Queen's, Kapiolani Maternity hosps.; clin. asst. prof. pediatrics U. Hawaii, 1973—. Diplomate Am. Bd. Pediatrics. Fellow Am. Acad. Pediatrics (Hawaii chpt. alt. chmn. 1973-74); mem. Honolulu County Med. Assn., A.M.A. Home: 653 Wyllie St Honolulu HI 96817 Office: 1374 Nuuanu Ave Honolulu HI 96817

SOO, DIXIE L. BONEY (MRS. LIANG YEE SOO), physician; b. Clinton, N.C., Aug. 3, 1933; d. Landron Clifford and Jessie (Cashwell) Boney; A.B., U. N.C., 1955; M.D., Bowman Gray Sch., 1959; m. Liang Yee Soo, June 16, 1957; children—Kenneth Alexander, Michael Landron, Jeffrey Derrick, Catherine Elizabeth. Intern, Queens Hosp., Honolulu, 1959-60; resident N.C. Meml. Hosp., Chapel Hill, 1961-64; instr. neurology U. N.C., Chapel Hill, 1964-65; practice medicine, specializing in neurology, Lima, O., 1965—; mem. staff St. Rita's Hosp., Lima Meml. Hosp.; cons. Lima State Hosp., 1968—. Diplomate Am. Bd. Psychiatry and Neurology. Mem. A.M.A., Am. Acad. Neurology, Phi Beta Kappa, Alpha Omega Alpha. Home: 1533 Fairway View Dr Lima OH 45805 Office: 310 S Cable Rd Lima OH 45805

SOPER, FRANCES ELIZABETH (MRS. RICHARD SOPER), office mgr.; b. Ellsworth, Me., Nov. 21, 1917; d. Frank F. and Eva L. (Curtis) Soper; grad. high sch.; m. Richard Soper, June 29, 1935; children—Richard, Brent H. With St. Regis Paper Co., Bucksport, Me., 1940-45, Town of Orland (Me.), 1946-73, P.B. Husters Co., Belfast, Me., 1967-68; with Thurston Boat Co., Orland, 1968—, office mgr., 1972—. Lectr. rocks and minerals to local schs., 1964—; chmn. Orland Fish Com., 1967—; dir. Civil Def., 1969-72; active Cub Scouts, 1951-61, Boy Scouts, 1948-63, Girl Scouts, 1968-70. Chmn. Sch. Bd., Orland, 1946-62; town clk., excise tax collector, Orland, 1964-68; Democratic candidate for Me. Ho. of Reps., 1958. Mem. Me. Archeol. Soc. (2d v.p. 1973—), Penobscot Geol. and Mineral. Soc., Penobscot Farm and Garden Assn. (pres. 1964-65), Castine Sci. Soc. (trustee 1965-73, treas. 1967-73), Orland Hist. Soc. (dir. 1965-73). Methodist (supt. ch. sch. 1972-73). Mem. Order Eastern Star. Home: Box 435 Orland ME 94472 Office: Thurston Boat Co Orland ME 04472

SOREL, CLAUDETTE, pianist; b. Paris, France, Oct. 10, 1932; d. Michel Maximilian and Elizabeth Sorel; came to Am., 1940, naturalized, 1947; B.S., Juilliard Sch. of Music, 1947; student with Sigismund Stojowski, Sari Biro, Olga Samaroff Stokowski, Mieczyslaw Horszowski, Rudolf Serkin, ensemble with Felix Salmond, musicology with Dr. Robert Tangeman, music history with Marian Bauer; spl. scholar Juilliard Grad. Sch. Music, 1943; grad. Curtis Inst. Music; B.S. cum laude, Columbia, 1954. Debut Town Hall, N.Y.C., 1943, since appeared in leading cities of Am.; performed with N.Y. Philharmonic, N.Y. Little Symphony, R.I., Reading symphony orchs., Little Orchestral Soc., NBC, Phila., New Orleans and Cin., Am. Youth Orch.; appeared at Aspen, Berkshire, Chautauqua festivals; European Concert tour, 1956, 57, 58, to Eng., Sweden, Holland, Germany, Switzerland, France; appeared on various radio, television programs; made recs. for R.C.A. Victor Rec. Co., Monitor Records. Music faculty, vis. prof. Kan. U., 1961-62; asso. prof. music Ohio State U., 1962-64; prof. music, head piano dept. State U. N.Y., Fredonia, 1964-69, Distinguished Univ. prof., 1969—. Mem. internat. jury Van Cliburn Internat. Piano Competition, Tex., 1966, Que. Music Festivals, 1967. Solo appearances with some 85 orchs. U.S., Europe. Fulbright scholar, 1951; Ford Found. Concert grantee 1962. Recipient Harry Rosenberg Meml., Frank Damrosch prizes, 1947; winner Phila. Orch. Youth Auditions, 1950, to appear with orch. under direction Eugene Ormandy; Nat. Fedn. Music Clubs Young Artist award, 1951; citation for service to Am. music Nat. Fedn. Music Clubs, 1966; named Outstanding Young Woman in U.S.A., 1965; citation Nat. Assn. Composers and Condrs., 1967, Mu Phi Epsilon, 1968. Bd. dirs. Olga Samaroff Found., Jr. com. aux. bd. N.Y. Philharmonic Symphony Orch.; N.Y. State Nat. Fedn. Music Clubs. Mem. adv. bd. U. Library Soc. Mem. Nat. Music Council (dir. 1973—), Pi Kappa Lambda, Mu Phi Epsilon (dir. Meml. Found., nat. chmn. Sterling Staff Concert Series, citation 1968). Author: Compendium of Piano Technique, 1970; Mind Your Musical Manners-Off and On Stage, 1972; The 24 Magic Keys, 3 vols., 1974; The Three Nocturnes of Rachmanioff, 1974. Linguist, painter of oil portraits; contbr. articles to profl. mags. Compiler: The Modern Music of Today, 1947; Serge Prokofleff--His Life and Works, 1947; The Ornamentations in Mozart's Music, 1948. Home: 333 West End Av New York City NY 10023 Office: State U NY Fredonia NY 14063

SORENSEN, ERLENE ANNE, accountant; b. Lakeview, Ore., Aug. 17, 1939; d. Eugene Wesley and Helen Irene (Angstead) Whitehouse; B.S., U. Ore., 1961; m. Donald Eldon Sorensen, Sept. 22, 1962 (div. Nov. 1973); children—Kala Rae, Brock O. Staff accountant Erickson & Eiseman, C.P.A.'s, Portland, Ore., 1962-64; accountant Dawson, Turner & Jenkins advt., Portland, 1964-67; asst. bus. mgr., chief accountant Med. Sch., U. Ore., Portland, 1967—. C.P.A., Ore. Mem. Hosp. Financial Mgmt. Assn., Ore. Soc. C.P.A.'s. Home: 7033 SW Garden Home Rd Portland OR 97223 Office: 3191 SW Park Rd Portland OR 97201

SORENSEN, JANE, occupational therapist; b. Cleve., Dec. 23, 1942; d. Clark Clarence and Hazel Rowe (Dunn) Sorensen; student Skidmore Coll., 1960-62; B.S., Tufts U., 1965. Occupational therapist Manhattan State Hosp., N.Y.C., 1965-66, Queens-Hillside Hosp., N.Y.C., 1966-67, Bellevue Hosp., N.Y.C., 1967, Harlem Hosp., N.Y.C., 1968-71; cons., pvt. practice as occupational therapist, N.Y.C., 1971—; tng. cons. Rikers Island Prison, N.Y.C., 1971-72. Grad. instr., div. rehab. edn. Sch. Edn., N.Y. U., 1974—. Mem. Am., N.Y. State (legislative chmn. 1972-74) occupational therapy assns., Nat. Orgn. Women (chmn. consciousness-raising N.Y. chpt. 1971-72), Nat. Women's Polit. Caucus (mem. original steering com. 1971), Women's Polit. Caucus N.Y.C. (chmn. speakers bur. 1971-72). Author: (with Edythe Cudlipp) The New Way To Become the Person You'd Like to Be: The Complete Guide to Consciousness Raising, 1973. Address: 418 E 73d St New York City NY 10021

SORENSEN, JEAN HART (MRS. RALPH JAMES SORENSEN), artist; b. San Diego, Nov. 18, 1920; d. William James and Hallie (Moran) Hart; student San Jose State Coll., 1938, 39, U. Cal. at Santa Cruz, 1969-73; m. Ralph James Sorensen, Sept. 1, 1939; children—Ellen (Mrs. Eugene Pacchetti), Ann (Mrs. Stephen Coons), James Christian. One woman shows include Upstairs Gallery, Sunnyvale, 1968, 71, Betchel Internat. Student Center, Stanford U., 1971, North Light Gallery, Burlingame, 1972, Palo Alto Cultural Center, 1972; exhibited in group shows M.H. de Young Museum, San Francisco, 1969, 70, 71, Nat. Acad. Gallery, N.Y.C., 1971, 72, 74, Palazzo Vecchico, Florence, Italy, 1972, Salvator Rosa, Naples, Italy, 1972; represented in permanent collection Okayama (Japan) Mus., Palo Alto Times, San Diego Women's Club. Recipient John Alden Walker award Nat. Assn. Women Artists, 1972, 1st watercolor award Nat. Acad. Gallery Annual Exhbn., N.Y.C., 1972. Mem. Soc. Western Artists (hon. degree 1971), Nat. Assn. Women Artists, Santa Clara Valley, Marin, Monterey watercolor socs., Los Altos, Palo Alto art clubs. Home: 23160 Mora Glen Dr Los Altos CA 94022 Office: 315 State St Los Altos CA 94022

SORENSEN, MARY ELIZABETH (MARY HART), home economist; b. Woodlake, Minn., Apr. 18, 1923; d. Peter C. and Emily (Kitchen) Engelhart; B.S., U. Minn., 1945; m. Franklin L. Sorensen, Jr., Apr. 12, 1947; 1 son, Peter. Home economist Mpls. Star and Tribune, 1945—, women's editor, 1969—. Mem. Minn. Home Econs., Assn. Home Economists in Bus., Minn. State Nutrition Council, Sigma Delta Chi. Phi Upsilon Omicron. Episcopalian. Home: 5121 Dupont Av S Minneapolis MN 55419 Office: 425 Portland Av Minneapolis MN 55415

SORGE, NAOMI YVONNE MCGEHEE (MRS. ALFRED F. SORGE), advt. agy. exec.; b. Sharon, Tenn., Dec. 14, 1925; d. Robert Wayne and Dora (Wright) McGehee; student Wheaton Coll., 1944-45, Memphis State U., 1945, U. Tenn., 1946-48; m. Alfred F. Sorge, Nov. 24, 1960. Sec., William Henry Fisher, Jr., marketing counsellor, Memphis, 1946-50; copywriter Rosengarten & Steinke, Memphis, 1950; copy chief John Gerber Co., Memphis, 1951-55; advt. and sales promotion mgr. Kennington's, Jackson, Miss., 1955-59; creative dir. Ridgway Hirsch Advt. Co., Memphis, 1960; with Gordon Marks & Co., Jackson, Miss., 1960—, sr. v.p., 1970—. Bd. dirs. Jackson Symphony League; bd. dirs. Miss. Art Assn., 1965—, pres. 1968-69. Named Miss. Advt. Woman of Year, Advt. Club Miss., 1962; recipient Silver medal Jackson Advt. Club, 1973. Home: 5509 Wayneland Dr Jackson MS 39211 Office: Bailey and Bailey Plaza PO Box 1757 Jackson MS 39205

SORGEN, ROSALIND B. SWILLER (MRS. JESSE SORGEN), social worker; b. Bklyn., July 18, 1919; d. Jacob R. and Anna (Housenbold) Swiller; A.B., N.Y. U., 1940; M.S.W., Adelphi U., 1961; m. Jesse Sorgen, Oct. 15, 1940; children—Deborah N. (Mrs. Kenneth J. Schuman), Jacqueline R. Psychiat. social worker Meadowbrook Hosp. Mental Health Clinic, East Meadow, N.Y., 1961-63; caseworker Family Service Assn., Mineola, N.Y., 1963-64; caseworker, group worker Brookwood Child Care, Bklyn., 1964-68; supr., field work instr. Adelphi U. Grad. Sch. Social Work, Bklyn., Brookwood Child Care, Bklyn., 1968-70; social work supr., field instr. Columbia U. Grad. Sch. Social Work, Bklyn., 1970—, pediatric psychiatry clinic Jewish Hosp. and Med. Center, Bklyn., 1970—. Home: 651 Lakeview Av Rockville Centre NY 11570 Office: 555 Prospect Pl Brooklyn NY 11238

SOROKA, MARGERY, artist; b. N.Y.C., May 30, 1920; d. Sam and Henrietta (Shindel) Soroka; student Hunter Coll., 1936-38, Art Students League, 1952-53, Sch. Visual Arts, N.Y.C., 1954-55, 62, Pratt Inst., 1960-61. Exhibited group shows Am. Watercolor Soc., 1964-70, Audubon Artists, 1963, 66, 68, 69, 72, Nat. Arts Club, 1960-68, 70-72, Am. Artists Profl. League, 1960-66, Nat. Assn. Women Artists, 1966-70, Catherine Lorillard Wolfe Club, 1962-65 (all N.Y.C.), Hudson Valley Art Assn., White Plains, N.Y., 1964, Watercolor U.S.A., Springfield, Mo., 1968, Wichita (Kan.) Centennial, 1970; exhibited traveling exhibits through museums, colls., various cities in U.S.; represented in permanent collections Forbes, Inc., N.Y.C., Va. State Coll.; art dir. Planned Parenthood Fedn. Am., Inc., N.Y.C. Recipient Forbes Indsl. award and Travel Exhibit, Anna G. Morse Meml. award, Gwen McClung Meml. award, Grumbacher award, Nat. Arts Club Artists Material award, William B. Connor Travel grant, Lena Newcastle Meml. award Am. Watercolor Soc., 1968, Winsor Newton award, Catherine Lorillard Wolfe Art Club, 1968; Lena Newcastle Meml. award Nat. Assn. Women Artists, 1969; Nat. Spl. award Nat. Arts Club, 1970; Samuel Mann Meml. prize, 1972. Mem. Am. Watercolor Soc., Nat. Assn. Women Artists, Knickerbocker Artists, Salmagundi Club. Featured in Am. Artist mag., Feb. 1971. Home: 200 E 16th St New York City NY 10003 Office: 810 7th Av New York City NY 10019

SOROKIN, HELEN PETROVNA, biologist; b. St. Petersburg, Russia, 1894; d. Peter A. and Claudia (Nicholsky) Baratinsky; B.S., U. Leningrad, 1917; Ph.D., U. Minn., 1925; student Charles U., Prague, Czechoslovakia, 1922-23; m. Pitirim A. Sorokin, June 3, 1917; (dec. Feb. 1968); children—Peter P., Sergei P. Came to U.S., 1924, naturalized, 1929. Instr. botany U. Leningrad, 1917-22; research cytologist U. Minn., Mpls., 1925-30, Harvard, Cambridge, Mass., 1930-31, 55—. Prof. botany Hamline U., St. Paul, 1925-30. Fellow Radcliffe Inst.; mem. Bot. Soc. Am., A.A.A.S., Sigma Xi. Russian translator Hunger as a Factor, 1974. Contbr. to profl. jours. Home: 8 Cliff St Winchester MA 01890

SOROKIN, JANET LEVIN (MRS. RAYMOND L. SOROKIN), artist; b. Hartford, Conn., Apr. 2, 1932; d. William Harry and Rose Irene (Cohen) Levin; student Simmons Coll., 1950-52, U. Hartford, 1950-72, Trinity Coll., 1972; m. Raymond L. Sorokin, June 8, 1952; children—Emily Beth, Judith Ellen. One woman shows Serendipity II Gallery, Hartford, 1970, Slater Meml. Mus., Norwich, Conn., 1973-74; exhibited in group shows Wadsworth Atheneum, Hartford, Conn., 1964-66, 68, 70, 72-73, Berkshire Mus., Pittsfield, Mass., 1966-69, 71; Mus. Fine Arts, also George Walter Vincent Smith Art Mus., Springfield, Mass., 1968-71, 73; represented in permanent collection Prosser Pub. Library, Bloomfield, Conn. Vol. instr. art Hartford Hosp., 1967-69; mem. Gallery on Green, 1963-73, Brookfield (Conn.) Craft Center, 1973—. Recipient various awards, including 3d prize Plaza 7 Arts Festival, Essex Art Assn. awards, 1966, 67, Slater Meml. Mus. award, 1973. Mem. Nat. Assn. Women Artists (Goldie Paley award 1970, travelling exhbn. 1973—), Conn. Acad. Fine Arts (nominating com. 1972), Conn. Women Artists (1st prize 1966), New Haven Paint and Clay Club, Berkshire, Essex, Stamford art assns., Springfield Art League.

SORRELLS, BEATRICE FARMER, realtor; b. Wichita, Kan., Mar. 14, 1918; d. Ole N. and Luna (Corbin) Farmer; student U. Ida., 1936-37, U. Cal. at Los Angeles and Irvine, 1968—, Lumbleau Real Estate Sch., 1966-70; m. Lester E. Sorrells, Aug. 6, 1946; children—Sandra Lynette (Mrs. George Elgart Morff), S. Leslie, Carol Lynne. Owner, prin. Bea Sorrells, Realtor, Cypress, Cal., 1969-70, Real Estate Shoppe, Cypress, 1970—, La Palma, Cal., 1971—, Cerritos, Cal., 1972—, Artesia, Cal., 1973—, Escrow Office, Artesia, 1974—, Marko, Inc., Norco, Cal., 1973—; dir. Silver Key, Inc., La Palma. Columnist, Cypress-La Palma News Enterprise, 1969-70. Chmn., Cultural and Ednl. Com. La Palma, 1966-69, Civic Pride Com., 1969-70; mem. Kennedy High Booster Club, 1971—, Children's Home Soc., La Palma, 1972—. Mem. La Palma C. of C. (founder, dir. 1965-68, Mrs. La Palma 1969), Cal. Real Estate Assn., Am. Legion Women's Aux. Republican. Mem. Ch. Religious Sci. Home: 8222 Suffield St La Palma CA 90623 Office: 5551 Orangethorpe Av La Palma CA 90623

SORTOR, KATHERINE MAIDA (MRS. JAMES D. PROKOP), lawyer; b. New London, Conn., Mar. 20, 1934; d. Charles Raymond and Catherine (McCarthy) Sortor; B.A., Smith Coll., 1955; LL.B., U. Va., 1959; LL.M., N.Y. U., 1969; m. James D. Prokop, Sept. 19, 1970. Admitted to Conn. bar, 1961, N.Y. bar, 1964; atty. law dept. RCA, N.Y.C., 1963-69; sr. counsel, asst. sec. legal dept. Internat. Tel. & Tel., N.Y.C., 1969—. Mem. Assn. Bar City N.Y., Conn. Bar Assn. Club: Oak Ridge Hunt (Darien, Conn.). Home: 5 Hatfield Mews New Canaan CT 06840 Office: Internat Tel & Tel 320 Park Av New York City NY 10022

SOSA, MARIA ISABEL VEGAS, psychologist; b. Caracas, Venezuela, July 15, 1921; d. Pedro and Luisa Vegas; licienciada, Central U. Venezuela, 1963; Ph.D., Spanish Am. U., Mexico, 1966; m. Luis Sosa, Feb. 19, 1941 (dec. July 1961); children—Luis, Jose, Teresa (Mrs. Rafael Bocaranda), Luisa, Morella (Mrs. Gustavo Melchert, Pedro, Gonzalo. Sch. psychologist, mem. staff dirs. Institutos Educacionales Asociados, Caracas, 1969—; mem. staff dirs. Avepane, Caracas, 1969—. Adviser Spanish Am. U., 1965—. Mem. Am. Assn. Mental Deficiency, Assn. del Preescolar, Assn. Children with Learning Disabilities. Contbr. articles to profl. publs. Home: Calle 555 D Caurimare Caracas Venezuela Office: Institutos Educacionales Asociados PO Box 80798 Caracas Venezuela

SOSBY, JACKIE ANN, journalist; b. Toccoa, Ga., Mar. 9, 1948; d. Walter Jackson and Evelyn Catherine (Whitworth) Sosby; A.A., Young Harris Jr. Coll., 1968; B.A., U. Ga., 1970. Staff writer local law enforcement, health, ednl. and govt. affairs The Daily Times, Gainesville, Ga., 1970—. Mem. Hall County Family Planning Adv. Com., 1971-73; volunteer photographer Hall County Fire Dept., 1971—. Mem. Women in Communication, Ga. Fireman's Assn. Baptist. Home: 3100 Esther Dr Gainesville GA 30501 Office: PO Box 838 Gainesville GA 30501

SOSKIN, MARIAN ROBERTA PENN (MRS. WILLIAM SOSKIN), lawyer; b. Phila., Aug. 18, 1946; d. Hyman B. and Charlotta (Lipschutz) Penn; A.B. with distinction, Cornell U., 1968; J.D. cum laude, Harvard, 1971; m. William Soskin, Oct. 1, 1972. Admitted to Cal. bar, 1972; with Mass. Law Reform Inst., Boston, 1969; with Ralph Nader U.S. Dept. Agr. study project, Washington, 1970; dep. pub. defender Monterey County Pub. Defenders Office, Salinas, Cal., 1971—. Cons. to local youth orgns., Office Econ. Opportunity youth group, Behavioral Sci. Inst. Juvenile Study group. Mem. State Bar Cal., Phi Beta Kappa. Jewish religion. Home: 183 La Ventana St Carmel Valley CA 93924 Office: Public Defenders Office Courthouse Salinas CA 93901

SOTO, CHARLOTTE ELIZABETH (MRS. MAXIMILIANO FRANCISCO SOTO), psychologist; b. South Orange, N.J., June 13, 1928; d. Leslie Orvis and Mary Alice (Cheston) Tupper; A.B., Bryn Mawr Coll., 1950; M.A., N.Y. U., 1952, postgrad., 1952-61; m. Maximiliane Francisco Soto, June 16, 1951; children—Stephen Henry, Robert Mark, Frank Clifford. Psychologist, N.Y. U. Testing Advisement Center, 1950-61; individual practice psychology, South Orange, 1965—; psychologist in charge testing Short Hills (N.J.) Country Day Sch., 1972-74; cons. psychologist The Pingry Sch., Hillside, N.J., 1974—. Mem. test adv. com. Ednl. Records Bur., Framingham, Mass., 1973—. Mem. Am., N.J. psychol. assns., Kappa Delta Pi, Pi Lambda Theta. Home: 341 Redmond Rd South Orange NJ 07079

SOUDERS, HELEN JEANETTE, research adminstr.; b. Red Lodge, Mont., May 14, 1912; d. Samuel Mott and Margaret Thomas (Jones) Souders; B.S., Mont. State Coll., 1932, D.Sc. (hon.), 1971; M.S., U. Mich., 1935; Ph.D., U. Cal. at Berkeley, 1955. Research asso. nutrition Childrens Fund of Mich., Detroit, 1935-36, 37-40; tchr. sci.

All Saints Sch. for Girls, Sioux Falls, S.D., 1936-37, Carbon County High Sch., Red Lodge, Mont., 1941-46; teaching and research asst. nutrition U. Cal. at Berkeley, 1948-52, instr., asst. prof. nutrition, Davis, 1952-57; asso. prof., prof. nutrition U. Wyo., Laramie, 1957-60; prin. human nutritionist Coop. State Expt. Sta. Service, U.S. Dept. Agr., Washington, 1960-63, asst. to dep. adminstr. Agrl. Research Service, 1964-70, asst. to dir. human nutrition research div., 1971-72, staff specialist nat. program staff, 1972—. Fellow A.A.A.S., Am. Inst. Chemists; mem. Am. Home Econs. Assn., Am. Chem. Soc., Am. Dietetics Assn., Mortar Bd., Sigma Xi, Iota Sigma Pi, Omicron Nu, Phi Kappa Phi, Pi Beta Phi. Contbr. articles to profl. jours. Home: 955 S Columbus St Arlington VA 22204 Office: Nat Program Staff ARS Agricultural Research Center W Beltsville MD 20705

SOULES, BETTY JANE, occupational therapist; b. Berkeley, Cal., Oct. 17, 1922; d. Guilford Harrison and Dagmar (Klitgaard) Soules; student U. Ore., 1940-41; A.A., U. Cal. at Berkeley, 1943, B.A., 1944; grad. Mills Coll. Sch. Occupational Therapy, 1946; postgrad. upper extremity prosthetics U. Cal. at Los Angeles, 1962, orthopedic univ. clinic, Muenster and Annastiff, Hanover, Germany, 1964, N.Y.C., 1966. Occupational therapy aide U.S. Army hosps., 1945-46; chief occupational therapy VA Hosp., Martinsburg, W.Va., 1947-49; dir. occupational therapy VA Hosp., Fresno, Cal., 1950-54; field craft dir. Spl. Services sect. U.S. Army Europe, Bad Kreuznach, Germany, 1954-57; occupational therapist sect. phys. medicine and rehab. dept. U. Cal. San Francisco Med. Center, 1958-60, sr. occupational therapist, 1960—; dir. beschaeftigungstherapie Kurort and Rehab. Centre, Rad Ragaz, Switzerland, 1960. Fulbright lectr., cons. occupational therapy Ministry Health, Cairo, Egypt, 1966-67; lectr., Nat. Inst. Rehab., Lima, Peru, 1972, univs. Pretoria, Witwatersrand, S. Africa, 1973. Mem. World Fedn. Occupational Therapy (expert adviser), Am., No. Cal., Peruvian (hon.) occupational therapy assns., German, Swiss assns. beschaftigungstherapie, Internat. Soc. for Prosthetics and Orthotics. Home: 1725 Taylor St San Francisco CA 94133 Office: U Cal Med Center San Francisco CA 94143

SOULIER, CARLA-BETH MCKENZIE (MRS. LOUIS RAY SOULIER), film librarian; b. Abbeville, La., Dec. 4, 1931; d. Paul and Effie (Greene) McKenzie; B.A., N.E. La. U., 1954; m. Louis Ray Soulier, June 6, 1951; 1 son, Paris Louis-Paul. Film librarian N.E. La. U., Monroe, 1954—. Film librarian P.T.A.; patron mem. Little Theatre. Mem. La. Tchrs. Assn., La. Library Assn., Nat. Commemorative Soc., La. Assn. Ednl. Communications and Tech., La. Assn. Higher Edn., Phi Sigma Alpha. Democrat. Episcopalian. Home: 519 Eason Pl Monroe LA 71201

SOUSER, ROSLYN COSKERY (MRS. KENNETH SOUSER, JR.), plastic surgeon; b. Phila., Mar. 27, 1939; d. Eugene Campbell and Lois Bertram (Day) Coskery; A.B. in Music, Duke, 1961; student U. Munich, Germany, 1959-60; M.D., Woman's Med. Coll. Pa., 1966; m. Kenneth Souser, Jr., May 9, 1964; children—Kenneth III, Eugene Coskery. Researcher hematology Bryn Mawr (Pa.) Hosp., 1961-62, resident gen. surgery, 1967-71, asst. plastic surgeon out-patient clinic, 1973—; intern surgery Hosp. Woman's Med. Coll. Pa., Phila., 1966-67; resident gen. surgery VA Hosp., Wilmington, Del., 1969-70; resident plastic surgery Temple U. Hosp., Phila., 1971-72, Hosp. U. Pa., 1972-73; practice medicine specializing in plastic surgery, Bryn Mawr, 1973—; cons. plastic surgery N. Penn Hosp., Lansdale, Pa.; instr. surgery Thomas Jefferson U. Sch. Medicine, Phila. Diplomate Am. Bd. Plastic Surgery. Mem. A.M.A., Internat., Am. med. women's assns., Montgomery County, Pa. med. socs., Am. Coll. Surgeons (candidate), Am. Soc. for Plastic and Reconstructive Surgery (candidate), Alumnae Assn. Woman's Med. Coll. Pa., Delta Delta Delta. Home: 738 Coopertown Rd Haverford PA 19041 Office: Bryn Mawr Med Bldg Bryn Mawr PA 19010

SOUTH, MARY ANN, physician; b. Portales, N.M., May 23, 1933; d. John Anderson and Carrie (Schumpert) South; student Baylor U., 1951-53; B.A., Eastern N.M. U., 1955; M.D., Baylor Coll. Medicine, 1959. Intern, Presbyn.-St. Lukes Hosp., Chgo., 1959-60; resident pediatrics Baylor Affiliated Hosp., Houston, 1960-62, fellowship infectious diseases, 1962-64; fellowship immunology U. Minn., instr. pediatrics, 1964-66; asst. prof. pediatrics Baylor Coll. Medicine, 1966-70, asso. prof., 1970-73; asso. prof. pediatrics U. Pa., 1973—; dir. pediatric immunology Children's Hosp. Phila., 1973—. Recipient NIH Research Career award, 1968-73. Diplomate Am. Bd. Pediatrics. Mem. Am. Assn. Immunologists, Soc. Pediatric Research, Infectious Diseases Soc. Am., Am. Med. Womens Assn., Am. Assn. U. Profs., Assn. Women Sci., Women's Equity Action League, Alpha Omega Alpha. Home: 557 Forest Rd Wayne PA 19087 Office: Childrens Hosp Philadelphia PA 19174

SOUTHAM, ANNA L. SKOW, physician; b. Cocolalla, Ida., Nov. 14, 1915; d. Peter N. and Josephine (Lawrence) Skow; B.S., U. Ida., 1942; M.D., Columbia, 1947; m. Chester M. Southam, Sept. 24, 1939; children—Lawrence, Leneve, Arthur. Intern, Bellevue Hosp., N.Y.C., 1947-48; resident Presbyn. Hosp., N.Y.C., 1952-53; acad. medicine specializing in obstetrics and gynecology, N.Y.C., 1954-65; mem. staff Columbia Presbyn. Med. Center, 1953-56, Presbyn. Hosp., 1956-67; instr. obstetrics and gynecology Columbia, 1954-57, asso. prof., 1959-67; med. cons. Population Council, 1963-65; program cons., program specialist Ford Found., N.Y.C., 1965, program adviser, 1966-67, program officer internat. div. population, 1967—. Recipient Ortho award Am. Fertility Soc., 1970. Diplomate Am. Bd. Obstetrics and Gynecology. Mem. Am. Coll. Obstetricians and Gynecologists, Am. Fertility Soc., A.A.A.S., A.M.A., N.Y. Obstet. Soc., N.Y. Acad. Scis., Am. Assn. Obstetricians and Gynecologists. Home: 50 Orchard Rd Demarest NJ 07627 Office: Ford Found 320 E 43d St New York City NY 10017

SOUTHERN, EILEEN (MRS. JOSEPH SOUTHERN), educator; b. Mpls., Feb. 19, 1920; d. Walter Wade and Lilla (Gibson) Jackson; B.A., U. Chgo., 1940, M.A., 1941; Ph.D., N.Y. U., 1961; m. Joseph Southern, Aug. 22, 1942; children—April, Edward. Concert pianist, 1940—; instr. Prairie View U., Hempstead, Tex., 1941-42; asst. prof. So. U., Baton Rouge, 1943-45, 49-51; tchr. N.Y.C. Bd. Edn., 1954-60; instr. Bklyn. Coll., City U. N.Y., 1960-64, asst. prof., 1964-69; asso. prof. York Coll. City U. N.Y., 1969-71, prof., 1972—. Active Girl Scouts U.S.A., 1954-63; chmn. mgmt. com. Queens Area YWCA, 1970-73. Mem. Internat., Am. (dir. 1974—) musicological socs., Renaissance Soc., N.A.A.C.P., Alpha Kappa Alpha. Author: The Buxheim Organ Book, 1963; The Music of Black Americans: A History, 1971; Readings in Black American Music, 1971. Editor, pub. The Black Perspective in Music, 1973—. Contbr. articles to profl. jours., encys. Home: 115-05 179th St St Albans NY 11434 Office: York Coll Jamaica NY 11432

SOUZA, DOROTHEA LOUISE, physician; b. East Boston, Mass., Sept. 8, 1918; d. Joseph and Louise (Silva) Souza; B.S., Tufts U., 1941, M.D., 1947. Intern, Mt. Auburn Hosp., Cambridge, Mass., 1947-48; fellow in pathology New Eng. Med. Center Hosp., Boston, 1948-49; asst. resident obstetrics New Eng. Hosp., Roxbury, Mass., 1949-50; asst. resident obstetrics and gynecology Chgo. Lying-In Hosp., 1951; asst. Margaret Hague Maternity Hosp., Jersey City, 1951-52; asst. resident gynecology Jersey City Med. Center, 1952; practice medicine specializing in obstetrics and gynecology, Medford, Mass., 1953—; mem. active staff Lawrence Meml. Hosp., Medford, sec.-treas. 1959-60; mem. courtesy staff Winchester (Mass.) Hosp., Malden (Mass.) Hosp., New Eng. Meml. Hosp., Stoneham, Mass. Diplomate Am. Bd. Obstetrics and Gynecology. Fellow Internat. Coll. Surgeons; mem. A.M.A., Am. Med. Womens Assn., Mass., Medford (pres. 1968) med. socs., Mass. Physicians Art Soc., Am. Coll. Obstetrics and Gynecology, New Eng. Obstet. and Gynecol. Soc., Rockport Art Assn. Club: Zonta. Home: 11 Daly Rd Medford MA 02155 Office: 11 Daly Rd Medford MA 02155

SOWA, ELIZABETH LEE CLARK (MRS. RONALD W. SOWA), physician; b. Flint, Mich., Oct. 11, 1933; d. George Eldred and Leadelle (Gray) Clark; B.S., Mich. State U., 1955; postgrad. U. Mich., 1958-59; M.D., Washington U., St. Louis, 1963; m. Ronald W. Sowa, Mar. 26, 1960; children—Erik C., Kurt E., Melissa K., Karl A. Med. technologist Wayne County Gen. Hosp., Eloise, Mich., 1955-57, intern, 1963-64; med. technologist dept. surgery U. Mich., 1957-59; resident Kresge Eye Inst., Wayne State U., Detroit, 1964-67; practice medicine specializing in ophthalmology, Detroit, 1967-68, Phila., 1968-70, Evansville, Ind., 1970—; clin instr. ophthalmology Wayne State U., 1967-68; asso. in opthalmology U. Pa. Med. Sch., 1968-70; mem. staffs St. Mary's, Welborn, Deaconess hosps., Evansville; courtesy staff Methodist Hosp., Henderson, Ky. Diplomate Am. Bd. Opthalmology. Fellow A.C.S., Am. Acad. Ophthalmology and Otolaryngology; mem. A.M.A., Ind., Vanderburgh County med. socs., Am., Ind. acads. ophthalmology, Evansville Musicians Club Choral Soc., Phi Kappa Phi. Home: 122 W Main St Newburgh IN 47630 Office: 1015 Hulman Bldg Evansville IN 47708

SOWA, EVA INGERSOLL LONG (MRS. WALTER D. SOWA), social worker; b. Birmingham, Ala., Sept. 4, 1910; d. John Hamner and Fannie (Ingersoll) Long; B.A., U. Pitts., 1930, M.A., 1933; M.S. in Social Service Adminstrn., 1941; m. Walter D. Sowa, Apr. 4, 1942; children—Peter William, Thomas Michael. Tchr., Bentleyville (Pa.) High Sch., 1930-32; social worker Allegheny County (Pa.) Emergency Relief Bd., Pitts., 1934-36, Mothers' Assistance, Old Age Pension, Blind Pension, Pitts., 1936-38, Travelers Aid Soc., Pitts., 1938-40; probation officer Allegheny County Junenile Ct., Pitts., 1940-43; case worker Childrens Aid Soc., Birmingham, Ala., 1960-67; supr. Travelers Aid Soc., Birmingham, 1967-72, acting dir., 1972—. Active P.T.A. Mem. Nat. Assn. Social Workers, Acad. Certified Social Workers, Sigma Kappa Phi, Pi Lambda Theta. Club: Social Workers. Home: 2121 16th Av S Birmingham AL 35205 Office: 3600 8th Av S Birmingham AL 35222

SOWA, PATRICIA ANN, psychologist; b. Chicopee, Mass., Dec. 11, 1945; d. Max and Genevieve Nellie (Cyran) Sowa; B.A., Am. Internat. Coll., 1967; M.Ed., Springfield Coll., 1968; certificate in Drug Addiction, Washingtonian Center for Addictions, 1972. Personnel research analyst John Hancock Ins. Co., Boston, 1968-71; research psychologist Washingtonian Center for Addictions, 1972—. Mem. Am. Psychol. Assn., Psi Chi. Home: 580 Adams St Dorchester MA 02122 Office: 41 Morton St Jamaica Plain MA 02130

SOWA, ROSE, educator; b. McKeesport, Pa., Sept. 22, 1914; d. Peter and Anna (Jankowski) Sowa; B.S., State Coll., Slippery Rock, Pa., 1937; M.Ed., U. Pitts., 1942. Tchr. pub. schs., Arnold, Pa., 1937-43; pub. schs., Miami, Fla., 1947-50, Am. Dependent Schs., Tokyo, Japan, 1950-54, Stuttgart, Germay, 1954-55, Wiesbaden, Germany, 1955-59, Clark AFB, Phillipine Islands, 1959-64; engr. asst. Wright Aero Corp., Cin., 1944-45; instr., critic women's health and phys. edn. State Coll., Dickinson, N.D., 1946; instr., phys. edn. U. Ore., 1946-47; dir. Miami Edison Cadet Corp., 1947-48; edn. advisor U.S. Army Edn. Center, Seoul, Korea, 1965; edn. officer U.S. Army Camp Carroll Depot, Waegwam, Korea, 1965-66; edn. services officer, dir. gen. ednl. devel. program Dept. Army, Madigan Gen. Hosp., Tacoma, 1966-71; vocational devel. specialist Hdqrs. U.S. Army, Okinawa, 1971—. Active A.R.C., YWCA. Recipient Dept. of Army Commendation, Outstanding Performance Rating and Sustained Superior Performance award Madigan Gen. Hosp., Tacoma, 1968, Certificate of Achievement as edn. officer, 1968. Mem. Am. Personnel and Guidance Assn., Nat. Employment Counselors Assn., Assn. U.S. Army, Am. Fedn. Govt. Employees, Fed. Employed Women, Nat. Vocational Guidance Assn. Office: Educ Br PO Box 546 USARBCO APO San Francisco CA 96331

SOWELL, BETTY MOLVIG (MRS. LEMUEL LEWIS SOWELL), newspaper editor; b. Glasgow, Mont., Dec. 23, 1925; d. Ole Christopher and Susan Amelia (Walde) Molvig; grad. high sch.; m. Lemuel Lewis Sowell, Aug. 3, 1945; children—Sally S. Shenton, Gary L., Janet Sue. With Pageland (S.C.) Jour., 1955-60, 66—, editor, 1958—; with Charlotte Observer, 1960-66. Recipient awards for feature writing S.C. Press Assn. Mem. C. of C. Methodist (mem. adminstrv. bd. 1965, chmn. Chesterfield County Coop. parish). Home: 609 W Maynard St Pageland SC 29728 Office: Box 218 Pageland SC 29728

SOWELL, HELEN VIENNE MILLER (MRS. JERRY F. SOWELL), banker; b. Southport, Fla., Mar. 22, 1936; d. Alvin Lee and Louise (Fuller) Miller; grad. high sch.; m. Jerry F. Sowell, July 23, 1953; children—Gretchen, Jerry F., Mark. With Beach State Bank, Panama City Beach, Fla., 1963—, cashier, 1968-70, v.p. loan dept., 1970—, also dir. Bd. dirs. United Fund, 1974—. Mem. Beta Sigma Phi (Girl of Year award 1960-61). Home: 1135 Balboa Av Panama City FL 32401 Office: PO Drawer J Panama City Beach FL 32401

SOWELL, KATYE MARIE OLIVER (MRS. JESSE CLARENCE SOWELL), educator; b. Winston-Salem, N.C., Apr. 6, 1934; d. William Manton and Katye (Price) Oliver, Sr.; B.A., Flora Macdonald Coll., 1956; M.S., U. S.C., 1958; postgrad. U. So. Miss., 1961-62; Ph.D., Fla. State U., 1965; m. Jesse Clarence Sowell, Sept. 7, 1957 (dec. Feb. 1961); 1 son, David Clarence. Instr., Flora Macdonald Coll., Red Springs, N.C., 1958; asst. prof. Elon Coll. (N.C.), 1958-60; instr. U. So. Miss., Hattiesburg, 1960-63, Fla. State U., Tallahassee, 1965; faculty E. Carolina U., Greenville, N.C., 1965—, asso. prof. math., 1967-71, prof. math., 1972—, supr. student teaching math., 1966—, dir. NSF Inst. for Secondary Tchrs. Math., 1968-69, 70-71, 72-73. Lectr., cons.; mem. adv. council div. math. N.C. Dept. Pub. Instrn. Mem. Math. Assn. Am., Am. Math. Soc., Nat. Council Tchrs. Math., Am. Assn. U. Profs., N.C. Assn. Educators, N.C. Council Tchrs. Math. (pres. Eastern region 1971-73), Pi Mu Epsilon, Democrat. Presbyn. Contbr. to Math. Tchr. jour. Home: 103 Garrett St Greenville NC 27834

SOWELL, THELMA LARSSON, city ofcl.; b. Monterey, Cal., Sept. 29, 1913; d. Louis Hjalmer and Elizabeth Anne (Fawcett) Larsson; student Mira Costa Jr. Coll., 1959-60, San Diego State U., 1963-64; m. Jack Rickman Sowell, Aug. 15, 1937 (div. Feb. 1971); children—Jack Richman, Karen (Mrs. Robert Barclay Newlin). Supr. So. Pacific Co., San Francisco, 1939-43; asst. to comptroller, produce accounting div. Safeway Stores, Inc., Oakland, Cal., 1956-58; finance dir. City of Carlsbad (Cal.), 1965—. Mem. Nat. Accounting Assn., Municipal Finance Officers Assn. Club: Soroptimist (pres. 1971-72) (Oceanside-Carlsbad, Cal.). Home: 2885 Wilson St Carlsbad CA 92008 Office: 1200 Elm Av Carlsbad CA 92008

SPACKS, PATRICIA MEYER, educator; b. San Francisco, Nov. 17, 1929; d. Norman B. and Lillian (Talcott) Meyer; B.A., Rollins Coll., 1949; M.A., Yale, 1950; Ph.D., U. Cal., 1955; m. Barry Spacks, June 10, 1955; 1 dau., Judith Elizabeth. Instr., Ind. U., 1954-56, U. Fla., 1958-59; instr. to prof. English, Wellesley Coll., 1959—. Cons., Nat. Endowment for Humanities. Shirley Farr fellow Am. Assn. U. Women, 1962-63; Guggenheim fellow, 1969-70; Nat. Endowment for Humanities sr. fellow, 1974. Mem. Modern Langs. Assn., Am. Soc. 18th-Century Studies. Author: The Varied God, 1959; The Insistence of Horror, 1962; John Gay, 1965; The Poetry of Vision, 1967; An Argument of Images, 1971; The Female Imagination, 1975. Editor: Eighteenth-Century Poetry, 1964; Late Augustan Prose, 1971; Late Augustan Poetry, 1973. Home: 16 Abbott St Wellesley MA 02181 Office: Wellesley Coll Wellesley MA 02181

SPADARO, CHARLOTTE, lawyer; b. N.Y.C., June 29, 1941; d. Sol and Eva (Malach) Rubinfeld; student U. Cal. at Los Angeles, 1958-60; B.A., Cal. State U., 1962; J.D., U. So. Cal., 1969; m. George Spadaro, Apr. 8, 1960; children—Michele, Jonathan. Tchr. English, Portola Jr. High Sch., Orange, Cal., 1962-63; substitute tchr. English and French, Santa Ana (Cal.) Unified and Orange (Cal.) Unified Sch. Dists., 1963-64; admitted to Cal. bar, 1970; law clk. Dist. Court of Appeals, Los Angeles, 1969; mem. firm Eliot B. Feldman, Profl. Corp., Los Angeles, 1970—. Recipient Speaker award Lions Club, 1965. Mem. Women Lawyers Assn., Ephebian Soc., League Women Voters (finance chmn. 1965, mem. speakers bur. 1964-65), Phi Delta Delta. Home: 221 S El Camino Dr Beverly Hills CA 90212 Office: 221 S El Camino Dr Beverly Hills CA 90212

SPAGNOLI, HARRIETT HELEN HANKE (MRS. GENE LOUIS SPAGNOLI), educator; b. Nanuet, N.Y., Dec. 16, 1918; d. Carl C. and Effie (Bahr) Hanke, Sr.; A.B., Wash. Sq. Coll., 1941; M.S., N.Y. U., 1946, Ph.D., 1951; m. Gene Louis Spagnoli, Jan. 23, 1949; children—Cathy Jean, Susan Ann, Gene Louis, Carl Christian. Instr. children's sch. Woods Hole Marine Biol. Labs., 1948; research asst. Lederle labs. Am. Cynamid, Pearl River, N.Y., 1952; instr. dept. biol. scis. Fairleigh Dickinson U., Teaneck, N.J., 1958-61, asst. prof., 1961-63, asso. prof., 1963-67, prof., 1967—, acting chmn., 1964-66, acting dean Coll. Liberal Arts, 1974—. Active various community orgns.; pres. League Women Voters Nyack, N.Y., 1954-55. Mem. Am. Inst. Biol. Scis., N.Y. Acad. Scis., Sigma Xi. Home: 29 Highview Av Nanuet NY 10954 Office: Fairleigh Dickinson U Dept Biol Scis Teaneck NJ 07666

SPAGNOLO, MARCIA ADAMS (MRS. ANTHONY SPAGNOLO), civic worker; b. Hibbing, Minn., July 24, 1937; d. Jacob Anthony and Agnes J. (Grivest) Adams; B.A., Coll. St. Catherine, 1959; m. Anthony Spagnolo, Oct. 29, 1960; children—Mark, Lauren. Cons., Scott County Welfare Bd., 1966—. Dir. Shakopee Bd. Edn., 1972—; leader Girl Scouts Am., 1972—. Vice chmn. Scott County Rep. party, 1972—. Bd. dirs. Scott-Carver Inebriety Com., 1973—. Mem. Am. Assn. U. Women, Am. Occupational Therapy Assn. Home: 949 Main St Shakopee MN 55379

SPAHT, KATHERINE SHAW (MRS. PAUL HOLDEN SPAHT), educator; b. Shreveport, La., Jan. 20, 1946; d. William Marshall and Jean (Craighead) Shaw; B.A., U. Miss., 1968; J.D. (Am. Assn. U. Women fellow), La. State U., 1971; m. Paul Holden Spaht, Aug. 7, 1971. Admitted to La. bar, 1971; atty. La. Legislative Council, Baton Rouge, 1972; asst. prof. law La. State U., Baton Rouge, 1972—. Vice pres. Young Women's Christian Orgn., Baton Rouge, 1973-74. Mem. Am., La., Baton Rouge bar assns., Mortar Bd., Order of Coif, Kappa Kappa Gamma, Phi Delta Delta. Home: 1479 Kenmore Baton Rouge LA 70808

SPAIN, HATTIE BELLE, restaurateur; b. Crockett, Tex., Aug. 22, 1902; d. James Robert and Lucy (Douglas) Turner; student Sam Houston U., 1921-22; m. Walter Adkin, Dec. 23, 1923; children—Charles A., Ann. Sch. tchr., 1922-25; owner, mgr. Modern Cleaners, Crockett, 1944-55, Royal Restaurant, Crockett, 1955—. Orgn. chmn. Dale Carnegie Course, 1962. Chmn., Tourist Com. on Council, 1961—; chmn. restoration com. Stage Coach Inn, 1961-62; mem., treas. Library Bd. Mem. Friends of Library (orgn. chmn. 1962), Pilot Club, Carnegie Alumni Assn. (orgn. chmn. 1962), Internat. Platform Assn. Mem. Order Eastern Star (past worthy matron). Club: Red Bud Garden. Home: 201 Pecan Dr Crockett TX 75835

SPAIN, JAYNE BAKER (MRS. JOHN A. SPAIN), govt. ofcl.; b. San Francisco; d. Lawrence Ian and Marguerite (Buchanan) Baker; student U. Cal. at Berkeley, 1944-47, Music U. Cin., 1947-50; LL.D., Edgecliff Coll., Cin., 1969; Dr. Pub. Service, George Washington U., 1970; LL.D., U. Cin., 1971, Dumbarton Coll., 1972, Springfield (Mass.) Coll., 1973, Gallaudet Coll., Washington, 1973; L.H.D., Bryant Coll., 1972, Russell Sage Coll., Troy, N.Y., 1973; m. John A. Spain, July 14, 1952; children—Jeffry Alan, Jon Kimberly. Pres., Alvey-Ferguson Co., Cin., 1952-66, pres. Alvey-Ferguson Operations div. Litton Industries, Inc., 1966-70, also dir. parent co., 1970—; vice chmn. U.S. Civil Service Commn., 1971—. Vice chmn. Pres.'s Com. on Employment Handicapped, 1966—; participant internat. trade fairs U.S. Depts. State, Commerce, Europe, North Africa, 1961-66, mem. trade and investment mission, India, 1965; mem. U.S. com. Internat. Council Social Welfare; mem. Internat. Soc. Rehab. Disabled; mem. adv. com. sheltered workshops U.S. sec. labor; mem. bldg. com. Children's Med. Center, Cin. Bd. dirs., past pres. Convalescent Hosp. Children, Cin., Greater Cin. Hosp. Council, Children's Neuromuscular Diagnostic Center, Cin., Cin. Sci. Center. Recipient Distinguished Service award for work overseas blind People to People Com., Washington, 1965; Migel medal Am. Found. Blind, N.Y., 1966; Golden Plate award industry Acad. Achievement, Dallas, 1967; Top Hat award Bus. and Profl. Women's Clubs. Am., N.Y., 1967. Mem. Conveyor Equipment Mfrs. Assn. (sec., treas. 1960-63), Machinery and Allied Products Inst., Internat. Platform Assn. Episcopalian. Contbr. articles to profl. jours. Office: 1900 E St Washington DC 20415

SPALDING, MYRNA JO-AN OAK, lawyer; b. Fort Frances, Ont., Can., Aug. 20, 1941; d. John and Anna (Pedersen) Oak; came to U.S., 1960, naturalized, 1966; B.Sc., U. Ariz., 1964, J.D., 1969. Admitted to Cal. bar, 1969, Ariz. bar, 1969, Nev. bar, 1969, practice in Stateline, 1970—. Tchr. pvt. painting lessons, 1973—. Mem. Tahoe Art League (gallery chmn. 1973-74, pres. 1974-75). Home and office: PO Box 2111 Stateline NV 89449

SPALDING, ROMALDA BISHOP, author, educator; b. Santa Rosa, Honduras, Feb. 1, 1899; d. Gilbert Curtis and Catherine (Rohrig) Bishop; B.A., U. Ill., 1922; M.A., Columbia, 1932; m. Walter Talbot Spalding, Jan. 25, 1941. Classroom tchr., Bronxville, N.Y., 1931-41; tchr. Shady Hill Sch., Cambridge, Mass., 1941-45; tchr. of tchrs. in 14 states and Can., 1951—; reading cons. 28 Catholic schs. in Hawaii, 1956-60. Mem. Nat. League Am. Pen Women (treas. Honolulu br. 1964-70). Author: The Writing Road to Reading, 1957, rev. edit., 1962, 69. Home: 3340 Pacific Heights Rd Honolulu HI 96813

SPAN, MIRIAM NUSBAUM (MRS. GERALD SPAN), lawyer; b. Newark, May 12, 1942; d. Marcus C. and Frances B. (Blumenthal) Nusbaum; B.A., Rutgers U., 1964, J.D., 1966; postgrad. Hague Acad. Internat. Law, 1964; m. Gerald Span, July 14, 1965; children—Henry, Jenny. Admitted to N.J. bar, 1966; asst. dir. N.J. Legal Services, Trenton, 1966-67; 1st asst. dep. pub. defender Union County, N.J., 1967-73; asst. U.S. Atty., Newark, 1973-74; Cons. Dept. Pub. Adv. N.J., Trenton, 1974—. Instr. Inst. Continuing Legal Edn., Newark, 1972-73. Mem. N.J., Union County (chmn. prison reform com. 1972-73) bar assns., Zionist Orgn. Am. Mem. Hadassah. Home: 1 Fair Hill Rd Westfield NJ 07090

SPANGLER, DAISY KIRCHOFF (MRS. FRANCIS R. COSGROVE SPANGLER), educator; b. Lancaster, Pa., Jan 27, 1913; d. Frank Augustus and Lida Flaharty (Forewood) Kirchoff; B.S., Millersville State Coll., 1963; M.Ed., Pa. State U., 1966, Ed.D., 1972; m. Francis R. Cosgrove Spangler, June 3, 1939; children—Stephen Russell, Michael Denis. Tchr. rural sch., Providence, Pa., 1933-35, Rapho Twp., Pa., 1935-42, Mastersonville, Pa., 1942-51; elementary sch. prin. Manheim Central, Pa., 1952-66; tchr., Manheim, Pa., 1967-68; asso. prof. elementary edn. Millersville (Pa.) State Coll., 1968—. Dist. chmn. A.R.C., 1965-66; mem. Hempfield P.T.A., 1966-67. Mem. Pa. Edn. Assn., Pa. Elementary Prins. Assn., Assn. Pa. State Coll. and U. Profs., Nat., Lancaster (pres. 1963-64) prins. assns., Pa. Outdoor Edn. and Conservation Assn., Nat., Pa. councils for social studies, Am. Ednl. Research Assn., Manheim Tchrs. Assn. (pres. 1964-65, Hempfield Profl. Women, Pi Lambda Theta, Delta Kappa Gamma. Lutheran (pres. Lutheran women 1966-67). Order Eastern Star. Home: Route 7 Box 238 Manheim PA 17545 Office: Millersville State College Millersville PA 17551

SPANGLER, SISTER MARY MICHAEL, educator; b. Woodsfield, O., Jan. 27, 1924; d. Otto Paul and Agnes Marie (Hoeffler) Spangler; B.S. summa cum laude, Coll. of St. Mary of the Springs, 1944; M.A., U. Notre Dame, 1957, Ph.D. (scholar), 1964. Joined Sisters of Dominican Order, 1944; primary tchr., prin. Ohio parochial schs., 1946-54; prof. philosophy edn., adminstr. Ohio Dominican Coll., Columbus, 1955—. Mem. Franklin County Tchr. Preparation Adv. Bd. Mem. Ohio Coll. Assn. (sec. tchr. edn. sect. 1968-69), Am. (faculty rep. 1968—), Ohio (pres. 1973-74) assns. colls. tchr. edn., Nat. Cath. Ednl. Assn., Tchr. Edn. Com. Franklin County (sec. 1969, chmn. 1968), Assn. Tchr. Edn., Delta Epsilon Sigma. Democrat. Author: Educational Psychology, 1965. Address: 1216 Sunbury Rd Columbus OH 43219

SPANIER, LELA MARSH, editor; b. Annapolis Royal, N.S., Can., July 18, 1922; d. Alfred Edward and Almeda Bernice (Rayfuse) Marsh; B.S., Simmons Coll., Boston, 1944; m. John L. Spanier, Aug. 6, 1951. Compiler Biomed. Serials, Washington, 1960-61; editor catalog Nat. Library of Medicine, 1961-63; librarian FDA, 1963-65; asst. editor New Serial Titles, Washington, 1966-70, editor, 1971—. Recipient award Nat. Library Medicine, 1962. Mem. Spl. Libraries Assn., Profl. Assn. Library of Congress. Office: Library of Congress Washington DC 20540

SPANIERMAN, LEATRICE SLOTE (MRS. ELLIOT SPANIERMAN), editor; b. N.Y.C., Aug. 16, 1934; d. Morris Tashman and Rosalyn Parker (Ballot) Slote; student Alfred U., 1952-54; B.S. cum laude, N.Y. U., 1956; m. Elliot Spanierman, Apr. 13, 1957; children—Clifford Slote, Brooke Slote. Columnist, Nassau Herald, Lawrence, N.Y., 1962-72; women's editor Nassau Herald and Rockaway Jour., 1963-65; editor Rockaway (N.Y.) Jour., 1965-68, Nassau Herald, 1968-73; exec. editor Bi County Pubs., Lawrence, N.Y., 1973—. Editorial cons. Youthquake, 1969-71, Sisterhood Week Women's Feminist Newspaper, 1971-73. Vice-pres. Willow Way Civic Assn., Woodmere, N.Y., 1960-64; founder Five Towns Beautification Com., 1965; founder, v.p. Lawrence Cedarhurst Youth Center, 1970-73; mem. Lawrence Ecology Com., 1970; mem. Lawrence Narcotics Guidance Council Com., 1971-72; youth commr. Lawrence, 1971-73. Trustee spl. events and services div. Five Towns Community Chest; bd. dirs., sec. Peninsula Child Guidance Center; bd. dirs. Lawrence-Cedarhurst Youth Center. Recipient Founder's Day award N.Y. U., 1956; award of merit Village Lawrence, 1972; Pub. Relations award Five Towns Community Chest, 1965; citations for Service, Am. Cancer Soc., 1967, March of Dimes, 1966. Mem. Beta Gamma Sigma, Alpha Kappa Delta, Mu Kappa Tau. Home: 233 Ocean Av Lawrence NY 11559 Office: 379 Central Av Lawrence NY 11559

SPANNBAUER, THELMA WILBUR (MRS. GODFREY K. SPANNBAUER), educator; b. Fairfax, Va., July 12, 1918; d. John Wesley and Orpha Grade (Walker) Wilbur; student Cortland State Normal Sch., 1935-38; B.S., Oneonta State Tchrs. Coll., 1952; M.S., Butler U., 1962, postgrad., 1963-69; m. Godfrey K. Spannbauer, Apr. 4, 1942; 1 son, David Godfrey. Tchr. pub. schs., Drydeh, N.Y., 1938-40, Scotia, N.Y., 1940-44, 49-55, Shelbyville, Ind., 1956—. Mem. Ind. Adv. Council for Tchr. Edn., 1971-72. Recipient Meritorious Alumni award Oneonta State Tchrs. Coll., 1971. Mem. N.E.A. (vice chmn.) legislative commn. 1969-72, council on human relations 1971-72), Ind. (pres. 1968, chmn. tchr. edn. and profl. standards 1970—), Shelbyville Central (pres. 1966) tchrs. assns., Delta Kappa Gamma. Home: Rural Route 2 Crest Dr Shelbyville IN 46176 Office: 115 Colescott St Shelbyville IN 46176

SPARBER, JOAN ELIZABETH, advt. agy. exec.; b. N.Y.C., Oct. 6, 1942; d. Irwin and Johanna (Kramer) Sparber; certificate N.Y. Sch. Interior Design, 1965; student Pratt Inst., 1965-69. Asst. to mgr. personnel benefits Genesco, Inc., N.Y.C., 1960-67; personnel dir. Con-Data Systems, Inc., N.Y.C., 1967-68; personnel mgr. Carl Ally, Inc., advt., N.Y.C., 1968-71; office mgr., personnel dir., account exec. Geer, DuBois Inc., advt., N.Y.C., 1971—. Mem. Advt. Agy. Personnel Assn. (founder; pres., 1970—), Advt. Agy. Office Mgmt. Assn. (sec.-treas. 1972—). Home: 355 E 72d St New York City NY 10021 Office: 1 Dag Hammarskjold Plaza New York City NY 10017

SPARE, PAULINE PAULSON (MRS. RAYMOND V. SPARE), librarian; b. Rochester, N.Y., July 13, 1914; d. Paul S. and Ruby B. (Unger) Paulson; B.A., U. Rochester, 1935; M.L.S., Syracuse U., 1964; m. Raymond V. Spare, Apr. 3, 1937 (dec.); children—John Paulson, Stephen Vigneron. Asst. dir. Wayne County Library System, Newark, N.Y., 1964-67, dir., 1967—. Mem. Phi Beta Kappa, Sigma Alpha Iota, Beta Phi Mu. Conglist. Home: 3402 W Lake Rd Canandaigua NY 14424 Office: 503 W Union St Newark NY 14513

SPARENBLEK, MATILDA VALENTINA, librarian; b. Indpls., Jan. 14, 1916; d. John and Anna (Hren) Sparenblek; A.B., Butler U., 1938; B.L.S., U. Chgo., 1947. Med. sec. City Hosp., Indpls., 1939-42; clk. Army Air Forces Storage Depot, Indpls., 1942-43; sec. Stewart-Warner Corp., Indpls. 1943-46; br. librarian Buffalo and Erie County Pub. Library, Buffalo, 1947-61; reference librarian Indpls.-Marion County Pub. Library, Indpls., 1961—. Tchr., Butler U. Evening Div., Indpls., 1939-40. Leader, South Buffalo council Girl Scouts U.S.A., 1947-48; active YWCA, Buffalo, 1946-50. Mem. A.L.A., Ind. Library Assn., Slovene Nat. Benefit Soc. (sec. 1937-38). Roman Catholic. Home: 1221 N Hawthorne Lane Indianapolis IN 46219 Office: 40 E St Clair St Indianapolis IN 46204

SPARGER, YVONNE, judge; b. Shawnee, Okla., Oct. 27, 1930; d. Delbert Franklin and Vinita Mary (Giles) Cravens; B.S., S.W. Mo. State Coll., 1953; postgrad. Georgetown Law Sch., 1956-58; LL.B., U. Okla., 1959; div.; children—Tiger, Ricky, Robin. Admitted to Okla. bar, 1959; law clk. U.S. Circuit Ct. Appeals, Oklahoma City, 1959-60; practice law, Oklahoma City, 1964-66; asst. atty. gen. State of Okla., 1971-73; judge Okla. State Indsl. Ct., Oklahoma City, 1973—. Home: 631 NE 18th Dr Oklahoma City OK 73105 Office: Industrial Court Oklahoma City OK 73105

SPARKS, MELBA DAY, educator; b. Portland, Ore., Jan. 4, 1915; d. Edward Hugh and Rose Meta (Fischer) Day; student Northwestern U., 1934; B.A. magna cum laude, Pacific U., 1935; postgrad. Portland U., Portland State Coll.; m. Victor E. Sparks, June 11, 1939; children—Jean (Mrs. Claude Gates), James Edward. Free lance model, Chgo., 1934; tchr. drama Eagle Point (Ore.) High Sch., 1936-38; instr. drama Meglin Studios, Seattle, 1938-39, drama tchr. Enterprise (Ore.) High Sch., 1939; owner, instr. Pvt. Dance and Drama Studio, Fallon, Nev., 1940-41; supr. time office Ore. Ship Yards, Portland, 1942-45; tchr. drama, dir. Jefferson High Sch., Portland, 1945-61, Madison High Sch., Portland, 1961—. Co-owner, pres. Sparks Food Products, Inc., Portland. State dir. Thespian Soc., Ore., 1947-68, trustee, 1968—; asst. dir. Internat. Thespian Soc., 1968-70, internat. dir., 1970-72; program chmn. for cons., 1947-68, produced pageant for drama conf., Portland, 1966—; stage mgr. Nat. Prins.' Conf. Pageant, Portland; dir. Pageant for N.E.A., 1956; dir. workshop Drama Conf., Ind. U., 1962, 64, 68. Recipient Jr. Achievement award to Portland Citizen for outstanding contbn. to achievement for youth, 1956-57; awards for play programs Nat. Thespian Soc., 1953, 54, 57. Mem. Profl. Women's League (v.p. Portland 1963-64, pres. 1964-65), Am. Edn. Theatre Assn., Secondary Theatre Assn., Children's Theatre Assn., Ore. Theatre Arts Assn., Zeta Phi Eta. Contbr. articles and pictures to Dramatics mag., Portland Sch. Bull., Photogravieure mag. sect. Oregonian newspaper, Ore. Photograph N.W. Mag. Home: Route 3 Box 1018 Troutdale OR 97060 Office: James Madison High Sch 2735 NE 82d St Portland OR 97220 also Internat Thespian Soc College Hill Station Box E Cincinnati OH 45224

SPARKS, MEREDITH PLEASANT (MRS. WILLIAM J. SPARKS), patent lawyer; b. Palestine, Ill.; d. John L. and Laura (Bicknell) Pleasant; A.B. with distinction, Ind. U., 1927, A.M., 1928; Ph.D., U. Ill., 1936; J.D., Rutgers U., 1958; m. William J. Sparks, Dec. 31, 1930; children—Ruth (Mrs. James W. Foster), Katherine (Mrs. Richard L. Albrecht), Charles, John. Tchr. chemistry Rochester (Ind.) High Sch., 1928-29; chemist DuPont Co., Niagara Falls, N.Y., 1929-34, Northam Warren Co., N.Y.C., 1939; chem. patent agt. Am. Cyanamid Co., Bound Brook N.J., 1941-46; admitted to Fla. bar, 1958, U.S. Dist. Ct. So. Dist. Fla., U.S. Ct. Customs and Patent Appeals, U.S. Supreme Ct. bar; patent atty., 1958—. Mem. Assn. Ind. U. Chemists (pres. 1950-51), Am., Fla., Dade County bar assns., Am., N.J. patent law assns., Internat. Patent and Trademark Assn., Am. Chem. Soc., Nat. Assn. Women Lawyers (dir. S.E. region), Am. Assn. U. Women, Phi Beta Kappa, Sigma Xi, Iota Sigma Pi, Kappa Delta. Contbr. articles to profl. jours. Patentee in field. Address: 5129 Granada Blvd Coral Gables FL 33146 Office: Alfred I DuPont Bldg 169 E Flagler St Miami FL 33131

SPARLING, EVANGELINE MARIE (MRS. CLARENCE DANILE SPARLING), automobile agy. exec.; b. Spearfish, S.D., Mar. 31, 1901; d. Vincent Samuel and Clara Jane (Morden) Johnson; grad. Black Hills State Coll., 1919; student Detroit Bus. Coll., 1941; m. Clarence Daniel Sparling, Aug. 17, 1921; children—Robert Daniel, Helen Clair (Mrs. Walter A. Terpenning). Elementary sch. tchr., S.D. and Wyo., 1919-21; bookkeeper, treas., dir. C.D. Sparling Co., Detroit, 1946-65; bookkeeper, treas. Sparling Plastic Industries, Plymouth, Mich., 1960-72, now dir.; treas., dir. Les Dallas Dodge Agency, Tecumseh, Mich., 1967—. Trustee Chelsea Methodist Home, 1940-50; sec., bd. dirs. Boulevard Methodist Home, 1960-65. Republican. Methodist. Mem. Order Eastern Star. Club: Detroit New Century. Home: 43753 Galway Dr Northville MI 48167 Office: 9229 General Dr Plymouth MI 48170

SPARLING, SEDA ARONIAN, pathologist; b. Istanbul, Turkey, Sept. 16, 1919; d. Arshag and Aroosiag (Opsoian) Aronian; came to U.S., 1920, naturalized, 1927; B.A., Boston U., 1942, M.D., 1944; m. Harold Sparling, Jr., Dec. 27, 1941 (div. Dec. 1969); children—Susan, Patricia, Sharon, Pamela, Martha, Nancy. Intern, Univ. Hosp., Boston, 1944-45; resident Salem (Mass.) Hosp., 1945-47; asso. pathologist Burbank Hosp., Fitchburg, Mass., 1947—, Henry Heywood Hosp., Gardner, Mass., 1948-60; asso. pathologist Leominster (Mass.) Hosp., 1949-65, cons. in pathology, 1965—. Mem. exec. bd. Mental Health and Mental Retardation Region II Area Bd., 1969—, Fitchburg, pres., 1972—; bd. dirs. Fitchburg unit Am. Cancer Soc. Fellow New Eng., Mass. socs. pathologists; mem. Mass., Worcester No. Dist. med. socs., League Women Voters, Fitchburg Art Mus., Worcester No. County Assn. for Retarded Citizens, Montachusett Women's Center, Friends of Fitchburg Pub. Library, N.C. Mental Health Assn. Office: Burbank Hospital Fitchburg MA 01420

SPARROW, MARGARET ELIZABETH WILLIS (MRS. CHARLES EDWARD SPARROW, JR.), assn. exec.; b. Balt., Aug. 21, 1919; d. Charles Fountain and Margaret (Norris) Willis; A.B., Goucher Coll., 1940; M.A. in Teaching (Ford Found. fellow, Johns Hopkins U., 1958; m. Charles Edward Sparrow, Feb. 1, 1941; children—Dorothy Talmadge, Constance Norris. Dir. vol. services Mental Hygiene Soc., Balt., 1955-56; exec. dir. Balt. council Camp Fire Girls, 1958-65; exec. dir. Southwestern Conn. council Girl Scouts, Wilton, 1966-68; asst. dir. div. community services Nat. League Nursing, N.Y.C., 1968-71, dir. div. community planning, 1971—. Mem. adv. council Am. Assn. for Comprehensive Health Planning, 1973—; dep. dist. coordinator Balt. Civil Def., 1952-55; pres. Md. Women's Council, Balt., 1953-55; mem. adv. com. Md. Conf. Citizenship, Balt., 1958-61; pres. Legislative Clearing House Md., 1960-61. Mem. Am. Soc. Tng. and Devel., Assn. Vol. Action Scholars, Am. Assn. U. Women (pres. Balt. br. 1956-58), Adult Edn. Assn., Nat. Assn. Female Execs., Md. Geneal. Soc. Clubs: Coll. (dir. 1968-70), Woman's, Westchester Hills Golf (White Plains, N.Y.); Hopkins of Balt. Editor: The Handbook for Constituent Leagues, 1972; Organizational Behavior-Conflict and its Resolution, 1973; Community Planning for Nursing-A Selected Bibliography, 1974. Contbr. articles to profl. publs. Home: 44 Prescott Av White Plains NY 10605 Office: 10 Columbus Circle New York NY 10019

SPARROW, SARA STELLE HAYCRAFT (MRS. DOMENIC CICCHETTI), research psychologist; b. Mpls.; d. Kenneth C. and Alberta (Smith) Haycraft; B.A., Montclair State Coll., 1958; M.A., U. Fla., 1962; Ph.D., 1968; m. Domenic Cicchetti, Feb. 22, 1969. Speech and hearing therapist, Orlando, Fla., 1958-61; coordinator speech and hearing program Orange County Schs., Orlando, 1962-64; fellow psychology dept. Yale, 1968-69, research staff psychologist child devel. dept. psychology Child Study Center, 1969-72, research asso., 1972-74, chief psychologist, 1972-73, 74—. Vis. prof. Conn. Coll., New London, 1973—; cons. psychologist Foote Sch., New Haven. Mem. Am., Eastern psychol. assns., Internat. Neuropsychology Assn. Home: PO Box 272 Stony Creek CT 06405 Office: 333 Cedar St New Haven CT 06510

SPATH, PATRICIA ANN, sch. psychologist; b. Cleve., Apr. 19, 1910; d. Charles Edward and Gertrude Elizabeth (Murphy) Spath; B.S. in Edn., St. John Coll., Cleve., 1949, M.A., 1952; A.M., John Carroll U., Cleve., 1960, postgrad., 1972-73; postgrad. St. Louis U., 1956-58. Joined Sisters of St. Joseph of Cleve., Roman Catholic Ch., 1936; tchr. Cath. Bd. Edn., Cleve., 1936-63, vice prin., then prin., 1964-65, secondary counselor, 1965-68, psychologist, dir. psychol. services, 1969—; adult counseling mem. Kent State Center for Ednl. Devel. and Strategic Services, also instructional supervision study team. Active local United Appeal, I.R.C., Neighbor Youth Corps. Governing bd. Cuyahoga Spl. Edn. Service Center. Mem. N.E. Ohio Guidance and Personnel Assn. (sec. 1968-69), Nat., Cleve. assns. schs. psychologists, Ohio Sch. Psychologists, Cleve. Psychol. Assn. Democrat. Co-author: Christian Child Reading Series, 1956. Contbr. articles to profl. jours. Home: 3529 E 118th St Cleveland OH 44105 Office: 5103 Superior Av Cleveland OH 44103

SPAULDING, JEAN MARIE, educator; b. Newberg, Ore., Sept. 29, 1918; d. H. Clifford and Mary E. (Baker) Spaulding; B.S., Ore. Coll. Edn., 1941; M.A., Colo. State Coll., 1949, postgrad., 1960; postgrad. Stanford, summer 1955, U. Ore., 1966. Tchr. elementary schs., Springfield, Ore., 1939-42, Salem, Ore., 1942-45, 46-48, 49-50, Seattle, 1945-46, Colo. State Lab. Sch., 1947-49; Eastern Wash. Coll. Lab. Sch., 1950-51; coordinator presch.-primary projects State Dept. Edn., Salem, 1951—. Mem. Nat. Assn. Edn. Young Children (task force 1970), Am. Assn. U. Women, Assn. Childhood Edn. Internat. (chmn. pub. affairs com. 1966-68), N.E.A., Ore. Edn. Assn., Nat. Council State Cons. in Elementary Edn. (treas. 1972-74), Ore. Assn. Sch. Suprs. (pres. 1956), Assn. for Supervision and Curriculum Devel., Ore. Dept. Elementary Sch. Prins., Delta Kappa Gamma (chpt. pres. 1964-66, state 2d v.p. 1969-71, 1st v.p. 1971-73, pres. 1973—), Phi Lambda Theta. Republican. Presbyn. Home: 1165 Chemeketa St Salem OR 97301

SPAULDING, NANCY LOUISE HALL, mus. ofcl.; b. Racine, Wis., Nov. 14, 1933; d. Earl Herman and Helen Leona (James) Hall; grad. high sch.; children—Jeffery, Steven, Julie. Registrar, Racine County Hist. Mus., Racine, Wis., 1966—. Mem. Racine Zool. Soc., Nat., Racine County hist. socs. Home: 1806 Summit Av Racine WI 53404 Office: 701 S Main St Racine WI 53403

SPAULDING, ROMA ALMA, state legislator; b. Woodstock, Vt., Oct. 16, 1914; d. John Wilhelm and Eveline Victoria (Bourdon) Magnusson; grad. high sch.; m. Bedford T. Spaulding, Dec. 24, 1937; children—Diane, Cynthia (Mrs. Douglas Dutilley). Mem. N.H. Ho. of Reps. from 4th Dist., 1967—, chmn. pub. health and welfare com., 1971—. Mem. N.H. Comprehensive Health Planning Council, 1971—. Mem. Claremont Hist. Soc. Republican. Methodist. Home: 8 Maple Av Claremont NH 03743

SPEAR, BARBARA ELLEN HINES, speech and lang. pathologist; b. St. Johnsbury, Vt., Aug. 28, 1921; d. Ernest Frank and Ellen (Kellogg) Hines; B.A., U. Me., 1949; M.A., Northwestern U., 1957; m. Harlan S. Spear, June 24, 1950 (div. July, 1963). Speech therapist South Portland (Me.) Schs., 1949-55; speech therapist Santa Ana (Cal.) United Sch. Dist., 1955-64, speech cons., 1964—. Mem. Cal. Speech and Hearing Assn. (v.p. so. region 1968-69, bd. dirs. 1971—). Home: 1820 Park Newport Dr Newport Beach CA 92660 Office: 1405 N French St Santa Ana CA 92701

SPEAR, R. JENELLE, educator; b. Kinston, N.C., Dec. 4, 1929; d. Herbert and Ruth (Spence) Spear; B.A., Agnes Scott Coll., 1951; M.A., Syracuse U., 1958; postgrad. U. Denver, 1963-66. Research asst. Oak Ridge Nat. Lab., 1952-55; asst. dean women Longwood Coll., Farmville, Va., 1958-63, U. Fla., Gainesville, 1966-67; dean students Converse Coll., Spartanburg, S.C., 1967—. Bd. dirs. Spartanburg County Mental Health Assn., 1968—, v.p., 1969-70. Mem. Nat., S.C. assns. women deans and counselors, S.C. Coll. Personnel (sec. 1970-73), Assn. Kappa Delta Pi, Delta Kappa Gamma. Office: Converse Coll Spartanburg SC 29301

SPEARMAN, DORIS WARREN, editor; b. Santa Rosa, Mo., Aug. 24, 1925; d. George Everette and Grace Alice (Henderson) Warren; grad. high sch., Famous Writers Sch., 1964; m. Daniel E. Spearman; children—Phylis (Mrs. David Barnard), Eddie, Danny, Marty, Jimmy, Sonny, Karyn, Rachel, Doris Danette. Free lance writer, 1944-64; editor, pub. Spearman Publs., Los Angeles, 1964—; staff writer Southside Jour., Los Angeles, 1967; editor Watts Star Rev., Los Angeles, 1968; editorial asst. Monist, 1971; founder Angel Publs., Los Angeles, 1964—. Pres., Graham Sch. P.T.A., Los Angeles, 1964-69; inspiration chmn. council Cub Scouts, 1967-68; founder Internat. Writers Fellowship, 1965—. Recipient various poetry awards. Office: Spearman Publs 392 Viewpark Circle San Jose CA 95136

SPEARS, FREDONIA WHITE SIKES (MRS. FLOYD D. SPEARS), coll. librarian; b. Big Sandy, Tex., May 20, 1918; d. Joseph Dial and Fredonia (Revill) White; B.A., N. Tex. State U., 1944, postgrad., 1969; M.Ed., Stephen F. Austin State U., 1958; postgrad. U. Tex., 1962-64, U. Mich., 1968, E. Tex. State U., 1970-71; m. Thomas B. Sikes, Jr., Oct. 12, 1935 (dec. July 1938); 1 son, Thomas Bryant III; m. Floyd D. Spears, Oct. 17, 1971. Asst. librarian Sul Ross State Coll., 1941-42; librarian, Mt. Pleasant Sr. High Sch., 1942-43, Gaston Sr. High Sch., 1943-47, Kilgore Coll., 1947-70; dir. library Grayson Coll., Denison, Tex., 197—. Mem. Am., Southwestern, Tex. library assns., Tex. Jr., Tex. State tchrs. assns., Alpha Lambda Sigma. Mem. Order Eastern Star. Clubs: Altrusa (Sherman, Tex.); Business and Professional Women's (Kilgore, Tex.). Home: 104 N Wood St Denison TX 75020

SPECIALE, THERESA MARY, editor; b. N.Y.C., Oct. 4, 1931; d. James and Helen (Chiapetta) Speciale; B.A., Hunter Coll. City N.Y., 1953; postgrad. Emory U., 1967. Statistician, Nat. Securities & Research Corp., N.Y.C., 1953-55; editor, mut. fund researcher Arthur Wiesenberger & Co., Investment Bankers, N.Y.C., 1955-60; asso. editor Dealers Digest Pub. Co., N.Y.C., 1960-62; computer programmer N.Y. State Employees' Retirement System, Albany, 1963-66; editor N.Y. Div. Budget, Albany, 1967—. Chmn. adv. com. Interdeptl. Com. on Research, 1970-71, sec.-treas. Mem. Am. Statis. Assn. (exec. com., sec. communications chmn. Albany chpt.). Editor: N.Y. State Statis. Reporter, 1969-71, N.Y. State Statis. Yearbook, 6 edits., 1967—. Home: Couse Corners East Greenbush NY 12061 Office: State Capitol Albany NY 12224

SPECKER, VIOLA MARIE MERRIMAN (MRS. EVERETTE LELAND SPECKER), educator; b. Prescott, Kan., Apr. 3, 1916; d. Samuel James and Kizzie (Coon) Merriman; B.S., Kan. State Coll., 1947, M.S., 1952; postgrad. U Warrensburg, 1965-73; m. Everette Leland Specker, June 9, 1957. Tchr., Pleasanton (Kan.) High Sch., 1947, Schell City (Mo.) High Sch., 1948, Kansas City (Mo.) Pub. Schs., 1949-54; supr. tng. program Higginsville (Mo.) State Sch. and Hosp., 1962-64, tchr., 1964-67, spl. edn. tchr., 1967—. Mem. exec. com. Lafayette County Cerebral Palsy Group, 1970; chmn. Lafayette County Council on Aging, 1972; vice chmn. Older Adults Transp. Service Steering Com., 1973. Mem. Am. Assn. Mental Deficiency (regional council developmental disabilities 1973—), Mo. Assn. Retarded Children (bd. dirs. 1973—), Mo. Tchrs. Assn. (life), Mo. Assn. Social Welfare, Lafayette County Assn. Retarded Children (corr. sec. 1973), Municipal Employees Union, Kappa Delta Pi, Phi Alpha Theta. Methodist (sec. commn. on minimum salaries 1972—, lay speaker 1970—). Home: Route 1 Box 71 Odessa MO 64076 Office: Box 522 Higginsville MO 64037

SPECTHRIE, MARY KLEINERMAN (MRS. SAMUEL W. SPECTHRIE), civic worker; b. Starokonstantinov, Russia; d. Frank and Clara (Bixgorn) Kleinerman; brought to U.S., 1921, naturalized, 1926; student Augustana Coll., 1927; tchrs. certificate Western Ill. U., 1929; m. Samuel W. Specthrie, June 14, 1931;children—Jared, Ida Rae (Mrs. Myron Laserson), Myra May (Mrs. David Wilson). Tchr. pub. schs., Rock Island, Ill., 1929-31. Pres., Esther and Phillip Bernick Meml. Aux., Hebrew Theol. Coll., 1940—; mem. Womens Scholarship Assn. Roosevelt U. Mem. Mizrachi Women Am. Mem. Hadassah, B'nai B'rith. Address: 3843 White Cloud Dr Skokie IL 60076

SPECTOR, BERTHA AWERBACH, judge; b. Russia, Sept. 28, 1918; d. Solomon and Anna (Rabinowitz) Awerbach; came to U.S., 1921, naturalized, 1942; J.D., U. Balt., 1939; m. Herman Spector, Jan. 7, 1943; children—Reeva (Mrs. Sheldon C. Simon), Sheila A., Stanley J., Sidney A. Admitted to Md. bar, 1942; practiced in Balt., 1946-58, 64-68; social worker Balt. Dept. Pub. Welfare, 1958-64; social worker dept. social services U. Md. Hosp., 1968-70; pub. welfare supr. Baltimore County Dept. Social Service, 1970-71; adminstrv. law judge Md. Dept. Social Services, Balt., 1971—. Home: 7300 Park Heights Av Baltimore MD 21208 Office: 1315 St Paul St Baltimore MD 21201

SPECTOR, JOAN (MRS. RALPH SPECTOR), pub. relations exec.; b. Mt. Vernon, N.Y., Oct. 19, 1929; d. Ben H. and Helen E. (Kest) Freedenberg; student Syracuse U., 1947-48, Columbia U., 1948-49; grad. Tobe Coburn Sch. of Fashion, 1949; m. Ralph Spector, Jan. 16, 1957; 1 dau., Andrea Jean. Editorial work Universal Pub. and Distbg. Corp., N.Y.C., 1951-56; owner, pres. Joan Spector/Pub. Relations Inc., Miami, Fla., 1957—. Mem. Nat. Womens Polit. Caucus, Women in Communications, Fla. Pub. Relations Assn., N. Miami C. of C. (dir. 1970-73). Home and office: 12472 Keystone Rd North Miami FL 33161

SPEECE, WINIFRED DOROTHY HUBLER (MRS. HARRY L. SPEECE), pub. relations exec.; b. Marshalltown, Ia., Sept. 1, 1917; d. Walter Trotter and Florence Dee (Pepper) Hubler; B.S., Drake U., 1939; m. Harry L. Speece, Jan. 3, 1945; children—Gretchen (Mrs. Frank Rich), Peter L., Todd Hubler, Dorothy (Mrs. Howard Shields). Receptionist Zaiser's Stationers, Des Moines, 1935-38; performer radio sta. KRNT, Des Moines; women's dir., broadcaster radio sta. WNAX, Yankton, S.D., 1939-73; dir. pub. relations and marketing First Dakota Nat. Bank, Yankton, 1973—. Bd. dirs. St. Mary's Sch. for Indian Girls, Springfield, S.D., 1968—. Recipient Lifeline of Am. award Grocery Mfrs. Am., 1959, 60, Eminent Citizens award East River Electric Co., 1973. Mem. Am. Women in Radio and Television, Am. Home Econs. Assn., Zeta Phi Eta. Club: Federated Women's (Yankton). Author: Your Neighbor Lady Book, 1941-72. Home: 314 E 15th St Yankton SD 57078 Office: 3d and Walnut Sts Yankton SD 57078

SPEED, CYNTHIA AGNES, educator; b. Santa Maria, Cal., Jan. 18, 1941; d. Carter Coleman and Lillian Jeanette (Freitas) Speed; B.A., Cal. State U., Sacramento, 1962; postgrad. U. Cal. at Berkeley, 1962-63; M.A. (fellow) Stanford, 1967; postgrad. U. Cal. at Davis, 1971-72. Teaching asst. U. Cal. at Berkeley, 1963; tchr. math. high sch. Sacramento, 1963-67, John F. Kennedy High Sch., Sacramento, 1967-69; lectr. math. Cal. State U., Sacramento, 1969; prof. math. Cal. State Poly. U., San Luis Obispo, 1969-71; tchr. math Santa Rosa (Cal.) Jr. Coll., 1973; math. instr. Mendocino Coll., Ukiah, Cal., 1973—. Tchr. computer programming to tchrs. and gifted students, 1967-69. Mem. Math. Assn. Am., Nat. Council Tchrs. Math., Cal. Math. Council Community Colls., Am. Assn. U. Women, Pi Mu Epsilon. Democrat. Roman Catholic (tchr. Confraternity Christian Doctrine 1964-71). Home: 1818 8th Av Sacramento CA 95818

SPEER, PAMELA CAROL, librarian; b. Little Rock, Ark., Oct. 16, 1942; d. William Dixon and Dixie Dean (Wyatt) Speer; B.Ed. in Edn., U. Mo., 1967, M.A. in Library Sci., 1973. Library supr. Berkeley (Mo.) Sch. Dist., 1967-69; librarian Mo. Inst. Psychiatry, St. Louis, 1968-69; head librarian Columbia (Mo.) Coll., 1970—. Ruth Tandy Royse grantee, 1969. Mem. Am., Mo. library assns., Mo. Sch. Library Assn., Zeta Tau Alpha. Home: 3400 Balboa No 8 Columbia MO 65201 Office: 8th and Rogers Columbia MO 65201

SPEETH, KATHLEEN RIORDAN, psychologist; b. N.Y.C., Feb. 12, 1937; d. John and Mavis (McIntosh) Riordan; student Barnard Coll., 1955-59; M.A., Columbia, 1963, Ph.D., 1967; m. Thomas Charles O'Keefe, Jr., 1954 (div. 1957); 1 dau., Deborah; m. 2d, Sheridan D. Speeth, 1961 (div. 1964); 1 dau., Lauren. Sr. systems analyst Basic Systems, Inc., N.Y.C., 1963-66; ednl. psychologist Xerox Edn., N.Y.C., 1966-68; materials mgr. Ind. Learning Systems, San Rafael, Cal., 1970-71; v.p. Individual Learning Systems, San Rafael, 1971-72; tchr. psychology Indian Valley Coll., 1971-72, Coll. Marin, 1971-72; sec., treas., mediation instr. SAT Inst., 1972—; tchr. Nyingma Inst., Berkeley, Cal., 1973—. Cons., Responsive Environments, Inc., Fort Lee, N.J., 1968-69, Ludi Edn., Inc., N.Y.C., 1968—, Ednl. Design, Inc., N.Y.C., 1968-73, Cybern Edn., Inc., N.Y.C., 1968-69, New Century, N.Y.C., 1969-72, Appleton Crofts, N.Y.C., 1969-72, various govt. agys. Barnard fellow, 1959. Mem. Am., Cal. psychol. assns., Nat. Soc. Programmed Instruction, Sigma Xi. Author: Supplement to Basic Psychology, 1971. Editor (with P. Ratoosh) Introductory Psychology, 1971. Contbr. chpt. to Spiritual Psychology, 1974. Home: 1199 Santa Fe Albany CA 94706 Office: SAT Inst 89 Kensington Rd Kensington CA 94707

SPEIDEN, HELEN ERLIK (MRS. ROBERT THOMAS SPEIDEN), artist; b. Cleve., Feb. 27, 1922; d. John and Mary (Shinko) Erlik; student Cleve. Mus. Sch. Art, 1934-38, Melbourne Sch. Art, Englewood, N.J. 1946, Workshop Sch. Comml. Art, 1947-48, Flower-Fifth Ave. Sch. Nursing, 1950-51; m. Robert Thomas Speiden, Jan. 19, 1957. Apprentice to Alfred Feinberg, med. artist, N.Y.C., 1953-58; asst. in art prodn. depts. Am. Book Co., N.Y.C., 1947, Alfred A. Knopf, book pubs., N.Y.C., 1946, Mus. Natural History, N.Y.C., 1949-50, A.M. Sneider Advt., N.Y.C., 1948-49, Designers 3, N.Y.C., 1951-53; free-lance med. artist, 1953—. Mem. Assn. Med. Illustrators. Club: Cranford Dramatic. Illustrator: Animal Structure and Function (by D.R. Griffin), 1962; Microbial Life (by W.R. Sistrom), 1962; The Living Plant (by P.M. Ray), 1963; Life Goes On (by Burnett, Clemensen, Hoyman), 1959; Exploring Biology (by Ella Thea Smith, 5th edit., 1959; Your Health and Safety (by Clemenson, Lawrence, Horman, LaPorte), 1958; Experiences in Biology (by Merholt), 1960; Radiographic Atlas of the Human Skull (by G.S. Schwarz and C.R. Golthamer), 1966; Physical Diagnosis (by Hochstein and Rubin), 1964. Address: 1216 Denmark Rd Plainfield NJ 07062

SPEIGHT, VELMA RUTH, educator; b. Snow Hill, N.C., Nov. 18, 1932; d. John Thomas and Mable L. (Edwards) Speight; B.S., Agrl. and Tech. State U., 1953; M.Ed. in Guidance, U. Md., 1965; postgrad. Am. U., Morgan State Coll., U. Md., Va. State Coll., Boston U., U. Md.; 1 dau., Trevillian Chineta Kennedy. Tchr. math and French, Kennard High Sch., Centreville, Md., 1954-60, counselor, 1960-66, adminstr. asst., 1964-66; counselor Queen Anne's County Hgh Sch., Centreville, 1966-68; curriculum resource specialist, family life-sex edn. Title III Project for Queen Anne's, Talbot, Caroline and Kent Counties 1969; adv. specialist civil rights Md. Dept. Edn., Balt., 1969; dir. equal opportunity recruitment program U. Md., College Park, 1971; specialist in guidance Md. Dept. Edn., Balt., 1972—, also mem. Human Relations Com., Career Edn. Task Force. Adj. prof. Loyola Coll., Balt., 1973; ednl. cons. N.A.A.C.P. Active various community drives; organizer Youth for Communication not Confrontation, Centreville, 1963, chmn., 1963-68; pres. Community Action Group, 1968; pres. Kent-Queen Anne's-Talbot Area Council, 1970—; chmn. state edn. com. N.A.A.C.P., 1971-72, 1st v.p. Queen Anne's County br., 1971-72; mem. Negro History Commn. Md.; chmn. Nat. Alumni Recruitment Com. NSF grantee, 1957-58, 59, Nat. Def. Edn. Act grantee, 1963, Gen. Electric Co. fellow, 1968. Mem. Am., Md. (chmn. policy com. 1967-69, exec. com. 1973), Upper Shore (sec. 1964-65, publicity com. 1966-68) personnel and guidance assns., N.E.A., Md. State Tchrs. Assn., Queen Anne's County Edn. Assn. (pres. 1965-66), Assn. Classroom Tchrs., Eastern Shore Profl. Group, Am. Assn. Sex Educators and Counselors, Delmarva Alumni Assn. A. and T. State U. (pres. 1964-65). N.A.A.C.P., Alpha Kappa Mu, Pi Delta Phi, Alpha Kappa Alpha. Democrat. Episcopalian. Home: 5373 Brookway Columbia MD 21044 Office: Friendship Internat Airport Baltimore MD 21240

SPEIRS, ANNE BONNELL, educator; b. Phila., July 26, 1923; d. Harold Frederic and Emily (Young) Speirs; student U. Del., 1941-42; B.A., U. Pa., 1945, M.S., 1950, postgrad., 1959—. Personnel dir. Franklin Square Hosp., Balt., 1945-46; sales Hutzler Bros. Co., Balt., 1946-47; asst. to dean of women U. Pa., Phila., 1947-53, asst. dean of women, 1953-54, vice dean of women, 1954-65, acting dean of women, 1954-55; v.p., sec. Coll. Entrance Exam. Bd., N.Y.C., 1965—. Mem. budget sect. Boys Club, 1952-58, Nat. Health Agys., 1958-65, United Fund, 1952-65; mem. bd. Phila. Camden Social Service Exchange, 1960-65, U. Pa. Assn. Alumnae, 1952-65, rec. sec., 1954-58, chmn. nominating com., 1960-62; mem. Episcopal com. Christian Assn. of U. Pa., 1959-65. Mem. Nat. (conv. local arrangements chmn. 1960, conv. program chmn. 1966, chmn. fellowship com. 1972), Pa. (chmn. by-laws and handbook com. 1954-57, chmn. conv. program com. 1962, 2d v.p. 1962-64) assns. women deans and counselors, Am. Assn. U. Women, Kappa Kappa Gamma, Pi Lambda Theta. Episcopalian (vestrywoman). Home: 240 W Ivy Lane Englewood NJ 07631 Office: 888 7th Av New York City NY 10019

SPEIRS, DORIS HUESTIS (MRS. J. MURRAY SPEIRS), artist, author; b. Toronto, Ont., Can.; d. Archibald Morrison and Florence Gooderham (Hamilton) Huestis; student Toronto Model Sch., 1900-02, Havergal Ladies Coll., 1902-15, U. Toronto, 1914-16, U. Ill., 1940-41; m. Wilfrid Gordon Mills, May 2, 1916 (div. June 1939); children—Adele Barbara (Mrs. Norman J. Hearn), Iris Florence (Mrs. John Leslie Weir); m. 2d, John Murray Speirs, Aug. 1, 1941. Exhibited one-man shows studio J.E.H. MacDonald, Toronto, 1925, Prouts Neck, Me., 1929, Jerrold Morris Gallery, Toronto, 1970, Toronto Heliconian Club, 1970, Robert McLaughlin Gallery, Oshawa, Ont., 1971; exhibited in group shows Art Gallery of Toronto, Bklyn. Mus. Art, Albright Art Gallery, others; represented in permanent collections Nat. Mus. Can., Art Gallery Ont., McMichael Canadian Collection, Kleinburg, Ont. Mem. Royal Ont. Mus., Art Gallery Ont., Fedn. Ont. Naturalists, Am., Brit. ornithologists' unions, Wilson Ornithol. Soc., World Federalists Can., Theta Beta Sigma. Clubs: Hamilton Nature, Heliconian of Toronto, Margaret Nice Ornithological. Author: Exercise for Psyche, 1922-72, 1973. Translator: The Forehead's Lyre (poems from Swedish of Lars von Haartman), 1962; Life History of the Evening Grosbeak, 1968. Contbr. poems, essays to mags., profl. jours. Home: Cobble Hill 1815 Altona Rd Pickering ON Canada

SPELLER, MAXINE ELLIOTT WATKINS (MRS. ROBERT E. B. SPELLER), book publisher; b. Roseboro, N.C., Oct. 25, 1906; d. Daniel Anderson and Margaret Louise (Patterson) Watkins; student Louisburg Jr. Coll., 1926; A.B., Duke U., 1932; m. Robert E. B. Speller, 1935; children—Robert E. B., Jon Patterson. Designer, Fashion Form Mfg. Corp., 1938-55; sec.-treas. Robert Speller & Sons, pub., Inc., 1955—; treas. East Europe Pub. Co., 1970—. Trustee Hough's Encyclopedia of Am. Woods Found. Patentee in field of design. Home: 115 E 9th St New York City NY 10003 Office: 10 E 23d St New York City NY 10010

SPENCE, HOLLY DEE (MRS. DONALD L. FERGUSON), editor; b. Pender, Neb., Jan. 24, 1943; d. Harold Leroy and Stella Leone (Lucier) Spence; B.A., U. Neb., 1965; m. Donald L. Ferguson, Dec. 19, 1968. Entertainment editor, critic, feature writer Lincoln (Neb.) Evening Jour. and Sunday Jour. and Star, 1965—. Program com. adviser YMCA-YWCA City Wide, 1967; mem. West Central Area Council YMCA, 1968; adviser Youth in Govt., 1968; adviser Neb. Human Resources Research Found., 1968-69; membership chmn. Lincoln (Neb.) Community Concert, 1968-69; mem. ad hoc com. on music Lincoln Pub. Schs., 1972. Del. county conv. Democratic party, 1971-72, alternate to state conv., 1971-72. Recipient writing awards Neb. Press Women, 1970-73, 3d pl. award Nat. Fedn. Press Women, 1970. Mem. Nat. Fedn. Press Women, 1970. Mem. Nat. Fedn. Press Women, Neb. Press Women, Omaha Press Club, Neb. Art Assn., Sigma Delta Chi, Alpha Chi Omega. Home: 7611 Englewood Dr Lincoln NE 68510 Office: 926 P St Lincoln NE 68501

SPENCE, JANET BLAKE CONLEY (MRS. ALEXANDER PYOTT SPENCE), civic worker; b. Upper Montclair, N.J., Aug. 17, 1915; d. Walter Abbott and Ethel Maud (Blake) Conley; grad. Masters Sch., 1933; student Vassar Coll., 1933-35; certificate Katharine Gibbs Sch., 1936; m. Alexander Pyott Spence, June 10, 1939; children—Janet Spence Kerr), Robert Moray, Richard Taylor. Active Jr. League, Neighborhood House, A.R.C., Girl Scouts U.S.A.; active various community drives; chmn. Darien (Conn.) Assembly, 1955-56; sec., chmn. Wilton Jr. Assembly, 1961-63; subscription chmn. Candlelight Concerts Wilton, Conn., 1963-65; rec. sec. Pub. Health Nursing Assn. Wilton Bd., 1964-67; corr., rec. sec. Royle Sch. Bd., Darien, 1952-55; mem. Washington Valley Community Assn., 1973—; vol. N.J. Symphony Orch., 1974—. Mem. Vassar (council rep. from Class of '37 1973—), Dobbs alumnae assns. Conglist. Home: Washington Valley Rd Morristown NJ 07960

SPENCE, ROANN ETHEL, occupational therapist; b. Washington, Dec. 3, 1940; d. Liter Estill and Ethel May (Woody) Spence; student U. Md., Munich br., 1960-61; B.S., U. Ida., 1964; certificate in Occupational Therapy, Colo. State U., 1967. Dir. occupational therapy Woodrow Wilson Rehab. Center, Fishersville, Va., 1967—. Program dir. Girls Camp program, waterfront dir. Family Camp, Boise (Ida.) YMCA, summers 1962-65. Mem. Am. Occupational Therapy Assn., Nat. Wildlife Fedn., Fellowship of the Crown. Home: Route 1 Box L42 Lyndhurst VA 22952 Office: Occupational Therapy Dept Woodrow Wilson Rehab Center Fishersville VA 22939

SPENCER, CATHERINE LLEWELLYN VAN WART (MRS. FREDERICK ALBERT SPENCER), rancher, civic worker; b. Balt., Nov. 19, 1914; d. Roy McLean and May Llewellyn (Jones) Van Wart; student Holmby Jr. Coll., 1931-32, U. Cal. at Los Angeles, 1932-34; m. John Woods Norcross, May 15, 1940 (div. 1944); m. 2d, Frederick Albert Spencer, June 1947; 1 son, F.A. Phineas. Sec., Inter-Am. Def. Bd., Washington, 1942-43; vol. translator Am. Internat. Red Cross, Washington, 1944-47; rancher, Descanso, Cal., 1949—. Case adv. bd. Travelers Aid, Los Angeles, 1936-37; vol. Childrens Hosp., Los Angeles, 1935-36, Family Welfare, Los Angeles, 1936-38; mem. Descanso Dist. grazing adv. bd. San Diego County Grazing Adv. Bd., 1965—. Bd. dirs. El Cajon Valley Research Found., San Diego Farm Bur., Del Mar Thoroughbred Club. Mem. Los Angeles Assistance League, Los Angeles Jr. League, San Diego County Cattlemens Assn., Cal. Thoroughbred Breeders Assn., Am. Nat. Cattlemens Assn., Kappa Alpha Theta. Club: Sulgrave (Washington). Home: Rancho Samataguma Box 407 Descanso CA 92016

SPENCER, DOROTHY M., speech and hearing therapist, educator; b. Port Arthur, Tex., Mar. 13, 1924; d. Walter Morgan and Florence (Morris) Spencer; B.S., Wayne State U., 1945; M.A., U. Mich., 1953; m. Paul J. Garry, Sept. 30, 1964. Speech therapist, directing tchr. Schs. for Orthopedically Handicapped, Detroit Pub. Schs., 1945-61; speech therapist U. Mich. Speech and Hearing Clinic, 1952-53, maj. therapist U. Mich. Speech Camp, Northport, summers 1947-53, Detroit Pub. Schs. Pre-Sch. Clinic, 1953-55; instr. night sch. Wayne State U., 1957-58; vocational rehab. speech therapist pvt. practice, Detroit, 1948-59; dir. Sunnyside Speech and Hearing Center, Port Arthur, 1961-64; exec. dir. Thomas W. Hughen Center for Crippled Children and Adults, Port Arthur, 1964—. Mem. Jefferson County Commn. to Hire Handicapped; vol. Dearborn (Mich.) VA Hosp., summer 1955; mem. cons. bd. Jefferson County Assn. for Parents Retarded Children, 1963; mem. Gov.'s Commn. to Study Needs of Retarded, 1965-66. Mem. Am. Speech and Hearing Assn., Council for Exceptional Children, Nat. Rehab. Assn., Nat., Tex., Port Arthur socs. for crippled children and adults, Tex. State Tchrs. Assn., Delta Gamma Chi, Sigma Alpha Epsilon. Episcopalian (Sunday sch. tchr. physically handicapped 1967). Home: 300 Emory Lane Port Arthur TX 77640 Office: 3620 28th St Port Arthur TX 77640

SPENCER, ELIZABETH FRANCES, educator; b. Edina, Mo., Apr. 4, 1922; d. Harry Francis and Ella (Linkenfelder) Spencer; student Quincy Coll., 1939-40; B.S., N.E. Mo. State Tchrs. Coll., 1945; M.S., U. Mo., 1950; Ed.D., U. Ill., 1962. Tchr. rural sch., Knox County, Mo., 1941-43; tchr. elementary sch., Hannibal, Mo., 1944-49, Quincy, Ill., 1949-51; tchr. class for educable mentally retarded, Quincy, Ill., 1951-60; mem. faculty Ball State U., Muncie, Ind., 1962—, prof., chmn. dept. spl. edn., 1967—. Cons. pub. schs., Bremen, Daleville, Elkhart, Muncie, New Castle, Rochester, Selma, Ind., 1962-69; cons. Muscatatuck State Sch., 1963-64, Fort Wayne State Sch., 1968-69. Mem. bd. Delaware County Assn. Retarded Children, 1969—, Delaware County Child Guidance Clinic, 1970—; mem. Ind. legislative com. to study multiple handicapped, 1968-69; mem. Ind. Spl. Edn. Adv. Com. on Mental Retardation, 1964-65. Recipient scholarship Delta Kappa Gamma, 1960, fellowship U.S. Office Edn., 1960-62. Mem. Am. Assn. Retarded Children, Council Exceptional Children (pres. Ind. fedn. 1966-67, nat. gov. 1970-73), Nat. Soc. Study Edn., Nat. Assn. for Retarded Children, Am. Assn. Mental Deficiency, Delta Kappa Gamma. Home: 2208 Yorkshire Dr Muncie IN 47304

SPENCER, JEAN AILEEN, gastroenterologist, gastrointestinal endoscopist; b. Cape Girardeau, Mo., May 25, 1925; d. Edwin Rollin and Adella Aileen (Hunter) Spencer; A.B. (Danforth fellow), U. Ill., 1946; M.D. U. Chgo., 1950; M.Sc., U. Minn., 1955. Intern, Bridgeport (Conn.) Hosp., 1950-51; resident in internal medicine Mayo Found., Rochester, Minn., 1952-55; instr. U. Chgo., 1955-56, asst. prof. internal medicine, 1956-63; practice medicine specializing in gastroenterology, Chgo., 1963-69, specializing in gastroenterology and gastrointestinal endoscopy, Arcadia, Cal., 1970-73; asst. clin. prof. internal medicine U. Cal. at Los Angeles, 1971—. Chgo. adviser Mayo Clinic, 1960-69; examiner Minn. Mining & Mills Co., 1964-69, 73—; multiple life ins. examiner, 1970—; cons. social security, 1969—; founder, dir. Walter L. Palmer vis. professorship U. Chgo., 1960-69, mem. council U. Chgo. 1964-69. Schweppe grantee, 1956, NIH grantee, 1959-63, Upjohn grantee, 1963-69, Squibb grantee, 1957; Mayo Found. fellow. Diplomate Am. Bd. Internal Medicine. Fellow A.C.P., Pan Am. Assn. Internal Medicine and Gastroenterology; mem. Am. Gastroenterol. Assn., Am. Soc. for Gastrointestinal Endoscopists, Am. Assn. for Study Liver Diseases, Am. Geriatrics Assn., A.M.A., Cal., Los Angeles County med. assns., Chgo. Inst. Medicine, So. Cal. Assn. Gastroenterology, Los Angeles Soc. Internal Medicine, So. Cal. Soc. Gastrointestinal Endoscopy, Sigma Xi, Alpha Lambda Pi, Alpha Pi Delta, Alpha Omicron Pi. Home: 385 S Los Robles St Pasadena CA 91101 Office: Foley Medical Group Inc 4220 W 3d St Los Angeles CA 90020

SPENCER, JEAN CLINTON BALLARD (MRS. JAMES ABNER SPENCER), editor, information specialist; b. Natchez, Miss.; d. James Clinton and Saluda (Bowman) Ballard; B.A., State U. Ia., 1934; M.S. in Journalism, Northwestern U., 1952; postgrad. U. Tex., 1934; m. James Abner Spencer, May 12, 1962. With Ala. State Tax Commn., Montgomery, 1935-36; with Ala. Dept. Pub. Welfare (name changed to State Dept. Pensions and Security, 1955), Montgomery, 1936—, information specialist, 1939-71, pub. information officer, 1971—. Mem. Ala. Conf. Social Work (sec. 1953, publicity chmn. 1954—), Am. Pub. Welfare Assn. (state membership chmn. 1966—, sec. div. pub. information office 1969—, Internat., So., Montgomery (sec. 1965-66, treas. 1972—) assns. bus. communicators, Ala. Conf. Child Care (publicity chmn. 1969—), U.D.C., Phi Beta Kappa, Chi Omega, Theta Sigma Phi. Episcopalian. Home: 1451 Marlowe Dr Montgomery AL 36111 Office: 807 Union Bank Bldg Montgomery AL 36104

SPENCER, JEAN MARIE MORGAN (MRS. W. BRUCE SPENCER), geologist, educator, editor; b. Ft. Sam Houston, Tex., Mar. 3, 1927; d. John Ross and Marie A. (LaRiviere) Morgan; student John Sealy Coll. Nursing, 1944-45; B.S. cum laude in Geology, Baylor U., 1961, M.S. in Geology, 1964; m. W. Bruce Spencer, Sept. 29, 1945; children—John Morgan, Robert Bruce. Research asso. dept. geology Baylor U., Waco, Tex., 1966-68, instr. dept. geology, 1968-71, asst. prof., 1971—, editor Baylor Geol. Studies Bull., 1966—. Fellow Tex. Acad. Sci. (v.p. earth sci. 1972); mem. Assn. Earth Sci. Editors (charter), Environmental Geochemistry and Health Soc. (charter), Nat. Assn. Geology Tchrs. (editor Tex. sect. 1971, sec.-treas. 1972, v.p. 1973, pres. 1974), A.A.A.S., Baylor Geol. Soc., Alpha Chi. Methodist (steward 1967-69). Author: Geological Factors Controlling Mutation and Evolution—A Review, 1964; Surface Waters of Waco, 1966; Geological Influence on Regional Health Problems 1970; Geology, Health and Phosphorus, 1974. Co-editor Environmental Phosphorus Handbook, 1973. Home: 4113 Pine Av Waco TX 76710

SPENCER, JOANN ROSS, educator; b. Morgantown, W.Va., Jan. 18, 1950; d. John David Ross and Marjorie Ann (White) Spencer; student Agnes Scott Coll., 1967-68; B.F.A., W.Va. U., 1971; M.F.A., U. Ga., 1973. Tchr., Athens (Ga.) Creative Theatre, 1971-73, dir. children's plays, asst. dir. Playhouse of Possibilities, 1971; dir. puppet mobile W.Va. U., Morgantown, 1973-74, creator, dir. The Stage Shoppe, 1973—. Dir. Children's Theatre, Mars Hill (N.C.) Coll., summer 1972. Mem. Am. Theatre Assn., Children's Theatre Assn., Puppeteers of Am., Nat. Collegiate Players, Chimes, Mortar Bd. Author adult and children's plays produced by Athens (Ga.) Creative Theatre, 1971-73. Home: 621 Grand St Morgantown WV 26505

SPENCER, LELA MAUD STULTING, educator, civic worker; b. Gonzales, Tex., Feb. 20, 1900; d. Willie Christopher and Alice Maye (Dismukes) Stulting; B.S., S.W. Tex. State U., 1926; postgrad. Colo. State U., 1927; M.Ed., U. Houston, 1952; m. Bryan Spencer, June 6, 1930; children—Bryan Stulting, Patricia Lee. Tchr. S.W. Tex. State U., San Marcos, 1925; tchr. Galveston (Tex.) Ind. Sch. Dist., 1942-48. Pres. Galveston Classroom Tchrs. Assn., 1948-50, 63-66. Mem. Galveston Mayor's Com. Sr. Citizens; participant White House Conf. on Aging; rep. Mission Home Aux., home for unwed mothers and mentally retarded, 1974; active A.R.C. Named Woman of Year Am. Assn. U. Women, 1963; recipient 20 year pin A.R.C. Mem. Galveston Ret. Tchrs. Assn. (pres. 1970-73, chmn. community affairs 1973), Tex. Ret. Tchrs. (co-chmn. pub. relations com. 1972, regional chmn. 1973), Alpha Delta Kappa. Methodist (dir. youth activities 1938-53). Mem. Order Eastern Star. Home: 1305 Houston Dr West La Marque TX 77568

SPENCER, LILA, pub. relations exec.; b. Murphysboro, Ill., Apr. 24, 1928; d. Merwin K. and Villa (Gates) Spencer; B.S., U. Ill., 1949. Tchr. home econs., Mt. Vernon, Ill. and Plant City, Fla.; home economist Dairy Council of St. Louis, 1949-52; with home econs. dept. Pet, Inc., St. Louis, 1953-64, product publicist, pub. relations dept., 1964-68, dir. pub. relations, 1968—. Publicity chmn. Common Cause-St. Louis Steering Com., 1970—; mem. pub. relations adv. com. Cancer Research Center Fund Campaign, 1972, St. Louis Regional Commerce and Growth Assn., 1972. Mem. Pub. Relations Soc. Am., Am. Home Econs. Assn., Home Economists in Bus. Author: Exciting Careers for Home Economists, 1967. Home: 4400 Lindell St St Louis MO 63108 Office: 400 S 4th St St Louis MO 63166

SPENCER, LORRAINE BARNEY, biologist; b. Odgen, N.Y., Jan. 26, 1924; d. Elmer Cecil and Edna Justine (Zinter) Barney; B.S. (Dana scholar), Guilford Coll., 1966; M.A. (Univ. scholar), Wake Forest U., 1970, Ph.D. (Research fellow), 1973; m. Richard Earl Spencer, Sept. 12, 1942 (div. 1961); children—Linda, Susan S. Foushee, Deborah (Mrs. Curtis L. Mitchell), Nancy (Mrs. Charles L. Hertlein). Instr. biology lab. Wake Forest U., Winston Salem, N.C., 1968-72, research fellow, 1972-73; biol. researcher, Greensboro, N.C., 1973—; adj. prof. Guilford Coll., Greensboro, 1974; asst. prof. St. Augustine's Coll., Raleigh, N.C., 1974—. Mem. So. Appalachian Bot. Club, Soc. Econ. Botany, Phycol. Soc. Am., N.C. Acad. Sci., Internat. Assn. Plant Taxonomy, Bot. Soc. Am., Assn. S.E. Biologists, A.A.A.S., Am. Inst. Biol. Scis., Sigma Xi. Contbr. articles to profl. jours. Home: 104 Batchelor Dr Greensboro NC 27410 Office: Box 554 Dept Biology St Augustine's Coll Raleigh NC 27611

SPENCER, MADELINE ELLEN WHITE, journalist; b. Chickasha, Okla., Feb. 11, 1907; d. James Edward and Myrtle Pearl (Plateau) White; grad. Okla. Presbyn. Coll., 1925; m. John F. Spencer, Oct. 13, 1930 (dec. Jan. 1971); 1 dau., Patricia (Mrs. Joe Webb). Dental asst., Rogers, Ark., 1953-60; proof reader Rogers (Ark.) Daily and Sunday News, 1960-61, soc. editor, 1960-63, woman's editor, 1963—. Recipient 1st pl. for Woman Talk column Ark. Press Conf., 1969. Mem. Nat. League Am. Pen Women (pres. N.W. Ark. br. 1970-72, pres. Ark. 1974—), League Women Voters, Beaver Lake Bus. and Profl. Women's Club. Home: 117 S 115th St Rogers AR 72756 Office: 313 S 2d St Rogers AR 72756

SPENCER, MARY JANE (MRS. JOHN ROBERT SPENCER), newspaperwoman; b. Garrett, Ind., Aug. 2, 1926; d. Rollie Hanlon and Fleta May (Schumaker) Crothers; A.B., U. Toledo, 1948; student Am. Press Inst., 1962; m. John Robert Spencer, Apr. 19, 1949. Reporter The Blade, newspaper, Toledo, O., 1948-60; fashion editor, 1960-68, asst. women's news editor, 1960-63, women's news editor, 1963-68, Sunday mag. editor, 1968-71, Sunday editor, 1971—. Recipient Nat. Headliner award, 1970; named Bus. Woman of Yr., Toledo Area Bus. and Profl. Women, 1967. Mem. Ohio Newspaper Women's Assn., Am. Assn. Sunday and Feature Editors, Toledo Mus. Art, Women in Communication, Chi Omega. Clubs: Zonta (Toledo), Press Toledo. Home: 4015 N Lockwood Toledo OH 43612 Office: 541 Superior Toledo OH 43660

SPENCER, MARY JOSEPHINE MASON (MRS. DONALD JAMES SPENCER), physician; b. Joliet, Ill., Oct. 19, 1936; d. Ray Miller and Marjorie Elizabeth (Tedens) Mason; B.A., U. Colo., 1958; postgrad. U. Tex. Med. Br., 1958-60; M.D., U. Cal. at Los Angeles, 1964; m. Donald James Spencer, June 3, 1960; children—Kenneth, Marjorie, Katherine. Intern Los Angeles County Gen. Hosp., 1964-65; health officer Los Angeles County Health Dept., 1965-66; gen. practice medicine So. Cal. Kaiser Permanente Group, Los Angeles, 1966-69; resident pediatrics Harbor Gen. Hosp., U. Cal. Hosp., Los Angeles, 1969-71; practice medicine specializing in pediatrics, Los Angeles, 1971—; mem. staff U. Cal. at Los Angeles, clin. instr. pediatrics, 1971-73, acting dir. pediatric outpatient dept., 1973, fellow pediatric infectious disease, 1973—. Mem. Los Angeles County Pediatric Soc. Episcopalian. Home: 615 Palisades Av Santa Monica CA 90402 Office: 5830 Overhill Dr Los Angeles CA 90043 also 11633 Hawthorne Blvd Los Angeles

SPENCER, MARY LOUISE BRADEN (MRS. WILLIAM GREGORY SPENCER), sch. adminstr.; b. Monette, Ark., Oct. 21, 1919; d. Robert David and Zephia Louise (Watkins) Braden; student Ark. State U., 1936-38; B.A., U. Ark., 1940, M.Ed., 1965, Ed.D., 1970; m. William Gregory Spencer, Apr. 1, 1942; children—Cynthia (Mrs. James A. Henderson), William Gregory. Dir. Polk County Dept. Pub. Welfare, Mena, Ark., 1965-67; dean of women Ark. Poly. Coll., Russellville, 1969-73; djr. Rich Mountain Vocational-Tech. Sch., Dept. Edn., Mena, Ark., 1973—. Mem. Gov.'s Adv. Com. on Drug Abuse Edn., 1970-71, Gov.'s Commn. on Status of Women, 1971—, Gov.'s Ednl. Task Force, 1973—. Bd. dirs. Mena Pub. Schs., 1959-67. Mem. Am. (senator 1973, mem. br. council So. region 1972—), Ark. (pres. 1973-74) personnel and guidance assns., Ark. Assn. U. Women (dir. 1972-73), Ark. Sch. Bds. Assn. (hon. life mem., pres. 1965-66), Ark. Assn. Women Deans and Counselors (pres. 1971-73), P.E.O., Delta Gamma. Methodist (mem. ofcl. bd. 1959-67). Home: PO Box 149 Mena AR 71953 Office: Rich Mountain Vocational-Technical School PO Box 69 Mena AR 71953

SPENCER, MARY LOUISE WAKEFIELD (MRS. HARRY CHADWICK SPENCER), civic worker; b. St. Louis; d. Ralph and Mary C. (Black) Wakefield; A.B., Northwestern U., 1930; M.A., U. Chgo., 1932; m. Harry Chadwick Spencer, May 26, 1935; children—Mary Grace (Mrs. James Robert Lyman, Jr.), Ralph Wakefield. Circle leader Woman's Soc. Christian Service, Calvary Meth. Ch., Nashville, 1954-56, pres., 1956-58, v.p., 1970-72, mem. ch. adminstrv. bd., 1967-71, vice chmn. commn. on missions, 1968-70, chmn. ecumenical affairs com., 1973—, chmn. coop. com. Hillsboro Rd. chs., 1973—; pres. United Ch. Women Nashville and Davidson County, 1959-61, chmn. nominating com., 1965-67; v.p. Nashville Assn. Chs., 1959-61; pub. relations chmn. United Ch. Women Tenn., 1958-61, pres., 1962-65, constn., by-laws chmn., 1965-70, area chmn. Middle Tenn., 1970-73, editor Tidings, state paper, 1973—; v.p. Tenn. Council Chs., 1962-65; lead tchr. ch. sch., 1955—. Vol. tchr. remedial reading program Buena Vista Sch., 1964-65, enrichment program for tchrs. Carter Lawrence Sch., 1965-71; mem. Nashville Mental Health Assn., Nashville Community Relations Council, Tenn. Council on Human Relations, Internat. Christian U. Tokyo Women's Planning Com., Goodwill Industries Aux., Scarritt Aid (nominating chmn. 1964, pres. 1968-70), Wesley Found. Aid; chmn. personnel com. Wesley House Centers Bd., 1968-70; active YWCA. Bd. dirs. Bethlehem Center, sec. 1963-67, chmn. nominating com. 1968-70; Mem. UN Assn. U.S. (state bd. 1964-65), UN Assn. Nashville, Tenn. Bot. Gardens and Fine Arts Center, Northwestern U. Alumni Assn., P.E.O. (pres. 1965-67, historian 1968-69, rec. sec. 1973-74), World Fedn. Meth. Women (del. 1966, 72), Alpha Omicron Pi. Club: Nashville Woman's (dir. home dept. 1969-71, pres. 1971-73, hospitality chmn. 1973—). Contbr. to religious publs. Home: PO Box 15063 610 Westview Av Nashville TN 37215

SPENCER, MARY MILLER, civic worker, club woman; b. Comanche, Tex., May 25, 1924; d. Aaron Gaynor and Alma (Grissom) Miller; B.S., North Tex. State U., 1943. 1 dau., Mara Lynn. Cafeteria dir. Mercedes (Tex.) Pub. Schs., 1943-46; home economist coordinator All-Orange Dessert Contest, Fla. Citrus Commn., Lakeland, 1959-62, 64. Tchr. purchasing sch. lunch dept. Fla. Dept. Edn., 1960. Clothing judge Polk County (Fla.) Youth Fair, 1951-68, Polk County Federated Women's Clubs, 1964-66; pres. Dixieland Elementary Sch. P.T.A., 1955-57, Polk County Council P.T.A.'s, 1958-60, dist. 7. Fla. Congress Parents and Tchrs., 1961-63; chmn. pub. edn. com. Polk County unit Am. Cancer Soc., 1959-60, mem. bd. dirs., 1962—; charter mem., bd. dirs. Lakeland YMCA; sec. Greater Lakeland Community Nursing Council, 1965—; trustee, vice chmn. Polk County Eye Clinic, Inc., 1962-64, pres., 1964—; pub. relations chmn. Fla. Congress Parents and Tchrs., 1962-66; bd. dirs. Polk County Scholarship and Loan Fund, 1962—; mem. exec. com. West Polk County (Fla.) Community Welfare Council, 1960-62, 65-68; mem. budget and audit com. Greater Lakeland United Fund, 1960-62, bd. dirs., 1967-70, residential chmn. fund drive, 1968; mem. adv. bd. Polk County Juvenile and Domestic Relations Ct., 1960-69; worker children's services Dist. II, Unit 3, Div. Family Services, Dept. Health and Rehab. Services, State Fla., 1969-70, social worker region 7, Unit 62, 1970-72, Unit 83, 1972—. Mem. exec. com. Suncoast Health Council, 1968-71; mem. Polk County Home Econs. Adv. Com., 1965-71; sec. bd. dirs. Fla. West Coast Ednl. Television, 1960—. Mem. Fla. Congress Parents and Tchrs. (hon. life), Am. Assn. U. Women (pres. Lakeland br. 1960-61), Polk County Mental Health Assn., Fla. Health and Welfare Council, N. Tex. State U. Alumni Assn. Democrat. Methodist. Mem. Order Eastern Star. Office: PO Box 2161 Lakeland FL 33803 Home: 535 W Beacon Rd Lakeland FL 33803

SPENCER, ROSEMARY E. HANNON, govt. ofcl.; b. Neb., Nov. 20, 1920. Sec. to exec. v.p. Title Guaranty Co., 1940-41; sec. War Dept., Detroit, Cin., 1941-46; with U.S. Mission to UN, 1946—, sec. to U.S. rep. to UN disarmament com., 1955, sec. to U.S. rep. to UN, 1956-62, chief protocol, 1962—. Office: US Mission to UN 799 UN Plaza New York City NY 10017

SPENCER, SALLY LOUISE, educator; b. Wilkinsburg, Pa., Apr. 1, 1931; d. Herbert Lincoln and Mildred (Pollard) Spencer; A.B. cum laude in English and History, Bucknell U., 1953; certificate Katharine Gibbs Sch., 1954; postgrad. Glassboro State Tchrs. Coll., 1955-56, Stroudsburg State Tchrs. Coll., 1956, Wilkes Coll., 1956, Tchrs. Coll., Columbia, 1957-58; M.A. in Student Personnel Adminstrn., 1958; postgrad. N.Y.U., 1960—; m. David L. Hurwitz. Sec., asst. to pub. relations dir. Conv. and Visitors Bur., Phila. C. of C., 1954-55; tchr. English and history Pennsauken (N.J.) Jr. High Sch., 1955-57; sec. Tchrs. Coll., Columbia, 1957-58; counselor Cornell U., Ithaca, N.Y., 1958-59; dean of women, asst. dean of students So. Conn. State Coll., New Haven, 1956-63, asst. prof. history, asst. to pres., 1965—. Mem. Am. Hist. Assn., Orgn. Am. Historians, Am. Acad. Polit. and Social Scis., Am. Assn. U. Profs., Modern Lang. Assn., Nat. Assn. Women Deans and Counselors, Am., Conn. (exec. bd. 1962-63), New Haven (pres. 1962-63) personnel and guidance assns., Am. Assn. U. Women, North Castle Hist. Soc. (treas.), Middle Patent Assn. (v.p.), League of Women Voters, Mortar Bd., New Haven Colony Hist. Soc., Phi Beta Kappa, Pi Delta Epsilon, Sigma Tau Delta, Phi Alpha Theta, Delta Delta Delta. Presbyn. Home: Hickory Kingdom Rd Bedford NY 10506 Office: So Conn State Coll New Haven CT 06515

SPENCER, SARA, pub.; b. Louisville, Feb. 18, 1908; d. Joseph and Julia (Vaughan) Spencer; B.A., Vassar Coll., 1930; postgrad. summers Emerson Coll., 1931, Am. Acad. Dramatic Arts, 1932; m. Clarence A. Campbell, May 14, 1943. Editor, Anchorage Press, Inc. (Ky.), 1935—, pres., 1960—. Chmn., Children's Theatre Found., Inc., 1965—. Recipient Thanksgiving award Clarke Coll., Dubuque, Ia., 1966; Davis award Southeastern Theatre Conf., 1965. Fellow Am. Theatre Assn.; mem. Internat. Children's Theatre Assn. (exec. council 1964-66, hon. chmn. U.S. Centre 1972—), Jr. League Louisville. Club: Pendennis (Louisville). Home: Cloverlot Anchorage KY 40223

SPENCER, VAINO HASSAN, judge; b. Los Angeles, July 22, 1920; d. Abdul and Nona (Taylor) Hassan; grad. summa cum laude, Los Angeles City Coll., 1949; LL.B., Southwestern Sch. Law, 1952; m. Lorenzo Spencer, Oct. 15, 1949 (div. 1967). Gen. real estate bus., Los Angeles, 1938-47; admitted to Cal. bar, 1952; pvt. law practice, Los Angeles, 1952-61; judge Municipal Ct., Los Angeles, 1961—. Mem. Cal. Law Revision Commn., 1960-62, Cal. Atty. Gen. Constl. Rights Commn., 1959-61. Mem. Democratic State Central Com., 1958-62, mem. exec. bd., 1958-60, pres. minority conf., 1957-60. Dir. at large, Cal. Mental Health Assn., 1962-65; mem. adv. com. Bank of Finance, 1963-67; adviser re integrated housing Consol. Realty Bd., 1961-66, Los Angeles Commn. Justice, 1971—. Mem. Cal. Conf. Judges, Am., Los Angeles bar assns., Am. Judicature Soc., Nat. Bar Assn., N.A.A.C.P., Women's Lawyers Assn. Office: 110 N Grand St Los Angeles CA 90012

SPENO, MARY VIRGINIA, theatrical dir., actress; b. St. Louis, Aug. 25, 1952; d. Leo Frank and Catherine Marie (O'Leary) Speno; student St. Louis U., 1970-74. Mem. Noah M. Ludlow Theatre Assn. (formerly Corpus Christi Players), St. Louis, 1968—, asst. bus. mgr., 1969, 70, bus. mgr., 1970-73, also actor, dir. Home: 908 Delaird St St Louis MO 63137 Office: Noah M Ludlow Theatre Assn Box 4016 Jennings Station St Louis MO 63136

SPERBER, ANN MARGARET, editor, writer; b. Vienna, Austria, June 20, 1935; d. Fred and Liselotte (Suss) Sperber; came to U.S., 1939, naturalized, 1945; B.A., Barnard Coll., 1956; postgrad. (Fulbright fellow) Free U. West Berlin, 1956-57. Editorial asst. Meridian Books, World Pub. Co., N.Y.C., 1960-62; asst. editor Collier Books, Crowell-Collier, N.Y.C., 1962; editor juvenile books G.P. Putnam's Sons, N.Y.C., 1963-68; sr. editor jr. books McGraw-Hill Book Co., 1968-70; cons. editor Franklin Watts, Inc., McGraw-Hill Jr. Books, 1970-73. Music critic Am. Record Guide, N.Y.C., 1964—. Mem. Women's Nat. Book Assn., N.Y.C. Opera Guild (v.p.). Record reviewer Sch. Library Jour.; book reviewer N.Y. Times. Address: 160 West End Av New York City NY 10023

SPERL, SISTER AUGUSTA, hosp. adminstr.; b. Springfield, Ill., Mar. 8, 1923; d. August Carl and Elizabeth (Beckman) Sperl; R.N., St. Johns Sch. Nursing, 1945; Registered Records Adminstr., St. Scholastica, 1953; postgrad. Milikin Coll., 1959-61. Staff nurse St. Francis Hosp., Springfield, 1945-47, St. Mary's Hosp., Streator, Ill., 1947-48, St. John's Sanatorium, Springfield, 1948-49; chief med. record librarian St. Mary's Hosp., Decatur, Ill., 1949-61; adminstr. St. Francis Hosp., Washington, Mo., also adminstrv. asst. to bd. dirs. Hosp. Sisters of Third Order of St. Francis, Springfield, Ill., 1968-69; adminstr. St. Nicholas Hosp. Sheboygan, Wis., 1969—. Mem. Cath. (mem. com. on evolving health care system 1969), Mo. (mem. com. to establish nursing care requirements 1967) hosp. assns., Sheboygan County Agy. for Comprehensive Health Planning, Northeastern Wis. Health Planning Council, Lake Mich. Council Hosp. Adminstrs. (sec. 1972-73). Home: St Nicholas Convent Sheboygan WI 53081 Office: St Nicholas Hospital Sheboygan WI 53081

SPERL, VIRGINIA R., librarian; b. Orange, N.J., Jan. 3, 1920; d. Adolph A. and Olga J. (Linn) Sperl; B.A., Randolph-Macon Woman's Coll., 1942; B.S. in L.S., U. Minn., 1945. Library asst. New Britain (Conn.) Inst., 1942-43; asst. order dept. Harvard Law Library, 1945-46; library asst. Pa. Sch. Social Work, Phila., 1947; serials cataloger, then asst. catalog librarian med. Columbia, 1947-58; chief cataloger Albert Einstein Coll. Medicine, N.Y.C., 1958-60; catalog librarian, then asst. librarian, asso. prof. Dowling Coll., Oakdale, N.Y., 1961—. Mem. Am., N.Y. State, Suffolk County library assns., Spl. Libraries Assn., N.Y. Tech. Services Librarians, Am. Assn. U. Profs., Am. Assn. Univ. Women, Am. Soc. Information Scis. Home: Sayville NY 11782 Office: Dowling Coll Oakdale NY 11769

SPERLINE, ELNORA ELIZABETH, exec.; b. LaMesa, Tex., Dec. 16, 1934; d. Horace Homer and Hazel (Starr) Van Meter; grad. Nat. Nurses Inst., 1950, Cerritos Coll., 1965; m. Vergil Arthur Sperline, Jr., May 2, 1953 (div. 1973); children—Donald Arthur, Jean Marie, Victoria Elizabeth, Marcella Kathleen. Treas., Coast & Sperline, Inc., Los Angeles, 1966-73; pres. Internat. Product Mgmt., Inc., Newport Beach, Cal., 1971-73; Cattle rancher, Fillmore, Utah; sec. Cal. Consumer Products, Inc., Santa Ana, Cal., 1971-72. Spl. cons. Ariz. to Office Econ. Opportunity, 1969-71; mem. White House Conf. Food, Nutrition and Health, 1969; mem. Pres.'s Commn. on Personnel Interchange. Mem. Republican State Central Com., 1971; nat. committeewoman Cal. Young Republicans, 1971, state chmn., 1972; alternate Los Angeles County Central Com., 1971, youth chmn., 1971, bd. dirs., 1973-74; candidate State Senate, 1970; mem. Electoral Coll., 1972. Mem. bd. Cal. Indian Edn. Assn., 1969; founding bd. Downey Rehab. Hosp. Aux., Friends San Antonio Regional Library. Recipient 1st pl. award Cal.-Americanism-Federated Womens Clubs, 1970, Cal.-Youth-Gen. Federated Womens Clubs, 1969; Outstanding Service to Democracy award Anaheim Young Reps. Mem. Bus. and Profl. Womens Federated Club, Huntington Park C. of C. (sec. 1971). Home: 5342 Stonehedge Ct Yorba Linda CA 92686

SPERLING, ADELLE BERNICE, ophthalmologist, educator; b. Birmingham, Ala., May 26, 1932; d. Alexander and Rose (Feigelson) Sperling; B.S. summa cum laude, Birmingham So. Coll., 1952; M.D., U. Ala. Sch. Medicine, 1956. Intern, resident U. Ala. Hosps. and Clinics; asst. prof. ophthalmology U. Ala. Sch. Medicine, Birmingham, 1963-64, clin. asst. prof., 1965—; chief ophthalmology service VA Hosp., Birmingham, 1963-64; pvt. practice medicine specializing in ophthalmology, Birmingham, 1965—; mem. staff U. Ala., Eye Found. hosps. Heed Ophthalmic fellow Mass. Eye and Ear Infirmary, Columbia-Presbyn. Hosp., 1962. Diplomate Am. Bd. Ophthalmology. Fellow Am. Acad. Ophthalmology and Otolaryngology; mem. Soc. Heed Fellows, Jefferson County Med. Soc., Med. Assn. State Ala., Alpha Omega Alpha, Phi Beta Kappa, Alpha Epsilon Iota. Republican. Jewish religion. Home: 111 Yorkshire Dr Birmingham AL 35209 Office: 1033 S 17th St Birmingham AL 35205

SPERLING, LILLIAN (MRS. IRVING LESLIE SPERLING), artist; b. Bklyn., Feb. 18, 1921; d. Samuel and Bessie (Zelikow) Schechter; B.A., Hunter Coll., 1942; postgrad. Rutgers U., also Upsala U., Montclair State Coll., Fairleigh Dickinson, New Sch. for Social Research; m. Irving Leslie Sperling, Jan. 30, 1944; children—Arnold, Linda (Mrs. Edwin Saladin), Michael. Tchr. Suburban Y, Livingston, N.J., 1967-72; exhibited one-man shows at Maplewood (N.J.) Library, 1969, Summit (N.J.) Art Centre, 1971, Drew U., Madison, N.J., 1973; others; exhibited in group shows at Trenton (N.J.) State Mus., Morris Mus. Arts and Scis., Morristown, N.J., Bergen Community Mus., Paramas Gallery 9, Chatham, N.J., Montclair (N.J.) Mus., Union Coll., Cranford, N.J., others. Recipient Medal of Honor award Nat. Assn. Women Artists, 1969, 70, 72. Mem. Nat. Assn. Women Artists, N.J. Water Color Soc., Artists Equity. Home and office: 24 Walnut Court South Orange NJ 07079

SPERLING, SALLY EDITH, educator; b. Mpls., May 7, 1930; d. Abe Jerome and Frieda (Juster) Sperling; B.A., U. Minn., 1954, M.A., 1956; postgrad. Columbia, 1955-56; Ph.D., U. Mich., 1961. Lectr., U. Mich., 1959-60; vis. asst. prof. U. Minn., 1960-61; lectr. U. Cal., Riverside, 1961-62, asst. prof. psychology, 1962-67, asso. prof., 1967-72, prof., 1972—. NSF predoctoral fellow, 1955-56; NSF research grantee, 1963-65, 66-68, 70-72. Mem. Am., Western psychol. assns., Psychonomic Soc. Home: 6825 Palomar Way Riverside CA 92504

SPERRY, SISTER LUCILE, artist, educator; b. Bay City, Mich., Nov. 24, 1907; d. George E. and Marguerite (McLean) Sperry; student Coll. of St. Catherine, U. Loyola (Chgo.), U. Notre Dame, U. Detroit, 1932-35; B.A., Nazareth Coll., 1942; B.F.A., Art Inst. Chgo., 1947, M.F.A., 1947. Tchr., St. Augustines Sch., Kalamazoo, 1930-32, St. Bernard High Sch., Detroit, 1932-45; became chmn. art dept. Nazareth Coll., Kalamazoo, 1947; tchr. art Flint (Mich.) Pub. Sch. System, 1968-70; art dir. New Cath. Central in Flint Luke M. Powers Ednl. Center, 1970—; exhibited one-man show Nazareth Coll. 1965; exhibited group shows Art Inst. Chgo., Gilmore Art Center, Kalamazoo, U. Ill., Cath. Art Assn.; represented in pvt. collections. Bd. dirs. Kalamazoo Fine Arts Program. Mem. Coll. Art Assn. Am., Cath. Art Assn. (regional dir. 1951-53, chmn. nominating com. 1954-55, dir. pub. relations 1956-57), Western, Mich. edn. arts assns. Home: 524 W Pierson Rd Flint MI 48505

SPERRY, PATRICIA FRANCES, lawyer; b. Sheridan, Pa., June 24, 1907; d. Patrick Francis and Mary Miriam (Mills) O'Malley; grad. in Law, Southwestern U., Los Angeles, 1957. With City Atty., Huntington Beach, Cal., 1932-41, pvt. law firm, 1941-43, Orange County Dist. Atty., 1943, IRS, 1943-49; with U.S. Dist. Ct., Los Angeles, 1949—, now career law clk.; admitted to Cal. bar, 1959. Home: PO Box 54 Huntington Beach CA 92648 Office: 231 US Courthouse Los Angeles CA 90012

SPICER, ELEANOR W. (MRS. DONALD SPICER), orgn. exec.; b. Key West, Fla.; d. Raymond B. and Eleanor Russell (Chamberlin) Sullivan; m. Donald Spicer; children—Donald, Raymond, Rolf, Nancy Eleanor. Civilian supr. U.S. Naval Air Sta., San Diego, World War II. Active A.R.C. Successively chmn. geneal. records Cal. Soc. D.A.R., then corr. sec., vice regent, regent, 1966-68, historian gen., 1968-71, pres. gen., 1971-74, hon. life pres., 1974—. Mem. Coronado Women's Club (past pres.), Daus. Founders Patriots, Nat. Soc. Colonial Dames Am., Magna Carta Dames, Soc. Washington Family Descs., Mayflower Soc. Episcopalian. Address: 6251 Old Dominion Dr McLean VA 22101

SPICER, LYNETTE JONES (MRS. JERRY LEE SPICER), newspaper exec.; b. Sioux City, Ia., Aug. 18, 1948; d. Orlie Jay and Fern Elizabeth (Steinhoff) Jones; B.S., Ia. State U., 1971; m. Jerry Lee Spicer, June 4, 1972. Bus. mgr. Ia. State Daily newspaper Ia. State U., Ames, 1971—. Mem. Women in Communications, Alpha Omicron Pi. Home: 509 E 16th St Ames IA 50010 Office: Iowa State Daily Iowa State Univ Ames IA 50010

SPIEGEL, JEANNE SHAPIRO (MRS. HARRY SPIEGEL), librarian; b. Fall River, Mass.; d. Samuel and Fannie (Avrutsky) Shapiro; A.B., Brown U., 1937; M.S., Simmons U., 1962; m. Harry Spiegel, May 4, 1942; children—Glenn Stephen, Mark Alan. Tchr. English, Durfee High Sch., Fall River, 1940-42; head acquisitions and cataloging Concord (N.H.) Pub. Library, 1962-66; librarian, staff dir. Bus. and Profl. Women's Found., Washington, 1966—. Trustee, Concord Pub. Library, 1955-62; bd. dirs. N.H. Council for Better Schs., 1956-65. Mem. A.L.A., Spl. Libraries Assn. (chmn. social sci. Washington chpt. 1971-72), Oral History Assn. (pub. relations com. 1971), Phi Beta Kappa. Home: 3900 16th St NW Washington DC 20011 Office: 2012 Massachusetts Ave NW Washington DC 20036

SPIER, PATRICIA EVELYN (MRS ROY WATSON), physician; b. N.Y.C., May 20, 1917; d. Oscar Agnew and Helen (Murphy) Spier; student Barnard Coll., 1934-36; B.S., Wheaton Coll., 1938; M.D., N.Y. Med. Coll., 1942, postgrad., 1950-51; m. Roy Watson, May 27, 1942; children—Gary, Paul. Intern Met. Hosp., N.Y.C., 1942-43; pediatric resident St. Luke's Hosp., 1943-44; practice specializing in pediatrics, Bronxville, N.Y., 1944—; dir., pediatric cons. Wickersham Hosp., 1945-47; mem. med. bd. St. Luke's Hosp., 1966—, asso. attending staff pediatrics, 1962—; courtesy staff Flower Fifth Av., Columbus, Lawrence hosps.; med. dir. Conservative Baptist Fgn. Mission Soc., 1946-51; examiner pediatrics N.Y. State Med. Bds., 1961-63; med. coordinator Bronxville Pub. Schs., 1968—; pediatric cons. Heartease Home, 1952-54. Mem. A.M.A., Westchester County (com. on child and sch. health 1970—), N.Y. State med. socs., Christian Med. Soc. Internat. Club: Zonta. Home: 8 Boulder Trail Bronxville NY 10708

SPIESS, JOHANNA MARGARETE, librarian; b. Bklyn., Apr. 5, 1927; d. Fredrick Bernhard and Margarete Elise (Czerwinski) Spiess; B.A., Bklyn. Coll., 1949; M.L.S., Pratt Inst., 1950. With Bklyn. Pub. Library, 1949—, prin. librarian, 1961—. Exchange librarian Hamburger Oeffentliche Buecherhallen, Hamburg, Germany, 1956-57. Mem. N.Y. Library Club, Theatre Library Assn. Lutheran. Home: 7520 Ridge Blvd Apt 4C Brooklyn NY 11209 Office: Brooklyn Pub Library Grand Army Plaza Brooklyn NY 11238

SPIESS, MARY LOUISE (MRS. CHALMERS D. SPIESS), county ofcl.; b. Delta, O., July 1, 1922; d. Robert Albert and Thelma Margaret (Lilley) Willey; student Davis Bus. Sch., Toledo, 1940; m. Chalmers D. Spiess, June 26, 1942; children—Roger D., Cheryl (Mrs. Adelbert Kempf). Sec., Comml. Credit Corp., Toledo, 1941-43, Willys Overland, Toledo, 1943-44, Grace E. Smith Cafeteria, Toledo, 1944-45; dep. clk. Office Probate Judge Fulton County, 1953—. Mem. Aetna Grange, 1948—. Mem. Order Eastern Star (dep. matron 1952). Clubs: Delta Literary, Delta Country. Home: Route 2 Box 235 Delta OH 43515 Office: Court House Wauseon OH 43567

SPIETH, ALDA MAY, educator; b. Jeffersonville, Ind., Apr. 5, 1898; d. Joseph Theodore and Martha Elizabeth (Gray) Spieth; B.A., Huntingdon Coll., Montgomery, Ala., 1918; M.S., U. Chgo., 1925, Ph.D., 1931. Tchr. biology Mansfield Coll., La., 1919-23, Statesville, N.C., 1924-25, Randolph-Macon Coll., Lynchburg, Va., 1925-28; chmn. dept. sci. and math. Livingston (Ala.) U., 1930-68; ret., 1968. Alda May Spieth Hall dedicated at Livingston U., 1969. Mem. A.A.A.S., Am. Biol. Inst., Bot. Soc. Am., Ala. Acad. Sci., Assn. Southeastern Biologists, Am. Assn. U. Women, Sigma Xi, Delta Kappa Gamma. Home: 1704 Springhill Av Mobile AL 36604

SPIEWAK, STELLA NANCY, educator; b. Steubenville, O., Nov. 8, 1927; d. Stephen Francis and Anastasia S. (Szydlowski) Spiewak; B.S. in Bus. Adminstrn., Coll. Steubenville, 1966; M.S. in Gen. Edn., Duquesne U., 1970; postgrad. (NSF fellow) Purdue U., 1971. Mgr.'s sec. Ohio Power Co., Brilliant, 1945-68; asst. prof. Jefferson County Tech. Inst., Steubenville, 1968—. Past sec. Jefferson County Republican Party. Mem. N.E.A., Ohio Higher Edn. Assn., Am. Tech. Edn. Assn., Ohio Assn. Marketing Mgmt. Educators, Ohio Assn. Two-Year Colls. Home: 1507 Pershing Av Steubenville OH 43952

SPIKES, CLEO HUBBARD (MRS. OLIN EDWARD SPIKES), nursing home dir.; b. Glenn, Ga.; d. Wilson Edward and Martha Victoria (O'Neal) Hubbard; R.N., Dunson Hosp. Sch. Nursing, 1926; m. Olin Edward Spikes, Mar. 8, 1931 (dec.); children—Billie Louise (dec.), Patricia Ann. Pvt. duty nurse, Auburn, Ala., 1926-60; supr. Auburn U. Infirmary, 1960-63; dir. Lee County Nursing Home, Opelika, Ala., 1963-72; dir. nursing Royal Elaine Nursing Home, LaGrange, Ga., 1972—. Vol. worker Auburn Hosp. Aux., Boy Scouts Am., Girl Scouts U.S.A.; occupational guidance vol. Meth. Youth Found. Recipient Achievement certificate Am. Nursing Home Assn. Mem. Am., Ala. nursing assns., Ala. Nursing Home Assn., A.M.A. (achievement certificate). Methodist (Sunday sch. tchr. 1951-52). Home: R-3 Moody Bridge Rd LaGrange GA 30240 Office: 2110 Hogansville Rd LaGrange GA 30240

SPILDE, LULU MARY CASLEY (MRS. OTIS SPILDE), educator; b. Flandreau, S.D.; d. Hugh and Elizabeth (Lane) Casley; B.S., S.D. State U., 1914; M.A., U. S.D., 1925; Ed.D., N.Y. U. 1942; m. Otis Spilde, June 8, 1921. Prin. pub. schs., Bryant, S.D., 1914-21, Vienna, S.D., 1921-23; dean women, dir. tchr. tng. U.S.D., Springfield, 1925-39, Fordham U., N.Y.C., 1944-46; prof. edn., dir. tchr. tng. St. John's U., Jamaica, N.Y., 1946-65; prof. edn. Niagara U., Niagara Falls, 1966-68, Ft. Lauderdale (Fla.) U., 1968—. Lectr., dir. testing and guidance, dir. extension centers; cons. state dept., Pierre, S.D.; active sch. surveys Nassau County, N.Y., 1961-62. Pres. So. dist. P.T.A., S.D., 1937-39, Am. Legion Aux., Vienna, S.D., 1923-25; supreme nat. dir. edn. Cath. Daus. Am., 1940-65. Mem. Am. Assn. U. Women, Am. Assn. U. Profs., N.E.A., Nat. Cath. Edn. Assn. Author: Audio-Visual Aids in Education, 1958, Observation and Student Teaching, 1961, Techniques of Oral Book Reviews, 1963. Contbr. articles to profl. mags. Home: 1201 SE 2d St Fort Lauderdale FL 33301

SPINDLER, LOUISE SCHAUBEL (MRS. GEORGE D. SPINDLER), anthropologist; b. Chgo., Mar. 4, 1917; d. Louis and Cora (Field) Schaubel; B.A. (Am. Assn. U. Women scholar), Carroll Coll., 1938; postgrad. U. Wis., 1947-49, U. Cal. at Los Angeles, 1949-50; M.A., Stanford, 1952; Ph.D., 1956; m. George D. Spindler, May 29, 1942; 1 dau., Sue S. Walker. Tchr. English and dramatics Park Falls (Wis.) High Sch., 1940-42; research asst. in anthropology U. Wis., Madison, 1947-49, U. Cal. at Los Angeles, 1949-50; teaching asst. in anthropology Stanford, 1950-54, asst. coordinator culture change program, 1954-57, research asso., lectr., 1957—. Wenner-Gren research grantee, 1952. Mem. Am. Anthrop. Assn., Am. Sociol. Assn., Sigma Xi. Asst. editor Am. Anthropologist; joint editor Culture Case Study Series, 70 books, 1959—; studies in Education and culture series, 12 books; author: (with others) Culture in Process, 1967, rev. edit., 1973; (with G. Spindler) Dreamers Without Power: Menomini Indians of Wisconsin, 1971; chpt. in American Indian Sorcery, 1971. Contbr. articles to profl. jours. Home: 4750 Alpine Rd Portola Valley CA 94025 Office: Dept Anthropology Stanford U Stanford CA 94305

SPINGARN, NATALIE DAVIS (MRS. JEROME SPINGARN), author, urban cons.; b. N.Y.C., May 26, 1922; d. Aaron Wise and Helen Miller (Obstler) Davis; B.A., Vassar Coll., 1943; m. Jerome Spingarn, June 14, 1944; children—Jeremy Davis, Jonathan Edward. Free lance journalist, 1943-60; staff asst. to Sec. Health, Edn. and Welfare, 1961-62; exec. asst. to Senator Abraham Ribicoff, 1962-67; asst. dir. Center for Community Planning, Office of Sec. Dept. Health, Edn. and Welfare, 1967-69; free lance writer, urban cons., Washington, 1969—. Cons. Ford Found., Met. Applied Research Center Mayor's Office D.C., Nat. Urban Coalition, 1969. Del. Democratic Conv., 1960, 64. Author: To Save Your Life, 1963. Asst. editor Chronicle of Higher Education, 1973—. Contbr. articles to mags. and profl. jours., newspapers. Home: 1409 29th St NW Washington DC 20007

SPISSINGER, SUSAN RUTH LANDERS, coll. adminstr.; b. Lansing, Mich., Sept. 18, 1946; d. Francis Michael and Arlene Margaret (Springman) Landers; B.A., Mich. State U., 1969, postgrad., 1969; M.Ed., U. Vt., 1971; m. John Gerald Spissinger, Jr., Aug. 21, 1971. Resident adviser U. Vt., 1969-71; asst. dean students Skidmore Coll., Saratoga, N.Y., 1971—, acting dean students, 1973, dir., adminstr. liaison acad. opportunity program, 1973—; coordinator Skidmore-State U. N.Y. at Albany and Vt. Intern Program, 1973-74; instr. in field. Mem. campaign com. Skidmore United Fund, 1973. Mem. Am. Assn. Higher Edn., Nat. Assn. Student Personnel Adminstrs., Nat. (mem. commn. profl. employment practices 1974—), N.Y. (area coordinator 1974-75) assns. women deans, adminstrs. and counselors. Home: Apt 3 71 Hamilton St Saratoga NY 12866

SPITLER, MARY EARLINE UTTER (MRS. ROBERT MERVIN SPITLER), occupational therapist; b. Carthage, Mo., Sept. 22, 1918; d. Earl Wayne and Inez Amosette (Corley) Utter; B.S., Kan. State Coll., 1942; registered occupational therapist U. So. Cal., 1945; postgrad. Cal. State U., San Jose, 1965, Cal. State U., Hayward, 1972-74; m. Robert Mervin Spitler, June 12, 1948; children—Gregg Corley, Kim. Occupational therapist VA Hosp., Oakland, Cal., 1947-50, Agnews State Hosp., San Jose, 1965-66, 68-73; asst. program dir. Sonoma State Hosp., Eldridge, 1973—. Den mother Boy Scouts, 1960-61; leader Girl Scouts, 1962-64; counselor Resources for Women, Palo Alto, 1973; pres., treas. Lawrence Tract Assn., 1962-65. Exec. bd. League Women Voters, Richmond, Cal., 1953-55, P.T.A., Pinole, Cal., 1955-56, Palo Alto, Cal., 1960-64; adv. bd. Rehab. Mental Health Services, San Jose, 1970-72. Del. Santa Clara County Democratic Conv., 1962, Cal. Dem. Conv., 1964. Recipient award Am. Assn. U. Women, 1941. Mem. Am. Occupational Therapy Assn., Nat. Rehab. Assn., Council for Exceptional Children, Phi Upsilon Omicron. Home: Palo Alto CA 94303 Office: Program II Sonoma State Hosp Eldridge CA 95431

SPITTLER, BETTY JANE, motel mgr.; b. Terre Haute, Ind., Nov. 12, 1922; d. John Thomas and Nellie (Brough) Jones; grad. high sch.; m. Fenton Eugene Spittler, Feb. 19, 1942 (div. July 1968); children—Robert Eugene, Karen Lynn. Mgr., Terrace Inn and Restaurant, Terre Haute, 1964-65, Hickory Manor Hotel, Crystal Lake, Ill., 1965; mgr., buyer St. Mary's Motel, Evansville, Ind., 1965-72; mgr. Donna Ct. Motel, Evansville, 1972—; owner Riverboat Motor Inn, Evansville, 1974—. Mem. Evansville C. of C. (com. mem. 1969—). Republican. Lutheran (ch. council 1962-65, mem. parish bd. 1951-65, supt. Sunday sch. 1950-65). Address: Riverboat Motor Inn 2804 S Kentucky Av Evansville IN 47714

SPIVACK, CHARLOTTE ROSCOE (MRS. BERNARD SPIVACK), educator; b. Schoharie, N.Y., July 23, 1926; d. William and Laura (Snyder) Roscoe; B.A., State N.Y. at Albany, 1947; M.A., Cornell U., 1948; Ph.D., U. Mo., 1954; m. Bernard Spivack, Oct. 17, 1956; children—Carla Naomi, Loren Adlai. Asst. prof. English dept. Coll. William and Mary, Richmond, Va., 1954-56; asso. prof. English dept. Fisk U., Nashville, 1956-64; prof. English, U. Mass. (Amherst), 1964—. Am. Assn. U. Women nat. fellow, 1959-60; So. Fellowship Found. grantee, 1961, 62. Mem. Renaissance Soc. Am., Dante Soc., Modern Lang. Assn. Author (with William Bracy) Early English Drama, 1966; George Chapman, 1967. Home: 209 Alpine Dr Amherst MA 01002

SPIVAK, GLORIA HELENE, mfg. co. exec.; b. N.Y.C., Nov. 17, 1935; d. Irving S. and Mollie (Epstein) Spivak; B.A. in Edn., Hunter Coll., 1956; postgrad. New Sch. for Social Research, U. Cal. at Berkeley, N.Y. Inst. Finance. Tchr., N.Y.C. Bd. Edn., 1956-63; tech. analyst Dines Chart Co., N.Y.C., 1963-66; portfolio analyst Boise Cascade, N.Y.C., 1966—. Mem. N.Y. Soc. Security Analysts. Home: 110 E 87th St New York City NY 10028 Office: 345 Park Av New York City NY 10022

SPIZIZEN, LOUISE FLEUR MYERS (MRS. JOHN SPIZIZEN), musician; b. Lynn, Mass., Aug. 24, 1928; d. Louis Samuel and Lilliam (Gordon) Myers; A.B., Vassar Coll., 1949; M.A., U. Cal. at San Diego, 1972; m. Eugene Schlesinger, June 19, 1948 (div. June 1967); children—Louis Myers, Thomas Roger, Kenneth Gordon, Kathryn Ann; m. 2d, John Spizizen, Apr. 26, 1968. Mus. dir. Interplayers, Inc., 1948-50; singer Westchester County (N.Y.) County Civic Opera Co., 1954-58; singer, accompanist Westport (Conn.) Madrigal Singers, 1959-66; composer, performer piano, harpsichord Monday Evenings on the Roof, U. Cal. at San Diego, Los Angeles, 1970; harpsichordist La Jolla Civic Orch., 1970—, Josef Marx Baroque Ensemble, 1970—, U. Cal. at San Diego, 1971-72, San Diego Symphony, 1973—; performer Athanaeum Library Series; co-founder, harpsichordist San Diego Community Concourse Mini-Concerts. Lectr. adult edn. courses Jewish Community Center Norwalk, Conn., 1963-66, Soc. for Edn. Gifted Children, 1963-66; pvt. tchr. theory and piano, 1964—; lectr. music San Diego Community Coll.; instr. harpsichord U. Cal. at San Diego Extension. Co-producer, weekly radio series Norwalk Symphony Soc., sta. WNLK. Active Nat. Council Jewish Women, established Sr. Citizens Center, White Plains, N.Y., 1954-59. Performing mem. Composer's Group, Friday Morning, Music Club Washington. Composer: Weary with Toil, 1969. Editor: Sonata for Two Oboes and Continuo (Fasch); Three Baroque Sonatas for Violin and Continuo. Home: 925 Havenhurst Dr LaJolla CA 92037

SPLAVER, SARAH, psychologist; b. N.Y.C.; d. Morris and Rose (Farber) Splaver; Ph.D., N.Y.U., 1953. Pvt. practice counseling psychologist and guidance cons., 1950—; dir. guidance Rhodes Sch., N.Y.C., 1946-50; personnel supr. U.S. War Dept., 1943-45; editor, pub. Occu-Press, 1953-70. Originator, editorial cons. Socio-Guidrama Series. Recipient certificate from Mayor LaGuardia for service as supr. of interviewers for Civilian Defense Vol. Office in World War II. Fellow Internat. Council Psychologists (co-chmn. com. on problems of children); mem. Am. Psychol. Assn., Am. Personnel and Guidance Assn., Nat. Vocational Guidance Assn., Acad. Religion and Mental Health. Authors Guild, Am. Sch. Counselor Assn., A.A.A.S. Mem. B'nai B'rith (v.p. educators chpt.). Author: Your Career-If You're Not Going to College, 1963, rev. edit., 1971; Your College Education-How to Pay for it, 1964, rev. edit., 1968; Your Personality and You, 1965; Your Handicap--Don't Let It Handicap You, rev. edit., 1974; Someday I'll Be An Aerospace Engineer; Some Day I'll Be A Doctor: Someday I'll Be A Librarian; The High School Students Guide To Summer Jobs (all 1967); You and Today's Troubled World, 1970; Paraprofessions: Careers for the Future and the Present, 1972; Nontraditional Careers for Women, 1973. Dir. Guidance Exchange, 1960—. Book rev. editor The School Counsel. Address: 3310 Rochambeau Av Bronx NY 10467

SPODAK, RUTH BAILYN (MRS. WILLIAM M. SPODAK), ednl. cons.; b. Paterson, N.J., Jan. 28, 1942; d. Edward and Sylvia (Grossman) Bailyn; B.A. in Psychology Pembroke Coll., Brown U., 1962; M.A. in Psychology, George Washington U., 1965; Ph.D. in Human Devel., U. Md., 1972; m. William M. Spodak, Mar. 30, 1963; children—Douglas Adam, Jeffrey Todd. Program asso. Center for Applied Linguistics, Washington, 1966-68; instr. U. Md., College Park, 1971-72; dir. research and tng. TRI-Services Center, Rockville, Md., 1974—, ednl. cons. to early childhood centers, 1972—. Coordinator Conf. on Child Abuse, Rockville, Md., 1973-74. Chmn. Parent Vol. Program Wayside Elementary Sch., Potomac, Md., 1974—; mem. Citizens for Child Advocacy Montgomery County, Md. Mem. Am. Psychol. Assn., Am. Ednl. Research Assn.

SPOMER, ANN EVANS (MRS. LOUIS SPOMER), county ofcl.; b. Coal Creek, Colo., Jan. 7, 1904; d. Richard and Susie (Jessop) Evans; A.B., Colo. State Coll. Edn., 1925; M.A., U. Ia., 1927; m. Louis Spomer, Sept. 10, 1928; children—Louis, Elizabeth Louise (dec.), Charles Howard (dec.). Mem. faculty exptl. sch. U. Ia., 1926-27; supr. tchrs. Colo. State Coll. Edn., Greeley, 1927-31; clk., recorder Weld County Colo., Greeley, 1941—. Mem. Gov.'s Love's 100 Man Commn., 1966; mem. budget com. United Fund; mem. Weld County Agrl. Adv. Council; charter mem. League Women Voters. Mem. Weld County Library Bd. Named Woman of the Year, Bus. and Profl. Women, also Soroptimists. Mem. Internat. Assn. Clks., Recorders, Election Ofcls., Treasurers (pres., 1973-74), Nat. Assn. Clks. and Recording Clks. (pres., 1967, dir., 1968-72), Bus. and Profl. Women's Club, Am. Assn. U. Women (legis. chmn.), Am. Legion Aux., Pi Lambda Theta, Delta Zeta. Mem. Order Eastern Star. Clubs: Soroptomist, Home Demonstration. Home: 902 5th St Greeley CO 80631 Office: PO Box 459 Court House Greeley CO 80631

SPONGBERG-HOLMBERG, VIOLA HILDUR, educator, musician; b. N.Y.C.; d. Axel Elof and Hildur (Emelijen) Hogberg Spongberg; A.B., Hunter Coll.; M.A., Columbia; Mus.D., N.Y. Coll. Music; Ph.D., N.Y. U.; 1 son, Anders A. Holmberg. Debut as violinist Town Hall, N.Y.C.; concert tours as violinist, pianist, soprano, organist, U.S., Can., Europe; prima donna with leading opera cos. in U.S., Europe; former lectr., entertainer overseas U.T.W.A.C., U.S.O.; dir. music therapy Bklyn. State Hosp., 1947-48; head music dept. Pilgrim Sch., Hastings, N.Y., 1956-57, Trinity Christian Sch., Scarsdale, N.Y., 1961-63; dir. music Augustana Lutheran Ch., 1963—; pvt. tutor; guest lectr. to schs., colls.; cons. philosophy and music Funk & Wagnalls Co., N.Y.C., 1953-57; writer articles New Internat. Year Book, 1953-57. Mem. Am. Security Council, 1972. Bd. dirs. Percy Grainger Library Soc., 1971—. Presser scholar with Henry Holden Huss. Recipient Libbie Van Arsdale Meml. prize Hunter Coll., U.S. Treas. Dept. citation, recipient A.R.C. medal; named hon. gen. Blue Star Brigade. Mem. Swedish Cultural Soc. (pres. N.Y. chpt. 1955—), Am. Philos. Assn., Am. Guild Mus. Artists, A.F.T.R.A., Am. Soc. for Art and Aesthetics, N.Y. U. Alumnae (dir. 1958—). Author: The Philosophy of Erik Gustaf Geijer; also articles on philosophy and music. Home: Hasthallen on Nannyhagen Rd Thornwood NY 10594 Office: PO Box 177 Thornwood NY 10594

SPONSLER, MARILYN PAULINE, mag. editor; b. Garden Grove, Ia., June 2, 1935; d. Arnold Thomas and Grace Ann (Nordstrum) Lovett; B.S., Ia. State Coll., 1956; m. Robert Lee Sponsler, Aug. 31, 1957 (div. Apr. 1962); children—John Robert, Michael Paul. Editorial, prodn. asst. Western Livestock Jour., Los Angeles, 1956-60; free-lance writer Ia. State Coll. Vet. Clinics, Ames, also Des Moines Register and Tribune, 1961-62; mng. editor Polled Hereford World mag., Kansas City, Mo., 1962—. 4th Dist. v.p. Ia. Young Republicans, 1961; committeewoman 1st ward, Kansas City, 1964-68. Mem. Am. Nat., Mo. cattlemen's assns., Mo. Poll-ettes, Nat. Wildlife Fedn., Am. Saddle Horse Breeders Assn., Am. Agrl. Editors Assn., P.E.O. Home: 9815 E 73d St Raytown MO 64133 Office: 4700 E 63d St Kansas City MO 64130

SPRAGUE, CLAIRE SACKS, educator; b. N.Y.C.; d. Albert and Mollie (Teich) Sacks; B.A., U. Wis., 1946, MA.A, 1947, Ph.D., 1955. Faculty, U. Wis., 1946-51, Reed Coll., 1955-56; faculty City U. N.Y., 1956—, faculty Bklyn. Coll., 1956-70, 73—, prof. English, asso. dean grad. studies John Jay Coll., 1970-73; Fulbright prof. Am. lit. U. Zaragoza (Spain), 1961-62. Am. Philos. Soc. research grantee, 1964; Am. Council Learned Socs. grantee-in-aid, 1965; Am. Assn. U. Women fellow, 1964-65. Mem. Modern Lang. Assn., Am. Assn. U. Profs., Am. Studies Assn., Columbia U. Faculty Seminar on Am. Lit. (co-chmn. 1965-67), P.E.N. Author: Hamlet: Enter Critic, 1960; Edgar Saltus, 1968; Van Wyck Brooks: The Early Years, 1968; Virginia Woolf, 1971. Contbr. articles, revs. to pubs. including Publs. Modern Lang. Assn., Am. Quar. Home: 61 W 9th St New York City NY 10011 Office: Dept English Brooklyn College Brooklyn NY 11210

SPRAGUE, ELIZABETH F(ERN), educator; b. San Diego, Sept. 23, 1911; d. George L. and Fern (Helm) Sprague; B.A., U. Cal. at Los Angeles, 1933, M.A., 1935; postgrad. (fellow) Claremont Grad. Sch., 1955-57, Ph.D., 1960. Tchr. biology Hoover High Sch., San Diego, 1936-39; faculty Fullerton (Cal.) High Sch. and Jr. Coll., 1939-41; liaison officer Convair, San Diego, 1942-44; active U.S.O., Abilene, Brownwood, Tex., 1944-46; faculty Sampson (N.Y.) Coll., 1946-49; faculty Sweet Briar (Va.) Coll., 1949—, asst. prof. biology, 1950-61, prof., 1961—. Sec., Amherst chpt. A.R.C., 1959-60. So. Found. fellow, 1955. Fellow San Diego Soc. Natural History, A.A.A.S.; mem. Am. Inst. Biol. Scis., Ecol. Soc. Am., So. Appalachian Bot. Club, Assn. Southeastern Biologists, Cal. Acad. Scis., Nature Conservancy (dir. Va. chpt. 1964—), Cons. Council Va. (dir.). Contbr. articles to profl. jours. Address: Sweet Briar Coll Sweet Briar VA 24595

SPRAGUE, ISABELLE BAIRD, educator, biologist; b. Manila, P.I., May 30, 1916; d. Henry Welles and Elizabeth (Tower) Baird; A.B., Mt. Holyoke Coll., 1937, M.A., 1939; Ph.D., U. Kan., 1953; m. James Baird Sprague, 1940 (div. 1950). Mem. faculty Mt. Holyoke Coll.,

1945—, chmn. dept. biol. scis., 1963—, prof. biol. scis., 1964—. Home: 88 Woodbridge Terrace South Hadley MA 01075*

SPRAGUE, MARY LOUISE DULL (MRS. WALLACE ARTHUR SPRAGUE), newspaper pub.; b. Orange, N.J., Sept. 5, 1918; d. Charles Elwood and Kathryn Louise (Brenizer) Dull; B.A., Oberlin Coll., 1938; A.M., Columbia, 1939; m. Wallace Arthur Sprague, Mar. 17, 1942; children—Charles Wallace, John Arthur. Instr. English Upsala Coll., East Orange, N.J., 1946-50; pres., mgr. Item Press, Millburn, N.J., 1969—; pub. The Item of Millburn, Short Hills, N.J., 1968—, Cranford (N.J.) Citizen & Chronicle, 1971—; pres., Quality Weeklies N.J., 1969-71; dir. Statesman Pub. Co., Salem, Ore. Pres., Short Hills (N.J.) Hosp. Aux., 1964, Neighborhood Assn., Millburn, N.J., 1965-67. Republican. Episcopalian. Home: 33 Birch Lane Short Hills NJ 07078 Office: 18 Main St Millburn NJ 07041

SPRAGUE, NANCY KUNZMAN (MRS. BRUCE LEIGHTON SPRAGUE), artist; b. N.Y.C., Sept. 27, 1940; d. Charles Marshall and Helen (Horwedel) Kunzman; student R.I. Sch. Design, 1958-59; B.F.A., U. Pa., 1962, postgrad., 1962-63; postgrad. Temple U., 1964, U. Kan., 1966; M.A., M.F.A., U. Ia., 1969; m. Bruce Leighton Sprague, Dec. 29, 1961; 1 dau., Jennifer Kunzman. One-man show Ruth White Gallery, N.Y.C., 1969; exhibited group shows The Sculptors Guild, Bryant Park, N.Y.C., 1969, Ball State U., Muncie, Ind., 1970, Goldsmith Civic Garden Center, Memphis, 1973, numerous others; represented in permanent collections Fairleigh Dickinson U., Rutherford, N.J., Tenn. State Capitol, Nashville. Instr. U. Kan. Extension, Lawrence, 1966-67; grad. asst. U. Ia., Iowa City, 1968-69. Mem. Coll. Art Assn. Home: Windham Way Route 1 Box 214a Iowa City IA 52240

SPRAKER, EILEEN CAMERON (MRS. RICHARD A. SPRAKER), editor; b. Dorchester, Ill., Sept. 3, 1920; d. Everett Lyle and Sarah Enza (Combes) Cameron; B.S., U. Ill., 1943; postgrad. U. Del., 1963-66; m. Richard Allen Spraker, Dec. 28, 1944; children—Sarah (Mrs. Albert J. Tigani, Jr.), Jean Ellen, Nancy Eileen, Carol Marie. Tchr. elementary sch., Gillespie, Ill., 1940-41; continuity writer WILL radio U. Ill., Urbana, 1942-43; society editor, mng. editor The News Virginian Waynesboro, 1943-48; mem. pub. relations staff Evanston (Ill.) Hosp., 1953-56; reporter News-Jour. Papers, Wilmington, Del., 1959—, editor, 1969—. Active Oak Lane Civic Assn. Recipient 2d place feature writing Va. Press Assn., 1945, 1st place feature series award Md., Del., D.C. Press Assn., 1970, Layman's community leadership award Mt. Joy Meth. Ch., 1972. Mem. Am. Assn. U. Women, Women in Communications (regional rep. 1959-61), Del. Press Club, Religion Newswriters Assn., Kappa Tau Alpha. Presbyn. Home: 1908 Shipley Rd Wilmington DE 19803 Office: 831 Orange St Wilmington DE 19899

SPRANDEL, HAZEL LAVONNE ZINK (MRS. LOUIS WALTER SPRANDEL), psychologist; b. Panama, Neb., Jan. 14, 1922; d. Roscoe M. and Mamie (Johnson) Zink; B.A., Neb. U., 1942; M.A., Washington U., St. Louis, 1965, Ph.D., 1969; m. Louis Walter Sprandel, Nov. 26, 1942; children—Richard Douglas, Robert Walter, James Kimberly, Gary Lynn. High sch. tchr. Stratton (Neb.) High Sch., 1942-43; mathematician Ballistics Research Lab., Aberdeen Proving Ground, Md., 1944-45; substitute tchr. St. Louis Pub. Schs., 1961-62; tchr. Ascension Luth. Sch., St. Louis, 1962-65; grad. asst. Office Student Services Washington U., St. Louis, 1965-67, counselor, 1967-69, counseling psychologist, 1969—; asst. prof. edn. U. Mo., summer and fall 1972; counseling supr. Fontbonne Coll., St. Louis, 1972-73; pvt. practice marriage counseling, intelligence testing, 1973—. Mem. commn. on edn. St. Louis Council Luth. Chs., 1968-70. Bd. dirs. Spl. Luth Sch. for Retarded Children. Mem. Am. (conv. com. 1972-73), St. Louis (trustee) personnel and guidance assns., Assn. for Ednl. Data Systems, Am. Psychol. Assn. (asst. mng. editor div. 17 Counseling Psychologist), Am. Edn. Research Assn., Am. Assn. for Higher Edn., Am. (conf. program com. 1969-70), Mo. (organizational com.) coll. personnel assns., Nat. Assn. Women Deans and Counselors, Pi Mu Epsilon, Kappa Delta Pi. Lutheran. Home: 8115 University Dr Clayton MO 63105 Office: Washington U St Louis MO 63130

SPRANGER, MARCIA J., librarian; b. Cleve., Mar. 19, 1942; d. Charles E. and Dorothy B. (Kucinski) Zeeck; B.A., St. Mary of the Woods Coll., 1964; M.A. in L.S., Rosary Coll., 1969; postgrad. Northwestern U., 1973—; div.; 1 son, Christopher. Chem. lit. searcher, asst. librarian Universal Oil Products Co., Des Plaines, Ill., 1964-67; mgr. corp. library and information center De Soto, Inc., Des Plaines, 1967—. Mem. Spl. Libraries Assn., Am. Mgmt. Assn., Am. Chem. Soc., Nat. Microfilm Assn., Am. Soc. Information Sci., Nat. Assn. Female Execs. Home: 1315 Wasdale Av Elk Grove Village IL 60007 Office: 1700 S Mt Prospect St Des Plaines IL 60016

SPRATT, BRENDA GAYE (MRS. CRAIG MONROE SPRATT), educator; b. Bradshaw, W.Va., Sept. 3, 1942; d. Jessie Leon and Shirley Gaye (Pippin) Roberts; B.S. W.Va. Legislature scholar), Concord Coll., 1964; M.A., W.Va. U., 1971; postgrad., U. Va., 1969-71; m. Craig Monroe Spratt, Aug. 15, 1964; 1 son, David Howard. Tchr. Bradshaw (W.Va.) Elementary Sch., 1964-65, Fairfax (Va.) Elementary Sch., 1965-68, June Ravensworth Elementary Sch., Fairfax, 1968, Fairfax Elementary Sch., 1968-69, Jermantown Elementary Sch., Fairfax, 1970—. Vice pres. Fairfax Elementary P.T.A., 1968-69; Named Concord Coll. Tchr. of the Year, 1964. Mem. Nat. Va. (del. 1967-70), Fairfax (del. 1967-70) edn. assns., Classroom Tchrs. Assn. (del. 1966-67), Mantua Civic Assn., Am. Assn. Mental Deficiency, Council Exceptional Children, Assn. Classroom Tchrs., Nat. Assn. Classroom Tchrs., Alpha Sigma Tau. Mem. Rebekah Lodge. Home: 3614 Glenbrook Rd Fairfax VA 22030 Office: 3616 Jermantown Rd Fairfax VA 22030

SPRAY, PAULINE ETHA MELLISH (MRS. RUSSELL ELBERT SPRAY), author; b. Byron Center, Mich., July 9, 1920; d. John Earl and Mary Rachel (Twining) Mellish; student Lapeer County Normal, 1938-39, Bethany Nazarene Coll., 1940, Central Mich. U., 1949-52; m. Russell Elbert Spray, Mar. 8, 1940; children—Sybil (Mrs. Wayne Louis Musatics), Sue (Mrs. David Earl Smith). Writer devotional column Benton Harbor (Mich.) News Palladium, 1961-64. Tchr. grade schs. Lapeer County, Mich., 1939-40, Shiawassee County, Mich., 1949-52. Mem. Mich. dist. council, Nazarene World Missionary Soc., 1955-65. Author: Daily Delights, 1968; Planned Programs for Women's Groups, 1968. Contbr. to Support the Church series; also numerous articles to religious publs. Address: 651 13 Mile Rd Sparta MI 49345

SPRAYBERRY, BARBARA LEE, educator; b. Washington, Dec. 20, 1930; d. Frank L. and Dorothy M. (Sprinkle) Sprayberry; B.S., Colo. State U., 1953; M.S., Ill. State Normal U., 1954. Instr. Colo. State U., 1951-53, Ill. State Normal U., 1953-54; tchr. pub. schs., New Lenox, Ill., 1954-58, Flossmoor, Ill., 1959-62; cons. for girls' and women's sport orgns. Am. Assn. for Health, Phys. Edn. and Recreation, Washington, 1962-66; tchr. Homewood-Flossmoor (Ill.) High Sch., 1966—, asso. dir. girls and boys phys. edn., 1974—. State chmn. Ill. div. Girls and Women's Sports, 1970—. Fellow A.A.H.P.E.R.; mem. N.E.A., Ill. Assn. Health, Phys. Edn. and Recreation (mem. exec. council girls and women's sports), Am. Assn. U. Profs., Midwest Assn. for Coll. Tchrs. Phys. Edn., Ill. Guidance and Personnel Assn. Author articles profl. jours. Home: 1326 W Thomas St Homewood IL 60430 Office: Homewood-Flossmoor High Sch Flossmoor IL 60422

SPRENGLING, ANN FRESTADIUS, newspaper corr.; b. Tampere, Finland; d. Alfred and Leni (Urbin) Frestadius; law degree U. Helsinki (Finland), 1930; m. Gerhard Ray Sprengling, Aug. 24, 1946 (div. 1959). Came to U.S., 1947, naturalized, 1955. Reporter, Uusi Suomi, daily newspaper, Helsinki, 1939-46, U.S. corr., 1946-69; U.S. corr. Aamulehti newspaper, 1969—. Vol. worker Children's Hosp., Pitts.; sec. Swedish Forum of Western Pa., 1955-56; sec. Longue Vue Civic Club, 1957; chmn. Penn Twp. Summer Library Com., 1956. Mem. Nat. League Am. Pen Women, UN Assn. Pitts., Pitts. Council for Internat. Visitors, Am.-Scandinavian Found., Women in Communications. Clubs: Zonta (internat. relations com. chmn. 1956-57, 65-67, dir. 1957-58), Finlandia (sec. 1955-57) (Pitts.). Home: 8168 Lincoln Rd Verona PA 15147

SPRINGBORN, ROSEMARY KELLY (MRS. BRUCE ALAN SPRINGBORN), editor; b. South Bend, Ind., June 2, 1932; d. Edward Joseph and Hazel Jeannette (Thompson) Kelly; B.S., Purdue U., 1953; postgrad. Northwestern U., 1958-59, U. Mich., 1960; m. Bruce Alan Springborn, Dec. 19, 1964. Mng. editor Brewers Digest, Siebel Pub. Co., Chgo., 1955-58; sr. tech. writer Bendix Corp., Ann Arbor, Mich., 1960-63; editor-in-chief, books div. Soc. Mfg. Engrs., Dearborn, Mich., 1965-69; dir. contracts, copyrights and subsidiary rights Harper & Row, Pubs., Inc., N.Y.C., 1969-73; mng. editor Research and Devel. Tech. Pub. Co., Barrington, Ill., 1973—. Mem. Copyright Soc. U.S.A., Chgo. Book Clinic, No. Ind. Hist. Soc. Home: 225 Francis Lane Barrington IL 60010 Office: 1301 S Grove Av Barrington IL 60010

SPRINGER, ADELE I., lawyer; b. N.Y.C., Dec. 30, 1907; d. Nathaniel and Cecilia (Palew) Springer; LL.B., St. John's U., 1930, LL.M., 1931; grad. work, Columbia, 1931-33, Sch. Internat. Studies, Geneva, Switzerland, 1933, U. of Geneva, 1933, Acad. Internat. Law, The Hague, 1934. Admitted to N.Y. State bar, 1931, Calif. bar, 1950; asso. law firm Battle, Levy, Van Tine & Fowler, N.Y. City, 1931-39; gen. law practice specializing in admiralty and internat. law, own firm, N.Y. City, 1939—; pioneer woman counsel to any U.S. Senate inquiry, 1935; admiralty counsel U.S. Senate sub-com. investigating Morro Castle and Mohawk sea disasters, 1935; admiralty counsel to congressional com. investigation patent pooling, 1936; drafted and helped in enactment shipowner liability laws, 1935-36; counsel Morro Castle Survivors Assn., 1935. Mem. Fed. Bar Assn. N.Y., N.J. and Conn. (mem. exec. bd. past officer), Am. Bar Assn. (mem. adminstrv. law com.; mem. Ho. of Dels. 1948), N.Y. Co. Lawyers Assn. (mem. fed. courts com.), Nat. Assn. Women Lawyers (nat. chmn. adminstrv. law coms., 1939-45; 1st v.p. 1945-46, pres. 1946-47), Nat. Taxpayers and Property Owners Assn. (mem. bd. govs., chmn. women's div.), Internat. Bar Assn. (mem. Ho. of Deputies 1948). Organizer and nat. dir. pioneer women lawyers div. Dem. Nat. Com., 1936. Active in civic, polit. and philanthropic orgns. Author (articles); The Growth of Administrative Process (Women Lawyers), 1945. Editor and publisher Women Lawyers Jour., 1946-47. Home: 3198 W 7th St Los Angeles CA 90005 Office: 3460 Wilshire Blvd Los Angeles CA 90005 also 60 Wall St New York City NY 10005*

SPRINGER, KATHRYN GRACE, editor; b. Greenport, N.Y., June 10, 1928; d. H. Otis and Ida Mae (Neil) Dickerson; grad. high sch.; m. Albert W. Springer, Sept. 1, 1946; children—Clifford, Arthur, Eric. With Shelter Island (N.Y.) Reporter, 1962—, asst. editor, 1965-69, editor, 1969—. Mem. conservation adv. council Town of Shelter Island, vice chmn., 1971; bd. dirs. Shelter Island Assn., 1967—. Mem. D.A.R. Republican. Lutheran. Home: 47 N Midway Rd Shelter Island NY 11964 Office: 9 Grand Av Shelter Island NY 11964

SPRINGER, MARTHA E., educator; b. Sunnyvale, Cal., Jan. 24, 1916; d. John E. and Ollie (Maxwell) Springer; A.B., Stanford, 1935, M.A., 1936; Ph.D., U. Mich., 1944. Tchr. high sch., Daly City, Cal., 1936-42; acting instr. biology Stanford, summers 1942-43; instr. botany Ind. U., Bloomington, 1944-45, 46-47, Conn. Coll., New London, 1945-46; asso. prof. Willamette U., Salem, Ore., 1947-53, prof. biology, 1953—, acting chmn. dept. biology, 1948-50, 65, curator Peck Herbarium, 1967—. Vis. prof. biology Alaska Meth. U., Anchorage, summer 1967. Mem. Am. Inst. Biol. Sci., A.A.A.S., Am. Assn. U. Profs., Bot. Soc. Am., Ore. Acad. Sci., Mycol. Soc. Am., Am. Assn. U. Women, P.E.O., Phi Beta Kappa, Sigma Xi. Presbyn. Home: 3441 Neef Av Salem OR 97302

SPROUSE, ANN LOVINGOOD, educator; b. Gaffney, S.C., Apr. 16, 1934; d. Urgel Hill and Lula Mae (McSwain) Lovingood; B.S., Limestone Coll., 1958; M.A., Western Carolina U., 1966; m. Walter Young Sprouse, Sept. 15, 1954; children—Michael Young, Timothy Scott. Girls phys. edn. dir. Wray Jr. High Sch., Gastonia, N.C., 1958-59; girls phys. edn. dir., basketball coach Gaffney Jr. High Sch., 1959-68; guidance dir., basketball coach East Jr. High Sch., Gaffney, 1968-72; guidance dir. East Jr. High Sch., Gaffney, 1972—; basketball coach Gaffney Sr. High Sch., 1972—. Dir. Clinton Camp Fire Girls Resident Camp, 1968—, Tate's Locke Tiger Basketball Camp, 1970—. Staff mem. at various basketball camps, 1969—. Recipient Wakan award for camping Camp Fire Girls, 1970. Mem. Nat., S.C., Cherokee County edn. assns., S.C. Assn. Sch. Counselors, Am. Personnel and Guidance Assn., Classroom Tchrs. Assn., Chi Beta Phi. Democrat. Baptist. Home: 110 Country Club Dr Gaffney SC 29340

SPRUCE, JILL ELAINE, rehab. counselor; b. Gulfport, Miss., May 24, 1944; d. Hearne Webster and Ophelia Anne (Hilliard) Spruce; B.S. in Psychology, Bethany Nazarene Coll., 1966; M.A. in Psychology (Social Rehab. Services fellow), Tex. Tech U., 1971. Counselor, dir. Hotline for Youth, Family and Children's Service, Kansas City, Kan., 1971-72; rehab. counselor Kan. Div. Vocational Rehab., Kansas City, 1973—. Mem. Wyandotte Region Developmental Disabilities Council, 1972—. Bd. dirs. Youth Drop-In Center, Kansas City, 1971-72. Mem. Am. Psychol. Assn., Nat. Rehab. Assn. Mem. Ch. of the Nazarene. Research in juvenile delinquency and time perspective. Home: 516 Splitlog St Kansas City KS 66101 Office: Gateway II Center Kansas City KS 66101

SPRUTE, RUTH ELIZABETH, personnel exec.; b. S.I., N.Y., Dec. 1, 1925; d. William F. and Elizabeth (Thomas) Sprute; B.A., Wellesley Coll., 1948. Adminstrv. asst. St. Vincent's Hosp., N.Y.C., 1955-60; personnel manager George B. Buck Cons. Actuaries, Inc., N.Y.C., 1960—. Sec.-treas. Village Neighborhood Com., Greenwich Village, 1961—; dir. Jacques Marchais Center of Tibetan Arts, Inc., S.I., 1972—. Mem. N.Y. County Rep. Com., 1965-70. Recipient prizes for paintings Wall Street Art Assn., 1963, 64, 67, 69. Mem. Eastern Coll. Placement Officers. Office: 2 Pennsylvania Plaza New York City NY 10001

SPURLOCK, JEANNE, psychiatrist; b. Sandusky, O., 1921; M.D., Howard U., 1947; grad. Chgo. Inst. Psychoanalysis. Intern, Provident Hosp., 1947-48; resident in psychiatry Cook County Psychopathic Hosp., 1948-50; fellow Inst. Juvenile Research, 1950-51; dir. child psychiatry clinic Michael Reese Hosp., 1960-68 (all Chgo.); clin. asst. prof. psychiatry U. Ill., 1953-59; chmn. dept. psychiatry Meharry Med. Coll., Nashville, 1968-73; vis. scientist spl. mental health programs Nat. Inst. Mental Health, 1973-74; dep. med. dir. Am. Psychiat. Assn., 1974—. Diplomate in psychiatry and child psychiatry Am. Bd. Psychiatry and Neurology. Mem. A.M.A., Am. Psychiat. Assn. Address: 1700 18th Av N Washington DC 20009

SPURLOCK, LUCILLE, librarian; b. Kleinwood, La., Mar. 28, 1920; d. Ernest Percival and Nellie Helm (Marshall) Spurlock; B.A., Northwestern State Coll., 1943; B.L.S., La. State U., 1950. Librarian, Tioga (La.) High Sch., 1943-69, Bolton High Sch., Alexandria, La., 1969—. Library sch. supr. coll. students La. Coll., Pineville, interim librarian, summers 1962-63. Mem. Assn. Classroom Tchrs., La. Tchrs. Assn., Alpha Beta Alpha. Address: Route 1 Box 262 Moreauville LA 71355

SPURLOCK, VIRGINIA SMITH, psychol. services worker; b. Louisville, Tenn., Mar. 3, 1926; d. Summers and Polly Tarter (Spangler) Smith; B.A., U. Ga., 1949; M.S., Tenn. State U., 1972; m. Charles Hughes Spurlock, Dec. 23, 1950; children—Charles Hughes, Dianne, Jefferson, Stacy, John. Tchr., Blount County (Tenn.) Schs., 1949-50; psychometrist U. Tenn. Guidance Center, 1950; real estate agt. John S. Fry Co., Nashville, 1963—; psychol. services worker Met. Nashville Pub. Schs., 1966—, Waverly Belmont Learning Center, Nashville, 1973-74. Mem. Am. Assn. U. Women (chmn. ways and means com. Nashville chpt. 1962-63, 2d v.p., membership chmn. 1971-72), Nat. Assn. Sch. Psychologists (charter), Tenn. Assn. Psychology in Schs., Nat., Tenn., Middle Tenn. edn. assns. Democrat. Methodist. Club: Ravenwood Country (Nashville). Author: A Study of Early Adolescent Rejection of Parents, 1972; also articles. Home: 1352 Cardinal Dr Nashville TN 37216 Office: 2601 Bransford Av Nashville TN

SPURRIER, MARGARET NORVELL (MRS. KEITH MCCAULEY SPURRIER), mem. Republican Nat. Com.; b. Nashville, Apr. 7, 1919; d. Richard and Margaret (Parker) Norvell; ed. Wellesley Coll., Vanderbilt U.; m. Keith McCauley Spurrier, June 26, 1940; children—Lucia Parker (Mrs. William Lee Drier), Irene LeJau (Mrs. John Alan Pendergrast). Co-chmn. Shelby County (Tenn.) Republican party, 1962-66; mem. Tenn. Rep. Exec. Com., 1966-70, Rep. Nat. Com. for Tenn., 1968—; chmn. program com. Rep. Nat. Conv., 1972; mem. Nat. Fedn. Rep. Women. Mem. Tenn. Commn. on Status of Women. Bd. dirs. Shelby United Neighbors, Tenn. Bot. Gardens and Fine Arts Center. Mem. Memphis Symphony League, Memphis Jr. League, Kappa Alpha Theta, Chi Delta Phi. Episcopalian. Address: 89 Goodwyn St Memphis TN 38111

SQUAIRES, GLADYS MARJORIE, dean, nursing edn. adminstr.; b. Long Beach, Cal., Aug. 24, 1912; d. Herman A. and Kate (Thorne) Prior; diploma in nursing Seaside Coll. Nursing, 1933; B.A., Long Beach State U., 1957, M.A., 1961; m. Robert M. Squaires, 1934 (div. 1966); children—Roberta (Mrs. C. Swanson), Nancy Moore, R. Michael. Head nurse Seaside Hosp., Long Beach, Cal., 1933-34; sch. nurse Long Beach Unified Schs., 1949-57, supervising nurse, 1957-64; coordinator of continuing edn. in nursing U. Cal. at Los Angeles, 1962-67; asso. dean U. Wis. Sch. of Nursing, Milw., 1973—. Cons. So. Cal. Med. TV Network, 1966-71; nat. cons. Continuing Edn. in Nursing, 1970—; chmn. So. Cal. Nurse Race Relations Com., 1969-71; v.p. Cal. Bd. Nursing Edn. and Nurse Registration, 1971-72; mem. task force continuing edn. Nat. Commn. Nursing and Nursing Edn., 1970-71. Mem. Cal. Congress Parents and Tchrs., 1962—. Fellow Royal Soc. for Promotion of Health; mem. Am. Nurses Assn., Am. Assn. U. Profs., Nat. League Nursing, Internat. Platform Assn., Am. Women in Radio and TV, Alpha Tau Delta. Mem. editorial bd. Nursing Digest, 1971—. Home: 1626 N Prospect Av Milwaukee WI 53202 Office: Univ of Wis PO Box 413 Milwaukee WI

SQUIRE, JEANNE C., club woman; ed. Ohio State U.; widow; 1 dau. Bus. mgr., sec.-treas. Merrick Chevrolet Co., Berea, O. Former nat. 1st v.p. and pres. Nat. Fedn. Bus. and Profl. Women's Clubs; pres. Retirement Living, Ohio BPW Retirement Found., Bus. and Profl. Women's Found.; bd. dirs. Keep Am. Beautiful. Mem. Berea C. of C., League of Women Voters. Conglist. Mem. Order Eastern Star. Clubs: Berea Women's; Women's City (Cleve.). Address: 6 Parkview Dr Berea OH 44017

SQUIRE, LUCY FRANK (MRS. RICHARD F. DEFENDINI), physician, educator; b. Washington, May 10, 1915; d. Leslie C. and Clara E. (Harris) Frank; B.A., George Washington U., 1936; M.D., Woman's Med. Coll. Pa., 1940; m. Charles Squire, Sept. 23, 1937 (div. June 1947); 1 son, Gordon; m. 2d, Richard F. Defendini, Dec. 14, 1963. Intern, Women's Hosp. West Phila.; resident radiology Mass. Gen. Hosp., Boston, 1942-44, New Eng. Med. Center, Boston, 1945; practice medicine specializing in radiology, Syracuse, N.Y., 1946-48; instr. radiology U. Rochester (N.Y.) 1950-60; asst. prof. radiology Downstate Med. Sch., Bklyn., 1966-68, prof., 1972—; lectr. radiology Harvard Med. Sch., Boston, 1965-72; mem. staff radiology Mass. Gen. Hosp., 1965-72. Recipient First Alumni citation for teaching U. Rochester, 1957. Diplomate Am. Bd. Radiology. Mem. Radiol. Soc. N.Am. (Gold medal 1972), Am. Coll. Radiology, N.Y. Roentgen Ray Soc., Mass. Med. Soc. Democrat. Author: Fundamentals of Roentgenology, 1964; Exercises in Diagnostic Radiology, vol. I: The Chest, vol. II: The Abdomen, vol. III: Bone, vol. IV: The Total Patient, vol. V: Pediatrics, vol. VI: Nuclear Radiology. Address: The Dakota 1 W 72d St New York City NY 10023

SQUIRES, JANICE, pub. relations exec.; b. Franklin, O., Jan. 22, 1927; d. Omer Gaynor and Marjorie Darragh (Hankinson) Squires; B.F.A., U. Cin., 1949; A.A., Gulf Park Jr. Coll., 1946; grad. Miami-Jacobs Coll., 1944; postgrad. La. State U., summers 1945, 46; m. Anson Adams Mount, Sept. 27, 1947 (div. July 1950). Radio actress Crosley Broadcasting System, Cin., 1948-50; publicity dir. station WCPO, Cin., 1949-51; asst. to v.p. Columbia Artists Mgmt., Inc., N.Y.C., 1951-54; consumer-dealer relations dir., built-up roofing dept. Phillip Carey Mfg. Co., Cin., 1954-56; asst. to pres. Milton Rubin Assos., Inc., 1956-58; pub. relations dir. Greenwich House, 1958-62, mgr. Greenwich Village Antiques Show, 1960-62; personal and confidential sec. to v.p. orgn. Federated Dept. Stores, 1962-70; dir. pre-sch. L'Acadamie Montessori, Atlanta, 1970—. Mem. Nat. Assn. Fund Raising Dirs., Delta Alpha Epsilon. Episcopalian. Home: 7156 Stonington Dr NW Atlanta GA 30328

SQUIRES, JO ANNE SMIT (MRS. CHARLES CARTER SQUIRES), psychologist, educator; b. Wilkinsburg, Pa., Sept. 2, 1926; d. Herbert Harris and Myrtle (Goldman) Smit; B.S., Ohio U., 1947; M.S., U. Pitts., 1949, Ph.D., 1951; m. Charles Carter Squires, Mar. 1, 1958; children—Herbert Bradshaw, Anne Catherine Teresa. Lectr., U. Pitts., 1948-49; research asst. Am. Inst. for Research, Pitts., 1948-49; instr. Alleghany Coll., 1950-52; sr. research asso. Personnel Research Inst., Cleve., 1952-53; lectr. Western Reserve U., 1952-53; sr. psychologist U.S. Govt., Washington, 1953-58; dir. psychol. services Hampton Rds. Speech and Hearing Center, Newport News, Va., 1962-67; psychologist Peninsula Assn. for Retarded Children, Hampton, Va., 1962-65, adviser to bd. 1966-70; asst. prof. Coll. William and Mary, 1964-67; asso. prof. Christopher Newport Coll., Newport News, Va., 1967-69, asso. prof., 1972-73, prof., 1973—, acting chmn. dept. psychology, 1970-71, chmn., 1971-72; supr. adjustive services Sarah B. Hudgins Regional Center, Hampton, Va., 1969-70. Cons., Newport News Sch. System, 1966-67; asso.

professorial lectr. George Washington U., Hampton, Va., 1972-73, professorial lectr., 1973—; cons. Learning Devel. Services, 1972-74, supervising and cons. psychologist, 1974—. Mem. Peninsula United Fund Bd. Com., Newport News, 1966-67. Mem. Am., Va. psychol. assns., Sigma Xi. Home: 239 Christopher Wren Rd Williamsburg VA 23185 Office: Christopher Newport Coll of Coll William and Mary PO Box 6070 Newport News VA 23601

SQUIRES, LINDA LEE, educator; b. San Francisco, Aug. 1, 1944; d. Alan Francis and Edna May (Rafael) Squires; B.A., San Jose (Cal.) State Coll., 1966, M.A., 1969. Teaching asst. San Jose State Coll., 1966-67; instr. speech Humboldt (Cal.) State Coll., 1968-69, Am. Inst. Banking, San Francisco, 1972—; instr. speech City Coll. San Francisco, 1969-75, dir. pub. relations, 1975—. Mem. Western Speech Communications Assn. (vice chmn. community coll. interest group 1972), Speech Communication Assn., Internat. Communication Assn., San Francisco Bay Area Speech Tchrs. Assn. (co-founder 1971). Home: 490 23d Av San Francisco CA 94121 Office: 50 Phelan Av San Francisco CA 94112

STAATS, MRS. J. RILEY, educator, club woman; b. Vermilion, Ill., June 26, 1905; d. John R. and Clara (Braden) Meadows; student Eastern Ill. State Tchrs. Coll., 1926-27; B.S. in Edn., California (Pa.) State Tchrs. Coll., 1937; M.Ed., U. Miami, 1955; m. J. Riley Staats, Dec. 24, 1935. Tchr. pub. schs., Edgar County, Ill., 1923-26; tchr. English, art, Orlando, Fla., 1927-35; tchr. English, California, Pa., 1945-46; tchr. poetry writing U. Miami, 1948-49; tchr. English, journalism, Miami, Fla., 1954-72. Tchr. Poetry workshops Gen. Fedn. Women's Clubs, Estes Park Fine Arts Festival, 1951; v.p. Coral Gables (Fla.) Youth Center, 1957-63, pres., 1963-65; mem. Miami Internat. Hospitality Com., Children's Service Bus. case com.; vol. service chmn. Dade County chpt. A.R.C., 1952-54. Pres. Greater Miami (Fla.) Council Ch. Women, 1953-54, Washington (Pa.) County Fedn. Women's Clubs, 1941-44; fine arts chmn. Fla. Fedn. Women's Clubs 1950-54, dist. dir., 1954-56; state resolutions chmn. D.A.R., 1952-53, regent Monogahela Valley chpt., 1947, Coral Gables (Fla.) chpt., 1950-52; pres. Coral Gables Women's Club, 1948-50, Univ. Woman's Club, 1948-49; Meth. dist. sec. Missionary Edn., 1950-54; Fla. club chmn. Nat. Poetry Day, 1959; state Fedn. Poetry chmn., 1954-59; state v.p., war bond chmn. Pa. Fedn. Women's Clubs, 1945-47. Recipient Freedoms Found. award, 1959, 61; U.S. Treasury war Bond medal, 1947; gold honor key Fla. Scholastic Press, gold honor key Columbia Scholastic Press, 1969; Honor award Fla. English Council, 1970, Alpha Delta Kappa, 1973; named Outstanding Woman Dade County, 1953, Tchr. of Year, Fla., 1963, in top ten U.S. Office Edn., 1963; Illustrious Alumna, California (Pa.) State Coll., 1973. Mem. League Am. Pen Women (pres. Miami br. 1950-52), Fla. English Council (state sec. 1957-59, editor 1965—), Dade County Council English Tchrs. (pres. 1960-62), Am. Assn. U. Women (nat. conv. press chmn.), Nat. Council Tchrs. English (nat. conv. chmn. 1962), Fla. Fedn. Women's Clubs (press chmn. 1960-62, poet laureate 1960—), U. Miami Grad. Sch. Alumni Assn. (pres. 1963-64, Outstanding Alumni 1963), Fla. Scholastic Press Assn. (v.p.), Kappa Delta Pi (v.p. 1950-51), Pi Gamma Mu, Alpha Delta Kappa (chmn. nat. conv., internat. publicity chmn. 1959—), Theta Sigma Phi (community headliner 1964). Author: Bright Quarry (poems); (workbook) Lord Jim. Contbr. to articles edn. jours., poems to mags., anthologies. Home: 5110 San Amaro Dr Coral Gables FL 33146

STABILE, ROSE (MRS. FRED STABILE), bldg. and mgmt., pub. relations cons.; b. Sunderland, Eng.; d. Stephen and Amelia Bergman; student English schs., Tchrs. Coll., Columbia; m. Wilfred Kermode (dec. Feb. 1934); m. 2d, Arthur Whittlesey Towne, May 29, 1926 (dec. July 1954); m. 3d, Norbert Le Veillie, June 10, 1961 (div. Feb. 1969); m. 4th, Fred Stabile, May 30, 1970. Formerly auditor Brit. War Office, Whitehall, London; activities and membership dir. N.Y. League of Girls Clubs, N.Y.C.; now real estate exec., also bldg. mgr. State Tower Bldg., Syracuse, N.Y.; office designer and decorator; lectr. real estate dept. Syracuse U. An initiator Syracuse Peace Council; mem. area sponsoring com. Assn. for Crippled Children and Adults. Mem. Syracuse Real Estate Bd., English Speaking Union (membership com.), Nat. N.Y. assns. real estate bds., Nat. Assn. Bldg. Owners and Mgrs., N.Y. Soc. Real Estate Appraisers, Syracuse C. of C., League Women Voters, Assn. UN, Women of Rotary, Bus. and Profl. Women's Clubs, Friends of Reading. Unitarian (chmn. service com. 1956-57.). Club: Corinthian. Home: 304 Malverne Dr Syracuse NY 13208 Office: State Tower Bldg Syracuse NY 13202

STACEY, EVA DRUMM (MRS. MARO HUNTING STACEY), journalist; b. Cedar Vale, Kan., Apr. 29, 1904; d. Frank Tilden and Myrta Lodema (Cross) Drumm; B.A., U. Kan., 1925, postgrad., 1926; m. Maro Hunting Stacey, Apr. 17, 1927; children—Martha (Mrs. William A. King), Donald Norman. English tchr. Lawrence (Kan.) Jr. High, 1925-27; freelance feature writer for various newspaper and mags., 1934—; now hist. writer St. Matthew's Episcopal Ch., Cedar Vale. Mem. Cedar Vale Hist. Soc. (book editor), Tuesday Writers Club, Tulsa, Okla. writers clubs, Women in Communications. Home and office: 402 Maple St Cedar Vale KS 67024

STACHLER, RUTH ANN, lawyer; b. Cleve.; d. Charles Joseph and Esther Dorothy (Goffene) August; student U. Dayton; J.D., U. Cin., 1958. Admitted to Ohio bar, 1958, Cal. bar, 1966, Supreme Court U.S., 1973; practiced law, Shelby County, O., 1958-59, Palo Alto, Cal., 1966—; asst. city atty. City of Sunnyvale, Cal., 1964-65. Mem. Am., Palo Alto, San Mateo County, Santa Clara (correctional reform and criminal justice com.) bar assns., Am. Judicature Soc., Bar Assn. San Francisco, Cal., San Mateo County trial lawyers assns., Phi Alpha Delta. Club: Commonwealth (San Francisco). Home: Menlo Park CA 94025 Office: 550 Hamilton Av Palo Alto CA 94301

STACKHOUSE, ELLA BERNICE (MRS. EDWARD STACKHOUSE), home economist; b. Alligator, Miss., Apr. 5, 1909; d. Andrew and Missouri (King) Mason; B.S. in Home Econs., Lincoln U., 1944; M.S. in Clothing and Textiles, Cornell U., 1954; m. Edward D. Stackhouse, Aug. 26, 1927. Tchr. pvt. music lessons, Springfield and St. Louis, Mo., 1934-40; sec. agr., asst. mgr. sch. cafeteria Lincoln U., Jefferson City, Mo., 1940-44; extension home economist S.E. Mo., U. Mo., Kansas City, 1944-70; urban home economist Extension Center, Kansas City, 1970—. Cons. Western Region U.S.A. on Low Income Families, 1963-65, Environmental Research Devel. Found., 1970-71. Adv. bd. Mid City Congress Reps., Kansas City, Mo. Recipient citation Bd. Curators Lincoln U., 1968; Alumni Achievement award for serving needy families in Bootheel, Mo. and hopeless in inner core area Kansas City, Mo., City County Office Aging, 1971. Mem. Nat. Assn. Extension Home Economists, Nat. Am. Home Econs. Assn., Mo. Home Econs. Assn. (chmn. health and welfare com. 1971), Kansas City Consumer Assn. (membership com. 1971—), U. Mo. Extension Assn., Alpha Kappa Alpha, Alpha Tau Epsilon, Sigma Phi. Home: 5240 Cypress Kansas City MO 64130

STACKOWSKI, MARY JANE, radiologist; b. Phila., July 23, 1933; d. Benjamin L. and Ruth Louise (Giltner) Stackowski; student Gettysburg Coll., 1951-53; B.A., Temple U., 1955, M.D., 1961. Intern, Harrisburg (Pa.) Polyclinic Hosp., 1961-62, resident pathology, 1962-63, radiology Robert Packer Hosp., Sayre, Pa., 1965, 69; practice medicine specializing in radiology, Lewisburg, Pa., 1969—; chief radiol. services Evang. Community Hosp., Lewisburg, 1969—; cons. radiologist Fed. Penitentiary, Lewisburg, 1971—, Shamokin State Hosp. (Pa.), 1969—; staff radiologist Sunbury (Pa.) Community Hosp., 1971-72. Mem. Milton (Pa.) Sch. Bd., 1970—. Diplomate Am. Bd. Radiology. Mem. Pa., Union County (sec. 1969—) med. socs., Pa. Radiol. Soc., Am. Coll. Radiology. Office: Evang Hosp Lewisburg PA 17837 Home: RD 1 Milton PA 17847

STACKPOLE, HENRIETTE ELIZABETH ABEL (MRS. ROBERT HAYES STACKPOLE), physician; b. Elizabeth, N.J., Apr. 28, 1934; d. Henri Ernest and Alice Stearns (Gibb) Abel; B.A., Vassar Coll., 1955; M.D., Cornell U., 1959; m. Robert Hayes Stackpole, Sept. 7, 1957; children—Sarah, Elizabeth, Jane, Alice. Intern Lenox Hill Hosp., N.Y.C., 1959-60; resident in dermatology Cornell U. Med. Coll., N.Y. Hosp., 1960-63; practice medicine specializing in dermatology Elizabeth, N.J., asst. attending Elizabeth Gen. Hosp., 1963-70, asst. prof. medicine, dermatology Cornell U. Med. Coll., N.Y., 1963—. Diplomate Am. Bd. Dermatology. Mem. A.M.A., Am. Assn. Dermatology, N.J. Med. Soc. Home: 29 Scotland Rd Elizabeth NJ 07208 Office: 360 Elmora Av Elizabeth NJ 07208

STACY, ESTELLE MABRY (MRS. JACK LEONARD STACY), drilling co. exec.; b. nr. Anderson, Tex., Sept. 3, 1913; d. David D. and Rosa (Miller) Mabry; grad. high sch.; m. Jack Leonard Stacy, Dec. 24, 1933 (dec. May 1963); 1 son, Richard Allen; m. 2d, John Baldwin Carrier, Mar. 2, 1974. Vice pres. Stacy Drilling Co., Douglas, Wyo., 1948-63, pres., 1963—; v.p., sec. Teno United, 1957-63, pres. 1963—. Treas., Converse County. (Wyo.) Found., 1953—; mem. Def. Adv. Com. on Women in Services, 1970—, chmn., 1972—; mem. adv. com. for Western area pub. opinion Dept. State, 1971-73. Vice chmn. Wyo. Republican State Com., 1960-66; mem. Wyo. Fedn. Rep. Women (past pres.); Rep. Nat. committeewoman, 1965—, mem. exec. com. Rep. Nat. Com., 1969-72, sec. nat. com., 1972—; Wyo. mem. Rep. Nat. Com. Women, 1966—. Pres. bd. trustees Converse County Library, Douglas, 1965—; bd. dirs. Wyo. Safety Council, vice chmn., 1972—. Mem. Wyo. Drilling Assn., C. of C., Epsilon Sigma Alpha. Mem. Order Eastern Star (past matron). Clubs: Douglas Civic (past pres.), Federated Women's. Home: 3 Hilltop Rd Douglas WY 82633 Office: PO Box 96 Douglas WY 82633

STADLER, ARETA CHRISTINE, sch. psychologist; b. Veteran, Nev., Aug. 4, 1912; d. Harry Elias and Nina Adelaide (Tewksbury) Wolters; A.B., Stanford, 1933; M.S., Cal. State U., San Jose, 1966; m. William A. Wilkes, Nov. 14, 1933 (div. 1943); m. 2d, Erman Stadler, Nov. 26, 1943 (dec. 1966); children—Mae, David Wilkes, Dorothy (Mrs. Dempster Leech), Catherine (Mrs. Robert A. Smith), Judy. Psychologist Sunnyvale (Cal.) Sch. Dist., 1966—; pvt. practice marriage, family and child counseling ednl. psychologist, 1968—. Mem. Cal. exec. bd. Camp Fire Girls, 1948-53; pres. San Jose br. World Affairs Council, 1962-64, Community Council Central Santa Clara County, 1960-62; del. Nat. Conf. Children and Youth, 1960. Bd. dirs. Family Service Assn., San Jose, 1954-60. Mem. Cal. Assn. Sch. Psychologists and Psychometrists, Am. Psychol. Assn. (asso.), Council Exceptional Children, Am. Assn. U. Women (pres. chpt. 1959). Conglist. (moderator 1961). Home: 16395 Belmont Av Los Gatos CA 95030 Office: 750 E Arques St Sunnyvale CA 94088

STADLER, FRANCES CORDELL HURD (MRS. ERNST ANTON STADLER), curator; b. St. Louis, Dec. 13, 1917; d. Carlos Fayette and Katherine Stewart (Cordell) Hurd; student Drury Coll., 1934-35; A.B., Washington U., St. Louis, 1938; student U. Munich (Germany), 1937; m. Ernst Anton Stadler, Dec. 23, 1954. Reference librarian St. Louis Post-Dispatch, 1942-43, writer, 1945-49; club and area club dir. U.S. Army Spl. Services, Germany, 1949-55; archivist, curator manuscripts Mo. Hist. Soc., St. Louis, 1956—. Mem. Assn. St. Louis Area Archivists (pres. 1972—), St. Louis Press Club. Conglist. Author: St. Louis-From Laclede to Land Clearance, 1962. Editor: Tenderly to Jerusalem (R.W. Raber), 1968. Home: 5802 Waterman St St Louis MO 63112 Office: Jefferson Meml Bldg St Louis MO 63112

STADLEY, PAT ANNA MAY GOUGH (MRS. JAMES M. STADLEY), author; b. El Paso, Tex., Aug. 31, 1918; d. Thomas and Leona (Plitt) Gough; A.A., Chaffey Jr. Coll., 1936; m. James M. Stadley, Aug. 15, 1936; children—William T., Jerry M. Author: The Black Leather Barbarians, 1960; Autumn of a Hunter (Edgar Allen Poe spl. award 1970, produced as The Deadly Hunt TV Friday Night Movie Week 1971), 1970; also numerous short stories including The Doe and The Gantlet, 1957, The Waiting Game, 1961, Kurdistan Payload, 1962; Something for the Club, 1963. Democrat. Mem. Christian Ch. Club: Cal. Writers (v.p. 1967) (Citrus Heights). Home: 6439 Donegal Dr Apt 2 Citrus Heights CA 95610

STAFFORD, EMILY-MAE, editor; b. Haverhill, Mass., Dec. 11, 1934; d. Charles Gilbert and Leona May (Stout) Stafford; B.S. in Journalism, Tex. Woman's U., 1956, postgrad. in govt., 1958-60; postgrad. in journalism U. Tex., 1961-62. Publs. editor Continental Supply Co., Dallas, 1956-57; pub. relations specialist Tex. Woman's U., 1957-61; research asso. U. Tex., 1962-66; copy editor Ft. Worth Star-Telegram, 1966, makeup editor, 1967—. Tchr., U. Tex., Tex. Christian U. Bd. dirs. Ft. Worth Opera, 1973; officer alumnae bd. Tex. Woman's U. Mem. Women in Communications, Inc. (sec. Dallas 1957-59, pres. Austin 1965-66, treas. Ft. Worth 1969-72, pres. 1973-74, named adviser of year 1961), Kappa Tau Alpha. Methodist. Home: 2418-B Refugio St Fort Worth TX 76106 Office: 400 W 7th St Fort Worth TX 76102

STAFFORD, HELEN ADELE, educator; b. Phila., Oct. 9, 1922; d. Morton O. and Ethel (Scherer) Stafford; B.A., Wellesley Coll., 1944; M.A., Conn. Coll., 1948; Ph.D., U. Pa., 1951. Research asso. biochemistry U. Chgo., 1951-54, instr. botany, 1951-53; asst. prof. Reed Coll., Portland, Ore., 1954-58, asso. prof., 1958-65, prof., 1965—. Guggenheim fellow, 1958-59, NSF postdoctoral fellow, 1963-64. Mem. Am. Soc. Plant Physiologists, Bot. Soc. Am., Am. Soc. Biol. Chemists. Asso. editor Jour. Plant Physiology, 1964—. Contbr. articles on plant biochemistry to profl. jours. Home: 5426 SE 45th St Portland OR 97206

STAFFORD, JOANNA BARTLETT ROGERS (MRS. PHILIP TRUESDALE STAFFORD), editor; b. Lake Forest, Ill., Mar. 2, 1918; d. George Thomas and Belle Joyce (Bartlett) Rogers; student U. Chgo., 1936, 37, 39; m. Philip Truesdale Stafford, Sept. 7, 1940; children—Anabel (Mrs. Kritos Demetriu), Jonathan T., Philip B. Dir. pub. relations Child Guidance Centers, Chgo., 1944-46; corr. Lake County (Ind.) Star, 1949-50; Hobart (Ind.) editor Herald Newspapers, 1954-56, 58-59; corr. Hobart City news Gary Post Tribune, 1960-64; realtor Harrigan Real Estate, Hobart, 1965-67; editor, pub. Hobart (Ind.) Gazette, 1968—. Pres., Sr. High P.T.A., 1955-56. Vice-chmn. Democratic party, 1957-58. Named Woman of Year, Hobart Jr. C. of C., 1973. Mem. Hobart Hist. Soc., Hobart C. of C. (mem. bd. 1968-73), League Women Voters (pres. 1963-65). Unitarian. Home: 605 Wabash Pl Hobart IN 46342 Office: 607 E 3d St Hobart IN 46342

STAFFORD, MERRILEE ANNE, educator; b. Chgo., Mar. 24, 1926; d. Clifford and Rosalie Aloisia (Jirik) Reese; B.A. with high honors, Cal. State U. at Los Angeles, 1957, M.A. in Speech and Drama, 1961; Ph.D. in Speech Communication, U. So. Cal., 1973; m. Graham Grey Stafford, Dec. 23, 1952. Free-lance radio and TV work, 1943-59; tchr. Thomas S. King Jr. High Sch., Los Angeles, 1960-67; mem. faculty Los Angeles S.W. Coll., 1967—, inaugurated speech dept., 1967, prof. speech, 1972—, inaugurated theatre arts dept., 1973, chmn. dept. speech and theatre arts, 1973—. Asso. Students Grad. Summer scholar, 1959. Mem. Speech Communication Assn., Western Speech Assn., Am. Ednl. Theatre Assn., Pi Lambda Theta. Roman Catholic. Dir., author materials in field.

STAGG, CAMILLE JANET STAGG, editor; b. Chgo., Apr. 6, 1942; d. Stanley Stephen and Jeanette (Heynatt) Stagg; student Mundelein Coll., 1959-61; B.S., U. Ill., 1963. Home service rep. People's Gas Co., 1963-65; reporter-writer food dept. Chicago Sun-Times, 1965; food editor Chicago Sun-Times, 1965—; mem. adv. bd. College of DuPage, 1967—. Recipient Merit award for excellence in food journalism, Am. Meat Inst. Mem. Am. Home Economics Assn., Home Economists in Bus., Confrerie de la Chaine des Rotisseurs (exec. mem. bd.). Club: Chicago Press. Office: 401 N Wabash Av Chicago IL 60611

STAGG, LURA DEAN WINSTEAD (MRS. PAUL LYNWOOD STAGG), physician; b. Roxboro, N.C., Feb. 21, 1942; d. Carl Coltrane and Emma Dean (Rogers) Winstead; B.A., U. N.C. at Greensboro, 1964; M.D., Bowman Gray Sch. Medicine, 1968; m. Paul Lynwood Stagg, June 3, 1967; children—Paul Lynwood III, Carl Coltrane. Rotating intern St. Francis Hosp., Hartford, Conn., 1968-69, resident pediatrics, 1969-71, mem. staff dept. ambulatory services, 1971-73; practice medicine, specializing in pediatrics, Hartford, 1971-73, Springfield, Mass., 1973—. Mem. Golden Chain. Home: 669 Frank Smith Rd Longmeadow MA 01106

STAHL, BARBARA JAFFE (MRS. DAVID G. STAHL), educator; b. Bklyn., Apr. 17, 1930; d. Samuel and Sophie (Kalison) Jaffe; B.A., Wellesley Coll., 1952; M.A., Radcliffe Coll., 1953; Ph.D., Harvard, 1965; m. David G. Stahl, July 7, 1951; children—Susan E., Nancy R., Sarah A., John S. Prof. biology St. Anselm Coll., Manchester, N.H., 1954—. Trustee, Derryfield Sch., Manchester, 1964—. Mem. Soc. Vertebrate Paleontology, Am. Assn. U. Profs., A.A.A.S., Phi Beta Kappa, Sigma Xi. Home: 100 Magnolia Rd Manchester NH 03104

STAHL, EVA BAMBERGER, dermatologist; b. May 5, 1933; d. Curt and Alice E. (Guttmann) Bamberger; B.A., Douglass Coll. Rutgers U., 1954; M.D., Med. Coll. Pa., 1958; m. Theodore J. Stahl, Aug. 18, 1957; children—Douglas, James, Lauren. Intern, Albert Einstein Med. Center, Phila., 1958-59; resident in dermatology Pa. Hosp., 1959-60, Columbia Presbyn. Hosp., N.Y.C., 1960-62; practice medicine specializing in dermatology, New Brunswick, N.J., 1963—; sr. attending physician, chief dermatology St. Peters Gen. Hosp., New Brunswick; attending physician, chief dermatology Middlesex Hosp., New Brunswick; asst. dermatologist Columbia Presbyn. Med. Center, N.Y.C.; asst. clin. prof. Rutgers Med. Coll. N.J. Diplomate Am. Bd. Dermatology. Fellow Royal Soc. Health (Eng.), N.J. Acad. Medicine, Pan Am. Soc. Dermatology, Dermatology Found. Editorial bd. Middlesex Hosp. Med. Jour. Home: 54 Ross Hall Blvd Piscataway NJ 08854 Office: 130 Easton Av New Brunswick NJ 08991

STAHL, JOYCE SIEBER (MRS. LEE A. STAHL III), mayor; b. Pitts., Aug. 2, 1941; d. John and Margaret Amelia (Whited) Sieber; student Valparaiso (Ind.) U.; m. Lee A. Stahl III, Aug. 20, 1960; children—Kelly Lee, Wendy Lee. Corporate sec. Cook County Sch. Bus, Inc., Arlington Heights, Ill., 1961-62; city clk., Darien, Ill., 1971-73, mayor, 1973—. Mem. DuPage Mayors and Mgrs. Club: Darien Woman's (rec. sec.). Office: 1702 Plainfield Rd Darien IL 60559

STAHLMAN, HELEN ABBOTT, nursing adminstr.; b. Boise, Ida., Aug. 3, 1921; d. Charles Whitin and Bessie Katherine (Byrd) Abbott; student U. Md., 1963, 67-71, Catholic U. Am., 1965; m. Emory George Stahlman, June 3, 1944; children—Kathryn Grimaldi, C. Ingrid, Carl, Claire. Staff nurse Nat. Inst. Neurology and Blindness, 1958; head nurse Martha Elliot Infirmary, D.C. Childrens Center, 1959-60, nurse supr. Cottage Life Program, 1960-67, asst. dir. nursing services, 1967-71; chief nursing services Central Services Office, Bur. Youth Services, Dept. Human Resources, Laurel, Md., 1972—. Mental health counselor family systems therapy Prince Georges County Mental Health Clinic. Served as 2d lt., Nurse Corps, AUS, 1943-44. Mem. Am., D.C. nurses assns., Nat. Assn. Mental Deficiency. Mem. Order Eastern Star. Home: 7 Shaw Av Silver Spring MD 20904

STAIHAR, JANET BARNES, journalist; b. Wilton, N.D., Nov. 11, 1938; d. Mike and Alice (Skoropat) Staihar; B.A., U. Ia., 1961; m. Richard L. Barnes, Apr. 23, 1971. Reporter, Vancouver (Wash.) Columbia, 1961-63, Portland Oregonian, 1963-65; staff writer A.P., Newark, also Balt., Atlantic City, N.J., Washington, 1965—; chmn. bd. Rock Creek Pub. Co., Washington, 1970—. Mem. Journalists for Profl. Equality. Club: Washington Press. Co-author Capital Feasts, 1970—. Home: 1739 1/2 Corcoran St NW Washington DC 20009 Office: 2021 K St NW Washington DC 20006

STAINES, MARY ANN REILLY (MRS. CHARLES E. STAINES, JR.), social worker; b. Bklyn., Sept. 29, 1928; d. Adelbert Richard and Anna (Scheibel) Reilly; student Adelphi U., 1966; B.A., Notre Dame Coll., 1950; M.S.W., Fordham U., 1964; m. Charles E. Staines, Jr., Dec. 1, 1951. Jr. caseworker Angel Guardian Home, Mineola, N.Y., 1954-61, provisional caseworker, 1961-64, sr. caseworker, 1964-66, supr., 1966-67, supr., group discussional leader, 1967-69, chmn. staff devel. program, 1969-70, asst. dir. Suffolk br., 1970-74, dir. foster home dept. Nassau-Suffolk br., 1974—. Mem. Nat. Assn. Social Workers, Acad. Certified Social Workers. Home: 1400 N Monroe Av West Islip NY 11795 Office: 110 Main St Mineola NY 11501

STAIR, LYNDA FAY, mathematician; b. Heber Springs, Ark., Sept. 18, 1941; d. Stanley and Ruby Mae (Powell) Stair; B.A., U. Ark., 1963, M.A., 1965; postgrad. Stevens Inst. Tech., 1966-67. Instr. math. Midwestern U., Wichita Falls, Tex., 1964-65; mem. tech. staff ABM def. systems research Bell Tel. Labs., Whippany, N.J., 1965-73; engr. Southwestern Bell Telephone Co., 1973—. Vol. tchr. English to fgn.-born residents, Dover, N.J., 1970—; tutor underprivileged children, Paterson, N.J., 1969-70. Mem. Math. Assn. Am., Phi Beta Kappa. Baptist. Home: 7823 Willow Lake Ct Apt 232 Dallas TX 75230 Office: Southwestern Bell Room 1832 308 S Akard St Dallas TX 75202

STAKES, MARJORIE LOUISE (MRS. WILLIAM SMITH STAKES), sorority exec.; b. Flint, Mich., Mar. 12, 1915; d. William Charles and Jean Irene (Crichton) Rowles; student U. Mich., 1934-35; B.A., Albion Coll., 1936; postgrad. Merrill-Palmer Sch., 1936-37; m. William Smith Stakes, July 17, 1937; children—William Smith, James Crichton, John Edward. Tchr. pvt. nursery sch., Detroit, 1937-38; case worker Detroit Welfare Dept., 1938-39; dir., tchr. Weekday Kindergarten and Nursery Sch., St. Andrew's Meth. Ch., San Antonio, 1957-62. Treas., Indian Shores Civic Assn., Crosby, Tex., 1970—. Mem. Assn. Childhood Edn. (v.p. nursery sch. div., 1960-61), Kappa Delta (nat. alumnae v.p., 1969—). Methodist. Clubs: Terrell Heights Garden (past pres.) (San Antonio); San Antonio Garden Center (past rec. sec.); Indian Shores Garden (pres. 1974-75) (Crosby, Tex.). Home: 20627 Appaloosa Trail Crosby TX 77532

STALBAUM, BERTHA ALICE (MRS. TREVOR LAVEL STALBAUM), mus. curator; b. Porter County, Ind., May 28, 1916; d. Frederick William and Edith Mariette (Bull) Wohlenberg; grad. high sch., 1935; m. Trevor Lavel Stalbaum, Feb. 27, 1936; children—Earl Frederick, Edith Fairy (Mrs. Roy Renshaw Thatcher). Part-time curator Porter County Hist. Soc. Mus., Valparaiso, Ind., 1963-66, curator, 1967—, also trustee. Mem. D.A.R. (past regent William Henry Harrison chpt.), Children Am. Revolution (sr. pres. 1970-74), Duneland, Porter County, Ind. State, Hasbrouck. New Paltz Huguenot, hist. socs. Home: 957 West St Valparaiso IN 46383 Office: Old Jail Mus 153 Franklin St Valparaiso IN 46383

STALEY, LINDA CAUTHEN (MRS. WILLIAM CHANNING STALEY), surgeon, plastic surgeon; b. Miami, Fla., Feb. 1, 1935; d. Marx D. and Clementine (Norman) Cauthen; student Gulf Park Coll., 1952-53, Barry Coll., 1958-61; M.D., U. Miami, 1965; m. William Channing Staley, Feb. 17, 1966; 1 son, Duke Cauthen Barnes (dec.). Surg. intern Vanderbilt U. Hosp., Nashville, 1965-66; practice medicine, specializing in surgery, Lewisburg, Tenn., 1967-70; plastic and gen. surg. resident Orange Meml. Hosp., Orlando, Fla., Lakeland (Fla.) Gen. Hosp., 1970—. Breeder Tenn. Walking Horses and cattle. Mem. A.M.A., Tenn., Marshall County (sec.-treas. 1969-70) med. socs., Marshall County Saddle Club, Marshall County Horseman's Assn., Marshall County Women's Club, Central Fla., Fla. walking horse assns., Tenn. Walking Horse Breeder's and Exhibitor's Assn. Clubs: Racquet (Miami Beach, France). Home: 123 Variety Tree Circle Spring Valley Farms Altamonte Springs FL 32701 also 210 Martin Av Lewisburg TN 37091 Office: PO Box 1842 Sanford FL 32771 also 210 Martin Av Lewisburg TN 37091

STALEY, MARTHA MCHENRY GREEN (MRS. WALTER G. STALEY), civic worker; b. Kirkwood, Mo., Oct. 22, 1905; d. Allen Percival and Josephine (Brown) Green; A.A., Hardin Coll., 1925; postgrad. Art Student's League N.Y.C., 1925-28, 50, Acad. Julian, Paris, 1950; m. Walter Goodwin Staley, Dec. 25, 1928; children—Martha (Mrs. Smith), Walter Goodwin, Allen Percival Green. First v.p. Mo. Assn. Mental Health, 1960-64, bd. dirs., 1958-64; v.p. East Central Mo. Mental Health Assn., 1969—; v.p. Presbyn. Home for Children Mo., 1962-63, bd. dirs., 1968-71; chmn. Audrain Fine Arts Council, 1965-70; pres. Audrain County Hist. Soc., 1965-70; mem. adv. council Mo. Arthritis Center, 1971—. Bd. dirs. Allen P. and Josephine B. Green Found; trustee Mexico-Audrain County Library, 1959-66. Mem. Nat. Soc. Colonial Dames Am., Nat. Soc. Magna Charta Dames, Huguenot Soc. S.C. Democrat. Presbyn. Home: 15 S Jefferson Rd Mexico MO 65265 also (winter) Sea Urchin Frederiksted St Croix VI 00840

STALEY, MILDRED WILKERSON (MRS. JOSEPH HARDIN STALEY), polit. party exec.; b. Meridian, Miss., Mar. 14, 1913; d. Forrest Edd and Beatrice Lucille (Clement) Wilkerson; student Randolph-Macon Woman's Coll., 1929-30; B.A., So. Methodist U., 1933; postgrad. Instituto Tecnologico de Monterrey, 1957, Midwestern U., 1965-66; m. Joseph Hardin Staley, Sept. 5, 1933; children—Nancy (Mrs. William Joseph Friedman), Joseph Hardin, Delia (Mrs. Benjamin Clark Mullins). Chmn. County Red Cross Motor Corps, 1942-44; sec. bd., 1941-44. Bd. dirs. Wichita Falls (Tex.) Symphony, 1960—. Del. Tex. Fedn. Republican Women convs., 1967, 69, 71, 73, pres., 1968, dir. 1967-71, 73-75, exec. bd. 1968-71, 73-75, Rep. county and state convs., 1968, 72; mem. Wichita Rep. Exec. Bd., 1970-74; del. Nat. Fedn. Rep. Women Convention, 1967, 69, 71; mem. exec. bd. Wichita County Rep. Women's Club, 1966—, dir. Nat. Fedn. Rep. Women's Clubs, 1969-71, 71-74. Mem. YWCA, Symphony Women's League, Mus. Guild, Am. Horticulture Soc. Zeta Tau Alpha (pres. local chpt. 1932-33). Clubs: Colony, Century. Home: 2205 Clarinda St Wichita Falls TX 76308 Office: PO Box 810 Wichita Falls TX 76308

STALLARD, ELINOR RUTH, sch. psychologist; b. Trenton, Neb., Oct. 21, 1921; d. Samuel Edmond and Pleasant Ethel (Hammond) Tarvin; B.A., U. Cal. at Los Angeles, 1943; M.S., Cal. State U. at Los Angeles, 1965; m. Thomas Brown Stallard, Sept. 27, 1946; children—Susan L., Rebecca J., Thomas Jonathan Paul. Primary sch. tchr. in Cal., 1943-64; sch. psychologist Rialto (Cal.) Unified Sch. Dist., 1964-65, Ontario (Cal.)-Montclair Sch. Dist., 1965—; guest lectr. LaVerne Coll., Redlands U.; organizer 1st summer session for mentally gifted children in Ontario, 1973. Panelist Nat. Assn. Gifted Children, 1972—; pres. West End Council Community Service, 1968—; Originator Title VI projects for prescriptive and remedial techniques for handicapped children, 1968-69; mem. Cal. State Audit Task Force for Mentally Gifted Minor Programs, 1975; presenter joint conf. Cal. State Psychologists Assn./Cal. Assn. Sch. Psychologists, 1975. Bd. dirs. First Methodist Nursery Sch., 1953-56, Bethany Pre Sch., 1957-58, West End Parents for Gifted, 1969-74, West End Mental Hygiene Assn., 1960-75; bd. advisers Gateway Youth Service Center, 1970-71, Am. Field Service, 1966-71. Mem. Southeastern Counties Sch. Psychologists Assn. (sec. 1965-67, pres. 1967-68), Chaffey Coll. Wives (v.p. 1950-51). Home: 325 E Rosewood Ct Ontario CA 91764 Office: 950 W D St Ontario CA 91761

STALLINGS, NELL ALLEN, educator; b. Louisburg, N.C., July 15, 1915; d. George B. Haywood and Christiana (Lacy) Stallings; B.S., U. N.C. at Greensboro, 1936; M.A., U. N.C. at Chapel Hill, 1942. Tchr. sr. high sch., High Point, N.C., 1936-42; Lenoir Rhyne Coll., Hickory, N.C., 1942-43; faculty East Carolina U., Greenville, N.C., 1943—, prof. phys. edn., 1963—. Staff mem. Nat. Aquatic Sch., 1958-72. Water safety chmn. Pitt County chpt. A.R.C., 1962—. Fellow A.A.H.P.E.R.; mem. N.E.A., Am. Assn. U. Women (pres. 1953-54), Nat., So. assns. phys. edn. for coll. women, N.C. Edn. Assn., N.C. Assn. Health, Phys. Edn. and Recreation (pres. 1954-55, recipient Honor award 1968). Home: 2411 Umstead Av Greenville NC 27834

STALTE, MARIE ELEANOR, personnel mgr.; b. Phila., June 13, 1929; d. Ralph Paul and Eleanor Letita (Mathers) Piccirilli; m. Edward A. Stalte, Nov. 16, 1948; children—Linda (Mrs. Craig Cunningham), Paula, Richard. Personnel mgr. IMS Am., Inc., med. market research, Ambler, Pa., 1967—; notary public, 1971—. Active local chpt. Girl Scouts. Mem. Am. Soc. Personnel Adminstrn., Adminstrv. Mgmt. Soc. Mem. Order Eastern Star. Home: 1471 Balboa Bend Norristown PA 19403 Office: IMS America Inc Butler and Maple Sts Ambler PA 19002

STALTER, SISTER ROSE CLEMENT, coll. adminstr.; b. Somerset, O., Aug. 28, 1922; d. Harry John and Rose M. (McGonagle) Stalter; B.A., Coll. St. Mary of Springs, 1954; M.A., Cath. U. Am., 1960. Tchr. grade schs. N.Y., Ohio, 1943-48; high sch. bus. tchr., New Haven, 1948-49, N.Y.C., 1949-54, 57-59, Zanesville, O., 1959-61, Marietta, O., 1954-57, 61-64; grade sch. prin., religious superior St. Mary Sch., Marietta, 1961-64; high sch. prin., religious superior Bishop Fenwick High Sch., Lancaster, O., 1964-67; high sch. bus. tchr., chmn. dept. St. Mary High Sch., New Haven, 1967-70; registrar Albertus Magnus Coll., New Haven, 1970—. Mem. Am., New Eng. assns. collegiate registrars and admissions officers. Conn. Assn. Collegiate Registrars. Address: 700 Prospect St New Haven CT 06511

STALVEY, LOIS MARK (MRS. BENNETT STALVEY, JR.), journalist; b. Milw., Aug. 22, 1925; d. Aloysius Leo and Gertrude Katherine (Wolf) Mark; grad. high sch.; m. Bennett Stalvey, Jr., May 14, 1955; children—Bennett III, Noah Wolf, Sarah Lois. Pres., Lois Mark & Assos. advt., Milw., 1946-54; radio/TV writer-producer McCann-Erickson advt., Chgo., 1954-55; contbr. to nat. mags. including Woman's Day, 1963—; book reviewer St. Louis Post-Dispatch, 1970—, Phila. Inquirer, 1974—. Coordinator, Panel of Am. Women, Phila., 1961-69, mem. nat. steering com., 1970-72; mem. Pa. state adv. com. U.S. Civil Rights Commn., 1965-71, Phila. Urban Coalition Ednl. Task Force, 1974—. Mem. Democratic Exec. Com. Phila., 1964. Recipient Erma Proetz award, 1949; Meritorious Service citation Frontiers Internat., 1965; Phila. Human Relations award, 1971. Mem. Soc. Mag. Writers. Author: The Education of a WASP, 1970; Getting Ready, 1974. Address: 821 Westview St Philadelphia PA 19119

STAMBAUGH, HARRIETT WYNN MCCARDELL (MRS. JAMES STAMBAUGH), social worker; b. Philipsburg, Pa., May 10, 1922; d. Horace A. and Vivian A. (Wynn) McCardell; B.A., Juniata Coll., 1942; M.S. in Social Service, Boston U., 1947; m. James Arthur Stambaugh, May 1, 1954; children—James Arthur, David Monroe, Richard Thomas. Tchr. history, Curwensville, Pa., 1942-44; social worker A.R.C., Lancaster, Pa., 1945-46, social work supr., Cin., 1947-54; adminstr. social work Dept. Pub. Welfare, Lexington, Va., 1958-61; area supr. social work State Dept. Child Welfare, Frankfort, Ky., 1962; intake social worker Hope Cottage, Children's Bur., Dallas, 1963; adminstr., mental health and mental retardation cons. Dallas County Health Dept., Dallas, 1963-66; dir. social work dept. Childrens Med. Center, Dallas, 1966—. Instr., Southwestern Med. Sch., Dallas, 1966-67, asst. prof. pediatrics, 1967—; exec. dir. Southwestern Cons., Inc., Dallas, 1968—; cons. Terrell State Hosp., Dallas Assn. Retarded Children, 1966-68. Mem. Mental Health-Mental Retardation Profl. Adv. Bd. Dallas County, Tex., 1966—, Mental Health Assn. Profl. Adv. Bd., Dallas, 1968-72, Dallas County Community Action Com. Bd., Dallas, 1967-68; mem. med. adv. com. Dallas chpt. Nat. Found., 1973; mem. profl. adv. com. Creative Learning Center, 1968, Epilepsy Assn., 1972—; mem. Abortion Edn. Com. Dallas, 1970-71. Bd. dirs. Dallas Mental Health Assn., Routh St. Center, Family Center, Parents Anonymous. Recipient Arete award, 1969. Mem. Nat. Assn. Social Workers (Social worker of Year, Dallas chpt. 1969), Acad. Certified Social Workers, Am. Assn. Marriage and Family Counselors, Dallas Assn. for Children with Learning Disabilities. Republican. Methodist. Home: 5935 Copperwood Lane Dallas TX 75240 Office: 1935 Amelia St Dallas TX 75235

STAMM, GAIL ELAINE LASH (MRS. STEPHEN FORREST STAMM), occupational therapist, health service adminstr.; b. Martins Ferry, O., Sept. 14, 1948; d. Albert Wells and Hester Lois (Stobbs) Lash; B.S. in Occupational Therapy, Ohio State U., 1971; m. Stephen Forrest Stamm, Dec. 26, 1970. Founder, dir. occupational therapy Good Samaritan Med. and Rehab. Center, Zanesville, O., 1971—. Instr. stroke workshop Muskingum Area Vocational Coll., Zanesville, 1972—; internship supr. adult edn. classes Ohio State and Columbus 1973—; cons. in designing rehab. unit. Mem. Am., Ohio occupational therapy assns., Good Samaritan Rehab. Club (founder 1973), Welcome Wagon (social chmn. 1972-73, editor 1973-74, parliamentarian 1974—), Pilot Club (extension dir. outreach div. Zanesville), Good Samaritan Charity Circle (baby photo chmn.), Kappa Delta. Presbyn. (Sunday sch. tchr. since 19—). Home: Route 1 Norwich OH 43767 Office: 800 Forest Av Zanesville OH 43701

STAMM, SISTER MARGARET, hosp. adminstr.; b. Chgo., Mar. 4, 1930; d. James Joseph and Clara (Dompke) Stamm; R.N., Little Co. of Mary Sch. Nursing, 1955; B.S., St. Xavier Coll., Chgo., 1959; M.H.A., St. Louis U., 1961. Med.-surg. supr. Little Co. of Mary Hosp., Evergreen Park, Ill., 1956-59, adminstr., 1962—; adminstrv. resident St. Vincent's Hosp., Erie, Pa., 1961-62; preceptor for adminstrv. residents Sch. Hosp. Adminstrn., St. Louis U. Sec., bd. dirs. Little Co. of Mary Hosp., Inc. Speaker, panel moderator Cath. Hosp. Assn. Conv., Chgo. Hosp. Council, Blue Cross-Blue Shield Services, St. Louis U. Symposium, St. Louis U. Alumni Confs. Hosp. Adminstrn., Council Mental Health, A.M.A.; vis. lectr. U. Chgo., Little Co. of Mary Hosp. Sch. Nursing; mem. Medcome Faculty of Nursing, N.Y.C. Mem. health scis. adv. com. Moraine Valley Community Coll. Recipient Outstanding Achievement award for winning Alumni Case Problem Contest Alumni Assn. St. Louis U., 1963, Service to Mankind award Evergreen Park Sertoma Club, 1970. Mem. Congregation Little Co. of Mary, Am. Coll. Hosp. Adminstrs., Chgo. Hosp. Council, Catholic (mem. program com. 1967 ann. conv.) Ill. (trustee; treas. 1970) hosp. assns., Alumni Assn. St. Louis U., Archdiocesan Conf. Cath. Hosps. (pres. 1966-68). Home: Little Co of Mary Convent 9350 S California Av Evergreen Park IL 60642 Office: 2800 W 95th St Evergreen Park IL 60642*

STANDEN, DONNA SONDRA KOMAR (MRS. JOHN L. STANDEN), editor; b. Red Bank, N.J., Dec. 1, 1936; d. Herman Harvey and Margaret Casper (Goldfarb) Komar; student Wellesley Coll., 1955-56; m. Maurice Gordon Stempler, Nov. 24, 1956 (div. July 1963) m. 2d, John Lucas Standen, July 15, 1965; children—Charles Jacob, Margaret Blair. Reporter Red Bank Register daily, 1955-56, 64-65; reporter, women's reporter Asbury Park (N.J.) Press, 1965-66; feature writer Trenton Times, 1966-68; copy editor Phila. Bulletin, 1968-73, asst. editor spl. sect. Focus, 1973—. Mem. Women in Communications, Wellesley Coll. Alumnae Assn., Sigma Delta Chi. Home: 303A Kingston Terrace RD 4 Princeton NJ 08540 Office: Philadelphia Bulletin 30th at Market St Philadelphia PA 19101

STANDEN, ILENE WOLKOFF, educator; b. Bklyn., Feb. 12, 1946; d. Sidney and Rose (Abrams) Wolkoff; B.S. in Bus. Edn., State U. N.Y. at Albany, 1967; M.S. in Spl. Edn., Hofstra U., 1970; m. Rodney John Ashby Standen, June 27, 1973. Tchr., W.C. Mepham High Sch., North Bellmore, N.Y., 1967-73; spl. edn. tchr. of educable mentally retarded, 1967—. Campaign worker for Democratic candidates, 1960—. Grantee to study spl. edn. tchr. certification N.Y. State, 1967. Mem. Am. Assn. Mental Deficiency, N.Y. State Tchrs. Mentally Handicapped, N.Y. State Tchrs. Assn., N.Y. Congress Tchrs., Council L.I. Educators, Tchrs. Assn. Central High Sch. Dist. 3. Address: 1550 N Hobart Blvd Los Angeles CA 90027

STANDS, TALMADGE HORN, cultural orgn. exec.; b. Beaumont, Tex., Oct. 29, 1921; d. Carroll Anderson and Mary Josephine (Withers) Horn; A.B. in Speech, Bethany Coll., 1947; postgrad. Rice U., U. Okla.; m. Jacob Eugene Stands, June 22, 1942; children—Catherine Sue (Mrs. Richard Hayward Buffett), Kahla Joy. Tchr. drama, speech Bethany Coll.; radio shows KOME, Tulsa, KFDM, Beaumont, Tex.; free lance, Houston; mem. repertory co. KTRK-TV; actress Alley Theatre, Shakespeare Soc.; San Antonio World's Fair; sec.-treas. Stands Enterprises; workshop drama dir. Country Playhouse, Houston, 1956-61; adminstrv. asst. Okla. Arts and Humanities; arts program dir., dir. community devel., 1969-73. Lectr., book reviewer; cons. Nat. Endowment Arts in Community Arts Councils, 1974. Div. chmn. fund raising Houston Bapt. Coll.; sect. chmn. Am. Cancer Soc. drives; publicity chmn. P.T.A.; community awareness chmn. Arts-in Edn. project Oklahoma City Arts Council; project dir. Poet-in-Residence, Artist-in-Residence, Okla. Pub. Schs. Named Outstanding Alumnus, Bethany Coll.; Best Actress (3), Best Dir. (4), Women in Communications. Bd. dirs. Civic Music, Ballet Soc. Oklahoma City, Okla. Theatre, Okla. Community Theatres. Democrat. Methodist. Mem. Current Lit. Club (pres. Houston 1965-67), Fedn. Womens' Clubs (v.p. Houston 1967-68), Coll. Women's Club, Hosp. Aux., Deliphian Soc. (program chmn. Houston 1967), Am. Women in Radio and Television (chmn. nat. conv. 1968, S.W. Area v.p., mem. nat. bd., pres. 1970), Okla. Fedn. Theatres (dir.), Bus. and Profl. Women, Coll. Women., D.A.R. Editor: Drift By Sometime, 1973; World of Your Own, 1973. Home: 701 Mockingbird Lane Norman OK 73069 Office: 4440 N Lincoln Oklahoma City OK 73609

STANFORD, ANN, educator, author; b. LaHabra, Cal.; d. Bruce and Rose (Corrigan) Stanford; B.A., Stanford, 1938; M.A. in Journalism, U. Cal. at Los Angeles, 1958, M.A. in English, 1961, Ph.D., 1962; m. Ronald Arthur White, Sept. 18, 1942; children—Rosanna (Mrs. William Norton, Jr.), Patricia, Susan, Arthur Bruce. Asst. prof. English, Cal. State U., Northridge, 1962-66, asso. prof., 1966-68, prof., 1968—, co-founder, co-editor Renaissance Edits., 1969—. Recipient Lit. award Am. Acad. Arts and Letters-Nat. Inst. Arts and Letters, 1972; Silver medal Commonwealth Club Cal., 1959. James D. Phelan fellow 1938-39. Mem. Modern Lang. Assn., Poetry Soc. Am. (Shelley Meml. award poetry 1969, v.p. West Coast 1970—), P.E.N., Internat., Wilderness Soc., Phi Beta Kappa. Author: (poetry) in Narrow Bound, 1943, The White Bird, 1949, Magellan: A Poem to Be Read by Several Voices, 1958, The Weathercock, 1966, The Descent, 1970, The Bhagavad Gita: A New Verse Translation, 1970. Editor The Women Poets in English: An Anthology, 1972. Editorial bd. Early Am. Lit., 1971-74. Home: 9550 Oak Pass Rd Beverly Hills CA 90210

STANFORD, BARBARA LYNN, educator; b. Santa Marie, Cal., Sept. 4, 1943; d. Alvin Gordon and Wilma Evelyn (Daily) Dodds; B.A., U. Ill., 1964; M.A., Columbia, 1966; Ph.D., U. Colo., 1973; m. Gene Howey Stanford, Jr., July 25, 1969. Tchr., Vashon High Sch., St. Louis, 1964-70, Fairview High Sch., Boulder, 1970-72; asso. faculty edn. dept. Utica (N.Y.) Coll. of Syracuse U., 1973—. Ednl. cons., 1970-73. Mem. Nat. Council Tchrs. English, Internat. Council Edn. for Teaching, World Council for Curriculum and Instrn., Women's Internat. League for Peace and Freedom, Phi Beta Kappa, Phi Kappa Phi. Democrat. Mem. Soc. Friends. Author: Learning Discussion Skills Through Games, 1969; (with Gene Stanford) Changes, Mix Jour. 3, Jour. 4, 1971; Myths and Modern Man, 1972; (with D. Turner) Theory and Practice in the Teaching of Literature by Afro-Americans, 1973; Strangers to Themselves, 1973; I Too Sing America, 1973; Love Has Many Faces, 1973; On Being Female, 1974. Home: 25 Talcott Rd Utica NY 13502

STANICK, KATHERINE LEE COULTER, librarian; b. Marshall, Ark., Jan. 19, 1917; d. Edward Herbert and Bird Anne (Pate) Coulter; B.A., Hendrix Coll., 1937; B.S. in L.S., George Peabody Coll., 1942; m. Bernard Louise Stanick, Dec. 24, 1943; 1 dau., Virginia Ann. Tchr. high sch. in Ark., 1937-45; acting librarian Troop Information and Edn. Library, Tokyo, summer 1948; acting med. librarian VA Hosp., Little Rock, 1963-65; adminstrv. asst. to dir. ESEA, Title II, Ark. Dept. Edn., 1967-72; exec. sec. Ark. Library Assn., 1974—. Mem. Charlie Mae Simon Book Award Com., 1971—; pres. Williams Sch. P.T.A., 1966. Mem. Am., Ark., S.W. library assns., Women's Nat. Book Assn., Nat. Assn. Lit. Advance, Hendrix Coll. Alumni Assn. (dir.), Ark. P.T.A. (life, dir. 1970—), League Women Voters. Methodist (vol. librarian). Editor: Learning to Read: Parents Can Help, 1973. Editor Ark. Library Quar. Address: 701 N McAdoo St Little Rock AR 72205

STANICKI, M. JANE, univ. adminstr.; b. Roselle, N.J.; B.A., Montclair State Coll., 1955; M.Ed., Springfield Coll., 1956; Ed.D., (Sara Sturdevant fellow), Columbia. Successively asst. dean students State U. N.Y. at Cortland; dean freshmen Elmira Coll.; adminstrv. asst. to dir. grad. programs in counseling City U. N.Y.; asso. dean students State U. N.Y. at Geneseo; dean students Rockland Community Coll.; dean women Syracuse U., 1969-71, now v.p. for student affairs, residential life, asst. prof. edn., 1971—. Address: Syracuse Univ Syracuse NY 13210

STANKE, FRANCES MARIAN, city ofcl.; b. Buffalo Grove, Ill., May 19, 1935; d. John Thomas and Alma Alvina (Loeding) Stanke; grad. high sch. Exec. sec. Willard F. Miner Agy., Barrington, Ill., 1955-63; village clk. Village of Wauconda, Ill., 1963—. Mem. Wauconda-Island Lake Hosp. Aux., 1972—. Mem. Lake County Clks. Assn., Lake County Municipal League (rec. sec. 1972-73), Wauconda C. of C. Club: Council Catholic Women (Wauconda). Home: 322 Brown St Wauconda IL 60084 Office: 100 Main St Wauconda IL 60084

STANLEY, CAROLYN ROWZEE (MRS. DANIEL SINGLETON STANLEY), youth specialist; b. Ft. Worth, Sept. 25, 1946; d. Mack Andrew and Kathryn Dexter (Howle) Rowzee; B.S., Miss. State Coll. for Women, 1968; student Miss. State U., summers 1964, 65; m. Daniel Singleton Stanley, Nov. 29, 1969; 1 son, Robert Daniel. Extension youth agt. N.C. Agrl. Extension Service, Henderson, 1968—. Publicity dir. Henderson-Vance County United Fund, 1971. Sec. bd. dirs. A.R.C., 1972—. Named Henderson's Young Careerist, 1974. Mem. Am., N.C. assns. extension home economists, Nat. Assn. Extension 4-H Agts., Henderson Bus. and Profl. Women's Club (pres. 1969-71), Phi Upsilon Omicron, Phi Tau Chi. Methodist. Home: 417 N Clark St Henderson NC 27536 Office: PO Box 1028 Henderson NC 27536

STANLEY, DOROTHY EVELYN, educator, artist, author, lectr.; b. Nuremberg, Germany, Sept. 18, 1909; d. William H. Sellings and Lucie (Danziger) Peiser; came to U.S., 1937, naturalized, 1943; B.A., Maidenhead Coll., London, 1928; M.A., Hunter Coll., 1951; postgrad. Columbia, 1946-47, U. Heidelberg, U. Munich, U. Paris, 1930-34; m. Jan. 31, 1932; children—Brigitte Strauss Saunders, Frank Strauss. Head proofroom George Grady Press, N.Y.C., 1939-42; asst. head monitoring sect. Overseas Radio div. U.S. State Dept., N.Y.C., 1942-45; tchr. French, English, Lycee Francais, N.Y.C., 1945-46; tchr. French, Latin, Acad. Sacred Heart, N.Y.C., 1946-49; tchr. French, German, Acad. Lang., N.Y.C., 1949-52; translator, interpreter 1st Nat. City Bank N.Y., 1952-59; asst. prof. modern langs. Old Dominion U., Norfolk, Va., 1960—. Exhibitor art galleries N.Y.C., 1954-59, Va., 1960—; lectr. creative living, 1959—; translator local orgns., bus., 1940. Recipient Grand Nat. Finalist award Am. Artists Profl. League, 1956, 57. Mem. Am. Fedn. Astrologers, Va. Astrol. Assn. (dir.), Am. Assn. Ret. Persons, Am. Assn. U. Women, Alliance Francaise. Lutheran. Author: Die Kunterbunte Spielkiste, 1929, Das Lustige Kinderbuch, 1931, They Call It Courage, 1968. Home: 330 W Brambleton Av Norfolk VA 23510

STANLEY, JUDITH A., psychologist; b. Buffalo, N.Y., Apr. 1, 1944; d. Stanley A. and Phyllis C. (Surma) Stanley; student Villa Maria Coll., Buffalo, 1961-66; B.A. cum laude, D'Youville Coll., 1969; M.S., State U. N.Y. at Buffalo, 1971. Tchr., Villa Maria Acad. Buffalo, N.Y., 1965-66; intern supr. E.J. Meyer Meml. Hosp., Buffalo, 1970-73, rehab. counselor, 1970-73; psychologist Adirondack Correctional Treatment and Evaluation Center, Dannemora, N.Y., 1973-74, Attica

Correctional Facility (N.Y.), 1974—. Cons., Roswell Park Meml. Inst., 1972-73. Mem. Am. Psychol. Assn. (asso.), Nat. Rehab. Assn., Council Arts Clinton and Essex Counties, Phi Lambda Theta. Roman Catholic. Home: 4 Swan St Batavia NY 14020 Office: Attica Correctional Facility Classification Attica NY 14011

STANLEY, KIM (MRS. JOSEPH S. SIEGEL), actress; b. Tularosa, N.M., Feb. 11, 1925; d. Dr. J. T. and Ann (Miller) Reid; grad. U. N.M., 1946; m. Curt Conway; children—Lisa, Jamison; m. 2d, Alfred Ryder; m. 3d, Joseph S. Siegel, 1964. Actress with winter stock company, Louisville, 1946, summer stock, Pompton Lakes, N.J., 1947; first appeared on Broadway in play Montserrat, 1949; other Broadway plays include House of Bernarda Alba, The Chase, Picnic (Pulitzer prize), Traveling Lady, 1954, Bus Stop, 1955; Clearing in the Woods, 1957; Cheri, 1959; A Far Country, 1961; has appeared in TV prodns. including: The Bridge, You Are There, The Brownstone, A Young Lady of Property, Omnibus, Big Story, The Goddess, 1958, A Touch of the Poet, 1958. Recipient N.Y. Drama Critics award for performance in Picnic, 1953, Donaldson award, 1953, N.Y. Newspaper Guild ann. Page One award (with Albert Salmi), 1955; Emmy award for A Cardinal Act of Mercy, 1963. Home: Laurel Dr Centerport NY 11721 Office: 119 W 57th St New York City NY 10019*

STANLEY, MARY K. GAFFORD (MRS. HAROLD A. STANLEY), educator; b. Coriscana, Tex., Jan. 24, 1924; d. Richard Homer and Mary (Philipi) Gafford; diploma Wichita-St. Joseph Hosp. Sch. Nursing, 1947; student Compton Coll., 1953-54, Long Beach City Coll., 1954; B.S., U. Cal. at Los Angeles, 1956, M.S., 1957; m. Harold Allen Stanley, Mar. 22, 1947; 1 dau., Mary Paula. Office nurse for dr., Compton, Cal., 1947-48; staff nurse Seaside Meml. Hosp., Long Beach, Cal., 1949-50, head nurse, 1950-53; pvt. nursing practice Long Beach Profl. Registry, 1953-55; staff nurse Torrance Health Center, Los Angeles County Health Dept., 1957-60; instr. pub. health nursing Sch. Nursing U. Cal. at Los Angeles, 1960-63; asso. prof. psychiat. nursing Los Angeles Harbor Coll., Wilmington, Cal., 1964—; information-receptionist Visitors' Center, Lassen Volcanic Nat. Park, Mancanita Lake, Cal., summers 1969—. Mem. Long Beach (pres. 1952-54), Lakewood Area (pres. 1957-59), Cal. (pres. 1965-67) nurses assns., Cal. League for Nursing, U. Cal. at Los Angeles (life), U. Cal. at Los Angeles Sch. nursing alumni assns., Alpha Tau Delta. Mem. Order Eastern Star. Contbr. articles to profl. jours. Home: 1908 Moray Av San Pedro CA 90732 Office: 1111 Figueroa Pl Wilmington CA 90746

STANLEY, NANCY NELL, librarian; b. Blum, Tex., Nov. 26, 1924; d. James Harvey and Sadie Pearl (Luton) Stanley; student Southwestern Baptist Theol. Sem., 1952-53; B.A., Mary Hardin-Baylor Coll., 1956; postgrad. in library sci. Va. Commonwealth U., 1960-61. Dir. religious edn. First Bapt. Ch., Belton, Tex., 1956-57; dir. religious edn. for youth First Bapt. Ch., Brownwood Tex., 1957-58; supr. library and archives Fgn. Mission Bd., So. Bapt. Conv., Richmond, Va., 1958—. Dean women, counselor Bapt. ch. camps in Tex., 1954-58. Mem. A.L.A., Soc. Am. Archivists, Va. Library Assn., So. Baptist Hist. Soc., Alpha Chi, Sigma Tau Delta. Contbr. articles to religious jours. Home: 3501 Idlewood Av Richmond VA 23221 Office: 3806 Monument Av Richmond VA 23230

STANLEY, VIOLET INEZ MARTIN (MRS. JOHN ALBERT STANLEY), civil engr.; b. Sheffield, Ala., Sept. 27, 1920; d. Herbert and Pearl (Webb) Martin; student Auburn U., 1941-43, Internat. Corr. Schs.; m. John Albert Stanley, Nov. 4, 1939; 1 dau., Carol Faye Bruchac. Office engr. Knox Kershaw Engring. Co., Montgomery, Ala., 1950-57; design engr. A.E. Asso., Montgomery, 1957-59; civil engr. Maxwell AFB, Montgomery, 1959-60; hwy. design engr. Ala. Hwy. Dept., Mobile, 1961-66, civil engr., Montgomery, 1966-69; civil engr. York Engring. Co., Inc., Montgomery, 1969-72, Goodwyn Engring. Co., Inc., Montgomery, 1973—; sec. Summerfield Corp., 1973—; sec.-treas. So. Engring. Co., Inc., 1954-56. Vice pres. Montgomery Little Theatre, 1956. Registered profl. engr., Ala., Miss., Tenn., Fla. Home: 2015 Beverly Dr Montgomery AL 36111 Office: 525 Augusta PO Box 945 Montgomery AL 36102

STANLEY, WINIFRED CLAIRE, lawyer; b. N.Y.C.; d. John Francis and Mary Winifred (Gill) Stanley; B.A. magna cum laude, U. Buffalo, 1930, J.D. (Edward Thompson Co. award), 1933. Admitted to N.Y. bar, 1934; asso. firm Finch & Huber, Buffalo, 1934-37; asst. dist. atty. Erie County, N.Y., 1938-42; N.Y. State rep. at large U.S. Congress, 1943-44; chief counsel N.Y. State Employees Retirement System, Albany, 1945-55; asst. atty. gen. N.Y. State, Albany, 1955—. Vice pres. Young Womens Rep. Club, Erie County, N.Y., 1933-34; mem. Women's Nat. Rep. Club, Frontier Rep. Women's Club Buffalo, Albany County Rep. Women's Club. Mem. Nat. Assn. Women Lawyers, Former Mems. Congress, Am., N.Y. (mem. com. on appellate courts and practice 1973—), Erie County bar assns., Buffalo (pres. 1938-39), N.Y. State (vice chmn. legislative com. 1973—) bus. and profl. Women's clubs, Cap and Gown Soc., Kappa Beta Pi. Club: Zonta (Albany, N.Y.). Office: The Capitol State St Albany NY 12224

STANMAR, MARGARET MARY VIDAS, physician; b. Chgo., Mar. 12, 1915; d. Klement E. and Gertrude (Byon) Vidas; student Mundelien Coll., 1932-35, Lewis Inst., 1935; M.D., Chgo. Med. Sch., 1939; m. Stanley Stanmar, June 23, 1938; children—Greg, Reg, Michele (Mrs. David Neill). Intern Grace Gen. Hosp., Windsor, Ont., Can., 1939-40, resident East Moline State Hosp., 1940-42; gen. practice medicine, LaSalle, Ill., 1942—; mem. staff St. Mary's Hosp., LaSalle, Peoples Hosp., Peru, Ill. Fellow Am. Acad. Gen. Practice; mem. A.M.A., Am. Med. Womens Assn., LaSalle Country (past sec.-treas., pres. 1959-60), Ill. med. socs., LaSalle Bus. and Profl. Women's Club (pres. 1950), Hammond Organ Soc., Zonta (past pres. LaSalle). Home: 1608 St Vincent St LaSalle IL 61301 Office: 555 2nd St LaSalle IL 61301

STANOJEVIC, PATRICIA SUSAN BOURCHIER, ednl. adminstr.; b. Newmarket, Ont., Can., July 6, 1931; d. Alexander Bourchier and Edith Winifred (Gillespie) Anderson; diploma in nursing Sch. Nursing, Hosp. for Sick Children, Toronto, Ont., 1955; B.S. in Nursing, U. B.C., 1957; M.S., McGill U., 1967; m. Miodrag Stanojevic, Mar. 8, 1969. Inst., in-service supr. Hosp. for Sick Children, Toronto, 1955-61; insp. nursing br. Ont. Ministry of Health, Toronto, 1962-63; asst. dir. Coll. of Nurses of Ont., Toronto, 1963-68; lectr. Queens U., Kingston, Ont., 1968-69; asst. research officer Ont. Ministry of Health, 1969-70; dir. Toronto Gen. Hosp. Sch. Nursing, 1971-74; dir. Toronto Gen. Hosp. Campus, George Brown Coll., 1974—. Provost Whittaker scholar, 1950, Nat. Red Cross fellow, 1965. Mem. Registered Nurses Assn. Ont. Home: Apt 1507 511 The West Hall Etobicoke ON M9C 1G5 Canada Office: 90 Gerrard St W Toronto ON Canada

STANSBURY, KATHELYNNE MACKIEWICZ, educator; b. Lafayette, La., Nov. 27, 1945; d. Joseph and Aubrey Agnes (Burleigh) Roman; B.A. in Psychology, U. Southwestern La., 1966; M.A., Stephen F. Austin State U., 1968; m. Michael Grant, Sept. 2, 1967; 1 son, Christian. Psychometrist, Lafayette Parish Sch. Bd., summer 1967; instr. spl. edn. and psychology, psychologist U. Southwestern La., 1968-70; ednl. psychologist, instr. spl. edn. U. New Orleans, 1971, St. Mary's Dominican Coll., New Orleans, 1972—. Mem. Am., Southeastern psychol. assns., Nat. Assn. Retarded Citizens, La. Assn. Sch. Psychologists, Psi Chi. Roman Catholic. Research on time perception, modeling theory. Home: 2216 Manson Av Metairie LA 70002 Office: 7214 St Charles Av New Orleans LA 70118

STANTON, GRETA WERTHEIMER (MRS. HERBERT G. STANTON), social work educator; b. Vienna, Austria; d. Richard and Klara (Deutsch) Wertheimer; B.A., Hunter Coll., 1945; M.S., Columbia, 1946; m. Herbert G. Stanton, Sept. 17, 1963; stepchildren—Andrew Y., Priscilla A. Came to U.S., 1939, naturalized, 1945. Caseworker Wiltwyck Sch. for Boys, 1947, Jewish Childcare Assn., 1948-54; supr. Edwin Gould Found., 1955-57; supr., adminstr., therapist Childville, Inc., 1958, 59; field instr. Columbia Sch. Social Work, N.Y.C., 1960, 61, 62; lectr. casework, human growth, acting dir. fieldwork, chmn. admissions, Hunter Coll. Sch. Social Work, N.Y.C., 1962-68; asso. prof. behavioral sci. (human growth sequence) Sch. of Social Service Fordham U., N.Y.C., 1968-71; asso. prof., dir. student affairs and admissions Grad. Sch. of Social Work, Rutgers U., 1971—. Dir. project U.S. Children's Bur. program Hunter Coll., 1964-67; trainer Headstart Program, 1967. Fellow Am. Orthopsychiat. Assn.; mem. Nat. Assn. Social Workers, Am. Assn. U. Profs., Acad. Certified Social Workers. Home: 34 Holly Lane Piscataway NJ 08854

STANTON, HARRIET LESLIE (MRS. GILBERT STANTON), artist; b. N.Y.C.; d. Jack N. and Gladys (Goldberg) Cooper; student Cornell U., summer 1941; grad. Richmond Profl. Inst., Coll. William and Mary, 1944; student Art Students League, 1946-47; m. Gilbert Stanton, Jan. 20, 1946; children—Joyce P., Janet B. Exhibited in group shows at Ward Eggelston Gallery (Emily Lowe Found. award), 1960, Pa. Acad. Fine Arts, 1961, Butler Inst. Am. Art, Youngstown, O., 1961, Silvermine Guild Artists, 1961, Pitts. Plan for Art, 1961, 63, Heckcher Mus., 1962, San Francisco Mus. Art, 1962, Argus Gallery, Madison, N.J., 1962, 64, Ball State Tchrs. Coll., 1963, Denker-Simon Gallery, 1962-63, North Shore Art Center, 1963, World's Fair, N.Y.C., 1964, Profl. Artists Guild, Adelphi Coll.-Molloy Coll., 1964, Greenwich St. Gallery, 1966, Guild Hall, East Hampton (First prize), 1966, Community Arts Council of S. Shore, 1966, 67, Excergian Gallery, 1966, Frankel Gallery, Roslyn, N.Y., 1967, Nat. Assn. Woman Artists, 1967, Les Semaines Internationales de la Femme, 1st prize Cannes, France, 1969, The Gallery, Ft. Lauderdale, Fla., 1972, Van Straaten Gallery, Chgo., 1974, represented in permanent collections at Post Coll. Mus., Atlantic Richfield collection; art tchr. Community Arts Council of South Shore, 1958-72, N.Y. U., 1967-70, Hofstra U., 1968-74. Participating artist Office of Cultural Devel., County of Nassau. Mem. Profl. Artists Guild, Nat. Assn. Women Artists, Art Students League. Address: 119 Malverne Av Malverne NY 11565

STANTON, JANE TRAPNELL (MRS. KENNETH E. STANTON), music co. exec.; b. Athens, Ga., July 8, 1921; d. James Comer and Eula (Mercer) Trapnell; B.S., Ga. State Coll. for Women, 1941; m. Robert W. Dale, Sept. 19, 1943 (dec. Feb. 1956); children—Dana D. Lamer, Nancy (Mrs. C. Wayne DeLoach); m. 2d, Kenneth E. Stanton, Aug. 2, 1957; 1 son, Kenneth Edwin. Office sec. Bell Aircraft Corp., Marietta, Ga., 1942-45; exec. sec. Lockheed Aircraft Corp., Marietta, 1951-58; asst. Ken Stanton Music, Inc., Marietta, 1959-67, v.p., 1967—, sec., 1974—; sec. Hutson-Stanton, Inc., Marietta, 1972—. Presbyn. Home: 440 Keeler Woods Dr NW Marietta GA 30060 Office: 777 Roswell St NE Marietta GA 30060

STANTON, JEANNE FRANCES, lawyer; b. Vicksburg, Miss., Jan. 22, 1920; d. John Francis and Hazel (Mitchell) Stanton; student George Washington U., 1938-39; B.A., U. Cin., 1940; J.D., Salmon P. Chase Coll. Law, 1954. Admitted to Ohio bar, 1954, So. Ohio Fed. Dist. Ct., 1956; chief clk. Selective Service Bd., Cin., 1940-43; instr. USAAF Tech. Schs., Biloxi, Miss., 1943-44; with Procter & Gamble, Cin., 1945—, legal asst., 1952-54, head advt. services sect. legal div. Trade Practices Dept., 1954-73, mgr. advt. services, legal div., 1973—. Team capt. Community Chest Cin., 1953. Mem. A.A.A.S., Am., Ohio (chmn. uniform state laws com. 1968-70), Cin. (sec. law day com. 1965-66, chmn. com. on preservation hist. documents 1968-71) bar assns., Vicksburg and Warren County, Cin. hist. socs., Internat. Oceanographic Found., Otago Early Settlers Assn. (asso.), Intercontinental Biog. Assn. Clubs: Cincinnati Lawyers, Cincinnati Women Lawyers (treas. 1958-59), Terrace Park Country. Home: 2302 E Hill Av Cincinnati OH 45208 Office: 306 E 6th St Cincinnati OH 45202

STANTON, JEANNETTE ELIZABETH, educator; b. Atlanta, Dec. 20, 1919; d. Guy Newton and Mary Elizabeth (Park) Stanton; A.B., Wesleyan Coll., 1941; diploma in radiography Emory U., 1942; M.A., Ohio State U., 1947, Ph.D., 1951. Mem. faculty Ohio Wesleyan U., Delaware, 1952—, prof. psychology, 1958—. Asso. prof. research Ohio State U., Columbus, 1955—, vis. asso. prof. psychology, 1955-60, 62-63; vis. prof. psychology U. Colo., Boulder, 1964; cons. Ohio Wesleyan U. Upward Bound Program, 1967-68; cons. area of exceptional child Ohio Dept. Edn., 1960-61. Research grantee U.S. Dept. Health Edn. and Welfare, 1957, 59, Ohio Dept. Edn., 1961. Mem. Mem. Am., Midwest psychol. assns., Am. Assn. Mental Deficiency, Internat. Gerontological Soc., A.A.A.S. Home: 250 W Riverglen Dr Worthington OH 43085 Office: Dept Psychology Ohio Wesleyan U Delaware OH 43015

STANTON, JULIET ELLEN (MRS. JOHN SCHOEDINGER), physician; b. Columbus, O., Nov. 9, 1914; d. Frederic M. and Nellie Darling (Swartzel) Stanton; A.B., Ohio State U., 1935, M.D., 1938; m. John Frederic Schoedinger, June 11, 1938; children—John A., David S., Steven P. Intern, Grant Hosp., Columbus, 1938-42, tchr. family practice sect., 1973—; practice medicine, specializing in gen. practice, Columbus, 1939—; physician Planned Parent Clinic, Columbus, 1940, Univ. Sch., Columbus, 1942-48, Juvenile Ct., Franklin County, 1947-59. Adv. bd. Girl Scouts U.S.A., Columbus, 1939-42, Planned Parenthood, Columbus, 1942-50. Fellow Am. Acad. Gen. Practice, Acad. Family Physicians; mem. Am., Pan Am., Ohio med. assns., Am. Women's Med. Assn. (pres. br. 1952, 62), Columbus Acad. Medicine, Delta Gamma, Alpha Epsilon Iota, Delta Gamma Alumni Assn. (pres. 1942). Presbyn. Club: Pilot (Columbus). Home: 4167 Nottinghill Gate Rd Columbus OH 43220

STANTON, PHOEBE BAROODY, art historian, educator; b. Freeport, Ill., Dec. 5, 1914; d. Elijah Tannous and Eleanor Elizabeth (Johnson) Baroody; B.A., Mt. Holyoke Coll., 1937, Litt.D., 1971; M.A., Radcliffe Coll., 1939; Ph.D., Courtauld Inst., U. London (Eng.), 1950; m. Daniel J. Stanton, Feb. 21, 1948 (dec. Apr. 1966); 1 son, Michael. Instr., Reed Coll., Portland, Ore., 1945-47; cultural affairs officer U.S. Fgn. Service, London, Eng., 1950-53; lectr. Bryn Mawr (Pa.) Coll., 1953-54, Goucher Coll., Towson, Md., 1954-62; lectr. Johns Hopkins, Balt., 1954-62, asst. prof., 1962-67, asso. prof., 1967-70, prof., 1970—, William R. Kenan prof., 1971. Cons. urban design city Balt., 1969—; archtl. critic Balt. Sun, 1971—. Am. Council Learned Socs. fellow, 1947-50, Am. Philos. Soc. fellow, 1958, Chapelbrook Found. fellow, 1969, Nat. Endowment Humanities sr. grantee, 1972-73. Mem. Soc. Archtl. Historians (dir. 1969-71), Victorian Soc. (v.p. 1972-73), Am. Assn. U. Women, Coll. Art Assn., Phi Beta Kappa. Author: Gothic Revival in American Church Architecture, 1968; Pugin, 1971. Contbr. articles in field to publs. Home: 114 W University Pkwy Baltimore MD 21210

STANTON, VIVIAN RITA JOAN BRENNAN (MRS. ERNEST STANTON), guidance counselor; b. Waterbury, Conn.; d. Francis P. and Josephine (Ryan) Brennan; B.A., Albertus Magnus Coll., 1939; M.S., So. Conn. State Coll., 1962, postgrad., 1965; postgrad. Columbia; m. Ernest Stanton, May 31, 1947; children—Pamela L., Bonita F., Kim Ernest. Tchr. English, history, govt. Milford (Conn.) High Sch., 1940-48; tchr. English, history Fgn. Born Night Sch., New Haven, 1948-54, Simon Lake Sch., Milford, Conn., 1960-62; guidance counselor, psychol. examiner Jonathan Law High Sch., Milford, 1962-73. Nat. Honor Soc. adviser, 1966-73, mem. Curriculum Councils, Graduation Requirement Council, Gifted Child Com., others, 1940-48, 60-73; guidance dir. Foran High Sch., Milford, 1973—. Active various community drives; mem. exec. bd. Ridge Rd. P.T.A., 1956-59; mem. Parent-Tchr. Council, Hopkins Grammer Sch., New Haven; mem. Human Relations Council, North Haven, 1967-69. Mem. Am. Assn. U. Women, Conn. Personnel and Guidance Assn., Conn. Sch. Counselors Assn., Conn. Assn. Sch. Psychol. Personnel, Conn., Milford (pres. 1945-47) edn. assns. Home: 44 Marlborough Rd North Haven CT 06473 Office: Foran High School Foran Dr Milford CT 06460

STANZIALE, INEZ MARIE, judge; b. Newark; d. Edward B. and Anna Antonetta (Russomaho) Stanziale; B.A., Coll. St. Elizabeth, Convent, N.J., 1932; LL.B., Rutgers U., 1948. Admitted to N.J. bar, 1949; practiced in Newark, 1949—; freeholder Essex County, 1964-67; judge State Div. Tax Appeals, 1966—. Tchr. probate practice and procedure Inst. Continuing Legal Edn., Rutgers U. Parliamentarian, Newark Essex Archdiocese, 1964-70; pres. Holy Rosary Nursery Guild, 1968-70. Ward chmn. Republican Party, 1936-43, chmn. 1st Voters, 1936-40. Served as 1st lt. U.S. Army, 1946. Recipient Amita Achievement award, 1965, Outstanding Citizen Achievement and Accomplishments award Earl Harris Assos., 1973. Mem. N.J., Essex County bar assns., Rutgers U. Alumni Assn. (exec. bd.), N.J. Profl. Women. Home: 505 Lake St Newark NJ 07104 Office: 744 Broad St Newark NJ 07102

STAPEL, JANE SCHNEIDER (MRS. PAUL F. STAPEL), pub. relations exec.; b. Dayton, O., Aug. 26, 1942; d. Robert C. and Mildred E. (McManaman) Schneider; B.A., Ohio State U., 1964; postgrad. Xavier U., 1967-68; m. Paul F. Stapel, Dec. 20, 1969. Pub. relations dir. Paul Werth Assos., Columbus, O., 1965-66; copywriter Union Central Life Ins. Co., Cin., 1966-67; dir. publs. Cin. Symphony Orch., 1967-70; asst. supr. marketing First Nat. Bank of Commerce, New Orleans, 1970-73; asst. marketing officer Kan. State Bank & Trust Co., Wichita, 1973-74. Mem. Internat. Assn. Bus. Communications, Women in Communications. Address: care Toledo Symphony Orchestra 1 Stranahan Sq Toledo OH 43604

STAPLETON, JEAN (JEANNE MURRAY), actress; b. N.Y.C., Jan. 19, 1923; d. Joseph E. and Marie (Stapleton) Murray; ed. Hunter Coll., N.Y.C.; m. William H. Putch, Oct. 26, 1957; 2 children. Sec., Greenwood Playhouse, Peaks Island; appeared in numerous theatre plays, 1941—, including Call Me Madam, Fayetteville, Pa., summer 1959, The Solid Gold Cadillac, summer 1960, Rhinoceros, N.Y.C., 1961, The Miracle Worker, Apple in the Attic, A Thurber Carnival, Everybody Loves Opal, Oklahoma, Fayetteville, summer 1962, Come Blow Your Horn, Gentlemen Prefer Blondes, All for Mary, summer 1963, A Rainy Day in Newark, Picnic, George Washington Slept Here, Speaking of Murder, My Fair Lady, Papa is All, The Sound of Music, summer 1964, Funny Girl, N.Y.C., 1964; appeared in numerous motion pictures including Damn Yankees, 1958, Bells Are Ringing, 1960, Something Wild, 1961; appeared on TV shows Camera Three, Danger, Studio One, Philco Television Playhouse, Omnibus, Woman With a Past, Today Is Ours, Naked City, Armstrong Circle Theatre, The Defenders, The Nurses, Eleventh Hour, Dr. Kildare, Dennis the Menace, Jackie Gleason Show, Car 54 Where Are You?, All in The Family. Mem. Actors' Equity (mem. council 1958-63), Screen Actors' Guild, A.F.T.R.A. Address: 244 W 74th St New York City NY 10023*

STAPLETON, MAUREEN, actress; b. Troy, N.Y., June 21, 1925; d. John P. and Irene (Walsh) Stapleton; student Siena Coll., 1943; m. Max Allentuck, July 1949 (div. Feb. 1959); children—Daniel Katharine. Debut appearance, Playboy of the Western World, 1946; other plays include tour with Barretts of Wimpole Street, 1947, Anthony and Cleopatra, 1947, Detective Story, The Bird Cage, Rose Tatoo, 1950-51, The Sea Gull, Orpheus Descending, The Cold Wind and the Warm, 1959, Amanda and the Glass Menagerie; motion pictures include Lonely Heart, The Fugitive Kind, A View from the Bridge, Bye Bye Birdie. Address: 15 W 70th St New York City NY 10023

STAPP, WILLIE LEE, accountant; b. Synder, Okla., Mar. 4, 1913; d. William Benjamin and Kate (Ross) Broome; grad. Draughan's Bus. U., 1935; student Okla. State U., 1936-37, U. Okla., 1936-44, 57-69; m. Carl Herbert Stapp, Nov. 23, 1938; children—Bruce Michael, Patricia Kay (Mrs. Bert Walker Jr.), Roger Leon. Sec. to pastor Bible Baptist Ch., Oklahoma City, 1935-36; office sec. Okla. Congress of Parents and Tchrs., Oklahoma City, 1936-44, asst. editor, bus. mgr., 1936-44, asso. exec. sec., 1957-59, exec. sec., 1959-69, mng. editor Okla. Parent-Tchr., 1963-69; real estate salesperson Carl H. Stapp Co., Oklahoma City, 1948-56; chief accountant, account sponsor athletic dept. U. Okla., Norman, 1969—. Mem. Okla. Edn. Assn. (asso.), Okla. Congress Parents and Tchrs. (life). Democrat. Baptist. Mem. Order Eastern Star. Home: 200 W Symmes Norman OK 73069

STAR, SHIRLEY ANN (MRS. WINSTON I. BRESLIN), sociologist; b. Chgo., Feb. 18, 1918; d. Harry Israel and Esther Florence (Eagle) Star; A.B., U. Chgo., 1939, Ph.D. with distinction, 1950; A.A. with highest honors, Merritt Coll., 1972; m. Winston I. Breslin, Sept. 16, 1961 (dec. Mar. 1962). Sr. analyst, research br. information and edn. div. War Dept., Washington, 1942-46; sr. analyst spl. com. for re-analysis of research br. experience Social Sci. Research Council, Washington, 1946; sr. study dir. Nat. Opinion Research Center, U. Chgo., 1947-60, project dir. Center for Urban Studies, 1964-66, research asso. univ. dept. sociology, 1951-60, 64-66; asso. prof. dept. mental hygiene Johns Hopkins Sch. of Hygiene and Pub. Health, Balt., 1961-62; vis. prof. sociology U. Cal. at Berkeley, 1966-68; sr. research asso. Bur. Social Sci. Research, Inc., Washington, 1973—. Research cons. 1960-61, 62-64, 68-72. Social Sci. Research Council fellow, 1946-47. Mem. Internat. Sociol. Assn., Am. Sociol. Soc. (council 1959-61), Am. (exec. council 1960-62, 67-68), World assns. for pub. opinion research, Soc. for Study Social Problems, World Assn. for Mental Health, Am. Civil Liberties Union, Editorial cons., asso. editor: Sociometry, 1956-63; adv. editor: Sociol. Methodology, 1971—. Home: 2710 Macomb St NW Washington DC 20008 Office: Bur Social Science Research 1990 M St NW Washington DC 20036

STARA, NANCY JOYCE (MRS. DENNIS CHARLES), lawyer; b. Jefferson City, Mo., Nov. 2, 1943; d. Maurice Joyce and Pearl Grace (Baker) Ayres; B.A., Park Coll., 1964; J.D., U. Neb., 1967; postgrad Coll. Bus. Adminstrn., 1973—; m. Dennis Charles, Feb. 10, 1973. Admitted to Neb. bar, 1967, Colo. bar, 1970; atty. Neb. Tax Commr.

Office, Lincoln, 1967-68; dep. county atty. Hall County, Grand Island, Neb., 1968; law clk. firm Ray, Owens, Keil & Hirsch, Columbus, Ga., 1968-69, McCoy, Weaver, Wiggins, Cleveland & Raper, Fayetteville, N.C., 1969; inheritance tax analyst, inheritance tax div. Colo. Dept. Law, Denver, 1970; legal counsel Neb. Dept. Revenue, Lincoln, 1970-73; sr. legal counsel, 1972-73; with Snyder, Grant & Muehling C.P.A.'s, Lincoln, 1974—. Mem. Neb., Colo., Am. bar assns., Republican. Episcopalian. Mem. Order Job's Daus. Home: 3727 Mohawk St Lincoln NE 68510 Office: 823 Sharp Bldg Lincoln NE 68508

STARBUCK, SHIRLEY, artist; b. Bklyn.; d. Sidney Hilton and Maria Ponce de Leon (French) Starbuck; student Art Students League, 1945-46; m. Baxter Ragsdale Still, Jr., May 27, 1949 (div. Apr. 1954); 1 dau., Susan. Art dir. Ted. Bates & Co., N.Y.C., 1944-49, Doherty, Clifford, Steers & Shenfield, N.Y.C., 1954-59, Norman, Craig & Kummel, N.Y.C., 1959-62; free lance designer, illustrator. Red Cross vol., sketching patients in mil. hosps. Mem. D.C. League Republican Women. Mem. D.A.R., Soc. Mayflower Descs. in State N.Y. Club: Tavern Cay Sailing (Abaco, Bahamas). Address: 2022 Columbia Rd NW Washington DC 20009

STARIKOFF, IREYNE (MRS. RAYMOND JONNARD), concert pianist; b. Odessa, Russia; d. Saul and Marie (Rosentover) Starikoff; scholar Conservatoire Marseilles, France, 1921-25; Ecole Normale de Musique, Paris, France, 1927; M.Mus. under Isidore Philipp, 1930; m. Dr. Raymond Jonnard, Mar. 7, 1935; 1 son, Claude. Came to U.S., 1937, naturalized, 1945. Concert pianist, France, Germany, Eng., 1930-37; instr. piano courses, music critic Courrier Mus. and Art Mus., 1932-37; appeared at Sorbonne Amphitheatre before Pres. French Republic, 1937; appeared with Bklyn. Mus. Concert Series, 1950, Paterson Symphony, N.J., 1957, Erie, Pa. and New London, N.H., 1958, Carnegie Hall, 1960; played before Chopin Soc., 1961, 62, 63, 65, played before many notables since; recital Paterson Pub. Library, 1959, lecture-recital Chopin and French Composers, 1960; radio programs sta. WNYC and WABC; pvt. piano studio, 1940—; chmn. Paterson area auditions. Recipient gold medal and cash award Piano Rec. Festival, 1955-56, Biennial Piano Rec. Competition, 1961-63, Guild Founders medal, 1973; Hall of Fame, Nat. Guild Piano Tchrs. Mem. Nat. Guild Piano Tchrs. (faculty mem., adjudicator), Chopin Soc. N.Y. (program chmn. 1960-63, dir. 1964-66, music dir. 1966), Piano Tchrs. Congress, Asso. Music Tchrs. League, League Women Voters, UN Assn. N.Y., Mus. Modern Art, Nat. Opera Club Am. Address: 465 West End Av New York City NY 10024 also summer Wayne NJ 07470

STARK, ALICE MAY SEITZMAN (MRS. CLAUDE ALAN STARK), mining co. exec.; b. Newark, Mar. 31, 1935; d. Louis Sidney and Esther (Esther) Seitzman; A.B., Barnard Coll., 1956; M.A., Columbia, 1960; m. Claude Alan Stark, Feb. 20, 1958; children—Victor Lowell, Veda Anne, Roland Bradley. Mem. faculty Cape Cod Community Coll., 1969; dir. Sodesmir, The Devel. Co. in the Congo, Zaire, 1972—; co-founder, treas. Claude Stark, Inc., pubs., 1973—. Corporator Cape Cod Conservatory Music and Art. Club: International (Washington). Office: Cape Cod MA 02670

STARK, NELLIE MAY (MRS. OSCAR ELDER STARK), educator, research scientist; b. Norwich, Conn., Nov. 20, 1933; d. Theodore Benjamin and Dorothy Josephine (Pendleton) Beetham; A.B., Conn. Coll., 1956; M.S., Duke, 1958, Ph.D., 1962; m. Oscar Elder Stark, Oct. 31, 1962. Botanist, U.S. Forest Service, Stanislaus Exptl. Forest, Pinecrest, Cal., 1958-62; research asso. Desert Research Inst., U. Nev., Reno, 1964-72; asso. prof. forestry, research asso. U. Mont. Sch. Forestry, Missoula, 1972—. Mem. Alpha Helix Expdn. to Amazon, 1967. Mem. Nev. Opera Guild, 1970-73, Met. Opera Guild, 1968—. Recipient Office of Water Resources grantee; NSF, Internat. Biol. program U.S. Forest Service grantee. Mem. Am. Inst. Biol. Scis., Inst. Tropical Ecology, Bot. Soc. Am., Assn. Tropical Biology, Ecol. Soc. Am. (chmn. com. on ethics 1970-72), Inst. Ecology (chmn. com. on hemisphere cooperation), Sigma Xi, Phi Beta Kappa. Author: Highway Planting Information Appropriate to Nevada, 1966; Nutrient Cycling in a Jeffrey Pine Forest, 1973. Contbr. articles to profl. jours. Home: Rural Route 2 Evoro Hill Missoula MT 59801 Office: Sch Forestry U Mont Missoula MT 59801

STARKE, HELEN, educator, physician; b. N.Y.C., Jan. 2, 1918; d. Edward William and Maude Duryea (Keating) Starke; A.B., Duke, 1938, M.D., 1942. Intern, Duke Hosp., 1942-43, resident, 1944-45; resident Strong Meml. Hosp., U. Rochester, 1943-44; asst. prof. internal medicine Duke Med. Center, Durham, N.C., 1945-53; internal medicine staff Queen of World Hosp., Kansas City, Mo., 1956-65; asst. prof. cardiology U. Neb. Med. Center, Omaha, 1969—. NIH fellow U. Kan. Med. Center, Kansas City, 1965-68. Diplomate Am. Bd. Internat. Medicine, Am. Bd. Cardiology. Fellow A.C.P., Am. Coll. Cardiology; mem. Council Clin. Cardiology Am. Heart Assn., Alpha Omega Alpha, Pi Mu Epsilon. Home: 1308 N 40th St Omaha NE 68131 Office: Univ Neb Med Center Omaha NE 68105

STARKE, KATHLEEN ANN, pub. co. exec.; b. Bklyn., Apr. 18, 1919; d. Joseph and Kathleen Ann (O'Brien) Starke; B.A., Bklyn. Coll., 1959; M.B.A. Coll. City N.Y., 1966. Asst. treas. Reinhold Pub. Corp., N.Y.C., 1960-68; dir. personnel Litton Publs., Oradell, N.J., 1970, v.p. personnel, 1971—. Home: 266 Bedford Park Blvd Bronx NY 10458 Office: 550 Kinderkamack Rd Oradell NJ 07649

STARKEY, PEARL (MRS. ROGER STARKEY), psychologist; b. Phila., Sept. 8, 1930; d. Victor and Anna (Lerner) Steinberg; B.S., Temple U., 1954; M.A. (Dept. Vocational Rehab. grantee 1961-62), Columbia, 1961, Ed.D., 1966; m. Roger Starkey, Oct. 9, 1966. Tchr., Phila., Burlington, N.J. pub. schs., 1954-60; psychology intern N.Y. U.-Bellevue Inst. for Rehab. Medicine, N.Y.C., 1963-64; supr., counselor, tng. Vocational Adv. Service, N.Y.C., 1964-67; asst. prof. dept. counseling San Francisco State Coll., 1967-69; dir. Vocational Rehab. Service, San Francisco Community Mental Health Services, Dept. Pub. Health, 1969—. Psychologist, Conard House; faculty Cal. Sch. Profl. Psychology; cons. San Francisco Unified Schs., Cal. Rehab. Planning Project, 1968-69. Pres., Coordinating Council on Mental Retardation; bd. dirs. Nat. Rehab. Assn., San Francisco, 1968-71. Nat. Inst. Mental Health fellow, 1963. Mem. Am., Cal., Western psychol. assns., Am. Personnel and Guidance Assn., No. Cal. Guidance Assn., Soc. for Research in Psychotherapy, San Francisco Municipal Psychologists Assn. (v.p.). Club: Altrusa. Home: 1730 Jackson St San Francisco CA 94109 Office: 1182 Market St San Francisco CA 94102

STARKEY, ROBERTA NELL JOHNSTON (MRS. JOHN DOW STARKEY), educator; b. Eskota, Tex., June 13, 1921; d. Clarence Beaman and Fannie Irene (Hassell) Johnston; B.S., Tex. Technol. Coll., 1942, Ed.D., 1961; M.A., Eastern N.M. U., 1956; m. John Dow Starkey, Nov. 3, 1943; children—David Joe, Bill Clarence, Marilyn Elaine. Tchr. various schs., 1942-44; tchr. Clovis (N.M.) Lincoln-Jackson Elementary Sch., 1956-59; tchr. Mil. Heights Elementary Sch., prof. Roswell Community Coll., 1961-63; asst. prof. U. Wyo., Laramie, 1964-67; prof. elementary edn. No. Ill. U., DeKalb, 1967—. Mem. summer faculty Eastern N.M. U., 1961-63. Active Girl Scouts U.S.A. Mem. Am. Assn. U. Women (Laramie pres. 1965-67, editor state bull. 1958-60), N.E.A. (sectional chmn. 1959), Internat. Reading Assn. (state chmn. 1966-67), Am. Personnel and Guidance Assn., Student Personnel Assn. for Tchr. Edn. (nat. editor newsnotes 1968-72, pres. 1974), Nat. Soc. Coll. Tchrs. Edn., Ill., N.M. edn. assns., Nat. Assn. Tchrs. Sci., Ill. Assn. Sci. Tchrs., Pi Lambda Theta (pres. 1972-74), Delta Kappa Gamma (pres. 1966-67). Democrat. Methodist (chmn. bd. edn. 1959-61). Home: 2906 Route 23S DeKalb IL 60115

STARKS, RENEE LEE (MRS. BENJAMIN F. LEE), fashion designer; b. Savannah, Ga., Aug. 10, 1914; d. Joseph and Lovevinia (Miller) Gregory; grad. Simplex Beauty Sch., 1937, McDowell's Sch. Fashion, 1942, Ecole-Guerre Lavigne Acad., De Coupe Paris, France, 1952; m. Benjamin F. Lee, May 21, 1929; 1 son, Billy F. Mgr. N.Y. Hat Shoppe, Newark, 1965, also Rental Service, Newark; owner Renee's Sch. French Design-Modeling, Newark, 1955—. Adv. bd. City Nat. Bank, 1973—. Bd. dirs. N.J. Community Drug Addiction. Recipient award Alpha Phi Alpha; Achievement award N.A.A.C.P., 1965, Community Service award Nat. Council Negro Women, 1971, many others. Democrat. Home: 595 High St Newark NJ 07102 Office: 591-93 High St Newark NJ 07102

STARKS, VIRGINIA MARY, social worker; b. Mpls., Nov. 5, 1914; d. Harvey A. and Lulu (Wilcox) Starks; R.N., B.S., U. Buffalo, 1938; M.Social Sci., Smith Coll., 1939. Child guidance clinic social worker Meyer Meml. Hosp., 1939-40; social worker Children's Aid Soc. Allegheny County, Pitts., 1940-45; asst. dir. social service Torrance (Pa.) State Hosp., 1943-63; chief med. social worker St. Vincent Hosp. Rehab. Center, Erie, Pa., 1964-69, dir. social service, 1969—. Field instr. State U. N.Y. Buffalo, 1965-70. Bd. dirs. Erie County Council Alcoholism. Mem. profl. adv. bd. Stairways, 1968-72. Mem. Acad. Certified Social Workers, Nat. Assn. Social Workers (chpt. treas. 1965-67), N.W. Pa. Heart Assn., Soc. for Hosp. Social Work Dirs., Nat. Conf. Cath. Charities, Erie County Hist. Soc., Presque Isle Audubon Soc. Episcopalian. Club: Zonta (sec. 1970-72) (Erie). Home: 720 N Park Av Erie PA 16502 Office: 232 W 25th St Erie PA 16512

STARKWEATHER, ELIZABETH KEZIA, educator; b. Knoxville, Tenn., Dec. 12, 1914; d. Richard Holmes and Lucy (Leal) Starkweather; B.A., Brown U., 1936; M.A., U. Ia., 1938; Ph.D., Cornell U., 1957. Teaching fellow Merrill Palmer Inst., Detroit, 1938-39; psychologist Child Guidance Clinics in New Eng., 1939-42; psychologist Child Guidance Clinic, Oklahoma City, 1943; psychologist State Child Welfare Div., Okla., 1944-54; asso. prof. child devel. Okla. State U., Stillwater, 1957—; mem. U.S. Nat. Com., World Orgn. on Early Childhood Edn.; colleague Creative Edn. Found. Mem. Okla. adv. bd. on Day Care for Children. Fellow Am. Orthopsychiat. Assn.; mem. Soc. for Research in Child Devel., Am. Home Econs. Assn., Sigma Xi, Omicron Nu. Contbg. editor Jour. of Creative Behavior. Home: PO Box 246 Stillwater OK 74074

STARR, BARBARA LOU, librarian; b. Boston, Oct. 1, 1937; d. DeWayne Edward and Sadie (Schneider) Nolting; B.A., Emory U., 1958, M.L.S., 1960; m. Robert Stephen Starr, May 8, 1964; children—James Edward, Michael Wayne. Cataloger, reference librarian Emory U. Library, Atlanta, 1959-62; with Peace Corps, 1962-70, vol., Jamaica, 1962-66, librarian, Washington, 1966-70; regional librarian Fairfax County Pub. Library, Alexandria, Va., 1970—. Mem. Va. Library Assn. Home: 3151 Woodland Lane Alexandria VA 22309 also 2501 Sherwood Hall Lane Alexandria VA 22306

STARR, JANICE LEIGH (MRS. RALPH PAUL STARR), educator; b. Gilman, Colo., Oct. 16, 1942; d. George Albert and Margaret Ella (Brown) Carlow; B.A., U. No. Colo., 1965; postgrad., Western State Coll., 1972-74; m. Ralph Paul Starr, May 21, 1961; children—Deena Ann, Danelle Marie, Dale Patrick. Tchr. bus. edn., English, Eagle Valley High Sch., Gypsum, Colo., 1965—. Pres. S & C, Inc., Eagle, Colo., 1963—. Treas. Town of Eagle, 1971-73. Mem. Nat., Colo., Eagle County edn. assns., Nat. Bus. Edn. Assn. Democrat. Roman Catholic. Home: PO Box 326 Eagle CO 81631 Office: PO Box 188 Gypsum CO 81637

STARR, JOY ELOISE SMITH (MRS. NICHOLAS STARR), writer; b. Rockford, Ill.; d. George Leonard and Bradie (Baker) Smith; B.A. in History of Art, Wheaton Coll., 1953; postgrad. George Washington U., 1957-58; m. Nicholas Starr, Aug. 17, 1963; children—Richard Kimball, Peter Tristram. Expeditor, Kiplinger Agy., Washington, 1955-57; sec. Nat. Acad. Scis., Washington, 1959-61; sec. Sylvania Electric Products, Washington, 1961-64, asst. security officer, 1962-64, staff asst. to mgr. navy relations, 1961-64; columnist Va. Sentinel, Fairfax, 1969; free lance writer, 1969—. Organizing rec. sec. Navy-Vale Community League, 1968-69; mem. Fairfax County Oakton Study Group, 1969-70; mem. Hist. Soc. Fairfax County (Va.), 1964-67, Fairfax Heritage Soc., 1968-69. Mem. D.A.R. (chpt. rec. sec. 1968-70, chmn. press and scrap book com., publicity com. 1968-70, dist. chmn. Jr. Am. citizens com. 1969, state chmn. jr. membership com. 1962-63). Contbr. articles to newspapers, mags. Home: 3000 Fox Mill Rd Oakton VA 22124

STARR, LETHIA WOOD, physician; b. New Straitsville, O., Oct. 22, 1905; d. Harry Kilborn and Cora Belle (Webb) Starr; student Ohio U., 1922-24; M.D., U. Cin., 1928. Intern, Good Samaritan Hosp., 1928-29, U. Chgo., Chgo. Lying-In Hosp., 1930; practice medicine, Logan, O., 1931—; mem. staff Hocking Valley Community, Lancaster-Fairfield, Grant hosps. Trustee Ohio Valley Health Services Found. Fellow Am. Acad. Family Physicians; mem. A.M.A., Ohio Med. Assn., Am., Ohio med. women's assns., Am., Ohio (Bronze plaque for 25 years postgrad. study) acads. gen. practice, Am. Legion, Hist. Soc., Am. Assn. U. Women, Pi Beta Phi. Republican. Methodist (Shriner). Mem. Order Eastern Star. Home: 109 S Mulberry St Logan OH 43138

STARRATT-WARD, PATRICIA ELIZABETH, energy analyst, author, actress; b. Boston, Nov. 7, 1943; d. Alfred Byron and Anna (Mazur) Starratt; A.B., Smith Coll., 1965; grad. prep. dept. Peabody Conservatory Music, 1961; m. R.L. Hubbard, June 19, 1965 (div. Feb. 1970); m. 2d, B. Van Winkle, Mar. 21, 1970 (div. Sept. 1971); m. 3d, L.T. Ward, V, June 1, 1973. Teaching asst. Harvard Grad. Sch. Bus. Adminstrn., 1965-67; mng. dir. INS Assos., Washington, 1967-68; adminstrv. asst. George Washington U. Hosp., 1970-71; legal asst. Morgan, Lewis & Bockius, Washington, 1971-72; profl. staff energy analyst Nat. Fuels and Energy Policy Study, U.S. Senate Interior Com., 1972-74; cons., exec. asst. energy resource devel. Fed. Energy Adminstrn., Washington, 1974—. Appeared Off-Broadway in To Be Young, Gifted and Black; performed as Amy in Dinny and The Witches; as Columbina in Servant of Two Masters; as Singer in Death of Morris Biederman; as Joan in Joan of Lorraine; as Mado in Amadee; as Mrs. Rowlands in Before Breakfast; as the girl in Hello Out There; as Angela in Bedtime Story; as Hannah in Night of the Iguana; as Lavinia in Androcles and the Lion; as Catherine in Great Catherine; as Julie in Lilliom; as First Nurse in Death of Bessie Smith; appeared at Detroit Summer Theatre in Oklahoma, Guys and Dolls, Carousel, Brigadoon, Kiss Me Kate, Finnian's Rainbow. Asst. to dir. Broadway plays A Cry Of Players, A Way Of Life; asst. to dir. in Off-Broadway play To Be Young, Gifted, and Black. Mem. Actors Equity. Episcopalian. Contbr. articles to profl. jours. Home: 309 12th St SE Washington DC 20003

STARRETT, AGNES LYNCH (MRS C. V. STARRETT), educator, author, editor; b. Peru, Ind.; d. Jerome and Nancy X. (ReMine) Lynch; A.B., U. Pitts., 1920, M.A., 1925; Litt.D., Waynesburg Coll., 1960; m. Clare V. Starrett, July 29, 1923; children—Clare (Mrs. Walter L. Thompson III), David D. Tchr. Lemington Sch., 1918-22; prof. dept. English, U. Pitts. 1922-64, prof. emeritus English and humanities, 1964—, dir. Univ. Press, 1952-64, emeritus dir. and editor, 1964—, editor Pitt, 1939-59; mem. Irish Scholarship Awards Com. Free lance editor, writer, book designer, 1964—. Named Distinguished Dau. of Pa. by Gov., 1954. Mem. Hist. Soc. Western Pa. (dir. 1960—), Gaelic Art Soc., Quens, Mortar Bd., Women in Communications, Phi Beta Kappa, Phi Alpha Theta. Roman Catholic. Clubs: Faculty (U. Pitts.). Womens Press, Zonta. Author: Through One Hundred Fifty Years, 1937; Falk Foundation, A Private Fortune, A Public Trust, 1967. Books represented in Fifty Books of Year selection, 1954, 64. Contbr. articles to jours. Address: 544 Bigham Rd Pittsburgh PA 15211

STARRITT, MARY EMILY WRIGHT (MRS. WILLIAM ANDREW STARRITT, JR.), club woman; b. Herrin, Ill., June 26, 1907; d. William Henry and Ema Gertrude (Bandy) Wright; student Oxford Female Acad., 1926— Va. Intermont Coll., 1927-28, East Tenn. State U.; m. William Andrew Starritt, Jr., Sept. 24, 1928; children—Marylou Nadyne (Mrs. William Hawthorne Conant), Emily Elizabeth (Mrs. George DuBose Sells). Tchr. music high schs., Johnson City, Tenn., 1941-58; dir. music Appalachian Preaching Mission, 1955, 56, 57; pres. Tipton-Haynes Hist. Living Farm, Johnson City, 1971—. Adviser Monday Club Aux., 1937-38; mem. Park and Recreation Bd., Johnson City, sec., 1944-48; sponsor Jr. and Juvenile Music Clubs, Johnson City, 1943-46; pres. Community Concert Bd., Johnson City, 1941-49, 2d v.p., campaign mgr., 1950-74; pres. Johnson City council Girl Scouts U.S., 1945-53, First Appalachian Area Council, 1953-57, Dixie V Regional Bd. dir., 1961-64. Bd. dirs. United Fund, 1961-62, Carroll Reece Museum, 1968-70. Recipient Certificate Girl Scouts, 1966, 35 year pin, 1971. Mem. D.A.R. (regent local chpt. 1960-62, dir. Appalachian dist. 1965-68, Tenn. chaplain 1968-71, mem. nat. speakers bur. 1971-74, chmn. Tenn. chpt. Am. Heritage 1971-74, chaplain Tenn. 1972-74, v.p. Officers Club 1971-74), Fedn. Music Clubs (pres. 1939-40), Dilettantes (pres. 1937-38), Daus. Colonial Wars (v.p. Tenn. 1971-74), Nat. Fedn. Garden Clubs (pres. local club 1962-64, 68-69), U.S. Power Squadron, Va., Tipton Haynes (pres. 1971-76), Rocky Mount (dir. 1971-74), Hist. assns., United Daus. 1812, So. Dames Am. (pres. 1969-72), Nat. Soc. Daus. Am. Colonists, Sons and Daus. Pilgrims, Assn. Preservation Tenn. Antiquities (sec.-1967-74), Colonial Dames Am., P.E.O., Kappa Delta, Kappa Delta (pres. adv. bd.), Delta Kappa Gamma. Baptist. Office: Tipton-Haynes Living Historical Farm Erwin Hwy 19 W Johnson City TN 37601

STASSER, DOROTHY ANN, educator; b. St. Francis, Kan., Oct. 13, 1942; d. Marvin and Cora Lou (Rockwell) Stasser; B.S., Bethany Nazarene Coll., 1964; M.S. (Nat. Def. Edn. Act fellow), Okla. State U., 1966, Ed.D., 1970. Asst. head resident Murray Hall, Okla. State U., 1966-67; faculty Bethany (Okla.) Nazarene Coll., 1967—, asst. prof. psychology, 1968-71, asso. prof., 1971-73, prof., 1973—, also dir. testing, 1970—. Mem. Ch. of Nazarene. Home: 8208 NW 27th St Bethany OK 73008

STATEN, BLANCHE LOUISE (MRS. GEORGE STATEN), horsebreeder; b. Wellston, O., June 5, 1921; d. Fred Guy and Thelma Pauline (Partlow) Saltsman; student pub. schs.; m. George F. Staten, Mar. 6, 1937; children—Kay (Mrs. Robert West), Betty (Mrs. Elmo Sherman), Jean (Mrs. Harold Davis), Martha (Mrs. Larry Martin), Harold, George. Breeder standardbred racing horses, Wellston, O., 1970—. Mem. U.S. Trotters Assn., Ohio Harness Horseman, Jackson County Harness Horseman Assn. (treas. 1971—). Democrat. Mem. Evang. U.B. Ch. Address: Route 3 Box 140 Wellston OH 45692

STATLAND, SUZANNE G. (MRS. HARRY STATLAND), human relations worker; b. Kansas City, Mo., July 20, 1931; d. A. Morris and Zora (Taxman) Ginsberg; B.A., Vassar Coll., 1952; M.A., Radcliffe Coll.-Harvard, 1953; m. Harry Statland, Feb. 26, 1957. Research asst. The Child Welfare League Am., N.Y.C., 1954; jr. press rep. Columbia Broadcasting Co., WCBS-TV, N.Y.C., 1955-57; asst. dir. publicity U. Kansas City, 1959-62; lectr. English history U. Mo. at Kansas City, 1963-65; script writer The City Meets the Eye, Kansas City Arts Commn., 1966; asst. to dir. Kansas City human relations dept., 1968; counselor Young Adult First Offenders Service, 1973—. Mem. Greater Kansas City Urban Policy Planning Program, 1973-74. Bd. dirs. Am. Heart Assn., Kansas City, 1957-69, v.p., 1959-61; mem. steering com. Women's Com. for Bonds, 1964-65; founder, pres. Friends of Library, U. Mo. at Kansas City, 1965-68, bd. dirs., 1965—; bd. dirs. Coaches Council for Job Action, 1968—, Landmarks Commn., Kansas City, 1970—, Union Sta. Commn., Kansas City, Mo., 1973—. Radcliffe Coll., Cambridge, Mass., 1965-71. Contbr. articles to Kansas City Star. Address: 1016 W 69th Terrace Kansas City MO 64113

STATON, BETTY ANNE SHIVER (MRS. ULYSSES G. STATON), polit. orgn. exec.; b. Orlando, Fla., Nov. 8, 1925; d. Samuel Wyatt and Sara Elizabeth (Stegar) Shiver; B.S. in Commerce, Fla. State U., 1946; student Rollins Coll., summer 1944; m. Ulysses Grant Staton, Aug. 24, 1946; children—Suzanne Brooks, Sara Elizabeth, Samuel Wyatt. Sec. to dept. psychology U. Fla., Gainesville, 1946-48; ins. sec. Tucker & Branham, Inc., Orlando, Fla., 1948-55. Pres. League Women Voters Orange County, 1964-66, nominating chmn., 1973-74; treas. League Women Voters Fla., 1966-69, 1st v.p., 1969-71, pres., 1971-73, cons., 1973—; edn. chmn. Jr. League Orlando, legislative and bylaws chmn., chmn. pub. relations, provisional chmn., editor Newsheet; mem. Orange County Local Govt. Study Commn., 1965-67; mem. Orange County Sch. Bd. Bi-racial Adv. Com., 1969-71; mem. steering com. Orange County Lay Curriculum Com.; mem. Gov.'s Citizens Com. on Edn., 1971-73; co-chmn. Orange County Com. for Better Constn., 1968, Citizens for Tax Reform, 1971, Citizens for Jud. Reform, 1972; chmn. Citizens Conf. on Edn., 1973; mem. Gov.'s Orange County Adv. Com., 1973—; mem. Dem. Women's Club Orlando. Bd. dirs. Fla. Symphony Soc., Orange County Econ. Opportunity; met. bd. dirs. Orange County YMCA. Recipient Liberty Bell award Orange County Bar Assn., 1970. Mem. Delta Delta Delta (pres. Alumnae Club 1951), Phi Kappa Phi. Presbyn. Home: 1217 Reading Dr Orlando FL 32804 Office: 1310 W Colonial Dr Orlando FL 32804

STATON, SUE KAREN, orch. adminstr.; b. Indpls., Aug. 28, 1932; d. Fayne E. and Veronica Elizabeth (Doyle) Staton; B.S. in Music, Ind. U., 1954. Lectr. and women's dir. radio TV dept. Ind. U., Bloomington, 1960; dir. sales and service WFBM-TV, Indpls., 1960-65; dir. pub. relations Indpls. Symphony Orch., 1965-71, asst. mgr., 1971-72; gen. mgr. Tulsa Philharmonic Orch. 1972-73; dir. pub. relations Cin. Symphony Orchestra, 1973-74; dir. audience, concert devel. Indpls. Symphony Orch., 1974—. Mem. Women in Communications, Alpha Gamma Delta, Sigma Alpha Iota. Home: 3644 Nobscot Ct #3B Indianapolis IN 46222 Office: Indpls Symphony Orch Clowes Meml Hall 4600 Sunset Av Indianapolis IN 46208

STATS, JEANETTE (MRS. HERBERT E. STATS), govt. ofcl.; b. Chgo.; d. Emil and Minna Rosenbery; student Weber Coll,, 1928-29, U. Minn., 1934-35; m. Herbert E. Stats, Nov. 14, 1932. Dir. edn. and pub. relations Washington Heart Assn., 1955-60; pub. relations cons., Washington, 1961-63; press rep. Nat. Ballet, Washington, 1962-63; reporter Environmental Health News Service, Washington, 1963-64; writer, editor fed. govt. agys. Dept. Health, Edn. and Welfare, Dept. Labor, Washington, 1964—, cons., co-founder Forum Profls. and Execs., Washington Sch. Psychiatry, 1966-67. Mem. Presdl. Inagural Com. U.S., 1965; bd. govs., exec. com. Women's Nat. Democratic Club, 1961-71. Mem. Am. Newspaper Women's Club. Unitarian. Home: Box 248 Bethany Beach DE 19930 Office: 14530 Kelmscot Dr Silver Spring MD 20906

STAUDER, SISTER FRANCIS BORGIA, educator; b. Witt, Ill., Apr. 7, 1911; d. Frank and Frances Margaret (Mast) Stauder; A.B., St. Louis U., 1937; M.S., U. Notre Dame, 1943, Ph.D., 1947. Tchr., St. Francis High Sch., Washington, Mo., 1937-45; adminstr. high sch., Westphalia, Mo., 1949-51, Aviston Community High Sch., Aviston, Ill., 1951-53; faculty Notre Dame Coll., St. Louis, 1954—, prof. math., 1960—. Recipient NSF grant, 1960. Mem. Math. Assn. Am., Am. Math. Soc., Soc. Sigma Xi. Home: 320 E Ripa St St Louis MO 63125

STAUFFER, BARBARA ALICE, banker; b. Durand, Ill., May 27, 1931; d. William Hiram and Mabel Alice (Crowley) Stauffer; grad. Nat. Grad. Trust Sch., 1973. With 1st Nat. Bank & Trust Co. Rockford (Ill.), 1948—, supr. operations, 1961-70, asst. trust officer, 1970-74, trust officer, 1974—. Methodist. Soroptimist (v.p.). Office: 401 E State St Rockford IL 61101

STAUFFER, DONNA LOIS FREDERICKSON (MRS. LEE D. STAUFFER), village ofcl.; b. Tyler, Minn., May 12, 1932; d. Howard Milton and Dagny (Ostergaard) Frederickson; student Grand View Coll., 1949-50, U. Neb., 1950-51; B.S., U. Minn., 1954; m. Lee D. Stauffer, Aug. 27, 1952; children—Karl, Lisa, Dane, Kristian. Occupational therapist Univ. Hosps., U. Minn., Mpls., 1954-55; councilman St. Anthony Village (Minn.), 1973—. Mem. St. Anthony Village Human Relations Adv. Com., 1972-73, vice chmn., 1973, chmn. edn. subcom., 1972-73; mem. St. Anthony Village Human Rights Study Com., 1968; mem. met. significance adv. com. Met. Council Twin Cities, 1974—. Bd. dirs. Mercy Hosp., Coon Rapids and Anoka, Minn., 1963, House of Faith Nursery Sch., Mpls., 1969—. Mem. Am., Minn. occupational therapy assns., League Women Voters, Mpls. Soc. Fine Arts, Danish-Am. Fellowship. Democrat. Club: University Faculty Women's (Mpls.). Home: 3000 Croft Dr Minneapolis MN 55418

STAUFFER, MARY RUTH SCHUH (MRS. FLOYD RANDALL STAUFFER), physician, surgeon; b. Toledo, Aug. 26, 1917; d. Henry Fredrick and Amelia Charlotte (Koerner) Schuh; B.S., Capital U., 1939; M.D., Ohio State U. Med. Sch., 1943, M.S., 1943; m. Floyd Randall Stauffer, Dec. 18, 1943; children—Dorothy (Mrs. Aldon Blowers), James Henry, Judith (Mrs. Robert Sanders), Janet Marie (Mrs. Masa Suzuki), John Henry. Intern Cleve. City Hosp., 1943, Franklin Roosevelt Hosp., Bremerton; Wash., 1944; resident Sacred Heart Hosp., Pensacola, Fla., 1948-49; practice medicine, Bremerton, 1944-47, Pensacola, 1948-53, Downey, Cal., 1954—; chief staff Downey Community Hosp., 1971-72. Mem. Downey-Guadalajara Sister City Assn. Mem. A.M.A., Cal., Los Angeles County med. assns., Alpha Omega Alpha, Sigma Xi. Home: 7207 Rio Flora Pl Downey CA 90241 Office: 11411 Brookshire Rd Downey CA 90241

STAVE, ANNA MONTEDONICO (MRS. HOLGER STAVE), orgn. exec.; b. Memphis, Oct. 16, 1943; d. Edward LeMaster and Anna (Rea) Montedonico; student Inst. for Am. Univs., Aix-en-Provence, France, 1963-64; B.A., St. Louis U., 1965; M.F.A. (Univ. scholar), Ohio U., 1967; m. Holger Stave, May 23, 1970. Grad. asst. creative drama, children's theatre Ohio U., Athens, 1966-67; tchr. drama, honors English, Highland Park (Mich.) High Sch., 1967-69, tchr. English, adult edn., 1968-69; dir. youth theatre Karamu House, Cleve., 1969-72, Salt City Playhouse, Syracuse, N.Y., 1972-73; dir. youth program YWCA, Syracuse, N.Y., 1973—. Tchr. pilot drama programs, schs. in Cleve., 1972, Syracuse, 1973-74; instr. creative drama for tchrs. Bur. of Sch. Services, Syracuse U., 1973; asst. camp dir. Girl Scouts Am., Syracuse, 1973; drama tchr. Athens Arts Council, 1966. Mem. Am., Theatre Assn., Children's Theatre Conf., Kappa Beta Gamma, Alpha Gamma Omega, Eta Sigma Phi. Office: 339 E Onondago Syracuse NY 13202

STAVRIDES, RIA, educator, philosopher; b. Weissenburg, Bavaria, Dec. 14, 1911; d. Karl Joseph Gistel and Babetta (Wansch) S.; ed. J. W. Goethe U., Frankfurt, Germany, 1933, U. Lausanne (Switzerland), 1934; Ph.D., Columbia, 1952. Came to U.S., naturalized, 1950. Prof. philosophy Vassar Coll., 1946-67, chmn. dept., 1966-67; prof. philosophy Temple Buell Coll., Denver, 1967—. Fellow Council Learned Socs., 1950-51; fellow Vassar Coll., 1957-58; scholar in residence Inst. Humanistic Studies, Aspen, Colo., 1966, 67. Mem. Am. Assn. U. Profs., Am. Philos. Assn., Metaphys. Soc. Am., Am. Soc. Phenomenology and Existential Philosophy, Am. Soc. Theatre Research, ANTA. Contbr. articles in field to profl. jours. Home: 45 Dexter St Denver CO 80220

STAYTON, JOSEPHINE SULLIVAN, newspaper librarian, researcher; b. McKinney, Tex., Apr. 4, 1918; d. Walter Lee and Johnie Jo (Waters) Sullivan; student Wichita Falls Jr. Coll., 1934-35, U. Okla., 1936-37; m. Logan Wilton Stayton, June 16, 1938; children—Robert Lee, Susan (Mrs. Pinkerton). Asst. librarian Times Pub. Co., Wichita Falls, Tex., 1969-70, head librarian, 1970—. Active A.R.C., United Fund, March Dimes, P.T.A.; mem. Wichita Gen. Hosp. Aux. Mem. So. Newspaper Pubs. Assn. Librarians Assn., Woman's Forum, Pi Beta Phi. Baptist. Democrat. Clubs: Colony, 1938 Century (Wichita Falls). Home: 2202 Harrison Wichita Falls TX 76308 Office: Times Sq PO Box 120 Wichita Falls TX 76307

STEAD, CHRISTINA (ELLEN), author; b. Rockdale, Sydney, New South Wales, Australia; d. David George and Ellen (Butters) S.; Tchr.'s certificate Sydney U. Tchrs. Coll.; m. William James Blake. Tchr. pub. schs., tchr. abnormal children, demonstrator psychology lab. Sydney (Australia) U.; clk. grain co., London, Eng., 1928-29, bank, Paris, France, 1930-35; sr. writer Metro-Goldwyn-Mayer, 1943; instr. workshop in novel N.Y. U., 1943-44. Recipient Aga Khan prize, Paris, 1967. Fellow creative arts Australian Nat. U., Canberra, 1969. Author: The Salzburg Tales, 1934 (with others) The Fairies Return, 1934; Seven Poor Men of Sydney, 1935; The Beauties and Furies, 1936; House of All Nations, 1938; The Man Who Loved Children, 1940; For Love Alone, 1944; Letty Fox: Her Luck, 1946; A Little Tea, A Little Chat, 1948; The People with the Dogs, 1952; Dark Places of the Heart, 1966 (pub. in Eng. as Cotters' England, 1966); The Puzzleheaded Girl and Other Stories, 1967; The Little Hotel, 1974. Editor: (with husband) Modern Women in Love, 1946; South Sea Stories, 1955. Translator: Colour of Asia (Fernand Gigon), 1955; The Candid Killer (Jean Giltene), 1956; In Balloon and Bathyscaphe (August Piccard), 1956. Contbr. short stories to Southerly, Kenyon Rev., Sat. Eve. Post, New Yorker, Paris Rev., others, revs. to various papers. Home: care Stead 10 Donald St Hurstville New South Wales 2220 Australia Office: care Cyrilly Abels 119 W 57th St New York City NY 10019

STEADMAN, MRS. HAROLD A. (L. ALICE TUTTLE STEADMAN), sculptor, author, painter; b. King, N.C., Mar. 10, 1907; d. John Walter and Alice (Slate) Tuttle; diploma in art Meredith Coll., 1928; postgrad. Naum Los Sch. Sculpture Pa. Acad. Fine Arts, Breckenridge Sch. Art, studied watercolor under Elliot H'Hara; m. Harold Alton Steadman, Dec. 25, 1936. Tchr. art. The Ark, Southern Pines, 1930-31, Queen's Coll., Charlotte, N.C., 1954, 55, Mint Mus., 1936—, Alexander Sch., 1942, 45; pvt. tchr., 1959—. Lectr. on astrology and emotionally induced ailments. Represented in pvt. collections U.S., Eng. Recipient Raleigh Studio Club Gold Medal award, 1935, Margaret Graham Silver Cup for Water Color, 1936; prize winner Blowing Rock, Spring's Show. Mem. Am. Assn. U. Women, N.C. State Art Soc., Guild Charlotte Artists. Baptist. Club: Opti-Mrs. (head girls work 1950-55, pres., lt. gov.). Author: Who's the Matter with Me, 1966. Address: 2500 Cloister Dr Charlotte NC 28211

STEADMAN, ROSE YEVTICH (MRS. MELVIN C. STEADMAN), real estate broker; b. Portland, Ore., July 8, 1928; d. Mike and Gabrielle (Jerep) Yevtich; student U. Ore., 1947-48, Santa Rosa Jr. Coll., 1950, U. Cal. at Berkeley, 1953, Portland State Coll., 1955; m. Melvin C. Steadman, Feb. 6, 1961; 1 dau., Sharon Rose. Secretarial positions with various firms, 1946-60; with Borrego Valley Realty, Inc., Julian, Cal., 1960—, v.p., sec., 1966—. Chmn. Borrego Springs (Cal.) Desert Festival, 1966, Mem. Nat. Assn. Real Estate Bds., San Diego Bd. Realtors, Borrego Springs C. of C. (dir. 1964-65). Club: DeAnza Players (Borrego Springs). Home: 200 Palm Canyon Dr Borrego Springs CA 92004 Office: 1934 Main St Julian CA 92036

STEAHLY, VIVIAN EUGENIA EMRICK, educator, author, cons.; b. Wapakoneta, O., July 10, 1915; d. Daniel and Katharine (Bush) Emrick; B.S., Ohio State U., 1936, B.A. cum laude, 1936; M.A., U. Cin., 1941; m. Frank Lester Steahly, Oct. 17, 1936 (dec. May 1967); 1 son, Lance Preston. Tchr. Latin, French, English, Grant High Sch., Georgetown, O., 1936-39; instr. English, Seaford (Del.) High Sch., 1942-43; instr. English, U. Tenn., Knoxville, 1948; tchr. Latin, French, English, Winfield (W.Va.) High Sch., 1955-58; asst. prof. English, French, Morris Harvey Coll., Charleston, W.Va., 1958-66, chmn. dept. modern langs., 1962-64, asst. prof. edn., 1964-65; asst. prof. English, Ohio State U., 1967—; editing cons. W.Va. U. bd. govs., W.Va. Dept. Edn., 1966-67. Free-lance writer; book reviewer, monologuist, tech. writing cons. Mem. Modern Lang. Assn., Am. Assn. Higher Edn., A.A.A.S., Ohio Acad. Sci., Ohio State U. Assn., U. Cin. Alumni Assn., Scholaris, Phi Beta Kappa, Pi Lambda Theta, Eta Sigma Phi. Republican. Presbyn. Author: Fanny Burney; Seven Steps to Sensible Structure and Style; Stories for Little People; I Always Wanted to Live in the Chicken Yard; The Gift and Other Tales. Home: 206 Stinebaugh Dr Wapakoneta OH 45895 Office: Ohio State U Lima OH 45804

STEALEY, MARY LOUISE (MRS. SYDNOR L. STEALEY JR.), social worker; b. Providence, Aug. 30, 1930; d. John Ivan and May (Bailey) Twombly; A.B., Boston U., 1952; M.S., Columbia, 1954; m. Sydnor L. Stealey, Jr., Nov. 24, 1960; children—Katherine Louise, Jessica Lynn, Laura Anne. Social worker Mass. Soc. for Prevention Cruelty to Children, Boston, 1954-58; head social worker Medfield (Mass.) State Hosp., 1958-60; psychiat. social worker Div. Mental Health, Fairbanks, Alaska, 1960-62; social work cons., 1962-66. Bd. dirs. Community Property and Service Corp. Mem. Nat. Assn. Social Workers, Acad. Certified Social Workers, Alaska, Fairbanks (sec. 1961, mental health assns. Clubs: Zonta (pres. 1972-73), Republican Woman's. Home: 937 8th Av Fairbanks AK 99701 Office: 604 Barnette St Fairbanks AK 99701

STEARNS, BETTY JANE, pub. relations exec.; Ph.B., U. Chgo., 1945, M.A., 1948; Certificate of Advanced Studies, U. London, 1949. Editor Chgo. Stagebill, copywriter Chas. A. Stevens & Co., also sec. U. Chgo. Cancer Research Found., 1948-50; with Pub. Relations Bd., Chgo., 1950—, v.p., dir. women's dept., 1953-63, sr. v.p., 1963; stationery accessories as EJS Enterprises. Bd. dirs. Drexel Home. Recipient 1st award, Publicity Club Chgo., 1959, 64, 68, 69, 70, Honor award, 1962, 64, 72. Mem. Art Inst. Chgo., Pub. Relations Soc. Am. (Silver Anvil award 1972), Home Fashions League Ill., Nat. Home Fashions League, Fashion Group Ill. (regional dir. 1967-69). U. Chgo. Alumni Assn. Home: 5427 Hyde Park Blvd Chicago IL 60615 Office: 150 E Huron St Chicago IL 60611

STEARNS, ISABEL SCRIBNER, educator; b. Manchester, N.H., June 23, 1910; d. Hiram Austin and Elisabeth (Scribner) Stearns; B.A., Smith Coll., 1931; M.A., Bryn Mawr Coll., 1933, Ph.D., 1938; student Radcliffe Coll., 1933-34, U. Cal. at Berkeley, 1939-40, Oxford U., 1935-36, U. Zurich, 1947-48. Instr. philosophy Smith Coll., Northampton, Mass., 1936-38, asst. prof., 1938-44; asso. prof. philosophy Bryn Mawr Coll., Bryn Mawr, Pa., 1944-52, prof., 1952—; vis. lectr. Barnard Coll., Columbia U., 1951-52. Mem. Emergency Aid of Pa.; vol. worker Muscular Dystrophy Assn. Mem. Am. Assn. U. Women (fellowship chmn. Conn. Valley br.), Charles Pierce Soc. (pres.), Am. Philos. Assn., Ancient Greek Philosophy Soc., Am. Metaphys. Assn., Soc. for Phenomenology and Existential Philosophy, Assn. for Philosophy of Math., Renaissance Soc. Am. Club: Fullerton (pres. 1948-49) (Bryn Mawr). Contbr. articles to scholarly jours. Contbg. author Studies in the Philosophy of Charles S. Pierce, 1952; Experience, Existence and the Good, 1961. Editor: Retreat from Reason, 1938. Home: Arnecliffe Gulph Rd Bryn Mawr PA 19010*

STEARNS, JESSIE E., journalist; b. Ft. Scott, Kan.; d. Andrew B. and Emma D. (Gunn) Stearns; B.S., U. Neb., 1929; student Northwestern U., 1938-39, U. Cal. Sch. Journalism, 1940-41, Kwanhua U., Shanghai, China, 1946; m. Edward C. Nixon, Sept. 30, 1929 (div. May 1934); m. 2d, Joseph Thomas Buscher, Mar. 29, 1958. Writer radio sta. WLS, Chgo., 1934-39, KYA, San Francisco, 1940, Lee & Losh, pub. relations, 1941-43; fgn. corr. Pittsburg (Kan.) Sun Headlight and other papers, Shanghai, China, 1946-47; writer radio sta. WEAM, Arlington, Va., 1948; free-lance writing various publs. and newspapers, 1949-51; writer Senate Judiciary Subcom. Internal Security, 1952-53; Washington corr. Pittsburg Headlight & Sun, 1954, Overseas Press Club Bull., 1951—, Midwest and internat. publs., 1958—, Columbus (O.) Dispatch, 1960-65, N.Am. Newspaper Alliance, Topeka Capital-Jour.; Washington editor Bus. Internat., 1955-58; columnist Neb. Alumnus, 1937—, Capital Hill Spectator; Washington corr. The Pacific Jour., Guam, WLAC-TV, Nashville, WBIR-TV, Knoxville, Tenn., KLIN, Lincoln, Neb., WX11-TV, Winston-Salem, N.C. Dir., mem. exec. com. Nat. Press Bldg. Corp. Served from pvt. to tech. sgt. WAC, writer for fgn. radio stas., 1943-46. Recipient nat. award Overseas Press Club, distingusihed service award U. Neb. Mem. U.S. Hist. Soc. (charter mem.), Women's Advt. Club, Capitol Hill Citizens Assn., White House Corrs. Assn., Capitol Hill Restoration Soc. (named Mem. of Year 1969), China-Burma-India Vets. Assn., Am. Legion, U. Neb. Alumni Assn. (bd. mem.), Neb. State Soc., Kans. State Soc., Dept. State Corrs. Assn., Japanese-Am. Soc., U.S. Senate and House Press Galleries, Women in Communications (hon.). Episcopalian. Clubs: Overseas Press, China Tiffin, Washington Press, Nat. Press, Am. Newspaper Womens (gov.). Author: LBJ Settles In in I Can Tell It Now. Home: 100 5th St SE Washington DC 20003 Office: Nat Press Bldg Washington DC 20004

STECHER, EMMA DIETZ, chemist, educator; b. Bklyn., Sept. 23, 1905; d. Nicholas and Emma (Weidt) Dietz; B.A., Barnard Coll., 1925; M.A., Columbia, 1926; Ph.D., Bryn Mawr Coll., 1929. Research asso. Harvard, 1929-34; research chemist Hercules Powder Co., Wilmington, Del., 1935-37, General Aniline Co., Easton, Pa., 1943-45; instr. Conn. Coll., 1941-43; instr. chemistry Barnard Coll., 1945-47, asst. prof., 1947-50, asso. prof., 1950-59, prof., 1959-71; adj. prof. Pace Coll., N.Y.C., 1971—. War gas expert Civil Def. Recipient fellowship Am. Assn. U. Women, 1934-35. Mem. Am. Chem. Soc., A.A.A.S., Iota Sigma Pi, Sigma Delta Epsilon. Home: 423 W 120th St New York City NY 10027

STECK, JACQUELINE, educator; b. Phila., Sept. 13, 1921; d. John Joseph and Alice Elizabeth (McTague) Steck; B.S. in Journalism, Temple U., 1944, M.A. in Am. History, 1947. Mng. editor Suburban Newspapers, Inc., Ardmore, Pa., 1943; pub. information writer, dir. student publs. Temple U., 1944-49, faculty dept. journalism 1949—, asso. prof. communications, 1969—. Editor, Cross Currents, Blue Cross of Greater Phila., 1961-72; editorial cons. Luth. Ch. Women, 1963-73. Recipient Lindback award for distinguished teaching, 1967; gold key for service to student journalists Columbia Scholastic Press Assn., 1971. Newspaper Fund Inc. grantee for work in journalism with minority high sch. students, 1972-74. Mem. Women in Communications, Assn. for Edn. in Journalism, Sigma Delta Chi. Home: 14 N Belfield Av Havertown PA 19083 Office: Communications and Theatre Temple U Philadelphia PA 19122

STECKEL, TIANNE ABRAMOVITZ, sch. psychologist; b. Palo Alto, Cal., July 5, 1930; d. Gordon B. and Sadie (Schwartz) Paris; B.A., U. Wash., 1952; M.A., U. Cal. at Berkeley, 1967; m. Jess Abramovitz, Nov. 19, 1954 (dec. Apr. 1964); children—Maria, David; m. 2d, Sheldon Steckel, Sept. 2, 1967. Tchr., Oakland (Cal.) Pub. Schs., 1953-55; social worker Wash. Dept. Welfare, 1955-56; tchr. Danville (Cal.) Union Schs., 1956-58; guidance cons. Head Start program Marin County (Cal.), 1966-67; psychologist Fremont (Cal.) Schs., 1969—; bd. dirs., therapist Cathersis Inst., Alamo, Cal., 1973—. Pres. ORT, Lafayette, Cal., 1965-66; co-chmn. fund drive Jewish Welfare Fedn., 1967; v.p. Hadassah, Walnut, Cal., 1963-64, mem. regional bd., 1964-65; founder City Hopemates br. John Muir Hosp., Walnut Creek, 1962; pres. Hillel Found., Seattle, 1951-52. Mem. Nat., Cal. assns. sch. psychologists and psychometrists, N.E.A., Contra Costa Mental Health Assn., Jules Magnus Museum, Valley Art Center, Brandies Women, Diablo Light Opera, Mensa, Phi Beta Kappa, Phi Theta Pi, Phi Sigma Sigma. Democrat. Jewish religion (dir. congregation 1973-74). Home: 3050 Bowling Green Dr Walnut Creek CA 94595 Office: Kennedy High Sch Fremont CA

STECKL, LISELOTTE RUTH SANDER (MRS. RUDOLPH STECKL), physician; b. Jihlava, Czechoslovakia, Aug. 30, 1925; d. Franz and Margarete (Buchsbaum) Sander; M.D., U. Vienna (Austria) Med. Sch., 1954; m. Rudolph Steckl, Mar. 6, 1955; children—Peter, Judy. Came to U.S., 1956, naturalized, 1962. Intern, Wilmington (Del.) Meml. Hosp., 1956-57; resident pediatrics Mericopa County Gen. Hosp., Phoenix, 1961-63; practice medicine specializing in pediatrics, Mesa, Ariz., 1963-66; pediatrician Children and Youth Project, Phoenix, 1966—; mem. staff Maricopa County Gen. Hosp., Phoenix. Diplomate Am. Bd. Pediatrics. Fellow Am. Acad. Pediatrics; mem. Pediatric Soc. Ariz., Assn. Fgn. Med. Grads. Home: 3826 N 59th Pl Phoenix AZ 85018 Office: 715 S 1st Av Phoenix AZ 85003

STECKLER, PHYLLIS BETTY SCHWARTZBARD (MRS. STUART J. STECKLER), pub. co. exec.; b. N.Y.C., May 15, 1933; d. Irwin H. and Bertha (Fellner) Schwartzbard; B.A., Hunter Coll., 1954; M.A., N.Y. U., 1957; m. Stuart J. Steckler, June 3, 1956; children—Randy, Sharon. Editorial dir. R.R. Bowker Co., N.Y.C., 1954-69, Crowell Collier Macmillan Information Pub., N.Y.C., 1969-71, Holt, Rinehart & Winston Information Systems, N.Y.C., 1971-73; pres., editorial dir. Oryx Press, Scottsdale, Ariz., 1973—. Home: 7632 E Edgemont Av Scottsdale AZ 85257 Office: 7077 E Main St Scottsdale AZ 85251

STEEGER, SHIRLEY MEEKER (MRS. HENRY STEEGER), civic worker; b. Denver; d. Lincoln Roy and Josephine (Voght) Meeker; grad. Albany Acad. for Girls, 1927; m. Henry Steeger, June 1, 1928; children—Henry Steeger, Jr., Susan Shirley (Mrs. John Herbert Hall), Nancy Victoria (Mrs. Richard B. Jennings). Chmn. editorial bd. The Garden, publ. of N.Y. Bot. Garden, 1949-50; chmn. N.Y. Bot. Garden Vol. Assos., 1950-51; mem. bd. Spence-Chapin Adoption Services, 1952, sec. bd., 1954-56, pres., 1960-63, v.p., 1963-66; mem. bd. Trail Blazers Camps, 1960-63; mem. devel. com. N.Y. Community Blood Center, 1962-65; adv. bd. Nat. Council on Illegitimacy, 1962—, chmn. adv. bd., 1964; bd. dirs. Child Welfare League Am., 1966—, v.p., 1972. nat. bd. Nat. Conf. Social Welfare. Home: 1060 Fifth Av New York City NY 10028

STEELE, BARBARA ANN (SISTER MARY CHRISTOPHER), coll. dean; b. Detroit, Aug. 11, 1932; d. Faye Albert and Helen Gertrude (Welch) Steele; student Western Res. U., 1949-50; B.A., Mercy Coll. Detroit, 1955; M.A., Cath. U. Am., 1962; Ph.D., U. Mich., 1967. Instr. English, Muskegon (Mich.) Cath. Central High Sch., 1955-57; chmn. English dept. Mercy High Sch., Detroit, 1957-63; profesorado de Ingles Mater Misericordiae, Buenos Aires, Argentina, 1964-66; acting chmn. English dept. Mercy Coll. of Detroit, 1968-69, acad. dean, 1969—. Cons. Nat. Assn. Ednl. Broadcasters, 1962-64. Judge Nat. Scholastic Writing Awards Competition, 1958-63. Commn. on English fellow, 1962; Am. Council on Edn. fellow, 1967-68. Mem. Am. Conf. Acad. Deans, Am. Assn. Higher Edn., Modern Lang. Assn., Lambda Iota Tau, Phi Kappa Phi. Home: 339 S Ardmore Los Angeles CA 90020

STEELE, CHERYL DIANNE, journalist; b. Warren, O., Oct. 13, 1949; d. John Lawrence and Dollie Irene (Herriott) Steele; B.S., Ohio U., 1971; postgrad. Youngstown State U., 1971. Youth edn. editor Niles (O.) Suburban Newspapers, 1971-73, City Hall and police reporter, 1972-73; reporter Columbia (S.C.) Record, 1973-74; editorial asst. dept. information services U.S.C., 1974—. Mem. Women in Communications, Phi Gamma Nu, Sigma Kappa. Home: 1065 Aylesford St Columbia SC 29210

STEELE, CHRISTINE NEWMAN (MRS. HARRY BLANCHARD STEELE, JR.), librarian; b. Shamokin, Pa., July 12, 1926; d. Malcom Joseph and Christine (Kompare) Newman; x-ray technician student U. Tex. Med. Schs., 1946; m. Harry Blanchard Steele, Jr., Feb. 9, 1946; children—Harry Blanchard III, David Newman, Charles Stephen, Margaret Susan, Christopher Patrick, Thomas Malcolm. Librarian Willow Springs (Mo.) Pub. Library, 1962—. Council mem. Girl Scouts Am., 1958-64; vice chmn. mayor's spl. centennial com., 1968-69; also active community drives; pres. Cath. Ladies Guild, 1969-70; bd. mem. Dogwood Library System, 1969. Mem. Howell County Hist. Soc., Howell County Council Fine Arts (charter), Willow Springs C. of C., Bus. and Profl. Womans Club, Women's C. of C., P.E.O. Clubs: Willow Springs Garden, Tuesday Study (pres. 1967-68), S.F. State and Federal Wives; Willow Springs Country (treas. women's club 1970). Home: 302 N Walnut St Willow Springs MO 65793 Office: Box 68 Pub Library Willow Springs MO 65793

STEELE, HILDA HODGSON, home economist; b. Wilmington, O., Mar. 24, 1911; d. George and Mary Jane (Rolston) Hodgson; certificate Wilmington Coll., 1932, B.S., 1935; M.A. in Home Econs. Edn., Ohio State U., 1941; postgrad. Ohio U., 1954, Miami U., 1959; m. John C. Steele. Tchr., Brookville (Ohio) Elementary Sch., 1931-36; tchr. home econs., Lincoln Jr. High Sch., Dayton Pub. Schs., 1936-40, coordinator home econs. dept., travelling exptl. home econs. tchr., 1940-45, supr. home econs., 1945—. Mem. Ohio Farm Electrification Com., 1964-66. Mem. town and country br. career com. Miami Valley br. YMCA, 1948-59. Adv. bd. Dayton Sch. Practical Nursing, 1951—; adv. com. Dayton Miami Valley Hosp. Sch. Nursing, 1951-67; jr. adv. com. Montgomery County chpt. A.R.C., 1940—. Mem. Montgomery County Nutrition Council (Dayton area. 1st vice-chmn. 1967), Am. (del. 1961), Ohio (chmn. elementary and secondary edn. com. 1947-51, co-chmn. ann. conv. 1961, mem. housing, equip. com. 1965-68), Dayton Met. (pres. 1949-50, 60-61) home econ. assns., Am. Vocational Home Econs. Assn., Nat., Ohio edn. assns., Dayton Sch. Adminstrs. Assn. (past sec., past v.p., pres. 1960-61), Dayton Sch. Mgmt. Assn. (program com. 1971), Elec. Women's Round Table, Ohio Assn. Childhood Edn. Mem. Ch. of Christ. Mem. Order Eastern Star. Club: Zonta (pres. Dayton 1950-52). Research in pub. sch. food habits, 1957. Home: 1443 State Route 380 Xenia OH 45385 Office: 348 W 1st St Dayton OH 45402

STEELE, LENORA ANN MCKENZIE (MRS. EDWARD E. STEELE), newspaper editor; b. Manchester, Mich., Aug. 3, 1932; d. James and Naomi Fay (Griffith) McKenzie; grad. high sch.; m. Edward E. Steele, July 21, 1950; children—Raymond G., Michael J., Thomas F. With Manchester (Mich.) Enterprise, 1971—, editor, 1971—. Bd. dirs. Manchester Area Community Chest and Red Cross Drive, 1973—. Mem. United Ch. Christ. Member Order Easter Star. Home: 305 Beaufort St Manchester MI 48158 Office: 305 Beaufort St Manchester MI 48158

STEELE, MARGARET MARY RYAN, dietitian; b. Mitchell, S.D., Oct. 21, 1925; d. Daniel James and Ida (Spear) Ryan; B.S., Saint Mary Coll., 1947; m. Raymond R. Steele, Dec. 30, 1954 (div. 1958); children—Mary Ann, Ellen Marie. Intern Ancker Hosp., St. Paul, 1947-48; therapeutic dietitian VA Hosp., Hot Springs, S.D., 1949-51, Saginaw (Mich.) Gen. Hosp., 1951-52; therapeutic dietitian VA Hosp., Tucson, 1958-64, asst. chief dietetic service, 1964-71, chief dietetic service, 1971—. Del. Tucson Community Council, 1965—. Mem. Am., Ariz. (pres. 1967-68; chmn. nominating com. 1969-70), So. Ariz. Dist. (pres. 1961-62) dietetic assns. Home: 1001 W Thurber St Tucson AZ 85705 Office: VA Hosp Tucson AZ 85723

STEELE, MARGARET THERESE, parliamentarian, corp. exec.; b. Kansas City, Kan., Aug. 2, 1910; d. Edward Francis and Therese (Hensmentle) Murphy; student Conservatory Music, Kansas City, Mo., 1929-32; B.A., U. Kan., 1933; m. James Warren Steele, Jr., Sept. 12, 1936; children—Judith (Mrs. William J. Springer), James Warren III, Donald E., David E. Editor, Adverette, Kansas City, Mo., 1942-44, Nat. Parliamentarian mag., Kansas City, Mo., 1951-57, 73—; pres. J.W. Steele & Co., Kansas City, Mo., 1958-68; v.p. Athena Corp., Bethesda, Md., 1972—. Parliamentary cons., Instr. in field, chmn. Council Standards Registered Parliamentarians, 1963-65. Trustee Oakwood, Mo., 1954-56, 60-62. Registered parliamentarian. Recipient civic beautification award Mo. K.C.'s, 1968. Mem. Nat. (Service award 1969, pres. 1965-67), Mo. (pres. 1956-57) assns. parliamentarians, Nat. League Am. Pen Women (pres. 1970-72; Distinguished Service award 1966), Internat. Platform Assn., Am. Rose Soc. (nat. accredited show judge), UN Assn., English Speaking Union, Gen. Fedn. Womens Clubs. Roman Catholic. Home: 1707 Strine Dr McLean VA 22101 Office: Athena Corp 5423 Audubon Rd Bethesda MD 20014

STEELE, MARY BRYAN, elementary sch. librarian; b. Louisville, Jan. 12, 1914; d. Volney Hewitt and Suzanne (Werne) Bryan; B.S. in L.S., U. Ky., 1936, M.Ed., 1957; m. John William Steele, June 24, 1939; children—Susan (Mrs. James W. Biddle), Jane (Mrs. Courtney E. Little), Frances (Mrs. Charles P. Jones). Librarian, Valley High Sch., Jefferson County, Ky., 1936-39, Glendover Elementary Sch., Lexington, Ky., 1957—. Chmn. Woodford County Girl Scout Leaders, 1948-55; pres. Woodford County Farm Bur. Women, 1941-43, Little Garden Club Woodford County, 1941-75. Mem. Am., Ky. library assns., Am. Assn. U. Women (past chpt. pres.), Alpha Delta Kappa (past chpt. pres., past state pres.), Pi Beta Phi (past chpt. pres.). Democrat. Mem. Christian Ch. Clubs: Central Ky. Woman's, Lexington Cotillion, Woodford Hills Country. Home: 2081 Mt Tabor Rd Lexington KY 40502 Office: Calendover Elementary Sch Glendover Rd Lexington KY 40503

STEELE, NANCY JANE SAUNDERS (MRS. JAMES BRUCE STEELE), editor; b. Kansas City, Mo., Nov. 14, 1943; d. Everett Lewis and Martha Jane (Fletcher) Saunders; student U. Kan., 1961, U. Cal. at Santa Barbara, 1962, U. Mo., 1964, B.J., 1966; m. James Bruce Steele, June 25, 1966. Soc. editor, Ind. (Mo.) Examiner, 1960; reporter, Kansas City (Mo.) Star, 1963-64; dir. publs. Kansas City (Mo.) Art Inst., 1966-67; asso. editor Parks and Recreation mag., Nat. Recreation and Park Assn., Washington, 1968-69; editor Research Bull., Georgetown U., Washington, 1969-70; editor, Frontiers Mag., Acad. Natural Scis. Phila., 1971—. Home: 2410 Panama St Philadelphia PA 19103 Office: 19th and Parkway Sts Philadelphia PA 19103

STEELE, VLADISLAVA JULIE NEJEDLY (MRS. DONALD H. STEELE), educator; b. Prague, Czechoslovakia, July 8, 1934; d. Vladislav and Julie (Exnarova) Nejedly; B.S., McGill U., Montreal, Que., 1957, M.S., 1959, Ph.D., 1965; m. Donald H. Steele, Apr. 28, 1959; 1 son, Sean Alexander. Came to Can., 1950, naturalized, 1956. Sessional lectr. zoology McGill U., 1960-61; vis. lectr. biology Meml. U. Nfld., St. John's, 1962-63, lectr. biology, 1963-65, asst. prof. biology, 1965-72, asso. prof., 1972—. Mem. Canadian Soc. Zoologists, Am. Mus. Natural History, Am. Inst. Biol. Scis. Home: 48 Wicklow St St John's NF Canada

STEELMAN, LALA CARR (MRS. JOSEPH FLAKE STEELMAN), educator; b. Milledgeville, Ga.; d. Iverson Curry and Ruth (Hardie) Carr; A.B., Ga. Woman's Coll., 1943; M.A., U. N.C., 1946, Ph.D., 1950; m. Joseph Flake Steelman, Aug. 30, 1947; children—Lala Carr, Joseph Flake. Tchr. French, history Madison (Ga.) High Sch., 1943-45; instr. U. N.C., Chapel Hill, 1947-50; asst. prof. history E. Carolina Univ., Greenville, 1955-61, asso. prof., 1961-65, prof., 1965—. First v.p. Democratic Women Pitt County, 1960—. Mem. Pi Gamma Mu. Contbg. author: Essays in Am. History, 1964, Essays in Southern Biography, 1965; Studies in The History of The South, 1875-1922. Home: 1703 Knollwood Dr Greenville NC 27834

STEEN, JUDITH ARLENE, librarian; b. Bremerton, Wash., Nov. 20, 1940; d. Matias Sefanias and Nanny Ottilia (Nelson) Kippola; student Wash. State U., 1958-59; B.A., U. Wash., 1962; M.L.S., U. Portland, 1965; m. Harold Karl Steen, June 16, 1962. Spl. services librarian U. Portland, 1964-65; librarian history and govt. dept. Seattle Pub. Library, 1966-69; librarian, research asso. Forest History Soc., Santa Cruz, Cal., 1969-73; reference librarian U. Cal. at Santa Cruz, 1972—. Trustee Santa Cruz County Pub. Library, 1973—. Mem. A.L.A., Cal. Library Assn., Internat. Assn. Agrl. Librarians and Documentalists, Victorian Soc. in Am., Finnish-Am. Hist. Soc. West, Santa Cruz Geneal. Soc. Home: 114 Escalona Dr Santa Cruz CA 95060 Office: Library U Cal Santa Cruz CA 95064

STEENSMA, GERALDINE JACQUELINE JAARSMA (MRS. RICHARD STEENSMA), educator; b. Grand Rapids, Mich., Jan. 27, 1919; d. Cornelius and Johanna (Huisman) Jaarsma; B.S. magna cum laude, Slippery Rock State Coll., 1939; M.A., Columbia Tchrs. Coll., 1967; m. Richard Steensma, Dec. 24, 1940; children—Nancy (Mrs. John Fennema Jr.), Kathleen (Mrs. Howard Doornbos), Kenneth. Elementary tchr., Wampum, Pa., 1939-40; tchr., prin. Rockland County Christian, Monsey, N.Y., 1953-58; tchr., prin. Eastern Christian Elementary and Jr. High Sch., Paterson, N.J., 1958-67; asso. prof. edn. Covenant Coll., Lookout Mountain, Tenn., 1968—. Tutor Florence Christian Home, Paterson, N.J., 1960-62. Mem. Assn. for Advancement Christian Scholarship, Assn. Supervision and Curriculum Devel., Assn. Tchr. Educators, Kappa Delta Pi (pres. Delta Tau chpt. 1938-39). Author: To Those Who Teach: Keys for Decision-Making. Home: 822 Murrell Rd Signal Mountain TN 37377 Office: Covenant Coll Lookout Mountain TN 37350

STEER, HELEN VANE, drama dir., educator; b. Manchester, Eng., 1926; d. C. Burrell and Dorothy A. (Rice) Steer; came to U.S., 1944, naturalized, 1955; B.A., La. State U., 1954, M.A., 1958, Ph.D., 1967. Drama dir. Samford U., Birmingham, Ala., 1956-59, dir. numerous shows including The Heiress, Pygmalion, Harvey, The Importance of Being Earnest, Amahl and the Night Visitors; teaching asst. La. State U., 1960-63; asso. prof. drama and speech dept. East Carolina U., Greenville, N.C., 1963—, appeared summer stock Wyo. Summer Theatre, Laramie, E. Carolina U. Summer Theatre; producer show Concepts WNCT, TV sta., Greenville. Mem. Speech Communication Assn., So. Speech Communication Assn., N.C. Speech and Drama Assn. (pres. 1971), Am. Assn. U. Profs., Am. Theatre Assn., Phi Kappa Phi. Drama editor: So. Speech Jour., 1966-69. Contbr. articles to profl. jours. Home: 2306 E 3d St Greenville NC 27834

STEERE, ELLEN DEWOLFE (MRS. HARRY HAVELOCK STEERE), educator; b. Portland, Me., June 6, 1934; d. James Codman and Doris Smith (Greenlaw) DeWolfe; A.B., Radcliffe Coll., 1956; student U. Grenoble, France, summer 1954; M.A., Middlebury Coll., France, 1958; postgrad., Columbia U., 1962-63; m. Harry Havelock Steere, Aug. 25, 1956. Remedial reading asst. The Fessenden Sch., West Newton, Mass., 1957; lang. lab. asst. Concord (Mass.) High Sch., 1958-59; library asst. Radcliffe Coll., Cambridge, Mass., 1960; tchr. French FLES program Thornwood & Hawthorne, N.Y., 1961-63; French tchr. White Plains (N.Y.) High Sch., 1963-64; library asst. Upsala Coll., East Orange, N.J., 1965-66; lectr. French, 1966-68; lectr. French, Bates Coll., Lewiston, Me., 1969-70, 73; pvt. instr. French, 1968—. Mem. Central Me. Gen. Woman's Hosp. Assn., Lewiston, 1972—. Mem. Am. Assn. Tchrs. of French, L'Alliance Francaise, Middlebury Amicale Francaise. Editor: Radcliffe Newsletter for State of Me., 1972—. Home: 55 Bardwell St Lewiston ME 04240

STEERS, NINA GORE AUCHINCLOSS (MRS. MICHAEL A. STRAIGHT), journalist; b. Washington, Jan. 10, 1937; d. Hugh D. and Nina (Gore) Auchincloss; B.A., Bryn Mawr Coll., 1959; M.S. in Journalism, Columbia, 1961, M.A. in Am. History, 1964; m. Newton Ivan Steers, Jr., June 8, 1957 (div. Jan. 1974); children—Ivan, Hugh, Burr; m. Michael W. Straight, May 1974. With pub. information officer Internat. Bank for Reconstruction and Devel., 1962; Washington corr. Chattanooga Times, 1962-71. Contbg. writer, feature articles, book reviews Sunday Star, Balt. Sun, Show, The Americas, Washington, 1962—; researcher, reporter New Focus, Washington, part-time, 1959-62. Episcopalian. Home: 5910 Bradley Blvd Bethesda MD 20014 Office: Nat Press Bldg Washington DC 20004

STEEVES, DOROTHY L., lawyer; b. Somerville, Mass., Apr. 9, 1926; A.B., U. Cal. at Berkeley, 1952, J.D., 1955. Admitted to Cal. bar, 1955, since practiced in Arcata; partner firm Stokes, Steeves, Calligan & Warren. Chmn. Humboldt County Civil Service Commn., 1966-69; city atty. City of Blue Lake, 1968—. Mem. Humboldt County Bar Assn. (pres. 1973), State Bar. Cal., Phi Beta Kappa. Office: 76 Sunny Brae Centre Arcata CA 95521

STEFANSSEN, STEPHANIE, writer, pub. relations cons.; b. N.Y.; m. Charles Moase Wilmarth (div.); children—Christopher Mallory, Alison Anne. Asso. editor Bonanza Sunday mag. San Francisco Chronicle, 1963-65; owner Stephanie Stefanssen, N.Y.C., San Francisco, 1965-66; account exec. Grey Advt., N.Y.C., 1966; account group supr. Batton, Barton, Durstine & Osborn, N.Y.C., 1967-70; pres. Stephanie Stefanssen, Inc., communications, N.Y.C., 1970-73; contbg. food editor Playgirl mag., N.Y.C., 1973—; pub. relations cons., 1973—; writer articles on travel, food, and gen. interest items for various publs., including Venture, Vista, Bon Appetit, West, Apt. Ideas, Time-Life books div., Humble Travel Guide, Cycling Today. Recipient gold medal, indsl. and ednl. category N.Y. Film and TV Festival, 1969. Mem. Pub. Relations Soc. Am., UN Assn. U.S.A., Alliance Francaise. Home: 300 E 40th St New York City NY 11016

STEFKOVICH, JACQUELINE ANNE, guidance counselor; b. Washington, Pa., June 19, 1947; d. Albert Paul and Betty Anne (Williams) Stefkovich; B.A. in Psychology, Duquesne U., 1969; M.A. in Counseling and Pupil Personnel, U. Conn., 1970. Recreation work Mayview State Hosp., Bridgeville, Pa., summers 1966-69; kindergarten tchr., Swissvale, Pa., 1969; guidance counselor Pennsville (N.J.) Jr. High Sch., 1970-73, Ocean City (N.J.) High Sch., 1972—. Mem. Nat. Assn. Women Deans, Adminstrs. and Counselors, N.J. Edn. Assn., Psi Chi, Alpha Gamma Delta. Home: 5539 Simpson Av Ocean City NJ 08226 Office: Ocean City High Sch Ocean City NJ 08226

STEG, DOREEN ETHEL RAY (MRS. LEO STEG), educator; b. Antwerp, Belgium; d. Nicolas Michel and Pauline (Printz) Ray; came to U.S., 1941, naturalized, 1950; B.A., N.Y. U., 1948; M.A., Cornell U., 1951; Ph.D., U. Pa., 1962; m. Leo Steg, June 12, 1947; children—Paula Jamie, Ellen Leslie, Audrey Leigh. Teaching fellow dept. modern langs. Cornell U., 1948-51; tchr. French, Cayuga Heights Elementary Sch., Ithaca, N.Y., 1952-54, Miquon (Pa.) Sch., 1956-59, Cheltenham Sr. High Sch., Wyncote, Pa., 1961-62; lectr. philosophy, history found. of edn. dept. Temple U., 1962-63; NSF fellow, lectr. dept. philosophy of edn. U. Pa., 1963-64; asso. prof. edn. Glassboro State Coll., 1964-66; asso. prof., chmn. dept. human behavior, devel. Drexel U., Phila., 1966-73, also dir. Responsive Environment Project; adviser Elsemere Project, Glassboro; lectr. Haifa Inst. Tech., 1966, Nat. Edn. Research Assn., Tokyo, 1967, U. Tokyo, 1967, U. Jammu and Kashmir, 1967. Cons. Phila. Bd. Edn. Bd. dirs. Long Beach Found. Arts and Scis., Loveladies, N.J. Fellow Philosophy of Edn. Soc., A.A.A.S.; mem. Am. Philos. Assn., Am. Assn. U. Profs., Am. Acad. Polit. and Social Sci., N.Y. Acad. Scis., Soc. Philosophy and Philosophy of Edn. (co-founder Eastern div.), John Dewey Soc., Comparative Edn. Soc., Middle States Philosophy of Edn. Soc., Nat. Soc. for Study Edn., Nat. Assn. for Edn. of Young Children, Nat. Hon. Soc. Biology, Assn. Internationale de Cybernetique, Am. Ednl. Research Assn., Soc. Research in Child Devel., Am. Cybernetic Soc. (asso. editor forum), Orgn. Mondiale pour Enfance Primaire. Author: A Philosophical and Cybernetic Model of Thinking. Editorial bd. Kubernetes Jour. (Eng.). Home: 1616 Hepburn Dr Villanova PA 19085 Office: Drexel U 32d and Chestnut Sts Philadelphia PA 19103

STEIGER, ALAYNE ROBERTS (MRS. SHERWIN STEIGER), personnel and pub. relations exec.; b. N.Y.C., Sept. 24, 1925; d. Moe and Florence G. Rabinowitz; student in journalism U. Minn., 1942-45; B.A., Ohio State U., 1946, M.A., 1948; teaching certificate Morris Harvey Coll., 1959; m. Sherwin Steiger, Mar. 16, 1948; children—Stephanie, James Gary. Tchr. Kanawka County (W.Va.) Schs., 1960-61; polit. sci. instr. Morris Harvey Coll., Charleston, W.Va., 1961; with Teledyne Econ. Devel. Co., Charleston, 1965—, personnel and pub. relations mgr., 1973—. Mem. W.Va. Press Women, Panel of Am. Women, Hadassah, Theta Sigma Phi. Home: 205 McKinley Av Charleston WV 25314 Office: Virginia and Summers Sts Charleston WV 25301

STEIGER, CLARA LOUISE GOSS (MRS. W. SELDEN STEIGER), educator; b. Columbus, O.; d. Leonard Whittlesey and Florence (Joyce) Goss; B.S., Ohio State U., 1932, M.A., 1939; m. W. Selden Steiger, Feb. 14, 1943; children—Walter Selden, Carl Whittlesey. Tchr. pub. schs., Ohio, 1932-49; instr. fine arts Starling High Sch., Columbus, 1936-48, Ohio State U., Columbus, 1948-49; tchr. pub. schs., Fla., 1960-73; tchr. Silver Bluff Sch., Miami, 1960-73. Chmn. United Fund, Cleve., 1958; active fund drives various civic orgns. Mem. Sigma Kappa Alumnae (pres. 1970-72). Home: 4135 Pamona Av Coconut Grove FL 33133 Office: Silver Bluff Sch Miami FL 33133

STEIGNER, A. MARGARET, ins. co. exec.; b. Phila., Oct. 2, 1912; d. Clayton S. and Mary R. (Hallman) Steigner; grad. Bible Inst. Pa. (now Phila. Coll. Bible), 1936. Stenographer, Fidelity Mut. Life Ins. Co., Phila., 1930-48, sec., 1948-51, supr. contract sect., 1951-69, mgr. investor and agy. services, 1969-72, dir. investor and agy. services, 1972—, mgr. investor and agy. services FML Funds Distbn. Co., subsidiary, 1969-72, dir. investor and agy. services, 1972—, asst. sec., asst. treas., 1971—. Republican. Baptist (organist 1943—, ch. clk. 1961-63, missionary treas. 1945-60, tchr. Sunday sch. 1942—). Home: Wyndmoor Gardens 219 E Willow Grove Av Philadelphia PA 19118 Office: Fidelity Mutual Life Bldg Philadelphia PA 19101

STEIMEL, EVA JUNE (MRS. CLARENCE AUSTIN STEIMEL), banking exec.; b. Creal Springs, Ill., Feb. 27, 1923; d. Lawrence Lealand and Nettie Bell (Pennington) McIntire; grad. Am. Inst. Banking, 1970; m. Clarence Austin Steimel, Aug. 2, 1941; children—James Austin, Thomas Lee. Reporter, Mt. Vernon (Ill.) Register News, 1942; asso. Alice Wilhoit & Assos., Phoenix, 1952-63; research asst. First Nat. Bank of Ariz., Phoenix, 1963-72, asst. v.p., 1972—. Mem. Am. Marketing Assn. (sec., treas. 1970-71), Ariz. Statis. Assn., C. of C. (indsl. and bus. devel. com. 1970—). Home: 3928 W Myrtle Dr Phoenix AZ 85021 Office: 100 W Washington St Phoenix AZ 85004

STEIN, ADLYN ROBINSON (MRS. HERBERT ALFRED STEIN), jewelery co. exec.; b. Pitts., May 8, 1908; d. Robert Stewart and Pearl (Geiger) Robinson; Mus.B., Pitts. Mus. Inst., U. Pitts., 1928; m. J. Francis Hollearn, 1929 (dec.); children—Adlyn (Mrs. Brandon J. Hickey), Frances (Mrs. Thomas M. Kidd); m. 2d, Allen Burnett Williams, Dec. 5, 1955 (dec.); m. 3d, Herbert Alfred Stein, Nov. 28, 1963; 1 adopted dau., Rachel Lynn. Treas., R.S. Robinson, Inc., Pitts., 1947—. Charter mem. Women's Symphony Soc., 1954; mem. Pitts. Symphony Soc., Tuesday Musical Club, Pitts. Mem. D.A.R. Republican. Episcopalian. Clubs: Duquesne, University, Rolling Rock Country (Ligonier); Lakewood Country; Clifton; South Hills Country. Home: 22200 Lake Rd Cleveland OH 44116 Office: Clark Bldg Pittsburgh PA 15222

STEIN, ADRIENNE, lawyer; b. N.Y.C., Nov. 15, 1924; d. Isidore and Lena (Florea) Bakst; B.B.A., City U. N.Y., 1944; J.D., Pacific Coast U., 1967; m. Jack M. Stein, June 18, 1946; children—Gilbert, Peggy, Harvey. Admitted to Cal. bar, 1967, since practiced in Long Beach; with firm Gyler & Gottlieb, Inc., Long Beach, 1967-73; partner Gottlieb, Gottlieb & Stein, 1974—. Mem. faculty Pacific Coast U., 1968—. Mem. Los Angeles Selective Service Law Panel, 1970-73. Bd. dirs., v.p. Long Beach Jewish Community Center; bd. dirs. Long Beach Jewish Community Fedn., Long Beach chpt. Am. Civil Liberties Union, United Crusade. Mem. Cal., Los Angeles County, Long Beach bar assns. Home: 3815 Gaviota Av Long Beach CA 90807 Office: 675 E Wardlow Rd Long Beach CA 90807

STEIN, CAROL B., mus. curator, zoologist; b. Columbus, O., Jan. 1, 1937; d. Henry E. and Elizabeth (Saiter) Stein; A.B. with honors Lake Erie Coll., 1958; M.S. (NSF Grad. fellow, 1961-63), Ohio State U., 1963, Ph.D. (Ohio Co-op Fisheries Unit Grad. fellow), 1973. Grad. asst. Ohio State U., Columbus, 1960-61, grad. fellow Ohio Co-op Fisheries Unit Dept. Zoology and Entomology, 1966-68, asst. curator Mus. of Zoology, 1970-72, curator Mus. of Zoology, 1972—; mus. technician Ohio Hist. Soc., div. of natural history, Columbus, 1964-66. Mem. Am. Malacological Union (mem. conservation com. 1972—), Ecol. Soc. of Am., Am. Inst. Biol. Scis., Ohio Acad. Sci., Columbus Audubon Soc. (trustee 1972-75), Rivers Unltd. (dir. 1973—), Nature Conservancy, Darby Creek Assn. (pres. 1972), Sierra Club, Sigma Xi. Contbr. articles on ecology and distribution of various fauna to profl. publs. Home: 1050 1/2 Parkway Dr Columbus OH 43212 Office: Museum of Zoology The Ohio State University 1813 N High St Columbus OH 43210

STEIN, ELANE, radio broadcaster; b. Balt.; d. Isadore Abraham and Yetta (Kirson) Stein; B.S., Johns Hopkins U.; postgrad. Am. Acad. Art; m. Merrill Rosenfeld, Dec. 31, 1968. Dir. U.S. Spl. Services, Germany, France, 1948-50; radio producer Voice of Am., 1958-60; with radio sta. WCBM, Balt., 1961—, women's editor, 1962—, founder, dir. WCBM Art Gallery, 1965—. Officer, Outdoor Arts Festival, 1965-72. Bd. dirs. Muscular Dystrophy, Young Audiences, Save Heart Found. Recipient Md. Community Achievement award, 1969; named Patron of Arts of Md., 1968; Outstanding Program award Radio-TV Mirror, 1968, 69, 70. Mem. Md. Heart Assn., Young Audiences. Home: 1101 Saint Paul St Baltimore MD 21202 Office: Music Fair Rd Owings Mills MD 21118

STEIN, ELIZABETH ANN, librarian; b. Cleve., Aug. 16, 1917; d. Harry Wade and Leola (Smith) Stein; A.B., Grove City Coll., 1939; M.S. in L.S., Western Res. U., 1950, Med. Librarian Certificate, 1955. Asst. librarian Euclid (O.) Pub. Library, 1939-40; librarian Wickliffe (O.) Pub. Library, 1940-47, Bailey Meter Co., Cleve., 1947-49, Luth. High Sch., Cleve., 1949-50; reference librarian Zanesville (O.) Pub. Library, 1950-51; circulation reference librarian U.S. Nat. Archives, Washington, 1951-53; med. librarian St. Luke's Hosp., Cleve., 1953-59; asst. librarian Cleve. Med. Library, 1959-63; librarian Brittingham Meml. Library, Cleve. Met. Gen. Hosp., 1963—. Mem. Med. Library Assn. No. Ohio. Home: 171 E 216th St Cleveland OH 44123 Office: 3395 Scranton Rd Cleveland OH 44109

STEIN, GERTRUDE EMILIE, educator, soprano, pianist; b. Ironton, O.; d. S.A. and Emilie M. (Pollach) Stein; Mus. V., Capitol Coll., 1927; B.A., Wittenberg Coll., 1929, M.A., 1931, B.S. in Edn., 1945; Ph.D., U. Mich., 1948; piano and voice student Cin. Coll. Conservatory Music. Music supr. Centralized County Schs. Ohio, Williamsburg, 1932-37; dir. jr. high sch. music, 1937-68; mem. faculty Adult Evening Sch. Springfield (O.) Pub. Schs., 1951-68; head dept. music, asso. prof. piano and music edn. Tex. Luth. Coll., Seguin, 1948-49. Donor, founder Rev. Dr. and Mrs. S.A. Stein Meml. Fund, 1955—. Mem. Am. Assn. U. Women, Am. Symphony Orch. League, Nat., Ohio edn. assns., Asso. Council Arts, Met. Opera Guild, Assn. Tchr. Educators, Am. Film Inst., Ohio Music Tchrs. Assn., Nat. Story League, Music Tchrs. Nat. Assn., Music Educators Nat. Conf., N.Y. Writers' Guild (Local pres.), Nat. Assn. Ednl. Broadcasters, Nat. Assn. Schs. Music, Nat. Fedn. Music Clubs (spl. mem. Ohio, Tex.), Amateur Chamber Music Players, Nat. Fedn. Bus. and Profl. Women, Zonta Internat., Phi Kappa Phi, Pi Lambda Theta. Lutheran. Contbr. articles to profl. jours. Home: 133 N Lowry Av Springfield OH 45504

STEIN, JANET RUTH, educator; b. Denver; d. Hermann B. and Mindell (Winter) Stein; B.A., U. Colo., 1951; M.A., Wellesley Coll., 1953; postgrad. Ind. U., 1956-57; Ph.D., U. Cal., Berkeley, 1957. Lab. technician U. Cal., Berkeley, 1957-59; instr. dept. biology and botany U. B.C., Vancouver, 1959-62, asst. prof., 1962-66, asso. prof., 1966-71, prof. botany, 1971—. Dir., Western Bot. Services Ltd. Recipient Darbaker award in phycology. Mem. Phycol. Soc. Am. (pres.), Canadian Bot. Assn. (pres.), Internat. Phycol. Soc. Author: (with others) Plant Diversity: An Evolutionary Survey, 1965; An Evolutionary Survey of the Plant Kingdom, 1969. Editor: Handbook of Phycological Methods, 1973; Jour. Phycology, 1975—; asso. editor Canadian Jour. Botany, 1970—, Phycologia, 1969-73. Office: Dept Botany U BC Vancouver BC U6T 1WS Canada

STEIN, LONA GOODMAN (MRS. GERALD HERBERT STEIN), educator; b. Phila., Jan. 12, 1942; d. Allan A. and Laura (Baylin) Goodman; B.A., Emerson Coll., 1962; postgrad. U. Vienna, 1960-61, U. Freiburg, Germany, 1961-62; M.A. Teaching in Theatre, U. Fla., 1967; m. Gerald Herbert Stein, May 30, 1963; children—Alexander, Lauren. Dir. creative dramatics Cultural Enrichment Center, Gainesville, Fla., 1967-70; instr. speech and children's theatre Sante Fe Community Coll., Gainesville, 1970—. Mem. Alachua County Bicentennial Commn., 1973—. Mem. Am., Southeastern theatre assns., Fla. Speech Communication Assn., Common Cause. Home: 1221 NW 28th St Gainesville FL 32605 Office: Sante Fe Community College PO Box 1530 Gainesville FL 32601

STEIN, MARGUERITE BLACKWELL, lawyer; b. Evanston, Ill., Oct. 16, 1924; d. George Robert and Marguerite Loyola (Keegan) Blackwell; student Hunter Coll., 1940-46, Fordham U., 1948-50; B.S., U. San Francisco, 1960; J.D., U. San Diego, 1966; m. Alfred Ferdinand Stein, Sept. 3, 1950 (div. June 1962); children—Janet (Mrs. Paul Roche), Laura, Frederic T., Karen E., Christopher B. Sec., W.R. Grace Co., N.Y.C., 1942-44; ofcl. reporter war crimes trials and courts martial U.S. Army, Italy, Austria, Germany, 1946-48; sec. to atty. P. Zimet, N.Y.C., 1948-50; court reporter, N.C., Ore., Va., D.C., N.Y., N.J., Cal., 1950-67; admitted to Cal. bar, 1967, U.S. Dist. Ct., 1967; dep. dist. atty. San Diego County, Cal., 1967—. Instr. Southwestern Jr. Coll., Chula Vista, 1968—, San Diego Evening Coll., 1968—, Cal. Western U. Sch. Law, San Diego, 1974—. Pres., South Bay Cities League Women Voters, San Diego County, 1973—. Bd. dirs. Family Service North County San Diego, 1958-59, Marian High Sch., 1971-73, Adult Protective Services, San Diego, 1971—; Evening Coll. Found., 1973—. Served with USNR, 1944-46. Mem. Am. Legion (condr. 1973), Bus. and Profl. Women, Am. Assn. U. Women, Soroptimist Internat., Am. Bus. Women's Assn., Cal. Ct. Reporters' Assn. (hon.), San Diego County Bar Assn., Lawyers' Club San Diego, San Diego Dist. Atty's Assn., Phi Alpha Delta, Phi Delta Delta (chpt. charter pres.). Editor San Diego Law Rev., 1965-66. Home: 1536 Melrose Av Chula Vista CA 92011 Office: 7002 County Courthouse San Diego CA 92101

STEIN, MARY KATHLEEN, tax. cons., accountant; b. Kansas City, Mo., Jan. 18, 1922; d. Jerry D. and Lillian L. (Tanner) Raggos; student U. Mo.-Columbia; grad. specialized schs.; m. Conrad A. Stein, Nov. 1, 1946; children—Michael J., Joseph C., James R. (dec.), Mary Kay (Mrs. Donald Soetaert), Sharon C. Self-employed ins. broker, Kansas City, Mo., 1939—; paymaster ins. div., timekeeper Lake City Ordnance Plant, Independence, Mo., 1941-46; motor vehicle agt. State Mo., 1962-73; owner-mgr. H&R Block & Stein Bookkeeping, West Plains, Mo., 1962—. Chmn. Howell County Democratic Central Com. Mem. West Plains C. of C. Home: Route 3 Box 454 West Plains MO 65775 Office: 400 Washington Av West Plains MO 65775

STEIN, NANCY LOU SOLOMON, psychologist; b. Youngstown, O., July 16, 1943; d. Howard and Sylvia (Berkowitz) Solomon; student Pa. State U., 1961-63; B.A. in Math., U. Cal. at Berkeley, 1965; Ph.D. in Child Devel., Stanford, 1969; m. Paul Stuart Greenbaum Stein, Sept. 12, 1965; children—Lisa Ruth, Joshua David. Asst. research psychologist, postdoctoral fellow U. Cal. at San Diego, 1969-71; asst. prof. psychology Washington U., St. Louis, 1971—; vis. scholar Stanford, 1973-74. Cons. CRM Books, Dorsey Press, San Diego Unified Sch. Dist., Far West Labs. for Ednl. Research and Devel. Mem. Am. Psychol. Assn., Soc. for Research in Child Devel. Author: Project Head Start: Research and Evaluation, 1967. Contbr. articles to profl. jours. Home: 8 N Tealbrook St St Louis MO 63141

STEIN, PEARL PAULA, social worker; b. N.Y.C., June 9, 1928; d. Samuel and Rae (Simon) Stein; B.A., Bklyn. Coll., 1949; M.S.W. (fellow), Columbia, 1951; M.A. in Edn., N.Y. U., 1970. Field supr., community organizer Bklyn. Zionist Youth Commn., 1956-61, United Synagogue Youth, N.Y.C., 1961-67; social worker Hudson Sch., N.Y. State Dept. Social Services, Hudson, N.Y., 1954-67; youth parole worker, Community Services Bur., N.Y.C., 1967-71; dir., psychologist Student Guidance Center, N.Y.C., 1970—; social worker N.Y. State Div. Youth, N.Y.C., 1971-74, ednl. coordinator, 1974—. Cons. social work State U. N.Y. at New Paltz, 1967-68. Mem. Bklyn. Community Planning Bd., 1964, adv. bd. Aware drug program, 1974. Ednl. Found. Jewish Girls scholar, 1949; Zionist Orgn. Am. summer scholars to Israel, 1961; N.Y. State travel grantee to P.R., 1963, summer scholar U. P.R. Sch. Social Work, 1963. Mem. Am. Psychol. Assn., Nat. Conf. Social Welfare. Research on halfway house recreational program for Women's Prison Assn., 1961, on health and welfare of Puerto Ricans in N.Y. for N.Y. state, 1963. Home: 2865 Ocean Av Brooklyn NY 11235 Office: NY State Div Youth 96 Duane St New York City NY 10007

STEIN, PEGGY LOUISE PUGH, computer co. exec.; b. Shreveport, La., Dec. 3, 1934; d. Paul David and Edna Louise (Alexander) Pugh; student Trinity U., 1955-56; children—Michael Lee, Patricia Suzanne. Policy and procedure writer Pacific Architects & Engring., Saigon, Vietnam, 1966-68; pub. relations rep. Volvo Southwest, Houston, 1972; asst. to dir. Service Computation Center, U. Tex. Med. Br., Galveston, 1973—. Mem. Nat. Assn. Female Execs. Author: Key Punching, 1967. Home: 1429 Bonanza Rd Clear Lake City TX 77058 Office: U Tex Med Br Galveston TX 77550

STEIN, ROSE LEHMAN (MRS. SIMON STEIN), lawyer; b. N.Y.C.; d. Isaac and Molly (Brill) Lehman; LL.B., N.Y. U., 1922, LL.M., 1938; m. Simon Stein, Dec. 22, 1923; children—Ellen (Mrs. Leonard L. Ostreich), Myron L. Admitted to N.Y. bar, 1923; practiced in N.Y.C., 1923—. Co-chmn. lawyers div. State of Israel Bond Orgn., 1956—, mem. exec. com., 1967—, also trustee. Trustee N.Y. U. Jewish Culture Found., 1960—, hon. pres. women's div., 1969—; mem. nat. exec. bd. women's div. Albert Einstein Med. Coll., 1965—. Mem. N.Y. Womens Bar Assn. (1st pres. 1935-40), N.Y. County Lawyers Assn. (bd. dirs. 1956-62), N.Y. U. Law Alumni Assn. (life dir., pres. 1952), N.Y. U. Fedn. Alumni (life dir. emeritus), Hadassah Yeshiva Orgn., Internat. Synagogue (dir. women's div.), N.Y. U. Gallatin Assos., Arbitration Assn., N.A.A.C.P., N.Y. U. Medalion Soc. (pres. 1972—). Club: N.Y. University (chmn. bd. govs. 1967-68). Home: 1401 NE Miami Gardens Dr North Miami Beach FL 33162 Office: 220 Madison Av New York City NY 10016

STEIN, VIRGINIA KRAMER, clin. psychologist; b. N.Y.C., July 22, 1924; d. Sidney David and Nora Dinah (Atkins) Kramer; A.B., Hunter Coll., 1944; postgrad. in occupational therapy Tufts U., 1945; M.A., San Francisco State Coll., 1954; certificate sch. psychology, Newark State Coll., 1967; m. Jerome David Stein, Jr., Sept. 7, 1947; children—Christopher David, Jonathan Atkins. Cons. psychologist Bur. Vocational Rehab., Oakland, Cal., 1948-57, Princeton (N.J.) Day Sch., 1954—, Bonnie Brae Farm Boys, Millington, N.J., 1958-69; fellow in clin. psychology Langley Porter Neuropsychiat. Clin., U. Cal. Sch. Medicine, San Francisco, 1954-55; pvt. practice clin., sch. and vocational psychology, 1954—. Vis. lectr. in psychology Vis. Homemakers Assn. Rutgers U., 1960-62. Mem. profl. adv. com. Somerset County Mental Health Assn., 1968—, trustee, 19. Chmn. Bridgewater Twp. Citizens for Kennedy, 1959-60. Mem. Am., N.J. psychol. assns., Nat., N.J. assns. sch. psychologists, Orton Soc., Council Advancement Psychol. Professions and Scis., Assn. Women in Psychology, Psychologists in Pvt. Practice, Nat. Rehab. Assn., Nat. Rehab. Counseling Assn., Assn. Advancement Psychology. Democrat. Mem. Reformed Ch. Home: 357 William St Somerville NJ 08876 Office: Princeton Day Sch PO Box 75 The Great Rd Princeton NJ 08540

STEINBERG, DORA ELLEN (MRS. ROY DAVID STEINBERG), librarian; b. Newburg, Mo., Mar. 31, 1906; d. John Jacob and Dora Charlotte (Delashmit) Brown; B.S., U. Mo., 1940; M.S., Central Mo. State U., 1964; m. Roy David Steinberg, Nov. 29, 1941; children—David Lee, Tchr., librarian Newburg (Mo.) Schs., 1923-38, 40-42, 47-55, 71—; tchr. Pub. Schs., Caryle, Ill., 1938-40, Waynesville, Mo., 1955-60; sch. library supr. Waynesville-Ft. Leonard Wood Sch., Ft. Leonard Wood, Mo., 1961-71. Cons. library media to various libraries and school in several states; instr. library sci. U. Mo., Columbia, 1967-72; asso. Encyclopedia Britannica Ednl. Corp., Mo., 1971-74. Mem. Nat., Mo. edn. assns., Am., Mo. library assns., Democrat. Baptist. Mem. Order Eastern Star. Home: PO Box 176 Newburg MO 65550

STEINBERG, JEAN ROSE, coll. adminstr.; b. Atlantic City, Dec. 15, 1934; d. Isadore and Rose Anne (McDonald) Steinberg; B.S., St. Joseph's Coll., 1959; M.A., Villanova U., 1963; postgrad. U. Pa., 1959-61, U. Mich., 1964. Sec. bus. offices, Phila., 1952-59; tchr. Harcum Jr. Coll., Bryn Mawr, Pa., 1959-61, Ferris State Coll., Big Rapids, Mich., 1963-65; grad. asst. Villanova U., 1961-63; tchr. St. Joseph's Coll., Phila., 1965-67, part-time 1967—, registrar, 1967—, Recipient Recognition of Outstanding Service, Twilight Players, 1956, 59, 71, 72. Mem. Assn. U. Evening Colls. (sec.-treas. local region 1970-73), Am. Assn. Collegiate Registrars and Admissions Officers, Cross Keys (nat. pres. 1969-71), Alpha Psi Omega. Home: 142 Summit Av Upper Darby PA 19082 Office: 54th St and City Line Av Philadelphia PA 19131

STEINBERG, URSULA WERTHON (MRS. NATHAN G. STEINBERG), plastic surgeon; b. Berlin, Germany, Mar. 17, 1926; d. Kenneth and Annie (Rosenthal) Werthon; A.B., Hunter Coll., 1952; M.D., Woman's Med. Coll. Pa., 1956; m. Nathan G. Steinberg, June 19, 1947; children—Vivian, Gregory. Intern Kings County Hosp., Bklyn., 1956-57; resident in surgery Kings County Hosp.-State U. N.Y. Med. Center at Bklyn., 1957-60, resident in plastic surgery Downstate Med. Center, 1960-62; asso. attending John F. Kennedy Hosp., Edison, N.J.; attending Muhlenberg Hosp., Plainfield, N.J.; cons. plastic surgery Somerset Hosp., Sommerville, N.J.; clin. instr. plastic surgery State U. N.Y. Med. Center at Bklyn., 1963—; clin. asst. prof. Rutgers U. Fellow A.C.S.; mem. Am. Soc. Plastic and Reconstructive Surgeons, N.J., N.Y. Regional socs. plastic and reconstructive surgery, A.M.A., N.J. Med. Soc. Office: 1024 Park Av Plainfield NJ 07060

STEINBERGH, JUDITH WOLINSKY, poet, educator; b. Louisville, Oct. 18, 1943; d. Mayer and Rosalyn (Levin) Wolinsky; A.B. in Econs., Wellesley Coll., 1965; m. Alex M. Steinbergh, Sept. 5, 1965; children—Shauna, David. Mgr. research McKinsey & Co., Cleve., 1965-71; part-time poetry writing tchr. pub. schs., East Cleveland, O., 1971; research asso. Cambridge (Mass.) Research Inst., 1971-72; poet, free-lance journalist Poet in Schs. program Mass. Council on the Arts and Nat. Endowment for the Arts, Brookline, 1972—. Ednl. dir. Calliope Children's Theatre, Brookline, 1972—. Mem. Poets Who Teach, Inc. Democrat. Jewish religion. Author: (with Cary Wolinsky) Marshmallow Worlds, 1972. Contbr. poems to mags. and anthologies, articles to newspaper. Home: 34 Park St Brookline MA 02146

STEINEM, GLORIA, writer; b. Toledo, Mar. 25, 1934; d. Leo and Ruth (Nuneviller) Steinem; B.A. in govt. magna cum laude, Smith Coll., 1956; postgrad. (Chester Bowles Asian fellow), U. Delhi, U. Calcutta (India), 1956-58. Dir., Ind. Research Service, Cambridge, Mass., N.Y.C., 1959-60; free-lance writer various nat. mags., 1961—; TV writer That Was the Week That Was, NBC-TV, N.Y.C., 1964-65; contbg. editor Glamour mag., 1962-69. Editorial cons. Curtis Pub., N.Y.C., 1964-65, Conde Nast Publs., N.Y.C., 1962-69, N.Y. Mag., 1968—, Seventeen Mag., 1969-70; founder, editor Ms. Mag. Mem. various coms. of arts, 1964—; mem. Student Non-Violent Coordinating Com. Founding mem. Nat. Women's Polit. Caucus, 1971—. Bd. mem. Women's Action Alliance, N.Y.C., 1971—. Named McCall's Woman of Yr., 1971. Mem. Author's Guild, Author's League Am., Writer's Guild Am., Nat. Acad. TV Arts and Scis., Soc. Mag. Writers, Washington Press Club, Phi Beta Kappa. Author: The Thousand Indias, 1957; The Beach Book, 1963. Address: care Sterling Lord Agy 660 Madison Av New York City NY 10021

STEINER, ANNE KERCHEVAL (MRS. EUGENE F. STEINER), educator; b. Warrensburg, Mo., Aug. 5, 1936; d. Frank M. and Mary Virginia (Humphreys) Kercheval; A.B., U. Mo., 1958, M.A., 1963; Ph.D., U. N.M., 1965; m. Eugene F. Steiner, Aug. 22, 1963. Asst. prof. Tex. Technol. Coll., 1965-66, U. N.M., 1966-68; asst. prof. Ia. State U., Ames, 1968-69, asso. prof. math., 1969-72, prof. math., 1972—; vis. asso. prof. U. Alta.; 1970-71. Mem. Am. Math. Soc., Math. Assn. Am., Phi Beta Kappa, Sigma Xi, Pi Mu Epsilon, Chi Omega. Editorial bd. Ia. State Jour. Research. Contbr. articles to math. jours. Home: 2327 Baker St Ames IA 50010.

STEINER, GITTA HANA, composer, pianist, poetess; b. Prague, Czechoslovakia, Apr. 17, 1932; came to U.S., 1939, naturalized, 1945; d. Eric Erhard and Erna (Bondy) Steiner; diploma composition (Abraham Ellstein scholar) Juilliard Sch. Music, 1963, Mus.B., 1967, M.S., 1969; studied with Vincent Persichetti, Gunther Shuller, Elliot Carter. Compositions include: Suite for Flute Clarinet and Bassoon, 1958; Suite for Orch., 1958; Three Songs for Medium Voice, 1960; Three Pieces for Piano, 1961; Concerto for Violin and Orch., 1963; String Trio, 1964; Pages From A Summer Jour., 1963; Piano Sonata, 1964; Fantasy for Clarinet and Piano, 1964; Brass Quintet, 1964; Jouissance for Flute and Piano, 1965; Five Choruses, 1965; Movement for Eleven, 1966; Tetrark for String Orch., 1965; Fantasy Piece for Piano, 1966; Two Songs, 1966; Concerto for Piano and Orch., 1967; Refractions for Solo Violin, 1967; String Quartet, 1968; Percussion Quartet, 1968; Three Pieces for Solo Vibraphone, 1968; Concert Piece for Seven, 1968; Interludes for Voice and Vibraphone, 1968; Concert Piece for Seven II, 1968; Trio for Two Percussionists and Piano, 1969; Four Bagatelles for Solo Vibraphone, 1969; Five Poems for Mixed Chorus, 1970; Duo for Horn and Piano, 1970; Four Songs for Medium Voice and Vibes, 1970; Settings for Chorus, 1970; Duo for Cello and Percussion, 1971; Percussion Music for Two, 1971; Trio for Voice Piano and Percussion, 1971; Four Choruses, 1972; Four Settings for A Capella Chorus, 1973; New Poems for Voice and Vibes, 1974; Dream Dialogues for Voice and Percussion, 1974; commd. N.Y. Percussion Trio, 1969, mems. Boston Symphony Orch., 1971, various soloists; works included in Lincoln Center Repertoire Project, 1967; performed orchestral, chamber music throughout U.S.A., abroad. Pvt. tchr. piano, 1960—; faculty Bklyn. Conservatory Music, 1963-65. Co-dir. Composer's Group for Internat. Performance, 1968. Recipient Gretchaninoff Meml. prize for string orch. work, 1966; Marion Freschl award for vocal works with original texts, 1966, 67; Standard Ann. award A.S.C.A.P., 1972; awarded Composer's Forum, Donell Library, 1966; fellow Berkshire Music Center, Tanglewood, 1967. Address: 71-81 244th St Douglaston NY 11362

STEINER, MONICA WILLIAMS (MRS. FRANKLIN STEINER), woman's editor; b. Venedocia, O., Mar. 2, 1921; d. Edwin Mathias and Veronica Elizabeth (Sever) Williams; grad. Northwestern Sch. Commerce, 1940; postgrad. Ohio No., 1941-42, U. Fla., 1954-55, Fla. State U., 1959-60; m. Franklin Gideon Steiner, Sept. 5, 1942; children—Jane (Mrs. Wayne Boynton), Franklin W., William H. Clk., Timmerman Sales Co. Inc., Lima, O., 1940, asst. sec. treas. corp., 1941-46; women's editor Sarasota (Fla.) Jour., 1955-64, Sarasota Herald-Tribune, 1964—. Mem. Ringling Mus. Mems. Council, 1965—, Asolo Theater Festival Assn., 1965—. Mem. bd. Sarasota County Program Aids. Named Outstanding Woman of Yr., Bus. and Profl. Women of Sarasota, 1973. Mem. Fla. Congress Parents and Tchrs. Assns. (hon. life), Fla. Women's Press (awards 1958-70; pres. 1967-69), Women in Communications. Editor, compiler 9 ann. cookbooks of readers' recipes, also spl. sect. on holiday entertaining and furniture fashions. Home: 280 Bird Key Dr Sarasota FL 33577 Office: PO Box 1719 Sarasota FL 33578

STEINHART, CAROL ANN ELDER (MRS. JOHN SHANNON STEINHART), biologist; b. Cleve., Mar. 27, 1935; d. Clayton Thomas and Carolyn (Kalkbrenner) Elder; A.B., Albion Coll., 1956; Ph.D., U. Wis., 1960; m. John Shannon Steinhart, Dec. 20, 1958; children—Gail, Martha, Geoffrey. Biologist Lab. Gen. and Comparative Biochemistry, Nat. Inst. Mental Health, Bethesda, Md., 1961-66; biologist Office Research Analysis and Evaluation, div. research grants, NIH, Bethesda, 1966-70; freelance writer, editor, 1970—. Mem. Med. Com. for Human Rights, 1965-67. Mem. Bot. Soc. Am., Am. Soc. Plant Physiologists, Internat. Soc. Plant Morphologists, N.Y. Acad. Scis., Am. Inst. Biol. Sci., Amateur Chamber Music Players, Phi Beta Kappa, Sigma Xi. Club: Gordon Setter of America. Author: (with John S. Steinhart) Blowout: A Case Study of the Santa Barbara Oil Spill, 1972; Energy: Sources, Use, and Role in Human Affairs, 1974; The Fires of Culture: Energy Yesterday and Tomorrow. Home: 104 Lathrop St Madison WI 53705

STEINHEIMER, LEODA, advt. exec.; b. St. Louis; d. Arthur D. and Della (Hance) Steinheimer; student City Coll., 1930-33. Promotion mgr. Martiz Sales Builders, St. Louis, 1937-42, Walk Easy Food Rest Mfg. Co., 1943-44; advt. mgr. Mary Muffet, Inc., 1945, Rosenthal-Ackerman Millinery Co., 1946-48; exec. asst., copy chief Marjorie Wilten Advt., 1949-50; owner Leoda Steinheimer Advt. Agy., St. Louis, 1951—. Bd. dirs. St. Louis League for Hard of Hearing. Mem. Am. Advt. Fedn. (recipient Nat. Advt. Woman of Yr. award 1972), Fashion Group, Inc. (sec. St. Louis), Advt. Women of St. Louis (2d v.p. 1971-72, recipient St. Louis Advt. Woman of Year award 1971). Home: 4949 Wise Av St Louis MO 63110 Office: Shell Bldg 1221 Locust St St Louis MO 63103

STEINKAMP, RUTH CHRISTINE, physician, educator; b. Little Rock; d. William Frederick and Sophie Louise Christine (Riegler) Steinkamp; B.S., U. Tex., 1940, M.S., 1940; M.D., U. Ark., 1950. Research nutrionist Vanderbilt U. Sch. Medicine, 1941-45; intern Barnes Hosp., St. Louis, 1950-51, resident, 1951-52; fellow internal medicine and hematology Washington U., St. Louis, 1952-54; practice medicine specializing in hematology, St. Louis, 1954-58, La Mesa, Cal., 1968-70; attending physician Barnes, St. Louis County, Jewish, Mo. Bapt. hosps., 1954-58; hematologist Donner Lab., Berkeley, 1958-61; dir. cancer program Ark. Regional Med. Program, Little Rock, 1971-73; pub. health physician adminstr. Ark. State Health Dept., 1973—; instr. medicine Barnes Hosp., St. Louis, 1950-58, Washington U., St. Louis, 1952-58, U. Cal. at San Diego, 1968-70; instr. pub. health and nutrition U. Cal. at Berkeley, 1960-68; asst. prof. medicine U. Ark. Med. Sch., Little Rock, 1971—. Cons. WHO, Geneva, Switzerland, 1958, Cowell Hosp., Berkeley, 1958-61, Cal. Dept. Pub. Health, 1961-68. Chmn. Ark. div. Am. Cancer Soc. Uterine Task Force, 1972—, also bd. dirs. Diplomate Am. Bd. Internal Medicine, Am. Bd. Clin. Nutrition. Fellow A.C.P.; mem. Altrusa, Alpha Omega Alpha, Phi Mu (alumni pres. East Bay 1964-65), Omicron Nu, Iota Sigma Pi. Contbr. articles in field to med. jours. Home: 409 Fairfax Av Little Rock AR 72205 Office: Ark State Health Dept W Markham St Little Rock AR 72204

STEINKULLER, JOAN MURIEL SOMMERS, physician; b. Weymouth, Mass., July 21, 1942; d. Waldo Stepler and Cordelia Lucille (Schmidt) Sommers; student U. Miami, 1959-62; A.B., George Washington U., 1964, M.D., 1967; m. Paul Gilbert Steinkuller, May 7, 1966; children—Anne-Marie, Paul David, John Erik. Intern, Washington Hosp. Center, 1967-68; practice gen. medicine. Cons., A.R.C., Beaufort, S.C., 1969; welfare dir. Naval Officers Wives, Marine Fighter Attack Squadron 333, 1969-70. Mem. Am. Med. Women's Assn. (pres. jr. br. 19b6-67), Alpha Epsilon Delta. Home: 5104 Battery Lane Bethesda MD 20014

STEINMAN, EDNA LOUISE, univ. adminstr.; b. Aberdeen, S.D.; d. Carl W. and Emma (Haselhorst) Steinman; student Huron Coll., 1948-50; B.J., U. Mo., 1953. Instr. journalism U. Mo., 1953-54; reporter American-News, Aberdeen, S.D., 1954-60, Albuquerque Jour., 1960-64; dir. news, publs. U. Redlands (Cal.), 1964-68, instr. journalism, 1965-66; dir. pub. affairs Cal. State Coll., San Bernardino, 1968—. Bd. dirs. San Gorgonio council Girl Scouts U.S., 1972-75. Mem. San Bernardino C. of C. (v.p. 1973, pres. women's div. 1973), Am. Assn. U. Women (bd. dirs. Aberdeen br. 1955-60, N.M. pub.

relations chmn., 1961-64, treas. Redlands br. 1966-68, 1st v.p. 1968-70, Cal. publicity chmn. 1968-70, pres. Redlands br. 1970-72, Cal. State bd. 1971-74), Twin Counties Press Club (bd. dirs. 1967-68), Cal. Am. Coll. Pub. Relations Assn. (editor and sec. Far West Dist. Bull. 1966-68), Women in Communications (v.p. chpt. 1963-64, treas. Inland Cal. chpt. 1973-74), Kappa Tau Alpha, Kappa Alpha Mu, Sigma Delta Chi. Club: Zonta (editor bull. 1966-67, pres. 1970-71, dir. Area V 1972-74). Home: 133 University St Redlands CA 92373 Office: 5500 State College Pkwy San Bernardino CA 92407

STEINMANN, ANNE (MRS. HERBERT R. STEINMANN), psychologist, psychotherapist; b. N.Y.C., Jan. 3, 1907; d. Harry and Rebecca (Comer) Gelof; B.A., Hunter Coll., 1927; M.A., N.Y.U., 1953, Ph.D., 1957; m. Herbert R. Steinmann, June 26, 1927; children—Shelley (Mrs. List), Peter, Daniel. Clinic affiliate, psychotherapist, research psychologist N.Y. Clinic Mental Health, N.Y.C., 1958-64; psychotherapist Soc. Psychoanalytic Study and Research, Inc., 1958-65; pres., prin. investigator female-male role research maffer Found., Inc., 1965—; with research dept. Postgrad. Center for Mental Health, N.Y.C., 1969—; pvt. practice individual and family clin. psychology, 1969—; with N.W. Ackerman Family Inst., 1967-68, summer 1972; adj. asst. prof. psychology Hofstra U., 1958-61; tchr. Human Relations Center, New Sch. for Social Research, 1969—; tchr. English pub. high schs. Co-founder and co-organizer Five Towns Music and Art Found., 1949-53; co-founder and co-organizer N.Y. Clinic Mental Health, 1955-58; mem. mayor's com. N.Y. Shakespeare Festival, 1963; sponsor Eleanor Roosevelt Meml. Found., 1964; mem. adv. bd. Internat. Inst. Women Studies. Fellow A.A.A.S., Internat. Council Psychologists; mem. Am. Psychiat. Assn., Am., N.Y. State, Eastern psychol. assns., N.Y. Soc. Clin. Psychologists, Interam. Soc. Psychology, Am. Personnel and Guidance Assn., Nat. Vocational Guidance Assn., Nat. Council Family Relations, N.Y. Acad. Scis., Soc. Sci. Study of Sex, N.Y. League Bus. and Profl. Women, Am. Assn. U. Women, Soc. Founding Fellows of Center for Human Devel. Hebrew U., Pi Lambda Theta. Author: (monograph) A Study of the Concept of the Feminine Role 51 Middle Class American Families; (with David J. Fox) The Male Dilemma, 1973. Contbr. articles to profl. jours. Research on concept of feminine and masculine role, 1952—. Home: 9 E 81 St New York City NY 10028 Office: 124 E 28th St New York City NY 10016

STEINMETZ, ELVA LUCILLE (MRS. WILLIAM F. STEINMETZ), realtor; b. nr. Wellington, Kan., July 14, 1914; d. George Oscar and Nora Faye (Shore) Kleier; grad. high sch.; m. William F. Steinmetz, Jan. 12, 1933; children—Jack, Seanne (Mrs. Kenneth E. Tonkovich), Jay D. Purchasing agt. Franks Mfg. Co., Compton, Cal., 1952-57; salesman Harold Lloyd Realtor, Hacienda Heights, Cal., 1959-61; owner Steinmetz Realtors, Hacienda Heights, 1961—. Named Woman Citizen of Year Greater La Puente Valley C. of C., 1973. Mem. Bus. and Profl. Women's Club (pres. 1965-66), La Puente Valley Women's Club (pres. 1970-71), C. of C. (pres. women's div. 1971), Women in Chambers of Commerce (state dir. 1973), United Selling Service (pres. 1967), San Gabriel Valley Bd. Realtors (dir. 1972-73), Cal. Real Estate Assn. (state dir. 1972-73, state del. 1974), Delta Pi. Mem. Order Eastern Star. Home: 2609 Vallecito Dr Hacienda Heights CA 91745 Office: 15922 E Gale Av Hacienda Heights CA 91745

STEINMETZ, GRACE ERNST TITUS (MRS. ROLLIN C. STEINMETZ), artist; b. Lancaster, Pa., Apr. 17, 1911; d. John and Anna (Ernst) Titus; student Pa. Acad. Fine Arts, 1932-33, Barnes Found., 1936-37; B.S., Millersville State Coll., 1953; M.S., U. Pa., 1957; m. Rollin C. Steinmetz, Aug. 15, 1937. One-man shows Millersville State Coll., Franklin and Marshall Coll., Elizabethtown Coll., Hager Gallery, Lancaster, Pa., Lesley Frost Studio Gallery, N.Y.; exhibited in group shows Ind. State U., Riverside Mus., Am. Watercolor Soc., Nat. Arts Club, N.Y., Pa. Acad. Fine Arts, Moore Coll. Art, Phila., Quarryville Festival of Arts, Knickerbocker Art Assn., Woodmere Art Galleries, Germantown, William Penn Meml. Mus., Harrisburg; represented in permanent collections Millersville State Coll., Franklin and Marshall Coll., U. So. Fla. Prof. oil painting, art history, appreciation of art Elizabethtown (Pa.) Coll., 1964-65; adj. prof. painting Elizabethtown Coll., 1969, 73—. Recipient awards Lancaster County Art Assn., Southeastern Pa. Regional Exhibit, 1960, Lancaster Area Regional Open Award Show, 1960, 64, 68, 70, Harrisburg Art Assn., 1965, Assn. Delaware Valley Art Centers, 1965, 69, 1st Grumbacher prize Nat. Soc. Painters in Casein, 1969, Zaccone award for non-traditional watercolor N.J. Painters and Sculptors Soc., 1968. Fellow Royal Soc. Arts, London, Eng.; mem. Pa. Acad Fine Arts, Nat. Soc. Painters in Casein and Acrylics, Lancaster County (charter mem., past sec.), Echo Valley art assns., Delta Kappa Gamma. Presbyn. Home: Box 340 RD 7 Manheim PA 17545

STEINMETZ, JOHANNA (MRS. GARY PEARSON CUMMINGS), journalist; b. Trenton, N.J., July 2, 1941; d. Edward George and Dorothy Grace (Sainsbury) Steinmetz; student Internat. Christian U., Tokyo, Japan, 1961-62; B.A. cum laude, Lawrence U., 1963; postgrad. Stockholm (Sweden) U., 1967; m. Gary Pearson Cummings, Apr. 18, 1970; 1 son, Ian Christian Dane. Aide, Japanese Mission to UN, N.Y., 1963-65; free lance journalist, Tokyo, 1966; stringer Time, Inc., others, Stockholm, part-time, 1967-68; feature writer Chgo.'s Am., 1968-69; radio-TV columnist Chgo. Today newspaper, 1969-73; freelance writer, 1973—; critic-at-large WBBM Radio, 1973—; contbg. editor Chicagoan mag., 1973-74, theater columnist, 1974—. Recipient Nat. Headliner award, 1972. Home: 641 Michigan Av Evanston IL 60202

STEJSKAL, SALLY ANN, data processing corp. exec.; b. Cedar Rapids, Ia., Sept. 20, 1941; d. Leo W. and Mamie E. (Schlueter) Asenbrener; grad. Cedar Rapids Bus. Coll., 1960; m. Kenneth J. Stejskal, Sept. 9, 1961; children—Lynette Sue, Brent Douglas. Office mgr. installment loan dept. Mchts. Nat. Bank, Cedar Rapids, 1960-61; sec. trust dept. Bank Am., Salinas, Cal., 1961-62; corporate sec., dir. Network Data Processing Corp., Cedar Rapids, 1967-70, corporate sec., treas., Oak Brook, 1970-71, Cedar Rapids, 1971—; corporate dir. Stejskal Florist's Inc. Mem. C. of C. (personnel mgrs. com. 1967—). Home: 2545 N Av NW Cedar Rapids IA 52405 Office: 321 3d St SE Cedar Rapids IA 52407

STEKERT, RUTH, physician; b. Jersey City, Jan. 2, 1918; d. Harold and Sarah (Fletcher) Stekert; M.D., Temple U., 1949. Pediatric fellow, resident St. Christopher's Hosp. Children, Phila., 1950-53; practice medicine specializing in pediatrics, Canton, O., 1953-56, Levittown, Pa., 1958—; mem. staffs Aultman Hosp., Canton, 1953-56, Lower Bucks County Hosp., Bristol, Pa., 1956-72, St. Christopher's Hosp. Children, Phila., 1958-67, courtesy staff, 1967—; instr. pediatrics Temple U. Med. Sch., 1968—; chief bur. child health, div. med. assistance and health service Dept. Instns. and Agys., State of N.J., 1971—. Cons., county, Valley Day Sch. for Children with Learning Problems, 1960-72; cons. physician Bristol Twp. Head Start program, 1967-70. Mem. N.J. Learning Disabilities Council, 1973—; mem. maternal and infant care com. State Health Planning Council N.J., 1973. Bd. dirs. Pa. Mental Health, 1966—, exec. com., 1968-69; bd. dirs. Radcliffe Cultural and Hist. Soc., Am. Cancer Soc. Bucks County, Valley Day Sch. for Children with Learning Difficulties; hon. chmn. Vols. Bucks County Easter Seal Soc., 1968-71. Mem. Am. Women's Med. Soc., Phila. Pediatric Soc., Ambulatory Pediatric Soc., N.J. Assn. Am. Acad. Pediatrics, Mercer County Med. Soc. (chmn. sch. health com. 1972—). Episcopalian. Home: 85 Thimbleberry Lane Levittown PA 19054

STELE, MARGARITA, physician; b. N.Y.C., Jan. 15, 1937; d. David and Frieda (Herzfeld) Stele; B.S. in Chemistry, U. Cal. at Los Angeles, 1957; student U. So. Cal. Sch. Medicine, 1958-62; m. John R. Thompson, June 20, 1965 (div. May 1969). Intern, U. So. Cal. Med. Center, Los Angeles, 1962-63, resident internal medicine, 1963-66, fellow hematology, 1967-69, instr. medicine, 1968-71, asst. prof. medicine, 1971—, asst. prof. emergency medicine, 1974—; staff hematologist U. Cal. at Irvine, 1966-67. NIH fellow hematology, 1968-69. Mem. Soc. Grad. Internists, Profl. Staff Assn. Home: 4455 Los Feliz Blvd Los Angeles CA 90027 Office: 1200 N State St Los Angeles CA 90033

STELLY, YVONNE JUANITA (MRS. GEORGE MABRY ANDERSON), physician; b. Lake Charles, La., June 22, 1921; d. Aurelie Michael and Juanita (Herbert) Stelly; B.S., Ursuline Coll., 1942; M.D., Loyola U., Chgo., 1946; m. George Mabry Anderson, Apr. 26, 1948; children—Linda Anne, George Mabry II. Intern Charity Hosp., New Orleans, 1946-47, resident, 1948-49; practice medicine, specializing in anesthesiology, Lake Charles, La., 1949-61; mem. staff St. Patrick Hosp., Lake Charles Meml. Hosp. Vice pres. Calcasieu Parish Heart Assn., 1968-70, pres., 1970—; bd. dirs. La. Heart Assn., 1970—, v.p., 1971. Mem. La. State, Calcasieu Parish med. socs. Roman Catholic. Home: 3820 Bluff Lane Lake Charles LA 70601 Office: Weber Bldg Lake Charles LA 70601

STEMCOSKY, LOIS M. (MRS. NORBERT STEMCOSKY), city ofcl.; b. Port Washington, N.Y., Feb. 5, 1934; d. John and Natalie (Truskowski) Kremski; grad. Skinners Bus. Sch., 1951; student Adelphi Coll., 1951-52; m. Norbert Stemcosky, May 3, 1958; children—John, Michael, Sheryl. City clk. City of Glen Cove, N.Y., 1968—. Democratic committeewoman 17th Election Dist. Glen Cove, N.Y., 1963; pres. Glen Cove Dem. Club, 1969-71. Elk. Home: 24 High Av Glen Cove NY 11542 Office: City Hall Bridge St Glen Cove NY 11542

STENDER, FAY ETHEL ABRAHAMS (MRS. MARVIN EDWARD STENDER), lawyer; b. San Francisco, Mar. 29, 1932; d. Samuel Albert and Ruby Fay (Lefkovitz) Abrahams; student Reed Coll., 1949-52; B.A. with honors, U. Cal. at Berkeley, 1953, postgrad., 1958; J.D., U. Chgo., 1956; m. Marvin Edward Stender, Jan. 5, 1954; children—Neal Aviron, Oriane. Admitted to Cal. bar, 1956; law clk. Cal. Supreme Ct., San Francisco, 1956-57; mem. firm Garry, Dreyfus, McTernan & Brotsky, San Francisco, 1961-69, Franck, Hill, Stender, Ziegler & Hendon, Berkeley, Cal., 1969-71, Stender, Lapides, Stender & Weinberg, San Francisco 1973—. Adv. atty. Prisoner's Union, San Francisco, 1971—. Trustee Prison Law Project Charitable Trust; bd. dirs. Women's History Research Library. Named Citizen of Merit, Sun Reporter Newspaper, San Francisco, 1973. Mem. Nat. Lawyers Guild, Internat. Childbirth Edn. Assn., Am. Civil Liberties Union (dir. No. Cal.). Jewish religion. Author: Intro to Maximum Security, Letters From California Prisoners, 1972. Editorial bd. Forum for Contemporary History, 1973—, Prison Law Reporter, 1973—. Office: Pier 37 The Embarcadero San Francisco CA 94133

STENHOLM, KATHERINE ALEE CORNE (MRS. GILBERT RALPH STENHOLM), motion pictures producer, dir.; b. Hendersonville, N.C., June 19, 1917; d. George Few and Luvenia (Heaton) Corne; B.A. in Speech, Bob Jones U., 1939; M.A. in Speech, Northwestern U., 1944, postgrad., 1945-49; postgrad. U. So. Cal., 1950; m. Gilbert Ralph Stenholm, June 4, 1941; 1 son, Gilbert Ralph, Jr. With Bob Jones U., Greenville, S.C., 1939—, chmn. dramatic prodn., 1939-50, founder Unusual Films studios, 1950, adminstr., 1950—, producer, 1950—, dir., 1950—, chmn. div. Cinema, 1950—. Dir. numerous stage and opera prodns., 1939-67; cons., supr. interior decoration Bob Jones U. Art Gallery, 1965; dir. numerous films including Wine of Morning, Red Runs the River, Flame in the Wind. Recipient Inter-collegiate Film award Screen Producer's Guild, 1959; named Dir. of Year Nat. Evangelical Film Found., 1953, 55, 64. Home: 211 Stadium View Dr Greenville SC 29609 Office: Unusual Films Bob Jones U Greenville SC 29614

STENNIS, COY HINES (MRS. JOHN STENNIS), wife of U.S. senator; m. John Stennis, Dec. 24, 1929; children—John Hampton, Margaret Jane. Wife of U.S. Senator from Miss. Address: 3609 Cumberland St Washington DC 20008*

STEPHAN, SHERYL JO, educator; b. Cedar Rapids, Ia., Aug. 6, 1934; d. Joseph A. and Mildred A. (Babbitt) Stephan; B.S., MacMurray Coll., 1956; M.A., State U. Ia., 1963; D. Recreation, Ind. U., 1973. Field tchr. Long Beach (Cal.) Outdoor Schs., 1956-57; phys. edn. instr. pub. schs., Biwabik, Minn., 1957, St. Charles, Ill., 1957-58, L'Anse, Mich., 1958-61, State U. Ia. Lab. Sch., Iowa City, 1962-63; field tchr. Cleveland Heights (O.) Outdoor Sch., 1963-66, coordinator outdoor edn., dir. Outdoor Sch., 1967-69; prof. recreation Ind. State U., Terre Haute, 1972-73; prof. recreation and outdoor edn. Eastern Ky. U., Richmond, 1973—. Co-dir. Title 1 Summer Outdoor Edn. Programs, Amherst, Wis., 1969; dir. Camp Hitaga, Camp Fire Girls, Cedar Rapids, Ia., 1971-72. Mem. Nat. Recreation and Park Assn., Am. Camping Assn., Mortar Bd. Home: 24-C Route 7 Brooklyn Richmond KY 40475

STEPHANS, ALICE PAULINE COLEMAN (MRS. JOSEPH P. STEPHANS), assn. exec.; b. East Pitts., Dec. 8, 1931; d. Thomas H. and Alyce E. (Pyles) Coleman; secretarial certificate, Bus. Tng. Coll., 1941; m. Joseph P. Stephans, Aug. 31, 1956; children—Craig Paul, Gary Jay. Sec., U.S.O., Pitts., 1948-49; stenographer, Union R.R. Co., Pitts., 1949-51, adminstrv. sec., 1951-55, cost accountant, 1955-58; adminstrv. asst. Edn. Writers Assn., Bloomington, Ind., 1968—. Mem. adv. council Bloomington sch. system Univ. Middle Sch., 1972-73. Chmn. collection gifts for Christmas Mental Health Assn., Bloomington, 1968—; den mother Cub Scouts Am., Bloomington, 1966-69; pres. Marlin Elementary Sch. P.T.A., 1967, P.T.A.-O Council 1972-73. Mem. Kappa Sigma (pres. 1966). Baptist (mem. com. 1972—). Mem. Dames Malta (queen 1956-57); mem. Order Eastern Star. Home: Rural Route 1 Audubon Dr Bloomington IN 47401 Office: PO Box 1289 Bloomington IN 47401

STEPHEN, MAE, sociologist; b. Manchester, N.H.; d. Simon Y. and Victoria (Saigh) Estfan; A.B., U. N.C., 1940; postgrad. U. Chgo., 1939-41, U. Buffalo, 1942, Am. U., 1959; children from former marriage—Anita Joan, Franklin David, Lisa Jeanne, Sharon E., Robert Michael. Group worker, Greensboro, N.C., 1936-37, Hiram House Settlement Camp, summer 1937; departmental asst. psychology dept. U. N.C., 1937-39, sociology dept. U. Chgo., 1940; social worker Internat. Inst., Buffalo, 1941-42; vocational adviser VA, Manchester, 1945-46; personnel technician AGO Dept. Army, 1942-44, 47-48; social sci. analyst Nat. Inst. Mental Health Dept. Health Edn. and Welfare, Bethesda, Md., 1959-61, pub. health analyst, 1966-67, program analyst Nat. Inst. Child Health and Human Devel., 1967-70; sociologist Stanford Research Inst. Edn. Policy Research Center, 1970-73, Edn. Research dept. Stanford Research Inst., Menlo Park, Cal., 1973—. Leader, Capitol council Girl Scouts U.S.A., 1959-62, organizer, 1962. Recipient Superior Service award Dept. Health, Edn. and Welfare, 1967. Mem. Am. Sociol. Assn., Am. Edn. Research Assn., Pacific Sociol. Assn., A.A.A.S., Alpha Kappa Delta. Author: A Brief Look at the State of Reading Research, 1961, rev. 1962; Career Education: Limitations and Possibilities, 1971; Early Childhood Education: Perspectives on the Federal and Office of Education Roles, 1972. Contbr. articles to profl. publs. Home: 1611 Castilleja Av Palo Alto CA 94306 Office: Education Research Dept Stanford Research Inst Menlo Park CA 94025

STEPHENS, CHARLENE BARR, otolaryngic researcher; b. Jackson, Miss., Sept. 2, 1936; d. Jacob Dexter and Charlene Brumfield (Vetter) Barr; student Miss. State Coll. for Women, 1954-56; B.A., U. Miss., 1958, M.S., 1966, Ph.D., 1970; Speech and hearing therapist Jackson Pub. Schs., 1958-59; tchr. English and choral music Florence (Ala.) Jr. High Sch., 1959-60; speech and hearing therapist Memphis Pub. Schs., 1960-62, Oxford (Miss.) Pub. Schs., 1962-64; speech pathologist, audiologist U. Miss. Med. Center, Jackson, 1964-65, asst. to dir. Communicative Disorders lab., 1965-67, instr. dept. surgery (otolaryngology), research asst. to dir., 1967-70, asst. prof. otolaryngology, asso. dir. research and grad. tng., 1970—, asso. mem. grad. faculty, 1970-72, mem., 1972—. Cons. speech pathology Easter Seal Soc., Vicksburg, Miss., 1966, Methodist Children's Home, Jackson, 1965-67. Counselor, Episcopal Young Churchmen, 1969-70. Mem. A.A.A.S., Am., Miss. speech and hearing assns., Miss. Acad. Scis., U. Miss. Alumni Assn., U. Miss. Med. Alumni Assn., D.A.R., Children Am. Revolution, Sigma Xi, Sigma Alpha Eta, Kappa Delta. Episcopalian. Contbr. articles to profl. publs. Home: 220 Edgewood Terrace Dr Jackson MI 39206 Office: 2500 N State St Jackson MI 39216

STEPHENS, ELIZABETH MEADOWS (MRS. PAUL STEPHENS, JR.), ednl. adminstr.; b. Columbus, Miss., July 26, 1918; d. John Cassius and Mary Emma (Andrew) Meadows; B.A., U. Ga., 1938; M.A., George Peabody Coll., 1949; postgrad. Fla. State U., 1966, U. South Fla., 1966-70; m. Paul B. Stephens, Jr., Feb. 23, 1939. Tchr. Ocoee (Fla.) Jr.-Sr. High Sch., 1940-43; asst. Chattanooga Pub. Library, summer 1940; librarian Chapman High Sch., Appalachicola, Fla., 1943-47, White County High Sch., Sparta, Tenn., 1947-51; librarian, audio-visual dir. Dependents Sch., Guantanomo (Cuba) Naval Operations Base, 1951-52; librarian St. Petersburg (Fla.) High Sch., 1952-62; library supr. Pinellas County (Fla.) Schs., 1962-65; dir. ednl. media Sch. Bd. Pinellas County, 1965—; instr. U. Ky., summer 1965, U. Ga., 1968; adj. prof. U. South Fla., 1971—. Cons. Paperback Conf. Columbia, 1965. Mem. Pinellas Dist. Fla. Library Devel. Council, 1970—; mem. Ednl. Media Curriculum Guide Devel. Com. Fla. State Dept. Edn., 1971-72. Mem. A.L.A., Am. Assn. Sch. Librarians (standard task force com. 1971; publs. com. 1972-74, chmn. suprs. sect. 1974-75), Fla. Assn. Sch. Librarians (pres. 1964-65), Assn. for Ednl. Communication and Tech. (standard task force com. 1971), Fla. Library Assn. (chmn. 1958-59), Alpha Omicron Pi, Kappa Delta Pi, Delta Kappa Gamma (pres. Beta Iota chpt. 1970-72). Presbyn. Home: 713 66th St N St Petersburg FL 33710 Office: 1956 E Druid Rd Clearwater FL 33516

STEPHENS, IRLENE ROEMER, librarian; b. nr. Jeffers, Minn., Jan. 28, 1928; d. Earl Loui and Minnie (Wagner) Roemer; B.S., Rutgers U., 1949, M.Ed., 1952; M.S., Columbia, 1954, D.L.S., 1973; m. Sheldon De Witt Stephens, June 29, 1944 (div.); children—Irlene, Shel'lene, Sheldon. Asst. to dir. research Schering Corp., Bloomfield, N.J., 1949-52; chief librarian Bristol-Myers Co., Hillside, N.J., 1952-54; dir. libraries Celanese Corp., Summit, N.J., 1954-60; instr. Bklyn. Poly. Inst., 1957-60; vis. lectr. Columbia, 1956-60; cons. Amherst Cons. and Lit. Services, 1960-63; library dir. South Orange (N.J.) Pub. Library, 1963-65; prof., chief librarian Ednl. Resources Center of Richmond Coll. of City U. N.Y., 1966—. Instr., U. So. Cal., summer 1966, Sch. Librarianship, U. Cal. at Berkeley, summer 1968, Pratt Inst. Grad. Sch. Library and Information Sci., N.Y.C., summer 1969, fall and spring 1969-70; acad. adviser Borough Planning Bds. for Richmond Borough, 1968—; condr. numerous library surveys. Mem. Am. Chem. Soc., A.A.A.S., Am. Documentation Inst., A.L.A., Med. Writers Assn., Am. Soc. Information Sci., N.Y. Acad. Scis., Spl. Libraries Assn., Drug Information Assn., Phi Beta Kappa, Kappa Delta Pi, Beta Phi Mu. Author: The Organization of Intramural Research Reports, 1954. Editor: (with M.F. Tauber) Library Surveys, 1967. Contbr. articles to profl. jours. Home: 15 Amherst Ct Maplewood NJ 07040 Office: 130 Stuyvesant Pl Staten Island NY 10301

STEPHENS, JEANNE HIBBARD (MRS. JAMES THOMAS STEPHENS), physician; b. Columbia, Mo., June 2, 1911; d. Herbert Wade and Mary Coleman (Davis) Hibbard; A.B., Oberlin Coll., 1933; B.S. in Medicine, U. Mo., 1935; M.D., U. Mich., 1937; m. James Thomas Stephens, June 21, 1937; children—Sally (Mrs. George A. Bracht), John B., Ann (Mrs. John W. Molyneaux). Intern City Hosp., Cleve., 1937-38, resident, 1938-39; pvt. practice medicine specializing in pediatrics, Oberlin, O., 1942-62; co-founder-group, pediatrician Oberlin Clinic, 1962—; asst. clin. prof. community medicine Case Western Res. Med. Sch., 1969—; mem. staff Allen Hosp., Oberlin, 1942—, pres. staff, 1950-51, 62. Mem. Oberlin Bd. Edn., 1948-54. Trustee Oberlin Coll., 1968—. Mem. Lorain County Med. Soc., Am., Ohio med. assns., Alpha Epsilon Iota, Alpha Omega Alpha. Republican. Mem. United Ch. of Christ. Home: 374 Morgan St Oberlin OH 44074 Office: Oberlin Clinic Oberlin OH 44074

STEPHENS, MARGARET ELENORA MCKOWN (MRS. FRANK STEPHENS), book editor; b. Peoria, Ill., Apr. 29, 1912; d. Charles Skelton and Elizabeth (Beatty) McKown; B.S., Kan. State U., 1936; m. Frank Stephens, Feb. 14, 1942; children—Ference Charles, Jeanette Elizabeth, Christopher T. Sch. tchr., Kan., 1936-37; asst. editor Scott, Foresman & Co., Chgo., 1937-40; asso. editor Lyons & Carnahan, Chgo., 1940-43; editor Standard Ednl. Corp., Chgo., 1943-46; book saleswoman Child's World, Chgo., 1947-59; editor Follett, Chgo., 1959-61; editor Rand McNally & Co., Skokie, Ill., 1962-70, Consol. Book Pubs., Chgo., 1972—. Mem. Womans Nat. Book Assn., Childrens Reading Round Table (chpt. pres. 1968-69), Chgo. Book Clinic. Republican. Presbyn. Author: (with Paul E. Blackwood) The World and Its Wonders, 1949. Office: 1727 S Indiana Av Chicago IL 60616

STEPHENS, MARGARET JOY BRANDENBURG, librarian; b. Elizabeth, N.J., Feb. 3, 1927; d. Arthur Henry and Margaret (Leonard) Brandenburg; B.A., Woman's Coll. U. N.C., 1948; M.L.S., Rutgers U., 1969; m. William Gustave Stephens, Dec. 18, 1948; 1 dau., Lee Elizabeth (Mrs. Robert William Wollenberg). Jr. high sch. librarian Elizabeth Bd. Edn., 1958-61; high sch. librarian Roselle Park (N.J.) Bd. Edn., 1961—. French horn player Elizabeth Civic Orch, 1958—, v.p., 1970—; French horn player Union County Symphony, 1972—. Co-chmn. library com. N.Y. Soc. for Ethical Culture, 1969-72, library dir., 1973—, del. Am. Ethical Union Assembly, 1971, 72. Mem. A.L.A., N.E.A., N.J. Edn. Assn., Roselle Park Edn. Assn. League Women Voters Roselle (treas., 1969-71). Home: 416 Birch St Roselle Park NJ 07204 Office: 185 W Webster Av Roselle Park NJ 07204

STEPHENS, NANCY GUNN, govt. ofcl.; b. Chgo., Sept. 28, 1916; d. Glenn Dillard and Bessie (Bracken) Gunn; student Chgo. Art Inst., 1933-34, Chgo. Conservatory of Music, 1936-39, Am. U., 1944-47; m.

Joseph S. Stephens, May 23, 1940; 1 son, John Anthony. Asst. music critic Chgo. Herald and Examiner, 1938-39; office asst. Ga. Warm Springs Found., 1939-40; clk. U.S. Dept. Agr., 1940-43; budget clk. Nat. Housing Agy., 1943-47; budget analyst, AEC, 1947-51; budget officer USIA, Washington, 1951-61, dep., 1961-64, agy. budget officer, 1964-72, cons. fed. budgeting, 1972—. Recipient meritorious service award USIA, 1961. Episcopalian. Home: Box 117 Ocean View DE 19970

STEPHENS, NATALIE (MRS. LAWRENCE LYNN TURNER), obstetrician and gynecologist; b. Orange, N.J., Nov. 13, 1920; d. Claude Edwin and Irma (Hughes) Stephens; A.B., Syracuse U., 1942, M.D., 1944; m. Lawrence Lynn Turner, Sept. 18, 1942; children—Stephen Park, Martha Lynn. Intern Balt. City Hosps., 1944-45; resident in obstetrics and gynecology Children's Hosp., San Francisco, 1945-46; resident Women and Children's Hosp., Chgo., 1946-48, attending staff, 1948-61; attending staff Passavant Meml. Hosp., Chgo., 1961—; asso. obstetrics and gynecology dept. Northwestern U. Med. Sch., 1957—. Diplomate Am. Bd. Obstetrics and Gynecology. Fellow Am. Coll. Obstetrics and Gynecology (founding); mem. Am. Med. Womens Assn. (pres. br. 2 Chgo. 1968-70), A.M.A., Ill., Chgo. med. socs. Clubs: Colony, Prairie (Chgo.). Home: 5840 Stony Island Av Chicago IL 60637 Office: 30 N Michigan Av Chicago IL 60602

STEPHENS, RUBY CHRISTINE, occupational therapist; b. Cocoa, Fla., Apr. 17, 1938; d. William Hualpha and Ruby (McDermed) Stephens; B.S. in Occupational Therapy, Tex. Woman's U., 1960; M.A. in Psychology, St. Mary's U., 1972. Staff occupational therapist Dallas Soc. for Crippled Children, 1961-63, Timberlawn Hosp., Dallas, 1963-64; acting chief occupational therapy VA Hosp., McKinney, Tex., 1964-65; chief occupational therapist VA Center, Temple, Tex., 1965-68; dir. occupational therapy Bexar County Hosp. Dist., San Antonio, 1968-73, adminstrv. dir. phys. rehab., 1973—. Cons. Bihl Rehab. Center, New Braunfels, Tex., 1968-70, Morningside Manor, San Antonio, 1971-73, Villa Rosa Hosp., San Antonio, 1972-73, Goodwill Industries, San Antonio, 1973—. Instr. occupational therapy St. Philips Coll., San Antonio, 1970—. Mem. Am. (com. for basic profl. edn. 1970-73), Tex., Southcentral Dist. (chmn. 1970-71) occupational therapy assns., Tex. Hosp. Assn. Home: 1715 Searcy St San Antonio TX 78232 Office: Bexar County Hosp 4502 Medical Dr San Antonio TX 78284

STEPHENS, WILL BETH DODSON (MRS. JACK HOWARD STEPHENS), psychologist, educator; b. Van Horn, Tex., July 14, 1918; d. John Lester and Almeda (Garner) Dodson; B.F.A., U. Tex., 1942, M.Ed., 1958, Ph.D., 1964; m. Jack Howard Stephens, Feb. 18, 1944; children—Jack Howard, Jill Johnstone. Asst. dir. U.S.O., Del Rio, Tex., 1942-45; asst. dir. YWCA, Austin, 1946-47; spl. edn. tchr., Tyler, 1956-60; research asso. U. Tex., 1962-64; research asst. prof. Inst. for Research on Exceptional Children, U. Ill., Urbana, 1965-66; prof. ednl. psychology Temple U., Phila., 1966—; researcher on devel. reasoning, moral judgment and moral conduct in normals retardates, analysis of reasoning in congenitally blind. Mem. Pres.'s Com. on Mental Retardation, 1971—, chmn. community services work group. Vocational Rehab. Adminstrn. post-doctoral fellow U. Geneva, Switzerland, 1964-65. Fellow Pa. Psychol. Assn.; mem. Am. Assn. Mental Deficiency (research com.), Council for Exceptional Children (pres. elect div. mental retardation 1974—), Am. Psychol. Assn., Soc. Research Child Devel., Am. Ednl. Research Assn., N.E.A., Internat. Assn. for Scientific Study Mental Deficiency, Nat. Assn. Retarded Children, Jean Piaget Soc. (internat. adv. bd.), Pi Lambda Theta. Episcopalian. Author and editor books and monographs. Contbr. articles to profl. jours. Home: 358 Winding Way Merion Station PA 19066 Office: Ritter Hall Temple U Philadelphia PA 19122

STEPHENSON, BETTY PEARCE (MRS. CHARLES STEPHENSON), anesthesiologist; b. Abilene, Tex., Jan. 31, 1927; d. Eugene Conrow and Ruth Isabel (Farris) Pearce; B.A., Hardin-Simmons U., 1947; postgrad. U. Colo., 1947-48; M.D., Baylor U., 1953; m. Charles T. Stephenson, Sept. 1, 1951; children—Patricia, Karen, Tom, John. Intern City Hosp., St. Louis, 1953-54; resident in anesthesiology Baylor Affiliated Hosps., Houston, 1955-57; practice medicine specializing in anesthesiology, Los Angeles, 1958, Houston, 1959—; clin. faculty Baylor Coll. Medicine, 1955—. Del. nat. council Girl Scouts U.S.A., 1969—; del. White House Conf. on Children, 1970. Bd. dirs. San Jacinto Girl Scouts U.S.A., 1966-72, chmn. bd. personnel com., 1967-72; bd. dirs. Sch. for Little Children; budget panel United Fund Houston-Harris County. Recipient Thanks Badge San Jacinto Girl Scouts, 1969. Diplomate Am. Bd. Anesthesiology. Mem. Am., Tex. socs. anesthesiology, Gulf Coast Anesthesia Soc., Aircraft Owners and Pilots Assn., Alpha Omega Alpha. United Methodist. Home: 5661 Flack St Houston TX 77036 Office: 6441 High Star Houston TX 77036

STEPHENSON, HELEN ROSE GIBSON, writer; b. Pitts.; d. Charles E. and Ruth (Bowers) Gibson; B.A., U. Pitts., 1936, postgrad. Grad. Sch. Retail Tng., 1936-37; m. Charles E. Ruch, Sept. 7, 1938 (div.); children—Rosalind, Karen; m. 2d, George M. Stephenson, June 10, 1961. Account supr. Ketchum, MacLeod & Grove, Inc., advt. agy., Pitts., 1948-61; free-lance writer, 1961-64; supr. printed materials service Gen. Foods Kitchens, White Plains, N.Y., 1964—. Recipient Golden Quill award for distinguished journalism in Western Pa., 1961, 1st place awards Pitts. Women's Press Club, 1953, 60. Mem. Nat. Home Fashions League, Sons and Daus. of Pioneer Rivermen. Club: Women's Press (Pitts.). Author: Adventure of a City, 1963. Contbr. articles to Town and Country, This Week, Better Homes and Gardens, Esquire, Editor and Publisher. Office: 250 North St White Plains NY

STEPHENSON, MARION, broadcasting co. exec.; b. Green Bay, Wis., Feb. 2, 1921; d. Marvin Schutte and Louise (Cykler) Stephenson; A.B., Antioch Coll., 1943; M.B.A., N.Y. U., 1948; D.Sc. Bus. Adminstrn. (hon.), Bryant Coll., 1963. With Standard Oil Co. N.J., 1943-44; with NBC, 1944—, dir. bus. affairs radio network, 1959-62, v.p. adminstrn. radio network, 1962-66, v.p. adminstrn. radio div., 1966-73, v.p. planning, radio, 1973—. Mem. adv. council on Latin Am., Dept. State, 1972-74. Trustee Hartwick Coll., Oneonta, N.Y., vice chmn. bd., 1974, chmn., 1974—. Recipient Marcus Nadler key for excellence in finance Money Marketeers of N.Y.U. Grad. Sch. Bus., 1948; sr. fellow Woodrow Wilson Nat. Fellowship Found., 1973-74. Mem. Internat. Radio and TV Soc., Am. Mgmt. Assn. (mfg. div. Council 1974—), Am. Women in Radio and TV. Home: 1352 Midland Av Bronxville NY 10708 Office: NBC 30 Rockefeller Plaza New York City NY 10020

STEPHENSON, MATILDE KEJNER, psychologist; b. Tucuman, Argentina, June 25, 1927; d. Aaron and Eva (Koifman) Kejner; Ph.D. in Math., U. Cordoba, 1947, Ph.D. in Psychology, 1959; M.A. in Psychology, Northwestern U., 1954; m. Robert William Stephenson, Aug. 19, 1968. Came to U.S., 1967, naturalized, 1975. Prof. psychology, chmn. dept. U. Cordoba, 1956-66; vis. prof. Cornell U., 1960-63, U. Pitts., 1967; social scientist Standard Oil Co. N.J., 1963-64; research scientist Am. Inst. Research, 1968-70; sr. research scientist, prof. Am. U., 1970-73; mgr. research and devel. div. Urban Bus. Edn. Assn., 1973—; prof. Grad. Sch. Bus., Fed. City Coll., 1973—. Vice pres., sec. Program Devel. Inc. Chmn. edn. and health coms. Commn. Concerns for Spanish Speaking Peoples, 1972; mem. Montgomery County Pub. Sch. Hispanic Task Force, 1973. Mem. Am. Psychol. Assn., Interam. Psychol. Assn., Soc. Humanistic Mgmt., Internat. Council Psychology, Bus. and Profl. Women's Club. Contbr. articles to profl. jours. Address: 6007 Bradley Blvd Bethesda MD 20034

STEPHENSON, MURIEL LOIS (MRS. LONNIE FRANKLIN STEPHENSON), educator; b. St. Paul, Jan. 15, 1923; d. Jacob Ernest and Daisy Victoria (Hanson) Janzen; student, N.D. State U., 1940-41; B.S., Moorhead State Coll., 1944; M.A., U. N.D., 1968, Ph.D., 1972; m. Lonnie Franklin Stephenson, Mar. 29, 1948; children—Melissa Lynne, Lonnie Franklin III. Tchr. English and Spanish, Fergus County High Sch., Lewistown, Mont., 1944-45; adminstrv. asst. Am. Consulate Gen., Frankfurt, Germany, 1946-48, U.S. Army, Nurnberg, Germany, 1949-52; tchr. Spanish, Am. High Sch., Taipei, Taiwan, 1956-57; asst. prof. English and humanities U. Albuquerque, 1969—, chmn. faculty senate, 1973—. Mem. Am. Assn. U. Profs., Am. Assn. U. Women, Modern Lang. Assn., Kappa Delta Pi, Sigma Tau Delta, Gamma Phi Beta. Home: 12441 Chelwood Place NE Albuquerque NM 87112

STEPNEY, JOYCE HARRIETTE, educator; b. Columbia, Miss., July 3, 1940; d. George Frank and Catherine Elizabeth (Brown) Stepney; B.S., Jackson State Coll., 1962, M.S., 1970; postgrad. U. So. Miss., 1972. Tchr. Marion Central High Sch., Columbia, Miss., 1962-68, Jefferson Middle Sch., 1968-72; spl. edn. tchr. Columbia Elementary, 1972—. Mem. N.A.A.C.P., 1970—; pres. Marion County Civicette Federated Club, 1973—. Sec., Marion County Democratic party, 1972—. Bd. dirs. Miss. Rural Center, 1973—. Mem. Marion County Dept. Classroom Tchrs. (sec. 1971-73), Marion County, Dist. 6, Miss. tchrs. assns., N.E.A., Am. Assn. Mental Deficiency, Marion County Assn. for Retarded Children, Miss. Assn. Federated Clubs, Nat. Assn. Colored Women Clubs, Southeastern Assn. Mental Deficiency. United Methodist (sec. Miss. conf. United Meth. Women 1973—, youth coordinator Miss. conf. 1973—). Home: Route 2 Box 313 Columbia MS 39429 Office: 401 Mary St Columbia MS 39429

STERLING, JO ANN, psychologist; b. Chgo., May 7, 1927; d. Nicholas A. and Maria M. (Mihalopulos) Chapralis; B.A., DePaul U., 1957, M.Ed., 1959; postgrad. Northwestern U., 1958-60; m. Carl V. Sterling, Jan. 26, 1946 (div. Dec. 1960); children—Maria Ann, Dean Nicholas. Clin. psychology trainee VA, Hines, Ill., 1959-61; psychologist Bur. Child Study, Chgo. pub. schs., 1961-63, Villa Park (Ill.) Sch., 1963-66; chief psychologist N.W. Coop. Mental Health Clinic, Arlington Heights, Ill., 1966-68; cons. Psychiat. Inst., Chgo., 1969—. Instr. Grad. Sch. Edn., DePaul U., part time 1961, 62, Elmhurst Coll., part time 1964—; individual practice Elmhurst (Ill.) Psychol. Center, 1966-69, Chgo., 1973—; psychologist Mt. Prospect (Ill.) schs., 1968-71; chief clin. psychologist Stickney (Ill.) Mental Health Clinic, 1971—; cons. Div. Vocational Rehab., Fed. Disability Program, Springfield, Ill., 1965—. Active Young Democrats Oak Park, Ill., also Dems. for McGovern, 1972-73. Mem. Am., Ill., Chgo. (sec. 1972-73) psychol. assns., Chgo. Psychol. Club (sec. 1972-73). Unitarian. Home: 1700 E 56th St Apt 3305 Chicago IL 60637 Office: 6721 W 40th St Stickney IL 60402

STERLING, JOANNE WINIFRED, psychologist, educator; b. Titusville, Pa., Nov. 29, 1934; d. George W. and Anne Elizabeth (Dowling) Sterling; B.A., Chatham Coll., 1956; postgrad. U. Colo., summer 1954; Ph.D. (Dept. Health, Edn. and Welfare fellow), U. N.M., 1970. Probation officer Allegheny County Juvenile Ct., Pitts., 1956-58; asst. clin. dir. Girls Welfare Home, Albuquerque, 1958-63; devel. and rehab. project dir. Ft. Logan Mental Health Center, 1963-65; asst. prof. U. N.M. Sch. Medicine, asst. dir. County Mental Health Center, Albuquerque, 1968—. Mem. Gov.'s Council on Criminal Justice Planning, 1972—, Met. Criminal Justice Coordinating Council, 1972—. Mem. profl. adv. bd. All Faith's Receiving Home. Mem. Am., N.M. (treas. 1973-75) psychol. assns., N.M. Correctional Assn., N.M. C. of C. (task Force on crime), N.M. Womens Polit. Caucus, Phi Kappa Phi. Contbr. articles to profl. jours. Office: 2600 Marble St NE Albuquerque NM 87106

STERN, CAROL SUE, dermatologist; b. N.Y.C., Mar. 4, 1943; d. Marvin and Libby (Rifkin) Stern; B.A., N.Y. U., 1963, M.D., 1967. Med. intern Kings County Hosp., Bklyn., 1967-68; resident dermatology N.Y. U., N.Y.C., 1968-71; practice medicine specializing in dermatology, Beth Page, N.Y., 1971-73; staff Univ. Health Service, State U. N.Y. at Stony Brook, 1971-73, acting dir., 1973—. Mem. Am. Med. Women's Assn., Am. Acad. Dermatology, Soc. Investigative Dermatology (asso.), Am. Soc. Dermatol. Surgery. Office: care Univ Health Service State U NY Stony Brook NY 11790

STERN, DORIS LISITZ, lawyer; b. N.Y.C.; d. Sam and Anna (Shaffer) Lisitz; B.A., Hunter Coll.; M.A., U. Cal. at Los Angeles, J.D., 1960; div.; children—Nancy, Elizabeth. Admitted to Cal. bar, 1960; asso. counsel USN, Los Angeles, 1960-61; practice law, Marina del Rey, Cal., 1961—. Bd. dirs. Los Angeles council Am. Youth Hostels. Mem. State Bar Cal., Los Angeles County, Marina del Rey bar assns., Women Lawyers Assn. Los Angeles, League Am. Wheelmen, Mensa, Phi Beta Kappa. Office: 4519 Admiralty Way Marina del Rey CA 90291

STERN, ELLEN GOTTLIEB (MRS. SAMUEL EDWARD STERN), educator; b. Balt., Apr. 7, 1942; d. William and Ada (Bargrosser) Gottlieb; B.S., U. Wis., 1964; M.A. (Mental Retardation fellow), U. Neb., 1966, Ph.D. (Nat. Def. Edn. Act fellow, Regents Tuition fellow), 1970; m. Samuel Edward Stern, Sept. 3, 1963; 1 dau., Jennifer Anne. Tchr. mentally retarded Hayward Elementary Sch., Lincoln, Neb., 1965-67; instr., psychologist U. Neb., Lincoln, 1968-69; asst. prof. edn., dir. mental retardation program Hunter Coll., N.Y.C., 1970-72; dir. Metro-West Center/Ga. Learning Resources System, Atlanta, 1972—. Cons. N.Y. State Psychiat. Inst., 1971-73, N.Y.C. Neighborhood Youth Corps for Retarded, 1971-72, Atlanta Regional Commn.-Task Force on Mental Health, 1973, Met. Atlanta Mental Health Assn., 1973—. Mem. Am. Assn. on Mental Deficiency, Am. Assn. U. Women, Am. Psychol. Assn., Council for Exceptional Children, Ga. Psychol. Assn., Ga. Assn. Educators, Assn. for Spl. Edn. Tech., Nat. Assn. Retarded Children, Phi Lambda Theta. Home: 1634 Ponce de Leon Av NE Atlanta GA 30307 Office: Metro-West Center GLRS 771 Lindbergh Dr NE Atlanta GA 30324

STERN, JOAN GABRIELLE, psychiatrist; b. N.Y.C., June 21, 1943; d. Victor and Grete (Metzger) Stern; B.A., N.Y. U., 1964; M.D. (Nat. Inst. Mental Health fellow), Woman's Med. Coll. Pa., 1968. Intern pediatrics Stanford U. Hosp., 1968-69; resident adult psychiatry Med. Coll. Pa., Phila., 1969-71, fellow child psychiatry, 1971-73, instr. child psychiatry, 1973—; cons. psychiatry Cath. Home for Girls, Phila., Germantown Friends Sch., Phila.; in tng. Phila. Psychoanalytic Inst., 1970—; pvt. practice adult and child psychiatry. Mem. Am. Psychiat. Assn., A.M.A., Am. Med. Women's Assn., Pa. Psychiat. Soc., Am. Psychoanalytic Soc., Pa. Med. Soc. Home: 6100 Henry Av Philadelphia PA 19128 Office: Dept Psychiatry Med Coll Pa 3300 Henry Av Philadelphia PA 19129

STERN, LORAINE MARSHA, pediatrician; b. Chgo., Aug. 26, 1944; d. Leopold and Trude (Samuel) Stern; B.A., U. Chgo., 1965, M.D., 1969. Intern dept. pediatrics U. Cal. at Los Angeles, 1969-70, resident pediatrics, 1970-72; pvt. practice medicine, specializing in pediatrics, Newhall, Cal., 1972—; mem. staff Golden State Meml. Hosp., Newhall; mem. clin. faculty U. Cal. at Los Angeles. Mem. Am. Acad. Pediatrics, Zero Population Growth. Home: 465 Mesa Rd Santa Monica CA 90402 Office: Valencia Med Group 23550 Lyons Av Newhall CA 91321

STERN, MADELEINE BETTINA, author, rare books dealer; b. N.Y.C., July 1, 1912; d. Moses R. and Lillie (Mack) Stern; A.B., Barnard Coll., 1932; M.A., Columbia, 1934. Tchr. English high schs., N.Y.C., 1934-43; partner Leona Rostenberg Rare Books, 1945—. Guggenheim fellow, 1943-45. Mem. Antiquarian Booksellers Assn. Am., Antiquarian Booksellers Assn. (Eng.), Internat. League Antiquarian Bookmen, Modern Lang. Assn., Authors League, Phi Beta Kappa. Author: The Life of Margaret Fuller, 1942; Louisa May Alcott, 1950; Purple Passage: The Life of Mrs. Frank Leslie, 1953; Imprints on History: Book Publishers and American Frontiers, 1956; We the Women: Career Firsts of Nineteenth-Century America, 1963; So Much in a Lifetime: The Story of Dr. Isabel Barrows, 1964; Queen of Publishers' Row; Mrs. Frank Leslie, 1965; The Pantarch: A Biography of Stephen Pearl Andrews, 1968; Heads and Headlines: The Phrenological Fowlers, 1971; (with Leona Rostenberg) Old and Rare: Thirty Years in the Book Business, 1974; also articles in field. Editor: Women on the Move, 1972; The Victoria Woodhull Reader, 1974; Louisa's Wonder Book: An Unknown Alcott Juvenile, 1974; Behind a Mask: The Unknown Thrillers of Louisa May Alcott, 1975. Address: 40 E 88th St New York City NY 10028

STERN, MARIE LOUISE, lawyer; b. Saarbrucken, Germany, Aug. 27, 1911; ed. Saarbrucken Coll., U. Geneva (Switzerland); LL.B., N.Y.U., 1951. Admitted to N.Y. bar, 1952, U.S. Supreme Ct. bar, 1960; with firm Netter, Lewy, Dowd, Fox, Ness & Stream, N.Y.C. Mem. Fed., N.Y. bar assns., Assn. Bar City N.Y., Internat. Fedn. Women Lawyers, Internat. Assn. for Protection of Indsl. Property. Office: 660 Madison Av New York City NY 10021

STERN, MIRIAM ROSE, exec.; b. Jersey City, Mar. 29, 1912; d. Isador V. and Anne (Van Doren) Stern; grad. high sch. Road mgr. Sammy Kaye Orch., 1941-47; exec. dir. Am. Guild Authors and Composers, N.Y.C., 1947-69; cons. James Van Heusen; officer Van Heusen Music Corp., 1969—; pres. Miriam Rose Stern Agy., Inc., 1970—. Home and office: 301 E 69th St New York City NY 10021

STERN, MRS. MORDECAI, religious orgn. exec.; b. Union City, N.J., Nov. 28, 1909; d. Barnet Isaac and Bessie (Rogosin) Gordon; grad. Hebrew Tchrs. Sem., 1928; postgrad. Bklyn. Coll., 1952; m. Mordecai A. Stern, Feb. 7, 1928 (dec. Dec. 1963); children—Ariel, Pnina (Mrs. Henry Grinberg). Exec. v.p., exec. dir. women's br. Union Orthodox Jewish Congregations Am., nat. pres., 1954-56, chmn. editorial and edn. com., 1964-74; founder L.I. region Mizrachi Women Am.; pres. women's div. Rabbinical Council Am. Home: 210 E 15th St New York City NY 10003 Office: 84 Fifth Av New York City NY 10011

STERN, SANDRA SILVERSTONE (MRS. ROBERT LOWELL STERN), television actress; b. London, Eng.; d. Arthur Joseph and Pearl (Finkelstein) Silverstone; A.B., Vassar Coll., 1955; m. Robert Lowell Stern, June 19, 1955; children—Antony Ian, Michael Keith, Wendy Joy, Peter Jonathan, Valery Jennifer. Summer stock actress, Ogunquit, Me., 1954; apprentice actress, 1955-56; writer, performer childrens tv program Jr. Clubhouse, Sta. CHCT-TV, Calgary, Alta., Can., 1957-59, Romper Room hostess, 1959-60, writer, producer, performer Teddy Bear Quiz and 12 and Under, 1960-61; writer, producer childrens tv program TV Partytime, CFCN-TV, Calgary, 1962-65, writer, producer, hostess Rocket IV Club, 1965-67; pres. R.L. Stern Mgmt. Co. Ltd., Calgary, 1967—. Childrens theatre chmn. Jr. League Calgary, 1970—. Mem. Nat. Council Jewish Women. Home: 15 Eagle Ridge Pl Calgary AB Canada

STERNBERG, HARRIET ELAINE, social worker; b. Greensboro Bend, Vt.; d. Celon Charles and Isabel (Silver) Sternberg; B.A., U. Mass., 1948; M.A., Clark U., 1953; M.S.W., U. Conn., 1961. Tchr. Orange (Mass.) High Sch., 1948-49, Arms Acad., Shelburne Falls, Mass., 1949-52, Exeter Acad. (N.H.), 1953-54, Greeley (Colo.) High Sch., 1954-55; social worker Foxboro State Hosp. (Mass.), 1955-58, Children's Services Conn., Torrington, 1958-59, Windsor County Mental Health Services, Springfield, Vt., 1961-67, Psychiat. Outpatient Clinic, Waterbury, Conn., 1967-68, Franklin County Mental Health Center, Greenfield, Mass., 1968—; pvt. practice as social worker, Greenfield, 1969-71; co-dir. Learning Center, 1972—. Sec. Project Help, Springfield, Vt., 1966-67; mem. Naugatuck Valley Mental Health Council on Alcoholism, Waterbury, Conn., 1968. Mem. Nat. Assn. Social Workers, Soc. Advancement Behavior Therapy, Council Social Agys. (bd. mem. Springfield 1965-67), Phi Kappa Phi. Club: Senior Citizens (bd. mem. 1965-67) (Springfield). Home: 28 James St Greenfield MA 01301

STERNBERG, STELLA (MRS. EDWARD SCHEER), lawyer; b. N.Y.C.; d. Adolph and Bertha (Holdner) Sternberg; student Hunter Coll.; LL.B., St. Johns U.; m. Edward Scheer, Aug. 20, 1940. Admitted to N.Y. State bar, since practiced in N.Y.C.; tax commr. City N.Y.; hearing officer Parking Violations Bur., N.Y.C., 1972—; arbitrator Small Claims Ct., N.Y.C., 1962—. Chmn. parks and recreation com. Community Planning Bd. 7, N.Y.C.; chmn. lawyers div. Fedn. Jewish Philanthropies, also bd. dirs. Bronx-Riverdale women's div.; chmn. lawyers div. United Jewish Appeal. Del. Constl. Conv., Albany, N.Y., 1967. Mem. Bronx Women's (past pres.), Bronx County (dir.) bar assns. Home: 222 Bedford Park Blvd Bronx NY 10458 Office: 500 Fifth Av New York City NY 10036

STERNE, HEDDA, artist; b. Bucharest, Rumania; d. Simon and Eugenia (Wexler) Lindenberg; studied art Paris, Bucharest, Vienna; m. Saul Steinberg, 1944. Came to U.S., 1941, naturalized, 1944. One-man shows: Wakefield Gallery, N.Y., 1943, Betty Parsons Gallery, 1947, 48, 50, 53, 54, 57, 58, 61, 63, 66, 68, 70, Galleria dell'Obelisco, Rome, 1953, 61, Museo de Arts, Sao Paulo, Brazil, 1953, Vassar Coll., 1956, Arts Club Chgo., 1955, Saidenberg Gallery, 1956, Rizzoli Gallery, 1968, others; represented in collections Met. Mus., Whitney Mus., Mus. Modern Art. Met. Mus. (all N.Y.C.), Chgo. Art Inst., Carnegie Inst., Pitts., Va. Mus. Richmond, U. Ill., Urbana, Rockefeller Inst., Detroit Inst. Art, Pa. Acad., Toledo Mus. Art, others; travelling show Mus. Modern Art, 50 years Am. Art; numerous group shows include: Molton Gallery, London, 1962, N.Y. Art Found., Rome, 1959, 61, Roswell (N.M.) Mus., 1963. Venice Biennale, 1956, Mexico City Biennial, 1960, Cin. Art Mus., 1964, Colorado Springs Art Center, 1964, Flint Inst., 1966, 68. Tchr. Art history Carbondale (Ill.) Coll., 1964. Recipient 2d prize, Art Inst. Chgo. Ann., 1957; 1st prize Art Inst. Newport Ann., 1967; Fulbright fellow, Venice, 1963. Mem. Am. Acad. Arts and Letters. Office: 24 W 57th St New York City NY 10019*

STERNER, WANDA ELAINE BEGLEY, educator; b. Boswell, Pa., Aug. 20, 1927; d. Robert C., Jr. and Verda (Yoder) Begley; student Juniata Coll., 1944-46; B.S., Whittier Coll., 1957, M.S., 1959;

postgrad. U. So. Cal., 1961, N.M. Highlands U., 1964, U. Cal. at Los Angeles, 1964; m. Karl H. Sterner, June 1, 1947 (dec.); children—Gretchen, Wanda. Instr. sci. Robertsdale (Pa.) Jr. High Sch., 1946-47; instr. Whittier (Cal.) Coll., 1956-60, 67-68; co-author script, presented TV program on SCOPE on KABC on Cerritos Cosmetology Chemistry Course, 1965; instr. chemistry Cerritos Coll., Norwalk, Cal., 1959-66, 67—, head chemistry dept., 1962-63, 65-66, cons. phys. scis., math., engring. div., 1967; pres. ProgramMedia Assos., Inc. Instructional systems analyst instructional materials div. Litton Industries, Anaheim, Cal., 1965-66; cons. Intron Assos., Downey, Cal., 1967—; instr. gen. chemistry Rio Hondo Jr. Coll., Whittier, 1967; lectr. chemistry Cal. State Coll., Los Angeles, 1967; tchr. hard core unemployed for Gen. Edn. Devel. exam. Central City Occupational Center, Los Angeles City Schs.; instr. U. Cal. Los Angeles Edn. Extension, Self-Instrn. and Vocational Edn. Corr. sec. Norwalk Coordinating Council, 1967-68. Mem. Cal. Assn. Chemistry Tchrs. (chmn. So. sect. 1968-69, state sec. 1967-71, dir. 1970-73), Am. Chem. Soc. (councilor 1973—, sec. So. Cal. sect. 1971-73), Cal. Tchrs. Assn., A.A.A.S., N.E.A., Metrication Forum Assn. Ednl. Communications and Tech., Cerritos Coll. Faculty Assn. (past pres.), Juniata Coll. Alumni Assn. (past sec. Cal. br.), League Women Voters (bd. dirs. Downey). Author: Science in Cosmetology, 1964; Newton's Laws of Motion, 1966; Chemical Bonding and Structure, 1966; Solid and Liquid States of Matter, 1966; Basics of Chromatography, 1966; Laboratory Procedures of Chromatography, 1966; Matter and Energy, 1966; Chemical Kinetics, 1966, Basic Atmospheric Circulation, 1966; Chemical Equilibrium pH Calculation. Home: 15612 Claretta Av Norwalk CA 90650 Office: 11110 Alondra Blvd Norwalk CA 90650

STERRETT, AUTUMN TYNDALL (MRS. EDWARD BLACKMAN STERRETT), club woman, civic worker; b. Union City, Pa., Oct. 28, 1904; d. Leighton E. and Maude (Rice) Tyndall; diploma Pa. State Tchrs. Coll., 1921; postgrad. Pa. State U., summer 1925, U. Pitts. 1926-27; m. Edward Blackman Sterrett, Aug. 18, 1928; 1 dau., Susan. Tchr. pub. schs., Lawrence Park, Erie, Pa., 1922-28; pub. welfare supr. Erie, 1930-34. Pres., Lake View Camp Bd., 1954-57, Peoria (Ill.) Council Sch. Clubs, 1957-58, Greater Peoria Area Council Ch. Women, 1959-61, U. Ill. Mothers Assn., 1959-61; v.p. Carver Center Bd., 1958-59; v.p. Peoria Area Council Chs., 1964-66, Peoria chpt. Am. Cancer Soc., 1963-64 (sec. 1965-66); Ill. rep. UNICEF, 1963-67; mem. com. to select outstanding Bradley U. alumni, 1965-67; parish visitor First Federated Ch., Peoria, 1970—, dir. parish activities, 1970-72. Leader, Republican Workshops, Peoria. Exec. bd. dirs. Florence Crittenton Home, 1968—. Mem. P.E.O. (officer 1969-72). Presbyn. (deaconess, Sunday Sch. supt. 1950-61). Home: 304 Mooseheart Rd North Aurora IL 60542

STERRETT, FRANCES SUSAN KRAUSS (MRS. ANTHONY H. STERRETT), educator; b. Vienna, Austria; d. Edmund and Klara (Handl) Krauss; came to U.S., 1939, naturalized, 1945; Matura, Realgymnasium, Austria, 1933; Ph.D., U. Vienna, 1938; m. Anthony H. Sterrett, May 27, 1939; children—Jane E., Elizabeth A. Research chemist Laboratoire du Dr. Grimberg, Paris, France, 1938-39, Columbia U. Med. Center, N.Y.C., 1939-40, Van Amerigen & Haebler Inc., Elizabeth, N.J., 1940-41, Woburn Degreasing Co., Harrison, 1943, Fritzsche Bros. Inc., N.Y.C., 1943-49; mem. faculty Hofstra U., Hempstead, N.Y., 1953—, asso. prof. chemistry dept., 1968-73, prof., 1973—, chmn. Senate faculty com., 1967-71, Mem. premed. adv. com., 1966—. Lectr. biochemistry NSF Inst. for High Sch. Tchrs., 1965, 66, 67. Mem. Garden City (N.Y.) Adv. Com. on Edn., 1965-68; mem. adv. com. Garden City Pub. Sch. Adult Edn., 1968-69. Fellow Am. Inst. Chemists; mem. Am. Chem. Soc. (mem. div. chem. edn. curriculum com. 1969), N.Y. Acad. Sci., A.A.A.S., Sigma Kappa Alpha (pres. 1973-74), Alpha Epsilon Delta. Author: (with others) A Laboratory Investigation of Concepts in Chemistry, 1968, Chemical Quantitative Analysis, 1972. Contbr. chpt. to book, articles for profl. jours. Home: 64 Hathaway Dr Garden City NY 11530 Office: Chemistry Dept Hofstra U 1000 Fulton Av Hempstead NY 11550

STEVENS, ANITA (MRS. JOHN S. HARPER), psychiatrist; b. Germany; came to U.S. 1938, naturalized, 1942; d. Martin and Rosa Stevens; M.D., U. Bonn, 1937; m. John Sanford Harper, June 12, 1971. Intern Bonn U. Hosp., 1937; resident Bellevue Psychiat. Hosp., N.Y.C., 1955-58; pvt. practice medicine specializing in psychiatry; attending psychiatrist Gracie Sq. Hosp., N.Y.C.; cons. psychiatrist Med. Arts Center Hosp., N.Y.C.; dir. psychiatry Nat. Soc. Prevention Juvenile Delinquency; spl. cons. N.Y. Joint Legislative Com. Mental Retardation; vis. prof. psychiatry U. Guadalajara, Mexico. Adv. bd. Adams Sch. for children with learning disabilities; mem. Narcotics Guidance Council of Putnam Valley. Recipient William Randolph Hearst Found. award, 1965. Fellow Am. Soc. Adolescent Psychiatry, Am. Soc. Psychoanalytic Physicians, Academy of Psychoanalysis; mem. Am. Psychiatric Assn., Pan Am. Med. Assn. (past pres. sect. psychiatry), Am. Med. Womens Assn., Assn. Advancement Psychoanalysis, N.Y. Soc. Clin. Psychiatry, Am. Group Psychotherapy Assn., Eastern Group Psychotherapy Soc., Gerontol. Soc., Alumna Bellevue Psychiat. Hosp. N.Y.C.; hon. mem. Quito (Ecuador) Psychiat. Soc., Guayquil (Ecuador) Psychiat. Assn., Argentine Soc. Psychiatry and Psychology in Infants and Adolescents. Author: I Hate My Parents!; Your Mind Can Cure. Editor: Adolescent Psychiatry of the Jour. Neuropsychiatry, Jour. Argentine Soc. Psychiatry and Psychology in Infants and Adolescents. Address: 60 Sutton Pl S New York City NY 10022

STEVENS, BARBARA JOAN, educator; b. Providence, Apr. 4, 1946; d. John Mitchell and Lillian (Birzell) Stevens; B.A., Wellesley Coll., 1968; Ph.D. in Econs., Mass. Inst. Tech., 1973. Fellow Joint Center for Urban Studies, Mass. Inst. Tech.-Harvard, Cambridge, 1971-72; quantitative analyst N.Y.C. Environmental Protection Adminstrn. Agy., 1970; asst. prof. bus. econs. Columbia Grad. Sch. Bus., 1972—. Cons. N.J. Housing Finance Agy., 1970-72; instr. Mass. Inst. Tech., 1970-71, Bernard Baruch Coll., 1970. NSF fellow, 1968-70. Mem. Am. Econ. Assn., Phi Beta Kappa. Home: 560 Riverside Dr New York City NY 10027

STEVENS, CALLIE LENTZ, educator; b. Bon Air Mountain, Tenn., Nov. 4, 1926; d. Dave Henry and Nellie (Johnson) Lentz; B.S., A. and I. U., Nashville, 1947; M.A., Northwestern U., 1951; postgrad. N.Y. U., summer, 1959, U. Tenn., 1964-66; m. George Allen Stevens, Aug. 20, 1953 (div. May 1971). Tchr., Lewis Bus. Coll., Detroit, summer 1947; Tchr. high schs., Festus, Mo., 1947-49, St. Joseph, Mo., 1949-50, St. Louis, 1950-51, Memphis, 1954-60; asso. prof. bus. edn. A. and I. State U., 1951-54; prin. Melrose Elementary Sch., Memphis, 1960-62, Florida Elementary Sch., Memphis, 1962-70; area dir. Memphis City Schs., 1970-71, asst. supt., 1971—; counselor Booker T. Washington High Sch., 1958-60; Head Start personnel interviewer Memphis City Schs., summers 1965-66; dir. social services Head Start Program, Memphis, 1967. Pres. 14th Ward Civic Club, 1959-61; mem. Tenn. Tax Modernization and Reform Commn., 1973-74; sec. com. adminstrn. Sarah Brown br. YWCA, 1963-66; mem. Memphis City Sidewalk Bd., 1965-68; mem. Tenn. Bd. Edn., 1971—; mem. Memphis Bicentennial Celebration Com., 1974—. Mem. adv. com. Nat. Elementary Prin. Mag. Recipient Achievement award Omega Psi Phi, 1961; Outstanding Community Service award Second Congl. Ch. Mens Fellowship, 1965. Mem. N.E.A., Tenn., Memphis edn. assns., Am. Assn. Sch. Adminstrs., Assn. for Supervision and Curriculum Devel., Assn. for Childhood Edn., Internat. Reading Assn., Dept. Elementary Sch. Prins. N.E.A., Nat. Council Negro Women, Alpha Kappa Alpha (Good Citizenship award 1962), Delta Pi Epsilon. Home: 800 E McLemore Av Memphis TN 38106

STEVENS, CARLA MCBRIDE (MRS. LEONARD A. STEVENS), pub. co. editor; b. N.Y.C., Mar. 26, 1928; d. Charles James and Marie (Minon) McBride; B.S., N.Y. U., 1949, M.A., 1952; m. Leonard A. Stevens, Dec. 18, 1954; children—Timothy, Brooke, Sara, April. Chmn. primary sch. Daltes Sch., N.Y.C., 1948-54; editor Young Scott Books div. Addison Wesley, N.Y.C., 1954-73. Instr., The New Sch.; cons. Parsons Inst. Bd. dirs. Regional Ednl. Services Center, Conn., 1967-70; trustee Pratt Edn. Center, New Milford, Conn. Author: Rabbit and Skunk, 1962; Scary Rock, 1962; Catch A Cricket, 1964; Rabbit and Skunk and The Big Fight, 1966; Spooks, 1968; Birth of Sunset's Kittens, 1969; Hooray for Pig, 1974; Pets for City Children, 1974; Your First Pet, 1974. Home: Christian St Bridgewater CT 06752

STEVENS, CAROL (MRS. ANDREW PETER KNER), writer, art dir.; b. N.Y.C., Aug. 18, 1937; d. George and Laura (Brandt) Stevens; student Universita degli Studi, Florence, Italy, 1956-57; B.A., Smith Coll., 1958; m. Andrew Peter Kner, Sept. 16, 1961; children—Anne Elizabeth, Peter Alexander. Asst. art dir. Doubleday & Co., Inc., N.Y.C., 1959-63; asso. art dir. Print Mag., 1963—; free lance writing on art topics, 1963—. Mem. Smith Coll. Alumnae Assn. Contbr. articles in field to profl. jours. Office: 19 W 44th St New York City NY 10036

STEVENS, CONNIE (CONCERTA ANN INGOLIE), singer, actress; b. Bklyn., Aug. 8, 1933; ed. Sacred Heart Acad., Hollywood Profl. Sch. Debut in Finaian's Rainbow, Hollywood Repertory Theatre; films include: Eighteen and Anxious, Young and Dangerous, Drag Strip Riot, Rock-a-Bye Baby, Parish, Susan Slade, Palm Springs, Weekend, Never Too Late, The Grissom Gang, Two on a Guillotine; TV work includes Hawaiian Eye, Wendy and Me; appeared on Broadway in Star Spangled Girl; rec. artist Kookie, Kookie, Lend Me Your Comb, 16 Reasons, What Did You Make Me Cry For, From Me to You, They're Jealouse of Me, A Girl Never Knows. Address: care Shane Prodns 148 S Beverly Dr Beverly Hills CA 94712

STEVENS, ELISABETH GOSS (MRS. ROBERT SCHLEUSSNER, JR.), journalist; b. Rome, N.Y., Aug. 11, 1929; d. George May and Elisabeth (Stryker) Stevens; B.A., Wellesley Coll., 1951; M.A. with high honors, Columbia, 1956; m. Robert Schleussner, Jr., Mar. 12, 1966; 1 dau., Laura Stevens. Editorial asso. Art News Mag., 1964-65; art critic and reporter Washington Post, Washington, 1965-66; freelance art critic and reporter, 1966—; contbr. art critic The Wall Street Jour., N.Y.C., 1969-72; art critic Trenton (N.J.) Times, 1974—. Recipient art critics' fellowship, Nat. Endowment for the Arts, 1973-74. Mem. Coll. Art Assn. Am., Soc. Mag. Writers, Authors Guild, Sigma Delta Chi. Contbr. articles to national newspapers and popular mags. Home: 289 Carter Rd Route 2 Princeton NJ 08540

STEVENS, HOLLY, mag. exec.; b. Hartford, Conn., Aug. 10, 1924; d. Wallace and Elsie Viola (Kachel) Stevens; student Vassar Coll., U. Conn.; m. John Martin Hanchak (div.); 1 son, Peter Reed; m. 2d, Duncan Stephenson (div.). Fire underwriter Aetna Life Affiliated Cos., Hartford, 1942-46; purchasing asst. Trinity Coll., Hartford, 1955-64; sec. Yale, 1966-68, advt. mgr. Yale Rev., 1968-69, bus. mgr., 1969—; fellow Timothy Dwight Coll. Founder, dir. New Eng. Poetry Circuit, 1963-68; founder, dir. Conn. Poetry Circuit, 1968-72, mem. selection com., 1972—; founding mem. Poetry Center Trinity Coll., Hartford. Ingram Merrill Found. grantee, 1964, supplemental award, 1965. Nat. Endowment for Humanities sr. fellow, 1972-73. Mem. English Inst. Club: Elizabethan (Yale). Editor: Letters of Wallace Stevens, 1966, 67; The Palm At The End Of The Mind: Selected Poems And A Play By Wallace Stevens, 1971. Home: 60 Ardmore St Hamden CT 06517 Office: Yale Rev New Haven CT 06520

STEVENS, ICLE JEAN, librarian; b. Lincoln, Neb., Aug. 21, 1925; d. Harry Evert and Gladys May (Scharton) Selders; B.A., U. Neb., 1947; M.A., U. Denver, 1948; m. Jackson W. Stevens, June 13, 1948; children—James Evert, Jeffrey Scott, Jay Thomas. Librarian, Denver Pub. Library, 1948-51, Pueblo (Colo.) Pub. Library, 1952; sch. librarian El Paso (Tex.) Ind. Sch. Dist., 1958-67; asst. prof. library sci. U. Tex., El Paso, 1967—. Mem. Am., Tex., Border Regional (2d v.p. 1966, sec. 1971, mem. bd. 1967-69) library assns., N.E.A., Tex. Tchrs. Assn. Mem. Christian Ch. Democrat. Mem. Order Eastern Star. Home: 312 Encino Dr El Paso TX 79905 Office: Edn Bldg 809 Univ Tex El Paso TX 79968

STEVENS, JOCELYN EDWYNA, librarian; b. Waco, Tex., Sept. 5, 1919; d. William Milton and Anita (Weston) Cain; B.S. in Edn., Northwestern U., 1941; M.S. in Library Sci., N.C. Central U., 1959; summer student library sci. U. Mich., 1963, Tex. Woman's U., 1972; m. James A. Stevens, Sept. 25, 1941; children—James, Robert, Edwin (dec.). Circulation librarian N.C. Central U., Durham, 1960-64, reference librarian, 1964—. Bd. dirs. Durham County Tb Assn., 1967-70. Mem. Am., Southeastern, Tex., N.C., Durham County (v.p.) library assns., Alpha Kappa Alpha. Democrat. Roman Catholic. Home: 623 Dupree St Durham NC 27701

STEVENS, MURIEL PORT (MRS. STANFORD S. STEVENS), orch. exec.; b. Providence, Dec. 26, 1919; d. Eli and Anna (Silverstein) Port; B.A., Pembroke Coll., 1940; Mus.B., Yale, 1945; m. Stanford S. Stevens, Feb. 22, 1942; children—Peter Jay, Ruth Faith. Exec. sec. children's concerts and ednl. programs R.I. Philharmonic Orch., Providence, 1964-65, acting mgr. orch., 1965-66, gen. mgr., 1966—. Mem. exec. com. Friends of Boston Symphony, 1955-60, Community Concerts Assn., 1953-60; v.p. Schubert Club, Providence, 1957-59. Bd. dirs. R.I. Philharmonic, 1951-65, mem. founding com., 1952, chmn. children's concerts, 1960-61, v.p. bd. dirs. 1960-62, pres. bd., 1962-64. Home: 42 Scott St Pawtucket RI 02860 Office: 39 The Arcade Providence RI 02903

STEVENS, NANCY DUNCAN, educator; b. Passaic, N.J.; d. Herbert Chester and Anna (Dunn) Stevens; A.B., Barnard Coll., 1947; M.A., N.Y.U., 1950, Ph.D., 1960. Asst. vocational bur. Vassar Coll., 1947-48; sec., asst. placement office Coll. City N.Y., 1949-50; asst. registrar N.J. State Tchrs. Coll., Newark, 1950-53; research asso. div. advanced studies N.Y. U., 1953-54, asst. dir. placement services, 1954-60; asso. dir. career counseling placement Hunter Coll., N.Y.C., 1960-68, 70—, asst. prof. counseling and student devel., 1968-70, asso. prof. counseling and student devel., 1971—, coordinator acad. counseling and advisement, 1968-70, dir. H.E.O. project for educationally disadvantaged students, 1969-70; vis. asst. prof. dept. guidance and student personnel N.Y.U., summers 1957-68, adj. asso. prof. dept. counselor edn., 1972-73. Recipient Gordon A. Hardwick award Middle Atlantic Placement Assn., 1968. Mem. Am. Coll. Personnel Assn. (chmn. placement commn. 1973—, mem. career counseling and placement com. 1971-74), Nat. Vocational Guidance Assn. (mem. editorial bd. quar. 1972—), Am. Personnel and Guidance Assn., Eastern Coll. Personnel Officers, Met. N.Y. Assn. Applied Psychology, N.Y. State (mem. exec. council 1967-68), N.Y. (pres. 1967-68) personnel and guidance assns., N.Y. U. Edn. Alumni Assn. (v.p. 1964-67), Met. N.Y. Coll. Placement Officers Assn. (chmn. profl. standards com. 1962-66, historian 1971-73), Personnel Assn. of N.Y. (2d v.p. 1966-67). Author articles in field. Home: 14 Albion St Passaic NJ 07055 Office: 695 Park Av New York City NY 10021

STEVENS, RISE, mezzo-soprano; b. N.Y.C.; d. Christian Steenberg; student Juilliard Sch. Music, N.Y.C., Mozarteum, Salzburg, Austria; studied singing with Mme. Anna Schoen Rene and Mme. Vera Schwartz; H.H.D. (hon.), Russell Sage Coll.; Mus.D., Hobart Coll., Smith Coll.; m. Walter G. Surovy, Jan. 6, 1939; 1 son, Nicolas Vincent. Made debut as Mignon, Prague, Czechoslovakia, 1938; 1st appearance with Met. Opera Co. in Mignon, 1938; has sung at Prague Opera, Vienna State Opera, Teatro Colon, Buenos Aires, Cairo, Egypt, Glynbourne Mozart Festivals, England, San Francisco Opera Co., Athens, Greece, Paris Grand Opera; created title-role in world-premiere of Virgilio Mortari's opera La Figlia del Diavolo at LaScala, Milan, 1954; prin. roles of Mignon, Der Rosenkavalier, Carmen, Samson et Delilah, La. Gioconda, Hansel and Gretel, Le Nozze di Figaro, Die Walkure, Cosi Fan Tutte, Orfeo ed Euridice, Khovanchina (Met. opera premiere), Tales of Hoffman, in Die Federmaus; created Carmen in new Met. Opera prodn.; in motion pictures The Chocolate Soldier, Going My Way, Carnegie Hall; co-gen. mgr. Met. Opera Nat. Co., 1964—. Traveled extensively with Hollywood Victory Caravan during World War II. Headed own radio programs; stars regularly on TV programs. Concertizes yearly throughout U.S. and Can. Recs. for Columbia Records and RCA Victor. Honors and awards: Citation for U.S. Treasury Dept.; Certificate of Honor from A.R.C.; Citation from Greater N.Y. Fund; Distinguished Service award N.Y. Cancer Com.; Box Office Blue Ribbon Award for picture, Going My Way; voted best female vocalist in radio by Motion Picture Daily and Musical America, 1947 and 1948; Spirit of Achievement award Albert Einstein Coll. of Medicine, 1965; Woman of Year, Cal., 1965. Established Rise Stevens Scholarship, Adelphi Coll., 1947. Hon. mem. Wagnerian Soc. (Buenos Aires), Sigma Alpha Iota. Address: Woodrow Wilson Dr Hollywood CA 90046 also Metropolitan Opera Assn New York City NY 10020*

STEVENS, SUE CASSELL, chemist; b. Roanoke, Va.; d. Edward B. and Dora (Fox) Stevens; A.B., Goucher Coll., 1930; M.A., Columbia, 1931, Ph.D., 1940. Research biochemist N.Y. Skin and Cancer Hosp., N.Y.C., 1932-35; biochemist Fifth Av. Hosp., N.Y.C., 1935; research chemist Coll. Phys. and Sugr., Columbia, 1935-39; research chemist N.Y. Orthopaedic Hosp., N.Y.C., 1940-41, Cal. Milk Products Co., Gustine, 1941-43; research dairy chemist Golden State Co. Ltd., San Francisco, 1943-46, Swift & Co., Chgo., 1946-47; dir. research and quality control Steven Candy Kitchens, Chgo., 1947-48; asso. prof. chemistry, biology MacMurray Coll., 1948-49; chief biochemist VA Center, Dayton, O., 1949-52, research biochemist, 1952-56; supr. research lab. VA Hosp., Lincoln, Neb., 1956-65; dir. div. endocrine chemistry Jewish Hosp. of St. Louis, 1965—; asst. prof. pathology Washington U. Sch. Medicine, 1967—. Fellow Am. Inst. Chemists, A.A.A.S.; mem. Am. Chem. Soc., Am. Assn. Clin. Chemists (chmn. Midwest sect. 1965), Am. Soc. Quality Control (treas. St. Louis sect. 1973-74, sec. 1974—), N.Y. Acad. Scis., Am. Assn. U. Women, Am. Soc. Clin. Pathologists, Sigma Xi, Sigma Delta Epsilon (nat. pres. 1964). Home: PO Box 4854 Field Sta St Louis MO 63108 Office: Jewish Hosp of St Louis 216 S Kingshighway St Louis MO 63110

STEVENS, SUSAN GREGG (MRS. DAVID BRANT STEVENS), journalist; b. Dayton, O., July 7, 1945; d. Robert Quinley and Wilma Louise (McCollum) Gregg; B.A., Tex. Christian U., 1967; m. David Brant Stevens, Apr. 29, 1967; 1 son, David Randolph. Journalism intern Beeville (Tex.) Bee Picayune, summer, 1965; family, foods, amusements editor The Herald Banner, Greenville, 1968—. Recipient 2 1st place awards Tex. Press Women's, 1969, 1 2d place award, 1970. Mem. City Fedn. Women's Clubs, Theta Sigma Phi, Phi Alpha Theta. Clubs: Altrusa of Greenville (rec. sec.); Jr. Federated Women's. Home: 1105 Commerce Dr Greenville TX 75401 Office: PO Box 1047 King St Greenville TX 75401

STEVENS, SYBIL, personnel adminstr.; b. Chgo., Nov. 29; d. Ithiel Silsby and Edith H. (Martin) Stevens; B.S., Bradley U., 1953; postgrad. U. Chgo., 1953-55. Personnel relations asst. Union Tank Car Co., Chgo., 1953-62; asst. personnel mgr. Reuben H. Donnelley Corp., Chgo., 1962-68, personnel mgr., 1968-71, regional personnel mgr., 1971-74, regional mgr. personnel devel., 1974—. Mem. personnel com. Girl Scouts Chgo., 1966-70, bd. dirs., 1970-73, asst. treas., 1971-73; corr. sec. Alliance Bus. & Profl. Women Chgo., 1968-69, 2d. v.p., 1969-70, 1st v.p. 1970-71. Mem. Women In Personnel (corr. sec. 1964, 1st v.p. 1971-72, pres. 1972-73), Indsl. Relations Assn. Chgo., Employers' Assn. Chgo. (mem. communications com. 1969-70), Am. Soc. Personnel Adminstrs., Internat. Assn. Personnel Women, Soc. Personnel Adminstrs. Chgo., Chgo. Assn. Commerce and Industry, Pi Beta Phi. Republican. Presbyn. Home: 9550 S Hamilton Av Chicago IL 60643 Office: 33 E Congress Pkwy Chicago IL 60605

STEVENSON, ALMIRA ABBOT (MRS. H. E. STEVENSON), adminstrv. law judge; b. Fayetteville, W.Va., July 8, 1916; d. Alois Bahlmann and Nona (Reynolds) Abbot; B.A., Randolph-Macon Women's Coll., 1937; student Student's Internat. Union, Geneva, Switzerland, 1937; J.D., U. Chgo., 1948; m. Henry Edwin Stevenson, Oct. 15, 1949; children—Henry Edminster, Abbot. Admitted to W.Va., D.C. bars, 1948; research analyst Office Def. Transp., Washington, 1942, Office Civilian Def., Washington, 1941; atty. office solicitor U.S. Dept. Labor, Washington, 1949-50; atty. adviser to NLRB, Washington, 1951-72, trial Examiner, 1972, adminstrv. law judge; 1972—; equal employment opportunity appeals examiner Civil Service Commn., 1970-72. Served from 2d lt. to maj. USMC Res., 1943-54. Mem. Federally Employed Women, Nat. Orgn. Women, Women Marines Assn. Home: 5512 30th St NW Washington DC 20015

STEVENSON, BARBARA LOU, editor; b. Oakland, Cal., Feb. 9, 1925; d. Austin K. and Florence (Frey) Stevenson; B.A., U. Cal., Berkeley, 1946. Soc. editor Lodi (Cal.) News-Sentinel, 1946; asst. soc. editor Oakland Post-Enquirer, 1946-50; womens editor Alameda (Cal.) Times-Star, 1951—. Mem. publicity com. Alameda County Health and Tb. Assn., 1950-58. Mem. adv. bd. Alameda Girls Club, Alameda chpt. Am. Field Service, Alameda chpt. A.R.C. Recipient 1st awards for womens pages in daily papers Cal. Newspaper Pubs. Assn., 1962, 63, 65, 66, 67, 69. Mem. East Bay Womens Press Club, Theta Sigma Phi. Club: Soroptimist (past pres., state chmn. pub. relations 1968-72, State Chmn. youth citizenship) (Alameda). Home: 3118 El Paseo Alameda CA 94501 Office: Alameda Times-Star Alameda CA 94501

STEVENSON, CLARA LEIS, educator; b. Houston, Dec. 5, 1929; d. Timothy and Eunice Minnette (Emanuel) Gibson; B.S., Howard U., 1951, M.S., 1958; Ph.D., U. Md., 1974; children—Karen L., Keely E. Instr. psychology So. U., Baton Rouge, 1958-62, Howard U., 1963-65; sch. psychologist, then clin. psychologist D.C. pub. schs., 1965-72, supervisory dir. placement-tuition office, 1972—. Co-founder Concerned Citizens for Exceptional Children, 1968. Bd. dirs. Iona Whipper Home. Grad. fellow Howard U., 1957-58; recipient Concerned Citizens award Concerned Citizens for Exceptional Children. Mem. D.C. Assn. Psychologists (founding pres. 1970).

STEVENSON, FLORENCE BYRD, ednl. adminstr.; b. Weldon, N.C., Jan. 1, 1922; d. Daniel Brian and Florence (Cazort) Byrd; B.A., U. Ark., 1943; M.A., Ohio State U., 1963; Ph.D., Mich. State U., 1973; children—Gardner, Brian Byrd. Adminstrv. asst. Women's Residence Halls, Ohio State U., Columbus, 1962-63; dean of women U. Tulsa, 1963-70; cons. for women's studies, U. Cin., 1972-73; coordinator Western Center Endowment for the Humanities, U. Cal. at Los Angeles, 1973—; cons. women's Resource Center, Mich. State U., 1970-72; tchr. women's studies. Chmn. A.R.C. Com. on Service to Mil. Families, Tulsa, 1970. Recipient Vicki award Gamma Epsilon Alpha, 1970. Mem. Nat. Assn. Women Deans, Adminstrs. and Counselors (mem. com. on continuing edn. for women 1970-72), Kappa Kappa Gamma. Home: 11090 Strathmore No 5 Westwood CA 90024 Office: 10995 Le Conte Av Los Angeles CA 90024

STEVENSON, GRACE EMELINE HOPE (MRS. KENNETH CAMPBELL STEVENSON), social worker, writer, artist; b. Bradford, Eng.; d. Archibald Campbell and Mary (Robson) Hope; came to U.S., 1935, naturalized, 1956; B.A., U. B.C., 1927, diploma in Social Work, 1930; postgrad. Columbia, 1936-38; M.S.W., U. Pa., 1964; m. Kenneth Campbell Stevenson, Dec. 21, 1939 (dec. Dec. 1940); 1 son, Kenneth Campbell II. Social case worker, dist. sec. Family Welfare Assn., Montreal, Can., 1930-35; asst. dist. sec. Bklyn. Bur. Charities, 1935-38; case supr. Family Service of Episcopal City Mission Soc., N.Y.C., 1938-40; case cons. Youth Consultation Service of N.J. Diocese, Trenton, 1945-47; supr. adoption placement Children's Home Soc. N.J., Trenton, 1947-58; dir. rehab. services Donnelly Hosp., Trenton, 1959-63; dir. research project St. Peter's Hosp., New Brunswick, 1964-66; mental health cons. Div. Mental Health and Hosps., State of N.J., Trenton, 1966-72. Writer series of radio plays, popular articles; exhibited one-man show water colors Trenton State Coll., 1956, Hun Sch., Princeton, 1958, S.S. Young Am., 1973, also group shows. Del.-at-large Princeton Social Service Council, 1959—. Mem. Acad. Certified Social Workers, Nat. Assn. Social Workers, U. Pa. Alumnae Assn. Home: Box 275 Mechanicsville PA 18934

STEVENSON, GUSSIE LEE, trust adminstr.; b. Tuxedo, Tex., May 9, 1915; d. Fred Marshal and Minnie B. (Coleman) Stevenson; student Tex. Woman's U., 1932-33, Draughon's Bus. Coll., Tex., 1933-34, Am. Inst. Banking, 1946-66, U. Colo., 1965-73; m. Owen Paul Korb, July 9, 1944, (div. Apr. 1955). Sec. to dist. engr., dist. sales mgr. United Gas Pipe Line Co., Wichita Falls, Tex., 1936-39; sec. to div. supt. Tex. Pipe Line Co., Wichita Falls, 1939-40; sec. to pres. First Nat. Bank, Wichita Falls, 1940-44; stenographer Farmers State Bank, Hays, Kan., part-time 1944-45; sec. to v.p., cashier Merc. Nat. Bank, Dallas, 1946-56; staff asst., account counselor Denver U.S. Nat. Bank (name now United Bank of Denver Nat. Assn.), Denver, 1956-65, trust adminstr., 1965—. Treas., hostess com. chmn. Gov.'s Conf. on Air and Water Pollution, 1967-68; rep. Colo. Clean Streams Com., Denver. Bd. dirs. Colo. Partners of Alliance, Denver. Mem. Nat. Secs. Assn., John Robert Powers Sch. Alumnae Assn. (past pres.), Bus. and Profl. Women's Club Denver, Colo. (state pres. 1966-67), Nat. (dir. 1966-67, mem. nat. membership com. 1967-68) fedns. bus. and profl. womans' clubs, Beta Sigma Phi (past pres.), Phi Chi Theta. Mem. Order Eastern Star (Worthy Matron 1970-71). Club: Cameo. Home: 269 Logan St Denver CO 80203 Office: PO Box 5247 Denver CO 80217

STEVENSON, JOAN SUZANNE WELCH, librarian; b. Rochester, N.Y., Oct. 9, 1936; d. Gordon Alman and Ella Phebe (Jewett) Welch; A.B., Syracuse U., 1958; M.A., U. Denver, 1960; m. James W. Stevenson, June 13, 1961. Young adult librarian N.Y. Pub. Library, 1960-62; head readers adv. dept. White Plains (N.Y.) Library, 1962-65; head young adult dept. Yonkers (N.Y.) Pub. Library, 1965-69, adminstr. Coyne Park br., 1969—. Pres. Your Own Floral Printing Co., Inc., Rochester, 1973—. Mem. N.Y. State, Westchester (pres. 1966-67), library assns., Yonkers Pub. Library Staff Assn. (pres. 1970-72, chmn. negotiating com. 1973—), Hist. Soc. Rockland County, Am. Assn. U. Women (chmn. legislature com. 1974-75, chmn. bicentennial com. 1974-75). Reviewer Library Jour., 1966—. Home: 224 Van Wyck Rd Blauvelt NY 10913 Office: 783 McLean Av Yonkers NY 10704

STEVENSON, LOIS WELLMAN HADDOCK (MRS. FREDERICK LEON STEVENSON), journalist; b. Mpls., Jan. 1927; d. Royal Wellman and Jean (Emmerick) Haddock; B.A., U. Cal. at Berkeley, 1949, B.S., 1960; m. Frederick Leon Stevenson, Apr. 8, 1944; 1 dau., Elizabeth Ann. Sec. to mayor and city council City of San Diego, 1952-53; analytical chemist Bendix Aviation Corp., Burbank, 1954-55; math. computer Poroloy Equipment Co., Van Nuys, 1956-57; pet columnist Courier-News, Somerville, N.J., 1968—, Star-Ledger, Newark, 1971—. Tchr. non-fiction writing, adult sch., Watchung, N.J., 1973—; free-lance writer for various mags., newspapers. Mem. Women in Communications, Outdoor Writers Assn. Am., Dog Writers Assn. Am. (awards for best feature articles 1971, 72, 73), Quill and Scroll. Address: 49 Rock Road W Green Brook NJ 08812

STEVENSON, NANCY (MRS. ADLAI E. STEVENSON III), wife of U.S. Senator; grad. Smith Coll., 1955; m. Adlai E. Stevenson III, June 25, 1955; children—Adlai E. IV, Lucy, Katie, Warwick. Wife of U.S. Senator from Ill. Home: 1519 N Dearborn St Chicago IL 60610*

STEVENSON, SALLY ROGERS, ednl. adminstr.; b. Augusta, Me., Oct. 27, 1931; d. Allan Harvard and Edith Valentine (Robinson) Rogers; A.B., Wellesley Coll., 1953; M.A., Boston U., 1957; m. Robert Findlay Stevenson, Mar. 19, 1960. Tchr. social scis. House in the Pines, Norton, Mass., 1953-55, tchr. history, acad. dean, 1958-60; tchr. Beverly (Mass.) High Sch., 1955-57; tchr., adminstrv. asst. Everglades Sch. for Girls, Miami, 1957-58; tchr. adminstrv. asst., MacDuffie Sch., Springfield, Mass., 1960-61; tchr., history, head lower and middle schs., dir. admissions Barnard Sch. for Girls, N.Y.C., 1961—. Research asst. Nat. Inst. Mental Health Research grant, Abidjan, Ivory Coast, 1965-66; mem. planning com. Buck Hill Falls Conf. I, Council for Religion in Ind. Schs., 1968—, chmn., 1972. Home: Box 399 Main St Stony Brook NY 11790 Office: 554 Fort Washington Av New York City NY 10033

STEWART, ALICE CORDELIA EICHHORN (MRS. FRANK STEWART), civic worker; b. Miles City, Mont., July 6, 1913; d. Arthur Campbell and Lucile (Prigg) Eichhorn; student Sullins Coll., 1931-32; B.S., Northwestern U., 1935, M.A., 1936; m. Frank Stewart, June 19, 1941; 1 son, Jerry. Tchr. Thornton Twp. High Sch., Harvey, Ill., 1935-41. Nurses aide A.R.C., 1942-43; organizer, mem. bd. Family Service and Mental Health Center S. Cook County, 1955-67, v.p., 1962-65; mem. Ill. Commn. on Children, 1958—, vice chmn., 1970-74, chmn., 1974—, chmn. com. comprehensive plan for hearing impaired children, 1965-68, chmn. com. location and treatment handicapped children, 1969-71; bd. dirs. Community Chest, Harvey, Ill., 1956-58; bd. dirs. Ill. Com. Child Welfare Legislation, 1958—, pres., 1962-64; del. White House Conf. on Children, 1960; bd. dirs. Child Care Assn. Ill., 1964-71, chmn. adoption sect., 1966-68; mem. pub. welfare div. pub. policy com., Welfare Council Met. Chgo., 1966-68; bd. dirs. Midwest Adoption Facilitating Service, Mpls., 1966-68; mem. adv. com. social service curriculum Thornton Jr. Coll., 1967—; hearing office on standards Ill. Dept. Children and Family Services, 1966; mem. Cook County Pub. Health Council bd., 1960-64; active P.T.A.; del. White House Conf. Children, 1970; mem. Thorton Twp. Youth Com., 1968—; mem. Cook County Adv. Com. Spl. Edn., 1968—; mem. task force on probation Council on Diagnosis and Evaluation Criminal Defendants, 1971—. Mem. Am. Assn. U. Women (pres. 1951-53, state div. legislative chmn. 1955-57, social econ. issues chmn. 1959-61), League Women Voters (chmn. welfare item 1964-66), Pi Lambda Theta, Alpha Omicron Pi. Republican. Presbyn. Address: 900 Sunset Dr Glenwood IL 60425

STEWART, ALICE HAMILTON, physician; b. Frame, W. Va., Mar. 1, 1907; d. Charles Lewis and Virginia Lee (Jackson) Stewart; B.S., W. Va. U., 1929; M.D., U. Chgo., 1933. Intern, Mt. Vernon Hosp., 1933-34, Bellevue Hosp., N.Y.C., 1933-34, L.I. Coll. Hosp., 1934-35; resident obstetrics Women's Hosp., Newark, 1935, Norwegian Hosp., Bklyn., 1935-36; practice medicine specializing in gynecology and obstetrics, N.Y.C., 1935—; clinician social hygiene N.Y.C. Dept. Health, 1936—; mem. staffs N.Y. Infirmary, N.Y.C., Swedish Hosp., Bklyn.; fellow Strang Clinic for Cancer Detection, N.Y.C., 1942-43. Fellow Am. Coll. Obstetrics and Gynecology; mem. A.M.A., N.Y., New York County med. socs., N.Y. Women's Med. Soc., N.Y. League of Girls Clubs, W. Va. Grange and All Stars, North River Power Squadron. Mem. Order Eastern Star. Home: 115 Henry St Brooklyn NY 11201 Office: 58 W 9th St New York City NY 10011

STEWART, ANITA (MRS. ANITA S. BACH), interior designer; b. Chgo., Oct. 25, 1921; d. Winfred Eric and Wilma (Lucas) Stewart; student MacMurray Coll., 1940-42; certificate of engring. drawing and machine design, Ill. Inst. Tech., 1942; certificate Parsons Sch. Design, 1948; m. Alfons Bach, May 23, 1953; children—Alfons S., Alexander S. Chief draftsman Power Plant Engring. Mag., 1942-45; decorator with Frederick P. Victoria, 1949-50, Melanie Kahane, 1950-51; instr. Parsons Sch., 1952-53; pres. Anita Stewart Interiors, Stamford, Conn., 1950—; v.p. Alba Investment & Devel. Corp., Delray. Sec. bd. dirs. YWCA. Mem. Am. Inst. Decorators, Stamford Mus. (sec. of aux.), Flagler Museum. Presbyn. Clubs: Beach (Palm Beach); Palm Trail Yacht; Sailfish of Fla. Home: 201 Sandpiper Dr Palm Beach FL 33480 Office: Palm Trail Plaza Delray Beach FL 33444

STEWART, ANNETTE, lawyer; b. Paris, Tex., Jan. 1, 1928; d. Ray Bryan and Mary Christine (Plumer) Stewart; Asso. B.A., Brownsville Jr. Coll., 1947; B.A., U. Tex. at Austin, 1949, M.Ed., 1952; LL.B. summa cum laude, So. Meth. U., 1966. Tchr. jr. high sch., San Benito Tex., 1949-51, counselor, 1952-53; dep. court reporter U.S. Dist. Ct. for So. Dist. Tex., Corpus Christi, 1955-56; ofcl. court reporter State Dist. Ct., Ellis County, 1956-57, Court Domestic Relations, Dallas, 1957-66, 67—; admitted to Tex. bar, 1966; mem. firm Parnass, McGuire & Handy, Irving, Tex., 1966-67. Mem. State Bar Tex., Am. Bar Assn. (adv. edit. bd., family law newsletter 1973—), Nat. Assn. Women Lawyers, Phi Beta Kappa, Bus. and Profl. Womens Club. Democrat. Presbyn. Home: 1822 Marydale Dr Dallas TX 75208 Office: 428 Dallas County Courthouse Dallas TX 75202

STEWART, BETTY KIRKE, statistician; b. Edgewood, Pa., Feb. 9, 1921; d. Elias Everett and Pamela Y'Morrill (Scott) Stewart; student Bethany (W.Va.) Coll., 1937-39; A.B., U. Pitts., 1955, postgrad., 1959-61; M.S., Ia. State U., 1959. Sec. Bethany Coll., 1939-41, FBI, Pitts., 1941-53; statistician U.S. Steel Research Lab., Monroeville, Pa., 1959—. U. Pitts. Grad. Sch. Pub. Health fellow, 1955-56. Mem. Am. Statis Assn., Am. Soc. Quality Control (chmn. 1969-70). Office: 125 Jamison Lane Monroeville PA 15146

STEWART, BEVERLY JOANNE, librarian; b. Macomb, Ill., June 18, 1924; d. Harold Victor and Gertrude Christina (Black) Johnson; student Western Ill. U., 1942-44; B.S., Bradley U., 1961; M.L.S., U. Ill., 1962; m. Charles Willard Stewart, June 4, 1949 (dec. Sept. 1956); children—William C., Robert G. Librarian, U. Ill. at Urbana, 1962-63; head librarian Parlin Ingersoll Library, Canton, Ill., 1964—. Mem. Am., Ill. library assns., Am. Assn. U. Women. Home: PO Box 135 110 Middle Park Dr Canton IL 61520 Office: 205 W Chestnut St Canton IL 61520

STEWART, CATHERINE HILL (MRS. JOHN ALEXANDER STEWART), newspaper editor; b. Washington, Jan. 22, 1923; d. John Phillip and Suzanne Howell (Carroll) Hill; asso. Washington Sch. for Secs., 1940-41; student U. Pa. extension, 1960-61; m. John Alexander Stewart, Feb. 15, 1943; children—John A., David Eugene. Customer rep. IBM, Washington, 1941-43; reporter Conn. Shore, weekly, Saybrook, 1943-45; reporter Phoenix-Times Pub. Co., Bristol, R.I., 1960-61, dir., 1960-61; editor Barrington (R.I.) Times, 1964—. Tchr. journalism Barrington pub. schs., 1972, 73. Chmn. Aged in Barrington, 1957-61; del. White House Conf. for Aged, 1962-63. Bd. dirs. Edwards Housing for Aged, Providence, 1956-59; bd. dirs., chmn. publicity R.I. Family Service, 1956-61. Recipient awards for excellence in newspapers New Eng. Press Assn., 1968—. Mem. New Eng. Press Assn. (sec.-treas. 1972-73, 2d v.p. 1973-74), Episcopalian (vestryman 1960-63). Editor Episcopal Diocesan Year Book of R.I., 1957-61. Home: 14 Harbour Rd Barrington RI 02806 Office: Box 227 Barrington Times Barrington RI 02806

STEWART, CATHLEEN BRADY, advt. exec.; b. Pitts., Dec. 20, 1946; d. Brady Wilson and Marjorie (Zapp) Stewart; student Muskingum Coll., 1964-65, U. Pitts., 1965-66; grad. Direct Mail Advt. Inst., 1971, N.Y. Advt. Inst., 1969. Advt. mgr. Nat. Union Ins. Co., Pitts., 1965-68; dir. advt. and promotion Am. Internat. Group, ins., N.Y.C., 1968-72; account exec. Della Femina Travisano, advt. agy., N.Y.C., 1972-73, Dusenberry, Ruriani, Kornhauser, N.Y.C., 1973-74; v.p., account supr. Clyne-Dusenberry, N.Y.C., 1974—. Exec. sec. Ins. Advt. Conf., 1967—. Home: 240 E 35th St New York City NY 10016 Office: 245 Park Av New York City NY 10017

STEWART, (CLARA) MAE SATTERFIELD (MRS. EARL STEWART, SR.), educator; b. Worth, W.Va., June 23, 1913; d. Oscar and Ida (Doss) Satterfield; B.S., W.Va. State Coll., 1934; M.A., W.Va. U., 1957; M.A., Marshall U., 1964, postgrad. 1966; m. Earl Stewart, Sr., June 22, 1935; children—Sandra Stewart (Mrs. Henry Carroll, Sr.), Earl. Tchr. biology, physics, chemistry Northfork High Sch., McDowell County Bd. Edn., 1935-40; tchr. sci. math. Northfork Jr. High Sch., 1940-60; counselor Elkhorn High Sch., Powhatan, W.Va., 1960-66, dir. Elkhorn Jr. High Sch., 1966—. Mem. McDowell County Sub-com. Curriculum Council, 1969-70. Troop leader Girl Scouts U.S.A., 1942-55, mem. exec. council McDowell County, 1942-50; supr. Neighborhood Youth Corp., 1968-69; election clk., McDowell County, 1968. Bd. dirs., coach W.Va. Golden Horseshoe Contest, 1973—. Named Tchr. of Month, Elkhorn High Sch., 1960. Mem. N.E.A., Classroom Tchrs. Assn. McDowell County, Am., W.Va. personnel and guidance assns., W.Va. Edn. Assn., Links of So. W.Va. (program chmn. 1950-60), Internat. Platform Assn., Delta Sigma Theta. Club: Les Precieuse (pres. McDowell County 1942). Author: Architectural Design, Family Residence, 1960; Handbook Cumulative Record for Counselors, 1960. Home: Box 3 Northfork WV 24868 Office: Box 207 Powhatan WV 24877

STEWART, CYNTHIA JORDAN (MRS. JAMES E.M. STEWART), horse breeder; b. Altoona, Pa., Jan. 31, 1941; d. Paul J. and Mildred E. (Kyle) Brickley; grad. high sch.; m. James E.M. Stewart, July 11, 1964. Owner, trainer, racer standard bred horses, Churchville, N.Y., 1968—. Owner, Past and Present Antique Shop, Churchville, 1970-72. Address; 1260 Johnson Rd Churchville NY 14428

STEWART, DOROTHY ANNA (MRS. DAVID RONALD STEWART), artist; b. Bklyn.; d. Henry Brewster and Marion Elsie (Green) Shotwell; student Art Student's League N.Y., 1942-43, 64-68, Nat. Acad. Sch. Fine Arts, 1967, 69, N.Y. U. (scholar), 1974; m. David Ronald Stewart, Oct. 20, 1944; children—Robert Ronald, Allan Michael. Exhibited in numerous group shows including Nat. Arts Club, Hudson Valley, N.Y., Parrish Art Mus. Southampton, N.Y., Allied Artists Am., Nat. Acad., Grand Nat. Am. Artists Profl. League, Lever House Gallery, N.Y.C., Am. WaterColor Soc., Washington Sq. Outdoor Art Exhibit, N.Y.C., Gregory Mus., Hicksville, N.Y., others. Mem. staff art dept. Am. Can Co., N.Y.C., 1945-46; instr. painting Malverne (N.Y.) Sr. High Sch., 1965-66, Nassau (N.Y.) Women's Club, 1966-67. Recipient Malvern Artists awards, 1962, 70, 71, 72, Bruce Stevenson Meml. award Washington Sq. Outdoor Art Exhibit, 1973, First prize Art League Nassau County, N.Y., 1971, first prize Gregory Art Mus., 1972, Kent (Conn.) Art Assn. award, 1974, numerous others. Mem. Allied Artists Am. (pub. relations chmn. 1972-74), Art League Nassau County (treas. 1959-61), Am. Artists Profl. League, Nat. Art League, Malverne Artists Assn. (corr. sec. 1966-67), Catharine Lorillard Wolfe Art Club (dir. 1971, v.p. 1971-74). Home: 14 Club Dr Candlewood Trails New Milford CT 06776

STEWART, ELIZABETH BRYAN (MRS. ISAAC DANIEL STEWART), psychologist; b. Pacatello, Ida., Jan. 14, 1931; d. Donald Norton and Geraldine (Smyth) Bryan; B.A., U. Utah, 1953, M.A., 1954, Ph.D., 1958; m. Isaac Daniel Stewart; children—Elizabeth Ann, Shannon. Chief psychologist Rehab. Center, U. Utah Coll. Medicine, Salt Lake City, 1957-62, chief child psychologist dept. psychiatry, 1967-68; resident psychologist St. Elizabeth's Hosp., Washington, 1962-64, staff psychologist, 1964-65; pvt. practice psychotherapy, 1968—; lectr. dept. psychology U. Utah, Salt Lake City, 1966-67. Chmn. Bd. Examiners for Licensure Psychologists, Utah, 1973-74, mem., 1970—. Diplomate Am. Bd. Examiners Profl. Psychology. Mem. Utah Psychol. Assn. Utah Psychologists Pvt. Practice, Sigma Xi. Mem. Ch. of Jesus Christ of Latter Day Saints. Contbr. articles to profl. jours. Home and office: 2900 Millicent Dr Salt Lake City UT 84108

STEWART, ELIZABETH LEE (MRS. CHARLES F. SELLE, JR.), dentist; b. nr. Annapolis, Md., Aug. 27, 1928; d. Edgar Lee and Esther Gladys (Roese) Stewart; student Johns Hopkins, 1952-54; D.D.S., U. Md., 1958; m. Charles F. Selle, Jr., Feb. 26, 1959. Pvt. practice dentistry, Sweet-Air Estates, Md., 1959-62; mem. staff Springfield Hosp. Center, Sykesville, Md., 1958—, sec.-treas., 1969—. Mem. Am., Md. dental assns., Baltimore County Dental Soc., Balt. Coll. Dental Surgery Alumni Assn. Home: 1205 Doves Cove Rd Towson MD 21204 Office: Springfield Hosp Center Sykesville MD 21784

STEWART, (ESSIE) MARIE (MRS. VIRGIL M. STEWART), editor; b. South Bend, Ind., Feb. 16, 1922; d. A. David and Gladys (Jeffries) Collins; certificate Topeka Bus. Coll., 1940; student, U. Neb., 1954-55; m. Virgil M. Stewart, May 9, 1941; children—Virgil M., Milton R. Pub. service dir. KOLN-TV, Lincoln, Neb., 1953-61; production asst., office mgr. MPATI, Inc., Lafayette, 1961-64; radio-TV mgr., women's editor Univ. News Service, Purdue U., Lafayette, Ind., 1964—, now sr. editor. Pres. Lakeview Sch. P.T.A., Lincoln, Neb., 1949-51. Recipient Mankind Service award Greater Lafayette United Fund, 1969; Sycamore council Girl Scout award, 1973. Mem. Women In Communications (chpt. pres. 1973-74), Tippecanoe Bus. and Profl. Womens Club (pres. 1971-72). Home: Box 581 Rural Route 2 Monticello IN 47960 Office: University News Service Purdue University Lafayette IN 47907

STEWART, EVELYN JUANITA, sem. dean; b. Ft. Smith, Ark., Nov. 15, 1926; d. Orvie Rufus and Gladys Beatrice (Efurd) Stewart; B.A., Ouachita Bapt. Coll., 1948; M.R.E., Southwestern Bapt. Theol. Sem., 1953. Asso. tng. union dept. Miss. Bapt. State Conv., Jackson, 1953-60; dir. jr. and intermediate work First Bapt. Ch., Tulsa, 1960-62; children's cons. Bapt. Sunday Sch. Bd., Nashville, 1962-69; dean of women, dir. student activities Southwestern Bapt. Theol. Sem., Ft. Worth, 1969—. Mem. Southwestern Bapt. Religious Edn. Assn. (sec. 1970), So. Bapt. Religious Edn. Assn. (v.p. 1971). Clubs: Seminary Woman's (v.p. 1971, 73), Fort Worth Woman's, Knife and Fork (Ft. Worth). Editor jr. sect. Builder mag., 1962-69. Contbr. to publs. in field. Home: 4536 Stanley St Barnard Hall Fort Worth TX 76122 Office: PO Box 22000-3F Fort Worth TX 76122

STEWART, KATHERINE ELIZABETH (MRS. HERBERT M. AITKEN), physician; b. Jacksonville, Fla., Sept. 28, 1911; d. Maurice DeWitt and Dorcas (Kester) Stewart; B.S., U. Cin., 1932, M.B., 1934, M.D., 1935; m. Herbert M. Aitken, Jan. 12, 1937. Intern U. Hosps., Madison, Wis., 1934-35; intern, resident Bellevue Hosp., N.Y.C., 1942-43; practice medicine, Ogdensburg, N.J., 1943-49; physician Student Health Dept., U. Wis., Madison, 1949-52; asst. prof., 1950-52; med. cons. No. Colony and Tng. Sch., Chippewa Falls, Wis., 1954—. Pres., Eau Claire Mental Health Assn., 1955-56; pres., bd. dirs. Eau Claire County Guidance Clinic, 1960-61; bd. dirs. Eau Claire Pub. Library, 1964-72, v.p., 1968-70, pres., 1970-72; bd. dirs. United Fund Eau Claire. Republican. Episcopalian. Home: 532 Summit Av Eau Claire WI 54701 Office: No Colony and Training Sch Chippewa Falls WI 54729

STEWART, LINDA JOAN WILLIAMS, educator; b. Monterey Park, Cal., Oct. 17, 1938; d. Ralph F. and Maude (Spicer) Williams; B.A. in Edn., Northwestern State Coll., 1962, M.Ed., 1964; Ed.D., Okla. State U., 1970; m. Douglas Stewart, Dec. 22, 1962 (div. 1973). Tchr. English, speech Medicine Lodge (Kan.) High Sch., 1963; tchr., counselor Harper (Kan.) High Sch., 1964-66; instr. speech Northwestern State Coll., Alva, Okla., 1968, acting chmn. speech dept., 1969-71, asst. prof., 1971—. Sponsor Castle Players; dir. coll. drama prodns. Mem. Bus. and Profl. Women's Club, Am. Personnel and Guidance Assn., Vocational Guidance Assn., Am. Ednl. Theatre Assn., Speech Assn. Am., N.E.A., Okla. Edn. Assn., Nesatunga Arts and Humanities Council, Alva C. of C., Am. Assn. U. Women, Am. Assn. U. Profs., Political Sci. Forum, Am. Assn. Female Execs., Alpha Psi Omega (sponsor). Republican. Conglist. Home: 1202 2d St Alva OK 73717

STEWART, LLOYD MAY, newspaper editor; b. Port Arthur, Tex., Jan. 15, 1924; d. Lloyd Martin and May (Cowart) Stewart; B.J., U. Tex., 1945. Reporter, Wichita Falls (Tex.) Record News, 1945, Marshall (Tex.) News Messenger, 1946-47; editor Cleburne (Tex.) Times-Rev., 1947-49; with Ft. Worth Star-Telegram, 1949—, soc. editor, 1950—, art editor, 1959-63, woman's editor, fashion editor, 1963—. Recipient 1st place award for women's news Tex. A.P. Mng. Editors Assn., 1966. Mem. Am. Assn. U. Women, Tex. Congress Parents and Tchrs., Theta Sigma Phi (chpt. pres. 1962-64, mem. nat. bd. 1964—, nat. pres. 1968-71). Episcopalian. Clubs: Woman's of Fort Worth; Woman's Shakespeare; Zonta Internat.; Fashion Group.

Home: 710 N Main St Cleburne TX 76031 Office: 400 W 7th St Fort Worth TX 76101

STEWART, LOIS ANN (MRS. WILLIAM WOLMAN), editor; b. Albion, Mich., Sept. 5, 1924; d. Lowell and Mary Gladys (Comfort) Stewart; B.S., Ia. State U., 1946; M.S. in Journalism, Columbia, 1947; M.A. in Econs., N.Y. U., 1954; m. William Wolman, June 30, 1962; 1 dau., Ann Elizabeth. Asst. news editor Elec. World mag., N.Y.C., 1948-51; staff writer, press relations Am. Mgmt. Assn., 1951-59; asst. mgmt. editor Bus. Week, 1959-61; editor mgmt. controls dept. Peat, Marwick, Mitchell & Co., 1961-63; mng. editor Mgmt. Adviser mag., 1964-71; mgr. pub. information Am. Nat. Standards Inst., N.Y.C., 1973—. Mem. Park Slope Civic Council, Park Slope Health Coalition; mem. exec. com. Park Slope Conservation Council. Mem. Ia. State U. Alumni Assn. (past pres. N.Y. chpt.), Overseas Press Club Am., Phi Kappa Phi, Theta Sigma Phi. Contbr. chpts. to Management Games, 1961; Simulation and Gaming, 1962. Contbr. articles bus. mags. Home: 508 7th St Brooklyn NY 11215 Office: 1430 Broadway New York City NY 10018

STEWART, MARGARET MCBRIDE, educator; b. Guilford County, nr. Greensboro, N.C., Feb. 6, 1927; d. David Henry and Mary (Morrow) Stewart; A.B., U. N.C., 1948, M.A., 1951; Ph.D., Cornell U., 1956; m. George E. Martin, Dec. 19, 1969. Lab. instr. biology U. N.C. at Greensboro, 1950-51; instr. biology Catawba Coll., Salisbury, N.C., 1951-53; research asst. oceanography Cornell U., Ithaca, N.Y., 1953, extension botanist, 1954-56; asst. prof. biology State U. N.Y. at Albany, 1956-58, asso. prof., 1958-65, prof. vertebrate biology, 1965—. Recipient U. N.C. Research grant, 1950, N.Y. Sci. Service award, 1954, State U. N.Y. Grant-in-aid, Research Found., 1958-61, 1965-67, 1967-69, 70-72, 73-74. Mem. A.A.A.S., Am. Inst. Biol. Scis., Am. Soc. Ichthyologists, Herpetologists, Am. Soc. Mammalogists, N.C. Acad. Sci., Soc. Systematic Zoology, Nature Conservancy, Herpetologists League, Soc. Study Amphibians and Reptiles, Herpetological Assn. Africa, Assn. Tropical Biology, Soc. Study Evolution, Ecol. Soc., Sigma Delta Epsilon, Phi Kappa Phi, Sigma Xi. Author: Keys to the Vertebrates of the Northeastern States, 1965; Amphibians of Malawi, 1967. Contbr. articles to profl. jours. Home: RD 1 Beaver Dam Rd Voorheesville NY 12186

STEWART, MARIE MCCAFFERY (MRS. SAMUEL E. STEWART), author; b. Stonington, Conn., Aug. 17, 1899; d. John Henry and Mary Ellen (Egan) McCaffery; B.S., Central Conn. Coll., 1944; M.A., U. Conn., 1948, Ph.D., 1958; m. Samuel E. Stewart, July 27, 1921; children—Eileen (Mrs. Albert LaLime), Maryann (Mrs. Albert R. Bessette). Tchr. elementary, secondary schs., colls. and bus. coll., 36 years. Corr. cons. G. Fox & Co., Hartford, Conn.; lectr. to numerous orgns. Recipient 1st Woman of Year award Westerly R.I. chpt. Bus. and Profl. Women, 19—. Author numerous books including Business English and Letter Writing, 1953; Business English and Communication, 1961, 4th edit., 1972; College English and Communication, 1964, 2d edit., 1969. Address: Alpha Av Stonington CT 06378

STEWART, MARY FLORENCE ELINOR (MRS. FREDERICK H. STEWART), author; b. Sunderland, County Durham, Sept. 17, 1916; d. Frederick A. and Mary Edith (Matthews) Rainbow; B.A., Durham U., 1939, M.A., 1941; m. Frederick H. Stewart, 1945. Asst. lectr. in English, Durham U., 1941-45; part-time lectr. English, St. Hild's Tng. Coll., Durham, also Durham U., 1948-56. Created lady Order Brit. Empire. Author: (novels) Madam, Will You Talk?, 1954; Wildfire at Midnight, 1956; Thunder on the Right, 1957; Nine Coaches Waiting, 1958; My Brother Michael, 1959; The Ivy Tree, 1961; The Moonspinners, 1962; This Rough Magic, 1964; Airs Above the Ground, 1965; The Gabriel Hounds, 1967; The Wind Off The Small Isles, 1968; The Crystal Cave, 1970; The Little Broomstick, 1971; The Hollow Hills, 1973; Ludo and the Star Horse, 1974; also poems, articles. Fellow Royal Soc. Arts; mem. Soc. Authors, Author's League Am., P.E.N. Address: 79 Morningside Park Edinburgh Ehio 5EZ Scotland

STEWART, MARY FRANCES, author; b. San Gabriel, Cal., May 6, 1911; d. Charles William and Annetta (Langsdale) Bean; student Occidental Coll., 1930-32; A.B., Whittier Coll., 1934, M.Ed. in Child Research, 1935; Ed.D., U. So. Cal., 1948; m. Robert Ernest Stewart, Jr., June 15, 1949; 1 son, Stephen Robert. Instr. emergency edn. program U. So. Cal., 1943-45; asso. prof. edn. Whittier Coll., 1945-46; asst. prof. edn. Cal. State U. at Sacramento, 1948-50; asst. prof. Cal. State U. at San Francisco, 1951-52. Fellow Royal Hort. Soc. Eng.; mem. Gleeson, U. San Francisco library assos., Friends of Huntington Library, Hist. Soc. So. Cal. Episcopalian. Author: (with Robert Ernest Stewart, Jr.) Adolph Sutro: A Biography (Silver medal Commonwealth Club Cal.), 1962. Home: 3634 Brockway Ct Sacramento CA 95818

STEWART, MARYALICE HARVEY, archivist; b. Banff, Alta., Can., Mar. 23, 1923; d. Ralph Strathie and Elizabeth (Brewster) Harvey; student Banff Sch. Fine Arts, 1939; div. Planner, developer Archives of Canadian Rockies, Banff, 1965, dir., 1968—. Adv. bd. Nat. Library, Ottawa, Ont., Can. Mem. Canadian Museums Assn., Canadian, Alta. hist. socs., Prairie Archivists, Alta. Archaeol. Soc., Am. Assn. Museums, Am. Assn. State and Local History, Gilcrease Inst. Club: Alpine (Can.). Home: 439 Muskrat St Banff AB Canada Office: 111 Bear St Banff AB Canada

STEWART, PATRICIA BROOKS, psychologist; b. Richmond, Va., Oct. 23, 1942; d. Leonard Gregory and Fay Elizabeth (Mackey) Brooks; student Richmond Profl. Inst., 1960-61; B.S., Longwood Coll., 1964; M.S., Va. Commonwealth U., 1970; m. William Allen Stewart, Apr. 17, 1971. Tchr. 4th grade Colonial Heights (Va.) Sch. System, 1964-68; asst. dir. Psychol. Services Center, Va. Commonwealth U., Richmond, 1970-71, tchr. human devel. Sch. Edn., 1971-72, acting dir. Child Study Center, 1971-73; sch. psychologist Henrico Sch. System, Highland Springs, Va., 1973—. Counselor Night Counseling Clinic, Bon Air, Va., 1970-72. Campaign worker Democratic Party, 1966. Recipient Pat Britton Citizenship award John Marshall High Sch., Richmond, 1960. Mem. Am. (asso.), Va., Richmond psychol. assns., Va. Assn. Sch. Psychologists, Longwood Alumnae Assn. (fund raising chmn. Richmond chpt. 1966-68), Colonial Heights Edn. Assn. (membership chmn. 1966-67), Sigma Sigma Sigma, Psi Chi. Episcopalian. Home: 5905 Willow Oaks Dr Richmond VA 23225 Office: Henrico Sch System PO Box 40 Highland Springs VA 23075

STEWART, PATRICIA RHODES, clin. psychologist; b. Vallejo, Cal., Feb. 11, 1910; d. Butler Young and Sarah Virginia (Ryan) Rhodes; A.B. with great distinction, Stanford, 1930; M.A., San Jose (Cal.) State Coll., 1959; Ph.D., U. London (Eng.), 1963; m. John K. Stewart, Aug. 15, 1930 (div.); children—John K., Nancy Shea. Teaching asst. in psychology San Jose State Coll., 1959-60; clin. psychologist Napa State Hosp., Imola, Cal., 1964—. Mem. exec. com. No. Cal. region Am. Friends Service Com., 1970-74. Mem. Am., Western psychol. assns., Am. Anthrop. Assn., Phi Beta Kappa. Mem. Soc. of Friends (clk. 1972-74). Home: 48 Gravatt Dr Berkeley CA 94705 Office: Napa State Hosp Imola CA 94558

STEWART, ROBERTA A., educator; b. Rochester, N.H., Aug. 24, 1923; d. Donald Harvey and Anna (Lowe) Stewart; B.S., U. N.H., 1944; A.M., Smith Coll., 1946, Ph.D., 1949. Research asso. Smith Coll., 1948-49; instr. chemistry Wellesley Coll., 1949-53; asst. prof. chemistry Hollins Coll. (Va.), 1953-56, asso. prof., 1956-70, prof., 1970—, chmn. dept. chemistry, 1963-66, 1969-73, chmn. div. natural scis. and math., 1967-73, asst. to pres., 1969—. Fellow Am. Inst. Chemists; mem. League of Women Voters, Am. Chem. Soc. (chmn. Blue Ridge sect. 1971), Va. Acad. Sci., A.A.A.S., Am. Assn. Univ. Profs., Sigma Xi, Phi Kappa Phi. Contbr. articles in field to profl. jours. Home: PO Box 9685 Hollins College VA 24020

STEWART, SALLY JEAN, assn. exec.; b. Painesville, O., Jan. 12, 1947; d. Robert Asa and Isla Eleanor (Ford) Stewart; B.S., Kent State U., 1970. Tchr. remedial reading, English, Painesville City Schs., 1970; aquatic dir. YMCA, Red Bank, N.J., 1970-73; asso. health and phys. edn. dir. YMCA, Balt., 1973—. Dir. Middle Atlantic Region Leadership Sch., 1974—, Aquatic Inst., 1972-73. Mem. Mid East Region Assn. Profl. Dirs., Middle Atlantic Region Phys. Dirs. Soc., Alpha Omicron. Home: 57 E Burke Av Towson MD 21204 Office: 600 W Chesapeake Towson MD 21204

STEWART, SHEILA (MRS. ERIC HAROLD STEWART), author; b. Devon, Eng., June 1, 1928; student Bishop Otter Tchr.-Tng. Coll., Chichester, Eng., 1946-48; m. Eric Harold Stewart, Apr. 16, 1952; children—Sarah, Timothy, Matthew. Tchr., Oxon, Eng., 1952-62; founder Temple Close Nursery Sch., Bloxham, Oxon, 1962. Author: A Home from Home, 1967; Country Kate, 1971. Address: Combe Rising Ascott nr Shipston-on-Stour Warwickshire England

STEWART, VESTA GENEVA, educator; b. Mills County, Tex., Sept. 16, 1925; d. Jesse D. and Jessie Pearl (Henry) Stewart; B.S., W. Tex. State U., 1951, Ed.M., 1956; postgrad. Fresno State Coll., 1966. Tchr. Union Sch., Terry County, Tex., 1944-47; elementary sch. tchr., Whitharral, Tex., 1947-48, Muleshoe, Tex., 1948-51, Petersburg, Tex., 1951-55; elementary tchr., spl. edn. tchr. Roosevelt Sch., Lubbock, Tex., 1955—. Mem. Tex., Lubbock County tchrs. assns., Tex., Roosevelt classroom tchrs. assns., Exceptional Children Council of Am. Mem. Order Eastern Star. Home: 1807 E Brown St Lubbock TX 79403 Office: Route 1 Roosevelt Sch Lubbock TX 79401

STEWART, WINIFRED GRAY (MRS. EVERETT E. STEWART), mus. ofcl.; b. Brockton, Mass., Dec. 2, 1901; d. Winfield Scott and Minnie Louise (Packard) Benson; student Wash. State Coll., 1924-25, Otis Art Inst., 1927, Coll. of Marin, 1950-55; m. Everett E. Stewart, Sept. 27, 1920. Lapidary and hand crafted jewelry Winifred's Gift Shop, Bolinas, Cal., 1959-64; archeol. lab. technician San Bernardino County Mus., Bloomington, Cal., 1966—, Calico Archeol. Site, Yermo, Cal., 1966-69; sec., asst. to San Bernardino County archeologist, 1968—. Mem. Marin Mineral Soc. (sec. 1954-55). Author: Poems, 1969. Contbr. poetry to lit. mags., anthologies. Home: 18855 Park St Bloomington CA 92316 Office: 18860 Orange St Bloomington CA 92316

STICKNEY, LORRAINE PHYLLIS OSBERG (MRS. FREDERIC HASKELL STICKNEY), librarian; b. Spicer, Minn., Sept. 2, 1936; d. Edgar Albin and Ella Sophie (Orson) Osberg; B.A., Augsburg Coll., 1958; M.L.S., U. Me., 1967; m. Frederic Haskell, June 25, 1960. Tchr., librarian Thornton Acad., Saco, Me., 1958-59; librarian Kenyon (Minn.) Pub. Schs., 1959-60, Gorham (Me.) High Sch., 1961—; tchr. Falmouth (Me.) High Sch., 1960-61. Asst. F.H. Stickney Assos., Standish, Me., 1970—. Named Outstanding Young Women Am. Augsburg Coll., 1971. Mem. Me. (sec. 1963-65, mem. exec. bd. 1971-73), New Eng. (mem. com. 1967-69) sch. library assns., Me. Tchrs. Assn., N.E.A., A.L.A., Lambda Iota Tau. Democrat. Lutheran. Home: Box 134 Standish ME 04084 Office: 41 Morrill Av Gorham ME 04038

STIDHAM, ANN BARTHOLD, educator, psychologist; b. Steubenville, O., May 24, 1935; s. Charles Raymond and Madge (Paisley) Barthold; B.S. in Edn. summa cum laude, Muskingum Coll., 1957; M.A. (fellow), Northwestern U., 1958; Ed.D. (fellow), U. Tenn., 1966; postgrad. U. Miami (Fla.), 1972; m. James D. Stidham, Aug. 27, 1960; children—James Barth, Thaddeus Jon. Asst. prof., coll. counselor Milligan (Tenn.) Coll., 1958-60; vis. prof. Muskingum Coll., summer 1959; staff psychologist Cambridge (O.) State Hosp., summer 1960; asst. prof. Maryville (Tenn.) Coll., 1960-63; U. Tenn. Eve. Sch., 1965; asso. prof. psychology Presbyn. Coll., Clinton, S.C., 1967—; pvt. practice counseling psychology, 1968—. Active local Cub Scouts, P.T.A. Muskingum Coll. Alumni Assn. fellow, Ohio P.T.A. fellow, NIH fellow. Mem. Am., Southeastern psychol. assns., Psi Chi. Home: E Walnut St Clinton SC 29325

STIEG, SALLY RUTH MARIE ANDERSON (MRS. HENRY P. STIEG), civic worker; b. Topeka, May 4, 1913; d. Emil and Lydia (Nordling) Anderson; student Kansas City Jr. Coll., 1931-32; R.N., Trinity Luth. Hosp. Nursing Sch., Kansas City, Mo., 1934; m. Henry P. Stieg, July 15, 1936; children—Jolane (Mrs. Frank Rogers), Norma Lee (Mrs. Bill Alley), John, David. Nurse supr. Trinity Luth. Hosp., 1934; sch. nurse North Phoenix High Sch., 1939-40; welfare supr. United Fund, Scottsdale, Ariz., 1953-56; co-owner Scottsdale Meat Packing Co., 1946—. Nurse instr. A.R.C., 1939-41; trustee Scottsdale Sch. Dist. 48 and 212, 1956-65, pres., 1959-64; pres. Scottsdale United Fund, 1954; vol. welfare worker, Scottsdale Area, 1950-60; pres. Scottsdale Sch. Dist. and County P.T.A., 1955-56; mem. Scottsdale Sch. Bd., 1956-64; P.T.A. rep. State Sch. Bd. Assn., 1962-64; mem. adv. com. to Bd. Edn. Rep., 1961-64; active cultural exchange programs, 1968-74. Recipient merit citation Scottsdale Sch. Bd., 1964; leadership and meritorious service award Ariz. Sch. Bds. Assn., 1965; Meritorious Civic Leader Nat. award, 1969; Nurse Recognition award, 1970. Mem. Am., Ariz. nurses assns., Nurses Assn. Dist. 18, League Women Voters, Bus. and Profl. Women's Club (Outstanding Citizen award 1952), Internat. Platform Assn. Democrat. Mem. Order Eastern Star. Club: Phoenix Exchangettes. Home: 7240 E Wilshire Dr Scottsdale AZ 85257 also 397 Arbol Av Chapalita Guadalajara Jalisco Mexico

STIER, ELIZABETH FLEMING (MRS. E. THEODORE STIER), educator; b. Riverton, N.J.; d. Walter Ernest and Eugenie (Jamison) Fleming; B.S., Douglass Coll., 1947; M.S., Rutgers, 1949, Ph.D., 1951; m. Eugene Theodore Stier, Dec. 27, 1947; children—Richard Fleming, Priscilla, Betsy. Research asso. food sci. Rutgers, New Brunswick, N.J., 1951-60, asst. prof., 1960-66, asso. prof. food sci., 1966-72, prof., 1972—. Cons. sensory testing to food industry, 1955. Capt. United Fund, New Brunswick, 1950—. Mem. A.A.A.S., Inst. Food Technologists, Am. Assn. U. Profs., N.Y. Inst. Food Technologists (dir., 1956—), Nat. Inst. Food Technologists (mem. edn. com.; councillor 1958), Am. Assn. U. Profs., N.Y. Acad. Sci., Sigma Xi, Phi Tau Sigma. Contbr. articles to profl. jours. Home: 5 Orchard Rd Piscataway NJ 08854 Office: Food Sci Dept Rutgers U New Brunswick NJ 08901

STIGOL, LUISA CORA (MRS. FLORIAN WEISSENBORN), physician; b. Buenos Aires, Argentina, Feb. 23, 1930; d. Abraham and Eugenia (Polnoroff) Stigol; Baccaleaureat, Liceo Nacional, Buenos Aires, 1946; M.D., Nat. U. Buenos Aires, 1954; m. Florian Weissenborn, Aug. 26, 1966; children—Georgina, Marcelo (by previous marriage), Odile. Came to U.S., 1965, naturalized, 1970. Intern, Univ. Hosp., Buenos Aires, 1952-53, hon. physician 1st chair pediatrics, 1954-60, chief out-patient service of infancy, 1959, instr., 1954-61; resident in pediatrics Nat. Inst. for Rehab. of Invalid, Buenos Aires, 1956-58; hon. physician Gastroenterology Center, Buenos Aires, 1957; asst. physician dept. physiopathology Center Respiratory Rehab., Buenos Aires, 1958-62, pediatrician, 1962-64; fellow Nat. U. Buenos Aires, 1960-61; research fellow physiology dept. Harvard Sch. Pub. Health, 1962, research asso. in physiology, 1965-70; career sci. researcher Nat. Council Sci. and Tech. Investigations, Buenos Aires, 1963-64; research fellow in medicine Children's Hosp. Med. Center, Boston, 1965-68, fellow in pathology, 1968-70, research asso. in pathology, 1970—, asst. in medicine, 1971—; fellow Radcliffe Inst., 1960-71; teaching fellow in pathology Harvard Med. Sch., Boston, 1970-72, asso. in pathology, 1972—; practice medicine, specializing in pediatrics, Dedham, Mass., 1971—; courtesy staff pediatrician Boston Hosp. for Women, 1971—. Mem. Mass. Med. Soc. Contbr. articles to med. jours., chpts. to books. Home: 150 Court St Dedham MA 02026 Office: Dedham Med Assos 743 High St Dedham MA 02026

STIKA, ELAINE ANNA, advt. exec.; b. Kenosha, Wis., July 3, 1924; d. Alexander and Paulina L. (Janota) Stika; student Kenosha Coll. Commerce, 1943, Mgmt. Center Marquette U., Milw., 1960, U. Wis., Kenosha, 1963, De Paul U., Chgo., 1963, Kenosha Tech. Inst., 1970. Asst. to mgr. market list div. sales dept. Macwhyte Wire Rope Co., Kenosha, 1943-49, asst. to advt., sales promotion, pub. relations, marketing mgr., 1949-65, advt. and sales services adminstr., 1966-73, marketing services adminstr., 1974—. Sec., treas. Kenosha Civil Council, 1955—; mem. Kenosha County health planning com. Comprehensive Health Planning Agy. Southeastern Wis., 1969—. Bd. dirs. Kenosha County council Girl Scouts U.S.A., 1962-68; bd. dirs. Kenosha County Blood Center, 1964—, v.p., 1968-70, pres., 1971—; bd. dirs. Kenosha County United Fund, 1966-72. Mem. Milw. Assn. Indsl. Advertisers, Constrn. Equipment Advertisers, Kenosha-Bradford Alumni Assn. (bd. dirs. 1968—, v.p. 1970-71, pres. 1971-73), Wis. Tb and Respiratory Disease Assn. (br. adv. bd. 1970—), Sigma Alpha Sigma (dir. 1953, pres. 1962-64). Club: Kenosha Advertising (dir. 1959-70, pres. 1963-64). Home: 922 48th St Kenosha WI 53140 Office: 2906 14th Av Kenosha WI 53140

STILES, ELIZABETH CONNELLY, coll. adminstr.; b. Chgo.; d. Harrington John and Barbara Cassilda (Mayer) Connelly; B.A., St. Xavier Coll., 1941; M.Ed., Chgo. State U., 1964; children—Elizabeth Ann, Barbara Carol, Patricia Jean. Personnel counselor and research Western Electric Co., Chgo., 1942-50; tchr., counselor Mother McAuley High Sch., Chgo., 1958-62, Oak Lawn (Ill.) Community High Sch., 1962-68; dir. financial aid and placement Moraine Valley Community Coll., Palos Hills, Ill., 1968—. Cons., Dept. Health, Edn. and Welfare. Miseracordia scholar, 1938-41. Mem. Am. Assn. Community and Jr. Colls., Midwest, Ill. (v.p.) assns. financial aid adminstrs., Placement Assn. Community Colls. and Employers (sec.), Kappa Gamma Pi. Home: 9311 Utica Av Evergreen Park IL 60642 Office: 10900 S 88th Av Palos Hills IL 60465

STILES, MARTHA BENNETT (MRS. MARTIN STILES), author; b. Manila, P.I. (parents American citizens); d. Forrest Hampton and Jane McClintock (Bennett) Wells; student Coll. William and Mary, 1950-52; B.S., U. Mich., 1954; m. Martin Stiles, Sept. 18, 1954; 1 son, John Martin. Recipient Avery Hopwood award, 1956, 58. Mem. Clements Library Assos., Authors Guild, S.C. Hist. Soc., Friends of Ann Arbor Pub. Library, Detroit Women Writers, Audubon Soc., Mich. Thoroughbred Breeders and Owners Assn., Washtenaw County Humane Soc. Author: One Among the Indians, 1962, The Strange House at Newburyport, 1963, Darkness Over the Land, 1966, Dougal Looks for Birds, 1972, James the Vine-Puller, 1975.

STILES, MURIEL ELIZABETH HOLM, librarian; b. Gardner, Mass., Sept. 8, 1927; d. Alvin Colbjorn and Catherine Maude (MacDonald) Holm; B.A., Jackson Coll., 1949; postgrad. Mass. State Coll., Worcester, 1967-70; m. David Stiles, June 25, 1949 (div.); children—Catharine, Dana Whitney. Group leader Friendly House, Worcester, Mass., 1949-50; librarian's asst. Beaman Meml. Pub. Library, West Boylston, Mass., 1962-68, acting librarian, 1968-69, head librarian, 1969—. Asst. leader troop Girl Scouts Am., 1958-60; den mother Cub Scouts Am., 1961-63; mem. Central Regional Adv. Council, 1969-71; 2d. v.p. Woman's Club, West Boylston, Mass., 1970-71, 1st v.p., 1971-73, pres., 1973—. Mem. Am., Mass., New Eng. library assns., Bay Path Library Club. Republican. Home: 36 Woodland Heights Rd West Boylston MA 01583 Office: 8 Newton St West Boylston MA 01583

STILLMAN, JUNE ELIZABETH SMITH (MRS. DONALD ALBERT STILLMAN), librarian; b. Webster, Fla., June 27, 1929; d. Phillip Ferg and Elizabeth (Akins) Smith; B.A., Fla. State U., 1951, M.A., 1966; m. Donald Albert Stillman, Apr. 19, 1957; children—Elizabeth June, Dorothy Lynne. Librarian Williston (Fla.) High Sch., 1951-54, Naval Air Sta. and Rogers Jr. High Sch., Ft. Lauderdale, Fla., 1954-57, Orlando (Fla.) Jr. Coll., 1963-68; with Fla. Tech. U. Library, Orlando, 1968—, head ref. librarian, 1969—. Mem. Am., Fla., Southeastern library assns., Beta Phi Mu. Home: 2851 Wright Av Orlando FL 32803 Office: Fla Tech U PO Box 25000 Orlando FL 32816

STILLWELL, JANET EVELYN O'BRIEN, educator; b. Saginaw, Mich., Dec. 12, 1936; d. J. George and Evelyn (MacArthur) O'Brien; B.A., U. Mich., 1958, M.A. in Edn., 1961, M.A. in Speech, 1963, Ph.D. in Speech, 1973. Tchr., Livonia Pub. Schs., 1958-61, Ann Arbor (Mich.) Pub. Schs., 1962-65, Kalamazoo Pub. Schs., 1965-67; asso. prof. dept. dance Coll. Fine Arts, Western Mich. U., Kalamazoo, 1967—, costume designer dept. speech, 1967—. Dance and creative dramatics tchr. Ann Arbor Recreation Dept., 1959-64; dir. Homestead Acres Children's Theatre Camp, Chelsea, Mich., summers 1962-64; instr. art appreciation Washtenaw Community Coll., Ypsilanti, Mich., summers 1967—; area coordinator Dance Residency Touring Programs, 1969, 70, 73, 74. Asst. dir. Kalamazoo Jr. Civic Center, 1965-67; state chmn. Mich. Children's Theatre Conf., 1967-69. Bd. dirs. Am. Coll. Dance Festival. Mem. Am. Edn. Theatre Assn., Sr. Soc., Kalamazoo Art Center, Kalamazoo Civic Players, Am. Assn. U. Profs., Mich. Acad. Sci., Arts and Letters, A.A.H.P.E.R., Zeta Phi Eta. Home: 2507 Harvard St Kalamazoo MI 49001

STILLWELL, MARGARET BINGHAM, bibliographer, writer; b. Providence; d. Edward Augustus and Mary Elizabeth Bingham (Pindar) Stillwell; spl. student R.I. Sch. Design, 1899-1905; A.B., Brown U., 1909, A.M. (hon.), 1925, Litt.D., 1942, U.R.I., 1952. Asst. John Carter Brown Library, Providence, 1909-14; cataloguer rare book div., N.Y. Pub. Library, 1914-17; curator and librarian The Annmary Brown Memorial, 1917-53; prof. bibliography Brown U., 1948-53, emerita prof., 1954—; President's fellowship Brown U., 1951. Lectr. Sch. Library Service, Columbia U., 1927-31. Designer, chmn. bldg. com. Greenville Pub. Library, 1955, 66. Mem. Colonial Dames Am., Bibliog. Soc. Am., Institut d'Etudes Europeenes et Mondiales (corr.), Phi Beta Kappa (pres. woman's sect. R.I. Alpha chpt. 1925-26). Episcopalian. Clubs: Hroswitha (N.Y.); Providence Art, Rhode Island Short Story (past pres.). Author: The Influence of William Morris and the Kelmscott Press, 1912; The Heritage of the

Modern Printer, 1916; Washington Eulogies, 1916; General Hawkins as He Revealed Himself to His Librarian, 1923; The Fasciculus Temporum, 1924; The Annmary Brown Memorial (descriptive essay), 1925; Incunabula and Americana, 1450-1800, A Key to Bibliographical Study, 1931; Gutenberg and the Catholicon, 1936; The Seventeenth Century (in The Dolphin History of the Printed Book), 1938; The Annmary Brown Memorial, A Booklover's Shrine, 1940; Noah's Ark in Early Woodcuts and Modern Rhyme, 1942; Bibliographical Survey: 15th and 16th Century books in The Hunt Botanical Collection, 1958; The Awakening Interest in Science During the First Century of Printing, 1450-1550, 1970; The Beginning of the World of Books: A Chronological Survey of the Texts Chosen for Printing during the First Twenty Years of the Printing Art, 1972. Author and illustrator: While Benefit Street Was Young, 1943; The Pageant of Benefit Street Down Through the Years, 1945; Librarians Are Human: Memories in and out of the Rare-Book World, 1907-1970, 1973. Compiler, editor: Incunabula in American Libraries, A Second Census, 1940. Home: Elfendale Greenville RI 02828 Office: care Annmary Brown Meml Providence RI 02912

STIMM, TRUDY W., pub. co. exec.; b. Stuttgart, Germany, Sept. 6, 1937; d. Fritz Herman and Emma Hilda (Bantle) Stimm; student Coll. for Bus. and Adminstrn., Stuttgart, U. Cal. at Berkeley Extension. Mgr. fgn. lang. dept., specialist fgn. lang. book imports Herder & Herder, Inc., N.Y.C., 1961—, controller, 1968-72; controller, treas. Stein & Day, Inc., N.Y.C., 1972-73; controller Seabury Press, Inc., N.Y.C., 1973—. Home: #O 15 E 36th St New York City NY 10016

STIMPSON, ANNE DILLEN (MRS. CLIFFORD L. STIMPSON), librarian; b. Mars Hill, Me., Aug. 24, 1910; d. Herrick Lufkin and Rachel E. (Kearney) Dillen; student Aroostook State Tchrs. Coll., 1928, U. N.H., summers 1962-66; m. Clifford Leslie Stimpson, June 9, 1929 (dec. 1973); children—Don Dillen, Darla Dawn (Mrs. Earl Chafin). Asst. librarian Presque Isle (Me.) Free Library (now Emily and Mark Turner Meml. Library), 1951-55, librarian, adminstr., 1955—; mem. faculty continuing edn. div. U. Me., 1969, 70. Organized catalogued med. library at Arthur R. Gould Meml. Hosp., 1961, now cons. librarian. Mem. exec. com. Northeastern Me. Library Dist., 1973. Mem. Urban Renewal Bd. Del., N.H. Republican Conv., 1962; mem. City Rep. Com. Recipient citation for interest and support Girl Scouts U.S.A., 1957. Mem. Me. Press and Radio Women, A.L.A., Me. Library Assn. (continuing edn. com. 1974), Bus. and Profl. Women, Beta Sigma Phi (dir. Tau chpt. 1954-58; hon. mem. Psi chpt.: exemplar). Conglist. Club: Pierian (hon.). Research on Presque Isle as a city for Ency. Americana, 1962. Condr. children's radio program, 1942-55, TV programs, 1955-60. Home: 23 Barton St Presque Isle ME 04769 Office: 39 2d St Presque Isle ME 04769

STINE, SISTER ANNE MARIE, educator; b. New Orleans; d. George Benton and Adrienne (Miller) Stine; B.S. cum laude, Loyola U., 1951; M.Ed., Xavier U., Cin., 1960; M.A. in English, Tulane U., 1963. Tchr. St. Michael's Sch., Crowley, La., 1942-44, 51-53, St. Joseph's, Gretna, La., 1944-48, Our Lady of Victories, Pascagoula, Miss., 1948-50; tchr. Pineville (La.) Sacred Heart Sch., 1950-51; tchr. English, Annunciation High Sch., New Orleans, 1953-60, prin., 1960-70; tchr. St. Mary's Dominican Coll., New Orleans, 1970-71; instr. English, Xavier U., New Orleans, 1970-72; instr. in edn. Our Lady Holy Cross, New Orleans; tchr. Orleans Parish Pub. Schs., 1973-74. Mem. Nat., La. edn. assns., Nat. Cath. Edn. Assn., Nat. Council Tchrs. English, English Speaking Union, Nat. Cath. Theatre Conf. Address: 336 30th St New Orleans LA 70124

STINE, ESTHER CORNELIUS (MRS. DONALD M. STINE), educator; b. Pitts., May 7, 1927; d. Maxwell and Esther Estelle (Davis) Cornelius; B.A., Maryville Coll., 1948; M.A., McCormick Theol. Sem., 1952; M.A., Northwestern U., 1957, Ph.D., 1960; children by previous marriage—William Howard, Esther Estelle; m. 2d, Donald M. Stine, July 21, 1972. Instr. Maryville (Tenn.) Coll., 1948-50, 1962-63, asst. prof., 1963-65, asso. prof., 1965-69, prof. philosophy and religion, 1970-73; counselor in edn. Program Agy., United Presbyn. Ch. U.S.A., N.Y.C., 1973—; asst. philosophy, theology McCormick Theol. Sem., Chgo., 1952-57, instr. philosophy, theology, 1957-60; instr. philosophy Northwestern U., Chgo., 1959-60. Religious emphasis week speaker U. Tenn., 1963, U. Mont., 1964, Davis and Elkins Coll., 1965; speaker religious assemblies, 1963-64. Bd. dirs. U. Tenn. Presbyn. Found., 1963-65, McCormick Theol. Sem., 1970—. Mem. Ontoanalytic Soc., Tenn. Philos. Assn. United Presbyn. Author: Man Before Chaos, 1968. Home: 6 Ell Rd Hillsdale NJ 07642

STINE, MARY ETTA, ednl. adminstr.; b. Monterey, Va., Mar. 15, 1924; d. Fred Bloom and Sophie Virginia (Johnson) Wyand; student Blackstone Coll., 1941-42, Ky. Wesleyan, 1942-43; A.B., Marshall U., 1946-48; M.A., Am. U., 1962; postgrad. U. Mich., 1962-63; m. David Augustus Stine, Feb. 16, 1945 (div. 1956); 1 dau., Virginia Morrison. Tchr., Fairfax (Va.) County Pub. Schs., 1951-62, helping tchr. math., 1963-64, asst. supr. math., 1964-65, supr. math., 1965-67, curriculum specialist math., 1968-73, curriculum specialist, compensatory edn., 1973—. Cons. various schs. and universities, 1964—; extension tchr. U. Va., 1965-67, Coll. William and Mary, 1964-66; lectr. Am. U., 1965-68. Recipient fellowship A.A.A.S., 1959, grants, NSF, 1962. Mem. Math. Assn. Am., A.A.A.S., N.E.A., Fairfax Edn. Assn., Va. Suprs. Math. Group (treas. 1967-69), Nat. Council Tchrs. Math. (dir. 1969-72). Methodist (pres. women's soc. 1953-55, bd. mem. 1952-55). Author (with others) Experiences in Mathematical Discovery, 1969. Editor: Fairfax County Curriculum Guides and Research Project, 1966—. Home: 9451 Lee Highway Fairfax VA 22030 Office: 10700 Page Av Fairfax VA 22030

STINSON, BESS, state senator; ed. Okla. U. Asst. v.p., dir. spl. service First Nat. Bank Ariz., 1952-67; home service adviser Dist. State Pub. Service Co., 1938-52; mem. Ariz. Ho. of Reps., 1967-70, Ariz. Senate, 1970—. Served with WAC. State women's chmn. U.S. Savs. Bonds; mem. Goodwill Aux., Asso. Women for Pepperdine Coll., Womens Med. Coll. Phila. Mem. League of Bus. and Profl. Women, Nat. Assn. Bank Women, Ariz. Fedn. Woman's Clubs (initiated Miss Stinson's Have-Flag-Will-Fly Program). Republican. Address: 2618 W Pierson Apt 4 Phoenix AZ 85017

STINSON, ETHELYN LENORE, musician; b. Harrisburg, Pa., June 7, 1904; d. William Henry and Melvina E. (Bretz) Stinson; diploma in violin Williamsport Dickinson Sem., 1927; tchrs. diploma piano Combs Coll. Music, Phila., 1938, Mus.B., 1939. Head music dept. Woods Schs., Langhorne, Pa., 1929-46; pvt. studio, Langhorne, 1946-50; chief music therapist Phila. State Hosp., 1950-70, chief music therapist psychotic mentally retarded patients N.E. unit, 1970-72. Tchr. piano, Phila. 1950—; lectr. music therapy. Adjudicator Nat. Guild Piano Tchrs., also mem. Hall of Fame. Mem. nat. bd. dirs. Am. Youth Symphony and Chorus. Registered music therapist. Mem. Nat. Assn. Music Therapy (sec., chpt. regent), Am. Coll. Musicians (faculty), Phila. Music Tchrs. Assn. Author: How to Teach Children Music, 1942. Composer: (music for piano) Climbing the Jungle Gym, 1938. Home: 9215 Annapolis Rd Philadelphia PA 19114

STINSON, HARRIETT LESLIE HILLS (MRS. RALF HALE STINSON), civic worker; b. San Francisco, Apr. 17, 1926; d. Leslie William and Ethel (Lee) Hills; B.S., Stanford, 1947; m. Ralf Hale Stinson, June 9, 1950; children—Ralf Hale II, Nell Lee, Leslie Balchen. Technician vascular research U. Cal., Franklin Hosps., 1947-49. Asst. chmn. San Mateo service unit Salvation Army, 1959-68, welfare sec., 1959; sec. Family Service Agy. San Mateo, 1967; founder Hillsborough Family Service League, 1965; chmn. youth behavior task force Comprehensive Health Planning Council San Mateo County, 1969-71; chmn. policy adv. com. Family Planning Project, Planned Parenthood Assn. and Dept. Health, Edn. and Welfare. Mem. information and edn. com. Planned Parenthood/World Population. Bd. dirs., v.p., founder Planned Parenthood Assn. San Mateo County, pres., 1972-73; bd. dirs. Damien House in San Mateo, v.p., 1970-71; bd. dirs. San Mateo County Service League. Mem. Jr. League San Francisco, Inc., Soroptimist (Burlingame-San Mateo Woman of Achievement, 1971). Episcopalian (mem. com. on violence Think Tank, metro. planning br. Diocese Cal.). Club: Burlingame Country (Hillsborough). Home: 249 Bridge Rd Hillsborough CA 94010

STINSON, THELMA JUNE, camp dir.; b. Butler, Pa., June 27, 1915; d. Melvin and Mary Elva (Linamen) Huselton; student Kent State U., 1943-45, Youngstown U., 1946-48; m. Lloyd E. Hetrick, June 26, 1935; children—Merry Anne (Mrs. Ronald Harrison), Melvin Wayne; m. 2d, Cecil E. Stinson, Nov. 1, 1945; children—Elizabeth Sue (Mrs. Barron Breakey), Jack, Jill (Mrs. Edward Stewart). Dir., Trumbull County (O.) Children's Home for Infants, 1941-45; family caseworker, Blackhawk County, Ia., 1946-47; bus. adminstrn. N. Ia. region Sears Co., 1948-49; kindergarten tchr., art instr., Warren, O., 1950-53; program dir. Rebecca Williams Settlement House, Warren, 1954-58; social services dir. Neighborhood Center, Columbus, O., 1958-61; exec. dir. Community Camps, Inc., Columbus, 1961—. Cons. camp program Nat. Council Chs.; cons. innercity and handicapped programs Franklin County, O. Bd. dirs. Friendly Town, Franklin County. Mem. Am. Camping Assn. (nat. bd.), A.A.H.P.E.R. (chmn. camping div.), Interpretive Naturalists, Audubon Soc. Contbr. articles to profl. publs. Home: 819 S Cassingham Rd Columbus OH 43209 Office: 4965 N High St Columbus OH 43214

STIREWALT, MARGARET AMELIA (MRS. DAVID RICHARD LINCICOME), med. research parasitologist; b. Hickory, N.C., Jan. 18, 1911; d. William Jacob and Mabel (Rhodes) Stirewalt; B.A. cum laude, Randolph-Macon Woman's Coll., 1931; M.A., Columbia, 1935; Ph.D., U. Va., 1938; m. David Richard Lincicome, Dec. 29, 1953. Research asso. U. Va., 1938-40; asso. prof. zoology Flora Macdonald Coll., 1941-43; commd. ensign Med. Service Corps, USN, 1943, advanced through grades to comdr.; acting dir. parasitology dept. Naval Med. Research Inst., Bethesda, Md., 1970-71, dir. div. parasitology, 1968-71; ret., 1971; research parasitologist Biomed. Research Inst., Rockville, Md., 1971—. Dairy farmer New Market, Va., 1966—. Recipient Du Pont fellowship, 1934-40; Commendation medal Sec. Navy, 1971; Emeritus Scientist award D.C. chpt. Soc. Exptl. Biology and Medicine, 1974. Diplomate in pub. health and med. lab. parasitology Am. Bd. Microbiologists. Fellow A.A.A.S., Royal Soc. Tropical Medicine and Hygiene (London); mem. Washington Helminthological Soc. (pres. 1959-60), Washington Assn. Tropical Medicine (pres. 1969-70), Am. Soc. Parasitologists (program officer 1962-67, council mem. 1962-67, 68-71, v.p. 1972—), Am. Soc. Tropical Medicine and Hygiene (membership com. 1963-64), Cell Biology, Am. Inst. Biol. Scis., Sigma Xi. Club: Potomac-Appalachian Trail. Mem. editorial bd. Jour. Parasitology, 1962-67, Exptl. Parasitology, 1974—. Home: 7118 Cedar Av Takoma Park MD 20012 Office: Biomed Research Inst Americal Found for Biomed Research 12111 Parklawn Dr Rockville MD 20852

STIRLING, LEONA STEIN (MRS. PAUL STIRLING), educator; b. Bklyn., Sept. 21, 1929; d. Gaston and Elsie (Eysman) Kintzburger; B.A., N.Y. U., 1962; M.A., C.W. Post Coll., 1970; m. Paul S. Stirling, Jan. 21, 1951; children—Jerold, Cary, David. Tchr. art East Meadow (N.Y.) Sch., 1962-69; asso. in tchr. edn. Hofstra U., Hempstead, 1967-68; instr. art history Nassau Community Coll., Hempstead, N.Y., 1969-70; chmn. elementary art dept. pub. schs. Great Neck, N.Y., 1974—. One woman shows Brookville, N.Y., Prudhoe Gallery, London, Eng., Art Guild, Smithtown, N.Y.; exhibited in group shows Nat. Acad. Galleries, N.Y.C., 1970-73. Recipient Charles Pfizer award Nassau County Office Performing and Fine Arts, 1970. Mem. Nat. Assn. Women Artists. Home: 15 Beach Rd Great Neck NY 11204 Office: 10 Hawthorne Lane Great Neck NY 11023

STIRN, ALVA RUTH (MRS. OSCAR WILLIAM STIRN), chem. co. exec.; b. Manning, Ia., Feb. 22, 1900; d. Grant W. and Molly L. (Myatt) Hockett; student Simpson Coll., 1918-20; diploma, certificate, Ia. State Tchrs. Coll., 1924; m. Oscar William Stirn, Feb. 16, 1934; 1 son, Oscar Nicholas. Tchr. pub. schs., Ia., 1921-23, Chgo., 1931-37; sec., treas. Reliable Paste & Chem. Co., Chgo., 1954-68, treas., 1968-73, v.p., 1973—, also dir. Mem. Mu Phi Epsilon. Methodist (mem. ch. bd. 1956-60, 63-65). Mem. Order Eastern Star (worthy matron 1944 grand Esther Ill. 1952). Club: Prairie (Chgo.). Home: 1018 Spruce Dr Manning IA 51455 Office: 3560 S Shields St Chicago IL 60609

STITES, M(ARY) ELIZABETH GAERTNER (MRS. RAYMOND S. STITES), educator; b. N.Y.C., July 28, 1915; d. Otto and Olivia (Stites) Gaertner; B.Arch., N.Y. U., 1940; student U. Vienna, summer 1961; m. Raymond S. Stites, July 29, 1938; 1 dau., Mary Elizabeth (Mrs. Paul B. Moyer II). Statistician research dept. Compton's Advt. Co., N.Y.C., 1936-37; free lance archtl. designer, Yellow Springs, O., 1940-49; asst. art dept. Antioch Coll., 1938-41; faculty dept. art, U. Md. Coll. Arts and Scis., 1949—, adminstrv. asst., 1959—, asso. prof., 1967—; lectr. religious architecture, history architecture, archtl. studies of Leonardo da Vinci. Mem. Yellow Springs, Town Planning Commn., 1944-45. Mem. Coll. Art Assn., Soc. Archtl. Historians, Archaeol. Inst. Am., A.I.A. Episcopalian. Archtl. research, drawings The Arts and Man (R.S. Stites), 1940; (with R.S. Stites) The Sublimations of Leonardo da Vinci, 1970. Contbr. articles to Book of Knowledge Grolier Soc., 1952, New Cath. Ency., 1965. Address: 11212 Kenilworth Av Garrett Park MD 20766

STITH, ANN CARTER SEE (MRS. RICHARD T. STITH, JR.), civic worker; b. Nashville, Nov. 21, 1920; d. Frank Montgomery and Ann Carter (Smith) Sec; student Vassar Coll., 1938-40; A.B., Washington U., 1942; m. Richard T. Stith, Jr., Nov. 27, 1943; children—Richard, Carter, Kate, Laura, Rebecca. Chmn., Jail Relocation Com., 1965, County Charter Com., 1968; mem. bd. Grand Jurors Assn. St. Louis County, 1963-72, pres., 1964-66; chmn. bd. County Jail Visitors, 1965—; mem. bd. Lakeside Center for Boys, 1967—; chmn. Corrections Task Force Mo. Assn. for Social Welfare; mem. Justice Task Force East-West Gateway Council; bd. mem. St. Louis-St. Louis County White Ho. Conf. on Edn., St. Louis Alliance for Shaping Safer Cities; mem. citizens adv. com. State Legislature. Bd. dirs. Am. Correctional Assn. Named Woman of Year for social responsibility Globe-Democrat, 1966; recipient John Augustus Meml. award St. Louis Parole Assn., 1966, Matrix award Theta Sigma Phi, 1966, Fleur de Lis award Maryville Coll., 1968. Home: 37 Aberdeen Pl Clayton MO 63105

STITT, KATHLEEN R., educator; b. Roanoke, Ala., Dec. 27, 1926; d. Mabrey and Bertha (Green) Stitt; B.S., U. Ala., 1946, M.S., 1955; Ph.D., Ohio State U., 1965. Dietetic intern U. Hosps., Cleve., 1946-47, adminstrv. dietitian, 1947-49; chief dietitian Selma (Ala.) Bapt. Hosp., 1949-54; instr., research asso. U. Ala., 1955-59, asst. prof., research asso., 1959-63, prof., head foods and nutrition dept., 1965—. Recipient Mead Johnson Grad. award, 1964-65. Mem. Am. (sect. chmn. 1970—, chmn. scholarship com., chmn. acad. requirements com. 1972—), Ala. (pres. 1955-56), Tuscaloosa (pres. 1967-68) dietetic assns., Am., Ala. (sect. chmn. 1955-63, pres. elect 1974-75) home econs. assns., A.A.A.S. (life), Am. Sch. Food Service Assn., Soc. Nutrition Edn., Sigma Xi, Sigma Delta Epsilon (chmn. scholarship com. 1969-70), Phi Upsilon Omicron, Delta Kappa Gamma (pres. chpt. 1972—). Contbr. articles to profl. jours. Home: 6 Wood Manor Apts Tuscaloosa AL 35401 Office: Box 3344 U Ala University AL 35486

STITT, PAULINE GEORGE, physician; b. Frewsburg, N.Y., May 28, 1909; d. Austin W. and Allene (Davis) Stitt; M.D., U. Mich., 1933; M.P.H., U. Cal., 1954. Student intern Ypsilanti (Mich.) State Hosp., 1932-33; jr. resident pediatrics and acute communicable diseases Buffalo City Hosp., 1933-34; staff pediatrician, attending physician W.C.A. Hosp. and Jamestown (N.Y.) Gen. Hosp., 1934-40; pvt. practice pediatrics, Jamestown, 1934-40; asst. physician Newton Meml. Hosp., Tb worker Chautauqua County, N.Y., 1940-41; pediatric staff mem., asst. med. supt. Edward J. Meyer Meml. Hosp., Buffalo, 1941-43; instr. pediatrics, psychiatry U. Buffalo Sch. Medicine, 1941-43; asst. surgeon USPHS, 1943; asst. chief Bur. Maternal and Child Health, also Bur. Crippled Children's Services, Honolulu, 1943-45, 47-48, chief, 1948-51; regional med. cons. Atlanta office U.S. Children's Bur., 1945-56; lectr. in developmental pediatrics, sr. pediatrician Children's Hosp. of East Bay, Sch. Pub. Health, U. Cal., Berkeley, 1951-53; acting asst. health officer in charge Maternal and Child Health, also Crippled Children's Services, Alameda County, Cal., 1953; asst. prof. maternal child health Harvard Sch. Pub. Health, Boston, 1954-61; asso. prof. preventive medicine and pediatrics, chief home med. service Mass. Meml. Hosps., Boston U. Sch. Medicine, 1961-62; chief Children's Bur., child health studies br., Washington, 1962-66; chief home care sect., home health and related services DMCA, BSS, U.S. Dept. Health, Edn. and Welfare, Washington, 1966-70; health forums coordinator White House Conf. Children, 1970; prof. pub. health U. Hawaii, 1972—, also chmn. maternal and child health; practice as physician, 1961; med. officer, maternal and infant health Boston Lying-in Hosp., 1954-62; part time lectr. Simmons Coll. Sch. Nursing, also Sch. Social Work, Boston U. Sch. Nursing, Boston Coll. Sch. Social Work. Recipient WHO fellowship for study in Far East in orgn. pub. health teaching methods, 1957. Diplomate Am. Bd. Pediatrics, Am. Bd. Preventive Medicine and Pub. Health. Mem. Am. Pub. Health Assn., Am. Acad. Pediatrics. Home: 3900 Watson Pl NW Washington DC 20016

STIVER, MYRTLE PEARL, nurse, bus. exec.; b. Osprey Twp., Ont., Can., Nov. 9, 1908; d. Henry and Abbie Olga (Smith) Stiver; R.N., Toronto Western Hosp., 1932; certificate Pub. Health Nursing, U. Toronto, 1940; B.S. in Nursing, Columbia, 1947. Individual practice nursing, Toronto, Ont., 1932-39; staff nurse Victorian Order Nursing, Toronto, 1940-41; staff nurse Toronto Dept. Health, 1941-43; nurse cons. Ont. Dept. Health, 1943-48; dir. pub. health nursing Ottawa Dept. Health, 1948-52; gen. sec.-treas. Canadian Nurses Assn., Montreal, 1952-60, hon. life mem., 1966—, exec. dir., Ottawa, 1960-63; exec. sec.-treas. Canadian Nurses' Found., 1963-64; co-owner Croft, Canadian handcraft shop, Baysville, Muskoka, Ont., 1963—. Mem. nat. nursing adv. com. Victorian Order Nurses Can., 1952-63, Can. Civil Def., 1952-62; mem. dental med. services adv. bd. Canadian govt., 1955-62; mem. vocational adv. com. Dist. Muskoka Bd. Edn., 1969—. Bd. dirs. Canadian Citizenship Council. Recipient Centennial medal Govt. Can., 1968. Fellow Am. Pub. Health Assn.; mem. Bus. and Profl. Women's Club (v.p. Bracebridge 1969-71, pres. 1971-73), Zonta Internat. (pres. Ottawa 1961-63), Venerable Order St. John Jerusalem (comdr. sister), Ont. Pub. Health Assn. (hon. life mem.). Baptist (deacon). Club: University Women's (Toronto, Montreal). Author: (with Christine Livingston) Patient Care in the Home, 1965. Address: Moosewood Baysville Muskoka ON Canada

STIVERS, CAMILLA DAY MCDOWELL, ednl. adminstr.; b. Evanston, Ill., Apr. 10, 1938; d. James Peter and Virginia Agnete (Schonlau) McDowell; B.A., Wellesley Coll., 1960; M. Liberal Arts, Johns Hopkins, 1967; m. George Spencer Stivers, June 12, 1959 (div.); children—Peter Lloyd, Carl Erickson. Exec. dir. Higher Edn. Council Urban Affairs, Balt., 1968-71; project dir. Title I Project, Towson (Md.) State Coll., 1971-72; coll. relations officer, mem. faculty Marymount Coll., Arlington, Va., 1972-74; Coordinator Anacostia Community Devel. Consortium, Washington, 1974—. Project dir. Washington area Women's Colls. Project Women's Higher Edn., 1973-74. Founding mem., mem. edn. task force St. George's Community Council, Balt., 1971-72. Sec. bd. Urban Observatory Balt., 1969-71; founder, mem. bd. Recruitment Task Force, Inc., Balt., 1971—. Mem. Phi Beta Kappa. Home: 6216 Western Av Chevy Chase MD 20015 Office: 2906 Martin Luther King Av SE Washington DC 20032

STOCK, FRANCES PATRICIA PECHANEC (MRS. VINCENT EUGENE STOCK), educator; b. Portland, Ore., July 31, 1937; d. Frank Mark and Josephine L. (Piazza) Pechanec; student Lewis and Clark Coll., 1955-56, Portland State Coll., 1956-57; B.S., U. Ore., 1959; postgrad. San Francisco State Coll., 1961, U. Cal. at Berkeley, 1961, Fresno State Coll., 1962-64; M.S., U. Ore., 1963; m. Vincent Eugene Stock, Aug. 17, 1963. IBM proof operator Fed. Res. Bank San Francisco, Portland, Ore., 1955; clk., janitress Russell Stover Co., Portland, Ore., 1956-57; ratio assessor Lane County Ct. House, Eugene, Ore., 1957-58; typist, bus. machine operator Bur. Bus. Research, Eugene, 1958; tchr. Thomas Downey High Sch., Modesto, Cal., 1960-61; tchr., chmn. women's phys. edn. dept. Coalinga (Cal.) Joint Union High Sch., 1961-65; asso. supr. dept. phys. activities, master tchr. U. Cal., Santa Barbara, 1965—, rep. faculty legislature acad. senate, 1971—, chmn. open registration phys. activities dept., 1970—. Lectr. colls., univs., high schs., assns., clubs, ednl. tv, others; cons. ednl. film on women's self def., 1972. Recipient award Wadsworth Pub. Co., 1969. Mem. Am. Assn. U. Profs., Am., Cal. (treas. tri-counties chpt. 1966-69) assns. health, phys. edn. and recreation, Western (chmn. by-laws com., exec. bd. 1969-71), Nat. (chmn. bylaws com. 1972-73) assns. phys. edn. for coll. women, Nat. Fedn. Bus. and Profl. Women's Clubs, Goleta Valley Bus. and Profl. Women's Club. Author: (with W. Hammer, A. Gallon, K. Hogarth, J. Luccio) Curriculum Design for Physical Activities, 1966; Personal Safety and Defense for Women, 1968. Contbr. articles to profl. jours. Home: 35 Morada Lane Santa Barbara CA 93105 Office: Dept Phys Activities Robertson Gymnasium U Cal Santa Barbara CA 93106

STOCK, MARY-JULE SCHRAUFNAGEL (MRS. BERNARD J. STOCK), psychologist; b. Ashland, Wis., Dec. 14, 1927; d. Michael and Mary Catherine (Ruby) Schraufnagel; B.A., Coll. St. Scholastica, 1959; M.Ed., Xavier U., 1965; Ph.D. (grad. asst.), St. Louis U., 1969; m. Bernard J. Stock, June 4, 1966. Reporter, Ashland (Wis.) Daily Press, 1945-46; tchr. St. Scholastica Priory, Duluth, Minn., 1949-62, Mother of Sorrows, Cin., 1962-65; counselor St. Louis U., 1965-68, asst. dir. counseling, 1967-68; dir. counseling Fontbonne Coll., St.

Louis, 1968-70; research asso. Mo. Inst. Psychiatry, 1970-71; clin.-counseling psychologist VA Hosp., St. Louis, 1971—. Cons., U. Mo. sch. medicine, St. Louis, 1970-73. VA trainee, 1965-66. Mem. Am., S.W., Mo. psychol. assns. Am. Personnel and Guidance Assn. (dir. St. Louis chpt. 1969-70). Roman Catholic. Home: 12856 Big Bend Blvd Kirkwood MO 63122 Office: VA Hospital Jefferson Barracks Division St Louis MO 63125

STOCKBAR, LINDA LOUISE, educator; b. Joliet, Ill., July 3, 1945; d. John Joseph and Lillian Lucy (Long) Stockbar; B.S. in Edn., Eastern Ill. U., 1968, M.S. in Edn., 1974. Tchr. jr. high sch. English, speech, drama and math., Kankakee, Ill., 1969—. Vice pres. Kankakee Valley Theatre, 1974-75, bd. dirs., 1975—; treas. Community Arts Council Kankakee, 1974—. Mem. Speech Communications Assn., Am. Fedn. Tchrs., Kappa Delta, Pi Kappa Delta. Home: 991 River Dr Kankakee IL 60901 Office: 240 Warren Av Kankakee IL 60901

STOCKBURGER, CASSANDRA NAOMI, charitable orgn. exec.; b. Ga., June 28, 1925; d. Walter Green and Bessie Bell (Boyd) Stockburger; B.A., Bethel Coll., 1947; M.A., Scarritt Coll., 1952. Tchr., Colegio Americano, Cali, Colombia, 1947-50; program dir. YMCA, Chattanooga, 1952-53; tchr. Montreat (N.C.) Prep. Sch., 1953-54; area dir. migrant ministry Nat. Council Chs., Memphis, 1954-63; exec. dir. Nat. Com. on Edn. Migrant Children, N.Y.C., 1963—. Cons., U.S. Office Edn., Vista. Bd. dirs. Child Devel. Asso. Consortium. Mem. Nat. Council Orgns. for Children and Youth (dir.), Nat. Council Agrl. Life and Labor (dir.). Presbyn. Home: 245 E 19th St New York City NY 10003 Office: 145 E 32d St New York City NY 10016

STOCKMAN, EDITH (MRS. MURRAY STOCKMAN), artist; b. N.Y.C., Aug. 12, 1906; d. Simon and Anna (Cohen) Blum; student Parsons Sch. Design, 1929-31, Art Students League, 1934-40; m. Murray Stockman, June 25, 1929; 1 son, Lewis. One woman show Eggleston Gallery, N.Y.C., 1952, Fairleigh Dickinson U., N.J., 1959; exhibited in group shows Jersey City Mus., Audubon Artists, Nat. Arts Club, Soc. Painters in Casein, Allied Artists, Met. Mus., Riverside Mus., N.Y. City Center; represented in permanent collections Troy, N.Y., Boulder, Colo., Miami, Fla., Washington. Recipient awards L.I. Artists, Nat. Assn. Women Artists, Queens Bar Assn. Mem. Nat. Assn. Women Artists (co-chmn. travelling oil show 1970—; dir. 1974—). Home: 125-10 Queens Blvd Kew Gardens NY 11415

STOCKSTROM, GERTRUDE TODD SCHAEFFER (MRS. CARL STOCKSTROM), civic worker; b. St. Louis; d. Louis and Amy (Tivy) Schaeffer; student Washington U., St. Louis, 1959; m. Carl Stockstrom, Dec. 12, 1917; children—Sherril (Mrs. Charles Richard Jacoby), Charles Louis. Mem. Aux. Good Shepherds, 1958-64. Bd. dirs. Med. Mission House Studies, St. Joseph Sch. for Deaf. Mem. U.D.C., Confederate Dames (dir. 1958-64), Friends of St. Louis Sch. Nursing (dir.), Friends St. Louis City Hosp., Mo. Hist. Soc., Jefferson County Heritage and Landmarks Corp., Jr. League. Home: White Oaks Montebello Rd Imperial MO 63052

STOCKTON, DORIS GROVE SKILLMAN (MRS. FRED D. STOCKTON), educator; b. New Brunswick, N.J., Feb. 9, 1924; d. Roland H. and Mary (Grove) Skillman; B.Sc., Douglass Coll., 1945; M.Sc., Brown U., 1947, Ph.D., 1959; m. Fred D. Stockton, Aug. 7, 1948; children—Frederick Richard, Thomas Todd. Instr. math. Rutgers, The State U., 1946, U. Conn., 1947-52, Brown U., 1952-53; mem. faculty U. Mass., Amherst, 1954—, asso. prof. math., 1973—. Cons. math. to pub. cos. Active Boy Scouts Am., Belchertown, Mass., 1963—. Mem. Am. Math. Soc., Math. Assn. Am., Nat. Council Tchrs. Math., Phi Beta Kappa, Sigma Xi. Author: (with H.M. Roberts) Elements of Mathematics, 1956; Essential Mathematics, 1972; Essential Algebra, 1973; Essential Algebra with Functions, 1973. Home: RFD 1 Belchertown MA 01007 Office: Dept Math U Mass Amherst MA 01002

STOCKTON, RUTH SMALL (MRS. TRUMAN ALEX STOCKTON, JR.), state senator; b. Ridgefield Park, N.J., June 6, 1916; d. Arthur Everett and Mary Rose (Hart) Small; ed. Vassar Coll., Columbia, Colo. U.; m. Truman Alex Stockton, Jr., Nov. 1, 1937; 1 dau., Alexe (Mrs. Bo G. Vikstrom). Co-chmn. 11 Western States Council of Young Republicans, 1946-47; nat. co-chmn. Young Reps., 1947-49; Rep. nat. committeewoman, 1955-56; mem. Colo. Ho. of Reps., 1961-65; mem. Colo. Senate, 1965—. Mem. Gov.'s Com. on Mental Health and Mental Retardation, 1966, Gov.'s Com. on Vocational Rehab., 1966, Gov.'s Council on Alcohol and Drug Abuse, 1971—; adv. council Colo. Workman's Compensation Fund, 1971—. Bd. dirs. Child Welfare Council. Named Woman of the Year, East Jefferson Sentinel, 1969; recipient Golden Bus. and Profl. Women's award, 1966. Methodist. Office: 1765 Glen Dale Dr Lakewood CO 80215

STOCKWELL, DOROTHEA VIVA BOUTWELL (MRS. PAUL STOCKWELL), educator; b. Boston; d. Herbert Raymond and Viva (Drew) Boutwell; B.S., Tchrs. Coll. City of Boston, 1929, M.Ed., 1930; Certificate in Advanced Grad. Specialization, Boston U., 1965; m. Paul Stockwell, June 18, 1938. Tchr. secondary schs., Boston, 1930-35; tchr. spl. class, pub. sch., Portsmouth, N.H., 1935-38; metall. research work Springfield (Mass.) Armory, 1942-44; statis. work Cornell U., Ithaca, N.Y., 1944-45; founder, dir. Brattleboro (Vt.) Adult Edn. Program, 1947-53; tchr. rural sch., Guilford, Vt., 1951-53; demonstration tchr. Lyndon Campus Sch., Lyndon Center, Vt., 1953-56; instr. Lyndon State Coll., Lyndon Center, 1956-58, asso. prof. psychology, 1958-70, counselor, 1958-70; faculty, counselor Antioch-Putney Grad. Sch., 1970—; counselor Woolman Hill, Deerfield, Mass., 1970—; mem. faculty Vt. Community Coll., 1973—, Mark Hopkins Coll., 1972—; mem. field faculty Goddard Coll.; pvt. practice psychotherapy, 1960—. Research coll. cons., 1965-68; pres., counselor Heifer Hill Learning Center, West Brattleboro, Vt. Mem. Assn. for Humanistic Psychology, Am. Guidance and Personnel Assn., Assn. World Colls. and Univs., Adult Edn. Assn. Am., Am. Assn. Higher Edn., Am. Assn. U. Profs. Home: Bonnyvale Rd RD 2 Box 196 A West Brattleboro VT 05301

STODDARD, GRACE IRENE JENKINS (MRS. HERBERT C. STODDARD), sculptor; b. Green Bay, Wis.; d. Wyburn C. and Mary (Tellor) Jenkins; student St. Xaviers Coll., 1915, Acad. Fine Arts Chgo., 1921, Ringling Art Sch., Sarasota, Fla., 1951; m. Joseph V. Sullivan, June 2, 1922 (dec. Jan. 1951); children—Colette (Mrs. Andrew Matosky), Joseph W.; m. 2d, Herbert C. Stoddard, Mar. 17, 1953. One man shows Longboat Art League, 1967, Hilton Leech Gallery, 1964—, Sarasota (Fla.) Art Assn., 1964—; exhibited in group shows Manatee Art League, Brodenton, Fla., 1961—. Mem. Nat. League Am. Penwomen (recipient first prize sculpture, 1972), Longboat Key Art Assn., Sarasota Art Assn., Manatee Art League, Fine Arts Assn. Sarasota. Home: 1543 Palmetto Lane Sarasota FL 33580

STODOLSKY, SUSAN SILVERMAN (MRS. MARVIN STODOLSKY), educator; b. N.Y.C., June 7, 1940; d. Abner H. and Ruth (Paskin) Silverman; A.B., Antioch Coll., 1961; M.A. (Nat. Def. Edn. Act fellow), U. Chgo., 1963, Ph.D., 1965; m. Marvin Stodolsky, Sept. 19, 1965; children—Amalia, Daniel. Research asso. Pre-Sch. Project, Harvard Research and Devel. Center, 1965-66, asst. prof. Harvard Grad. Sch. Edn., 1966-67; asst. prof. edn. U. Chgo., 1967-72, asso. prof. edn., 1972—, asst. prof. Com. Human Devel., 1970-72, asso. prof. Com. Human Devel., 1972—. Mem. Soc. Research in Child Devel., Am. Ednl. Research Assn. Editor Elementary Sch. Jour., 1967-72. Office: Dept Education U Chicago 5835 S Kimbark Chicago IL 60637

STOERTZ, CYNTHIA RIGGS (MRS. GEORGE E. STOERTZ), sci. writer, editor; b. Martha's Vineyard, Mass., June 15, 1931; d. Sidney Noyes and Dionis (Coffin) Riggs; B.A. in Geology, Antioch Coll., 1953; postgrad. George Washington U., 1965-66, Dept. Agr. Grad. Sch., 1964-69; m. George E. Stoertz, Aug. 10, 1952; children—William S., James C., Mary W., Ann C., Robert R. Free lance writer, 1953-64; mus. aide Smithsonian Oceanographic Sorting Center, 1964-65; asso. editor Ocean Sci. News, news editor Geo-Marine Tech., 1965-67; oceanography asst., press sec. Congressman Hastings Keith, 1967; mng. editor Marine Tech. Soc. Jour., 1967-71; editor MTS Memo, 1967-71, Marine Resources Digest, Washington, 1968—; free lance writer, editor, researcher Nat. Geographic Soc., Washington, 1971—; editor Petroleum Today, 1972—. Mem. Com. Needs and Opportunities for Disadvantaged in Marine Sci., 1968-69; cons. Ocean Sci. & Engring., Inc., Riviera Beach, Fla., 1968-69, Marine bd. Nat. Acad. Engring. 1972—. Pres. recreation dept. Parents Club, Washington, 1959-61. Sec. Amateur Fencers League Am., Washington, 1960. Recipient Antarctic Service medal U.S. Dept. Def., 1965, Sch. Betterment award D.C. Pub. Sch. System, 1968-69, Named Outstanding Women in Marine Sci., New Eng. sec. Marine Tech. Soc., 1971. Mem. A.A.A.S., Am. Geol. Inst., Am. Geophys. Union, Antarctic Press Club, Assn. Earth Sci. Editors, Geol. Soc. Am., Geol. Soc. Washington, Marine Tech. Soc. Unitarian. Club: Gonzaga Mothers' (Washington). Contbr. articles and photographs to numerous publs. Home: 2518 Que St SE Washington DC 20020 Office: Am Petroleum Inst 1801 K St NW Washington DC 20006

STOESSEL, CAROLE JEAN (MRS. ALEXANDER W. ZVONAR), physician, pianist; b. Salisbury, N.C., July 14, 1936; d. Frank William and India Beatrice (Aldredge) Stoessel; student piano with Raymond Lewenthal, 1954-55; B.A. magna cum laude, Catawba Coll., 1959; M.D. (Nancy Lybrook Lasater Reynolds scholar), Bowman Gray Sch. Medicine, Wake Forest U., 1963; m. Alexander W. Zvonar, Nov. 2, 1963. Concert pianist recitals, concerts, 1950-59, 71—; various tv and radio appearances, 1950-55; intern pathology Columbia Presbyn. Med. Center, N.Y.C., 1963-64, resident fellow dept. microbiology, 1964-65; physician Rowan County (N.C.) chpt. A.R.C. Blood mobile Unit, 1972—; dealer in antique dolls, 1967—. Mem. spl. adv. com. to trustees Historic Salisbury Found., Inc., also charter mem. Mem. Children Am. Revolution. Democrat. Lutheran. Address: 329 S Fulton St Salisbury NC 28144

STOGSDILL, CHARLENE GRACE (MRS. BYRON A. STOGSDILL), educator; b. Cheyenne, Wyo., June 20, 1925; d. Anthony Martin and Grace Lillian (Thomas) Ries; B.A. in Edn., U. Wyo., 1950, M.A., 1966, profl. diploma, 1969; m. Willard Roth, Apr. 14, 1945 (div. Nov. 1947); 1 son, James Paul; m. 2d, Byron A. Stogsdill, July 26, 1952; 1 dau., Kym Meroa. Reporter, Wyo. State Tribune, Cheyenne, 1944, Laramie (Wyo.) Republican Boomerang, 1944-45; tchr. pub. schs., Basin, Wyo., 1945-47, Sheridan, Wyo., 1947-48, Cheyenne, 1948-50, 1957-66; psychometrist Ruth Chaplin Center, Cheyenne, 1966—; reporter Wyo. Eagle, Cheyenne, 1951; instr. U.S. Air Force, 1951-57; instr. adult basic edn., Cheyenne, 1965-68. Bd. dirs. Wyo. Assn. Mental Health, also county pres., 1962, Cheyenne Community Council, 1971—; mem. Cheyenne Community Concert Assn., Cheyenne Little Theatre. Republican candidate for Wyo. Ho. of Reps., 1964, 66. Recipient Cheyenne's Young Woman of Yr. award, 1960; Elsie M. Spaulding scholarship local br. Am. Assn. U. Women, 1963. Mem. N.E.A., Wyo. Edn. Assn., Am. Assn. U. Women (past br. pres.; div. pres. 1969-71, legislative com. 1971-73, Nat. (regional dir. 1969-71, 2d v.p. 1971-73), Wyo. (pres. 1965-67) fedns. press women, Am., Wyo. personnel and guidance assns., Colo.-Wyo. Assn. Women Deans and Counselors, Cheyenne Classroom Tchrs. Assn. (parliamentarian 1957-69; editor; welfare chmn.), Cheyenne Adminstrs. and Spl. Personnel Assn., D.A.R. (chpt. regent 1964-66), Am. Legion Aux., Daus. Am. Colonists (Wyo. regent 1964-66), Psi Chi, Theta Alpha Phi, Kappa Kappa Iota (conclave pres. 1970-71, state pres. 1973-74), Phi Sigma Alpha (hon.). Methodist (charter mem.; Sunday sch. supt. 1958-60; trustee 1963-66). Club: First Nighters (pres. 1968-70, pres. interclub council 1970-71). Mem. Order Eastern Star. Home: 3457 Essex Rd Cheyenne WY 82001

STOHRER, SISTER MARY BAPTIST, musician; b. Urbana, Ill., Apr. 13, 1927; d. Walter Albert and Elvera Emily (Glanner) Stohrer; B.A. magna cum laude, Rosary Coll., River Forest, Ill., 1957; M.Mus. magna cum laude, Inst. Pius XII, Florence, Italy, 1961; Ph.D., U. Wis., 1974. Joined Dominican Sisters of Sinsinawa, Wis., Roman Catholic Ch., 1944; profl. tchr. music, 1947—, recently specializing on song lit. of 19th Century; mem. faculty Edgewood Coll., Madison, Wis., 1965-69; prof., chmn. dept. music Rosary Coll., 1973—; performing mezzo-soprano, 1958—. Mem. Am. Musicol. Soc., Liturgical Conf. Address: Rosary Coll 7900 W Division St River Forest IL 60305

STOICA, LUCRETIA LETITIA, assn. exec.; b. Youngstown, O.; d. George and Elena (Grovu) Stoica; M.A., U. King Ferdinand I, Cluj, Romania, 1945. With Nationalities Services Center, Cleve., 1947—, dep. dir., 1959-63, exec. dir., editor News Bull., 1963—. Vice chmn. Christian Orthodox drive, 1966-67; mem. Interracial-Intercultural Com. Cleve. Welfare Fedn., 1965-67; cons. Cleve. Urban Coalition Community Relations Task Force, 1969; mem. Mayor's Commn. on Aging, 1970—; mem. Manpower and Devel. Commn., 1971—; mem. Bi-Centennial Commn. Trustee Cleve. Internat. Program, Fedn. for Community Planning, 1970—, Cleve. Area Arts Council, 1971—, Ohio Citizens Council, 1971—; bd. overseers Case Western Res. U., 1972—. Recipient Internat. Service award Rotary Club Cleve., 1963. Mem. Nat. Assn. Intergroup Relations Ofcls. (co-chmn. program com. Cleve. chpt.). Romanian Orthodox. Club: Zonta Internat. (Cleve.). Home: 4401 Oak Park Av Cleveland OH 44109 Office: 1001 Huron Rd Cleveland OH 44115

STOKES, BETTIE EUGENE GREEN (MRS. CHARLES G. STOKES), educator; b. New Orleans, July 18, 1907; d. Lawrence and Matilda (Taylor) Green; B.S., Tuskegee Inst., 1949, M.Ed., 1963; postgrad. Ohio State U., 1966; m. Gladstone Hodge, Jan. 9, 1944 (div. June 1948); m. Charles G. Stokes, Nov. 10, 1952. Clerical, adminstrv., sec. VA Hosp., Tuskegee, Ala., 1928-62; career devel. guidance Tuskegee Inst., 1964-71. Trustee, sec. bd. Greenwood Cemetery Assn. Mem. State Steering com. Ala. Women's Polit. Caucus, 1972-74, vice chmn., 1973-74; mem. steering com. Nat. Women's Polit. Caucus. Recipient Outstanding Performance award VA, 1958, Incentive award 1959. Mem. Nat. Vocational Guidance Assn., Coll. Personnel Assn., Am. Assn. U. Women, Am. Fedn. Govt. Employees (pres. 1950-52), N.A.A.C.P. (sec. Tuskegee br. 1944-46), Am. Civil Liberties Union, Nat., Ala. personnel and guidance assns., Southeastern Council on Family Relations (chmn. resources and materials com. 1973—), Tuskegee Civic Assn. Home: PO Box 477 Tuskegee Institute AL 36088

STOKES, DORIS MARSONE NICKEL (MRS. CECIL GAINES STOKES), univ. dean; b. Brazil, Ind., July 16, 1914; d. John H. and Ethel (Beaton) Nickel; B.S., Ind. State U., 1939; M.S. Ind. U., 1945, postgrad., 1959; postgrad. Columbia, 1941, Northwestern U., 1950; m. Cecil Gaines Stokes, Aug. 6, 1960; step-children—Cecil Gaines, J. Burt, T. Eugene. Tchr. bus. Warrensburg (Ill.) High Sch., 1939-42; tchr. bus., dean girls Charleston (Ill.) High Sch., 1942-47; instr. secretarial sci. U. Louisville, 1947-53, asst. prof. edn., 1953—, asst. dean women, 1953-55, acting dean women, 1955-58, dean women, 1958-70, asso. dean students, 1970—. Bd. dirs. Louisville Area Mental Health Center, sec. bd., 1966-69; mem. personnel com. Louisville chpt. A.R.C., 1966-70; personnel com. YWCA, Louisville, 1967—, bd. dirs., 1971—. Mem. Nat. Ky. (pres. 1960-62) assns. women deans and counselors, Am. Assn. U. Women (sec. 1953-55), Nat. Soc. Cwens (adv. dean), Mortar Bd., P.E.O., Delta Pi Epsilon, Pi Lambda Theta, Delta Kappa Gamma. Clubs: University Louisville Women's (pres. 1964-65); Altrusa (chmn. internat. relations 1960, 64, chmn. vocational services com. 1968-69, 71-72, dir. 1967-69) (Louisville). Home: 4711 Kitty Hawk Way Louisville KY 40207

STOKES, ELIZABETH EARLE HENDON (MRS. WILLIAM G. STOKES), educator; b. Richland, Tex., June 5, 1922; d. Walter Lee and Gertrude (McCord) Henden; B.S., Sam Houston State Coll., 1942, M.A., 1947; Specialist in Edn. degree, George Peabody Coll. for Tchrs., 1956; Ed.D., North Tex. State U., 1960; m. William G. Stokes, May 1, 1942; children—William Glenn III, Sara Lynne. Field Worker Tex. Dept. Pub. Welfare, 1942-44; tchr. Tex. Pub. Schs., 1945-46, 51-53; VA appraiser Navarro Jr. Coll., Corsicana, Tex., 1949-50, instr. sociology, 1948-49; sch. psychologist Clarksville (Tenn.) City Schs., 1955-57; asst. prof. Northwestern State U., Natchitoches, La., 1957-58; instr. N.Tex. State U., Denton, 1959-60; mem. faculty Austin Peay State U., Clarksville, 1960—, prof. psychology, 1964—. Therapist Harriet Cohn Guidance Center, Clarksville, 1961-64; Head Start psychol. cons. Clarksville-Montgomery County Schs., 1965-69; dir. Nat. Def. Edn. Act Inst. for Tchrs. of Disadvantaged Children, 1968. Pres. Montgomery County Council Retarded Children, 1960-63; chmn. mental health com. Regional Planning Commn., Clarksville, 1966-68; chmn. Human Relations Council, Clarksville, 1968—. Mem. Am., Southeastern psychol. assns., Am., Tenn. (pres. 1966-67, editor newsletter 1965-66, 67-68) personnel and guidance assns., Southeastern Assn. Counselor Educators and Supervisors, Tenn. Edn. Assn., N.E.A. Home: 316 Irene Dr Clarksville TN 37040

STOKES, PEG LEE EWING (MRS. LYALL N. STOKES), author, lectr.; b. Walkerton, Ind.; d. Sid C. and Marie (Mikesell) Ewing; student South Bend Conservatory Music, Christian Writers Inst., 1952; m. Lyall N. Stokes, Mar. 21, 1941. Dir. Med. Service, Wright Field, Dayton, O., 1942-45; Community Club awards dir. WFBM-TV, Indpls., 1957-60; dir. Town and Country div. Wilking Music Co., Indpls., 1963; lectr. Redpath Lecture Bur., Chgo., 1963—. Dir. Dorothy Carnegie Course for Central Ind., 1968-70; free lance newspaper columnist. Bd. dirs. Lakeland Humane Soc., Warsaw, Ind., 1955-60, bd. dirs. emeritus, 1962—. Recipient awards Booth Tarkington Civic Theatre, 1968, 69; several Dorothy Carnegie awards. Mem. Nat. League Am. Pen Women (1st v.p. Indpls. br. chpt. 1966-68, editor newsletter 1965-67), Internat. Platform Assn., Nat. Fedn. Press Women, Women's Nat. Book Assn., Theta Sigma Phi. Clubs: Women's Press (Ind.), Women's Four-F (pres. 1969-71), Masquers (dir. 1970-71). Author: Out of the Darkness, 1951; I Am Anthony, 1961; Think and Grow Slim, 1963. Home: 124 Dogwood Lane Bayside Estates Fort Myers Beach FL 33931

STOKES, MRS. WILLIAM E. D., JR. (LUCIA HOBSON STOKES), social worker; b. Washington, July 7, 1909; d. Richmond P. and Grizelda H. (Hull) Hobson; student N.Y. Sch. Applied Design Women, N.Y.C., 1927, U. Cal. at Los Angeles, 1928, Chouinard Sch. Art, Los Angeles, 1929; m. William E. Dodge Stokes, Jr., Aug. 16, 1938; children—Houston Hobson, Sylvia Hobson. Partner Freeman & Hobson, costume design shop, N.Y.C., 1931-32; sec. to pres. World Narcotic Def. Assn., 1933-34; display dept. Jay Thorpe, N.Y.C., 1937-38. Vol. social work Navy Relief Soc., 1942-44; bd. dirs., exec. com. Berkshire County chpt. A.R.C., 1967-71; dir. Pittsfield Gen. Hosp., mem. exec. com., 1956-59, 61-67, chmn. pub. relations com., 1959-67, mem. bldg. com., 1956-63, mem. bldg. and grounds com., 1964-67, chmn. decorating com., 1964-67; bd. mgrs. Daus. of Cin., 1968-71; trustee, v.p. Berkshire Garden Center, Stockbridge, Mass., 1948-62; pres. Friends of Lenox Sch., 1957-58. Mem. exec. com. So. Berkshire Women's Republican Club, 1965. Clubs: Lenox Garden (pres. 1955-58), Mahkeenac Boating (pres. 1947—) (Lenox); Country (Pittsfield); Colony (N.Y.C.). Editor Pittsfield Gen. Hosp. Aux. Newsletter, 1955-62. Judging rep. Zone 1, Garden Club Am., 1971-74, also nat. judging chmn., certified life judge flower arrangements. Home: Thistlewood Lenox MA 01240

STOLLMACK, RUBY ELLEN (MRS. FREDRIC H. STOLLMACK), occupational therapist; b. N.Y.C., Jan. 12, 1931; d. Benjamin and Rose (Lazarus) Weisbrod; B.S., N.Y. U., 1952; m. Fredric Herbert Stollmack, Aug. 30, 1953; children—Jody Alison, Kyle Lisa, Noele. Occupational therapist L.I. Home, South Oaks, 1952-54; acting asst. dir. occupational therapy dept. Essex County (N.J.) Hosp. Center, Cedar Grove, 1968—. Jr. Girl Scout leader, Montclair, N.J., 1965-66. Mem. exec. bd. Montclair (N.J.) Action Com., 1969-72; mem. Kimberley Home Sch. Assn., 1965-73. Bd. dirs. Montclair YWCA, 1974—. Mem. Profl. Assn. North Essex, Nat. Council Jewish Women. Home: 53 Stonebridge Rd Montclair NJ 07042 Office: Essex County Hospital Center Fairview Av Cedar Grove NJ 07009

STOLPEN, BEULAH HARRIS (MRS. A. ANTON STOLPEN), pub. co. exec., ednl. cons.; b. Long Island, N.Y.; d. Reuben and Flossie (Haft) Harris; student Hunter Coll., 1951-52, Vassar Coll., 1953, U. Conn., 1968; m. A. Anton Stolpen, Jan. 1, 1946; children—Adam Douglas, Rodger Haft. Buyer infants' and children's wear and toys Saks, N.Y.C., 1942-44; merchandiser infants and children's wear and toys J. Anstendig, N.Y.C., 1944-47; free lance designer and innovator of childrens fashions, N.Y.C., 1941—; pres. Psych-Ed Games, N.Y.C., 1958—; pres. Rolling Reader Pub. Co., Westport, Conn., 1960—; author, program developer Scott Foresman & Co., 1963—. Cons. Nat. Reading Center, 1972-73, Migrant Center, Geneseo, N.Y., 1973—, Children's TV, 1972—. lectr. at universities, clubs and teaching confs. Mem. founding bd. Women's div. United Cerebral Palsy, 1952-54; founder Riverdale, N.Y., chpt. United Cerebral Palsy, 1953. Founder Interfaith Jr. Olympics. Mem. Internat. Reading Assn., Nat. Council Tchrs. of English, Internat. Platform Assn. Patentee teaching devices; creator Johnny Can Read game, 1956; inventor The Rolling Reader, 1958, The Rolling Phonics, 1960, Linguistic Blocks Series, 1963, New Linguistic Blocks Series, 1968, 70, Geome-Trics, 1972, Sum Antics, 1974. Home: 282 North Av Westport CT 06880 also 2301 E St NW Washington DC 20037 Office: 41 W 72d St New York City NY 10023

STOLPIN, DOROTHY FLORENCE MITCHELL (MRS. WILLIAM STOLPIN), registered stock rep.; b. Flint, Mich., June 12, 1917; d. Roger Earl and Neva Marie (Ketrow) Mitchell; A.S., Flint Jr. Coll., 1938; student Mich. State Coll., 1938, Internat. Corr. Schs., 1948-50, Wis. Coll. Music, 1950-53; diploma in higher accounting Baker Bus. U., 1956; B.A. in Bus. Adminstrn., U. Mich. at Flint, 1967; certificates N.Y. Inst. Finance, 1956, 57, 69, Gen. Motors Inst., 1969,

Investment Bankers Assn. Am., 1962; m. William Stolpin, Dec. 24, 1938; children—William R., Roger Mitchell. Pharm. trainee Hurley Hosp. Pharmacy, Flint, 1935-36; pvt. piano tchr., 1930-45; clk. Colony Shop, Whitefish Bay, Wis., 1952, Plimpton Music Shop, Whitefish Bay, 1952; rep. Fahnestock & Co., stock brokerage house, Flint, 1956—. Mailing chmn. Flint Community Players, 1961-68. Sponsor, Things Theatrical. Fellow Harry S. Truman Library Inst. (hon.); mem. Women's Stockbrokers Assn., Am. Assn. U. Women, Internat. Platform Assn., Am. Soc. Archeology, Am. Mgmt. Assn., League Women Voters, Mus. Performing Arts Assn. (charter), UN Assn. U.S., Postal Commemorative Soc., Mich. (sec. Genesee chpt.), Mo. Archeol. socs., Flint Inst. Arts Founders Soc., Am. Anthrop. Assn., Flint Coll. and Cultural Devel. Assn., Genesee County Hist. Mus. Soc., Univ. Musical Soc., Greater Flint Arts Council, Intercontinental Biog. Assn. (life), Internat. Graphoanalysis Soc., Hist. Soc. Mich., Alpha Chi Omega Club (life), Pi Mu, Sigma Chi Lambda. Club: Zonta (treas. 1961, dir. 1965-66), Composer: Four Ducks On A Pond. Home: 140 E Carpenter Rd Flint MI 48505 Office: 346 Saginaw St Flint MI 48502

STOLZ, STEPHANIE BALOG, psychologist, educator; b. Syracuse, N.Y., June 27, 1938; d. Max Landsberg and Clotilda Catherine (Balog) Stolz; B.A., Reed Coll., 1959; M.A., U. Wash., 1961, Ph.D. (USPHS fellow), 1963. Instr. psychology Beloit (Wis.) Coll., 1963-65, asst. prof., 1965-67; dep. chmn. psychology, 1965-67; dir. research Jewish Found. for Retarded Children, Washington, 1967-70; chief Mental Health Small Grants Sec., Nat. Inst. Mental Health, Rockville, Md., 1970—; asst. prof. behavioral analysis dept. psychiatry Johns Hopkins U. Med. Sch., Balt., 1969—. USPHS postdoctoral fellow, 1966-67. Fellow Behavior Therapy and Research Soc.; mem. Am., Md. (mem. exec. council 1970-73) psychol. assns., Psychonomic Soc., Assn. for Advancement Behavior Therapy (sec.-treas. 1974—), Md. Civil Liberties Union (dir. 1970-72), Phi Beta Kappa, Sigma Xi. Asso. editor, Jour. Applied Behavior Analysis, 1973—. Contbr. articles to profl. jours. Home: 10109 Windstream Dr Columbia MD 21044 Office: National Institute Mental Health Fishers Lane Rockville MD 20852

STONBERG, SELMA FRANKS (MRS. ABRAHAM STONBERG), educator; b. Lawrence, Mass.; d. Samuel and Frances (Fishman) Franks; student Radcliffe Coll., 1933-34; A.B., Smith Coll., 1935; postgrad. Boston U., 1951-52; m. Abraham Stonberg, Aug. 13, 1935; children—Jane (Mrs. Jane Rakatansky), Barbara (Mrs. Robert W. Morrison), Margery S. (Mrs. Alberto Berti). Asso. prof. English, Newton Jr. Coll., Newtonville, Mass., 1956—, chmn. dept. humanities, 1973—. Vis. prof. Honolulu Community Coll., 1967; research asst. U. Health Services, Psychiat. Service, Harvard, 1963-68. Mem. Nat. Council Tchrs. English (dir. 1969-72), Assn. English Tchrs. in Two-Year Colls. (exec. sec. 1964-67), Conf. on Coll. Composition and Communication (exec. com. New Eng. region 1966-67), Am. Assn. Jr. Colls. (New Eng. commn. on under achiever 1963), Coll. English Assn., Am. Assn. U. Profs., Nat., Mass., Newton tchrs. assns., English Tchrs. in New Eng. Jr. Colls. (editor newsletter 1963). Author: From Start to Finish, 1970. Home: 280 Boylston St Chestnut Hill MA 02167 Office: Park Pl Newtonville MA 02160

STONE, BARBARA DOROTHY SHELL (MRS. HARRY WEDGEWOOD STONE), educator; b. Los Angeles, Sept. 2, 1942; d. Joseph Claude and Barbara (Morton) Shell; B.A., U. So. Cal., 1964, M.A., 1965, Ph.D., 1968; m. Harry Wedgewood Stone, June 12, 1963; children—Robert William, Steven Edward. Teaching asst. U. So. Cal., Los Angeles, 1964-65; instr. Pepperdine Coll., Los Angeles, 1965-69; asst. prof. polit. sci. Cal. State Univ., Fullerton, 1969-71, asso. prof., 1971—, chmn. dept., 1973—. Bd. dirs. So. Cal. Center for Edn. in Pub. Affairs. Mem. Am., Western, So. Cal. polit. sci. assns., Phi Beta Kappa, Phi Kappa Phi, Pi Sigma Alpha, Delta Gamma. Home: 15840 Arbela Dr Whittier CA 90603 Office: Cal State Univ 800 N State College Blvd Fullerton CA 92631

STONE, BARBARA HASKINS (MRS. OLIVER ELLIS STONE), ednl. cons.; b. Plymouth, Devon, U.K., June 25, 1924; d. Nicholas Henry Hopkins and Meta Malcolm (McCaull) Haskins; B.Sc. (Econs.), U. London, 1950; postgrad. U. Zarogoza, Spain, 1953, U. Sorbonne, France, 1950-53; m. Oliver Ellis Stone, Oct. 9, 1970. Editor, writer, translater, compiler Hutchinson's Sci. and Tech. Pubs., London, Eng., 1950-51, Marshall Plan, Paris, France, 1952-53, food and agrl. tech. OEEC, Paris, France, 1954; sec. The Wildfowl Trust, Slimbridge, U.K., 1955-56; Econometric Soc., Yale U., 1957, A.A.H.P.E.R., Washington, 1958-60, World Confedn. Orgn. of Teaching Profession, Washington, 1960-62, Brookings Instn., Washington, 1963-67; coordinated student planned jour. and projects N.E.A., Washington, 1967-72; freelance writer, editor, ednl. cons., 1972—. Cons., adviser Brit. Fgn. Service and Adminstrn. Office. Mem. Edn. Press Assn. Am. (treas. 1961-62), Washington Film Council, Jevons Soc. Contbr. articles to profl. jours. Home: 1732 Church St NW Washington DC 20036 Office: Box 255 Route 2 Hollywood MD 20636

STONE, DOROTHY MAHARAM (MRS. A. H. STONE), educator; b. Parkersburg, W. Va.; d. Max and Ella (Soloway) Maharam; B.S., Carnegie Inst. Tech., 1937; Ph.D., Bryn Mawr Coll., 1940; m. Arthur H. Stone, Apr. 12, 1942; children—David, Ellen. Asst. lectr. Manchester U., 1952-61; prof. math. Rochester (N.Y.) U., 1961—. Mem. at large NRC, 1972—. Mem. Math. Assn. Am. (mem. commn. undergrad. program 1969-72, Am. Math. Soc. (mem. at large council 1972—). Home: 120 Oakdale Dr Rochester NY 14618

STONE, ELAINE MURRAY (MRS. F. COURTNEY STONE), author, musician, advt. exec.; b. N.Y.C., Jan. 22, 1922; d. H. Murray and Catherine (Fairbanks) Murray-Jacoby; student Juilliard Sch. Music, 1939-41; diploma N.Y. Coll. Music, 1942; licentiate in organ Trinity Coll. of Music, London, Eng., 1947; student U. Miami, 1952, Fla. Inst. Tech., 1963; m. F. Courtney Stone, May 30, 1944; children—Catherine Margaret (Mrs. Robert Louis Rayburn), Pamela Elizabeth (Mrs. Don Webb), Victoria Francis. Organist, choir dir. St. Ignatius Episcopal Ch., 1940-44; accompanist Strawbridge Ballet on Tour, N.Y.C., 1944; organist All Saints Episcopal Ch., Ft. Lauderdale, Fla., 1951-54, St. John's Episcopal Ch., Eau Gallie, Fla., 1956-59, First Christian Ch., Melbourne, Fla., 1962-63, United Ch. of Christ, Melbourne, 1963-65; piano studio, Eau Gallie, 1955-70; editor-in-chief Cass, Inc.; dir. continuity radio sta. WTAI, AM-FM, Melbourne, 1971—. Vice pres. pub. relations consol. Cybertronics, Inc. Exec. bd. Women's Assn., Brevard Symphony, 1967—. Recipient 1st place in piano Ashley Hall, 1935-39, S.C. State Music Contest, 1939. Mem. Children Am. Revolution (past N.Y. State Chaplain), Am. Guild of Organists (organizing warden Ft. Lauderdale), D.A.R. (Fla. chmn. music 1962-64), Nat. League Am. Penwomen (1st pl. journalism award Fla. Conv. 1967, orgn. pres. Cape Canaveral br. 1968-70, sec. 1970-72, v.p. 1972-74, pres. 1974—), Fla. Press Women's Assn., A.S.C.A.P., Space Pioneers. Episcopalian (Ch. women exec. bd. 1964-67). Author: The Taming of The Tongue, 1954; Love One Another, 1957; Menendez de Aviles, 1968; Bedtime Bible Stories, Travel Fun, Sleepytime Tales, Improve Your Spelling for Better Grades, Improve Your Business Spelling, Tranquility Tapes, 1970. Contbr. feature articles to nat. mags., newspapers including N.Y. Herald Tribune, Guidepost Mag., Logos Jour.; space corr. Cape Kennedy, for Religious News Service, 1962—. Home: 1945 Pineapple Av Melbourne FL 32935 Office: Box 1560 Melbourne FL 32935

STONE, FLORENCE UTLEY PIERCE (MRS. WALTER C. STONE), newspaper pub.; b. New Britain, Conn., Oct. 8, 1903; d. Frederick Ernest and Elizabeth (Brown) Pierce; student Elmira Coll., 1918-19, Columbia, 1919-20; m. Walter C. Stone, Apr. 19, 1929 (dec.); children—Ellen (Mrs. Kenneth C. Parkes), Philip R., Gregory. News editor, reporter, feature writer, photographer Camden (N.Y.) Advance-Jour., 1948—, pub., 1969—. Mem. N.Y. Press Assn., Camden C. of C. Home: 110 Main St Camden NY 13316 Office: 82 Main St Camden NY 13316

STONE, HAZEL LUCY ROTH (MRS. NORREL L. STONE), purchasing exec., educator; b. Des Moines; d. William and Verne (Fessler) Roth; student U. Ia., 1937-39; Drake U., 1939-41, U. Kansas City Sch. Law, 1941-43; m. Norrel L. Stone, Jan. 8, 1954. Buyer regional office Montgomery Ward, 1941-43; citrus grower, Haines City, Fla., 1943-48; buyer Mass Bros., St. Petersburg, Fla., 1950-72. Instr. marketing Jr. Coll., St. Petersburg, evenings 1950-55; prof. econs., English, Am. Inst. Banking, St. Petersburg, evenings 1956—. Mem. women's com. Republican Com., Winter Haven, Fla., 1945-46; active various community fund drives; state adviser distributive edn., 1949-72. Named Outstanding Bus. and Profl. Woman of Year, 1956. Mem. Common Cause, Am. Inst. Banking, Mus. Fine Arts, Fla. League of Arts, Smithsonian Assos., Kappa Alpha Theta. Republican. Club: Bath. Contbg. author to textbooks. Home: 1330 North Shore Dr NE St Petersburg FL 33701

STONE, JOYCE LAVINIA WILSON (MRS. DELMER ELTON STONE), librarian; b. Batavia, N.Y., Dec. 23, 1924; d. Herbert Guy and Thirza Ora (Marriott) Wilson; student Bethany Coll., 1942-44; B.A., Lake Erie Coll., 1946; M.A. in Religious Edn., Hartford Sem. Found., 1949; M.L.S., Carnegie Library Sch., 1956; m. Delmer Elton Stone, Dec. 3, 1966; children—Suzanne (dec.), Cynthia, Ricky D., Steven G. Young adult coordinator Topeka Pub. Library, 1956-58; regional librarian N.M. State Library, Silver City, 1958-61; librarian Blytheville AFB, Blytheville, Ark., 1961-64, Andersen AFB, Guam, 1964-67, Naval Sta., Guam, 1968-73; researcher, photographer Marine Lab., U. Guam. Organist Andersen AFB Chapel, Guam, 1965-67, Naval Sta. Chapel, Guam, 1968-70. Recipient Outstanding Library award Naval Sta., Guam, 1969, 70, 71. Mem. A.L.A. (life). Methodist. Clubs: Guam Shell, Marianas Yacht, Marianas Divers (Guam). Home: PO Box 3434 Agana GU 96910 Office: Naval Sta Library Naval Sta Box 174 FPO San Francisco CA 96630

STONE, MARGARET GRIFFITH JONES, mathematician; b. Culpeper, Va., June 20, 1929; d. Hal Roberts and Bertha Catherine (Smith) Jones; B.A., Duke U., 1950, M.A., 1959; postgrad. N.C. State U., 1961-63, U. Tenn., 1969; m. Joseph Donald Stone, Apr. 28, 1951 (div. Apr. 1958); 1 dau., Catherine (Mrs. Edward Bernard Dorsey). Tchr. pub. schs., Culpeper, 1954-57; instr. math Duke U., Durham, N.C., 1957-59; mathematician U.S. Army Research Office, Durham, 1959-60; instr. math. U. S.C., Columbia, 1960-61, N.C. State U., Raleigh, 1961-64, Coll. William and Mary, Williamsburg, Va., 1964-67; mathematician Computing Tech. Center, Union Carbide Nuclear Div., Oak Ridge, 1967—. Mem. Oakridge Playhouse, 1967—, Tenn. Citizens for Wilderness Planning, 1972—. Bd. dirs. Oak Ridge Civic Music Assn., 1965—. Mem. Am. Math. Soc., Soc. Indsl. and Applied Math., U.D.C., Am. Phys. Soc., Math. Assn. Am., Am. Canoe Assn., Alpha Chi Omega. Democrat. Episcopalian. Mem. Order Eastern Star. Clubs: East Tennessee White Water, Carbide Canoe, Oak Ridge Chorus, Knoxville Ski. Home: 109 Cedar Lane Oak Ridge TN 37830 Office: Oak Ridge Gaseous Diffusion Plant PO Box P Oak Ridge TN 37830

STONE, MARGUERITE BEVERLEY, univ. dean; b. Norfolk, Va., June 10, 1916; d. James L. and Clara (Thompson) Stone; B.A. in Chemistry, Randolph-Macon Woman's Coll., 1936; M.A. in Student Personnel Adminstrn., Columbia, 1940, profl. diploma, 1956. Tchr., Norfolk High Sch., 1936-41; instr. Tusculum Coll., 1941-43; asst. dean women U. Ark., 1946-50, asso. dean women, 1952-54, dean women, 1954-55; asst. dean women Purdue U., 1956-67, asso. dean women, 1967-68, dean women, 1968-74, dean students, 1974—. Served with USNR, 1943-46, 52-55. Mem. Am. Assn. U. Women (past pres. Fayetteville, Ark.), Nat. (chmn. liaison com. with Nat. Panhellenic Conf. 1964-65, treas., chmn. hdqrs. adv. com. 1973—), Ind. assns. women deans and counselors, Ind. Personnel and Guidance Assn., Women's Equity Action League, Women's Polit. Caucus, Purdue Women's Caucus, Bus. and Profl. Women, Am. Coll. Personnel Assn., Am. Assn. Higher Edn., Mortar Bd., Phi Beta Kappa, Alpha Lambda Delta (dist. adviser, mem. nat. council 1973—), Kappa Delta Pi, Delta Kappa Gamma, Pi Lambda Theta, Zeta Tau Alpha. Methodist (trustee). Clubs: Lafayette Country; Purdue Women's, Purdue University, Parlor. Home: 1808 Summit Dr West Lafayette IN 47906 Office: Exec Bldg Purdue U Lafayette IN 47907

STONE, MARILYN ESTELLE, pedodontist; b. Atlanta, Feb. 9, 1925; d. A. Neal and Mary (Eggler) Stone; A.B., Huntingdon Coll., 1947; Med. Tch. certificate Emory U. Hosp., 1948, D.D.S., Emory U., 1955; m. Otto Lamar Cantrall, Jr., Oct. 19, 1951 (div. May 1953); m. 2d, Karl E. Moore, May 22, 1969 (div. Apr. 1974). Practice dentistry specializing in pedodontics, Atlanta, 1955—; asso. in clin. pedodontics Emory U., 1957-68. Trustee, treas. Gillette Hayden Meml. Found., 1967—. Fellow Ga. Dental Assn. (hon.), Internat. Coll. Dentists, Am. Coll. Dentists; mem. Ga. Soc. Dentistry for Children (v.p. 1966, pres. 1968), Assn. Am. Women Dentists (pres. 1966), No. Dist. Dental Soc. (exec. council 1972-74), Am. Dental Assn., Am. Soc. Dentistry for Children (award Merit 1955), Am. Acad. Pedodontics, Fedn. Dentaire Internationale, Pilot Internat., Omicron Kappa Upsilon.

STONE, MARJORIE HANSON (MRS. FRANCIS WARREN STONE), editor; b. Santa Maria, Cal., Nov. 29, 1927; d. Andrew Brandt and Margaret (Tracy) Hanson; B.A., Stanford, 1948; m. Francis Warren Stone, Feb. 10, 1952; children—Tracy Ann, Peter Andrew. Reporter, Honolulu Star-Bull., 1948-50, columnist, 1956-58; reporter U.P.I., San Francisco, 1951; writer troop information and edn. sect. U.S. Army, Tokyo, 1952-54; editor Valley Publs., Los Angeles, 1954-56; treas. Ad-Mail, Honolulu, 1958-67; editor Hawaiian Travel News, 1967—; editor Hawaii Tourist News, Honolulu, 1969—. Club: Junior League (Honolulu). Home: 44-006 Aumoana Pl Kaneohe HI 96744 Office: Box 32 Honolulu HI 96810

STONE, (MARY) KATHARINE GANN (MRS. ERNEST STONE), educator; b. Sylacauga, Ala.; d. William C. and Mary (Twilley) Gann; B.S., Jacksonville State U., 1933; M.A., U. Ala., 1944, postgrad., 1960, 62; m. Ernest Stone, Aug. 18, 1934; 1 son, William Ernest. Prin., tchr., DeKalb County Schs., 1934-44; tchr. U. Ala., summers 1940-43; tchr. Jacksonville (Ala.) State U., 1944-46, dir. elementary lab. sch., 1948-74. Condr. workshops for tchrs. Jefferson, Calhoun, Marshall, Butler, Cherokee counties; tchr. inst. numerous counties, cities; Mem. course study com. Ala. Dept. Edn., 1946-48, 72—, Title II adv. council, 1960—, state textbook com., 1945-49. Recipient Alumnus of Year award Jacksonville State U., 1961-62; named Merit Mother Ala., 1971, Honor Mother, 1972. Mem. Ala. Edn. Assn. (dist. pres. 1944-46), Edn. Profl. Standards Commn. (tchr. 1944-50), Am. Assn. U. Women (pres. 1950-52), N.E.A. (pres. dist.), Dept. Elementary Prins., Childhood Edn., Nat. Assn. Parliamentarians, Ala. Assn. Parliamentarians (historian 1966-70, sec. 1971-73, v.p. 1973—), Mary Haislip Parliamentary Law Unit (historian 1972-73, treas. 1973-74), Nat. Council Tchrs. Math., Am. Assn. Sch. Adminstrs., Delta Kappa Gamma (pres. chpt. 1940-44), Kappa Delta Pi, Alpha Xi Delta. Clubs: Alabama Federation Women's (exec. bd. 1945—, Kitty Stone scholarship established 1969), Progressive study (pres. 1951-52). Home: President's Home Jacksonville State U Jacksonville AL 36265

STONE, MILDRED MARY-ANNE SIMON, physician; b. Sturgeon Bay, Wis.; d. Peter John and Catherine (Merget) Simon; B.A., U, Wis., 1934, M.D., 1938; m. Grant Clifford Stone, Feb. 7, 1933 (div. July 1952); children—Kathleen (Mrs. Frank Fox), Karen (Mrs. Robert C. Anderson), Bonnie, Linda, Rebecca. Intern U. Hosps., Madison, Wis., 1938-39; practice medicine specializing in allergy, Berlin, Wis., 1939-51; staff sec. Red Cross Blood Bank, Madison, 1951-52; head allergy clinic VA Hosp., Madison, 1952-60, Cuba City (Wis.) Med. Center, 1960—; chief staff Cuba City Hosp., 1967—. Health officer Berlin, 1941-51. Mem. A.M.A., Am. Thoracic Soc., Am. Heart Assn., Am. Acad. Allergy, Am. Acad. Gen. Practice, Am. Coll. Allergists, Wis., Grant County med. socs., Theta Sigma Phi. Home: 507 E Webster St Cuba City WI 53807 Office: 808 S Jefferson St Cuba City WI 53807

STONE, MINNA ADOLPH (MRS. SAMUEL J. STONE), civic worker; b. New Philadelphia, O., Dec. 23, 1907; d. Elias and Rosa Bauman (Abraham) Adolph; ed. pub. schs.; student law with judge, 1923-26; m. Samuel J. Stone, Apr. 24, 1927; children—Virginia (Mrs. Theodore Stern Gup), Dorothy (Mrs. David Newman), Barbara (Mrs. Lawrence D. Landy). Comdr. in chief ladies div. Jewish Welfare campaign, Canton, 1938; sec. McKinley Av. Temple, Canton, 1935-38, pres. Sisterhood, 1932-36; treas. Ohio Fedn. Temple Sisterhoods, 1938, v.p., 1940; chmn. Ohio Synagogue of Air, 1941, 16th Ohio Congl. dist. Women's Action Com. for Victory and Lasting Peace, 1945; mem. com. by-laws Nat. Fedn. Temple Sisterhoods, 1947-49, speakers bur., 1943-47; mem. WAC Recruiting Com., Canton, 1945; dir. Brit. War Relief Soc., Canton, 1940-42; field worker div. women vols. def. and service Ohio Council Def., 1941-43; dir. women's activities Office Civilian Def., Canton, 1941-42, asst. exec. dir., 1942-43; pres. Sorosis Book Club, Canton, 1945-46; mem. speakers bur. Union Am. Hebrew Congregations; chmn. fund drives A.R.C., Golden Beach, Fla., 1951, 52, Community Chest, Golden Beach, 1951, 52; founder, chmn. Sick Loan Cupboard Nat. Council Jewish Women, 1956, rec. sec., Broward County, Fla., 1956-57, dir. Bay div., 1958-61, 73; sec. aux. Miami Heart Inst., 1960, v.p., 1961-62, life chmn. bd. dirs., 1960—, mem. devel. fund corps Inst., also bd. dirs.; lay chmn. Internat. Symposium on Anti-coagulants, 1964. Bd. dirs. Jewish Center, Canton, 1940-44. Recipient award U.S. Dept. Treasury and War Finance Com. Ohio, 1945; service award Dade County Community Chest, 1951; Silver medallion distinguished service award Miami Heart Inst., 1970. Mem. League Women Voters (dir. Miami 1955). Club: Vizcayans, Jockey (Miami). Home: 10245 Collins Av Bal Harbour FL 33154

STONEBACK, DIANE WILLIAMSON (MRS. BRUCE THOMAS STONEBACK), editor; b. Phila., June 16, 1950; d. Richard Hadwin and Frances Jeanne Molitor Williamson; B.S., Ohio U., 1972, postgrad., 1972; m. Bruce Thomas Stoneback, Oct. 28, 1972. Editor tabloid for young people Call-Chronicle Newspapers, Inc., Allentown, Pa., 1972-73, spl. features editor, 1973—. Asst. instr. journalism Ohio U., 1972. Mem. Women in Communications, Inc., Pa. Women's Press Assn. (award 1974), Ohio U. Alumni Assn., Mortar Bd., Sigma Delta Chi, Tau Kappa Alpha. Home: 2911 Ithaca Apt F Allentown PA 18103 Office: 101 N 6th St Allentown PA 18105

STONE-DELATTRE, VIVIANE M., psychologist, artist; b. Paris, France, 1926 (came to U.S. 1940, naturalized 1950); d. S. and Y. Delattre-Seguy Labourcatte Bomanji; B.A. cum laude, Coll. St. Elizabeth, 1944; M.A., Miami U., Oxford, O., 1948; student Academie du Port Royal, Paris, 1972-73; m. Carl Henry Stone, 1945; children—Claudia Ann, Douglas Fernald. Grad. asst. psychology Miami U., 1947-48, instr. psychology, 1948-49; instr. psychology Earlham Coll., Ind., 1948-49, U. Tex., Austin, 1949-50, Mass. Bay Community Coll., 1966-67, Am. Coll. Paris, 1968-69; sec., dir. Compu-Centers, Inc., Knoxville, 1961-62. One man show Galerie Marcel Bernheim, Paris, 1974; exhibited group shows Salon des Artistes Francaises, Automne, Independents, Surindependants, Neuilly, Internat. des Beaux-Arts Galerie Bernheim Jeune, Galerie Marcel Bernheim Galerie Ror Volmar, all Paris, 1970-74. Bd. dirs. Ecole Billingue, Paris, 1967-70. Am. Womens Group, Paris, 1968-69, Am. Wives of Europeans, 1968-69; société Internationale des Beaux Arts, Paris, 1970—. Mem. Am. Psychol. Assn., Salon des Artists Francais (hon. mention 1971), Paris. Club: Wellesley Country (Mass.); Union Interalliée (Paris). Home: 2 Bis rue Scheffer Paris 16 France

STONEK, BERNICE JANE (MRS. LEO R. STONEK), printing co. exec.; b. Milw., May 1, 1913; d. Walter Henry and Clara Jeanette (Boehm) Hofherr; student Marquette U., 1930-32, U. Wis. at Milw., 1932-33; m. Leo Robert Stonek, Aug. 17, 1935; children—Robert Lee, Donald James, Dale Kenneth. Joint editor, pub. Reminder-Enterprise Press weekly, Cudahy, Wis., 1935-72; sec. Reminder-Enterprise Printing, Cudahy, 1972—. Active P.T.A., Community Fund, Am. Cancer Soc., others. Mem. Theta Sigma Phi. Home and office: 3643 E Barnard Av Cudahy WI 53110

STONER, CARROLL GRATHWOL (MRS. ROBERT BERGAZYN), newspaper editor; b. Fort Snelling, Minn., Feb. 6, 1943; d. Warren William and Elva Margaret (Mayhew) Grathwol; B.A., U. Minn., 1964; m. Garrick Rowan Stoner, May 1966 (div. Jan. 1970); 1 son, Garrick Rowan; m. 2d, Robert Bergazyn, Dec. 23, 1972. Columnist Fairbanks (Alaska) Daily News-Miner, 1964-68; women's editor Hartford (Conn.) Times, 1968-70; women's editor, Phila. Inquirer, 1970-73; asst. trends editor, 1973—. Bd. dirs. Alaska Camp Fire Girls, 1964-66, World Affairs Council Phila., 1972-74. Mem. Women in Communications, Sigma Delta Chi. Club: Soroptimist. Home: 2643 Aspen St Philadelphia PA 19130 Office: 400 N Broad St Philadelphia PA 19101

STONER, DOROTHY ELEANOR CURTIS (MRS. ROSS ARNOLD STONER), journalist; b. Rowan, Ia., Feb. 25, 1916; d. Leon L. and Mabel (Henry) Curtis; grad. high sch.; m. Ross Arnold Stoner, Sept. 26, 1936 (dec. Aug. 1960); 1 dau., Sybil Jeanne (Mrs. Paul Donald Carter). Owner, operator Curtis grocery, Charles City, Ia., 1933-39; bookkeeper, office sec. Scott Barnett Plumbing & Heating, Charles City, 1948-61; bookkeeper Dobbs Coal and Oil Co., Charles City, part-time 1950-53; woman's page editor Charles City Press, 1961—. Leader troop Girl Scouts Am., 1945-50; pres. P.T.A., 1945-47; treas. YWCA, 1955-62. Republican. Mem. Christian Ch. (ch. clk. 1948-54). Rainbow Girls, Pythian Sisters. Soroptimist (mem. com. 1966—). Home: 1002 1/2 Hulin St Charles City IA 50616 Office: 100 N Main St Charles City IA 50616

STONER, ELIZABETH J(ANE) TIMMONS (MRS. RAY N. STONER), home economist; b. Erie, Pa., Apr. 15, 1941; d. James D. and Beatrice M. (Kelly) Timmons; B.S. in Home Econs. Edn., Villa Maria Coll., 1963; M.S. in Home Econs. Edn., N.Y. State U. Coll., Buffalo, 1971; m. Ray N. Stoner, Oct. 26, 1968; children—Michael Nicholas (dec.), Thomas. Home service and lighting rep. Niagara Mohawk Power Corp., Buffalo, 1963-67, dir. home service, 1963-65; extension home economist N.Y. State Co-op. Extension, Buffalo, 1967—. Cons. Erie County Consumer Protection Bd., Buffalo. Mem. Adult Edn. Assn., Am., N.Y. (consumer adviser 1973—), home econ. assns., Nat. Extension Home Econs. Assn. (recruitment chmn. 1968-69). Club: Zonta (Olean, N.Y.). Home: 406 Roycraft Blvd Snyder NY 14226 Office: 238 Main St Buffalo NY 14102

STONER, JOYCE ELAINE PUGH (MRS. ROGER ROYER STONER), journalist; b. Chambersburg, Pa., Apr. 13, 1945; d. Melvin Arthur and Miriam Elizabeth (Byers) Pugh; B.A., Elizabethtown Coll., 1967; postgrad. North Tex. State U., 1970-71; m. Roger Royer Stoner, June 15, 1968. Tchr. English, Central Dauphin Sch. Dist., Harrisburg, Pa., 1967-68, Lake Worth Ind. Sch. Dist., Ft. Worth, 1968-69; staff writer Lancaster (Pa.) Newspapers, Inc., 1972—. Corr. sec. New Holland Welcome Wagon, 1972-73. Mem. Women in Communications, Elizabethtown Alumni Assn., Sigma Delta Chi. Lutheran. Home: 1650 Princess Anne Dr Lancaster PA 17601 Office: 8 W King St Lancaster PA 17604

STONESIFER, KAREN ANNE ELLIS (MRS. JEFFREY CRAIG STONESIFER), occupational therapist; b. Gainesville, Fla., Apr. 11, 1946; s. Harlan Reed and Helen Constance (Chard) E.; B.S., U. Fla., 1968; M.S. cum laude, Boston U., Sargent Coll. Allied Health Professions, 1972; m. Jeffrey Craig Stonesifer, Sept. 11, 1971; 1 dau., Heidi Ann. Sr. occupational therapist Trenton (N.J.) State Hosp., 1968-70; occupational therapist Newington (Conn.) Children's Hosp., 1971—. Cons. Skillman Tng. Sch. for Boys, Princeton, N.J., 1970. Bd. dirs. Family Service Assn. Meriden, Conn., 1972—, chmn. counseling com., 1973. Am. Occupational Therapy Assn. grantee, 1970-71. Mem. Am., Conn. occupational therapy assns. Conglist. Home: Townhouse 36 184 Gravel St Meriden CT 06450 Office: 181 Cedar St Newington CT 06111

STOOP, NORMA MCLAIN, author, photographer; b. Panama, C.Z.; b. Harry Edward and Gladys (Brandon) McLain; student Penn Hall Jr. Coll., Carnegie Inst. Tech., New Sch., N.Y. U.; m. William J. Stoop, Jr., Sept. 20. Contbg. editor Dance Mag. and After Dark, N.Y.C., 1969-71, asso. editor, 1971—, also photographer, film critic. Mem. Poetry Soc. Am., Dance Masters Am. Contbr. poems to Tex. Quar., Chgo. Rev., N.Y. Times, Arts in Society, Quest, Atlantic Monthly, Christian Sci. Monitor, others, 1958—, essays to Book Week in N.Y. Herald Tribune; represented in Best Poems of 1973. Home: 1 Lincoln Plaza 23D New York City NY 10023 Office: 10 Columbus Circle New York City NY 10019

STOOPS, LOUISE, librarian; b. Honolulu; d. Robert Earl and Ethel (Saunders) Stoops; B.A., U. Ariz.; M.S., Simmons Coll., 1952. Asst. librarian Popular Library, 1952-53; bus. and econs. div. Enoch Pratt Free Library, Balt., 1953-54; librarian, advt. and information services and office of adviser non-theatrical films Eastman Kodak Co., Rochester, N,Y., 1954-57; librarian Wilson, Haight, Welch & Grover, advt. agy., Hartford, Conn., 1957-58; asst. librarian U.S. Steel Corp., N.Y.C., 1958-60, head librarian, 1960-68; chief librarian Bache & Co., Inc., N.Y.C., 1968-70, chief librarian Cities Service Co., N.Y.C., 1970-71; chief librarian Dominick & Dominick, Inc., N.Y.C., 1971-72; librarian Baker, Weeks & Co., N.Y.C., 1972—. Mem. Spl. Libraries Assn. (editor Conn. Valley Chpt. News 1957-58; hospitality chmn. N.Y. chpt. 1959-60, sec. 1960-61, dinner chmn. 1961-62, chmn. internat. vis. librarians 1960-62, recruitment com. 1960-61, program chmn. N.Y. chpt. 1965-66, sec. advt. and marketing div. 1964-67, chmn. bus. and finance div. 1968-69), Chi Omega. Indexed English-Speaking Union International Cookbook, 1962, The Dollars and Sense of Business Films (Assn. Nat. Advertisers), 1954. Home: 7 W 96th St New York City NY 10025 Office: One Battery Park Plaza New York City NY 10004

STOPOL, LEONORA MUELLER (MRS. MURRAY S. STOPOL), lawyer; b. St. Louis, Sept. 7, 1927; d. Mark and Mary (Kahan) Mueller; B.S., Washington U., St. Louis, 1949; J.D. cum laude, San Fernando Valley Coll., 1970; m. Murray S. Stopol, Jan. 31, 1953; children—Richard, Elizabeth, Michael, Kathryn. Occupational therapist St. Louis City Hosp., 1949-50; admitted to Cal. bar, 1971; pvt. practice law, Woodland Hills, Cal., 1971-72; atty. Cal. Dept. Social Welfare, Los Angeles, 1972—; asso. counsel Cal. Fair Employment Practices Commn., 1974—. Chmn. community adv. council Hughes Jr. High Sch., Woodland Hills, 1971-72. Mem. Am., Los Angeles County bar assns., State Bar Cal., Nat. Council Jewish Women, Women Lawyers Assn., Constl. Rights Found. Home: 5901 Capistrano Av Woodland Hills CA 91364 Office: 322 W 1st St Los Angeles CA 90012

STORCH, RUTH ELSIE MARTIN (MRS. RONALD CHARLES STORCH), pub., editor; b. Phila., Dec. 15, 1934; d. George Theodore and Ruth Anna (Lewis) Martin; grad. high sch.; m. Ronald Charles Storch, July 5, 1951; children—Stephen, Frederick, Deborah, Barbara, Suzanne, Laura, Gregory. Pub., editor Halifax Shopping News, Daytona Beach, Fla., 1966—. Recipient Certificate Award Daytona Beach Civitan Club, 1970; certificate appreciation U.S. Navy Recruiting Service, 1971. Mem. Fla. Advt. Pub. Assn., Nat. Assn. Advt. Pubs. Home: 5 Granville Circle Daytona Beach FL 32018 Office: PO Box 7235 Daytona Beach FL 32016

STOREY, JANET MARIE KINSEY (MRS. WILLIAM GEORGE STOREY), newspaperwoman; b. Gideon, Mo., Feb. 2, 1942; d. Everett Eldon and Evelyn Fern (Oates) Kinsey; grad. high sch.; m. William George Storey, Dec. 27, 1963; children—Gary Paul, Craig William, Carrie Marie. With Internat. Shoe Co., Sikeston, Mo., 1960-62; supr. Daily Standard, Sikeston, Mo., 1962—. Mem. Sikeston Bus. and Profl. Women (sec. 1963-64), V.F.W. Baptist. Home: 907 Sikes St Sikeston MO 63801 Office: 205 S New Madrid St Sikeston MO 63801

STORM, DORIS FAITH (MRS. FRANK DAVID JACOBY), film producer; b. N.Y.C., July 1, 1926; d. Manheim and Fannie B. (Shafsky) Rosenzweig; B.A. magna cum laude, Bklyn. Coll., 1955; m. Frank David Jacoby, Mar. 9, 1946; children—Douglas Evan, Bruce Hale, Jeffrey Mann. Film and TV actress, 1948—; commentator WPIX, N.Y.C., 1953-56; staff dir. WATV, Newark, 1948-49; asso. producer NBC series, 1949-51; free-lance producer and dir. TV and films, 1951-61; sr. v.p., exec. producer Guidance Assos., Pleasantville, N.Y., 1961-71; partner Jacoby/Storm Prodns., documentary, indsl. and ednl. films, Westport, Conn., 1971—. Pres. Citizens Adv. Com. for Edn., Freeport, N.Y., 1966-67, exec. bd., 1960-66. Mem. Democratic Com., Freeport, 1964-66. Bd. dirs. Project Renaissance, drug rehab. center, Westport. Recipient award Am. Film/TV Festival, 1966-69, Nat. Ednl. Film Festival, 1971-72, Internat. Film Festival N.Y., 1971. Mem. Screen Actors Guild, Am. Fedn. Radio and TV Artists, Actors Equity, Phi Beta Kappa. Home: 8 W Branch Rd Westport CT 06880 Office: 101 E State St Westport CT 06880

STORM, ETHEL PAINE GORTON (MRS. ERIC FOSTER STORM), assn. exec.; b. Bridgeport, Conn.; d. Henry H. and Carrie Hanna (Paine) Gorton; A.B., Middlebury Coll., 1916; postgrad. Inst. Mus. Art, 1920, Sorbonne, Paris, France, 1929; m. Willard Duncan Carpenter, Oct. 6, 1917 (dec. July 1947); m. 2d, Eric Foster Storm, Feb. 14, 1951. Concert singer, 1924-30; ch., oratorio singer Roxy Theatre, 1930-34; soloist mus. prodns. Student Prince, Blossom Time, Friends Music and Schola Cantoram; organizing pres. Vt. Soc. Dames of Ct. Honor, West Castleton, 1961—; organizing pres. Conn. Soc., Milford, 1963, recording sec. gen., 1963-65, organizing sec. gen., 1965—. Mem. Magna Charta Dames Conn. (regent), D.A.R., Nat. Soc. Colonial Dames Am., Colonial Order Crown, Plantagenet Soc., Castleton Hist. Soc., Nat. Soc. Daus. of Founders and Patriots, Rutland Humane Soc. (trustee), So. Vt. Art Center, Huguenot Soc., Descs. of Knights Order of Garter, Nat. Soc. New Eng. Women, Pi Beta Phi. Clubs: Middlebury (Vt.) Garden (past pres.), Fair Haven Garden (past pres.), Home: West Castleton VT also 111 5th Av Milford CT 66464

STORM, FREEDA MAE WILSON, educator; b. Elmer, Okla.; d. Alfred S. and Lillie (Schrimsher) Wilson; student Southwestern Extension U.; m. Feb. 19, 1927; children—Terrell E., H. Lynn, Lawanna Gay (Mrs. Bob Phillips). Asst. to Dr. John Coburn, Altus, Okla., 1956-59; opthalmic dispenser, mgr. G.T. Optical Dispensing Co., Houston, 1962-69; instr. U. Houston, Coll. of Optometry, 1969—. Tex. chmn. New Eyes for the Needy. Fellow Internat. Acad. Opticianry, Nat. Acad. Opticianry, Am. Bd. Opticianry; mem. Certified Opthalmic Dispensers Assn. Tex. (ednl. chmn.), Houston Area Tchrs. Assn. Mem. Unity Ch. of Christianity (dir.). Editor: Lens Craft, 1964. Research, developed prosopic lab. Home: 5940 Dashwood St Apt 22 Houston TX 77036 Office: 4415 Cullin Blvd Houston TX 77004

STORM, LEOTA BOHNENBLUST (MRS. WILLIAM M. STORM), librarian; b. Larimore, N.D., Feb. 21, 1928; d. Roy and Hazel Dell (Henderson) Bohnenblust; student U. N.D., 1947-49; B.A. with library certificate Kan. State Tchrs. Coll., 1949-51; m. William M. Storm, Oct. 23, 1960. U.S. Army librarian Fort Sill (Okla.), 1951-53; post librarian Fort Knox (Ky.), 1954, Fort Meade (Md.), 1954-57, Fort Hood (Tex.), 1957-61; librarian Harry S. Truman Library, Independence, Mo., 1961-62, Los Angeles Pub. Library, 1962—. Mem. Am. Fedn. State, County and Municipal Employees. Mem. Order of Eastern Star. Home: 1077 Superba Av Venice CA 90291 Office: 2906 S LaBrea Av Los Angeles CA 90016

STORM, MARY ELIZABETH, lawyer; b. Frederick, Md., Jan. 11, 1940; d. Edward Daniels and Mildred Elizabeth (Raum) Storm; student St. John's Coll., Annapolis, 1958-60; B.A., Hood Coll., 1962; J.D., George Washington U., 1966. Admitted to Md. bar, 1967; mem. firm Storm & Storm, Frederick and Emmitsburg, Md., 1967—. Instr. estate planning Frederick Community Coll., 1969-70, mem. adv. com. asso. degree nursing program, 1970—, recorder, 1970-72. Mem. League of Women Voters, 1967—, Hosp. Aux., 1967—, Md. Comprehensive Health Planning Council, 1971—. Second v.p. Md., Young Democrats, 1961. Bd. dirs., sec. Girl Scout council Central Md., 1972-73; bd. dirs. Frederick Orgn. for Rehab., 1970-71. Mem. Nat. Assn. Women Lawyers (del. Md. 1969-73), Frederick County (rec. sec. 1971—), Am., Md. (council, com. family and juvenile law 1968-70) bar assns., Am. Assn. U. Women, Md. Fedn. Women's Clubs (dir. jr. clubs 1970-72), Phi Delta Delta. Democrat. Presbyn. Clubs: Hood, Frederick Women's Civic, Zonta (pres. 1971-72, lt. gov. dist. 3 1974—). Home: 103 Record St Frederick MD 21701 Office: 114-A W Church St Frederick MD 21701

STORMSON, JACQUELINE ELLEN POZAR, librarian; b. San Andreas, Cal., Oct. 15, 1930; d. John Frank and Martha Ellen (Primrose) Pozar; A.A. in Humanities, San Bernardino Jr. Coll., 1951; postgrad. U. Nev., 1964; B.A. in History and Polit. Sci., U. Cal. at Los Angeles, 1955; m. Geoffrey Paul Stormson, Mar. 19, 1955 (div. Feb. 1972);children—Eric Paul, Christina, Julia Ellen. Project dir. reclassification U. Nev. Library, Las Vegas, 1963-64; elementary and secondary sch. librarian, 1965-66, Las Vegas, 1966-67; instructional media dir. Variety Sch. Spl. Edn., Las Vegas, 1968—. Mem. Nev. central Com. Dem. party, 1971-72, mem. Legislative Subcom., 1971-72, Rules Reform Com., 1971. Recipient Fed. Internship Program grant U.S. Dept. Edn., 1968, 73. Mem. League Women Voters (dir. Nev. 1965—), Am. Assn. U. Women, Clark Tchrs. Assn., N.E.A., Council Exceptional Children, Clark County Instructional Media Specialists. Home: 3062 Vegas Valley Dr Las Vegas NV 89121 Office: 2601 Sunrise Lane Las Vegas NV 89101

STORRS, ELEANOR EMERETT, research inst. exec.; b. Waterbury, Conn., May 3, 1926; d. Benjamin Porter and Alta Hyde (Moss) Storrs; B.S. with distinction in botany, U. Conn., 1948; M.S. in Biology, N.Y. U., 1958; Ph.D. in Chemistry, U. Tex., 1967; m. Harry Phineas Burchfield, Jr., Nov. 29, 1963; children—Sarah Storrs, Benjamin Hyde. Asst. biochemist Boyce Thompson Inst. for Plant Research, Yonkers, N.Y., 1948-62; research scientist Clayton Found. Biochem. Inst., U. Tex., Austin, 1962-65; biochemist Pesticides Research Lab., USPHS, Perrine, Fla., 1965-67; dir. dept. biochemistry Gulf South Research Inst., New Iberia, La., 1967—. Cons. in rehab. and prevention deformities leprosy Pan Am. Health Orgn., WHO, Venezuela, Argentina, Brazil, 1972—. NIH grantee, 1968—; Center for Disease Control grantee, 1969-73. Fellow Am. Inst. Chemists, A.A.A.S., N.Y. Acad. Scis.; mem. Internat. Leprosy Assn., Am. Chem. Soc., Internat. Soc. Tropical Dermatology, Bot. Soc. Am., Reticuloendothelial Soc., Sigma Xi. Episcopalian (vestryman). Clubs: Appalachian (Boston); Green Mountain (Bear Mountain, N.Y.). Author: (with H. P. Burchfield) Biochemical Applications of Gas Chromatography, 1962; (with Burchfield, D. E. Johnson) Guide to the Analysis of Pesticide Residues, 2 vols., 1965; also articles, book chpts. Pioneer devel. leprosy in exptl. animal (armadillo). Home: 303 Duperier Av New Iberia LA 70560 Office: PO Box 1177 New Iberia LA 70560

STORY, ADELINE ELIZABETH WEISGERBER (MRS. ALLAN H. STORY), banker; b. Chgo.; d. Charles H. and Anna (Usack) Weisgerber; grad. Bryant and Stratton Bus. Coll., 1930; student Am. Inst. Banking, 1934-40; m. Allan H. Story; 1 dau., Caryl (Mrs. Patrick F. VanKeuren). Exec. sec. Upper Av. Nat. Bank Chgo., 1946-48, asst. cashier, 1948-60, asst. v.p., 1960-63, v.p., 1963-69, v.p., trust officer, 1969—. Counsellor Suburban Youth Groups; judge awards scholarships Jr. Achievement Chgo. Recipient First Lady of Day tribute with certificate Sta. WAIT, Chgo. Mem. Nat. Assn. Bank Women, Assn. Chgo. Bank Women (dir.), Chgo. Council on Fgn. Relations, Chgo. Ednl. Television. Presbyn. Home: 6851 N Tripp Av Lincolnwood IL 60646 Office: 875 N Michigan Av Chicago IL 60611

STOTLER, ALICEMARIE HUBER (MRS. JAMES ALLEN STOTLER), lawyer; b. Alhambra, Cal., May 29, 1942; d. James Russell and Loretta (Montoya) Huber; A.B., U. So. Cal., 1964, J.D., 1967; m. James Allen Stotler, Sept. 11, 1971. Admitted to Cal. bar, 1967; prosecutor Orange County Dist. Atty.'s Office, Santa Ana, Cal., 1967-73; mem. firm Stotler & Stotler, Tustin, Cal., 1973—. Mem. Mortor Bd., Kappa Alpha Theta. Office: 17291 Irvine Blvd Tustin CA 92680

STOUT, JUANITA KIDD, judge; b. Wewoka, Okla., Mar. 7, 1919; d. Henry M. and Mary A. (Chandler) Kidd; student Lincoln U., 1935-37; A.B., State U. Ia., 1939; postgrad. U. Colo., U. Minn.; J.D., Ind. U., 1948, LL.M., 1952; m. Charles Otis Stout, June 23, 1942. Tchr. music elementary sch., Seminole, Okla., 1939-41, high sch., San Springs, Okla., 1941-42; instr. bus. law and ins. Fla. A. and M. U., 1948, Tex. So. U., 1949; administrv. sec. U.S. Ct. Appeals 3d Circuit, Phila., 1949-54; asst. dist. atty., 1956-57, chief appeals, pardons and paroles divs., 1957-59; judge Municipal Ct., Phila., 1959-62, judge County Ct., 1962-69, Ct. Common Pleas, 1969—. Recipient Jane Addams medal Rockford Coll., 1966. Mem. Am. Judicature Soc., Am., Pa., Phila. bar assns., Nat. Assn. Women Lawyers (named outstanding woman lawyer year 1965). Democrat. Episcopalian. Home: 1919 Chestnut St Philadelphia PA 19103 Office: City Hall Philadelphia PA 19107

STOUT, LENA MINNIE JONES, city ofcl.; b. Weiser, Ida., Feb. 16, 1919; d. Elmer McKinnley and Martha Lina (Coats) Jones; student Vancouver Washington Bus. Coll., 1962-63; m. Robert Lee Stout, Mar. 5, 1939 (div.); children—Marvin, Glenn, Carolyn (Mrs. Larry VanLaeken). Bookkeeper, Bank Washougal, Wash., 1963-65; city treas., Washougal, 1966—. Mem. Ch. Nazarene (treas. 1966—). Club: Soroptimist (Washougal). Home: 3021 H St Washougal WA 98671 Office: 1701 C St Washougal WA 98671

STOVALL, MARGARET O. (MRS. JAMES DONALD GUNDERSON), newspaperwoman; b. nr. Philomath, Ore., Sept. 3, 1911; d. Dennis H. and Odessa (Freed) Stovall; grad. high sch.; m. James Donald Gunderson, July 5, 1969. Reporter Pasadena Evening Post, 1929-32, Pasadena Star-News, 1932-35, San Diego Tribune, 1935-37; free-lance writer comml. and portrait photography, Los Angeles and Santa Barbara, Cal., 1940-45; reporter, photographer Pasadena Star-News, 1946-65, chief photographer, feature writer, 1965—. Freelance writer, photographer Christian Sci. Monitor, Desert Mag., Sunset Mag., House and Garden Bldg. Guide, Book of Homes, Am. Home, U.S. Nat. Forest, 1929—. Recipient 1st nat. award A.I.A., 1953; Am. Journalism award Am. Legion, 1962, Jeane Hoffman Unique Coverage award Theta Sigma Phi, 1967; Community Service award Pasadena Womens' Civic League, 1972; certificate of appreciation Pasadena Tournament of Roses, 1973; named Newspaperman of Year, Pasadena Elks, 1971. Home: 725 Earlham St Pasadena CA 91101 Office: 525 E Colorado Blvd Pasadena CA 91109

STOVALL, MARY KATE SANDERS (MRS. TURNER STOVALL), librarian; b. Uniontown, Ala., Dec. 13, 1921; d. Tim and Estella (Billingsley) Sanders; B.S. in Elementary Edn., Ala. State Coll., 1949, M.Ed., 1955; M.L.S., Atlanta U., 1969; m. Turner Stovall, May 9, 1953; children—Kathleen, Audrey. Tchr. elementary schs., Perry County, Ala., 1943-51; librarian Russell County Tng. Sch. Library, Hurtsboro, Ala., 1951—. Owner, operator Stovall Funeral Home, Hurtsboro, 1953—; reporter Union Springs (Ala.) Herald. Mem. Ala. League for Advancement Edn., Ala., Russell edn. assns., N.E.A., Nat. Funeral Dirs. and Morticians Ala., Ala. Instructional Media Assn., Am., Southeastern, Ala. Library assns., Order Eastern Star, N.A.A.C.P. Home: PO Box 154 Hurtsboro AL 36860 Office: Russell County Tng Sch Library Hurtsboro AL 36860

STOVALL, THELMA L. (MRS. LONNIE RAYMOND STOVALL), state ofcl.; b. Munfordville, Ky., Apr. 1, 1919; d. Samuel Dewey and Addie Mae Hawkins; student LaSalle Extension U., U. Ky., Eastern State Coll.; m. Lonnie Raymond Stovall, Sept. 30, 1936. Mem. Ky. Ho. of Reps., sec. of state, Ky., 1956-60, 64-68, 72—; state treas. Ky., 1960-64, 68-72. Active State Labor Movement; sec. Tobacco Workers Internat. Union; liaison officer Louisville Community Chest and labor unions; state chmn. Muscular Dystrophy, 1957-73; v.p. Muscular Dystrophy Assns. Am., Inc., 1970-71, 72-73; mem. Ky. Commn. on Women, 1973; chmn. Ky. Bd. Election Commrs. Nat. committeewoman Young Democratic Clubs Ky., 1952-56, pres., 1956-58. Bd. dirs. edn. dept. Ky. Fedn. Labor. Mem. Bus. and Profl. Women's Club. Democrat. Baptist. Moose; mem. Order Eastern Star. Club: Altrusa. Home: 104 Valley Rd Louisville KY 40204 Office: State Capitol Room 150 Frankfort KY 40601

STOVER, ANN SPEARS (MRS. RICHARD FREDERICK STOVER), civic worker; b. Brazil, Ind., Sept. 8, 1910; d. Andrew Allen and Laura Mae (Morgan) Spears; A.B., Ind. State Tchrs. Coll., 1933; m. Richard Frederick Stover, Mar. 30, 1935; children—Sally Elisabeth (Mrs. James Dalton Little), Simon Frederick, Karl Richard. Social Worker YWCA, Indpls., 1934-35; caseworker Fla. Welfare Bd., Miami, 1942-43; pres. Woman's Aux. Dade County Med. Assn., 1948-49; chmn. Woman's Aux. Fla. Med. Assn., 1949-53, v.p., 1953-54, pres., 1954-55; pres. Woman's Aux. So. Med. Assn., 1953-54; chmn. Fla. Gov.'s Adv. Com. on Mental Health, 1952-53; com. chmn. Woman's Aux. A.M.A., 1952-56, bd. dirs., 1956-59, 1st v.p., 1958-59; vol. conv. chmn., 1960; bd. dirs. Nat. Assn. for Mental Health, 1951-58, 67-70, 70-73, Fla. Assn. Mental Health (gold medallion 1965), Greater Miami Assn. Mental Health; recipient Plaque 15 Years Service and Leadership, 1964; vol. conv. chmn. Nat. Assn. for Mental Health, 1961; legislative chmn. Fla. Assn. Mental Health, 1964, pres.-elect, 1965-66, pres. 1966-67, recipient 1st life membership, 1970; bd. dirs. Mental Health Assn. Dade County, pres., 1968-69; hon. life mem. Woman's Aux. to Fla. Med. Assn.; past mem. Fla. Conf. Social Workers, U. Miami Sch. Medicine Faculty Wives Assn.; active mem. Doctors Hosp. Aux. Active in gubernatorial and senatorial campaigns. Vice pres. Democratic Woman's Club Date County, 1964-65, former mem. Fla. Dem. Woman's Club; del. at large State Fla., Dem. Nat. Conv., 1964. Recipient Social Conscience award Ft. Pierce (Fla.) br. Am. Assn. U. Women, 1968, Ann Spears Stover Ann. Vol. award Mental Health Assn. Dade County, 1971. Home: 6145 SW 92d St Kendall Miami FL 33156

STOVER, SHIRLEY VERE-SMITH (MRS. JORDAN HOMER STOVER III), bus. exec.; b. N.Y.C., July 15, 1918; d. Sidney and Mildred (Merriman) Vere-Smith; student Columbia, 1936-37; m. Jordan Homer Stover III, Sept. 20, 1941; 1 dau., Sandra. Vice-pres., treas., dir. Stover Locknut & Machinery Corp., Easton, Pa., 1942-54; adminstrv. mgr. Stover Labs., Bloomfield, Mich., 1954-68, Tucson, 1968—. Mem. Indsl. Coll. Armed Forces. Clubs: Skyline Country, Old Pueblo (Tucson); Oakland Hills Country (Birmingham, Mich.); Recess, Detroit Athletic; Greenwich (Conn.) Country. Address: 4951 Winged Foot Dr Tucson AZ 85718

STOWELL, HELEN SMITH, librarian; b. Rochester, N.Y., Sept. 30, 1913; d. Louis Charles and Catherine Gertrude (Hahn) Smith; A.B., N.Y. State Coll. Tchrs., 1935, B.S. in L.S., 1936; m. Cecil Bernard Stowell, Apr. 27, 1946; children—Carolyn (Mrs. Robert C. Harden), William Charles. Tchr. English, librarian Savannah (N.Y.) High Sch., 1936-38; asst. librarian, then librarian Hackett Jr. High Sch., Albany, N.Y., 1939-48; asst., then organizer 3 elementary libraries Albany pub. sch. system, 1956-57, librarian schs. 20 and 21, 1957-62, librarian, audio visual coordinator sch. 16, 1962-72; ret., 1972; organizer children's library 1st Lutheran Ch., Albany, 1973—. Mem. Willowbrook Civic Assn., Guilderland, N.Y. Hon. life mem. N.Y. State Congress P.T.A.; mem. Am. Assn. U. Women, Am. Assn. Ret. Persons, Eastern N.Y. Sch. Librarians Assn. (pres. 1964-66), Hudson-Mohawk Library Assn., N.Y. State Ret. Tchrs. Assn., State

U. N.Y. at Albany Alumni Assn., Friends Albany, Schenectady County pub. libraries. Lutheran (pres. Ch. Women 1971-74, chmn. Christian edn. com. 1971-74). Home: 17 Hite Ct Schenectady NY 12303

STOZEK, SISTER MARY ALODIA, ednl. adminstr.; b. Chgo., Dec. 15, 1922; d. John and Mary (Kuczaj) Stozek; B.S., Loyola U., Chgo., 1958; M.A., Marquette U., Milw., 1962; Ph.D., U. Chgo., 1966. Joined Sisters Saint Felix of Cantalice, 1941; tchr. elementary sch. Archdiocese Chgo., 1943-60; asst. to dir. Marquette U. Reading Center, Milw., 1960-63; dir. psychoednl. center Felician Coll., Chgo., 1966—. Mem. adv. com. Ill. Right to Read Commn., 1972-73. Mem. Am., Ill. psychol. assns., Psychologists Interested in Religious Issure, Internat. Reading Assn. Contbr. articles to profl. jours. Home and office: 3800 Peterson Av Chicago IL 60659

STRAAT, PATRICIA ANN, research biochemist; b. Rochester, N.Y., Mar. 28, 1936; d. Harold William and Marcelline (Hetzler) Straat; B.A., Oberlin Coll., 1958; Ph.D. (Univ. fellow and scholar 1958-61, USPHS fellow 1961-64), Johns Hopkins, 1964; postgrad. U.S. Dept. Agr. Grad. Sch., 1969-72. Lab. asst. Mass. Inst. Tech., 1957; lab. instr. dept. biology Johns Hopkins, Balt., 1958-59, USPHS postdoctoral fellow dept. radiol. sci., 1964-67, research asso., 1964-68; asst. prof. radiol. sci., 1968-70, lectr., part time, 1970-72; sr. reserch biochemist Biospherics, Inc., Rockville Md., 1970—. Mem. A.A.A.S., Am. Chem. Soc., Internat. Oceanographic Soc., Am. Inst. Biol. Scis., N.Y. Acad. Scis., Sigma Xi. Club: Sierra. Contbr. articles to profl. jours. Home: 5497 Harpers Farm Rd Columbia MD 21044 Office: 4928 Wyaconda Rd Rockville MD 20852

STRACENER, MARY HELEN LANGLOIS, savs. and loan exec.; b. Baton Rouge, Oct. 30, 1922; d. Joseph Aubin and Elizabeth Mae (Netterville) Langlois; B.A. in Journalism, La. State U., 1943, postgrad., 1943-44; m. Nealon Stracener, June 2, 1943; children—Douglas Nealon, Carol Elizabeth. Editor West Side Jour., Port Allen, La., 1941; society editor, court reporter Morning Advocate, Baton Rouge, 1942-43; mem. adv. staff La. Press Assn., Baton Rouge, 1944-46; sec. La. Dept. Commerce and Industry, Baton Rouge, 1946-48; sec.-mgr. Guaranty & Fed. Savs. & Loan, 1960-72, exec. v.p., 1972—, also dir. Alternate del. Republican Nat. Conv., 1956. Mem. U.S. Savs. and Loan League (chmn. com. on federally chartered assns. 1973-74), La. Savs. and Loan League (co-chmn. edn. com. 1973-74), Am. Savs. and Loan Inst., Alpha Xi Delta Mothers (chpt. pres.), Phi Lambda Pi. Baptist. Mem. Order Eastern Star. Home: 9461 Woodbine Dr Baton Rouge LA 70815 Office: 3155 Weller Av Baton Rouge LA 70805

STRACHSTEIN, HARRIET WOLF (MRS. ABRAHAM STRACHSTEIN), psychologist; b. N.Y.C., Dec. 23, 1906; d. Samuel and Rose (Held) Wolf; B.S., N.Y. U., 1925, M.S., 1955, Ph.D., 1960; m. Abraham Strachstein, Mar. 21, 1924; children—Marjorie (Mrs. Seymour Miller), Judith (Mrs. Jack Davis). Staff psychologist Alfred Adler Consultation Center, 1956-62; cons. psychologist Bklyn. VA Hosp., 1963-65; lectr. tng. dept. Postgrad. Center for Mental Health, N.Y.C., 1963—, sr. supr. group therapy dept., 1968—, sr. supr. family therapy dept., 1970—; pvt. practice psychology, 1945—. Mem. Am. Psychol. Assn., N.Y. Soc. Clin. Psychologists, Am. Group Psychotherapy Assn., Council Psychoanalytic Psychotherapists. Club: N.Y. U. Alumni. Home: 155 W 68th St New York City NY 10023

STRACNER, BONNIE DEAN, govt. ofcl.; b. Kennett, Mo., Feb. 7, 1939; d. Ellis James and Letha Faye (Swain) Ward; B.S.E., Ark. Tchrs. Coll., 1964; M.S.E., State Coll. Ark., 1970; m. Elbert J. Stracner, Mar. 24, 1959 (div. Apr. 1974); children—Kathy Jo, Sonja Ann. Tchr. bus. edn., pub. schs., Scotland, Ark., 1959-61, 64-66, Alread, Ark., 1961-63, Wonderview, Ark., 1963-64, 66-69; tng. supr. Ark. Children's Colony, Conway, 1969-73; tng. coordinator pub. service careers, Ark. Dept. Social and Rehab. Services, Little Rock, 1973-74, dir., 1974—. Mem. Am. Assn. Mental Deficiency. Home: 2206 Broadview St Conway AR 72032 Office: 1220 W 6th St Little Rock AR 72201

STRAEB, ELIZABETH GRACE JOHNSON (MRS. CHARLES H. STRAEB), ednl. adminstr.; b. Colorado Springs, Colo., Jan. 22, 1925; d. Oscar Klepser and Grace (Lord) Johnson; student Colo. Coll.; grad. U. Denver, 1966; postgrad. U. Colo., 1968-69; m. Charles H. Straeb, Mar. 14, 1943; children—Carol (Mrs. Rodney J. Griffin), Charles Heinz, Robert Frederick Lord. Tchr. kindergarten Guardian Angel Day Nursery, St. Louis, 1943, Franzhurst, Colorado Springs, 1945; head dir. Nursery Sch. Denver U. Campus, 1946-47, San Louis Day Nursery, Colorado Springs, 1948-49; founder Miss Betty's Nursery Sch., Colorado Springs, 1949, Pre-Sch. for Y Wives, Colorado Springs, 1949-50; pres., dir. Jr. Acad. Nursery Sch., Ltd., Colo. Coll., Colorado Springs, 1950—, ABC Nursery Sch., Colorado Springs, 1961—. Entertainer, USO Traveling Unit, 1942; Grey lady A.R.C., 1949-54; co-chmn. 1969 Colorado Springs Opera Festival; v.p. Opera Guild Colorado Springs, 1972-73. Bd. dirs. Am. Childhood Edn.; bd. dirs. Rocky Mountain Ballet Founds., Colorado Springs, 1964—, pres., 1967. Mem. regional bd. Taft for Pres. Club, El Paso County, Colo., 1951; mem. Republican Women's Round Table Colorado Springs, 1966—. Recipient Service award U.S.O., 1943, award Y Wives for 1st pre-sch., 1950, Outstanding Service award Rocky Mountain Ballet Found. Bd. and Co., 1967. Mem. Am. Music Soc., Colorado Springs Nat. Fedn. Music Club (sec. 1948), Colorado Springs Fine Arts Center (docent), Women's Edn. Soc. Colo. Coll. (life), D.A.R. (pres. 1949, Good Citizenship medal 1941), Alpha Chi Omega. Episcopalian (soprano soloist 1955-64). Founder 1st pvt. day camp in Colorado Springs, 1954; originator 1st pvt. ungraded primary in Colo., 1966. Home: 24 E Fontanero St Colorado Springs CO 80907 Office: 1311 N Nevada St Colorado Springs CO 80903 and 1511 N Weber St Colorado Springs CO 80907

STRAETER, JANE KENNEY, pub. relations ofcl.; b. St. Louis, Dec. 9, 1919; d. Hal James and Inez Celeste (Howe) Kenney; student Columbia, 1960; m. Edwin Charles Straeter, Aug. 18, 1940 (dec.); children—Terry, Ted III. Program dir. Am. Cancer Soc., St. Louis, 1959-60; dir. pub. relations Goodwill Industries, St. Louis, 1960-63; dir. continuing edn. and cultural affairs YMCA, St. Louis, 1966-67; program dir. Mayor's Council on Youth, St. Louis, 1967-68; dir. community relations St. Mary's Health Center, St. Louis, 1968—. Bd. dirs. Cerebral Palsy Assn. Recipient publs. award United Fund, 1969; awards for internal pub. relations program Midwest Hosp. Assn., 1971-73, award for interpretive pub. relations program, 1970; MacEachern award for hosp. publs. Am. Hosp. Assn., 1971-73. Mem. Acad. Hosp. Pub. Relations Dirs. (dir.), Community Service Pub. Relations Council (v.p.), Mo. Hosp. Assn. (pub. information com.), St. Louis Hosp. Pub. Relations Dirs. (pres.), St. Louis Women in Advt., St. Louis Press Club (dir.). Home: 4400 Lindell Blvd Lane St Louis MO 63108 Office: 6420 Clayton Rd St Louis MO 63117

STRAHLER, ELLEN LOUISE, ret. librarian; b. Dayton, O., May 1, 1909; d. Ezra Frederick and Bertha (Daniels) Strahler; A.B., Wittenberg U., 1941; B.S. in L.S., Western Res. U., 1943. Children's librarian Cleve. Pub. Library, 1943-60; br. librarian Burkhardt br. Dayton and Montgomery County Pub. Library, 1960-67, head lit. and fine arts div., 1968-74; evening instr. children's lit. U. Dayton, 1964-67; librarian Grace United Meth. Ch. Mem. Dayton Art Inst. Mem. A.L.A., Ohio Library Assn., Staff Assn. Dayton Pub. Library (pres. 1968-69). Republican. Home: 19 W Siebenthaler Av Dayton OH 45405

STRAHLER, VIOLET RUTH, educator, author; b. Dayton, O., Sept. 30, 1918; d. Ezra Frederick and Bertha (Daniels) Strahler; A.B., Wittenberg U., 1944; M.A., Miami U., 1959; Ed.D., Ind. U., 1972. Tchr. sci. and math. Miamisburg (O.) High Sch., 1944-51; tchr. sci. and math., counselor Dayton Pub. Schs., 1951-66, tchr. cons. secondary instrn. and curriculum, 1967-69, supr. sci., math. and curriculum publs., 1969-70, supr. curriculum design and publs., 1970-72, exec. dir. curriculum devel. dept., 1972—; indsl. chemist, summers 1944-58; vis. instr. sci. and edn. Miami U., Oxford, O., summers, 1959-61. Mem. planetarium com. Dayton Mus. Natural History, 1961-63. Ford Found. fellow, 1952-53. Fellow Ohio Acad. Sci. (chmn. sect. on edn. 1950-51, editor Jr. Acad. Newsletter 1951-53), Nat. Sci. Tchrs. Assn. (alternate dir. 1956-58), N.E.A., Am. Chem. Soc., Nat. Assn. for Research in Sci. Teaching, Nat. Soc. for Study Edn., Ohio Edn. Assn., Am. Assn. Sch. Adminstrs., Assn. Supervision and Curriculum Devel., Delta Kappa Gamma (chmn. research com. 1962-64). Author jr. high sch. sci. text books; also articles profl. jours. Home: 5340 Brendonwood Lane Dayton OH 45415 Office: Bd Edn 4280 N Western Av Dayton OH 45427

STRAIN, PAULA MARY, librarian; b. Brooke County, W.Va.; d. Paul Russell and Margaret (Evans) Strain; A.B., Bethany Coll., 1937; B.S., Carnegie Inst. Tech., 1938; student U. Pitts., 1940-41. Asst. librarian Westminster Coll., 1939-40; asst. librarian Carnegie-Ill. Steel Corp., Pitts., 1940-42, librarian, 1942-44; librarian U.S. Naval Photog. Interpretation Center, Washington, 1946-48, liaison and selection officer Library of Congress, 1948-57; sr. research analyst Library of Congress, 1957-60; tech. librarian Electronics Systems Center, IBM, Owego, N.Y., 1960-68; head librarian Booz Allen Applied Research, Inc., Bethesda, Md., 1968-70; mgr. library services MITRE Corp., McLean, Va., 1970—. Served with USNR, 1944-46. Mem. bd. mgrs. Finger Lakes Trail Conf., 1962-68, editor, 1962-66, pres., 1966-67. Mem. Am. Assn. U. Women, Women's Nat. Book Assn., Appalachian Trail Conf., Spl. Libraries Assn. (editor geography and map div. 1962-65, chmn. 1968-69, pres. Upstate N.Y. chpt. 1967-68, nat. employment policy com. 1969-73). Clubs: Potomac Appalachian Trail (pres. 1970-72, Washington); Adirondack Mountain. Author articles various periodicals and jours. Home: 8315 N Brook Lane Bethesda MD 20016 Office: 1820 Dolley Madison Blvd McLean VA 22101

STRAIN, SIBYL MARJORIA SHIPP (MRS. NUMA ALONZO STRAIN), educator; b. Hiram, Ga.; d. John Seaborn and Nell (Barber) Shipp; A.B. summa cum laude, Berry Coll., 1942; M.A., Columbia, 1955; postgrad. U. So. Cal., Whittier Coll., U. Cal. at Los Angeles, Cal. State Coll., Loyola U. at Los Angeles; m. Numa Alonzo Strain, Aug. 19, 1944 (dec. July 1969); 1 dau., Laura Marjoria. Tchr., Hiram (Ga.) High Sch., 1942-43; exec. sec. research dept. J.M. Mathes, Inc., N.Y.C., 1947-49; reading specialist John Muir High Sch., Pasadena, Cal., 1957-60, John Marshall Jr. High Sch., Pasadena, 1960-66; asst. dir. Nat. Charity League, U. So. Cal. Reading Center, Los Angeles, 1966-67; prof. psychology and reading, chmn. dept. Los Angeles S.W. Coll., 1967—, sec. acad. senate, 1967-68, exec. council, 1970—. Active various community drives. Asso. mem. Am. Mus. Natural History. Center for Study Dem. Instns., Smithsonian Instn. Served to lt. WAVES, 1943-47. Mem. Nat. Soc. for Study Edn., N.E.A., Internat., Western reading assns., Am. Assn. U. Women (br. newsletter editor 1965-66), Pasadena Assn. Career Tchrs. (co-founder 1964, sec.-treas. 1964-65), Internat. Platform Assn., U. So. Cal. Hon. Assn. Women in Edn. (charter mem.), Cal., Los Angeles (exec. council 1967—) tchrs. assns., Am., Cal. (del. S.W. Community Coll. 1969—) higher edn. assns., Am. Assn. U. Profs., Nat. Hist. Soc., U. So. Cal., Berry Coll. (v.p. 1944-45) alumni assns., Kappa Delta Pi, Pi Lambda Theta (chpt. pres. 1962-63), Phi Delta Gamma. Democrat. Presbyn. Author: (with Regina Moses, Meredith Meadows) Tips on Teaching the Slow Learner, 1965. Home: 2236 Las Lunas St Pasadena CA 91107 Office: 11514 S Western Av Los Angeles CA 90047

STRAMSKI, GERALDINE ANNE (MRS. WILLIAM HYMAN), physician; b. Salem, Mass., Feb. 28, 1928; d. Wladyslaw and Bronislawa Anne (Wronkowski) Stramski; B.S., Tufts U., 1948, M.D., 1952; m. William Hyman, Dec. 28, 1954; children—Robert Douglas, Eric Alan. Intern, Queens Gen. Hosp., Jamaica, N.Y., 1952-53; resident Buffalo Children's Hosp., 1952-55; pvt. practice medicine specializing in pediatrics, Long Beach, Cal., 1956—; med. dir. chronic disease service Children's Hosp., Long Beach, 1971—; mem. staff Children's, Harbor gen. hosps. Adj. asso. prof. Cal. State Coll., Long Beach, 1968—; asst. clin. prof. U. Cal. at Los Angeles, 1968—. Home: 6361 Vera Crest Dr Long Beach CA 90815 Office: Children's Hosp 2801 Atlantic Av Long Beach CA 90801

STRAND, FLEUR LILLIAN EMANUEL (MRS. CURT R. STRAND), educator; b. Republic of S.Africa, Feb. 24, 1928; d. Stanley V. and Vera (Gross) Emanuel; came to U.S., 1945, naturalized, 1948; A.B., N.Y. U., 1948, B.S., 1950, Ph.D., 1952; m. Curt R. Strand, June 14, 1946; 1 dau., Karen. Instr. Bklyn. Coll., 1951-57; researcher, lectr. Free U., Berlin, Germany, 1957-59; mem. faculty N.Y. U., N.Y.C., 1961—, asso. prof. biology, 1967-73, prof., 1973—. Mem. N.Y. Acad. Scis., Am. Physiol. Soc., Soc. Exptl. Biology and Medicine, A.A.A.S., Soc. Neurosci., Sigma Xi. Author: Modern Physiology, 1965. Contbr. articles to profl. jours.

STRAND, ROBERTA MARY (MRS. JESSE R. STRAND), educator; b. Pasadena, Cal., Apr. 27, 1924; d. Calver Oram and Harriet Flora (Sweet) Mace; student Santa Barbara State Coll., 1942-43; B.A., Stanford, 1946; postgrad. Stanford, Sacramento State Coll., Cal. Poly. Coll., U. Ore., U. Minn.; m. Jesse R. Strand, June 24, 1972; children—Robert A., David C. Tchr. Carpinteria (Cal.) High Sch., 1947-57; prep sports writer Santa Barbara (Cal.) News-Press, 1947-57; sports corr. for various So. Cal. newspapers, 1949-58; tchr. phys. edn., English and journalism San Luis Obispo (Cal.) High Sch., 1958-72. Ex-officio mem. Helms Athletic Found. Bd. Prep Writers, Los Angeles, 1949-58; summer workshop instr., 1964-71; yearbook conf. speaker various univs., 1964—. Corr. sec. S. Atascadero (Cal.) Suburban Soc., 1971-72. Newspaper Fund fellow, 1963; Josten's Yearbook scholar, 1968. Recipient Nat. medal of merit Journalism Edn. Assn., 1972; Golden Eagle award Am. Yearbook Co., 1972; Nat. Scholastic Press Assn. Pioneer Journalism award, 1970. Mem. Nat. Educators Fellowship (area rep. 1959-60), Journalism Edn. Assn. (pres. 1970-71, v.p. So. Cal. 1970-72), Theta Sigma Phi. Home: PO Box 1255 Sparks NV 89431 also 305 W 6th Av Sun Valley NV 89431

STRANG, MARY SOPHIA, radiologist; b. Phila., Feb. 6, 1929; d. Fowler Smythe and Hilda Francis (Elble) Strang; B.S., Guilford Coll., 1949; M.D., Woman's Med. Coll., 1956; div. Intern St. Luke's Hosp., Bethlehem, Pa., 1956-57, then resident; gen. practice medicine, Flourtown, Pa., 1960-65; resident in radiology Germantown Dispensary and Hosp., Phila., 1966-68; fellow nuclear medicine Hahnemann Hosp., Phila., 1969; chief nuclear medicine div. Hamot and St. Vincent hosps., Erie, Pa., 1970—; practice medicine specializing in nuclear medicine. Diplomate Am. Bd. Radiology, Am. Bd. Nuclear Medicine. Office: 104 E 2d St Erie PA 16512

STRANG, RUTH HANCOCK, physician; b. Bridgeport, Conn., Mar. 11, 1923; d. Robert Hallock Wright and Ruth (Hancock) Strang; B.A., Wellesley Coll., 1944, postgrad., 1944-45; M.D., N.Y. Med. Coll., 1949. Intern, Flower and Fifth Av Hosp, N.Y.C., 1949-50, resident pediatrics, 1950-52; mem. faculty N.Y. Med. Coll., N.Y.C., 1952-57; fellow cardiology Babies Hosp., N.Y.C., 1956-57, Harriet Lane Cardiac Clinic, Johns Hopkins Hosp., Balt., 1957-59, Children's Hosp., Boston, 1959-62; mem. faculty U. Mich., Univ. Hosp., Ann Arbor, 1962—, prof. pediatrics, 1970—; dir. pediatrics Wayne County Gen. Hosp., Eloise, 1965—; mem. staff Univ. Hosp., Wayne County Gen. Hosp., Eloise, Mich. Mem. med. adv. com. Wayne County chpt. Nat. Found., 1966—; chmn. med. adv. com. Nat. Cystic Fibrosis Research Found., Detroit, 1971—; cons. cardiology Plymouth (Mich.) State Home and Tng. Sch., 1970—. Mem. citizen's adv. council to Juvenile Ct., Ann Arbor, Mich., 1968—; mem. med. adv. bd. Ann Arbor Continuing Edn. Dept., 1968—; mem. Diocesan Com. for World Relief, Detroit, 1970—. Trustee Episcopal Med. Chaplaincy, Ann Arbor, 1971—. Diplomate Am. Bd. Pediatrics. Mem. Am. Acad. Pediatrics, Am. Coll. Cardiology, Detroit Pediatric Soc., Mich., Washtenaw County med. socs., A.M.A., N.Y. Acad. Medicine, N.Y. Acad. Sci., Am., Mich. heart assns., Women's Research Club (membership sec. 1966-67), Am. Assn. Maternal and Child Health, Ambulatory Pediatric Assn., Am. Assn. Child Care in Hosps., A.A.A.S., Assn. Am. Med. Colls., Mich. Soc. Study Adolescents. Episcopalian (mem. Bishop's Com. 1966-69, sec., 1966-68). Author: Clinical Aspects of Operable Heart Disease, 1968. Contbr. numerous articles to profl. jours. Home: 4500 E Huron River Dr Ann Arbor MI 48104 Office: Dept Pediatrics Wayne County Gen Hosp Eloise MI 48132

STRANGE, LETHA BELLE (MRS. CURTIS STRANGE), hist. mus. curator; b. Kaukauna, Wis., May 28, 1895; d. Charles Gottlieb and Sophia (Wendel) Dauber; student Oshkosh (Wis.) Normal Sch., 1919; postgrad. Stevens Point (Wis.) Coll.; m. Curtis Strange, Dec. 25, 1920; 1 dau., Alice (Mrs. William Klymko). Tchr. pub. schs. Oshkosh, 1918-20, pub. schs., Kenosha, Wis., 1921-23, then substitute tchr.; tchr. Kenosha Orthopedic Sch., 1953-60; acting curator Kenosha County Hist. Mus., 1967—. Active Kenosha council Girl Scouts Am., 1933-73, pres., 1940-44, also active nat. com.; active United Fund, A.R.C. Bd. dirs. Friends of City Mus., 1970-72. Recipient Thanks Badge award Girl Scouts Am., 1949, Girl Scout Stauette, 1968. Mem. State Hist. Soc., League of Women Voters (charter). Republican. Home: 7410 7th Av Kenosha WI 53140 Office: 6300 3rd Av Kenosha WI 53140

STRASSMAN, TONI, authors rep.; b. N.Y.C.; d. Joseph Solomon and Pauline (Gottlieb) Strassman; grad. high sch. Sec. Harold Bell Wright, Tucson; sec., asst. to mgr. Provincetown Playhouse and Cape Playhouse, Dennis, Mass.; legal sec. Viking Press, N.Y.C., 1931-44; agt. for various authors, 1945—, including Harry Mark Petrakis, Brian Garfield, Joseph Hayes, Gina Berriault, John Bell Clayton, Robert N. Winter-Berger. Home and office: 130 E 18th St 7D New York City NY 10003

STRATAS, TERESA, soprano; b. Toronto, Ont., Can., May 26, 1939; d. Emanuel and Argero (Teregis) Stratas; student Royal Conservatory Music with Irene Jessner, 1955-59; student U. Toronto, 1959. Radio debut, 1953, TV debut, 1954, operatic debut as Mimi in La Boheme, Canadian Opera Co., 1958; Am. debut with Houston Symphony Orch., 1958; winner Met. Opera auditions, 1959; Met. Opera debut as Pousette in Manon, 1959; appeared as Mimi at Covent Gardens-Royal Opera House, London, Eng., 1961; appeared with symphony orchs. Houston, Toronto, Montreal, Ottawa, Detroit; featured role in motion picture The Canadians, 1960; title role world premiere opera Nausica, Herod Atticus Theatre, Athens, Greece, 1961; appeared as Madam Butterfly Vancouver Internat. Festival, 1960; operatic debut in Atlantida, La Scala Opera, 1962; German debut with Munich Opera, 1964; debut Berlin Opera, 1966, San Francisco Opera, 1966; debut Bolshoi, Riga and Talinn Operas during tour U.S.S.R., 1963, 64; prodns. include La Traviata, Munich, 1964, Queen of Spades, Met. Opera, 1965, Hansel & Gretel, 1967. Home: 19 Brooksihe Dr Toronto 13 ON Canada Office: Met Opera Co New York City NY 10023*

STRATE, MAY LEORA VAN TRIES (MRS. CLARENCE LEROY STRATE), writer; b. Maroa, Ill., May 2, 1900; d. Isaak Frank and Mabel Camelis (Bowzer) Van Tries; m. Clarence Leroy Strate, June 5, 1920. Writer radio scripts, 1945-55; writer dramatizations of service programs of vets. and civic orgns., gen. advt. and radio plays, 1945-55; writer dir. patriotic pageant, 1944, hist. pageant, 1945, religious pageant, 1958; lectr. various groups, including schs., churches, vets. and civic groups; prose pub. in mags., including Am. Legion mag., This Day, Ia. Legionnaire, others; poetry pub. Orphic Lute, Am. Bard, also numerous newspapers. Recipient George Washington medal Freedoms Found., 1953; named Poet of the Present, Poets' Roundtable of Ark., 1970. Mem. Am. Legion Aux. (unit pres. 1938, 52, county pres. 1940, dist. pres. 1945), Poets' Roundtable Ark. (br. pres. 1968-69, 69-70). Rebekah (noble grand 1924); mem. Order Eastern Star (past matron). Clubs: Study (Garner, Ia. and Hot Springs); Hot Springs (Ark.) Poets. Author: The Tree That Talks With God (book of poetry), 1967. Home: 116 Suburban Dr Hot Springs AR 71901

STRATHMEYER, NANCY CHARLOTTE MILLS (MRS. CHARLES RUTLAND STRATHMEYER), realtor, environmentalist; b. Toledo, Nov. 4, 1923; d. James Foulds and Dorothy Ormond (Thomas) Mills; student Miami U. (Ohio), 1941-42, Barnard Coll., 1942-43; A.B., U. Cal. at Berkeley, 1951; m. Lowell Foltz Dennis, June 14, 1943 (div. Aug. 1949); 1 son, Jeffrey A.; m. 2d, Charles Rutland Strathmeyer, Dec. 7, 1952; 1 dau., Kevan Ann, 1 stepdau., Kristi L. Real estate broker, Carmel Valley, Cal., 1959—; co-owner Strathmeyer Real Estate. Mem. citizen's adv. com. Monterey Peninsula Area Planning Commn., 1962-66, 71-72; mem. Carmel Valley Property Owners Assn., 1955—, sec., 1955-56, v.p., 1957, dir., 1958-59, zoning com. chmn. 1965; mem. Monterey County Low Income Housing Study Commn., 1968-71, Monterey County Mental Health Assn. Vice chmn. Monterey County Dem. Central Com. Bd. dirs. Carmel Area Coalition. Mem. Nat. Assn. Realtors, Cal. Assn. Realtors (dir. 1961), Carmel Bd. Realtors (sec. 1960, dir. 1961-62, chmn. community planning com. 1966—, v.p. 1974), League Women Voters, Community Hosp. Women's Aux., Carmel Art Assn., Panhellenic of Monterey Peninsula, Delta Delta Delta Alumni. Democrat. Episcopalian. Address: 27890 Dorris Dr Carmel CA 93921

STRATTON, ARLENE DALE BERGER (MRS. RICHARD HAROLD STRATTON), photographic engr.; b. Ringoes, N.J., Nov. 27, 1933; d. Ralph Owen and Helen Catherine (Higgins) Berger; B.S., Douglass Coll., 1954; M.S., Rutgers U., 1962, postgrad., 1968-72; m. Richard Harold Stratton, Feb. 20, 1958. Technician photog. products dept. E.I. du Pont de Nemours & Co., Inc., Parlin, N.J., 1954-57, physicist analytical equipment, 1957-59, physicist computer services, 1959-67, supr. math. services, 1967-69, research supr. engrng. research, 1969—. Vol. reader Rec. for Blind, Inc., 1972—. Mem. Soc. Photographic Scientists and Engrs. (service award 1968), Soc. Women Engrs., Assn. for Computing Machinery, Douglass Alumnae Assn. Presbyn. (ruling elder 1968-70). Mem. Order Eastern Star. Editor:

Thesaurus of Photographic Science and Engineering Literature, 1968. Mem. publs. bd. Abstracts of Photog. Sci. and Engring. Lit., 1966-69, chmn. thesaurus and indexes subcom., 1968-69. Home: 304 Brunswick Av Sportwood NJ 08884 Office: Cheesequake Rd Parlin NJ 08859

STRAUSS, DOROTHY BRANDFON, marital and family therapist; b. Bklyn.; d. Marcus and Beatrice (Wilson) Brandfon; B.A., Bklyn. Coll.; M.A., N.Y. U., Ph.D., 1963; m. Hyman Strauss, Oct. 19, 1947; 1 dau., Josette. Research asst. Center For Human Relations Studies N.Y. U., 1962, instr., 1963; instr. Hunter Coll., 1964; prof. Kean Coll. N.J., 1964—; spl. instr. U.S. Army Signal Corps Sch., 1967-71; instr. dept. psychiatry U. Pa. Sch. Medicine; lectr. dept. psychiatry State U. N.Y. Downstate Med. Sch.; cons. sch., community and ch. agys; pvt. practice marital and sex therapy and family counseling, Bklyn., 1963—. Mem. Am., N.J. psychol. assns., Am. Assn. Marriage and Family Counselors, Eastern Acad. Sex Therapy, Am. Assn. Sex Educators and Counselors, Soc. Clin. and Exptl. Hypnosis, N.J. Gerontologic Soc., Kappa Delta Pi, Pi Lambda Theta. Home: 1700 Ditmas Av Brooklyn NY 11226

STRAUSS, HELEN, media ofcl.; b. N.Y.C., Feb. 8, 1924; d. Albert and Gertrude V. (Greenwald) Strauss; A.B., Colby Coll., 1945. With Kastor, Hilton, Chesley, Clifford & Atherton, advt. agy., N.Y.C., 1960-69, Macmillan Co., N.Y.C., 1967-69; media dir. Franklin Spier Advt. Agy., N.Y.C., 1969—. Mem. Colby Coll. Alumni Assn. (pres. N.Y.C. 1970-72). Home: 240 E 79th St New York City NY 10021 Office: Franklin Spier Inc 270 Madison Av New York City NY 10016

STRAUSS, JUDITH FEIGIN (MRS. HARRY W. STRAUSS), pediatrician; b. N.Y.C., Mar. 7, 1942; d. Milton Mordechai and Blanche Estelle (Tobias) Feigin; student U. Vt., 1959-61; B.S., Cornell, 1963; M.D., State U. N.Y. Med. Center, 1967; m. Harry William Strauss, June 14, 1964; children—Cheryl Beth, Marcy Jill. Intern State U. N.Y. Kings County Hosp., N.Y.C., 1967-68; resident Sinai Hosp., Balt., 1968-69; fellow pediatrics and child psychiatry Johns Hopkins Hosp., 1969-70; pvt. practice pediatrics, Sacramento, 1970-72, Balt., 1972—; mem. staff Sinai Hosp., Balt.; asst. in pediatrics Johns Hopkins Hosp.; cons. pediatrics Bur. Disability Ins., Social Security Adminstrn.; instr. pediatrics, U. Cal. Med. Sch. at Davis, 1971-72. Diplomate Am. Bd. Pediatrics. Mem. Baltimore County Med. Assn., Am. Acad. Pediatrics, A.A.A.S., Alpha Lambda Delta. Home: 2019 W Rogers Av Baltimore MD 21209

STRAUSS, RUTH LOUISE (MRS. MAX R. GUTENSTEIN), color cons.; b. Lima, Peru, May 5, 1910 (parents Am. citizens); d. Lester Wallack and Bertha (Miller) Strauss; B.A., Hunter Coll., 1930; B.A., Parsons Sch. Design, 1932; postgrad. Design Lab., 1939; m. Max R. Gutenstein, Sept. 3, 1931; children—Robert G., Gerald P. Art dir. Nat. Bellas Hess, N.Y.C., 1930-33; package designer A.L. Siegel Co., N.Y.C., 1940-46; owner Ruth L. Strauss, Inc., N.Y.C., 1942—. Cons. interior designs, colors for architects and builders, 1948—. Lectr. N.Y. Inst. Tech., N.Y.C., 1966-69, N.Y. U., N.Y.C., 1970-71. Co-chmn. Restoration com. Old Merchant's House, N.Y.C., 1964. Fellow Am. Inst. Interior Designers, Nat. Home Fashions League; mem. Decorator Club (v.p. 1965), Color Marketing Group (v.p. 1970), Inter-Soc. Color Council, Designers Lighting Forum, League Women Voters. Author: (with Samuel Paul) AIA Complete Book of Home Modernizing, 1964. Contbr. articles to newspapers. Home: 45 Sutton Pl S New York City NY 10022 Office: 127 E 59th St New York City NY 10022

STRAWN, DOROTHY ROSEVEAR (MRS. LOREN GLENN STRAWN), ret. univ. adminstr.; b. Glenns Ferry, Ida., Mar. 16, 1916; d William Joseph and Minnie M. (Board) Rosevear; B.A., U. Ida., 1937; M.Ed., U. Wash., 1959; m. Loren Glenn Strawn, Dec. 18, 1937; children—Claire Louise (Mrs. Michael S. Floan), Evelyn Dorothy Strawn. Tchr. high sch., Kooskia, Ida., 1937-38, Model High Sch., Dickenson, N.D., 1939; women's editor Univ. Herald, Seattle, 1939-40; chief clk. SSS, Corvallis, Ore., 1941-43; counselor Shreline Sch. Dist., Seattle, 1954-60; dean women U. Wash., 1960-70, dir. women's continuing edn., 1968-70, dir. Women's guidance center, 1970-74; cons. Nat. Def. Edn. Act Insts., 1959-63; lectr.; dir. workshops Continuing Edn. Women, 1963-73; cons. to community colls. Mem. bd. King County council Camp Fire Girls, 1948-49, chpt. Am. Cancer Soc., 1962-64, Puget Sound Multiple Sclerosis Assn., 1969-73. Mem. adv. bd. Ednl. Policies Commn. Named Woman of Year, Bus. and Profl. Women, 1966, Golden Key award, 1970. Mem. N.E.A., P.T.A. (life), Am. Assn. U. Women, Nat. Assn. Women Deans and Counselors (Wash. pres. 1967-68, chmn. nat. com. on women's continuing edn. 1968-71), Am. Personnel and Guidance Assn., N.W. Coll. Personnel Assn., Women's Equity Action League, Audubon Soc., Seattle Zool. Soc., Mortar Bd., Nat. Def. Exec. Res., Alpha Phi, Alpha Lambda Delta, Kappa Phi. Club: Faculty Women's (pres. 1967-68). Contbr. articles to popular mags. and profl. publs. Home: 11039 Dayton Av N Seattle WA 98133

STRAYER-PRIEMER, DOROTHY S., civic worker; b. S.I., N.Y., Mar. 28, 1912; d. William Henry and Emma (Klinger) Schneider; grad. N.J. Bus. Coll.; m. Mar. 28, 1925; 1 son. Pres., Prince Bay Woman's Club, S.I. Woman's Club, Richmond County (N.Y.) Community Assn., Priors and Formers, N.Y. State Fedn. Women's Clubs; now pres. N.Y.C. Fedn. Women's Club; dir. Civic Congress S.I., Tb and Respiratory Assn.; mem. planning bd., N.Y.C.; initiator, producer radio program New Yorker of the Week, 1943; developer musical program Social Communications through Music, Geriatric Hosp., N.Y.C. Bd. dirs. Sea View Hosp. and Home. Recipient citations Gov. Dewey of N.Y., Mayor Wagner of N.Y.C., Mayor Lindsay of N.Y.C., Gen. Fedn. Women's Clubs, N.Y. State Chiropractic Orgn. Mem. St. Vincent's Woman's Aux., Richmond Meml. Hosp. Aux., S.I. Hist. Soc., S.I. Museum Aux., Port Richmond Woman's Club. Home: 354 Deere Park Pl Staten Island NY 10301

STRAYHORNE, PAULINE ALLEN, savs. and loan exec.; b. Birmingham, Ala., Nov. 12, 1926; d. Willie Edward and Hattie (Carter) Allen; student Chase Coll., 1946-47, U. Cin., 1961-63; grad. diploma Am. Savs. & Loan Inst., 1962; m. Willie L. Strayhorne, May 24, 1952 (div.); 1 dau., Charlotte Maria. With Major Fed. Savs. & Loan Co., Cin., 1947—, exec. v.p., sec., 1970—, also dir. Trustee Savs. & Loan League Southwestern Ohio, 1966-68, 72-74; bd. dirs. Am. Savs. and Loan League, Washington, 1969—. Bd. dirs. Met. Cin. YWCA, 1964-70, chmn. finance com., 1966-70; bd. dirs. Jr. Achievement Greater Cin., 1970-72; mem. North Frame Planning and Review Com., City Cin., 1971-72. Trustee Jennie D. Porter Ednl. Fund, 1965—; adv. bd. Therapeutic Recreation Project for Aged, 1966-68. Recipient Black Excellence award Cin. chpt. PUSH, 1972. Mem. Nat. Soc. Controllers and Financial Officers Savs. Instns., Am. Soc. Women Accountants, Cin. Bus. and Profl. Women's Club (named Outstanding Bus. Women Cin. chpt. 1972), Credit Women Internat. (treas. 1968-69), Greater Cin. C. of C. Clubs: Lady Wonders Federated, Cosmopolitan (Cin.). Office: 2917 Gilbert Av Cincinnati OH 45206

STRECKER, SHERRY FLO, city ofcl.; b. Arcadia, Kan., June 29, 1932; d. Raymond Cecil and Emma (Pearce) Strecker. Bookkeeper Mackie-Clemens Fuel Co., Pittsburg, Kan., 1951-55; dispatcher Pittsburg Police Dept., 1955-59; pbx and clk.-typist Pittsburg Finance Dept., 1959-63; dep. city clk. City of Pittsburg, 1963-64, city clk., 1964-73, city commr., 1973—. Owner Sentinel Creditors Service. Organizer S.E. Kan. Humane Soc., 1973, charter v.p., 1973-74, pres. 1974-75. Bd. dirs. Pittsburg United Fund, 1970-72. Recipient Woman of Year in Service award City of Pittsburg, 1970, Outstanding Woman of Yr., award, 1970; Woman of Yr. award Pittsburg chpt. Am. Bus. Women's Assn., 1969. Mem. Internat. Inst. Municipal Clks., City Clks. and Municipal Finance Officers Assn. Kan. (pres. 1971), Am. Bus. Women's Assn. (pres. 1969), Crawford County Geneol. Soc. (charter). Mem. Christian Ch. Mem. Order Eastern Star. Club: Altrusa (dir. 1968-70, rec. sec. 1974-75) (Pittsburg). Home: 406 Fieldcrest Dr Pittsburg KS 66762 Office: 1007 S Locust St PO Box 282 Pittsburg KS 66762

STREET, DOROTHY ROUSE, occupational therapist, mil. officer; b. Chgo., Feb. 12, 1928; d. Charles Larrabee and Mary Louise (Rouse) Street; B.A. magna cum laude, Smith Coll., 1950; certificate occupational therapy Boston Sch. Occupational Therapy, 1954; M.A., U. Tex., 1963; M.H.A., Baylor U., 1969. Commd. officer Med. Specialist Corps, U.S. Army, 1953, advanced through grades to lt. col., 1968; staff occupational therapist various army hosps., 1954-62, chief occupational therapist, 1963-67, 69-70; resident hosp. adminstr. Letterman Gen. Hosp., San Francisco, 1968-69; personnel staff officer Office Surgeon Gen. Dept. Army, 1971, dir. personnel occupational therapy sect., 1973—, cons. occupational therapy, 1971—; chief occupational therapist sect., asst. chief Army Med. Specialist Corps, Washington, 1971—, also chief career activities office, 1973—. Decorated Meritorious Service medal. Mem. Am. Occupational Therapy Assn., Am. Hosp. Assn., Assn. Mil. Surgeons U.S., Phi Beta Kappa.

STREET, JUDY RICHEY (MRS. ED H. STREET, JR.), psychol. examiner; b. Chattanooga, Oct. 28, 1940; d. Claude Leonard and Minnie Thelma (McCamish) Richey; student Stetson U., 1958-59; B.S., E. Tenn. State U., 1963; M.Ed., U. Tenn. at Chattanooga, 1967; postgrad. Case Western Res. U., 1970; m. Ed H. Street Jr., Aug. 28, 1960; children—Ed Hobart III, Julie Richey. Tchr. pub. schs. Chattanooga, 1963-67; dir. psychology dept. Greene Valley Developmental Center, Greenville, Tenn., 1968-71. Bd. dirs. Central Bapt. Day Care Center, Johnson City, Tenn., 1971—. Nat. Def. Edn. Act fellow, 1965-66. Mem. N.E.A., Nat. Assn. Retarded Children, and Adults, Kappa Delta Pi, Phi Gamma Mu. Baptist. Home: 301 Ivanhoe Dr Johnson City TN 37601 Office: Box 3561 CRS Johnson City TN 37601

STREET, JULIA MONTGOMERY (MRS. CLAUDIUS AUGUSTUS STREET), writer; b. Concord, N.C., Jan. 19, 1898; d. Samuel Lewis and Elizabeth Blanche (Norris) Montgomery; A.B., U. N.C., Greensboro, 1923; m. Claudius Augustus Street, Sept. 13, 1924; children—Carol (Mrs. Archibald Alexander McMillan), Claudius Augustus. Tchr. pub. schs. N.C., 1918-20, 23-24; field worker N.C. Children's Home Soc., Greensboro, 1924; faculty U. N.C., Greensboro, 1922-23. Cons. N.C. History-in-Sch. Radio, 1970—; script writer N.C. History (radio) State of N.C., 1970—. Mem. Winston-Salem (N.C.) Radio Council, 1940—. Recipient award Am. Assn. U. Women, 1956, 63, 66; Alumni Service award U. N.C., Greensboro, 1967. Mem. N.C. Poetry Soc., N.C. Folklore Soc., N.C. Lit. and Hist. Assn. Author: Fiddler's Fancy, 1955; Moccasin Tracks, 1958; Candle Love Feast, 1959; Drovers' Gold, 1961; Dulcie's Whale, 1963; (with Richard Walser) North Carolina Parade, 1966; (poetry) Street Lights, 1949; Salem Christmas Eve, 1955. Contbr. mag. articles to various mags. Home: 545 Oaklawn Av Winston-Salem NC 27104

STREETER, MARJORIE MALCOLM (MRS. ROBERT AUGUSTUS STREETER, JR.), pub. co. exec.; b. N.Y.C., Sept. 9, 1934; d. MacKay and Louise Anna (Bailey) Malcolm; student Bard Coll., 1951-53, Columbia, 1954-58; m. Robert Augustus Streeter, Jr., Sept. 4, 1959; 1 dau., Wendy Bailey. Editor univ. publs. Columbia, N.Y.C., 1956-65; editor-in-chief Crossbeat. Mag., Potts Point, Sydney, Australia, 1965-67; with Spectrum Books, Prentice-Hall, Inc., Englewood Cliffs, N.J., 1971—, editorial prodn. mgr., 1973—. Home: 34 Huntting Dr Dumont NJ 07628 Office: Englewood Cliffs NJ 07628

STREETER, RUTH COOPER, lawyer; b. New Rockford, N.D., July 16, 1918; d. George William and Julia Anna (Busch) Streeter; B.A., Grinnell Coll., 1939; J.D., U. N.M., 1953. Tchr. social sci., Akron, Ia., Windsor, Colo., Glenrock, Wyo., Green River, Wyo., and Alamogordo, N.M., 1939-50; admitted to N.M. bar, 1953; pvt. practice law, Albuquerque, 1953-54; law clk. to U.S. Dist. Ct. Judge Hatch, 1954-57; asst. U.S. atty., Albuquerque, 1957-69, U.S. atty., 1969, 1st asst., 1970—; lectr. Vice pres. Albuquerque Council Pres.'s Civic Orgns., 1963-64; active YWCA, Albuquerque Opera Guild, Albuquerque Women's Symphony. Mem. Better Bus. Bur. N.M. (hon.), Am., Fed. (pres. N.M. chpt. 1973-74), Bernalillo County, N.M. bar assns., Am. Judicature Soc., D.A.R. Episcopalian. Mem. P.E.O., O.E.S. Club: Albuquerque Altrusa (pres. 1963-64, gov. internat. 1969-71, dir.). Home: 2825 Cuervo Dr NE Albuquerque NM 87110 Office: PO Box 607 Albuquerque NM 87103

STREISAND, BARBRA, singer, actress; b. Bklyn., Apr. 24, 1942; student acting schs., N.Y.C.; m. Elliott Gould; 1 son, Jason. Played stock, then Greenwich Village clubs; appeared N.Y.C. night clubs Bon Soir, Blue Angel; starring role Broadway musical I Can Get It for You Wholesale, 1962, Funny Girl, 1964; coast-to-coast tour including Coconut Grove, Hollywood, Cal., McCormick Place, Chgo., Basin Street East, N.Y.C.; appeared in films Funny Girl, Hello Dolly, What's Up Doc, The Way We Were, others; rec. artist for Columbia Records. RecipientOscar for best actress for Funny Girl, 1968.*

STREIT, MAE HELEN GLASCOCK (MRS. JOHN SAM STREIT), editor; b. Hamilton, Ala., June 27, 1914; d. James Oscar and Lula (Owen) Glascock; student pub. schs.; m. John Sam Streit, Aug. 27, 1939 (dec. June 1953); 1 son, Samuel Allen. With Franklin County Times, Russellville, Ala., 1961—, soc. editor, 1962-63, city editor, 1963-65, editor, 1965—; corr. Birmingham (Ala.) Post-Herald newspaper, 1962—. Bd. dirs. Franklin County chpt. A.R.C. Named Outstanding Bus. Woman for Russellville, 1973-74; recipient 1st place Newspaper Contest, Ala. Press Assn., 1973. Mem. Sigma Delta Chi. Mem. Ch. of Christ. Clubs: Cultura Garden (pres. 1956-57). Home: 408 High St Russellville AL 35653 Office: PO Box 1088 Russellville AL 35652

STRICKLAND, ALICE DENINGTON (MRS. CLARENCE A. STRICKLAND), savs. and loan exec.; b. nr. Clinton, Ky., May 21, 1919; d. William Edward and Lovie Marie (Dean) Denington; student Manatee Jr. Coll., 1966-68; m. Clarence A. Strickland, Aug. 2, 1936; children—John Edward, William T. Bookkeeper, ins. clk. DeSoto County Hosp., Arcadia, Fla., 1948-52, asst. bookkeeper, 1952-56; teller First Fed. Savs. & Loan Manatee County, Bradenton, Fla., 1957-59, asst. head teller, 1959-60, asst. controller, 1960-61; treas., controller Manatee Fed. Savs. & Loan, Bradenton, 1961-72, v.p., treas., 1972—. Tchr. ednl. classes Am. Savs. & Loan Inst., Bradenton, 1968-71, instr. Sarasota Manatee chpt., bd. govs., 1966, sec., 1967. Named Boss of Year, Credit Women Bradenton, 1964. Mem. Beta Sigma Phi (pres. 1968, service chmn. 1969). Baptist (supt. Young Peoples Dept. 1959-61, tchr. girls class 1973-74). Club: Zonta (sec. Bradenton 1969). Home: 4903 26th Av W Bradenton FL 33505 Office: PO Box 4166 Cortez Plaza Bradenton FL 33507

STRICKLAND, ALLEN MCGILL (MRS. GEORGE M. STRICKLAND), artist; b. Washington; d. I.J. Nota and Frances M. (Maloy) McGill; student pvt. schs.; m. George Marlon Strickland. Salon in Paris Artistes Francais, 1924—; one-man shows Daytona Beach, 1958, 59, Ormand Beach, 1955; numerous group shows including Daytona, 1972; represented in pvt. collections in U.S. and France. Recipient numerous awards in painting and sculptures. Mem. Nat. League Am. Pen Women (pres. Daytona Beach br., 1961-64), Fla. Fedn. Art, Daytona Beach Art League, St. Augustine Art Assn., Am., Halifax County (pres. 1962-64) garden clubs. Home: 487 John Anderson Hwy Ormond Beach FL 32074

STRICKLAND, CAREY HILL (MRS. ARTHUR DANIEL STRICKLAND), educator; b. Gaffney, S.C., Dec. 12, 1925; d. George William and Florence Vallaree (Hammett) Hill; B.S., Berry Coll., 1948; M.A., Peabody Coll. for Tchrs., 1959; Edn. Specialist, U. Ga., 1966; m. Arthur Daniel Strickland, May 30, 1948; children—Valeria (Mrs. Daniel L. Moore), Karen. Bus. tchr., N. Ga. Bus. Coll., Rome, 1947-48, Waresboro High Sch., Waycross, Ga., 1949-52, Morven (Ga.) High Sch., 1952-53; elementary tchr. Bickley Jr. High Sch., Nicholls, Ga., 1953-55; bus. tchr. Bacon County High Sch., Alma, Ga., 1955-56, Blackshear (Ga.) High Sch., 1956-59, Jefferson (Ga.) High Sch., 1959-60, Hoboken (Ga.) High Sch., 1960-61, Terrell County High Sch., Dawson, Ga., 1961-65, Oconee County High Sch., Watkinsville, Ga., 1965-66; asst. prof. bus. edn. Sch. of Bus., Ga. So. Coll., Statesboro, 1966-72; bus. and career edn. tchr. Washington-Wilkes Comprehensive High Sch., Washington, Ga., 1972—. Mem. Nat., Ga., So. business edn. assns., Nat., Ga. edn. assns., Am. Assn. U. Women (treas. Statesboro br. 1969-72), Wilkes Assn. Educators (sec. 1973-74), Pi Omega Pi, Delta Pi Epsilon, Kappa Delta Pi. Home: PO Box 856 Washington GA 30673 Office: Washington-Wilkes Comprehensive High School Gordon St Washington GA 30673

STRICKLER, JANE ANN METZ (MRS. DONALD WARD STRICKLER), radiologist; b. Merchantville, N.J., Oct. 27, 1933; d. Victor Hoch and Mae Elizabeth (Hellick) Metz; B.S., Pa. State U., 1955; M.D., Temple Med. Sch., 1959; m. Donald Ward Strickler, June 21, 1957; children—Thomas Craig, Dale Edward. Intern, Western Pa. Hosp., Pitts., 1959-60, resident radiology, 1960-63; asso. radiologist with Dr. H. D. Lykens, State College, Pa., 1964—; chief radiologist Ritenour Health Center, Pa. State U., State College, 1970—. Diplomate Am. Bd. Radiology and Nuclear Medicine. Mem. A.M.A., Am. Coll. Radiology, Radiol. Soc. North Am., Pa., Center County med. socs., Pa. Radiol. Soc. Home: Box 59 Boalsburg PA 16827 Office: 253 Easterly Parkway State College PA 16801

STRICKLER, JOAN CAROLE, pub. information cons.; b. St. Louis, July 21, 1935; d. Edward Francis and Constance Agnes (Lippy) Mulholland; B.J., U. Mo., 1957; m. John Strickler, Sept. 7, 1957; children—John Edward, Carole Jean. Free lance writer; pub. information cons. Gov.'s Council on Developmental Disabilities, 1974—. Pres., Kan. Assn. Retarded Children, 1973—; chmn. council state presidents Nat. Assn. for Retarded Citizens. Bd. dirs. Fedn. for Handicapped Children, Riley County Assn. for Retarded Children; chmn. bd. dirs. Big Lakes Developmental Center. Mem. Women in Communications, Nat., Kan. press women. Editor: Tracks, 1967-70. Address: 1523 University Dr Manhattan KS 66502

STRICKLER, MARY JANE, mag. editor; b. Columbia, Pa., Mar. 4; d. George C. and Rosaline (LeFevre) Kurtz; ed. privately; m. Earl T. Strickler, Apr. 25, 1969; children—Thomas R., Richard A. Stenographer Nat. Assn. Watch and Clock Collectors, Columbia, Pa., 1965-67, sec. to mng. dir., 1967-71, librarian, 1970-72, adminstrv. asst., 1971—, asso. editor, 1973—. Mem. Order Eastern Star. Office: PO Box 33 Columbia PA 17512

STRIGHT, MARJORIE IONE LOWRY (MRS. DANIEL H. STRIGHT), newspaper editor; b. Carbondale, O., Dec. 8, 1921; d. Chester Clinton and Elizabeth (Shingler) Lowry; student Washington Sch. Secs., 1943-44; m. Daniel H. Stright, May 18, 1944; children—Daniel H., Jr., Karin (Mrs. Larry Michael Coon), Marilee, Melanie. Clerical worker Dept. Agr., Athens, O., 1940-41, U.S. Maritime Commn., Washington, 1941-43; sec. Athens County Soil Conservation, 1957-58; editor Athens Messenger, 1966—; tchr. reporting Ohio U., Athens, part-time, 1969—. Presbyn. (mem. Christian edn. com. 1961-71). Home: Route 1 Box 321 Athens OH 45701 Office: Route 33N Johnson Rd Athens OH 45701

STRINGER, MARY EVELYN, art historian; b. Huntsville, Mo., July 31, 1921; d. William Madison and Charity (Rogers) Stringer; A.B., U. Mo., 1942; A.M., U. N.C., 1955; postgrad. (Fulbright fellow) U. Freiburg im Breisgau (West Germany), 1955-56; Ph.D., Harvard, 1973. Asst. prof., asso. prof. art Miss. U. for Women, Columbus, 1947-73, prof., 1973—. Danforth Tchr. Study grantee, 1959-60, 64-65; Harvard Travel fellow, 1966-67. Mem. Coll. Art Assn. Am., Internat. Center Medieval Art, Medieval Acad. Am., Southeastern Coll. Art Conf., Nat. Orgn. Women, Sierra Club, Phi Beta Kappa. Address: Box W-1109 Columbus MS 39701

STRINGER, PAULA L., realtor; b. McKinney, Tex., Oct. 9, 1924; d. Samuel Haven and Lillian (Duncan) Lemons; student So. Meth. U., 1942-43; m. Charles F. Stringer, Dec. 20, 1943 (div.); children—Stephen Charles, Suzanne, Patricia Kay. Asso. Stewart Smith, Realtor, Houston, 1954-56; co-owner Suburban Realtors, 1958-60; owner Paula Stringer Realtors, 1960—. Mem. Woman's Council Dallas Real Estate Bd. (chmn.), Dallas Real Estate Bd., Nat. Assn. Real Estate Brokers, Nat. Inst. Real Estate Brokers, Internat. Traders Assn., Tex. Real Estate Assn., Tex. Real Estate Assn., Collin County Bd. Realtors (v.p. women's council), Dallas Home Builders Assn., League Women Voters (adv. bd.), Kappa Alpha Mothers. Clubs: Delta Delta Delta Mothers, Canyon Creek Country, Tanglewood Country. Sponsor Richardson Symphony Orchestra, Hurricane Creek Country, Willow Bend Polo and Hunt. Home: 6744 Harvest Glen Dallas TX 75240 Office: 750 S Central Expressway Richardson TX 75080 also 4230 LBJ Freeway Dallas TX 75234 also 2121 W 15th St Plano TX 75075

STRINGFELLOW, WILMA VIRGINIA, social worker; b. Des Moines; d. Ervin E. and Myrtle (Blake) Stringfellow; A.B., Drake U., 1933; M.S.W., U. Pitts., 1949. Girl res. sec. YWCA, Marshalltown, Ia., 1935-39, Colorado Springs, Colo., 1939-42, young adult sec., Peoria, Ill., 1942-47, nat. adv. sec. YWCA of Egypt, Cairo, 1949-53, field staff nat. bd. YWCA, Chgo., 1953-62, mett. exec. dir., Phila., 1962—. Bd. dirs. Adult Edn. Council Phila., 1968—; mem. adv. bd. Phila. Internat. Youth Hostel, 1968, Mem. United Fund Profl. Adv. Com., 1963-66, 69—. Mem. League Women Voters, Am. Assn. U. Women, Nat. Assn. Social Workers. Mem. Christian Ch. Club: Zonta Internat. Home: The Mermont Plaza Bryn Mawr PA 19010 Office: 2027 Chestnut St Philadelphia PA 19130

STRINGHAM, MARY ELIZABETH FLOOD, educator; b. Mpls., June 7, 1937; d. Roger Shannon and Clara Mae (Celine) Flood; B.A., St. Olaf Coll., 1958; M.A., W.Va. U., 1966; postgrad. U. Vienna, U.

Toronto, Luther Coll.; m. R. Scott Stringham, June 15, 1958. Elementary sch. music tchr., Trumansburg, N.Y., 1958-60; vocal music tchr., Millersburg, O., 1963-64; string instr. Luther Coll., 1961-63; instr. German, Davis and Elkins Coll., 1966-67; asst. prof. music edn. W.Va. U., 1967-74, asso. prof., 1974—. Cons., Fearon Publs., W.Va. Dept. Edn.; tchr. Orff-Schulwerk classes and Suzuki violin program. Recipient Univ. Senate grant for project in elementary music, 1971-72; W.Va. U. Outstanding Prof. award, 1973. Mem. Danforth Assos., Music Educators Nat. Conf., Am. String Tchrs. Assn., Internat. Soc. Music Edn., Orff-Schulwerk Assn. Club: Morgantown Woman's Music (pres. 1969-71). Contbr. articles profl. jours. Home: 1217 Corvet St Morgantown WV 26505

STRNAD, EDNA LOUISE DAWLEY (MRS. JAMES JOHN STRNAD), civic worker; b. Cleve.; d. William Jay and Helen (King) Dawley; B.A., Vassar Coll., 1945; m. James John Strnad, Apr. 7, 1951; children—James Frank, Lyse Stuart, Nina Phelps. Copy editor Social Spectator, N.Y.C., 1945-46, Mellor & Wallace Advt., Washington, 1947-48; account exec. Leech Advt., Cleve., 1949-51; dir. Lempco Industries Inc., Cleve., 1968—; dir. devel. Hathaway Brown Sch., 1973—. Founder, 1st pres. Unitarian Coop. Nursery Sch., 1954; mem. womens bd. Hiram House Camp, 1956-64; bd. Jr. League Cleve., 1963-66; co-founder Lake Erie Opera Theatre, 1964—, v.p., 1968—; womens bd. Cleve. Orch., 1965-68; founder Lake Erie Opera Theatre Womens Council, 1966, 1st pres., 1966-68. Trustee Cleve. Music Sch. Settlement, 1969—, Hathaway Brown Sch., 1973—. Mem. Cleve. Coll. Womens Assn. (bd. 1953-55). Clubs: Vassar (pres. 1961-63), Intown (Cleve.). Home: 2963 Courtland Blvd Shaker Heights OH 44122

STROBACH, JOAN M., marketing exec.; b. Los Angeles, July 16, 1922; d. John Bente and Leola May (Burroughs) Marshall; grad. high sch.; div.; children—Richard Craig, Jeffrey Scott. Interviewer, coordinator Field Research Corp., Los Angeles, 1959-61, asso. dir., 1966-68; dir. consumer research, sec.-treas. Ward J. Jenssen, Inc., Los Angeles, 1961-66; v.p. Tele-Research, Inc., Los Angeles, 1963-66; v.p., partner MSI Internat., Los Angeles, 1968—. Mem. Am. Marketing Assn., Marketing Research Assn. (expansion chmn. 1972-73). Home: 6836 Lasaine Av Van Nuys CA 91406 Office: 3440 W 8th St Los Angeles CA 90005

STROBER, MYRA HOFFENBERG (MRS. SAMUEL STROBER), educator; b. N.Y.C., Mar. 28, 1941; d. Julius William and Regina (Scharer) Hoffenberg; B.S., Cornell U., 1962; M.A., Tufts U., 1965; Ph.D., Mass. Inst. Tech., 1969; m. Samuel Strober, June 23, 1963; children—Jason, Elizabeth. Lectr., U. Md., College Park, 1967-69, asst. prof. econs., 1969-70, U. Cal. at Berkeley, 1970—; asst. prof. econs. Stanford (Cal.) U., 1972—. Mem. Am. Econs. Assn. (mem. com. on the status of women in the profession 1972—), Indsl. Relations Research Assn., Mortar Bd., Phi Kappa Phi. Contbr. articles to profl. jours. Home: 892 Lathrop Dr Stanford CA 94305 Office: Grad Sch Bus Stanford Univ Stanford CA 94305

STROCK, EILEEN CORTELYOU (MRS. ARTHUR STROCK), newspaper editor; b. Los Angeles, Aug. 28, 1910; d. Louis VanZandt and Fay (Pulliam) Cortelyou; B.A., U. Cal. at Los Angeles, 1932, postgrad., Berkeley, 1933; m. Arthur Strock, June 25, 1938; children—Arthur VanZandt, John Edgar. With Newporter-Mesa News, Newport Beach, Cal., 1965—, soc. editor, 1967-69, editor, 1969—. Bd. dirs. Orange County Philharmonic Soc., 1963-68; adv. bd., 1968—. Mem. Cal. Press Women, Theta Sigma Phi. Home: 225 Via Lida Nord Newport Beach CA 92660 Office: 350 N Newport Blvd Newport Beach CA 92660

STROLLO, JOHANNA CHRISTINE, ednl. adminstr.; b. Scranton, Pa., Feb. 5, 1937; d. Vincent and Josephine Louise (Brunnetti) Strollo; B.S., Kutztown State Coll., 1958; M.Ed., Pa. State U., 1962, D.Ed., 1972. Tchr. area schs., Reading, Pa., 1958-66; reading cons. Eastern Lebanon County, Myerstown, Pa., 1966-69; asst. prof. spl. edn., prin. Demonstration Sch. at Cresson (Pa.) State Sch. & Hosp., 1971-73, asst. dir., 1973—. Edn. cons. Cresson State Sch. and Hosp., 1969-71. Mem. Central Pa. Reading Council (pres. 1970-71), Pi Lambda Theta. Home: 31 Clover Dr Hollidaysburg PA 16648 Office: Cresson State Sch and Hosp Cresson PA 16630

STROM, INGRID MATHILDA, educator; b. Duluth, Minn., Dec. 8, 1912; d. John and Mary (Gragg) Strom; B.E., State Tchrs. Coll., Duluth, 1935; M.A., U. Minn., 1944, Ph.D., 1955. Tchr. Minn. and Wis. pub. schs., 1935-42; grad. asst. U. Minn., 1942-44; instr. in edn. and critic tchr. English, speech and journalism U. Sch., Ind. U., 1944-53, head English dept., 1946-53, asst. dir. student tchrs., sch. edn., 1955—, asst. prof. edn., 1955-61, asso. prof. edn., 1961—; dir. summer conf. English Lang. arts in secondary schs., 1957-68. Mem. nat. adv. bd. Lit. Cavalcade of Scholastic Mag., 1952-54; mem. nat. adv. textbook com. U.S. Armed Forces Inst., 1949-50. Mem. Ind. State Tchrs. Assn. (pres. English sect. 1949-50), Nat. Soc. Coll. Tchrs. Edn., N.E.A., Assn. Student Teaching (chmn. research com. 1960-64), Nat. Council Tchrs. English, Am. Assn. U. Profs., Assn. for Supervision and Curriculum Devel., Nat. Soc. for Study Edn., Nat. League Am. Pen Women (chpt. pres. 1960-62), Delta Phi Lambda, Pi Lambda Theta, Delta Kappa Gamma (pres. Alpha chpt. 1953-54). Author: The Teaching Load of Teachers of English in Indiana, 1956; The Role of Literature in the Core Curriculum, 1958; co-author An Analysis of the Instructional Utility of 319 Programs of the National Education Television and Radio Center, Ford Found. Project Editor: Leadership through Research. Home: 3801 E 3d St Bloomington IN 47401 also 3718 Grand Av Duluth MN 55807

STROM, SUEANN PECORA, ednl. adminstr.; b. Cleve., Dec. 12, 1946; d. Paul Frank and Margaret Viola (Regal) Pecora; B.A. in English, Ohio U., Athens, 1966; M.A. in Guidance and Counseling, John Carroll U., Cleve., 1972; m. Robert Jay Strom, Apr. 26, 1969; 1 dau., Mara Elizabeth. Substitute tchr., 1968-69; instr. pre-employment tng. Chrysler Corp., Twinsburg, O., 1969; tchr. English, Bedford (O.) Pub. Schs., 1969-71; freshman adviser Miami U., Oxford, O., 1972-74, coordinator campus events, 1974—. Mem. Nat., Ohio assns. women deans, adminstrs. and counselors, Am. Coll. Personnel Assn., Am. Personnel and Guidance Assn., Nat. Entertainment Conf., Alpha Xi Delta. Jewish religion. Home: 719 Marcia Dr Oxford OH 45056

STROMAN, CONNIE ELIZABETH, social agy. exec.; b. Edgemont, S.D., Mar. 14, 1917; d. Ruel Homer and Lela Mena (Barton) Stalcup; student Neb. Wesleyan U., 1934-35, Lincoln Sch. Commerce, 1955; m. J. Oakland Sidell, Nov. 17, 1940; children—Susan (Mrs. Roger D. Brandt), Joel Ruel; m. 2d, Vincent J. Stroman, Sept. 5, 1970. Govt. relations rep. Sperry and Hutchinson Co., N.D. and S.D., 1961-66; mdse. cons. J.P. Stevens Co., 1966-67; women's dir. radio sta. KMMJ, Grand Island, Neb., 1967-69; exec. dir. Grand Island United Way, 1969—. N.D. rep. to Nat. Commn. on Status of Women, Washington, 1963-64. Mem. Nat. Assn. Parliamentarians, Grand Island C. of C. (pres. women's div. 1970), Bus. and Profl. Women's Club, League Women Voters. Republican. Methodist. Clubs: Grand Island Women's, Grand Island Toastmistress. Home: 1324 North Huston St Grand Island NE 68801 Office: 2020 W 7th St Grand Island NE 68801

STRONER, JOAN HANNAH, theatrical adminstr.; b. Chgo., Feb. 10, 1940; d. William Fred and Myrtle Maria (Granzig) Stroner; B.A., Alverno Coll., 1961; M.A., Northeastern U., 1970. Chmn. drama dept. Alvernia High Sch., Chgo., 1961-69; children's theatre dir. Grand Rapids (Mich.) Civic Theatre, 1970-72; cons. ednl. service region office N.W. Area Service Center, Ill. State Gifted Program, Rockford, 1972-74; adminstrv. asso. New Am. Theatre, Rockford, 1974—. Creative drama instr. War on Poverty Program, Chgo., summers 1965, 66. Mem. Internat. Assn. Theatre Movement Program, Am., Children's theatre assns. Home: 2020 Forest View Rd Rockford IL 61108 Office: 108 N 2d St Rockford IL 61101

STRONG, ALDA (MRS. LAVERN STRONG), club woman, realtor; b. Menan, Ida., Sept. 22, 1911; d. William D. and Margaret (Hunting) Watson; grad. of high school; m. LaVern Strong, June 14, 1930; children—Nalda (Mrs. Richard C. Powell), Harvey, Deanna (Mrs. Douglas Vollmer). Active Internat. Toastmistress Clubs, 1951—, organizer 4 local clubs, pres. council number 9, No. region, 1959-60, parliamentarian No. region, 1960-61; legislative chmn. Ida. Bus. and Profl. Women's Clubs, 1958-59, chmn. pub. relations, 1959-61, pres.; safety chmn. Ida. Gen. Fedn. Women's Clubs, 1960-61, Ida. chmn. crime prevention, 1964, state safety chmn.; sec. dist. South Central, Bus. and Profl. Clubs, 1967; pres. 20th Century, Twin Falls, Idaho, 1962-63; bd. dirs. Twin Falls Salvation Army; state rep. to President's Safety Conf. Mich. State U. Organizer 5 safety clubs Nat. Safety Council; safety chmn. So. Ida. Citizens Safety Council; regional dir. Ida. Women's Hwy. Safety Leaders, 1971-74; bd. dirs. Twin Falls Civic Auditorium, 1959-61; chmn. Twjn Falls County chpt. Nat. Found.; sec. Ida. Hosp. Auxiliaries, 1959-60; pres. Twin Falls (Ida.) YWCA; sponsor Sigma chpt. Beta Sigma Phi; sec.-treas. Twin Falls County Civil Def.; past pres. Gem. State Writers Guild, editor Gem State News Letter, 1970-71; mem. Nat. Assn. Parliamentarians. Democratic candidate Ida. Ho. of Reps., 1960. Recipient Certificate of Merit award Nat. Safety Council, 1959; named Woman of Year, Bus. and Profl. Women's Clubs, 1960, Magic Toastmistress Club, Number 1002, No. region, 1959; Distinguished Service award Jr. C. of C., 1960, merit award Ida. Safety Council. Clubs: Altrusa (internat. chmn.); 20th Century Federated (fine arts chmn. 2d v.p.) Home: 2016 Stadium Blvd Twin Falls ID 83301

STRONG, ANNE J. ELMER (MRS. GEORGE W. STRONG), social worker; b. Fargo, N.D., Nov. 10, 1915; d. Manuel Conrad and June (Ashley) Elmer; B.A., U. Pitts., 1936, M.A., 1937, Ph.D., 1947; m. George W. Strong, Mar. 30, 1940 (dec. July 1943); children—Georgeanna (Mrs. Charles L. Beck), Patricia (Mrs. Roger M. Rathbun). Sr. visitor Dept. Pub. Welfare, Pitts., 1937-41; sch. social worker Pitts. Bd. of Edn., 1946-48, dist. supr., 1948—. Lectr. LaRoche Coll., 1969. Mem. Nat. Assn. Social Workers, Acad. Certified Social Workers, N.E.A., Adminstrv. Women in Edn., Delta Kappa Gamma, Pi Lambda Theta, Zeta Tau Alpha. Home: 427 Elmer St Pittsburgh PA 15218 Office: 302 Zara St Pittsburgh PA 15210

STRONG, CATHERINE ROBINSON (MRS. CEYLON PERSEUS STRONG, JR.), journalist, educator; b. Pensacola, Fla., Feb. 25, 1948; d. Clement J. and Mary Elizabeth (Twitchell) Robinson; B.A., U. Washington, 1970; M.A., Kent State U., 1974; m. Ceylon Perseus Strong, Jr., Mar. 21, 1970. Athletic and program dir. Alliance (O.) YMCA, 1971; prof. journalism East Liverpool (O.) br. of Kent State U., 1972-73; writer, photographer Akron (O.) Beacon Jour. Newspaper, 1972—. Bd. dirs. Stark County (O.) Mental Health Assn. Mem. Women in Communications, Profl. Soc. of Journalists, Women's Equity Action League (mem. state exec. bd.), Sigma Delta Chi. Roman Catholic. Home: Cunningham Hall Mt Union College Alliance OH 44601 Office: State Desk Akron Beacon Journal 44 East Exchange St Akron OH 44308

STRONG, JOAN M. TENGZELIUS (MRS. JOHN GRAHAM STRONG), civic worker; b. Far Rockaway, N.Y., Sept. 8, 1933; d. Archie E. and Angela (Prochaska) Tengzelius; B.A., Mary Washington Coll., U. Va., 1956; m. John Graham Strong, June 4, 1956; children—Michelle Kathrine, Mary Beth, John Graham, Noelle. Tchr., Bridgehampton (N.Y.) Sch., 1956-57. Corr. sec. Assn. Help Retarded Children, 1956-58; founder Am. Symphony, N.Y.C., 1968-70; founder, sponsor, dir. YMCA, East Hampton, N.Y., 1969-72; v.p. Ft. Lauderdale (Fla.) Civic Ballet Co., 1972-73. Mem. Am. Assn. U. Women (br. treas. 1956-69, 2d v.p. 1969-70, Fla. div. fellowships chmn. 1973-74), Alpha Phi Sigma, Psi Chi. Baptist. Clubs: Le Club Internat. Yacht and Tennis, Lighthouse Point Yacht and Tennis, Landings Boat (editor publ.). Home: 81 Bay Colony Dr Fort Lauderdale FL 33308

STRONG, LEAH AUDREY, educator; b. Buffalo, Mar. 14, 1922; d. Robert Leroy and Dorothy Sinclair (Kennedy) Strong; B.A., Allegheny Coll., 1943; M.A., Cornell U., 1944; Ph.D., Syracuse (N.Y.) U., 1953. Instr. English Syracuse U., 1947-52; asst. prof. English Cedar Crest Coll., Allentown, Pa., 1953-61; prof. Am. Studies Wesleyan Coll., Macon, Ga., 1961—. Mem. Am., Southeastern Am. (sec.-treas. 1973—) studies assns., So. Humanities Conf. (chmn. 1974-75), South Atlantic Modern Lang. Assn., Am. Assn. U. Profs., Pi Delta Epsilon (2d v.p. 1973—). Mem. Order Eastern Star. Club: Altrusa (Macon). Author: Joseph Hopkins Twichell: Mark Twain's Friend and Pastor, 1966. Contbr. articles to profl. jours. Home: 1173 Forest Hill Rd Macon GA 31204 Office: Am Studies Wesleyan Coll Macon GA 31201

STRONG, MARGARET I., steel co. exec.; b. Fowler, Ind., Mar. 19, 1920; d. James Oliver and Henrietta E. (Rhoades) Michaels; student Gary (Ind.) Bus. Coll., 1935-36; also extension courses in accounting La Salle Coll.; m. Howard F. Strong, June 6, 1936; children—James H., Judy K. (Mrs. Jacob Pater, Jr.). Statis. sec. to purchasing agt. Colyear Motor Sales, Phoenix, 1950-60; head bookkeeper Lou Regester Furniture, Phoenix, 1960-63; deptl. bookkeeper Madison Industries, Phoenix, 1963-69; office mgr. PEDCO, Inc., Mesa, Ariz. and Atlanta, 1969-71, controller, 1971—, sec.-treas., 1973—.

STRONG, MARILYN HARRIET, librarian; b. Batavia, N.Y., July 10, 1937; d. Stuart M. and Frances (Bauer) Strong; B.S. in Elementary Edn. State U. N.Y. Coll. at Brockport, 1958; M.L.S., State U. N.Y. Coll. at Geneseo, 1964. Tchr. Elba (N.Y.) Central Sch., 1958-62, Jackson Sch., Batavia, N.Y., 1962-63; asso. librarian Drake Meml. Library State U. N.Y. at Brockport, 1964—. Reviewer books Am. Ref. Books Ann., 1971—. Mem. A.L.A. Home: 209 Ellis Dr Brockport NY 14420

STROOP, CHRISTINE, educator; b. Nashville, Dec. 22, 1913; d. John Erskine and Ethel May (Brinkley) Stroop; B.S., Middle Tenn. State U., 1935; M.A., George Peabody Coll., summers 1936, 37, 39; D.Ed. (scholar) N.Y. U., 1951; postgrad. Bowling Green Bus. U., Northwestern U., U. Pitts. Tchr., Magnolia High Sch., Lumberton, N.C., 1935-37, Biloxi (Miss.) High Sch., 1937-40; instr. Bowling Green (Ky.) Bus. U., 1940-41; prof. bus. edn. Salem (W.Va.) Coll., 1942-43; asso. prof. bus. edn. West Liberty (W.Va.) State Coll., 1943-45; asst. prof. bus. edn. Paterson (N.J.) State Tchrs. Coll., 1946-52; prof. bus. edn. Austin Peay State U., Clarksville, Tenn., 1952—. Mem. Tchrs. Edn. Assn. (pres. bus. edn. sect. 1971—), Delta Pi Epsilon, Pi Omega Pi, Kappa Delta Pi. Editor: Business Education Observer, 1950-52. Contbr. articles in field to profl. jours. Home: 1655 Valley Rd Clarksville TN 37040

STROTHER, HAZEL B., accountant; b. Akron, O., June 29, 1929; d. Lawrence McCauley and Josie (Friend) Beall; student W.Va. Wesleyan Coll., 1947-49; A.A., George Washington U., 1951, A.B., 1952; m. Samuel L. Strother, Oct. 23, 1953 (div. Feb. 1971). Sec., jr. accountant C.B. Stovall & Co., Washington, 1951-52; sec., ins. underwriter Washington Ins. Agy., Inc., 1952-57; accountant U.S. AEC, 1957-62; accountant, asst. chief, accounting and analysis br. Hdqrs. Marine Corps, Washington, 1962-66; staff accountant Hdqrs. NASA, Washington, 1966-68; staff accountant Hdqrs. Dept. Health, Edn. and Welfare, Washington, 1968—. Mem. Am. Accounting Assn., Fed. Govt. Accountants Assn. (nat. chmn. pub. relations com. 1972—), George Washington U. Alumni Assn., W.Va. U. Alumni Assn. (treas.), W.Va. State Soc., Internat. Platform Assn., Alpha Beta Gamma. Democrat. Club: George Washington University (charter mem.). Home: 1600 S Eads St Arlington VA 22202 Office: 300 Independence Av SW Washington DC 20201

STROUD, BILLIE JANE, telephone co. engr.; b. Montgomery, La., July 14, 1929; d. Edwin and Edna Mae (Johnson) S.; student Famous Artist Sch., Westport, Conn., 1952-54, U. Houston, 1960-61. Asst. chief operator Southwestern Bell Telephone Co., Houston, 1954-63, chief operator, Victoria, Tex., 1963-64, staff asst., Austin, 1964-65, supervising chief operator, Austin, 1966-68, engring. asst., San Antonio, 1968-69, staff engr., 1970-73, supr. network design, 1974—; co-owner E&S Quick Clean Center, Port O'Connor, Tex., 1964-71. Recipient Vail awards Bell System, 1961, 67, 70, El Paisano award, 1970. Mem. San Antonio Soc. Telephone Engrs., Internat. Pilot Club (safety chmn. Victoria 1964). Composer. Address: 8607 Jones Maltsberger San Antonio TX 78216

STROUT, JANIS LYNN, educator; b. Altadena, Cal., Dec. 24, 1947; d. George Augustus and Dorothy Deane (Wiseman) Strout; B.A. in History and Sociology, Cal. State U., Long Beach, 1970, secondary credential, 1972; M.S. in Edn., Counselor Edn. and Human Services, So. Ill. U., 1975. Grad. asst., night mgr. student union Cal. State U., Long Beach, 1972-73; asst. program dir. So. Ill. U., Edwardsville, 1973—. Mem. Assn. Coll. Unions Internat. (pres. region XV, 1972-73 coordinator women's affairs region 9, 1974—), Nat. Assn. Women Deans, Adminstrs. and Counselors. Address: Program Dept Univ Center Box 67 So Ill Univ Edwardsville IL 62025

STRUBLE, DARLENE, quartz co. exec.; b. Pompton Lakes, N.J., Aug. 31, 1936; d. Edward Phillip and Beatrice (Pellington) Weatherwalks; grad. high sch.; m. Richard Joseph Struble, May 6, 1956; children—Brenda, David. Sec. Paragon Woven Label Co., Haskell, N.J., 1954-55, Artistic Weaving Co., Pompton Lakes, 1958-60; office mgr., personnel dir. U.S. Fused Quartz Co., Inc., Fairfield, N.J., 1960—. Sec. ladies aux. Pompton Lakes Fire Dept., 1970-71, 73-74. Sec. West Milford Democratic Orgn., 1957-58. Home: 289 Germantown Rd Butler NJ 07405 Office: 7 Spielman Rd Fairfield NJ 07006

STRUIK, RUTH REBEKKA, educator; b. Worcester, Mass., Dec. 15, 1928; d. Dirk Jan and Sally Ruth (Ramler) Struik; B.A. with high honors, Swarthmore Coll., 1949; M.A., U. Ill., 1951; Ph.D., N.Y. U., 1955; m. Dec. 1952 (div. Sept. 1969); children—Marion, Margo, Louise. Teaching asst. U. Chgo., 1952, Upsala Coll., 1953; lectr. Columbia, 1955; asst. prof. maths. Drexel Inst. Tech., 1956-57; lectr. U. B.C., 1957-61; acting asst. prof. U. Colo., 1961-62; asst. prof. maths. U. Colo., 1962-63, 64-65, asso. prof., 1965—; reviewer Math. Reviews; translator Russian translation project Am. Math. Soc. Mem. Nat. Orgn. Women, Math. Assn. Am., Am. Math. Soc., Assn. for Women in Math., Am. Fedn. Tchrs. Am. Assn. Univ. Profs. Contbr. articles profl. jours. Home: 3130 E Aurora St Boulder CO 80303

STRUTZ, GLORIA MARIE, surgeon; b. Richmond, Mich., Apr. 5, 1933; d. William Louis and Marie (Christensen) Strutz; B.S., U. Mich., 1954; M.D., Woman's Med. Coll. Pa., 1964. Med. technologist St. Joseph Hosp., Mt. Clemens, Mich., 1954-56; J.F. Juliar, M.D., 1956-59, U. Mich. Med. Center, 1959-60, intern physician, surgeon Riverside Meth. Hosp., Columbus, O., 1964-65; resident surgeon Henry Ford Hosp., Detroit, 1965-69; resident thoracic surgeon U. Ia. Hosps., Iowa City, 1969-71; emergency room physician E.R. Doctor, Mt. Clemens, Mich., 1972—; vol. instr., coordinator local Emergency Med. Technician Tng. Program, 1973—. Instr. U. Ia., Iowa City, 1969-70, asso. dept. surgery, 1970-71. Mem. Detroit Surg. Assn., Mich., Macomb County med. socs., A.M.A., Am. Med. Women's Assn., Roy D. McClure Surg. Soc., Nat. Assn. Residents and Interns, Alumnae Assn. Woman's Med. Coll. Pa., Gamma Delta. Lutheran. Home and office: Colonial Country Club Apts 28123 23 Mile Rd New Baltimore MI 48047

STRUZINSKY, ALYCE JEANNE, coll. adminstr.; b. New Haven, Feb. 3, 1932; d. Bernard and Pauline Mary (Zdanowicz) Struzinsky; student New Haven State Tchrs. Coll., 1949-51; Asso. Sci., Quinnipiac Coll., 1953, B.S., 1953. Asst. office mgr. Greater New Haven C. of C., 1954-66; placement dir., prelaw adviser Quinnipiac Coll., Hamden, Conn., 1966—. Mem. Nat. Wildlife Fedn., Eastern Coll. Personnel Officers, Quinnipiac Coll. Alumni Assn. Home: 65 Home Pl Branford CT 06405 Office: Mount Carmel Av Hamden CT 06518

STRYKER, MARIAN ANDERSON, ret. ednl. adminstr.; b. Green Springs, O., May 6, 1909; d. James Arthur and Elnora (Lynch) Anderson; A.B. in English, Modern Lang., Hope Coll., 1931; student Tiffin Bus. U., 1931-32; m. John Alvin Stryker, Oct. 15, 1936 (dec. 1946); children—John Alvin II, James William, David Philip. Sec. law office, Muskegon, Mich., 1932-33; sec. to sec. of state of Mich. Adminstrv. Bd., Lansing, 1933-36; corr. Grand Rapids (Mich.) Herald, 1953-58; alumni exec. sec. Hope Coll., Holland, Mich., 1947-74, also alumni editor, 1949-74. Pres. Holland Concert Assn., 1970-72; sec. Holland Arts Council, 1973—. Mem. Am. Alumni Council (treas. dist. 1959-63, editorial achievement award 1961). Club: Holland Century (pres. 1966-67). Home: 105 West 26th St Holland MI 49423 Office: 112 East 12th St Holland MI 49423

STUART, FRANCES LOUISE (MRS. THOMAS BLAINE STUART), dir. library services; b. Cameron, S.C., June 7, 1919; d. Marion Emile and Lizzie Rebecca (Haigler) Crook; B.A., U. S.C., 1940; B.S. in L.S., George Peabody Coll. Tchrs., 1943, M.L.S., 1971; m. Thomas Blaine Stuart, Nov. 10, 1945; 1 son, Wayne Dukes. Circulation librarian S.C. Library, U. S.C., Columbia, 1941-45; asst. librarian Carnegie Pub. Library, Sumter, S.C., 1946-48, librarian, 1949-51; departmental librarian Post Library, Fort Jackson, S.C., 1951-53; asst. librarian Atlas Chems. Industries, Wilmington, Del., 1954; cataloger State Library Bd., Columbia, S.C., 1957-66; dir. library services Midlands Tech. Coll., Columbia, 1966—. Mem. evaluation team So. Assn. Colls. and Schs., 1969-74. Mem. Am., S.C. (mem. com. 1962-64, 73—), So. library assns., S.C. Tech. Center Librarians (cons. 1967—), Beta Phi Mu. Home: 3546 Greenleaf Rd Columbia SC 29206 Office: PO Box Q 316 Beltline Blvd Columbis SC 29205

STUART, JANE KATHERINE, home economist; b. Raleigh, N.C., Feb. 22, 1943; d. Archie David and Katherine Lelia (Bennett) Stuart; B.S., U. Ga., 1965; M.Ed., N.C. State U., 1972. Asst. home econs. extension agt., Danbury, N.C., 1965-67; home econs. extension agt., Reidsville, N.C., 1968—. Mem. Nat., N.C. assns. extension home economists, Am., N.C. home econs. assns., Nat. Assn. Extension 4-H Agts., Epsilon Sigma Phi. Home: 1018 Cypress Dr Reidsville NC 27320 Office: Route 4 Box 1 Reidsville NC 27320

STUART, MARGARET MARTIN, state govt. ofcl.; b. Butte, Mont., Dec. 1, 1926; d. William Henry and Mary Ann (Sullivan) Martin; B.A. cum laude, St. Mary Coll., 1948; M.S.W., U. Wash., 1960; m. Harold Stuart, June 15, 1950; children—William Glenn, Joyce (Mrs. James Andersch), Harold Sanders. Child welfare worker Social and Rehab. Services, Butte, 1955-58, Silver Bow County, Mont., 1960-65; dist. child welfare supr., then asst. dir. social service programs Mont. Dept. Social and Rehab. Services, 1965-73, chief Child Welfare Services Bur., Helena, 1973—; lectr. Carroll Coll., 1972—; cons. in field. Mem. admissions com. Casey Family Program; mem. bd. Model Cities, 1966-68. Social Service Reform grantee, 1973. Mem. Am. Pub. Welfare Assn., Child Welfare League Am., Council Social Work Edn., Am. Assn. U. Women, Kappa Gamma Pi. Home: 1805 Joslyn St Apt 121 Helena MT 59601 Office: 836 Front St Helena MT 59601

STUART, SUSAN WELLS, real estate and ins. broker; b. Visalia, Cal., July 11, 1914; d. Delaware B. and Clara Irene (Swanson) Wells; A.B., U. Cal. at Berkeley, 1936; postgrad. real estate U. Cal. extension, 1937, Armstrong Coll., 1937; m. Gerald E. Stuart, May 29, 1938; children—Geraldine (Mrs. Herbert Foster), James M., John E. Salesman various firms, 1954-71; broker Stuart Realty, Hayward, Cal., 1971—; registered rep. Investment Programs, Inc., Oakland, Cal. Mem. Oakland, So. Alameda County bd. realtors, D.A.R. (regent chpt.), Am. Assn. U. Women, Am. Bus. Women's Assn., Eagles Aux. Republican. Mem. Order Eastern Star (past matron). Home: 7 Edgemont Way Oakland CA 94605

STUART, VIRGINIA HEIDE, state ofcl.; b. Kenosha, Wis., Aug. 25, 1914; d. John Martin and Anna Christine (Huus) Heide; Litt.B., Douglass Coll., 1936; postgrad. Columbia, 1936, 37, 38-40; m. Douglas E. Stuart, Oct. 31, 1942 (dec. Nov. 1970); children—Alison (Mrs. Frederic A. deP. Todd), Anne Kristine, Douglas Reed. Asst. editor Princeton U. Press., 1937-43; pub. relations dir. Chestnut Hill Hosp., Phila., 1951-54; dir. pub. relations Princeton Hosp., 1957-66; mental health information officer N.J. Div. Mental Health and Hosps., Trenton, 1966—. Active Girl Scouts U.S.A., Am. Cancer Soc., Nat. Found., other charity drives. Mem. Nat. Assn. Mental Health Information Officers (pres. 1973-74), Am. Soc. Hosp. Pub. Relations, Nat. Fedn. Press Women, Phi Beta Kappa. Home: Feather Bed Lane Hopewell NJ 08525 Office N J Div Mental Health and Hosps Dept Instns and Agys 136 W Hanover St Trenton NJ 08625

STUBBLEFIELD, MARY FRANCES, educator; b. Viola, Tenn., Aug. 12, 1925; d. Will Locke and Annie Clara (Gessler) Stubblefield; B.S., Tenn. Technol. U., 1946; M.A., Peabody Coll., 1949, postgrad., 1959—. Tchr. algebra Livingston (Tenn.) Acad., 1946-47, McMinnville (Tenn.) High Sch., 1947-51; tchr. math., physics Tullahoma (Tenn.) High Sch., 1951-59; asso. prof. math. Middle Tenn. State U., Murfreesboro, 1959—. Engring. aide Arnold Engring. Devel. Center, summers 1954-59. Recipient Outstanding Tchr. award Middle Tenn. State U., 1967-68. Mem. Nat. Council Tchrs. Math., Math. Assn. Am., Tenn. Math. Tchrs. Assn., N.E.A. (life), Tenn., Middle Tenn. (sec. 1969-70) edn. assns., Am. Assn. U. Women (past treas.), Bus. and Profl. Womens Club, D.A.R. (past Murfreesboro vice regent and treas.), Delta Kappa Gamma. Mem. Ch. of Christ. Clubs: Tullahoma Junior Woman's, Dames. Home: Apt 32 Mercury Manor Murfreesboro TN 37130

STUBBS, ALICE CAMILLA, educator; b. Waco, Tex., Jan. 27, 1916; d. James Thomas and Alice (Jett) Stubbs; B.S., U. Tex., 1938; M.S., Columbia, 1944; Ph.D., Purdue U., 1957. Asst. prof. home econs. U. Ga., 1945-48; asso. prof. Centenary Coll., 1949-51; instr., research asst. U. Ill., 1951-52; asst. grad. tchr. Purdue U., 1952-53, grad. research asst., U., 1956-57; head home econs. dept. Mary Hardin-Baylor Coll., 1953-54; asso. prof. home econs. Ala. Coll., 1954-56; asst. prof. to asso. prof. home econs. research dept. Agrl. Expt. Sta. of Tex. A. and M. U., 1957—, head Consumer Research Center, 1961—. Vis. prof. Miss. So. U., 1957. Sec. Brazos County Community Action Com. Fellow A.A.A.S.; mem. Am. Assn. Housing Educators, Am. Assn. U. Profs., Am. Assn. U. Women, Am., Tex. (Tex. sec. 1971—) home econs. assns., Bus. and Profl. Women's Club, Tex. Nutrition Council, Assn. Adminstrs. Home Econs. (regional chmn. 1969-71), Tex. Inst. Food Technologists, Omicron Nu, Phi Tau Sigma. Club: Bryan Altrusa (local pres. 1971-72). Contbr. articles profl. jours., agrl. expt. sta. bulls. Home: 204 Inlow St Bryan TX 77801

STUBBS, DORETHA LAVERN BEAVER (MRS. EVERETT WALTER STUBBS), newspaper editor; b. Paden, Okla., Feb. 14, 1922; d. Joe Martin and Effie Gretchen (Powers) Beaver; m. Everett Walter Stubbs; children—Barbara Caywood, Donna Powders, Shelly Crow. Editor, Tulsa County News, Tulsa, 1965—. Home: 4839 S 35 W Av Tulsa OK 74107 Office: 1801 W 51st St Tulsa OK 74107

STUBBS, LUCILLE HILDA, editor; b. Seguin, Tex., Aug. 17, 1908; d. William Ernst and Olga Mary (Blumberg) Koepsel; grad. Tex. Chiropractic Coll., 1928; student U. Houston, 1961; m. Frank L. Stubbs, Feb. 17, 1929; 1 son, Donald W.K. Pvt. practice chiropractic medicine, 1928; asst. mgr. Vivreux Gift Shop, Seguin, 1947-54; with radio sta. KWED, Seguin, 1954-55; with Guadalupe County Pub. Co., Seguin, 1955—, women's editor, 1955—. Chmn. Guadalupe County March of Dimes, Seguin, 1959-74; commr. Seguin Housing Authority, 1970-74. Sec. Guadalupe County Dem. Womens Forum, 1969-74. Bd. dirs. Seguin Conservation Soc., 1969-74. Recipient Community award City of Seguin, 1972. Mem. Women in Communication, Daus. Republic of Tex. (reporter 1972-74), Tex. Press Assn. Methodist. Clubs: Seguin Study; Delphian. Contbr. articles in field to profl. jours. Home: 931 N Austin St Seguin TX 78155 Office: 1100 N Camp St Seguin TX 78155

STUCKE, DORIS GENEVA, educator; b. Malta, Mont., Jan. 31, 1918; d. Herbert August and Esther Marie (Stark) Stucke; student No. Mont. Coll., 1935-37; B.S., Am. U., 1949; diploma Sibley Meml. Hosp. Sch. Nursing, 1948; M.Ed., U. Minn., 1956; Ed.D., Columbia, 1967. Nursing arts instr. Sibley Meml. Hosp., Washington, 1948-49, Deaconess Hosp., Grand Forks, N.D., 1949-53; evening clin. instr. Swedish Hosp., Mpls., 1953-55; chmn. dept. nursing Gustavus Adolphus Coll., 1956-67; prof., dir. Pacific Luth. U. Sch. Nursing, 1967—. Luth. Nurses's Guild scholar, 1955; Martin Luther fellow, 1964. Mem. Am. Nurses Assn., Nat. League Nursing, Delta Kappa Gamma, Kappa Delta Pi, Pi Lambda Theta. Lutheran. Home: 13219 E B St Tacoma WA 98445

STUCKEY, IRENE HAWKINS, plant physiologist; b. Griffin, Ga., Apr. 6, 1911; d. Henry Perkins and Cornelia Childress (Martin) Stuckey; B.A., Vanderbilt U., 1932; Ph.D., Cornell U., 1936. Prof. plant physiology U. R.I., 1937—. Author: Rhode Island Wildflowers, 1967. Home: 28 Cherry Rd Kingston RI 02881 Office: Dept Plant and Soil Sci U RI Kingston RI 02881

STUCKY, OLGA BEATA EVA (MRS. HENRY FRANK STUCKY), librarian; b. Freeman, S.D., Dec. 25, 1905; d. Fred and Christina Fredrica (Walz) Jundt; student Dakota Wesleyan U., Mitchell, S.D., 1923-25; student U. S.D. Sch. Library Sci., 1969, Springfield, 1971—; m. Henry Frank Stucky, July 25, 1927; children—Loren, Allen, John Henry. Tchr. pub. schs., Freeman and Hurley, S.D., 1925-27; librarian Freeman Pub. Library, 1961—. Mem. S.D. Library Assn., Home Extension Homemakers, Freeman Community Hosp. Aux. Lutheran. Home: 400 S Dewald St Freeman SD 57029 Office: Box 235 Freeman SD 57029

STUDWELL, ANN MARIE STROIA (MRS. WILLIAM EMMETT STUDWELL), editor; b. Detroit, Feb. 23, 1944; d. John Alex and Ruth Ada (Peregrine) Stroia; B.A., Kalamazoo Coll., 1965; M.A., U. Mich., 1969; m. William Emmett Studwell, Aug. 28, 1965. Tech. editor Peat, Marwick, Livingston & Co., mgmt. cons., Washington, 1966-68; instr. English and French, Kirtland Community Coll., Roscommon, Mich., 1968-70; editor Golf Supt. trade mag. Golf Course Supt.'s Assn. Am., Des Plaines, Ill., 1972-74; asst. dir. Ednl. Resources Information Center Clearinghouse in Career Edn., Northern Ill. U., DeKalb, 1974—. Mem. Modern Lang. Assn., Soc. for Tech. Communication, Phi Beta Kappa. Club: University Women's (No. Ill. U.). Home: Route 1 Box 88A Sycamore IL 60178 Office: Northern Ill Univ DeKalb IL 60115

STUERMER, VIRGINIA MAE, surgeon, educator; b. Lincoln, Neb.; d. Max J. and Pauline H. (Sander) Stuermer; B.A., U. Neb., 1945, M.D., 1948. Intern, Jersey City Med. Center, 1948-49; resident obstetrics and gynecology State U. Ia., Iowa City, 1949-52; pvt. practice medicine specializing in obstetrics and gynecology, Los Angeles, 1952-54, New Haven, 1955—; mem. staff Yale New Haven Hosp.; mem. faculty Inst. Yale Sch. Medicine, New Haven, 1954-55, asso. clin. prof. obstetrics, 1969—. Med. dir. Planned Parenthood League Conn., 1965-69, chmn. med. adv. com., 1969—. Mem. A.A.A.S., Am. Fedn. Clin. Research, Conn. Med. Soc., Conn. Soc. Obstetrics, New Haven Obstetrics Soc. Home: 605 Ridge Rd Hamden CT 06517 Office: 2 Church St S New Haven CT 06519

STUFF, MARJORIE ANN, librarian; b. Lincoln, Neb., July 14, 1906; d. Frederick Ames and Minnie Julia (Moore) Stuff; B.A., U. Neb., 1929; M.A., Bryn Mawr, 1931; postgrad. U. London, 1932-33, Sorbonne U., summer 1933, State U. Ia., 1933-36; B.S., Columbia, 1938. Cataloger, Stetson U., DeLand, Fla., 1938-39; library asst. U. Neb., Lincoln, 1939-40; serials cataloger, 1940-43; cataloger spl. collections, acting curator rare books Ind. U., Bloomington, 1943; asst. catalog librarian U. Neb., 1944-46; head order and catalog dept. Stephens Coll., Columbia, Mo., 1946-52; head librarian Neb. Wesleyan U., Lincoln, 1952-54; head reference dept. Omaha Pub. Library, 1954-56; librarian, history of medicine div. Nat. Library of Medicine, Bethesda, Md., 1956—. Mem. Am. (mem. council 1952-56), Med., D.C. library assns., Assn. Coll. and Research Libraries, Am. Assn. History Medicine, Wash. Soc. Hist. Medicine, Potomac Tech. Processors, Phi Beta Kappa, P.E.O., Alpha Chi Omega. Home: 8200 Wisconsin Av Bethesda MD 20014 Office: 8600 Rockville Pike Bethesda MD 20014

STUFF, PATRICIA JANE (MRS. WILLIAM WESLEY GROVER, JR.), physician; b. Dixon, Ill., May 11, 1929; d. Ralph Maynard and Marjorie Melviron (Cashman) Stuff; student Coe Coll., 1947-48; B.S., U. Denver, 1951; M.D., Med. Coll. Pa., 1951; m. William Wesley Grover, Jr., Oct. 5, 1957; children—Sara Watt, Thea Diehl, William Wesley Grover, III. Intern St. Luke's Hosp., Chgo., 1955-56; resident U. S.D., Yankton, 1956-57; practice medicine Bonduel (Wis.) Clinic, 1957—; mem. staffs Shawano (Wis.) Community Hosp. Organizer Citizens' Com. Shawano County for Mental Health Clinic, 1964-66; vice-chmn. Unified Mental Health Bd. of Shawano and Waupaca Counties, 1974, chmn. planning com., 1974; bd. dirs. Wolf River Mental Health Center, 1966-73, pres., 1966—; mem. family life edn. com. Shawano County, 1967-68; co-founder Bonnie Club, 1969—. Recipient Woman of Year award Shawano County Bus. and Profl. Women's Assn., 1971. Mem. A.M.A., State Med. Soc. Wis. (vice-speaker ho. of dels. 1973—), Shawano County Med. Soc. (county del. 1967-72). Presbyn. Club: Woman's (Bonduel). Home: 135 Elm St Bonduel WI 54107 Office: 401 Mill St Bonduel WI 54107

STULL, SARAH LOUISE, librarian; b. Thompsonville, Ill., Aug. 3, 1917; d. Carl Kinison and Sarah Isabel (McCreery) Stull; B.A., U. Ill., 1957, M.L.S., 1958. Clk. asst. Urbana (Ill.) Pub. Library, 1941-44; chief clk. undergrad. U. Ill. Library, 1944-55; sch. librarian pub. schs., Evanston, Ill., 1958-59; curriculum librarian Fresno State Coll. Library, 1959-66; chief social scis. U. Ariz. Library, Tucson, 1966-67; librarian, prof., curriculum library Sch. Edn., Cal. State U., Fresno, 1967—. Mem. A.L.A., Internat. Relations Roundtable, Am. Assn. Sch. Librarians, Assn. Coll. and Research Libraries, Cal. Library Assn., Cal. Assn. Sch. Librarians, Cal. Tchrs. Assn., Photographic Soc. Am. Clubs: Fresno Camera, San Joaquin Valley Council of Camera Clubs. Contbr. articles to profl. pubs. Home: 1274 East Vartikian St Fresno CA 93710

STULL, VIRGINIA ELIZABETH, physician; b. Springfield, O., May 7, 1939; d. Robert and Ruth Estelle (Callahan) Stull; B.S., Tex. So. U., 1960; postgrad. Am. U., 1960-61; M.D., U. Tex., 1966; postgrad. Capital U. Law Sch., 1970—. Intern Grant Hosp., Columbus, O., 1966-67; practice gen. medicine, Columbus, 1967-68; sch. physician Columbus Bd. Edn., 1968-73; field med. cons. Bur. Vocational Rehab., 1970—; examining physician Bur. of Disability Determination, 1973—; adminstrv. med. cons. Ohio Rehab. Services Commn., 1974—; mem. staffs Grant, St. Anthony hosps., Columbus. NIH grantee Baylor U. Med. Sch., 1961-62; fellow. Am. U., 1960-61; cardiology research fellow Ohio State U., 1965. Mem. Am. Med. Women's Assn., Acad. Medicine of Columbus and Franklin Counties, Nat. Rehab. Assn., Beta Kappa Chi, Alpha Kappa Alpha. Home: Redbridge and E Ringold Rd Ashville OH 43103 Office: 1825 Bryden Rd Columbus OH 43205

STULTZ, MARGUERITE, mus. ofcl.; b. Frankfort, Ind., Nov. 11, 1894; d. William Allen and Elizabeth (Rhodes) Stultz; B.S., Ind. State Tchrs. Coll., 1931. Tchr. Tippecanoe, Boone and Whitley Counties, Ind., 1913-63; curator Whitley County Hist. Mus., Columbia City, Ind., 1963—. Mem. D.A.R., P.E.O. Home: 114 W Jefferson St Columbia City IN 46725 Office: 108 W Jefferson St Columbia City IN 46725

STUNKEL, EVA BARBARA RUSSELL, research psychologist; b. N.Y.C., Aug. 22, 1923; d. Irwin and Marion (Axelrod) Russell; B.A., Hunter Coll., 1944; M.A., N.Y. U., 1947; m. Kenneth Stunkel, 1951 (div. 1961); children—Sally Melissa, Reagan Myron. Research psychology worker Central Islip (N.Y.) State Hosp., 1944-46; research psychologist Personnel Research Br., U.S. Dept. Army, Washington, 1948-52, U.S. Civil Service Commn., 1952-55, 55-57, 61-63, Met. Police, Washington, 1955, U.S. Dept. Health Edn. and Welfare, Washington, 1957-59; research psychologist Social Security Adminstrn., Balt., 1963-67, personnel research psychologist, 1963-67, dep. chief personnel research and employee evaluation br., 1967—. Panel mem. bd. U.S. Civil Service Examiners for rating psychologists, 1963-67. Bd. dirs. Modern Dance Council Washington, 1958-60. Mem. Am. Psychol. Assn., Soc. Personnel Adminstrn. Contbr. articles to profl. jours. Home: 5152 Endymion Lane Columbia MD 21044 Office: 6401 Security Blvd Baltimore MD 21235

STUPACK, BETTI MILDRED (MRS. IRWIN STUPACK), occupational therapist; b. Bklyn., Jan. 5, 1932; d. Joseph Louis and Helen Betti (Straus) Hamburger; student Centenary Jr. Coll., 1949-50; B.S. in Occupational Therapy, N.Y. U., 1953; m. Irwin Sheldon Stupack, Oct. 16, 1953; children—Robert Louis, Barbara Lynn. Staff registered occupational therapist N.J. State Hosp., Trenton, 1953-54; occupational therapist rehab. dept. Kings County Hosp., Bklyn., 1954-56; psychiat. sr. occupational therapist Nassau County Med. Center, East Meadow, N.Y., 1969-70, sr. occupational therapist dept. rehab., 1970—. Participant profl. workshops. Mem. P.T.A., Baldwin, N.Y., Rockville Centre, N.Y., 1962—; leader Baldwin council Girl Scouts Am., 1968; mem. Civic Assn., Baldwin, 1965-68, edn. com. Central Synagogue of Nassau County, Rockville Centre, 1973. Mem. Am. Occupational Therapy Assn., League of Women Voters (voters service chmn. 1966-67, Interfaith Council 1973-74), Hadassah. Mem. B'nai B'rith. Address: 61 Banbury Rd Rockville Center Long Island NY 11570

STUPP, VICKI O'DONNELL, educator; b. Greensburg, Pa., Feb. 12, 1938; d. Victor Clarence and Helen Alyne (Detar) O'Donnell; B.A., Pa. State U., 1959, M.A., 1961, Ph.D., 1968; m. William Eugene Stupp, June 13, 1959; children—Christopher O'Donnell, Browning William. Instr. Pa. State U., 1961-65; asst. prof. Midwestern U., Wichita Falls, Tex., 1965-67, research grantee, 1966-67; asso. prof. speech communication North Tex. State U., Denton, 1967—, research grantee, 1974-75. Lectr., Detlesenschule, Gluckstadt, Germany, 1960-61. Pub. relations dir. Denton County Democratic campaign, 1972; mem. steering com., student coordinator Farenthold for Gov. Campaign, 1972. Mem. Speech Communication Assn., Rhetoric Soc. Am., Tex. Speech Communication Assn. (chairperson coms.), Tex. Assn. Coll. Tchrs. (chpt. pres. 1973-74), Nat. Orgn. Women, Women for Change, Nat., Tex. women's polit. caucuses, Delta Sigma Rho-Tau Kappa Alpha, Pi Kappa Delta (hon.). Lutheran. Contbr. articles to profl. jours. Home: 314 Magnolia St Denton TX 76201

STURDIVANT, LAURA DRAKE SATTERFIELD (MRS. EDWIN COLEMAN STURDIVANT), hist. and med. writer; b. Port Gibson, Miss., Aug. 31, 1913; d. Milling Marion and Laura (Drake) Satterfield; B.A. magna cum laude, Millsaps Coll., 1934; m. William Harrell, Oct. 12, 1933 (dec. 1969); m. 2d, Edwin Coleman Sturdivant, Nov. 17, 1973. Research and editorial asst. Miss. Dept. Archives and History, Jackson, 1941-47, 50, research asst., 1961-73, asst. dir. information and edn. div., 1973—; med. sec. VA Hosp., Little Rock, 1950-52; publs. writer med. scis. army med. service Army Med. Service Sch., Brooke Army Med. Center, San Antonio, 1952-58; publs. writer med. scis. bur. state services Communicable Disease Center, USPHS, Atlanta, 1959-60. Mem. Miss. history adv. com. Miss. Authority Ednl. TV, 1973—. Recipient Gautier Hist. Article award South Miss. Festival of Arts, 1967, Old Spanish Fort Poetry award, 1968, 69. Mem. Soc. Am. Archivists, Am., So. hist. assns., Miss. Folklore Soc. (pres. 1971-72), Internat. Platform Assn., Am. Med. Writers Assn., Nat. League Am. Pen Women (pres. Magnolia br. 1971-74), Millsaps Coll. Alumni Assn. (dir. 1971-74), Med. Library Assn., Miss. Hist. Soc., Miss. Geneal. Soc., Colonial Dames Am. (chpt. v.p.), A.A.A.S., D.A.R., Kappa Delta. Methodist (archives and history commn.). Club: Jackson Yacht. Author: (with J.H. Hendrix, Jr.) A History of the American Association of Plastic Surgeons, 1971. Asst. editor Jour. Miss. History, 1963—; cons. editor Enchantment of Am. series; asst. editor, contbr. to A History of Mississippi, 2 vols., 1972; indexer, author preface reprint Recollections of Mississippi and Mississippians (Reuben Davis), 1972. Contbr. to hist. publs. Home: 820 Arlington St Jackson MS 39202 Office: Miss Dept Archives and History PO Box 571 Jackson MS 39205

STURGEON, MIRIAM JOY (MRS. ROBERT RAY STURGEON), editor; b. Waldron, Ind., Aug. 27, 1916; d. James Henry and Pearl Ethel (Haymond) Meloy; A.B. with honors, Ind. U., 1938, A.M., 1940; m. Robert Ray Sturgeon, Aug. 6, 1943; children—William, Sally, Barbara, Margaret (Mrs. Bradford Meador). Editor, The Review, Ind. U., Bloomington, 1957—, Hoosier Bus. Women, Nashville, Ind., 1967—. Pres. Southeastern Ind. Area Library Services Authority, 1973—. Recipient Golden Statuette, Girl Scouts Am., 1971. Mem. Women in Communications (nat. pres. 1961-63, pres. Bloomington chpt. 1974-75), Nat. Soc. Arts and Letters (pres. 1973-75), Nat. Fedn. Press Women (chmn. scholarship com. 1963-70), Women's Press Club Ind. (chmn. internat. com. 1972, chmn. scholarship com. 1972-74). Home: Route 3 Nashville IN 47448 Office: Box 368 Nashville IN 47448

STURGEON, PAULINE, journalist; b. Centralia, Mo., Sept. 4, 1907; d. William Arthur and Ruth Jane (Cook) Sturgeon; B.J., U. Mo., 1929. Proofreader, press checker Ovid Bell Press, Fulton, Mo., 1930-33; copy editor, news writer Centralia Fireside Guard, 1956-60; asst. womens dept., feature writer Columbia (Mo.) Daily Tribune, 1960-64; womens editor Independence (Mo.) Examiner, 1966-67; editor Russell (Kan.) Record, 1967—. Mem. Centralia Library Bd., 1960-61. Mem. Nat. Fedn. Press Women, Mo. (northeast dist. v.p. 1963), Kan. (northwest dist. v.p. 1973) press women, Bus. and Profl. Womens Club (Woman of Year, Centralia, 1963, Russell, 1971), Am. Assn. U. Women. Methodist. Home: PO Box 86 Russell KS 67665 Office: 802 Maple St Russell KS 67665

STURGES, CHRISTINE ANNE, educator; b. Danbury, Conn., Jan. 29, 1945; d. John Carter and Marjorie Ethel (Wight) Sturges; A.B. with honors, Coll. William and Mary, 1967; M.A., Northwestern U., 1969, Ph.D., 1971. Tchr. reading and lit. Vogel Jr. High Sch., Torrington, Conn., 1967-68; tchr. creative dramatics Haven Jr. High Sch., Evanston, Ill., 1969; pub. relations mgr. Theatre 65, Evanston, 1969-70; asst. prof. theatre arts U. No. Colo., 1971—; stage mgr. The Common Glory, summer 1968; dir. Polly Pockets Children's Theatre project of Zeta Phi Eta, 1970-71. Mem. Am. Theatre Assn. (chmn. research panel on theatre edn.), Phi Beta Kappa, Theta Alpha Phi, Zeta Phi Eta, Kappa Delta. Home: PO Box 728 Windsor CO 80550

STURGES, FLORENCE MARGARET (MRS. DWIGHT RICHARD STURGES), librarian; b. Boston, July 2, 1908; d. Edgar Saxon and Charlotte Jane (Case) Stanley; student New Eng. Conservatory, 1928-30; student Boston Pub. Library Tng. Sch., 1931-33; diploma Curry Coll., 1940; m. Dwight Richard Sturges, Oct. 12, 1935. Children's librarian Boston Pub. Library, 1932-41; children's librarian Wellesley (Mass.) Free Library, 1943-70, reference librarian, 1943-70; children's librarian, asst. librarian Skidompha Library, Damariscotta, Me., 1970—. Cons. in establishment of library at Children's Hosp., Boston, 1956-60; pres. New Eng. Round Table of Children's Librarians, 1960-62; mem. Sci. Mus. Book Com., Boston, 1962-68; Caroline M. Hewins lectr., Boston, 1959. Mem. Bronte Soc. of Eng., Nat. Book League, Am. Pen Women (book rev. editor 1968-70). Clubs: Saturday Morning of Boston, Women's Club. Contbr. articles to lit. publs. Home: Old County Rd Damariscotta ME 04543 Office: Skidompha Library Damariscotta ME 04543

STURM, RUTH FOSTER, lawyer; b. Bklyn., Jan. 3, 1911; d. Ernest and L. Elsie (Foster) Sturm; B.A., Vassar Coll., 1932; LL.B., Columbia, 1935; summer study U. Lausanne (Switzerland), 1929, U. Berlin, 1931. Admitted to N.Y. bar, 1936, pvt. practice N.Y.C., 1936-42, asso. with Walter F. O'Malley, Esq.; law asst. Ct. of Appeals State N.Y., 1942-44; U.S. Customs Ct., 1944—. Mem. Gov.'s Com. Edn. and Employment Women, 1964-65, adv. com. Hudson River Valley Commn., 1965-66. Mem. N.Y. County Lawyer's Assn., Fed. Bar Assn., Bus. and Profl. Women's Club Tarrytowns (pres. 1948-50) N.Y. State safety chmn., 1950-52, (by-laws chmn., 1953-58, 2d v.p. 1958-60, 1st v.p., 1960-62, pres. 1962-64, parliamentarian 1972—), Nat. Council Women, Phi Beta Kappa, Kappa Beta Pi. Republican. Presbyn. Author: A Manual of Customs Law, 1974. Home: Hudson House Ardsley-on-Hudson NY 10503 Office: 1 Federal Plaza New York City NY 10007

STUTZ, GERALDINE (MRS. DAVID GIBBS), corp. exec.; b. Chgo., Aug. 5, 1924; d. Alexander H. and Estelle (Tully) Stutz; B.A. cum laude, Mundelein Coll., Chgo., 1945; m. David Gibbs. Asso. fashion editor Glamour mag., 1947-52; fashion and promotion dir. I. Miller & Sons, Co., N.Y.C., 1953-54, v.p., gen. mgr., 1954-57; pres. Henri Bendel, Inc., 1957—, dir., 1956—. Office: 10 W 57th St New York City NY 10019 35 E 61st St New York City NY 10021*

STYNES, MARCIA ANNE, braillist; b. Appleton, Wis., Mar. 17, 1932; d. Paul Robert and Ruth Helen (Holz) Meyers; B.S. in Occupational Therapy, Wayne State U., 1955; m. Stanley Kenneth Stynes, Aug. 27, 1955; children—Peter Casey, Pamela Kay, Suzanne Elizabeth. Occupational therapist Rehab. Inst. Met. Detroit, 1955-56; hand transcription of ink print into braille. Registered occupational therapist; certified braillist. Mem. Am., Detroit Dist. (past pres.) occupational therapy assns., Wayne State U. Occupational Therapy (past pres.), Wayne State U. (dir.) alumni assns., Faculty Wives of Wayne State U., Tri-County Braille Vols., Sisterhood of Temple Beth El, Alpha Omicron Pi. Methodist. Home: 35260 Scone St Livonia MI 48154

SUAREZ, BARBARA (MRS. JOSEPH SUAREZ), specialist mental retardation; m. N.Y.C., Mar. 22, 1927; d. Max and Hannah (Sprayragon) Silberbusch; B.S., Bklyn. Coll., 1949; M.S., Yeshiva U., 1963; m. Herman B. Fleishman, Mar. 1949 (div. Nov. 1960); children—Marc Fleishman, Ivan Fleishman; m. 2d, Joseph Suarez, Oct. 8, 1966. Dir. Rehab. Center for Children, Bronx, Albert Einstein Coll. Medicine, 1960-67; program specialist mental retardation Westchester County Community Mental Health Bd., White Plains, N.Y., 1967—. Fellow Am. Orthopsychiat. Assn. Home: Route 1 Journey's End Rd Lewisboro NY (PO) New Canaan CT 06840 Office: West Chester County Community Mental Health Bd County Office Bldg White Plains NY 10601

SUAREZ-MURIAS, MARGUERITE C., educator; b. Havana, Cuba, Mar. 23, 1921; d. Eduardo R. and Marguerite (Vendel) Suarez-Murias; came to U.S., 1935, naturalized, 1959; B.A., Bryn Mawr Coll., 1942; M.A., Columbia, 1953, Ph.D., 1957. Lectr. Spanish, Columbia, 1954-56; pub. relations officer med. div. Johns Hopkins, 1957-58; asst. prof. Spanish and French, Sweet Briar Coll., 1958-59, Hood Coll., 1960-61; lectr. Cath. U., 1960-63, asst. prof., summers 1960-62, asso. prof., summer 1964-66; asst. prof. dept. langs. and linguistics Am. U., 1961-63, asso. prof., 1963-66; prof. dept. classical and modern langs. Marquette U., Milw., 1966-68; prof. Spanish and Portuguese U. Wis., Milw., 1968—, chmn., 1972—. Mem. Modern Lang. Assn., Am. Assn. Tchrs. Spanish and Portuguese, Wis. Council Latin Americanists, Marquis Biog. Library Soc. (adv. mem.), Instituto Internacional de Literatura Iberoamericana. Roman Catholic. Author: La novela romantica en Hispanoamerica, 1963; Antologia estilistica de la prosa moderna espanola, 1968; also various articles profl. jours. Editor: Gironella's Los cipreses creen en Dios, 1969. Home: 3904 St Paul St Baltimore MD 21218 Office: U Wis Milwaukee WI 53201

SUBOCZEWSKI, IRENE (MRS. GEORGE E. SUBOCZEWSKI), educator; b. Kaunas, Lithuania, Sept. 1, 1923; s. Klemas and Viera (von Budde) Pogozelskis; came to U.S, 1950, naturalized, 1954; B.A. magna cum laude, Hunter Coll., 1967; M.A., U. Md., 1968, Ph.D., 1970; m. George E. Suboczewski, Sept. 3, 1949. Asst. prof. comparative lit. Fed. City Coll., Washington, 1971—. Nat. Def. Edn. Act fellow, 1967-70. Mem. Phi Beta Kappa, Phi Kappa Phi. Home: 25 E Wayne Av Apt 815 Silver Spring MD 20901 Office: Dept English Federal City College Washington DC 20001

SUCHARA, HELEN THERESA, educator; b. Detroit, Jan. 2, 1919; d. Frank and Veronica (Urbanik) Suchara; B.A., Wayne U., 1942, M.A., 1947; Ed.D., Columbia, 1956. Tchr. various Mich. schs., 1942-50; instr. Columbia Tchrs. Coll., 1950-53; asso. prof. Wheelock Coll., Boston, 1953-56; faculty Wayne State U., Detroit, 1956—, prof. edn., 1965—. Faculty spl. summer sessions U. Va., 1951, U. Del., 1954-56; cons. spl. edn. programs Detroit Met. Area sch. systems, 1958—. Mem. Nat. (exec. com. 1965-67), Mich. (pres. 1962-63) assns. student teaching, Am. Edl. Research Assn., Am. Assn. U. Profs;, N.E.A., Am. Mich. assns. for higher edn. Assn. Childhood Edn. Internat. (contbr. mags. 1968—), Kappa Delta Pi, Beta Sigma Phi. Address: 14360 Farmington Rd Livonia MI 48154

SUCHY, GREGORIA KARIDES (MRS. RAYMOND WILLIAM SUCHY), composer, educator; b. Milw.; d. George Peter and Maruly Alexander (Stratigos) Karides; B.S., Milw. State Tchrs. Coll., 1945; M. Music, Northwestern U., 1951, postgrad, summer 1957, 59, 60, DePaul U., 1959-60, 60-61, Roosevelt U., 1961-66, U. Chgo., 1967-69; m. Raymond William Suchy, Dec. 28, 1947; children—Jessica, Mara. Tchr. instrumental music Milw. Pub. Schs., 1943-44; tchr. piano and instrumental Northwestern Conservatory of Music, 1944-47; tchr. theory, instrumental teaching Carroll Music Studios, Milw., 1945; mem. faculty U. Wis., Milw., 1946—, prof. theory and composition dept. music Sch. Fine Arts, 1969—. Recipient Star award Delta Omicron, 1957, certificate of recognition Greek Orthodox Archidiocese of North and South Am., 1967, research grant Grad Sch. U. Wis., 1960, 63, 65, 69, numerous prizes and awards including 1st prize Musicians Club of Women, Chgo., 1960, Nat. Fedn. Music Clubs, 1973, Milw. Profl. Panhellenic Achievement award, 1973. Faculty fellow U. Wis., 1967. Mem. Am. Music Center, Inc., Delta Omicron, Internat. Soc. Contemporary Music, Wis. Fedn. Music Clubs, Wis. Contemporary Composers Forum, Milw. Civic Concert Assn. (dir. 1948-59, pres. 1956-57, pres. ex officio, 1959), Kappa Delta Pi. Mem. Greek Orthodox Ch. Home: 2601 E Newton Av Milwaukee WI 53211

SUDDUTH, MARTHA COOPER, educator; b. Winchester, Ky., Feb. 13, 1914; d. Thomas Goff and Frances (Edmondson) Sudduth; B.S., Eastern Ky. U., 1934; M.A., U. Ky., 1954; postgrad. U. Ore., 1953-55; Ed.D., Ind. U., 1962. Tchr. elementary pub. schs. Winchester, Ky., 1937-41, Covington, 1941-42; exec. sec. Codell Constrn. Co., Winchester, 1942-44; tchr. elementary schs. Winchester, 1944-53, Eugene, Ore., 1953-55; supr. elementary curriculum Madera Sch. Dist. (Cal.), 1955-57; prof. edn. U. Ky., Lexington, 1959—. Vis. prof. U. Ind., Bloomington, summer 1966. Mem. Am. Assn. U. Women, N.E.A. (life), Nat. Council Tchrs. Math., Ky. Edn. Assn., Ky. Council Tchrs. Math (pres. 1965, 74, v.p. coll. sect. 1966-73), Central Ky. Edn. Assn. (pres. 1969-70), Delta Kappa Gamma, Pi Lambda Theta, Kappa Delta Pi. Presbyn. Club: Spindletop Alumni U. Ky. Author: Help Yourself Mathematics Board, 1965; (with others) Computerized Instruction in Mathematics versus Other Methods of Mathematics Instruction, 1972. Home: 205 W Lexington Av Winchester KY 40391 Office: Coll Edn Univ Ky Lexington KY 40506

SUDJIAN, MARY, mfg. co. exec.; b. Phila., Aug. 2, 1926; d. David and Maritza (Mooradian) Sudjian; grad. Moore Coll. Art, 1947. Designer, Nannette Mfg. Co., Phila., 1947-53, head design, 1953-68, v.p., 1968-72, sr. v.p., 1972—. Office: 3800 Frankford Av Philadelphia PA 19024

SUDRANN, JEAN, educator; b. Bklyn., June 24, 1919; d. Abram Henry and Ida (Bernhard) Sudrann; B.A., Mt. Holyoke Coll., 1939; M.A., Columbia, 1940, Ph.D., 1950. Instr., Wheaton Coll., Norton, Mass., 1940-45; mem. faculty Mt. Holyoke Coll., 1947—, prof. English, 1964—, chmn. dept., 1963-69, 71-72. Mem. Am. Assn. U. Profs., Am. Assn. U. Women, Am. Civil Liberties Union, Internat. Assn. U. Profs. English, Phi Beta Kappa. Contbr. profl. jours. Mem. editorial bd. Mass. Rev., 1962-70. Home: 51 Collegeview Heights Chapel Hill South Hadley MA 01075

SUEDKAMP, HARRIET NEWELL, publ. co. exec.; b. Ames, Ia., Nov. 26, 1917; d. George Nelson and Mattie Myrtle (Johnson) Graves; B.S., Ia. State U., 1940; m. George Raymond Suedkamp, Aug. 20, 1940 (div. Mar. 1968); children—Stephen, Stanley, Sarah (Mrs. James Eral), Stuart, Susan, Stafford, Stacey, Sherwin. Editor, Lake Wilson (Minn.) Pilot, 1950-55; dir. publicity St. Paul Dispatch and Pioneer Press, 1963—. Mem. Internat. Assn. Bus. Communicators (recipient awards for professionalism in editing, dir. Northstar chpt. 1966-67), Women in Communications, Phi Upsilon Omicron. Home: 1445 Wilson Av St Paul MN 55106 Office: 63 E 4th St St Paul MN 55101

SUGHRUE, KATHRYN EILEEN, home economist; b. Oketo, Kan., May 2, 1913; d. John William and Charlotte (Cook) Peterman; B.S., Kan. State U., 1936; M.S. (Epsilon Sigma Phi scholar), Colo. State U., 1962; m. Herbert Sughrue, May 3, 1941; children—Kathleen Mary (Mrs. Harry Hoff), Margaret Helen (Mrs. Calvin Carlson), Patricia Anne (Mrs. Charles Sprincin), John, Timothy. Tchr. home econs., Kan., 1936-37; extension home economist, Ford County (Kan.), 1937-41, Reno County, 1949-55, Finney County, Kan., 1955-61; dist. supr. extension home econs., Manhattan, Kan., 1961-67; asso. leader home econs., Manhattan, 1967-69; state leader extension home econs. Coop. Extension Service, N.D. State U., Fargo, 1969—. Home econs. adviser Andra Pradesh U., Hyderabad, India, 1968. Home: 2610 11th St S Moorhead MN 56560 Office: State Univ Station Fargo ND 58102

SUHRHEINRICH, JEANNE BEELER (MRS. ROBERT LOUIS SUHRHEINRICH), journalist; b. Evansville, Ind., July 23, 1919; d. Jerome Durham and Helen (Tucker) Beeler; grad. high sch.; m. Robert Louis Suhrheinrich, Aug. 7, 1937; children—Robert Jerome, Jerry William. Columnist, Evansville (Ind.) Press, 1937; publicity dir. Council of Churches, Evansville, 1953-55; entertainment editor Evansville Courier, 1955—. Pres. Community Players, Evansville, 1948-52. Mem. D.A.R., Jr. League. Mem. United Ch. of Christ. Home: 610 S Alvord Blvd Evansville IN 47714 Office: 201 NW 2d St Evansville IN 47701

SUITS, ESTELLE DUPONT (MRS. LEONARD SUITS), ret. sch. adminstr.; b. Forest Port, N.Y.; d. Joseph Francis and Estella (Lyon) Dupont; B.Ed., Oswego State Tchrs. Coll., 1946; M.S., Syracuse U., 1950; m. Leonard Suits, July 9, 1934 (dec. Aug. 1953). Elementary sch. tchr. Camden (N.Y.) Bd. Edn., 1932-47; tchr. Syracuse (N.Y.) Bd. Edn., 1947-52; prin. Merrick Sch., 1952-61, Danforth Sch., 1961-65, Nichol Sch., 1966-73 (all Syracuse); prin., elementary tchr. summer session Syracuse U., 1949-53; instr. elementary lang. arts, human relations Syracuse U. summers 1954, 1955; lectr. creative thinking, 1960-73; v.p. Dorothy Carnegie Continuation Class, Dale Carnegie, 1967; mem. evaluating elementary schs. Temple U., 1960, 62. Recipient Oswego State Tchrs. Coll. award for Outstanding Tchr. N.Y. State, 1959. Mem. N.E.A., N.Y. State Tchrs. Assn. Childhood Edn. (v.p. 1951-52, pres. 1953, state chmn. 1960), Dept. Elementary Sch. Prins. (state publicity chmn. 1958-62), Am. Assn. U. Women (publicity chmn. 1967—, area regional chmn. 1967), Syracuse Assn. Adminstrs. and Suprs. (sec. 1960, v.p. 1963, pres. 1964), Nat. League Am. Pen Women (corr. sec. 1966—, br. pres. 1970-72), Authors League (v.p. membership 1974—), Zonta Internat. (local program chmn. 1972-73, music com. chmn. 1972-73, exec. bd. 1972-74), Profl. Women's League (pres. 1972-74). Recorded album Health and Safety Through Music, 1962; Good Manners Through Music, 1965. Home: 753 James St Syracuse NY 13203

SULLENBERGER, ARA BROOCKS COX (MRS. HAL J. SULLENBERGER), educator; b. Amarillo, Tex., Jan. 3, 1933; d. Carl Clarence and Ara Frances (Broocks) Cox; student Randolph-Macon Woman's Coll., 1951-52, So. Meth. U., 1952-53, Arlington State Coll., 1953, Amarillo Coll., 1953-54; B.A., Tex. Technol. U., 1955, M.A., 1958; postgrad. Tex. Christian U., 1963-64, N. Tex. State U., 1969—; m. Hal Joseph Sullenberger, Nov. 2, 1952; children—Hal Joseph, Ara Broocks. Tchr. math. Lubbock (Tex.) High Sch., 1955-56; instr. math. Tex. Technol. Coll., 1956-63; chmn. dept. math. Ft. Worth County Day Sch., 1964-67; instr. Tarrant County Jr. Coll., Ft. Worth, 1967-70, asst. prof. math., 1970-74, assoc. prof., 1974—; cons. math. Project Change, 1967-68. Sec. Alcoholics United, 1970-71; speaker Conf. Advancement Math. Teaching, Austin, Tex., 1973. Recipient award for teaching excellence Gen. Dynamics of Ft. Worth, 1966. Mem. Math. Assn. Am. (speaker Tex. sect. 1971), Nat. Council Tchrs. Math. (speaker ann. meeting 1970, 72, 73), Tex. Jr. Coll. Tchrs. Assn., Am. Assn. U. Profs., Jr. League, Pi Beta Phi. Episcopalian. Club: Ft. Worth Architects Wives. Home: 600 Eastwood Av Ft Worth TX 76107 Office: 5300 Campus Dr Ft Worth TX 76119

SULLENS, IDELLE DEPERE, educator; b. Prairie City, Ore., June 28, 1921; d. Russell Harrison and Madeleine (Barlow) Sullens; secretarial certificate Northwestern Sch. Commerce, Portland, Ore., 1939; A.B. with distinction in Humanities, Stanford, 1943, Ph.D., 1959; M.A., U. Wash., 1954. Sec., accountant with various firms, Portland, 1939-41; owner, mgr. Rockline Kennels, Bremerton, Wash., 1948-50; instr. English Stanford (Cal.) U., 1955-56; instr. English and humanities Monterey (Cal.) Peninsula Coll., 1958—, chmn. dept., 1968-69. Served with USNR, 1943-48, 50-54; now comdr. Res. ret. Nat. Endowment for Humanities fellow, 1974-75. Mem. Am. Assn. U. Women, Cal. Tchrs. Assn., Modern Lang. Assn., Early English Text Soc., Nat. Council Tchrs. English. Author: Principles of Grammar, 1966; The Whole Idea Catalog: College Writing Projects, 1971; (with Edith Karas and Raymond Fabrizio) The Inquiring Reader, 1967, 2d edit., 1974; The Inquiring Reader: Essays, 1969. Home: Box 4418 Carmel CA 93921 Office: Monterey Peninsula Coll 980 Fremont St Monterey CA 93940

SULLINS, DOROTHY MAY LANG, pub. relations exec.; b. Pasadena, Cal., Mar. 18, 1921; d. Frank and Bertha Lee (Cribbs) Lang; B.S., N.M. State U., 1974; children—James Lee, Nancy Grace. Free-lance agrl. writer, Las Cruces, N.M., 1967-72; information dir., editor N.M. Farm and Ranch mag., 1972—; dir. N.M. Farm and Livestock Bur., 1974—. Mem. N.M. Commn. Status Women. Mem. N.M. Press Women's Assn. Club: Las Cruces Press. Office: 421 N Water St Las Cruces NM 88001

SULLIVAN, DOROTHY DOUGLAS, educator; b. Indpls., Feb. 2, 1924; d. Wilks Hargrave and Elaine Ardell (Williams) Douglas; student Moore Inst. Art, 1940-41; A.B., U. Md., 1945, M.Ed., 1960, D.Ed., 1965; m. Eugene John Sullivan, Aug. 1, 1945 (div. 1960); children—Eugene John, Mark M., Peter A., Kathleen, Brian D., Matthew, Arthur J. Tchr. elementary schs. Kent and Prince George counties, Md., 1958-62; asst. prof. edn. U. Md., College Park, 1965-70, asso. prof., 1970—. Cons. pub. schs., 1965—, Kimbo Records, Deal, N.J., 1969—. Mem. Internat. Reading Assn., N.E.A., Md. Tchrs. Assn., Coll. Reading Assn. (sec.-treas., 1973—), Phi Kappa Phi, Mortar Bd., Pi Delta Epsilon, Delta Delta Delta, D.A.R. Author: (with James Humphrey, Robert Wilson) Teaching Reading Through Creative Movement, 1969; (with J. Humphrey) Teaching Slow Learners Through Active Games, 1970; (with J. Humphrey) Teaching Reading Through Motor Learning, 1973. Home: 8304 Curry Pl Adelphi MD 20783 Office: Reading Center Coll Edn Md College Park MD 20742

SULLIVAN, DOROTHY RONA, state ofcl.; b. Boston, Jan. 7, 1941; d. Lewis Robert and Dorothy (Hopkins) Sullivan; B.A., Boston U., 1963, C.A.G.S., 1972; M.Ed., State Coll. Boston, 1966; postgrad. Northeastern U. Research asst., lay med. editor Boston Lying-in Hosp., 1963-64; employment counselor Mass. Div. Employment Security, Boston, 1964-66, sr. employment counselor, 1966-67, prin. employment counselor, 1967-70, employment office mgr., 1970—. Supr. community counselor interns and rehab. adminstrn. intern Northeastern U. Grad. Sch. Edn., 1968-72; mem. regional adv. subcom. on mental retardation Mass. Dept. Mental Health, 1969. Mem. Jamaica Plain Community Council Health, Edn. and Welfare Subcom., 1967-69; recorder Gov.'s Conf. on Rehab., 1970; asso. mem. Gov.'s Commn. on Employment Handicapped, 1972—; mem. Boston Task Force on Employment of Handicapped, 1972—. Bd. dirs. Greater Boston council Camp Fire Girls, 1972—; exec. bd. local chpt. Am. Fedn. State, County and Municipal Employees, AFL-CIO, 1972-73. Mem. Nat. Vocational Guidance Assn., Nat. Rehab. Assn. (sec. Mass. chpt. 1971-72, exec. bd. chpt. 1971-74, v.p. 1974—, recorder, awards chmn. Northeast Regional Conf. 1971), Nat. Employment Counselors Assn., Am. Personnel and Guidance Assn. (nat. recorder conf. 1968), Rockport Art Assn., Cape Cod Art Assn., Chatham Conservation Found., Essex County Greenbelt Assn., Internat. Platform Assn. Author: Boston Employment Service Guide, 1969. Contbr. articles to profl. jours. Home: 33 Morey Rd Roslindale MA 02131 Office: Employment Security Bldg Govt Center Boston MA 02114

SULLIVAN, ELEANOR REGIS, editor; b. Cambridge, Mass., Oct. 19, 1928; d. Timothy Joseph and Katherine Irene (Dowd) Sullivan; B.S. in Edn., Salem State Coll., 1950. Tchr. elementary schs., Clinton, Conn., 1950-53, Cambridge, 1953-57, White Plains, N.Y., 1957-60; editorial asst. Pocket Books, Inc., N.Y.C., 1961-62; editor Charles Scribner's Sons, N.Y.C., 1962-69; mng. editor Ellery Queen's Mystery Mag., N.Y.C., 1970—. Vol., A.R.C., 1968-72, Euphrasion Residence, N.Y.C., 1970—. Mem. Mystery Writers Am. (dir.), Dramatist Guild. Democrat. Roman Catholic. Contbr. stories, articles to mags., newspapers. Home: 7 Stuyvsant Oval New York City NY 10009 Office: 229 Park Av S New York City NY 10003

SULLIVAN, HELEN BLAIR, educator; b. Fall River, Mass.; d. Eugene J. and Emma (Blair) Sullivan; B.S., Boston U., 1926, M.A., (teaching fellow), 1937; Ed.D., Harvard, 1943. Pub. sch. tchr., supr., Concord and Winchester, Mass., 1926-34; grad. asst. Harvard, 1936-38; asst. prof. Boston U., 1938-42, asso. prof., 1942-46, prof., from 1946, now prof. emerita; psychol. cons. slow learning and drop-outs, N.Y., Vt., Cal., Hawaii, 1968-69. Vis. lectr. Mexico, Europe, Can. Mem. bd. govs. Internat. Council Exceptional Children, 1945—. Trustee, Mass. Spl. Class Tchrs., 1940-50; bd. dirs. Co-op Nat. Banks-Children's Fund. Mem. Am., Eastern psychol. assns., A.A.S., Am. Assn. U. Women, Boston League Women Voters, Nat. Assn. Remedial Tchrs. (pres. 1952, dir. 1953—), Assn. Childhood Edn., Nat. Soc. Study Edn., Am. Ednl. Research Assn., Internat., New Eng. reading assns. Club: College of Boston. Pub. tests intelligence, basal readers reading tests for children and adults World Book Co., 1938—, Harcourt, Brace World, Inc., 1938—. Research on academically talented students, also slow learners and sch. dropouts. Address: Elmcroft 21 Centre St Yarmouth Port MA 02675

SULLIVAN, LEONOR KRETZER (MRS. JOHN B. SULLIVAN), congresswoman; b. St. Louis; d. Frederick William and Nora (Jostrand) Kretzer; student Washington U., St. Louis; numerous hon. degrees; m. John Berchmans Sullivan, Dec. 27, 1941 (dec. Jan. 1951). Formerly adminstr. St. Louis Comptometer Sch.; adminstrv. aide office of husband, Rep. Sullivan, Washington, 1942-51, Rep. Irving, 1951-52; mem. 83d-93d Congresses, 3d dist. Mo.; mem. banking and currency com.; chmn. mcht. marine and fisheries com.; chmn. sub-com. consumer affairs; sec. Democratic caucus; mem. Dem. Steering Com. Mem. Joint Com. Def. Prodn.; chmn. U.S. Territorial Expansion Commn. Mem. League Women Voters, Am. Legion Aux. Democrat. Home: 2 River Bluff Plaza St Louis MO 63111 Office: Rayburn Bldg Washington DC 20515

SULLIVAN, MARGARET ELIZABETH JACKSON (MRS. J. MINOR SULLIVAN III), realtor; b. S.C., Mar. 5, 1918; d. Ernest and Elizabeth Bess (McCall) Jackson; student Washington Bus. Inst., 1935-36; certificate Traphagan Sch. Design, 1937; A.A. in Bus. Adminstrn., Rider Coll., 1958, B.S. in Commerce, 1960, also postgrad.; m. J. Minor Sullivan III, Mar. 5, 1941; 1 child (dec.). Bookkeeper, Carl Schneider Fur Co., N.Y.C., 1938-40; supr. tech. order dept. and airplane parts dept. LaGuardia Air Depot Detachment, L.I., N.Y., 1941-44; sec. social service dept. Sydenham Hosp., N.Y.C., 1944; bus. mgr. Dr. J. Minor Sullivan III, Trenton, N.J., 1945-63; propr. Margaret E. Sullivan Real Estate & Ins. Co., Trenton, 1964—; mem. Multiple Listing Brokerage Service. Pres., N.J. Med. Assn. Woman's Aux., 1958-60, chmn. exec. bd., 1960-62; an organizer vol. aides for N.J. State Hosp., 1949; rec. sec. to exec. bd. Mercer County Med. Soc. Woman's Aux., 1949-51; mem. N.J. Civil Rights Commn., 1955, former pres., v.p., sec.; vice chmn. Trenton Landmarks Commn., 1973; rec. sec. Central N.J. Links, 1962-64; v.p. Girl Friends, Inc., 1970-72; mem. Model Cities Policy Com.; mem. citizens adv. com. Trenton Bd. Edn.; lectr. on air def. missilery and survival, 1967-68. 13th ward committeewoman Mercer County Democratic Com., 1948, vice chmn., 1954-64. Trustee N.J. State Mus. Named Woman of Year for outstanding services and contbns. to welfare and progress of blacks in N.J., N.J. Herald News, 1955; recipient merit award U.S. Army Air Def. Command, 1967. Mem. Nat. Assn. Real Estate Bds., N.J. Ins. Brokers Assn., Mercer County Bd. Realtors, Omega Psi Phi Quette Aux. Designer leather gloves and ceramics. Home: 6 Renfrew Av Trenton NJ 08618 Office: 200 Spring St Trenton NJ 08618

SULLIVAN, MARGARET PATRICIA, physician; b. Lewiston, Mont., Feb. 7, 1922; d. William A. and Mabel (Conrad) Sullivan; B.A., Rice Inst., 1944; M.D., Duke, 1950. Intern Duke Hosp., Durham,

N.C., 1950-51, asst. resident pediatrics, 1951-52; asst. resident pediatrics St. Louis Children's Hosp., 1952-53; pediatrician Atomic Bomb Casualty Commn., Hiroshima and Nagasaki, Japan, 1953-55; asst. resident pediatrics Tex. Children's Hosp., Houston, 1955; asst. pediatrician U. Tex. M.D. Anderson Hosp. and Tumor Inst., Houston, 1956-61, asso. pediatrician, 1961-73, pediatrician, prof. pediatrics, 1973—; asst. prof. pediatrics Postgrad. Sch. Medicine, U. Tex., Houston, 1956-61, asso. prof. Grad. Sch. Biomed. Scis., 1961—. Diplomate Am. Bd. Pediatrics. Mem. A.M.A., Am. Assn. Cancer Edn., Am. Assn. Cancer Research, Am. Med. Women's Assn. (nat. sec. 1967, nat. treas. 1971, nat. pres. 1973), Am. Acad. Pediatrics, Am. Soc. Clin. Oncology, Harris County Med. Soc., A.A.A.S., Houston Pediatric Soc., So. Soc. Pediatric Research, Tex. Med. Assn., Phi Beta Kappa, Sigma Xi, Alpha Omega Alpha. Mem. editorial bd. Yearbook of Cancer, 1959—. Contbr. articles to profl. publs. Home: 5353 Institute Lane Houston TX 77005 Office: MD Anderson Hosp and Tumor Inst Houston TX 77025

SULLIVAN, MARGARET RITA, librarian; b. Fall River, Mass., Oct. 12, 1916; d. Algernon Desmond and Abbie Angela Sullivan; B.S., Boston U., 1935, M.Ed., 1945; postgrad. Bristol Community Coll., 1970-71. Tchr. English, Joseph Case High Sch., Swansea, Mass., 1937-68, librarian, 1968—. Women's Program radio sta. WALE, Fall River, 1942-45; recreation supr. Fall River, 1946-71; chmn. Recreation of Model Cities, 1967-71. Sec. Fall River Park Bd., 1956—. Mem. women's bd. Union Hosp., 1956—. Mem. Am., Mass., New Eng. library assns., Mass., Swansea (sec. 1965-67) tchrs. assns., South Shore Librarians Assn., Am. Assn. U. Women, Boston U. Alumni Assn., Fall River Little Theater, Fall River Friends of Library, Holy Name Women's Guild, Pi Lambda Theta, Pi Alpha Epsilon. Clubs: College, Catholic Woman's (Fall River). Home: 860 President Av Fall River MA 02720 Office: Joseph Case High Sch Swansea MA 02777

SULLIVAN, SISTER MARY CATHARINE, coll. dean; b. South Amboy, N.J., Apr. 28, 1934; d. Edward David and Nora Catherine (Coleman) Sullivan; B.A., Georgian Ct. Coll., 1955; M.A., Middlebury Coll., 1965. Joined Sisters of Mercy of N.J., 1955; tchr. lang. Mt. St. Mary Acad., Plainfield, N.J., 1955-59, Notre Dame High Sch., 1959-65; asst. prof. Spanish, Georgian Ct. Coll., Lakewood, N.J., 1965—, chmn. dept. modern and classical langs., 1968—, dean women, 1970—. Nat. Def. Edn. Act grant, 1962. Mem. Am. Assn. Tchrs. Spanish and Portuguese, N.E. Conf. Lang. Teaching, Nat. Assn. Women Deans and Counselors, Eastern Assn. Deans. Home and office: Georgian Court College Lakewood NJ 08701

SULLIVAN, MARY MARGARET, lawyer; b. Escanaba, Mich., Dec. 22, 1933; d. Charles Michael and Eleanor Louise (Bergeron) Gallaher; A.B., St. Mary's Coll., Notre Dame, Ind., 1955; postgrad. Golden Gate Coll., 1966-68; J.D., U. San Diego, 1970; m. William S. Sullivan, June 8, 1954; children—Kathleen, William, Edward, David, Joyce, Patrick, Jean. Social worker San Diego County Dept. Pub. Welfare, 1963-66, 68-70; admitted to Cal. bar, 1971; staff atty. San Diego Legal Aid Soc., 1971-73; practice law, San Diego, 1973—. Active Imperial council Girl Scouts U.S.A., 1969-73; legislative chmn. Lakeview Sch. P.T.A., 1970-72. Mem. Am., Cal., San Diego County bar assns. Home: 12633 Casa Vista Rd Lakeside CA 92040 Office: 964 5th Av San Diego CA 92101

SULLIVAN, MARY ROSE, educator; b. Boston, May 13, 1931; d. John Joseph and Elinor Mary (Crotty) Sullivan; B.A., Emmanuel Coll., 1952; M.A., Catholic U. Am., 1958; Ph.D., Boston U., 1964. Faculty, Emmanuel Coll., Boston, 1960-65; prof. U. Colo., Denver, 1966—. Served to capt. USNR, 1952-56; comdr. Res. Am. Council Learned Socs. fellow, 1973. Mem. Modern Lang. Assn., English Speaking Union, Am. Assn. U. Profs., Am. Assn. U. Women, Naval Res. Assn. Club: Altrusa Internat. (Denver). Author: Browning's Voices in The Ring and The Book, 1969. Mem. editorial bd. English Language Notes, 1971—. Contbr. articles profl. jours. Home: 2445 S Colorado Blvd Denver CO 80222 Office: 1100 14th St Denver CO 80222

SULLIVAN, RUTH MAE SIMPSON (MRS. CHARLES STANTON SULLIVAN), lawyer; b. Louisville, Feb. 23, 1931; d. Sam Paul and Estelle Boone (Merrifield) Simpson; B.A., Vanderbilt U., 1952; postgrad. Western Reserve U., 1952-54; LL.B., U. Ala., 1955; m. Charles Stanton Sullivan, Sept 29, 1956; children—Charles Stanton, Jr., Paul Wesley. Admitted to Ala. bar, 1955; law clk. Ct. of Appeals Ala., Montgomery, 1955-57; practiced in Opelika, Ala., 1958-61, Dadeville, Ala., 1961—. Mem. exec. com. Ala. Rep. Party, 1970—. Bd. dirs. House Corp., Gamma Phi chpt. Gamma Phi Beta, Auburn (Ala.) U., 1966—. Mem. Am. Bar. Assn., Ala., Fifth Circuit, Tallapoosa County bar assns., Bus. and Profl. Women, Ala. Assn. Women Lawyers, Gamma Phi Beta. Methodist. Home: Box 176 Camp Hill AL 36850 Office: Box 332 Dadeville AL 36853

SULLIVAN, RUTH MARGARET, librarian; b. Quincy, Mass., Nov. 25, 1913; d. Daniel Philip and Ruth Patrice (Phelan) Sullivan; Mus.B., Boston U., 1950; M.L.S., U. R.I., 1969. Commd. ensign WAVES, 1943, advanced through grades to lt. comdr., 1952, released from active duty, 1966; officer in charge communications center U.S. Naval Communication Sta., Boston, 1950-54; ready res., to 1966; adminstrv. asst., Children's Hosp. Med. Center, Boston, 1954-57; sec. editorial asst. dept. physics Mass. Inst. Tech., Cambridge, 1958; asst. to sales control mgr., sec. to pres. Harper-Atlantic Sales, Inc., Boston, 1958-61; library asst. Boston Pub. Library, 1962; librarian New Eng. Deaconess Hosp., Boston, 1963—. Mem. 1st violin sect. Hingham Civic Orch., 1960-72; mem. Plymouth Philharmonic Orch., 1973—. Mem. Spl. Libraries Assn. (mem. local arrangements com. 63d Conf., Boston 1972), New Eng. Mass. library assns., Ret. Officers Assn. Home: 15 Winslow Rd Duxbury MA 02332 Office: 185 Pilgrim Rd Boston MA 02215

SULLIVAN, SANYA MAE, dean, educator; b. Mineral Well, Tex., Apr. 24, 1936; d. Jerry Kern and Ruby Mae (Bumgarner) Sullivan; B.A., Baylor U., 1958; M.Edn., N. Tex. State U., 1959, postgrad., 1967-71; postgrad. U. Tex., 1963. Tchr. Monnig Jr. High Sch., Ft. Worth, 1959-63; dir. student personnel Ranger (Tex.) Jr. Coll., 1963-67; asst. prof. psychology Tarrant County Jr. Coll., Ft. Worth, Tex., 1967-71, vocational counselor, 1968-71; asst. prof. psychology McMurry Coll., Abilene, Tex., 1971—, asso. dean students, 1971—. Chmn. counseling sect. vis. so. assn. accrediting team to Eastern Hills High Sch., 1969. Mem. Nat., Tex. vocational guidance assns., Am., Tex. personnel and guidance assns., Jr. Coll. Student Personnel Assn. Tex. (dir. 1967-71), Am. Coll. Personnel Assn., Nat., Tex. assns. women deans, adminstrs. and counselors, Am. Assn. U. Women, Delta Kappa Gamma, Pi Gamma Mu, Beta Sigma Phi. Baptist. Home: 4600 Coachlight Rd No 177 Abilene TX 79601 Office: Box 716 McMurry College Abilene TX 79605

SULZER-AZAROFF, BETH WINER (MRS. LEONID VLADIMIROVITCH AZAROFF), psychologist, educator; b. N.Y.C., Sept. 6, 1929; d. Ben-Zion and Celia (Horwitz) Winer; B.S. in Edn., City Coll. N.Y., 1950, M.A., 1953; postgrad. Tchrs. Coll., Columbia, 1953, 54; Ph.D. (Nat. Inst. Mental Health tng. fellow), U. Minn., 1966; m. Edward Stanton Sulzer, Oct. 11, 1953 (dec. Feb. 1970); children—David, Richard, Lenore; m. 2d. Leonid Vladimirovitch Azaroff, Mar. 4, 1972. Tchr. elementary schs., N.Y.C., 1950-55, Washington, 1955-56; teaching asst. U. Minn., 1961-62; asso. prof. dept. guidance and ednl. psychology So. Ill. U., Carbondale, 1966-72; asso. prof. dept. psychology, area coordinator ednl. psychology U. Mass., Amherst, 1973—. Cons. to sch. systems, 1966—, U. Conn. Dental Sch., 1972-73. Mem. Am. Psychol. Assn., Am. Ednl. Research Assn., Soc. for Exptl. Analysis of Behavior, Am. Assn. for Advancement Behavior Therapy, Soc. for Research in Child Devel., Nat. Soc. for Study Edn. Author: (with L. Chovanic) A Guide to the Development of Mathematical Instructional Activities, 1968; (with G. Roy Mayer) Behavior Modification Procedures for School Personnel, 1972. Contbr. articles and book revs. to profl. jours. Home: PO Box 103 Storrs CT 06268 Office: Dept of Psychology University of Mass Amherst MA 01002

SUMMERS, ANNIE RUTH (MRS. WALTER JEROME SUMMERS), realtor; b. Bradley Junction, Fla., Feb. 25, 1915; d. Lonnie Edward and Alice Elmina (Allen) Harvey; student Fla. State Coll. for Women, 1930-31; m. Walter Jerome Summers, Nov. 9, 1933 (dec.); 1 dau., Mary Alice (Mrs. Harry L. Pender). Sales mgr. Arboretum Lychee Orchards, Laurel, Fla., 1946-66; real estate broker, mgr. branch office H.N. Wimmers, Venice, Fla., 1956-60; pres., mgr. Summers Nursery & Landscaping, Inc., Laurel, Fla., 1960-65; mgr. Basswood, Inc., Okeechobee, Fla., 1965-68; owner, broker and realtor Summers Realty, Nokomis, Fla., 1968—. Mem. Venice C. of C. (dir. 1965—), Venice Bd. Realtors (pres. 1973—). Inventor spl. propogation container for growing plants. Home: 205 E Palm Av Nokomis FL 33555 Office: 229 N Tamiami Trail Nokomis FL 33555

SUMNER, ELAINE MARY GERHARD, educator; b. Pasadena, Cal.; d. C.F. and I.M. Gerhard; B.A., Cal. State Coll. at Los Angeles, 1962, M.A., 1968; postgrad. Whittier Coll., 1969, U. Cal. at Los Angeles, 1970; children—Valerie Elaine, Richard Joseph. Sec. Cal. Inst. Tech., 1951-52; elementary tchr. Los Angeles City Schs., 1962—. Brownie leader Pasadena council Girl Scouts U.S., 1960. Mem. Assn. for Childhood Edn. (v.p. 1963), Am. Assn. U. Women. Home: 8502 Los Olivos Dr San Gabriel CA 91775 Office: 450 N Grand St Los Angeles CA 91775

SUMNER, EVA SMITH, educator, accountant; b. Manassa, Colo.; d. Elias Austin and Jessie (Block) Smith; B.S., U. Utah, 1927; postgrad. Utah State U., Brigham Young U., Utah U.; m. Cecil G. Sumner, Dec. 29, 1931; children—Cecil Smith, Eve, Lois (Mrs. Reed F. Christensen), Robert Smith. Tchr. bus. North Summit High Sch., Coalville, Utah, 1929-30; accountant Penzoil Co., Los Angeles, 1930-32, C.E., U.S. Army, Salt Lake City, 1942-44, Z.C.M.I., 1945; tchr. bus. Stevens Heneger Coll. Bus., 1946; tchr. bus., vocational counselor Granite High Sch., 1947-51, Olympus High Sch., 1951-59; counselor Valley Jr. High Sch., 1959-65; coordinator bus. edn. Granite Sch. Dist., 1964-69. Bd. dirs. Granite Tchrs. Credit Union. Pres. Hanna (Wyo.) Women's Relief Soc. Pres. bd. trustees Utah Boys Ranch. Mem. Utah Bus. Tchrs. Assn. (v.p. 1951-52), N.E.A., Utah Edn. Assn., Utah Assn. Sch. Counselors, Granite Guidance Assn., Am. Assn. U. Women, Phi Chi Theta (nat. exec. bd. 1958, 62, 68, 70, 72). Democrat. Mem. Ch. of Jesus Christ of Latter-day Saints. Home: 1314 E Stratford Av Salt Lake City UT 84106

SUMNER, LOUISE OWEEN, librarian; b. Orlando, Fla., June 18, 1907; d. Robert Lawson and Julia (Mellown) Sumner; A.B., Fla. So. Coll., Lakeland, 1929; B.S. in L.S., George Peabody Coll., 1932; M.A. in L.S., 1958; student Grad. Library Sch., U. Chgo., summers 1938, 40. Librarian Fla. So. Coll., 1929—, instr. library sci., 1934-49. Mem. Am., Southeastern, Fla. (chmn. coll. and univ. sect. 1948) library assns., Am. Assn. U. Women, Nat. Fedn. Bus. and Profl. Women's Clubs (dist. dir. Fla. 1939-40, pres. Pionette club 1936-37), Delta Kappa Gamma, Pi Gamma Mu, Delta Zeta (alumnae chpt. pres. 1959-60). Democrat. Methodist. Home: 717 Success Av Lakeland FL 33801

SUMNERS, RUTH, journalist; B.A., Vassar Coll.; M.A., U. Denver. Teaching fellow English, U. Denver, 1966-68; dir. pub. relations U.S. Ski Team, 1969-70; reporter Rocky Mountain News, Denver, 1970-74; press rep. Santa Fe Opera, 1973, 74; freelance writer, editor, pub. relations cons. Home: 1144 Humboldt St Denver CO 80218 Office: Denver Rocky Mountain News 400 West Colfax Av Denver CO 80204

SUN, RUTH QUINLAN, editor; b. Elmira, N.Y., May 16, 1907; d. Daniel and Margaret Ellen (Doherty) Quinlan; B.A., Elmira Coll., 1928; M.S. in Journalism, Northwestern U., 1945; M.A. in Asian Studies, U. So. Cal., 1947; postgrad. Harvard, 1950, U. Mo., 1951-53; m. Norman Sun, Oct. 30, 1947. Editor, Gannett Newspapers, 1936-40, Charles E. Tuttle Pub. Co., Tokyo, Japan, 1959-61; Fulbright fellow, faculty Thammasat U., Bangkok, Thailand, 1956-57, U. Saigon (South Vietnam), 1964-65; vis. Fulbright prof. Am. lit. U. Md. in Far East, Tokyo, 1961-68; with Temple U. Press, Phila., 1970—, editor, 1971—. Lectr. continuing edn. program Kansas City U., 1955—. Active League Women Voters. Bd. dirs. Urban League Kansas City. Recipient prize Elmira Coll., 1928; Theta Sigma Phi Nat. award, 1947; Fulbright fellow, China, 1948-49; Am. Council Learned Socs. grantee, 1950; Chinese Cultural scholar, 1946-47. Mem. Theta Sigma Phi. Club: Elmira College of Chemung County (N.Y.) (pres. 1939-41). Author: Land of Seagull and Fox: Folk Tales of Vietnam, 1967; A China Journey, 1973; The Asian Animal Zodiac: The Yellow Road of the Sun, 1974. Home: 1052 Ollerton Rd Sherwood-on-the-Green Woodbury NJ 08096 Office: Temple U Press 305-6 Denny Hall Philadelphia PA 19122

SUNDBERG, NORMA ELIZABETH JOHNSON (MRS. COLLINS Y. SUNDBERG), funeral dir.; b. Rockford, Ill.; d. Conrad Walfred and Olga (Pierson) Johnson; student Brown's Bus. Coll., 1928-30; m. Collins Y. Sundberg, June 20, 1942. Partner Sundberg Funeral Home, Rockford, 1952—. Sec.-treas. Col-Nor Corp., Rockford, 1961—. Dep. coroner, Winnebago County, Ill., 1952—. Mem. Winnebago County Women's Republican Club, 1948—, v.p., 1956, 57. Mem. Nat., Ill. funeral dirs. assns., Am. Legion Aux., Women of Moose, Rockford Humane Soc. Aux. (v.p.). Lutheran. Mem. Order Eastern Star, Order White Shrine of Jerusalem. Clubs: Zonta (dir.), Rockford Woman's, Ostende, Forest Hills Country. Home: 5431 Einor Av Rockford IL 61108 Office: 215 N 6th St Rockford IL 61107

SUNDERLAND, ISABEL KLEIN, librarian; b. Freeburg, Ill.; d. August Frank and Martha Maria (Heiligenstein) Klein; B.S., So. Ill. U.; M.L.S., U. So. Cal.; m. Harold Busick Sunderland, Jan. 27, 1951; 1 son, Steven Klein. Jr. high sch. tchr. English, Bement, Ill. and Avenal, Cal.; elementary sch. librarian, Avenal; secondary sch. librarian Porterville (Cal.) Union High Sch. Dist.; dir. library and media services Kern Community Coll. Dist., Porterville, 1969—. Mem. Am., Cal. library assns., N.E.A., Cal. Tchrs. Assn., Porterville Coll. Faculty Assn. (pres. elect 1974), Delta Kappa Gamma. Mem. Order Eastern Star, Daus. of Nile. Home: 749 W Kanai Av Porterville CA 93257

SUNDERLIN, SYLVIA SWEETMAN (MRS. CHARLES EUGENE SUNDERLIN), editor; b. Lakeside, Mont., Sept. 22, 1911; d. Luke Decatur and Alice May (Waterman) Sweetman; B.A., U. Mont., 1933; m. Charles Eugene Sunderlin, July 8, 1936; children—Elizabeth, Mary, Katherine, William. Asst. editor Assn. for Childhood Edn. Internat., Washington, 1964-66, asso. editor, 1966-69, cons. asso. editor, 1970-72; editor, staff asso. Am. Assn. for Gifted Children, 1973—. Pres. Jackson Elementary Sch. P.T.A., Washington, 1956-57; del. Fedn. Am. Womens Clubs Overseas, Paris, 1959, The Hague, 1961; mem. ad hoc com. on Copyright Law Revision, 1965-69; research vol. with fine arts com. U.S. Dept. Interior, 1966. Recipient All-Am. award for excellence in editing Ednl. Press Assn. Am., 1969. Mem. Delta Gamma. Democrat. Episcopalian. Editor: Migrant Children: Their Education, 1971; others. Home: 1161 York Av New York City NY 10021 Office: Am Assn Gifted Children 15 Gramercy Park New York City NY 10003

SUNDERMAN, CAROLYN REYNOLDS, physician; b. Bryn Mawr, Pa., Jan. 17, 1940; d. Hal Kearns and Frances (Lambeth) Reynolds; B.A., Mount Holyoke Coll., 1961; student U. Pa. Med. Sch., 1961-64; M.D., U. Fla., 1965; m. Frederick William Sunderman, Jr., Aug. 24, 1963; children—Frederick, Elizabeth, Emily. Intern pediatrics U. Fla. Coll. Medicine, 1965-66, resident, 1966-68; asso. in pediatrics U. Conn. Sch. Medicine, Hartford, 1968—. Bd. dirs. Farmington (Conn.) Recreation Assn. Diplomate Am. Bd. Pediatrics. Episcopal (vestryman 1969-72). Home: 139 Mountain Springs Rd Farmington CT 06032 Office: U Conn Health Center 2 Holcomb St Hartford CT 06111

SUNDSTROM, MARY INGRID, reporter; b. Sault Ste Marie, Mich., Aug. 13, 1946; d. Eugene Joshua and Doris Lillian (Babington) Sundstrom; student Lake Superior State Coll., 1964-66; B.A., Mich. State U., 1968. Reporter Sault Ste. Marie Evening News, 1962-66, Lansing (Mich.) State Jour., 1967-68; reporter circuit ct., govt., edn. Oakland Press, Pontiac, 1968—. Home: 752 Ann St Birmingham MI 48009 Office: PO Box 9 Pontiac MI 48056

SUNSHINE, NANCY JEAN, psychologist; b. N.J., May 2, 1935; d. Kenneth Hastings and Amy May (Colbeth) Van Valkenburg; B.S., Cornell U., 1956; M.A., Queens Coll., 1967; Ph.D., City U. N.Y., 1971; m. Robert Milton Sunshine, Aug. 10, 1957 (dec. Dec. 1965); children—Winifred Joyce, Christopher James. Psychol. clk. Manhattan State Hosp., N.Y.C., 1968-70; instr. psychologist Kings County Hosp., Bklyn., 1970-71; psychotherapist L.I. Consultation Center, N.Y.C., 1971—. Individual practice psychotherapy, 1971—; psychol. asso. Psychol. Service Center, 1972—; asst. editor Found. for Interdisciplinary Biocharacterization, 1972. Mem. Am., Eastern, N.Y. psychol. assns., N.Y. Soc. Clin. Psychologists. Contbr. articles to profl. jours. Home: 61-41 Saunders St Rego Park NY 11374

SUPINSKI, CATHERINE JOSEPHINE CURRAN (MRS. EDMUND SUPINSKI), librarian; b. N.Y.C., Aug. 27, 1915; d. Francis Joseph and Mary (Jordan) Curran; B.A., Hunter Coll., 1936; M.A., Columbia, 1937, B.S. in Library Sci., 1943; m. Edmund Supinski, June 2, 1951. Asst. librarian Nat. Indsl. Conf. Bd., N.Y.C., 1943-48; librarian N.Y. C. of C., N.Y.C., 1948-64, Dumont (N.J.) High Sch., 1964—. Mem. Spl. Libraries Assn. (N.Y. pres. 1950-51, internat. 2d v.p. 1953-54), A.L.A., N.E.A., N.J., Bergen County, Dumont edn. assns., N.J., Bergen County (rec. sec. 1967-68) sch. librarians assns., N.J. Secondary Tchrs. Assn. Home: 30 Kinderkamack Rd Woodcliff Lake NJ 07675 Office: Dumont High Sch New Milford Av Dumont NJ 07628

SURGEN, OLIVE ROSALIA RICE (MRS. RAYMOND CHARLES SURGEN), mgmt. cons.; b. Danbury, Conn., Apr. 1, 1917; d. Ralph I. and Rosalia W. (Marcioch) Rice; student Crandall Bus. Coll., 1934-35; grad. Danbury (Conn.) Hosp. Sch. Nursing, 1939; student spl. courses Am. U., U.S. Dept. Agr. Grad. Sch., Cath. U.; m. Raymond Charles Surgen, July 23, 1939; children—Louis Gerald, Olive Ramona. Records mgmt. specialist, cons. paperwork and office mgmt. Dept. Health, Edn. and Welfare, USPHS, Washington, 1942-49, WHO, Geneva, Switzerland, 1951, Pam Am. San. Bur., Washington, 1949-51, Small Def. Plants Adminstrn., Small Bus. Adminstrn., Washington, 1951-54, Pan Am. Union, Washington, 1954-56; owner, mgr. Olive R. Surgen, cons., records mgmt., West Hyattsville, Md., 1956-69; sr. cons., div. dir. Commonwealth Services, Inc., N.Y.C., 1965—, mgr. records mgmt. dept.; mgmt. cons. div. Gilbert Assos., Inc., 1969-70, dir. adminstrv. systems, 1972-73; pres. Information & Bus. Systems, Inc., 1973—. Cons. subcontracts Leahy & Co., mgmt. cons., N.Y.C., 1956-59; mgmt. cons. records archives City of Houston, 1959-65, NIH, Bethesda, Md., 1958-60; cons. records mgmt. NSF, Washington, 1959-60; lectr. Am. U., 1955, George Washington U., 1955-56, Inst. on Paperwork Mgmt., 1954-55, Lehigh U., 1971-72. Mem. Am. Soc. Archivists, Am. Mgmt. Assn., Am. Records Mgmt. Assn. (seminar speaker, chpt. pres.; nat. sec. 1971-73, exec. v.p., 1973-74; Record Mgr. of Year, Region I, 1971, chmn. certified records mgr. com.), Kappa Gamma (pres. 1947-49). Club: Am. Sealyham Terrier. Author: Records Management Fundamentals, 1973. Contbr. articles to profl. publs. Home: 16716 Cavalry Dr Rockville MD 20853 Office: 7100 Baltimore Av College Park MD 20740

SURRAN, EDNA M. WALSH (MRS. CARL ALGER SURRAN), writer, clubwoman; b. Chgo., Jan. 27, 1895; d. Francis Walter and Ida May (Wiley) Walsh; grad. N.J. State Tchrs. Coll., 1912; m. Carl Alger Surran, Sept. 26, 1916 (dec. June 1970); 1 son, Carl Robert. Tchr., Atlantic City Pub. Sch., 1912-16, 18-19. Mem. hostess com. Miss Am. Pageant, 1935-53; chmn. fund raising Children's Seashore House; founder Edna M. Surran Award for Good Citizenship, 1943; mem. Rent Control Bd.; pres. Women's Aux. Atlantic County Med. Soc., 1935-36; chmn. Atlantic unit Am. Woman's Vol. Services, 1943-45, v.p. N.J., 1944, nat. bd. dirs., 1944; pres. Beta Delphian, 1929-45. Worker, Republican Party; adviser Volusia County Rep. Club. Recipient awards for vol. services USAAF, City of Atlantic City, USO, A.R.C. Club: Atlantic City Woman's (charter mem., pres. 1956-57). Mem. Am. Mothers Assn., Am. Legion Aux., Internat. Platform Assn., Nat., Fla. audubon socs. clubs: Deland Women's, Deland Bridge, Deland Tourists. Home: 1050 Lindley Blvd DeLand FL 32720

SURRELL, HELEN MYRA WEBB (MRS. JACK SURRELL), social worker; b. Charleston, Ark.; d. Roy L. and Essie M. (Waters) Webb; A.B., Ark. State Coll., 1947; M.S.W., Wayne State U., 1962, postgrad., 1964-65, U. Detroit Law Sch., 1968—; m. Jack Surrell, Dec. 19, 1959. Tchr., Eliza Miller High Sch., Helena, Ark., 1947-50, Drew County High Sch., Monticello, 1950-51; with Barthwell Drug Stores, Inc., Detroit, 1951-52, Henry Ford Hosp., Detroit, 1952, J.L. Hudson, Detroit, 1952-54; caseworker foster homes Children's Aid Soc., Detroit, 1954-60; with Wayne County Juvenile Ct., Detroit, 1962—, unit dir. field work instrn., intensive casework and tng. unit, and supr. trainee program, 1967—, referee adoption releases and consents, part time, 1967-72, program dir., psychiat. social work supr. Pub. Act 54, 1973-74, adminstrv. asst. to dir. ct. and clinic services, 1974—. Vice pres. alumni exec. bd. Wayne State U. Sch. Social Work, 1967-69, editor alumni publ., 1967-68. Recipient various awards. Nat. Inst. Mental Health scholar, 1960-62. Mem. Nat. Assn. Social Workers, Nat. Council Crime and Delinquency, Mich. Soc. Mental

Health, Am. Bar Assn. (student mem.), Social Workers Club Met. Detroit, Acad. Certified Social Workers, Internat. Platform Assn., Delta Sigma Theta. Home: 14870 Piedmont Av Detroit MI 48223 Office: 1025 E Forest Av Detroit MI 48207

SUSE, RUTH E., data processor; b. Jackson, Mich., Jan. 11, 1910; d. Howard A. and Bessie (Oliver) Matthews; student MacMurray Coll., Jacksonville, Ill., 1928-29, U. Mich., 1929-33; A.B., U. So. Cal., 1942; certificate Los Angeles Sch. Lab. Tech., 1946; postgrad. Am. U.; m. Edmund T. Suse, July 20, 1935 (div. Sept. 1940); 1 dau., Barbara J. Tchr., Am. Sch., Colombia 1933-35, schs. in Guatemala, 1939-40; geodesist U.S. Govt., 1942-44, 54-57, 58-61; clin. pathologist Pasadena (Cal.) Hosps., 1945-54; med. technologist, tchr. Am. Hosp., La Paz, Bolivia, 1957-58; math. linguistics U.S. Govt. and Gen. Elect., 1961-62; educator langs. U.S. Army, Okinawa, 1962-64; tech. asst., dept. dir. biomed. div. Documentation, Inc., Bethesda, Md., 1964-66; systems analyst U.S. Army, Washington, 1966; tech. dir. edn. resources br. Nat. Naval Med. Sch., Bethesda, Md., 1967-68; computer systems analyst Naval Air Systems Div. Integrated Logistics Support Center, 1968-70; computer specialist U.S. Army Computer Systems Support and Evaluation Command, Washington, 1970-72, computer systems br. U.S. Forest Service, 1972-73, now cons. data processing; tchr. data processing; substitute tchr. Va. Schs. Fairfax County, 1966. Bd. govs. U. Mich. Alumni Club, Alumni Devel. Council. Active Girl Scouts U.S.A.; mem. Linguistic U. Mich. Alumni Club, devel. council U. Mich. Recipient citation for meritorious service Dept. Army. Mem. Linguistic Soc. Am., Am. Documentation Inst., Am. Fedn. Information Processing, Federally Employed Women, Soc. for Applied Learning Tech., Sigma Kappa, Phi Delta Gamma. Club: Univ. Mich. Alumni of Washington (bd. govs. 1967—). Home: 1239 Delaware Av SW Washington DC 20024

SUSSMAN, MARION BEATRICE BAUM (MRS. IRVING SUSSMAN), counseling psychologist, ednl. cons.; b. Paterson, N.J.; d. Samuel and Adele (Gerstein) Baum; student U. Ala., 1940-42; B.Ed. cum laude, U. Miami, 1953, M.Ed., 1956, Ph.D. in Counseling Psychology, 1973; postgrad. U. N.C., 1969; m. Irving Sussman, Nov. 21, 1943; children—Nicki (Mrs. Steve Charles Horowitz), Roberta Joy. Sci. tchr. Kinloch Park Jr. High Sch., Miami, Fla., 1953-56, counselor, guidance chmn., test chmn., 1956-63, asst. prin. for guidance 1969-73; pvt. counseling practice, 1973—; counselor, test chmn. S.W. Miami High Sch., 1963-68; grad. asst. U. Miami, Coral Gables, Fla., 1968-69; mem. staff Piedmont summer program Wake Forest U., Winston-Salem, N.C., 1972, 73; dir. Piedmont winter program Biscayne Coll., Miami, Fla., 1974; sch. services specialist N.C. Advancement Sch., 1974—. Active various community drives. Mem. Assn. Humanistic Psychology, N.E.A., Am., Fla., S. Fla., Dade County (pres. 1967-68) personnel and guidance assns., Fla. Edn. Assn. Mem. B'nai B'rith Women. Home: 317 Hanover Arms Ct Winston-Salem NC 27104

SUSSMAN, SALLY BRAGINSKY, contractor; b. Copenhagen, Denmark, May 21, 1911; d. Max and Esther (Bunenova) Braginsky; came to U.S., 1917, naturalized, 1942; student N.Y. U., 1953, Queens Coll., 1964, Cooper Union Coll., 1967; m. Max Sussman, Feb. 21, 1932 (dec. 1952); children—Marvin, Gerald, Stephen. Pres. Greater N.Y. York Air Conditioning Co., Inc., 1950; pres. Greater N.Y. Mech. Contractors, Inc., N.Y.C., 1967—. Recipient award for achievement Gen. Electric Inst., 1955, Recognition award Carrier Co., 1965. Registered profl. engr., N.Y. Mem. Soc. Women Engrs. (life), L.I. Bldg. Congress, Mech. Contractors N.Y., Bldg. Trades Employers' Assn. N.Y., Syossit Bus. and Profl. Womens Club L.I. (pres. 1968), Hicksville C. of C. (treas. 1966-69), L.I. Assn. Commerce and Industry. Home: 58-59 206th St Bayside NY 11364 Office: 9 Midland Av Hicksville NY 11801

SUSTER, BARBARA JANE, art gallery and framing co. exec.; b. Des Plaines, May 21, 1921; d. John E. and Rose (Donbek) Suster; B.A., Wellesley Coll., 1942; M.A., Columbia, 1944. Treas. Newcomb-Macklin Co., Inc., framing and art gallery, Chgo., 1949—. Mem. Ill. Mfg. Assn., Lyric Opera Guild, Ravinia Assn., Chgo. Symphony Soc., Art Inst. Chgo. Republican. Conglist. Club: Chicago Wellesley. Home: 1221 Prairie Av Des Plaines IL 60016 Office: 400 N State St Chicago IL 60610

SUTHERLAND, JOAN, coloratura soprano; b. Sydney, Australia, Nov. 7, 1926; d. McDonald Sutherland; student Royal Coll. Music, London, 1951; m. Richard Bonynge, 1954; 1 son. Appeared concert performance Purcell's Dido and Aeneas; concerts, oratorio performances, Australia; appeared in opera Judith, Sydney (Australia) Conservatory of Music; debut Covent Garden in Magic Flute, 1952, other operatic performances include Lucia Di Lammermoor, La Traviata, La Sonnambula, Handel's Acis and Galatea, heroine roles operas by Bellini and Donizetti; debuts include Handel's Alcina, Teatro la Fenice, Venice, 1960, appeared in Bellini's Puritani, Glyndebourne Festival, Sussex, Eng., 1960, Barcelona, Spain, 1960, Antwerp, Belgium, 1962, Amsterdam, Holland, 1962, Dallas, 1960, Met. Opera, N.Y.C., 1961, Vancouver Opera, 1964, Teatro Colon, 1969, Lyric Opera of Chgo., 1971, San Francisco Opera, 1972, Met. Opera, 1973. Winner Sun Aria competition; recipient Mobil Quest award, 1951. Decorated comdr. Order Brit. Empire. Rec. artist London Records. Address: care Colbert Artists Mgmt 11 W 57th New York City NY 10019

SUTHERLAND, LINDA BARRETT, actress; b. Chgo.; d. John and Marie (LaVicka) Dubsky; student Northwestern U., 1927-29, Bush Conservatory, Chgo., 1927-29; m. Victor C. Sutherland, Oct. 19, 1940 (dec. Aug. 1968). Actress in radio programs Hollywood Romance, 1928, First Nighter, 1928-29; stock and Broadways appearances with Al Jackson Players, 1929-32; tour with Arsenic and Old Lace, 1942-43, Man and Superman, 1949; films include Star, 1968, Doctor's Wives, 1970; author, actress radio show Adventures in Living, 1952; interior designer, 1958-69; residence dir. St. Vincent's Coll. Nursing, Los Angeles, 1971-73. Mem. Phi Beta Kappa. Address: 916 N Alfred St Los Angeles CA 90069

SUTHERLAND, ZENA BAILEY (MRS. ALEC SUTHERLAND), editor; b. Winthrop, Mass., Sept. 17, 1915; d. Jacob and Lena (Cowen) Karras; B.A., U. Chgo., 1937, M.A., 1968; m. Alec Sutherland, July 30, 1965; children by previous marriage—Stephen, Thomas, Katherine. With U. Chgo., 1958—, editor bull. Center for Children's Books, Grad. Library Sch.; children's book editor Chgo. Tribune, 1972—. Lectr. U. Chgo., 1973—; cons. NBC, 1966-70. Pres. P.T.A., 1950-52. Mem. Reading Round Table, 37 Players, Phi Beta Mu. Unitarian (pres. Women's Alliance 1950). Clubs: Colony, Quadrangle. Author: History in Children's Books, 1967; Children and Books, 1972; The Best in Children's Books, 1973. Contbg. editor Saturday Rev., 1966-72. Contbr. to encys. Home: 1418 E 57th St Chicago IL 60637 Office: 1100 E 57th St Chicago IL 60637

SUTKER, PATRICIA BOWDEN, clin. psychologist; b. Lynn, Mass., May 23, 1942; d. Richard William and Eleanor Ernestine (Parmalee) Foley; B.A., Oglethorpe U., Atlanta, 1965; M.S., U. Ga., 1967, Ph.D., 1969; 1 dau., Kim. Asst. prof. dept. psychiatry Tulane U. Sch. Medicine, 1969-72, Med. U. S.C., Charleston, 1972—; staff psychologist VA Hosp., Charleston, 1972—; exec. dir. Charleston County Substance Abuse Commn., 1973—, Charleston Alcohol Safety Action Program, 1973—. Mem. Am., Southeastern psychol. assns., Neuropsychology Soc., Phi Kappa Phi, Phi Beta Kappa, Sigma Xi. Contbr. articles to profl. jours. Home: 1275 Oldwanus Dr Mount Pleasant SC 29464 Office: Psychology Service VA Hosp 109 Bee St Charleston SC 29403

SUTLIFF, LINDA LEE, educator; b. Elyria, O., July 11, 1944; d. Obert Francher and Carolyn (Guthrie) Sutliff; B.A., Baldwin Wallace Coll., 1966; M.A., Bowling Green State U., 1967. Instr. N.Y. State U., Oswego, 1967-69; mgr. Melody Ranch, Inc., Wakefield, Mass., 1969-70; asst. prof. English and speech Endicott Jr. Coll., Beverly, Mass., 1970—; dir. drama Shore Country Day Sch., Beverly, 1974—. Active in creative drama program as therapy for retarded and disturbed children Alice A. Mackin Sch., Oswego, N.Y., also Hathorne State Regional Center, Danvers, Mass. Mem. Speech Communications Assn., Am. Ednl. Theatre Assn., New Eng. Theatre Conf., Internat. Platform Assn. Contbr. drama reviews to various local newspapers. Home: 1106 Windsor Ct Beverly MA 01915 Office: 362 Hale St Beverly MA 01915

SUTTENFIELD, VIRGINIA, physician; b. Roanoke, Va., Mar. 27, 1917; d. Warner C. and Anna G. (Ward) Suttenfield; A.B., Agnes Scott Coll., 1938; M.D., Med. Coll. Ga., 1944. Resident psychiatry R.I. State Hosp. Mental Diseases, 1945-48; child psychiatry tng. U. Md., 1950-52; psychoanalytic tng., Balt. and Western New Eng., 1952-58; instr. psychiatry U. Md. Sch. Medicine, 1952-53; dir. mental health Baltimore County Health Dept., 1953-55; dir. Psychiat. Clinic for Children, Stamford, Conn., 1955-66; pvt. practice medicine, specializing in psychiatry, Stamford, 1966—. Cons., Southwestern Conn. Mental Health Planning Council, 1969-72; also cons. to agys. Mem. Am. Psychiat. Assn., Am. Orthopsychiat. Assn., Am. Acad. Child Psychiatry. Address: 500 Wire Mill Rd Stamford CT 06903

SUTTER, ELIZABETH HENBY (MRS. RICHARD A. SUTTER), civic leader, mgmt. co. exec.; b. St. Louis, May 15, 1912; d. William Hastings and Alvina (Steinbreder) Henby; A.B., Washington U., 1931; m. Richard A. Sutter, June 15, 1935; children—John Richard, Jane Elizabeth, Judith Ann (Mrs. William Hinrichs). Sec.-treas. Sutter Mgmt. Co., St. Louis; sec. Sutter Clinic; v.p. Downtown Med. Bldg., Inc. Chmn. com. on mental health A.M.A. Aux., 1960-62, v.p., 1962-63, 64-64, pres. 1965-66, editor Direct Line newsletter, 1967-74; asso. editor MD's Wife, 1973—; mem. adv. bd. Deaconess Hosp. Sch. of Nursing, St. Louis; trustee John Burroughs Sch., 1958-61, v.p. 1959, devel. commn., 1960-61; mem. Historic Bldgs. Commn. St. Louis County, 1957—, chmn., 1973-74; chmn. Com. for Preservation Children's Teeth; sec., treas. Sutter Clinic, St. Louis; mem. planning bd. Health, Hosp. Health, Welfare Council Met. St. Louis, 1955-64; pres. Aux. Central States Soc. Indsl. Medicine and Surgery, 1960-61; pres. St. Louis County Med. Soc. Aux., 1948-49, Mo. Med. Soc. Aux., 1952-53; sec. St. Louis County Health and Hosp. Bd., 1956-60, chmn., 1961; bd. dirs. Tb Soc. St. Louis, exec. com., 1956—, v.p., 1960-61; pres. Tb and Health Soc. of St. Louis, 1962-65; adv. council vol. services Nat. Assn. Mental Health, 1962-64; bd. dirs. Am. Cancer Soc., St. Louis, exec. com., 1954-64; bd. dirs. Mental Health Assn. St. Louis, 1960-61; mem. Practical Nursing Edn. Council, chmn. exec. com., 1959-60; mem. A.M.A. Council on Mental Health Planning for Nat. Conf. on Mental Health, 1961; mem. adv. com. on women in services Dept. Def., 1969-72, vice chmn., 1971; participant 24th ann. global strategy discussion U.S. Naval War Coll., 1972; bd. govs. Washington U. Alumni, 1970-71, pres. Washington U. Arts and Scis. Century Club, 1970-71. Named one of 10 Women of Achievement in good citizen category St. Louis Globe-Democrat, 1961; Alumna of Year, Gamma Phi Beta, St. Louis, 1966; recipient St. Louis County Med. Soc. award of merit, 1964; Distinguished Alumni citation Washington U., St. Louis, 1968. Presbyn. (chmn. finance com. Women's Assn. 1954-60). Mem. Mo. Hist. Soc., St. Louis Symphony Soc., Mo. Assn. Social Welfare, Am., Mo. pub. health assns., Women's Aux. Mo. Med. Assn. (hon. life). Home: 7215 Greenway Dr St Louis MO 63130

SUTTER, MARIAN DOROTHY, museum curator; b. Pitts., July 26, 1943; d. William G. and Margaret Estelle (McNally) Sutter; B.S., Slippery Rock State Coll., 1965, postgrad., 1971-73; M.Ed., East Stroudsburg State Coll., 1971. Tchr. health and phys. edn. Wilkins Jr. High Sch., Pitts., 1965-68; grad. teaching asst. East Stroudsburg State Coll., Pa., 1968-69; instr. health and phys. edn. Allegany Community Coll., Cumberland, Md., 1969-71; curator health sci. Buhl Planetarium and Inst. Popular Sci., Pitts., 1971—. Ednl. cons., mem. Speakers Bur., Planned Parenthood Center of Pitts., 1971—. Water safety instr. trainer A.R.C., 1970-71. Mem. Am., Pa. assns. health, phys. edn. and recreation, Am. Sch. Health Assn., Am. Assn. Health and Med. Museums (rep.). Home: 175 Pennsylvania Av Pittsburgh PA 15202 Office: Allegheny Sq Pittsburgh PA 15212

SUTTIN, DORIS BETH, wholesale co. exec.; b. Chgo., July 5, 1940; d. Saul S. and Pearl (Goldberg) Siegal; B.S., U. Ill., 1961; m. Eugene N. Suttin, Feb. 1, 1961; 1 son, Adam. Advt. mgr. Goldblatt's Dept. Store, Champaign, Ill., 1961-62; pub. relations, real estate sales Grand Bahama Devel. Co. Ltd., Freeport, 1963-65; asst. sales mgr. Coral Beach Ltd., Freeport, 1967-69; showroom sales dir. Saul S. Siegal Co., Miami, Fla., 1970—. Mem. Women in Communications, Nat. Soc. Interior Designers. Club: Jockey. Office: 95 NE 40th St Miami FL 33137

SUTTLE, EDITH FRANCES DUCROW (MRS. WILLIAM E. SUTTLE), educator; b. St. Louis; d. George and Julia (Millender) Ducrow; grad. Moody Bible Inst., 1932; B.S., Northeastern State Coll., 1961, Ed.M., 1963; postgrad. St. Louis U., 1965; m. William E. Suttle, Dec. 3, 1937; stepchildren—Mildred (Mrs. Sherman Chastain), Enola (Mrs. LaVere Marple), Geraldine (Mrs. James L. McCoy). Ordained to ministry Meth. Ch., 1949; minister, Spavinaw, Okla., 1946-49, Wyandotte, Okla., 1949-56, Miami, Okla., 1956-58, Ochelata, Okla., 1958-59, Cookson, Okla., 1959-61, Bethel, Okla., 1962-64; tchr., St. Louis, 1961-62; guidance counselor, Hazelwood, Mo., 1964—. Psychol. examiner N. County Day Sch., Ferguson, Mo., 1968—. Devotional chmn. Brown Elementary Sch. P.T.A., Hazelwood, 1968-73. Mem. Nat. Guidance Assn., Moody Bible Inst. Alumnae Fellowship (sec. St. Louis area 1966-74), Woman's Soc. Christian Service (pres. Bartlesville dist. 1947-49), Spanish Internat. Pavilion, Assn. Founders, Rho Theta, Alpha Chi. Republican. Author: (poetry) The Garden Gate, 1971. Home: 3202 Cross Keys Dr Florissant MO 63033 Office: 15985 New Halls Ferry Rd Florissant MO 63033

SUTTON, BEVERLY JEWELL (MRS. H. ELDON SUTTON), psychiatrist; b. Rockford, Mich., May 27, 1932; d. Beryl Dewey and Cora Belle (Potes) Jewell; M.D., U. Mich., 1957; m. H. Eldon Sutton, July 7, 1962; children—Susan, Caroline. Intern, St. Joseph's Hosp., Ann Arbor, Mich., 1958; resident child psychiatry Hawthorne Center, Northville, Mich., 1958, 62; resident pediatrics Univ. Hosp., Mich. Med. Center, Ann Arbor, 1959-61; resident adult psychiatry Austin (Tex.) State Hosp., 1962-64, chief child psychiatry, 1964—; dir. Children's Psychiat. Hosp., Austin, 1966—; instr. spl. edn. U. Tex. Grad. Sch., Austin, 1967-70; dir. child psychiatry tng. Austin State Hosp., 1971—; mem. clin. faculty U. Tex. Med. Sch., San Antonio, 1970—. Mem. Tex. Gov.'s Council on Early Childhood Devel., 1971. Diplomate Am. Bd. Pediatrics, Am. Bd. Psychiatry and Neurology. Fellow Am. Acad. Child Psychiatry; mem. Am. Psychiat. Assn., Am. Soc. Human Genetics, Am., Tex. med. assns., Travis County Med. Soc., Tex. Soc. Child Psychiatry (sec.-treas. 1971). Contbr. to publs. in field. Home: 1103 Gaston St Austin TX 78703 Office: 4110 Guadalupe St Austin TX 78751

SUTTON, CAROL (MRS. CHARLES EDWARD WHALEY), newspaperwoman; b. St. Louis, June 29, 1933; d. Dallas Monroe and Marie (Marler) Sutton; B.J., U. Mo., 1955; m. Charles Edward Whaley, Nov. 23, 1957; children—Carrie, Kate. With Courier-Jour., Louisville, 1955—, news and feature writer, 1955-63, women's editor, 1963-74, mng. editor, 1974—. Mem. Kappa Alpha Theta. Unitarian. Home: 2531 Cherokee Pkwy Louisville KY 40204 Office: 525 W Broadway Louisville KY 40202

SUTTON, CLARA MIDDLETON, ret. educator; b. Pine Bluff, Ark., June 25, 1907; d. Willie Joseph and Annie Elizabeth (Harris) Middleton; B.S., U. Ark. at Pine Bluff, 1936; B.A., Pratt Inst., 1955; M.A., Columbia U., 1959; m. John M. Sutton, June 26, 1940 (div. Nov. 1947); children (adopted)—Roselyn, Magdelyn. Tchr. pub. schs., Rison, Ark., 1930-35, Morrilton, Ark., 1940-44, Crossett, Ark., 1936-40; free lance clothing designer Coats & Clark Thread Co., N.Y.C., also Cunningham Welch Advt., N.Y.C., 1950-52, Hattie Carnigie Custom Shop, N.Y.C., 1953; home econs. tchr., Vineland (N.J.) Tng. Sch., 1955-59; instr. clothing and design U. Ark., Pine Bluff, 1959-73, ret., 1973. Mem. Vols. in Pub. Schs., Pine Bluff. Mem. Nat. Coll. Women Assn. (chpt. v.p. 1964), Am. Home Econs. Assn. (coll. counselor 1959—), Am. Assn. Mental Deficiency, Council of Exceptional Children, Am. Assn. U. Profs. Presbyn. (deacon 1966—). Home: 1801 W 11th Av Pine Bluff AR 71601

SUTTON, EVELYN MCCRACKEN (MRS. PAUL ALLISON SUTTON), librarian; b. Lake Juanluska, N.C., July 21, 1926; d. Albert Johnson and Myrtle (Medford) McCracken; student Western Carolina U., 1943-46; m. Paul Allison Sutton, Dec. 26, 1946; children—Cynthia (Mrs. Howard Lee Williams), William Gregg, Mark Allison. Librarian Assn. Methodist Hist. Socs., Lake Junaluska, N.C., 1957-60; librarian Commn. Archives and History United Methodist Ch., Lake Junaluska, 1968—. Mem. United Methodist Women. Democrat. Methodist. Home: 19 Holston Village Rd Waynesville NC 28786 Office: World Methodist Bldg Lakeshore Dr Lake Junaluska NC 28745

SUTTON, JULIA SUMBERG, musicologist, educator; b. Toronto, Ont., Can., July 20, 1928; d. Samuel L. and Anne R. (Rubin) Sumberg; A.B. summa cum laude, Cornell U., 1949; M.A., Colo. Coll., 1952; Ph.D., U. Rochester, 1962. Instr. music history New Sch. for Social Research, 1962-63; instr. music Queens Coll., Coll. City N.Y., 1963-66; chmn. dept. music lit. New Eng. Conservatory of Music, 1967—, chmn. faculty senate, 1971-73. Vis. asst. prof. George Peabody Coll. for Tchrs., 1966-67; instr. N.Y.U., summers 1963, 66; pvt. tchr. piano, 1949-65; dance dir. N.Y. Pro Musica prodn. An Entertainment for Elizabeth, Caramoor, N.Y., Saratoga, N.Y., U. Ariz., Stanford, U. Cal. at Los Angeles, 1969, nationwide tours, 1970, 71, 72, 73; dance dir. Descent of Rhythm and Harmony, Colo. Springs, Colo., 1970, Renaissance Revisited, Phila., 1972, An Evening of Renaissance Music and Dance, York U., Toronto, 1974; lectr., cons., research dir. in music lit., music as related to the dance. Mem. Am. Musicological Soc., Music Library Assn., Phi Beta Kappa, Phi Kappa Phi. Editor: (Thoinot Arbeau) Orchesography, 1966. Contbr. articles and book revs. to profl. jours. Address: New England Conservatory 290 Huntington Av Boston MA 02115

SUTTON, WILMA JEAN (MRS. CLARENCE E. SUTTON), savs. and loan exec.; b. Murphysboro, Ill., Nov. 11, 1933; d. Edward and Hattie D. (Jennings) Hopkins; student So. Ill. U., 1951-52, Wilson Jr. Coll. Night Sch., 1959-60, U. Ill., 1967, Central YMCA Nigh Sch., 1968, U. Conn., 1969-70; m. Clarence E. Sutton, May 22, 1953; 1 dau., Michele I. With Chgo. Title & Trust Co., 1952-63; sec. John Foster Dulles Sch., Chgo., 1963; with Hyde Park Fed. Savs. & Loan Assn., Chgo., 1964—, v.p., 1968—; mem. supervisory bd. Hyde Park Fed. Coop. Credit Union, 1973. Active Mother McAuley Liberal Arts High Sch. P.T.A.; mem. Field Mus. Natural History. Bd. dirs. Loretto Adult Edn. Center, 1973. Mem. Am., U.S. savs. and loan leagues, Cosmopolitan C. of C., Urban League. Roman Catholic (sec. finance com. 1970—). Home: 9551 S Michigan Av Chicago IL 60628 Office: 5250 Lake Park Av Chicago IL 60615

SUZUKI, JOY SUEMI, educator; b. Honolulu, Sept. 11, 1948; d. Jack Soichi and Teruyo (Takafuji) Suzuki; B.A., U. No. Colo., Greeley, 1969. Tchr. speech and English, Moanalua Intermediate Sch., Honolulu, 1970—, tchr. drama, 1973—. Mem. Speech Communications Assn., Hawaii, Nat. councils tchrs. English, Nat. Soc. Lit. and Arts, Alpha Psi Omega. Democrat. Buddhist. Home: 105 Kawananakoa Pl Honolulu HI 96817 Office: 1289 Mahiole St Honolulu HI 96819

SVAGR, VIRGINIA BAILEY, psychologist, educator; b. Jackson, Mich., Apr. 4, 1923; d. William Everett and Gladys (Smith) Bailey; student Jackson Jr. Coll., 1941-43; B.S., U. Mich., 1948; M.Ed., Wayne State U., 1960, Ph.D., 1965; m. John Svagr, June 15, 1947 (div. June, 1971); children—Gladys Elizabeth, John Joseph, Teresa Jean. Instr. U. Mich. at Ann Arbor, 1949-50; asst. prof. chemistry Detroit Inst. Tech., 1956-60; instr. Wayne State U., Detroit, 1961-65; lectr. U. Detroit Grad. Sch., 1967-69; dir. reading clinic Oakland Schs., Pontiac, Mich., 1965-69; dir. diagnostic center and learning systems Oakland Community Coll., Bloomfield Hills, Mich., 1969—, also prof. psychology. Ednl. cons. to Neuro-Ednl. Center William Beaumont Hosp., Birmingham, Mich.; adviser Mich. Assn. for Children with Learning Disabilities. Mem. Mich. Assn. Clin. Psychologists, Am., Mich. psychol. assns., Mich. Reading Assn., Mich. Assn., Sch. Psychologists. Home: 26502 W 14 Mile Rd Franklin MI 48025 Office: Oakland Community College 2480 Opdyke Rd Bloomfield Hills MI 48013

SVAJIAN, PERGROUHI NAJARIAN, educator; b. Harput, Turkey, Nov. 11, 1918; d. Haroutune Toross and Nevart Touma (Kevorkian) Najarian; came to U.S., 1961, naturalized, 1966; B.A., Am. U. in Beirut, 1948; M.S., Cornell U., 1950, Ph.D., 1952; m. Stephen G. Svajian, Aug. 20, 1961; 1 dau., Sylva. Chmn. child devel. and family relations Beirut Coll. Women, 1952-56, dean faculty, 1965-66; asso. prof. edn. Am. U. Beirut, 1956-61; prof. edn. Bklyn. Coll., 1963—, coordinator div. secondary edn. Sch. Edn., 1972—; coordinator research Eastern Mediterrean group Cross Cultural Group Middle East, Rice U.-Ford Found., 1953-57; cons. FAO, 1957—. Bd. dirs. Armenian Gen. Benevolent Union; v.p. Howard Karakheusian Found. Mem. Am. Psychol. Assn., Am. Ednl. Research Assn., Soc. Study Child Devel., Omicron Nu, Phi Kappa Phi, Phi Lambda Theta. Author: Adolescence—Studies in Human Development, 1974. Contbr. articles to profl. jours. Home: 524 3d St Brooklyn NY 11215

SVARE, KIRSTEN LOUISE, polit. orgn. exec.; b. Fergus Falls, Minn., May 21, 1943; d. Bjarne Nathaniel and Vivian Mae (Johnson) Svare; B.A. in English and Journalism, U. N.D., 1966. Tchr. Lakeville High Sch., Otisville, Mich., 1966-67; asst. editor Donnelley Printer Mag., R.R. Donnelley & Sons Co., Chgo., 1967-69; account exec.

Morton B. Stone & Assos., Chgo., 1969-71; office mgr. Citizens for Joseph R. Lundy for State Rep., Chgo., 1971-72; free lance pub. relations cons., Chgo., 1972—; adminstrv. asst. to State Rep. Bruce L. Douglas, Chgo., 1972-74; exec. dir. Ind. Voters Ill., Chgo., 1974, Project LEAP (Legal Elections in All Precincts), Chgo., 1974—. Pub. relations advisor Loop Center YWCA, Chgo., 1969-70. Vol. ind. polit. campaigns, 1972—. Recipient Cub's Cup Chgo. chpt. Women in Communications, 1971. Mem. Ind. Voters Ill. (vice chmn. pub. relations 1973-74; sec. 1972-73; bd. dirs. 1972-74), Ind. Precinct Orgn., Nat. Orgn. for Women, Women's Polit. Caucus, Am. Civil Liberties Union, Women in Communications (pres. Chgo. chpt. 1974-75). Club: Publicity (chmn. com. 1970-71) (Chgo.). Home: 420 W Surf St Chicago IL 60657 Office: 22 W Monroe St Chicago IL 60603

SVENDSEN, LOUISE AVERILL (MRS. THORALF SVENDSEN), curator; b. Old Town, Me., Nov. 22, 1915; d. Albert Guy and Louise Norris (Pierce) Averill; B.A., Wellesley Coll., 1937; M.A., Yale, 1941, Ph.D., 1949; m. Thoralf Svendsen, July 3, 1950. Docent, Met. Mus. Art, N.Y.C., 1941-42; lectr. dept. edn. Boston Mus. Fine Arts, 1942; instr. history art Duke, 1943-45; instr., asst. prof. history art Goucher Coll., 1945-50; asst. prof. history art Am. U., Washington, 1950-51; lectr. Solomon R. Guggenheim Mus., N.Y.C., 1954—, asso. curator, 1962-66, curator, 1966—. Decorated knight 1st class Royal Norwegian Order St. Olav, 1965. Mem. Am. Assn. Mus. Home: 16 Park Av New York City NY 10016 Office: 1071 Fifth Av New York City NY 10028

SVILAND, MARY ANN PETRICH, psychologist; b. Milw., July 1, 1937; d. Slavko John and Ann Rose (Boldin) Petrich; B.S. with honors, U. Wis.-Madison, 1959; M.A., Cal. State U. at Northridge, 1967; Ph.D., U. So. Cal., 1971. Predoctoral intern Cedars-Sinai Med. Center, Los Angeles, 1968-69, research psychologist, investigator, 1971; psychology trainee Wadsworth VA Hosp., Los Angeles, 1969-71; clin. psychologist VA Hosp., Sepulveda, Cal., 1971—; clin. asso. dept. psychology U. So. Cal., 1972—; asst. prof. Cal. State U., Northridge, 1973—. Mem. Am., Los Angeles County, San Fernando Valley (chmn. pub. relations 1974—), Western psychol. assns., Cal. Inst. for Human Sexuality (adv. bd., exec. com. 1974—). Contbr. articles to profl. jours. on drug addiction, sexual behavior and dysfunction, chronic illness and dying. Home: 24021 Victory Blvd Canoga Park CA 91304 Office: VA Hosp 16111 Plummer St Sepulveda CA 91343

SVOBODA, LOIS VATNE (MRS. WILLIAM BANCROFT SVOBODA), physician; b. Elizabeth, N.J., Oct. 16, 1939; d. Nils Eriksen and Naomi (Johnsen) Vatne; B.S., Evang. Coll., 1961; M.D., U. Chgo., 1966; m. William Bancroft Svoboda, Dec. 22, 1962; children—Karen, Heather, David. Intern, St. Francis Hosp., Evanston, Ill., 1966-67; emergency room physician Victory Meml. Hosp., Waukegan, Ill., 1967-68; practice medicine Olmstead Med. Group, Rochester, Minn., 1969-71; mem. staff Univ. Health Service, U. W.Va. Med. Center, Morgantown, 1971—. Presbyn. Home: 1461 Dogwood Av Morgantown WV 26505 Office: Univ Health Service WVa U Med Center Morgantown WV 26505

SWAB, PATRICIA JEAN (MRS. GEORGE LOUIS SWAB), educator; b. Bloomfield, Ia., Aug. 31, 1924; d. George Weston and LaRue (Anderson) Smith; B.A. (Music scholar), Grinnell Coll., 1947; M.A., U. Ia., 1953; postgrad. summers Northwestern U., 1948, Ind. U., 1949; m. George Louis Swab, June 19, 1954. High sch. tchr. vocal, instrumental music Seymour (Ia.) Pub. Sch., 1945-46; tchr. speech, dir. drama, Cedar Rapids, Ia., 1947-58; tchr. jr. high sch., 1958-73. Speech judge Ia. High Sch. Forensic League, Ia. High Sch. Speech Assn., 1949—. Active YWCA. Recipient Spl. pin award Am. Fedn. Tchrs., Cedar Rapids, 1972. Mem. Am. Assn. U. Women (chmn. drama group, 1957, chmn. fine arts 1957-58), Ia. Council Tchrs. Speech (chmn. speech curriculum, 1973-74), N.E.A., Ia. Edn. Assn., Am. Ednl. Theatre Assn., D.A.R. (Good Citizen award 1942), Speech Communication Assn. Am., Phi Mu Gamma. Methodist. Clubs: Toastmistress (pres. 1963-64), Zonta Internat., Camera. Home: 3215 Dairydale Ct SE Cedar Rapids IA 52403

SWAIM, ALICE MACKENZIE (MRS. WILLIAM THOMAS SWAIM, JR.), author; b. Aberdeen, Scotland, June 5, 1911; d. Donald C. and Alice (Murray) Mackenzie; student Chatham Coll., 1928-30; B.A. Wilson Coll., 1932; m. William Thomas Swaim, Jr., Dec. 27, 1932: children—Elizabeth Anne, Kathleen Mackenzie. Came to U.S., 1928, naturalized, 1939. Author: (books of poetry) Let the Deep Song Rise, 1952; Up to the Stars, 1954; Poetry Calendar, 1956; Sunshine in a Thimble, 1958; Crickets Are Crying Autumn (award prize Pageant Press), 1960; The Gentle Dragon, 1962; Beneath a Dancing Star, 1967; Beyond My Catnip Garden, 1970; (books) Pennsylvania Profile, 1966; Here on the Threshold, 1966; Honeysuckle Scented Days, 1966; also children's articles, 1950-54; also brochures, 1959-60. Critic Nat. Writers Club, 1952-53; poetry columnist Cornucopia, 1955, Carlisle Evening Sentinel, 1965-70, Tejas mag., 1969-70; judge in various state and nat. contests; featured poet Am. Bard, The Muse, Scimitar & Song and others. Active A.R.C., Girl Scouts Am. Recipient Anna Hempstead Branch Lyric award, 1959; 1st prize N.Y. Writers Guild Contest, 1959, Silver medal Esternaux award, 1959 medal of merit Studie Scambi, Italy, Internat. Contest, 1970, N.Y. Poetry Forum, 1969-70, Jesse Stuart Contest, 1970, Pa. Poetry Soc. Contest, 1953-71; Poet-Laureate of the Sonnet; Cyclofame award, 1971; 2d prize Am. Poets Fellowship, 1972; numerous other poetry awards. Mem. Am. Assn. U. Women, Am. Poetry League (nominating com. 1964, 1st v.p. 1964-67, 67-70), Poetry Soc. Am., Nat. Fedn. State Poetry Socs., Midwest Chaparral, Ida. Poets and Writers' Guild, Pa. (v.p. Mary O'Conner chpt.), N.H. poetry socs., World Poetry Day Assn., Eng.-Am. Bard Family, Centro Studie Scambi, Book Club for Poetry, U.S.A., Hymn Soc. Am., N.Y., Writers Guild, Pa. Folklore Soc., Am. Poets' Fellowship Corp., Avalon, Assn. for Poetry Therapy. Presbyn. Club: Nat. Writers'. Home: 322 N 2d St Apt 1606 Harrisburg PA 17101

SWAIM, JOAN HEWATT (MRS. JOHNNY RAY SWAIM), librarian; b. Ft. Worth, Oct. 2, 1934; d. Willis Gilliland and Elizabeth Georgina (Harris) Hewatt; B.A., Tex. Christian U., 1966, M.A., 1968; postgrad. North Tex. State U., 1973—; m. Johnny Ray Swaim, Nov. 7, 1953; children—Michael Ray, Susan Elizabeth. Asst. faculty social dir. Tex. Christian U., Ft. Worth, 1960-63, teaching asst. English dept., 1967-68, file personnel, catalog dept. Univ. Library, 1968-70; instr. reading dept., basic studies div. Tarrant County Jr. Coll., Ft. Worth, 1968; head librarian, dir. audio-visual services Tex. Coll. Osteo. Medicine, Ft. Worth, 1970—. Cons. to med. library Ft. Worth Osteo. Hosp., 1970—. Pres. Metroplex Council Med. Librarians, Dallas-Tarrant Counties, 1974-75. Mem. TCU Women Execs. Mem. Christian Ch. Club: Faculty Woman's (pres. 1970-72) (Tex. Christian U.). Home: 3721 Fenton St Fort Worth TX 76133 Office: 3516 Camp Bowie St Fort Worth TX 76107

SWAIN, ALICE MARIE MCNEELY, reading specialist; b. Oklahoma City, Feb. 3, 1924; d. William Henry and Lucy Bruce (McCuiston) McNeely; B.S., Langston U., 1946; M.E., U. Okla, 1952; m. Robert Alphonso Swain, Aug. 24, 1946; children—Robert Alphonso II, Lecia Danee. Tchr. schs., Oklahoma City, 1950—; Alice's Together Charm and Modeling Sch., Oklahoma City, 1971—; asst. prof. div. edn., coordinator reading Langston (Okla.) U.; social columnist Black Dispatch, 1974—. Recipient S.W. Regional Sigma of Year award, 1962, U. Okla. math. grantee, 1963, Livingtext book grantee, 1964; named one of 10 outstanding nat. Sigma women, 1965. Mem. Urban League Guild, N.A.A.C.P., YWCA, Okla. Edn. Assn., N.E.A., Nat. Pan-Hellenic Council (sec. 1970-72, v.p. 1972-74, pres. 1974—), Sigma Gamma Rho (past chmn. bd. dirs., youth services dir., pub. relations chmn., grand epistoleus 1974—). Mem. Christian Ch. Club: Tes Trams Social (Oklahoma City). Editor: Silver Quota. Short Stories, 1972. Address: 3016 Norcrest Dr Oklahoma City OK 73111

SWAIN, CLEONE BEATRICE, banker; b. Columbia, S.C., Feb. 23, 1918; d. Lawrence Jefferson and Blanche Aileen (Waites) Perry; grad. high sch.; m. Marriett Don Swain, June 10, 1944. Sec., Fort Jackson, S.C., 1941-44, U.S. Army, Memphis Gen. Depot, 1946-47, Prosperity Laundry Machines, Memphis, 1948-51; with Union Planters Nat. Bank, 1951—, asst. cashier, 1964—, br. mgr., 1971—. Mem. Nat. Assn. Bank Women (chmn. Tenn. group 1973-74, asst. v.p. 1972, nat. bd. dirs. 1970-71), Beta Sigma Phi. Club: Whitehaven Quota. Home: 5486 Park Av Memphis TN 38117 Office: PO Box 30010 Air Terminal Br Memphis TN 38130

SWAIN, MARIAN LOUISE BOATMAN (MRS. THERON RICHARD SWAIN), social worker; b. Cedar Falls, Ia.; d. John Harlan and Bertha (Williams) Boatman; B.A. magna cum laude, U. Ia., 1935; postgrad. U. Chgo., 1935-36, Pa. Sch. Social Work, 1938-39; M.S.W., Portland State U., 1969; m. Theron Richard Swain, Feb. 5, 1941 (dec. May 1968); children—Harlan J., Scott Terry. Pub. welfare worker Ia. Dept. Social Welfare, 1936-38, children's worker, 1939-42; sr. children's worker King County Welfare Dept., Wash., 1945-46; exec. sec. Planned Parenthood Center, Seattle, 1946-47; housemother Children's Instn., Ketchikan, Alaska, 1955-56; child welfare worker, Ketchikan, 1956-68; social worker, supr. services Alaska Div. Family and Children Services, Ketchikan, 1968—. Chmn., Ketchikan Community Council, 1964-66; chmn. Gateway Community Mental Health Center Bd., 1968-70. Named Profl. Woman of Year, Ketchikan Bus. and Profl. Women, 1960. Mem. Nat. Assn. Social Work, Acad. Certified Social Workers, Phi Beta Kappa, Eta Sigma Phi. Club: Soroptimist (Ketchikan). Home: 2725 5th St Box 592 Ketchikan AK 99901 Office: Box 257 Ketchikan AK 99901

SWAIN, MYRTLE THOMPSON, educator; b. Cookeville, Tenn., Jan. 10, 1926; d. Albert Lee and Sara Emma (Dyer) Thompson; B.S., Tenn. Tech. U., 1947; M.A., George Peabody Coll. Tchrs., 1952, Ed.S., 1956; Ed.D., Duke, 1970; m. George Harry Swain, Aug. 15, 1948; children—George Harry, Albert Craig, Kevin Thompson (dec.). Tchr. Marion County (Fla.) Pub. Schs., 1947-49, Cnipola Jr. Coll., Marianna, Fla., 1952-53; asst. prof. Atlantic Christian Coll., 1954-65; asso. prof. math. edn. Old Dominion U., 1969-73, Duke, 1973—. Mem. Internat. Platform Assn., Nat. Council Tchrs. Math., Tidewater Council Tchrs. Math., Am. Assn. Higher Edn., Kappa Delta Pi, Kappa Mu Epsilon, Sigma Sigma Sigma. Methodist. Club: Norfolk Altrusa (pres. 1972). Home: 505 Brentwood Dr Wilson NC 27893 Office: Duke U Durham NC 27706

SWAIN, NANCY JANE COX (MRS. JAMES OBED SWAIN), former educator; b. Elwood, Ind., Dec. 19, 1901; d. Alfred Thomas and Emma (Allen) Cox; A.B. with high distinction, Ind. U., 1923, postgrad., 1928; M.A., U. Tenn., 1951, postgrad., 1953; m. James Obed Swain, June 24, 1923; children—J. Maurice, J. Robert. Teaching missionary M.E. Ch., Costa Rica, 1923-28; instr. U. Tenn., Knoxville, 1943, 45, non-resident instr. corr. Extension Div., 1959-71; tchr. Oak Ridge High Sch., 1943-67, Hollins Coll., 1967. Mem. Am. Assn. Tchrs. Spanish and Portuguese, E. Tenn. Edn. Assn., S. Atlantic Modern Lang, Assn., Phi Beta Kappa, Phi Kappa Phi, Sigma Delta Pi, Pi Delta Phi, Pi Lambda Theta. Republican. Methodist. Mem. P.E.O. Home: 414 Forest Park Blvd Knoxville TN 37919

SWAIN, OLIVE, librarian; b. South Bend, Wash., July 3, 1896; d. Ernest Dyson and Emma Theresa (Lackie) Swain; B.S., U. Wash., 1922, B.S. in L.S., 1927; M.A., U. Cal. at Berkeley, 1940. Med. technologist Tacoma (Wash.) Gen. Hosp., 1923-26; sr. librarian, catalog dept. U. Wash. Library, Seattle, 1927-43; head catalog dept. Cal. State Library, Sacramento, 1943-61. Lectr. U. Cal., summer 1941. Mem. A.L.A., Alpha Phi. Author: Notes Used On Catalog Cards, 1940, rev. edit., 1964. Home: 11 W Aloha St Seattle WA 98119

SWAINBANK, LOUISE ROBINSON, state legislator; b. Ware, Mass., Nov. 3, 1917; d. Philip Weeks and Lois Cleveland (Gould) Robinson; B.A., Smith Coll., 1939; m. John A. Swainbank, June 28, 1941; children—John Allen, Anne Cleveland (Mrs. Arthur S. Brooks), Daniel Robinson, Joseph Gould. Tchr., Morning Face Sch., Richmond, Mass., 1939-40, Brookfield (Mass.) High Sch., 1940-41; substitute tchr. St. Johnsbury (Vt.) Acad., 1957-66; tchr. St. Johnsbury Jr. High Sch., 1966-69; mem. Vt. Ho. of Reps., 1970—. Mem. Gov.'s Juvenile Delinquency Council, 1969-71; pres. Brightlook Hosp. Aux., St. Johnsbury, 1955-56; mem. state adv. com. U.S. Civil Rights Commn., 1972—; mem. Gov.'s Commn. on Status Women, 1972—, Gov.'s Energy Adv. Com. Sec. Caledonia County Republican Com., 1969—. Bd. dirs. Vt. YWCA, Burke Mountain Acad.; trustee U. Vt.; mem. adv. bd. Lyndon State Coll. Clubs: St. Johnsbury Women's, Smith Coll. (pres. 1962-64). Home: 49 Summer St St Johnsbury VT 05819

SWAN, CLARA LINCOLN, coll. adminstr.; b. Princeton, Me., Apr. 28, 1912; d. Andrew Coburn and Grace (Coffin) Swan; tchr. tng. diploma Husson Coll., 1933; B.S., Am. Internat. Coll., 1939; M.Ed., U. Me., 1951; Ped.D., Fort Lauderdale U., 1971. Tchr. Mexico (Me.) High Sch., 1933-35, Foxcroft (Me.) Acad., 1935-38; faculty Husson Coll., Bangor, Me., 1939—, dir. summer session, 1941-69, dir. dept. secretarial sci., 1941-51, exec. dir., 1946-53, 3d v.p., 1954-59, 1st v.p., 1959-68, v.p. acad. affairs, 1968-72, v.p., asst. to pres., 1972-73; v.p., dir. Casco Bay Coll., Portland, Me., 1973—. Recipient Sports Hall of Fame award Bangor Daily News, 1960. Mem. United Bus. Schs. Assn., Am. Assn. U. Profs., Nat. Judges Women's Basketball, Nat. Assn. Coll. and U. Summer Sessions (mem. audit com. 1965-67), Eastern Bus. Tchrs. Assn. (state membership chmn. 1962-69), New Eng. Bus. Educators Assn. (1st v.p. 1965-66, pres. 1966-67), Bangor Execs. Club, Pi Rho Zeta (gov. gen. 1968—). Club: Altrusa (1st v.p. 1972-74, pres. 1974—) (Bangor, Me.). Home: Mounted Route C Box 42B Bangor ME 04401 also 11 Depot Rd Falmouth ME 04105

SWAN, EVELYN ANNE, data processor; b. Washington, Feb. 17, 1943; d. Charles Frederick and Eleanore (Hobson) Swan; B.S. in Math., U. Okla., 1964. Research engr. Gen. Dynamics/Convair, San Diego, 1964-69; chief programmer, analyst myocardial infarction research unit U. Cal. Med. Sch., San Diego, 1969—. Mem. Assn. for Computing Machinery (chpt. chmn. 1973-74; treas. 1971-72; chmn. nat. conv. com. 1973-74), Kappa Delta. Home: 2453 Geranium St San Diego CA 92109 Office: 225 W Dickinson St AID 8115 San Diego CA 92103

SWAN, FRANCES ELIZABETH ARROWOOD (MRS. RAYMOND W. SWAN), social worker; b. Union, S.C., Sept. 6, 1939; d. Robert Henry and Mary (Hall) Arrowood; student Isabella Thoburn Coll., Lucknow, India, 1959-60; B.A., Winthrop Coll., 1961; M.S.W., Fla. State U., 1963; m. Raymond W. Swan, Nov. 23, 1972. Psychiat. social worker Spartanburg (S.C.) Mental Health Clinic, 1963-65, Childrens Psychiat. Center, Miami, Fla., 1965-67, VA Hosp., Miami, 1967-71, VA Hosp., New Orleans, 1971—; social worker Big Bros. Am., 1967-71. Field instr. grad. students Fla. State U., 1969-71, So. U., 1971-73, Tulane U., 1973—. Mem. Acad. Certified Social Workers, Nat. Assn. Social Workers, (sec. Piedmont chpt. 1964), Alpha Kappa Delta. Home: 1205 Dauphine St New Orleans LA 70116 Office: 1601 Perdido St New Orleans LA 70146

SWAN, MARGARET MUELLER, educator; b. San Antonio, June 13, 1919; d. Emil and Emma (Schneider) Mueller; B.S., Trinity U., 1960, M.Ed., 1961; postgrad. U. Tex.; m. George Henry Swan, Mar. 20, 1938; children—George Henry III, Margaret Anne (Mrs. Donald J. Huppert), Robert David, Timothy Lawrence. Dir. health, phys. edn. and recreation San Antonio YWCA, 1958-60; tchr. MacArthur High Sch., 1960-62; asst. prof. phys. edn. San Antonio Coll., 1962—, also coach swim team. Dir., coach Cygnets of San Antonio; mem., sec. U.S. Olympic Synchronized Swimming Com.; vice chmn. Nat. Amateur Athletic Union synchronized swimming com.; team mgr. Pan Am. Games synchronized swimming team, 1972; water safety instr. trainer A.R.C. Named Outstanding Sportswoman of Yr., Express-News Pub. Co.; named to United Savs. Helms Athletic Hall of Fame, 1973. Mem. Am., Tex. assns. health, phys. edn. and recreation, Tex. Jr. Coll. Assn. Episcopalian (dir. Canterbury House diocese W. Tex.). Contbr. articles mags. Home: 9303 Perrin Beitel Rd San Antonio TX 78217

SWANDAL, BONNIE JEAN (MRS. AUSTIN SWANDAL), lawyer; b. Sheffield, Ia., July 18, 1929; d. Webb and Caroline (Bina) Brogan; LL.B., LaSalle Extension U., 1965; m. Austin Swandal, Sept. 29, 1946 (dec.); children—Patrick, William Nels, Ronald Stuart, Cynthia. Admitted to Mont. bar, 1967, individual practice in Livingston, 1967-72; partner Swandal & Douglass, Livingston, 1973—. Mem. Park County (Mont.) Planning Bd., Livingston, 1973—; Park County women's chmn. Farm Bur., 1963. Republican State com. woman, Park County, 1960-62. Mem. Am., Mont., Park-Sweet Grass (chmn. 1971-73) bar assns., Am. Legion, Bus. and Profl. Women, Am. Luth. Ch. Women. Clubs: Toastmistress, Soroptomist (Livingston). Home: Basin Meadow Ranch Wilsall MT 59086 Office: Box 507 113 W Callender St Livingston MT 59047

SWANK, GLADYS RAE HISER (MRS. LEWIS RAY SWANK), journalist, photographer, former legislator; b. Adrian, Mo.; d. George W. and Mary (Lemaster) Hiser; student summers U. Wash., Lewiston Normal Sch.; m. Lewis Ray Swank, Jan. 17, 1925; 1 son, Robert M. Free-lance writer, 1945—; editor Clarkston Herald, weekly newspaper, 1958-65; area reporter Spokane Daily Chronicle. Mem. adv. bd. Port of Lewiston, 1965—. Mem. bd. YWCA, 1930-36; mem. govs. adv. council on health, 1967—, commn. on status women, 1965—, Legislative Council Revision Ida. Criminal Code. Mem. Ida. Ho. of Reps., 1965-69. Recipient 25 Year award Ida. Cancer Soc., 1965; nat. awards Nat. Fedn. Press Women; Achievement award Ida. Press Women, 1972; named Women of Year, Altrusa Club, Lewiston, 1950. Mem. Nat. Press Photographers Assn., Lewiston C. of C., Ida. Press Women, Nat. Fedn. Press Women (youth chmn.), Ida. Writers League (state pres. 1941), Theta Sigma Phi (achievement award). Contbr. articles to mags., hist. pubs. Home: 119 16th Av Lewiston ID 83501

SWANKE, (DOROTHY) PRATT WILLIAMS (MRS. ALBERT HOMER SWANKE), editor; b. New Orleans; d. Herschel V. and Lillian E. (Strickland) S.; student Barnard Coll., 1935-36; m. Albert Homer Swanke, Feb. 5, 1969; children—Charles King Mallory III, Addison O. Wood, Jr. Fashion editor New Orleans Times-Picayune, 1942-45; asst. promotion dir. Vogue Pattern Service, Conde Nast Publs., 1946-48; fashion dir. D.H. Holmes Co., New Orleans, 1948-49; ind. cons. interior decoration, New Orleans, 1950-62; asso. decorating editor House & Garden mag., N.Y.C., 1963-68, decorating editor, 1968-69, contbg. editor, 1969—. Former vice chmn. La. Republican Central Com.; pres. La. Fedn. Women's Rep. Clubs, 1956-62; chmn. women's com. Rep. Nat. Finance Com., 1971-74. Mem. D.A.R., Jr. League. Club: Sulgrave (Washington). Home: 416 E Charlton St Savannah GA 31401 Office: care House and Garden 350 Madison Av New York City NY 10017

SWANKER, ESTHER MOREY (MRS. HENRY J. SWANKER), ednl. research exec.; b. Syracuse, N.Y., Oct. 15, 1927; d. Arthur H. and Alice (Cash) Morey; A.B., Syracuse U., 1950; M.L.S., State U. N.Y., 1962, postgrad., 1964-67; m. Henry J. Swanker, Feb. 23, 1952. Field dir. Girl Scouts U.S.A., Albany, N.Y., 1950-52; tech. writer, editor Gen. Electric Co., Schenectady, 1952-58; jr. high sch. librarian Burnt Hills (N.Y.) Pub. Schs., 1958-63; library supr. Schenectady Pub. Schs., 1963-65; coordinator Title III Elementary and Secondary Edn. Act, N.Y. State Edn. Dept., Albany, 1965-66, asst. to dept. commr., 1966-67, asst. dir. urban edn., 1967-69; partner Center for Urban Redevel. in Edn., Latham, N.Y., 1969—; pres. Donovan & Swanker Asso. Research in Edn., Inc., Latham, 1971—. Chmn. emergency blood com. A.R.C., 1958-63, publicity chmn., 1955-58. Bd. dirs. Euphrasian Residence, N.Y.C. Mem. Am., N.Y. State library assns., N.E.A., Am. Assn. Sch. Adminstrn., N.Y. State Tchrs. Assn. Club: Faculty Women's (Union Coll.). Home: 1470 Grenoside Av Schenectady NY 12308 Office: 8 Wade Rd Latham NY 12110

SWANKIN, HARRIET REBECCA SHUR, psychotherapist; b. Bangor, Me.; d. Jacob and Violet (Rubin) Shur; B.A. cum laude with distinction in psychology, Brandeis U., 1954; M.S., Columbia, 1956; Certificate in Group Psychotherapy, Washington Sch. Psychiatry, 1973; m. David Arnold Swankin, Aug. 12, 1956; 1 dau., Sheryl Robin. Caseworker, Mendota State Hosp., Madison, Wis., 1956-57, Family and Child Services, Washington, 1957-58, 61-70; psychotherapist in pvt. practice, Washington, 1970—; mem. faculty Washington Sch. Psychiatry, 1974—. Mem. Nat. Assn. Social Work, Acad. Certified Social Workers, Am. Group Psychotherapy Assn., Women's Nat. Democratic Club. Home: 334 N St SW Washington DC 20024

SWANN, MARY EDNA GOLDSMITH, educator; b. San Diego, July 3, 1920; d. Charles Thomas and Florence (Adams) Goldsmith; student San Diego State Coll., 1938-40, Kendall Coll., 1940-41; A.B., Scarritt Coll., 1945, M.A., 1946; jr. coll. credential U. of Pacific, 1965; postgrad. U. Denver, 1965—; m. Arthur William Swann, June B, 1945; children—Anna Florence, David Sutherland, Helen Mary. Typist, Convair Aircraft Corp., 1942-43; dir. Bus. and Profl. Women YWCA, Nashville, 1945-46; program dir. Bethlehem Center, Atlanta, 1946-47; supr. social work students Atlanta Sch. Social Work, 1946-47; alumni sec. Scarritt Coll., Nashville, 1947-48; dir. publicity, editor monthly newspaper San Diego County Council Chs., 1957-60; tchr. adult edn. Stockton (Cal.) Unified Sch. Dist., 1960-65; sch. social worker, 1965-68; social worker Head Start program Denver pub. schs., 1966; instr. sociology Arapahoe Jr. Coll., Littleton, Colo., 1966-68; dir. Community Pre Sch., Sunnyvale, Cal., 1969-70; instr. home econs. and sociology Delta Community Coll., Stockton, 1970—; instr. sociology U. Cal. at Davis, 1973. Dir., Christian edn. 1st Congl. Ch., Stockton, 1971-74; sponsor, Stockton Symphony Orch. Chamber Music Assn., 1960-65; mem. Community Concerts, Pioneer Mus. and Art Gallery, 1960-65, Stockton Youth Symphony, 1963-65, Denver Art Mus., 1965-69; chmn. parent edn. P.T.A., 1961-62. Bd. dirs. Stockton council Girl Scouts U.S.A.; bd. dirs., chmn. dept. Christian edn., camping So. and No. Cal. Conf. United Ch. of Christ; bd. dirs.

Planned Parenthood Stockton. Mem. Nat. Council Family Relations, Am., Cal. home econs. assns., Am. Assn. U. Women, Cal. Home Econs. Assn. (bd. dirs. Valley dist.). Democrat. Editor Newsletter Scarritt Coll. Alumni Assn., 1947. Home: 434 Bristol Av Stockton CA 95204

SWANNER, GRACE MAGUIRE (MRS. ROY O. SWANNER), physician; b. Albany, N.Y., Dec. 5, 1901; d. Joseph A. and Mary D. (Stevens) Maguire; B.S., State U. of N.Y., 1923; M.A., Columbia U., 1927; postgrad. U. Chgo., 1929; M.D., Albany Med. Coll., 1933; m. Roy O. Swanner, Apr. 25, 1936; children—Roy Stevens, Katherine Vaughn. Intern, Albany Med. Center, 1933-34; resident Jersey City Med. Center, 1934-35, Margaret Hague Hosp., Jersey City, 1934-35, Overlook Hosp., Summit, N.J., 1935-36; gen. practice medicine, Saratoga Springs, N.Y., 1936—; mem. staff Saratoga Hosp., also bd. mgrs.; health officer town of Wilton (N.Y.), 1937-39, town of Greenfield (N.Y.), 1948—. Lectr. pub. health Skidmore Coll., Saratoga Springs, 1944-46; acting med. dir. Saratoga Spa, 1953, 55-58, med. cons., 1969—. Bd. dirs. Am. Cancer Soc. Mem. A.M.A., N.Y., Saratoga County med. socs., N.Y. Health Officers Assn., Am. Assn. U. Women (chpt. pres. 1959-61). Home and office: 107 Lake Av Saratoga Springs NY 12866

SWANSON, ANNCHEN TILL (MRS. ROY G. SWANSON), librarian; b. East Orange, N.J.; d. John Walter and Edna (Stanwood) Till; A.B., Upsala Coll., 1934; postgrad. Columbia, 1939-41; m. Roy G. Swanson, Nov. 13, 1943. With Chase Manhattan Bank Library, N.Y.C., 1938—, library asst., 1938-40, reference librarian, 1940-42, 46-52, asst. chief librarian, 1952-56, chief librarian, 1956—. Served from apprentice seaman to lt. comdr., WAVES, 1942-46. Mem. Spl. Libraries Assn., Theta Beta Gamma. Home: 85 Washington St East Orange NJ 07017 Office: 1 Chase Manhattan Plaza New York City NY 10015

SWANSON, AUDREY ELAINE (MRS. STUART KENNETH SWANSON), librarian; b. Mpls.; d. Henry Richard and Jessie Elizabeth (Kenyon) Hanson; B.S., U. Minn., 1943, postgrad., 1956-60; m. Stuart Kenneth Swanson, June 29, 1946; children—Deborah Elaine, Stephen Kenyon. With editorial dept. St. Paul campus U. Minn., 1943-48; librarian Hennepin County Libraries, Mpls., 1957—. Active P.T.A. Mem. Am., Minn. library assns., Nat. League Am. Pen Women, Minn., Hennepin County, Ramsey County, Richfield hist. socs., Minn. Geneal. Soc., Bus. and Profl. Women. Lutheran. Office: 7000 Nicollet Av S Minneapolis MN 55423

SWANSON, ELLEN ESTHER, editor; b. Rehoboth, Mass., May 20, 1921; d. Carl O.F. and Esther Blanche (Pierce) Swanson; A.B., Brown U., 1942; postgrad. U. Wis., 1942-43. Tchr. math., Stevens Point, Wis., 1943-44; adminstrv. asst. Bur. Econ. Research, Rutgers U., New Brunswick, N.J., 1946-49, Brown U., Providence, 1952-54; editorial asst., dir. editorial services Am. Math. Soc., Providence, 1954—. Supt. Rehoboth Conglist. Ch. Sch., 1950-66. Mem. Am. Assn. U. Women (br. treas. 1970-73). Home: Locust Av Rehoboth MA 02769 Office: Box 6248 Providence RI 02904

SWANSON, FERN ROSE (MRS. WALTER E. SWANSON), educator; b. Kalmar Twp., Minn.; d. Henry E. and Susie (Hastings) Rose; student Winona (Minn.) Normal Coll., 1918-20; B.S., St. Cloud (Minn.) State Coll., 1955, M.S., 1958; m. Walter E. Swanson, June 24, 1928. Tchr. high sch. English, Latin, Eyota, Minn., 1920-21; tchr. jr. high sch. English, Appleton, Minn., 1921-22; tchr. elementary schs., Harmony, Minn., 1922-23; tchr. high sch. English, Latin, Augusta, Wis., 1923-24, South Haven, Minn., 1924-26; tchr. elementary and high sch. dramatics, Waterville, 1926-27; tchr. elementary schs., South Haven, 1927-41, 43-51, Silver Creek, Minn., 1941-43; tchr. elementary schs., Annandale, Minn., 1951-53, prin., 1953-67; tchr. elementary reading, Belgrade, Minn., 1967-71. Organizer, South Haven council Girl Scouts U.S.A., 1927, leader, 1927-30. Mem. Minn. Elementary Sch. Prins. Assn. (charter mem. 25 Year Club), N.E.A., Minn. Edn. Assn., Nat. Council Tchrs. English, Central Minn. Reading Council (past dir.), Internat., Minn. reading assns., D.A.R., Ladies of Grand Army Republic (pres. Lookout Circle, jr. v.p. Minn.), Minn. Hist. Soc., Rebekah, Delta Kappa Gamma (chpt. pres.). Episcopalian. Home: 541 Fairhaven Av South Haven MN 55382 Office: South Haven MN 55382

SWANSON, PRISCILLA MARIE, dermatologist; b. Sioux Falls, S.D., July 1, 1938; d. Elmer C. and Elizabeth (Haglund) Swanson; A.A., North Park Coll., 1958; B.A. cum laude, St. Olaf Coll., 1960; M.D., U. Wis., 1965; m. Donald A. Dahlstrom, Apr. 1, 1967. Intern, Ill. Masonic Hosp., Chgo., 1965-66; resident dermatology, chief resident U. Wis., 1967-70; practice medicine, specializing in dermatology, Sioux Falls, 1971—; mem. staff Sioux Valley Hosp., McKennan Hosp. Recipient Physicians Recognition award A.M.A. Diplomate Am. Bd. Dermatology. Contbr. articles to profl. jours. Office: 1320 S Minnesota St Sioux Falls SD 57105

SWANSON, SUSAN BLAKE (MRS. WALTER C.J. SWANSON), realtor; b. Fort Dodge, Ia., Oct. 10, 1894; d. Fred Jarvis and Effie (Scofield) Blake; Ph.G., State U. Ia., 1915; LL.B., Loyola U., 1931, J.D., 1969; m. Walter C.J. Swanson, Oct. 11, 1930; children—Joan Patricia (Mrs. Dale P. Scannell). Pharmacist Oleson Drug Co., Fort Dodge, Ia., 1915-22, pharmacist, asst. store mgr. MacLean Drug Co., Chgo., 1922-28; admitted to Ill. bar, 1931; practiced in Chgo., 1931-42; real estate salesman Crawford Realty & DeWitt Jenkins Co., Akron, O., 1944-62; broker Susan B. Swanson, Realtor, 1962—. Mem. Delta Delta Delta, Kappa Beta Pi. Republican. Home: 733 Roslyn Av Akron OH 44320 Office: 733 Roslyn Av Akron OH 44320

SWANSON, VIRGINIA LEE, pathologist; b. Sioux City, Ia., June 15, 1922; d. Clarence W. and Millicent (Hermanson) Swanson; B.A., U. So. Cal., 1947; M.D. (tuition scholar) Yale, 1952; m. Martin D. Kamen, Apr. 29, 1967. Intern Yale-New Haven Med. Center, New Haven, 1952-53, resident, 1955-57; instr. pathology Yale, New Haven, 1957-59; pathologist M.C., U.S. Army, Far East, S.E. Asia, P.R., 1957-66, also Australian Pub. Health Service, Terr. Papua and New Guinea, 1961; asso. prof. U. So. Cal. Med. Sch. and Children's Hosp., Los Angeles, 1966-70, prof., 1970-71; chief lab. services VA Hosp., La Jolla, Cal., 1971-73. Prof. pathology U. Cal. at San Diego, 1971-73, U. So. Cal. Med. Sch. and Childrens Hosp., Los Angeles, 1973—. USPHS fellow, Copenhagen, Denmark, 1953-55; Prof. ad honorem U. P.R., 1964-66. Diplomate Am. Bd. Pathology. Mem. A.A.A.S., Sigma Xi, Alpha Omega Alpha. Contbr. to profl. jours. Research in pathology of tropical diseases. Home: 5698 Holly Oak Dr Los Angeles CA 90068 Office: Childrens Hosp Los Angeles CA 90027

SWANSTROM, KATHRYN RAYMOND (MRS. LUTHER D. SWANSTROM), conv. mgmt. exec.; b. Milw., Sept. 5, 1907; d. William Hyland and Jessie Viola (Bliss) Raymond; student Bryant and Stratton Bus. Coll., 1927-28; m. Luther D. Swanstrom, Aug. 27, 1937; 1 son, William Hyland Raymond. Caterer, Racine, Wis., 1926; field rep., asst. mgr. Master Reporting Co., 1936-52; dir., sec. Diesel-Ritter Corp., 1942-46; pres. Kay C. Raymond Assos., 1952—; v.p., treas. Kenneth G. Mackenzie Assos., 1954—. Asst. sec. nat. com. U.S.A. 3d World Petroleum Congress, 1950-51. Sec. Ridge Civic Council, 1940-69, Police Traffic Safety Com., Mayor's Com. Keeping Chgo. Clean; state chmn. legislation Ill. Congress Parents and Tchrs. Rep. Ill. Central Republican party committeewoman, 1938-44; asst. ofcl. reporter Rep. Nat. Conv., 1940-48. Mem. Anti-Cruelty Soc., A.I.M., Soc. Mayflower Descs., D.A.R., Nat. Geographic Soc., Am. Soc. Testing and Materials, Ladies Oriental Shrine N. Am., Founders, Patriots and Aux. Ancient Honorable Arty. Co. of Boston (nat. treas. 1971—), John Alden Kindred, Colonial Dames Am., Magna Charta Dames, Internat. Platform Assn., Hugenot Soc., Pi Omicron (nat. pres. 1950-54). Episcopalian. Clubs: Beverly Hills Woman's Crescendo; Ridge Book. Address: 9027 S Damen Av Chicago IL 60620 also 3 Old Hill Farms Rd Westport CT 06880

SWANTON, IRENE WRAY (MRS. WALTER F. SWANTON), librarian; b. Rochester, N.Y., Dec. 4, 1911; d. Delos H. and Irene (Warner) Wray; B.A., U. Rochester, 1934, M.S., 1936; M.A., State U. of N.Y. at Geneseo, 1962; m. Walter F. Swanton, Sept. 28, 1940; children—Susan Irene, Carolyn. Library dir. Avon (N.Y.) Free Library, 1951-61; asst. dir. Livingston County Library System, Avon, N.Y., 1962—. Pres. Avon (N.Y.) Central Sch. Bd., 1964-69; chmn. environmental council Town of Avon, N.Y., 1971—. Mem. Am., N.Y. library assns., Sigma Xi. Home: 86 E Main St Avon NY 14414 Office: 303 E Main St Avon NY 14414

SWANTON, MARY ELLEN CASHIN (MRS. DONALD JACKSON SWANTON), research statistician; b. Modesto, Cal., Feb. 3, 1915; d. Frances Patrick and Leone (Allison) Cashin; B.A., U. Hawaii, 1967, M.A., 1968; m. Lester J. Newell, Apr. 8, 1932 (div. Jan. 1942); children—Lester James II, Michael Gerald, Patricia Ellen (Mrs. James Frank); m. 2d, Donald Jackson Swanton, Jan. 5, 1942. With Monterey (Cal.) Peninsula Herald, 1932; agt. So. Pacific Ry., Reno, 1946-54; exec. sec. to Wilbur D. May, May Dept. Stores, Reno, 1954-59; travel agt. Reno, Honolulu, 1959-63; student sec. astro-geophysics U. Hawaii, 1963-65; now research statistician Hawaii Dept. Health. Chmn. Gov.'s Adv. Bd. State Insts., Nev., 1958-59; chmn. Hawaii Gov.'s Commn. on Status of Women, 1964-68; mem. Citizen's Com. on Ethics, 1966, 1967, pub. relations chmn., 1966; chmn. Honolulu Mayor's Commn. Status of Women, 1971—; mem. Constl. Conv. Conf. Com., 1967. Sec. 17th Dist. Democratic precinct, 1964-68, pres. 13th Dem. precinct, 1964-68; treas. Women Dems. of Hawaii. Mem. Nat., Hawaii (pres. 1970-71) fedns. bus. and profl. women's clubs, Western Regional Sci. Assn., Hawaii Econ. Assn. (2d v.p.), Hawaii Assn. Parliamentarians (1st v.p.), Am., Hawaii statis. assns., Nat. Orgn. for Women. Home: 91-357 Ewa Beach Rd Ewa Beach HI 96706 Office: State Dept Health Surveillance Program PO Box 3378 Honolulu HI 96801

SWANTON, SUSAN IRENE, librarian; b. Rochester, N.Y., Nov. 29, 1941; d. Walter Frederick and Irene (Wray) Swanton; A.B., Radcliffe Coll., 1963; M.L.S., Columbia, 1965; m. Wayne Ronald Holman, Apr. 12, 1969 (div. June 1973); 1 son, Michael Walter. Library dir. Warsaw (N.Y.) Pub. Library, 1963-64, Gates Pub. Library, Rochester, N.Y., 1965—. Home: 284 Gatewood Av Rochester NY 14624 Office: 1605 Buffalo Rd Rochester NY 14624

SWARD, MARCIA PETERSON (MRS. GILBERT L. SWARD), educator; b. Maywood, Ill., Feb. 1, 1939; d. Walter Edward and Marjorie Alice (Keiler) Peterson; B.A., Vassar Coll., 1961; M.A., U. Ill., 1963, Ph.D., 1967; m. Gilbert L. Sward, July 16, 1960; children—Douglas Gilbert, David Reeve. Asst. prof. math. Trinity Coll., Washington, 1968-73, asso. prof., 1973—. Asst. prof. Cath. U., Washington, summers 1968-71. Mem. Math. Assn. Am., Am. Math. Soc., Phi Beta Kappa. Home: 9101 LeVelle Dr Chevy Chase MD 20015 Office: Dept Math Trinity College Washington DC 20017

SWART, HANNAH WERWATH (MRS. GEORGE J. SWART), museum curator; b. Milw., Mar. 21, 1913; d. Oscar and Hannah (Seelhorst) Werwath; student Milw. Downer Coll., part-time 1931-34, U. Wis., 1933-36, Milw. Sch. Engring., 1933-46; m. George Jerry Swart, Oct. 7, 1937; children—Greta Toni, JoHannah Werwath Nickolai, George Jerry Jr., Paul Oscar. Head dept. records, registrar coll. engring. Milw. Sch. Engring., 1931-51, mem. corp., 1952—, also cons. dept. alumni affairs; curator Hoard Hist. Mus., Fort Atkinson, Wis., 1967—. Co-chmn. heritage Wis. Bicentennial Commn. Bd. dirs. Girl Scouts Am. Recipient Bronze Statue, Girl Scouts U.S.A., Nat. Thanks badge, 1967. Mem. State Hist. Soc. Wis. (past pres. women's aux., life mem.), Watertown (hon. life), Fort Atkinson (program chmn.) hist. socs., Wis. Acad. Scis., Wis. Council Writers, Nat. Trust for Historic Preservation. Clubs: Tuesday, Quarter Century. Author: Footsteps of our Founding Fathers, 1963; Biography of General Henry Atkinson, 1964; Margarethe Meyer Schurz, 1967; Koshkonong Country: A History of Jefferson County. Home: Rural Route 3 Box 27 Fort Atkinson WI 53538 Office: Hoard Historical Museum Merchants Av Fort Atkinson WI 53538

SWARTOUT, GLENDA MUHLENBURG, occupational therapist, educator; b. Joplin, Mo., July 13, 1922; d. Burr Franklin and Winnifred Evelyn (Featheringill) Muhlenburg; A.A., Joplin Jr. Coll., 1942; B.S., Western Mich. U., 1945; postgrad. U. So. Cal., 1952-56; m. Roy Swartout III, Dec. 25, 1944; children—Michael, Roy IV, Kathryn, Laurie, Kurt. Staff occupational therapist Santa Barbara County Hosp., 1945-46; occupational therapist Nat. Inst. Infantile Paralysis, 1948-49, Childrens div., 1952-54; tchr. Jr. High and High Sch., Pasadena, Cal., 1967-73; co-chmn. Jr. Coll. Trustee Election, Temple City (Cal.) Schs., 1966, 69, 71, chmn. Family Life Com., 1965—, co-chmn. tax override, 1970, mem. steering com. curriculum and early childhood edn., 1970-73. Mem. Am. Occupational Therapy Assn. Home: 5723 N Primrose St Temple City CA 91780

SWARTWOOD, SUSAN HUNTER, sch. psychologist; b. Elmira, N.Y., Dec. 15, 1943; d. James Edwin and Mabel Alberta (Stebbings) Swartwood; B.A. in Music and Psychology, Lake Erie Coll., 1965; M.S. in Ednl. Psychology, Case Western Res. U., 1969, doctoral student, 1971—; m. Robert Jerome Berk, Sept. 30, 1973. Nursery sch. tchr., Cleve., 1965-67, sch. librarian, 1967-68; sch. psychologist Cleve. Bd. Edn., 1969—; psychol. cons. Portage County Welfare Dept., Ravenna, O., 1972—; owner, instr. Clarkwood Dance Workshop, Cleve., 1966-68; program commentator Cleve. Philharmonic Orch., 1966-68; mem. The Temple, semi-profl. choir, Cleve., 1966-68. Mem. Nat. Assn. Sch. Psychologists (charter), Ohio, Cleve. (sec. 1972-73) sch. psychol. assns., Ohio, Cleve. psychol. assns., Am. Civil Liberties Union, Friends of the Earth, Sierra Club. Home: 2729 Edgehill Rd Cleveland OH 44106 Office: 10600 Quincy Av Cleveland OH 44106

SWARTZ, LILLIAN BURTON, editor; b. Ansonia, Conn., Mar. 16, 1897; d. James and Caroline (Prisk) Williams; student George Washington U.; m. Bert O. Swartz, July 7, 1921 (dec. Sept. 1959); 1 dau., Jean E. (Mrs. Ivan B. Colburn). Chief sect. Civilian Personnel div. Office Sec. Army, Washington, then chief Policy, Regulations and Procedures br.; editor weekly Community Reporter, Mt. Airy, Md., 1966—. Recipient achievement award Sec. Army. Mem. Md., Del., D.C. Press Assn. Mem. Order Eastern Star (grand matron Md. 1964-65, chmn. cancer research gen. grand chpt. 1973—). Home: Route 2 Mount Airy MD 21771 Office: Main St Mount Airy MD 21771

SWARTZ, PATSY CURTIS (MRS. CHARLES C. SWARTZ), city ofcl.; b. nr. Elizabethton, Tenn., July 19, 1928; d. William Erving and Mary Christine (Kyte) Curtis; student Steed Coll., 1951-52, Massey Tech. Inst., 1967-69; m. Charles Clifford Swartz, Aug. 1, 1947. With finance office, City of Johnson City, Tenn., 1949—, tax assessor, 1970-71, tax clk., 1956—. Dep. tax assessor Washington County, 1972—. Mem. Tenn. Bus. and Profl. Women's Club (state dist. dir. 1964-65). Home: Route 7 Ridgefield Dr Johnson City TN 37601 Office: 601 E Main St Johnson City TN 37601

SWAYNE, CLEO RUTH (MRS. SAMUEL A. SWAYNE), mus. ofcl.; b. Wabash, Ind., June 20, 1914; d. William Homer and Georgia Mae (Schoby) Speieher; student, N.W. State Tchrs. Coll. at Kirksville, Mo., 1932-34, Inter Am. U., 1960; m. Samuel A. Swayne, Feb. 7, 1943; children—William Daniel, Betty (Mrs. Ted Keith), Bruce Richard. Nurse, Dr. Samuel A. Swayne, Nampa, Ida., 1965-73; with Cleo's Ferry Mus., Nampa, 1966—, mus. dir. 1965—. Speaker at various clubs and church groups. Pres. Mercy Hosp. Aux., Nampa, 1953-54; mem. Mayor's Com. for the Handicapped, 1973-74. Mem. Order Eastern Star. Clubs: Women's Century; Fidelis (pres. 1969-70); Jeudi (pres. 1966-67) (Nampa). Home and office: 311 14th Av S Nampa ID 83651

SWEARENGEN, MARY-B MOSLEY, edn. cons.; b. Lacasa, Tex., June 12, 1911; d. Garrett Benjamin and Margaret Ann (Eubanks) Mosley; B.S., Hardin-Simmons U., 1950; M.A., N.M. State U., 1957, Ed.S., 1959; Ed.D., U. N.M., 1966; m. Alvin Henry Swearengen, Oct. 11, 1930; 1 dau., Marilyn (Mrs. James Basler). Tchr. pub. schs., Tex. and N.M., 1929-58; counselor, guidance center dir., Las Cruces, N.M., 1959-67; asso. prof. edn. McGill U., 1967-68, U. Tulsa, 1968-71; cons. Region XIX Edn. Service Center, El Paso, Tex., 1971—. Mem. Tex. Tchrs. Assn., N.E.A., Am. Personnel and Guidance Assn., Assn. Phi Kappa Phi. Baptist. Home: 10449 Seawood St El Paso TX 79925 Office: 6611 Boeing St El Paso TX 79997

SWEARINGEN, ANETTE WILDMAN, clergyman; b. St. Paul, Mo., May 21, 1897; d. Fritz and Josephine (Boehmer) Schulte; ed. Jr. Coll., Kansas City U., Unity Sch. Christianity; m. Mitchell Soutee, Mar. 29, 1915; 1 son, ReVorre Soutee; m. 2d, Dick Swearingen, Jan. 27, 1967. Student, tchr. Unity Southside Center, Unity Sch. Christianity, Lee's Summit, Mo., 1925-47; instr. adult edn., counselor, leader jr. ch., tchr. Bible sch., Sunday sch. Unity Temple on the Plaza, 1948-63; co-founder, minister Unity N.E. Ch., Kansas City, 1963-67; minister edn. Unity Valley Ch., Hemet, Cal., 1968; ordained minister, 1966. Mem. Assn. Unity Chs., Unity Alumni, Christian Women's Temperance Union, Nat. League Am. Pen Women (pres. Kansas City Westport br. 1956-68, pres. Mo. 1958-60, v.p., historian Hemet br. 1972—), Intercontinental Biog. Assn. (life fellow), Ladies Vets. World War I Aux., Hemet Woman's Club (co-chmn. religion 1973—). Republican. Author: (poetry) Mosaic of Living, 1951; Sonnettones, 1951; Moments of Mood, 1952; Of Heart and Home, 1956. Home: 25124 Yale St Hemet CA 92343

SWEDBURG, WILMA ADELINE, educator, author; b. Nora Springs, Ia.; d. Lee Henry and Laura (Ellingson) Swedburg; B.S., U. Minn., 1954, M.A., 1956, specialist in edn., 1962. Supt., nursery classes, Edina Bapt. Ch., Mpls., 1952-62; tchr. kindergarten Mpls. Pub. Schs., 1954-58, 1st grade, 1958—. Adult tchr. for tng. nursery sch. classes Council Chs., Mpls., 1959-60, 62-64; workshop tchr. Nat. Ch. Confs., Columbus, O., summers 1960—; asst. prof. edn. Augsburg Coll., Mpls., 1969—; asst. prin. Irving, Clinton and Greeley Elementary Schs., Mpls., 1972-73; resource tchr., culturally disadvantaged children program, Mpls., summer 1965. Mem. N.E.A., Minn., Mpls. edn. assns., Assn. for Childhood Edn., Internat. Platform Assn. Author: Christmas Donkey, 1962; Jeannie Goes to Sunday School, 1962; Just Like Me, 1962; The World Around Johnnie, 1966; The World Around Me, 1969; also packet materials for use by pre-sch. and head start programs Cook Pub. Co., Chgo. Home: 5720 27th Av S Minneapolis MN 55417 Office: 2736 17th Av S Minneapolis MN 55417

SWEEDEN, CELIA, city ofcl.; b. Greenbay, Wis., Dec. 26, 1916; d. Harry and Ida (Paykel) Kristol; student Santa Monica Bus. Coll., 1935; div.; 1 son, Daniel S. Mistriel. Med. social service stenographer County of Los Angeles Health Centers, 1938-42; with City of El Centro, Cal., 1945—, city clk., 1955—. Sec. Imperial Valley div. League of Cal. Cities, 1973—. Mem. Internat. Inst. Municipal Clks., Cal. City Clks. Assn. Club: Soroptimist (El Centro, Cal.). Home: 1015 Commercial Av El Centro CA 92243 Office: PO Bin 1701 1275 Main St El Centro CA 92243

SWEENEY, BEATRICE MARCY (MRS. PAUL H. LEE), educator; b. Boston, Aug. 11, 1914; d. Henry Orlando and Eleanor Hunniwell (Nichols) Marcy; A.B., Smith Coll., 1936; Ph.D., Radcliffe Coll., 1942; m. A. Randolph Sweeney, Jr., Mar. 1937 (div. May 1950); children—Eleanor (Mrs. John DeMarco), Randolph, John, Wendy (Mrs. Paul Constans); m. 2d, Paul H. Lee, Nov. 3, 1961. Research biologist Scripps Instn. Oceanography, La Jolla, Cal., 1947-61; lectr. biology Yale, 1961-67; faculty U. Cal. at Santa Barbara, 1967—, asso. prof. 1969-71, prof., 1971—. Mem. Nat. Com. on Photobiology, 1972—. Nat. Research Found. grantee, 1960—. Mem. Am. Soc. Plant Physiologists, Soc. Gen. Physiologists, Am. Soc. Cell Biology, Bot. Soc. Am., A.A.A.S. (chmn. 1973), Sigma Xi, Phi Beta Kappa. Author: Rhythmic Phenomena in Plants, 1969. Contbr. articles to profl. jours. Home: 6877 Del Playa Goleta CA 93017 Office: Dept Biol Scis U Cal Santa Barbara CA 93106

SWEENEY, SISTER MARGARET MARY, hosp. adminstr.; b. N.Y.C., Oct. 24, 1921; d. Jeremiah and Mary J. (Dougherty) Sweeney; B.S. in Bus. Edn., Coll. Mt. St. Vincent, 1953; M.B.A., St. John's U., 1966; M.S. in Hosp. Adminstrn., Columbia, 1970. Joined Order Sisters of Charity; tchr. St. Joachims Sch., 1946-50; asst. controller St. Vincent's Hosp., N.Y.C., asst. adminstr., adminstrv. asst., supr. bus. office; dep. exec. dir. St. Vincent's Hosp. and Med. Center N.Y., N.Y.C., 1970—; mem. faculty City U. N.Y. Adv. bd. St. Vincent's Hosp., Harrison, N.Y.; trustee St. Joseph's Hosp., Yonkers, N.Y. Mem. Am. Coll. Hosp. Adminstrs., Hosp. Financial Mgmt. Assn., Pub. Health Assn., Delta Mu Delta. Home: 130 W 12th St New York City NY 10011 Office: 153 W 11th St New York City NY 10011

SWEENY, RUTH EVANS, coll. adminstr.; b. Orange, N.J., Jan. 21, 1922; d. Edward Francis and Gertrude (Evans) Sweeny; B.A., Smith Coll., 1943; M.Ed., Rutgers U., 1970; m. Richard B. Perkins, Nov. 27, 1970; children—Alexandra Johnson, Evan Johnson, Craig Johnson, Randall Johnson. Asst. editor U.S. News and World Report, Washington, 1945-46; asst. dir. N.J. Heart Assn., Union, 1967-69; counselor St. Peters Coll., Jersey City, 1970—. Chmn., N.J. Community Mental Health Adv. Council, 1964-67; vice chmn. N.J. Community Mental Health Bd., 1967-70; chmn. Bd. Recreation, Chatham Borough, 1958, Mental Health Com. N.J., State Health Planning Council, 1974—; pres. Morris County Mental Health Assn., 1960-62. Mem. Am. (asso.), N.J. psychol. assns., Am. Personnel and Guidance Assn. Home: 117 Green Av Madison NJ 07940 Office: St Peters Coll Jersey City NJ 07306

SWEET, CODY, behavioral scientist; b. Chgo.; d. Charles Wheeler and Alice Naomi (Grush) S.; B.S., Northwestern U., also Ph.D.; M.A., Northeastern U.; postgrad. Harvard. Pres. Nonverbal Communications, Inc., Wilmette, Ill.; moderator syndicated radio series Dr. Body Talk, 1974—; guest TV shows; lectr. in field. Mem.

Nat. Speakers' Assn. (dir.), Sales and Marketing Execs. Internat., Am. Soc. Tng. Dirs., Women Speakers Internat. (pres.). Author: World Beyond Words, 1973. Contbr. column World Beyond Words to nat. newspapers. Address: 606 Locust Rd Suite 101 Wilmette IL 60091

SWEET, DEE (MRS. HERBERT A. SWEET), day camp exec.; b. Muskogee, Okla., June 3, 1913; d. Walter Oliver and Lola R. (Morris) McDaniel; student Butler U., 1931, 33; m. Herbert A. Sweet, Aug. 28, 1935; children—Judee Lo, Jill B. (Mrs. Alfred P. Bowles). Asst. to interior decorator, L.S. Ayres & Co., Indpls., 1930-33; co-dir. Acorn Farm Camp, Carmel, Ind., 1933—; owner Acorn Farm Antiques, Carmel, 1960—; dir., TV programs WFBM, Indpls., 1949-54, WISH, Indpls., 1955-60; lectr. adult edn. Ind. U., Purdue U. Mem. Appraisers Assn. Am., Antique Dealers Nat. Assn., Am. Camping Assn., Am. Women in Radio and Television, Ind. Hist. Soc., C. of C. Author newspaper column. Home: Rural Route 1 Box 810 Carmel IN 46032

SWEET, LUCY MARGUERITE, assn. exec.; b. Marcellus, N.Y., Dec. 11, 1907; d. Myron Andrew and Allie May (Howe) Sweet; student Cortland (N.Y.) Normal Sch., 1929-31, Syracuse U., 1940-42. Tchr. elementary schs. Pompey, N.Y., 1927-29, Marcellus, 1931-73. Historian, Marcellus Town and Village, 1953—; sec. Marcellus Hist. Soc., 1957—. Active Onondaga council Girl Scouts U.S.A., 1924-60, N.Y. State Christian Endeavor, 1925—, Onondaga Pomona Grange, 1931—, Marcellus Community Council, 1947—. Mem. N.Y. State Tchrs. Assn. Presbyn. Home: 1 Park St Marcellus NY 13108

SWEET, MARY DOLORES HAMMITT, educator; b. Seibert, Colo., May 29, 1918; d. Floyd Lewis and Fernelle Esther (Boyd) Hammitt; B.A. with honors, U. Mo., 1963, M.A., 1963, Ph.D., 1969; m. children—Suzanne, Kenneth Joseph. Instr. philosophy No. Ariz. U., Flagstaff, 1963-66, Woodbury Coll., Los Angeles, 1966-68; asso. prof. Cal. State Poly. U., San Luis Obispo, 1968—. Mem. Am. Philos. Assn. Home: 1197B Ella St San Luis Obispo CA 93401

SWEETSER, MARY CHISHOLM (MRS. SIDNEY M. SWEETSER), author; b. Malden, Mass., June 11, 1894; d. William Frank and Nellie (Hopkins) Chisholm; student Sch. Practical Art, 1919-21; m. Sidney M. Sweetser, June 11, 1921 (dec. Sept. 1963); children—Donald Arthur, Jean Carol (Mrs. Walter Eugene Kelley). Writer articles and juvenile stories appearing in various publs., including Boston Globe, Lewiston Evening Jour., Hearthstone mag., Christian Sci. Monitor, Galaxy mag., Yankee mag.; (under pseudonymn Ted Sweester) articles and juvenile stories in various publs., including Hearthstone mag., No. Sportsman, Forest and Outdoors; Hwy. Traveler, Am. Forests; author book: The Extra Gift, 1969. Founder, dir. Star Island Writer's Conf., 1957-73. Recipient Eleanor Widger award Manuscript Club of Boston, 1949, 55, 63. Methodist. Club: Manuscript (pres. 1956-58) (Boston). Home: 10 Kneeland St Maiden MA 02148

SWEITZER, DOROTHY IRENE STEPHENSON (MRS. MARK W. SWEITZER), librarian; b. Corning, Ia., June 13, 1913; d. Walter Bryant and Edith Juliette (Roland) Stephenson; B.A., U. Colo., 1934; postgrad. U. Chgo., 1938, 39, U. Cal., 1959, 68, U. So. Cal., 1962; M.A., Immaculate Heart Coll., 1972; m. Mark Walter Sweitzer, Dec. 26, 1938; children—Marion Sue (dec.), Terry (Mrs. John L. Emmett), Valerie (Mrs. Stephen B. Castor). Tchr. Corning Sch. Dist., 1934-38; pottery finisher Scio Pottery Co. (O.), 1940-42; tech. lit. searcher, librarian Jet Propulsion Lab., Pasadena, Cal., 1956—; partner ownership and mgmt. apts. Active P.T.A., YWCA, Campfire Girls, Girl Scouts, World Federalists U.S.A., UN Assn. U.S.A. Mem. A.A.A.S., Am. Chem. Soc., Math. Asn. Am., Smithsonian Assos., Am. Inst. Physics, Cal. Library Assn., Am. Soc. Information Sci., Spl. Library Assn., Sigma Pi Sigma, Alpha Delta Pi. Unitarian. Mem. P.E.O. Home: 747 N Mentor Av Pasadena CA 91104 Office: 4800 Oak Grove Dr Pasadena CA 91103

SWENSON, ANN MARIE, mag. editor; b. Buenos Aires, Argentina, Dec. 29, 1932; d. Erhardt Sven and Anna (Granberg) Swenson; A.B., Wheaton Coll., 1955; M.A., U. Wis., 1957; M.R.E., Southwestern Baptist Theol. Sem., 1962; M.Ed., U. Tex., El Paso, 1970. Missionary Fgn. Mission Bd., So. Baptist Conv., El Paso, Tex., 1962—, editor Ensayo sobre la Obra Estudiantil Bautista, Baptist Spanish Publishing House editor La Preparacion de Los Jovenes de la Iglesia Mag., pres. bd. trustees, 1973—; editor Ancla, Adelante!. Pres. Union Nacional Femenil Bautista Misionera Sara Alicia Hale, Mexico, 1971—. Mem. Asociacion de Universitarias de Cd. Juarez, Am. Personnel and Guidance Assn., Kappa Delta Pi. Home: 4204 Edgar Park El Paso TX 79904 Office: Box 4255 El Paso TX 79914

SWENSON, ANNE BEATRICE, piano tchr., artist; b. Conn.; d. Leonard and Josephine (Pontino) Ruggiello; student N.Y. Sch. Indsl. Art, 1941, Art Students League, 1943, 8th St. Art Sch., 1948-52, William Fisher Kennebunkport Art Inst., 1956-58; m. Raymond A. Swenson, Apr. 11, 1942; 1 dau., Anita (Mrs. Anthony De Stefano). Pianist, tchr. arts and crafts U.S.O., 1945; piano tchr., 1954—; tchr., head art dept. St. Peters Elementary Sch., 1963-65; exhibited at Little Art Gallery, N.Y.C., 1946-48, S.I. Mus., 1955-61, Art and Sci. Mus., Statesville, N.C., 1967, Civic Art Center, Rapid City, S.D., 1968, Nat. Arts Club, N.Y.C., 1969, Washington Mus. Fine Arts, Hagerstown, Md., 1971, Met. Mus. Art, N.Y.C., 1975; represented in permanent collection at St. Peters Rectory, S.I. Recipient 250 hour medal for vol. service U.S.O., Waynesville, Mo., 1945, Am. Accordion Assn. award for mus. composition, 1959, Haiku award in poetry Japan Airlines, 1963. Mem. Burr Artists (dir. 1967—), Composers, Authors and Artists of Am. (treas. N.Y.C. chpt. 1970-72, historian 1974—, 2d place Watercolors 1969), Gotham Painters (treas. 1974—, Anna B. Morse Gold medal 1966), N.Y. Poetry Forum, Artists Equity. Home: 10 Phelps Pl Staten Island NY 10301

SWENSON, MAY, poet; b. Logan, Utah; d. Dan Arthur and Anna Margaret (Hellberg) Swenson; B.S., Utah State U. Writer-in-residence Purdue U., 1966-67; lectr. and poetry readings to colls. throughout country. Judge for Lamont Poetry award, 1964, 66, Nat. Book award in poetry, 1964, 72, U.S. Poetry award, 1970, Devins poetry award, 1971, Mademoiselle Poetry competition, 1971, Bollingen prize in poetry, 1973. Recipient Creative Arts award and citation Brandeis U., 1967; Distinguished Service medal Utah State U., 1967; Nat. Inst. Arts and Letters Award, 1960; Nat. Endowment Arts award, 1974. Guggenheim fellow, 1959; Amy Lowell Travelling scholar, 1960; Ford Found. Theatre-Affiliated grantee, 1964; Lucy Martin Donnally fellow, 1968-69; Rockefeller Writing fellow, 1967-68. Fellow Yaddo, Edward MacDowell Colony; mem. Nat. Inst. Arts and Letters. Author: Another Animal, 1954; A Cage of Spines, 1958; To Mix with Time, New and Selected Poems, 1963; Half Sun Half Sleep, 1967; Poems to Solve, 1966; Iconographs, 1970; More Poems To Solve, 1971. Translator: Windows and Stones (Tomas Transtromer), 1972. Contbg. poet anthologies including Twentieth Century American Poetry, 1963; The Modern Poets, 1963; A Country in the Mind, 1962; New Poets of England and America, vol. 1, 1957; A Treasury of Great American Poetry, 1955; The New Modern Poetry, 1967; Poems of Our Moment, 1968; The Contemporary American Poets, 1969; The Voice That Is Great Within Us, 1970; The New Yorker Book of Poems, 1969. Contbr. poetry, prose, critical revs. to mags. including Poetry, Nation, Saturday Rev., New Yorker, Hudson Rev., Paris Rev., Western Rev., New Directions in Prose and Poetry, Harpers, Atlantic, others. Address: 73 Boulevard Sea Cliff NY 11579

SWICK, LUCILLE, performing artist; b. Athens, Ala., Aug. 31, 1930; d. James H. and Agnes E. (Neely) Sims; student, Orlando Fla. Jr. Coll., 1949-50, Orlando Fla. Sch. of Modelling, 1951; m. Thomas Swick, Mar. 22, 1958; children—Nanette M., Mark S., Harrison, Carol Anne. Singer, guitarist Radio Sta. WORZ, Orlando, Fla., 1956-58, WLOF, Orlando, Fla., 1955-56, WDBO, Orlando, Fla., 1950-54. Recipient numerous awards for country and western music performances. Mem. So. Quartets Assn. Club: Pomfret (Easton, Pa.). Home and office: 651 Elder Av Phillipsburg NJ 08865

SWICK, MARYBELLE, banker; b. Franklin, O., May 31, 1919; d. William Landon and Cecile Lena (Bell) Swick; grad. high sch. Teller, Comml. Savs. Bank, Galion, O., 1937-42; teller 1st Nat. Bank, Galion, 1942-44, asst. cashier, 1944-67, v.p., 1967-74, v.p., cashier, 1974—; dir. Galion Real Estate Investment Corp. Trustee Galion Pub. Library. Mem. Nat. Assn. Bank Women (Ohio chmn. 1970-71), Ohio Bankers Assn. (vice chmn. women's activities), Bankers Adminstrn. Inst. (dir. chpt.), Ohio Fedn. China Painters. Mem. Ch. of Christ (mem. financial bd. 1967, trustee). Home: 228 N Boston St Galion OH 44833 Office: 1st Nat Bank Pub Square Galion OH 44833

SWIFT, DOLORES MONICA MARCINKEVICH (MRS. MORDEN LEIB SWIFT), pub. relations exec.; b. Hazleton, Pa., Apr. 3, 1936; d. Adam Martin and Anna Frances (Lizbinski) Marcinkevich; student McCann Coll., 1954-56; m. Morden Leib Swift, Dec. 18, 1966. Pub. relations coordinator Internat. Council Shopping Centers, N.Y.C., 1957-59, Wendell P. Colton Advt. Agy., N.Y.C., 1959-61, Sydney S. Baron Pub. Relations Corp., N.Y.C., 1961-65, Robert S. Taplinger Pub. Relations, N.Y.C., 1965-66; prin. Dolores M. Swift, Pub. Relations, Chgo., 1966—. Bd. dirs. Welfare Pub. Relations Forum, 1971—; mem. pub. relations adv. com. Mid-Am. chpt. A.R.C., 1973—; mem. women's com. Mark Twain Meml., 1968-69; pub. relations dir. N.J. Symphony, Bergen County, 1969-70; mem. Wadsworth Atheneum, 1968-69. Bd. dirs. Youth Guidance, 1972—. Mem. Pub. Relations Soc. Am. (accredited, chmn. subcom. Nat. Center for Vol. Action 1971-72, pub. service com. Chgo. chpt. 1971-72, counselors sect. 1973—). Clubs: Women's (publs. chmn. Englewood, N.J., 1970-71); Publicity (Chgo.). Address: 5701 N Sheridan Rd Chicago IL 60660

SWIFT, ELIZABETH GILE PEIRCE (MRS. HENRY ROBINSON SWIFT), editor; b. New Haven, Jan. 21, 1921; d. Clarence Appleton and Marion Emblien (Walsh) Peirce; B.A. with high honors, Swarthmore Coll., 1942; m. Henry Robinson Swift, Mar. 25, 1944; children—Elizabeth Hawley, Henry Robinson, James Peirce, Richard Hamilton. Editor, Books in Spl. Edn., John Day Co., N.Y.C., 1963—, Human Relations Area Files Press, New Haven, 1964—. Mem. Am. Assn. on Mental Deficiency. Democrat. Conglist. Clubs: Lawn (New Haven); Copper Valley (Cheshire, Conn.). Author: (with Henry Swift) Running A Happy Family, 1960, Community Groups and You, 1964. Editor: Behavior Sci. Research, 1966—. Home: 470 Whitney Av New Haven CT 06511 Office: Box 2054 Yale Sta New Haven CT 06520

SWIFT, ELIZABETH ROSS THOMPSON (MRS. GARFIELD CHRISTIAN SWIFT), bus. exec.; b. Washington, Oct. 16, 1916; d. John William and Elizabeth Noyes (Hempstone) Thompson; certificate Kelsey-Jenney Bus. Sch., San Diego, 1937; m. Garfield Christian Swift, Sept. 16, 1939; children—Theodore Noyes, Justin Ransom II, Garfield Christian, William Byrne III. Sec. to drama critic Washington Star, 1938-40; asst. to Eastern advt. mgr. Charm Mag., 1941-43; owner Request Records, 1943-46; picture researcher, photog. br., internat. press and publs. div. State Dept., Washington, 1950-51; communications and records supr. Mutual Security Agy., Hague, Holland, 1952-54, Army-Navy-Air Force Register, Washington, 1955-58; service club dir. Soesterberg Air Base, Huis Ter Heide, Holland, 1958-61; adminstrv. asst. Cath. Coll. Admissions and Information Center, Washington, 1964-66; co-dir., pres. Edu-Data Service Center, Washington, 1966—. Recipient Letter of Commendation for outstanding service USAF, 1960. Republican. Episcopalian. Home: Highfield House Highfield MD 21753

SWIFT, EVANGELINE WILSON (MRS. GEORGE LEE SWIFT), govt. ofcl.; b. San Antonio, May 2, 1939; d. Raymond Erskin and Josephine (Woods) Wilson; student So. Meth. U., 1956-59, U. Hawaii, summer 1957, U. So. Cal., U. Cal. at Los Angeles, summer 1959, U. Denver, 1960; LL.B., St. Mary's U., San Antonio, 1963; m. George Lee Swift, June 27, 1963; 1 son, Justin Lee. Gen. atty., non-hearing examiner Bur. Operating Rights ICC, Washington, 1964-65, atty. Headstart, Office Econ. Opportunity, 1965; spl. asst. to vice chmn. Equal Employment Opportunity Commn., Washington, 1965-71, chief decisions div., 1971-74, legal counsel to chmn., 1974—. Pub. mem. U.S. delegation UN Commn. on Status Women, 1970—. Recipient Meritorious Service award Equal Employment Opportunity Commn., 1967, Presdl. Civilian citation, 1972. Mem. Nat. Assn. Women Lawyers, Tex. Bar Assn., Delta Zeta. Methodist. Home: 2836 Arizona Terrace NW Washington DC 20016 Office: 1800 G St NW Washington DC 20506

SWIFT, JANE HASTINGS NICHOLS (MRS. DAVID EVERETT SWIFT), coll. adminstr.; b. Binghamton, N.Y., Sept. 3, 1917; d. Robert Hastings and Marjorie Newton (Wallace) Nichols; A.B., Mt. Holyoke Coll., 1939; M.A., Columbia, 1941; m. David Everett Swift, July 5, 1941; children—Jonathan G., James E., Gordon N., Ellen S. Apprentice tchr. English, Fieldston Sch., Riverdale, N.Y., 1939-40; intern tchr. English, drama coach Leland Jr. High Sch., Bethesda, Md., 1940-41; head English dept. Arnold Coll. Phys. Edn., New Haven, 1941-42; tchr. English, Ogontz Sch. for Girls, Rydal, Pa., 1942-43; head resident Pendle Hill, Wallingford, Pa., 1943-45; lectr. English, Middlesex Community Coll., Middletown, Conn., 1966-70; dir. admissions Hartford (Conn.) Coll. for Women, 1970—. Mem. Middletown (Conn.) Youth Services Commn., 1972-74. Bd. dirs. Greater Middletown Homemaker Service, 1965—, pres., 1972-74. Mem. New Eng., Conn. assns. coll. admissions counselors. Conglist (deacon 1966, steward 1972-75). Democrat. Home: 390 Coleman Rd Middletown CT 06457 Office: 1265 Asylum Av Hartford CT 06105

SWIFT, MARJORIE ANN, educator; b. Lexington, Ky., Oct. 8, 1916; d. William Alpheus and Irene (Kieser) Swift; A.B., Lambuth Coll., 1938; M.A., George Peabody Coll., 1941; Ph.D., Northwestern U., 1947. Librarian Mercer (Tenn.) High Sch., 1938-41; tchr. English and Latin, Sardis (Miss.) High Sch., 1941-42; librarian Huntington (Tenn.) High Sch., 1942-44; dean of women, prof. edn. Drury Coll., Springfield, Mo., 1946-49, Wesleyan U., Salina, Kan., 1950-51; dean women Carroll Coll., Waukeshau, Wis., 1949-50; prof. edn. U. Ala., Tuscaloosa, 1951—. Coordinator, cons. for Ala. and Montgomery depts. edn. evaluation programs for secondary schs.; coordinator West Blocton High Sch., Ozark (Ala.) Jr. High and High Sch., 1967-68; dir. guidance clinics for high schs. U. Ala., 1951; cons. U.S. office edn. Bur. of Higher Edn., 1966-68; mem. gov.'s Commn. on Status of Women, 1964—; mem. com. on employment policies and practices in state supported instn. of higher learning and state supported hosps. Mem. Am. Assn. U. Profs., Am. Assn. U. Women (chmn. edn. com. 1957, chmn. higher edn. com. 1958), Ala. Edn. Assn. (sec. treas. 1953-57, Dist. VII pres. 1959, mem. state TV com. 1958), Bus. and Profl. Women's Club (chmn. research com. 1958), Kappa Delta Epsilon (nat. 1st v.p. 1972-74), Pi Lambda Theta, Delta Kappa Gamma, Kappa Delta Pi. Methodist. Club: Quota. Home: 187 Woodland Hills Tuscaloosa AL 35401

SWIFT, SISTER MARY GRACE, educator; b. Bartlesville, Okla., Aug. 3, 1927; d. Frank William and Helen (Moran) Swift; student St. Mary's Coll., Notre Dame, 1945-47; B.A., Creighton U., 1956, M.A., 1960; Ph.D. (Nat. Def. Edn. Act fellow), U. Notre Dame, 1967. Elementary sch. tchr. Kan. Schs., 1948-57; secondary sch. tchr., Kan., Okla., 1957-62; faculty Loyola U., New Orleans, 1966—, asso. prof. history, 1970—. Nat. Def. Fgn. Lang. grantee, summers 1968, 69. Mem. Am. Assn. U. Profs., Am. Assn. for Advancement Slavic Studies. Author: The Art of Dance in the USSR, 1968; A Loftier Flight, 1974. Address: Box 192 Loyola U New Orleans LA 70118

SWIGER, ELINOR PORTER, lawyer, author; b. Cleve., Aug. 1, 1927; d. Louie Charles and Mary Isabelle (Shank) Porter; B.A., Ohio State U., 1949, J.D., 1951; m. Quentin G. Swiger, Feb. 5, 1955; children—Andrew, Calvin, Charles. Admitted to Ohio bar, 1951; atty. chief counsel's office Dept. Internal Revenue, Washington, 1951-56; free lance author, 1970—. Mem. Am. Bar Assn., Children's Reading Round Table, Chgo., Nat. League of Am. Pen Women, Off-Campus Writer's Workshop, Mortar Bd., Pi Sigma Alpha, Alpha Gamma Delta. Author: Mexico for Kids, 1971; Europe for Young Travelers, 1972; The Law and You: A Handbook for Young People, 1973. Contbr. articles to magazines and newspapers. Home and office: 1933 Burr Oak Dr Glenview IL 60025

SWIGERT, ALICE HARROWER (MRS. JAMES MACK SWIGERT), civic worker; b. Montrose, Pa., Dec. 18, 1908; d. Lewis Titcomb and Margaret (Ayars) Harrower; student U. Tenn., 1927-29; m. James Mack Swigert, July 7, 1931; children—Oliver, David Ladd, Sally Harper (Mrs. Swigert Hamilton). Sec. to profs. Harvard Law Sch., Cambridge, Mass., 1932-35; pub. relations U. Chgo. Press, 1935-36. Mus. panoramas chmn. Cin. Symphony Orch. Womens Com., 1963-65; founder, treas. Citizens Crusade, 1967—; vol. Childrens Convalescent Hosp., 1969—; corr. sec. New Life for Girls, Inc., Cin., 1971—, also trustee; mem. adv. council Ohio Presbyn. Home, Trustee, sec. bd. Cin. Speech and Hearing Center, Citizens Crusade, 3 Arts Scholarship Fund. Mem. D.A.R., Chi Omega. Republican. Presbyn. Clubs: Cincinnati Womans, Cincinnati Country, Queen City, Town. Home: 196 Green Hills Rd Cincinnati OH 45208

SWIHART, BEVERLY JANE (MRS. JOHN J. SWIHART), lawyer; b. Detroit, Nov. 11, 1930; d. Arvid Olaf and Cordia Elizabeth (Brehm) Holmberg; A.B., Wayne State U., 1952, LL.B., 1954; m. John J. Swihart, Oct. 19, 1955; 1 dau., Sharon Ann. Admitted to Mich. bar, 1955, Ind. bar, 1964; out of state asso. mem. Detroit firm Victor G. Hanson, Argos, Ind., 1963—, also individual practice, Argos. Co-owner, mgr. Swihart Dairy Farms, Argos, 1964—. Mem. Winnetka assos., woman's bd. Art Inst. Chgo., 1973—. Bd. dirs. Women's Republican Club New Trier Twp., Winnetka. Mem. Ind., Mich. bar assns., Phi Delta Delta. Club: Pine Street Circle. Co-founder (with Gilbert Frimet) Wayne State U. Law Rev., 1953-54. Contbr. articles to newspapers. Home: Route 1 Argos IN 46501 also 882 Pine St Winnetka IL 60093

SWIRNOFF, LOIS (MRS. JULE GREGORY CHARNEY), artist, educator; b. Bklyn., May 9, 1931; d. Harold and Fannie (Goldstein) Swirnoff; certificate with honors Cooper Union, 1951; B.F.A. with honors, Yale, 1953, M.F.A., 1956; 1 son, Joshua Avram Boyce; m. 2d, Jule Gregory Charney, Dec. 29, 1967. Instr. art Wellesley (Mass.) Coll., 1954-58; asst. prof. art U. Cal. at Los Angeles, 1963-68; vis. critic in architecture U. So. Cal., Los Angeles, 1966-68; lectr. visual and environmental studies Harvard, Cambridge, Mass., 1969—; exhibited one-man shows at Hyman Swetzoff Gallery, Boston, 1962, Farnsworth Mus. 1958, Wellesley Coll., Wheaton Coll., 1961; exhibited in many group exhbns., U.S., abroad; represented in permanent collections at Addison Gallery of Am. Art, Andover, Mass., Jewett Art Center, Radcliffe Inst., pvt. collections. Home: 80 Monmouth St Brookline MA 02146 Office: Carpenter Center for Visual Art Harvard 19 Prescott St Cambridge MA 02138

SWITZER, WILDA PEARLINE, sch. adminstr.; b. Gulfport, Miss., Dec. 26, 1939; d. Calvin Myers and Emma Pearl (Gill) Switzer; A.S., Gulf Coast Jr. Coll., 1960; B.S., U. So. Miss., 1962, Ed.M., 1967. Home econs. evaluator vocational unit Good Samaritan Hosp., Gulfport, Miss., 1962-65, tchr. Good Samaritan Sch., 1965-66, prin., 1967-70; dir. Harrison County Tng. Center for Exceptional Children, Gulfport, 1970—. Cons. DDTA Human Resource Network, 1973—. Mem. adv. com. Harrison County Family Ct., Gulfport, 1971—. Recipient Laurel Wreath award as Outstanding Citizen Harrison County, 1972. Mem. Am. Assn. Mental Deficiency, Gulf Coast Mental Health Assn., Council for Exceptional Children, Gulf Coast United Cerebral Palsy, Miss. Assn. Retarded Children (dir.), Miss. Edn. Assn. (pres. spl. edn. 1969-70), Nat. Rehab. Assn., Smithsonians Instns. (asso.), U. So. Miss. Alumni (dir.), Epsilon Sigma Alpha, Kappa Delta Pi, Kappa Omicron Phi. Club: Gulfport Garden. Home: 3002 8th Av Gulfport MS 39501 Office: PO Drawer J Gulfport MS 39501

SWOPE, MARY MARGARET RICHARDS (MRS. KING SWOPE), club woman; b. Morganfield, Ky.; d. Lewis and Margaret Blue (Cromwell) Richards; student Centre Coll., 1912-15, Pa. Coll. for Women, 1915-18; m. King Swope, Mar. 22, 1918 (dec. Apr. 1961); children—William Richards, King. Sec., Nat. Soc. Daus. Barons of Runnemede; nat. councillor Daus. Founders and Patriots Am., 1958-62; Ky. pres. Daus. Colonial Wars, 1959-62; pres. chpt. IX Colonial Dames Am., 1952-58. Mem. Lexington Jr. League, Daus. Am. Colonists, D.A.R., Order of Crown (3d v.p.), Colonial Daus. 17 Century (chpt. pres., nat. councillor), Ams. of Royal Descent, Magna Charta Dames, Burgess First Families of Va., Ky. Hist. Soc., Surety Nat. Soc. Daus. Barons Runnemede, Nat. Soc. Arts and Letters. Republican. Presbyn. Clubs: Lexington (Ky.) Country; Congressional (Washington); Idle Hour Country; Filson. Home: 247 S Hanover Av Lexington KY 40502

SWORD, SUE ELLA JONES, r.r. exec.; b. Rosebud, Tex., Nov. 4, 1924; d. Roy Allen and Luna Vera (Slay) Jones; student Central City Comml. Coll., 1942-43; m. Erl J. Sword, Nov. 23, 1946. Accountant Santa Maria Valley R.R. Co., Santa Maria, Cal., 1948-60, chief clk., 1961-67, asst. auditor, 1968, auditor, sec., treas., 1968-69, v.p., mgr., 1969—, also dir., mem. exec. com.; auditor, sec., treas. La Brea Ice Co., Santa Maria, 1969, v.p., 1969—, also dir.; comptroller S.M. Land Co., Santa Maria, 1971—. Asso. mem. Children's Home Soc., 1965—; charter mem. bd. dirs. Boys' Club Santa Maria Valley, 1966—, sec., asst. treas., 1966-70, v.p., 1971-73, pres., 1973—, mem. ladies aux., 1969—; bd. dirs. United Fund No. Santa Barbara County, 1972, mem. budget com., 1972, v.p., 1974. Mem. Santa Maria Valley Republican Women's Club, 1969—. Mem. Assn. Am. Railroads, Am. Short Line R.R. Assn. (dir. 1972), Pacific Coast Claim Conf., Santa Maria Valley C. of C. (co-chmn. com. 1972, v.p. 1974), U.S. C. of C. Episcopalian. Club: Soroptimist (pres. 1967-68) (Santa Maria). Home: 200 Linda Dr Santa Maria CA 93454 Office: PO Box 340 Santa Maria CA 93454

SWORDS, RUTH CLIFFORD RILEY (MRS. HENRY LOGAN SWORDS), dentist, univ. ofcl.; b. Itasca, Tex., Nov. 1, 1916; d. Philip Eugene and Ruth (Love) Riley; B.A., East Tex. State U., 1938; B.S., Tex. Wesleyan Coll., 1961; D.D.S., Baylor U., 1961; m. Henry Logan Swords, June 20, 1940; children—Henry Logan II, Sylvia Lorraine. Tchr., Ft. Worth Pub. Schs., 1938-42; engring. draftsman Gen. Dynamics Co., Ft. Worth, 1942-48; dir. Caruth Sch. Dental Hygiene, Baylor Coll. Dentistry, Dallas, 1962—. Named Alumna of Year, Tex. Wesleyan Coll., 1964, Distinguished Alumna, East Tex. State U., 1974. Fellow Internat., Am. colls. dentists; mem. Am., Tex. dental assns., Ft. Worth Dist. Dental Soc., Am. Assn. Dental Schs., Baylor Odontological Honor Soc. (charter), Tex. Dental Hygienists Assn. (hon.), Dallas Dist. Dental Hygienists Soc. (hon.), Sigma Tau Delta, Alpha Chi, Sigma Phi Alpha, Omicron Kappa Upsilon (chpt. pres. 1969), Alpha Delta Pi, Upsilon Alpha. Methodist. Rotarian (pres. Ft. Worth woman's chpt. 1954-56). Club: Rejebian Afternoon (treas. 1956-57). Home: 5808 Blueridge Dr Fort Worth TX 76112 Office: Baylor College Dentistry 800 Hall St Dallas TX 75226

SYBURG, JANE MITCHELL (MRS. FREDERIC W. SYBURG), educator, author; b. Des Moines, Aug. 29, 1927; d. Robert John and Alice Josephine (Duffy) Mitchell; A.B., Clarke Coll., Dubuque, 1949; M.A., U. Notre Dame, 1969; m. Frederic Winkler Syburg, June 17, 1950; children—Nancy, Robert, Ellen. Tchr. English, St. Mary's Acad., South Bend, Ind., 1959—, religion Little Flower Ch.; author: People, 1968; Principles, 1969; Partners, 1970; Pilgrims, 1971, The Lit Book, 1973 (with manuals). Mem. Council Tchrs. English. Democrat. Roman Catholic. Home: 918 Whitehall Dr South Bend IN 46615

SYKORA, SYLVIA ESTHER, mus. ofcl.; b. Windom, Minn., Apr. 21, 1898; d. William Wesley and Ella Della (Peterson) Hunter; student Expert Sch. Bus., 1915-16; m. Frank Sykora, Nov. 26, 1919; children—Charlotte (Mrs. Thomas Vucinovich), Harley, Richard, Donna (Mrs. Glenn Grahn), Lucy (Mrs. Wayland Madson), Merle. With Cottonwood County Hist. Soc., Windom, 1947—, sec., 1951—, curator, 1968-74, dir., 1969-70. Democrat. Baptist (deaconess 1970). Home: 1157 River Rd Windom MN 56101 Office: 641 4th Av Windom MN 56101

SYLVESTER, BARBARA BOLEN (MRS. JOSEPH G. SYLVESTER), civic worker; b. Florence, S.C., Mar. 8, 1929; d. Hugh Bernard and Ola Mae (Williamson) Thornton; student Mars Hill Coll., 1946, also Western Carolina U., summers; m. Joseph Georg Sylvester, June 30, 1954; children—Pamela Mae, Elsa April. Sec., S.C. Bd. Juvenile Corrections, 1969-71; chmn. S.C. Bd. Youth Services, 1971-74; chmn. First Step-Red Brick Bd., 1972—; chmn., Florence County White House Conf. on Children and Youth, 1970. Mem. Democratic Nat. Com. from S.C., 1968—, mem. O'Hara (rules) commn., subcom. on credentials. Bd. dirs. S.C. Assn. Retarded Children, 1968-70; pres. Florence County Assn. for Retarded Children, 1969. Home: 510 Camellia Circle Florence SC 29501

SYLVESTRI, TONIA CAMILLE (MRS. CHARLES FLOOD, JR.), constrn. co. exec.; b. Yonkers, N.Y., July 16, 1949; d. Anthony James and Amalia Theresa (D'Anna) Sylvestri; grad. high sch.; m. Charles Flood, Jr., Sept. 9, 1973. Exec. sec. Sylron Constrn. Co., Yonkers, N.Y., 1969, sec.-treas., 1971—. Mem. heart fund com. Westchester County, Mem. Spl. Indsl. Radio Service Assn. (mem. exec. bd.) ACIM, Yonkers Toppers Bowling Assn. (pres. 1972-74), Westchester County Assn. Home: 50 Linn Av Yonkers NY 10705 Office: 865 Nepperhan Av Yonkers NY 10703

SYMINGTON, EVELYN WADSWORTH (MRS. STUART SYMINGTON), wife of U.S. senator; m. Stuart Symington, Mar. 1, 1924; children—William Stuart, James Wadsworth. Wife of U.S. Senator from Mo. Address: 3263 N St Washington DC 20007

SYMINGTON, JANEY STUDT (MRS. STUART SYMINGTON, JR.), biologist; b. St. Louis, June 29, 1928; d. Sidney Melchior and Jane Belle (Sante) Studt; A.B., Vassar Coll., 1950; Ph.D., Radcliffe Coll., 1959; m. Stuart Symington, Jr., June 21, 1949; children—Anne, Stuart, Sidney, John. Research asst. Washington U., St. Louis, 1958-60, research asso., 1961-65, research asst. prof., 1965-69, lectr. biology, 1969-70, asst. prof. research, 1971-72, biology research asso. microbiology, 1972—. Mem. A.A.A.S., Am. Soc. Plant Physiologists, Am. Inst. Biol. Sci., Mid States Electron Microscope Soc., Bot. Soc. Am., N.Y. Acad. Sci., Am. Soc. Cell Biology, Womens Soc. Washington U. (dir., v.p. 1967-68, 70-71), Sigma Xi, Phi Beta Kappa. Club: St. Louis Country. Contbr. articles to profl. jours. Home: 745 Cella Rd St Louis MO 63124

SZEGO, CLARA MARIAN (MRS. SIDNEY ROBERTS), biologist, educator; b. Budapest, Hungary, Mar. 23, 1916; d. Paul Stadler and Helen Elek Szego; brought to U.S., 1921, naturalized, 1927; B.A., Hunter Coll., 1937; M.S., U. Minn., 1939, Ph.D., 1942; m. Sidney Roberts, Sept. 14, 1943. Instr. physiology Sch. Medicine, U. Minn., Mpls., 1942-43; Cancer research fellow Minn. Med. Found., U. Minn., 1943-44; research scientist Office Sci. Research and Devel., Nat. Bur. Standards, Washington, 1944-45; research asso. Worcester Found. for Exptl. Biology, Shrewsbury, Mass., 1945-47; research instr. dept. physiol. chemistry Yale Sch. Medicine, 1947-48; research asso. dept. biophysics, U. Cal., Los Angeles, 1948-49, asst. prof. dept. zoology, 1949-54, asso. prof. dept. zoology, 1955-59, prof. dept. biology, 1960—. John Simon Guggenheim Meml. fellow, 1956-57. Recipient Ann. Ciba award Endocrine Soc., 1953; named Woman of Year in Sci., Los Angeles Times, 1958. Fellow A.A.A.S.; mem. Am. Physiol. Soc., Soc. Exptl. Biology and Medicine (sect. pres. 1953-54), Soc. for Endocrinology, Endocrine Soc., Soc. for Study of Reproduction, Biochem. Soc., Soc. Cell Biology, Phi Beta Kappa, Sigma Xi. Editorial bd. Endocrinology, 1959-67; Annual Reviews of Physiology, 1960-63. Home: 1371 Marinette Rd Pacific Palisades CA 90272 Office: Dept Biology U Cal Los Angeles CA 90024

SZENTIVANYI, JUDITH, dermatologist; b. Miskolc, Hungary, Apr. 4, 1928 (came to U.S. 1957, naturalized 1965); d. Charles and Magda (Rosenberg) Szasz; M.D., U. Debrecen (Hungary), 1952; m. Andor Szentivanyi, July 14, 1948; children—Peter, Edward. Intern Woodlawn Hosp., Chgo., 1957-58; resident in dermatology Sch. Medicine U. Colo., Denver, 1962-65; fellow Children's Asthma Research Inst. and Hosp., Denver, 1960-61; practice medicine specializing in dermatology, Aurora, Colo., 1966-67, Cogley Clinic, Council Bluffs, Ia., 1967-71, Tampa, Fla., 1972—; mem. staff Tampa Gen. Hosp., St. Joseph's Hosp., Tampa, Univ. Community Hosp., Tampa, Centro Espanol Meml. Hosp., Tampa. Clin. instr. dermatology Creighton U., Omaha, 1967-70, clin. asst. prof., 1970-71; clin. asst. prof. dermatology U. South Fla. Coll. Medicine, 1973—. Home: 11603 Carrollwood Dr Tampa FL 33618 Office: 10549 N Florida Av Tampa FL 33612

SZERLIP, BARBARA LESLIE, editor, poet; b. Newark, Nov. 28, 1949; d. Stewart and Ziril (Weinstein) Szerlip; student U. Miami, 1967-69, U. Cal., Santa Barbara, 1969-71. Actress, dancer, later asst. tech. dir. Summer Stock Theater, White Lake and East Monticello, N.Y., 1963-69; leather craftsman, Montreal, Que., Can., 1969; instr. Hatha Yoga and Kirtan Mantras, Sivananda Ashram, Val Morin, Que., 1969; profl. masseuse, San Francisco, 1973—; editor Tractor mag., 1971—. Coordinating Council Lit. Mags. grantee for continuing publ. of Tractor, 1973. Author: Teopantiahuac, 1971; Four Young Women: Poems, 1973; Bear Dancing, 1974; Sympathetic Alphabet, 1975. Home: 1900 Eddy St #18 San Francisco CA 94115 also Apt #223 NE 195th St North Miami Beach FL 33162

SZESKO, LENORE RUNDLE, artist; b. Galesburg, Ill., Mar. 13, 1933; d. James Urvin and Helen (Crawford) Rundle; B.F.A., Art Inst. Chgo., 1961, M.F.A., 1966; m. Robert Stanley Szesko, May 2, 1961. Exhbtd. group shows Audubon Artists, 1969, 70, 71, 72, 73, Nat. Acad. Design, N.Y.C., 1968-70, Woodcut U.S.A., 1967, Mercyhurst Coll., 1969,70, Boston Printmakers, 1968, 72, Print Club Albany, N.Y., 1967, 69, 71, Miniature Painters, Sculptor and Gravers Soc., Washington, 1967-73, Hunterdon Co. Print Exhbn., 1967, 70, 71, 72, 73, 75; group shows maj. cities U.S.; exhbt. regularly Art Inst. Chgo. Sales and Rental Gallery, Galaxy Original Print Gallery, Hollis, N.H. Mem. Painters and Sculptors Soc. N.J., Hunterdon Art Center, Boston Printmakers, Miniature Art Soc. N.J., Audubon Artists, Delta Phi Delta. Home: 835 S Ridgeland Av Oak Park IL 60304

SZIEDE, EDNA BAKEOVEN (MRS. HOWARD SZIEDE), ret. adminstrv. sec.; b. Phila., Dec. 31, 1908; d. George W. and Ella C. (Moylan) Bakeoven; student Phila. Coll. of Bible, 1927-28, Hartwick Theol. Sem., 1930-31, Pratt Inst., 1931; m. Albert F. Harkins, June 14, 1930; m. 2d, Louis F. McCreedy, Aug. 7, 1937 (dec. Feb. 1967); 1 dau., Frances H.; m. 3d, Howard Sziede, 1970. Exec. sec. lt. gov. Pa., Montgomery County Republican Hdqrs., 1951-56; exec. sec. office mgr. Linear, Inc., Phila., 1956-61; exec. sec. to v.p. marketing and pub. relations Univac, Blue Bell, Pa., 1962, Foote Mineral Co., Phila., 1962-63; coordinator N.Y. Stock Exchange Investors Information Program, 1963; asst. treas. Greenfield Realty Co., Inc., Phila., 1962-63; exec. sec. dean Coll. Engring. Drexel U., Phila., 1963, also sec. Engring. Faculty Com.; adminstrv. asst. to pres., instr. English, Holy Family Coll., Phila., 1964-65; asst. pub. relations dir. St. Luke's Hosp., Phila., 1966; adminstrv. sec. to Mr. Courtlandt S. Gross, Lockheed Aircraft Corp., Phila., 1967-73; asst. treas. Greenfield Realty Co., Inc., Phila., 1963-64; partner, sec., treas. Elkins Park Health Salon, 1947-61; tchr. masso-theraphy, 1947-61. Dir. Adult Edn. Council of Phila., 1962-66; adv. bd. mem. Bus. Belles, Montgomery County, 1962-66; 1st chmn. Old York Rd. dist. campaign Salvation Army Old York. Chmn., Career Group Hannah Penn House Republican Women of Pa., 1967-72, bd. dirs., publicity dir. Eastern Montgomery County Council Rep. Women, 1968—, Rep. Woman Pa., past sec. Profl. and Business Women's Rep. Club of Phila. Mem. Order Eastern Star. Lutheran. Contbr. poetry to mags. Home: Neshaminy Woods Apts Comanche Bldg 815 Croydon PA 19020 Office: Girard Trust Bldg Philadelphia PA 19102

SZIGETHY, MARION C., librarian; b. Budapest, Hungary; d. Janos Gy and Colette (Belatiny) Szigethy; came to U.S., 1956, naturalized, 1962; M.S. in L.S. with honors, Columbia, 1965, postgrad., 1971—; children—Frank, Peter. Librarian Nat. Szechenyi Library, Budapest, 1950-56; librarian Free Europe Research Library, N.Y.C., 1966-75; librarian N.Y. U., 1975—; lectr. in field. Mem. A.L.A., Spl. Libraries Assn. (chmn. newspaper group 1970-71), N.Y. Library Club (scholarship 1962), Beta Phi Mu (chmn. chpt. publns. com. 1969—). Author: Maurice Falcolm Tauber: A Bibliography, 1974. Contbr. articles to profl. jours. Home: 169 E 92d St New York City NY 10028

SZMANT, ALINA MARGARITA (MRS. PHILIP N. FROELICH, JR.), marine biologist; b. Dayton, O., June 18, 1946; d. Herman Harry and Adelina (Mesa) Szmant; B.S., U. P.R., 1966; M.S. in Marine Biology, Scripps Instn. Oceanography, 1970; m. Philip N. Froelich, Jr., Dec. 1971. Aquanaut-scientist Tektite II, summer 1970; research asso. dept. marine scis. U. P.R., 1970-71, radioecology div. P.R. Nuclear Center, Mayaguez, 1971-73; research scientist Raytheon Co., Portsmouth, R.I., 1973—. Recipient Conservation award U.S. Dept. Interior, 1970; Meritory awards Los Angeles County Mus. Natural History, 1970, County of Los Angeles, 1970; named hon. citizen City of Chgo. Mem. Internat. Oceanographic Found., Am. Soc. Limnologists and Oceanographers, Marine Biol. Assn. U.K. Democrat. Address: Oceanographic and Environmental Services Raytheon Co PO Box 360 Portsmouth RI 02871

SZOSTAK, MARY ISABELLE (MRS. EDWARD JOSEPH SZOSTAK), librarian; b. Buffalo, Aug. 13, 1925; d. William and Frances (Kryta) Pijanowski; student Nazareth Coll., 1944-45; B.A., U. Buffalo, 1959; M.L.S., Rutgers U., 1960; m. Edward Joseph Szostak, Aug. 13, 1946. Library clk. Erie County Pub. Library, Buffalo, 1948-50; sr. library clk. Cheektowaga Pub. Library (N.Y.), 1950-59, library dir., 1969—; jr. librarian Buffalo & Erie County Pub. Library, Buffalo, 1960-62; sr. librarian, 1962-69, mem. exec. bd., 1964-66, 73—. Recipient Buffalo & Erie County Pub. Library scholarship, 1959. Mem. Internat. Platform Assn., Am., N.Y. library assns., Cheektowaga Hist. Soc. (dir. 1973—), Soc. for the Prevention of Cruelty to Animals, U. Buffalo Alumni Assn., Rutgers U. Alumni Assn. Roman Catholic. Clubs: Polish Arts (Buffalo); Quota of Checktowaga. Home: 398 Curtiss St Buffalo NY 14212 Office: Cheektowaga Public Library 2580 Harlem Rd Cheektowaga NY 14225

TABACHNICK, BARBARA JOYCE, educator; b. Paterson, N.J., May 20, 1936; d. William J. and Lillian (Salzberg) Gerson; A.B. in Psychology, U. Cal. at Los Angeles, 1964, M.A., 1968, Ph.D. (NSF fellow), 1971; m. Kenneth Tabachnick, Aug. 28, 1955. Sr. research asst. Human Factors Research, Inc., Los Angeles, 1959-64; project asso. Serendipity Assos., Chatsworth, Cal., 1964-67; research and teaching asst. dept. psychology U. Cal. at Los Angeles, 1967-71; asst. prof. psychology Cal. at U. at Northridge, 1971—; dir. research Cal. Center Ednl. Therapy, Los Angeles, 1972—. Bd. dirs. Bell Canyon (Cal.) Assn., 1972-73, Cal. Found. to H.E.L.P. Mem. Am., Western psychol. assns., Western Assn. Women in Psychology, A.A.A.S., Am. Assn. U. Women. Contbr. articles to profl. jours. Office: Dept Psychology Cal State U Northridge CA 91324

TABER, JACQUELINE, judge; b. Portland, Ore., Nov. 21, 1922; d. John T. and Etta (Johnson) T.; A.B., U. Cal. at Berkeley, 1945, LL.B., Boalt Hall of Law, 1947. Admitted to Cal. bar, 1947; clk. 9th circuit ct. appeals, San Francisco, 1947; pvt. practice, 1947-65; judge Municipal Ct. Oakland-Piedmont Jud. Dist., Oakland, Cal., 1965—; instr. real estate law Merritt Coll., Oakland, 1963-64. Pres. vol. bur. Alameda County, Oakland, 1966-71; adv. com. Commn. Status of Women, State Cal., 1968-72; adv. com. John F. Kennedy U. Law Sch., Martinez, Cal., 1968-72. Bd. dirs. Alameda County Legal Aid Soc., Nat. Safety Council Alameda County, Oakland, Jr. Statesman Am., Bay Area Soc. Planning. Named one of 10 distinguished women for 1967, San Francisco Examiner. Home: 4689 Lincoln Av Oakland CA 94602 Office: Municipal Ct Oakland-Piedmont Judicial Dist 600 Washington St Oakland CA 94607

TABER, LINDA PERRIN (MRS. ALLAN D. TABER), pub. relations co. exec.; b. Marshalltown, Ia., Dec. 30, 1941; d. Burr H. and Luella M. (Memler) Perrin; B.A., U. Ia., 1964; M.A. (Nat. Inst. Mental Health fellow), Syracuse U., 1969; m. Allan D. Taber, Apr. 26, 1969. Women's editor Cedar Rapids (Ia.) Gazette, 1964-67; mem. editorial staff Inst. of Life Ins., Health Ins. Inst., N.Y.C., 1968-69; account supr. Ketchum, MacLeod & Grove, Inc., N.Y.C., 1969-73; v.p. Carol Moberg, Inc., N.Y.C., 1973—. Bd. dirs. Elec. Women's Round Table. Mem. Women in Communications, Home Fashions League, Home Economists in Bus. (asso.), Am. Home Econs. Assn. (asso.), Alpha Phi. Home: 160 West End Av New York City NY 10023

TABOR, HANNAH ROSE, realtor; b. Butte, Mont., Dec. 30, 1919; d. Samuel and Ester Mollye (Shindell) Ladon; student Balt. Jr. Coll., 1935-36, Johns Hopkins U., 1941-42, 56-58, U. Md., 1968-70; m. Donald Tabor, Jan. 31, 1937; children—Merle (Mrs. Barry Stern), Susan (Mrs. Stern), Neil, Gary. Saleswoman Mal Sherman Realty, Balt., 1951-55; owner Hannah Tabor Co., real estate, Pikesville, Md., 1955-60, pres. Hannah Tabor Co., 1960—. Pres. Lou-Hannah investment Co., Glen Bernie, Md., 1961—; partner Hannah Tabor Mgmt. Co., Glen Bernie, 1963-74. Instr. water safety A.R.C., 1949-52. Recipient Professionalism citation Apt. House Owners Assn., 1971. Mem. Home Builders Assn. Md. (million dollar circle 1970—), Anne Arundel County Real Estate Bd. (pres. women's council 1967-68, treas. 1966-68), Real Estate Bd. Greater Balt. (bd. dirs. 1969-71), Nat. Real Estate Bd., Nat. Fedn. Bus. and Profl. Women's Club, C. of C., Nat., Balt. home builders assns., Baltimore County Brokers Round Table, Pi Sigma Tau. Home: 2511 Willow Glen Dr Baltimore MD 21209 Office: 8 Church Lane Pikesville MD 21208

TABRAH, RUTH MILANDER, state ofcl., author; b. Buffalo, Feb. 28, 1921; d. Henry and Ruth (Harwood) Milander; B.A., U. Buffalo, 1941; postgrad. U. Washington, 1945-46; m. Frank Tabrah, May 8, 1943 (div. Aug. 1971); children—Joseph Garner, Thomas. Mem. Hawaii Sch. Adv. council, 1962-66, chmn., 1964-66; mem. Hawaii State Bd. of Edn., 1966—; Pacific area v.p. Nat. Assn. State Bds. Edn., 1969-72, dir. at large, 1970-71; cons. to U.S. office of edn., 1969-71. Recipient Woman in Edn. award Am. Assn. U. Women, 1971. Mem. Phi Beta Kappa. Author: Pulaski Place, 1949; The Voices of Others, 1959; Hawaiian Heart, 1964; Hawaii Nei, 1967; Buddhism: A Modern Way of Life and Thought, 1970; The Red Shark, 1970; The Old Man and The Astronauts, 1974. Cons. editor Island Heritage Press, 1972-74. Home: 108 Puako Beach Dr Kamuela HI 96743 Office: PO Box 2360 Honolulu HI 96804

TACHMINDJI, DIANE ELIZABETH PRIMEAU (MRS. ALEXANDER J. TACHMINDJI), civic worker, assn. exec.; b. Davenport, Ia., Dec. 3, 1936; d. Carl Donald and Fern (Elofson) Primeau; B.A., Marygrove Coll., 1962; m. Alexander J. Tachmindji, Dec. 4, 1965. U.S. congl. sec., 1957-59; legislative liaison, librarian Gen. Motors Corp., Washington, 1962-63; exec. sec. Inst. for Def. Analyses, Washington, 1963-64; asst. to dir. community relations service U.S. Conf. Mayors, Washington, 1964-65. Vol. canteen worker A.R.C., 1962-63; vol. Albert Deutsch Center, 1967-69, dir. vols., 1967-69, mem. policy com., 1967-68, bd. dirs., 1968-72, sec., 1968-69, v.p., 1969-72; chmn. membership and vol. recruitment com. D.C. Mental Health Assn., 1968-69, mem. publicity com., 1969, bd. dirs., 1970-72, vice chmn. Mental Health Ball, 1971, del. Health and Welfare Council, 1970-72; rec. sec. Womens Com. Nat. Ballet, 1967-68, corr. sec., 1968-69, vice chmn., 1969-71; womens com. Nat. Symphony, 1967-68; bd. dirs., mem. finance com. Washington Area Council on Alcoholism and Drug Abuse, 1972. Mem. D.C. Mental Health Assn., Nat. Ballet Soc., Women's Com. for Nat. Ballet (asso.). Home: 4915 Sedgwick St Washington DC 20016

TACKETT, VIRGINIA ONSTEAD (MRS. RICHARD LOWELL TACKETT), lawyer; b. Foreman, Ark., Nov. 12, 1919; d. Charles Frederick and Isabelle Elva (Emerick) Onstead; student Ouachita Baptist Coll., 1939-40, U. Ark., 1961-62; LL.B., Ark. Law Sch., 1964; m. Richard Lowell Tackett, Nov. 7, 1937; children—Richard, Fred. Admitted to Ark. bar, 1965; staff atty. Ark. State Hwy. Dept., Little Rock, 1965—. Mem. substantive com. Criminal Code Revision Commn. Ark., 1973—; mem. Gov.'s Commn. on Status of Women, Legal Task Force. Mem. Ark. Bar Assn. (law day chmn. 1974, del. 1973—). Democrat. Methodist. Home: 4815 B St Little Rock AR 72205 Office: PO Box 2261 Little Rock AR 72203

TADLOCK, FRANCES AYERS (MRS. WILLIAM RAY TADLOCK), educator; b. Pickens County, S.C., May 2, 1926; d. Frank Jackson and Lucy Elizabeth (Blackerby) Ayers; B.S., Winthrop Coll., 1946; postgrad., 1947, 49, 52-53; postgrad. Furman U., 1965-67, U. S.C., 1967, La Verne Coll., 1971, Clemson U., 1973-74; m. William Ray Tadlock, Apr. 27, 1946; children—William Ray, Connie Lorraine. Tchr. home econs. Greenville County (S.C.) Sch. Dist., 1946-57, tchr. 1965-74. Mem. Childhood Edn. Assn. (state v.p. 1970-72), Internat. Reading Assn., N.E.A., Greenville County, S.C. edn. assns., Delta Kappa Gamma. Baptist. Home: 20 Westbrook Lane Greenville SC 29605 Office: East Gantt Elementary School Route 4 Greenville SC 29605

TADLOCK, LILA CLEMENTA SWINDELL (MRS. WILLIAM LAWTON TADLOCK), poet; b. Cummingsville, Tenn., Jan. 13, 1903; d. Edward Thulus and Martha Frances (Plumlee) Swindell; student Hardin Baylor U., 1921-23, Austin Coll., 1928-28; B.S., East Tex. State U., 1940, M.S., 1945; m. William Lawton Tadlock, Sept. 1, 1923; 1 son, Theodore Gamaliel (dec.). Tchr., Bells High Sch., 1942-43, North Fannin Sch., 1943-46, Gober High Sch., 1947-54, Bartley Woods Primary Sch., 1954-55, 1955-68, Windom Primary Sch., 1968-69 (all in Tex.), ret., 1969. Active A.R.C. Recipient Humerous Prize Poetry Soc. Tex., 1954. Mem. Fannin County Tchrs. (3d v.p.), Poetry Soc. Tex., Woodmen of World, Nat. Ret. Tchrs. Club. Presbyn. Club: Fannin County Republican, Bonham Women's, Triple L, Poet's Study, Lannius Community. Contbr. poetry to Visions in Verse, 1968, Contemporary Poets, 1969. Composer Forever Yours, Belated Love, Angels Unaware, To the Class of 21. Address: Box 334 Franklin Av at Denison Av Bonham TX 75418

TAEGE, MARLYS LAVONNE SCHMIDT (MRS. JACK F. TAEGE), editor; b. Milbank, S.D., Mar. 21, 1928; d. Daniel A. and Lulu Irene (Hoy) Schmidt; student La Escuela Interamericana de Verano, Saltillo, Coahuila, Mexico, 1949; Ph.B., Marquette U., 1950; m. Jack F. Taege, Sept. 6, 1952; children—Linda, Lauren, James. Tchr. journalism, sr. English Barron (Wis.) High Sch., 1950-51; women's news editor Badger Luth. Newspaper, 1951-53, editor, 1970—; corr. Lake Country Reporter, 1958-59; corr., spl. features writer Waukesha Daily Freeman, 1957-59, home sect. editor, 1968-70; mission editor Luth. Woman's Quar., St. Louis, 1963-66, editor-in-chief, 1966—; internat. pub. relations dir. Luth. Women's Missionary League, 1964-66. Co-chmn. Zion Kindergarten Com., 1958-59, West Central High Sch. Citizens' Com. 1963-64; v.p., program chmn. Zion P.T.A., 1961-63; photography instr. Zion 4-H Club, 1961-63, 64-67, gen. leader, 1967-71; chmn. Kettle Moraine High Sch. Curriculum Com., 1964-65; sec. Long Range Planning Com. Kettle Moraine Sch. dist., 1967-69. Republican precinct committeewoman, Delafield, Wis., 1964-68. Bd. dirs. Kettle Moraine Scholarship Found., 1972—. Recipient Hawks Inn award of honor, 1969. Mem. Bethlehem Luth. Ladies Guild, Luth. Women's Missionary League (zone pres. 1958-60, dist. pub. relations dir. 1960-64), Hawks Inn Hist. Soc. (charter), Women in Communications (chpt. treas. 1951), Gamma Pi Epsilon, Kappa Tau Alpha, Sigma Delta Pi, Delta Zeta. Author: Hawks Inn Revisited; Delafield Heritage Trail Guide. Home: N5W29116 Venture Hill Rd Waukesha WI 53186 Office: 6914 W Appleton Av Milwaukee WI 53216

TAEUBER, ALMA FICKS, demographer; b. Seattle, Sept. 19, 1933; d. George and Alma (Beveridge) Ficks; B.A., Wash. State U., 1954; M.A., U. Chgo., 1960, Ph.D., 1962; m. Karl Taeuber, Mar. 17, 1960; children—Shawn, Stacy, Wendy. Research asst. Population Research Center, U. Chgo., 1956-61, research asso., 1961-64; research asso. U. Wis., Madison, 1964—, Inst. for Research on Poverty, 1966—. Mem. Sociol. Research Assn., Population Assn. Am., Am. Sociol. Assn. Author: (with K. Tauber) Negroes in Cities, 1965. Contbr. articles to profl. jours. Home: 1911 Vilas Av Madison WI 53711 Office: Inst for Research on Poverty U Wis Madison WI 53706

TAEUBER, IRENE BARNES (MRS. CONRAD F. TAEUBER), demographer, sociologist; b. Meadville, Mo., Dec. 25, 1906; d. Ninevah C. and Lily D. (Keller) Barnes; A.B., U. Mo., 1927; M.A., Northwestern U., 1928; Ph.D., U. Minn., 1931; LL.D., Smith Coll., 1960; D.Sc., Western Coll. for Women, 1965; m. Conrad Taeuber, July 1929; children—Richard Conrad, Karl Ernst. Instr. sociology, econs. U. Minn., 1928-30, Mt. Holyoke Coll., 1931-34; research demographer Office Population Research, Princeton, 1936—; cons. Internat. Statistics Bur. Census, 1940-50; cons. demography Pacific Sci. Bd., 1955-70, AID, 1963-71. Dir. census library project Library of Congress and Bur. of Census, 1941-44; v.p. UN World Population Conf., 1965. Mem. Population Assn. Am. (pres. 1953-54), Internat. Union (v.p.), Am. Assn. U. Women, Social Sci. Research Council (subcom. on Chinese soc. 1961-70). Author: General Censuses and Vital Statistics in the Americas, 1943; The Population of Tanganyika, 1949; The Population of Japan, 1958; (with F.W. Notestein), The Population of Europe and the Soviet Union, 1943; (with others) Public Health and Demography in the Far East, 1949; (with Conrad Taeuber) The Changing Population of the United States, 1958; Population Trends in the United States, 1900-1960, 1964; The People of the United States in the Twentieth Century, 1972. Died Feb. 24, 1974. Home: 4222 Sheridan St Hyattsville MD 20782 Office: Office of Population Research Princeton U Princeton NJ 08540

TAFFEL, LIBBY BLEK (MRS. CHARLES TAFFEL), clin. psychologist; b. N.Y.C., Jan. 23, 1921; d. Max and Ida (Rosenfeld) Blek; B.A., Bklyn. Coll., 1941; M.A., Ohio State U., 1946; Ph.D., U. Conn., 1952; m. Charles Taffel, 1971. Clin. psychologist Norwich (Conn.) State Hosp., 1947-48, VA Mental Hygiene Clinic, Milw., 1950-52, VA Hosp., American Lake, Tacoma, 1952-53; supervising clin. psychologist VA Hosp., Canandaugua, N.Y., 1954-55, VA Hosp., Brockton, Mass., 1955-57; clin. psychologist Child Guidance and Speech Correction Clinic, Jacksonville, Fla., 1957-58; chief clin. psychologist Palm Beach County Guidance Center, West Palm Beach, Fla., 1958-70; clin. psychologist So. Ariz. Mental Health Center, Tucson, 1970-71; clin. psychologist West Yavapai Guidance Center, Prescott, Ariz., 1972-74; child clin. psychologist Guidance Center of Camden County, West Collingswood, N.J., 1974—. Mem. Am., Western, Ariz., Palm Beach County (pres. 1969) psychol. assns. Contbr. articles to profl. jours. Home: 308-7 Echelon Dr Voorhees NJ 08043 Office: 322 White Horse Pike North Collingswood NJ 08107

TAFT, FRANCES PRINDLE (MRS. SETH CHASE TAFT), educator; b. New Haven, Dec. 12, 1921; d. William Edwin and Mildred (Bradley) Prindle; B.A., Vassar Coll., 1942; M.A., Yale, 1948; m. Seth Chase Taft, June 19, 1943; children—Frederick I., Thomas P., Cynthia B., Seth Tucker. Tchr., Gateway Sch., New Haven, 1945-48; prof. art history, chmn. dept. history of art Cleve. Inst. Art, 1954—. Mem. Jr. council Cleve. Mus. Art, 1950—, Cleve. Inst. Art Womens Com., 1949—; mem. adv. com. Jennings Found., 1973—. Bd. dirs. Shaker Heights League Women Voters, 1955; trustee Karamu House, 1950-65, Cleve. Mus. Art, 1973—, Western Res. Acad., 1973—, Vassar Coll., 1973—; trustee Laurel Sch., 1960—, pres. bd., 1965-71; mem. vis. com. Case-Western Res. U. Mem. Soc. Archtl. Historians, Coll. Art Assn., Cleve. Art Assn. (dir. 1964-67), Asso. Alumnae Vassar Coll. (dir. 1959-61, pres. bd. 1966-72), Western Res. Archtl. Historians (pres. 1972), Phi Beta Kappa (trustee Cleve. chpt. 1969—, pres. 1972). Club: Cleveland Print. Home: 6 Pepper Ridge Rd Cleveland OH 44124

TAGER, RAMONA MARIE (MRS. HAROLD BERNARD TAGER), state ofcl.; b. Osage, Ia., Oct. 7, 1930; d. Edgar Charles and Marie Elizabeth (Ulfers) Schmidt; B.A., U. Ill., 1954; m. Harold Bernard Tager, Feb. 9, 1957; children—Patricia Ann, Alison Marie. Statistical analyst div. highways, State Ill., 1960-66; statis. analyst, dept. health State Ariz., Phoenix, 1966—. Democrat. Roman Catholic. Home: 353 E Thomas Rd Phoenix AZ 85012 Office: 1740 W Adams St Phoenix AZ 85007

TAGGART, MADGE, former judge; b. Buffalo, Feb. 1, 1897; d. William James and Margaret A. (McGuire) Taggart; LL.B., U. Buffalo, 1920; m. Walter E. Doyle, Oct. 6, 1917 (dec.). Admitted to N.Y. Bar, 1920, practiced law, Buffalo; apptd. asst. dist. atty. Erie County (N.Y.), 1952; judge City Ct., 1952-62; judge Family Ct., Buffalo, 1963-73. Active Cath. Charities; organizer, pres. Inter Club Council Western N.Y., 1938-41. Chmn. speaker's bur., writer radio, TV scripts for polit. campaigns Erie County Republican Com., 1938-52. Named One of Ten Outstanding Citizens Buffalo, 1953. Mem. Nat. Assn. Women Lawyers (regional dir. 1930-36), Bus. and Profl. Women's Clubs (Susan B. Anthony award 1952, Woman of Year Buffalo 1942, 43), Zonta (pres. Buffalo 1952-53). Home: 1615 SE 7th Ct Deerfield Beach FL 33441

TAGIURI, CONSUELO ADELA KELLER (MRS. RENATO TAGIURI), physician; b. San Francisco; d. Cornelius H. and Adela (Rios) Keller; A.B., U. Cal. at Berkeley, 1941; M.D., U. Cal. at San Francisco, 1944; m. Renato Tagiuri, May 5, 1946; children—Robert, Peter, John. Intern, Fajardo Dist. Hosp., P.R., 1944-45; resident, clin. fellow Royal Victoria Hosp., Montreal, Que., Can., 1945-47, Mass. Gen. Hosp., Boston, 1947-49, Boston Thom Clinic, 1947-51, Mass. Meml. Hosp., Boston, 1948-49, Judge Baker Guidance Center, Boston, 1949-55, James Jackson Putnam Childrens Center, Boston, 1950-51, Boston Children's Hosp., 1950-56; practice medicine specializing in psychiatry, Cambridge, Mass., 1961—; mem. staff Cambridge Guidance Center, Gifford Sch.; clin. instr. psychiatry Harvard Med. Sch., 1967—. Diplomate Am. Bd. Psychiatry and Neurology. Fellow Am. Orthopsychiat. Assn.; mem. New Eng. Council Child Psychiatrists, Phi Beta Kappa. Home: 432 Concord Rd Weston MA 02193 Office: 5 Sacramento St Cambridge MA 02138

TAGRIN, EDITH SWEEDER (MRS. MARVIN S. KAPLAN), med. artist; b. Boston; d. David and Anna (Morillo) Sweeder; student Museum of Fine Arts, Boston, 1942-46, Boston U., 1945-46, Sch. Med. Illustration, Mass. Gen. Hosp., 1946-49; m. Ralph Tagrin, Nov. 14, 1948 (dec. July 1958); m. 2d, Marvin S. Kaplan, Oct. 23, 1966. Free-lance med. artist, Boston, 1949-58; staff artist Mass. Gen. Hosp., Boston, 1958-60, dir. med. art unit, 1960—, dir. Sch. Med. Illustration, 1966—. Mem. Soc. Tech. Writers and Pubs., Assn. Med. Illustrators (editor directory, chmn. finance, bd. govs.; v.p. 1969, chmn. scholarship, chmn. archives). Club: Art Directors (Boston). Illustrator: Violence and the Brain, 1970; Gynecology, Principles and Practice, 1971; Human Design, 1971; Surgery of Upper Respiratory System, 1971; Fundamentals of Colon Surgery, 1974; also numerous other med. books, jours. Office: Med Art Dept Mass Gen Hosp Boston MA 02114

TAICHER, BETTE TOMAR (MRS. LEONARD L. TAICHER), mfg. co. exec.; b. Camden, N.J.; d. Morris and Kate (Sadinsky) Tomar; student Temple U., 1931-33, U. Pa., 1933-34; D.F.A. honoris causa, Internat. Fine Arts Coll. Fashion; m. Leonard L. Taicher, July 17, 1935; children—L. Donald, Robert. Vice-pres., treas., designer Pan Am. Import Export Co., Vineland, N.J., 1944-49; v.p., sec., designer Pan Am. Modes, Miami, Fla. 1949-55; co-founder, v.p., sec., dir. fashion Caressa, Inc., Miami, 1955—; sec. treas. Allure Shoe Corp., Miami, 1964—; sec.-treas. Caressa of P.R., 1963—; dir. Teb, Inc., Miami. Co-founder Mt. Sinai Hosp.; staff asst. Vineland chpt. A.R.C., 1941-44; sec. Vineland Sr. Council, 1939-41. Recipient designer's award Leather Industries Am., 1964. Mem. Shoe Women Execs., Nat. Shoe Mfrs., Lowe Art Galleries, Friends of the Earth, Miami Art Alliance, Hadassah (program and edn. chmn. 1945-46). Home: 3690 Chase Av Miami Beach FL 33140 Office: 3601 NW 54th St Miami FL 33142

TAIT, CORNELIA DAMIAN (MRS. JOY NELSON TAIT), artist; b. Phila., Dec. 22, 1922; d. Mihai Traian and Sofia Maria (Bogdan) Damian; student Stella Elkins Tyler Sch. Fine Arts, 1940-46; B.F.A. (scholar), Temple U., 1944, B.S. in Edn., 1945, M.F.A., 1946; m. Joy Nelson Tait, Feb. 27, 1953. One-woman shows Temple U., 1946, Phila. Art Alliance, 1950, Woodmere Art Gallery, 1966, 73, also in Bucharest, Cluj and Timisoara, Romania, 1973, Romanian Library, N.Y.C., 1974; exhibited art in nat. traveling exhibitio exhbns., represented in permanent collection Temple U.; art commissions various religious groups; faculty supr. Abington (Pa.) Cultural Center, 1962-63. Organizer internat. exhbn. Romanian Contemporary Art, Phila., 1973. Mem. Artists Equity Assn., Phila. Art Alliance, Woodmere Art Gallery, Violet Oakley Meml. Found., Internat. Platform Assn. Home and studio: 10 Armour Rd Hatboro PA 19040

TAIT, ELAINE ANN BRAZZ (MRS. CHARLES ALBERT TAIT II), editor; b. Nesquehoning, Pa., Apr. 17, 1936; d. John Charles and Anne (Labick) Brazz; B.S., Drexel U., 1957; m. Charles Albert Tait II, Dec. 28, 1957. Market devel. specialist Am. Viscose Corp., 1958-60; advt. writer Strawbridge & Clothier, 1960-63; food editor Phila. Inquirer, 1963-74, fashion editor, 1974—. recipient 1st prize for advt. copy Phila. Club Advt. Women, 1961, Vesta award for outstanding newspaper food pages Am. Meat Inst., 1966. Mem. Sigma Delta Chi (dir. 1973—). Home: 771 Conestoga Rd Malvern PA 19355 Office: 400 N Broad St Philadelphia PA 19101

TAIT, MARION, educator; b. Saskatoon, Sask., Can., Nov. 4, 1911; d. Robert and Jane (West) Tait; B.A., Victoria Coll., U. Toronto (Ont. Can.), 1934, M.A., 1935; fellow Am. Sch. Classical Studies, Rome, 1938-39; Ph.D., Bryn Mawr Coll., 1941. Teaching fellow Victoria Coll., U. Toronto, 1934-35; instr. Bryn Mawr Coll., 1939-40, Sweet Briar Coll., 1940-41; successively instr., asst. prof., asso. prof. Mt. Holyoke Coll., 1941-48; prof. Vassar Coll., 1948—, dean, 1948-61, dean of faculty, 1961-65, acting dean faculty, 1970-71, now dean faculty. Mem. Am. Philol. Assn., Am. Assn. U. Profs. Home: 77 Raymond Av Poughkeepsie NY 12601

TAIT, NANCY JOAN, coll. dean; b. Duluth, Minn., Feb. 26, 1939; d. William and Evelyn J. (Martin) Tait; A.A., Penn Hall Jr. Coll., 1959; B.S., Lake Erie Coll., 1961; M.S., No. Ill. U., 1963; Ed.D., Ind. U., 1973. Residence hall counselor Eastern Ill. U., Charleston, 1964-69; dean women California (Pa.) State Coll., 1971—. Mem. Nat. Assn. Student Personnel Adminstrs., Center for Study Democratic Instns., Am. Assn. Higher Edn., California State Coll. Assn. Women Faculty (sec., 1972-73, pres. 1974—), Phi Theta Kappa, Pi Lambda Theta. Home: 73 Skyline Dr California PA 15419

TAITANO, MAGDALENA SANTOS (MRS. RICHARD F. TAITANO), librarian; b. Guam, July 1, 1928; d. Jose S. and Josefa (Ignacio) Santos; B.A., Mt. Marry Coll., 1955; M.L.S., Tex. Woman's U., 1959; m. Richard Flores Taitano, June 20, 1959; children—Taling Maria, Richard Flores, John Joseph, Carmen Teresita. Asst. librarian Nieves M. Flores Meml. Library, Agana, Guam, 1955, chief librarian, 1959-61, territorial librarian, 1966—, reference librarian Office Tech. Services Dept. Commerce, 1963-64; chief librarian U. Guam, 1964-66. Chmn., Nat. Library Week, 1970. Mem. Am., Guam (publicity chmn. 1968-69, vice chmn. 1971-72, chmn. 1972—) library assns., U. Wives's Club, Guam Women's Club, Exec. Wives' Club, Juvenile Conf. Com. Home: Dededo GU 96910 Office: PO Box 652 Agana GU 96910

TAKACH, EILEEN THERESE BUTKUS, research mathematician; b. Evergreen Park, Ill., Sept. 26, 1946; d. Benedict Anton Eugene and Anne Therese (Bolf) Butkus; B.S., Marian Coll., 1968; postgrad. Purdue U., 1970-71; m. John Andrew Takach, June 7, 1969. Research mathematician Naval Avionics Facility, Indpls., 1968—; tutor coll. math. Vol. Heart Fund drive, 1970-71; mem. com. Marian Coll. Alumni Fund drive, 1970-72. Mem. Math. Assn. Am., Applied Research Investment Club. Roman Catholic. Research on numerous aerodynamic simulations for digital computer, method for math. modeling large quantities of data by parametric optimization. Home: 8220 Crousore Rd Indianapolis IN 46219 Office: Naval Avionics Facility Dept 823 21st and Arlington Sts Indianapolis IN 46218

TAKAFUJI, JUNE H., lawyer; b. Honolulu, June 6, 1942; d. Charles and Akiko (Tasaki) Takafuji; B.A., U. Chgo., 1964; LL.B., U. San Francisco, 1967; m. Robert E. Lall, Jr., May 20, 1972. Admitted to Cal. bar, 1967, since practiced in San Francisco; asso. Charles Morgan, atty., 1967-72; asst. gen. counsel, asst. sec. Castle & Cooke, Inc., food co., San Francisco, 1972—. Mem. Am., San Francisco bar assns. Soroptimist (dir. San Francisco club). Home: 30 Ardendale St Daly City CA 94014 Office: 50 California St San Francisco CA 94111

TAKASAKI, MYRA MIYOKO AKIYAMA (MRS. MAURICE ISAMI TAKASAKI), savings and loan exec.; b. Lahaina, Maui, Hawaii, Apr. 13, 1930; d. Yoichi and Katsuno (Tanabe) Akiyama; grad. high sch.; m. Maurice Isami Takasaki, Nov. 8, 1958; children—Valerie, Stuart, Peter, Corinne, Naomi. Exec. v.p. 1st Financial Savs. & Loan Assn., Honolulu, 1966-67, pres., 1968—, also dir. Mem. Honolulu Police Commn., 1971-74. Mem. Japanese, Honolulu chambers commerce. Home: 92 Coelho Way Honolulu HI 96817 Office: 77 Merchant St Honolulu HI 96813

TALBERT, DOROTHY GEORGIE BURKETT, social worker; b. Rison, Ark.; d. Booker T. and Dorothy (Ragan) Burkett; A.B., Ark. State A.M. and N. Coll., 1946; M.S.W., Atlanta U., 1948; postgrad. U. Pa., 1962, Tulane U., 1965; m. Ernest Talbert, May 14, 1949; children—Ernest George, Dorothy Ernette. Caseworker child welfare services Miss. Dept. Pub. Welfare, 1948-49, Ill. Pub. Aid Commn., Chgo., 1951-53; probation counselor Family Ct. Del., 1956-58; with Del. State Dept. Pub. Welfare, Dover, 1958-71, unit supr., 1962-64, supr. licensing and day care services, 1964-67, chief program devel. Child Welfare Services, 1967-68, chief services to families and children, 1968-71; asst. dir. family services, div. social services Del. Dept. Health and Social Services, 1971—. instr. continuing edn. program U. Del., part time, 1968—. Mem. social services adv. com. Del. Adolescent Program, 1969—, bd. dirs., 1969—; mem. State Adv. Council on Alcoholism, 1972—. Mem. Nat. Assn. Social Workers, Am. Pub. Welfare Assn., N,A.A.C.P., Delta Sigma Theta. Home: 3007 W 3d St Wilmington DE 19805 Office: PO Box 309 Wilmington DE 19899

TALBOT, MARTHA LEONE THOMAS, real estate, advt. and pub. relations exec.; b. Little Rock, Oct. 13, 1926; d. David Vista and Anna Bay (Howell) Thomas; student Memphis State U., 1942-44, Draughton's Bus. Coll., 1943-45, Art Inst. Chgo., 1957-60, U. Ill., 1961-62, Prairie State Coll., 1964-65; grad. Realtors Inst. Ill., 1970; m. Allan David Talbot, Sept. 26, 1948 (div. Jan. 1969); children—Patricia Anne, Martin David. With Merrill Lynch, Pierce Fenner & Smith, 1942-46; asst. buyer Denver Dry, 1946-47; office mgr. Rainen's, Kansas City, Mo., 1948-52; part owner, treas. Integraphics, Inc., 1962-65; broker, saleswoman Park Forest Realty, 1965-69; v.p., dir. Thorn Creek Realty, 1969-71; dir. pub. relations and advt. Continental Real Estate, Inc., Chicago Heights, Ill., 1971—, asst. v.p. So. region, 1971—; partner Dillenbeck-Talbot, realtors, Park Forest South, Ill., 1972—; dir. U.S. Life Ins. Co. Ill. Instr. adult edn. real estate Prairie State Coll., 1967-70, vice chmn. real estate adv. bd.; sec. South Suburban Bd. Realtors, 1972-73. Pres. P.T.A., Westwood Jr. High Sch., 1960-61; leader Park Forest council Girl Scouts U.S., 1956-58; vice-chmn. citizens adv. com. Prairie State Coll., 1972; Park Forest area chmn. March of Dimes Found., 1972. Named Bus. Woman of the Year, Am. Bus. Women's Assn., 1969; recipient Plaque for outstanding leadership Nat. March of Dimes Found., 1970-71, citation, Prairie State Coll., 1971. Mem. Nat. Inst. Real Estate Brokers (bd. rep. 1971-72), Nat., Ill. (vice chmn. asso. div. 1969-70, state award 1971) assns. real estate bds., Real Estate Securities and Syndication Inst., Am. Bus. Women's Assn. (membership, scholarship and courtesy chmn. 1969-72, charter pres. Ill. chpt. 1969-70), League Women Voters, South Suburban Bd. Realtors (asso. dir. 1969-70, pub. relations and membership chmn. 1970-72). Club: Lincolnshire Country (Crete, Ill.). Contbr. articles to profl. jours. Home: 239 Grant St Park Forest IL 60466 Office: 850 Exchange Av Park Forest South IL 60466

TALBOT, MARTHA WALCOTT HAYNE (MRS. LEE MERRIAM TALBOT), conservationist, biologist; b. San Francisco; d. Francis Bourn and Anna Walcott Hayne Likins; B.A., Vassar Coll., 1954; m. Lee Merriam Talbot, May 16, 1959; 1 son, Lawrence Hayne. Co-founder, co-dir. student conservation program U.S. Nat. Parks Assn., Washington, 1955-59; asst. dir. East African Ecol. Research Project, U.S. Nat. Acad. Scis., N.Y. Zool. Soc., Govts. of Kenya and Tanzania, East Africa, 1959-64; asst. dir. S.E. Asia Project, Internat. Union for Conservation, various Asian countries, 1964-65; research asso. Office of Ecology, Smithsonian Instn., Washington, 1966-70, cons., 1971. Cons. Club Tours, N.Y.C., 1969—; mem. organizational staff internat. scientific and tech. confs. in Africa, Asia, U.S.; leader tour to East Africa, 1969-70. Mem. Fairfax County Park Authority, Va., 1972—. Bd. dirs. Student Conservation Assn., Inc., also sec., mem. exec. com.; bd. dirs. Defenders of Wildlife, 1974—. Mem. Soc. Women Geographers (exec. council, 1972—), Nat. Parks Assn., Vassar Alumni Assn. Co-recipient Outstanding Publs. award Wildlife Soc., 1963, Cine Golden Eagle award, 1969. Club: Sierra (San Francisco). Co-author: An Introduction to the Landscape of East Africa, 1961; The Wildebeest in Western Masailand, 1963; Renewable Natural Resources in the Philippines, 1964; Meat Production Potential of Wild Animals in Africa, 1965; Conservation of the Hong Kong Countryside, 1966. Co-editor: Conservation in Tropical South East Asia, 1968. Contbr. articles to profl. jours. Home: 6656 Chilton Ct McLean VA 22101

TALBOTT, MARY ELLEN, judge; b. Aurora, Ill., Nov. 23, 1921; d. John F. and Lucille D. (Miller) Weiss; B.S. in Econs., U. Ill., 1942; J.D., U. Pa., 1963; m. James N. Talbott, May 1, 1947 (dec. Aug. 1959); children—Jane (Mrs. Robert Reid Barbor), Mary Katherine (Mrs. James Jester), Barbara H., James N. Admitted to N.J. bar, 1963; practiced in Camden, N.J., 1963-71, Haddonfield, N.J., 1971-73; dist. ct. judge Camden County, 1973—. Pres., Camden County Mental Health Assn., 1973-74. Bd. dirs. United Way Camden County. Served with USNR, 1943-48. Mem. N.J., Camden County bar assns., Zonta Internat. Home: 324 Knoll Top Lane Haddonfield NJ 08033 Office: Room 212 Court House Camden NJ 08101

TALCOTT, RONA LYNNE (MRS. EDWARD LEE KLINENBERG), photographer, audio-visual producer; b. Chgo., Mar. 3, 1944; d. Martin and Esther Eta (Jaffe) Talcott; B.S., So. Ill. U., 1965; m. Edward Lee Klinenberg, May 13, 1967; children—Eric, Danielle. Account exec. Charles Feldstein Co., Chgo., 1969-71; partner Audio-Visual Impact Group Co., Chgo., 1971—; owner Rona Talcott Photography Co., Chgo., 1971—; dir. Precise Communications, Inc. Chgo. Bd. dirs. Chgo. Focus, Chgo. Forum of Chgo. Council on Fgn. Relations, Menomonee Club for Boys and Girls, Mary Meyer Sch. Recipient Communications award Family Service Assn. Am., 1972; Helen Cody Baker award, 1972-74; Golden Trumpet award Publicity Club Chgo., 1972, 73. Mem. Women in Communications (dir.). Home: 1758 North Park Av Chicago IL 60614 Office: 233 E Erie Chicago IL 60611

TALESE, NAN AHEARN, editor; b. N.Y.C., Dec. 19, 1933; d. Thomas James and Suzanne Sherman (Russell) Ahearn; B.A., Manhattanville Coll. of Sacred Heart, 1955; m. Gay Talese, June 10, 1959; children—Pamela Frances, Catherine Gay. Fgn. exchange student 1st Nat. City Bank, London, Eng., also Paris, France, 1956; editorial asst. Am. Eugenics Soc., N.Y.C., 1957-58; editorial asst. Vogue mag., N.Y.C., 1958-59; copy editor Random House Pubs., N.Y.C., 1959-64, asso. editor, 1964-67, sr. editor, 1967-73; sr. editor Simon & Schuster Publishers, N.Y.C., 1973—. Home: 109 E 61st St New York City NY 10021 Office: 630 Fifth Av New York City NY 10020

TALLEY, CAROLYNN (MRS. AUGUSTUS W. ANDERSON), physician; b. Dallas, Sept. 14, 1917; d. Lynn Porter and Martha (Downs) Talley; A.B., Vassar Coll., 1939; M.D., Tulane U., 1943, M.P.H., 1956; m. Augustus W. Anderson, Apr. 10, 1944 (dec. July 1948); 1 son, Robert Edward. Intern, Charity Hosp., New Orleans, 1943-44, resident pediatrics, 1944-45; practice medicine specializing in pediatrics, Hammond, La., 1948-50; fellow dept. pediatrics Tulane U. Sch. Medicine, New Orleans, 1947-48, instr., 1948-54, clin. asst. prof. pediatrics, 1954-63, clin. asso. prof. pediatrics, 1963—; dir. div. maternal and child health La. Div. Health Maintenance, New Orleans, 1951—. Diplomate Am. Bd. Pediatrics. Mem. Am. Acad. Pediatrics, La., New Orleans pediatric socs., La. Heart Assn. Contbr. articles to profl. jours. Home: 6220 Ackel St Apt 447 Metairie LA 70003 Office: La Div Health Maintenance Box 60630 New Orleans LA 70160

TALLEY, ISABEL DURON (MRS. JAMES D. TALLEY, JR.), TV journalist; b. Salinas, Cal., Apr. 14, 1947; d. Eligio and Maria Jesus (Salgado) Duron; B.A., San Jose State U., 1970; m. James D. Talley, Jr., June 3, 1972. Asst. information officer Cabinet Com. on Opportunities for Spanish Speaking, Washington, 1970; TV news writer KNXT-CBS, Los Angeles, 1970-71, KRON-NBC, San Francisco, 1971; TV news reporter intern KPIX-Westinghouse, San Francisco, 1971-72; with KTVU-COX Broadcasting, Oakland, 1972—, staff news reporter, 1973—. Minority media specialist East Oakland Devel. Center, Merritt Jr. coll., 1973—. Recipient Communications Achievement award Cal. Classroom Tchrs. Assn.,

1974; fellow Washington Journalism Center, Washington, 1970. Mem. Women in Communications, Nat. Chicano Media Coalition, Nat. Chicano Anti-Defamation Com., Cal. Raza Media Coalition. Office: 1 Jack London Sq Oakland CA 94607

TALLEY, NEVA BENNETT (MRS. J.H. MORRIS), lawyer; b. Judsonia, Ark., Aug. 12, 1909; d. John W. and Erma (Rhew) Bennett; B.A. magna cum laude, Ouachita Coll., 1930; M.Ed., U. Tex., 1938, postgrad., 1939-41; m. Cecil C. Talley, Jan. 1, 1946 (dec. Oct. 1948); m. 2d, Joseph H. Morris, Mar. 22, 1952. Tchr. high sch., prin. White County, Ark., 1930-42; student asst. U. Tex., summers, 1937-41; ordnance insp. war service appointment U.S. Army Service Forces, 1942-45; law office apprentice, pvt. tutorship, North Little Rock, Ark., 1945-47; admitted to Ark. bar., 1947, pvt. practice in Little Rock. Chmn. Ark. Council of Children and Youth, 1952-54. Pres., Nat. Women Lawyers Assn., 1956-57; Recipient ann. award Nat. Assn. Women Lawyers, 1962; distinguished service award Ark. Bar Assn., 1970. Fellow Am. Acad. Matrimonial Lawyers (gov. 1971—); mem. Nat. (life, council del., pres. 1956-57, hon. chmn. family law com. 1970-71), Little Rock (pres. 1950-51) assns. women lawyers, North Little Rock Bus. and Profl. Women's Club (pres. 1951-52), Am. Assn. U. Women (life mem.), Am. (mem. family law council 1958—, chmn. family law sect. 1969-70, mem. ho. of dels. 1970—), Ark. (chmn. family law reform com. 1960-61, U.P.L. coms., 1966-70, ho. of dels. 1973—), Pulaski County bar assns., Am. Judicature Soc., Nat. Conf. Lawyers and Social Workers (mem. nat. exec. bd. 1962-66), Delta Kappa Gamma, Phi Alpha Delta. Author: Family Law Practice and Procedure Handbook, 1973; Appellate Civil Practice and Procedure Handbook. Contbr. articles to profl. publs. Home: 101 N State St Little Rock AR 72201 Office: 722 W Markham St Little Rock AR 72201

TALLEY, RUTH GENTRY, lawyer; b. Bogalusa, La., Aug. 27, 1921; d. Bascom Destrehan and Maude H. (Gentry) Talley; B.A., Hollins Coll., 1942; J.D., La. State U., 1953; postgrad. Tulane U., 1942-43. Admitted to La. bar, 1953, since practiced in Bogalusa; jr. partner law firm Talley, Anthony, Hughes and Knight, Bogalusa, 1959—. Asst. sec. Columbia Rd. Land Co., Bogalusa, 1957—, dir., 1956—; dir. Parish Nat. Bank Bogalusa. Mem. La. Commn. on Status of Women. Mem. Am. Judicature Soc., Am. (mem. council of family law sect. 1970-74), La., Washington Parish bar assns., Nat. Assn. Women Lawyers (pres. 1968-69), Phi Alpha Delta. United Methodist. Home: 922 Mississippi Av Bogalusa LA 70427 Office: 322 Columbia St Bogalusa LA 70427

TALLMAN, JOHANNA ELEONORE ALLERDING (MRS. LLOYD A. TALLMAN), librarian; b. Lubeck, Germany, Aug. 18, 1914 (father Am. citizen); d. Friedrich Franz and Johanna (Voget) Allerding; A.A., Los Angeles Jr. Coll., 1934; A.B., U. Cal. at Berkeley, 1936, certificate in librarianship, 1937; m. Lloyd A. Tallman, May 8, 1954. Asst. librarian San Marino (Cal.) Pub. Library, 1937-38; various positions Los Angeles County Pub. Library, 1938-40, tech. reference librarian, 1940-42; asst. librarian Pacific Aero. Library, Hollywood, Cal., 1942-43, head librarian, 1943-44; librarian Engring. and Math. Scis. Library, U. Cal. at Los Angeles, 1945-73, coordinator phys. scis. libraries, 1962-73; faculty Sch. Library Service, 1961-73; dir. libraries Cal. Inst. Tech., Pasadena, 1973—. Dir. re-cataloging project U.S. Naval Ordnance test Sta. Library, China Lake, Cal., 1951; cons. to indsl., research, ednl. instns.; chmn. com. Civil Service Examining Bd., Los Angeles; mem. trade adv. com. for library assts. Los Angeles Trade Tech. Coll., 1958-73; Fulbright lectr. on sci. documentation, Brazil, 1966-67. Mem. A.L.A. (chmn. engring. sch. libraries sect. 1949-50), Cal. Library Assn. (chmn. coll., univ. and research libraries sect. So. dist. 1954), Spl. Libraries Assn. (joint compiler subject headings for aero. engring. libraries N.Y. 1949, pres. So. Cal. chpt. 1965-66, chmn. sci.-tech. div. 1969-70), Librarians Assn. U. Cal. (pres. 1971). Contbr. articles to profl. jours. Home: 4731 Daleridge Rd LaCanada CA 91011

TALMAGE, HARRIET (MRS. HARRY TALMAGE), educator; b. Chgo., May 11, 1923; d. Nathan and Lucy (Hurwitz) Talmage; A.B., U. Chgo., 1945; M.A., U. Wis., 1947; Ph.D., Northwestern U., 1967; m. Harry Talmage, Dec. 15, 1948; children—Gita, Roberta. Instr. Barron County (Wis.) Normal Sch., 1946-47; field dir. Chgo. area Camp Fire Girls, 1949-52; jr. high sch. tchr., Maywood, Ill., 1958-65; prof. edn., asso. Office of Evaluation Research, U. Ill. at Chgo. Circle, 1966—; cons. to sch. dists. on in service tng., tchr. evaluation, curriculum evaluation, research design. Recipient Silver Circle award for excellence in teaching, U. Ill., 1969. 5th Cycle Tchrs. Corps Project grantee 1970-72; Bur. Research of Office Edn. grantee, 1969; NSF grantee, 1974-75. Mem. Am. Ednl. Research Assn., Nat. Soc. for Study of Edn. (commn. on extended publs.), Profs. Curriculum. Contbr. articles profl. jours. Home: 1011 N Hayes St Oak Park IL 60302 Office: Box 4348 Chicago IL 60680

TALMEY, ALLENE, editor, writer; b. Boston; d. George and Rosa (Broad) Talmey; B.A., Wellesley Coll., 1924; m. Richard L. Plaut, Dec. 13, 1927; 1 son, Richard L. Reporter, feature writer, columnist N.Y. Morning World, 1924-27, feature writer Evening World, 1927-28; movie critic Time mag., 1929-30; asso. editor Stage mag., 1932-35; mng. editor Vanity Fair, 1935-36; feature editor Vogue, 1936-50, sr. editor, 1950-63; asso. editor, 1963-71, contbg. editor, 1972—, book reviewer, 1973—, columnist on politics and econs., 1974—. Former mem. jury Albert Lasker awards in med. journalism. Author: Doug and Mary and Others, 1927; also profiles and articles in mags. Editor: People Are Talking About...People and Things in Vogue, 1969. Home: 975 Park Av New York City NY 10028 Office: 350 Madison Av New York City NY 10017

TAMBURINE, JEAN HELEN (MRS. EUGENE BERTOLLI), artist, author; b. Meriden, Conn., Feb. 20, 1930; d. Paul Daniel and Helen Martha (Marks) Tamburine; student Art Student's League, N.Y.C., 1948-50, Traphagen Sch. Fashion, N.Y.C., 1948-49; m. Eugene E. Bertolli, Apr. 21, 1956; children—E. Robert, Lisa Marie. Designer, Norcross, Inc., N.Y., 1948-50, Rust Craft, Dedham, Mass., 1955-57; free-lance artist, painting portraits, landscapes, still lifes, 1950—; exhibited in one-woman shows Meriden Pub. Library, Town & County Club, Hartford, Conn., also group shows; represented in pvt. collections. Lectr. drawing talks in Eastern areas. Mem. Conn. Commn. Arts; chmn. arts appts. City of Meriden, 1966-74. Mem. Allied Artists of Am., Women's Nat. Book Assn., Soc. Children's Book Writers, Author's Guild, Inc., Internat. Platform Assn. Clubs: Women's; Zonta. Author, designer, illustrator: Almost Big Enough, 1963; I Think I Will Go to the Hospital, 1965; Who Wants Willy Wells, 1965; illustrator: It's Nice To Be Little, 1965; The Complete Peddler's Pack (May Justus), 1966; See Me Grow (Mary Sue White), 1966; 5 Busy Bears (Sterling North); Smoky Mountain Sampler (May Justus); How Now Brown Cow, 1967; Something Was Missing (Helen Guittard), 1969. Home: 73 Reynolds Dr Meriden CT 06450

TANCEK, ANNA EVELYN, physician; b. Cleve.; d. Frank and Barbara (Heisz) Tancek; A.B., Flora Stone Mather Coll., 1917; M.D., Case Western Res. U., 1931. Tchr. langs. and Americanization work, Cleve., 1913-25; with Standard Oil Co., Cleve., 1918, U.S. Army Ordnance, 1919; appraiser Hydraulic Pressed Steel Co., Cleve., 1919; tchr. high sch., Cleve., 1920-25; intern Womans Hosp., Cleve., 1931-32; practice medicine, Cleve., 1932-67; clinic physician Pub. Health, Pediatrics, Cleve., 1959-71; indsl. physician Kinsman Accident Clinic, Cleve., 1971-72; pvt. practice, 1972—. Fellow Royal Soc. Health. Home: 1618 Newman Av Lakewood OH 44107

TANCIN, CHARLOTTE ELIZABETH (MRS. STEPHEN TANCIN), health service supr., educator; b. Newark, Mar. 7, 1925; d. Gerrit Lawrence and Anna Catherine (Wolfe) de Vries; grad. St. James Hosp. Sch. Nursing, 1946; student Pa. State U., 1966-73, Bloomsburg State Coll., 1973-74; m. Stephen Tancin, Aug. 3, 1946; children—Charlotte Ann, Stephen. Nurse pvt. duty Hazleton, Pa., 1948-64; psychiat. nurse White Haven (Pa.) State Sch. and Hosp., 1964-69, also head nurse, 1966-69, supr. pediatric ward, 1969-70, supr. adult non-ambulatory unit, 1970-71, clin. instr. nursing edn., 1971—. Pres. Mining and Mech. Inst. Aux., 1970-73. Mem. Am., Pa. (treas. 1973-74) nurses assns., Am. Assn. Mental Deficiency, Luzerne County Assn. for Retarded Children (mem. N.Am. com. on services for deaf-blind children and youth 1972—), St. Mary's Parent Tchrs. Guild (pres. 1962-63). Democrat. Roman Catholic. Home: 1020 Carbon St Freeland PA 18224 Office: White Haven State School and Hospital White Haven PA 18661

TANCZAK-DYCIO, MARY, physician; b. Rybnyky, Ukraine, July 10, 1922; d. Basil and Helen (Cisyk) Tanczak; student U. Lviv, 1940-41, Med. Sch., 1942-44, U. Erlangen (Germany), 1945-49; m. George Dycio, Nov. 11, 1949; children—George Myron, Mark Roman. Came to U.S., 1950, naturalized, 1955. Resident Contagious Disease Hosp., Belleville, N.J., 1951-52; intern Mercy Hosp., Canton, O., 1952-53, resident anesthesia, 1952-55; practice medicine specializing in anesthesiology, 1955-58; mem. staffs Irvington (N.J.) Gen. Hosp., 1955-58; staff St. Mary's Gen. Hosp., Lewiston, Me., 1958—, chief anesthesia dept., 1960—, chief inhalation therapy dept., 1966. Fellow Am. Coll. Anesthesiologists; mem. A.M.A., Am.-Ukrainian, Me., Androscoggin County med. socs., Am., Me. socs. Office: 300 Pine St Lewiston ME 04240 also 3 Bayberry Lane Lewiston ME 04240

TANENBAUM, HELGA WEISS, clin. psychologist; b. Cologne, Germany; d. Harry S. and Henriette (Heymann) Weiss; B.A., City U. N.Y., 1951; M.A., Columbia, 1953; postgrad. St. John's U., 1973—; m. Marc Herman Tanenbaum, May 22, 1955; children—Adena, Michael, Susan. Tchr., Yonkers (N.Y.) Elementary Sch., 1951-52, N.Y.C., 1952-53; psychologist Bur. Child Guidance, N.Y.C., 1954-55; clin. psychologist Queens Coll. Ednl. Clinic, Flushing, N.Y., 1955-58, Retarded Infants' Service, N.Y.C., 1967, Roosevelt Hosp., N.Y.C., 1970-71; psychotherapist Jamaica (N.Y.) Center Psychotherapy, 1972—. Script writer, actress TV show "4thR" sta. WNBC, 1954-55; Active parents' groups UN Internat. Sch., 1970—. Mem. Am., N.Y. State psychol. assns., Phi Beta Kappa, Pi Lambda Theta, Alpha Chi Alpha, Kappa Delta Pi. Home: 33-15 80th St Jackson Heights NY 11372

TANENBAUM, LESLIE BLACK (MRS. GEORGE G. TANENBAUM), journalist; b. Sterling, Kan.; d. William and Clara (Snyder) Black; B.S., Kan. State U., 1948, M.S., 1949; m. George G. Tanenbaum, June 28, 1952 (dec. Aug. 1954). Writer-editor Seaton Publs., Manhattan, Kan., 1947-49, Capper Publs., Topeka, Kan., 1950-51; asst. publs: dir. N.D. State U., 1951-52; publs. editor U.S. Dept. Agr., Beltsville, Md., 1957-63, tech. editor biol. scis., 1963-72, nat. tech. editor, 1972—. Bd. dirs. World Wide Baraca Philathea Union, pres., 1969-71. Mem. Soc. Tech. Writers and Publs., Fed. Editors Assn., Nat. League Am. Pen Women, V.F.W. Aux., D.A.V. Aux., Am. Legion Aux., Women in Communications (treas. nat. capital chpt. 1965-67), Phi Kappa Phi. Mem. Christian Ch. Mem. Order Eastern Star. Club: Nat. Press. Home: Box 7395 Washington DC 20044 Office: 131-No-P ARS Agrl Research Center Beltsville MD 20705

TANGRI, SANDRA SCHWARTZ, psychologist; b. St. Louis, Aug. 27, 1936; d. Hyman and Ruth B. (Levine) Schwartz; B.A., U. Cal., Berkeley, 1961; M.A., Wayne State U., 1964; Ph.D., U. Mich., 1969. Tchr. sociology and psychology depts. U. Mich., Douglass Coll. Rutgers U. and Richmond Coll. City U. N.Y.; now dir. research U.S. Commn. on Civil Rights, Washington. Cons., Am. Psychol. Assn., Nat. Inst. Edn., NIH. Recipient Labor Dept. postdoctoral grant. NIH fellow, Ford Found. fellow in population. Mem. Am. Psychol. Assn., Soc. for Psychol. Study Social Issues, Nat. Orgn. Women, Assn. for Women in Psychology, A.C.L.U. Contbr. articles to profl. jours. Mem. editorial bd. Jour. Psychology of Women. Home: 6211 E Halbert St Bethesda MD 20034 Office: US Commn on Civil Rights Washington DC

TANK, CYNTHIA LORAINE, ednl. adminstr.; b. Detroit, Sept. 1, 1948; d. Robert Genrich and Bernice Lois (Honold) Tank; B.A., Valparaiso U., 1970; postgrad. Ball State U., 1970-71. Asst. to dir. Valparaiso (Ind.) U. News Bur., 1968-70; grad. asst. Ball State U., Muncie, Ind., 1970-71; gen. reporter Banning (Cal.) Record Gazette, 1971-72, city editor, 1972; dir. news services U. Redlands (Cal.), 1972—. County reporter San Bernardino (Cal.) Sun Telegram, 1972—. Mem. Am. Coll. Pub. Relations Assn., Soc. Profl. Journalists (chpt. sec. 1974-75), Alpha Phi Gamma, Theta Sigma Phi. Democrat. Home: 132 B N 4th St Banning CA 92220 Office: 1200 E Colton Av Redlands CA 92373

TANNEHILL, COURTNEY RHEA (MRS. JACK LONG TANNEHILL), publisher; b. Pulaski, Tenn., Nov. 15, 9121; d. David Rankin and Vernon Louise (Porter) Rhea; B.A., George Peabody Coll., 1943; M.A., Miss. State U., 1973; m. Jack Long Tannehill, Jan. 14, 1944; 1 son, Jack Rhea. Tchr., art supr. St. Tammany Parish, La., 1950-54; asso. editor Neshoba Democrat Pub. Co., Philadelphia, Miss., 1954-66; asso. editor The Appeal Pub. Co., Inc., Union, Miss., 1967-68, pub., 1968—, also dir. Librarian Newton County (Miss.) Schs., 1972—. Bd. dirs. Neshoba County Fair Assn., Inc., 1968—. Mem. Nat. (award 1959, 1960, 1968), Miss. (v.p. 1962-64) press women, Bus. and Profl. Women (pres. 1962). Home: PO Box 207 Philadelphia MS 39350 Office: 105 Main St Union MS 39365

TANNER, ANNE STEARNS (MRS. P. HANS TANNER), editor; b. Grand Rapids, Mich., Dec. 29, 1938; d. William F. and M. Leora (Cornell) Stearns; B.A. with honors, U. Ia., 1961; postgrad. Pa. State U., 1962-64; m. P. Hans Tanner, Nov. 11, 1967; With Gannett Co., Inc., Rochester, N.Y., 1964—, copy editor, 1970-74, asst. met. editor, 1974—. Recipient award N.Y. State Bar Assn., 1967. Mem. Women in Communications, Nat. Newspaper Guild (dir. Rochester chpt. 1967-68), P.E.O. Home: 5990 Groveland Hill Rd Geneseo NY 14454 Office: 55 Exchange St Rochester NY 14614

TANNER, CLARA LEE (MRS. JOHN FREDERICK TANNER), educator; b. Biscoe, N.C., May 28, 1905; d. Joseph Conrad and Clara Dargon (Lee) Fraps; B.A., U. Ariz., 1927, M.A., 1928; postgrad. Nat. U. Mexico, Mexico City, 1929, U. Chgo., 1934; m. John Frederick Tanner, Jan. 22, 1936; 1 dau., Sandra Lee (Mrs. Karl Emerson Elers). Instr. dept. anthropology U. Ariz., Tucson, 1928-35, asst. prof., 1935-57, asso. prof., 1957-68, prof., 1968—. Asst. prof. U. Denver, summer 1949. Judge, Indian Art Shows. Fellow Am. Anthrop. Assn.; mem. Soc. for Am. Archeology, Am. Ethnol. Soc., Ariz. Acad. Sci., Ariz. Press Women, Nat. Fedn. Press Women, Sigma Xi, Delta Kappa Gamma, Theta Sigma Phi. Author: Southwest Indian Painting, 1957; Southwest Indian Craft Arts, 1968; Southwest Indian Painting, A Changing Art, 1973. Contbr. articles to profl. jours. Home: PO Box 4606 Tucson AZ 85717

TANOUS, HELENE MARY, physician; b. Zanesville, O., Oct. 22, 1939; d. Joseph Carrington and Rose Marie (Mokarzel) Tanous; B.A., Marymount Coll., 1961; M.D., U. Tex., 1967. Intern County Hosp., Los Angeles, 1967-68; resident in radiology U. So. Cal. Hosp., Los Angeles, 1969-72; instr. radiology U. So. Cal. Med. Sch., Los Angeles, 1972-73; practice medicine specializing in radiology Los Angeles, 1972-73; asst. prof. diagnostic radiology Baylor Med. Sch., Houston, 1973—; dir. med. student elective in diagnostic radiology Ben Taub Hosp., Houston, 1973—. Diplomate Am. Bd. Radiology. Mem. Am. Med. Women's Assn. (del. to Internat. Med. Women's Assn., Paris). Home: 15 Park Av New York City NY 10016 Office: Dept Radiology Baylor Med Coll Med Center Houston TX 77025

TANSER, CATHERINE LYDIA, physician; b. Shawville, Que., Can., Jan. 24, 1933; d. Jacob Hamilton and Phyllis Helen (Cavill) Weaver; grad. lab. technologist; M.D., U. Ottawa, 1967; m. Paul Harry Tanser, Sept. 1, 1962; children—Christopher Paul John, Carl Rodney Harry. Intern Royal Victoria Hosp., Montreal, Que., 1967-68; clin. and research in hematology, 1968-71; practice gen. medicine, 1971-72; resident Royal Victoria Hosp.-McGill U., Montreal, 1973-74, attending staff, 1974-75. Kaufmann scholar, 1971. Contbr. articles to med jours. Office: Royal Victoria Hosp Pine Av Montreal PQ 112 Canada

TANTAQUIDGEON, GLADYS IOLA, mus. curator; b. New London, Conn., June 15, 1899; d. John W. and Harreit W. (Fielding) Tantaquidgeon; student U. Pa., 1923-27. Community worker Sioux area Bur. Indian Affairs, 1934-37; specialist in Indian arts and crafts No. Plains area Interior Dept., 1938-45; co-owner, curator Tantaquidgeon Indian Mus., Uncasville, Conn., 1931—. Mem. Conn. Archaeol. Soc., Delta Kappa Gamma. Conglist. (trustee 1970). Contbr. material to profl. lit. Address: 1819 Norwich-New London Turnpike Uncasville CT 06382

TANZMAN, MARY (MRS. JACK TANZMAN), social worker; b. Bialystok, Poland, Sept. 29, 1915; d. Jacob and Bertha (Cohen) Grodman; came to U.S., 1920, naturalized, 1921; B.A. in Social Work, Wayne U., 1939; M.A., U. Chgo., 1964; m. Jack Tanzman, Feb. 22, 1942; children—Elaine, Edward. Social worker, dist. supr. Jewish Family and Community Service, Chgo., 1942-49, 55-61; dir. social work marital dept. Forest Hosp., Des Plaines, Ill., 1959-64; pvt. practice with ind., family and marital problems, Chgo., 1955—, Evanston, Ill., 1964—. Condr. tng. programs in marital, family and group therapy; lectr., tchr. schs. and community agys. Mem. Transactional Analysis Inst., Am. Assn. Marriage and Family Counselors, Nat. Assn. Social Workers, Am. Orthopsychiat. Assn. Home: 1103 Seward Evanston IL 60202 Office: 55 E Washington St Chicago IL 60602

TAPLEY, FRANCES PORTER PRATT (MRS. GEORGE OTIS TAPLEY), civic worker, ret. educator; b. Rogers Park, Ill., May 8, 1908; d. George Erskine and Martha Pearl (Porter) Pratt; grad. in piano New Eng. Conservatory Music, 1931, Mus.B., 1946, postgrad., 1960; m. George Otis Tapley, Apr. 22, 1951. Supr. music elementary schs., Leominster, Mass., 1935-55, dir. elementary sch. music program, 1955-73; piano instr. Wheelock Coll., Boston, 1937-55, also lectr.; lectr. Boston U., Fitchburg State Coll., 1937—. Co-founder Sterling Hist. Soc., 1963, trustee, 1963—, clk., 1963-64, curator, 1965—; mem. program com. Leominster (Mass.) Hist. Soc., 1967-68, hist. events com. City Leominster Twin anniversary Year, 1965; chmn. Sterling Hist. Commn., 1968—; chmn. Sterling Bicentennial Com., 1973—. Mem. D.A.R. (state chmn. Am. Heritage com. 1965-68, state organizing sec. 1968-71, state chmn. membership com. 1971-74, mem. state bylaws com. 1971-73, state registrar 1974—), Daus. Founders and Patriots, Daus. Am. Colonists (state registrar 1970—), Children Am. Revolution (state lineage com. 1968-71, sr. state registrar 1970-73, sr. state chmn. music com. 1973-74, sr. state membership com. 1974—), Soc. Mayflower Descs., Daus. Colonial Wars, New Eng. Hist.-Geneal. Soc., Mu Phi Epsilon, Delta Kappa Gamma. Home: 5 North Row Sterling Box 206 Rural Route Lancaster MA 01523

TAPPAN, MARY ELLEN, advt. exec.; b. Port Huron, Mich., Apr. 8, 1922; d. Bruce Nicholas and Verna (Derck) T.; B.A., Mich. State U., 1944. Art apprentice Florez, Inc., Detroit, 1944-45; art traffic J. Walter Thompson Co., Detroit, 1945-47, asst. traffic and prodn. mgr., 1947-51; prodn. editor PS mag., Aberdeen Proving Grounds, Md., 1952-54; traffic mgr. Grant Advt., Inc., Detroit, 1955-60; traffic mgr. Batten, Barton, Durstine & Osborn, Inc., Detroit, 1960-62, supr., budget control and billing, 1962-68, office mgr., 1968—. Mem. Founders Soc. Detroit Inst. Arts. Mem. Women's Advt. Club Detroit (dir. 1964-70, treas. 1964-65, v.p. 1965-67 pres. 1967-69, named Detroit Advt. Woman of Year 1972), Women's Econ. Club Detroit (dir. 1970-72, pres. 1973-74), Detroit Hist. Soc., Photog. Soc. Am., Alpha Phi. Mem. Christ Ch. Club: Grosse Pointe Camera (asso. 1968, dir. 1964-66, 67-69, sec. 1964-65, 67-68). Home: 8 Alger Pl Grosse Pointe MI 48230 Office: 211 W Fort Detroit MI 48226

TARANTOLA, CHARLSIE LOVELL (MRS. MICHAEL NICHOLAS TARANTOLA), educator; b. Weatherford, Tex., Aug. 16, 1920; d. James Thomas and Pauline (Harris) Bradshaw; B.S., Smith Hughes, 1945; postgrad. George Washington U., U. Va., Am. U. Washington, Trenton State Tchrs. Coll., North Tex. State U.; M.S. in Edn., Va. Poly. Inst., 1973; m. Michael Nicholas Tarantola, June 3, 1944; children—Michael Roy, John Terry. Tchr., Muenster (Tex.) Pub. Schs., 1941-43, Breckenridge (Tex.) Pub. Schs., 1945, Farwell (Tex.) Pub. Sch., 1947, Sasebo (Japan) Am. Sch., 1948-49; adult ednl. instr. TI & E Div., Gelenhausen, Germany, 1954; elementary tchr. Gelenhausen Am. Sch., 1952-54, Pemberton (N.J.) Twp., 1954-57, Fort Myer (Va.) Elementary Sch., 1957-65; sci. tchr. Oakridge Elementary Sch., Arlington, Va., 1965-72, Thomas Jefferson Jr. High Sch., Arlington, 1972—. Mem. Assn. for Supervision and Curriculum Devel., Nat., Va., Arlington edn. assns., Nat. Sci. Tchrs. Assn., Delta Kappa Gamma. Roman Catholic. Home: 515 N Longfellow St Arlington VA 22203

TARBOX, CHRISTINA KAY (MRS. FREDERICK CHARLES TARBOX), data processor; b. Cleve., Sept. 7, 1942; d. Stanley Joseph and Mary Agnes (Patena) Kay; B.S. in Math. (W.S. Richardson scholar, Lindsay scholar), Case Inst. Tech., 1964; M.S. in Exptl. Statistics, N.C. State U., 1966; m. Frederick Charles Tarbox, Nov. 28, 1964. Jr. programmer IBM, Owega, N.Y., 1964; programmer Battelle Meml. Inst. Columbus, O., 1964-65, N.C. State U., Raleigh, 1966; mathematician Chemstrand Research Triangle Park, N.C., 1967-68; systems analyst Hydra Computer Corp., Raleigh, 1968—. Sponsor Indsl. Co-op Tng. Enloe High Sch., Raleigh, 1970-71. Mem. Am. Statis. Assn., Data Processing Mgmt. Assn., Assn. for Computing Machinery. Mem. Christian Ch. Republican. Home: 300 Cedar Crest Court Raleigh NC 27609 Office: PO Box 17883 Raleigh NC 27609

TARBOX, RUTH WADDELL, library cons.; b. Mellen, Wis., Oct. 16, 1911; d. Reuben Lathrop and Goldie (Dunn) Tarbox; B.A., Northland Coll., 1932; B.S. in L.S., U. Minn., 1941. High sch. tchr. Drummond, Wis., 1932-33, Shell Lake, Wis., 1932-35; librarian Roosevelt Sch., McKinley Sch., Wauwatosa, Wis., 1935-40, 41-42, Roxboro Jr. High Sch., Cleveland Heights, O., 1942-43; dir. work with children Pub. and Sch. Libraries, River Forest, Ill., 1943-46; dir. sch. and library service Field Enterprises Ednl. Corp., Chgo., 1946-65; exec. sec. children's and young adult services divs. A.L.A., Chgo., 1966-73; library cons., 1974—. Mem. Chgo. bd. UNICEF, 1967—, Chgo. bd. Reading is Fundamental, 1972—. Mem. A.L.A., Women's Nat. Book Assn. (bd. Chgo. chpt. 1968-70), Beta Phi Mu. Address: 1360 Lake Shore Dr Chicago IL 60610

TARCHER, MARY BRAGER (MRS. JACK D. TARCHER), lawyer; b. Vilna, Russia; d. Joseph and Cecelia (Deutsch) Brager; B.S., N.Y.U., 1928, LL.B., 1938; M.A., Columbia, 1933; m. Jack D. Tarcher, Oct. 27, 1924; children—Judith (Mrs. Stephen F. Krantz), Miriam (Mrs. Jacques G. Brien), Jeremy. Admitted to N.Y. bar, 1938; asso. N.Y.C. Legal Aid Soc., 1938—, atty.-in-charge main office and asst. atty.-in-chief, 1957—; treas. J. D. Tarcher & Co., advt. agy., 1946-52. Bd. dirs. United Jewish Appeal, United Hias Service. Mem. Assn. Bar City N.Y., N.Y. County Lawyers. Home: 475 Park Av New York City NY 10022 Office: 11 Park Pl New York City NY 10007

TARGAN, JUDY, artist; b. N.Y.C., Oct. 12, 1931; d. Benjamin Harrison and Evelyn (Schlessinger) Plesser; B.A. magna cum laude, Smith Coll., 1953; postgrad. Rutgers U., 1955, Fairleigh Dickenson U., 1956-60; m. Ronald George Targan, Feb. 14, 1954; children—Amy Beth, Adam Joseph. Eight one-woman shows N.J. art galleries, 1966-73; exhibited in numerous group shows including N.J. State Mus. at Trenton, Boston Mus. Fine arts, Audubon Artists, N.Y.C., Morris (N.J.) Mus. Arts and Scis., Newark Pub. Library, Painters and Sculptors Soc., Hunterdon Art Center, Monmouth Coll., Brewster Gallery, N.Y.C.; prints included traveling exhbns., U.S. and Europe; represented in permanent collections Newark Mus., also pvt. collections U.S., Europe and Japan. Recipient numerous award including Purchase prize Newark Mus., 1970, Theme award Rochester (N.Y.) Festival Religious Art, 1971, Best in Show, Summit (N.J.) Art Center, 1970, Rubi Roth award Nat. Assn. Women Artist, 1970, 1st prize Art Gallery South Orange and Maplewood, N.J., 1969-71, 1st prize N.J. Council Arts, 1971. Mem. Atelier 3 (co-founder graphic workshop), Artists Equity N.J., Nat. Assn. Women Artists, Print Club Phila., Summit Art Center, Phi Beta Kappa. Home: 40 Glenside Rd South Orange NJ 07079 Office: Atelier 3 Maplewood NJ 07040

TARGOVNIK, SELMA E. KAPLAN, physician; b. N.Y.C., Apr. 22, 1936; d. Harry A. and Helen (Goodstein) Kaplan; B.A., N.Y.U., 1957; M.D., Albert Einstein Coll. Medicine, 1961; m. Jerome H. Targovnik, Dec. 2, 1961; children—Nina Rebecca, Labe Eric, Diane Michelle. Intern, Kaiser Found. Hosp., San Francisco, 1961-62; tng. internal medicine Bellevue Hosp.-N.Y.U. Med. Center, 1962-63 U. Colo. Med. Center, Denver, 1963-64; tng. dermatology Boston U. Med. Center, 1964-66; practice medicine, specializing in dermatology, Flushing, N.Y., 1966-68, Brookline, Mass., 1968-69, Phoenix, 1969—; spl. research fellow Boston U. Med. Center, 1968-69; mem. staff St. Joseph's Good Samaritan, Doctor's, St. Luke's hosps.; chief div. dermatology Maricopa County Gen. Hosp., Phoenix. Diplomate Am. Bd. Dermatology. Fellow Am. Acad. Dermatology; mem. Dermatology Found., Sonora, Southwestern dermatologic socs., Pacific Dermatologic Assn., Eclectic, Caducean Soc., Am. Civil Liberties Union (dir. Ariz. chpt., Central Ariz. chpt.), Phi Beta Kappa, Beta Lambda Sigma, Mu Chi Sigma, Pi Delta Phi. Jewish religion (dir. temple). Home: 51 E Hayward Av Phoenix AZ 85020 Office: 909 E Brill St Phoenix AZ 85006

TAROWSKY, MARY JUDITH (MRS. THOMAS JOSEPH TAROWSKY), journalist; b. Latrobe, Pa., Oct. 27, 1949; d. Guy Bayard and Mary Grace (Mullen) Young; B.S. in Journalism, W. Va. U., 1971; m. Thomas Joseph Tarowsky, June 20, 1970. Account exec. WEIR, Weirton, W. Va., 1971-72; reporter The Intelligencer, Wheeling, W. Va., 1972; news reporter Weirton Bur., Steubenville, O., 1972—. Mem. Women in Communications, Nat. Orgn. for Women (sec. Ohio chpt. 1972—). Home: 3700 Brightway St Weirton WV 26062 Office: Sinclair Bldg Steubenville OH 43952

TARPLEY, PATRICIA ANN GAY, ednl. adminstr.; b. San Antonio, Oct. 26, 1935; d. Charles Thomas and Ida Helen (Blackburn) Gay; A.A., Del Mar Coll., 1955; B.S., Trinity U., 1957; m. Ernest Davis Tarpley, June 29, 1957 (div. Apr. 1968); 1 dau., Deborah Gay. Sec. bus. office Del Mar Coll., 1958-61, sr. sec. to controller, 1968-69, dir. financial aid and placement, 1969—. Mem. Hinson-Hazelwood Coll. Student Loan Adv. Com., 1973; rev. panel mem. Dept. Health, Edn. and Welfare regional office, 1971-72. Mem. Nat. (com. on certification 1972—), Tex. (newsletter editor 1972-73, rec. sec. 1970-72), Southwest (exec. com. 1972-73) assns. student financial aid adminstrs., Alumni Council Trinity U., Order of Rainbow for Girls. Episcopalian (v.p. women All Saints Ch. 1964). Home: 4821 French St Corpus Christi TX 78411 Office: Baldwin & Ayers Corpus Christi TX 78404

TARRANTS, MARY ELIZABETH HOUSE (MRS. GENE TARRANTS), physicist; b. Lewistown, O., July 29, 1918; d. Olaf C. and Claribel (Philips) House; B.A., Ohio State U., 1940; postgrad. U. Cin., 1943, Boston Coll., 1957, Air Force Inst. Tech., 1958-59, Mass. Inst. Tech., 1969; m. Gene Tarrants, July 9, 1955. Tech. sec. William S. Merrell Co., Cin., 1940-41; chemist, bacteriologist Kroger Food Found., Cin., 1941-44; analytical chemist Ohio State U. Research Found., 1945-51; chemist electronic tech. lab. USAF, Wright-Patterson AFB, O., 1954-61, physicist avionics lab., 1961-67, physicist materials lab., 1967—. Mem. Electrochem. Soc., Soc. Women Engrs., Am. Inst. Mining, Metall. and Petroleum Engrs., Research Soc. Am., Dayton Execs. Club. Club: Soroptimist (past pres. Dayton). Home: 2747 Ater Dr Xenia OH 45385 Office: Air Force Materials Lab Wright-Patterson AFB OH 45433

TARS, SANDRA EMILIE, clin. psychologist; b. Westfield, Mass., June 20, 1944; d. Martin and Emilie Helen (Pietrowski) Eidinger; B.A. magna cum laude, Cornell U., 1966; Ph.D., U. Mich., 1972; m. Arvo Tars, June 24, 1967. Asst. project dir., then research investigator Inst. Gerontology, U. Mich., Ann Arbor, 1971-73, lectr. psychology, 1972-73; asso. psychologist Hutchings Psychiat. Center, Syracuse, N.Y., 1973—; instr. psychiatry Upstate Med. Center, State U. N.Y. at Syracuse, 1973—. Mem. Nat. Council Aging, 1973—. USPHS trainee, 1966-68; Vocational Rehab. Adminstrn. trainee, 1966. Mem. Am. Psychol. Assn., Assn. Women in Psychology, Gerontol. Soc., Phi Beta Kappa, Psi Chi. Contbr. articles to profl. jours. Home: 202 Byron Rd Fayetteville NY 13066 Office: Hutchings Psychiat Center 650 Madison St Syracuse NY 13210

TARTOUE, CASSIE EUGENIA (MRS. PIERRE TARTOUE), ins. co. exec., poet; b. Buffalo, Okla., June 9, 1931; d. Earl I. and Emily E. (Rogers) Dixson; student Panhandle A. and M. Coll., 1950-51, Northwestern State Coll., Okla., 1951-52; m. Pierre Tartoue, Oct. 9, 1961 (dec.). Sec. claims disbursements Standard Life Ins. Co., Oklahoma City, 1959-66; policy writer Hartford Ins. Co., Oklahoma City, 1966-72. Recipient Critics and Editors award Midwest Chaparral, 1966; award for peace and brotherhood through poetry Poetry Assn., 1967. Mem. Internat. Platform Assn., Okla. Writers Assn., Cath. Poetry Soc. Am., Ida. Poets and Writers Guild, Legion of Mary. Roman Catholic. Author: (poetry) These Things of Beauty, 1966; Reflections, 1966; Poetic Ponderings, 1967; This Gift of Love, 1967; Silhouette of the Heart, 1968; Silver Etchings, 1968; Fragments, 1969; Old Crystal-New Wine, 1971; Silver Etchings; Gypsy Shadows, 1972; (Cookbook) Palette and Palate, 1972. Address: Apt 311 Hotel Moscow Moscow ID 83843

TARVER, CONSTANCE BEZANT (MRS. WILLIAM NEWTON TARVER), social worker; b. Ocala, Fla., Dec. 3, 1924; d. Henry Robert and Eva Maude (Seager) Bezant; B.S., Fla. State U., 1949; Certificate Social Work, La. State U., 1953; m. William Newton Tarver, June 5, 1953; 1 son, Roland Wayne, Children's caseworker La. Dept. Pub. Welfare, Tallulah, 1953-56; clin. social worker State Colony and Tng. Sch., Pineville, La., 1959-60; clin. social worker Villa Feliciana Geriatric Hosp., Jackson, 1962-68; dir. social service and parent tng. program Columbia (La.) State Sch., 1970—. Mem. Am. Assn. Mental Deficiency, Caldwell Parish Assn. for Retarded Children (sec. 1972). Home: PO Box 897 Columbia LA 71418 Office: PO Box B Columbia LA 71418

TARWATER, JEAN CATE, physician; b. Maryville, Tenn., July 1, 1924; d. William H. and Dixie (Cate) Tarwater; B.A. cum laude, Maryville Coll., 1947; M.D., U. Tenn., 1951. Intern, Erlanger Hosp., Chattanooga, 1952, resident, 1954-55; mem. staff Laird Meml. Hosp., Montgomery, W.Va., 1952-54; student Kennedy Sch. Missions, Hartford, Conn., 1955; med. missionary Meth. Ch., Kolar, India, 1956-58; practice medicine, New Tazewell, Tenn., 1960-73; staff physician Oak Ridge Gaseous Diffusion Plant, U.S. AEC, 1973—; mem. staff Claiborne County Hosp. Mem. Tenn. Heart Assn., Am., Tenn. Indsl. Med. Assn., Knoxville Acad. Medicine, Christian Med. Soc., Alpha Epsilon Iota. Methodist. Home: Emory Heights Route 2 Knoxville TN 37918 Office: Box P Oak Ridge TN 37830

TASHJIAN, VIRGINIA (MRS. JAMES H. TASHJIAN), librarian; b. Brockton, Mass.; d. Vahan H. and Zvart (Shushian) Agababian; B.S., Simmons Coll., 1943, M.S., 1969; m. James H. Tashjian, Feb. 11, 1946; 1 son, Douglas. Childrens librarian Newton (Mass.) Free Library, 1943-45, br. librarian, 1945-68, asst, librarian, 1968-70, city librarian, 1970—; city storyteller for childrens groups, book reviewer for publs., 1943—; tchr. childrens lit. Bridgewater State Coll., 1969-70, Framingham State Coll., 1972—. Chmn. New Eng. Roundtable of Childrens Librarians. Mem. New Eng. (exec. bd.), Mass. (exec. bd., pres. 1973—) library assns., Armenian Relief Soc., Friends of Armenian Culture Soc., Womens Nat. Book Assn., Boston Authors Club. Author: Once There Was and Was Not, 1966; Juba This and Juba That, 1969; Miller-King, 1969; Three Apples Fell From Heaven, 1971; With a Deep Sea Smile, 1974. Home: 278 Belmont St Watertown MA 02172 Office: 414 Centre St Newton MA 02158

TATA, LORRAINE POWERS (MRS. ROMEO TATA), realtor; b. New Haven, Jan. 13, 1907; d. John J. and Flora (Chase) Powers; student Lauralton Hall, 1919-21, 1922-25; Coll. d'Hulst (Versailles, France), 1921-22; Mus.B., Yale U., 1930; M.A., Ariz. State U., 1940; student Mich. State U., 1942-43; m. Romeo Tata, June 22, 1933; children—Armin Chase, Geri Ann. Head music dept. St. Joseph Coll., 1931-36; instr. Ariz. State U., 1938-40; instr. English Mich. State U., 1946-57; with Westdale Co., Lansing, Mich., 1968—, broker, 1962—. Chmn. advt. Lansing Symphony Orch. Program, 1943-60; vice-chmn. Gov.'s Com. Keep Mich. Beautiful, 1971—. Mem. Nat. Soc. Real Estate Appraisers (chmn. pub. relations 1971, Nat. award), Nat. Fedn. Bus. and Profl. Womens Clubs Inc. (pres. 1971-73, chmn. membership 1973-74), Am. Assn. U. Women, D.A.R., Daus. Am. Colonists, Lansing Bd. Realtors, Mich. Real Estate Assn., Nat. Assn. Real Estate Bds. (pres. 1970-71, Nat. award, Lansing chpt. Woman of Year award 1971, 72), Kappa Delta Pi. Home: 1736 Hitching Post Rd East Lansing MI 48823 Office: 719 Abbott Rd East Lansing MI 48823

TATE, DOROTHY ZETS (MRS. MARVIN R. TATE), nursing adminstr.; b. Earlville, Ill., Dec. 17, 1920; d. Erwin O. and Grace (Sargent) Kaminky; student U. Cal. at Los Angeles, 1952; B.A., LaVerne Coll., 1962; M.A., U. Redlands, 1970; m. John J. Zets, Aug. 3, 1946 (dec. Dec. 1962); 1 dau., Dianna; m. 2d, Marvin R. Tate, Sept. 29, 1967. Night supr. Silver Cross Hosp., Joliet, Ill., 1942-43; staff nurse San Antonio Community Hosp., Upland, Cal., 1943-44, supr., 1948-49; office nurse, Upland, 1944-47; sch. nurse Ontario (Cal.) Sch. Dist., Ontario Health Dept., 1951-56, supr., 1956-57; supr. sch. nurses Ontario Sch. Dist., 1957—. Sec., West End Council Community Services, 1962-64, West End Child Devel. Centers, 1970-72; Upland chmn. Muscular Dystrophy Dr., 1962, 63; Brownie leader, Girl Scouts, 1956-57. Bd. dirs. San Antonio Community Hosp. Dental Center. Mem. Assn. Cal. Sch. Adminstrs., Am., Cal. sch. health assns., Am. Pub. Health Assn., Cal. Sch. Nurses Orgn., Cal., Ontario tchrs. assns., N.E.A., A.A.H.P.E.R., Council Exceptional Children (sec. San Bernardino chpt. 1962-63), Cal. Nurses Assn. (dist. pres. 1948-49), Am. Assn. U. Women. Lutheran. Club: Zonta (sec. 1963-64) (Ontario-Upland, Cal.). Home: 8651 E Foothill Blvd Cucamonga CA 91730 Office: 432 West J St Ontario CA 91762

TATE, MERZE, educator; b. Blanchard, Mich.; d. Charles E. and Myrtle K. (Lett) Tate; B.A., Western Mich. U., 1927; M.A., Columbia, 1930; Litt.B., Oxford U., 1935; Ph.D., Radcliffe Coll., 1941; postgrad. Geneva Sch. Internat. Studies, summer 1931, Berlin U., summer 1935; D.Litt., Western Mich. U., 1948; LL.D., Morgan State Coll., 1968. Prof. history, dean women Barber-Scotia Coll., 1933-36; prof. charge social sci. div. Bennett Coll., 1936-41; prof. history, dean women Morgan State Coll., 1941-42; prof. history Howard U., 1942—; Fulbright lectr. India, 1950-51; vis. prof. Wayne State U., summer 1953, Western Mich. U., summer 1955; Am. Council Learned Socs. grant-in-aid of research, 1959; Washington Eve. Star research grant, 1960; Rockefeller Found. grant-in-aid of research, 1961. U.S. rep. UNESCO Seminar, 1948. Mem. nat. bd. Radcliffe Coll. Recipient Radcliffe Coll. Grad. chpt. Alumnae medal, 1953; Louis Knott Koontz award, 1963; Distinguished Alumna award Western Mich. U., 1970. Alpha Kappa Alpha fellow, 1932; Julius Rosenwald fellow, 1939-40; Fulbright award, 1950. Established Radcliffe Inst. grad. fellowship, 1971. Mem. Am. Hist. Assn., Am. Assn. U. Women, Am. Bridge Assn., Phi Beta Kappa, Pi Gamma Mu, Alpha Kappa Alpha, Phi Delta Kappa. Clubs: Howard U. Faculty Womens; Radcliffe, Writers (Washington); Round Table. Author: The Disarmament Illusion—The Movement for a Limitation of Armaments to 1907, 1942; The U.S. and Armaments, 1948; United States and the Hawaiian Kingdom, 1965; Hawaii: Reciprocity or Annexation, 1968; Diplomacy in the Pacific, 1973. Home: 1314 Perry St NE Washington DC 20017

TATLOW, ROSE ETHEL, editor; b. Olsen Lake, B.C., Can., Apr. 25, 1915; d. Otto Bernard and Elise (Merz) Lasser; grad. high sch.; m. Clarence Elmer Tatlow, June 29, 1935; children—Beth (Mrs. Gary Kershaw), Delores (Mrs. Robert George Mason). Editor, Squamish (B.C.) Advance, 1951-57; editor, asst. pub. Squamish Times, 1963—. Sec., treas. Squamish Library Bd., 1964—. mem. Squamish Adv. Planning Commn., 1966—. Mem. Order Eastern Star. Home: Box 21 Squamish BC V0N 3G0 Canada Office: Box 107 Squamish BC V0N 3G0 Canada

TATMAN, BARBARA KAY SMITH, advt. and pub. relations exec.; b. Scottsbluff, Neb., Oct. 2, 1938; d. Howard Arthur and Robbie (Twiggs) Johnson; B.F.A. cum laude, U. Denver, 1960; postgrad. U. Coll., 1963-64; M.A., Colo. State Coll., 1967; m. Richard A. Smith, Sept. 5, 1959 (div. June 1968); children—Brian Richard, Keri Lyn (dec.); m. 2d, Richard L. Tatman, Aug. 1, 1970. Program dir. KYOU Radio, 1959; artist KRMA-TV, 1959-60; tech. illustrator Martin Marietta Corp., 1960-61; editor women's page, Broomfield Star-Builder, 1964; advt. mgr. Jour. Publs., 1965-66; marketing officer Weld County Bank, 1967-68; alumni sec. Colo. State Coll., Greeley, 1968-69; asst. exec. dir. Colo. State Coll. Found., 1968-69; asso. dir. Colo. State Coll. Manual High Sch. Project, Denver, 1969-70; partner Jour. Group Journeys, 1969—; sec.-treas. Jour. Pub. Co., Greeley. Instr. Aims Jr. Coll., 1967-69; cons. pub. relations, 1967—. Campaign mgr. Dem. Candidate for State Senate, 1968. Recipient Golden Coin award Bank Pub. Relations and Marketing Assn., 1968. Mem. C. of C. (retail com. 1967-68), Soroptimist Internat., Delta Gamma. Author: The First Hundred Years: Greeley, Colorado, 1870-1970, 1970. Home: 2020 26th Av Greeley CO 80631 Office: 720 14th St Greeley CO 80631

TAUB, ETHEL BETTY FLECKER (MRS. RONALD H. TAUB), advt. exec.; b. Bklyn., Sept. 10, 1931; d. Moses and Minnie (Feldman) Flecker; B.S., Rutgers U., 1950; postgrad. N. Y. U., 1951; M.B.A., U. Chgo. Exec. Program, 1974; m. Ronald H. Taub, June 1, 1952; children—Liba, Marcia, Susan. Asst. fashion coordinator Spiegel, Inc., 1950-54; exec. v.p. Creative Displays, Inc., Chgo., 1958—. Dir. Point of Purchase Advt. Inst., 1969—, recipient Man of Year award, 1974; dir. U. Chgo. Grad. Sch. Bus. Exec. Program Club, 1974—. Mem. Am. Marketing Assn., Women's Advt. Club Chgo. Home: 1154 Sheridan Rd Highland Park IL 60035 Office: 230 E Ohio St Chicago IL 60611

TAUBENECK, ANNE DALLMAN (MRS. G. GREGORY TAUBENECK), editor; b. Springfield, Ill., Oct. 21, 1946; d. Vincent Young and Greta Mae (Reid) Dallman; B.S., U. Ill., 1968; postgrad., U. N.C., 1968-69; m. G. Gregory Taubeneck, June 28, 1969. Copy editor Ency. Britannica Ednl. Corp., Chgo., 1969; pub. relations staff Michael Reese Hosp., Chgo., 1970-71; sr. editor LADYCOM Mag., Chgo., 1972—. Mem. Women in Communications, Alpha Lambda Delta, Kappa Tau Alpha, Pi Beta Phi. Episcopalian. Home: 1825 N Lincoln Plaza Chicago IL 60614 Office: 520 N Michigan Av Chicago IL 60611

TAUBENHAUS, BARBARA ALPERN, lawyer; b. Boston, Dec. 29, 1924; d. Henry and Anna (Weintraub) Alpern; A.B. magna cum laude, Radcliffe Coll., 1946; LL.B., Yale, 1949; m. Leon J. Taubenhaus, Sept. 6, 1969 (dec. Nov. 1973). Admitted to Mass. bar, 1949; asso. firm of Ropes, Gray, Best, Coolidge & Rugg, Boston, 1949-54; pvt. law practice, Boston, 1954-66; asso. firm Ely, Bartlett, Brown & Proctor, Boston, 1966-72, partner, 1972-74; partner firm Gaston Snow & Ely, Bartlett, Boston, 1974—. Sec., Brookline Taxpayers Assn., 1954-57; dir. Brookline Forum, Inc., 1953-55. Mem. Brookline Rep. Town Com., 1952-60, Brookline Rep. Town Meeting, 1950-68, Brookline Council on Planning and Renewal, 1964-68. Trustee Brookline Pub. Library, 1957—, sec., 1958-65. Mem. Am., Mass., Boston (mem. com. on jr. bar 1951-53, mem. admissions com. 1957-58, legislation com. 1959-69, com. substantive law, 1963-69) bar assns., Mass. Assn. Women Lawyers (chmn. membership com. 1951-52, newsletter editor 1955-57, corr. sec. 1952-53, chmn. legislative com. 1957-58, director 1958-59, treas. 1960-61, chmn. publicity com. 1961-62), Yale Law Sch. Assn. Boston (mem. exec. com. 1951-53, 56-57), Radcliffe Coll. Alumnae Assn. (dir. 1956-58), League Women Voters, Jewish Family and Children's Service (dir. 1960-66); Women's Rep. Club of Brookline (v.p. 1958-60), Phi Beta Kappa (Radcliffe chpt. sec. 1961-69). Club: Radcliffe (corr. sec. 1955-59, councillor 1959-61, chmn. budget and finance com. 1961-62). Home: 1559 Beacon St Brookline MA 02146 Office: 225 Franklin St Boston MA 02110

TAUCH, WALDINE, sculptor; b. Schulenburg, Tex., Jan. 28, 1892; d. William and Elizabeth (Heiman) Tauch; ed. Brady (Tex.) High Sch.; pupil of Pompeo Coppini (sculptor); hon. D.F.A., Howard Payne Coll., Brownwood, Tex., 1941. Asso. prof. fine art dept. Trinity U., San Antonio, 1943-45. Works include: Henderson Meml., Richmond, Ky.; Soldiers, Sailors and Pioneer Monument, Bedford, Ind.; Le Seuer Smith Children, portrait fountain group, Pelham Manor, N.Y.; portrait bust Mrs. Eli Hertzberg, Tuesday Musical Club, San Antonio; bas-relief, Children's Reading Room, Jersey City Library; portrait relief George Washington, Washington Jr. High Sch., Mt. Vernon N.Y., Tex. Independence Monument, Gonzales, Tex.; portrait monument Mr. and Mrs. Isaac Van Zandt, Canton, Tex.; Moses Austin Monument, San Antonio; Gulf Breeze, Witte Meml. Mus., San Antonio; Innocence, ideal head, Woman's Club, San Antonio; meml. relief John Allen Walker, Howard Payne Coll., Brownwood, Tex.; Genius of Music, Anna Hertzberg Meml., San Antonio; bust of Mirabeau Lamar, Alamo Library, San Antonio; heroic portrait statue group Buckner Ranch for Boys, Burnet, Tex.; Louis Kocurek children, garden group, San Antonio; life size figure of Pippa Passes, Baylor U.; heroic figure The Texas Ranger of Today, Dallas; portrait fountain group Louis Kocurek, Jr. children, San Antonio; portrait figure R.L. Thornton, former mayor of Dallas; heroic figure of Gen. Douglas MacArthur, Brownwood, Tex., large heroic sized ideal figure representing Higher Edn. Trinity U., San Antonio, The Doughboy in front Am. Legion Bldg., Austin, Tex., heroic size bust Ernest Altgelt, founder Comfort, Tex., others. Recipient citation for outstanding contbn. to art Tex. Senate. Charter mem. (sponsor) Coppini Acad. Fine Arts. Fellow Nat. Sculptor Soc., Am. Artists Profl. League; mem. Nat. Soc. Arts and Letters, Artists and Craftsmen San Antonio Art League. Methodist. Clubs: Tuesday Musical, Women's (San Antonio); Brady (Tex.) Tuesday. Address: 115 Melrose Pl San Antonio TX 78212

TAUSSIG, ELLEN MEREDITH, journalist; b. Phila., July 13, 1906; d. John Hawley and Meredith (Ball) Taussig; grad. Springside Sch., 1924; student Am. Acad. Dramatic Art., N.Y.C., 1925. Reporter, Phila. Evening Ledger, 1938-42, Phila. Daily News., 1942-43, Phila. Record, 1943-47, Courier-Post Newspapers, Camden, N.J., 1947-48, Phila. Evening Bull., 1948; reporter, feature writer Buffalo Evening News, 1949-74; freelance writer, 1974—. Recipient Front Page award Buffalo Newspaper Guild, 1953, 54. Mem. Am. Pen Women, Frontier Press Club, Sigma Delta Chi. Episcopalian. Home: 555 Breekenridge St Buffalo NY 14222

TAUSSKY, OLGA (MRS. JOHN TODD), mathematician, educator; b. Olomouc, Czechoslovakia; d. Julius David and Ida (Pollach) Taussky; student Zurich (Switzerland) U., 1930, Bryn Mawr Coll., 1934-35; M.A., U. Cambridge (Eng.), 1937; Ph.D., U. Vienna (Austria), 1939; m. John Todd, Sept. 29, 1938. Came to U.S., naturalized, 1953. Asst. U. Vienna and Goettingen U., 1931-34; lectr. London U., 1937-44; sci. officer Ministry of Aircraft Prodn., London, Eng., 1943-46; cons. Nat. Bur. Standards, Washington, 1948-57; research asso. Cal. Inst. Tech., 1957-71, prof., 1971—; mem. Inst. Advanced Study, Princeton, 1948; editor jours. Linear Algebra, Jour. Number Theory. Fulbright vis. prof. Vienna U., 1965. Mem. Com. of Space of Mayor of Los Angeles, 1964. Named Los Angeles Times Woman of the Year, 1963; recipient Ford prize of Math. Assn. of Am., 1971. Mem. Am. Math. Soc., Math. Assn. Am., Sigma Xi. Research publs. to math. periodicals. Office: Dept Math Cal Inst Tech Pasadena CA 91109

TAVES, ISABELLA (MRS. DAN MICH), author; m. Dan Mich (dec. 1966). Formerly entertainment editor Look mag.; now free-lance writer. Recipient Headliner award Women in Communications, 1974. Author: Successful Women, 1944; Harriet Hubbard Ayers, 1957; The Quick Rich Fox, 1959; (with Virgil Damon) I Learned About Women from Them, 1962; Woman Alone, 1968; (with Katherine de Jersey) Destiny Times Six, 1970; Not Bad for a Girl, 1972; Love Should Not Be Wasted, 1974. Contbr. to mags., including Reader's Digest, McCall's, Redbook, Ladies' Home Jour.;

columnist Women Alone, Des Moines Register and Tribune Syndicate. Home: 137 E 38th St New York City NY 10016 Office: care Julian Bach Agy New York City NY 10017

TAVRIS, CAROL ANNE, editor; b. Los Angeles, Sept. 17, 1944; d. Samuel and Dorothy (Marcus) Tavris; A.B., summa cum laude, Brandeis U., 1966; Ph.D. in Social Psychology (Rackham prize fellow), U. Mich. at Ann Arbor, 1971. Articles editor Psychology Today mag., Del Mar, Cal., 1968-69, asso. editor, 1969-72, sr. editor, 1971-72, asst. mng. editor, 1972—; cons., lectr. in field. Ford Found. fellow, 1969-71; Nat. Def. Edn. Act fellow, 1966-68. Mem. Nat. Orgn. Women, Am. Civil Liberties Union, Assn. Women in Psychology, U.S.-China Friendship Assn., Phi Beta Kappa. Editor: The Female Experience, 1973. Contbr. articles to profl. jours. Writer filmstrips on psychology and biology of women. Office: 317 14th St Del Mar CA 92014

TAYLOE, MARJORIE ELLEN ZAERR (MRS. RALPH CHESTER TAYLOE), harpist, singer; b. Los Angeles, Feb. 15, 1930; d. John L. and Eleanor (Jones) Zaerr; tchrs. diploma Samoiloff Opera Acad., Los Angeles, 1952; student Whittier Coll., Los Angeles Valley Coll., Occidental Coll.; studied in Europe; m. Ralph Chester Tayloe, June 18, 1955; children—Mary Ellen, David Chester, Sarah Lee and Susan Marie and John Dannie (triplets). Harpist, Phil Kerr's Harmony Chorus, 1949-53; appeared as organist, harpist various radio and TV broadcasts, U.S., fgn. countries; 8 concert tours Europe. appeared Seattle World's Fair Concert, 1963; sang various opera roles; star Music Until Midnight, 1948-62; rec. artist Young Records; soloist, harpist Beverly Hills Symphony, 1962—; builder, player first Welch Triple String harp U.S. Founder, Mus. Arts Acad., North Hollywood, Cal., 1950, dir., 1950—. Mem. Minstrel Harpers Soc. Am. (pres. 1962-68), Am. Harpist Soc., English Hand Belle Ringers Am., Pen Women Am., D.A.R. Presbyn. Clubs: West Shore Music, Los Angeles Opera Reading, Southern Cal. Componology. Author: Irish Songs for Irish Harpers. Editor, pub.: A Harpers Notebook, 1960—. Home: 4527 Kraft Av North Hollywood CA 91602

TAYLOR, ADELIA EMILIA GEBAUER, realtor; b. Northport, Neb.; d. Ernest Julius and Emilie (Krause) Gebauer; certificate Chadron State Tchrs. Coll., 1924; B.A. magna cum laude, Ariz. State U., 1942, M.A., 1943; postgrad. Boulder U., 1934, Denver U., 1939; m. Donald G. Taylor, Sept. 9, 1940. Tchr. pub. schs., Scotts' Bluff, Neb., 1924-27, Los Angeles, 1944; librarian Phoenix City Schs., 1928-42; social worker Maricopa County (Ariz.) Bd. Welfare, Phoenix, 1943; pres., chmn. bd. Gay Taylor Realty Co., Scottsdale, Ariz., 1956-64; pres. Gay Land Co., 1964—. Dir. Real Estate Bd., Phoenix, 1961-64. Mem. Scottsdale Real Estate Bd. (life), Ariz. Assn. Realtors, Nat. Assn. Real Estate Bds., Phi Gamma Mu. Club: Paradise Valley Country. Home: 6050 N 52d Pl Paradise Valley AZ 85253 Office: 849 S 91st Pl Mesa AZ 85208

TAYLOR, AILENE SMITH (MRS. RICHARD RAYMOND TAYLOR), civic worker; b. Oklahoma City, May 27, 1923; d. Claude Layfette and Julia (Alexander) Smith; student Oklahoma A. and M. Coll., 1940-41; B.A. cum laude, U. Tulsa, 1944; m. Richard Raymond Taylor, Aug. 16, 1947; children—Gary Allen, Richard Lee. Records sec. Kappa Delta Sorority nat. office, Springfield, Mo., 1944-48, pres. met. bd., Cleve.; bd. dirs. League Women Voters, Cleve., 1964-65, 2d v.p., 1965-67, pres., 1967-69; pres. Valley View Elementary P.T.A., 1962-63, Newton D. Baker Jr. High P.T.A., 1965-66; legislation chmn. Cleve. Council P.T.A.'s, 1966-67; mem. Cleve. Bd. Edn., 1970-73, chmn. edn. com., 1971-72; chmn. large cities commn. Ohio Sch. Bds. Assn., 1972; mem. legislative com., former trustee Citizens League. Bd. dirs. YWCA Cleve., Council of Gt. Cities Schs., 1971-73; trustee, chmn. women's com. Cleve. Scholarship Programs, Inc. Mem. Kappa Delta. Mem. United Ch. of Christ. Address: 1902 Martingale Rd Wheaton IL 60187

TAYLOR, ALICE LEE BENNETT, hotel exec., lawyer; b. Weston, W.Va., May 11, 1927; d. Hunter McCauley and Madge (Hinzman) Bennett; B.A., U. Miami, 1951, LL.B., 1955; m. Marion Vance, Aug. 31, 1946 (div. Jan. 1963); children—James McCauley, Suzanne, Jonathan B.; m. 2d, Robert R. Taylor, Apr. 4, 1974. Admitted to Fla. bar, 1955, W.Va. bar, 1956, Ky. bar, 1958; asso. firm Helen Tanos Hope, Miami, Fla., 1964-68; individual practice, Weston, 1968-73; city atty. City of Weston, 1971-73; owner Webster Springs (W.Va.) Hotel, 1973—. Mem. rules com. W.Va. Democratic party, 1972—. Mem. D.A.R., Law Alumni Asn. U. Miami, Kappa Beta Pi. Address: Webster Springs Hotel Webster Springs WV 26288

TAYLOR, ALICE L(OUISE), geographer, author, editor; b. N.Y.C., Aug. 4, 1911; d. Norman and Bertha (Fanning) Taylor; baccalaureates, Ecole Alsacienne, Paris, France, 1929, 30, U. Paris, France, 1932; grad. study geography Columbia, 1942-44; m. Louis Lubrano, May 17, 1941 (div. 1945). Sec. to dir. Am. Geog. Soc., N.Y.C., 1941-49, editor, Focus, 1950—, Around the World series, Doubleday, 1955-73; Know Your America series, Doubleday, 1956-74. Author: Egypt, 1953; Union of South Africa, 1954; Iran, 1955; Switzerland, 1955; France, 1956; India, 1957; Boston, 1957; Philadelphia, 1958; New York City, 1958; Maryland and Delaware, 1959; Egypt and Syria, 1960; N.Y. State 1962; United Arab Republic, 1964; Syria, 1965; Taiwan, 1967; Iraq, 1968; Algeria, 1968; Hong Kong, 1969; Iran, 1970; Western Europe, 1972. Editor: Focus on the Middle East, 1971; Focus on Southeast Asia, 1972; Focus on South America, 1973. Mem. Soc. Internat. Devel. (chmn. chpt. membership com. 1972—), Soc. Woman Geographers (chmn. program com. 1952, chmn. chpt. membership com. 1972—), Assn. Am. Geographers, Nat. Council Social Studies, Am. Acad. Polit. and Social Sci., A.A.A.S. Home: 120 E 36th St New York City NY 10016 Office: Am Geog Soc Broadway at 156th St New York City NY 10032

TAYLOR, ANNE PANNELL (MRS. GEORGE A. TAYLOR), govt. ofcl.; b. Durham, N.C., Sept. 15, 1910; d. Alexander Henry and Anne Roche (Thomas) Gary; A.B., Barnard Coll., 1931; D.Phil., Oxford, 1935; postgrad. Inst. Hist. Research, U. London, 1932-33; LL.D., U. Ala., 1952, Women's Coll. U. N.C., 1960, Cedar Crest Coll., 1968, Washington Coll., 1972; Litt.D., Western Res. U., 1963; D.H.L., U. Chattanooga, 1963, Women's Med. Coll. Pa., 1968; m. Henry Clifton Pannell, Sept. 2, 1935 (dec. 1946); children—Henry Gary, Clifton Wyndam; m. 2d, George Alfred Taylor, June 12, 1971. Instr. history Montevall U., Ala., 1934-36; mem. faculty U. Ala., 1935-49, asst. prof., 1946-47, asso. prof., 1948-49; prof. history, acad. dean Goucher Coll., 1949-50; pres., prof. history Sweet Briar (Va.) Coll., 1950-71; mem. U.S. Bd. Fgn. Scholarships, 1971—. Vice chmn. bd. Am. Council on Edn., 1968-69; mem. scholarship bd. Ford Motor Co. Fund, 1959-62, internat. fellowship bd., 1961-66; mem. Va. com. Fulbright scholarships; mem. adv. council Marchall Aid Commemoration Commn., 1966-71. Chmn. Amherst County (Va.) Health and Welfare Council, 1963-64. Bd. visitors Womans Coll. Duke U., Durham, 1964; trustee Barnard Coll., N.Y.C., 1968-72, Mt. Vernon Coll., Washington, 1972—, Talbot Free Library, Easton, Md., 1972—, Phi Beta Kappa Found., 1967-70; bd. dirs. Alumnae Adv. Center, N.Y.C. Barnard Internat. fellow, 1931; decorated comdr. Order Palmes Academiques (France), 1966; recipient Gerard Gold medal in Am. history, Mother Gerard Phelan Gold medal, Marymount Coll. Va., 1968. Mem. Am., So., Ala. hist. assns., Am. Assn. U. Women (nat. pres., 1967-71), So. Assn. Colls. for Women (pres., 1961-62), Assn. Va. Colls. (pres., 1964-65), Assn. Am. Colls., So. Univ. Conf. (v.p., 1956-57), Tchrs. Ins. and Annuity Conf., Protestant Colls. and Univs. (dir., 1967-70), Phi Beta Kappa. Author: Julia S. Tutwiler and Social Progress in Alabama, 1961; Political and Economic Relations of English and American Quakers, 1750-85, 1936; (with Dorothea Wyatt) Canada: Our Northern Neighbor, 1951. Contbr. profl. jours. Home and office: 514 Trippe Av Easton MD 21601

TAYLOR, BARBARA JO ANNE HARRIS (MRS. RICHARD POWELL TAYLOR), civic and polit. worker; b. Providence, Sept. 9, 1936; d. Ross Cameron and Anita (Coia) Harris; student Tex. Christian U., 1952, Salve Regina Coll., 1952-53, Our Lady of the Lake Coll. and Convent, 1953-54, St. Mary's U., summer 1954, Incarnate Word Coll., 1954-55; student, Georgetown U., 1956-59, B.S., 1963; m. Richard Powell Taylor, Dec. 19, 1959; 1 son, Douglas Howard. Adminstrv. asst. profl. devel. and welfare N.E.A., Washington, 1956-59; asst. to dir. Georgetown U., Washington, 1956-59; exec. asst. All Am. Conf. to Combat Communism, Washington, 1960. Mem. exec. bd. Salvation Army Aux., D.C., 1967—, chmn. fund-raising, 1968, chmn. membership com., 1969-70, co-chmn., 1972-74, mem. exec. com. of exec. bd., 1970—, treas., mem. finance com., 1970-71, v.p., 1971-72, historian, 1972-73, editor Our Watchword Newsletter, 1968-69, chmn. Christmas Toycenter com., 1972—; mem. exec. bd. Welcome to Washington Internat., 1969-72, bd. advisers, 1969-72, dir. workshop, 1969—, tchr. English and Spanish lit., 1970—; exec. bd. Am. Opera Sch. Soc., Washington, 1970—, v.p., program chmn., 1973—; exec. bd. Women's Aux., St. David's Episcopal Ch., Washington, 1970—, v.p., 1970-71, 73—, chmn. program com., 1970-71, 73—; exec. bd. Women's Aux. Episcopal Center for Emotionally Disturbed Children, Washington, 1970—, Women's Aux. Episcopal Ch. Home for Aged, 1970—. Mem. exec. bd. League Republican Women D.C., 1964-67, treas., 1964-67; mem. nat. council Womens Nat. Rep. Club, N.Y.C., 1969—; mem. Nat. Fedn. Rep. Women, 1964—, Md. Fedn. Rep. Women, 1969—. Mem. Internat. Platform Assn., Spanish-Portuguese Study Group (dir. 1969—, treas. 1970—, finance chmn. 1972), D.A.R. (state vice chmn. Nat. Def. Com. 1972—, vice chmn. flag com. 1973—, state bd. mgmt. 1973—, nat. congl. com. 1973, nat. museum docent com. 1973—), Am. Austrian Soc., Lawyers Wives D.C. Clubs: Internat., Nat. Lawyers Wives, Capitol Hill, Capital Speakers, Congressional Country, Washington (internat. com. 1971—). Home: 6007 Corewood Lane Sumner Washington DC 20016

TAYLOR, BETH HOBBS (MRS. MORRIS HARDING TAYLOR), convalescent center adminstr.; b. Nephi, Utah, Apr. 21, 1917; d. George Lloyd and Jennie V. (Malmgren) Hobbs; student U. Utah, 1935-36; grad. Latter-day Saints Hosp. Sch. Nursing, Salt Lake City, 1938; student George Washington U. Extension, 1966; B.S., Utah State U., 1971; m. Morris Harding Taylor, June 5, 1940; children—Gordon Morris, Gary Lloyd, Loren Graig, Genan, Grant Paul, Mary Gay. Nurse gen. duty, Salina (Utah) Hosp., 1938-39, Cache Valley Hosp., Logan, Utah, 1944, Logan Latter-day Saints Hosp., 1951-55; pub. health nurse, Utah Health Dept., Manti, 1939-40, Logan, Utah, 1949, Madison (Wis.) Bd. Health, 1957-58; tchr. Red Cross nursing classes, N.D. Agrl. Coll., Fargo, 1941, Logan High Sch., 1955, Utah State U., Logan, 1956-57; adminstr. Sunshine Terrace Found., Logan, 1959-68; adminstr. Hillhaven Convalescent Center, Ogden. Chmn. Nursing Home Task Force on Study Nursing, Utah. Pres., North Cache council P.T.A., 1955-57. Recipient award and pin North Cache council P.T.A., 1959. Fellow Am. Coll. Nursing Home Adminstrs. (sec.-treas. Rocky Mountain region); mem. Utah, Cache County (pres. 1963) councils on aging, Farm Bur. Women (pres. 1955), Extension Women's Orgn. (pres. 1955), Utah State Nurses Assn. (chmn. geriatric sect.), Utah State Nursing Home Assn., Utah State U. Faculty Woman's Assn., Asso. Extension Women's Assn. Mem. Ch. of Jesus Christ of Latter-day Saints (Sunday Sch. tchr.). Clubs: Hyde Park (Utah) Home Makers; Soroptimist (Logan, del. to conv. 1966). Home: 131 E 2d S Hyde Park UT 84318 Office: 3430 Harrison Blvd Ogden UT 84403

TAYLOR, BETTY KAYE, orgn. exec.; b. Freeport, N.Y.; d. Harry and Anna (Brisk) Kaye; B.A., U. Wis., 1946; m. Alexander L. Taylor, Jan. 22, 1950 (div. July 1966); children—David, Seth. With Jewish Labor Com., N.Y.C., 1948—, asst. dir., 1968—; exec. sec. Nat. Trade Union Council for Human Rights, N.Y.C., 1964—; exec. sec. Ad Hoc Com. on Human Rights and Genocide Treaties, 1964—. Mem. Assn. Jewish Community Relations Workers (exec. bd. 1965—, pres. 1974—). Home: 61 E 86th St New York City NY 10028 Office: 25 E 78th St New York City NY 10021

TAYLOR, BETTYE HACKER (MRS. MATHEWS C. TAYLOR), banker; b. nr. Athens, Ala.; d. Homer H. and Jeannette (Peete) Hacker; student pub. schs.; m. Mathews C. Taylor, Jan. 10, 1947; children—Deborah (Ms. Ashford), John David. Sec., Malone & Malone attys., Athens, 1945-47, Ernst & Ernst, C.P.A.'s, Athens, 1960; head proof operator State Nat. Bank, Athens, 1952-64; asst. br. mgr. Peoples Nat. Bank, Huntsville, Ala., 1965-69, head bookkeeper, 1964-65, asst. cashier, 1967-70, mgr. proof and transit dept., 1969-70, asst. cashier, 1970-72, asst. comptroller, personnel mgr., 1972—. Bd. dirs. Cerebral Palsy, Huntsville-Tenn. Valley, Inc., 1968—, treas. bd., 1970—, exec. dir.; treas. Ala. Cerebral Palsy Assn., 1973-74, exec. bd. dirs. Mem. Nat. Secs. Assn. (pres. chpt. 1969-70), Nat. Assn. Bank Women, Am. Inst. Banking, Bus. and Profl. Women's Clubs (com. chmn.). Baptist. Club: John Hunt Pilot (Huntsville). Home: 817 Loukell Av SE Huntsville AL 35802 Office: PO Box 267 Huntsville AL 35804

TAYLOR, CLELLIE MIZELLE (MRS. PHILLIP WYNNE TAYLOR), ednl. adminstr.; b. nr. Ahoskie, N.C., Sept. 28, 1923; d. Elemuel Lafayette and Phay (Liverman) Mizelle; B.A., E. Carolina U., 1944, M.A. in Edn., 1970, M.L.S., 1972; m. Phillip Wynne Taylor, June 5, 1946; children—Phillip Wynne, Richard Mizelle. Tchr. pub. schs., N.C., 1944-68; dir. Learning Resources Center Halifax County Tech. Inst., Weldon, N.C., 1968—. Instr. reading Lenoir Community Coll., Kinston, N.C., 1967. Mem. Assn. Community Coll. Pub. Information Officers (sec. 1972-73), N.C. State Library Assn., N.C. Educators Assn., Ednl. Media Assn., N.C. Community Coll. Adult Educators Assn. Asso. editor For Adults Only, 1970—. Home: Eastern Shores Littleton NC 27850 fOffice: Box 809 Weldon NC 27890

TAYLOR, D. JANE, biologist, research coordinator; b. Waco, Tex., June 3, 1921; d. Mat E. and Sulee (Damon) Taylor; B.A., Rice U., 1943; M.S., Ia. State U., 1947; Ph.D., George Washington U., 1957. Chem. technician Humble Oil Co., 1943-45; instr. zoology and physiology Ia. State U., 1945-47; parasitologist lab. tropical diseases NIH, Bethesda, Md., 1947-58, biologist Nat. Cancer Inst., 1958-61, head exptl. biology projects asst. br. chief breast cancer program coordinating br., div. cancer biology and diagnosis, 1961—. Fellow A.A.A.S., N.Y. Acad. Scis.; mem. Am. Assn. Cancer Research, Soc. for Exptl. Biology and Medicine, Sigma Xi, Sigma Delta Epsilon. Editor monograph on endocrine-related tumors. Contbr. articles on research in malaria, amoebiasis and cancer biology and therapy to sci. jours. Home: 4500 Connecticut Av NW Washington DC 20008 Office: Landow Bldg NIH Bethesda MD 20014

TAYLOR, ELINOR MARCINE MCILVAINE (MRS. JAMES NELSON TAYLOR), newspaper editor; b. Wooster, O., Dec. 10, 1916; d. Benjamin Marsh and Candace Amy (Tuttle) McIlvaine; grad. high sch.; m. James Nelson Taylor, Aug. 14, 1948; children—Lynn S., Theodore M., James B. Dep. county treas. Wayne County, 1936-43; reporter Akron (O.) Beacon Jour., 1944-46; reporter Canton Repository, 1944-47; reporter Wooster (O.) Daily Record, 1945-70, editor, 1970—. Recipient numerous awards in journalism writing; award Internat. Newspaper Pubs. Assn., 1968, 71; Ohio Photo-Journalism award Ohio News Photographers Assn., 1972. Mem. World Assn. Women Journalists, Nat. Fedn. Press Women, Ohio Newspaper Women's Assn. (pres. 1970, 71), Ohio Press Women (treas. 1969-72), Ohio Blue Pencil (pres. 1971). Home: 1522 Overlook Dr Wooster OH 44691 Office: 212 E Liberty St Wooster OH 44691

TAYLOR, ELIZA JANE, physician; b. Columbia, Va., Feb. 19, 1936; d. Dean Franklin and Pinkie Julia (Riddle) Taylor; nurse's certificate, Freedmen's Hosp. Sch. Nursing, 1956; B.S., Howard U., 1963, M.D. (Nat. Med. Assn. scholar 1965, 66), 1967; M.P.H. in Adminstrn., Johns Hopkins, 1974. Profl. nurse, Saginaw, Mich., 1957, Washington, 1957-66; intern D.C. Gen. Hosp., Howard U. Med. div., 1967-68, resident, 1968-70, chief resident, 1970-71; chief med. officer emergency div., 1971-72, chief ambulatory services, 1972—. Chmn., Dr. Emile C. Nash. Meml. Trust Fund. Mem. D.C. Med. Soc., Met. Assn. Emergency Dept. Dirs. Home: 641 Constitution Av NE Washington DC 20002 Office: DC Gen Hosp 19th and E St SE Washington DC 20003

TAYLOR, ELIZABETH PASSMORE (JILL TAYLOR), author; b. Swarthmore, Pa., Mar. 27, 1917; d. Norman Sumner and Sarah Eastburn (wood) Passmore; student Swarthmore Coll., 1935-36; m. John Howard Taylor, Jan. 18, 1936; 1 son, Richard Wood. Free lance writer, 1964—; free lance promotional writer Widener Coll., Chester, Pa., 1970-72, Am. Trauma Soc., Chester, 1973—. Moderator Writers' Workshop Our Lady of Angels Coll., Glen Ridle, Pa., 1970—. Sec. Concord Twp., Delaware County, Pa., 1972-73. Recipient first prize for juvenile fiction Phila. Writers Conf., 1971. Mem. Nat. League Pen Women, Delaware County Writers Club. Mem. Soc. of Friends (treas. Concord monthly meeting 1959-69). Contbr. articles, poems and short stories to mags. and newspapers.

TAYLOR, ETHEL MAE HENDERSON (MRS. JOHN BENJAMIN TAYLOR), educator, broadcaster; b. nr. Laurens, S.C.; d. James William and Ella (Dendy) Henderson; B.A., Benedict Coll., 1946; summer study U. S.C., 1966, 69, 71-72; Ph.D. (hon.), Hamilton State U., Tucson, 1973; m. John Benjamin Taylor, Feb. 10, 1946; children—John B., Gwendolyn Bernice (Mrs. Robert Hall), James Howard, Ludwald Clifton, Audriene Denice, Deborah Elizabeth, Melonie Joyce, Cheryl Kaye, Melissa Carol. Sec., Hampton Printing Co., Columbia, S.C., 1949-52; tchr. Richland Co. Sch., Eastover, S.C., 1953-60, Columbia city schs., 1961—; part-time radio announcer WOIC radio sta. Columbia, 1954—. Pub. relations dir. Fairwold Jr. High Sch., 1967—; sec. Lincoln Park Community Club. Mem. Columbia Urban League, Nat., Richland County ednl. assns., Nat., S.C. councils tchrs. English, S.C. Tchr. Assn., Nat. Assn. Broadcasters, Nat. Assn. Television and Radio Announcers, Nat. Women's Aux. Nat. Alliance Postal and Fed. Employees. Baptist (organist). Home: 2221 Mance St Columbia SC 29203 Office: 1129 Washington St Columbia SC 29201

TAYLOR, FLONNIA CHAMBERS (MRS. RHEA A. TAYLOR), social worker; b. Williamsburg, Ky.; d. James Henry and Lassafaye (Hicks) Chambers; A.B. cum laude, Carson-Newman Coll., 1926; M.A., Ohio State U., 1933; M.A., U. Chgo., 1952; m. Rhea A. Taylor, June 26, 1930. Tchr. English and dramatics Bethel Coll., 1931-32, U. Ky., 1945, English, Georgetown Coll., 1955-56; social work cons. Ky. Child Welfare Div., Frankfort, 1937-42; area rep. A.R.C., Alexandria, Va., 1942-46; psychiat. social worker VA, Lexington, Ky., 1946-51; spl. supervisory and adminstrv. work A.R.C., Washington chpt., Family Service, Lansing, Mich., 1952-55; social worker Shriners Hosp., Lexington, Ky., 1955-57; exec. dir. United Cerebral Palsy of Bluegrass Agy., 1958—. Mem. Gov.'s Adv. Com. Child Welfare of Ky., 1960—, v.p., 1970; chmn. Gov.'s Adv. Com. Day Care, Ky., 1963—; mem. Nat. Adv. Com. on Social Service to Nat. United Cerebral Palsy Assn., 1959—; profl. cons. coms. on children and family Ky. White House Conf. Bd. dirs. Community Chest, Family Service, County Child Welfare, Florence Crittenden Home (pres.); bd. dirs. Lexington Philharmonic Orch., 1961—, sec. bd., 1961-62. Named Outstanding Woman of Lexington, 1945. Mem. Am. Assn. U. Women (pres. 1960-62), Ky. Welfare Assn. (pres. 1959-60), League Women Voters, Am. Assn. Social Workers, Nat. Assn. Social Workers, Acad. Certified Social Workers, State Mental Health Orgn., P.E.O. Clubs: Zonta (pres.), University of Kentucky Woman's. Home: Tayraf Hill Route 2 Harrodsburg Rd Lexington KY 40504 Office: 465 Springhill Dr Lexington KY 40503

TAYLOR, GILDA ROSENBLUM, psychologist; b. Bklyn., Sept. 14, 1931; d. Morris and Pauline (Levine) Rosenblum; R.N., Jewish Hosp. Sch. Nursing, Phila., 1951; B.S. in Nursing Edn., Temple U., 1966; M.Ed. in Counseling, 1967, D.Ed., in Counseling Psychology, 1973; m. Charles Everett Taylor, Apr. 5, 1952; 1 son, Neil Stuart. Gen. duty nurse Albert Einstein Med. Center, 1954-61; acting inservice edn. supr. Moss Rehab. Center, Boston, 1964-65; counselor Phila. Bd. Edn., 1967-74; individual practice psychol. counseling, Phila., 1973—; instr. Antioch Putney U., 1971. Mem. Am., Eastern psychol. assns. Address: 5021A S Convent Lane Philadelphia PA 19114

TAYLOR, IMOGENE PATRICK (MRS. J. NELSON TAYLOR), pub. relations exec.; b. Crosses, Ark., Mar. 12, 1923; d. John Burtis and Charlotte (Cravens) Patrick; B.A., U. Ark., 1943; m. J. Nelson Taylor, Aug. 21, 1954. Reporter, N.W. Ark. Times, Fayetteville, 1943, Tulsa World, 1943-45; spl. writer, med. writer Daily Oklahoman, Oklahoma City, 1945-58; dir. pub. relations U. Okla. Health Scis. Center, Oklahoma City, 1958-73; pub. information rep. Okla. Dept. Instns., Social and Rehabilitative Services, Oklahoma City, 1973—. Mem. Nat. Assn. Sci. Writers, A.A.A.S., Am. Soc. Hosp. Pub. Relations, Women in Communications (Byliner award 1959). Democrat. Home: 724 NE 20th St Oklahoma City OK 73105 Office: PO Box 25352 Oklahoma City OK 73125

TAYLOR, JANE URBAN, market analyst; b. Sacramento; d. Clarence Urban and Virginia (Doron) Taylor; certificate studeies U. Valencia (Spain), 1960; B.A., Northwestern U., 1962; Fulbright scholar U. Madrid (Spain), 1962-63; M.A. (Univ. fellow), U. Ill., 1964; M.B.A., U. Chgo., 1971. Market analyst Davee Koehnlein & Keating, Chgo., 1964-69; mgr. client services, pharm. market research IMS America Ltd., Chgo.-Des Plaines, 1969-71; abstractor, translator, free-lance A.M.A., Chgo., 1965-71; free-lance pharm. market research IMS America Ltd., 1971—; bus. mgr., treas., med. edn]. cons. Natresources, Inc., Chgo., 1971-73; market analyst G.D. Searle & Co., Chgo., 1973—. Mem. Modern Lang. Assn., Am. Marketing Assn., Council Fgn. Relations, Chgo. Art Inst., Phi Beta Kappa. Club: Columbia Yacht (Chgo.). Author: New Drugs on Clinical Trial, annually 1969—. Home: 860 N DeWitt Pl Chicago IL 60611 Office: PO Box 5110 Chicago IL 60680

TAYLOR, JEANNE D'HERETE, editor; b. Bridgeport, Conn., Feb. 13, 1943; d. Larison Holcombe and Lucille (Maestri) Taylor; B.A., Manhattanville Coll., 1965. Asst. shopping editor Mademoiselle mag., N.Y.C., 1965-67; shopping editor Seventeen mag., N.Y.C., 1967—. Author: Where the Boutiques Are, 1967. Home: 220 East 73d St New York City NY 10021 Office: 320 Park Av New York City NY 10022

TAYLOR, JO, social worker; b. nr. Maiden, N.C., Nov. 8, 1930; d. Clyde O. and Connie (Brown) Taylor; A.B., Lenoir-Rhyne Coll., 1955; M.S.W., U. N.C., 1965. Clin. lab., dr.'s office asst., Hickory, N.C., 1955-61; caseworker Catawba County Dept. Pub. Welfare, Newton, N.C., 1961-63; clin. social worker VA Hosp., Salisbury, N.C., 1965-70, coordinator inpatient social work services and student tng., 1970—; field instr. U. Ga. Sch. Social Work, Athens, 1968-71; adj. asst. prof. U. S.C., Columbia, 1971—. Mem. Nat. Assn. Social Workers, Acad. Certified Social Workers, Mu Sigma Epsilon. Home: Apt 18 2802 W Innes St Salisbury NC 28144 Office: VA Hosp Salisbury NC 28144

TAYLOR, JO SMITH (MRS. ROBERT B. TAYLOR), artist; b. Big Sandy, Tex.; d. James Dennis and Nancy Pearl (Faulk) Smith; student N. Tex. State U., 1944-47, U. Guanajato, Mexico, 1946; studied portrait painting under Ramon Froman, 1956-62, water color painting under Gerry Peirce, summers 1953-59, Edgar A. Whitney; m. Robert Bonner Taylor, Apr. 4, 1947; children—Mary, Beth, Robert Bonner. One-man shows Tex. Panhandle Plains Mus., Canyon, Paris (Tex.) Jr. Coll., 107 Gallery, Nacogdoches, Tex.; exhibited in group shows at Southwestern Water Color Soc. Regional Exhbn., So. Meth. U., Dallas, Witte Mus., San Antonio, Laguna Gloria Mus., Austin, Tex., 103d, 105th ann. Traveling Exhbn., Am. Water Color Soc. Judge art shows Gregg County Art Guild, Gladewater, Marshall, Tex., Tex. Art League, Festival Arts, Little Rock; lectr. art guilds, Gladewater, Longview, Jefferson, Gilmer, Henderson, Tyler, Lubbock, Austin, Dallas (all Tex.). Recipient Carl Folke Sahlin award Am. Watercolor Soc., 1968; 1st award Nat. Show at Canyon Mus., 1966; others. Mem. Am. (Grumbecher award 1971), Tex., Southwestern (1st award 1968) watercolor socs., Gregg County Art Guild. Home: Box 539 Pittsburg TX 75686

TAYLOR, JOAN KOSLOSKY, clin. psychologist; b. Mpls., Nov. 7, 1929; d. Ione Elizabeth Koslosky; B.A., Coll. St. Catherine, 1951; M.A., Cath. U. Am., 1954; Ph.D., Columbia, 1968; m. Richard Wirt Taylor, July 6, 1957; children—Laura Lee, Martha Caroline. Mem. staff Family Service and Child Guidance Center of the Oranges, Maplewood and Millburn, Orange, N.J., 1962—, chief supervising psychologist, 1973—; individual practice psychotherapy, Chatham, N.J., 1961—. Cons. Orange Day Care Center, 1973-74. Founder, trustee, officer Unitarian Coop. Nursery Sch., Summit, N.J., 1961-63, 64-66; mem. Summit Drug Adv. Com., 1972-73. Bd. dirs. Child Care Center, Summit, 1960-61. Mem. Am., N.J., Eastern, Essex County (pres. 1973-74) psychol. assns., Am. Orthopsychiat. Assn., Am. Group Psychotherapy Assn. Home: 33 West End Av Summit NJ 07901 Office: 12 Parrott Mill Rd Chatham NJ 07928

TAYLOR, JUDITH HELEN MUNDLAK (MRS. IRVIN S. TAYLOR), physician; b. London, Eng., July, 1934; d. Max and Fanny (Shapiro) Mundlak; B.A., M.A., Somerville Coll., Oxford, 1956; B.M., B.Ch., Oxford U., 1959; m. Irvin S. Taylor, Nov. 23, 1961; children—David, Hugh. Came to U.S., 1959, naturalized, 1964. Intern, Bklyn. Hosp., 1959-60; resident neurology Kings County Hosp., 1960-61; resident neurology Albert Einstein Coll. Medicine, 1962-65, asst. clin. prof., 1966—; practice medicine specializing in neurology, Scarsdale, N.Y., 1965—; asst. attending neurologist Brox Municipal Hosp. Centre, 1965—; attending neurologist Lawrence Hosp., Bronxville, 1965—, White Plains Hosp., 1965—. Chmn. med. adv. bd. Westchester chpt. Multiple Sclerosis Soc.; med. adviser Westchester chpt. Muscular Dystrophy Assn. Am. Mem. A.M.A., Am. Assn. Neuropathologists, Am. Acad. Neurology, Assn. for Research in Nervous and Mental Diseases. Home: 27 Hampton Rd Scarsdale NY 10583 Office: Harwood Bldg Scarsdale NY 10583

TAYLOR, LINDA ELIZABETH, psychologist; b. Sumter, S.C., Mar. 8, 1945; d. Reese Joye and Elizabeth Ann (Wilkes) Taylor; B.A., Furman U., 1967, M.A., 1969; postgrad. U. S.C., 1971—. Grad. asst. dept. psychology, dean women Furman U., Greenville, S.C., 1967-69; psychologist Vocational Rehab. Sch. Program, Sumter, 1969-70, Sumter Sch. Dist., 1969-72; chief psychologist Pee Dee Center, S.C. Dept. Mental Retardation, Florence, 1972-74, dir. diagnostic and evaluation service, 1974—. Itinerant instr. Coll. Gen. Studies, U. S.C., Columbia, 1969-71; psychometrist Whitten Village, S.C. Dept. Mental Retardation, Clinton, summer 1968; research asst. Adolescent Resources Center for Prevention Emotional Disturbance, summer 1969; vis. prof. Morris Coll., Sumter, summer 1971; in service tng. for local Headstart staff, summers 1973, 74; participant U. Ala. at Birmingham, Mgmt. Tng. Program, 1972-73. Membership chmn. Sumter County Mental Health Assn., 1970-72; mem. health services com. Florence County Headstart, 1973—. Mem. Am. (asso.), S.C. psychol. assns., S.C. Assn. Sch. Psychologists, S.C. Assn. Children with Learning Disabilities, Nat., S.C., Sumter County (sec., v.p. 1969-72) assns. retarded children, Am. Assn. Mental Deficiency, Council for Exceptional Children, S.C. Employees Assn., S.C. Farm Bur. Baptist. Home: 1807 Citadel Florence SC 29501 Office: 714 National Cemetery Rd Florence SC 29501

TAYLOR, LISA SUTER, museum dir.; b. N.Y.C., Jan. 8, 1933; d. Theo and Martina (Weincerl) von Bergen-Maier; student Corcoran Sch. Art, 1958-65, Georgetown U., 1958-62, Johns Hopkins, 1956-58; m. Bertrand L. Taylor III, Oct. 30, 1968; children—Lauren, Lindsay. Adminstrv. asst. President's Fine Arts Com., 1958-62; membership dir. Corcoran Gallery Art, 1962-66; program dir. Smithsonian Instn., 1966-69; dir. Cooper-Hewitt Mus. Decorative Arts and Design, Smithsonian Instn., 1969—. Mem. adv. bd. N.Y. State Assn. Museums, Museums Collaborative, Global Village, Am. Works, Center for Defensible Space Design, Resources Council, Friends of Zoo, N.Y. Recipient Exceptional Service award Smithsonian Instn., 1969, also Gold medal, 1972; Bronze plaque Johns Hopkins YMCA, 1958; medal of honor Am. Legion, 1951. Mem. Am., N.Y. State, N.Y.C. museum assns., Am. Craftsman's Council, Ceramics Circle, Needle and Bobbin Club, hon. mem. Am. Inst. Interior Designers, Nat. Soc. Interior Designers. Co-dir. (film) A Living Museum, 1968. Home: 1115 Fifth Av New York City NY 10028 Office: 9 E 90th St New York City NY 10028

TAYLOR, LYNNETTE DOBBINS (MRS. HOBART TAYLOR, JR.), educator, civic worker; b. Birmingham, Ala.; d. Albert Greene and Louise (Brown) Dobbins; B.S., Ala. State U., 1938; M.Ed., Wayne State U., 1948; m. Hobart Taylor, Jr., Jan. 26, 1950; children—Albert, Hobart III. Tchr. Detroit Pub. Schs., 1945-49; adminstr. elementary schs., 1949-63; exec. dir. Delta Sigma Theta; program analyst, field rep. Midwest region Office Econ. Opportunity, Washington, 1965—; woman's editor N.Y. edit. Chgo. Defender, Detroit Tribune; edn. editor children's page feature and columnist Mich. Chronicle. Adv. com. Truth in Lending, Fed. Res. Bd. Mem. exec. bd. United Found., 1960—. Bd. dirs. Hillcrest Children's Center, A.R.C. Mem. Friends Soc. Detroit Inst. Arts, Nat. Council Vol. Action, Nat. Friends Pub. TV. Mem. Internat. Soc. Women Educators, N.A.A.C.P., Urban League, Washington Ednl. TV Assn. (bd. dirs.), Am. Newspaper Women's Club, Women in Community Service (dir.), Delta Kappa Gamma, Phi Delta Kappa, Delta Sigma Theta. Democrat. Unitarian. Club: Nat. Women's Democratic (Washington), Old Acquaintance (Detroit). Home: 2500 Virginia Av NW Washington DC 20037 Office: 1707 New Hampshire St NW Washington DC 20009

TAYLOR, MARGARET KIRKWOOD (MRS. JOHN LANING TAYLOR), pub. relations cons.; b. Harding, Pa., Jan. 20, 1899; d. Thomas A. and Harriet (Welter) Kirkwood; student Cornell U., 1917-21; m. John Laning Taylor, Jan. 19, 1924; children—John Laning III, Jean Kirkwood. Condr. community radio program sta. WHCU, Cornell U., 1941-42; pub. relations and field rep., United Dairy Com., 1942-43; legislative rep. Nat. Milk Producers Fedn., Washington, 1943-44, ednl. dir., 1944-54; free-lance pub. relations cons., 1954—; exec. dir. Am. Parents Com., Inc., 1961-64. Cons. White House Conf. on Children and Youth, 1958-60; mem. Nat. Leadership Council Nat. Com. on Children and Youth, 1965-72; partner Conv. and Conf. Coordinators, 1960-70; cons. on programs for aging minorities, 1971—. Trustee Washington Hosp. Center, bd. dirs. women's aux. 1957—, pres. Women's Aux., 1968-70; bd. dirs. Hyman Research Found. Mem. exec. com. N.Y. Rep. State Com., 1936-42, vice chmn., 1938-42; alternate del.-at-large N.Y. Rep. Nat. Conv., 1940; nat. legislative chmn. Nat. Fedn. Rep. Women, 1961-63; mem. Women's Nat. Rep. Club; mem. League Rep. Women D.C., 1953—, pres., 1963-65, mem. Rep. Central Com. D.C., 1969—; mem. D.C. Mayor's Commn. on Food, Nutrition and Health, 1971—; mem. Equal Rights Amendment Ratification Council, 1972—. Recipient Bus. Woman citation, D.C. State Fedn. Bus. and Profl. Women's Clubs, 1957; award for vol. service to Washington Hosp. Center, 1973. Mem. Am. Legion Aux., 8 and 40 (Spl. Service award 1969), Nat. Fedn. Bus. and Profl. Women's Clubs, Pan Am. Liaison Com. Women's Orgns. Clubs: Cornell of Washington, Class '21 Women Cornell U. (reunion chmn. 1961-66, pres. 1966—); Cosmopolitan Business and Professional Women's (dir. 1966—); Alpha Phi. Episcopalian. Research on D.C. nursing homes for elderly. Home: The Woodner 3636 16th St NW Washington DC 20010

TAYLOR, MARIAN CATHERINE FAHS (MRS. ARTHUR D. TAYLOR), sch. adminstr.; b. Nazareth, Pa., July 15, 1921; d. John H., Jr. and Mae Evans (Luckenbach) Fahs; student Columbia; grad. Mandl Sch. Med. Technicians, N.Y.C., 1940; M.Ednl. Adminstrn., U. Mass., 1973, postgrad., 1973—; m. Arthur D. Taylor, Sept. 26, 1943 (dec. July 1970); children—Susan Lynn (Mrs. David Gottesman), Deborah Jane (Mrs. Alfred Fredricks), Richard James. Office mgr., technician doctor's office, Forest Hills, L.I. and N.Y.C., 1940-46; adminstr. Prospect Sch., North Bennington, Vt. 1967-72; adminstr. Antioch Grad. Sch., Harrisville, N.H., 1973—. Pres. P.T.A. local elementary, jr. high, high schs., 1954-62; troop leader, pres. council Girl Scouts, 1954-63; mem. Vt. Bd. Edn., 1969-73, chmn., 1968-73; active citizens com. for high sch., Bennington; mem. Gov.'s Commn. on Regional Community Colls., 1970—, Edn. Commn. of States, 1971-73; Nat. Com. For Support Pub. Schs. Life mem. bd. corporators Putnam Meml. Hosp., Bennington, 1965—; dir., chmn. finance com. United Counseling Service Bennington County, 1970-72; bd. dirs. Bennington Community Resources Center, 1970-71; mem. bd., also chmn. Mt. Anthony Union High Sch., 1963-67; bd. dirs. Bennington South Supervisory Union, 1964-67, N.H.-Vt. Blue Cross, 1972-73. Recipient Laymen's award Vt. Edn. Assn., 1965, Pres.'s citation outstanding service edn. Greater Bennington Assn., 1965. Mem. Nat. Assn. State Bds. Edn. (dir.-at-large 1968-73), Dollars for Scholars (bd. dirs. Bennington chpt. 1967-68). Home: 4 Summit Rd Keene NH 03401 Office: Antioch Grad Sch Harrisville NH 03450

TAYLOR, MARY ALICE (MRS. WALTER E. TAYLOR), editor; b. South Bend, Ind., Apr. 20, 1916; d. James and Isabella (Power) Smith; grad. high sch.; m. Walter E. Taylor, May 17, 1936; children—Walter Alexis, John Stacy. Social news Potter Enterprise, Inc., Coudersport, Pa., 1954-57; reporter Olean (N.Y.) Times Herald, 1954-57; editor, co-pub. Oregon (O.) Pub. Co., Inc., 1967—. Mem. com. on drug abuse Concerned Citizens Core, Oregon, 1971-73. Recipient certificate of award Oregon Fraternal Order of Police, 1972; Osman C. Hooper editorial award Ohio Newspaper Assn., 1970, other awards. Mem. Oregon Bus. and Profl. Women's Club (career achievement award 1970, pres. 1974—), Toastmistress Club (pres. 1971, sec. 1972-73). Home: 562 S Wheeling St Oregon OH 43616 Office: 2460 Navarre Av Oregon OH 32515

TAYLOR, MARY CATHERINE (MRS. JACK FRANCIS MAHON TAYLOR), food mfg. co. propr., author; b. Mt. Vernon, Ill., July 24, 1904; d. William Bogan and Nelle Maude (Sullivan) Goodrich; student schs. U.S. and abroad; m. Jack Francis Mahon Taylor, Dec. 31, 1927; children—Ursula Taylor Schorer, James M., Judith Taylor Cant. Co-owner, operator Mayacamas Vineyards, Napa County, Cal., 1941-68; propr. Mayacamas Foods, Ltd., Sonoma, Cal., 1971—; dir. Impi Highland Pty., Victoria, Australia. Author: Catch That Catch Can, 1945; Rounds and Rounds, 1946; Rounds for Recorders, 1969; Mushroom Magic, 1963; Mayacamas Sampler, 1962. Address: 215 Stuyvesant Dr Sleepy Hollow San Anselmo CA 94960

TAYLOR, MARY CURTIS SMITH (MRS. JOHN GORDON TAYLOR), musician; b. Shepherdsville, Ky., Jan. 9, 1937; d. Curtis Waldo and Hazel Dell (Trunnell) Smith; student U. Louisville, 1955; B.S. in Music, Murray State U., 1958, M.Ed., 1960; m. John Gordon Taylor, Aug. 16, 1958; children—John Gordon, Tiffany May, Whitney Adams. Soloist, Louisville Orch., 1954, mem., 1963-71; music educator, Benton, Ky., 1958-60, Jefferson County, 1960-64; concertmaster Louisville Civic Orch., 1963—; pvt. violin instrn.; mem. profl. strolling violinists; instr. music appreciation Alice Lloyd Coll., Pippa Passes, Ky., summer 1967; violinist Ky. Opera Assn., 1967-70; 1st violinist Nashville Symphony, 1969-71, prin. 2d violin, 1971—; mem. faculty music dept. Murray (Ky.) State U., 1974—. Mem. Nat. Soc. Colonial Dames XVII Century, Sigma Alpha Iota. Club: Murray Woman's. Home: Route 7 Box 13 Murray KY 42071

TAYLOR, (MARY) EMILY, univ. adminstr.; b. Columbia, Ala., Apr. 13, 1915; d. Lee R. and Laura Pearle (Rollins) Taylor; certificate Urbana Coll., 1935; B.S., Ohio State U., 1937, M.A., 1944; Ed.D., Ind. U., 1955. English tchr., DeGraff, O., 1937-38; chmn. English dept. Deer Park High Sch., Cin., 1938-44; counselor Ind. U., Bloomington, 1944-46; dean women No. Mont. Coll., Havre, 1946-51, U. Kan., Lawrence, 1956—; asso. dean women Miami U., Oxford, O., 1952-56. Nat. adviser Intercollegiate Assn. Women Students, 1969-72, 73—; cons.-evaluator North Central Assn. Colls. and Secondary Schs., 1973—; cons., workshop leader on affirmative action, 1973—. Legislative chmn. Kan. Gov.'s Commn. on Status of Women, 1968—; mem. nat. adv. com. Com. for Re-election Pres. Bd. dirs. Meml. Union Corp.; trustee Status of Women Research and Edn. Fund, 1974—, also v.p. Named to Women's Hall of Fame, U. Kan., 1970, Kansan of Year for Women's Rights, Topeka Capital-Jour., 1971. Mem. Nat., Kan. (pres. 1966-70) assns. women deans, adminstrs. and counselors, Nat. (editorial bd. jour. 1969-71), Kan. (pres. 1970) assns. student personnel adminstrs., Am. Assn. U. Women (pres. North Mont. br. 1950, pres. Lawrence br. 1973—), Nat., Kan. women's polit. caucuses, Nat., Kan. councils women, Women's Equity Action League (state convenor 1972, trustee 1973—), Nat. Orgn. for Women, Nat. Soc. Owens (dir. 1962-70), Interstate Assn. Commns. on Status of Women (dir. 1970—, v.p. 1974—), C. of C., Mortar Board, Kappa Alpha Theta. Republican. Episcopalian. Editor: Breakthrough, 1972. Home: 847 Avalon Rd Lawrence KS 66044

TAYLOR, MARY JOAN (MRS. EDWARD MCKINLEY TAYLOR JR.), lawyer; b. Kenton, O., Dec. 24, 1926; d. Maurice A. and Martina (Dolan) McMahon; student St. Mary Springs Coll., 1944-45; Asso. Degree in Bus. Administrn. Franklin U., 1946-49; J.D. with high distinction, Ohio No. U., 1951; postgrad., U. Wyo., 1954-56; m. Edward McKinley Taylor, Jr., Apr. 23, 1952; 1 dau., Mary Margaret. Admitted to Ohio bar, 1951; gen. practice law, Kenton, 1951-52, Wichita Falls, Tex., 1953—; mem. law firm Taylor and Taylor, Dayton, O., 1957—; law librarian Franklin U., 1948-49. Mem. Ohio Bar Assn., Montgomery County Law Library Assn., Ohio No. U. Alumni Assn. (sec. Miami Valley 1958-60), Iota Tau Lambda, Kappa Beta Pi. Club: Soroptimist. Address: 7417 N Main St Dayton OH 45415

TAYLOR, MARY OLA DREW (MRS. WALTER T. TAYLOR), poet; b. Old Washington, Tex., Apr. 10, 1880; d. John Melvin and Lola (Monroe) Drew; student Sam Houston Tchrs. Coll., 1896-97, Baylor U., 1900-01; m. Walter T. Taylor, June 3, 1904; children—Lola Anita (Mrs. Edwin F. Rea), Mary Ola (Mrs. James Ford Hoke), Walter. Contbr. poetry and articles to many mags., jours. and daily newspapers. Mem. Key Women Am. (hon.), Poetry Soc. Tex. (life). Democrat. Methodist. Mem. Order Eastern Star. Club: Shakespeare (organizer 1920, 1st pres. 1920-21). Author: Life's Meditation, 1958; Texas History in Poetry. Contbg. author: Greater Anthology of Verse, 1939; Anthology of American Poetry, 1962; Vision in Verse, 1967. Home: 167 Oak Dr Lake Jackson TX 77566

TAYLOR, ROSLYN DONNY, physician; b. Columbia, S.C., Feb. 14, 1941; d. Otto Gary and Roslyn Elizabeth (Alfriend) Donny; B.A., Emory Coll., 1963; M.D., Emory U., 1967; m. Benjamin Thomas Taylor, June 10, 1962; children—Cynthia Gambill, Kevin Emroy. Intern U.S. Naval Hosp., Jacksonville, Fla., 1967-68; practice medicine, Green Cove Springs, Fla., 1968-70; physician U.S. Naval Hosp., Rota, Spain, 1972-73; resident family practice Spartanburg (S.C.) Gen. Hosp., 1974—. First aid counselor Boy Scouts Am. Mem. Nat. Assn. Residents and Interns, Am. Med. Women's Assn., Phi Beta Kappa, Alpha Omega Alpha, Phi Sigma. Presbyn. Home: 13 Elmhurst St Inman SC 29349 Office: 43 N Main St Inman SC 29349

TAYLOR, VERA COOK (MRS. GLENN LAVERN TAYLOR), educator; b. Sioux City, Ia., June 4, 1924; d. Clarence R. and Mabel (Morrell) Cook; B.S., Ia. State U., 1946, M.S., 1949; postgrad. summers U. Cal. at Berkeley, 1959, Ore. State U., 1964; Ph.D., U. So. Cal., 1970; m. Glenn Lavern Taylor, June 6, 1948; children—Jeannette, Carol, Walter. High Sch. tchr., Ia., 1944-45, 47-49, 54-55; extension home economist Ia. State U., 1955-58; instr., dept. chmn. Coll. of Sequoias, Visalia, Cal., 1958-65; asst. prof. Cal. State U. at Fresno, 1965-69, asso. prof., 1969-73, prof., 1973—, coordinator interdisciplinary child devel. program, 1969—. Vis. lectr. U. Alta., Edmonton, Can. 1960, U. So. Cal., 1969; cons. Early Childhood Edn., 1966—; mem. U.S. Nat. Com. for Early Childhood Edn. Mem. Cal. Coll. and U. Faculty Assn., Am. Assn., for Higher Edn., Am. Home Econs. Assn. (past pres. Central dist., past state dir.), Nat. Assn. for Edn. Young Children (state pres.), Phi Kappa Phi, Omicron Nu, Kappa Delta Pi, Delta Phi Upsilon. Editor: Readings in Child Development, 1968. Home: 205 Krest Way Madera CA 93637 Office: Fresno State Coll Fresno CA 93726

TAYLOR, VIRGINIA LEE HOOVER (MRS. JOHN THERROTT TAYLOR), assn. exec.; b. Balt., June 8, 1946; d. Sterling Wilmer and Dorothy Virginia (Phillips) Hoover; B.A. (Sears Roebuck scholar), U. Md., 1968; postgrad. (Danforth summer fellow) Western Md. Coll., 1970—; m. John Therrott Taylor, Aug. 15, 1970. Program and club dir. Spl. Services, 8th U.S. Army, Seoul, Korea, 1968-69; tchr. social studies Carroll County Bd. Edn., Westminster, Md., 1969-70; Carroll County program dir. Balt. Area-Met. YMCA, Balt., 1970—. Youth and govt. coordinator Greater Balt. Area 1971—; mem. Carroll County Council Social Agys., 1972—. Mem. Assn. Profl. YMCA Dirs. Democrat. Lutheran (publicity chmn. for bldg. program 1973—). Home: 176 Pennsylvania Av Westminster MD 21157 Office: 84 E Main St Westminster MD 21157

TAYLOR, YVONNE WALKER (MRS. R. HARVEY TAYLOR), educator; b. New Bedford, Mass.; d. D. Ormonde and Eva (Revallion) Walker; B.S., Wilberforce U., 1936; M.A., Boston U., 1938; hon. D.H., Monrovia Coll., Liberia, 1950; Ed.S., U. Kan., 1964; m. R. Harvey Taylor, Aug. 28, 1963. Asst. prof. English, adminstrv. asst. to pres. Wilberforce U., 1956-64; asso. prof. edn., chmn. dept. 1964—, asst. acad. dean, 1967, acting acad. dean, 1968, dean instrn., 1969-72, acad. dean, 1973—; Danforth asso., 1968—. Mem. Wilberforce Property Owners and Voters Assn., Com. on Juvenile Delinquency, Xenia, O. Named Tchr. of Year, Kappa Alpha Psi, 1966, 67. Mem. Am. Assn. Higher Edn., Nat. Council Tchrs. English, Nat. Assn. Acad. Deans, Nat. Assn. Women Deans and Counselors, Links Inc. (pres. 1966-68), Am. Assn. U. Women (sec. 1957-60), Alpha Kappa Alpha (basileus 1959-61). Methodist. Clubs: Cliques, Gourmets, Podners. Address: Box 336 Wilberforce OH 45384

TAYLOR-BRASLOW, EDITH MAE ELIZABETH (MRS. LAWRENCE BRASLOW), physician; b. Melrose, Mass., Dec. 23, 1916; d. Lyndon Elmer and Beulah Evelyn (Steele) Taylor; student Redlands U., 1934-37; M.D., Loma Linda U., 1941; m. Lawrence Braslow, Dec. 22, 1941; children—Judith Elizabeth (Mrs. Christian Zacher), Jonathan Steele, Norman, Lawrence, Devorah Evelyn (Mrs. David McIntosh), Joel Tupper, Rebekah Arletta. Intern, Los Angeles County Gen. Hosp., 1941-42; resident in pediatrics Los Angeles Children's Hosp., 1942-43; resident in anesthesiology Loma Linda U. Sch. Med., Loma Linda, Cal., 1961-64; practice medicine, specializing in pediatrics, Riverside, Cal., 1954-61, specializing in anesthesiology, 1964—; staff Loma Linda White Meml. Hosp., 1948-49; Parkview Community Hosp., 1964—. Recipient gold medal Am. Physicians Art Assn., 1968. Home: 2915 Las Flores Av Riverside CA 92503 Office: 3875 Jackson Av Riverside CA 92503

TEAGARDEN, FLORENCE MABEL, educator; b. Dallas, W.Va., Sept. 5, 1887; d. William David and Sarah Ella (Braddock) Teagarden; A.B., U. Pitts., 1915, M.A., 1916; Ph.D., Columbia, 1924. Mem. faculty, instr. to prof. psychology U. Pitts., 1915-57, prof. emeritus, 1957—; practice clin. psychology, Pitts. Summer teaching Mills Coll.; lectr. to various orgns. An organizer United Fund. Bd. dirs. numerous civic socs. Diplomate Am. Bd. Examiners in Profl. Psychology. Fellow A.A.A.S., Am. Psychol. Assn., Am. Orthopsychiat. Assn.; mem. Am. Assn. U. Profs., Pa. Psychol. Assn., Child Devel. Assn., Sigma Xi, Pi Lambda Theta, Kappa Delta Pi. Club: South Hills College (Mt. Lebanon, Pa.). Author: Child Psychology for Professional Workers, 1940, rev. edit., 1946; also numerous articles. Home: 726 Gypsy Lane Pittsburgh PA 15228

TEAGUE, CAROL LYNN JOYCE, research programmer; b. Cleve., May 26, 1941; d. Robert Emmett and Carolyn Iola (Leverett) Joyce; B.S., Ohio U., 1965, M.S., 1965; m. Charles Dwight Teague, Aug. 29, 1964; children—Andrew Franklin, Nancy Joyce. Computer programmer United Aircraft Research Labs., Hartford, Conn., 1963;

instr. math. Eastern Ky. U., 1965-67, research programmer, 1970—; systems programmer U. Rochester, 1967-69, asst. lectr. bus. adminstrn., 1968-69. Mem. Ky. Acad. Sci., League of Women Voters. Home: 117 Hammons Dr Richmond KY 40475

TEAGUE, SARAH ANN CRUMBLEY (MRS. DONALD WAYNE TEAGUE), journalist; b. Holly Pond, Ala., Aug. 17, 1938; d. James Burr and Alma (Reid) Crumbley; B.A., Howard Coll., 1959; m. Donald Wayne Teague, Feb. 20, 1960. Asst. in pub. relations Howard Coll., Birmingham, Ala., 1959-64; fashion editor Birmingham Post-Herald, 1964-72, women's editor, 1972—. Co-chmn. state publicity Birmingham Festival Arts, 1963-64; nat. sec. Howard Coll. Alumni Assn., 1963-64; mem. U. Alumni Assn. Scholarship Com., 1964-67; mem. Birmingham's Fall Fashion Time Com., 1964—. Mem. Chi Omega, Sigma Delta Chi. Baptist. Home: 1429 S 28th St Birmingham AL 35205 Office: 2200 4th Av N Birmingham AL 35202

TEAL, ERIN HOWELL (MRS. ROBERT BURNS TEAL), univ. adminstr.; b. Ozark, Ala., Mar. 13, 1918; d. Alvie R.V. and Sarah Emmie (Belcher) Howell; student Riley Bus. Sch., 1936; m. Robert Burns Teal, Oct. 13, 1946; 1 dau., Ann (Mrs. Billy Wayne Kelton). Sec., Ozark (Ala.) Prodn. Credit Assn., 1937-46; claims clk. Ala. Employment Service, Alexander City, 1947-48; sec. Ala. Hwy. Dept., Troy, 1951-55; sec., placement office Troy (Ala.) State U., 1956-65, placement asst., placement office, 1965-67, dir. placement, 1967—. Mem. So. Coll. Placement Assn., Ala. Edn. Assn., Troy State U. Edn. Assn. Baptist. Club: Mid-Century (Troy). Home: 1408 S Brundidge St Troy AL 36081 Office: Room 105 Bibb Graves Troy State U Troy AL 36081

TEANEY, BEVERLY ANN BILAS (MRS. ROBERT J. TEANEY), educator; b. Passaic, N.J., May 1, 1936; d. Joseph and Helen (Ziptko) Bilas; B.S., Boston U., 1958; M.A., William Paterson State Coll., 1962; D.Ed., Pa. State U., 1971; m. Robert J. Teaney, Nov. 25, 1973. Tchr., Bd. Edn., Pequannock, N.J., 1958-60, East Orange (N.J.) Bd. Edn., 1960-65; radio and television spokeswoman Singer Mfg. Co., N.Y.C., 1965-67; tchr., South Orange (N.J.)-Maplewood Bd. Edn., 1967-68; asst. prof. early childhood edn. Grad. Sch. Edn., Fordham U., N.Y.C., 1970-74, early childhood program writer, 1970—, fellow, 1972—. Research evaluator N.Y.C. Corrective Reading Programs, N.Y.C. Bd. Edn., 1970-73; cons. early childhood programs Urban Edn., Inc., 1972—. Sec., N.J. Young Republicans, 1962; vice-chmn. Passaic County Young Republicans, 1957-58; county com. woman, Passaic County, N.J., 1964-66. Palmer scholar, 1956-57, Charles Howard scholar, 1957-58. Mem. Phi Lambda Theta. Home: 2200 Victory Pkwy Cincinnati OH 45206 Office: Sch Edn Fordham U 113 W 60th St New York City NY 10023

TEANY, SUSAN CALDWELL (MRS. GEORGE W. TEANY), sch. librarian; b. Roanoke, Va., Oct. 15, 1942; d. Tazewell Harvey and Elva Mae (Altizer) Caldwell; B.S., Radford Coll., 1964, M.S., 1967; m. George William Teany, Jan. 8, 1972. Librarian, Pulaski (Va.) High Sch., 1964-68, Radford (Va.) High Sch., 1968—. Mem. Va. (chmn. dist. M. librarians), Radford (sec.) edn. assns., Kappa Delta Pi, Pi Gamma Mu, Phi Kappa Phi. Mem. Ch. of Christ. Home: Route 1 Box 539 Christiansburg VA 24073 Office: Radford High Sch DeHaven Dr Radford VA 24141

TE ATA, actress, folklore interpreter; b. nr. Tishomingo, Okla.; A.B., Okla. Coll. Women; student theatre sch. Carnegie Inst. Tech. Pub. relations asst. Okla. Coll. Women, 1957; numerous roles on Broadway, also Okla., Pitts., Ark.; tours with folklore program colls., other orgns., U.S., Europe; participated Indian Workshop, Idyllwild (Cal.) Sch. Music and the Arts, 1950; presented folklore Chickasaw Centennial, Tishomingo, Okla., 1957. Named to Okla. Hall of Fame, 1957, Okla. Coll. Liberal Arts Hall of Fame, 1972; Lake Te Ata, Palisades Interstate Park, named in her honor. Mem. Soc. Woman Geographers, Nat. Congress Am. Indians, Okla. Hist. Soc., Okla. Heritage Center, Five Tribes Museum. Zeta Phi Eta. Address: 121 S Dillon St Moore OK 73060

TEATER, DOROTHY JANE SEATH (MRS. ROBERT WOODSON TEATER), housing and home furnishings specialist; b. Manhattan, Kan., Feb. 11, 1931; d. Dwight Moody and Minnie Martha (Stahnke) Seath; student La. State U., 1947-48; B.S. in Home Econs. Edn., U. Ky., 1951; M.S. in Home Mgmt., Ohio State U., 1954; m. Robert Woodson Teater, May 24, 1952; children—David D., James S., Donald R., Andrew S. Tchr. home econs. Georgetown (Ky.) City Schs., 1951-53; tchr. adult clothing Columbus (O.) City Schs., 1965; housing, home furnishings specialist Ohio Co-op. Extension Service, Ohio State U., Columbus, 1967-73. Mem. Local Draft Bd. 41, Columbus, 1968-71; mem. SSS Appeal Bd., So. dist. State Ohio, 1972; pres. Dominion Jr. High Sch. P.T.A., Columbus, 1972-73; mem. City Columbus Consumer Protection Commn., 1972—. Mem. Am., Ohio home econs. assns., Mortar Bd., Phi Upsilon Omicron, Delta Zeta, Alpha Lambda Delta, Kappa Delta Pi. Republican. Methodist. Home: 286 W Weisheimer Rd Columbus OH 43214

TEBALDI, RENATA, opera singer; b. Pesaro, Italy, Jan. 2, 1922; d. Teobaldo and Giuseppina (Barbieri) Tebaldi; student Arrigo Bolto Conservatory, Pesaro Gioacchino Rossini Conservatory, Parma, Italy; pupil of Carmen Melis, Giuseppe Pais. Lyric soprano profl. debut in Mefistofele, Rovigo, 1944; debut at LaScala, 1946; singer opera houses of Naples, Rome, Venice, Bologna, Florence, Modena, Cesana, Turin, Venice, Pompeii; Am. debut in Aida, San Francisco Opera Co., 1950; debut in Otello, Met. Opera House, N.Y.C., 1955; singer operatic roles in La Boheme, Madame Butterfly, Tosca. Roman Catholic. Home: 1 Piazza Gusatalla Milan Italy Office: care Metropolitan Opera House Lincoln Center New York City NY 10019

TEBERG, ANNABEL JEAN (MRS. LORIN C. SPENCER), pediatrician; b. St. Paul, Feb. 25, 1926; d. Laurence E. and Annabel D. (Drenckhabor) Teberg; B.A., U. Minn., 1948, B.S., 1949, M.D., 1952; m. Lorin C. Spencer, July 19, 1952; children—Suzanna, Lucinda, Daniel, Marsha, Stuart, Amanda. Intern, Los Angeles County Gen. Hosp., 1951-52, resident pediatrics, 1952-53; resident pediatrics U. Cal. at Los Angeles, 1954-55; pediatrician Kaiser Permanente, North Hollywood, 1955-56; practice pediatrics, Pomona, 1958-61; asst. clin. prof. pediatrics U. So. Cal.-Los Angeles County Med. Center, 1961—; dir. presch. handicapped Casa Colina Hosp., Pomona, 1961—; pediatric cons. mental retardation clinic Pomona and El Monte Health Dept., 1969-72; cons. educable handicapped program Alta Loma and Cucamonga Sch., 1967-72; cons. multiply handicapped sch., Asuza, 1968-72; cons. maternity-infant care program Los Angeles, 1969-71. Sec. Upland Environmental Task Force, 1972. Bd. dirs. Casa Colina Hosp., 1960-67, East End Symphony Assn., 1971-72. Roman Catholic. Home: 1894 N Euclid St Upland CA 91786 Office: 318 N Indian Hill Claremont CA 91711

TEC, NECHAMA (MRS. LEON TEC), sociologist; b. Lublin, Poland, May 15, 1931; d. Roman and Esther (Finkelstein) Bawnik; came to U.S., 1952, naturalized, 1960; B.S. cum laude, Columbia, 1954, M.A., 1955, Ph.D. (Social Sci. Research fellow), 1963; m. Leon Tec, Feb. 14, 1950; children—Leora, Roland. Lectr., Columbia, N.Y.C., 1957-60, 68-71; vis. prof. sociology Trinity Coll., Hartford, Conn., 1972-73; dir. research Mid-Fairfield Child Guidance Center, Norwalk, Conn., 1968—. Fellow Am. Sociol. Assn.; mem. Phi Beta Kappa. Author: Gambling in Sweden, 1964; Grass is Green in Suburbia, 1974. Contbr. numerous articles on social problems, social sci. and medicine to profl. jours. Home: 11 Rockyfield Westport CT 06880

TEDDLIE, STELLA MAYE HARWELL (MRS. HORACE TEDDLIE), educator; b. Cedar Hill, Tex.; d. Josiah Clayton and Myrtle Mae (Trees) Harwell; B.A., U. Wyo., 1945; postgrad. So. Methodist U., 1953-56, 63—; Ph.D. (hon.), Hamilton State U., 1973; m. Horace Teddlie, Apr. 1, 1926; children—Albert Harwell, Merritt Bonar. Binding librarian Dallas Pub. Library, 1934-42; tchr. pub. schs., Okla., Colo., Wyo., Tex., 1945-53, Dallas Pub. Schs., 1953-56, 60—; tchr. Basic Education Program; manager Preston Center Travel Office, Dallas, 1956-57, Dallas Travel Service, 1957-60. Chmn. bd. dirs. Thorp Spring Christian Coll.; chmn. Dallas Tchrs. Blood Bank com. Mem. N.E.A. (textbook com. for Dallas schs.), Tex. Tchrs. Assn., Tex. Council Geography Tchrs., (pres. 1969-71), Dallas Classroom Tchrs. Assn. (rep.), Phi Kappa Phi, Psi Chi, Alpha Delta Kappa (charter Kappa chpt. 1956, internat. transp. chmn. 1957—, organizer Mexico City chpt. 1963, state historian 1974—). Democrat. Mem. Ch. of Christ. Clubs: Dallas Export-Import, Zonta (program chmn. Dallas 1958-59). Author: (handbook) Practical Handicraft, 1942. Home: 2718 Over Crest Dallas TX 75211 Office: 2940 Singleton Blvd Dallas TX 75212

TEDROW, MARY ETHEL (MRS. MYRON E. TEDROW), food product co. exec.; b. Griggsville, Ill., Nov. 11, 1919; d. Robert Leander and Elizabeth Dora (Butler) Walker; grad. Gem City Coll., 1938; m. Myron E. Tedrow, Oct. 4, 1953. Stenographer M.D. King Milling Co., Pittsfield, Ill., 1939-68, asst. sec., 1968-71, v.p., sec., 1971—. Sec. Pike King Feed Co., Griggsville, 1968—, King Transit Co., Pittsfield, Ill., 1970—, King Feed Co., Blandinsville, Ill., 1973—. Republican. Mem. Christian Ch. Mem. Order Eastern Star. Home: 220 Piper Lane Pittsfield IL 62363 Office: 502 N Madison Pittsfield IL 62363

TEECHER, JUNE ELAINE, lawyer; b. Los Angeles, June 14; d. Mack and Stella (Feinstein) Teecher; student Pomona Coll., 1942-44; B.A., U. So. Cal., 1947; J.D., Southwestern U., 1950; m. Freddie Slack, Feb. 11, 1953 (dec. Aug. 1965); 1 son, Robert Frederic Slack. Admitted to Cal. bar, 1951, U.S. Ct. Claims, 1965, Tax Ct. U.S., 1965, U.S. Supreme Ct. bar, 1965; practiced in Beverly Hills, 1951-65, Los Angeles, 1965—. Pres., Studio City-Ajijic (Mexico) Sister City Assn., 1972—. Bd. dirs. Nat. Audubon Soc. Mem. Assn. Am. Trial Lawyers, Cal. Trial Lawyers Assn., Los Angeles Trial Lawyers' Assn. Advocate, Nat. Assn. Women Lawyers, Am. Judicature Soc., State Bar Cal., Internat., Am., Los Angeles County, Hollywood bar assns., Studio City C. of C. (pres. women's div. 1972-74, bd. dirs. 1972—), Nat. Bus. and Profl. Women (v.p. Studio City br. 1972-73), Iota Tau Tau. Home: 3905 Eureka Dr Studio City CA 91604 Office: 8019 Melrose Av Los Angeles CA 90046

TEEL, DONA RUTH MCINTOSH (MRS. WILLIAM TEEL), civic worker; b. Denver, Dec. 29, 1932; d. Donald M. McIntosh and Ruth (Hollister) Smith; B.A., Conn. Coll., 1954; postgrad. U. Denver, 1955-56; m. Peter Kerr Buchan, Jan. 9, 1962 (div. Jan. 1970); 1 dau., Holly Kerr; m. 2d, William Teel, Oct. 2, 1971; 1 son, William McIntosh. Apprentice, Thornton Fuller Studio, Denver, 1955-57; sales, decorator Sarkisian's, Denver, 1957-58; mgr. Sarkisian's Marco Polo Shop, Colorado Springs, Colo., 1959-62. Chmn. historic bldg. survey com. Jr. League of Denver, 1968-69; mem. Nat. Trust for Historic Preservation. Trustee, Historic Denver. Mem. State Hist. Soc. Colo. (dir.), Nat. Soc. Colonial Dames Am., Denver Botanic Gardens Guild. Club: Connecticut College (pres. 1968-70). Home: 3 Lynn Rd Englewood CO 80110

TEELE, DORIS CORINNE HEADRICK, realtor, author, artist; b. Springfield, Ill., Feb. 13, 1926; d. John Raymond and Corinne (Burch) Headrick; ed. Lincoln Land Community Coll., Sangamon State U., Realtors Inst. Ill., Mag. Inst. N.Y.; m. Paul Edward Teele, Nov. 27, 1945; children—Cheryl S., Stephan Paul. Salesman Al Sokolis Realtor, Springfield, Ill., 1955-57; owner Doris Teele Realtor, Springfield, 1958-60, 66-72; salesman James D. Call Realtor, Springfield, 1960-64, Charles Dunseth Realtor, Springfield, 1964-66; owner D'Eleet Residential Rentals; notary pub. Served with USMC, 1945. Mem. Springield Bd. Realtors, Ill. Assn. Real Estate Bds., Nat. Inst. Real Estate Brokers, Nat. Assn. Real Estate Bds., Christian Bus. and Profl. Women's Club, Family Motor Coach Assn., Clayville Folk Arts Guild, Women Marine Assn., Lincoln Meml. Gardens, Smithsonian Inst., Alpha Omega. Lutheran. Home: 4004 Hazelcrest Rd Springfield IL 62703 Office: 430 W Edwards St Springfield IL 62704

TEEPEN, NANCY ROUX, educator; b. Perrysburg, O., Mar. 15, 1935; d. Dale Jearum and LaDonna Ruth (Helman) Roux; B.S., Ohio U., 1957; M.A., Ohio State U., 1963; m. Feb. 2, 1957 (div.); children—Kristina Lynn, Jeremy Roux. Research asst. Fels Research Inst., 1961-65; lectr. Central State U., 1965-67; lectr. psychology Wilberforce (O.) U., 1969-71, research asso., 1973—; lectr. psychology Antioch Coll., Yellow Springs, O., 1971—. Mem. U.S. Trotting Assn., Am. Craft Council, Am., Ohio, Miami Valley (mem. exec. bd. 1973—) psychol. assns. Home: Box 54B Route 1 Yellow Springs OH 45387

TEER, BARBARA ANN, dir., actress, author, educator; b. St. Louis, June 18, 1937; d. Fred L. and Lila B. (Benjamin) Teer; B.A. in Dance, U. Ill., 1957; studied drama with Sanford Meisner, Paul Mann, Phillip Burton and Lloyd Richards; studied dance in Berlin, Paris and Wigman Sch. of Dance; 1 son, Omi. Founder Nat. Black Theatre, 1968—; dir. Me and My Song for Black Heritage Series for CBS-TV; writer, dir., co-producer film Rise / A Love Poem for a Love People based on life of Malcolm X; dir. (Off-Broadway musical) The Believers, Day of Absence (award winner), Who's Got His Own at Am. Place Theatre, Home Movies (Vernon Rice award); dance capt. (on Broadway) for Agnes DeMille in musical Kwamina (Antoinette Perry award); adapted, produced We Sing a New Song; appeared in Slaves, 1968, Angel Levine, 1969; appeared on Broadway in Where's Daddy?, 1967; appeared on TV show SOUL; guest lectr. on contemporary Black art for Black Heritage Series CBS-TV. Cultural dir. teenage workshop Dorothy Maynor's Harlem Sch. Arts, 1967; founder (with Robert Hooks) Group Theatre Workshop. Contbr. to Black Power Revolt, 1968. Contbg. editor Black Theatre Mag., 1969—. Contbr. numerous articles to drama sect. Sunday N.Y. Times, Negro Digest. Creator new art form called Revival. Home: 792 Columbus Av New York City NY 10025 Office: care of Nat Black Theatre 9 E 125th St New York City NY 10035

TEES, MIRIAM HADLEY, librarian; b. Montreal, Que., Can., Feb. 24, 1923; d. Frederick James and Beatrice Mary (Armstrong) Tees; B.A., McGill U., 1944, B. L.S., 1951. Asst. librarian Internat. Civil Aviation Orgn., Montreal, 1951-53; with Royal Bank Can., Montreal, 1953—, chief librarian, 1953—. Dir. Corp. Profl. Librarians Que., 1969-73, pres., 1971-72; sessional lectr. McGill U., 1971-75. Commr. Girl Guides Can., 1960-66. Mem. Spl. Libraries Assn. (chpt. pres. 1957-58; dir. 1970-73, pres. elect 1974-75), Que. Library Assn. (treas. 1964-65; pres. 1965-66), Commn. des Bibliothéques Publiques du Québec, Am. Recorder Soc. Home: 1 Rosemount Av Montreal PQ H3Y 3G6 Canada Office: 1 Place Ville Marie Montreal PQ H3C 3A9 Canada

TEESE, LORRAINE MACLEAN (MRS. PHILIP ALANSON TEESE), psychologist; b. Newark, Nov. 6, 1924; d. Nicholas Michael and Rose Marie (Rank) MacLean; B.S., N.J. State Tchrs. Coll., 1946; M.A., Columbia Tchrs. Coll., 1947; certificate in Sch. Psychology, Seton Hall U., 1972; m. Philip Alanson Teese, Aug. 7, 1954; children—Jeffrey Stuart, Gregory Duncan, Martha Ellen. Tchr., Chatham Borough, N.J., 1946-47; tech. specialist Psychol. Corp., N.Y.C., 1947-49; tchr., Summit, N.J., 1949-56; clin. psychologist Child Evaluation Center, Morristown (N.J.) Meml. Hosp., 1972; sch. psychologist, Parsippany-Troy Hills, N.J., 1972—. Staff asst. Red Cross of Oranges and Maplewood, 1941. Mem. Am., N.J. psychol. assns., N.J., Morris County assns. sch. psychologists, Summit Tchrs. Assn., Kappa Delta Pi. Republican. Conglist. Clubs: Maplewood (N.J.) Junior Women's (chmn. Am. home dept. 1952); Racquets (Short Hills). Home: 88 Stewart Rd Short Hills NJ 07078 Office: PO Box 52 Parsippany NJ 07054

TEFFERTELLER, RUTH SINOVOY (MRS. RALPH B. TEFFERTELLER), social worker; b. Albany, N.Y., Aug. 28, 1917; d. Samuel and Jennie (Katz) Sinovoy; B.A., N.Y. State Coll. for Tchrs., 1939; postgrad. Ia. U., 1939-40; M.S.W., Columbia, 1955; m. Ralph B. Tefferteller, Sept. 5, 1941. Social worker A.R.C., St. Louis, Denver, Roswell, N.M., Ft. Bragg, N.C., 1942-46; dir. Children's div., camp dir., program dir., dir. spl. project for delinquency prevention and control Henry Street Settlement, N.Y.C., 1946-68; asst. chief Unitarian-Universalist Service Com. Project in Vietnam, in cooperation with U.S. AID Mission, 1968-71; asso. area dir. Danvers-Salem area Mass. Dept. Mental Health, 1971—. cons. Astor Project, 1961-62. Mem. Nat. Assn. Social Workers. Contbr. articles to profl. jours. Address: 127 Front St Marblehead MA 01945

TEICHMAN, JUDITH LEONE, lawyer, city ofcl.; b. Benton Harbor, Mich., June 24, 1938; d. William W. and Leona L. (Dahnke) Teichman; B.A., Mich. State U., 1959; LL.B., U. Mich., 1966; m. Chester F. Relyea, Apr. 15, 1971. Admitted to Cal. bar, 1966; asst. regional atty., U.S. Dept. Health, Edn. and Welfare, San Francisco, 1967-72; dep. city atty. City of San Francisco, 1972—. Mem. Cal., San Francisco bar assns., Nat. Lawyer's Guild. Home: 2558 Clay St San Francisco CA 94115 Office: City Hall San Francisco CA 94102

TEIGEN, DOROTHY MARIE RUSSELL (MRS. FERDINAND AUSTIN TEIGEN), author, journalist, pub. relations cons.; b. Galveston, Tex.; d. Charles Percival and Claire (Pritchard) Russell; B.A., Hunter Coll.; postgrad. Columbia, Sorbonne, Paris; m. Ferdinand Austin Teigen, Dec. 31, 1962 (dec. Dec. 1971). Formerly reporter European edition N.Y. Herald Tribune, Paris, France, staff writer Asso. Press of Am., London, Eng. spl. UPI, N.Y.C., dir. pub. relations U.S. Lines, London, Eng., Am. Friends of France, Paris, also internat. hdqrs., N.Y.C.; formerly dir. pub. relations women's div. Am. Soc. for Brit. War Relief, N.Y.C.; formerly information specialist, feature writer Office of Coordinator of Inter-Am. Affairs, Washington, and U.S. Dept. State, Washington, pub. relations cons. women's div. A.R.C. War Fund, N.Y.C., also Nat. Women's Party, Washington, Pilot Club Internat., Washington, others; chief of news bur., mgr. press relations Investors Diversified Services, Inc., Mpls., 1953-67, pub. relations cons., 1967-69; free lance writer, pub. relations cons., Mpls., 1969—; also co-producer, broadcaster, guest on network programs. Mem. women's assn. Minn. Symphony Orch. Mem. Am. Newspaper Women's Club, Minn. Press Club (charter). Contbr. to nat. mags.; editor mags. and house organs; scriptwriter. Address: 1767 Humboldt Av S Minneapolis MN 55403

TEIZERIS, HELENA (MRS. OSMAN TEIZERIS), physician; b. Wilno, Poland, Sept. 2, 1905; d. Adam and Eva (Safarewicz) Murza-Murzicz; M.D., Stefan Batory U., Wilno, 1933; m. Osman Teizeris, June 9, 1958. Came to U.S., 1959, naturalized, 1963. Asst. to prof. of anatomy U. Stefan Batory, 1933-39; sr. med. hosp. officer Ministry of Health Hosp., Isloyd Park, Eng., 1946-55; med. officer, blood transfusion centre, Edgware, (illegible), Middlesex Eng., 1955-59; house physician Daus. of Jacob Geriatric Center, Bronx, N.Y., 1963—. Home: 2185 Hone Av Bronx NY 10461 Office: 321 167th St Bronx NY 10456

TELFER, MARGARET CLARE, physician; b. Manila, Philippines, Apr. 9, 1939; d. James Gavin and Margaret Adele (Baldwin) Telfer; A.B., Stanford, 1961; M.D., Washington U., 1965. Intern Michael Reese Hosp., Chgo., 1965-66, resident, 1966-69, fellow in hematology, 1969-70; practice medicine, specializing in hematology, Chgo., 1970—; acting asst. dir. div. hematology Michael Reese Hosp. and Med. Center, Chgo., 1970-71, acting dir., 1971—, asso. attending physician, 1971-72, attending physician, 1972—; asst. prof. Pritzger Sch. Medicine, U. Chgo., 1973—. Recipient Research fellowship Dept. Health, Edn. and Welfare, Nat. Heart and Lung Inst., NIH, 1970. Diplomate Am. Bd. Internal Medicine. Home: 4800 Chicago Beach Dr Apt 2301 Chicago IL 60615 Office: 29th and Ellis Av Chicago IL 60616

TELFER, NANCY, physician, educator; b. San Francisco, Apr. 15, 1930; d. Warren John and Helen Isabelle (Michaelis) Telfer; B.S., Stanford, 1951; M.D., Med. Coll. Pa., 1956. Intern Los Angeles County Gen. Hosp., 1956-57, resident in internal medicine, 1960-67; asst. prof. medicine U. Cal. at Los Angeles, 1961-67; chief outpatient dept. Harbor Gen. Hosp., Torrance, Cal., 1960-67; research fellow Hosp. Cantonal, Geneva, Switzerland, 1961; asst. prof. radiology (nuclear medicine) and medicine Los Angeles County/U. So. Cal. Med. Center, Los Angeles, 1967-68, asso. prof., 1968—, asst. head physician div. nuclear medicine, 1967—. Kate Mead Hurd Research fellow, 1960-61, Los Angeles County Heart Assn. research fellow, 1960-61. Diplomate Am. Bd. Internal Medicine, Am. Bd. Nuclear Med. Research. Fellow A.C.P.; mem. Am. Fedn. Clin. Research, A.A.A.S., Soc. Nuclear Medicine, Los Angeles Soc. Internal Medicine (sec.-treas.), Western Soc. for Clin. Research). Home: 3346 Griffith Park Blvd Los Angeles CA 90027 Office: 1200 N State St Los Angeles CA 90033

TELFORD, RUTH JANE, physician; b. Stamford, N.Y., Sept. 8, 1920; d. Johnson Lee and Henrietta (Welsh) Telford; B.S., Fla. State Coll. for Women, 1942; M.S., Emory U., 1943; M.D., Baylor U., 1950. Fellow in biochemistry Emory U., 1942-43; research chemist nutrition dept. U. Ala., 1943-44; research asst. Baylor U., 1944-46; intern Rochester (N.Y.) Gen. Hosp., 1950-51, resident, 1952-54; asso. pharmacology U. Louisville, 1951-52; practice medicine, specializing in anesthesiology, Houston, 1955—; instr. anesthesiology Baylor Med. Sch., 1955-57, asst. prof., 1957-61, asso. prof., 1961-69, prof., 1969—; cons. Tex. Children's Hosp., Houston, Tex. Inst. Rehab. and Research, Houston. Diplomate Am. Bd. Anesthesiology. Mem. Am. Soc. Anesthesiologists, A.M.A., Harris County Med. Soc., Gamma Sigma Epsilon, Alpha Omega Alpha. Contbr. to profl. publs. Home: 606 Baywood Dr Seabrook TX 77586 Office: 1200 Moursund Av Houston TX 77025

TELLEFSEN, BETTY LOU STRANGE, assn. exec.; b. Diagonal, Ia., Oct. 14, 1929; d. Lewis A. and Effie Myrtle (Ruby) Strange; student Los Angeles City Coll., 1956-62; grad. Inst. Orgn. Mgmt., U.

Santa Clara; m. Donald E. Tellefsen, Apr. 1, 1961; 1 dau., Tanya Annette; stepchildren—Susan Kay, Jennifer Ann. Stenographer, Ia. Social Welfare Dept., Des Moines, 1948-50; sec. Hoffman Radio & TV, Los Angeles, 1950-51; sec. Gen. Services Adminstrn., Los Angeles, 1951-53; adminstrv. asst. ICA, Djakarta, Indonesia, 1953-56; pub. relations asst. Matson Navigation Co., Los Angeles, 1956-61; exec. dir. The Life Underwriters Assn., Los Angeles, Inc., Los Angeles Gen. Agts. and Mgrs. Assn., Inc., Los Angeles County chpt. C.L.U.'s, Inc., Employee Benefit Planning Assn. So. Cal., Cal. Transplant Found., Life Ins. Leaders Round Table, 1962—. Mem. Los Angeles Area C. of C., Am. Soc. Assn. Execs., Publicity Club Inc. Clubs: LaQuinta (Cal.) Desert; Publicity, Soroptimist (Los Angeles). Home: 16412 Heathfield Dr Whittier CA 90603 Office: 417 S Hill St Los Angeles CA 90013

TELLER, BARBARA GORELY (MRS. GRAHAM PRESCOTT TELLER), writer, cons.; b. Wellesley, Mass., Mar. 14, 1920; d. Charles Percival and Jean Niven (Watt) Gorely, Jr.; B.A., Wellesley Coll., 1943, M.A. in Am. Social and Cultural History, 1944, postgrad., 1946; m. Graham Prescott Teller, Dec. 14, 1950; children—Grafton, Diana, Christopher. Registrar, Soc. for Preservation New Eng. Antiquities, Boston, 1969-74, asst. to curator, 1970-74; asso. editor Old-Time New Eng., 1970-74. Researcher, writer, cons. hist. socs., mus. on decorative arts exhbns., house mus. interior restoration projects; lectr. mus. seminars and forums, hist. socs., clubs, groups. Contbr. articles on ceramics, other aspects of decorative arts in colonial, fed. period of New Eng. to hist., antique jours. Home: Wellesley MA 02181

TELLER, JANE SIMON (MRS. WALTER TELLER), artist; b. Rochester, N.Y., July 5, 1911; d. Joseph and Florence (Miller) Simon; student Barnard Coll., 1933; B.A., Rochester Inst. Tech.; m. Walter Teller, Apr. 7, 1933; children—Raphael, Joseph, David, Walter. One man shows Parma Gallery, N.Y.C., Berresford Gallery, Martha's Vineyard, Mass., Princeton Gallery Fine Arts; two man shows Parma Gallery, N.Y.C., Phila. Art Alliance, Osgood Gallery, N.Y.C.; exhibited in group shows Mus. Modern Art, N.Y.C., Lyman-Allyn Mus., New London, Conn., Whitney Mus., N.Y.C., Phila. Mus. Art, Riverside Mus., N.Y.C., Phila. Art Alliance, Pa. Acad., N.J. State Mus., Trenton, Newark Mus., Bertha Scaefer Gallery, N.Y.C., Stable Gallery, N.Y.C., Nat. Assn. Women Artists, Gallerie Claude Bernard, Paris, France, Holland-Goldowsky Gallery, Chgo., Sculptors Guild Annuals, Lever House, N.Y.C.; represented in permanent collections Olsen Found., Stamford, Conn., N.J. State Mus., Trenton, Temple Judea, Doylestown, Pa.; various commns. Recipient Purchase award N.J. State Mus., 1971; 50th Anniversary prize Nat. Assn. Women Artists. Mem. Sculptors Guild, Artists Equity Assn., Am. Art Therapy Assn. Address: 200 Prospect Av Princeton NJ 08540

TEMMER, HELENA WELLISZ, psychologist; b. Warsaw, Poland, Jan. 8, 1920; d. Leopold T. and Jadwiga A. (Landau) Wellisz; came to U.S., 1941, naturalized, 1947; M.A., Tchrs. Coll., Columbia, 1944; M.A., Yale, 1949; Ph.D., N.Y. U., 1957; div.; 1 son, Michael L. Staff psychologist Md. State Tng. Sch. for Girls, Reisterstown, 1953-56; sch. psychologist pub. schs., Balt. County, 1956-57; sr. psychologist Camden (N.J.) Area Mental Hygiene Clinic, 1957-62; prin. clin. psychologist children's unit Neuropsychiat. Inst., Princeton, N.J., 1962—; pvt. practice psychology, Princeton. Cons., Youth and Family Services N.J., 1958—; lectr. acad. and health instns. Sweden and Poland, 1973; cons. N.J. Rehab. Commn., 1962—; N.J. State Sch. for Boys, Jamesburg, 1974—. Mem. Am., N.J. psychol. assns., Assn. N.J. Instnl. Psychologists (sec.), A.A.A.S. Democrat. Club: Princeton YWCA Internat. (past pres.). Contbr. research articles on exptl. psychology, personality, childhood psychopathology and treatment to profl. jours. Home: Cherry Valley Rd RD 5 265 Princeton NJ 08540 Office: New Jersey Neuropsychiatric Institute Box 1000 Princeton NJ 08540

TEMPLE, H. ROSE (MRS. SIDNEY E. TEMPLE), psychologist; b. N.Y.C.; d. Joseph and Cecelia (Merezky) Weitzman; R.N., Beth Israel Hosp. Sch. Nursing, 1945; A.B., San Diego State Coll., 1951; M.A., San Francisco State Coll., 1959; postgrad. Universidad de las Américas, Mexico, 1967, U. Cal. at Hayward, 1969; m. Sidney E. Temple, Aug. 10, 1947; children—Edmond S., Sabrina R. Pub. health nurse San Diego Pub. Health Dept., 1945-47; with San Francisco Unified Sch. Dist., 1952—, successively asst. supt. child welfare and attendance, acting head counselor, tchr., 1952-69, sch. psychologist Emergency Evaluation Center, 1969—. Mem. Am. Psychol. Assn., Cal. Assn. Sch. Psychologists and Psychometrists, Psychologists Assn. San Francisco, San Francisco Personnel and Guidance Assn. Office: 1945 Washington St San Francisco CA

TEMPLE, LILLY SCHULTZ (MRS. JACK B. TEMPLE), lawyer; b. Chgo., May 23, 1920; d. Israel Hersch and Ida (Blumenthal) Schultz; Ph.B., Loyola U., Chgo., 1942; J.D., DePaul U., 1945; m. Jack B. Temple, Apr. 28, 1949; 1 dau., Iris Lee. Tchr., Chgo. Comml. Coll., 1942-47; admitted to Ill. bar, 1946; practiced in Chgo., 1948—; partner firm Temple & Temple, 1949—. Mem. Chgo. Jewish Bd. Edn. Mem. Women's Bar Assn., Nat. Assn. Claimants' Compensation Atty., Chgo. Art Inst., Chgo. Mus. Natural History. Home: 6849 N Francisco Chicago IL 60645 Office: 111 W Washington Av Chicago IL 60602

TENBRINCK, MARGARET DOROTHY SCHAFFNER (MRS. EDUARD JOHAN TENBRINCK), physician; b. N.Y.C., Feb. 28, 1911; d. Charles Edward and Ethel Martha (Scharff) Schaffner; A.B., Barnard Coll., 1932; M.S., N.Y. U., 1934, M.D., 1939; m. Eduard Johan Tenbrinck, Nov. 4, 1933; children—Jean Dorothy (Mrs. Joseph A. Daubenas), Ethel Elizabeth (Mrs. Fahad Saqr Al Hazzam). Intern, house physician Bellevue Hosp., N.Y.C., 1940-41, asso. resident pediatrics, 1941-43; practice medicine, specializing in pediatrics, N.Y.C., 1944-72; asso. attending physician Bellevue Hosp., 1955-72, Univ. Hosp., N.Y.C., 1955-72; asst. clin. prof. pediatrics N.Y. U. Coll. Medicine, 1955-71, asso. prof. clin. pediatrics, 1971-72; asst. med. dir. Met. Life Ins. Co., N.Y.C., 1962-69, asso., 1969-72; dir. Child Evaluation Center, Phoenix, 1972—; physician Hospital Albert Schweitzer, Lambaréné Gabon, 1961, 64, Hospital Amazonico A. Schweitzer, Pucallpa, Peru, 1963, Spafford Children's Hosp., East Jerusalem, 1968; contract pediatrician USPHS, Indian Hosp., Whiteriver, Ariz., 1966. Bd. dirs., treas., v.p. Am. Women's Hosp. Service; bd. dirs. Binder Schweitzer Amazonian Hosp. Found., 1963-70, Am. Colony Charities; mem. physicians' com. A. Schweitzer Fellowship. Recipient Lovejoy award, 1972. Diplomate Am. Bd. Pediatrics. Mem. Am. Acad. Pediatrics (life), A.M.A., Am. Med. Women's Assn. (life), Maricopa County Med. Soc. Episcopalian. Contbr. articles profl. jours. Home: 7447 E Indian Bend Scottsdale AZ 85253 also RD 1 Hillsdale NY 12529

TENBROECK, NANCY PENNINGTON, educator; b. Phila., May 21, 1943; d. Edward Hanzsche and Mary (Atmore) Tenbroeck; B.A., Pa. State U., 1965; M.F.A., Stanford, 1968. Instr. East Stroudsburg (Pa.) State Coll., 1969-71; asst. prof. Ind. U., South Bend, 1971—. Mem. U.S. Inst. for Theatre Tech. Home: 2500 Topsfield Rd South Bend IN 46614

TENCZYNSKI, DOLORES HELENE, psychologist; b. Scranton, Pa., Nov. 5, 1943; d. Leon Francis and Helen Dolores (Tomaszewski) Tenczynski; B.A. cum laude, Seton Hill Coll., 1966; M.A., Fordham U., 1968, postgrad. Vocational counselor Cath. Charities, N.Y.C., 1967-69; psychol. cons. N.Y. U. Med. Center, 1968-69; psychologist Counseling Center Fordham U., Bronx, N.Y., 1969-73, asst. dir., 1974—. Instr. psychology Coll. New Rochelle, 1968-69, Fordham U., 1969-73. Mem. Am. Psychol. Assn., Am. Group Therapy Assn., Met. Coll. Mental Health Assn., Am. Personnel and Guidance Assn., Kosciuszko Found., UN Assn. Clubs: Chalet, Sandbar. Home: 341 E 81st St New York City NY 10028 Office: Counseling Center Fordham U Bronx NY 10458

TENHAAF, EDNA RUTH, realtor; b. St. Francisville, Mo., Sept. 27, 1928; d. Emmett Pritchett and Lois Hortense (Atteberry) Wayland; grad. Realtors Inst. Ill., 1969; m. Harry E. Tenhaaf, June 9, 1946; children—Linda (Mrs. Jerry Spence), Steven Allen, Douglas William. Saleswoman Peck Real Estate, Galesburg, Ill., 1966-69, Deets Realty Corp. and Western Estates Corp., Galesburg, 1969-70; owner Home Realty Co., Galesburg, 1970—. Leader Brownies, 1954-57, Girl Scouts, 1957-61; den mother Boy Scouts Am., 1958; active Heart Fund, March of Dimes, Community Chest, 1957-64; pres. Mothersingers Galesburg High Sch., 1964-65. Election judge, 1960-67. Bd. dirs. Girl Scouts, 1960-61. Mem. Ill. Assn. Real Estate Bds. (legis. com. 1972-73), Galesburg C. of C. Home: 3255 Morningside Dr Galesburg IL 61401 Office: 501 E Losey St Galesburg IL 61401

TEN HOOR, ELVIE MARIE MORTENSEN (MRS. PERRY J. TEN HOOR), artist; b. Watseka, Ill.; d. John and Emma (Kemnitz) Mortensen; student Sch. Art Inst. Chgo., 1917-19, Academie Notre Dame Des Champs, Paris 1970; m. Perry J. Ten Hoor, Oct. 11, 1917; children—Gloria Jean (Mrs. Walter D. Scheihing), Perry John II. One-man shows at Univ. Club Gallery, Bibo Gallery, Peoria, Ill., Hefner's Art Gallery, Grand Rapids, Mich., Dunes Theater Gallery, Mich. City, Ind., Raymond Duncan Galleries, Paris, France, 1967, Harper Galleries, Covenant Club of Ill., 1968, 72, 74, Rubino Galleries, many others; exhibited in group shows at Quint Assos. Gallery, Park Forest Art Rental and Sales Gallery, 1st Fed. Gallery, Chgo. Sun Times Gallery, Town Gallery Munster (Ind.), Ligoa Duncan Gallery, N.Y.C., numerous others; represented in permanent collections, Toronto, Can., Los Angeles, Dayton, O., Israel. Mem. Alumni of Sch. Art Inst. Chgo., All-Ill. Soc. Fine Arts, N. Shore Art League, Artists Equity Assn., Art Inst. Sales and Rental Gallery, Chgo. Soc. Artists, Renaissance Soc., Sigma Kappa (chpt. pres. 1946-66). Club: Arts of Chicago. Author: (with Dona Meilach) Collage and Found Art, 1963, Collage and Assemblage, 1974. Address: 6740 Oglesby Av Chicago IL 60649

TENNANT, DAISY MAE ELMORE, poet; b. Senatobia, Miss., Aug. 27, 1910; d. Charlie and Nora (Wimberly) Elmore; student U. Tex., 1930, Odessa (Tex.) Evening Coll., various periods, Rutherford Bus. Coll., 1967; m. Tracy W. Tennant, Feb. 17, 1934 (div. 1945); children—Nancy Jo (Mrs. James E. Stiles), Sharon Annora (Mrs. Mitchell R. Gause). Office mgr. Ormand Idustries, Inc., Odessa, Tex., 1955-64, Dallas, 1964-70, Dallas office Main Lafrentz & Co., 1970—. Poetry workshop leader Odessa Evening Coll., 1957-59; poetry chmn. Odessa Coll. Writer's Roundup, 1957-63; spl. adv. com. services women's dept. Tex. Bank and Trust Co., Dallas, 1966—; judge various poetry contests. Recipient numerous poetry awards, including Hadra Meml. award, 1965, Chapbook award, 1963, Globe Peace award, 1966, Lyric award, 1966, Grand Prix award Nat. Fedn. State Poetry Socs., 1966, Old South award, 1967, Hurley Meml. award, 1967, Siegel Ecology award, 1971, many others. Mem. Poetry Soc. Am., Nat. Fedn. State Poetry Socs., Acad. Am. Poets (affiliate), Poetry Soc. Tex. (rec. sec. 1968, treas. 1969, chmn. Tex. Poet's Meml. Collection Baylor Coll., 1966-69, program chmn. 1967), Writer's Workshop (pres. Odessa 1961-62), Shakespeare Club (v.p. Odessa Coll. 1962), Avalon World Arts Acad., Vachel Lindsay Assn., Compatriots Dallas. Author books of verse: Shifting Sands, 1954, Miss Fitts and Miss Cellany, 1960; contbr. poems to anthologies, including Anthology of American Poetry, 1959; Avalon Anthologies, 1962; National Federation Anthology, 1968; also to newspapers, mags., radio, television. Home: 13526 Winterhaven St Dallas TX 75234 Office: Bryan Tower Dallas TX 75201

TENNANT, HAZEL MARY, psychologist; b. Albia, Ia., Aug. 13, 1907; d. William Emmett and Anna Margaret (Manley) Bennett; B.A., William Penn Coll., 1930; M.A., Western Mich. U., 1961, Specialist in Edn., Sch. Psychology, 1963; m. Cloyd Fidelus Tennant, Oct. 10, 1932 (dec. 1971); 1 dau., Hazel Anne (Mrs. Roland Hart). Elementary sch. tchr. Bd. Edn., Lovilia, Ia., 1925-27; tchr. Bd. Edn., Albia, 1927-30, Bd. Edn., Ames, Ia., 1930-32; statis. supr. dept. agrl. econs. La. State U., Baton Rouge, 1939-41; tchr., elementary guidance Bd. Edn., Hartford, Mich., 1946-61; sch. psychologist Van Buren Intermediate Sch. Dist., Bd. Edn., Lawrence, Mich., 1961—. Instr. psychol. testing Western Mich. U., Kalamazoo, 1967-68, instr. spl. edn., 1972-73, supr. sch. psychology interns, 1963—. Mem. Gov.'s Com. Kalamazoo Regional Com. on Mental Retardation and Devel. Disabilities, 1969—. Bd. dirs. McKercher Rehab. Center, Kalamazoo, 1968-71. Mem. Am., Mich. psychol. assns., Nat., Mich. edn. assns., Council for Exceptional Children, Mich. Assn. for Emotionally Disturbed Children, Mich. Assn. for Children with Learning Disabilities, Nat., Mich. assns. for retarded children. Home: PO Box 97 Hartford MI 49057 Office: 704 Paw Paw St Lawrence MI 49064

TENNERY, ELIZABETH, lawyer; b. Marietta, Okla., Apr. 7, 1926; d. Claude V. and Perle (Brooks) Tennery; B.A., Am. U., 1961, J.D., 1962; (div. June 1957); 1 son, Brian A. Admitted to Md. bar, 1963, since practiced in Rockville; partner Welsh and Tennery, 1963—. Adj. professorial lectr. Am. U., Washington, 1967—. Mem. Nat. Assn. Women Lawyers, Am., Md. State, Montgomery County bar assns., Bus. and Profl. Women's Club. Home: 9909 Silverbrook Dr Rockville MD 20850 Office: 22 W Jefferson St Rockville MD 20850

TENNYSON, JEAN, soprano; b. Chgo., Sept. 15, 1905; ed. pub. schs.; studied under Cattone in Italy, Madame Gilly and Mary Garden in Paris, Florence Easton in N.Y.C.; m. Dr. Camille Dreyfus, Sept. 18, 1931; m. 2d, Ernest Boissevain, May 22, 1958. Began as a singer in operetta; went to Italy, 1929-30; made operatic debut as Mimi in La Boheme at La Fenice Theatre, Venice, 1930, and sang in many Italian theaters; sang 2 seasons with San Carlo Opera Co. in Can. and U.S., 1934-35; with Chgo. Civic Opera Co., 1935, 36, 38; sang in Salzburg Festival with Vienna Symphony, 1935; made operatic tour of continent, singing in all leading opera houses including Prague, Budapest, Vienna, Bucharest, Belgrade and Sofia, 1936-37, with San Francisco Opera Co., 1942; featured on program, Great Moments in Music, CBS, 1942-46; exec. vice chmn. Stadium Concerts, Inc., 1946—; nat. chmn. Artists Vet. Hosp. Program, MEF, 1947. Pres. The Jean Tennyson Found., 1949—; mem. central com. aux. bd., patron Philharmonic-Symphony Soc. N.Y. Bd. dirs. Spoleto Festival; trustee City Center of Music and Drama. Decorated Stella della Solidarieta Italiana (Italy); St. Olaf Medal (Norway). Hon. mem. Delta Omicron. Address: 5 Crosby St Brattleboro VT 05301

TENOPYR, MARY LOUISE WELSH (MRS. JOSEPH TENOPYR), psychologist; b. Youngstown, O., Oct. 18, 1929; d. Roy Henry and Olive (Donegan) Welsh; A.B., Ohio U., 1951, M.A., 1951; Ph.D., U. So. Cal., 1966; m. Joseph Tenopyr, Oct. 30, 1955. Psychometrist, Ohio U., Athens, 1951-52, also housemother, Sigma Kappa; personnel technician to research psychologist USAF, 1953-55, Dayton, O., 1952-53, Hempstead, N.Y.; indsl. research analyst to mgr. employee evaluation N.Am. Rockwell Corp., El Segundo, Cal., 1956-70; asso. prof. Cal. State Coll. at Los Angeles, 1966-70; asso. research educationist U. Cal. at Los Angeles, 1970-71; program dir. U.S. Civil Service Commn., 1971-72; mgr. human resources research Am. Tel. & Tel., N.Y.C., 1972—; lectr. U. So. Cal., Los Angeles, 1967-70. Vice chmn. research com. Tech. Adv. Com. on Testing, Fair Employment Practice Commn. Cal., 1966-70; adviser on testing Office Fed. Contract Compliance, U.S. Dept. Labor, Washington, 1967-73. Mem. Nat. Mgmt. Assn., Am., Western, Cal. psychol. assns., Internat. Council Psychologists, Nat. Council on Measurement in Edn., Nat. Vocational Guidance Assn., Psychonetic Soc., Met. N.Y. Assn. for Applied Psychology, Am. Ednl. Research Assn., Sigma Xi, Sigma Kappa, Psi Chi, Alpha Lambda Delta, Kappa Phi. Contbr. articles to profl. jours. Home: 557 Lyme Rock Rd Somerville NJ 08876 Office: 195 Broadway New York City NY 10007

TEPPER, BRENDA, clin. psychologist; b. N.Y.C., Apr. 18, 1940; d. Michael and Pauline (Lerner) Schlossberg; B.A. magna cum laude, Coll. City N.Y., 1965; Ph.D., U. City N.Y., 1970; postgrad. N.Y. U., 1970—; m. Jesse Tepper, Aug. 20, 1967. Instr. Coll. City N.Y., 1969; clin. psychologist Comprehensive Community Mental Health Center, Meadowbrook (N.Y.) Hosp., 1970-72; asst. prof. psychologist Bergen Community Coll., Paramus, N.J., 1972-73; pvt. practice psychoanalysis, N.Y.C., 1970—; supr., faculty Inst. Contemporary Psychotherapy, 1974—. County committeewoman Borough Manhattan, 1972-73. Dissertation fellow Am. Assn. U. Women, 1969-70; Nat. Def. Edn. Act fellow, 1965-69. Mem. Am., N.Y. State psychol. assns., Am. Assn. U. Profs., N.Y. Soc. Clin. Psychologists, Phi Beta Kappa. Home: 165 Bennett Av New York City NY 10040 Office: 315 Central Park West New York City NY 10025

TEPPER, NANCY BOXLEY, lawyer; b. Richmond, Va., Mar. 7, 1933; d. Joseph Harry and Mathilda (Appell) Boxley; student U. Richmond, 1950-51; B.A. magna cum laude, Radcliffe Coll., 1953; LL.B. magna cum laude, Harvard, 1958; children—Amanda, Eliza and Nicholas (Twins). Admitted to N.Y. bar, 1958, Cal. bar, 1969; asso. firm Simpson Thacher & Bartlett, N.Y.C., 1958-63; free lance writer, editor Columbia Law Sch., N.Y.C., Prentice-Hall, Inc., Englewood, N.J., 1963-69; asso. firm Robertson, Howser & Garland, Laguna Hills, Cal., 1969-70, Kindel & Anderson, Laguna Hills, 1970—; instr. U. Cal. at Irvine, 1971-72; lectr. on estate and tax planning for several local orgns. Mem. Orange County Bar Assn., Phi Beta Kappa. Club: Harvard (dir. 1970-72) (Orange County). Editor: Harvard Law Rev., 1956-58. Home: 331 Vista Suerte Newport Beach CA 92660 Office: 23521 Paseo de Valencia Laguna Hills CA 92653

TERANIS, MARA ZARINS (MRS. ZIGURDS BERNHARTS TERANIS), librarian; b. Daugavplis, Latvia, Apr. 9, 1944; d. Rudolfs and Nina (Petersons) Zarins; student Mil. Downer Coll., 1962-64; B.A. in Biology and Chemistry, Lawrence U., 1966; M.S. in L.S., U. Wis., 1973; m. Zigurds Bernharts Teranis, June 11, 1965; 1 son, Eriks. Librarian Lakeside Labs., Milw., 1966—. Mem. A.L.A., Med. Library Assn., Spl. Libraries Assn. Home: 4428 N Oakland Av Shorewood WI 53211 Office: Lakeside Labs Milwaukee WI 53201

TEREBELO, SHERYL LYNN, radio broadcasting co. exec.; b. Detroit, Dec. 28, 1947; d. Lawrence and Rita Alice (Bakst) Terebelo; B.A., Mich. State U., 1970, M.A., 1973. Staff counselor, trainer drug edn., staff coordinator Drug Edn. Center, East Lansing, Mich., 1970-71; drug edn. coordinator, coordinator drug media programs 4-H Youth Programs, State Mich., East Lansing, 1970-71; crisis center and methadone center counselor Hegira Drug Center, Inkster, Mich., 1971; dir. program, counselor Hearing Aide Crisis Intervention Center, Dearborn, Mich., 1971-73; community affairs coordinator, dir. community switchboard WRIF Radio, Southfield, Mich., 1973; counselor, therapist Providence Hosp. Drug Abuse Program, Southfield, Mich., 1973; advt. salesperson Fifth Estate newspaper, Detroit, 1974—. Cons. Office Drug Abuse State Mich., 1970-73, cons. for amorphia, drug edn., drug cons. drug law reform group, 1973—. Mem. Detroit Met. Substance Abuse Council, 1971—; Crisis Center Council, Detroit, 1971—. Bd. dirs. Narcotics Addists Rehab. Coordinating Orgn. Mem. Women in Communications, Mich. Assn. Crisis Centers (council), Iota Beta Sigma. Home: 20084 Northrop St Detroit MI 48219 Office: 4403 Second Detroit MI 48219

TEREY-SMITH, MARY (MRS. CHARLES ANTHONY C. SMITH), musician; b. Budapest, Hungary; d. Emil and Lillian (Wooland) Terey; B.A., Liszt Acad. Music, 1950; M.A., U. Vt., 1964; Ph.D. in Musicology, U. Rochester Eastman Sch. Music, 1971; m. Charles Anthony C. Smith, June 21, 1959. Came to U.S., 1965. Vocal and orchestral coach Hungarian Opera, 1952-56; resident condr. Tatabanya Symphony, nr. Budapest, 1952-56; instr. summer courses Folklore Inst., 1950-56; music specialist Protestant Sch. Bd. of Greater Montreal, 1957-64; asst. prof. music Western Wash. State Coll., Bellingham, 1967-73, asso. prof., 1973—, coll. research grantee for European travel, summer 1972. Mem. Am., Internat. musicological socs., Am. Soc. Aesthetics, Am. Assn. U. Profs., Coll. Music Soc. Contbr. articles in field to profl. jours. Home: 1809 Harris Av Bellingham WA 98225

TERRAZAS, HENRIETTA LOWE, pub. relations exec.; b. Chgo., Apr. 5, 1928; d. Henry Jacob and Irene (Coffee) Lowe; grad. high sch.; m. Carlos Terrazas, Aug. 28, 1953; children—Carlos, Ana Luisa, Alex. Womans page editor El Paso Herald-Post; spl. sects. editor Tucson Newspapers, Inc.; creative dir., copywriter, photographer, pub. relations dir. Terrazas & Terrazas, Tucson. Pub. relations United Way Campaign, 1973, Tucson chpt. Los Amigos de las Americas. Mem. Pub. Relations Soc. Am., Tucson Advt. Agy. Council. Home: 930 W Wanda Vista Pl Tucson AZ 85704 Office: 101 W Drachman St Tucson AZ 85705

TERRELL, CATHERINE FLEMING, state ofcl.; b. Augusta, Ga., Nov. 29, 1945; d. Samuel Preston and Florence (Anderson) Fleming; B.A., Baylor U., 1968; m. James Oscar Terrell, June 8, 1968. Secondary tchr. Robinson (Tex.) Ind. Sch. Dist., 1968-69; asso. dir. sales promotion, family div. Success Motivation Inst., Waco, Tex., 1969-71; copywriter Word, Inc., publishing, Waco, 1971-73; coordinator comprehensive health planning Heart of Tex. Council Govts., Waco, 1972-74, dir. Area Agy. Aging, 1974—. Mem. McLennan County Drug Abuse Steering Com., McLennan County Home Health Agy. Adv. Bd., Waco Inter-agy. Council Smoking and Health. Adv. bd. Providence Hosp., Waco. Mem. Women in Communication, Am. Assn. Comprehensive Health Planning (dir. region VI, 1973—), Tex. Women's Polit. Caucus, Downtown Waco Bus. and Profl. Women's Club, Nat. Orgn. Women, Waco Civic Theatre, Historic Waco Found. (docent, dir.). Contbr. articles to jours. Office: 216 N 5th St Waco TX 76701

TERRELL, SARA ELDORA HAWORTH (MRS. THOMAS EUGENE TERRELL), physician; b. High Point, N.C., Oct. 4, 1929; d. Chester Carl and Sara (Richardson) Haworth; B.S., Guilford Coll., 1949; M.D., Duke U. Sch. Medicine, 1953; m. Thomas Eugene Terrell, Sept. 8, 1951; children—Sara Elizabeth, Thomas Eugene, William Hunt, Richard Green, John Timothy, Amanda Jane. Intern Duke Hosp. and Durham (N.C.) VA Hosp., 1953-54, resident internal medicine, 1954-55; practice medicine specializing in internal medicine, High Point, 1957—; mem. staff High Point Meml. Hosp. Staff physician Guilford County Mental Health, High Point, part-time, 1963-66. Mem. High Point Human Relations Commn., 1971—. Bd. dirs., pres. Family Service Bur., 1969-70, High Point Family Life Council, 1969-70; pres. High Point Med. Aux., 1971-72; bd. dirs. Friends Homes, Inc., 1969—, N.C. Family Life Council, 1971—. Recipient Sperry award N.C. Family Life Council, 1971. Mem. N.C., Guilford County med. socs., A.M.A. Mem. Soc. of Friends (mem. exec. com. N.C. yearly meeting 1972—), Guilford Coll. Alumni Assn. (pres. 1974—). Club: Altrusa (pres. 1973-74) (High Point). Home: 514 Hayworth Circle High Point NC 27262 Office: 624 Quaker Lane High Point NC 27262

TERRIS, SUSAN (MRS. DAVID WARREN TERRIS), author; b. St. Louis, May 6, 1937; d. Harold William and Myra Rae (Friedman) Dubinsky; B.A., Wellesley Coll., 1959; M.A., San Francisco State Coll., 1966; m. David Warren Terris, Aug. 31, 1958; children—Daniel, Michael, Amy. Researcher, 1962-66; substitute tchr., vol. librarian, 1964-68; free lance writer Chandler Pub. Co., San Francisco, 1966-70; free lance writer, 1970—. Mem. Authors Guild. Author: The Upstairs Witch and the Downstairs Witch, 1970; The Backwards Boots, 1971; On Fire, 1972; The Drowning Boy, 1972; Plague of Frogs, 1973; Pickle, 1973; Whirling Rainbows, 1974; Amanda, The Panda, and The Redhead, 1974. Address: 11 Jordan Av San Francisco CA 94118

TERRY, ANGELA OWEN (MRS. ELBERT ARNOLD TERRY), psychol. cons.; b. Memphis, Feb. 13, 1941; d. William Franklin and Addie Seay (Griffin) Owen; certificate psychology U. Vienna, 1963; B.A., Spelman Coll., 1962; M.A., Fisk U., 1964; Ph.D., U. Conn., 1973; m. Elbert Arnold Terry, June 9, 1967; 1 dau., Angela Daphne. Asst. prof. psychology Albany (Ga.) State Coll., 1964-69; sch. psychologist Bd. Edn., Memphis, 1969-71; cons. psychol. services Conn. Dept. Edn., Hartford, 1973—. Edn. Professions Devel. Act fellow, 1971-73. Mem. Am. Assn. Mental Deficiency, Council Exceptional Children, Tenn. Psychol. Assn., Conn. Assn. Sch. Psychologists, N.A.A.C.P., Urban League, Delta Sigma Theta. Mem. Disciples of Christ Ch. Home: Patriot Rd Windham Center CT 06280 Office: State Office Bldg 165 Capitol Av Hartford CT 06501

TERRY, EMALITA NEWTON, artist, educator; b. San Angelo, Tex., Jan. 15, 1909; d. William Isaac and Mary Emma (Williamson) Newton; diploma Howard Payne Coll., Tex. Instr. painting and drawing Tex. A. and M. U., 1949-59, dir. Art Gallery, 1950-59; instr. painting and drawing Terry's Art Studio, Las Vegas, Nev., 1960—; exhibited in numerous one-man shows in Tex. and Nev.; represented in permanent collections museums and galleries throughout U.S., also pvt. collections. Spl. tng. for Jr. League Art Groups, Las Vegas, 1971-72. Recipient Distinguished Service awards M. Grumbacher, 1954, 57, 58, Spl. Art award Tex. A. and M. U., 1952-53, Emily Goldman Meml. award Nat. Assn. Women Artists, N.Y.C., 1958. Mem. Tex. Watercolor Soc., Art League of Las Vegas. Home: 3215 Medicine Man Way Las Vegas NV 89109

TERRY, ESTHER MCCLARD (MRS. EUGENE TERRY), educator; b. Warrenton, N.C., Dec. 8, 1938; d. Richard and Mary Ella (Greene) Alexander; B.A., Bennett Coll., 1961; M.A., U. N.C., 1962; Ph.D. (Esso grantee), U. Mass., 1973; m. Eugene Terry, May 12, 1966; 1 son, Jules Michael Eugene. Instr., St. Augustine's Coll., Raleigh, N.C., 1962-65, prof. English, 1967-68; teaching asst. English dept. U. Mass., Amherst, 1965-67, asst. asso. prof. Afro-Am. studies dept., 1970—, dir. Black Repertory Theatre, 1969—. Mem. Gov.'s Council on Arts, 1971—. Danforth asso. U. Mass., 1971; named Tchr. of the Year, St. Augustine's Coll., 1969. Mem. Coll. English Assn., Nat. Theatre Assn. Home: 97 Meadow St Amherst MA 01002 Office: Univ of Massachusetts Amherst MA 01002

TERRY, POLLY E., public relations exec.; b. Waterloo, Ia., July 20, 1940; d. Gleyn W. and Betty Lou (Farnum) Singleterry; student U. Ia., 1959, Phoenix Coll., 1963-65. Editor publs., then adminstrv. asst. to pres. Arcoa Internat., Phoenix, 1965-71; reporter Morning Democrat, Davenport, Ia., 1957-59; copy writer John W. Shaw Advt., Chgo., 1959-60, L.W. Ramsey Advt., Davenport, 1960-61; press pub. relations rep. Valley Nat. Bank, Phoenix, 1971-72; owner, pres. pub. relations firm Polly E. Terry & Assos., Phoenix, 1973—. Participant Lion's Rec. for Blind program; past chmn. for AMERCO system United Fund campaign, 1970; pub. relations com. Wayland Child Care Center. Pres., bd. dirs. CARES; past bd. dirs. Phoenix Little Theatre. Mem. Ariz. Press Club, Phoenix Press Club, Nat. Indsl. Editors, Phoenix Ad Club (man/woman of yr. com. 1973). Republican. Address: 1143 E Rovey St Phoenix AZ 85012

TERSUHOW, CECELIA, retail store exec.; b. Phila., Apr. 6, 1908; d. Nathan and Anna (Pickholtz) Tersuhow; student Pa. State U., 1925-26, U. Pa., 1926-28. With Tersuhow's Miracle Store, women's and children's apparel, Reading, Pa., 1928—, pres., 1936-42, owner, 1942—; partner Tersuhow Realty, 1950—. Club: Wyomissing. Home: 1212 Parkside Dr S Reading PA 19602 Office: 404-406 Penn St Reading PA 19602

TERVALON, ADRIENNE CALLISTA, univ. adminstr.; b. New Orleans, Feb. 5, 1928; d. Harry Peter and Anita Louise Benedicta (Mercadel) Tervalon; B.S., Xavier U., New Orleans, 1948; M.Ed., Loyola U., New Orleans, 1959. Tchr. sci. J.S. Clark High Sch., Orleans Parish Sch. System, 1950-63; lectr. edn. Dillard U., New Orleans, 1959-60, asst. prof. edn., 1963—, dir. Upward Bound Project, 1965—, asso. dean students, 1968—. Tchr., In-Service Tng. classes for sci. high sch. tchrs. 1959-61; cons. Ednl. Assos., Inc., Washington, 1966-67; Office Edn., Dept. Health, Edn. and Welfare, Dallas, 1974. Mem. Human Relations Com. New Orleans, 1970—. Bd. dirs. Friends of New Orleans Pub. Library, 1967-70, Social Welfare Planning Council; bd. dirs., asst. sec. Opportunities Industrialization Center, New Orleans. Mem. La. (sec.), S.W. assns. student assistance programs, Nat. Assn. Student Personnel Adminstrs., Am. Assn. for Higher Edn., Alpha Kappa Alpha. Democrat. Roman Catholic. Clubs: Dillard Women's (treas.), Les Dames du Bridge. Home: 4616 Annette St New Orleans LA 70122

TERWILLIGER, GLORIA HELEN (MRS. JOHN W. TERWILLIGER), ednl. adminstr.; b. Springfield, Mass., Sept. 30, 1927; d. Guido and Alfea (Molinari) Pasquini; student Boston U., 1945-46; B.A. (Dwight Morrow scholar) cum laude, Smith Coll., 1950; M.A., Ind. U., 1953; M.L.S., Catholic U., 1966; postgrad. U. Md., 1969—; m. John W. Terwilliger, Oct. 21, 1950; children—Constance Kay, Eric William. Free lance musician, 1955-66; librarian Mary Washington Coll., Fredericksburg, Va., 1966-68; librarian N. Va. Community Coll., Alexandria, 1968, dir. learning resources, 1969—. Instr. Canterbury Sch., Accokeek, Md., 1962-63; cons. ednl. tech., 1971—. Pres. Music Tchrs. Guild, Prince William County, Va., 1964-65. Mem. Va. Jr. and Community Coll. Assn. (chmn. 1970-71), Community Coll. Assn. for Instrn. and Tech. (sec. 1972-74), A.L.A., Assn. for Ednl. Communications and Tech., Am. Assn. Community and Jr. Colls., Nat. Council Learning (steering com. 1972-73, pres. 1973-74), So. Assn. Schs. and Colls., Alpha Phi Kappa Psi. Home: 4716 Exeter St Annandale VA 22003 Office: Northern Virginia Community College 3001 N Beauregard St Alexandria VA 22311

TESCHNER, JOY GRIESBACH (MRS. RICHARD R. TESCHNER), county ofcl., club woman; b. Prairie du Chien, Wis., Sept. 21, 1909; d. George L. and Harriet (Walker) Griesbach; student St. Mary's Coll., Prairie du Chien, 1927-28; B.A. in Journalism, U. Wis., 1931; m. Richard R. Teschner, Sept. 24, 1932; 1 son, Richard Vincent. Trustee, Village of Whitefish Bay (Wis.), 1951-54; alderman City of Mequon (Wis.), 1957-58; bd. suprs. Ozaukee County, Mequon, 1957-63; mem. Milw. County Park Commn., 1971—, sec., 1972-73, v.p., 1973—. Sec., bd. dirs. Milw. Protestant Home for Aged, 1954-71, Ozaukee-Washington County Guidance Center, 1960-63; sec. Ozaukee County Park Commn., 1960-68; bd. dirs. Milwaukee-Downer College Endowment Assn., 1959-65, pres. 1963-65; bd. dirs. Wis. Planned Parenthood Assn., 1966—, sec., 1970-73; bd. dirs. Riveredge Nature Center, 1970-73. Mem. Whitefish Bay Planning Commn., 1952-54. Mem. League Women Voters (v.p. Milw. 1949-50, dir. 1947-51, sec. Ednl. Found. 1948-62, pres. 1962-64), Wis., Ozaukee County hist. socs., Ozaukee County History Found., Women in Communications, Phi Kappa Phi, Coranto. Republican. Presbyn. Club: Woman's of Wis. Home: 929 N Astor St Milwaukee WI 53202

TESELLE, SALLIE MCFAGUE, educator; b. Quincy, Mass., May 25, 1933; d. Maurice G. and Jessie N. (Reid) McFague; B.A. magna cum laude, Smith Coll., 1955; B.D. magna cum laude, Yale, 1959, M.A., 1960, Ph.D., 1964; m. Eugene A. TeSelle, Jr., Sept. 12, 1959; children—Elizabeth Reid, John Graeme. Lectr., Yale Div. Sch., New Haven, 1962-65; asst. prof. theology Vanderbilt Div. Sch., Nashville, 1971—. Mem. Belmont-Hillsboro Neighbors, 1970—; mem. Concerned Citizens for Improved Schs., 1970—. Kent fellow, 1959—. Mem. Am. Acad. Religion, Soc. Religion in Higher Edn., Am. Civil Liberties Union, Common Cause, Phi Beta Kappa. Author: Literature and the Christian Life, 1966. Editor: The Family, Communes and Utopian Societies, 1972; The Rediscovery of Ethnicity, 1973. Editor Soundings, An Interdisciplinary Jour., 1967—; mem. editorial council Theology Today, 1973—, Jour. Theol. Ethics, 1973—. Home: 2007 Linden Av Nashville TN 37212

TESKE, JUNE ELIZABETH (MRS. EDWARD FIELDS TESKE), ednl. adminstr.; b. Detroit, June 24, 1927; d. Heber Knight and Catherine Elizabeth (Jones) Fisk; B.S., Wayne State U., 1949; M.S., Cal. State U., 1968; postgrad. U. So. Cal., 1969—. m. Edward Fields Teske, Aug. 25, 1952; children—Steven Knight, James Fields. Tchr., phys. edn., Madison (Wis.) Pub. Schs., 1949-52; supr. health edn. YWCA, Pasadena, Cal., 1952-56, Glendale, Cal., 1956-68; psychologist Los Angeles County (Cal.) Supt. Schs., 1968-72, supr. psychol. services and admission, 1972—. Mem. Am. Psychol. Assn., Assn. Cal. Sch. Adminstrs., Council Exceptional Children, Am. Assn. Mental Deficiency. Home: 3315 Mills Av La Crescenta CA 91214 Office: Office of Los Angeles County Supt Schs 9200 E Imperial Hwy Downey CA 90242

TEST, JANE GLASS, constrn. co. exec.; b. San Angelo, Tex., Sept. 9, 1928; d. Frank Patton and Lula Emiline (Vickers) Glass; grad. San Angelo High Sch., 1946; m. James William Strother, Aug. 9, 1946 (dec. May 1953); 1 dau., Carol (Mrs. Walter G. Berry III); m. 2d, Bramwell Collins Test, Feb. 7, 1958 (div. Jan. 1968). Office mgr., bookkeeper San Angelo By-Products Co., 1954-62, Kmart Co., San Angelo, 1963-66; corporate treas. Gene Murphree Corp., Houston, 1967—, Demco Corp., Houston, 1967—. Republican. Presbyn. Home: 1811 Stoney Brook No 102 Houston TX 77042 Office: 7900 Westglen Houston TX 77042

TESTER, SYLVIA ROOT (MRS. N. EUGENE TESTER), writer; b. Phoenix, Oct. 6, 1939; d. Ralph Orrin and Thelma Judson (Aldridge) Root; student Cin. Bible Coll., 1957-59; m. N. Eugene Tester, July 18, 1959; children—Rachael Anne, Julia Linette. Asst. editor Standard Pub. Co., 1959-60, editor, 1961; free-lance writer, Germantown, Ky., 1961-63; editor religious products David C. Cook Pub. Co., Elgin, Ill., 1963-68, editor sch. products, 1968-74; free lance writer; 1974—. Author: Health and Cleanliness Teaching Pictures, 1966; But I Can't See Him, 1967; Plants and Seeds Teaching Pictures, 1967; Moods and Emotions Teaching Pictures, 1970; Creative Adventures Teaching Pictures, 1972. Home: 1001 Cedar St Elgin IL 60120

TETA, LILLIAN MORAN, TV exec.; b. Balt., Aug. 5, 1918; d. Lee Summers and Sara Melinda (Kogler) Moran; student voice with Jean Peters, 1936-41, Elsa Baklor, 1941-43, Lillian Mann, 1943-47, Louise Rush, 1943-47; student diction with Blanche Yurka, 1948-49; m. William B. Halbert, May 3, 1941 (div. Mar. 1947); 1 son, William B.; m. 2d, Nicholas R. Teta, June 30, 1952. Profl. singer, 1946-52; appeared nightclubs, 1949-51; with Papermill Playhouse, 1946-48; TV traffic mgr., broadcaster Poole Broadcasting, sta. WTEN and predecessor, Albany, N.Y., 1958—; fashion show coordinator, soloist ch. choir. Bd. dirs. N.Y. Assn. Brain Injured Children, Rensselaer County chpt. Am. Cancer Soc. Recipient award Grocery Mfrs. Assn., 1962, Dairymen's League, 1964, Conservation Alliance League, 1967, Clairol Co., 1972. Mem. Am. Women in Radio and TV (chpt. pres. 1961, sec. 1965, treas. 1974—), Women's Press Club N.Y. State (pres. 1968-69), Opera Buffs. Home: 25 Phillip St Troy NY 12180 Office: 341 Northern Blvd Albany NY 12201

TETLOW, KARIN COCUZZI (MRS. TIMOTHY CHADWICK TETLOW), journalist; b. London, Eng., Mar. 23, 1936; d. Luigi and Rachel (Pinney) Cox; B.A. with honors, Keele U., Eng., 1958; m. Timothy Chadwick Tetlow, Aug. 17, 1968; children—Sam Chadwick, Georgia Katherine. Came to U.S., 1959. Editorial asst. Leather Trades Rev., Benn Bros., London, 1958-59; econ. asst. Fortune Mag., N.Y.C., 1962-64; reporter, researcher, 1964-70; free lance journalist New York Mag., House and Garden Mag., 1970—. Vice pres., finance chmn. Children's Underground Day Care Center, N.Y.C., 1972—. Mem. Art Students League. Address: 101 W 80th St New York City NY 10024 also Peterskill Heights Alligerville NY 12440

THACKER, BARBARA JEWELL, educator; b. Denver, Oct. 15, 1941; d. Frank and Ethel Evelyn (Ames) Curtis; A.A., Diablo Valley Coll., 1968; B.A., Cal. State U. at Hayward, 1970; postgrad., Fresno State U., 1972—; m. (div. Oct. 1972); 1 dau., Barbara Jo Ann. Tchr. various treatment centers Contra Costa County, Cal., 1971-72; tchr. educable mentally handicapped students, Clovis, Cal., 1972—. Counselor to parents with handicapped children, 1972—. Mem. Am. Assn. on Mental Deficiency, Cal. Speech Assn. Home: 4811-114 N Winery Circle Fresno CA 93726 Office: 902 5th St Clovis CA 93612

THACKER, JOANN KERR (MRS. ROBERT RICHARD THACKER), psychologist; b. Gettysburg, Pa., Aug. 20, 1943; d. John Richard and Saranna Ruth (White) Kerr; B.A., U. Md., 1965; M.A., Am. U., 1969; m. Robert Richard Thacker, May 29, 1965. Personnel, mgmt. research NASA, Goddard Space Center, Greenbelt, Md., 1966-69; psychologist Community Mental Health, Dept. Human Resources, Washington, 1969-74, Montgomery County Detention Center, Rockville, Md., 1974—. Counselor, Bowie (Md.) Involvement Program for Parents and Youth, 1972—; adviser Bowie Hotline, 1973; group therapist Washington Free Clinic, 1970-71; birth control counselor Prince Georges County Free Clinic, 1972, health research com. Nat. Orgn. Women, 1971, D.C. Abortion Alliance, 1972, Zero Population Growth, 1971. Campaign worker for McGovern, 1972. Mem. Am. Psychol. Assn., Wilderness Soc., Common Cause, Am. Personnel and Guidance Assn., Am. Correctional Assn., Psi Chi, Phi Kappa Phi. Home: 8312 Garland Av Takoma Park MD 20012

THACKERY, DONNA KAY SCHRAKE (MRS. LEONARD EUGENE THACKERY, JR.), state ofcl.; b. Chillicothe, O., Oct. 11, 1948; d. Warren Kenneth and Cora Elizabeth (Cutright) Schrake; student Otterbein Coll., 1967-68; B.A. in Journalism, Ohio State U., 1970; m. Leonard Eugene Thackery, Jr., June 2, 1973. News reporter WOSU Radio, Columbus, O., 1970-71; FM traffic dir. continuity WMNI Radio, Columbus, 1972-73; programming asst. Ohio Ednl. TV Network Commn., Columbus, 1973-74; information writer Ohio Dept. Natural Resources, Columbus, 1974—. Pres. Waste Watchers, 1970-72; coordinator Ohio Waste Watchers, Inc., 1972. Mem. Women in Communications. Baptist. Home: 2634 Neil Av Columbus OH 43202 Office: Ohio Dept Natural Resources Fountain Sq Columbus OH 43224

THACKERY, SHERA LYNNE (MRS. DENNIS E. BAKE), systems analyst; b. Greensburg, Ind., Sept. 1, 1943; d. Roger Lavelle and Edythe Eloise (Jones) Thackery; B.S., Birmingham-So. Coll., 1965; M.A., Samford U., 1967; m. Dennis E. Bake, Jan. 13, 1973. Asso. research engr. programming aerospace Boeing Co., Cocoa Beach, Fla., 1967-69; programmer, analyst Computer-Time-Sharing Systems, Inc., Cocoa Beach, 1970; systems analyst Compu-Time div. ACTS Computing Corp., Daytona Beach, Fla., 1971—. Linly Heflin scholar, 1962-65. Mem. Am. Math. Assn., Data Processing Mgmt. Assn. (bd. dirs., 1969-70), Pi Mu Epsilon. Home: 1140 S Ridgewood St Apt 121 Daytona Beach FL 32014 Office: 327 Orange Av Daytona Beach FL 32014

THACKREY, JESSIE DEAN (MRS. FRANKLIN THACKREY), editor; b. Princeton, Kan., June 14, 1913; d. John Gillette and Eva Logan (Bice) Dean; B.S., Kansas State U., 1934; m. Franklin Thackrey, Mar. 31, 1935; children—Janet (Mrs. Wayne Daugherty), Karen, Kent Dean, Maureen (Mrs. John G. Adams), Sue, Keith Richards. Editor home econs. and 4-H clubs Kan. Extension Service, Manhattan, 1934-35; editor Falls Church (Va.) Ch. Sch. Report Card, 1967-73, School-Community Publs., 1973—. Pres. P.T.A., Falls Church, 1949-50, 61; chmn. United Givers Fund, Falls Church, 1962-69. Mem. Falls Church Sch. Bd., 1962-70, vice chmn., 1965-70. Bd. dirs. No. Va. Ednl. TV, 1969-73. Mem. Women in Communications, League of Women Voters, Ch. Women United (chpt. pres. 1973—). Episcopalian. Address: 102 W Rosemary Lane Falls Church VA 22046

THADEN, LOUISE MCPHETRIDGE, plastic mfg. co. exec.; b. Bentonville, Ark., Nov. 12, 1905; d. Roy Fry and Edna (Hobbs) McPhetridge; student U. Ark., 1921-25; m. Herbert von Thaden, June 19, 1928 (dec. Feb. 1969), children—William, Patricia (Mrs. Frederic William Frost). Mgr. D. C. Warren Co., airplane distbr., 1928-29; pub. relations Pitts. Aviation Industries, Inc., 1930-31; codeveloper Nat. Air Markings Program, Bur. Air Commerce, Dept. Commerce, 1935-36; factory rep. Beech Aircraft Corp., 1937-39; purchasing agt. Thaden Engring. Co., 1945-46, plastics research and devel., 1953-55, co-partner, 1959-69, owner, mgr., 1969—, research and devel. reinforced plastics processes and machines mfg.; v.p. Thaden Molding Corp., 1955-59, dir. 1955-59. Mem. adv. com. on women in services Dept. Def., 1959-61, chmn. pub. information subcom., 1960-61. Active motor Corps A.R.C., 1946-52, Lt. col. Civil Air Patrol, 1949-70, ret., 1970, chmn. Nat. Comdr.'s Tng. Com., Coordinator for Women Middle E. region, command pilot. Recipient Harmon trophy. Fedn. Aeronautique Internationale, 1936; winner 1st Woman's Air Derby, 1929, Bendix Trophy Race, 1936; recipient Distinguished Service Award, Meritorious Service Award with Oak Leaf Cluster, Exceptional Service award, Civil Air Patrol; Silver Wings aviation award, 1973. Mem. Ninety Nines (sec. 1930-33, bd. dirs. Amelia Earhart Meml. Scholarships 1962-65), Civil Air Patrol (mem. nat. scholarships com. 1963-69), Vet Air Pilots, Nat. Aero. Assn. (sec. 1937-38), Airplane Owners and Pilots Assn., Antique Airplane Assn., Delta Delta Delta. Club: Silver Wings OX5 of America (Broadwick award 1963, Hall of Fame 1974). Author: High, Wide and Frightened, 1938, repub., 1973. Holder airplane records for altitude, 1928, solo endurance 1929, speed 1929, refueling endurance 1932, light plane speed 1934, East-West speed 1936, 100 kilometer speed 1938. Home: 1101 N Main St High Point NC 27262

THAL, HELEN M., educator; b. Lakota, N.D.; d. Abraham and Ida (Ellingboe) Thal; B.A., St. Olaf Coll., 1938; M.A., State U. Ia., 1940; Ed.D., Columbia, 1966. Instr., Colo. Womans Coll., Denver, 1940-42; counselor Stephens Coll., Columbia, Mo., 1942-43; asst. prof. Hood Coll., Frederick, Md., 1943-45; asst. dir. ednl. div. Inst. Life Ins., N.Y.C., 1945-70, dir. edn. services, 1970—. Lectr., Tchrs. Coll. Columbia, 1963-68. Sec., Interfaith Council for Family Financial Planning. Regent St. Olaf Coll. Recipient Distinguished Alumni award St. Olaf Coll., 1965. Mem. Am. Home Econs. Assn., Am. Econs. Assn., Am. Vocational Assn., Nat. Council on Family Relations, Omicron Nu. Lutheran (pres. bd. trustees ch.). Club: Eaglehead Golf and Country (Md.). Author: Your Family and its Money, 1968, rev. edit, 1973. Home: 350 1st Av New York City NY 10010 Office: 277 Park Av New York City NY 10017

THALER, JANICE M. FOSTER (MRS. DONALD MURRAY THALER), retail exec.; b. Fremont, O., July 27, 1934; d. John William and Lola Marabelle (Cypher) Foster; B.Sc., Ohio State U., 1956, M.Sc. in Nursing (govt. fellow), 1957; m. Donald Murray Thaler, Mar. 26, 1955; children—David John, Kathleen Lynn, Jennifer Lee. Instr. sch. nursing Ohio State U., Columbus, 1957-58; instr. med. surg. nursing U. Buffalo (N.Y.), 1958-60; asst. prof. nursing, 1960-62; instr. sr. med. surg. nursing Holzer Hosp. Sch., Gallipolis, O., 1963-64, med. surg. nursing cons., 1967-68; pres. P.J.'s Inc., Gallipolis, 1972—; sec. Ventures IV, Inc., Gallipolis, 1972—. Active French Art Colony, 1964—, curator, 1971—, acting coordinator, 1973—; liason person Ohio. Arts Council and Gallipolis City Schs., 1972—. Bd. dirs. Community Concert Assn.; trustee French Art Colony. Mem. Retail Mchts. Assn., R.N.'s Assn., Nat. League Nursing, Am. Assn. U. Women (v.p. 1965-66), Newcomer's Club (pres. 1963-64), Frency City Investment Club, Sigma Theta Tau. Presbyn. Philomathean. Home: Route 2 Box 112 Gallipolis OH 45631 Office: 330 2nd Av Gallipolis OH 45631

THALHEIM, BETH MARILYN TARSHIS (MRS. JAY RICHARD THALHEIM), trade show mgmt. exec.; b. N.Y.C., Feb. 17, 1926; d. Arthur and Raina (Goldmann) Tarshis; B.A., N.Y. U., 1947; m. Jay Richard Thalheim, June 25, 1950; children—David Tarshis, Amy Susan, Neil Tarshis. With Thalheim Expn. Mgmt. Corp., Great Neck, N.Y., 1951—, v.p., 1961—, sec., treas., 1968—. Dir. Variety Mdse. Show, Premium Show, Nat. Mdse. Show, Western

Mdse. Show, Phys. Fitness, Health & Diet Show. Mem. Nat. Premium Sales Execs., Premium Merchandising Club N.Y., Nat. Assn. Expn. Mgrs. Home: 15 Shore Dr Kings Point NY 11024 Office: 98 Cutter Mill Rd Great Neck NY 11021

THAL-LARSEN, MARGARET WILSON (MRS. HERMAN THAL-LARSEN), manpower researcher; b. Dunsmuir, Cal., Apr. 15, 1913; d. Jeremiah Judd and Emma Louise (Smith) Wilson; A.B., U. Cal. at Berkeley, 1934, Ph.D., 1941; m. Herman Thal-Larsen, Mar. 23, 1934. Employment interviewer, research technician U.S. War Manpower Commn. No. Cal., San Francisco, 1942-44, chief div. reports and analysis, 1944-46; coastal area analyst Cal. Dept. Employment, San Francisco, 1946-60; regional economist Bur. Employment Security, U.S. Dept. Labor, San Francisco, 1961-66; exec. sec. Cal. Commn. on Manpower, Audomation and Tech., 1961-66; project dir. bay area labor market study Inst. Indsl. Relations, U. Cal. at Berkeley, 1966-70, project dir. human factors research group, dept. indsl. engring. and operations research, 1970-73; sr. cons. Man-Technology, mgmt. cons., Berkeley, 1973—. Mem. Am. Statis. Assn., Sierra Club, Phi Beta Kappa. Home: 2390 Vine St Berkeley CA 94708 Office: 1611 Scenic Av Berkeley CA 94709

THAMM, CHRISTINE ELIZABETH (MRS. CONRAD A. THAMM), coll. adminstr.; b. Newark, Mar. 13, 1945; d. Peter Paul and Verne Marie (Vasilik) Piontek; B.A., Kean Coll. N.J., 1967, M.A., 1972; postgrad. U. Alaska, 1969; m. Conrad A. Thamm, Oct. 3, 1971. Tchr. Mt. Arlington (N.J.) schs., 1967-70; asst. to placement dir. Middlesex County Coll., Edison, N.J., 1971; counselor and adminstr. Douglass Coll., Rutgers U., New Brunswick, N.J., 1972—. Resident counselor Kean Coll. N.J., Union, 1969-71. Active 1st aid squad Twp. of Passaic. Mem. Am. Assn. Univ. Women, Nat. Assn. Women Deans, Counselors and Adminstrs., Am. Assn. U. Adminstrs., Sierra Club N.J. Home: 111 Gates Av Gillette NJ 07933 Office: PO Box 2751 New Brunswick NJ 08903

THARP, DEBRA SUE, advt. exec.; b. Iola, Kan., May 13, 1949; d. Dale and Lillian Romaine (Russell) Tharp; B.S. in Journalism, U. Kan., 1971. Advt. intern Harris Paper Co., Chanute, Kan., 1970; sales rep. Rockland Jour. News, Nyack, N.Y., 1971-73; advt. account exec. Westchester Rockland Newspapers, White Plains, N.Y., 1973—. Mem. Women in Communications, Rockland Found. for the Arts. Home: 1523 Central Park Av Yonkers NY 10710 Office: 1 Gannette Dr White Plains NY 10604

THATCH, LAURA BELLE, merchant; b. Jerico Springs, Mo., Mar. 15, 1912; d. Wyatt and Nettie Belle (Alexander) Hazelwood; grad. high sch.; m. Luther Seborn Thatch, Nov. 26, 1932; 1 dau., Peggy Belle (Mrs. Orville Dean Sibley). Sch. tchr., 1931-32; owner, partner Thatch's Market, El Dorado Springs, Mo., 1944—; treas., dir. Sibley & Thatch, Inc., El Dorado Springs, 1956—; dir. Lee & Thatch, Appleton City, Mo., Bolivar U.S. Mart (Mo.), El Dorado Springs Community Nursing Home, El Dorado Springs Laminated Beams Corp. Vol., A.R.C., 1963-71. Dep. circuit clk., Cedar County, Mo., 1938-42. Mem. Federated Garden Clubs of Mo. (dir. S.W. dist. 1973-75), Osage Valley Fine Arts Guild. Republican. Mem. Ch. of God-7th Day (trustee). Rotary Ann. Clubs: Cedar County Art; Iris Belles Garden (pres. 1967-68); Ladies Shrine, Busy Bees Garden (Springfield, Mo.). Home: 405 N Main St El Dorado Springs MO 64744 Office: Hwy E 54 El Dorado Springs MO 64744

THATCHER, JUDITH ANNE, lawyer; b. Phillipsburg, N.J., Feb. 17, 1945; d. Donald Castner and Catherine Josephine (Pence) Thatcher; B.A. cum laude, Moravian Coll., 1967; postgrad. Washington U., 1967-69; J.D. Rutgers U., 1971. Admitted to N.Y. bar, 1971; practiced in N.Y.C., 1971-73; asso. firm Donovan, Leisure, Newton & Irvine, 1971-73; atty. Am. Airlines, N.Y.C., 1973—. Mem. Am., N.J., N.Y., N.Y.C. Women's bar assns., Assn. of Bar City N.Y., Pi Delta Epsilon, Phi Alpha Theta. Home: 245 E 72d St New York City NY 10021 Office: c/o Am Airlines 633 3d Av New York City NY 10017

THAU, ROSEMARIE BRIGITTE ZISCHKA, scientist; b. Vienna, Austria, Mar. 15, 1936 (came to U.S. 1963); d. Leopold F. and Wilfriede (Kern) Widl; B.S., U. Vienna, 1954, Ph.D., 1963. Research asso. Duke, Durham, N.C., 1963-65; instr. N.Y. State U., Bklyn., 1965-69, asst. prof., 1970-72; staff scientist Rockefeller U., 1972—. Mem. A.A.A.S., Sigma Xi. Home: 400 Central Park W New York City NY 10025 Office: Population Council Rockefeller U York Av 66th St New York City NY 10021

THAYER, DOROTHY THERESA, statistician; b. Somerville, N.J., July 25, 1939; d. Martin Joseph and Mary (Bartolanzo) Spinelli; B.S., Purdue U., 1961; m.S., Rutgers U., 1963; m. Richard Thayer, June 29, 1963. Asst. prof. math. Radford (Va.) Coll., 1963-66; asst. statistician ednl. testing service Ednl. Testing Service, Princeton, N.J., 1966—, data analyst, 1969—. Mem. Am. Statis Assn. Home: RD 1 Rocktown Rd Hopewell NJ 08825 Office: Educational Testing Service Princeton NJ 08540

THAYER, ETHEL STANSBURY, ednl. adminstr., educator; b. Sayre, Pa., July 21, 1925; d. James Stansbury and Sarah Ethel (Mullan) Thayer; B.S., U. Md., 1948, M.Bus. Edn., 1971; postgrad. John Hopkins, 1953, Western Md. Coll., 1955, Am. U., 1958, Columbia, 1963. Accountant, Celanese Fiber Co., 1948-49, B.&O. R.R., Balt., 1950-53; supr. United Meth. Ch. High Sch., Cumberland, Md., 1953—; tchr. bus. Allegany County High Schs., Md., 1953-71; instr. adult edn. program Allegany County, Cumberland, 1960-70; asst. prof. accounting; dir. bus. services Garrett Community Coll., McHenry, Md., 1971—, coordinator vocational bus. programs, 1974—. Staff replacement First Fed. Savs. & Loan Assn. of Cumberland, 1960-70. Mem. Md. Bus. Officer's Community Coll. Com., 1971—. Mem. Am. Assn. U. Adminstrs., Md. Assn. Coll. and U. Bus. Officers, Am. Assn. U. Women. Mem. Order Eastern Star. Home: 219 N 11th St Oakland MD 21550 Office: Garrett Community Coll McHenry MD 21541

THAYER, HENRIETTA WRIGHT (MRS. WALTER G. NEWNAM), civic worker, columnist; b. Klamath Falls, Ore. Nov. 16, 1913; d. George Irving and Annette (Vahldieck) Wright; B.S., Northwestern U., 1934; D.Litt. (hon.), Hamilton U. Ariz., 1973; m. Robert Henry Thayer, May 28, 1938 (dec. 1967); children—Annette Susan (Mrs. Michael Tjong), Patricia Ann (Mrs. Dale Marrou), Thomas Wright; m. 2d, Walter G. Newnam, Apr. 3, 1971; stepchildren—Nancy (Mrs. Dennis Noak), Rebecca (Mrs. Richard Santeler). Employment interviewer personnel dept. Montgomery Ward, Chgo., 1934-36, asst. dept. head mdse. literature, 1936-39, dept. head, 1939-42; weekly columnist Beverly Review, Chgo., 1955—. Sec. state bd. dirs. Ill. Div. Am. Cancer Soc., 1963—, chmn. standards com., 1962—, v.p. Chgo., 1963—, sec. Chgo. council, 1956-59, lay v.p., 1959-63; vol. nurse's aide Walter Reed Hosp., Washington, 1943-45; chmn. opportunity dept. Vol. Office, Washington, 1943-45, dir., 1943-45; dir. Far South Side br. Am. Cancer Soc., 1956-63, chmn. bd., 1956-63; sec. Beverly Hills Community Concerts Assn., 1962—, dir., 1958—; dir. Southtown Youth Concerts Assn., 1957-61; treas. Beverly Aux. of Mary Barteime Home for Girls of Met. Chgo., 1962—, v.p., 1964-65, pres., 1965, v.p. home, 1968—; pres. Chgo. City Panhellenic, 1967-68; chmn. women's bd. Beverly Art Center; mem. Chgo. Citizens Com. Pub. Library Survey; bd. dirs. United Charities Calument dist.; mem. Ridge Service Guild Aux., treas., 1968—; bd. dirs. Beverly YMCA, 1958—, Beverly Art Center, 1968—; v.p., pres. Clissold P.T.A., 1953-56; pres. Morgan Park High Sch. PTA, 1961-63. Recipient ann. nat. divisional award Am. Cancer Soc., 1964, Woman of Year, Beverly-Morgan Park area. Mem. South Side Chgo. Alumni Assn., Met. Chgo. Council of Kappa Delta (v.p. 1952-54), Chgo. City Panhellenic (treas. 1963, sec. 1965, pres. 1966-67), Morgan Park Bapt. Ch. Woman's Soc. (treas. 1959-63, financial sec. 1963-65, treas. 1966-68), Mortar Bd, Kappa Delta (pres. 1950-52). Clubs: Ridge Book of the Hour (sec. 1952-54, librarian 1954-56), Mother's (v.p., pres. 1947-50), Ridge Country; Beverly Hills University. Home: 2208 W 110th St Chicago IL 60643 also Box 54 Clearwater Lake WI 54518

THAYER, JANE HILLIS, psychologist; b. N.Y.C., June 17, 1930; d. Harold Lee and Ruth Evelyn (Caldwell) Hillis; B.A., Cornell U., 1952; M.A. in Clin. Psychology, George Washington U., 1956, Ph.D. in Clin. Psychology, 1969; m. Roger Eugene Thayer, June 16, 1952; children—Peggy, David, Cynthia. Clin. intern St. Elizabeth Hosp., Washington, 1965-66, research intern, 1966-68; staff psychologist Alexandria (Va.) Community Mental Health Center, 1968-71, acting chief psychologist, 1969-70; individual practice psychotherapy, Washington, 1971—. Cons. in field. Pres., Gestalt Inst., Washington, 1973. Mem. D.C., Am. psychol. assns., Sigma Xi, Psi Chi. Contbr. articles to profl. jours. Home: 4621 Chevy Chase Blvd Chevy Chase MD 20015 Office: 2430 Pennsylvania Av NW Washington DC 20037

THAYER, MARCIA CLAIRE (MRS. DAVID LEWIS THAYER), educator, choreographer; b. Boise, Ida., Nov. 27, 1935; d. Milton William and Claire (Stone) Belsher; B.A., Mills Coll., 1956; M.A., U. Ia., 1960; m. David Lewis Thayer, Sept. 9, 1956. Choreographer, Ore. Shakespearean Festival, Ashland, 1957-58, Highfield Summer Theatre, Falmouth, Mass., 1960; dir. Dance Theatre U. Ia., Iowa City, 1960—, head program in modern dance, 1964—. Guest lectr., choreographer Portland (Ore.) State U., 1965; cons. artist Conf. on Dance and Related Arts, U. Ill., Urbana, 1968; mem. com. on dance research Office of Edn., Am. Dance Guild, N.Y.C., 1966—. Mem. Am. Dance Guild, Iowa Dance Council, Am. Theatre Assn., A.A.H.P.E.R. (chmn. dance aesthetics sect. 1968—), Phi Beta Kappa. Choreographer numerous plays, operas, concert dances. Home: 435 Lee St Iowa City IA 52240

THEBOM, BLANCHE, concert and opera singer; b. Monessen, Pa., Sept. 19, 1919; d. Carl Gustav and Caroline (Lindberg) Thebom; student Canton (O.) Actual Bus. Coll., 1933; study of voice dramatics, dance, langs. with pvt. instrs. in N.Y.C., 1939—; m. Richard E. Metz, Nov. 9, 1950 (div.); m. 2d, Albert D'Errico (div.). Debut with Phila. Orch. (Brahms Alto Rhapsody), condr. Eugene Ormandy, Nov. 1941; appeared in Town Hall recital, N.Y.C., 1944; Met. Opera, Fricka in Walkure, 1944; Stockholm Opera, Sweden, 1950; Glyndebourne Mozart Festival, Eng., 1950; extensive European appearances, 1954; created role Baba, the Turk in Rake's Progress by Stravinsky at Met. Opera, 1953; created role Adelaide in Arabella by Strauss in Met. Opera, 1953; under contract to Met. Opera, 20 years; rec. artist Victor Records; concert singer, 1941—; artistic dir. for opera Municipal Theatre of Atlanta; founder, dir. So. Regional Opera, Atlanta; creator Carmen Caravan, opera in streets; distinguished prof. U. Ark. at Little Rock, 1974—, also dir., tchr., translator, arranger, producer for opera. Gen. dir. Hot Springs (Ark.) Found. for Performing Arts. Founder and sole contbr. Blanche Thebom Scholarship Found., Inc., 1948. Recipient Order of Vasa (Sweden). Office: University of Ark at Little Rock University at 33d St Little Rock AR 72204

THEDE, MARION DRAUGHON (MRS. JOHN FREDERICK THEDE), writer, violinist, violist; b. Davis, Okla., Nov. 11, 1903; d. James and Lena (Erdwurm) Draughon; B. Mus., U. Okla., 1922; postgrad. Chgo. Mus. Coll., 1929, Murray Sch. Agr., 1923-24, Okla. City U., 1938-39; pvt. study violin with Leon Sametini, 1929, Max Fischel, 1929; m. John Frederick Thede, Mar. 12, 1960; children—Johnston Murray, Jr., James H. Buchanan. Violinist, violist Oklahoma City Symphony Orch., 1937-67, Oklahoma City Lyric Theatre, 1961-66, Tulsa Philharmonic, 1967-70; various radio, TV appearances; rec. artist; producer folk festivals. Music historian folk and ethnic music U.S., 1929—. Chmn. Okla. State folk music Okla. Fedn. Music Clubs, 1964—; organizer Okla. Folk Council, 1965; nat. chmn. Folk Music and Folk Archives for Nat. Fedn. Music Clubs, 1968-71, mem. nat. com., 1971—. Recipient Merit awards Nat. Fedn. Music Clubs, 1965—, Okla. Fedn. Music Clubs, 1968. Mem. Soc. Ethonomusicology, Internat. Musicol. Soc., Nat. Folk Festival Assn., Okla. Old Time Fiddlers' Assn. (organizer 1971, sec., editor newsletter), Am. Fedn. Musicians, Mu Phi Epsilon, Alpha Gamma Delta. Democrat. Author: The Fiddle Book, 1967. Contbr. articles to mus. publs., Western mags. Address: 1824 NW 23d St Oklahoma City OK 73106

THEES, SISTER ALICE MATTHEW, ednl. adminstr.; b. Jersey City, Aug. 22, 1926; d. Matthew Jerome and Alice Genevieve (Cousins) Thees; B.A., Caldwell Coll., 1953; M.A., Villanova U., 1959; Ph.D., Columbia, 1971. Joined Order Sisters of St. Dominic; tchr. St. Virgil's Sch., Morris Plains, N.J., 1948-53, St. Dominic Acad., Jersey City, 1953-63; faculty Caldwell (N.J.) Coll., 1963—, acad. dean, 1970—. Mem. Values Clarification Assn. Address: Ryerson Av Caldwell NJ 07006

THEILKAS, DOROTHY MILDRED (MRS. GOTTFRIED THEILKAS), civic leader; b. Kansas City, Sept. 27, 1908; d. Louis William and Hannah B. (Shoemaker) Klein; student U. Mo., 1929-30, U. Minn., 1942; m. Gottfried Theilkas, Feb. 27, 1932; children—Sharon Kay (Mrs. James Hadley Templin), Dorothy Lynn. Exec., Pheonix Research Inst. Mgmt. Edn., 1972—; dir. Citizens Com. for Tax Stblzn. and Revenue Sharing, 1972—. Mem. regional adv. council Small Bus. Adminstrn., 1970—; city councilwoman, City Phoenix, 1968-70. Asst. to mayor Phoenix Youth Council, 1968-70; mem. Phoenix Youth Commn., 1971—, chmn. com. on career edn., 1972—. Mem. Phoenix Pub. Library Bd., 1955-68, pres., 1959-68. Recipient Rosenzweig Pub. Library award for service to all Ariz. Libraries, 1966. Author: Your City Government, 1973. Home: 2046 W Windsor Phoenix AZ 85009

THEIS, CATHERINE FRANCES CARNEY (MRS. JOHN H. THEIS), bus. exec.; b. Gardner, Mass.; d. Joseph P. and Catherine F. (Murray) Carney; B.A., Vassar Coll., 1934; m. John H. Theis, Apr. 22, 1939 (dec. Feb. 1967); children—John H., Joseph C., James M. With Thayer, Inc., Gardner, 1950—, pres., 1962—; pres. Wiley Mfg. Inc., Gardner, 1964—; clk. asst. treas. Thayer Furniture Corp., Gardner, 1958—. Mem. Gardner C. of C. (dir. 1971—). Home: 65 Parker Hill Rd Gardner MA 01440 Office: 205 School St Gardner MA 01440

THEIS, GENEVA M., nursing cons.; b. Lawrenceburg, Ind., Dec. 22, 1905; d. George W. and Anne (Draut) Theis; student Bradley U., 1923-24, U. Minn., 1935, 37, 40, 43, B.S. in Pub. Health Nursing, certificate in pub. health nursing, 1952; student Meth. Hosp. Sch. Nursing, 1924-27. Supr. nurse med. floor Passavant Hosp., Jacksonville, Ill., communicable disease; staff nurse, asst. supr. student affiliates Vis. Nursing Assn., Peoria, Ill.; sr. pub. health nurse Silver Bow, Fergus, Lewis, Clark counties, Mont.; nursing cons. U. Ill., div. service Crippled Children, 1947—. Chmn. tech. adv. com. Macoupin County Health Study; bd. dirs. Macoupin County Mentally Retarded Assn., sec.; sec. Macoupin County Assn. Retarded Children, 1970-71, pres., 1971-72. State recruitment officer U.S. Cadet Nurse Corps, World War II. Mem. Ill., 9th Dist. (past pres., dir., rec. sec.) nurses assns., Bus. and Profl. Women's Clubs (Carlinville pres. 1954-56, 68-70, finance chmn. 1970—, chmn. scholarship fund for sr. girls, 1970—, chmn. pub. relations com.; past dist. chmn. Ill., v.p.), Am. Assn. U. Women (past pres.), Ill. Fedn. Bus. and Profl. Womens Clubs, Inc. (recorder Golden Book of Memory). Methodist. Mem. Order Eastern Star (past matron). Contbr. articles nursing mags. Home: 503 E 2d S St Carlinville IL 62626 Office: 230 E Main St Carlinville IL 62626

THEISS, WILDA JUNE SNOW (MRS. DARRYL FLOYD THEISS), educator; b. Marshall, Tex., June 1, 1932; d. Corbin Lee and Lela Mae (Bassett) Snow; B.A. in Speech and Drama (radio-TV scholar), North Tex. State U., 1961; M.A., Baylor U., 1964; postgrad. La. State U., 1968-70; m. Darryl Floyd Theiss, Jan. 25, 1969. Tchr. West Orange High Sch., Orange, Tex., 1963-65; instr., Tex. Agrl. and Indsl. U., Kingsville, 1967-68; grad. asst. La. State U., Baton Rouge, 1968-70; tchr. San Antonio Ind. Sch. Dist., 1973-74, Schertz-Cibolo-Universal City (Tex.) Ind. Sch. Dist., 1974-75. Mem. Speech Communication Assn. Clubs: Elks Wives, U.S. Army Officers Wives. Home: Apt 247 520 McCarty St San Antonio TX 78216

THELANDER, MARION FUNK (MRS. PETER VICTOR THELANDER), ednl. psychologist; b. Phila., June 17, 1905; d. Martin Engle and S. Agnes (Kreider) Funk; B.S., U. Pa., 1931; M.S., Franklin and Marshall Coll., 1956; postgrad. Temple U., 1957-62; m. John Herr Smith, June 19, 1931; 1 dau., Glenna Mary (Mrs. Edgar David McClure); m. 2d, Peter Victor Thelander, Nov. 28, 1963. Tchr. spl. edn. Bd. Edn., Lancaster, Pa., 1931-34, 46-56; tchr. spl. edn., jr. high sch. English, Bd. Edn., Haverford, Pa., 1935-38; psychol. intern Millersville (Pa.) State Coll., 1957; dir. spl. services, psychologist Bd. Edn., Roselle, N.J., 1958-65; psychologist Bd. Edn. of Charlotte County (Fla.), Punta Gorda, 1965-68; mem. Council Tng. and Research in Mental Health, Dept. State, Fla., 1970—; writer column Herald News, Punta Gorda, Fla. Cons., psychologist on mental retardation various states, 1954—; cons. Charlotte County Mental Health Assn., 1967, v.p., 1969; pres. Charlotte County Health Plus Community Action, Inc., 1969-71, exec. dir., 1972—; chmn. rehab. facilities adv. com.-area of retarded Lee, Collier, Charlotte counties div. vocational rehab. Fla. Dept. Edn., Tallahassee, 1967-70; tchr. lip reading Port Charlotte U., 1970—. Fla. del. White House Conf. on Aging, 1971. Bd. dirs. West Central Comprehensive Health Planning Council, Inc., 1971-73; sec. South Central Comprehensive Health Planning Council, 1972, pres., 1973; v.p. Southwest Comprehensive Health Planning Council, 1973; pres. Charlotte County (Fla.) Comprehensive Health Planning Council, 1974. Named One of Women of Achievement, N.J. Zeta Tau Alpha, 1963. Mem. Am. Assn. Sch. Adminstrs., N.E.A., Provisional League Women Voters (Charlotte County pres. 1966), Am. Speech and Hearing Assn., Speech Assn. Eastern States, Internat. Council Exceptional Children (pres. Lancaster chpt. 1934), N.J., Fla. psychol. assns., Psi Chi. Republican. Author: Children at the Window, 1953; Teaching the Slow Learning Child, 1954; ednl. series, documentary film for TV. Contbr. articles to publs. Home: 809 NE Conway Blvd Port Charlotte FL 33950

THEODORE, ATHENA RENTOUMIS (MRS. CHRIS A. THEODORE), educator; b. Nashua, N.H., Jan. 24, 1919; d. Michael and Mary (Karvelas) Rentoumis; B.S., Salem State Coll., 1941; M.Ed., Boston U., 1950, M.A., 1951, Ph.D., 1956; m. Chris A. Theodore, Sept. 8, 1951; children—Arthur, Suzanne, Stuart. Instr., asso. prof. Simmons Coll., Boston, 1956-74, prof. sociology, 1974—, dir. program in community affairs, 1969-72. Mem. Am., Mass., Eastern sociol. assns., Am. Econ. Assn., Am. Statis. Assn. Author: The Professional Woman, 1971. Home: 27 Turning Mill Rd Lexington MA 02173 Office: 300 The Fenway Boston MA 02173

THERESE, SISTER MARY (FLORENCE MAE LENTFOEHR), educator, author; b. Oconto Falls, Wis.; d. George F. and Florence Mae (Brooks) Lentfoehr; student Wis. Conservatory music, 1921; grad. in piano St. Joseph Conservatory Music, 1926-28; B.A., Marquette U., 1933, M.A., 1938, postgrad., 1939-47. Mem. Sisters of the Divine Savior; lectr. English, St. Clare Coll., Milw., summer, 1944; lectr. English, Marquette U., 1946-51; instr. philosophy, English, Divine Savior Coll., Milw., 1951-52; lectr. poetry Loretto Heights Coll., Denver, summer 1960; lectr. poetry Georgetown U., summer 1963, poet in residence, 1966; asso. prof. English Mt. St. Paul Coll., Waukesha, Wis., 1965-69, Coll. of Racine (Wis.), 1969—. Mem. Milw. Mayor's Council on The Arts. Mem. Gallery Cath. Living Authors, Cath. Poetry Soc. Am. (charter mem., founder Milw. chapter 1938), Sigma Tau Delta (hon.). Author: (books of poetry) Now There is Beauty, 1940; Give Joan a Sword, 1944; Moment in Ostia, 1959; Marianne Moore, 1969. Editor: I Sing of a Maiden, 1947. Address: 4042 N Main St Racine WI 53402

THIBAUDEAU, SISTER YVETTE, hosp. adminstr.; b. Lowell, Mass., Aug. 18, 1922; d. Armand J. and Medora (Carrier) Thibaudeau; grad. St. Joseph's Sch. Nursing, 1943; student Ottawa U., part-time 1949-53; B.A. in Nursing, Rivier Coll., 1955. Joined Order of Grey Nuns of the Cross, 1945; asst. adminstr. Ottawa Gen. Hosp., 1952-54; asst. adminstr. St. Joseph's Hosp., Lowell, 1954-62, adminstr., 1962—, trustee, treas., 1962—. Cons. on hosp. mgmt., 1956—. Trustee Grey Nurses, Inc., Lowell. Fellow Am. Coll. Hosp. Adminstrs. Address: St Joseph's Hosp 220 Pawtucket St Lowell MA 01854

THIBAULT, ROBERTA LOUISE (MRS. EDWARD ALLEN THIBAULT), educator; b. Buffalo, Nov. 8, 1940; d. Preston Lewis and Eleanor Louise (Stevenson) Walbridge; A.B. (N.Y. Regents scholar) magna cum laude, Syracuse U., 1962; M.A. in English (teaching fellow), State U. N.Y. at Buffalo, 1966; m. Edward Allen Thibault, Jan. 23, 1965; 1 son, Robert Edward. Editorial asst. William J. Keller, Inc., Buffalo 1963-64; tchr. English Wakefield High Sch., Arlington, Va., 1965-66; accessions librarian Folger Shakespeare Library, Washington, 1966-67; teaching fellow Geroge Washington U., 1967-68; asst. curator Syracuse U. Manuscripts Library, 1968-69; instr. English Onondaga Community Coll., Syracuse, N.Y., 1969-72, asst. prof., 1972—. Mem. Modern Lang. Assn., Syracuse U. Library Assos. Author: Edward Corsi: Inventory of His Papers, 1969. Editor: Social Science Research Manual, 1971; Kul Wicasa Oyate, 1971. Home: 125 Vincent St Syracuse NY 13210

THIELE, MILDRED DORCAS BRADFORD (MRS. WALTER H. THIELE), nurse; b. Walnut, Miss.; d. Blythe Thompson and Ellen (Davis) Bradford; diploma in nursing Bapt. Hosp., Memphis, 1938; student U. Mich., 1940; B.S., U. Wash., 1950; m. Walter H. Thiele, Apr. 15, 1968. Pub. health nurse, Miss., 1938-40; head nurse to chief nurse VA hosps., Jackson, Miss., Grand Island, Neb., N.Y.C., Chgo., Mpls., Lake City, Fla., Gainesville, Fla., 1945-69. Served to capt. U.S. Army Nurse Corps, Korean War. Recipient commendation Dir. VA Hosp., Grand Island, 1953. Mem. Am., Fla. (chmn. membership com., 1968, dir.) nurses assns., Bus. and Profl. Womens Club Lake City (past pres.), Alpha Tau Delta. Republican. Episcopalian. Club: Ponte Vedra (Fla.). Address: 5347 Noble Circle S Jacksonville FL 32211

THIELEMANN, ELIZABETH NORTH, educator; b. Schenectady, Aug. 22, 1923; d. Frank E. and Ruby (Clark) North; A.B., Allegheny Coll., 1945; M.A., U. Ill., 1948; postgrad. Ind. U., 1960. Northeastern Ill. State Coll., 1968-71, De Paul U., 1968-71, Northwestern U., 1969-70; children by previous marriage—Kathleen, George III, James, Gerald, Patricia. Tchr., U. Ill., Urbana, 1946-48, theatre dir. Faculty Players, 1948-49; tchr. and debate coach St. Benedict's Coll., Atchison, Kan., 1957-59, N. Central High Sch., Indpls., 1960-62; tchr. and adviser chmn. New Trier Twp. High Sch., Northfield, Ill., 1962—. Mem. Nat. Assn. Women Deans, Adminstrs. and Counselors, Ill. Assn. Women Deans, Nat., Ill. edn. assn., New Trier High Schs. Edn., Am. Assn. Univ. Women, Ill. Tchrs. English. Roman Catholic. Home: 2324 Central St Evanston IL 60201 Office: 7 Happ Rd Northfield IL 60093

THIELEN, DELLA KRAUSE, civic worker; b. Lake Charles, La., July 11, 1930; d. Rudolph Edward and Della (Bel) Krause; B.A., Cornell U., 1951; m. Jack Edwin Thielen, July 28, 1951; children—Katherine Bel (Mrs. H.M. Julian), John Chadick. With land dept. Humble Oil & Refining Co., New Orleans, 1951-52; pres. Jr. League of Lake Charles, Inc., 1963-64; pres. Lake Charles Ballet Soc., 1969-71, pub. relations chmn., 1975—; chmn. Southwestern Regional Ballet Festival, 1972; pres. Womans Aux., La. Med. Soc., 1972-73, conv. co-chmn., 1974; corr. Alumni News, Cornell Assn. Class Officers, 1974. Bd. dirs. Lake Charles Civic Symphony; trustee Calcasieu Parish Pub. Library System; bd. dirs. La. Boys Village, sec. 1975. Mem. Kappa Kappa Gamma. Episcopalian. Home: 320 Drew Park Dr Lake Charles LA 70601

THIELEN, SISTER MARIE, hosp. adminstr.; b. Elkton, S.D., June 19, 1925; d. John Andrew and Regina Agnes (Ferrie) Thielen; B.S. in Nursing Edn., Mercy Coll., Detroit, 1957; M.Ed. in Psychology, U. Detroit, 1960; M.H.A., St. Louis U., 1965. Joined Religious Sisters of Mercy, 1948; asst. adminstr. St. Joseph Mercy Hosp., Sioux City, Ia., 1965-66; adminstr. St. Joseph Mercy Hosp., Detroit, 1966—. Trustee Mercy Sch. Nursing, Detroit. Home: 2200 E Grand Blvd Detroit MI 48211

THIGPEN, ELLA ROSE (MRS. BENNY THIGPEN), lawyer; b. Lancaster, S.C., Dec. 9, 1937; d. Grady and Mary (Scarborough) Mercer; student Meredith Coll., 1956-57, E. Carolina Coll., 1957-60, Duke, 1963; LL.B., U. N.C., 1963; m. Benny Thigpen, Aug. 20, 1961; children—Ben, Rose. Admitted to N.C. bar, 1963, since practiced in Kenansville; mem. firm Mercer, Thigpen & Mercer, 1964—. Chmn., A.R.C. Kenansville; mem. U. N.C. Med. Found., 1970—. Mem. N.C. State Bar Assn., N.C. Acad. Trial Lawyers, Philaretian Soc., U. N.C. Alumni Assn., Delta Chi, Phi Alpha Delta. Mem. Order Eastern Star. Club: Ramblewood Country. Home: Beulaville NC 28518 Office: Kenansville NC 28349

THIRD, BETTIE JANE (MRS. JOEL H. THIRD), librarian; b. Fort Bragg, N.C., Aug. 29, 1929; d. James Alfred and Julia Boyd (Flint) Dougherty; B.S., E. Carolina U., 1954; M.L.S., Columbia, 1962; m. Joel H. Third, Mar. 14, 1970. Librarian, N.C. Dept. Edn., Burlington, 1954-56; asst. documents librarian U. N.C., Chapel Hill, 1956-58; reference librarian First Nat. City Bank, N.Y.C., 1959-60; librarian Gen. Electric Co., N.Y.C., 1960-62; librarian Port of N.Y. Authority, N.Y.C., 1962-71; cons. N.Y. World Trade Information Center, 1972-73. Mem. Am., Spl. library assns., Am. Soc. Information Sci., Soc. Am. Indexers. Editor Bus. Periodical Index, 1973—. Home: 2077 Center Av Fort Lee NJ 07024 Office: HW Wilson Co 950 University Av Bronx NY 10452

THIRKILL, EVELYN STUCKI (MRS. HOWARD E. THIRKILL), educator; b. Paris, Ida.; d. Joseph S. and Mary (Price) Stucki; B.S., Ricks Coll., 1955; M.S., Utah State U., 1956; Ed.D., U. Md., 1972; m. Howard E. Thirkill, Feb. 18, 1926 (dec.); children—Mary Lou (Mrs. John Lambourne), Evelyn Jean (Mrs. Dennis E. Skinner). Tchr. elementary sch. Bear Lake County, Ida., 1924-27, 29-30; elementary prin. Soda Springs, Ida., 1942-47, Bancroft, Ida., 1947-54, instr. Ricks Coll., Rexburg, Ida., summers 1953, 54, Utah State U., 1955; elementary coordinator pub. schs., Pocatello, Ida., 1955-59, dir. elementary edn. pub. schs., 1959; former prin. Soda Springs Elementary Sch.; now asst. prof., dir. Lab. Diagnosis and Treatment Learning Disabilities, Coll. Edn., Ida. State U.; mem. state guidance com. State Dept. Edn. Mem. Curriculum Devel. and Textbook Commn. for Ida., 1952-55; resource person Nat. Safety Council, 1957—; bd. dirs. Bannock County Mental Health Assn.; adv. bd. Human Devel. Council, Pocatello, Ida., sec., 1973—. Speaker at Parent Tchr. Meetings, tchr. assemblies, convs., other functions, 1950—. Ida. Congress Parents and Tchrs. scholar for study exceptional children, 1952. Pres., Caribou County chpt. Nat. Found. for Infantile Paralysis, 1947-49. Mem. N.E.A. (life), Ida. Edn. Assn. (pres. classroom tchrs. of 5th dist. 1950-52), Assn. Supervision and Curriculum Devel. (state pres. 1959—, nat. dir.), Ida. Congress Parents and Tchrs. (state bd. mem.), Am. Ednl. Research Assn., Council for Exceptional Children (chpt. pres. 1973—), Kindergarten-Primary Edn., Internat. Reading Assn. (pres. elect 1973), Nat. Assn. Adminstrv. Women Edn., Nat. Assn. Sch. Psychologists, Delta Kappa Gamma (past state scholarship chmn.). Mem. Ch. of Jesus Christ of Latter-day Saints. Club: Soroptimist. Address: 110 Stanford Pocatello ID 83201

THODE, E. BLODWEN, rancher, civic worker, state senator; b. Bankhead, Alta., Can., July 5, 1909; d. Joseph John and Lillian (Gahn) Cole; R.N., Holy Cross Hosp., Calgary, 1929; m. Earl Ernest Thode, July 13, 1931 (dec.); children—Ernest J., Thomas A. Came to U.S., 1931, naturalized, 1941. Farming and cattle ranching enterprises, Casa Grande and Vernon, Ariz. Mem. Ariz. Ho. of Reps., 21st to 25th sessions; mem. Ariz. Senate, 1964—. Chmn. Pinal County Polio Assn., 1948, 49; dir. Pinal County Tb Assn., 1950—; dir. at large Ariz. Tb Assn., 1955-57, pres., 1960-61; past pres. Western States Tb Conf.; mem. Casa Grande Community Hosp. Assn., 1948-55, bd. dirs., 1948—, pres., 1948-54; charter mem. adv. bd. Ariz. Dept. Vocational Edn.; bd. dirs. Surgicenter, Phoenix, 1970—, bd. dirs. Patterdell Sch.; mem. Gov.'s Com. Mental Health. Treas., Pinal County Indsl. Devel. Authority, 1971—; mem. Ariz. Employment Security Council; Recipient bronze plaque for community service V.F.W., 1949; distinguished citizen award Casa Grande Rotary Club, 1949; bronze dedication plaque Bd. Dirs. Hoemako Hosp., 1954; service award Brunstein Meml. Casa Grande, U.H.S. Council, 1955; named hon. chpt. farmer Future Farmers Am., 1955; hon. State Farmer Degree Service to Youth, 1956. Am. Vocational Edn. Assn. award merit, 1959; certificate of appreciation Ariz. Edn. Assn., 1961, recognition plaque, 1973; 1st Humanitarian award Ariz. Conf. Social Welfare, 1962; certificate of commendation Nat. Assn. Mental Health, 1962; plaque for outstanding service Central Ariz. Coll., 1971; plaque for service to handicapped Indoor Sports Club, 1970. Mem. Ariz. Hosp. Assn. (legislative chmn. 1954-57), Zonta (hon.). Home: PO Box 999 Casa Grande AZ 85222

THOMAN, MAXINE MAE WATT (MRS. CHARLES ELWOOD THOMAN), hosp. ofcl.; b. Crestline, O., Feb. 23, 1923; d. Ralph Austin and Esther Marie (Swarer) Watt; grad. high sch.; m. Charles Elwood Thoman, Aug. 22, 1941; 1 son, Charles Leslie. Pvt. sec. to v.p. Autocall Co., Shelby, O., 1941-42; pvt. sec. to ofcl. Revere Brass & Copper Co., Rome, N.Y., 1943; sec. Shelby Air Depot (O.), 1944-45; office mgr. Crestline Meml. Hosp. (O.) 1948-52, adminstr., 1952-74, office mgr., personnel mgr., 1974—. Bd. dirs. Crawford County Tb and Health Assn., Bucyrus, O., 1970, Crawford County Health Planning Council, 1971—. Home: 747 Gearhart Av Crestline OH 44827 Office: 291 Heiser Ct Crestline OH 44827

THOMAS, ANN VAN WYNEN, lawyer; b. The Netherlands, May 27, 1919; d. Cornelius and Cora Jacoba (Daansen) Van Wynen; brought to U.S., 1921, naturalized, 1926; B.A. with distinction, U. Rochester, 1940; J.D., U. Tex., 1943; LL.M., So. Meth. U., 1952; m. A. J. Thomas Jr., Sept. 10, 1948. U.S. fgn. service officer, Johannesburg, London, The Hague, 1943-47; research atty. Southwestern Legal Found., So. Meth. U. Sch. Law, Dallas, 1952-67, asst. prof. polit. sci., 1968-73, asso. prof., 1973—. Mem. Tex. Bar Assn., Am. Soc. Internat. Law., London Inst. World Affairs. Author: Communist versus International Law, 1953; (with husband) International Treaties, 1950, Non-Intervention—The Law and its Import in the Americas, 1956, OAS: The Organization of American States, 1962; (with husband) Internat. Legal Aspects of Civil War in Spain 1936-1939, 1967; (with husband) Legal Limitations on Chemical and Biological Weapons, 1970; (with husband) The Concept of Aggression, 1972, An International Rule of Law—Problems and Prospects, 1974. Home: 3404 Stanford St Dallas TX 75225

THOMAS, BERTHA FAY COMBS (MRS. EUGENE PRESTON THOMAS), advt. exec.; b. Eldorado, Okla., Jan. 6, 1918; d. William David and Bertha (Simmons) Combs; student (coll. scholar), Okla. Coll. for Women, 1936; m. Eugene Preston Thomas, Feb. 24, 1946; children—Linda Gene (Mrs. Paul L. Sherman), David Mitchell. Tchr. pvt. piano and violin, Louis Hill and Midway sch. systems, Eldorado, 1940-41; advt. mgr., soc. writer Eldorado Courier, 1941-45; advt. mgr., soc. writer Duke (Okla.) Times, 1946—. Recipient editorial awards Okla. Natural Gas Co., 1957, 61. Mem. Am. Legion Aux. (pres. 1947), Okla. Press Assn. Baptist (organist, pianist 1948—). Club: Wednesday (reporter Duke, Okla. 1946—). Address: Box 189 Duke OK 73532

THOMAS, BETH EILEEN WOOD (MRS. RAYMOND O. THOMAS), editor; b. North Vernon, Ind., May 12, 1916; d. Fayette J. and Emma J. (Ream) Wood; grad. Bedford High Sch., 1934; comml. diploma Lockyear Bus. Coll., 1936; m. Raymond O. Thomas, Feb. 28, 1941; 1 son, Stephen W. Sec., WPA, Vincennes, Ind., 1935-36, Evansville, Ind., 1937-38, Indpls., 1939-41; sec. to adj. AAF Storage Depot, Indpls., 1941-44; sec. Coll. Life Ins., Indpls., 1957-58, Indpls. Sch. Bd., 1958-59; classified office mgr. North Side Topics Newspaper, Indpls., 1960-67; editor Child Life Mag., Indpls., 1967-71, Brownie Reader, 1971-73, Children's Playmate mag., Indpls., 1968—; editorial asso. Saturday Evening Post, Indpls., 1971—; exec. editor Jack and Jill mag., 1971—, Young World mag., 1971—, Child Life mag., 1971—. Clubs: Indianapolis Press, Thetis. Home: 6172 Compton B Indianapolis IN 46220 Office: 1100 Waterway Blvd Indianapolis IN 46202

THOMAS, CAROL LOUISE JOSEPH (MRS. CHARLES RAYMOND THOMAS), community planning co. exec.; b. Poughkeepsie, N.Y., Aug. 29, 1923; d. Harold Kritzman and Charlotte Carolyn (Freiberg) Joseph; student Vassar Coll., 1941-43, Boston U., 1943, 49; A.B. cum laude, Syracuse U., 1948; M.A., U. Conn., 1950; postgrad. Mass. Inst. Tech., 1950; m. Charles Raymond Thomas, Mar. 21, 1943; children—Charles Joseph, Katharine Louise. Free-lance community planner, 1950-58; partner Sonthoff & Thomas, community planners, 1958-61; pres., treas. Thomas Assos., community planners, 1961-69; dir. Thomas Assos. div. Universal Engring. Corp., Boston, 1969—. Dir. Summer Inst. in Community Planning for Minority Groups, Dept. Housing and Urban Devel., 1969; vis. lectr. U. R.I. Grad. Curriculum in Community Planning and Area Devel., 1964-65, asst. prof. community planning and area devel., 1965-71, adj. prof., 1971—; lectr. Boston State Coll., 1970—. Active various community drives; mem. Gov.'s Adv. Com. on Planning, 1963-68. Gov.'s Adv. Com. on Civil Def., 1966-68, Wayland (Mass.) Town Govt. Com., 1958-72; chmn. scholarship awarding com. P.T.A., Wayland, 1965-72. Pres., Arlington (Mass.) Women's Republican Club, 1954-55; vice-chmn. town com. Rep. party, Arlington, 1953-55; sec. town com. Rep. party, Wayland, 1957-59, 68-70, vice-chmn., 1959-61; del. state conv. Rep. party, 1954-58. Mem. Am. Soc. Planning Ofcls., Am. Assn. U. Profs., Am. Soc. Pub. Adminstrs., Am. Inst. Planners (pres. New Eng. chpt. 1965-67, chmn. jury of awards 1969-71), Mass. Fedn. Planning Bds. (dir. 1970—), Internat. Platform Assn. Republican. Unitarian (mem. parish com. 1958-60, adult edn. com. 1973). Author articles in field. Home: 17 Fayette St Boston MA 02116 Office: 100 Boylston St Boston MA 02116

THOMAS, DELLA PAULINE FARMER (MRS. JOHN E. THOMAS), librarian, cons.; b. nr. Mitchell, S.D., Mar. 27, 1913; d. Charles Lester and Della Dolly (Tullis) Farmer; B.Ed., Wis. State Coll., 1935; B.S. in L.S., U. Wis., 1942; m. John E. Thomas, Feb. 1, 1942; children—Susan (Mrs. Joel Lynd), Tommy, Peter. Tchr., librarian Lone Rock (Wis.) High Sch., 1935-37, Oconomowoc (Wis.) High Sch., 1937-39, Dodge County Normal Sch., Mayville, Wis., 1937-41, Platteville (Wis.) State Coll., summer 1940; librarian Emerson Elementary Sch., Madison, Wis., 1942-43; mem. library staff Madison Pub. Library, 1943-45; bibliographer, cons. Scott-Foresman, Chgo., 1945-56; asst. prof. Okla. State U., Stillwater, 1956-65, asso. prof., 1965-69, head edn. area library, 1956-59, coordinator library sci. dept., 1959-65, head curriculum materials lab., 1956-69, dir. internat. study tours in children lit., 1967-74; cons. H.W. Wilson Pub. Co., Bronx, N.Y., 1968—. Mem. A.L.A. (chmn. children's services div. internat. relations com. 1970—, mem. Newbery-Caldecott com. 1970-71), Okla. (pres. 1965; Distinguished Service award 1969), S.W. (mem. exec. bd. 1962-64, part-time exec. sec. 1969-72) library assns., Beta Phi Mu. Contbr. articles to nat. profl. jours. Home: 217 N Stallard St Stillwater OK 74074 Office: Okla State U Library Stillwater OK 74074

THOMAS, DIANE COULTER, journalist; b. Oakland, Cal., Apr. 22, 1942; d. Charles Mitchell and Mildred Melinda (Coulter) Thomas; student Emory U., 1960-61; B.A., Ga. State U., 1965; M.F.A., Columbia, 1969. Reporter, Atlanta Constn., 1965-66, entertainment editor, 1966-69; editorial asso. Atlanta mag., 1970-74; free-lance journalist, 1974—. Mem. Inman Park Restoration, Atlanta, 1972—. Home: 838 Virgil St NE Atlanta GA 30307

THOMAS, DONNA RUTH TAG (MRS. ALLEN DANIEL THOMAS), lawyer; b. Houston, Dec. 9, 1932; d. Lee Reinhold and Verna Ray (King) Tag; B.S., Tex. Woman's U., 1953, B.A., 1953; J.D., Bates Coll. Law, U. Houston (Kappa Delta Pi legal scholar 1972; Fulbright, Crooker & Jaworski legal scholar 1972), 1973; m. Allen Daniel Thomas, June 7, 1954; children—Jane Allen, John Daniel, Anthony King. Admitted to Tex. bar, practice in Deer Park, 1973—; adj. asst. prof. law U. Houston, 1973-74. Adminstrv. cons. City Deer Park, Tex., 1969-70; mem. Deer Park Ladies Civic Club, 1957-65, chmn., 1958, 65; with Pasadena-LaPorte Neighborhood Centers Assn., Pasadena, Tex., 1961-64, chmn., 1964; chmn. bd. trustees Deer Park Pub. Library, 1964-70. Recipient Certificate of Appreciation Deer Park C. of C., 1969. Mem. Am. Library Trustee Assn. (mem. legislative com. 1967-70, chmn. 1970, del. to conf. with Pres. Nixon 1969), Tex. Library Assn. (mem. legislative com. 1970; named Library Trustee of Year 1970), Tex. Library Trustee Assn. (dist. chmn. 1968, state chmn. 1970), Am., Houston, Pasadena bar assns., Tex. Criminal Def. Lawyers Assn., Order Barons, Phi Alpha Delta, Phi Upsilon Omicron. Articles editor Houston Law Rev., 1972-73. Home: 354 Linda St Deer Park TX 77536

THOMAS, DORIS WORK (MRS. CHARLES WILBUR THOMAS), home economist; b. Lancaster, Pa., Oct. 31, 1928; d. Howard Benton and Ada Pearl (Jackson) Work; B.S., Hood Coll., 1950; postgrad., Pa. State U., 1966; m. Charles Wilbur Thomas, June 17, 1950; 1 dau., Debora Lynn. Home service dir. Lancaster County (Pa.) Gas Co., 1950-52; dietitian Slater Foods, Phila., 1952-53; tchr. home econ. Solanco Sch. dist., Quarryville, Pa., 1953-56, 60-63; extension home economist, Lancaster County, 1963—. Mem. Nat., Pa. Assn. extension home economists (v.p. 1967-69, pres.-elect 1974), Lancaster County Home Econs. Assn. (pres. 1962-63), Epsilon Sigma Phi. Home: 43 Valleybrook Dr Lancaster PA 17601 Office: 1383 Arcadia Rd Lancaster PA 17601

THOMAS, ELEANOR LOUISE SHEPHERD (MRS. MARVIN E. THOMAS), broadcasting co. exec.; b. Brookfield, Mo., Sept. 18, 1925; d. John Davis and Abbie Lou (Gilman) Shepherd; grad. high sch.; m. Marvin E. Thomas, Mar.27, 1971. With Civil Service in Air Transport Command, Rosecrans Army Air Base, St. Joseph, Mo., 1941-43; producer daily program for women KFEQ-Radio, 1943-55; producer puppet shows, ventriloquist KUSN-AM-FM, St. Joseph, 1955—. Recipient Golden Slipper award Am. Footwear Inst., 1965. Mem. Am. Women in Radio and Television, Nat., Mo. press women, St. Joseph Area C. of C. (pres. women's div. 1973), P.E.O. Mem. Order Eastern Star. Club: Fortnightly Musical (St. Joseph). Address: 4502 Gene Field Rd St Joseph MO 64506

THOMAS, ELLIDEE DOTSON (MRS. ULYSSES GORDON THOMAS), physician; b. Huntsville, Ark., July 20, 1926; d. Ewell and Vera Taylor Dotson; B.A., U. Ark., 1947, B.S. in Medicine, M.D., 1958; certificate Sch. Phys. Therapy, U. Tex., 1948; m. Ulysses Gordon Thomas, Jan. 9, 1960; 1 dau., Ardel Marie. Phys. therapist Ark. Assn. for Crippled, 1949-50, Moody State Sch. for Cerebral Palsied Children, Galveston, Tex., 1950-52; intern Jefferson Davis Hosp., Houston, 1958-59; resident pediatrics Baylor U. Coll. Medicine, 1959-61, fellow newborn neurology, 1961-62, resident neurology, 1962-63; resident neurology-pediatric U. Okla. Health Sci. Center, Oklahoma City, 1963-65, asst. prof. pediatrics and neurology, 1965-68, asso. clin. prof., 1968—, asso. prof. pediatrics, 1969—, dir. child study center, 1969—; pediatric neurologist Children's Med. Center, Tulsa, 1968—. Med. adviser Oklahoma County chpt. Nat. Found., 1965-68; mem. adv. bd. Area Centers for Deaf-Blind Children. Served with USAF, 1952-54. Diplomate Am. Bd. Pediatrics. Mem. Am. Med. Women's Assn., A.M.A., Okla., Tulsa County med. socs., Am. Acad. Neurology, So. Soc. Pediatric Research. Author: Muscle Tone in Newborn Infants, 1964. Home: 2524 NW 121st St Oklahoma City OK 73120 Office: Dept Pediatrics Coll of Medicine U of Okla Health Science Center Oklahoma City OK 73104

THOMAS, SISTER ELOISE, educator; b. Chgo., Apr. 7, 1924; d. Joseph S. and Agnes (Latowski) Thomas; B.A., Mundelein Coll., 1947; M.A., U. Notre Dame, 1955, Ph.D., 1960. Tchr., Nazareth Acad., LaGrange Park, Ill., 1947-48; part-time instr. Clarke Coll., Dubuque, Ia., 1948-51; tchr. Muscatine Cath. High Sch., Muscatine, Ia., 1951-54; instr. Mundelein Coll., Chgo., 1954-56, asso. prof., chmn. dept. econs., 1959-66, prof., chmn. dept. econs., 1966-68, prof. econs., div. social scis., 1968—, chmn. div. social scis., 1970-72. Bd. dirs. Edgewater Community Council, Project Equality of Ill. Recipient fellowship Case Inst. Tech., Cleve., 1960, U. Chgo., 1961, Claremont Inst. Higher Edn., 1970. Mem. Am. Econ. Assn., Assn. Social Econs., Religious Research Assn. Address: 6363 Sheridan Rd Chicago IL 60660

THOMAS, ELOISE MITCHELL (MRS. RONALD FRANCIS THOMAS), mus. adminstr.; b. Harbor Beach, Mich., June 3, 1907; d. Omer Alva and Frances Magdalena (Wulfekotter) Mitchell; student Flint Jr. Coll., 1926-27; m. Ronald Francis Thomas, Nov. 29, 1927; children—Mary Frances (Mrs. Carl H. Justice, Jr.), Omer (Mrs. Arthur H. Lynds). Office mgr. Mich. Credit Bur., Flint, 1933-40; sec., crafts instr. U.S.O., Southern Pines, N.C., 1944; choir dir., soloist St. Anthony Ch., Southern Pines, 1944-45; chorus dir., instr. Sacred Heart Coll., Tokyo, Japan, 1950-51, also soloist Sacred Heart Ch., Tokyo, 1949-51; dir., curator, co-founder Yesteryears Mus., Sandwich, Mass., 1961—. Lectr., collector old dolls, Tokyo, 1949-51, Stuttgart, Germany, 1954-57. Graylady Tokyo Army Hosp., 1950-51. Mem. Internat. Art Soc., Doll Collectors Am., Sandwich Hist. Soc., Anti-Vivisection Soc., Japanese Cultural Soc., Doll Study Club of Boston (pres. 1969-71). Clubs: Falmouth Outlook (pres. 1972-74). Home: 130 Old Main Rd North Falmouth MA 02556 Office: Main and River Streets Sandwich MA 12563

THOMAS, ETHEL COLVIN NICHOLS (MRS. LEWIS VICTOR THOMAS), educator; b. Cranston, R.I., Mar. 31, 1913; d. Charles Russell and Mabel Maria (Colvin) Nichols; Ph.B., Pembroke Coll. in Brown U., 1934; M.A., Brown U., 1938; postgrad. Boston U., Fisk U., Rutgers U.; m. Lewis Victor Thomas, July 26, 1945 (dec. Oct. 1965); 1 son, Glenn Nichols. Tchr. English, Cranston High Sch., 1934-39; social dir. and adviser to freshmen, Fox Hall, Boston U., 1939-40; instr. to asst. prof. English Am. Coll. for Girls, Istanbul, Turkey, 1940-44; dean freshman, dir. admission Women's Coll. of Middlebury, Vt., 1944-45; tchr. English, Robert Coll., Istanbul, 1945-46; instr. English, Rider Coll., Trenton, N.J., 1950-51; tchr. English, Princeton (N.J.) High Sch., 1951-61, counselor, 1960-62, 72—, coll. counselor, 1962-72. Mem. N.E.A., Am. Assn. U. Women, Nat. Assn. Women Deans and Counselors, Am. Personnel and Guidance Assn., Met. Mus. Art, Kappa Delta Pi. Presbyn. Club: Brown University (N.Y.C.); Nassau. Home: 154 Prospect Av Princeton NJ 08540 Office: Princeton Regional Schs Box 711 Princeton NJ 08540

THOMAS, EVA GLADYS BUNDY (MRS. FRANKLIN DELANO THOMAS), media specialist; b. Starke, Fla., Mar. 8, 1936; d. Marvin Oliver and Oweida Lucille (Hall) Bundy; A.A., Fla. Coll., 1958; B.A., U. Fla., 1962; postgrad. Fla. State U., 1966; m. Franklin Delano Thomas, Aug. 25, 1961; children—William Barry, Brian Bundy, Maria Elena. Stenographer U. Fla., Gainesville, 1954-56; librarian Starke (Fla.) Elementary Sch., 1963, Southside Elementary Sch., Starke, 1963-68; media specialist Bradford Middle Sch., Starke, Fla., 1968-73; media coordinator Learning Resources Center Bradford County Pub. Schs., 1973—. Chmn. Bradford County Library Com., 1964—. Mem. Bradford Edn. Assn. (pres. 1969-71), N.E.A., Fla. Assn. Media Edn., Ladies Golf Assn., Alpha Delta Kappa, Delta Kappa Gamma. Club: Golf and Country (Starke, Fla.). Home: 1404 N Ree St Starke FL 32091 Office: Sch Bd Office Bldg 582 N Temple Av Starke FL 32091

THOMAS, GAIL GRIFFIN (MRS. ROBERT HYER THOMAS), univ. dean; b. Princeton, Tex., Aug. 24, 1937; d. James Isaac and Electra Gibson (West) Griffin; B.A., So. Methodist U., 1958; M.A., U. Dallas, 1973; m. Robert Hyer Thomas, Dec. 14, 1957; children—Victoria, Stewart, Electra. Counselor of students So. Meth. U., Dallas, 1958-59; dean of women U. Dallas, 1971-73, tchr., 1971—, dean of students, 1973—. Bd. dirs. Dallas Mus. Fine Arts, YMCA, Dallas Soc. for Crippled Children (v.p. 1965—). Mem. Tex. Assn. Women Deans and Counselors (research com. 1972), Nat. Assn. Women Deans and Counselors, Jr. League Dallas, Kappa Kappa Gamma. Club: Rush Creek Yacht (dir.). Home: 4537 Lorraine Dallas TX 75205

THOMAS, GEORGELLE, educator; b. Jacksonville, Fla., July 5, 1928; d. George Leonard and Mary Elizabeth (McNair) Thomas; A.B., Queens Coll., Charlotte, N.C., 1949; M.S., U. Ga., 1965, Ph.D., 1967; Dean of residence Salem Acad., 1953-55; admissions counselor Queens Coll., 1955-57; research asst. U. Ga., 1963-67; asst. prof. psychology Ga. So. Coll., Statesboro, 1967-69, asso. prof., 1969—. Mem. Am., Southeastern psychol. assns., Psi Chi, Phi Kappa Phi, Phi Mu. Contbr. articles to profl. jours. Home: Route 1 Grove Lakes Statesboro GA 30458 Office: Ga So Coll Statesboro GA 30458

THOMAS, GEORGIANA ARCHER, county extension home economist; b. Huntsville, Tex., Sept. 14, 1922; d. Virgil and Mae Dell (Walker) Archer; student Mary Allen Jr. Coll., 1940-41; B.S. in Home Econs., Bishop Coll., 1942; M.S. in Extension Edn., Prairie View A. & M. Coll., 1956; m. Theodore Calvin Thomas, June 29, 1943 (div. 1955); children—June Marie, Fleur Ann. Tchr. Mt. Prairie Elementary Sch., Huntsville, Tex., 1942-43, Booker T. Washington Sch., Turkey, Tex., 1949-51; kindergarten tchr. Presidio Army Base, San Francisco, 1945-46; county home demonstration agt., Richmond, Tex., 1951—. Cons. Agrl. Extension Service, 1961-62. Chmn. Houston Youth Com., 1954-72. Mem. County Home Demonstration Agts. Assn., Nat. Assn. Extension Home Economists, Epsilon Sigma Phi (Alpha Zeta chpt.). Democrat. Baptist. Address: PO Box 163 Richmond TX 77469

THOMAS, GERTRUDE, systems analyst; b. Natchez, Miss., Aug. 30, 1946; d. Sidney and Mildred (Wright) Thomas; B.S., Tenn. State U., 1969. Systems analyst data systems div., A.O. Smith Corp., Milw., 1969-72, Wis. Electric Power Co., Milw., 1972—. Mem. Math. Assn. Am., Beta Kappa Chi, Alpha Kappa Mu. Baptist. Home: Apt 109 833 N 24th St Milwaukee WI 53233 Office: Wis Electric Power Co 231 W Michigan St Milwaukee WI 53201

THOMAS, GRACE FERN, physician, psychiatrist; b. Gothenburg, Neb., Sept. 23, 1897; d. George William and Martha C. (Johnson) Thomas; B.S., U. Neb., 1924; M.A., Creighton U., 1926; M.D., U. So. Cal., 1935; postgrad. study, U. Colo., 1942-43, Inst. of Living, 1943, U. So. Cal., 1946, U. Cal. at Los Angeles, 1947-50, Columbia, 1953; M.A. in Religion, U. So. Cal., 1968. Instr. chemistry, biology Duchesne Coll., 1924-27; lab. technician various hosps., 1927-32; intern Los Angeles County Hosp., 1934-35; resident physician Riverside County Hosp., 1935-36; resident psychiatrist Los Angeles County Psychopathic Hosp., 1936-37; staff psychiatrist Cal. State Hosp. System, 1937-42, Glenside Hosp., 1943-44; pvt. practice neuropsychiatry, Long Beach, Cal., 1946-51; chief mental hygiene clinic VA, Albuquerque, N.M., 1951-54; dir. psychiatric edn. Miss. State Hosp., Jackson, 1955; dir. Stark County Guidance Center, Canton, O., 1956-58; dir. Huron County Guidance Center, Norwalk, O., 1958-61, Arrowhead Mental Health Center, San Bernardino, Cal., 1962-64; dir. Mendocino County Mental Health Services, Ukiah, Cal., 1964-65; chief psychiat. edn. Porterville (Cal.) State Hosp., 1965-66; dir. Tuolumne County Mental Health Services, Sonora, Cal., 1966-70; psychiatrist-cons. Emanuel Hosp. Mental Health Center, Turlock, Cal., 1970-71; pvt. practice psychiatry, Turlock, 1970-73, Modesto, Cal., 1973—; cons. psychiatrist Stanislaus County Mental Health Dept., Modesto, 1972-73; alienist to Stanislaus County Superior Ct., Modesto, 1972—. Ordained to ministry Meth. Ch., 1963. Served as capt. M.C., AUS, 1944-46. Diplomate Am. Bd. Psychiatry and Neurology. MEm. A.M.A., Cal., Stanislaus med. assns., Central Cal., Psychiat. Soc., Inst. Religion and Health, Am. Psychiat. Assn., Am. Med. Women's Assn., Am. Legion, Am. Assn. U. Women, Internat. Platform Assn., Soroptimists, Phi Delta Gamma, Phi Beta Kappa, Sigma Xi, Phi Kappa Phi, Nu Sigma Phi. Methodist. Home: 1900 N Denair Av Turlock CA 95380 Office: 801 17th St Modesto CA 95354

THOMAS, JUSTINE NAHALA HILL (MRS. J. EDGAR THOMAS), funeral home exec.; b. nr. Muskogee, Okla., May 30, 1911; d. John and Emma (Pamdrill) Hill; B.S., Md. State Coll., 1940; M.S., Temple U., 1942, Ph.D., 1954; grad. Eckels Embalming Sch., Phila., 1947; m. Charles E. Clark, Apr. 15, 1925, children—Charles Edward, Marie (Mrs. Clifton C. Humbles); m. 2d, J. Edgar Thomas, Oct. 27, 1940 (dec. Feb. 1961). Home demonstration agt., Somerset County, Md., 1930-41; tchr. Mary Nottingham Sch., Accomac, Va., 1942-61; partner J. Edgar Thomas Funeral Home, Accomac, 1942-61, owner, mgr., 1961—. Pres., mgr. Central Agrl. Fair, Accomac, 1961—, Accomack County Civic Orgn., 1942—. Mem. Lambda Zeta Nu. Address: Box 243 Accomac VA 23301

THOMAS, KATHLEEN CAMARA (MRS. VERN R. THOMAS), ednl. adminstr.; b. New Bedford, Mass., Nov. 15, 1946; d. Joseph Nicolau and Lillian Anne (Mendes) Camara; B.A. cum laude, Bridgewater State Coll., 1968; M.A. in Speech and Theatre, Northwestern U., 1969; m. Vern R. Thomas, Nov. 21, 1970. Instr. speech, drama Bemidji (Minn.) State Coll., 1969-70, dir. child devel. tng. program, 1971—. Actress, Paul Bunyan Playhouse, Bemidji, 1970-72. Mem. Assn. for Childhood Edn. Internat., Assn. for Edn. Young Children, Soc. for Research in Child Devel., Am. Assn. U. Women, Kappa Delta Pi. Home: 1019 America Av Bemidji MN 56601

THOMAS, KATRINA, photographer; b. N.Y.C., Jan. 25, 1927; d. Frederic C. and Roberta G. (Roelker) Thomas; A.B., Bryn Mawr Coll., 1949. Free-lance photographer, N.Y.C., 1966—. Photo. publs.: My Skyscraper City, 1963; Chito, 1969. Address: 17 E 96th St New York City NY 10028

THOMAS, LAURA JEAN MCKAMY (MRS. DOUGLAS FAIRBANKS THOMAS), univ. dean; b. Atlanta, Oct. 12, 1922; d. William Edwin and Frances McInnis (Kilgore) McKamy; student Ga. State U., 1942-44; B.S., U. Ga., 1945, M.Ed., 1968, D.Ed., 1972; m. Douglas Fairbanks Thomas, Dec. 25, 1946; children—David Edwin McKamy, Laura Lynn. Tchr., Atlanta Pub. Schs., 1945-47; interior design apprentice Rich's Dept. Store, 1952; tchr., dir. Head Start, community relations, library summer programs, inservice tchr. tng. Atlanta Pub. Schs., 1952-68; asst. dean women Ga. State U., Atlanta, 1968-72, dean women, 1972—. Cons. Atlanta Pub. Schs. Head Start Program and Tchr. Corps work, 1967-67. Bd. founders Sparks Scholarship Fund; bd. dirs. Nell Hamilton Trotter Scholarship Bd., Tri-Cities Girls Club. Am. Assn. U. Women grantee, 1973. Recipient Gen. Council award Ga. State U., 1969; named Woman of Year in Edn. in Atlanta, 1973. Mem. N.E.A., Am. Assn. U. Women (state leadership dir. 1969-71), Nat. Assn. Women Deans and Counselors (arranger local conv. 1970), So., Ga. coll. personnel assns., Ga. Presch. Assn., Ga. Assn. Edn. Young Children, Nat. Ga. Art Assn., Ga. Council on Crime and Delinquency, Ga. Assn. Edn. (pres. local unit 1971-72), Kappa Delta Pi, Mortar Bd., Phi Chi Theta (Alumna of Year 1972), Alpha Phi, Mu Rho Sigma. Clubs: Altrusa (Atlanta); Opri-Mrs. (pres. Tri-city 1964-65). Home: 1158 Cardinal Way SW Atlanta GA 30311

THOMAS, LYNN CAROL, mag. editor, writer; b. Berkeley, Cal., Dec. 19, 1939; d. William Donald and Marjorie Lorraine (White) Thomas; B.A. in English, U. Cal. at Berkeley, 1961. Asso. editor San Francisco mag., 1967—; contbr. to Cal. Living, Better Homes and Gardens, Ebony, Reader's Digest; cons. Perspective mag., 1974—. Fund for Investigative Journalism grantee, 1972.

THOMAS, MARGARET HAY DUDLEY, pub. relations exec., society columnist; b. Kingman, Ariz., July 22, 1921; d. Brooks and Margaret Jones (Hay) Dudley; grad. Phoenix Coll., 1941; m. Jared Evans Thomas, Mar. 13, 1943 (div.); children—Jared Evans, II, Brooks Dudley, Betty Brooks. Pub. relations dir. Camelback Inn, Scottsdale, Ariz., 1955-61, Goodwill Industries, Phoenix, 1969; feature writer Republic, Phoenix, 1961-63; owner Margaret Thomas Pub. Relations, Phoenix, 1963—; soc. columnist Ariz. Republic, Phoenix, 1971—; pub. relations coordinator Met. YMCA, Phoenix, 1963-69; publs., social dir. Phoenix Country Club, 1963-69; Rep. Laurence Laurie & Assos. and McCulloch Properties, Phoenix, 1964-71. Pres. Pottstown (Pa.) Jr. Service League, 1949-50, Parents Assn. Wyndcroft Sch., Pottstown, Pa., 1954-55. Mem. Pub. Relations Soc. Am. (state sec. 1971-72, mem. bd. 1970-73), Ariz. Press Women (v.p. 1970-71), Phoenix Press Club, Nat., Ariz. press women, Phoenix Execs. Club, Daus. of Nile, Theta Sigma Phi (chpt. pres. 1968-70), Sigma Delta Chi. Home: 1336 E Vermont Av Phoenix AZ 85014 Office: Margaret Thomas Pub Relations 1336 E Vermont Av Phoenix AZ 85014 also Carefree Ranch PO Box 708 Carefree AZ 85331

THOMAS, MARION IRENE PETERSON (MRS. JOSEPH M. THOMAS), assn. exec.; b. Winnebago, Ill., Oct. 29, 1916; d. John and Edith Victoria (Larson) Peterson; grad. high sch.; m. Joseph M. Thomas, May 2, 1936; d. Patricia (Mrs. Thomas G. Peterson), Dorothy (Mrs. Dennis Baker), Deborah (Mrs. Douglas J. Wheeler). Inventory clk. J. L. Clark Mfg. Co., Rockford, Ill., 1955-64; bookkeeper, Rockford YMCA, 1964-67, bus. dir., 1967—. Mem. Fraternal Order Police Aux. Republican. Moose. Club: Serah's Investment (Rockford). Home: 2014 12th Av Rockford IL 61108 Office: 200 Y Blvd Rockford IL 61101

THOMAS, MARJORIE EVALYN, librarian; b. Oak Hill, O., Feb. 13, 1920; d. Gomer and Orpha Lois (Hanes) Thomas; student Ohio U., 1938-42, Kent State U., summers 1960-63. Tchr. Oak Hill High Sch., 1942-65, librarian, 1960-65; asst. librarian Portsmouth (O.) Pub. Library, 1965-66, head librarian, 1966—. Mem. Community Concert Assn., 1950-63, Council Humanities, Portsmouth, 1971—. Bd. dirs. Am. Cancer. Soc., Jackson County, O., 1958-63. Mem. Am., Ohio, Ohio Valley library assns., Portsmouth Area Mgmt. Assn. (v.p. 1970), Bus. and Profl. Women's Club (dir. 1970-71), Phi Beta Kappa, Delta Kappa Gamma, Beta Phi Mu. Home: 1307 Bihlman Dr Portsmouth OH 45662 Office: 1220 Gallia St Portsmouth OH 45662

THOMAS, MARTHA JANE BERGIN, chem. engr.; b. Boston, Mar. 13, 1927; d. John A. and Augusta Martha (Harris) Bergin; B.A. with honors, Radcliffe Coll., 1945; M.A., Boston U., 1950, Ph.D., 1952; m. George R. Thomas, Oct. 29, 1955; children—Augusta, Abbigail, Anne Marie, Susan. Jr. technician GTE Sylvania, Inc., Danvers, Mass., 1945-47, jr. engr., 1947-51, sr. engr., 1951-58, research and devel. engr., 1958, 65, sect. head, 1965-69, engring. mgr. Phosphor-Chem. Lab., 1969-72, engring. mgr. Tech. Assistance Labs., 1972—. Named Women Engr. of Year, recipient Golden Plate Am. Acad. Achievement. Fellow Am. Inst. Chemists; mem. Am. Chem. Soc., Soc. Women Engrs. (chmn. Boston sect., nat. corr. sec., nat. recording sec., trustee 1961-64; recipient Achievement award 1965), Eletrochem. Soc., Sigma Xi. Clubs: Radcliffe, Altrusa. Contbr. articles to profl. jours. Patentee in field. Home: 18 Cabot St Winchester MA 01890 Office: 100 Endicott St Danvers MA 01923

THOMAS, MARTHA RODGERS, educator; b. Yeso, N.M., May 19, 1922; d. Samuel Franklin and Lillian (O'Connor) Rodgers; B.S., Tex. Women's U., 1945; M.A., Denver U., 1954; Ph.D., U. Tex., 1968; m. William Ray Thomas, Oct. 19, 1946 (div. July 1957); 1 son, Gary D. Tchr. Dumas, Tex., 1943-44, Bovina, 1945-46, Perryton, 1957-66; Fulbright exchange tchr. Australia, 1959-60; asso. prof. edn., English, U. Tex., Austin, 1966-68, Lamar St. Coll. Tech., Beaumont, Tex., 1968-70, Tex. Arts and Industries U., Laredo, 1970—; inservice, consulting Beaumont, Silsbee, Nederland, Eastland, Hamblin, Laredo, Tex., and Liberal, Dodge City, Meed, Kan. Mem. Tex. joint English Com., 1973—, chmn. dists. 1 and 2, 1974, Tex. sec., 1974. Delta Kappa Gamma scholar, 1966. Mem. Assn. for Supervision and Curriculum Devel., Am. Ednl. Research Assn., Nat. Council Tchrs. English, N.E.A., Tex. State Tchrs. Assn. Author: Outlook, 1960; So. Australian Teacher, 1961, 69. Home: 1601 Fremont St Laredo TX 78040

THOMAS, SISTER MARY EVANGELINE, coll. adminstr.; b. Carbondale, Pa., Dec. 16, 1904; d. John W. and Lida M. (Coggins) Thomas; A.B., Marymount Coll., 1932; M.A., Cath. U. Am., 1934, Ph.D., 1936. Prin. grade sch., Plainville, Kan., 1926-31; prof. history, chmn. dept. Marymount Coll., Salina, Kan., 1936-68, dean students, 1941-48, dir. devel., 1960-66, dir. coll. relations and spl. projects, 1962—. Mem. Salina (Kan.) Cultural Arts Commn., 1966-70; mem. exec. com. Coop. Coll. Devel. Program, 1966-70. Sister Evangeline Thomas Alumni scholar, 1970; named Woman of Achievement, Bus. and Profl. Women's Club, 1972. Mem. Am. Assn. U. Women (v.p. br. chpt. 1968), Am. Cath. Hist. Assn. (mem. exec. bd. 1962-66), Kan. Hist. Soc. (mem. exec. bd. 1956-70), Kan. Tchrs. History (pres. 1962), Salina C. of C. (mem. community action and edn. coms. 1967-69). Author: Nativism in Old Northwest, 1936; Footprints on the Frontier, 1948. Home: 523 S Santa Fe Salina KS 67401

THOMAS, MIRIAM MASON HIGGINS, chemist; b. Chgo., June 22, 1920; d. William Henry and Mame Charlotte (Mason) Higgins; B.S., Bennett Coll., 1940; M.S., U. Chgo., 1942; m. Lucius Howard Thomas, Jr., Sept. 6, 1947; 1 son, Brian Kevin. Research asst. U. Chgo., 1942-45; research chemist U.S. Army Q.M. Food and Container Inst., Chgo., 1945-62; research chemist food scis. lab. nutrition div. U.S. Army Natick (Mass.) Labs., 1962—. Vol., Internat. Tech. Assistance. Mem. adv. com. Framingham (Mass.) Human Relations Council, 1971—. Mem. Assn. Vitamin Chemists, A.A.A.S., Inst. Food Tech., Animal Research Council, Soc. Nutrition Edn., Armed Forces Mgmt. Assn. (sec. 1972-73), Am. Soc. Mil. Comptrollers, Waltham Community Concert Assn., League Women Voters, Coblentz Soc., Sigma Xi, Sigma Delta Epsilon. Contbr. numerous articles to profl. jours. Home: 163 Eaton Rd Framingham MA 01701 Office: US Army Natick Labs Food Sciences Lab Natick MA 01760

THOMAS, MURIEL GRAY (MRS. DONALD ROSS THOMAS), librarian; b. Sherbrooke, Que., Can., Dec. 21, 1909; d. George Howell and Esther Elizabeth (Hope) Gray; B.S., Syracuse U., 1931; m. Donald Ross Thomas, Dec. 8, 1934. Librarian Syracuse (N.Y.) U. Coll. Medicine, Library, 1931-34, Syracuse U. Chemistry Library, 1931-34; librarian Rockingham Free Pub. Library, Bellows Falls, Vt., 1936—. Mem. Vt. Library Bd., 1973—; Vt. dir. Nat. Library Week, 1974. Mem. Am. (Vt. councillor 1962), New Eng. (an incorporator 1963, sec., 1962-63), Vt. (pres. 1951, mem. exec. bd. 1964-68, 73-74) library assns., Kappa Kappa Gamma, Pi Lambda Sigma. Home: Bramley Way Bellows Falls VT 05101 Office: 65 Westminster St Bellows Falls VT 05101

THOMAS, NORMA JEAN, banker; b. Lawrence, Kan., Apr. 28, 1934; d. John Eugene and Margie Fay (Hutsler) Goble; grad. high sch.; m. Theodore Rayford Thomas, Feb. 27, 1956; children—Teri Ann, Raejean, Jerry Wayne. Bookkeeper Balt. Bank, Kansas City, Mo., 1953-56; with Farmers State Bank, Schell City, Mo., 1966—, bookkeeper, teller, 1966-69, asst. cashier, 1969-72, cashier, 1972—. Pres. Walker Sch. Dist. P.T.A., 1960-61; officer Schell City Sch. Dist. P.T.A., 1964—; sec. Schell City Amateur Sports Assn., 1969—. Democrat. Baptist. Mem. Order Eastern Star. Home: Box 126 Schell City MO 64783 Office: Box 98 Schell City MO 64783

THOMAS, PATRICIA ELINDA GRAFTON (MRS. LEWIS EDWARD THOMAS), educator; b. Michigan City, Ind., Sept. 30, 1921; d. Robert Wadsworth and Elinda (Opperman) Grafton; student Stephens Coll., 1936-39, Purdue U., summer 1938; B.Ed. magna cum laude, U. Toledo, 1966; postgrad. (fellow) Bowling Green U., 1968; m. Lewis Edward Thomas, Dec. 21, 1939; children—Linda L. (Mrs. John R. Collins), Stephanie A., (Mrs. Andrew M. Pawuk), I. Kathryn (Mrs. James N. Ramsey), Deborah. Tchr., Toledo Bd. Edn., 1959—, tchr. lang. arts Harvard Sch., 1966—. Mem. lit. curriculum com. Toledo Pub. Schs., 1969. Dist. capt. A.R.C., 1954-55. Mem. Toledo Soc. Profl. Engrs. Aux., Helen Kreps Guild, Phi Kappa Phi, Kappa Delta Pi, Pi Lambda Theta, Delta Kappa Gamma (chpt. v.p. 1968-70). Republican. Episcopalian. Home: 4148 Deepwood Lane Toledo OH 43614 Office: 1949 Glendale St Toledo OH 43614

THOMAS, PATRICIA LOUISE KRESHA (MRS. H. EUGENE THOMAS), newspaper exec.; b. Osceola, Neb., Aug. 31, 1929; d. Adolf Frederick and Eva Frances (Karges) Kresha. Student Neb. U., Midland Coll., 1947, Mesa Jr. Coll., 1963; Colo. U., 1967-68; m. H. Eugene Thomas, May 17, 1956; children—Joseph, Teresa, Karen, Gloria. Co-pub. Fruita (Colo.) Times, 1957-63, 65-66, Huerfano World, Walsenburg, Colo., 1964-65, Pleasant Hill (Mo.) Times, 1969—. Mem. Citizen's Sch. Com., 1972-73; treas. W. Central Mo. Dist. Fair, 1973—. Bd. dirs. Pleasant Hill Community United Funds. Mem. Mo. Press Women, Better Bus. Assn. (sec. 1970—). Democrat. Club: Rooster Booster (Pleasant Hill). Home: 603 Olive St Pleasant Hill MO 64080 Office: 126 1st St Box 8 Pleasant Hill MO 64080

THOMAS, ROBERTA HELENA CARTER (MRS. STANLEY E. THOMAS), former coll. adminstr.; b. Coronado, Cal., Aug. 23, 1946; d. Robert Ross and Margaret Helena (Zabriskie) Carter; B.A., Seton Hill Coll., 1968; M.Ed., Boston U., 1970; m. Stanley E. Thomas, Nov. 27, 1972; 1 dau., Donna Ross. Dir. placement counseling Mass. Coll. Art, Boston, 1970-73; owner, operator R.H. Carter Gallery, Cape Cod, Mass., 1972. Counselor N.A.A.C.P., Boston chpt., 1971-73; chmn. Mass. Com. on Placement for State Colls. and Univs., 1973; coordinator/chmn. Fulbright-Hayes Grant, 1970-73; rep. Marshall Grant, 1973. Mem. Am. Personnel and Guidance Assn., N.A.A.C.P., New Eng. Assn. State Colls. and Univs. (mem. com. cons. on confidentiality of student records 1970-73). Club: Art Directors (Boston). Home: 5 Wiget St Boston MA 02113

THOMAS, SANDRA CAROL, former coll. dean; b. Eagle Lake, Tex., July 11, 1941; d. Ralph and Mary (Hight) Thomas; B.A., U. Tex. at Austin, 1963; M.S., Ind. U., 1967-68; Ph.D., St. Louis U., 1973. Teacher Lakewood High Sch., Denver, 1963-65; tchr. English Briam Inst. Acad., Madrid, Spain, 1965-66; pvt. tutor English, Madrid, Spain, 1965-66; asst. head counselor Willkie Quadrangle Ind. U., 1967-68; asst. dean women So. Methodist U., 1968-69; dean students Lindenwood Coll., 1969-70, dean coll., 1970-72. Bd. dirs. St. Charles Y.M.C.A.; bd. dirs. St. Louis Council Experiment in Internat. Living. Named Outstanding Young Woman Met. St. Louis, 1972. Mem. Nat. Assn. Women Deans, Adminstrs. and Counselors, Nat. Edn. Assn., Mo. Assn. Women Deans and Counselors, Am. Assn. Higher Edn., Nat. Assn. Student Personnel Adminstrs., St. Louis Council on World Affairs, St. Louis Symphony Soc., Sociedad Hispano-Americana of St. Louis, Alpha Phi, Alpha Lambda Delta. Home: 1606 Watson St St Charles MO 63301

THOMAS, SHARON LYNN, ednl. adminstr.; b. Chgo., Oct. 30, 1949; d. Henry I. and Gloria D. (Ward) Thomas; B.A., U. Ill., 1970, M.A. in History, 1971, postgrad., 1974—. Tchr., Chgo. Bd. Edn., 1970-71; asst. prof. history George Wiliams Coll., Downers Grove, Ill., 1971—, asst. dean students, 1972—. Mem. Nat. Assn. Women Deans, Adminstrs. and Counselors, Nat. Council Negro Women, Alpha Kappa Alpha. Office: 555 31st St Downers Grove IL 60515

THOMAS, SHIRLEY (MRS. WILLIAM C. PERKINS), author, bus. exec.; b. Glendale, Cal.; d. Oscar Miller and Ruby (Thomas) Annis; student pvt. schs.; m. W. White, Feb. 22, 1949 (div. June 1952); m. 2d, William C. Perkins, Oct. 24, 1969. Actress, writer, producer, dir. numerous radio and TV stas., 1942-46; v.p. Commodore Prodns., Hollywood, Cal., 1946-52; pres. Annis & Thomas, Inc., Hollywood, 1952—; Hollywood corr., NBC, 1952-56; motion picture editor CBS, Hollywood, 1956-58; corr. Voice Am., 1958-59; now free lance writer. Cons. George Washington U. Biol. Scis. Communication Project, 1965-66, Stanford Research Inst., 1967-68, Jet Propulsion Lab., 1969-70. Organizer, chmn. City Los Angeles Space Adv. Com., 1964-73, Women's Space Symposia, 1962-73. Recipient Frances Holmes award, 1950, 51; Aviation Edn. Assn. award, 1962. Mem. Am. Inst. Aero. and Astronautics, Internat. Soc. Aviation Writers, Air Force Assn. (Airpower Arts and Letters award 1961), Nat. Aero. Assn. A.A.A.S., Nat. Assn. Sci. Writers, Am. Astronautical Soc., Nat. Geog. Soc., Am. Soc. Pub. Adminstrs. (com. for sci. and tech. in govt. 1972—), Aviation and Space Writers Assn., Air Force Hist. Assn., Achievement Rewards for Coll. Soc. (nat. bd.), Muses of Cal. Mus. Sci. and Industry, Theta Sigma Phi, Phi Beta. Author: Men of Space, vols. 1-8, 1960-68, translated into Spanish, 1961, Italian, 1962; Space Tracking Facilities, 1963; Computers - Their History, Present Applications and Future, 1965; The Book of Diets, 1974. Home: 8025 Hollywood Blvd Hollywood CA 90046

THOMAS, UNA BRYANT (MRS. WALTER J. THOMAS), steel co. exec.; b. Rohnerville, Cal., July 27, 1912; d. Calvin Harvin and Mayme (Jessen) Bryant; grad. high sch., 1930; m. Walter J. Thomas, Jan. 22, 1944; children—Marily (Mrs. Richard Huysman), Alice Reina. Exec. sec. Western Pipe & Steel Co., San Pedro, Cal., 1941-44; accountant, sec. Nat. Parts Co., 1944-50; with Riverside Steel Constrn. Co., Santa Fe Springs, Cal., 1951—, sec., treas., 1952—, also chmn. employees pension plan; dir. Greenstone Devel. Co., Radio Towers, Inc., Riverton Indsl. Steel Constrn. Co., Thermal Instruments, Inc., Rudine Steel Constrn. Co. Mem. Nat. Secs. Assn. (past treas.). Home: 10127 Van Ruiten St Bellflower CA 90706 Office: 11400 Greenstone St Santa Fe Springs CA 90670

THOMAS, WILMA JEAN CLARK (MRS. JAMES L. THOMAS), govt. ofcl.; b. Dill, Okla., Aug. 25, 1931; d. Joel Peter and Grace (Williams) Clark; B.S., Southeastern State Coll., 1953; m. James L.

Thomas, Aug. 27, 1954; children—Philip Thomas, David. Sec. Okla. Edn. Assn., Oklahoma City, 1953-54, Dept. of Air Force, Vance AFB, Okla., 1954-55, City Clerks Office, Wichita Falls, Tex., 1963-64; city clk. Wichita Falls, Tex., 1964—. Second v.p. Hirschi Jr.-Sr. P.T.A., 1968-70; mem. Rider High Sch. Band Parents Club, 1972—, sec., 1974-75. Mem. Assn. City Clerks and Secs. of Tex., Internat. Inst. Municipal Clks. Mem. Ch. of Christ. Home: 2513 Elmwood Circle N Wichita Falls TX 76308 Office: 1300 7th St Wichita Falls TX 76301

THOMASON, BERENICE MILLER, microbiologist; b. Birmingham, Ala., Mar. 10, 1924; d. Henry Herbert and Lillian Irene (Martin) Miller; student Huntingdon Coll., 1941-43; B.S., Ga. State U., 1960; m. Earl Luther Thomason, Dec. 4, 1944 (div. 1948); 1 son, Thomas Stephen. Med. technologist War Dept., Stat. Hosp., Ft. Benning, Ga., 1943-45; pub. health technologist Muscogee County Health Dept., Columbus, Ga., 1948-51; bacteriologist Communicable Disease Center, Atlanta, 1951-53, 3rd Army med. lab., Ft. McPherson, Ga., 1953-54; microbiologist Center for Disease Control, Atlanta, 1954-61, research microbiologist, 1961—. Mem. Am. Forestry Assn., Nat. Wildlife Assn., Am. Soc. for Microbiology, DeKalb Humane Soc., Sigma Xi. Baptist. Research and publs. on techniques of detecting pathogenic microorganisms. Home: 4202 Hambrick Way Stone Mountain GA 30083 Office: 1600 Clifton Rd Atlanta GA 30333

THOMPSON, AMANDA MEADE BREWER (MRS. JAY VERNON THOMPSON), editor; b. Inez, Ky.; d. William T. and Estella (Sammons) Meade; A.B., Marshall U., 1961; m. Lee Roy Brewer, Dec. 5, 1936 (dec. Dec. 1959); m. 2d, Jay Vernon Thompson. Tchr., Mingo County Sch. System, Kermit, W.Va., 1921-69, prin. Kermit Grade Sch., 1933-40. Mem. Gov.'s Antiquities Commn., 1968, 69; mem. Gov.'s Travel Commn., 1966—, W.Va. Centennial Commn., 1960-63, Black Diamond Jubilee Commn., 1969; mem. Mingo County (W.Va.) Health Council, 1971-72. Mem. Democratic County Exec. Com., 1924-36. Bd. dirs. Mingo County Cancer Soc. Recipient Best Tchr. certificate NBC, 1941, Decoration of Chivalry medal Odd Fellows lodge, 1946, Silver Clover Leaf award 4-H Club, 1947, medal Valley Forge Freedoms Found., 1963. Mem. N.E.A., W.Va. Edn. Assn., World Poetry Soc., Am. Assn. U. Women, Ky. Poetry Soc., Nat. Fedn. State Poetry Socs., Mingo County Hist. Soc. (pres. 1965—), W.Va. State Poetry Soc. (2d v.p. 1967—), Appalachian Poetry Guild, Nat. Soc. D.A.R. (founder 1950, regent Jennie Wiley chpt. 1968-73), World Poetry Soc., Delta Kappa Gamma (2d v.p. 1966—). Methodist (pres. Alpha Circle 1951-55). Club: Kermit Area Woman's (pres. 1969-71). Mem. Order Eastern Star (past worthy matron), Rebekahs, Pocahontas, White Shrine. Author: Romantic West Virginia, 1963; I Sing of Appalachia, 1967, 2d edit., 1972; (song) Ballad of Roseanna McCoy, 1961; also hist. plays, numerous poems. Editor Appalachian Poets, 1950—; poetry editor Williamson Daily News, 1950—, W.Va. Sch. Jour., 1965-73. Address: 73 Elm St Kermit WV 25674 also 210 Palmetto St New Smyrna Beach FL 32069

THOMPSON, SISTER ANN, educator; b. Cleve., Apr. 25, 1929; d. John Ignatius and Margaret (Kelly) Thompson; A.B., Coll. Mt. St. Joseph, 1951; M.A., Marquette U., 1962; Ph.D., Cath. U. Am., 1966; postgrad. Western Res. U., 1951-52. Tchr., Cleve. Bd. Edn., 1951-52; tchr. secondary schs. Sisters of Charity, Cin., 1954-56, Lima, O., 1956-60; faculty dept. history and polit. sci. Coll. Mt. St. Joseph, Mt. St. Joseph, O., 1966-71; exec. sec. Sisters of Charity, 1971—. Ednl. observer World Acad. Fgn. Study, 1969; coordinator Stanford Research Inst. Project, 1969-70. Mem. Am., Am. Cath. hist. assns., Soc. for Ch. History, Am. Polit. Sci. Assn., Nat. Ohio councils for social studies, Am. Assn. Higher Edn., Phi Alpha Theta, Kappa Gamma Pi. Address: Office of the Generalate Mount St Joseph OH 45051

THOMPSON, ANNE ELISE (MRS. WILLIAM HENRY THOMPSON), judge; b. Phila., July 8, 1934; d. Leroy Henry and Mary Elise (Jackson) Jenkins; B.A., Howard U., 1955, LL.B., 1964; M.A., Temple U., 1957; m. William Henry Thompson, June 19, 1965; children—William Henry, Sharon Annette. Staff atty. U.S. Dept. Labor, Chgo., 1964-65; admitted to D.C. bar, 1965, N.J. bar, 1966; practiced in Trenton, 1966—. N.J. asst. dep. pub. defender, Trenton, 1967-70; pros. atty. Lawrence Twp., Trenton, 1972—. Mem. N.J. Commn. on Vocational Edn. in Correctional Instns., 1971-72. Del. to Democratic Nat. Conv., 1972. Recipient achievement award Mercer County Polit. Action Council, 1967. Mem. Am., N.J., Mercer bar assns. Club: Girl Friends. Home: 123 Renfrew Av Trenton NJ 08618 Office: 484 Princeton Av Trenton NJ 08618

THOMPSON, ARLUVENE GROSSMAN (MRS. JAMES DISNEY THOMPSON), librarian; b. Cullison, Kan., Jan. 21, 1927; d. Forrest Ross and Orra Margaret (Covey) Grossman; B.S. in Occupational Therapy, Washington U., St. Louis, 1950; certificate teaching St. Mary of Plaines, 1968; M.S., Emporia Kan. State Tchrs. Coll., 1971; m. James Disney Thompson, Apr. 2, 1951 (dec. July 1965), children—James, Barbara, John, Marguerite, Charles, Mark, Brian, Alan. Occupational therapist St. Anthony Hosp., St. Louis, 1950-51, Occupational Therapy Workshop, Richmond, Va., 1952-53; lab. asst. Plastics Research Co., Richmond, 1955-65; librarian and media specialist Concordia (Kan.) pub. schs., 1971—. Sec., Cloud County Child Care Assn., 1972—, dir., 1972—. Mem. Am., Kan. Occupational Therapy assns., Nat., Kan., North Cloud County (sec. 1973-74) edn. assns., A.L.A., Kan. Spl. Libraries Assn., Am. Pub. Health Assn., Am. Assn. Univ. Women. Roman Catholic. Home: 612 Iowa St Holton KS 66436 Office: 9th and New York Sts Holton KS 66436

THOMPSON, AUDREY MARIE, social worker; b. Poughkeepsie, N.Y., Oct. 13, 1930; d. Lawrence Vincent and Stephanie Lucille (Isaacs) Thompson; B.A., Hunter Coll., 1961; M.S.W., Fordham U., 1964. Caseworker foster care div. N.Y. Foundling Hosp., N.Y.C., 1964-66; therapist Children's Day Treatment Center and Sch., N.Y.C., 1966-69; therapist Manatee County Mental Health Center, Bradenton, Fla., 1969-73, coordinator children's services, 1973—; adj. prof. U. South Fla. Pres., Manatee County Health and Welfare Council, 1973—, Early Childhood Devel. Council Manatee County, 1973—; mem. adv. council Manatee County Head Start Program, 1973—. Bd. dirs. Manatee Opportunity Council. Mem. League Women Voters, N.A.A.C.P., Am. Assn. U. Women, Nat. Assn. Social Workers (treas. Fla. state council 1973—, v.p. Tampa Bay chpt. 1973—). Home: 2420 Bayshore Gardens Pkwy Bradenton FL 33507 Office: 1300 9th St E Bradenton FL 33505

THOMPSON, BARBARA COOPER, state ofcl.; b. Rochester, N.H.; d. Burt Randall and Lillian (Foss) Cooper; A.A., Colby Jr. Coll. for Women, 1937; B.S., Boston U., 1939; m. Charles C. Thompson, June 8, 1941 (div.); children—Sandra (Mrs. James W. Grigg), Mark Cooper, C. Boyen, Betsy (Mrs. Ronald C. Booth). Social worker N.H. State Hosp., 1940-43; social worker Rochester Sch. System, 1965-68; rep. N.H. Gen. Ct., 1969—. Bd. dirs. Rochester Assn. Retarded Children, Strafford Guidance Center, N.H. Family Planning Assn., Blodgett Farm for Intellectually Handicapped, Day Care and Child Devel. Council N.H., N.H. Mental Health Assn. Mem. Nat. Order Women Legislators, Delta Delta Delta. Republican. Conglist. Home: 77 Rochester Hill Rd Rochester NH 03867

THOMPSON, BARBARA STORCK, state ofcl., educator; b. McFarland, Wis., Oct. 15, 1924; d. John C. and Marie Ann (Kassabaum) T.; B.S., Wis. State U.-Platteville, 1956; M.S., U. Wis.-Madison, 1959, Ph.D., 1969; postgrad. U. Ia., Mt. Mary Coll., U. Wis.-Milw.; m. Glenn T. Thompson, July 1, 1944; children—David C., James T. Tchr. elementary schs., Mt. Horeb, Wis., 1944-56; instr. Green County Tchrs. Coll., Monroe, Wis., 1956-57; curriculum coordinator Monroe pub. schs., 1957-60; instr. U. Wis.-Platteville, 1960; supr. schs., psychologist, reading specialist Waukesha (Wis.) pub. schs., 1960-62; adminstr., prin. Fairview Elementary Schs., Brookfield, Wis., 1962-64; adminstrv. cons. Wis. Dept. Pub. Instrn., Madison, 1964-72, state coordinator innovations and program devel., 1971-72, state supt. pub. instrn., 1973—; instr. supervision instrn. U. Wis.-Madison, 1972. Participant White House Conf. Children, Washington, 1970; mem. Wis. Gov.'s Com. State Conf. Children and Youth, 1970—; mem. Wis. State Adv. Bd. Early Childhood Edn., 1971—. Recipient State Conservation award Lions, Madison; named Your Madisonian, Wis. State Jour., 1970. Mem. Nat. Council Adminstrv. Women in Edn. (Woman of Year), Nat. Council State Cons. in Elementary Edn. (pres.), Wis. Assn. Sch. Dist. Adminstrs., Nat., Wis. assns. supervision and curriculum devel., Nat., Wis. elementary sch. prins. assns., P.T.A., Nat., Wis. (life), So. Wis. edn. assns., Wis. Ednl. Research Assn., Internat. Assn. Childhood Edn., Pi Lambda Theta, Alpha Beta. Home: 1 Springwood Circle Madison WI 53717 Office: Supt Pub Instrn Dept Pub Instrn 126 Langdon St Madison WI 53702

THOMPSON, BERTHA BOYA (MRS. JOHN L. THOMPSON), educator; b. New Castle, Pa., Jan. 31, 1917; d. Frank L. and Kathryn (Park) Boya; B.S., Slippery Rock (Pa.) State Coll., 1940; M.A., Miami U., Oxford, O., 1954; Ed.D., Ind. U., 1961; m. John L. Thompson, Mar. 27, 1942; children—Kay Lynn (Mrs. W. W. Koolage, Jr.), Scott McClain. Tchr. elementary schs., New Castle, 1940-45; coordinator social studies, tchr. secondary schs., Oxford, 1954-63; asso. prof. edn., geography, chmn. dept. edn. Western Coll. for Women, Oxford, 1963-71; prof. and co-dir. Tchr. Edn. Center, Western Coll., Oxford, 1971-74; asso. prof. edn. Miami U., Oxford, O., 1974—. Mem. Nat. Council Geog. Edn. (exec. bd. 1966-69), Nat. Council Social Studies, Soc. Women Geographers, Assn. Am. U. Profs., Nat. Soc. for Study Edn., Assn. Am. Geographers, Internat. Reading Assn., Pi Lambda Theta, Kappa Delta Pi, Gamma Theta Upsilon, Pi Gamma Mu, Zeta Tau Alpha. Contbr. articles to profl. jours. Home: 6073 Contreras Rd Oxford OH 45056

THOMPSON, BETTY ANNE, communications exec.; b. Atlanta, Feb. 4, 1926; d Joseph Rodgers and Anna (Jamerson) Thompson; A.B. cum laude, Wesleyan Coll., Macon, Ga., 1947; postgrad. Kenyon Sch. English, Gambier, O., 1948-49. Dir. pub. relations Wesleyan Coll., Macon, 1947-49; staff writer Methodist Bd. Missions, N.Y.C., 1950-55; publicity sec. World Council Chs., Geneva, Switzerland, 1955-56, dir. pub. relations, N.Y.C., 1956-64, attended assemblies in New Delhi, India, 1961, Uppsala, Sweden, 1968, also Geneva, Canterbury, Eng., mem. communications com., Geneva, 1968—; asst. gen. sec., head of communications United Meth. Bd. Missions, N.Y.C., 1965-74; asso. gen. sec., head edn. and cultivation div. United Meth. Bd. Global Ministries, 1974—. Bd. mgrs. Friendship Press. Recipient Distinguished Achievement award Wesleyan Coll., 1970. Mem. Religious Pub. Relations Council (awards chmn., bd. govs.). Author: Turning World, 1960; The Healing Fountain, 1973. Contbr. to Fifty Years of South Atlantic Quarterly, 1950; Enigma of Thomas Wolfe, 1953; Christianity and Crisis, Christian Century, World Outlook. Editor at large Christian Century, 1964—. Office: 475 Riverside Dr New York City NY 10027

THOMPSON, CAROL GWEN, artist, educator; b. Pasadena, Cal., May 10, 1944; d. Sumner Comer and Cordelia (Whittemore) Thompson; student Pasadena City Coll., summer 1963; B.A. with distinction, U. Redlands, 1966; postgrad. Stanford, summer 1966; M.A., Cal. State Coll. at Los Angeles, 1967; M.F.A., Claremont Grad. Sch. and Univ. Center, 1969. Student asst. Cal. State Coll., 1966-67; head resident Pitzer Coll., Claremont, Cal., 1967-70; instr. art Mt. San Antonio Coll., Walnut, Cal., 1968—, dir. coll. art gallery, 1972-73; exhibited one-man show M.F.A. Exhbn., Scripps Coll., Claremont, 1969, Covina Pub. Library, 1971; exhibited in shows U. Redlands, 1964, 65, 70, Sr. Thesis Exhibit, U. Redlands, 1966, Cal. State Coll., 1967, Rio Hondo Coll. Design div. Am. Ceramic Soc., 1968, faculty exhibits Mt. San Antonio Coll., 1968, 70, 72, Am. Ceramic Soc. Design Div. Mem. Show, 1969, Cal. State Poly. Coll., Pomona, 1972. Reader, Henry E. Huntington Library and Art Gallery, 1967-68. Recipient Curved Bar award Girl Scouts U.S.A., 1958, Forensic award Lions Club, Region finalist, 1962. Womans Aux. Am. Legion scholar Alhambra Post, 1962, Cal. State Grad. fellow, 1968. Mem. Cal. Scholarship Fedn. (life), Faculty Assn. Mt. San Antonio Coll., Am. Ceramic Soc., Coll. Art Assn. Am., Friends Huntington Library, Internat. Platform Assn., Sigma Tau Delta. Republican. Presbyn. Home: 1212 N Hidalgo Av Alhambra CA 91801 Office: Mt San Antonio Coll Grand Av Walnut CA 91789

THOMPSON, CHARLOTTE ANNE, librarian; b. Lansing, Mich., Nov. 10, 1909; d. James Herbert and Mary Elizabeth (Ardis) Thompson; student Hollins Coll., 1927-30; A.B., U. Mich., 1931, A.B. in L.S., 1932, summer student, 1944; M.S. in L.S., Columbia, 1955. Librarian, U. Tampa (Fla.), 1933-70, head spl. collections div. Merl Kelce Library, 1970-74, acting dir. Merl Kelce Library, 1974—. Mem. A.L.A., Fla., Southeastern, Hillsborough County (pres. 1964-65) library assns., Am. Assn. U. Women, P.E.O., Zeta Tau Alpha, Delta Kappa Gamma. Democrat. Presbyn. Clubs: Pilot, Woman's (Tampa). Home: 4015 Bayshore Blvd Tampa FL 33611

THOMPSON, CHERYLE, country music singer; b. Jacksonville, Fla. Rec. artist, 1966—; most popular recs. include her compositions 3d Person (nominated for Most Popular Song of Year), Stranger on the Hwy. (award, 1963), also Top 20, Wall to Wall Heartaches. Nominated for Grammy award Nat. Acad. Rec. Arts and Scis., 1969; one of 2 country music singers named as Top Female Artist of Year; nominated for Most Popular Female Country Star, 1969; named Miss Las Vegas, Miss Nevada, semi-finalist in Miss America Contest, 1963. Address: 1634 E Lewis Av Las Vegas NV 89101

THOMPSON, CONSTANCE PURTELL (MRS. LOVELL THOMPSON), editor; b. Brookline, Mass., Nov. 20, 1915; d. Lawrence and Elizabeth Howes (Streamberg) Purtell; B.A. cum laude, Radcliffe Coll., 1935; postgrad. U. Munich (Germany), 1935-36; m. Darcy Crenshaw Coyle, 1941 (div. Jan. 1969); m. 2d, Lovell Thompson, Mar. 14, 1969. With art dept. Houghton Mifflin Co., pubs., Boston, 1936-69, advt. mgr., 1943-69; dir., fgn. lang. editor Gambit, Inc., pubs., Boston, 1969—. Mem. Soc. Mayflower Descs. Contbr. poems and articles to lit. and trade publs. Home: 142 Argilla Rd Ipswich MA 01938 Office: 53 Beacon St Boston MA 02108

THOMPSON, DORIS ELIZABETH WELLS (MRS. ROBERT DAVID THOMPSON), splty. oil mfg. co. owner; b. Elizabeth, N.J., July 27, 1914; d. Richard Harvey and Louise Christine (Sauer) Wells; student N.J. Law Sch., 1935-36; grad. Chgo. Coll., 1941; m. Robert David Thompson, Mar. 16, 1957. With G.S. Miller Co., splty. oil mfr., Treasure Island, Fla., 1941—, partner, 1948-50, owner, 1950—. Mem. Treasure Island Library Study Com., 1963; mem. Treasure Island Personnel Adv. Bd., 1966—, chmn., 1967—; mem. Treasure Island Election Bd., 1966—, clk., 1968—; mem. Treasure Island Municipal Complex Com., 1973—. Bd. dirs., treas. Isle of Capri Civic Assn., Inc., 1964-68. Chmn. Ruby Lee Minar Loan Fellowship of So. Region, Soroptimist Internat. of Ams., 1968-74, lt. gov. So. region, 1972-74, gov., 1974—. Mem. Am. Council Automotive Women, Leonardy Parliamentarians of Pinellas County, Fla. Assn. Parliamentarians. Republican. Roman Catholic. Clubs: Bath, Soroptimist Internat. Holiday Isles (pres. 1964-66). Home: Heartstone Apts 210-126th Av Treasure Island FL 33706 Office: PO Box 9202 Treasure Island FL 33740

THOMPSON, DOROTHY BROWN, writer; b. Springfield, Ill., May 14, 1896; d. William Joseph and Harriet (Gardner) Brown; A.B., U. Kan., 1919; m. Dale Moore Thompson, July 2, 1921; 1 son, William Brown. Began writing professionally, 1931; contbd. verse to nat. mags. and newspapers including Saturday Rev., Sat. Eve. Post, Va. Quar. Rev., Poetry (Chgo.), Commonweal, Good Housekeeping, others; author research articles for hist. jours.; poems pub. in numerous collections and textbooks, mags. and textbooks in Eng., Can., Australia, Sweden, New Zealand, 26 in Braille; 10 poems pub. as songs. Leader poetry sect. Writers' Conf., U. Kan., 1953-55, McKendree Coll., 1961, 63, Creighton U., 1966, Am. Poets Series, Kansas City, Mo., 1972-73. Recipient Mo. Writer's Guild award, 1941, awards poetry socs. Ga., 1955, Va., 1956, La., 1958, also Poetry Soc. Am. and various local awards. Mem. Diversifiers, Poetry Soc. Am., Am. Hist. Assn., Nat. Soc. Colonial Dames. Mem. Christian Ch. Clubs: Woman's City, University Women's, Filson. Author: (poetry) Subject to Change, 1973. Address: 221 W 48th St Kansas City MO 64112

THOMPSON, EDITH MILLINA (MRS. MORTON C. STEVENSON JR.), physician; b. N.Y.C., Aug. 31, 1931; d. Percival Micheson and Edith Lenore (Smith) Thompson; B.A., Hunter Coll., 1952; M.D., MeHarry Med. Coll., 1956; m. Morton C. Stevenson, Jr., Apr. 28, 1962. Intern Grasslands Hosp., Valhalla, N.Y., 1956-57; resident anesthesiology L.I. Jewish Hosp., New Hyde Park, N.Y., 1957-59; asst. in anesthesiology Horace Harding Hosp., Queens, N.Y., 1959-60; asst. anesthesiologist Hosp. Med. Center, Bklyn., 1962-66, attending anesthesiologist, 1966—. Diplomate Am. Bd. Anesthesiology. Mem. Am., Nat. med. assns., Am., N.Y. socs. anesthesiologists, N.Y. Acad. Scis. Address: 2767 E 66th St Brooklyn NY 11234

THOMPSON, EDNA MAY, librarian; b. Stephentown, N.Y., Jan. 17, 1917; d. Harry Edmund and Phoebe (Livingston) Thompson; B.Ed., State U. N.Y., 1942, B.S. in L.S., 1947. Tchr. one room sch., Fayette, N.Y., 1942-43; librarian in various positions N.Y.C. Pub. Library, 1947-49; librarian U.S. Army, Fort Dix, 1949-51, Chief Camp Drum, 1951-53, Field Bremerhaven, Germany, 1954, cataloger, Frankfurt, Germany, 1954, Sect. LaRochelle and Verdun, France, 1954-57, Vicenza, Italy, 1957-58, Supt. Schs. Office, Kaiserslautern, Germany, 1958-61, acquisitions librarian Directorate U.S. Dependents Schs., Karlsruhe, Germany, 1961—, acting chief, 1964-67. Served with Waves, 1943-45. Mem. N.E.A., A.L.A., Armed Forces Librarian Assn., Spl. Libraries Assn. Home: 251 Union St Bennington VT 05201 Office: Directorate USDESEA APO NY 09164

THOMPSON, EILEEN JANET (MRS. JOHN BRUCE PANOWSKI), author; b. Lincoln, Neb., Mar. 17, 1920; d. Hugh and Nelle Josephine (Masters) Thompson; B.A. cum laude, Miami U., Oxford, O., 1941; M.A., U. N.M., 1971; m. John Bruce Panowski, Sept. 7, 1942; children—Thomas Michael, Bruce Philip, Lynn Eileen (Mrs. Lawrence M. Sherman) and Daryl Anne (twins). Radio chemistry technician Los Alamos Sci. Lab., 1956-64; guide Bradbury Sci. Mus., Los Alamos, 1969—. Vice-pres. P.T.A., 1957-58; mem. staff fund drives and clinic Cancer Soc. and Polio Found., 1953-56. Recipient 1st Prize Short Story Project, Am. Assn. U. Women, 1962, Scroll, Mystery Writers Am., 1966. Mem. Writers Guild, Western Writers Am., Audubon Soc., Am. Mus. Natural History, Common Cause. Methodist (mem. bd. 1965-67). Club: Women's (v.p. Los Alamos 1949-51). Author: The Blue-Stone Mystery, 1963; The Spanish Deed Mystery, 1964; The Apache Gold Mystery, 1965; The Dog Show Mystery, 1966; The Golden Coyote, 1971. Home: 1267 46th St Los Alamos NM 87544

THOMPSON, ELLEN MARIE WILLIAMS (MRS. ROBERT H. THOMPSON), banker; b. Dell Rapids, S.D., Sept. 19, 1921; d. Lowell L. and Zeo Ramona (Bowles) Williams; student McKennan Sch. Nursing, 1940-41; m. Robert H. Thompson, Mar. 19, 1941; children—Sylvia Joy (Mrs. Edward Q. Wood), Robert Kenton. Bookkeeper, Miner County Bank, Howard, S.D., 1953-57, teller, 1957-58, asst. cashier, 1958-62, cashier, 1962—, sec., 1962—, also dir.; dir. Security State Bank, Canova, S.D., Miner Ins. Agency, Howard, S.D. Mem. Am. Legion Aux. (pres. 1955-57). Mem. Order Eastern Star, PEO, Eight and Forty (pres. Kingsbury County chpt., 1960, 61, state pres. 1967-68). Club: Miner County Extension. Home: PO Box 1 Howard SD 57349 Office: Miner County Bank Box 1 Howard SD 57349

THOMPSON, EMMA JEAN, sch. counselor; b. Ind., Nov. 23, 1900; d. Anthony J. and Anna C. (Formento) Jakeno; A.A., Western Ill. State Tchrs. Coll.; B.S., Wayne U., Detroit, 1937; postgrad. U. Mich., U. Mexico, U. Ill.; m. Thomas T. Thompson, Dec. 22, 1952. Tchr. rural schs., Cuba, Ill., 1923-28; tchr. elementary and jr. high sch., also head audio-visual work, Dearborn, Mich., 1928-52; exchange tchr., Honolulu, 1940-41; tchr. for U.S. Army, Germany, 1949-50. Recipient certificates of Honor in Best Tchr. Contest, 1947, 48, certificate for meritorious service Bd. Edn., Dearborn, 1952. Mem. Am. Assn. U. Women, Women's Overseas Service League. Mem. Disciples of Christ Ch. Home: 500 Wall St Seattle WA 98121

THOMPSON, ERA BELL, editor; b. Des Moines; d. Stewart C. and Mary (Logan) Thompson; student (Wesleyan Service Guild scholar 1931) U. N.D., 1929-31, L.H.D., 1969; B.A., Morningside Coll., 1933, LL.D., 1967; postgrad. Northwestern U., 1938, 40. Sr. interviewer U.S. and Ill. State Employment Service, 1942-47; asso. editor Ebony, Johnson Pub. Co., Chgo., 1947-51, mng. editor, 1951-64, internat. editor, 1964—, mng. editor of Ebony Africa, 1964. Mem. North Central Manpower Adv. Comn., 1965-68. Bd. dirs. Chgo. Pub. Library, 1959-60, Hull House, 1963-64. Recipient Newberry Library fellowship write autobiography, 1945; Bread Loaf Writers' Conf. fellow, 1949; named Iota Phi Lambda's Outstanding Woman of Year, 1965. Mem. Soc. Midland Authors (dir. 1961-72, recipient Patron Saints award 1968), Urban League (Chgo.), N.A.A.C.P., Sigma Gamma Rho (hon.). Methodist. Author: American Daughter, 1946, reissued 1967; Africa, Land of My Fathers, 1954. Co-editor: White on Black, 1963. Home: 2851 King Dr Chicago IL 60616 Office: 820 S Michigan Av Chicago IL 60605

THOMPSON, ESTHER LEE JOHNSON, poet; b. Wolfe City, Tex., Apr. 7, 1919; d. Claro Nelson and Christa Miller (Spencer) Johnson; student Tex. Bus. Coll., 1953-54, Dallas Theater Center, 1961-64, Newspaper Inst. Am., 1967-69, So. Meth. U., 1972, Tarrant County Jr. Coll., 1973; m. George Thompson, Oct. 17, 1951 (dec.). Ins. underwriter Universal Life Ins. Co., Dallas, 1948-52; feature writer Dallas Star Post Newspaper, 1949-56; asso. editor Good Pub. Co., Fort Worth, 1955-57; feature writer Bronze Texan Newspaper Fort Worth, 1968-69; editor, pub. A Galaxy of Verse, quar., 1974—. Recipient John C. Klien award journalism Newspaper Inst. Am., 1968; Popular Prize Poetry Soc. Tex., 1971, Eva Willes Wangsgaard Lyric award, 1973, Naylor award, 1974. Mem. N.A.A.C.P., Poetry Soc. Tex. Democrat. Baptist. Club: F.B. Brooks and L. Gray Literary and Art (lit. chmn. 1973—). Contbr. poetry to numerous mags. including Poet Lore, Poetry Soc. Tex. Yearbook. Home: 200 S Chandler Dr Fort Worth TX 76111

THOMPSON, HARRIETTE LINE (MRS. CHARLES SYDNOR THOMPSON), pianist; b. Carlisle, Pa., Mar. 27, 1923; d. James Harvey and Harriet Rebecca (Brenneman) Line; Mus., Syracuse U., 1947; Mus.M., U. N.C., 1966; grad. Vienna Conservatory Music, 1967; m. Charles Sydnor Thompson, June 2, 1947; children—Darcy (Mrs. Michael A. Craddock), Charles Sydnor III, Harriet, Brenneman, Mary Katherine. Piano faculty Boston U., 1948-50; N.Y.C. debut, 1955; Vienna debut, 1967; piano faculty Queens Coll., Charlotte, N.C., 1968-69, U. N.C., Charlotte, 1970-71; world tour, 1972-73. Mem. Sigma Alpha Iota. Home: 34 Balthassar Kraussgasse Perchtoldsdorf A-2380 Wien Austria Office: 1100 Cameron Brown Bldg Charlotte NC 28204

THOMPSON, SISTER HELEN ELIZABETH, coll. dean; b. San Francisco, Jan. 19, 1933; d. Howard E. and Gertrude Helen (Riordan) Thompson; A.B., Mundelein Coll., 1960; A.M., U. Chgo., 1961, Ph.D. (LaVerne Noyes scholar), 1963; grad. Inst. Ednl. Mgmt., Harvard, 1970. Tchr. elementary, jr. high sch., Chgo., 1953-59; instr. edn. Mundelein Coll., Chgo., 1963-64, asst. prof., acting chmn. edn. dept., 1965-68; prof. edn., acad. dean Clarke Coll., Dubuque, Ia., 1968-71, prof. edn., acad. dean, 1971—. Instr. Camp Minwanca, Am. Youth Found., 1974. Mem. budget com. United Way, Dubuque, 1972—. Mem. Am. Ednl. Research Assn., Am. Assn. Higher Edn. Address: Clarke Coll Dubuque IA 52001

THOMPSON, HELEN MULFORD, orchestra exec.; b. Greenville, Ill.; d. Job Herbert and Lena (Henry) Mulford; student DePauw U., 1926-27; A.B. cum laude, U. Ill., 1932; Litt.D., Conservatory of Music Cin., 1961; Mus.D., Marshall U., 1967; m. Carl D. Thompson, Apr. 8, 1933; 1 son, Charles D. Agy. dir., casework supr. pub. and pvt. agys., Ill., Wis., N.Y., 1932-40; mgr. Charleston Symphony Orch., 1940-50; exec. sec. Am. Symphony Orch. League, 1950-63, exec. v.p., 1963-70; mgr. N.Y. Philharmonic, N.Y.C., 1970—. Exec. vice chmn. Pres.'s music com. of People-to-People Program, 1956-59; mem. study panel Rockefeller Bros. Fund study on Performing Arts in U.S. Recipient Laurel Leaf award Am. Composers Alliance, 1961. Mem. Am. Fedn. Musicians, Nat. Music Council (mem. exec. com.), Phi Beta Kappa, Alpha Chi Omega, Sigma Alpha Iota. Presbyn. Author: The Community Symphony Orchestra—How to Organize and Develop it. Co-author: Organization and Presentation of Symphony Orchestra Concert Activities. Editor: Newsletter of Am. Symphony Orch. League, 1948-70. Contbr. articles to profl. jours. Office: NY Philharmonic Orch Lincoln Center New York City NY 10023

THOMPSON, HELEN STEPHANIE, govt. ofcl.; b. East Walpole, Mass., Oct. 4, 1923; d. Felix Robert and Helen Terese (Geigle) Thompson; B.S. in Bus. Adminstrn., 1945, M.A., 1947; postgrad. London Sch. Fgn. Langs., 1945, Indsl. Coll. Armed Forces, 1963, U. Md., 1969. Editorial asst. W.R. Grace & Co., N.Y.C., 1947-48; instr. Ft. Trumbull br. U. Conn., New London, 1948-49; financial economist FDIC, Washington, 1950-56; jr. economist Fed. Res. Bank, Cleve., 1956; bus. economist FTC, Washington, 1957-62; labor economist U.S. Dept. Labor, Washington, 1962—. Program economist AID, Saigon, Vietnam, 1966-67. Recipient Meritorious Service award FTC, 1961. Mem. Am. Econ. Assn., English Speaking Union, Epsilon Pi Epsilon. Home: 2000 N St NW Washington DC 20036 Office: Patrick Henry Bldg 601 D St NW Washington DC 20213

THOMPSON, HELEN TARKO (MRS. JOHN MURRAY THOMPSON), govt. ofcl.; b. Collier, Pa., Mar. 6, 1923; d. Mike and Mary (Woodmaska) Tarko; student George Washington U., 1958-64; m. John Murray Thompson, May 15, 1965. Sec., War Dept., Washington, 1941-45; prodn. and marketing adminstr. Dept. Agr., Washington, 1945-47, indsl. analyst Agrl. Stablzn. and Conservation Service, 1947-66, program officer food stamp div. Food and Nutrition Service, 1966—. Analyst, Pres.'s Commn. on Assassination of Pres. Kennedy, 1964; dir., sec.-treas. Camp Appalachia, Inc., Covington, Va., 1968—. Recipient Superior Accomplishment award Dept. Agr., 1952, Outstanding Performance ratings, 1955, 56, Spl. Achievement award, 1971, Superior Performance award, 1973, Superior Service award 1974. Mem. Am. Pub. Welfare Assn. Home: 2 Midhurst Rd Silver Spring MD 20910 Office: Dept Agr Food and Nutrition Service Food Stamp Div Washington DC 20250

THOMPSON, IRENE POWELL (MRS. ROBERT L. THOMPSON), assn. exec.; b. Arcadia, La., June 23, 1908; d. Aaron A. and Sarah Elizabeth (James) Powell; grad. Tyler Comml. Coll., 1927; m. Robert L. Thompson, Sept. 6, 1944; children—Glenda (Mrs. Robert W. McDonald), Charles A. Robertson. Stenographer, file clk. Remington Rand, Homer, La., 1936—; file clk. Agrl. Stabilization and Conservation, Minden, La., 1932; bookkeeper Shreveport (La.) C. of C., 1963-67; office mgr. Homer C. of C., 1967—. Sec. Claiborne Parish Cancer Found., Homer, 1969; chmn. Homer chpt. A.R.C., 1966; active Beautification Found. Mem. Am. Legion Aux. (pres. 1969-70, Thelma Ashley award), Art Club, Ceramic Club, Rebekah Assembly La. (pres. 1970-71), Internat. Assn. Rebekah (rep. fron from La. to Vancouver, Canada, 1971, regional chmn. Region 8, 1971-72). Democrat. Baptist (sec., ch. aux.). Club: Women's Department. Home: 607 Fulmer St Homer LA 71040 Office: 502 N 2nd St Homer LA 71040

THOMPSON, JESSIE E. THAYER (MRS. JOHN E. THOMPSON), banker; b. Meeteetse, Wyo., Nov. 4, 1926; d. Harry W. and Susan (Van Ben-Thysen) Thayer; student pub. schs.; m. John E. Thompson, Jan. 19, 1947. Stenographer, mortgage loan dept. Nat. Bank of Alaska, Anchorage, 1956-60, 61-68, supr., 1968, operations officer, 1968—. Home: 8231 Spruce Rd Anchorage AK 99503 Office: Box 4-J Spenard AK 99503

THOMPSON, JULIE MORSE (MRS. H. SHELDON THOMPSON), theater dir.; b. Chgo., Dec. 5, 1914; d. Watt Drew and Lucille (Petrillo) Morse; student Edinburgh Jr. Coll., 1930-31; m. H. Sheldon Thompson, May 27, 1939; children—Wendy (Mrs. Arthur Davenport), H. Sheldon III, Julianne (Mrs. Walter Trepashko), Penny. Actress, Clare Tree Major Children's Theatre, 1935-40; dir. Charleston (W.Va.) Children's Theatre, 1941-43; founder, dir. Springfield (O.) Jr. Civic Theatre, 1944-47; a founder, producer Children's World Theatre, N.Y.C., 1947-49; founder, dir. Young Peoples Theatre Workshop, Levittown, N.Y., 1953-58; acting tchr. Adelphi Children's Centre for Creative Arts, Garden City, N.Y., 1956-60, asso. dir., 1960-71, dir., 1971—. Mem. Am. Ednl. Theatre Assn. (regional vice-gov. 1967-69). Christian Scientist (trustee local ch.). Home: 4 Mulford Pl Hempstead NY 11550 Office: Adelphi U Garden City NY 11530

THOMPSON, KATHLEEN, educator; b. Goodwater, Ala., Feb. 18, 1920; d. Aldrich R. and Urbie (Bailey) Thompson; B.S., U. Ala., 1942; postgrad. Ala. Coll., Montevallo, 1942, U. Tenn., summers 1954-55; M.S., Pa. State U., 1961. Tchr. vocational home econs. Liberty High Sch., Pickens County, Ala., 1942-44; with Coop. Extension Service U.S. Dept. Agr., 1944—, asst. home demonstration agt., Randolph, Walker and Calhoun counties, 1944-46, home demonstration agt., Pickens County, 1946-47, asso. home demonstration agt., St. Clair County, 1947-48, home demonstration agt., Fayette County, 1948-52, specialist in clothing, handicraft State Office, Auburn, Ala., 1952-69, specialist in clothing, 1969—; cons. State Maid of Cotton; appeared on ednl. TV sta. Auburn U.; adviser Fayette County Home Demonstration Council. Mem. Am. (past com. chmn.), Ala. (com. chmn.) home econs. assns., Bus. and Profl. Womens Club Fayette (past pres.). Contbr. chpt. to Consumers All, The Yearbook of Agriculture, 1965. Contbr. articles to profl. publs. Home: 121 S Ross St Auburn AL 36830 Office: Coop Extension Service Auburn U Auburn AL 36830

THOMPSON, KATHRYN FRANCES (MRS. WILLIAM STONE THOMPSON), librarian; b. Center, Tex., Nov. 26, 1918; d. Robert Francis and Lily May (Williams) Broadway; B.A., Rice Inst., 1938; M.A., U. Denver, 1963; m. William Stone Thompson, Dec. 20, 1941; children—Frances (Mrs. Hal Shure), Kathryn (Mrs. William Haskell Cathey). Elementary and high sch. tchr., Bay City, Tex., 1938-39; elementary and jr. high sch. tchr., Houston, 1939-56; audio-visual coordinator, librarian, jr. high schs., Houston, 1956-68; supr. learning media services Spring Branch Schs., Houston, 1968—. Teaching cons. Gulf Coast Scis. Ednl. Resources Center, 1965-68. Mem. N.E.A., Tex. State Tchrs. Assn., Tex. Assn. for Ednl. Tech. (pres. 1972-74), Tex. Assn. Sch. Librarians, Tex. Assn. Supervision and Curriculum Devel., Assn. for Ednl. Communications and Tech. Republican. Home: 310 Bunker Hill St Houston TX 77024 Office: PO Box 19432 Houston TX 77024

THOMPSON, KAY F. (MRS. RALPH P. KRICHBAUM), dentist; b. Pitts., Aug. 22, 1930; d. Lony C. and Bertha E. (Porter) Thompson; B.S., U. Pitts., 1951, D.D.S., 1953; m. Ralph P. Krichbaum, Jan. 10, 1959. Pvt. practice dentistry, Pitts., 1953—; dir. course clin. hypnosis Sch. Dentistry, U. Pitts., 1960—, faculty continuing edn. dept., 1968—, asst. prof. Dept. Behavioral Scis., Sch. Dental Medicine, 1971—; lectr. hypnosis Pa. Med. Sch., 1965—. Lectr., tchr. hypnosis and psychology in dentistry, 1959—. Fellow Am. Soc. Clin. Hypnosis (hon. fellow, trustee Edn. and Research Found., ann. award 1970, workshops faculty, v.p. 1967-68, sec. 1968-69, pres. 1972-73, asso. editor jour.), Seminars on Hypnosis Found. (life), Soc. Clin. and Exptl. Hypnosis (faculty workshops, Am. Dental Assn. liaison 1968—); mem. Am., Pa., Pitts. dental assns., Acad. Gen. Dentistry, A.A.A.S., Am. Assn. Women Dentists, Am. Bd. Hypnosis in Dentistry, Council Socs. in Dental Hypnosis (pres. 1966-71), Zeta Tau Alpha. Lutheran. Contbr. articles to profl. publs. Office: 247 Gulf Bldg Pittsburgh PA 15219

THOMPSON, LAURETTA NAYLOR (MRS. GEARS H. THOMPSON), educator; b. Chgo.; d. Arthur W. and Ada (Ferrell) Peterson; grad. Wilson Jr. Coll., 1944; B.E., Chgo. Tchrs. Coll., 1949; M.E., Northwestern U., 1953; m. Gears H. Thompson. Tchr., McCosh Elementary Sch., Chgo., 1949-60, adjustment tchr., 1954-60; asst. prin. McCosh Primary Sch., 1960-70; area A sch. mental health dir. Chgo. Bd. Edn., 1970-73; parent coordinator Dumas and McCosh Spl. Summer Schs., 1965, 67; asst. prin. Wendell Smith Sch., 1973—. Mem. adv. bd. Woodlawn Mental Health Center, 1964, vice chmn. community bd., 1970; faculty adviser McCosh Sch. P.T.A., 1954-69; mem. Beatrice Caffrey Youth Service. Mem. Chgo. Assn. Elementary Asst. Prins., Mental Health Assn. Greater Chgo., Chgo. Ednl. Dirs. Assn., N.A.A.C.P., Nat. Council Negro Women, Alpha Kappa Alpha (nat. sec. 1966-70 financial sec. 1970—), Chgo. Urban League, Alpha Gamma Pi. Baptist (gen. supt. Sunday sch. 1971—). Home: 7257 S Dr M L King Dr Chicago IL 60619

THOMPSON, LIBBIE MOODY (MRS. CLARK W. THOMPSON), civic worker; b. Galveston, Tex., Nov. 22, 1897; d. William Lewis and Libbie Rice (Shearn) Moody; student Holton-Arms, Washington, 1915; m. Clark W. Thompson, Nov. 16, 1918; children—Clark W., Libbie (Mrs. James I. Stansell) (dec.). Past dir. YWCA, A.R.C., Galveston, chpt. Mem. nat. bd. Med. Coll. Pa.; mem. fine arts com. State Dept., Washington; mem. chancellor's council U. Tex.; mem. pres.'s club U. Tex. Med. Br.; founding mem. Jr. Welfare. Bd. dirs. Meridian House Internat. Mem. Plantagenet Soc., Colonial Dames Am., Daus. Republic of Tex., Am. Legion Aux., Am. Newspaper Women's Club, League of Women Voters (past dir.), Huguenot Soc., U.D.C., Soc. Sponsors USN (life), Magna Charta Dames, Smithsonian Soc. of Assos. (life), Order of Washington, Descs. Most Noble Order of Garter, Salvation Army Aux. Washington, Friends of Kennedy Center, Friends of Rosenberg Library, Galveston, Jr. League (hon.), Friends of LBJ Library, Fine Arts Soc. Tex. (dir.), Presidents Assos. of Med. Coll. Pa., Friends of Am. Philos. Soc., A.R.C. Aux. Clubs: Women's Nat. Democratic, Sulgrave, 1925 F Street (Washington); Georgetown; Galveston Artillery. Home: 1616 Driftwood Lane Galveston TX 77550 also 3301 Massachusetts Av NW Washington DC 20008

THOMPSON, LOIS ADELE, coll. adminstr., educator; b. Chickasha, Okla., Apr. 21, 1925; d. Jordan Alvy and Roxie Lou Emma (Graham) Thompson; B.S., Okla. Coll. Liberal Arts, 1946; M.Comml. Edn., U. Okla., 1951, Ed.D., 1961; postgrad. summers Okla. State U., 1947, Ore. State Coll., 1963, 73. Profl. photographer; 1943-53; instr. bus. Verden (Okla.) High Sch., 1947-48, No. Okla. Coll., Tonkawa, 1948-49; asst. prof. bus., dir. audio-visual center Okla. Coll. for Liberal Arts, Chickasha, 1949-60; asst. prof. bus. Kan. State Coll. Pittsburg, 1960-62; asso. prof. bus. So. Ore. Coll., Ashland, 1962-66; dean of women, prof. bus. Coll. So. Ida., Twin Falls, 1966—. Ednl. adviser coll. bus. orgns., 1949—; also cons. Mem. med. adv. bd. Tri-County Head Start, 1973—. Bd. dirs. YWCA, Twin Falls, 1971—. Mem. Okla., Ore. bus. edn. assns., Nat., United, Western, Mountain-Plains bus. edn. assns., Nat. Women Deans and Counselors Assn., Ida. Guidance and Personnel Assn., Bus. and Profl. Women, Northwest Coll. Personnel Assn., Magic Valley Guidance Assn., Kappa Delta Pi, Delta Pi Epsilon. Club: Soroptimist. Contbr. to Roses along Your Pathway (Frank Briggs), 1973. Home: Route 2 Elizabeth Blvd E Twin Falls ID 83301

THOMPSON, LULA BELLE (MRS. GORDON THOMPSON), author, educator; b. Birmingham, Ala., Oct. 19, 1889; d. R. Whitfield and Mary Frances (Wood) Beck; student East Lake Athenaeum Coll.; m. Gordon Thompson, Dec. 31, 1914; 1 son, Robert Gordon. Tchr. pub. schs., Jefferson, Montgomery Counties, Birmingham, 1908-13; free lance writer, 1925—; lectr. Birmingham City Schs., Masonic Home, Montgomery; tchr. writing VA Hosp., Birmingham, 1969—. Mem. staff Internat. Fair, Birmingham, 1970—; mem. speaker's bur. Birmingham Centennial celebration, 1971. Mem. Women in Communications, Nat. League Am. Pen Women (pres. Birmingham br. 1960-62), Berean Club (Woman of Year 1962, 64, plaque award 1973). Baptist (tchr. 1906—). Contbr. numerous articles, stories to various publs. Home: Essex House 605 N 21st St Birmingham AL 35203

THOMPSON, M. GLADYS (MRS. W. STUART THOMPSON), club woman; b. N.Y.C.; d. John and Isabel (Rhind) Slade; B.A., Barnard Coll., 1913; student Am. Sch. Classical Studies (Athens, Greece), 1913-14, 22-25, N.Y. Sch. Social Work, 1934-35; m. W. Stuart Thompson, Aug. 22, 1913; children—W. Stuart, George C., Isabel F. (dec.). Exec. sec. Bklyn. League of Nations Assn., 1925-27. Worked with Greek Refugees, 1923-25; helped establish, mem. 1st bd. dirs., YWCA, Athens, Greece, 1922-24. Mem. Women's Aux. N.Y. Acad. Scis. (exec. bd. 1951—), Am. Assn. U. Women. Presbyn. Clubs: Barnard and Greenwich College; Indian Harbor Yacht (Greenwich); Knollwood Garden; Women's Aux. Columbia U. Home: North St Greenwich CT 06830

THOMPSON, MARGARET M., mus. curator; b. Trenton, N.J., Feb. 22, 1911; d. Albert Gillingham and Hannah (Booth) Thompson; B.A., Radcliffe Coll., 1931. Mem. staff Agora Excavations, Athens, Greece, 1937-40, 48; field dir., publicity dir. Greek War Relief Assn., 1942-46; curator Greek coins Am. Numis. Soc., N.Y.C., 1949-69, now chief curator; adj. prof. art history and archaeology Columbia U., 1965—. Mem. Bur. Internat. Numis. Commn., 1970—; chmn. Internat. Numis. Congress, 1973. Medallist, Am. Numis. Soc., 1961, Royal Numis. Soc., 1967. Fellow Am., Royal, French (hon.), Rumanian (hon.) numis. socs.; mem. Archaeol. Inst. Am. (pres. 1964-68; trustee), German Archaeol. Inst., Am. Philos. Soc., Phi Beta Kappa. Author: The Athenian Agora, vol. 2, Coins, 1954; The New Style Silver Coinage of Athens, 1961; Sylloge Nummorum Graecorum, The Burton Y. Berry Collection, 1961-62; The Agrinion Hoard, 1968; (with others) An Inventory of Greek Coin Hoards, 1973. Asso. editor Archaeology, 1954-58, mem. editorial adv. bd., 1958-67. Home: 140 Cabrini Blvd New York City NY 10033 Office: Am Numis Soc Broadway at 156th St New York City NY 10032

THOMPSON, MARGARET M., educator; b. nr. Falls Church, Va., Aug. 1, 1921; d. Lesley L. and Madeline (Shawen) Thompson; B.S., Mary Washington Coll., U. Va., 1941; M.A., George Washington U., 1947; Ph.D., U. Ia., 1961. Tchr., supr. phys. edn. Staunton (Va.) City Schs., 1941-44; tchr. jr. high sch. phys. edn., Arlington County, Va., 1944-47; instr. womens phys. edn. Fla. State U., Tallahassee, 1947-51; instr., asst. prof., asso. prof. phys. edn. Purdue U., Lafayette, Ind., 1951-65; asso. prof. phys. edn. U. Mo., Columbia, 1965-68, prof., 1968—, dir. Cinematography and Motor Learning Lab. Dept. Health and Phys. Edn., 1965-71; prof. phys. edn. U. Ill., Urbana, 1971—. Mem. Am., Ill. assns. health, phys. edn. and recreation, Nat., Midwest assns. phys. edn. for coll. women, Nat. Found. Health, Phys. Edn. and Recreation, Am. Sch. Health Assn., N.E.A., Am. Assn. Higher Edn., Am. Assn. U. Profs., Am. Assn. U. Women, Internat. Assn. Phys. Edn. and Sports for Coll. Women, Pi Lambda Theta. Author: (with Barbara B. Godfrey) Movement Pattern Checklists, 1966; also film strips. Contbr. articles to profl. jours., books. Home: 3 Wildwood Lane Mahomet IL 61853

THOMPSON, MARGARET SMALL, med. sch. adminstr.; b. St. Charles, Minn., Feb. 28, 1918; d. Walter Edward and Lenore (Tuper) Small; student Winona State Coll., 1935-36; m. William R. Thompson, Dec. 31, 1936 (div. Oct. 1944); children—Richard D., James A. Registrar, Mayo Clinic, Rochester, Minn., 1945-47, asst. mng. editor Mayo Clinic Proc., 1947-49, exec. asst. sect. of publs., 1949-71; registrar Mayo Med. Sch., Rochester, 1971—. Mem. Gov.'s Com. on Fair Campaign Practices, 1962, Gov.'s Commn. on Status of Women, 1964; editorial cons. PORT of Olmsted County, 1970—, bd. dirs., 1971—; v.p. Five Oaks Assn., 1973—. Mem. Nat. Adv. Com. on Polit. Orgn. of Democratic Nat. Com., 1957; mem. exec. com. Minn. Dem.-Farmer-Labor party, 1958-64, vice chmn., 1958-62, del.-at-large, 1962-64; state chmn. Operation Support for Johnson-Humphrey, 1964; alternate del. Dem. Nat. Conv., 1964; spl. asst. to vice chmn. United Democrats for Humphrey, 1968; spl. asst. to vice chmn. Dem. Nat. Com., 1968. Bd. dirs. Rochester Better Chance, Inc., 1973—. Mem. Am. Med. Writers Assn. (dir. 1970-71), Am. Assn. Coll. Registrars and Admissions Officers. Unitarian-Universalist. Home: 317 6th Av SW Rochester MN 55901 Office: Mayo Found-Mayo Med Sch Rochester MN 55901

THOMPSON, MARY ANN MIGHTON, banker; b. Laing, W.Va., Jan. 8, 1922; d. Joseph Mighton and Christine Emma (Schaaf) Thompson; grad. Cannon Assos. Trust Tng. Sch. Brevard Coll., 1968. With New River Coal Co., Price Hill, W.Va., 1939-41; sec. Claims div. Social Security Adminstrn., Washington and Phila., 1941-44; sec. to dir. W.Va. Dept. Health, Charleston, W.Va., 1945-54; trust dept. Nat. Bank Commerce Charleston, (W.Va.), 1954-69, trust adminstrv. officer, 1969-70, asst. trust officer, 1970-73, trust officer, 1973—. Mem. Community Council Kanawha Valley. Mem. Am. Inst. Banking, Nat. Assn. Bank Women (W. Va. group). Lutheran (deaconness 1968-71, pres. altar guild 1974—). Home: 209-B Beauregard St Charleston WV 25301 Office: PO Box 633 Charleston WV 25322

THOMPSON, SISTER MARY EILEEN, educator; b. Mpls., Dec. 21, 1928; d. Albert Charles and Blanche (McAvoy) T.; B.A., Coll. St. Catherine, 1953; M.S., U. Minn., 1958; Ph.D., U. Cal. at Berkeley, 1964. Instr. Coll. St. Catherine, 1953-57; teaching asst. U. Minn., 1957-58; research asst. U. Cal., Lawrence Radiation Lab., 1960-64; asst. prof. Coll. St. Catherine, St. Paul, 1964-69, asso. prof. chemistry, chmn. dept., 1969—. Cons. Center for Ednl. Affairs, Argonne Nat. Lab., 1968-71. Fellow Am. Inst. Chemists; mem. Am. Chem. Soc., Chem. Soc. London, A.A.A.S., Minn., N.Y. acads. scis., Phi Beta Kappa, Sigma Xi. Address: 2004 Randolph Av St Paul MN 55105

THOMPSON, MAXINE MARIE, horticulturist, educator; b. Bloomington, Ill., Nov. 3, 1926; d. Earnest William and Marie Amelia (Cowan) Moeller; B.S., U. Cal. at Davis, 1948, M.S., 1951, Ph.D., 1960; m. Harry S. Thompson, Jr., Apr. 3, 1953 (div. Apr. 1959); children—Michael Allen, Laurie Marie. Asst. prof. biology Wis. State Coll., Oshkosh, 1963-64; asst. prof. horticulture Ore. State U., Corvallis, 1964-71, asso. prof., 1971—. Mem. A.A.A.S., Bot. Soc. Am., Am. Soc. for Hort. Sci. Home: 2715 NW Frazier Creek Dr Corvallis OR 97330

THOMPSON, SISTER MIRIAM, coll. adminstr.; b. Sidney, O., Mar. 3, 1906; d. Alexander Claybourne and Philomena Josephine (Koverman) Thompson; A.B., Xavier U., 1938; M.F.A., Cath. U. Am., 1948. Counselor in resident sch. Brown County Ursulines, 1934-46, headmistress, 1946-58; co-founder, dir. Chatfield Coll., St. Martin, O., 1969—. Address: Ursuline Center St Martin OH 45170

THOMPSON, MYRNA RIVERS, psychologist; b. Lawrenceville, Va., Sept. 27, 1937; d. Jarratt Daniel and Annie Lee (Manson) Rivers; B.A., Fisk U., 1958, M.A., 1960; postgrad. U. Cal. at Long Beach, 1970, U. Cal. at Los Angeles, 1972, Cal. Sch. Profl. Psychology; m. James F. Thompson, Dec. 27, 1960; children—Danny, Traci, Angela, Jay, Kelli. Asst. psychologist pediatrics dept. Meharry Med. Sch., Nashville, 1959-60, cons., psychiatry dept., 1963-65; intern psychologist Crownsville (Md.) State Hosp., 1960; psychologist Central State Hosp., Nashville, 1961-65; psychologist VA Hosp., Long Beach, Cal., 1967-68; sch. psychologist intern Long Beach Sch. Dist., 1968-69; psychologist Watts Health Center, Los Angeles, 1969—. Cons., Headstart program, Los Angeles, 1965. Mem. Long Beach C. of C., Long Beach Fair Housing Found., N.A.A.C.P., Fisk

U., Long Beach State U. alumni assns., Delta Sigma Theta. Democrat. Home: 3307 Daisy Av Long Beach CA 90806 Office: 2051 E 103d St Los Angeles CA 90002

THOMPSON, NELDA MARIE SNOW (MRS. DEWITT P. THOMPSON), assn. exec.; b. Roswell, N.M., Sept. 8, 1922; d. Morris F. and Ovella (Elmore) Snow; student Eastern N.M. U., 1940-41; B.B.A., Tex. Technol. Coll., 1948; M.B.A., U. Denver, 1952; m. DeWitt P. Thompson, Aug. 12, 1966; stepchildren—Molly Ann, Jon Quinn. Chief clk. AC Supply, Clovis (N.M.) Army Air Base, 1942-46; instr. Tex. Technol. Coll., Lubbock, 1948-57; dir. Community Planning Council, 1957-65; dir. United Fund, Lubbock, 1965—. Mem. Am. Inst. Banking (faculty), Nat. Secs. Assn. (hon.), P.E.O., Delta Pi Epsilon, Phi Gamma Nu (hon.). Methodist. Home: 5414 28th St Lubbock TX 79407 Office: 2201 19th St Lubbock TX 79401

THOMPSON, NORMA HOYT (MRS. WILLIAM PAUL THOMPSON), educator; b. Burlington Junction, Mo., Oct. 7, 1915; d. James Albert and Jennie Myrtle (Halfhill) Hoyt; diploma Jackson Sch. Bus., 1935, Moody Bible Inst., 1941; student St. Lawrence U., 1942, Baylor U., 1942-44; A.B., Hunter Coll., 1946; postgrad. Union Theol. Sem., 1946-47; postgrad. Columbia, 1947-48, M.A., 1955; Ph.D., N.Y. U., 1961; m. William Paul Thompson, Dec. 28, 1961. Supr. vacation weekday church schs. Greater N.Y. Fedn. of Churches, N.Y.C., 1944-47; dir. children's work Fifth Av. Presbyn. Ch., N.Y.C., 1944-45; exec. sec. Bronx div., The Protestant Council of the City of N.Y., 1947-54; instr. religious edn. N.Y. U., 1954-61, asst. prof., 1961-63, asso. prof., 1963-72, prof., 1972—, mem. faculty council Sch. of Edn., 1971-74, mem. curriculum com., com. on degree requirements, 1971-72, chairperson faculty-student com., 1973-74, mem. edn. council, 1973-74. Curriculum adviser vis. prof. Christian Edn., Thailand Theol. Sem., Chiengmai, Thailand, 1965. Mem. bd. mgrs. Manhattan div., The Protestant Council of the City of N.Y., 1964-66; mem. exec. com. professors and research sect., Nat. Council of Churches, 1966-71; mem. N.Y. adv. com., World Council of Christian Edn., 1969-70. Recipient Religious Edn. Fellowship citation, N.Y. U., 1966. Mem. Religious Edn. Assn. (mem. exec. com. N.Y. chpt.), N.Y. U. Liaison, Am. Assn. U. Women, Soc. for Sci. Study of Religion, Am. Acad. Religion. Contbr. articles to profl. jours. Home: 600 W 111th St New York City NY 10025 Office: Dept of Religious Edn NY U 737 E Bldg 239 Greene St New York City NY 10003

THOMPSON, NORMA JONES (MRS. VERNON RAY THOMPSON), univ. dean; b. nr. Pembroke, N.C., Dec. 13, 1932; d. Walter and Alverdia (Maynor) Jones; B.S., Pembroke State U., 1957; M.A., Appalachian State U., 1965; Ph.D., Ga. State U., 1972; m. Vernon Ray Thompson, Sept. 8, 1951; children—Lydia Jean, Lori, Verl Radcliff, Vernon Ray II. Tchr., Pembroke High Sch., 1957-59; sec., Pembroke State U., 1959-63, prof. bus. edn., 1963-72, dean admissions and registration, 1972—. Active 4-H, Girl Scouts Am., Boy Scouts Am. Ford Found. grantee 1970. Mem. Pembroke Bus. and Profl. Women's Club, Pembroke State U. Alumni Assn. (exec. sec. 1963—), Delta Pi Epsilon. Methodist (council on ministries 1973—). Home: PO Box 85 Pembroke NC 28372

THOMPSON, OLGA CZORNY, innkeeper; b. Holyoke, Mass., July 23, 1918; d. Elias and Bessie (Wermenchuk) Czorny; Ed.B., R.I. Coll. Edn., 1939; m. DeWolf Cook Thompson, Oct. 13, 1945 (dec. 1967); children—Kenneth DeWolf, Douglas Ross. Tchr., Providence Schs., 1939-45; partner Menemsha Inn and Cottages, Martha's Vineyard Island, Mass., 1945-67, owner, mgr., 1967—. Pres., Chilmark Community Club, 1960-62; mem. Chilmark Finance Com., 1962-64, Tisbury Planning Bd. Com., 1973—. Mem. Martha's Vineyard C. of C., New Eng. Innkeepers Assn., Mass. Hotel and Motel Assn. Home: Box 485 Skiff Av Vineyard Haven MA 02568 Office: Menemsha Inn Menemsha MA 02552

THOMPSON, PATRICIA, journalist; b. N.Y.C., July 27, 1950; d. Joseph and Anna (Kidora) Thompson; B.S., Syracuse U., 1972. Darkroom technician Judy Buck Livingston, Fayetteville, N.Y., 1972; prodn. asst. Redbook Mag., N.Y.C., 1972-73; sportswriter, Daily Record, Morristown, N.J., 1973—. Mem. Syracuse U. Alumni Assn., Sigma Delta Chi, Alpha Xi Delta. Home: 39 Stony Brook Rd Rockaway NJ 07866 Office: 55 Park Pl Morristown NJ 07960

THOMPSON, PATRICIA JUSTICE, educator; b. St Helens, Ore., Mar. 17, 1944; d. Leroy Arthur and Johanna (Schuring) Kallberg; B.S., Portland State U., 1966, M.S. (Alpha Chi Omega grad. fellow, Ednl. fellow), 1970, postgrad., 1970-73; m. Alfred R. Thompson, June 30, 1973. Tchr. English, speech Curtis High Sch., Tacoma, 1966; information and edn. receptionist U.S. Forest Service, Vancouver, Wash., 1967; grad. teaching asst., speech Portland State U., 1968-70; tchr. Mt. Hood Community Coll., Gresham, Ore., 1970—, competitive speech coach, 1970-72, instr. communication and speech edn., 1972—. Precinct committeewoman Democratic party, Portland, 1968-72, legislative research aid, 1970. Ore. State U. Personnel Devel. Funds research grantee, 1974. Mem. Speech Communication Assn. Am., Western, Ore., speech assns., Mt. Hood Community Coll. Faculty Assn. (officer), Am. Assn. Women in Community and Jr. Colls., Phi Kappa Delta, Alpha Chi Omega. Home: Route 1 Box 543 Troutdale OR 97060 Office: 26000 SE Stark Gresham OR 97030

THOMPSON, PAULINE JANET (MRS. SIDNEY R. THOMPSON), editor; b. Thornton Heath, Surrey, Eng., July 14, 1931; d. Alfred John and Elizabeth (Aldridge) Brooks; student Clark's Coll., Eng., 1945-46; m. Sidney R. Thompson, July 14, 1964; 1 son, James P. Came to U.S., 1953, naturalized, 1959. Promotion mgr. sta. KPLC-TV, Lake Charles, La., 1953-57; owner Publici-Tips Co., Littleton, Colo., 1958—. Free lance writer rodeo and other mags., 1961-70; editor Am. Cat Fanciers Assn. Bull., Littleton, 1970-72, Cat World Mag., Littleton, 1973—; co-owner Bodante Cattery, Littleton, 1967—. Mem. English Speaking Union. Address: 5395 S Miller St Littleton CO 80123

THOMPSON, PHEBE KIRSTEN, physician; b. Glace Bay, N.S., Can., Sept. 5, 1897; came to U.S., 1923, naturalized, 1937; d. Peter and Catherine (McKeigan) Christianson; M.D., C.M., Dalhousie U., Halifax, N.S., 1923; m. Willard Owen Thompson, M.D., June 21, 1923 (dec. Mar. 1954); children—Willard Owen, Frederic, Nancy, Donald. Intern Children's Hosp., Halifax, N.S., 1922-23; asst. bio-chemistry, dept. applied physiology Harvard Sch. Pub. Health, 1924-26; asst. research fellow in medicine, thyroid clinic Mass. Gen. Hosp., Boston, 1926-29; asst. in metabolism dept., endocrinology Rush Med. Coll. U. Chgo. and The Central Free Dispensary, Chgo., 1930-46; asso. with husband in pvt. practice medicine, Chgo., 1954-56; mng. editor Jour. Clin. Endocrinology and Metabolism, 1954-61, cons. editor, 1961-65; cons. editor Endocrinology, 1961-65; editor Jour. Am. Geriatrics Soc., 1954—; freelance editor and writer, 1961—. Recipient Appreciation award Am. Thyroid Assn., 1966. Fellow Am. Geriatrics Soc. (Thewlis award 1966), Gerontological Soc., Am. Med. Writers Assn. (adv. com. 1958-61, v.p. Chgo. 1962-63); mem. Endocrine Soc., A.A.A.S., World Med. Assn., Am. Genetic Assn., Ill. Acad. Scis., Alliance Bus. and Profl. Women Chgo., Am. Pub. Health Assn., Chgo. Hist. Soc. (life), Art Inst. (life). Clubs: Harvard; Canadian (Chgo. corr. sec. 1968-73, dir. 1973—). Address: 2337 Commonwealth Av Chicago IL 60614

THOMPSON, REGINA, educator; b. Beckley, W. Va.; d. Elder Lee and Grace Maie (Allen) Thompson; B.S., Bluefield State Coll., 1951; diploma Lincoln Sch. for Nurses, 1955; M.A., Columbia U., 1958, postgrad. 1963—. Clin. instr., acting asst. ednl. dir. Sea View Hosp., S.I., N.Y., 1955-57; staff nurse, acting head nurse, Walter Reed Gen. Hosp., Washington, 1958-60; staff nurse USPHS, S.I., 1960-61; instr. Wagner Coll. Sch. Nursing, S.I. 1961-63, asst. prof., adviser to student nursing fellowship, 1963-65, 67-69, 1963-69; asst. prof. nursing Clemson (S.C.) U., 1969—, adviser Student Nurse Assn. Sch. of Nursing, 1970—. Mem. S.C. Inter-Agy. Council on Aging, 1970; mem. regional adv. group S.C. Regional Med. Program, Joint Practice Commn. Bd. dirs. A.R.C.; budget and control bd. United Fund. Served to 1st lt. Army Nurse Corps, 1958-60. N.Y. Regents fellow, 1967-68. Mem. S.C. Council on Human Relations, S.C. League for Nursing (program com.), Am. Heart Assn., Tb and Respiratory Diseases Assn., N.A.A.C.P., Am., S.C. nurses assns., Nat. League for Nursing, Am. Assn. U. Profs., Am. Assn. U. Women, Delta Sigma Theta. Home: Rural Route 1 Box 276 Walhalla SC 29631 Office: Strode Tower Box 72 Clemson U Clemson SC 29631

THOMPSON, VIVIAN L. (MRS. DANIEL THOMPSON), author; b. Jersey City; d. Harry J. and Letty B. (Lendrum) Laubach; B.S., Tchrs. Coll., Columbia, 1939, M.A., 1943; m. Daniel Thompson, Mar. 17, 1951. Tchr. pub. schs., Nutley, Millburn and Union, N.J., 1930-37, Ossining, N.Y., 1937-43, 46-47, La Jolla, Cal., 1945-46, 47-49, Paauilo and Honolulu, Hawaii, 1949-51; faculty mem. Christian Life Seminar, Hilo, 1966; made video tape on story-telling for Dept. Edn., 1966, video tape Hawaii Stories Old and New for U. Hawaii, 1967. Del. Gov's conf. on Libraries, 1966. Active Girl Scouts, 1951-61 Mem. Hawaii Island Library Adv. Commn., 1960-70; dist. membership chmn. Friends of Pub. Library, 1967; tchr., supt. Christian edn. St. Columba's Ch., 1959-68. Served with USMC Women's Res., 1943-45. Mem. Author's Guild. Republican. Episcopalian. Author: Camp-in-the-Yard, 1961; Sad Day, Glad Day, 1962; The Horse That Liked Sandwiches, 1962; Kimo Makes Music, 1962; Ah See and the Spooky House, 1963; Faraway Friends, 1963; George Washington, 1964; Hawaiian Myths of Earth, Sea, and Sky, 1966; Keola's Hawaiian Donkey, 1966; Meet The Hawaiian Menehunes, 1967; Hawaiian Legends of Tricksters and Riddlers, 1969; Maui-Full-of-Tricks, 1970; Hawaiian Tales of Heroes and Champions, 1971; Aukele the Fearless, 1972. Address: Box 297 Paauilo HI 96776

THOMSON, BETTY FLANDERS, educator; b. Cleve., May 10, 1913; d. James Bewick and Bess (Whitmore) Thomson; B.A., Mount Holyoke Coll., 1935, M.A., 1938; Ph.D., Columbia, 1942. Instr. botany U. Vt., Burlington, 1941-43; instr. botany Conn. Coll., New London, 1943-46, asst. prof., 1946-56, asso. prof., 1956-61, prof. botany, 1961—, chmn. dept., 1970—. NSF Faculty fellow, 1958-59. Fellow A.A.A.S.; mem. Bot. Soc. Am., Ecol. Soc. Am., Soc. for Developmental Biology, Sigma Xi. Author: The Changing Face of New England, 1958. Research on exptl. morphology of plants. Home: 10 Dunbar Rd Quaker Hill CT 06375 Office: Box 1538 Conn Coll New London CT 06320

THOMSON, IRENE TAVISS, educator; b. N.Y.C., Dec. 10, 1941; d. David and Ruth (Geller) Taviss; B.A. in Sociology, Bklyn. Coll., 1962; Ph.D. (Woodrow Wilson fellow), Harvard, 1967; m. Michael Thomson, Feb. 8, 1974. Research asso. program on tech. and soc. Harvard, Cambridge, Mass., 1966-72, lectr. sociology, 1972-74; Exec. asso. Am. Acad. Arts and Scis., 1974—. Mem. A.A.A.S., Am. Sociol. Assn., Phi Beta Kappa, Alpha Kappa Delta. Author: Our Tool-Making Society, 1972. Editor: The Computer Impact, 1970; (with E. Mendelsohn and J. Swazey) Human Aspects of Biomedical Innovation, 1971. Home: 740 W 7th St Plainfield NJ 07060

THOMSON, JEANNE EADIE, coll. ofcl.; b. Nashville, June 19, 1918; d. Charles Douglas and Cherie Lillian (Bashaw) Eadie; student Wheaton Coll., 1936-39; B.A., Judson Coll., 1970; m. Clinton Youle, May 17, 1941 (div. June 1970); children—Jessica (Mrs. Robert Elliott), Susan (Mrs. David Millstein), John Clinton; m. 2d, John F. Thomson, Nov. 22, 1973. Newspaper reporter, columnist, soc. editor Lombard (Ill.) Spectator, 1938-42, mng. editor 1941-42; co-owner, pub. Youle Newspapers, Jo Daviess County, Ill., 1950-60; editor-dir. news bur., dir. pub. relations Judson Coll., Elgin, Ill., 1967-70, instr. in journalism, summer writers confs., 1967, 68; dir. devel. Elgin Acad., 1970-72; dir. alumni relations Rockford (Ill.) Coll., 1972—. Actor, NBC-TV, Chgo., 1949-57; midwest rep., cons. asso. Bernd, Brecher & Assos., N.Y.C., 1973—. Sec. Ill. Coll. Relations Conf., 1969; mem. Religious Pub. Relations Council, 1968-72. Republican campaigner, 1965. Served to capt. Women's Def. Corps Am., World War II; also Civil Air Patrol. Mem. Fellowship Christians in Arts and Media, Nat. Assn. Woman Deans, Adminstrs. and Counselors, D.A.R., Quota Club Internat. Home: 1115 Nassau Pkwy Rockford IL 61107

THOMSON, JOAN ALBERTA, editor; b. Chgo., July 6, 1912; d. Mark Hopkins and Ellen (Crandall) Place; B.A. cum laude, Milton (Wis.) Coll., 1933; postgrad. (Regents fellow) U. Wis., 1933-34; M.A., Colo. Coll., 1962; m. Godfrey Edward Thomson, Nov. 20, 1948 (dec. Feb. 1974); children—Alice Ellen (Mrs. James Salazar), George Edward. State supr. hist. records survey WPA, Madison, Wis., 1938-39; owner Community Bookshop, Chgo., 1949-52; instr. English So. Colo. State Coll., Pueblo, 1965-73; founder Midway Book Shop, Pueblo, 1966; editor Pueblo Regional Planning Commn., 1973—, also editorial asst. commn. mag. Pueblo Design quar. Exec. sec. Am. League Peace and Democracy, Madison, 1938-39; organizer Communist Party U.S.A., Chgo., 1940-52; candidate for alderman, Chgo., 1943; pres. Women's Internat. League Peace and Freedom, Pueblo, 1969-71. Recipient certificate appreciation March of Dimes, 1964. Mem. Am. Assn. U. Profs., Pueblo Impossible Players. Unitarian. Editor poetry mag. Expression, 1973—. Home: Box 66 Beulah CO 81023 Office: 1 City Hall Pl Pueblo CO 81002

THOMSON, MARIAN JOYCE (MRS. WILLIAM L. SCHEIRMAN), writer; b. Irving, Kan.; d. Reginald Gray and Irl (Browning) Thomson; B.S. with honors, U. Kan., 1946; m. William L. Scheirman, Oct. 6, 1951; children—David, John, Margaret, Kathleen. Asst. editor The Torch, Kansas City, Mo., 1946-51; editor Kansan Cookbook, Kansas City, Kan., 1970, 72; free lance contbr. articles and poetry Sat. Eve. Post, Presbyn. Life, Scouting Mag., Christian Life Mag., Orbit, Edmonton Jour., others, 1960—. Asst. precinct chmn. Republican Party, Oklahoma City, 1965-69. Mem. adv. bd. Kansas City Chamber Choir, 1970—; bd. dirs. Oklahoma City Civic Music Assn., 1966-69. Mem. Women in Communications (pres. Okla. chpt. 1954-56), Choristers Guild. Presbyn. Club: Johnson County (Kan.) Christian Womens (dir. 1970—). Home: 5201 W 99th St Overland Park KS 66207

THOMSON, RUTH A., assn. exec.; b. Syracuse, Neb., Oct. 23, 1913; d. John and Bertha (Klein) Thomson; B.S., U. Neb., 1935; M.S.W., Washington U., St. Louis, 1952. Tchr. elementary schs., Neb., 1935-41; group worker YWCA, Waterloo, Ia., 1941-50; br. exec. YWCA, Cleve., 1952-58, nat. staff, N.Y.C., 1958-63; exec. Neighborhood Center, N.Y.C., 1963-64; exec. dir. YWCA of Hartford (Conn.) Region, Inc., 1964—. Field supr. U. Conn., Hartford, 1966—, mem. adv. com. Sch. Social Work, 1973-74. Mem. Gov.'s Commn. on Status of Women, Conn., 1967-68. Bd. dirs. Times Camps, Inc., New Hope—Counselling and Residency Service; past pres. bd. Hartford Campus Ministry. Recipient Boss of Year award Jaycees, 1972. Mem. Nat. Assn. Social Workers, Acad. Certified Social Workers, League Women Voters. Home: 7 Westview Dr Bloomfield CT 06002 Office: 135 Broad St Hartford CT 06103

THOMSON, RUTH FIMBEL (MRS. JAMES H. LAUBACH, JR.), social worker; b. Newark, Dec. 12, 1917; d. Edward and Carlotte (Niver) Fimbel; B.S., Douglass Coll., 1938; M.S., Columbia, 1953; certificate community psychiatry Harvard, 1969; m. K. Jefferson Thomson, May 25, 1957 (dec. Dec. 1965); children—Constance E. Nickel, Jane J., (Mrs. Harry Weinhagen), Ann J. (Mrs. Philip G. True); m. 2d, James H. Laubach, May 13, 1972. Acting program dir. Assn. for Aid Crippled Children, N.Y.C., 1954-58; program asst. N.Y.C. chpt. Nat. Assn. Social Workers, 1962-63; exec. dir. Counseling Service, Middlebury, Vt., 1963-68; asst. prof. psychiatry U. Vt. Coll. Medicine, Burlington, 1969—. Bd. dirs. Vt. Assn. Mental Health. Mem. Nat. Assn. Social Workers, Am. Pub. Health Assn., Council on Social Work Edn., Am. Orthospychiat. Assn. Home: Box 936 Brattleboro VT 05301 Office: U Vt Coll Medicine Burlington VT 05401 also 6 Park Pl Brattleboro VT 05301

THOMSON, SANDRA JOAN, pediatric orthopedic surgeon; b. Boston, June 28, 1937; d. Stuart Warburton and Elizabeth Veronica (Cloney) Thomson; A.B., Newton Coll. Sacred Heart, 1958; M.D., Med. Coll. Pa., 1962. Intern Boston City Hosp., 1962-63; resident, 1963-64; resident Lahey Clinic, 1964-67, Children's Hosp., Boston, 1967-68; practice medicine specializing in pediatric orthopedic surgery Boston, 1968—; asso. orthopedic surgeon Children's Hosp. Med. Center, Boston, 1968—; instr. orthopedic surgery Harvard Med. Sch., 1968—. Fellow Am. Acad. Orthopedic Surgery; mem. Mass. Med. Soc. Home: 30 Clinton Rd Brookline MA 02146 Office: 300 Longwood Av Boston MA 02115

THOMSON, THYRA GODFREY, state ofcl.; b. Florence, Colo., July 30, 1916; d. John and Rosalie (Altman) Godfrey; B.A. cum laude, U. Wyo., 1939; m. Keith Thomson, Aug. 6, 1939 (dec. Dec. 1960); children—William John II, Bruce Godfrey, Keith Coffey. With dept. agronomy and agrl. econs. U. Wyo., 1938-39; writer weekly column Watching Washington pub. in 14 papers, Wyo., 1955-60; planning chmn. Nat. Fedn. Republican Women, Washington, 1961; sec. state Wyo., Cheyenne, 1962—. Mem. Marshall Scholarships Com. for Pacific Region, 1964-68; del. 72d Wilton Park Conf., Engl., 1965; mem. youth commn. UNESCO, 1970-71, Allied Health Professions Council Dept. Health, Edn. and Welfare, 1971-72. Recipient distinguished alumni award U. Wyo., 1969; named internat. woman of distinction Alpha Delta Kappa; Recipient citation Omicron Delta Epsilon, 1965, Beta Gamma Sigma, 1968, Delta Kappa Gamma, 1973. Mem. N.Am. Securities Adminstrs. (pres. 1973-74), Nat. Assn. Secs. of State, Council State Govts. (chmn. natural resources com. Western States 1966-68), Am. Assn. U. Women, Wyo. Press Women, Zeta Psi, P.E.O., Pi Beta Phi, Alpha Kappa Psi, Psi Chi. Home: 204 E 22d St Cheyenne WY 82001 Office: Capitol Bldg Cheyenne WY 82001

THOR, LINDA MARIA, pub. relations exec.; b. Los Angeles, Feb. 21, 1950; d. Karl Gustav and Mildred Dorrine (Hofius) Thor; B.A. magna cum laude, Pepperdine U., 1971; postgrad. Cal. State U., Fullerton, 1973—; m. Robert Paul Huntsinger, Nov. 22, 1974. Dir. pub. information Sch. Continuing Edn., Pepperdine U., Los Angeles, 1971-72, cons., 1972-73; partner Thor Assos., pub. relations, Monterey Park, 1972-74; communications officer Los Angeles Community Coll. Dist., 1974—. Cons. LeMot Ednl. Services, Los Angeles, 1972-73. Mem. Women in Communications (nat. chmn. for new profls. 1971-72, v.p. Los Angeles chpt. 1974—). Home: 634 Sefton Av Monterey Park CA 91754 Office: 2140 W Olympic Blvd Los Angeles CA 90006

THORBURN, CAROLYN COLES (MRS. ANDREW THORBURN), educator; b. Newark, Dec. 20, 1941; d. Charles Edward and Dorothy (Walker) Coles; B.A., Douglass Coll., 1962; M.A. (scholar), Rutgers U., 1964, Ph.D., 1972; m. Andrew Thorburn, June 26, 1965. Bi-lingual sec. Office Temporaries, N.Y.C., 1962-63; tchr. Spanish, Barringer High Sch., Newark, 1964-66; teaching asst. Rutgers U., New Brunswick, N.J., 1966-67; faculty Upsala Coll., East Orange, N.J., 1967—, asst. prof. Spanish, 1972—, coordinator Black studies, 1973—. Pres., Alumni Class of 1962 Douglass Coll., 1970-72. Mem. Modern Lang. Assn., Am. Assn. Tchrs. Spanish and Portuguese, Am. Assn. U. Profs., Amateur Athletic Union U.S., Phi Sigma Iota. Club: Central Jersey Track and Field. Home: 293 Branch Brook Dr Belleville NJ 07109 Office: Upsala Coll Prospect St East Orange NJ 07019

THORESON, ALLISON KAY (MRS. DONALD L. THORESON), journalist; b. Auckland, New Zealand, Sept. 19, 1941; d. William Allison and Jessie Edna (Law) Kelly; B.A. summa cum laude in History, U. Wash., 1972; m. Donald L. Thoreson, Nov. 12, 1965; children—Eric Kelly, Allison Christine. Came to U.S., 1965, naturalized, 1969. Journalist, Auckland Star, 1961; editor Thames (New Zealand) Star, 1962-63; journalist Vancouver (B.C., Can.) Sun, 1963-65, Seattle Post Intelligencer 1965-68; free lance writer, 1968—. Recipient Sugar Plum award for outstanding achievement and community service Wash. State Press Women, 1967, 8 journalism awards, 1966-68. Mem. Women in Communications, Mortar Bd., Phi Beta Kappa, Sigma Delta Chi (awards 1965-68). Lutheran. Club: Women's University. Address: 3055 Magnolia Blvd W Seattle WA 98199

THORHAUG, ANITRA LOUISE K., marine ecologist, biophysicist; b. Chgo.; d. Thorleif Harald and Helene Louise (Heman) Thorhaug; student Smith Coll., 1958-59, U. Chgo., 1960, Roosevelt U., 1960-61, U. Oslo, Norway, 1961; B.S., U. Miami (Fla.), 1963, M.S., 1965, Ph.D. (NASA fellow, Koczy Sr. fellow), 1969; postgrad., Stanford, 1966. Research scientist U. Miami, Fla., 1970—. Cons. Coll. Physicians and Surgeons, Columbia, N.Y., 1969; vis. scientist Polymer dept. Weizman Inst. Sci., Rehovot, Israel, 1970-71; research scientist U. Cal., Berkeley, 1971; guest lectr. Marine Biol. Lab., Eilat, Israel, 1971, Duke U., Beaufort (N.C.) Marine Sta., 1971, Woods Hole (Mass.) Oceanographic Inst., 1971. Mem. Hoover Commn. on Thermal Pollution, 1969, conf. critical problems of coastal zone, Woods Hole, 1972. NSF grantee, 1972—, Fla. Power and Light grantee, 1969-74, Nat. Oceanographic and Atmospheric Adminstrn. grantee, 1971-74, AEC grantee, 1971-74. Mem. Am., European biophys. socs., Am. Bot. Soc. (chmn. physiology 1974—), Am. Soc. Plant Physiology, Am., Brit. socs. phycologists, Am. Soc. Microbiologists, Am. Soc. Protazoologists, Fla. Acad. Scis., Sigma Xi. Contbr. articles on marine ecology and biophysics to sci. jours. Office: 10 Rickenbacker Causeway Miami FL 33149

THORN, SUZIE SCHAPIRO, lawyer; b. San Francisco, June 17, 1932; d. Esmond and Gussye (Goldberg) Schapiro; A.B., U. Cal., 1954; J.D., Hastings Coll. of Law, 1958; M.L.S., U. Cal. at Berkeley, 1964; m. Joe W. Thorn, Mar. 28, 1958; 1 son, Joe W. Thorn. Admitted to Cal. bar, 1959; practiced in San Francisco, 1961—, Pacifica, Cal., 1972—; asso. Schapiro and Thorn, 1961-62, partner, 1963-74, pres.,

1974—. Reference librarian U. Wash., Seattle, 1959-60. Chmn. Diamond Heights Neighborhood Assn., 1972. Bd. dirs. San Francisco Bay council Girl Scouts Am., 1970—. Mem. Am., Cal., San Francisco (mem. family law com., 1971—), San Mateo County bar assns., Queens Bench (dir. 1973—), Nat. Orgn. Women, Order of the Coif, Phi Beta Kappa. Unitarian (dir. 1968—). Office: 110 Sutter St San Francisco CA 94104 also 45 W Manor Dr Pacifica CA 94044

THORNBROUGH, EMMA LOU, educator; b. Indpls., Jan. 24, 1913; d. Harry Cloud and Bess M. (Tyler) Thornbrough; A.B., Butler U., 1934, M.A., 1936; Ph.D., U. Mich., 1946. Asst. prof. history Butler U., Indpls., 1946-49, asso. prof., 1949-57, prof., 1959—. Visiting prof. Ind. U., Bloomington, 1971. Nominated rep. Ind. Gen. Assembly, 1952. Bd. dirs. Indpls. Council World Affairs. Recipient faculty fellowship Ford Found., 1955-56. Mem. Am., So. hist. assns., Orgn. Am. Historians (exec. bd. 1973—), Assn. Study Negro Life and History, Ind. Hist. Soc., Am. Assn. U. Profs., Phi Beta Kappa, Phi Kappa Phi, Ind. Civil Liberties Union (bd. dirs. 1966-73), N.A.A.C.P., League Women Voters. Author: Negro in Indiana, 1957, Indiana in the Civil War Era, 1965, Since Emancipation, 1963, T. Thomas Foretune, Militant Journalist, 1972. Editor: Booker T. Washington, 1968; Black Reconstructionists, 1972. Contbr. numerous articles to profl. pubs. Home: 3012 Cold Spring Rd Indianapolis IN 46222

THORNBURG, MARY LOU, educator; b. Waukesha, Wis.; d. William Howard and Eleanor (Sawyer) Thornburg; B.S., Wis. State U., LaCrosse, 1958; M.S., U. N.C., 1962; postgrad. U. Colo., 1964, Boston U., 1964-66; Ph.D., U. Ia., 1967. Tchr., Nicolet High Sch., Milw., 1958-61; grad. asst. U. N.C., 1961-62; instr. U. Ia., 1962-64; instr., asst. prof., asso. prof., prof. Bridgewater (Mass.) State Coll., 1964—. Water safety instr. trainer A.R.C., 1962-72. Mem. Am. (past chmn. So. Mass. bd.), Mass. (pres.) assns. health, phys. edn. and recreation, U.S. Field Hockey Assn. (dir., pres. Boston, pres. North East Coll. chpt.), Nat., Eastern assns. phys. edn. for coll. women, Am. Assn. U. Profs. Home: 64 Carey Rd Needham MA 02194 Office: Bridgewater State Coll Bridgewater MA 02324

THORNE, EVELYN E. JENKINS (MRS. WILLIAM LESTER THORNE), social worker; b. Cleve., Mar. 19, 1907; d. Thomas Henry and Mildred Edith (Jacobs) Jenkins; R.N., Youngstown Hosp., 1928; A.B., Youngstown U., 1961; M.S.W., U. Pitts., 1964; m. William Lester Thorne, Mar. 30, 1941 (dec. Nov. 1966); 1 son, William J. Pvt. duty nurse, Youngstown, O., 1928-35; indsl. nurse Youngstown Steel Door Co., 1935-41, Republic Steel Corp., Youngstown, 1943-54; exec. sec. Am. Cancer Soc., Youngstown, 1954-58; caseworker Mahoning County Welfare Dept., Youngstown, 1958-61, Childrens and Family Service, Youngstown, 1961; pub. assistance supr. Ohio State Dept. Welfare, Columbus, 1964-66, staff devel. cons., 1966-67, chief Bur. Child Welfare, 1967-69, coordinator Fed. Child Welfare Services Funds, 1969-70, staff devel. specialist, 1970—. Mem. Ohio Commn. on Mentally Retarded. Bd. dirs. Fairfield County Vision Center. Mem. Am. Assn. Ret. Persons, Youngstown Hosp. Alumni Assn., Am. Nurses Assn., Nat. Assn. Social Workers, Ohio Child Welfare Assn., Ohio Welfare Conf., Am. Assn. U. Women. Episcopalian. Mem. Order Eastern Star; Order White Shrine Jerusalem. Home: Colonial Estates Route 3 Lancaster OH 43130 Office: 80 S 6th St Columbus OH 43215

THORNE, JOAN, educator; b. Bklyn., Aug. 3, 1943; d. Irving J. and Rose (Lehman) Thorne; B.S., N.Y. U., 1965; M.A. in Fine Arts, Hunter Coll., 1968. Instr. painting and drawing Bklyn. Mus., 1973—; instr. art R.I. Sch. Design, Providence, 1973—, N.Y. U., 1974—; exhibited one artist shows Corcoran Gallery Art, Washington, Fischbach Gallery, N.Y.C., 1974; exhibited group shows Whitney Ann. Am. Painting, N.Y.C., Aldrich Mus., Gemeinschaft der Kunstlerinnen und Kunstfreunde, Hamburg, Germany, Warren Benedict Gallery, N.Y.C., Univ. Art Gallery, Albany, N.Y., 1974, Bklyn. Mus., Phila. Mus.; represented in permanent collections Mus. Modern Art Lending Library, N.Y.C., Aldrich Mus. Named Artist of Year, Aldrich Found., 1972. Author: From Eye to Moon, 1971. Home: 169 Mercer St New York City NY 10013

THORNTON, BARBARA ANN, stage designer; b. Macon, Ga., Sept. 21, 1946; d. William Bryan and Verna Louise (Van Landingham) Thornton; B.F.A., U. Ga., 1968, M.F.A., 1970. Photog. asst. Ga. Center for Continuing Edn., Athens, 1968-69; tech. asst. Univ. Theatre, U. Ga., Athens, 1969-70; scene artist Milw. Repertory Theatre, 1971; photog. asst. U. Wis., Milw., 1971; summer stock properties designer Milw. Melody Top Theatre, 1971, 72; tech. asst. Centre Stage Dinner Playhouse, Milw., 1972-73, properties mistress, 1972-73; set designer Milw. Opera Co., 1972-74; with prodn. dept. WTMJ-TV, Milw., 1974—. Theatrical adviser Village Guild, 1972-74. Mem. Am. Theatre Assn., Art Students League, Theatre Communications Group, Zeta Tau Alpha. Home: 1212 N Van Buren Milwaukee WI 53202 Office: 720 E Capitol Dr Milwaukee WI 53212

THORNTON, CAROL RAUEN, journalist, civic leader; b. Chgo., July 30, 1933; d. Sidney and Clara Marie (Rauen) Radley; attended U. Chgo., 1955-59; 1 son, Matthew Rauen. Customer relations rep. Lockheed Aircraft Corp., Burbank, Cal., 1968-70; account exec. Steven L. Wells Pub. Relations, Los Angeles, 1970-73; soc. editor Valley News and Green Sheet subsidiary Chgo. Tribune, Van Nuys, Cal., 1973-74. Mem. Assistance League So. Cal. Women's com. Los Angeles Philharmonic Orch. Mem. Theta Sigma Phi. Home: 15272 1/2 Sutton St Sherman Oaks CA 91403

THORNTON, FLORENCE EMMA (MRS. LAURANCE C. THORNTON), lectr.; b. Boston, May 9, 1897; d. August L. and Emma (Ericson) Tobin; student Emerson Coll., Boston, 1917-18; m. Laurance C. Thornton, Oct. 19, 1946 (dec. 1952). With U.S. Govt. in Alaska, 1921-53; sec. Bethlehem Shipbuilding Corp., 1917-19; bookkeeper Granite Trust Co., Quincy, Mass., 1920-21; chief civilian personnel USCG, 1940-51; acting mgr. OPS, Fairbanks, Alaska, 1952-53; pvt. tchr. of Violin 1921-30; co-founder Orthopedic and Tech. Center, Kottayam, Kerala, India, 1963-64; lectr. on her extensive world travels, also art and religion, U.S., Alaska, 1953—; columnist local newspaper, 1965—; humorist. Pres., Alaska Fedn. Music Clubs, 1928-34. Mem. Dept. of Alaska Am. Legion Aux. (life, pres. 1935-36), W.C.T.U. (sec. Alaska 1950-53), Nat. Assn. Ret. Civil Employees (past pres.), World War I Vets. Aux. Republican. Methodist. Clubs: Alaska (Woodburn, also Salem). Home: 1291 Princeton Rd Woodburn OR 97071

THORNTON, JEAN ROBINSON TYROL, state legislator; b. Glastonbury, Conn., Sept. 28, 1921; d. Edward Howard and Frances Olive (Bidwell) Tyrol; grad. high sch.; div.; children—Malcolm E., Kirk R., Barbara J. Mem. Conn. Ho. of Reps., 1963—. Registrar voters, 1956-62; vice-chmn. Republican Town Com., Glastonbury, 1958-65; alternate del. Rep. Nat. Conv., 1968. Served to 2d lt. WAC, 1942-44. Home: 28 Gayfeather Lane Glastonbury CT 06033 Office: State Capitol Hartford CT 06115

THORNTON, JUDITH GROUSE, educator; b. Kansas City, Mo., Oct. 17, 1935; d. S. Tom and Helene Dorothy (Bjornson) Grouse; B.A., Vassar, 1956; M.A., Radcliffe, 1958, Ph.D., 1960. Mem. faculty dept. econs. U. Wash., Seattle, 1961—, prof. econs., 1972—. Home: 3338 43d Av NE Seattle WA 98105

THORNTON, KATHLEEN BAUER (MRS. DAVID FESS THORNTON), television producer; b. Bismarck, N.D., Sept. 22, 1930; d. Otto R. and Laura Lucille (Pearson) Bauer; B.A., Roanoke Coll., 1952; m. David Fess Thornton, Aug. 25, 1951. Advt. mgr., soc. editor, columnist Times Register, Salem, Va., 1953-59; asst. to Nelson Bond, Nelson Bond Assos., Roanoke, Va., 1959-61; free lance photographer, Salem, 1961-66; television producer/host daily interview show WDBJ-TV, Roanoke, 1966—. Co-founder Showtimers, Salem, 1951, bd. dirs., 1950s, pres., 1955; sec., bd. dirs. Roanoke Valley Mental Health Services; bd. dirs. English Speaking Union; bd. advisers Craft Program, OEO, Roanoke, 1972. Recipient 1st Pl. award Va. Press Assn., 1964; Golden Mike award Am. Women in Radio and Television, 1967. Mem. Foremost Women in Communications, Writers Hall of Fame, So. Furniture Assn., 2000 Women of Achievement. Republican. Writer, producer, actress Emily of Amherst, an Impression, produced for TV, 1971. Home: 324 Hawthorn Rd Salem VA 24153 Office: PO Box 227 Roanoke VA 24002

THORNTON, KAYE ELISE (MRS. ZWINGLI JOE THORNTON), journalist; b. Ft. Worth, July 2, 1941; d. Jesse Maurice and Martha Anna (Barnes) Dysart; B.S. in Edn., North Tex. State U., 1963; m. Zwingli Joe Thornton, June 29, 1963; 1 son, Zwingli Bartholomew. Asst. editor employee publ. Sun Oil Co., Dallas, 1963-64; tchr. journalism and English, Kimball High Sch., Dallas, 1964-66, Paschal High Sch., Ft. Worth, 1966-67, Southwest High Sch., Ft. Worth, 1968-70, Southwest High Sch., 1974-75; writer columns Colonial Country Club, Ft. Worth, 1972—, Shady Oaks Country Club, 1974—. Vice pres. Friends of Library, Ft. Worth, 1967-68; area chmn. Mothers March of Dimes, 1973. Mem. Women in Communications (v.p. 1973, scholarship chmn. 1973). Home: 2013 Carleton St Fort Worth TX 76107

THORNTON, LEOTA JOPLING, banker; b. Henrietta, Tex., Sept. 23, 1922; d. Jodie Clifford and Bessie Q. (Covington) Jopling; student Lippert's Sch. Bus., Plainview, Tex., 1938-39, Wayland Bapt. Coll., 1968; student numerous Am. Inst. Banking courses children—Charles Edwin II, Travis Glen, Linda Kay. With Hale County State Bank, Plainview, Tex., 1944—, v.p., 1969—, trust officer, 1967—. Pres. Highland P.T.A., Plainview, Tex., 1956-57. Treas., exec. bd. Central Plains office Econ. Opportunity Orgn., 1970—. Named Mother of the Year, College Heights Bapt. Ch., 1970. Mem. Nat. Assn. Bank Women. Baptist (youth coordinator 1971-72). Clubs: Plainview Women's (treas. 1962-63); Les Progres' Study (charter mem.). Home: 1608 W 8th St Plainview TX 79072 Office: 201 W 6th St Plainview TX 79072

THORNTON, SISTER MADELENA, educator, journalist; b. De Witt, Ia.; d. James Lewis and Anna (Devitt) Thornton; A.B., Clarke Coll., 1928; A.M., U. Ill., 1934; postgrad. U. Minn., Fordham U., Harvard, Fribourg (Switzerland), U. Ky. Joined Sisters of Charity of Blessed Virgin Mary, 1928; tchr. journalism, dir. pub. relations Mundelein Coll., Chgo., 1935-57; chmn. journalism dept., dir. pub. relations Clarke Coll., Dubuque, Ia., 1957—; free lance writer, 1973—. Staff mem. Journalism Inst., Catholic U. Am., Washington, 1969. Bd. dirs. Little Cloud council Girl Scouts. Recipient Moderator's award Catholic Sch. Press Assn., 1950, Distinguished Service award Dubuque Area C. of C., 1968. Mem. Am. Assn. Univ. Women, Assn. for Edn. in Journalism. Author: (with others) Principles of Advertising, 1964. Contbr. feature articles and revs. to ednl. and religious jours. Address: 1550 Clarke Dr Dubuque IA 52001

THORNTON, RUBY HOWELL (MRS. BROWN D. THORNTON), educator; b. Baxter, Tenn., Jan. 20, 1922; d. Hershal W. and Preshia (Callis) Howell; B.S., Tenn. Tech. U., 1949; M.S., U. Tenn., 1955, postgrad., 1957; Edn. Specialist, George Peabody Coll., 1962; m. Charles W. Wilson, 1942 (dec. Dec. 1957); children—Charles Warren, E. Floyd, J. LeRoy; m. 2d, Brown D. Thornton, Jan. 26, 1959; children—Susan I., Brown D. Tchr., prin. elementary and secondary schs., Crossville, Tenn., 1946-59; tchr. Central Elementary Sch., Haines City, Fla., 1960-61; supr. instrn. Wilson Co. Sch. System, Lebanon, Tenn., 1962-67; prof. psychology Cumberland Coll. Tenn., Lebanon, 1967—. Summer dir. Headstart Program Wilson Co., 1966-69. Mem. Am. Assn. U. Women, N.E.A., Assn. Supervision and Curriculum Devel., Delta Kappa Gamma Democrat. Baptist. Club: Cumberland Women's. Home: 420 Vosswood Dr Lebanon TN 37087

THORNTON, SUE BONNER, librarian; b. nr. Fairfield, Tex.; d. John Carder and Mary (Bonner) Thornton; A.B., U. Okla., 1920, A.B. in L.S., 1938, Mus. B. in Piano, 1921; M.A., Columbia, 1932; postgrad. U. Hawaii, summer 1936. Music supr. Okla. pub. schs., 1921-25; head music dept. Northeastern State Coll., Tahlequah, Okla., 1925-32, librarian, 1932—, prof. emeritus. Chmn. Hist. Marker and Landmarks Com. Freestone County, 1964—. Mem. Tex. Hist. Found., N.E.A., A.L.A., Daus. of Am. Colonists (State historian), Colonial Dames of 17th Century, Tahlequah C. of C., Nat. Soc. U.S. Daus. 1812, Ams. Royal Descent and Colonial Order Crown, Tex. Fed. Women's Clubs (chmn. edn. dept.), Freestone County Mus., Plantagenet Soc., Huguenot Soc. S.C., Soc. Descs. Knights of Garter, Nat. Soc. Magna Charta Dames, United Ch. Women Tahlequah (chmn. 1960), D.A.R. (chmn. good citizens com. for state 1958-60, chmn. N.E. Dist. Okla.), Daus. Colonial Wars, Order of Washington, Okla., Tex. geneal. socs., Pan Am. Round Table of Corsicana, History Club (Fairfield), Tex. and Southwestern cattle raisers assns., Central Tex. Area Mus., P.E.O., Alpha Gamma Delta. Democrat. Presbyn. (chmn. Women's Assn.). Clubs: Freestone Country; Harvey Woman's (Palestine, Tex.). Author: The Bonner Family. Home Fairfield TX 75840

THORPE, HELENE SMITH (MRS. JAMES H. THORPE), physician; b. N.Y.C., June 18, 1930; d. Maurice and Sara (Smith) Smith; B.A. cum laude, Elmira Coll., 1951; M.D., Woman's Med. Coll. Md., 1955; M.P.H., U. Cal. at Berkeley, 1966; m. James H. Thorpe, Mar. 24, 1957; children—Sara, Edward, Carol, Susan, Christopher. Rotating intern, Phila. Gen. Hosp., 1955-56; resident pediatrics Cin. Children's Hosp., 1956-57, Rochester (N.Y.) Gen. Hosp., 1957-58; fellow pediatric cardiology U. Rochester, 1958-59, research asso. pediatrics, 1958-59; pediatrician U.S. Civil Service, 36th TAC Hosp., USAF, Bitburg, Germany, 1959-63, Rochester (N.Y.) Child Guidance Clinic, 1963-65; pediatric cons. Sutter Diagnostic and Treatment Center, Sacramento, 1967-69; Sutter Speech and Hearing Center, 1968-70; pediatric cons. Project Head Start, Am. Acad. Pediatrics, 1967—; staff physician Cowell Student Health Center, U. Cal. at Davis, 1967—; asst. clin. prof. pediatrics, U. Cal. Sch. Medicine, at Davis, 1969—; mem. profl. adv. bd. Yolo County Mental Health Assn., 1968—, chmn., 1968-69; mem. Davis Joint Unified Sch. Dist. Com. Family Life, 1969—; conducted numerous workshops and seminars in child developmental assessment. Diplomate Am. Bd. Pediatrics. Fellow Am. Acad. Pediatrics (mem. sect. child devel. 1968, mem. community pediatrics 1969, chpt. chmn. mental health com. 1970—); mem. Am. Pub. Health Assn. Am. Orthopsychiat. Assn., Sacramento Pediatric Soc., Am. Assn. Child Care in Hosps. Author: The Thorpe Developmental Inventory. Edited proceedings annual meeting Am. Assn. Child Care in Hosps., 1970. Address: 805 Oak Av Davis CA 95616

THORPE, JO ANNE LEE, educator; b. Tampa, Fla., June 20, 1931; d. David McDonald and Johnnie Lee (Hancock) Thorpe; B.S., Fla. State U., 1953; M.Ed., U. N.C., 1958; postgrad. U. Ia., summer 1960; Ph.D., Tex. Womans U., 1964. Tchr., Winter Park (Fla.) Jr.-Sr. High Sch., 1953-54, N.E. Sr. High Sch., St. Petersburg, Fla., 1954-56; grad. asst. U. N.C., Greensboro, 1956-57; instr. phys. edn. Fla. State U., Tallahassee, 1957-58; prof. phys. edn. So. Ill. U., Carbondale, 1958—. Chmn., Volleyball Nat. Championships for Coll. Women, 1969-71; chmn. selection and implementation 5th Nat. Inst. Girls Sports, 1968-69. Mem. A.A.H.P.E.R. (v.p. 1971-72), Midwest Assn. Phys. Edn. Coll. Women (treas. 1969-71), Nat. Assn. Phys. Edn. Coll. Women (treas. 1974—), Alpha Xi Delta, Phi Kappa Phi. Contbr. articles to profl. jours. Home 1709 W Freeman St Carbondale IL 62901

THORPE, NEAL GILKYSON, newspaper editor; b. Mont Clare, Pa., Feb. 17, 1920; d. Hamilton H. and Phoebe (Hunter) Gilkyson; A.B. summa cum laude, Smith Coll., 1942; postgrad. Columbia, 1944; m. Robert B. Thorpe, June 20, 1970; children—Alfred I., James G., Leila B. Stuart. Editor women's page Ore. Jour., Portland, 1954-55; asso. editor, articles editor Ladies Home Jour., 1955-62; text editor Life Books, Time In., 1963-64; fiction editor Redbook mag., 1965-73; editor Phoenixville (Pa.) Daily Republican, 1974—; pres. Phoenixville Pub. Co., 1974—. Home: Box Q Mont Clare PA 19543 Office: Daily Republican Phoenixville PA 19453

THORSON, MARILYN COLLEEN MCCRUDDEN (LINN MASON) (MRS. ROBERT L. THORSON), actress; b. Rochester, Minn.; d. William Patrick and Beatrice (Johnson) McCrudden; student Northwestern U., 1954; B.A. cum laude, U. Minn., 1956; m. Robert L. Thorson, May 26, 1956; children—Blake, Bret. Featured, starred in various stage plays, including Wayward Stork, Don Juan in Hell, Third Best Sport, A Shot in the Dark, Disenchanted, The American Woman, others; various parts in radio, tv shows. Mem. A.I.A. Aux. (pres. N.Y. chpt. 1965-66), U. Minn. Alumni Assn. (chpt. v.p. 1961-62), N.Y. Jr. League, Episcopal Actors Guild (council), Alpha Chi Omega. Home: 360 E 65th St New York City NY 10021

THRASH, AGATHA MOODY (MRS. CALVIN LASSETTER THRASH II), pathologist; b. Baxley, Ga., May 15, 1931; d. Norwood Perry and Inez Geneva (Hicks) Moody; B.A., Woman's Coll. Ga., 1951; M.D., Med. Coll. Ga., 1955; m. Calvin Lassetter Thrash II, June 14, 1953; children—Carol Ann, Calvin Lassetter III. Intern Louisville Gen. Hosp., 1955-56; resident Emory U. Hosp., Atlanta, 1956-60; asso. pathologist Atlanta VA Hosp., 1959-60; pathologist in chief St. Francis Hosp., Columbus, Ga., 1960-67; pathologist-dir. Thrash Labs., Columbus, 1961—. Biology tchr. Columbus Coll., 1963-71. Head leukemia com. Am. Cancer Soc., 1964-72; active Tb and Respiratory Disease Assn., Civil Def. and Disaster Preparedness. Bd. dirs. Archeol. Research Found. N.Y., Yuchi Pines Inst. for Med. Missionaries. Recipient award for excellence in community service Tb and Respiratory Disease Assn., 1971. Seventh-day Adventist (health and welfare dir. 1966-71). Home: Box 273 Seale AL 36875 Office: Box 591 Columbus GA 31902

THRASHER, EMMA REID (MRS. HAROLD MORGAN THRASHER), city extension agt.; b. East Orange, N.J., Nov. 8, 1921; d. William Albert and Hope (Forman) Reid; B.S. in Child Devel. and Home Econs., Pa. State U., 1940-44; student Coll. William and Mary, 1955, 58, U. Va., 1957, Va. Poly. Inst., 1962; m. Harold Morgan Thrasher, June 22, 1944; children—Henry Taylor, William Seay, Lee-Hope. Tchr. Friend's Community Sch., West Chester, Pa., 1944-45; tchr. Chesapeake (Va.) Pub. Sch., 1951-53, 55-61; extension agt. Extension div. Va. Poly. Inst. and State U. Coop. Extension Service, 1961—, supr. 4-H youth program, 1970—; saleswoman, unit mgr. Tupperware Home Parties, Inc., 1953-56; treas. Seay Hope Taylor Corp., Chesapeake, Va., 1970-74; adv. bd. J.C. Penney, Inc. Pres. Gt. Bridge Band Parents Assn., 1968; patron Norfolk Civic Ballet, 1968-74; mem. Chrysler Museum, Norfolk, Va. Museum, Richmond. Bd. dirs. 4-H Camp Farrar, Chesapeake. Mem. Nat. (Distinguished Service award 1973), Va. (mem. policy com. 1971, 4-H com. 1971) assns. extension home economists, Nat., Va. (dir. 1964-69, dist. chmn. 1962-65) home econs. assns., Nat., Va. (v.p. 1972-73) assns. extension 4-H agts., Va. Extension Service Assn., Pa. State U. Alumni Assn. (life mem., area chmn. 1969-70), Epsilon Sigma Phi. Home: 710 Sign Pine Rd Chesapeake VA 23322 Office: Agrl Dept 300 Cedar Rd Chesapeake VA 23320

THRASHER, HELEN RAYE, physician; b. West Blocton, Ala., Feb. 15, 1939; d. George Martin and Edna Elizabeth (Gilbert) Thrasher; B.S., U. Ala., 1959; M.D., Med. Coll. Ala., 1963. Intern, Univ. Hosp., Birmingham, Ala., 1963-64, resident ophthalmology, 1964-67; practice medicine specializing in ophthalmology, Birmingham, 1967—; mem. staffs Univ., East End Meml., Brentwood, South Highlands hosps.; cons. VA. Hosp., Birmingham, Adult Dept. for Blind, Talladega, Ala.; part time clin. instr. Dept. Ophthalmology, Univ. Hosp., U. Ala. Med. Center, Birmingham, 1964—. Mem. Am. Acad. Ophthalmology and Otolaryngology, Ala. Acad. Ophthalmology (state sec. 1969—), A.M.A., Med. Soc. Ala., Jefferson County Med. Soc., Birmingham Eye, Ear, Nose and Throat Soc. Home: 4316 Corinth Dr Birmingham AL 35213 Office: 7714 2d Sts Birmingham AL 35206

THRASHER, JEAN HARMON, sociologist; b. Canton, Mo., June 20, 1934; d. Henry Gadd and Helen Bernice (Sherman) Harmon; B.A., Drake U., 1956; M.A., U. N.C., 1959, Ph.D., 1961; m. George Charles Thrasher, Jr., June 21, 1960 (dec. Aug. 1963). Asst. prof. dept. sociology U. N.C., 1961-67, asst. dir. social research sect., 1963-67, clin. asst. prof. dept. psychiatry, Sch. Medicine, 1963-67; asso. prof. sociology Drake U., Des Moines, 1967-70; research scientist, dir. div. program evaluation N.C. Dept. Mental Health, Raleigh, 1970—. Bd. dirs. Ia. Children's and Family Services, 1966-67. Mem. Am. Sociol. Assn., Soc. for Study Social Problems, Jr. League, Phi Beta Kappa. Home: 325 Glendale Dr Chapel Hill NC 27514 Office: Box 7532 Raleigh NC 27611

THREATT, HELEN VIOLA KILPATRICK, librarian; b. Dover, N.C., Dec. 31, 1928; d. Randolph and Lucy Kilpatrick; B.A., St. Augustine's Coll., Raleigh, N.C., 1949; M.L.S., N.C. Central U., Durham, 1952; m. Robert Threatt, Dec. 25, 1966. Librarian, Ninth Av Sch., Hendersonville, N.C., 1952-57, Allen U., Columbia, S.C., summer 1957; pub. service librarian Ft. Valley (Ga.) State Coll., 1958—. Mem. Ga. Library Assn., Ga. Edn. Assn., Beta Phi Beta. Episcopalian. Home: 601 University St Atlanta GA 30314 Office: Box 432 Fort Valley GA 31030

THRELKELD, JEAN EDITH (MRS. CHARLES EVAN THRELKELD), library adminstr.; b. Detroit, Mar. 20, 1928; d. George and Edith Rose (Martin) Cary; B.A., Wayne State U., 1951; M.L.S., U. Wash., 1969; m. Charles Evan Threlkeld, Dec. 20, 1952; children—Jon, Hugh, Leslie, Bonnie, Scott. Head librarian King County (Wash.) Library, Issaquah, 1969-72, Newport Way, 1972, adminstr. library services, Bellevue, 1969—. Bd. dirs. Thalia Conservatory Music, 1973—. Mem. Am., Wash. State, Pacific N.W. library assns., Fedn. Am. Scientists, E. Lake Thalia Guild Youth Symphonies (chmn. 1973-74), People to People. Home: 5303 231 Av

SE Issaquah WA 98027 Office: 14250 Newport Way Bellevue WA 98006

THRON, ANN LUKACH (MRS. WOLFGANG J. THRON), physician; b. N.Y.C., Apr. 24, 1927; d. Arthur S. and Marion L. (Long) Lukach; B.A., Smith Coll., 1949; M.D., N.Y. U., 1953; m. Wolfgang J. Thron, June 7, 1953; children—Jonathan Louis, Penelope Helen, Peter Andreas, Karin Elizabeth, Rajnder Michael. Intern, St. Louis City Hosp., 1953-54; physician Well Baby Clinics, Boulder City (Colo.) County Health Dept., 1955—; physician Women's Clinic, People's Free Clinic, Boulder, Colo., 1971—; with Planned Parenthood, 1972—; pvt. practice pediatrics, 1973—; asst. at dispensary Mindanao State U., Marawi, Philippines, 1966-67; guest doctor Children's Hosp., Erlangen, Germany, 1970-71. Mem. Religious Soc. Friends. Home: 430 Christmas Tree Dr Boulder CO 80302

THROOP, BEATRICE TERRY, educator; b. Raymond, Ill.; d. John Charles and Therese (Mathis) Terry; B.E., Ill. State U., 1930; M.S., U. Chgo., 1938; postgrad. U. Ore., summer 1939, Ore. State U., summer 1953, Colo. U., summers 1955-56, U. Caen (France), summers 1965-66, U. Md., summer 1963, 65-66; m. Vincent Medville Throop, May 29, 1940 (dec. Oct. 1968); children—Medville Jay, Alice Milberry, David Edmund, Annette Beatrice, Julian. Tchr. Lima (Peru) High Sch., Women's Fgn. Missionary Soc. of Meth. Ch., 1930-36; instr. Stephens Coll., 1938-40; tchr. pub. schs., Portland (Ore.) Air Base, 1941; bibliographer Library of Congress, Washington, 1960-61; tchr. Prince George's County Schs., Brandywine, Md., 1961—; George Washington U., summers 1967-69. Mem. Am. Assn. U. Women, Assn. Am. Geographers, N.E.A., Md. Edn. Assn., Prince George's County Tchrs. Assn., Am. Assn. Tchrs. Spanish and Portuguese, Alliance Francaise, Sigma Delta Epsilon. Contbr. articles to local publs. Home: 5609 Delaware Dr Forest Heights Washington DC 20021

THROOP, DORIS E., univ. adminstr.; b. Irvington, N.J., Feb. 16, 1916; d. Ray Edmund and Bessie (Morgan) Throop; B.S., Syracuse U., 1939. Advt. asst. Schering Corp., Bloomfield, N.J., 1939-57; asst. headmistress Gill Sch., Bernardsville, N.J., 1957-59; dir. financial aid Fairleigh Dickinson U., Madison, N.J., 1959—. Financial aid evaluator Ednl. Assistance Fund, Morris County, N.J., 1970-73. Mem. Am. Assn. U. Women, Bus. and Profl. Womens Club (Woman of Achievement award 1974), Eastern, N.J. assns. student financial aid adminstr., Phi Mu. Republican. Presbyn. Home: 34 Peachtree Rd Basking Ridge NJ 07920 Office: 285 Madison Av Madison NJ 07940

THU, ANNE BERNADETTE, psychologist, city ofcl.; b. Hankow, China; d. Francis K.S. and Mary (Luke) Thu; M.A., U. Detroit, 1956; postgrad. Catholic U. Am., 1957-58. Psychologist, Nat. Inst. Mental Health, Bethesda, Md., 1958-59; human resources specialist Human Resources Adminstrn. N.Y.C., 1964-68; sr. psychologist Health Services Adminstrn., N.Y.C. Dept. Corrections, 1969—. Mem. Am. Psychol. Assn. Office: 1 Court Sq Long Island City NY 11101

THULIN, BARBARA WASSON (MRS. WILLIAM J. THULIN), physician; b. Harrisburg, Ill., Feb. 21, 1926; d. Loran Arthur and Wilma Alice (Reese) Wasson; B.S., Northwestern U., 1948; postgrad. U. Ill., 1948-49, Woman's Med. Coll. Pa., 1949-51; M.D., U. Colo., 1953; m. William J. Thulin, Sept. 5, 1952; children—Lauren, Lucy, Andrew. Intern, Denver Gen. Community Hosp., 1953-54; resident neurology U. Colo., 1954-57; child neurologist Children's Hosp., Denver, 1958-69; dir. student health Temple Buell Coll., Denver, 1959-60; instr. neurology U. Colo. Sch. Medicine, 1958-59; attending neurologist Denver VA Hosp., 1958—; dir. EEG Lab., Children's Hosp., Denver, 1962-69; neurologist Wallace Village for Children, Broomfield, Colo., 1961-74; neurologic cons. Denver Gen. Hosp., 1958-63, Pueblo State Hosp., 1959-60; mem. Office of Comprehensive Health Planning, State of Colo., 1971; mem. med. review bd. State of Colo. Motor Vehicle Div., 1965-73. Bd. dirs. Summit County Citizens Assn., 1971—; bd. dirs. Spalding Rehab. Hosp., 1970—; Colo. Health Careers Council; med. adv. bd. Colo. Epilepsy Soc., Colo. Speech and Hearing Assn., 1960-62, Multiple Sclerosis Soc., 1966-67. Mem. Am. Med. Women's Assn. (branch pres. 1968), Colo. Neuro-Psychiat. Soc. (sec.-treas. 1964-65), Am. Acad. Neurology, Am. Epilepsy Soc., Internat. League Against Epilepsy, Colo. Diabetes Assn., Nat. Orgn. for Women (chpt. pres. 1971-72). Contbr. articles to profl. pubs. Home: 5505 S Steele St Littleton CO 80121 Office: 3535 S Lafayette St Englewood CO 80110

THUM, MARCELLA LAURA, librarian, author; b. St. Louis, Sept. 7, 1924; d. Frank and Louise Marie (Holle) Thum; B.A., Washington U., St. Louis, 1948; M.L.S., U. Cal. at Berkeley, 1954. Advt. copywriter Olian Advt. Agy., St. Louis, 1948-49; civilian writer U.S. Army Pub. Information Office, Okinawa, 1949-50, hist. div., Heidelberg, Germany, 1951-52, Karlsruhe, Germany, 1952-53; civilian librarian USAF, Korea, 1954-55, Scott AFB, Ill., 1955-56, Schofield Barracks, Hawaii 1957-58, Hickam AFB, Hawaii, 1958-60; sch. librarian Affton (Mo.) Sr. High Sch., 1962-67; reference librarian Meramec Community Coll., Kirkwood, Mo., 1968—. Recipient Edgar award Mystery Writers Am., 1964, Competition award Dodd, Mead, 1964. Mem. St. Louis (pres. 1967), Mo. writers guilds, Mo. Library Assn. Author: Mystery at Crane's Landing, 1964; Treasure of Crazy Quilt Farm, 1965; Anne of the Sandwich Islands, 1967; Librarian with Wings, 1968; Secret of the Sunken Treasure, 1969; The Persuaders (with Gladys Thum) 1972; Fernwood, 1973; Exploring Black America, 1975. Home: 6716 Smiley Av St Louis MO 63139 Office: Meramec Community College Library 11333 Big Bend Kirkwood MO 63122

THUNBERG, URSULA HELGA, psychiatrist; b. Wismar, Germany, Oct. 18, 1934; d. Otto Heinrich and Charlotte Bernhardine (Karlsen) Luddemann; student U. Hamburg (Germany), 1957-62, M.D., 1964; student U. Freiburg (Germany), 1962; m. Erling Thunberg, Dec. 13, 1957; 1 son, Jari Michael. Came to U.S., 1964, naturalized, 1970. Rotating intern Mt. Sinai Hosp. Services, Elmhurst, N.Y., 1965-66, resident psychiatry, 1966-67, 68-69, resident child psychiatry, 1967-68; fellow child psychiatry State. N.Y. Downstate Med. Center, Bklyn., 1969-70, clin. instr. child psychiatry, 1970—; asst. attending staff in child psychiatry Pediatric Oncology Clinic, Kings County Hosp., Bklyn., 1970—, attending child psychiatrist dialysis and transplant unit, 1970—; practice medicine specializing in child psychiatry, N.Y.C., 1970—; mem. joint cancer com. State N.Y. Downstate Med. Center-Kings County Hosp.; attending in child psychiatry Arthur C. Logan Meml. Hosp., N.Y.C., 1974—, acting dir. dept. psychiatry, 1974—; asso. Found. Thanatology, N.Y.C., 1974—. Vol. med. service The Door-Free Youth Clinic, N.Y.C., 1972—. Mem. Med. Soc. County N.Y., A.M.A., Am. Psychiat. Assn., Internat. Center for Integrative Studies (asso.), Found. Thanatology, Soc. for Gen. Systems Research, Soc. for Adolescent Psychiatry, N.Y. Council for Child Psychiatry. Office: 186 W 4th St New York City NY 10012

THURMAN, RUTH FLEET, lawyer; b. St. Petersburg, Fla., Sept. 27, 1929; d. Charles Carvel and Ruth (Harvey) Fleet; A.A., St. Petersburg Jr. Coll. 1949; B.A., Smith Coll., 1951; LL.B., Stetson U., 1963, J.D., 1967; m. James Endicott Thurman, June 10, 1952 (div. 1965); 1 son, James Endicott. Admitted to Fla. bar, 1964, since practiced in St. Petersburg; partner Collins, Hallett, Ford and Thurman, 1969—; asst. to state atty. for Pinellas and Pasco counties, Fla., 1967-68. Mem. Fla. Bd. Bar Examiners. Bd. dirs. Civic Music Assn. of St. Petersburg, sec., 1969-70; bd. dirs. South Pinellas chpt. A.R.C., 1967-72, Fla. West Coast Ednl. TV, 1967—. Mem. Fla. Assn. Women Lawyers (pres. 1969-70), St. Petersburg Bar Assn. (sec. 1970-71), St. Petersburg Legal Aid Soc. (dir. 1965-67), Jr. League St. Petersburg. Mem. First Ch. Christ Scientist (trustee 1967-68). Club: West Fla. Smith College Club (pres. 1960-61, 66-68). Home: 2411 Brevard Rd NE St Petersburg FL 33704 Office: 33 4th St N Petersburg FL 33701

THURSBY, MARILYN PEARCY (MRS. GENE ROBERT THURSBY), ednl. specialist; b. Evanston, Ill., Oct. 1, 1940; d. Noah Clyde and Louise (Barth) Pearcy; B.A., Oberlin Coll., 1962; M.Ed., Harvard, 1963; Ph.D., Duke, 1970; m. Gene Robert Thursby, June 9, 1963. Tchr. Newton (Mass.) pub. schs., 1962-63, Oberlin (O.) pub. schs., 1963-64, Durham (N.C.) pub. schs., 1964-65; research coordinator Durham County Schs., 1967-68; spl. project evaluation specialist Sch. Bd. Alachua County, Gainesville, Fla., 1970—. Cons. ednl. testing and evaluation. Chmn. Gainesville and Alachua County chpt. Am. Civil Liberties Union, 1973, also mem. bd. dirs. Fla. chpt.; mem. Alachua County Coordinated Child Care Bd., 1971-73. Mem. Nat. Soc. for Study of Edn., Am. Ednl. Research Assn., Phi Beta Kappa, Kappa Delta Pi. Mem. United Ch. Christ (mem. council Fla. conf. 1973, moderator 1973-74). Home: 2049 NW 7th Lane Gainesville FL 32603 Office: School Board of Alachua County Gainesville FL 32601

THURSTON, ALICE JANET STOUFFER, coll. pres.; b. Milw., Mar. 20, 1916; d. Karl J. and Nellie Ann (Smith) Stouffer; B.A., Denison U., 1937; M.A., Northwestern U., 1938; Ph.D., George Washington U., 1960; children—Anne Catherine, Robert William. Instr. psychology U. Md., 1941-45; lectr. George Washington U., 1947-49; prof. psychology Montgomery Coll., Takoma Park, Md., 1950-64, dean students, 1964-65; dir. counseling Cuyahoga Community Coll., Cleve., 1965-66, dean students Western campus, 1966-68; vis. lectr. U. Ill., 1968-69; dir. instl. research and student personnel services Met. Jr. Coll. Dist., Kansas City, Mo., 1969-71; pres. Garland Jr. Coll., Boston, 1971—. Trustee Franklin-Suffolk Bank, Boston. Mem. Community Coll. Adv. Bd., Am. Coll. Testing Program, 1970-73; mem. Mass. Regional Community Coll. Bd., 1972—. Mem. Am. Coll. Personnel Assn., N.E.A., Mortar Bd., Kappa Alpha Theta. Club: Zonta (v.p. Boston 1973-75). Editor: (with Terrence O'Banion) Student Development Programs in the Community Junior College, 1972. Home: 59 Richdale Rd Needham Heights MA 02194 Office: 409 Commonwealth Av Boston MA 02215

THURSTON, BONNIE MAY LINDEN (MRS. WILLIAM EUGENE THURSTON), computer co. exec.; b. Thiensville, Wis., Sept. 3, 1936; d. Matthew Fred and Lydia Catherine (Ellenbecker) Linden; B.S., Marquette U., 1958; postgrad. Cal. State Coll., 1960-63; M.S., U. So. Cal., 1971; postgrad. Southwestern U. Law, 1971-73; m. William Eugene Thurston, May 5, 1962. Program dir. U.S. govt., Augsburg, Germany, 1959-60; asso. Planning Research Corp., Los Angeles, 1962-66; market planning analyst Internat. Tel. & Tel., Los Angeles, 1966-67; long range planning analyst McDonnell Douglas, Los Angeles, 1967-68; mgr. market research Computer Sci. Corp., Los Angeles, 1968-73; mgr. market devel. System Devel. Corp., computer software, Santa Monica, 1973—. Marketing cons. several computer related firms, 1962—. Mem. Am. Marketing Assn., So. Cal. Planners Assn., Human Factors Soc., Pacific Area Travel Assn. (mem. research com. 1964-68), Air Transp. Assn. (mem. ad hoc com. 1965-66). Home: 531 Esplanade Redondo Beach CA 90277 Office: 2500 Colorado Av Santa Monica CA 90406

THURSTON, HELEN MARIE DUNTON (MRS. MARLIN OAKES THURSTON), editor; b. Cheyenne Wells, Colo., Dec. 13, 1921; d. Jessie Carey and Lenora Wilhelmina (Schuelke) Dunton; student U. Colo., 1939-42; B.A., Ohio State U., 1959, M.A., 1961; B.Sc. cum laude in Edn., 1964; m. Marlin Oakes Thurston, Mar. 15, 1942; children—Richard Ben, Kenneth Paul, Charles Marlin. Instr. history Otterbein Coll., Westerville, O., 1961-63, Capital U., 1964; asst. editor Ohio History, 1965-66, editor-mgr., 1966—. Mem. N.W. Area Council for Human Relations, 1967—. Mem. League Women Voters, Ohio Acad. History, Ohio Hist. Soc., I.E.E.E. Aux., Upper Arlington Civic Assn., Nat. League Am. Pen Women, Pi Lambda Theta. Home: 3751 Kioka Av Columbus OH 43220 Office: 1982 Velma Av Columbus OH 43211

THURSTON, MARGARET DILWORTH FELL (MRS. THOMAS WATSON THURSTON), educator; b. Shawnee, Okla., July 30, 1931; d. Daniel Ackley and Ruth (Dilworth) Fell; B.S., U. Okla., 1953, M.Ed., 1966; m. Thomas Watson Thurston, Aug. 17, 1953; children—Thomas Watson, Catherine Ann. Tchr. Taft Jr. High Sch., Oklahoma City, 1953-57; tchr. courses in gen. health, first aid, camp leadership, phys. edn. U. Okla., Norman, 1963—. Camp counselor, dir. camp for underpriviledged children, 1955—. Mem. Norman Park and Recreation Bd., chmn., 1969—; mem. mayor's hist. com., 1972—. Bd. dirs. Camp Fire Girls, Norman, 1965—. Mem. Am., Okla. assns. health, phys. edn. and recreation, Am. Camping Assn., Nat. Recreation Assn., PEO (pres. 1970-72), Phi Delta Kappa, Pi Beta Phi. Presbyn. (deacon 1970—, Sunday sch. tchr. 1964—). Home: 531 E Boyd Norman OK 73069 Office: 441 W Brooks Norman OK 73069

THURSTONE, PHYLLIS BAILEY (MRS. CONRAD THURSTONE), physician, educator; b. Watsonville, Cal., Sept. 15, 1933; d. Clarence N. and Leona A. (Trafton) Bailey; A.A., U. Cal. at Berkeley, 1954; B.S., Northwestern U., 1955, M.D., 1958; m. Conrad Thurstone; children—Elizabeth, Andrew, Christian. Intern San Francisco Gen. Hosp., 1958-59; resident in internal medicine Stanford Med. Center, Cal., 1960-63; practice medicine specializing in internal medicine, San Mateo, Cal., 1963—; staff H.D. Chope Hosp., San Mateo, 1963—; mem. clin. faculty Stanford U. Sch. Medicine, 1965—. Diplomate Am. Bd. Internal Medicine. Fellow A.C.P.; mem. Am. Assn. Univ. Women. Republican. Presbyn. Home: 51 Cragmont Way Woodside CA 94062 Office: 222 W 39th Av San Mateo CA 94403

THUSS, LOUISE BENEDICT (MRS. WILLIAM GETZ THUSS), civic worker; b. Nashville, Feb. 8, 1899; d. Chauncey B. and Sara (Byrns) Benedict; student Ward-Belmont Coll., 1916; Vandervilt U., 1920; m. William Getz Thuss, Sept. 25, 1923; children—William Getz, Chauncey Benedict, Robert Wilkey. Organizer, 1st pres. Vis. Nursing Assn., Birmingham, Ala., 1937, bd. dirs., 1937-43, 1949-55; bd. mgrs. Gateway Home, 1930—, pres., 1953-55, treas., 1964-68, hon. mem. bd., 1970; mem. Jefferson County Coordinating Council, 1950—, pres. children's com., 1929-39; mem. spl. com. on juvenile delinquency Jefferson County Assn. for Mental Health, 1960-67, mem. planning com., 1963-64; mem. edn. com. Jefferson County unit Am. Cancer Soc., past v.p. Radio-TV Council; mem. Home Garden Club; active A.R.C., 1942—, co-chmn. Women's div. fund raising; charter mem. Univ. Hosp. Aux., Cauldron Lit. Club; pres. Jefferson County Med. Soc. Woman's Aux., 1952-53, bd. dirs., 1956-62, hon. mem., 1965—; pres. Ala. Med. Assn. Woman's Aux., 1955-56, bd. dirs., 1956-62, hon. mem., 1967—; mem. nat. bd. dirs. A.M.A. Woman's Aux., 1954-57, 1st v.p., nat. membership chmn., 1960-61, nat. pres., 1962-63, bd. dirs., 1963-64, nat. chmn. 1972 Golden Anniversary; 1st v.p. So. Med. Assn. Woman's Aux., 1963-64, pres., 1965-66; v.p. U.S. sect. Internat. Coll. Surgeons Woman's Aux., 1958-60, 61-63, pres., 1963-64, bd. dirs., chmn. Southeastern region, 1958-60; 2d v.p. Southeastern Surg. Congress Woman's Aux., 1960-61, Ala. councilor, 1955-62; chmn. luncheons, corr. sec. Women's Com. of 100 for Birmingham, bd. dirs., pres., 1972-74; mem. adv. council Women's com. Spain Rehab. Center; mem. Birmingham Area Land-Marks Com.; mem. steering com. Comprehensive Mental Health Planning Com. 1964-65; chmn. Salvation Army Entertainment Festival of Arts. Recipient various certificates of appreciation; named Birmingham Woman of Year, 1972. Mem. Am., Internat. needlepoint guilds, Birmingham Art Mus., Birmingham Art Assn. (corr. sec. 1966-69), Birmingham Music Club, Ala. Opera Assn., Family Counseling Assn. Jefferson County, Arlington Hist. Assn. (pres. 1972-74), Nat. Trust for Historic Preservation, Am. Heritage Soc., Kenmore Hist. Soc., Nat. Hist. Assn., Birmingham Bot. Soc., English Speaking Union, Internat. Platform Assn., Am. Assn. U. Women, Birmingham Jr. League (sustaining), Kappa Alpha Theta. Methodist. Home: 2837 Southwood Rd Birmingham AL 35223 Office: 2124 4th Av S Birmingham AL 35233

THYSEN, JANICE DARROW, pub. relations exec.; b. Hammond, Ind., Mar. 24, 1941; d. Jack M. and Ruth Thelma (Bush) Darrow; B.J., U. Mo., 1963; m. Benjamin Thysen, Aug. 12, 1962 (div. Feb. 1970); 1 son, Gregory Eden Darrow. Asst. editor Bus. Week Mag., 1963-66; creative dir. Frank Block Assos., 1966-69; account exec. Wright & Manning, Inc., St. Louis, 1970—; founder, dir. U.S. Metric Plans Bd., 1974—; pres. Thysen Communications Cons., 1970—, Thysen Imports, 1971—, J. D. Thysen & Assos., 1972-74. Mem. CLASP sect. St. Louis White House Conf. on Edn., 1973—. Recipient award of commendation U. Mo. Sch. Journalism, 1963, Hon. Scholarship, U. Mo. Curators, 1960; William Randolph Hearst fellow, 1963. Mem. Nat. Sch. Pub. Relations Assn., St. Louis Women's Advt. Club, Women in Communications, Sigma Delta Tau. Republican. Book reviewer Kansas City Star, 1963-64, St. Louis Globe Democrat, 1974—. Home: 5 W Walling Dr St Louis MO 63141 Office: 515 Olive St St Louis MO 63101

TIBBETTS, MARY OVERBY (MRS. CARL FREDERICK TIBBETTS), coll. adminstr.; b. Buford, Ga., Feb. 19, 1911; d. James Floyd and Sallie Mae (Thomas) Overby; B. Oratory, Brenau Coll., 1932; m. Carl Frederick Tibbetts, June 8, 1935; children—Carl Frederick, Ruth Marie (Mrs. Floyd Murray Whetstone, Jr.). Instr. speech U. Ga., Athens, 1960-65; instr. speech Brenau Coll., Gainesville, Ga., 1965-71, dir. alumnae affairs, 1971—. Mem. Am. Legion Aux. (pres. 1950-52), Ga. Fedn. Women's Clubs (pres. 1950-52), Fine Arts Study Club (pres. 1959-61), Ga. Speech Communication Assn. (pres. 1967-69), Ga. Theater Conf. (pres. 9th dist. 1967), Gainesville Arts Council, Am. Alumni Council (treas. 1973—), Delta Kappa Gamma, Zeta Phi Eta. Home: 847 Memorial St Gainesville GA 30501 Office: Brenau College Gainesville GA 30501

TIDBALL, M(ARY) ELIZABETH PETERS (MRS. CHARLES S. TIDBALL), educator; b. Anderson, Ind., Oct. 15, 1929; d. John Winton and Beatrice (Ryan) Peters; B.A., Mt. Holyoke Coll., 1951; M.S., U. Wis., 1955, Ph.D., 1959; Sc.D., Wilson Coll., 1973, Trinity Coll., 1974; m. Charles S. Tidball, Oct. 25, 1952. Teaching asst. physiology dept. U. Wis., 1952-55, 58-59; research asst. anatomy dept. U. Chgo., 1955-56, research asst. physiology dept., 1956-58; USPHS postdoctoral fellow NIH, Bethesda, Md., 1959-61; staff pharmacologist Hazleton Labs., Falls Church, Va., 1961, cons., 1962; asst. research prof. pharmacology dept. George Washington U. Med. Center, 1962-64, asso. research prof., physiology dept., 1964-70, research prof., 1970-71, prof., 1971—. Cons., FDA, 1966-67, asso. sci. coordinator sci. assos. tng. program, 1966-67; mem. com. on NIH tng. programs and fellowships Nat. Acad. Scis., 1972—; lectr. on human sexuality, edn. of women; faculty summer confs. Am. Youth Found., 1967—. Rep. to D.C. Commn. on Status of Women, 1972—. Trustee Mt. Holyoke Coll., 1968-73, vice chmn., 1972-73; trustee Hood Coll., 1972—. Shattuck fellow, 1955-56; Mary E. Woolley fellow Mt. Holyoke Coll., 1958-59; USPHS postdoctoral fellow, 1959-61; recipient Alumnae Medal of Honor, Mt. Holyoke Coll., 1971. Mem. A.A.A.S., Am. Physiol. Soc. (chmn. task force on women in physiology), Histamine Club, Sigma Delta Epsilon, Sigma Xi, Mt. Holyoke Alumnae Assn. (dir. 1966-70). Episcopalian. Contbr. sci. articles to profl. jours. Home: 4100 Cathedral Av NW Washington DC 20016 Office: 2300 Eye St NW Washington DC 20037

TIEDEMAN, GRETCHEN THOMAS, artist; b. Washington, June 9, 1919; d. Dorsey Opie and Gretchen (Gorton) Thomas; student Mt. Vernon Jr. Coll., Washington, 1936-38, Corcoran Sch. Art, 1939-40; m. Robert Komfort Tiedeman, Aug. 23, 1941; children—Trudi (Mrs. John A. Puravs), Thomas Van Dohlen. Art tchr. Mt. Vernon Jr. Coll., 1939-40; designer, 1943-45; founder, tchr. Packahack Coop. Nursery Sch., Wayne, N.J., 1953-59; exhibited paintings in shows including Wayne Library; pvt. art tchr.; portraits in collections Navy Mus., Packanack Community Ch., St. Michael's Episcopal Ch., Wayne. Mem. Wayne Hist. Commn., 1969—, chmn., 1972; Wayne chmn. Am. Bicentennial Commn., 1973—. A founder Wayne chpt. Fedn. Republican Women; mem. county com. Rep. Party, 1960-68; chmn. Nixon Now, 1968; co-chmn. Nixon campaign, 1968; bd. govs. Rep. Club. Bd. dirs. United Givers Packanack Lake. Mem. D.A.R., Daus. Am. Colonists, Colonial Dames 17th Century. Episcopalian. Club: Packanack Lake Golf. Home: 23 Spruce Terrace Wayne NJ 07470

TIEDT, IRIS MCCLELLAN, educator, editor; b. Dayton, O., Feb. 3, 1928; d. Raymond Hill and Ermalene (Swartzel) McClellan; B.S., Northwestern U., 1950; M.A., U. Ore., 1962; Ph.D., Stanford, 1972; m. Sidney Willis Tiedt, Sept. 17, 1949; children—Pamela Lynne, Ryan Sidney. Tchr., pub. schs., Chgo., 1950-51, Anchorage, 1952-57, Eugene, Ore., 1960-61; teaching fellow U. Ore., Eugene, 1959-61; vis. prof. elementary edn. San Jose Cal. State U., 1961-66; dir. tchr. edn. U. Santa Clara (Cal.), 1968-72, asst. prof. edn., 1968—, dir. grad. reading program, 1972—. Mem. Bay Area Tchr. Edn. Commn., 1968-72. Mem. Santa Clara County Pace Center Bd., 1969—. Am. Assn. U. Women grantee, 1966. Mem. Nat. Council Tchrs. English (editor ofcl. jour. 1972—), Internat. Reading Assn., Nat. Women's Polit. Caucus, Pi Lambda Theta, Sigma Delta Pi. Author: Contemporary English in the Elementary School, 1967; The Elementary Teacher's Complete Ideas Handbook, 1965; Sexism in Education, 1974. Contbr. numerous articles to profl. jours. Editor: Elementary Tchrs. Ideas and Materials Workshop, 1968—. Home: 1654 Fairorchard Av San Jose CA 95125 Office: Univ of Santa Clara Santa Clara CA 95053

TIEMAN, JULIA ANN DAVIS (MRS. OSCAR H. TIEMAN), educator; b. Sayre, Pa., May 23, 1911; d. Ralston K. and Julia (Martin) Davis; student Ohio Wesleyan U., 1929-31, U. Wis., 1931-32; B.S., Miami Jacobs Bus. Coll., 1933; B.S. in Secondary Edn., U. Dayton, 1954; M.Ed., Miami U., 1959, Specialist in Edn., 1966; m. Oscar H. Tieman, Sept. 25, 1933 (dec. Jan. 1972); 1 dau., Judith Marie. Intake investigator div. aid for aged Dept. Pub. Welfare, Dayton, O., 1938-40; clk. stenographer Police Dept., Dayton, 1940-44; tchr. pub. schs., Trotwood, O., 1954-58, guidance counselor, 1958-61, dir. guidance, 1961—, dir. elementary guidance Madison Twp.,

Trotwood. Mem. bd. parish edn. Am. Lutheran Ch., 1970-73. Mem. Am. Personnel and Guidance Assn., Am., Ohio schs. counselors assns., Nat., Ohio, Western Ohio edn. assns., Montgomery County Tchrs. Assn. Lutheran. Mem. Order Eastern Star. Contr. articles to profl. jours. Research in field. Home: 2020 Wayne Av Dayton OH 45410 Office: 444 S Broadway Trotwood OH 45426

TIEMANN, KATHLEEN ELLEN, communications exec.; b. Fremont, Neb., July 14, 1943; d. Alvin Ernest and Lorna (Bahle) Tiemann; B.S., U. Colo., 1965. Pub. editor Financial Programs, Inc., Denver, 1965-71; corporate communications Petro-Lewis Corp., Denver, 1971—. Mem. Colo. Indsl. Press Assn. (sec. 1968-69, dir. 1970-72, pres. 1972), Internat. Assn. Bus. Communicators, Chi Omega, Theta Sigma Phi. Republican. Lutheran. Home: Apt 214 1225 S Oneida St Denver CO 80222 Office: 1600 Broadway Denver CO 80202

TIEMEYER, HOPE ELIZABETH JOHNSON, advt. co. exec., club woman; b. Ft. Wayne, Ind., May 20, 1908; d. Edward Tibbens and Burton (Meyers) Johnson; B.A., U. Cin., 1932; m. Edwin H. Tiemeyer, Oct. 30, 1929 (dec. Apr. 1955); children—Ann Elizabeth (Mrs. G. L. Lewin, Jr.), Edwin Houghton (dec.). Pres., owner Mail-Way Advt. Co., Cin., pres., 1955—. Regent, Cin. chpt. D.A.R., 1956-58, chmn. nat. sch. survey com., 1961-62, nat. vice chmn. Americanism Manual for Citizenship, 1962-65, Continental Congress program com., 1962-65, Congress Marshall Com., 1966-68, mem. Congress hostess com., 1969—; rec. sec. Nat. Chmn.'s Assn., 1969-71; sr. nat. membership chmn. Children Am. Revolution, 1958-60, sr. nat. rec. sec., 1960-62, nat. chmn. Mountain Sch., 1962-64, hon. sr. nat. v.p., 1963-64, sr. nat. 1st v.p. 1964-66, sr. nat. pres., 1966-68, hon. nat. life pres., 1970—, 1st v.p. Nat. Officers Club, 1965-69, pres., 1970-73, hon. sr. life pres. Ohio soc.; hon. life mem. Ohio Congress P.T.A., treas., 1957-62, v.p., dir. dept. health, 1962-63; hon. life mem. Nat. Congress P.T.A.; life mem. Kappa Alpha Theta Mothers Club, pres., 1958-59; v.p. women's com. Cin. Symphony Orch., 1964-65; pres. U. Cin. Parents Club, 1959-61, v.p., 1963-64; area chmn. State House Conf. on Edn., 1953; dir. Am. Assn. U. Women, 1963-64; mem. Cin. Social Health Bd., 1950—, exec. com., 1965-70, v.p., 1973—; pres. Singleton's of Cin. Club, 1969-71, 73—, mem. travelers bd., pres., 1973-74, art com., 1971—, mem. membership com., 1973—; pres. Newtown Garden Club, 1947-49, City Panhellenic Assn., 1951-52, Ohio Hobby Club, 1958-59, Sigma Nu Mothers Club, 1963-65, pres. Alumnae chpt. Alpha Omicron Pi, 1930-32, nat. admissions com., 1933-35; life mem. Craftshops for Handicapped; chmn. Amelia Earhart Fellowship com. Zonta Club, Cin., 1963-64, program chmn., 1964-65, orientation chmn., 1965-67, internat. relations chmn., 1967-68, dir., 1969—, mem. exec. com., 1969—, mem. nat. nominating com., 1970—, v.p., 1971-73; mem. music com., mem. tea room com. Cin. Woman's Club, 1969—; treas. Queen City chpt. Nat. Assn. Parliamentarians, 1965-69; mem. Nat. Platform Assn., Nat. Gavel Assn. Recipient Jonathon Moore citation and award Ind. Soc. Sons Am. Revolution, 1967; Good Citizenship medal Nat. Soc., 1967. Home: 2786 Little Dry Run Rd Cincinnati OH 45244 Office: 229 426-30 Plum St Cincinnati OH 45202

TIERNEY, MURIEL, travel cons.; b. Milw., Sept. 5, 1908; d. John and Freda (Kortum) Laursen; student San Diego State Coll., 1926-27; m. Norman W. Tolle, Aug. 18, 1929 (div. 1961); children—Lynn Edith, Norman W. (dec.); m. 2d, Roger R. Tierney, Oct. 9, 1965. Legal sec., 1928-30; prodn. asst. Campbell Co., 1930-31; partner Norman Tolle & Assos., now Tolle Co., 1932-47, v.p., 1947-61; account exec. Floats, Inc., 1961-62; mgr. Centre City Travel Service, Inc., 1964-66; v.p. Cabrillo Travel Service, Inc., San Diego, 1966-73; v.p. Acacia Travel, Inc., 1973—. Commr., Mission Bay Park, 1954-57; mem. Nat. Rivers and Harbors Congress rep. 30th dist. Cal. Del. Internat Advt. Conf., London, Eng., 1951; Nat. Resources Conf. Indsl. Coll. Armed Forces, 1957. Bd. dirs. Fiesta del Pacifico, 1956, 57, Aztec Coll. Trust, San Diego Aero-Space Mus., 1973—; chmn. San Diego-Yokohama Friendship Com. Named San Diego Advt. Woman of Year, 1958. Mem. San Diego Assn. Advt. Agencies (past pres.), San Diego State Coll. Alumni Assn. (past pres.), San Diego Pub. Relations Club, San Diego Advt. and Sales Club (past pres.) Advt. Assn. of the West (v.p. at large), C. of C., Service Clubs Presidents' Council (dir.), San Diego Better Bus. Bur. (dir.), Air Force Assn. (comdr.). Home: 2955 McCall St San Diego CA 92106 Office: 4250 Pacific Hwy San Diego CA 92110

TIERS, MARY LOWBER, photographer, retail trade co. exec.; b. Bryn Mawr, Pa., Apr. 20, 1915; d. William Twells and Alice (Welsh) Tiers; student Bennington Coll., 1934-35; certificate in comml. photography, N.Y. Inst., 1938; certificate Sch. Modern Photography, N.Y.C., 1942; postgrad. N.Y. U. 1945. Free lance photographer, 1939—; instr. Sch. Modern Photography, N.Y.C., 1943-49; photographer spl. services U.S. Army, Japan, 1950-54, Korea, 1950; photographer Orlando Sentinel Vero Beach, Fla., 1973-74; propr. Photog. Products, Vero Beach, 1962—. Recipient numerous photog. awards, 1940—. Mem. Profl. Photographers Am., Profl. Photographers Fla., Nat. Audubon Humane Soc., Art Club Vero Beach, Art Club Ft. Pierce. Contbr. numerous photographs to books and mags. including Life and articles on photography to profl. publs. Address: 1718 34th St Vero Beach FL 32960

TIFFANY, LOIS HATTERY (MRS. F. H. TIFFANY), botanist, educator; b. Collins, Ia., Mar. 8, 1924; d. Charles R. and Blanche (Brown) Hattery; B.S., Ia. State Coll., 1945, M.S., 1947, Ph.D., 1950; m. F. Henry Tiffany, May 14, 1945; children—Charles Ray, Jean Marie, David Henry. Instr. botany Ia. State U., Ames, 1950-56, asst. prof., 1956-58, asso. prof., 1958-65, prof., 1965—. Mem. Am. Phytopath. Soc., Mycol. Soc. Am., Sigma Xi, Phi Kappa Phi. Home: Route 4 Ames IA 50010

TIFFANY, MARGUERITE BRISTOL, artist; b. Syracuse, N.Y.; d. Ernest Livingston and Clara Frances (Bristol) Tiffany; B.S., Syracuse U., 1922; M.A. Columbia, 1930, also postgrad.; postgrad. Parsons, N.Y., Fawcett, Newark, N.Y. U., Montclair (N.J.) State Coll. Tchr. grade and high sch. arts, music, Sidney and Herkimer, N.Y., 1919-21; supr. arts, West Orange, N.J., 1921-26; tchr. arts jr. high sch., Montclair, N.J., 1926-29; asso. prof., head art dept. William Patterson (N.J.) Coll., 1929-56; faculty art dept. Fairleigh Dickinson U., 1956-64; exhibited one-man shows at Forest Grove, Ore., 1948, Grant Lee Theatre, Fort Lee, N.J., 1960, 61, Schine Inn, Massena, N.Y., 1963, Maplewood (N.J.)Women's Club, 1966, Peterson Mus., 1967, Paterson Woman's Club, 1967, N.Y., 1968; paintings exhibited N.Y., N. J., Ore., Ariz., Me.; exhibited weavings Newark Museum, 1969, 70, 72; represented in numerous pvt. collections; Judge local and scholastic art exhibits, Pa., N.J., 1950, 51, 60, 62; summer sch. lectr. Rutgers U., Ariz. State Coll., Flagstaff, YMCA, YWCA art courses. Mem. Ridgewood (N.J.), Fair Lawn art assns., Met. Art Mus., Sch. Art League, ANTA, Met. Opera Guild (N.J. chmn. Arts-in-Opera contests 1952-58), Nat. League Am. Pen Women (past N.J. pres.), English-Speaking Union, D.A.R., Am. Artists Profl. League (corr. sec.), Panhellenic Bd., N.Y.-Paterson Mus. Art League (past pres.), Am. Assn. U. Profs., Women's Press Club, Montclair Museum Art Tchrs. Assn. (past pres.), N.E.A., Eastern Arts Assn., National, N.J. art edn. assns., Am. Assn. U. Women (dir.), Assn. Hand Weavers (past pres. 1968-70), Chi Omega (past pres.), Kappa Delta (hon.), Pi Lambda Theta (hon.). Clubs: Century Theatre (past pres.) (N.Y.C.); Paterson Women's (chmn. lit. com.). Author articles ednl. jours. Home: 330 E 33d St Paterson NJ 07504

TIFFIN, MARY ELIZABETH (MRS. JOHN G. CLEGG), pediatrician; b. Pueblo, Colo., Sept. 21, 1911; d. Charles C. and Mary O. (Barr) Tiffin; B.S., U. Wash., 1932; M.D., Stanford, 1937; m. John G. Clegg, May 4, 1940 (dec. July 1967); children—Charles Tiffin, John Gibson, Helen, Hugh. Intern Stanford Hosp., San Francisco, 1931-37, resident, 1937-39; practice medicine specializing in pediatrics, Los Angeles, 1942—. Mem. staff sch. medicine U. So. Cal., Los Angeles, 1943-48, 68—, Children's Hosp., Los Angeles, 1942—. Cons. Los Angeles Child Care Centers, 1957-67. Mem. Los Angeles Pediatric Soc., Alpha Omega Alpha, Delta, Delta Delta, Phi Beta Kappa, Sigma Xi. Contbr. articles in field to profl. jours. Office: 321 N Larchmont St Los Angeles CA 90004

TIGUE, ETHEL ERKKILA (MRS. RALPH TIGUE), author; b. Virginia, Minn., Feb. 19, 1916; d. Oscar John and Serafia (Sarvela) Erkkila; B.Ed., U. Minn., 1938, postgrad., 1945-50; m. Ralph Tigue, June 30, 1941; children—Randall, Kevin. Tchr. high sch., Shakopee, Minn., 1938-41; city editor Women's News, Duluth, 1942-43; advt. mgr. Duluth Glass Block Store, 1943-45; high sch. counselor, Burley, Ida., 1945-48; freelance layout artist, St. Paul 1953-60; editorial asst. Farmer Mag., St. Paul, 1965-66. Tchr., dir. Writer's Workshop, Adult Edn., St. Paul, 1959-65. Recipient humanities award McKnight Found. Mem. Democrat Farmer Labor Party. Author: Betrayal, 1958; Looking Forward to a Career in Writing, 1971; Stranger Come Home, 1962; (with Louise Bower) The Secret of Willow Coulee, 1966, Packy, 1968. Home: 2067 Shepard Rd St Paul MN 55116

TILDEN, LORRAINE FREDERICK (MRS. WESLEY R. TILDEN), educator; b. Peoria, Ill., May 16, 1912; d. Milo Grover Frederick and Anna C. (Hebert) Frederick; student DePaul U., summer 1929; A.A., Ill. State U., 1931; postgrad. U. Ill., summer 1932, Universidad de La Habana (Cuba), 1937-41, Cornell U., 1944-45; U. Wis., 1940, Washington U., St. Louis, 1935-37, B.A., U. Cal. at Los Angeles, 1948, postgrad. 1956-57; M.A., Claremont Grad. Sch., 1954; postgrad. Whittier Coll., summer 1954, Universidad de Madrid (Spain) summer 1955, U. Redlands, 1960-61, Universidad de Guanajuato, Mexico, summer 1964, U. Cal., Riverside, 1967, Cal. State U. at San Francisco, summer 1971; m. Wesley R. Tilden, June 20, 1948. Various coll. teaching positions in English and Spanish, 1937-61; debate coach La Verne (Cal.) Coll., 1960-62; asso. prof. humanities Upland (Cal.) Coll., 1962-65; profl. interpreter Spanish, Claremont, Cal., 1948—; lectr. Latin Am. Lit. various univs., 1948—; lectr. travelogues with husband to colls., civic groups, 1948—; staff Glendora (Cal.) High Sch., 1967—. Counseling intern vocational guidance Cal. State Poly. Coll., 1961-62. Made hon. citizen of Guanajuato, Mex., 1963; recipient Best Single Project award People-to-People, Nat. League of Cities and Reader's Digest Found., 1964, Best Overall Program award 1965; 8 citations from Gt. Britain; Distinguished Pub. Service citation Claremont City Council, 1965. Mem. Am. Assn. U. Women (various positions held), Am. Assn. Tchrs. Spanish and Portuguese, Nat. Council Tchrs. English, Vachel Lindsay Assn., Associacion de Escritores y Artistas Panamericanos, Claremont Grad. Sch. Alumni Council (pres. 1973-74), Cornell Alumni Club Council (gov. 1960-62), U. Cal. at Los Angeles Alumni Assn. (mem. scholarship com. 1952), Town Affiliation Assn. of Claremont (pres. 1964-65), Sigma Delta Pi, Pi Lambda Theta. Author: Modernism in the Poetry of Jose Asuncion Silva, translated Streamlined English (Laubach) to Spanish, 1967; contbr. numerous dramatic, music and lit. revs. to mags., profl. jours., newspapers, including Atlantic and Hispania. Home: 351 Oakdale Dr Claremont CA 91711 Office: Glendora High Sch 1600 E Foothill Blvd Glendora CA 91740

TILGER, BESSIE ZORA, city ofcl.; b. Yorktown, Tex., May 21, 1918; d. Willie Moore and Minnie Sophie (Boesche) Harryman; m. Orville Lee Tilger, Aug. 6, 1938; 1 son, Dale Martin. Employed various positions, 1946-73; mem. Morton (Tex.) City Council, 1972—, County Park and Recreation Adv. Bd., 1973—. Active Cub Scouts; pres. Ladies Hosp. Aux., Morton, 1969-72; spl. dep. to sheriff Cochran County, mem. Cochran County Sheriff Posse, 1948-68. Sec., Democratic party Women, 1956-62. Bd. dirs. Cochran County Community Action Center, Cochran County Overall Econ. Devel. Plan. Recipient 4-H award of Clover, 1963-65; Fight Against Crime certificate Nat. Police Officers Assn.; 1st place in oil painting Morton Art Show, 1968. Baptist (Sunday sch. tchr. 1963—). Home: 901 E Grant St Morton TX 79346 Office: 107 W Taylor St Morton TX 79346

TILL, IRENE, economist; b. Syracuse, N.Y.; d. Edward Francis and Frances (Wehner) Till; B.A., Syracuse U., 1928; M.A., Radcliffe, 1929; Ph.D., Columbia U., 1937; postgrad. Yale, 1937-39; m. Walton Hale Hamilton, July, 1937 (dec. Oct. 1958); children—Robert, Douglas, Leslie. Economist, Senate Antitrust and Monopoly Subcom., Washington, 1955-66; prof. econs. Howard U., 1964-68; head drug study staff Social Security Adminstrn., 1968-71; economist Corporate Accountability Research Group, 1971—. Mem. Am. Econ. Assn., Am. Political Sci. Assn. Club: Washington Golf and Country. Author: (with others) Prices and Price Policy, 1937, (with W.H. Hamilton) Antitrust in Action, 1941. Editor: In a Few Hands (Senator Estes Kefauver), 1965. Contbr. to The Monopoly Makers, 1973. Home: 4630 N 32d Rd Arlington VA 22207 Office: 1832 M St NW Washington DC 22207

TILLER, MARGARET FAYE YEAGLEY (MRS. WAYNE KEITH TILLER), editor; b. San Antonio, May 4, 1939; d. Frank Winton and Margaret (Kirkpatrick) Yeagley; B.J., U. Tex., 1961; m. David Ragsdale Ellison, Sept. 2, 1961 (div. Apr. 1967); 1 dau., Lisa Claire; m. 2d, Wayne Keith Tiller, Feb. 8, 1969. Admissions com. sec. Soc. Petroleum Engrs., Dallas, 1961; editorial asst. Line, Tenneco, Inc., Houston, 1961-63; pub. relations, advt. Gulf & Western Industries, Inc., Houston, 1966; librarian Trunkline Gas Co., Houston, 1966, editor, 1966-69; exec. editor, sec.-treas. Editors, Inc., Austin, Tex., 1969—; editor Todays Family mag., 1969-71, also free lance writing, editing; pub. relations asst. Tex. Credit Union League, Dallas, 1971; cons., pub. relations specialist, Tulsa 1972—. Vol., Tulsa Republican Com., 1972—. Mem. S.E. Tex. Indsl. Editors, Theta Sigma Phi, Kappa Kappa Gamma. Methodist. Contbr. articles to various mags. Home: 13123 Conifer St Houston TX 77024

TILLER, MARTHA AMELIA RUSSELL (MRS. DAVID CLYDE TILLER), broadcasting co. exec.; b. Temple, Tex., Jan. 2, 1940; d. John Lafayette and Olle Cleo (Davidson) Russell; B.F.A. cum laude, U. Tex., 1961; student Nat. U. Mex., 1959; m. David Clyde Tiller, Nov. 26, 1966; 1 son, John Russell. Comml. coordinator, asst. to producer cultural specials CBS-TV, N.Y.C., 1961-64; asst. to producer Password, Goodson-Todman Prodns., N.Y.C., 1964-66; dir. publs. Tex. Fine Arts Commn., Austin, 1967-69; chief media design Southwest Ednl. Devel. Lab., Austin, 1969-72; spl. asst. to Pres., and now Mrs. Lyndon B. Johnson, Tex. Broadcasting Corp., Austin, 1972—. Free-lance writer, producer, pub. relations cons., 1966—. Docent Austin Natural Sci. Center, 1969-70, project chmn., 1970-71, v.p., 1971-72; auction week chmn. Ednl. TV Auction, 1971, city chmn., 1972; active United Fund, 1970, 72; publicity chmn. Mayor's Town Lake Beautification Com., 1972—. Bd. dirs. Austin Symphony Orch. Soc., 1972—, v.p., 1972, mem. exec. com., 1973. Recipient scholarship Am. Women Radio and TV, 1960, Outstanding Young Woman of Tex. award, 1972. Mem. Women in Communications, Art Guild Laguna Gloria Museum, Mortar Board, Alpha Epsilon Rho, Delta Zeta. Mem. Ch. of Christ. Club: Junior Austin Woman's. Home: 900 W 17th St Austin TX 78701 Office: 2313 Red River St Austin TX 78705

TILLERY, MARGIE FREEMAN (MRS. LEE ROY TILLERY, JR.), banker; b. West Point, Ga., Aug. 9, 1921; d. Arthur Roy and Sadie (Clem) Freeman; grad. LaGrange (Ga.) Bus. Coll., 1939; student U. Ga., 1946-47; m. Lee Roy Tillery, Jr., July 19, 1947; 1 son, Roy Lewis. Sec., Callaway Mills, LaGrange, Ga., 1939-47; legal sec. Cantey & Huff, Attys., West Point, 1947-48; bookkeeper First Nat. Bank, West Point, 1949-50; mgr. bus. office Valley Med. Group, Langdale, Ala., 1950-55; asst. cashier Valley Nat. Bank, Lanett, 1956-63; cashier Citizens Nat. Bank, Shawmut, Ala., 1963—. Early treatment edn. chmn. West Point area Am. Cancer Soc. Sec., bd. dirs. United Fund, Inc., West Point; bd. dirs. Troup County unit Am. Cancer Soc., United Fund, Inc., West Point. Named Key Banker, Chambers County. Ga. Mem. Nat. (membership chmn. Central Ala., regional v.p. 1971-72, nominating com. 1972-73), Ala. assns. bank women, Ala. Bankers Assn., Am. Inst. Banking, Beta Sigma Phi. Mem. Christian Ch. Clubs: West Point Junior Woman's (charter), Contemporary. Home: 400 E 4th St West Point GA 31833 Office: Citizens Nat Bank of Shawmut PO Box 708 Shawmut AL 36876

TILLEY, CAROLYN PATRIA NELSON (MRS. HUGH MACKENZIE TILLEY), ednl. adminstr.; b. Escalon, Cal., June 26, 1918; d. George Andrew and Mildred Rose (Barth) Nelson; A.B., U. Cal. at Berkeley, 1939; M.S. (Jordan Marsh fellow 1949-50), Simmons Coll., 1950; m. Hugh MacKenzie Tilley, Nov. 21, 1954; children—Elizabeth Barth, Jean Elsie. Tchr. Coalinga (Cal.) sch. dist., 1940-43, Mt. Diablo sch. dist., Concord, Cal., 1943-44; tng. dir. H.C. Capwell Co., Oakland, Cal., 1944-49; mgr. interior decorating studio The Emporium, San Francisco, 1950-51; tchr. Vallejo (Cal.) Jr. Coll., 1951-64; placement and financial aids officer Solano Community Coll., Suisun City, Cal., 1964—. Mem. Cal. Tchrs. Assn., Community Coll. Assn. Financial Aid Dirs. (dir. 1965—), N.E.A., (legislative liaison 1954—), Delta Kappa Gamma. Presbyn. (elder 1971—). Mem. Order Eastern Star. Home: 156 Mountain View Av Vallejo CA 94590 Office: Box 246 Suisun Valley Rd Suisun City CA 94585

TILLEY, ELIZABETH ROBERTS CORNWALL (MRS. THOMAS CLARK TILLEY), astronomer, civic worker; b. New Haven, Sept. 23, 1914; d. Charles Edward and Millicent (Johnson) Cornwall; B.A., Vassar Coll., 1935; postgrad. Yale, 1935-36; M.A., Wellesley Coll., 1939; Ph.D., U. Mich., 1942; m. Thomas Clark Tilley, Oct. 31, 1942; children—Thomas Clark III, Anne Bradford. Computer, Mt. Wilson Obs., Pasadena, Cal., 1936-37; asst. tchr. Wellesley (Mass.) Coll., 1937-40, U. Mich. at Ann Arbor, 1940-42; editor, supr. computers OSRD Rocket Project, Cal. Inst. Tech., Pasadena, 1943-44; tchr. St. John's Prep. Sch., San Juan, P.R., 1958-60; supr. lab. tests Analysts, Inc., San Juan, 1961-63. Bd. dirs. Ladies Aux. Presbyn. Hosp., San Juan, 1964—, pres., 1966-70, trustee, 1970—. Mem. Am. Astron. Assn., Phi Beta Kappa. Episcopalian. (mem. altar guild 1964—, pres. 1968-69, mem. bishop's council advice Diocese P.R. 1968-69). Club: Garden of P.R. (dir. 1963-66). Home: 510 Tintillo Rd Bayamon PR 00619

TILLIM, MURIEL SHARON (MRS. SIDNEY TILLIM), educator, theatre dir.; b. Cleve., Dec. 24, 1924; d. Benjamin Jay and Ella (Schwartz) Schochen; student Ohio State U., 1942-44; B.S., Western Res. U., 1946; Fulbright fellow Bristol (Eng.) U., 1952-53; m. Sidney Tillim, June 17, 1956. Dir. children's drama dept. 92d St YM-YWHA, N.Y.C., 1947-70; dir. The Pocket Players, Inc., profl. adults performing for children, N.Y.C., 1956—; artistic dir. Jr. Sch. of Neighborhood Playhouse Sch. of Theatre, N.Y.C., 1966-72; staff Moreno Inst. Psychodrama, N.Y.C., 1971—; lectr. Cornell U., Ithaca Coll., Brit. Drama League, Sarah Lawrence, Bennington Coll., State U. N.Y., U. Vienna. Cons. Project Create, Title III Program, 1967; mem. exec. com. U.S. Center of ASSITEJ, 1966—. Mem. Am. Ednl. Theatre Assn. (regional chmn. children's theatre conf. 1961-63), Am. Soc. Group Psychotherapy and Psychodrama. Author: (children's plays) Master of All Masters, 1957. Dir. motion picture The Unborn, 1965, dir. Histoire du Soldat, (mus. drama), 19—. Contbr. articles to profl. publs. Home: 166 E 96th St New York City NY 10028 Office: 92d St YM-YWHA Lexington Av New York City NY 10028

TILLIN, ALMA MAY (MRS. ISRAEL TILLIN), media specialist; b. Calgary, Alta., Can., Dec. 4, 1916; d. Solomon and Jennie Rachel (Shapiro) Bercov; came to U.S., 1939, naturalized, 1944; B.A., U. Alta., 1938; postgrad. Sorbonne, U. Paris, 1938-39; M.A., U. Cal. at Berkeley, 1940, certificate in librarianship, tchrs. credential, 1941; m. Israel Tillin, Mar. 28, 1942; children—Sandra, Pauline (Mrs. William Franklin Johns). Librarian, Burlingame (Cal.) Sch. Dist., 1942-45; cataloging asst. Alameda County Tchrs. Profl. Library, Oakland, Cal., 1950-55; librarian Madison Jr. High Sch., Oakland, 1959-61; tech. services media specialist Library Center, Berkeley (Cal.) Sch. Dist., 1961—. Ednl. workshop leader; lectr. and cons. in orgn. nonprint media; speaker and program participant in nat. library and audiovisual insts., confs. Mem. A.L.A. (descriptive cataloging com. 1971—, audiovisual com. 1973—), Assn. Ednl. Communications and Tech. (chmn. com. nonprint media storage, information systems div. 1970-72, spl. cons. information sci. com. 1973—), Cal. Assn. Sch. Librarians (conf. registrar 1968), Cal. Library Assn., Audiovisual Edn. Assn. Cal., N.E.A., Cal. Tchrs. Assn. Democrat. Mem. Jewish religion. Author: The Organization of Nonbook Materials in School Libraries, 1967, Developing Multi-Media Libraries, 1970, Standards for Cataloging Nonprint Materials, 3d edit., 1972; School Library Media Center Procedures, 1973. Contbr. articles to profl. pubs. Home: 1326 Portland Av Albany CA 94706 Office: 1720 Oregon St Berkeley CA 94703

TILLION, DIANA RUTZEBECK (MRS. CLEM V. TILLION, JR.), artist; b. Paradise, Cal., June 1, 1928; d. H. Hjalmar and Margaret R. (Johnson) Rutzebeck; corr. student U. Neb., 1946-47; studied with Barbara Morgan and Hans H. Hoffman, N.Y.C., 1951; student Alaska Community Coll., Juneau, 1963; m. Clem V. Tillion, Jr., Nov. 5, 1952; children—William David, Marian Ingrid, Martha Belle, Clement Vincent III. Exhibited one-man shows Anchorage, Internat. Gallery, 1963, Alaska State Bank, 1963-67, Stockbridge, Mass., 1966, Lenox (Mass.) Library, 1967, Amherst (Mass.) Gallery, 1967, Alaska State Mus., 1970, Anchorage Hist. and Fine Arts Mus., 1971, U. Alaska Gallery, 1972; exhibited in group show Abercrombie and Fitch's Alaska Show, N.Y.C., Chgo., San Francisco, 1967; represented in permanent collections Internat. Gallery, Anchorage, Vic Power Gallery, Juneau, Amherst Gallery; instr. Kenai Community Coll. Art, 1966-67. Recipient Gov.'s award Alaska Meth. U. Show, 1968. Mem. Nat. League Am. Penwomen (state pres. 1967), Kachemak Bay Arts and Crafts Guild (pres.), Alaska Poetry Soc., Alaska State Council on Arts. Co-author: Alaska in Haiku, 1972. Home: Halibut Cove Homer AK 99603

TILTON, BERNICE ELIZABETH SHEPPARD (MRS. EARLE BARTON TILTON), civic worker; b. Chgo.; d. Samuel Charles and Elizabeth (Keith) Sheppard; Mus.B., Wis. Coll. Music, 1954; m. Earle

Barton Tilton, Mar. 12, 1940. Performed as soloist and two-piano team for orgns., Ill., Wis., Fla., 1947—. Pres., Symphony Club, Clearwater, Fla., 1958-60; founder Mus. Arts Soc., Clearwater, 1960, pres., 1960-62; chpt. pres. Delta Omicron, 1964-66, Fla. chmn. alumnae-at-large, 1965-67, internat. v.p. alumnae, internat. bd. dirs., 1967-71; Fla. W. Coast pres. Panhellenic Assn., 1967-68, chpt. adv. bd., 1968—. Bd. dirs., v.p. Clearwater Community Concert Assn., 1963—. Recipient Gold Star Delta Omicron, 1967, Recognition award, 1971. Mem. Nat. Soc. Arts and Letters (local sec., v.p. 1972—), Delta Omicron (alumnae chpt. pres. 1973—). Home: 405 Orangewood Av Clearwater FL 33515

TILTON, ELEANOR MARGUERITE, educator, author; b. Boston, Aug. 20, 1913; d. Rufus H. and Marguerite (Verne) Tilton; B.A., Mt. Holyoke Coll., 1934; M.A., Boston U., 1935; Ph.D., Columbia, 1947. Tchr. Mt. Holyoke Coll., 1937, Vassar Coll., 1939-43, MacMurray Coll., 1944-47; asst. prof. English, Temple U., 1948-50, Barnard Coll., 1950-54, asso. prof., 1954-59, prof., 1959—, chmn. dept., 1961-63. Fellow Am. Assn. U. Women, 1943-44; Guggenheim fellow, 1963-64; Radcliffe Inst. fellow, 1969-70. Mem. Modern Lang. Assn., Am. Assn. U. Profs., N.Y. Hist. Soc., Phi Beta Kappa. Author: Amiable Autocrat, 1947; (with T. F. Currier) Oliver Wendell Holmes, a Bibliography, 1953. Contbr. articles profl. jours. Home: 401 W 118th St New York City NY 10027

TIMBERLAKE, MARY ESTELLE, librarian; b. Durham, N.C., Dec. 2, 1910; d. Joe Elmore and Estelle (Flintom) T.; student Winthrop Coll., 1929-30; A.B., U. S.C., 1932; M.A., George Peabody Coll. Tchrs., 1943. File clk. Fed. Land Bank, Columbia, S.C., 1933-42; librarian Lander Coll., Greenwood, S.C., 1943-45; reader's services librarian Vassar Coll., Poughkeepsie, N.Y., 1950-54; librarian Newberry (S.C.) Coll., 1954-57; reference librarian U. S.C., Columbia, 1957-59, asst. reference librarian, 1945-50, 60-71, documents librarian Undergrad. Library, 1971—. Mem. Am., Southeastern, S.C. library assns., Am. Assn. U. Women, D.A.R. Republican. Methodist. Club: Adirondack Mountain (Poughkeepsie). Home: 1041 Marion St Columbia SC 29201 Office: Univ Library University of South Carolina Columbia SC 29208

TIMBERS, ELAINE BEATTY (MRS. HARLEY CLARK TIMBERS), librarian; b. Glen Ridge, N.J., Aug. 6, 1925; d. Lloyd Graham and Mary-Elizabeth (Scheffey) Beatty; B.A., Vassar Coll., 1946; M.A., U. Wis., 1952; m. Harley Clark Timbers, Dec. 26, 1953; children—Jill Graham, Bradford Clark. Editorial asst. Glamour Mag., Conde Nast Pubs., N.Y.C., 1947-48; library asst. Bloomfield (N.J.) Pub. Library, 1948-51; research librarian World Book Ency., Field Enterprises, Chgo., 1952-54; reference librarian Summit (N.J.) Pub. Library, 1959-63, Allentown, (Pa.) Pub. Library, 1964-66; librarian Emmaus (Pa.) High Sch., 1966-67; dir. Emmaus Pub. Library, 1967—. Mem. Am., Pa. library assns., D.A.R. Home: 915 Turner St Emmaus PA 18049 Office: Ridge and Main Sts Emmaus PA 18049

TIMCHICK, MARY ROBERTA, journalist; b. Cleve., June 28, 1942; d. Michael and Bertha Clare (Smith) Timchick; B.S., Ohio U., 1964. Children's book reviewer, chmn. Cleve. Book Fair for Boys and Girls, dir. World Friends Club, investigative reporter, feature writer and reviewer adult books, writer on aging Cleve. Press, 1964—. Mem. Mayor's Commn. on Aging, Cleve., 1973—. Mem. Women's Nat. Book Assn. (sec. Cleve. chpt. 1967-69), Newspaper Guild (sec. Cleve. Press unit 1968-69, del. Nat. Conv. 1970, rec. sec. exec. bd. Cleve. local 1), Ohio Newspaper Women's Assn. Club: Ohio U. Womens (Cleve.). Home: 5719 Chevrolet Blvd Parma OH 44130 Office: 901 Lakeside Av Cleveland OH 44114

TIMKO, JUANITA ELIZABETH FLETCHALL, bus. exec.; b. Evansville, Ind., Mar. 18, 1908; d. Frank and Mary (Record) Fletchall; grad. high sch.; m. Lewis Timko, Nov. 23, 1927 (div. Aug. 1946); 1 son, Lewis T. With Temme Spring div. Maremont Corp., Chgo., 1937—, office mgr., 1968—. Instr. first aid A.R.C., Chgo., 1950-60, comdr. first aid corps, 1954-55; pres. adult program council Central YMCA, Chgo., 1969-70; vol. worker Hines Vaughn VA hosps., 1956-60. Served as 1st lt. Civil Air Patrol, 1952-54. Mem. Bus. and Profl. Women's Club. Home: 434 Melrose St Chicago IL 60657 Office: 1515 S Wabash St Chicago IL 60605

TIMM, DOROTHY JEAN, music therapist; b. Wood Lake, Minn., Jan. 16, 1929; d. Julius Christian and Augusta Hannah (Todt) Timm; Mus.B., MacPhail Coll. of Music, Mpls., 1952; Mus.B. Therapy, Fla. State U., 1966. Instr. music Conservatory, LaCross, Wis., 1952-55, Dr. Martin Luther Coll., New Ulm, Minn., 1957-64; music therapist Faribault (Minn.) State Hosp., 1967—. Mem. Nat. Assn. for Music Therapy, Am. Orff-Schulwerk Assn., Fla. State U. Alumni Assn. Home: 14A 3d St NE Faribault MN 55021 Office: Faribault State Hosp Faribault MN 55021

TIMMER, ELLEN, physician; b. Tallinn, Estonia, Jan. 19, 1912; d. Gustav and Aline (Israel) Timmer; M.D., U. Tartu (Estonia), 1937; postgrad. N.Y. U., 1949-50; m. Karl Saar, July 1, 1960. Came to U.S., 1947, naturalized, 1949. Resident, N.Y.-Bellevue Med. Center, 1949-51; intern Meth. Hosp., Peoria, Ill., 1952-53; practice medicine specializing in ear, nose and throat, Estonia, 1937-44, Peoria, 1954—; mem. staff Meth., St. Francis, Proctor Community hosps.; instr. U. Tartu, Estonia, 1940-44. Mem. Am., Ill., Peoria med. assns., Peoria Mus. Soc. Club: Pilot. Home: 716 Highview Rd East Peoria IL 61611 Office: 331 Fulton St Peoria IL 61602

TIMMERMANN, SANDRA, ednl. adminstr.; b. Orange, N.J., Mar. 25, 1941; d. Bernhard and Matilda (Schaaf) Timmermann; B.A., U. Colo., 1963; M.A., Columbia, 1967, postgrad. (Kellogg fellow), 1971—. Account exec. Rowland Co., N.Y.C., 1964-67; dir. information services Ednl. Communications Network, State U. N.Y., N.Y.C., 1967-72; prin. S. Timmermann, pub. relations bus. and cons. service, N.Y.C., 1972-74; asso. dean Instr. Lifetime Learning, Am. Assn. Ret. Persons and Nat. Ret. Tchrs. Assn., Washington, 1974—. Mem. Am. Assn. Higher Edn., Phi Beta Phi, Pi Lambda Theta, Kappa Delta Pi, Phi Delta Kappa. Address: 4201 Cathedral Av NW Washington DC 20016

TIMMERMANS, DEANNA D. (MRS. JOHN J. TIMMERMANS), former pharmacist; b. Rapid City, S.D., Feb. 5, 1939; d. Bernard Briggs and Luella (Olson) Dodds; B.S., State U. Ia., 1961; m. John J. Timmermans, June 24, 1961; 1 son, Jeffrey Jay. Pharmacist, Race Drug, Ketchikan, Alaska, 1961-63, St. Vincent's Hosp., N.Y.C., 1965-66, S.I. Hosp., 1966-71. Mem. Jr. Guild S.I., 1970—; treas. Women's Guild S.I. Mental Health Assn., 1970-71; toy chmn. Christ Ch. Day Sch. Fair, N.Y.C., 1971. Mem. Women for Rockefeller, S.I., 1970; mem. com. Republican party, Richmond County, 1970-71; chmn. credentials com. Women's Rep. Conf., Phila., 1972; mem. Met. Rep. Club, 1972—. Bd. dirs. Women's Aux. N.Y. U. Coll. Dentistry. Mem. Pharm. Soc. State N.Y., Assn. Hosp. Pharmacists, Am., Ia. pharm. assns., Acad. Pharm. Scis., Fgn. Policy Assn., Parents League N.Y., Jr. League City N.Y., Kappa Alpha Theta Alumni Assn., Kappa Alpha Theta (past v.p.), Kappa Epsilon. Lutheran. Home: 59 E 72d St New York City NY 10021

TIMMNER, GEORGIA RITA, pub. relations agy. exec.; b. St. Paul, Apr. 7, 1941; d. Folmer Lynn and Gertrude Marie (Lynch) Lauritzen; student, U. Minn., 1959-61; married. Continuing edn. and in service tng. researcher Am. Rehab. Found., Mpls., 1962-67; data processor Cal. Inspection Rating Bur., San Francisco, 1967-69; adminstrv. asst. Conley, Knollin & Strain Advt., San Francisco, 1970-71, media/marketing dir., 1971—. Office: 494 Jefferson St San Francisco CA 94109

TIMMONS, DOROTHY LOU, city ofcl.; b. Edmonson, Tex., Dec. 31, 1943; d. Van Earl and Erlene Bernice (Brooks) Barbour; grad. with honors, Draughon's Bus. Coll., 1963; m. Patrick Walker Timmons, Dec. 13, 1963 (dec. Nov. 1969); children—Patrick Noble, Gregory Blake. Utility and billing clk., sec. to city mgr., Tulia, Tex., 1967-70, deptl. bookkeeper, 1968-70; utility clk. City of Coppell, Tex., 1972, acting city adminstr., 1972, city sec., tax assessor-collector, 1972—, head dept. tax assessing, 1973—. Mem. City Secs. Assn., Tex. Assn. Assessing Ofcls., Beta Sigma Phi (award as girl of year 1970). Home: PO Box 416 Coppell TX 75019 Office: PO Box 478 Coppell TX 75019

TINCH, HELEN MOSS PEARL (MRS. HARRY H. TINCH), mus. adminstr.; b. Houston; d. Edgar Winfield and Elma Marie (Huebner) Pearl; student Sinclair Sch. Bus. Adminstrn.; m. Burrell B. Liles, Jan. 23, 1934; dec. June 1940); m. 2d, Harry H. Tinch, Nov. 30, 1947. Sec.-treas. Pipe Line Engrng. & Equipment Co., Houston, 1947-72, pres., 1972—. Archivist, curator Mus. Houston Baptist Coll. (name now changed to Houston Bapt. U.), 1964-68, dir., 1968—. Mem. Harris County Hist. Survey Com., Tex. Hist. Found., Harris County Heritage Soc., Am. Assn. Mus. Episcopalian. Author: Days of Colonial Texas, 1967. Contbr. articles to profl. jours. Home: 2921 Rice Blvd Houston TX 77005 Office: PO Box 25121 Houston TX 77005

TINGLE, DOLLI E. (MRS. WARD GORDON BRACKETT), author, artist; b. Chgo.; d. Horace Berchard and Mabel Viola (Ermen) Tingle; B.A., Chgo. Acad. Fine Arts, 1937; postgrad. Am. Acad. 1938, Bklyn. Mus. Sch. Art, 1960-61; m. Ward Gordon Brackett, May 4, 1940; 1 son, Gordon. Free lance artist, designer, author, painter, Chgo., 1938-40, N.Y.C., 1940-47, Westport, Conn., 1947—; one man shows at Kaymar Gallery, N.Y.C., 1963, Nat. Audubon Show, N.Y.C., 1961, New Eng. Show, Silvermine, Conn., 1961, Bruce Mus., Stamford, Conn., 1960, Conn. Gallery, Westport, 1971, Cape Cod Gallery, Dennis, Mass., 1961, 72. Art chmn. Wesport Women's Club, 1954-58. Named Woman of Year Am. Needlepoint Guild, 1974. Mem. Rowayton Arts Center, Silvermine Guild Artists. Author: Our Baby's First Book, 1967; Expecting, 1968; Going to Be a Bride?, 1969; Look Who's a Grandma, 1971; Baby's Health Record, 1972. Designed U.S. Govt. Christmas Postage Stamp, 1973. Home and studio: 7 Woodland Dr Westport CT 06880

TINKER, CAROL WICKS (MRS. GEORGE EDWARD TINKER III), state legislator; b. Claire City, S.D., Dec. 21, 1920; d. LeRoy Soren and Alta Ruth (Ness) Wicks; student N.M. Highlands U., 1938-41; m. George Edward Tinker III, Oct. 17, 1942; children—George Edward IV, Anne (Mrs. Willard Robert Baker, Jr.), Tanya, Randy, Christy. Sec., Horwath & Horwath, C.P.A.'s, Chgo., 1941-42, U.S. Army Logistics, Salzburg, Austria, 1948-49, N.M. Cattle Growers Assn., 1965. Pub. relations coordinator for consolidation of East and West Las Vegas, Nev., 1966; chmn. San Miguel County (N.M.) chpt. March of Dimes, 1966-68. Sec. to gubernatorial candidate Merle H. Tucker, San Miguel County, N.M., 1964; San Miguel County campaign mgr. Clifford Hawley, gubernatorial candidate, 1966, Anderson Carter, U.S. Senate candidate, 1966; chairwoman San Miguel County Republican Party, 1966; sec. N.M. State Republican Party, 1973-74, exec. dir. central com.; mem. N.M. State Legislature, 1968-72, mem. legislative drug abuse com., 1971-72, legislative corrections study com., 1969-70, edn. com., 1970-72, natural resources com., 1968-72, rules and order of bus. com., 1971-72. Bd. dirs. N.M. Regional Med. Program, 1971-74, N.M. Adult Basis Edn., 1970-74, N.M. Mental Health Assn., 1969-72, Alcoholic Commn., 1970-72. Mem. San Miguel County C. of C. (bd. dirs. 1970-74), Delta Zeta. Lutheran. Club: Business and Professional Women's (Las Vegas). Home: 902 3d St Las Vegas NM 87701

TINKHAM, CATHERINE WILLIAMS, pub. health nurse educator; b. Boston, Apr. 16, 1916; d. Harry G. and J. Winona (Williams) Tinkham; grad. St. Luke's Hosp., 1937; B.S., Simmons Coll., 1948; M.P.H., U. Mich., 1953. Staff nurse Brockton Vis. Nurse Assn., 1940-42; pub. health nurse USPHS, 1942; field supr. Cambridge Vis. Nurse Assn., 1948-51; instr. Boston U. Sch. Nursing, 1953-55, asst. prof., 1955-60, asso. prof., 1960-67, prof., 1967—, coordinator pub. health nursing program, 1959-74. Mem. steering com. New Eng. Regional Conf. for Pub. Health Nursing Edn., 1956-59, chmn.-elect, 1963-64; mem. exec. com. New Eng. Council Higher Edn. for Nursing, New Eng. Bd. Higher Edn., 1965-67. Pres., Rockne Assn., Inc. Served from ensign to lt. comdr. Nurse Corps, USNR, 1942-45, 51-52. Fellow Am. Pub. Health Assn. (membership com. pub. health nursing sect. 1969-71); mem. Am. Nurses Assn. (certification bd. for community health nursing 1971—), Nat. (mem. sub-com. pub. health nursing edn. 1960-65), Mass. leagues for nursing, Mass. Pub. Health Assn., Delta Omega, Pi Lambda Theta, Sigma Theta Tau. Co-author: Community Health Nursing: Evolution and Process, 1972. Home: 65 Strathmore Rd Brookline MA 02146 Office: Boxton U Sch Nursing Boston MA 02215

TINKLE, MAYBELLE, educator; b. Henrietta, Tex., Dec. 20, 1909; d. George and Carrie Mae (Heindel) Tinkle; B.S., Tex. Wesleyan Coll., 1931; M.Ed., U. Tex., 1932; postgrad. U. Colo., 1937, U. Wis., 1938; D.Ed., U. Mich., 1955. Co-owner, M.B. Tinkle Dept. Store, Ft. Worth, 1932-38; asst. prof. phys. edn. Tex. Wesleyan Coll., Ft. Worth, 1937-46; asso. prof. phys. edn. Tex. Christian U., Ft. Worth, 1946—. Summer camp counsellor Camp El Tesoro, Granbury, Tex., 1942, Camp Waldemar, Hunt, Tex., 1943-49. Mem. Am. Assn. U. Women (pres. 1959-61), Am., Tex. assns. health, phys. edn. and recreation, Nat., So. assns. phys. edn. coll. women, Ft. Worth Womens Phys. Edn. Assn., English Speaking Union, Delta Psi Kappa, Alpha Chi, Pi Lambda Theta, Delta Kappa Gamma, Kappa Delta Pi. Methodist. Clubs: Womans, Altrusa (pres. Ft. Worth 1973-74). Home: 4900 Staples Av Fort Worth TX 76133

TINKLEPAUGH, WENDY RUTH (MRS. NORMAN P. SOLOWAY), pediatrician; b. Manhattan, N.Y., Aug. 25, 1942; d. Frost L. and Ruth Starbuck (Cooper) Tinklepaugh; B.A., Wellesley Coll., 1964; M.D., Albany Med. Coll., 1968; m. Norman P. Soloway, June 2, 1968; children—Robin, Christopher. Intern pediatrics Roosevelt Hosp., N.Y.C., 1968-69, sr. resident pediatrics, 1969-70, fellow, community pediatrics, 1970-71; practice medicine specializing in pediatrics, Manchester, N.H. 1971—, pediatric cons. Dept. Pub. Health, Concord, N.H., 1971—; cons. adolescent medicine Community Guidance Center, Manchester, N.H., 1971—. Mem. Am. Women's Med. Assn., League of Women Voters. Home: Baboosic Lake Rd Amherst NH 03031 Office: Dept Pub Health 61 S Spring St Concord NH 03301

TINKLIN, GWENDOLYN LAVERNE, educator; b. Corning, Kan., May 8, 1910; d. Chauncey E. and Effie (Sanders) Tinklin; A.A., Mt. St. Scholastica Coll., 1930; B.S., Kan. State U., 1940, M.S., 1944; postgrad. Ia. State U., 1947-48, U. Wis., 1956-57. Tchr. pub. schs. Atchison County Kan., 1930-43; grad. asst. Kan. State U., Manhattan, 1943, asst. home economist agrl. expt. sta., 1943-45, instr. foods, nutrition, 1945-47, asst. prof., 1949-56, asso. prof., 1956-63, prof., dept. foods and nutrition, 1963—, acting head foods and nutrition, 1953-55, 63-66; adviser home sci. Kan. State U., U.S. AID-India, Andhra Pradesh Agrl. Coll., Hyderabad, India, 1966-67. Mem. Am., Kan. home econs. assns., Inst. Food Technologists, Soc. for Nutrition Edn., Am. Assn. U. Women (rec. sec. Manhattan br. 1967-71), Sigma Xi, Omicron Nu (prin. adviser Theta chpt. 1970—), Phi Upsilon Omicron, Gamma Sigma Delta (pres. Eta chpt. 1971-72). Contbr. articles to profl. jours. Home: 721 Elling Dr Manhattan KS 66502

TINNIN, HELEN LOU, community health scientist; b. Austin, Tex., Feb. 1, 1933; d. Hugh and Mattie May (Carter) Tinnin; A.B., U. Cal. at Berkeley, 1952, M.P.H., 1961; Ph.D., Ohio State U., 1964. Pharm. mfrs. rep. Pfizer Lab. of N.Y., Youngstown, O., 1952-54, Ayerst Lab. of N.Y., Birmingham, Ala., 1954-59; instr. personal and community health Ohio State U., 1961-63; health edn. cons., project dir. Tri-Agy. Health Edn. Council, Canton, O., 1963-64; asst. prof. preventive medicine and pub. health, cons. scientist Univ. Hosp. and Clinics, U. Ala. Med. Center, 1964-66; asso. prof. health edn. and asst. to dean program planning U. Tex. Grad. Sch. Biomed. Scis., Tex. Med. Center, Houston, 1966-67; prof. community health and med. practice U. Mo. Med. Sch., Columbia, 1967-70; exec. dir. Forsyth Health Planning Council, also prof. community medicine Bowman Gray Sch. Medicine, Wake Forest U., Winston-Salem, N.C., 1970—. Cons. Westinghouse Learning on Population Dynamics, program methodology U. Mo. regional med. program Health Service Research sect. Adviser youth groups Episcopal Ch. Mem. Assn. Am. Med. Colls., Am. Assn. U. Profs., N.C. Pub. Health Assn., Soc. Pub. Health Educators, Am. Sch. Health Assn., Council on Med. TV, Assn. Tchrs. Preventive Medicine, Am. Pub. Health Assn., Assn. Sch. Allied Health, Am. Assn. U. Women, League Women Voters. Home: 2934-B St Mark's Rd Winston-Salem NC 27103 Office: Suite 200 811 W 5th St Winston-Salem NC 27103

TINSLEY, ADRIAN, coll. dean; b. N.Y.C., July 6, 1937; d. Theodore Adrian and Mary Ethel (White) T.; A.B., Bryn Mawr Coll., 1958; M.A., U. Wash., 1962; Ph.D. (U. Grad. fellow, U. sr. fellow), Cornell U., 1969. Lectr. English, Cornell U., 1966-68; asst. prof. English, U. Md., College Park, 1968-72; dean William James Coll., Grand Valley State Coll., Allendale, Mich., 1972—. Fulbright fellow, 1958-59; Woodrow Wilson teaching fellow, 1961-62. Mem. Women's Caucus for Modern Langs. (chairwoman discrimination com. 1971-72), Modern Lang. Assn. (mem. commn. on status of women in profession 1972—), Phi Beta Kappa, Phi Kappa Phi. Author: Academic Women, Sex Discrimination and the Law, 1971, 72. Editor: (with Hoffman, Secor) Female Studies VI, 1972. Home: 201 S 5th St Grand Haven MI 49417 Office: William James Coll Allendale MI 49401

TINSLEY, MONA GAIL, counselor; b. Hugo, Okla., Mar. 20, 1935; d. Cecil V. and Claudia E. (Bright) Tinsley; B.S., Okla. Coll. Women, Chickasha, 1957; grad. student E. Tex. State U., 1962, also Tex. Tech. U., Sul Ross State U. Vocational, home econs. and girls counselor Pauls Valley (Okla.) Jr. High Sch., 1957-59; tchr. phys. edn. and head, girls guidance counselor, Graham, Tex., 1959-61; dormatory counselor E. Tex. State U., 1961-62; high sch. counselor, Andrews, Tex., 1962—. High sch. counselor Menninger Found. Mem. Nat. Assn. Women Deans and Counselors, Andrews Classroom Tchrs. Assn., Am., Tex. personnel and guidance assns., Tex. State Tchrs. Assn. (life), Gamma Phi Beta. Home: 401 NW 8th St Andrews TX 79714 Office: 405 NW 3d St Andrews TX 79714

TINSLEY, NORMA ELISE ROBINSON (MRS. JAMES MADISON TINSLEY), mfg., wholesale co. exec.; b. Shreveport, La., July 18, 1909; d. James Malcolm and Effie (Estes) Robinson; A.B. magna cum laude, Centenary Coll., 1930; postgrad. U. Colo., 1931; m. James Madison Tinsley, Apr. 26, 1943; 1 son, James Robinson. Asso. prof. English, psychology Dodd Coll., Shreveport, La., 1930-41; mng. partner Robinson-Tinsley Co., Shreveport, 1936—. Sec., Little Theater Guild, 1936-37; mem. com. Preservation Fort Hudson Battlefield, 1959-61; mem. Soc. Preservation Fort Del., 1959-61. Mem. U.S., Shreveport chambers commerce, L'Alliance Francaise, La., North La. (dir. 1959-61, sec. 1959) hist. assns., Am. Assn. U. Women (hospitality chmn. Shreveport), Ky. Hist. Soc., Centenary Coll. Alumni Assn. (dir. chpt. 1965-67), Internat. Platform Assn., Hon. Order Ky. Adms., Hon. Order Ky. Cols., Chi Omega (chpt. pres. 1935-37), Alpha Chi, Pi Gamma Mu. Baptist. Home: 1039 Sheridan Av Shreveport LA 71104 Office: 2101 Seymour St Shreveport LA 71104

TIOCO, NARCISA FELIX, librarian; b. Tondo, Manila, Mar. 18, 1919; d. Jose F. and Gavina (Felix) Tioco; grad. Philippine Normal Coll., 1936; student Far Eastern U., 1950; M.A. in L.S., Simmons Coll., Boston, 1959. Elementary sch. tchr. Div. City Schs., Manila, 1939-41; jr. librarian U.S. Armed Forces, 1945-47; library asst. U. of East Library, Manila, 1947-50, cataloger, 1951-57, chief librarian, 1959—, dir. Summer Inst. Library Sci., 1971; library trainee Widener Library, Harvard, 1957-59. Recipient Nat. award Philippine Normal Coll., 1970. Mem. Philippine Library Assn. (named Most Outstanding Librarian Pvt. Schs. 1968, One of Top Ten Filipino Librarians 1968), Assn. Spl. Libraries Philippines (past pres.), Assn. Tchrs. Library Sci. (past pres.), Philippine Normal Sch.-Philippine Normal Coll. Alumni Assn. (pres.). Author: Looking at Ourselves: A Survey of the Book Collection, 1957; The University of the East Library: Status and Accessibility of the Science and Technology Collection, 1967; The Organization and Administration of the Book Collection, 1969; Financing Libraries, 1969; The Library in the 70's, 1971; Library Personnel Management, 1971; The Fear of Change: A Test of a Librarian, 1972. Home: 49 E Fernandez San Juan Rizal Philippines Office: C M Recto Manila D408 Philippines

TIPPETT, SUSAN RANDALL PINCOFFS (MRS. J. ROYALL TIPPETT, JR.), civic worker; b. Balt., Mar. 17, 1922; d. Maurice Charles and Katharine (Randall) Pincoffs; grad. Johns Hopkins Hosp. Sch. Nursing, 1946; A.B., Vassar Coll., 1943; spl. student Johns Hopkins Sch. Hygiene and Pub. Health, 1947; m. J. Royall Tippett, Jr., Apr. 20, 1951; children—J. Royall III, Susan Randall, Ann Thornton. Staff nurse out-patient dept. Johns Hopkins Hosp., Balt., 1947, instr. pub. health nursing, 1952; asst. dir. med. care clinic U. Md., 1948-51; instr. gen. sci. Roland Park Country Sch., 1965-68. With religious edn. dept. Cathedral of Mary Our Queen, Balt., 1960-72, chmn. high sch. religion, 1968-70; mem. Mayor's Task Force on Nutrition, 1969-70; pres. Md. Food Com., Inc., 1969-71, exec. dir., 1971—. Mem. Am. Nurses Assn., Catholic Evidence League. Club: Md. Vassar. Home: 4801 Keswick Rd Baltimore MD 21210

TIPTON, DIANE MARIE, library exec.; b. Helena, Mont., July 6, 1950; d. Walter H. and Mary Ellen (Wetzstein) Tipton; student Carroll Coll., 1968-69; B.A. in Radio-TV and Elementary Edn. (Honor scholar, Cable TV Ednl. TV scholar), U. Mont., 1972. Prodn. asst., traffic mgr. U. Mont. radio, Missoula, 1969-72; actress Old Brewery Theatre, Helena, 1972; counselor career edn. Helena Pub. Schs., 1972-73; community relations dir. Helena Pub. Library, 1973—. Pub. relations chmn. Camp Fire Girls, 1973-74; treas. Community Recipient Chet Huntly award Brewery Theatre, 1968.

Mem. Nat., Mont. edn. assns., Women in Communications (treas. U. Mont. 1970-71, pres. U. Mont. 1971-72), Friends Helena Library, Lewis and Clark Reading Assn. (pres. 1974), Mortar Bd., Phi Kappa Phi. Home: 809 N Warren St Helena MT 59601 Office: 325 N Park Helena MT 59601

TIPTON, PAULA M. (MRS. GEORGE ALICESON TIPTON), lawyer; b. N.Y.C., Apr. 2, 1936; d. Samuel S. and Doris (Fromkin) Edelman; B.A., Hunter Coll., 1957; J.D., Loyola U., Los Angeles, 1967; m. George Aliceson Tipton, Sept. 19, 1969. Admitted to Cal. bar, 1967; practiced in North Hollywood, Cal., 1967-70, Wrightwood, Cal., 1971—; law clk. Hurley and Grassini, North Hollywood, Cal., 1963-67, asso. firm, 1967-69. Mem. Am. (com. copyright div. 1973-74), Los Angeles County, San Bernardino County bar assns., Cal. Trial Lawyers Assn., Environmental Def. Fund, Center for Law in Public Interest. Home: Star Route Box 40 Wrightwood CA 92397 Office: 1576 State Hwy 2 Wrightwood CA 92397

TIREBUCK, BETTY IRENE, nurse; b. West Garafraxa Twp., Wellington County, Can., July 3, 1937; d. Benson Orton and Margaret Irene (Byers) Boys; grad. Guelph (Ont.) Gen. Hosp. Sch. Nurses, 1958; diploma in nursing edn. U. Western Ont., 1961-62; m. Trevor Tirebuck, Oct. 19, 1973. Gen. duty nurse Guelph Gen. Hosp., 1958-60, asst. head nurse operating room, 1960-61, tchr. operating room, 1962-63, head nurse operating room, 1963—. Partner, Espada Internat. Mem. Registered Nurses Assn. Ont., Guelph Gen. Hosp. Nurses Alumnae (pres. 1966-68), U. Western Ont. Alumnae, Beta Sigma Phi (chpt. treas. 1971-72, pres. 1973-74). Clubs: Guelph Racquets (treas. 1970-71). Home: 37-7 Wilsonview Av Guelph ON N1G 2W5 Canada Office: 115 Delhi St Guelph ON Canada

TIRRE, BARBARA CARAMELLA (MRS. JOSEPH C. TIRRE), educator; b. Paterson, N.J., May 5, 1935; d. William Joseph and Mafalda Erminia (Benedetto) Caramella; B.S., Syracuse U., 1957; M.A., 1966; postgrad. Washington U., 1971; m. Joseph C. Tirre, July 12, 1958; children—J. Conrad, William C. Women's editor, continuity dir. WWBZ radio, Vineland, N.J., 1957-58; dir. publicity Conti Advt. Co., Ridgewood, N.J., 1958; copywriter KCNY, San Marcos, Tex., 1959; tchr. Henninger High Sch., Syracuse, N.Y., 1966-67; mem. faculty So. Ill. U., Edwardsville, 1967—, instr. broadcasting, mass communications, 1970—. Instr. speech and English, Belleville (Ill.) Area Jr. Coll., 1967-68; instr. speech Washington U., St. Louis, 1967-70. Bd. dirs. So. County Jr. Football, 1963—. Mem. Speech Communications Assn., Nat. Acad. TV Arts and Scis., Am. Women in Radio and TV, Delta Sigma Rho, Zeta Phi Eta, Alpha Chi Omega. Home: 6 Hawthorne Ct Oakland MO 63122 Office: Southern Illinois University Edwardsville IL 62225

TISCHLER, ROSE HANDLER (MRS. LOUIS PRIMUS TISCHLER), civic worker; b. Amsterdam, N.Y., Nov. 19, 1910; d. Louis and Esther (Weinberg) Handler; A.B., N.Y. State Coll. Edn., Albany, 1930; m. Louis Primus Tischler, Dec. 23, 1931; children—Judith (Mrs. William Marks Goldstein), Howard, Paul, Emily (Mrs. Kim LeVasseur). Tchr., Wilbur H. Lynch Sr. High Sch., Amsterdam, 1930-35. Chmn. women's div. Schenectady County Community Chest Campaign, 1950, bd. dirs., Schenectady, 1950-52; mem. nominating com., 1961, co-chmn. spl. gifts, 1963, 66; pres. Schenectady County Med. Soc. Woman's Aux., 1957-58; chmn. press and publicity com. N.Y. State Med. Soc. Aux., 1958-59, councilor 4th dist., 1961-62, 66-68, nominating com., 1960, chmn. health careers, 1963-64, corr. sec., 1964-66, pres. elect 1968-69, pres., 1969-70, chmn. nominating com., 1970-71; pres. Schenectady County Sr. Citizens Center, 1959-61, bd. dirs., 1970—, v.p., 1973-74, chmn. capital campaign, 1975, pres. Nat. Council Jewish Women, Schenectady, 1959-62, mem. nat. overseas com. 1963-67, hon. v.p., 1966—; chmn. women's div. Schenectady Federated Welfare Fund, United Jewish Appeal, 1963-68, 70; chmn. residential div. of Schenectady County Cancer Crusade, 1959; mem. adv. bd. Vol. Bur. Community Welfare Council, Schenectady, 1959-63; mem. organizing com. Schenectady Citizens Com. for Pub. Schs., 1960; mem. Schenectady County Com. to Study Chronic Illness, 1960-62; del. N.Y. State Regional Conf. on Aging, 1960; mem. nominating com. Schenectady Community Welfare Council, 1961-62; mem. organizing com. Schenectady Found., 1962-64; chmn. organizing com. Home Care Program Schenectady County, 1962-64; mem. City Council Youth Guidance Commn., 1961-63, Schenectady Community Leaders Conf., 1968—. Bd. dirs. Capitol Dist. Travelers Aid Soc. (v.p. 1966-68), bd. dirs. Am. Cancer Soc., Schenectady, 1959-65; mem. organizing com. Schenectady United Fund, 1965, v.p., dir., 1966-68, co-chmn. spl. gifts, 1967, 1st v.p., 1970-71; pres., 1971-72, chmn. residential div., 1972. Named Vol. of Year United Fund, 1972; recipient numerous awards including Distinguished Alumnus award State U. N.Y. at Albany, 1974, Distinguished Service award B'nai B'rith, 1974. Mem. N.A.A.C.P., League Women Voters, Alumni Assn., N.Y. State Coll. Edn., Hadassah, Pi Gamma Mu, Pi Alpha Tau. Jewish religion (pres. Sisterhood 1948-50, 51-53, hon. dir. 1958, chmn. bldg. fund campaign 1955-58, trustee congregation 1957-60). Home: 1177 Ruffner Rd Schenectady NY 12309

TISDALE, BARBARA, librarian; b. Boston, Dec. 24, 1913; d. Charles Henry and Nancy (Wood) Tisdale; A.B. cum laude, Radcliffe Coll., 1935, postgrad., 1942-43; B.S. in L.S., Syracuse U., 1940; postgrad. Queens Coll., 1958-65; M.A., N.Y.U., 1971; postgrad. Cath. U. of Milan, Rome, 1970. Asst. catalogue dept. Harvard U. Library, 1936-39; librarian various schs., Mass., 1940-42; asst. librarian, cataloger Northeastern U. Library, Boston, 1942-43; librarian high sch., Bristol, Conn., 1943-45; reference and circulation asst. bus. dept. Columbia U. Library, N.Y.C., 1945-46; extension librarian Great Neck (N.Y.) Library, 1946-50, Lakeville br. librarian, 1951—. Mem. A.L.A., Nassau County Library Assn., League Women Voters Great Neck, Nat. Trust for Historic Preservation, Internat. Platform Assn. Club: Radcliffe (L.I. and N.Y., L.I. book sale chmn. 1961-62). Home: 24 Terrace Circle Apt 4A Great Neck NY 11021 Office: 475 Great Neck Rd Great Neck NY 11021

TISDALE, MARILYN ELIZABETH, occupational therapist; b. Wilmington, Del., May 24, 1928; d. Wendell Holmes and Elizabeth Emma Wilhelmina (Koch) Tisdale; B.A. in Psychology, Ohio Wesleyan U., 1949; B.S. in Occupational Therapy, Ohio State U., 1951; postgrad. Columbia, 1958. Asst. dir. then acting dir. occupational therapy Buffalo Children's Hosp., 1951-52; occupational therapist Meadowbrook Hosp., Hempstead, N.Y., 1953-55; supr. occupational therapy Parkview Meml. Hosp., Ft. Wayne, Ind., 1955-66; supr. occupational therapy Leach Sch., New Castle, Del., 1966—. Mem. Am., Del. occupational therapy assns., Phi Beta Kappa, Theta Alpha Phi. Home: 402 Faulk Rd Apt 2A7 Wilmington DE 19803 Office: Leach School Landers Lane New Castle DE 19720

TISINGER, CATHERINE ANNE, coll. adminstr.; b. Winchester, Va., Apr. 6, 1936; d. Richard Martin and Irma (Ohl) Tisinger; B.A., Coll. Wooster, 1958; M.A., U. Pa., 1962, Ph.D., 1970. Asst. prof. Asian studies State U. N.Y. Coll. at Oneonta, 1964-67; asst. prof. social sci., Asian studies Callison Coll., U. Pacific, Stockton, Cal., 1967-70, asso. prof., 1970-72, acting provost, 1971-72; v.p. adminstrv. affairs, treas., dean learning resources Minn. Met. State Coll., St. Paul, 1972—. Cons. non-traditional studies. Nat. Def. Fgn. Lang. fellow, 1959-63; Am. Council Learned Socs. fellow, 1972. Mem. Assn. Asian Studies, Am. Acad. Polit. and Social Sci., Women Historians of Midwest. Home: 62 S Dale St St Paul MN 55102

TISZA, VERONICA ELIZABETH BENEDEK, physician; b. Szeged, Hungary; M.D., U. Budapest (Hungary), 1937; m. Laszlo Tisza, 1938 (div. 1963). Came to U.S., 1941, naturalized, 1946. Intern, New Eng. Hosp., Boston, 1942-43; resident Boston Floating Hosp., Mass. Gen. Hosp.; practice medicine specializing in pediatrics and psychiatry, Boston, 1947—; asst. prof. pediatrics and psychiatry Tufts U. Med. Sch., 1952-59, asso. prof. psychiatry, 1959-61; asso. prof. child psychiatry U. Pitts. Med. Sch., 1961-68; asst. prof. psychiatry Harvard Med. Sch., 1969-73, asso. prof., 1973—; dir. psychiat. services for children New Eng. Med. Center, 1952-61; sr. asso. psychiatry Childrens Hosp. Med. Center, 1969—, dir. tng., 1969; dir. tng. Judge Baker Guidance Center, 1969—. Vis. psychiatrist Hampstead Health Nursery, London, Eng., 1968-69. Diplomate Am. Bd. Pediatrics, Am. Bd. Psychiatry, Nat. Bd. Med. Examiners. Mem. Am. Acad. Pediatrics, Am. Acad. Child Psychiatry, Am. Psychiat. Assn., Am. Orthopsychiat. Assn., Boston Psychoanalytic Soc. and Inst., Pitts. Psychoanalytic Soc. Home: 221 Mount Auburn St Cambridge MA 02138 Office: 300 Longwood Av Boston MA 02115

TITELBAUM, OLGA ADLER (MRS. SYDNEY TITELBAUM), translator, editor; b. Petrograd, Russia, Feb. 2, 1916; d. Michael and Sophie (Gunther) Adler; brought to U.S., 1921, naturalized, 1927; B.A. in Geography, U. Chgo., 1937, Ph.D. in Slavic Linguistics, 1967; m. Sydney Titelbaum, Mar. 20, 1939; 1 son, Daniel Ethan. Statis. sec. grad. library sch. U. Chgo., 1935-41; research asst. atlas Ency. Brit., 1941, 55, asst. geography editor, 1967-73; editor, translator NSF Survey of East European Math. Lit., U. Chgo., 1959-61; cons., editor Follett Pub. Co., Chgo., 1964-65; lectr. Geography of USSR, U. Chgo. Downtown Coll., 1959, 60. Mem. Assn. Am. Geographers, League Women Voters (chmn. Chgo. Southwest Water Resources com. 1957-58, editor Chicago Voter 1958-60, mem. Ill. Water Resources Com.). Translations from Russian include: Natural Regions of the USSR (L.S. Berg), 1950; (with Robert M. Hankin) Economic Geography of the USSR (Balzak, Feigin, Vasyutin), 1949; (with Alfred K. Henn) Mistakes in Geometric Proof (Dubnov), 1963; (with Norman D. Whaland, Jr.) The Fibonacci Numbers (Vorobyov), 1963; (with A.W. Goodman) Induction in Geometry (Golovina and Yaglom), 1963; (with Norman D. Whaland, Jr.), Random Walks (Dynkin and Uspenskii), 1963, trans. from Macedonian, also author Glossary Handbook for the Study of the Macedonian Language (Ruzha Punoska and Aleksandar Dzhukeski), 2d edit., 1971; also trans. articles in jours. Author: Glossary of Water Resource Terms, 1970. Contbr. articles to profl. publs. Home: 2003 W 102d St Chicago IL 60643

TITMUS, ALETHA RIEDEL (MRS. THOMAS JOSEPH TITMUS), lawyer; b. San Francisco, Dec. 23, 1933; d. George H. and Aletha Lee (Ellsworth) Riedel; A.B. in Art and Speech, U. Cal. at Berkeley, 1959; postgrad. Heidelberg (Germany) U., 1957, Hastings Coll. of Law, 1966; J.D., Golden Gate U., 1963; m. Thomas Joseph Titmus, July 9, 1960. Admitted to Cal. bar, 1964, U.S. Ct. of Appeals bar, 1964, U.S. Dist. Ct. bar, 1964, U.S. Supreme Ct. bar, 1971; asst. to v.p. and gen. counsel Regents of U. Cal., Office of the Gen. Counsel, Berkeley, 1964-65, asst. to Gen. Counsel, atty. residence matters, 1965-67, asst. counsel of regents, 1967—. Mem. faculty San Francisco Law Sch., 1973—. Chmn. Children's Hosp. Med. Center, Oakland, Cal., 1969-70; mem. San Francisco Mus. Art Assn., 1960—, Oakland (Cal.) Symphony Guild, 1964—, San Francisco Opera Guild, 1969—. Exhibited paintings in group shows at U. Cal. Art Mus., 1958-59, 65, ann. art shows State Bar Cal., 1965, 67, 70. Bd. dirs. Alumni Council Golden Gate U., 1973—, Women's Faculty Club, U. Cal. at Berkeley, 1968-72. Mem. Nat. Assn. Women Lawyers, Alameda County Bar Assn., State Bar Cal. (mem. com. on continuing edn. of the bar 1972—), U. Cal. Alumni Assn., Queen's Bench. Home: 9 La Punta Orinda CA 94563 Office: 590 University Hall 2200 University Av Berkeley CA 94720

TITO DE MORAES, MARIA PALMIRA, internat. nurse council exec.; b. Lisbon, Portugal; d. Augusto and Caroline Loureiro (deMacedo) Tito deMoraes; M.A., Columbia, 1959; Licence es Lettres, U. Lisbon, Faculty of Letters, 1950; certificate pub. health nursing U. Toronto (Ont., Can.) Sch. Nursing, 1939. Chief Pub. Health Nursing Services, Centro de Saude de Lisboa, Dept. Health, Lisbon, 1939-50; prof. pub. health nursing Escola Tecnica de Enfermeiras, Lisbon, 1940-50; nursing adviser WHO, missions in Syria, Iran, Central Am., Egypt, Brazil, Geneva, Switzerland, 1951-66, regional officer for nursing Regional Office for Europe, Copenhagen, Denmark, 1966-72; nurse adviser Internat. Council Nurses, Geneva, 1972—. Rockefeller Found. fellow, 1935-39, 58-60. Mem. Grad. Nurses Assn. (Lisbon), Am. Sociol. Assn., Nat. Soc. Study Edn., The Soc. for Applied Anthropology, A.A.A.S., Kappa Delta Pi, Pi Lambda Theta. Home: 52 rue de Moillebeau Geneva Switzerland Office: Internat Council Nurses 37 rue de Vermont Geneva Switzerland

TITUS, CATHERINE FONTELLE, educator; b. Lexington, Mo., Dec. 13, 1909; d. William Eben and Myrtle (Patton) Titus; A.B., Central Coll., Fayette, Mo., 1931; M.A., U. Mo., 1950, Ph.D., 1955. Tchr. Richmond (Mo.) High Sch., 1932-43, 46, Trenton (Mo.) Jr. Coll., 1947-52; instr. U. Mo., 1953-55; asst. prof. English, Central Mo. State U., Warrensburg, 1956-58, asso. prof., 1959-63, prof., 1964—, head English dept., 1969—, dir. honors program, 1958-69. Mem. Mo. Assn. Tchrs. English (past pres.), Alpha Gamma Delta (alumna sponsor Central Mo. State Coll. chpt. 1959-68), Delta Kappa Gamma (v.p. 1952), Sigma Tau Delta (sponsor Central Mo. State Coll. chpt. 1961-68). Home: 104 Meadow Lane Warrensburg MO 64093

TJELTA, (INGA) TOMINE, educator; b. Radcliffe, Ia., Sept. 6, 1909; d. Torger and Inger (Ravnaas) Tjelta; student Luth. Bible Inst., Mpls., 1926-27, Ia. State Agrl. Coll., Ames, summer 1942; R.N., Swedish Hosp. Sch. Nursing, Mpls., 1946; postgrad. U. Minn., summer 1950; B.S., U. Wash., 1954, M.A., 1958, Ph.D., 1965. Tchr. pub. schs. Hardin, Hamilton Counties, Ia., 1927-43; staff nurse Meml. Hosp., Eldora, Ia., 1946-47; asst. nursing arts instr. Ia. Meth. Hosp., Des Moines, 1947-48, clin. instr. surg. nursing, 1949; instr. nursing arts Allen Meml. Hosp., Waterloo, Ia., 1949-52; staff nurse Swedish Hosp., Seattle, 1952-54; instr. med. nursing Sch. Nursing U. Wash., Seattle, 1954-59, instr., 1963-64, pre-doctoral asso., 1964-65, asst. prof., 1965-70, project dir. Program for Nursing Care Patients with Coronary Disease with Dept. Health, Edn. and Welfare, USPHS Nat. Center for Chronic Disease Control, Heart Disease and Stroke Control Program, 1967-70; prof., chmn. dept. nursing Coll. St. Benedict, St. Joseph, Minn., 1970-74; prof., dir. nursing Oral Roberts U., Tulsa, 1974—. Recipient Tng. grant USPHS, 1957-58, Sigma Theta Tau research grant, 1965-67; USPHS Spl. Nurse research fellow, 1959-63. Mem. Am. Nurses Assn., Nat. League Nursing, Am. Edn. Research Assn., Nat. Council Measurement in Edn., Am. Sci. Affiliation, Am. Heart Assn., Alpha Tau Delta, Sigma Theta Tau, Pi Lambda Theta. Lutheran. Home: 11762 S 76th East Av Bixby OK 74008 Office: Oral Roberts University Tulsa OK 74102

TOAL, JEAN HOEFER (MRS. WILLIAM THOMAS TOAL), lawyer; b. Columbia, S.C., Aug. 11, 1943; d. Herbert Wellington and Lilla Florence (Farrell) Hoefer; B.A., Agnes Scott Coll., 1965; J.D., U. S.C., 1968; m. William Thomas Toal, Aug. 27, 1967; 1 dau., Jean Hoefer. Admitted to S.C. bar, 1968; asso. firm Haynsworth, Perry, Bryant, Marion & Johnstone, Greenville, S.C., 1968-70. Belser, Belser, Baker, Barwick & Toal, Columbia, S.C., 1970—; dir. Am. Exec. Life Ins. Co. Mem. S.C. State Commn. on Human Affairs, 1972—; mem. indsl. adv. bd. S.C. Dept. Corrections. Bd. dirs. Opportunities Industrialization Centers Columbia. Mem. S.C. State Bar, S.C., Richland County bar assns. Democrat. Roman Catholic. Clubs: Columbia Business and Professional Women, Zonta (Columbia). Mng. editor S.C. Law Rev., 1968. Home: 2418 Wheat St Columbia SC 29205 Office: PO Box 11690 1213 Lady St Columbia SC 29201

TOBIAS, ARLENE RUTH, organizer; b. Alsask, Sask., Can., June 4, 1933 (parents Am. citizens); d. Andrew Alert and Gunda Elvira (Johnson) Tobias; B.S., U. Wis. at Superior, 1961; postgrad. in Theatre Arts, U. Minn. Tchr. speech and drama, pub. schs., Wausau, Wis., 1961-67; editor Wis. Ednl. Assn., Madison, 1967-73, tchr. rep., 1973—. Publicity chmn. Madison Theatre Guild, 1971. Bd. dirs. Wausau Community Theatre. Mem. N.E.A., Reno Classroom Tchrs. (pres. elect 1957), Wausau Edn. Assn. (pub. relations chmn. 1964), Alpha Psi Omega (pres. 1960), Zeta Phi Eta. Home: 1116 Crocker St Wausau WI 54401 Office: 3303 Terrace Ct Wausau WI 54401

TOBIAS, JEAN FRANCES, city ofcl.; b. Pulaski County, Ill., June 15, 1922; d. Francis John and Eleanor Lucille (Tilley) Campbell; m. Lloyd Delmore Tobias, Jr., Apr. 17, 1943; children—Lloyd Delmore III, Gregory J., Jane (Mrs. James Miller), James R., Celeste M. Former dep. dir. Fairfield County Bd. Elections; now city treas. Lancaster, O. Sec. treas. Fairfield County Democratic exec. and central coms. Recipient Adult of Year award Camp Fire Girls, 1972. Mem. Fairfield County Heritage Assn. Home: 219 Wilson Av Lancaster OH 43130 Office: City Bldg E Main St Lancaster OH 43130

TOBIAS, SHEILA, coll. adminstr.; b. N.Y.C., Apr. 26, 1935; d. Paul Jay and Rose (Steinberger) Tobias; B.A., Radcliffe Coll., 1957; M.A., Columbia, 1961, M.Phil., 1974; m. Carlos Stern. Journalist, The Am. Weekend, Frankfurt, Germany, 1958-60, Nat. Ednl. TV, ABC-TV, 1963-64; lectr. history Coll. City N.Y., 1965-67; asst. to the v.p. acad. affairs Cornell U., Ithaca, N.Y., 1967-70; asso. provost Wesleyan U., Middletown, Conn., 1970—. Pres. Alert, Inc. Mem. Nat. Council Hampshire Coll., Amherst, Mass., 1972—. Bd. dirs. Women's Action Alliance, Women's Law Fund, Assn. Am. Colls. Project on Women, Nat. Orgn. Women Legal Def. and Edn. Fund. Mem. Profl. Women's Caucus (pres. 1971-72), Phi Beta Kappa. Editor: Cornell Conf. on Women, 1969; Female Studies I, 1970. Home: Macht Rd Columbia CT 06237 Office: Provost Office Wesleyan Univ Middletown CT 06457

TOBIN, AVIS ANN, assn. exec.; b. Helena, Mont.; d. Richard D. and Blanche H. (Sites) Tobin; student U. Mont., 1939-40. With Mont. Hardware and Implement Assn., Helena, 1954—, exec. sec., 1964—. Dir. Home Fed. Savs. and Loan Assn. Dir. Mont. Hwy. Users Conf. Mem. Mont. Unemployment Adv. Council, 1967—; mem. adv. council Helena Vo-Tech Sch. Treas. Mont. Govs. Prayer Breakfast. Mem. Daus. of Nile. Clubs: Metropolitan Dinner (pres., dir.) (Helena), Helena Soroptimist (dir.). Home: 1525 Beaverhead Rd Helena MT 59601 Office: 506 Lamborn PO Box 1152 Helena MT 59601

TOBIN, CLARA MATILDA, mag. pub. co. exec.; b. Willard, Wash., Mar. 17, 1900; d. Emil and Barbara Elizabeth (Egger) Willard; student Western Wash. Coll. of Edn. 1919-21, U. Wash., 1924; m. Emery Fridolf Tobin, Oct. 15, 1926; 1 dau., Doris Lorraine (Mrs. Gordon Wesley Bordine). Tchr. pub. schs., Willard, Wash., 1921-24, Seattle, 1924-25, Seldovia, Alaska, 1925-26. Ketchikan, Alaska, 1928-29; mng. editor Alaska Sportsman mag., 1935-58; partner Alaska Mag. Pub. Co., 1935-67. Treas. Ketchikan Women's Rep. Club 1955-56. Organized first troop Girl Scouts, Ketchikan, 1928. Mem. C. of C. Pioneers of Alaska Auxiliary, Mazamas, Am. Legion Auxiliary (pres. 1928), Skamania County, Ore., Tongass (charter mem.), Ft. Vancouver hist. socs. Club: Soroptimist (life, pres. 1953). Home: 4304 Willamette Ct Southcliff Vancouver WA 98661

TOBIN, MARGARET MARY, librarian; b. Scranton, Pa., Oct. 11, 1928; d. Thomas Henry and Mary F. (Ferrick) Tobin; B.A., Marywood Coll., 1950; M.Ed., Duquesne U., 1958; postgrad. Pa. State U. 1962—. Instr. St. Francis Coll., Loretto, Pa., 1950-58, asst. prof., 1958-62, asso. prof., 1963—, asst. librarian, 1950-62, asso. librarian, 1962-66, head librarian, 1966—. Cons. Barnesboro (Pa.) Pub. Library, 1960. Mem. Am. Assn. U. Profs., Am., Pa., Cath. library assns., Bus. and Profl. Women's Club. Roman Catholic. Author: (with V.R. Negherbon) Bibliographic and Library Manual, 1953; rev. edit., 1962. Contbr. articles to profl. jours. Home: 8A College Heights St Loretto PA 15940

TOBIN, MARILYN, editor; b. Plainfield, N.J., Nov. 8, 1936; d. Vincent Nelson and Muriel (Packard) Tobin; A.S. cum laude, Keystone Jr. Coll., 1956. Editor, Lab. Equipment, Gordon Publs., Inc., Morristown, N.J., 1966—, Archtl. Products, 1966-71, Industria Quimica, 1971-73, Heating and Plumbing Merchandiser, 1974—. Computer, Morris County Civil Def., 1966-68. Recipient Kitzbuhel (Austria) Gold star for 50 different ski runs, 1968. Mem. Am. Bus. Press. Club: Madison Ski (rec. sec., trustee). Home: 1133 Evergreen Av Plainfield NJ 07060 Office: 20 Community Pl Morristown NJ 07960

TOBIN, MARY HELEN (RIV) (MRS. ALBERT KIEFER TOBIN), journalist; b. Chgo., Feb. 15, 1919; d. Harry Gilman and Helen Mary (Taylor) Jordan; B.S. in Edn., U. Ill., 1940; M.A. in Edn., Northwestern U., 1946; m. Albert Kiefer Tobin, Jan. 2, 1947; 1 son, Gilman Taylor. Soc. editor, feature articles writer, Honolulu Advertiser, 1961-67; columnist Copley News Service, San Diego, 1969—. Bd. dirs. Hawaii chpt. Easter Seal Soc., 1965-73; bd. dirs. Hawaii chpt. A.R.C., sec., 1963-64. Mem. Nat. League Am. Pen Women (pres. Hawaii chpt. 1972), Freedoms Found. at Valley Forge (charter mem. Hawaii chpt.), Theta Sigma Phi, Gamma Phi Beta. Home: 32 Antigua Villa Coronado CA 92118 Office: Box 190 San Diego CA 92112

TOBOLOWSKY, HERMINE DALKOWITZ (MRS. HYMAN M. TOBOLOWSKY), lawyer; b. San Antonio, Jan. 13, 1921; d. Maurice and Nora (Brown) Dalkowitz; student Incarnate Word Coll., 1938-39, U. San Antonio, 1939-40; LL.B., U. Tex., 1943; m. Hyman M. Tobolowsky, Aug. 19, 1951. Admitted to Tex. bar, 1943; mem. firm Lang, Byrd, Cross & Lodon, San Antonio, 1943-47; pvt. practice law, San Antonio, 1947-51, Dallas, 1951—. Mem. Nat. Health Adv. Council, Surgeon Gen. U.S., Washington, 1966-69. State chmn. for passage Equal Legal Rights Amendment to Tex. Constn. and Ratification Equal Rights Amendment to U.S. Constn., 1971-72. Mem. Nat. Assn. Women Lawyers, Bus. and Profl. Women's Club (state pres. 1959-60, chpt. pres. 1958-59, legislation chmn. Tex. fedn. 1961—), Dallas Citizens Traffic Assn. (dir.), Dallas Women's Forum (parliamentarian 1972-74), State Bar Tex., Delta Kappa Gamma. Address: 6247 Desco Dr Dallas TX 75225

TOBRINER, ALICE LENA, educator; b. Honolulu, May 17, 1922; d. Leon and Anna Cecilia (Monihan) Tobriner; A.B., Holy Names Coll., 1943; M.A., Stanford U., 1960, Ph.D. (scholar 1964), 1966. Tchr., counselor Marin Cath. High Sch., Kentfield, 1961-64, Ramona Convent High Sch., Alhambra, 1966-68; dean of students Holy Names Coll., Oakland, Cal., 1953-61, asso. prof. edn., chmn. edn. dept., 1970—; asst. prof. edn. Cal. State U. at Los Angeles, 1967-70. Del. White House Conf. on Children, Washington, 1970. Recipient Impact Tchr. Award, Nat. Cath. Edn. Assn., 1967. Mem. Holy Names Order, Renaissance Soc. Am., Am. Hist. Assn., History of Edn. Soc. Author: J.L. Vives' Introduction to Wisdom, 1968; A Sixteenth Century Urban Report, 1971. Address: 3500 Mountain Blvd Oakland CA 94619

TOCZEK, ARIADNE MAYAKIS (MRS. STANISLAW K. TOCZEK), pediatric neurologist; b. Athens, Greece, Oct. 31, 1927 (parents Am. citizens); d. Eros Alexander and Maria (Dagdelenis) Mayakis; student Coll. St. Rose of Lima, 1943-44; B.A., U. Cal. at Los Angeles, 1946; M.D., Woman's Med. Coll., 1955; m. Stanislaw K. Toczek, Feb. 27, 1961; children—Andrzej, Maria Tekla. Research asst. AEC, U. Cal. at Los Angeles, 1950-51; intern Misericordia Hosp., Phila., 1955-56; resident pediatrics Highland Alameda County Hosp. Oakland, Cal., 1956-57; with Kaiser-Permanente Med. Services of So. Cal., Los Angeles, 1957-59; resident pediatrics U. Cal. at Los Angeles, 1960-61; United Cerebral Palsy Post Doctoral Research fellow pediatric neurology U. Cal. at Los Angeles Med. Center, 1961; physician Army Presidio, San Francisco, 1962-63; pediatric neurologist Presbyn. Hosp., San Francisco, 1962; physician Modesto (Cal.) State Hosp., 1963; with Bur. Medicine, Investigative Neurosycho-Pharmacology, FDA, Arlington, Va., 1966-67; pvt. practice medicine specializing in pediatric neurology, Arlington, 1968—; mem. staff Fairfax (Va.) Hosp.; cons. United Cerebral Palsy Nursery Schs., Los Angeles, 1961. Mem. Am., Am. Womens med. assns., Women's Med. Coll. Alumni Assn., Arlington County Med. Soc. Mem. Greek Orthodox Ch. Contbr. articles to profl. jours. Address: 4833 Yorktown Blvd Arlington VA 22207

TODD, DELLA PEPPER, educator; b. Marshall, Tex., Dec. 3, 1925; d. Elisha Joshua and Faith Lamar (Cirlot) Pepper; B.A., Southwestern U., 1946; M.S., East Tex. State U., 1965, Ph.D., 1970; postgrad. Tex. Woman's U., 1965-66, Tex. U., 1966-67; m. Harold C. Todd, Oct. 19, 1947; children—Harold C., Lela Lamar. Vocational adjustment coordinator Longview (Tex.) Sch. Dist., 1961-66; dir. spl. edn. Pine Tree Ind. Sch., Longview, 1966-73; asst. prof. spl. edn. East Tex. State U., Commerce, 1970—, head dept., 1973—. Bd. dirs. Windamere Sch. for Children With Learning Disabilities, Longview. Named Outstanding Educator of Tex., Civitans, 1973. Mem. Tex. Assn. Ednl. Diagnosticians (bd. advisers 1972—), Council for Exceptional Children (pres., bd. advisers 1970-72), Tex. Council for Adminstrs. Spl. Edn. (sec. 1970). Mem. Order of Eastern Star (matron 1963-64). Home: 3002 Tanglewood St Commerce TX 75428 Office: Special Education Dept East Texas State University Commerce TX 75428

TODD, DOROTHY ANN, social worker; b. Lexington, Ky., Mar. 30, 1940; d. Joseph Joplin and Jean (Johnson) Todd; B.A., Wake Forest Coll., 1961; M.S.W., U. Denver, 1963. Psychiat. social worker U. Colo. Med. Center, Denver, 1963-70, instr, dept. psychiatry U. Colo., 1967-70; clin. social worker Contra Costa County Mental Health Clinic, Martinez, Cal., 1970-71; asst. dir., treatment leader Denver Childrens Home, 1971—. Cons. Denver pub. schs. Fellow Am. Orthopsychiat. Assn.; mem. Nat. Assn. Social Work, Acad. Certified Social Workers. Home: 2555 Dahlia St Denver CO 80207 Office: 1501 Albion St Denver CO 80206

TODD, DOROTHY VAUGHN, occupational therapist; b. Herrin, Ill., Jan. 10, 1918; d. William Richard and Bridget Hanora (Slattery) Todd; student So. Ill. U., 1947-48; B.S., Western Mich. U., 1951; postgrad. Syracuse U., 1954, U. Ill., 1970-71, Western Ill. U., 1971. Dir. occupational therapy St. John's Sanitorium, Springfield, Ill., 1951-53; occupational therapist Springfield (Ill.) pub. schs., 1953—. Mem. Am., Ill. Occupational Therapy assns., Council for Exceptional Children (life), Assn. for Study Perception (life). Home: 1516 Fairfield Dr Springfield IL 62702 Office: Hay Edwards School 400 W Lawrence St Springfield IL 62704

TODD, ESTHER STEVENS (MRS. OWEN WILLIAM TODD), librarian; b. Wenatchee, Wash., Dec. 5, 1914; d. Edward Francis and Loraine Emily (Johnson) Stevens; A.A. (Lanham Found. scholar), Wenatchee Jr. Coll., 1947; B.A., U. Wash., 1949, teaching certificate, 1950; postgrad. U. Minn., 1955; M.L.S., U. Wash., 1964; m. Owen William Todd, June 12, 1960. With traffic dept. Interstate Telephone Co., Wenatchee, Wash., 1933-54, instr. traffic dept. employees, 1941-45; tchr. typing and lang. arts, librarian Peshastin (Wash.) High Sch., 1950-56, also adviser drama; librarian Eastmont High Sch., East Wenatchee, Wash., 1956—. Mem. Columbia River Information Specialists. Active Nat. Polio Week campaign, 1955. Mem. Ind. Telephone Women Employees Assn. (pres. 1935), Nat., Wash., Eastmont edn. assns., Wash. Assn. Sch. Librarians (area-chmn. 1960-62, mem. state constn. com. 1962-64), Adminstrv. Women in Edn. (chmn. North Central council 1967-69, treas. Wash. council 1971-72), A.L.A., Wash. Christian Endeavor Union (devotional chmn. 1935), Wash. Chess Fedn., Wenatchee Valley Humane Soc. Baptist (chmn. local Pioneer Girls 1956-71, mem. library com. 1970—). Home: 2 S Garfield Av Wenatchee WA 98801 Office: 270 9th St NE East Wenatchee WA 98801

TODD, KAREN IRIS ROHNE PRITCHETT (MRS. RONALD D. TODD), educator; b. nr. Cranfills Gap, Tex., Dec. 21, 1936; d. Ernest J. and Clarice (Bertelson) Rohne; B.S., N. Tex. State U., 1957, M.S., 1961; Ph.D., U. Ia., 1965; student Fla. State U., 1962; m. Tom Pritchett, Dec. 22, 1957 (div. June 1967); 1 son, T. Gordon; m. 2d, Ronald D. Todd, May 30, 1969; 1 dau., Roni Kristin; 1 stepdau., Stephanie Todd. Tchr., Roswell (N.M.) Jr. High Sch., 1957-58, Andrews (Tex.) Sch. System, 1958-59; nursery sch. asst. N. Tex. State U., Denton, 1960-61, asst. prof. psychology, 1964-65; research, asst. U. Ia., Iowa City, 1962-64; asst. dir. dept. psychology Ednl. Research Council of Am., Cleve., 1965-68; asst. prof. edn., dir. master's degree program for elementary tchrs. Cleve. State U., 1968-70; adj. prof. N.Y. U., 1972—; research and evaluation specialist Ednl. Improvement Center N.W. N.J., 1973—. Cons., Ednl. Research Council Am., Creative Learning Systems Ednl. Alliance. Mem. Am. Psychol. Assn., Nat. Soc. Study Edn., Am. Ednl. Research Assn., League Women Voters, Common Cause. Democrat. Presbyn. Home: 12 Holmes Av New Providence NJ 07974

TODD, MARY ELIZABETH (MRS. ALVA CRESS TODD), ednl. adminstr.; b. Lafayette, Ind., Aug. 26, 1920; d. Christian Frederick and Anna Marie (Mahlke) Schelle; diploma Ind. Bus. Coll., 1940; m. Alva Cress Todd, Apr. 17, 1941; children—Richard Schelle, Carol (Mrs. Everett Andrew Biegalski), Joanne (Mrs. Louis Edward Horton), Elizabeth Ann. Sec. Sears Roebuck & Co., Lafayette, 1940, Riley Poultry Farm, Lafayette, 1940-41; treas. Todd Assos., engrs., Villa Park, Ill., 1961-67; bus. mgr., treas. Midwest Coll. Engring., Lombard, Ill., 1967—, trustee, 1973—. Mem. Meml. Hosp. Guild, Elmhurst, Ill., 1963—. Mem. Nat. Assn. Coll. and Univ. Bus. Officers, Lombard C. of C., Delta Sigma Kappa. Home: 827 S Summit Av Villa Park IL 60181 Office: 440 S Finley Rd Lombard IL 60148

TODD, MARYSNOW STONE (MRS. ZANE G. TODD), educator; b. Owensville, Ind., Apr. 6, 1920; d. Clarence Edgar and Mary Pearl (Knowles) Stone; student Lockyear Bus. Coll., 1945-46, Ind. Central Coll., 1958-62; m. Zane G. Todd, Feb. 8, 1950; 1 dau., Betty (Mrs. William Hudson). Bookkeeper, Mo. Valley Bridge & Iron Co., Evansville, Ind., 1942-45, McCrory's Stores, Indpls., 1947-51; asst. editor Research and Rev. Publs., Inc., Indpls., 1951-55, asso. editor, 1956-58; tchr. Perry Twp. schs., Indpls., 1968—. Counselor in edn., 1965-67. Mem. com. Ind. Symphony Soc., 1960—; area leader Am. Cancer Soc., 1968; mem. Winchester Civic Assn., 1962—, Ind. Hist. Soc., 1959—; volunteer A.R.C., 1970-72; mem. Lions Aux., 1956—. Bd. dirs. Muscular Dystrophy Assn., 1969. Mem. Soc. Comml. Journalists, Internat. Platform Assn. Republican. Presbyn. Clubs: Riviera, Indianapolis Athletic. Contbr. articles to ins. jours. Home: 1941 Remington Dr Indianapolis IN 46227

TODER, FRANCINE ANN, clin. psychologist; b. Bklyn., June 13, 1940; d. Max and Sylvia (Kaby) Toder; B.B.A. in Indsl. Psychology, Coll. City N.Y., 1961; M.A., Mich. State U., 1964, Ph.D., 1968; m. Ira Weinstein, Aug. 20, 1961 (div.); 1 son, Matthew. Tchr. elementary sch., Lansing, Mich., 1961-64; counselor, dir. testing and research Lansing Community Coll., 1964-66; vis. lectr. dept. ednl. psychology U. Tenn. Knoxville, 1970-72, sch. psychologist Santa Barbara County Schs., 1972-74; counseling psychologist Cal. State U., Sacramento, 1974—. Postdoctoral clin. intern in psychology Camarillo State Hosp., 1971; lectr. U. Cal. at Santa Barbara, 1973-74; cons. Cal. State Dept. Edn., 1973-74. Mem. Am. Psychol. Assn., Am. Assn. for Humanistic Psychology. Contbr. chpt. to textbook; editor vol. on autism.

TOEPPE, JOAN M. (MRS. GERALD TOEPPE), librarian; b. Clyde, O., May 14, 1924; d. Karl A. and Anna (Bookmyer) Hutchinson; B.S., Coll. St. Teresa, 1946; M.A. in L.S., U. Mich., 1950; m. Gerald Toeppe, Oct. 12, 1968. Food chemist Kellogg Co., Battle Creek, Mich., 1946-49; cataloger, reports library Los Alamos Sci. Lab., 1950-52; librarian Nat. Lead Co. of Ohio, Cin., 1952-61; research librarian Diamond Shamrock Corp., Painesville, O., 1961—. Mem. Am. Chem. Soc. (sec. North Eastern Ohio sect. 1963), Spl. Libraries Assn. (chmn. Documentation Div., 1968). Club: Altrusa (pres. Painesville 1966—). Home: 28784 Johnson Dr Wickliffe OH 44092 Office: PO Box 348 Painesville OH 44077

TOLAN, SISTER PROVIDENCIA, educator; b. Anaconda, Mont., Feb. 24, 1909; d. John H. and Alma (Deschamps) Tolan; B.A., Coll. Great Falls, 1945; M.A., Catholic U. Am. Joined Sisters of Charity of Providence, 1928; tchr. Des Plaines, Ill., 1936-37, Seattle, 1931-33; Indian missionary DeSmet, Ida., 1937-41; tchr. Great Falls, Mont., 1941-45; with Coll. Great Falls, 1949—, instr., 1949-51, asst. prof., 1951-56, asso. prof. sociology, 1956—; cons. Am. Indian tribes, orgns. Northwest U.S., also community Action Programs, cons. VISTA Vols. on Pacific Northwest Indian reservations, Providence Resocialization Center, Great Falls, N.Am. Indian Alliance, Mont. Com. Humanities program. Mem. Mayor's Com. on Indian Research, Great Falls, 1963-64; sec. Mayor's com. Housing and Relocation, Great Falls, 1967-68; com. co-chmn. Great Falls Air Base-Community Council, 1968; mem. Indian task force Mont. Council Chs., 1968—; corr. sec. Great Falls br. N.A.A.C.P., 1968-69; vice chmn. Mont. Low-Income Health Task Force; mem. exec. com. Great Falls Yokefellow Prison Ministry; dir. Great Falls Emergency Food Program, 1973-74. Bd. mgrs., v.p. Tri-County Ch. Women United, 1970-72; bd. dirs. Opportunities, Inc., 1971—; mem. bd. Great Falls Wesley Youth Center. Mem. Mont. Acad. Sci. (asso. editor procs. 1968, mem. bd. 1971—), Cascade County Social Workers Assn., Am. Sociol. Soc., Pi Gamma Mu. Address: Coll Great Falls Great Falls MT 59401

TOLBERT, ROSA JEAN FURR (MRS. CHARLES MADDEN TOLBERT), librarian; b. Fernwood, Miss., Apr. 26, 1925; d. Luther A. and Rosa (Simrall) Furr; B.A., Miss. Coll., 1947; M.L.S., Tex. Women's U., 1965; m. Charles Madden Tolbert, June 2, 1949; 1 son, Charles Madden II. Tchr. high sch. social studies Copiah-Lincoln Jr. Coll., 1947-49; asst. librarian Miss. Coll., 1950-53; jr. librarian La. State U. Library, Baton Rouge, 1954-57; asst. serials librarian Baylor U. Library, Waco, Tex., 1957-64, tchr. library sci., part-time 1966-67, religion librarian, 1964-69, religion-reference librarian Baylor U. Moody Library, 1969—; librarian Tidwell Bible Library, Waco, 1964-68. Danforth asso., 1964—. Mem. A.L.A., Southwestern, Tex. library assns., Am. Assn. U. Women. Clubs: Baylor Round Table, Baylor University Faculty Wives (pres. 1969-70). Home: 5206 Lake Arrowhead Dr Waco TX 76710 Office: Baylor U Moody Library Waco TX 76706

TOLBERT, VIRGINIA STANSEL (MRS. EARL PEEBLES TOLBERT), physician; b. Ruleville, Miss., Aug. 10, 1918; d. Horace Sylvan and Dovie Pearl (High) Stansel; B.A. magna cum laude, Miss. State Coll. for Women, 1937; med. certificate, U. Miss., 1948; M.D., U. Tenn., 1950; m. Earl Peebles Tolbert, June 7, 1953; 1 son, Henry Lawrence. Intern U. Ala. Hosp., Birmingham, 1950-51; general practice medicine, Ruleville, 1951—; mem. staff North Sunflower County Hosp., Ruleville; cons. physician Sunflower County Health Dept. Pres. Sunflower County Heart Assn., 1960—; mem. exec. com. Miss. Municipal Assn., 1973—. Alderman, mem. town. bd. Ruleville, Miss., 1970-73, mayor, 1973—. Mem. Am., Miss. med. assns., Delta Med. Soc., Alpha Omega Alpha. Methodist. Home: 220 E Oscar St Ruleville MS 38771 Office: 601 N Oak St Ruleville MS 38771

TOLCHIN, SARA DEBORAH (MRS. RICHARD ORRIN TOLCHIN), pediatrician; b. N.Y.C., July 20, 1941; d. Joseph and Edna (Kinzler) Nemser; B.A., Barnard Coll., 1962; M.D., State U. N.Y. Downstate Med. Center, 1966; m. Richard Orrin Tolchin, Apr. 15, 1965; children—Robert Joseph, David William, Andrew Michael. Intern Kings County Hosp., Bklyn., 1966-67; resident Bronx Municipal Hosp. Center, N.Y.C., 1967-69; instr. pediatrics Albert Einstein Coll. of Medicine, Bronx, 1969-72, asst. prof., 1972—; mem. staff Bronx Municipal Hosp. Center. Diplomate Am. Bd. Pediatrics. Fellow Am. Acad. Pediatrics. Office: 1600 Tenbroeck Av Bronx NY 10461

TOLINS, SELMA JOAN, psychologist; b. Flushing, N.Y., Aug. 6, 1930; d. Emanuel and Sally Lillian (Weinstock) Leifer; B.A., Queens Coll., 1952; M.Ed., Temple U., 1967; m. David Bruce Tolins, Jr., May 30, 1951; children—Madeline Hani, Andrew Marshall. Tchr. elementary schs., N.Y., 1952-56; guidance counselor Centennial Sch. Dist., Warminster, Pa., 1964-67, sch. psychologist, 1967-71; dir. psychol. services Upper Moreland Sch. Dist., Willow Grove, Pa., 1971—; cons., speaker in field. Mem. Am., Pa. psychol. assns., Council Exceptional Children, Phila. Psychoanalysis Soc., Nat., Pa. edn. assns., Upper Moreland Adminstrs. Assn., Women's Am. Ort (com. chmn. 1962-65), Maple Glen Homeowners Assn. (charter), Sigma Alpha (award 1952). Editor: Practical Applications of Behavior Modifications for the Classroom Teacher, 1974. Home: 1881 Dillon Rd Maple Glen PA 19002 Office: Adminstrn Bldg Terwood Rd Willow Grove PA 19090

TOLLER, GLADYS SCHWARTZ, educator; b. Phila., Sept. 6, 1925; d. Samuel Simon and Dorothy (Elgart) Schwartz; B.S. in Bus. Adminstrn., Temple U., 1948, Ed.M., 1951, Ed.D., 1967; m. Benjamin Esia Toller, Mar.30, 1950; 1 dau., Gale Elgart. Supr. jr. unit Temple U. Lab. Sch. reading clinic, Phila., 1956-60; reading cons. in pvt. practice, 1960-66; corrective reading tchr. Rosetree Media Sch. Dist., Media, Pa., 1966-67; asso. prof. elementary and secondary edn. Cheyney (Pa.) State Coll., 1967-70, prof. reading, 1970—, also mem. com. for new dean, 1973-74. Reading cons. Media Friends' Sch., 1963-64; head reading tchr. Chester City Sch. Dist., 1965-66. Recipient silver medallion Mental Health Assn. S. Eastern Pa., Mem. Am., Pa. (com. on tng. and standards) psychol. assns., Phila. Soc. Clin. Psychologists, Internat., Delaware Valley reading assns., Am. Assn. Univ. Profs., N.E.A., Pa. State Edn. Assn., Assn. Pa. Colls. and Univ. Faculties, Del. Assn. for Children with Learning Disabilities, S.E. Pa. Mental Health Assn. Jewish religion (trustee temple 1965-68, pres. Couples Club 1966-68, mem. social action com. 1973-74). Club: Knowlton Swim. Home: 109 Roberts Rd Brookhaven PA 19015 Office: Cheyney State College Cheyney PA 19319

TOLLETTE, SAMMIE NELL (MRS. SANFORD B. TOLLETTE), librarian; b. Karnack, Tex., May 10, 1928; d. Wesley and Dorothy B. (Coleman) Irving; B.A., Wiley Coll., 1949; M.A. in L.S., Ind. U., 1963, postgrad. U. Cal. at Irvine, U. Ark., 1973; m. Sanford B. Tollette, Apr. 2, 1951; children—Sanford Irving, Frederick Wesley. Pub. sch. tchr., Hope, Ark., 1951-53, Union Grove, Ark., 1953-56, Stamps, Ark., 1949-51; sec. to librarian U. Ark., Pine Bluff, 1955; tchr., librarian Smackover (Ark.) sch. system, 1956-60; librarian Camden (Ark.) schs., 1961-63; librarian Little Rock sch. dist., 1963—. Mem. Little Rock Classroom Tchrs. (v.p. 1970-71, pres. 1971-72, recipient Honor Edn. award 1970-71), Ark. Assn. Sch. Librarians (v.p. 1971-72, pres. 1972-73), N.E.A., Ark. Assn. Sch. Librarians, Ark. Edn. Assn., Urban League Guild (sec. 1974—), Top Ladies of Distinction, Alpha Kappa Alpha. Home: 2715 Chester St Little Rock AR 72206 Office: 21st and Barber Sts Little Rock AR 72206

TOLMACH, JANE LOUISE MCCORMICK (MRS. DANIEL MICHAEL TOLMACH), city ofcl.; b. Havre, Mont.; d. Robert Francis and Veronica (Tracy) McCormick; A.B., U. Cal. at Los Angeles, 1943; M.S.S., Smith Coll., 1945; m. Daniel Michael Tolmach, Sept. 9, 1946; children—James, Richard, Eve Alice, Adam, Jonathan. Psychiat. social worker A.R.C. Field Service, 1945-46; mem. Oxnard (Cal.) City Planning Commn., 1957-62, vice-chmn., 1959-62; mem. Oxnard City Council, 1970—, mayor, 1970-74. Mem. Ventura County Grand Jury, 1958; dir. S. Coast Area Transit. Mem. Ventura County Democrat Central Com., 1953-70, chmn., 1959-62; mem. Cal. Dem. State Central Com., 1958-74, women's chmn. south, 1966-70; del. Dem. Nat. Conv., 1960, 68, alternate, 1956, 64. Trustee Camarillo State Hosp., 1959-68, chmn., 1966-68. Home: 656 Douglas Av Oxnard CA 93030 Office: 305 W 3d St Oxnard CA 93030

TOLMAN, SUZANNE NELSON, psychologist; b. Omaha, Nov. 8, 1931; d. Raymond LeRoy and Lottie (Kerns) Nelson; B.A. with distinction in Spanish, U. Neb., Omaha, 1951; M.A., U. Neb., Lincoln, 1952, Ph.D., 1957; m. Dan Edward Tolman, June 8, 1957; 1 dau., Kimberly Suzanne. Research asst. U. Neb., Lincoln, 1951-52; tchr. Omaha Pub. Schs., 1952-53, counselor, high sch. instr. history and English, 1953-59; instr. psychology U. Neb., Omaha, 1957-59; social service worker Mayo Clinic, Rochester, Minn., 1959-60; instr. psychology U. Tampa, 1962-63; sch. psychologist Sch. Dist. 535, Rochester, 1966—. Bd. dirs. Jefferson PTA, Rochester, 1966-68; bd. dirs., sec. Family Consultation Center, Rochester, 1970—; bd. dirs. Olmsted County (Minn.) Council Coordinated Child Care, 1971-75, pres., 1973-75; bd. dirs. Olmsted County Assn. Mental Health. Mem. Minn., Rochester edn. assns., Minn. Sch. Psychologists, Am. Psychol. Assn., Am. Assn. U. Women, Zumbro Valley Dental Aux. (pres. 1970-71), Alpha Lambda Delta, Alpha Delta Kappa, Psi Chi, Chi Omega. Presbyn. Mem. Order Eastern Star. Home: 2709 Merrihills Dr Rochester MN 55901 Office: Ind Sch Dist 535 Rochester MN 55901

TOLNAI, SUSAN ROBERT (MRS. GEORGE TOLNAI), scientist; b. Budapest, Hungary, Nov. 29, 1928; M.D., Univ. Med. Sch. (Budapest) 1953; m. George Tolnai, June 30, 1950; children—Peter, Ronald. Postdoctoral fellow Nat. Acad. Scis., Hungary, 1953-56; biologist Dept. Nat. Health and Welfare, Ottawa, Ont., Can., 1957-62; lectr. asst. prof. dept. histology and embryology U. Ottawa, 1962-66, asso. prof., 1966-71, prof., 1971—. Mem. Tissue Culture Assn., Am., Canadian socs. for cell biology, Canadian Assn. Anatomists, N.Y. Acad. Scis. Home: 1954 Lauder Dr Ottawa ON K2A 1B1 Canada Office: 275 Nicholas St Ottawa 2 ON K1N 6N5 Canada

TOLOR, BELLE (MRS. ALEXANDER TOLOR), psychologist; b. Queens, N.Y., Mar. 24, 1930; d. William and Gertrude (Schneider) Simon; B.A., Bklyn. Coll., 1951; M.S., U. Bridgeport, 1961; postgrad. Fairfield U., 1962-72; m. Alexander Tolor, Sept. 2, 1951; children—Karen Beth, Lori Ann, Diana Susan. Tchr., N.Y.C. Bd. Edn., 1952-55, Newtown (Conn.) Bd. Edn., 1964-65; psychologist Waterbury (Conn.) Bd. Edn., 1969, Trumbull (Conn.) Bd. Edn., 1969—. Mem. League Women Voters, 1961-73, v.p., 1965. Treas., Newtown Bd. Edn., 1965-69. Mem. Am., Eastern psychol. assns., Conn. Assn. Sch. Psychologists. Home: Route 3 Saw Mill Ridge Rd Newtown CT 06470 Office: Middlebrook Sch Middlebrooks Av Trumbull CT 06611

TOLPO, LILY (MRS. CARL TOLPO), painter, sculptor; b. Chgo., Sept. 13, 1917; d. Sing Hong and Mary (Labuda) Mark; student (scholar) Chgo. Acad. Fine Art, 1935-39; m. Carl Tolpo, June 1, 1941; children—Christine (Mrs. R. Ossanna), Carolyn, Vincent. One-woman shows Ill. Soc. Fine Arts, 1941, State Bank, Palatine, Ill., 1964; spl. show Freeport (Ill.) Country Club; represented in permanent collections at Thomas Jr. High Sch., Arlington Heights, Ill., Glenbrook South High Sch., Northbrook, Ill., Lake County (Ill.) Bldg., Waukegan, Palatine Library; numerous portraits including Mrs. Pat Nixon; also symbolic sculpture including Law and Justice, Lake County Courthouse; represented in numerous pvt. collections. Mem. Heritage League NW Ill., Beta Sigma Phi, Xi Beta Lambda. Address: Route 2 Box 180 A Sky Ridge Rd Stockton IL 61085

TOMASELLO, ANN MUNI (MRS. FRANK A. TOMASELLO), writer; b. Cleve., Apr. 4, 1912; d. Tom C. and Mary Ann (Caracciolo) Muni; M.A., Cleve. Coll., 1957; postgrad. Western Res. U., 1965, John Carroll U., 1968; m. Frank A. Tomasello, July 30, 1938; 1 dau., Joyce Ann (Mrs. Paul E. Litvin). Tchr., Cleve. Schs., 1933-38, Cleveland Heights Schs., 1957-61, Orange (O.) Schs., 1961-66; sch. psychologist Rocky River (O.), 1967-68; sch. psychologist, coordinator pupil services Beachwood (O.) City Schs., 1968-73. Free lance writer, 1954—. Title I grantee, 1970-73. Mem. Am. Psychol. Assn., Nat. Assn. Sch. Psychologists, Ohio Assn. Sch. Psychologists. Unitarian. Contbr. articles to profl. jours., juvenile stories and plays to mags. Home and office: 563 Shorely Dr Apt 201 Barrington IL 60010

TOMBERLIN, IRMA GORDON RAYNE (MRS. ROBERT WENDELL TOMBERLIN), educator; b. Baton Rouge, Aug. 23, 1920; d. Stanford and Selene Anne (Mahier) Rayne; B.A., La. State U., 1940, B.S. in Library Sci., 1941; M.L.S., U. Okla., 1958; m. Robert Wendell Tomberlin, Dec. 22, 1945; 1 son, Brion. Asst. librarian Bossier (La.) Parish Library, 1941-43; parish librarian, Natchitoches, La., 1943-44; art librarian U. Okla., Norman, 1948-53, asst. reference librarian, 1953-57, asst. prof. Sch. Library Sci., 1957-60, information librarian, 1962-63, asst. prof. Sch. Library Sci., 1963-70, asso. prof.,

1970—. Mem. Am. Assn. Library Schs., Am., Southwestern, Okla. (pres. 1957) library assns., Phi Kappa Phi, Beta Phi Mu, Alpha Lambda Delta. Home: 825 W Timberdell St Norman OK 73069 Office: 401 W Brooks St Norman 73069

TOMCZYKOWSKA, WANDA BRONISLAWA, found. exec.; b. N. Bytom, Poland, Aug. 29, 1921; d. Leon and Paulina (Fichna) Krawczyk; ed. Polish and German schs., spl. courses Harvard, U. Cal.; m. Sigmund P. Tomczykowski, Apr. 25, 1946 (dec. 1950); 1 dau., Caria (Mrs. Andrzej Szykier). Reporter Everybody's Daily, Buffalo, 1948-50; meteorol. lexicographer U.S. Air Force contract, Boston, 1952-54; librarian Widener Library, 1951, Farlow Library Cryptogamic Botany, Harvard, 1954-55, Main Library of U. Cal., 1955-64, Center for Research and Devel. Higher Edn. of U. Cal., 1966-69; dir. Internat. Arts and Crafts Gallery, Internat. Center, San Francisco, 1970; co-dir. UN Center, San Francisco, 1972-74; founder, pres. Polish Arts and Culture Found., San Francisco, 1966—; dir. Internat. Arts Prodns., 1969—. Program dir. People to People, Berkeley, 1959-64; dir. 25th Ann. of UN, San Francisco, 1970; writer, producer radio and TV; lectr. on Polish subjects No Cal. univs. and colls.; translator and ct. interpreter. Recipient Kosciuszko Order, 1968, People to People award, 1961, 600th Anniversary medal Jagiellonian U., Cracow, 1963, Coopernicus medal, 1973, others. Mem. World Affairs Council, UN Assn. San Francisco, Artists Embassy San Francisco, Internat. Hospitality Center. Club: Univ. Cal. Faculty. Home: 3308 Claremont Av Berkeley CA 94705 Office: 50 Oak St San Francisco CA 94102

TOMECEK, CAROLYN LOUISE, data processing co. exec.; b. Chgo., Dec. 12, 1944; d. Frank Joseph and Louise Mary (Belihar) Tomecek; B.S., Coll. St. Francis, 1965; M.A. in Math., U. Chgo., 1967. Tchr., Bloom High Sch., Chicago Heights, Ill., 1966-68; systems engr. IBM Corp., Chgo., 1968-72, marketing rep., 1972—. Cons. mgmt. devel. working woman. Mem. Art Inst. Chgo., 1971—, Chgo. Symphony Assn., 1970—, U.S. com. UN, Chgo., 1970—, Center for Study Democratic Instns., Santa Barbara, Cal., 1967—. Mem. Soc. for Study Edn. Home: 2518 W 59th St Chicago IL 60629 Office: 1 IBM Plaza Chicago IL 60611

TOMEH, AIDA K. (MRS. H. AL AMIRE), educator; b. Nabik, Syria; d. Kaiser and Nabeha (Najjar) Tomeh; B.A., Am. U. Beirut (Lebanon), 1954; M.A., U. Mich., 1958, Ph.D., 1962; m. H. Al. Amire, Nov. 25, 1965; children—Rannie, Roula. Postdoctoral fellow U. Mich., Ann Arbor, 1962; asst. prof. Beirut (Lebanon) Coll. for Women, 1963-65; asso. prof. Bowling Green (O.) State U., 1965-71, prof., 1971—. Recipient Fulbright award, 1955. Mem. Am., Mich., North Central sociol. assns. Contbr. articles to profl. jours. Home: 1127 Charles St Bowling Green OH 43402

TOMICH, LILLIAN, lawyer; b. Los Angeles, Mar. 28, 1935; d. Peter and Yovanka P. (Ivanovic) Tomich; A.A., Pasadena City Coll., 1954; B.A. (LaVerne Noyes scholar 1955, 56), U. Cal. at Los Angeles, 1956, gen. secondary teaching credential (Charles Fletcher Scott fellow), 1957, M.A., 1958; J.D. (Univ. scholar), U. So. Cal., 1961. Admitted to Cal. bar, 1961; practice law, 1961-66, 66-68; mem. firm Hurley, Shaw & Tomich, San Marino, Cal., 1968—; counsel Mfrs. Bank, Los Angeles, 1966. Recipient Nat. 1st award debating Phi Rho Pi, 1954, Pacific Coast 1st award debating, 1953, 54; Nat. 1st award debating Pi Kappa Delta, 1955. Mem. Cal. State Bar, Am., Los Angeles bar assns., Women Lawyers Assn., U. Cal. at Los Angeles Alumni Assn., Order Mast and Dagger, Iota Tau Tau, Alpha Gamma Sigma (life), Pi Kappa Delta (pres. 1955-56), Phi Rho Pi (pres. 1953-54), Pi Sigma Alpha (v.p. 1957). Mem. Serbian Orthodox Ch. (trustee). Home: 501 N Del Mar Av San Gabriel CA 91775 Office: 2540 Huntington Dr San Marino CA 91108

TOMKINS, MURIEL AGNES, banker; b. Weehawken, N.J., June 4, 1919; d. Henry and Agnes (Evers) Krusius; bus. diploma Wash. Sch. for Secretaries, 1937; m. John Orr Tomkins, Feb. 19, 1949. Registrar, Washington Sch. Secretaries, N.Y.C., 1938-56; with Manhattan Savs. Bank, N.Y.C., 1956—, asst. sec., 1961-64, asst. v.p., 1964-69, v.p.-sec., 1969—. Republican. Lutheran. Home: 8 Cardinal Way Wayne NJ 07470 Office: 385 Madison Av New York City NY 10017

TOMLINSON, ARLIA OLGA, banker; b. Mayday, Ga., July 23; d. Charles Applin and Eugenia (Griffin) Tomlinson; grad. Ga.-Fla. Comml. Coll., 1932; grad. Nat. Grad. Trust Sch. Northwestern U., 1971. Cashier The Famous Store, Valdosta, Ga., 1933-41; bookkeeper office mgr. Rhodes, Inc., Valdosta, 1941-55; with The First Nat. Bank of Valdosta, 1955—, asst. trust officer, 1965—. Mem. Nat. Assn. Bank Women Inc., Valdosta Bus. and Profl. Women's Club. Democrat. So. Baptist (pres. woman's missionary union 1965-67, ch. finance com. 1970-74). Home: 511 N Ashley St Valdosta GA 31601 Office: 300 N Patterson St Valdosta GA 31601

TOMLINSON, HELEN IRENE CHUNN (MRS. JAMES H. TOMLINSON), mag. editor; b. Winston-Salem, N.C., Dec. 3, 1922; d. Thomas Matthew and Myrtle (Jackson) Chunn; B.A., Appalachian State Coll., 1945; postgrad. Guilford Coll., 1957-59; m. James H. Tomlinson, July 14, 1940; children—Gary, Jimmy, Steven, Leslie. With Western Electric Co., 1946-68, editor, engring. asst., 1960-68; editor, gen. mgr. Am. Salesman and Supervision mags. Nat. Research Bur., 1968—. Democrat. Baptist. Home: 4049 MacEachen Blvd Sarasota FL 33581 Office: 1970 Main St Sarasota FL 33577

TOMLINSON, JULIETTE, mus. exec.; b. N.Y.C., Mar. 13, 1921; d. John Canfield and Katharine Hyde (McAuley) Tomlinson; grad. pvt. sch. Dir., Connecticut Valley Hist. Mus., Springfield, Mass., 1947—. Mem. Hist. Commn. City of Northampton, Mass., 1974—. Am. Philos. Soc. (Phila.) fellow. Mem. Bay State Hist. League, Am. Assn. Museums, Am. Assn. for State and Local History (chmn. Mass.). Episcopalian. Clubs: Colony (N.Y.C.); Colony (Springfield). Author: The Pynchons of Springfield (1636-1702) Founders and Colonizers, 1970; Thus Out of Small Beginnings: A History of Christ Church Cathedral, 1972. Home: 35 Woodlawn Av Northampton MA 01060 Office: William Pynchon Meml Bldg Springfield MA 01103

TOMLINSON, MURIEL DOROTHY, educator; b. Manchester, Conn.; d. George and Sarah (McConnell) Tomlinson; B.A., Bates Coll., 1937; M.A., Duke, 1944, Ph.D. (Angier Duke Meml. fellow), 1947; postgrad. summers Laval U., Que., Can., 1947, U. Poitiers, Tours, France, 1950, U. Montreal, Can., 1967; certificat l'Institut de Phonetique, U. Paris (France), 1966. Tchr., Bridgewater (Me.) Classical Acad., 1938-40, Pratt (Conn.) High Sch., 1940-43; asst. prof. Marshall Coll., 1946-47; asso. prof., chmn. modern fgn. lang. dept. Guilford Coll., 1947-56; prof. French, chmn. modern fgn. lang. dept. U. Tenn., Martin, 1959—; asso. dir. Sch. Affiliation Service, Paris, France, 1956-59. Fulbright grantee, Ghent, Belgium, 1953-54, So. Fellowship Fund summer grantee, Geneva, Paris, 1960. Mem. Am. Assn. Tchrs. French (past pres. N.C. chpt.), Am. Assn. U. Profs. (past pres. Martin br.), Tenn. Edn. Assn., Tenn. Philol. Assn., So. Conf. Lang. Teaching (adv. council), U. Tenn. Martin Hon. Soc. (past pres.), Am., South Atlantic, South Central modern lang. assns., Phi Beta Kappa, Phi Kappa Phi, Phi Sigma Iota, Sigma Delta Pi, Delta Phi Alpha. Contbr. articles to profl. jours. Home: 242 Oakland St Martin TN 38237

TOMLJANOVICH, ESTHER MOELLERING (MRS. WILLIAM TOMLJANOVICH), lawyer, state ofcl.; b. Galt, Ia., Nov. 1, 1931; d. Chester William and Thelma Leone (Brooks) Moellering; B.S. in Lang., William Mitchell Coll., 1953, LL.B., 1955; m. William Tomljanovich, Dec. 26, 1957; 1 son, William Brooks. Admitted to Minn. bar, 1955; group claims mgr. Minn. Mut. Life Ins., St. Paul, 1955-57; asst. revisor statutes State of Minn., St. Paul, 1957-66, revisor statues, 1974—; pvt. practice law, St. Paul, 1966-73; atty. State of Minn. legislature, 1973-74. Legal cons. Minn. County Attys. Assn., 1971-73. Pres., Minn. Council on Status of Women, 1964; mem. Bd. Edn. North St. Paul Maplewood Schs., 1972-73, Planning and Zoning Commn., Village of Lake Elmo, Minn., 1968-71, Gov.'s Commn. on Constl. Revision, 1961-63, Gov.'s Commn. on Status of Women, 1964-67. Mem. Minn. State Bar Assn., Nat. Assn. Women Lawyers St. Paul Bus. and Profl. Womens Assn. (pres. 1958-60), Phi Delta Delta (pres. Minn. chpt. 1967). Club: St. Paul Gavel (pres. 1963). Home: 8533 Hidden Bay Trail North Lake Elmo MN 55042 Office: State Capitol St Paul MN 55155

TOMPKINS, DOROTHY LOUISE CAMPBELL (MRS. JOHN BARR TOMPKINS), former pub. adminstrn. analyst; b. St. Paul; d. Harry Arthur and Alta (Hayes) Campbell; A.B., U. Cal. at Berkeley, 1929, M.A., 1937; m. John Barr Tompkins, June 2, 1941. Library asst. Bur. Pub. Adminstrn. (name changed to Inst. Govtl. Studies), U. Cal., Berkeley, 1927-30, asst. librarian, 1930-43, sr. research technician, 1943-47, asst. pub. adminstrn. analyst, 1947-52, pub. adminstrn. analyst, 1952-74, editor Cal. Pub. Survey, bimonthly digest, 1949-72. Recipient Joseph Andrews Bibliog. award Am. Assn. Law Libraries, 1971-72. Mem. Western Govtl. Research Assn., Am. Soc. Criminology, Am. Soc. Indexers, Mus. Soc. San Francisco. Author: The Offender: a Bibliography, 1963; Probation Since World War II: a Bibliography, 1964; Juvenile Gang and Street Groups: a Bibliography, 1966; White Collar Crime: a Bibliography, 1967; Strikes by Public Employees and Professional Personnel, 1967; The Confession Issue: a Bibliography, 1968; Poverty in the United States During the Sixties: a Bibliography, 1970; Sentencing the Offender: a Bibliography, 1971; Research and Service: A Fifty Year Record, 1971; The Prison and the Prisoner: a Bibliography, 1972; Local Public Schools: How to Pay For Them, 1972; Power From the Earth: Geothermal Energy, 1972; Strip Mining for Coal, 1973; Court Organization and Administration, 1973; Furlough From Prison, 1973; Selection of the Vice President, 1974. Contbg. editor Criminology, 1966-73. Home: 909 Regal Rd Berkeley CA 94708

TOMPKINS, PAULINE, coll. pres.; b. Rhinelander, Wis., Mar. 5, 1918; d. Robert Freeman and Mae (Browne) Tompkins; student Pine Manor Jr. Coll. 1936-38; A.B., Mt. Holyoke Coll., 1941, LL.D., 1957; A.M., Fletcher Sch. Law and Diplomacy, 1942, Ph.D., 1948; LL.D., Hood Coll., 1960, Western Coll., 1968, Wilson Coll., 1969; L.H.D., Muhlenberg Coll., 1970. Instr. history Pine Manor Jr. Coll., Wellesley, Mass., 1941-42, 44-46; lectr., then asst. prof. polit. sci. Wellesley Coll., 1944-46, 48-52; research asso. Mass. Inst. Tech., 1947-49; asso. prof. history, dean of women Colby Coll., 1952-57; prof. polit. sci. Tunghai U., Taiwan, 1958-59; vis. cons. in Asia, United Bd. Christian Higher Edn. in Asia, 1958-59; gen. dir. Am. Assn. U. Women, 1959-67; bd. dirs. Am. Council on Edn., 1972—; pres. Cedar Crest Coll., Allentown, Pa., 1967—. Mem. U.S. adv. com. Internat. Ednl. and Cultural Affairs, 1964-69. Pres. Pa. Assn. Colls. Univs., 1972-73. Trustee Dana Hall Schs., 1950-57, Pine Manor Jr. Coll., 1960-74, Hood Coll., 1961-73, Mt. Holyoke Coll., 1969-74, Carnegie Found. for Advancement Teaching, 1970—. Recipient Carnegie Corp. young administrs. travel grant, 1955-56, grant for survey Australian and New Zealand univs., 1957-58. Mem. Am. Assn. U. Women. Mem. United Ch. of Christ. Author: American-Russian Relations in the Far East, 1949. Home: 2868 College Dr Allentown PA 18104 Office: Cedar Crest Coll Allentown PA 18104

TOMPKINS, VIRGINIA ARMS (MRS. AVERY TOMPKINS), social worker; b. Detroit; d. Floyd Gready and Henrietta (Swan) Arms; A.B., A.M., U. Mich., J.D., U. Mo.; M.S.W., Washington U., St. Louis; postgrad. U. Cal. at Berkeley; m. Avery Tompkins. Former exec. dir. Detroit office children's div. Mich. State Dept. Social Welfare, Children's Service, Kansas City; Family and Children's Service, Kansas City, Family and Children's Service of Berkeley (Cal.); former referee Juvenile Ct. of San Francisco; faculty U. Cal. Sch. Social Welfare, Berkeley; former cons. child guidance clinics San Francisco Schs., Contra Costa County Schs. Mem. aux. Community Hosp. Monterey Peninsula, Monterey, Cal., Monterey Peninsula Vol. Services. Bd. dirs. Monterey Peninsula Mus. Art, Monterey Peninsula Lyceum, Peninsula chpt. Monterey County Symphony Guild, now pres. Mem. Acad. Certified Social Workers, Nat. Assn. Social Workers, Cal. Assn. Health and Welfare, Am. Assn. U. Women, Save the Redwoods League, Nat. Soc. Colonial Dames, San Francisco Symphony Assn., Women's Faculty Club U. Cal., Berkeley, Collegiate Sorosis. Episcopalian. Clubs: Monterey Peninsula Country, Beach and Tennis, Casa Abrego; Town and Country (San Francisco). Author: Future Interests—Executory Devises to Children; Adopted Child as Legal Heir; Wartime Recruitment of Foster Homes for Children of Working Mothers. Home: PO Box 1775 Carmel CA 93921

TOMS, DOLORES C. (MRS. GEORGE LEE ROBINSON), educator; b. Washington, Dec. 26, 1926; d. Walter Dympsie and Deella (Broome) Toms; B.S., Howard U. 1947, M.S., 1948; Ph.D., U. Mich., 1956; postgrad. U. Ill., 1956-57; m. George Lee Robinson, June 3, 1960; children—Georgette Lea, Gregory Toms. Psychologist, Lapeer (Mich.) State Home, 1948-50; instr. Howard U., Washington, 1950-51; psychologist Balt. Pub. Schs., 1951-54; psychologist, asst. clin instr. U. Utah, 1957-58; psychologist Children's Health Center, Salt Lake City, 1957-58; asso. prof. So. U., La., 1958-60; dir. psychol. services Jarvis Christian Coll., Hawkins, Tex., 1960-62; dir. freshman studies Jackson (Miss.) State Coll., 1962-63; dir. counseling and guidance Tex. So. U., Houston, 1964-70, prof. psychology, 1964-70; prof. spl. edn. Central Mich. U., 1970—. Mem. Am. Psychol. Assn., Assn. on Mental Deficiency, Council Exceptional Children, Am. Assn. U. Profs. Home: 155 W Remus Rd Mount Pleasant MI 48858

TONELLI, MARY J. O'DELL, physician; b. St. Louis, Jan. 17, 1925; d. Clifton B. and Lucy Mae (Smith) O'Dell; B.A., U. Tex., 1946; M.D., Baylor U., 1950; M.P.H., U. Cal. at Berkeley, 1953; m. Jerome Tonelli, 1951 (div. Nov. 1961); children—Paul, Stanford, Bradford. Intern, San Diego County Hosp., 1950-51; resident Children's Hosp. East Bay, 1951-52; asst. health officer Marin County, Cal., 1953-64; health dir. Denison-Shoman Grayson County, Sherman, Tex., 1964—, Denton County, Denton, Tex., 1969—. Chmn., Mental Health, Sherman. Mem. Tex., Grayson County med. assns., Am., Tex. pub. health assns., Tex. Pub. Health Physicians, Tex. Health and Respiratory Disease Assn. Club: Seroptimist. Home: 2702 Devonshire St Sherman TX 75090 Office: Box 1295 Sherman TX 75090

TONEY, MYRNA MAE, educator; b. Richland Center, Wis., Oct. 22, 1937; d. Henry Melvin and Margaret Louise (Jewel) Toney; B.S. in Edn., Wis. State U., 1963, M.S. in Edn., 1967; Ph.D. in Ednl. Adminstrn. (Delta Kappa Gamma scholar), U. Wis., 1971. Grad. asst. Oak Ridge Rural Sch., Muscoda, Wis., 1957-61; tchr. Jefferson Elementary Sch., Richland Center, 1961-63, 68-70, Wilson Sch., Beaver Dam, Wis., 1963-66, Boscobel, Wis., 1966-68, asst. prof. edn. Ill. State U., Normal, 1971, clin. supr. Peoria (Ill.) tchr. edn. center, 1971-74; program asst. Wis. improvement program/tchr. internship U. Wis., Madison, 1970-71; dir. McLean County Tchr. edn. Center, Normal, also Bloomington, Ill., 1974—. Cons. career edn. Peoria pub. schs., 1972-73, head start tchrs. Rock Island, Ill., 1973. Mem. Nat., Ill. (sec. 1973-74), assns. elementary, kindergarten and nursery educators, Nat., Ill. Edn. assns., Ill. Assn. Higher Edn., Am. Assn. Univ. Profs., Am. Assn. Tchr. Educators, Assn. Supervision and Curriculum, Am. Assn. Univ. Women, Kappa Delta Pi, Delta Kappa Gamma (treas. 1967-70). Lutheran. Contbr. articles to profl. jours. Home: 705 S University St Apt 208 Normal IL 61761

TONIETTE, SALLYE JEAN, physician; b. Sulphur, La.; d. Eugene Augusta and Sallye (Tanner) Toniette; student John McNeese Jr. Coll., 1946-47; B.S., La. State U., 1949; tchrs. certificate La. State U., 1950, M.D., 1955. Intern, Crawford W. Long Meml. Hosp., Emory U., Atlanta, 1955-56, resident obstetrics and gynecology, jr., sr., chief residencies, 1956-59; practice obstetrics and gynecology, Sulphur, La., 1959—; bd. dir. Holly Hill Nursing Home; mem. med. staff West Calcasieu Cameron Hosp., 1959—. Dir. Calcasieu Parish Cancer Soc. 1963-67. Named Woman of Dinstinction, Calcasieu Parish Police Jurors, also Bus. and Profl. Women's Club of West Calcesieu, 1969. Fellow Am. Coll. Obstetrics and Gynecology; mem. Am., So. med. assns., La., Calcasieu Parish med. socs., La. Wildlife Fedn., Am. Quarter Horse Assn., Assn. Am. Physicians and Surgeons, Alpha Chi Omega, Beta Tau Mu, Iota Sigma Pi, Phi Theta Kappa. Democrat. Methodist. Contbr. articles to profl. jours. Home: 301 W Verdine St Sulphur LA 70663 Office: 521 Cypress St Sulphur LA 70663

TONJES, CONSTANCE REBECCA UNDERWOOD (MRS. M. DODD TONJES), editor; b. Fostoria, O., Sept. 30, 1924; d. C. Alton and Thelma Rebecca (Tefft) Underwood; B.S., U. Toledo, 1945; m. M. Dodd Tonjes, July 13, 1946; children—Stephen Dodd, Craig Louis, Douglas Glenn, Rebecca Sue, Katherine Elizabeth, Matthew Alton. Stringer, feature writer Toledo Blade, 1962-69; corr., asst. editor Anthony Wayne Standard, 1964-69; asst. editor Maumee Valley Pub. Co., Waterville, O., 1969-70, editor, advt. mgr., 1970-74. Presbyn. (elder 1966-69, 74—). Home: 1185 Farnsworth Rd Waterville OH 43566 Office: 217 South St Waterville OH 43566

TONNE, ELIZABETH VAN DERVEER (MRS. HERBERT A. TONNE), editor; b. Manasquan, N.J., Mar. 19, 1908; d. Charles E. and Anna C. (Crosby) Tilton; student N.J. State Normal Sch., 1928, Trenton State Tchrs. Coll., 1944; M.A., N.Y. U., 1946, Ed.D., 1951; m. J. Nivison Van Derveer, July 8, 1934 (dec. 1943); m. 2d, Herbert A. Tonne, Aug. 8, 1966. Tchr., Freehold High Sch., 1928-47; prof. N.J. State Coll., Upper Montclair, 1947-66; editor Jour. Bus. Edn., Wilkes Barre, Pa., 1951—. Mem. Internat. Soc. Bus. Edn. (pres. U.S. chpt. 1961-62), Delta Pi Epsilon. Contbr. articles to mags. Home: Box 12 Northvale NJ 07647 Office: 15 S Franklin St Wilkes Barre PA 18701

TONRA, SISTER MARY FIDELIS, psychologist; b. Bklyn.; d. Patrick and Mary (Glynn) Tonra; B.A., St. Joseph's Coll. for Women, Bklyn., 1960; M.A., Fordham U., 1963; Ph.D. cum laude, U. Ottawa, 1966. Joined Missionary Servants of the Most Blessed Trinity, 1935; staff psychologist child guidance clinic Cath. Welfare Bur., Trenton, N.Y., 1962-63; staff research asst. Astor Home for Emotionally Disturbed Children, Rhinebeck, summer 1964; staff psychol. services U. Ottawa (Ont., Can.), 1963-66; gen. supr., practitioner Cath. Welfare Bur., Trenton, N.J., 1966-68; dir. psychol. services child guidance clinic Cath. Social Services, Phila., 1968-72; dir. Dr. Margaret Healty Research Center, Phila., 1966-72; staff mem. Diocesan Counseling Services for Religious Women, Phila., 1968—. Dir. experimentation programs of religious community Missionary Servants of the Most Blessed Trinity, 1966-72, dir. Trinity Research Center, 1972—; bd. dirs. Diocesan Pastoral Council, Trenton, N.J., 1967-68; exec. dir. Croagh Patrick Youth Center, Cambridge, Mass., 1948-54, Dr. White Settlement House, Bklyn., 1954-59; v.p. Navy Yard Dist. Neighborhood Council, Bklyn., 1955-59; bd. dirs. Vis Nurses Assn., Trenton, 1966-68. Mem. Am., Canadian psychol. assns., Soc. for Psychol. Studies Social Issues, Am. Personnel and Guidance Assn., Personnel and Guidance Assn. Greater Phila., Soc. Sc. Study Religion, Psychologists Interested in Religious Issues, Religious Research Assos. Home: 3501 Solly Av Philadelphia PA 19136

TOOKER, ELISABETH JANE, anthropologist, educator; b. Bklyn., Aug. 2, 1927; d. Clyde and Amy (Luce) Tooker; B.A., Radcliffe Coll., 1949; Ph.D., 1958; M.A., U. Ariz., 1953. Instr., U. Buffalo, 1957-60; teaching asst. Harvard, 1960-61; asst. prof. Mount Holyoke Coll., South Hadley, Mass., 1961-65; asst. prof. Temple U., Phila., 1965-67, asso. prof. anthropology, 1967—. Fellow Am. Anthrop. Assn., A.A.A.S.; mem. Northeastern Anthrop. Assn. (sec. 1966-68), Phila. Anthrop. Soc. (pres. 1969). Office: Dept Anthropology Temple U Philadelphia PA 19122

TOOKS, KATHERINE VAUGHNS, lawyer; b. Oakland, Cal., Mar. 27, 1945; d. James Henry and Millie (Wilcox) Vaughns; student U. Cal. at Davis, 1963-64; A.B., U. Cal. at Berkeley, 1967, J.D., 1970; postgrad. Howard U. Sch. Law, 1967-69; m. Lloyd Edward Tooks, Dec. 20, 1969. Law clk. Alameda County Legal Aid Soc., Oakland, 1969-70; admitted to Cal. bar, 1971; legal research asst. Earl Warren Inst. Housing and Urban Devel., Berkeley, 1969-70; atty. Pacific Telephone Co., Los Angeles, 1971—. Mem. Am., Los Angeles County bar assns., Queens Bench San Francisco, Am. Right-of-Way Assn. Methodist. Club: Commonwealth (San Francisco). Home: 3087 Manning Av Los Angeles CA 90064 Office: 740 S Olive St Los Angeles CA 90055

TOOLE, DONNA RIGDON, occupational therapist, educator; b. Fort Leavenworth, Kan., July 3, 1933; B.S. in Occupational Therapy, U. Kan., 1955; M.Ed. in Rehab. Counseling, U. Ga., 1969, Ed.D., 1975; m. Michael G. Toole, June 20, 1958; children—William Robert, McDonald Michael. Dir. occupational therapy Augusta VA Hosp., 1955-58; sr. staff therapist Northport VA Hosp., 1958-60; instr. dept. psychiatry Med. Coll. Ga., Augusta, 1963-69, asst. prof. dept. occupational therapy, 1973—; mem. clin. faculty occupational therapy, U. Fla., Gainesville, 1964-69; pvt. practice as occupational therapist, 1969-73; cons. Chulalongkorn U., Bangkok, Thailand, 1973, Kowloon Rehab. Center, Hong Kong, 1973, Tokyo U. (Japan), 1973, Gracewood State Sch. and Hosp., 1973—. Lectr., participant numerous seminars throughout U.S., Australia, Japan, Israel; mem. faculty continuing edn. workshop Columbia (S.C.) Area Mental Health Center, 1972-74; vice chmn. Gov.'s Permanent Com. on Arthritis Health Edn. Sect.; mem. com. for Health Services to Mentally and Emotionally Handicapped Georgians; recruitment chmn. exec. bd. Allied Health Profession; mem. exec. bd. Ga. Interagy. Com. for Exceptional Children, Augusta Psycho-Ednl. Center Profl. adv. bd. Recipient Gov.'s award of excellence, 1969; named Outstanding Citizen Ga., 1973. Mem. Am. (assembly del. 1970—), Ga. (past pres.) occupational therapy assns., World Fedn. Occupational Therapists, Augusta Area Mental Health Assn. (profl. adv. bd. 1973—), Ga. Arthritis Found. (chmn. patient services com.), Am. Assn. Mental Deficiency, Am. Assn. Univ. Women, Augusta Choral Soc., Augusta Music Club, Episcopal Day Sch. Parents' Assn., Historic Augusta, U. Kan. Alumni Assn. (life), U. Ga. Alumni Assn., Mu Rho Sigma. Episcopalian. Club: Augusta Junior Women's (outstanding citizen award 1973). Contbr. articles to profl. jours. Collaborator on film In the Beginning. Home: 2350 Kings Way Augusta GA 30904 Office: Medical College of Georgia Augusta GA 30902

TOOMEY, JEANNE ELIZABETH (MRS. JIM R. GRAY), journalist; b. N.Y.C., Aug. 22, 1921; d. Edward Aloysius and Anna Margaret (O'Grady) Toomey; student Hofstra U., 1938-40, Fordham Law Sch., 1940-41; m. Peter E. Terranova, Sept. 29, 1951 (dec. Sept. 1968); children—Peter, Sheila; m. 4th, Jim R. Gray, Dec. 5, 1972. With N.Y. local desk A.P., 1963-64, stringer East End L.I., 1970—; editor weeklies, Al Tahoe, Cal., 1964-65; editor Bronx Home News, 1966-67; writer for mags. Family Weekly, Modern Maturity, Family Circle, Cats. Chmn. com. to establish wildlife refuge in Hackensack Meadows, 1968-69. Recipient N.Y. Women's Press Club award for best series pub. by N.Y.C. newspaper, 1960; Patrolmen's Benevolent Assn. award, 1960; Nev. Press Assn. Best Feature award, 1961. Mem. Wilderness Soc., Defenders of Wildlife, Overseas, N.Y. press clubs, Newswomen's Club N.Y., Silurians. Address: Gondola Gardens North Sea Rd Southampton NY 11968

TOOMIM, MARJORIE KAWIN (MRS. HERSHEL TOOMIM), psychologist; b. Los Angeles, Feb. 25, 1923; d. Elias Victor and Mildred (Firth) Rosenkranz; student Pomona Coll., 1940-42; B.A., U. So. Cal., 1945, Ph.D., 1966; m. Hershel Toomim, Feb. 14, 1969; children—Bruce F. Kawin, Elise (Mrs.George Osner), Pamela J. Kawin. Staff psychologist Los Angeles Psychiat. Service, 1964-66; cons. Los Angeles Council of Chs. Project Head Start, 1967-70; coordinator consultation div. Los Angeles Psychol. Center, project coordinator Mental Health Consultation Program, Los Angeles County Project Head Start, 1966-67; chief psychologist, adminstr. Asso. Counseling Services, 1967-71; pvt. practice as clin. psychologist, Los Angeles, 1966—. Lectr., Cal. State U. at Los Angeles, summers 1967-68; dir. research and clin. applications biofeedback instruments Biofeedback Research Inst., 1969-73. Mem. Am., Cal., Los Angeles County psychol. assns., Los Angeles Soc. Clin. Psychologists, Assn. for Humanistic Psychology, Biofeedback Research Soc., Phi Beta Kappa, Phi Kappa Phi, Alpha Kappa Delta. Contbr. to book, articles to profl. jours. Address: 6542 Hayes Dr Los Angeles CA 90048

TOOP, JUDITH LYLA, educator; b. Almonte, Ont., Can., June 1, 1942; d. Harry Gordon and Grace Jean (Howard) Toop; came to U.S., 1961; B.A., Walla Walla Coll., 1963, M.A., 1969. Sci. tchr. Monterey Bay Acad., Watsonville, Cal., 1963-66; asso. dean women Walla Walla Coll., College Place, Wash., 1966-71; sci. tchr. Auburn (Wash.) Acad., 1971—. Mem. Internat. Oceanographic Found., Nat. Assn. Biology Tchrs., Am. Soc. Botany, Nat. Audubon Soc., Western Wash. Assn. Seventh-Day Adventist Educators (sec. 1973—). Address: Auburn Acad Auburn WA 98002

TOOPER, VIRGINIA OLIPHANT (MRS. EDWARD BENJAMIN TOOPER), educator; b. Nashville, June 25, 1928; d. Thomas Alfred and Catherine (Holt) Oliphant; B.S., La. State U., 1949; O.T.R., Tex. Womens U., 1953; M.A., Columbia, 1954; Ed.D., U. Cin., 1973; m. Edward Benjamin Tooper, Aug. 6, 1955; 1 son, Jon Edward. Tchr. pub. schs., Laton Rouge, 1949-52; tchr. VA Hosp., Hines, Ill., 1955-58, Child Guidance Home, Cin., 1963-65; instr. Cleve. State U., 1970-72; asst. prof. spl. edn. San Jose (Cal.) State U., 1972—. Recipient grants Dept. Mental Hygiene and Correction, 1969, Am. Occupational Therapy Assn., 1970. Nat. Tb. scholar in occupational therapy, 1952-54. Mem. Ohio Occupational Therapy Assn. (ednl. dir.), Am. Assn. Mental Deficiency (regional sec.-treas.), Council Exceptional Children (chpt. pres. elect). Author: Motor Skills, 1971; Communication Skills, 1973. Home: 7953 Stonehurst Ct Pleasanton CA 94566 Office: Room 201 Edn Bldg 7th and San Carlos Sts San Jose CA 95192

TOPALIS, MARY, ednl. adminstr.; b. N.Y.C.; d. George and Nota (Cosmos) Topalis; diploma Cornell U.-N.Y. Hosp. Sch. Nursing, 1944; B.S. in Nursing, Tchrs. Coll. Columbia, 1946, M.A., 1950, Ed.D., 1968. Staff nurse, asst. head nurse Payne Whitney Clinic, N.Y.C., 1944-46; head nurse, instr. psychiat. nursing Westchester div. N.Y. Hosp., 1946-49; ednl. adminstr. psychiat. nursing Central State Hosp., Lakeland, Ky., 1950-51; supr. neuropsychiat. nursing VA Hosp., Albany, N.Y., 1951-53; instr. psychiat. and med. surg. nursing, chmn. dept. Fairleigh Dickinson U., Rutherford, N.J., 1953-68; dean U. Bridgeport (Conn.) Coll. Nursing, 1968—. Cons. in nursing VA Hosp., New Haven, 1969—. Mem. nursing tng. rev. com. Nat. Inst. Mental Health, 1968—, chmn., 1970-71; bd. dirs. Conn. Hosp. Planning Commn., 1969-73; mem. Conn. Bd. Examiners for Nursing, 1969—, pres., 1972—; mem. Conn. Regional Med. Planning Commn., 1969—; mem. council New Eng. Bd. Higher Edn., 1968—; mem. steering com. Conn. Family Health Plan, 1972—. Mem. Am. Assn. U. Women, N.E.A., Nat., Conn. leagues for nursing, Am. Nurses Assn., Am. Assn. Allied Health Professions, Kappa Delta Pi. Author: (with R. Matheney) Psychiatric Nursing, 5th edit., 1970. Home: 570 Burr St Fairfield CT 06430 Office: 75 Linden Av Bridgeport CT 06602

TORCZYNSKI, ELISE, ophthalmologist; b. Chgo., July 2, 1933; d. Vincent Francis and Helen Ann (Nowogrodski) Torczynski; B.S. in Nursing, St. Mary's Coll., 1956; postgrad. Marquette U., 1963-65; M.D., Marquette Sch. Medicine, 1969. Instr. nursing Cook County Hosp., Chgo., 1956-58; nurse Chgo. Vis. Nurse Assn., 1958-61; nurse, social worker Kpandu (Ghana) Hosp., 1961-63; intern Evanston (Ill.) Hosp., 1969-70; resident ophthalmology Med. Coll. Wis., Milw., 1970-73; fellow ophthalmic pathology Armed Forces Inst. Pathology, Washington, 1973—. Heed Ophthalmic fellow, 1973-74. Mem. Assn. for Research in Vision and Ophthalmology, A.M.A., Alpha Omega Alpha. Office: Armed Forces Inst Pathology Washington DC 20306

TORF, JANE HAMILTON, antiques dealer; b. Marshall, Ill., Aug. 29, 1916; d. George and Ethel Rosa (Bennett) Beuhler; student Acad. Fine Arts, Chgo., 1935; m. Allen Britt Hamilton, Feb. 26, 1940 (dec. Feb. 1957); children—Judith (Mrs. William Cappello), Janet (Mrs. Larry Agajanian); m. 2d, Al Torf. Saleswoman, Marshall Field Co., Chgo., 1935-40; propr. Hamilton House Antiques, Glendora, Cal., 1951—. Lectr. on antiques, 1960-65; exhibitor at antiques shows, So. Cal., 1957—. Mem. So. Cal. Antique Assn. (v.p. 1968, show chmn. 1968-69, program chmn. 1968-69), Antiquarian Soc., Los Angeles County Mus., Wesleyan Service Guild, Women's Club of Glendora. Methodist (past pres. parsonage com.). Home: 603 N Doheny Dr Beverly Hills CA 90210 Office: 1030 E Alosta St Glendora CA 91740

TORNABENE, NORMA ROGERS (MRS. LOUIS F. TORNABENE), univ. dean; b. Carthage, Tex., Nov. 18, 1924; d. James T. and Jessie Mae (Hobby) Rogers; student McNeese State Coll., 1954-57, U. Md., 1958-59; B.S., U. N.M., 1961; postgrad. Stephen F. Austin U., 1966-67; M.Ed., McNeese State U., 1969, postgrad., 1970-72; m. Louis F. Tornabene, Oct. 2, 1942; children—Louis F., Charles J., Anne (Mrs. Ronald Kemerly). Tchr., U.S. Dependents Sch., Scotland, 1958-59, Albuquerque pub. schs., 1962-64, Calcasieu Parish Schs., Lake Charles, La., 1964-70; dean women McNeese State U., Lake Charles, 1970—. Mem. Status Women Commn. La., 1972—. Mem. Am. Assn. Univ. Women (pres. 1970-72, regional v.p. 1973—), Am., La., Tex. assns. women deans and counselors, La. Tchrs. Assn., Quota Club, Phi Lambda Theta, Alpha Delta Kappa. Home: 4726 Ponderosa St Lake Charles LA 70601 Office: McNeese State University Lake Charles LA 70601

TORNATORE, CONNIE CRIMI (MRS. JAMES-JOSEPH TORNATORE), librarian; b. Randazzo, Sicily, Italy, Feb. 12, 1927; came to U.S. 1928; naturalized 1938; d. Nunzio and Gaetana (Ruttino) Crimi; B.S. (Nat. Def. Edn. Act. scholar 1964), Syracuse (N.Y.) U., 1965, M.S. in L.S., 1972; m. James-Joseph Tornatore, Oct. 7, 1950; children—Kathleen Mary, Douglas J. and Charles W. (twins). Exec. sec. to v.p. Canastota div., Oneida Ltd., Canastota, N.Y., 1944-55; exec. sec. to treas. Syracuse U., 1958-59; tchr. Canastota Central Sch. Dist., 1965-69; librarian, tchr. South Side Elementary Sch., Canastota, 1969—; librarian Elementary Secondary Edn. Act Summer reading program, 1970-71. Troup leader Girl Scouts Am., 1963-66; mem. exec. com. Boy Scouts Am., 1967-69; chmn. N.Y. Home Extension unit, 1957-60, v.p., sec., 1969—; mem. exec. com. local P.T.A., Canastota, 1967—. Am. Newspaper Pubs. Assn., 1966. Newspaper in the Classroom scholar. Mem. Nat. Edn. Assn., N.Y., Canastota tchrs. assns., A.L.A., Am. Assn. Sch. Librarians, Syracuse U. Coll. Alumni Assn., Central N.Y. Librarian's Assn., Beta Phi Mu, Kappa Epsilon. Republican. Lionette. Clubs: Syracuse University Alumni. Writer of script Elvis-the Educated-Elf, 1965. Home: 216 Prospect St Canastota NY 13032 Office: Canastota Central Schs Roberts St Canastota NY 13032

TORO, AMALIA MARIE, lawyer, state ofcl.; b. Hartford, Conn., Nov. 6, 1920; d. Frederick and Mary (Casale) Toro; B.A., U. Conn., 1942; J.D., Yale, 1944. Admitted to Conn. bar, 1944; practiced in New Haven, 1944-46; asso. firm Wiggin & Dana., 1944-46; elections atty. Office of Sec. State, Hartford, 1946—. Parliamentarian nat. conv. Nat. Assn. Ins. Women, 1966. Mem. Conn. State Employees Retirement Commn., 1960—, Ford Found. Com. on Election Systems, 1971; chmn. elections panel ann. conf. Internat. Inst. Municipal Clks., Phoenix, 1973. Recipient Woman of Year award Greater Hartford Bus. and Profl. Women's Clubs, 1969; Nat. award, 1970; Outstanding State Employee award Conn. State Employees Assn., 1973. Mem. Conn. Assn. Municipal Attys. (pres. 1973-74). Home: 17 Clarkridge Rd Wethersfield CT 06109 Office: 234 Pearl St Hartford CT 06103

TORRENCE, LOIS E., educator; b. McCune, Kan., July 5, 1924; d. Ira W. and Madge (Chamberlain) Torrence; B.A., Kan. Wesleyan U., 1945; M.A., So. Meth. U., 1948; Ph.D., Am. U., 1961. Instr., Am. history So. Meth. U., Dallas, 1947-48; asst. prof. history Kan. Wesleyan U., Salina, 1948-51, asst. prof., 1954-60, asso. prof., 1960-66, prof., 1966—, dir. admissions, 1951-54, asst. registrar, 1954-57, univ. registrar, 1957-63; dir. Office of Instl. Studies, Am. U., Washington, 1963—. Cons. Office Edn., Dept. Health, Edn. and Welfare, 1966-69. Trustee Kan. Wesleyan U., Salina. Mem. Am. Assn. U. Women, Internat. Fedn. U. Women, Assn. for Instl. Research (pres. 1974-75), Am., Canadian polit. sci. assns., Am. Assn. Collegiate Registrars and Admissions Officers, Am. Assn. U. Profs., Phi Kappa Phi, Pi Sigma Alpha, Phi Alpha Theta. Home: 1931 N Cleveland St Arlington VA 22201 Office: Am U Washington DC 20016

TORRES, LORRAINE BOVARD (MRS. EMILIO TORRES), govt. ofcl.; b. Denver, Jan. 1, 1927; d. Francis Albert and Charlotte (Andrews) Bovard; B.A., U. Denver, 1949, M.A., 1951; postgrad. George Washington U. Law Sch., 1956-58; m. Emilio Torres, June 6, 1960. Officer, U.S. Dept. State, Washington, 1951-53, 55-58; staff asso. Am. Assn. U. Women, Washington, 1958-63; program analyst research grants br. Nat. Inst. Mental Health, Bethesda, Md., 1963-66, exec. sec. social sci. sect. Behavioral Scis. Research Br., 1966-69, chief sect., 1969-74, chief planning br., 1974—. Congressional fellow, 1972-73. Mem. Am. Polit. Sci. Assn., Am. Sociol. Assn., Am. Antrhop. Assn., Am. Acad. Polit. and Social Sci. Home: 3531 Hamlet Pl Chevy Chase MD 20015 Office: 5600 Fishers Lane Rockville MD 20852

TORREY, JANE WHEELWRIGHT, educator; b. Atlanta, Oct. 3, 1925; d. William Wheelwright and Dorothy Minot (Greene) Torrey; B.A., Swarthmore Coll., 1947; M.A., U. Cal. at Berkeley, 1949, Ph.D., 1951. Research asso. Student Counseling Bur., U. Minn., 1951-53; instr. psychology Conn. Coll., New London, 1953-56, asst. prof., 1956-63, asso. prof., 1963-69, prof., 1969—. Mem. Am., Eastern, Conn. (sec. 1963-66), New Eng. psychol. assns., Soc. for Psychol. Study Social Issues, Am. Ednl. Research Assn., Internat. Reading Assn., Linguistic Soc. Am., Phi Beta Kappa, Sigma Xi, Psi Chi. Research in fgn. lang. learning, social dialects, psychology of women. Home: 3 Winchester Rd New London CT 06320

TORRIANI, ANNAMARIA GORINI (MRS. LUIGI GORINI), educator; b. Milan, Italy; d. Carlo and Ada (Forti) Torriani; Ph.D., U. Milan, 1942; m. Luigi Gorini, Dec. 6, 1959; 1 son, Daniel. Came to U.S., 1955, naturalized, 1964. Research asso. Istituto Chimica e Biochimica, G. Ronzoni, Milan, 1942-48; charge de recherche dept cellular physiology, Institut Pasteur, Paris, France, 1948-56; Fulbright postdoctoral fellow dept. microbiology N.Y. U., 1956-58; research asso. Harvard Med. Sch., Boston, 1958-59, research asso. Harvard biology dept., 1959-60; research asso. Mass. Inst. Tech., Cambridge, 1960-71, asso. prof. microbiology, 1971—. Mem. Am. Soc. Microbiology. Contbr. articles to profl. jours. Home: 115 Longwood Av Brookline MA 02146 Office: Dept Biology Mass Inst Tech Cambridge MA 02114

TORVEND, EVELYN SOPHIA, educator; b. Silverton, Ore., Sept. 18, 1919; d. Samuel and Gjertina Renettie (Refsland) Torvend; B.S., Mt. Angel (Ore.) Coll., 1950; M.S., Pacific U., 1960; postgrad. Ore. State U., 1963-68, Ore. Coll. Edn., 1966-72. Tchr., Marion County (Ore.) Elementary Schs., 1938-46, B.W. Barnes Jr. High Sch., Hillsboro, Ore., 1946-60, Judson, Leslie Jr. High Sch., Salem, Ore., 1960—. Mem. N.E.A. (N.W. regional dir. dept. classroom tchrs. 1956-59), Ore. (sec. dept. classroom tchrs. 1951-53, tchr. edn. and profl. standards commn. 1952-55, v.p. 1953-55), Salem (parliamentarian 1962-66, bull. editor 1962-66, tchr. edn. and profl. standards com., chmn. 1971-73) edn. assns., Delta Kappa Gamma (pres. Nu chpt. 1972-74). Lutheran (mem. world mission comm. 1972—). Home: 225 Judson S Salem OR 97302

TOULMIN, MARGARET CLARISSE, sculptor; b. Filton, Bristol, Eng., Oct. 2, 1916; d. Christopher and Dorothy (Wilkins) Hayes; student St. Faith's, Weston-super-Mare, 1928-31, West of Eng. Sch. Art, 1931-40; m. William Toulmin, Nov. 2, 1940; children—Christopher, Alastair, Nicholas. Came to Can., naturalized, 1960. Exhibited sculptures and paintings in Britain, Iran, Nigeria and Can., 1938—; represented in permanent collections chs. Western Eng., also in Can. Academician, Royal Canadian Acad. Arts; asso. Royal West of Eng. Acad. Mem. Lakeshore Artists Assn., Montreal. Home: 273 Shore Rd Beaconsfield PQ Canada

TOUSIGNANT, DOROTHY WILTAMUTH (MRS. LEONARD A. TOUSIGNANT), mgmt. exec.; b. East Moline, Ill., Jan. 7, 1920; d. Edward W. and Eleonora (Struss) Wiltamuth; B.S., U. Ill., 1941; M.E., State Tchrs. Coll., Fitchburg, Mass., 1951; postgrad. Am. U., 1959-61; m. Leonard A. Tousignant, June 11, 1949; 1 dau., Carmen Louise. Chief dietitian U.S. Army Hosps., CBI, 1942-45; served to capt.; food service tng. supr. Air Transport Command Hdqrs., Washington, 1946-47; cons. Office Surgeon Gen., Washington, 1948, Inflight Feeding Manual Air Quartermaster, 1948, Office Q.M. Gen.; ednl. promotion, sales work Basic Vegetable Products, Inc., San Francisco, 1947-49; dietitian resident halls State Tchrs. Coll., Fitchburg, Mass., 1950; ednl. promotion work Dehydrated Food Industries, San Francisco, also Washington, 1950-53; instr. home econs. U. Md., College Park, 1954; nutritional cons., Washington, 1955; asst. prof. nutrition Cath. U. Am., Washington 1954-55; dist. mgr. United Food Mgmt. Services, Inc., Washington, 1955-64, v.p. Hosp. Dietetics, Inc. div. Interstate United Corp., Washington, 1964-67; pres. D.W. Tousignant & Assos., Inc., Washington, 1967—. Served with AUS, 1942-45. Decorated Bronze Star medal. Mem. Am. Home Econs. Assn. (pres. Washington 1958), Home Economists in Bus., Nursing League, Washington Women's Advt. Club, Washington Advt. Club, Am. Dietetics Assn., Nat. Restaurant Assn., English-speaking Union, Bus. and Profl. Women's Club. Contbr. articles profl. jours. Research in dehydrated foods. Address: 4020 49th St NW Washington DC 20016

TOUTON, BEATRICE HUPPERT, textile mill exec.; b. Waukesha, Wis., Aug. 30, 1919; d. Raynard E. and Elsa T. (Jones) Huppert; B.S., U. Wis., 1941, postgrad., 1942; m. Louis L. Touton, Aug. 29, 1942 (dec. Feb. 1970); children—Richard, Charles, Mary, Louis. Instr. chemistry U. Wis.-Milw., 1941-44; bookkeeper Oil Seed Products, Co., Fresno, Cal., 1945-47, with research and devel. dept., 1947-48; pres. Sosawagaming Corp., Parlier, Cal., 1970—; pres. Windigo Mills, Hanford, Cal., 1970—; gen. mgr. Calspun Mills, Parlier. Mem. Am. Assn. U. Women, Phi Beta Kappa. Clubs: University-Sequoia; Sunnyside (Fresno). Home: 935 Park Circle Dr Fresno CA 93727 Office: 625 Zediker St Parlier CA 93648

TOVEY, EVELYN MARY, nurse, educator; b. Akron, O.; d. Frederick George and Mary Ellen (Underwood) Tovey; diploma Akron City Hosp. Sch. Nursing, 1936; B.S., Western Res. U., 1940, M.S. in Nursing, 1950. Staff nurse Akron City Hosp., 1936-37, mem. nursing adv. com., 1952-67; staff nurse U. Hosps., Cleve., 1937-39; instr. sci. Christ Hosp. Sch. Nursing, Cin., 1940-45; asst. dir. Sch. Nursing Mt. Sinai Hosp., Cleve., 1945-48, acting dir., 1948-49; asso. prof. nursing Coll. Edn., U. Akron, 1950-67, Coll. Nursing, 1967-70, prof., 1970—. Mem. adv. com. Akron Sch. Practical Nursing, 1956-63, Akron Gen. Hosp. Sch. Nursing, 1957-67. Mem. Springfield Twp. Improvement League, 1957—; mem. nursing service com. Akron chpt. A.R.C., 1958—, chmn. nursing service com., 1970. Bd. dirs. Summit County chpt. Multiple Sclerosis Soc. Recipient 15 Year Service award A.R.C., 1974. Mem. Am. (past dist. pres.), Ohio nurses assns., Nat., Ohio leagues for nursing, Am. Assn. U. Profs. Club: Altrusa (Akron). Home: 936 Onondago Av Akron OH 44312

TOWER, JANET KENDALL (MRS. ALBERT HIGGINS TOWER), civic worker; b. Oak Park, Ill., Mar. 20, 1921; d. William Eugene and Jessie May (Thorpe) Kendall; B.S., Purdue U., 1942; m. Albert Higgins Tower, July 15, 1943; children—Barbara (Mrs. James Marshall Williams), Jacqueline (Mrs. James Martin Jarrard). Vice pres. nat. collegiate programs Alpha Xi Delta, 1968-71, asst. to nat. expansion dir., 1971-73; dir. vols. Bedford Med. Center, 1973—. Active Girl Scouts Am. since 1954-71, pres. Tulip Trace Council, 1962-66, mem. bd. dirs., 1962-71. Mem. Panhellenic Assn. (pres. 1956), Am. Assn. U. Women. Methodist (mem. bd. stewards 1960-66). Home: 218 Westwood Dr Bedford IN 47421

TOWER, JOAN PEABODY, composer, pianist; b. New Rochelle, N.Y., Sept. 6, 1938; d. George Warren and Anne (Robinson) Tower; B.A., Bennington Coll., 1961; M.A., Columbia U., 1967, D.Mus. Arts. Concertized Da Capo Chamber Players, Inc, N.Y.C., 1970—, Carnegie Recital Hall, 1971,72, N.Y.U., 1972, Mass. Inst. Tech., 1972, State U.N.Y. at Potsdam, 1972, State U.N.Y. at Purchase, 1972, Town Hall, N.Y.C., 1973, Alice Tully Hall, 1974, others; compositions performed Composers Forum, N.Y.C., 1968, Buffalo Philharmonic, 1971, Ann. Conf. Am. Soc. Univ. Composers, 1972, Women in the Arts, 1972; radio show, univs., others, 1972— grad. asst. Columbia U., 1964-71; lectr. at C. W. Post Coll., Greenvale, N.Y., 1968—; piano instr. Greenwich House Music Sch. N.Y.C., 1961-71; faculty Bard Coll., Annandale-on-Hudson, N.Y., 1972—. Recipient Naumburg Chamber Music award, 1973; Nat. Endowment grantee, 1974. Mem. Am. Soc. U. Composers (sec. exec. com. 1971—), Am. Composers Alliance (sec. bd. 1971—), Internat. Soc. Contemporary Music (dir. 1972—). Composer: Percussion Quartet, 1963; Brimset, 1965; Movement for Flute and Piano, 1968; also recordings. Home: 545 W 111 St New York City NY 10025 Office: Bard Coll Annandale-on-Hudson NY 12504

TOWER, LOU BULLINGTON (MRS. JOHN G. TOWER), wife of U.S. Senator from Tex.; m. John G. Tower, Mar. 21, 1952; children—Penelope, Marian, Jeanne. Address: 4100 Cathedral Av NW Washington DC 20016

TOWER, MARGENE VALERIE, mental health adminstr.; b. Portland, Ore., Sept. 21, 1939; d. Gordon Eugene and Marjorie LaVelle (Tryon) Tower; student Ore. State Coll., 1957-59; R.N., U. Ore., 1961; postgrad. Portland State Coll., summer 1965; M.S. in Psychiat. Nursing (Nat. Inst. Mental Health grantee), U. Colo., 1967. Instr. psychiat. nursing, chmn. mental heatlh integration project U. Colo., 1967-68; dir. nurses Community Mental Health Center, Denver Gen. Hosp., also asst. dir. nursing, 1968-70; dep. chief area mental health services br. USPHS Indian Health Service, Billings, Mont., 1971-73, chief, mental health services, 1973—. Mem. adj. faculty Rocky Mountain Coll., Billings. Named Outstanding Grad. Student Psychiat. Nursing U. Colo., 1967. Mem. Am. Nurses Assn. (mem. interim cl certification bd., div. psychiat. mental health nursing practice), Council Advanced Practitioners Psychiat. and Mental Health Nursing, Alpha Tau Delta, Sigma Theta Tau. Democrat. Methodist. Author: (with Carol DeYoung) The Role of the Nurse in Community Mental Health Centers: Out of Uniform and Into Trouble, 1971. Office: PO Box 2143 Billings MT 59103

TOWER, SALLY ARMITAGE METCALF, iron co. exec.; b. Utica, N.Y., Oct. 17, 1922; d. Francis Marion and Marion (Elliott) Metcalf; grad. high sch.; m. Tripp Tower, June 6, 1942 (div. 1965); children—Tripp, Sally Victoria, Deborah. Dir. Westmoreland Malleable Iron Co., Ltd. (N.Y.), 1959-61, sec., dir., 1961-63, sec., treas., 1963-66, pres., treas., 1966—. Mem. 17th Ward Republican Com., Utica, 1954-62, ward chmn., 1958-62; chmn. Utica Rep. Com., 1960-62, vice chmn. Oneida County, 1960-62. Presbyn. Clubs: 100,000 (v.p. 1959-60), Lincoln (chmn. 1959-60) (Utica, N.Y.); Women's Republican. Home: 2811 Oneida St Utica NY 13501 Office: Westmoreland Malleable Iron Co Westmoreland NY 13490

TOWERS, DIXIE ANN RICE (MRS. JOSEPH ANTHONY TOWERS), buyer; b. Los Angeles, Aug. 23, 1939; d. Richard Sidney and Margaret (Chapton) Rice; B.S., U. So. Cal., 1961; postgrad. Hunter Coll., 1962; m. Joseph Anthony Towers, Feb. 4, 1965; 1 son, David Brent. Asst. buyer Ohrbach's, N.Y.C., 1961-63, buyer, Los Angeles, 1963-66; buyer D.H. Holmes, New Orleans, 1966—. Mem. Ephebian Soc. Los Angeles, Cal. Scholarship Fedn. Named Woman of Year, Gamma Alpha Chi, 1961. Mem. Fashion Group, Am. Assn. U. Women, Advt. Assn. of West, U. So. Cal. Alumni Assn. Alpha Chi

Omega. Home: 2336 Holiday Dr New Orleans LA 70114 Office: PO Box 60160 New Orleans LA 70160

TOWN, (JO) OSTA CLARICE HAMILTON (MRS. ALBERT RAY TOWN), banker; b. St. John, Wash.; d. Oscar Charles and Minnie (Miller) Hamilton; student Edison Inst. Tech., 1952; m. Albert Ray Town, Aug. 31, 1934; children—Charlene Lorraine (Mrs. Kaestner), Richard Lee, David Ray. With W. L. Anderson, Mayor, Moscow, Ida., 1944-50; clk., cashier dept. store, Moscow; clk.-cashier Bon Marche-Northgate, Seattle, 1950; clk.-stenographer Blake, Moffitt & Towne, Seattle, 1951-53; bookkeeper Wockner Pontiac, Seattle, 1953-54; asst. cashier, loan officer Nat. Bank of Alaska, Anchorage, 1954-72, mgr. Internat. Airport br., 1972—, asst. v.p., 1973—. Mem. Am. Inst. Banking (chpt. pres. 1966-67, asso. councilman 1967—), Nat. Assn. Bank Women (group chmn. 1969-70). Club: Quota (pres. 1968). Home: 4000 Iowa Dr Anchorage AK 99503 Office: PO Box 4-J Anchorage AK 99503

TOWNES, WILLA MAE CRAWFORD (MRS. JOHN B. TOWNES), civic worker; b. Lamont, Okla., Nov. 25, 1897; d. Charles C. and Elmira (Nelson) Crawford; B.Sc., Northwestern State U., 1926; M.L.S., Okla. U., 1954; m. John B. Townes, Sept. 11, 1924; 1 dau., Willa Ann (Mrs. Jack L. Bostwick). Instr. home econs. Nowata (Okla.) High Sch., 1918-20, Tonkawa (Okla.) High Sch., 1920-25; librarian Seminole (Okla.) High Sch., 1954-63, Jr. Coll., 1954-63; owner, mgr. Townes Newcomer Service, 1949—. Mem. Okla. Arts and Humanities Council, 1969—; v.p. Seminole Arts and Humanities Council, 1968—. Mem. Okla. Sch. Librarians (pres. 1960-61), Seminole C. of C. (chmn. cultural affairs 1970—), Seminole Hist. Soc. (dir. 1970—), D.A.R. (regent Cedar River chpt. 1970-72), P.E.O. Methodist. Home: 1220 Van Dr Seminole OK 74868

TOWNS, EVA ROSE, psychiatrist; b. Ellwood City, Pa., Feb. 3, 1927; d. Albert and Mattie (Flagg) Rose; B.S., U. Pitts., 1948; M.D., Howard U., 1953; postgrad. Freedmen's Hosp., 1947-52, Johns Hopkins Hosp., 1952-54; children—Ronald V., Shaaron R., James A., Jennifer R. Intern, Homer Phillips Hosp., St. Louis, 1953-54; civilian physician Travis AFB, Fairfield, Cal., 1955-56; resident adult psychiatry Freedmen's Hosp., Washington, 1958-62; fellow child psychiatry Johns Hopkins Hosp., Balt., 1962-64, cons. in pediatrics, psychiatry, 1964—; cons. Nat. Inst. Mental Health, 1964-73; staff dept. pediatrics Howard U., 1966-73; dir. area mental health program D.C. Dept. Human Resources. Fellow Am. Psychiat. Assn.; mem. D.C. Psychiat. Assn., Alliance for Psychiat. Progress, Nat. Med. Assn., Med. Chirurg. Soc. D.C. Address: 7739 16th St NW Washington DC 20012

TOWNSEND, BESSIE WHALEY (MRS. BUFORD A. TOWNSEND), former motel owner; b. Gatlinburg, Tenn., Mar. 27, 1906; d. John Mitchel and Charity (Ogle) Whaley; student U. Tenn. Coll. Edn., 1926-30; m. Buford A. Townsend, June 18, 1926. Tchr., Sevierville (Tenn.) Elementary Sch., 1930-59; sec. to chancellor 13th Jud. Circuit, 1959-71; co-owner, mgr. Edgewater Motel, Gatlinburg, 1960-73. Active P.T.A.; mem. library bd. Sevier County, Tenn., 1960-63. Mem. U. Tenn. Gen. Alumni Assn. Baptist. Republican. Clubs: Manthano (pres. Sevierville 1955-56, 70-71); Century, Univ. Tenn. (Knoxville, Tenn.). Home: PO Box 191 Gatlinburg TN 37738

TOWNSEND, DEBORAH, coll. dean; b. Jackson, Mich., Aug. 22, 1934; d. Richard Emory and Edna (Wiers) Townsend; B.A., U. Mich., 1956, M.A., 1961; postgrad. U. Wis. Asst. dean students Beloit (Wis.) Coll., 1957-62; asst. dean women U. Wis., Madison, 1962-66, asst. dir. housing, 1966-67; intern, student counseling center, 1967-68, asst. to dean Coll. Letters and Sci., 1968-69; dean women Swarthmore (Pa.) Coll., 1969—. Mem. Nat., Pa. assns. women deans adminstrs. and counselors, Eastern Assn. Coll. Deans and Counselors, Am. Assn. Higher Edn., Pi Lambda Theta. Home: 512 Elm Av Swarthmore PA 19081

TOWNSEND, DORIS ANN MCFERRAN (MRS. WILLIAM PORTER TURNER TOWNSEND), editor; b. Mpls., Apr. 1, 1914; d. Robert Bayard and Edith Elisabeth (Hoar) McFerran; B.A., U. Minn., 1934; M.S., U. Kan., 1940; m. Floyd Raymond Cogswell, Mar. 15, 1935 (div. Nov. 1937); m. 2d, William Porter Turner Townsend, May 20, 1944; stepchildren—Lynne Mary (Mrs. Frank Turley), Karen Ann (Mrs. Thomas McLaughlin). Asst. dir. women's activities radio sta. WTCN, Mpls., 1934-35; program dir. radio sta. WDGY, 1936-37; free-lance writer, free-lance actress, 1937-42; editor Radio-TV Mirror Mag., Macfadden Publs., N.Y.C, 1942-52; free-lance writer, 1952-60; editor-in-chief Rutledge Books Inc., N.Y.C., 1961—. Counselor disturbed high sch. boys, 1942-60. Mem. Authors Guild, Authors League, Alpha Delta Pi, Delta Phi Lambda. Author: Your Career in Civil Service, 1942; Your Career in Retailing, 1942; Dinny and Dreamdust, 1961; 1000 Fabulous Sandwiches Cookbook, 1965; (under pseudonym Ann McFerran) Poems to Be Read Aloud, Stories to Be Read Aloud, 1965; Elizabeth Blackwell, First Woman Doctor, 1966; The Joy of Family, 1969; Big and Little ABC, Ten Trained Bears, 1969; The Family Cookbook: Desserts, 1971; The Fish and Game Cookbook, 1974. Home: 301 E 48th St New York City NY 10017 Office: 25 W 43d St New York City NY 10036

TOWNSEND, ELIZABETH SERRE, social agy. adminstr.; b. Phila., May 22, 1914; d. Charles and Antoinette (Serre) Townsend; B.S. in Edn., U. Pa., 1935, M.S.W., 1938. Formerly social worker Sleighton Farm Sch. Girls, Darling, Pa.; social worker Children's Bur. Del., Wilmington, 1939-40, supr., 1940-47, asst. dir., 1947-48, exec. dir., 1948—. Chmn. Del. Inter-Agy. Com. on Adoption; Bd. dirs. Child Welfare League Am., Wilmington YMCA, Episcopal Ch. Home Found.; adv. bd. Adoption Resource Exchange N. Am. Mem. Nat. Assn. Social Workers, Acad. Certified Social Workers, Kappa Alpha Theta. Home: 14 Bedford Ct Wilmington DE 19805 Office: 2005 Baynard Bldv Wilmington DE 19802

TOWNSEND, FLORENCE OCTAVIA ALEXANDER (MRS. WALTER L. TOWNSEND), educator; b. Prentiss, Miss., May 2, 1939; d. Robert and Hattie Mae (Barnes) Alexander; B.S., Tenn. Agrl. and Indsl. State U., 1962, M.S., 1967; m. Walter L. Townsend, Jan. 15, 1963; children—Olatunde, Audarshia. Psychol. examiner Peabody Coll., Nashville, 1964-67; psychologist-unit dir. Clover Bottom Hosp. and Sch., Donelson, Tenn., 1967-70; instr. psychology Malcolm X Coll., Chgo., 1970-73, asst. prof. psychology, chmn. social sci. dept., 1973—. Recipient Ujima and Umoja award Malcolm X Coll. Sisterhood, 1973; named Outstanding Tchr. of Year, Malcolm X Coll. Students, 1970. Mem. Am. Assn. Mental Deficiency, Am., Chgo. Area assns. Black psychology. Office: 1900 W Van Buren St Chicago IL 60612

TOWNSEND, JANE KALTENBACH (MRS. ROBERT LESLIE TOWNSEND), educator; b. Chgo., Dec. 21, 1922; d. Robert William and Frances (Rayner) Couffer; B.S., Beloit Coll., 1944; M.A., U. Wis., 1946; Ph.D., U. Ia., 1950; m. Robert Leslie Townsend, Aug. 30, 1966. Research asst. U. Wis., 1950-53; Am. Cancer Soc. postdoctoral fellow Wenner Grens Institut, Stockholm, Sweden, 1953-56; asst. prof. biol. scis. Northwestern U., 1956-58; asst. prof. biol. scis. Mt. Holyoke Coll., 1958-64, asso. prof. 1964-70, prof., 1970—. Mem. A.A.A.S., Am. Inst. Biol. Scis., Am. Assn. Anatomists, Soc. for Devel. and Growth, Am. Soc. Zoologists (program officer 1965-67, chmn. publs. bd. 1968-70 div. comparative endocrinology), Tissue Culture Assn., Phi Beta Kappa, Sigma Xi, Pi Beta Phi. Contbr. articles to profl. jours. Home: 139 Cold Hill Granby MA 01033 Office: Dept Biol Sci Mount Holyoke Coll South Hadley MA 01075

TOWNSEND, JEANNETTE KATHRYN, psychologist; b. Los Angeles, May 30, 1939; d. James R. and Annabel Jean (Fischer) Townsend; B.A., Stanford, 1962; Ph.D., U. N.C., 1968. Psychologist, Umstead Hosp., N.C., 1966-68; postdoctoral fellow Reiss Davis Child Study Center, Los Angeles, 1968-70; staff psychologist Orange County Med. Center, 1970-73; chief childrens services East Central Regional Mental Health Service, Orange County, Santa Ana, Cal., 1973—; clin. instr. med. psychology, dept. psychiatry and human behavior U. Cal. at Irvine, 1971—. Cons., Easter Seal Rehab. Center, Orange, 1971; pvt. practice, Newport Beach, Cal., 1973—. Founding mem. Orange Sch. Attendance Rev. Bd., Orange County chpt. Momma. Mem. Am., Western, Cal., Orange County psychol. assns. Home: 14185 Paseo Corto Tustin CA 92680 Office: 2110 E 1st St Santa Ana CA 92701

TOWNSEND, JOAN BROOM, anthropologist, educator; b. Dallas, July 9, 1933; d. Turner I. and Pauline (Paulk) Broom; A.A., Christian Coll., 1952; B.A., U. Cal. at Los Angeles, 1959, Ph.D., 1965; m. Edwin O. Anderson, Aug. 14, 1970; children (of previous marriage)—Paula Lynn, Wayne. Tutor phys. anthropology U. Cal., Los Angeles, 1959-60, 61-62, research asst., 1959, 61-62, teaching asst. dept. anthropology, 1962-63; instr. cultural anthropology E. Los Angeles Coll., 1962-63; asst. prof. dept. anthropology Los Angeles State Coll., 1963; instr. dept. anthropology So. Ill. U., Carbondale, 1963-64; lectr. dept. anthropology U. Man., Winnipeg, Can., 1964-65, asst. prof., 1965-72, asso. prof., 1972—. Fellow Am. Anthrop. Assn., Royal Anthrop. Inst., Arctic Inst. N. Am., Soc. Applied Anthropology; mem. Soc. Am. Archaeology, Canadian Archaeol. Assn., Current Anthropology (asso.), A.A.A.S., N.Y. Acad. Sci., Sigma Xi, Phi Beta Kappa, Pi Gamma Mu, Phi Theta Kappa. Contbr. articles to profl. jours. Address: 85 Tunis Bay Winnipeg MB R3T 2X2 Canada

TOWNSEND, MARJORIE TREES RHODES (MRS. CHARLES EBY TOWNSEND), electronic engr.; b. Washington, Mar. 12, 1930; d. Lewis Boling and Marjorie (Trees) Rhodes; B.E.E., George Washington U., 1951; m. Charles Eby Townsend, June 7, 1948; children—Charles Eby, Lewis Rhodes, John Cunningham, Richard Leo. Phys. sci. aid Nat. Bur. Standards, 1948-51; electronic scientist Naval Research Lab., Washington, 1951-59; electronic engr. aero-space tech. Goddard Space Flight Center, Greenbelt, Md., 1959—, project mgr. Small Astronomy Satellite, 1966—. Mem. Joint Bd. on Sci. Edn. for Greater Washington Area, 1964-69, vice chmn. secondary sch. contacts com. and planning council, 1964-68, contact at Alice Deal Jr. High Sch., 1963-69. Bd. dirs. George Washington U. Engr. Alumni Assn., 1973—. Mem. I.E.E.E. (sr. mem., program chmn. group aerospace and electronic systems Washington chpt. 1964-68, chmn. 1969-70; program chmn. Washington sect. 1969-70, exec. com. 1971, treas. 1971-72, sec. 1972-73, vice chmn. 1973-74), Am. Inst. Aero. and Astronautics, D.A.R., A.A.A.S., N.Y. Acad. Scis., Daus. Colonial Wars, Sigma Kappa. Episcopalian. Home: 3529 Tilden St NW Washington DC 20008 Office: Code 405 2 Goddard Space Flight Center Greenbelt MD 20771

TOWNSEND, PATRICIA ANN, educator; b. Lufkin, Tex., May 25, 1933; d. Paul Monarch and Clifford (Carson) Townsend; B.S., Stephen F. Austin State Coll., Tex., 1953, M.A., 1956; Ph.D. (U. fellow), U. Wis., 1959. Speech tchr. Blocker Jr. High Sch., Texas City, Tex., 1954-56; research asst. U. Wis., 1956-57; asst. prof. speech U. No. Ia., Cedar Falls, 1959-66; asso. prof. speech Wis. State U., Whitewater, 1966-68, prof., 1968—. Dir. Speakers Bur., United World Federalists, Cedar Falls, 1963-65, Whitewater, 1965-69. Bd. dirs. Whitewater chpt. A.R.C., 1971—, chmn., 1972—. Mem. Speech Assn. Am., Central States, Wis. speech assns., Am. Assn. U. Profs. (pres. 1973—), Rhetoric Soc. Am., Am. Civil Liberties Union (dir. Whitewater 1971-72), Wis. Speech Communication Assn. (treas.), Soc. Historic Preservation, Common Cause, Zeta Phi Eta, Pi Kappa Delta, Alpha Psi Omega, Phi Kappa Phi, Alpha Chi. Editor: Iowa State Speech Newsletter, 1963-65, News and Notes, Central States Speech Jour., 1970-73. Home: 417 S Prince St Whitewater WI 53190

TOWSLEY, ALICE CATHERINE GOLDSMITH, editor; b. N.Y.C., July 26, 1924; d. George Everett and Alice Sophie (Kunkeli) Goldsmith; student U. Hawaii, 1943; m. Harold Dulmage Towsley, Jan. 4, 1941 (div. Sept. 1942). Writer Honolulu Advertiser, 1942-47; advt. mgr. Paterson (N.J.) Morning Call, 1949-52; contbg. editor Med. World News, Rudder, Welcome, Mayfair, Internat. Design, Parents, 1953-69; pub. editor Jr. League Mag., 1954-59; editor, asst. pub. Drs. Wife Mag., 1959-64; dir. information services, editor Am. Field Service Internat. Scholarships, N.Y.C., 1967—. Cons. N.Y. Herald Tribune, 1953-54, Ida. Free Press, 1948-49. Active Henry St. Settlement, Nat. Assn. Retarded Children, Arthritis and Rheumatism Found. Mem. Advt. Women N.Y. Club: Overseas Press Am. Home: 325 E 41st St New York City NY 10017 Office: 313 E 43d St New York City NY 10017

TRACEY, MILDRED WHITE (MRS. PATRICK A. TRACEY, JR.), lawyer; b. Providence; d. John A. and Mary Frances (Sweeney) White; B.S., U. R.I., 1941; LL.B., Portia Law Sch., 1958; LL.M., Suffolk Law Sch., 1960; m. Patrick A. Tracey, Jr., Aug. 8, 1945; children—Elaine, Michelle, Seanna, Austine, Patrick Austin III. Admitted to Mass. bar, 1959; practiced law, Boston, 1959-69; mem. firm McGee, Gifford, Farrelly & Keough, Providence, 1969—. Mem. Nat. Assn. Women Lawyers, R.I. Women Lawyers Assn., R.I., Mass. bar assns. Home: 197 Taber Av Providence RI 02903 Office: 10 Dorrance St Providence RI 02906

TRACY, JEAN CAROL, banker; b. Bklyn., Nov. 11, 1930; d. Frank W. and Irene (Crewe) Tracy; A.B., N.Y. U., 1962. Adminstrv. asst. to v.p. for devel. N.Y. U., N.Y.C., 1951-64; with Beverly Hills Nat. Bank (Cal.), 1964, asst. v.p., 1969—, corporate sec., 1970—; corp. sec. Beverly Hills Bancorp., 1971—. Home: 2112 Camden Av Los Angeles CA 90025 Office: 9600 Santa Monica Blvd Beverly Hills CA 90210

TRACY, LOUISE TREADWELL (MRS. SPENCER TRACY), educator; b. New Castle, Pa.; d. Alliene Wetmore and Bright (Smith) Treadwell; student Lake Erie Coll., 1915-17; D.Sc. (hon.) Northwestern U., 1951; L.H.D. (hon.), U. So. Cal., 1953, MacMurray Coll., 1956, Whitworth Coll., 1974; D. Liberal Arts (hon.), Lake Erie Coll., 1955; Litt.D. (hon.), Gallaudet Coll., 1966; m. Spencer Tracy, Sept. 12, 1923 (dec.); children—John, Louise. Founder John Tracy Clinic, pre-sch. deaf and hard of hearing children and their parents, 1942, pres. bd. dirs., 1943—; 2d v.p. Alexander Graham Bell Assn. for Deaf, 1957-64, now mem. hon. bd.; mem. Nat. Adv. Council Vocational Rehab., 1956-60; mem. Nat. Adv. Bd. on Establishment of Nat. Tech. Inst. for Deaf, 1965-66; mem. Presdl. Task Force on Physically Handicapped, 1969-70. Recipient Ann. award Save the Children Fedn., 1956; distinguished service citation Conf. Execs. of Ams. Schs. for Deaf, 1963; 1st honors award Internat. Parents Orgn., 1968. Hon. mem. Am. Orthopsychiatric Assn. Episcopalian. Home: 700 S Beverly Glen Blvd Los Angeles CA 90024 Office: 806 W Adams Blvd Los Angeles CA 90007

TRACY, MARY ELIZABETH, librarian; b. Joliet, Ill., Aug. 18, 1922; d. Charles Joseph and Catherine (Fay) Tracy; B.A. cum laude, Coll. St. Francis, 1944; M.A. in L.S., Rosary Coll., River Forest, Ill., 1958. Tchr., Joliet grade schs., 1944-52, 54-61, Am. schs., Bremerhaven, Frankfurt, Germany, 1952-54; librarian Joliet Twp. Central High Sch., 1961—, dist. dir., 1972-73; instr. library tech. Joliet Jr. Coll., 1973—. Pres., Joliet Jr. Catholic Woman's League, 1950-51. Mem. Am., Ill., Chicagoland library assns., Am., Ill. sch. library assns., Ill. Audio-visual Assn., Chgo. Suburban Audiovisual Roundtable, Alumnae Assn. Coll. St. Francis (sec. 1946-48, v.p. 1957-59, bd. advisers 1965-67). Home: 353 Wilson St Joliet IL 60433 Office: 201 E Jefferson St Joliet IL 60432

TRACY, SISTER MARY JOANNA, educator; b. Newark; d. Edward J. and Helen E. (Brady) Tracy; B.S., Fordham U., 1928; M.A., Cath. U., Washington, 1933; Ph.D. (NSF summer grantee), St. Thomas Inst. Exptl. Medicine, 1963. Prof. biology and chemistry Caldwell (N.J.) Coll., 1941—, chmn. sci. dept., 1941-71. Regional dir. N.J. Jr. Acad. Sci., 1966—. Mem. Am. Chem. Soc., A.A.A.S., N.J. Acad. Scis., Albertus Magnus Assn., Caldwell Coll. Alumnae Assn. (dir.). Address: Caldwell Coll Caldwell NJ 07006

TRACY, PAULINE ALOISE SOUERS (MRS. JAMES RICHARD TRACY), author; b. Bridgeport, Ill., Nov. 20, 1914; d. William Fitch and Carrie (Milhouse) Souers; B.Ed., Eastern Ill. U., 1937; m. James Richard Tracy, Sept. 18, 1946 (dec. Aug. 1972). Mem. Nat. Ret. Tchrs. Assn., Eastern Ill. Alumni Assn. (life), P.E.O. Sisterhood, Nat. League Am. Pen Women, Am. Poets Fellowship Soc. (hon. life mem.), New World Poets Club, The Pensters, Pleasure Island Sr. Citizens Club (charter), Am. Poetry League, Ill. Pen Women, Ill. Women's Press Assn., Nat. Fedn. Press Women, Ill. Poetry Soc. (charter), Book Club for Poetry. Republican. Baptist. Author: His Handiwork, 1954; Memory is a Poet, 1964; The Silken Web, 1965; A Merry Heart, 1966; In Two or Three Tomorrows, 1968; All Flesh Is Grass, 1971; Beyond The Edge, 1973. Address: 447 Chestnut St Bridgeport IL 62417 also Box 382 Gulf Shores AL 36542

TRACY, RUTH MARY, nursing adminstr.; b. Parry Sound, Ont., Can., Jan. 10, 1928; d. Charles Edward and Mary Annie (Little) Bushey; R.N., Peterborough (Ont.) Civic Hosp., 1948; m. Ralph Tracy, May 6, 1950; children—Gary, Brian, Kelly. Mem. staff Parry Sound Dist. Gen. Hosp., 1948—, dir. nursing, dir. nursing asst. centre, 1964—, also dir. home care program, infection control program, 1974—. Mem. Ont. Hosp. Assn. (chmn. dist. council 10, 1970, mem.-at-large to Provincial Nursing Adminstrn. 1971), Registered Nurses Assn. Ont. Home: 15 Adelaide St Parry Sound ON P2A 1H2 Canada

TRAEGER, BARBARA SHIELDS (MRS. JOHN E. TRAEGER), pub. relations exec.; b. Pitts., Oct. 19, 1932; d. Marshall Charles and Margaret Helen (Ward) Shields; B.A. in English, Ripon Coll., 1954; postgrad., U. Chgo., 1971; m. John E. Traeger, Apr. 30, 1971; children by previous marriage—Cynthia, Charles R., Henry. Dir. pub. relations Chgo. unit Am. Cancer Soc., 1964-65; asst. bur. pub. information Am. Hosp. Assn., Chgo., 1966-68; dir. pub. relations U. Chgo. Hosps. and Clinics, 1968-72; dir. pub. relations Evanston (Ill.) Hosp., 1972—. Recipient excellence award, Am. Inst. Graphic Arts, 1971, MacEachern award, 1972, 73, award Type Dirs. Club, 1970, excellence award Modern Publicity, 1972. Mem. Assn. Am. Med. Colls., Am. Soc. Hosp. Pub. Relations Dirs., Acad. Hosp. Pub. Relations (seminar chmn. 1974), Ill. Hosp. Assn. Pub. Relations Soc. Chgo. Hosp. Council Pub. Relations Assn. Home: 1830 Balmoral Lane Glenview IL 60025 Office: 2650 Ridge Av Evanston IL 60201

TRAEGER, LYDIA ELSIE (MRS. MARVIN C. TRAEGER), educator; b. Gladstone, Neb., Oct. 29, 1917; d. Gustave Herman and Emma Adeline (Starck) Dux; B.S., Peru State Coll., 1959; postgrad. Kearney State Coll., 1968, U. Neb., 1964, 66, 70; m. Marvin C. Traeger, Aug. 3, 1947. Tchr. rural and small town schs. in Neb., 1938-63; elementary prin., Steele City, Neb., 1959; elementary tchr., Hasting, Neb., 1963-69, Deshler, Neb., 1970—. Pres. Muscular Dystrophy Found. Neb., 1953—. Named Midwest Good Neighbor of Year, Radio Sta. KFAB, Omaha, 1956. Mem. N.E.A., Neb., Deshler edn. assns., Fairbury Bus. and Profl. Women's Club, Methodist. Club: Woman's (Deshler). Home: Rural Route 3 Box 147 Fairbury NE 68352

TRAEGER, MILDRED (MRS. LAWRENCE E. TRAEGER), assn. exec.; student N.Y. U., 1944-46, U. Cal. at Los Angeles, 1960-62, Pierce Coll., 1958; m. Lawrence E. Traeger, Feb. 8, 1947 (dec. Sept. 1972); children—Suzanne, Jamie (Mrs. Lloyd McGowan). Free lance pub. relations, Spokane, also Los Angeles; owner Mildred Traeger Pub. Relations, WoodlandsHills, Cal., 1956-65; pub. relations dir. So. Calif. div. Salvation Army, Los Angeles, 1966—. Mem. Pub. Relations Soc. Am., Los Angeles Advt. Women (Merit award 1966, Spl. Anniversary award 1971, dir. 1970), Los Angeles Publicity Club, Los Angeles Press Club. Home: 6121 Scenic Av Hollywood CA 90068 Office: The Salvation Army So Calif Div Hdqtrs 900 W 9th St PO Box 15899-Del Valle Sta Los Angeles CA 90015

TRAHAN, ELIZABETH WELT (MRS. DONALD TRAHAN), educator; b. Berlin, Germany; d. Albert and Selma (Silberstein) Welt; came to U.S., 1947, naturalized, 1954; B.A., Sarah Lawrence Coll., 1951; M.A., Cornell U., Ithaca, N.Y., 1953; Ph.D., Yale, 1957; m. Donald Trahan, Aug. 31, 1957; 1 dau., Jennifer. Reader, contbr. Der neue Weg, Vienna, Austria, 1945-47; tchr. Am. Joint Distbrn. Com., Vienna, 1946-47; asst. reader Vienna Burgtheater, 1946-47; stenographer-typist Imperial Linens, Inc., N.Y.C., 1947-49; teaching fellow in German, Cornell U., Ithaca, N.Y., 1951-53; instr. German, Russian, U. Mass., Amherst, 1956-60; asst. prof. Russian, U. Pitts., 1960-64, asso. prof., 1965-66; asso. prof. humanities, chmn. dept. translation and interpretation Monterey (Cal.) Inst. Fgn. Studies, 1968—. Mem. Modern Lang. Assn., Internat. Arthur Schnitzler Research Assn., Am. Comparative Lit. Assn., Am. Assn. Tchrs. German, Am. Assn. Tchrs. Slavic and East European Langs., Am. Assn. for Advancement Slavic Studies, Am. Translator Assn. Editor 2 German readers; fiction, translations. Contbr. articles to profl. jours. Home: 79 Via Ventura Monterey CA 93940

TRAHEY, JANE, advt. agy. exec.; b. Chgo., Nov. 19, 1923; d. David and Margaret (Hennessy) Trahey; B.A. Mundelein Coll, 1943; postgrad. U. Wis., 1945. With survey dept. Chgo. Daily News, 1946; copywriter Carson Pirie Scott & Co., 1947; copywriter Neiman-Marcus, Dallas, 1947-55, advt. dir., 1951-53, sales promotion dir., 1953-55; with 425 Advt. Assos., Inc., N.Y.C., 1955—; pres. Trahey Advt., Inc. Mem. Fashion Group (mem. bd. govs.). Advt. Assn. Women, Am. Inst. Graphic Arts. Author: Taste of Texas; The Martini Cookbook; Life with Mother Superior, 1962; 100 Years from Harper's Bazaar, 1967; Pecked to Death, 1970; Ring Round the Bathtub, 1972. Home: 180 E 79th St New York City NY 10021 Office: 919 3d Av New York City NY 10022

TRAINER, SISTER DESIRÈE, coll. ofcl.; b. Malden, Mass., Dec. 23, 1905; d. Owen Christopher and Alice Sarah (O'Donnell) Trainer; B.A. in English and Music, St. Mary-of-the-Woods Coll., 1937; M.A. in English, U. Notre Dame, 1955. Joined Order Sisters of Providence; elementary music instr., band dir., 1925-36; instr. English, French, social studies, religion secondary schs., Ind., Ill., Mass., 1939-65; lectr. English, moderator campus news Immaculata Coll. of Washington, 1965-71, dir. coll. and alumnae relations, 1971—. Lectr. lit. Am. U., Washington, 1969-72. Newspaper Fund fellow, summer 1962; Nat. Def. Edn. Act grantee, 1965. Mem. Nat. Council Tchrs. English, Notre Dame English Assn. Home: 4344 Wisconsin Av NW Washington DC 20016

TRAINOR, MARY ROSALEEN, educator; b. Nelson, B.C., Can., May 20, 1931; d. George Edwin and Nora Christina (Murphy) Trainor; B.Ed., Seattle U., 1958, M.A., St. John's U., 1963, Ph.D., 1966. Came to U.S. 1954, naturalized 1960. Tchr. B.C. pub. schs., 1951-54, St. Teresa, Seattle, 1958-59, St. Joseph Sch., Wenatchee, 1959-61; asso. prof. philosophy Seattle (Wash.) U., 1965—, dir. honors program, 1972—. Mem. Sisters of St. Joseph of Peace, Seattle Archdiocese Sisters Council (sec. 1970-72, chmn. 1972-73). Home: 1663 Killarney Way Bellevue WA 98004 Office: Seattle U Seattle WA 98122

TRAIS, MARY (MRS. JACK TRAIS), editor; b. Chgo., Apr. 4, 1919; d. Nathan and Marcia (Arkis) Trais; student Herzl Jr. Coll., 1950-52, Northwestern U., 1953-58, U. Chgo., 1955-56; m. Jack Trais, Mar. 2, 1936; children—Stuart, Richard, Karen. Mem. pub. relations staff First Comml. Bank, Chgo., 1960; with Chgo. Park Dist., 1967—, editor Parkways, 1967—, pub. relations writer, 1967—. Sec. Rest Have Convalescent Home Soc., 1946-48; pres., Sumner Sch. P.T.A., 1954-56. Mem. Am. Women in Radio and TV, Internat. (sec.-treas. dist. 4), Chgo. (v.p. 1972) assns. bus. communicators. Club: ALPHA Bridge (Chgo.). Contbr. articles and fiction to mags. Home: 1245 W Farwell Chicago IL 60626 Office: 425 E McFetridge Dr Chicago IL 60605

TRAKS, ELMERICE (MRS. ANDREAS A. TRAKS), internist; b. Estonia, Dec. 5, 1924; d. Voldo and Leonore (Mauser) Teetsmaa; student U. Tartu (Estonia), 1942-44; M.D., U. Tübingen (Germany), 1950; m. Andreas A. Traks, Dec. 24, 1949. Intern, St. Joseph's Hosp., Paterson, N.J., 1953-54; resident Cleve. Met. Gen. Hosp., 1954-57; teaching fellow Western Res. U., Cleve., 1957-58, asst. prof. medicine, 1965—, asst. prof. pediatrics, 1971—; research fellow Am. Heart Assn., 1958-60. Mem. Heart Assn. N.E. Ohio, A.C.P., Am. Fedn. Clin. Research, Sigma Xi. Home: 6495 Big Creek Parkway Cleveland OH 44130

TRANTHAM, GRACE ELEANOR MACDOUGAL (MRS. WALTER E. TRANTHAM, JR.), writer; b. Washington; d. John and Grace Kimball (Douglass) MacDougal; student Dunbarton Coll., 1933-35, Columbia (Tenn.) Inst., 1935-37; m. Walter Earl Trantham, Jr., Oct. 30, 1943; children—Walter Earl III, Duffey Douglass. Publicist, Navy Dept., 1943-45; columnist, reporter Camp Pendleton (Cal.) Scout, Oceanside (Cal.) Blade Tribune, 1947-51; staff columnist Oceanside Blade Tribune, 1952-54; free-lance writer, including ednl. monographs for use in secondary and coll. edn., 1954—. Area co-chmn. March of Dimes campaign, 1966-70, Am. Cancer Soc., 1962-69; co-chmn. Montclair Prep. Sch. Assn., 1968-69. Recipient Merit award Cal. Press Women's Assn., 1955. Republican. Mem. Anglican Ch. (co-chmn. Altar Guild 1961-70). Home: 2605 Faber Ct Falls Church VA 22046

TRASTER, JOAN FLORA-CLOTILDE (MRS. RICHARD J. TRASTER), investment co. exec.; b. Castropignano, Province de Campobasso, Italy, Jan. 8, 1915; d. Nicola and Maria (Tagliaferri) Zinni; came to U.S., 1917, naturalized, 1940; B.A., Case-Western Res. U., 1936, Med. Technologist, 1938; m. Richard J. Traster, Dec. 3, 1940 (dec. Nov. 1965). Med. technologist St. Joseph Hosp., Ft. Wayne, Ind., 1938-40; lab. adminstr. Irene Byron Hosp., Ft. Wayne, 1940-44; co-owner Traster Ins. Agy., Ft. Wayne, 1940-70, Ft. Wayne Loan-Discount Co., 1944-60, Suburban Motors, Inc., Ft. Wayne 1944-66, Traster Securities Co., Ft. Wayne, 1959-63; co-founder Bankers Investment Corp., Ft. Wayne, Ind., 1959, exec. adminstr., 1960—. Mem. Am. Soc. Clin. Pathologists, Am. Soc. Med. Technologists, Am. Assn. U. Women, Nat. Assn. Mut. Ins. Agents, Ind. Mut. Agts. Assn. Ind. (conv. chmn. 1962-63), Alumni Assn. Case-Western Reserve U. Presbyn. Elks Ladies Assn. Clubs: Orchard Ridge Country, Summit (Ft. Wayne). Home: Three Rivers Apts E 1205 Fort Wayne IN 46802 Office: 4740 Coldwater Rd Fort Wayne IN 46825

TRAUBE, SYLVIA GOULD, psychiatrist; b. Bangor, Me., Oct. 16, 1909; d. Daniel Israel and Florence (Speare) Gould; A.B., U. Me., 1930; Ed.M., Boston U., 1942, M.D., 1950; postgrad. U. Chgo., 1944-45; m. Serge Vladimir Traube, Feb. 1, 1935 (div. May 1943); 1 son, Richard Serge. Interne medicine Kings County Hosp., Bklyn., 1950-51; research fellow dept. medicine Columbia Coll. Phys. and Surg., 1951-55; clin. fellow medicine Presbyn. Hosp., N.Y.C., 1951-53, asst. physician, 1953-55; spl. fellow medicine Meml. Hosp. for Cancer, N.Y.C., 1955-56, clin. asst. physician preventive medicine, 1955-57, clin. asst. physician gen. medicine, 1957-58; co-dir. research project Sloan-Kettering Inst. for Cancer Research, N.Y.C., 1955-61; research asso. geriatric project Cold Spring Inst., Cold Spring-on-Hudson, N.Y., 1955-58; research asso. preventive medicine Sloan-Kettering div. Cornell U. Med. Coll., 1956-60; resident psychiatry VA Hosp., Montrose, N.Y., N.Y. Hosp. Payne Whitney Clinic, N.Y.C., 1956-59; staff psychiatrist N.Y. State, also cons. psychiatrist Suffolk County Mental Health Bd., Holtsville and Babylon, N.Y., 1960-62; asst. psychiatrist N.Y. Hosp., 1960-64, asst. attending psychiatrist, 1964—; psychiat. cons., personal health service N.Y. Hosp., 1963-64; pvt. practice psychiatry, N.Y.C., 1959—; asst. psychiatry Cornell U. Med. Coll., N.Y.C., 1960-63, clin. instr. psychiatry, 1963—. Mem. Am. Psychiat. Assn., A.M.A., Am. Group Psychotherapy Assn., Assn. Am. Med. Colls., N.Y. Soc. Clin. Psychiatry, N.Y. State Med. Soc., N.Y. Acad. Scis., Hawk Mountain Sanctuary Assn., Delta Delta Delta. Address: 200 East End Av New York City NY 10028

TRAUERNICHT, KAY ANTHANY SNODGRASS (MRS. STANLEY R. TRAUERNICHT), garment co. exec.; b. Flat River, Mo.; d. Anthany and Sarah (Meade) Snodgrass; student Flat River Jr. Coll., 1936; m. Stanley A. Trauernicht, Oct. 21, 1936; 1 dau., Rita (Mrs. William Snyder). With Nat. Garment Co., St. Louis, 1937-42, Carfree Sportwear, St. Louis, 1942-55; with Lowenbaums Mfg. Co., 1955—, plant mgr., Mounds, Ill., 1959—, Cape Girardeau, Mo., 1972—. Home: East Cape Park McClure IL 62957 Office: 100 S Minnesota St Cape Girardeau MO 63701

TRAUERTS, HELEN MARIE (MRS. ERNEST J. PETRULIO), pediatrician; b. Bklyn., Mar. 4, 1931; d. Theodore Richard and Gerritze Aleida (Van Bree) Trauerts; A.B., N.Y. U., 1951; M.D., N.Y. Med. Coll., 1955; m. Ernest J. Petrulio, Oct. 16, 1954; children—Karen, Richard. Intern Ellis Hosp., Schenectady, 1955-56; resident in pediatrics St. Christopher's Hosp. for Children, Phila., 1956-58; with Sacramento County Health Dept., 1959-61; pediatrician Cal. Children's Home Soc., Sacramento, 1961—, Sacramento County schs., 1965—; med. cons. in spl. edn. for San, Juan, Rio Linda, Folsum Sch. dists. Health careers chmn. Sacramento Women's Med. Aux., 1965—. Episcopalian. Home: 4960 Sudbury Way Carmichael CA 95608 Office: 1813 Professional Dr Sacramento CA 95825

TRAUTNER, MARILYN PICKERING (MRS. DEAN TRAUTNER), physician; b. Jackson, Mich., Apr. 6, 1926; d. Clay and Pauline (Blair) Pickering; A.B., Marietta Coll., 1948; M.D., U. Colo., 1958; m. Dean Trautner, Mar. 5, 1948; children—Christopher, Paula, Clay, David. Intern Gen. Rose Meml. Hosp., Denver, 1958-59; resident Denver Gen., Colo. Gen., Nat. Jewish hosps., Denver, 1960-61; practice medicine specializing in anesthesiology, Denver, 1962—; anesthesiologist Swedish, Porter, Children's hosps.; asst. clin. prof. surgery (anesthesia) U. Med. Center. Diplomate Am. Bd. Anesthesiology. Fellow Am. Coll. Anesthesiologists; mem. Am., Colo. (pres. 1974), Denver socs. anesthesiologists, Phi Beta Kappa. Home: 3370 W Union Av Englewood CO 80110 Office: 3601 S Clarkson St Englewood CO 80110

TRAVAGLINI, BARBARA CARLSON (MRS. ALFONSO FREDERICK TRAVAGLINI), steel co. exec.; b. Easton, Pa., Nov. 4, 1925; d. Gunard Oscar and Margaret Bailey (Berry) Carlson; Bryn Mawr Coll., 1943-44, Moore Coll. of Art, 1944-48; m. Alfonso Frederick Travaglini, June 15, 1946; children—Gunard Carlson, Frederick Carlson, Mark Carlson. Dir., asst. v.p., sec. G.O. Carlson, Inc., Thorndale, Pa., 1956—. Pres. Coatesville Hosp. Aux., 1967-72, 1st v.p., 1972—; treas. Chester County Airport authority. Vice pres. bd. mgrs. Coatesville Hosp.; sec., treas. Gunard Berry Carlson Meml. Found. Trustee Saint Francis Coll. Republican. Roman Catholic. Author: The Kelly Green Cow, 1949; Henry Hippo, 1972. Home: 4000 Hazelwood Av Thorndale PA 19372 Office: G O Carlson Inc Thorndale PA 19372

TRAVELSTEAD, ANN THOMAS, pub. relations and marketing exec.; b. Nashville; d. John Isaac and Elizabeth (Henderson) Thomas; student U. Tenn., 1938-41; m. Frank Charles Welshan, Aug. 20, 1940 (div. Apr. 1942); 1 son, John Thomas; m. 2d, Elmer Charles Pearson, Dec. 26, 1947 (div. June 1958); m. 3d, Will Gooch Travelstead, Dec. 2, 1972. Divisional advt. mgr. Bullocks, Los Angeles, 1949-56; account exec. Botsford-Constantine & Gardner, Portland, Ore., 1956-59; copy dir. Edwin C. Huster, Inc., Knoxville, Tenn., 1960-61; copy supr. Stockton-West-Burkhart, Inc., Cin., 1962-63; feature events dir. Burdines, Miami, Fla., 1963-70; dir. spl. marketing McCormick & Co., Hunt Valley, Md., 1970-72, dir. spl. projects, 1972—; editor Partner Social Calendar Pub. Co., Miami, 1965-67. Chmn., Downtown Improvement Com., Miami, 1964-66. Dir. Women's Orgn., Miami Philharmonic Soc., 1965-66; case com. Children's Service Bur., Dade County, Fla., 1963-66. Mem. Fashion Group (sec.), Vizcayans, Advt. Assn. of Balt., Balt. Symphony, Balt. Art Mus., English Speaking Union, Urban Living Council, Nat. Press Club. Home: 1942 W Northern Pkwy Baltimore MD 21209 Office: 11350 McCormick Rd Hunt Valley MD 21031

TRAVERS, DOROTHY CLAYTON, pub. co. exec.; b. Wilmington, Del., Nov. 19, 1923; d. Frederick George and Helen Grace (Merrick) Clayton; student U. Del., 1941-62; m. Major Nicholas Travers, Jr., Jan. 10, 1942; children—Major Nicholas III, Frederick George, James William. Singer lead roles Wilmington Opera Soc., 1948-62; pres. New Castle (Del.) Independent Press, Inc., 1968—; pres. Fryday's Gift Box, Inc.; v.p. The Marketeers, Inc. Sec., Wilmington Opera Soc., 1947-48; pres. Arasapha Garden Club, 1961-62; chmn. Del. Flower Show, 1961. Pres. Found. House, Inc., Travers Found. Candidate for mayor, New Castle, 1969, City Council, 1971, Trustees New Castle Common, 1972. Address: 112 W 6th St New Castle DE 19720

TRAVERS, MARY ALLIN, folk singer; b. Louisville, Nov. 9, 1936; d. Robert John and Virginia (Allin) Travers; grad. pvt. high sch.; student Art Inst. N.Y.; m. Gerald Taylor, June 1, 1969; children—Erika Allin, Alicia Alice. Sang on 1st records at age 14 as mem. The Songswappers; made albums Talking Union, Folksongs of Four Continents, Banjo Coral; appeared in chorus Broadway show The Next President, 1957; later worked with various lit. and advt. agys.; mem. trio (with Paul Stockey and Peter Yarrow) Peter, Paul and Mary, appearing in concerts U.S. and abroad, on TV and in 5 record albums; now appearing solo. Vice pres. Trio Concerts, Inc. Pres., Artist Civic Rights Assistance Fund, 1964-65. Recipient 4 Gold Albums, Grammy awards Nat. Acad. Rec. Arts and Scis. Office: 75 E 55th St New York City NY 10022

TRAVIS, ANN MARIE, physician; b. Birmingham, Ala., June 19, 1928; d. William Henry and Nettie (McDowell) Travis; B.S., Birmingham-So. Coll., 1948; Ph.D., U. Wis., 1952, M.D., 1955. Rotating intern Birmingham Bapt. Hosps., 1955-56; resident neurology Nat. Hosp., London, Eng., 1956-57, Univ. Hosp., Mpls., 1957-58, VA Hosp., Coatsville, Pa., 1964-65; research asso. neurophysiology U. Wis., 1952-53; staff neurologist VA Hosp., Tomah, Wis., 1965-68, VA Center, Wood, Wis., 1968-71; asst. prof. neurology Marquette Med. Sch., 1968-71; practice medicine, Pinson, Ala., 1971—. Recipient Eva Comer Math. prize, 1948; Phi Sigma Research award, 1952, Charles W. Mayo award, 1955. Mem. Am. Acad. Neurology, A.M.A., Milw. Neuro-Psychiat. Soc., Wis. Neurol. Soc., Phi Beta Kappa, Sigma Xi, Alpha Omega Alpha, Sigma Delta Epsilon. Contbr. articles to profl. jours. Home: Route 3 Box 363 Pinson AL 35126

TRAVIS, IDA, banker; b. Scales Mound, Ill., July 9, 1905; d. William and Eliza (Kuchemann) Travis; grad. pub. schs. Bookkeeper Millhouse Bros. Hardware, Galena, Ill., 1924-28; asst. cashier State Bank of Scales Mound (Ill.), 1928-43, cashier, 1943-69, pres., 1969—, dir., 1953—. Treas. Scales Mound Schs., 1945-54. Club: Contract Bridge Club. Home: Scales Mound IL 61075 Office: State Bank of Scales Mound Scales Mound IL 61075

TRAVIS, MARY EILEEN (MRS. ARTHUR J. TRAVIS), librarian; b. New Glasgow, N.S., Can., Mar. 16, 1931; d. Louis Michael and Mary Cummane (Hallisey) Connolly; B.A., St. Francis Xavier U., 1952; B.L.S., McGill U., 1953; m. Arthur J. Travis, Sept. 1, 1958; children—Mary Patricia, John Louis. Librarian bookmobile Pictou County Library, New Glasgow, 1953-55, head children's dept., 1955-58; head children's dept. St. John (N.B.) City Library, 1960-63, city librarian, 1963-67, regional librarian, since 1969—. Condr. radio show Book Review, CFBC-FM, St. John, 1966—, TV show Magazine CHSJ-TV, St. John, 1966—. Mem. St. John Mayor's Com., 1972—, St. John Bd. Trade, 1970—. Bd. dirs. Netherwood Sch. for Girls, 1969—, Sch. Dist 19, Kings County, N.B., 1968—, N.B. Opera Co., 1965-73, St. John Arts Council, 1968—. Named Woman of Year, St. John, 1973. Mem. Can., Nat. (mem. adv. bd. 1972-74), Ottawa, Atlantic Provinces (pres. 1969-70) library assns., Can. Assn. Children's Librarians (sec. 1967), Catholic Women's League (pres. Rothesay, N.B. chpt. 1966), N.S. Drama League (pres. 1957), Can. Pony Club, Eclectic Club. Roman Catholic. Home: PO Box 302 Rothesay NB Canada Office: Saint John Regional Library 20 Hazen Av Saint John NB Canada

TRAVIS, NEVENNA TSANOFF (MRS. DON C. TRAVIS), realtor; b. Houston, Apr. 16, 1916; d. Radoslav Andrea and Corrinne (Stephenson) Tsanoff; B.A. with distinction, Rice Inst., 1936; M.A., U. Wis., 1938; m. Don C. Travis, June 13, 1940; children—Neven Don Tsanoff, Andrew David Tsanoff. Asso. Bob Bright, Austin, Tex., 1955-57; asso. Ann Miller Crockett, Austin, 1957-66; owner N. T. Travis Real Estate, Austin, 1966—. Texas System Natural Labs., Inc., dir., sec. bd., 1967, sec. treas., dir., 1968—, acting system coordinator, 1973—; v.p., asst. sec., dir. Travis Ecology, Inc., 1973—. Pres. P.T.A. Am. Dependents Sch., Berlin, Germany, 1952-53; mem. Gov's. Commn. on Status of Women, 1970. Recipient Salesman of Yr. 1962 award Austin Real Estate Bd., 1963. Mem. Austin Real Estate Bd. (pres. women's council 1962), Nat Assn. Real Estate Bds. (women's council), Soc. Certified Master Brokers and Certified Master Salesmen (mem. bd. dirs. 1961-64, 66, pres. 1965), Pan Am Round Table, Tex. Real Estate Assn. (chmn. edn. promotion commn. 1963, historian 1966), Phi Beta Kappa. Address: 900 Bluebonnet Lane Austin TX 78704

TRAYLOR, MARGARET HENRIETTA, librarian; b. Atlanta, Aug. 27, 1944; d. Amater Zeale and Margaret Henrietta (Brown) Traylor; B.A., Bennett Coll., 1964; M.L.S., Atlanta U., 1965. Reference librarian Bridgeport (Conn.) Pub. Library, 1965-66; librarian N. Peralta Community Coll., Oakland, Cal., 1967—. Mem. Community Black History Com. No. Cal., 1973—; spl. exhibits and edn. com. Oakland Mus., 1972—. Mem. A.L.A., Cal. Library Assn., Black Librarian Caucus. Home: 1750 Walnut St Berkeley CA 94709 Office: 5714 Grove Oakland CA 94609

TREADWELL, BETHEL PORTER (MRS. NORWOOD CLYDE TREADWELL), city ofcl.; b. Enfield, Me., Dec. 12, 1925; d. John Barker and Laura Salome (Smith) Porter; student Husson Coll., 1942-43; m. Norwood Clyde Treadwell, May 11, 1947; children—Amelia Faye (Mrs. Norman W. Hurlburt), Karl Norwood. Sec. to mgr. Atlas Plywood Corp., Howland, Me., 1943-47; tax collector Town of Burlington, Me., 1954-55; selectman, assessor Burlington, 1960-66, town clk., 1966—; librarian Angie G. Wakefield Meml. Library, 1960-62. Tchr. aide Burlington Elementary Sch., 1967—; registrar voters, 1968—; notary pub., 1970—. Trustee, treas., co-founder Stewart M. Lord Hist. Mus., 1968—. Mem. V.F.W. Aux., N.E. Folklore Soc., Grange. Democrat. Baptist (mem. choir). Home: Box 33 Burlington ME 04417

TREADWELL, HELEN, artist; b. Chihuahua, Mexico, July 27, 1902; ed. Vassar Coll., Sorbonne, Paris, France. Came to U.S. Exhibited one-woman shows Arthur Newton Gallery, 1934, Rockefeller Center, N.Y.C., Archtl. League, 1946, 49, 50, 56, Crespi Gallery, 1959, Contemporaries Gallery, N.Y.C., 1956; executed murals for Hotel New Yorker, N.Y.C., Hotel Utah, Salt Lake City, Hotel Tourraine, Boston, Hotel Bermudiana, Hotel Southern, Balt., Cipango Club, Dallas, Roslyn Country Club, L.I., N.Y., Burlington Ry. coach panels, S.S. Uruguay, Chase Manhattan Bank, San Juan P.R., Bklyn. Sav. & Loan Bank, Bensonhurst, L.I., Marine Midland Trust Co., N.Y.C., Valeria Club, N.Y.C., Sun and Surf Club, Atlantic Beach, L.I. Guggenheim Dental Clinic for Children, N.Y.C.; also executed indsl. murals for Okonite Cable Co., Passaic, N.J., Standard Vacuum Oil Co., Harrison, N.Y., Trinity Office Bldg., N.Y.C.; executed mosaics in schs. N.Y.C., Bronx, N.Y., Bklyn., also Lutheran Ch. of Incarnate Word, Rochester, N.Y. Treas. U.S. com. Internat. Assn. Art. Recipient spl. awards for mural paintings in Municipal Bldgs., Chile. Mem. Nat. Soc. Mural Painters (dir., past pres.), Archtl. League N.Y. (past 1st v.p.; recipient Pres.'s medal, mem. bd.). Studio: 33 W 67th St New York City NY 10023

TREADWELL, YVONNE, psychologist; b. Knoxville, Ia., May 8, 1928; d. Ernest William and Leda Myrle (Fletcher) Thoman; B.A., U. Cal., Los Angeles, 1962, M.A. (Navy Salary fellow), 1966; div.; 1 son, William Alan. Employee devel. officer Naval Weapons Center, China Lake, Cal., 1957-62, research psychologist, 1962-67; research psychologist USAF Hdqrs., Washington, 1968-69, equal employment opportunity specialist, fed. womens program coordinator, 1969-73; research analyst Dept. Housing and Urban Devel., Washington, 1973—. Chmn., Family Counseling Service Bd., China Lake, 1964. Mem. Am. Psychol. Assn. (asso.), Federally Employed Women, Inc. (exec. bd. D.C. charter chpt. 1971—, treas. 1971-72, nat. exec. bd. 1972—, treas. 1972-73). Contbr. articles profl. jours. Home: 410 G St SE Washington DC 20003

TREBACH, SHIRLEY LOUISE (MRS. ARNOLD S. TREBACH), photographer, portrait artist; b. Bklyn., Dec. 14, 1927; d. Israel and Bess (Seigel) Zuckerman; student Rutgers U., 1952-55, Roosevelt U., 1963-64, Am. U., 1964-67; m. Arnold S. Trebach, Feb. 6, 1954; children—David J., Paul L. Profl. photographer, mgr.-owner Trebach Studio, Washington and Bethesda, Md., 1967—; mgr.-owner Artisan's Gallery, Bethesda, 1972-73; dir. photography Justice Mag., 1972. Mem. Profl. Photographers Assn. Am. Home: 7 Carderock Ct Bethesda MD 20034 Office: 7687 MacArthur Blvd Bethesda MD 20731

TREECE, ELEANOR MAE WALTERS (MRS. JAMES WILLIAM TREECE, JR.), nursing cons., author; b. Mansfield, O., Feb. 11, 1921; d. Clarence Samuel and Helen LaDonna (Marmet) Walters; grad. Mansfield Bus. Tng. Sch., 1939; diploma in missions Nyack Coll., 1944; R.N., Manfield Gen. Hosp. Sch. Nursing, 1948; B.A., Ashland Coll., 1952; M.Ed., U. Minn., 1962, Ph.D., 1967; m. James William Treece, Jr., Apr. 11, 1954. Asst. instr. Mansfield Gen. Hosp. Sch. Nursing, 1949, asst. evening supr. hosp., 1950-51, asst. to dir. nurses, 1951-52, instr. Sch. Nursing, 1952-53; asst. dir. nursing service Meml. Hosp., Casper, Wyo., 1953-54; office nurse Dental Clinic, Casper, 1954-56; instr. practical nursing Casper Coll., 1956; pvt. duty nurse, Casper, 1957-58; dir., instr. Mpls. Vocational Sch. Practical Nursing, 1958-61; instr. St. Paul Bible Coll., 1965-67, St. Mary's Jr. Coll., Mpls., 1965-66; adminstrv. head St. Paul unit S.D. State U., 1967-68; curriculum coordinator Arthur B. Ancker Meml. Sch. Nursing, St. Paul-Ramsey Hosp. and Med. Center, 1968-71; nursing cons., Mpls., 1971—. USPHS spl. nurse trainee, 1961-62; USPHS nurse predoctoral fellow, 1963-65. Mem. Internat. Platform Assn., Am. Ednl. Research Assn., Asm. Assn. Higher Edn., Am., Minn. nurses assns., Nat., Minn. leagues nursing, Am., Minn. vocational assns. Co-author: Elements of Research in Nursing, 1973; author: Internship in Nursing Education: Technoterm, 1974. Address: 1809 E 41st St Minneapolis MN 55407

TREFETHEN, FLORENCE NEWMAN (MRS. LLOYD MACGREGOR TREFETHEN), writer, editor; b. Phila., Sept. 18, 1921; d. Otto Carl-Johann and Emma Martha (Paessler) Newman; A.B. magna cum laude, Bryn Mawr Coll., 1943; M. Litt., Cambridge U., 1950; m. Lloyd MacGregor Trefethen, May 17, 1944; children—Gwyned, Lloyd Nicholas. Operations analyst, operations research office Johns Hopkins, Chevy Chase, Md., 1950-54; instr. English, Tufts U., Medford, Mass., 1959-66; lectr. Northeastern U. Grad. Sch. Arts and Scis., Boston, 1967-69, Radcliffe Inst., Cambridge, Mass., 1969-70, 72-73; columnist Poet's Workshop, Writer, Boston, 1967—; free lance writer, rewrite editor, Boston, 1966—. Served to lt. (j.g.) WAVES, 1943-45. Recipient Arthur Davison Ficke award Poetry Soc. Am., 1969; Ann. Lyric prize New. Eng. Poetry Club, 1971. Mem. Nat. Orgn. for Women (dir. Lexington), Poetry Soc. Am., New Eng. Poetry Club (bd. mem. 1972—), Bryn Mawr Alumnae (editorial bd. mem. Bull. 1966—). Author: Writing a Poem, 1970; (with Joseph F. McCloskey) Operations Research for Management, vol. 1, 1954. Contbr. revs., poems to lit. jours. Address: 23 Barberry Rd Lexington MA 02173

TREGELLAS, PATRICIA SKIDMORE (MRS. S. STALEY TREGELLAS), marketing exec.; b. Summit, N.J., Dec. 28, 1930; d. James Bond and Emma (Pattison) Skidmore; A.B., Sarah Lawrence Coll., 1952; m. S. Staley Tregellas, Dec. 20, 1952; children—Sandra Bond, Staley Tylor. Retail rep. Merchandising Group, N.Y.C., 1960-64; editorial promotion mgr. Ladies Home Jour., 1964-68, promotion dir., 1973—; promotion writer Life Mag., 1968-69, merchandise mgr., 1969-70, advt. mgr., 1970-72; market mgr. marketing services dept. Time Mag., N.Y.C., 1973. Home: 1165 Park Av New York City NY 10028 Office: 641 Lexington AV New York City NY 10022

TREI, ALICE ROSALIE, occupational therapist; b. Estonia, Oct. 17, 1909; d. Prüdu and Müna (Kraun) Roost; came to U.S., 1929, naturalized, 1938; certificate occupational therapy, Columbia, 1948; B.S., N.Y. U., 1954; m. Peter Trei, Sept. 20, 1928 (dec. Jan. 1962); children—Astra (Mrs. Felix Bottenhorn), Alan. Occupational therapist N.Y. State Psychiat. Inst., N.Y.C., 1948-53, head occupational therapist, 1953—. Mem. Am., N.Y. State (treas. 1959-62, 69-73) occupational therapy assns., Met. N.Y. Dist., World Fedn. Occupational Therapists. Home: 15 Sickles St New York City NY 10040 Office: 722 W 168th St New York City NY 10032

TREIMAN, EDNA, ins. co. exec.; b. River Forest, Ill., May 21, 1932; d. William D. and Thelma (Gibbs) Treiman; student Denison U., 1950-52. Mgmt. trainee Eckhart Co., Forest Park, Ill., 1953-55; salesman Livernois Ins. Co., Stone Park, Ill., 1955-63, office mgr., 1963-68, asst. v.p., 1968—. Active Girl Scouts U.S. Trustee Hersheimer Home for Aged. Mem. Ins. Assn. Am., Round Table. Address: 2918 W Fargo St Chicago IL 60645

TREIMAN, JOYCE WAHL (MRS. KENNETH TREIMAN), artist; b. Evanston, Ill., May 29, 1922; d. Rene and Rose (Doppelt) Wahl; A.A., Stephens Coll., 1941; B.F.A. (Grad. fellow 1943), State U. Ia., 1943; m. Kenneth Treiman, Apr. 25, 1945; 1 son, Donald. One-man shows include Paul Theobald Gallery, Chgo., 1942, John Snowden Gallery, Chgo., 1945, Art Inst. Chgo., 1947, North Shore Country Day Sch., Winnetka, Ill., 1947, Fairweather-Garnett Gallery, Evanston, 1950, Edwin Hewitt Gallery, N.Y.C., 1950, Palmer House Galleries, Chgo., 1952, Glencoe (Ill.) Library, 1953, Elizabeth Nelson Gallery, Chgo., 1953, Charles Feingarten Gallery, Chgo., 1955, 58, Marian Willard Gallery, N.Y.C., 1960, Felix Landau Gallery, Los Angeles, 1961, 64, Adele Bednarz Gallery, Los Angeles, 1969, 74, Forum Gallery, N.Y.C., 1970, La Jolla (Cal.) Mus. 10 year retrospective, 1971; exhibited group shows at Met. Mus., 1950, Carnegie Internat., 1955, 57, Whitney Mus., 1951, 52, 53, 58, John Herron Art Inst., 1953, Art Inst. Chgo., 1954-59, Library of Congress, 1954, Corcoran Gallery, 1957, Pa. Acad. Fine Art, 1958, Mus. Modern Art, 1962, Whitney Mus., 1962, Penelope Gallery, Rome, 1964, numerous others; represented in permanent collections Denver Mus. Art, State U. Ia., Ill. State Mus., Tupperware Art Mus., Orlando, Fla., Art Inst. Chgo., Utah State U., Abbott Labs., Oberlin Allen Art Mus., Internat. Mineral Corp., Pasadena Art Mus., U. Ore., Whitney Mus. Am. Art, Long Beach Mus. Art; also pvt. collections; artist in residence San Fernando Valley State Coll., 1968; vis. artist Art Center Sch., Los Angeles, summer 1968; vis. prof. San Fernando Valley State Coll., Northridge, Cal., 1969; vis. lectr. U. Cal. at Los Angeles, 1969-70. Recipient numerous awards including Logan prize and purchase prize Art Inst. Chgo., 1951; Martin B. Cahn prize, 1959, 60; Pauline Palmer prize, 1953; Saratosa Am. Painting Exhbn. award, Ford Found. purchase prize, 1960; Ball State Coll. purchase prize, 1961; La Jolla Art Mus. prize, 1961; Pasadena Art Mus. purchase prize, 1961; named Woman of Year for Arts, Los Angeles Times, 1965. Tiffany fellow, 1947, Tupperware Art Fund fellow, 1955. Tamerino Lithography fellow, 1961. Home: 712 Amalfi Dr Pacific Palisades CA 90272

TRELEASE, PAULINE ARMSTRONG (MRS. SIDNEY BRIGGS TRELEASE), social worker; b. Urbana, Ill., Aug. 26, 1904; d. Thomas Arthur and Ida (Besore) Burt; B.S., U. Ill., 1926, M.S.W., 1955; m. John Harold Armstrong, Mar. 17, 1926 (dec. June 1952); children—Thomas, Dorothy (Mrs. Harold Baker), John; m. 2d, Sidney Briggs Trelease, Dec. 11, 1963. Exec. dir. Planned Parenthood Family Service, Danville, Ill., 1953; psychiat. social worker Psychol. Clinic, U. Ill., Champaign, 1955-71, cons., 1971—. Mem. 708 Bd. Pres., League Women Voters, 1938-40. Bd. dirs. Planned Parenthood Assn., 1946-53. Fellow, Am. Orthopsychiat. Assn.; mem. Ill. Welfare Assn., Nat. Assn. Social Workers, Acad. Certified Social Workers. Home: 1118 W Armory St Champaign IL 61820 Office: 51 E Gerty St Champaign IL 61820

TREMAINE, MARY M., educator; b. Eagle Grove, Ia., July 31, 1912; d. Ralph and Ethel (Willard) Tremaine; A.A., Stephens Coll., 1932; B.A., U. Wyo., 1935; M.S., U. Ia., 1952, Ph.D., 1954. Med. technologist Mercy Hosp., Mason City, Ia., 1938-41; sr. serologist Ia. State Health Dept. Labs., Iowa City, 1943-51; instr. micbrobiology State U. N.Y. Downstate Med. Center, Bklyn., 1954-60; asst. prof. med. microbiology U. Neb. Coll. Medicine, Omaha, 1960-65, asso. prof., dir. Antibiotic Research Lab., 1965—. Free lance wildlife photographer. Mem. Neb. Ornithol. Union, Wilson Soc., Sigma Xi, Phi Theta Kappa. Home: 3860 Harney St Omaha NE 68131 Office: 42d and Dewey Sts Omaha NE 68105

TREMBLAY, CAL CALHOUN (MRS. LEO EDWARD TREMBLAY), advt. exec.; b. Annawan, Ill.; d. John Paul and Maye (Riel) Calhoun; B.A., U. Ill.; grad. Am. Press Inst., Columbia, 1959; m. Leo Edward Tremblay, Mar. 1, 1952; children—Carolyn (Mrs. Daryl Lauppe), Stephen Eubanks, Linda (Mrs. Grant Schleiger), John Eubanks (by previous marriage). Advt. sales, mgmt. South Bay Daily Breeze, Torrance, Cal., 1947-53, mgr. classified advt. dept., 1953-72; corporate dir. Harte-Hanks Newspapers, Inc., San Antonio, 1972-73; pres. Van/De Pub. Co., Huntington Beach, Cal., 1973—. Mem. Redondo Beach (Cal.) Community Devel. Com. and Model City Program, 1968. Mem. So. Cal. Classified Advt. Mgrs. Assn. (past pres.). Western Classified Advt. Assn. (past pres.). Internat. Newspapers Advt. Execs., Asso. Newspaper Classified Advt. Mgrs. (regional adviser, bd. dirs.). Author booklet: Tips on Writing Real Estate Advertising, 1962. Home: 24205 Robledo Circle Mission Viejo CA 92675 Office: PO Box 1940 Huntington Beach CA 92647

TREMBLE, STELLA CRAFT, author, editor, poet; b. Frenchburg, Ky.; d. Levi and Mary (Sexton) Craft; student State Tchrs. Coll., Charleston, 1922, Ypsilanti Tchrs. Coll., 1928; D.Lit., Free U. Asia, 1968; H.H.D., Acad. Culture, Hull, Eng., 1970; D.Liberal Arts, Hong Kong World U., 1970; m. Walter Shirley Tremble, Nov. 26, 1926. Tchr. elementary schs., Ashmore, 1922-23, Joliet, 1923-25, Charleston, 1942-47, Royal Oak, Mich., Mattoon, Ill., 1947-50; editor Prairie Press, Charleston, 1961—. Author books including The Silver Chain, 1953; Thorns and Thistledown, 1954; Wind in the Reed, 1957; The Crystal Prism, 1958; Loom and Lyre, 1961; The Prairie Poet Anthology, 1961; Telescope of Time, 1962; Happy Holidays, 1963 (2d place Nat. Fedn. Press Women 1964), Vol. II, 1974; Miss Anne's Country School; Songs of the Prairie (book verse), 1964, volume II, 1965; Isles of Silence (1st place Nat. Fedn. Press Women contest, also 1st place Ill. Woman's Press Assn. 1969); Bells of Autumn, 1967; Paths to Parnassus, 1969 (2d prize Ill. Woman's Press Assn.); Center and Circumference, 1971; Unmeasured Moments, 1972; Clod and Cloud, 1974; also three anthologies, 1965; poetry analyst, sec.-treas. Am. Poetry League, 1958-64, pres., 1964—. Recipient Book of Year award Am. Poets Fellowship Soc., 1958; 1st prize Nat. Fedn. Press Women (for The Crystal Prism), 1960; George Washington medal Freedoms Found., 1963; Gold Cup, Am. Poets Fellowship Soc., 1965; Gold medal Scambi Internat., Rome, Italy, 1966; Poet Laureate Philippines, 1966; citation United Poets Laureate Internat., 1967; Laurel wreath and medal Pres. Philippines, 1965; Gold Cup and trophy Eastern div. London Poetry Soc., 1970. Mem. World Poetry Soc. Intercontinental, Am. Poets Fellowship Soc. (nat. adviser 1966—, pres. 1965—), Ill. Woman's Press Assn., Nat. League Am. Penwomen (annual high school contest chmn., pres. Mattoon br.), Ill. Poetry Soc. (founding pres.), D.A.R. (chpt. Chaplain), United Poets Soc. Am. (v.p.), Cosmosynthesis Poetry League Australia (life), Am. Poets, Ill. Poetry Soc. (founding pres. 1972—). Pub., editor: The Am. Poet (2d mate Palmer award 1964), Prairie Poet, United Poets (mags.), Prairie Poet Anthology. Home: 902 10th St Charleston IL 61920

TRENARY, DIANA SIMMS, educator; b. Indpls., Jan. 4, 1943; d. Thomas Steve and Lydia Helen (Ylitalo) Simms; B.A., State U. N.Y. Coll. at Cortland, 1968; M.A., Syracuse U., 1970, Ph.D., 1971; m. Paul Gene Trenary, Jan. 21, 1961 (div. Sept. 1963); children—Kimberly, Lynn. Asst. dir. Day Camp of Assn. Retarded Children, Cortland, 1968-69; head tchr. Liverpool (N.Y.) Lab. Nursery Sch., 1969-70; sch. psychologist intern, Skaneateles, N.Y., 1971; asst. prof. psychology U. Wis.-LaCrosse, 1971-74, coordinator child devel. fieldwork program, 1972-74; asst. prof. psychology Eastern Ky. U., Richmond, 1974—. Cons. Head Start, LaCrosse, 1971. Mem. Am. Ednl. Research Assn., Am. Psychol. Assn., Soc. Research Child Devel., Nat. Orgn. Women. Contbr. articles to profl. jours. Office: Dept Psychology Eastern Ky U Richmond KY 40475

TRENNER, KATHRYN THERESA, lawyer; b. Westfield, N.J., Oct. 19, 1941; d. Nelson Richard and Kathryn Theresa (Farrell) Trenner; B.S., Pa. State U., 1963; J.D., Rutgers U., 1969. Admitted to N.J. bar, 1969; hearing officer N.J. Dept. Community Affairs, 1969-70, enforcement officer, 1970-71; jud. clk. to judge Appellate Div. N.J. Superior Ct., 1971-72; practiced in Princeton, N.J., 1972—. Hearing officer Dept. Civil Service State N.J., 1973-74; atty. Rocky Hill Boro Zoning Bd. Adjustment, 1974—. Mem. N.J., Mercer County, Princeton bar assns. Office: 245 Nassau St Princeton NJ 08540

TRENNT, EVELYN LADENE, educator; b. Miller, Neb.; d. William Carl and Alura (Chartraw) Trennt; B.A., U. Omaha, 1942; M.A., U. Ill., 1946. Tchr. math. Gaza (Ia.) High Sch., 1942-43, Walnut (Ia.) High Sch., 1943-45; instr. math. Springfield (Ill.) Jr. Coll., 1946-53; tchr. math. Milw.-Downer Sem., 1953-55; asso. prof. math. Monticello Coll., Godfrey, Ill., 1955-71; prof. math. Lewis and Clark Community Coll., Godfrey, 1971—. Judge math. div. ann. State Sci. Exposition of Ill. Jr. Acad. Sci., 1958—. Mem. Nat., Ill. (mem. bd. 1960-61) councils tchrs. math., Math. Assn. Am., Am. Assn. U. Profs., Alton Bus. and Profl. Women's Club, Sigma Pi Phi, Pi Mu Epsilon. Home: 1012 Richard Dr Godfrey IL 62035

TRENT, ALTHEA, realtor; b. Savannah, Okla., Aug. 29, 1916; d. James Francis Rogers and Dorothy (Lewis) Templeton; student Ind. U., 1961-62; m. Theodore Anderson, Aug. 3, 1935, (div. 1948); 1 dau., Phyllis Jean Anderson (Mrs. Trowbridge Calloway III); m. 2d Henry D. Trent, Jan. 11, 1954. Mgr. Lincoln Hwy. Inn, Mishawaka, Ind., 1940-60; broker B & F Realty Inc., Elkhart, Ind., 1962-65, sales mgr., 1965-69, v.p., treas., 1969—. Mem. Elkhart Bd. Realtors (treas. 1968), Ind. Real Estate Assn., Nat. Assn. Real Estate Brokers, Nat. Fedn. Bus. & Profl. Women's Clubs. Republican. Episcopalian. Clubs: Elks (treas. Lady Elks 1969-70), Four Lakes Country Club (Adamsville, Mich.). Home: 1102 Laverne Ct Elkhart IN 46514 Office: 1300 Cassopolis St Elkhart IN 46514

TRENT, EVA MAE MANES (MRS. HORACE MAYNARD TRENT), mathematician; b. Bloomfield, Ind., Mar. 11, 1909; d. Charles Edgar and Eliza (Abrams) Manes; A.B., Ind. U., 1930, postgrad., 1931, Miss. State U., 1936-37; m. Horace Maynard Trent, July 29, 1933; children—Marilyn (Mrs. Jerome Roger Grunkemeyer), Sandra (Mrs. Charles John Rothwell). Counselor, Westminster Found., Bloomington, Ind., 1930-31; rate procs. analyst Pub. Service Co. Ind., Indpls., 1931-33; instr. math. Ind. U., Boomington, 1934; instr. edn. Miss. State U., State College, 1937; mathematician U.S. Naval Research Lab., Washington, 1956—. Mem. Washington Acad. Sci., Sci. Research Soc. Am., Acoustical Soc. Am., Internat. Oceanographic Found., Philos. Soc., Washington Nat. Social, Zeta Tau Alpha, Gamma Zeta (hon. installation initiate). Contbr. articles in field to profl. jours. Research in atmospheric electricity and its relation to meterology, U.S. Naval research reports. Home: 413 Tennessee Av Alexandria VA 22305 Office: US Naval Research Lab Washington DC 20375

TRENT, NELLIE JANE, psychologist; b. St. Louis, July 5, 1921; d. Richard Wesley and Helen Elizabeth (Kuhn) Mellow; A.B., Wellesley Coll., 1943; M.A., Washington U., St. Louis, 1944; m. John Brabson, Apr. 9, 1946; children—Elizabeth (Mrs. Peter D.W. Heberling), John Brabson. Tchr., Mary Inst., St. Louis, 1944-46; grad. asst. psychology Washington U., 1963-65; psychologist Kirkwood (Mo.) Sch. Dist., 1965—; lectr. psychology Meramec Community Coll., St. Louis, 1969-70; lectr. spl. edn. St. Louis U., 1970. Founder, pres. greater St. Louis Women's Assn. of Freedoms Found. at Valley Forge, 1968; residential chmn. St. Louis and St. Louis County United Fund, 1968. Founder, pres. bd. Ladue Chapel Nursery Sch., 1957; bd. dirs. Campbell House, Girls Home, Multiple Sclerosis Soc. St. Louis. Recipient Wellesley Coll. award of year, 1968; Liberty Bowl, Freedoms Found., 1968. Mem. Am. Psychol. Assn., Nat. Assn. Sch. Psychologists (charter), Assn. Children with Learning Disabilities, Council Exceptional Children, Am. Personnel and Guidance Assn., St. Louis Jr. League (dir. 1950-53), Mo. Hist. Soc. (pres. women's assn. 1963-64, trustee soc. 1968-71), Kirkwood Community Tchrs. Assn. (dir. 1970-75), Nat. Soc. Colonial Dames in Mo. (dir. 1967-69). Presbyn. (deaconess). Clubs: Wellesley, St. Louis, Woman's (St. Louis). Contbr. article to pubis. Home: 70 Fair Oaks St St Louis MO 63124 Office: 516 S Kirkwood Rd St Louis MO 63122

TRENT, SOPHIE C. (MRS. RONALD B. STEVENS), physician; b. New Britain, Conn., Oct. 3, 1917; d. George A. and Stella (Kawiecka) Tenerowicz; B.A., Brown U., 1939; M.D., Yale, 1943; m. Ronald B. Stevens, June 1, 1970. Intern, Vanderbilt U. Hosp., Nashville, 1943-44, U. Hosp., San Juan, P.R., 1944-45; resident in pathology Sch. Tropical Medicine, San Juan, P.R., 1945-46; resident in medicine Duval Med. Center, Jacksonville, Fla., 1948-49; sr. research fellow NIH, Bethesda, Md., 1946-47; chief medicine Municipal Hosp., St. Thomas, V.I., 1947-48, Fajardo (P.R.) Dist. Hosp., 1948; asso. physician U. Conn., 1949-50; practice medicine specializing in internal medicine, Meriden, Conn., 1954-73; mem. sr. staff Meriden, Vets. Meml. hosps.; chief Tropical Disease Clinic, clin. physician VA, Hartford, Conn.; clin. staff physician Newington VA Hosp., 1958—; med. cons. Undercliffe Hosp., Meriden, 1966-73. Mem. tax bd. City of Meriden, 1968-69. Trustee Brown U., 1968-78; bd. dirs. Family Service Assn., Meriden. Served to lt. col. M.C., AUS. Diplomate Nat. Med. Examiners. Mem. Am. (1st v.p. 1966-67), Conn. (dir. 1959-67) med. women's assns., Pan Am. Med. Women's Alliance (v.p. U.S. 1965-67), Am. Assn. U. Women, A.M.A., Am. Soc. Tropical Medicine and Hygiene, Meriden Med. Assn., Am., Conn. physicians art assns., Mil. Surgeons U.S., Pembroke Alumnae Assn. (dir. 1968-71), New Haven Paint and Clay Assn., Phi Beta Kappa. Author: (anthology verse) Bird of Passage, 1965; (poetry) My New England, 1970. Contbr. articles in field to profl. mags. Home: 96 Boylston St North Meridan CT 06450

TREPP, GLORIA FERNE, community service exec.; b. Chgo., Nov. 18, 1924; d. John Theodore and Millicent (Bartos) Johnson; student Art Inst. Chgo., 1944-45, Northwestern U., 1947-49; m. LaVern Oliver Trepp, May 10, 1952; children—Devereaux, Laird, Wendell, Erik, Andrea. Sec. asst. Am. Farm Bur. Fedn., Chgo., 1949-52; mgr. duties Pine Mountain Corp. resort, Iron Mountain, Mich., 1952-70. Mem. Memominee Range Hist. Commn., 1974—; mem. Dickinson County Overall Econ. Devel. and Planning Com., 1972—, exec. sec., 1974—; exec. sec., mem. bd. Dickinson County Council Arts, 1966—; mem. Meml. Hosp. League, 1964—, chmn. nominating com., 1974; pres. Iron Mountain-Kingsford Women's Club, 1972-74, Iron Mountain Music Club, 1966; mem. Central UP Planning and Devel. Region Commn., 1974—. Vice chmn. Dickinson County Republican Party, 1970. Mem. Menominee Range Hist. Soc., Phi Gamma Nu. Lutheran. Address: 1126 Bay Shore Dr Iron Mountain MI 49801

TRESMONTAN, OLYMPIA DAVIS, counselor; b. Boston, Nov. 27, 1925; d. Peter Konstantin and Mary (Hazimanolis) Davis; B.S., Simmons Coll., 1946; M.A., Wayne State U., 1960; Ph.D. (Schaefer Found. grantee), U. Cal. at Berkeley, 1971; m. Dion Marc Tresmontan, Sept. 15, 1957 (dec. Mar. 1961); m. 2d, Robert Baker Stitt, Mar. 21, 1974. Child welfare worker San Francisco Dept. Social Service, 1964-66; sensitivity tng. NSF Sci. Curriculum Improvement Study, U. Cal. at Berkeley, 1967-68; individual practice psychol. counseling, San Francisco, 1970—. Dir. Studio Ten Counseling Services, San Francisco; tchr. U. Cal. extension at San Francisco, 1971-72. Active Cal. Tomorrow, San Francisco Soc. Mental Health, Friends San Francisco Pub. Library, Internat. Hospitality Com. Bay Area. Mem. Am. Psychol. Assn., Am. Orthopsychiat. Assn., Nat. Assn. Social Workers, Am. Assn. Marriage Counselors, Cal. Assn. Marriage, Family and Child Counselors, Nat. Orgn. Women (mem. Task Force Older Women). Author: (with J. Morris) The Evaluation of A Compensatory Education Program, 1967; (Karplus edit.) What is Curriculum Evaluation, Six Answers, 1968. Home: 14 Allen St San Francisco CA 94109

TREUDE, MAI (MRS. ARVI T. TREUDE), librarian; b. Tartu, Estonia, July 2, 1935; d. John and Marta (Ponna) Naadel; came to U.S. 1951, naturalized 1957; B.A., U. Minn., 1957, M.A., 1963; m. Arvi T. Treude, Aug. 3, 1957. Head catalog dept. Weyerhaeuser Library, Macalester Coll., St. Paul, 1963-66; map curator Wilson Library, U. Minn., Mpls., 1966—. Mem. Spl. Libraries Assn., Minn. Library Assn. Contbr. articles to profl. jours. Home: 316 Westwood Dr N Minneapolis MN 55422 Office: U Minnesota Minneapolis MN 55455

TREVASKIS, JANE LOUISE, pub. relations exec.; b. Pitts., Jan. 12, 1941; d. John Lewis and Isabella Berryhill (Muir) Trevaskis; B.A., Pa. State U., 1962. Pub. relations dir. Penn Fed. Savs. & Loan Assn., Phila., 1969-71; pub. relations dir. Girl Scouts of Phila., 1971-73; dir. community relations Montgomery County Assn. for Retarded Citizens, Silver Spring, Md., 1973; pub. relations exec. Girl Scouts Council of Nations Capital, Washington, 1973—. Free lance writer, photographer, pub. relations cons. Bd. dirs. D.C. Striders. Mem. Internat. Assn. Bus. Communicators, Am. Women in Radio and Television, Women in Communications, Pub. Relations Soc. Am., Nat. Pub. Relations Council. Home: 919 E Capitol St SE Washington DC 20003 Office: 2133 Wisconsin Av NW Washington DC 20007

TREVINO, BERTHA GAMEZ, educator; b. Laredo, Tex., Nov. 27, 1908; d. Leonardo and Francisca (Garza) Gamez; B.A., Our Lady of the Lake Coll., 1930; M.A., Mich. State U., 1962; M. Ed., U. Tex., 1950, Ph.D., 1968; m. Desiderio Trevino, Dec. 26, 1930 (dec. Aug. 1961); children—Dorotea (Mrs. Richard M. Robinson), Desiderio. Tchr. math. Laredo (Tex.) pub. schs., 1947-58; chmn. dept. math. Laredo Jr. Coll., 1958—; cons. Bilingual edn. Kingsville (Tex.), Zapata (Tex.) schs., Our Lady of the Lake Coll., San Antonio, U. Tex., Austin. NSF Summer Inst. grantee, 1958. Named Tchr. of the Year, Laredo Jr. Coll., 1968. Mem. Am. Assn. U. Women (pres. 1964, state treas. 1968-70), Cath. Daus. Am. (grand regent 1961, state treas. 1970), Tex. Jr. Coll. Tchrs. Assn. (state treas. 1971-72), Nat. Council Tchrs. of Math., Math. Assn. Am., Tex. State Tchrs. Assn. (local pres. 1958), Altar Soc. Christ the King (pres. 1966-67), Our Lady Lake Alumnae (pres. 1969). Club: A & M Mothers (pres. 1960, state treas. 1962) (Laredo). Contbr. articles to profl. jours. Home: 1620 Cortez St Laredo TX 78040 Office: PO Box 738 Laredo TX 78040

TREVOR, MERIOL, author; b. London, Eng., Apr. 15, 1919; d. Arthur Prescott and Lucy May Eleni (Dimmock) Trevor; B.A., St. Hugh's Coll., Oxford U., 1942. Fellow Royal Soc. Literature. Author (novels) The New People, 1957, A Narrow Place, 1958, Shadows and Images, The Last of Britain, 1956, The City and the World, 1970, The Holy Images, 1971, The Two Kingdoms, 1973, The Fugitive, 1973; (biography) Newman: The Pillar of the Cloud, 1962, Newman: Light in Winter, 1962 (Jams Tait Black Meml. prize biography 1962); Apostle of Rome, 1966; Pope John, 1967; Prophets and Guardians, 1969; The Arnolds, 1973; also books for children. Roman Catholic. Address: care Bolt & Watson Ltd 8 Storey's Gate London SW1 England

TREWHELLA, CLAIRE CONOVER (MRS. ARTHUR P. TREWHELLA), data processing co. exec.; b. New Brunswick, N.J., Mar. 19, 1928; d. Frank Hayward and Geraldine (Brown) Conover; B.A., Wellesley Coll., 1950; m. Arthur P. Trewhella, Feb. 21, 1953; children—Andrew, Timothy. Sr. project dir. Alfred Politz Research, Inc., N.Y.C., 1950-58; mgr. market research Computers for Industry and Business, Inc., N.Y.C., 1961-63; sr. staff analyst, prin. analyst Computer Usage Corp., N.Y.C., 1964-69; adminstrv. mgr. research data processing Data Sta. Corp., N.Y.C., 1969-70; prin., Trewhella/Cohen/Arbuckle, Inc., N.Y.C., 1970—. Cons. Ted Bates & Co., Grey Advt., Inc., 1963-64. Home: 522 E 20th St New York City NY 10009 also Fox Hunt Lane Amagansett NY 11930 Office: 500 Fifth Av New York City NY 10036

TREXLER, PATRICIA DOOLAN (MRS. JACK P. TREXLER), journalist; b. Little Rock, Dec. 14, 1926; d. James Patrick and Betty (VanSickle) Doolan; student Stevens Coll., 1944-45, U. S.C., 1945; m. Jack P. Trexler, Jan. 12, 1945; children—Connie (Mrs. William F. Michael), Jimmy, Jack Pinkney, Tommy. Newspaper columnist, Charlotte (N.C.) Observer, 1964—, Publishers-Hall Syndicate, 1966—; v.p. Trexler World Travel Service, Charlotte, 1970—. Mem. Women in Communications, Fashion Group. Club: Westport Golf and Country (Denver, N.C.). Author: Knit and Crochet Ideas, 1967; Knit Knacks, 1970. Home: Route 1 Island Forest Dr Davidson NC 28036 Office: 515 Charlottetown Mall Charlotte NC 28036

TREXLER, VIRGINIA HAMILTON (MRS. JOHN PETER TREXLER), dentist; b. Allentown, Pa., June 9, 1928; d. Earl Ezekiel and Ruth Stover (Detweiler) Hamilton; student Swarthmore Coll.,

1946-47; B.A., Cedar Crest Coll., 1951; D.D.S., U. Pa., 1954; m. John Peter Trexler, Jan. 29, 1950; children—Margaret Ruth Hamilton, Virginia Pennock. Pvt. cons. practice dentistry, Allentown, Pa., 1954—. Vol. worker Republican Com., Washington, 1960. Recipient Certificate of Merit, Internat. Jour. of Anesthesia, 1957. Mem. Matthew H. Cryer Soc., U. Pa. Women's Dental Soc. (charter mem.), Internat. Assn. Anesthesiology, Am. Assn. U. Women, League Women Voters, Huntingdon Community Theater. Republican. Presbyn. Contbr. articles to profl. jours. Home: Stone Creek Rd R D 2 Huntingdon PA 16652 Office: 36 S 11th St Allentown PA 18102

TREZISE, ROSE MALFAIRE, psychologist, educator; b. Donora, Pa., June 18, 1922; d. Arthur and Rose Mary Louise (Lachien) Malfaire; student Ellen Cushing Jr. Coll., 1941-44; B.S., Grand Canyon Coll., 1960; M.A. in Edn., Ariz. State U., 1967; m. John Mack Trezise, Aug. 26, 1944 (dec. July 1974); children—Miriam (Mrs. Jack Bowles), John Mack. Personnel mgr. F.W. Woolworth Co., Phoenix, 1950-55; tchr. elementary schs., Phoenix, 1960-67; sch. psychologist Mesa (Ariz.) pub. schs., 1968—. Tchr. evening div., Mesa Community Coll., 1970—. Bd. dirs. Marc Sch., Mesa, 1970-72. Mem. Nat. (western dir. 1971-73, treas. 1974—), Ariz. (news letter editor 1971-73) assns. sch. psychologists, Ariz. Personnel Guidance Assn., Nat., Ariz., Mesa edn. assns., Mesa Assn. Sch. Adminstrs. (sec.). Republican. Baptist. Clubs: Caliente, Dance. Home: 808 East La Jolla Tempe AZ 85282 Office: 39 South Hibbert Mesa AZ 85202

TRIBBLE, DAGMAR HEGGSTROM (MRS. ELSTON J. TRIBBLE), artist; b. N.Y.C.; d. Olaf Albin and Ida (Sabini) Haggstrom; student Parsons Sch. Design, N.Y. and Paris, 1928, Art Students League, 1930-32, Farnsworth Sch. of Painting, 1949-50; m. Elston J. Tribble, July 15, 1933; 1 dau., Martha Watkins (Mrs. James Malcolm McKinnon). Tchr. fashion illustration Parsons Sch. Design, 1929-32; designer sportswear and beachwear Travelo Corp., N.Y.C., 1933-45. Exhibited one-man shows at The Beard Sch., Orange, N.J., Monmouth Coll., West Long Branch, The Present Day Club, 1968, 71, M.S. Kungsholm, 1971, M.S. Sagafjord, 1971, United Nat. Bank, Fenwood, N.J., 1972, others; exhibited in group shows at Cape Cod Art Assn., 1963, Knickerbocker Artists Ann. Exhbn., 1963, Westfield Art Assn. State Show, 1963, 64, Hunterdon County Art Center Ann., 1963, 64, Catherine Lorillard Wolfe Art Show, 1964, Nat. Arts Club shows, also Met. Mus. Art, Nat. Acad., N.Y.C., Am. Water Color Soc. Ann., Nat. Assn. Women Artists Ann., 1967—, Nat. Assn. Women Artists Internat., Paris, France, 1969, Am. Watercolor Soc. anns., 1967—, Garden State Watercolor Soc. anns., 1970—, Am. Watercolor Soc. Ann. Traveling Exhbn., 1972, represented in pvt. collections. Recipient Agnes B. Noyes award, 1962; Windsor Newton award, 1963; Captain's Barn award for Watercolor Westfield Art Assn. State Show, 1964; Steinback Co. award for watercolor Festival of Fine Art Exhbn., 1964; Am. Artist medal merit, Am. Watercolor Soc., 1965; Jane C. Stanley Meml. prize, Nat. Assn. Women Artists, 1966. Mem. Am. Watercolor Soc., Garden State Watercolor Soc. (pres. 1970—), Nat. Assn. Women Artists, Princeton Art Assn. (pres. 1968-69). Club: Nat. Arts (N.Y.C.). Home: 12 Battle Rd Princeton NJ 08540

TRIBBLE, MILDRED F., home economist; b. Navasota, Tex., Oct. 5, 1923; d. Cornelius Asher and Helena (Archer) Tribble; B.S., Tex. Womans U., 1945; M.S., La. State U., 1970. Home service adviser Gulf States Utilities Co., Navasota, 1945-51, Baton Rouge, 1951-69, home service coordinator, Beaumont, Tex., 1969-72, home service dir., 1972—. Mem. Am., Tex. home econs. assns., South Tex. Home Economists in Bus., D.A.R. Baptist. Home: 2556 Broadway Beaumont TX 77702 Office: 285 Liberty Av Beaumont TX 77704

TRICE, DOROTHY LOUISE, city health ofcl.; b. Bklyn.; d. George Cooper and C. Rosella (Payne) Trice; B.S. in Edn., Hunter Coll., 1947; postgrad. U. Cal. at Berkeley, 1949-52; M.D., Woman's Med. Coll. Pa., 1956; M.P.H., Columbia, 1959; m. James E. Willie, Sept. 15, 1957. Intern, L.I. Coll. Hosp., Bklyn., 1956-57; health officer-in-tng. N.Y.C. Dept. Health, 1957-59, asst. health officer, 1959, pub. health physician, 1959-61, sr. pub. health physician, 1961-70, borough dir. health services Borough of Bklyn., 1970-72, dep. commr. health, 1972-74. Bd. dirs. Ch. Charity Found. of L.I., 1971—, Kings County Hosp. Center Community Bd.; pres.-elect Provident Clin. Soc. Bklyn., 1972—. Mem. Am. Cancer Soc. (dir. Bklyn. div. 1969—, N.Y. div. 1972—), N.Y. Diabetes Assn. (dir. 1968—). Office: 335 Central Av Brooklyn NY 11221

TRICE, EVA JONES GARLAND (MRS. JAMES ERNEST TRICE), hotel exec.; b. Halifax, Va., Mar. 12, 1910; d. Junior Hayes and Ruth Kirby (Moore) Jones; grad. high sch.; m. Nolan Henry Garland, Nov. 14, 1928 (dec. Jan. 1949); m. James Ernest Trice, Feb. 20, 1965 (dec. Sept. 1966). Waitress, Hotel Weyanoke, Farmville, Va., 1926, dining room mgr., 1926-41, asst. mgr., 1941-61, hotel mgr., 1961—. Mem. Am., Va. hotel and motel assns., Va. State, Farmville chambers commerce. Presbyn. Office: 202 High St Farmville VA 23901

TRIEFLER, JUDITH ANN BURKE (MRS. EDWARD TRIEFLER), summer sch. dir.; b. Bklyn., Nov. 15, 1944; d. Myron Allen and Beatrice Mildred (Olkin) Burke; B.A., Long Beach State Coll., 1966; postgrad. U. Cal. at Los Angeles, 1966; m. Edward Triefler, Oct. 13, 1970; 1 dau., Kimberly Beth. Owner, Mimi Mini Mini Mini, Los Angeles, 1966, N.Y.C., 1967; piece goods buyer Encore Fashions, Eilen Tracy, 1967-70; dir. Fox Hill Sch. Horsemanship, Greenfield Park, N.Y., 1970—, operator children's summer camp program, 1970—. Vol., Narcotics Half-Way House for Women, 1968-69. Mem. Am. Horse Shows Assn., Am. Camping Assn. Club: Windy Hollow Hunt (Florida, N.Y.). Composer: Lets Make Love Not War, 1965. Address: Fox Hill Ranch Greenfield Park NY 12435

TRIESCHMANN, ROBERTA BARBARA, psychologist, educator; b. Milw., Nov. 16, 1939; d. Robert E. and Bertha M. (Rysticken) Trieschmann; B.S., U. Wis.-Milw., 1961; Ph.D., U. Minn., 1966. Asst. prof. rehab. medicine and psychology U. Wash., 1966-70; rehab. psychologist S.W. Regional Spinal Cord Injury Center, Phoenix, 1971-72; asso. prof., chief psychologist phys. medicine and rehab. U. Cin., 1972-74; practice psychol. counseling, 1974—. Mem. Am. (exec. bd. rehab. psychology div. 22 1971—), Cin. (sec. 1973—) psychol. assns., Am. Congress Rehab. Medicine, Internat. Med. Soc. Paraplegia, Phi Kappa Phi. Author: (with Ernest R. Griffith) Sexual Function Associated with Physical Disabilities, 1974. Editor: Rehab. Psychology News, 1971—. Home: PO Box 2465 Culver City CA 90230

TRIGGS, FRANCES ORALIND, psychologist; b. Coal Creek, Colo., Aug. 26, 1910; d. Lewis Clay and Eva Lena (Osterhoudt) Triggs; B.A., Lawrence Coll., 1933; M.A., U. Chgo., 1935; Ph.D., Syracuse U., 1937. Dean women Asheville (N.C.) Coll., 1937-38; clin. counselor Minn. U., 1939-42; clin. counselor, asso. psychologist U. Ill., 1942-44; chmn. Com. on Diagnostic Reading Tests, Inc., Mountain Home, N.C., 1942—; chief psychologist Roosevelt Hosp., N.Y.C., 1942-51; lectr. Rutgers U., 1942-51; adj. prof. psychology Pace Coll., N.Y.C., 1958—; personnel researcher Ednl. Records Bur., N.Y.C., 1946-48; asso. prof. psychology, acting dir. student counseling center U. Md., 1950-52. Chmn. Henderson County Mental Health Clinic Adv. Bd.; bd. dirs. N.C., Henderson County mental health assns., N.C. Tng. and Edn. Autistic and Communications Handicapped Children. Diplomate Am. Bd. Examiners Profl. Psychology. Mem. A.A.A.S., Am. Psychol. Assn., Am. Personnel and Guidance Assn., Nat. Soc. for Study Edn., Am. Ednl. Research Assn., Nat. Soc. for Study Communication, Nat. Council Measurements in Edn. Clin. Techniques. Author several text books, tng. manuals. Contbr. articles to profl. jours. Home: Mountain Home NC 28758

TRIMBLE, HELEN MIRICH (MRS. JERRY MAX TRIMBLE), occupational therapist, educator; b. Gebo, Wyo., May 3, 1936; d. Sam N. and Anja (Raicevich) Mirich; B.S. in Occupational Therapy cum laude, Colo. State U., 1958; Ed.M., Boston U., 1968, Ed.D., 1974; m. Jerry Max Trimble, Dec. 20, 1969; 1 son, Derek Laurence. Occupational therapist Los Angeles County Med. Center, 1959-67; clin. instr. Los Angeles County Med. Center, 1962-67; adj. clin. instr. U. So. Cal. Med. Sch., 1966-67; tchr. occupational therapy Boston U., 1968-69, 70-71, cons. and human relations trainer, 1968—; instr. Salve Regina Coll., Newport, R.I., 1972—. Cons. to U. Ala. U. Year for Action, 1972-73. Recipient Marian Carnes Hendric award, 1958. Vocational Rehab. Services fellow, 1958, 59, 68-70; Human Relations Center affiliate and fellow Boston U., 1968-70. Mem. Am. Occupational Therapy Assn. (student affiliation com. 1964-65, profl. edn. com. 1965-66), Adult Edn. Assn., Kappa Alpha Theta. Mem. Serbian Orthodox Ch. Home: 61 Church St Newport RI 02840

TRIMBLE, LORA NELLE GARRETSON (MRS. JAMES CURTIS TRIMBLE), pub. relations exec.; b. Wichita Falls, Tex., Aug. 12, 1935; d. Jesse Columbus and Alma Geneva (Higgenbottom) Garretson; student Sul Ross State Tchrs. Coll., 1954, Midwestern U., 1956; B.A., So. Meth. U., 1961; m. James Curtis Trimble, Sept. 4, 1954; children—James Curtis, Mary Christiana. Free lance writer, 1961—; dir. Royal Lane Lang. Center, Dallas, 1969—; English lang. tchr. to fgn. adults, 1969—. Mem. Internat. Platform Assn., Theta Sigma Phi. Address. 9445 Hunters Creek Dallas TX 75231

TRIMMER, ELLEN CHRISTENA, probation officer; b. London, Ont., Can., Mar. 5, 1915; d. Donald Alexander and Evelyn Elizabeth (Simpson) McKay; grad. Ont. Bible Coll., 1939; m. Vincent D. Trimmer, July 6, 1940; children—David Donald, Ruth Ellen. Probation officer, now sr. officer, Islington, Ont., 1962—; sessional lectr. Ont. Bible Coll., 1964-68; lectr. on family life, chs. of many denominations; mem. faculty Decision Sch. Christian Writing (Billy Graham). Mem. Ont. Civil Service Assn., Probation Officers Assn., Evang. Fellowship Can., Delta Epsilon Chi. Author: The Cup; Tiny Tales 'N Tunes; You and Yours. Contbr. articles and poetry to profl. publs. Home: 25 Widdicombe Hill Apt 809 Weston ON Canada Office: 5233 Dundas St W Islington ON Canada

TRINER, ALMA, pub. relations exec.; b. N.Y.C., Feb. 17, 1926; d. Abraham Carl and Frances (Tennenbaum) Triner; B.A., Bklyn. Coll., 1944. Pub. relations account supr. Daniel J. Edelman, Inc., Chgo., 1953-57, v.p., mgr., N.Y.C., 1957-62; dir. pub. relations, gen. pub. div. Macmillan, Inc., N.Y.C., 1963-64, dir. pub. relations, 1964—, asst. v.p., 1968—; dir. Cornwall Corp., Boston; mem. adv. bd. mag. Present Tense. Mem. Pub. Relations Soc. Am. Office: 866 3d Av New York City NY 10022

TRINITY, SISTER MARY, hosp. adminstr.; b. Humboldt, Kan., Nov. 22, 1923; d. Arthur Franklin and Mabel Minnie (Lyons) Jackson; student Mercy Sch. Nursing, 1942-45; B.S. in Nursing, St. Mary Coll., Xavier, Kan., 1957; M.H.A., St. Louis U., 1968. Entered Order Sisters of Mercy, 1946; supr. med. surg. Mercy Hosp., Ft. Scott, Kan., 1948-56, adminstr., 1968—; supr. operating room St. Elizabeth Hosp., Hutchinson, Kan., 1957-62, Mercy Hosp., Vicksburg, Miss., 1962-63; supr. emergency room St. John's Hosp., St. Louis, 1963-66. Bd. dirs. St. John's Med. Center, Joplin, Mo. Named Bus. Woman of Week, Ft. Scott Tribune-Monitor, 1968. Mem. Am. Coll. Hosp. Adminstrs., Kan. Hosp. Assn. (treas. 1974, dir.), Bourbon County Heart Assn. (sec. 1973), Soc. Bus. and Profl. Women. Address: 821 Burke St Fort Scott KS 66701

TRIPLETT, JUNE LAVONNE, educator; b. Stewart, Minn., Jan. 5, 1921; d. William Henry and Gladys (Adams) Triplett; B.S., U. Minn., 1943; M.P.H., U. Mich., 1955, Ed.D., 1968. Pub. health nurse Martin County Nursing Service, Fairmont, Minn., 1943-45, Hawaii Health Dept., Lihue, Kauai, 1946-48, Steele County Nursing Service, Owatonna, Minn., 1948-50; pub. health nurse, supr. Minn. Dept. Health, Winona, 1950-54; gen. pub. health nursing cons. Fergus Falls (Minn.) Dept. Health, 1955-58; instr. pub. health nursing in pediatrics U. Ia., Iowa City, 1958-62, asst. prof. dept. pub. health nursing Coll. Nursing, 1962-66, asso. prof. pediatrics, 1968-72, prof. pediatrics, 1972—. Mem. Am. Assn. Mental Deficiency, Nat. Assn. for Retarded Children, Am. Pub. Health Assn., Am. Nurses Assn., Nat. League for Nursing, Delta Omega, Sigma Theta Tau. Home: 608 9th Av Coralville IA 52241 Office: Coll Nursing U Ia Iowa City IA 52242

TRIPP, GRACE DELORIS (MRS. WILLARD WAYNE TRIPP), educator; b. St. Louis, July 17, 1912; d. Frank Herbert and Ida Emma (Burst) Marlott; A.B., Harris Tchrs. Coll., 1934; M.A., Wash. U., 1936; m. Willard Wayne Tripp, June 20, 1953. Sec. Universal Aviation Schs. St. Louis, 1929-30; sec., mgr. Mo. Inst. of Accountancy and Law St. Louis, 1932-42; tchr. St. Louis Bd. of Edn., 1936-57; tchr. Normandy, Mo. schs. 1957-64; prof. philosophy and humanities, Florissant Valley Community Coll., St. Louis, 1964—. Lectr. English, Washington U., St. Louis, part time, 1947-64. Author: (with E.R. Magnus) Refrigeration and Air Conditioning, 1948. Home: 2805 Country Side Dr Florissant MO 63033 Office: 3400 Pershall Rd Ferguson MO 63135

TRIPP, LENA ELVINA FLACK (MRS. ELMER TRIPP), author; b. Churdan, Ia., Sept. 30, 1899; d. Samuel Marion and Wilhelmina (Bjornson) Flack; A.B., U. Wash., 1923; M.A., U. Cal. at Berkeley, 1924; m. Elmer Tripp, Aug. 24, 1935 (dec. Nov. 1959). First grade tchr., Plymouth, Cal., 1953-69. Author: Verses, 1968; More Verses, 1970; The Broken Tree, 1971; Those Pets of Mine, 1971; Two Years Old, 1972; Words are Wonderful, 1972; Autumn Leaves, 1973. Contbr. poetry to profl. jours. Home: Box 124 Plymouth CA 95669

TRIPP, MARIAN RUTH BARLOW (MRS. JAMES EDWARD TRIPP), advt. exec.; b. Lodgepole, Neb.; d. Lewis Rockwell and Cona (Davis) Barlow; student Doane Coll., 1939-40; B.S., Ia. State U., 1944; m. James Edward Tripp, Feb. 9, 1957; children—Brendan Michael, Kevin Mark. Head product promotion div., pub. relations Swift & Co., Chgo., 1945-55; with J. Walter Thompson Co., 1956—, v.p., Chgo., 1972—, dir. consumer affairs, 1973—. Bd. dirs. Chgo. Conv. and Tourist Bur. Mem. U.S. C. of C. (consumer affairs com.), Pub. Relations Soc. Am., Am., Ill. home econs. assns., Chgo. Home Economists in Bus., Chgo. Consumer Profls., Confrerie de la Chaine Des Rotisseurs, Women's Advt. Club Chgo. Home: 560 Arlington Pl Chicago IL 60614 Office: 875 N Michigan Av Chicago IL 60611

TRISTER, BARBARA, pub. relations exec.; b. Redlands, Cal.; d. Aaron and Sophia (Koegingheim) Leipsic; B.A., U. So. Cal.; m. Harry Trister, Mar. 6, 1952. Editor, Cal. Fashion Publs. Los Angeles, 1946-58; prin., pres. Barbara Trister Pub. Relations, Los Angeles, 1958—. Adviser to mayor Los Angeles for retailing, mfg. and textiles, 1973—. Bd. dirs. U. So. Cal. Sch. Journalism, 1958—; past gov. U. So. Cal. Recipient Distinguished Service award U. So. Cal., 1967; Spl. Recognition plaque Women For, 1968. Founder U. So. Cal. Journalism award, 1959. Mem. Women in Communications (spl. commendation 1969, pres. 1969-71), Journalism Alumni Assn. U. So. Cal. (pres. 1959-60, 66-68, Fashion Group (treas. Los Angeles 1960-62, past dir.), Fashion Circle West (co-founder 1964), Colleagues Fashion Aux. (pres. 1972-73), Gamma Alpha Chi. Home: 581 Lorna Lane Los Angeles CA 90049 Office: 819 Santee St Los Angeles CA 90014

TRIVETTE, FRANCES CLEVELAND SMITH (MRS. WILLIAM H. TRIVETTE), museum ofcl.; b. Lexington, Ky., 1916; d. John Thomas and Myrtle Frances (Cleveland) Smith; A.B., U. Ky., 1938; m. William H. Trivette, Aug. 13, 1949; 1 son, William H. III. Staff, Waveland Mus., Lexington, 1965-72; dir. Waveland State Shrine, Lexington, 1972—. Mem. Nat. Soc. Arts and Letters (treas. local chpt. 1964-67), D.A.R., U.D.C., Alpha Gamma Delta. Clubs: Lexington Womans (program chmn. 1960-64), Woman's of Central Ky., Alumni of Spindletop Hall. Home: 307 E Maxwell St Lexington KY 40508 Office: Waveland State Shrine Higbee Mill Rd Lexington KY 40503

TRIVISON, SISTER MARY ST. LOUIS, educator; b. Cleve., Apr. 11, 1928; d. Amelio Salvator and Louise Mary (Zaccagnini) Trivison; B.A., Notre Dame Coll., 1950; diploma theology, Pontifical Inst. Regina Mundi, Mundi Rome, 1958; M.A., Case Western Reserve U., 1955, Ph.D., 1971. Instr. Notre Dame Acad., Cleve., 1950-55; instr. Elyria Catholic High Sch., Ohio, 1958-60, St. Mary High Sch., Warren, Ohio, 1960-62; instr. lang. and religion Cardinal Mooney High Sch., Youngstown, Ohio, 1962-64; asso. prof. theology, romance lang., philosophy Notre Dame Coll., Cleve., 1964—; prof. theology Notre Dame Inst. Advanced Studies in Religious Edn., Middleburg, Va., 1971-74. Mem. Coll. Theology Soc., Am. Classical League, Ohio Classical Conf., Religious Edn. Assn., Greater Cleve. Classical Assn., Am. Assn. Tchrs. Spanish and Portuguese, Catholic Biblical Assn., Assn. Catholic Religious Edn. Editor: The Herald of Catholic Teaching. Home: 4545 College Rd Cleveland OH 44121

TROCKMAN, RACHEL ETA WEINER (MRS. MITCHELL D. TROCKMAN), physician; b. Mpls., Jan. 22, 1942; d. Phillip J. and Bernice (Wasser) Weiner; B.A. magna cum laude, U. Minn., 1962, B.S., 1964, M.D., 1966; m. Mitchell D. Trockman, July 1, 1962; children—Mark Alan, Daniel Gary, Steven Jay. Intern, Hennepin County Gen. Hosp., Mpls., 1966-67; resident pediatrics U. Minn., 1967-70, instr. pediatrics, 1971-72, asst. prof. pediatrics, 1972—, asst. prof. Sch. Pub. Health, 1972—; tng. pediatric neurology U. Minn. Hosp., 1970-71; asso. physician Hennepin County Gen. Hosp., Mpls., 1971—; physician Pilot City Health Care Center, Mpls., 1969; dir. Child Behavior and Learning Clinic, 1971—; cons. spl. edn. Mpls. Pub. Schs., 1972—; mem. faculty Pediatric Nurse Asso. Program, 1971—; co-dir. Community Pediatric Tng. Program, Mpls., 1972—. Diplomate Am. Bd. Pediatrics. Mem. Twin City, Northwest pediatric socs., Phi Beta Kappa. Home: 8026 Plymouth Av N Minneapolis MN 55427 Office: Hennepin County Gen Hosp Minneapolis MN 55455

TROISE, AUDREY HELENA FLAVIN (MRS. FRANK TROISE), corp. exec.; b. Schenectady, Sept. 22, 1934; d. George H. and Emma (Relyea) Flavin; student pub. schs.; m. Frank Troise, Aug. 1, 1964. Steno-sec. Gen. Electric Co., Waterford, N.Y., 1951-52; sec. Taft Hotel and Republic Pictures, N.Y.C., 1952-54; sec. Walter Schneider Assos., Inc., N.Y.C., 1954-57; sec. William G. Moore & Son, Inc. of Del., N.Y.C., 1957-64, corp. sec., dir. 1965-69, v.p., dir., 1969—. Office: 5 World Trade Center New York City NY 10048

TROJAK, THERESE ANNE (MRS. EDWARD V. TROJAK), banker; b. Chgo., Nov. 17, 1929; d. Robert Roger and Anne Marie (Loula) Du Monte; corr. course Chg. Sch. Nursing, 1950-51; student N. Central Tech. Inst. Adult Edn., 1971—; m. Edward V. Trojak, June 13, 1953; children—Gregory Edward, Maureen Ann. With State Bank Phillips (Wis.), 1950-55, 61—, comml. and savs. teller, 1962—, bookkeeper and bank officer, 1970—. Sec. Ladies Drum and Bugle Corps, 1951-53; treas. So. Price County chpt. A.R.C., 1966-68, mem. Bloodmobile Com., 1968; chmn. reunion day Lugerville Sch. P.T.A., 1969—, treas., 1962-63, sec.-treas., 1970—, chmn. publicity, 1962—, pres., 1963-65, 68-70; chmn. Friendship Campaign for Mentally Handicapped Children, 1972. Instr. snowmobile safety Wis. Dept. Natural Resources, 1972. Acting sec. Price County adv. com. New Concepts Found. Mem. V.F.W. (treas. ladies aux. 1967—). Roman Catholic (mem. adult choir 1942-53). Home: Luger Route Box 97 Phillips WI 54555 Office: Drawer 67 Phillips WI 54555

TROMBLY, CATHERINE ANNE, occupational therapist, educator; b. Manchester, N.H., July 14, 1936; d. Frank Herbert and Mary Ellen (Shea) Trombly; B.S., U. N.H., 1958; M.A., (Am. Occupational Therapy Assn. fellow), U. So. Cal., 1964; postgrad. (Am. Occupational Therapy Assn. fellow) Case Western Res. U., 1963-64; 1 son, Christopher Frank. Clinician and clin. educator Highland View Hosp., Cleve., 1959-62, researcher orthotics, 1963-67, adminstr. and clin. educator, 1968-71; asst. prof. U. N.H., Durham, 1967-68; asst. prof. occupational therapy Boston U., 1971—. Mem. Am., Mass. (editor Newsletter 1972), Cleve. (chmn. 1965-67) occupational therapy assns., World Fedn. Occupational Therapists, Am. Assn. U. Profs., Phi Kappa Phi, Phi Sigma. Editorial bd. Am. Jour. Occupational Therapy, 1968-71. Contbr. articles to profl. jours. Office: Sargent College Boston University Boston MA 02115

TROSSELLO, MARY THERESA, occupational therapist; b. Queens, N.Y., Nov. 27, 1946; d. John Edmund and Joan Theresa (Broderick) Singleton; B.A., Marymount Manhattan Coll., 1968; M.S. (N.Y. State Trusteeship for Occupational Therapy scholar), Columbia Coll. Phys. and Surg., 1970; m. Vincent Anthony Trossello, Apr. 27, 1968; 1 dau., Elizabeth Marie. Occupational therapist Bronx State Hosp., 1970-72; head occupational therapy dept. St. Joseph's Day Treatment Center, Yonkers, N.Y., 1972—. Chairwoman arts and crafts Pelham Manor (N.Y.) Newcomers Club, 1971—; cons. activities dept. Portchester (N.Y.) Nursing Home, 1971—. Mem. Am. Occupational Therpy Assn. Home: 991 Plymouth St Pelham Manor NY 10803 Office: St Josephs Hosp Psychiatric Day Treatment Center 8 Guion St Yonkers NY 10701

TROTT, JUDITH DAVIS, ednl. adminstr.; b. Blue Mountain, Miss., May 15, 1939; d. George Richard and Helen Adair (Davis) Trott; B.S. in Phys. Edn., U. Miss., 1961, M.Ed. in Guidance and Counseling, 1964, Ed.D. in Student Personnel Services, 1972. Tchr., Stuart Hall Sch., Staunton, Va., 1961-63; counselor Balt. (Md.) County Schs., 1964-66; dir. residence life student personnel women's activities U. Miss., University, 1966—. Nat. adviser Intercollegiate Assn. Women Students, 1973—. Active Girl Scouts Am., 1969-72. Mem. Nat. Assn. Women Deans, Adminstrs. and Counselors (mem. liason com. 1972-74), Miss. Assn. Women Deans and Counselors (pres. 1974—), Am. Assn. Univ. Women, Miss. Personnel and Guidance Assn., Oxford C. of C., Delta Gamma (pres. Alpha Psi alumni chpt. 1967-69). Club: Oxford Country (sec. bd. dirs. 1973—). Home: Box 523 University MS 38677

TROTT, ROSEMARY CLIFFORD (MRS. JAMES E. TROTT), author; b. Mt. Vernon, N.Y., Mar. 8; d. Edward Farnsworth and Beatrice (Wright) Clifford; student Bates Coll., 1942, Columbia, 1947-48; L.H.D., Internat. U. Coll. Therapeutics, Ceylon, 1973; m. James Edwin Trott, Feb. 8, 1930; children—Donald Victor, Rosemary Diane. Feature writer Portland (Me.) Evening News, 1930; reporter, feature writer Gannett Publs. 1942-46, Brunswick (Me.) Record, 1942-47; feature writer Lewiston (Me.) Jours., 1945—; radio copy writer, WPOR, 1948-49; news reporter, WLOB, 1957—, also writer; Me. corr. Dealerscope Mag. (N.E.), 1969—; guest appearances

WABI-TV, WCSH-TV WRKD, WJTO, WLAM; lectr. Dir. Maine Women's State Relief Corps, 1948-50, treas. G. W. Randall Relief Corps, 1960-62; women's dir. Cumberland County Civil Def. and Pub. Safety, 1959—; founder Poetry Day in Me.; Me. state chmn. Poetry Day mem. world com., nat. com.; founder Me. Poetry Sunday, 1968; head of com. for Am. Poetry Sunday, 1969; Me. chmn. Authors' Nat. Library Week, 1959; judge Me. State Writers' Conf., juvenile fiction contest, 1960; judge, chmn. state poetry competition Me. Poetry Week, 1969, 72; Me. chmn. Am. Art Week, 1964, also dir.; state chmn. Maine Poetry Week, 1964, 69, 70, 72, Me. Poetry Day, 1969; chmn. World Poetry Day, 1968, Nat. Poetry Day; sponsor, judge essay contest schs. Maine; dir. pub. relations World Congress Poets, Taiwan, 1973. Dir. World Poetry Center, Freeport, Me., Poetry Exhbns. of Portland (Me.) Players, Am. Art Week New Eng. States, Am. Artists' Profl. League, N.Y.C.; tchr. Woodfords Sch., 1968—; columnist Freeport Post, Eastland Pub. Co., Lisbon Falls, Me., 1972—. Recipient 1st prize Nat. Poetry Exhbn.; 1st prize World Poetry Competition, 1967; 1st prize (free form) Poetry Soc. N.H., 1967; 1st Nat. Poetry Day, State of N.J.; 3d prize Am. Poetry League, 1968; E. Centro Studi Internazionalia, Italy, 1972; 1st prize Northeastern U.S.A., World Congress Poets, 1973, Decretum of award, 1973; gold medal 1st Lady of Philippines, 1973; others. Mem. Nat. League Am. Pen Women (N.E. regional chmn. of poetry 1954, pres. Pine Tree br. 1960, nat. lyric chmn. 1959, nat. poetry chmn., northeastern regional chmn. 1962), Maine Poetry Day Assn. (pres. 1959—), Internat. Platform Assn., Poetry Fellowship (sec. 1948), Me. Hist. Soc., Am. Poetry League (judge contest 1960), United Poets' Laureate Internat. (hon.), Cosmosynthesis League Australia (life), Centro E. Scambi Internazionali (honorary). Maine Writers Research Club, Maine Press Radio Women, Nat. Grange, Congress Am. Housewives. Author: Sea Mist and Balsam, 1958; Diaries of John Hill White, 13th Mass. Volunteers; Blue Through Tears; Sea to Sea in Song, 1968; American Poets, 1968; By Wind and Water, 1970; also poetry in magazines. Editor: From One Bright Spark, 1959. Mem. editorial bd. As Maine Writes, 1948, Maine Indians in Story and Legend, 1950; The Pen Woman's Year, 1954. Contbr. articles to mags. including Maine Life, Lewiston Jour., Christian Herald, others. Home: Blueberry Hill Freeport ME 04032

TROTTER, ANN BECK (MRS. CHARLES DAVID TROTTER), educator; b. Duluth, Minn., June 6, 1935; d. Edwin Oscar and Vivian Angela (Olessen) Beck; student Northwestern U., 1953-55; B.A. magna cum laude, U. Minn., 1957, M.A., 1958; Ph.D., U. Wis., 1965; m. Charles David Trotter, Aug. 26, 1961. Instr., research asst. U. Minn., Mpls., 1958-61; rehab. counselor U. Wash., Seattle, 1961-63; asst. prof. rehab. counseling U. Wis., Milw., 1965-69, prof., 1972—, project dir. rehab. counseling, 1965—. Cons. Rehab. Services Adminstrn., U.S. Dept. Health, Edn. and Welfare, 1971. Mem. med. adv. bd. Curative Workshop, Milw., 1967—. Rehab. Services Adminstrn. fellow, 1959-61, Recipient Nat. Merit award Amvets Aux., 1970. Mem. Am. Psychol. Assn., Am. Personnel and Guidance Assn., Council Rehab. Counselor Educators (sec.-treas. 1973—), Nat. Rehab. Assn., Phi Beta Kappa, Pi Lambda Theta, Psi Chi, Alpha Omicron Pi. Author: (with G.N. Wright) Rehabilitation Research, 1968. Home: 9600 N Lake Dr Milwaukee WI 53217

TROTTER, NANCY LOUISA, educator; b. Monaca, Pa., July 26, 1934; d. Robert James and Mary Lou (Braham) Trotter; A.B., Oberlin Coll., 1956; Sc.M., Brown U., 1958, Ph.D., 1960. Instr. dept. anatomy Columbia, 1961-64, asst. prof., 1964-68; asso. prof. dept. anatomy Thomas Jefferson U., Phila., 1968—. Mem. Am. Assn. Anatomists, Sigma Xi. Home: Box 95 RD 1 Enon Valley PA 16120

TROTTER, VIRGINIA YAPP, univ. vice chancellor; b. Boise, Ida., Nov. 29, 1921; d. Rockford Glenn and Lena Idylla (Topliff) Yapp; B.S., Kan. State U., 1943, M.S., 1949; Ph.D., Ohio State U., 1959; m. Robert Talbot Trotter, July, 1943 (dec.); 1 son, Robert Talbot. Instr., dir. home mgmt. U. Utah, Salt Lake City, 1948-50; chmn. dept. home econs., asst. to dean Coll. Agr. and Home Econs., U. Vt., 1955-63; asst. prof., head family econs. U. Neb., Lincoln, 1950-55, dir. Sch. Home Econs., asso. dean, 1963-70, dean Coll. Home Econs., asso. dir. Agrl. Expt. Sta. and Agrl. Extension Service, 1970-72, vice chancellor acad. affairs, prof. edn. and family resources, 1972—; mem. Nat. Advt. Review Bd., 1971—. Cons. President's Com. on Employment of Handicapped, 1967—; cons. home econs. Neb. Mission in Colombia, So. Am., 1966-73, Hacettepe U., Ankara, Turkey, 1967; cons. J.C. Penney Research, 1966—. Mem. adv. council N.Y. State Coll. Home Econs., Cornell U., 1967-71; mem. Gov.'s Com. on Employment of Handicapped, 1971—. Recipient Melvin McArtor Dist. Service award, 1971. Mem. Am. (v.p. 1970-72), Neb. (pres. 1968-70) home econs. assns., Neb. Heart Assn. (chmn. bd. 1970-72). Contbr. articles to profl. jours. Home: 3223 S Summit Lincoln NE 68502

TROUPIN, ROSALIND HILSEN (MRS. ALLAN S. TROUPIN), radiologist; b. N.Y.C., Feb. 11, 1937; d. Irving and Claire (Weizelberg) Hilsen; B.S., City Coll. of N.Y., 1956; M.D., Columbia, 1960; m. Allan S. Troupin, Dec. 29, 1957; children—Mark W., Barbara Elaine. Spl. tng. radiology, U. Mich., 1962-65; instr. radiology U. Wash., Seattle, 1965-66, asst. prof. radiology, 1968-73, asso. prof., 1973—, coordinator Dept. Radiology, Sch. of Medicine, 1968—; asst. prof. radiology Med. Coll. Ga., Augusta, 1966-68; cons. Hall Health Service, 1965-66. Recipient Outstanding Tchr. award U. Wash. Med. Sch., 1971, 72. Mem. Radiologic Soc. No. Am., Assn. U. Radiologists, Wash. State Radiological Assn., Wash., King County med. socs. Home: 2672 168th Av SE Bellevue WA 98008 Office: Dept Radiology University Hosp Seattle WA 98105

TROUT, CARRIE ALICE, city ofcl.; b. Lake Andes, S.D., Mar. 19, 1913; d. Charles Reynier and Blanche Myrtle (Copple) Wilson; student Wayne State Tchrs. Coll., 1932-33, Lincoln Sch. Commerce, 1936; m. Lester Lowell Trout, Nov. 19, 1959; 1 stepson, Larry L. Sec. Lincoln (Neb.) Water and Light Dept., 1938-41; adminstr. Neb. accounting dept. U.P.R.R. Co., Omaha, 1942-56; city clk. and finance officer Chadron, Neb., 1957-65, city clk., finance officer, 1968—. Mem. Bus. and Profl. Women's Club (pres. 1963-64), Neb. League Municipalities (sec.-treas. city clks. sect. 1972-74), Internat. Inst. Municipal Clks. Methodist. Home: PO Box 262 Alliance NE 69301 Office: PO Box 390 Chadron NE 69337

TROUT, SYLVIA MARION FESSLER (MRS. ROBERT D. TROUT), librarian; b. Cressona, Pa., Nov. 11, 1931; d. William McKinley and Viola Mae (Sticher) F.; B.S., Kutztown State Coll., 1953; m. Robert D. Trout, July 2, 1955. Librarian, Palisades Joint Jr. and Sr. High Sch., Kintnersville, Pa., 1953-55; children's librarian D.C. Pub. Library, 1955-67; librarian St. Croix (U.S. V.I.) Country Day Sch., 1967—. Mem. A.L.A., St. Croix Library Assn. Home: Box 1136 Christiansted St Croix US Virgin Islands 00820

TROUTMAN, MARY OLENA FLESHER (MRS. EDWIN GLENN TROUTMAN), physician; b. Rochester, Minn.; d. Clinton G. and Mary (Dyer) Flesher; A.A., Pasadena Jr. Coll., 1945; B.A., U. So. Cal., 1947, M.D., 1954; m. Edwin Glenn Troutman, Sept. 4, 1949; children—Clinton Edwin, David Glenn. Dir. employees health service James Ewing Hosp., N.Y.C., 1956-57; intern Los Angeles County Harbor Gen. Hosp., Torrance, Cal., 1953-54; resident Manhattan VA Hosp., N.Y.C., 1955-56, U. Tex. Med. Br., Galveston, 1957-58; practice medicine specializing in allergy, Ft. Worth, 1967—. Vice pres. Tex. Allergy Labs., Inc., Ft. Worth, 1967—, Med. Computers, Inc. Ft. Worth, 1969—. Home: 2026 Ward Pkwy Fort Worth TX 76110 Office: 712 7th Av Fort Worth TX 76104

TROUTWINE, CHARLOTTE TEMPERLEY, ednl. counselor, psychologist; b. Newton, Mass., Nov. 27, 1906; d. Joseph and Libbie (Kempton) Temperley; B.S., Simmons Coll., 1927; grad. student Boston U., 1947-49; M.A., Northeastern U., 1966; m. Arklay S. Richards, Nov. 28, 1928 (div. 1942); children—Whitman Albin, Lincoln Kempton, Sylvia Caroline; m. 2d, Harry Troutwine, May 3, 1945 (div. 1954); m. 3d, Lester Lewis Walsh, Feb. 16, 1968 (div. 1972). Pvt. sec. pres. Hygrade Sylvania Electric Corp. Salem, Mass., 1927-28; pvt. and dept. exec. sec. Dr. Stanley Cobb, Bullard prof. of neuropathology Harvard Med. Sch., 1928-31; part-time work, various positions, 1931-51; exec. dir. Postgrad. Med. Inst., 1951-57; mgr. Postgrad. Information Service, Lederle Labs., a div. of American Cyanamid Co., Pearl River, N.Y., 1957-61; exec. sec. postgrad. med. edn. Hahnemann Med. Coll. and Hosp., also exec. dir. Mary Bailey Inst. Cardiovascular Research, Phila., 1961; high sch. counselor; instr. psychology Holliston High Sch., 1965-66, Falmouth (Mass.) High Sch., 1966—. Friends of Framingham Reformatory; speaker, organizer Am. Epilepsy League. Mem. Simmons Coll. Alumnae Assn., Am. Assn. U. Women, Mass. Psychol. Assn., Mass. Sch. Psychologists Assn., Am. Assn. Psychical Research, Spiritual Frontiers Assn., N.E.A. (life), Mass. Sch. Counselor Assn., League Women Voters, Cape Cod Guidance Assn., States Med. Postgrad. Assn. (sec.), Am. Assn. Med. Soc. Execs. (emeritus), Mass. Tchrs. Assn. (life), Nat. Ret. Tchrs. Assn., Am., Mass. personnel and guidance assns., Mass. Assn. Women Deans and Counselors, Falmouth Educators Assn., Nat. Sch. Counselors Assn. (life and charter), Cape Cod Mental Health Assn., Northeastern Alumni Assn., Soc. Mayflower Descs. (life), Assn. Research and Enlightenment. Mem. Soc. Friends. Author articles in field. Home: 10 Waterside Dr North Falmouth MA 02556

TROVINGER, ETHEL MARIE (MRS. LAWRENCE B. TROVINGER), sch. psychologist; b. Spruce, Wis., May 25, 1920; d. John Paul and Barbara Cecelia (Levash) LeClair; student U. Wis., Whitewater, 1938-40; B.S., Wis. State U., Milw., 1943; M.A., U. Wis., Madison, 1948; postgrad. U. Wis.-Milw., 1960-68, U. Chgo., 1965-66; m. Lawrence B. Trovinger, June 5, 1940; children—Anne Marie, William Henry II. First tchr. mentally retarded Milw. County, 1943-54; sch. psychologist Milw. County Schs., 1960-66; psychologist Nicolet High Sch., Milw., 1965—; instr. psychology Milw. Area Tech. Coll., 1963—. Dir. summer reading clinics U. Wis., Madison, 1945-46. Leader, Milw. Area council Girl Scouts U.S.A., 1944-66; leader Mental Health Assn., 1966—. Mem. Am., Wis., Milw. County psychol. assns., Wis. Assn. Sch. Psychologists, Suburban Sch. Psychologists, Nat., Wis. edn. assns., Psi Chi, Pi Lambda Theta (past pres., sec.). Conglist. Clubs: Ausblick, Dansette, Lake Shore. Home: 6600 N Birch Hill Fox Point Milwaukee WI 53217

TROY, ANNETTE ORANTAS (MRS. JAMES MATTHEWS TROY), educator; b. Waterbury, Conn., Jan. 15, 1937; d. Anthony and Anna (Malinauskas) Orantas; B.S., U. Conn., 1958; M.S., Central Conn. State Coll., 1967; m. James Matthews Troy, Aug. 23, 1958; children—Lisa Wright, Sanders Martin, Maura Rivers. Head bus. dept. Wolcott (Conn.) High Sch., 1958-61; instr. Post Jr. Coll., Waterbury, Conn., 1962-65, asst. prof., 1965-73, asso. prof., 1973—, div. chmn. secretarial scis. div., 1966—. Mem. Eastern, Conn. bus. tchrs. assns., U. Conn. Alumni Assn. (sec. 1961-64), Delta Pi Epsilon, Alpha Delta Pi. Home: 327 Nova Scotia Hill Rd Watertown CT 06795 Office: 800 Country Club Rd Waterbury CT 06708

TROY, MARGARET MARY HASSON, librarian; b. Medford, Mass., Aug. 30, 1921; d. John P. and Julia A. (MacFarland) Hasson; A.B., Radcliffe Coll., 1943; certificate U. London (Eng.), 1950; m. John Grannan Troy, Nov. 23, 1963. Research asst. Harvard Med. Sch., 1943-51; librarian Nat. Research Corp., Cambridge, Mass., 1951-54, United Fruit Co., Boston, 1954-55; research adminstrv. asst. Sloan Kettering Inst. Cancer Research, N.Y.C., 1955-59; head librarian Bolt Beranek and Newman, Inc., Cambridge, 1959—. Vol. work for blind in Boston area, 1960—. Recipient award merit OSRD, 1948. Mem. Spl. Libraries Assn., Nat. Geog. Soc., Marine Tech. Soc., Sigma Xi. Clubs: Radcliffe, Appalachian Mountain (Boston). Home: 52A Charlesbank Way Waltham MA 02154 Office: 50 Moulton St Cambridge MA 02138

TROY, NANCY S., social worker; b. Uhrichsville, O., Apr. 23, 1930; d. Ray Ellis and E. Dorothy (Petry) Troy; B.A., Lake Erie Coll., 1951; M.S. S.A., Western Res. U., 1955. Med. social worker Univ. Hosps., Cleve., 1955-62; psychiat. social worker Cal. Dept. Mental Hygiene, Sacramento, San Jose, 1962-66; supr. State Dept. Social Welfare, San Jose, 1966-68; supr. Santa Clara County Div. Social Services, Family and Childrens Program, San Jose, 1968-73, supr. placement unit, 1973—; student supr. Sch. Applied Social Scis., Western Res. U., 1960-61, Sch. Social Work, U. Cal. at Berkeley, 1966-68. Profl. vol. Am. Cancer Soc., 1967—, bd. dirs. Santa Clara unit, 1972—. Mem. Nat. Assn. Social Workers, Am. Acad. Certified Social Workers, Cal. Social Workers Orgn. Home: 125-85 Connemara Way Sunnyvale CA 94087 Office: 55 W Younger St San Jose CA 95110

TROYER, EDITH BRAUN (MRS. RICHARD P. TROYER), social worker; b. Vienna, Austria (came to U.S. 1938, naturalized 1943); d. Rudolf and Josefine (Huss) Braun; student Tchrs.'s Coll., Vienna, Austria, 1927, Summer Sch. Inst. J.J. Rousseau, Geneva, Switzerland, 1928; Internatinal Montessori diploma, London, England, 1929, Vienna Psychoanalytic Inst., 1930-38; M.A., Bryn Mawr Coll., 1942; m. Richard P. Troyer, Oct. 28, 1938. Tchr. Vienna Children's House, 1932-38; case worker Family Service of Phila., 1939-45, dist. dir., 1945-52; case worker Family Service of the Main Line, Ardmore, Pa., 1960-62; psychiat. social worker Pathway Sch. for Brain Injured Children, Narberth, Pa., 1962-63; psychiat. social worker Lankenau Hosp., Child Guidance Clinic, Phila., 1963-72; pvt. practice personal and family counseling, Merion, Pa., 1972—. Active, Tri-county Concerts Assn., Wayne, Pa., 1946-52, Antonia's Music Shelf, supplying music materials to rural sch. children, Shrewsbury, Vt., 1955-60. Mem. Nat. Assn. Social Workers (active com. work), Acad. Certified Social Workers, Orthopsychiatric Assn., Pa. Soc. Clin. Social Work, Bryn Mawr Alumna Assn. Home: 637 S Highland Av Merion PA 19066

TRUAX, ANNE THORSEN, ednl. adminstr.; b. Mpls., Mar. 21, 1925; d. Melford Bernhard and Sylvia Amelia (Utter) Thorsen; B.A., U. Minn., 1963, postgrad., 1968—; children by previous marriage—Thomas, David, Steven, John, Richard. Adminstrv. asst. KTCA-TV, St. Paul, 1965-68; asst. to dean students U. Minn., Mpls., 1968-69, dir. Minn. women's center, 1969—, instr. family social sci., 1969—, instr. women's studies, 1974—. Mem. Women's Equity Action League (trustee 1973—), Minn. Women's Polit. Caucus, Democratic-Farmer Labor Feminist Caucus, Nat. Orgn. Women, Council for U. Women's Progress, Profl. Women's Caucus, Assn. Am. Colls. (mem. adv. com. project on status and edn. women 1973—), Am. Assn. U. Profs. (mem. com. on status women in profession 1971-74, dir. Twin Cities chpt.), Nat. Coalition on Research in Women's Edn. and Devel. (v.p. 1974—), Nat. Assn. Women Deans, Adminstrs. and Counselors (mem. continuing edn. com. 1971-72). Home: 65 Clarence Av SE Minneapolis MN 55414 Office: 306 Walter Library University Minnesota Minneapolis MN 55455

TRUBE, MARY DUNN, museum ofcl.; b. Abilene, Tex., Nov. 14, 1909; d. Proctor Orr and Eunice (Dunn) Cole; student Tex. Christian U., 1935-37, Juilliard Sch. Music, N.Y.C., summer 1937; m. Edwin A. Trube, Feb. 15, 1947. Music tchr., Dallas, Waco and Temple, Tex., 1936-37; violinist So. Meth. U. Symphony Orch., Dallas, 1944-47; now owner Trube House Mus., Galveston, Tex. Clubs: Galveston Garden (v.p. 1966—), Galveston Musical (treas. 1968—). Home: 1627 Sealy Av Galveston TX 77550

TRUDEAU, GWENDOLYN DOLORES CAMPBELL (MRS. ANDRE N. TRUDEAU), physician; b. Columbus, O., Mar. 6, 1923; d. Clare L. and Avis (Elder) Campbell; B.A., Ohio State U., 1946; M.D., 1949; m. Andre N. Trudeau, June 11, 1949; children—Michael David, Gregory Daniel, Marie Claire, Phillip Andre, Martha Estelle, James William, Laura Louise, Charles Campbell. Rotating intern St. Luke's Hosp., New Bedford, Mass., 1949-50; preceptorship anesthesia St. Luke's, 1950-51; resident anesthesia Ohio State U. hosp., 1951-53; anesthesiologist Ohio Tb Hosp., 1953-62; instr. anesthesia Ohio State U. Hosp., 1951—; active staff anesthesia St. Ann's Hosp., Columbus, 1962—, chmn. dept., 1967-73, sec., treas. med. staff, 1968-69, chmn. com. on intensive care, 1970-72. Diplomate Am. Bd. Anesthesiology. Mem. Am., Ohio med. assns., Columbus Acad. Medicine Internat. Anesthesia Research Soc., Am. Ohio socs., anesthesiologists, Columbus Soc. Anesthesiologists, Am. Med. Women's Assn. (br. pres. 1971). Methodist. Republican. Address: 1943 Collingswood Rd Columbus OH 43221

TRUE, JEAN DURLAND (MRS. HENRY A. TRUE, JR.), bus. exec.; b. Olney, Ill., Nov. 27, 1915; d. Clyde Earl and Harriet Louise (Brayton) Durland; student Mont. State U., 1935-36; m. Henry Alfonso True, Jr., Mar. 20, 1938; children—Tamma Jean (Mrs. Donald G. Hatten), Henry Alfonso III, Diemer Durland, David Lanmon. Partner, True Drilling Co., Casper, Wyo., 1951—, True Oil Co., Casper, 1951—; treas., dir. True Service Co., Casper, Toolpushers Supply Co., Casper, White Stallion Ranch, Inc., Tucson; dir. Black Hills Oil Marketers, Casper, Belle Fourche Pipeline Co., Casper, Camp Creek Gas Co., Casper. Mem. steering com. YMCA, Casper, 1954-55, bd. dirs., 1956-58; mem. exec. bd. trustees Gottsche Rehab. Center, Thermopolis, Wyo., 1966—, v.p., 1973—; mem. adv. bd. for adult edn. U. Wyo., 1966-68. Mem. Nat. Fedn. Republican Women's Clubs; del. Rep. nat. conv., 1972. Mem. Rocky Mountain Oil and Gas Industry, Casper Area C. of C., Alpha Gamma Delta. Episcopalian. Club: Casper Country; Petroleum Women's (Casper). Home: 6000 S Poplar St Casper WY 82601 Office: Riverside Rd PO Box 2360 Casper WY 82601

TRUE, MARION (MRS. LAURENCE M. TRUE), civic worker; b. Franklin, N.H., Feb. 16, 1902; d. Ichabod S. and Mary K. (Dunlap) Williams; B.S. in Chemistry, U. N.H., 1923; m. Laurence M. True, Sept. 3, 1927 (dec.); children—Lavinia (Mrs. Paul H. Plough, Jr.), David, Gilbert, Melbern, Katharine (Mrs. Douglas Logan). Tchr. Sanborn Sem., 1923-24, Braintree High Sch., 1924-27. Active Cleve. Girl Scouts, 1942-69, mem. bd. dirs., mem. regional com. 1951-61, mem. group services council, 1943-61, vice chmn., 1943-58, mem. exec. bd., 1955-58; mem. personnel com. Welfare Fedn. of Cleve., 1954-56; mem. Com. on Older Persons; chmn. Com. on Homes for Aged; alumni dir. U. N.H., 1964-70; pres. Aux. Bapt. Home Ohio. Trustee, house chmn., sec. of bd. Judson Park. Recipient Alumni Meritorious award 1961; Thanks badge, Lake Erie Girl Scouts. Mem. Nat. Soc. New Eng. Women (pres. Cleve. colony), New Eng. Soc. Western Res. Daus. Am. Colonists (treas.), Am. Soc. Mech. Engrs. (woman's aux.), Alpha Xi Delta. Baptist (trustee 1958-61, 64-70, 73, 74, cabinet 1970-73, stewardship com. 1972—). Clubs: College dir.); Canterbury Golf. Home: Jordan-Gardner Tower 2181 Ambleside Rd Cleveland OH 44106

TRUEHEART, HELEN ELIZABETH LAKIN (MRS. HERBERT L. TRUEHEART), artist, bus. exec.; b. Boonsboro, Md., Oct. 2, 1912; d. Robert Thompson and Lenora (McLaughlin) Lakin; B.S., Md. Coll. Women, 1935; art student Paul Roache and Grace Graff, 1938-41; postgrad. investment banking Johns Hopkins, 1960-62; m. Herbert Lee Trueheart, June 19, 1937; 2 children (dec.). Free-lance dress designer, fashion model, artist, sculptor, 1935-41; operator food business, 1941-45, dress designer, 1945—; conducted pvt. art sch., 1945-54, research in ceramic chemistry, 1945-54; ceramic sculptress, 1945—, made original models for Dalmatian, Beagle, Scottie and German Shepherd clubs, 1956-60, one-of-a-kind series 19th century fashion figurines, 1950—; painter, 1954—; owner, operator food brokerage, 1961— (all Balt.). Sec., Belvedere Improvement Assn., Balt., 1947-57; organizer nat. movement Service Through the Creative Arts, 1965; mem. Star Spangled Banner Flag House Assn., Soc. Prevention Cruelty to Animals, Women's Civic League, Ft. McHenry Nat. Shrine Mission, Gov.'s Commn. for Creation Replica Original Star Spangled Banner, Gov.'s Commn. Star Spangled Banner Sesquicentennial, Balt. Mus. Art. Recipient Mayor's Citation of Merit award City of Balt., 1965; named hon. Chief Creek Indian Nation for life, hon. lt. col. aide-de-camp Ala. State Militia. Fellow Royal Soc. Arts (London); mem. Md. Coll. Alumnae Assn., Nat. League Am. Pen Women (br. pres. 1962-64, state pres. 1960-62, 66-68, nat. 2d v.p., regional coordinator 1964-66, nat. 1st v.p. 1968-70, nat. membership 1970-72, nat. pres. 1972-74), Fashion Congress, Nat. Soc. Arts and Letters, Md. State Fedn. Arts, Md. Poetry Soc., Internat. Platform Assn., English Speaking Union (chmn. various groups women's sect. 1952-62), D.A.R. (vice regent dir. Gen. Mordecai Gist chpt. 1958-60, vice regent 1961-64), U.S. Daus. 1812 (state 2d v.p. 1970—), Daus. Am. Colonists, Alpha Psi Omega. Mem. Evang. Ref. Ch. Clubs: Woman's of Govans (past dir.), Thalia; Washington. Address: 816 E Belvedere Av Baltimore MD 21212

TRUEMAN, INEZ GENEVA GANDRUD (MRS. K. R. TRUEMAN), legislator; b. Glenwood, Minn., Apr. 8, 1917; d. Gustav M. and Ida E. (Disrud) Gandrud; R.N., Kahler Sch. Nursing, 1938; student U. Winnipeg (Man.), 1969-71; m. K. R. Trueman, Dec. 29, 1938; children—Robert, David, Donald, Martha (Mrs. Edward Kennedy). Pres. Jr. League Winnipeg (Man., Can.), 1951-52; pres. Community Welfare Planning Council, 1965-67; mem. Winnipeg City Council, 1968-69; mem. Legislative Assembly Province Man., 1969-73. Named Woman of Yr. Women's Sales and Advt. Club, 1968. Progressive-Conservative. Mem. United Ch. Can. Clubs: St. Charles Country (Winnipeg); Winnipeg Winter. Home: 179 Oxford St Winnipeg MB Canada

TRUETT, BEVERLY ANN, ednl. adminstr.; b. Dallas, June 25, 1941; d. Sam Langston and Ida (Meier) Truett; B.A., Tex. Tech. U., 1963; M.Ed., U. Okla., 1964. Counselor, U. Okla., Norman, 1963-64; dir. residence hall, asst. dean Ariz. State U., Tempe, 1964-69, Angelo State U., San Angelo, Tex., 1969-72; counselor Tex. Technol. U., Lubbock, 1972—. Mem. Tex. Assn. Women Deans and Counselors, Nat. Assn. Women Deans, Adminstrs. and Counselors, Tex. Technol. Ex-Students Assn., U. Okla. Alumnae Assn., Mortar Bd., Mortar Bd. Alumnae Clubs, Gamma Phi Beta. Lutheran. Home: 6741 N 45th Av Glendale AZ 85301

TRUEX, DOROTHY ADINE, univ. ofcl.; b. Sedalia, Mo., Oct. 6, 1915; d. Chester Morrison and Madge (Nicholson) Truex; A.B., William Jewell Coll., 1936; M.A., U. Mo., 1937; Ed.D., Columbia, 1956. Asst. and later dean of women N.W. Mo. State Coll., Maryville, 1939-45; dean of women Mercer U., Macon, 1945-47; dean of women U. Okla., Norman, 1947-69, asso. prof. higher edn., dir. research and program devel., 1969-70, prof. edn., dir. grad. program in student personnel services, 1970-74; vice chancellor for student affairs U. Ark.

at Little Rock, 1974—. Nat. adviser, mem. resource personnel bd. Intercollegiate Assn. Women Students. Mem. Am. Assn. U. Women, Nat. Assn. Women Deans, Adminstrs. and Counselors (pres. 1973-74), So. Coll. Personnel Assn. (pres. 1970), Okla. Coll. Personnel Assn. (pres. 1972-73), William Jewell Coll. Alumni Assn. (pres. 1970-73), Pi Beta Phi, Alpha Lambda Delta, Mortar Bd., Sigma Tau Delta, Cardinal Key, Gamma Alpha Chi, Kappa Delta Pi, Pi Lambda Theta, Alpha Psi Omega, Pi Gamma Mu, Phi Delta Kappa, Delta Kappa Gamma. Home: 1912 Green Mountain Dr Apt 250 Little Rock AR 72205

TRUEX, RUTH BREWSTER OLMSTED (MRS. EDWARD HAMILTON TRUEX), state senator; b. East Hartford, Conn., Aug. 10, 1912; d. Horace Bigelow and Julia Augustine (Williams) Olmsted; B.A., Mount Holyoke Coll., 1932, M.A., 1934; m. Edward Hamilton Truex, July 6, 1935; children—Ann Elizabeth (Mrs. Robert H. Steele), Joan (Mrs. John H. Barton), Edward Hamilton IV, Richard H. Grad. asst. Mt. Holyoke Coll., 1932-34, faculty, 1934-37; research asst. Inst. Internat. Studies, Yale, 1938-41; mem. Conn. Ho. of Reps., 1967-72, asst. minority leader, 1971; mem. Conn. senate, 1973—, chmn. edn. com. Del. White House Conf. on Aging, 1971. Mem. bd. edn., Wethersfield, Conn., 1956-60. Bd. dirs. New Eng. Bd. Higher Edn., Edn. Commn. of States, Community Council, Ch. Homes. Mem. Gerontology Soc. (dir. 1971). Home: 37 Farmingdale Rd Wethersfield CT 06109

TRUITT, CANDACE SUSAN YORK, newspaperwoman; b. Jefferson, N.C., Feb. 2, 1950; d. Samule William and Wanna (Pennington) York; B.S. in Journalism, U. Md., 1972; m. Roy L. Truitt, Jr., Dec. 30, 1972. Reporter, Hagerstown (Md.) Daily Mail, summer 1971; reporter, make-up and layout editor Balt. News-Am., 1972-74; asst. to dean Coll. Journalism, U. Md., 1974—. William Randolph Hearst scholar, 1971. Mem. Women in Communication. Home: 428 Hillview Dr Linthicum MD 21090 Office: Coll Journalism U Md College Park MD 20742

TRUITT, (MARY) ANN, sch. psychologist; b. Washington, Aug. 31, 1941; d. Stephen and Ruth May (Moreland) Truitt; B.S., D.C. Tchrs. Coll., 1962; M.A., Columbia, 1963; Ph.D., Heed U., 1974. Tchr. spl. edn. in jr. high schs. Prince Georges County (Md.) Pub. Schs., 1963-68, sch. psychologist, 1968—. Instr. Western Md. Coll. Grad. Sch., Westminster, 1971—. Mem. N.E.A., Nat. Assn. Sch. Psychologists, Md., Prince Georges County psychol. assns., Md., Prince Georges County tchrs. assns. Author: Read Better with Jim King, 1969. Home: 5101 River Rd Chevy Chase MD 20016 Office: 4913 Tilden Rd Bladensburg MD 20710

TRUJILLO, JOSEPHINE CATHERINE DE FRANCESCO, physician; b. Phila., June 26, 1923; d. Nicholas Anthony and Santa (Vitullo) DeFrancesco; A.B., Temple U., 1944, M.D., 1948; m. Hernando Trujillo, June 30, 1962 (div. May 1968); 1 son, Hernando Trujillo II. Intern, Albert Einstein Med. Center No. div., Phila.; resident Columbia-Presbyn. Med. Center, 1951-53; anesthesiologist St. Christopher's Hosp. for Children, Phila., 1953-54; anesthesiologist Chester (Pa.) Hosp., Crozer Hosp., Chester, Pa., Taylor Hosp., Ridley Park, Pa., 1954-65, Sacred Heart Hosp., Chester, Pa., 1960-65; anesthesiologist St. Francis Hosp., Trenton, N.J., 1965—. Diplomate Am. Bd. Anesthesiology; fellow Am. Soc. Anesthesiologists; mem. A.M.A., Pa. Med. Soc., Phila., Pa., N.Y. State socs. anesthesiologists, Pan Am. Med. Assn. Home: 368 Green Valley Rd Langhorne PA 19047 Office: 2667 Nottingham Way Trenton NJ 08619

TRULOCK, MILLIE WARD (MRS. ELBERT P. TRULOCK, JR.), hosp. adminstr.; b. Donalsonville, Ga., Sept. 23, 1919; d. Jack S. and Martha Prudence (Martin) Ward; grad. high sch.; m. Elbert P. Trulock, Jr., Sept. 18, 1939; children—Elbert Powell III, Franklin Ward. Bookkeeper, Crosby Aeromarine Co., 1960-61, dept. head, office mgr., 1961-71; hosp. adminstr. Donalsonville (Ga.) Hosp., 1971—. Pres., P.T.A., 1958-59. Baptist. Club: Woman's (v.p. Donalsonville). Home: 800 S Woolfork St Donalsonville GA 31745 Office: 102 Hospital Circle Donalsonville GA 31745

TRUNZ, CECILIA AMALIE, educator, village ofcl.; b. Bklyn., Feb. 14, 1906; d. Maximilian and Amalie (Herold) Trunz; B.A., St. Joseph's Coll. for Women, 1927; M.A., Columbia, 1930; Ph.D., Albert Ludwig U., Freiburg in Breisgau Baden, Germany, 1933. With St. Joseph's Coll., 1928-50, prof., head German dept., 1933-50, head modern lang. dept., 1942-50; dir. Trunz, Inc., Bklyn., 1938-69, v.p., sec., 1945-69. Trustee Village Millerton (N.Y.), 1967-69, mayor, 1969-71; v.p., dir. Trunz Food Stores, Inc., Greenvale, N.Y., 1971—. Bd. visitors N.Y. Tng. Sch. Girls at Hudson. Mem. Modern Lang. German tchrs. assns. Nat. Cath. Philos. Assn. (life) Brit. Inst. Philosophy (life), Cath. Lawyers Guild (hon.), Delta Epsilon Sigma. Author: Die Autobiographien von deutschen Industrier-Arbeitern, 1934 (Germany). Home: Highland Dr Millerton NY 12546 Office: 9 Northern Blvd Greenvale NY 11158

TRUSSELL, ELLA MAY, educator; b. Santa Rosa, Cal., July 29, 1939; d. Rhodes and Margaret Southerland (Brown) Trussell; A.A., Santa Rosa Jr. Coll., 1948; B.A., U. Cal., 1950, M.A., 1952, Ed.D., 1966; postdoctoral studies Stanford U., 1967. Instr. phys. edn. Stockton Coll., 1952-54, Mt. San Antonio Coll., 1954-63, Merritt Coll., 1963-65; prof. phys. edn. Cal. State Coll., Sonoma, 1965—, currently prof. health sci. and phys. edn., chmn. div. edn., 1971-74, chmn. acad. senate, 1973-74, acting dean acad. planning, 1974-75. Guest instr. Cal. Poly. Workshop. Mem. Am., Cal (unit pres.) assns. health, phys. edn. and recreation, Western Soc. Phys. Edn. Coll. Women, Am. Coll. Sports Medicine, Am. Assn. Phys. Edn. Coll. Women, Internat. Council Health, Phys. Edn. and Recreation, N.E.A., Pi Lambda Theta, Delta Psi Kappa. Contbr. articles profl. jours. Home: 1232 Fair Oaks St Santa Rosa CA 95404 Office: Sonoma State College Rohnert Park CA 94928

TRUST, ESTELLE LOUISE, author; b. New Orleans, Nov. 1, 1915; d. Cyril Januarius and Catharine Estelle (Unsworth) Trust; B.A., St. Vincents Coll., 1933. Formerly tchr. St. Vincent's Coll., St. Mary's Sch. and pub. schs. Recipient Certificate of Appreciation for outstanding contbn. to lit. Hayden Library, Ariz. State U., 1970. Mem. Eugene Field Soc., Mark Twain Soc., Bronte Soc. Author: Anne Bronte, A Biography, 1954; (poetry) Hour of Happiness, 1961; (novel) Wine and Roses, 1962; Glorious Day, 1966; Shadow Lace of Years, 1968; April Rose, 1970; Black Lace Mantilla, 1971; Wildwood, 1972; (poetry collection) The Wine and Roses, 1973. Editor Quintessense, 1963—. Home: 166 Albany Av Shreveport LA 71105

TSALTAS, MARGARET ELIZABETH OWEN (MRS. THEODORE TSALTAS), physician, educator; b. Springfield, O., July 16, 1922; d. Daniel Joseph and Dorothy (Owen) Cave; A.B., Vassar Coll., 1942; postgrad. Columbia, 1944-45; M.D., N.Y. U., 1949; certificate in psychoanalysis William A. White Inst. for Psychoanalysis, 1958; m. Theodore Tsaltas, May 19, 1956; children—Theodore Theodosius, Penelope Elizabeth. Intern Grasslands Hosp., Valhalla, N.Y., 1949-50, resident, 1950-52; resident children's psychiat. ward Bellevue Hosp., N.Y.C., 1952-53; staff psychiatrist Postgrad. Center Psychotherapy, N.Y.C., 1953-55; practice medicine specializing in psychiatry, N.Y.C., 1953-58; dir. psychiatry clinic Jefferson Med. Coll. Phila., 1958-59; faculty coll., 1958—, asst. prof. psychiatry, 1969—; asso. attending Coll. Hosp., Phila. Gen. Hosp. Cons. pub. agys., instns. Recipient Outstanding Alumna citation Moravian Sem. for Girls, Bethlehem, 1967. Mem. A.M.A., Phila. County Med. Soc., Phila. Psychiat. Soc., Am. Psychiat. Assn., Acad. Psychoanalysis, N.Y. Acad. Scis., Regional Council Child Psychiatry (com. mem.). Republican. Episcopalian. Club: Philadelphia Hemodialysis. Home: 1314 Prospect Hill Rd Villanova PA 19085 Office: 1301 Spencer St Philadelphia PA 19120

TSCHAPPAT, DONNA BELLE, coll. ofcl., pub. relations exec.; b. Chgo., Oct. 25, 1936; d. Robert William and Rena Louise (Morgan) Tschappat; A.A., William Woods Coll., 1956; B.S., U. Houston, 1958; postgrad. U. Colo., 1961. Tchr. Wheatridge High Sch., Jefferson County (Colo.) pub. schs., 1958-62; coordinator of field services William Woods Coll., Fulton, Mo., 1962-68, asst. dean of students, 1968-72, dir. pub. relations and alumnae affairs, 1972—. Instr. adult edn. program Denver pub. schs., summer, 1959. Mem. Fulton (Mo.) Plan Town Council and Housing Com., 1971-73; William Woods Coll. rep. for Callaway County United Fund Drive, 1972, publicity chmn., 1974. Recipient Order of the Green Owl award William Woods Coll. Alumnae Assn., 1969, Soc. Centennial Fellows medallion William Woods Coll., 1972. Mem. Callaway County League of Women Voters (dir. 1972-75), Am. Alumni Council, U. Houston Alumni Fedn., Fulton Area C. of C. (pres. 1975), Am. Assn. U. Women (pres. 1966-69, world problems area rep. 1969-70), William Woods Nat. Alumnae Assn. (dir. 1966—), Bd. Assos. Fulton Colls., Phi Kappa Phi, Phi Theta Kappa, Kappa Delta Pi. Mem. Christian Ch. Clubs: Callaway County Alumnae, Denver William Woods Coll. Alumnae (chmn. 1959-61). Address: William Woods College Fulton MO 65251

TSE, ROSE LOU (MRS. HAROLD FOO HENG), physician, educator; b. Shanghai, China, July 27, 1929; d. Chak Wann-Wei and Winnie Oi-Chun (Yung) Lou; B.S., St. John's U., China, 1948; M.A., Mt. Holyoke Coll., 1950; Ph.D., Yale, 1953; M.D. magna cum laude, Med. Coll. Pa., 1960; m. Harold Foo Heng Tse, June 16, 1953. Intern Phila. Gen. Hosp., 1960-61, resident 1961-64, sr. attending physician, 1970—, dir. sect. rheumatology, 1971—; practice medicine specializing in internal medicine, Phila., 1964—; cons. Med. Coll. Pa., Phila., 1960-63, clin. instr., 1964-68; asso. in medicine U. Pa., Phila., 1968-71, asst. prof. medicine, 1971—. Diplomate Am. Bd. Internal Medicine, Am. Bd. Rheumatology. Fellow A.C.P., Am. Inst. Chemists, Am. Coll. Angiology. Home: 130 E Levering Mill Rd Bala Cynwyd PA 19004 Office: 700 Civic Center Blvd Philadelphia PA 19104 also 206 Maloney Hosp U Pa 36th and Spruce Sts Philadelphia PA 19104

TSELOS, BEATRICE PALLISTER, psychologist; b. Bklyn., Oct. 20, 1910; d. Stanley Wilson and Elizabeth May (Jackson) Pallister; B.A., Adelphi Coll., 1932; M.A., Columbia, 1933, postgrad., 1933-35; postgrad. U. Minn.; m. Dimitri Theodore Tselos, June 11, 1935; children—George Dimitri, Susan Elizabeth. Psychologist, Brearley Sch., N.Y.C., 1948-49, Summit Sch., St. Paul, 1949-55; sch. psychologist Ind. Sch. Dist. 280, Richfield, Minn., 1957—, coordinator dept., 1969—. Bd. dirs. Internat. Inst. Minn., mem. travel com., 1972—, personnel com., 1971-74, edn. com., 1974—. Diplomate Am. Bd. Examiners Profl. Psychology. Mem. Am., Minn. psychol. assns., Assn. for Gifted, Minn. Sch. Psychologists Assn. (sec.-treas. 1962-63), Assn. Children with Learning Disabilities. Home: 1494 Branston St St Paul MN 55108 Office: Sheridan Sch 6400 Sheridan Av South Richfield MN 55423

TSUJIMURA, LILLIE YURIKO (MRS. RICHARD SHIGERU TSUJIMURA), hotel exec.; b. Honolulu, May 30, 1923; d. Unosuke and Yu (Ishikawa) Yamamoto; m. Richard Shigeru Tsujimura, Dec. 5, 1943; 1 son, Rickey Brian. Reservations mgr. Matson Navigation Co., 1951-53, Waikiki Biltmore Hotel, 1953-57; sales mgr. Island Holidays Resorts, 1957-67; adminstrv. asst. Ambassador Hotel, 1967-69; gen. mgr. Pagoda and Pacific Beach Hotel, Honolulu, 1970—. Dir. H.T. Enterprises; trustee Hawaiian Mfr. Center. Mem. mayor's commn. Status of Women, 1972—, Gov.'s Commn. on Manpower and Full Employment. Mem. Hawaiian Hotel Assn., Japanese C. of C., Travel Women Club. Democrat. Home: 760 Hao St Honolulu HI 96821 Office: Pacific Beach Hotel 2490 Kalakaua Av Honolulu HI 96815

TSUSAKI, EDNA KIKUE OGATA (MRS. JUN TSUSAKI), librarian; b. Honolulu, Hawaii, Dec. 7, 1931; d. Harold Tsuyoshi and Kimiye (Yamasaki) Ogata; B.A., U. Hawaii, 1953; M.S. in L.S., Syracuse U. 1955; m. Jun Tsusaki, June 6, 1954; children—Wayne Harold, Chris Alyn, Verne Jorge, Roseanne Midori. Reference librarian Chgo. Pub. Library, 1955-57; librarian Hawaii State Library System, Honolulu, 1958-69; head librarian Pearl City Regional Library, 1969—. Budget chmn. P.T.A., 1971-72; troop sec. Boy Scouts of Am., 1971-72; den mother Cub Scout, 1972-74. Bd. dirs. Pearl City Community Assn., 1971; bd. dirs. Momilani Community Assn., 1973, sec., 1974; chmn. Community Club Awards, 1971. Mem. Am., Hawaii library assns., Beta Phi Mu. Club: Pearl City Aquatics (treas. 1970-71). Home: 1916 Hoolehua St Pearl City HI 96782 Office: 1138 Waimano Home Rd Pearl City HI 96782

TUCHMAN, BARBARA WERTHEIM (MRS. LESTER R. TUCHMAN), writer; b. N.Y.C., Jan. 30, 1912; d. Maurice and Alma (Morgenthau) Wertheim; B.A., Radcliffe Coll., 1933; D.Litt. (hon.), Yale, Columbia, N.Y. U., Williams Coll., others; m. Lester R. Tuchman, June 18, 1940; children—Lucy, Jessica, Alma. Research asst. Inst. Pacific Relations, N.Y.C., 1934, Tokyo, 1935; editorial asst. The Nation, N.Y.C., 1936, Spain, 1937; staff writer The War in Spain, London, 1937-38; Am. corr. New Satesman and Nation, London, 1939; writer Far East news desk OWI, N.Y., 1944-45. Trustee Radcliffe Coll., 1960-72. Mem. Author's League (mem. council), Soc. Am. Historians (pres.), Am. Acad. Arts and Letters. Club: Cosmopolitan. Author: The Lost British Policy, 1938; Bible and Sword, 1956; The Zimmerman Telegram, 1958; The Guns of August, 1962 (Pulitzer prize 1963, Book-of-the-Month Club selection); The Proud Tower, 1966 (Book-of-the-Month Club selection); Stilwell and the American Experience in China 1911-45, 1971 (Book-of-the-Month Club selection) (Pulitzer prize 1972); Notes from China, 1972. Contbr. to numerous periodicals. Home: Cos Cob CT 06807 Office: care Russell & Volkening 551 Fifth Av New York City NY 10017

TUCHMAN, MICHELLE BECKER (MRS. MARC ELLIOT TUCHMAN), editor; b. Los Angeles, Nov. 21, 1950; d. Bernard I. and Frances (Rosenbaum) Becker; B.A., Cal. State U., Northridge, 1972; m. Marc Elliot Tuchman, Oct. 29, 1972. Writer, pub. relations asst. Office of Pub. Affairs, Cal. State U., Northridge, 1971-72; reporter Beverly Hills (Cal.) Ind., 1972; asst. society editor Thousand Oaks (Cal.) News Chronicle 1972—. Mem. Women in Communications, Sigma Delta Chi, Alpha Chi Omega. Home: 17830 Sherman Way Reseda CA 91335 Office: 2595 Thousand Oaks Blvd Thousand Oaks CA

TUCK, MIRIAM LYONS, educator; b. Bklyn.; d. William W. and Irene (Lyons) Tuck; R.N., Cumberland Hosp. Sch. Nursing, 1945; P.H.N., Cal., 1948; B.S., N.Y. U., 1954; M.A., Columbia, 1956, Ed.D., 1961 Pub. health nurse Bklyn. Vis. Nurse Assn., 1945-56, Dept. Pub. Health, San Francisco, 1946-52; tng. supr. A.R.C., San Francisco, 1947-52; indsl. nurse, partial mgmt. Feurer Emblem Works, Inc., Bronx, 1952-56; sch. nurse, instr. Great Neck (L.I.) Pub. Schs., 1956-62; instr. summer session Springfield (Mass.) Coll., 1961-62; asso. prof. health edn., chmn. undergrad. maj. div. U. Ore., Eugene; 1962-66, prof., 1966-70; asso. prof., coordinator health edn. Herbert H. Lehman Coll., City U. N.Y., Bronx, 1970-71; prof., coordinator health edn. Tex. Woman's U., Denton, 1971-72; prof., dir. health edn. Russell Sage Coll., Troy-Albany, N.Y., 1972—. Cons. Job Corps Centers, 1966—; mem. White House Conf. Health, 1965; cons. Pres.'s Com. on Health Edn., White House Conf. Nutrition and Health. Former bd. dirs. N.Y. Interagy. Council Smoking and Health, Lane County Mental Health Assn., Lane County Council on Alcoholism, Lane County Community Health Council; exec. bd. Ft. Worth Regional Council Alcoholism. Recipient citation for community service Gov. of N.Y. State. Fellow Am. Pub. Health Assn. (governing council, past chmn. sch. health (sect.), Royal Soc. Pub. Health, Soc. Pub. Health Educators, Am. Sch. Health Assn.; mem. A.A.H.P.E.R. (v.p.). Author: Consumer Health, 1972; co-author Health, 1969. Contbr. articles to profl. jours. Home: 129 2d St Troy NY 12180

TUCKER, BARBARA BEBE LOU MUEHLE (MRS. RICHARD WALTER TUCKER), civic worker, fashion cons.; b. Des Moines; d. Louis John and Harriett (Shilke) Muehle; student Drake U. Music Sch.; B.S., Ia. State U.; m. Richard Walter Tucker; 1 dau., Pamela Helen. Fashion writer W.T. Grant, N.Y.C., 1946-47, Kresge Newark, Newark, 1947-50, Best & Co., N.Y.C., 1950-51; millinery designer Chez Nous, Detroit, 1954-57; instr. fashion design Detroit Bd. Edn., 1960-63; fashion lectr. John Robert Powers Sch., Detroit, 1965-68; fashion coordinator Armo Co. of N.Y., 1968-72; v.p. Richard Tucker & Co., Detroit, 1969—. Mem. speakers bur. United Found., Detroit, 1967; mem. Met. Opera Com., Detroit, 1962—; v.p., workshop chmn. Am. Symphony Orch. League Women's Council, 1966-70, nat. pres., 1971-73; pres. Jr. Women's Assn. for Detroit Symphony, 1957. dirs. Womens Assn. Detroit Symphony Orch., 1960—, pres., 1963, bd. dirs. Orch., 1969—; bd. dirs. Womens Com. Tb and Health Soc., 1967—, Womens Com. for Project Hope, 1966—, Detroit Opera Theatre, 1962-64; mem. nat. women's bd. Northwood Inst., 1972—. Mem. Am., Mich. home econs. assns., Founders Soc. Detroit Inst. Arts, Fashion Group Detroit (sec. 1973—), Theatre Arts Detroit, Internat. Platform Assn., Alpha Gamma Delta. Home: 3335 Burning Bush Rd Birmingham MI 48010

TUCKER, BETTY JO MAYER (MRS. LAWRENCE W. TUCKER), ednl. adminstr.; b. Pueblo, Colo., Mar. 19, 1931; d. Rudolph and Josephine (Donahue) Mayer; A.A., Pueblo Jr. Coll., 1955; A.B. cum laude, Colo. Coll., 1958, M.A., 1963; Ed.D., U. No. Colo., 1972; m. Lawrence W. Tucker, Jan. 13, 1951; children—John Kelly, Susan Claire. Tchr., Pueblo Schs., 1955-62, jr. high sch. counselor, 1962-64; dean women So. Colo. State Coll., Pueblo, 1964-70, asst. dean student services, 1973-74, asso. prof. edn., 1974—, dir. Upward Bound Program, 1965-67, chmn. day nursery adv. bd., 1965-69. Staff dir. Help Anonymous, 1968—; dir. Nat. Tng. Program for Crisis Telephone Workers, 1971-72; cons. Virginia Neal Blue Resource Center for Colo. Women, 1972—. Mem. Pueblo City Council Adv. Com. on Human Relations, 1966-69; mem. Bd. Edn. of Pueblo Sch. Dist. 60, 1969-71. Bd. dirs. Spanish Peaks Mental Health Center, Pueblo, 1965-71, pres. bd. dirs., 1966-67; bd. dirs. Women's Information Service of Pueblo, 1973—; Colo. topic chmn. Woman Searching for Self, Am. Assn. U. Women, 1973-75. Mem. Am. Coll. Personnel Assn., Am. Personnel and Guidance Assn., N.E.A., Nat. Assn. Women Deans and Counsellors. Contbr. articles to profl. publs. Home: 70 Stanford St Pueblo CO 81005

TUCKER, BILLIE ANNE, lawyer; b. Anniston, Ala., Aug. 11, 1936; d. Lemuel Bill and Anne (Tatum) Crouch; B.S., U. Ala., 1956, J.D., 1959; m. Mose Allen Tucker, Mar. 7, 1959; children—Mose Allen, Joseph McNamee, Stanley Thornton, John Sterling. Admitted to Ala. bar, 1959; asso. firm William O. Walton, Jr., Lafayette, Ala., 1959-72. Vice chmn. Chambers County Republican Exec. Com., 1962—. Mem. Am., Chambers County, Ala. bar assns. Republican. Methodist. Home: Lafayette AL 36862 Office: 213 Av A SE Lafayette AL 36862

TUCKER, C(YNTHIA) DELORES (MRS. WILLIAM L. TUCKER), state ofcl.; b. Phila., Oct. 4, 1927; d. Whitfield and Captilda (Gardiner) Nottage; grad. Phila. Sch. for Girls, 1946; student Temple U., Pa. State U., U. Pa., N. Phila. Sch. Realty; m. William L. Tucker, July 21, 1951. Pres., C. DeLores Tucker Assos. pub. relations, Phila.; sec. Commonwealth Pa., Harrisburg, 1971—. Vice pres. Penn. N.A.A.C.P., 1967—; mem. Nat. Assn. Minority Consultants, Urban League, participant Martin L. King Selma-Montgomery March, 1965; del. White House Conf. on Civil Rights. Mem. arrangements com. Dem. Nat. Conv., 1972, exec. com. Dem. Nat. Com., 1972—; sec. Phila. Zoning Bd. Adjustment, 1968-70; vice chmn. Pa. Dem. State Com., 1970—, Women for Democratic Action. Bd. dirs. Phila. Tribune Charities, YWCA, Phila., Med. Coll. Phila., Urban Coalition, New Sch. Music, United Fund; mem. exec. bd. Equal Rights Council. Recipient Achievement award Nat. Assn. Real Estate Brokers, 1971, Community Service award Opportunities Industrialization Center, Emma V. Kelley Achievement award Nat. Elks, 1971, Phila. Tribune Charities Annual award, 1971, Service and Achievement award N.A.A.C.P., 1964; named one of 100 most influential blacks in Am. Ebony mag., 1973. Mem. Nat. Assn. Real Estate Brokers (bd. dirs., 1967—), Nat. Assn. Market Developers, Bus. and Profl. Women's Club. Author jour. The Suburban Noose. Home: 6700 Lincoln Dr Philadelphia PA 19119 Office: Office Bldg Harrisburg PA 17120

TUCKER, DAISY SNELLGROVE (MRS. WILLIAM C. TUCKER), librarian; b. Pinckard, Ala., Dec. 11, 1912; d. LaFayette and Jessie (Bryant) Snellgrove; grad. Columbus (Ga.) City Hosp. Sch. Nursing, 1934; student U. Ga., 1952-67; m. William Clifford Tucker, Jan. 12, 1935 (dec. Apr. 1961); children—William Clifford, Frances (Mrs. Eugene Dobson, Jr.). Librarian Ledger-Enquirer Newspapers, Columbus, Ga., 1952—; book review editor Columbus Enquirer, 1954—; head research dept. Ledger-Enquirer, 1952—. Mem. Gov.'s Adv. Com. Mental Instns., 1959-62; bd. dirs. Muscogee Mental Health Assn., 1957-64; bd. dirs. Ga. Assn. Mental Health, sec., 1962. Recipient Cup of Hope award Georgia Assn. Mental Health, 1958. Baptist. Club: Country (Columbus). Home: 1915 Wildwood Av Columbus GA 31906 Office: Ledger-Enquirer Newspapers Columbus GA 31902

TUCKER, DOROTHY LOUISE MCNEILL, educator; b. Racine, Wis., Sept. 1, 1923; d. Frank J. and Bess (Phillips) McNeill; B.S., U. Minn., 1945; M.S., Ill. State U., 1949; Ed.D., U. Cal. at Los Angeles, 1959; m. Elbridge Ashcraft Tucker, Nov. 26, 1958. Recreation dir. Study and Treatment Center for Emotionally Disturbed Children, Hennepin County, Minn., 1945-46; tchr. Racine pub. schs., 1946-48; instr. supervising tchr. Western Ill. U., Macomb, 1949-52, tchr. San Bernardino (Cal.) city schs., 1952-54; counselor, instr. psychology San Bernardino Valley Coll., 1955-57; coordinator secondary preparation program Cal. State Poly. U., Pomona, 1957-72, asso. prof. psychology, 1957-66, prof. psychology, 1966—, dir. Tchr. Preparation Center, 1972-73. Bd. dirs. East Hills Homeowners' Assn., Edgewood Family Counseling Agy. Mem. Am., Western, Cal. psychol. assns., Am. Assn. U. Profs. (chpt. sec.-treas. 1959-60, sec. 1964-66), Delta Kappa Gamma (sec. 1968-70), Pi Lambda Theta, Zeta Tau Alpha. Republican. Episcopalian. Club: South Hill Women's Golf (chmn.

1968-70). Home: 2915 Mesa Dr West Covina CA 91791 Office: Cal State Polytechnic U Pomona CA 91768

TUCKER, HELEN WELCH (MRS. WILLIAM T. BECKWITH), author; b. Raleigh, N.C., Nov. 1, 1926; d. William Blair and Helen Mae (Welch) Tucker; A.B., Wake Forest U., 1946; postgrad. Columbia, 1957-58; m. William T. Beckwith, Jan. 9, 1971. Reporter Burlington (N.C.) Times-News, 1946-47, Twin Falls (Ida.) Times-News, 1948-49, Boise (Ida.) Statesman, 1950-51; continuity writer Radio KDYL, Salt Lake City, 1952-53; continuity supr. Radio WPTF, Raleigh, N.C., 1953-55; reporter Raleigh (N.C.) Times, 1955-57; editorial asst. Columbia U. Press, N.Y.C., 1959-60; dir. publicity and publs. N.C. Museum Art, Raleigh, 1967-70. Recipient Distinguished Alumni award Wake Forest U., 1971. Mem. Authors Guild. Episcopalian. Author: The Sound of Summer Voices, 1969; The Guilt of August Fielding, 1971; No Need of Glory, 1972; The Virgin of Lontano, 1973. Contbr. short stories and articles to mags. Home: 2930 Hostetler St Raleigh NC 27609

TUCKER, JANICE CLARE, educator; b. Washington, Apr. 25, 1939; d. William Clarke and Helene Frances (Strobl) Tucker; B.S., Ohio State U., 1961, M.A., 1971. Tchr., Woodcrest Elementary Sch., Columbus, O., 1961-66; enrichment tchr. Siebert Elementary Sch., Columbus, 1966-67; speech tchr. Hastings Jr. High Sch., Upper Arlington, O., 1967—. Dir. children theatre Columbus Jewish Center, 1964-66. Named Outstanding Tchr. of Year, Hastings Jr. High Sch., 1971-72. Mem. N.E.A., Am. Theatre Assn., Speech Communication Assn., Ohio Theatre Alliance, Ohio, Upper Arlington edn. assns., Ohio State U. Alumni Assn. (life). Home: 1455-D W Lane Av Columbus OH 43221 Office: 1850 Hastings Lane Upper Arlington OH 43220

TUCKER, JULIA WARREN, motion picture script. supr.; b. Boston, Nov. 21, 1933; d. Richard and Shirley Warren (Keene) Tucker; B.A., Smith Coll., 1955. Free-lance motion picture script supr., 1961—; supr. film continuity For Love of Ivy, 1967, Goodbye, Columbus, 1968, Last Summer, 1968, Cotton Comes to Harlem, 1969, Diary of A Mad Housewife, 1970, Doc, 1970, Gordon's War, 1973, The Gambler, 1973, The Other Side of the Mountain, 1974, The Barony, 1974; others; co-producer, co-dir. film on Pomo Indian culture, 1973—. Mem. Internat. Alliance Theatrical and Stage Employees, Common Cause. Writer, dir., producer Cat, film for children (Bronze award Internat. Film and TV Festival of N.Y.), 1972. Home: 126 E 28th St New York City NY 10016 also 520 S Kelton Av Los Angeles CA 90024

TUCKER, MAE SUETTA, librarian; b. Mt. Holly, N.C., Oct. 5, 1922; d. Walter Lee and Mamie Lantz (Shuford) Tucker; B.S. in Edn., Appalachian State U., 1943; B.S. in L.S., U. N.C., 1945. Reference asst. Pub. Library Charlotte and Mecklenburg County, Charlotte, N.C., 1945-56, head Main Library Pub. Services, 1956-73, asst. dir., 1973—. Mem. Women's Democratic Club. Mem. A.L.A., N.C. (chmn. devel. com. 1971-73), Southeastern, Spl. library assns., Am. Assn. U. Women, Bus. and Profl. Women's Club, Women's Polit. Caucus, Beta Phi Mu. Methodist. Home: 108 W Catawba Av Mt Holly NC 28120 Office: 310 N Tryon St Charlotte NC 28202

TUCKER, MILDRED ALYENE, county ofcl.; b. Altus, Okla., Oct. 10, 1921; d. Jasper Milton and Edna Loraine (Taylor) Tucker; student Lippert's Bus. Coll., 1940, Wayland Bapt. Coll., 1958, 67. Sec., Green Machinery Co., Plainview, Tex., 1941; dep. county clk. Hale County Clk.'s Office, Plainview, 1942-52, county clk., Tex., 1952—. Pres., Las Camaradas, 1961-62, v.p., 1963-64, 67-68. Mem. Plainview Hist. Soc., Plainview Bus. and Profl. Women's Club (1st v.p. 1959; pres. 1960-61, 2d v.p. 1967-68), Tex. Fedn. Bus. and Profl. Women (state finance com. 1972-73). Democrat. Presbyn. (sec. Sunday sch. 1952-62). Home: 508 W 10th St Plainview TX 79072 Office: Box M Plainview TX 79072

TUCKER, PATRICIA, journalist, pub. relations counsel, lawyer; b. Red Lodge, Mont.; d. Royal Kenneth and Juliet (Luttrell) Tucker; student Tulane U., La. State U.; m. Nelson Jackson, Apr. 6, 1934 (dec.); 1 dau., Lael Hollister; m. 2d, Edward Stuart, Jr., July 16, 1958. Admitted to Tex. bar, 1940; Research Labs. 1940-41; researcher, reporter Time Mag., Fortune mag., 1941-44; mng. editor Science Illustrated, 1944-45; free-lance pub. relations counsel, journalist 1946—. dir., officer Dwight Corp., 1955-56, Eastern Forestry, Inc., 1956-60, Craftsmen of Chelsea Court, Inc., 1972—; information officer Central Fla. Regional Planning Council, 1965-68. Mem. Com. for Effective Use of Internat. Ct., 1961. Mem. Kappa Kappa Gamma. Democrat. Episcopalian. Clubs: Overseas Press. Home: 888 16th St NW Washington DC 20006 also 2917 Timberlake Dr Orlando FL 32806

TUDBURY, PATRICIA BREED, physician; b. Washington, Mar. 8, 1918; d. Warren Chamberlain and Ethel Putnam (Wheeler) Tudbury; A.B., Mills Coll., 1938; M.A., U. Cal. at Berkeley, 1941; M.D., Yale U. 1947. Intern, Hosp. for Women and Children, San Francisco, 1947-48, resident, 1948-49; practice medicine specializing in internal medicine, San Francisco, 1949-51, Visalia, Cal., 1951-55, Pomona, Cal., 1955—; clin. instr. medicine U. So. Cal. Med. Sch., 1958—; mem. staffs Pomona Valley Community Hosp., Casa Colina Hosp., Los Angeles, U. So. Cal. Med. Center. Bd. dirs. Mount San Antonio Council Camp Fire Girls, 1966-72; bd. dirs. Greater Pomona Valley YWCA, 1971—. Diplomate Am. Bd. Internal Medicine. Fellow A.C.P.; mem. A.M.A., Cal., Los Angeles County med. assns., Am. Assn. Internal Medicine, Los Angeles Soc. Internal Medicine, World Med. Assn., Am. Med. Women's Assn. (sec. 1971-72, councilor 1973—), Phi Beta Kappa, Bus. and Profl. Women's Club. Episcopalian (vestryman 1971-74). Clubs: Soroptimist (Pomona, Cal.); Sierra (Cal.). Home: 844 Highpoint Dr Claremont CA 91711 Office: 142 Nemaha St Pomona CA 91767

TUETING, PATRICIA ANN, research scientist; b. Blooming Prairie, Minn., Jan. 26, 1941; d. Thomas Christian and Lucille Evelyn (Basness) Peterson; B.A., St. Olaf Coll., 1963; M.A., Columbia, 1964, Ph.D., 1968; m. William F. Tueting, June 11, 1966; 1 son, Jonathan Lief. Postdoctoral fellow N.Y. State Psychiat. Inst., N.Y.C., 1968-69; asst. prof. Herbert H. Lehman Coll., Bronx, N.Y., 1969-71; asst. research scientist biometrics research N.Y. State Dept. Mental Hygiene, N.Y.C., 1971-72, asso. research scientist, 1973—. Lectr. psychiatry Columbia, 1971—. Mem. A.A.A.S., Soc. Neurosci., Soc. Psychophysiol. Research, Am. Psychol. Assn., N.Y. Acad. Sci., Phi Beta Kappa, Sigma Xi. Contbr. articles to profl. jours. Home: 730 W 183d St New York City NY 10033 Office: Biometrics Research 722 W 168th St New York City NY 10032

TUFELE, PAMELA HARRIET ADAM (MRS. SENI SU'ATELE TUFELE), lawyer; b. North Canaan, Conn., Apr. 11, 1938; d. Forbes Sampson and Eleanor Sedgwick (Tracy) Adam; B.A., Ohio Wesleyan U., 1960; LL.B., U. Conn., 1964; m. Seni Su'atele Tufele, Sept. 8, 1972. Admitted to Conn. bar, 1964, Mich. bar, 1968; practiced in Canaan, Conn., 1964-67, East Lansing, Mich., 1968-69; town atty., Town of Canaan, Conn., 1966-67; atty. Treas. office, State Mich., 1967-68; VISTA atty. Oklahomans for Indian Opportunity, Norman, 1970-71, Am. Samoa, 1972. Republican registrar voters, Canaan, Conn., 1964-67. Bd. dirs. Robert C. Geer Meml. Hosp., Canaan. Mem. Nat. Assn. Women Lawyers, Am., Mich., Conn., Minn., Lansing, Litchfield County, Am. Samoa bar assns., Canaan C. of C. (dir. 1964-67). Mem. Order Eastern Star. Home: 221 4th Av N Sauk Rapids MN 56379

TUFTS, EMILY, med. educator; b. Pinehurst, N.C., May 23, 1925; d. Albert Sise and Frances (Easton) Tufts; B.A., U. N.C., 1944; M.D., Temple U., 1950, M.S., 1954. Intern, Charlotte (N.C.) Meml. Hosp., 1950-51; resident pediatrics St. Christophers Hosp. for Children, Phila., 1951-54; practice medicine specializing in pediatrics, Moore County, N.C., 1954-64; fellow U. Ore. Med. Sch., 1964-65, asst. prof. medicine, 1966—; clin. faculty U. N.C., 1955-64. Dir. Ore. Poison Control Center. Active Tb Seal Sale, Moore County, 1955, A.R.C., Moore County, 1955-64. Diplomate Am. Bd. Pediatrics. Fellow Am. Acad. Pediatrics; mem. Ore., Portland pediatric socs., Sierra Club, Mazamas. Home: 3929 SW Mount Adams Dr Portland OR 97201 U Ore Med Sch Portland OR 97201

TUFTY, BARBARA JEAN TAEUSCH (MRS. HAROLD GUILFORD TUFTY), author; b. Iowa City, Ia., 1923; d. Carl Frederick and Mary (Hamen) Taeusch; student Vassar Coll., 1941-42, Cath. U., 1943-44; B.A., Duke, 1945; postgrad. New Sch. for Social Research, 1946; Sorbonne, 1948, U. Colo., 1948-50; m. Harold Guilford Tufty, Dec. 29, 1948; children—Christopher Guilford, Karen, Steven. Information writer U. Colo. Extension Center, Denver, 1948-50; free lance writer newspapers, tech. jours. from Europe, India, Africa, 1948-62; translator, writer various instns., including Mus. of Abidjon, Ivory Coast, Bombay (India) Natural History Soc., 1957-62; staff writer Sci. News of Sci. Service, part-time 1948-68; author books Dodd, Mead & Co., N.Y.C., 1966-69, Putnam Pubs., N.Y.C., 1973—; sci. writer Nat. Acad. Scis., 1970-72. Recipient Thomas Stokes hon. mention award, 1964, Catherine O'Brien hon. mention award, 1964. Mem. Nat. Assn. Sci. Writers, Authors Guild, Washington Press Club, A.A.A.S., (hon. life) Bombay Natural History Soc., Nat. Wildlife Fedn., Wilderness Soc., Smithsonian Assos. Author: 1001 Questions Answered About Natural Land Disasters, 1969; 1001 Questions Answered About Storms, 1970; Cells: Units of Life, 1973. Home: 3812 Livingston St NW Washington DC 20015 Office: Mosaic Mag Nat Science Found Washington DC 20550

TUFTY, MARY ELIZABETH WHITE (MRS. JAMES VANWAGONER TUFTY), advt. exec.; b. Hammond, Ind.; d. Cecil Valentine and Vesta Ivern (Bradley) White; B.S., So. Ill. U., 1957; m. James VanWagoner Tufty, June 3, 1967; children—James VanWagoner, Valentina Ivern. Sec., Library of Congress, Washington, 1957-58; FDA, Washington, 1958-59; social sec. U.S. Senate, Washington, 1959-69; sec.-treas. Ad. Agy., Inc., Washington, 1971—. Mem. Ind. Soc. Washington, Mich. Soc. Washington. Democrat. Club: Senate Staff. Home: 3209 Military Rd NW Washington DC 20015

TULIN, MARILYN BERNSOHN (MRS. STEPHEN WISE TULIN), psychotherapist; b. N.Y.C., Feb. 23, 1930; d. Irving and Gloria (Turner) Bernsohn; B.A., Washington Sq. Coll., N.Y.U., 1960; M.S.W., N.Y. Sch. Social Work Columbia, 1962; m. M. Harold Klingbeil, Feb. 14, 1948 (div. May 1952); 1 dau., Deborah (Mrs. Wayne Ralph Donnell); m. 2d, Stephen Wise Tulin, Jan. 31, 1959; children—Douglas Wise, Andrea Wise. Caseworker, Community Service Soc., N.Y.C., 1962-63; caseworker Jewish Child Care Assn., N.Y.C., 1964-67, psychotherapist Psychiat. Clinic, 1967-70. Dealer, collector early am. primitive furniture. Bd. dirs. Bloomingdale House of Music, N.Y.C. Mem. Nat. Assn. Social Workers, Pi Sigma Alpha. Home: 16 Walnut Av Larchmont NY 10538

TULLIS, DIANNE NELSON, painter; b. Tucson, Jan. 18, 1940; d. Dines and Anne Comfort (Chatillon) Nelson; student Sch. Simi, Florence, Italy, 1961; B.A., Briarcliff Coll., 1960; m. Edwin E. Tullis, Jr., Dec. 26, 1963 (div. Feb. 1974); children—Ivan, Luke. Exhibited one-woman shows at Benson Gallery, Bridgehampton, N.Y., 1970, Graham Gallery, N.Y.C., 1971, 72, 73; exhibited in group shows at Huntington (L.I.) Mus., 1972, Parish Art Mus., Southampton, N.Y., 1972, others. Recipient Purchase award Parish Art Mus., 1972. Address: 5 Sierra Vista Dr Tucson AZ 85716

TUNISON, ELIZABETH LAMB, educator; b. Belfast, Ireland, Jan. 7, 1922; d. Richard Ernest and Ruby (Hill) Lamb; came to U.S., 1923, naturalized, 1943; B.A., Wittier Coll., 1943, M.A., 1963; postgrad. U. So. Cal., 1961—; m. Ralph W. Tunison, Jan. 24, 1947; children—Eric, Christine (Mrs. Gregory Wait), Dana. Tchr. pub. schs., Compton and Los Angeles, Cal., 1943-45; exec. dir. Student YMCA, Pasadena, Cal., 1945-48; tchr. pub. schs., East Whittier, 1951-57, curriculum cons., 1957-61; TV tchr. Los Angeles County Sch., 1961—; dir. curriculum Bassett Unified Sch., La Puente, Cal., 1962-65; prin. Yorbita Sch., Rowland Heights, 1965-68; asso. prof. edn. Cal. Poly. State U., Pomona, 1968-71, Whittier (Cal.) Coll., 1971—. Cal. scholar, 1939; Helen Heffernan scholar, 1961. Mem. Nat. Assn. Elementary Sch. Adminstrs. (mem. resolutions com., 1972-73), Los Angeles County Sch. Adminstrs. Assn. (pres. 1969-70), Whittier Area Sch. Adminstrs. (sec., v.p. 1971-73, pres. 1973-75), P.E.O., Delta Kappa Gamma. Me. Christian Ch. Home: 5636 S Ben Alder St Whittier CA 90601

TUNSTALL, GEORGE LUCILLE HAWKINS, educator; b. Thurber, Tex., Jan. 17, 1922; d. Harry and Ruth (Martin) Hawkins; B.S., U. Colo., 1943; M.S., Wayne State U., 1959, Ph.D., 1963; m. William Neal Brown, Jan. 19, 1944 (div. Mar. 1946); m. 2d, Edward Haney Tunstall, June 19, 1947 (div. Apr. 1962); children—Ruth Neal, Leslie Diane. Med. tech. U. Colo. Med. Sch., Denver, 1943-45, Presbyn. Hosp. Colo., Denver, 1946-47, Evang. Deaconess Hosp., Detroit, 1950-52, Sinai Hosp. Detroit, 1952-55, Brent Gen. Hosp., Detroit, 1955-58; research teaching asst. biology dept. Wayne State U., 1958-62; asst. prof. Delta Coll., Univ. Center, Mich., 1963-65; asso. prof. Saginaw Valley Coll., Univ. Center, 1965-67; chmn. biology dept. Bishop Coll., Dallas, 1967-71; asso. dir. United Bd. for Coll. Devel., Atlanta, 1971-72; prof., dir. allied health programs Clark Coll., Atlanta, 1972—; adj. prof. biology dept. Atlanta U., 1972—. Ednl. cons. Saginaw (Mich.) C. of C., 1966-67, Nat., State, Regional confs., N.A.A.C.P., 1965-67. Active Girl Scouts Am., 1952-62; edn. chmn. Mich. Conf. N.A.A.C.P. brs., 1964-67, pres. Bay City br. 1965-67); exec. sec. Human Relations Commn. Bay City, 1965-67; trustee Mich. Tb. Respiratory Disease Assn., 1965-67; mem. personnel com. YWCA, 1966-67, mem. nominating com. exec. bd., 1967; exec. com. Bay City chpt. Ship Hope, 1966-67. NSF faculty research grants, summer 1969-71. Mem. Am. Soc. Cell Biology, Am. Assn. U. Women, Tex. Acad. Sci., Bay City Bus. Profl. Women's Club, Am. Soc. Microbiology, Am. Soc. Clin. Pathologists, Mich. Acad. Sci. Arts Letters, A.A.A.S., Am. Inst. Biol. Sci., Am. Assn. U. Profs., Am. Acad. Polit. Social Sci., N.Y. Acad. Scis., Am. Soc. Allied Health Professions, Sigma Xi, Alpha Kappa Alpha. Methodist. Contbr. articles profl. jours. Home: 2909 Campbellton Rd SW Atlanta GA 30311

TUNSTALL, VELMA BARRETT, poet; b. Vidette, Ark., Aug. 11, 1914; d. Sterling Isam and Cecil Anna (Jack) Barrett; student pub. schs.; m. Earl Archer Tunstall, Oct. 30, 1934; children—Patricia, Deanna. Author: Shadows on My Soul, 1970, also poetry appearing in anthologies, numerous mags. including El Viento, CQ, The Archer, Headlight, West Plains Daily Quill, also newspapers. Mem. Cal. State Poetry Soc., Cal. Fedn. Chaparral Poets, Internat. Platform Assn., Hall of Fame. Home: 928 3d Pl Upland CA 91786

TUPPER, ELEANOR (MRS. GEORGE O. BIERKOE), coll. pres.; b. Fitchburg, Mass.; d. Clarence E. and Ella G. (Webster) Tupper; student Bancroft Acad. Worcester, Mass., Wheaton Coll.; A.B. (E. Benjamin Andrews fellow), Brown U.; A.M. and Ph.D., Clark U.; advanced study New York U., Columbia; m. Rev. George O. Bierkoe, June 21, 1933; children—Priscilla Tupper (Mrs. Semans), Barbara Tupper. Prof., dept. head history and govt. 1929-30, head of history dept., Lindenwood Coll., St. Charles, Mo., 1933; coll. adminstr. Pine Manor Jr. Coll., and Dana Hall Schs., Wellesley, Mass.; academic dean Stoneleigh Coll., Rye, N.H.; academic head, Emma Willard Sch., Troy, N.Y.; adminstr. Lay Council, Teacher Coll., Columbia U.; dean, v.p. Endicott Jr. Coll., 1939-71, pres., 1971—. Lectr. current events, European travels. Mem. div. adminstrn. and communications N.E. Synod Luth. Ch. in Am. Trustee Upsala Coll. Mem. Am. Acad. Polit. and Social Scis., Am. Assn. U. Women, Am. Hist. Assn., Am. Geog. Assn., YWCA, Beverly C. of C., Internat. Platform Assn., Nat. Council Women U.S., N.E.A., Beverly Hist. Soc., Beverly Improvement Soc., Nat. Soc. D.A.R., Salem Hosp. Aid Assn., Sandwich Hist. Soc., Rotary Women, Phi Beta Kappa, Phi Beta Kappa Assos., Pi Gamma Mu, Phi Theta Kappa (dir. nat. bd.). Clubs: North Shore Wheaton (past pres.); Women's (N.Y., Mass.). Author: Syllabus on European History, 1931; Japan in American Public Opinion (with George E. McReynolds), 1937; Tupper Family Genealogy, 1972. Home: 375 Hale St Beverly MA 01915

TURANO, JEAN MARIE, banker; b. Trenton, N.J.; d. Martin A. and Jennie (Gantiosa) Turano; certificate Sch. Financial Pub. Relations, Northwestern U., 1955. Office mgr. Trenton (N.J.) Area chpt. A.R.C., 1945-52, chmn. pub. relations, 1955-66, sec., 1965—; community relations rep. Trenton Sav. Fund Soc., 1952-53, asst. to pres., 1953-66, v.p., 1966—, mem. bd. mgrs., 1965—. Sec. Dunn Scholarship Fund, 1952—, Delaware Valley (N.J.) United Fund, 1956, 57; mem. Social Service Council of Greater Trenton. Bd. dirs. Community Found. Trenton. Recipient Trenton Woman of Year award, 1958; award civic achievement and community service Unico Club of Trenton, 1958, award Trenton-Mercer County C. of C., 1971, Distinguished Citizenship award Sales and Marketing Execs. Central N.J., 1971, award Savs. Instns. Marketing Soc. Am., 1970. Mem. Heart of Trenton Businessmen's Assn. (dir., sec. 1962-67), Greater Trenton C. of C. (chmn. women's div. 1958, 59, chmn. task force on ambulance and emergency service 1971-72, mem. Trenton Mag. com. 1971—), Nat. Secs. Assn. (pres. Trenton chpt. 1951-53), Am. Bankers Assn. (mem. savs. adv. council 1965-69), Savs. Banks Assn. N.J. (mem. pub. relations and personnel coms. 1961—), Nat. Assn. Bank Women. Club: Soroptimist (pres. 1962-63) (Trenton). Contbr. articles to profl. jours. Home: 502 Columbus Av Trenton NJ 08629 Office: Trenton Savings Fund Soc 123-125 E State St Trenton NJ 08602

TURBOW, SANDRA RUTH, owner, mental health center, psychotherapist; b. Los Angeles, Oct. 28, 1938; d. Arthur O. and Eva C. (Flam) Turbow; B.S. in Occupational Therapy, U. So. Cal., 1960. Innovator, dir. dept. psychiatry adj. services Cedars of Lebanon Hosp., Los Angeles, 1960-65; spl. cons. phys. rehab. div. Einstein Hosp., Phila., also group psychotherapist Inst. Study Psychotherapy, Phila.; dir. Geriatric Day Care Center, Cedars-Sinai Med. Center, Los Angeles, 1966-69; owner, dir. Adult Day Treatment Center (formerly known as Geriatric Day Care Center), Beverly Hills, Cal., 1969—; individual practice psychotherapy, 1968—. Guest lectr. U. Cal., Los Angeles Extension, 1972; discussion leader Nat. Council on Aging Health Services Workshop, 1974; tchr. Beverly Hills City Dept. Recreation, 1975—. Mem. Gerontol. Soc. (speaker ann. meeting 1970, 72, 73), Am. Occupational Therapy Assn. Am., Beverly Hills C. of C. Club: Cameos (pres. 1958) (Beverly Hills). Office: 280 S Beverly Dr Beverly Hills CA 90212

TURCZYN, JANE ELLEN, orgn. exec.; b. LaSalle, Ill., July 27, 1950; d. Frank C. and Agnes A. (Spelich) Turczyn; B.S.J., Northwestern U., 1972. Editorial asst. Summy-Birchard Music Pub. Co., Evanston, Ill., 1970-71; teaching asst. in music Northwestern U., Evanston, 1970-71; asst. pub. information officer Ill. Arts Council, Chgo., 1971, dir. spl. projects, 1974-75; exec. dir. Young Friends of the Arts, Chgo., 1971-74. Freelance writer Chgo. Tribune, 1973-74. Nat. Endowment for Arts grantee, 1973-74. Mem. Women in Communications. Home: 59 E Cedar St #3A Chicago IL 60611 Office: 22 111 N Wabash Chicago IL 60602

TURETSKY, JUDITH, librarian; b. Bklyn., Jan. 19, 1944; d. Samuel and Ruth (Moskowitz) Turetsky; M.S., L.I. U., 1969; student U. Bridgeport, 1961-63; B.S., Boston U., 1965. Tchr. Bridgeport (Conn.) Bd. of Edn., 1966-67; librarian Darien (Conn.) Bd. of Edn., 1968-69; librarian Albert Einstein Coll. of Medicine, Bronx, N.Y., 1969—. Mem. N.Y. Regional Med. Library Assn., Med. Library Assn. Author: The History and Development of the D. Samuel Gottesman Library of the Albert Einstein College of Medicine, 1970. Home: 496 W McKinley Av Bridgeport CT 06604 Office: Albert Einstein College of Medicine Eastchester Rd and Pelham Pkwy Bronx NY 10461

TURK, MARY JANE, educator, lectr.; b. Corydon, Ind.; d. Jesse Thomas and Lovia (Denbo) Jones; ed. Ind. U., U. Chgo.; m. Donovan A. Turk (dec. Dec. 1959); 1 dau., Marjorie (Mrs. Carter W. Eltzroth). Mem. Marion County (Ind.) Bd. Tax Review, 1944-51; tchr. Indpls. Pub. Sch., 1960—, coordinator open classroom concept, individually guided edn.; lectr. Internat. Travel, 1965—. Mem. women's interests sect. Bur. Pub. Relations War Dept., 1943-45; founder Indpls. Hist. Council, 1945, pres., 1946-48. Mem. exec. bd. camp and hosp. com. Indpls. chpt. A.R.C. Recipient citation U.S. Treasury Dept. for patriotic work on behalf of War Finance Program, 1946. Mem. Internat. Platform Assn., Indpls. Council Women (past pres.), Nat. Soc. Arts and Letters (pres. Ind. chpt., 1953-55, nat. pres. 1958-60, life mem., nat. adv. bd. 1971—), N.E.A., Ind. Tchrs. Assn., Indpls. Edn. Assn., Narrators (life). Episcopalian. Club: Indianapolis Parliamentary Law (pres. 1965). Home: 5869 Guilford Av Indianapolis IN 46220

TURKEL, ANN RUTH (MRS. LEON LEFER), physician; b. N.Y.C., Nov. 28, 1928; d. Henry Lewis and Betty (Rosenweig) Turkel; A.B., Barnard Coll., 1947; M.D., Albany Med. Coll., 1952; certificate in psychoanalysis Wm. Alanson White Inst., 1964; m. Leon Lefer, July 4, 1954; 1 dau., Heidi Sara. Intern, Montefiore Hosp., Bronx, N.Y., 1952-53; resident Bronx VA Hosp., 1953-54, VA Research Hosp., Chgo., 1954-55; asst. psychiatrist Womens and Childrens Hosp., Chgo., 1955-56; sr. staff psychiatrist Manhattan VA Hosp., N.Y.C., 1956-62; practice medicine specializing in psychiatry, N.Y.C., 1956—; mem. attending staff St. Vincents, Bronx VA hosps.; cons. N.Y. State Div. Vocational Rehab., 1962—; faculty William Alanson White Inst., 1970—; adj. asst. prof. dentistry Coll. Physicians and Surgeons, Columbia, 1971-73, asso. in psychiatry, 1973—. Mem. exec. council Found. for Thanatology, 1969—. Diplomate Am. Bd. Psychiatry and Neurology. Mem. Am. Acad. Psychoanalysis (asso. editor Newsletter 1966-70, mem. com. psychoanalysis and women 1974—), Am. Psychiat. Assn. (asso. editor Bull. 1965—), N.Y. Soc. for Clin. Psychiatry, World Fedn. for Mental Health, White Psychoanalytic Soc. Co-editor: White Inst. Newsletter, 1963—.

Contbr. articles to profl. jours. Address: 350 Central Park W New York City NY 10025

TURKISH, FRANCES JOAN BILOFSKY (MRS. NORMAN A. TURKISH), financial cons.; b. Loch Arbor, N.J.; d. Maxwell M. and Betty (Keller) Bilofsky; B.A., Finch Coll., 1968; student N.Y. Inst. Finance, 1968-69; m. Norman A. Turkish, Aug. 13, 1966; children—Harry Wayne, Jenny Beth. Dir., comptroller Indsl. Electronics Corp., Newark, 1968—; asst. exec. v.p., dir. Magno-Tronic Corp., Newark, 1968—; sec.-treas. Gold Seal Radio Tube & Electronics Corp., Newark, 1969—; dir., financial cons. Magno-Tronic Corp., Secnarf Realty Co., Inc., Crown Starter Co., Inc. (all Newark). Vol. worker Finch Coll. Scholarship Fund, 1964-69. Mem. Monmouth Coll. Library Assn. Clubs: Finch (N.Y.C.); Allenhurst (N.J.) Beach. Home: 4 Spier Av Allenhurst NJ 07711 also 301 E 64th St New York City NY 10019 Office: 295 Halsey St Newark NJ 07102

TURLI, IRENE ANNA, newspaperwoman; b. Brockway, Mont., Sept. 9, 1926; d. Lars and Ingeborg (Hamre) Turli; B.A. in Journalism, U. Mont., 1949. Reporter Williston (N.D.) Daily Herald, 1949; former asst. to editor McClusky (N.D.) Gazette; former editor women's page Mandan Daily Pioneer; soc. editor Mitchell (S.D.) Daily Republic, 1968-72; editor The Gazette, 1974—; domestic agt. Kansas City Life Ins. Co., 1974—. Exhibited art works in shows at galleries, Minot, N.D., Williston, N.D., Fargo, N.D., Custer, S.D., others. Leader, Girl scouts, 1950-51. Named honorary mem. U.S.A.F., 1959; recipient award Lewis and Van Nuys, 1970. Mem. Press Assn. Club: Toastmistress. Author: Uncollected Poems, 1971; also numerous plays. Home: 512 S Sanborn Mitchell SD 57301

TURNER, ADELE TUPPER (MRS. ERWIN TURNER), educator; b. Brewster, Wash., Dec. 9, 1916; d. Emmett Oren and Lula Mae (LittleJohn) Tupper; B.A., Central Wash. Coll., 1952; M.A., U. Mo., 1954; Ed.D., U. No. Colo., 1960; m. Erwin Turner, Feb. 1, 1935; 1 son, Bruce Erwin. Prof. sociology Coll. of Ozarks, Clarksville, Ark., 1960-62; asso. prof. sociology So. State Coll., Magnolia, Ark., 1962-64; prof. sociology Northeastern State Coll., Tahlequah, Okla., 1964—. Fellow Am. Sociol. Assn.; mem. Southwestern Sociol. Assn., Midwest, So. sociol. socs., Nat. Council Family Relations, Am. Acad. Polit. and Social Scis., Pi Lambda Theta, Kappa Delta Pi. Home: 200 North St Tahlequah OK 74464

TURNER, ALBERTA TUCKER (MRS. WILLIAM ARTHUR TURNER), educator; b. N.Y.C., Oct. 22, 1919; d. Albert Chester and Marion Watson (Fellows) Tucker; B.A., Hunter Coll., 1940; M.A., Wellesley Coll., 1941; Ph.D., Ohio State U., 1946; m. William Arthur Turner, Apr. 9, 1943; children—Prudence Mab (Mrs. Sidney David Comings), Arthur Brenton. Lectr., Oberlin (O.) Coll., 1947-69; lectr. Cleve. State U., 1964-70, asst. prof., 1970-73, asso. prof. English, 1973—, dir. Poetry Center, 1964—. Oberlin Coll. grantee, 1968. Mem. Ohio Poets Assn., Milton Soc. Am., Midwest Modern Lang. Assn., Acad. Am. Poets. Author: North, 1970; Need, 1971; Learning to Count, 1974. Asso. editor periodical Field: Contemporary Poetry and Poetics, 1970—. Contbr. poems to various periodicals, articles to publs. Home: 482 Caskey Ct Oberlin OH 44074 Office: Cleve State U Euclid at 24th St Cleveland OH 44115

TURNER, ALICE WILLARD, educator; b. Norval, Ont., Can.; d. William David and Margaret (Scott) Turner; B.A., McGill U., 1927, M.A., 1928; Ph.D., U. Toronto (Ont.), 1932. Statistician, Wood, Gundy & Co., Toronto, 1937-60; asst. prof. math. York U., Toronto, 1960-64, asso. prof. math., 1964-70; prof. math. York U., 1970—. Dir. Toronto Mut. Life Ins. Co. Mem. adv. bd. Toronto YWCA, Girl Guides Can. Fellow Royal Statis. Soc.; mem. Am. Statis. Assn., Am. Math. Assn., Canadian Math. Congress. Club: University Women's. Author: We all Own Canada, 1944; Canadian Investors Handbook, 1948. Contbr. articles to profl. jours. Home: Apt 607 77 St Clair Av E Toronto M4T 1M5 ON Canada

TURNER, BARBARA PRESS (MRS. WILLIAM STEPHEN TURNER), ednl. equipment export co. exec.; b. Chgo., Mar. 24, 1943; d. John Elmer and Betty Schroeder (Grace) Press; B.S., Cornell U., 1965; A.M. (Nat. Def. Edn. Act grantee), U. Chgo., 1966; m. William Stephen Turner, June 26, 1965; children—Lisa Anne, Christopher Ian. Research asst. Nat. Bur. for Cooperation in Child Care, London, Eng., 1966-70; tech. adviser Ministry Edn., Santiago, Chile, 1967-70; asst. to dean U. Chgo. Dept. and Grad. Sch. Edn., 1970-73; corporate sec. Ednl. Innovations Systems, Inc., Chgo., 1969—, Ednl. Innovation Systems Internat., Inc., Chgo., 1972—. Mem. Chgo. Soc. Fund Raising Execs., Pi Lambda Theta, Kappa Kappa Gamma. Editor: Education at Chicago, 1971-73. Address: 4858 S Greenwood Chicago IL 60615

TURNER, BESSYE LEE TOBIAS, educator; b. Liberty, Miss.; d. Aaron and Bessie (Smith) Tobias; A.B., Rust Coll., 1939; M.A. in English, Columbia, 1954, M.A. in Speech, 1964, postgrad., 1968. Tchr. English, Burgland High Sch., 1939-44; clk. Internal Revenue, 1945-48; tchr. English, drama coach Alexander High Sch., 1950-55; asst. prof. English, dir. dramatics Alcorn A. and M. Coll., 1955-62; asst. prof. English, So. U., Baton Rouge, 1962-63; asst. prof. English and speech Tex. So. U., Houston, 1963-68, Miss. Valley State Coll., 1968—. Cons., Phelph Stokes Project, Natchez, Miss., 1955-58; coordinator Communication Workshop, Natchez City Sch. System, 1961-62; cons. English and lit. Miss. Tchrs. Assn.; drama judge, cons. Big Eight Dramatic Tournament, 1958-62. Speaker numerous schs., also orgns. Recipient Speech award R.C. Speech Club, Holly Springs, Miss., 1938, numerous awards of merit. Fellow Internat. Poetry Soc. (founder); mem. N.E.A., Am. Assn. U. Profs., Speech Assn., Nat. Council Tchrs. of English, Conf. Coll. Composition and Communication, Centro Studie Scambi Internazionale, Smithsonian Instn., Internat. Platform Assn., Dir. Am. Scholars English-Speech Internat. Reading Assn., Am. Civil Liberties Union, Intercontinental Biog. Assn., N.Y. Poetry Forum, M.B.L.S. (adv. mem.), Alpha Kappa Alpha, Kappa Delta Pi. Mem. Order Eastern Star. Methodist. Author: LaLibrae (poetry), 1969; Peace and Love, 1972; songwriter, also contbr. to poetry mags. Home: 829 Wall St McComb MS 39648

TURNER, CLARICE PATRICIA (MRS. CHARLES HYGHE DEBNAM), physician; b. Wilmington, Del.; d. Patrick William and Helen (Henderson) Turner; B.S., Temple U., 1944; M.D., Meharry Med. Coll., 1949; m. Charles Hyghe Debnam, Oct. 15, 1950; children—Charlene Patricia, Christopher Charles Patrick. Intern, Hubbard Hosp., Nashville, 1949-50, resident St. Agnes Hosp., 1950-51; psychiat. resident Del. State Hosp., New Castle, 1952-55; psychiat. cons. Dept. Research, New Castle, Del., 1955-57, Del. Dept. Mental Health, Wilmington, 1960-61; cons. Del. League for Planned Parenthood, 1965—. Bd. dirs. Childrens Bur. Del., 1965-66. Mem. New Castle County Med. Soc., Am. Acad. Family Physicians, Del. Acad. Gen. Practice, A.M.A. Episcopalian. Home: 1809 Newport Rd Wilmington DE 19808 Office: 1214 French St Wilmington DE 19801 also 825 Washington St Wilmington DE 19801

TURNER, CORNELIA MCDUFFIE, newspaperwoman; b. Mobile, Ala., Nov. 17, 1916; d. John and Cornelia Annette (Hixon) McDuffie; student Sweet Briar Coll., 1934-36; m. Richard Felder Turner, Mar. 27, 1937 (div. June 1946); children—John McDuffie, Richard Felder, Cornelia Annette (Mrs. John Caldwell Gaillard). Staff Mobile (Ala.) Press-Register, 1947—, women's editor, 1952—. Pres. Mobile County Assn. for Mental Health, 1970-71, So. Ala. Arthritis Found., 1970-72. Bd. dirs. Mobile chpt. A.R.C., 1962-66, Vis. Nurses Assn., 1962-64, Mobile Gen. Hosp., 1966-69, Nat. Arthritis Found., 1972—; mem. adv. bd. Mastin Sch. Nursing, 1969—. Mem. Ala. Women's Press Assn. (1st v.p. 1970-72, pres. 1973—), Jr. League, Sigma Delta Chi (pres. Mobile chpt. 1974—). Home: 2016 A North Portier Ct Mobile AL 36607 Office: PO Box 2488 Mobile AL 36630

TURNER, DIANE, journalist, educator; b. Ft. Worth, Jan. 7, 1943; d. Samuel Donel and June Inez (Jackson) Turner; B.A. in Journalism, Tex. Christian U., 1965; M.A. in Journalism, East Tex. State U., 1970. Reporter, photographer Ft. Worth Press, 1966-68; instr. journalism Tarrant County Jr. Coll. South, Ft. Worth, 1968—; cons. journalism, 1971—. Mem. Lena Pope Aux., 1970—; active summer program for Blind Children, Civic Arts Com., 1968—. Mem. Women In Communications, Nat. Council Coll. Publs. Advisers, Asso. Collegiate Press, Tex. Jr. Coll. Tchrs. Assn. (sect. sec. 1973—), Tex. Jr. Coll. Journalism Tchrs. (sec.), Delta Gamma (named Outstanding Alumnae 1968; v.p. 1968-70, Rush cons. 1970—, chmn. adv. bd. 1973—; writer songs for nat. conv. 1972, also chpt. songs). Mem. Jr. Woman's Club (annual show writer 1972—, show co-ordinator 1973, jour. reporter 1971). Home: 809 Griggs Fort Worth TX 76103 Office: 5301 Campus Drive Fort Worth TX 76119

TURNER, ELMA JUANITA (MRS. FRED F. TURNER), polit. party ofcl.; b. Milton, Ore., Oct. 13, 1919; d. Elmer and Millie Sabrina (Modrell) Shipp; student U. Nev. Extension; m. Fred F. Turner, June 21, 1938; children—Patricia (Mrs. George Wallace Farren), Fred. Cons. to motel mgmt. and gen. bldg. firm. Sect. head Republican presdl. campaign for Goldwater, 1964; vice chmn., mem. exec. bd. Rep. County Central Com., 1966-70; vice chmn., mem. exec. bd. Rep. State Central Com., 1970-72; del. to county, state Rep. convs., 1966, 68, 70, 72; del. to Nat. Rep. Conv., 1968; Washoe County Rep. campaign coordinator for gov., 1970; co-chmn. No. Nev. campaign for re-election Pres., 1972; No. dir., mem. exec. bd. Nev. Fedn. Rep. Women; mem. bd. Reno Rep. Women's Club, 1973-74. Clubs: Toastmistress, Craft. Home: 515 Stearns Circle Reno NV 89502

TURNER, FRANCES BERNADETTE, clergyman, lectr., author; b. Superior, Wis., June 28, 1903; d. Fyler Bedell and Eleanor Dolores (Donaly) Rainsford; B.S. in Edn., U. Minn., 1926; M.A. in Sociology, Northwestern U., 1938; postgrad. social service adminstrn. U. Chgo., 1941-44; Ph.D. in Sociology and Social Work, Washington U., St. Louis, 1948; m. Delos Ashley Turner, Dec. 8, 1936. Tchr. high sch., Bessemer, Mich., 1924-28; field rep. nat. staff A.R.C., chpt. exec. sec. Kan., Wash., Nev., 1929-36; psychiat. social worker Chgo. State Hosp., Inst. Ill. Research, Chgo., 1938-41; chief social service Dixon (Ill.) State Hosp., 1945; asso. prof. sociology and social work Ariz. State Coll., Tempe, 1946-56, also student counselor nursing schs. Good Samaritan, Meml. hosps., Phoenix, 1946-56; individual practice marriage and family counseling, Phoenix, 1950-62; programmer radio programs radio stas. KTAR, Phoenix, KYND, Tempe, WEAW, WRSV, Chgo., WFIR, Roanoke, Va., 1953-68, KICT, Wichita, Kan., 1974—; ordained to ministry Divine Sci. Ch., 1965; founder Divine Sci. Center, Evanston, Ill., 1965; pastor Divine Sci. Ch., Roanoke, 1971-72, Evanston, 1971-72; resident counselor Retirement Home, Wichita, Kan., 1974—. Lectr. in field. Bd. dirs. Maricopa Council Campfire Girls, Phoenix, 1955-61. Fellow Am. Sociol. Assn.; mem. Nat. Assn. Social Workers (charter), Internat. Assn. Women Ministers, Am. Assn. Pastoral Counselors, Nat. League Am. Pen Women, Am. Poetry League, Kan. Authors Club, Divine Sci. Internat. Fedn., Internat. New Thought Alliance. Mem. Daus. of Nile. Author: Happy is the Man, 1965; God-centered Therapy, 1968; Faith of Little Creatures, 1972, also poetry. Contbr. articles, poetry to newspapers, mags. Address: 155 N Market St Defenders Townhouse Wichita KS 67202

TURNER, JANICE CATHERINE TROTTER (MRS. JOHN TURNER), ednl. adminstr.; b. Paoli, Ind., Sept. 7, 1923; d. Bert Ermin and Helen Pauline (Heard) Trotter; B.A. cum laude, Ind. U., 1945, M.S., 1963; m. John Turner, Feb. 27, 1949; 1 dau., Joana (Mrs. Larry Jones). Editor mag. sect. Lafayette (Ind.) Jour. & Courier, 1945-49; free-lance writer for mags., 1949-53; news editor Mitchell (Ind.) Tribune, 1954-59; tchr. English, Paoli (Ind.) High Sch., 1959-67; dir. pub. relations, mem. dept. English, Northwood Inst., West Baden, Ind., 1967—, asso. prof. English, 1972—. Nat. Council Tchrs. English fellow, 1961. Mem. Nat. Fedn. Press Women, Women's Press Club Ind., Theta Sigma Phi. Kappa Kappa Kappa, Alpha Omicron Pi. Mem. Christian Ch. Contbr. articles to various mags. Home: Route 2 Orleans IN 47452 Office: Northwood Inst West Baden IN 47469

TURNER, JEANNETTE WINIFRED BAUMERT (MRS. JOHN HAROLD TURNER), opera exec.; b. McAlester, Okla., Feb. 5, 1913; d. Charles Carter and Maud Mae (Evans) Baumert; grad. Christian Coll. for Women, 1932; B.A., U. Okla., 1934; postgrad. U. Okla., 1934-36. Tulsa U., 1957-58; m. John Harold Turner, Aug. 25, 1933 (dec. Dec. 1960); children—John Baumert, Sharron Charlene. Pub. relationist Kerr's, Oklahoma City, 1936-68; pub. relationist, bridal cons. Levy Bros., Houston, 1938-40; mgr. Tulsa Opera, Inc., 1958—; dir., 1951-58. Extensive European travel. Mem. P.E.O., Theta Sigma Phi. Methodist. Home: 1207 S Urbana St Tulsa OK 74112 Office: 1610 S Boulder St Tulsa OK 74119

TURNER, KATHERINE JEANETTE DUPREE (MRS. JOHN W. TURNER), club woman; b. Hawkinsville, Ga., July 3, 1901; d. John Daniel and Martha Ann (Turner) Dupree; student Agnes Scott Coll., 1918-19; m. John W. Turner, Dec. 29, 1920. Organizing pres. DuPree Dist. Home Demonstration Club, 1945, pres. Pulaski council, 1947-48; historian Am. Legion Aux., Hawkinsville, 1934-39, pres., 1939, 43, 45, 56-57, 61, 63—, Americanism chmn. dept. Ga., 1939-40, 3d dist. Ga., 1962-63. Named Woman of Year, Am. Legion Aux., 1966. Mem. D.A.R. (sec. Hawkinsville chpt. 1962—), U.D.C. (pres. Hawkinsville 9 years). Baptist (pres. Women's Missionary Union 1942-44, circle chmn. 1931, 33). Columnist DuPree News, Hawkinsville Dispatch and News, 1943-55. Address: RFD 3 Hawkinsville GA 31036

TURNER, LELIA AIKEN FRIEND (MRS. CHARLES G. TURNER), civic leader; b. Richmond, Va., May 12, 1900; d. William Waverley and Susan (Holland) Friend; student pvt. schs.; m. Charles Green Turner, June 22, 1922; children—Charles Green, Lelia (Mrs. Robert de Treville Lawrence). Sec., Community League, The Plains, Va., 1960—; pres. Antiquarian Soc., Warrenton, Va., 1963-65; v.p., 1965—; mem. bd. advisers Facquier Hist. Found., Warrenton, 1965—; sec., mem. bd. dirs. Am. Cancer Soc., Warrenton, 1965—; grey lady Facquier Hosp., A.R.C., 1966—; co-chmn. Fauquier County Am. Revolution Bicentennial Commn., 1970—. Mem. Preservation Soc. Charleston (S.C.) Episcopalian (mem. teaching staff, 1966—; pres. Women). Clubs: Charleston Garden, Facquier. Home: The Plains VA 22171 also 47 Tradd St Charleston SC 29401

TURNER, LOUISE BONDS, realtor; b. Pasadena, Cal., Apr. 6, 1915; d. John Pruit and Dorothy Louise (Hasty) Bonds; student Mills Coll., 1933-34, U. So. Cal., 1934-36; m. Robert Lewis Turner, June 15, 1935 (div. 1973); children—Nancy (Mrs. Gary Wynn), Susan (Mrs. Richard Cortese). Engaged in real estate bus., 1957—; propr. Turner Assos. Realtors, Laguna Beach, Cal., 1964—; mem. adv. com. Westlands Bank, Santa Ana, Cal., 1974—. Mem. Am. Field Service Com., 1958-70, Laguna Beach Beautification Com., 1965—; adv. com. Laguna Beach Sch. Art and Design, 1974—. Named Realtor of Year, Laguna Beach Bd. Realtors, 1969, Top Salesman, 1967, 71. Mem. Cal. Real Estate Assn., Laguna Beach Bd. Realtors, Internat. Real Estate Fedn., C. of C. (pres. women'd div. 1966-68), Nat. Assn. Realtors. Clubs: Big Canyon Country (Newport Beach, Cal.); El Niguel Country (S. Laguna). Home: 178 Emerald Bay Laguna Beach CA 92651 Office: 1105 N Coast Hwy Laguna Beach CA 92651

TURNER, LYNNE ALISON (MRS. PAUL H. SINGER), harpist; b. St. Louis, July 31, 1941; d. Sol and Evelyn (Klein) Turner; student Paris Conservatory, 1959-60;; m. Paul H. Singer, June 2, 1963; children—Bennett Lloyd, Rachel Elise. Harpist, Chgo. Symphony Orch., 1962—. Recipient first prize Second Internat. Harp Contest, Jerusalem, Israel, 1962. Home: 1993 Westgate Terrace Highland Park IL 60035 Office: 220 S Michigan Av Chicago IL 60604

TURNER, MARTHA ANNE BONNER, author, professor; b. Warren, Tex., Jan. 31, 1904; d. Archibald King and Cora Louella (Ketchum) Bonner; B.A., Stephen F. Austin U., 1930; M.A. (Grad. fellow), U. Tex., 1945; postgrad. U. So. Cal., summer 1943, U. Tex., 1951-52. Head English dept. Dayton (Tex.) High Sch., 1930-37; dir. English program David Crockett Sr. High Sch., Conroe, Tex., 1940-46; prof. English Sam Houston State U., Huntsville, Tex., 1946—, univ. publicist, 1946-64. Gen. chmn. Tex. Joint English Com. for Schs. and Colls., 1966. Recipient research grants Sam Houston U., 1967-69; Plaque for 25 years outstanding service to Sam Houston State U.; named Outstanding Woman Huntsville chpt. Am. Assn. U. Women, 1971. Author: White Dawn, 1943; The City and Other Poems, 1946; Tools of the Earthmover, 1951; Sam Houston and His Twelve Women, 1966; The Life and Times of Jane Long, 1969; William Barret Travis: His Sword And His Pen, 1972; The Yellow Rose of Texas: The Story of A Song, 1971; Women in Texas, 1972; Texas Epic: An American Story, 1974; Mark Twain's 1601, 1974; Old Nacogdoches of the Jazz Age, 1975. Contbr. articles to profl. jours. Home: 2114 Av S Huntsville TX 77340

TURNER, MARY LOUISE, librarian; b. Quincy, Ill., Oct. 13, 1925; d. Thelbert Russel and Ellen Evelyn (Tucker) Turner; A.B., U. Mo., 1967, M.A. (Mo. State Library scholar 1967), 1968; postgrad. St. Louis Sch. Pharmacy, 1971. Library asst. U. Mo., Columbia, 1962-68; cons. for instl. library services Mo. State Library, Jefferson City, 1968-69; librarian Mo. State Tng. Sch. for Boys, Boonville, 1969-71; learning resource librarian Parkway North Sr. High Sch., Creve Coeur Mo., 1971-73; head librarian El Paso Community Coll., 1973—. Vol. Mid-Mo. Mental Health Center, 1967-68; cons. library services Am. Correctional Assn., 1970—. U.Wis. at Madison grantee, 1968, 71, 72; U.Ky., Lexington, grantee, 1970. Mem. A.L.A., Border Regional, Tex., Mo. library assns., Mo. State Tchrs. Assn., Mo. Assn. Sch. Librarians (publicity chmn. 1970-71), Assn. Hosp. and Instl. Libraries (chmn. Bibliotherapy com. 1970-71), Am. Assn. Sch. Librarys, N.E.A., Kan. U.-Instructional Materials Center, Am. Correctional Assn., Am. Assn. U. Women, Bus. and Profl. Women, Beta Phi Mu. Home: 299 Kings Point Dr Apt 103 El Paso TX 79912 Office: El Paso Community Coll Learning Resource Center 6601 Dyer St El Paso TX 79904

TURNER, MARY PAULINE CURTIS (MRS. JAMES CASTLE TURNER), artist, educator; b. Lincoln, Neb., Feb. 14, 1916; d. William Clapp and Nellie (Lee) Curtis; student Wilson Tchrs. Coll., 1940, Corcoran Sch. Art, 1950-54, Am. U., 1955; m. James Castle Turner, Apr. 14, 1934; children—Vivian Lee (Mrs. Gershom Kekst), Daniel Castle, Brian, Lisa, Lauran. Exhibited at Corcoran Gallery, 1951, Rockville Art Center, 1968, bronze sculpture of Esther Peterson, asst. sec. labor under Kennedy and Johnson at Rehoboth Beach Art League, 1968; art tchr. for ret. persons Sargent House Project, 1965-69. Mem. budget com. D.C. Schs., 1969; mem. D.C. Council Arts and Humanities, 1974. Housing chmn. League Women Voters, 1950. Recipient Ronshein award, 1951, prizes Corcoran Sch., 1951, Area award, 1952. Episcopalian (vestry 1969-71, pres. all women's activities 1969, mem. ch. centennial com.). Home: 6961 32d St NW Washington DC 20015

TURNER, MILDRED COZZENS (MRS. HUNTINGTON M. TURNER), composer; b. Pueblo, Colo., Feb. 23, 1897; d. Harmon and Johanna Augusta (Wehrhane) Cozzens; student Gulliford Acad., 1912, U. Wis. Sch. Music, 1916, U. Louisville, 1917; m. Huntington M. Turner, Jan. 31, 1934; 1 son by previous marriage, L. Philip Ewald. Supr. music pub. schs., Mineral Point, Wis., 1916. Vol. worker A.R.C., 1940-60. Recipient numerous commendations from various agys. and orgns. Mem. A.S.C.A.P., Famous Song Writers, Nat. Inst. Social Scis., English Speaking Union; Alliance Francaise, Pi Beta Phi. Composer: Wish They Didn't Mean Goodbye, 1960 (performed at Carnegie Hall, N.Y.C., also recorded), Dalmation Lullaby, Geisha. Home: 45 East End Av New York City NY 10028

TURNER, MYRA BROOKS (MRS. RONALD JOSEPH TURNER), composer; b. Knoxville, Tenn., Jan. 13, 1936; d. Paul David and Lillie Mary (Ray) Brooks; student Juilliard Sch. of Mus., 1947-51; Mus. B., So. Meth. U., 1955, Mus. M., 1956; m. Ronald Joseph Turner, June 11, 1960; children—Stacy Lynn, Cheryl Leigh, Teresa Jeanne. Mus. specialist Dallas schs., 1956-60; mus. dir. choral music, Knoxville, 1960-64; composer-in residence Birmingham (Ala.) Children's Theatre, 1967-69; composer, lectr., performing artist, Atlanta, 1969—. Choral dir. St. Cecilia Choir, St. Martin-in-the Fields Ch., Atlanta, 1973—. Recipient award Seattle Nat. Playwriting Contest, 1968. Mem. Nat., Ga. (dist. festival chmn. 1970—; state festival chmn. 1972) federated mus. clubs, Nat., Ga., Atlanta (v.p. 1972) music tchrs. assns., Mu Phi Epsilon (pres. Atlanta alumnae 1972-74), Pi Kappa Lambda, Alpha Delta Pi. Composer: (three act plays) Cinderella, 1966, Pinocchio, 1965, The Green Dragon, 1965, Mid-Summer Nights Dream, 1965, Flibbertygibbet, 1972, Javoho Junction, 1959; (piano solos) Praise The Lord, Christ Jesus, 1966, Man Speaks Through Music, 1965, The Jazz Man Suite, 1968, Fantasy in A Minor, 1968. Club: Atlanta Woman's. Address: 2433 MacLaren Circle Atlanta GA 30340

TURNER, ROSALIE LAURIE (MRS. EDWARD TURNER, JR.), physician; b. Havre de Grace, Md., Dec. 3, 1941; d. John Benjamin and Nina Rosina (Freeman) Laurie; B.S., Morgan State Coll., 1963; M.D., Meharry Med. Coll., 1967; m. Edward Turner, Jr., Dec. 5, 1970; 1 dau., Nicole Ray. Externship pub. health U. Ky. Med. Sch., Lexington, 1965, externship medicine Hubbard Hosp., Nashville, 1966, intern, medicine, 1967-68; resident, resident fellow dermatology Freedmen's Hosp., Washington, 1968-71, now chief dermatology med. officer Community Health Center South, D.C. Gen. Hosp., Washington. Recipient Dermatology Resident of Yr. award Dome Pharm. Co., 1970. NIH fellow in dermatology, 1968-70. Mem. Soc. Investigative Dermatology, Assn. Former Interns and Residents Freedmen's Hosp., D.C. Med. Soc. Baptist. Home: 5710 Eastern Av NE Washington DC 20011

TURNER, SUSAN JANE, educator; b. Kansas City, Mo., Sept 7, 1913; A.B., U. Ky., 1934, M.A., 1936; Ph.D., Columbia, 1956. Tchr. English, Margaret Hall Sch. for Girls, Versailles, Ky., 1936-41; instr. U. Tenn., 1942-44; instr. English, Vassar Coll., Poughkeepsie, N.Y., 1944-49, 51-55, asst. prof., 1955-57, asso. prof., 1957-63, prof., 1963-73, emeritus, 1973—. Mem. Am. Studies Assn., Modern Lang. Assn. Author: A. History of The Freeman: Literary Landmark of the Early Twenties, 1963. Research on Am. lit. after 1870, lit. and literary criticism. Address: 124 Elm St Versailles KY 40383

TURNER, SUZANNE PAULINE WILBERT (MRS. BERT S. TURNER), civic worker; b. Plaquemine, La., Jan. 16, 1927; d. Louis Joseph and Gertrude Louise (Pope) W.; student Our Lady of the Lake Coll., 1943-46; B.A., La. State U., 1947; diploma Woodlawn Preservation Seminar, 1973; m. Bert S. Turner, Sept. 21, 1947; children—Suzanne Louise, Robert Louis, Mary Margaret, Thomas Holmes, John Grover. Asst. children's room Boston Pub. Library, 1947-49; with La. State Dept. Edn., 1949. Mem. East Baton Rouge Parish Curriculum Study Com., 1969—; chmn. East Baton Rouge City Parish Beautification Commn., 1970-71; sec.-treas. La. State Arts and Sci. Commn., 1963—; mem. La. Bi-Centennial Commn., 1971-72; regional adviser Nat. Archives, 1971—; coordinator La. Regional Preservation Conf., 1971; mem. Found. for Hist. La., 1961—. Chmn. bd. dirs. Catholic Social Services, 1972-73; bd. dirs. Family Counseling; trustee La. Arts and Sci. Center, Friends of Cabildo, Magnolia Mound, St. Joseph's Acad., Jr. League Baton Rouge (pres. 1965-66). Mem. Kappa Kappa Gamma, La. Landmarks Soc., Nat. Trust for Hist. Preservation, Baton Rouge Assembly. Democrat. Roman Catholic. (mem. diocesan liturgical commn. 1969-70). Club: Baton Rouge Country. Contbr. articles on preservation and beautification to local publs. Home: 741 Delgado Dr Baton Rouge LA 70808

TURNER, VIRGINIA KELLEY (MRS. RICHARD TURNER), media specialist; b. Riverside, Cal., Apr. 22, 1919; d. William Eugene and Myrtle Edith (Johnson) Kelley; A.A., Riverside Jr. Coll., 1938; student U. Cal. at Santa Barbara, 1938-40; B.A., Lake Forest Coll., 1954; postgrad. Oriel Coll., Oxford (Eng.) U., summer, 1965; M.A., No. Ill. U., 1967; m. Richard Turner, Feb. 2, 1939; children—Lawrence Kelley, Renee Dorothy (Mrs. Thomas Becker). Tchr. Mundelein (Ill.) Dist. 75, 1948-59, librarian, 1959-70; material resource coordinator Lincolnshire Prairie View Dist. 103, Lake Forest, Ill., 1970—. Chmn. library groups Area Insts., 1968, 71. Mem. A.L.A., N.E.A., Assn. for Communication and Ednl. Tech., Am. Assn. Sch. Librarians (div. ednl. media and materials), Ill. Edn. Assn., Ill. AudioVisual Assn., Ill. Library Assn. Club: McHenry (Ill.) Country. Home: 17 East Park Mundelein IL 60060 Office: 1370 Riverwoods Lake Forest IL 60045

TURNER, WANDA ANN BUNDICK (MRS. FREDIE LAMAR TURNER), city ofcl.; b. Smiley, Tex., June 18, 1945; d. Athel Boone and Mayme Ione (Rhodes) Bundick; certificate N. Tex. State U., 1973; m. Fredie Lamar Turner, Apr. 10, 1963; 1 son, Brett Lamar. Typist, Retail Credit Co., Austin, Tex., 1964; sec. Yorktown (Tex.) Ind. Sch. dist., 1967-68; city sec. Yorktown, 1968—. Liaison officer City Tex. Parks and Wildlife, 1972—, City and Nat. Flood Control Com., 1973—. Mem. DeWitt Assn. for Retarded Children Citizen's Adv. Com., 1968—, City Planning Commn., 1968—. Mem. Asso. Pub.-Safety Communications Officers, Assn. City Clks. and Secs. Tex., Internat. Inst. Municipal Clks., Coastal Bend Assn. City Clks. and City Secs. (pres. 1971-72, sec., treas. 1972-73), Tex. Assn. Assessing Officers, Sheriffs' Assn. Tex. Baptist. Club: Country (Yorktown). Home: PO Box 183 Yorktown TX 78164 Office: PO Box 605 Yorktown TX 78164

TURNER, YOUTHA BELL (MRS. HERBERT MACK TURNER, JR.), home economist; b. Bedford, Va., Apr. 28, 1930; d. Henry Robert and Alice Louise (Brown) Bell; B.S., Va. State Coll., 1951; postgrad. Cornell U., 1959-61; m. Herbert Mack Turner, Jr., Dec. 31, 1965; 1 son, Herbert Mack III. Spl. tng. Henrido County, Va., 1952; extension agt. Prince Edward County, Va., 1952-56; home economist extension agt. Amherst Va., 1956—. Mem. adminstrv. com. Phyllis Wheatley YWCA, 1960-66, 69-72. Bd. dirs. Lynchburg Community Action Orgn., 1969-71, Amherst chpt. A.R.C., 1956, 58-60; bd. dirs. central region Va. Lung Assn., 1973-76, chmn. Christmas Seal Campaign. Recipient Outstanding service award, Central Va. Tb and Health Assn., 1965; Distinguished Service award, Nat. Assn. Extension Home Eonomists, 1967. Mem. Nat., Va., East Central assns. extension home economists, Va. Farm and Home Agts. Assn., Am. Home Econs. Assn., Nat. Honorary Extension Fraternity, Nat. 4H Agts. Assn., Negro Coll. Women, Amherst Health and Welfare Council, Amherst Parent-Tchrs. and Citizens Assn., Friends of Amherst County Pub. Library, Am. Cancer Soc. (dir. 1962-65), Alpha Kappa Alpha. Baptist. Home: 4120 Audubon Place Lynchburg VA 24503 Office: PO Box 373 Courthouse Amherst VA 24521

TURNIPSEED, JORJA POUND (MRS. J. LARRY TURNIPSEED), educator; b. Tupelo, Miss., July 28, 1939; d. George Thompson and Bill (Sneed) Pound; B.A., Blue Mountain Coll., 1960; Mus.M., U. So. Miss., 1967, Ph.D., (grad. fellow 1962-64, 66-68), 1968; m. J. Larry Turnipseed, Mar. 13, 1964; 1 son, Terry Lynn. Elementary music tchr. East Tallahatchie Sch. Dist., Charleston, Miss., 1960-61; part time faculty U. So. Miss., Hattiesburg, 1961-62, coordinator of curriculum material center, 1966-68; asso. prof. music edn. Miss. State U., State College, 1968—. Cons. elementary classroom music with Miss. Ednl. Services Center, contemporary and jr. coll. music. Mem. exec. com. Miss. Gov.'s lt. col. staff, 1964-68; mem. Gov.'s staff, 1972—. Recipient Outstanding Woman Faculty award Miss. State U., 1972. Mem. Nat., Miss. edn. assns., Music Edn. Nat. Conf., Miss. Music Edn. Assn., Kappa Delta Pi, Mu Phi Epsilon, Phi Delta Kappa. Baptist (dir. youth week 1957-58). Clubs: Pilot (dir. 1971, chmn. edn., internat. relations com. 1971, v.p. 1972, pres. 1973) (Starkville, Miss.). Author: An Analytical Analysis of the Keyboard Toccatas of G. Frescobaldi, 1967; Academic Success of Jr. College Transfer Students at U.S.M., 1968; A Study of the Economic Conditions of Harrison County, Miss., 1969. Collaborator: The Sniveling Civil War (musical play), 1961; The Talented Cat (musical childrens play), 1962. Home: 2105 Plum Rd Starkville MS 39759 Office: Box 2952 Mississippi State MS 39762

TURNS, DANIELLE MARTHE MARIE FLORIO, psychiatrist, epidemiologist; b. Toulouse, France, Dec. 26, 1936; d. Rene and Lucienne (Lasgourgues) Florio; M.D., U. de Lyon (France), 1963; m. Calvin Newton Turns, May 26, 1962 (div. 1974); children—Calvin Patrick, Martine Lucienne. Came to U.S., 1961, naturalized, 1971. Resident Manhattan State Hosp., N.Y.C., 1961-65, early drug evaluation research unit, 1965-69; asso. research scientist Hudson River State Hosp., psychiatrist, epidemiology research unit, 1969—; practice medicine specializing in adult psychiatry, Poughkeepsie, N.Y., 1969—. Home: 11 Riverview Circle Poughkeepsie NY 12601 Office: Hudson River State Hospital Branch B Poughkeepsie NY 12601

TURRELL, EUNICE ALICE RAE (MRS. RAYMOND S. TURRELL), physician; b. Townsville, Australia, Nov. 16, 1918; d. Lester James and Elizabeth (Fox) Dowzer; M.B.B.S., U. Queensland, Faculty of Medicine, 1943; m. Raymond S. Turrell, Nov. 30, 1944; 1 dau. Anne (Mrs. Hamilton Graham Lamont). Came to the U.S., Apr. 1946, naturalized, 1954. Intern, Brisbane Gen. Hosp. Queensland, Australia, 1943-44, Cedars of Lebanon Hosp., Los Angeles, 1952-53; resident Townsville Gen. Hosp., Australia, 1944-45; practice medicine specializing in family medicine, Brisbane, Australia, 1945-46; volunteer work YWCA, Red Cross, U.S.O., Community Chest, Los Angeles, 1946-52; sch. physician Los Angeles Unified Sch. Dist., 1955-68, coordinator physician services, 1968—, med. cons., 1968—. Mem. adv. council Family Service of Los Angeles, 1962-65. Fellow Royal Soc. of Health; mem. Sch. Physicians and Dentists Assn. (pres. 1964-65), Am. Sch. Health Assn., Los Angeles Pediatric Soc., Am. Med. Womens Assn. Republican. Episcopalian. Home: 7435 E Quinn St Downey CA 90241 Office: 1208 Magnolia Av Gardena CA 90247

TUSTIN, KAREN KLEIV (MRS. DOUGLAS TUSTIN), lawyer; b. Bremerton, Wash., Dec. 9, 1942; d. Ole O. and Anna C. (Lyndahl) Kleiv; B.A., Stanford, 1964, LL.B., 1968; m. Douglas Tustin, June 20, 1965; children—Ole, Jason. Admitted to Cal. bar, 1970; law clk. Jorgenson, Cosgrove, Flickinger, attys., Menlo Park, 1967-68; mem. firm Hillyer & Irwin, San Diego, 1970-74; dep. pub. defender El Dorado County, 1974—; with law office Daryl J. McKinstry, Placerville, Cal., 1974—. Mem. Placerville Citizen's Adv. Com. to Create a Gen. Plan for City of Placerville, 1973-74. Mem. Am., San Diego County bar assns., State Bar Cal., Am. Assn. U. Women (status of women rep. 1973-74), Order of Coif, Phi Beta Kappa. Home: 1702 Country Club Dr Placerville CA 95667 Office: 3003 Bedford Av Placerville CA 95667

TUTEN, SIMONA MORINI (MRS. FREDERIC TUTEN), philologist, editor; b. Naples, Italy, Aug. 20, 1932; d. Bruno and Eleonora (Aidinyan) Morini; Litt.D., U. Rome, Italy, 1957; m. Frederic Tuten, Sept. 9, 1962. Came to U.S., 1960. Translator, UN Italian Mission, N.Y.C., 1961-64; reader fgn. books Farrar, Straus & Giroux, N.Y.C., 1964-65; asst. editor Fgn. Rights New Am. Library, N.Y.C., 1965-66; head researcher Vogue mag., N.Y.C., 1966-69, editor, writer, 1969-71, contbg. editor, 1971-73. Cons. transl. fgn. publs. McGraw-Hill Pub., N.Y.C., 1973—. Author: Body Sculpture, Plastic Surgery from Head to Toe, 1972. Translator 12 children's books into Italian for Ency. Brit., 1964; The House of Farnese, 1968; Charles Baudelaire, Letters From His Youth, 1970. Address: 319 E 10th St New York City NY 10009

TUTEUR, CIVIA MARLENE (MRS. PAUL TUTEUR), librarian; b. Ware, Mass., Sept. 24, 1937; d. Berton B. and Ruth (Schnitman) Weiss; B.A. in History, U. Mich., 1959; M.L.S., Pratt Inst., 1961; postgrad. U. Americas, Mexico, 1973; m. Paul Tuteur, Sept. 6, 1971. Librarian children's books Franklin Square (NY) Pub. Library, 1961-64; employment counselor Blvd. Employment Co., Chgo., 1964-69; catalogue librarian Mundelein Coll., Chgo., 1969-74; asst. cataloger Roosevelt U., Chgo., 1974—. Mem. Am., Ill. Library assns., Am. Assn. U. Profs., Art Inst. Chgo., Beta Phi Mu. Democrat. Home: 6312 N Paulina St Chicago IL 60660 Office: 430 S Michigan Av Roosevelt U Chicago IL 60605

TUTINO, ROSALIE JACQUELINE, pub. relations exec.; b. Bklyn., Dec. 28, 1937; d. Peter R. and Rose J. (Oliva) Tutino; student Coll. Mt. St. Vincent, 1954-55; B.A., St. Joseph's Coll., 1955-59; M.A., N.Y. U., 1964. Mgr. Equitable Life Assurance Soc., N.Y.C., 1959-62; tchr. Our Lady of Perpetual Help High Sch., Bklyn., 1962-70; dir. pub. relations St. Joseph's Coll., Bklyn., 1970—. Prin. R. J. Tutino, ins. broker Bklyn., 1966—. Mem. Coll. Entrance Examination Bd., 1970—, Catholic Coll. Coordinating Council, 1970—. Mem. Young Republicans. Mem. N.Y. Personnel and Guidance Assn., Bklyn. Ins. Brokers Assn., Am. Coll. Pub. Relations Assn. Home: 1412 64th St Brooklyn NY 11219

TUTT, LOUISE THOMPSON, lawyer; b. Centerville, Ia., Nov. 10, 1937; d. Lawrence Eugene and Alice Helen (Thompson) Tutt; B.A. in English, U. Ariz., 1963, J.D., 1969. Admitted to Cal. bar, 1972; practiced law, San Diego, 1972-73, La Jolla, Cal., 1973—; prin. Louise Tutt, atty., La Jolla, 1972—. Mem. Fine Arts Soc. San Diego. Mem. State Bar Cal., Bar of U.S. Dist. Ct. So. Dist. Cal. Home: 4036 Shasta St San Diego CA 92109 Office: 7924 Ivanhoe Av Suite 7 La Jolla CA 92037

TUTTLE, HELEN IRENE, ednl. adminstr.; b. Newton, Kan., Apr. 10, 1922; d. Ralph A. and Sarah Helen (Harley) Tuttle; B.S., Kan. State Coll., 1954, M.S., 1955; Ed.D., U. Miss., 1968. Tchr., Truesdale (Kan.) Schs., 1942-43, Garfield Elementary Sch., Abilene, Kan., 1943-45, Lincoln Sch., El Dorado, Kan., 1945-47, Alta Vista Jr. High Sch., Carlsbad, N.M., 1955-57; asst. prof. English, Upper Ia. Coll., Fayette, Ia., 1957-60, dean women, 1961-68; dean women Ripon (Wis.) Coll., 1968—. Served with USAF, 1949-53. Mem. Nat. Assn. Women Adminstrs., Deans and Counselors, Am. Assn. U. Women, Am. Assn. Higher Edn., Delta Kappa Gamma. Methodist. Mem. Order Eastern Star. Home: 603 S Grove St Ripon WI 54971 Office: Ripon Coll Ripon WI 54971

TUTTLE, LEAH JANE, librarian; b. Lansing, Mich., Nov. 18, 1921; d. Harold C. and Ruth I. (Eason) Tuttle; B.A., Mich. State U., 1945; M.A., U. Mich., 1955, M.A. in L.S. (Margaret Mann scholar), 1958. Prodn. asst. WOOD, Grand Rapids, Mich., 1945-46; dir. radio advt. Herpolsheimer's Grand Rapids, 1946; women's editor WILS, Lansing, 1947-52; writer U. Mich. Television Office, Ann Arbor, 1953-54; writer WJIM, Radio-TV, Lansing, 1954-55; communications skills instr. Heidelberg Coll., Tiffin, O., 1955-56; instr. communications skills Mich. State U., 1956-57; reference librarian, publicity, group services, gen. asst. Baldwin Pub. Library, Birmingham, Mich., 1958-62, head, reference dept., publicity, 1962—. Vice chmn. Birmingham Hist. Commn., 1964-66; mem. finance adv. com. Birmingham-Bloomfield League Women Voters, 1972—. Mem. A.L.A., Spl. Libraries Assn., Mich. Library Assn. (reference sect. chmn.-elect 1973-74, chmn. 1974-75), Alpha Xi Delta, Beta Phi Mu, Alpha Epsilon Rho, Phi Kappa Phi. Home: 525 Watkins St Birmingham MI 48009 Office: 351 Martin St Birmingham MI 48012

TWEDDLE, MARGARET ALICE, graphic arts co. exec.; b. Richmond, Mich., Apr. 3, 1915; d. Earl and Armeda (Upplegar) Fenton; R.N., Highland Park (Mich.) Gen. Hosp., 1936; m. Edmund B. Tweddle, Sept. 9, 1939; children—Janice (Mrs. Clark Lincoln), Michael E. Treas. Tweddle Litho Co., St. Clair Shores, Mich., 1954—, pres., chief officer, 1967—. Club: Womens Economic Club. Home: 2003 Shore-Pointe Rd Grosse Pointe Woods MI 48236 Office: 24000 Harper St St Claire Shores MI 48080

TWIGGS, MARGARET SINKLER, newspaper reporter; b. Augusta, Ga., Mar. 31, 1919; d. John David and Meta Huger (Sinkler) Twiggs; student Jr. Coll. Augusta, 1936-38, Winthrop Coll., 1938-39; B.A. in Journalism, U. Ga., 1940. Soc. editor Augusta Chronicle, 1941-44, 46-49; with A.R.C., ETO, 1944-45; woman's editor Ft. Lauderdale (Fla.) Daily News, 1949-51; soc. editor Augusta Herald, 1951-56, govt. and polit. reporter, 1956—. Mem. Richmond County Republican Exec. Com., 1952-64; mem. Ga. Rep. Exec. Com., 1954-60, vice chairwoman, 1956-60; mem. platform com. from Ga., Nat. Rep. Com., 1956. Mem. Augusta League Women Voters (pres. 1953), Jr. League Augusta, Ga. Soc. Colonial Dames, Richmond County Hist. Soc. (v.p. 1962). Episcopalian. Club: Augusta Country. Home: 1014 Hickman Rd Apt D Augusta GA 30904 Office: News Bldg Augusta Herald Augusta GA 30904

TWISDOM, JOAN MARY, editor; b. Phila., Feb. 9, 1926; d. William Joseph and Mary Mildred (Rice) Twisdom; B.S., St. Joseph's Coll., 1962; postgrad. Phila. Coll. Art, 1968. Research asst. Henry Phipps Inst. for Tb. Research, Phila., 1954-58; research asst. U. Pa. Moore Sch. Elec. Engring., Phila., 1958-60; librarian asst. Smith Kline Labs., Phila., 1960-62; med. corr. Cliggott Pub. Co., Greenwich, Conn., 1963, writer, editor, 1963-70, acting editor-in-chief, 1970, sr. editor, 1970—. Mem. Nat. Audubon Soc., Nat. Wildlife Fedn., Defenders Wild Life, Wilderness Soc., Acad. Natural Scis. Phila. Contbr. articles to profl. jours. Home: 3192 Tilton St Philadelphia PA 19134 Office: 500 W Putnam Av Greenwich CT 06830

TWISS, SUZANNE, statistician; b. Phila., Apr. 8, 1934; d. Richard Mathew and Grace Isabel (Richardson) Free; B.S., Fla. State U., 1954; M.A., U. Cal. at Berkeley, 1968; m. Robert H. Twiss, Jr., Sept. 30, 1956; children—R. Gregory, Gail. Tchr. math. Victor Valley Jr. High Sch., Victorville, Cal., 1957-58; statistician Ford Motor Co., Dearborn, Mich., 1958-60; statistician behavioral and attitude research projects on med. attitudes Cal. Dept. Health, Berkeley, 1963-65, statistician birth defects research, 1965-67, air pollution research statistician Air and Indsl. Hygiene Lab., 1968—; USPHS trainee, 1967-68. Served to lt. (j.g.) U.S. Navy, 1954-56. Mem. Am. Pub. Health Assn., A.A.A.S., Biometric Soc., Delta Omega, Sigma Pi Sigma. Contbr. to publs. in field. Home: 739 Pierce St Albany CA 94706 Office: 2151 Berkeley Way Berkeley CA 94704

TWITTY, HELEN COOK, banker; b. Kershaw, S.C., June 12, 1932; d. William Culp and Addie Mae (Poole) Cook; student Draughon's Bus. Coll., 1951-52; student courses Am. Inst. Banking; m. Glen Tillman Twitty, Apr. 22, 1951. Office worker S.C. Area Trade Sch., West Columbia, 1953-54; billing clk. Spring Mills, Lancaster, S.C.; bookkeeper, asst. mgr. bookkeeping, mgr. bookkeeping, asst. v.p. operations administrn. S.C. Nat. Bank, Columbia. Mem. Nat. Assn. Bank Women. Baptist (tchr.). Home: 901 12th St Cayce SC 29033 Office: 900 Assembly St Columbia SC 29202

TWYFORD, BARBARA JEAN, pub. relations exec., editor; b. Montebello, Cal., July 6, 1945; d. Henry Harrison and Genevieve Lee (Pieratt) Twyford; B.A. in Journalism, Polit. Sci., Syracuse U., 1967. Sec., Am. Assn. U. Women, Washington, 1967-68; sec. press relations U.S. senator, Washington, 1968-69, press aide, 1969-70; sec. press relations Brewer & Co., Ltd., Honolulu, 1970—. Loaned mgmt. person Aloha United Fund, 1972. Mem. Women in Communications, Hawaii Communicators Assn. (sec. 1972), Honolulu Pres Club, Gamma Phi Beta. Office: PO Box 3470 Honolulu HI 96801

TYAU, FRANCES SIU LAN, educator; b. Honolulu, July 19, 1919; d. Henry and Hannah (Aiau) Tyau; B.Ed., U. Hawaii, 1941, 5th year diploma, 1941; M.A., Columbia U. Tchrs. Coll., 1957, 6th yr. Profl. Degree, 1958. Tchr. Honolulu Dept. Pub. Instrn., 1941-55; intern tchr. supr. Dept. Edn. U. Hawaii, 1951-56; instr. Western Ill. U., 1958-59; asso. prof. State U. Coll. at Buffalo, 1959—. Mem. finance com. Western N.Y. United Ministry Higher Edn. Dir. Buffalo Area People to People High Sch. Ambassador Travel Program, 1970—. Mem. Nat. Edn. Assn., Am. Assn. Higher Edn., Assn. Tchr. Edn., Chinese Lang. Assn., Assn. Supervision Curriculum Devel., N.Y. Tchrs. Assn., Am. Assn. U. Profs., Internat. House N.Y.C., Kappa Delta Pi (counselor 1959), Pi Lambda Theta. Club: Altrusia Internat. of Buffalo (dir. 1971, 72, sec. 1974). Office: 1300 Elmwood Av Buffalo NY 14222

TYLER, ANN GLENN, advt. exec.; b. Winston-Salem, N.C., May 21, 1932; d. Robert Perry and Lucille (Glenn) Tyler; A.B. with honors, Hollins Coll., 1953. With Merrill Lynch, Pierce, Fenner & Smith, Inc., N.Y.C., 1954-60; reporter, asso. editor, editorial staff Fortune Mag., Time, Inc., N.Y.C., 1961-72, advt. sales rep., 1972—. Mem. Financial Communications Soc., Financial Advt. and Marketing Assn. N.Y. Club: Bankers (N.Y.C.). Home: 330 E 43d St New York City NY 10017 Office: Fortune Mag Time Inc Time & Life Bldg Rockefeller Center New York City NY 10020

TYLER, ANNE (MRS. TAGHI M. MODARRESSI), author; b. Mpls., Oct. 25, 1941; d. Lloyd Parry and Phyllis (Mahon) Tyler; B.A., Duke U., 1961; postgrad. Columbia U., 1962; m. Taghi M. Modaressi, May 3, 1963; children—Tezh, Mitra. Author novels: If Morning Ever Comes, 1964; The Tin Can Tree, 1965; A Slipping-Down Life, 1970; The Clock Winder, 1972; Celestial Navigation, 1974. Contbr. short stories to nat. mags. Home: 222 Tunbridge Rd Baltimore MD 21212

TYLER, BARBARA ANN, museum ofcl.; b. Rockdale, Tex., Jan. 6, 1938; d. Henry Alexander and Mary Pearl Tyler; B.A., Tex. Christian U., 1960, M.A. in Am. Frontier History, 1965; postgrad. Seminar for Hist. Adminstrs., Colonial Williamsburg (Va.), 1967. Exhibit research Amon Carter Museum Western Art, Ft. Worth, 1961, bursar and registrar, 1962-63, research historian, 1963-64, curator history, 1964-68; asst. chief operations div. in charge intrepretation Nat. Historic Sites Service Dept. Indian Affairs and No. Devel., Ottawa, 1969; chief communications div. Nat. Museum Man, Nat. Mus. Can., Ottawa, Ont., 1969—; Canadian rep. Joint Com. Devel. Nat. and Hist. Parks, U.S. and Can., Washington, 1969; cons. ad hoc adv. com. Commr. for establishment N.W. Terr. Museum, 1971; lectr. in field. Mem. Am. Assn. State and Local History, Canadian Museums Assn., N.E. Museums Assn., Western History Assn., Ft. Worth Corral Westerners, Tex. Christian U. Alumni Assn. Contbr. articles to profl. jours. Home: 28 Leeming Dr Ottawa ON K2H 5P7 Canada Office: Nat Museum of Man Century Bldg 360 Lisgar St Ottawa ON Canada

TYLER, BETTY SESSLER (MRS. GEORGE BOYD TYLER, JR.), newspaperwoman; b. Richmond, Va.; d. Grover C. and Hannah (Engelberg) Sessler; B.A., U. Richmond, 1942; postgrad. U. Bridgeport, 1964; m. George Boyd Tyler, Jr. July 25, 1954. Reporter Richmond Times-Dispatch, 1942-51, asst. to Sunday editor, 1951-54; with Bridgeport (Conn.) Sunday Post, 1955—, teen-age editor, 1957-72, arts editor, 1960—, travel writer, 1966—, asst. to editor, 1968—. Chmn. Monroe (Conn.) Library Bd., 1968-70; pres. Friends of Library, Monroe, 1965-66; sec. Town Hall Complex Bldg. Com., Monroe, 1970—, Community Devel. Action Plan, Monroe, 1968-70. Named New Eng. Newspaper Woman of Yr., New Eng. Woman's Press Assn., 1960, 61. Home: 233 Old Newtown Rd Monroe CT 06468 Office: 410 State St Bridgeport CT 06602

TYLER, CAROLYN BUTLER, newspaper editor; b. Grand Island, Neb., May 4, 1935; d. Vance L. and Bessie (Heuring) Butler; student Wayne State Tchrs. Coll., Neb., 1953-55; B.A. in Journalism U. Neb., 1957; m. Robert H. Tyler, July 31, 1960; 1 stepson, H. Bruce Tyler. Editor, Goldenrod newspaper, Wayne State Tchrs. Coll., 1953-55; soc. editor Wayne (Neb.) Herald, 1955; editor Ainsworth (Neb.) Star-Jour., 1957-60; editor Riverton (Wyo.) Daily Ranger, 1961—, newspaper desk editor, columnist, free-lance writing and photography. One-man photography show Wyo. Capitol Bldg., 1966. Recipient over 200 state and nat. newspaper writing and photography awards, 1957-74; named Neb. Press Woman of Year, 1959; Riverton High Sch. Wally award, 1972. Mem. Working Women's Orgn. (pres.

1960), P.E.O. Methodist. Home: 1103 Sierra Dr Riverton WY 82501 Office: 421 E Main Riverton WY 82510

TYLER, CAROLYN SMITH (MRS. JOSIE LEE TYLER, JR.), librarian; b. Culverton, Ga., Jan. 30, 1923; d. Marvin Henry and Emmie Frank (Waller) Smith; B.A., Ga. State Coll. for Women, 1944; B.A. in L.S., Emory U., 1945; m. Josie Lee Tyler, Jr., Aug. 31, 1954; 1 son, Josie Lee III. Librarian Emory U., Atlanta, Ga., 1945-56; serials cataloger Duke U., Durham, N.C., 1956-57; cataloger Colleton County Meml. Library, Walterboro, S.C., 1957-58; librarian, instr. Coll. of Edn., U. S.C., Columbia, 1960—, instr. library edn., 1960-70. Mem. Am., S.C. library assns., Am. Assn. U. Women. Methodist. Home: 1100 Eastminster Dr Columbia SC 29204

TYLER, GLADYS ELLEN (MRS. RONALD ANTHONY TYLER), librarian; b. London, Eng., Nov. 20, 1920; d. Ernest Edward and Mathilda Gladys (Schmidt) Brockwell; B.Sc., U. London, 1942; B.L.S., U. Ottawa, 1968, M.L.S., 1972, M.Ed., 1973; m. Ronald Anthony Tyler, Sept. 12, 1942; 1 son, Jeremy. Tchr., Bristol, Eng., 1942-47; research asst. dev. biology NRC Can., Ottawa, Ont., 1953-58; tchr. Ottawa schs., 1958—, head librarian Fisher Park High Sch., Ottawa Bd. Edn., 1968—. Mem. Ont. Library Assn., Ont. Secondary Sch. Tchrs. Fedn. Home: 728 Lonsdale Rd Ottawa ON K1K 0K2 Canada Office: Fisher Park High School 250 Holland Av Ottawa ON K1Y 0Y6 Canada

TYLER, HELEN (MRS. TRACY F. TYLER), social worker; b. Fulda, Min., Oct. 3, 1918; d. Sanke and Ida (Johnson) Behr; B.S., Mankato State Tchrs. Coll., 1940; M.A. in Psychiat. Social Work, U. Minn., 1950; m. Willard P. Comstock, May 27, 1942 (dec. June 1945); children—Patricia Ann; m. 2d, Tracy F. Tyler, Nov. 17, 1950; adopted children—Fletcher W., Ralph S. Tchr. 1st grade Alden, Minn., 1940-41, Waterville, Minn., 1941-42; jr. clk-typist U.S. Naval Air Sta., Corpus Christi, Tex., 1942; vis. tchr. Mpls. Pub. Schs., 1948-58, cons. in social work, 1958-68, asst. dir. for sch. social work, 1969—, also chmn. human relations com. 1963—. Mem. edn. com. Mpls. Mayor's Com. on Human Relations, 1964—; mem. edn. task force Hennepin County Econ. Opportunity Com., 1964—; pres. bd., co-chmn. Midwest Sch. Social Work Conf., 1970; mem. adv. bd. Hennepin County Community Health and Welfare Council Agys., Vol. Service Bur., Holiday Bur., Children's Dental Services, Pub. and Parochial Child Welfare. Mem. Nat. Assn. Social Workers (dir. Minn. chpt.), Acad. Certified Social Workers, Council for Exceptional Children, Nat., Minn. edn. assns., Midwest Sch. Social Work Assn. (dir.), Minn. Adminstrs. Spl. Edn., Minn. Sch. Social Workers Assn. (dir.), Mpls. Assn. Retarded Children, City of Mpls. Adminstrn. Assn., Nat. Conf. Social Welfare, Minn. Welfare Assn., Am. Orthopsychiat. Assn., Delta Kappa Gamma. Clubs: Quota (corr. sec. 1965-66, chmn. service com. 1964-65), Faculty Women's (U. Minn.). Home: 1564 Fulham St St Paul MN 55108 Office: 807 NE Broadway Minneapolis MN 55413

TYLER, JANICE LUELLA, educator, coll. dean; b. Montebello, Cal., Sept. 10, 1942; d. Rufus Lloyd and Shirley Ellen (Blackmer) Tyler; B.S., Brigham Young U., 1964; student Salzburg, Austria, 1965; M.A. in Edn., Counseling, Ariz. State U., 1969. Sec., Hansen's Accounting Firm, Walla Walla, Wash., 1965-67; personnel coordinator, inst. dir., adminstrv. asst. Ariz. State U., Tempe, 1967-71; asst. dean students, founder, dir. Women's Environ. Inst., Weber State Coll., Ogden, Utah 1971-74, asst. prof. student personnel 1971-74; coordinator Family Consultation Center, asst. prof. child devel. and family relationships Brigham Young U., 1974—. Cons. women's orgns., programs, 1971—. Mem. Phoenix Symphony Chorale, 1969-71; mem. adv. bd. Odyssey House, 1971—; mem. subcom. Utah Gov.'s Com. on Status of Women, 1972—. Recipient Silver Chalice award Asso. Women Students Weber State Coll., 1973; named Outstanding Young Woman State of Utah, 1973. Mem. Nat. Assn. Women Deans, Adminstrs. and Counselors, Internat. Platform Assn., Women's Equity Action League (Utah state convenor 1970—), League of Women Voters, Am. Assn. U. Women (corr. sec. Utah State Bd. 1973), Beta Sigma Phi. Bd. editors Dialogue: A Jour. of Mormon Thought. Home: 351 E Center 104 Provo UT 84601 Office: Brigham Young U Provo UT 84601

TYLER, JOHNNIE MAE WEEKS (MRS. E.J. TYLER), ret. educator, civic worker; b. Ozark, Ala., July 28, 1913; d. John Calvin and Lena Lee (Boyett) Weeks; B.S. in Edn., Troy State Coll., 1946; postgrad. Auburn U., 1955-57; diploma in Christian tng. Baptist Sunday Sch. Bd., Nashville, 1961; m. Saxon DeWitt Dykes, Sr., Sept. 23, 1933 (div. Oct. 1963); children—Saxon DeWitt, Catherine Malissa; m. 2d, William Deval Barefoot, Nov. 25, 1964 (dec. Oct. 1968); m. 3d, E.J. Tyler, June 12, 1969. Tchr. elementary schs. Barbour county, Dale county, Ozark, Ala., 1940-69, 6th group Emma P. Flowers Elementary Sch., Ozark, Ala., 1955-69. Grey lady Dale county chpt. A.R.C., Ozark, 1942-45, 1st aid instr., 1942-69; instr. Civil Def., Ozark, 1963-65; co-ordinator Ariton Civil Def., 1967-68. Notary pub., justice of peace Barbour County, 1963-64. Founding fellow So. Soc. Geneologists, Inc.; mem. Internat. Platform Assn., Ala. Ret. Tchrs. Assn., N.E.A., Ala. Edn. Assn., Fedn. Women's Clubs (chmn. Dale County 1949-51), Beta Sigma Phi. Baptist (librarian ch. 1963-64). Clubs: Clio Study (pres. 1956-57), Progressive Study (Clio) (pres. 1959-60); Maud Martin Study (charter mem., Ozark). Contbr. papers to tech. lit., book reviews Ch. Paper Monthly Publ., Clio, 1963-64. Home: Route 2 PO Box 186 Ariton AL 36311

TYLER, JUNE ELIZABETH DAVIS (MRS. ROBERT K. TYLER), educator; b. Ithaca, Wis., Apr. 25, 1911; d. Roscoe Vincent and Leone Ella (Van Dusen) Davis; teaching certificate Richland County Normal, 1929; diploma Meth. Sch. Nursing, Madison, Wis., 1941; B.S., U. Wis., 1964; postgrad. Platteville State Tchrs. Coll., U. Chgo.; m. Enoch A. Jewel, Dec. 20, 1930 (div. Jan. 1932); 1 dau., Yvonne (Mrs. Marvin Hottmann); m. 2d, Robert K. Tyler, May 22, 1948; stepchildren—Robert R., Shirley (Mrs. Henry DeBruin). Elementary and rural sch. tchr., Richland County, Wis., 1929-31, 32-38; obstetric supr. nursing, instr. Meth. Hosp. and Sch., Madison, Wis., 1941-45, 47-57, Milw. Columbia Hosp. and Sch., 1945-47; instr., coordinator Madison Area Tech. Coll., 1957-65; coordinator div. health occupations edn. N.E. Wis. Tech. Inst., Green Bay, 1965—. Cons. health career programs in high schs., 1972—; mem. Licensed Practical Nursing Exam. Council, State of Wis., 1966-72. Recipient Sr. High Honors, U. Wis., 1964; Recognition of Service award State Wis. Bd. Vocational, Tech. and Adult Edn. Mem. Wis. Assn. Vocational and Adult edn. (dir. 1970-72), Green Bay Dist. Nurses (dir. 1966-72). Mem. Order Eastern Star. Club: Green Bay Altrusa (pres. 1971-73). Home: 409 S Webster St Green Bay WI 54301 Office: 2740 W Mason St Green Bay WI 54303

TYLER, MARGO HILLS (MRS. CONVERSE TYLER), found. exec.; b. Salt Lake City, Sept. 4, 1921; d. Harold Haven and Mary Edith (Roberts) Hills; B.A., U. Utah, 1942; m. Converse Tyler, Sept. 30, 1950. Asst. city editor Salt Lake Telegram, Salt Lake City, 1942-45; adminstrv. asst. safety service Am. Nat. Red Cross, Washington, 1945-55; dir. pub. relations Am. Cancer Soc., Washington, 1957-65, Am. Assn. Motor Vehicle Adminstrs., Washington, 1966-68; dir. pub. information Coll. V.I., St. Thomas, 1968-70; dir. communications Nat. 4-H Found., Washington, 1970—. Mem. community outreach com., adv. council nat. orgns. Corp. for Pub. Broadcasting, Washington, 1971—, chmn., 1973-74; co-founder Pub. Information Assn. St. Thomas, V.I., 1969, sec., 1969. Mem. Pub. Relations Soc. Am. (mem. nat. bd. 1962-64, 1967, 72-73), Mortar Bd., Phi Beta Kappa, Phi Kappa Phi, Delta Gamma. Club: Montgomery County Press (Silver Spring, Md.). Office: 7100 Connecticut Av Washington DC 20015

TYLER, PRISCILLA, educator; b. Cleve., Oct. 23, 1908; d. Ralph Sargent and Alice Lorraine (Campbell) Tyler; B.A., Radcliffe Coll., 1932; M.A., Case Western Res. U., 1934, Ph.D., 1953. Tchr., English, Cleveland Heights, O., 1935-45; asst. prof. English, asst. dean Case-Western Res. U., 1945-50; asst. prof. edn. Harvard, 1959-63; asso. prof. English, dir. freshman rhetoric, U. Ill., 1963-67; prof. edn. and English, U. Mo., Kansas City, 1967—. Recipient award for distinguished teaching, Case Western Res. U., 1962. Mem. Nat. Council Tchrs. English (2d v.p. 1963, trustee research found. 1970-73), African Studies Assn., Linguistic Soc. Am., Modern Lang. Assn., Delta Kappa Gamma, Pi Lambda Theta. Editor: Writers the Other Side of the Horizon, 1964; Writers in the World Tradition of English, 1971. Contbr. articles to profl. mags. Home: Rural Route 1 Stilwell KS 66085 Office: School of Education Univ of Missouri Kansas City MO 64110

TYLUTKI, BEATRICE STELLA, lawyer; b. N.Y.C., Dec. 23, 1936; d. Stanley and Katherine (Kocul) Tylutki; B.A., Temple U., 1958; LL.B., Georgetown U., 1961. Law clk. to atty. gen. N.J., 1960; N.J. bar, 1961; dep. atty. gen. N.J., 1962-67; asst. counsel to gov. N.J., 1962-69; counsel Hackensack Meadowlands Commn., 1969-71; practiced law, Irvington, N.J., 1971-72; chief Office Legal Research, Adminstrv. Office Cts. N.J., Trenton, 1972-74; dep. dir. N.J. Lottery Commn., 1974—. Exec. sec. Gov.'s Commn. on Status of Women, 1964-67; mem. Del. Valley Regional Planning Commn., 1969-71. Mem. N.J., Mercer County bar assns., Kappa Beta Pi. Home: 22 Wedge Dr Trenton NJ 08610 Office: Taxation Bldg Trenton NJ 08625

TYNER, DOROTHY DAVIDSON, judge; b. Kan., Nov. 15, 1913; s. Fred and Ida Katie (Donecker) Davidson; A.B., Washburn U., LL.B.; m. E. Radley Stangl, Dec. 14, 1946 (div.); 1 son, Franz F. With War Labor Bd., Kansas City, Mo., OPA; individual practice law Anchorage, 1946-50; atty. Rent and Price Stabilization Anchorage, 1950-53; pvt. practice, Seward, Alaska, 1953-57, Anchorage, 1957-61; law clk. U.S. Dist. Ct., 1961-69; dist. judge, Anchorage, 1969—. Instr. Washburn Law Sch., Topeka, 1942-43; tax cons., Topeka; asst. editor Cyclopedic Tax service, Chgo. City atty., Seward, 1953-57. Bd. dirs. YMCA, Anchorage, 1947-52. Mem. Bus. and Profl. Women's Club, Am., Alaska, bar assns., Conf. Alaska Judges, Nat. Conf. Spl. Ct. Judges, Phi Delta Delta. Home: 400 E 24th Av Anchorage AK 99503 Office: 941 4th Av Anchorage AK 99501

TYNER, ROBERTA SARA COLE (MRS. SAMUEL M. TYNER), occupational therapist; b. Brinklow, Md., July 2, 1933; d. Robert Allen and Mary Elizabeth (Ames) Cole; student Howard U., 1952-54; B.S., Columbia, 1956; certificates for various courses in mgmt. and rehab. field; m. Samuel M. Tyner, Aug. 23, 1958; 1 dau., Yvette Alethia. Staff occupational therapist Freedmen's Hosp., Washington, 1957-62; supr. occupational therapy Community Mental Health, Washington, 1963-69, coordinator rehabilitative therapies, Area Community Mental Health Center, 1969—. Mem. Am. Occupational Therapy Assn. Home: 4957 12th St NE Washington DC 20017 Office: 1905 E St SE Washington DC 20003

TYREE, LANA JEANNE, lawyer; b. Oklahoma City; d. James Edward and Eula Mae (Ditmore) Brown; student Okla. State U., 1963-64; B.A., Okla. City U., 1968; J.D., U. Okla., 1971. Admitted to Okla. bar, 1971; legal intern Legal Aid Soc., Oklahoma County, 1970-71; atty. Benefield Shelton Lee Wilson & Tyree, Oklahoma City, 1971—. Republican precinct chmn., Oklahoma City, 1973-74; chmn. Okla. County Rep. candidate recruitment com., 1973, Okla. state candidate recruitment com., 1973; parliamentarian Rep. county conv., 1972, congl. dist. Rep. conv., 1971. Mem. adv. bd. Oklahoma County Juvenile Ct., 1971-74. Mem. Am., Okla. (civil rights and responsibilities com. 1974-75), Oklahoma County (mem. legal internship com. 1971, law day com. 1973, profl. fitness and conduct com. 1974-75) bar assns., Phi Alpha Delta (pres.). Home: 4204 NW 50th St Oklahoma City OK 73112 Office: 2700 City National Bank Tower Oklahoma City OK 73102

TYRER, LOUISE BRINES, physician; b. Shanghai, China, Apr. 11, 1921; s. Rolland J. Celia (Richmond) Brines (parents American citizens); student La Sierra (Cal.) Coll., 1937-39; B.S., Pacific Union Coll., 1940; M.D., Loma Linda U.; m. Austin Roy Tyrer, Jr., Dec., 1927 (div. May, 1948); children—Robson Brines, Richard Clay. Intern Los Angeles County Hosp., 1944, resident, 1945-48; practice medicine, specializing in obstetrics, gynecology, San Jose, Cal., 1948-56; clin. prof. Med. Sch., U. Cal. at San Francisco, 1956-60; practice medicine, specializing in obstetrics and gynecology, Reno, 1960-70; dir. div. family planning Am. Coll. Obstetricians and Gynecologists, Chgo., 1971—; mem. staff Rush-Presbyn.-St. Lukes, Cook County hosps. Bd. dirs. Reno chpt. Am. Cancer Soc., 1965-70. Mem. Am. Coll. Obstetrics and Gynecology, Schufelt Soc. San Jose (hon.), Am. Fertility Soc., Am. Assn. Planned Parenthood Physicians, N.Y. Acad. Scis., Am. Pub. Health Assn., Am. Women's Med. Assn., Soc. Advanced Med. Systems, Am. Assn. Sex Educators & Counselors, Nat. Family Planning Forum (bd. dirs.), Am. Assn. Gynecol. Laparoscopists, Family Planning Assn. Americas, Bus. and Profl. Women's Club. Home: 225 W Menomonee St Chicago IL 60614 Office: 1 E Wacker Dr Chicago IL 60603

TYROLER, CAROLYN PIERPONT WILLIAMS (MRS. CHARLES TYROLER II), civic worker; b. Savannah, Ga., July 9, 1915; d. Herschel Victor and Lilian Eliza (Strickland) Williams; student pvt. schs.; m. Edmund Burke Games, June 22, 1932 (div. 1946); children—Sara Doane (Mrs. Ronald Dean Forster), Edmund Burke; m. 2d, Charles Tyroler II, Apr. 10, 1946. Research analyst New Orleans Archives, 1942-43; asst. dir. records div. Ochsner Clinic, New Orleans, 1943-44; dir. engring. resources Higgins Aircraft, New Orleans, 1944-45. Pres. Loudoun Valley Recreation Council, 1968-69; vice chmn. Waterford Humane Ednl. Center, Va., 1967. Founding pres. Loudoun County Democratic Women, 1961-63, pres., 1967-69, chmn. exec. com., 1963-67. Bd. dirs. Loudoun County chpt. A.R.C., 1957-66; state bd. dirs. Va. Mental Health Assn., 1966-69; state bd. dirs. Tb and Respiratory Disease Assn., 1968—, chpt. dir., 1965—; bd. dirs. Loudoun County Humane Soc., Va., 1964-68; bd. dirs., com. sec. Nat. Policy Com., Pockets of Poverty, Washington, 1965-67; bd. dirs. Nat. Pollution Control Found., N.Y.C., 1967—. Mem. Humane Soc., Am. Boxwood Soc., Loudoun County Hist. Soc., Nat. Cathedral Assn. (chmn. No. Va. 1971—). Episcopalian. Clubs: Millwood Country (Va.); Goose Creek Country (Leesburg, Va.); Sulgrave (Washington); Regency-Whist (N.Y.C.); Tail-Waggers (Washington, dir. 1964). Home: Point Nine Bluemont VA 22012 also 1028 Connecticut Av Washington DC 20036

TYRRELL, ROSALIE ANN FINK, nurse; b. Renton, N.J., Feb. 19, 1946; d. Herman Alfred and Rosalie Rita (Fisher) Fink; B.S., Niagara U., 1968; M.S., Boston U., 1971; m. Wayne Francis Tyrrell, June 20, 1970. Staff nurse, pediatrics Boston Floating Hosp., Tufts U.-New Eng. Med. Center, 1968-69; head nurse pediatrics Malden Hosp., Malden, Mass., 1971-73; clin. specialist child psychiatry Boston City Hosp., 1973—; trainee Boston Family Inst., 1973—. Nat. Inst. Mental Health trainee, 1969-71. Mem.Am. Orthopsychiat. Assn., New Eng. Region Advocates for Child Psychiat. Nursing, Nat. Orgn. Women. Home: 77 Wentworth St Malden MA 02148 Office: 818 Harrison Av Boston MA 02118

TYSON, MARTHA HARALSON (MRS. JOHN EDWARD TYSON), educator, psychologist; b. Birmingham, July 20, 1919; d. Jonathan and Mattie Moran (Jones) Haralson; B.A., Birmingham-So. Coll., 1939; M.A., U. Houston, 1967, Ph.D., 1968; m. John Edward Tyson, Aug. 8, 1941; children—Jon Edward, William Mabry, Edward Page. Mem. faculty S. Tex. Jr. Coll., Houston, 1968-74, asso. prof. psychology and related courses, 1973-74; asso. prof. U. Houston, 1974—. With Ednl.-Psychol. Consultants, Bellaire, Tex., 1971—; lectr. U. Houston, 1968; cons. Head Start, 1968. Mem. Am., Southwestern, Tex., Houston psychol. assns., Phi Beta Kappa, Phi Sigma Iota, Theta Sigma Lambda, Psi Chi, Zeta Tau Alpha. Democrat. Episcopalian. Home: 3526 Bluebonnet Houston TX 77025 Office: 6300 W Loop South Bellaire TX 77401

TYTELL, PEARL LILY (MRS. MARTIN KENNETH TYTELL), examiner disputed documents; b. N.Y.C., Aug. 29, 1918; d. Harry and Yetta (Feigenbaum) Kessler; student St. John's U., 1941-43; B.S., N.Y. U., 1962, M.A., 1968; m. Martin Kenneth Tytell, May 23, 1943; children—Peter, Pamela. Examiner disputed document, N.Y.C., 1950—; lectr. on handwriting, typewriter identification, detection forgery colls., univs., 1955—; lectr. N.Y. U., 1955-57; mem. faculty N.Y. Inst. Criminology, N.Y.C., 1958; cons. govtl. agys., law firms; expert witness in city, state, fed. cts., U.S. and Commonwealth P.R. Sec. Along The Hudson Home Owners Assn., 1960—. Mem. A.A.A.S., Internat. Assn. Chiefs of Police (asso.), Eastern Bus. Tchrs. Assn. Club: New York University. Co-author: The Confrontation of Anonymous Letter Writers. Home: 3031 Scenic Pl Riverdale NY 10463 Office: 116 Fulton St New York City NY 10038

UCELAY, MARGARITA, educator, author; b. Madrid, Spain, May 5, 1916; d. Enrique and Pura (Maortua) Ucelay; B.A., Inst. Escuela, Madrid, 1933; student U. Madrid Sch. Law, 1933-36; M.A., Columbia, 1942, Ph.D., 1950; m. Ernesto DaCal, Oct. 28, 1936 (div. 1965); 1 son, Enrique. Came to U.S., 1939, naturalized, 1945. Instr. Spanish, Vassar Coll., 1940-42, Hunter Coll., 1942-43; mem. faculty Barnard Coll., 1943—, prof. Spanish, 1967—, chmn. dept., 1962-70, 73—; active exptl. theatre groups, 1933—. Recipient Hispanic medal Am. Assn. Tchrs. Spanish, 1942. Author: Los espanoles pintados por si mismos: estudio de un genero costumbrista, 1951; (with E. DaCal) Literatura del Siglo XX, 1968; (with A. del Rio) Vision de Espana, 1968. Home: 300 Riverside Dr New York City NY 10025

UGGAMS, LESLIE, singer; b. N.Y.C., May 25, 1943; student Juilliard Music Sch.; m. Grahame Pratt, 1963. Began singing career, age 5; appeared on (radio) Peter Lind Hayes-Mary Healy Show, Milton Berle, Star Time, Arthur Godfrey, (TV) Milton Berle Show, Jack Paar Show, Name That Tune, Garry Moore, Sing Along with Mitch; now singer in Broadway show HallelujahBaby; rec. artist with Columbia Records.*

UHL, SISTER MARY CAPISTRANA, nursing adminstr.; b. Germany; d. Xavier Francis and Maria (Brenner) Uhl; came to U.S., 1927, naturalized, 1936; diploma Mercy Hosp. Sch. Nursing, 1935; B.S. in Nursing Edn., Coll. St. Teresa, 1938. Head nurse Mercy Hosp., Oshkosh, Wis,, 1936, dir. nursing edn. and nursing services, 1941-60, sec. bd. govs., 1953-60, asst. dir. nursing edn., nursing instr. Hosp. Sch. Nursing, 1938-41; dir. sch. nursing St. John's Hosp., Tulsa, 1960-66, mem. bd. govs., 1960-66; chief exec. officer St. Mary's Hosp. and Extended Care Facility, Roswell, N.M., 1966-72, pres. bd. govs., 1966-72; supr. med. nursing div. St. Francis Hosp., Wichita, Kan., 1972—, bd. govs., 1973—. Mem. N.M. Bd. Examiners Nursing Home Adminstrs., 1970-72. Mem. disaster com. Oshkosh area chpt. A.R.C., 1956-58, Tulsa area chpt., 1960-65. Bd. dirs. N.M. Conf. Cath. Hosps. Mem. Am. Hosp. Assn., Eastern N.M. Hosp. Council (v.p. 1969-70, pres. 1970-71), Am. (Kan. Nurse Assn. del. to conv. 1974), N.M. nurses assns., A.R.C. Nursing Service, Mercy Hosp. Sch. Nursing Alumni Assn. (Nurse of Year 1972). Address: St Francis Hosp 929 N St Francis St Wichita KS 67214

UHLAND, RUTH ELLEN, educator; b. Escondido, Cal., May 4, 1925; d. William and Ruth (Rooker) U.; A.A., Mira Costa Coll., 1945; B.A., San Diego State Coll., 1947, postgrad. 1948-49, 61, 62, 64, 70-72, San Jose State Coll., 1966-67, Fresno State Coll., 1956-57, U. San Diego, 1969, Internat. U., 1971—. Tchr. jr. high sch., Brawley (Cal.) Elementary Sch. Dist., 1947-50, 53-54, 56-64, elementary tchr., 1950-53, 55, 65—, chmn. health-phys. edn. dept., 1960. Active various community drives. Adv. bd. Rainbow Girls, 1972—. Mem. N.E.A., Internat. Reading Assn. (sch. rep. 1969-72), Cal., Brawley tchrs. assns., Imperial Valley Girls Phys. Edn. Assn. (pres. 1967-68), Brawley Bus. and Profl. Women's Club (v.p. desert sect. 1968-69, pres.'s ecology citation 1972), Desert Protective Council (life), Imperial Photog. Soc., Nat. Audubon Soc., Cooper Ornithological Soc. (life), Am. Assn. U. Women, Delta Kappa Gamma. Mem. Order Eastern Star. Club: Venture (pres. 1954-55) (Brawley); Sierra (San Diego). Home: 158 G St Brawley CA 92227 Office: 261 D St Brawley CA 92727

UHLIR, GLADYS ANN, educator; b. Kokomo, Ind., Aug. 13, 1934; d. George Cleigh and Gladys Eleanor (Young) Uhlir; B.S., Ball State U., 1955; M.A., Columbia, 1956, postgrad. (alumni fellow), 1959-60, Ed.D., 1962. Math. Bendix Aviation, Teterboro, N.J., 1956; asso. prof. phys. edn. State U.N.Y., Brockport, 1956-65; prof., chmn. dept. women's phys. edn. Eastern Ky. U., Richmond, 1965—, mem. faculty senate, 1970-73, mem. grad. council, 1971-74. Mem. Nat., Southern assns. of phys. edn. for coll. women, Am. (chmn. profl. preparation council 1973-74), Ky. (pres., 1971-72) assns. for health, phys. edn. and recreation, Ky. Women's Intercollegiate Conf., Ky. Bd. of Women Officials, Sigma Zeta, Kappa Delta Pi. Editorial bd. Ky. Jour. of Health, Phys. Edn. and Recreation, 1965-71. Home: Barnes Mill Rd Richmond KY 40475 Office: Eastern Ky U Richmond KY 40475

UHLRICH, HELEN MARIE, educator; b. Bozeman, Mont., Mar. 29, 1913; d. Joseph Andrew and Mary (Hagen) Uhlrich; B.A., St. Louis U., 1940; M.S., Fordham U., 1945, Ph.D., 1947. Chmn. sci. div., head biology dept. Viterbo Coll., LaCrosse, Wis., 1947-65; prof. biology Carlow Coll., Pitts., 1965—. Mem. A.A.A.S., Am. Inst. Biol. Scis., Bot. Assn. Western Pa., Pa. Acad. Sci. Home: 5320 5th Av Pittsburgh PA 15232

UHRHANE, LUELLA JANE, educator; b. Marietta, O., Jan. 20, 1915; d. Francis Joseph and Honora (Trapp) Uhrhane; R.N., St. Joseph's Hosp. Sch. Nursing, 1939; B.S. in Edn., U. Cin., 1947; M.P.H., U. N.C., 1951; postgrad. N.Y. Hosp.-Cornell U., 1942. Staff nurse, supr. Good Samaritan Hosp., Dayton, O., 1940-42; staff nurse, head nurse N.Y. Hosp., N.Y.C., 1942-45; with student health service U. Cin., 1945-47; instr. health edn. Duke, Durham, N.C., 1947-50, asst. prof., 1951-56, asso. prof., 1957—. Mem. com. on tchr. edn. and certification N.C. Dept. Pub. Instrn., 1962; mem. steering com. N.C. Coll. Conf. on Health Edn. and Phys. Edn. in Elementary Schs., 1967-68; certification program evaluation panel Am. Coll. Health

Assn., 1969-72; adv. com. Dept. Health Edn., Sch. Pub. Health U. N.C., 1969—. Mem. Durham Community Planning Council, 1959. Fellow N.C. Dept. Health, 1950; N.C. Alcoholic Rehab. program fellow Yale, 1955; WHO fellow, Ethiopia, Malawi, Uganda, Ghana, 1967. Fellow Am. Pub. Health Assn., Am. Sch. Health Assn., Soc. Pub. Health Educators; mem. Royal Soc. for Health (life, Eng.), N.C. Assn. Health Educators-N.C. Soc. Pub. Health Edn. (pres. 1972-73), Am. Coll. Health Assn., Health Edn. Pub., Gerontol. Soc., Internat. Union Health Edn. Pub., Kappa Delta Pi. Home: 2712 Circle Dr Durham NC 27705 Office: 6446 College Station Durham NC 27708

UHRMAN, CELIA, artist, writer; b. New London, Conn., May 14, 1927; d. David Aaron and Pauline (Schwartz) Uhrman; B.A., Bklyn. Coll., 1948, M.A., 1953; postgrad. Tchrs. Coll., Columbia, 1961, U. City N.Y., 1966, Bklyn. Mus. Art Sch., 1956-57, Ph.D. (hon.), Litt.D., 1973. One man shows Leffert Jr. High Sch., Bklyn., 1958, Flatbush C. of C., N.Y.C., 1963, Conn. C. of C., New London, 1962; exhibited in group shows at Smithsonian Instn., Washington, 1958, Springfield (Mass.) Mus. Fine Arts, 1959, Bklyn. Mus., 1959, Old Mystic (Conn.) Art Center, 1959, Carnegie Endowment Internat. Center, N.Y.C., 1959, Lyman Allyn Mus., New London, Conn., 1960, Palacio de La Virreina, Barcelona Spain, 1961, YWCA, Bklyn., 1962, UFT Art Exhibit, N.Y.C., 1963, Soc. of 4 Arts, Palm Beach, Fla., 1964, Perspective 68, Monte-Carlo, Monaco, 1968, George W. Wingate High Sch., Bklyn., 1967, Premier Salon Internat., Charleroi, Belgium, 1968, Palme dor Beaux Arts, Monte-Carlo, 1970, 72, Dibuix-Joan Miro Premi Internacional, Barcelona, Spain, 1970; N.Y. Art Festival, 1970, Internat. Platform Assn. Art Show, Washington, 1971, 73, Ouar Mus., Portugal, 1974, others; represented in permanent collections Bklyn. Coll., Ch. of Evangel, Bklyn.. Tchr., N.Y.C. Sch. System, 1948—; partner Uhrman Studio, 1973—; hon. rep. U.S., Centro Studi E Scambi Internazionali, Rome, Italy, mem. internat. com., 1969—. Recipient award Freedoms Found., George Washington medal of honor, 1964; Diplome d'Honneur Palme d'Or des Beaux Arts Exhbn., Monaco, 1969, 72, Diploma and Gold medal, 1972; decorated Order of Gandhi Award of Honour, Knight Grand Cross, 1972; personal poetry certificate WEFG Stereo, 1970; named Poetry Translator Laureate World Acad. Lang. and Lit., 1972; Poet of Mankind Acad. Philosophy, 1972. Mem. Internat. Arts Guild (Monte-Carlo), World Poetry Soc. Intercontinental (rep. at large 1970—), Internat. Platform Assn. Author: Poetic Ponderances, 1969; A Pause for Poetry, 1970; Poetic Love Fancies, 1970; A Pause for Poetry for Children, 1973; The Chimps Are Coming, 1974; also poems. Home: 1655 Flatbush Av Apt C210 Studio B811 Brooklyn NY 11210

ULLMEN, MARY AGNES, realtor, ins. broker; b. Chgo., June 4, 1912; d. John Baptist and Helen Agnes (Mick) Ullmen; B.A., Rosary Coll., 1934; student St. Mary's Coll. of Notre Dame, 1930-32; postgrad. U. Chgo., 1935-36. Tchr. Morton (Ill.) High Sch., 1934-35, Trinity High Sch., River Forest, Ill., 1935-36, Niles (Ill.) Grammar Sch., 1937-40; sec. Lyon & Healy, Chgo., 1937-40, Schieff, Dahlstream, Terhunde & Harding, Chgo., 1940-45, John E. Colnon & Co., Chgo., 1945-55; asso. Fager Homes, Maywood and Elmhurst, 1955-65; pvt. practice real estate and ins., Oak Park, Ill., 1955-65; owner, broker Ullmen Real Estate, Glen Ellyn, Ill., 1965—. Founder, dir., sec.-treas. Ellyn Corp. custom homes, Glen Ellyn, 1967—. Mem. bd. to assist Chairwomen Ill. 14th Congl. Dist. Democratic party, 1965-66; bd. dirs. The Ellyn Corp. Founder, mgr. Friends of St. Francis animal shelter, 1967—; alumnae bd. Rosary Coll., River Forest, 1945-50. Mem. DuPage Bd. Realtors, Ill., Nat. assns. real estate bds. Democrat. Home: 1917 Summit St Wheaton IL 60187 Office: 485 Forest St Glen Ellyn IL 60137

ULLOM, FAYE MARIE TRAPP (MRS. ROBERT LEE ULLOM), home economist; b. San Bernardino, Cal., May 28, 1925; d. William J.C. and Edith Hazel (Hill) Trapp; A.A., San Bernardino Jr. Coll., 1945; B.A., U. Cal. at Santa Barbara, 1947; m. Robert Lee Ullom, Dec. 23, 1949 (dec. Nov. 1969). Home economist Cal. Electric Power Co., Hemet, Cal., 1947-49, San Bernardino, 1951-64, named changed So. Cal. Edison Co. (merged), Rialto, Cal., 1964-70, Corona, Cal., 1970—. Mem. Am., Cal. (treas. citrus dist. 1971-73) home econ. assns., Pacific Coast Elec. Assn. (home econs. com. 1960—), Home Economists in Bus. (chmn. ways and means com.). Clubs: Altrusa (pres. 1956-58, dir. 1971-72), Interservice Club Council (treas. 1961-62). Home: 548 E Etiwanda Av Rialto CA 92376 Office: 2885 Foothill Blvd San Bernardino CA 92410

ULLOM, MADELINE MARIE, army nurse; b. O'Neill, Neb., Jan. 1, 1911; d. John and Mary Louise (Jones) Ullom; B.S., Incarnate Word Coll., 1947; M.S., Cath. U. Am., 1951 Staff nurse Jefferson Hosp., Phila., 1937-38; commd. 2d lt. Nurse Corps, U.S. Army, 1938, advanced through grades to lt. col., 1958-64; served as ednl. co-ordinator, instr., sch. dir., supr., asst. chief nurse, chief of nursing Service Hosp. Bd. dirs. McCall Day Nursery, El Paso, Tex., 1960. Tucson br. Am. Assn. U. Women rep. Tucson Council Aging, 1968-72, sec., 1969-70, chmn. awards com., 1970. Recipient Commendation medal; decorated Bronze Star. Mem. Internat. Platform Assn., Women's Overseas Service League (pres. Tucson unit 1969-70), Am. Legion (post comdr. 1968; dist. exec. com. 1968-70), Colo. (chmn. pract. nursing council 1961-64), Tex. (career com. 1958-60), El Paso (pres. 1958-60, chmn. dist. coordinating com.) leagues for nursing, Tex. Grad. Nurses Assn., Am. Assn. U. Women, A.A.A.S., El Paso Mental Health Assn. (dir.), Tucson Ret. Officers Assn. (2d v.p. 1969), Acad. Polit. Sci., Am. Acad. Polit. and Social Sci., Tucson Art Center, Santa Cruz Valley Art Assn., Nat. Trust Historic Preservation, Ariz. Acad. Sci., Am. Nurses Assn., Am. Defenders Bataan and Corregidor, Mont., Ariz. hist. socs., Tucson Art Center League, Pi Gamma Mu, Sigma Theta Tau. Clubs: Pilot (2d v.p. Denver 1963-64); Tex. Federation Business and Professional Women's (dir. dist. 8). Home: 2901 E Waverly St Tucson AZ 85716

ULMAN, LUCY THIMANN, educator; b. Vienna, Austria, Jan. 21, 1933; d. Joseph and Maria (Tauber) Thimann; came to U.S., 1939, naturalized, 1945; B.S., Boston U., 1958, Ed.M., 1965; Ed.D., 1974; Ph.D., Heed U., 1973; m. Theodore B. Ulman, Feb. 20, 1954 (div. June 1971); children—Karen Sue, Janet Lee, Geoffrey Samuel, Linda Ann. Sch. adjustment counselor Needham (Mass.) Pub. Schs., 1964-67; staff psychologist Leslie B. Cutler Child Guidance Clinic, Norwood, Mass., 1965-69; asst. prof. Lesley Coll., Cambridge, Mass., 1967-72; v.p., cons. Universal Freedom, Inc., Newton, Mass., 1970—; asso. prof. Newton Coll. Sacred Heart, 1972—; individual practice psychol. counseling, Newton, 1962—. Vis. prof. Heed U., 1972—, Mass. Coll. Optometry, Framingham State Coll., 1973—. Mem. exec. bd. P.T.A. Mason Rice Sch., Newton, 1966-69. Bd. dirs. Washingtonian Hosp., Jamaica Plain, Mass. Mem. Heed U. Alumnae Assn. (dir.), Am., Mass., N.E. psychol. assns., Am. Group Psychotherapy Assn., Am. Personnel and Guidance Assn., Am. Assn. Sex Educators and Counselors, Am. Assn. Marriage and Family Counselors, Am. Assn. U. Profs. Address: 30 Locke Rd Waban MA 02168

ULRICH, RENEE SANDRA, endocrinologist; b. N.Y.C., Aug. 26, 1940; d. Charles and Anna (Granat) Ulrich; B.A., U. Cal. at Los Angeles, 1960, Ph.D., 1966; m. Herbert J. Harwick, Apr. 4, 1971 (dec. July, 1974); 1 dau., Bethany Elise. USPHS postdoctoral fellow U. So. Cal., 1966-67, U. Cal. at Los Angeles, 1968; asst. prof. biology San Fernando Valley State Coll., 1969-70; asst. research neuroendocrinologist dept. psychiatry U. Cal. at Los Angeles, 1971—; cons. Neurobiochemistry Lab VA Hosp., West Los Angeles. Mem. Phi Beta Kappa, Sigma Xi. Contbr. articles to profl. jours. Home: 10750 Wellworth Av Los Angeles CA 90024 Office: 601/t-85 Neurobiochemistry Lab VA Center Wilshire and Sawtelle Blvds Los Angeles CA 90073

ULSHAFER, TRUDY L., assn. exec.; b. Shenandoah, Pa., Jan. 3, 1916; d. Raymond Leo and Violet Mae (Hughes) Ulshafer; grad. McCann's Bus. Coll. Adminstrv. asst. Pa. Assn. for Blind, Harrisburg, 1954-60, exec. sec., 1960—, editor, pub. The Seer, pub. in inkprint and Braille, 1960—. Cons. to programs and services for blind and visually handicapped. Recipient Community Service citation Pa. Acad. Opthalmology and Otolaryngology, 1973. Mem. Internat. Assn. Rehab. Facilities, Am. Assn. Opthalmology, Am. Assn. Workers for Blind (chpt. dir. 1967—), Nat. Rehab. Assn. Home: 2417 Jericho Dr Harrisburg PA 17110 Office: 2843 N Front Harrisburg PA 17110

UMBREIT, LUCILE BURDELLA, educator; b. Kobe, Japan, Nov. 19, 1911; d. Samuel John and Mary Amanda (Bauernfeind) Umbreit; B.A., Radcliffe Coll., 1933; M.A. (Marston fellow in music 1934-36), Vassar Coll., 1936; Barrett fellow in music Wellesley Coll., 1936-37 Asst. music dept. Vassar Coll., 1934-36; with Sweet Briar (Va.) Coll., 1937—, successively instr., asst. prof., asso. prof., 1937-59, prof. music, 1959—, also chmn. dept. music. Mem. Am. Assn. U. Profs., Am. Musicological Soc. Address: Sweet Briar VA 24595

UMSCHEID, SISTER THEOPHANE, nurse educator; b. Manhattan, Kan.; d. Albert A. and Gertrude (Bach) Umscheid; R.N., St. Joseph Sch. Nursing, Concordia, Kan., 1938; A.B., Marymount Coll., 1942; M.S. in Nursing Edn., Cath. U. Am., 1949; postgrad. U. Cal. at San Francisco, 1963-64, 65-66. Dir. schs. of nursing, Kan., 1938-47; head dept. nursing edn. Marymount Coll., Salina, Kan., 1949-64, prof. nursing and psychiat. nursing, also mental health coordinator, 1964-70; dir. mental health services St. Joseph Hosp., El Paso, Tex., 1971—. Vice pres. Kan. Bd. Nursing, 1968-71. Chmn., Salina Council on Human Relations, 1969-70; sec. for bd. dirs. Central Kan. Found. on Alcoholism, 1967-71. Mem. Am. (com. on legislation 1954-56, com. on intergroup relations 1956-58), Kan. (Nurse of Year 1958, dir. pres. 1954-58, state v.p. 1956-58) nurses assns., Nat. League for Nursing, Diocesan Council Cath. Nurses, Nat. Council Cath. Nurses, Kan. Mental Health Assn. (dir.). Contbr. articles to profl. jours. Address: 1837 Grandview Av El Paso TX 79902

UNANGST, FLORENCE BECK (MRS. AUSTIN UNANGST), editor, author; b. N.Y.C., Dec. 31, 1911; d. Peter Petersen and Anna Wilhelmena (Kriegeskotten) Beck; grad. high sch.; D. Humane Lit., Internat. Acad., Hull, Eng., 1971; D. Liberal Arts, Gt. China Arts Coll., Kowloon, Hong Kong, 1972; m. Austin Unangst, Nov. 14, 1941; children—Patricia (Mrs. Vincent Quintalino), Gladys (Mrs. Pat Fedele), Sandra (Mrs. Robert Chizmadia). Reporter Teaneck (N.J.) Times, 1928-30; editor, pub. Poetry Prevue, Bklyn., 1966-73; secretarial position Van Heusen Co., N.Y.C., 1969—. Recipient Clover award Danae, Poetry Club, 1971. Mem. Eastern Centre Poetry Soc. London, Mich. Poetry Soc., Grand Rapids Bards, N.Y. Poetry Forum, Assn. Poetry Therapy (membership chmn.), Ancient Mystical Order Rosae Crucis, Mayans. Author: Mainly Laughter, 1964; Mainly Quatrainly, 1965; The Searching Soul, 1966; Past & Present, 1967; Love and Stuff, 1967; Mellowing Years, 1970; Memos to Myself, 1972; Lines and Points, 1968. Editor anthologies. Asst. editor Driftwood East; contbg. editor Ocarina. Home: 88 Church Av Brooklyn NY 11218 Office: 417 Fifth Av New York City NY 10016

UNDERHILL, ANNE BARBARA, astrophysicist; b. Vancouver, B.C., Can., June 12, 1920; d. Frederic Clare and Irene Anna (Creery) Underhill; B.A., U. B.C., 1942, M.A., 1944; Ph.D., U. Chgo., 1948; D.Sc., York U., Toronto, Ont., Can., 1969. Came to U.S., 1970. Astrophysicist Dominion Astrophys. Obs., Victoria, B.C., 1949-62; prof. astrophysics U. Utrecht (Netherlands), 1962-70; chief lab. optical astronomy Goddard Space Flight Center, Greenbelt, Md., 1970—. Canadian Fedn. U. Women fellow, 1944-45, 47-48; NRC fellow, 1948-49. Mem. Am., Royal astron. socs., Astron. Soc. Pacific. Episcopalian. Author: The Early Type Stars. Contbr. articles to profl. jours. Home: 9004 Breezewood Terrace Apt 302 Greenbelt MD 20770 Office: Code 670 Goddard Space Flight Center Greenbelt MD 20771

UNDERWOOD, JANE HAMMONS (MRS. JOHN W. UNDERWOOD), educator; b. Ft. Bliss, Tex., Oct. 30, 1931; d. Frank and Lydia (Williams) Hammons; A.A., Imperial Valley Coll., 1957; B.A., U. Cal. at Riverside, 1960; M.A., U. Cal. at Los Angeles, 1962, Ph.D., 1964; m. Van K. Hainline, Oct. 20, 1947 (div. Apr. 1966); children—Michael K., Susan J.; m. 2d, John W. Underwood, July 4, 1968; 1 dau., Anne K. Asst. prof. U. Cal., Riverside, 1963-68; research anthropology Yap Islands, 1964, 65-66; prof. anthropology U. Ariz., Tucson, 1968—. Woodrow Wilson fellow, 1960-61; UCR jr. faculty fellow, 1968. Fellow Am. Anthrop. Assn., A.A.A.S.; mem. Am. Assn. Phys. Anthropologists, Assn. for Study Human Biology, Internat. Assn. Human Biologists, Sigma Xi. Contbr. articles to profl. jours. Home: 2228 E 4th St Tucson AZ 85719

UNDERWOOD, MARY BETTY (MRS. RAYMOND P. UNDERWOOD), author; b. Rockford, Ill., July 4, 1921; d. Clarence Scott and Ethel (Todd) Anderson; A.B., Pa. State U., 1942; m. Raymond P. Underwood, Nov. 6, 1943; children—Douglas Mark, Jeffrey Kirk, Barbara Lael. Publs. analyst Dept. Justice, Washington, 1942-43; asst. editor Houghton Mifflin Pub. Co., Boston, 1944-48; pub. relations, mem. editorial staff George Washington U. Med. Center, 1969; adminstrv. asst. Lane County Council on Alcoholism, Eugene, Ore., 1970-71; office mgr., editor Ore. Civil Liberties Union, Portland, 1972. Chmn., Multnomah County Welfare Adv. Com., 1960-62; mem. regional com. Am. Friends Service Com., 1971; mem. Ore. Council for Women's Equality, 1971—, Ore. Gov.'s Com. on Status Women, 1972—. Bd. govs. U. Ore. Art Mus., 1970-72. Recipient John W. White Grad. award, 1942. Mem. Am. Assn. Univ. Women (com. chmn.), Reed Coll. Women's Com. (life), League Women Voters, Planned Parenthood, Common Cause, Women's Internat. League for Peace and Freedom, Phi Beta Kappa, Kappa Alpha Theta, Phi Kappa Phi, Alpha Lambda Delta, Pi Gamma Mu. Democrat. Mem. Soc. Friends. Author: The Tamarack Tree, 1971 (Nat. Jane Addams Book award 1972); The Forge and the Forest, 1975. Contbr. to Childcraft Ency., 1963. Home: 6236 SW Tower Way Portland OR 97221

UNDERWOOD, SUSIE, ednl. cons.; b. Rome, Ga., Oct. 6, 1917; d. James Thomas and Emma Nevada (Evans) Underwood; A.B., Shorter Coll., 1940; M.Ed., U. Ga., 1949; postgrad. (NSF fellow), U. Wyo., 1957, 58, 60, Columbia U., 1964-66. Tchr. 2d grade Rome City Sch. System, 1940-44, high sch. math., 1944-61, tchr. math., math. cons., 1961-66; math. cons. Ga. State Dept. Edn., Atlanta, 1966-67, elementary and migrant edn. cons., 1967—. Tchr. Vets. Night Sch., 1950-55, U. Ga. Campus Center, Rome, 1958-66. Mem. N.E.A., Ga. Assn. Educators, Ga. Assn. Curriculum Dirs., Nat. Council Tchrs. Math., Nat. Assn. State Elementary Edn. Cons., Ga. Dept. Elementary Sch. Prins., Delta Kappa Gamma, Kappa Delta Pi. Office: 156 Trinity Av SW Atlanta GA 30303

UNGER, BERTHA MAE BROWN (MRS. MAX UNGER), nurse; b. Ellenville, N.Y., Apr. 20, 1916; d. Walter and Cora (Stedner) Brown; B.S., Columbia Tchrs. Coll., 1956, M.A., 1958; m. Max Unger, Dec. 30, 1937; children—Nancy T., David Gibbs. Instr. nursing Columbia, 1956-59; staff nurse Neurol. Inst., Presbyn. Hosp., N.Y.C., 1953-56; lectr. nursing Hunter Coll., 1961; asst. supt. nursing Neuropsychiat. Inst., U. Cal. at Los Angeles, 1962-68, supt. nursing services, 1968—, clin. instr. psychiat. nursing, 1963—, lectr. faculty of medicine dept. psychiatry; lectr. psychiat. nursing. Mem. Cal. Nurses Assn. (bd. mem. 1965-66), Nat. League Nursing, Am., Internat. assns. suicidology, Hosp. Council So. Cal. (dir. nurses council), Alumni Assn. Div. Nursing Edn. Tchrs. Coll. Columbia (life), Pi Lambda Theta, Kappa Delta Pi. Home: 940 N Bundy Dr Los Angeles CA 90049 Office: 760 Westwood Plaza Los Angeles CA 90024

UNTERBERGER, BETTY MILLER (MRS. ROBERT RUPPE UNTERBERGER), educator; b. Glasgow, Scotland (parents Am. citizens); d. Joseph C. and Leah (Miller) Miller; B.A. (Forensic scholar) magna cum laude, Syracuse U., 1943; M.A., Radcliffe Coll., 1946; Ph.D., Duke, 1950; m. Robert R. Unterberger, June 29, 1945; children—Glen Alan, Gail Lynn, Gregg Russell. Asst. prof. history East Carolina Coll., Greenville, N.C., 1948-50; lectr. history Whittier Coll., summers 1950-54, dir. Liberal Arts Center for Adults, 1954-61, asso. prof. history, polit. sci., 1957-61; asso. prof. history Cal. State Coll., Fullerton, 1961-65, prof. history, 1965-67, grad. coordinator dept. history, 1966-67; vis. prof. U. Hawaii, 1967; prof. history Texas A and M U., 1967—; cons. Fund for Adult Edn., 1959-60. Exec. sec. U. Seven Seas, Whittier, Cal., 1958-60. Recipient Pacific Coast award Am. Hist. Assn., 1956; research grants Am. Philos. Soc., 1960, 62; distinguished teaching award Cal. Legislature 1966. Mem. Am. Assn. Advancement Slavic Studies, Far Western Conf. on Slavic Studies (founding mem.) History Guild, Am. Hist. Assn., Am., Pacific hist. assns., Rocky Mountain, Southwestern social sci. assns., Conf. on Peace Research in History, Rocky Mountain Slavic Studies Assn. (v.p. 1972—), Soc. Historians Am. Fgn. Relations, Orgn. Am. Historians, Pi Sigma Alpha, Phi Beta Kappa, Phi Alpha Theta, Delta Sigma Rho. Author: America's Siberian Expedition, 1918-20, 1956; American Intervention in the Russian Civil War, 1968; articles profl. jours. Home: 3706 Oak Ridge Dr Bryan TX 77801 Office: Tex A and M U College Station TX 77843

UNTERBERGER, HILMA, psychologist; b. Wilkes-Barre, Pa., Feb. 28, 1927; d. Maurice and Mary (Mittleman) Unterberger; B.A., Bryn Mawr Coll., 1948, M.A., 1950. Alcoholism coordinator Mass. Dept. Pub. Health, Boston, 1959-69; asso. area dir. Cambridge-Somerville Mental Health and Retardation Center, Cambridge, Mass., 1969—; cons. in field. Bd. dirs. Flynn House, Boston, 1963—, pres., 1969-71. Mem. Am. Psychol. Assn., Am. Pub. Health Assn. Contbr. articles to profl. jours. Home: 64 Halifax St Jamaica Plain MA 02130 Office: 9 Sacramento St Cambridge MA 02138

UNTERKOEFLER, FRANCES AGNES, stock broker; b. Phila., Apr. 29, 1934; d. Emil E.J. and Frances J. (Raith) Unterkoefler; student U. Pa., 1966-69. Asst. underwriter Liberty Mutual Ins., Phila., 1951-55; exec. sec. Pacific Nat. Ins., Phila., 1955-58; regional sec. Waddell & Reed, Inc., Phila., 1958-69; corporate sec., asst. treas. Interamerica Investors Services, Inc., Phila., 1969—, dir. 1971—; dir. Puerto Rican Investors Fund, Inc., San Juan, I.I.S. Corp. and subsidiaries, San Juan. Republican jr. committeewoman, Springfield Twp., Pa., 1966-72. Mem. Ind. Broker Dealers Assn. Home: 911 Springhave Rd Springfield PA 19064 Office: 2000 McLeary Santurce PR 00911

UPRICHARD, MURIEL, educator; b. Regina, Sask., Can., Nov. 21, 1911; d. Joseph and Frances (Murphy) Uprichard; B.A. with honors, Queens U., Kingston, Ont., 1943; M.A., Smith Coll., 1944; Ph.D., U. London, 1947. Elementary tchr. Sask. Pub. Schs., 1930-42; research in edn., 1943-47; dir. study Florence Nightingale, Internat. Found. for Internat. Council of Nurses, 1947-48; nat. dir. Canadian Jr. Red Cross, 1949-55; asst. prof. U. Toronto Sch. Nursing, 1955-59, asso. prof., 1959-65; asso. research psychologist, lectr. nursing U. Cal. at Los Angeles, 1965-71; prof., dir. Sch. Nursing, U. B.C., Vancouver, 1971—. Cons. in field of nursing. Brit. Council scholar, 1944-47. Mem. Canadian Assn. U. Schs. Nursing, Canadian, B.C. psychol. assns., Vancouver Inst., Canadian, Vancouver University Women's Club, Nat. League for Nursing, Royal Soc. for Promotion of Health, Canadian, B.C. tchrs. assns. Contbr. articles to profl. jours. Home: 4858 W 2d Ave Vancouver BC V6R 1K9 Canada

UPTON, LUCILE MORRIS (MRS. EUGENE V. UPTON), writer; b. Dadeville, Mo., July 22, 1898; d. Albert G. and Veda (Wilson) Morris; student Drury Coll., 1915-16, S.W. Mo. State Coll., 1917-20; m. Eugene V. Upton, July 22, 1936 (dec. July 1947). Pub. sch. tchr. Dadeville Mo., 1917-19, Everton, Mo., 1920-22, Roswell, N.M., 1921-23; tchr. creative writing Adult Edn. div. Drury Coll., 1947-52; reporter Denver Express, 1923-24, El Paso (Tex.) Times, 1924-25, Springfield (Mo.) Newspapers, Inc., 1926-64, writer weekly hist. column, 1964—. Mem. Springfield City Council, 1967-71, Springfield Hist. Sites Bd., 1972—. Named Woman of Achievement Woman's div. Springfield C. of C., 1967. Mem. Mo. Writers Guild (past pres.), State Hist. Soc. Mo., Greene County (Mo.), White River Valley hist. socs. Conglist. Author: Bald Knobbers, 1939; (booklet) Battle of Wilson's Creek, 1950. Contbr. short stories, articles to mags., newspapers. Home: 1305 S Kimbrough Springfield MO 65807

URBAN, EVA AMALIE, ophthalmologist; b. Berlin, Germany, Sept. 30, 1924; d. Fritz Albert and Helene (Schall) Urban; M.D., U. Med. Sch., Berlin, Germany, 1951. Came to U.S., 1952, naturalized, 1957. Intern, St. Joseph Hosp., Ann Arbor, Mich., 1952-53; resident Univ. Hosp., Oklahoma City, 1953-55; practice medicine, specializing in ophthalmology, East Lansing, Mich.; mem. staffs St. Laurence, Ingham Med. hosps.; ophthalmic cons. Mich. Sch. for Blind, Lansing, 1958—. Violinist, Lansing Symphony Orch., 1955—. Diplomate Am. Bd. Ophthalmology. Lutheran. Club: Zonta (Lansing, Mich.). Home: 540 Glenmoor Rd East Lansing MI 48823 Office: 241 E Saginaw St East Lansing MI 48823

URBANSKI, ANNA FRANCES, savs. and loan exec.; b. Victoria, Mich., Aug. 25, 1905; d. Joseph Peter and Anna (Mravinec) Wertin; certificate bus. adminstrn. Platt Comml. Coll., 1925; m. Leo J. Urbanski, Oct. 6, 1945; m. Lloyd E. Richardson, June 23, 1973. Bookkeeper Provident Savs. & Loan Assn., St. Joseph, Mo., 1925-50, mgr.-sec., 1950—, dir., 1962—, sec. bd. dirs., 1972—. Active local charitable orgns. Mem. Mo. Savs. and Loan League (dir. 1944-45, 48-49, 50-52), Kansas City Savs. and Loan Controllers (sec. 1952-68), St. Joseph Woman's Bowling Assn. (dir. 1940-68, sec. 1940-68), Daus. of Isabella (regent 1945-47), Cath. Order Foresters, St. Ann's Altar Soc., Phi Eta. Clubs: St. Joseph Camera, Elizabeth Prescott (pres. 1972—). Home: 3101 Floral Av St Joseph MO 64506 Office: 513 Francis St St Joseph MO 64501

URDANG, CONSTANCE HENRIETTE (MRS. DONALD FINKEL), author; b. N.Y.C.; d. Harry Rudman and Annabel (Schafran) Urdang; A.B., Smith Coll., 1943; M.F.A., State U. Ia., 1956; m. Donald Finkel, Aug. 14, 1956; children—Elizabeth Antonia, Thomas Noah, Amy Maria. Recipient Carleton Coll. Centennial award for prose, 1967. Author: Charades and Celebrations, 1965; (novel) Natural History, 1969; The Picnic in the Cemetery, 1975. Contbr. poetry to numerous anthologies. Home: 6943 Columbia Pl St Louis MO 63130

URE, BARBARA ANN, physician; b. Mpls., Mar. 11, 1928; d. William and Carolyn (Jensen) Ure; B.A., Ohio Wesleyan U., 1948; B.S., U. Minn., 1951, M.D., 1953. Intern Kings County Hosp., Bklyn., 1953-54; resident Bronx VA Hosp., 1954-56, Lenox Hill Hosp., 1956-57; Child Devel. Center, N.Y.C., 1957-59; supr. Hillside Hosp., N.Y.C., 1959-62, chief Adolescent Pavillion, 1962-64; coordinator Mental Health Planning for Alaska, 1964-65; dir. children's services Alaska Div. Mental Health, 1965-67; pvt. practice child psychiatry, 1967-69. Dir. Anchorage Childrens Center, Inc., 1970—; mem. Anchorage Child Abuse Bd. Diplomate in psychiatry and child psychiatry Am. Bd. Neurology and Psychiatry. Mem. Am. Psychiat. Assn., Am. Acad. Child Psychiatry. Home: 2108 Roosevelt Dr Anchorage AK 99501

URE, HELEN DAVIS BOWRING (MRS. JAMES W. URE III), civic worker; b. Salt Lake City, Feb. 23, 1913; d. William D. and Hannah (Davis) Bowring; student Latter-day Saints Bus. Coll., U. Utah; m. James W. Ure III, Jan. 17, 1938; children—James W. IV, Martha (Mrs. Orson Niederhauser), Jonathan D., Joseph McCune. Sec., Home Owners Loan Corp., Salt Lake City, 1935-38; clk. Bd. 13 Selective Service, 1941-43; pres. Libbie Edward Elementary P.T.A., 1951-53, Granite Council P.T.A.'s, 1955-57; v.p. Utah Congress Parents and Tchrs., 1957-58, pres., 1961-64; bd. mgrs. Nat. Congress Parents and Tchrs., 1961-64, v.p., 1965-68; mem. Utah Womens Legislative Council, 1958-64, edn. chmn., 1973-75; mem. Salt Lake County Bd. Health, 1961—, Utah Council Econ. Edn., 1961—; mem. legislative council Com. on Sch. Finance, 1963-64; sec.-treas. Salt Lake City Center for Prevention Suicide, 1964-66; mem. Utah Bd. Edn., 1964-72, vice chmn., 1969-71, chmn., 1971-72; chmn. State Head Start Coordinating Council, 1968-70; vice chmn. bd. dirs. Model Cities, 1969-70; state chmn. Nat. Library Week, 1965; mem. State Adv. Com. for Head Start, 1965-70; chmn. Utah Com. on Children and Youth, 1965-69; chmn. Gov.'s com. White House Conf. Children and Youth, 1969-71; mem. Nat. Com. for Support Pub. Schs., 1966—; chmn. sub-com. finance and econs. 8 State Project Designing Edn. for future, 1968-70; mem. adv. com. Utah Tng. Center for Prevention and Control Juvenile Delinquency; mem. City-County Bd. Health; mem. Utah Gov.'s Task Force on Venereal Disease, 1973-74; chmn. Salt Lake County Commn. on Youth, 1974—. Bd. dirs. Salt Lake Area League Women Voters, Community Services Council, Big Brothers Am.; trustee Youth Tobacco Adv. Council. Recipient U.S. Treasury Dept.'s citation for support sch. savs. program, 1964; Distinguished Service award Utah Library Assn., 1966; named Man of Year in Edn. for Utah, Phi Delta Kappa, 1964, Woman of Yr., Delta Kappa Gamma, 1971. Mem. Utah Pub. Health Assn. (dir., pres.-elect 1973, pres. 1974—), Mut. Improvement Assn. (speech and drama dir., activities councilor to pres.), Alpha Delta Kappa (hon.). Mem. Ch. of Jesus Christ of Latterday Saints. Home: 3105 Imperial St Salt Lake City UT 84106

UREN-STUBBINGS, HILDA RUBENA, bibliographer; b. Hayle, Cornwall, Eng., Dec. 14, 1914; d. John Percival and Florence Mary (Williams) Uren; B.A. summa cum laude, Stetson U., 1960, M.A. in Am. Studies, 1962; Ph.D. in Comparative Lit., Vanderbilt U., 1968; m. George A. Stubbings, Nov. 16, 1935; children—Katharine (Mrs. Stanley Mott), Robert George, Carl Herbert, Suzanne (Mrs. David Willis). Asst. prof. Warner Pacific Coll., 1967-68, Willamette U., 1968-70, Clackamas Community Coll., 1970-72; bibliographer Internat. Scholarly Book Services, Inc., Portland, Ore., 1974—. Charles E. Merrill grantee Am. studies, 1957-59; recipient Harry L. Taylor prize humanities, 1958. Mem. Scroll and Key, Phi Beta Kappa. Author: Renaissance Spain in Its Literary Relations with England and France: A Critical Bibliography, 1969. Address: Route 1 Box 40A Beaver Creek OR 97004

USDIN, VERA RUDIN, biochemist; b. Vienna, Austria, May 31, 1925; d. Robert and Natalie (Adlersburg) Rudin; came to U.S., 1941, naturalized, 1947; B.S., Sterling Coll., 1945; M.A., Duke, 1947; Ph.D., Ohio State U., 1951; m. Earl Usdin, Dec. 12, 1949; children—Barbara, Theodore, Sylvia, Steven. Research asso. U. Pa., 1951-54; guest investigator Medicinska Nobel Institutet, Stockholm, Sweden, 1955-56; research chemist Rohm & Haas, Phila. 1956-59; asso. prof. N.M. Highlands U., 1959-62; head br. Melpar, Inc., Falls Church, Va., 1962-67; group leader Gillette Research Inst., Rockville, Md., 1967—. Recipient Sigma Delta Epsilon nat. award, 1962. Mem. Am. Chem. Soc., Am. Inst. Biol. Scis., Soc. Exptl. Biology and Medicine (sec.-treas. D.C. sect. 1971-74), Am. Soc. Cell Biology, Internat. Assn. Dental Research, A.A.A.S., Sigma Xi. Contbr. articles to profl. jours. Home: 2924 N Oxford St Arlington VA 22207 Office: Gillette Research Inst 1413 Research Blvd Rockville MD 20850

USHER, ELIZABETH REUTER (MRS. HARRY T. USHER), librarian; b. Seward, Neb.; d. Paul and Elizabeth (Meyer) Reuter; diploma Concordia Tchrs. Coll., Seward; B.S. in Edn., U. Neb., 1942; B.S. in Library Sci., U. Ill., 1944; m. Harry Thomas Usher, Feb. 25, 1950. Tchr. Zion Luth. Sch., Platte Center, Neb., St. Paul's Luth. Sch., Paterson, N.J.; library asst. charge res. book reading room U. Neb., 1942-43; asst. circulation librarian Mich. State U., 1944-45; librarian Cranbrook Acad. Art, Bloomfield Hills, Mich., 1945-48; catalog and reference librarian Met. Mus. Art, N.Y., 1948-53, head cataloger and reference librarian, 1953-54, asst. librarian, 1954-61, chief of the art reference library, 1961-68, chief librarian, 1968—, acting librarian, 1954-57. Trustee N.Y. Met. Reference and Research Library Agy., 1968—, sec. bd. trustees, 1971—. Mem. Spl. Libraries Assn. (chmn. mus. div. 1954-55; pres. N.Y. chpt. 1957-58, dir. 1963-65; assn. pres. 1967-68, dir. 1960-63, 66-69), Am. Assn. Museums, Coll. Art Assn. (chmn. libraries session 1972-73), N.Y. Library Club, ARLIS/NA. Lutheran. Contbr. articles to profl. periodicals. Home: 5 Peter Cooper Rd New York City NY 10010 Office: Fifth Av at 82d St New York City NY 10028

USINGER, DOROTHY MARIE RHODES (MRS. PHILIP C. USINGER), ret. govt. ofcl.; b. Seattle; d. Frederick N. and Julia (Wetherbee) Rhodes; B.A., U. Wash.; J.D., Golden Gate Coll., 1951; m. Philip C. Usinger, May 14, 1949. Agt., U.S. Treasury Dept., San Francisco, 1943-51, auditor, 1951-58, chief audit and statutory notice sect. Appellate Div., Internal Revenue Service, San Francisco, 1958-70. Mem. D.A.R. (regent San Francisco chpt. 1955-57), Nat. Soc. Colonial Dames XVII Century (2d v.p. Cal. 1957-59, nat. publicity chmn. 1960-65, pres. chpt. 1964-66), Sonoma County Geneal. Soc. (dir. 1973-74), Piscataqua Pioneers Me. and N.H., Desc. Colonial Clergy New Eng., Daus. Founders and Patriots Am. (Cal. treas. 1956-58), Magna Charta Dames, Huguenot Soc. London, New Eng. Women, Soc. Descs. Knights of Garter, Jedediah Smith Hist. Soc., Nat. Huguenot Soc. (registrar chpt. 1968-74), Ams. Royal Descent, Cal. Heritage Council, Am. Assn. U. Women, Nat. Assn. Ret. Fed. Employees (editor newsletter Santa Rosa chpt.), Cal. Geneal. Soc., Zeta Tau Alpha. Conglist. Club: Internat. Knife and Fork (Santa Rosa). Home: 510 Country Club Dr Santa Rosa CA 95401

UTZ, KATHRYN ELIZABETH, educator; b. Attica, O., Sept. 1, 1910; d. George Frederick and Lorena Belle (Cook) Utz; student Tiffin Bus. U., 1927-28; Toledo U., 1929-30; A.B., Capital U., 1941, B.S. in Edn., 1941; M.A., Ohio State U., 1947, Ph.D., 1952; postgrad. U. Cin., 1941-42, Western Res. U., 1953. With DeVilbiss Co., Toledo, 1928-30; teletype operator Owens-Ill. Glass Co., Toledo, 1930-37; tchr. rural high schs., Trenton, O., 1941-42, Bucyrus, O., 1942-43, Shaker Heights (O.) High Sch., 1952-53; asst. Ohio State U., 1947-51, instr., 1951-52; faculty U. Wis., Whitewater, 1953—, asso. prof., 1955-59, prof. English, 1959—; Smith-Mundt Act vis. prof. U. Recife (Brazil), 1957-58, Instituto da Educacao, Belo Horizonte, Brazil, 1957-58. Served with Signal Corps, WAC, 1943-46. Mem. Nat., Wis. councils tchrs. English, Modern Lang. Assn., Coll. English Assn., Wis. Acad. Scis., Arts and Letters, Am. Assn. U. Profs., Am. Assn. U. Women, The Assn. U. Wis. Faculties, Am. Studies Assn., Ohio Hist. Soc., Ohio Geneal. Soc., D.A.R., Phi Kappa Phi (hon.). Democrat. Lutheran. Home: 968 W Conger St Whitewater WI 53190

UZMAN, BETTY GEREN, physician, educator; b. Ft. Smith, Ark., Nov. 17, 1922; d. Benton Asbury and Myra Estelle (Petty) Geren; student Ft. Smith Jr. Coll., 1939-40; B.S., U. Ark., 1942; M.D., Washington U., St. Louis, 1945; m. Lahut Uzman, Dec. 17, 1955 (dec. Nov. 1962); 1 dau., Betty Tuba. Intern, pathology Children's Hosp., Boston, 1945-46; resident Barnes Hosp., St. Louis, 1946-48; Am. Cancer Soc. research fellow Mass. Inst. Tech., Cambridge, 1948-50; chief ultrastructure lab. Children's Cancer Research Found., Boston, 1950-71; asso. prof. pathology Harvard Med. Sch., Boston, 1967-71, prof., 1971-72; prof. pathology La. State U.-Shreveport Med. Sch., 1974—; vis. prof. zoology U. Ark., Fayetteville, 1972-74; cons. cancer research program St. Edward Mercy Hosp. and head research dept. Sparks Regional Med. Center, Ft. Smith, 1972-74. Recipient Weinstein award United Cerebral Palsy, 1964; decorated Order Andres Bello 3d class (Venezuela). Address: La State U-Shreveport Med Center PO Box 3932 Shreveport LA 71130

VACCA, LINNEA BRANDWEIN (MRS. ROBERT ANDREW VACCA), educator; b. Chgo., Apr. 18, 1939; d. William Albert and Ida (Roppolo) Brandwein; M.A. (Univ. fellow 1965-68), U. Chgo., 1969, postgrad., 1969—; m. Robert Andrew Vacca, Dec. 14, 1968; children—David, Thomas. Various office positions Orthogenic Sch. of the U. Chgo., 1959-65; asst. prof. English and humanistic studies St. Mary's Coll., Notre Dame, Ind., 1969—. Editor and researcher for Bruno Bettelheim, 1970—. Bd. dirs. Early Childhood Devel. Center, 1974—. U. Paris Exchange fellow, 1967-68. Mem. Am. Assn. U. Profs. (del. nat. conv. 1973), Am. Philol. Assn. Home: 525 Napoleon St South Bend IN 46617 Office: Box 71 Madeleva Hall Saint Mary's College Notre Dame IN 46556

VACCARA, BEATRICE LILLY NEWMAN (MRS. JOHN F. VACCARA), govt. ofcl.; b. N.Y.C., Sept. 20, 1922; d. Wilfred and Gussie (Newman) Newman; B.A., cum laude, Bklyn. Coll., 1943; M.A., Columbia, 1944; m. John F. Vaccara, June 15, 1944; 1 son, Richard John. Instr. econ. Bklyn. Coll., 1944; research asst. Nat. Bur. Econ. Research, N.Y.C., 1944-49; economist U.S. Dept. Agr., Washington, 1949-50; bus. economist, U.S. Dept. of Labor, Washington, 1950-54; research asso. Brookings Instn., 1954-59; asst. chief Nat. Econ. Div. Office of Bus. Econs. U.S. Dept. Commerce, Washington, 1959-65, coordinator econ. growth studies, 1965-71, chief econ. growth div., 1971—. Exec. com. conf. on research in income and wealth Nat. Bur. Econ. Research. Fellow Am. Statis. Assn.; mem. Am. Econ. Assn., Washington Statis. Soc. (pres. 1971-72). Author articles and books in field. Home: 700 New Hampshire Av NW Washington DC 20037 Office: US Dept Commerce Washington DC 20230

VACHA, KATHRYN HARRIET, educator; b. Washington County, Ia., July 18, 1919; d. Melo G. and Myrtle (Murdock) Vacha; B.A., Ia. State Teachers Coll., 1947; M.A., Columbia U. Teacher's Coll., 1956, Ed.D., 1961. Tchr. Joint Oil Co. Schs., Maracaibo, Venezuela, 1946-50, Des Moines, 1944-46, Wapello, Ia., 1942-44, Washington County (Ia.) Schs., 1937-41; asst. to coordinator student teaching, prof. edn. State U. N.Y. at Oswego, 1957-61; asst. dir. grad. studies, prof. edn. Western Conn. State Coll., 1962—; elem. edn. cons. Row-Peterson Pub. Co., 1950-55. Bd. dir. No. Fairfield County chpt. A.R.C. Mem. Eastern States Assn. Tchr. Edn. (program chmn. 1965-68, v.p. 1968-69, pres. 1969-70), Assn. Student Edn. (mem. publs. com. 1967-69), Am. Assn. U. Women, Nat., Conn. edn. assns., Comparative Edn. Soc., New Eng. Assn. Tchr. Educators (membership chmn.), Delta Kappa Gamma (chpt. chmn. profl. devel. and chmn. publicity), Pi Lambda Theta, Kappa Delta Pi. Home: 203 R Southern Blvd Danbury CT 06810 Office: Western Conn State Coll Danbury CT 06810

VACHON, VIRGINIA LEA STOWE (MRS. NORMAN J. VACHON), social worker; b. Balt.; d. Thomas Godwin and Susan (Hobbs) Stowe; B.A., The Kings Coll., 1951; M.S., Boston U., 1953; m. Norman J. Vachon, Aug. 20, 1966. Psychiat. social worker Akron (O.) Child Guidance Center, 1953-55; case worker Family and Childrens Soc., Balt., 1955-60; sch. social worker So. Berkshire Regional Sch. Dist., Sheffield, Mass., 1960—. Social work cons. Pines Nursing Home, Great Barrington, Mass., Geer Meml. Convalescent Hosp., North Canaan, Conn.; part-time family counsellor Family and Childrens Service, Pittsfield, Mass., 1961-63; cons. social work group therapist Avalon Sch., Monterey, Mass., 1974—. Bd. dirs., mem. area bd. Berkshire Mental Health Center, Pittsfield. Named alumni of the year The King's Coll., 1968. Mem. Nat. Assn. Social Workers (chpt. sec. 1967—), Acad. Certified Social Workers, Mass. Assn. Sch. Adjustment Counsellors (chpt. sec.-treas. 1966—, exec. com. 1972—, chpt. pres. 1972-73, 1st v.p. 1973-74), Nat. Assn. Christians in Social Work (dir. 1954-57), Mass. Conf. on Social Welfare. Home: S Main St Sheffield MA 01257 Office: Box 384 Sheffield MA 01257

VACHULE, JO ANN (MRS. JAMES FRANCIS VACHULE), newspaperwoman; b. Port Arthur, Tex., Nov. 14, 1926; d. Joe Nelson and Annie Pearl (Matthews) Eidom; B.J., U. Tex., 1950; m. James Francis Vachule, July 7, 1950; children—Joan Frances, Jan Kathryn. Newspaper reporter Port Arthur (Tex.) News, 1944-47; reporter Austin (Tex.) Am.-Statesman, 1948-50; reporter Ft. Worth Star-Telegram, 1950-53, food editor, 1963—. Recipient Tex. Headliner Club award, 1966. Mem. Mortar Bd., Theta Sigma Phi. Democrat. Methodist. Home: 7308 Madiera St Fort Worth TX 76112 Office: 400 W 7th St Fort Worth TX 76102

VADALA, JULIA ANN, govt. ofcl.; b. N.Y.C., July 27, 1942; d. Anthony Joseph and Shirley Donaline (Harris) V.; B.A., U. Colo., 1964, M.A., 1969. Program coordinator Western Interstate Commn. for Higher Edn., Boulder, Colo., 1967-70; White House fellow for v.p. White House, Washington, 1970-71; spl. asst. for external affairs Office Sec. Dept. Health, Edn. and Welfare, Washington, 1971-73, dep. asst. sec. for human devel., 1973—; dep. dir. Cabinet Com. on Human Resources, White House, Washington, 1973. Mem. White House Fellows Assn., Am. Polit. Sci. Assn., Alpha Omicron Pi, Pi Sigma Alpha. Republican. Episcopalian. Editor (with Kevin P. Bunnell) Medical Edn. for Sparsely Settled States, 1968; (with K. P. Bunnell) Effective State Board Leadership on Community College Devel., 1969; Hispano Library Service for Arizona, Colorado and New Mexico, 1970. Home: 308 Kentucky Av Alexandria VA 22305 Office: 330 Independence Av Washington DC 20201

VAIDEN, CAROL KELLY (MRS. H. WAYNE VAIDEN JR.), journalist; b. N.Y.C., July 1, 1943; d. Albert Bolling and Dorothy (Holton) Kelly; B.S., Miss. State Coll. for Women, 1965; m. H. Wayne Vaiden Jr., Jan. 25, 1969. With Memphis Press-Scimitar, 1965—, writer Chatterbox column, 1971—. Team capt. Memphis Women's Tennis League, 1974. Mem. Women in Communication (pres. 1972-73), Subsidium, Memphis Bar Aux., St. Augustines Guild, Les Passees, Memphis Symphony League, D.A.R. Episcopalian. Home: 3253 N Waynoka Circle Memphis TN 38111 Office: 495 Union Memphis TN 38101

VAIL, BETH, educator; b. Forrest, Ill., Sept. 20, 1920; d. Charles McKinley and Mary Mae (Horine) Vail; B.S., Eastern Ill. U., 1947; M.S., U. Denver, 1948; postgrad. U. Ill., 1944-46, Syracuse U., 1951-52; Ed.D., Ind. U., 1956. Elementary sch. tchr., Ill., 1940-43, Lab. Sch., Muncie, Ind., 1948-50; with Ball State U., Muncie, Ind., 1948—, prof. philosophy and psychology, 1957—. Mem. Ohio Valley Philos. Soc. (sec.-treas. 1965-68), Comparative Edn. Assn. (charter), N.E.A., Internat. Arabian Horse Assn., Philosophy Soc., Delta Zeta. Republican. Author: The Elementary Education Selection Research Project, 1968. Research in selection and retention tchr. candidates. Home: Rural Route 9 Muncie IN 47302 Office: Ball State U TC Room 312 Muncie IN 47306

VAILLANCOURT, PAULINE MARIETTE, med. librarian; b. Fall River, Mass.; d. Leo E. and Rhea (Godbout) Vaillancourt; B.S. in Biology, St. John's U., Bklyn., 1947; M.S. in Library Sci., Columbia, 1953, Ph.D., 1968 Periodicals librarian Nat. Health Library, 1949-51; librarian Sch. Nursing Library, Mary Immaculate Hosp., Jamaica, N.Y., 1951-58, Kings Park (N.Y.) State Hosp., 1958-60; med. librarian Meml. Sloan-Kettering Cancer Center, N.Y.C., 1960-68; pvt. library cons., 1968—; editor Scientific Information Notes, Sci. Assos. Internat., N.Y.C., 1969-70; vis. asso. prof. librarianship State U.N.Y. at Albany, 1962, asso. prof. library sci., 1970—; lectr. Sch. Library Service, Columbia, 1968; vis. asso. prof. L.I. U., 1969; Cons. Queensboro Tb and Health Assn., 1952-54, United Hosp. Fund N.Y., 1955. Mem. Spl. Libraries Assn. (chmn. biol. scis. 1951-52, chmn. scholarship and student fund com. 1953-54, sec. N.Y. chpt. 1956-57), Med. (chmn. hosp. sect. 1956-57), Am. library assns., A.A.A.S., N.Y. Acad. Scis., St. John's U. Alumni Fedn., Assn. Computing Machinery, Columbia Alumni Assn., A.A.A.S., Delta Psi Gamma. Clubs: N.Y. Library (counselor 1964-68), Young Rep. (2d v.p. 7th dist. N.Y. 1951); Soroptimist (sec. 1959-60) (Huntington, N.Y.). Author: Bibliographic Control of the Literature of Oncology, 1800-1860, 1969. Contbr. articles profl. publs. Home: 89-14 34th Av Jackson Heights NY 11372 also 124 Lexington Av Albany NY 12206 Office: Sch Library Scis State U NY at Albany Albany NY 12222

VAILLOT, SISTER MADELEINE CLEMENCE, coll. dean; b. Bourdan, France, May 27, 1907; d. Jules Alexandre and Madeleine Marguerite Eugenie (Soubies) Vaillot; M.Ed., Boston Coll., 1953, Ph.D., 1960. Came to U.S., 1939, naturalized, 1945. Nurse, French Hosp., Barcelona, Spain, 1936; staff nurse Clinica della Presentazione, Roma, Italy, 1936-39; dir. St. Anne's Hosp., Sch. of Nursing, Fall River, Mass., 1940-69; asst. prof. nursing Boston Coll., 1960-67; dean Coll. Nursing, Southeastern Mass. U., North Dartmouth, 1969—. Mem. nursing adv. com. Boston Bd. Higher Edn., 1967-70, mem. nursing steering com., 1973—; mem. council Comprehensive Health Planning, Fall River, Mass., 1969—. Bd. dirs. Region VII Comprehensive Health Planning, 1972—; trustee St. Anne's Hosp., Fall River, Mass., 1947—. Mem. Nat. League Nursing, Am. Nurses Assn. Contbr. articles to profl. jours. Home: 3012 Elm St Dighton MA 02715 Office: Southeastern Massachusetts University College of Nursing North Dartmouth MA 02747

VAINSTEIN, ROSE, educator; b. Edmonton, Alta., Can., Jan. 7, 1920; d. Nathan and Jane (Simenstein) Vainstein; A.B., Miami U, Oxford, O., 1941; B.L.S., Western Res. U., 1942; M.S., U. Ill., 1952. Came to U.S., 1924, naturalized, 1931. Jr. librarian Cuyahoga County Library, Cleve., 1942-43; young people's librarian Bklyn. Pub. Library, 1943-44; armed forces librarian U.S., Hawaii and Japan, 1944-48; br. librarian Contra Costa County Library, Martinez, Cal., 1948-51; library cons. Cal. State Library, Sacramento, 1953-55; head extension dept. Gary Pub. and Lake County Library, Gary, Ind., 1955-57; pub. library specialist U.S. Office Edn., Washington, 1957-61; asso. prof. Sch. Librarianship, U. B.C., Vancouver, 1961-64; dir. Bloomfield Twp. Pub. Library, Bloomfield Hills, Mich., 1964-68; prof. library sci. U. Mich., Ann Arbor, 1968—, dir. Middle Mgmt. Inst. for Pub. Librarians, 1969. Dir. Pub. Libraries Research Study of British Columbia (Can.), 1963-64. Fulbright Research scholar, England, 1952-53; Council on Library Resources fellow, 1974-75. Mem. Adult Edn. Assn., Am. (chmn. pub. library standards com. 1969-74), Canadian, Mich., Spl. library assns., Am. Assn. Higher Edn., Am. Assn. U. Profs., U. Mich. Womens Research Club (treas. 1971-72), League Women Voters. Club: Altrusa Internat. (Ann Arbor-Ypsilanti, Mich.). Contbr. articles to profl. jours. Home: 2013 Medford Rd Apt 261 Ann Arbor MI 48104

VAITKUS, ALDONA PAULIUS (MRS. RIMANTAS L. VAITKUS), statistician; b. Lithuania, Nov. 3, 1940; d. Simas and Ona (Geguzaitis) Paulius; came to U.S., 1949, naturalized, 1960; B.S., U. Ill., 1962; M.S., Ill. Inst. Tech., 1970; m. Rimantas L. Vaitkus, Feb. 2, 1963. Chief of biometrics mental health dept. Inst. for Juvenile Research, Chgo., 1962-68; supr. biometry cons. lab. U. Minn. Sch. Pub. Health, Mpls., 1968-69, statistician child devel. study, dept. pediatrics and med. sch. curriculum evaluation program Med. Sch., 1969-72; dir. Evidence for Community Health Orgn., Ariz. Dept. Health, Phoenix, 1972-73; statistician Ariz. Health Planning Authority, Phoenix, 1973—. Cons. Minn. Dept. Mental Health, 1971-72. Mem. Am., Ariz. (v.p. 1973-74) statis. assns. Home: 1819 E Colter St Phoenix AZ 85016 Office: 1740 W Adams St Phoenix AZ 85007

VALDES, LAURA, lawyer; b. Havana, Cuba; d. Abelardo and Panfila (Valde) Valdes; student Coll. City N.Y., 1941; B.S., N.Y. U., 1943; J.D., N.Y. Law Sch., 1960. With N.Y. State Dept. Labor, N.Y.C., 1935-73; employment security supt., 1973; admitted to N.Y. bar, 1960. Mem. Community Planning Bd. #13, Bronx, N.Y., 1974; mem. Community Sch. Bd. Dist. #11, Bronx, 1962-73; pres. Williamsbridge Sr. Citizens Assn., N.Y.C., 1972-74; vice chmn. community adv. bd. Bronx Municipal Hosp. Center, 1974. Recipient Woman Year award Bronx Schoolmens Lodge, 1973; Human Rights award N.Y. State Div. Human Rights, 1970. Mem. N.A.A.C.P. (life mem., pres. co-op. city br. 1973—, pres. Williamsbridge br. 1963-72), Bronx County Bar Assn. (dir. 1972—), Bronx Women's Bar Assn. Home: 3820 Paulding Av Bronx NY 10469

VALDES-DAPENA, MARIE AGNES (MRS. ANTONIO M. VALDES-DAPENA), pathologist; b. Pottsville, Pa., July 14, 1921; d. Edgar Daniel and Marie Agnes (Rettig) Brown; B.S., Immaculata Coll., 1941; M.D., Temple U., 1944; m. Antonio M. Valdes-Dapena, Apr. 6, 1945; children—Victoria Maria (Mrs. Bruce Grefe), Deborah Anne (Mrs. Frank Malle), Maria Cristina (Mrs. Glenn Heck), Andres Antonio, Antonio Edgardo, Carlos Roberto, Marcos Antonio,

Ricardo Daniel, Carmen Patricia, Catalina Inez, Pedro Pablo. Intern Phila. Gen. Hosp., Phila., 1944-45, resident pathology, 1945-49; asst. pathologist Fitzgerald-Mercy Hosp., Darby, Pa., 1949-51; dir. labs. Womans Med. Coll. Pa., Phila., 1951-55, instr. pathology, 1947-51; asst. prof., 1951-55, asso. prof., 1955-59; asso. pathologist St. Christopher's Hosp. for Children, Phila., 1959—; cons. div. pathology Lankenau Hosp., Phila., 1971—; cons., lectr. U.S. Naval Hosp., Phila., 1972; instr. pathology Sch. Medicine, U. Pa., 1945-49, instr. pathology Sch. Dentistry, 1947, instr. pathology Grad. Sch. Medicine, 1948-55, vis. lectr. pathology, 1960-62; asst. prof. pathology Temple U. Sch. Medicine, 1959-63, asso. prof., 1963-67, prof. pathology, 1967—, prof. pediatrics, 1967—. Cons. pediatric pathology, div. med. examiner Dept. Pub. Health, Phila., 1967-70; mem. perinatal biology and infant mortality research and tng. com. Nat. Inst. Child Health and Human Devel. NIH, 1971-73. Vice pres. Nat. Found. for Sudden Infant Death, Inc., N.Y.C., 1970—, chmn. med. bd., 1970—. NIH grantee. Diplomate Am. Bd. Pathology. Mem. Internat. Acad. Pathology, Am. Assn. Pathologists and Bacteriologists, Pathol. Soc. Phila., Phila. Pediatric Soc., Pediatric Pathology Club, Path. Soc. Gt. Britain and Ireland, Coll. Physicians Phila., Alpha Omega Alpha. Roman Catholic. Contbr. to publs. in field. Home: 214 Plush Mill Rd Wallingford PA 10986 Office: 2600 N Lawrence St Philadelphia PA 19133

VALDIVIA, MARTHA A., librarian, educator; b. Cochabamba, Bolivia, Sept. 8, 1925; d. Franklin A. Valdivia, and Angela (Sujet); B.S. in Edn., Nat. Tchrs. Coll., Sucre, Bolivia, 1946; L.S. degree (scholar) W. Va. U., 1958; postgrad. Cal. State U., Los Angeles, 1972—; m. divorced. Came to U.S., 1960, naturalized, 1966. Tchr. elementary schs., Bolivia, 1947-55; asst. librarian Bolivian-Am. Center USIS U.S. Dept. State, La Paz, Bolivia, 1950-55, chief librarian Bolivian-Am. Center USIS, 1955-59, tchr. Spanish Fgn. Lang. Inst., La Paz, 1959-60; asst. librarian law library George Washington U., 1960-61; regional children's librarian Los Angeles County Pub. Library, Montebello, 1961-63; med. librarian Harbor Gen. Hosp., Torrance, Cal., 1963-71, Los Angeles County-U. So. Cal. Med. Center Gen. Hosp., 1971-73, Los Angeles County Harbor Gen. Hosp., 1973—. Sec. cultural affairs YWCA, Bolivia, 1959. Mem. Med. Librarians Group So. Cal., Med. Library Assn., Western Hosp. Assn., Alliance Francaise. Clubs: Bolivian Woman's (press sec. 1967), Women's Internat. (corr. sec. 1968) (Los Angeles). Editor, Bolivian Bull., Los Angeles; translator med. articles Eng.-Spanish. Home: 5860 Spring Oak Dr Hollywood CA 90068 Office: Harbor Gen Hosp 1000 W Carson St Torrance CA 90509

VALENCIK, MAY VIRGINIA KUNZ (MRS. GUS VALENCIK), librarian; b. Newark, Mar. 25, 1909; d. Edward and Helen (Reilly) Kunz; A.B., Douglass Coll., 1931; postgrad. U. Chgo., 1936-38, N.Y. Sch. Social Research, 1934, Columbia U., 1935; LL.D., Cedar Crest Coll., 1952; m. Gus Valencik, Jan. 19, 1943. Library asst. Passaic (N.J.) Pub. Library, 1931-36; sr. reference asst. Utica (N.Y.) Pub. Library, 1936-41; state supr. W.P.A., Ky., 1941-42; librarian Allentown (Pa.) Free Library, 1942-63; library dir. White Plains (N.Y.) Pub. Library, 1963—; exec. bd. Pub. Library Dirs., 1969—. Pres., Middle Atlantic States Regional Library Conf., 1953-58; N.Y. commr. Nyquist's Com. on Library Access, 1973—. Sec. Westchester County Easter Seals Soc., 1969—; jury of awards, Freedoms Found., 1952; adviser Winbrook Study Center, 1964-66; mem. pres. Eisenhower's civil defense adv. bd., 1955-57, pres. Eisenhower's traffic safety com., 1955-57. Trustee Meml. Methodist Ch., 1972—, METRO, 1970—. Mem. A.L.A. (council 1950-52), Pa. (pres. 1950-52, state lobbyist 1950-52), Westchester (exec. bd. 1966-70), N.Y. library assns., Smithsonian Inst., Historic Preservations, Wild Life Fedn. White Plains C. of C. (bd. dirs. 1971—), League of Women Voters, Am. Assn. U. Women, Delta Kappa Gamma. Club: Quota (life, internat. pres. 1955-57). Contbr. articles to profl. jours. Home: 10 Nosband Av White Plains NY 10605 Office: 100 Martine Av White Plains NY 10601

VALENSTEIN, ALICE STARR (MRS. LAWRENCE VALENSTEIN), artist, interior decorator; b. N.Y.C., Feb. 12, 1904; d. Morris and Theresa (Isidor) Sternberg; B.S. (Arthur Wesley Dow scholar), Columbia Tchrs. Coll.; m. Lawrence Valenstein, May 10, 1934; children—Linda (Mrs. Jerome Elkind), John. Owner, Alice Starr Interior Decorating, N.Y.C.; exhibited one man shows Krasner Galleries, Miami (Fla.) Modern Mus., Katonah (N.Y.) Galleries; exhibited in group shows Yonkers (N.Y.) Art Mus., Hudson River Mus., N.Y.C.; represented in permanent collections Hofstra S.I. Mus., Mills Coll., Coral Gables U. Founder, bd. dirs. Alice Valenstein Fund. Recipient painting prizes Scarsdale Art Soc., Westchester Arts, Brandeis Art Assn. Mem. Nat. Soc. Women Artists. Club: Westchester Art (N.Y.C.). Contbr. articles to profl. jours. Home: 20 Heathcote Rd Scarsdale NY 10583

VALENTINE, MILLIE STROH (MRS. RALPH EDWARD VALENTINE), psychologist; b. Piketown, Pa., Sept. 26, 1910; d. Simon Henry and Alice (Feaser) Stroh; A.B., Ohio No. U., 1932; M.Ed., Temple U., 1958, postgrad., 1958-64; m. Ralph Edward Valentine, June 17, 1931; children—Paul Arthur, Ralph Edward. Tchr., Dauphin (Pa.) Boro Sch., 1955-58; tchr. county class physically handicapped children Dauphin County, 1958-62, county supr. spl. classes, 1962-70; sch. psychologist Capital Area Intermediate Unit 15, Harrisburg, Pa., 1970—. Pres., P.T.A., Huntington, W.Va., 1946-50. Bd. dirs. Tri-County Easter Seal Soc., Council Chs. Greater Harrisburg. Mem. Nat. Assn. Sch. Psychologists, Pa. Psychol. Assn., Council Exceptional Children, Ohio No. Social Orgn., Xi Beta Chi. Republican. Mem. Soc. of Friends. Club: Women's of Fishing Creek Valley (Harrisburg). Home: Linglestown Route 4 Box 941 Harrisburg PA 17112 Office: 2994 N 2d St Harrisburg PA 17112

VALERIO, MARY E., nutritionist, social worker; b. Cin.; d. Alfredo and Massimilla (Fiorda) Valerio; B.S. in Nutrition, U. Cin., 1927, postgrad. social work, 1930; postgrad. Columbia, 1929. Instr. nutrition, chemistry U. Cin., 1927-28; nutritionists, social worker Juvenile Ct., Cin., 1928-48; case work supr. Hamilton County (O.) Welfare Dept., 1948—. Co-owner Valerios Italian Restaurant, Cin., 1956-65. Mem. food stamp program food and nutrition edn. com. U.S. Dept. Agr., 1972—. Mem. Nat. Assn. Social Workers, U. Cin. Sch. Household Adminstrn. Alumnae Assn. (pres.). Editor monthly booklet nutrition, home econs. Hamilton and Montgomery (O.) Counties, 1939-56. Home: 1 Madison Lane Cincinnati OH 45208 Office: 628 Sycamore St Cincinnati OH 45202

VALERO, DENISE JOSEPHINE LUCIENNE, author, photographer; b. Algiers, Algeria, Feb. 22, 1923; d. Andre Jean Joseph and Marie-Louise Denise Paulet; ed. Faculte des Lettres d'Alger, 1943-45; pvt. schs. Casablanca and Rabat, 1950-52; m. Henri-Emile Marechal, 1941; 1 dau., Colette; m. 2d, François Valero, Aug. 23, 1951; children—Jean Louis, Romain. Journalist, Paris, France, 1945; dir. Editions Moliere, Nice, France, 1960-62; free lance writer, photographer, 1946—; lectr. 1957—. Founder, owner Internat. Mus. Malacology, Nice, 1969—. Mem. Horizons 2000, paramunicipal commn., 1971—; mem. Nat. Commn. of Inquiry into Nat. Edn., 1973—. Senatorial delegate, Nice, 1971. Decorated chevalier du merite social Ministere du Travail. Mem. Assn. National Fracais Afrique du Nord section Nice (chmn. 1957-60), Artistic Fedn. Cote d'Azur (chmn. 1962), French and Internat. Center for Malacology, Assn. Parents Students Secondary Schs. and Colls. Nice (chmn. 1969-71), Am. Malacological Union, Loyola High Sch. Paleontology Assn., Profl. Women's Union, Women's Civic and Social Union, Soc. Friends of Univ., Internat. Collectors' Club, French Golf Fedn. Author: Petite Histoire des Ruines Portugaises au Maroc, 1952; Peintereset Sculpteurs de la Cote d'Azur, 1961; Pes Pelicani, 1973; Le Nouveau Pes Pelicani, 1974. Contbr. articles to mags., profl. jours. Home: 3 rue Alfred-Binet Nice 06100 France Office: 3 cours Saleya Nice 06300 France

VALERO, LUCY ANN, ednl. assn. exec.; b. Delmont, Pa., Sept. 27, 1917; d. Joseph and Mary (Cerrutt) Valero; B.S., California (Pa.) State Tchrs. Coll., 1942; M.Ed., Pa. State U., 1949; postgrad. U. Pitts., 1955-56. Mem. adv. council Pa. Dept. Pub. Instrn., 1950; prof. edn. State Tchrs. Coll., California, Pa., 1951-56; asst. exec. sec. Student Edn. Assn. Pa., 1957—, state cons., 1957—; asst. exec. sec. Pa. Future Tchrs. Am., 1957—, state cons., 1957—. Mem. White House Conf. Edn., 1955, Northeast U.S. Regional confs. Dept. Classroom Tchrs., 1949-56; N.E.A. del. World Confedn. Orgns. Teaching Profession, Manila, P.I., 1956; del. Gov.'s Conf. Edn. in Pa., 1958; del. UNESCO, 1949; mem. Gov.'s Forum Planning Com., 1958, Gov.'s White House Conf., 1960-61; mem. Gov.'s Task Force on Council for Human Services; mem. Pa. Youthpower Conf. Com., 1966. Recipient Illustrious Alumni award Cal. State Coll., 1972; named Woman of Year Harrisburg. Mem. Pa. Future Homemakers of Am. (hon.), Am. Assn. U. Women (pres. Harrisburg br.), Assn. State Pres.'s in Edn. (v.p. 1956), N.E.A. (life), Assn. Childhood Edn. Internat., Pa. (state pres. 1956), Washington County (exec. com. 1950-57) edn. assns., Classroom Tchrs. Pa. (pres. 1949), Rural Edn. Pa. (pres. 1949), Assn. Student Teaching, Delta Kappa Gamma, Pi Lambda Theta. Home: Slickville PA 15684 Office: 400 N 3d St Harrisburg PA 17101

VALK, JANICE BORDANARO (MRS. CHARLES WILLIAM VALK), real estate broker; b. Phoenix, Apr. 30, 1925; d. Joseph Charles and Auda (Pingree) Bordanaro; A.A., Coll. of Marin, 1942; m. Charles William Valk, May 7, 1944; children—Kenneth W., Karen (Mrs. Fred Nastasuk), Keith W., Kathleen. With Pingree & Co., Corte Madera, Cal., 1959—, owner, 1973—. Sec., Village Square Assn., Corte Madera, 1969—. Bd. dirs. Little League, 1959-60, Pony League, 1962-63. Named Mother of Year, 1960; Salesman of Year, Marin County Bd. Realtors, 1969. Mem. Marin County Bd. Realtors (dir. 1968-70), Corte Madera C. of C. (pres. 1972), Women Council Realtors, Bus. and Profl. Womens Club. Home: 412 Oakdale Av Corte Madera CA 94925 Office: 206 Tamalpais Dr Corte Madera CA 94925

VALLE, MARTA, social worker; b. N.Y.C., May 12, 1934; d. Jose and Gloria (Ponce de Leon) Valle; B.A., Hunter Coll., 1954; M.S.W., Columbia, 1961; 1 son, Carlos J. Active Puerto Rican affairs, N.Y.C.; organizer N.Y.C. Mayor's Puerto Rican Community Conf., 1967; founding mem. Puerto Rican Forum; asst. dep. adminstr. community relations Human Resources Adminstrn., N.Y.C.; commr. N.Y.C. Youth Services Agy.; exec. dir. N.Y.C. Youth Bd. Bd. dirs. Community Health Inst.; mem. Bd. Higher Edn.; trustee Carnegie Corp. John Hay Whitney fellow. Home: 42-12 196th St New York City NY 11358 Office: Valle Consultants Ltd 42-12 196th St Flushing NY 11358

VALSAMOULIS, CATHERINE, mfg. co. exec.; b. Chgo., Aug. 19, 1932; d. William John and Afrodite (Pantazapoulos) Valsamoulis; student Wright Jr. Coll., 1963-64. With Warners, Chgo., 1948-61, supr. data processing dept., 1948-61; supr. data processing dept. Bear Brand Hosiery, Chgo., 1961-63; mgr. data processing dept. Pioneer Screw & Nut Co., Elk Grove Village, Ill., 1963—, chmn. shortages com., 1972-73. Mem. Data Processing Mgrs. Assn., Socrates Alumni Assn. Mem. Greek Orthodox Ch. Office: 2700 York Rd Elk Grove Village IL 60007

VAN ALLEN, MARTHA INEZ, educator; b. Little Falls, N.Y., Mar. 13, 1929; d. Leland C. and Helen (Kennedy) Van Allen; B.S., State U. N.Y., 1950; M.Ed., St. Lawrence U., 1958; D.Phys. Edn., Springfield Coll., 1966. Tchr., Little Falls Pub. Schs., 1950-54, Argyle Central Sch., 1954-56; asst. prof. State U. N.Y., Potsdam, 1957-63, Springfield (Mass.) Coll. 1963-70; asso. prof. Westfield (Mass.) State Coll., 1970—. head counselor Camp Red Wing, Adirondack, N.Y., 1950-67. Mem. A.A.H.P.E.R., Eastern Assn. Phys. Edn. for Coll. Women, Assn. Phys. Edn. Women N.Y. State, N.Y. State, Mass. phys. edn. assns., Creative Practices Council Mass., Alpha Delta. Home: Sycamore Apts Sycamore St Westfield MA 01085

VAN APPLEDORN, MARY JEANNE, educator, musician; b. Holland, Mich., Oct. 2, 1927; d. John and Elizabeth (Rinck) van Appledorn; Mus.B., Eastman Sch. Music, U. Rochester, 1948, Mus.M., 1950, Ph.D., 1966. Piano debut Carnegie Recital Hall, N.Y.C., 1957; chmn. dept. music, lit. and theory Tex. Tech. U., Lubbock, founder, chmn. Symposium of Contemporary Music. Mem. Mu Phi Epsilon, Alpha Chi Omega, Delta Kappa Gamma (Scholar, 1959-60). Presbyn. Author: Keyboard Singing and Dictation Manual, 1968. Composer various vocal and instrumental selections. Home: 1629 16th St Lubbock TX 79401

VAN ARSDALE, DOROTHY LANGFORD THAYER (MRS. STUART FRANK VAN ARSDALE), mus. adminstr.; b. Malden, Mass., Jan. 14, 1917; d. Arthur Langford and Dorothy (Clark) Thayer; B.S., Simmons Coll., 1938; m. Howard Charles Pritham, Aug. 31, 1939 (dic. Sept. 1947); children—Howard George, Eleanor (Mrs. Serge Liros); m. 2d, Stuart Frank Van Arsdale, Aug. 25, 1951 (dec. July 1958); 1 son, Stuart Frank. Sec., Filene's Boston, 1946-48; exec. sec. Macy's, N.Y.C., 1948-51; sec. John Fox, publisher Boston Post, 1952-54, spl. promotions Boston Post, 1954-55; exec. sec. N.E. Industries, Boston, 1957-60, adminstrv. asst., 1960-62, treas., 1960-64, also. dir.; financial mgr. Smithsonian Traveling Exhbn. Service, Washington, 1962-64, chief, 1964-70; head Dorothy T. Van Arsdale Assos. Traveling Exhbn. and Art Gallery, 1971—. Mem. So. Lake Meml. Hosp. Aux. Created Knight Denmark, 1971. Mem. Am. Assn. Museums, Internat. Council Museums, Simmons Coll. Alumni Assn. Club: Internat. (Washington). Address: 501 Slaters Lane Alexandria VA 22314

VAN ARTSDALEN, MARTHA JEAN, newspaper editor; b. Darby, Pa., June 1, 1950; d. James Truxton and Eunice Ann (McCart) Van Artsdalen; B.A. in Journalism, Syracuse U., 1972. Copyeditor, Charlotte (N.C.) Observer, 1971; copyeditor, entertainment editor Today's Post, King of Prussia, Pa., 1972—. Newspaper Fund Editing intern, 1971. Mem. Women in Communications, Pa. Women's Press Assn. Home: 152 E Marshall Rd Lansdowne PA 19050 Office: 750 Moore Rd Box 426 King of Prussia PA 19406

VANASSE, SARAHJANE PAULSON, sorority ofcl.; b. Seattle, Jan. 29, 1911; d. Paul and Ida (Hutchinson) Paulson; student Wash. State U., 1929-31; m. Horace Jesmer Vanasse, Aug. 24, 1932; children—Joy (Mrs. William H. Goodenough), Julianne (Mrs. William W. Vaux). Pres. John Hay Elem. PTA, 1946-48; pres. Queen Anne Sr. High Sch. PTA, 1952-53; pres. Seattle Pi Beta Phi Alumnae Club, 1952-53; alumnae province pres. Pi Beta Phi, 1956-60, nat. dir. chpt. programs, 1964-67, grand. v.p., 1967-69, grand pres., 1969-73. Bd. dirs. YWCA, United Good Nabor, Seattle Milk Fund, Childrens Orthopedic Hosp., Seattle Jr. Programs, Seattle Women's Symphony, Diocesan Council of Sacramento, Sacramento Womens Symphony, Sacramento Opera Guild. Republican. Episcopalian (pres. Women's Guild 1962, 1964). Clubs: San Francisco Metropolitan; Seattle Women's University. Club. Home: 3401 25th St W Apt 520 Seattle WA 98199

VANBIBER, BELVA DELL DAVIS (MRS. RUSSELL CARL VANBIBER), poet; b. Salem, W.Va., July 31, 1913; d. Albert Nelson and Flora Dell (Bailey) Davis; student grad. schs.; m. Russell Carl Vanbiber, Sept. 11, 1928; children—Loretta (Mrs. Stanley Carson), Russell Carl. Saleslady, Pallissard Jewelry, Perry, Okla., 1947-48; buyer, saleslady J.C. Penny Co., Perry, 1948-66; contbr. poetry to Daily Oklahoman, Oklahoma City, Household Mag., Perry Pub. Co., also to Exchange Bank, Lintz's Dept. Store (both Perry). Pres. vol. hosp. aux. Parker Funeral Home, Perry, 1973—; mem. hosp. governing bd. Perry Hosp., 1973—. Mem. Bus. and Profl. Women, Internat. Platform Assn. Baptist. Author: Keep Looking Up, 1966; Hold Up the Cross, 1966; Step Out of the Shadows, 1971. Address: 1002 Hillside St Perry OK 73077

VANBUREN, ABIGAIL (PAULINE FRIEDMAN PHILLIPS), columnist, writer, lectr.; b. Sioux City, Ia., July 4, 1918; d. Abraham and Rebecca (Rushall) Friedman; student Morningside Coll., Sioux City, 1936-39; m. Morton Phillips, July 2, 1939; children—Edward Jay, Jeanne. Vol. worker for causes of better mental health, Nat. Found. Infantile Paralysis, tng. Gray Ladies A.R.C., 1939-56; columnist Dear Abby, San Francisco Chronicle, 1956, syndicated McNaught Syndicate, N.Y.C., 1956—, now appears in newspapers U.S., Brazil, Australia, Japan, Germany, Holland, Denmark, Can.; radio program CBS, 1963—. Nat. chmn. Crippled Children Soc., 1962. Author: Dear Abby, 1957 (also translated Japanese, Dutch, German, Spanish); Dear Teen Ager, 1959; Dear Abby on Marriage, 1962. Home: Beverly Hills CA 90213 Office: 132 Lasky Dr Beverly Hills CA 92012

VANCE, BARBARA JANE, instructional psychologist; b. Salt Lake City, Utah, Mar. 5, 1934; d. Reed and Vidella (Rushton) Vance; B.A., U. Utah, 1956; M.A., Brigham Young U., 1959; Ph.D. (Henry Newell fellow), Stanford, 1967; instr. child devel. Brigham Young U., 1959-62, asso. prof., 1967-72, instructional psychologist instructional research and devel., 1972—; instr. early childhood edn. Tufts U., 1962-63; resident asst., dean students staff Stanford U., 1963-66, research asst., 1966-67; lectr. child devel. San Jose State Coll., 1966-67; dir. research ednl. program, Fremont Unified Sch. Dist., 1966-67. Charter mem. Utah Valley Symphony Orchestra. Recipient honorary spur Brigham Young U., 1962, outstanding achievement and service award Asso. Students Brigham Young U., 1972. Mem. Am. Psychol. Assn., Am. Ednl. Research Assn., Soc. for Research in Child Devel., Nat. Assn. for Edn. Young Children (conf. chmn. 1969), Phi Kappa Phi, Pi Lambda Theta, Mu Phi Epsilon, Omicron Nu. Mem. Ch. of Jesus Christ of Latter-day Saints. Author: Teaching the Prekindergarten Child, 1973; also articles. Home: 2204 N 200 E Provo UT 84601

VANCE, CARMEN LEE, coll. dean; b. St. Louis, May 19, 1942; d. Ira Earnest and Helen Carlene (Milner) Vance; B.S., U. Mo., 1964; M.Ed., Pa. State U., 1968. Tchr. math., psychology George Mason Jr. and Sr. High Sch., Falls Church, Va., 1964-67; asst. dean students Capitol campus Pa. State U., Middletown, 1968-71; asso. dean students Frostburg (Md.) State Coll., 1971—. Mem. Nat. Assn. Student Personnel Adminstrs., Assn. Coll. and U. Housing Officers (regional pres. 1973-74), Nat. Assn. Women Deans and Counselors (mem. placement com. 1973-74), Am. Ednl. Studies Assn., Pi Lambda Theta, Alpha Chi Omega. Home: 160 W Main St Frostburg MD 21532

VANCE, ELEANOR GRAHAM, author; b. Pitts., Oct. 16, 1908; d. Joseph Paul and Sarah Margaret (Hargrave) Graham; A.B., Westminister Coll., 1930, Litt.D., 1952; M.A., Medill sch. journalism Northwestern U., 1931; postgrad. Columbia, summer 1934, U. Pitts., 1933-34; m. William Silas Vance, Nov. 22, 1945; children—Eleanor Margaret, Dale Lines. Proofreader Akron (O.) Typesetting Co., 1931-32; tchr. Pitts. pub. schs., 1933-37, 39-43, Dormont (Pa.) High Sch., 1943-44; organized home teaching handicapped children, Pitts., 1935-37; mem. research dept. Colonial Williamsburg (Va.), 1944-45; poetry lectr. Pitts. schs., H.C. Frick Edn. Commn., 1945-66, lectr. lit. related subjects, 1935—. Attended Bread Loaf Writers Conf., 1937. Recipient award of merit Alumni Assn. Northwestern U., 1938; achievement award Westminster Coll. Alumni, 1956; ann. contest prizes Poetry socs. Tex. and Okla., 1947-73. Mem. Poetry Soc. Tex., Chi Omega, Delta Kappa Gamma (hon.). Author: (poems) For These Moments, 1939, Store in Your Heart, 1950, It Happens Every Day, 1962; (operettas) Christmas in Old England, 1938; A Musical Calendar, 1940, Hammer in His Hand, 1966; adaptations of French, Spanish, Italian, Portuguese and German folk-songs for music texts, Latin Am. folksongs, Canciones Pan-Americanas, 1942; (children's books) Henry the Helicopter, 1945; Tweets, The Story of a Cat, 1956; Jonathan, 1966; Famous Fairy Tales, 1946; Favorite Nursery Tales, 1946; Bedtime Stories, 1946; Tall Book of Fairy Tales, 1947; Black Beauty, 1949; Robin Hood, 1953; Treasured Memories: Our Baby, 1970; The Everything Book, 1974; biog. introduction to Arthur Guiterman's posthumous collection of poems Brave Laughter, 1943; compiler From Little to Big: A Parade of Animal Poems, 1972. Contbr. Sat. Eve. Post, New Yorker, Ladies Home Jour., Good Housekeeping, Parents, Sat. Rev., N.Y. Times and N.Y. Herald Tribune, McCall's, childrens publs. Address: 109 Austin Blvd Edinburg TX 78539

VANCE, JUDITH ELLEN, ednl. adminstr.; b. Anderson, Ind., Mar. 27, 1943; d. Charles Ernest and Juanita Lucille (Morris) Vance; B.S., Ball State U., 1965, M.A., 1967. Secondary tchr. LaVille (Ind.) Jr.-Sr. High Sch., 1965-67; with student personnel services Ball State U., Muncie, Ind., 1967-70; asst. dean of students Ill. Wesleyan U., Bloomington, 1970-72, dir. student programs, 1972—. Mem. Nat. Assn. Women Deans, Adminstrs. and Counselors (mem. continuing edn. adv. bd. 1973—), Ill. Assn. Women Deans and Counselors (program chmn. 1971—), Alpha Lambda Delta. Club: Altrusa Internat. (mem. govs. commn. on vol. action 1970-71) (Bloomington, Ill.). Home: 1511 North Fell Bloomington IL 61701 Office: Memorial Center University St Illinois Wesleyan University Bloomington IL 61701

VANCE, LINDA SUSAN, journalist; b. Columbus, O., Mar. 24, 1949; d. William Chaney and Jane Roberta (Simon) Vance; student, U. Sao Paulo, Brazil, 1970; B.S. in Journalism, Ohio State U., 1971. With, Commodity News Services, Inc., Chgo., 1971, Washington, 1971—, bur. chief, 1973—. Mem. Women in Communications, Nat. Press Club (mem. bd. govs. 1973—). Home: 1600 S Eads St Arlington VA 22202 Office: Suite 400 777 14th St NW Washngton DC 20005

VANCE, MAE HOWARD, artist; b. Rushsylvania, O.; d. William and Minnie Mae (Slater) Vance; student Cleve. Inst. Art, 1919-21, Corcoran Art Sch., 1923-25, Renshaw Sch. Speech, 1930-31. Marine mural painter, ceramic designer; painter, author pictorial illustrations depicting birthplaces of presidents of U.S.; exhibited group shows Robert Lee Hall, N.C., Statler Hotel, Cleve., Carlton Hotle, Washington, Ind. Washington Artists, Nat. League Am. Pen Women, many pvt. exhibits; represented in F. D. Roosevelt ship collection.

Mem. D.A.R., Nat. League Am. Pen Women, Internat. Platform Assn. Republican. Presbyn. Home: 3702 Northampton St NW Washington DC 20015

VANCE, MARGARET H. ALEXANDER (MRS. KIRBY VANCE), physician; b. Temple, Tex., Dec. 5, 1907; d. Hartwell and Alwilber (Bouldin) Alexander; B.A., Mary Hardin Baylor, 1931; M.D., Baylor Med. Coll., 1931; m. Kirby Vance, May 14, 1944; children—Margaret Ruth (Mrs. Chris Cahill), James. Intern, Meth. Hosp., St. Joseph, Mo., 1931-32; resident eye, ear, nose and throat, New Orleans, 1932-33; practice medicine specializing in ophthalmology and otolarygology, Taylor, Tex., 1934—; mem. staff Johns Community Hosp. Diplomate Am. Bd. Otolaryngology. Mem. A.M.A., Am. Acad. Ophthalmology and Otolaryngology, Tex. Med. Assn., Am. Assn. U. Women, Alpha Epsilon Iota, Delta Kappa Gamma (hon.). Home: 720 Talbot St Taylor TX 76574

VANCE, MARY ANN, social work exec.; b. Ponca City, Okla., July 26, 1929; d. Lloyd Clifford and Amanda Faye (Stewart) Vance; B.S. U. Okla., 1950; M.Ed., Wayne State U., 1966. Exec. dir., camp dir. Camp Fire Girls, Ada, Okla., 1950-52, field dir., camp dir., Oklahoma City, 1952-55, exec. dir., camp dir. Albuquerque, N.M., 1955-61, dist. dir., camp dir. Detroit, 1961-66, regional adviser Nat. Field Staff, 1966-69; dir. vol. services Detroit Gen. Hosp., 1969—. Mem. Nat. Assn. Social Workers, Acad. Certified Social Workers, Alpha Gamma Delta. Home: 18280 Whitby Livonia MI 48152 Office: 1326 St Antoine St Detroit MI 48226

VANCE, MARY ELISABETH ZELT, editor; b. Washington, Pa.; d. Adam C. and Dorothy (McCutcheon) Zelt; student Mt. Mercy Jr. Coll., 1928-29, U. South Fla., 1966-67, U. Tampa, 1973; m. Carl A. Vance, Aug. 13, 1935 (dec. Feb. 15, 1963); children—David C., Mary Melissa (Mrs. Jack Abelard Harnett), James Zelt, Carl Alexander II. Women's editor Sarasota (Fla.) Herald Tribune, 1949-55, News, Sarasota, 1955-59; family editor Tampa (Fla.) Times, 1959-68; women's editor Tampa Tribune, 1968—. Recipient numerous state and nat. awards, including Fashion Reporters Award N.Y., 1968, Gen. Elec. Writing award, 1963, 64. Mem. Theta Sigma Phi. Clubs: Fla. Press, Tampa Yacht and Country. Home: 84 Davis Blvd Tampa FL 33606 Office: 505 E Kennedy Blvd Tampa FL 33601

VANCE, NINA ELOISE WHITTINGTON, theatrical exec.; b. Yoakum, Tex.; d. Perry and Minerva (Dewitt) Whittington; B.A., Tex. Christian U.; postgrad. U. So. Cal., Columbia, Am. Acad. Dramatic Art. Dir., Players Guild, Houston, 1944-46; founder, permanent dir., artistic dir. Alley Theatre, Houston, 1947—; guest dir. Arena Stage, Washington, Playhouse-in-the-Park, Phila. Participant Am. Assembly meeting Asian-Am. Assembly, Kuala Lumpur, Fedn. Malaya. Adv. com. Nat. Cultural Center; adv. com. on arts U.S. Adv. Commn. Ednl. and Cultural Affairs. Recipient grant English Speaking Union, 1958; Matrix award for contbn. to field of fine arts Theta Sigma Phi; Personal Dir.'s grant for travel and study Ford Found. Home: 1400 Hermann Dr Houston TX 77004 Office: Alley Theatre 615 Texas Av Houston TX 77002

VAN CLIEF, MARGARET LOUISA ROBERTSON (MRS. DANIEL G. VAN CLIEF), civic worker; b. Balt.; d. Frank Barry and Helen (Kriel) Robertson; B.A., Vassar Coll., 1945; m. Daniel Good Van Clief, May 22, 1946; children—Daniel Good and Barry Robertson (twins), Jan Courtlandt, Alan Sterling. Vice-pres. Blue Ridge Sch. Parents' Assn., 1966-67; mem. Albemarle-Charlottesville (Va.) spl. gifts com., 1967-74, co-chmn. Flamingo Ball, Hialeah, Fla., 1968-74, Am. Cancer Soc.; sponsor Charlottesville-Albemarle chpt. Planned Parenthood Assn.; patron U. Va. Hosp. Aux.; active various community drives. Chmn. Women's Com. to elect Van Clief to Ho. Dels., 1967, 69, 71. Bd. dirs., founding mem. Belfield Sch., 1955-57, 62-64, 68-70; trustee, founding mem. Tros-Dale Home for Boys, Scottsville, Va., 1964-68. Recipient Leone Ladson Perry award Albemarle Garden Club, 1968, 69. Mem. Nat. Geog. Soc., Nat. Trust Historic Preservation, Internat. Women's Fishing Assn. U. League, Oratorio Soc. Democrat. Episcopalian. Clubs: Baltimore Country; Keswick (Va.) Hunt; Chub Cay (Bahamas); Ocean Reef; Saratoga Golf; Edgartown Yacht; N.Y. Yacht; Va. Yacht; Farmington Country, Farmington Hunt, Albermarle Garden (corr. sec. 1966-68, program chmn. 1969-71, pres. 1971-73, dir. 1966-68, 73-76) (Charlottesville); Garden of Am.; Garden of Va. (judge, Eleanor Truax Cup, 1966, 67); Vassar Alumni of Va. (Richmond). Home: Nydrie Farms Esmont VA 22937

VANDEN BRINK, MARY LUCILE NICKLE (MRS. GEORGE ERNEST VANDEN BRINK), potter; b. Sioux City, Ia., Feb. 9, 1910; d. Orla Daniel and Grace (Batman) Nickle; student State Tchrs. Coll. Neb., 1929-30, N.Y. U., 1960; m. George Ernest Vanden Brink, June 6, 1931; children—John Anthony, Mary Sue (Mrs. Donald Register Loweree). Exhibited in group shows at Rockville (Md.) Art Center, Md. Fedn. Arts at Annapolis, Balt. Art Mus., U. Md., Western Md. Coll., Smithsonian Instn., Dept. Interior Art Gallery, Washington, others. Dir., Pottery Studio, Towson, Md., 1958—; mem. Chesapeake Potters Corp. Leader, Girl Scouts of Am., Sioux City, Ia., 1944-49. Organizer Ia. Watercolor show, 1948. Recipient Woman of Achievement award Sioux City Jour.-Tribune, 1950, 1st prize, pottery, Rockville, Md., 1963-65, sculpture, Am. Fedn. Arts, Annapolis, Md., 1964, Internat. Platform Assn., 1966, pottery, Wheaton, Md., 1967, Towson Bi-Centennial, 1968; 1st prize pottery, Annapolis, 1969, honorable mention pottery, Salt Lake City, 1970. Mem. Nat. League Am. Pen Women (1st prize pottery Md. 1971), Internat. Platform Assn., Am., Md. craft councils, League Women Voters (dir. 1955-59). Republican. Unitarian. Home: 405 Carolina Rd Towson MD 21204 Office: 600 W Chesapeake Av Towson MD 21204

VANDENBURGH, BEVERLY ANN HIBBOTT (MRS. EDWARD C. VANDENBURGH), lawyer; b. Chgo., Oct. 25, 1930; d. John W. and Florence (Wallen) Hibbott; student Denison U., 1948-50; B.S., Northwestern U., 1952; J.D., DePaul U., 1958; m. Edward C. Vandenburgh, Apr. 11, 1959; children—Lynn, Derek. Admitted to Ill. bar, 1958, U.S. Patent Office, 1959; patent lawyer, law dept. Swift & Co., Chgo., 1958-61; individual practice law, Barrington, Ill., 1961—. Mem. Barrington aux. Countryside Center for Handicapped. Mem. Am. (chmn. publs. com., also editor sect. patent, trademark and copyright law), Chgo. bar assns., Phi Beta Kappa, Chi Omega. Baptist. Club: Barrington (Ill.) Woman's. Home: 31 Elizabeth Lane Barrington IL 60010

VAN DEN HONERT, DOROTHY HAYWARD JOHNSON (MRS. LEONARD VAN DEN HONERT), educator; b. Greensboro, N.C., Apr. 23, 1924; d. Gerald Whyte and Kathryn (Hayward) Johnson; A.B., Vassar Coll., 1945; m. Leonard van den Honert, June 12, 1948; children—Peter, Christopher, Ann Kathryn, Gerald, Louisa. Weekly columnist Berkshire Evening Eagle, Pittsfield, Mass., 1962-64; tchr. perceptually handicapped children at jr. high sch. level Pittsfield Pub. Sch. System, 1969—. Columnist Berkshire Sunday Sampler, 1972—. Charter mem., sec. Action for Opportunity, Pittsfield, 1964-69. Mem. League Women Voters. Democrat. Author: Demi, the Baby-Sitter, 1960. Home: 115 Mountain Dr Pittsfield MA 01201

VANDERBEKE, LOIS MARIE, coll. dean; b. Detroit, May 7, 1936; d. Joseph Adolph and Leontine (Blomme) Vanderbeke; B.A., Dominican Coll., 1960; M.S., Marquette U., 1962; Ph.D., U. Ill., 1968; student Fla. State U., 1969. Mem. Sisters of St. Dominic, Roman Catholic Ch., 1958—; tchr. St. Mary's Sch., Racine, Wis., 1958-59; sr. high sch. math. tchr. St. Catherine's High Sch., Racine, Wis., 1960-63; instr. math. Dominican Coll., 1966-68, asst. prof., 1968-70, assoc. prof., 1970, acting v.p. for acad. affairs, 1970-71, dean grad. studies and continuing edn., 1971—. Treas. Big Sisters of Greater Racine, 1969—. NSF postdoctoral fellow Fla. State U., 1969. Mem. Am. Conf. Academic Deans, Nat. Council Teachers of Mathematics, Math. Assn. Am., Wis. Educators of Math., Kappa Delta Pi. Roman Catholic. Home: 5635 Erie St Racine WI 53402

VANDERBILT, GLORIA (MRS. WYATT E. COOPER), artist; b. N.Y.C., Feb. 20, 1924; d. Reginald and Gloria (Morgan) Vanderbilt; student pvt. schs.; m. Wyatt E. Cooper, Dec. 24, 1963; children—Stan S., Christopher S., Carter V., Anderson H. Exhibited Hammer Gallery, N.Y.C., Reading (Pa.) Mus., Monterey (Cal.) Peninsula Mus., Nashville Mus. Fine Arts, Cheekwood, Tenn. Designer textiles. Recipient Neiman-Marcus Fashion award, 1969. Mem. Author: Love Poems; The Gloria Vanderbilt Book of Collage. Address: 870 United Nations Plaza New York City NY 10017

VANDERBILT, HELEN CUMMINGS (MRS. WILLIAM H. VANDERBILT), educator; b. Skowhegan, Me., May 31, 1918; d. Willard Howe and Helen (Warren) Cummings; A.B., Bennington Coll. 1941; m. John R. Cook, Mar. 21, 1942; children—Warren Cummings, Rebecca I. John R., Helen Warren, Averill, Willard; m. 2d, William H. Vanderbilt. With Mus. Modern Art, Boston, 1938-40; mem. Hoover com., 1939-40, Fight for Freedom, 1940-42; salvage div. WPB, 1942-44; editorial work Young & Rubicam, 1944-46, Berkshire Agrl. Conservation Group, 1945; prof. English lit. Berkshire Community Coll., 1962—. Vice pres. South Forty Corp. Trustee Fisk U., Nashville, Mass. State Coll. System. Home: Oblong Rd Williamstown MA 01267

VAN DERBUR, MARILYN (MRS. LAWRENCE A. ATLER), TV personality, pub. speaker; b. Denver, June 16, 1937; d. Francis S. and Gwendolyn (Olinger) Van Derbur; B.A., U. Colo., 1960; m. Lawrence A. Atler, Feb. 14, 1964; 1 dau., Jennifer. Selected Miss America, 1958; TV spokeswoman Am. Tel. & Tel. Co., 1959-63; appeared on various TV shows including Ed Sullivan, Tonight Show, Mike Douglas Show, To Tell the Truth, others; TV hostess Thanksgiving and Cotton Bowl parades, 1964-73; hostess NBC Monitor Program, 1968—; guest lectr. Gen. Motors Corp., 1966-73; cons. Best Foods on Youth Affairs, 1966-72. Mem. President's Adv. Council on Edn., 1973—. Named Saleswoman of Yr., Direct Selling Assn., 1970, Outstanding Woman Speaker in Am. Meeting Planners Internat., 1973. Mem. Phi Beta Kappa. Home: 718 17th St Denver CO 80222

VANDERBURG, SISTER MARY LAWRENCE, hosp. adminstr.; b. Columbus, O., Sept. 25, 1925; d. Joseph John and Mary Ruth (Appl) Vanderburg; B.S. in Bus. Adminstrn., U. Dayton, 1956; M.H.A., Xavier U., 1965. Joined Franciscan Sisters of the Poor, 1949; personnel dir., bookkeeper Our Lady of Bellefonte Hosp., Ashland, Ky., 1957-59, adminstr., 1965—; bus. mgr. St. Mary's Hosp., Cin., 1959-65. Mem. Alcoholic Council Greenup County (Ky.), 1971-73; mem. Fivco Area Planning Commn. Boyd, Greenup and Lawrence Counties (Ky.), 1971-73. Bd. trustees St. Elizabeth Hosp., Covington, Ky., 1971—. Home and office: Our Lady of Bellefonte Hospital St Christopher Dr Ashland KY 41101

VANDERGRIFF, LOLA AOLA (MRS. WILLIAM PALMER VANDERGRIFF), writer; b. LeMars, Ia., May 7, 1920; d. Cecil Reno and Lola Hazel (Dannelley) Seery; student Am. River Coll., 1971-72; m. William Palmer Vandergriff, July 11, 1942; children—Jacquelyn (Mrs. Vance H. Yount), William Ladd, Rebecca (Mrs. Charles L. Williams), Jamie, Michael, Patrick. With Program KTOK, Oklahoma City, 1937-38; columnist Minuteman Messenger, Grand Forks, N.D., 1964-65; free lance writer of short stories to slicks, sports, religious, confession mags., farm publs. and newspapers, 1966—. Tchr. short story Am. River Coll., Sacramento, 1973—. Mem. CAPES, 1972—. Mem. Cal. Republican Assembly. Recipient numerous writing awards. Mem. Suburban Writers (pres. 1967-68), Cal. Writers. Author: Golden Harvest (poetry), 1936; novels Sisters of Sorrow, House of Dancing Dead, Witch of Wyndspelle, Bell of Wyndspelle. Address: Box 176 La Luz NM 88337

VANDERMEULEN, ALICE JOHN (MRS. DANIEL C. VANDERMEULEN), educator; b. Denver, Colo., Oct. 3, 1918; d. William Mestrezat and Alice Margaret (Schleter) John; A.B., Bryn Mawr Coll., 1939; A.M., Radcliffe Coll., 1946; Ph.D., Harvard, 1947; m. Daniel C. Vandermeulen, Sept. 3, 1941; 1 son, David John. Instr. Simmons Coll., Boston, 1942-43; Wellesley (Mass.) Coll., 1943-45; Harvard, Cambridge, Mass., 1947-48; asst. prof. econs., Claremont Men's Coll., Cal., 1949-50, asso. prof., 1950-51; lectr. Claremont (Cal.) Grad. Sch., 1956-58; vis. asso. prof. econs., U. Cal., Los Angeles, 1960—, lectr., 1961-65, sr. lectr., 1966-70, prof. in residence, 1970—. Cons. Cal. Assembly Interim com. on revenue and taxation, 1963-64; Cal. adv. commn. on tax reform, 1968. Recipient John Randolph and Dora Haynes Found. grant, 1951; Social Sci. Research Council grant, 1954. Mem. Am., So. Cal. (pres., 1956-57), Western (exec. com., 1967-73), econ. assns., Econometric Soc., Phi Beta Kappa. Author: National Income, 1956; California's Fee and License Structure, 1964. Editor: Western Economic Jour., 1966-73. Contbr. articles to econ. jours. Office: Dept Economics Univ California Los Angeles CA 90024

VANDER MEY, CAROL DIANE, ins. mag. editor; b. Chgo., July 3, 1948; d. Richard Robert and Ruth G. (Zeigler) Vander Mey; student No. Ill. U., 1966-68; B.J., U. Mo., 1970. Editor, Nat. Safety Council, Chgo., 1970-72; asso. editor Kemper Agt. Mag., Long Grove, Ill., 1973—. Mem. Women in Communication. Office: Kemper Insurance Long Grove IL 60049

VAN DER VOORT, AMANDA VENELIA (MRS. MAYNARD I. LANDA), artist; b. Alliance, O.; d. Frederic Miller and Venelia Penrose (Clarendon) Van Der Voort; student Pratt Inst., 1928-31, Met. Sch. Art, 1938-41, Nat. Acad. Sch. of Fine Arts, 1945-48, Columbia, N.Y.U., 1949-50, 1951; m. Maynard I. Landa, Sept. 12, 1934. Exhibited in group shows including Nat. Acad. Design, N.Y., Allied Artists Am., N.Y.C., Hudson Valley Art Assn., N.Y., Springfield (Mass.) Mus., Am. Artists Profl. League, Nat. League Am. Pen Women (rec. sec. Bridgeport chpt. 1974—), Nat. Arts Club, Catharine Lorillard Wolfe Art Club, Burr Galleries, N.Y.C., Bruce Mus., Greenwich, Conn.; represented in numerous pub., pvt. collections. William H. Fogg scholar Nat. Acad. Sch. Fine Arts, 1952-54. Joseph I. Isadore Meml. scholar. Nat. Acad. Sch. Fine Arts, 1956-57. Recipient numerous awards. Fellow N.A.D., Royal Soc. Arts (Eng.) (life); mem. Am. Artists Profl. League (nat. dir. 1970—), Art League L.I. (dir.), Nat. League Am. Pen Women 1st prize for portrait 1962), Hudson Valley Art Assn. (dir. 1966—, chmn. awards 1968—, rec. sec. 1970—), Acad. Artists Assn., Women of '76 (chmn. mus. standing com. 1960-65), D.A.R., Nat. Wildlife Fedn., Met. Mus. Art, Washington Hdqrs. Assn., Nat. League Watch and Clock Collectors, Greenwich Art Soc., Art Assn. Old Greenwich. Republican. Clubs: Contemporary Arts (Greenwich, Conn.); Catherine Lorillard Wolfe Art (dir. 1960—, publicity dir. 1961-66), Pen and Brush (dir. 1967-72, 1st v.p. 1972—, publicity dir. 1964-65), Nat. Arts, Travel, Woman's of Greenwich (chmn. ann. arts and crafts exhbn.). Address: 17 Stonehedge Dr S Greenwich CT 06830

VAN DER ZEE, SISTER MAUREEN, hosp. adminstr.; b. Grand Forks, N.D., Feb. 22, 1917; d. John and Josephine (Riley) Van der Zee; R.N., St. Vincent Coll., Nursing, 1939; student in adminstrn. St. Louis U., 1965— summers. Dir. nursing service St. Luke Hosp., Pasadena, Cal., 1950-53; supr. obstets. dept. Santa Rosa Meml. Hosp., Santa Rosa, Cal., 1953-57, dir. nursing service, 1957-60; hosp. adminstr. St. Mary Plains Hosp., Lubbock, Tex., 1960—. Chmn., S. Plains Hosp. Area, 1965; local superior Sisters St. Joseph, Lubbock, 1960—. Sec. Tex. Conf. Cath. Hosps., 1966; chmn. S. Plains Hosp. Area, 1972-73. Bd. dirs. Lubbock Heart Assn., South Plains Guidance Center; mem. South Plains Area U. Affiliation Council, 1972—. Mem. Am. Coll. Hosp. Adminstrs., Lubbock Hosp. Council (chmn. 1962-65), Lubbock C. of C. (mem. hosp. planning council 1964—). Address: 4000 24th St Lubbock TX 79410

VAN DE VATE, NANCY JEAN HAYES (MRS. DWIGHT VAN DE VATE, JR.), educator, composer; b. Plainfield, N.J., Dec. 30, 1930; d. John Fleming and Anna Martha (Tschudi) Hayes; student Eastman Sch. Music, 1948-49, summer 1950; A.B., Wellesley Coll., 1952; Mus. M., U. Miss., 1958; Mus. D., Fla. State U., 1968; m. Dwight Van de Vate, Jr., June 9, 1952; children—Katherine, Barbara, Dwight III. Faculty U. Miss., Oxford, 1960, Memphis State U., 1964-66, U. Tenn., Knoxville, 1967; asso. prof. music Knoxville Coll., 1968-69, 71-72, Maryville Coll., 1973—. Violist Knoxville Symphony Orch., 1970-73. Alumnae admissions rep. Wellesley Coll., 1967—. Recipient commn. for composition Knoxville Choral Soc. Mem. A.S.C.A.P. (Standard award 1974), Am. Soc. U. Composers, Southeastern Composers League (sec. 1965-68, 70-73, pres. 1973—), Nat. Orgn. for Women (chpt. convenor 1971-73). Unitarian (chmn. music com. 1971-72). Editor: Music Now, 1965-68, 70-73. Composer Concerto for Piano and Orch.; An Am. Essay for mixed chorus, piano and percussion. Home: 5610 Holston Hills Rd Knoxville TN 37914

VANDIVERT, RITA ALICE ANDRE (MRS. WILLIAM VANDIVERT), author; b. London, Eng.; d. Frank and Alice (Matthes) Andre; intermediate commerce exam., London U. School Econs., 1924; m. William Vandivert, June 7, 1940; 1 dau., Susan. Came to U.S., 1946, naturalized, 1950. Translator RKO Radio Films, European distbn. dir., London, Paris, 1933; editorial asst., Time, Inc., London, Paris, 1935-41; film editor, Brit. Information Service, N.Y.C., 1942-44; war corr., March of Time, Life mags., Germany, 1944-46; pres., Magnum Photos, Inc., N.Y.C., 1947-48; free-lance writer, researcher, 1948—. Author: Common Wild Animals & Their Young, 1957, The Porcupine Known as J.R., 1959, Young Russia, 1960, Barnaby, 1963, Chicken As You Like It, 1968; Favorite Wild Animals of North America, 1973. Home: 21 E 10th St New York City NY 10003

VAN DOOREN, ADA ALEID, psychiatrist; b. Renkum, Netherlands, Feb. 20, 1925 (came to the U.S. 1953, naturalized 1968); d. Johan and Aaltje (deJong) Visser; student U. Groningen, 1947; U. Leiden, 1949; M.D., U. Amsterdam, 1952; m. Hugo Van Dooren, Aug. 7, 1952 (div. 1970); children—JoAnn Maureen, Ivan Mark, Michael Neal, Gwendolyn Ann. Rotating intern, Holland, 1952-53, Tacoma (Wash.) Gen. Hosp., 1953-54; biochem. research, U. Utah, 1955-57; in patient tng. Western State Hosp., Tacoma, 1963-65, VA Hosp., Seattle, 1965-67; out patient tng. U. Wash., 1967-68; practice medicine specializing in psychiatry and community psychiatry, Tacoma, 1968—; cons. Aberdeen (Wash.) Mental Health Center, 1968-69; Div. Vocational Rehab., Tacoma Sch. system, 1969-70; staff psychiatrist Pacific Lutheran U., 1968—, Child Devel. Center, Fort Lewis, Wash., 1968—, U. Puget Sound, Tacoma, 1970—; cons. Drug. action coordinating council, Pierce County, 1971. Lectr. occupational therapy students U. Puget Sound, student nurses Tacoma Gen. Hosp. Mem. P.T.A., Tacoma, 1960—, originated Meeker Coop. Nursery, Tacoma, 1960; mem. adv. bd. Community Mental Health Clinic, Tacoma, 1968-69. Mem. Wash. State Med. Assn., Am. Psychiat. Assn., Am. Coll. Health Assn., Tacoma Art Museum, Wash. Assn. for Retarded Children, N.W. Assn. Adolescent Psychiatry. Club: Holland American (Seattle). Home: 10908 Meadow Rd SW Tacoma WA 98499 Office: 10908 Meadow Rd SW Tacoma WA 98499

VAN DOREN, RUTH MAE, librarian; b. Cleve., Aug. 1, 1915; d. Francis Mack and Lillian (Moore) Van Doren; B.A., Cleve. Coll. of Western Res. U., 1937; postgrad. Western Res. U., 1937-38; M.L.S., Rutgers, 1968. Asst. to head pub. relations Cleve. Coll. Western Res. U., 1938-39; sec. Citizens Tax League O., Inc., Cleve., also Columbus, 1939-40; registrar Frances Payne Bolton Sch. Nursing, Western Res. U., Cleve., 1940-41; reporter-clk. Heights Press, Cleveland Hieghts, O., 1942; asst. dir. pub. information Western Res. U., Cleve., 1942-45; dir. pub. relations Cleve. YWCA, 1945-47; asst. dir. pub. relations Coll. Wooster (O.), 1948-51; adult activities program dir. Jackson (Mich.) YWCA, 1951-52; dir. pub. information Wilson Coll., Chambersburg, Pa., 1952-61; information officer Woodrow Wilson Nat. Fellowship Found., Princeton, N.J., 1961-68; head librarian Coyle Free Library, Chambersburg, Pa., 1969-70; dir. Conococheague Dist. Library, Chambersburg, 1970-74; adult services librarian Western Md. Libraries, Hagerstown, 1974—. Dep. foreman Mercer County (N.J.) Grand Jury, 1967. Bd. dirs. Princeton (N.J.) YWCA, 1962-65, v.p., 1964; mem. bd. Franklin County Soc. Crippled Children and Adults, 1959-61, Community Actions, Inc., Chambersburg, 1969-72. Mem. Geneal. Soc. N.J., Am., Pa., Cumberland Valley library assns. Presbyn. (deacon 1967-69). Club: Soroptimist (pres. Chambersburg 1960). Home: 1628 Scotland Av Chambersburg PA 17201 Office: 100 S Potomac St Hagerstown MD 21740

VANDOW, EVA SHRIBMAN (MRS. JULES VANDOW), physician, psychiatrist; b. Malden, Mass., Mar. 4, 1909; d. Samuel and Menicha (Stasel) Shribman; student Simmons Coll., 1926-28; M.D., Boston U., 1932; m. Jules Vandow, Dec. 21, 1930 (dec. Jan. 1971); 1 son, Michael E. Intern. Met. Hosp., N.Y.C., 1932-33; resident Willard Parker Hosp., N.Y.C., 1933; exec. physician Sea View Hosp., S.I., N.Y., 1935-37; practice medicine specializing in gynecology, 1937-39; dep. med. supt. Kingston Av. Hosp., Bklyn., 1940-47, N.Y.C. Hosp., 1947-50; med. supt. Willard Parker Hosp., 1950-54, Francis Delafield Hosp., N.Y.C., 1954-56; sr. med. supt. Coney Island Hosp., Bklyn., 1956-63; hosp. adminstr. City Hosp. Center at Elmhurst, N.Y.C., 1963-65; ret. as hosp. adminstr. Bronx Municipal Hosp. Center, 1967, attending psychiatrist, 1970—; asst. prof. psychiatry Albert Einstein Coll. Medicine. Preceptor for adminstrv. resident Columbia Sch. Pub. Health and Adminstrv. Medicine, 1963—. Mem. sr. faculty adv. com. R.F. Kennedy Center for Mental Retardation; asst. dir. Throgs Neck Community Services, 1970—. Recipient certificate pub. service State of N.Y., 1958, award for 25 years service N.Y.C. Dept. Hosps., 1962. Fellow Am. Coll. Hosp. Adminstrs., Am. Pub. Health Assn.; mem. A.M.A. N.Y. State, N.Y. County med. socs., N.Y.C. Pub. Health Assn. (dir. 1963-65), Profl. Assn. Pub. Execs., Am. Psychiatric Assn., Assn. Clin. Faculty Albert Einstein Coll. Medicine, Hosp. Council Bklyn., L.I. and S.I. (sec. 1958-59, v.p. 1959-60, pres. 1961-62), Hosp. Adminstrs. Assn. Dept.

Hosps. City of N.Y. (sec. 1955-56, 56-57, chmn. edn. com. 1961-62, exec. com. 1961-62, pres. 1962-63). Club: Zonta, Woman's City (N.Y.). Contbr. articles to profl. publs. Home: 750 Kappock St Riverdale NY 10463 Office: 750 Kappock St Riverdale NY 10463

VAN DUYN, CARROLL LORRAINE (MRS. OTTO MARION VAN DUYN), ednl. adminstr.; b. Laramie, Wyo., Nov. 15, 1946; d. John Carroll and Esther Lorraine (Eurich) Clay; B.A. in Edn., U. Wyo., 1970; postgrad. Purdue U., 1972—; m. Otto Marion Van Duyn, June 1, 1969. Student asst. Ross Hall U. Wyo., Laramie, 1968-69. Fiscal mgr. Snowy Range Community Action Agy., 1969-71; asst. mgr. Meredith Hall, Purdue U., Lafayette, Ind., 1971-72, McCutcheon Hall, 1972-74, Windsor Halls, 1974—. Mem. Am. Personnel Guidance Assn., Nat. Assn. Women Deans, Adminstrs. and Counselors, Am., Ind. coll. personnel assns., Nat. Assn. Student Personnel Adminstrs. Republican. Episcopalian. Home: 2601 Soldiers Home Rd West Lafayette IN 47906 Office: Windsor Halls Purdue University West Lafayette IN 47906

VAN DUYNE, FRANCES OLIVIA, educator; b. Newark, Sept. 16, 1912; d. Philip R. and Lucy (Harrison) Van Duyne; B.A., Vassar Coll., 1934; M.A., 1936; Ph.D., Columbia, 1940. Asst. in physiology Vassar Coll., Poughkeepsie, N.Y., 1934-36; asst. in chemistry Columbia, N.Y.C., 1936-40; asso. in home econs. U. Ill., Urbana, 1940-45, asst. prof. foods, 1945-49, asso. prof., 1949-53, prof., 1953—. Fellow A.A.A.S.; mem. Am. Chem. Soc., Am. Dietetic Assn., Am. Home Econs. Assn., Inst. Food Tech., Phi Beta Kappa, Sigma Xi, Iota Sigma Pi, Phi Kappa Phi, Phi Upsilon Omicron, Sigma Delta Epsilon. Contbr. articles to profl. jours. Home: 604 S Gregory Pl Urbana IL 61801

VAN DYKE, ANNY MARION, tel. co. exec.; b. Howard, Ont., Can., Sept. 30, 1928; d. Anthony and Anna (Koolen) Van Dyke; C.F.A., U. Va., 1969; B.A., Sir George Williams U., 1959. Teacher Lanoraie Sch. Bd., 1946-47; sec. Can. Nat. Rys., Montreal, Que., Can., 1947-51; sec. Sorel Industries Ltd., Sorel, Que., Can., 1952-53; with Bell Canada, Montreal, Que., Can., 1953—, common stock investment mgr., 1974—. Mem. Inst. Chartered Financial Analysts, Montreal Soc. Financial Analysts (program chmn., pres. 1974-75), Cercle Finance-Placement. Home: 305 St Charles St W Apt 104 Longueuil PQ J4H 1H2 Canada Office: Bell Canada Treasury Dept 1050 Beaver Hall Hill Montreal PQ Canada

VAN DYKE, JUNE MAREE CALDWELL, fashion exec.; b. Cleve.; d. William Robert and Gertrude Vivian (Cantwell) Caldwell; grad. Am. Acad. Dramatic Arts (N.Y.C.), 1950; m. Truman Van Dyke, Jr., July 14, 1951 (div.); children—Truman III, Richard Robert. Producer fashion spectaculars for large charitable, polit., nat. corporate accounts including Am. Mining Congress, Kiwanis Internat., Max Factor Internat; coordinator-producer fashion show prodns. Edith Head, designer, Hollywood, Cal., 1960—. Chmn., So. Cal. Automobile Show Premiere, 1968; mem. Los Angeles Orphanage Guild, 1966—; mem. costume council Los Angeles County Art Mus., 1964—. Bd. dirs. Assistance League So. Cal., 1968—, chmn. Mannequins Aux., 1967-68. Mem. Mannequins Assn. Los Angeles (adv. bd. 1967—), Los Angeles Fashion Group. Office: 6922 Hollywood Blvd Hollywood CA 90028

VAN DYKE, WILHELMINA MARIE (MRS. RICHARD COLLINS LORD), pediatrician; b. Chgo., Oct. 10, 1913; d. John and Catherine (Vandermeer) Van Dyke; student Ypsilanti State Normal Coll., 1934; M.D., U. Mich., 1938; m. Richard Collins Lord, June 5, 1943; children—Diana (Mrs. Scott U. Adam), Susan (Mrs. Charles M. Lundt), Margaret (Mrs. John Sacco), Catherine. Intern U. Hosp., Boston, 1939-41; asst. resident Mass. Gen. Hosp., Boston, 1941-42, resident in pediatrics, 1942-43; practice medicine specializing in pediatrics, Milton, Mass., 1943—; asst. pediatrician Harvard Med. Sch., 1953-62, instr. in pediatrics, 1962—; asst. to children's med. services, Mass. Gen. Hosp., 1944-65; clin. asso. in pediatrics, 1965—; chief of pediatrics Milton (Mass.) Hosp., 1959—; mem. staffs Milton Hosp. (sec., treas., 1961-64, pres. 1973-75), St. Margaret's Hosp., Boston; sch. physician, Milton, 1968—; pediatrician, well baby and pre-sch. clinics, Brookline, Dedham, Westwood, Holbrook, Randolph, Canton, Milton, Mass. Mem. A.M.A., Norfolk Dist. Med. Soc., New Eng. Pediatrics Soc., Mass. Inst. Tech. Matron. Club: Milton Women's. Home: 16 Spafford Rd Milton MA 02186 Office: 16 Spafford Rd Milton MA 02186

VANE, FLOIE MARIE, chemist; b. Dawson, Minn., Nov. 25, 1937; d. Alvin and Jessie (Olson) Vane; B.S., Gustavus Adolphus Coll., 1959; Ph.D., Mich. State U., 1963; postgrad. Mass. Inst. Tech., 1963-64. Vis. asst. prof. Baylor Coll. Medicine, Houston, 1968-69; sr. chemist Hoffmann-LaRoche Inc., Nutley, N.J., 1964-72, research group chief, 1973—. Recipient Jr. Research award Sigma Xi, 1962, First Decade award Gustavus Adolphus Coll., 1969. Mem. Am. Chem. Soc., Sierra Club, A.A.A.S., Sigma Xi. Contbr. articles to profl. jours. Home: 380 Mountain Rd Union City NJ 07087 Office: Hoffmann-LaRoche Inc Roche Park Nutley NJ 07110

VANE, JULIA RUTH RANDLE (MRS. ROBERT J. VANE), educator; b. Bklyn.; d. Harry T. and Mary (Stoddard) Randle; B.A., Bklyn. Coll., 1941; M.A., Columbia, 1942; Ph.D., N.Y. U., 1951; m. Robert J. Vane, Apr. 15, 1944. Psychologist, Mallon Consultation Service, 1942-43; chief psychologist Cath. Charities Psychiat. Clinic, N.Y.C., 1943-51, Hempstead (N.Y.) Pub. Schs., 1952-62; asso. prof. Hofstra U., 1962—, prof. psychology, 1968—, coordinator doctoral programs in psychology, 1967—. Cons. Seaford Pub. Schs., 1968-69, Hempstead Pub. Schs., 1969-71, Nassau County Headstart Program, L.I., N.Y., 1967-70. Diplomate in clin. and sch. psychology Am. Bd. Examiners in Profl. Psychology. Mem. Am. Assn. U. Profs., Am. (pres. div. sch. psychologists), N.Y. State, Nassau County (pres. 1956) psychol. assns. Author: Vane Kindergarten Test, 1968. Home: 141 Elmwood Av Hempstead NY 11550

VAN ECK, GERTRUDE JOAN VERMANDE (MRS. WILLIAM FREDERICK VAN ECK), physician; b. Hoorn, Netherlands; d. Jan and Jacoba (Van Maanen) Vermande; M.D., U. Amsterdam, 1939; m. William Frederick Van Eck, May 10, 1943; children—Walter John, Herman Jan. Came to U.S., 1949, naturalized, 1956. Intern, Univ. Hosp. Amsterdam, 1937-39; resident Univ. hosps. Rotterdam (Holland), Vienna (Austria), 1939-43; research asst. Yale Sch. Medicine, 1950-52, research asso., 1952-61; practice medicine specializing in obstetrics and gynecology, East Haven, Conn., 1961—; mem. staff Yale-New Haven Hosp. Mem. Internat. Soc. Fertility and Sterility, Am. Soc. Sterility, Am. Coll. Obstetrics and Gynecology, N.Y. Acad. Scis., Conn., New Haven County med. socs., New Haven Obstet. Soc. Home: 494 Thompson Av East Haven CT 06512 Office: 228 Main St East Haven CT 06512

VAN EEDEN, CONSTANCE (MRS. CHARLES HALL KRAFT), educator; b. Delft, The Netherlands, Apr. 6, 1927; d. Willem and Constance (Boer) van Eeden; candidaatsexamen, U. Amsterdam (The Netherlands), 1949, doctoral examen, 1954, Ph.D., 1958; m. Charles Hall Kraft, Dec. 8, 1960; 1 dau., Kari. Came to U.S., 1960. Mathematisch Centrum, Amsterdam, The Netherlands, 1951-60; vis. asso. prof. Mich. State U., East Lansing, 1960-61; research asso. U. Minn., Mpls., 1961-64, asso. prof., 1964-65; asso. prof. U. Montreal, Que., Can., 1965-68, prof., 1968—. Vis. prof. Math. Research Center, U. Wis., Madison, 1969, U. Rennes (France), spring 1970. Mem. N.Y. Acad. Scis., Inst. Math. Statistics, Am. Statis. Assn., A.A.A.S., Actuarial Soc. Netherlands, Statis. Soc. Netherlands, Canadian Math. Congress. Author: (with Charles H. Kraft) A Nonparameteic Introduction to Statistics, 1967. Contbr. articles to profl. jours. Home: 3438 Draper Av Montreal 261 PQ Canada

VAN EPPS, RUTH HANSEN, lawyer; b. Manitowoc, Wis., Sept. 1, 1906; d. Hans Andreas and Abigail (Haggerty) Hansen; grad. high sch., 1923; m. Kenneth P. Van Epps, Sept. 22, 1945; children—Mary (Mrs. Duane Schultz), Jean (Mrs. Roderick Thomson), Karen (Mrs. David Otto). Admitted to Wis. bar, 1936; practiced in Manitowoc, 1936-45, Weyauwega, Wis., 1945—; mem. firm Van Epps, Gull & Werth, Weyauwega. Mem. Am., Wis., Waupaca County bar assns., Weyauwage C. of C., Kensington Club. Roman Catholic. Home: Orchard Hill Weyauwage WI 54983 Office: 108 W Main St Weyauwage WI 54983

VANEVENHOVEN, MAXINE TOLER, assn. exec.; b. Redfield, Ia., Mar. 19, 1921; d. Clarence Victor and Mary Rose (Paardekooper) Toler; student U. Ia., 1939-40; sensitivity tng. course Lake Geneva (Wis.) campus George Williams Coll., 1965; certificate YMCA Program Profl. Devel., 1968, 69, 70; student U. Wis., 1968-74; m. Louis J. Vanevenhoven, Jan. 19, 1946. Bus. mgr., fashion model A. Held Exclusives, Des Moines, 1939-42; bus. mgr. Samuel Binghams' Co., Des Moines, 1942-45; pvt. sec. Stearns Rogers Co., Denver, 1946-47; interviewer loans VA, Appleton, Wis., 1947-48; pvt. sec. Appleton YMCA, 1949-52, bus. mgr., 1952-58, pre-sch. dir., 1958—, health club dir., 1958—, girls and womens dir., 1958-70, adult exec. dir., 1970—; YMCA tour guide; cons. health and beauty; tchr. weight control and exercise classes. Dir. youth in govt. program Wis. YMCA, 1960—, mem. nat. com., 1974. Organizer, chmn. bd. community beautification project, 1973-74, Kaukauna (Wis.) Community Council, 1971-73; chmn. Leadership Tng. Clinic for Club Officers, Appleton Area, 1970; organizer lectr. series Office Girl & Job Dinner, 1958—. Mem. Assn. Profl. YMCA Dirs., Internat. Toastmistress Clubs (dist. pres. 1972), Altrusa Club (community service chmn. Appleton 1972-74), Assn. Theatres, YMCA Health Club, Elks Ladies Club (pres. 1964-65). Methodist (v.p. women's orgn. 1970-73). Editor: Model for Recruiting Women Volunteer Group Leaders in YMCA, 1970; Maxine's Luscious Low Cal Recipes, 1974-75; Dynamic Exercises for Health and Beauty, 1975; Relaxation and Agility Exercises for Older Americans, 1975. Home: 18 Idlewild St Kaukauna WI 54130 Office: 218 E Lawrence St Appleton WI 54911

VAN FLEET, JOSEPHINE, physician; b. Trenton, N.J., Jan. 1, 1917; d. Peter and Stella (Kise) Van Fleet; A.B., Ind. U., 1941, M.D., 1943. Instr. pathology Ind. U. Sch. Medicine, 1944-50; chief lab. service VA Hosp., Indpls., 1952-55; dir. bur. labs. Ind. Bd. Health, Indpls., 1957—. Named a Sagamore of the Wabash, Gov. Ind. Diplomate Am. Bd. Pathology. Fellow Coll. Am. Pathologists, Am. Soc. Clin. Pathologists, Am. Pub. Health Assns; mem. Ind. Pub. Health Assn., A.M.A., Ind. Assn. Pathologists, Indiana, Local medical societies. Home: 3320 W 62d Pl Indianapolis IN 46208 Office: 1330 W Michigan St Indianapolis IN 46206

VANFOSSEN, BETH ELAINE ENSMINGER, sociologist, educator; b. Birmingham, Ala., Dec. 11, 1935; d. Ross Emmanuel and Margaret (Goodhue) Ensminger; B.A., Blackburn Coll., 1957; M.A., Pa. State U., 1958; Ph.D., Emory U., 1960; m. Marion Gilbert Vanfossen, June 3, 1956 (div. 1973). Asst. prof. sociology Furman U., Greenville, S.C., 1960-66; lectr. Grinnell Coll., Ia., 1967; asso. prof. sociology Old Dominion U., Norfolk, Va., 1968-69; asso. prof., chmn. dept. sociology Wells Coll., Aurora, N.Y., 1971—. Mem. Williamsburg-James City County League Women Voters (dir. 1970-72), Am. Assn. U. Women, Am. Civil Liberties Union, Am. Sociol. Assn., So., Midwest, Eastern sociol. socs., Alpha Kappa Delta. Contbr. articles in field to profl. jours. Home: Lansing Apts West Ithaca NY 14850

VAN FOSSEN, HELEN KEY, physician; b. Lake Providence, La., May 19, 1926; d. Harry Thomas and Maude Olivia (McPhate) Van Fossen; B.S., La. State U., 1948; M.D., 1955. Intern, Charity Hosp., New Orleans, 1955-56; resident internal medicine La. State U. Med. Service New Orleans, 1956-59, fellow in gastroenterology, 1959-62; practice medicine, specializing in internal medicine and gastroenterology, Memphis, 1962—; mem. staffs Bapt. Hosp., Memphis, St. Joseph Hosp., Memphis. Bd. dirs. Memphis Ballet Soc.; v.p. bd. dirs. Ballet South of Memphis. Fellow Am. Coll. Gastroenterology, Am. Soc. Gastro-intestinal Endoscopy; mem. A.M.A., Tenn., So., Women's med. assns., Memphis, Shelby County med. socs. Episcopalian. Home: 4317 Burgundy Rd Memphis TN 38111 Office: 969 Madison Suite 1000 Memphis TN 38104

VAN GELDER, LINDSY EVANS, journalist; b. Plainfield, N.J., Sept. 19, 1944; d. Lester John and Marilynn (Chamberlain) Evans; B.A., Sarah Lawrence Coll., 1966; student Northwestern U., 1962-64; m. Lawrence Ralph Van Gelder, Feb. 26, 1966; children—Sarah Chamberlain, Miranda Jordan. Editorial asst. N.Y. World-Telegram & Sun, summers 1963-65; reporter U.P.I., N.Y.C., 1967-68; reporter N.Y. Post, N.Y.C., 1968—. Free lance work for United Nations Radio, 1970, WNET-TV, 1971. Mem. Internat. Wizard of Oz Club, Am. Civil Liberties Union, Friends of the Animal Med. Center, Newspaper Guild. Contbr. articles in field to profl. jours. Office: 210 S St New York City NY 10002

VANGEN, DOROTHY BARNETT (MRS. HANS KENNETH VANGEN), supt. schs.; b. Fountain Prairie, Wis., Dec. 26, 1919; d. Edwin Julius and Blanche Macelle (Loomis) Sauer; B.A., Whitewater State Tchrs. Coll., 1960; M.A., U. Wis., 1965; m. Hans Kenneth Vangen, June 10, 1961; 1 son, Philip. Tchr. elementary schs. Columbus County, 1940-55, first grade, 1955-60, Wautoma, 1960-65; supt. schs., Princeton, Wis., 1966-70, supr. guidance, 1970—. Assn. Curriculum Devel., Wis. Edn. Assn., Phi Beta Theta. Home: Rural Route 2 Wautoma WI 54982 Office: Princeton WI 54968

VAN HOESEN, BETH MARIE (MRS. MARK ADAMS), artist; b. Boise, Ida., June 27, 1926; d. Enderse Gross and Freda Marie (Soulen) Van Hoesen; B.A., Stanford, 1948; student Escuela Esmaralda, Mexico, Acad. Julian, Grande Chaumier, Fontainbleau, France, San Francisco Art Inst.; m. Mark Adams, Sept. 12, 1953. Exhibited one-man shows including DeYoung Mus., San Francisco Mus., Cal. Palace of Legion of Honor, San Francisco, Santa Barbara (Cal.) Mus.; represented in permanent collections including San Francisco Mus., Achenbach Collection, Mus. Modern Art, N.Y.C., Bklyn. Mus., Smithsonian Instn., Victoria-Albert Mus., London. Recipient purchase awards San Francisco Mus., Pasadena (Cal.) Mus., Achenbach Found., U. Hawaii. Home: 3816 22d St San Francisco CA 94114

VAN HOOK, VIOLA LOUISE (MRS. LEWIS JOHN VAN HOOK), dept. store exec.; b. Millville, N.J., Sept. 10, 1913; d. Emil Joseph and Harriet May (Chapman) Fath; student Immaculata Coll., 1931-32; Vineland Bus. Coll., 1939-41; m. Lewis John Van Hook, Apr. 10, 1944; 1 son, Emil Lewis. With Armstrong Cork Co., Millville, N.J., 1941-46; sec. Millville Glass Mfg.; with Fath's Dept. Store, Millville, 1967—, pres., 1971—. Pres. Millville Hosp. Aux., 1952-68; Millville P.T.A., 1959-60; Parent's Music Booster Club, 1962-63; den mother local council Boy Scouts Am., 1957-58. Club: Woman's (pres. 1954-56, pres. evening dept. 1966-68) (Millville). Home: 102 Harrison Av Millville NJ 08332 Office: 120-24 High St Millville NJ 08332

VAN HORN, FRANCES RUTH, coll. adminstr.; b. Macon, Ga., Feb. 3, 1932; d. David Frank and Hattie Ruth (Swan) Bruce; A.B., Wesleyan Coll., Macon, 1953; m. Richard Dean Van Horn, Feb. 1, 1953; children—Lauri, Cris, Tracy, Miriam. Tchr. elementary schs., Macon, 1954-55, 66-69; alumnae dir. Wesleyan Coll., Macon, 1969—. Swimming instr. A.R.C., Macon, 1951-54; v.p. P.T.A., Macon, 1962-63; leader Girl Scouts, Macon, 1962-66. Bd. dirs. Central br. Ga. Lung Assn., 1970-73, pres., 1973-74; bd. dirs. Am. Alumnae Council. Methodist. Club: Garden (pres. 1963-64) (Macon). Home: 5854 Forsyth Rd Macon GA 31204 Office: Wesleyan Coll Macon GA 31201

VAN HORN, (HARRIET) EDITH, union ofcl.; b. Rangoon, Burma, Feb. 7, 1919 (parents Am. citizens); d. Clarence Eugene and Alice (Owells) Van Horn; B.A., Denison U., 1941; postgrad. Oberlin U., 1941-42. With Goodyear Aircraft Corp., Akron, O., 1942-44, Douglas Aircraft Corp., Santa Monica, Cal., 1944-45, Chrysler Corp., Hamtramck, Mich., 1946-63; mem. internat. staff U.A.W., Detroit, 1963—. Committeewoman UAW local 856, Akron, 1942-44, chief steward local 17, Santa Monica, 1944-45, chief steward and exec. bd. mem. local 3, Hamtramck, 1946-63. Mem. N.A.A.C.P., Nat. Women's Polit. Caucus (founding mem.), Nat. Orgn. for Women (charter mem.), Coalition of Labor Union Women (founder, midwest co-chmn. nat. coordinator 1973—), Am. Civil Liberties Union, Women's Internat. League for Peace and Freedom, Women's Action Alliance (dir.). Democrat. Home: 586 Ashland Av Detroit MI 48215 Office: 8000 E Jefferson St Detroit MI 48214

VANLANDINGHAM, MARY NELL, r.r. co. exec.; b. McGregor, Tex., May 30, 1916; d. Eugene Castleman and Hallie (Oliver) Clark; student U. Tex., 1933-35; B.A., Baylor U., 1940; m. Marshall Addie Vanlandingham, June 15, 1947. Teacher Elk Sch., McLennan County, Tex., 1935-40, Bosqueville Sch., McLennan County, Tex., 1940-42; sec. Bluebonnet Ordnance Plant, McGregor, Tex., 1942-45; sec. So. Pacific R.R. Co., Waco, Tex., 1945-60; chief clk. So. Pacific Transp. Co. and Cotton Belt Ry. Co., Waco, Tex., 1960—. Sec.-treas., trustee Evergreen Cemetery Assn. McLennan County. Clubs: Altrusa of Waco (chmn. ways and means 1969-70, v.p. 1970-71, pres. 1971-72, dir. 1970-72, dist. membership chmn. 1972-74, dist. exec. bd. 1973-74, award 1972). Hammond Organ. Home: Rt 2 Box 890 Waco TX 76710 Office: 301 S 8th St Waco TX 76701

VAN LEER, ELLA WALL (MRS. BLAKE R. VAN LEER), artist, engr., educator, civic leader; b. Berkeley, Cal., Nov. 21, 1893; d. A. Conrad and Mary Elizabeth (Leaf) Wall; A.B., U. Cal., 1914, M.A. in Art and Architecture, 1915; m. Blake Ragsdale Van Leer, Sept. 6, 1924 (dec.); children—Blake Wayne, Maryly (Mrs. Jordan Brown Peck, Jr.), Samuel Wall. Instr. U. Cal., 1914-15, summer 1916, Glendale High Sch., 1915-17, San Mateo High Sch., 1917-18, 20, Oakland Tech. High Sch., 1920-25, 27-29; condr. sketching classes, Gainesville, Fla., 1935-37. Illustrator Rand-McNally Lit. Maps, also various short stories; executed murals Women's Athletic Club (Oakland), Nursery Sch. U. Cal., Rockefeller Recreation Center (Washington); collaborator on murals Men's Faculty Club, U. Cal.; painter numerous portraits, Cal., Washington, Fla., N.C.; represented in juried exhbns., N.Y., Cal., Washington and so. states. Recipient art prizes and winner art competitions. Mem. motor corps. A.R.C., 1944-48; pres. Henrietta Egleston Hosp. Children's Aux., 1957-59, v.p. charge vols., 1959—; trustee Henrietta Egleston Hosp. for Children; scenery and costume designer Little Theatre, Cal., Fla., N.C. Served during World War I. R.A.P.T., 15 A.E.F. World War II O.O.M.G. prin. draftsman and technologist, research and development br., 1942-44. Recipient citation of commendation. Mem. Am. League Pen Women, Gainesville Fine Arts Assn., Am. Artists Profl. League, So. Art League, Atlanta Art Assn. (docent 1957—), Soc. Women Engrs. (treas. Atlanta 1956—), Service Group Atlanta (pres. 1953-55), Ret. Officers Assn. (hon.), Alpha Xi Delta (nat. chaplain 1955, pres. Atlanta alumnae 1953-55), Delta Epsilon Art Hon. (founder. hon. nat. pres.), Women's Big C Soc. (U. Cal.). Democrat. Episcopalian. Clubs: Capital City (Atlanta); Woman's Athletic (hon.) (Oakland, Cal.); Ga. Tech. Woman's Planters Garden (pres. 1963-65), Ft. McPherson Officers, Altrusa. Lectr.; ofcl. hostess as wife of pres. Ga. Tech., 1944-56. Home: 847 Techwood Dr NW Atlanta GA 30313

VAN LEEUWEN, JEAN (MRS. BRUCE DAVID GAVRIL), editor, author; b. Glen Ridge, N.J., Dec. 26, 1937; d. Cornelius and Dorothy Elizabeth (Charlton) Van Leeuwen; B.A., Syracuse U., 1959; m. Bruce David Gavril, July 7, 1968; children—David Andrew, Elizabeth Eva. Editor Random House, N.Y.C., 1963-68, Viking Press, N.Y.C., 1968-70, Dial Press, N.Y.C., 1971-73. Author: Timothy's Flower, 1967; One Day In Summer, 1969; The Great Cheese Conspiracy, 1969; I Was A 98 Pound Duckling, 1972; Too Hot for Ice Cream, 1974. Editor: A Time of Growing, 1967. Home: 444 E 75th St New York City NY 10021

VAN LYDEGRAF, MARY ELLEN WILLIAMS (MRS. LESTER L. VAN LYDEGRAF), counselor; b. Phila.; d. Fredrick Eugene and Emma (Henderson) Williams; B.A., U. Ore., 1939; M.A., U. Nev., 1962; Ph.D., Neotarian Coll. Philosophy, 1969; N.D. cum laude, Bernadeau U., 1971, Th.D. cum laude; m. Lester L. Van Lydegraf, June 5, 1939; children—Robert Eugene, JoAnn Dea, Jay Frank. Tchr. Washoe County sch. system, Reno, Nev., 1958-59, counselor Central Jr. High Sch., Reno, 1962-64, Sparks (Nev.) High Sch., 1964-69; counselor Spl. Services, 1965, Upward Bound Counselor, U. Nev., owner pvt. counseling service, Reno, 1970—; dir. County Counseling Service, 1971—; tchr. Sparks High Sch., 1971—; regular lectr., vis. prof. Bernadeau U., Las Vegas, 1972—; tchr. transcendental meditation. Mem. Profl. Counselors Assn., N.E.A., Congress Med. Equality, Washoe Assn. Retarded Children, Internat. Platform Assn., Nat. Vocational Guidance Assn., Internat. Naturopathic Assn., Washoe County Tchrs. Assn., Nat. Hemophiliac Found., Am. Assn. U. Women, Reno Panhellenic, Zeta Tau Alpha, Democrat. Mem. Baha'i World Faith. Home: 5445 W 4th St Reno NV 89503 Office: 5445 W 4th St Reno NV 89503

VAN MAANEN, HENRIETTA, home economist; b. Sioux Center, Ia., Mar. 24, 1936; d. Bert and Gertrude (Dykstra) Van Maanen; A.A., Northwestern Jr. Coll., 1955; B.S., Ia. State U., 1959; M.Ed., U. Md., 1964. Tchr. Orange City, Ia., 1955-57; county extension home economist, Eldora, Ia., 1959-63; home economist Cedar Rapids, Ia., 1964-69; dist. program leader Wash. State U. Extension Service, Prosser, Wash., 1969-74; area extension dir. Ia. State U. Extension Service, 1974—. Dir. Home and Family Living Service, Cedar Rapids, 1966-68. Mem. Family Life Edn. com., Cedar Rapids, 1966-68; mem. Headstart Planning, 1965-68, Linn County Family Planning, 1967-68. Bd. dirs. YWCA, 1967-68, Common Ministries, 1969-74. Mem. Am. Home Econ. Assn., Nat. Council Family Relations, Adult Edn. Assn. Presbyn. (elder 1972-74). Editorial bd. Extension Jour., 1972-74.

Home: 1435 1st Av N Fort Dodge IA 50501 Office: Fed Bldg Fort Dodge IA 50501

VAN METER, MARY MCNEAL, educator; b. Knox County, Ind., Feb. 5, 1919; d. Vernie and Anna Mary (Stanley) McNeal; B.S., Ind. State U., Terre Haute, 1950, M.A. in Fine Arts with honors, Ind. U., 1956; m. Charles L. Van Meter, Aug. 24, 1940. Instr., critic tchr., Ind. U., 1954-56; elementary art supr. Vincennes (Ind.) city schs., 1956-57; art tchr. Washington (Ind.) High Sch., 1956-57; mem. faculty Vincennes U., 1967—, prof. art, 1972—. Participant Ednl. Profl. Devel. Act Workshop Ind. U., 1973, Purdue Artists/USA, 1970-71. Sec. Vincennes Art Guild, 1967-69. Pres. Northwest Terr. Art Guild, 1969, bd. dirs., 1975. Recipient honor certificate Ind. U., 1956. Presbyn. Mem. Order Eastern Star. Contbr. articles to profl. publs. Home: R 1 Vincennes IN 47591

VAN METER, RUTH FRANCES, social work adminstr.; b. Moscow, Ida., Feb. 6, 1911; d. Claude Henry and Charlotte (Fogle) Van Meter; student Northwestern Sch. Commerce, 1930; diploma Cascade Coll., 1931-34; A.B., Asbury Coll., 1947; postgrad. Sch. Social Work, U. So. Cal., 1947, Nr. and Middle East Inst., Columbia, 1956-57. Sec., Ore. Dept. Mines and Geology, Portland, 1937-42; clk. Western Pacific and Santa Fe Rys., 1942-44; exec. dir. YWCA, Vallejo, Cal., 1944-46, Ogden, Utah, 1947-52, Berkeley, Cal., 1952-54, adv. sec., Istanbul, Turkey, 1957-62; dir. Fernhurst YWCA, Honolulu, 1962-63; adviser to YWCA's of Latin America, Montevideo, Uruguay, 1964-70, YWCA cons. Iran, Sri Lanka (Ceylon), India, Pakistan, Ethiopia, 1970-73. Fulbright tchr. Sch. Social Work, Athens, Greece, 1954-56; asso. gen. sec. woman's div. Bd. Missions, Methodist Ch., N.Y.C., 1963-64. Adviser to teen-age refugees, Greece, 1954-55. Recipient award for vol. work U.S.O. Club, Istanbul, 1962. Mem. Nat. Assn. Social Workers, Internat. Conf. Social Work, Am. Acad. Polit. and Social Sci., Acad. Certified Social Workers. Club: Soroptmist. Home: 3217 SW Ridge Dr Portland OR 97219 Office: care Internat Div YWCA 600 Lexington Av New York City NY 10022

VAN NESS, MARGUERITE DICKERSBACH (MRS. ROBERT C. VAN NESS), newspaper editor; b. New Rochelle, N.Y.; d. Peter and Elsa (Lang) Dickersbach; student pub. schs.; m. Robert C. Van Ness, Nov. 15, 1940; children—Marguerite D., Roberta C. (Mrs. James D. Elmore), Robert C. Asst. to publisher, profiel writer Scott Stamp & Coin Co., N.Y.C., 1942-47; with Richardson Publs., Carpentersville, Ill., 1968—, editor, 1969—. Dir. Midwest Mfg. Co., 1969—. Mem. N.Y. State P.T.A. (life). Home: 717 Webster St Algonquin IL 60102 Office: 451 Maple Av Carpentersville IL 60110

VANNIER, MARYHELEN, educator, author; b. Decatur, Ill., June 18, 1915; d. William H. and Maude (Rockwood) Vannier; B.A., James Millikin U., 1938; M.A., Tchrs. Coll., Columbia, 1943; Ed.D., N.Y.U., 1950. Dir. womens phys. edn. Drake U., Des Moines, 1940-42, St. Lawrence U., Canton, N.Y., 1948-50, Wellesley High Sch., 1940-41; dir. women's health and phys. edn. So. Meth. U., Dallas, 1950—. Mem. Internat. Congress Phys. Edn. Tchrs. Girls and Women, Nat. Conf. Research in Therapeutic Recreation, Am. Sch. Health Assn., A.A.H.P.E.R., Am. Assn. U. Profs., Park and Recreation Assn., Nat. Assn. Phys. Edn. Coll. Women. Author: Teaching Physical Education in Elementary Schools, 1973; Methods and Materials in Recreation Leadership, 1974; Individual and Team Sports for Girls and Women, 1974; Physical Activities for College Women, 1968; Physical Activities for the Handicapped, 1975; many others; articles in profl. jours. Home: 7006 Stefani St Dallas TX 75225

VAN NOSTRAND, JOAN FEDELL (MRS. LYMAN G. VAN NOSTRAND), statistician, govt. ofcl.; b. Pitts., Oct. 1, 1944; d. John Charles and Rose M. (Madia) Fedell; B.S. cum laude, Am. U., 1966; m. Lyman G. Van Nostrand, Aug. 25, 1972. Statistician, Office Dir. Nat. Center Health Statistics, Dept. Health, Edn. and Welfare, Washington, 1966-67, survey statistician health facilities statistics br., 1968-70, asst. chief br., Rockville, Md., 1971-74, acting chief long term care statistics br., 1974—. Mem. Young Profls. Adv. Council to Adminstr. Health Services and Mental Health Adminstrn., 1971-72. Mary Graydon scholar, 1962-66. Mem. Am. Statis. Assn., Internat. Statis. Inst., Internat. Assn. Survey Statisticians, Am. Pub. Health Assn., Phi Kappa Phi, Psi Chi. Contbr. articles and statis. surveys on nursing facilities and costs to profl. publs. Home: 10765 Deborah Dr Potomac MD 20854 Office: 5600 Fishers Lane Rockville MD 20852

VAN ORSDELL, MARJORIE L. TERWILLIGER (MRS. ELBERT L. VAN ORSDELL), educator; b. Walden, N.Y.; d. Daniel J. and Anne (Doherty) Terwilliger; B.Ed., State U. N.Y., 1943; M.A., N.Y. U., 1958; postgrad. U. Cal. at Berkeley, 1966, also Cornell U., San Diego State U., Trinity U.; m. Elbert L. Van Orsdell, Feb. 1, 1942; children—John Jeffrey, Anne Katherine. Tchr., Greenport Sch., Hudson, N.Y., 1940-43, Cornwall-on-Hudson (N.Y.) High Sch., 1943-46, 53-56, Mountainville Sch., Cornwall, N.Y., 1950-53; sci. coordinator Cornwall Central Elementary Schs., 1958-67; chmn. sci. dept., tchr. Cornwall Central High Sch., 1965—; mem. Fla. Inst. Tech. eclipse expdn., 1973. Cons., regional instr. program N.Y. State Edn. Dept., 1961-63. Mem. Orange County Med. and Radiol. Corps. of Civil Def., 1957—. Active boy and girl scouts' programs. Adviser, past trustee Mus. Hudson Highlands. Mem. N.Y. State Sci. Tchrs. Assn., N.Y. State, Cornwall (pres. 1957-58) tchrs. assns., N.E.A., League Women Voters. Democrat. Episcopalian. Mem. Order Eastern Star. Club: Cornwall Womens, Cornwall Garden. Home: Robert Arms Newburgh NY 12550 Office: 122 Main St Cornwall NY 12518

VAN OVERBEEK, THELMA TAYLOR (MRS. JOHANNES VAN OVERBEEK), lawyer; b. San Francisco, Jan. 28, 1918; d. Harold Frederick and Ann Elizabeth (Lawler) Taylor; B.S., U. Cal. at Berkeley, 1939; J.D., U. of Pacific, 1967; m. Johannes van Overbeek, July 24, 1948; children—Thomas Taylor, Marina Elizabeth, Frederick Octavius, William Dominic. Admitted to Tex. bar, 1968; mem. firm Cofer, Dillon, Giesenschlag, Bryan, Tex., 1969-71, Cofer and van Overbeek, Bryan, 1972—. Chmn., Brazos County Child Welfare Bd., 1971—. Mem. Am., Brazos County (v.p.) bar assns., State Bar Tex., Am. Assn. Women Lawyers. Home: 3615 Sunnybrook Lane Bryan TX 77801 Office: 200 E 33d St Bryan TX 77801

VAN PATTEN, MURIEL MAY, educator; b. Quincy, Mich., Apr. 27, 1932; d. Lloyd Delmar and Edwina (Parsons) Van Patten; B.S., Eastern Mich. U., 1954, M.A., 1962; student Wayne State U., 1967—. Art tchr. Fenton (Mich.) Pub. Schs., 1954-56; arts, crafts instr. Chgo. Park Dist., 1955-56; tchr. Wayne (Mich.) Community Sch. Dist., 1956-60, dir. art, 1960-67, elementary sch. prin., 1968—. Dir. secondary edn., coordinator student tchrs. Eastern Mich. U., 1962, vis. guest lectr. edn., art depts.; supr. summer art program City Wayne. Mem. Nat., Nat. Art, Mich., Mich. Art edn. assns., Mich. Dirs. Pub. Sch. Art Edn. (chmn. 1966-67), Mich. Assn. Supervision and Curriculum Devel., Mich. Assn. Elementary Prins., Sigma Nu Phi (v.p. 1954). Club: Soroptimist Fedn. Ams., Soroptimist of Wayne (rec. sec. 1967). Home: 34935 Ash St Wayne MI 48184 Office: 3712 Williams St Wayne MI 48184

VAN RIPER, SUE ELLEN FOUKE (MRS. EDWARD L. VAN RIPER, JR.), psychometrist; b. Indpls., Dec. 19, 1943; d. Myron Tyler and Jean Ellen (Storen) Fouke; B.A., DePauw U., 1965; M.S. (grad. fellow), Butler U., 1968; m. Edward L. Van Riper, Jr., Aug. 12, 1967; 1 son, Edward Stewart. Fourth grade tchr. Noblesville (Ind.) Pub. Schs., 1965-67, 68-70, psychometrist, tchr. jr. high sch. spl. edn., 1970-71; 4th grade tchr. Indpls. Pub. Schs., 1967-68; psychometrist Hamilton County Spl. Services Coop., Carmel, Ind., 1971—. Sales cons. Yarn Shoppe, Etc., Zionsville, Ind., 1971—. Sec. profl. group Jr. League Indpls., 1973-74. Mem. Nat. Assn. Sch. Psychologists, Council Exceptional Children. Democrat. Methodist. Club: Dramatic (Indpls.). Home: 4740 Washington Blvd Indianapolis IN 46205 Office: 420 E Main St Carmel IN 46032

VAN SLYKE, HELEN LENORE VOGT, author; b. Washington, July 9, 1919; d. Frederick H. and Lenore (Siegel) Vogt; m. William Woodward Van Slyke, Aug. 9, 1946 (div. Jan. 1952). Beauty editor Glamour Mag., N.Y.C., 1945-55, promotion dir., 1955-60; promotion and advt. dir. Henri Bendel, N.Y.C., 1960-62; v.p. Norman, Craig & Kummel, Advt. Agy., N.Y.C., 1962-63; pres. House of Fragrance, N.Y.C., 1963-68; internat. pres. The Fashion Group, Inc., 1966-67; v.p. advt. Helena Rubinstein, 1968-71; novelist, lectr., 1971—. Vol. worker Lighthouse for the Blind, 1963-71. Home: 350 E 57th St New York City NY 10022

VAN SLYKE, JUDY KULSTAD (MRS. TODD BRIAN VAN SLYKE), pub. relations exec.; b. St. Paul, Feb. 23, 1948; d. William Martin and Alberta Jane (Applen) Kulstad; B.S. with honors, Northwestern U., 1970; m. Todd Brian Van Slyke, July 25, 1970. Reporter, editor Asso. Press, Chgo., 1970-72; staff writer, editor Dept. of Univ. Relations, Northwestern U., Evanston, Ill., 1972-74; press relations asso. Continental Bank, Chgo., 1974—. Pres. Northwestern U. Young Alumni Council, Evanston, 1973—. Mem. Women in Communications, Quill and Scroll, Mortar Bd., Kappa Delta, Kappa Tau Alpha. Home: 2152 C Rugen Rd Glenview IL 60025 Office: 231S LaSalle St Chicago IL 60693

VAN SOELEN, ESTHER LYNEILLE (MRS. THEODORE VAN SOELEN), lawyer; b. Clovis, N.M., Apr. 4, 1928; d. Otto and Eva May (Burge) Smith; A.A., Cottey Coll., 1947; B.A., U. Okla., 1949, LL.B., 1951; m. Theodore Van Soelen, Oct. 25, 1969; children—Marian Burge Smith, Beverly Anne Smith, Fred Travis, Darrell Theodore. Admitted to N.M. bar, 1951; mem. firm Van Soelen & Sheehan, Clovis, 1951—. Mem. gen. com. Nogal Mesa Ranchman's Camp Meeting Assn., Clovis, 1961; legal adviser Ranchman's Camp Meeting Assn. S.W., 1970. Bd. dirs. Wesley Found., 1965—, Inst. Family Dynamics, Eastern N.M. U., Portales, 1971—. Mem. P.E.O. Republican. Methodist (trustee 1961-65, 72—. Home: Rural Route 2 Box 285 Clovis NM 88101 Office: 409 Pile St PO Drawer 1080 Clovis NM 88101

VAN STRATEN, SISTER MARY PETRONIA, educator; b. DePere, Wis., Mar. 3, 1913; d. Peter John and Louise (De Cleene) Van Straten; B.A., Mt. Mary Coll., 1944; Ph.D., U. Notre Dame, 1947; student Marquette U., 1948, U. Wash. (NSF grant), 1962, U. Ariz., summer 1963. Mem. Sch. Sisters of Notre Dame, 1932—; tchr. St. Peter & Paul Sch., Wisconsin Rapids, Wis., 1932-41, St. Mary's Sch., Elm Grove, Wis., 1941-43; with Mt. Mary Coll., 1947—, instr. math., 1947-49, asst. prof., 1949-51, asso. prof., 1951-69, prof., 1969—, chmn. math. dept., 1965—. Named Outstanding Educator of Am., 1972. Mem. Wis. Math. Council (sec. 1959-62, mem. exec. bd. 1964-66, v.p. elem. sect. 1965-66, treas. 1970-74, pres.-elect 1974-75), Nat. Council Teachers of Math. Conv. (mem. program com. 1970), Wis. Math. Council, Math. Assn. Am. Nat. Council Teachers of Math., Math. Educators of Wis., Kappa Mu Epsilon. Home: 2900 N Menomonee River Pkwy Milwaukee WI 53222 Office: Mt Mary Coll Milwaukee WI 53222

VAN TIEM, FLORENTINE URBAN STEWART (MRS. RICHARD L. VAN TIEM), bus. exec.; b. Detroit, Sept. 15, 1928; d. Joseph Stephen and Helen (Reinowski) Urban; A.B., Wayne U., 1948; m. John Slagle, June 15, 1950 (dec.); 1 son, John Gerard (dec.); m. 2d, Dr. Maitland Newman Stewart, May 4, 1957 (div. 1965); children—Joseph Gerald, Victoria Helen; m. 3d, Richard L. Van Tiem, Apr. 22, 1972. Copywriter and publicity dir. of the W. B. Doner Co., 1946-48; account exec. Wolfe, Jickling, Dow & Conkey, 1948-51; exec. v.p. Ruse & Urban, Inc., 1951-55; pres. Splty. Bakers Services, Inc., 1954—; owner Scope Advt. Agy., 1955—, Christopher Gerard & Asso., 1963—, Hilltop Farm Products Inc., 1968—, Specialized Investment Co., 1968—, Victoria Farms, Inc., 1968—. Dir. Ednl. Found., trustee Louis K. Buell Scholarship and Award Found. Recipient numerous awards including Crusade for Freedom, Capital V Viscountess. Mem. Catholic Theatre Detroit, Navy League, Am. Inst. Mgmt., Am. Bakers Assn., Am. Women Radio and TV, Women's Advt. Club, Fashion Group, Detroit Symphony Orch. Women's Assn., Theta Sigma Phi. Republican. Roman Catholic. Clubs: Pilot, Western Golf and Country, Women's City, Young Republicans, Bakers of Chicago, Edgewood Country; Lapeer Golf and Country. Home: 1779 Brocker Rd Metamora MD 48455 Office: 280 N Washington St Oxford MI 48051

VAN TUYL, MARCELLA LEONA, ret. city ofcl.; b. Warren County, Ill., Aug. 10, 1895; d. Elmer and Rosenia (Shotty) Van Tuyl; student in pub. speaking Monmouth Coll., 1913-14, Knox Coll., 1911-12; student Macomb Normal Coll., 1914; grad. Mosher Bus. and Adminstrn. Coll., Chgo., 1920; postgrad. N.Y. Sch. Social Work, N.Y.C., 1933-34 Tchr. rural schs., Warren County, Ill., 1916-18; asst. edn. dir. Ill. Tb and Pub. Health Assn., Springfield, 1922-24; health educator N.Y.C. Tb and Pub. Health Assn., 1924; exec. sec. State Charities Aid Assn., Rensselaer County, Troy, N.Y., 1924-30; with Emergency Relief Bur., N.Y. State and N.Y.C., 1932-35; field organizer State Charities Air Assn., N.Y.C., 1935-36; adminstr. Dept. of Welfare, N.Y.C., 1936-50, field pub. relations rep., 1950-57, adminstr. community relations, 1957-65; ret., 1965; lectr., cons. on pub. health, welfare. Past mem. bd. dirs., policy making com. nat. citizens com. WHO. Mem. Am. Pub. Health Assn., Am. Pub. Welfare Assn., Nat. and Internat. Council Women, Nat. Conf. Social Work, Nat. Council Chs., Internat., Nat. fedns. bus. and profl. women, N.Y. State Bus. and Profl. Women's Clubs (state bd. chmn. internat. relations com.), N.Y. League Bus. and Profl. Women's Club (pres. N.Y.C. 1956-58, chmn. hospitality com. N.Y. State 1972—), Am. Found. Religion and Psychiatry (bd. govs.), Am. Assn. Advancement of UN, Fgn. Policy Assn. Mem. Dutch Reform Ch. (past pres. of bus. and profl. women). Home: 10 Stuyvesant Oval New York City NY 10009

VAN VELZER, VIRGINIA CLAIRE, editor, writer, librarian; b. State College, Pa., Sept 19, 1927; d. Harry Leland and Golda Lillian (Cline) Van Velzer; B.S. magna cum laude, U. Ill., 1950; postgrad. Syracuse U., 1955. Personnel technician Wright-Patterson AFB, Ohio, 1952-53; library asst. Battelle Meml. Inst., Columbus, O., 1953-54; asst. statistician Syracuse (N.Y.) Bd. Edn., 1954-55; reference and cataloging librarian Electronics lab., Gen. Electric Co., Syracuse, 1955-56, tech. writer-editor, 1956-57, tech. writer-editor Gen. Electric Microwave lab., Palo Alto, Cal., 1957-61; founder, head tech. publs. and library Microwave Electronics Corp., Palo Alto, 1961-63; sr. tech. writer-editor, lead writer, librarian Western Div. Electronic Systems group GTE Sylvania, Inc., Mountain View, Cal., 1964—, Recipient Bronze plaque U. Ill. Mem. Soc. Tech. Writers and Pubs. (sr. mem. bd. dirs. 1965-69, chpt. sec. 1965-66, chmn. referral services 1965-69, membership com., historian and chmn. procedures documentation, chmn. registration com. Stanford Seminar 1966, recipient Merit award for publ. 1965), Soc. Tech. Communication (sec. 1974, chmn. Stanford Seminar registration com. 1974), I.E.E.E. (chmn. publicity and public relations profl. tech. group on engring. writing and speech, bd. dirs. 1965-66, acting sec. 1966, coms.), Assn. Old Crows, Joint Council for Sci. and Math. Edn., Internat. Soc. Gen. Semantics, Am. Bus. Writing Assn. (nat. conf. com. 1967), Special Libraries Assn., Cal. Library Assn., U. Ill. Illini Alumni Assn., A.A.A.S., Sierra Club, Phi Beta Kappa, Alpha Lambda Delta, Phi Kappa Phi, Psi Chi, Alpha Theta Upsilon. Also mem. numerous theater player groups, camera clubs, wildlife socs., Borzoi clubs, cat fancier clubs, gem and mineral socs. Author: Sylvania Style Guide; profl. reports. Contbr. articles to profl. jours. Home: 4048 Laguna Way Palo Alto CA 94306 Office: GTE Sylvania Inc PO Box 188 Mountain View CA 94040

VAN VLACK, MELVA BULLINGTON (MRS. WILLIAM CLARK VAN VLACK), home economist; b. Vesta Community, Charleston, Ark., Apr. 3, 1909; d. Baxter Lee and Ella Emma (McConnell) Bullington; B.S., U. Ark., 1932, M.S., 1966; postgrad. U. Cal., at Berkeley, 1939, U. Ala., 1948, Jacksonville State U., 1949; m. William Clark Van Vlack, Aug. 9, 1946. Home econs. instr., Prairie Grove, Ark., 1932-33; elementary tchr., Liberty-Tulsa County, Okla., 1933-34; home demonstration agt., Magnolia, Ark., 1934-36, Hope, Ark., 1936-39, Pine Bluff, Ark., 1939-47; jr. high sch. home econs. instr., Atalla, Ala., 1949-59; extension home economist, Ft. Smith, Ark., 1959—. Ofcl., Ark.-Okla. Dist. Fair, 1958-72. Recipient Distinguished Service award Nat. Assn. Extension Home Economists, 1970, Ark. Farm Bur., 1970, Ark. Extension Homemakers Council, 1971. Mem. Am. Home Econs. Assn., Ark. Assn. Extension Home Economists (dist. counselor), Bus. and Profl. Women Pine Bluff and Ft. Smith, Epsilon Sigma Phi, Delta Gamma Sigma. Methodist (life mem. Weslyan Service Guild). Clubs: Sorosis (Magnolia); Soroptimist, Garden (Ft. Smith); Altrusa (Pine Bluff, Ark.). Home: 11 Salome St Fort Smith AR 72901 Office: Courthouse Bldg Fort Smith AR 72901

VAN VOORHIS, LINDA LYON, poet; b. Rochester, N.Y., May 7, 1902; d. Edmund and Carolyn H. (Talcott) Lyon; student Masters Sch., Dobbs Ferry; m. John Van Voorhis, June 2, 1928; children—Emily (Mrs. Edward Ridgway Harris), June Allis (Mrs. Louis D'Amanda), Eugene. Propr. Wawheek Inn, Upper Saranac Lake, N.Y. Mem. Women's com. Rochester (N.Y.) Art Gallery, Bausch Meml. Mus. (now Rochester Mus. and Sci. Center), Japan Internat. Christian U. Found., Inc., N.Y.C., Rochester (N.Y.) Civic Music Assn. Dir. Rochester (N.Y.) Sch. for Deaf. Fellow Rochester Acad. of Medicine (hon. life); mem. Poetry Soc. of Am., Rochester Poetry Soc., Rochester Jr. League, English Speaking Union, Sigma Alpha Iota. Republican. Episcopalian. Clubs: Century, Chatterbox. Author: June's Verses, 1924, More June's Verses, 1935; June in September, 1973. also numerous poems pub. in popular anthologies. Home: 714 Rock Beach Rd Rochester NY 14617

VAN WECHEL, AVIS NAAS (MRS. WILLARD L. VAN WECHEL), clubwoman; b. McVille, N.D., Feb. 7, 1926; d. Tom L. and Agness M. Naas; student Standard-Mayville State Tchrs. Coll., 1950; m. Willard L. Van Wechel, June 26, 1949; children—Wendel, Lynndel, Vickie. Sch. tchr., Luverne, N.D.; pres. Gran, Am. Lutheran Ch. Women, 1953-64, supt. Sunday Sch., 1957-72, pres. Mayville Conf., 1972—; pres. N.D. Fedn. Womens Clubs, 1972-74. Sec. Community Council, 1968—. Clubs: Pioneer Daughters (pres. Goose River chpt. 1968), Goose River Ski (sec.-treas. 1969—), Mayville Womens. Home: Mayville ND 58257

VAN WERT, ALICE ANDERSON (MRS. J. S. VAN WERT), civic worker; b. Worthington, Minn., Nov. 27, 1912; d. Erick and Natalie (Carlson) Anderson; B.S., Ia. State U., 1934; m. J. S. Van Wert, June 20, 1935 (dec. Mar. 1954); children—Jay Stanley, David Walter, Sondra Lee, Patricia Alice. Tchr. home econs., Thompson, Ia., 1934-35; Judge 4-H exhibits, also culinary arts, Ia. county fairs, 1945-58; lectr. travelogs and philosophy, Ia., Minn., Ill., Neb., Wis., 1956—. Midwest regional chmn. Am. Farm Bur. Women's Com., 1965—; state chmn. Ia. Farm Bur. Women, 1960-66, dist. chmn., 1954-60; mem. bd. Ia. Farm Bur., 1960-66; mem. Ia. Farm Bur. Mutual Ins. Bd., 1960-66; mem. adv. com. Inst. Agr. Medicine, State U. Ia., 1960-66; mem. adv. council to dean home econs. Ia. State U., 1956-60; mem. Pres. Kennedy's Farm Safety Program Planning Com., 1962; mem. Am. Field Service Com., 1962-64; mem. Franklin County Planning Commn., Hampton, Ia., 1960-62; mem. County Zoning Adjustment Bd., 1972-75, Ia. Commn. Status of Women, 1972—; mem. Franklin County Extension Council, 1955-58, sec., 1956; chmn. Franklin County 4-H Girls Com., 1952-53; mem. sch. bd. Washington Valley-Hampton, 1955—, pres., 1959-60; mem. Gov.'s UN Com., 1964-65, Gov.'s Adv. Com. Day Care of Children, 1965-66, Gov.'s Hwy. Safety Com., 1965-67; mem. bd. 1st Christian Ch., Hampton, 1958-60, supt. vacation Bible sch., 1959; mem. State Environmental Health Com., 1971—, Gov.'s Ednl. Adv. Com., 1969-71, adv. council U.S. Postal Service, 1971-73, service com. Nat. 4-H, 1972—, state adv. com. FHA, 1971-74; mem. O.S.H.A. Adv. Com. on Agrl. Standards-U.S.A., 1972—. Bd. dirs. Ia. State U. Found., Ia. Health Planning Council. Recipient Nat. 4-H Alumni Recognition award, 1966, Ia. State U. Alumni Merit award, 1963, Ia. Soil Conservation award, 1960, Ia. State U. Centennial award, 1958; named Ia. Mother of Year, Ia. Mothers' Assn., 1965; recipient Golden Year award Ia. Farm Bur., 1968. Mem. Nat. Safety Council (mem.-at-large women's conf. 1965-66, womens conf. exec. com.), Ia. State U. Alumni Assn. (sec. exec. com. 1960-61, bd. trustees), Nat. Soc. Arts and Letters (state sec. 1965—), Asso. Country Women of World (conf. del. Ceylon 1957, Scotland 1959, Ireland 1965, Norway, 1971), Am. (adv. bd. 1968—), Ia. (pres. 1967-68, advisor 1968-69) mother's assns., Ia. Young Mother's Council Service (chmn. 1964-65), Am. Assn. U. Women (chpt. pres. 1943-44), Des Moines Women's C. of C., Ia. Home Econs. Assn., P.E.O. (sec. 1968-69). Republican. Mem. Order Eastern Star. Club: Hampton (Ia.) Federated Women's (pres. 1949). Home: Route 3 Box 112 Hampton IA 50441 Office: Am Farm Bur 225 Touhy Park Ridge IL 60068

VANWINKLE, ADELAIDE SHAFFER (MRS. ARTHUR D. VANWINKLE), realtor; b. Hackensack, N.J., Jan. 21, 1917; d. Louis William and Adelaide (Applebee) Shaffer; student Lasell Jr. Coll., 1934-35, Columbia, 1941-42, Rutgers U., 1963; m. Nicholas Demarest Campbell, Jr., Nov. 19, 1949 (div. Oct. 1973); m. 2d, Arthur Decker VanWinkle, Nov. 1, 1973. Sec., Vanderwart & Scharnikow, attys., Hackensack, 1935-40; head drug and dept. store sales Sales Affiliate, Inc., N.Y.C., 1940-42; account exec. Bendix Aviation Corp., Teterboro, N.J., 1942-47; sales mgr. Louis W. Shaffer, Inc., Hackensack, 1947-68, pres., 1968—; dir. Garden State Nat. Bank, Hackensack. Bd. mgrs. YMCA, Central Bergen br., 1963-73, The Residence, Hackensack, 1969—. Mem. Central Bergen County Bd. Realtors (past pres.), N.J. Assn. Realtor (past pres.), Nat. Assn. Realtors (v.p. 1969, dir. 1968, 72), Nat. Inst. Real Estate Brokers (state membership chmn. 1967), Am. Inst. Real Estate Appraisers, Soc. Real Estate Appraisers (v.p.), Lasell Alumni Assn. Clubs: Hackensack Woman's (v.p. 1963), Lasell (past pres.). Home: 125 Prospect Av Hackensack NJ 07601 Office: 725 Main St Hackensack NJ 07601

VANZANDT, DOROTHY PERKINS (MRS. MORDECAI MOORE VANZANDT), nutritionist; b. Wilmington, Del., Sept. 4, 1913; d. Charles Furry and Florence Ella (Porter) Perkins; B.S., Pa. State U., 1935; teaching certificate, U. Md., 1956; M.S., Tex. Woman's U., 1967, Ph.D., 1969; m. Mordecai Moore VanZandt, July 3, 1937; children—Suellen, Stephen Charles, John Michael. Home econ. rep. Pa. Coop. Extension Service, New Bloomfield, Pa., 1935-37; Farm Security Adminstrn., Lewisburg, Pa., 1938-40; tchr. Pimmit Hills Elementary Sch., Fairfax County, Va., 1956-57; tchr. home econs. Gurrie Central Jr. High Sch., LaGrange, Ill., 1959-66; food and nutrition specialist Md. Coop. Extension Service, College Park, Md., 1969—. Mem. Md., Am. home econ. assns., Md., Am. dietetic assns., Am. Assn. U. Women, Kappa Kappa Gamma, Omicron Nu, Iota Sigma Pi, Epsilon Sigma Phi. Home: 11809 Stonington Pl Silver Spring MD 20902 Office: 1210 Symons Hall Univ Md College Park MD 20742

VAN ZANTE, SHIRLEY M. (MRS. DIRK C. VAN ZANTE), mag. editor; b. Elma, Ia.; d. Vernon E. and Georgene (Woodmansee) Borland; A.A., Grandview Coll., 1950; B.A., Drake U., 1952; m. Dirk C. Van Zante, 1970. Asso. editor Mchts. Trade Jour., Des Moines, 1952-55; copywriter Meredith Pub. Co., Des Moines, 1955-60, book editor, 1960-67, home furnishings editor Better Homes and Gardens Spl. Interest Publs. Meredith Corp., 1967—. Named Advt. Woman of Year, Des Moines, 1961; recipient Dorothy Dawe home furnishings award, 1970, 72. Mem. Am. Inst. Interior Designers (press affiliate), Nat. Home Fashions League, Am. Fedn. Advt., Alpha Xi Delta, Theta Sigma Phi. Club: Women's Advt. (Des Moines). Office: 1716 Locust St Des Moines IA 50336

VARADIAN, ROXIE MARY, librarian; b. San Francisco, July 12, 1916; d. Levon and Veron (Azarian) Varadian; A.B., Fresno State Coll., 1938; student U. Cal. at Berkeley, 1938-39. Social service caseworker Cal. State Relief Adminstrn., Fresno, Cal., 1939-40; teacher Clovis (Cal.) High Sch., 1940-66, counselor, 1961-63, librarian, 1942-51, dept. head, 1955-62, div. head, 1964-66; dir. compensatory edn. Clovis (Cal.) Unified Sch. Dist., 1966-73, dir. dist. libraries, 1967—. Mem. Assn. Cal. Sch. Adminstrs., Cal. Assn. Sch. Librarians, Am. Assn. U. Women, Am. Library Assn., Fresno Area Library Council, Central Sierra Library and Media Assn., Fresno State Coll. Alumni Assn., Alpha Delta Kappa. Co-author: Library Personnel Handbook for Clovis Unified Sch. Dist. 3d edn., 1971. Home: 620 DeWitt Av Clovis CA 93612 Office: 914 4th St Clovis CA 93612

VARANESE, MAUREEN HELEN, banker; b. Fall River, Mass., Nov. 11, 1942; d. Pasquale William and Helen (Flannery) Varanese; student U. Mass., 1971. With Fall River (Mass.) Savs. Bank, 1960—, teller, 1961-62, mortgage teller, 1962-64, br. mgr., 1964-70, vice treas., 1970-72, asst. v.p., corporator, 1972—. Task Force volunteer youth motivation Fall River C. of C., 1974—. Mem. Savings Bank Women of Mass. (mem.-at-large 1972—, chmn. southeastern group 1973). Home: 1010 High St Fall River MA 02720 Office: 141 N Main St Fall River MA 02720

VARDAMAN, HAZEL CLARE (MRS. HOWARD VARDAMAN), educator; b. Utica, N.Y., Sept. 12, 1913; d. Charles W. and Rose (Struve) Clare; A.B., Smith Coll., 1935; postgrad. U. Leipzig (Germany), 1935-36; M.A., U. Minn., 1937; Ph.D., Northwestern U., 1941; m. Howard F. Vardaman, Nov. 20, 1940 (dec. June 1973). Tchr. Jeffersonville (N.Y.) High Sch., 1937-39; faculty Doane Coll., Crete, Neb., 1941-42, Smith Coll., Northampton, Mass., 1942-46; asst. prof. U. Ill. at Chgo., 1946-53, asso. prof., 1953-59, prof. German, 1959—. Mem. Am. Assn. U. Profs., Am. Assn. Tchrs. German, Ill. Modern Lang. Tchrs. Assn., Modern Lang. Assn., Am. Council Teaching Fgn. Langs. Home: 700 Roslyn St Evanston IL 60201 Office: 1625 Univ Hall U Ill Circle Campus Chicago IL 60680

VARIAN, ELAYNE HANLEY (MRS. JOHN VARIAN), mus. ofcl.; b. San Francisco; d. William and Florence R. (Shull) Hanley; M.A., U. Chgo., 1947; M.F.A., Art Inst. of Chgo., 1946-47; postgrad. N.Y. U., 1953-55; m. John Varian, Oct. 10, 1940; 1 son, Alfred Wright. Asst. to pres. Duveen Bros., N.Y.C., 1953-62; exec. dir. Village Art Center, N.Y.C., 1962-64; with Finch Coll. Mus. of Art, N.Y.C., 1964—, dir. Contemporary Wing, 1964—. Instr. Chgo. Art Inst., 1946-48, Ill. Inst. of Tech., Chgo., 1946-48; cons. N.Y. State Council on the Arts, 1967-73, Everson Mus., 1969—. Mem. Mayor Lindsey's Citizen's Adv. Com., N.Y.C.,1967-69. Bd. dirs. Gallery Assn. of N.Y. State, 1972—; founder Am. Friends of Attingham, N.Y.C., 1967, pres., 1967-68. MacDowell Colony fellow, 1970. Mem. Internat. Council of Museums, Am. Assn. Museums, Nat. Trust for Historic Preservation, Nat. Trust (Great Britain), Coll. Art Assn. Home: 1310 Lakeshore Dr Orlando FL 32803 Office: 62-64 E 78th St New York City NY 10021

VARKONYI, CHARLYNE ANNETTE, editor; b. Easton, Pa., Mar. 29, 1949; d. Charles Michael and Nancy Yvonne (Frinzi) Varkonyi; B.J., U. Mo., 1970. Asst. women's editor Easton Express, 1970-71, Evening Chronicle, Allentown, Pa., 1971-73; consumer editor Morning Call and Evening Chronicle, Allentown, 1973—. Recipient Outstanding Performance certificate U.S. Consumer Product Safety Commn. Mem. Women in Communications, Pa. Women's Press Assn. (2d pl. award Better Newswriting Contest, 1973, hon. mention 1974), Sigma Delta Chi. Home: 1334 N Nelson St Allentown PA 18103 Office: 6 and Linden Sts Allentown PA 18105

VARNAY, ASTRID, soprano; b. Stockholm, Sweden; d. Alexander and Maria (Yavor) Varnay; received musical tng. in U.S.; m. Herman O. Weigert. Came to U.S.; naturalized, 1943. Concerts in U.S., Can., Europe; appeared in opera Chgo., Cin., Rio., San Francisco and West Coast; made debut, Met. Opera, 1941-42; sang major roles for 12 consecutive seasons, interpreting all Wagnerian soprano repertoire, Elektra, Salome, Santuzza, Amelia, Marschallin, at Met. Opera House, N.Y.; star of Florence (Italy) May Festival and Bayreuth (Germany) Wagner Festival, 1951, 52, leading soprano, 1953; Berlin Arts Festival, 1951, 52; Munich Staatsoper, 1952. Home: 375 Riverside Dr New York City NY 10025 Office: care Rosset 570 7th Av New York City NY 10018

VARNER, CHARLEEN LAVERNE MCCLANAHAN (MRS. ROBERT B. VARNER), educator, adminstr., nutritionist; b. Alba, Mo., Aug. 28, 1931; d. Roy Calvin and Lela Ruhama (Smith) McClanahan; student Joplin (Mo.) Jr. Coll., 1949-51; B.S. in Edn., Kan. State Coll. Pittsburg, 1953; M.S., U. Ark., 1958; Ph.D., Tex. Woman's U. 1966; postgrad., Mich. State U., summer, 1955, U. Mo., summers, 1952, 1962; m. Robert Bernard Varner, July 4, 1953. Apprentice county home agt. U. Mo., summer 1952; tchr. Ferry Pass. Sch., Escambia County, Fla., 1953-54; tchr. biology, home econs. Joplin Sr. High Sch., 1954-59; instr. home econs. Kan. State Coll., Pittsburg, 1959-63; lectr. foods, nutrition Coll. Household Arts and Scis., Tex. Woman's U., 1963-64, research asst. NASA grant, 1964-66; asso. prof. home econs. Central Mo. State U., Warrensburg, 1966-70, adviser to Colhecon, 1966-70, adviser to Alpha Sigma Alpha, 1967-70, 72, mem. bd. advisers Honors Group, 1967-70; prof., head dept. home econs. Kan. State Tchrs. Coll., Emporia, 1970-73; prof., chmn. dept. home econs. Benedictine Coll., Atchison, Kan., 1973—. Cons. dietitian Medi-Center also other hosps. and rest homes, Topeka, 1973—. Mem. Joplin Little Theater, 1956-60. Mem. N.E.A., Mo., Kan. state tchrs. assns., Am. Assn. Univ. Women, Am., Mo., Kan. dietetics assns., Am., Mo., Kan. home econs. assns., Mo. Acad. Scis., Am. Assn. U. Profs., U. Ark. Alumni Assn., Alumni Assn. Kan. State Coll. of Pittsburg, Am. Vocational Assn., Assn. Edn. Young Children, Sigma Xi, Beta Sigma Phi, Beta Beta Beta, Alpha Sigma Alpha, Delta Kappa Gamma, Kappa Kappa Iota, Phi Upsilon Omicron. Methodist (organist). Home: Main PO Box 1009 Topeka KS 66601

VARNEY, SHARON ARLEN (MRS. RALPH H. VARNEY), librarian; b. Portland, Ore., Feb. 1, 1945; d. Lawrence Russell and Elizabeth (Bruckel) Tippie; B.A., U. Alta., 1965; B.L.S., U. Toronto, 1967; m. Ralph H. Varney, Mar. 20, 1971; 1 dau., Sarah Elizabeth. Library asst. Calgary (Alta., Can.) Pub. Library, 1965-66; reference librarian U. Alta. 1967-68; archivist Provincial Archives B.C., Victoria, Can., 1969-73; reference librarian Vancouver (B.C.) Island Regional Library, 1973—. Mem. B.C. Library Assn. Home: 482 St Andrew St Nanaimo BC Canada Office: 10 Strickland St Nanaimo BC Canada

VARRO, BARBARA JOAN, newspaperwoman; b. East Chicago, Ind., Jan. 25, 1938; d. Alexander Richard and Lottie Rita (Bess) Varro; B.A., Duquesne U., 1959. Asst. fashion editor Chgo. Sun Times, 1959-64; fashion editor, 1964—. Mem. Fashion Group of Chgo., Chgo. Press Club, Am. Newspaper Guild, Duquesne U. Alumni Club. Home: 900 N Lake Shore Dr Chicago IL 60611 Office: 401 N Wabash Av Chicago IL 60610

VASCHAK, MATHILDA R. (MRS. L. ROBERT OAKS), indsl. physician; b. Youngstown, O., Aug. 30, 1910; d. Joseph G. and Mary (Matyskwicz) Vaschak; A.B., Western Res. U., 1932; M.D., Women's Med. Coll., 1936; postgrad. Psychoanalytic Inst., 1950, N.Y. U., 1957, Columbia-Presbyn. Med. Center, 1957; m. L. Robert Oaks, Dec. 24, 1940; 1 son, John Quincy Adams. Intern, Jersey City Med. Center, 1937-38; physician, instr. hygiene Albany State Tchrs. Coll., 1938, State Tchrs. Coll., Fredonia, N.Y., 1938-41; clin. asst. out-patient dept. Meml. Hosp. for Cancer and Allied Diseases, N.Y.C., 1947-51; staff physician N.Y. Telephone Co., 1946-51, Pratt Inst., Bklyn., 1947-51, Am. Tel. & Tel. Co., N.Y.C., 1951-52; practice medicine, specializing in internal medicine, Bklyn., 1947-53; plant physician E. R. Squibb & Sons, Bklyn., 1952-53, physician in charge plant med. services, New Brunswick, N.J., 1953-70, dir. med. services, 1970—; mem. staff Middlesex Rehab. and Polio Hosp. Mem. adv. bd. Raritan Valley Workshop, 1967—; trustee Am. Woman's Hosps. Named woman of yr. N.J. br. Am. Med. Women's Assn., 1969. Diplomate Am. Bd. Preventive Medicine and Pub. Health. Fellow Indsl. Med. Assn.; mem. Acad. Occupational Medicine, N.J. Indsl. Med. Assn. (sec. 1953, pres. 1964), Am. (publicity chmn. 1964, chmn. med. edn. and research com. 1968-71), N.J. (pres. 1963-64) med. women's assns., Pan Am. Med. Women's Alliance, Med. Women's Internat. Assn. (publicity chmn. 1966 congress, del. 1972 congress), Med. Soc. N.J. (mem. com. on occupational health, workmen's compensation and rehab.). Club: Quota (pres. Plainfield 1960). Home: 104 Myrtle Av North Plainfield NJ 07060 Office: E R Squibb & Sons New Brunswick NJ 08903

VASILEFF, ESTHER ISABEL (MRS. VASIL VASILEFF), sch. psychologist; b. Bloomington, Ill., June 25, 1919; d. Eugene and Mabel Claire (Jones) Pitts; B.Ed., Ill. State U., 1941; M.A., Washington U., 1966; m. Vasil Vasileff, Nov. 19, 1941; children—Michael, Thomas. Music supr. Madison (Ill.) Pub. Schs., 1941; kindergarten tchr., Venice, Ill., 1946-51; elementary tchr., Granite City, Ill., 1955; 3d grade tchr. Washington Sch., 1956-58; violinist St. Louis Philharmonic Orch., 1960-66; tchr. music dist. 9 elementary schs., 1966; elementary counselor Logan, Emerson schs., Granite City Dist. 9, 1966-68; sch. psychologist region 1 spl. edn. dist., Granite City, 1969—. Mem. Jr. Service Club, Madison, Ill., 1941-50. Mem. Nat. Assn. Sch. Psychologists, So. Ill. Psychol. Assn., Nat. Psychol. Assn., Bus. and Profl. Women's Club, Delta Kappa Gamma. Mem. Order Eastern Star. Home: 154 Barnett Dr Edwardsville IL 62025 Office: 2801 State St Granite City IL 62040

VASQUEZ, LUTGARDA ABAD (MRS. GIL VASQUEZ), pediatrician; b. Manila, Philippines, June 16, 1934 (came to U.S. 1964, naturalized 1971); d. Moises Buenaflor and Fidela Colendrino (Sion) Abad; A.A., U. Philippines, 1952, M.D., 1957; m. Gil Vasquez, June 16, 1958; 1 son, Daniel. Intern Philippine Gen. Hosp., Manila, 1956-57; resident pediatrics L.I. Coll. Hosp., Bklyn., 1957-59; practice medicine, specializing in pediatrics, Bklyn., 1968—; attending pediatrician, dir. nurseries L.I. Coll. Hosp., Bklyn., 1968—; clin. instr. pediatrics State U. N.Y. Downstate Med. Center, Bklyn., 1968—. Diplomate Am. Bd. Pediatrics. Fellow Am. Acad. Pediatrics; mem. A.M.A., Med. Soc. State N.Y., Kings County Med. Soc., Am. Acad. Pediatrics, Phi Kappa Phi. Office: 340 Henry St Brooklyn NY 11201

VAUGHAN, ANN HELDERMAN (MRS. LESLIE CRANDALL VAUGHAN, JR.), ednl. orgn. adminstr.; b. Gold Hill, N.C., Jan. 19, 1941; d. Charlie Lentz and Kathleen (Stikeleather) Helderman; B.S. with honors, U. Tenn., 1963; m. Leslie Crandall Vaughan, Jr., Aug. 7, 1965. Home economist Va. Electric & Power Co., Alexandria, 1963-65; tchr. home econs. Roanoke County, (Va.) Sch. System, 1965-66; exec. dir. Dairy Council of Roanoke (Va.), 1966-74; free lance home economist, 1974—. Vice pres. Adult Activities Council of Roanoke Valley, 1967, pres., 1968. Recipient Alumna Leadership award 4-H Clubs Roanoke County, 1969. Mem. Am., Va. (sec. 1970-72, conv. chmn. 1973) home econs. assns., Am. Women in Radio and TV (pres. 1970-71), Va. Home Economists in Bus. (foods and nutrition chmn. 1968-69, newsletter editor 1971-72). Home: 1901 Pelham Dr Roanoke VA 24018

VAUGHAN, BARBARA M., gas leakage detection surveys exec.; b. Malden, Mass., July 8, 1922; d. George Percy and Wilhelmenia Blanche (Steadman) Vaughan; B.S., U. Mich., 1944. Cashier Singer Sewing Machine Co., Boston, 1944-59; controller Heath Survey Cons. Inc., Wellesley, Mass., 1959-64, v.p., 1964—; v.p. Heath Survey Consultants, Ltd., Can., 1964—, treas., dir., 1973—; dir., sec. Heath Consultants Australia Pty., Ltd., 1971—. Active United Fund, Melrose Mass., 1959-61; Heart Fund, Melrose, 1958-61. Mem. U. Mich. Alumni Assn. (dir. 1955-58, v.p. 1957-58), Adminstrv. Mgmt. Soc. (pres. 1969-70), Internat. Fiscal Assn., Tax Execs. Inst., Am. Soc. Women Accountants, Alpha Xi Delta. Office: 100 Tosca Dr Stoughton MA 02072

VAUGHAN, EDITH GIBBS (MRS. EARLE RUSSELL VAUGHAN), sch. adminstr.; b. Los Angeles; d. Robert Adams and Della (Page) Gibbs; A.B., U. So. Cal., 1934; m. Earle Russell Vaughan, Jan. 18, 1936; children—Russell Gibbs, Robert Page, Charles Julian, Charaline Page. Tchr. Page Mil. Acad., Los Angeles, 1929-35, exec. officer, 1935-43, supt., 1943—; supt. Page Sch. of Beverly Hills, Cal. 1959—, Page Sch. of Garden Grove, Cal., 1972—. Founder mem. Los Angeles Cultural Heritage Commn. 1962—, pres., 1965-67; mem. Mayor's Adv. Com., 1961—; spl. rep. Cal. Bicentennial Celebration Commn., 1968—. Bd. dirs., charter mem. Freedoms Found., women's div. Los Angeles County chpt.; charter bd. mem., com. profl. Women Los Angeles Philharmonic Orch.; trustee So. Cal. Youth Leadership Found., Youthpower U.S.A. Found, Lt. Col. Women's Ambulance and Def. Corps., 1941-46; youth leadership adv. council Los Angeles County Schs., Los Angeles, 1960—. Bd. dirs. Della P. Gibbs Found., Los Angeles, 1939—. Recipient Americanism medal Am. Legion, 1958, Merit medal, 1964. Mem. Nat. Apt. Owners Assn. (pres. women's div. 1961-62), D.A.R. (regent Los Angeles 1962-64), Miracle Mile Bus. and Profl. Women's Club (pres. 1959-61, pres. Los Angeles-Sunset dist. 1964-65), Apt. Assn. Los Angeles County (dir. 1960—), Internat. Platform Assn., Mortar Board, Kappa Delta, Delta Psi Kappa, Phi Beta (nat. 1st v.p., nat. bd. mem.). Republican. Episcopalian. Mem. Order Eastern Star, Daus. Nile, White Shrine Jerusalem. Club: Euterpe Opera (dir. 1958-61). Author: A Christmas Story, 1934; Pageant of Nations, 1946; The Magic Mountain, 1947; The Golden Empire, 1949; Pageant of Mother Goose, 1950; Flags of Am., 1951; Flags of Cal., 1951; Heroes of Am., 1952; Am.-Then-Now-Forever, 1957; No Greater Love, 1960. Home: 276 S Lorraine Blvd Los Angeles CA 90004 Office: 565 N Larchmont St Los Angeles CA 90004 also 419 S Robertson St Beverly Hills CA 90211

VAUGHAN, SARAH LOIS, vocalist; b. Newark, Mar. 27, 1924; d. Asbury and Ada (Baylor) Vaughan; student pub. schs.; m. George Treadwell, Sept. 17, 1946; m. 2d, Clyde Brook Atkins. Joined Earl Hines Orchestra, 1942; Billy Eckstein Band, 1943; vocalist Mercury Records, Columbia, Em Arcy Records, Roulette Records. Winner Apollo amateur contest, 1942; recipient ann. vocalist award Downbeat, 1946-52. Home: Englewood NJ 07631

VAUGHAN, WANDA THERESA (MRS. RICHARD J. VAUGHAN), music co. ofcl.; b. Scranton, Pa., Mar. 14, 1928; d. John S. and Mary Ann (Borowski) Dende; A.B., Marywood Coll., 1949; m. Richard J. Vaughan, July 28, 1973. Office mgr. Dende Press, Inc., Scranton, Pa., 1949-73; sec. Otto Stein Music Co., Phoenix, 1973—. Mem. Am. Bus. Women's Assn., Marywood Coll. Alumnae Assn., Polish Am. Frats., Paderewski Univ. Club. Home: 2417 E Campbell Av Phoenix AZ 85016 Office: Otto Stein Music Company 1327 E McDowell Rd Phoenix AZ 85016

VAUGHEN, JUSTINE LIESEL (MRS. RICHARD M. FRY), physician; b. Wilmington, Del., Apr. 21, 1930; d. John and Charlotte (Leicht) Vaughen; B.S., Stetson U., 1950; M.D., Temple U., 1954; m. Richard M. Fry, June 26, 1956; children—Martha Hilary, Amanda Florence. Intern St. Joseph Mercy Hosp., Ann Arbor, Mich., 1954-55; resident U. Hosp., Ann Arbor, 1955-59; clin. asso. Div. Orthopaedic Surgery, U. Fla. Teaching Hosp., Gainesville, 1963-68; practice medicine specializing in phys. medicine and rehab., Gainesville, Fla., 1961—; mem. staffs, Fla. Hosp., Orlando, Alachua Gen. Hosp., Gainesville, North Fla. Regional Hosp.; chief phys. medicine and rehab. VA Hosp., Gainesville, 1971—. Nat. Found. for Infantile Paralysis fellow, 1955-58. Mem. A.M.A., Fla., Alachua County med. assns., Am. Congress, Fla. (pres. 1974) phys. medicine and rehab. socs. Office: 926 North West 13th St Gainesville FL 32601

VAUGHN, BETTY JANE (MRS. HAROLD ALBERT VAUGHN), librarian; b. Rochester, N.Y., Jan. 10, 1926; d. William F. and Clara R. (Jacobs) Bittner; A.B., State U. N.Y. at Albany, 1948, M.A., 1956, M.S., 1957; m. Harold Albert Vaughn, Feb. 22, 1946; children—Karen Ruth (Mrs. Thomas C. Schlendorf), Constance Anne, Eric, Melanie Louise, Jason Paul, Allen Peck, Claude Christopher, Elizabeth Noel. Tchr. social studies Coxsackie (N.Y.)-Atherns Central Sch., 1948-50, So. Glen Falls (N.Y.) Central Sch., 1951-56, Saratoga Springs High Sch., Saratoga, N.Y., 1957-58; Ft. Edward (N.Y.) High Sch., 1958-60, serials librarian N.Y. State Library, Albany, 1948-50; circulation librarian U. Chgo., 1955-57; dir. Library of Continuing Edn., Syracuse U., 1961—, social sci. bibliographer E.S. Bird Library, 1972—, adj. prof. Sch. Information Sci., 1975—, asso. dir. Ednl. Resources Information Center in Adult Edn., 1964-68. Mem. Mayor's Com. on Libraries, Syracuse, N.Y., 1970-72; mem. County Exec's. Com. on Parks and Recreation, 1971—; pres. Salt City Playhouse Performing Arts Center, 1974—. Bd. dirs. Salt City Playhouse, 1972—. Mem. Am. Assn. U. Women (sec. 1954), N.Y. State P.T.A. (corr. sec. 1961), N.Y. State Adult Edn. Assn., Am. Library Assn., Am. Edn. Assn. Home: 351 Bruce St Syracuse NY 13224

VAUGHN, BETTY (MRS. LEWIS DAVIS), pub. relations exec.; b. El Paso, Tex., Apr. 24, 1926; d. Edward Vaughn and Mabel (Bowden) Vaughn; B.S., Ohio U., 1948; m. Lewis Davis, Jan. 20, 1970. With Time, Inc., N.Y.C., 1952-55; pub. relations dir. Sandgren & Martha, Inc., N.Y.C., 1960-65; owner Vaughn Assos., N.Y.C., 1965—. Mem. Pub. Relations Soc. Am. Home: 33 E End Av New York City NY 10028 Office: 450 Park Av New York City NY 10022

VAUGHN, EMMA JUAN BELL (MRS. ERASMUS ROSCOE VAUGHN), librarian; b. Cartwright, Ky., Aug. 23, 1908; d. Henry Clay and Nannie (Cooper) Bell; student Transylvania U., 1925-28, Western State U., 1928; B.S., Tenn. Poly. U., 1940; postgrad. Memphis State U., 1950-52, Catheryn Spalding U., 1957-60; m. Erasmus Roscoe Vaughn, Sept. 25, 1928; children—George Clay, Ann (Mrs. Jere Calvin Robertson), James Erasmus. Prin., Three Forks Sch., Warren County, Ky., 1942-44, Lamont Sch., Robertson County, Tenn., 1944-46; tchr. Alamo (Tenn.) High Sch., 1946-49, pub. schs., Dyer County, Tenn., 1950-54; tchr. English and French, Heath High Sch., Paducah, Ky., 1948-49; librarian Ballard County High Sch., LaCenter, Ky., 1949-50, Hickman High Sch., Clinton, Ky., 1956-57, Fulton County High Sch., Hickman, Ky., 1957-58; tchr. French, biology Byars Hall High Sch., Covington, Tenn., 1954-56; librarian Lowes (Ky.) High Sch., 1958-69. Trustee Stinnett (Ky.) Settlement Sch. Recipient honor award Lowes High Sch. chpt. Future Farmers Am., 1969. Mem. N.E.A., Ky. Edn. Assn., Ky. Hist. Soc., D.A.R. Democrat. Mem. Christian Ch. (pianist 1959-69). Clubs: Woodville (Ky.) Home Makers (charter mem.). Home: 827 W Broadway Mayfield KY 42066

VAUGHN, JANET LEE, educator; b. Waterman, Ill., Mar. 28, 1934; d. James Ramon and Ethel Harriet (Schoener) Vaughn; B.S. with honors, U. Ill., 1956; M.S., Purdue U., 1960; Ph.D., 1967; certificate Internat. Marketing Inst., Harvard, 1969. Grad. teaching asst. Purdue U., Lafayette, Ind., 1958-59, grad. asst., instr., 1961-67, asst. prof. home mgmt. and family econs., 1967-71; project dir. Dept. Health, Edn. and Welfare research project, 1969-71; home mgmt. specialist Vt. Extension Service, Burlington, 1959-61; asso. prof. home econs., asso. family economist, chmn. family econs. and home mgmt. div. U. Ariz., Tucson, 1971—; mem. consumer edn. steering com., Ind. Vocational Home Econ. curriculum project, 1970-71; mem. com. family econs. Agr. Expt. Sta. com., also sec., 1969-71. Served to 1st lt. WAC, 1956-58; maj. Res. Mem. Am. Home Econ. Assn. Editor Family Econ. Home Mgmt. Research abstracts, 1970, 71. Home: 137 N Norton Av Tucson AZ 85719

VAUGHN, PEARL HENDERSON, educator; b. Chattanooga; d. Cicero C. and Fannie (Strickland) Henderson; B.S., Tenn. A. & I. State U., 1956, M.S., 1957; m. Roy O. Vaughn, Sept. 10, 1930, (div. May 1942); 1 son, Roy Orlando II. Tchr. pub. schs., summer playground dir., city of Chattanooga, 1940-42; community recreation dir. and organizer, also first aid and water safety instr., A.R.C., Chattanooga, 1942-54; water safety instr. Southeast Nat. Aquatic Sch., Nashville, 1954; asst. prof. phys. edn. and recreation, profl.

counselor, asst. dean women Tenn. A. & I. State U., Nashville, 1957-60; asso. prof. phys. edn. Lemoyne Coll., Memphis, 1960-62; head tennis counselor Camp Kokosin, Bedford, Vt., summer 1961; asso. prof. phys. edn. and recreation Grambling Coll., 1962—, coordinator recreation majors curriculum soc., 1963—, sec. library com., 1964-66, mem. student union bd., 1964—, mem. curriculum com., 1967-68, mem. edn. com., 1965-68, cons. high sch. phys. edn. and recreation career days. Recreation coordinator dept. health, phys. edn. and recreation Grambling Coll., 1970—. Dir. Recreation Leadership Tng. Workshop, 1968-69, 69-70, 70-71; recreation cons., specialist Lincoln Parish Emergency Assistance Program, summer 1972. Leader Pelican council Girl Scouts Am., 1966—. coordinator recreation com. Town Grambling, La., 1964-66; pres. North La. br. Mental Health Program, 1967-72. Mem. Nat. Recreation and Park Assn. (nat. council membership services task force 1971-72), La. Recreation and Parks Assn. (chmn. 6th dist. 1970-71), Am. Park and Recreation Soc. (chmn. minority groups relation com. 1971-73), A.A.H.P.E.R., Nat. Recreation Park Assn., Am. Forestry Assn., Am. Camping Assn., Am. Assn. U. Profs., Delta Psi Kappa (hon.), Delta Sigma Theta (pres. 1972-73). Home: 301 Medgar Evers St PO Drawer V Grambling LA 71245

VAUGHT, MAXINE HARRIS (MRS. WILLIAM VAUGHT), educator; b. Elkins, Ark.; d. James A. and Daisy (Laymon) Harris; B.S., U. Ark., 1954, M.Ed., 1955; Specialist Spl. Edn., Peabody Coll. Tchrs., 1965; m. William C. Vaught, Sept. 15, 1940; 1 dau., Kimberly S. Tchr., New Zion, Ark., 1943-46, Durham, Ark., 1947-48, West Fork, Ark., 1949-50, Elkins, Ark., 1950-54, Bates Sch., Fayetteville, Ark., 1954-56, Root Sch., Fayetteville, Ark., 1956-57; spl. edn. U. Ark., Fayetteville, 1957-66, tchr., dir. primary edn., 1966-70, asst. prof. elementary edn., 1970—. Mem. Internat. Reading Assn., N.E.A., Nat. Soc. Study Edn., Nat. Council Tchrs. English, Assn. Childhood Edn. Internat. (state chmn. project in the arts 1966-68), Soc. on Mental Retardation, Council Exceptional Children, Dept. Classroom Tchrs., Ark. Edn. Assn., Fayetteville Mental Health Soc. (charter), Phi Sigma Alpha, Kappa Delta Pi, Alpha Delta Kappa, Kappa Kappa Iota. Home: 1415 Crestwood Dr Fayetteville AR 72701

VAVAK, RUBYE LEE MCMURTREY, bank exec.; b. Belleview, Mo., Apr. 18, 1916; d. Samuel A. and Minta M. (Sutton) McMurtrey; grad. Chillicothe Bus. Coll., 1937; m. Estel Edwin Vavak, Oct. 9, 1938; children—Judy (Mrs. Harold J. Crowe), Jay, Jennifer. With Commercial Bank of Gideon (Mo.), 1937-43, asst. cashier, 1945-46; owner Rubye's Grocery, Gideon, 1948-49; chief teller Farmers & Mchts. Bank, Long Beach, Cal., 1955-56; office mgr. Bunny Bread, Inc., Anna, Ill., 1961-69; cashier Irondale (Mo.) Bank, 1969—. Bookkeeper Potosi (Mo.) Auction, 1956—, Bulk Fertilizer & Feed Store, Bismarck, Mo., 1965—, Wright's Feed Store, Bismarck, 1962-72. Mem. Women's Soc. Christian Service, pres., 1963-65. Methodist. Clubs: Needlecraft (Bismarck, Mo.). Home: Rural Route 1 Box 383 Bismarck MO 63624 Office: Irondale Bank Irondale MO 63648

VAZQUEZ, MARTHA DELIA (MRS. JACINTO J. VAZQUEZ), pathologist; b. Cuba, May 4, 1921 (came to the U.S. 1950, naturalized 1955); d. Horacio H. and Delia G. (Robainas) Sierra; M.D., Havana U., 1948; m. Jacinto J. Vazquez, Aug. 19, 1948; children—Flavia I. (Mrs. Hanna Sarji), Rachel. Intern St. Mary's Hosp., Kansas City, Mo., 1950-51; resident Menorah Hosp. Med. Center, Kansas City, Mo., 1951-52, Ohio State U. Hosp., Columbus, 1952-55; asso. Dept. of Pathology, U. Pitts. Sch. Medicine, 1956-61; asst. prof. pathology Duke U., Durham, N.C., 1963-70; asst. prof. pathology U. Ky. Med. Center, Lexington, 1970-73, asso. prof., 1973-74; chief lab. service VA Hosp., Lexington, 1972-74. Diplomate Am. Bd. Pathology. Fellow Am. Soc. Clin. Pathologists, Coll. Am. Pathologists; mem. Internat. Acad. Pathology, A.M.A. Home: 2676 Caminito Prado La Jolla CA 92037

VEATCH, JEANNETTE, educator; b. Ada, O., Apr. 12, 1910; d. Reese F. and Maude (Marks) Veatch; teaching certificate Western Mich. U., 1931, A.B., 1937; M.A., N.Y.U., 1947, Ph.D., 1953. Tchr. pub. schs. Kalamazoo, Mich., 1937-39, Grand Rapids, 1939-46; mem. staff edn. dept. Am. Mus. Natural History, N.Y.C., 1946-47; research specialist N.Y. State Dept. Edn., Albany, 1947-48; mem. faculty elementary edn. dept. N.Y.U., 1948-53; mem. faculty Goucher Coll., Balt., 1953-54; dir. program devel. div. Girl Scouts U.S.A., 1955-58; summer teaching Univs. Mich., Wis., Ind., Syracuse, Milw., Lehigh U., Macdonald Coll., McGill U.; vis. asso. prof. U. Ill., 1958-59; asso. prof. Pa. State U., 1959-64; prof. English, Jersey City State Coll., 1964-67; vis. prof. edn. U.S.C., Los Angeles, 1967-68; prof. edn. Ariz. State U., Tempe, 1968—. Mem. N.E.A., Assn. Childhood Edn., Nat. Council of Tchrs. English, Am. Civil Liberties Union, Nat. Assn. Edn. Young Children. Author: Individualizing Your Reading Program, 1959; Reading in Elementary School, 1966; How To Teach Reading With Children's Books, 2d edit., 1968; For Love of Teaching, 1973; co-author: Creativity in Teaching; Curriculum for Today's Boys and Girls, 1963; New Frontiers in Education, 1966; Key Words To Reading, 1973. Mem. nat. editorial adv. bd. Young Children mag. Home: 2007 E Balboa Dr Tempe AZ 85282

VEDDER, CAROL LEE, pub. relations co. exec.; b. San Francisco, Feb. 25, 1947; d. Ralph Fred and Florence Nadine (Nielsen) Vedder; student San Francisco State U., 1964-67. With Robert Ebey Co., Menlo Park, Cal., 1967—, traffic mgr., 1972—. Home: 1401 Floyd St Sunnyvale CA 94025 Office: Robert Ebey Company Inc 770 Menlo Park CA 94025

VEEDER, ELIZABETH, physician; b. Schenectady, Sept. 2, 1917; d. Carl William and Florence (McMurray) Veeder; A.B., Smith Coll., 1939; M.D., Albany Med. Coll., 1946; certificate in internal medicine U. Pa. Grad. Sch. Medicine, 1953. Intern Ellis Hosp., Schenectady, 1946-47, resident in internal medicine, 1947-48, 61-62; physician Skidmore Coll., 1948-52, Indsl. Clinic, Gen. Elec. Co., Schenectady, 1953-60, Duke Health Service, Durham, N.C., 1962-63, Wellesley Coll. Health Service, Wellesley, Mass., 1963—. Bd. dirs. Girls Clubs Am., 1970—. Fellow Am. Coll. Health Assn.; mem. A.M.A., Mass., Charles River Dist. med. socs., Jr. League. Home: 670 Washington St Wellesley MA 02181 Office: Health Service Wellesley Coll Wellesley MA 02181

VEELEY, SISTER EILEEN, mag. editor; b. Columbus, O., Dec. 7, 1924; d. James Aloysius and Estella Frances (Rubadue) Veeley; B.S., Our Lady of Cin. Coll., 1952; M.Ed., Xavier U., 1958; postgrad., Cin. Art Acad., 1959, Catherine Spalding Coll., 1960. Tchr. Elementary Schs., Cin., 1945-55; prin. Assumption Sch., Cin., 1955-59; tchr. Our Lady of Mercy Acad. High Sch., Louisville, 1959-62; asso. dir. of mgmt. adv. services Sisters of Mercy, Cin., 1962-70, dir. publs. services and editor Mercy Profile Mag., 1971—. Home: 2317 Grandview Av Cincinnati OH 45206 Office: 2303 Grandview Av Cincinnati OH 45206

VEGSO, KATHRYN ARMSTRONG (MRS. RICHARD E. VEGSO), educator; b. Peoria, Ill.; d. Ralph C. and Reba (Vail) Armstrong; B.S., U. Ill., 1951; M.S., U. Akron, 1964; m. Brady L. Kimble, Oct. 26, 1945 (dec. Dec. 1958); children—Gary L., Daniel R.; m. 2d, Richard E. Vegso, Apr. 18, 1962. Instrn. dietetics U. Akron (O.), 1946-50, dir. Student Center, 1959-60, adviser of women, mem. gen. faculty, 1960-67, dir. woman's activities, adviser of women, after 1967, now asst. to v.p., dean student services; tchr. Akron pub. schs., 1958. Officer pub. relations Western Res. council Girl Scouts U.S.A., 1962—, now trustee; cons. Akron Internat. Inst., 1962—; active various coms. Akron Area Adult Edn. Council, 1960—; coordinator Akron Area Vis. Internat. Student Program, 1962—; European leader Expt. in Internat. Living, 1960; vol. agys. United Community Council United Fund. Charter mem. Ohio Commn. Status Women. Trustee YWCA; aux. bd. dirs. Internat. Inst. Mem. Am. Assn. U. Women, Nat., Ohio assns. women deans and counselors, Akron Altrusa, Altrusa Internat., Pi Lambda Theta, Alpha Lambda Delta, Delta Kappa Gamma. Presbyn. (trustee). Club: Akron Coll. Home: 438 Vaughn Trail Akron OH 44319

VEHLOW, EDNA LUCILLE, pub. co. exec.; b. Pittsburg, Kan., July 7, 1907; d. Albert W. and Nettie (Kelly) Vehlow; B.S., Kan. State Coll., 1928, M.S. 1933. Editor Ulysses (Neb.) Dispatch, 1934-35; ednl. therapist Menninger Clinic Topeka, 1935-36; occupational therapist Galveston (Tex.) Research Hosp., 1936-41, Scottish Rite Hosp., Dallas, 1941-42, San Antonio, 1942-43; sr. occupational therapist McCloskey Gen. Hosp., War Dept., Temple, Tex., 1943-47; exec. asst. Winter VA Hosp., Topeka, 1947-55; operator composition room Stauffer Pub., Topeka, 1955—. Teaching fellow Kan. Coll., 1933. Mem. Am. Assn. Rehab. Therapists, Pilot Internat., Sigma Tau Delta, Kappa Delta Pi, Sigma Phi Mu. Home: 2020 Randolph St Topeka KS 66604 Office: 616 Jefferson St Topeka KS 66607

VEITCH, CAROL JEAN, librarian; b. Irwin, Pa., Oct. 27, 1942; d. Charles J. and Henrietta B. (Slack) Veitch; B.S. in Edn., Clarion (Pa.) State Coll., 1964; M.L.S., U. Pitts., 1966, postgrad., 1973—. Librarian, Norwin Sch. Dist., Irwin, 1964—; prof. children's lit. McKeesport campus Pa. State U., part-time 1969—. Mem. Am., Pa. library assns., Pa., Westmoreland County sch. librarians assns., Pitts. Suburban Librarians Assn., Nat. Pa., Norwin edn. assns., Friends of Norwin Pub. Library, Beta Phi Mu, Pi Gamma Mu. Home: 18 Hempfield Highlands Jeanette PA 15644 Office: Sixth St Jr High Sch Irwin PA 15642

VEITH, ILZA, educator; b. Ludwigshafen, Germany; came to U.S., 1937, naturalized, 1945; student med. schs., Geneva, Switzerland, Vienna, Austria, 1934-36; M.A., Johns Hopkins, 1944, Ph.D., 1947; m. Hans von Valentini Veith, Oct. 20, 1935. Cons. Oriental medicine Armed Forces Med. Library, Washington 1947-57; lectr. in history of medicine U. Chgo., 1949-51; editor Biology and Medicine, U. Chgo. Press, 1951-53; asst. prof., history of medicine U. Chgo., 1953-57, asso. prof., 1957-64, prof., vice chmn. dept. history health scis., 1964—; prof., vice-chmn. dept. history of health scis., prof. dept. psychiatry U. Cal. Med. Center, San Francisco, 1967—; D. J. Davies Meml. lectr. U. Ill. Sch. Medicine 1958; Alfred P. Sloan vis. prof. Menninger Sch. Psychiatry, Topeka, Kan., 1963, 65; lectr. U. Kan. Med. Center, Kansas City, 1966, 69, Logan Clendening lectr., 1971; vis. prof. Mayo Clinics, Rochester, Minn., 1966, 71; George W. Corner lectr. med. history U. Rochester; John Shaw Billings lectr. U. Ind. Sch. Medicine, 1970; hon. mem. Inst. History of Medicine and Med. Research, New Delhi, India, 1970. Decorated officer's cross of merit Fed. Republic of Germany. Fellow Am. Psychiat. Assn. (hon.), World Fedn. Neurology, Royal Soc. Medicine (London); mem. Am. Assn. History of Medicine (council mem. 1958—, Fielding H. Garrison lectr. 1974), A.A.A.S., William Osler Soc. Am. (charter, gov. 1974—), Soc. History of Medicine Chgo. (pres. 1954-64), Soc. History Med. Scis. Los Angeles (hon.), History Sci. Soc., A.M.A. (asso.), Bay Area Med. History Soc. (v.p. 1970), Spanish Soc. History of Medicine (hon. corr. mem.), Johns Hopkins U. Alumni Assn. (Ill. pres. 1956-58), German Soc. History Medicine, Natural Scis. and Tech. (corr.), Sigma Xi. Co-author: Great Ideas in the History of Surgery, 1961; author Hysteria, the History of a Disease, 1965, Phoenix edit., 1970; The Yellow Emperor's Classic Internal Medicine, 1966; L'histoire de l'hystérie, 1974. Mem. bd. editors Am. Jour. Medicine, 1959—, Perspectives in Biology and Medicine, 1974—; adviser to editorial bd. Ency. Brit., 1959—. Many articles. Home: 2235 Centro E Tiburon CA 94920 Office: U Cal San Francisco San Francisco CA 94122

VELDWYK, JEAN DELORES, ins. co. exec., real estate co. exec.; b. Seattle, July 2, 1931; d. Harry John and Minnie Vander (Sanden) V.; student, U. Wash., 1948-49. With Lawyers Title Co., 1948, Allstate Ins. Co., 1949-59, Pallis Realty, 1959-62; owner Jean Vel Dyke Realty, Seattle, 1962—, Veldwyk Ins. Agy., Seattle, 1962—. Chmn. housing and phys. improvements S.E. Seattle Model Cities, 1970-73; chmn. women's conf. Nat. Safety Council, 1973-75. Mem. exec. bd. Seattle 2000 Commn., 1972-73. Named Bus. Woman of Year, Greater Seattle Bus. and Profl. Women's Club, 1964; named Woman of Year, Seattle Quota Club, 1969. Mem. Nat. Assn. Ins. Women (internat. pres. 1968-69), Seattle King County Bd. Realtors (1st v.p. 1973—), So. Seattle C. of C. (pres. 1973—). Home: 5423 Lake Washington Blvd S Seattle WA 98118 Office: 5500 Rainier Av S Seattle WA 98118

VELENOVSKY, MARIE JOSEPHINE, auditor; b. Annapolis, Md., Feb. 1, 1921; d. Thomas Joseph and Josephine Rose (Charvat) Velenovsky; student Annapolis Bus. Coll., 1937-38, Am. Inst. Banking, 1958-64. With Farmers Nat. Bank of Annapolis (Md.), 1943—, auditor, 1964—. Mem. Nat. Assn. Bank Women, Cath. Daus. of Am. Home: 525 Burnside St Annapolis MD 21403 Office: 5 Church Circle Annapolis MD 21404

VELEZ, NORA ADAMS (MRS. VENTURA VELEZ, JR.), educator; b. Santa Clara, Cuba, June 29, 1946; d. Jeronimo Miguel and Rafaela (Rizo) A.; came to U.S., 1965, naturalized, 1972; B.A. (Paterson Spanish Apostolate scholar), Montclair State Coll., 1971, M.A., 1973; m. Ventura Velez, Jr., May 1, 1971. Tchr. Spanish, Our Lady of Lourdes Sch., Paterson, N.J., 1968-69; counselor Spanish, English as 2d lang. Youth Devel. Program Paterson, 1971; asso. prof./designate Spanish, and English as 2d lang., counselor Passaic County Community Coll., Paterson, 1971—. Mem. Nat. Assn. Women Deans and Counselors, Am. Personnel and Guidance Assn., Am. Assn. Tchrs. Spanish and Portuguese, Passaic County Guidance Assn. (exec. bd. 1971—). Home: 85 9th Av Hawthorne NJ 07506 Office: 170 Paterson St Paterson NJ 07505

VELLEMAN, RUTH ANN, librarian; b. N.Y.C., Apr. 12, 1921; d. Joseph and Celia (Applebaum) Saltman; B.A. in Intellectual History, Smith Coll., 1942; M.S. in L.S., L.I. U., 1965; m. Moritz Velleman, June 11, 1944; children—Paul Flor, James David, Daniel Jon. Dir. libraries Human Resources Center, Albertson, N.Y., 1963—. Speaker, panelist, cons. in field. Bd. dirs., editor newsletter P.T.A., 1960-62, League Women Voters, 1960-63. Mem. Council for Exceptional Children, Med., Am. (com. on library service to exceptional children), Nassau-Suffolk Sch. library assns. Contbr. articles to profl. publs. Home: 15 Cliffway Port Washington NY 11050 Office: Human Resources Center Albertson NY 11507

VELLER, MARGARET PAXTON, physician; b. Beaver Dam, Ky., Dec. 14, 1925; d. Darrell K. and Gladys (Myers) Veller; B.A., Vanderbilt U., 1947, M.D., 1950. Intern, resident Vanderbilt U. Hosp., Nashville, 1950-54; pvt. practice, 1954—. Mem. Am., Miss. (com. maternal and child care 1956-72) med. assns., Miss. Obstet. and Gynecol. Soc., Adams County Med. Soc., Natchez Assn. Commerce, Phi Beta Kappa, Alpha Omega Alpha. Baptist. Club: Pilgrimage Garden. Home: 28 S Circle Dr Natchez MS 39120 Office: Natchez Med Clinic 49 Sgt S Prentiss Dr Natchez MS 39120

VENABLE, MARTHA JOE (MRS. JAMES EDWARD VENABLE, III), home economist; b. New Albany, Miss., Nov. 12, 1943; d. Joe Shawn and Ottis Ophelia (Brown) Davis; B.S., Delta State Coll., 1965; postgrad. Miss. State U., 1966, U. Miss., 1969; m. James Edward Venable, III, Feb. 26, 1966. Asst. home economist Miss. Extension Service, Charleston, 1965-70, asso. home economist, 1970—. Mem. Tallahatchie County Fair Assn., 1965-72. Recipient Outstanding Agt. in Miss. award, 1968. Mem. Bus. and Profl. Women's Club, Miss. Extension Home Economist Assn. (vice councilor 1970-72), Am., Miss., home econs. assns., Miss. Assn. Extension H-H Youth Agts. (pres.-elect), N.W. Dist. Assn. Extension Home Economists (dir. 1973-74), Presbyn. Women (sec. 1970-71, com. chmn. 1972, v.p. women of ch. 1973-74, Sunday sch. supt. 1973-74). Home: Route 1 Charleston MS 38921 Office: Box 308 Charleston MS 38921

VENDRELY, DOROTHY MAE (MRS. ERVING ROY VENDRELY), real estate broker; b. Allen County, Ind., Mar. 17, 1915; d. Ezriah E. and Elizabeth Elbertie (Oberholtzer) Hursh; student Ind. Tech. Inst., 1963; m. Erving Roy Vendrely, Dec. 17, 1932; children—B. Ronald, Nancy Jo (Mrs. Frederic L. Romero). Lab. technician St. Joseph Hosp., Ft. Wayne, Ind., 1953-56, Duemling Clinic, Ft. Wayne, Ind., 1956; insp. ITT Research Lab., Ft. Wayne, 1957-62; real estate broker Vendrely Real Estate, Spencerville, Ind., 1965—. Bd. dirs. DeKalb County Chpt. A.R.C., 1970-72; mem. Make Am. Better, 1972. Mem. Nat. Assn. Realtors, Ind., N.E. Ind. (mem. Nat. Realtor Week com. 1971) bds. realtors. Democrat. Lutheran. Home: State Rd Spencerville IN 46788 Office: Box 12 Main St Spencerville IN 46788

VENEKLASEN, RUTH MATCHNER, psychologist; b. Harrisburg, Pa.; d. Horace Appel and Vinnie Edna (Bear) Matchner; student Am. U., Jerusalem, 1939; B.A., Wayne State U., 1939; M.A., U. Mich., 1941; postgrad. Utah State U., 1962, Am. Internat. Coll., 1963, Springfield Coll., 1963-64, Framingham State Coll., 1965, Syracuse U., 1967—; m. Rodger D. Veneklasen, July 6, 1945 (dec. Feb. 1962); 1 dau., Sharon Lee. Tchr., Detroit Pub. Schs., 1939-40, Grosse Pointe (Mich.) Pub. Schs., 1943-45, Longmeadow (Mass.) Pub. Schs., 1962-65; counselor, psychologist Wayland (Mass.) Pub. Schs., 1965-66; dir., psychologist Lochland Sch., Geneva, N.Y., 1966-67; psychologist North Syracuse (N.Y.) Central Sch. Dist., 1967—. Mem. Ontario chpt. Mentally Retarded Children. Mem. New Eng. Psychol. Assn., Mass. Sch. Counselors Assn., Am. Personnel and Guidance Assn., Am. Psychol. Assn., Nat. Commn. on Tchr. Edn. and Profl. Standards, Assn. for Measurement and Evaluation of Guidance, Nat., N.Y. State assns. sch. psychologists, Omega Upsilon, Pi Lambda Theta, Phi Kappa Phi Home: 5562 Bear Rd North Syracuse NY 13212 Office: North Syracuse Central Sch Dist North Syracuse NY 13212

VEN HORST, SISTER MARIE, educator; b. Pleasant Valley, Ia., Feb. 8, 1916; d. John R. and Helena (Venes) Ven Horst; B.S., Marycrest Coll., 1942; M.S., St. Louis U., 1943; Ph.D., U. Ia., 1952. Faculty mem. chemistry dept. Marycrest Coll., Davenport, Ia., 1943-49, 52—, chmn. div. natural sci. and math., 1965—. Lectr. Ia. Vis. Scientists Program, 1962-65; campus coordinator Regional Computer Center, U. Ia. and area colls.; mem. adv. bd. health edn. Eastern Ia. Community Coll., 1967—. Mem. Am. Chem. Soc. (treas. Ill.-Ia. sect. 1969), Am. Assn. Physics Tchrs., Research Soc. Am., Rock Island-Scott Counties Math. and Sci. Tchrs. Assn., Sigma Xi, Phi Theta Kappa, Iota Sigma Pi. Democrat. Roman Catholic. Contbr. articles to profl. jours. Home: 1607 W 12th St Davenport IA 52804

VENNEBERG, BINA CLARICE (MRS. WILLIAM HENRY VENNEBERG), civic and polit. worker; b. Meyers Falls, Wash., July 1, 1912; d. George Harvey and Bina Josephine (Bartlett) Hammer; grad. high sch.; m. William Henry Venneberg, Aug. 19, 1931; children-Leonard, Shirly (Mrs. Dana A. Meier), Christina (Mrs. Alvan K. Sampson), Marlene (Mrs. Dale D. Badgley), Rachel (Mrs. Kevin G. Imper). Guardian Camp Fire Girls, Manson, Wash., 1956-61; pres. Manson P.T.A., 1965-66; general chmn. Manson Apple Blossom Festival, 1962; Vice chmn. Chelan County, Democratic Com., 1970-72; del. Nat. Dem. Conv., 1964; mem. precinct com. Manson Dem. Central Com., 1960—. Mem. Grange Aux., Eagles Aux. Clubs: Manson Garden (pres. 1958-59); Fortnightly (pres. 1969-72) (Lake Chelan, Wash.); Wash. Fedn. Women's (Manson). Home: Box 196 Boetzkes Av Manson WA 98831

VENNER, KATHRYN DODDS HILL (MRS. ROBERT BROWNING VENNER), physician; b. Council Bluffs, Ia.; d. Chalmers A. and Christine (Ericksen) Hill; student Lindenwood Coll., 1934-37; M.D., U. Neb., 1941; m. Robert Browning Venner, July 7, 1942; children—Mary Ann (Mrs. Herman Albert Schmidt), Amanda Jane (Mrs. Michael A. Yoder), Robert Hill, Sarah Elizabeth, (Mrs. Hughes J. Rhodes III), William Hunter, John Orlin, James Alexander. Intern, N.Y. Infirmary for Women and Children, N.Y.C., 1941-42, N.Y. Hosp., N.Y.C., 1942-43; practice medicine specializing in pediatrics, Council Bluffs, Ia., 1943-47, Virginia Beach, Va., 1947—; mem. staffs Gen. Hosp., Virginia Beach, Virginia Beach-De Paul Hosp., Leigh Meml. Hosp., Norfolk, Va. Mem. A.M.A., Med. Soc. Va. (child health com. 1967), Virginia Beach Med. Soc. (pres. 1952-53). Republican. Presbyn. Home: 2260 Princess Anne Rd Virginia Beach VA 23456 Office: 4144 Holly Rd Virginia Beach VA 23451

VENTURA, STEPHANIE JOAN (MRS. JACK SAL VENTURA), demographer; b. Cambridge, Mass., Sept. 13, 1942; d. Joseph Stevenson and Rosamond Helena (Goldberg) Leavitt; A.B., Brandeis U., 1964; A.M. (Population Council fellow 1964-65), U. Pa., 1965; m. Jack Sal Ventura, May 29, 1966; children—Daniel Reuben, Jerome Hosea. Statistician Nat. Center for Health Statistics, U.S. Dept. Health, Edn., and Welfare, Washington, 1965—. Mem. Population Assn. Am., Am. Econ. Assn., Montgomery County Assn. for Retarded Citizens, Brandeis U. Nat. Women's Com., B'nai B'rith Women. Jewish religion. Author: (with Alice Clague) Trends in Illegitimacy: United States, 1940-1965, 1968. Home: 1025 Chiswell Lane Silver Spring MD 20901 Office: 5600 Fishers Lane Rockville MD 20852

VENTURI, DENISE SCOTT BROWN, architect, planner; b. Nkana, No. Rhodesia (now Zambia), Oct. 3, 1931 (came to the U.S. 1958, naturalized 1971); d. Simon and Phyllis (Hepker) Lakofski; student U. Witwatersrand, 1948-51; student Archtl. Assn. London, 1952-55, A.A. certificate tropical architecture, 1955, A.A. diploma, 1956; M.C.P., U. Pa., 1960, M.Arch., 1965; m. Robert Scott Brown, July 21, 1955 (dec. 1959); m. 2d, Robert Venturi, July 23, 1967; 1 son, James Charles. Asst. prof. Sch. Fine Arts, U. Pa., Phila., 1960-65; vis. prof. Sch. Environmental Design, U. Cal. at Berkeley, 1965; asso. prof., head urban design program, U. Cal. at Los Angeles, 1966-68; vis. prof. Yale U., 1967-70; with Venturi and Rauch, architects and planners, Phila., 1967—, partner, 1969—. Cons. on planning projects for South Central Phila., bicentennial, poplar community and city edges, 1968-74; adviser Am. Civil Liberties Union. Found., Phila., 1971—; vis. com. Sch. Arch. and Planning Mass. Inst. Tech., 1973-76.

Mem. admissions com. for environmental design Am. Acad. in Rome, 1974, Com. of Friends Environmental Design Collection Cooper-Hewitt Mus. of Smithsonian Instn., 1974. Morse Coll. fellow Yale U., 1970. Registered architect, U.K. Asso. Royal Inst. Brit. Architects, mem. Archtl. Assn. London, Alliance of Women in Architecture. Democrat. Jewish religion. Author: (with Robert Venturi, Steven Izenour) Learning From Las Vegas, 1972. Contbr. articles to profl. jours. Home: 6904 Wissahickon Av Philadelphia PA 19119 Office: 333 S 16th St Philadelphia PA 19102

VENUTOLO, ELISABETH CHARLOTTE (MRS. FELIX J. VENUTOLO), physician; b. Barmen, Germany, Aug. 16, 1923; d. Paul H. and Felicitas (Möller) Willemsen; Abitur, U. Hamburg Med. Sch., Germany, 1946-50; M.D., U. Munich, 1950; m. Felix J. Venutolo, Jan. 31, 1959; children—Elisabeth, Felicia, Maria, Catherine. Came to U.S., 1953, naturalized, 1962. Intern, U. Hosp., Hamburg, 1950-52, resident, 1952-56; practice medicine specializing in opthalmology, Paramus, N.J., 1961—; mem. staffs Newark Eye, Ear, Nose and Throat Infirmary, Bergen Pines Hosp., Paramus. Am., Bergen County med. socs., Am. Med. Womens Assn., Internat. Platform Assn. Address: 410 Farview Av Paramus NJ 07652

VERA, HARRIETTE DRYDEN, microbiologist; b. Washington, Pa., Feb. 22, 1909; d. Theodore D. and Marian D. (Thomas) Vera; A.B., Mount Holyoke Coll., 1930; Ph.D., Yale, 1938. Asst. zoology Mt. Holyoke Coll., 1930-31; tchr. biology New Haven High Sch., 1931-37; fellow Yale, 1937-38; instr. Goucher Coll., 1938-42, asst. prof., 1942-43; research microbiologist Balt. Biol. Lab., 1943-60; dir. quality control lab. products Becton, Dickinson Co. (name changed to Bioquest div. Becton, Dickinson & Co.) Balt., 1960-62, dir. quality control, 1962—; cons. U.S. Balt., 1960—; cons. U.S. Army, 1955—. Named Woman of Year, Balt. Bus. and Profl. Women, 1965. Diplomate Am. Bd. of Microbiology. Fellow Am. Acad. Microbiology, A.A.A.S., Am. Pub. Health Assn.; mem. Am. Soc. Microbiology (recipient of the Barnett L. Cohen award Md. branch 1963), Am. Inst. Biol. Sci. (governing bd. 1964-68), Brit. Soc. Gen. Microbiology, Am. Soc. Biologists (v.p. eastern U.S. 1954-55, treas. 1957-65), Conf. State and Provincial Pub. Health Lab. Dirs., Md. Pub. Health Assn., Md. Soc. Bacteriologists (pres. 1942, councilor 1951), N.Y. Acad. Sci., Parenteral Drug Assn., Royal Soc. for Promotion of Health, Soc. for Indsl. Microbiology, Bus. and Profl. Women, Sigma Xi. Democrat. Presbyn. Clubs: Quota (pres. 1961), Mt. Holyoke. Contbr. numerous articles to scientific jours. Home: 204 E Joppa Rd Apt 315 Baltimore MD 21204 Office: Box 243 Cockeysville MD 21030

VERDY, VIOLETTE, ballerina; b. Pont-L'Abbe, France, Dec. 1, 1933; d. Renan and Jeanne (Chateaureynaud) Guillerm; ed. in Paris; m. Clark C. Verdy, Apr. 1961. With Ballet des Champs Elysees, 1945-51, then Ballet de Paris de Roland Petit; headed London Festival Ballet on tour U.S.; appeared La Scala, Milan, 1955-56, also Ballet Rambert Co., Eng., Am. Ballet Theatre on tour U.S., Europe and Iron Curtain countries, 1957-58; prin. ballerina N.Y. City Ballet, 1958—; guest ballerina Royal Ballet, 1958—; guest appearances include Munich, Stuttgart opera ballets, Jacob's Pillow Festival, others; roles include Miss Julie, Cinderella, Sleeping Beauty, Nutcracker, Romeo and Juliette, Carmen, Giselle; movie roles in Ballerina, 1948, The Glass Slipper, 1954; TV appearances in U.S., Eng., France, Belgium, Germany. Office: NY City Ballet Broadway at 64th St New York City NY 10020

VERIN, TERESA YOUNG (MRS. ELSO VERIN), city ofcl.; b. Irvington, N.J., Nov. 6, 1928; d. Charles McKay and Florence Gertrude (Leonard) Young; Med. Secretarial certificate Essex County Adult Tech. Sch., 1947; certificates in municipal finance Rutgers U., 1973; m. Elso Verin, May 26, 1951. Secretarial positions Prudential Ins. Co., Newark, 1947-52, Hoffmann-LaRoche Inc., Nutley, N.J., 1953-59; dep. borough clk., asst. treas. Borough of Kinnelon (N.J.), 1960-71, borough clk., treas., 1972—. Mem. N.J., Morris County municipal clks. assns., Municipal Finance Officers Assn. N.J., Municipal Receivers, Tax Collectors and Treasurers Assn. N.J. Roman Catholic. Club: Soroptimist of Pequanoc Valley (Butler, N.J.). Home: 154 Kiel Av Kinnelon NJ 07405 Office: Municipal Bldg Kinnelon NJ 07405

VERKIN, ROBYN KAY RUSSELL (MRS. WINTFORD EVANS VERKIN, JR.), telephone co. exec.; b. St. Joseph, Mo., Nov. 1, 1947; d. Robert V. and Junaita N. (Burrier) R.; student Stephens Coll., 1965-66; B.J., U. Tex., 1969; m. Wintford Evans Verkin, Jr., May 3, 1969. Mgmt. trainee Southwestern Bell Telephone Co., Austin, Tex., 1969-70, supr. bus. office, staff instr., 1970-75. Free-lance writer, photographer, Range-Finder, Austin C. of C. mag., Go mag., Austin World. Vol. pub. relations work Humane Soc. Austin and Travis County. Mem. Women in Communications, Austin Heritage Soc., Women's Symphony League Austin. Episcopalian. Club: Austin Lawyer's Wives. Home: 8008 Seawall Blvd Apt 225 Galveston TX 77550 Office: PO Box 2901 Austin TX 78767

VERNICE, SISTER MARY (MAKOVIC), coll. dean; b. Cleve., Aug. 2, 1910; d. John Joseph and Anne (Gresh) Makovic; B.S. in Edn., St. John Coll., 1938; M.A., St. Louis U., 1942; Ph.D., Case Western Res. U., 1968. Joined Sisters of Notre Dame of Cleve., 1929; tchr. elementary and secondary schs., Los Angeles, 1936-37, Cleve. and Elyria, O., 1929-36, Memphis, 1938-41; asst. prof. edn. Grad. Sch. Arts and Scis., Catholic U. Am., Washington, 1943-57; prin. Elyria Cath. High Sch., 1957-58, Notre Dame Acad., Los Angeles, 1958-63; asso. prof. edn. Notre Dame Coll., Cleve., 1963-66, dean acad. affairs, 1966—, prof. edn., 1968—. Lectr. in edn. U. San Francisco, summers 1961-62, Mt. St. Mary Coll., Cal., summers 1959-60; supr. secondary schs., Warren and Youngstown, Cleve., Elyria, O., also Middleburg, Va., 1963-66; mem. coll. and univ. evaluating team Ohio Dept. Edn., 1972-73; mem. Bd. Cath. Edn. Diocese of Cleve., 1973—. Mem. Am., N. Central confs. acad. deans, Am. Assn. Higher Edn., Am. Ednl. Research Assn., Ohio Coll. Assn., Nat. Cath. Ednl. Assn. (sec. Midwest coll. and univ. region 1972, chmn. 1973), Phi Alpha Theta, Pi Delta Phi. Author: Teacher's Manual for American Neighbors, 1951; co-author Geography Work book for North American Neighbors, 1952. Asso. editor Cath. Ednl. Rev., 1947-58. Address: 4545 College Rd Cleveland OH 44121

VERNON, MARY, home economist; b. Tangipahoa, La., Jan. 22, 1908; d. Daniel Edgar and Nancy Ellen (Bond) Vernon; B.S., Northwestern State Coll., Natchitoches, La., 1928; M.S., La. State U., 1956. Home econs. tchr., Loranger, La., 1929-30; home demonstration agt. La. Coop. Agrl. Extension Service, various parishes in La., 1931—. Recipient Farm Bur. Freedom award Ascension Parish, La., 1971. Mem. Am. Home Econs. Assn., Nat. Assn. Extension Home Economists (Distinguished Service award 1958), Epsilon Sigma Phi. Mem. Order Eastern Star. Home: 103 Anthony Dr Box 463 Donaldsonville LA 70346 Office: PO Box 29 Donaldsonville LA 70346

VERNON, ROSE MARIE, real estate broker; b. Hudson, N.Y., Apr. 25, 1937; d. John and Anne (Focca) Marie; grad. high sch.; m. Leonard Vernon, Aug. 27, 1954; children—Bambi, Marc Todd. With XPO Realty Corp., N.Y.C., 1972—, pres., 1974—. Host, TV show Real Estate with Rose Marie, N.Y.C., 1972—. Mem. Real Estate Bd. of N.Y.C., Women's Bd. Realtors. Jewish religion. Home and office: 155 E 80th St New York City NY 10021

VERROS, ATHENA PAPPAS (MRS. ANTHONY A. VERROS, JR.), coll. adminstr.; b. Charlton, Mass., Jan. 8, 1924; d. Michael Steven and Thelma (Boyatzi) Pappas; B.S., Clark U., 1967; M.A., Assumption Coll., 1970; student U. Florence, Italy, 1962, Pierce Coll., Athens, Greece, 1966, Alliance Fracaise, Paris, France, 1963; m. Anthony A. Verros, Jr., Jan. 14, 1970. Registrar, Worcester (Mass.) Polytech. Inst., 1957-70; head dept. Eng. bus., dir. pub. relations Am. Lisan ve Sanat Dersanesi, Istanbul, Turkey, 1970-72; registrar and transfer coordinator Lasell Jr. Coll., Newton, Mass., 1972—. Dir. Howard Johnsons Motor Lodge, W. Boylston, Mass., 1967—, Sheraton Yankee Drummer Inn, Auburn, Mass., 1961—. Mem. New Eng. Assn. Collegiate Registrars and Admissions Officers (sec. 1962-64, pres. 1969-70), Turkish-Am. Assn. Home: Charlesbank Garden Apts 5 Charlesbank Way Waltham MA 02154 also 64 Beytulmalci Sokak Ayazpasa Istanbul Turkey Office: 5 Cheswick Rd Auburndale MA 02166

VERSCHOOR, HELEN LYON (MRS. IRVING ALTON VERSCHOOR), librarian; b. White Plains, N.Y., Oct. 23, 1914; d. William Henry and Helen (Oram) Lyon; B.A., Vassar Coll., 1935; B.S., Columbia Sch. Library Service, 1948; m. Irving Alton Verschoor, Sept. 26, 1943; children—Karin, Adriana. Real estate saleswoman, small house designer, landscaper Edward I. Margolin, also Gilchrest Realty Corp., Great Neck, N.Y., 1936-40; library asst., then reference librarian Great Neck Library, 1940-46, asst. dir. then acting dir., 1948-51; reference librarian N.Y. State Library, Albany, 1947; cataloger Sch. Library Sci., State U. N.Y., Albany, 1960-61; cataloger Jr. Coll. Albany and Russell Sage Evening div. (both divs. Russell Sage Coll., Troy, N.Y.), 1960-65, head librarian Albany Campus Russell Sage Coll., 1965—. Trustee, Ravena (N.Y.) Free Library. Mem. Albany Inst. History and Art, Dudley Obs., Am. Assn. U. Profs., Albany, No. N.Y. Vassar Club, Northeastern N.Y. Orchid Soc. Home: Rural Route #2 Ravena NY 12143 Office: 140 New Scotland Av Albany NY 12208

VERSO, MARIE ANTONIETTE (MRS. DONALD M. BURT), endocrinologist; b. Buffalo, Dec. 18, 1940; d. Joseph Archimedes and Mary Antonetta (Panasci) Verso; B.S. cum laude, St. Bonaventure U., 1962; M.D., Woman's Med. Coll. Pa., 1966; m. Donald M. Burt. Intern and resident Buffalo Gen. Hosp., N.Y., 1966-68; practice medicine specializing in endocrinology, Buffalo, N.Y., 1969-70; dir. health dept. Rosary Hill Coll., Buffalo, 1969-70; endocrinology fellow, Hosp. for Sick Children, Toronto, Can., 1971-72; asst. prof. medicine Yale, 1973—. Recipient fellowship State U. N.Y., Buffalo, 1968-69, U. Toronto, 1971-72. Mem. Am. Med. Woman's Assn., Mensa. Home: 569 A Prospect St New Haven CT 06511 Office: Hill Health Center 428 Columbus Av New Haven CT 06519

VER VALEN, LORETTA CAROLINE LEE (MRS. ALFRED CARSON VER VALEN), civic worker, musician; b. New Castle, Pa.; d. William Henry and Loretta C. (Miller) Lee; tchrs. certificate in voice, Peabody Conservatory Mus., 1925, artist diploma in voice, 1926; m. Alfred Carson Ver Valen, June 25, 1928; children—Henry Clay III, Carolyn Lee (Mrs. Robert Govett Hopson). Tchr. Peabody Inst., preparatory dept., Balt., 1926-48; soloist DeFeo Opera Co., Md., Va., Pa., 1925-26; soloist Colombia Opera Co., Md., Va., Pa., 1936-37; owner pvt. vocal studio, 1940-48; lectr. music, lit. and travel. Soloist various chs., Balt., 1924-28, 34-48; pres. women's assn. Balt. Symphony Orch., 1959-61; v.p. Balt. Opera Inc., 1955—; head awards Balt. Opera Guild, Inc., 1955—, 1st v.p., 1970-72, pres., 1972—. Mem. women's aux. Johns Hopkins Hosp., Rosewood State Hosp.; mem. bd. classical music radio sta. WBAL, Balt. Recipient Juillard scholarship Peabody Conservatory of Music, 1922, vocal scholarship, 1923-26, Peabody award, 1973. Mem. Md. Fedn. Music Clubs (pres. 1955-57), English Speaking Union, Md. Hist. Soc., Woman's Civic League (pres. 1957-59), Walters Art Gallery, Balt. Mus. Art, Nat. Assn. Preservation of Antiquities, Nat. Trust Hist. Preservation. Clubs: Three Arts of Homeland (pres. 1948-51, historian 1971—), Baltimore Music (pres. 1951-55), Woman's of Roland Park (dir. 1953-57). Home: 5005 St Albans Way Baltimore MD 21212

VERZYL, JUNE CAROL, art gallery dir.; b. Huntington, N.Y., Feb. 5, 1928; d. Leo Daniel and Louise Caroline (Scherer) Convery; ed. Parsons Sch. Design, 1948; m. Kenneth Henry Verzyl, Mar. 6, 1953; 1 dau., Kim Greer. Owner, dir. Verzyl Art Gallery, Northport, N.Y., 1966—. Mem. bd. elections Village of Asharoken, N.Y., 1967—; co-founder Asharoken Citizens Party, 1966. Home: 25 Bevin Rd Asharoken Northport NY 11768 Office: 377 Route 25A Northport NY 11768

VETTER, BETTY MCGEE, orgn. exec.; b. Center, Colo., Oct. 25, 1924; d. William A. and Bonnie V. (Hunsaker) McGee; B.A., U. Colo., 1944; M.A., Stanford U., 1948; m. Richard C. Vetter, Sept. 4, 1951 (div. Oct. 1970); children—David Bruce, Richard Dean, Robert Alan. Chemist, Shell Devel. Co., Emeryville, Cal., 1944-45; instr. Fresno (Cal.) State Coll., 1948-50; instr. Far East div. U. Cal., Japan and Guam, 1950-51; adj. prof. Am. U., Washington, part-time 1951-64, No. div. U. Va., Arlington, part-time 1952-64, U. Md. Extension Div., College Park, 1960-61; exec. dir. Sci. Manpower Commn., Washington, 1964—. Bd. dirs. Coop. Coll. Registry, 1973—. Served with U.S. Navy Women's Res., 1944-45. Mem. Am. Theatre Assn., A.A.A.S., Parents Without Partners. Editor: Scientific, Engineering, Technical Manpower Cemments. Contbr. articles to profl. jours. Home: 4779 N 33d St Arlington VA 22207 Office: 1776 Massachusetts Av NW Washington DC 20036

VETTERLE, MAY ELIZABETH, audiologist; b. Fresno, Cal., May 1, 1905; d. George Leonard and Elizabeth (Baxter) Vetterle; B.A., San Jose State Coll., 1939; M.A., Western Res. U., 1948. Classroom tchr. Castro Valley Elementary Sch., 1925-30; exec. sec. Marin County Camp Fire Girls, San Rafael, Cal., 1930-31; classroom tchr. Petaluma Bd. Edn., Cal., 1932-37; office mgr., social worker Home of Benevolence, San Jose, Cal., 1941-47; exec. dir., audiologist Youngstown (O.) Hearing and Speech Center, 1948—. Pres., Tri-County Rehab. Council, 1962-64. Mem. Am., Ohio speech and hearing assns., Nat. Rehab. Assn. Club: Quota. Home: 1119 Bryson Youngstown OH 44505 Office: 69 Illinois Av Youngstown OH 44505

VEVERKA, MARY LOUISE ALMJELD (MRS. DONALD VEVERKA), educator, concert pianist; b. Tyler, Minn., Apr. 28, 1940; d. Floyd Joseph and Frances Mildred (Townswick) Almjeld; B.S., Mankato State Coll., 1962; M.Mus., Northwestern U., 1963; postgrad. Stanford, 1965; m. Donald Veverka, May 27, 1967; children—Tayna Marie, Holly Suzanne. Appearances as pianist throughout U.S., 1957—; tchr., pianist North Shore Country Day Sch., Winnetka, Ill., 1963-64; instr. music, pianist Concordia Tchrs. Coll., River Forest, Ill., 1964-67, Rosary Coll., River Forest, 1967—; mem. Bristol Trio, 1974—. Mankato Alumni scholar, 1958-62. Mem. Ill. State Music Tchrs. Assn. (chpt. pres. 1971-72; piano festival chmn. 1971-74), Soc. Am. Musicians (dir.), Western Springs Music Club. Home: 709 N Park Rd LaGrange Park IL 60525 Office: 7900 Division River Forest IL 60305

VEZEAU, SISTER JEANNETTE EVA, coll. pres.; b. Rochester, N.H., May 11, 1913; d. Edward U. and Laura Ann (Richey) Vezeau; B.S., Boston U., 1948, M.Ed., 1955, Ed.D., 1960. Joined Sisters of Holy Cross, 1933; tchr. high sch., Manchester, N.H., 1937-45, North Grosvenordale, Conn., 1945-49, New Bedford, Mass., 1949-57; prin. St. George High Sch., Manchester, N.H., 1960-64; supr. schs. for Sisters of Holy Cross in New Eng., Pittsfield, N.H., 1964-67; pres. Notre Dame Coll., Manchester, 1967—. Mem. Christian Unity Commn., 1965-71. Mem. Diocesan Sch. Bd., Manchester, 1965-71, Adv. Bd. Elliott Sch. Nursing, Manchester, 1968—; exec. bd. N.H., Coll. and Univ. Council, 1967—; mem. Gov.'s Commn. on Post Secondary Edn., 1973—. Recipient Woman of Achievement award N.H. Fedn. Bus. and Profl. Women's Clubs, Inc., 1974. Mem. Am. Council Edn. Author: (with others) 10,000 Legal Words, 1971. Address: 2321 Elm St Manchester NH 03104

VEZIE, MARY SOUTHWORTH (MRS. KRIEG STANTON VEZIE), occupational therapist; b. San Francisco, Apr. 19, 1930; d. Lawrence and Evelyn (Benham) Bull; student Pomona Coll., 1948-50; B.F.A., U. Colo., 1953; certificate in occupational therapy, U. So. Cal., 1957; certificate Center for Study Sensory Integrative Dysfunction; m. Krieg Stanton Vezie, Feb. 4, 1956; children—Eric, Kirk, David. Occupational therapist Shriner's Hosp., San Francisco, 1957-58, Marin Child Devel. Center, Tiburon, Cal., 1969—; pvt. practice in occupational therapy specializing in sensory integration, Mill Valley, Cal., 1972—. Mem. Am. Occupational Therapy Assn., Am. Assn. U. Women, Center for Study Sensory Integrative Dysfunction, Cal. Assn. Neurologically Handicapped Children, No. Cal. Occupational Therapy Assn., World Fedn. Occupational Therapists. Home: 6 Vasco Dr Mill Valley CA 94941 Office: 240 Tiburon Blvd Tiburon CA 94920

VICK, MARGARET MINA POTTER (MRS. ORVILLE A.C. VICK), real estate broker; b. Tipton, Ia., July 9, 1924; d. Elmer Junie and Emma Mae (Shreve) Potter; student Ill. Inst. Tech., 1944; m. Orville A.C. Vick, Feb. 22, 1946; children—Susan (Mrs. James Dennis Rohman), Barbara (Mrs. Larry McWilliams), James. Salesman, Paul Jones & Assos., real estate, Pomona, Cal., 1966-70; owner Vick Realty, Pomona, 1970-74. Leader, Girl Scouts U.S.A., 1957-60; v.p. North Side Civic Youth Welfare Club, Chgo., 1958, 59. Mem. Bus. and Profl. Women's Club (hospitality hostess 1969), Nat. Assn. Real Estate Bds., Photo-Engr. Women's Aux., Pomona Valley Bd. Realtors (dir. 1973-75), Pomona C. of C. Home: 2211 Las Vegas St Pomona CA 91767 Office: 551 W Holt Blvd Pomona CA 91767

VICK, MARY DORCAS WHEELER (MRS. EWALD AUGUST VICK), nurse educator; b. Oklahoma City, Oct. 20, 1909; d. Otis Earl and Clara Bell (Edwards) Wheeler; B.S. cum laude, Greenville Coll., 1932; postgrad. Eastern Ill. U., 1932-33; R.N. with honors, St. Mary's Hosp., Rochester, Minn., 1937; M.S., Marquette U., 1958; m. Ewald August Vick, July 23, 1938; children—Charles Ewald, Marna Jane (Mrs. Stanley Wiggam), John Edwards. Instr. sci. St. Mary Hosp. Sch. Nursing, Rochester, 1936, gen., pvt. duty nursing, 1937; instr. sci. Columbia Hosp. Sch. Nursing, Milw., 1937-38; gen. duty nurse, ednl. dir. Waukesha (Wis.) Meml. Hosp., 1953-54; coordinator-instr. practical nursing Milw. Tech. Coll., 1954-57; instr. Tb nursing Muridale Sanitarium, Wauwatosa, Wis., 1957-58; instr. sci. U. Wis., Milw., 1958-60; dean nursing and health occupations Milw. Area. Tech. Coll., 1960—. Troop leader, dir. Eastern dist. Gt. Blue Heron Area council Girl Scouts U.S.A., 1947-49; pres. Waukesha County P.T.A., 1949-52; instr. first aid Waukesha County chpt. A.R.C., 1950-52; mem. steering com. coordinating council Allied Health S.E. Wis., 1972—; mem. coordinating council Continuing Edn. for Nurses Greater Milw. Area, 1969—, council Nursing Service and Nursing Edn. Greater Milw. Area, 1972—; mem. Wis., Para-Dental Commn., 1962—, Wis. Para-Med. Commn., 1966-72; mem. accreditation teams N. Central Assn. Colls. and Secondary Sch., 1970—. Mem. Nat. League for Nursing, Am., Milw. (chmn. educators, adminstrs. counselors, and tchrs. sect. 1962-64) nurses assns., Am. Vocational assn. (sec. health occupations div. 1973). Methodist. Home: 2134 S Sunny Slope New Berlin WI 53151 Office: 1015 N 6th St Milwaukee WI 53203

VICKERS, ELIZABETH, banker; b. Wilkes-Barre, Pa., May 1, 1916; d. Jerry Thomas and Jessie Mabel (Reese) Vickers; grad. Wilkes-Barre Bus. Coll., 1935; certificate Am. Inst. Banking, 1952; postgrad. Stonier Grad. Sch. Banking, 1966. Asst. cashier Citizens Bank of Parsons (Pa.), 1945-51; cashier Citizens Bank of Wilkes-Barre (Pa.), 1951-67; v.p. Miners Nat. Bank of Wilkes-Barre, 1967-68; v.p., br. mgr., United Penn Bank, Wilkes-Barre, 1968—, sec., adv. com. East End (Pa.) and Parsons (Pa.) offices, 1968—. Mem. Luzerne County (Pa.) Savs. Bond Com., 1971—. Vice chmn. Wilkes-Barre Indsl. Devel. Authority, 1968—. Bd. dirs. Wyo. Valley (Pa.) United Fund, 1964-70, Wilkes-Barre Area Vocational Tech. Sch., 1969—. Mem. Am. Inst. Banking (pres. Wyo. Valley chpt. 1953-54), Greater Wilkes-Barre C. of C. (chmn. visitation com. 1970-72), Wilkes-Barre Bus. and Profl. Women's Club (pres. 1962-64), Bank Adminstrn. Inst. (pres. Pocono chpt. 1970-71), Soroptimist Club (pres. Wilkes-Barre 1968-70), Nat. Assn. Bank Women (chmn. Anthracite Group 1958, 68-69). Methodist. Home: 242 N Main St Wilkes-Barre PA 18702 Office: 341 Kidder St Wilkes-Barre PA 18702

VICKERS, NAOMI RUTH (MRS. ROBERT ROSS VICKERS), real estate mgr.; b. Anderson, Ind., Mar. 25, 1917; d. Floyd Leroy and Gertrude Marie (Richards) Stamm; grad. high sch.; m. Robert Ross Vickers, July 22, 1933; children—Robert Vernon, Richard Ross, Philip Leroy, Denise (Mrs. Michael Eugene Lennen). Sec., treas. Vickers Fine Homes, Anderson, Ind., 1951—, Vickers Apts., 1956—; mgr., co-owner Tower Apts., Anderson Apts., Inc., 1970—; sec., treas. Comml. Bldgs., 1958—; sec., mgr. Vickshire Corp., 1969—; co-owner Vic-Von Corp. (Perkins Pancake House). Sec., treas. Down Town Enterprises, 1970—. Mem. Bus. and Profl. Womens Club. Mem. Order Eastern Star, White Shrine. Home: 2003 E 7th St Anderson IN 46012

VICKERY, BYRDEAN EYVONNE HUGHES (MRS. CHARLES EVERETT VICKERY, JR.), ednl. adminstr.; b. Belleview, Mo., Apr. 18, 1928; d. Roy Franklin and Margaret Cordelia (Wood) Hughes; student Flat River (Mo.) Jr. Coll., 1946-48; B.S. in Edn., S.E. Mo. State Coll., 1954; M.L.S., U. Wash., 1964; postgrad. Wash. State U., 1969-70; m. Charles Everett Vickery, Jr., Nov. 5, 1948; 1 dau., Camille (Mrs. Larry Eugene Allaway). Tchr. Ironton, (Mo.) Pub. Schs., 1948-56; elementary tchr. Pasco (Wash.) Sch. Dist. 1, 1956-61, jr. high sch. librarian, 1961-68, coordinator libraries, 1968-69; asst. librarian Columbia Basin Community Coll., Pasco, 1969-70, head librarian, dir. Instructional Resources Center, 1970—. Mem. Am. Assn. U. Women (2d v.p. 1966-68, corr. sec. 1969), Wash. Dept. Audio-Visual Instrn., A.L.A., Wash. Library Assn., Am., Wash. assns. higher edn., Wash. State Assn. Sch. Librarians (state conf. chmn. 1971-72), Tri-Cities Librarians Assn., Am. Assn. Research Libraries, Soroptimist Internat. Assn. (rec. sec. Pasco-Kennewick chpt. 1971-72, treas. 1973-74), Columbia Basin Coll. Adminstrs. Assn. (sec.-treas. 1973-74), Pacific N.W. Assn. Ch. Libraries, Beta Sigma Phi, Delta Kappa Gamma. Author, editor: Library and Research Skills Curriculum Guides for the Pasco School District, 1967; author (with Jean Thompson), also editor Learning Resources Handbook for Teachers, 1969. Home: 4016 W Park St Pasco WA 99301 Office: 2600 N Chase St Pasco WA 99301

VICTOR, JANET MARSHALL (MRS. DONALD C. VICTOR), editor; b. Wichita, Kan., Jan. 27, 1914; d. Clifford Ormond and Claribel (Macomber) Bentley; A.A., Compton Coll., 1934; B.A., Whittier Coll., 1936, M.S. in L.S., 1938; m. Donald C. Victor, Oct. 22, 1961. Soc. editor, reporter Bell Indsl. Post, Cal., 1930-36; asst. br. librarian, head book reviewer Los Angeles County Library, 1930-41; propr. various photog. studios, also tchr., 1942-51; founder Rangefinder Mag., also editor, pub., Los Angeles, 1952—. Instr., Los Angeles Inst. Photog. Art, 1948-49. Mem. Whittier Alumni Found., 1948—, Los Angeles Press Club 8 Ball Found., 1954—, Los Angeles Mus. Art, 1971—. Recipient Achievement awards Profl. Photographers Am., Inc. Mem. Mont. Photographers Assn., Profl. Photographers Cal., Profl. Photographers West, Profl. Photographers So. Cal. (exec. mgr.), Am. Soc. Mag. Photographers, Indsl. Photographers So. Cal., Greater Los Angeles Press Club, Western Soc. Bus. Pubs., others. Contbr. articles to photog. jours. Home: 14231 Cohasset Van Nuys CA 91405 Office: 3511 Centinela Av Los Angeles CA 90066

VICTOR, WILMA LOUISE, govt. ofcl.; b. Idabel, Okla. (mem. Choctaw Indian Tribe); d. George Taafe and Nancy (Forbes) Victor; student U. Kan., 1937-39; B.S. in English, and Social Studies, U. Wis., 1941, M.A. in Sch. Adminstrn., Okla. U., 1952. With Bur. Indian Affairs, Dept. Interior, 1941—, acad. supr. Intermountain Indian Sch., 1949-60, 64-70, dep. area dir. Phoenix area office, 1970-71, spl. asst. to sec. interior, Washington, 1971—, supervisory edn. specialist, 1960-61, prin. Inst. Am. Indian Art, Santa Fe, 1961-64. Mem. Gov. Utah Commn. Indian Affairs. Mem. Utah Conf. Social Welfare, Council for Exceptional Children No. Utah, Nat. Fedn. Bus. and Profl. Women's Clubs, Kappa Delta Pi. Address: Interior Bldg Washington DC 20240

VIDAL, DAGMAR LUND (MRS. LEWIS LEONARD VIDAL), nat. Democratic committeewoman, civic worker; b. Hampton, Ia., Dec. 10, 1917; d. Peter Lauritsen and Mette Elizabeth (Miller) Lund; student Grandview Coll., 1935-36, U. No. Ia., 1938-39, U. Minn., summer 1940, Colo. State U., summer 1941, Los Angeles Govt. Tng. Sch., 1943; m. Lewis Leonard, June 22, 1944; children—Katherine (Mrs. Payton Edward Shaw), Robert, Peter, Leonard. Tchr. rural sch., Hampton, 1936-38; elementary sch. tchr., Garner, Ia., 1939-41, Cherokee, Ia., 1941-42, Mason City, Ia., 1941-42; weather observer U.S. Govt., Salt Lake City, 1943-44. Alternate del. Democratic Nat. Convs., 1960, 64, del., 1968, 70; 3d Congl. Dist. Dem. committeewoman, 1964-68, state vice chmn., 1968-70, nat. committeewoman, 1970—; mem. exec. com. Dem. Nat. Com., 1972. Mem. adv. bd. Ia. Center for Edn. in Politics, 1966—. Found. bd. mem. North Ia. Area Community Coll. Mem. Franklin County Community Hosp. Aux. (pres.). Lutheran. Home: Rural Route 2 Beeds Lake Hampton IA 50441

VIEHMANN, NANCY ELIZABETH HINES (MRS. GEORGE ANTHONY VIEHMANN), ednl. adminstr.; b. Hartford, Conn., Mar. 26, 1946; d. Thomas Francis and Muriel Virginia (McMahon) Hines; A.A., Hartford Coll. for Women, 1966; B.A., Marymount Coll., 1968; postgrad. Boston State Coll., 1972—; m. George Anthony Viehmann, Aug. 4, 1973. Admissions counselor Marymount Coll., Tarrytown, N.Y., 1968-70; asst. dir. admissions Newton (Mass.) Coll., 1970-72, dir. career counseling, 1971—. Ski instr. Ski Patrol, Okemo Mountain, Ludlow, Vt., 1970-74. Recipient Vol. Service award Mass. Gen. Hosp., 1972. Mem. Nat. Assn. Fgn. Student Affairs (regional team state rep. 1973), Eastern Coll. Personnel Officers. Home: 608 Watertown St Newtonville MA 02160 Office: 885 Centre St Newton MA 02159

VIETTI, TERESA JANE, physician; b. Ft. Worth; d. William V. and Grace (Christian) Vietti; A.B., Rice Inst., 1949; M.D., Baylor U., 1953. Intern, St. Louis Children's Hosp., 1953-54, asst. resident, 1954-55, chief resident, 1955-56; hematology resident Children's Hosp., Detroit, 1956-58; fellow Am. Cancer Soc. and USPHS trainee, 1958-60; instr. Wayne U., 1958; instr. U. Tex. Southwestern Med. Sch., 1958-60; vis. pediatrician Hacettepe Children's Hosp., Ankara, Turkey, 1960-61; asst. prof. pediatrics Washington U. Sch. Medicine, St. Louis, 1961-65, asso. prof., 1965-72, prof., 1972—, also dir. div. hematology and oncology; asst. pediatrician St. Louis Children's Hosp., 1961-65, asso. pediatrician, 1965—. Bd. dirs. Leukemia Soc. Am. and Ill., 1964—. Mem. Am., Internat. socs. hematology, Midwest Pediatric Research Soc., Am. Soc. Clin. Oncology, Am. Acad. Pediatrics, Am. Assn. Cancer Research, Am., St. Louis pediatric socs. Contbr. articles to med. jours. Home: 11701 Brookbend Des Peres MO 63131 Office: 500 S Kingshighway St Louis MO 63110

VIGLIOTTA, CELIA LEE, occupational therapist; b. Euphrates, Wash., Oct. 26, 1945; d. Thomas Grecenzo and Rosella Agnes (Pepping) Vigliotta; Asso. Sci., Mt. Aloysius Jr. Coll., 1965; B.S., Coll. St. Catherine, 1968. Asst. occupational therapy Bird S. Coler Hosp., N.Y.C., 1965-66; staff therapist N.Y. Med. Coll.-Met. Hosp. Center, N.Y.C., 1968-70, sr. therapist, 1970-71, supr. occupational therapy, 1971-73, chief occupational therapist, 1973—. Cons. occupational therapy Flower and Fifth Av. Hosp., N.Y.C., 1973. Vol. tchr. adult edn. Archdiocese of N.Y., 1970-71; vol. asst. to elderly Leisure Club, N.Y.C., 1973. Recipient grant Vocational Rehab. Adminstrn., 1966-68. Mem. Am., N.Y. State occupational therapy assns. Home: 220 E 63d St New York City NY 10021 Office: 1901 1st Av New York City NY 10029

VIKLINETZ, BARBARA ANN PARKER (MRS. EDWARD A. VIKLINETZ SR.), motel exec.; b. Nashua, N.H., Apr. 14, 1929; d. Lambert Achilles and Ruth Madelaine (Burnham) Parker; certificate in accounting, Internat. Corr. Schs., 1956; m. Edward A. Viklinetz, Sr., Oct. 15, 1949; children—Edward A., Gail Nancy. Officer mgr. and banquet sales Grantmoor Restaurant, Newington, Conn., 1959-62; dining room mgr. Windsor House Restaurant, Windsor, Conn., 1962-63; office Shoreham Hotels, Hartford, 1963-68, banquet sales, 1965-68, pub. relations and sales mgr., 1970-72; mgr. Howard Johnson's Motor Lodge, Hartford, Conn., 1972-74, area mgr., 1973-74; gen. mgr. Ramada Inn, Warehouse Point, Conn., 1974—. Active Girl Scouts Am., 1961-66. Mem. Hotel Sales Mgmt. Assn. (instr. 1973-74), Conn. Hotel Motel Assn. (dir. 1974—). Office: Ramada Inn Bridge St Warehouse Point CT 06088

VILA, ELIZABETH MILLER, civic worker; b. Wayne, Pa., July 23, 1911; d. Edgar T. and Norah (Schweyer) Miller; grad. Baldwin Sch., 1930; B.A., Vassar Coll., 1934; postgrad. Maria Ouspenskayo Sch. Acting, 1934-36; certificate N.Y. Sch. Design, 1972; m. George R. Vila, Oct. 4, 1941 (div. Feb. 1970); children—John Desmond, Richard Lawrence. Actress, Essex (N.Y.) Summer Theatre, 1937, Barter Theatre, Abingdon, N.Y., 1938-39, Drove Players, Greenwich Village, N.Y.C., 1939-41, Canton Workshop (Conn.), 1941, Woonsocket (R.I.) Theatre, 1940. Nurses' aide A.R.C., Waterbury Hosp., 1942-48; chmn. Planned Parenthood; pres. Woodbury (Conn.) P.T.A., 1951-53; mem. Citizens Com. to Evaluate Pub. Sch. and Tchr. Tng., 1954; mem. restoration com. Wallace House, Somerville, N.J., 1966-68; chmn. decorating, seminar coms. Wykeham Rise Sch. Festival, 1972-73. Bd. mem. Vis. Nurse Assn., Somerset Hills, N.J., 1962-68, Washington, Conn., 1972—; trustee Gunnery Sch., Washington, Conn. Episcopalian (vestry 1973—). Clubs: Somerset Hills Garden (historian 1967-69); Vassar, Cosmopolitan (N.Y.C.); Washington (Conn.) Garden (hort. chmn. 1971-73); Washington (Washington). Home: Meadow Wind Washington Depot CT 06794

VILHAUER, SANDRA LYNNE (MRS. JACOB ERNEST VILHAUER), pediatrician; b. Richmond, Cal., Jan. 13, 1944; d. Daryl Kline and Matilda Christine (Meyer) Armstrong; B.S., Ore. State U., 1965; M.D. cum laude, U. Ore., 1969; m. Jacob Ernest Vilhauer, Mar. 6, 1966; 1 dau., Allison. Rotating intern Emanuel Hosp., Portland, Ore., 1969-70; resident pediatrics U. Ore. Med. Sch., Portland, 1970-72; practice medicine specializing in pediatrics, 1972—; mem. staffs Emanuel, St. Vincents, Good Samaritan hosps. (all Portland); clin. instr. in pediatrics U. Ore. Med. Sch., Portland, 1972—. Mem. med. adv. bd. March of Dimes. Mem. Nat. Assn. Residents and Interns, Am. Med. Womens Assn., Portland Acad. Pediatrics, N. Pacific, Ore. pediatric socs., Multnomah County Med. Soc., Ore. Med. Assn., Washington County Med. Soc., Delta Delta Delta. Home: 8245 SW Canyon Lane Portland OR 97225 Office: Barnes Rd Profl Bldg 9340 SW Barnes Rd Portland OR 97225

VILLA, RITA FLYNN (MRS. JAMES G. VILLA), lawyer; b. N.Y.C., June 7, 1946; d. Daniel and Mary (Kelly) Flynn; B.A., Cath. U., 1967; J.D., Albany Law Sch., 1970; m. James G. Villa, May 30, 1970; 1 dau., Catherine Flynn. Admitted to Vt. bar, 1970; staff atty. Vt. Legal Aid, Burlington, 1970-71; individual practice, Hinesburg, Vt., 1971-73; partner Villa & Kohn, Hinesburg, 1973—. Mem. Hinesburg Planning Commn., 1971—. Mem. Vt. Com. on Individual and Human Rights, 1971-72. Mem. Chittenden County bar assns. Address: Box 136 Hinesburg VT 05461

VILLELLA, GAIL HOLLAND (MRS. VINCENT JAMES VILLELLA), coll. bus. adminstr.; b. Statesville, N.C., Mar. 14, 1940; d. Walter Columbus and Ruth Edith (Freudenthal) Holland; grad. high sch.; m. Vincent James Villella, Dec. 31, 1971. Agy. accounting supr. Hanover Ins. Co., Chgo., 1958-63; bookkeeper Link Belt/FMC Corp., Chgo., 1963-69, Field Enterprises, Chgo., 1969-71; controller, asst. treas., office mgr. Wis. Coll. Conservatory, Milw., 1972—. Home: 424 W Walters St Port Washington WI 53074 Office: 1584 N Prospect Milwaukee WI 53202

VILLWOCK, MARY K. SMITH (MRS. ARTHUR EUGENE VILLWOCK), psychologist; b. Barnesville, O., July 11, 1913; d. John Jeffrey and Nancy (Miller) Smith; B.A., Muskingum Coll., 1935; M.A., Ohio State U., 1936; Ph.D., Northwestern U., 1940; m. Arthur Eugene Villwock, June 29, 1957; children—John Eugene, Kenneth Arthur, Cynthia Martha. Asst. prof. Central State Tchrs. Coll., Mt. Pleasant, Mich., 1938-39, 40-41; psychologist State Bur. Juvenile Research, Columbus and Athens, O., 1941-47; asso. prof. U. Ill., Urbana, 1947-49; sch. psychologist, Whitefish Bay, Wis., 1949-52; asso. prof. Muskingum Coll., New Concord, O., 1952-54; psychologist, dir. Tuscarawas Valley Guidance Center, Dover, O., 1954-69; practice psychology, New Philadelphia, O., 1969—; dir. Family Service, Dover, 1970—. Fellow Am. Assn. Mental Deficiency; mem. Am. Psychol. Assn., Am. Assn. U. Women (br. pres. 1966-68), Sigma Xi. Methodist. Home: 243 Beaver Av NE New Philadelphia OH 44663 Office: 331 Beaver Av NE New Philadelphia OH 44663

VILOTT, CATHERINE LAVON ELDER (MRS. L. DALE VILOTT), real estate broker; b. Oregon, Mo., Feb. 25, 1911; d. David Harlen and Edith Mae (Culp) Elder; student Coll. of Desert, 1963-64; m. L. Dale Vilott, June 25, 1932; adopted children—Lawrence G., Theodore E. Buyer, J.C. Penney Co., Anaheim, Cal., 1933-43; owner Vilotts Variety Stores, Long Beach and Whittier, Cal., 1945-60; salesman Art Katje Realty, Yucca Valley, 1961-65; owner Circle K. Realty, Yucca Valley, 1965—. Chmn., House Beautiful Tour, 1963-72; area chmn. San Bernardino Heart Assn., 1965, 66. Mem. Bus. and Profl. Women's Club (charter pres. 1962-66), C. of C. Club: Soroptimist (charter pres. Yucca Valley 1963-64). Home: Fairway 1A Country Club Yucca Valley CA 92284 Office: 55379 29 Palms Hwy Yucca Valley CA 92284

VINCENT, CHARLOTTE JANE MCCARROLL (MRS. CHARLES RIDGELY VINCENT), fashion merchandiser; b. Detroit, Nov. 8, 1918; d. R. Hudson and Muriel (Channer) McCarroll; student Denison U., 1936-38, Vogue Sch. Design, 1938-39; m. Charles Ridgely Vincent, June 17, 1939; children—David Ridgely, Barbara Channer (Mrs. Gerald Henares), Peter McCarroll, Patricia Tiffany. Tchr., Forest Hill Sch., Carmel, Cal., 1959; mem. sales staff Boystown, Carmel, 1959-60; dept. mgr. I. Magnin & Co., Carmel, now San Francisco, 1960—. Mem. staff Gallery Americana, 1972; cons., free-lance interior designer, 1967-72. Membership chmn. Am. Women Vol. Services, 1942-45, Monterey Peninsula Vol. Services, 1955-59. Mem. Community Hosp. Women's Aux. Named Top Salesperson I. Magnin & Co., 1962, 66, recipient award for meritorious services, 1965, 73. Mem. Denison U., Stuart Hall alumnae assns., Kappa Alpha Theta. Republican. Episcopalian. Home: 219 Spruce St San Francisco CA 94118 Office: 1 Magnin Co Union Sq San Francisco CA 94111

VINCENT, DOROTHE LUISE HILDEGARD HEINRICH, editor; b. Berlin, Germany, Aug. 3, 1920; d. Johannes Christian and Frieda Bertha (Zickelbein) Meinrich; student Lette Coll., Berlin, 1936-40, Schiller theatre, Berlin, 1940-42; student in journalism U. Toronto, 1967-68. Free-lance journalist, writer, Germany and Can., 1963—; editor in charge German Publs., Scarborough, Ont., Can., 1972—. Tchr. German lang. German Lang. Schs., Toronto, Ont., 1971. Chmn. for recreation Canadian Safety Council, 1970. Mem. Media Club Can. Home: 5 High Park Av Toronto ON Canada Office: 46 Crockford Blvd Scarborough ON Canada

VINCENT, GERALDINE EVELYN, former missionary; b. Erie, Pa.; d. Carl John and Marie (Nunes) Vincent; B.A., Wheaton Coll., 1941; postgrad. Biblican Sem. N.Y., 1941-42; M.A. (Grad. fellow), Wheaton Coll., 1945. Head Christian edn. dept. London (Can.) Bible Coll., 1945-47; tchr. Anwhwei Province, China, China Inland Mission, 1947-51, Mwanza, Tanzania, East Africa, Africa Inland Mission, 1953-65; dean women, head missions dept. Buffalo Bible Inst. (name now changed to Houghton Coll.), 1965-70; asst. candidate sec. Africa Inland Mission, Pearl River, 1970—. Mem. student affairs com., Buffalo, 1965-69. Recipient Silver medal Nat. Oratorical Contest, Northfield, Mass., 1935. Honor mem. Christian Edn. Fellowship. Baptist. Author: Church History for African Youth, 1958; Great Men of the Bible, 1957; Panoramic View of the Bible, 1956; Acts of the Apostles, 1959; also interdenominational youth and camp lessons. Office: PO Box 178 Pearl River NY 10965

VINCENT, SISTER MARY CLAUDINE, educator; b. Balt. d. William Paul and Anna McCormick (Carroll) Vincent; A.B., Coll. Notre Dame of Md., 1936; M.A., Seton Hall U., 1944; postgrad. Notre Dame U., 1958, Johns Hopkins, 1943-60, U. Mich., 1967. Tchr. parochial schs., Annapolis, Md., 1923-33, Irvington, N.J., 1933-37, high sch., Balt., 1937-41; instr. Notre Dame Tchrs. Tng. Sch., Balt., 1941-49; directress of postulants Balt. Province Sch. Sisters Notre Dame, 1949-58; dir. student personnel, asso. prof. psychology Coll. Notre Dame of Md., Balt., 1958—. Mem. Am., Md. personnel and guidance assns., Nat. Vocational Guidance Assn., Am. Coll. Personnel Assn., Nat. Cath. Guidance Assn. (dir. 1967-68), Middle Atlantic Placement Assn., Md. Psychol. Assn. Home: 4701 N Charles St Baltimore MD 21210

VINCENT, ROSE HELEN (MRS. LYLE CLEMENT VINCENT), realtor; b. San Luis Potosi, Mexico, Aug. 8, 1923; d. Carl Richard and Hortensia Minerva (Esquivel) Samuelson; came to U.S., 1928, naturalized, 1944; student (Cal. Fedn. scholar), San Francisco State Coll., 1941-42; m. Lyle Clement Vincent, Mar. 17, 1956. Bus. mgr., profl. entertainer, 1945-56; with Lyle C. Vincent, Inc., Wahiawa, Hawaii, 1956—, corporate exec., 1961—. Mem. Nat. Assn. Real Estate Bds., Honolulu Bd. Realtors, Bus. and Profl. Womens Club (pres. 1964). Home: 98-1386 Kaonohi St Aiea HI 96701 Office: 55 Westervelt St Wahiawa HI 96786

VINING, CAROL JEANETTE, advt. exec.; b. Joliet, Ill., Jan. 1, 1941; d. Carl A. and Berniece K. (Rademacher) Vining; student Fenger Jr. Coll., 1957-59, U. Ariz., 1970, Mich. State U., 1971. With Evergreen Plaza, Chgo., 1960—, dir. advt. and promotion, 1968—. Mem. Internat. Council Shopping Centers. Office: Rm 312 9730 S Western Av Evergreen Park IL 60642

VINING, ELIZABETH GRAY (MRS. MORGAN FISHER VINING), writer; b. Germantown, Phila., 1902; d. John Gordon and Anne Moore (Iszard) Gray; A.B., Bryn Mawr Coll., 1923; B.S. in L.S., Drexel Inst. Library Sch., 1926; m. Morgan Fisher Vining, Jan. 31, 1929 (dec. Oct. 1933). Tutor to the Crown Prince of Japan in Tokyo, 1946-50. Vice pres. bd. trustees Bryn Mawr Coll. 1950-71. Recipient Third Order of the Sacred Crown (Japan), 1950; Distinguished Dau. of Pa., 1952; Am. Women's Assn. Eminent Achievement award, 1953; Constance Lindsay Skinner award, 1954; Phila. Atheneum Lit. award, 1964. Mem. Authors Guild. Mem. Religious Soc. of Friends. Author: Windows for the Crown Prince, 1952; The World in Tune, 1954; The Virginia Exiles, 1955; Friend of Life: The Biography of Rufus M. Jones, 1958; Return to Japan, 1960; Take Heed of Loving Me: A Novel about John Donne, 1964; Flora: A Biography, 1966; I Roberta, 1967; Quiet Pilgrimage, 1970; childrens' books Meggy MacIntosh, 1930; Young Walter Scott, 1935; Penn, 1938; Adam of the Road, 1942; The Cheerful Heart, 1959; I Will Adventure, 1962; The Taken Girl, 1972. Home: Kendal at Longwood Box 194 Kennett Square PA 19348

VINSON, LU OUIDA, assn. exec.; b. nr. Chgo., July 30, 1924; d. Thomas Clarion Vinson and Exer E. (Fincher) Vinson Pendergraft; B.A., Mary Hardin Baylor Coll., 1949; postgrad. U. Conn., 1957; M.A., U. Tex., 1963; M.L.S., Tex. Womans U., 1967. Tchr. pub. schs. Floyd County, 1941-42; tchr. Corsicana Orphans Home, 1942-45; tchr. pub. schs., Waco, Tex., 1945-59; librarian, Waco, 1959-63; sch. and library cons. Field Enterprises Ednl. Corp., Chgo., 1963-67; exec. sec. Am. Assn. Sch. Librarians, Chgo., 1967—. Master Tchr. Harvard-Newton Summer Program, 1960; dir. Tchr. Growth Workshop, U. Tex.; lectr. in field. Mem. Assn. for Childhood Edn. (pres.), Hist. Phila. Soc. (v.p.), N.E.A., A.L.A., Assn. Sch. Curriculum and Devel., Nat. Assn. Secondary Sch. Prins., Nat. Assn. Elementary Sch. Prins., Internat. Reading Assn., Internat. Assn. Sch. Librarianship (charter; asst. sec.), Delta Kappa Gamma. Contbr. regular column in Media Quarterly, 1967; articles to profl. jours. Home: Box 62 Lott TX 76656 Office: 50 E Huron St Chicago IL 60611

VINSON, WANDA MAY, youth dir.; b. Kansas City, Mo., Nov 25, 1916; d. Clarence C. and Maybelle Sarah (Prindle) Vinson; A.B., Baker U., 1938; postgrad. U. Wis., 1938-39; M.A., Kan. U., 1949 Prin. Antioch Grade Sch., 1938-42; instr. social Sci. Wellsville High Sch., 1942-45; tchr. social sci. and speech Wellington High Sch., 1945-46; instr. social sci. Wichita East High Sch., 1946; adminstrv. asst. Kan. High Sch. Activities Assn.; youth dir. Kan. Assn. for Youth, 1946—; dir. speech activities state, 1957-67, dir. student council program, 1950-56. State dir. 2 Kayette Leadership Camps; state citizenship chmn. White House Conf. on Youth; state 1st v.p. Kan. Sch. Health Adv. Com. Trustee, Baker U. Recipient Alumni citation Baker U., 1958; nat. citations Cerebral Palsy, CARE, Meals for Millions; Wanda May Vinson Scholarship Fund established by Kays and Kayettes; Wanda May Vinson Seminar Room given to 4-H Citizenship Bldg. by Kays and Kayettes; named Kan. Woman of Year, Cardinal Key Women of KSTC, 1971. Mem. State Tchrs. Assn., Am. Assn. U. Women, Pi Lambda Theta, Pi Kappa Delta, Delta Kappa Gamma (1st state v.p. 1971-73). Methodist. Clubs: Topeka Woman's; Kansas Dinner. Home: 1200 College St Topeka KS 66604 Office: 520 W 27th St Topeka KS 66601

VIOLA, JOY WINKIE (MRS. ALFRED VIOLA), editor; b. Kansas City, Mo., Aug. 19, 1936; d. Edward Ferdinand and Lilyon Marguerite (Sweet) Winkie; B.A., U. Minn., 1957, M.A., 1958; m. Alfred Viola, Oct. 19, 1963. Asst. dir. press bur. Northeastern U., Boston, 1958-60, asst. dir. office publs., 1960-65, asso. dir. office publs., 1965-66, editorial asst. to pres., 1966—; sr. editor Internat. Ency. Higher Edn., 1974—. Free lance nature writer, lectr. and photographer, 1969—; editor Newsletter Sudbury Valley Trustees, 1969—. Mem. Women in Communications (pres. Boston chpt. 1963-66, v.p. memberships Boston chpt. 1971), U. Minn. Alumni Club (dir. Boston chpt. 1966—). Author: Stepping Stones or Stumbling Blocks: Basic Decisions in College Life, 1965; contbg. author Handbook of College and University Administration, 1970. Home: 14 Glover Rd Wayland MA 01778 Office: Northeastern University Boston MA 02115

VIOLA, VIRGINIA WATSON (MRS. RALPH T. VIOLA), constrn. co. exec.; b. Los Angeles, Oct. 21, 1924; d. Willard Henry and Frances Josephine (Rock) Watson; grad. high sch.; m. Ralph T. Viola, Feb. 20, 1944; children—Michael Thomas, William Terrence, Timothy Robert. Jr. actuary Occidental Ins. Co., Los Angeles, 1942-48; accountant, gen. mgr. Corey's Super Shopping Center, Los Angeles, 1948-49; accountant, sec.-treas. Viola, Inc., Ralph T. Viola Co., Inc., Oxnard, Cal., 1949—; corporate officer Calaine Corp., Subin Developing Corp., M & T Concrete, Inc., Bond's Jewelers, Oxnard Milling Co. (all Oxnard), Treas., Ventura County chpt. Assistance League, 1953-63. Bd. dirs. Children's Home Soc. Club: Los Posas Country (Camarillo, Cal.). Home: 2944 Solimar Beach Dr Ventura CA 93001 Office: 1144 Commercial Av Oxnard CA 93030

VIRDEN, MAXINE FERRELL (MRS. ROBERT MILES VIRDEN), occupational therapist; b. Webster City, Ia., July 22, 1916; d. Walter Jason Roger and Maye Addo (Thompson) Ferrell; student Am. Bus. U., 1935, Drake U., 1935-36, U. Cal. at Los Angeles, 1936-37; B.S., Ia. State U., 1940; certificate occupational therapy U. Ill., 1946; m. Robert Miles Virden, May 22, 1955. Dir. art dept. Hertzberg Craftsman, Des Moines, 1940-45; occupational therapist U.S. Army Hosp., Brigham City, Utah, 1945-46; occupational therapist VA Hosp., Des Moines, 1946—, dir. occupational therapy, 1946—. Mem. Health Careers Council Ia., 1963-67; mem. Gov. Ia. Com. on Status Women, 1964. Mem. Am. (del. 1948-54, mem. bd. mgmt. 1951-53), Ia. (v.p. 1947, pres. 1961-63) occupational therapy assns., Phi Kappa Phi, Delta Phi Delta, Omicron Nu, Alpha Delta Pi. Home: 3108 26th Place Des Moines IA 50310 Office: 30th and Euclid Sts Des Moines IA 50310

VIRTUE, CONSTANCE COCHNOWER (MRS. CLARK W. VIRTUE), musician, composer, educator; b. Cin., Jan 6, 1905; d. Robert Stewart and Edith (Rankin) Cochnower; Mus.B., U. Cin., 1927; postgrad. Am. Conservatory, 1932-33; M. Sacred Music, Union Theol. Sem., 1945; m. Clark W. Virtue, July 3, 1928; adopted children, Jean Christie, Robert Clark. Pvt. tchr. piano, organ, theory; organist, dir. numerous chs. including Mt. Auburn Presbyn. Ch., Cin., 1927, St. Luke's Evang. Luth. Ch., N.Y.C., 1945, Mission Hills Congl. Ch., San Diego, Cal., 1955-57, First Unitarian Ch., San Diego, 1960-65; organ instr. Convent of Sacred Heart, El Cajon, Cal., 1960-68, Great Music Listening, also class piano Grossmont Coll., 1961-63; pianist local concerts; four opera program Alaska Music Trails, 1968; live music and lectr. courses U. Cal. Extension, San Diego, 1969-70, 72; originator Virtue NotaGraph, 1933 now editor, pres. Virtue NotaGraph Editions; composer music dramas: (text by Erna Kruckemeyer) What Gift to the King?, 1923, The Queen of Camelot, 1933; anthems, instrumental works, songs including Love is Like a Rose, 1941; new setting for America the Beautiful, 1938. Recipient 1st prize in 5 nat. composition contests, including Mu Phi Epsilon Silver Loving Cup, 1936, research award for new music notation plan, 1938 1st prize orchestral composition, 1940; gold medal theme, Pensacola's Ann. Fiesta, 1950. Mem. Am. Guild Organists, Am. Piano Tchrs. Assn., Music Tchrs. Assn. Cal., Music Educators Nat. Conf., Mu Phi Epsilon. Home: 4940 Beaumont Dr La Mesa CA 92041

VISCARDI, NAOMI YARMOLINSKY (MRS. JOHN EDISON VISCARDI), physician; b. Kishinev, Russia, July 31, 1896; d. Bezalel and Malka (Nemoy) Yarmolinsky; student Hunter Coll., 1914-18; M.D., N.Y. Med. Coll., 1925; m. John Edison Viscardi, Nov. 6, 1919. Intern Met. Hosp. N.Y.C., 1926-27; practice medicine, Washington, 1925-26, N.Y.C., 1927-40, 44-68, Wichita, Kan., 1941-43, Dayton, O., 1969-71, San Antonio, 1972—; physician pre-sch. and sch. children N.Y.C. Health Dept., 1927-40; chief physician Aero. Parts Mfg. Co., Wichita, Kan., 1941-43; mem. birth control and clin. service staffs Fordham Hosp., also Knickerbocker Hosp., N.Y.C., 1944-68, Miami Valley Hosp., Dayton, 1969-71. Life mem. Am., N.Y. State, N.Y. County med. socs. Address: 7039 San Pedro Av San Antonio TX 78216

VITORITTO, ELVIRA MARY LANZA (MRS. ANTHONY F. VITORITTO), poet; b. Trenton, N.J., Aug. 5, 1900; d. Frank Sebastian and Rose (Ferrari) Lanza; certificate of teaching Carroll Robbins Tng. Sch., 1915, Rider Bus. Coll., 1920; m. Anthony F. Vitoritto, Aug. 16, 1922. Social Worker Trenton Internat. Inst., settlement house, 1915-22; tchr. trenton Bd. Edn., 1918-53. Named Italo-Am. Poet Laureate in Residence for N.J., 1968; recipient Edna St. Vincent Millay award Com. of 100 Poets Laureate of Md., 1970. Mem. Centro Studie Scambi Internationale (hon. v.p. 1974-76 Rome, Italy). Author books of poetry including: Above The Roar Of Silence, 1968; Gentle On The Wind, 1969; Substance and Dreams, 1972; Another Dawn Another Flowering, 1973. Home: PO Box West Trenton NJ 08628

VITOUSEK, BETTY BELLE MORRISON (MRS. ROY ARNOLD VITOUSEK, JR.), judge; b. Wenatchee, Wash., Mar. 9, 1919; d. Raymond Redmond and Zelma (Reeves) Morrison; B.A., U. Wash., 1940; LL.B., Stanford, 1948; m. Roy Arnold Vitousek, Jr. Dec. 2, 1945; children—Peter Morrison, Roy Arnold III, Kelly Marquerite (Mrs. Gardner White Bemis). Sec. to Sec. State of Wash., 1942; admitted to Hawaii bar, 1948; practiced in Honolulu, 1952-70; asst. program dir. A.R.C., New Zealand, 1943-44, New Caledonia, 1944-45, Hawaii, 1945; exec. dir. Bar Assn. Hawaii, 1961-67; judge Circuit Ct. State of Hawaii, Honolulu, 1970—. Pres. Conf. of Conciliation Cts., 1973—. Bd. dirs. Child and Family Service, Mental Health Assn.; bd. dirs. Legal Aid Soc. of Hawaii, sec. 1951-52; bd. dirs. Health and Community Services Council of Hawaii; mem. adv. bd. Liliuokaland Trust. Mem. Am., Hawaii bar assns., Am. Judicature Soc. Jr. League Hawaii (pres. 1958-59), Phi Beta Kappa, Chi Omega. Episcopalian. Home: 4005 Round Top Dr Honolulu HI 96822 Office: PO Box 3498 Honolulu HI 96811

VITTENSON, LILLIAN KASS (MRS. ALBERT A. VITTENSON), psychologist, educator; b. Chgo.; d. Morris and Rebecca (Weiner) Kass; B. Music, Am. Conservatory Music, 1946; M.A., Northwestern U., 1962, Ph.D., 1964; m. Albert A. Vittenson, Nov. 18, 1945; children—Jeffrey, Richard, Barbara. Profl. musician, 1946-63; tchr. Sch. Dist. No. 107, Highland Park, Ill., 1956-63; pvt. practice clin. psychology, Skokie, Ill., also Highland Park, 1964—; clin. psychologist North Oto-Audiology Group, Skokie, Ill., 1964—, Winnetka Inst. Hearing and Speech, Winnetka, Ill., 1964—, Oak Therapeutic Sch., Chgo., 1967—; prof. spl. edn. and psychology Northeastern Ill. State U., Chgo., 1963—; cons., lectr. psychology Ill. Coll. Optometry, Chgo., 1969—; psychologist Ill. State Office Pub. Instruction, 1964-67; psychologist U. Minn. Minnemast Program, 1965-67. Psychol. cons. Oak Therapeutic Sch., Evanston, Ill., 1967-71, Beacon Sch., Chgo., 1969—, Libra Sch., Chgo., 1969—; psychologist, cons. State Office Pub. Instruction Ill., 1964-68; cons. Chgo. Center for Achievement Human Potential, 1969—; mem. profl. adv. bd. Reading Research Found., 1963-70, Oak Therapeutic Sch., 1967-71, Libra Sch., 1969—, Chgo. Assn. for Children with Learning Disabilities, 1969—. Mem. Orgn. for Rehab. Through Tng., 1955—. Fellow Internat. Acad. Forensic Psychology; mem. Am., Ill. psychol. assns., Am. Assn. U. Profs., Council for Exceptional Children, Am. Assn. Mental Deficiency, Am. Judicature Soc., N.Y. Acad. Scis. Contbr. articles to profl. jours. Home: 590 Rambler Lane Highland Park IL 60035 Office: 64 Old Orchard Rd Skokie IL 60076

VIVROUX, VIOLET SCHRAUB (MRS. ARTHUR VIVROUX), gift show owner; b. Seguin, Tex., Oct. 28, 1908; d. Albert August and Lydia Sophia (Mertz) Schraub; student Draughan's Bus. Coll., 1927-78; m. Arthur Vivrous, Jan. 29, 1932 (dec. Dec. 1966); children—Arthur Charles, Judy (Mrs. Fritz B. Scheffel, Jr.). Employed at Guadalupe County (Tex.) Abstract Office, Seguin, 1928-29, Seguin-Guadalupe County C. of C., Seguin, 1929; recorder Office of Guadalupe Clk., County 1930-31; bookkeeper Vivroux Hardware Co., Seguin, 1958-70, Sequin C. of C., 1931-32; city treas. City of Seguin, 1966-74; owner Vivroux Gift Shop, Seguin, 1974—. Mem. C. of C. Elk. Club: Lazy Daisy Garden (Seguin). Home: 113 E Live Oak St Seguin TX 78155 Office: 114 S Austin St Seguin TX 78155

VIZCARRA CASTELLON, GINORIS (MRS. CARLOS A. LOPEZ-LAY), lawyer; b. Mexico City, Mex., Feb. 7, 1934; d. Salvador and Edelmira (Castellon) Vizcarra; B.A., Bennington Coll., 1954; LL.B., Yale, 1957; m. Carlos A. Lopez-Lay, July 2, 1966; children—Carlitos, Ginorita, Gloriana. Admitted to Supreme Ct. P.R., 1958, Dist. Ct. P.R., 1960, U.S. Ct. Appeals, 1960, U.S. Supreme Ct., 1961; law clk. Supreme Ct. P.R., 1958-61; practice in San Furce, P.R., 1961-66; mem. firm Lopez-Lay and Vizcarra, Santurce, 1967—. Lectr. labor legislation U. P.R., 1960-61; legal adviser Infantila Paralisis of P.R., 1963. Trustee Family Inst., 1966; regent Colegio Puertorriqueno de Ninas, 1968-74; sec. bd. dirs. Colegio Puertorriqueno de Ninas, 1968-71. Club: Yale (v.p. 1960-61) (P.R.). Mem. editors commn. P.R. Bar Assn. Jour., 1962. Author: Digest of the Administrative and Judicial Decision Issued Under The Puerto Rico Labor Relations Law, 1960. Contbr. articles to legal jours. Home: Garden Meadows B-9 Georgetown Guaynabo PR 00619 Office: 407 Parque St Santurce PR 00912

VLADZIMIRSKA, HELEN, pharm. chemist.; b. Buhajivka, Ukraine, USSR, Nov. 22, 1929; d. Basil Vladzimirskyj and Anna Martyniuk Vladzimirska; Diplom of pharmaceutist, 1952; Candidate of pharm. scis. Pharm. Inst. Moscow, 1955; Doctor pharm. sci., Med. Inst. at Lviv, 1965. Asst., Med. Inst. at Lviv, 1955-60, asst. prof., 1960-67, prof. pharm. chemistry, 1967—. Recipient ensign of excellent sci. worker of pub. health service USSR, 1969. Mem. All-Union Chem. Soc., All-Union Pharm. Soc. Author 2 books on pharm. chemistry and drugs, 1972; also numerous publs. on chemistry of thiazolidines and I, 3-thiazanes. Home: 23/8 Nemyrovych-Danchenko Lviv Ukraine USSR Office: 69 Pekarska Lviv Ukraine USSR

VLAHAKOS, IRENE J., psychologist, educator; b. Biddeford, Me.; d. James and Pota J. (Pappas) Vlahakos; B.A., U. N.H., 1962; M.A., U. Kan., 1965; Ph.D., U. Conn., 1974. Psychol. cons. Biddeford Sch. system, 1966; instr. dept. psychology Central Conn. State Coll., New Britain, 1966—. Cons. to schs. in Central Conn. state region, 1967-69. Mem. Adv. Com. Inst. on Police Relations with Troubled Youth in Conn., 1973—. Bd. dirs. Police Athletic League of New Britain. U.S. Dept. Edn. fellow in mental retardation, 1970-71. Mem. Am., New Eng. psychol. assns., Conn. Assn. Sch. Psychol. Personnel, Council of Exceptional Children, Nat. Assn. Sch. Psychologists, Nat. Soc. for Study of Edn., Am. Assn. on Mental Deficiency, Am. Assn. Univ. Women, Am. Assn. Univ. Profs., Phi Beta Kappa, Phi Kappa Phi, Pi Kappa Alpha, Psi Chi. Home: 10 Walnut St New Britain CT 06051 Office: Psychology Dept Central Connecticut State College New Britain CT 06050

VLEREBOME, MARGARET ANN, editor; b. Dayton, O., Apr. 1, 1947; d. Robert Hughes and Glenna (Protsman) Vlerebome Sr.; A.B. in Journalism and Govt. (Poynter Fund scholar), Ind. U., 1969. Reporter, St. Petersburg (Fla.) Times, 1969-73, asst. met. editor, 1973—. Mem. Women in Communications (v.p. coll. chpt. 1968-69, sec. Fla. West Coast chpt. 1973-74). Home: 4892 B Beach Dr SE St Petersburg FL 33705 Office: Box 1122 St Petersburg FL 33701

VOCE, MARY FRANCES, lawyer; b. Flint, Mich., Feb. 4, 1944; d. Edgar Jesse and Helen Mary (Zenko) Voce; B.A., U. Mich., 1966; LL.B., U. Va., 1969; m. Stephen David Gardner, Sept. 19, 1973. Admitted to N.Y. bar, 1970; asso. atty. Breed, Abbott & Morgan, N.Y.C., 1969—. Mem. N.Y. Council of Law Assos., N.Y. State Bar Assn., Assn. Bar City N.Y., Phi Beta Kappa, Phi Delta Phi, Alpha Lambda Delta, Pi Sigma Alpha. Democrat. Home: 32 Gramercy Park New York City NY 10003 Office: care Breed Abbott & Morgan 1 Chase Manhattan Plaza New York City NY 10005

VOEGELIN, FLORENCE M. HARMON (MRS. CHARLES F. VOEGELIN), anthropologist; b. Colorado Springs, Colo., Sept. 26, 1927; d. Darell Boyd and Florence (Morrow) Harmon; A.B., Colo. State Coll. Edn., 1949; M.A., Ind. U., 1952, Ph.D., 1954; m. Ralph F. Robinett, Sept 1, 1946 (div. Jan. 1952); m. 2d, Charles F. Voegelin, Dec. 25, 1954. Instr., U. P.R., Rio Piedras, 1949-51; dir. Archives of Langs. of World, Ind. U., Bloomington, 1955—. Research asso. Mus. No. Ariz., Flagstaff, 1968—. Fellow Am. Anthrop. Assn.; mem. Linguistic Soc. Am. Editor: Anthrop. Linguistics, 1959—. Contbr. articles to profl. jours. Research on Am. Indian langs. Home: 500 Arbutus Dr Bloomington IN 47401 Office: Anthropology Dept Ind U Bloomington IN 47401

VOEKS, VIRGINIA WILNA, educator; b. Champaign, Ill., May 9, 1921; d. B. Forrest and Dorothy (Wade) Voeks; B.S., summa cum laude (Pres.' medalist 1943), U. Wash., 1943, M.S., 1944; Ph.D., Yale, 1947; m. William McBlair IV. Research asso. Yale U., New Haven, 1944-45; asst. prof. U. Wash., 1947-49; asst. prof. San Diego (Cal.) State Coll., 1949-55, asso. prof., 1955-58, prof., 1958—. Recipient Pres.'s medal U. Wash., 1943; Sterling award Yale, 1945. Fellow N.Y. Acad. Scis., Am. Psychol. Assn. (sec.-treas. div. I 1965—, editor Newsletter); mem. Western Pyschol. Assn., Am. Assn. U. Profs., A.A.A.S., Am. Civil Liberties Union, The Psychonomic Soc. (charter), UN Assn. San Diego, San Diego Ballet Assn. (charter), Phi Beta Kappa Sigma Xi, Psi Chi (pres. U. Wash., 1942-43), Phi Kappa Phi, Sigma Epsilon Sigma, Alpha Lambda Delta. Club: Heritage. Author: On Becoming an Educated Person, 1957, 64, 70; articles profl. jours. Home: PO Box 877 4319 Explorer Rd La Mesa CA 92041 Office: Dept Psychology San Diego State U San Diego CA 92115

VOELKER, JUDITH MAYO PENNEBAKER (MRS. ROBERT GORDON VOELKER), editor; b. Murray, Ky., July 17, 1938; d. Gordon Bennett and Dorothy Mayo (Printz) Pennebaker; B.A., U. Ky., 1960; postgrad. Vanderbilt U., 1961; m. Robert Gordon Voelker, Oct. 27, 1973; 1 son, Alfred Clay Ludlum III. Fashion editor The Nashville Tennessean, 1961-64; fashion publicist, pub. relations E. I. duPont de Nemours & Co., N.Y.C., 1964-66; fashion writer Pitts. Post-Gazette, 1967-73. The Cleve. Plain Dealer, 1973—. Mem. Women in Communications, The Fashion Group, Women's Press Club, Pitts. Press Club, Chi Omega. Episcopalian. Home: 19660 Roslyn Dr Rocky River OH 44116 Office: 1810 Superior St Cleveland OH 44114

VOELKER, LOUISE FROMM, civil engr.; b. Milw.; d. Edward William and Edna (Eadus) Fromm; B.S., U. Wis., 1939, M.S. in Math., 1951; M.S. in Engring. Mgmt., U. Alaska, 1966; m. Harry E. Voelker, Jan. 2, 1942 (div. Apr. 1959); 1 son, John Alan. Tchr. pub. schs., Two Rivers, Wis., 1939-43, Ashland, Wis., 1944-45; instr. U. Wis., 1946-48; asst. prof. Elmhurst Coll., 1954-55; civil engr. U.S. C.E., Camp Atterbury, Ind., 1943; cartographic engr. U.S. Lake Survey, Detroit, 1951; geodetic engr. Tokyo, Japan, 1952-53; computer Western Electric, Anchorage, 1955-56; with U.S. Army Corps Engrs., 1957-66, chief control and photogrammetry sect., Anchorage, 1958-66; project officer DMAAC Geodetic Survey Squadron, Warren AFB, Wyo., 1966—. Mem. Am. Assn. U. Women, Am. Soc. Photogrammetry, Soc. Am. Mil. Engrs. (treas. Anchorage Post 1965), Phi Beta Kappa. Club: Zonta Internat. (sec. Anchorage 1962-63, pres. Cheyenee 1972-73). Address: 1757 Oxford Dr Apt 2 Cheyenne WY 82001

VOGEL, MARION LACK (MRS. HARRY VOGEL), librarian; b. Jersey City, Feb. 8, 1921; d. Philip and Rose (Fondiller) Lack; B.A., Douglass Coll., Rutgers U., 1942; M.A., Columiba, 1946; m. Harry Vogel, Nov. 2, 1947; children—Nancy R. (Mrs. Paul Feldman), Joan E., Stephen H., Richard J. Children's librarian Newark Pub. Library, 1942; research and reference librarian Am. Geog. Soc., N.Y.C., 1942-46; librarian indsl. relations dept. Ebasco Services, Inc., N.Y.C., 1947-48; librarian Palmer Coll., Charleston, S.C., 1969—. Cons. St. Francis Hosp. Nursing Library, 1963; mem., Palmer Coll. rep. Trident Forum for Handicapped, 1973—. Mem. P.T.A. Steering Com., Bayside, N.Y. 19—; internat. relations chmn. Bayside Oaks Jewish Community Center, L.I.; rec. sec., chmn. library com. Jewish Community Center, Charleston, 1967—; parliamentarian Synagogue Emanu-El, Charleston, also v.p. edn. Synagogue sisterhood, 1966-70; v.p. Charleston Area Mental Health Assn., 1973—; pres. jr. congregation Temple Emanuel, Westwood, N.J., 1935; internat. relations chmn. So. Region United Synagogue, 1967-68; mem. steering com. Pub. Sch. 213 PTA, Bayside, 1958, chmn. library com., 1956-59. Recipient Citizenship award Synagogue Emanuel Talmud Torah, 1961. Mem. Am., S.C., Southeastern library assns., Rutgers U. Grad. Library Assn., Douglass Alumni Assn., League Women Voters, Grad. Alumni Assn. Columbia U., Nat. Council Jewish Women (pres. 1968-71), Hadassah Elk. Club: Family Y Bridge. Home: 624 Rebellion Rd Charleston SC 29407 Office: 125 Bull St Charleston SC 29401 Mem. P.T.A. Steering Com., Bayside, N.Y. 19—.

VOGEL, SUZANNE HALL (MRS. EZRA F. VOGEL), psychiat. caseworker; b. Dallas, Jan. 17, 1931; d. Clabe Washington and Tina (Gable) Hall; B.A., U. Tex., 1951; M.A., Northwestern U., 1953; M.S., Simmons Coll., 1954; m. Ezra F. Vogel, July 5, 1953; children—David, Steven, Eva. Psychiat. social worker Mass. Mental Health Center, Boston, 1954-56; research interviewer schizophrenia project Harvard Sch. Pub. Health, Boston, 1957-58; research interviewer, Japan, 1958-60; psychiat. social worker Child Study Center, Yale, 1960-61; field work supr., social work dept. Chung Chi Coll., Hong Kong, 1963-64; psychiat. caseworker McLean Hosp. Out-Patient Clinic, Belmont, Mass., 1965-72, casework supr., 1968-72; pvt. practice casework and marital counseling, 1969—; chief social worker in psychiatry Harvard Health Services, 1972—; spl. instr. field work Simmons Coll. Sch. Social Work, 1973—. Mem. Nat. Assn. Social Workers, Mass. Acad. Psychiat. Social Workers, Acad. Certified Social Workers, Phi Beta Kappa. Home: 46 Parker St Cambridge MA 02138 Office: 75 Mt Auburn St Cambridge MA 02138

VOGEL, VIRGINIA REYNOLDS, ednl. adminstr.; b. N.Y.C., Dec. 10, 1946; d. Robert Dwight and Louise Helen (Persina) Reynolds; B.A. in Sociology, Mary Baldwin Coll., 1968; M.A. in Counseling, N.Y. U., 1969; postgrad George Washington U., 1972—; m. John Henry Vogel, June 27, 1970. Admission counselor and financial aid counselor N.Y. U., N.Y.C., 1969-71; counselor George Washington U., Washington, 1971-73; dir. guidance Georgetown Visitation Prep. Sch., Washington, 1973—. Mem. Am. Personnel and Guidance Assn., Nat. Assn. Women Deans, Adminstrs. and Counselors, Jr. League. Home: 9213 Farnsworth Dr Potomac MD 20804 Office: 1524 35th St NW Washington DC 20007

VOGELE, RUTH, physician; b. Riesa, Germany, Aug. 16, 1923; d. Adolf and Frieda (Bossack) Vogele; came to U.S., 1926, naturalized, 1952; B.A., N.Y. U., 1944, M.D., 1946. Intern, Newark City Hosp., 1946-47; resident Albany (N.Y.) Hosp., 1947-49; practice medicine, specializing in anesthesiology, Utica, N.Y., 1949—; mem. staff St. Lukes-Meml. Hosp. Center, Faxton, Utica State hosps. Home: 106 Lyon Pl Utica NY 13502

VOGELER, MARTHA SALMON (MRS. ALBERT R. VOGELER), educator; b. N.Y.C., July 11, 1924; d. Joseph Jerome and Ruth (Taylor) Salmon; B.S., N.J. State Coll., 1946; M.A., Columbia, 1952, Ph.D., 1959; m. Albert R. Vogeler, June 5, 1962. Instr. Vassar Coll., Poughkeepsie, N.Y., 1959-62; asst. prof. L.I. U., Bklyn., N.Y., 1962-66; lectr. No. Ariz. U., Flagstaff, 1968-69; prof. English Cal. State U., Fullerton, 1969—. Recipient grants Am. Learned Socs., Am. Philos. Soc. Contbr. articles on Victorian lit. and cultural history to scholarly publs. Home: 403 Virginia Rd Fullerton CA 92631

VOGELPOHL, OLGA MARIA, city ofcl.; b. Hebron, N.D., Mar. 1, 1918; d. Wilhelm B. and Regina (Weisz) Ziegler; student Dakota Bus. Coll., 1937; m. Earl Vogelhohl, Oct. 26, 1946; 1 son, Steven. Sec. Kneer Dairy Co., Fargo, N.D., 1937; accountant Mandan Beverage Co. (N.D.), 1937-48, accountant Klein Motor Sales, 1948-50; office mgr. Mandan Hosp., 1950-51, 62-64; treas., city Mandan, 1964—. Owner Vogelpohl Apts., 1946—, Quick Clean Center Laundry, Mandan, 1968—. Methodist. Elk (honor degree). Home: 307 Division St N W Mandan ND 58554 Office: 112 Collins Av Mandan ND 58554

VOGEL-SPROTT, MURIEL DORIS (MRS. DAVID A. SPROTT), educator; b. Waterloo, Ont., Can.; d. Henry and Ellen (Stroh) Vogel; B.A., McMaster U., 1955; Ph.D., Toronto U., 1960; m. David A. Sprott, Dec. 16, 1961; children—Anne, Jane. Research asso. Addiction Research Found., Toronto, Ont., Can., 1956-60; prof. psychology U. Waterloo, 1961—, asso. dean grad. affairs, arts faculty, 1972—. Mem. Am., Canadian psychol. assns., Sci. Council of Canada. Home: 295 Ferndale Pl Waterloo ON Canada

VOGL, SISTER MARY JUDITH, educator; b. Dyersville, Ia., June 25, 1910; d. Wolfgang W. and Frances Margaret (Duschner) Vogl; B.A., Loras Coll., 1942; M.A., Cath. U. Am., 1952; postgrad. U. Northern Ia., 1950, (Asian Studies grant) U. Colo., 1961, (Delta Kappa Gamma scholar) U. Portland, 1971. Tchr., asst. prin. Holy Trinity Lab. Sch., Dubuque, Ia., 1934-49; prin. St. Peter & Paul Sch., Petersburg, Ia., 1949-53, Saint Michael's Sch., Sioux City, Ia., 1953-56; asso. prof. edn. Briar Cliff Coll., Sioux City, Ia., 1956—. Mem. Nat., Ia. State (sponsor of Briar Cliff chpt. of students, 1956—, dir. of elementary student teaching 1956—) edn. assns., Childhood Edn. Internat., Internat. Reading Assn., Nat. Assn. of Elementary Sch. Prins., Nat. Geog. Assn., Nat. Cath. Edn. Assn., Delta Kappa Gamma. Address: Noonan Hall Briar Cliff College 3303 Rebecca St Sioux City IA 51104

VOGT, ESTHER LOEWEN (MRS. CORNELIUS T. VOGT), writer; b. Collinsville, Okla., Nov. 19, 1915; d. Henry L. and Agnes (Penner) Loewen; student Tabor Coll., 1939; m. Cornelius T. Vogt, May 24, 1942; children—Shirley (Mrs. Danny Williams), Ranney, Naomi (Mrs. Lee Eitzen). Nursing aide Parkside Homes, Hillsboro, Kan., 1970—. Mem. Kan. Authors Club, Delta Kappa Gamma (hon.). Republican. Mennonite. Club: Mentor Study (Hillsboro). Author: Cry to The Wind, 1965; The Sky is Falling, 1968; High Ground, 1970; Ann, 1971; I'll Walk Again, 1972; Prairie Tales, 1971; Eight Wells of Elim, 1974. Contbr. short stories and articles to various publs., including Christian Life, Scripture Press, others. Home: 502 E 1st St Hillsboro KS 67063

VOHR, BETTY ROHLOFF (MRS. FRED VOHR), pediatrician; b. N.Y.C., July 14, 1940; d. Albert Frederick and Mary (Becker) Rohloff; B.A., Adelphi U., 1962; M.D., Albany Med. Sch., 1966; m. Fred Vohr, Mar. 28, 1964; children—Jennifer, Matthew. Intern R.I. Hosp., Providence, 1966-67, resident in pediatrics, 1967-68; resident Boston Children's Hosp., 1968-69; fellow in neonatology Providence Lying-In Hosp., 1969-70; practice medicine specializing in pediatrics, Barrington, R.I. , 1970—; mem. staff R.I. Hosp., 1970—, Providence Lying In Hosp., Roger Williams Hosp.; sch. physician R.I. Sch. Design, 1970-72. Cons. Meeting St. Sch., 1971-72. Mem. exec. bd. R.I. March of Dimes. Diplomate Am. Bd. Pediatrics. Mem. New Eng., R.I. pediatric socs., R.I., Bristol County med. socs. Home and office: 2 White Birch Lane Barrington RI 02806

VOILS, JESSIE WILEY (MRS. WILLARD H. VOILS), author; b. Caldwell, Kan.; d. Daniel Wesley and Lillie May (Hawks) Wiley; student Emporia Tchrs. Coll., 1919-20, Columbia, 1936, N.Y. U., 1940-57; m. Willard H. Voils, Mar. 3, 1920 (dec. July 1973); 1 dau., Patricia June (Mrs. John S. Tillman). Midwestern editor, columnist Delineator mag., N.Y.C., 1935-37; contbg. editor Pictorial Review mag., N.Y.C., 1937-39; writer, broadcaster NBC, N.Y.C., 1940-47, asso. editor Streamline Jour. of the Air, 1940-43, writer, co-producer childrens program, 1944-45; radio dir. Nat. Bd. YWCA, N.Y.C., 1949-54. Mem. Author's League of Am., Kan. State Hist. Soc., English Speaking Union, Kan. Authors Club. Author: Summer on the Salt Fork, 1969. Home: 609 Morningside Dr Wellington KS 67152

VOJTA, BARBARA ROTHMAN (MRS. JIRI T. VOJTA), dir. youth theatre; b. Bklyn., June 6, 1935; d. Max and Sylvia (Gordon) Rothman; B.A., Bklyn. Coll., 1957, M.A., 1962; student (scholar) Lester Polakov Studio of Stage Design, 1960-61; student Bklyn. Conservatory of Music, 1957-62; postgrad. Hunter Coll., Queens Coll., Syracuse U., State U. N.Y. at Oswego; m. Jiri T. Vojta, Nov. 29, 1969. Asst. to producer Jewish Theatre for Children, N.Y.C., 1957-58; box office treas. Sacandaga Summer Theatre, N.Y., summer 1958; liaison Phoenix Theatre, N.Y.C., 1958-59; box office treas. Town Hall, N.Y.C., 1959-60; costume coordinator Brooks-Van Horn Costumes, N.Y.C., 1960-61; costume designer Playhouse-in-the-Park, Phila., 1961; costume designer, instr. Queens Coll., Flushing, N.Y., 1961-63; costumer, lectr. Bklyn. Coll., 1963-66; instr. in theatre and speech, dir. children's theatre Chico (Cal.) State Coll., 1966-68; tchr., dir. drama activities Corning (Cal.) Union High Sch., 1968-69; asst. prof. speech, costumier State U. N.Y. at Oswego, 1969-70; drama specialist Sumner Sch., City Sch. Dist., Syracuse, N.Y., 1970-71; instr. communications Onondaga Community Coll., Syracuse, N.Y., 1971-72; tchr. creative dramatics Auburn (N.Y.) Children's Theatre, 1971—; dir. youth theatre spring prodn. Jewish Community Center, 1972; dir. creative dramatics workshop Dewitt (N.Y.) Parks and Recreation Commn., 1973-74. Recipient scholarship in costuming to San Diego Shakespeare Festival, 1957, scholarship in acting Barnard Coll. Summer Theatre Workshop, 1959. Mem. Onondaga Community Coll. Women's Assn., Am. Theatre Assn., Speech Communications Assn., Children's Theatre Assn., N.Y. State Speech Assn., Speech Assn. of the Eastern States, Am. Assn. U. Profs, ANTA, Co-author: The Magic Trunk (play), 1972. Contbr. articles in field to profl. jours. Home: PO Box 382 Jamesville NY 13078 Office: Dewitt Parks and Recreation Commn Dewitt NY

VOKES, EMILY ANN HOSKINS (MRS. HAROLD E. VOKES), educator, paleontologist; b. Monroe, La., May 21, 1930; d. Tom D. and Betty (Lundy) Hoskins; B.S., Tulane U., 1960, M.S., 1962, Ph.D., 1967; m. Harold E. Vokes, Mar. 7, 1959. Mem. staff Tulane U. New Orleans, 1953—, curator fossils, 1957-74, instr. phys. geography, 1969-74, asso. prof. geology, 1974—, asso. editor Tulane Studies in Geology and Paleontology, 1969—. Mem. Paleontol. Research Instn., Paleontol. Soc., Am. Malacol. Union, Sigma Xi, Sigma Gamma Epsilon. Home: 2501 Audubon St New Orleans LA 70125

VOLCKMANN, NANCY SORLEY, realtor; b. San Francisco, Jan. 11, 1914; d. Lewis Stone and Nan (Merrow) Sorley; student Pa. Museum Sch. Indsl. Art, 1931-34, Am. U., 1960; m. Russell William Volckmann, Aug. 25, 1934, (div. Sept., 1947); 1 son, Russell William Jr. Sec. U.S. Govt., Ft. Belvoir, Va., 1941-43; space control agt. Am. Airlines, Washington Nat. Airport, 1944-46; asst. press mgr. NBC, Washington, 1947-49; employed Kal Ehrlich-Merrick, Washington, 1949-51; advtg. copywriter Gustave Ring, Washington, 1951-58; sales mgr. J. F. Begg Inc., Washington, 1958-61; real estate sales mgr., broker firm H. A. Gill & Son, Washington, 1961-72; v.p. Burr N. Johnson Jr. & Co., Washington, 1972-74, Reuter's, Inc., Washington, 1974—. Mem. Nat. Assn. Real Estate Bds. (v.p. D.C. chpt. women's council 1967), Washington Bd. Realtors. Club: Army and Navy Club (Washington). Home: 4000 Cathedral Av NW Washington DC 20016 Office: 4614 Wisconsin Av NW Washington DC 20016

VOLIO, ALLENA ANNE MENOUGH (MRS. JAY ANGELO VOLIO), psychologist; b. Garrettsville, O., Aug. 25, 1931; d. Donald Jay and Margery McGee (Shope) Menough; B.S., Kent State U., 1953, M.A., 1957, B.S. in Edn., 1967, certificate sch. psychology, 1968; m. Jay Angelo Volio, Sept. 19, 1954; children—Jay Neil, Jon Kevin, Margery Elizabeth. Sch. psychologist intern Portage County Schs., Ravenna, O., 1967-68, sch. psychologist, 1968-69; sch. psychologist Crestwood Schs., Mantua, O., 1969-70, Ravenna (O.) City Schs., 1970—. Mem. Portage County Spl. Edn. Com., 1969—, chmn., 1970-71; mem. adv. bd. Spl. Edn. Planning Center, Medina, Portage, Summit counties, Ohio, 1970—. Mem. Portage County Devel. Disabilities Com., 1973—; mem. Adv. Council Family Counseling and Mental Health Center, 1972—. Mem. Nat. Council Exceptional Children, Nat., Ohio assns. sch. psychologists, Portage County Guidance Assn., Portage County Council Health and Social Agys., Kent Akron Area Sch. Psychologists (pres. elect 1973-74), Delta Gamma. Home: 2021 Rosewood Dr Kent OH 44240 Office: 507 E Main St Ravenna OH 44266

VOLIVA, FRANCES SANDERS (MRS. BOBBY LEE VOLIVA), home economist; b. Gaffney, S.C., Aug. 15, 1939; d. Woodrow Wilson and Virginia (Evans) Sanders; student Winthrop Coll., 1957-58; B.S., Limestone Coll., 1963; postgrad. U. N.C., 1968-69; m. Bobby Lee Voliva, Mar. 7, 1965; children—Elizabeth Evans, Robert Lee. Home economist N.C. Agr. Extension Service, Raleigh, 1963—; trainer agt. Expanded Nutrition Program, 1970—; coordinator County 4-H, 1966-72. County dir. N.C. Cystic Fibrosis Research Found., 1972; Heart Fund, 1970-71; chmn. County Cancer Fund, 1969; sec. Columbia (N.C.) Redevel. Commn., 1971; coordinator Adult Art Classes, 1969-70. Recipient State Founders award, Heart Fund, 1971. Mem. Am. (fund raising chmn. 1970), N.C. (area chmn. 1969) home econ. assns., Nat., N.C. (state fellowship chmn. 1971, exec. bd. 1968-74, state 3d v.p. 1973-74, Outstanding Young Agts. award 1973, nat. exhibits com. 1973-74) assns. extension home economists, Epsilon Sigma Phi. Club: Tyrrellinean (pres. 1974) (Columbia). Home: PO Box 196 Columbia NC 27925

VOLK, MARY JANE, librarian; b. Pitts.; d. Paul Godfrey and Mary Ann (Fisher) Volk; B.S., Carnegie Inst. Tech., 1944, B.S. in L.S., 1945. Asst. cataloger Carnegie Inst. Tech. Library, Pitts., 1945-47; asst. librarian Mellon Inst. Sci., Carnegie-Mellon U., Pitts., 1947-58, librarian, 1958, supr. library, 1958—. Vice pres. Bd. Crafton Pub. Library, 1969—. Mem. Spl. Libraries Assn. (chpt. pres. 1969-70), Am. Chem. Soc. (chem. lit. div.). Home: 103 Noble Av Pittsburgh PA 15205 Office: 4400 Fifth Av Pittsburgh PA 15213

VOLK, MARYANN SCHRAMM (MRS. DONALD GEORGE VOLK), psychologist; b. Perrysburg, O., July 29, 1938; d. Ernest John and Mary Margaret (Diebert) Schramm; student Ohio State U., 1956-59; B.S., Youngstown U., 1962; M.S., Kent State U., 1966, Edn. Specialist, 1971; m. Donald George Volk, June 18, 1960. Tchr., Champion High Sch., Warren, O., 1962-65; intern psychologist Columbiana County Bd. Edn., Lisbon, O., 1966-67; staff psychologist Mahoning County Bd. Edn., Youngstown, 1967—; pvt. practice psychology, Warren, 1973—; instr. ednl. psychology Shenango Valley campus Pa. State U., Sharon, 1969—. Adv. bd. Trumbull County Hearing Soc. Named Girl of Yr., Xi Eta Xi, 1969, 70, Beta Sigma Phi, 1970. Mem. Nat. Assn. Sch. Psychologists (charter mem.), Ohio Sch. Psychologists Assn., Ohio Psychol. Assn., Kent Area Sch. Psychologists. Home: 8428 Squirrel Hill Dr NE Warren OH 44484 Office: 21 W Boardman St Youngstown OH 44503

VOLKOMENER, HELEN, coll. pres.; b. Neilsville, Wis., June 13, 1923; d. James W. and Caroline (Mahlich) Volkomener; B.A., Coll. Great Falls, 1950; M.A., U. Notre Dame, 1955; Ph.D., St. Louis U., 1960 Tchr. elementary schs., Washington and Cal., 1945-55; prof. philosophy Seattle U., 1959-64; asst. dean Coll. of Providence Heights, Seattle, 1960-63; acad. dir. Center Intercultural Formation, Cuernavaca, Mexico, 1964-67; Ford Found. program Project Bridge, Cleve., 1967-68; ednl. cons. Migrant Edn. Office, Olympia, Wash. 1968-69; prof. philosophy So. Ore. Coll., Ashland, 1969-74; exec. sec. devel. edn., nat. office United Meth. Ch., N.Y.C., 1971-72; pres. Ft. Wright Coll., Spokane, Wash., 1974—. Mem. Am. Assn. U. Profs., Am. Philos. Assn. (pres. N.W. 1963), Am. Assn. Colls. Tchr. Edn. (regional dir.) Am. Anthropol. Assn., Found. for World Justice (Belgium). Author: Re-Founding a Community in Chile. Home: Ft Wright College Spokane WA 99204

VOLLENWEIDER, GRACE MARIAN LIVENGOOD, editor; b. Hillsdale, N.J., Dec. 15, 1927; d. William Winfred and Dorothy Grace (Edmed) Livengood; B.A. cum laude, Bucknell U., 1949. Free-lance writer, 1949-50; with Am. Cyanamid Co., Wayne, N.J., 1951—, mgr. tech. information, agrl. products Cyanamid Internat., 1968—. Recipient ann. award for excellence in tech. pub. N.Y. chpt. Soc. Tech. Writers and Editor, 1960, certificate of spl. merit Printing Industries Met. N.Y., 1962, 63, award of merit N.Y. chpt. Soc. Tech. Communication, 1972. Mem. Am. Med. Writers Assn., Nat., N.J. Audubon socs., Soc. for Tech. Communication, Phi Beta Kappa, Phi Sigma, Alpha Lambda Delta. Club: Ahdeek Tennis (Bergenfield, N.J.). Home: 725 Hillsdale Av Hillsdale NJ 07642 Office: Am Cyanamid Co Berdan Av Wayne NJ 07470

VOLLMER, VIRGINIA MARION MCMURRAY (MRS. BOB VOLLMER), educator; b. Birmingham, Ala., Aug. 29, 1923; d. Arthur Alexander and Frances Willard (Osborn) McMurray; student Ohio State U., 1940-42; R.N., Youngstown Hosp. Nursing Sch., 1945; B.A., U. Cin., 1945, M.S., 1949; Ph.D., State U. Ia., 1953; m. Bob Vollmer, Mar. 10, 1964. Fulbright scholar Hubrecht Lab., Utrecht, Holland, 1953-54; research asst. Rockefeller Inst., N.Y.C., 1954-56; asst. prof. physiology Mt. Holyoke Coll., 1956-57; asst. prof. physiology U. Mich. Med. Sch., Ann Arbor, 1957-59; research project analyst NIH, Bethesda, Md., 1959-60; asst. prof. anatomy U. Tenn. Med. Sch., Memphis, 1960-62; tech. communications dir. Alcon Labs., Fort Worth, 1962-64; asso. prof. nursing Tex. Womans U., Dallas, 1965-67; cons. health scis., 1967-70; asst. prof. instructional communications U. Tex. Health Sci. Center, Dallas, 1970—. Mem. Tex. League for Abortion Edn., Dallas, 1972—; Tex. Heart Assn., Dallas, 1970—. Bd. dirs. Dallas chpt. United Ostomy Assn. Mem. Am. Soc. Tng. and Devel., Am. Physiol. Soc., Am. Nurses Assn., Health Scis. Communications Assn. Presbyn. (mem. com. 1971—). Author: (with John Vanatta and William H. Briggs) Oxygen Transport, Hypoxia and Cyanosis, 1974. Contbr. articles to profl. jours. Home: 570 W Maple Pocatello ID 83201

VOLSTORFF, VIVIAN VIRGINIA, ret. ednl. adminstr.; b. Chgo., July 14, 1907; d. August William and Laura Louisa (Brugge) Volstorff; B.S., Northwestern U., 1928, M.A., 1929, Ph.D., 1932. Dean women, prof. history, dir. student activities, mem. grad. faculty S.D. State U., Brookings, 1932-74, dean of women emeritus, prof. history, 1974—. Recipient Civilian Service medal Dept. Army, 1973. Mem. Brookings Woman's Club, Faculty Women's Club, Panhellenic Assn., Am. Hist. Assn., Nat. Assn. Women Deans and Counselors (past state pres.), Am. Assn. Univ. Women (state div. pres., 1960-62), Mortar Bd., Phi Beta Kappa, Phi Kappa Phi, Pi Gamma Mu, Alpha Lambda Delta, Theta Upsilon. Republican. Baptist. Home: 1311 7th St Brookings SD 57006

VOLTZ, JEANNE APPLETON (MRS. LUTHER MANSHIP VOLTZ), mag. editor; b. Collinsville, Ala., Nov. 12, 1920; d. James Lamar and Marie (Sewell) Appleton; A.B., U. Montevallo, 1942; postgrad. Academie Cordon Bleu, Paris, 1960; m. Luther Manship Voltz, July 31, 1943; children—Luther Manship, Jeanne Marie. Corr. Birmingham (Ala.) News; reporter Mobile (Ala.) Press-Register, 1942-45; reporter The Miami (Fla.) Herald, 1947-51, food editor, 1951-60; food editor Los Angeles Times, 1960-73; food editor Woman's Day, 1973—. Agrl. adv. council, U. Cal., 1971-73; trade adv. com., Los Angeles Trade Tech. Coll., 1960-73; adv. com. Sch. Agr., Cal. Poly. U., Pomona, 1972. Recipient Vesta awards, Am. Meat Inst., 1963, 65, 66, 67, 68, Hon. Service award Cal. Home Econs. Assn., 1972. Mem. Inst. Food Technologists, Nat. Nutrition Exchange, Am. Home Econs. Assn., Citizens Commn. Sci. Law and Food Supply, Home Economists in Bus., Elec. Women's Round Table, Knights of the Vine, La Confrerie St. Etienne, Confrerie de la Chaine de Rotisseurs (dame), Theta Sigma Phi (chpt. v.p. 1970-72, corr. sec. 1972—). Methodist (adminstrv. bd., 1970-72). Club: The Nut (Chgo.). Author: Famous Florida Recipes, 1954; The California Cookbook, 1970; (with Burks Hamner) The L.A. Gourmet, 1971; The Los Angeles Times Natural Foods Cook Book, 1973. Home: 170 West End Av New York City NY 10023 also 3695 Bay Homes Dr Miami FL 33133 Office: Woman's Day 1515 Broadway New York City NY 10036

VON BERG, LOIS HELENE, univ. adminstr.; b. Albert Lea, Minn., Oct. 6, 1932; d. John Phillip and Helene Annette (Oliver) von Berg; B.A., U. No. Ia., 1955; M.A., U. No. Colo., 1962; postgrad. Springfield Coll., 1966. Tchr. high sch., Madelia, Minn., 1955-56; tchr. jr. high sch., Clinton, Ia., 1956-59; tchr. high sch., Rochester, N.Y., 1959-61; counselor Douglas High Sch., Ellsworth AFB, S.D., 1962-64; dir. guidance Sch. Nursing, Rochester, Minn., 1964-67; asst. dir. financial aids State Coll., St. Cloud, Minn., 1967-69; asst. dir. financial aid U. Wis., Stout, Menominie, Wis., 1969-71, dir. financial aid, 1971—. Mem. Am. Personnel and Guidance Assn., Am. Coll. Personnel Assn., Nat., Midwest, Wis. assns. student financial aid adminstrs., Assn. U. Wis. Faculties (mem. del. assembly 1972-74), Rochester C. of C. (mem. edn. com. 1965-67), Bus. and Profl. Women's Club (treas. 1968-69), Delta Kappa Gamma (v.p. 1972-74). Home: 511 16th St Menomonie WI 54751

VON BERG, SISTER RITA MARIE, hosp. adminstr.; b. Wheeling, W.Va., Aug. 27, 1922; d. Peter Paul and Anastasia Elizabeth (Kopp) Von B.; R.N., Wheeling Hosp. Sch. Nursing, 1944; B.S., Cath. U. Am., 1951. Supr. operating room St. Mary's Hosp., Clarksburg, W.Va., 1944-48, 51-53; dir. nursing St. Francis Hosp., Charleston, W.Va., 1953-56; dir. nursing Wheeling Hosp., 1956-58, adminstr., 1958-64; adminstr. St. Joseph's Hosp., Parkersburg, W.Va., 1964-69, pres., chief exec. officer, 1969—. Mem. Gov.'s Adv. Council Comprehensive Health Planning, 1968—, vice chmn., 1971—. Bd. dirs. Wood County Heart Assn., 1969-73, United Hosp. Center, Clarksburg, 1970—, St. Francis Hosp., Charleston, 1969—. Mem. Am., W.Va. (pres. elect 1974, dir. 1969—) Cath. hosp. assns., Am. Coll. Hosp. Adminstrs., Am. Nurses Assn., Nat. League Nursing, Parkersburg C. of C., Nat. Wildlife Assn., Nat. Rifle Assn., W.Va. Conservation Assn. Democrat. Club: Altrusa (mem. nursing scholarship com. Parkersburg, 1970—). Home: Route 5 Box 45A Parkersburg WV 26101 Office: PO Box 327 Parkersburg WV 26101

VON BEROLDINGEN, DOROTHY GUNDELFINGEN, lawyer; b. Oak Park, Ill.; d. A. R. and Anna E. (Stastney) Gundelfingen; student Northwestern U., U. Cal.; LL.B., U. San Francisco, 1954; J.D., San Francisco Law Sch., 1968; m. Linton von Beroldingen (div.); 1 son, Paul. Admitted to Cal. bar, since practiced in San Francisco; past pres., gen. counsel Internat. Direct Marketing Assn. Prof. tax law Lincoln U. Sch. Law, 1959-69, Hastings Coll. Law, 1973-74. Mem. Civil Service Commn., City and County of San Francisco, 1964-66; mem. San Francisco City and County Bd. Suprs., 1966—, chmn. finance com., 1968-72, 74—. Trustee Lincoln U. Mem. Cal. State Bar, San Francisco Lawyers Club, Queen's Bench, Am. Trial Lawyers Assn., League Women Voters, St. Thomas More Soc. Office: 1255 Post St Suite 700 San Francisco CA 94109

VON BRIESEN, DOROTHY ALICE CLARK (MRS. RALPH VON BRIESEN), lawyer; b. Moline, Ill., Sept. 1, 1912; d. William L. and Eva (Pratt) Clark; student Cornell U., 1930-31; A.B., Northwestern U., 1935; LL.B., U. Wis., 1937; m. Ralph von Briesen, June 10, 1939; children—Richard, Mary, Katherine, Ann. Admitted to Wis. bar, 1937; caseworker problems of legal residence County Welfare Dept., Racine, Wis., 1937-39; acting pub. defender Children's Ct., Milw. County; atty. Legal Aid Soc., Milw. County. Vol. Wis. rep. Am. Field Service Internat. Student Exchange Program, Milw., 1952-63. Nat. bd. dirs. COSERVE, Washington. Recipient Community Service Woman of Year award for work with fgn. students Theta Sigma Phi, 1963, for legal aid work Quota Club, 1970. Mem. Am. Assn. U. Women, Nat. Assn. Fgn. Student Affairs (regional community chmn.), Kappa Sigma Phi. Lutheran. Club: Woman's of Wis. Home: 3535 N Hackett St Milwaukee WI 53211 Office: 757 N Broadway Milwaukee WI 53202

VONDER LINDT, ALICE MARY, librarian; b. Phila., Nov. 4, 1919; d. Charles Nicholas and Bertha Jessie (Houseman) Vonder Lindt; B.A., U. Ky., 1958, M.S., 1960. Librarian, VA Hosp., Lebanon, Pa., 1959-62; chief librarian VA hosps., Beckley, W.Va., 1962-64, Martinsburg, W. Va., 1964-67, Coatesville, Pa., 1967—. Mem. Med. Library Assn., Soroptomist Internat. Office: US VA Hosp Coatesville PA 19320

VON DER LOHE, PATRICIA ANN, social worker; b. Los Angeles, Feb. 4, 1935; d. Arnold C. and M. Lucile (Trueblood) Von Der Lohe; A.B. with honors and distinction in Social Service, San Diego State Coll., 1957; M.S.W. (Nat. Inst. Mental Health trainee), U. So. Cal., 1961. Hosp. social worker San Diego County Hosp., San Diego, 1957-59; caseworker, supr. Evang. Welfare Agy., Whittier, Cal., 1961-69; clin. social worker Hollygrove Children's Home, Los Angeles, 1969—. Mem. Nat. Assn. Social Workers, Nat. Assn. Christians in Social Work, Acad. Certified Social Workers, Cal. Licensed Clin. Social Workers. Mem. Soc. of Friends. Address: 815 N El Centro Los Angeles CA 90038

VON DER PORTEN, AMY MARGUERITE (MRS. ARNOLD PAUL VON DER PORTEN), librarian; b. Kingston, Jamaica, Oct. 1, 1923 (came to the U.S. 1953, naturalized 1961); d. Herbert Frank and Olga Eva (Burrowes-Litherland) Barry; certificate Cambridge U., 1942; student Rutgers U., 1970—, Trenton State Coll., 1971; m. Arnold Paul Von Der Porten, Jan. 4, 1947; children—Michael Paul (dec.), Richard Arnold, Marguerite Kay, Christopher Paul, Arlene Elizabeth. Asst. librarian, Jr. Center, Inst. Jamaica, 1942-43; botanist, acting curator Sci. Museum, 1943-52; library chmn. Madison Twp. (N.J.) Sch. libraries, 1959-63, librarian Bd. Edn., 1962-63; P.T.A. Middlesex County library chmn., 1959-63; librarian Rutgers Prep. Sch. Library, Somerset, N.J., 1967—; Den mother Cub Scouts, 1967-71. Trustee Libraries of Madison Twp., 1970-75. Mem. N.J. Congress of the P.T.A. (life), Madison Twp. Hist. Soc. (curator, 1966—), Natural History Soc. Jamaica (sec. 1945-52), N.J. Assn. Ind. Sch. Librarians (chmn. 1973—), N.J. Sch. Media Assn., N.J. Edn. Assn., Am., N.J., Library assns., Assn. Ednl. Communications & Tech., Am. Assn. State and Local History. Mem. Soc. of Friends. Club: Rutgers U. Outing (New Brunswick, N.J.). Author: (with W.J. Chapman) Marine Algae of Jamaica (2 vols.), 1961-63. Editor (with R.P. Bengry and C. Bernard Lewis) Natural History Notes, 1949, Glimpses of Jamaica, Vol. I, 1946, Vol. II, 1949. Contbr. articles to profl. jours. Home: 71 Kensington Av Old Bridge NJ 08857 Office: Rutgers Prep Sch 1345 Easton Av Somerset NJ 08873

VON ELM, SISTER THEODORE MARY, librarian; b. El Reno, Okla., Apr. 26, 1921; d. Theodore Otto and Johanna Mary (Bestgen) Von Elm; B.A., Our Lady of the Lake Coll., 1947, M.A., 1953; M.S.W., Worden Sch. Social Service, 1963. Tchr. Catholic parochial schs., Okla., 1942-48, Tex., 1955-61; mistress of candidates of missionary catechists of divine providence, San Antonio, 1948-54; dir. Madonna Community Center, San Antonio, 1963-65; supr. Vols. in Service to Am., San Antonio, 1967-68; librarian St. Francis DeSales Center for Christian Renewal, Oklahoma City, 1968—. Mem. Am., Cath. library assns., Am. Theol. Library Assn. Address: PO Box 332 Oklahoma City OK 73101

VON KLEMPERER, ELIZABETH LEE GALLAHER (MRS. KLEMENS VON KLEMPERER), educator; b. Claremont, N.H., July 9, 1923; d. Hugh and Catharine (McCollester) Gallaher; A.B., Smith Coll., 1944; postgrad. Radcliffe Coll., 1946-48; Ph.D., Harvard, 1958; m. Klemens Von Klemperer, Dec. 19, 1953; children—Catharine, James. Teaching asst. Harvard, 1947-48, 51-52; faculty Smith Coll., Northampton, Mass., 1952—, asso. prof. English, 1967—. Served to lt. (j.g.) WAVES, 1944-46. Fulbright scholar, 1950-51. Mem. Phi Beta Kappa. Home: 23 Washington Av Northampton MA 01060

VON OESEN, (ANNA) ELAINE, librarian; b. Wilmington, N.C., Sept. 6, 1913; d. Martin and Adeline (Behrens) von Oesen; A.B., Lenior Rhyne Coll., 1938; B.A. in L.S., U. N.C., 1940, M.A., 1951. Asst. librarian Rockingham County Library, Leaksville, N.C., 1940-42; dir. libraries, Walker County, Lafayette, Ga., 1942-43; chief librarian Camp Davis, N.C., 1943-44; instr., asst. prof. library sci. U. N.C., Chapel Hill, N.C., 1947-52; field librarian N.C. Library Commn., Raleigh, 1952-56; head extension div. State Library, Raleigh, 1956-65, asst. N.C. state librarian, 1965—, also acting N.C. state librarian. Mem. Am. (editorial com. 1972-74), Southeastern (pres. 1968-70) library assns., Am. Assn. State Libraries (sec. 1961-62), N.C. Adult Edn. Assn. (mem. exec. bd. 1958-68), N.C. Library Assn. (chmn. com. on orgn. 1961-66), Beta Phi Mu, Alpha Psi Omega. Democrat. Lutheran (sec. ch. council 1964-67, 69-71). Home: 201 D Boylan Apts Raleigh NC 27603 Office: 109 E Jones St Raleigh NC 27611

VON ROHR, BEATRICE LOUISE CONNBERG (MRS. OSCAR E. VON ROHR), educator; b. St. Louis, Apr. 7, 1925; d. Jacob Lee and Sylvia (Broude) Cohnberg; A.B., Washington U., 1946; M.S., Gonzaga U., 1964; m. Oscar E. von Rohr, June 15, 1947. Assistantship in math. Washington U., St. Louis, 1946, instr. math., 1947-51, prof. math., 1952-58; math. researcher in thoracic physiology Barnes Hosp., St. Louis, 1951-52; head math. dept. Normandy (Mo.) Sr. High, 1958-59; prof. math. Hannibal LaGrange Extension Center, St. Louis, 1961-62, Shelton Coll., Cape May, N.J., 1966-67; prof. math., student counselor Mo. Bapt. Coll., St. Louis, 1967—, head math. and sci. div., 1968-70. Vice pres. Electrovision

Co. Cons. math. programs and texts. Mem. Friends of Shaw's Garden, St. Louis, 1957-62; mem. Cowles Museum Com., Spokane, Wash., 1964-66. Mem. Math. Assn. Am. (Mo. Baptist Coll. rep. 1973—), Soc. Indsl. and Applied Math., Women in Math., Pi Mu Epsilon. Home: 1119 Sanford Av St Louis MO 63139

VON RÜMKER, ROSMARIE, research and mgmt. cons.; b. Halberstadt, Germany, July 30, 1926; d. Arnold and Margret (Engel) von Rumker; M.S., Sc.D., U. Bonn (Germany), 1950. Came to U.S., 1954, naturalized, 1964. Research scientist Farbenfabriken Bayer A.G., West Germany, 1951-54; dir. research Chemagro Corp., N.Y.C., 1954-58, v.p. research and devel., Kansas City, Mo., 1958-69, sr. v.p. research and devel., 1969-71; mgmt. cons. RvR Cons., 1971—. Chmn. pesticides com. Agr. Research Inst., Washington, 1969-70, exec. com., 1970-71; mem. Nat. Tech. Adv. Com. Pesticides in Water Environments, 1971-72; mem. hazardous materials adv. com. Environmental Protection Agy., 1973—; mem. agrl. research program and facilities subcom. agrl. research policy adv. com. U.S. Dept. Agr., 1972-73. Mem. Entomol. Soc. Am., Am. Chem. Soc., Am. Soc. Agrl. Engrs., Agrl. Research Inst., Weed Sci. Soc. Am. Office: PO Box 553 Shawnee Mission KS 66201

VON SCHMIDT, BARBARA, pathologist; b. Alameda, Cal., Oct. 23, 1925; d. Roland and Elizabeth Cross (Redford) von Schmidt; A.A., U. Cal. at Berkeley, 1944, A.B., 1946; M.D., U. Buffalo, 1955. Intern, San Francisco County Hosp., San Francisco, 1955-56; resident surgery Stanford, San Francisco, 1956-57, resident pathology, 1957-59, resident pathology, Palo Alto, 1959-61; pediatric pathologist Children's Hosp. Med. Center, Oakland, 1961—. Mem. Am. Med. Women's Assn., Am. Soc. Clin. Pathologists, A.M.A., Cal., Alameda-Contra Costa med. assns. Home: 314 Panoramic Way Berkeley CA 94704 Office: 51st and Grove Sts Oakland CA 94609

VON WERSSOWETZ, MURIEL ELIZABETH WILFORD (MRS. ARTHUR J. VON WERSSOWETZ), physician; b. Tzeliutsing, Sze, China, Feb. 1, 1914; d. Edward C. and Claudia (Gaviller) Wilford; M.E.L., Ont. Ladies Coll., Whitby, 1932; M.D., U. Toronto, 1938; m. Arthur J. Von Werssowetz, Oct. 3, 1940 (dec. June 1962); children—Diana (Mrs. William F. Kelsay), Arthur J. Intern, St. Micheals Hosp., Toronto, Ont., 1938-39; resident St. Josephs Hosp., Hamilton, Ont., 1939-40; part-time clinician Chattanooga-Hamilton County (Tenn.) Health Dept., 1941-62, clinician, dir. maternal and child health, 1962—. Mem. Cath. Charities, 1963—; v.p. Newman Club Found., Chattanooga, 1966-67. Mem. A.M.A., Tenn. Med. Assn., Chattanooga-Hamilton County Med. Soc., Am., Tenn. pub. health assns., Cath. Bus. Women's Club (past pres.), Chi Omega Mothers Club (v.p. 1962-63), Lambda Chi Alpha Mother's Club (pres. 1967-68). Club: Altrusa (past pres.). Home: 3412 Alta Vista Dr Chattanooga TN 37411 Office: 921 E 3d St Chattanooga TN 37403

VOORHEES, HELEN MACMURTRIE, assn. ofcl.; b. Three Bridges, N.J., Nov. 16, 1892; d. Oscar McMurtrie and Alice Robertson (MacNair) Voorhees; B.A., Mt. Holyoke Coll., 1915; M.A., U. Wis., 1926. Asst. to sec. Phi Beta Kappa, 1916-20; asst. to dean Mt. Holyoke Coll., South Hadley, Mass., 1920-29, dir. appointment bur., 1929-59; pres. Van Voorhees Assn., 1961—; sec. New Brunswick Hist. Club, 1961—. Mem. Am. Assn. U. Women (pres. New Brunswick br. 1965-67). Author: History of the Eastern College Personnel Officers, 1926-52, 1952. Contbr. articles on coll. personnel work to profl. jours. Home: 151 George St New Brunswick NJ 08901

VORTMAN, BETTY MARJORIE LESLIE (MRS. LUKE J. VORTMAN), banker; b. LaGrange, Mo., July 10, 1922; d. Edward and Mae (Smith) Leslie; B.S. in Edn., Northeast Mo. State Tchrs. Coll., 1942; m. Luke J. Vortman, Dec. 22, 1946. Tchr. pub. high schs. Knox City, Mo., Chandlerville and Havana, Ill., 1942-47; stenographer U. Ill., 1947-49; with Albuquerque Nat. Bank, 1949—, bond teller, sec. to pres., 1950-55, personnel dir., 1955-58, asst. v.p., 1958-67, v.p., 1967—. Bd. dirs. Albuquerque Area Council on Alcoholism. Mem. Nat. Assn. Bank Women (v.p. Rocky Mountain Region 1959-60, rec. sec. 1968-69), Am. Inst. Banking (sec. 1953-54), Am. Soc. Personnel Adminstrn. (dist. dir. N.M. 1963, 64, 66, v.p. region 17, 1971-72), N.M. Personnel Assn. (sec. 1964-65, pres. 1968-69), Rocky Mountain Coll. Placement Assn., Am. Bankers Assn. (exec. com. personnel div. 1972—, adminstrv. com. edn. council 1973—, chmn. edn. com. personnel div. 1973—), Beta Sigma Phi (city sponsor 1961-67). Republican. Home: 3603 Calle del Sol NE Albuquerque NM 87110 Office: Albuquerque Nat Bank 123 Central St NW Albuquerque NM 87108

VOS, DONNA COUSINS (MRS. JOHN DIRK VOS), editor; b. Mpls., Aug. 11, 1948; d. C. Willis and S. Lorraine (Olson) Cousins; B.A., Northwestern U., 1970, M.S., 1971; m. John Dirk Vos, July 3, 1971. Editor, Curriculum Innovations, Inc., Highwood, Ill., 1971—, Synopsis, Evanston, Ill., 1971-72, Career World, Highwood, Ill., 1972—; contbg. editor Current Health, Highwood, 1974—. Mem. Chgo. Council on Fgn. Relations, 1971—. Mem. Northwestern U. Alumni Assn., Women in Communications, Kappa Kappa Gamma. Home: 1567 Ridge Av Evanston IL 60210 Office: First Nat Bank Chgo 6 Pl des Eaux-Vives 1207 Geneva Switzerland

VOSS, VERONICA JOAN HASSETT (MRS. TIDWELL R. VOSS), writer; b. McLeansboro, Ill., Oct. 21, 1909; d. James Jerome and Nellie Mary (Smith) Hassett; grad. piano Western Conservatory, 1925; student So. Ill. U., 1940; m. Tidwell R. Voss, Oct. 26, 1951. Bookkeeper, stenographer McLeansboro (Ill.) Hosp., 1927-40, 41-43, Dept. Pub. Welfare, McLeansboro, 1945; tchr. piano, McLeansboro, 1921-49; with Office of Town Clk., McLeansboro, 1953; tchr. piano and organ, Decatur, Ala., 1953-62; writer Times-Leader, McLeansboro, 1962—, Register News, Mt. Vernon, Ill. 1968—. Lectr. to various local groups. Mem. Nat. League Am. Pen Women (treas. Egypt br. 1974-76). Club: Altrusa (Decatur). Home: 610 E St Charles Av McLeansboro IL 62859

VRANIC, MAGDA PETRIC, physician; b. Zabreb, Yugoslavia, Oct. 18, 1932; d. Ivo and Zlata (Klein) Petric; M.D., Med. Faculty Zagreb, 1958; m. Mladen Vranic, Sept. 7, 1957; children—Iva, Maya. Intern Women's Coll. Hosp., 1963-64, Sick Children's Hosp., 1964-65; resident Wellesley Hosp., 1965-66, Lyndhurst Lodge Hosp., 1966-67; resident Sunnybrook Hosp., 1968, staff physician, 1970; asst. prof. rehabilitation medicine U. Toronto, Ont., Can., 1972—; cons. Toronto Rehab. Center, 1971. Mem. Ont. Med. Assn., Canadian Assn. Phys. Medicine and Rehab. Office: Sunnybrook Hospital Bayview Av Toronto Canada

VREDEVOE, DONNA LOU (MRS. JOHN PORTER), educator, researcher; b. Ann Arbor, Mich., Jan. 11, 1938; d. Lawrence E. and Verna (Brower) Vredevoe; B.A. in Bacteriology, U. Cal. at Los Angeles, 1959, Ph.D. in Microbiology (U. fellow, USPHS fellow), 1963; m. John Porter, Aug. 22, 1962; 1 dau., Verna. USPHS postdoctoral fellow Stanford, 1963-64; instr. dept. bacteriology U. Cal., Los Angeles, 1963, postgrad. research immunologist dept. surgery Center for Health Scis., 1964-65, asst. research immunologist dept. surgery, 1965-67, asst. research immunologist Sch. Nursing, 1967, asst. prof. sch. nursing Center Health Scis., 1967-70, asso. prof., 1970—, cons. to lab. nuclear medicine and radiation biology, 1967—. Post-doctoral fellow USPHS, 1963-64; Mabel Wilson Richards scholar U. Cal., Los Angeles, 1960-61; research grantee including Cal. Inst. Cancer Research, 1967-69, 72, Cal. div. Am. Cancer Soc., 1968-69, 69-70, 72 USPHS, 1969—, Am. Nurses Found., 1968, Cancer Research Coordinating Com. of U. Cal., 1967-68. Mem. Am. Soc. Microbiology, Am. Assn. Immunologists, Sigma Xi, Alpha Gamma Sigma. Contbr. articles to profl. publs. Home: 355 21st Pl Santa Monica CA 90402 Office: Sch Nursing U Cal Los Angeles CA 90024

VREELAND, JANE DAVENPORT, educator; b. Flocktown, N.J., Aug. 23, 1915; d. George Washington and Margaret Gladys (Stephens) Vreeland; B.S., Newark Tchrs. Coll., 1940; M.A., Columbia, 1966. Classroom tchr. Warren County, N.J., 1940, Essex County, N.Y., 1940-43; supr. elementary schs., Pearl River, N.Y., 1956-66; prin. Lincoln Av. Sch., Pearl River, 1955-66; faculty State U. N.Y. at New Paltz, 1966—, prof. edn., 1966—. Summer faculty U. Wis., Platteville, Wis., 1966, Duna Campus, St. John's, Newfoundland, 1969. Mem. Delta Kappa Gamma. Author: Learning About Our Country, 1967. Home: 9 C Village Arms New Paltz NY 12561

VUCKOVICH, CAROL YETSO (MRS. MICHAEL VUCKOVICH), librarian; b. East Liverpool, O., Sept. 23, 1940; d. Stephen A. and Louise (Sever) Yetso; B.S., Geneva Coll., 1966; M.L.S., U. Pitts., 1968; m. Michael Vuckovich, Sept. 24, 1970. Computation analyst Crucible Steel div. Colt Industries, Midland, Pa., 1958-62; library dir. Community Coll. Beaver County, Monaca, Pa., 1968—, instr. human anatomy and physiology, 1970—. Mem. Am., Pa. library assns., Spl. Libraries Assn., Am. Inst. Biol. Scis., Am. Anti-Vivisection Soc., Nat. Wildlife Fedn., Coll. and Research Libraries. Home: 21 Elm St Midland PA 15059 Office: Center Grange Rd Monaca PA 15061

VUILLEUMIER, MARION VIRGINIA RAWSON (MRS. PIERRE DUPONT VUILLEUMIER), educator, writer; b. Worcester, Mass.; d. Walter A. and Mary E. (White) Rawson; A.B. in Theology, Gordon Coll., 1940; postgrad. Boston U., 1940-41; m. Pierre DuPont Vuilleumier, May 3, 1942; children—Virginia Marian (Mrs. Louis Roger Lobo), Pierre DuPont II, Louis Edward. Asst. to claims insp. Liberty Mut. Ins. Co., Boston, 1940-42; dir. Christian edn. Wachague Community Ch., Springfield, Mass., 1951-53, 1st Congl. Ch., Westfield, Mass., 1953-54, 2d Congl. Ch., Holyoke, Mass., 1954-59; tchr. pub. schs., Holyoke, 1959-60, Barnstable, Mass., 1960-62; asst. dir. Craigville (Mass.) Inn and Conf. Center, 1960-73; exec. dir. Cape Cod United Ch. Homes, Falmouth, and Mashpee, 1962; free-lance contbr. to religious jours., 1946—; feature writer, book reviewer Sunday Cape Cod Standard Times, 1964—; hist. columnist Cape Cod Illustrated Mag. Exec. sec. Cape Cod Writers Conf., 1963—, sec., 1964—; sec. Ch. Mus. Conf., Craigville, 1962-72. Mem. Mass. Soc. Mayflower Descs., Pilgrim Soc., N.E.A., Plimoth Plantation. Author: Earning a Living on Olde Cape Cod, 1968; Boys and Girls on Olde Cape Cod, 1968; Indians on Olde Cape Cod, 1970; Sketches of Old Cape Cod, 1972; Craigville on Old Cape Cod, 1972; Churches on Old Cape Cod, 1974. Editor: Transformation mag., 1973—. Home: Green Dunes Dr West Hyannisport MA 02672

VULLO, BETTY JEAN BATTLES (MRS. JOHN P. VULLO), town ofcl.; b. Omaha, Nov. 21, 1927; d. Lyman Harvey and Dorothy Pauline (Rutt) Battles; grad. high sch.; m. John P. Vullo, Dec. 25, 1950; children—John L. and Valerie J. (twins), Teresa M. and Vincent J. (twins). Clk., County Registrar of Deeds, Hastings, Neb., 1945-46; clk. Cushing Wholesale, Hastings, 1947-49; credit sec. Bowman Biscuit Co., Denver, 1949-52; sec. Boeing Airplane Co., Wichita, Kan., 1953-56; town clk. Town of North Reading (Mass.), 1969—. Mem. North Reading Council on Aging, 1969-71; publicity chmn. United Fund, 1972, municipal chmn., 1973; agt. Bd. Health, 1969—; exec. bd. P.T.A., 1962-65. Justice of peace, 1969—; chief election officer, 1969—; clk. Bd. Voter Registrars, 1969—. Mem. New. Eng., Mass. town clks. assns., Internat. Inst. Municipal Clks. Conglist. Home: 21 Sunset Av North Reading MA 01864 Office: Town Clk's Office Flint Meml Hall North Reading MA 01864

VUYLSTEK, MARIAN ANNETTE (MRS. RAYMOND VUYLSTEK), hosp. adminstr.; b. Mitchell, S.D., Sept. 14, 1921; d. Leo and Lillian (Crawford) Disburg; grad U. Neb. Sch. Nursing, 1943; m. Raymond Vuylstek, June 3, 1943 (dec. Mar. 1949); 1 dau., Paula (Mrs. Robert Lott). Surp. U. Neb. Hosp., Omaha, 1943-51; hosp. adminstr., Tilden, Neb., 1951-58, Community Meml. Hosp., Missouri Valley, Ia., 1958—. Bd. dirs. Health Planning Council Midlands, 1972—; mem. exec. bd. Pottawatamie Mental Health Center, Council Bluffs, Ia., 1970—. Mem. Am. Acad. Med. Adminstrs., Nat. League Nursing. Home: 407 E St Clair St Missouri Valley IA 51555 Office: Community Memorial Hospital Missouri Valley IA 51555

WACKENHUT, RUTH J., business exec.; b. Phila., 1922; m. George Russell Wackenhut, Apr. 8, 1944; children—Janis Lynn (Mrs. John P. Thorsen), Richard Russell. Sec., Spl. Agt. Investigators, Inc., Spl. Agts. Security Guards, Inc., Security Services Corp., Miami, Fla., 1954-58; sec. Wackenhut Corp., Coral Gables, Fla., 1958—; dir. Wackenhut Services, Inc., Pan Am. Bank of Coral Gables, Inc. Designer. Home: 20 Casuarina Concourse Gables Estates Coral Gables FL 33143 Office: 3280 Ponce de Leon Blvd Coral Gables FL 33134

WADDELL, DOROTHY CHRISTINE, auditor; b. Decatur, Ill., Oct. 9, 1930; d. Elmer Bahner and Frances Mary (Guntern) Waddell; student Millikin U., 1948-50, Nabac Sch. Bank Audit Control and Operation, 1965-67. With Millikin Nat. Bank, Decatur, 1950—, auditor, 1970—. Mem. Am. Inst. Banking (bd. govs. 1967-70), Nat. Assn. Bank Women (membership chmn. 1969, program co-chmn. 1970, treas. 1973-74). Lutheran (financial sec. 1965-67, mem. audit com. 1969-73). Club: Altrusa (treas. 1971-73, membership chmn. 1973-74). (Decatur). Office: 100 S Water St Decatur IL 62525

WADDELL, SANDRA SUE, librarian; b. Lebanon, Ind., Mar. 24, 1940; d. Roderick R. and Helen B. (Snyder) Witt; B.S., Ball State U., 1962; m. James D. Waddell, Sept. 1, 1962; children—James Michael, Jeffrey Allen, Jennifer Robin. Librarian Northwhite Sch., Monon, Ind., 1962-64; head librarian Columbus (Ind.) High Sch., 1964-65; elementary sch. tchr. Hillsville Elementary Sch., Riceville, Tenn., 1967; librarian Riceville Elementary Sch., 1967-69; head librarian E.G. Fisher Pub. Library, Athens, Tenn., 1969—. Mem. Am., Tenn. library assns., Southeastern Library Trustees Assn., Wesleyan Service Guild (pres. 1973-74). Methodist. Home: 536 Brewer St Athens TN 37303 Office: Box 825 106 Hornsby St Athens TN 37303

WADDINGTON, BETTE HOPE (STAGE NAME ELIZABETH CROWDER), violinist; b. San Francisco, July 27, 1923; d. John and Marguerite (Crowder) Waddington; A.B., U. Cal. at Berkeley, 1945; postgrad. U. Cal. at Berkeley, Juilliard Sch. Music, 1950, San Jose State Coll., 1955; M.A., San Francisco State Coll., 1953. Violinist, St. Louis Symphony, 1958—. Home: 2800 Olive St St Louis MO 63103 Office: Powell Hall Grand Av and Delmar Blvd St Louis MO 63103

WADDINGTON, MIRIAM DWORKIN, poet, educator; b. Winnipeg, Man., Can., Dec. 23, 1917; d. Isaac and Mussia (Dobrusin) Dworkin; B.A., U. Toronto, (Ont., Can.), 1939, diploma social work, 1942, M.A., 1968; M.S.W., U. Pa., 1945; m. Patrick Donald Waddington, July 9, 1939 (div. 1965); children—Marcus, Jonathan. Caseworker, Toronto, 1942-44, Montreal, 1950-60; lectr. Mc Gill U. Sch. Social Work, Montreal, 1946-49; supr. North York Family Service, Toronto, 1960-62; tchr. English, York U., 1964—, prof., 1973—. Canadian Council sr. fellow in poetry, 1962-63, 71-72; Canadian Council acad. leave fellow, 1968-69. Mem. Modern Lang. Assn., Assn. Canadian U. Tchrs. of English. Author: Green World, 1945; The Second Silence, 1955; The Season's Lovers, 1958; The Glass Trumpet, 1966; Call Them Canadians, 1968; Say Yes, 1969; A.M. Klein, 1970; The Dream Telescope, 1972; Driving Home, 1972; John Sutherland, 1973. Editorial bd. Jour. Otto Rank Assn., Doylestown, Pa., 1971; editor The Collected Poems of A.M. Klein, 1974. Home: 32 Yewfield Crescent Don Mills Toronto ON M3B 2Y6 Canada

WADDLE, ROBERTA MARIE, educator, biologist; b. Schuyler County, Mo., Dec. 27, 1943; d. Sherman and Bernice Snowbarger; B.S. in Edn. cum laude, N.E. Mo. State U., 1965; M.A. in Botany, Ia. State U., 1968; m. Floyd Waddle, June 1, 1965; children—Margret, Julia. Sec., N.E. Mo. State U., summers 1962-63; grad. teaching asst. Ia. State U., 1965-68; file clk., Kirksville (Mo.) Coll. Osteopathy and Surgery, 1961-65; now instr. botany and biology Fayetteville (N.C.) State U., 1973-74. Sec., chmn. environmental quality com. League Women Voters, Fayetteville, 1973—. Home: 2714 Larry St Fayetteville NC 28306

WADE, CAROL RUTH (MRS. DANIEL L. WADE), psychologist, ednl. adminstr.; b. South Bend, Ind., Mar. 15, 1943; d. Cassell B. and Martha G. (Kurtz) Wieand; B.S. in Elementary Edn., Manchester Coll., 1965; M.Ed. in Ednl. Psychology (grad. fellow), Ind. U., 1967; m. Daniel L. Wade, June 19, 1966. Tchr., Elmhurst (Ill.) Pub. Schs., 1965-66; sch. psychologist Wheaton (Ill.)-Warrenville Pub. schs., 1967—, supr. interns, 1972—. Lectr., Nat. Coll. Edn., Evanston, Ill. Mem. Nat. Assn. Sch. Psychologists, Ill. Psychol. Assn. Home: 1001 Lorraine Rd Wheaton IL 60187 Office: 504 Naperville Rd Wheaton IL 60187

WADE, ESTELLE BETTY (MRS. DONALD WADE), psychologist; b. Bklyn., July 20, 1938; d. David and Selma Jobyna (Marks) Schwartz; student Bklyn. Coll., 1955-57; A.B., Clark U., 1959; M.A., Brandeis U., 1965; Ph.D., Columbia, 1971; m. Donald Wade, Oct. 20, 1963. Counselor, Inst. for Crippled and Disabled, N.Y.C., 1961-62, N.Y.C. Dept. Hosps., Bklyn., also Elmhurst, Queens, 1963-65; psychologist intern VA Regional Office, N.Y.C., 1966-68; lectr. City U. N.Y. Grad. Div., 1969-70; psychologist Queens County Neuropsychiat. Inst., N.Y.C., 1970—, chief psychologist, 1972—. Hostess weekly radio show WBAI-FM, 1973—. Mem. Am., N.Y. State psychol. assns., Am. Personnel and Guidance Assn., Country Dance and Song Soc. (program dir.), Phi Beta Kappa, Psi Chi. Home: 35-41 72d St Jackson Heights NY 11372 Office: 37-64 72d St Jackson Heights NY 11372

WADE, HENRIETTA MYERS (MRS. JOHN Q. WADE), educator; b. Crofton, Ky., Apr. 9, 1916; d. Benjamin Edward and Myrtle (West) Myers; A.B., Bowling Green Coll. Commerce, 1939; M.B.A., U. Ky., 1945; m. John Q. Wade, Aug. 20, 1950; 1 son, Ben Myers Wade. Teacher Crofton High Sch., 1939-44; instr. Northwest Miss. Jr. Coll., 1944; instr. Middle Tenn. State U., 1945-57, asst. prof., 1958-68, asso. prof., 1969—. Mem. Nat. Bus. Edn. Assn., Tenn., Middle Tenn. edn. assns., Pi Omega Pi. Home: 1907 Greenland Dr Murfreesboro TN 37130

WADE, JEWEL MILLSAP, educator; b. Fannin, Ga., June 20, 1937; d. Wallace James and Ida (Harkins) Millsap; A.B., Mercer U., 1959; M.Ed., U. Ga., 1965, Ed.D., 1967; m. Gerald W. Wade, Nov. 21, 1959; children—Rhonda Dynette, Garett Scott. Tchr. Hope Mills (N.C.) Pub. Schs., 1959-62; spl. edn. teacher Carroll County (Ga.) Schs., 1962-64; prof. Ga. So. Coll., 1966-69; prof. East Tenn. State U., 1969-70; prof. Atlanta U., 1970—; cons. tchrs. of mentally retarded or culturally deprived. Mem. Ga. Confedn. Council for Exceptional Children, Am. Assn. Mentally Deficient. Author: Pre-Vocational Reading for High School Educable Mentally Retarded, 1967. Home: 4750 W Hampton Dr Tucker GA 30084 Office: Atlanta U Chestnut St Atlanta GA 30314

WADE, JOAN HAGER GATLIN (MRS. LEWIS CLARK WADE), city ofcl.; b. Pikeville, Ky., Sept. 20, 1935; d. Russell Vervil and Alyce Mayo (Reynolds) Gatlin; B.A. in Polit. Sci., Coll. of William and Mary, 1958; m. Lewis Clark Wade, Aug. 1, 1961; children—John Clark, Andrea Lynn. Bd. dirs., sec. Harris County Water Control and Improvment Dist. #83, Houston, 1968-70; alderman City Council, Nassau Bay, Tex., 1970-71, councilman, 1972—. Mem. Nassau Bay Civic Club, 1966—, founder newsletter Foghorn, 1967, first editor, 1967-68, sec., treas., 1967-68. Mem. Bay Area League Women Voters, Clear Lake C. of C., Bayou Preservation Assn. (dir.). Home: 1526 Saxony Lane Houston TX 77058 Office: 18100 Upper Bay Rd Ste 102 Houston TX 77058

WADE, MABLE OPHELIA, author, genealogist; b. Scott County, Mo., Mar. 23, 1929; d. James Bertram and Erma Nata (Boswell) Richardson; student Harding Coll., 1947-48, corr. course Famous Writers Sch., 1968-70; m. Hamlet Jefferson Wade, Jr., June 19, 1948; children—Michael Richardson, Kevin Richardson. Writer, geneaologist, 1968—; pub. 11 source books of records from Pemiscot, Dunklin and New Madrid counties, Mo., Webster County, Miss., and Mississippi County, Ark.; tchr., researcher in field. Mem. Pemiscot Hist. Soc. (pres. 1970-71), D.A.R. (chmn. chpt. geneal. records 1972). Democrat. Mem. Ch. of Christ. Author: Lucius Families, U.S.A., Vol. I, 1971, Vol. II, 1971; Jacob Lillar Family, 1750-1972, 1972; Wade Ancestors and Related Families, 1973; The Heritage of Blytheville, Arkansas, 1973; Kimbriel Kith and Kin, 1974. Address: Route 1 Box 66 Bragg City MO 63827

WADE, MELVA JEAN, coll. dean; b. Noblestown, Pa., Oct. 17, 1923; d. John Hutchinson and Edith Elizabeth (Chalmers) Wade; B.A, Hunter Coll., 1955; M.A., N.Y. U., 1956. Ph. Ph.D., 1969. Instr./counselor evening div. N.Y.C. Community Coll., 1965-67, asst. prof., 1967-69, asso. prof., 1969-70, prof., 1970—, dean students, 1972—. Mem. Am., N.Y.C. personnel and guidance assns., Am. Coll. Personnel Assn., Common Cause, N.Y. State Assn. Jr. Colls., N.Y. U. Alumni Assn. Presbyn. Club: Women's City (N.Y.C.). Home: 175 Adams St Brooklyn NY 11201

WADE, RUTH ELIZABETH, psychiat. social worker; b. Elyria, O., Jan. 28, 1919; d. Horace E. and Margie Mae (Maupin) Wade; B.A. in Sociology, Roosevelt U., Chgo., 1970; M.A., U. Chgo., 1972. Began as community vol., then paraprofl. worker poverty program; paraprofl. social worker Harlem Hosp. Center N.Y.C., 1967-72, psychiat. social worker, 1972—. Mem. Nat. Assn. Social Workers, Orthopsychiat. Assn. Am., Am. Assn. U. Women. Home: 1335 Noble Av Bronx NY 10472

WADLER, PEARL NISSENBAUM (MRS. NATHAN H. WADLER), religious assn. ofcl.; b. Jersey City, Aug. 12, 1920; d. Samuel and Bella (Schaffermann) Nissenbaum; Hebrew Tchr.'s diploma with honors Yeshiva U. Tchr.'s Inst., 1937; B.A. with honors, L.I. U., 1939; M.A., Columbia, 1945; m. Nathan H. Wadler, June 15, 1941; children—Cheryl Jessica (Mrs. Norman M. Meskin), Barry A., Judith Marilyn. Tchr., Jersey City Bd. Edn., 1939-42; nat. pres. women's br. Union of Orthodox Jewish Congregations Am., N.Y.C., 1964-68, Mem. Nat. Conf. Race and Religion, Citizens' Crusade Against Poverty, Fair Housing Com.; mem. commn. on marriage and family life Synagogue Council Am. Bd. dirs. Jewish Braille Inst. Am.; pres. Alumnae Hebrew Tchrs. Tng. Sch. for Girls Yeshiva U.; v.p. Federated Alumni Tchrs.' Insts. Yeshiva U.; mem. nat. bd. Union Orthodox Jewish Congregations, Jewish Welfare Bd. Women's Orgn. Services; adviser Queens Jewish Center Sisterhood; del. 1st world conf. Ashkenazi and Sephardi Synogogues, Jerusalem, 1968. Lectr., also handbook publs. on assn.'s history and speakers' guides. Home: 112-35 69th Rd Forest Hills NY 11375 Office: 84 Fifth Av New York City NY 10011

WADLEY, CAPITOLA JOY (MRS. DEAN MCKENNON WADLEY), educator, librarian; b. Stonewall, Okla., July 26, 1916; d. William J. and Mollie J. (Thomas) Anderson; B.S., E. Central State U., Okla., 1938; postgrad. Columbia, 1939, La. State U., 1940; M.Ed., Northeastern State Coll., 1955; M.L.S., Okla. U., 1966; m. Dean McKennon Wadley, Jan. 20, 1940; children—Dean McKennon, Gregg Anderson, Timothy Durand. Elementary tchr. Seminole County, Okla., 1936-40, City Pub. Schs. San Diego, 1943-45, Cherokee County, Tahlequah, Okla., 1947-63; faculty, librarian Northeastern State U., Tahlequah, Okla., 1963—, asst. prof. library sci., 1966—. Rep., Field Enterprises Edn. Corp., Chgo., part-time 1961—. Pres., Friends-in-Council Study Club, Tahlequah, 1955, Northeastern State Coll. Aux., Tahlequah, 1952. Mem. Am., Okla. library assns., Nat., Okla. edn. assns. Democrat. Mem. Ch. of Christ. Home: 110 Garrison Tahlequah OH 74464

WADLOW, JOAN K. (MRS. RICHARD R. WADLOW), educator; b. LeMars, Ia., Aug. 21, 1932; d. R. John and Norma (Ihle) Krueger; B.A., U. Neb., 1953, Ph.D., 1963; M.A., Fletcher Sch. Law and Diplomacy, 1956; certificate Grad. Inst. Internat. Studies, Geneva, Switzerland; m. Richard R. Wadlow, July 27, 1958; children—Dawn, Kit. Reporter, Lincoln Star, 1952-53; pub. relations asst. U. Neb., Lincoln, 1955, 58-59, instr. polit. sci., part time 1963-66, asst. prof., 1966-71, asso. prof., 1971—, vice chmn. dept. polit. sci., 1970-72, asst. dean Coll. Arts and Scis., 1972—. Mem. Jr. League Lincoln; pres. adv. bd. U. Neb. YWCA, 1962-63. Mem. Am. Polit. Sci. Assn., Am. Assn. U. Profs., Pi Sigma Alpha, Delta Sigma Rho, Theta Sigma Phi, Gamma Alpha Chi, Gamma Phi Beta. Mem. United Ch. Christ. Home: 3940 S 40th St Lincoln NE 68506

WADSTROM, ANN KENNEDY, anesthesiologist; b. Slippery Rock, Pa., Aug. 5, 1931; s. James Alton and Eva Mildred (Flemming) Kennedy; B.S., Wheaton Coll., 1953; M.D., Woman's Med. Coll. Pa., 1958; m. Howard T. Wadstrom, June 23, 1956; children—Barbara, Jeffrey, Mark, Carol. Intern Chestnut Hill Hosp., Phila., 1958-59; resident anesthesiology Grad. Hosp. U. Pa., 1959-60, U. Utah Coll. Medicine, 1961; anesthesiologist Holy Cross Hosp., Salt Lake City, 1961-65; anesthesiologist Los Alamos Med. Center, 1965—. Clin. asst. prof. anesthesiology U. Utah Sch. Medicine, 1963-65. Diplomate Am. Bd. Anesthesiology. Fellow Am. Coll. Anesthesiologists; mem. A.M.A., N.M., Los Alamos County med. socs., Am., N.M. socs. anesthesiologists. Home: 42 Loma del Escolar Los Alamos NM 87544 Office: Los Alamos Med Center Los Alamos NM 87544

WADSWORTH, CAROL ECKBERG (MRS. JAMES W. WADSWORTH), librarian; b. Rochester, N.Y., Dec. 28, 1927; d. A. Ralph and Esther Lois (Reeves) Eckberg; B.A., Wellesley Coll., 1949; B.S., Geneseo (N.Y.) State Tchrs. Coll., 1950; M.L.S., Columbia, 1957; m. James W. Wadsworth, Aug. 27, 1966. Bookmobile librarian, Pittsfield, Mass., 1950-52; librarian to supervising librarian Queens Borough Pub. Library, Jamaica, N.Y., 1952-60; asst. dir. Mid York Library System, Rome, N.Y., 1961-63; adult services librarian Farmingdale (N.Y.) Pub. Library, 1963-65; supervising librarian Bklyn. Pub. Library, 1965—; book reviewer Library Jour. Mem. N.Y. Library Assn., N.Y. Library Club. Home: 102 W 85th St New York City NY 10024 Office: 7223 Ridge Blvd Brooklyn NY 11209

WADSWORTH, MARION FRANCES EDDY (MRS. LESLIE R. WADSWORTH), ednl. adminstr.; b. Swansca, Mass., Oct. 30, 1916; d. Robert Palmer and Hazel Frances (Baker) Eddy; student Columbia U., 1939, Simmons Coll., 1940-44; B.S., Boston U., 1950; m. Leslie R. Wadsworth, Oct. 5, 1951. Instr. nursing Union Hosp. Sch. Nursing, Fall River, Mass., 1940-44, dir. edn., 1945-49; instr. social studies New Eng. Bapt. Hosp. Sch. Nursing, Boston, 1950-52; inservice program dir. Belchertown (Mass.) State Sch., 1965—. Vis. lectr. social studies Childrens Hosp., Boston, 1950-51, Peter Bent Brigham Hosp., Boston, 1950-51. Mem. Am. Assn. Mental Deficiency, Pi Gamma Mu, Alpha Sigma Nu. Conglist. Home: 79 Taylor St Granby MA 01033 Office: PO Box 486 Belchertown MA 01007

WADSWORTH, RAE LYNN, banker; b. Kansas City, Mo., Jan. 8, 1943; d. Ray Thomas and Chloe (Deberry) Crane; student Anchorage Community Coll., 1961; m. Frank Dennis Wadsworth, Dec. 19, 1964; 1 son, Sean Thomas. Bookkeeper Matanuska Valley Bank, Anchorage, Alaska, 1962-64; teller Planters State Bank, Salina, Kan., 1965-66; teller First State Bank, Junction City, Kan., 1966-69, asst. cashier, 1969-72, v.p., 1972—. Mem. Credit Women Internat., Junction City of C. of C., Assn. U.S. Army, Beta Sigma Phi. Baptist. Home: 725 W Vine St Junction City KS 66441 Office: PO Box 247 904 W 6th St Junction City KS 66441

WAECHTER, ELISABETH (MRS. HEINRICH H. WAECHTER), sch. adminstr.; b. Nuremberg, Germany, Oct. 11, 1911; d. Siegfried and Helene (Wallersteiner) Schloss; grad. Lyceum and Nursery Tng. Sch. (Nuremberg), 1930; student U. Munich, 1930-32, M.Ed., U. Ore., 1961; m. Heinrich H. Waechter, May 7, 1935; children—Erika, Martin. Came to U.S., 1940, naturalized, 1946. Tchr. mentally retarded children, Germany, 1931-37, Holland, 1934, Boston, 1945-47, Blacksburg, Va., 1947-50, Eugene, Ore., 1951-53; dir. Pearl Buck Center For Retarded, Eugene, Ore., 1953—; instr. Sch. Edn., U. Ore., 1962-65; lectr. on retarded children at ednl. instns. Mem. govs. Adv. com. Vocational Rehab., 1967-68. Recipient Woman of achievement award Quota Club, Eugene, Ore., 1957, Distinguished Service award U. Ore., 1973. Fellow Am. Assn. Mental Deficiency; mem. Nat. (del.); workshop leader several convs.), Ore. (chmn. edn. com. 1957-58) assns. retarded children, Ore. Psychol. Assn., Assn. Retarded Children, N.E.A. (council exceptional children), Delta Kappa Gamma (hon.). Author: (with H. H. Waechter) Schools for the Very Young. Collaborator (with Pearl S. Buck) A Community Success Story. Home: 34994 E Danstrom Rd Creswell OR 97426 Office: 5100 W Amazon Blvd Eugene OR 97405

WAELTERMANN, RUTH CHRISTINA, high sch. tchr.; b. St. Louis, Dec. 5, 1941; d. Vincent J. and Henrietta Catherine (Dillon) Waeltermann; B.Journalism, U. Mo., 1964, postgrad., 1968-69; postgrad. U. Mo. at St. Louis, 1959-61. Journalism asst. U. Mo. at Columbia, 1963; copy editor Ark. Gazette, Little Rock, 1964; pub. relations rep., editor house organ Barnes Hosp., St. Louis, 1965-68; pub. relations dir. Goodwill Industries, St. Louis, 1968-69; tchr. journalism, Mehlville Sr. High Sch., St. Louis, 1969—; mem. curriculum planning com. English phase elective courses Mehlville R-9 Sch. Dist., 1972. Recipient photo awards Sigma Delta Chi, 1963, United Fund Greater St. Louis, 1967; Editorial Writing award United Fund Greater St. Louis, 1967. Mem. Sponsors Sch. Publs. Greater St. Louis (treas. 1973-74), St. Louis Cath. Alumni Club (editor newsletter, cultural chmn. 1966-74), St. Louis Suburban Tchrs. Assn., N.E.A., Kappa Tau Alpha, Theta Sigma Phi (sec. St. Louis 1965). Home: 2358 Tennessee Av St Louis MO 63104 Office: 3200 Lemay Ferry Rd St Louis MO 63125

WAGEMAN, DOROTHY GREENWOOD REED (MRS. CHARLES WILLIAM WAGEMAN), author, editor; b. Ossining, N.Y., Jan. 6, 1921; d. Prentiss Bishop and Eleanor Frey (Cochran) Reed; B.A., Smith Coll., 1941; m. Charles William Wageman, Dec. 29, 1956. Coll. cons. Dorothy Gray, Ltd., N.Y.C., 1941-43; mgr. promotion dept Abbott Kimball Co. Inc., N.Y.C., 1944-46; beauty editor McCall's mag., N.Y.C., 1946-52; promotion dir. Max Factor & Co., Los Angeles, 1952-58; account supr. Grey Advt., Beverly Hills, Cal., 1958-60; advt. dir. Revell, Inc., Culver City, Cal., 1960-62; owner DRW Creative Marketing and Pub. Relations, North Hollywood, Cal., 1962—; west coast editor Ladies Home Jour., 1966—. Area chmn. devel. fund Smith Coll., 1968-70; costume council Los Angeles County Mus. of Art, 1969—. Mem. Fashion Group, Am. Marketing Assn., Smith Coll. Alumnae Assn., Jr. League of Los Angeles. Club: Smith College (Los Angeles) (dir. 1962-74). Author: The Six-Week Make Yourself Over Plan, 1970. Home: 3833 Eureka Dr North Hollywood CA 91604

WAGEMAN, VIRGINIA FARLEY, editor; b. Jersey City, Feb. 18, 1941; d. James C. and Charlotte C. (Stebbins) Farley; student Douglass Coll., 1959-61; B.A., Bard Coll., 1964; m. James C. Wageman, Apr. 22, 1968; children—Melissa, Robinson, Sarah. Editorial asst. Am. Inst. C.P.A.'s, N.Y.C., 1964-66; prodn. mgr. U. Hawaii Press, Honolulu, 1966-68; asst. to dir. office univ. relations U. Md., Balt., 1968-70; publs. editor Princeton Art Mus., 1971—. Editor Record of the Art Mus., Princeton U., 1971—. Home: 184 Jefferson Rd Princeton NJ 08540 Office: Art Museum Princeton Univ Princeton NJ 08540

WAGENHALS, MARTHA RUTH (MRS. NILS DAVID WAGENHALS), photographer; b. Tulsa, Nov. 26, 1938; d. Russell Hall and Helen (Sheeks) Miller; B.S. in Mech. Engring., U. N.M., 1961; student ann. sessions West Coast Sch. Profl. Photography, 1972—; m. Nils David Wagenhals, Nov. 23, 1967. Engr., Lockheed, Burbank, Cal., 1961-65; engr., tech. information specialist Ill. Inst. Tech. Research Inst., Chgo., 1965-67; tech. information specialist Naval Weapons Center Tech. Library, China Lake, Cal., 1967-70; owner, propr. bookstore, Ridgecreast, Cal., 1971—, profl. photographer, owner studio, 1972—. Mem. assns. profl. photographers Am., Cal., Inland Empire. China Lake Photog. Soc. Republican. Home: PO Box 905 Ridgecrest CA 93555 Office: 205 Balsam Ridgecrest CA 93555

WAGENKNECHT, THERESE JEAN MUELLER (MRS. ROBERT EDWARD WAGENKNECHT), librarian; b. Chgo., Mar. 4, 1936; d. Florian Frederick and Jean Evangeline (Parkinson) Mueller; B.Mus., U. Mich., 1958, M.A., 1960; m. Robert Edward Wagenknecht, June 11, 1965; children—George Robert, Caroline Therese. Research asst. U. Mich. Sch. Medicine, Ann Arbor, 1958-60; music librarian Wellesley (Mass.) Coll., 1960-67; lectr. in L.S., Northeastern U., Boston, 1965-67, So. Ill. U., Edwardsville, 1968; asst. librarian Lincoln Land Community Coll., Springfield, Ill., 1969—. Lectr. in L.S., U. Ill., Urbana, 1973. Mem. Springfield Symphony Orch., 1967—. Bd. dirs. Springfield Community Concert Assn., 1970—. Mem. Ill. Library Assn., Music Library Assn. (chmn. New Eng. chpt. 1962-65, nat. dir. 1964-66), Sangamon County Hist. Soc., Mu Phi Epsilon (dist. dir. 1964-66). Club: Morning Etude (v.p. Springfield 1973—). Home: 716 Woodland St Springfield IL 62704 Office: Shepherd and Toronto Rds Springfield IL 62708

WAGENSCHEIN, MIRIAM, univ. dean; b. Kingsville, Tex., July 17, 1922; d. Carl Ferdinand and Joe Lee (Howard) Wagenschein; certificate Hockaday Sch., 1942; student Eastman Sch. Music, 1942-44; B.A., U. Tex., 1947; A.M., U. Chgo., 1950; Ed.D., Stanford U., 1963. Tng. instr. Foleys Dept. Store, Houston, 1947-49; instr. sociology Whitman Coll., Walla Walla, Wash., 1950-52, asst. prof., 1953-55, asso. prof., 1955-66, prof., 1967, dean women, 1951-67, chmn. office student affairs, 1963-67; asso. dean Ill. State U., Normal, 1967-69, dir. gen. student services, 1971-72, spl. cons. to pres., 1972—, prof. edn., 1973, dean coll. arts and humanities Tex. Agrl. and Indsl. U., Corpus Christi, 1973—. Mem. City Civil Service Commn., Walla Walla, 1965-67, 73; Republican Precinct committeeman, Walla Walla, also Normal Fellow Am. Sociol. Assn.; mem. Nat. Assn. Women Deans, Adminstrs. and Counselors, Am. Personnel Guidance Assn., Am. Assn. Univ. Women, Am. Assn. for Higher Edn., Nat. Assn. Student Personnel Adminstrs., Mortar Bd., Alpha Dappa Delta, Pi Lambda Theta, Sigma Alpha Iota, Alpha Lambda Delta. Home: 6810 Sahara Dr Corpus Christi TX 78412 Office: 6300 Ocean Dr Corpus Christi TX 78411

WAGERS, LOIS ELIZABETH HALL (MRS. LYMAN WAGERS), real estate devel. corp. exec.; b. Lexington, Ky., Dec. 14, 1922; d. Forest E. and Elizabeth (Hamilton) Hall; A.B., U. Ky., 1958, M.A., 1960; m. Lyman Wagers, Feb. 21, 1943; children—David L., Lyman Ellsworth, Susan E. Vice pres. Loman Inc., Lexington, 1959-69, pres., 1969—; pres. de Ly Ly Inc., Lexington, 1960-62. Mem. Eisenhowers People-to-People Program, 1958-60; chmn. Lexington-Deauville (France) Twinning Com., 1957-60. Pres., Fayette County Republican Womans Club, 1973. Bd. dirs. Youth Symphony Orch. Lexington, 1969—, pres. bd., 1969. Mem. Lexington Home Builders Assn., Philharmonic Guild Lexington, Kappa Delta Pi, Phi Sigma Iota. Republican. Club: Lexington Womans (pres. 1960-61). Home: 1040 Armstrong Mill Rd Lexington KY 40502 Office: 1044 Armstrong Mill Rd Lexington KY 40502

WAGGENER, LEXIE JEAN BROWN, archivist; b. Franklin, Tenn., Nov. 1, 1936; d. Lexie Gene and Nola Irene (Fristoe) Brown; student David Lipscomb Coll., 1955-59; B.A., Peabody Coll., 1960, M.L.S., 1967; postgrad. Am. U., 1969; m. Joseph Taylor Waggener, June 10, 1961. Tchr. English, Franklin (Tenn.) High Sch., 1960-61; sec. to dean David Lipscomb Coll., Nashville, 1961-62; research asst. Am. Finance Conf., Nashville, 1962-64; archivist manuscripts sect. Tenn. State Library and Archives, Nashville, 1964-66, 68-69, sr. archivist, 1968-70, reference librarian, 1970-71, dir. manuscripts sect., 1971—. Mem. steering com. Franklin (Tenn.) Sr. Citizens Assn., Mem. Nat. Trust for Historic Preservation, Soc. Am. Archivists, Tenn. Library Assn., So., Tenn., Williamson County (corr. sec. 1966-71) hist. socs., Assn. for the Preservation of Tenn. Antiquities, Franklin Heritage Found., Bus. and Profl. Women's Club (pres. Franklin br. 1970-71), Tenn. Fedn. Bus. and Profl. Womens Club (state historian 1973—), Sigma Tau Delta, Beta Phi Mu, Phi Sigma Iota. Home: 724 Fair St Franklin TN 37064 Office: 403 Seventh Av Nashville TN 37219

WAGGONER, MARGARET ANN, educator; b. Centerville, Ia., Aug. 27, 1926; B.A., U. Ia., 1946, M.A., 1948, Ph.D., 1950. Instr. physics Vassar Coll., 1950-54, asst. prof., 1954-58; mem. faculty Stanford, 1958-61; asso. prof. U. Md., 1961-65; asso. prof. U. Ia., 1965-70; prof. physics Smith Coll., Northampton, Mass., 1970—, dean coll., 1970-73. Address: Smith Coll Northampton MA 01060

WAGGONER, NANCY MANN (MRS. EDWARD L. WAGGONER), curator; b. Boston, Nov. 16, 1924; d. Alden T. and Olive A. (Huegely) Mann; B.A. magna cum laude, Smith Coll., 1946; M.A., Columbia, 1963, Ph.D. with distinction, 1968; m. Edward L. Waggoner, Mar. 27, 1948; children—Martha M., Amelia M. Asst. curator Greek coins Am. Numismatic Soc. Mus., N.Y.C., 1968-70, asso. curator, 1970—. Am. Numis. Soc. grad. fellow, 1966-67; Am. Philos. Soc. grantee, 1970. Fellow Am. Numis. Soc. (life); mem. Am. Inst. Iranian Studies, Am. Schs. Oriental Research, Archaeol. Inst. Am., Brit. Inst. Persian Studies. Episcopalian. Home: 184 Purchase St Rye NY 10580 Office: Broadway at 156th St New York City NY 10032

WAGLEY, MARJORIE IRENE CORLEY (MRS. ALTON CADE WAGLEY), educator; b. Florien, La., Nov. 4, 1914; d. Luther Franklin and Nancy (Miller) Corley; B.A., Northwestern U., 1936, U. Houston, 1950; postgrad. S.W. Tex., State Coll., 1946; Brigham Young U., 1958; m. Alton Cade Wagley, Jan. 16, 1937; children—Margie Katherine (Mrs. Gene Barry), Alton Carlin. Tchr. pub. schs., Sabine Parish, La., 1936-42, Beaumont, Tex., 1945-53; dir. spl. edn. S. Parks Schs., Beaumont, 1953—. Dir. Services Unlimited, Beaumont; Mem. adv. council Beaumont State Center for Human Devel. Mem. N.E.A., Tex. Tchrs. Assn., Council Adminstrs. Spl. Edn. (sec. 1967-69), Council for Exceptional Children, Tex. Council for Exceptional Children (pres. 1966, membership chmn. 1967-70), Delta Kappa Gamma. Baptist. Club: Soroptimist (charter; corr. sec., pres. 1972-74) (Beaumont). Author: Organizing and Administering Special Education. Home: PO Box 206 Nome TX 77629 Office: 1025 Woodrow St Beaumont TX 77705

WAGLEY, MARY FRANCES PENNEY (MRS. PHILIP FRANKLIN WAGLEY), educator; b. N.Y.C., May 28, 1927; d. James Cash and Caroline (Autenrieth) Penney; B.S., Mass. Inst. Tech., 1947; Ph.D., St. Hilda's Coll., 1950; m. Philip Franklin Wagley, June 20, 1953; children—Anne Paxton, Mary Kemper, James Franklin. Instr. Smith Coll., 1950-52, asst. prof., 1952-53; research asst. Johns Hopkins Sch. Medicine, Balt., 1953-54; instr. chemistry Goucher Coll., Balt., 1956-57; headmistress, regent St. Paul's Sch. for Girls, Brooklandville, Md., 1966—. Dir., Md. Nat. Corp., Md. Nat. Bank. Trustee Goucher Coll., 1959-71; mem. corp. Mass. Inst. Tech., 1969—. Home: 21 Meadow Rd Baltimore MD 21212 Office: St Paul's Sch for Girls Brooklandville MD 21022

WAGNER, ANABEL RATCLIFF, anesthesiologist; b. Lafayette, Ind., Sept. 6, 1933; d. Frank William and Mary Rovene (Holt) Ratcliff; A.B., Ind. U., 1955, M.D., 1959; 1 son, Warren Lee. Intern, Meth. Hosp., Indpls., 1959-60; resident anesthesiology Ind. U. Med. Center, Indpls., 1960-62; staff anesthesiologist VA Hosp., Indpls., 1962-63; practice medicine, specializing in anesthesiology, Lafayette, 1963—; mem. staff St. Elizabeth Hosp., Home Hosp., Purdue U. Hosp.; instr. Ind. U. Med. Center, Indpls., 1962—. Piano accompanist civic chorus, also combined civic vocal groups; mem. governing bd. Lafayette Symphony Orch., 1971—. Diplomate Am. Bd. Anesthesiology. Mem. Am. Soc. Anesthesiologists, Internat. Anesthesia Research Soc., Pan Am. Surg. Assn., Ind. Med. Assn., Ind. Soc. Anesthesiologists, A.M.A., Kappa Kappa Kappa, Delta Delta Delta. Methodist. Home: 1834 Summit Dr West Lafayette IN 47906 Office: Life Bldg Lafayette IN 47901

WAGNER, ANN CAPETILLO (MRS. CLARENCE H. WAGNER), investment co. exec.; b. Omaha, Sept. 19, 1926; d. Valentine Louis and Lois (Rickard) Capetillo; student Garner Secretarial Coll., 1944; m. Clarence H. Wagner, July 23, 1945; children—Ann Louise, Clarence H., Evalynne L. Divisional sec., cashier Investors Diversified Services, New Orleans, 1943-46; v.p., prin. C.H. Wagner & Co., Inc., Boston, 1969—; pres. Yankee Mortgage and Realty Corp., Wellesley, Mass. Pres. Palm Beach P.T.A., 1965-66. Mem. Nat. Assn. Securities Dealers, Am. Mothers Com. Mem. Order Eastern Star. Home: 2 Denton Rd Wellesley MA 02181 Office: 185 Devonshire St Boston MA 02110

WAGNER, ANNA ELIZABETH, ednl. adminstr.; b. Allison Park, Pa.; d. George Joseph and Elizabeth Catherine (Huber) Wagner; diploma St. John's Sch. Nursing, 1946; B.S. in Nursing Edn., U. Pitts., 1960, postgrad., 1973; M.Ed., Duquesne U., 1965. Joined USN Nurse Corps, 1947, advanced through grades to lt. (j.g.), 1950, ret., 1953; instr. St. Francis Sch. Nursing, Pitts., 1958-60; organizer Alvernia Sch. Practical Nursing, Pitts., 1960, dir., 1961—. Mem. Nat. Assn. for Practical Nurse Edn. and Service (accrediting rev. bd. 1973—), Am., Pa. nurses assns., Hosp. Assn. Pa. (patient care service com. 1972-73), Women's Overseas Service League, Am. Legion, St. Francis Sch. Nursing Alumni (hon.). Home: 4012 Kahn Av Allison Park PA 15101 Office: St Francis Gen Hosp 45th St off Penn Av Pittsburgh PA 15201

WAGNER, BETTY JOY, retail co. exec.; b. Chgo., Mar. 3, 1926; d. Percy E. and Elizabeth Cecelia (McGeeney) Wagner; student U. Chgo., 1942-44; B.A., Vassar Coll., 1947; postgrad. Katharine Gibbs Sch., 1947-48. With Marshall Field & Co., Chgo., 1950—, mem. real estate div., 1950-72, mgr. corp. ins., 1972—. Dir. dist. Republican assembly; asst. sec. ward Rep. Orgn., 1964—; sec. dist. state central com., 1968—; alternate del. Rep. Nat. Conv., 1968. Recipient Leadership certificate Women in Met. Chgo., YWCA, 1973. Mem. Vassar Alumnae Assn., Vassar Club Chgo., Katharine Gibbs Alumnae Assn. (past pres.), Am. Soc. Ins. Mgmt. (dir. Chgo. chpt.), Pewter Collectors Club Am., Midwest Pewter Collectors Club. Home: 1440 N Lake Shore Dr Chicago IL 60610 Office: 25 E Washington St Chicago IL 60602

WAGNER, ELAINE MARIE WEIMAR (MRS. DARRELL GABRIEL WAGNER), librarian; b. St. Paul, Mar. 8, 1939; d. Leroy George and Rose (Weiss) Weimar; B.A., Coll. St. Catherine, 1961; m. Darrell Gabriel Wagner, Dec. 30, 1961; children—Kristin, Douglas. Young adult librarian St. Paul Pub. Library, 1961-63, coordinator br. children's services, 1963-64, supr. publs. office, 1964-65, supr. community relations, 1965-67, supr. publs. office, 1967—. Mem. Delta Phi Lambda. Author: A Case of Bottled Murder, 1973. Home: 2152 St Clair Av St Paul MN 55105 Office: 90 W 4th St St Paul MN 55102

WAGNER, ELEANORA ROSE, lawyer; b. Chgo., July 29, 1941; d. Elmer Edward and Evelyn Lucille (Culp) Wagner; B.A., Boston U., 1964; J.D., Loyola U., Chgo., 1970; divorced. Admitted to Ill. bar, 1970; atty. Harris Trust & Savs. Bank, Chgo., 1970-71; staff atty. Am. Hosp. Assn., Chgo., 1971—. Mem. Am., Chgo. (chmn. subcom. medicolegal 1972), Ill. Women's (chmn. law day com. 1972) bar assns. Democrat. Home: 222 E Pearson St Chicago IL 60611 Office: 840 N Lake Shore Dr Chicago IL 60611

WAGNER, FRANCES JOAN ESTELLE, paleontologist; b. Hamilton, Ont., Can., 1927; d. Harold Wilfrid and Muriel G. (Konkle) Wagner; B.A., U. Toronto, 1948, M.A., 1950; M.S., Stanford, 1951, Ph.D., 1954. Geologist, Geol. Survey Can., Ottawa, Ont., 1950-67, Atlantic oceanographic lab. Bedford Inst., Dartmouth, N.S., Can., 1967-71, Atlantic Geosci. Centre, Bedford Inst., 1971—. Fellow Royal Can. Geog. Soc.; mem. Paleontol. Soc., Sigma Xi. Contbr. articles profl. jours. Home: 75 Lake Major Rd Westphal Rural Route 1 Dartmouth NS B2W 3X7 Canada Office: Box 1006 Dartmouth NS B2Y 4A2 Canada

WAGNER, GERALDINE ELIZABETH (MRS. HARRY LORAIN WAGNER, JR.), city ofcl.; b. Keller, Tex., Dec. 6, 1917; d. Charles Merida and Edna Gertrude (Grow) Clifton; student U. Redlands, 1936-38; m. Harry Lorain Wagner, Jr., June 23, 1938; children—Jane (Mrs. Robert L. Hunt), Joanna (Lawrence Lowell Lindsay), Deanna (Marvin Dennis Pitts). Mem. city council Prescott, Ariz; Co-owner Miller Valley Builders' Supply. Chmn., Ariz. Council, Resource Conservation and Development Areas; past pres. County Health Bd., United Fund, County Heart Assn.; past bd. dirs. Salvation Army supr. Chino-Winds Natural Resource Conservation Dist.; rep. North Ariz. on Ariz. Coordinating Council; mem. Parks-Recreation Bd., Library Bd., Ariz. League of Cities. Bd. dirs. Ariz. Safety Council, Ariz. Acad., Pacific Region Soroptimists. Named Citizen of the Year, Prescott C.of C., 1969. Mem. Internat. Platform Assn., Am. Assn. U. Women, Nat. Assn. Parliamentarians, Gen. Fedn. Women's Clubs (dir. 1964-68, past rec. sec., 3d v.p., 2d v.p. elect 1974—). Presbyn. (pres. Ariz. Synodical Soc.). Clubs: Garden (pres.), Torrance Jr. Women's (pres.), Mentone Women's (pres.), Prescott Monday (pres.). Home: 820 Fairview Av Prescott AZ 86301 Office: 609 Division St Prescott AZ 86301

WAGNER, JEANNETTE (MRS. PAUL G. WAGNER), state ofcl.; b. Wadsworth, O., Feb. 3, 1915; d. Sterling G. and Phoebe (Trew) Sechrist; student Ind. U., 1933; A.B. Akron U., 1937; m. Paul G. Wagner, Mar. 27, 1938; children—Christine, Sterling. Mem. Ohio Bd. Edn., 1958—, v.p. 1968-70, pres., 1970—. Treas. Wagner-Green Co., Cleve., 1945—. Sec. Ednl. TV Met. Cleve., 1963—. Mem. women's adv. bd. Fenn Coll.; past mem. area council Girl Scouts Am. past chmn. legislation Cuyahoga County P.T.A. Trustee Orange Community Library, Alternate del. Republican Nat. Conv., 1964. Mem. Council World Affairs, Citizens League Cleve., Delta Gamma. Republican (committeeman, bd. dirs. Western Res. Club). Mem. Federated Ch. Club: Womans City (Cleve.). Home: 37855 Jackson Rd Chagrin Falls OH 44022 Office: 12808 Drexmore Rd Cleveland OH 44120

WAGNER, KAREN MARGARET, ednl. adminstr.; b. Phila., Oct. 29, 1947; d. Paul Raymond and Ethel Marie (Ackerman) Wagner; B.A., Hood Coll., 1969; Mus.M., Manhattan Sch. Music, 1973. Sec. student services/placement office Manhattan Sch. Music, N.Y.C., 1969-70, spl. asst., controller, bus. mgrs. office, 1970-72, dir. student services/placement, 1972—. Mem. Nat., Eastern assns. student financial aid adminstrs., N.Y. State Financial Aid Adminstrs. Assn. Home: 21 W 74th St New York City NY 10023 Office: 120 Claremont Av New York City NY 10027

WAGNER, LINDA WELSHIMER (MRS. PAUL V. WAGNER), educator; b. St. Mary's, O., Aug. 18, 1936; d. Sam A. and Esther S. (Scheffler) Welshimer; Ph.D., Bowling Green U., 1963; m. Paul V. Wagner, Jan. 30, 1957; children—Douglas, Thomas, Andrea. Instr., Bowling Green U., 1962-65; asst. prof. Wayne State U., 1965-67; prof. English, Mich. State U., East Lansing, 1968—. Author: The Poems of William Carlos Williams, 1964; Denise Levertov, 1967; Intaglios: Poems, 1967; The Prose of William Carlos Williams, 1970; Phyllis McGinley, 1971; William Faulkner: Four Decades of Criticism, 1973; T.S. Eliot, 1974; Ernke Ernest Heminway: Five Decades of Criticism, 1974. Office: Mich State U East Lansing MI 48823

WAGNER, MARJORIE DOWNING (MRS. M. JOHN WAGNER), educator; b. N.Y.C., Mar. 16, 1917; d. Charles A. and Marguerite (Ohland) Coogan; B.A., Coll. Mt. St. Vincent, 1938; M.A., Catholic U. Am., 1939; Ph.D., Yale, 1942; m. Francis Downing, Sept. 8, 1952 (dec. Dec. 1964); children—Francis, Nicholas; m. 2d, M. John Wagner, June 6, 1974. Instr. English, Barnard Coll., 1942-47; asst. prof., asso. prof. Bklyn. Coll., 1947-61; dean of coll. Sarah Lawrence Coll., Bronxville, N.Y., 1961-65; dean of faculty Scripps Coll., Claremont, Cal., 1965-71, Frederick Hard prof. English lit., 1971-74; pres. Cal. State Coll., Sonoma, 1974—. Trustee Windward Sch., White Plains, N.Y., 1962-65. Mem. Am. Assn. U. Women, Modern Lang. Assn., Medieval Soc. of Pacific, Western Assn. Schs. and Colls. (bd. sr. accreditation commn. 1968-71). Home: 780 W 9th St Claremont CA 91711

WAGNER, MAZIE EARLE (MRS. HERMAN SCHUBERT), clin. psychologist, educator; b. Williamsville, N.Y., Oct. 28, 1901; d. Joseph and Laura (Lapp) Wagner; B.A., U. Buffalo, 1925, M.A., 1927; postgrad. U. Chgo., 1927-28; Ph.D., Columbia, 1932; m. Herman J. P. Schubert, July 1, 1931; 1 son, Daniel S. P. Research asso., asst. dean students U. Buffalo, 1931-49; asso. prof. State U. N.Y. State U. Coll., Buffalo, 1949, now prof. edn., emeritus, also dir. counselling and guidance emeritus, dir. research in student affairs, 1972—. Fellow Am. Psychol. Assn.; mem. N.Y. State Ednl. Research Assn., Soc. Projective Techniques, Phi Beta Kappa, Pi Lambda Theta. Author articles in field. Home: 500 Klein Rd Buffalo NY 14221 Office: 1300 Elmwood Av Buffalo NY 14222

WAGNER, PEGGY (MARGARET DALE), editor; b. Chgo., June 14, 1949; d. Vernon Milton and Marcia (Nierman) Wagner; B.A. cum laude, Tufts U., 1971. Editorial staff Ency. Brit., Inc., Chgo., 1971-73; art editor Houghton Mifflin Co., Boston, 1973—. Author: Hurrah for Hats, 1964; Arts of Central Africa, 1974. Home: 477 Monroe Av Glencoe IL 60022 also 35 Gorham St Cambridge MA 02138

WAGNER, SHARON BLYTHE, author; b. Wallace, Ida., Dec. 16, 1936; d. Moses Ross and Dorothy Agnes (Stephens) Wagner; student Colo. Women's Coll., 1955-56, Mesa Community Coll., 1968-71; grad. Famous Writers Sch., 1965. Short story writer, 1961-71, also novelist. Author: Prairie Wind, 1967; Dude Ranch Mystery, 1968; Curse of Still Valley, 1969; Country of the Wolf, 1970; Maridu, 1970; Circle of Evil, 1971; Silly Filly from Nowhere, 1971; Winter Evil, 1971; House of Shadows, 1972; Moonwind, 1972; Shadow on the Sun, 1972; Legacy of Loneliness, 1972; Cove in Darkness, 1972; Cry of the Cat, 1973; Haitian Legacy, 1973; Wind of Bitterness, 1973; Gypsy and Nimblefoot, 1973; Shades of Evil, 1974; Satan's Acres, 1974; Colors of Death, 1974; Havenhurst, 1974; Dark Waters of Death, 1974; Roses from Yesterday, 1974. Home: 2137 E Bramble Av Mesa AZ 85204

WAGNER, SHARON LEE SPENCE, constrn. co. exec.; b. Thermopolis, Wyo., Sept. 7, 1931; d. Henry Grant and Beula Sue (Harris) Spence; student Eastern Mont. Coll., 1949-51; m. William R. Wagner, May 31, 1952; children—Vicki Lee, Cindy Jo, Sheri Lynn, Kathleen Marie. Sec.-treas. Western States Constrn. Co., Inc., Loveland, Colo., 1964-69, v.p., 1969—; sec.-treas. Rocky Mountain Concrete and Constrn., Inc., Estes Park, Colo., 1967-73; interior decorator for Columbine Park; artist. Home: 1123 W Eisenhower St Loveland CO 80537

WAGNER, SHIRLEY WOOTAN (MRS. FRANK L. WAGNER), accountant; b. Paducah, Ky.; d. John Thomas and Minnie Florence (McNeil) Wootan; student pub. schs. and spl. courses; m. Frank L. Wagner, June 12, 1929. Pub. accountant Taylor-Wagner, Co., Sedalia, Mo., 1938-55; pvt. practice as pub. accountant, Sedalia, 1955—. C.P.A., Mo. Mem. Mo. Assn. Pub. Accountants (pres. 1959-60), Am. Inst. C.P.A.'s, Am. Woman's Soc. C.P.A.'s, Mo. Soc. C.P.A.'s, Bus. and Profl. Women's Clubs Sedalia Civic Council (pres. 1960), Sedalia C. of C. Altrusa, Sorosis. Baptist. Mem. Order Easter Star (past matron). Home: 1009 W Broadway Sedalia MO 65301 Office: 107 1/2 W 3d St Sedalia MO 65301

WAGSTAFF, MRS. MARIAN, educator; b. San Francisco, Apr. 23, 1912; d. Harry Alexander and Lillian (Hofers) Cavassa; A.B., San Francisco State Coll., 1933; M.A., Stanford, 1942, Ed.D., 1958; postgrad. U. Chgo., summer 1945, U. Mich., summer 1952, U. So. Cal., 1942-44; m. Wendell W. Wagstaff, June 28, 1940. Tchr. elementary and secondary schs., S. San Francisco Sch. Dist., 1933-42; adminstr., prin. Willowbrook Jr. High Sch., Compton, Cal., 1942-51; prof. edn. dept. Cal. State Coll. at Los Angeles, 1951—, also chmn. secondary dept. Sch. Edn.; edn. cons. Revell, Inc. Mem. nat. joint com. N.E.A.-Am. Legion Com., 1954-59, 62-65, chmn. TV com., 1964-65; edn. chmn. Los Angeles Mayor's Space Com., 1964-66, home base brochure and plan coordinator, 1963—; mem. Cal. aerospace edn. com. NASA, 1963—; dir. ednl. program 1st Woman's Space Symposium, 1962; instr. Columbia Peace Corp Adminstrv. Program, 1965, co-organizer, coordinator on campus program Project Incentive; cons. Cerritos Jr. Coll., Norwalk Los Angeles City Bd. Edn., U. Cal. at Los Angeles Extension; cons. Cassa Jr. High Com. Tchrs. Recipient Mrs. Robert Goddard Ann. award Am. Legion-N.E.A., 1965, Hobby Industry Assn. Am. award, 1973, Kappa Delta Phi award, 1973. Mem. Nat., Cal. (past pres, state scholarship chmn.) aviation edn. assns., U. Aviation Assns., Cal. Assn. Secondary Sch. Adminstrs. (sec. Jr. High Com., chmn. aviation com.), Cal. Student Tchrs. Assn. (co-sponsor Los Angeles State), Los Angeles Bus. and Profl. Women's Orgn. (chpt. vice chmn. legislative com.), N.E.A., Air Force Assn. (edn. cons.), Pi Lambda Theta, Delta Kappa Gamma. Office: 5151 State College Dr Los Angeles CA 90032

WAIDELICH, ANN ELIZABETH (MRS. MICHAEL W. WAIDELICH), librarian; b. Balt., Dec. 1, 1941; s. Joseph Robinson and Arrilla Katherine (Stadel) Ryan.; B.S., Miami U., Oxford, O., 1963; M.S., U. Denver, 1964; m. Michael W. Waidelich, Sept. 2, 1967. Librarian bus. and sci. div. Madison (Wis.) Pub. Library, 1964-71; librarian municipal reference service Madison and Dane County govts., Madison, 1972—. Lectr. U. Wis. Library Sch., Madison, 1972—. Mem. Wis. Library Assn., Madison Area Library Council (chmn. pub. com. 1973). Home: 2150 Lakeland Av Madison WI 53704 Office: Room 103 210 Monona Av Madison WI 53709

WAINERDI, ANGELA ELIZABETH LAMPONE (MRS. RICHARD E. WAINERDI), artist, civic worker; b. Buffalo, Mar. 31, 1928; d. Thomas and Angelina (Distefano) Lampone; student Albright Art Acad., Buffalo, 1946-49; m. Richard E. Wainerdi, June 2, 1956; children—Thomas Joseph, James Cooper. Free lance and advt. comml. artist, 1946-56. Organizer Brazos Amputee's Club for Rehab. and Encouragement, Club Handy, 1957, pres., 1957—; established shoe and glove exchange for amputees, 1958; residential chmn. Am. Cancer Soc. Crusade, College Station, Tex., 1963. Mem. Beta Alpha Sigma. Roman Catholic. Home: 1115 Langford Dr College Station TX 77840

WAINWRIGHT, MARY LEE SELLERS (MRS. NEWMAN DAVID WAINWRIGHT, JR.), composer; b. Ruby, S.C., Apr. 24, 1913; d. Samuel Joseph and Martha Ellen Sellers; student Sch. Music, Stetson U., 1947-48; m. Newman David Wainwright, Jr., Nov. 7, 1950; 1 dau., Dolores Ann (Mrs. Clint Kimbrough). Mem. Pres.'s Action Com., Washington, 1958-72; Democratic exec. committeewoman, Broward County, Fla., 1957-62; chmn. edn. Dem. Nat. Exec. Com., Fla., 1957-62. Recipient Spl. awards Fla. Folk Festival, 1957-60; award of merit South Fla. State Hosp., 1966; Superior awards Nat. Fedn. Music Clubs and ASCAP, 1955-72; certificate of appreciation Mayor of Hollywood, Fla., 1962; certificate of appreciation Nat. Police Officers Assn. Am., Police Hall of Fame, 1971. Mem. Am. Soc. Composers, Authors and Pubs., Song Writers Hall of Fame, Internat. Platform Assn., Hollywood Music Club (pres. 1957-59), Fla. Fedn. Music Clubs (pres. Royal Poincina dist. 1959-61), Nat. Fedn. Music Clubs (mem. nat. com. World of Music 1963-67, pres. Hollywood chpt. Past President's Assembly 1974—), World Home Bible League, Am. Security Council (bd. policy), New Spirit of '76 Found. Composer: Hollywood, Florida U.S.A., 1955; The Master Key, 1967; Education is the Master Key, 1967; Wake Up, Wake Up America, 1959; Our God of All, 1966; The March of Faith, 1965; Rise and Shine, 1964; The Masquerade is Over, 1964; Inspiration is Making all Things New, 1963; Thank You God, 1963; God is Love, 1972 (nat. award 1972); The Meek Shall Inherit The Earth, 1973; Wake Up World, 1974. Home: 1519 Dewey St Hollywood FL 33020

WAINWRIGHT, SARAH HARRIS BELL (MRS. THEA T. WAINWRIGHT), social worker; b. Evanston, Ill., June 28, 1918; d. Cleon M. and Gertrude (Carter) Bell; B.S., Coll. William and Mary, 1940; M.S.W., Richmond Profl. Inst. Sch. Social Work, 1961; m. Thea T. Wainwright, June 20, 1942; children—Edward Curtis, John Irving. With Family & Children's Service, Richmond, Va., 1961—, caseworker, 1961-63, caseworker, supr., 1963-71, dir. profl. services, 1971—, field instr., 1965—. Home service vol. A.R.C., 1957-59, bd. dirs., 1958-66. Mem. Nat. Assn. Social Workers (rec. sec. Central Va. chpt. 1962-64, chmn. ethics and certification com. 1964-68, mem. finance com. 1973—), Va. Council Social Welfare (rec. sec. Capitol Area dist. 1973—), Kappa Kappa Gamma. Home: 9400 University Blvd Richmond VA 23229 Office: Family and Children's Service 1518 Willow Lawn Dr Richmond VA 23230

WAITE, DOROTHY ELIZABETH, banker; b. Cheboygan, Mich., May 8, 1921; d. Clyde Edwin and Myrtle Elizabeth (Floury) Waite; student Mich. State Coll., 1963. Asst. mgr. LaLondes Inn, Cheboygan, 1936-52; with Cheboygan Bank, 1953—, asst. cashier, 1958-63, asst. v.p. personnel payroll, 1963—. Vice pres. Cheboygan County chpt. Am. Cancer Soc., 1960—; mem. Cheboygan Community Arts Council. Mem. Mich. Bank Women Assn. (chmn.), Nat. Assn. Bank Women (chmn. Mich. 1967-68), Cheboygan Area Bus. and Profl. Women's Club (pres.), Hist. Soc. Cheboygan County, Daus. Isabella. Roman Catholic. Club: Cheboygan Duplicate Bridge Club. Home: 618 Snow Apple Ct Cheboygan MI 49721 Office: 316 N Main St Cheboygan MI 49721

WAITE, SARITA CAMILLE, lawyer; b. San Jose, Cal., Apr. 27, 1941; d. Horace and Muriel (Scheffler) Waite; B.A., U. Cal. at Berkeley, 1963; J.D., Golden Gate Law Sch., San Francisco, 1969. Admitted to Cal. bar, 1970; partner firm Bender & Waite, Berkeley, 1970—. Mem. adj. faculty Hastings Coll. Law, 1973; extension tchr. U. Cal., 1973. Mem. Cal., Alameda County bar assns., Lawyers Guild, Am. Civil Liberties Union. Home: 1020 Miller Av Berkeley CA Office: 1905 Berkeley Way Berkeley CA 94708

WAKEFIELD, ANNE KAYE, coll. librarian; b. Norfolk, Va., Nov. 13, 1945; d. Truett Dwight and Anne Lee (Jordan) Wakefield; Asso. B.A., Emory U., 1964, B.A., 1967, M.L.S., 1968. Audio/visual librarian Augusta-Richmond County (Ga.) Pub. Library, 1968-69; chief librarian Atlanta Meml. Arts Center, Atlanta Coll. Art, 1969—. Mem. library dirs. com. U. Center in Ga., Atlanta, 1969—, audio/visual projects com., 1973—. Mem. Art Librarians Soc. N.Am. (chmn. Ga. chpt. 1973—), Spl. Libraries Assn., Ga. Library Assn., Coll. Art Assn., Mus. Modern Art, Theosophical Soc. Am., Ga. Astrological Assn. Editor: Bookman's Guide for Valuable Books (Edgar V. Kimsey), 1974. Home: 128 17th St Atlanta GA 30309

WAKEFIELD, CAROLINE CARUSO (MRS. CHARLES EDWARD WAKEFIELD), vending co. exec.; b. Bridgeport, Conn., Feb. 2, 1921; d. Frank and Frances (Passafiume) Caruso; B.A., Coll. St. Elizabeth, 1941; M.A., U. Conn., 1949; certificate advanced grad. study U. Hartford, 1960; m. Charles Edward Wakefield, Feb. 21, 1955. Tchr. math., sci. Williams Meml. Inst., New London, Conn., 1942-45; tchr. math., counselor Milford (Conn.) High Sch., 1945-52; dir. guidance Housatonic Valley Regional High Sch., 1945-52; dir. guidance Housatonic Valley Regional High Sch., Falls Village, Conn., 1952-73; sec. C & C Vending Corp., Falls Village, 1957—. Sec. Falls Village Pub. Health Nursing Assn., 1961-67; mem. Falls Village Planning and Zoning Commn., 1968—, sec., 1970-73; municipal agt. for elderly, 1973—, dir. Falls Village Sr. Center, 1974—; chmn. Northwestern Conn. Agy. on Aging. Chmn., Democratic Town Com., Falls Village, 1969—. Bd. dirs. N.W. Conn. Heart Assn., 1954-59, sec., 1955-59; bd. dirs. Housatonic Homemakers Health Aide Service. Recipient citation Nat. Assn. Women Deans and Counselors, 1973; Woman of Year award Bus. and Profl. Women, 1973; Coll. St. Elizabeth award, 1974. Mem. Conn. Sch. Counselors Assn. (treas. 1971—), Delta Kappa Gamma. Roman Catholic. Home: Box 43 Falls Village CT 06031 Office: Route 7 Falls Village CT 06031

WAKEHAM, MABEL IRENE, educator; b. Watford, Eng., June 28, 1912 (parents Am. citizens); s. William Henry and Mabel May (Pringle) Wakeham; B.A., Andrews U., 1934; M.A., U. So. Cal., 1939; Ph.D., Stanford, 1965. Tchr., English, French and commerce Mt. Vernon (O.) Acad., 1934-36; tchr., accountant, registrar, Loma Linda, Cal., 1936-40; tchr. Lynnwood (Cal.) Acad., 1940-41; Hawaiian Mission Acad., Honolulu, 1941-45, Pacific Union Coll., 1945-46; tchr., registrar, head English dept. Philippine Union Coll., Manila, 1946-54, tchr., dean Sch. Liberal Arts, dean Grad. Sch., 1965-70; head English dept., registrar Mountain View Coll., Philippines, 1954-64, acad. dean, acting pres., 1960-61; chmn. dept. English, chmn. humanities div. Oakwood Coll., Huntsville, Ala., 1971—. Named Outstanding Educator of Yr., Outstanding Educators Am., 1971; mem. Andrews U. Hall of Fame. Mem. Nat. Council Tchrs. English, Tchrs. English to Speakers of Other Lang., Am. Assn. U. Women. Seventh-day Adventist. Club: Faculty Women's (Huntsville). Author: Strictly Confidential, 1955; Oral English, 2d edit., 1956; Though The Heavens Fall, 1971; also articles. Home: 3922 Broadmor Rd Huntsville AL 35810

WAKERLIN, RUTH COLEMAN (MRS. GEORGE E. WAKERLIN), med. illustrator; b. Chgo., Mar. 2, 1917; d. George H. and Marcella (Montgomery) Coleman; A.B., Wellesley Coll., 1939; postgrad. Shady Hill Sch., 1939-40; certificate med. illustration U. Ill. Sch. Med., 1944; M.A., U. Mo., 1971; m. George E. Wakerlin, Feb. 14, 1952; children—Susan Helen, George E. Med. illustrator U. Ill., 1944-45, instr., 1945-47, asst. prof., 1947-53; free-lance med. illustrator, Chgo., 1953-57, Summit, N.J., 1963-66; med. illustrator U. Mo. Med. Center, 1966-69, chief illustration sect. med. ednl. services, 1969-74; coordinator div. med. illustration and graphics, asso. prof. med. illustration U. Cal. at San Francisco Med. Center, 1974—. Mem. Assn. Med. Illustrators (gov., chmn. amendments com., spl. study com., corr. sec. 1973-74), Health Services Communications Assn., Guild Nat. Sci. Illustrators. Med. art editor Continuing Edn. for Family Physician, 1973—. Home: 2120 Pacific Ave Apt 406 San Francisco CA 94115

WAKIN, BAYSHEA BERTHA, educator; b. Oneonta, N.Y., June 21, 1925; d. Chickri Abraham and Hattie (Nauseef) Wakin; B.S., State U. N.Y. at Albany, 1947, M.S., 1952; Ed.D., Pa. State U., 1962. Tchr. Homer (N.Y.) Central High Sch., 1947-54; Fulbright exchange scholar, Australia, 1956-57; tchr. bus. Norwich (N.Y.) High Sch., 1954-59; asso. prof. Elmira Coll., 1962-66; prof. State U. N.Y. at Albany, 1966—, chmn. dept. bus. edn., 1973—; curriculum cons. State Edn. Dept. Bur. Continuing Edn. Curriculum Devel.; edn. mem. Inst. Certifying Secs.; cons. Nat. Assn. Ednl. Secs. Bd. dirs. Capitol Artists Opera Co. N.Y. State. Found. for Econ. Edn. fellow, 1964; Grace LeGendre State BPW scholar, 1961. Mem. Am. Vocational Assn., Internat. Assn. Bus. Edn., Nat. Bus. Edn. Assn., Bus. Tchrs. Assn. N.Y. State, Eastern Bus. Tchrs. Assn., Nat. Edn. Assn., N.Y. State Tchrs. Assn., Bus. and Profl. Womens Club Inc. Asso. editor Jour. of Bus. Edn., 1966—; asst. editor Delta Pi Epsilon Jour., 1966—. Contbr. articles to profl. jours. Home: 10 Kimberly Pl Delmar NY 12054 Office: BA 366 State U NY at Albany 1400 Washington Av Albany NY 12222

WALBOM, PAMELA DEE (MRS. MICHAEL DAVID WALBOM), ednl. adminstr.; b. Cedar City, Utah, Dec. 12, 1944; d. James Gerald and Ruth Elvine (Cornwell) Hansen; student U. Utah, 1962-64; B.S. in Sociology, Brigham Young U., 1966; postgrad. U. So. Cal. at Los Angeles, 1974—; m. Michael David Walbom, June 20, 1968; 1 son, James Michael. Vocational counselor Cal. State Employment Service, Los Angeles, 1966-67; employment counselor, placement interviewer Utah Employment Security State Employment Service, Provo, 1967-69; vocational tng. specialist Lane County Welfare, Eugene, Ore., 1970; dir. financial aid U. So. Cal., Los Angeles, 1970—. Cons. Am. Coll. Testing Corp., Iowa City, Ia. Mem. Nat., Western assns. of coll. financial aid adminstrs. Mem. Ch. of Jesus Christ of Latter-day Saints. Home: 13499 Aclare Cerritos CA 90701 Office: Univ of Southern California University Park Los Angeles CA 90007

WALBOT, VIRGINIA ELIZABETH, educator, biochemist; b. Los Angeles, June 27, 1946; d. Henry Charles and Mary Elizabeth (Wehrly) Walbot; A.B. in Biology with honors and distinction, Stanford, 1967; M.Philosophy, Yale, 1969, Ph.D. in Biology (NSF fellow), 1972. Postdoctoral fellow NIH, U. Ga., Athens, 1972-74; asst. prof. biology Washington U., St. Louis, 1975—. Recipient Seymour award Cal. Scholarship Fedn., 1963. Mem. A.A.A.S. (pres. women's caucus 1971-73, mem. com. opportunities in sci. 1973—), Soc. Plant Physiology, Internat. Plant Tissue Culture, Soc. Devel. Biology (mem.-at-large 1974-77), Bot. Soc. Am. Founder Women in Cell Biology, 1970, since editor. Office: Dept Biology Washington Univ St Louis MO 63130

WALCH, MARY JOSEPHINE, lawyer; b. Lake Wales, Fla., Jan. 11, 1935; d. John William and Josephine Marie (Huebner) Woods; B.A., Trinity Coll., Washington, 1956; J.D., U. Md., 1966; m. Rudolph Carl Walch, Jr., Feb. 27, 1960; 1 son, John William. Chemist, W.R. Grace & Co., Curtis Bay and Clarksville, Md., 1956-59, reference librarian,

Clarksville, 1959-61, patent investigator, 1961-67, atty., 1967—; admitted to Md. bar, 1966. Active Parent-Tchrs. League. Mem. Am. Patent Law Assn., Md. Bar Assn. Democrat. Roman Catholic. Clubs: Rolling Road Golf, Tail of the Fox. Patentee tetrahydropyridazinium compounds, N-Aminophenind aminium salts. Office: 7379 Route 32 Columbia MD 21044

WALCH, SHIRLEY JANE, assn. exec.; b. Chgo., Sept. 3, 1938; s. Joseph James and Vera (Williamson) Horak; B.A., U. Ia., 1960; postgrad. U. Cal. at Los Angeles, 1968, 70; postgrad. Loyola Marymount U.; divorced. Tchr. art and social studies jr. high sch., Des Moines, 1960-61; art tchr., chmn. dept. sr. high sch., Bloomington, Minn., 1961-63; mem. staff San Fernando (Cal.) Valley Girl Scout council, 1964—, asst. exec. dir., 1973—. Instr. recreation dept. Cal. State U., Northridge, 1972; lectr., camping cons., 1971—; Girl Scout rep. to numerous orgns. in area. Recipient commendations for profl. work in serving youth. Mem. Assn. Girl Scout Profl. Workers, U. Ia. Alumni Assn., Am. Camping Assn. (chmn. standards com., bd. dirs. So. Cal. sect. 1969—, mem. nat. standards com. 1972—), Alpha Xi Delta. Home: 22125 Av Morelos Woodland Hills CA 91364 Office: 18700 Sherman Way Reseda CA 91335

WALD, ELLEN RASHKOW (MRS. ARNOLD WALD), physician; b. Bklyn., Sept. 29, 1943; d. Irving and Ethel (Jacobson) Rashkow; B.S., Bklyn. Coll., 1964; M.D., Downstate Med. Center, 1968; m. Arnold Wald, June 26, 1966; children—Elissa Karen, Eric Lawrence. Intern pediatrics Kings County Hosp., Bklyn., 1968-69, resident, 1969-71; pediatrician Sinai Druid Clinic, Balt., 1971-72, attending physician, 1972-73; fellow div. infectious diseases U. Md. Hosp., Balt., 1973—. Mem. Phi Beta Kappa, Sigma Xi, Pi Mu Epsilon, Alpha Omega Alpha. Home: 9464 Wandering Way Columbia MD 21045 Office: 29 S Greene St Baltimore MD 21201

WALD, FRANCINE JOY WEINTRAUB (MRS. BERNARD J. WALD), physicist; b. Bklyn., Jan. 13, 1938; d. Irving and Minnie (Reisig) Weintraub; student Bklyn. Coll., 1955-57; B.E.E., Coll. City N.Y., 1960; M.S., Poly. Inst. Bklyn., 1962, Ph.D., 1969; m. Bernard J. Wald, Feb. 2, 1964; children—David Evan, Kevin Mitchell. Engr., Remington Rand Univac div. Sperry Rand Corp., Phila., 1960; instr. Poly. Inst. Bklyn., 1962-64, adj. research asso., 1969-70; lectr. N.Y. Community Coll., Bklyn., 1969, 70. Nat. Def. Edn. Act. fellow, 1962-64. Mem. Am. Phys. Soc., Sigma Xi, Tau Beta Pi, Eta Kappa Nu. Home: 520 LaGuardia Pl New York City NY 10012

WALD, SYLVIA, artist; b. Phila., Oct. 30, 1914; ed. Moore Inst. Art, Sci. and Industry. Exhibited in one-man shows U. Louisville, 1945, 49, Kent State Coll., 1945, Nat. Serigraph Soc., 1946, Grand Central Moderns, 1957, Devorah Sherman Gallery, 1960, New Sch., 1967, Book Gallery, White Plains, N.Y. 1968, group shows Nat. Sculpture Soc., 1940, Sculpture Internat., Phila., 1940, Chgo. Art Inst., 1941, Bklyn. Museum, Library of Congress, 1943, 52, 58, Smithsonian Instn., 1954, Internat. Print Exhbn., Salzburg and Vienna, 1952, 2d Sao Paulo Biennial, 1953, N.Y. Cultural Center, 1973; represented in permanent collections Aetna Oil Co., Am. Assn. U. Women, Ball State Tchrs. Coll., Bibliotheque Nathionale, Bklyn. Mus., Howard U., State U. Ia., Library of Congress, U. Louisville, Nat. Gallery, Mus. Modern Art, Phila. Mus., N.C. Mus., Rose Mus. Art at Brandeis U., Whitney Mus., N.Y.C., Finch Coll. Mus., N.Y.C., U. Neb., Ohio U., U. Okla., Princeton, Victoria and Albert Museum, Walker Gallery, Worcester (Mass.) Art Museum. Contbr. to profl. publs. Address 37 E 4th St New York City NY 10003

WALDAU, HELEN FRANCES, educator; b. Torrington, Conn., Mar. 21, 1925; d. Teofil and Michaelena (Plaga) Budney; B.A., U. Conn., 1953, 6th yr. certificate, 1968; M.A., U. Hartford; divorced; children—Geoffrey, Christopher, Peter, Sandra. Mem. faculty Hopewell Sch., Glastonburg, Conn., 1966—, supr. U. Conn. open edn. interns, 1971—. Fellow U. Conn., 1967-68. Mem. Nat., Conn., Glastonbury edn. assns., Greater Conn. Council for Open Edn. (charter), Psi Upsilon Omicron. Home: 154 Wood Pond Rd Glastonbury CT 06033

WALDBUESSER, MARILYN ELAINE VERHAAGH (MRS. OTTO F. WALDBUESSER), home economist; b. Milw., Mar. 26, 1939; d. George I. and Elaine K. (Baughkman) VerH.; B.S., Stout State U., 1967, M. Home Econs. Edn., 1972; m. Otto F. Waldbuesser, Apr. 17, 1959; children—Susan Marilyn, Carolyn Louise. Extension home economist, Pepin County, Wis., 1967, Chippewa County, Wis., 1968—. Mem. Am., Wis. home econs. assns., Nat. (Florence Hall award 1970), Wis. (v.p. 1973-74) assns. extension home economists. Methodist. Office: Box 310 711 Bridge St Chippewa Falls WI 54729

WALDEN, AMELIA ELIZABETH, author; b. N.Y.C.; d. William A. and Elizabeth (Wanner) Walden; B.S., Columbia U., 1934; certificate Am. Acad. Dramatic Arts; m. John William Harmon, Feb. 9, 1946 (dec. 1950). Author: Gateway, 1946; Waverly, 1947; Sunnycove, 1948; Skymountain, 1950; A Girl Called Hank, 1951; Marsha, On-Stage, 1952; Victory for Jill, 1953; All My Love, Daystar, 1954; Three Loves Has Sandy, 1955; The Bradford Story, I Found My Love, My Sister Mike, Palomino Girl (all 1956); Flight into Morning, 1957; Today Is Mine, 1958; Queen of the Courts, 1959; Where Is My Heart, 1960; A Boy to Remember, 1960; Shadow on Devils Peak, 1961; When Love Speaks, 1961; How Bright the Dawn, 1962; So Near the Heart, 1962; My Dreams Ride High, 1963; To Catch a Spy, 1964; My World's the Stage, 1964; The Spy on Danger Island, 1965; Race the Wild Wind, 1965; The Spy with Five Faces, 1966; In Search of Ophelia, 1966; A Spy Called Michel-E, 1967, A Name For Himself, 1967, The Spy Who Talked Too Much, 1968; Walk In A Tall Shadow, 1968; A Spycase Built For Two, 1969; Same Scene, Different Place, 1969; The Case of the Diamond Eye, 1969; Basketball Girl of the Year, 1970; What Happened to Candy Carmichael, 1970; Valerie Valentine is Missing, 1971; Stay to win, 1971; Play Ball, McGill!, 1972; Where Was Everyone when Sabrina Screamed?, 1973; Go, Phillips, Go!, 1974; Escape on Skis, 1975. Pioneer young adult novel genre in Am. lit. Collected papers donated to Case-Western Res. U. Home: 89 N Compo Rd Westport CT 06880

WALDEN, BONNIE JEAN, clubwomen; b. Eau Claire, Wis., July 3, 1938; d. Miles F. Mathieu and Edna Mae (Lowry) Mathieu; A.A., Clark Coll., 1958; B.A., Western Wash. State Coll., 1960; M.Ed., Portland U., 1964; m. Paul R. Walden, June 10, 1961; children—Grant R., Matt F. Primary sch. tchr. Vancouver (Wash.) pub. schs., 1960-65. Bd. dirs. Clark Coll. Alumni Assn., 1962-64, sec. bd. dirs., 1963-64; sec. Battle Ground P.T.A., 1972-73; bd. dirs. Vancouver YWCA, 1969-72. Mem. Gen. Fedn. Women's Clubs, Silver Star Jr. Woman's Club (pres. 1967-68 Chrysanthemum award 1967, 71, Helping Hand award 1969, named Clubwoman of Yr. 1970), Federated Woman's Club (pres. Battle Ground, Wash. 1972-73, mem. state bd. 1965-68, dist. dir. 1970-71, dist. dean chmn. 1971-73). Methodist (membership sec. 1969-75). Address: 415 W Hawthorne St Battle Ground WA 98604

WALDER, LORETTA, clin. psychologist; b. N.Y.C., July 2, 1932; d. Jack and Fay (Wernilk) Berkowitz; B.A., Hunter Coll., 1953; Ph.D., Columbia, 1959; m. Eugene Walder, Sept. 29, 1954; children—Brian Evan, Noeleen Gywnbeth. Psychotherapist Bleuer Center, Jamaica, N.Y., 1961-64; pvt. practice clin. psychologist, 1962—; supervising psychologist Roosevelt Hosp., N.Y.C., 1964-68; chief sch. psychologist Bethpage (N.Y.) Pub. Schs., 1960-63; cons. psychologist Easton (Conn.)-Redding Schs., 1971-72. Mem. Am. Psychol. Assn., Sigma Xi. Contbr. articles to profl. jours. Address: 710 N Park Av Easton CT 06112

WALDMAN, ANNE LESLEY, poet; b. Millville, N.J., Apr. 2, 1945; d. John M. and Frances (LeFevre) Waldman; B.A. in Lit., Bennington Coll., 1966. Dir. poetry project St. Marks Ch. In-The-Bowery, N.Y.C., 1966—. Bd. dirs. Coordinating Council Lit. Magazines. Recipient Dylan Thomas Meml. prize, 1967; Poets Found. grantee, 1969; Nat. Literary Anthology grantee, 1970. Author: Baby Breakdown, 1970; Giant Night, 1970; No Hassles, 1971; Life Notes, 1973. Editor: The World Anthology, 1969; Another World, 1971. Co-editor Angel Hair Books and Mags., 1966—; editor The World, 1966—.

WALDMAN, BETTY KLUSNER (MRS. JACK LEON WALDMAN), librarian; b. Cleve., Dec. 15, 1917; d. Lazarus W. and Anna (Cohen) Klusner; B.A., Western Res. U. (now Case Western Res. U.), 1939, M.L.S. (Greater Cleve. scholar 1943), 1944; m. Jack Leon Waldman, Feb. 24, 1946; children—Barbara Lee, Susan Kay. Asst. to head sch. dept. Cleve. Pub. Library, 1941-44; librarian East High Sch., Cleve., 1944-46, John Hay Night Sch., Cleve., 1944-46, Cleve. Trade Sch., 1944-46, Temple Israel, Akron, O., 1958-66; children's librarian Ayres br. Akron Pub. Library, Akron, 1966-71, head Ayres br., 1971—. Mem. Am., Ohio library assns. Home: 2320 Thurmont Rd Akron OH 44313 Office: 1765 W Market St Akron OH 44313

WALDMAN, DIANE (MRS. PAUL WALDMAN), museum curator; b. N.Y.C., Feb. 24, 1936; d. Robert and Beatrice Rose (Albert) Deleson; B.F.A., Hunter Coll., 1956; M.A., Inst. Fine Arts, N.Y.U., 1965, certificate mus. tng., 1965, postgrad.; m. Paul Waldman, Sept. 26, 1957. With Solomon R. Guggenheim Museum, N.Y.C., 1965—, now curator exhbns. Author: Roy Lichtenstein, Drawings and Prints, 1970; Ellsworth Kelly, Drawings, Collages, Prints, 1971; Roy Lichtenstein, 1971. Contbr. articles to art jours. Office: Guggenheim Museum 1071 Fifth Av New York City NY 10028

WALDO, GEORGIA JEAN, lawyer; b. Los Angeles, Aug. 22, 1924; d. John Henderson and May O. (Hindsley) Waldo; B.S., U. Cal. at Los Angeles, 1946; M.A., U. So. Cal., 1955; certificate U. Oxford, 1959; student Loyola U., 1961-63, U. Cal. at Los Angeles Sch. Law, 1964-66. Instr. law Los Angeles Community Coll., 1963—; admitted to Cal. bar, 1971, prof. law, Los Angeles Community Coll. dist., 1971—. Mem. Cal. State Bar, Am., Los Angeles County bar assns., Women Lawyers' Assn. Nat. Orgn. Women, Lawyers Club, Cal. Tchrs. Assn., Los Angeles World Affairs Council, English-Speaking Union, Soc. Mayflower Descendants, Phi Alpha Delta. Office: PO Box 1933 Newport Beach CA 92663

WALDO, SALLY (MRS. CLAUDE A. WALDO), ins., real estate broker; b. Seattle, Jan. 8, 1903; d. Hyman and Lena (Kapian) Rosenstein; student Modesto Jr. Coll., 1930; m. Claude A. Waldo, Nov. 6, 1925 (dec. 1969). Exec. sec., co-owner firm Claude A. Waldo, land surveyor, Martinez, Cal., 1945-69, bus. opportunity broker, real estate broker, 1949—, ins. broker, 1950—. Mem. Cal. 50-50 Bill Conn., 1937; mem. constrn. revision com. nat. conv. Young Democratic Clubs Am., 1937, nat. committeewoman, 1937-39, 1st v.p., 1936-37, chmn. woman's activities, 1936; Cal. chmn. circulation Nat. Young Dem. Paper, 1937; adv. bd. women's div. Cal. Dem. Central Com., 1936-38; organizer three young Dem. clubs in Stanislaus County, 1935; mem. Cal. Dem. Campaign Com., 1936; v.p. San Joaquin dist. Fed. Dem. Women's Study Clubs, 1940. Mem. San Joaquin Dist. Conv. Fedn. Women's Clubs (pub. chmn. 1935, legislation chmn. Stanislaus County 1934), Women's Improvement Club, Modesto, Cal. (sec. 1933), Women's Progressive Club (charter), Modesto (sec. 1933), Tres Artes (organizer 1935), Modesto Art League (charter), Martinez Grange, Laguna Honda Home Vols., Patrons Art and Music, San Francisco, DeYoung Mus. Art, (San Francisco), U. Cal. Hosp. Aux., Internat. Hospitality Center Nat. League Women's Service Cal., World Affairs Council San Francisco, Internat. Platform Assn. Toastmistress (charter); mem. Order Eastern Star. Clubs: Woman's City (San Francisco); Berkeley, City Commons (Berkeley, Cal.). Address: Box 710 Lafayette CA 94549

WALDO, TOMMY RUTH BLACKMON (MRS. SELDEN FENNELL WALDO), educator; b. Dallas, Jan. 14, 1916; d. Gulie Hargrove and Mary Lee (Craig) Blackmon; B.A., Agnes Scott Coll., 1938; M.A., U. Fla., 1955, Ph.D., 1961; m. Selden Fennell Waldo, Oct. 28, 1941 (dec. Nov. 1950); children—George Selden (dec.), Andrew Blackmon. Grad. asst. U. Fla., Gainesville, 1952-55, instr., 1955-61, asst. prof. English, 1961-68, asso. prof. English, 1968—; pvt. tchr. piano and organ, 1938-55. Mem. So. Atlantic Modern Lang. Assn., Modern Lang., Assn., Fla., Gainesville music tchrs. assns., Southeastern Renaissance Conf., Phi Beta Kappa, Sigma Alpha Iota (patroness), Delta Kappa Gamma. Contbr. articles to profl. jours. Home: 719 NE 1st St Gainesville FL 32601

WALDRON, HELEN JEANETTE, librarian; b. Nampa, Idaho, Aug. 15, 1916; d. Fred Harrison and Ora (Hamilton) Waldron; B.A., U. of Wash., 1937; M.A., U. Cal., Berkeley, 1951. Cataloger, reference asst. Nat. War Coll., Washington, 1951-55; asst. librarian, head tech. documents sect., U.S. Naval Proving Ground, Dahlgren, Va., 1955-58; asst. librarian The RAND Corp., Santa Monica, Cal., 1958-62, library mgr., 1962—; occasional lectr., John Cotton Dana lectr., 1970. Mem. adv. com. Los Angeles Trade Tech. Coll., 1970—. Recipient H.W. Wilson award, 1972. Mem. Cal. Library Adv. Bd., 1969-72, U. So. Cal. Library Sch., Adv. Bd., 1964-70. Mem. Spl. Libraries Assn. (pres. So. Cal. chpt. 1963-64, conf. program chmn. 1968-69, chmn. adv. council 1968-70), A.A.A.S., Am. Soc. Information Scis. (co-editor Proc. Ann. Meeting 1973), Nat. Microfilm Assn., Friends of Santa Monica Pub. Library (sec. 1963-64). Contbr. to Acquisition of Special Materials, 1966. Home: 1145 Yale St Santa Monica CA 90403 Office: 1700 Main St Santa Monica CA 90401

WALDROP, CLARACY LEE MILLER (MRS. EARL LEO WALDROP), pub. relations co. exec.; b. Rothville, Mo.; d. Roscoe C. and Claracy (Hulett) Miller; student Baylor Coll., 1926-28; B.A. in Speech, Okla. Bapt. U., 1931, postgrad., 1931-40; m. Earl Leo Waldrop, Feb. 22, 1932 (dec. May, 1956); children—Elizabeth Lee (Mrs. Robert W. Rhoads), Robert Earl. Asst. mgr., dir. pub. relations Wichita (Kan.) Symphony Soc., Inc., 1952-57; exec. dir. U.S.O., Wichita, 1957-60; free lance writer, 1960-63; accountant, office mgr. Keller Heartt Fuel Oil Co., Clarendon Hills, Ill., 1963-64; editor home supplement Citizen Newspaper, LaGrange, Ill., 1964-66; nat. advt. mgr. Laidlaw Bros. div. Doubleday & Co., Inc., River Forest, Ill., 1966-70; account exec., also dir. pub. relations Moody & Harrison, Inc., Oak Brook, Ill., 1970-72; pres. Lee M. Waldrop & Assos., Westchester, Ill., 1972—; lectr. communications at coll. seminars. Organizer, 1st pres. women's assn. Wichita Symphony Soc., 1949-60; vol. A.R.C., 1940-48; mem. adv. com. Am. Security Council, Washington, also mem. nat. voter adv. bd.; mem. citizens com. U. Ill., 1973—. Bd. dirs., trustee Rev. R. C. Miller Trusteesship-Endowment Okla. Bapt. U.; trustee Earl Leo Waldrop Meml. Fund of Wichita Symphony Soc. Recipient certificate Merit and Distinguished Service Wichita Symphony Soc., 1949-60, Merit award House Beautiful, 1965, Nat. 1st place award Display Advt. Nat. Fedn. Press Women, 1965, 3d pl., 1969; 1st place awards Ill. Press Women, 1965, 66, 73, 74, Direct Mail Advt., 1969, 1st place award for feature article Deep South Writers Conf., 1973. Mem. Women's Advt. Club Chgo., Opera Guild, Nat. League Am. Pen Women (pres. Chgo. br. 1964-66, organizer and Ill. 1966-68, nat. 4th v.p. 1968-70; nat. editor Pen Woman 1970-74, nat. pres. 1974—, named Pen Woman of Year Chgo. br. 1972), Poets and Patrons Club Chgo., Internat. Platform Assn., Friends Am. Writers, Nat. Fedn. Press Women, Ill. Women's Press Assn. (communications contest chmn. 1974). Club: Women's Advertising (edn. com.) (Chgo.). Author pageants; Unto Us, 1957, It Came Upon the Midnight Clear, 1960. Were You There, 1958, also numerous articles, plays. Home: 765 Louise Dr Springfield PA 19064 Office: 1300 17th St NW Washington DC 20036

WALDROP, GRACE MARIE, physician; b. Winnett, Mont., Dec. 12, 1922; d. George Robert and Grace Greenwood (Marshall) Waldrop; B.A., U. Cal., 1946, M.D., 1949. Intern San Francisco City and County Hosp., 1949-50; resident St. Louis Maternity Hosp., 1950-51, U. Cal. Hosp. at San Francisco, 1951, St. Luke's Hosp., San Francisco, 1952, Highland-Alameda County Hosp., Oakland, Cal., 1952-53; asso. research cancer surgeon Roswell Park Meml. Inst., Buffalo, 1954-57; obstetrician and gynecologist Ross-Loos Med. Group, Los Angeles, 1957-61; practice medicine specializing in obstetrics and gynecology, Los Angeles, 1961—; mem. active staff Queen of Angels Hosp., Los Angeles, 1957—; mem. active staff Hosp. of Good Samaritan; clin. instr. Buffalo Med. Sch., 1955-57; asst. clin. prof. Cal. Coll. Medicine, 1964-67; dir. oncology clinic Queen of Angels Clinic, 1960-71; gynecologist Internat. Ladies Garment Workers Union Health Center, 1962-72. Mem. met. med. adv. com. A.R.C. Diplomate Am. Bd. Obstetrics and Gynecology. Fellow Am. Coll. Obstetricians and Gynecologists, A.C.S.; mem. A.M.A., Cal. Med. Assn., Los Angeles County Med. Assn., Los Angeles Obstet. and Gynecol. Soc. Home: 5744 Briarcliff Rd Los Angeles CA 90068 Office: 1127 Wilshire Blvd Los Angeles CA 90017

WALDROP, RUTH WIGGINS, librarian; b. May, Tex.; d. James Ernest and Della (Campbell) Wiggins; B.S., Livingston State Coll., 1939; M.S., U. Ala., 1960, Ed.S., 1970. Librarian, Shades Valley High Sch., Jefferson County, 1949-59; spl. instructional material cons. Jefferson County Bd. Edn., Birmingham, 1960-68; instr. library sci. U. Ala., 1961-67; instr. summers U. So. Cal., 1966, U. Tenn., 1967, Auburn U., 1968; cons. state sch. libraries Dept. Edn., Montgomery, Ala., 1968-69; chmn. dept. sch. librarianship U. Ala., 1969—. Mem. Am., Southeastern (chmn. childrens and sch. library sect. 1964-66), Ala. (pres. 1967-68) library assns., Ala. Sch. Librarians' Assn. (pres. 1963-64), Am. Assn. Sch. Librarians (dir. region 5, 1968-70), Alpha Beta Alpha, Delta Kappa Gamma. Home: PO Box 2469 University AL 35486

WALENSKY, LUCILE ROBERTS, librarian; b. Sioux City, Ia.; d. Homer Cramotte and Leah Olive (Jones) Roberts; B.A., Morningside Coll., 1943; student Grinnell Coll., 1940-42; M.L.S., Tex. Women's U., 1965; m. Theodore H. Walensky, Mar. 25, 1944 (div.); 1 son, Dana Grant. Copywriter Carson, Pirie, Scott, Inc., Chgo., 1943-44; reader's adviser Sioux City Pub. Library, 1964-66; adult services librarian Marshalltown (Ia.) Pub. Library, 1966-67; dir. Yankton (S.D.) Carnegie Library, 1967-73; regional adminstr./cons. S.W. Ia. Regional Library System, Missouri Valley, Ia., 1973—. Nat. Library Week chmn., S.D., 1970. Pres. Sioux City P.T.A. Council, 1958-59; program chmn. Yankton Civic Council, 1968-70. Mem. Ia. Library Assn., A.L.A., Jr. League Sioux City, Am. Assn. U. Women. Mem. United Ch. of Christ. Home: Missouri Valley IA 51555 Office: Box 327 Missouri Valley IA 51555

WALES, FLORENCE ALBERTA, librarian, writer; b. Niagara Falls, N.Y.; d. Charles C. and Christeana (Retallack) Wales; M.L.S., Syracuse U., 1954. Dir., Niagara Falls Pub. Library, 1954-73. Bd. dirs. Porta-Niagara Center Girls Club, 1955—, treas., 1967—. Mem. Assn. Profl. Women Writers, Am. Assn. U. Women, Beta Phi Mu. Club: Zonta (past sec., dir. Niagara Falls). Home: 711 8th St Niagara Falls NY 14301

WALES, NYM (HELEN FOSTER SNOW), writer; b. Utah, Sept. 21, 1907; d. John Moody and Hannah (Davis) Foster; student U. Utah, Yenching U. (Peking, China); m. Edgar Snow, Dec. 25, 1932 (div. 1949). Lived in China and P.I. and traveled in Far East, 1931-41; co-founder (with Edgar Snow and Rowi Alley) Gung Ho Chinese Indsl. Coops., China, 1938; exhibited photographs of China, Met. Mus., N.Y.C., 1972. Corr. UN Conf., San Francisco, 1945. Fellow Internat. Inst. Arts and Letters; mem. Natural Food Assos., Natural Hygiene Soc., Madison Conservation Trust, Soc. Women Geographers, Am. Acad. Social, Polit. Sci. Assn. for Asian Studies, Nat. Geog. Soc., Madison Hist. Soc., Soc. Genealogists Eng., Nat. Geneal. Soc., Internat. Platform Assn., Intercontinental Biog. Assn., Eng., Conn. Soc. Genealogists, Antiquarian and Landmarks Soc., Nat. Travel Club, English-Speaking Union, Soil Assn. Eng., Unitarian-Universalist Fellowship. Club: Shoreliners Square Dance. Author (in Chinese translation) Lives of Revolution (biographies), 1938; Women of China, 1938; (in English) Inside Red China, 1939; China Builds for Democracy, 1941; (with Korean, Kim San) Song of Ariran, 1941; The Chinese Labor Movement, 1945; Red Dust, 1952; Fables and Parables, 1952; The Christopher Foster Family History, 1953; The Dameron-Damron Genealogy, 1954; Ancestor Hunting, A Game of Skill and Chance, 1954; The Book of Moody Ancestry, 1958; Historical Notes on China, 6 vols., pub. 1962; My Yenan Notebooks, 1962; Notes on Korea and the Life of Kim San, 1962; Women in Modern China, 1967; Classics and New Adventures in Cooking, 1969; The Chinese Communists: Sketches and Autobiographies of the Old Guard, 1972; also pamphlets and chpts. on China in books and encys.; verse included in various anthologies. Contbr. numerous periodicals U.S., China, Eng., also book reviewer on Far East. Compiled Nym Wales Collection, Hoover Instn., Stanford U., 1958-62. Antiquarian researcher in local history, age of old houses. Certified genealogist. Address: 148 Mungertown Rd Route 1 Madison CT 06443

WALEVSKA, CHRISTINE TERESE, cellist; b. Los Angeles, Mar. 8, 1945; d. Hermann Anton and Marian (McIntyre) Walecki; ed. pvt. tutors; student Conservatoire Nat. Superieur de Musique de Paris, France, 1959-61. Solo cellist on concert tours with symphony orchs. throughout Europe, S.Am.; soloist with Nat. Symphony at Kennedy Center, 1972. Recs. include: Schumann's Cello Concerto, Bloch's Schelomo, Bruch's Kol Nidrei (with Monte Carlo Orch.); (with London Philharmonic) Dvorak Cello Concerto and Tschaikowsky's Rococo Variations, 1971; (with English Chamber Orch.) 2 Haydn Cello Concertos, 1972; (album) The Artistry of Christine Walevska, 1967; records (with Monte Carlo Orch.) Khachaturian Cello Concerto, Prokofiev Cello Concerto (both 1972); complete works for cello and orch. by Camille Saint-Saens, 1973. Home: 1910 Manning Av Los Angeles CA 90025

WALINSKA, ANNA, artist; b. London, Eng., Sept. 8, 1916; d. Ossip Joseph and Rosa (Newman) Walinsky; student Nat Acad. Design, Art Students League, Acad. Andre' L'Hôte, Paris, Grand Chaumiere, Paris; m. Louis Lazarin, May 1954. Founder, dir. Guild Art Gallery,

N.Y.C., 1936-37; asst. dir. Contemporary Art Bldg., World Fair, N.Y.C., 1940; one-man shows retrospective Jewish Mus., N.Y.C., 1957, Gres Gallery, Washington, Mari Gallery, Woodstock, N.Y., 1958, Sunken Meadows Gallery Contemporary Art, L.I., 1958, exhibited art in group shows at Balt. Mus., Mus. Modern Art, N.Y.C., Riverside Mus., N.Y.C., Lending Library Mus. Modern Art, Ann Ross Gallery, Pa. Acad., others including Audubon anns. and Pictures of Year Met. Mus. Art, also traveling shows Paris, Tokyo; tchr. Master Inst. United Arts, N.Y.C., 1956-71; represented in permanent collections throughout U.S., Europe and Asia; portrait painter Eleanor Roosevelt, President Truman, President Johnson, President Kennedy, Burmese Prime Minister U. Nu, others. Recipient First prize Nat. Assn. Women Art, 1957; First Prize Silvermine Guild, 1957; First Prize Soc. Contemporary Arts, 1959, 60. Mem. Am. Soc. Contemporary Artists, Audubon Soc., Nat. Soc. Women Artists, Casein Soc. Illustrator Merry Communist; The Gate Breakers. Home: 875 West End Av New York City NY 10025 Office: 310 Riverside Dr New York City NY 10025

WALKER, ANNE KISSEL, banker; b. Chgo.; d. Nestor and Pauline (Andrews) Kissel; student U. Chgo., 1930; m. Edward Eugene Walker, Aug. 15, 1931 (dec. 1947); 1 son, Lawrence E. With First Nat. Bank, Palm Beach, Fla., 1945—, beginning as sec., successively sec. to bd. dirs., adminstrv. asst., asst. v.p., v.p., 1949-65, v.p., cashier, 1965-69, sr. v.p., cashier, 1969—. Mem. Nat. Assn., Bank Women. Home: 2600 Flagler Dr West Palm Beach FL 33407 Office: 225 S County Rd Palm Beach FL 33481

WALKER, BARBARA BROOKS, journalist; b. Wellesly, Mass.; d. Napoleon Bonaparte Kneass and Maude (Waters) Brooks; student pvt. schs.; m. Harold D. Walker, Jan. 2, 1932 (dec. Apr. 1937). Asst. publicity Greater Boston U.S.O., 1941-45; free lance journalist Boston Globe, Boston Herald Am., Christian Sci. Monitor, others, 1941—; archtl. music and theater critic, Sarasota (Fla.) Jour. and Herald Tribune, 1955-56. Radio WCRB, Boston, 1957-60; tour leader, lectr. Ireland. Chmn. ladies com. Boston Archtl. Center 1938—; workshop leader Star Island (N.H.) Writers' Conf., 1964, 65. Bd. govs. Nicholas House Mus. Mem. Beacon Hill Civic Assn., Boston Council for Internat. Visitors, Boston Soc. Architects (hon.), Mass. Assn. Architects (hon.), Boston Archtl. Center (hon.), Boston Soc. Arts and Crafts, Soc. Descs. of Signers Declaration Independence (gov. Mass. chpt.). Unitarian. Home: 13 Walnut St Boston MA 02105

WALKER, CAROL LEE (MRS. ELBERT A. WALKER), educator; b. Martinez, Cal., Aug. 19, 1935; d. Fred Waldo and Alice Elizabeth (DeVinny) Hardy; B. Mus. Edn., U. Colo., 1957; postgrad. U. Denver, 1957-58; M.S., N.M. State U., 1961, Ph.D., 1963; m. Elbert A. Walker, Dec. 28, 1962; children—Diana Marie, David Elbert, Daniel Lawrence, Elaine Alice. Mem. Inst. Advanced Study, Princeton, N.J., 1963-64; mem. faculty N.M. State U., Las Cruces, 1964—, asso. prof. math., 1966-72, prof., 1972—. Nat. Def. Edn. Act fellow, 1960-63; NSF postdoctoral fellow, 1963-64, research grants, 1964-72. Mem. Am. Math. Soc., Pi Mu Epsilon, Sigma Xi, Phi Kappa Phi. Author: (with F. Richman and R.J. Wisner) Mathematics for the Liberal Arts Student, 1967, 2d edit., 1973; (with F. Richman and E.A. Walker) Trigonometry, 1970. Home: 1801 Imperial Ridge Las Cruces NM 88001

WALKER, SISTER CATHERINE, educator; b. Bartlesville, Okla.; d. Ethan Allen and Lula Mae (Kuhn) Walker; B.A., Our Lady of Lake Coll., 1942, B.S. in L.S., 1947; M.A., Cath. U. Am., 1951; Ph.D., Northwestern U., 1955. Jr. high sch. tchr., Alexandria, La., 1941-46; critic tchr. Demonstration Sch., Our Lady of Lake Coll., San Antonio, 1941-46, prin., dean of girls Demonstration Sch., 1946-53, prof. edn. Grad. Sch. Edn., 1955—, chmn. grad. edn., 1970-72, dir. student personnel services, 1955-63, dir. counselor edn., 1958—. Guidance cons. Nat. Cath. Edn. Assn., 1968-70; exec. sec. Archdiocesan Guidance Council, 1967-71; cons., speaker, panelist at local, state and nat. profl. meetings. Bd. mgrs. United Colls. of San Antonio, 1970-72. Mem. Nat. Cath. Guidance Conf. (dir. 1962-66), Am., Tex. (conv. coordinator 1968) personnel and guidance assns., Tex. Assn. Counselor Educators and Suprs. (sec.-treas. 1967-69, exec. bd. 1970-72), San Antonio Women Deans and Counselors (pres. 1962-63), South Tex. Personnel and Guidance (pres. 1968-69, exec. bd. 1968-73), Tex. Assn. Rehab. Counselors (sec. 1970-72), Pi Lambda Theta. Mem. editorial bd. The Cath. Counselor, 1958-60, asso. editor, 1960-62, chmn. editorial bd. and staff, 1962-65. Contbr. articles to profl. jours. Address: 411 SW 24th St San Antonio TX 78285

WALKER, CLARETA, extension specialist; b. Oswego, Ill., July 11, 1907; d. Fred Lewis and Clara Louise (Smith) Walker;; B.S., Ia. State U., 1932; postgrad. Columbia, 1939; M.S., U. Ill., 1947. Tchr. home econs. Amboy Twp. High Sch., 1933-35; extension adviser Macoupin County, Ill., 1935-42; Ill. rural youth extension specialist, 1942-57; family life extension specialist Univ. Coop. Extension Service and U.S. Dept. Agr., Urbana, Ill., 1957—. Recipient 25-year Service award Internat. Four-H Youth Exchange, 1973. Mem. Am., Ill. home econs. assns., Nat., Ill. (state bd. dirs.) councils on family relations, Am., Ill. assns. univ. profs., Am., Ill. camping assns., Bus. and Profl. Women's Club (state bd. 1944-46), Epsilon Sigma Phi, Gamma Sigma Delta, Phi Sigma, Alpha Gamma Delta. Presbyn. (elder). Home: 612 W Iowa St Urbana IL 61801 Office: 563 Bevier Hall Urbana IL 61801

WALKER, CONSTANCE MAE, librarian; b. Providence, July 22, 1928; d. Bayden Powell and MaeEliza (Hobson) Taylor; B.A., U. Tex. at Austin, 1954, M.L.S., 1956; m. Billy Jack Walker, Nov. 17, 1956. Reference librarian, Houston Pub. Library, 1956-60; asst. librarian South Tex. Jr. Coll., Houston, 1960-67, librarian, 1967—. Mem. A.L.A., Tex. Library Assn. (chmn. scholarship awards com., 1965-66), Phi Beta Kappa, Beta Phi Mu. Home: 8117 Albacore Dr Houston TX 77036 Office: 1 Main St Houston TX 77002

WALKER, DORA FOGARTY (MRS. HAROLD FRANCIS WALKER), librarian; b. New Haven, June 4, 1905; d. James Augustine and Grace (Hyland) Fogarty; B.S., Columbia, 1930; M.A., Yale, 1956, So. Conn. Coll.; diploma U. Conn., 1962; m. Harold Francis Walker, June 28, 1937 (dec. Nov. 1953); children—John James, Margaret Grace (Mrs. Edward Stowell Gaffney), Elizabeth Rose (Mrs. Armand Catelli), Francis Edward. Elementary sch. tchr., West Haven, Conn., 1923-29; training tchr. Danbury State Coll., 1930-42; reading tchr. Haley Sch., West Haven, 1952-57; library tchr. Bailey Jr. High Sch., West Haven, 1957-63; library head West Haven (Conn.) High Sch., 1963-72; sch. library cons., 1957-72; bldg. rep., recreation supr. Lake Clarke Gardens; library cons. St. Luke's Sch. Adminstrv. asst. Col. Park Sch., West Haven, 1951-52; spl. state cons. part-time, 1964-70; asst. prof. So. Conn. State Coll., New Haven, 1960-70. Water safety chmn. A.R.C., West Haven, 1967-72. Mem. Conn. Sch. Library Assn. (pres. 1961-62), Nat. Council Parents and Tchrs. (West Haven v.p. 1956-57), Conn. Ret. Tchrs. Assn., Fla. Ret. Tchrs. Assn., Am. Assn. U. Women, A.L.A., Fla., Southeastern, Catholic library assns., Fla. Assn. for Media in Edn. Club: New England (Lake Worth). Contbr. articles to publs. Home: Lake Clarke Gardens 2811 S Garden Dr Lake Worth FL 33460

WALKER, DORIS BRIN, lawyer; b. Dallas, Apr. 29, 1919; d. Sidney Thomas and Helen (Franklin) Brin; B.A., U. Cal. at Los Angeles, 1939; J.D., U. Cal. at Berkeley, 1942; m. Mason Alexander Roberson, Sept. 12, 1952; 1 dau., Emily Brin. Admitted to Cal. bar, 1942; practice in San Francisco, 1942-63, Oakland, 1963—; partner firm Treuhaft, Walker & Nawi. Mem. Nat. Lawyers Guild (pres. 1970-71), Alameda County Bar Assn. Home: San Francisco Office: 1440 Broadway Oakland CA 94612

WALKER, ELVA MAE DAWSON, cons. health, hosps., aging; b. Everett, Mass., June 29, 1914; d. Charles Edward and Mary Elizabeth (Livingston) Dawson; R.N., Peter Bent Brigham Hosp., Boston, 1937; student Simmons Coll., 1935, U. Minn., 1945-48; m. Walter Willard Walker, Dec. 16, 1939 (div. 1969). Supr. nursery Wesson Maternity Hosp., Springfield, Mass., 1937-38; asst. supr. out-patient dept. Peter Bent Brigham Hosp., Boston, 1938-40; supr. surgery and out-patient dept. Univ. Hosps., Mpls., 1945. Chmn. Gov.'s Citizens Council on Aging, Minn., 1960-68, acting dir., 1962-66, Econ. Opportunity Com. Hennepin County, 1964-69; v.p., treas. Nat. Purity Soap & Chem. Co., 1968-69, pres., 1969—; cons. on aging to Minn. Dept. of Pub. Welfare, 1962-67; mem. nat. adv. Council for Nurse Tng. Act, 1965-69, Com. Status on Women in Armed Services, 1967-70; dir. Nat. Council on the Aging, 1963-67, sec., 1965-67. Dir. Planning Agy. for Hosps. of Met. Mpls., 1963—, United Hosp. Fund of Hennepin County, 1955—, Nat. Council Social Work Edn., 1966-68; vice chmn. Hennepin County Gen. Hosp. Adv. Bd., 1965-68; sec. Hennepin County Health Coalition, 1973; chmn. bd. dirs. Am. Rehab. Found, 1962-68, vice chmn., 1968-70; pres. bd. trustees Northwestern Hosp., 1956-59, Children's Hosp. of Mpls., 1961-65; dir. Twin Cities Internat. Program for Youth Leaders and Social Workers, Inc., 1965-67; mem. Community Adv. council United Community Funds and council of Am., Inc., 1968, Nat. Assembly Social Policy and Devel., Inc., 1968—; mem. priorities determination com. United Fund of Mpls., 1971; vice chmn. govt. specifications com. Soap and Detergent Assn. Candidate for Congress, Third Dist., Minn., 1966. Trustee Macalester Coll., Archie D. and Bertha H. Walker Found.; chmn. St. Mary's Jr. Coll. Bd., 1970-74. Pres. U. Minn. Sch. Nursing Found., 1958-70. Mem. Am. Pub. Welfare Assn., Mpls. Med. Research Found., Minn. League for Nursing (pres. 1971-73), Jr. League of Mpls. Democrat. Presbyn. Home: 3655 Northome Rd Wayzata MN 55391 Office: Nat Purity Soap & Chem Co 110 SE 5th Av Minneapolis MN 55414

WALKER, EMMA MILLS CLEMENT (MRS. SAUNDERS E. WALKER), educator; b. Charlotte, N.C., May 19, 1909; d. George Clinton and Emma (Williams) Clement; A.B., Livingstone Coll., 1930, M.A., Atlanta U., 1941; postgrad. Louisville Municipal Coll.; Ph.D., Ohio State U., 1969; m. Saunders E. Walker, Aug. 28, 1945; 1 dau., Sandra Clementine. Tchr., Dinwiddie (Va.) Normal Sch., 1930-31, Fee High Sch., Maysville, Ky., 1932, Hunt High Sch., Ft. Valley, Ga., 1939-41; faculty Tuskegee Inst., Ala., 1941-67, asst. prof. English, 1943-67, acting chmn. dept. English, 1952-56, 66, 67; prof. coll. edn. achievement project Ft. Valley (Ga.) State Coll., 1967-70, asso. prof. edn., 1970—. Dir. Project Upward Bound, Ft. Valley, 1970-71; dir. communications Ednl. Workshop, U. Tenn., summer 1973. Sec. Peach County Community Action Program, Ft. Valley, 1970—; sec. Macon County (Ala.) Community Action Program, Tuskegee, 1966-67; chmn. adv. bd., pres. Tuskegee YM-YWCA, 1966-67; mem. Am. Security Council. Mem. Am. Assn. U. Profs., Nat. Council Tchrs. English, So. Atlantic Modern Lang. Assn., Am. Assn. Higher Edn., Am. Assn. U. Women, Ala. Tchrs. Coll. English, N.A.A.C.P., Links Inc. (area sec. 1968—), Phi Lambda Theta, Alpha Kappa Alpha, Lambda Iota Tau. Methodist (chmn. missions Ch. Women United 1965-67). Home: PO Box 1633 FVSC Fort Valley GA 31030

WALKER, ESTELLE HARRIS (MRS. MURISS LIVINGSTON WALKER), publisher; b. Duluth, Ga.; d. Jenner Winton and Florence Estelle (Smith) Harris; grad. high sch.; m. Muriss Livingston Walker; children—Mary Frances (Mrs. Alvin Heynen), Barbara Ann (Mrs. Frank Deady), Ralph Harris. Pres., Walker Pub. Co., Inc., Sedalia, Mo., 1971—; pub., editor Fullby mag., 1944—. Mem. Bus. and Profl. Women. Clubs: Altrusa Internat., Knife and Fork. Home: 1217 W 4th St Sedalia MO 65301 Office: 2016 W Main St Sedalia MO 65301

WALKER, ESTHER SUMNER, editor; b. Boulder, Mont.; d. Ernest and Viola (Southworth) Sumner; B.A. with honors, U. Cal. at Los Angeles, 1934; m. Edwin Walker; 1 child, Lynn. Reporter Lynwood (Cal.) Tribune, 1929-37; police reporter, soc. editor San Luis Obispo (Cal.) Telegram-Tribune, 1937-42; police reporter San Jose (Cal.) Mercury-News, 1942-45, woman's editor, 1949—. Recipient Nat. Footwear Inst. top award reporting, 1969, Am. Inst. Men's and Boys' Wear award, 1969, others. Home: 3973 Golf Dr San Jose CA 95127 Office: 750 Ridder Park Dr San Jose CA 95131*

WALKER, EUNICE MIRIAM ARNAUD, writer; b. Monett, Mo., June 17, 1908; d. Emile and Pauline (Barriquand) Arnaud; student Southwest Mo. State U., 1925-26; B.A., U. Ark., 1930; postgrad. George Washington U., 1956; m. Joseph Edward Walker, Nov. 24, 1933; children—Diane (Mrs. David Waldo Edward Smith), Carole Cecile (Mrs. Ross Kenneth Baker). Reporter, feature writer The Monett (Mo.) Times, 1930-31, The Kansas City (Mo.) Star, 1931-33; publs. writer Woodrow Wilson Centennial Celebration Commn., Washington, 1957; pub. relations writer Senator Joseph S. Clark, Washington, 1958-59; asst. pub. relations House of Reps. Com. on Sci. and Astronautics, 1959-61; information specialist U.S. Arms Control and Disarmament Agy., Washington, 1961-65; policy reports officer, Washington, 1965-70; pub. information officer U.S. Dept. Agr., Washington, 1970—; free lance writer, 1956—. Mem. League Women Voters, Nat. League Am. Penwomen, Nat. Fedn. Press Women, Assn. Agr. Coll. Editors, Nat. Hist. Soc., Am. Hist. Soc., Nat. Archives, Smithsonian Assos., Nat. Trust for Historic Preservation, Huguenot Soc. Club: National Press, City Tavern (Washington). Author: Woodrow Wilson, 1958. Contbr. articles to various publs. Home: 205 James Thurber Ct Falls Church VA 22046 Office: US Dept Agr South Bldg Washington DC 20250

WALKER, EVELYN, ednl. radio-tv broadcasting exec.; b. Birmingham, Ala.; d. Preston Lucas and Mattie (Williams) Walker; A.B., Huntingdon Coll., 1927, L.H.D., 1974; postgrad. Cornell U., 1927-29; M.A., U. Ala., 1963, postgrad., 1965—; spl. TV course U. Ill., summer 1953. Tchr. speech Phillips High Sch., Birmingham, Ala., 1930-34; head speech dept. Ramsay High Sch., Birmingham, 1934-52; chmn. schs. radio, TV, 1944—, producer, coordinator TV-radio Birmingham Pub. Schs., 1952-69; head instrnl. TV programming services, 1969—; broadcaster daily childrens program, Birmingham, 1946-57; staff producer Birmingham Ednl. TV Studio for Ala. Ednl. TV Network, 1954—. Mem. Def. Adv. Com. on Women in the Services, 1958-60; chmn. television and radio competition Festival of Arts, 1962-65; bd. dirs. Women's Com. of 100 for Birmingham, 1968—, Ala. Animal League; TV radio co-chmn. Gov's Adv. Bd. to State Safety Com., 1965-68; nat. del. Asian-Am. Women Broadcaster's Conf. 1966; mem. Salvation Army Aux.; audio visual chmn. Birmingham Council P.T.A., 1966—. Bd. dirs. Women's Army Corps Found. Recipient Educator's Medal award Freedoms Found., 1963; Spl. award for the Arts Birmingham Festival of Arts, 1962; Red Cross TV award, 1964; Nat. Headliner award Women in Communications, 1965; Key to City of Birmingham, 1966; Ala. service award Nat. Exchange Club, 1969; named Ala. Woman of Achievement, 1964, Birmingham Woman of Yr., 1965; Ala. Woman of Yr., Progressive Farmer mag., 1966; named hon. col. Ala. militia, hon. lt. a.d.c.; 20-Year Service award Ala. Ednl. Television Commn. Mem. Nat. League Am. Pen Women, Nat. Assn. Ednl. Broadcasters, Am. Women in Radio and Television (local pres. 1959-60; dir.), Marquis Biog. Library Soc., Ala. Hist. Assn., Colonial Dames XVII Century, Daus. Am. Colonists (state TV chmn. 1966—), Noble Order of Crown, Colonial Order of Crown, Am. United Daus. 1812 (TV chmn.), Huntingdon Coll. Alumnae Assn. (achievement award, 1958, 1st nat. v.p. 1959-60, internat. pres. 1961-63, 2d v.p. 1973—), Ams. Royal Descent, Royal Order Garter, Magna Charta Dames (sec.-treas. 1963-64), U.D.C., Plantagenet Soc., Freedom Ednl. Found. (bd. dirs.), Ala. Congress P.T.A. (audio visual chmn. 1966—), Arlington Hist. Assn. (mem. bd. 1969—), Women in Communications, Ala. Dist. Exchange Clubs (hon. life, bronze plaque award 1969), Art Assn., Art Mus., Bot. Soc., Symphony Women, Women for Patriotic Events Ala., Delta Delta Delta Alumna (past local pres). Methodist. Clubs: Press, The Club, Downtown, Birmingham Country. Home: 744 Euclid Av Birmingham AL 35213 Office: Ednl TV 2316 N 7th Av Birmingham AL 35203 also Birmingham Bd Edn PO Drawer 10007 Birmingham AL 35202

WALKER, FAYE EDRICE BALZEN (MRS. JOHN HARMON WALKER), city ofcl.; b. Upper Quibi, Tex., Feb. 12, 1932; d. Walter Gustav and Velma Mary (Bohlen) Balzen; grad. high sch.; m. John Harmon Walker, Sept. 7, 1949; 1 dau., Sandra Faye (Mrs. Ralph Christian Porter). Clk., City of Nondo (Tex), clk., 1952-63, city sec., assessor, collector, 1963—. Club: Band Boosters (sec., treas. Hondo 1968-70). Home: 2908 Av H Hondo TX 78861 Office: 1600 Av M Hondo TX 78861

WALKER, GENE ALDEN (MRS. CLARE J. CRARY), artist; b. New Albany, Ind.; d. Herbert Graham and Clara (Perry) Walker; grad. Pratt Inst., 1920; spl. courses N.A.D., 1940; m. Clare J. Crary, June 30, 1943. Exhibited in one-man shows at Grand Central Galleries, N.Y.C., 1946; exhibited in group shows at N.A.D., Nat. Arts Club, Grand Central Galleries, Allied Artists, Pen and Brush, Am. Water Color Soc., Carnegie Inst., Butler Mus., Phila. Water Color Soc., John Herron Art Inst., Toledo Mus., Speed Mus., Louisville, Wildenstein Galleries; represented in permanent collections N.A.D., N.Y.C., Montgomery Mus. Art, Ala., pvt. collections. Bd. dirs. Watson Meml. Home, The Warren Found. Recipient numerous art awards including Maynard prize for portrait N.A.D., 1943, Cooper prize Nat. Assn. Women Artists, 1943, First prize award John Herron Art Mus., 1950, Portrait prize Nat. Assn. Women Painters, 1946. Mem. Nat. Arts Club, Nat. Assn. Women Artists, Warren Art League, Grand Central Galleries, Allied Artists, Audubon Artists, Pen and Brush. Clubs: Woman's, Warren, Conewango Valley Country, Philomel (Warren, Pa.). Illustrator: Western Range Plant, 1939. Home: 508 Liberty St Warren PA 16365

WALKER, GERTRUDE QUIST (MRS. WALTER HENRY WALKER), city ofcl.; b. Weston, Conn., Sept. 14, 1917; d. Carl Edwin and Jennie Louise (Gustafson) Quist; student Bridgeport U., 1938; m. Walter Henry Walker, June 14, 1941 (dec. Apr. 1970); children—Kathleen (Mrs. Robert R. Boulware) and Kristine (Mrs. James S. Gavitt) (twins), Eileen (Mrs. Henry Jurand) and Kevin Sloane (twins). Ins. sec., salesman Howard Co., Norwalk, Conn., 1937-43, mgr., 1943-45, partner, 1945-50; owner Gertrude Walker, Ins., 1950-69; town clk. Weston, 1945—, clk. Planning and Zoning Commn., 1950-53, 58—, Zoning Bd. Appeals, 1950—; mem. Charter Commn. Weston, 1966-67, charter revision commn., 1971. Mem. town com. Republican party, 1938-40. Mem. Internat. Inst. Municipal Clks., New Eng., Conn. town clks. assns. Home: 4 Whippoorwill Lane Georgetown CT 06829 Office: 56 Norfield Rd Weston CT 06880

WALKER, GRACE MARY CLAYBORNE (MRS. WILBERT L. WALKER), social worker; b. Gloucester, Va.; d. George and Mary Otelia (Carter) Clayborne; A.B., Morgan State Coll., 1946; M.S.W., Atlanta U., 1950; m. Wilbert L. Walker, June 15, 1951; 1 son, Ronald Lee. Caseworker bur. family and children's services Balt. Dept. Social Service, 1950-52, supr. pub. assistance program, 1952-72, supr. services to adults, to families on aid, aid to dependent children, foster care and day care programs, 1972—; field instr. social work Howard U., 1962, 66, head spl. project Work Experience Program, 1967; head spl. project Work Incentive Program, 1969-71. Mem. adv. council Vocational Edn. Balt. City Schs. Recipient Certificate of Appreciation, Balt. City Pub. Schs. Mem. Acad. Certified Social Workers, Md. Conf. Social Welfare, Nat. Council Negro Women, Zeta Phi Beta. Presbyn. Home: 2704 Longwood St Baltimore MD 21216 Office: 1510 Gilford Av Baltimore MD 21202

WALKER, HELEN SMITH, realtor; b. Grovania, Ga.; d. George Washington and Mattie (Ellis) Smith; grad. in Commercial Sci., Ga. Wesleyan Coll., 1938; m. James Lee Walker, Apr. 21, 1946; 1 son, James Kenneth. Sales rep. Thornton Realty Co., Macon, 1959-68; vice-pres. Oneal-Willingham Realty, Macon, 1968-71, mgr. residential sales, 1968-71; asso. broker Fickling & Walker Inc., Macon, Ga., 1971—; co-owner, v.p. Warno Corp., 1964-69; owner, opr. Klondike Farms, Houston County, Ga., 1960—. Mem. State Ga. Make America Better Com., 1971. Mem. Nat. Assn. Real Estate Bds. (v.p. Macon chpt. 1971, women's council), League Women Voters of Macon. Baptist (supt. primary training 1950-65). Clubs: Quota Club Macon (dir. 1972—), Wesleyan Alumnae Club of Macon. Home: 2638 Stanislaus Circle Macon GA 31204 Office: 2378 Ingleside Av Macon GA 31204

WALKER, IRENE ELIZABETH BAKER (MRS. EARNEST ARTMAN WALKER), ret. govt. ofcl.; b. Niagara Falls, N.Y., Dec. 17, 1905; d. Chalice Whitmore and Mattie Louise (Weybright) Baker; student Johns Hopkins, summer 1925; A.B., Goucher Coll., 1927; M.A. (Harriet Remington Laird fellow 1928-29), U. Wis., 1928; postgrad. Am. U., 1949-52; m. Earnest Artman Walker, Aug. 28, 1929; 1 dau., Elizabeth Ann. Teaching asst. dept. history U. Wis., Madison, 1927-29; statistician Rural Electrification Adminstrn., Washington, 1936-42; economist WPB, Washington, 1942-45, policy analyst Civilan Prodn. Adminstrn., Washington, 1945-47; historian Office Chief of Engrs. Def. Dept., Balt., 1947-49; economist AID (and predecessors agy.), Washington, 1949-51, internat. trade and devel. economist, 1951-55, internat. relations officer, 1955-62, sr. mgmt. analyst, 1962-65, supervisory mgmt. analyst, 1965-67, acting chief Program Devel. div. Population Service, Office War on Hunger, AID, 1967-68, chief Program Implementation div., 1968-69, chief Program Grants div., Office Population, 1969-71, asst. dir. spl. projects, 1971-73, chmn. women's adv. com. AID, 1971-72; cons. on women, population and devel. programs, 1973—; sec., congl. rep. Greenbelt Consumer Services, D.C. Area Council, 1974—. Lectr. Career Devel. Sch., 1959-68, Mil. Assistance Inst., Washington, 1960-62; U.S. delegate XIII Pan American Child Congress, Quito, Ecuador, June 1968. Bd. dirs. Internat. Center for Dynamics of Devel., 1973—, Washington Forum. Mem. Soc. Internat. Devel. (pres. Washington chpt. 1969-70, council 1967-73), Polit. Sci. Acad., Am. Econs. Assn., Am. Statis. Assn., Am. Hist. Assn., Am. Assn. U. Women (various chairmanships 1933-42), Phi Delta Gamma (pres. Alpha chpt. 1955-57, 74-75, Nat. achievement award 1972), Goucher Coll. Alumnae Assn. (pres. 1970-71, exec. com. 1968-73), U. Wis. Alumni Assn., Delta Gamma. Methodist. Contbr. monographs and digests to profl. publs. Home: 6903 Carleton Terrace College Park MD 20740 Office: AID Dept State Washington DC 20523

WALKER, ISABELLA BROCKWAY (MRS. WALLACE HAYNES WALKER), artist, printmaker; b. Dunkirk, N.Y.; d. Thomas C. and Isabella (Parmelee) Brockway; student U. Vt., 1920-21; student Boston Mus. Sch. Fine Arts, 1921-25, Boston Designers Art Sch., 1925; m. Wallace Haynes Walker, June 16, 1928; children—Peter Brockway, Clinton Brockway. Cartographic-photo compiler Army Map Service, Washington, 1951-63; free lance illustrator and designer; one man shows Newport Art Assn., Silver Spring (Md.) Art Gallery, Longwood Sch., Arts Club; exhibited group shows D.C. Arts Club, Balt. Art Mus., Newport Art Assn., U. Va., Albany Print Club, Corcoran Gallery, Smithsonian Instn.; represented in permanent collections Nat. Collection of Fine Arts, Smithsonian Instn. Mem. Artists Equity, Washington Art League, Washington Water Color Assn., Arts Club D.C., Washington Print Club, Soc. Washington Printmakers (v.p., acting corr. sec. 1958-73). Home: 5315 Massachusetts Av NW Washington DC 20016

WALKER, JAN KATHERINE, advt. and public relations exec.; b. Jacksonville, Fla., Oct. 1, 1943; d. Thomas Garrett and Florence (Gregory) Walker; B.A. in Internat. Affairs, Fla. State U., 1965. Editor indsl. devel. div. Ga. Inst. Tech., 1965-66; staffer A.P., 1966-69; pub. relations with A.R.C., 1969-70; asst. to dean Sch. Medicine, U. Md., 1971-73; dir. pub. relations Luckie & Forney, Inc., Birmingham, Ala., 1973—. Mem. Women in Communications. Office: PO Box 7484-A Birmingham AL 35223

WALKER, JESSIE, writer; b. Milw.; d. Stuart Richard and Loraine (Freuler) Walker; B.S., Medill Sch. Journalism, Northwestern U., also M.S. First major feature article appeared in The Am. Home mag., 1950, since contbr. numerous articles in nat. mags. including Better Homes and Gardens, McCall's, House and Garden, Good Housekeeping, Parent's, others; midwest editor Am. Home mag.; contbg. editor Better Homes & Gardens. Mem. Ill. Opera Guild; mem. N. Shore jr. bd. Northwestern U. Settlement, 1949-59. Mem. Am. Inst. Decorators, Assn. Home Fashion League, Inc., Theta Sigma Phi. Author: How to Plan a Trend Setting Kitchen, 1962; How to Make Window Decorating Easy, 1969; Shaker Design-150-year-old Modern, 1972; Good Design—What Makes It Last?, 1973; Junking Made Easy, 1974. Address: 241 Fairview Rd Glencoe IL 60022

WALKER, KATHELEEN FAULK (MRS. HERBERT G. WALKER), home economist; b. New Iberia, La., Oct. 23, 1942; d. Dennis and Della Marie (Romero) Faulk; B.S., La. State U., 1964, M.S., 1970; m. Herbert Graham Walker, Oct. 23, 1965; children—Wesley Graham, Cinnamon Jill. Home economist Coop. Extension Service of U.S. Dept. Agr., Opelousas, La., 1964—. Parish dir. March of Dimes; pres. Civic Circle, 1965. Trustee, mem. exec. com. Nat. Kidney Found., 1972-74. Mem. Nat., La. assns. extension home economists, La. Quarter Horse Assn., Opelousas C. of C., La. Fedn. Women's Clubs (dir., rec. sec. 1972—, pres. council 1970), Gen. Fedn. Women's Clubs (home life jr. chmn. 1972-74, dir. jr. clubs 1974-76). Club: Opelousas Garden. Home: PO Box 352 Opelousas LA 70570 Office: PO Box 1030 Opelousas LA 70570

WALKER, LEE ANNE SEVERY (MRS. SCOTT BARTON WALKER), artist; b. Nashville, July 19, d. P. Lee and Sara M. (Baggott) Severy; B.S. in Art, Middle Tenn. State U., 1968; M.A., Peabody Coll., 1972; m. Scott Barton Walker, June 24, 1967. Tchr. art Nashville Met. Schs., 1969-71, Vol. State Community Coll., 1972, Watkins Inst., 1972—; exhibited one-man shows Peabody Coll., 1971, Centennial Park Art Center, 1972; exhibited group shows MTSU Gallery, 1968, Circle Theater Gallery, 1972, Gallery III, 1973, Studio S Gallery, 1973. Active Project Challenge. Recipient Purchase awards Ann. Tenn. Crafts Fair, 1972, 73, Crafts award Vanderbilt Gallery Arts and Antiquies Benefit, 1974. Mem. Tenn. Artists-Craftsmen Assn., Am. Crafts Council, Delta Zeta. Address: Millcreek 217 Margo Lane Nashville TN 37211

WALKER, LILLIAN WALKER, ins. exec.; b. Meridian, Miss., May 8, 1923; d. Rudolph Blanche and Elizabeth (George) Walker; grad. Meridian Jr. Coll.; m. Edward E. Walker, May 25, 1942; children—Edward T., Betti H. Owner, Baton Rouge Agy., 1956—; sec. Southland Concessions, Inc., mem. La. Ho. of Reps., 1964-72, chmn. contingent com., 1964-72; mem. exec. com. Baton Rouge Ins. Exchange. Capt. bldg. fund dr. YMCA, Baton Rouge, 1959, 73; treas. Audubon council Girl Scouts; pres. La. Assn. for Retarded Children, 1960; mem. La. Commn. Status Women. Del. Nat. Democratic Conv., Los Angeles, 1960. Vice pres. South Central region Nat. Assn. Retarded Children, 1972-73; bd. dirs. Baton Rouge chpt. Nat. Arthritis Found. Named Louisianian of Year, La. Assn. Broadcasters, 1964, Baton Rouge First Lady of Year Beta Sigma Phi, 1966; Nike award La. Fedn. Bus. and Profl. Women's Clubs; Man of the Quarter award, Am. Assn. Mental Deficiency; Pub. Ofcl. award. La. Assn. Retarded Children. Mem. Nat. Order Women Legislators, Nat. Soc. State Legislators, Am. Legion Aux., La. Assn. Ins. Agts., Baton Rouge Bus. and Profl. Women's Club (pres.), La. State U. Alumni Fedn. (hon.), Delta Kappa Gamma (hon.). Club: Zonta (dir.) (Baton Rouge). Presbyn. (capt. bldg. fund dr.). Home: 655 Cora Dr Baton Rouge LA 70815 Office: 778 Chevelle Dr Baton Rouge LA 70806

WALKER, LORRAINE, broadcasting exec.; b. Lewistown, Mont., Aug. 28, 1922; d. Irving and Georgia Minta (Pense) Wilber; student Sorbonne U. Paris, 1951-52, George Washington U., 1953; m. James O. Walker, Oct. 2, 1945 (div. June 1957); 1 son, William Warren. Office mgr., R.W. Dean M.D., Great Falls, Mont., 1960-64; account exec. radio sta. KFBB Great Falls, 1964-66; with KCNB radio sta., Reno, 1966—, pres., 1970—, gen. mgr., 1968—, owner, 1970—. Named Nev. Ad Man of Year by Reno Ad Club, 1971. Mem. Nev. Broadcasters Assn. (pres. 1971-72), Reno C. of C. (dir.), Reno Ad Club (1st v.p. 1971-72, pres. 1972-73). Office: 111 N Virginia St Reno NV 89504

WALKER, LUISE ELISABETH, librarian; b. Ferndale, Mich., Nov. 14, 1927; d. James Allen and Luise Melanie (Deutsch-Kussmann) Walker; A.B., U. Wash., 1951; A.M. L.S., U. Mich., 1955; M.S., State U. N.Y. Coll. Forestry, 1961. Head biology librarian U. Notre Dame, 1955-58; head math. librarian Syracuse U., 1958-60; teaching fellow botany State U. N.Y. Coll. Forestry, 1960-61; genetics technician Inst. für Forst Genetik, Schmalenbeck, W. Germany, 1961; head readers services librarian State U. N.Y. Coll. Forestry, 1961-67, editor faculty publs., 1963-67; head sci. librarian Ore., 1967—. Mgr., Walker's Tree Farm, Marlette, Mich., 1951—; mgr. Silverborg's Tree Farm, Lafayette, N.Y., 1962-64. Mem. Mt. Pisgah Arboretum Assn. (charter), Spl. Libraries Assn. (archivist Upstate N.Y. chpt. 1963-67), A.A.A.S., Am. Soc. Icthyologists and Herpetologists, Nat. Rifle Assn. Contbr. monthly column Jour. Forestry, 1965-67. Home: Route 4 Box 319-D Eugene OR 97405

WALKER, MARGOT JEAN (MRS. EDWARD JOHN WALKER), librarian; b. Montreal, Que., Can., Oct. 28, 1944; d. Walter Gordon and Jane (Francis) Donnelly; B.A., McGill U., 1965, M.L.S., 1969; m. Edward John Walker, May 19, 1973. Asst. librarian Imperial Tobacco Products, Ltd., Montreal, 1965-67, corporate librarian, 1969—. Lectr. library tech. Loyola Coll., Montreal, 1972—. Mem. Canadian Library Assn., spl. Libraries Assn., Corporation of Profl. Librarians Que., Nat. Microfilm Assn., Am. Mgmt. Assn., Canadian Mfrs. Assn., Conf. Bd. Home: 5207 MacDonald Montreal PQ Canada H3X 2V9 Office: PO Box 6500 Montreal PQ Canada

WALKER, MARGUERITE LUNDY, sociologist; b. Boise, Ida., Apr. 24, 1898; d. Maurice H. and Mary (Christensen) Lundy; A.B. in Sociology, Mundelein Coll., Chgo., 1934; A.M., Loyola U., Chgo., 1935; Ph.D., U. So. Cal., 1944; m. Louis O. Walker, Aug. 12, 1917. Sr. case worker Chgo. Relief Adminstrn., 1936-37; supr. adult psychiat. clinic Loyola U. Sch. Medicine, 1937-38; mem. faculty Loyola U. Grad. Sch. Social Work, 1937-38; research on adjustment problems of mentally ill in re-establishing selves in community, 1939-44; research analyst Mental Hygiene Soc. Union County, N.J., Plainfield, 1945—, exec. dir., 1945-49; dir. services for Manhattan children's and girls' term cts. Catholic Big Sisters, N.Y.C., 1952-57; cons. Cath. Charities Archdiocese N.Y., 1957-59, dir. research Cath. Charities Guidance Inst., 1959-62. Mem. N.Y.C. Youth Bd., 1959-62, Health and Welfare Council on Juvenile Delinquency, 1959-62, Coordinating Com. Cath. Lay Orgns., 1959-62, Com. for Establishment N.J. Dept. Mental Health, 1945-49. Recipient Cardinal Mundelein Gold Key award, 1934; Achievement award Mundelein Coll., 1957. Life fellow Am. Orthopsychiat. Assn.; mem. Am. Sociol. Soc. (charter), Nat. Assn. Social Workers, Fedn. World Mental Health, Ladies Charity Archdiocese N.Y., Cath. Women's League, Mental Health Assn. Ida., Am. Assn. Retired Persons, Alpha Kappa Delta, Phi Kappa Phi. Contbr. profl. jours. Research incidence and relationship of learning disabilities among emotionally disturbed children. Address: 1808 W Jefferson St Boise ID 83702

WALKER, MAXINE CANFIELD (MRS. JORDAN C. WALKER), real estate broker and developer; b. Boise, Ida., June 29, 1933; d. Max M. and Alice Irene (Chamberlin) Armstrong; student Williamette U., 1950-51, Sacramento Jr. Coll., 1951-52; m. Jordan C. Walker, Aug. 4, 1967; children—Karen Joanne (Mrs. William J. Brown), Mark A. Canfield, Leslie Canfield. Real estate salesman MacBride Realty, Sacramento, 1961-63; propr., broker Canfield and Assos. Realtors, Sacramento, 1963-66; partner Canfield Hurst & Walker Realtors, Sacramento, 1966-67; propr., broker Canfield & Assos. Realtors, Sacramento, 1968—. Mem. Cal. Real Estate Assn., Nat. Assn. Real Estate Bds., Sacramento Bd. Realtors. Home: 4330 Sierra Madre Dr Sacramento CA 95825 Office: Canfield and Associates Realtors 1721 Eastern Av Sacramento CA 95825

WALKER, MILDRED (MRS. MILDRED MERRIFIELD WALKER SCHEMM), writer, educator; b. Phila., May 2, 1905; d. Walter Milliken and Harriet Jane (Merrifield) Walker; B.A., Wells Coll., Aurora, N.Y., 1926; M.A., U. Mich., 1933; m. Ferdinand Ripley Schemm, Oct. 25, 1927; children—Margaret Ripley, George Walker, Christopher Merrifield. Prof. English lit. Wells Coll., Aurora, N.Y., now emeritus prof. Recipient Avery Hopwood award (fiction-essay), U. Mich., 1933. Mem. Phi Beta Kappa. Author: Fireweed, 1934; Light from Arcturus, 1935; Dr. Norton's Wife, 1938; The Brewers' Big horses, 1940; Unless the Wind Turns, 1941; Winter Wheat, 1944; The Quarry, 1947; Medical Meeting, 1949; The Southwest Corner, 1951; The Curlew's Cry, 1955; The Body of a Young Man, 1960; If ALion Could Talk, 1970; A Piece of the World, 1972. Home: Grafton VT 05146

WALKER, PAULINE ELAINE SCHOENAUER (MRS. MARTIN ELDON WALKER), poet; b. Red Lake Falls, Minn., Apr. 23, 1913; d. Paul Edward and Edythe Mae (Demann) Schoenauer; student MacPhail Coll. Music, 1930-31; m. Martin Eldon Walker, Aug. 2, 1948; 1 son, Martin Paul. Pvt. piano tchr., Plummer, Minn., 1934-41; 45-48, Gonvick, Minn., 1946-49, Oklee, Minn., 1945—; asst. to mgr. music dept. Donaldson's Dept. Store, Mpls., 1942-43; contbr. poems to various mags. including Ideals, Pen Grit, The Muse, The Am. Bard, Writer's Notes and Quotes, The Farmer, Haiku Highlights, Haiku West, Modern Haiku, On the Line, numerous others. Mem. bd. Northwest Regional Library, Thief River Falls, Minn., 1968—. Recipient 2d prize Nat. Camellia Poetry Contest Fed. Chaparral Poets, 1968, spl. mention Haiku West, 1970, award, 1971; hon. mention Modern Haiku, 1970, 73. Mem. Am. Legion Aux. Author: The Things I Love, 1973. Address: PO Box 165 Oklee MN 56742

WALKER, PAULINE MINTZ, real estate broker; b. Passaic, N.J., Apr. 2, 1923; d. Frederick and Marie (Perucki) Mintz; student Paterson (N.J.) State Tchrs. Coll., 1940, New Sch. for Social Research, 1953-54, real estate extension courses U. Cal. at Los Angeles, 1960-66; m. Paul Walker, Feb. 28, 1959; children—Lester, Jacqueline, Dale, Maria. Pres. Walker and Assos., Inc., income properties, Rancho Palos Verdes, Cal., 1969—. Mem. Nat. Inst. Real Estate Brokers, Cal. Real Estate Assn., Rolling Hills, Santa Barbara, Torrance bds. realtors. Home: 7325 Via Lorado Rancho Palos Verdes CA 90274 Office: 29941 Hawthorne Blvd Rancho Palos Verdes CA 90274

WALKER, PHYLLIS CUBBERLEY, pathologist; b. Lowell, Mass., Mar. 20, 1922; d. Heber Merle and Marjorie Sparling (Armstrong) Cubberley; A.B., U. So. Cal., 1944, M.D., 1950; m. Owen Ross Walker, Jan. 29, 1949. Resident internal medicine VA hosps., Long Beach, Cal., 1951-53, Seattle, 1953-54; practice medicine Long Beach, Cal., 1955-62; resident pathology Meml. Hosp., Long Beach, 1962-66; pathologist Meml. Hosp., Long Beach, 1966-69; pathologist No. Inyo Hosp., Bishop, Cal., 1969—, chief staff, 1972-74. Fellow A.C.P.; mem. Am., Cal. med. assns., Am. Soc. Clin. Pathologists. Home: Route 1 Rocking K Ranch Bishop CA 93514 Office: No Inyo Hosp Bishop CA 93514

WALKER, ROBERTA HAM (MRS. DAVID HONORE WALKER), health service exec.; b. Sumter S.C., Aug. 20, 1940; d. John Henry and Eliza (Pringle) Ham; B.A., Hampton Inst., 1962; postgrad. Temple U., 1968-70; m. David Honore Walker, Apr. 30, 1966. Speech clinician Easter Seal Soc. Phila., 1962-64, adminstr., 1966—; speech clinician Magee Meml. Rehab. Center, Phila., 1964-66; pvt. practice speech, Phila., 1965-70; cons. speech Inglis House, Phila., 1967—, Parents Network Delaware Valley, 1970-74. Recipient Legion of Honor award Chapel of Four Chaplins, 1973; Service award Optimist Club, 1972. Mem. Council for Exceptional Children, Phila. Speech and Hearing Assn. (v.p. 1965-66), Delaware Valley Assn. for Edn. Young Children, Del. Valley Assn. for Children with Learning Disabilities, Walnut Street Theatre Soc., Piaget Soc., Delta Sigma Theta. Home: 141 Woodshade Dr Newark DE 19711 Office: 2425 N 59th St Philadelphia PA 19131

WALKER, RUTH AMELIA, educator; b. Beacon, N.Y., Nov. 11, 1902; d. Frederick Eugene and Len Willah (Baxter) Walker; grad. Arnold Coll., 1923; student Dickinson Coll., 1924-25, Clark U., 1928-35. Dir. girls phys. edn., Dickinson Coll., 1923-26, YWCA, Carlisle, Pa., 1923-26; exec. dir. health edn. YWCA, Worcester, Mass., 1926-48. Mem. Women's Club, Orleans, Mass., 1950—, mem. scholarship com., 1957-59; membership com. Soroptomist Club, 1946-48; vol. Orleans Women's Community Exchange, 1970—; mem. Friends of Snow Library, Orleans, Mass. Audubron Soc., East African Wildlife Soc. Served as capt. Mass. Women's Def. Corps, 1941-46. Mem. U. Bridgeport Alumni Assn., Hawaiian Malacological Soc., Sierra Club. Clubs: Garden (Orleans); Hyannis (Mass.) Yacht. (asso.). Author articles on health and phys. edn., newspaper articles. Home: Unit 3A Sea Pines Dr Brewster MA 02631

WALKER, SARA ELIZABETH, banker; b. Dalton, Ga., Aug. 2, 1934; d. James Roy and Ruby (Steele) Dantzler; grad. Ga. Banking Sch., 1973; student U. Wis. Banking Sch., 1973—; m. Alvin Francis Walker, Oct. 18, 1952; children—Randall Lee, Joy Lynne. Asst. cashier First Nat. Bank of Dalton, 1970-71, operations officer, 1971—. Adviser Jr. Achievement, 1969-70, 71—. Mem. Nat. Assn. Bank Women, Inc. Home: 210 Royal Oak Dr Dalton GA 30720 Office: PO Box 1088 201 S Hamilton St Dalton GA 30720

WALKER, SHARPE CLEO BELLE, educator; b. LeGrand, Ala., July 25, 1918; d. Augusta Allen and Minnie Lee (Hazzard) Sharpe; B.S. (tuition scholarship), Tuskegee Inst., 1939, M.S., 1954; m. Andrew William Walker, Sr., Oct. 12, 1942; children—Patricia Elaine, Andrew William. Home econs. instr. Indsl. High Sch., Tuscalooga, Ala., 1939-41; home economist Booker T. Washington Sales Agy., Tuskegee (Ala.) Inst., 1941-42; home econs. tchr. Paul L. Dunbar High Sch., Little Rock, 1943; elementary grade tchr. Little Roxanna Elementary Sch., Montgomery, Ala., 1944-46; clothing instr. Tuskegee Inst., 1946-54; home economist Ala. Flour Mill, Decatur, 1955-58; with Ala. Coop. Extension Service, 1958—, Negro dist. home agt. Tuskegee Inst., 1958-65, dist. home demonstration agt. Auburn (Ala.) U., 1965-69, clothing specialist, 1969-71, asso. dist. extension chmn., 1971—. Nat. youth adminstrn. supr. Ala. State Tchrs. Coll., Montgomery, 1941. Mem. N.A.A.C.P., Am., Ala. home econs. assns., Alpha Kappa Mu, Pi Lambda Theta, Zeta Phi Beta. Home: 305 Logan St Tuskegee Inst Tuskegee AL 36088 Office: Duncan Hall Extension Service Bldg Auburn U Auburn AL 36088

WALKER, SHIRLEY CONSTANCE, educator; b. N.Y.C.; d. Harold Edward and Dagmar (McCabe) Cheatum; B.A. cum laude, Howard U., 1947; M.A. in Guidance and Counseling, Hunter Coll., 1956; M.S. in Edn., advanced certificate Bklyn. Coll., 1970; m. Melvin L. Walker, Apr. 4, 1953; 1 dau., Julie Patrice. Mem. staff N.Y.C. Bd. Edn., 1948-71, sch. psychologist Bur. Child Guidance, 1970-71; teaching asst. Bklyn. Coll., 1968-69, sr. counselor HEOP grant, 1969-70; instr. ednl. psychology York Coll., City U. N.Y., Jamaica, 1972—; cons., chmn. Protestant Bd. Guardians Remedial Reading Program for Delinquent Youth, 1963-68. Chmn. art exhibit United Negro Relief, 1963; mem. Flatbush Community Council, 1965-66; mem. guild Bklyn. Home Aged Colored People, 1968-69; chmn. art exhibit Willia Hardgrow Mental Health Clinic, 1966, 67, bd. dirs., 1963—. Mem. Nat. Assn. Sch. Psychologists, N.Y. State Psychol. Assn., N.A.A.C.P., Urban League, Jack and Jill Am., Bklyn. and L.I. Lawyers Wives (pres. 1967-69), Alpha Kappa Alpha. Author children's stories, hist. scripts, also newspaper column. Home: 183 Maple St Brooklyn NY 11225 Office: 150-14 Jamaica Av Jamaica NY 11432

WALKER, SUE ALBERTSON, librarian; b. Bloomsburg, Pa., May 1, 1943; d. Robert Wilson and Sara Ann (Porter) Albertson; B.S. in Edn., Millersville State Coll., 1964; M.S. in Library Sci., Syracuse U., 1967; m. Robert Smith Walker, Apr. 13, 1968. Librarian, Benton (Pa.) Area Sch. Dist., 1964-68; librarian Fairfax County (Va.) Sch. Dist., 1968-72, media coordinator, 1972-73; librarian McCaskey High Sch., Lancaster, Pa., 1973—; cons. Am. Vocational Assn., 1968. Mem. Nat., Va., Pa., Lancaster edn. assns., A.L.A., Pa. Library Assn. Club: Capitol Hill (Washington). Home: 6065 Parkridge Dr East Petersburg PA 17520 Office: Reservoir St Lancaster PA 17601

WALKER, SYLVIA HUTTER (MRS. JOSEPH R. WALKER), educator; b. St. Gallen, Switzerland, June 2, 1932; d. Paul and Laura (Schwegler) Hutter; ; student Conservatory Music, Zurich, Switzerland, 1945-47, Polyclinic Zurich, 1947-48; B.A., U. Cal. at Los Angeles, 1958, M.A., 1965, Ph.D., 1972; m. Joseph R. Walker, Feb. 16, 1950. Came to U.S., 1950, naturalized, 1954. Adminstrv. sec. Bircher Klinic, Zurich, 1948-50, Univ. Elementary Sch., U. Cal. at Los Angeles, 1952-53; teaching asst. U. Cal. at Los Angeles, 1961-63, 64-65, lectr. French, adminstr. Ecole Francaise, French dept., 1966—. Tchr. U.S. Grant High Sch., Los Angeles, 1963-64. Mem. Am. Assn. U. Profs., Am. Assn. Tchrs. French, U. Cal. Womens Faculty Assn., Pi Delta Phi. Home: 15306 Del Gado Dr Sherman Oaks CA 91403 Office: French Dept 405 Hilgard Av Los Angeles CA 90024

WALKER, URSULA GENUNG, ret. editor; b. Kansas City, Mo., Mar. 4, 1913; d. Harry Marion and Clara Louise (Matty) G.; A.B. in Philosophy, U. Mo., 1934; M.A. in English, Northwestern State U., Natchitoches, La., 1968; m. Kenneth J. Walker, June 14, 1941 (dec. 1965); 1 son, Kenneth J. Women's editor Kansas City (Mo.) Jour., 1939-41; mng. editor Bermuda Mid-Ocean News, 1943; editor, pub. Colfax (La.) Chronicle, 1946-58, Natchitoches Enterprise, 1958-65; instr. Lake Sumter Community Coll., Leesburg, Fla., 1968-72; editor Earth Day, newsletter, 1968-72; weekly travel column Journey to the East, 1974—. Pres. La. Press Women, 1966-67. Recipient state and nat. awards for newspaper work. Mem. Am. Studies Assn., Am. Dialect Soc., Modern Lang. Assn., Wilderness Soc., Sierra Club, Common Cause, Kappa Delta Pi, Delta Delta Delta. Address: Hotel Sea View Visakhapatnam 3 India

WALKER, VIRGINIA HARRIET, educator; b. Vossburg, Miss., Jan. 9, 1910; d. Dryden Lamar and Nannie Evelyn (Walker) Walker; diploma Meml. Hosp. Sch. Nursing, 1934; B.S., U. Tenn., 1947; M.A., U. Chgo., 1952; postgrad. Johns Hopkins, 1934, Sloan Hosp. N.Y.C., 1935. Pub. health nurse Miss. State Bd. Health, 1935-40; indsl. nurse, personnel adminstr. Flintkote Co., Meridian, Miss., 1941-45; dir. nursing service, asst. prof. U. Tenn., 1947-52; staff urban life research inst. Tulane U., 1952-54, project dir. research project in nursing function, 1954; asso. dir. Am. Nursing Assn., N.Y.C., 1954-56; dir. nursing, asso. prof. Ind. U., Indpls., 1956-65; asso. prof. nursing U. Tex., Galveston, 1965-70, former acting asst. dean Sch. Nursing; dir. nursing S.W. Gen. Hosp., Berea, O., 1970—. Condr. numerous workshops in nursing adminstrn. and supervision; pub. speaker at profl. meetings. Mem. Ohio Council for Hosps., 1972—. Mem. Indsl. Nurses Assn. (pres. Miss. 1945), Am. (chmn. nurses service adminstr. com. on research 1958-59, 62-64, mem. adv. com. for research critique session for nurses 1964-67), Ohio (com. on nursing service 1970-74), Ind. (award for journalism 1961, 62, 65) nurses assns., Internat. Platform Assn., Sigma Theta Tau. Contbg. Author: Change and Dilemma in Nursing Profession, 1957. Research and publs. on ritualism in nursing, nurse-doctor role relationship. Home: 15642 Indianhead Rd Strongsville OH 44136 Office: SW Gen Hosp Berea OH 44017

WALKER, WANDA HOLLINGSWORTH (MRS. EVERETTE C. WALKER, JR.), educator; b. Oakland, Ark., Mar. 28, 1918; d. Ira and Ollie (Hampton) Hollingsworth; B.A., U. Ark., 1938, M.S., 1950; Ed.D., U. Ark., 1953; m. Everette C. Walker, Jr., Sept. 3, 1938; children—Cloidette (Mrs. Joe Rios), Everette C. III, Bettye Karolyn (Mrs. Tom Strade). Substitute tchr. Flippin, Scranton, Mulberry, 1938-40; girls phys. edn. Rogers, Ark., 1951-53, English and spelling, 1953-55; prof. edn. Miss. State Coll. Starkville, summer 1955; asst. prof. edn. N.W. Mo. State Coll., 1955-60, asso. prof., 1960-66, prof. psychology, 1966—. Dir. psychol. services N.W. Mo. Dist. Office Econ. Opportunity, 1966—. Named Mo. Mother of Year, 1970. Mem.

Am. Assn. U. Women, Mo. State, N.W. Mo. Dist. tchrs. assns., Phi Beta Kappa, Delta Kappa Gamma. Author 2 books on philosophy, psychology; also Walker readiness tests for disadvantaged pre sch. children. Contrbr. articles to profl. jours. Home: 934 W 3d St Maryville MO 64468

WALKER, WILDA LUCINDA NICKELSON (MRS. HARLEY C. WALKER), educator; b. Orion, Okla., Oct. 27, 1919; d. Wesley A. and Ruby (Gould) Nickelson; B.S., Northwestern U., 1940; M.E., Phillips U., 1955; postgrad. (Nat. Def. Edn. Act grantee), U. Colo., 1966; m. Harley C. Walker, Jan. 4, 1943; children—Linda Kay, Joyce Fay. Tchr. Hunter (Okla.) High Sch., 1940-42, Mooreland (Okla.) High Sch., 1944-45, Sun City (Kan.) High Sch., 1945-46, Emerson Jr. High Sch., Enid, Okla., 1955-62, Enid (Okla.) High Sch., 1962—. Instr. creative writing Enid YWCA, 1973—. Mem. Am. Assn. U. Women (dir. creative writing workshops 1964-65, 74—, chmn. com. 1963-64), Nat. League Pen Women (pres. Enid br. 1966-69, 71-73), Okla. Poetry Soc., Okla. Classroom Tchrs. English (state chmn. lit. landmarks com. 1969-73), Nat. Council Tchrs. English, Okla. Fedn. Writers, Enid Writers (pres. 1959-61), Truitteers, Delta Kappa Gamma (chmn. personal growth and services com. 1970-73). Republican. Baptist. Contbr. articles and poetry to various publs. Home: 1216 Indian Dr Enid OK 73701 Office: 611 W Wabash St Enid OK 73701

WALKONEN, HELVI ESTHER, librarian; b. Skandia, Mich., Dec. 16, 1925; d. William and Selma (Lindbergh) Walkonen; A.B., No. Mich. U., 1946; M.A. in English, U. Mich., 1951, M.A. in L.S., 1955. Tchr., Manistique (Mich.) High Sch., 1946-47, 49-52, Ishpeming (Mich.) High Sch., 1947-49, Munich, Germany, 1953-54; head librarian Grosse Pointe (Mich.) High Sch., 1955-63; reference librarian No. Mich. U., 1963-64, head librarian, 1964—, also asso. prof. Mem. A.L.A., Am., Assn. U. Profs., Mich. Library Assn., Delta Kappa Gamma. Club: Zonta. Home: 1519 Lincoln St Marquette MI 49855

WALL, CAROL, librarian; b. N.Y.C., July 5, 1941; d. George and Lillian Marie (Goetz) Wall; B.S., East Stroudsburg State Coll., 1963; M.L.S., State U. N.Y. at Albany, 1966; M.Ed., State U. N.Y. at Oneonta, 1968. Asst. librarian Auburn (N.Y.) Community Coll., 1965-66; circulation and reference librarian Shippensburg (Pa.) State Coll., 1966-67, head reference librarian 1968-70, acting head librarian, 1970-71; undergrad. librarian Kent (O.) State U., 1971—; dir. computerized union list Area Coll. Library Coop., also mem. steering com. Mem. Am. Assn. U. Profs. (sec.-treas. 1969-70), Delta Kappa Gamma. Home: 182 Dale Dr Kent OH 44240

WALL, SISTER CLARE DOLORES, hosp. adminstr.; b. Peterson, N.J.; d. Stephen A. and Anna (Ryan) Wall; student St. Elizabeth's Coll., 1932-40; B.S., Catholic U. Am., 1946; M.A., Seton Hall U., 1952. Tchr. Our Lady of Sorrows Sch., South Orange, N.J., 1934-40, Sch. Nursing, Sanit Raphaels Hosp., New Haven, 1940-43; adminstr. St. Vincent's Hosp., Montclair, N.J., 1946-74. Dir. Hosp. Sch. Practical Nursing, 1953-56. Trustee Pontifical Chair Diocese of Paterson, N.J. Named Woman of Year Montclair N.J. Bus. and Profl. Women's Club, 1967; 1st Ann. Humanitarian award St. Vincent's Hosp., 1968; Outstanding Citizenship award Combined Service Clubs Montclair, 1969. Fellow Am. Coll. Hosp. Adminstrs.; mem. Am., N.J. (pub. relations council 1947-50, trustee 1950-52), Cath. (chmn. state conf. com. 1967) hosp. assns., N.J. Conf. Cath. Hosps. (pres. 1955-57), Internat. Platform Assn., Sigma Theta Tau. Contbr. article to profl. jour. Died Aug. 22, 1974. Address: St Vincent's Hosp 45 Elm St Montclair NJ 07042

WALL, FLORENCE ISABELLE, assn. exec.; b. Antigonish, N.S., Can., July 11, 1919; d. James Martin and Mary Rundle (Brown) Wall; B.A., Mt. St. Vincent U., Halifax, N.S., 1939; diploma in edn. Dalhousie U., 1940; M.A., Columbia, 1957. Tchr. St. Patrick's Boys' Sch., Halifax, 1942-55, vice prin., 56-62, 65-67; prin. St. Stephen's Annex, Halifax, 1955-56; pres. N.S. Tchrs. Union, Halifax, 1962-65, exec. asst., 1967—. Bd. govs. Mt. St. Vincent U., 1968—, chmn. 1971—. Mem. Canadian Coll. of Tchrs., Dalhousie U. Alumni Assn. (pres. womens div. 1952-53). Club: Zonta (Halifax). Editor The Teacher, 1967-69. Home: 6180 Regina Terrace Halifax NS B3H 1N5 Canada Office: 106 Dutch Village Rd Halifax NS B3L 4L7 Canada

WALL, HALLIE WYNNE (MRS. WILLIAM HERBERT WALL), coll. adminstr.; b. Mobile, Ala., Sept. 18, 1944; d. William Winfred and Hallie M. (Botter) Wynne; B.A., U. Ala., 1967, M.A., 1974; m. William Herbert Wall, July 8, 1972. Social worker Dept. Pensions and Security, Mobile County, Ala., 1967-68; area dir. univ. housing U. Ala., University, 1970-71, asst. dir. residence halls, 1971-74, asst. dir. univ. housing, 1974—. Mem. Nat., Ala. (sec. 1971-73, chmn. univ. sect. 1973—, pres. 1974—) assns. women deans, adminstrs. and counselors, Ala. Council Student Personnel Educators (sec., treas. 1973—), League Women Voters, Pi Tau Chi, Alpha Kappa Delta. Club: University Women's (University, Ala.). Home: Box 3234 University AL 35486

WALL, HELEN MARGARET, hosp. adminstr.; b. Akron, O., June 22, 1920; d. Arthur William and Edna Alberta (Norton) Durr; B.A. in Sociology, U. Akron, 1951, M.A. in Spl. Edn., 1969; m. John Christopher Wall, Jan. 15, 1944 (dec. 1967); children—Donavon, Lynne, Jon, Tony, Christopher, Jane, Julie. Tchr. of trainable retarded Summit County, O., 1966-69; curriculum coordinator, asst. prin., 1969-70; dir. retardation services Mental Health and Mental Retardation Center, Wichita Falls, Tex., 1970-73; adminstr. children's services Wichita Falls State Hosp., 1973—. Ednl. cons. spl. edn. Wichita County, 1970-73. Republican precinct capt., 1972. Served to 1st lt. USAAF, 1942-44. Mem. Am. Assn. Mental Deficiency, Council Exptl. Children, Assn. Retarded Children, Childhood Edn. Soc., Tex. Mental Health Assn., Orton Soc., League Women Voters, Zeta Tau Alpha. Soroptimist. Home: 2901 McNiel Av Wichita Falls TX 76309 Office: PO Box 300 Wichita Falls TX 76300

WALL, JEAN MARGARET, lawyer; b. Lansford N.D., May 15, 1919; d. George Edward and Linda Lou (Miller) Wall; B.A., U. Wash., 1947; M.A., Cal. State U. at San Francisco, 1956; J.D., Hastings Coll. Law, U. Cal. at San Francisco, 1970; m. David Ralph Wardell Jordan, Feb. 10, 1941 (dec. Dec. 1959). Advt. copywriter, Seattle and San Francisco, 1945-50; tchr. high sch. bus. and social studies, San Francisco, 1950-69; admitted to Cal. bar, 1969, since practiced privately in San Francisco; legal counsel Mary McCants Stewart Found. Trusts. Asso. mem. San Francisco County and Cal. Republican central coms.; candidate for Cal. Assembly, 1972. Mem. Am., San Francisco bar assns., Am. Assn. U. Women, Cal. Tchrs. Assn., N.E.A., Nat. Assn. Women Lawyers, San Francisco Lawyers Club. Address: 421 Moraga St San Francisco CA 94122

WALL, KATHLEEN JEAN MUNGER, lawyer; b. Mpls., May 11, 1940; d. Byron Frank and Kathleen Iola (Bowles) Munger; student Smith Coll., 1958-59; B.A., U. Minn., 1964; J.D., Hastings Coll. of Law, 1967. Admitted to Nev. bar, 1968; clk. for Chief Justice Nev. Supreme Ct., 1967-69; asst. chief dep. Washoe County Dist. Attys. Office, Reno, 1969—. Mem. Nev. Bar Assn., Nat., Nev. (sec. 1973-74) dist. attys. assns. Home: Star Route 1 Box 734B Carson City NV 89701 Office: Washoe County Courthouse Reno NV 89505

WALL, MARTHA, author; b. Alsen, N.D., Mar. 22, 1910; d. George G. and Christine (Loewen) Wall; grad. Tabor Acad., 1935; student Tabor Coll., 1936-38; R.N., Salem Hosp. Nuses Tng. Sch., 1931; student Alliance Francaise, Moyen Fort, 1950. With Sudan Interior Mission, Nigeria, West Africa, 1939-54, with Katsina Leper Settlement and Bush Dispensary, Jega, 1939-43, with bush dispensaries, Niger, 1943-54. Republican. Author: Splinters from an African Log, 1960; As a Roaring Lion, 1967; In Crossfire of Hate, 1970; Strong Tower, 1970. Contbr. articles to periodicals. Founder Throneroom Messages (religious tape service), 1973. Home: 3710 Gross Rd Santa Cruz CA 95062

WALLACE, ALICE LOCKWOOD INGALLS, educator; b. Washington, Kan., June 12, 1911; d. Claude Eugene and Eleanor (Caldwell) Ingalls; B.S. in Edn., Ore. State U., 1932; M.A. in Speech, Northwestern U., 1938; m. Stanton Willcox Wallace, Aug. 7, 1939; children—Barbara (Mrs. John F. Cullicot), Richard. Tchr., Corvallis (Ore.) High Sch., 1932-38, 42-47; exchange tchr. Central High Sch., Honolulu, 1936-37; mem. faculty Augustana Coll., Rock Island, Ill., 1938-39; mem. faculty Ore. State U., Corvallis, 1954—, asst. prof. speech communication, 1960—; speaker before many groups. Mem. alumni bd. dirs. Ore. State U. Mem. Am. Assn. U. Women, Speech Assn. Am., Western, Ore. speech assns., Phi Kappa Phi, Theta Sigma Phi, Kappa Delta Pi, Delta Sigma Rho, Zeta Phi Eta, Pi Beta Phi. Clubs: Corvallis Woman's; Faculty Women's Ore. State U. (pres. 1971-72). Contbr. articles. Home: 3855 SW Fairhaven St Corvallis OR 97330

WALLACE, ALICEANNE, city govt. ofcl.; b. Chgo., Sept. 28, 1925; d. Alexander and Mary (Zurek) Zalac; student De Paul U. Secretarial Sch., 1943, St. Teresa Coll., Winona, Minn., 1944-45, DePaul U., 1945-46, DePaul U. Law Sch., 1946-48; m. Henry Clay Wallace, Jr., Apr. 10, 1948; children—Laura (Mrs. Houston L. Cavin), Christine Claire. Legal sec. to attys. in Chgo. and Dallas, 1945-50; real estate broker, Irving, Tex., 1955-63; city sec., Southlake, Tex., 1969—. Certified municipal clk., Tex. Mem. Assn. City Clks. and Secretaries Tex. Home: 1616 E Continental Blvd Southlake TX 76051 Office: 667 N Carroll Av Southlake TX 76051

WALLACE, ANNA BYRD HARNESS (MRS. WILLIAM JEWELL WALLACE), univ dean; b. Colorado City, Tex., May 9, 1914; d. Conrad Tutt and Lillian (Blandford) Harness; B.A., Tex. Christian U., 1935; postgrad. U. Houston, 1947-48, U. Ariz., 1957-58; M.Ed., Trinity U., 1950-53; m. William Jewell Wallace, Mar. 8, 1935; 1 son, William Warren. Tchr., Tech. High Sch., El Paso, 1935-36; sec. El Paso High Sch., 1936-39; dir. Christian edn. Central Christian Ch., San Antonio, 1948-51; tchr., counselor San Antonio pub. schs., 1951-57; tchr., Tucson, 1957-58; dir. admissions Tex. Christian U., Fort Worth, 1958-68, asso. dean admissions, 1968-72, dean admissions, 1972—. Mem. Tex. Guidance and Personnel Assn., Am., Tex. assns. collegiate registrars and admission officers, Nat. Assn. Coll. Admissions Counselors (sec.), Great Plains Assn. Coll. Admissions Counselors, Tex. Christian U. Women's Ex-Student Assn. (co-founder Houston chpt. 1947, pres. Fort Worth chpt. 1963-65), Alpha Delta Kappa (past pres.). Mem. Christian Ch. (bd. deaconesses 1965-67, mem. gen. bd. 1965-67). Home: 4407 Bellaire Dr S Apt 114 Fort Worth TX 76109

WALLACE, BARBARA DAN, librarian; b. Arlington, Mass., Jan. 2, 1945; d. Dan and Elizabeth Ann (Criger) Wallace; B.A., Northwestern State Coll., 1967; M.S., La. State U., 1968; postgrad. U. Wyo., 1969. Page, br. asst. Shreve Meml. Library, Shreveport, La., 1962-63; children's librarian Barksdale AFB, La., summers 1965-66; monitor library Northwestern State Coll., 1963-67; librarian Lincoln Elementary Sch., Rock Springs, Wyo., 1968-70; vis. lectr. library sci. U. Wyo., summers 1969-70; librarian Johnson AFB, Japan, 1970-73; librarian Taegu (Korea) Am. Sch., 1973-74, Ansbach (Germany) Am. Sch., 1974—. Instr. U. Md. Far East Div., Yokota AFB, Japan. Mem. Wyo. Edn. Evaluation Team, 1969. Mem. Am. Assn. U. Women, Wyo. Library Assn., Phi Kappa Phi, Sigma Kappa. Methodist. Mem. Internat. Order Rainbow Girls. Club: Kanto Plains Aero (Yokota AFB). Home: 261 E Fairview St Shreveport LA 71104 Office: Ansbach American Sch APO New York City NY 09177

WALLACE, CLEO SPURLOCK (MRS. THOMAS R. WALLACE), adminstr.; b. Garo, Colo., July 29, 1914; d. Guy H. and Edith (Swope) Spurlock; B.A., U. Denver, 1937, M.A., 1943; m. Thomas R. Wallace, Sept. 4, 1937 (dec. July 1948). Founder, exec. dir. Wallace Village for Children, Broomfield, Colo., 1943—. Instr. U. Colo., 1949-58; cons. Switzer Center, Hermosa Beach, Cal., 1970; mem. Nat. Adv. Neurol. Diseases and Stroke Council, 1972—. Mem. White House Conf. on Services for Handicapped Children, 1950; mem. Gov.'s Commn. on Licensure of Child Care Instns., 1971—. Recipient Evans award U. Denver, 1955, Anthonian award St. Anthony Hosp., 1961. Mem. Assn. Med. Rehab. Dirs. and Coordinators, Royal Soc. Health, Colo. Assn. Child Care Instns. (sec.), Rosacrucian Order, Sertoma Internat. Home: 6795 W 26th Av Denver CO 80214 Office: PO Box 345 Broomfield CO 80020

WALLACE, CONNIE WADDELL (MRS. LAWRENCE DOUGLAS WALLACE), educator; b. Spangler, Pa., Aug. 25, 1942; d. Charles Edward and Gladys (Plymale) Waddell; B.S., M.A., W.Va. U.; m. Lawrence Douglas Wallace, Aug. 28, 1965. Counselor, counselor supr. U. Houston Placement Center, 1965-67; asst. dean women U. Houston, 1967-70, asst. dean students, 1970-74, asso. dean students, 1974—. Mem. adv. bd. Tex. Statewide Coordinating Bd. Project in Continuing Edn. for Women, 1973—. Mem. Nat., Tex. (univ. sect. recorder 1969) assn. womens deans and counselors, Nat. Assn. Student Personnel Adminstrs., Am. Coll. Personnel Assn., Am., Houston (sec. 1968-69) personnel and guidance assns., Mortar Bd. (sect. coordinator 1970-73, nat. 1st v.p. 1973-76), Delta Gamma, Kappa Delta Pi, Alpha Lambda Delta (hon.), Gamma Sigma Sigma (hon.). Home: 719 Seamaster Houston TX 77058

WALLACE, FRANCES MARIAN (MRS. DEANE D. WALLACE), savs. and loan assn. exec.; b. Lovelock, Nev., Oct. 10, 1917; d. John R. and Estelle (Sullivan) Russell; student Wash. State U., 1935-37; m. Deane D. Wallace, Nov. 29, 1945; children—Michael, Scott, Catherine, Deane Thomas, Susan. Pvt. sec. to pres. Western Gear Works, 1937-44; founder Capital Savs. & Loan Assn., Little Rock, 1962, sec., dir., 1962—. Chmn. Ark. State Savs. and Loan Bd., 1962; gen. mgr., ins. and tax adminstr., trustee profit sharing plan Obstetrics and Gynecology, Profl. Assn. Inc. Vice chmn. program com. of bd. govs. Am. Nat. Red Cross, 1966—; active United Fund, 1966—, co-campaign chmn., 1965. Trustee Ark. Art Center, St. Joseph's Orphanage, North Hills Exceptional Children's Sch., United Community Funds and Councils Am. Named Woman of Year, Ark. Democrat newspaper, Little Rock, 1965; hon. mem. City of San Diego, 1965, City of Oklahoma City, 1966. Home: 6 Edgehill Rd Little Rock AR 72207 Office: 500 S University Little Rock AR 72207

WALLACE, GLENN WALKER (MRS. JOHN MCCHRYSTAL WALLACE), civic worker; b. Salt Lake City; d. Mathew Henry and Angelena (Andrews) Walker; student Rowland Hall Sch. for Girls, 1905-13; grad. Miss Winsors Sch., Boston, 1916; D. Arts and Humanities (hon.), Westminster Coll.; L.H.D., Coll. Eastern Utah; m. John McChrystal Wallace, Sept. 18, 1920; children—Mathew Walker, John McChrystal. Founder, Utah Symphony, Salt Lake City, 1939-40, pres., 1947-52; mem. bd. Utah Art Inst., Salt Lake City, 1938-52; mem. Jr. League of Boston, Jr. League of Salt Lake, 1916 Sewing Circle Boston; assisted in organizing civic music; founder, pres. Ballet West. Decorated Grand Cross Dame Knightly Order St. Brigette; Order St. Jonh Jerusalem; named Woman of Year, to Hall of Fame, Salt Lake Council Women, 1968; Outstanding Community Leadership in the Arts award Am. Assn. U. Woman. Mem. Phi Beta Kappa (hon.). Republican. Clubs: Altrusa (hon.); Francisca (San Francisco). Home: 2520 Walker Lane Salt Lake City UT 84117

WALLACE, HELEN MARGARET, physician, educator; b. Hoosick Falls, N.Y., Feb. 18, 1913; d. Jonas and Ray (Schweizer) Wallace; A.B., Wellesley Coll., 1933; M.D., Columbia, 1937; M.P.H., cum laude, Harvard, 1943. Intern Bellevue Hosp., N.Y.C., 1938-40; child hygiene physician Conn. Health Dept., 1941-42; successively jr. health officer, health officer, chief maternity and new born div., dir. bur. for handicapped children N.Y.C. Health Dept., 1943-55; prof., dir. dept. pub. health N.Y. Med. Coll., 1955-56; prof. maternal and child health U. Minn. Sch. Pub. Health, 1956-59; chief profl. tng. U.S. Childrens Bur., 1959-60, chief of child health studies, 1961-62; prof. maternal and child health U. Cal. Sch. Pub. Health, Berkeley, 1962—. Dir. Knudson Corp. Cons. WHO in Uganda, 1961, Phillipines, 1966, 68, India, 1969, 70, Geneva, Switzerland, 1969, 70, 74, Iran, 1972; cons. U.S. Office Child Devel.; cons. to Panama Canal Zone, 1972; mem. med. adv. bd. Planned Parenthood Assn. Bd. dirs. Nat. League for Nursing, United Cerebal Palsy. Recipient traveling fellowship WHO. Fellow Am. Acad. Pediatrics, Am. Pub. Health Assn. (gov. council, chmn. med. adv. com.); mem. A.M.A., Am. Women's Med. Assn. (asst. editor jour.) Author: Health Services for Mothers and Children. Editorial bd. Human Sexuality Jour. Home: 1515 Oxford St Berkeley CA 93305

WALLACE, JANE YOUNG (MRS. DONALD H. WALLACE), editor; b. Geneseo, Ill., Feb. 17, 1933; d. Worling R. and Margaret C. (McBroom) Young; B.S. in Journalism, Northwestern U., 1955, M.S. in Journalism, 1956; m. Donald H. Wallace, Aug. 24, 1959; children—Robert, Julia. Editor House organ Libby McNeill & Libby, Chgo., 1956-58; prodn. editor Instns. Mag., Chgo., 1958-61, food editor, 1961-65, mng. editor, 1965-68, editor-in-chief, 1968—. Cons. Nat. Restaurant Assn., Nat. Inst. for Food Service Industry. Mem. U.S. Dept. Edn. Com. Investigation Vocational Needs for Food Service Tng., 1969; pres. Instnl. Food Editors' Conf., 1967. Recipient Jesse H. Neal award for best bus. press editorial, 1969, 73. Mem. Soc. for Advancement Food Service Research, Am. Inst. Interior Designers (asso.), Women in Communications (v.p. Chgo. 1957-58), Gamma Phi Beta, Kappa Tau Alpha. Editor: The Professional Chef, 1962; The Professional Chefs Book of Buffets, 1965. Contbr. to World Book Ency., 1974. Home: 186 Signal Hill Rd Barrington IL 60010 Office: 5 S Wabash Av Chicago IL 60603

WALLACE, JOAN EDAIRE SCOTT (MRS. JOHN WALLACE), social scientist; b. Chgo., Nov. 8, 1930; d. William Edouard and Esther (Fulks) Scott; A.B. with honors, Bradley U., 1952; M.S.W., Columbia, 1954; postgrad. U. Chgo. Sch. Social Service Adminstrn., 1963-64; Ph.D. in Psychology, Northwestern U., 1973; m. John H. Wallace, June 12, 1954; children—Mark Scott, Eric Matthew, Victor Paul. Social worker St. Mary's Home for Children, 1954-58, casework dir., 1965-67, also field instr.; social worker United Charities Family Service Bur., 1959-61; social work analyst Midway research project U. Chgo. Sch. Social Service Adminstrn., 1962-65; asso. prof. social work Jane Addams Grad. Sch. Social Work U. Ill., Chgo. Circle campus, 1967-73; lectr. psychology Barat Coll., U. Ill.; asso. dean, prof. Howard U. Sch. Social Work, Washington, 1973—. Mem. planning com. Midwest region Child Welfare League, 1968, 70; mem. council on tng., com. on short courses for child care workers Child Care Assn. Ill., 1967-68, bd. dirs., 1968-69, chmn. adoption sect., 1967-69, chmn. adoption workshop, 1968-69; chmn. planning com. Inst. Child Care Workers, 1968; bd. execs. Wilmette (Ill.) Human Relations Com., 1968-69; mem. adv. com. Fish (vols. in social service), 1969; mem. adv. com. Project for Emergency Care of Children, 1968-69; mem. Ill. Welfare Assn., 1967-69; mem. Council on Social Work Edn., 1968—; mem. Psychologists for Social Action, 1969-73. Cons. dept. children and family services Wilmette Schs., Ill. Children's Home and Aid Soc. Chmn. sect. Child Welfare League Conf., 1968; coordinator Inst. Child Care Workers, 1968. Vol. Wilmette Urban Gateways. Trustee St. Mary's Services for Children. Recipient Robert S. Abbott award, 1948; Episcopal Service for Youth fellowship in social work, 1952-54; Northwestern U. fellowship for grad. study, 1969-70; Outstanding Educators award, 1971. Mem. Nat. Assn. Social Workers, (membership com. Chgo. chpt. 1968-69, sec. North Suburban br. 1967-69), Acad. Certified Social Workers, Soc. for Psychol. Study Social Issues, Am. Sociol. Assn., Assn. Black Psychologists, Pi Gamma Mu. Home: 12118 Quorn Lane Reston VA 22091 Office: Howard University School Social Work Washington DC 20001

WALLACE, JOYCE IRENE MALAKOFF (MRS. LANCE ARTHUR WALLACE), physician; b. Phila., Nov. 25, 1940; d. Samuel Leonard and Henrietta (Hameroff) Malakoff; A.B., Queens Coll., City U. N.Y., 1961; postgrad. Columbia, 1962-64; M.D, State U. N.Y., 1968; m. Lance Arthur Wallace, Aug. 30, 1964; 1 dau., Julia Ruth. Intern St. Vincent's Hosp. Med. Center, N.Y.C., 1968-70; resident Manhattan VA Hosp., N.Y.C. and Nassau County Med. Center, East Meadow, N.Y., 1972-73; practice medicine specializing in internal medicine, N.Y.C., 1970-72, North Conway, N.H., 1974—; family physician Central Manhattan Med. Group, 1970-71; mem. attending staff Nassau County Med. Center, 1974. Asso. mem. Girl Scout Council Greater N.Y. Mem. Am. Med. Women's Assn., N.Y. County, N.Y. State med. socs. Address: Box J Intervale Rd North Conway NH 03860

WALLACE, JOYCE JEAN, educator; b. Louisville, Nov. 15; s. Sammy Lee and Martha (Winters) Wallace, Sr.; B.S., Jackson State Coll., 1971; M.A., Northwestern U., 1972. Instr. speech and drama Mary Holmes Coll., West Point, Miss., 1972—. Dir. Black Arts Theater, West Point, 1972—; oral interpreter local schs. Mem. Speech Communication Assn., People United to Save Humanity, Am. Assn. U. Profs. Home: 144 Afro Dr Kosciusko MS 39090 Office: Drama Dept Mary Holmes College West Point MS 39773

WALLACE, LAVERNA FAYE ICE (MRS. HAROLD BLAINE WALLACE), occupational therapist cons.; b. Lawrence, Kan., Apr. 4, 1924; d. La Vern Dexter and Lola Faye (Tobler) Ice; B.S., U. Kan., 1946; m. Harold Blaine Wallace, Oct. 20, 1946; children—Gary Alan, Karen Jean. Staff therapist VA Center, Wadsworth, Kan., 1946-48; dir. occupational therapy Kan. U. Med. Center, Kansas City, Kan., 1948-51, cons. occupational therapist, home care unit, 1963-70; dir. occupational therapy Florence Crittendon Home, Kansas City, Mo., 1956; occupational therapy cons. Jewish Geriatrics and Convalescent Center, Kansas City, Mo., 1970—, Cath. Family and Community Services, Kansas City, Mo., 1971—, Hillhaven Convalescent Center, Kansas City, Mo., 1971—. Asst. prof. preventive medicine Kan. U., Kansas City, Mo., 1966-70; mem. Kan. regional med. program Interprofl. Council of Related Health Profession, 1969-71; cons., lectr. occupational therapy dept. Kan. U., Lawrence, 1971; cons., instr. Research Hosp., 1972-73. Mem. adv. bd. Wyandotte County chpt. Am. Cancer Soc., 1966-70, Cath. Family and Community Services,

1969-71, Greater Kan. City Conf. Student Profl. Orgns., 1969-70. Mem. Am., Kan. (pres. 1948-50) occupational therapy assns., World Fedn. Occupational Therapy, Allied Health Profls. Arthritis Found., Kan. Pub. Health Assn. Home: 9002 Switzer St Overland Park KS 66214 Office: 7801 Holmes St Kansas City MO 64131

WALLACE, LILA ACHESON, editor; b. Virden, Man., Can.; d. Thomas Davis and Mary E. (Huston) Acheson; student Ward-Belmont Coll.; A.B., U. Ore.; m. DeWitt Wallace, Oct. 15, 1921. Co-founder (with husband) Reader's Digest. Presbyn. Home: High Winds Mount Kisco NY 10549 Office: Pleasantville NY 10570

WALLACE, MARY JAMIESON, journalist; b. Ann Arbor, Mich., Apr. 20, 1937; d. Clark Bostwick and Marion Cecilia (Crippen) Jamieson; B.A., Coll. William and Mary, 1959; M.A., U. Mich., 1962; m. Victor L. Wallace, June 23, 1962. Reporter, Ann Arbor News, 1962-69; bur. chief Orange County Bur., Durham Herald-Sun Papers, Chapel Hill, N.C., 1971—. Lectr. journalism U. N.C., 1973-74. Publicity chmn. Chapel Hill League Women Voters, 1971. Mem. Women in Communications. Home: 338 Wesley Dr Chapel Hill NC 27514 Office: 412 W Franklin St Chapel Hill NC 27514

WALLACE, MIRIAM, advt. co. exec.; b. Englewood, N.J., Apr. 7, 1932; d. Jerome and Helen (Hirsch) Kolberg; B.A., N.Y. U., 1954; 1 son, David. Asst. radio-TV comml. bus. mgr. Batten, Barton Durstine & Osborne, Inc., N.Y.C., 1955-62; talent agt. Lester Lewis Assos., N.Y.C., 1964-68; with Ted Bates & Co., Inc., N.Y.C., 1968—, v.p. in charge radio-TV comml. bus. affairs, 1973—; pres. Channelex, Inc., Calla Music, Inc., N.Y.C., 1973—. Home: 165 E 32d St New York City NY 10016 Office: 1515 Broadway New York City NY 10036

WALLACE, NAN JOY, realtor; b. King City, Cal., Aug. 28, 1914; d. Richard A. and Magdalene (Mather) Joy; grad. pub. schs.; m. Lawrence Wallace, Dec. 3, 1941; children—Gerald R., Barbara Joy. Adminstrv. sec. Glen Taylor Sch., Walnut Creek, Cal., 1949-51; saleswoman Lawrence Wallace, Realtor, Clayton, Cal., 1951-67, Clayton Real Estate Co., 1967-70, real estate broker, 1969—, owner, 1970—. Pres. bd. Mt. Diablo Therapy Center. Home: 1525 N Mitchell Canyon Clayton CA 94517 Office: 6000 Main St Clayton CA 94517

WALLACE, SARA KLIER (MRS. JACOB WALLACE), lawyer; b. Warsaw, Poland; d. Abraham and Rose (Mochedlover) Klier; came to U.S., 1911, naturalized, 1920; LL.B. magna cum laude, Portia Law Sch., 1930; m. Jacob Wallace, Aug. 23, 1931; children—David H., Marjorie Ruth (Mrs. Ira M. Potell), Deborah Ellen (Mrs. Roger D. Feldman). Admitted to Mass. bar, 1930; practiced in Boston, Brookline, Mass., 1930-40, 63—; spl. legal counsel Town of Brookline, 1964—, Federally Assisted Code Enforcement Program, 1966—. Mem. corp. Brookline Savs. Bank, 1971—. Vice chmn. Brookline Redevel. Authority, 1957-59; pres. Brookline Community Council, 1961-67; chmn. Brookline Community Action Program, 1966-70; vice chmn. Regional Anti-Poverty Program, 1967-70; mem. Mass. Meat and Pultry Hearing Bd., 1970—. mem. Town of Brookline Town Town meeting, 1958-72, adviser, 1958-66; mem. corporation Children's Hosp. Med. Center, 1946—. Mem. Mass. Bar Assn., Mass. Assn. Women Lawyers, League Women Voters (pres. 1952-56). Home: 115 Tappan St Brookline MA 02146 Office: 1674 Beacon St Brookline MA 02146

WALLACE, SARAH LESLIE, librarian; b. Kansas City, Mo., Oct. 28, 1914; d. Leslie Linn and Mary Louise (Shortall) Wallace; A.B., Coll. St. Catherine, 1935, B.S. in L.S., 1936. With Mpls. Pub. Library, 1936-63, pub. relations officer, 1958-63; publs. officer Library of Congress, Washington, 1963—. Instr. Coll. St. Catherine, 1944-60. Recipient St. Joan of Arc award Jr. Catholic League Mpls., 1963, Horace Hart award Edn. Council of Graphic Arts Industry, 1969, Alexandrine award Coll. St. Catherine, 1972. Mem. A.L.A. (membership chmn. 1962-63), D.C. Library Assn., Franklin Tech. Soc., Am. Inst. Graphic Arts, Fed. Editors Assn., Typophiles, Delta Phi Lambda, Kappa Gamma Pi. Author: So You Want To Be a Librarian, 1963; Definition: Library, 1961. Author, illustrator: Promotion Ideas for Small Public Libraries, 1953; Patrons Are People, 1956. Editor Quarterly Jour. Library of Congress, 1964—, Friends of Libraries. Home: 8705 Jones Mill Rd Washington DC 20015 Office: 10 1st St SE Washington DC 20540

WALLACE, VICTORIA, librarian; b. Wilkes-Barre, Pa., Sept. 26, 1933; d. Stephen and Josephine (Zurinsky) Zavatsky; B.Edn., Wilkes Coll., 1956; M.L.S., Pratt Inst., 1957-58. Sr. librarian Bklyn. Pub. Library, 1959-61; reference librarian Long Beach (N.Y.) Pub. Library, 1961-62; mem. library staff Northport (N.Y.) Pub. Library, 1962—, asst. dir., 1964-69, dir., 1969—. Librarian U.S. exhibit N.Y. World's Fair, 1964; field reader U.S. Office Edn., 1969—. Mem. Suffolk County (mem. exec. bd. 1964-70; editor Data jour. 1968-69), Am. (life; chmn. subcom. on Spanish materials, mem. membership task force, task force on pub. library standards), N.Y. (chmn. exhibits com. 1974—), Suffolk (chmn. exhibits com. 1974—) library assns., Suffolk County Dirs. Assn. (pres.). Home: 21 Bluff Point Rd Northport NY 11768 Office: 151 Laurel Av Northport NY 11768

WALLACE, VIRGINIA CHARLOTTE, publishing co. exec.; b. Dayton, O., Nov. 27, 1936; d. George Noble and Charlotte (Koring) Wallace; B.A., Denison U., 1958; m. John Stuart Beltz, Dec. 28, 1959 (div. Nov. 1971). Copywriter Halle Bros., Cleve., 1958-59; promotion asst. Highlights for Children, 1966; copy dir. Kight Cowman Abram, Columbus, O., 1959-65, account exec., 1968-73, pub. relations dir., 1971-73; communications/advt. dir. Zaner-Bloser, Inc., Columbus, 1973—. Mem. Columbus Soc. for Communicating Arts, Pi Beta Phi, Pi Delta Epsilon. Home: 184 E Willow St Columbus OH 43206 Office: 612 N Park St Columbus OH 43215

WALLACE, VIRGINIA WILSON (MRS. PAUL MACLELLAN WALLACE), club woman, educator; b. Waterloo, Ia., July 6, 1905; d. Edwin C. and Ellen (Cheseborough) Wilson; student U. Sask., 1926; B.A., U. Ia., 1930; M.A., U. Louisville, 1948; postgrad. Ind U., 1950-55; m. Paul Maclellan Wallace, July 17, 1930; 1 dau., Mary Wallbridge. Instr. U. Louisville, 1946-48; instr., lectr. Ind. U. Extension, 1948—. Mem. bd. Young Artists' Promotions, Inc. Mem. lit. com. Women's Club, 1942—; mem. Am. Assn. U. Profs., Am. Assn. U. Women, Arts Club, Monday Afternoon Club, Waldorf Sch. Assn., Internat. Order St. Luke, Internat. Platform Assn., So. Modern Lang. Assn., Nat. Council Tchrs. English, N.E.A,, Friends Camphill Movement, Pi Beta Phi, RotaryAnne, Ky. Opera Assn., 1955—, Jr. Art Gallery, 1950—, Women's Assn. Louisville Orch., 1949—; active A.R.C., 1944—; mem. Frontier Nursing Assn., 1935—; mem. hostess com. Farmington Found., 1961—; mem. women's bd. Norton Meml. Infirmary 1961—; mem. Jr. League, 1933—; mem. Nat. Soc. Colonial Dames Am. Episcopalian (charter mem. ch. 1945). Club: Hunting Creek Country. Author: articles in Coll. English, 1953. Home: 6505 Deep Creek Rd Hunting Creek Prospect KY 40059

WALLACE, VITALIA LEOLA (MRS. VINCENT ASTOR WALLACE), coll. dean; b. St. Thomas, V.I., Feb. 23, 1921; d. Henry and Delphine (Lindo) Richards; B.S. with highest honors, Hampton Inst., 1960; M.A., N.Y. U., 1965; m. Vincent Astor Wallace, Aug. 27, 1943; children—Vivian (Mrs. Liston Lewis), Valia (Mrs. Edward Clausell), Vincent Astor, Vernon, Vance, Viggo. Elementary tchr. Deischer's Pvt., Abraham Lincoln, Dober, George Washington Schs., 1938-44; secondary sch. tchr. Charlotte Amalie High Sch., St. Thomas, 1944-58, guidance counselor, 1958-60; coordinator guidance services V.I. Dept. Edn., 1960-63, dir. elementary schs., 1963-71; asso. dean, asso. prof. edn., financial aid officer Coll. V.I., St. Thomas, 1971—. Sec., Vocational Adv. Council V.I., 1973-74. Mem. N.E.A., Assn. Elementary Sch. Prins., Assn. Financial Aid Officers. Home: 2BA-3 Caret Bay Estates St Thomas VI 00801

WALLAS, LEE STEINBACH, artist; b. St. Louis, Feb. 10, 1911; d. Bernard and Mary (Brown) Steinbach; B.F.A., Wash. U., 1962, MFA, 1967; m. Seymour Jacob Wallas, May 1, 1936; children—Charles Henry, Eugenie. One-woman exhbns. include Harmon Gallery, St. Louis, 1962, Martin Schweig Gallery, St. Louis, 1963, Little Gallery, Kansas City, Mo., 1962, Contemporary Gallery, Kansas City, 1971, Ellis Art Center, Springfield, Mo., 1965; group exhbns. include Nelson-Atkins Mus., Kansas City, 1971, Joslyn Mus., Omaha, 1965, Ark. Art Center, Little Rock, 1965; rep. Mo. Pavillion at N.Y. World's Fair, 1964; traveling exhbn. 10 Mo. Painters, 1970-71; asso. with Painters Gallery, St. Louis, 1965-70. Recipient Purchase prize Springfield Art Mus., 1961, 62; medal of honor and Herbert Lehman award Nat. assn. Women Artists, 1964. Address: 4534 Pershing St St Louis MO 63108

WALLBROWN, JANE DOWNS (MRS. FRED HAROLD WALLBROWN), psychologist; b. New Brunswick, N.J., Sept. 27, 1935; d. Eulius Sheldon and Gladys Minor (Hall) Downs; B.A., Coll. Wooster, 1957; M.A., Ohio State U., 1959, Ph.D., 1972; m. Fred Harold Wallbrown, Aug. 6, 1973; 1 son (by previous marriage), Laurence Dean Rupp; stepchildren—Grace Marie, Amelia Ruth, Frank Frederick. Tchr. pub. schs., Sterling, O., 1957-58, Columbus, O., 1958-59; counselor jr. high sch., Weston, Mass., 1959-62; dormitory dir. Boston U., 1963-65; counselor elementary schs., Columbus, 1969-71; intern sch. psychologist Columbus Pub. Sch. System, 1971-72; sch. psychologist pub. schs., Worthington, O., 1972—. Lectr. Ohio State U., Columbus, 1972—; pvt. practice as psychologist, Columbus, 1972—. Mem. Council for Exceptional Children, Nat. Assn. Sch. Psychologists. Contbr. articles to profl. jours. Home: 871 Sheridan Av Columbus OH 43209 Office: 55 E Stafford St Worthington OH 43085

WALLE, PAULINE ANN, editor; b. Duluth, Minn., Jan. 23, 1936; d. Michael Paul and Josephine Margaret (Lewkiewicz) Walle; B.A., U. Minn., 1958. Women's editor Hibbing (Minn.) Daily Tribune, 1958-59; news service and alumni asst. U. Minn., Duluth, 1959-62, acting dir. United Campus Christian Fellowship, 1961-62; area editor Rochester (Minn.) Post-Bull., 1962-63, family editor, 1963—. Recipient awards Minn. Press Women. Mem. Minn. Press Women (treas. 1963-64). Methodist (mem. ofcl. bd. 1966-69). Home: 104 SW 16th Av Rochester MN 55901 Office: 18 SE 1st Av Rochester MN 55901

WALLEN, MARY ELIZABETH GRIER, psychologist; b. Waukesha, Wis., June 27, 1912; d. James Harold and Edith Rozetta (Jacobson) Grier; A.B., U. Chgo., 1936, M.S., 1938, Ph.D., 1947; m. Lawrence Jacques, 1938 (div. 1953); m. 2d, Richard Wallen, 1956 (div. 1969). Research fellow, instr. com. on human devel. and div. psychiatry U. Chgo., 1942-47; supervisory psychologist VA, Chgo., 1947-56, Cleve., 1956-67; chief psychologist youth services area C div. human resources Community Mental Health Center, Washington, 1968—. Fellow Cleve. Gestalt Inst., 1964-68. Pres. bd. govs. S.W. Day Care Assn., 1973-74. Mem. Am. Psychol. Assn. (fellow div. clin. abnormal psychology), Am. Orthopsychiat. Assn., Internat. Council Psychology, Parents without Partners. Mem. P.E. Ch. Club: Americana. Home: 560 N St SW Washington DC 20024 Office: 1905 E St SE Washington DC 20003

WALLER, CAROLYN ALLISON (MRS. ROWELL LUCIAN WALLER), librarian; b. East Providence, R.I., July 16, 1925; d. Walter Allen and Eva May (Luther) Adams; A.B., Brown U., 1946; M.S. in L.S., Columbia, 1952; m. Rowell Lucian Waller, June 6, 1953; children—Susan (Mrs. Alfred A. Quattrucci), Elizabeth Adams. Asst. librarian Pembroke Coll., Brown U., Providence, 1946-49, librarian, 1949-51, 52-53; librarian cons. nursing and med. library Roger Williams Gen. Hosp., Providence, 1959-60, Providence Lying-In Hosp., 1961-67, Providence Child Guidance Clinic, 1966-67; med. librarian Emma Pendleton Bradley Hosp., Riverside, R.I., 1967—. Bd. trustees Library, Seekonk, Mass., 1961-67, chmn., 1962-67; bd. dirs. Tannerhill, Inc., Providence, 1973—. Mem. New Eng. Library Assn. (hosp. sect. v.p. 1973, pres. 1974), R.I. Med. and Health Scis. Librarians. Conglist. Home: 17 Bradley St Seekonk MA 02771 Office: 1011 Veterans Memorial Pkwy Riverside RI 02915

WALLER, CARRIE ELLEN MCLAIN (MRS. J.C. WALLER, JR.), city ofcl.; b. Van Alstyne, Tex., Mar. 3, 1932; d. George Carry Dine And Amy Ellen (Russell) McLain; grad. high sch.; m. J.C. Waller, Jr., Oct. 2, 1970; children—Joe Henry, Elliott. Owner, Carrie's Dept. Store, Van Alstyne, 1969-70; sec. Howe (Tex.) State Bank, 1970—, asst. cashier, 1974—; first city councilwoman, Howe, Tex., 1972-74. Mem. Grayson County (Tex.) Bicentennial Com., 1974—. Bd. dirs., treas. Cannon Cemetery Assn., 1970—; bd. dirs. Grayson County Mental Health and Mental Retardation Assn., 1972-73. Designer, first ofcl. flag Howe, Tex., 1972, Centennial Seal, Howe, 1972. Mem. Howe C. of C. (dir., sec., treas. 1971-74), Howe Young Homemakers. Methodist. Clubs Band Booster (reporter, author by-laws 1973-74), Bulldog Booster (sec., treas. 1973-74), Sesame (Howe, Tex.). Author, editor: Howe's Centennial Book, 1972. Home: 609 Farmington Rd Box 335 Howe TX 75059 Office: 100 S Denney St Box 428 Howe TX 75059

WALLER, CLARELLA FREEMAN (MRS. LEONARD HARMON WALLER), city ofcl.; b. Oklaunion, Tex., Dec. 13, 1913; d. Ransom Wilbur and Amanda Maurine (Anderson) Freeman; student Draughon's Bus. Coll., 1928-29; m. Leonard Harmon Waller, Oct. 3, 1932 (dec.); children—Anna Maureene (Mrs. R.W. Capt), Mary Kathryn (Mrs. John R. White Jr.). Asst. bookkeeper Piggy Wiggly Store, Freeport, Tex., 1940-42; mgr. grocery store, Whitsett, Tex., 1932-34; bookkeeper Ruth's Dress Shop, Palacious, Tex., 1954-60; various clerical jobs Internat. Harvester Co., Three Rivers, Tex., 1945-48; city sec., tax assessor collector, Three Rivers, 1967—. Baptist (sec. 1934). Home: 303 Hill St Three Rivers TX 78071 Office: Hwy 72 and 281 Three Rivers TX 78071

WALLER, SISTER MARY CONCETTA, educator; b. Louisville, June 25, 1914; d. Andrew and Emma (Jacob) Waller; B.S., Creighton U., 1944; M.S., Marquette U., 1950; Ph.D., St. Louis U., 1961. Tchr., St. Martin Sch., Louisville, 1935-37, Blessed Sacrament Sch., Omaha, 1937-44; instr. chemistry Ursuline Coll., Louisville, 1951-57, 61-62, pres., 1962-64; prof. chemistry Bellarmine Coll., Louisville, 1965-68; mem. gen. council Ursuline Sisters Governmental Structure, Louisville, 1968—. Exec. sec., trustee Ursuline Soc. and Acad. of Edn., 1968-72, 2d v.p., 1972—. NSF grantee, 1960, 64-65; NSF fellow, 1957-58. Mem. Ky. Chemistry Tchrs. Assn. (pres. 1955-56, adv. bd. 1956-57), Am. Chem. Soc., Nat. Assn. Women Religious, Ky. Acad. Sci (sect. pres. 1957-58), Soc. Am. Archivists, Sigma Xi. Contbr. articles to profl. jours. Address: 3105 Lexington Rd Louisville KY 40206

WALLER, PATRICIA FOSSUM (MRS. MARCUS B. WALLER), psychologist; b. Winnipeg, Man., Can., Oct. 12, 1932 (parent Am. citizen); d. Magnus Samuel and Diana (Briggs) F.; A.B. cum laude, U. Miami, 1953, M.S., 1955; Ph.D., U. N.C., 1959; m. Marcus B. Waller, Dec. 27, 1957; children—Anna, Justin, Martha, Benjamin. Psychology intern VA Hosp., Roanoke, Va., 1956; instr. psychology N.C. Meml. Hosp., 1957; USPHS research fellow R.B. Jackson Meml. Lab., Bar Harbor, Me., 1958-60; staff psychologist VA Hosp., Brockton, Mass., 1961-62; lectr., research asso. U. N.C., Chapel Hill, 1962-64, lectr. at Greensboro, 1964-65; staff asso. U. N.C. Hwy. Safety Research Center, 1967—, also asso. prof. Sch. Pub. Health, U. N.C., Chapel Hill, 1970—. Mem. Am., Eastern, Southeastern, N.C. psychol. assns., A.A.A.S., Soc. Projective Techniques, Sigma Xi. Contbr. articles to profl. jours. Home: Rt 1 Box 394 Chapel Hill NC 27514

WALLER, WILHELMINE KIRBY (MRS. THOMAS MERCER WALLER), civic worker, orgn. ofcl.; b. N.Y.C., Jan. 19, 1914; d. Gustavus Town and Wilhelmine (Claflin) Kirby; ed. Chapin Sch., N.Y.C.; m. Thomas Mercer Waller, Apr. 7, 1942. Conservation chmn. Garden Club Am., 1959-61, pres., 1965-68, dir., 1968-71, chmn. nat. affairs com., 1968-74; mem. adv. com. N.Y. State Conservation Commn., 1959-70, dist. dir. Soil and Water Conservation, Westchester County, 1967—; mem. Nat. Adv. Com. Hwy. Beautification, 1965-68; mem. Lyndhurst council Nat. Trust Historic Preservation, 1965-74; mem. Conservation Adv. Council, Bedford, N.Y., 1968-70; mem. Westchester County Planning Bd., 1970—; dir. Westchester Council Social Agys., 1970-72; mem. Rachel Carson council Nat. Audubon Soc., 1964—; v.p. Bedford (N.Y.) Farmers Club, 1954—; mem. planning bd., Bedford, 1953-57; mem. adv. com. to sec. of state UN Conf. on Human Environment, 1971-72; mem. N.Y. State Parks Adv. Com., 1971-72; adviser Gov. Rockefeller's Study Commn. Future of Adirondacks, 1968-70; mem. Citizens Adv. Com. on Environmental Quality, 1973—. Bd. govs. Nature Conservancy; trustee Mianus River Gorge, Arthur W. Butler Meml. Sanctuary. Mem. Nat. Soc. Colonial Dames, Huguenot Soc. Am., Daus. Cincinnati. Episcopalian. Club: Colony (N.Y.C.). Address: Tanrackin Farm Bedford Hills NY 10507

WALLERSTEIN, JUDITH HANNAH SARETSKY (MRS. ROBERT S. WALLERSTEIN), social worker; b. N.Y.C., Dec. 27, 1921; d. Samuel and Augusta (Tucker) Saretsky; B.A. cum laude, Hunter Coll., 1943; M.S.W., Columbia U. Sch. Social Work, 1946; postgrad. Topeka Inst. for Psychoanalysis, 1955-61; m. Robert S. Wallerstein, Jan. 26, 1947; children—Michael Jonathan, Nina Beth, Amy Lisa. Asst. dir. Residential Treatment Center, Community Service Soc., N.Y.C., 1945-47; sr. psychiat. social worker, child therapist Menninger Found., Topeka, 1949-57; instr. Kan. U., Lawrence, 1965-66; lectr. U. Cal. Sch. Social Welfare, Berkeley, 1966—. Sr. cons. Community Mental Health Center, Marin County (Cal.), 1968—, prin. investigator Children of Divorce Project, 1970—; lect. dept. psychiatry U. Amsterdam, Holland, 1967; lectr. Paul Baerwald Sch. Social Welfare, Jerusalem, 1970. Bd. dirs. Homewood Terrace Adolescent Treatment Center, San Francisco, 1971-73. Recipient Distinguished Teaching award U. Cal. at Berkeley, 1970-71. Mem. Assn. for Child Psychoanalysis, Am. Orthopsychiat. Assn., Nat. Assn. Social Workers. Contbr. articles to profl. jours. Home: 290 Beach Rd Belvedere CA 94920 Office: Sch Social Welfare U Cal Berkeley CA 94720

WALLEY, HELEN J. VENOVITCH (MRS. ZENIS M. WALLEY), psychologist; b. Spirit Lake, Ida., Oct. 12, 1932; d. John and Mary (Rom) Venovitch; B.A., U. Cal. at Berkeley, 1959; M.S., Cal. State Coll., 1964; m. Zenis M. Walley, July 4, 1969; 1 step-son, Zenis M. Faculty English, Coll. of Guam, Agana, 1960-62; tchr., counselor Livermore (Cal.) High Sch., 1962-64; counselor James Logan High Sch., Union City, Cal., 1964-65, Santa Maria (Cal.) Joint Union High Sch. Dist., 1965-68; psychologist, dir. alcohol abuse program Community Mental Health Center, San Luis Obispo, Cal., 1968—; lectr. in field; Mem. exec. bd. Middle House, 1972—; mem. Coordinating Councils of All Areas of San Luis Obispo County, 1969—. Bd. dirs. A.R.C., 1966-69. Mem. Am. Assn. U. Women, Am. Personnel and Guidance Assn., Cal. Counseling and Guidance Assn., Bus. and Profl. Womens Club, Ladies Fleet Res. Assn., Nat. Council on Alcoholism. Mem. Order Eastern Star. Club: Minerva. Contbr. articles to profl. jours. Home: PO Box 276 Arroyo Grande CA 93420 Office: 2180 Johnson Av San Luis Obispo CA 93401 also 108 Bridge St Arroyo Grande CA 93420

WALLHAUSEN, MILDRED CAROLYN, newspaper publisher; b. Bklyn., Apr. 3, 1914; d. James Meroe and Frances (Bronson) Savell; grad. Brown's Bus. Coll., 1932; m. Arthur Louis Wallhausen, Sept. 25, 1936; children—Arthur Louis, Elizabeth (Mrs. James Anderson). Sec. to real estate co., N.Y.C., 1932-33; proofreader Daily Am. Republic, Poplar Bluff, Mo., 1933-36; co-owner Enterprise-Courier, Charleston, Mo., 1936—; dir. Cape Central Pub. Co. Mem. Gov. Mo. Adv. Council Comprehensive Health Planning, 1969-73; mem. Bootheel Comprehensive Health Planning Council, 1971—, Community Pub. Health Service Task Force, 1973, Mental Health Task Force, 1973, Regional Planning Commn., 1972-73, Charleston Park and Recreation bd., 1972-73; mem. bd. Sr. Citizen Housing Project, 1973; mem. rev. team for grants Mo. Div. Mental Health, 1972—; pres. Eugene Field Sch. P.T.A., 1948, Charleston High Sch. P.T.A., 1953; pres. Mississippi County Tb Assn., 1945-53, Mississippi County Child Welfare Council, 1971—. Bd. dirs. S.E. Archaeol. Assn., Mississippi County Cancer Soc., Mississippi County Recreation Assn. Recipient various awards for service; named Woman of Year, BPW Club, Charleston, 1973. Mem. Am. Legion Aux. Clubs: Athena Study (pres. 1955), K. Boone Music (Charleston). Lutheran (Sunday sch. tchr.). Home: 108 S Gilmore St Charleston MO 63834 Office: 206 S Main St Charleston MO 63824

WALLIN, JEAN ROGERS, polit. party worker; b. Hibbing, Minn., Jan. 13, 1934; d. William John and Rhea (Madison) Rogers; m. Donald Frank Wallin, June 12, 1954; children—Rikka Louise, Amy Suzanne. Mem. N.H. Ho. of Reps., 1967-70. Mem. Nashua (N.H.) Sch. Bd., 1968—, pres., 1974—. Del., mem. rules com. Dem. Nat. Conv., 1968; mem. Dem. Nat. Com., 1968-73; mem. credentials com. Dem. Nat. Conv., 1972; del. to Dem. Mid-year Conf., 1974; del. to N.H. Constl. Conv., 1974—. Mem. N.H. Civil Liberties Union, League of Women Voters, Order of Women Legislators. Home: 3 Durham St Nashua NH 03060

WALLING, GENEVA C. (MRS. LEDFORD WALLING), assn. exec.; b. St. Matthews, S.C., Oct. 3, 1927; d. Frank A. and Jessie (Rucker) Crim; grad. high sch.; m. Ledford W. Walling, Nov. 28, 1946; 1 son, Glenn Wilson. Sec., Shep Pearlstine Co., St. Matthews, 1945-48, Hicklin Motor Line, St. Matthews, 1955-64; exec. sec. Calhoun County C. of C., St. Matthews, 1964—. Mem. adv. com. Orangeburg-Calhoun Tech. Edn. Center, 1971-72, Home Health Services, Calhoun, Orangeburg and Bamberg counties, 1971-72; exec. sec. Calhoun County Planning Commn.; community and civic affairs chmn. Calhoun County Extension Council, Clemson U., 1969—; mem. Calhoun County Heart Unit; mem. Calhoun County Mental Retardation Commn., 1972; mem. comprehensive health planning com. Lower Savannah Regional Planning Council, 1973-74. Methodist (past treas. ch.). Club: St. Matthews Garden Council (pres.,

1968-69). Home: Route 1 Box 161A St Matthews SC 29135 Office: Railroad Av St Matthews SC 29135

WALLINGFORD, FRANCES AMBROSE (MRS. CHARLES A. WALLINGFORD), musician, educator; b. Eldorado, Kan., Dec. 28, 1904; d. George Franklyn and Ida (Scott) Ambrose; B.Mus., Southwestern Coll., Winfield, Kan., 1932, B.A., 1933; M.Mus., Wichita State U., 1956; m. Charles A. Wallingford, Dec. 24, 1939. Tchr. class piano El Dorado (Kan.) Pub. Schs., 1926-28; tchr. piano, history of music Southwestern Coll., Winfield, Kan., 1930-39; asst. prof. Wichita State U., 1963-72, asso. prof., 1972—; mem. Miller-Wellingford, one piano fourhand team recitalists and clinicians, 1953—. Vice pres., mem. exec. bd. Wichita Civic Music Assn., 1963—. Recipient award Internat. Piano Technicians, 1971. Mem. Kan. Music Tchrs. Assn. (state certification chmn. 1965—), Music Tchrs. Nat. Assn., Nat. Fedn. Music Clubs, Wichita Area Piano Tchrs. League, P.E.O., Sigma Alpha Iota. Episcopalian. Author: Piano Materials Syllabus, 1969. Contbr. articles to profl. jours. Home: 207 N Taylor St El Dorado KS 67042 Office: Wichita State U Wichita KS 67208

WALLIS, BONNIE RUTH LOW (MRS. RANDALL WALLIS), TV performer; b. Lake City, Ia.; d. Harold A. and Tena (Schulte) Low; B.S., U. Ida., 1934, postgrad., 1934; m. Randall Wallis, Apr. 6, 1935. Driver for base adj., Gowen Field, Boise, Ida., 1942-43; receptionist, 1944-46; star Bonnie Wallis Show, KBOI TV Sta., Boise, 1954—. Gray lady VA Hosp., Boise, 1946-48; chmn. Jr. Red Cross, Boise, 1949-52; mem. Def. Adv. Com. on Women in Services, 1963-66; active YWCA, Boise; mem. Legal Tenders, 1969. Mem. St. Lukes Hosp. Aux., 1967—. Recipient TV Native Son award Allied Stores, Boise, 1958, TV award as best local personality, 1958; March of Dimes Service award, 1964. Mem. Alpha Phi. Club: Internat. of Boise. Author: Bonnie's Cook Book, 1957. Home: 807 Wyndemere Dr Boise ID 83702 Office: Sta KBOI 10th and Jeffersons Sts Boise ID 83702

WALLIS, MARIE POPE, free-lance writer; b. Des Moines, July 18, 1901; d. Elwyn Almer and Adelaide (Harless) Pope; B.A., U. Cal. at Los Angeles, 1925; M.A., U. So. Cal., 1928, M.S. in Social Work, 1935; Ph.D., U. N.M., 1947, M.A., 1960; M.L.S., U. Okla., 1959; postgrad. U. Mexico, 1939, U. P.R., 1940, U. Mich., 1943, U. San Marcos, Lima Peru, 1941, U. Hawaii, 1963, 68, 73-74; M.A., N.M. State U., 1972. Profl. actress, N.Y., N.J., Cal., 1926-28, 31-33; dir. Wallis Players, Los Angeles, 1930-31; supr., dist. dir. Cal. Relief Adminstrn., Los Angeles, 1933-38; zone dir. WPA, Albuquerque, 1938-39; dir. social service tng., field rep. Sch. Inter-Am. Affairs, U. N.M., Albuquerque, 1942-44; welfare officer UNRRA, Europe, 1945; cons. N.M. Community Service, Santa Fe, 1951-52; asst. prof. Spanish and Portuguese, U. N.M., 1939-42, 45-50; prof. English, IBEU, Rio, 1950-51; librarian Sandia High Sch., Albuquerque, 1960-61, Taos (N.M.) High Sch., 1961-62, A. Montoya Sch., Albuquerque, 1962-64, Principia Coll., 1964-65; dir. Instructional Materials Center, Bur. Indian Affairs, Ft. Wingate, N.M., 1965-66; library coordinator, Hawaii, extension librarian Okinawa, 1966-67; media librarian dept. ednl. communications U. Hawaii, Honolulu, 1968-69; prof. speech El Paso Coll., 1969-70; free-lance writer, 1969—. Counselor, WAC, 1944-45; program chmn. Albuquerque Girl Scout Bd., 1946-49; mem. Albuquerque Civic Recreation Commn., 1948-49; cons. N.M. Commn. on Children and Youth, 1951-52; v.p. N.M. Conf. on Social Welfare, 1951-52; coordinator women's activities N.M. wing Civil Air Patrol, 1952-56; chmn. City-County In-Service Tng. Com., Socorro, N.M., 1953-54; mem. N.M. migratory Labor Conf., 1952-53; mem. N.M. Civil Def. Com. on Women's Activities, 1951-53. B'nai B'rith fellow in intercultural relations, 1957; recipient numerous other fellowship and scholarship awards. Mem. N.E.A., Am. Library Assn., Am. Assn. Social Workers (sec. N.M.), Mus. Navaho Ceremonial Art, D.A.R., Albuquerque Hist. Soc. (pres. 1963), Internat. Platform Assn., Travelers Century Club, Am. Legion, Mortar Bd., Phi Kappa Phi, Alpha Kappa Delta, Theta Alpha Phi, Tau Kappa Alpha, Sigma Delta Pi, Phi Sigma Iota, Pi Lambda Theta, Delta Kappa Gamma, Sigma Alpha Iota, Phi Alpha Theta, Alpha Epsilon Rho, Phi Delta Gamma. Author: Intersection, 1950. Contbr. articles to profl. jours. Address: Star Route 2 Box 59 Socorro NM 87801

WALLIS, SHARON KAPLAN (MRS. CHARLES S. WALLIS), lawyer; b. Phila., July 26, 1943; d. Louis S. and Kathryn (Madden) Kaplan; B.A., St. John's Coll., 1964; LL.B. (Reginald Heber Smith fellow), U. Pa., 1967; m. Charles S. Wallis, Mar. 14, 1970. Admitted to Pa. bar, 1968; staff atty., head housing law reform Community Legal Services, Inc., Phila., 1967-69; staff atty. Lawyers Com. for Civil Rights Under Law, Phila., 1969-70; pvt. practice law, Phila., 1970—. Supervising atty. N. Phila. Tenant Union, 1969—; lectr. U. Pa. Law Sch., Phila., 1973; lectr., cons. Temple U. Law Sch., Phila., 1973. Pres., Phila. Womens Polit. Caucus, 1971—; mem. Democrat Ward Exec. Com., 1971—. Recipient Human Rights award Phila. Human Relations Commn., 1973. Mem. Phila. Bar Assn. (chmn. consumer protection com. 1972), U. Pa. Law Alumni Soc. (treas. 1972-74). Address: 640 Rodman St Philadelphia PA 19147

WALLNER, MARY (MRS. FRANK WALLNER), Democratic nat. committeewoman. Art. tchr., pub. schs.; mgr. Dem. Hdqrs. Polit. Campaigns, S.D., 1958, 60; mem. S.D. Dem. Exec. Com.; Dem. nat. committeewoman from S.D., 1964—. Treas. S.D. Arts Council Bd. dirs. Sioux Falls Civic Fine Arts Center, Minnehaha County unit Am. Cancer Soc. Mem. Sioux Empire Arts Council, St. Mary's Altar Soc., Garden Hobbyists (v.p.). Address: 2605 Poplar Dr Sioux Falls SD 57105

WALLOCH, BETSY OGLESBY, psychiatrist; b. Ft. Smith, Ark., May 10, 1934; d. Charles W. and Mary Elizabeth (Robinson) Oglesby; student Little Rock U., 1957-59; B.S. in Medicine, M.D., U. Ark., 1963; m. Bob L. Walloch, Apr. 15, 1952 (div.); children—Robert Lee, Sandra Lynn, Kim Alan. Intern Ark. Bapt. Hosp., Little Rock, 1963-64; resident in gen. psychiatry U. Ark. Med. Center at Little Rock, 1964-66; resident in child psychiatry Children's Med. Center, Tulsa, 1966-68; practice medicine specializing in child and adolescent psychiatry Tulsa, 1968—; med. dir. Parkwood Clinic, 1972—; cons. Moton Health Center, 1969—, Tulsa County Juvenile Ct., 1968—; med. dir. Employer's Protective Life Assurance Co., Little Rock, 1966-67; dir. Hydroflow Corp., Little Rock. Bd. dirs. Tulsa County Assn. for Mental Health. Mem. Tulsa County Psychiat. Soc. (v.p. 1972—), Mid-Continent Psychiat. Assn., Am. Soc. Psychotherapy and Expression, Phi Theta Kappa. Office: 5579 S Lewis Av Tulsa OK 74105

WALLOP, LUCILLE FLETCHER (MRS. JOHN DOUGLASS WALLOP III), author; b. Bklyn., Mar. 28, 1912; d. Matthew Emerson and Violet Marie (Anderson) Fletcher; B.A., Vassar Coll., 1933; m. John Douglass Wallop III, Jan. 6, 1949; children—Dorothy Louise Herrmann, Wendy Elizabeth Hermann. With publicity dept. CBS, N.Y.C.; writer radio scripts, including Sorry Wrong Number, motion picture scripts, Broadway play, Night Watch. Author: The Daughters of Jasper Clay; Blindfold; And Presumed Dead; The Strange Blue Yawl; The Girl in Cabin B54. Address: Oxford MD 21654

WALLOWER, LUCILLE, author, librarian; b. Waynesboro, Pa., July 27, 1910; d. Roland Custer and Grace (Werdebaugh) Wallower; student Pa. Mus. Sch. Art, 1928-31, Traphagen Sch. Fashion, 1946. Sch. librarian Harrisburg (Pa.) Pub. Library, 1943-44, asst. children's librarian, 1944-46; fashion artist Pomeroy's Inc., Harrisburg, 1946-49, Bowman's, Inc., 1949-52; children's librarian Abington Library Soc., Jenkintown, Pa., 1959-71, librarian, 1971—. Dir. Harrisburg Art Assn. Studio, 1943-48. Mem. Hist. Soc. Pa., Old York Rd. Hist. Soc., Pa. Library Assn. Author-illustrator: A Conch for Molly, 1940; Chooky, 1942; The Roll of Drums, 1945; Your Pennsylvania, 1953; Old Satan, 1955; Indians of Pennsylvania, 1956; The Hippity Hopper, 1957; The Morning Star, 1957; All About Pennsylvania, 1958; They Came to Pennsylvania, 1960; The Lost Prince, 1963; Your State, 1963; Pennsylvania ABC, 1964; My Book About Abraham Lincoln, 1967; author: The Pennsylvania Primer, 1954; William Penn, 1968; Colonial Pennsylvania, 1969; The Pennsylvania Dutch, 1971; Introduction to Pennsylvania, 1974; illustrator of several other children's books. Home: 828 Greenwood Av Jenkintown PA 19046 Office: York and Vista Roads Jenkintown PA 19046

WALLRAFF, EVELYN BARTELS (MRS. CHARLES F. WALLRAFF), educator; b. Chgo., Oct. 21, 1920; d. Paul Peter and Bernice Agnes (Brown) Bartels; Mus.B., Rosary Coll., 1939, B.S., 1940; M.S. (Tchrs. scholar 1940-41), U. Chgo., 1942; Ph.D., U. Ariz., 1961; m. Charles F. Wallraff, Sept. 6, 1946; children—Dean Christopher, Barbara Jean. Instr., U. Ariz., Tucson, 1943-46, asst. prof. bacteriology, 1946-47, research asso., 1971-72; research asso. Southwestern Clinic and Research Inst., Tucson, 1947-51; research microbiologist VA Hosp., Tucson, 1961-72, cons. med. research, 1971—; mem. faculty Pima Coll., Tucson, 1972—, prof. microbiology 1972—, coordinator life scis., 1973—. Recipient fellowship NSF, 1946. Mem. Am. Assn. Immunologists, Am. Soc. Microbiology (br. pres. 1967-68), Am. Thoracic Soc., A.A.A.S. Contbr. articles to profl. jours. Home: 2708 E Mabel St Tucson AZ 85716

WALLS, ANNA ALICE, librarian; b. McComb, Okla., Oct. 4, 1937; d. Robert Earl and Grace (Spray) Walls; student Blackwood Bus. Coll., 1955, Oklahoma City U., 1958-60. Clk., Okla. Dept. Libraries, Oklahoma City., 1955-56, librarian asst. law div., 1956-63, legislative reference div., 1963-68, head legislative reference div., 1968—. Editor: Oklahoma State Agys., Bds., Commns., Cts., Instn., Legislature and Officers, 1961—; Short Biographies of Govs., Okla. Territory, State of Okla., 1967—; The Okla. Gazette, 1968—; Who Is Who in the Okla. Legislature, 1969—. Contbr. articles to profl. jours. Home: 1622 N W 21st St Oklahoma City OK 73106 Office: Room 109 State Capitol Oklahoma City OK 73105

WALLS, MARTHA ANN WILLIAMS (MRS. B. CARMAGE WALLS), newspaper exec.; b. Gadsden, Ala., Apr. 21, 1927; d. Aubrey Joseph and Inez (Cooper) Williams; student pub. schs., Gadsden; m. B. Carmage Walls, Jan. 2, 1954; children—Byrd Cooper, Lissa Williams. Pres., dir. Walls Newspapers, Inc., 1969-70; sec.-treas. Summer Camps, Inc., Guntersville, Ala., 1954-69, also dir; pres., dir. So. Newspapers, Inc., Baytown, Tex., 1970—; dir. Scottsboro Newspapers, Inc. (Ala.), Ft. Payne Newspapers, Inc. (Ala.); v.p., dir. Dixie Newspapers, Inc., Gadsden, Ala., McKinney Newspapers, Inc. (Tex.), Rev. Publs. Inc., Freeport, Tex., Bay City (Tex.) Tribune, Reidsville Newspapers, Inc. (N.C.), Brenham (Tex.) Banner; dir. Angleton (Tex.) Times, Alvin (Tex.) Sun, Terrell (Tex.) Tribune, Henderson (Tex.) News, Herald-Coaster, Rosenberg, Tex., Coastal Publs., Inc., Rosenberg, Tri-County Newspapers, Inc., Katy, Tex., Mangum Newspapers, Inc. (Okla.), Bayport Pubs. Inc., Deer Park, Tex., Bayshore Pubs. Inc., LaPorte, Tex., Royse City (Tex.) News-Am. Bd. dirs. Montgomery Acad., 1970-74. Methodist. Home: 18603 Upper Bay Rd Nassau Bay Houston TX 77058 Office: Suite 106 18100 Upper Bay Rd Houston TX 77058

WALLS, SARA LOUISE, editor; b. Bessemer, Ala., Sept. 10, 1917; d. Odie Clarke and Stella Louise (Taylor) Walls; student U. Ala., 1940. Chief clk. forestry div. Gulf States Paper, Tuscaloosa, 1948-54; asso. editor The News Bag mag., Tuscaloosa, 1954-63, editor, 1963—; editor newspaper The Green Tree, Tuscaloosa, 1966—. Recipient Award of Excellence Birmingham Assn. Indsl. Editors, 1966, 68; Award of Achievement So. Council Indsl. Editors, 1966, 67. Mem. Phi Chi Theta. Methodist. Club: Tuscaloosa Zonta (chmn. scrapbook and yearbook). Home: 1616 2d Av Tuscaloosa AL 35401 Office: PO Box 3199 Tuscaloosa AL 35401

WALSETH, KRISTI ELIZABETH, govt. ofcl.; b. Riverside, Cal., Mar. 12, 1950; d. John Einer and Kathryn Elizabeth (Flynn) Walseth; B.S. in Journalism, Tex. Woman's U., 1971; M.A. in Journalism, U. Tex., 1975. Gen. assignment reporter Grand Prairie (Tex.) Daily News, 1971-72; adminstr. asst. to a state senator, Austin, Tex., 1973—. Mem. Democratic Women Dallas Country. Mem. Tex. Woman's Polit. Caucus, Women in Communications, Phi Alpha Theta. Home: 2101 Elmont Austin TX 78701 Office: Room Capitol Bldg Austin TX 78711

WALSH, ANN WATSON (MRS. THOMAS DEWITT WALSH), cosmetics co. exec.; b. Cambridge, Mass., Feb. 8, 1932; d. Wallace and Marie (Dunn) Watson; B.A. in History, Smith Coll., 1953; m. Thomas deWitt Walsh, May 8, 1954; children—Gloria, Brooke, Thomas, Hughes. Asst. account exec. firm Barkan & Platt, N.Y.C., 1959-61; dir. pub. relations Helena Rubinstein Co., N.Y.C., 1961-68; dir. pub. relations and sales promotion Lentheric, Inc., 1968-69; creative dir. Germaine Monteil Corp. Cosmetics, 1970-72, v.p., 1972-74, exec. v.p., 1974—. Mem. The Fashion Group, N.Y.C., 1962—. Mem. Am. Women Radio and TV, Pub. Relations Soc. Am. Home: 1356 Madison Av New York City NY 10028 Office: 40 W 57th St New York City NY 10019

WALSH, ANNMARIE HAUCK, research assn. exec.; b. N.Y.C., May 5, 1938; d. James Smith and Ann-Marie (Kennedy) Hauck; student Smith Coll., 1956-58; B.A. cum laude, Barnard Coll., 1961; M.A., Columbia U., 1969, Ph.D., 1971; m. John F. Walsh, Jr., Aug. 20, 1960; 1 son, Peter Hauck Lillis. Editor Met. Area Problems: News and Digest, N.Y.C., 1961; with Inst. Pub. Adminstrn., N.Y.C., 1962-64, dir. internat. urban studies, 1964-72; dir. study pub. authorities 20th Century Fund, 1972—; asso. prof. Grad. Center, City U. N.Y., 1972—. Mem. N.Y. del. to Centennial Conf. on Met. Problems, Toronto, Ont., Can., 1967; cons. AID, State Dept., Pub. Adminstrn. div. UN, Com. for Econ. Devel. Herbert Lehmann fellow, 1966-69. Mem. Nat. Acad. Pub. Adminstrn. Phi Beta Kappa. Author: Urban Government for the Paris Region, 1968; Urban Government for Lagos, Nigeria; Urban Government for Zagreb, Yugoslavia, 1968; The Urban Challenge to Government, 1969. Editor: (with Lyle Fitch) Agenda for a City, 1970. Mem. editorial bd. Urban Affairs Quar., 1973—.

WALSH, BEATRICE PASSAGE (MRS. THOMAS JOSEPH WALSH), club woman; b. Schnectady, Mar. 6, 1917; d. William Riley and Jessamine (Littlefield) Passage; student Western Res. U., 1941-42; m. Thomas Joseph Walsh, July 12, 1941; 1 dau., Joan Beatrice (Mrs. Peter Michael Waltz). Vol. worker A.R.C., 1941-46, 47-53; leader council Cleve. Beachwood (O.) Girl Scouts, 1952-57; vol. worker Community Chest, 1947-50; mem. women's com. Cleve. Orch., 1962—; ladies program chmn. Am. Chem. Soc., 1960, Am. Inst. Chem. Engrs., 1961, ladies program conv. com., 1969; mem. Orange Community Arts Council, 1969—, Pepper Pike Civic League, 1966—; ladies program co-chmn. Nat. Heat Transfer Conf., 1964; mem. Shaker Heights League Women Voters, Case Faculty Wives (pres. 1958-59), Western Res. Rep. Women's Club, D.A.R. (Shaker chpt., corr. sec. 1962-64, registrar 1964-69, publicity chmn. 1968-70, chaplain 1969-71, librarian 1972-73, vice regent 1973-74, regent 1974—, del. state conv. 1963, 64, 66, 69, 73, 74 chmn. reception, del. nat. conv. 1964, 73, 74), Garden Center Greater Cleve. Presbyn. Clubs: The Hugenot Society (Ohio), Blackbrook Country, Landerhaven Golf, Moreland Hills Golf, Landerwood Swim, Suburban Garden, Green Valley Garden (club rep. 1972-73). Home: 32555 Creekside Dr Pepper Pike Cleveland OH 44124

WALSH, ETHEL BENT, govt. ofcl.; b. Bridgeport, Conn., Dec. 29, 1923; d. William Woodworth and Corrine Ethel (Secor) Bent; student Katherine Gibbs Sch., Boston, 1941-42; m. Robert John Walsh (div. 1949); children—Diane (Mrs. Alfred M. Broch), Robert John. Vice-pres. Aerosol Techniques, Inc., Bridgeport, 1955-63; pres. Adminstrv. Technical Services, Inc., Hartford, Conn., 1964-66; cons. to aerosol industry, Fairfield, Conn., 1966-67; plant mgr. Lanvin-Charles of the Ritz, Holmdel, N.J., 1967-69; dir. adv. councils Small Bus. Adminstrn., Washington, 1969-71; commr. Equal Employment Opportunity Commn., Washington, 1971—. Mem. Washington Forum, Exec. Women in Govt. (founding). Home: 318 Independence Av SE Washington DC 20003 Office: US Equal Employment Opportunity Commission 1800 G Street Rm 1249 Washington DC 20506

WALSH, HELENA TERESA, educator, librarian; b. Montreal, Que., Can., Apr. 24, 1938 (came to U.S., 1967); d. Joseph and Antonia (Zubrycka) Kaczkowski; B.Edn. (Que. Dept. Edn. scholar 1967), St. Joseph's Tchrs. Coll. (Montreal), 1967; B.Arts, Loyola Coll. (Montreal), 1967; M.S. in L.S., Catholic U., Washington, 1972; postgrad. Blackstone Sch. Law, 1970—; m. John Joseph Walsh, Nov. 6, 1954 (div. 1970). Tchr. elementary sch., Montreal, 1961-63, secondary sch., 1963-67; tchr. secondary sch. Capitol Heights, Md., 1968-71; tchr., librarian Suitland (Md.) Jr. High Sch., 1971—. Law clk. K. David, Washington, 1970—. Mem. Prince George's County Educators Assn., Md. Tchrs. Assn., N.E.A. Home: 3114 Wisconsin Av NW Apt 202 Washington DC 20016

WALSH, JULIA MARGARET CURRY (MRS. THOMAS M. WALSH), investment co. exec.; b. Akron, O., Mar. 29, 1923; d. Edward A. and Catharine U. (Skurkay) Curry; B.B.A. magna cum laude, Kent State U., 1945; postgrad. N.Y. Inst. Finance, 1956; grad. Advanced Mgmt. Program, Harvard, 1962; LL.D., Hood Coll., 1969, Regis Coll., 1973; m. John G. Montgomery, Apr. 7, 1948 (dec. Dec. 1957); children—John, Stephen, Michael, Mark; m. 2d, Thomas M. Walsh, May 18, 1963; 1 dau., Margaret; stepchildren—Mary Francis (Mrs. Steven Ferencie), Patrick Joseph, Kathleen, Thomas D., Joan, Daniel, Ann. Personnel officer Am. counsulate gen. Munich, Germany, 1945-48; probation officer Wash. State Sch. Girls, Centralia, 1948-50; exec. officer U.S. Ednl. Commn. Ankara, Turkey, 1952-54; registered rep. Ferris & Co., Inc., Washington, 1955-59, gen. partner, 1959-70, sr. v.p., 1971—; mem. Am. Stock Exchange, 1965—, bd. govs., 1972, exchange ofcl., 1973—; dir. Wayne-Gossard Corp.; adv. bd. 1st Nat. Bank Washington, Frank R. Jelleff's, Inc. Mem. Sec. State's Spl. Adv. Com. on Pub. Opinion; mem. adv. com. loan guarantee programs in health Dept. Health, Edn. and Welfare. Bd. dirs. Bus. Resources Center, Kent State U. Found., Christ Child Soc., Nat. Shrine Immaculate Conception, St. Mary of the Woods Coll., Georgetown U., Med. Coll. Pa.; dir.-at-large Met. Washington Bd. Trade; mem. Washington bd. Nat. Multiple Sclerosis Soc. Recipient Distinguished Alumna award Kent State U., 1967; Bus. and Profl. Leader in Finance award Religious Heritage Am., 1973. Mem. Financial Analysts Soc. Washington (chmn. women's conv. program, 1965), Bus. and Profl. Women's Club Potomac, Am. Assn. U. Women, Harvard Bus. Sch. Assn. (exec. council) Democrat. Clubs: Women's Nat., Am. Newspaper Women's, Harvard Business Sch. (past pres.), Zonta, Internat. (Washington). Home: 5001 Millwood Lane NW Washington DC 20016 Office: Ferris and Co 1720 Eye St NW Washington DC 20006

WALSH, MARY D. (MRS. F. HOWARD WALSH), civic worker; b. Whitewright, Tex., Oct. 29, 1913; d. William Fleming and Anna Maud (Lewis) Fleming; B.A., So. Meth. U., 1934; m. F. Howard Walsh, Mar. 13, 1937; children—Richard, Howard, D'Ann (Mrs. Wm. F. Bonnell), Maudi (Mrs. Geo. C. Porter III), William Lloyd. Pres. Fleming Found.; v.p. Walsh Found.; partner Walsh Co.; bd. dirs. Lloyd Shaw Found., Colorado Springs, Colo. Guarantor Fort Worth Arts Council, Fort Worth Opera, Fort Worth Symphony Orch.; v.p. Opera Bd., 1967-73. co-founder Am. Field Service in Ft. Worth; mem. Tex. Commn. for Arts and Humanities, 1968-72, mem. adv. council, 1972—. Bd. dirs. Van Cliburn Internat. Piano Competition, Colorado Springs Day Nursery, Colorado Springs Symphony. Recipient numerous awards, including Altrusa Civic award as 1st Lady of Ft. Worth, 1968; (with husband) Distinguished Service award So. Bapt. Radio and Television Commn., 1972; named (with husband) Patron of Arts in Ft. Worth, 1970, Edna Gladney Internat. Grandparents of 1972. Mem. Ft. Worth Boys Club, Ft. Worth Children's Hosp., Jewel Charity Ball, Ft. Worth Pan Hellenic (pres. 1940), Wm. Edrington Scott Theatre Guild, Opera Guild, Fine Arts Found. Guild, Girl's Service League, Am. Assn. U. Women, Goodwill Industries Aux., Child Study Center, Tarrant County Aux. of Edna Gladney Home, YWCA (life), Ft. Worth Art Assn., Ft. Worth Ballet Assn., Tex. Boys Choir Aux., Round Table, Colorado Springs Fine Art Center, Am. Automobile Assn., Southwestern Bapt. Theol. Sem. Wives, Rae Reimers Bible Study Class (pres. 1968), Tex. League Composers (hon. life), Chi Omega (pres. 1935-36), others. Baptist. Clubs: Bankers' Wives, Rejebian Book Review, Kappa Sigma Wives and Mothers, The Woman's (Club Fidelite), Roundelay, Dinner Dance (1st v.p. 1968). Home: 2425 Stadium Dr Fort Worth TX 76109 also 1801 Culebra Av Colorado Springs CO 80907

WALSH, NANCY BALLARD, librarian; b. Bedford, Va., Aug. 25, 1927; d. Henderson Suter and Ethel Blanche (Davis) Ballard; B.A. in Edn., Madison Coll., 1948; postgrad. Am. U., 1966-68; m. W. Michael Walsh, Mar. 3, 1973. Tchr. pub. schs., Bassett, Va., 1948-56; reference librarian Office Chief of Engrs. Library, U.S. Army, Washington, 1956-60; chief pub. services sect. Indsl. Coll. Armed Forces Library, Washington, 1960-64, asst. librarian, 1964-66, library dir., 1966—. Mem. Spl. Libraries Assn. (sec.-treas. mil. librarian's div. 1969-70), Am., D.C. library assns., D.A.R., U.D.C., Beta Sigma Phi. Episcopalian. Home: 4306 S 8th St Arlington VA 22204 Office: Industrial College of Armed Forces Library Fort Lesley J McNair Washington DC 20319

WALSH, SISTER PATRICIA MARIE, sch. adminstr.; b. Los Angeles, July 14, 1930; d. William Joseph and Blanche Ida (Parent) Walsh; B.A., Queen of the Holy Rosary Coll., 1955; M.A., Cath. U. Am., 1963. Joined Dominican Order, 1946; prin. St. Elizabeth Sch., Oakland, Cal., 1963-68; adminstr. St. Catherine's Mil. Sch., Anaheim, Cal., 1968—; pres. St. Catherine's Corp., 1968—. Mem. Bishop's Ecumenical Commn., Oakland, 1966-68. Mem. Nat. Council Tchrs. English, Nat. Catholic Edn. Assn. Home: 215 N Harbor Blvd Anaheim CA 92803

WALSH, RUTH BEECHER LAWSON, public relations exec.; b. Lancaster, Pa., Mar. 2, 1925; s. Raymond Sylvester and Alma Lamar (Myers) Lawson; B.F.A., Ohio U., 1946; M.Ed., Loyola Coll., Balt., 1959; m. Robert Vincent Walsh, Nov. 6, 1948; children—Eric Wyatt, Mark Lawson. Writer, women's broadcaster radio sta. WJIM, Lansing, Mich., 1946-47; women's program dir. radio sta. WPDX, Clarksburg, W.Va., 1947-49; free-lance radio and TV broadcasting, Balt., Washington and Phila., 1949—; dir. dramatics St. Timothy's Sch., Stevenson, Md., 1962-72; pub. relations dir., asst. to pres. Peabody Inst., Balt., 1970—; conductor TV show sta. WPTZ, Phila., 1951-52; actress, dir. local and regional theatre. Pres. Johns Hopkins Playhouse Assn., 1960-62. Vol. for Stevenson, 1952, 56, for Kennedy, 1960; program dir. City-County Democratic Club, Balt., 1958-62. Mem. Episcopal Soc. Cultural and Racial Unity (pres. 1963-64), Pub. Relations Soc. Am., A.F.T.R.A., Phi Mu. Home: 1706 Regent Rd Baltimore MD 21209 Office: 1 E Mt Vernon Pl Baltimore MD 21202

WALSHE, DOROTHY LEE (MRS. WILLIAM HOWARD SCHECKEL), psychologist; b. Washington, Nov. 2, 1932; d. Leo Augustus and Dorothy Eleanor (McCabe) Walshe; B.S., Va. Commonwealth U., 1955; M.A., Am. U., 1968, postgrad., 1968—; postgrad. Cath. U., 1965-66, Fairfield U., 1963-64; m. Francis Edward Dully, Jr., Nov. 21, 1956 (div. 1966); children—Kathleen Mary, Ann Margaret, Margaret Elizabeth, David Francis Walshe; m. William Howard Scheckel, June 27, 1970; stepchildren—Karen Vermont, Lisa Wood, Claudia Lynn, Tracy Lee. Staff occupational therapist NIH, Bethesda, Md., 1955-56; supr. dept. occupational therapy Hebrew Home Greater Washington, 1964-66; ednl. psychologist D.C. Soc. Crippled Children, Washington, 1971—. Recipient Grant, Pres. Commn. on Heart Disease, Cancer and Stroke, 1966, Grant, Rehab. Services Adminstrn., Am. Occupational Therapy Assn., 1968. Mem. Am. Assn. Mental Deficiency, Council Exceptional Children, World Fedn. Occupational Therapists, Am. Occupational Therapy Assn., Am. Psychol. Assn. (asso.), Am. Orthopsychiat. Assn., Common Cause, Smithsonian Assos., Found. Exceptional Children, D.C. Pub. Health Assn., Psi Chi, Phi Gamma Delta. Home: 9706 Eclipse Pl Gaithersburg MD 20760 Office: 2800 13th St NW Washington DC 20009

WALSTER, ELAINE CATHERINE (MRS. G. WILLIAM WALSTER), psychologist, educator; b. Detroit, Oct. 22, 1937; d. Charles E. and Eileen (Kalahar) Hatfield; B.A., U. Mich., 1959; Ph.D., Stanford, 1963; m. G. William Walster, Apr. 26, 1962. Asst. prof. U. Minn., 1963-64, asso. prof., 1964-66; asso. prof. U. Rochester, 1966-68, U. Wis., Madison, 1968-69, prof., 1969—. Fellow Am. Psychol. Assn.; mem. Am. Sociol. Assn. Author: Interpersonal Attraction, 1969. Contbr. articles to profl. jours. Home: 3033 Waunona Way Madison WI 53713

WALTER, ALICE CONRIED, psychologist; b. N.Y.C., June 20, 1914; d. Richard Gence and Margaret (Leith) Conried; B.S., Columbia Coll., 1950, M.A., 1952; m. Henry Glendon Walter, Jr., Apr. 29, 1936 (div. Apr. 1946); children—Henry Glendon, III, Margaret Wendy. Psychologist Home Term Ct., 1952-53; clin. child psychologist Columbia Presbyn. Med. Center, 1953-58; mem. bd. edn. Bur. Child Guidance, N.Y.C., 1958—, psychologist, 1970—. Psychologist N.Y. Sch. Edn. for Blind, 1954-56. Mem. N.Y. Soc. Clin. Psychologists, N.Y. State Psychol. Assn., Orthopsychiat. Assn., Am. Psychiat. Assn., Sch. Psychol. Assn. Home: 297 Riversville Rd Greenwich CT 06830 Office: 1199 Park Av St New York City NY 10028

WALTER, HELEN JESSIE HOLT (MRS. LAWRENCE G. WALTER), statistician; b. Greeneville, Tenn., Nov. 13, 1909; d. Albert Campbell and Mary (Ackerly) Holt; student Ward-Belmont Coll., 1925-27; B.A., Vanderbilt U., 1929; postgrad. Am. U., 1943-45, 1964-65; m. Lawrence G. Walter, Sept. 19, 1944; children—Anne Marie, Karolyne (Mrs. Ronald Roy Putnam). Statistician War Dept., Washington, 1943-44, Hdqrs. Army Air Forces, Washington, 1944-47; statis. asst. NSF, Washington, 1963-65; supervisory statistician Nat. Inst. Child Health and Human Devel., NIH, Bethesda, Md., 1965—. Treas. Republican Womens Club, Potomac, Md., 1960-61; Rep. precinct chmn. Montgomery County, Md., 1961-62. Recipient Civilian Meritorious Service award War Dept., 1944. Mem. Washington Statis. Soc., Am. Statis. Assn., Biometric Soc., P.E.O. (chpt. pres. 1959-60), Kappa Alpha Theta. Methodist (pres. Women's Soc. 1955). Home: 12408 Stony Creek Rd Potomac MD 20854 Office: Nat Inst Child Health and Human Devel NIH Bldg 31 9000 Wisconsin Av Bethesda MD 20014

WALTER, MAMIRUTH COLLINS (MRS. ALBERT FREDERICK WALTER), coll. counselor; b. Jacksonville, N.C., Nov. 10, 1907; d. William Mandrick and Nellie (Walton) Collins; B.A., East Carolina U., 1939; M.Ed., George Washington U., 1963; m. Albert Frederick Walter, May 23, 1942; children—Barbara Louise, William Albert. Elementary tchr. Columbus County Schs., Whiteville, N.C., 1925-39; instr. English, Latin, civics Hallsboro (N.C.) Sch., 1939-42; presch. reading coordinator, cons. Browne Acad., Alexandria, Va., 1948-60; reading specialist Fairfax County Pub. Schs., Fairfax, Va., 1960-64; counselor, Okaloosa-Walton Jr. Coll., Niceville, Fla., 1964—, coordinator counseling services, 1970—. Bd. dirs. Mental Health, Okaloosa Guidance Clinic. Recipient Guidance Inst. Grant, Nat. Defense Edn. Act, 1966. Mem. Am. Assn. U. Women (scholarship rep. 1970-72), N.E.A., Am. Assn. U. Profs., Am. Personnel and Guidance Assn., Internat. Reading Assn., Fla. Edn. Assn., Delta Kappa Gamma. Democrat. Baptist. Home: 425 Eastview Dr Fort Walton Beach FL 32548 Office: Okabosa-Walton Jr Coll Niceville FL 32578

WALTER, MARILYN E. (MRS. CARL H. CARLSON, JR.), security analyst; b. N.Y.C., Apr. 19, 1935; d. Julius G. and Ethel (Schwinn) Walter; A.B., Syracuse U., 1956; m. Carl H. Carlson, Jr., Nov. 4, 1972. Statistician J. & W. Seligman, N.Y.C., 1956-57; jr. security analyst Smith, Barney & Co., 1957-62; bus. mgr. Theodore Flohr, Jeweler, 1962-64; sr. security analyst Pickard & Co., Inc., N.Y.C., 1964-66; sr. security analyst W. E. Hutton & Co., N.Y.C. 1966-70, v.p. instnl. research, 1970-72; v.p. Shareholders Mgmt. Co., Los Angeles, 1972—, asso. dir. research, 1973—. Mem. Hemophilia Found. Mem. N.Y. Soc. Security Analysts, Internat. Platform Assn., Lambda of Alpha Chi Omega (treas. 1956). Republican. Episcopalian. Home: 1036 Chantilly Rd Los Angeles CA 90024 Office: 1888 Century Park E Los Angeles CA 90067

WALTER, MARY FRISHMUTH, pub. relations exec.; b. Bryn Mawr, Pa., Nov. 27, 1926; d. Clifford E. and Ann P. (Prettyman) Frishmuth; student Briarcliff Coll., 1946-48; B.A., U. Pa., 1948; m. Dawes Walter, Nov. 18, 1951 (div. May 1963); 1 son, John Frishmuth. Pub. relations dir. Holy Redeemer Hosp., Meadowbrook, Pa., 1967-70; pres. pub. relations, community relations MFW Communications Co., Richboro, Pa., 1970—. Mem. Women in Communications, Pub. Relations Soc. Am. (dir. 1974-76), N.J. Hosp. Assn., Hosp. Assn. Pa., Delaware Valley Hosp. Assn. (past pres.), Phila. Pub. Relations Assn., Soroptimist Club. Presbyn. (deacon 1972-73). Club: Huntingden Valley Country. Address: 98 Manor Dr Richboro PA 18954

WALTER, MAY ELIZABETH, retail co. exec.; b. N.Y.C.; d. Peter J. and Elizabeth (Schaub) Walter; student N.Y. U., Columbia, evenings, 1920-30. Co-founder, treas., exec. v.p., vice chmn. Mut. Buying Syndicate, Inc., 1931-65; pres. Retail Marketers Advt., Inc., N.Y.C., 1966-67, cons., adviser, 1968-71. Sec., trustee, mem. exec. com, Am. Crafts Council, N.Y.C., 1962—. Recipient Salute to Women award Republican Women in Bus. and Professions, 1962. Mem. Am. Fedn. Arts, Gallatin Assos., Thought Assos., Mus. Modern Art, Guggenheim Mus. Assos., Met. Mus., Art Gallery U. Notre Dame (adv. council). Home: 923 Fifth Av New York City NY 10021 also Siscowit Rd Pound Ridge NY 10576

WALTER, RUTH MARION, govt. ofcl.; b. Yonkers, N.Y., Oct. 3, 1916; d. Oliver Alonzo and Meta (Ehlenberger) Walter; B.A., Barnard Coll., 1937, M.A., Columbia, 1942. Research asst. Columbia U., N.Y.C., 1938-41; information and outpost rep. Office Govt. Reports, OWI, N.Y.C., 1941-45; fgn. press liaison officer U.S. Dept. State, N.Y.C., 1945-47, 48-53; internat. adviser Girl Scouts U.S.A., N.Y.C., 1947-48; mem. staff Voice of Am., USIA, Washington, 1953—, staff asst. to dir., 1958-66, pub. information officer, 1966—. Evaluator, Communications Conf. of Americas, U. Mich., 1968. Trustee, sec. Nat. Soc. Autistic Children, 1965-68. Mem. Am. Women in Radio and TV (trustee, sec., v.p. Ednl. Found. 1964-67), Pub. Relations Soc. Am. (mem. internat. affairs task force), Barnard-in-Washington (pres. 1969-74), Asso. Alumnae Barnard Coll. (dir.-at-large 1974—), Women's Equity Action League. Home: 6200 29th St NW Washington DC 20015 Office: 330 Independence Av SW Washington DC 20547

WALTERS, BARBARA, TV personality; b. 1931; d. Lou Walters; grad. Sarah Lawrence Coll.; LH.D., Ohio State U., 1971. Formerly writer producer WNBC-TV then with sta. WPIX and CBS-TV; joined Today Show, 1961, regular panel mem., 1963—, co-host, 1974—; moderator Not for Women Only, nationally syndicated television program. Hon. chmn. Nat. Assn. of Help for Retarded Children, 1970. Named to 100 Women of Accomplishment, Harper's Bazaar, 1967, 71; America's 75 Most Important Women, Ladies' Home Jour., 1970, Woman of Yr. in Communications, 1974; named Woman of Year, Theta Sigma Phi. Author: How to Talk With Practically Anybody About Practically Anything. Contbr. articles to Good Housekeeping, Family Weekly, Reader's Digest. Address: care NBC 30 Rockefeller Plaza New York City NY 10020

WALTERS, CYNTHIA ANN, educator; b. Roaring Spring, Pa., Dec. 13, 1940; d. Theodore and Thelma Pearl (Miller) Walters; B.S., Lockhaven (Pa.) State Coll., 1962; M.Ed., U. Pitts., 1963. Phys. dir. Sara Heinz House, Pitts., 1963-64; tchr. phys. edn. N. Allegheny High Sch., Pitts., 1964-66; asst. prof., dir. women's phys. edn. Grove City (Pa.) Coll., 1966—; condr. life saving and synchronized swimming clinics. Bd. dirs. Mercer County chpt. A.R.C. Mem. Pa. Assn. Health, Phys. Edn. and Recreation (chmn. nominating com.). Home: Box 95 Harrisville PA 16038 Office: Grove City Coll Grove City PA 16127

WALTERS, ELEANOR BOYD, mathematician, educator; b. Gunnison, Miss., Mar. 28, 1914; d. Jerry Edward and Loudie (Boyd) Walters; B.S. in Edn., Delta State Coll., 1934; M.A., Duke, 1939; Ed.D., Tchrs; Coll., Columbia, 1956. Tchr. math. Shelby Consol. Sch., Shelby, Miss., 1934-38, Hernando (Miss.) High Sch., 1939-41, Pensacola (Fla.) High Sch., 1941-43; grad. asst. in math. Duke, 1938-39; asso. prof. math. Delta State U., Cleveland, Miss., 1943-55, prof., 1955—, acting head dept. math., 1948-55, head dept., 1955—. Mem. adv. com. on secondary math., adv. com. on arithmetic Miss. Dept. Edn., 1960—; math. cons. various Miss. schs., 1961—. Fellow A.A.A.S.; mem. Am. Math. Soc., Math. Assn. Am. (chmn. La.-Miss. sect. 1973-74), Nat. Council Tchrs. Math., Am. Assn. U. Women (v.p. Miss. div. 1959-61, nat. conv. com., 1963, implementation com. 1963-64, br. v.p. 1958-64, sec. S.E. Central region 1963-64, v.p. 1967-71, chmn. nat. conv. com. 1965), Delta Kappa Gamma, Kappa Delta Pi, Pi Gamma Mu. Democrat. Methodist. Home: 1804 Delta State Univ Cleveland MS 38732

WALTERS, ELLEN SWEET (MRS. HAROLD CHARLES WALTERS), civic worker; b. Ullin, Ill., Feb. 7, 1916; d. Hiram Goodrich and Julia Maude (Kelley) Sweet; student U. Ill., 1934-35; m. Harold Charles Walters, June 9, 1945; children—William H. (dec.), James G. Sec., Isler-Tompsett Lithograph Co., St. Louis, 1935-38, Skrainka Constrn. Co., St. Louis, 1938-39, Talent Mgmt., St. Louis, 1945-46. Treas., League Women Voters of Webster Groves, Mo., 1962-64, pres., 1964-67; treas. League Women Voters Mo., 1967-69, pres., 1969-73; sec. League Women Voters U.S., 1974—. Presbyn. (elder). Club: St. Louis Kart (past sec.). Home: 829 Edgar Rd Webster Groves MO 63119

WALTERS, MARY DAWSON (MRS. VINCENT WALTERS), librarian; b. Mitchell County, Ga., Oct. 6, 1923; d. William Henry and Carrie Lou (Richardson) Dawson; B.S. cum laude, Savannah State Coll., 1949; M.S., Atlanta U., 1957; postgrad. Ohio State U., 1963; m. Vincent Walters, Feb. 14, 1964; children (by previous marriage)—Marjorie (Mrs. Quinten Ted Smith), Robert H. McCoy. Librarian, Carver Jr. High Sch., Albany, Ga., 1956-57; dir. library Albany (Ga.) State Coll., 1957-61; asst. prof. library adminstrn., head process div. Ohio State U. Libraries, Columbus, 1961-71, asso. prof., head acquisitions dept., 1971-74; asso. librarian, chief acquistions Cal. State U., Los Angeles, 1974—. Recipient Dirs. Citaiton of Merit, Ohio State U. Libraries, 1963. Mem. Am. Assn. U. Profs., Am., Cal. library assns., Cal. Employees Assn. Home: 3205 Los Feliz Blvd Los Angeles CA 90039 Office: 5151 State University Dr Los Angeles CA 90032

WALTERS, MAXINE BERNICE OYLER (MRS. ROBERT WILLIS WALTERS), sch. adminstr.; b. Columbus, O., June 4, 1921; d. Vernon William and Olga (Wade) Oyler; B.S. in Edn., Ohio State U., 1943, M.A., 1952; m. Robert Willis Walters, June 28, 1953. Tchr., Pickaway County, O., 1943-45, Ashville, O., 1945-46, Piqua, O., 1946-47, Cleve., 1947-49; elementary sch. tchr. Columbus Pub. Schs., 1949-52, elementary sch. prin., 1952—, mem. supt.'s adv. council, 1955-57. Mem. area planning com. Southwest Mental Health Center. Mem. N.E.A., Ohio Dept. Elementary Sch. Prins., Ohio Edn. Assn. (mem. constn. com. 1965), Columbus Elementary Prins. Assn. (v.p. 1954-55, mem. exec. bd.), Internat. Platform Assn., Alumni Assn. Ohio State U., Ohio P.T.A., Environmental Def. Orgn., Nat. Assn. for Female Execs., Nat. Council Adminstrv. Women in Edn., Pi Lambda Theta (Nu chpt. pres. 1952), Kappa Phi Epsilon. Mem. Order Eastern Star. (past matron). Club: Players. Home: 12 S High St Mount Sterling OH 43143 Office: 784 Georgian Dr Columbus OH 43224

WALTERS, NANCY ROCKHILL (MRS. ELWOOD WALTERS), educator; b. Greencastle, Ind.; d. Howard and Muriel (Rector) Rockhill; A.B., DePauw U., 1949; M.S., Ind. U., 1951, Ph.D., 1967; m. Elwood Walters, Nov. 22, 1950; children—Mark, Joel, John, Paul, Adam. Counselor, tchr. Greencastle High Sch., 1957-63; asso. prof. counselor edn. Central Mo. State U., Warrensburg, 1967—, dir. research grant, tng. grant, 1973—. Mem. Mo. delegation White House Conf. on Children and Youth, 1970; mem. Gov.'s Com. on Children and Youth, 1972—; chmn. 10-county Conf. Prevention Juvenile Delinquency. Recipient Coop. research grant, 1968-69. Mem. Am. Personnel and Guidance Assn., Am. Vocational Assn., Am. Psychol. Assn., Mo. Guidance Assn., Mo. Tchrs. Assn., Nat. Vocational Guidance Assn. Methodist (adminstrv. bd.). Contbr. articles to profl. jours. Home: 210 E North St Warrensburg MO 64093 Office: 406 Edn Bldg Warrensburg MO 64093

WALTNER, NELLIE LAIRD (MRS. ARTHUR WALTER WALTNER), librarian; b. Harper, Kan., Sept. 6, 1918; d. Irl Weaver and Fern Elizabeth (Titus) Laird; A.B., Bethel Coll., 1941; postgrad. Morehead State Coll., 1942, N.C. State U., 1962-66; M.S. in L.S., U. N.C., 1969; m. Arthur Walter Waltner, Apr. 10, 1941; children—Ann Beth (Mrs. Robert Anholt), Linda Ruth (Mrs. William MacDonald Neville). Catalog asst. D.H. Hill Library N.C. State U., Raleigh, 1969-71, head acquisitions, 1971—. Mem. A.L.A., Southeaster, N.C. library assns., Alumni Assn. Sch. Library Sci. U. N.C. (sec., exec. bd. 1972-75), Beta Phi Mu. Home: 1204 Westmoreland Dr Raleigh NC 27612 Office: Acquisitions Dept D H Hill Library North Carolina State University Raleigh NC 27607

WALTON, ELEANOR YINGER, educator; b. Bellvue, Mich., Nov. 11, 1908; d. George Daniel and Emma Mae (Bancroft) Yinger; A.B., Albion Coll., 1931; M.A., Boston U., 1948; postgrad. U. Mich., 1957-65; m. Edgar A. Walton, Aug. 9, 1951. Tchr. English, speech pub. high schs., Grand Ledge, Mich., 1931-40, Lansing,Mich., 1940-43; dir. Peabody Theatre, Boston, 1947-48, Wingspread Colon, Mich., 1955-62; asst. prof. speech, dir. dramatics Manchester (Ind.) Coll., 1949-51; vis. prof. speech and dramatics No. Mich. U., 1951; head speech, dir. dramatics Kellogg Community Coll., Battle Creek, 1958-65; asst. prof. Western Mich. U., Kalamazoo, 1965-68, asso. prof. communication arts, 1968—, chairperson oral interpretation, 1968—, dir. seminar Britain, 1969, 71, 73, 75. Program dir. A.R.C., North Africa, 1943-44, Italy, 1944-46, Germany, 1946-47. Mem. Mich. (chmn. theatre and oral interpretation sect. 1967-69), Central States speech assns., Nat. Assn. of Speech Communication Assn. Home: 1021 Farrell Kalamazoo MI 49007 Office: Sprau Western Michigan University Kalamazoo MI 49001

WALTON, HARRIETT JUNIOR, educator; b. Claxton, Ga., Sept. 19, 1933; d. Ester James and Mable Rose (Myrick) Junior; A.B., Clark Coll., 1952; M.S., Howard U., 1954; M.A., Syracuse U., 1957; student Ga. Inst. Tech., 1964-66, Emory U., summer 1966; m. James Harry Walton, June 7, 1958; children—Renee, Anthony, Jennifer, Cyrus. Asst. prof. math. Hampton Inst., 1954-55, 1957-58; asst. prof. math. Morehouse Coll., 1958—; dir. Math. Inst. Atlanta U., 1970—. Named Outstanding Educator of Am., 1971. Mem. Nat. Council Teachers of Math., Math. Assn. Am., Am. Assn. U. Profs., Pi Mu Epsilon, Beta Kappa Chi, Alpha Kappa Mu, Delta Sigma Theta. Baptist (clk. session 1966—). Home: 860 Venetta Pl NW Atlanta GA 30318 Office: Morehouse Coll Atlanta GA 30314

WALTRIP, ELIZABETH JANE NEWELL, educator; b. Denver, Feb. 1, 1921; d. Thomas VanBuren and Dora E. (Hull) Newell; B.S., U. Houston, 1945, M.A., 1950; Ed.D., Tex. Technol. Coll., 1955; m. V. Drexel Waltrip, July 21, 1942. Tchr. pub. schs., Houston, 1945, El Paso, Tex., 1946-56; tchr. Mt. Diablo Unified Sch. Dist., Concord, Cal., 1956—; guest asst. prof. San Diego State Coll. Del. Cal. Democratic Council, Fresno, 1963. Bd. dirs. Bi-County Epilepsy League, 1963-65, adv. com.; Council Exceptional Children, Contra Costa County, Cal., 1958-63, nat. treas.; pres. Cal. div. on mental retardation Cal. Council Exceptional Children; bd. dirs. Contra Costa Residents for Density Control; sec. Martinez Homeowners Assn. Recipient 6 A. Corey Communication's awards Cal. Tchrs. Assn., 1962-67; named Woman of Achievement, Menorah chpt. B'nai B'rith, 1966. Mem. N.E.A., Contra Costa Mental Health Assn., Cal. Assn. Neurologically Handicapped Children, Cal. Council for Retarded, Internat. Platform Assn., Assn. Childhood Edn. Internat., Zonta Internat., Alpha Delta Kappa. Baptist. Mem. Royal Arch Masons (pres. Keystone Club). Parttime author newspaper column; editor Mt. Diablo Edn. Assn. News, Cal. Assn. Childhood Edn. News. Home: 2814 Marion Terace Martinez CA 94553 Office: Mt Diabla United Sch Dist 1936 Carlotta Dr Concord CA 94520

WAMPLER, DORRIS MARIE BERRY (MRS. FREDERICK FRANCIS WAMPLER), librarian; b. Leaksville (now Eden), N.C., Sept. 13, 1927; d. Willie Albert and Flora (Bryant) Berry; B.A., Bridgewater Coll., 1947; library certificate Madison Coll., 1960; M.L.S., George Peabody Coll., 1970; m. Frederick Francis Wampler, June 20, 1947; children—Frederick Albert, Stephen Berry. Tchr. pub. elementary schs., Va., 1947-49; librarian Buffalo Gap High Sch., Swope, Va., 1962-65, Mt. Clinton (Va.) Elementary Sch., 1965-66, Wayland Intermediate Sch., Bridgewater, Va., 1966—. Instr. edn. Bridgewater Coll., 1970—; lectr. library sci. dept. Madison Coll., Harrisonburg, Va., 1972—. Mem. Sch. Supt.'s Adv. Council, 1971—; mem. Task Force for 5 Year Plan Local Schs., 1971—. Mem. Nat., Va. (mem. spl. services com. 1969-70), Rockingham County (v.p. 1967-69) edn. assns., Va. Mus. Fine Arts Assn., Va. (pres.-elect dist. G), Rockingham County sch. librarians assns., A.L.A., Delta Kappa Gamma, Beta Theta Mu. Mem. Ch. Brethren. Club: Dames of Bridgewater College. Home: Box 25 Bridgewater College Bridgewater VA 22812 Office: Wayland Intermediate Sch Bridgewater VA 22812

WAMPLER, MARGUERITE AUSHERMAN LONG (MRS. ROBERT FRANKLIN WAMPLER), educator; b. Harrisonburg, Va.; d. Jacob Owen and Clara (Ausherman) Long; diploma Shenandoah Coll., 1942; B.S. in Edn., Madison Coll., 1958, M.S., 1961; Ed.D., U. Va., 1972; m. Robert Franklin Wampler, Sept. 20, 1942; children—Claranell (Mrs. Phillip Branner), Carolyn L. (Mrs. Gregory Snow). Elementary sch. tchr., 1958-62; tchr. John C. Myers Intermediate Sch., Broadway, Va., 1963-65; prof. edn., supr. middle grades Anthony Seeger Sch., Madison Coll., Harrisonburg, 1966—. Rockingham County chmn. Vol. Services Western State Hosp., 1963-66. Bd. dirs. Harrisonburg-Rockingham Mental Health Assn., 1960—, sec. bd., 1962. Mem. Va. (chpt. chmn. personnel policies 1968), Rockingham County (chmn. pub. relations com. 1964-65) edn. assns., Madison Coll. P.T.A., Delta Kappa Gamma (sec. 1966—), Kappa Gamma. Mem. Ch. Brethren (tchr. jr. class 1966—). Clubs: Pilots Internat., Madison Coll. Woman's, Plains District Woman's (sec.-treas. 1961—, pres. 1963-65). Home: Route 3 Box 27 Broadway VA 22815 Office: Madison Coll Anthony Seeger Sch Harrisonburg VA 22801

WANDEL, ELSIE DELPHINE (MRS. LESTER J. WANDEL, SR.), psychologist; b. Soledad, Cal., June 9, 1918; B.A. cum laude in Psychology, Stanford, 1951; M.A., San Jose State U., 1952; postgrad. (fellow) U. Tex., 1952-53; m. Lester J. Wandel, Sr., Dec. 6, 1959. Pvt. practice as psychologist and marriage counselor Moraga, Cal., 1936-47, 59—; psychologist Kern and Alada (Cal.) County Sch. systems, 1952-59. Instr. mental health Kern County Jr. Coll., 1952-54, Fresno (Cal.) State U., 1954-56. Vol. Contra Costa County Suicide Answering Service, 1962-68. Bd. trustees Kern County YWCA, 1955-56. Mem. Kings County C. of C. (v.p. 1945), Nat., Internat., Cal., Kern County (v.p. 1956), Contra Costa County psychol. assns., Contra Costa County Mental Health Assn., Nat. Platform Assn., Psi Chi. Recipient National Gold Book for Women, 1967.

WANG, ANNIE TAK-AN HUNG (MRS. DAVID C. P. WANG), physician; b. Hong Kong, China, Sept. 8, 1938; d. Ko-Wong and Chow-Kut (Ho) Hung; came to U.S., 1955, naturalized, 1972; B.A., Wellesley Coll., 1959; M.D., Med. Coll. Pa., 1963; m. David C.P.

Wang, June 29, 1968; children—Enoch Yu-Hsin, Grace Yu-En. Intern Phila. Gen. Hosp., 1963-64, resident pediatrics, 1964-66, chief resident pediatrics, 1966-67; pediatric hematology fellow St. Christophers Hosp. for Children, Phila., 1967-69; practice medicine, specializing in pediatrics and pediatric hematology, Phila., 1969—; mem. staff Hahnemann Hosp.; asst. prof. pediatrics Hahnemann Med. Coll. and Hosp., 1969—. Mem. Phila. Soc. Pediatrics, Phila. Soc. Hematology, Am. Hematology Soc. Mem. Evangelical Ch. Contbr. articles to profl. jours. Home: Bala Cynwyd PA 19004 Office: care Hahnemann Hosp 215 N Broad St Philadelphia PA 19102

WANG, FRANCES DZO (MRS. TED T.H. WANG), librarian, curator; b. Soochow, Kiangsu, China, July 3, 1918 (came to U.S. 1946, naturalized 1961); d. T'ai Sun and Chu Fang (Yang) Dzo; grad. Ginling Coll., Nanking, China, 1938; M.A. in Social Work, U. Chgo., 1950; M.A. in Sociology, U. Wash., 1954, M.A. in Librarianship, 1958; m. Ted T.H. Wang, June 25, 1949; 1 son, Donald P. Head distbn. dept. OWI Chengtu br., Szechwan, China, 1943-45; head library pub. relations USIS Hdqrs., Shanghai, China, 1945-46; librarian for adminstrn. and acquisition Chinese Air Force Office, Washington, 1947-48; research asst. dept. sociology U. Wash., 1953-55, research asso. Far Eastern and Russian Inst., 1955-56, asst. librarian Far Eastern Library, 1956-69; curator-librarian Asian Studies Collection, Honnold Library, Claremont (Cal.) Colls., 1969—; vis. prof. Coll. Chinese Culture and Nat. Taiwan U., 1968-69. Hon. adviser Pacificulture-Asia Mus., Pasadena, Cal. Mem. Am. Sociol. Assn., A.L.A., Assn. Asian Studies, Internat. Assn. Orientalist Librarians, Alpha Kappa Delta, Beta Phi Mu. Contbr. articles to profl. jours. Home: 1662 Denver Av Claremont CA 91711

WANG, FRANCESCA ELIZABETH, computer programmer; b. Shanghai, China, Mar. 7, 1924; d. Robert Hsian-Sung and Stella Anne (Hu) Wang; B.S. in Math., Shanghai U., 1948; M.S. in Edn., Fordham U., 1957. Came to U.S., 1947, naturalized, 1965. Programmer, Stevens Inst. Tech., Hoboken, N.J., 1962-64; sci. programmer-analyst Internat. Tel. & Tel. Fed. Labs., N.J., 1964-67; sci. programmer-analyst Schering Corp., Bloomfield, N.J., 1967-68; staff programmer Reflectone Inc., Stanford, Conn., 1968-69; sr. programmer-engr. Raytheon Co., Burlington, Mass., 1969; programmer on Aurora project USAF Research Lab., Cambridge, Mass., 1972-74. Home: 1110 Commonwealth Av Boston MA 02215

WANG, LUCY YUNG-LING, author, assn. exec.; b. N. China (naturalized Am. citizen); M.A., Columbia; m. Joseph E.P. Wang; children—Anthony, Vincent. Author: Modern Chinese for the Elementary Sch. Vice pres. Chinese Women's Assn. Home: 1336 Ivanhoe St Alexandria VA 22304

WANG, YA-YEN LEE (MRS. CHI-WU WANG), educator; b. Peking, China, Mar. 1, 1930; d. Mong-Lin and Shu-Ming (Liu) Lee; B.S., Villa Maria Coll., 1956; M.S., U. Fla., 1958; Ph.D., U. Ida., 1965; m. Chi-Wu Wang, June 9, 1956; children—Ching-Pi, Ching-Chao, Ching-Yi. Came to U.S., 1952, naturalized, 1964. Instr. math. U. Ida., Moscow, 1960-62, asst. prof., 1965-72, asso. prof., 1972—, acting dir. Computer Center, 1967. Mem. Am. Math. Soc., Math. Assn. Am., Soc. Indsl. and Applied Math., Assn. for Computing Machinery, Am. Assn. U. Profs., Sigma Xi. Home: 2603 East D St Moscow ID 83843

WANGER, RUTH BETSY, psychologist; b. Bridgeport, Conn., July 17, 1938; d. Emil William and Hilda (Kaplan) Schwartz; B.A., Smith Coll., 1960; M.A., George Washington U., 1965, Ed.D., 1971; postgrad. Bethesda Naval Hosp., 1971-72; m. Stanley Wanger, Nov. 11, 1962. Asst. placement officer George Washington U., Washington, 1961-62, alumni placement officer, 1962-67, asst. dir. Continuing Edn. for Women program, 1967-68; psychologist Profl. Assos. Psychiatric Inst., Washington, 1973—. Asst. prof. counseling George Washington U., 1972—. Nat. Def. Edn. Assn. fellow, 1969-70. Mem. Am. Psychol. Assn., Am. Personnel and Guidance Assn., Smith Coll. Club of Washington, Pi Lambda Theta, Phi Delta Gamma. Home: 3536 Hamlet Pl Chevy Chase MD 20015 Office: 2141 K St NW Washington DC 20037

WANGLIN, ANN JEANNETTE (MRS. BYRON CHASE WANGLIN), civic leader; b. Spokane, Wash., May 10, 1922; d. John James and Maybelle Margaret (Gibson) Georgeson; B.A., U. Cal. at Los Angeles, 1944; m. Byron Chase Wanglin, Apr. 6, 1951; children—Ronald Chase, Valerie Ann, Michael James. Pres., Spastic Children League, 1961—; mem. Beverly Hills adv. bd. Assistance League; mem. women's com. Channel KCET; mem. Muses of Mus. Sci. and Industry. Pres., bd. dirs. Performing Fine Arts. Mem. Nat. Charity League, U. Cal. at Los Angeles Affiliates (past pres.), U. Cal. at Los Angeles Med. Center Aux., U. Cal. at Los Angeles Alumni Assn. (dir. 1965-67), Gold Shield, Sigma Kappa. Republican. Mem. Christian Ch. Rotary Annes (pres. W. Los Angeles 1959). Club: Beach. Home: 612 N Roxbury Dr Beverly Hills CA 90210

WANN, MARIE LOUISE DIMARIO (MRS. HARRY ARTHUR WANN), govt. ofcl.; b. N.Y.C., Dec. 13, 1911; d. Peter and Louise (Vandenhoeck) DiMario; B.A., Hunter Coll., 1931; M.A., Columbia U., 1934, Ph.D., 1943; m. Harry Arthur Wann, Oct, 9, 1942 (dec. May 1965). Tchr. math. N.Y.C. high schs., 1932-35; statistician N.Y.C. Dept. Health, 1935-39; statistician U.S. Govt., 1939—; statistician exec. office of pres. Bur. Budget, 1967-70, chief math. statistician Office Statis. Policy, Exec. Office of Pres., Office Mgmt. and Budget, 1970—; tchr. math and statistics, lectr. N.Y.U., Seton Hall Coll., Am. U., Queens Coll., George Washington U. Fellow A.A.S.; mem. Am. Statis. Assn., Am. Math. Soc. Author: Dependent Baggage, 1955. Contbr. articles to profl. jours. Home: 3457 S Leisure World Blvd Silver Spring MD 20906 Office: New Exec Bldg Washington DC 20503

WANTLAND, EVELYN KENDRICK (MRS. WAYNE W. WANTLAND), educator; b. Suffolk, Va., June 22, 1917; d. Marion Kelly and Mary (Causey) Kendrick; student Hollins Coll., 1934-35, U. Chgo., 1936-37; B.A., U. Ill., 1948, M.A., 1949, Ph.D., 1958; m. John R. Kinney, May 16, 1939 (div. 1949); 1 dau., Lois (Mrs. Lawrence Dimmitt); m. 2d, Wayne W. Wantland, Apr. 19, 1964 (dec. Mar. 1971). Prof. math. Ferrum Jr. Coll., 1949-51; asst. prof. math. Ill. Wesleyan U., Bloomington, 1951-57, prof., head math. dept., 1964—; asst. prof. math. Kan. State U., 1957-62; asso. prof. math. U. Miss., 1962-64. Mem. Math. Assn. Am., Am. Math. Soc., Sigma Xi, Pi Mu Epsilon, Sigma Delta Epsilon, Zeta Tau Alpha. Home: 110 E Beecher St Bloomington IL 61601

WARD, AILEEN, educator; b. Newark; d. Waldron Merry and Aline (Coursen) Ward; A.B., Smith Coll., 1940; M.A., Radcliffe, 1942, Ph.D., 1953. Teaching fellow Radcliffe Coll., 1943-45; instr. English, Wellesley Coll., 1946-47, Barnard Coll., 1947-49; asso. Inst. Internat. Edn., 1952, Fund for Advancement Edn., 1953; asst. prof. Vassar Coll., 1954-58; mem. faculty Sarah Lawrence Coll., 1960-64; prof. Brandeis U., Waltham, Mass., 1964—. Fulbright fellow at Girton Coll., Cambridge (Eng.) U., 1949-50; Guggenheim fellow, 1966-67; Radcliffe Inst. fellow, 1970-71. Recipient Duff Cooper Meml. prize for non-fiction, London, 1963; Rose Mary Crawshay prize Brit. Acad., 1964; Nat. Book award in arts and letters, 1964. Author: John Keats: the Making of a Poet, 1963. Home: 21 Alpine St Cambridge MA 02138 Office: Brandeis U Waltham MA 02154

WARD, ALICE MARIE, civic worker; b. New London, O.; d. Clyde Eugene and Daisy (White) Ward; B.A., Ohio Wesleyan U., 1932. Sec., asst. treas. C. E. Ward Co., New London, 1937-72, also dir. Mem. Huron County Republican Women's Club. Mem. New London Bus. and Profl. Women's Club (pres. 1967-68, 72-73), U.S. Lawn Tennis Assn., Mortar Board, Alpha Xi Delta. Methodist (trustee). Mem. Order Eastern Star. Composer songs In the Swim, 1959; Tennis for Everyone, 1963; I Hear a Bird Singing, 1963. Home: 139 E Main St New London OH 44851

WARD, AUDREY LORINE, realtor; b. Chalmbers, Ind., Aug. 22, 1936; d. Clarence Marris and Mary (Allen) Short; grad. high sch.; m. Apr. 10, 1954 (div. 1972); children—Terry Lane, Sherry Ann. Owner Lorine Ward Co., Realtor, Indpls., 1963—. Chmn. Burkhart Home and Garden Tour, 1964. Mem. Zonta Internat., Indpls. Real Estate Bd. (corp. sec.), Nat. (v.p. Ind. chpt. women's council), Indpls. (pres. women's council 1970) bds. realtors, S. Side Multiple Listing Assn. (chmn. 1970). Home: 319 Bennington Rd Indianapolis IN 46227 Office: 3020 S Meridian St Indianapolis IN 46217

WARD, BARBARA (LADY JACKSON), economist, educator, writer; b. York, Eng., May 23, 1914; d. Walter and Teresa (Burge) Ward; student Convent of Jesus and Mary, Felixstowe, 1921-29, Lycee Moliere and Sorbonne, Paris, 1929-31, Die Klause, Jungenheim A/D/B Germany, 1932. Somerville Coll., Oxford (exhibitioner 1932-35), 1935, hon. degrees include, Fordham U., 1949, Columbia, 1954, Keyon Coll., 1957, Harvard, 1957; m. Robert Gillman Allen Jackson, Nov. 16, 1950; 1 son. Lectured for univ. extension courses Cambridge U., 1936-39; joined staff The Economist, London, 1940; vis. lectr. Harvard, 1957-68, Carnegie fellow, 1959-68; Albert Schweitzer prof. internat. econ. devel. Columbia, 1968-73; pres. Internat. Inst. for Environmental Affairs, 1974—. Mem. Pontifical Commn. Justice and Peace; bd. govs. Internat. Devel. Research Center, Can.; bd. dirs. Adlai Stevenson Inst. Internat. Affairs. Mem. Cath. Women's League (nat. pres. 1948-50), Am. Acad. Arts and Scis. (hon.). Author: The International Share Out, 1938; Turkey, 1941; The West at Bay, 1948, Policy For the West, 1951; Faith & Freedom, 1954; The Interplay of East and West, 1957; Five Ideas That Change the World, 1959 (Christopher award 1960); India & The West, 1961; The Rich Nations and The Poor Nations, 1962; Nationalism and Ideology; Spaceship Earth, 1969; The Lopsided World, 1968; The Widening Gap, 1971; (with Rene Dubos) Only One Earth, 1972. Office: care The Economist 25 St James's St London SW1 England

WARD, BETTY LOU HICKS (MRS. JAMES B. WARD), realtor; b. San Pedro, Cal., Oct. 16, 1941; d. Clyde Otho and Elizabeth Clark (Ortis) Hicks; student Diablo Valley Coll., 1960, Anthony's Sch. Real Estate, 1969; m. James B. Ward, Aug. 16, 1970; 1 son, Edward Lu. Accountant, head refinance dept. Volk-McLain Co., Dublin, Cal., 1962-66; salesperson Valley Realty, Dublin, 1966-70; broker, partner, owner Tri-Valley Brokers, Dublin, 1970—. Recipient Salesman of Year award So. Alameda County, So. Alameda County Bd. Realtors, 1971, also named to 5 Million Dollar Club. Mem. Cal. Real Estate Assn. (dir. 1971), So. Alameda County Bd. Realtors (dir. 1970-71). Home: 45 Castlewood Dr Pleasanton CA 94566 Office: 8929 San Ramon Rd Dublin CA 94566

WARD, EVANGELINE HOWLETTE, educator; b. Portsmouth, Va., Apr. 27, 1920; d. Ernest Alonzo and Lillian Bysshe (Somerville) Jones; student Shaw U., 1935-36; B.S., Hampton Inst., 1940; M.A., Atlanta U., 1941; postgrad. Cornell U., 1948, 50; Ed.D., Columbia, 1955; postgrad. Oxford U. (Eng.), summer 1966, U. St. Andrews (Scotland), summers 1968, 73; 1 son, David Nathaniel. Tchr. pub. schs., 1941-45; asst. prof. Hampton Inst. (Va.), 1946-53; grad. research asst. Columbia U., N.Y.C., 1953-55; exec. dir. Nursery Found. of St. Louis, 1955-63; prof. early childhood edn. Temple U., Phila., 1963—. Guest prof. various colls. and univs.; del. White House Conf. on Children, 1970. Bd. dirs. Nat. Found. Improvement Edn. Mem. Nat. Assn. for Edn. of Young Chidlren (pres. 1970-74), World Orgn. for Early Childhood Edn., Assn. Childhood Edn. (mem. tchr. edn. com. 1970-73), Child Welfare League Am., Am. Assn. Elementary-Kindergarten-Nursery Edn., N.E.A. (dir. Nat. Urban League Edn. com. 1972), Pa. Assn. Higher Edn., Standards Com. for Day Care. Author: Early Childhood Edn., 1968. Home: 1220 E Mt Pleasant Av Philadelphia PA 19150

WARD, GERTRUDE LUCKHARDT, educator; b. Mt. Vernon, N.Y., May 27, 1923; d. Carl H. and Marguerite F. Luckhardt; A.B. cum laude, Mt. Holyoke Coll., 1944; postgrad. Ia. State U., 1944-46; M.S., U. Mich., 1948; postgrad. U. Minn., summer 1955, Purdue U., 1961-62; Ph.D., Purdue U., 1970. Instr. biology Earlham Coll., Richmond, Ind., 1949-61, asst. dir. coll. mus., 1952—, lectr. biology, 1961-68, asst. prof. biology, 1968-70, asso. prof., 1970—. Bd. dirs. Richmond Animal Welfare League, Zool. Soc. Wayne County. Mem. Am. Micros. Soc., Entomol. Soc. Am., Herpetologists League, Ind. Acad. Sci. (past sect. chmn.), Wilson Ornithol. Soc., Richmond Audubon and Nature Club (past pres.), Ind. Audubon Soc. (past asst. editor), Sigma Xi. Home: Rural Route 1 Box 194 Centerville IN 47330 Office: Earlham Coll Richmond IN 47374

WARD, INGEBORG LEHMANN (MRS. OTIS BYRON WARD, JR.), psychologist; b. Rotha, Germany, Aug. 14, 1940; d. Richard Herman and Annemarie Charlotte (Henke) Lehmann; came to U.S., 1950, naturalized, 1955; B.S., Westhampton Coll., 1960; M.S., Tulane U., 1965, Ph.D., 1967; m. Otis Byron Ward, Jr., Jan. 1963; children—Richard Byron, Michael Patrick. Asst. prof. psychology Villanova (Pa.) U., 1966-71, asso. prof., 1971—. Mem. small grants com. Nat. Inst. Mental Health, 1972—. Recipient research grants NSF, 1968, Nat. Inst. Child Health and Human Devel., 1970. Mem. Am. Psychol. Assn., Am. Assn. Univ. Profs., Soc. for Study Reprodn., Sigma Xi, Psi Chi. Contbr. articles to profl. jours. Office: Dept Psychology Villanova U Villanova PA 19085

WARD, ISABEL ROBBINS (MRS. WALTER EMERSON WARD), club woman; b. St. Paul, Mar. 9, 1906; d. Orison Benjamin and Mary Ednah (Fiske) Robbins; A.B. with high distinction, George Washington U., 1929; M.Ed., U. Md., 1951; m. Walter Emerson Ward, Aug. 29, 1931; children—Mary Frances (Mrs. Mary Frances Forrester), Elizabeth Louise (Mrs. Robert Lee Shelton). Sch. social worker D.C. Pub. Schs., 1942-66. Nat. vice chmn. Jr. Am. citizens com. D.A.R., 1965-68, D.C. regent, 1966-68, v.p. gen. Nat. Soc., 1970-73, nat. vice chmn. conservation, 1969-71, mem. resolutions com., 1969—, mem. adv. bd. Tamassee (S.C.) D.A.R. Sch., 1966-69, nat. chmn. Seimes Microfilm Center, 1974—; nat. chmn. resolutions com. Nat. Soc. Women Descs. of Ancient and Honorable Arty Co., 1966-68, pres. D.C. ct., 1969-71, nat. rec. sec., 1971-74, nat. pres. 1974—; nat. mus. chmn. Colonial Dames XVII Century, pres. Ft. Garrison chpt., 1973—. Recipient 2 medals of appreciation S.A.R. Mem. Kappa Delta. Republican. Baptist. Home: 4822 Drummond Av Chevy Chase MD 20015

WARD, JEAN (MRS. ERNEST C. SALCIDO), ret. journalist; b. St. Louis; d. Clayton Irving and Vitura (Barnes) Ward; B.A., U. Redlands, 1930; m. Ernest C. Salcido, Jan. 15, 1954. Club editor Los Angeles Examiner, 1945-62; staff writer Los Angeles Times, 1962-72. Mem. Women in Communications, Inc., D.A.R., Daus. Am. Colonists, Assistance League of So. Cal., P.E.O. (pres. 1964-65). Republican. Mem. Order Eastern Star. Address: 109 South Orange Dr Los Angeles CA 90036

WARD, KATHRYN PAINTER, educator; b. Phila.; d. Harry Hottel and Jetta (O'Connell) Painter; A.B., George Washington U., 1935, M.A., 1936, Ph.D., 1947; Docteur de l'Universite, Sorbonne U., Paris, France, 1937. Instr. English, U. Md., College Park, 1938-43, asst. prof., 1945-49, asso. prof. English, 1952—; asso. dir. English Sch., Office of Soviet Mil. Attache Washington, 1943-45; lectr. Grad. Sch., U.S. Dept. Agr., 1945-49; cultural attache Am. Embassy, Greece, 1949-51; chmn. U.S. Ednl. Commn. Greece, 1949-51; cons. Dept. State, 1951-52; lectr. Army Extension Program, 1952-65. Mem. Georgetown Citizens Assn. Mem. Am. Assn. U. Profs., Coll. English Assn., Modern Lang. Assn., D.A.R. (past regent Dolly Madison chpt., state historian), D.C. Fedn. Women's Clubs (past edn. chmn.), Greek-Am. Cultural Inst., Phi Kappa Phi, Phi Delta Delta, Delta Kappa Gamma, Phi Delta Gamma. Club: Women's City (past pres.). Contbr. articles to profl. jours. Home: 3622 Prospect St NW Washington DC 20007 Office: Dept English U Md College Park MD 20742

WARD, LUCY ANN, librarian; b. Joliet, Ill., Feb. 7, 1936; d. Marvin Edward and Margaret (Nickles) Ward; B.S. in Edn., Ill. State U., 1957; M.S. in L.S., U. Ill., 1964. Unit dist. librarian Herscher (Ill.) pub. schs., 1957-58, Plainfield (Ill.) pub. schs., 1958-60; librarian Lockport (Ill.) Twp. High Sch., 1960—. Reference cons. Chgo. Bridge & Iron Co. Research Lab., 1967-68; archives librarian Nat. Office of Christian Bros., Lewis Coll., Lockport, Ill., 1968—. Mem. Ill. Library Assn., Am. Fedn. Tchrs., Ill. Assn. Sch. Librarians, Am. Assn. U. Women, Joliet League Women Voters, Lockport Bus. and Profl. Women's Club (pres.), Will County Hist. Soc., Pi Gamma Mu. Democrat. Methodist. Home: 568 E 2d St Lockport IL 60441

WARD, MADELEINE REBECCA SUPLEE, interior decorator; b. Phila., Dec. 4, 1908; d. William Zerns and Emma Theresa (Ward) Suplee; student Temple U., 1927, Pa. State Coll., 1933-34, Pa. Mus. Sch. Indsl. Art, 1934-35, N.Y. Sch. Interior Decoration, 1935-36; m. Douglas Henry Ward, Mar. 2, 1940; 1 son, James Burton III. Interior decoratior, Hampton Bays, L.I., N.Y., Mem. Am. Assn. Ret. Persons, Hampton Bays Civic Assn. Democrat. Mem. Order Eastern Star. Address: Box 211 Private Rd Springville Rd Hampton Bays NY 11946

WARD, MARIE BARBER (MRS. JOHN PHILLIP WARD), educator; b. Gainesville, Tex., Oct. 18, 1912; d. John Manning and Minnie Estelle (Vestal) Barbar; student Mary-Hardin Baylor Coll., 1929-31; B.A., Tex. Women's U., 1937; M.A., Hardin-Simmons U., 1950; postgrad. Tex. Technol. U., 1964-68; m. John Phillip Ward, Apr. 21, 1938. Tchr., Aspermont (Tex.) Ind. Sch. System, 1937-62; faculty Sul Ross State U., Alpine, Tex., 1962-64; instr. English, Angelo State U., San Angelo, Tex., 1964—. Bd. dirs. Stonewall County March of Dimes, 1952. Named Woman of Year in Aspermont, C. of C., 1962. Mem. Tex. Fedn. Women's Clubs (Tex. Tchr. of Year 1958, sec. 1962-64, 1st v.p. Heart Tex. dist. 1974-76), Tex. Joint Council English Tchrs. (hon. life), Delta Kappa Gamma (chpt. pres. 1970-72). Mem. Order Eastern Star. Clubs: Literary Review (San Angelo); Phoenix (Aspermont). Address: Box 11070 ASU Station San Angelo TX 76901

WARD, MARTHA EADS, librarian; b. Quincy, Ill., July 21, 1921; d. Oliver Thomas and Gladys (Feagans) Eads; student Knox Coll., 1938-40; B.S., U. So. Cal., 1942; B.L.S., Pratt Inst. Library Sch., 1947; teaching certificate Quincy Coll., 1963; m. Vincent P. Ward, Feb. 3, 1951 (div. Aug. 1962). Children's librarian Quincy Pub. Library, 1947—. Mem. Ill. (chmn. children's sect. 1953, 65), Am. library assns. Conglist. (sec. bd. deacons 1969). Author: (with Dorothy A. Marguardt) Authors of Books for Young People, 1964; Adlai Stevenson: Young Ambassador, 1967; Ollie Ollie Oxen-Free, 1969; (with Dorothy A. Marquardt) Illustrators of Books for Young People, 1970; The Bugman, 1972. Home: 2300 Hampshire St Quincy IL 62301 Office: Quincy Pub Library 526 Jersey St Quincy IL 62301

WARD, MARY BEATRICE, educator; b. Bradford, Yorkshire, Eng., Nov. 5, 1904; d. Arthur and Florence (Thorpe) Ward; brought to U.S., 1904, naturalized, 1910; student Sarah Lawrence Coll., 1928-29, Fontainebleau Conservatoire Americana, France, 1930; B.S., Boston U., 1945, M.Ed., 1949. Music instr. Abbott Acad., Andover, Mass., 1930-31; head music dept. North Providence (R.I.) High Sch., 1939-59; dir. guidance North Providence Schs., 1957—, sch. psychologist, 1968—. Asst. dir. Fed. House Sch. Music, 1932-36; choir dir. Ch. of Master, Providence, 1935-52; choir dir., organist Mathewson St. Ch., Providence, 1952-59; organist 1st Ch. Christ Scientist, Providence, 1959—. Trustee Union Free Library, North Providence, R.I.; founder, bd. dirs. One Worlders, Fidelio Choral Soc. Named Woman of Year, Fruit Hill Jr. Women's Club, 1964, Bus. and Profl. Women's Club, 1963; recipient John Fitzgerald Kennedy award R.I. Coll. Alumni Assn., 1973. Mem. Nat. Assn. Sch. Psychologists, Delta Kappa Gamma, Pi Lambda Theta. Home: 112 Waterman Av North Providence RI 02911 Office: 1828 Mineral Spring Av North Providence RI 02904

WARD, MARY J. (MRS. DENNIS WARD), physician; b. Harrogate, Tenn., Sept. 6, 1924; d. LeRoy and Willa (Mitchell) Johnson; A.B., Lincoln Meml. U., 1944; M.D., U. Tenn., 1952; m. Dennis Earl Ward, June 19, 1950; children—Dennis Earl, Thomas Roy, Edmund Haynes. Rotating intern Scott-White Hosp., Temple, Tex., 1952-53; pvt. practice medicine, Iuka, Miss., 1953-56; chief pediatric resident Ga. Bapt. Hosp., 1956-58; pediatrician Forest Park and Atlanta, 1958-59; pvt. practice pediatrics, Corinth, Miss., 1961—; mem. staff Magnolia Hosp., Corinth; cons. staff Tishomingo County Hosp., Iuka, Miss. Diplomate Am. Bd. Pediatrics. Fellow Am. Acad. Pediatrics; mem. A.M.A., Miss. Med. Assn., Alcorn County Med. Club, Alpha Psi Omega Alpha Epsilon Iota. Address: Route 1 Old Kassuth Rd Corinth MS 33834

WARD, MAURICE BRADLEY, educator; b. Paxico, Kan., Apr. 27, 1923; d. Edgar Luther and Gertrude (Guillory) Bradley; B.S., Kan. State U., 1949, M.S., 1951; Ed.D., U. No. Colo., 1972; 1 dau., Wynona (Mrs. Gerald Eugene Black). Instr. citizenship edn. Kan. State U., Manhattan, 1952-53; supr. film reservations Wichita (Kan.) Pub. Schs., 1954-58, tchr. homemaking, 1958-61, counselor, 1961-70; asst. prof. and program specialist career devel. U. No. Colo., Greeley, 1970—. Named Outstanding Homemaking Tchr., Seventeen Mag., 1961. Mem. Am., Colo. Vocational assns., Nat. Assn. Women Deans, Adminstrs. and Counselors (mem. adv. council continuing edn. com. 1973), Delta Sigma Theta. Roman Catholic. Home: 1808 21st St Rd Greeley CO 80631

WARD, PEARL LEWIS, librarian, educator; b. Greeley, Colo., Nov. 30, 1920; d. Claude Thomas and Gertrude (Skinner) Lewis; B.A., Pepperdine Coll., 1951; M.S. in L.S., U. So. Cal., 1952, Ph.D., 1969; m. Ralph E. Ward, Aug. 29, 1940, 1 son, Paul. Librarian and tchr. Pepperdine Coll., Los Angeles, 1952-58; tchr. Los Angeles State Coll., 1959-61; catalog librarian Aerospace Corp., El Segundo, Cal., 1961-62; sch. librarian Los Angeles City Schs., 1962-64; reference librarian El Camino Coll., Torrance, Cal., 1964-66; faculty U. So. Cal., Los Angeles, 1966—, asst. prof., 1969—. Mem. Am., Cal. library

Assns., Assn. Am. Library Schs., Am. Assn. Sch. Librarians, Assn. for Ednl. Communication and Tech., Am. Assn. U. Women, Pi Lambda Theta, Beta Phi Mu. Author: The School Media Center, 1973. Home: 3211 W 78th Place Los Angeles CA 90043

WARD, RUTH SUTHERLAND, advt. and pub. relations exec.; b. Billings, Mont., Sept. 24, 1915; d. John and Evelyn (Sutherland) Ward; B.A., La. State U., 1937; Reporter, Ogden (Utah) Standard Examiner, 1937-39, Sacramento Bee, 1939-48; pub. relations dir. Sacramento area United Crusade, 1953-55, 58-60; news dir. KCRA-TV, Sacramento, 1955-57; advt. dir. Sacramento Municipal Utility Dist., 1965—, publs. editor, 1960-65. Pub. relations chmn. Sacramento Commn. for Women, 1972. Mem. Am. Advt. Fedn., Audubon Soc., Soroptimists Internat. (pub. relations chmn. Sacramento 1971-72), Pi Beta Phi. Author: For The People, The Story of the Sacramento Municipal Utility District, 1973. Home: 3428 Mesa Verde Dr El Dorado Hills CA 95630 Office: 6201 S St Sacramento CA 95813

WARDEBERG, HELEN L., educator; b. Barnesville, Minn.; d. Anton O. and Lillie (Bredemeier) Wardeberg; B.S., State Tchrs. Coll., Moorhead, Minn., 1945, M.A., U. Minn., 1948, Ph.D., U. Minn., 1951. Tchr., supr. Clay County, Minn., 1939-42; tchr. elementary sch. Browns Valley, Minn., 1942-43; elementary supr. Winona (Minn.) State Tchrs. Coll., 1944-47; asst. prof. elementary edn., supr. student tchrs. Cortland (N.Y.) State Tchrs. Coll., 1951-54; prof. edn. Cornell U., Ithaca, N.Y., 1954—, chmn. dept. edn., 1969—. Mem. Am. Ednl. Research Assn., Assn. Supervision and Curriculum Devel., Internat. Reading Assn., N.E.A., Nat. Soc. Study of Edn., Pi Lambda Theta. Contbr. articles in field to profl. jours. Home: 100 Fairview Square Ithaca NY 14850

WARDEN, MARGARET SMITH, library trustee; b. Glasgow, Mont., July 18, 1917; d. Thomas Wilson and Carrie (Johre) Smith; m. Robert Dickinson Warden, Aug. 9, 1942; children—Gary Sherman, Margaret Macintyre. Trustee Great Falls (Mont.) Pub. Library, 1957—, chmn. bd., 1963—. Mem. Civil Def. Womens Adv. Com., 1955; civil def. chmn. Great Falls Schs., 1955-58; chmn. Great Falls chpt. A.R.C., 1956-59; mem. pres.'s council Coll. Great Falls, 1967—; citizen's rep. to ad hoc bldg. com. for classroom office bldg. Mont. State U., 1969—; mem. Mont. Adv. Council on Libraries, 1973-74; mem. Mont. Com. for Humanities, 1973—; mem. Mont. State Library Com., 1974—, vice chmn., 1974-75. Del., Mont. Constl. Conv., 1971-72. Bd. dirs. Camp Fire Girls. Recipient 1st. Library Trustee award Mont. Library Assn., 1965, blood program award Mont. Kiwanis, 1959; named Woman of Year, Great Falls Bus. and Profl. Womens Club, 1955. Mem. Am. (membership chmn. Mont. 1962-64), Pacific N.W. (chmn. legislative com. 1965), Mont. (chmn. legislative com. 1961—, pres. 1973-74) library assns., Am. Library Trustees Assn. (chmn. legislative com., 1968-69, sec. 1974-75), League Women Voters. Contbr. Montana Libraries, 1962-68. Home: 208 3d Av N Great Falls MT 59401

WARDEN, PATRICIA, assn. exec.; b. Washington, Apr. 11, 1931; d. Robert Bruce and Elizabeth Vandergrift (Withers) Warden; student U. Tenn., 1949-50. Asst. editor Am. Automobile Assn., 1957-59; press sec. to Congressman Frank C. Osmers, Jr., 1964; feature and news writer Capital Hill and Georgetown Spectators, also Washington World mag., 1962-64; dir. sales and pub. relations Virgin Isle Hilton Hotel, St. Thomas, also St. Thomas editor Caribbean Beachcomber mag., 1965-68; dir. pub. relations Nat. Presbyn. Center, Washington, 1968-72; dir. community relations Montgomery County Assn. Retarded Citizens, Wheaton, Md., 1972-73; dir. pub. relations D.C. chpt. A.R.C., 1973—. Guest lectr. Virgin Islands Coll., 1967. Mem. Pub. Relations Soc. Am., Am. Women in Radio and TV. Home: 4000 Tunlaw Rd NW Washington DC 20007

WARDIN, LUCILE PEAK (MRS. ALBERT W. WARDIN, JR.), coll. dean; b. Long Island, Va., Jan. 31, 1925; d. Russell Nez and Mary Lee (Hodges) Peak; B.S., Madison Coll., 1946; M.R.E., So. Bapt. Theol. Sem., 1949; M.A. in Higher Edn., Ohio State U., 1967; m. Albert W. Wardin, Jr., May 31, 1969. Bapt. student dir. Longwood Coll., Farmville, Va., 1949-56, Mary Washington Coll., Fredericksburg, Va., 1956-61, U. Ill. at Urbana, 1961-63, Memphis State U., 1963-64; asst. dean of students Meredith Coll., Raleigh, N.C., 1964-68; dean of women Belmont Coll., Nashville, 1968—. Mem. Nat., Tenn. assns. women deans and counselors. Baptist. Home: 331 Gaywood Dr Nashville TN 37211 Office: Belmont Coll Nashville TN 37203

WARDLAW, BARBARA RUTH, librarian; b. Del Rio, Tex., June 6, 1930; d. Roy Lee and Anna Elizabeth (Walker) McCulley; B.A., Our Lady of the Lake Coll., San Antonio, 1967, M.S. in Library Sic., 1968; m. L.B. Wardlaw, Jr., Feb., 14, 1949 (div. 1962); children—Watt Lamar, Denise, Lawrence. Asst. librarian Bee County Coll., Beeville, Tex., 1968—. Mem. Southwestern, Tex. library assns., Tex. Jr. Coll. Tchrs. Assn., Alpha Chi. Republican. Episcopalian. Home: Route 1 Box 22F Beeville TX 78102 Office: Route 1 Beeville TX 78102

WARDLAW, CATHERINE CAROLINE MULLICAN, poet; b. Brigman, Tex., Dec. 6, 1902; d. Evan Bethel and Mary Caroline (Pepper) Mullican; certificate, North Tex. State U., 1926; B.A., Tex. State U., 1930; m. Robert Asa Wardlaw, Aug. 8, 1936; 1 dau., Caroline (Mrs. Abdulkader Abbas Muhalhal). Tchr. pub. schs., Tex., 1924-36, 58-67, Ark., 1942-44, 52-58, Los Angeles, 1944-45; contbr. poetry to U.S. and fgn. publs., anthologies, periodicals. Active A.R.C. Recipient numerous awards for poetry. Mem. Poetry Soc., Creative Writers, Delta Kappa Gamma. Mem. Order Eastern Star. Address: 1710 Royalty St Odessa TX 79761

WARDLAW, HELEN EMILY CRAIG (MRS. GEORGE MILLARD WARDLAW), banker; b. LaGrange, Ga., Nov. 15, 1916; d. Eldridge Jerome and Emily (Heath) Craig; B.S., Winthrop Coll., 1938; M.A. in Edn., Columbia, 1941; postgrad. Emory U., 1946; m. George Millard Wardlaw, June 12, 1942; 1 son, Craig Millard. Head bus. dept. Anderson (S.C.) Coll., 1938-40; instr. Queens Coll., Charlotte, N.C., 1940-42, also registrar, 1941-42; dir. So. Bus. U., Atlanta, 1945-47; diversified occupations coordinator Central High Sch., Charlotte, 1947-52; with First Union Nat. Bank N.C., Charlotte, 1952—, v.p., trust officer, 1971—. Named Charlotte Woman of Year in Banking, 1965. Mem. Charlotte C. of C. Episcopalian. Club: Myers Park Country (Charlotte). Home: 637 Wingrave Dr Charlotte NC 28211 Office: 301 S Tryon St Charlotte NC 28211

WARDLAW, JANET MELVILLE, univ. dean; b. Toronto, Ont., Can., 1924; d. J.M. and Mollie (Law) Wardlaw; B.A. in Household Econs., U. Toronto, 1946; M.S. in Pub. Health Nutrition, U. Tenn., 1950; Ph.D. in Nutrition, Pa. State U., 1963. Dietetic intern, Royal Victoria Hosp., Montreal, 1946-47; dietitian, Canadian Red Cross Sch. Meal Study, 1947-49; nutritionist, Mich. Dept. Health, 1950-53, Toronto Dept. Health, 1953-56; asst. prof., faculty household science U. Toronto, 1956-60, asso. prof., faculty food sci., 1963-66; prof. dept. foods and nutrition Coll. Family and Consumer Studies, U. Guelph (Ont., Can.), 1966-67, asso. dean-dean designate, 1968-69, dean, 1969—. Mem. Nutrition Soc. Can. (nominating com.), Canadian Dietetic Assn. (treas. 1965-67), Am. Dietetic Assn., Internat. Fedn. Home Econs., Am., Can. home econs. assns., Sigma Xi. Home: 20 Suffolk St W Guelph ON N1H 2H8 Canada

WARE, DOROTHY WAITERS (MRS. CHARLES EDWARD WARE), librarian; b. Charlotte, N.C., Feb. 8, 1943; d. Clifton and Lela (English) Waiters; B.A., Johnson C. Smith U., 1969; M.S. in L.S., Atlanta U., 1969; m. Charles Edward Ware, May 29, 1972. Adult community services librarian Pub. Library of Charlotte and Meck, 1965-68, coordinator spl. project, 1971-72, coordinator services to spl. groups, 1973—. Adviser, Appalachian Adult Edn. Center, Morehead (Ky.) State U., 1972—. Trustee N.C. State Library. Home: 1320 Fordham Rd Charlotte NC 28208 Office: 310 N Tryon St Charlotte N.C. 28202

WARE, FRANCES LEE, govt. ofcl.; b. Louisville, Dec. 13, 1919; d. Willie Lionel and Florence (Brown) Ware; A.B., U. Louisville, 1940; postgrad. George Washington U., Syracuse U. aide U.S. Govt. Printing Office, Washington, 1943-50, planner, 1950-60; printing specialist, publishing services br. Internal Revenue Service, Washington, 1960-62, mgmt. services officer, 1962-72, asst. operations mgr., 1972-73, operations mgr., 1973—. Recipient Career Ednl. award, 1969. Mem. Am. Soc. Pub. Adminstrn., Am. Assn. U. Women, Internat. Personnel Mgmt. Assn., Franklin Tech. Soc., Columbian Women George Washington U. (publicity chmn. 1967-72, treas. 1972-74, v.p. 1974-76), Bus. Profl. Women's Club D.C., Phi Delta Gamma (chpt. historian 1967-68, nat. editor 1963—, chpt. pres. 1969-70). Club: University Women's (v.p. D.C. 1960-62, pres. 1968-70). Home: 4201 Massachusetts Av NW Washington DC 20016 Office: 1111 Constitution Av NW Washington DC 20224

WAREK, SUE ANN, ednl. counselor; b. Schenectady, June 28, 1942; d. Joseph Paul and Beatrice Caroline (Warrington) Warek; B.A. in Speech Arts, Am. U., 1964. Counseling specialist for corr. students McGraw-Hill, Inc., Washington, 1968—. Free lance photographer. Vol. worker Corcoran Art Gallery. Vol. worker Democratic Polit. Campaign. Mem. East African Wildlife Soc., Wilderness Soc., Recorder Soc. Home: 2800 Wisconsin Av NW Washington DC 20007 Office: 3939 Wisconsin Av NW Washington DC 20016

WARENSKJOLD, DOROTHY, lyric soprano; b. San Leandro, Cal.; d. William E. and Mildred (Stombs) Warenskjold; B.A., Mills Coll.; student U. Cal., Berkeley; studied voice with Mabel Riegelman, San Francisco. Recital debut, San Francisco, 1943; opera debut as Agathe in Weber's Der Freischutz, 1947; debut in Falstaff, San Francisco Opera Co., San Francisco, Cal., 1948; guest soloist Voice of Firestone radio and TV; lyric soprano concert artist, concert tours throughout U.S., 1949—; singer-producer Dorothy Warenskjold's Mus. Theater; rec. artist Capitol Records, including Student Prince, Songs of Grieg and Dvorak, On Wings of Song; appeared with Cin. Summer Opera, also in New Orleans, San Antonio, Pitts., San Francisco, Los Angeles, Chgo., Fort Worth, Miami. Mem. Alpha Omicron Phi, Sigma Alpha Iota. Address: care Columbia Artists Mgmt Inc 165 57th St New York City NY 10019

WARFEL, RUTH ELIZABETH, coll. dean; b. Lancaster, Pa., Aug. 13, 1920; d. G. Earle and Mary (Breuninger) Warfel; B.S., State Tchrs. Coll., Millersville, Pa., 1941; M.S., Ind. U., 1948; postgrad. Tchrs. Coll., Columbia. Tchr. elementary schs. Lancaster, Pa., 1941-44; dean of women State U. Tchrs. Coll., Potsdam, N.Y., 1948-51, asso. dean of students, 1951-61; dean of women Miami U., Oxford, O., 1961-64; dean students Mt. Holyoke Coll., South Hadley, Mass., 1964—. Served as ensign WAVES, Bur. Naval Personnel, Washington, 1944-46. Mem. Am. Coll. Personnel Assn., Nat. Assn. Student Personnel Adminstrs., Nat. Assn. Women Deans, Adminstrs. and Counselors (treas. 1971-73), Pi Lambda Theta, Kappa Delta Pi. Club: Zonta (v.p. Potsdam). Home: 15 Ashfield Lane South Hadley MA 01075 Office: Mt Holyoke Coll South Hadley MA 01075

WARFIELD, GRACE LUCILLE JACOBSON (MRS. WALTER S. WARFIELD), educator, editor; b. Albert Lea, Minn., Feb. 27, 1910; d. John and Anna-Cena (Larsen) Jacobson; B.S., U. Minn., 1930, M.A., 1958, specialist in edn., sch. psychology services, 1962; m. Walter S. Warfield, Apr. 16, 1948; children—James D., Patricia Ann (Mrs. Bertram A. Coppock, Jr.), Wendy S. English tchr., Garden City, Minn., 1930-33; prodn. asst. U. Minn. Press, 1952-55; tchr. mentally retarded, Mpls., 1955-61; sch. psychologist, coordinator classes for mentally retarded-handicapped, 1962-65; prin. Dowling Sch. for Crippled Children, Mpls., 1965-66; asst. editor Exceptional Children, The Council for Exceptional Children, Washington, 1966-68, asst. exec. dir., editor, Exceptional Children, 1968—. Mem. Council for Exceptional Children, Ednl. Press Assn. Am., Am. Assn. Mental Deficiency, Nat. Assn. Sch. Psychologists. Democrat. Author: (with Harriet Blodgett) Understanding Mentally Retarded Children, 1959. Home: 7614 16th St NW Washington DC 20012 Office: 1920 Association Dr Reston VA 22091

WARGOTZ, HELEN, psychoanalyst; b. N.Y.C.; d. Louis and Eva (Weinglass) Wargotz; B.A., Hunter Coll., 1942; M.S.W., Columbia, 1946; m. Joseph DeMarco, July 4, 1942. Case worker foster home dept. Jewish Child Care Assn., N.Y.C., 1946-47; psychiat. social worker VA Mental Hygiene Clinic, N.Y.C., 1947-48; case worker Mental Retardation Clinic Flower Hosp. Mental Hygiene Clinic, N.Y.C., 1950-51; psychiat. social worker Youth Bd. P.S. 140, L.I., 1951-52; family counselor Jewish Family Service, 1952-55; psychoanalytic therapist L.I. Consultation Center, 1955-57; counselor N.Y. Guild for Jewish Blind, 1957-58; counselor, chmn. speakers bur. Jamaica Center for Psychotherapy, 1958-68; psychoanalytic group therapist Mental Health Inst., N.Y.C., 1959-60; chief psychiat. social worker Children's Clinic N.Y. Sch. Psychiatry, 1962-63; dir., coordinator Allied Teen-Age Guidance and Adult Counseling Service, N.Y.C., 1964—; counselor Shield David Sch. and Clinic, N.Y.C., 1966-69; chief psychiat. social worker 5th Av. Center for Counseling and Psychotherapy, N.Y.C., 1968-72; psychotherapist, supr. group therapy Theodore Reik and N.Y. Clinic for Mental Health, 1956-64; group discussion leader 92d St. YM-YWHA, Manhattan, 1967-68; lectr. in field family and child relationships and mental health. Mem. Internat. com. sci. and medicine Parents Without Partners, profl. adv. com., 1967. Mem. Nat. Assn. Social Workers (charter), N.Y. Acad. Scis., Am. (pub. relations, bus., social issues and finance coms. 1957—), Eastern group psychotherapy assns., Council Psychoanalytic Psychotherapists (rec. sec. 1963-64). Club: City. Home: 510 E 86th St New York City NY 10028

WARING, MARILYN MAE OLSON (MRS. RYDER C. WARING), real estate exec.; b. Salt Lake City; d. Dewey H. and Jennie D. (Dolmer) Olson; student U. Utah, 1953-56; m. Ryder C. Waring, Dec. 10, 1956; children—Kari, Mark, Stacie Ann. Office mgr. Olson Service & Constrn. Co., 1953-56, now dir.; office mgr. Frank & Thomas Advt., 1956-57; exec. v.p. Taft & Co., Inc., Salt Lake City, 1959—; real estate and investments Capson Investment & Realty Co., 1968—; office mgr. Mailliard & Schmiedell, 1965-67. Dir. publicity Crestview Sch. P.T.A., 1965, sec., 1968-69, pres., 1970-71; chmn. scholarship com. Girls League Granite High, 1965—. Mem. Salt Lake Bd. Realtors (mem. pub. relations com., salesmen's activities com. 1974—), Utah Assn. Realtors (mem. make Am. better com. 1974—), Kappa Kappa Gamma (pres. alumni assn. 1972). Republican. Mem. Ch. of Jesus Christ of Latter-day Saints. Club: Spa Athletic. Home: 1918 Severn Dr Salt Lake City UT 84117 Office: 1549 South 11th E care Capson Investment & Realty Co Salt Lake City UT 84105

WARMAN, MARY KATHERINE OCKERMAN, educator; b. Burgin, Ky., Sept., 1924; d. Everett Listen and Jenny Katherine (Scifres) Ockerman; student. U. Md., 1959-62; M.S., Murray State U., 1967, M.A. in Edn., 1969, Ed.S. in Sch. Adminstrn., 1972; m. James A. Warman, Apr. 5, 1942 (div. June 1962); children—James A., Everett Michael, Jenny Katherine, Arthur Louis. Substitute tchr. Hopkins County Bd. Edn., Madisonville, Ky., 1962-63; tchr. Outwood Hosp. and Sch., Dawson Springs, Ky., 1963-65, asst. prin., 1965-67, prin., 1967-69, program dir., 1969-72; unit dir. Oakwood, Somerset, Ky., 1972—. Mem. Am. Assn. Mental Deficiency, Am. Speech Assn., Bus. Profl. Women's Club, N.E.A., Ky. Guidance and Personnel Assn., Ky. Continuing Edn. Assn., Ky. Assn. for Tchr. Edn., Internat. Platform Assn., Kappa Delta Pi. Address: 110 Crab Orchard St Somerset KY 42501

WARMAN, RUTH EDGAR (MRS. MYRON WORK WARMAN), lawyer; b. Waynesburg, Pa., Mar. 24, 1918; d. Clarence and Etta Maria (Shirk) Edgar; A.B., Waynesburg Coll., 1941; postgrad. Rutgers U., 1947-48; LL.B., U. W. Va., 1952, postgrad., 1958-60; postgrad. Dartmouth U., 1961; m. Myron Work Warman, July 10, 1941; children—Philip, Ralph, Etta (Mrs. Willian Tantlinger), Mary (Mrs. James Terry). Tchr. various pub. schs. Pa., 1955-65; admitted to Pa. bar, 1962; mem. firm Warman & Warman, Uniontown, Pa., 1965—. Active in 4-H work, Uniontown, Pa., 1950-55. Bd. dirs. Outreach, 1973-74; mem. exec. bd. Fayette County Child Welfare Assn., 1969-74. Mem. Pa., Fayette County bar assns., Am. Civil Liberties Union, Nat. Orgn. Women, Am. Assn. U. Women, N.A.A.C.P. Club: Soroptimists (Uniontown, Pa.). Home: Box 464 Rural Delivery 6 Uniontown PA 15401 Office: 97 E Main St Uniontown PA 15401

WARMER, MARGERY ANN BRADEN (MRS. JAMES CRAIG WARMER), educator; b. Chanute, Kan.; d. Perry Marshall and Blanche (Barnes) Braden; A.B., U. So. Cal., 1943, M.S., 1947; Ph.D., U.S. Internat. U., 1973; m. James Craig Warmer, Dec. 19, 1943; 1 dau., Jennie Anne. Secondary tchr. pub. schs., San Diego, 1944-47, Compton, Cal., 1947-58, Arcadia, Cal., 1948-49, Orange, Cal., 1952-53; family life edn. counselor city schs., San Diego, 1953-56; asso. dean students San Diego State U., 1956-71, dean of students, 1971-73, prof. Sch. Family Studies and Consumer Scis., 1974—. Recipient certificate of appreciation for civilian service WAC, 1965; named Woman of Achievement, Pres.'s Council Women's Service and Bus. Clubs, San Diego, 1965. Mem. Nat. Assn. Women Deans and Counselors, Cal. Assn. Women Deans and Vice Prins. (pres. So. sect. 1964-66, mem. state bd. 1964-66), U. So. Cal. Alumni Assn., Mortar Bd., Phi Beta Kappa, Alpha Lambda Delta (nat. dist. adviser 1965-71, v.p. 1974—), Phi Sigma Alpha, Pi Lambda Theta, Phi Kappa Phi. Office: San Diego State U San Diego CA 92115

WARMS, RUTH HANSTEIN, fashion retail store exec.; b. Atlantic City, N.J., Aug. 26, 1925; d. Walter and Henrietta (Rauh) Hamstein; B.S. in Home Econs. and Edn., Pa. State U., 1946; m. Leon J. Warms, Jan. 4, 1947; children—Susan (Mrs. Steven Harris Lefkowitz), Carol Ruth, Lisa Janet. Buyer, Nat. Dept. Store, Atlantic City, 1947-48; co-owner, v.p., buyer, fashion coordinator The Clothers Tree, Inc., Youngstown, O., 1961—. Mem. Women's Com. for Children's Concerts, 1960-68; patron Youngstown Playhouse, 1961—; mem. Youngstown Heart Assn., Nat. Council Jewish Women, Planned Parenthood Assn., Friends Am. Art (life). Alpha Epsilon Phi. Republican. Jewish religion. Home: 207 Gypsy Lane Youngstown OH 44504 Office: 5090 Market St Youngstown HO 44512

WARNE, ALICE ELIZABETH, editor; b. Bellefonte, Pa., Sept. 23, 1916; d. Harold Alfred and Mary Pearl (Waite) Warne; A.B., Barnard Coll., 1938; M.A., Pa. State U., 1956. Asst. to supt. sample rooms Macy's, N.Y.C., 1941; editorial asst. Warner Publs. N.Y.C., 1942; asst. editor labor relations and govt. regulation bus. services Prentice-Hall, Inc., N.Y.C., 1942-48, editor Food and Drug Service, 1946-47; research asst. Center Research, Pa. State U. Coll. Bus. Adminstrn., University Park, 1948-56, author, co-author monographs, articles, 1949-55, 57-60, 64—, research asso., 1956—, editor Pa. Bus. Survey, 1958—, editor publs., 1956—, editor Coll. Bus. Adminstrn. Alumni News, 1973—. Guest econs. program for bus. sch. faculties Swedish Govt., 1966. Case Inst. Tech. Econs.-in-Action program fellow, 1964. Mem. Am. Assn. U. Profs., Beta Gamma Sigma, Pi Gamma Mu, Omicron Delta Epsilon. Home: Box 127 Pleasant Gap PA 16823 Office: Bus Adminstrn Bldg Pa State U University Park PA 16802

WARNER, ANNE RATHBUN (MRS. RICHARD C. WARNER), health assn. exec.; b. Detroit, Sept. 6, 1928; d. Irvin N. and Estelle (Kuhlman) Rathbun; B.A. in English and Polit. Sci., Heidelberg Coll., 1950; postgrad. Kent State U., 1949, U. Akron, 1960, Pace Coll., 1968; m. Richard C. Warner, Oct. 15, 1950. Asst. librarian North Canton (O.) Pub. Library, 1951-53; underwriter, group actuarial dept. Monarch Life Ins. Co., Springfield, Mass., 1953-55; staff asst. for pub. information Area Devel. Com., Akron, O., 1956-62; asst. dir. pub. relations Am. Nurses Assn., N.Y.C., 1962-66, dir. pub. relations, 1966-72; program and communications dir. Nat. Health Council, N.Y.C., 1972—. Mem. Pub. Relations Soc. Am. (accredited mem.), Nat. Pub. Relations Council of Health and Welfare Services, Women Execs. in Pub. Relations. Home: 124 Heather Hill Rd Cresskill NJ 07626 Office: 1740 Broadway New York City NY 10019

WARNER, EVELYN, educator; b. Pasadena, Cal., Oct. 8, 1925; d. William Henry and Alma Naomi (Allred) Warner; B.S., U. So. Cal., 1948; M.S. in Edn., U. So. Cal., 1965. Tchr. mentally retarded pub. schs., Pomona, Cal., 1966, San Gabriel, Cal., 1967—; 1st adminstr., tchr.-coordinator Devel. Center for Handicapped Minors, Los Angeles County Supt. Schs., 1968—; program specialist office supt. schs., Los Angeles County, 1971—. Mem. Am., So. Cal. occupational therapy assns., N.E.A., Cal. Tchrs. Assn.

WARNER, GERTRUDE CHANDLER, author; b. Putnam, Conn., Apr. 16, 1890; d. Edgar Morris and Jane Elizabeth (Carpenter) Warner; student Yale, 1936, 40. Tchr. elementary sch., Putnam, Conn., 1918-32; publicist A.R.C., 1917-50. Named Woman of Yr., Emblem Club, 1965; recipient Edgar Allen Poe award U. So. Miss., 1966. Mem. Women's Fellowship (pres. Putnam 1951). Conglist. (clk., Sunday sch. tchr.). Author (juveniles): House of Delight, 1916; Star Stories, 1918; (with Frances L. Warner) Life's Minor Collisions, 1921, Pleasures and Palaces, 1933; The World in a Barn, 1927; Windows into Alaska, 1929; World on a Farm, 1931; Henry Barnard, 1948; Boxcar Children, 1940; Surprise Island, 1949; Yellow House Mystery, 1953; Mystery Ranch, 1955; Mike's Mystery, 1960; Blue Bay Mystery, 1961; Lighthouse Mystery, 1963, Mountain Top Mystery, 1964; Schoolhouse Mystery, 1965; Caboose Mystery, 1966; Houseboat Mystery, 1967; Snowbound Mystery, 1968; Tree House Mystery, 1969; Bicyle Mystery, 1970; Mystery in the Sand, 1971; Mystery Behind the Wall, 1973; Bus Station Mystery, 1974. Address: 22 Ring St Putnam CT 06260

WARNER, GLORIA MARMAR (MRS. RICHARD R. PICHEL WARNER), psychiatrist; b. N.Y.C., July 24, 1933; d. William W. and Celia (Dantzig) Marmar; B.A., Barnard Coll., 1952; M.D., N.Y. U.,

1959; postgrad. Columbia Psychoanalytic Clinic for Tng. and Research, 1972—; m. Richard R. Pichel Warner, July 4, 1953; children—Jon J.P., Keith R.P., Douglas C.P., Lynn S.P. Intern Montefiore Hosp., N.Y.C., 1959-60; research fellow Mt. Sinai Hosp., N.Y.C., 1961-63, resident psychiatry, 1963-66, staff psychiatrist, 1966-69, asst. attending psychiatrist, 1969—; instr. Mt. Sinai Sch. Medicine, City U. N.Y., 1965-69, clin. asso. psychiatrist, 1967-73, asst. clin. prof. psychiatry, 1973—; sch. psychiatrist Mt. Sinai Hosp. Sch. Nursing, 1966-69. Diplomate Am. Bd. Psychiatry and Neurology. Mem. A.M.A., N.Y. State, N.Y. County med. socs., Am. Psychiat. Assn., Am. Fedn. Clin. Research, Am. Assn. Group Psychotherapy, Am. Med. Womens Assn., Assn. for Psychoanalytic Medicine, N.Y. Acad. Scis., Alpha Omega Alpha. Contbr. profl. jours. Office: 1160 5th Av New York City NY 10029

WARNER, JOANE DALE, occupational therapist; b. New Haven, May 10, 1947; d. Paul Malcolm and Barbara Stearn (Gray) Warner; student U. Conn., 1965-67, New Eng. Coll., 1967-68; B.S., U. N.H., 1970. Staff therapist Berkshire Rehab., Pittsfield, Mass., 1971-72; head dept. occupational therapy Lenox Hill Rehab. Hosp., Lynn, Mass., 1972—. Asst. basketball coach, girl's team Cath. Youth Orgn., Lawrence, Mass., 1972-73; asst. basketball coach and trainer, girl's team, Salem, N.H., 1973—, also No. Essex Community Coll., Haverhill, Mass.; player, trainer women's basketball team, Salem, 1972—. Mem. Am. Occupational Therapy Assn. Home: 64 Crescent St Lawrence MA 01841 Office: 70 Granite St Lynn MA 01914

WARNER, LUCILE MERTZ (MRS. HENRY CHESTER WARNER), club woman; b. Burnettsville, Ind., July 19, 1888; d. Peter H. and Catherine (Ferris) Mertz; student Ind. U., 1906-08; Ph.B., U. Chgo., 1911; m. Henry Chester Warner, Sept. 19, 1913; children—Myra Alice (Mrs. George F. Nichols), Louise, Nancy E. Mem. Dixon chpt. D.A.R., 1913, state historian 1947-49, state vice regent 1952-54, state regent 1955-57, v.p. gen. 1959-62, hon. v.p. gen. for life; pres. Assn. Wives Ill. Lawyers, 1944-45, 50-51; sec. trustees Ill. State Library Assn., Springfield; pres. trustees Dixon Pub. Library, 1951-52, 59-60; organizing mem. Dixon br. Am. Assn. U. Women, 1947; commr. Dixon Girl Scouts, 1927-30; pres. Dixon High Sch. P.T.A., 1928-29. Mem. Colonial Daus. 17th Century (1st v.p. Ill.; past sec. gen. nat. soc.), Colonial Dames Am., Nat. Soc. Daus. Founders and Patriots Am., Nat. Soc. New Eng. Women, Colonial Coverlet Guild Am., Nat. Soc. Magna Charta Dames. Home: 321 E Everett St Dixon IL 61021

WARNER, NANCY ELIZABETH, pathologist; b. Dixon, Ill., July 8, 1923; d. Henry Chester and Lucille (Mertz) Warner; B.S., U. Chgo., 1944, M.D., 1949. Intern U. Chgo. Clinics, 1949-50, asst. resident pathology, 1950-53; resident pathology Cedars of Lebanon Hosp., Los Angeles, 1953-54, asst. pathologist, 1954-58, asso. dir. div. labs., 1965-66; asst. prof. pathology U. Chgo., 1958-59, asso. prof. pathology, 1959-65, dir. Lab. Surg. Pathology, 1959-65; asso. prof. Wash. Sch. Medicine, 1966-67; asso. prof. pathology U. So. Cal. Sch. Medicine, 1967-69, prof. pathology, 1969—, chmn. dept. pathology, 1972—; att. physician U. So. Cal. Med. Center; chief pathologist Women's Hosp., Los Angeles County-U. So. Cal. Med. Center, 1968-72, dir. labs. and pathology, 1972—; cons. Barlow Sanatorium and Hosp., 1968—. Fellow Coll. Am. Pathologists, Am. Soc. Clin. Pathologists; mem. A.A.A.S., Chgo. Path. Soc., U. Chgo. Alumni Assn., D.A.R., Daus. Founders and Patriots, Am. Forestry Assn., Ann. Assn. Pathologists and Bacteriologists, Am. Assn. Anatomists, Endocrine Soc., Am. Soc. Cytology, Microcirculatory Soc., Am. Soc. Exptl. Pathology, European Soc. Microcirculation, Internat. Acad. Pathology, Los Angeles Acad. Medicine, Sigma Xi, Alpha Omega Alpha. Home: 1065 S San Rafael Av Pasadena CA 91105 Office: U So Cal 2025 Zonal Av Los Angeles CA 90033

WARNER, WAVERLY WESTERVELT, investment co. exec.; b. Plainfield, N.J., Feb. 23, 1943; d. Harris S. and Norma (Westervelt) Warner; student Upsala Coll., 1961-63, Union Coll., 1963-65, Wagner Coll., 1965-67. Sec. to pres. Handler Mfg. Co., 1958-60; asst. to ins. mgr. Weston Instruments, Inc., 1963-65; asst. treas., asst. sec. Nelson Fund, Inc., N.Y.C., 1968-69, treas., asst. sec., 1969-71, sec., treas., 1971—; sec. Tokyo Fund, Inc., 1968—, George J. Nelson Assos., 1968—. Home: 555 Ft Washington New York City NY 10033 Office: 345 Park Av New York City NY 10022

WARNOW, JOAN NELSON, librarian; b. Buffalo, Dec. 11, 1931; d. C. David and Edith G. (Sjolander) Nelson; student U. Buffalo, 1950-52; B.S., Simmons Coll., 1953; postgrad. Columbia Faculty Philosophy, 1953-55, Sch. Library Service, 1966-67; m. Morton Warnow, Jan. 28, 1955 (div. 1966); children—Tandy, Kimmen, Paul. Librarian, N.Y. Pub. Library, N.Y.C., 1953-55, Queensboro (Queens, N.Y.) Pub. Library, 1960-62; librarian Am. Inst. Physics, N.Y.C., 1965-74, acting dir. Center for History Physics, 1974—. Archival cons. N.Y. Psychoanalytic Inst., N.Y.C., 1971-72, Consumers Union, Mt. Vernon, N.Y., 1973—. Mem. Spl. Libraries Assn., Soc. Am. Archivists, Com. on Archives Sci., Mid-Atlantic Archives Regional Conf., History Sci. Soc., Oral History Assn. Editor: (with H. Wright and C. Weiner) The Legacy of George Ellery Hale, 1972. Home: 150-90 Village Rd Jamaica NY 11432 Office: 335 E 45th St New York City NY 10017

WARREN, BETTY DEANE, artist; b. N.Y.C., Jan. 12, 1920; d. Alonzo Vincent and Dorothy Deane (Devor) Warren; student N.A.D., N.Y.C., 1937-42; student Cape Sch. Art, 1937-42, 1949; m. Stuart Lancaster, May 12, 1950; children—John Warren, Michael Dean; m. 2d, Jacob H. Herzog, 1960. Tchr. drawing, painting Albany (N.Y.) Inst. History and Art, 1959-73; co-owner, dir. Malden Bridge (N.Y.) Sch. Art, 1964-73; one-person shows Albany Inst. History and Art, U. N.C., Berkshire Mus., Hartwick Coll., Sarasota Art Assn., Pen and Brush Club, Shaker Mus.; exhibited art in group shows Allied Arts Am., Tampa Mus., Am. Watercolor Soc., Knickerbocker Artist, Nat. Arts Club, Am. Artists profl. League, Cooperstown (N.Y.) Ann., numerous others; represented in permanent collections at numerous galleries and pvt. collections. Recipient Purchase prize Albany Inst. History and Art, 1964; Gold medal Catherine Lorrilard Wolfe Nat. Annual, 1964, grand prize Cooperstown Nat. Ann., 1966, Kathleen Grumbacher medal C. L. Wolfe Club, 1970. Mem. Grand Central Art Galleries, Portraits, Inc., Nat. Arts Club, Am. Artists Profl. League, Nat. League Am. Pen Women. Address: 76 Western Av Albany NY 12203

WARREN, DOROTHEA GRUBBS, librarian; b. Columbus, Kan., Feb. 3, 1919; d. Eyrle Vance and Ruth Cleveland (Hawkins) Grubbs; A.B., Kan. State Coll., 1939; J.D., Washburn U., 1942; m. Harold Hudson Warren, Nov. 20, 1944 (div. Sept. 1973); children—Barbara (Mrs. Vernon Hutton), Rebecca (Mrs. David Laney), Brenda. Admitted to Kan. bar, 1942; with govt. regulations dept. Seagram's Distillery, Louisville, 1942-44; with Postal Savs. & Loan, Topeka, Kan., 1955-56; asst. law librarian Kan. State Library, Topeka, 1956-67; law librarian, prof. law Washburn U. Law Sch., Topeka, 1967—. Part-time practice law, 1942—. Mem. Bar Assn. State Kan., Topeka Bar Assn. Home: 1434 Polk St Topeka KS 66612 Office: 1700 College St Topeka KS 66621

WARREN, GALE SUZANNE, mental health adminstr.; b. Pekin, Ill., Mar. 19, 1942; d. Bertis Everett and Ida Mae (Edwards) Capehart; B.A., Miami U., Oxford, O., 1964; M.S., Ind. U., 1966, Ph.D., 1972; m. Gordon Harris Warren, Aug. 20, 1966; children—Kevin G., Jason L. Research asst. Bur. Ednl. Studies and Testing, Ind. U., 1966-69; asst. dir. ednl. testing Counseling and Testing Center, So. Ill. U., 1969-70; dir. Kittitas County (Wash.) Mental Health/Mental Retardation Office, Ellensburg, 1972—. Mem. Am. Psychol. Assn., Am. Ednl. Research Assn., Nat. Council Measurement in Edn., Kittitas Valley League Women Voters. Author: (with Clinton I. Chase) Freshmen View the College Scene: Opinions Before and After the Initial Semester, 1969. Home: 1807 Regal Av Ellensburg WA 98926 Office: Kittitas County Mental Health/Mental Retardation Office 507 Nanum St Ellensburg WA 98926

WARREN, GERTRUDE LILLIAN, govt. ofcl., educator; b. Lockport, N.Y., Nov. 17, 1884; d. John Hepner and Lillie A. (Andrus) Warren; grad. Geneseo State Tchrs. Coll., 1906; student Cornell U., summer 1906; B.S., Columbia U., 1916, M.A., 1925. Tchr. elementary and high schs., 1906-14; instr. Tchrs. Coll., Columbia U., 1915-16, Simmons Coll., 1916-17; fed. leader 4-H Club work, coop. extension service, U.S. Dept. Agr., 1917-52; co-compiler documentary materials 4-H Hist. Library, 1960—. Mem. White House Confs. on children and youth, 1930, 40, 50; mem. Eighth sci. Conf. of the Americas, 1940, White House Conf. Rural Edn., 1944, 54, Nat. Conf. Rural Edn., 1954, 6th Internat. Grassland Congress, 1952, Internat. Confs. Asso. Country Women of the World, 1936, 53, Internat. Conf. Christian Edn., 1938, Conf. Profl. Leaders Character-Bldg. Agys., 1937, Nat. Nutrition Conf. for Def., 1941, 1st 4-H Leaders Conf. Caribbean Area, 1946, Nat. Conf. on Prevention and Control Juvenile Delinquency, 1946, Nat. Confs. on Citizenship, 1946-53, White House Conf. Hwy. Safety, 1954. Mem. com. on devel. Nat. 4-H Found. and 4-H Center, 1947-51; nat. adv. council Girl Scouts U.S.A., 1956—; nat. exec. com. Am. Youth Hostels, Inc., 1938-58; exec. com. Alliance for Rural Youth, 1938—; spl. program adviser O. Latham Hatcher Edn. Fund, 1946-62. Decorated Order of Three Stars (Latvia), 1938; recipient award for distinguished service U.S. Treasury Dept., 1945, Superior Service award U.S. Dept. Agr., 1949, Outstanding Service award Epsilon Sigma Phi; cited by Nat. 4-H Club Found., 1951; named one of 10 Pioneer 4-H Leaders, Nat. Com. for Rural Leaders, 1962. Mem. Am. Assn. U. Women, Am. Home Econs. Assn., Columbia U. Alumni Assn., Pan Am. Liaison Com. Women's Orgn., Am. Country Life Assn., Women's Nat. Farm and Garden Assn. (nat. pres. 1952-54, nat. adv. com. 1954—), Epsilon Sigma Phi (past chief). Episcopalian. Club: Washington. Author govt. bulls. and mag. articles. Contbr. Book of Rural Life, Careers for Women, Life Worth While. Home: 4201 Cathedral Av NW Washington DC 20016

WARREN, HELEN ROZELLE GUYTON (MRS. HAROLD WARREN), financial co. exec.; b. Hannibal, Mo., July 8, 1932; d. John R. and Oline A. (Kelby) Guyton; Asso. in Bus., St. Joseph Jr. Coll., 1957; B.S., Central Mo. State Tchrs. Coll., 1959; m. Harold Warren, Jan. 10, 1960; children—Harold, Helisa Oline. Sec., Land Clearance for Re-devel., Columbia, Mo., 1959-65; asst. project mgr. Housing Authority of Columbia, 1965-73, project mgr., 1973; service asst. CIT Financial Services, Columbia, 1973—. Funeral dir. Stuart Parker Funeral Home, Columbia, 1968. Historian West Blvd P.T.A., 1970-71, treas., 1972-74. Mem. Am. Legion. Mem. Order Eastern Star. Home: 10 N 4th St Columbia MO 65201 Office: 10 N 4th St Columbia MO 65201

WARREN, JANE BYRNS, newspaper editor; b. Babylon, L.I., N.Y., Jan. 24, 1925; d. Richard Stephen and Cora Osborn (Horton) B.; grad. Katharine Gibbs Secretarial Sch., 1943; m. Millard R. Warren, June 8, 1946; children—Millard R., Steven B., Paul H., Mary T., Elizabeth A. Sec., J. Walter Thompson Co., advt., N.Y.C., 1943-47; editor Beacon newspaper, Babylon, 1967—. Den mother local Cub Scouts, 1954-57; pub. relations Southside Hosp. Aux., Bayshore, N.Y., 1957-60. Recipient Pub. Service award Creative Art League. Home: 39 Cormact Ct Babylon NY 11702 Office: 45 Deer Park Av Babylon NY 11702

WARREN, JUDITH ANNE, coll. adminstr.; b. Chgo., June 6, 1935; d. Frank Herbert and Janet Elizabeth (Johns) Warren; B.A., Wells Coll., 1957. Adminstrv. asst. Northwestern Med. Sch., 1957-59; asst. dir. pub. relations Children's Meml. Hosp., Chgo., 1959-60; asso. dir. Cancer Research Found., U. Chgo., 1960-63; asst. to pres. Wells Coll., Aurora, N.Y., 1963—. Pres., Aurora Vol. Fire Dept., 1973—; chmn. Cayuga County Emergency Health Planning Council, 1972—. Presbyn. (elder 1972). Home: Moonshine Rd Aurora NY 13026

WARREN, MARY GRESHAM, newspaperwoman; b. Temple, Tex., Feb. 16, 1920; d. Oliver Pinkney and Willie Ellen (Chambliss) Gresham; B.S. in Home Econs., U. Tex., 1943, M.Journalism, 1951; m. Francis Albert Warren, Dec. 10, 1955. Tchr. home econs. Acad. High Sch., Temple, 1943-45; county home demonstration agt., Hays County, Tex., 1945-49; author homemaking column San Marcos (Tex.) Record, also Kyle (Tex.) News, 1945-49; Central Tex. women's editor Austin Am.-Statesman, also supr. reporting lab. U. Tex., Austin, 1950-51; tech. writer S.W. Research Inst., San Antonio, 1952-54, asst. dir. pub. relations, editor house organ, 1954-60; garden editor, feature writer women's news Waco (Tex.) Tribune Herald, 1970—. Sec. activities bd. Regis Retirement Center, Waco, 1967-69; publicity vol. Waco chpt. A.R.C., 1969-70; sec. to bd. Laura Edwards Community Center, Waco, 1969-70. Mem. Nell Pape Garden Center (life), Waco Council Garden Clubs (hon.), Women in Communication, Ex-Students Assn. U. Tex. Methodist. Editor: Manual on Volunteer Services in Homes for the Aging and Nursing Homes, 1970. Home: 2133 Lake James Dr Waco TX 76710 Office: 900 Franklin Av Waco TX 76701

WARREN, PAMELA S. (MRS. ROBERT SABELLA), librarian; b. Maryville, Mo., Dec. 31, 1940; d. Clyde Absalom and Ruth (Scamman) Warren; student Central Coll. (Fayette, Mo.), 1959-61; B.A., Neb. Wesleyan U., 1962; M.A. in Library Sci. (Mo. State Library scholar), U. Ill., 1963. Asst. librarian Trails Regional Library, Warrensburg, Mo., 1963-66; dir. Rolling Hills Regional Library, St. Joseph, Mo., 1966-74; asst. dir. users' services Broward County Library, Ft. Lauderdale, Fla., 1974—. Named Outstanding Young Woman, St. Joseph Jr. C. of C., 1971. Mem. Am., Mo. (chmn. jr. mems. round table, pres. pub. library div., sec.; pres. elect 1973-74) library assns., Altrusa Internat. (pres.), Bus. and Profl. Womens Club (pres. 1971), Am. Assn. U. Women (chmn. study group), St. Joseph C. of C. (1st v.p. womens div.), D.A.R., Beta Sigma Phi, Alpha Gamma Delta, Alpha Lambda Delta, Alpha Mu Lambda, Delta Kappa Gamma. Home: 5100 SW 90th Av Apt 407 Cooper City FL 33314 Office: 413 N Belt St St Joseph MO 64506

WARREN, PATRICIA ARMSTRONG, curator; b. Los Angeles, Jan. 29, 1932; d. Paul Lincoln and Marie (Collison) Armstrong; student Mills Coll., 1949-51, U. Cal. at Berkeley, 1951-52; B.A., Cal. State U. at Los Angeles, 1965, M.A., 1967; m. William Joscelyn Warren, Dec. 26, 1951; children—William, Tiffany, John, Wendy. Hist. curator County Los Angeles, Dept. Arboreta and Botanic Gardens, Arcadia, Cal., 1967—. Instr., Pasadena City Coll., 1968—, U. Cal. at Los Angeles, 1969—. Recipient Grant, Nat. Mus. Act, 1973. Mem. Am. Assn. Museum, Am. Assn. State and Local History, Orgn. Am. Historians, Nat. Trust Historic Preservation, Western History Assn., Cal. Hist. Soc. (merit award 1974), Asso. Hist. Socs. Los Angeles County (pres. 1971-73), Hist. Soc. So. Cal. (v.p. 1971), Conf. Cal. Hist. Socs. (awards chmn./museums chmn. 1971-73), Phi Alpha Theta. Author: California Architecture, 1971; Santa Anita Depot, 1970; Elias Jackson Baldwin, 1973; A Time of Change: Hugo Reid, 1973. Home: 245 W Colorado Blvd Arcadia CA 91006 Office: 301 N Baldwin Av Arcadia CA 91006

WARREN, PATRICIA NELL, editor; b. Helena, Mont., June 15, 1936; d. Conrad Kohrs and Nellie Bradford (Flinn) Warren; A.A., Stephens Coll., 1955; B.A., Manhattanville Coll. of Sacred Heart, 1957; m. George Orest Tarnawsky, June 21, 1957 (div. July 1973). Copy editor Reader's Digest, Pleasantville, N.Y., 1959-63, book editor, 1959—. Staff writer Runner's World, Mountain View, Cal., since 1971—. Clubs: Road Runners Club Am., Nat. Road Runners (publicity and women's dir. 1972), Amateur Athletic Union. Author: The Last Centennial, 1971; The Front Runner, 1974. Office: Reader's Digest Pleasantville NY 10570

WARREN, PATRICIA SUE STRICKLAND, lawyer; b. Columbus, O., Nov. 28, 1944; d. Crump Johnson and Ensley Sue (Osburn) Strickland; student Ohio State U., 1962-64; B.A., U. Fla., 1966; postgrad. Stetson U., 1966-67; J.D., Fla. State U., 1969; m. Richard Michael Warren, Nov. 18, 1973. Admitted to Fla. bar, 1969, practiced in Pensacola, 1969-70, Fort Walton Beach, 1970—; asso. firm Hahn and Reeves, Pensacola, 1969-70. Chmn. Okaloosa County Law Day, 1972. Mem. Okaloosa County Republican Club, 1970—, bd. dirs., 1972, treas., 1972; state coll. chmn. Fla. Fedn. Young Republicans, 1966-67; Recipient Merit award Fla. Fedn. Young Republicans, 1967. Mem. Fed., Fla., Okaloosa-Walton (treas. 1974) bar assns., Soc. Bar 1st Jud. Circuit, Fla. Assn. Women Lawyers, Phi Alpha Delta. Baptist. Home: E Kelly St Destin FL 32541 Office: 40 Beal St Fort Walton Beach FL 32548

WARREN, ROSLYN PAUKER (MRS. RICHARD M. WARREN), educator; b. N.Y.C., N.Y., Jan. 30, 1923; d. George and Henrietta (Fincle) Pauker; B.A., N.Y. U., 1944, M.S., 1947, Ph.D., 1954; postgrad. U. Kan., 1947-48; m. Richard M. Warren, Mar. 31, 1950. Research student Am. Mus. Natural History, N.Y.C., 1945-47, 50-54; research asso. dept. anatomy U. Kan., 1947-48, Brown U., 1954-56, instr. dept. neurology and psychiatry N.Y. U. Coll. Medicine, 1956-57; vis. scientist dept. zoology U. Cambridge (Eng.), 1957-59; asst. prof. zoology Howard U., 1959-61, Shimer Coll., 1961-64; asst. prof. zoology U. Wis., Milw., 1965, asso. prof., 1966-70, prof. 1970—, asso. dean scis. Coll. Letters and Sci., 1971—, on leave of absence as vis. scientist animal behavior research group zoology dept. Oxford (Eng.) U., 1969-70. Mem. A.A.A.S., Am. Psychol. Assn., Animal Behavior Soc. (mem. exec. com.), Am. Soc. Zoologists, Internat. Soc. Developmental Psychobiology (exec. sec.). Author (with Richard M. Warren) Helmholtz on Perception: its Physiology and Development, 1968. Home: 924 E Juneau Av Milwaukee WI 53202

WARREN, SHAR SOUTHALL (MRS. GUY SCOTT WARREN), editor; b. Holidays Cove, W.Va., Jan. 28, 1930; d. Edgar C. and Freda Bodell (Kay) Southall; B.A. in Journalism, Bethany Coll., 1952; m. Leech Key Cracraft, Dec. 10, 1956 (dec. Aug. 1961); 1 son, Stuart McLure; 2d. m., Guy Scott Warren, July 18, 1970. Reporter, columnist Wheeling (W.Va.) News Register, 1951-56; soc. editor Palm Springs (Cal.) Life Mag., 1959-61; social columnist Riverside (Cal.) Daily Enterprise, 1958-63; owner, editor, publisher Personages, social listings for leaders Palm Springs, Cal., 1972—; women's editor The Desert Sun, Palm Springs, Cal., 1967-70. Exec. v.p. Opera Guild of the Desert, 1972—; pres. Palm Springs (Cal.) Pathfinders, 1974—. Bd. dirs. Palm Springs (Cal.) Boys Club, 1972—. Mem. World Affairs Council, Phi Mu. Republican. Clubs: Press, Thunderbird Country (Palm Springs, Cal.). Home: 222 Chino Dr Palm Springs CA 92262 also Aldeia do Golf Vilamoura Algarve Portugal Office: PO Box 1004 Palm Springs CA 92262

WARREN, SUE ALLEN, psychologist, educator; b. Dunn, N.C.; d. Robert Lee and Jessie (Allen) Warren; A.B., East Carolina U., 1939; M.A., Duke, 1951; Ph.D., State U. Ia., 1955; m. Robert D. Little, Nov. 20, 1941 (div. May 1952); 1 son, Arthur Allen. Tchr. High Point (N.C.) Schs., 1939-41; psychologist Duke U. Med. Center, 1941-51, LaCrosse (Wis.) Child Guidance Center, 1951-53, U. Ia. Med. Center, 1953-55; coordinator research and psychol. service Williamsville (N.Y.) Schs., 1955-59; dir. psychology Ore. Fairview Home, Salem, 1959-63, Ill. State Pediatric Inst., Chgo., 1963-69; region V adminstr. Mass. Mental Health Dept., Dedham, 1969-70; Lectr. U. Buffalo, 1955-59, U. Portland, 1959-63, Boston U., 1969-70, prof., 1970—; asso. prof. U. Ill., 1963-69. Recipient Sylvia Capper award Ore. Assn. Retarded Children, 1964. Diplomate Am. Bd. Profl. Psychologists. Mem. Am. Psychol. Assn., (mem. council reps. 1961-63), Am. Assn. Mental Deficiency (mem. exec. com. 1966-68, v.p. 1969-71, 1st v.p. 1974—), Council for Exceptional Children, A.A.A.S., Soc. for Research in Child Devel., Internat. Soc. for Sci. Study Mental Deficiency, Sigma Xi. Contbr. articles to publs. Editor Ore. Psychol. Newsletter, 1961-63, Mental Retardation, 1970—. Home: 4 Seaway Rd Squantum MA 02171 Office: Boston U 765 Commonwealth Av Boston MA 02215

WARRICK, DOROTHY ANNE VOGEL (MRS. JAMES EDWARD WARRICK), fashion coordinator; b. Saginaw, Mich.; d. Stanley Edward and Blanche (Stewart) Vogel; student Wayne State U., 1953-56, Mich. State U., 1938-42, U. Cal. at Los Angeles, 1944-45; m. James Edward Warrick, Nov. 6, 1943; children—M. Starr, Brooke Harry. Dir., Fairlane Nursery Sch., Dearborn, Mich., 1953-60; corp. fashion trainer J.L. Hudson Co., Detroit, 1960-69; adminstrv. asst. Milgrin in Fisher Bldg., Detroit, 1969-70; store mgr. Himelhoch Bros., Detroit, 1970; dir. advt. and promotion Kresco, Inc., Detroit, 1970—; advt. and tng. dir., fashion coordinator Alvin's, Inc.-Lion Store, 1971-73. Mem. Detroit Tchrs. Assn. (pres. 1959-60), Am. Soc. for Tng. and Devel., Detroit Nursery Assn. (past pres.), Detroit Symphony Assn., Fashion Group. Episcopalian. Club: Womens City (Detroit), Kiwaniqueens (Dearborn). Home: 2111 S Telegraph Pontiac MI 48053

WARRICK, MARTHA HALTOM (MRS. WILLIAM EDGAR WARRICK), psychiatrist; b. Martinsburg, W.Va., Oct. 7, 1939; d. William Lorenz and Estelle (Armstrong) Haltom; A.B., Gettysburg Coll., 1961; B.S. in Occupational Therapy, Washington U., St. Louis, 1967; M.D., W.Va. U., 1967; m. William Edgar Warrick, Jr., Nov. 7, 1971; stepchildren—Laurie, Amy, Elaine. Intern, W.Va. U. Hosp., Morgantown, 1967-68, resident in psychiatry, 1968-70; resident in psychiatry John Ulmstead Hosp., Butner, N.C., 1970-71; staff psychiatrist W.H. Trentman Mental Health Center of Wake County, Raleigh, N.C., 1971-72, Orange-Person-Chatham Mental Health Center, Chapel Hill, N.C., 1972—; clin. asst. prof. psychiatry U. N.C., 1973—; cons. psychiatrist Dorothea Dix Hosp., Raleigh, 1971-72; mem. staff Wake Meml. Hosp., Raleigh. Mem. Am. Occupational Therapy Assn. Home: 4436 Sunny Ct Durham NC 27705 Office: 310 W Franklin St Chapel Hill NC 27514

WARRIN, HELEN BROWN, educator; b. Bklyn.; d. William and Clementine (Walcott) Brown; B.S., Rutgers U., 1929; M.A., Columbia Tchrs. Coll., 1933; Ph.D., N.Y.U., 1935; m. James J. Kelly, Apr. 28, 1958 (dec. Dec. 1962). Classroom tchr., Newark, 1927-37; sci. cons. curriculum, ednl. radio programs sta. WBGO., Newark, 1948-64; curriculum cons. Newark Bd. Edn., 1937-39; vice prin. 1st Av. Elementary Sch., Newark, 1939-45; prin. S. 8th St. Sch., Newark, 1945-64; field prof. N.J. State Coll., Paterson, 1954-64; asso. prof. edn. Seton Hall U., South Orange, N.J., 1964—, dir. environmental edn., 1972—. Research cons. Universal Edn. and Visual Arts, div. Universal City Studios, Inc., N.Y.C., 1958—; mem. N.J. Com. for Higher Edn. for Outdoor Edn., 1962—. Chmn. youth program Essex County (N.J.) chpt. A.R.C., 1955—, mem. adv. com. Eastern area A.R.C., Office Ednl. Relations, 1960-63, dir., dean women at leadership devel. centers in N.J. for high sch. A.R.C. dels., 1960-67. Grantee Dept. Health, Edn. and Welfare, 1972-74. Mem. Pi Lambda Theta (editor nat. jour. 1940-45). Author: (with Grace Maddux, Arthur Baker) Jr. Scientist Series, Grades 1-6, 1960. Home: 73 Hudson Av Maplewood NJ 07040 Office: Seton Hall U Dept Elementary Edn South Orange NJ 07079

WARRINGTON, FERN MARIE FISK, social worker; b. Farmington, Minn., Mar. 23, 1913; d. James Austin and Laura Blanche (St. John) Fisk; B.S. cum laude, U. Minn., 1933, M.A., 1941; certificate U. Pitts., 1949; certificate Inst. Psychoanalysis, Chgo., 1953, Menninger Found., 1950; m. Ronald J. Warrington, July 12, 1959 (div. Mar. 1964). Social worker mother's pension div. Ramsey County Juvenile Ct., St. Paul, 1934-35; with children's bur. Div. for Exceptional Children State Bd. Control St. Paul, 1935-38; field instr. U. Minn. Sch. Social Work, Mpls., 1938-41; case supr. Children's Bur., Dayton, O., 1941-42; asst. field dir. A.R.C., Washington, 1942-45; med. social worker demonstration project U. Chgo. Clinics, Chgo., 1946-48; cons. in child devel. Ravinia Nursery Sch., Highland Park, Ill., part time 1954-55; asso. in social work Gus Weinfeld Child psychiatrist, Highland Park, Ill., 1954-55; counselling service Assn. Family Living, Chgo., 1950-51; psychiat. social work mental hygiene clinic Women's and Children's Hosp., Chgo., 1951-53 (part-time); psychiat. social worker, Chgo., 1950-55 (part-time); asst. chief social worker Inst. Juvenile Research Ill. Dept. Pub. Welfare, Chgo., 1949-55; case supr. social service div. Agnews State Hosp., Dept. Mental Hygiene, Sacramento, 1955-56; research asso. lab. human devel. Stanford, 1956-58; chief social worker Child Guidance Clinic Mental Health Services San Mateo (Cal.) County Dept. Pub. Health and Welfare, 1958-66, supr. adoption program social service div., 1966—. Dir. San Mateo Mental Health Soc., 1960-63. Mem. Nat. Assn. Social Workers, Acad. Certified Social Workers, Am. Assn. U. Women, Kappa Delta. Home: 402 Portofino Dr San Carlos CA 94070 Office: 225 W 37th St San Mateo CA 94403

WARSAW, IRENE, ret. banker; b. Kawkawlin, Mich., Nov. 26, 1908; d. Herman August and Auguste (Malzahn) Warsaw; grad. high sch. With Bay Trust Co. (merged with People's Nat. Bank & Trust Co., 1957), Bay City, Mich., 1933—, v.p., trust officer, 1960-72, v.p., trust officer, 1972-74. Lectr. creative writing pub. schs., colls., profl. orgns.; editorial cons. Poetry Soc. Mich., 1962—; judge numerous poetry contests, 1966—. Active Community Chest, Bay City, Y.M.C.A., Bay City, Y.W.C.A., Bay City; mem. Bay City Players, 1955—, Studio 23, 1963—. Recipient 1st prize Shakespearean Sonnet contest Poets' Club Chgo., 1970; 1st prize Humorous Poetry contest Nat. League Am. Pen Women, 1968, numerous others. Mem. Nat. League Am. Pen Women (pres. Mich.), Mich. (rec. sec.), Pa. poetry socs., Detroit Women Writers, Bus. and Profl. Women's Club. Presbyn. Author: A Word in Edgewise, 1964. Contbr. numerous poems to nat. mags., 1950—. Home: 1309 6th St Bay City MI 48706

WARSHAW, ALEXANDRA ANNE, univ. adminstr.; b. San Francisco, Nov. 9, 1940; d. Murry F. and Rachel Alexandra (Hirshberg) Felds; student State U. N.Y., 1958-59; B.A., C.W. Post Coll., 1962; M.A., Temple U., 1964. Grad. asst. Temple U., Phila., 1962-64, instr. speech, 1964-67, trainer for Center for Community Studies, 1967-68, acad. adviser, 1968-70, asst. to dir. coll. relations, 1970-72, coordinator student orientation, high sch. Outreach programs, 1972-74, dir. coll. relations, 1974—, chmn. adminstrv. groups, 1974—. Cons. Am. Right-of-Way Assn., 1965-69. Chmn. Temple Women's Rights Coalition, 1972-73. Mem. Nat. Assn. Student Personnel Admintrs., Nat. Assn. Women Deans, Adminstrs. and Counselors, Phila. Coll. Council on Community Involvement. Contbr. to profl. publs. Home: 515 S 18th St Philadelphia PA 19146 Office: Temple Univ Owl's Nest Philadelphia PA 19122

WARSHAW, EDNA HOFFMAN (MRS. STANLEY W. WARSHAW), occupational therapy cons.; b. Boston, July 9, 1926; d. Irving L. and Julia (Fisher) Hoffman; certificate occupational therapy Tufts U., 1946, B.A., 1947; m. Stanley W. Warshaw, May 23, 1948; children—Deborah S., Ruth I. Cons. occupational therapy Elm Hill Nursing Home, Roxbury, Mass., 1965—, Star of David Convalescent Centre, West Roxbury, Mass., 1968—, Bapt. Home Mass., Newton, 1968—, Charles House Convalescent Centre, Boston, 1970—, Glover Meml. Hosp., Needham, Mass., 1970—, Green Grove Nursing Home, North Reading, Mass., 1970—, Greenery Nursing Home, Boston, 1970—, Briarwood Convelescent and Retirement Centre, Needham, Mass., 1972—, Brittany Towers Convalescent Centre, Natick, Mass., 1972—, Belmont Manor Nursing Home, Belmont, Mass., 1973—, Alpine Manor Nursing Home, Boston, 1973—; dir. Tech. Coatings, Inc., E-Z Flash, Inc. Cons. home health services div. Needham (Mass.) Vis. Nurse Assn., 1969—. Mem. Newton (Mass.) Republican City Com., 1969-72. Bd. dirs. P.T.A., Mason-Rice Sch., Weeks Jr. High Sch., Newton, Mass. Mem. Am. Occupational Therapy Assn., Mass. Assn. Occupational Therapy. Jewish religion (trustee temple 1961-70). Home: 19 Brentwood Av Newton Centre MA 02159

WARSON, JUDITH KAY PORTER (MRS. RUSSELL J. WARSON), charity exec.; b. Moberly, Mo., Oct. 3, 1940; d. Edward Elwood and Helen Marie (Lynch) Porter; A.A., Moberly Area Jr. Coll., 1960; m. Russell J. Warson, June 12, 1960; 1 son, Craig Anthony. Bookkeeper Uregas, Inc., Moberly, Mo., 1960-61; exec. sec. United Fund Randolph County, Inc., Moberly, 1969—. Pres. P.T.A., Moberly, 1971-72; chmn. Moberly (Mo.) Community Betterment, 1972-73; treas. Older Adults Transp. Systems, Randolph County, Moberly, 1973; judge Future Bus. Leaders Am., 1973, Mo. Campers Assn. Campvention, 1974, Bus. and Profl. Womens Club, 1974; pres. Little Dixie Concert Assn. Moberly, 1974; chmn. publicity Sr. Citizens Quilt-O-Rama, Moberly, 1974. Recipient Outstanding Service to Moberly award Moberly C. of C., 1973. Mem. C. of C. (chmn. banquet decorations 1973), Beta Sigma Phi. Baptist. Club: Altrusa (chmn. service com. 1973—) (Moberly). Home: 822 W Reed St Moberly MO 65270 Office: PO Box 576 201 Rollins St W Moberly MO 65270

WARWICK, MURIEL, accountant; b. Great Kills, N.Y., Jan. 20, 1920; d. Morris and Johanna (Mintus) Benjaminson; grad. high sch.; student bus. coll., 1940-43; m. Leonard Aberbach, Aug. 15, 1943 (div. Jan. 1946); 1 dau., Leah (Mrs. John Schultz); m. 2d, William E. Warwick, Apr. 17, 1958 (div. May 1970); 1 dau., Elizabeth Jo. Auditor Fort Montigue Beach Hotel, Bahamas, 1967, Dolphin Hotel, Bahamas, 1968; accountant Credit Bureau of San Mateo and Burlingame, Cal., 1973—. Mem. Am. Fuchsia Soc. (recording sec. br., 1966), African Violet Soc. Am. (life), San Mateo County (pres. 1970), San Francisco (pres. 1972) Hilltop Gardeners (pres., 1970), african violet socs., San Mateo Garden Center, Inc. (treas. 1971-72, rec. sec. 1973). Home: 2221 Fleetwood Dr San Bruno CA 94066 Office: 101 S Ellsworth Av San Mateo CA 94401

WARWICKE, DIONNE, singer; b. Orange, N.J., Dec. 12, 1940; d. Lee Warwick; student piano Hart Coll. Music, Hartford, Conn., 1959-61. Worked as background singer for vocal group; made debut on records 1962; appearances include Cannes (France) Film Festival, 1964, Olympia Theatre, Paris, France, 1964, 65, 66, Savoy Hotel, London, Eng., 1965, Carnegie Hall, N.Y.C., Symphony Hall, Boston, 1965, Lincoln Center Philharmonic Hall, N.Y.C., 1966, Copacobana Club, N.Y.C.; starred in motion picture The Slaves, 1969, Dionne Warwicke Chevy TV Spl., 1969. Recipient Grammy award, 1969, 71; Creative Achievement award B'nai B'rith, 1971; Alumna of Year award Hartt Coll. Music, 1971; named Woman of Year Harvard U. Hasty Pudding Club, 1970, Best Female Vocalist Nat. Assn. Record Mfrs., 1970. Best-known records include Anyone Who Had a Heart, Walk on By, Don't Make Me Over, I Say A Little Prayer, I'll Never Fall in Love Again, Who Can I Turn to, Message to Michael. Address: 144 S Beverly Dr Beverly Hills CA 90212

WASERMAN, BARBARA ANDERSON (MRS. MANFRED J. WASERMAN), librarian; b. Evanston, Ill., Jan. 17, 1925; d. Donald Kennedy and Kathryn Marie (Shields) Anderson; B.S., Northwestern U., 1948; M.L.S. (Va. State fellow 1962-63), Cath. U. Am., 1963; m. Roland D. Paine, Jr., July 30, 1944 (div. 1969); children—Mary Catherine, Jeremy Thomas; m. 2d, Manfred J. Waserman, May 31, 1970. Children's librarian Fairfax County (Va.) Pub. Library, 1963-69; br. librarian, 1969—. Mem. Va. Library Assn., Fairfax County Pub. Library Staff Assn. Home: 7412 Hastings St Springfield VA 22150 Office: 6400 Cumberland St Springfield VA 22150

WASH, MELBA EURYDICE WILSON (MRS. GEORGE THOMAS WASH), librarian; b. Benton, Tenn., Aug. 6, 1918; d. John Winkle and Marchia (Cook) Wilson; A.B., Berea Coll., 1939; B.S., George Peabody Coll., 1942; m. George Thomas Wash, Feb. 28, 1953 (dec. May 1964). Tchr., Old Fort (Tenn.) Elementary Sch., 1939-41, librarian Oneida (Tenn.) High Sch., 1941-42; asst. librarian McDonogh (Md.) Sch., 1942-43, librarian, 1943-46; spl. services librarian U.S. Army, Germany, 1946-48; regional librarian W. Tenn. Regional Library, Jackson, 1949-50; dir. Reelfoot Regional Library, Martin, Tenn., 1950—. Mem. Am. (mem. council 1951-54, membership com. 1974—), Tenn. (treas. 1954-55, sect. chmn. 1966), Southeastern, West Tenn. (pres. 1973-74) library assns., Am. Assn. U. Women. Democrat. Baptist. Home: 126 Fonville Av Martin TN 38237 Office: 408 Jackson St Martin TN 38237

WASHBURN, SHARON MARGARET, assn. exec.; b. Amarillo, Tex., May 1, 1935; d. Cromwell Arthur and Margaret (Floyd) Washburn; B.S., W. Tex. State U., 1957, postgrad., 1957-59, 63-65. Camp dir., field adviser Amarillo council Girl Scouts U.S.A., 1957-61, Sangre de Cristo council, 1961-62, dir. program services, camp dir. Caprock council, Lubbock, Tex., 1966—, also rep. nat. program change workshop, mem. staff 4 nat. events, bd. dirs. Quivera council, Pampa; tchr. Pampa Ind. Sch. Dist., 1962-66. Mem. St. Mary's Hosp. aux., Lubbock. Recipient Thanks badge Caprock council Girl Scouts U.S.A. Mem. Am. Camping Assn., Assn. Girl Scout Profl. Workers, N.E.A., Lubbock Humane Soc., Soil Conservation Soc., Sigma Phi Chi, Beta Sigma Pi, Kappa Kappa Iota. Roman Catholic (mem. choir). Home: 4205 38th St Lubbock TX 79413 Office: 2600 Av P Lubbock TX 79405

WASHBURN, URSEL IRENE (MRS. HOWARD C. WASHBURN), church worker; b. Ind., Apr. 22, 1900; d. Charles Evington and Blache (Griffith) McCoy; student Earham Coll., 1918-20, 21-22, Purdue U., 1922, U. Mich., 1925; B.A., Earlham Coll., 1926; m. Howard Caldwell Washburn, July 28, 1927; children—Angus David, Samuel Howard. Tchr., Washington Twp. High Sch., Logansport, Ind., 1920-22, Walton (Ind.) High Sch., 1922-26, Mt. Ayr (Ind.) High Sch., 1926-27, Kentland (Ind.) High Sch., 1950-51. Mem. nat. exec. com. United Presbyn. Women, 1954-58; pres. Ind. chpt. Ch. Women United, 1967-70, mem. nat. bd. mgrs., 1967-70; v.p. Ind. Council Chs., 1967-70; vice moderator Ind. Synod United Presbyn. Ch. U.S.A., 1972—, mem. Synod Lincoln Trails Council, 1973-74. dist. cookie chmn. Girl Scouts U.S., 1961-66; Ind. clothing chmn. Christian Rural Overseas Program, 1972—. Trustee Kentland Pub. Library, pres., 1973, 74. Mem. Ind. Library Trustee Assn. (pres. 1967, Library Trustee of Year 1972), Am., Ind. library assns., Ind., Newton Country hist. socs. Republican. Presbyn. (pres. Ind. Synodical 1957-60, mem. nat. bd. pensions, 1965-71). Club: Federated Womens (Kentland). Home and office: 307 6th St Kentland IN 47951 307 6th St Kentland IN 47951

WASIK, BARBARA HANNA, psychologist, educator; b. Douglas, Ga., May 29, 1942; d. Frank Joseph and Josephine (Nahoom) Hanna; B.A., U. Ga., 1963; M.A., Fla. State U., 1965, Ph.D., 1967; Nat. Inst. Child Health and Human Devel. postdoctoral fellow, Duke, 1967-68; m. John Louis Wasik, June 26, 1966; children—John Gregory, Mark Timothy. Dir. research edn. improvement program Duke, 1968-69, lectr., 1968-69, asst. prof. edn., 1969-73, asso. prof., 1973—, asst. dean Grad. Sch., 1972-73, asso. dean, 1973—; investigator Frank Graham Child Devel. Center, U. N.C., Chapel Hill, 1972—; cons. in field. Mem. Gov. N.C. Adv. Com. Youth Devel., 1972—. Bd. dirs. Janus House, Chapel Hill, N.C., 1971-72. USPHS fellow, 1963-66. Mem. Am., Southeastern psychol. assns., Soc. Research Child Devel. Author articles, chpts. in books. Bd. editors Jour. Applied Behavior Analysis, 1972, asso. editor, 1973. Home: 809 Emory St Chapel Hill NC 27514

WASSER, GLADYS ELVA, public relations and adv. counselor; b. Lebanon, Pa., July 5, 1935; d. Russell Orestes and Gladys Mae (Saltzer) Wasser; B.S., Ithaca Coll., 1957. Continuity dir. WKOP Radio, Binghamton, N.Y., 1957-60, WNBF Radio, 1960-61; supr. copy and traffic WNBF-AM-FM-TV, 1961-65; supr. TV copy and traffice WNBF-TV, 1965-70; partner pub. relations and advt. firm, Binghamton, 1970—. Publicity dir. Binghamton United Fund, 1967; publicity chmn. Broome County chpt. Am. Heart Assn., 1970—. Mem. Southside Republican Club, 1962-70, N.Y. State Women's Rep. Fedn., 1962-65. Bd. dirs. Girls Club Binghamton. Mem. Women in Communication. Presbyn. (elder, treas. 1963-65, clk. session 1973). Club: Zonta (dir., 1st v.p. Binghamton 1967—). Home: 25 Genesee Av Binghamton NY 13903 Office: 19 Chenango St Binghamton NY 13901

WASSERMAN, LILLIAN SCHWARTZ (MRS. MILTON WASSERMAN), educator; b. N.Y.C., Nov. 2, 1914; d. Morris and Rose (Markowitz) Schwartz; B.A., Bklyn. Coll., 1938; M.S., Hofstra U., 1961, postgrad., 1965-67, 70—; m. Milton Wasserman, Feb. 19, 1939; children—Amy (Mrs. Richard Alan Schwed), Bruce. Employment interviewer N.Y. State Employment Service, N.Y.C., 1938-40; classroom tchr. Levittown (N.Y.) Sch. Dist., 1957-61; reading tchr. North Merrick (N.Y.) Sch. Dist., 1961-63; reading cons. Hicksville (N.Y.) Sch. Dist., 1963-65. Hempstead (N.Y.) Sch. Dist., 1965-67; asso. prof. reading Nassau Community Coll., Garden City, N.Y., 1967—. Mem. adult edn. com. East Meadow Sch. Dist., 1971—. Mem. Internat. Reading Assn., Nat. Soc. Study Edn., N.E.A., N.E. Two Year Coll. Reading Assn. (treas. 1967-71, dir. 1971-73), N.Y. State Tchrs. Assn., Nassau Reading Council, Bklyn. Coll. Alumni Assn. Home: 1684 Meadow Lane East Meadow NY 11554 Office: Stewart Av Garden City NY 11530

WASSERMAN, SYLVIA KATZ, lawyer; b. Milw., Mar. 30, 1916; d. Abraham and Anna Esther (Dubin) Katz; B.A., U. Ill., 1937; LL.B., Northwestern U., 1939, J.D., 1970; m. Eugene Wasserman, Dec. 6, 1942 (dec. 1970); children—Barbara M., Louis. Admitted to Ill. bar, 1939, Wis. bar, 1952; practice with Daniel D. Carmell, Chgo., 1939-42; atty. N.Y. Ordnance Dist., N.Y.C., 1943-46; writer briefs for other lawyers, 1946-52; work with husband, 1952-70; pvt. practice law, Sheboygan, Wis., 1970—. Registrant adviser SSS, Sheboygan, 1971—; mem. Sheboygan Citizens Adv. Com., 1964-68. Bd. dirs. Wis. Equal Employment Opportunity Assn., 1968—, vice chmn., 1970; bd. dirs. Sheboygan United Fund, 1963—, treas., 1966—; bd. dirs. Sheboygan County Welfare Concil, John M. Kohler Arts Center, Sheboygan br. Big Sisters Am., Sheboygan br. Planned Parenthood Assn., Sheboygan br. Hadassah. Mem. Wis., Sheboygan bar assns., Am. Assn. U. Women (dir. Sheboygan). Home: 215 Superior Av Sheboygan WI 53081 Office: 2808 Memorial Dr Sheboygan WI 53081

WASSERSTROM, EVELYN YAFFE (MRS. DEXTER JEROME WASSERSTROM), civic worker; b. Boston, Sept. 11, 1927; d. Joseph Harry and Tena (Drew) Yaffe; student Kansas City Art Inst., 1946-47, Kansas City Jr. Coll., 1946-47; m. Dexter Jerome Wasserstrom, Dec. 25, 1948; children—Tena Lynn, Bruce Alan. Project dir. Housing Survey for Retarded, Kansas City Assn. for Retarded, 1969; pres. YWCA, Kansas City, Mo., 1964-65; co-chmn. Met. Action, 1969—; bd. dirs. Kansas City region Nat. Conf. Christians and Jews, 1963—, Jewish chmn., 1973—; bd. dirs. Jewish Community Relations Bur., 1969—; bd. dirs. Jewish Ednl. Council, 1970—, chmn., 1973—; mem. adv. group Met. Jr. Coll., 1967-69; co-chmn. High Sch. of Jewish Studies of Greater Kansas City, 1971-73; mem. Panel of Am. Women, 1966—; mem. adv. com. Ethnic, Black Awareness Center, U. Mo. at Kansas City; v.p. Jewish Fedn. and Council of Greater Kansas City. Recipient Citation and Brotherhood award Kansas City sect. Nat. Conf. Christians and Jews, 1971; named Woman of Valor Jewish Chronicle, 1969. Jewish religion (mem. bd. edn. 1970—). Mem. B'nai B'rith Women (internat. v.p.). Home: 449 W Dartmouth Rd Kansas City MO 64113

WASSON, BARBARA HICKAM (MRS. AUDLEY JACKSON WASSON), pianist, educator; b. Spencer, Ind., Feb. 12, 1918; d. Hubert and Ruth (Moffett) Hickam; student DePauw U., 1937-38; B.A., Vassar Coll., 1939; Mus.M., Chgo. Musical Coll., 1944; student Ind. U., summers 1963, 64; m. Audley Jackson Wasson, Aug. 29, 1942; children—Carol Ruth (Mrs. Anthony A. Pasquale), Steven. Tchr. piano Tudor Hall Sch., Indpls., 1940-41, Chgo. Musical Coll., 1942-44, Cedarville Coll., 1971-72; founder, co-dir. Wasson Piano Studio, Dayton, O., 1946—; piano tchr., workshops in Miss., Ohio, 1964—; piano soloist Dayton Philharmonic, 1953, Dayton Philharmonic Tng. Orch., 1957. Recipient Mason and Hamlin recognition award Music Tchrs. Nat. Assn., 1973. Mem. Nat. Guild Piano Tchrs. (judge 1965—), Ohio Music Tchrs. Assn., Mu Phi Epsilon, Kappa Kappa Gamma. Club: Dayton Music (v.p., 1968-72). Home: 1913 Harvard Blvd Dayton OH 45406 Office: 1175 Reibold Bldg Dayton OH 45402

WATANABE, RUTH, librarian, educator; b. Los Angeles, May 12, 1916; d. Kohei and Iwa (Watanabe) Watanabe; B.Mus., U. So. Cal., 1937; A.B., 1939, A.M., 1941, M.Mus., 1942; student Eastman Sch. Music, 1942-46, Columbia, 1947; Ph.D., U. Rochester, 1952. Instr. piano, music theory, Los Angeles, 1934-41; counselor, personnel work Eastman Sch. Music, U. Rochester, 1943-46, instr. music history, 1946-61, asso. prof. musicology, 1961—, instr. English, 1946-47, dir. music library workshop, 1956—, also lectr. music U. Sch.; staff mem. in charge circulation Sibley Music Library, Rochester, N.Y., 1943-47, acting librarian, 1947-48, librarian, 1948—; lectr. on music appreciation and music history, 1956—; lectr. Sch. Library Sci., Kent State U., summer 1968; cons. music libraries, 1968—; program annotator Rochester Philharmonic Orch., 1959—; in charge adult edn. Rochester Civic Music Assn. Recipient Pa.-Del. fellowship Am. Assn. U. Women, 1949-50. Mem. Am. Assn. U. Women (v.p. Rochester br. 1964-65, mem. state bd. N.Y. State div. 1965-66, pres. Rochester br. 1969-71, fellowship com. 1968—), Internat., Am. musicological socs., Music Library Assn. (v.p. 1968-69, program chmn. 1970), Internat, Assn. Music Libraries (2d v.p. commn. on conservatory libraries 1971—), Assn. Coll. and Reference Librarians, U. Rochester Alumni Fedn. (bd. govs. 1958-61), Rochester Oratorio Soc. (bd. dirs. 1961-63, 70-74), Delta Kappa Gamma, Phi Beta Kappa (bd. dirs. Iota of N.Y. 1962-65), Phi Kappa Phi, Mu Phi Epsilon (gen. chmn. nat. conv. 1956, nat. librarian, 1958-61), Pi Kappa Lambda, Delta Phi Alpha, Epsilon Phi. Club: Soroptimist (sec. 1956-57, pres. 1963-64). Author: Five Books of Italian Madrigals, 1956; Introduction to Research in Music, 1967. Contbg. author: Music Library Handbook, 1966. Editor: Music Received. Home: 300 Melville St Rochester NY 14609 Office: 26 Gibbs St Rochester NY 14604

WATERFALL, CORNELIA ELIZABETH LIEN, mag. editor; b. Johnson County, Ia., Oct. 13, 1929; d. Jacob Aall Ottesin and Cornelia Mae (Wahl) Lien; B.A., Luther Coll., 1951; M.A., Columbia Coll., Chgo., 1952; postgrad. Northwestern U., 1953; m. Wallace Knapp Waterfall, Oct. 31, 1958 (div. 1974); children—Ann Lien Riley, Clark Lien Riley, Eve Lien Riley. With CBS, Chgo., 1951-52, WBEZ, Chgo., free lance writer radio-tv., Hollywood, Cal., 1954-55; free lance writer, N.Y.C., 1955; with WISH-TV, Indpls., 1956-57, Indpls. Times, 1957-59, Mademoiselle mag., N.Y.C., 1959-60, Glamour mag., N.Y.C., 1960-63, Lady-Fare mag., N.Y.C., 1964-65; editor-in-chief Mothers' Manual mag., N.Y.C., 1965—. Chmn. sch. concerts Friends of Music, Croton-on-Hudson, N.Y., 1972—; pres. Croton Community Nursery Sch., Croton-on-Hudson, 1970-72. Mem. Soc. Mag. Editors, Sigma Delta Chi. Lutheran. Editor: Sounding Bd. Croton P.T.A., 1968-71. Home: 176 Cleveland Dr Croton-on-Hudson NY 10520 Office: 420 Lexington New York City NY 10022

WATERLOW, CHARLOTTE MARY, educator; b. Lewes, Sussex, Eng., May 31, 1915 (came to U.S. 1970); d. Sydney and Helen (Eckhard) Waterlow; B.A. 1st class, Newnham Coll., Cambridge U. (Eng.), 1936, M.A., 1953; Diploma Edn., London U., 1954. Head history dept. Guildford (Surrey, Eng.) Girl's Grammar Sch., 1954-67; asst. prof. history Notre Dame U., Nelson, B.C., Can., 1967-69; tchr. history Am. Coll. of Switzerland, Leysin, 1969-70, Concord (Mass.) Acad., 1970-72, Buckingham Sch., Browne Nichols Sch., Cambridge, Mass., 1972—. Decorated mem. British Empire, 1950; U.S. State Dept. grantee, 1965. Mem. Royal Inst. Internat. Affairs (London), Canadian Inst. Internat. Affairs (Toronto), European Tchrs. Assn. (hon. sec. Brit. sect. 1962-65). Author: Tribe, State and Community: Contemporary Systems of Government and Justice, 1967; India, 1969; Europe 1945 to 1970, 1973; Superpowers and Victims: The Outlook for World Community, 1974. Home: 205 Appleton St Cambridge MA 02138

WATERMAN, DOROTHY ANN FORRESTAL (MRS. DENISON R. WATERMAN), civic worker; b. Duluth, Minn., July 2, 1919; d. Martin Jennings and Angela (Fitzgerald) Forrestal; student Mundelein Coll., Chgo., 1936-38; m. Denison R. Waterman, July 5, 1941; children—Denison R., Martin John, Kevin Patrick, Daniel Forrestal, Matthew Gerard. Mem. Ia. League Women Voters, pres., 1969-71, nat. v.p., 1972—; mem. Gov.'s Com. on Status of Women, 1969-70, Gov.'s Com. for Internat. Edn., 1969—, Inner-City Conf. Com., 1968-70, League Women Voters Edn. Fund, 1968—; mem. governing bd. Common Cause, 1972—. Home: 1111 Oakland Dr Muscatine IA 52761 Office: League Women Voters US 1730 M St NW Washington DC 20036

WATERS, BETTY HALE (MRS. JULIAN LAFAY WATERS), educator; b. Atlanta, Dec. 21, 1927; d. Robert Lorin and Blondyne (Cooper) Hale; Mus.B., Converse Coll., 1949; M. Elementary Edn. (Optimist scholar 1966), Ga. State U., 1968, Edn. Specialist (Delta Kappa Gamma state fellow 1970, internat. fellow 1972), 1971; Ed.D., U. Ga., 1973; m. Julian Lafay Waters, June 3, 1950; 1 son, John Robert (dec.). Classroom tchr. Dekalb County (Ga.) Schs., 1956-70, in-service lectr., 1965-68, learning disabilities clinician, 1968-70; mem. faculty, coll. supr. Oglethorpe U., Atlanta, 1970-71; coll. supr. U. Ga., Athens, 1971-73; learning disabilities specialist Newton County Schs., Covington, Ga., 1973—. Co-chmn. Julian L. Waters Dr. For Retarded Children, Decatur, 1962. Recipient Tchrs. medal Freedoms Found., 1965, Tchr. of Year award, Dogwood chpt. Council Exceptional Children, 1970. Mem. Assn. Childhood Edn. (local pres. 1964-66, state v.p. 1968-70, state pres. 1974—), Am. Assn. U. Women, Assn. for Supervision and Curriculum Devel., Assn. Tchr. Educators, Assn. Children with Learning Disabilities, Delta Kappa Gamma, Kappa Delta Epsilon. Home: Route 1 Piedmont Rd Box 492 Hull GA 30646

WATERS, CAROL ARTH (MRS. DANIEL C. WATERS), civic worker; b. Emmett, Ida., Aug. 20, 1922; d. William Emmett and Marjorie (Alford) Renner; student U. Cal. at Los Angeles, 1939-40; m. Donald P. Arth, Sept. 4, 1940 (div. Dec. 1952); children—Nancy Catherine (Mrs. Harold K. Phillips), Carol Marie (Mrs. John L. Cowan); m. 2d, Daniel C. Waters, Nov. 17, 1962. Co-chmn. Young Republican Nat. Fedn., 1951-52, chmn., 1952-53; spl. asst. to Sec. Dulles and pub. affairs officer, U.S. Dept. of State, 1953-58; exec. sec. U.S. Commn. on Civil Rights, 1958-59; mem. nat. mgmt. group Nixon Presdl. Campaign, 1960, statewide mgmt. group Gubernatorial Campaign, 1962; pub. information dir. Los Angeles County Heart Assn., 1966-67. Vice pres. Los Angeles City Human Relations Commn., 1966-67, pres. 1967-68; bd. dirs. YWCA of Los Angeles, 1968-70; pres. Friends of Los Angeles YWCA; pub. relations dir. Los Angeles County Heart Assn., 1969—; bd. dirs. Law Enforcement and Its Needs, 1967—, Colorado River Assn., 1972—. Mem. Los Angeles Area C. of C. (dir., mem. exec. com. women's div. 1966-71, pres. 1972-73). Republican. Conglist. Home: 1842 1/2 N Normandie Av Los Angeles CA 90027 Office: 2405 W 8th St Los Angeles CA 90057

WATERS, DOROTHY LOOSE (MRS. PAUL R. WATERS), educator; b. Pitts., June 18, 1919; d. Otto Walter and Wilhelmina (Doepke) Loose; B.S. in Edn., U. Pitts., 1937, M.Ed., 1961; m. Paul R. Waters, June 29, 1946; children—Doreen, Paul David, Devin. Sec., Westinghouse, East Pittsburgh, Pa., 1942-47; tchr. Turtle Creek (Pa.) Pub. Schs., 1957-58, Gateway Union Sch., Monroeville, Pa., 1958—. Tchr., Westinghouse Tech. Night Sch., Turtle Creek, Pa., 1959-60; instr. Community Coll., Monroeville, 1967-68. Pres., Monroeville Women's Club, 1959-60. Mem. Eastern Bus. Tchrs. Assn., Western Pa. Bus. Educators Assn., Nat. Assn. Exec. Females, Internat. Platform Assn., Tri-State Educators, Delta Delta Lambda. Lutheran. Home: 1321 Corkwood Dr Monroeville PA 15146 Office: Gateway Union Sch Moss Side Blvd Monroeville PA 15146

WATERS, ELEANOR CONNORS, banker; b. N.Y.C.; d. Michael J. and Mary (Wachter) Connors; grad. Pratt Inst., 1937; student Am. Inst. Banking, 1940; m. Robert H. Water, July 19, 1949; stepchildren—Margaret (Mrs. Shardlow Hansen), Rolan. Sec. N.Y. Title & Mortgage Co., N.Y.C., 1933-36, Prudential Ins. Co., N.Y.C., 1936, Mortgage Commn. Servicing Corp., N.Y.C., 1936-39; with Seamen's Bank Savs., N.Y.C., 1939—, officer, asst. sec. pub. relations, 1954-58, asst. v.p., 1958-67, v.p., 1967—. Mem. com. on information and marketing Nat. Assn. Mut. Savs. Banks, 1967—; mem. exec. com. Savs. Bank Marketing and Pub. Relations Forum, Savs. Banks Assn. N.Y. State, 1970—. Bd. dirs. Spence-Chapin Adoption Service, 1960—, chmn. Spence Chapin Corner Shop, 1970—; adv. council Jr. Achievement of N.Y.; mem. Community Planning Bd. No. 1, Borough of Manhattan, 1971—; hon. mem. bd. mgrs. Mariner's Home for Aged Women of Sea, 1973—. Mem. Am. Inst. Banking (chmn. women's com. N.Y. chpt. 1941-42, nat. com. 1946-47, chmn. women's com. 1949-50), Savs. Bank Women Met. Area (program chmn. 1942-43, mem. exec. com. 1944-46, pres. 1953-54), Am. Pub. Relations Assn. (dir. 1955-59), Nat. Assn. Bank Women (chmn. N.Y. group 1959-60), Women Execs. in Pub. Relations, Mech. Bank Collectors Am., Pub. Relations Soc. Am., Wall St. Art Assn. (bd. govs. 1962-72), Navy League, U.S. Naval Inst., Women's Propeller Club U.S. Home: 227 E 57th St New York City NY 10022 Office: 30 Wall St New York City NY 10005

WATERS, ELEANOR LOIS YOUMANS, librarian; b. Waycross, Ga., Aug. 25, 1928; d. Jacob Edward and Hazel Lois (Hendrix) Youmans; student Perry Bus. Sch., 1944-45, U. Wis., 1966, Loyola U., 1968; m. Thomas Edward Waters, Mar. 28, 1948; children—Belinda (Mrs. Harold Richard Wheeler), Thomas Bruce, Sharon Lois, Steven Edward. Sec. to supt. shipbuilding Brunswick Marine Constrn. Corp., Brunswick, Ga., 1945; library technician Nat. Marine Fisheries Service, Brunswick Lab., 1959-73, Ga. Dept. Nat. Resources Coastal Fisheries, 1974—. Recipient Superior Performance award, U.S. Dept. Interior, 1965, 68. Mem. Ga. Library Assn., Soc. for Bibliography Natural History. Presbyn. Home: 2606 Starling St Brunswick GA 31520 Office: Ga Dept Natural Resources Game and Fish Div PO Box 1676 Brunswick GA 31520

WATERS, ETHEL, actress, singer; b. Chester, Pa., Oct. 31, 1900; d. John Wesley Waters and Louisa Tar Anderson. Began as singer, making first stage appearance at Lincoln Theatre, Balt., about 1917; sang in night clubs and Negro theatres; made first Broadway appearance at Daly's Theatre in Africana, 1927; appeared in Blackbird's of 1930, Rhapsody in Black, 1931, As Thousands Cheer, 1933, At Home Abroad, 1935; made debut as dramatic star in Mamba's Daughters, Empire Theatre, N.Y., 1939; starred in Cabin in the Sky, 1940-41; appeared in A Member of the Wedding (winner N.Y. Drama Critics award); radio artist, 1934—; now also on TV; on radio programs for U.S.O. Camp Shows, Inc., 1942; concert at Carnegie Hall, 1938; gained recognition for her singing of Dinah, Stormy Weather, Am I Blue, others; featured in motion picture On With the Show; also appeared in Tales of Manhattan, 1941, Cairo, Stage Door Canteen, 1943, Pinky, The Heart is a Rebel, 1956, The Sound and the Fury, 1958. Hon. capt. Cal. State Militia and 7th Women's Ambulance Corps, 1942. Council mem. Hollywood Victory Com., 1942; mem. exec. council Actors Equity Assn., 1942-43; v.p. Negro Actors Guild Am., 1942-43. Author: (with Charles Samuels) His Eye is on the Sparrow (autobiography), 1951. Address: c/o Sidney M Levee Agy 8721 Sunset Blvd Los Angeles CA 90069

WATERS, GRACE JOHNSON NICHOLS (MRS. WILLIAM J. WATERS), educator; b. Norfolk, Va., Sept. 8, 1916; d. Franklin Bradshaw and Gladys (Scott) Nichols; B.S., Radford State Tchrs. Coll., 1955; M.Ed., Coll. William and Mary, 1958; m. Walter R. Johnson, Sept. 21, 1940 (dec. Apr. 1956); children—Jacqueline Gay (Mrs. Stanley Lynn Shaw), Bonnie Gayle (Mrs. Paul S. Arthur); m. 2d, William J. Waters, Dec. 26, 1960. Elementary sch. tchr. Coleman Pl. Crossroads, Norfolk, Va., 1938-40, 46-57; dir. Ednl. TV, Norfolk, Va., 1957—. Cons. instructional TV State Dept. Edn., 1967. Girl Scout counselor various camps, 1938-40; swimming instr. pvt. and service club camps, 1935-39. Leader Girl Scout leader tng., 1935-37. Mem. C. of C. (Norfolk Women's Div.), So. Ednl. Communications Assn. (mem. instrnl. com.), Am. Assn. U. Women, Nat. Assn. Ednl. Broadcasters, Tidewater Suprs.' Group (sec. 1973—), Beta Sigma Phi. Methodist (pres. Wesley Bible Class 1966-68; vice chmn. ch. adminstrv. bd., 1969, chmn. 1970-72). Clubs: Junior Women's (Manteo, N.C., Norfolk, Va.), Tidewater Press. Contbr. articles various publs. Mem. editorial panel Using TV in the Classroom, 1961. Pub. speaker, 1957—. Home: 3555 Heutte Dr Norfolk VA 23518 Office: 5200 Hamton Blvd Norfolk VA 23508

WATERS, MARY ALICE, editor; b. Calinog, P.I., Jan. 12, 1942; d. Henry Scott and Anna (Martin) Waters; B.A., Carleton Coll., 1963; postgrad. U. Cal. at Berkeley, 1963-64. Mng. editor Militant, N.Y.C., 1969-70, editor, 1971—. Mem. polit. com. Socialist Workers Party, 1970—; nat. sec. Young Socialist Alliance, 1967-68, nat. chmn., 1968. Mem. Phi Beta Kappa. Author: GIs and the Fight Against War, 1966; The Politics of Women's Liberation, 1970; Attica: Why Prisoners Are Rebelling, 1971; Feminism and the Marxist Movement, 1972. Editor: Rosa Luxemburg Speaks, 1970. Office: 14 Charles Lane New York City NY 10014

WATERS, SISTER MARY ANN ELIZABETH, univ. dean; b. Washington; d. Joseph Borrows and Mary Catherine (Power) Waters; B.A., U. Notre Dame, 1924, M.S., 1930; Ph.D., Cath. U. Am., 1943. Sisters of Holy Cross, 1920—; mem. faculty Dunbarton Coll. Holy Cross, Washington, 1942—, prof. chemistry, 1952—, acad. dean, 1969—. Fellow Am. Inst. Chemists; Am. Chem. Soc., A.A.A.S. Home: 2935 Upton St NW Washington DC 20008

WATERS, MARY E., judge; b. Los Angeles; d. Frank Joseph and Ida (Baumann) Waters; student U. Cal. at Los Angeles, 1934-35; A.B., U. Cal. at Berkeley, 1938, postgrad., 1938-39; LL.B., U. So. Cal., 1949. Admitted to Cal. bar, 1949; practiced law, Los Angeles, 1949-65; judge Municipal Ct. Los Angeles, 1965—. Mem. bd. Rancho San Antonio. Served with USN, World War II, now comdr. Res. Mem. Nat. Bus. and Profl. Women Los Angeles (pres. 1960), League for Crippled Children, U. So. Cal., U. So. Cal. Law Alumni Assn. (pres. 1971-72), Am., Los Angeles County bar assns., Conf. Cal. Judges, Navy League, World Affairs Council, Phi Alpha Delta. Clubs: Zonta, Irish Setter of Southern Cal., Women Lawyers. Home: 549 N Wilcox Av Los Angeles CA 90004 Office: 110 N Grand St Los Angeles CA 90012

WATERS, MARY RUTH, nursing dir.; b. Pickaway County, O., July 12, 1927; d. Grover McClelland and Nellie Florence (Shoub) Dudleson; R.N. (outstanding nurse 1948), White Cross Hosp., Columbus, O., 1948; m. George Clarence Waters, Jr., Sept. 29, 1948; children—George McClelland, Ruth Rae Nell (Mrs. Randy D. Ross), Carlton Kenneth, Beth Yvonne. Asst. head nurse med. floor White Cross Hosp. (name now changed to Riverside Meth. Hosp.), 1948-50; spl. duty nurse Riverside Meth., Mt. Carmel and Grant hosps., Columbus, 1953-63; nursing dir. Orient (O.) State Hosp., Ohio Dept. Mental Retardation, 1961—. Cons., participant in tng. nurses for psychiat. duty. Mem. Am., Ohio nurses assn., Am. Assn. Mental Deficiency, Ohio League Nurses, Franklin County Mental Health Assn., Riverside Hosp. Alumnae Assn. Mem. Order Eastern Star, Ladies Oriental Shrine N.Am. Home: 3509 Beechgrove Dr Grove City OH 43123 Office: Orient State Inst Orient OH 43146

WATERS, MONA NELSON, real estate exec.; b. Faribault, Minn., Dec. 4, 1929; d. Raymond E. and Dorothy H. (Shaft) Nelson; student Foothill Coll., San Jose City Coll., San Jose State Coll., U. Cal., Lincoln U.; m. Willis E. Waters, Aug. 5, 1956; 1 son, Denny Ray. Owner, Mona's Dance Studio, 1949-64; owner Mona Waters & Co. Realtors, San Jose, Cal., 1964—; agt. S.S. Schmittmann, sculptor. Mem. Nat. Assn. Real Estate Bds., Cal. Real Estate Assn., San Jose Real Estate Bd. Home: 117 Callecita St Los Gatos CA 95030 Office: PO Box 6264 San Jose CA 95150

WATERS, NUALA MARY KILBRIDE (MRS. FRANCIS P. WATERS), physician; b. Longford, Ireland; d. Bernard J. and Anna (Ledwith) Kilbride; M.B., U. Coll., Dublin, Ireland, 1969, B.Ch., 1969, B.A.O., 1969; m. Francis P. Waters, Oct. 2, 1965. Mem. Irish Med. Assn. Address: 22 Trees Av Mount Merrion Blackrock Dublin Ireland

WATERS, VOULA DAVANIS (MRS. LAUGHLIN EDWARD WATERS), lawyer; b. Woodland, Cal., May 17, 1925; d. George A. and Theoni (Mihelis) Devanis; A.B., U. Cal. at Berkeley, 1946; J.D., U. San Francisco, 1949; m. Laughlin Edward Waters, Aug. 22, 1953; children—Laughlin, Maura, Deirdre, Megan, Brigid. Admitted to Cal. bar, 1950, Supreme Ct. U.S., 1953; dep. legislative counsel State Col., Sacramento, 1950-54; practiced in Los Angeles, 1954—. Bd. dirs. Los Angeles Orphanage, Ladies Charity, Assistance League; bd. regents U. San Francisco. Mem. Lawyers Wives. Address: 112 N June St Los Angeles CA 90004

WATERSTONE, MARY MANDANA, lawyer; b. St. Joseph, Mich., Nov. 19, 1939; d. Robert H. and Virginia E. (Clarke) Long; B.A., Northwestern U., 1961; J.D. cum laude, U. Mich., 1965. Admitted to Mich. bar, 1966, D.C. bar, 1966; law clk. firm Covington and Burling, Washington, 1964; law clk. U.S. Dist. Ct., Eastern Dist. Mich., Detroit, 1965-67; practiced in Detroit, 1967-68; atty. Mich. Bell Telephone Co., Detroit, 1968—. Adj. asso. prof. Wayne State U., Detroit, 1968-71. Mem. Am., Fed. (past sec., past asst. treas.), Detroit (mem. fed. dist. ct. com.) bar assns., State Bar Mich. (sec. civil liberties com., sec. criminal law sect., co-chmn. police trial bd. com. young lawyers sect.). Contbr. articles to profl. jours. Home: 3404 Seminole St Detroit MI 48214 Office: 444 Michigan St Detroit MI 48226

WATHEN, SISTER MARY ANTONIA, religious order adminstr.; b. Morganfield, Ky., Mar. 20, 1909; d. John Thomas and Caroline Lee (Manning) Wathen; A.B., Spalding Coll., 1946; M.A., Catholic U. Am., 1951, Ph.D., 1954. Joined Ursuline Sisters, 1929; tchr. Ky. pub. schs., 1932-44, 47-50, Neb. pvt. schs., 1944-47; mem. faculty Brescia Coll., Owensboro, Ky., 1954-70, acad. dean, 1955-70, mem. bd. govs., 1970—; mem. exec. council Mt. St. Joseph, Maple Mt., Ky., 1972—. Recipient Afro-Am. Tng. Program grant. Ky. Coll., 1971. Mem. Nat. Cath. Ednl. Assn., Am. Hist. Assn., Am. Cath. Hist. Assn. Home and office: Mt St Joseph Convent Maple Mount KY 42356

WATKINS, CAROL KERN (MRS. K. C. WATKINS), social worker; b. Windsor, Colo., Dec. 26, 1911; d. George Franklin and Isaphine D. (Cooper) Kern; A.B., Colo. Women's Coll., 1931; B.S., U. Denver, 1947; M.S.W., Loyola U., Chgo., 1954; postgrad. Art Inst. Chgo., 1950-53, 57, student-at-large, 1972-74; m. K.C. Watkins, May 1, 1934 (div. Apr., 1946). Psychiat. social worker Chgo. Bd. Health, 1954-56; psychiat. social worker Child Psychiatry Clinic, Northwestern U. Med. Sch. clinics, Chgo., 1957-63, supervisory social worker adult and child psychiatry clinics, 1963-69. Partner George F. Kern & Co., Windsor, Colo., 1944—. Mem. Nat. Assn. Social Workers. Home: Windsor CO 80550 also 1220 N State Pkwy Chicago IL 60610

WATKINS, CHARLOTTE CRAWFORD (MRS. MARK HANNA WATKINS), educator; b. New Haven, Apr. 21, 1913; d. George W. and Sadella (Donalson) Crawford; B.A., Wellesley Coll., 1933; Ph.D., Yale, 1937; m. Mark Hanna Watkins, June 16, 1951. Instr., asso. prof. Dillard U., New Orleans, 1937-43; asso. prof., prof., head dept. English, Morgan State Coll., Balt., 1943-48; prof. English, Howard U., Washington, 1948—. Mem. Am. Assn. U. Women, Am. Assn. U. Profs., Modern Lang. Assn. (del. assembly 1971-74), Linguistic Soc. Am., Nat. Council Tchrs. English, Coll. English Assn., Middle Atlantic Group Coll. English Assn. (pres. 1952-53, v.p. 1951-52, exec. com. 1953-54). Mem. United Ch. of Christ. Contbr. articles in field to profl. jours. Home: 1311 Delaware Av SW Washington DC 20024

WATKINS, CHARLOTTE JEAN METCALF, assn. exec.; b. Coffeyville, Kan., Mar. 24, 1921; d. Seward Estel and Amber (Maxson) Metcalf; student Kan. State Coll., 1938-39; R.N., St. Luke's Nursing Sch. (Kansas City, Mo.), 1942; m. Carlton Gunter Watkins, Mar. 21, 1943; children—Lloyd D.H., Carlton G., Jr., Mary Melissa (Mrs. William Best), Charlotte Lou. Pres. N.C. Congress Parents and Tchrs., 1968-70; v.p. region 3 Nat. PTA, 1970-72, also nat. commr. Nat. PTA, 1972—. Mem. adv. council Pres.'s Cabinet Com. on Edn., 1971—, Gov.'s Task Force on Child Advocacy, 1969-70, on Juvenile Delinquency, 1969-71, on Student Unrest, 1971-72, Gov.'s Com. on State Reorgn., 1970-71. Bd. dirs. PTA Mag., Inc., Chgo., Mecklenburg Nat. Conf. Christians and Jews, 1966-72, Mecklenberg Family Life Council, 1962-66. Mem. Charlotte Jaycettes (founder, past pres.), Nat. (life), N.C., Tenn., Fla., Ky. PTA's, Mecklenburg Med. Aux., Am. Social Health Assn. (mem. N.C. com.). Mem. P.E.O. Home and office: 6724 Constitution Lane Charlotte NC 28210

WATKINS, LOIS VIRGINIA DANIELS (MRS. PAUL FERGUSON WATKINS), publisher; b. Kansas City, Mo., Mar. 30, 1898; d. George Warren and Alice (Clark) Daniels; A.B., Ill. Coll., 1918; M.A., U. Ill., 1919; m. Paul Ferguson Watkins, Aug. 13, 1921 (dec. Dec. 1951); children—Marion (Mrs. Herget), George Daniels. Tchr., Robinson (Ill.) High Sch., 1919-20; instr. Ill. Coll., 1920-21; with advt. and circulations depts. Herald-Progress, Ashland, Va., 1933-51, editor, 1951-63, pub., mgr., 1951—. Pres. Ashland Community League, 1937-38; mem. Richmond area Citizens Community Study, 1972—, Va. Commn. of Outdoor Recreation, 1966—; sec. Ashland Indsl. Devel. Corp., 1960-64; bd. dirs. Hanover Arts and Activities Center, 1967-69. Trustee Pamunkey Regional Library, 1951-67, Ashland Rescue Squad, 1974—. Recipient Merit award Nat. Newspaper Assn., Emma McKinney award. Mem. Va. Press Assn. (pres. 1965, dir. 1955-67), Va. State Printers Assn. (dir. 1962-64), C. of C. (sec. 1957-65) Va. Press Women (bd. dirs.). Methodist (adminstrv. bd. 1952-72, trustee 1973—). Home: 316 S James St Ashland VA 23005 Office: 114 Thompson St Ashland VA 23005

WATKINS, LOTTIE HEYWOOD, real estate co. exec.; b. Atlanta; d. Eddie and Susie (Wilson) Heywood; student Reid's Bus. Coll., 1943-45; m. J. Elmo Watkins, 1947 (dec. 1951); children—Joyce Rankin (Mrs. Samuel W. Bacote), Judy Yvonne (Mrs. James A. Barnett). Sec., Alexander-Calloway Realty Co., Atlanta, 1945-54; teller-clk. Mut. Fed. Savs. & Loan Assn., Atlanta, 1954-60, now dir.; owner, pres. Lottie Watkins Enterprises, Atlanta, 1960—. Dir. Citizens Trust Bank. Mem. Ga. Gov.'s Commn. Voluntarism, 1972, mem. Ga. Residential Finance Authority, 1974. Co-chmn. bus. div. Community Chest, 1955-59; YMCA membership campaigns, 1960—, YWCA membership enrollment drive, 1962; active Am. Cancer Soc., 1958-59, N.A.A.C.P. membership drive, 1957-59, N.A.A.C.P. freedom fund banquet, 1964, program com. nat. conv., 1962, now mem. exec. com.; chmn. cheer fund Atlanta Inquirer, 1961-62; div. leader YMCA centennial fund drive, 1967-68; co-chmn. membership com. Greater Atlanta Council on Human Relations, 1965-66; asst. sec. Atlanta Bus. League, 1960-61; sec. Vis. Nurses Assn.; mem. exec. com. Fulton County Bd. of Registration and Election. Field dir. Fulton County Citizens Democratic Club, 1960-63; mem. exec. com. 5th Congl. dist. Ga., 1963; vice chmn. Fulton County Dem. party, 1967-68, mem. exec. com., 1967-69; mem. finance chmn.'s exec. bd. Dem. Nat. Com. Recipient award for citizenship and progressive bus. leadership College Park Civic League, 1963, YMCA leadership award, 1974, others; named Woman of Year and Bronze Woman of Year, Iota Phi Lambda, 1962, Woman of Year in bus. Atlanta Negro Bus. and Profl. Womens Club, 1964, Interracial Council Bus. Opportunity, 1974. Mem. Atlanta Summit Leadership Conf., Atlanta Women's C. of C., League Women Voters, Nat. Negro Bus. and Profl. Womens Club (regional sec.). Baptist. Home: 107 Mathewson Pl SW Atlanta GA 30314 Office: 1065 Gordon St SW Atlanta GA 30310

WATKINS, SUSAN CARY, editor; b. Daytona, Fla., Sept. 11, 1945; d. Robert Cantrell and Helen Louise (Greer) Feamster; B.S., Ia. State U., 1967; M.A., U. N.C., 1972; m. William Sherrill Watkins, June 16, 1973. Asst. dir. advt. and promotion KRNT Radio-TV, Des Moines, 1967-69; grad. sch. asst., tchr. U. N.C., 1969-71; multi-media ednl. writer/producer Data-Design Labs., engring. cons., Falls Church, Va., 1971-72; environmental editor, report prodn. mgr. Howard, Needles, Tammen & Bergendoff, cons. engrs., Alexandria, 1972—. Cons. ednl. designer Project LIFE, 1972; cons. media specialist U. N.C. Sch. Pub. Health and Interchurch Council Chapel Hill, 1970-71; asso. writer/producer multi-media show Greening of Am., 1971. Mem. Am. Advt. Fedn., Assn. for Ednl. Communications and Tech., Nat. Assn. Ednl. Broadcasters, Women in Communications. Republican. Presbyn. Mem. Order Eastern Star. Office: 201 N Washington St Alexandria VA 22314

WATLING, SYLVIA MARIAN, union ofcl.; b. Barcombe, Sussex, Eng., May 31, 1922; d. Robert Frank and Emily (Boaks) Heasman; m. Archibald William Watling, June 5, 1943; children—Yvonne Jean (Mrs. David Ingersoll), Lloyd Derek, Robert Heasman, Frank Archibald, Jasmin Beverley. Food service supr. Hotel Dieu Hosp., Chatham, N.B., Can., 1969—. Vice pres., chief shop steward Hosp. Employees Union, also dietary shop steward. Served with English Womens Land Army, 1940-41. Mem. Newcastle Chatham Labour Council (v.p. 1969-74), Chatham Sr. Citizens Club (2nd v.p. 1972-74), Home: 526 Main St Chatham Head Newcastle NB Canada Office: Hotel Dieu Hospital Chatham NB Canada

WATNIK, BETTE, lawyer; b. Bklyn., June 26, 1928; d. Albert Abraham and Meriam (Peckman) Ignatin; B.S., Temple U., 1950; J.D., N.Y. U., 1964; m. Morton M. Watnik, June 19, 1949; children—Winston B., Webster L. Admitted to N.J. bar, 1966; law clk. firm Porzio, Bromberg & Newman, Morristown, N.J., 1965-66; asso. atty. firm Mellinger & Rudenstein, Orange, 1966-69; legal rating specialist VA, Newark, 1969—. Sec., counsel Madison (N.J.) Community Pool Corp., 1970-71, counsel, 1971—. Madison committeewoman Morris County Republican Com., 1967-69, Madison chmn., 1968-69. Recipient Schaeffer award Phi Delta Delta,

1960; Writing and Scholarships awards Washington Coll. Law, 1960. Mem. Fed. Bar Assn., League Women Voters (chmn. Upper Derby, Pa., 1955-56, legislative chmn. Elizabeth, N.J. 1957-58), Bus. and Profl. Women's Club (legislative chmn. Madison 1967-68). Legal editor Morristown Municipal Code, 1966. Home: 16 Cross Gates Rd Madison NJ 07940 Office: 20 Washington Pl Newark NJ 07102

WATROUS, NAOMA D., clin. psychologist; b. Pauls Valley, Okla.; d. William Maddon and Almeda (Cosby) Dickson; student U. Md., 1957-59; M.S., Okla. State U., 1950; Ed.D., Okla. U., 1960; postgrad. Catholic U. Am., 1961-63. Sch. psychologist D.C. Pub. Schs., 1960-61; staff psychologist VA, Washington, 1963-69, chief psychologist, dept. human resources, area B in-patient services, 1970—. Pvt. practice Psychiat. Center, Washington, 1973—; cons. psychologist Prividence Hosp., Washington. Mem. Am., D.C. psychol. assns. Home: 2501 Calvert St NW Washington DC 20008 Office: 3000 Connecticut St Washington DC 20010

WATSON, ANN ELIZABETH, physician; b. San Diego, Cal., Nov. 12, 1941; d. Albert Orville and Nadia Florence (Herman) Watson; student U. Tex., Arlington, 1957, Ph.G., Austin, 1962, M.D., Galveston, 1967. Intern John Sealy Hosp., Galveston, John Peter Smith Hosp., Ft. Worth, 1968-69; pvt. practice medicine and surgery, Ft. Worth, 1969-71, Claude, Tex., 1971—; musician, author, dramatist, owner and breeder Quarter horses. Mem. A.M.A., Tex., Tarrent County, Potter County med. assns., Assn. Am. Physicians and Surgeons, Am. Acad. Gen. Practice, Tex. Pharmacy Assn., D.A.R., Gen. Soc. Mayflower Descs., Nat. Soc. Colonial Dames, of XVII Century, Nat. Soc. Dames of Court of Honor, U.S. Dau. War of 1812, Nat. Soc. Am. Colonists. Home: 805 Easley St Fort Worth TX 76108 Office: Armstrong County Med Center Claude TX 79019

WATSON, BARBARA M., govt. ofcl.; b. N.Y.C., Nov. 5, 1918; d. James S. and Violet (Lopez) Watson; B.A., Barnard Coll., 1943; LL.B., N.Y. Law Sch., 1962; L.H.D., Mt. St. Mary Coll., 1973; LL.D., U. Md., 1973. Owner, dir. Barbara Watson Models-Barbara Watson Charm and Model Sch., N.Y.C., 1946-56; fgn. student adviser Hampton (Va.) Inst., 1958-59; atty., bd. statutory consolidation City N.Y., 1962-63, asst. atty., law dept., 1963-64; exec. dir. N.Y.C. Commn. to UN, 1964-66; dep. adminstrn., bur. security and consular affairs Dept. State, Washington, 1966, acting adminstr., 1967-68, adminstr., 1968—. Dir. United Mut. Life Ins. Co., 1950-70. Trustee Barnard Coll., Fed. Women's Award; bd. dirs. Friendship House, Day Care and Child Devel. Council. Am., Greater Washington Ednl. Telecommunication Assn., Wolf Trap Found. for Performing Arts, Nat. Capital USO; bd. visitors Sch. Fgn. Service, Georgetown U.; adv. bd. Office Econ. Opportunity. Mem. Am. Bar Assn. N.Y. County, Women's Internat. lawyers assns., Harlem Lawyers Assn., Fed. Women's Bar Assn., Internat. Women's Lawyers Assn., Assn. Am. Fgn. Service Women, Urban League Guild, Bus. and Profl. Women's Club, Delta Sigma Theta (hon.). Clubs: International (Washington); Women's City (N.Y.C.). Office: Dept of State Washington DC 20525

WATSON, BEULAH CLARK (MRS. DAVID F. WATSON), social worker; b. Panama, C.Z.; d. Arthur B. and Miriam (Hanson) Clark; B.A., Hunter Coll., 1945; M.S.W., Atlanta U., 1947; m. David F. Watson, June 1, 1947; children—Glenda Maria, Kenneth Foster B. Caseworker Salvation Army Foster Home Service, N.Y.C., 1948-54, Bklyn. Home Children, 1954-59; housing cons. N.Y.C. Housing Authority, 1959-62; social worker Luther E. Woodward Sch. Disturbed Children, Freeport, N.Y., 1962-64; adviser health and welfare services Greater N.Y. Fund, 1964—; v.p. Youth Consultation Service Diocese L.I., 1967—. Mem. resources rev. bd. Human Resources Adminstrn. Mem. bd. Elmcor Youth and Adult Activities. Mem. E. Elmhurst Civic Assn., Nat. Assn. Social Workers, Sigma Gamma Rho. Home: 27-30 Butler St East Elmhurst NY 11369 Office: 99 Park Av New York City NY 10016

WATSON, DOROTHY MARGARET, editor; b. Little Rock, Sept. 5, 1912; d. Edward Bliss and Pearl (Jarnagin) Watson; B.A., La. State U., 1940; M.A., U. Cal. at Los Angeles, 1958. Reporter, Morning Advocate, Baton Rouge, 1940-42; city editor Hollywood (Cal.) Citizen-News, 1942-56; editor Mirror News, Los Angeles, 1956-58; city editor Daily News, Indio, Cal., 1960—. Dir. Asso. Desert Newspapers, Inc., Indio. Mem. Riverside County (Cal.) Bd. Edn., 1972—. Mem. Bus. and Profl. Women's Club, Sigma Delta Chi. Club: Soroptimist (Indio). Free-lance mag. writer, 1942—. Home: 81373 Palmyra Av Indio CA 92201 Office: 45140 Towne St Indio CA 92201

WATSON, GEORGIA BROWN, educator; b. Atlanta; d. George C. and Willie (Willingham) Watson; B.S., Ga., So. Coll., 1946; M.A., George Peabody Coll., 1947, Ph.D., 1949. Tchr. Ga. pub. schs., 1931-42; prof. psychology Ga. So. Coll., Statesboro, 1949—, also chmn. psychology dept.; postdoctoral research fellow Yale, 1961-62. Served to maj. with WAC, 1942-46. Mem. Am. Assn. U. Profs., Am., Southeastern psychol. assns., Kappa Delta Pi, Delta Kappa Gamma, Pi Gamma Mu. Methodist. Home: 4 Preston Dr Statesboro GA 30458

WATSON, GLADYS HAZEL, educator, polit. worker; b. Shiloh, Okla., Mar. 3, 1908; d. Thomas and Laura (Knowles) Dabner; grad. Kan. State Tchrs. Coll., 1933; m. Harold Edmond Watson, Dec. 27, 1937 (dec. Dec. 1967). Tchr. pub. schs., Kansas City, Mo., 1933-39, 68—; supply tchr. all grades, Kansas City, 1947-49; tchr. U.S. census takers, 1960. Speaker pub. meetings, ch. related schs. State committeewoman Mo. Republican Party, 1960-64. Vol. worker ednl., civic, charity orgns., 1953—. Sec. bd. dirs. Big Sister Home, 1955-58; life mem. Wheatley Provident Hosp. Assn., 1960—; mem. Univ. Assos., U. Mo., Kansas City. Recipient Franklin Delano Roosevelt citation, 1946. Baptist. Home: 2631 Tracy Av Kansas City MO 46108

WATSON, KATHERINE ALICE (MRS. PAUL ADAM WATSON), realtor; b. Chgo.; d. Alma Abbott and Mary Alice (Clark) Pitt; student Rockford Coll., 1921; B.S. cum laude, Beloit Coll., 1925; grad. Realtor's Inst., 1973; m. Paul Adam Watson, Sept. 2, 1927; children—Paul Clark, Mary Katherine (Mrs. Anthony Downs), Janice Elizabeth (Mrs. Frank Jenkins). Saleswoman, Koerner Real Estate Co., Park Ridge, Ill., 1956; with Barrington Realty Co. (Ill.), 1956—, partner, 1961—, v.p., dir., 1968—. Mem. sch. bd. Park Ridge Elementary Schs., 1953-56. Mem. Nat. (pres. state chpt. women's council 1972, gov. Ill. women's council 1974—), Ill. (mem. membership com. 1967-71, mem. edn. com. 1965-72, mem. Multiple Listing Service com. 1971-74) assns. realtors, Northwest Suburban (dir. 1961-67, pres. 1967), Barrington (dir. 1969-72, pres. 1972) bds. realtors, Barrington C. of C. (mem. membership com. 1972). Delta Gamma Alumni. Presbyn. Club: Barrington Hills Country (Barrington, Ill.). Home: 45 Brinker Rd Barrington IL 60010 Office: 131 W Main St Barrington IL 60010

WATSON, KIM MINER MORRIS, banker; b. Boston, Dec. 10; d. Joseph Daly and Louise (Malouf) Watson; A.A., Coll. San Mateo, 1956. Dept. sales mgr. The Emporium, Palo Alto, Cal., 1956-59; exec. sec., adminstrv. asst. nuclear sci. lab. Mass. Inst. Tech., Cambridge, 1960-66; dir. pub. relations Brookline Savs. Bank (Mass.), 1966—. Mem. World Affairs Council Boston, 1970—. Mem. Savs. Inst. Marketing Soc. Am., Publicity Club Boston, Internat. Inst. Boston, Mass. Soc. Mayflower Descs., D.A.R. Office: 160 Washington St Brookline MA 02147

WATSON, MARGARET LOUISE LIEBE (MRS. VINTON C. WATSON), educator; b. Cleve., Mar. 25, 1912; d. Adolph W. and Bertha (Burger) Liebe; B.A., Coll. Wooster, 1933; M.A., U. Mich., 1935, Ph.D., 1937; m. Vinton C. Watson, Dec. 18, 1938; children—Vinton Philip, James Liebe, Margaret Jo (Mrs. Howard Soroos). Mem. faculty Simpson Coll., Indianola, Ia., 1937-41, 1955—, prof. biology, 1965—. Mem. PEO, A.A.A.S., Am. Inst. Biol. Scis., Nat. Assn. Biology Tchrs., Am. Genetic Assn., Ia. Acad. Sci., Phi Beta Kappa, Sigma Xi. Home: 1102 North C St Indianola IA 50125

WATSON, NANCY B., judge; b. Pomona, Cal., July 14, 1926; d. Frank Baker and Ruth Barbara (Reynolds) Belcher; B.A, Stanford, 1946; J.D., U. Cal. at Los Angeles, 1958; m. Philip E. Watson, June 4, 1970; children from previous marriage—Marcia, Brian, Harvey, Diane. Admitted to Cal. bar; mem. firm Belcher, Henzie & Biegenzahn, 1959-68; judge Municipal Ct., Los Angeles Jud. Dist., 1968-72; judge Superior Ct., Los Angeles County, 1973—. Mem. Kappa Alpha Theta. Republican. Episcopalian. Office: 111 N Hill St Los Angeles CA 90012

WATSON, OPAL JEANNETTE PERRY (MRS. JAMES PARIS WATSON), educator; b. Pickens County, S.C., Oct. 31, 1922; d. Samuel Lee and Sallie Mae (Jewell) Perry; student Anderson Jr. Coll., 1941-43; B.S. in Elementary Edn., Oglethorpe U., 1955; m. James Paris Watson, Nov. 26, 1943; 1 son, James Paris. Elementary tchr. Gwinnett County (Ga.) Schs., 1948-57, Fulton County-Newtown Sch., 1957-63; field worker ch. tng. dept. Ga. Bapt. Conv., Atlanta, 1963—. Tutor pub. sch. tchrs., 1963—; substitute tchr. Duluth High Sch., 1971—. Dir. day camp Girl Scouts U.S.A., Duluth, Ga., 1957-62; leader Youth Temperance Council, 1968—, ch. tng. dir. Lawrenceville Bapt. Assn., 1956-63, dist. pres. ch. tng. Ga., 1960-65; dist. pres. Woman's Christian Temperance Union, 1964-69, pub. Ga. bull., 1968-72, del. world conv., 1971, state pres., 1968-72, pres. Duluth, 1971—; alternate mem. Nat. Temperance and Prohibition Council, 1970; mem. Ga. Safety Council, 1971-72; mem. Gov.'s Conf. on Edn. and Intellectual Enrichment, 1971-74; sec. Ga. Save Sunday Assn., 1973—; pre-sch. leader Lawrenceville Bapt. Assn., 1973—; mem. Gwinnett County Taxpayers Assn., 1971—, Foster Parents Gwinnett County, 1973—. Baptist (intermediate Sunday sch. supt. 1957-69, peoples dir. 1967-70, adult Sunday sch. tchr. 1973—, women's mission study chmn. 1973-74). Home: 2923 Pineview St Duluth GA 30136

WATSON, PEARL ALEXANDRINA, ophthalmologist; b. Washington, Jan. 13, 1924; d. Edwin Josiah and Mabel Etta (Taylor) Watson; B.S. with honors, Howard U., 1944, M.D., 1948; div.; children—Jualenda Ann Boschulte, Joseph Watson Boschulte. Intern, Freedmen's Hosp., Washington, 1948-49, resident gen. surgery, 1949-50, resident ophthalmology and otolaryngology, 1950-53, ophthalmic pathology Armed Forces Inst. Pathology, postgrad. tng. Episcopal Eye Hosp., 1950-53; practice medicine specializing in ophthalmology, Washington, 1954—; asst. prof. ophthalmology dept. surgery Howard U., 1955—. Cons., mem. panel on rev. ophthalmic drugs FDA; mem. Comprehensive Health Services and Hosp. Devel. Adv. Council; mem. Nat. Capital Med. Found. Chmn. adv. com. Caribbean-Am. Intercultural Orgn. Diplomate Nat. Bd. Med. Examiners, Am. Bd. Ophthalmology, Pan Am. Med. Assn. Fellow Am. Acad. Ophthalmology and Otolaryngology; mem. Am., Nat. med. assns., Med. Soc. D.C., Jack and Jill Am. Democrat. Home: 6217 16th St NW Washington DC 20011 Office: 1629 Columbia Rd NW Park Plaza Washington DC 20009

WATSON, PHOEBE ETHEL KRUGER (MRS. DEWANE L. WATSON), real estate broker; b. Mofatt County, Colo., Nov. 16, 1914; d. Fred O. and Ethel Alma (Rogers) Kruger; grad. Lee's Sch. Real Estate, 1956; m. Irven E. Azbill, 1932; children—Irven Marshall, Roy Gordon (dec.), Janet (Mrs. D.T. Gribble); m. 2d, Dewane L. Watson, Nov. 27, 1964. Real estate salesman Warren Douglas McTaggert Realty, Santa Monica, Cal., 1957-58; with George G. Ross Realty, San Luis Obispo, Cal., 1962-67; owner, real estate broker Ross Realty, 1967—. Mem. Nat. Assn. Real Estate Bds., Soc. Real Estate Appraisers (dir. 1967-69), San Luis Obispo Bd. Realtors (dir. 1968-69, sec., treas. bd. 1970-71), San Luis Obispo Multiple Listing Service (pres. 1972), San Luis Obispo C. of C. Club: Soroptimist (San Luis Obispo, Cal.). Home: 1317 Broad St San Luis Obispo CA 93401 Office: 1321 Broad St St San Luis Obispo CA 93401

WATSON, SARAH KEIL LITTLE (MRS. ARCHER HUNTER WATSON, JR.), educator; b. Des Moines, June 20, 1914; d. Albert Keil and Gladys (Ralston) Little; B.S. in Edn., U. Okla., 1936; M.S. in Spl. Edn., U. Ore., 1971; m. Archer Hunter Watson, Jr., May 28, 1938; children—Archer Hunter III (dec.), Albert Matlock, Catherine Keil (Mrs. Don. Lee Brown). Elementary tchr. pub. schs., Billings, Okla., 1937-38, Rolla, Mo., 1942, Medford, Ore., 1955-66; child resource tchr. specialist, Medford pub. schs., 1966-67; tchr. primary educable mentally retarded Howard Elementary Sch., Medford, 1967—. Instr. 1st aid A.R.C., 1942, 43, 59-61; emergency registrar Jackson County Civil Def., Medford, 1965—; vol. counselor Jackson County Family and Child Guidance Clinic, Medford, 1967-71. Democratic precinct chmn., Medford, 1958-59. Mem. N.E.A., Ore. (sec. county exec. bd. 1963), Medford edn. assns., Nat. Congress Parents and Tchrs., Internat. Reading Assn. (local treas. 1968-70), Jackson County Assn. Classroom Tchrs., Jackson County Mental Health Assn., Nat., Ore. assns. for retarded citizens, Jackson County Assn. for Retarded Citizens, Delta Gamma (v.p. local alumni chpt. 1969-70), Phi Beta Sigma, Kappa Delta Pi. Lutheran. Club: College Women's (Medford). Home: 2925 Comice St Medford OR 97501

WATT, LOIS BELFIELD (MRS. RALPH W. WATT), govt. ofcl.; b. Washington, Mar. 2, 1914; d. Julian Fillmore and May (Ellis) Belfield; B.A., U. Md., 1934, M.A., 1940; M.S. in L.S., Catholic U. Am., 1961; m. Ralph Wardlaw Watt, July 28, 1934; 1 son, Ward Belfield. Asst. librarian Sidwell Friends Sch., Washington, 1946-58; program specialist U.S. Office Edn., Dept. Health, Edn. and Welfare, Washington, 1958-59, chief ednl. materials center, 1960-72, chief information and materials br., 1973-74. Lectr. dept. library sci. Grad. Sch., Catholic U. Am., Washington, 1965-71; asso. prof. tchr. edn. Grad. Sch., Fed. City Coll., Washington, 1971-74. Mem. adv. com. Washington Book Fair, 1953—, also co-chmn., 1958; mem. Children's Book Guild, 1950—, pres., 1958-59. Mem. A.L.A., Assn. Childhood Edn. Internat. (chmn. lit. com.), D.C. Council Adminstrv. Women (pres. 1966-67), Nat. Council Adminstrv. Women in Edn. Editor: Told under the City Umbella, 1972. Chmn. children's book revs. Childhood Edn. mag. and Bibliography: Books for Children, 1971-74. Home: 1206 Parker Av Hyattsville MD 20782 Office: US Office of Education Washington DC 20202

WATT, LOUISE ROTHENBERGER (MRS. JOHN SIMMONS WATT), occupational therapist; b. Pennsburg, Pa., Apr. 13, 1922; d. Wayne Heebner and Margaret Myrtle (Meckley) Rothenberger; student Moravian Coll., 1939-41; certificate occupational therapy U. Pa., 1944; m. John Simmons Watt, May 6, 1967; children—Jane (Mrs. Bruce Wallace Topping), John Stanley. Civilian occupational therapist Dept. Army, Ft. Dix, N.J., 1944-46; occupational therapist VA Hosp., West Roxbury, Mass., 1946-48; chief occupational therapist VA Hosp., Newington, Conn., 1948-53, West Haven, Conn., 1953-67. Chief occupational therapist U.S. Army Res., 1949-67. Home: 161 Leopolds Dr Ottawa Ontario KIV 7E2 Canada

WATT, PATRICIA EVALYNN, univ. dean; b. Pitts.; d. L. Arnold and Gladys L. (Ireland) Watt; B.S., U. Pitts., 1945, M.Ed., 1948, candidate for Ph.D. Dean, Radford Women's Coll., 1960-62, Lock Haven (Pa.) State Coll., 1962-64, U. Wis.-Eau Claire, 1964-66; adminstr. Avco Corp., 1966-68; dean of women Duquesne U., Pitts., 1968-70, asso. dean students, 1970-73, dean students, 1973—; prof. continuing edn. Pa. State U., 1972—. Mem. Nat. Assn. Women Deans and Counselors, Nat., Pa. assns. student personnel adminstrs., Am. Personnel and Guidance Assn., Adminstrv. Women in Edn., Zeta Tau Alpha, Delta Psi Kappa. Club: Altrusa. Home: 325 Inglewood Dr Pittsburgh PA 15228

WATTENBERG, JOAN LOUISE DILLON (MRS. CARL A. WATTENBERG, JR.), lawyer; b. Melrose Park, Ill., Feb. 18, 1941; d. Harold Vincent and Gilberta (Bond) Dillon; B.S., Washington U., 1963, J.D., 1966; m. Carl A. Wattenberg, Jr., June 5, 1965. Admitted to Mo. bar, 1967; trademark atty. Ralston Purina Co., St. Louis, 1966-72; asso. law firm Klamen, Summers, Wattenberg & Compton, St. Louis, 1972—. Mem. Am., Mo. bar assns., U.S. Trademark Assn., Internat. Trademark Com., U.S. Capitol, Mo. hist. socs., St. Louis Jr. C. of C. Aux., Alpha Chi Omega. Club: Zonta (St. Louis). Home: 7235 Creveling Dr St Louis MO 63130 Office: 7820 Maryland Av St Louis MO 63105

WATTERS, JOAN BARTOW ANDREWS (MRS. WELLINGTON MORSE WATTERS), designer, civic worker; b. Englewood, N.J., Sept. 25, 1928; d. Joseph and Helen Hotchkiss (Davis) Andrews; B.A., Vassar Coll., 1950; m. Frederick Snare, III, Mar. 17, 1951; 1 son, Frederick, IV; m. 2d, Wellington Morse Watters, Mar. 19, 1966. Asst. to co-producer Tex and Jinx Show, NBC Radio, 1950-52; mgmt., devel. cons. to ednl. and cultural orgns. John G. Holmes, Assos., 1957-60; free-lance sportswear designer, 1960—. Chmn. Wilton (Conn.) Mid-Fairfield Child Guidance Benefit, 1956-57; bd. dirs. Parents Assn. Browning Sch., N.Y.C., 1968-70; asst. to publicity dir. Cherry Lane Theatre, N.Y.C., 1950; co-chmn. Mayor's Com. for N.Y. Shakespeare Festival Theatre Benefit, 1968-69; mem. adv. com., 1970; co-chmn. N.Y.C. Theatre Benefit for Silvermine Guild Artists, New Canaan, Conn., 1955-56; asso. met. field dir. Vassar Coll. Capital Campaign, 1971-72; chmn. 50th Anniversary scholarship benefit Vassar Club of N.Y., 1972. Mem. Snarks, Georgica Assn. (membership chmn. 1970-72), Asso. Alumni of Vassar Coll. (pres. bd. dirs. 1972—, dir. devel. Phoenix Theatre 1972-74). Episcopalian (dir. religious edn. 1974—). Club: Vassar (dir. membership chmn. 1951-57; publicity chmn. 1961-67; pres. 1968-70) (N.Y.C.). Address: 404 E 66th St New York City NY 10021

WATTLETON, OZIE GARRETT, clergyman; b. Farm Haven, Miss., Nov. 21, 1915; d. Eugene and Ola (Brown) Garrett; m. George Edward Wattleton, May 17, 1939; 1 dau., Alice Faye. Ordained to ministry Church of God, 1941; founding minister ch. Oak Grove, La., 1949-51; home missionary to La., Miss., 1951-52; pastor, Farm Haven, Miss., Laurel, Miss., 1952-53; pastor, Columbus, Neb., 1953-55; pastor radio ministry Ch. God., Cleve., 1959-62; pastor and radio ministry, Washington Court House, O., 1963-66, Liberty Road Ch. God, Houston, 1969—. Founder, exec. dir. Christian Campers and Crusaders, Inc., 1965—; mem. nat. com. race relations Ch. God, Wattleton's grocery, Washington Courthouse, 1965-69. Trustee Bay Ridge Christian Coll., Kendleton, Tex. Mem. Gen. Ministerial Assembly Ch. God. Democrat. Home: 405 Newberry St Washington Court House OH 43160 Office: 4221 Liberty Rd Houston TX 77026

WATTS, EMMA LOU HUBER (MRS. IKE WATTS), ednl. adminstr.; b. Albany, Tex., May 9, 1937; d. Dave and Clara R. (Wernecke) Huber; student Cisco Jr. Coll., 1959-61; m. Ike Watts, May 4, 1957; children—Ricky, Susan. Mem. faculty Cisco (Tex.) Jr. Coll., 1954—, bus. mgr., 1958—. Mem. Tex. Assn. Pub. Jr. Coll. Bus. Officers. Home: 709 E 21st St Cisco TX 76437 Office: Route 3 Box 3 Cisco TX 76437

WATTS, EVADEAN MARIE, social worker; b. Chgo.; d. William Henry and Eleanor Veronica (Maurer) Watts; B.A., Mundelein Coll., 1959; M.S.W., Loyola U., Chgo., 1962; postgrad. U. Chgo., 1963-64, Smith Coll., summer 1965. Part-time cons. Clearbrook Center, Rolling Meadows, Ill., 1965-66, dir. spl. services, 1966-69; social work supr. Ill. State Pediatric Inst., State of Ill. Dept. Mental Health, Chgo., 1962-66; field work instr. Jane Addams Sch. Social Work, 1963-64; adminstr. Augustana Nursery, Lutheran Welfare Services of Ill., Chgo., 1969—. State project coordinator mental retardation services survey Nat. Assn. of Pvt. Facilities UnderFed. Grant, 1972-74. Sec.-treas. N.W. Suburban Welfare Council, 1968-69. Fellow Am. Assn. Mental Deficiency (chmn. Ill. chpt. 1972-73); mem. Ill. Assn. Pvt. Residential Facilities for Mentally Retarded (dir. 1971-74), Alliance Bus. and Profl. Women of Chgo. (pres. 1971-72), Loyola Alumni Sch. Social Work. Office: 400 W Dickens Av Chicago IL 60614

WATTS, JUDITH GEISLER, info. scientist; b. Morenci, Mich., Mar. 6, 1941; d. Henry G. and M. Geraldine (Stanley) Geisler; student U. Vienna, 1962; B.A., Alma Coll., 1963; M.L.S., Pratt Inst., 1968; m. John M. Watts, Jr., Sept. 3, 1966; children—R. Judson, Alexis S. Spl. librarian Bendix Field Engrng. Corp., Adelphi, Md., 1964-66; librarian trainee, librarian I, reference librarian New York Pub. Library, 1966-68; asst. dir. tech. services Hampshire Coll. Library, Amherst, Mass., 1968-73; asst. librarian Program Library Computer Sci. Center, U. Md., College Park, 1973-74; chief librarian Martin Marietta Labs., Balt., 1974—. Mem. Am., New Eng. (chmn. coll. librarians sect. 1972-73) library assns., Am. Coll. and Research Libraries, Am. Soc. for Info. Sci. Home: 11100 Montgomery Rd Beltsville MD 20705 Office: Martin Marietta Labs 1450 S Rolling Rd Baltimore MD 21227

WATTS, MABEL, author; b. London, Eng., May 20, 1906; d. Ernest Henry and Edith Mary (Elias) Pizzey; ed. in Eng. and Can.; m. William Watts, Feb. 22, 1936; 1 dau., Patricia Linda (Mrs. Babcock). Came to U.S., 1927, naturalized, 1943. Club: Burlingame Writers (pres. 1962). Author children's books, 1950—, including Jr. Lit. Guild selections Cow in the House, 1956, Everyone Waits, 1959, Weeks and Weeks, 1962; also Henrietta and the Hat, 1962; The Boy Who Listened to Everyone, 1963; The Narrow Escapes of Solomon Smart, 1966; (film) The Story of Zachary Zween, 1967; The King and The Whirly Bird, 1969; The Elephant That Become a Ferryboat, 1971; The Basket That Flew Over the Mountain, 1972; While the Horses Galloped to London, 1973 (Soc. Illustrators show 1974, Children's Book Showcase 1974); Molly and the Giant, 1973 (Book of Yr. award Child Study Assn.). Home: 1520 Ralston Av Burlingame CA 94010

WATTS, MAY PETREA THEILGAARD (MRS. RAYMOND WATTS), naturalist, author; b. Chgo., May 1, 1893; d. Hermann and Claudia (Andersen) Theilgaard; B.S., U. Chgo., 1918; m. Raymond Watts, Dec. 27, 1924; children—Erica, Tom, Nancy, Peter. Staff naturalist Morton Arboretum, Lisle, Ill., 1942-61, naturalist emeritus, 1961—. Hon. mem. Friends of Our Native Landscape, 1950—; founder Ill. Prairie Path, 1965—. Recipient Douglas medal for conservation edn. Garden Club of Am., 1954; Presidents award

Dupage Audubon Soc., 1965; spl. citation award Ill. Parks and Recreation; May Theilgaard Watts Reading Garden named for her Morton Arboretum, 1963; Teaching citation Am. Hort. Soc., 1971; Hutchinson medal Chgo. Hort. Soc., 1972; Arthur Hoyt Scott medal Swarthmore Coll., 1972; Book award Chgo. Geog. Soc., 1972. Mem. Assn. Interpretive Naturalists (hon.), Phi Beta Kappa. Democrat. Clubs: Garden (hon.) (Ravinia and Naperville). Author: Reading the Landscape, 1957; Trees, 1964; Reading the Landscape of Europe, 1971; also handbooks. Columnist Nature Afoot, Chgo. Tribune, 1966. Home: 227 E Jefferson Av Naperville IL 60540

WATTS, NANCY BAYLY, mus. curator; b. Los Angeles, July 12, 1915; d. Roy Downer and Ada Belle (Seeley) Bayly; student Mills Coll., 1932, U. Cal. at Los Angeles, 1934; m. Leslie C. Watts, 1945 (div. June 1967); children—Joan Haradon, Fritz Howard Haradon, Jr., Luis Guevera. Art tchr., lectr. art edn., asst. to curator edn. Pasadena Art Mus., 1960-65, curator edn., 1969-73; dir. Childrens Art Workshop, Los Angeles County Museums, 1965-69; art edn. instr. Pasadena City Coll., 1968-74; instr. U. Cal., Los Angeles, 1969—. Home: 1439 Lida St Pasadena CA 91103

WATTS, SARAH EVELYN MILES, educator, journalist; b. Wellsville, N.Y., May 11, 1934; d. Sydney Henderson and Evelyn Eleanor (Gardner) Miles; B.A., U. Rochester, 1956; Troisième Degré de la langue française, Alliance Francaise, Brussels, Belgium, 1968; m. Ronald Alan Watts, Dec. 16, 1961; children—Valerie Louise, Sydney Evelyn, Alan Miles. Reporter, Times-Union, Rochester, 1956-62; founder, editor Journalist's World, Brussels, 1962-68; mag. editor, instr. journalism State U. N.Y. Coll. at Brockport, 1968—. Mem. Women in Communications (pres. Rochester chpt. 1973-74). Author: The Art of Belgium Cooking, 1971. Home: 46 King St Brockport NY 14420

WATUMULL, M'LOU, cafe exec.; b. Cedar Rapids, Ia., May 12, 1927; d. Jairus Harrison and Lula (Holland) Watson; B.A., U. Cal. at Los Angeles, 1949; m. David G. Watumull, Sept. 10, 1948 (div.); children—David G., Rann Jonathon, Teren, Denton, Melanie. Tchr. pub. schs., Hermosa Beach, Cal., 1947-48; treas. My House, Inc., 1964-66; personal sec. Elizabeth Dresser, 1967; mgr. Garden Cafe, Honolulu Acad. Arts, 1969—. Asst. chmn. Honolulu Symphony Childrens Concerts, 1956-57; fair chmn., treas., sec., pres. Hanahauoli Sch. P.T.A., 1958-63; asst. treas., by laws chmn. Jr. League, 1958-67; pres. Childrens Hosp. Aux., 1959-61; coordinator Council Hosp. Aux., 1961-62; treas. Punahou Sch. Swim Club, 1966-69; by laws chmn., ways and means budget chmn. Queens Med. Center Aux., 1967—. Del. Republican State Conv., 1964, 66, 68. Mem. Honolulu Acad. Arts. Mem. Christian Ch. Club: Outrigger Canoe. Home: 3661 Woodlawn Dr Honolulu HI 96822 Office: 900 S Beretania Honolulu HI 96822

WAUGH, DORIS HANNER, elementary librarian; b. Greensboro, N.C., June 4, 1928; d. Thomas Benton and Eliabeth (Hanner) Waugh; B.S., Appalachian State Tchrs. Coll., 1950; M.S., U. N.C., 1956. Librarian Black Mountain (N.C.) High Sch., 1950-51, Burlington (N.C.) City Schs., 1951-53, Greensboro Pub. Schs., 1953—. Active Girl Scouts, Brownies; program chmn. Ladies Aux. Climax Vol. Fire Dept. Mem. Southeastern, N.C. library assns., N.E.A., N.C. Assn. Educators, Assn. Childhood Edn. Methodist. Home: Box 40 Climax NC 27233 Office: 600 W Terrell St Greensboro NC 27406

WAUGH, ELIZABETH LOHRLI (MRS. SANFORD A. WAUGH), lawyer; b. Parma, Ida., May 1, 1913; d. Gottfried and Anna (Husser) Lohrli; B.A., U. Cal. at Los Angeles, 1937; gen. secondary teaching credential Claremont Grad. Sch., 1941; LL.B., LaSalle Extension U., 1962; m. Sanford A. Waugh, June 14, 1941; 1 son, Ernest Sanford. Tchr. adult edn. Long Beach City Schs., 1941-46; legal sec. Sanford A. Waugh, Lancaster, Cal., 1952-57; partner firm Waugh & Waugh, 1963—; admitted to Cal. bar, 1963; since practiced in Lancaster. Mem. adv. bd. Antelope Valley chpt. Salvation Army, 1969-72; chmn. Antelope Valley br. GEMCO Charitable and Scholarship Found., 1969—; chmn. Antelope Valley Hosp. Med. Center Gift Found., 1973. Trustee Lancaster (Cal.) Elementary Sch. Bd., 1954-56. Recipient award of merit Los Angeles County Bd. of Suprs., 1970; named Lancaster Woman of Year, Lancaster C. of C., 1969; certificate of honor Cal. State Assembly. Mem. Am. Assn. U. Women (pres. Antelope Valley br. 1956-57), Antelope Valley Bar Assn. (pres. 1967), So. Cal. Women Lawyers Assn., Antelope Valley Bus. and Profl. Women, Lancaster C. of C. (pres. 1969-70). Kiwaniannes. Club: Women's (Lancaster). Home: 39724 Makin Av Palmdale CA 93550 Office: 44822 Cedar Av Lancaster CA 93534

WAUGH, GENE BARNWELL (MRS. HOWARD WAUGH), research and information specialist; b. Johnson City, Tex., Oct. 7, 1920; d. James Franklin and Alma Irene (Lewis) Barnwell; B.J., U. Tex., Austin, 1938; m. Howard J. Waugh, Jan. 23, 1955; 1 stepson, Howard J. Asst. librarian Los Angeles Times, 1944-45; asst. editor Tex. Plumbing Contractor, 1949; reporter, head photography dept. San Antonio Express, 1942-43, women's club editor, 1957-63, editor, 1950-55; asso. editor Tex. Pub. Employees Assn., 1963-69; chief research and information br. Tex. Office Econ. Opportunity, Austin, 1969—, also editor ann. report and weekly newsletter. Mem. Women in Communications (charge publicity nat. conv. 1962). Democrat. Lutheran. Home: 608 Harthan St Austin TX 78703 Office: 510 S Congress St Austin TX 78701

WAUGH, MARY HESTER, hosp. adminstr.; b. Dighton, Kan., June 29, 1931; d. Harry Oscar and Lulu May (Morgan) Glenn; student Garden City Community Coll.; m. Vernon Robert Waugh, May 13, 1951; children—Vernon Robert, Sally Ann, Jack Lee, Mary Louise. Operator, United Telephone Co., Dighton, 1949-51; dep. county clk. Lane County, Kan., 1955-58; with Lane County Hosp., Dighton, 1960—, adminstr., 1968—. Sec. Far S.W. Comprehensive Health Planning Council, 1973; chmn. planning com. S.W. region Kan. Regional Med. Program, 1970, vice chmn., 1970-71; mem. Citizens Adv. Com. Lane County; adv. com., phys. therapy dept. Wichita (Kan.) State U., 1973-74. Mem. Kan. Hosp. Assn. (chmn. dist. 8 1972-73, mem. council manpower 1972-75), Kan. Assn. Hosp. Edn. and Tng. Coordinators (chmn. 1973-74), Dighton C. of C. Home: Box 11 Dighton KS 67839 Office: Box 718 Dighton KS 69839

WAY, ISABEL STEWART (MRS. THOMAS THOMSON), author, lectr.; b. Muskegon, Mich., Aug. 2, 1904; d. Harlow A. and Alice (Brown) Stuart; student pub. schs.; m. Scott Way, Jan. 20, 1922 (dec.); m. 2d, David Bonnard, Aug. 6, 1932 (dec.); 1 dau. Eve Felicity (Mrs. Bonnard North); m. 3d, Thomas Barclay Thomson, Nov. 2, 1965. Author: Seed of the Land, 1936; Paula Wayne, 1963; Nurse in Love, 1964; Doctor Jenny, 1964; Mountain Doctor, 1967; Lindy Haynes, M.D., 1967; Nurse Christy, 1968; Fleur Macabre, 1968; Mystery of Sky High Road, 1969; Bell, Book and Candleflame, 1970; Calling Nurse Lorrie, 1972; Fighting Doctor Diana, 1973; also numerous short stories, articles for mags. including Pictorial Review, New Yorker, Sat. Eve. Post, Redbook, This Week, Country Gentlemen, others; author radio continuity Gilmore Circus, 1933. Child def. chmn. Azusa (Cal.) Def. Council, 1942-45. Mem. 49th Dist. Democratic Council, 1944-45. Mem. Nat. Writers Club (dir. 1952-62), Cal. Writers Guild, Azusa Library Bd. Club: Soroptimist (pres. Azusa 1958-60). Episcopalian. Address: 733 Soldano St Azusa CA 91702

WAY, LULA ROSETTA, educator; b. nr. Mt. Pleasant, Mich., Dec. 3, 1912; d. C.O. and Nellie (Meginley) Way; B.S., George Peabody Coll. Tchrs., 1940, M.A., 1941; Ed.D., Mich. State U., 1958. Tchr. rural schs., Mich., 1931-36, Okemos Consol. Sch. (Mich.), 1936-39; tchr. social studies Pioneer Sch., W. Carrol Parish, La., 1942-45; elementary supr. campus sch. Neb. State Coll., 1945-49, jr. high sch. supr., 1951-54, prof. edn., 1954-62; prof. psychology, dir. psychol. reading clinic Florence (Ala.) State U., 1962—. Dir. N.E. Ala. Head Start tng. program, 1968—. Cons. Title III Spl. Edn. Project. Bd. dirs. Colbert Lauderdale Child Study Center, Florence, Ala., 1966—; pres. bd. Muscle Shoals (Ala.) Area Retarded Children, 1965-68; bd. dirs. dir. Ala. Assn. Retarded Children, 1966—. Named Neb. Outstanding Tchr. of Year, 1956; recipient Civic award for work with retarded children, 1969. Mem. P.T.A. (mem. Neb. planning bd. 1945-52), N.E.A. Delta Kappa Gamma, Phi Kappa Psi. Baptist. Author: (with Elizabeth Woolridge) Let's Play Arithmetic, 1960. Contbr. articles profl. jours. Home: 515 Sherwood Ct Florence AL 35630 Office: Box 502 Florence AL 35630

WAYNE, GAIL MOVENE, motion picture producer, real estate investment co. exec.; b. Calgary, Alta., Can., Oct. 11, 1922; d. Earl Ransom and Ida Movene (Helgeson) Tamblin; student Los Angeles City Coll., 1939, Lumbleau Real Estate Sch., 1956; m. Steve Wayne, May 28, 1948 (div. Nov. 1952); 1 son, Christopher Stephen. Motion picture actress, Hollywood, Cal., 1938-46; owner Gail Wayne Splty. Shop, Farmers Market, Los Angeles, 1946-54; real estate broker, Los Angeles, 1958—; pres. Sun State Lands, Inc., Los Angeles, 1958—; pres. Asia-Am. Land Investments, Ltd., Hong Kong, 1965—, chmn. bd., 1966—; exec. producer, v.p. Hagen-Wayne Prodns., Inc., Hollywood, Cal., 1973—; pres. Hagen-Wayne Film Orgn., Inc., Hollywood, 1974—. Del. Hawaii State Republican Conv., 1970. Bd. dirs. Hawaii chpt. WAIF div. Internat. Social Service. Mem. Honolulu Bd. Realtors, Nat. Assn. Realtors. Clubs: Hawaii Polo (social chmn. 1973-74) (Honolulu); Diamond Head Tennis, Outrigger Canoe (Waikiki, Hawaii). Home: 2957 Kalakaua Av Honolulu HI 96815 Office: 1040 N Las Palmas Av Hollywood CA 90038 also 407-409 Gloucester Bldg Hong Kong China

WAYNE, JUNE C., artist; b. Chgo., Mar. 7, 1918; d. Albert and Dorothy Alice (Kline) LaVine; m. George Jerome Wayne, June 18, 1941 (div. 1961); 1 dau., Robin Claire; m. 2d, Arthur H. Plone, 1964. Artist, 1935—; indsl. designer, N.Y.C., 1939-41; radio writer, staff mem. sta. WGN, Chgo., 1942-43; lithographer 1948—; founder, dir. Tamarind Lithography Workshop, Inc., 1959—; many solo shows 1936—, including Far Gallery, N.Y.C., 1969, Cin. Mus. Art, 1969, Ia. Art Mus., 1970, Gimpel Gallery, N.Y.C., 1972, La Demeure Gallery, Paris, France, 1972; exhibited numerous nat. and internat. group shows; represented in permanent collections including Los Angeles County Mus., San Diego Fine Arts Gallery, Library of Congress, N.Y.C. Pub. Library, Pasadena Art Mus., Mus. Modern Art, N.Y.C., Grunwald Found. of U. Cal. at Los Angeles, Phila. Mus. Art, Newberry Library, Art Inst. Chgo., Houghton Library, Harvard, Walker Art Center, Mpls., Bibliothetheque Nationale de France, Paris, Bibliotheque Royale de Belgique, Brussels, Le Musée d'Epinal (France), Cin. Mus. Art, Mus. Modern Art, Amon Carter Mus. of Ft. Worth, Smithsonian Instn., Rosenwald Collection, Nat. Gallery Art, Allen Art Mus., Oberlin, O., Baron Edmond de Rothschild Collection, Phila. Print Club, many others. Recipient purchase prize, Los Angeles County Museum, 1951; Los Angeles County Fair, 1950, also 1st prize, 1950; J. H. F. Knobloch prize for lithography Am. Graphic Artists, 1953; Mary S. Collins prize for lithography Phila. Print Club, 1955; prize for painting Laguna Beach Art Festival, 1956; purchase prize Los Angeles Art Festival, 1956; purchase prizes Library of Congress Pennel Fund, 1959, Soc. Washington Printmakers, 1960; 2d nat. print. exhbn. Pasadena Art Mus., 1960, Contemporary Am. Printmakers, DePauw U., 1960, Francesca Wood Prize, Am. Color Print Soc.; Prix de Bienale, Epinal, France, 1971; named Woman of Year for Modern Art, by editorial bd. Los Angeles Times, 1952. Bd. dirs. Grunwald Center for Graphic Arts, U. Cal. at Los Angeles, 1965—, mem. chancellor's adv. com., arts mgmt. program Grad. Sch. Adminstrn., 1969—; adviser Tamarind Inst. of U. N.M., 1970—; mem. vis. com. Sch. Visual and Environmental Studies of Harvard, 1972-73. Studio: 1108 N Tamarind Av Los Angeles CA 90038

WEACHTER, EVELYN, librarian; b. Akron, O., Apr. 12, 1908; d. William Clyde and Minnetta (McConnell) Weachter; A.B., Coll. of Wooster, 1932; B.S. in L.S., Columbia, 1940; postgrad. Fitchburg State Coll., 1960-64. With Akron Pub. Library, 1933-45, reference librarian, 1940-43, bus. reference librarian, 1943-45; reference librarian Fitchburg (Mass.) Pub. Library, 1945-55, asst. librarian, 1955-60; head librarian Fitchburg State Coll., 1960-66; head librarian Cocoa Beach (Fla.) Pub. Library, 1969—. Instr. reference course Clark U., Worcester, Mass., 1950-51, Mass. U. Extension Service, Cambridge, Mass., 1949-50; author corr. course in reference librarianship for Commonwealth Mass., 1958. Mem. Mass. (chmn. planning com. 1955-56), Fla. library assns., Council State Coll. Librarians (pres. Mass. 1963-64), Brevard County Librarians Assn. Home: Twin Towers 612 N 2020 N Atlantic Av Cocoa Beach FL 32931 Office: 55 S Brevard St Cocoa Beach FL 32931

WEARIN, LOLA IRENE, farmer, community worker; b. Strahan, Ia., Nov. 7, 1907; d. Thomas Marion and Rose Belle (Gipe) Brazelton; student Boyles Bus. Coll., 1926, Grinnell (Ia.) Coll., 1930; m. Otha Donner Wearin, Jan. 2, 1931; children—Martha (Mrs. Robert L. Rasmussen), Rebecca (Mrs. Allen F. Pulk). 4-H leader, 1944-56; bd. dirs. Ia. Soc. for Preservation Historic Landmarks, 1956, Local Hist. and Mus. Assn., 1958; pres. 73d Club, 1933; womens pres. Mills County Farm Bur., 1950; mem. County Extension Family Living Council, 1953; mem. Ia. Bd. Pub. Instrn., 1960; mem. bd. Terrace Hill Commn., 1970. Democratic county vice chmn., 1952, dist. vice chmn., 1954-56. Bd. curators Ia. Hist. Soc.; bd. dirs. Grinnell Coll. Recipient Alumni award Grinnell Coll., 1959; named Ia. Master Farm Homemaker, 1957. Club: Mills County Federated Womens (pres. 1933). Home: Rural Route 1 Hastings IA 51540

WEATHERBY, LOIS MAXINE FLETCHER (MRS. JOSEPH NORMAN WEATHERBY), civic worker; b. Temple, Tex.; d. Omar Lester and Sarah Belle (McDonald) Fletcher; A.A., Ward-Belmont Coll., 1928; B.A. in English, Tex. U., 1930; postgrad. Mary Hardin Baylor Coll., 1931-32, Howard Payne Coll., 1950-51; m. Joseph Norman Weatherby, Feb. 23, 1933; children—Joseph Norman, Sarah Maxine (Mrs. Homer Hilton Stephens). Gray lady Vol. Service, A.R.C., 1942-46; officer, mem. bd. Women's Missionary Union First Bapt. Ch., 1965-69; regent Mary Garland chpt. D.A.R., 1957-60; sec. Hon. Phillip Livingston chpt. Daus. Am. Colonists, 1963-65; charter mem. Feur de Lis chpt. Huegenot Soc. (Austin, Tex.); corr.-sec. Maj. James McGregor chpt. Colonial Dames of XVIII Century (Dallas); mem. San Antonio-Austin chpt. Nat. Soc. Magna Charta Dames, Sovereign Colonial Soc. Am. Royal Descent, Colonial Order of Crown, Descs. Knights of Garter, Plantaganet Soc., Clan Donald Soc. Tex., Sterling C. Robertson chpt. Daus. Rep. of Tex. (Waco), Jr. Service League; charter mem., div. chmn. Women's Aux. Brownwood (Tex.) Community Hosp., 1968—; organizing sr. pres. Tejas Soc. Children Am. Revolution, 1944—; mem. bd. Brownwood Civic Music Assn., 1955-69; officer Women's Assn. Brownwood Country Club, 1950—. Recipient Gen. D. MacArthur Acad. Freedom medal Howard Payne Coll., 1968. Mem. Tex. Ex-Student Assn., Am. Assn. U. Women (past officer), Ashbel Lit. Soc., Brown County Hist. Soc., Pi Beta Phi. Rotary Ann. (div. chmn. 1967-69). Clubs: Knife and Fork, Investment, Junior 20th Century Study (Brownwood). Home: 2110 Belmeade St Brownwood TX 76801

WEATHERFORD, MERLE VIVIAN GIBSON (MRS. OLEN KALMATH WEATHERFORD), educator, former city ofcl.; b. Enville, Tenn., Dec. 18, 1913; d. Poney and Lelia Blaine (Kerby) Gibson; student Freed-Hardeman Coll., 1932-35; B.S., Memphis State U., 1956; m. Olen Kalmath Weatherford, Dec. 24, 1936; children—Kalmath Gene, Winfred Roger, Charles Neal, Fred Anthony. Tchr., McNairy County Schs., 1935—, librarian's asst., 1969—; city recorder, treas., sec. Town of Eastview, Tenn., 1968-72. Active P.T.A. Mem. Nat., Tenn., McNairy Tchrs. edn. assns. Home: Route 2 Box 496 Selmer TN 38375

WEATHERLY, MARGARET BROOKS HISCOCK (MRS. BRUCE A. WEATHERLY), museum ofcl.; b. New Haven, Jan. 27, 1926; d. Ira Vaughan and Margaret McConway (Scoville) Hiscock; B.A., Smith Coll., 1947; postgrad. Yale, 1947-50, Barnes Found., Merion, Pa., 1968-70; m. Bruce A. Weatherly, June 3, 1950; children—John A., Christopher B., Margaret E., Mark A., Peter B. Asst. div. of arts Yale, 1947-48, registrar Art Gallery, 1948-50; substitute tchr., asst. librarian Moorestown Pub. Schs., 1965-70; dir. Hist. Soc., edn. program Mus. and Camden County Hist. Soc., Camden, N.J., 1970—. Leader, Girl Scouts U.S.A., 1961-62; Cub Scout leader Boy Scouts Am., 1964-65; program chmn. P.T.A., 1964-66. Bd. dirs. Childrens Program, Ancora State Hosp., 1966-71, chmn. program, 1969-71; founder, bd. dirs. No. Ky. Mental Health Assn. Aux., 1957-59; Mem. Phila., N.J. mus. councils, League Hist. Socs. N.J. (del.), Nat. Trust for Historic Preservation. Episcopalian. Club: Appalachian Mountain (Delaware Valley chpt.). Home: 324 E 2d St Moorestown NJ 08057 Office: Park Blvd and Euclid Av Camden NJ 08103

WEATHERS, EMILY BECK (MRS. ARTHUR K. WEATHERS), coll. dean; b. Griffin, Ga., Mar. 20, 1919; d. Lewis Hicks and Ethel Emily (Williams) Beck; B.S., U. Ga., 1940; M.Ed., Midwestern U., 1964; m. Arthur K. Weathers, May 30, 1942; children—Arthur Kitchings, Seaborn Beck, James Daniel. Asst. dean women Midwestern U., Wichita Falls, Tex., 1965-66; dir. womens activities Memphis State U., 1967-71, asst. dean students, 1971-72, asso. dean students, 1973—. Recipient Centennial award Pi Beta Phi, 1968; Woman of Year award Phi Mu, 1972, Alpha Lambda Delta, 1971. Mem. Nat., Tenn. (pres. 1972-73) women deans, counselors and adminstrs., Am. Assn. U. Women, So. Coll. Personnel Assn., Phi Mu, Club: Zonta International Home: 1231 Cherrydale Cove Memphis TN 38111 Office: Memphis State University 114 Scates Hall Memphis TN 38152

WEATHERS, PEARL AMELIA, journalist; b. Shelby, N.C., May 22, 1922; d. Lee Beam and Williewee (Wiseman) Weathers; A.B., Greensboro (N.C.) Coll., 1943. Gen. advt. Shelby Daily Star, 1946-51, gen. news reporter, 1958-61; asso. dir. Presbyn. News Service, Atlanta, 1952-58, 62—; dir. interpretation and promotion Presbyn. Women's Work, 1961-62. Mem. Pres.'s Council of Atlanta, Atlanta Womens C. of C., Atlanta Press Club, Women in Communications. Presbyn. (deacon). Club: Altrusa International (Atlanta). Home: 710 Peachtree St NE Atlanta GA 30308 Office: 341 Ponce de Leon Av NE Atlanta GA 30308

WEAVER, BARBARA FRANCES, govt. ofcl.; b. Boston, Aug. 29, 1927; d. Leo Francis and Nina (Durham) Weisse; B.A. in Math., Radcliffe Coll., 1949; M.L.S. (F. J. Barnard scholar 1964), U. R.I., 1968; m. George B. Weaver, June 6, 1951 (dec. Feb. 1970); 1 dau., Valerie Susan. Tech. writer EG & G Inc., Boston, 1951-59; librarian Thompson (Conn.) Library, Inc., 1961-69; asst. dir. Conn. State Library Service Center, Willimantic, 1969-71, dir., 1971-72; regional adminstr. Central Mass. Regional Library System, Worcester, 1972—. Pres. Thompson Raceway Inc., 1970-71. Exec. dir. Nat. Library Week, Conn., 1969-72; mem. adv. com. religious edn. Roman Catholic Diocese Norwich, Conn., 1969-71. Mem. New Eng. (chmn. continuing edn. task force 1970-71), Conn. (dir. 1968-69) library assns., Thompson Hist. Soc. (sec. 1971—), Am. QuarterHorse Assn. Club: Sports Car of America (Denver). Home: East Thompson Rd PO Box 295 Thompson CT 06277 Office: Worcester Public Library Salem Sq Worcester MA 01608

WEAVER, DE LORES, news reporter, photographer; b. Memphis, Dec. 9, 1947; d. George Milton and Margaret Louise (Madden) Weaver; B.A. in Journalism, Memphis State U., 1971. News reporter sta. WREC-TV, Memphis, 1969-72, sta. WJXT-TV, Jacksonville, 1972-73, also photgrapher, film editor; account exec. WVOJ-Radio, Jacksonville, Fla., 1974—. Mem. Am. Women in Radio and TV, Theta Sigma Phi, Sigma Delta Chi. Home: 2447 Spring Park Rd Jacksonville FL 32207 Office: 1435 Ellis Rd S Jacksonville FL 32205

WEAVER, JOSEPHINE ELIZABETH, librarian; b. McSherryston, Pa., Sept. 28, 1923; d. John William and Bernadina (Horwedel) Weaver; B.S. in Edn., Millersville State Tchrs. Coll., 1949; M.L.S., Rutgers U., 1957. Post librarian Army Chem. Center, Md., 1949-54, Ft. Greeley, Alaska, 1954-56, Ft. Hancock, N.J., 1956-57; chief librarian post library Ft. Devens, Mass., 1958—. Librarian Ayer (Mass.) Library, 1968—. Chmn. pub. relations com. Central Mass. Regional Library Bd., 1970-71. Mem. A.L.A. (pres. armed forces library sect. 1961-62). Home: 17 Nashua St Ayer MA 01432 Office: Davis Library Fort Devens MA 01433

WEAVER, KITTY DUNLAP, author; b. Frankfort, Ky., Sept. 24, 1910; d. Arch Robertson and Rebecca (Johnson) Dunlap; student Sorbonne, Paris, summer 1930; A.B., William and Mary Coll., 1932; M.A., George Washington U., 1933; B.S., U. Md., 1947; postgrad. Georgetown U., U. Pa., George Washington U., 1964-67; m. Henry Byrne Weaver, June 29, 1933. Jr. high sch. tchr., 1931-32; poultry farmer, 1947-55; author, 1970—. Mem. founding bd. Fauquier-London Day Care Center. Mem. O.M.E.P., U.S.-China Friendship Soc. Episcopalian. Clubs: Middleburg (Va.) Tennis; Washington, Sulgrave (Washington); River (N.Y.C.). Author: Lenin's Grandchildren, 1971. Home: Glengyle Aldie VA 22001

WEAVER, L. RUTH RUNDLE (MRS. C.H. WEAVER), lawyer; b. St. Joseph, Mo.; d. Charles Vail and Anna (Wist) Rundle; B.A., Neb. State Tchrs. Coll., 1923; J.D., Akron Law Sch., 1955; m. Clyde Hulbert Weaver, Feb. 28, 1931 (dec. June 1951). Tchr. Chase County High Sch., Imperial, Neb., 1923-24, Biwabik (Minn.) High Sch., 1924-25, Child High Sch., Edgerton, Wis., 1925-28, Central High Sch., Akron, O., 1928-30; supr. personnel record sect. Goodyear Tire and Rubber Co., Akron, 1942-47; teller Evans Savs. Assn., Akron, 1951-56; admitted to Ohio bar, 1956, since in practice, Akron. Mem. adv. com. Coll. of Law, Akron U. Named Woman of Year, Summit chpt. Am. Bus. Women's Assn., 1961. Mem. Am. Judicature Soc. Fedn. Women's Clubs, Am. Trial Lawyers Assn., Am. (com. estate and gift tax 1962—), Ohio, Akron (chmn. speakers bur. com. 1958-61,

65—, probate court com. 1967-68, mem. ethics com., inquiry com. 1967—, chmn. necrology com. 1973—) bar assns., Cuyahoga Falls League Women Voters, Am. Bus. Women's Assn., Akron Dist. Golf Assn., (tournament chmn. 1939-41, pres. 1941-49), Phi Delta Delta (pres. Beta Xi chpt. 1969-70). Clubs: Quota (chmn. community service 1964-65), Woman's City (chmn. six-thirty sect.), Business Women's Current Events (1st v.p. 1959, pres. 1964-66). Home: 2453 16th St Cuyahoga Falls OH 44223 Office: United Bldg Akron OH 44308

WEAVER, MARGARET DUNLOP (MRS. ROBERT G. WEAVER), newspaper columnist; b. Springfield, Ill., Aug. 28, 1909; d. George C. and Pearl (Rogers) Dunlop; student U. Cin., 1928-30, Cin. Art Acad., 1930-32; m. Robert G. Weaver, Nov. 4, 1934; children—Andrew, Randall, Michael. Columnist Cin. Post, 1932-34, columnist, soc. editor, 1956-58; columnist, soc. editor Cin. Post and Times Star, 1958—. Mem. Ohio Newspaper Women's Assn., Kappa Alpha Theta, Episopalian. Clubs: Mt. Lookout Swim, Queen City Figure Skating, Cincinnati. Home: 1215 Halpin Av Cincinnati OH 45208 Office: 800 Broadway Cincinnati OH 45202

WEAVER, MARILYN LEWIS (MRS. JAMES E. WEAVER, JR.), ednl. aminstr.; b. Pitts., May 29, 1938; s. Joseph Edwards and Mary Elizabeth (Dolan) Lewis; B.S., U. Houston, 1959, M.A., 1962; m. James E. Weaver, Jr., Jan. 28, 1970; children—Joseph Lewis, Jefferson Lee, Robert Christopher. Therapist Houston Speech and Hearing Center, 1960-62; dir. Spl. Care Sch., Dallas, 1964-68; dir. edn. and day care service Dallas County Mental Health and Mental Retardation Center, 1968-70; program dir. Children, Inc., Dallas, 1970-72, Angels, Inc., Dallas, 1971—. Instr. community service div. El Centro Jr. Coll., Dallas, 1968—. Mem. Adv. Bd. Helping Hand Sch., Irving, Tex., 1969—. Mem. Am. Assn. Mental Deficiency, Council for Exceptional Children, Gamma Phi Beta. Home: 4321 Mill Creek Dallas TX 75234 Office: PO Box 18581 Dallas TX 75218

WEAVER, PATSY A., cultural orgn. exec.; b. Oklahoma City, Mar. 17, 1935; B.F.A. in Advt. Design, U. Okla., 1957; postgrad. painting Kansas City Art Inst.; m. Robert Richard Weaver; 1 dau., Amy Marie. Designer greeting cards Hallmark Cards, Inc.; free-lance advt. artist; pub. information dir. Okla. Arts and Humanities Council, editor newsletter, coordinator conf. community Justice and Traditions, summer 1972. Paintings exhibited Nelson-Atkins Gallery, Hallmark Mezzanine Gallery, Kansas City Art Inst., others; bus. mgr. Cedwarwood Gallery. Mem. Outreach Adv. Bd.; staff asst. Mid-Del Youth and Family Center, Oklahoma City; mem. steering com. Vol. Action Center; vol. Golden Door Nursery; sec. Oklahoma City Arts Festival, com. chmn.; active other charity drives. Bd. dirs. Oklahoma City Arts Council; bd. dirs., mem. arts com. Okla. Sci. and Arts. Found. Mem. Delta Gamma, P.E.O. Methodist (mem. edn. commn.). Home: 1140 N W 63d St Oklahoma City OK 73116

WEAVER, PATSY JEAN, ednl. adminstr.; b. Waterloo, Ark., May 30, 1932; d. Luther P. and Vida (Polk) Weaver; B.S., So. State Coll., Magnolia, Ark., 1954; M.Ed., U. Ark., 1957; postgrad. Auburn U., 1959, 60, U. Ala., 1961-62. Tchr. Harmony Grove High Sch., 1954-55, Camden High Sch., 1955-61; asst. dean of women So. State Coll., Magnolia, Ark., 1962-67, dean of women, 1967—. Mem. Nat., Ark. assns. women deans and counselors, N.E.A., Ark. Edn. Assn., Am., Ark. personnel and guidance assns., Am., Ark. coll. personnel assns., Am. Assn. U. Women, Delta Kappa Gamma. Baptist. Home: 1725 Dogwood Dr Magnolia AR 71753

WEBB, ANNE KAVANAUGH (MRS. ROBERT REED WEBB), supr. schs.; b. Shelbyville, Ky., June 26, 1937; d. William Lackey and Mary Anna (Beard) Kavanaugh; A.B. (Am. Assn. U. Women scholar), Centre Coll., 1959; M.S. in Edn., Ind. U., 1962, Ed.S. in Supervision and Curriculum Devel., 1969; m. Robert Reed Webb, June 27, 1967; 1 son, Allen Randolph. Tchr. elementary schs. Mentor, O., 1959-61; tchr. elementary grades Ind. U. Lab. Sch., Bloomington, 1962-67; tchr. elementary grades Shelbyville (Ky.) Ind. Sch. Dist., 1967-69, supr. Shelbyville Ind. Sch. System, 1973—. Lectr. edn. dist. and student tchrs. Ind. U., 1969-71, 73—. Mem. Am. Assn. Tchr. Educators, Ky. Assn. Supervision and Curriculum Devel., Ky. Assn. Sch. Adminstrs., N.E.A., Ky. Edn. Assn., Delta Kappa Gamma, Pi Lambda Theta. Contbr. articles to profl. jours. Home: 1402 W Main St Shelbyville KY 40065 Office: 418 E Main St Shelbyville KY 40065

WEBB, ARDELLA MAE (MRS. LAWRENCE M. WEBB), educator; b. Orleans, Neb., Nov. 14, 1912; d. Asher Woolman and Lillie Mae (Reynolds) Thomas; B.A., Kearney (Neb.) State Coll., 1934, M.A., 1957; postgrad. U. Neb., summer 1959, U. So. Cal., summer 1959, Nat. Coll. Edn. at Evanston, summer 1960, Kearney State Coll., summer 1967; m. Lawrence M. Webb, Dec. 31, 1934; children—Ardienne (Mrs. Gale McNulty), Lawrence L., Thomas F. Tchr. pub. schs., Hazard, Neb., 1935; prin. Odessa Pub. Sch., 1939-41; tchr. West Kearney High Sch., 1941-45, tchr., librarian, 1955-56; sec. Dir. Edn., 1941-45; instr. edn., elementary supr. Campus Sch., Kearney State Coll., 1957, asst. prof. English, 1958-60, asst. prof. edn., supr. kindergarten 1961-64; tchr. Bryant Sch., Kearney, 1965-66; tchr. theatre and English, Kearney Pub. Schs., 1967-68, tchr. English, 1969—. Dir. Sch. Bd. Dist. 114, 1946-56; leader Nat. 4-H Clubs, 1947-57. Sec.-treas. Webb Implement, 1945-48. Mem. Am. Assn. U. Women (lit. group), Nat., Neb., Kearney edn. assns., Nat. Council Tchrs. English, P.T.A. (life mem., pres. 1935), Kappa Delta Pi, Pi Gamma Mu, Sigma Tau Delta, Beta Pi Theta, Alpha Delta Kappa (state chaplin 1974-76), Delta Zeta, Iota Sigma. Methodist. Home: Route 2 Box 278 Kearney NE 68847

WEBB, BERNICE LARSON (MRS. ROBERT M. WEBB), educator; b. Ludell, Kan.; d. Carl Godfred amd Ida (Tongish) Larson; A.B., U. Kan., 1956, M.A. 1957, Ph.D. in English, 1961; m. Robert M. Webb, July 14, 1961; children—William Carl Schear, Rebecca Rae Schear (Mrs. Cowan E. Gentry, Jr.). Asst. prof. English, U. Southwestern La., Lafayette, 1961-67, asso. prof., 1967—. Foreign exchange scholar U. Aberdeen (Scotland), 1959-60, numerous others; vis. prof. World Campus Afloat, 1972, coordinator, cons. Poetry in schs. program Lafayette Parish, La., 1974. Com. mem. Girl Scouts U.S.A., 1961-66. Mem. Modern Lang. Assn., South Central Coll. English Assn., Coll. English Assn., La. Folklore Soc., Deep South Writers Conf. (poetry panel), La. Council Tchrs. English, South Central Modern Lang. Assn., Am. Assn. U. Women (state officer), La. State, S.W. La. poetry socs., Lafayette Little Theatre, Internat. Platform Assn., Phi Beta Kappa (sec.-treas. S.W. La. assn. 1965-71), Pi Delta Phi. Author: The Basketball Man, 1973. Editor: Cajun Chatter, 1964-66, The Magnolia, 1967-71, Louisiana Poets, 1970—. Contbr. poems, articles, stories to various publs. Home: 159 Whittington Dr Lafayette LA 70501

WEBB, BRENDA BEARCE (MRS. JAMES W. WEBB), educator; b. Hartford, Conn., June 29, 1914; d. Alexis W. and Maude W. (Smith) Bearce; A.B., Vassar Coll., 1936; B.S., U. Buffalo, 1954; M.A., Columbia, 1968; m. James W. Webb, Nov. 5, 1938 (dec. May 1950); children—Alexis B., Jane W. (Mrs. Allan J. Evelyn). Asst. to bond analyst E. W. Axe Co., N.Y.C., 1936; clerk market research dept. Am. Sales Book Co. (name now changed to Moore Bus. Forms, Inc.), Niagara Falls, N.Y., 1936-38; accountant Billings Mut. Agy., Inc., Niagara Falls, N.Y., 1954-59, 63-64; jr. accountant James William Heary & Co., Niagara Falls, N.Y., 1959-63; asst. prof. Niagara County Community Coll., Sanborn, N.Y., 1964-67, asso. prof., coordinator accounting dept., 1967-74, prof., 1974—. Recipient award N.Y. State Soc. C.P.A.'s, 1954, Am. Inst. C.P.A.'s, 1954. Mem. Am. Accounting Assn., Am. Soc. Women Accountants, Nat. Bus. Edn. Assn., Beta Gamma Sigma, Delta Pi Epsilon. Unitarian. Home: 151 Buffalo Av Niagara Falls NY 14303

WEBB, CORA HELEN, home economist; b. Boston, Nov. 9, 1919; d. George Eddy and Margaret (Weaver) Webb; B.S. in Edn., State Tchrs. Coll., Framingham, Mass., 1941; M.S. in Edn., Cornell U., 1952. Home econs. tchr., Topsfield, Mass., 1941-42; 4-H Club agt. Kennebec County (Me.), 1942-45; home demonstration agt. Tolland County (Conn.) Extension Service, Rockville, 1945-57; women's adviser community devel. ICA, Iraq, 1957-58, home economist, Washington, 1959; extension home economist Tolland County Extension Service, Rockville, Conn., 1959—, field coordinator, 1972—. Recipient Award for Distinguished Service Nat. Home Demonstration Agts. Assn., 1954, State Coll. at Framingham, Mass. Alumnae Assn. award, 1963. Mem. Am., Conn. (pres. 1962-64) home econs. assns., Conn.-R.I. Home Demonstration Agts. Assn. (past pres.), Nat. Assn. Extension Home Economists, Conn. Consumer Assn., Conn.-Framingham Alumnae Assn. (pres. 1962-64), Alumnae Assn. State Coll. at Framingham, Natick (Mass.) Grange, Conn. Gerontology Soc., Epsilon Sigma Phi (chpt. sec.-treas. 1956-57). Conglist. Club: Greater Hartford Home Economics (past sec.). Home: RFD 4 Rockville CT 06066 Office: 24 Hyde Av Route 30 Rockville CT 06066

WEBB, HELEN MARGUERITE, educator; b. N.S., Can., July 7, 1913; d. James Everett and Emma (Minahan) W.; came to U.S., 1928, naturalized, 1932; B.S., Northwestern U., 1946, M.S., 1948, Ph.D., 1950. Asst. prof. Boston Coll., 1950-52; mem. faculty Goucher Coll., 1952—, prof. biology, 1966—; research Marine Biol. Lab., Woods Hole, Mass., summers 1950-70; vis. investigator La Stazione Zoologica, Naples, Italy, 1960. Mem. corp. Marine Biol. Lab. Mem. Am. Soc. Gen. Physiologists, Am. Soc. Zoologists, A.A.A.S., Sigma Xi, Roman Catholic. Spl. research invertebrate endocrinology, biol. rhythms. Home: 1 Warren Lodge Ct Cockeysville MD 21030 Office: Dept Biol Scis Goucher Coll Towson MD 21204

WEBB, JOYCE ALDENE WILEY (MRS. ROBERT R. WEBB), state ofcl.; b. Portland, Me., May 30, 1920; d. William Carroll and Marian Alberta (Rankin) Wiley; B.A., U. Wis., 1942; m. Robert R. Webb, July 7, 1946. News editor Santa Paula (Cal.) Chronicle, 1942-43; loan analyst Wis. Dept. Vets. Affairs, Madison, 1947—. Mem. Women in Communications, Wis. Fellowship Poets (pres. 1966-68). Author: Dark Earth, 1965; Return to Lincolnville, 1968. Editor: Hawk and Whipporrwill Recalled, 1973. Home: 53 S Midvale Blvd Madison WI 53705 Office: 1 W Wilson St Madison WI 53702

WEBB, MARGARET LEA, librarian; b. Phila., June 14, 1936; d. Prosper Nehemiah and Margaret Cecelia (Quinn) Webb; A.B. (tuition scholar), Chestnut Hill Coll., 1957; M.A. in History, St. John's U., 1960; M.L.S., Rutgers U., 1963. Tchr., English, Wildwood (N.J.) High Sch., 1957-58; grad. asst. St. John's U., 1959-60; library trainee, Plainfield, N.J., 1962-63; reference librarian N.J. State Library, Trenton, 1963-64, asst. lending services librarian, 1964-67; librarian in charge N.J. Dept. Transp. Library, Trenton, 1967—. Mem. N.J. Library Assn. (publicity com. 1963-67), Spl. Libraries Assn. (constn. com. 1968-69; asst. editor Newsletter 1970-73, chairperson chpt. employment com. 1973-74), Cath. Alumni Club (sec. 1968). Roman Catholic. Home: 130 W Farrell Av Trenton NJ 08618 Office: 1035 Parkway Av Trenton NJ 08625

WEBB, MARIANNE (MRS. DAVID N. BATEMAN), educator, organist; b. Topeka, Kan., Oct. 4, 1936; d. Samuel Earl and Margaret (Shafer) Webb; Mus.B. summa cum laude, Washburn U., 1958; Mus.M., U. Mich., 1959; m. David N. Bateman, Oct. 3, 1970. Organist, instr. organ and piano Ia. State U., 1959-61; asst. prof. organ and music literature Madison Coll., 1963-65; univ. organist, asso. prof. organ and theory So Ill. U., Carbondale, 1965—. Concerts given throughout U.S. and Europe. Recipient Fulbright Grant, 1961-62. Mem. Am. Guild of Organists (chpt. dean 1965-67, 73—, chpt. dir. 1960-61), Music Tchrs. Nat. Assn., Am. Assn. U. Profs., Sigma Alpha Iota (chpt. v.p. 1957-58), Pi Kappa Lambda, Phi Kappa Phi, Delta Gamma. Contbr. articles in field to profl. jours. Address: Sch Music So Ill U Carbondale IL 62901

WEBB, MARY ELIZABETH ROBERTS, media coordinator; b. Porter, Okla., Nov. 16, 1914; d. H.V. and Retta Mae (Tacker) Roberts; B.S., Northeastern State Coll., 1947; A.B., Okla. U., 1952, M.L.S., 1968; m. Samuel F. Webb, Jan. 10, 1937; children—Mary Elizabeth, Franklin Roberts. Prin. rural schs., Wagoner County, 1942-45; tchr. mathematics Wagoner Jr.-Sr. High Sch., 1945-46; tchr., librarian, Moore, Okla., 1946-49; tchr. Norman (Okla.) Elementary Sch., 1949-52; librarian U. Okla., 1952-60, Ponca City (Okla.) Jr. and Sr. High Sch., 1960-71; media coordinator, librarian McLain Sr. High Sch., Tulsa, 1971—. Precinct chmn. Tulsa Dem. Party, 1971-72. Mem. N.E.A., Okla. Edn. Assn., A.L.A., Okla. Library Assn., Okla. Assn. Audiovisual Media and Tech., Am. Assn. U. Women, Internat. Platform Assn., Tulsa Classroom Tchrs., P.T.A., Kappa Kappa Iota, Beta Phi Mu. Mem. Ch. of Christ. Home: 7398 E 24th St Tulsa OK 74129 Office: 4929 N Peoria St Tulsa OK 74126

WEBB, NANCY ANN LYONS (MRS. GEORGE G. WEBB), ednl. adminstr.; b. Crowley, La., Feb. 20, 1937; d. Claude C. and Nancy (Myers) Lyons; student Centenary Coll., 1955-56; B.S., La. State U., 1959, M.Ed., 1963; m. George G. Webb, Sept. 2, 1961; 1 son, George G. Jr. Tchr. high sch., St. Mary Parish, 1959, Acadia Parish, 1959-60, Lafayette Parish, 1960-61; guidance counselor and sci. tchr., Lafayette Parish, 1961-62; Camp Fire day camp dir., Acadia Parish, 1964-66; guidance counselor Iota High Sch., 1963-64, Acadia Parish Adult Edn. Program, 1965-67, Rayne High Sch., 1964-68 (all Acadia Parish); adminstr. Office Student Affairs La. State U. at Eunice Acadia Parish, 1968—, now dir. student affairs. Bd. dirs. Acadia Parish Camp Fire Girls, Am. Legion Hosp. Nursing Scholarship Program. Recipient citation for outstanding contribution in counseling and guidance USAF, 1965. Mem. So. Assn. Schs. and Colls. (ann. mem. evaluation com.), D.A.R. (historian), S.W. Rally Assn. (exec. sec.), La. Assn. for Higher Edn. (mem. com. on pub. relations), La. Guidance Assn., La. Tchrs. Assn., Nat. Assn. Coll. Women Deans, S.W. Assn. Student Personnel Adminstrs., Kappa Kappa Iota (sec., v.p.), Delta Delta Delta. Presbyn. Home: 726 E 6th St Crowley LA 70526 Office: Box 1129 Eunice LA 70535

WEBB, THELMA ELIZABETH, educator, librarian; b. Bethlehem, Pa., Mar. 24, 1914; d. Ernest and Beatrice Maud (Elwell) Hooper; B.A. cum laude, Baldwin-Wallace Coll., 1936; postgrad. Pestalozzi-Froebel Sch., Chgo., 1962, Concordia Tchrs. Coll., River Forest, 1974; M.A. in L.S., Rosary Coll., River Forest, Ill., 1969; m. Harold W. Webb, Sept. 14, 1940; children—Paul Kent, Margaret Eileen (Mrs. Margaret St. John). Tchr., pub. schs., Wellington, O., 1936-40, Lincoln Sch., Maywood, Ill., 1961-63; tchr., librarian Jane Addams Sch., Melrose Park, Ill., 1963—; coordinator library media dist. 89 Ill., 1974—. Sec. Irving Sch., Maywood, 1960-61; finance officer, mgr. Mid-Am. chpt. A.R.C., 1942-43. Mem. Nat., Ill. edn. assns., Am., Ill. library assns., Am. Assn. Sch. Librarians, Bus. and Profl. Women's Club (chpt. treas.), Oak Park (Ill.) P.T.A. (life), Gamma Sigma (treas. 1938-40), Alpha Phi Gamma (v.p. 1939-40). Baptist (sec., tchr. Sunday sch.). Home: 913 N 9th Av Maywood IL 60153

WEBB, ZADIE OZELLA THOMPSON (MRS. HARVEY WEBB, JR.), pediatrician; b. Washington; d. John Vera and Zadie Ozella (Sizemore) Thompson; B.S., Howard U., 1954, M.D., 1958; certificate contemporary pediatrics Harvard, 1965; M.P.H., Johns Hopkins Sch. Hygiene and Pub. Health, 1974; m. Harvey Webb, Jr., June 8, 1957; children—Tomai, Harvey III, Hoyt. Intern, Freedmens Hosp., Washington, 1958-59, resident, 1959-62; med. officer pediatrics D.C. Gen. Hosp., 1963, D.C. Health Dept., 1964-68; pub. health and pediatric cons. Howard U. Med. Sch., Washington, 1964-68; med. dir. health services br. Social Services Adminstrn., Washington, 1968-72, mem. adminstrv. staff, resources div., 1970-72; med. cons. Social Rehab. Adminstrn., Washington, 1972; chief med. assistance unit Adminstr. Medicaid Program, Washington, 1973—; clin. asst. prof. pediatrics Georgetown U., Washington, 1968—; attending pediatrician Hosp. for Sick Children, Washington, 1969—; cons. Head Start, 1969-72. Mem. Pub. Welfare Com. D.C., 1969—, Interdepartmental Com. on Battered and Mistreated Children, 1969—. Recipient grant NIH, 1956, 57, 59-60. Mem. Am. Pub. Health Assn., Nat. Med. Assn., Former Internes and Residents of Freedmens Hosp., Med. and Chirurgical Soc. D.C., Howard U. Med. Alumni, Am. Med. Women's Assn. (br. chmn. membership com. 1969-70, br. program chmn. 1972—), N.A.A.C.P., Washington Urban League. Clubs: Capezios Social (pres. 1968, treas. 1970-74), Wijamii Social, Jack and Jill of Am. Home: 11108 Swansfield Rd Columbia MD 21044 Office: 614 H St NW Washington DC 20001

WEBBER, ELIZABETH JEAN, editor; b. Evanston, Ill., Feb. 1, 1921; d. S. Arthur and Mary (Park) Webber; B.A., Lawrence Coll., 1942; M.A., U. Wis., 1943. Tchr., Am. history, English high sch., Norwalk, Wis., 1943-44; research asst. Ency. Brit., Chgo., 1944-45, asst. dir. library research, 1945-47; asst. editor F.E. Compton Co., Chgo., 1947-51; asst. editor trade books Rand McNally & Co., Chgo., 1951-56, asso. editor adult non-fiction, 1956-62, editor trade map dept., 1962—. Pvt. cons. book manuscripts. Mem. Am. Assn. U. Women, Women's Nat. Book Assn. (nat. treas. 1957-61), Chgo. Book Clinic. Club: Zonta (pres. N.W. Cook County 1961-63). Home: 3055 Park Pl Evanston IL 60201 Office: Rand McNally PO Box 7600 Chicago IL 60680

WEBBER, GALE ROSE NEWCOMB, editor; b. Great Bend, Kan., Jan. 20, 1940; d. Charles Earl and Lola Bell (Stephenson) Newcomb; student Allegheny Coll., 1958-60; B.S. in Tech. Writing, Carnegie Inst. Tech., 1962; m. Donald Webber, July 29, 1964 (div. May 1970). Tech. writer, editor Jersey Prodn. Research Co., Tulsa, 1962-64; tech. reports librarian Esso Prodn. Research Co., Houston, 1964-66; asst. editor Univ. Bull., Tex. Tech U. Lubbock, 1967-69, editor, 1970—. Cons. Research Editorial Service, Internat. Center for Arid and Semi-Arid Land Studies, 1971. Mem. Women in Communications (pres. Lubbock chpt. 1972—), Soc. Tech. Writers and Pubs., Am. Coll. Pub. Relations Assn., League Women Voters, W. Tex. Mus. Assn., Theta Sigma Phi. Republican. Clubs: University Women's, Faculty, Quarterly, Greater Lubbock Press. Editor: Mus. Jour., 1971—, Flashes of Fashion, 1973. Home: 3810 26th St Lubbock TX 79410 Office: Box 4210 Texas Tech Univ Lubbock TX 79409

WEBER, AUDREY REITER (MRS. ROBERT JOHN WEBER), ednl. adminstr.; b. Milw., Nov. 16, 1922; d. Charles Otto and Rose Margaret (Brahm) Reiter; Ph.B., Marquette U., 1944, postgrad., 1944-46; postgrad. U. Wis., 1968; m. Robert John Weber, Nov. 6, 1948; children—Robert Francis, Mark Charles, Rosanne. Editor Catholic Sch. Press Assn., Milw., 1944-46; instr. journalism Loretto Heights Coll., Denver, 1946-47; pub. relations asst. Milw. Sch. Engring., 1947-48; reporter, women's editor Waukesha (Wis.) Freeman, 1969-70; instr. journalism, publs. adviser Mt. Mary Coll., 1970-73, dir. pub. relations, 1973—. Mem. Women in Communications, Am. Coll. Pub. Relations Assn. Home: 12805 Dunwoody Dr Elm Grove WI 53122 Office: 2900 N Menomonee River Parkway Milwaukee WI 53222

WEBER, CAROL WAKSMAN, women's apparel co. exec.; b. Anspach, Germany, Nov. 22, 1947; d. Leib and Bella (Shper) Waksman; came to U.S., 1951, naturalized, 1956; grad. Fashion Inst. Tech., N.Y.C., 1967; m. Mike Weber, Apr. 29, 1973. Field dir. market research Oxtoby-Smith, N.Y.C., 1967-68; account exec. apparel industry Graphic Workshop, N.Y.C., 1968-70; sales and marketing mfg. IFT Internat., N.Y.C., 1970—; speaker radio and TV. Co-author articles. Home: 25 E 86th St New York City NY 10028 Office: Beldoch Industries Corp 1411 Broadway New York City NY 10018

WEBER, CECILIA ELIZABETH, scenic designer; b. Milw., Apr. 1, 1943; d. Kenneth E. and Eva S. (Scharmach) Weber; B.F.S., U. Wis.-Milw. Designer sets for TV stas. WMVS and WMVT, Milw., 1973; free-lance designer for Pick-A-Pack Players, Am. Dance Repertory, Wis. Contemporary Theatre; choreographer Ballermaters Inc., U. Wis.-Milw.; tchr. Milw. Area Tech. Coll., Adele Artinian Sch. Dance, Cecilia Weber Sch. Dance. Bd. dirs., sec. Wis. Children's Theatre. Dance scholar Jacob's Pillow, 1962. Mem. Am. Theatre Assn., U.S. Inst. Theatre Tech., Nat. Collegiate Players. Address: 3554 N Prospect St Milwaukee WI 53211

WEBER, CHARDELLE ANN, editor; b. Middletown, O., Dec. 18, 1924; d. Walter John and Marie Elizabeth (Holland) Weber; grad. high sch. With Wright Patterson AFB, Dayton, O., 1942-45; with Middletown Jour., 1945—, women's editor, 1957—. Mem. women's com. Middletown Symphony Orchestra. Recipient award for services Nat. Fedn. Music Clubs, 1959, certificate recognition of service Daus. Penelope, 1962. Mem. Phi Beta Psi. Democrat. Roman Catholic. Home: 3307 Wildwood Rd Middletown OH 45042 Office: Middletown Journal Broad St Middletown OH 45042

WEBER, CYNTHIA (MRS. JAMES C. FARAH), advt. co. exec.; b. L.I., N.Y., June 2, 1949; d. Andrew John and Aria Emma (Jelnikova) Weber; B.A. in Communications, Stanford, 1971; m. James C. Farah, Jan. 12, 1974. Cinematographer, producer sta. KROD-TV El Paso, Tex., 1971-73; v.p. Sanders Co. Advt., El Paso, 1973-74; free lance writer, photographer, 1974—; dir. publicity El Paso Plaza Performing Arts. Film critic El Paso Times, 1972—. Mem. Found. Devel. Bd. Tex. System Sch. Nursing. Mem. Women in Communications, Stanford Alumni Assn. Home: 192 Sir Lancelot Dr El Paso TX 79902 Office: 1511 E Missouri El Paso TX 79941

WEBER, FELICE MARIETTE, pediatrician, geneticist, epidemiologist; b. Kenton, Middlesex, Eng., Aug. 1, 1931; d. Charles Eugene and Mariette (Helfer) Weber; M.B., B.S., Royal Free Hosp. Sch. Medicine, London U. (Eng.), 1957; M.P.H., U. Cal. at Los Angeles, 1966. Came to U.S., 1962. House officer Royal Free Hosp. Group, London, 1957-58; intern West Middlesex Hosp., Iselworth, Middlesex, 1959-61; resident Glendale (Cal.) Sanatarium and Hosp., 1962-63; resident in pediatrics U. Cal. at Los Angeles, 1963-65, fellow 1966-70, acting asst. prof., 1970-71, asst. clin. prof. pediatrics, 1971—; dir. Med. Genetics Clinic Ventura County Health Dept., Loma Vista and Ventura, Cal., 1970—. Mem. Los Angeles Pediatric Soc., Western Soc. Pediatric Research, Am. Soc., Human Genetics, Environmental Mutagen Soc. Club: Westwood Ski (Los Angeles). Home: 11728 Darlington Av Los Angeles CA 90049

WEBER, HARRIETTE B. SKLADD, bus. exec., real estate broker; b. Detroit; d. Alexander and Victoria (Lesnik) Skladd; student Wayne U., 1937-39, U. Mich., 1950-52; m. E. George Weber. Real estate broker H. B. Weber, Realtor, Detroit, 1953—; fee appraiser, per diem appraiser FHA, Detroit, 1958—. Mem. Detroit Real Estate Bd., Nat. Assn. Real Estate Bds., Internat. Platform Assn., Founders Soc. Detroit, Inst. Arts. Club: Detroit Yacht. Inventor beaute specs, turkey jackets. Home: 18230 Ten Mile Rd East Detroit MI 48021 Office: 12323 Kelly Rd Detroit MI 48224

WEBER, HULDA see Hilda Katz

WEBER, JEAN MACPHAIL (MRS. RICHARD BAKER WEBER), mus. ofcl.; b. Boston, Apr. 2, 1933; d. Harold Percy and Dorothy Norma (Mutch) MacPhail; student R.I. Sch. Design, 1950-52, Edinburgh (Scotland) U., 1952-53; B.A., Brown U., 1954; postgrad. (Danforth scholar), State U. Ia., 1954-55; m. Richard Baker Weber, June 26, 1955; children—Julia Lee, Karin MacPhail, Laurie Stewart. Mgr. Lane Bryant Splty. Shop, Denver, 1956-57; campus advisor Saratoga Springs (N.Y.) Council Chs., Skidmore Coll., 1960-64; art dir. Our Lady of Peace Hosp., Louisville, 1964-65; dir. Jr. Art Gallery, Louisville, 1965-69, Parrish Art Mus., Southampton, N.Y., 1969—. Adj. asso. prof. art history Southampton (N.Y.) Coll., L.I. U., 1971—; mus. cons. N.Y. Council on the Arts, 1970-74. Mem. cultural affairs adv. com. Suffolk County, N.Y., 1974—. Met. Mus. grantee Internat. Mus. Program, 1971. Mem. Am. Assn. Mus., Internat. Council Mus., N.Y. State Assn. Mus., Phi Beta Kappa. Mem. Religious Soc. of Friends. Home: Henry St Sag Harbor NY 11963 Office: 25 Jobs Lane Southampton NY 11968

WEBER, MARILYN BAUM, artist; b. N.Y.C.; d. Albert and Betty (Savat) Baum; student Pratt Inst., 1951-52, Traphagen, 1953-54, Art Students League, 1954-55, Sch. Visual Arts, 1967-68; m. Robert Weber, Oct. 11, 1953 (div. 1966); children—Peter, Lee. Exhibited one-man shows at DeMena Gallery, 1967, 69; Orpheus Ascending, 1972, Westside Gallery, 1972; exhibited in group shows at Westbeth, 1970, 72, Roko Gallery, 1971, 72, N.J. Soc. Painters and Sculptors, 1970, N.J. Art of Our Time, 1972, Hechtlinger Gallery, 1973. Artist, Am. Mus. Natural History, N.Y.C., 1954-56; paintings in pvt. collections; various travelling shows Italy, U.S.A. Recipient Silver Medal award Grande Prix de Peinture de la Côte D'Azur, 1974. Mem. Nat. Assn. Women Artists (Molly Morpeth Canaday Meml. award 1974). Illustrator: 177 Favorite Poems for Children, 1974. Contbr. drawings to various publs. Address: 463 West St New York City NY 10014

WEBER, MARTHA GESLING, educator; b. Lancaster, O., Apr. 10, 1912; d. William and Sue (Crump) Gesling; A.B., Ohio No. U., 1935, Pd.D. (hon.), 1971; A.M., Ohio State U., 1941; fellow edn. Duke 1944-46, Ph.D., 1951; m. Dr. Joseph Elliott Weber, Dec. 1956. Tchr. history and music, grad. schs., 1933-40, history, English, debate, high schs., 1940-44; asst. prof. edn., ednl. psychology Bowling Green State U., 1946-49, asso. prof. edn., 1949-53, prof. edn., 1953—, dir. reading center, 1946-65. Reading cons. basic reading series for slow learners. Recipient Distinguished Alumnus citation Ohio No. U., 1954; Distinguished Faculty award Bowling Gree U., 1963, Coll. of Edn. Outstanding Teaching award, 1968. Mem. Am. Assn. U. Women, Internat. Reading Assn. (pres. Ohio council 1957-58), Am. Ednl. Research Assn., Nat. Soc. Study Edn., Nat. Council Tchrs. English, Coll. Reading Assn. (nat. dir. 1965-68), Ohio Edn. Assn., Mortar Board, Phi Kappa Phi (chpt. pres. 1965-67), Chi Omega, Kappa Delta Pi, Delta Kappa Gamma. Home: 816 E Wooster Bowling Green OH 43402 Office: Bowling Green State U Bowling Green OH 43402

WEBER, MILADA PAUK (MRS. JOSEF WEBER), librarian; b. Brno, Czechoslovakia, Mar. 2, 1911; d. Frantisek and Milada (Stransky) Pauk; came to U.S., 1952, naturalized, 1957; diploma Konsularakademie, Vienna, Austria, 1933; Dr. Law, Masaryk U., Brno. 1939; certificate U. Parana, Curitiba, Brazil, 1949; M.S. in L.S., L.I. U., 1964; m. Josef Weber, Oct. 23, 1948; 1 son, Thomas Michael. Mem. Czechoslovakian Deplomatic Service, Rio de Janeiro, Brazil, 1945-48; tchr. Eng. and French, Sr. High Sch., Paranagua, Brazil, 1948-51; sec. to consulate gen. Venzuela, Houston, 1955-58; library asst. Poly Prep Country Day Sch., Bklyn., 1962; cataloger Elmont (N.Y.) Meml. Library, 1963-65; catalogue librarian Hofstra U., Hempstead, N.Y., 1965-68; head cataloger Northwestern U. Law Sch. Library, Chgo., 1968—. Mem. Am. Law Library Assn. Home: 8842 Lavergne Av Skokie IL 60076 Office: 357 E Chicago Av Chicago IL 60611

WEBER, NATALIE ANNE, educator; b. Evanston, Ill., Dec. 14, 1932; d. Carl Joseph and Natalie (Purcell) Weber; B.S., Northwestern U., 1954; A.M., Stanford, 1955. Tchr. secondary sch. Fremont Union High Sch. Dist., Sunnyvale, Cal., 1955—; instr. Nat. High Sch. Inst., Northwestern U., 1958-68; asst. prof. speech-communication Cal. State U., Hayward, 1969, San Jose, 1965-66. Mem. Western Speech Communication Assn. (v.p. 1973, councillor oral interpretation 1964-65), Nat. (dist. chmn. 1967-73; Double Diamond Key award 1968, Distinguished Service plaque 1969, chmn. nat. tournament com. 1971), Coast (pres. 1958-59) forensic leagues, Nat. U. Extension Assn., Cal. High Sch. Speech Assn. (curriculm dir. 1968-73, v.p. 1974), Speech Communication Assn., Zeta Phi Eta. Contbr. articles to profl. jours. Home: 366 W Olive St Sunnyvale CA 94086 Office: Box F Homestead High Sch Sunnyvale CA 94087

WEBER, ROSEMARY, educator; b. Lancaster, Pa., Aug. 25, 1926; d. David Wenger and Violet (McVey) Weber; B.S. in Edn., U. Pa., 1948, M.S. in Edn., 1951, Ed.D., 1973; M.S. in Library Sci., Drexel U., 1957. Tchr., Trainer Borough Sch. Dist., Chester, Pa., 1948-56; elementary library supr. Upper Merion Twp. Sch. Dist., King of Prussia, Pa., 1956-60; elementary librarian Radnor Twp. schs., Wayne, Pa., 1960-67; asso. prof. West Chester (Pa.) State Coll., 1967-68; asst. prof. library sci. Drexel U., Phila., 1968—. Recipient Teaching fellowship U. Pa., 1965-66. Mem. Am., Pa. (treas. 1971-73) library assns., Internat. Reading Assn., Am. Assn. Univ. Profs., Nat. Council Tchrs. English, Phila. Children's Reading Round Table, Internat. Assn. Sch. Librarians, Pi Lambda Theta, Beta Phi Mu, Phi Delta Kappa. Mem. Ch. of Christ, Scientist (treas. 1969-72). Home: 421 E Lancaster Av St Davids PA 19087 Office: Grad Sch Library Sci Drexel U Philadelphia PA 19104

WEBER, RUTH JOANN, lawyer; b. Fairbank, Ia., Mar. 16, 1936; d. John F. and Ruth O. (Kauffeld) Weber; B.A., Valparaiso U., 1959; J.D., 1962. Admitted to Wis. bar, 1962; mem. Byrne, Bubolz & Spanagel, Appleton, Wis., 1962—. Dir. Universal Travel Service, Inc., Appleton. Subrogation atty. Home Mut. Ins. Co., Appleton, 1962-74, asst. v.p., asso. legal counsel, 1974—. Mem. Am., Outagamie County (sec., treas. 1965-66), bar assns., State Bar Wis. (com. on communications 1973—), Am. Judicature Soc., Am. Assn. U. Women. Home: 725 E Brewster St Appleton WI 54911 Office: 2401 S Memorial Dr Appleton WI 54911

WEBKES, SISTER LILLIAN, library cons.; b. Ft. Madison, Ia., June 6, 1896; d. John and Josephine (Guenther) Webkes; Ph.B., De Paul U., 1939, M.A. in Edn., 1944; certified librarian Cardinal Stritch, 1959, certified audio visual dir., 1961 Joined Sch. Sisters of St. Francis, 1916; tchr. Sacred Heart Sch., Peoria, Ill., 1916-23, St. John, Monroeville, Ind., 1923-30; prin. Sacred Heart, Allenton, Wis., 1930-34; tchr. St. Nicholas Grade Sch., Chgo., 1934-40, St. Ludger Sch., Creighton, Neb., 1940-45, St. John's High Sch., Rubican, Wis., 1945-50; prin. St. John's Sch., Petersburg, Neb., 1950-59; library, audio visual dir. St. Benedict High Sch., Chgo., 1959-70, library cons., tutuor spl. edn., 1970—. Mem. Telecare Red Cross Vol. for Sr. Citizens, 1973-74. Recipient plaque in appreciation 10 yrs. service St. Benedict High Sch., 1970; grantee Gallaudet Coll., Washington, 1965. Mem. Ill. Library Assn., High Sch. Librarians Chgo. Land, A.L.A., Apostolate of Handicapped. Home: 2222 W Byron St Chicago IL 60618

WEBSTER, BERTHA EVELYN, physician; b. Tracy, Cal., Aug. 2, 1914; d. Benjamin Ferdinand and Lillian Ruth (Rich) Webster; student George Washington U., 1940-42; A.B. (Phoebe A. Hearst scholar, Iota Sigma Pi scholar) U. Cal. at Berkeley, 1948, postgrad., 1949-51; M.D., Hahnemann Med. Coll., 1955. With U.S. Dept. Agr., Watsonville and Berkeley, Cal., 1936-40, U.S. War Dept., Washington, 1940-42, Hammond Gen. Hosp., Modesto, Cal., 1942-43; tchr. Garfield Grammar Sch., Selma, Cal., 1946-47; intern Seaside Meml. Hosp., Long Beach, Cal., 1955-56; resident surgery VA Hosp., Albuquerque, 1956-57; resident gen. practice Stanislaus County Hosp., Modesto, Cal., 1957-60; resident internal medicine San Joaquin County Hosp., Stockton, Cal., 1960-63, Kaiser Hosp., Oakland, Cal., 1966-67; fellow medicine, rheumatic fever research unit Hosp. Good Samaritan, Children's Hosp. Med. Center and Harvard Med. Sch., Boston, 1969-71; practice medicine, specializing in internal medicine, Modesto (Cal.) State Hosp., 1963-66, Scenic Gen. Hosp., Modesto, 1967-68, Gen. Hosp. Monterey County, Salinas, Cal., 1968-69; now mem. staff Drs. Hosp., Meml. Hosp. North, Scenic Gen. Hosp.; mem. staff Modesto City Hosp., chmn. med. dept., 1973-74. Mem. council YWCA, Watsonville, 1938-39; chmn. pub. edn./pub. relations com. Central Cal. Heart Assn., 1966. Bd. dirs. Stanislaus County Heart Assn., Modesto, 1963-66, Vis. Nurses Assn., 1972—. Mem. Am., Cal. med. assns., Stanislaus County Med. Soc., Am. Med. Women's Assn., Am. Assn. U. Women, Cal. Alumni Assn., Hahnemann Alumni Assn. Democrat. Home: PO Box 3984 Modesto CA 95352 also 1712 Carver Rd Modesto CA 95350 Office: 801 17th St Suite B Modesto CA 95354

WEBSTER, CARMEN JACQUELINE (MRS. HARRY M. KELLY), railroad co. exec.; b. Houston, Apr. 25; d. Jefferson Charles and Nettie Alice (Fitchett) Duncan; B.S., Coll. Bus. and Pub. Adminstrn., N.Y. U., 1941; m. Harold Franklyn Webster, May 20, 1940; m. 2d, Harry M. Kelly, June 21, 1973. Asst. sales mgr. Scholl Mfg. Co., N.Y.C., 1938-39; supr. N.Y.C. Dept. Welfare, 1939-40; pres. Model Railroad Equipment Corp., N.Y.C., 1942—, also co-publisher The News, 1950-60, drama editor, 1954—, publisher, 1960-62; pres. Rail Chief Products Co., N.Y.C., 1944-52; dir. Dunjen Publishing Corp., Hartsdale, N.Y., 1950-62. Permanent patron Bellevue Med. Center, N.Y. U., 1950-52. Pub. relations co-chmn. Greenburgh Republican Com., 1954-60; mem. N.Y. State Legislative Adv. Com., 1971-72. Bd. dirs. Myopia Internat. Research Found., Futura Home Found. Recipient Madden Meml. award, N.Y. U., 1953, N.Y. U. Alumni Meritorious Service award, 1969. Mem. Hobby Indsl. Assn. Am. (packaging award 1950, best promotional idea award 1952, dir. retail div. 1968-71), N.Y. U. Commerce Alumni Assn. (v.p. 1950-52), N.Y. U. Club (founder 1957), N.Y. U. Alumnae Club (pres. 1940-41), Outer Circle of Drama Critics of N.Y. Theatre Working Press, Soroptimist Internat. (pres. Central Westchester Club 1959-60, dir. 1960-63), Nat. Assn. Model Railroad Mfgrs. (dir., sec. 1943-47), Nat. Model Railroad Assn., Hobby Industry Assn. Am. (dir. retail div. 1974—), N.Y. U. Alumni Fedn. (dir. 1952-55, dir. emeritus 1966), Beta Gamma Sigma (dir. 1969—), Am. Contract Bridge League. Club: Northern Westchester (N.Y.) Country. Editor: Manual and Catalog for all Gauges, 1950; Handbook and Catalog for HO Model Railroaders, 1953. Patentee in field. Home: 76-15 35th Av Jackson Heights NY 11372 Office: Model Railroad Equipment Co 23 W 45th St New York City NY 10036

WEBSTER, ELEANOR RUDD, educator; b. Cleve., Oct. 11, 1920; d. George Davis and Mary (Spink) Webster; A.B., Wellesley Coll., 1942; M.A., Mt. Holyoke Coll., 1944; M.A., Radcliffe Coll., 1951, Ph.D., 1952. Chemist, Eastman Kodak Co., Rochester, N.Y., 1944-47; instr. Wellesley Coll., 1952-53, asst. prof., 1953-60, asso. prof., 1961-67, prof., 1967—, chmn., 1964-67, dir. Inst. Chemistry, 1964-72, dir. continuing edn., 1969-70. Mem. Am. Chem. Soc., History Sci. Soc., A.A.A.S., Am. Assn. U. Profs., Brit. Soc. History Sci., New Eng. Assn. Chemistry Tchrs., Phi Beta Kappa, Sigma Xi. Home: 162 Western Av Sherborn MA 01770 Office: Chemistry Dept Wellesley Coll Wellesley MA 02181

WEBSTER, ISABEL GATES (MRS. DONALD G. WEBSTER), lawyer; b. Henderson, N.C., Apr. 16, 1931; d. Caswell Jerry and Rowena (Gregory) Gates; student N.C. Coll., 1948-49; B.S., Boston U., 1953, J.D., 1955; m. Donald G. Webster, Jan. 28, 1956; children—Donald E., Jerry G., Karen E., Michael G. Admitted to Ga. bar, 1958; practiced in Atlanta, 1960—; asso. firm Jackson, Patterson, Parks and Franklin, Atlanta, 1972—. Mem. adj. faculty Emory U. Law Sch., Decatur, 1973—. Second v.p. Atlanta Urban League, 1972-73, pres., 1974-75. Bd. dirs. Gate City Day Nursery Assn. Recipient Community Service award United Appeal, 1962, Certificate of Merit, N.A.A.C.P., 1964, Certificate of Appreciation, Boy Scouts Am., 1971. Mem. State Bar Ga., Am., Gate City bar assns. Home: 371 Fielding Lane SW Atlanta GA 30311 Office: First Federal Bldg Atlanta GA 30303

WEBSTER, JEAN LOUISE, lawyer; b. Santa Ana, Cal., July 4, 1926; d. J. Leonard and Alice Mary (Carlson) Cole; B.B.A., Woodbury Bus. Coll., Los Angeles, 1946; A.B. cum laude in Econs., U. So. Cal., 1952, J.D., 1955; m. Warren M. Webster, Apr. 6, 1946 (dec. Sept. 1948). Admitted to Cal. bar, 1956; practiced in Los Angeles, 1956-57; asso. firm Reed & Kirtland; staff atty. Universal Pictures, Inc., Hollywood, Cal., 1957-58; atty. Office of County Counsel, Los Angeles County, 1958—. Mem. State Bar Cal., Am. Judicature Soc., Am., Los Angeles, Pasadena bar assns., Cal. Scholarship Fedn., U. Cal. Law Alumni Assn. Legion Lex (dir. 1969—), Order of Artus, Latin and Greek Soc. U. So. Cal., Kappa Delta, Phi Delta Delta, Phi Alpha Delta. Home: La Canada CA 91011 Office: 648 Hall of Administration Los Angeles CA 90012

WEBSTER, JOSEPHINE MARIA, financial analyst, banker; b. Shelbyville, Ind., Dec. 19, 1924; s. William Roscoe and Alma (Isley) Webster; student N.Y. Inst. Finance, 1960-61. With Chambers Corp., Shelbyville, Ind., 1943-58, nat. service corr., 1951-58; investment research asst. Indpls. Bond and Share Corp., 1958-66; v.p., trust investment officer Am. Fletcher Nat. Bank & Trust Co., Indpls., 1966—. Mem. Indpls. Soc. Financial Analysts, Inst. Chartered Financial Analysts, Indpls. C. of C., Nat. Assn. Bank Women. Home: 1102 Meridian St Shelbyville IN 46176 Office: 101 Monument Circle Indianapolis IN 46204

WEBSTER, NORMA KATHLEEN STAMPS (MRS. RONALD L. WEBSTER), lawyer; b. Kansas City, Mo., Jan. 13, 1945; d. Norman LaVaun and Mary Lenore (Harline) Stamps; B.A., Maryville Coll., 1966; J.D., U. Mo., 1971; m. Ronald L. Webster, May 29, 1967; children—Nathan Addison, Daphne Renee, Jason Christopher. Admitted to Mo. bar, 1971; asso. William K. Poindexter, Lee's Summitt, Mo., 1971; asst. city counselor Kansas City, Mo., 1971—. Mem. Bar U.S. Dist. Ct. Western Dist. Mo., Mo., Kansas City bar assns., Phi Alpha Delta. Home: 138 E 132d St Kansas City MO 64145 Office: 414 E 12th St Kansas City MO 64106

WEBSTER, ROSALIND MARIE HELTON (MRS. ALAN HUNTLEY WEBSTER), assn. exec.; b. Champaign, Ill., Aug. 22, 1925; d. Carl Vernon and May Ella (Maxwell) Helton; grad. high sch.; m. Alan Huntley Webster, Aug. 23, 1962; children—Peter, Karen, David. Field dir. Camp Fire Girls, Oshkosh, Wis., 1950-57; display librarian Oshkosh Pub. Library, 1959-62; with Oshkosh YMCA, 1962—, program dir., 1962—. Chmn. Friends of Library, Oshkosh, 1968, Oshkosh Community Council, 1970; bd. dirs. Oshkosh Sch., 1973; v.p., sec., treas. Oshkosh Council Chs., 1964-68. Methodist (bd. edn. 1970-72; bd. discipleship 1972—). Clubs: Republican, Fireside Antique (Oshkosh). Home: 3843 Red Oak Ct Oshkosh WI 54901 Office: 324 Washington Av Oshkosh WI 54901

WECHSLER-GAINER, CECILE, physician; b. Warsaw, Poland, Oct. 1, 1907; d. Mathias and Lea (Emden) Rotkel; B.A., U. Basel (Switzerland), 1937; M.D., U. Paris, 1949; m. Irving Gainer, Dec. 18, 1959; 1 son, (by previous marriage), Felix Leneman. Came to U.S., 1949, naturalized, 1954. With Prophylactic Inst., Paris, 1932-40; dir. underground hosp., Bourboule, France, 1943-45; in charge home for war orphans, France, 1946-49; intern Knickerbocker Hosp., N.Y.C., 1951-52; practice medicine, specializing in allergy, N.Y.C., 1959—; asso. attending Knickerbocker Hosp. Diplomate Am. Bd. Clin. Immunology and Allergy. Fellow Am. Coll. Allergy, Am. Assn. Clin. Immunology and Allergy; mem. Am. Acad. Gen. Practice, Am. Womens Med. Assn., Israeli Med. Assn., Med. Histadrut for Israel, Jewish Physicians from Poland. Home: 140 Wadsworth Av New York City NY 10033

WECHTER, VIVIENNE THAUL (MRS. NATHAN WECHTER), artist, educator; b. N.Y.C.; d. Samuel Joshua and Hilda (Thaul) Rosenthal; B.Pedagogy, Jamaica Tchrs. Coll.; postgrad. Columbia, N.Y. U., New Sch. for Social Research, Art Studesnt League, Sculpture Center, Pratt Inst. Graphic Center; m. Nathan Wechter; 1 dau., Robyrta Joan (Mrs. Bernard R. Rapoport). Exhibited one-man shows including Castellane Gallery, East Hampton Gallery, N.Y.C., Cornell U., Ithaca, Neville Pub. Mus., Green Bay, Wis., Nashville Fine Arts Center, Fairleigh Dickinson U., Rutgers U., Waterloo (Ia.) Municipal Galleries, Bodley Gallery, represented in permanent collections Corcoran Gallery, Washington, Houston Mus. Fine Arts, Jewish Mus. N.Y.C., Fordham U., N.Y.C., Univ. Art Mus., Berkeley, Cal., Mus. Art and Sci., Norfolk, Va., N.Y. U., Ohio State U., Phoenix Mus. Fine Arts, Fairleigh Dickinson U., Madison, N.J., UN, others. Artist-in-residence Fordham U., 1964—, asst. prof. art and esthetics, 1964, now prof. fine arts, chmn. acquisitions and exhbns.; moderator weekly radio broadcast U. Roundtable, WFUV, 1951—. Chmn. coll. liaison div. Bronx Council on Arts. Bd. dirs. Urban Arts Corps; founder, trustee Bronx Mus. Art. Recipient awards from various orgns. including Am. Acad. Arts and Letters, Am. Soc. Contemporary Art. Mem. Am. Assn. U. Profs., Coll. Art Assn., Artists Equity Assn., Am. Soc. Contemporary Artists, Urban League Greater N.Y. (bd. dirs., mem. adv. bd. 1952—), United World Federalists (1st chmn.), Fedn. Modern Painters and Sculptors, Alpha Mu Gamma, Kappa Pi. Illustrator book cover Park of Jonas (Alfeo Marzi), 1965. Author: A View From the Ark, 1973. Contbr. introductory essays to Five Museums Come to Fordham and Fordham in the Arts. Home: 4525 Henry Hudson Pkwy New York City NY 10471

WECKLER, NORA LOEB, educator; b. Toronto, Ont., Can.; d. Bernard and Alice (Heslewood) Loeb; B.A., Toronto U., 1937, M.A., 1938, Ph.D., 1941; m. Joseph E. Weckler, Oct. 25, 1941 (dec. Nov. 1963); children—Linda Ann (Mrs. Anthony Advokaat), David Alan. Came to U.S., 1941, naturalized, 1945. Instr. U. Md., 1942-43; research asso. U. Chgo., 1944-45; lectr. human devel. U. So. Cal. and U. Cal. at Los Angeles, 1947-55; asst. prof. psychology Cal State Coll. at Los Angeles, 1955-58; asso. prof., chmn. psychology dept. Cal. State U. at Northridge, 1958-61, prof. psychology, 1963—, dean acad. affairs Cal. Sch. Profl. Psychology, 1973—; cons. in field. Mem. Am. (chairperson membership, dir. div.), Western chairperson com. status women), Cal., Los Angeles County (pre. 1969-72), Los Angeles County (sec.-treas. 1964-65) psychol. assns. Home: 12434 Rochedale Lane Los Angeles CA 90049 Office: 18111 Nordhoff St Northridge CA 91324

WEDDINGTON, SARAH RAGLE, lawyer, state legislator; b. Abilene, Tex., Feb. 5, 1945; d. Herbert Doyle and Lena Catherine (Morrison) Ragle; B.S. magna cum laude, McMurry Coll., 1965; LL.B., U. Tex., 1967. Admitted to Tex. bar, 1967; mem. firm Weddington & Weddington, Austin, 1970-74, Sarah Weddington Law Offices, 1974—; mem. Tex. Ho. of Reps., 1972—. Mem. Joint Conf. Reps. Am. Bar Assn. and A.M.A. Nat. bd. dirs. Zero Population Growth. Recipient Woman of Year award Tex. Women's Polit. Caucus, 1973. Mem. Am., Tex. bar assns., Nat. Orgn. Women, Am. Assn. U. Women, Women's Equity Action League. Address: 709 W 14th St Austin TX 78701

WEDEEN, SHIRLEY ULLMAN (MRS. PETER WEDEEN), educator; b. N.Y.C., May 29, 1926; d. Hugo L. Esther (Forschein) Ullman; B.A., Bklyn. Coll., 1946; M.A., N.Y.U., 1947, Ph.D., 1951; m. Peter Wedeen, Jan. 13, 1952; children—Van, Glenn. Substitute tchr. edn. Bklyn. Coll., 1948-49, psychology, 1949-50, edn., 1950-51, instr. edn., 1951-58, asst. prof., 1958-66, asso. prof., 1966-72, prof., 1972—, coordinator Basic Skills Center, 1961-64, coordinator gen. counseling program, 1965-66, asst. dean students, 1966-68, curriculum coordinator Sch. Edn., 1971—. Mem. Am. Psychol. Assn., Internat. Reading Assn., Internat. Platform Assn., Coll. Reading Assn., Am. Psychol. Assn. (N.Y. div.) Am. Assn. U. Profs., Kappa Delta Pi. Club: Woman's Press. Author: College Reader; Advanced College Reader. Contbr. articles in field to profl. jours. Home: 116 Buckingham Rd Brooklyn NY 11226 Office: Brooklyn College Bedford Av Brooklyn NY 11210

WEDEL, CYNTHIA CLARK, psychologist; b. Dearborn, Mich., Aug. 26, 1908; d. Arthur Pierson and Elizabeth (Haigh) Clark; B.A., Northwestern U., 1929, M.A., 1930; Ph.D. in Psychology, George Washington U., 1957; L.H.D., Western Coll. Women 1958, Elmhurst Coll., 1970, Moravian Coll., 1971, Fordham U., 1971, Smith Coll., 1972; m. Rev. Theodore O. Wedel, May 4, 1939 (dec. July 1970). Profl. ch. work Episcopal Ch., 1931-39; tchr. Nat. Cathedral Sch., 1939-48; nat. exec. bd. Woman's Aux., Episcopal Ch., 1946-52, mem. nat. council Episcopal Ch., 1955-62; asso. gen. sec. Nat. Council Chs., 1962-69; asso. dir. Center for a Voluntary Soc., Washington, 1969—. Lectr. Am. U., 1958-61. Cons. Nat. Office Vols. 1945-72, nat. chmn. vols. A.R.C., 1973—; mem. nat. bd. Girl Scouts of U.S.A., 1960-66, President's Commn. Status Women, 1961-63, citizen's adv. com., 1963-68. Mem. United Ch. Women (nat. pres., 1955-58), Nat. Council Chs. (gen. bd. 1954-62; v.p. 1957-60, pres. 1969-72), Dept.

of World Council Chs., Am. Psychol. Assn., Phi Beta Kappa, Kappa Delta. Episcopalian. Author: Citizenship, Our Christian Concern, 1952; What of the Women?, 1953; Women in the Church, 1955; The Glorious Liberty, 1958; Employed Woman and the Church, 1959. Contbr. articles mags. Home: 4800 Fillmore Av Alexandria VA 22311 Office: Center for Vol Soc 1785 Massachusetts Av NW Washington DC 20036

WEDEL, MARY CATHRYN (MRS. OSCAR E. WEDEL), banker; b. Brazil, Ind., July 19, 1905; d. Watkin William and Lola Augusta (Whittington) Jones; student pub. schs.; m. Linus E. Brooks, Jan. 16 (dec. May 1947; m. 2d, Oscar E. Wedel, Oct. 5, 1951. With Riddell Nat. Bank Brazil, Ind., 1923—, successively file clk., asst. cashier, cashier, cashier and v.p., 1923-69, exec. v.p., 1969—, also dir. Mem. adv. com. A.R.C., 1969-72; treas. fund drives Girl Scouts U.S., 1964—, Clay County Easter Seal campaigns, 1965—. Recipient Outstanding Career Woman Clay County award, 1971. Mem. Ind. Bankers Assn. (pres. region 6 1958-59, council 1957-59), Nat. Assn. Bank Auditors and Comptrollers (chpt. pres. 1963-64). Mem. Daus. of Nile (past queen), Order Eastern Star. Clubs: Women's Democratic (pres. 1937-41) Brazil Business and Professional Women's (pres. 1929-30, 46), Kee Wana (Brazil, Ind.). Christian Scientist. Home: Route 1 Brazil IN 47834 Office: 2 E National Av Brazil IN 47834

WEDOW, SHIRLEE ANN COLLIER (MRS. WALTER F. WEDOW), civic worker; b. Kansas City, Mo.; d. John J. and Florence (Quaries) Collier; A.B., U. Mo., Kansas City, 1938; tchr. certificate, U. Nev., 1956; m. Walter F. Wedow, Feb. 1, 1939; children—Frederick J., Michael W. Mem. Govs. Com. on Edn., 1959-61, 65-66, 66-68; adv. com. S.W. Regional Lab. for Edn. Devel. and Research, 1967-69; mem., sec. Sparks (Nev.) Recreation Commn., 1965-68; mem., sec. Washoe County Community Action Program, 1965-68; sec. Mayors Com. on Children and Youth, 1964-66, Washoe County Study Com. on Drug Abuse, 1967-68, Govs. Adv. Commn. Juvenile Concerns, 1968-69; del. White House Conf. on Children and Youth, 1960; mem. Nev. Ednl. Devel. Council, 1966-68, chmn., 1969—; mem. Govs. Safety Com., 1961-63; chmn. Gov.'s Adv. Council on Children and Youth, 1971—. Bd. dirs. Nev. Safety Council, 1963-65. Named Outstanding Citizen Working for Edn., 1969. Mem. Am. Assn. U. Women, Nat. Assn. Parliamentarians (state sec. 1966-68), Nat. (life) (bd. mgrs. 1960-67, membership chmn. 1964-67, chmn. adv. com. Designing Edn. for the Future 1966-69), Nev. (life) (pres. 1960-63, bd. mgrs. 1954—, legislation chmn. and lobbyist 1963—, state coordinator 1968-72) parent-tchrs.-assns., State Adult Edn. Assn., P.E.O. Roman Catholic. Home: 11811 Av of PGA Palm Beach Gardens FL 33403 Office: Whalen Studio Tanglewood Plaza Palm Beach Gardens FL 33403

WEDUM, BERNICE GOLDEN (MRS. ARNOLD G. WEDUM), pediatrician; b. Oakland, Cal., Aug. 17, 1915; d. Frank Joseph and Bernice M. (Naggs) Golden; A.B., U. Cal. at Los Angeles, 1935; M.D., U. Cin., 1941; m. Arnold G. Wedum, Aug. 26, 1936; children—Ellen, Eric. Intern, Cin. Gen. Hosp., 1941-42; resident Children's Hosp., Cin., 1942-43; instr., asst. dir. Denver Rheumatic Fever Diagnostic Service, U. Colo. Sch. Medicine, 1944-47; visitor cardiac clinic Johns Hopkins Hosp., Balt., 1947; visitor cardiac catheterization lab. Johns Hopkins, 1951; pediatrician Harriet Lane Home, Balt., 1952-54; prin. investigator, grant USPHS, 1958-63; med. officer D.C. Health Dept., 1963-65, 68—; staff Children's Hosp., Washington, 1967—; guest worker NIH, 1968—; cons. cardiology Children's Hosp., Phila., 1951-71; cons. Nat. Heart Inst., 1965-66, U.S. Children's Bur., 1966, D.C. Tchrs. Coll. Health Service, 1972; vol. physician for Vietnam, summer 1970. Mem. tech. adv. com. Montgomery County Tb Assn., 1971. Bd. dirs. Denver Tb Assn., 1946. Mem. Frederick County Med. Assn., Phi Beta Kappa, Sigma Xi, Alpha Omega Alpha. Contbr. articles to profl. jours. Home: 3114 Wisconsin Av Washington DC 20016

WEED, HELEN HALE (MRS. WILLIAM HOWELL WEED), ednl. adminstr.; b. Eklo, Md., July 5, 1914; d. John Henry and Carrie Estelle (Cooper) Hale; A.B., Goucher Coll., 1935; student Cornell U., summers 1936-39; M.A., Johns Hopkins, 1952; m. William Howell Weed, Dec. 29, 1973. Faculty, Dundalk Jr. High Sch., 1935-38, Towson (Md.) High Sch., 1938-49; supr. sci. pub. schs. Baltimore County (Md.), 1949-65, coordinator Office Sci., 1965—; faculty Evening Sch., Western Md. Coll., 1957, McCoy Coll. of Johns Hopkins, 1959-61, U. Md., Baltimore County, 1969, 71; mem. tech. adv. bd. Harper & Row Pubs. Del. World Confedn. Orgns. Teaching Profession Editorial Cons. series of trade books on sci. topics Lippincott Co.; chmn. operating com. achievement awards for students, recognition awards for tchrs. Future Scientists Am. Found., 1954-56; lectr. Engrs. Council Profl. Devel., 1956-57; mem. coms. Balt. Sci. Fair, 1956—; chmn. registration Nat. Sci. Fair, 1964—; mem. ednl. adv. bd. Am. Cancer Soc., 1971—, trustee Baltimore County unit, 1973—. Trustee Am. Sci. Film Assn., 1968-72. Recipient Macalaster award for distinguished leadership in sci. teaching, 1966; named Towsontowne Woman of Year, 1966; citation for distinguished service to sci. edn. Nat. Sci. Tchrs. Assn., 1973. Fellow A.A.A.S.; mem. N.E.A., Nat. Assn. Research in Sci. Teaching, Nat. Sci. Suprs. Assn., Assn. Edn. Tchrs. Sci., Md. Acad. Scis. (sci. council 1960—, v.p.). Assn. Supervision and Curriculum Devel., Council Elementary Sci., Nat. Sci. Tchrs. Assn. (dir. Workshop for improvement sci. teaching 1957, chmn. exploration com. Yearbook 1958, pres. 1964-65), Pi Lambda Theta. Contbr. articles to profl. publs. Home: 505 Woodbine Av Towson MD 21204 Office: Greenwood Towson MD 21204

WEEHUNT, ETHEL AVIS MACKEY (MRS. GEORGE RILEY WEEHUNT), rancher, poet; b. Okemah, Okla., Mar. 2; d. Burt and Ruth (Marcellus) Mackey; B.A., Okla. U. Sch. Corr., 1965-68; m. George Riley Weehunt (dec. 1970); children—Marie Wilma (Mrs. John McHenry), George Leonard. Poultry farmer, Okemah, 1939-50; establisher cattle ranch, Okemah, 1930-70, farmer, rancher, Okemah, 1970—. Mem. Okfuskee County Livestock Assn., Southwestern Peanut Growers Assn., D.A.R. Methodist. Clubs: Study, Redbud Garden (Okemah). Author: The Clover Collection of Verse, 1971; Special Honors, 1972; Academia Internazionale, 1971; Year Book of Modern Poetry, 1971; The Best of Gato, 1972. Address: Route 3 Box 122 Okemah OK 74859

WEEKS, ALICE MARY DOWSE (MRS. ALBERT WILLIAM WEEKS), educator, geologist; b. Sherborn, Mass., Aug. 26, 1909; d. Charles Arthur and Jessie M. (Parker) Dowse; B.A., Tufts Coll., 1930; M.A., Radcliffe Coll., 1934, Ph.D., 1949; resident fellow Bryn Mawr Coll., 1934-35; m. Albert William Weeks, May 20, 1950. Instr., asst. prof., asso. prof., dept. geology Wellesley Coll., Wellesley, 1936-49; research geologist, br. exptl. geochemistry and mineralogy U.S. Geol. Survey, Washington, 1949—; asso. prof. Temple U., 1962-64, prof., 1964—, chmn. dept. geology, 1962—. Mem. geology panel Bd. Civil Service Examiners, 1958-63; mem. 21st Internat. Geol. Congress, Copenhagen, 1960, 23d Congress, Prague, 1968, 24th Congress, Montreal, 1972. Fellow Geol. Soc. Am., Mineral. Soc. Am., A.A.A.S., Am. Geog. Soc.; mem. Geochem. Soc., Mineral. Assn. Can., Nat. Clay Minerals Soc., Nat. Assn. Geology Tchrs., Geol. Soc. Washington, Phila. Geol. Soc. (pres. 1967-68), Phila. Mineral. Soc., Marine Tech. Soc. (mem. council of Delaware Valley chpt. 1969-70), Sigma Xi. Unitarian. Clubs: Appalachian Mountain (life), Philadelphia Trail. Contbr. numerous articles in field to profl. jours. Home: 1029 Nicholson Rd Wynnewood PA 19096 Office: Dept Geology Temple U Philadelphia PA 19122

WEEKS, FRANCES MCMURTRAY (MRS. LEROY WEEKS), city ofcl.; b. Murchison, Tex., Feb. 4, 1924; d. Benjamin Allan and Mary Margaret (Norris) Mayfield; grad. high sch.; b. Raymond W. McMurtray, Jan. 23, 1945 (dec. Sept. 1965); children—Wayne, Clark, Betty (Mrs. Raymond Smith), Janette (Mrs. Allen Talley); m. 2d, Leroy Weeks, June 17, 1972. Short stop mgr. James Connally Base Exchange, Waco, Tex., 1965-68; with Morgan Sign Co., Waco, 1968-69; city sec. City of Beverly Hills, Tex., 1969—. Vol. worker United Fund, 1972—. Mem. Rebekah. Home: Route 5 Box 994 Waco TX 76705 Office: 3418 Memorial Dr Waco TX 76711

WEEKS, JEANNE Q. GARTRELL (MRS. ROBERT L. OPPENHEIMER), editor; b. Atlanta; d. Robert Derby and Nancy Hayes (Reynolds) Gartrell; B.A., Salem Coll., 1939; student N.Y. Sch. Interior Design, 1956-57; m. Willet Weeks, Nov. 28, 1941 (div. Feb. 1955); 1 son, Willet III; m. 2d, Robert L. Oppenheimer, Nov. 26, 1961. Asst. editor Harper's Bazaar, N.Y.C., 1954-55, Am. Home mag., 1955-59; asso. editor Interiors mag., N.Y.C., 1959, mng. editor, 1959-71; asso. Kirk-Brummel Assos., Inc., N.Y.C., 1971-72; dir. advt. and pub. relations Harvey Probber, Inc., N.Y.C., 1973—; sometimes lectr. Recipient Jesse H. Neal award for editorial achievement, 1965. Mem. Am. Inst. Interior Designers, Nat. Home Fashions League, Designer's Saturday Assn. (exec. bd.). Author: (with others) Rugs and Carpets of Europe and the Western World. Home: 250 E 87th St New York City NY 10028 Office: 979 3d Av New York City NY 10022

WEEKS, MARILYN ARVIDSON (MRS. J. STEPHEN WEEKS), writer; b. Hastings, Neb., Sept. 15, 1937; d. Otto Leo and Mary Marjorie (Stunkard) Arvidson; B.S., certificate journalism U. Neb., 1959; m. J. Stephen Weeks, Mar. 11, 1967; 1 son, Geoffrey Michael. Womens dept. reporter Waterloo (Ia.) Daily Courier, 1959-63; womens dept. feature writer Miami (Fla.) Herald, 1963-68; reporter, med. writer Suffolk Sun, Deer Park, N.Y., 1968-69; free lance writer, 1969—. Recipient Distinguished Service award Jackson Meml. Hosp., 1968. Mem. Theta Sigma Phi. Home: 1 Squirrel Lane Newark DE 19711

WEEKS, MARY LYLE CHILDS (MRS. JAMES TAYLOR WEEKS), educator, editor; b. Gainesville, Tex., Apr. 9, 1934; d. William Lyle and Nella Mae (Beavers) Childs; B.A. in Journalism, U. Okla., 1956, M.A., 1974; m. James Taylor Weeks, Jan. 22, 1956; 1 dau., Deborah Susan. Journalism librarian U. Okla., Norman, 1955-56, pub. information asst. 1967-70, instr. journalism, 1970—; tchr, nursery sch., Babenhausen, Germany, 1957; women's reporter Daily Okla. and Oklahoma City Times, 1957; tchr. U.S. Army Edn. Center, Babenhausen and Darmstadt, Germany, 1957-58; typist Shell Oil, Midland, Tex., 1958-59; continuity writer, traffic dir. KOSA-TV, Odessa, Tex., 1959-60; free-lance writer, 1961-73; editor Sooner State Press., Norman, 1970—. Sponsor, Student Press Assn., Norman, 1970-73, Soc. Black Journalists, Norman, 1972—. Pres. Chi Omega Alumnae, Norman, Okla., 1966, Norman Alumnae Pan-Hellenic, 1967. Bd. dirs. Cleve. County Planned Parenthood Assn., 1965. Mem. Women in Communications, Assn. for Edn. in Journalism, Chi Omega. Democrat. Mem. Christian Ch. Contbr. articles to profl. jours. and mags. Home: 1833 Vine St Norman OK 73069

WEEKS, SUSAN ANN, journalist; b. Commerce, Okla., Mar. 20, 1948; d. Marvin Earl and Helen Katherine (Heffner) Weeks; A.A., Northeastern Okla. A. and M. Jr. Coll., 1968; student Catholic U. Milan, Rome, Italy, 1969; B.J., U. Mo., 1970. Advt. copywriter J.C. Penney Co., Inc., N.Y.C., 1970-73; exec. dir. Composers and Choreographers Theatres, Inc., N.Y.C., 1973; dir. publ. Caudill Rowlett Scott, architects, planners, engrs., N.Y.C., 1973—. Free lance publicity dir. Central Arts Cabaret, N.Y.C., 1971-72. Mem. Women in Communications, A.I.A., Pub. Relations Soc. Am. Democrat. Presbyn. Home: 150 E 78th St New York City NY 10021 Office: 299 Park Av CRS New York City NY 10017

WEESNER, BETTY JEAN, newspaper publisher; b. Danville, Ind., Jan. 22, 1926; d. Edward Jabin and Ruth Leah (Daugherty) Weesner; A.B., Ind. U., 1951. Sec.-treas. Hendricks County Republican, Danville, 1951-61, pres., treas., 1961—. Mem. Ind. Republican Editorial Assn. Mem. D.A.R., Nat. Fedn. Press Women, Am. Legion Aux., Woman's Press Club Ind., Ind. U. Alumni Assn. Women in Communications. Home: 48 Maple Row Danville IN 46122 Office: PO Box 6 E Main St Danville IN 46122

WEGERBAUER, MARGARET ELIZABETH (MRS. KARL A. WEGERBAUER), occupational therapist; b. Detroit, May 13, 1931; d. Gervase Joseph and Emma Mary (Bammel) Schultz; student Mercy Coll., Detroit, 1949-50; B.S., Milw-Downer Coll., 1953, diploma in occupational therapy, 1954; m. Karl A. Wegerbauer, June 12, 1954; children—Carol, Patricia, John, Linda, Robert, Joan, Margaret. Occupational therapist Curative Workshop Milw., 1954-55, Trinity Meml. Hosp., Cudahy, Wis., 1968—. Mem. Am., Wis. occupational therapy assns., Lawrence U. Alumni Assn. (sec. Milw. Downer sect.). Home: 331 E Wynbrook Dr Oak Creek WI 53154 Office: 5900 S Lake Dr Cudahy WI 53110

WEGERT, MARY MAGDALENE HARDEL (MRS. DENNIS HAROLD WEGERT), educator; b. Knox, Ind., Nov. 3, 1942; d. Adam Alford and Lucy (Fletcher) Hardel; student Ball State U., 1960-61; B.S., Ark. State U., 1964, M.S. (Ark. Edn. Dept. fellow), 1967, postgrad., 1968-70; postgrad. Nicholls State U., 1971, U. S.W. La., 1972; m. Dennis Harold Wegert, Dec. 20, 1964. Tchr. spl. edn., Knox, Ind., 1964-65; primary tchr. South Elementary Sch., Jonesboro, Ark., 1965-66; tchr. spl. edn. Dudley Elementary Sch., Jonesboro, 1967—; tchr. adult basic edn. extended day classes, Jonesboro, 1970—. Mem. Ark. Adult Edn. Adv. Com., 1974—. Mem. Council for Exceptional Children (chpt. pres. 1969), Ark. Assn. for Pub. Continuing and Adult Edn. (pres. 1973-74), Ark. Edn. (pres. 1973-74), Ark. Edn. Assn., Jonesboro Classroom Tchrs. Assn. Home: 1200 Dana St Jonesboro AR 72401 Office: 1311 Logan St Jonesboro AR 72401

WEGFORTH, RUTH VIRGINIA PETERS (MRS. ROBERT ARTHUR WEGFORTH), educator; b. Olivet, Ill., Mar. 20, 1934; d. Bryan Alonzo and Margaret Eliza (Collins) Peters; B.S. (Coll. scholar, (Kathryn Ruth Howe scholar), Olivet Nazarene Coll., 1956; M.Ed. (Gen. Foods fellow 1960-61), U. Ill., 1962; postgrad. Ill. Tchrs. Coll., 1966; Ed.D., No. Ill. U., 1970; m. Robert Arthur Wegforth, June 16, 1967; children—Robert Scott, Gayl Lynette, John Peter. Tchr. bus. East Jr. High Sch. and Kankakee High Sch., Kankakee, Ill., 1956-63; chmn. bus. edn. dept., dist. supr. vocational bus. edn. Bremen High Sch. Dist., Midlothian, Ill., 1963-67; supr. student tchrs., asst. prof. No. Ill. U., DeKalb, 1967—. Ednl. cons. Stenography, Inc., Skokie, 1966-69; mgr., treas. Kankakee Fedn. Tchrs. Credit Union, 1958-63; v.p., treas. Dist. 228 Fed. Credit Union, 1964-71. Mem. Nat. (life), Ill. edn. assns., Assn. Tchrs. Educators, Assn. Higher Edn., Nat., Ill. (mem. program com. 1972, 73), N. Central, Chgo. Area bus. edn. assns., Am. Assn. U. Women, Kappa Delta Pi, Delta Kappa Gamma, Delta Pi Epsilon, Phi Delta Lambda, Pi Lambda Theta. Home: 10035 W 125th St Palos Park IL 60464 Office: Northern Illinois U DeKalb IL 60115

WEGMANN, JANE RUTH WHITE (MRS. GERALD PATRICK WEGMANN), occupational therapist; b. Waterloo, Ia., Oct. 10, 1948; d. Leighton S. and Wava E. (Barfels) White; B.S., U. Ia., 1971; m. Gerald Patrick Wegmann, June 9, 1973. Dir. occupational therapy Immanuel Med. Center, Omaha, 1971; dir. cardiac occupational therapy Ia. Meth. Hosp., Des Moines, 1972-73; dir. occupational therapy dept. St. Joseph's Hosp., Ottumwa, Ia., 1973—. Mem. Am., Ia. occupational therapy assns. Roman Catholic. Home: Route 1 Ottumwa IA 52501

WEGRZYNOWICZ, CAROL ANN, operations research analyst; b. Jersey City, Oct. 13, 1945; d. Joseph Albert and Jean Ann (Osiecki) Wegrzynowicz; B.A., Holy Family Coll., 1967; postgrad. Catholic U. Am., 1967-68; M.S. in Operations Research, George Washington U., 1974; m. Thomas J. Mooney, Dec. 21, 1968. Geodesist, Army Topographic Command, Washington, 1967-68; mathematician Naval Oceanographic Office, Washington, 1969-73, operations research analyst, 1973—. Mem. Operations Research Soc., Washington Operations Research Council, Nat. Orgn. for Women. Home: 4132 Suitland Rd Suitland MD 20023 Office: Naval Research Lab 4555 Overlook Av SW Washington DC 20390

WEIANT, ELIZABETH ABBOTT, educator; b. New Britain, Conn.; d. William Armstrong and Flora (Abbott) Weiant; student Westbrook Jr. Coll., 1939-40; B.S., Tufts Coll., 1943, M.S., 1943; M.A., Radcliffe Coll., 1952; Ed. D., Boston U., 1970. Mem. faculty Tufts U., Medford, Mass., 1943-61, asst. prof. biology, 1956-61; asst. prof. biology Simmons Coll., Boston, 1961-72, asso. prof., 1972—. Research asso. Orgn. Sci. Research and Devel., 1945, CWS, 1945-55, NSF and USPHS, 1955-60; biol. research Arthur D. Little, Inc., Cambridge, 1959-61; sec. New Eng. Biol. Conf., 1962-73. Bd. dirs., chmn. activities com. Stone Inst., Newton Home for Aged People; alumna trustee Tufts U., 1974—. Recipient Sheriffs Assos. award, Dedham, Mass., 1966. Mem. A.A.A.S., Am. Soc. Zoologists, N.Y. Acad. Sci., Am., Mass. (sec. 1966-67) orchid socs., Sigma XI (chpt. sec.-treas. 1957-60), Alpha Omicron Pi. Conglist. Club: College (dir., asst. treas.) (Boston). Home: 48 Prince St West Newton MA 02165 Office: Simmons Coll 300 The Fenway Boston MA 02115

WEICHNER, THELMA GERTRUDE CLEVELAND, banker; b. Saginaw, Mich., Sept. 27, 1919; d. Vernon Bruce and Lola (Orser) Cleveland; grad. pub. high sch. (valedictorian); m. Roy E. Weichner, Mar. 26, 1966; stepchildren—Marlene, Roy, Jr., Gary. With Shiawassee County Bank (merged into Citizens Comml. & Savs. Bank), Durand, Mich., 1937—, asst. mgr., 1961-64, asst. cashier, 1964—. Active United Fund, Durand, 1960—. Mem. Am. Inst. Banking (gov.), Nat. Assn. Bank Women (state membership chmn. 1971, met. Detroit group chmn. 1966), Greater Durand C. of C., Durand High Sch. Alumni Assn. (pres. 1973—). Free Methodist (organist; sec. ofcl. bd.; treas.). Home: 418 Fitzgerald St Durand MI 48429 Office: 201 N Saginaw St Durand MI 48429

WEIDEN, SISTER ROBERTINE, educator; b. Bklyn.; d. Charles Robert and Josephine (Weiskittle) Weiden; A.B., St. Joseph Coll. for Women, 1923; M.A., Fordham U., 1927; Ed.D., Johns Hopkins U., 1941. Tchr. various schs., 1923-38; mem. faculty St. Joseph Coll., Emmitsburg, 1941-47, 50—, prof. edn., 1954—, chmn. dept., 1967-69, dir. student teaching, 1954-69, dir. summer sessions, 1954—. Mem. Assn. Tchr. Educators (sec.-treas. Md.-D.C. unit 1968-69). Home: 5715 Emerson St Bladensburg MD 20710

WEIDMAN, MARGARET LILLIAN (MRS. GILBERT LOUIS WEIDMAN), ednl. adminstr.; b. Bedford, Ind., Jan. 13, 1913; d. Martin Hubbard and Arla Louise (Wagner) Inman; student Ind. U., 1931-33, Butler U., 1937-38, Quincy Coll., 1951-52; B.S., Culver Stockton Coll., 1953; Ed.M., U. Ill., 1955; postgrad. Seton Hall U., 1958, Newark State Coll., 1958, West Mich. U., 1968, Nat. Coll. Ed., 1972; m. Gilbert Louis Weidman, June 14, 1937; children—Linda (Mrs. Richard Schurman), Larry. Tchr. elementary schs., Hillsdale, Ind., 1933-34, St. Bernice, Ind., 1934-37; tchr. mentally handicapped classes Emerson and Franklin Schs., Quincy, Ill., 1952-57, Edison Sch., West Orange, N.J., 1957-58, Washington Sch., Montclair, N.J., 1958-60, Stevenson and Melrose Park (Ill.) schs., 1960-64; supr. mentally retarded Proviso Twp., Maywood, Ill., 1964—. Instr. Culver Stockton Coll., Canton, Mo., 1966; student tchr. counselor No. Ill. U., DeKalb, 1972—. Mem. Ill. Council for Exceptional Children, Ill. Adminstrs. Spl. Edn., Am. Assn. Mentally Deficiency, Alpha Delta Kappa. Mem. Christian Ch. Home: 617 N Taylor Av Oak Park IL 60302 Office: 1000 Van Buren St Maywood IL 60153

WEIGAND, EVA MAE (MRS. PALMER H. WEIGAND), librarian; b. Freedom, Okla., July 20, 1918; d. Loren Elsworth and Edna Susan (Merideth) Bruner; B.S., Northwestern State Coll., 1942; M.S. in L.S., U. So. Cal., 1966; m. Palmer H. Weigand, Apr. 3, 1938; children—Pamela (Mrs. Charles A. Husk), Randal. Tchr. lang. arts Alva City (Okla.) Schs., 1948-49; tchr. Whittier (Cal.) City Schs., part-time 1958-65; dist. librarian Buena Park (Cal.) Elementary Sch. Dist., 1966—. Mem. adv. bd. Sch. Library Sci., U. So. Cal., 1968-71, div. Library Sci., Fullerton (Cal.) Coll., 1969-71, 73-74. Mem. Am., Orange County Library assns., Cal. Assn. Sch. Librarians, Buena Park Sch. Adminstrs. Assn., Assn. Cal. Sch. Adminstrs., Gen. Alumni Assn. U. So. Cal., Pi Lambda Theta. Baptist. Office: 6885 Orangethorpe Av Buena Park CA 90620

WEIHRER, ANNA LEA (MRS. ARTHUR H. WEIHRER, JR.), mathematician; b. Clarksburg, W.Va., Feb. 28, 1927; d. Roscoe and Ruth (Waters) Allman; A.B., W.Va. U., 1948, M.S., 1949; m. Arthur H. Weihrer, Jr., Dec. 25, 1950; 1 dau., Carol Jo. Instr., Sweet Briar (Va.) Coll., 1948-51; high sch. tchr. Walton, W.Va., Dublin, Va., 1952-55; instr. math. W.Va. U., 1955-56; mathematician USN Propellant Plant, Indian Head, Md., 1956-62; mathematician USPHS, Washington, 1962-69; asst. prof. dept. clin. engring. George Washington U. Med. Center, Washington, 1969-71; chief system devel. br. Data Systems Agy., U.S. Army, 1971—. Part-time instr. Charles County Jr. Coll., LaPlata, Md., 1958-64. Mem. Assn. Computing Machinery, Pattern Recognition Soc., Assn. for Advancement Med. Instrumentation, Soc. for Computerized Medicine, Phi Beta Kappa, Alpha Delta Pi. Baptist. Contbr. articles to profl. jours. Research field computer programming for analysis electrocardiograms and other med. signals. Home: Rt 2 Thurmont MD 21788 Office: Data Systems Agency Fort Detrick Frederick MD 21701

WEILER, VIVIAN LOUISE STRICKLER (MRS. EMIL HENRY WEILER), occupational therapist; b. Lander, Wyo., July 16, 1921; d. George Leslie and Mary Rosalind (Youngs) Strickler; B.S., Colo. State Coll., 1943; certificate occupational therapy Milw.-Downer Coll., 1946; m. Emil Hemry Weiler, Mar. 1, 1953; children—Karen Lynn, George Emil. Instr. homemaking Loveland (Colo.) High Sch., 1943-46; occupational therapist Medi-Therapy Services, San Francisco, 1968-70; cons. occupational therapy Sonoma (Cal.) Convalescent Hosp., 1971; mgmt. cons. Acacia Grove Mobile Park, Sonoma, 1972—. Pres., P.T.A., Winfield Scott Sch., 1963-64; tng. chmn. San Francisco council Camp Fire Girls, 1963, day camp chmn.,

1964. Served to 1st. lt. Women's Med. Specialist Corps, U.S. Army, 1945-53. Recipient Service award Camp Fire Girls, 1966; Sponsor award P.T.A., 1964. Mem. Am. Occupational Therapy Assn., P.E.O., Delta Delta Delta. Presbyn. Mem. Order Eastern Star. Address: 740 3d St E Sonoma CA 95476

WEIMER, RUTH MEISTER (MRS. RAE O. WEIMER), journalist; b. Oklahoma City, Nov. 21, 1909; d. Melvin George and Helen Harriet (Gay) Meister; B.A., U. Okla., 1931; m. Rae O. Weimer, Nov. 5, 1942; children—Rae O. II, Ann (Mrs. James Edward Moxley). Reporter, Oklahoma City Times, 1931-33; women's dept. reporter, editor Daily Oklahoman, 1933-38; women's editor Akron (O.) Times Press, 1938-39; columnist, women's editor Gainesville (Fla.) Sun, 1950-55, 62-66. 1st v.p. Friends of Library, 1973-74; mem. Gainesville City Recreation Com., 1962-66. Mem. Alachua Gen. Hosp. Aux., Suwannee Presbytery of Women of Ch. (corr. sec.), Women in Communications (charter pres. Gainesville profl. chpt.), Nat. League Am. Pen Women (past pres. Gainesville), Chi Omega, Sigma Delta Chi. Presbyn. (past pres. women of ch.). Clubs: University of Florida Women's, Gainesville Woman's. Home: 2042 N W 7th Lane Gainesville FL 32603

WEINBERGER, PEARL RICKLESS (MRS. MARCUS WEINBERGER), educator; b. Derby, Eng., Apr. 20, 1926; d. Isaac H. and Rosina (Greenberg) Rickless; B.S., Manchester U. (Eng.), 1948, M.S., 1951; Ph.D., Ottawa (Ont., Can.) U., 1962; m. Marcus A. Weinberger, Aug. 29, 1948; children—Ruth S., Jeffrey M. Demonstrator botany Leeds (Eng.) U., 1948-49; editorial asst. Nat. Research Council, Ottawa, 1949-50, research officer applied biology, 1950-52; lectr. biology Ottawa U., 1955-62, asst. prof., 1962-67, asso. prof., 1967—. Fellow Brit. Biophys. Soc., Internat. Soc. Ecologists; mem. Ottawa Biochem. and Biol. Soc., Canadian, Am. socs. plant physiology, Canadian Bot. Soc., Canadian Genetics Soc., N.Y. Acad. Sci., Canadian Soc. Cell Physiology, Canadian Soc. Photobiology. Research, publs. in environmental control plant growth with spl. reference to Arctic research, vernalization, pollution, audible and ultrasound. Jours. Patentee sonic plant growth. Home: 290 Buena Vista Rd Ottawa ON Canada

WEINBLATT, MARGARET DEE SHERWIN (MRS. ALAN WEINBLATT), educator; b. Charleston, S.C., Oct. 29, 1943; d. Herbert and Ida Delle (Silverman) Sherwin; B.A., Radcliffe Coll., 1965; M.A., U. Pa., 1968. ph.D.. 1970; m. Alan Winblatt. May 10, 1970. Tchr. math. Am. Coop. Sch.. La Paz. Bolivia. 1965-66: teaching fellow math. U. Pa.. Phila.. 1966-70: asst. prof. math. Simmons Coll.. Boston. 1970-71, Babson Coll., Wellesley, Mass., 1971—. Mem. Am. Math. Soc., Math. Assn. Am., Assn. Women in Math., Assn. Tchrs. Quantitative Methods, Am. Inst. Decision Scis. Club: Radcliffe (co-chmn. Saturday Seminar program). (Boston). Home: 287 Harvard St Cambridge MA 02139 Office: Babson Coll Wellesley MA 02157

WEINER, BETH RICHTER, health service adminstr., educator; b. Madison, Wis., May 25, 1930; d. Walter Allen and Hazel (McConnell) Richter; B.S. in Occupational Therapy, U. Ill., 1954; M.A., U. South Fla., 1969; div.; children—Kathy, Eugene. Dir. Cerebral Palsy Treatment Center, Greenville, S.C., 1954-56; chief occupational therapy Roger Huntington Center of Greenville Gen. Hosp., 1962-66; counselor mental health div. Vocational Rehab., Tampa, Fla., 1970-73; chief rehab. services Community Health Center, Tampa, Fla., 1973; asst. prof. Fla. Internat. U. Miami, 1973—; trainee Getalt Inst. Miami, 1973—. Ill. Fedn. Women's Club scholar, 1949-52; U.S. Adminstrn. on Aging grantee, 1968. Home: 13824 Kendale Lakes Dr Miami FL 33143 Office: Occupational Therapy Program Florida International University Miami FL 33144

WEINERT, ARLA ELAINE, govt. ofcl., data processor; b. Highland Park, Mich., May 27, 1920; d. Richard Henry and Rilla Ruth (Trathen) Weinert; B.A., Wayne State U., 1942, M.Pub. Adminstrn., 1947. Personnel technician Wayne County Civil Service Commn., Detroit, 1943-47; research psychologist Dept. of Army, Washington, 1948-50, analytical statistician, 1951-52; tech. staff mem. Research Analysis Corp., McLean, Va., 1953-67; systems analyst Naval Command Systems Support Activity, Washington Navy Yard, 1967—. Mem. Assn. for Computing Machinery, Soc. for Indsl. and Applied Math. (treas. Washington chpt. 1958-59), Conf. on Data Systems Langs. (systems com. 1968-74), Washington Operations Research Council, Psychometric Soc.

WEINHOLT, RUBY MAUDE CALDWELL (MRS. FRANCIS E. WEINHOLT), credit agy. exec.; b. Butler, Ky., Mar. 4, 1918; d. Sylvan Smith and Mary Edith (Gray) Caldwell; student U. Cin., 1936-37, Southwestern Sch. for Credit Union Personnel, U. Houston, 1968-73; m. Francis Edward Weinholt, Nov. 25, 1937 (dec.); children—Francis Edward, Mary Beth, Margaret Anne (Mrs. Wayne J. Mabry). Cost clk. Watsworth Watch Case Co., Dayton, Ky., 1936-42; united fund clk. Henshaw Brothers Oil Co., San Antonio, 1942-45; Sec., clk. Mortgage Investment Corp., San Antonio, 1945-49; treas., mgr. St. Josephs Credit Union, San Antonio, 1959—. Mem. City Council, Town Hollywood Park, Tex., 1970-72, mayor, protem, 1973—. Bd. dirs. San Antonio chpt. Credit Unions, 1968-72. Mem. Adminstrv. Mgmt. Soc. (bd. dirs. 1973—), Soc. Cajun Luau. Club: Woman's (pres. Hollywood Park 1969-70). Home: 235 Sequoia Dr San Antonio TX 78232 Office: 206 San Pedro Av San Antonio TX 78205

WEINIG, SISTER MARY ANTHONY (JEAN WEINIG), educator; b. N.Y.C., May 19, 1920; d. Anthony Joseph and Elizabeth Leo (O'Brian) Weinig; B.A., Rosemont Coll., 1942; M.A., Fordham U., 1951, Ph.D., 1957. Tchr., Sch. Holy Child, Suffern, N.Y., 1943-56; mem. faculty Rosemont (Pa.) Coll., 1956—, prof. English lit., 1970—. Recipient research grant Am. Philos. Soc., 1965. Mem. Soc. of Holy Child Jesus, Modern Lang. Assn., Nat. Council Tchrs. English, English Inst., Coll. English Assn. Author: Fire in the Well, 1966; Rain in the Chimney, 1972. Contbr. articles to profl. jours. Address: Rosemont Coll Rosemont PA 19010

WEINKAUF, MARY LOUISE STANLEY (MRS. ALAN DALE WEINKAUF), educator; b. Eau Claire, Wis., Sept. 22, 1938; d. Joseph Michael and Marie (Holzinger) Stanley; B.A. in Secondary Edn. magna cum laude, Wis. State U., 1961; M.A., U. Tenn., 1962, Ph.D., 1966; m. Alan Dale Weinkauf, Oct. 12, 1962; children—Stephen Alan, Xanthippe Elizabeth. Organist, St. Johns Luth. Ch., Eau Claire, Wis., 1957-61; mem. faculty U. Tenn. at Knoxville, 1961-66; asst. prof. English, Adrian (Mich.) Coll., 1966-69; prof., chmn. dept. English, Dakota Wesleyan U., Mitchell, S.D., 1969—, also chmn. Div. Humanities. Mem. Mitchell (S.D.) Community Arts Council. Mem. bd. Mitchell Concert Series, Teen-Aid Phone. Mem. Tenn. State Rep. Com., 1965-66. Mem. Modern Lang. Assn. Am., Midwest Modern Lang. Assn., Milton Soc. Am., Nat. Council Tchrs. English, Am. Assn. U. Women, Sci. Fiction Research Assn., S.D. Coll. English Assn., Monday Musicale (treas.), Middle Border Chorus (sec.), Sigma Pi Kappa, Phi Kappa Phi, Sigma Tau Delta, Pi Kappa Delta, Kappa Delta Pi, Delta Kappa Gamma. Lutheran. Home: 914 University Blvd Mitchell SD 57301

WEINLANDER, ALBERTINA ABRAMS (MRS. MAX M. WEINLANDER), educator; b. Mecosta, Mich., July 21, 1919; d. Edward and Albertina (Mantai) Abrams; B.S., Central Mich. U., 1942; M.A., U. Mich., 1947; Ph.D., 1955; m. Max M. Weinlander, June 4, 1945; children—Bruce, Annette. Tchr., prin. Mecosta (Mich.) High Sch., 1942-46; tchr. Sherman Twp. Rural Agrl. Sch., Weidman, Mich., 1946-48; instr., asst. prof. edn. and integrated studies Miami U., 1948-55, lectr. extension service, 1955-56; asst. prof. Wittenberg U., 1956-59, asso. prof. edn., 1960-69, prof., 1969—. Mem. N.E.A., Author's Guild (pres. Sprinfield chpt. 1968-70), Ohio Edn. Assn., Nat. Aerospace Edn. Council, Assn. Learning Disabilities, Am. Assn. U. Women (pres. Springfield br. 1962-64), Pi Lambda Theta, Kappa Delta Epsilon, Kappa Delta Pi. Clubs: Springfield Women's, Zonta (pres. 1968-70). Author: Your Child in a Scientific World, 1959; How to Prepare for the National Teacher, Examination, 1968, rev. edit., 1970. Education in the Elementary School, 1970; also articles in profl. jours. Home: 290 Ridge Mall Springfield OH 45504

WEINMANN, BERT MILLICENT LANDES (MRS. RICHARD A. WEINMANN), artist; b. N.Y.C., July 20, 1924; d. Harry and Esther (Lurie) Landes; student Hunter Coll., 1941-43, Queens Coll., 1958-59, Bklyn. Mus. Art Sch., 1959, New Sch. for Social Research, 1963; grad. Fashion Inst. Tech., 1943; also pvt. student art; m. Richard A. Weinmann, Dec. 26, 1944; children—Harriet, Elaine. Fashion illustrator, designer with Mainbocher, Maurice Rentner, Tabin Picker, others, 1942-50; exhibited one-woman shows Six Trees Gallery, Edgartown, Mass., 1971, Kron Gallery, Mattituck, N.Y., 1972, Firehouse Gallery, Garden City, N.Y., 1975, Unicorn Gallery, N.Y.C., 1974; exhibited in group shows at Palazzo Vecchio, Florence, Italy, 1972, Nat. Acad. Art, 1969, 72, 73, Hecksher Mus., Huntington, N.Y., 1971, Salvator Rosa, Naples, Italy, 1972, Port Washington (N.Y.) Pub. Library, 1972, Fairfield (Conn.) U., 1973, also numerous art galleries; works represented in numerous pvt. collections; tchr. drawing and painting North Shore Community Arts Center, Great Neck, N.Y., 1973—. Mem. exec. bd. Great Neck Com. for Human Rights, 1962-73. Recipient awards from numerous juried art exhbns., purchase award Nassau Coll. Assn., 1973. Mem. Nat. Assn. Women Artists (co-chmn. fgn. exhbns. com. 1973-74, Ziuta G. and Joseph James Akston prize 1972), Women in Arts, Artists in Am. Home: 61 Franklin Pl Great Neck NY 11023 Office: 807 Middle Neck Rd Great Neck NY 11024

WEINREB, ILENE SPACK, city ofcl.; b. Kansas City, Mo., 1931; d. Henry and Mary (Botwinik) Spack; M.A., U. Chgo., 1953; postgrad. San Jose State U., summer 1959, Cal. State U., Hayward, U. Cal. at Berkeley, 1966-68; m. Marvin S. Weinreb, 1951; children—Rachel, Deborah, Judith. Mayor, Hayward, Cal., 1974—; City Council liaison Hayward Area Recreation Dist., East Bay Regional Park Dist.; City Council rep., chmn. Hayward Area Shoreline Planning Joint Agy.; Mem. Hayward Beautification Com., Save the Bay Assn.; vol. coordinator East Bay Community Housing.; mem. Cal. Central Coastal Commn.; chmn. Alameda County Joint Manpower-Office Econ. Opportunity Bd. Pres., Hayward Area League Women Voters, Alameda County Mental Health Assn., Friends of Library-Cal. State U., Tennyson Parent Nursery Sch.; v.p. Central Alameda County Family Service, Fargo Sr. Center; mem. exec. com. Satellite Sr. Homes, Project Eden, Jewish Welfare Fedn. Alameda and Contra-Costa County. Bd. dirs. ACCMA Med. Aux.; Mem. League Cal. Cities. Club: Sierra. Home: 30504 Prestwick Av Hayward CA 94544

WEINSHIENK, ZITA LEESON (MRS. HUBERT T. WEINSHIENK), dist. judge; b. St. Paul, Apr. 3, 1933; d. Louis and Ada (Dubov) Leeson; student U. Colo., 1952-53; B.A. magna cum laude, U. Ariz., 1955; LL.B. cum laude, Harvard, 1958; Diploma in Law (Fulbright grantee), U. Copenhagen (Denmark), 1959; m. Hubert T. Weinshienk, July 8, 1956; children—Edith Blair, Kay Anne, Darcy Jill. Admitted to Colo. bar, 1959; probation counselor, legal adviser, referee Denver Juvenile Ct., 1959-64; judge Denver County Ct., Denver, 1964-71; judge Denver dist. ct., 1972—. Mem. Denver Anti-Crime Council. Precinct committeewoman Denver Democratic Com., 1963-64. Mem. Am., Colo., Denver bar assns., Nat. Conf. State Trial Judges, Denver League Women Voters, Adult Edn. Council, Denver A.D.L. (exec. com.), Bus. and Profl. Women's Club Denver, Harvard Law Sch. Assn., Colo. Assn. Dist. Judges, Order of the Coif (hon.). Soroptimist. Home: 1881 S Niagara Way Denver CO 80222 Office: Denver Dist Court City and County Bldg Denver CO 80202

WEINSTEIN, LAURA KAGAN, educator; b. N.Y.C.; d. Sol and Mollie (Moshinsky) Kagan; B.A., Cornell U., 1949; M.A., Vanderbilt U., 1961, Ph.D., 1963; children—Richard Gordon, Steven Andrew. Asst. prof. psychology George Peabody Coll. Tchrs., 1963-66, asso. prof., 1966-72, prof., 1972-73; dir. research and evaluation Edwin Gould Services for Children, 1973—. Mem. Am., Southeastern, Tenn. psychol. assns., Am. Assn. U. Profs. Home: 28P Edison Court Monsey NY 10977

WEINSTEIN, PAULINE (MRS. HYMAN LEDEEN), lawyer, social service worker with convicts; b. Boston, July 28, 1910; d. Louis H. and Esther F. (Adelberg) Weinstein; J.D., Southwestern U., 1933; m. Hyman Ledeen. Admitted to Cal. bar, 1935, since practiced in Los Angeles; gen. counsel Engring. Products Co., also Ledeen Mfg. Co., Los Angeles, 1941-53; gen. counsel, personnel dir. Ledeen Inc., Los Angeles and El Monte, Cal., 1953-65; field rep. prisoners' aid and rehab. program Jewish Com. for Personal Service, Los Angeles, 1967—. Bd. dirs. Jewish Com. for Personal Service, 1947—, Gateways Hosp., Los Angeles, 1947—. Mem. Criminal Cts. Bar Assn., Universala Esperanto Asocio, Esperanto League N.Am., Women's Orgn. for Rehab. Through Tng., United Order of True Sisters, Southwestern Univ. Alumni Assn., Themis Soc., Lawyers Club. Home: 1620 Poppy Peak Dr Pasadena CA 91105 Office: 1891 Effie St Los Angeles CA 90026

WEINTRAUB, ANNA AVA (MRS. MICHAEL J. WEINTRAUB), broadcasting exec., journalist; b. Hackensack, N.J., July 7, 1946; d. Seymour and Dorothy (Richman) Malkin; B.A., Am. U., 1968; m. Michael J. Weintraub, Aug. 17, 1969. Feature writer Record, Hackensack, 1968-69, Cin. Enquirer, 1969-70; reporter, feature writer Cin. Post and Times Star, 1970-71; asst. to dir. information services N.J. Pub. Broadcasting, Trenton, 1971—. Recipient first place award Corp. for Pub. Broadcasting, 1971-72, 72-73. Mem. Women in Communications, Kappa Tau Alpha. Office: 1573 Parkside Av Trenton NJ 08638

WEIR, CLARA BILLS, speech clinician, educator; b. Macedon, N.Y., Aug. 27, 1905; d. Samuel Walter and Marion Elizabeth (Bills) Weir; B.A., Syracuse U., 1927; M.A., Tchrs. Coll., Columbia, 1933; postgrad. St. Lawrence U., 1932, Columbia, 1933-45, U. Conn., 1951. Tchr. speech, English elementary and secondary schs., N.Y. State, 1928-45; asso. prof. speech, English Ithaca (N.Y.) Coll., 1945-51; asso. prof. and dir. speech and hearing clinic, Bloomsburg (Pa.) State Tchrs. Coll., 1952-55; tchr. speech and hearing Bd. Edn., Waterbury, Conn., 1955-57; clinician of speech, lang. and hearing Bd. Edn., Hartford, Conn., 1957—. Recipient Community Leaders of Am. award News Pub. Co., Inc., 1969. Mem. Am. Speech and Hearing Assn. (state del. 1970), Speech Assn. Am. (chmn. 1962), Speech Assn. Eastern States (exec. council 1964), Nat., Conn. (mem. legislative com. 1965-75) edn. assns., Am. Assn. U. Women, New Eng. Speech Assn. (mem. exec. council 1965), Nat. Orgn. Women, League of Women Voters (exec. council 1954, 69), Sigma Alpha Eta. Contbr. articles and revs. on speech to profl. jours. Home: 94 Jefferson St Hartford CT 06106 Office: 249 High St Hartford CT

WEIR, GLORIA JANE (MRS. N. LYLE EVANS), physician; b. Baton Rouge, Jan. 18, 1921; d. Claude Arnold and Peggy (Downing) Weir; student Sullins Coll., 1936-37; B.S., La. State U., 1940, M.D., 1943; m. N. Lyle Evans, July 26, 1952; children—Peggy Jane, David Lyle. Intern Charity Hosp. La., New Orleans, 1944, resident in pediatrics, 1949-51; pvt. practice medicine specializing in pediatrics, Baton Rouge, 1952—; staff mem. Baton Rouge (La.) Gen. Hosp., vice-chief staff, 1965, vice-chief pediatrics, 1969, chief pediatrics, 1970-71; mem. staff Our Lady of Lake Hosp., Baton Rouge, vice chief pediatrics, 1959-60; mem. staff Women's Hosp., chief pediatrics, 1969-70; mem. staff Drs. Meml. Hosp.; mem. cons. staff Mary Bird Perkins Treatment Center of Cancer, Radiation and Research Found.; vis. staff Earl K. Long Meml. Hosp.; clin. instr. pediatrics La. State U. Med. Sch.; pediatric cons. Baton Rouge Gen. Hosp. Child Day Care Center, Disability Determination and Rehab., State of La. Licentiate Am. Bd. Pediatrics. Fellow Am. Acad. Pediatrics; mem. A.M.A., La. 6th Dist., East Baton Rouge Parish med. socs., La. Heart Assn., La., Baton Rouge pediatric socs. (v.p. 1968-69, pres. 1969-70), Cancer Soc. Baton Rouge (dir. 1963-67), Sullins Alumnae Assn., Am., La. med. polit. action coms., Baton Rouge Civic Symphony Aux., Delta Zeta, La. State U. Alumni Fedn. Episcopalian. Clubs: Harlequins, Bocage Racquet. Home: 5885 Eastwood Dr Baton Rouge LA 70806 Office: 3955 Government St Baton Rouge LA 70806

WEIR, JANET DOUTHIT (MRS. WALTER D. WEIR), advt. exec.; b. Lincoln, Neb., Sept. 14, 1923; d. Harold Kenneth and Edith Christina (Benjamin) Douthit; student U. Neb., 1941-45; B.A., U. Colo., 1964; m. Walter D. Weir, May 11, 1945; children—Charles Hood II, Ellen Tiffany. Free lance writer, pub. relations cons., Portland, Ore., 1952-56, Boulder, Colo., 1956-64; prin., exec. v.p., Wolff & Weir, Inc., Boulder, Colo., Denver, 1965-70; copy dir. Henderson-Bucknam Advt., Denver, 1970-71; prin., creative dir. Mefford Wolff Weir, Inc., Denver, 1972—; dir. Fontana Media Corp. Exec.-in-residence U. Colo. Coll. Bus., 1973. Mem. Colo. Commn. on Status of Women, 1970—; historian Colo. Gen. Assembly, 1965. Bd. dirs. Multnomah County (Ore.) Women Democrats, 1953-56; pres., Boulder County (Colo.) Women Democrats, 1962-64; mem. Colo. State Dem. Central Com., 1964-68. Bd. dirs. Women's Resource Center, Colo. Women's Coll. Recipient Golden Lulu award Los Angeles Advt. Women, 1968, awards Am. Advt. Fedn., 1965-74; named Copywriter of Year, Denver Advt. Club, 1966, 67, 68, Denver Woman of Year, Nat. Orgn. Women, 1971. Mem. Am. Women in Radio and TV, Am. Assn. Advt. Agys., Am. Advt. Fedn., Friends Nat. Libraries, Advt. Club Denver (1st v.p. 1974), Alpha Omicron Pi, Sigma Alpha Iota. Democrat. Author: An American Odyessy, 1974. Home: 5949 Southvale Rd Boulder CO 80303 Office: 555 17th St Denver CO 80202

WEIR, WINNIFRED ARIEL BEALE (MRS. THOMAS NIVEN WEIR), newspaper editor; b. Cranbrook, B.C., Can., Aug. 16, 1909; d. Myles Ariel and Marjorie Frances (Armstrong) Beale; student Alice Ottley Sch., Worcester, Eng. 1927-28, Victoria (B.C.) Normal Sch., 1928-29; m. Thomas Niven Weir, May 21, 1932; children—Christine Elizabeth (Mrs. David Nish McDonald), Judith Ariel (Mrs. Trevor Ray Matthias), John Myles. Primary tchr. Invermere (B.C.) Elementary Sch., 1929-32; editor Lake Windermere Valley Echo, Invermere, 1956—. Free lance writer various Canadian newspapers, mags., hist. and travel material, 1940—. Coordinator, Civil Def., Invermere, 1966—; v.p. B.C. Cancer Soc., 1964-68; dist. commr. Girl Guides, 1948-57. Mem. Windermere Dist. Hist. Soc. (pres. 1964—), Windermere Dist. C. of C. (hon.). Home: Box 548 Invermere BC V0A 1K0 Canada Office: Box 70 Invermere BC V0A 1K0 Canada

WEISBERGER, BARBARA, tchr., choreographer, artistic dir.; b. Bklyn., Feb. 28, 1926; d. Herman and Sally (Goldstein) Linshes; B.S., Pa. State U., 1945; L.H.D., Swarthmore Coll., 1970; D.F.A. (hon.), Temple U., 1972; m. Sol Spiller, 1945 (div. 1948); m. Ernest Weisberger, Nov. 15, 1949; children—Wendy, Steven. Performed Met. Opera Ballet, N.Y.C., 1937, 38, Mary Binney Montgomery Co., Phila., 1940-42; tchr., dir. Wilkes-Barre (Pa.) Ballet Theatre, 1953; artistic dir., founder Wilkes-Barre Ballet Guild, 1957; ballet mistress, choreographer Ballet Co. of Phila. Lyric Opera, 1961-62; artistic dir., founder Sch. Pa. Ballet Co., also Pa. Ballet Co., 1962—, choreographic works include: Judgment of Paris (Debussy, Griffes); Gingko Tree (Mendtner, Schubert); The Sorceress (Chopin); Quintet in Gay Minor (Gould); The Endless Curve (Debussy); Symphonic Variations (Franck); Italian Concerto, Bach; also operas for Phila. Lyric Opera Co., choreography for contemporary musical theatre. Ford Found. grantee, 1963, 65, 68, 71. Named Distinguished Dau. Pa., 1972. Mem. Psi Chi. Home: 571 Charles Av Kingston PA 18704 Office: School Pa Ballet Co 2333 Fairmount Av Philadelphia PA 19130

WEISBURGER, ELIZABETH KREISER, scientist; b. Greenlane, Pa., Apr. 9, 1924; d. Raymond Samuel and Amy (Snavely) Kreiser; B.S., Lebanon Valley Coll., 1944; Ph.D., U. Cinn., 1947; m. John H. Weisburger, Apr. 7, 1947; children—William Raymond, Diane Susan, Andrew John. Research asso., U. Cin., 1947-49; postdoctoral research fellow Nat. Cancer Inst., Bethesda, Md., 1949-51; commd. 1st lt. to col. USPHS, research scientist, 1951-73, chief carcinogen metabolism and toxicology br., 1973—. Trustee, Lebanon Valley Coll. Recipient Meritorious Service medal USPHS, 1973. Fellow Ohio Acad. Sci., A.A.A.S., Chem. Soc., London; mem. Chem. Soc. Washington (program, women's, membership, entertainment coms. 1950-73, chmn. dinner arrangements com. 1966, bd. mgrs. 1967-69), Am. Chem. Soc., Soc. Toxicology, Am. Assn. Cancer Research, Alpha Chi Sigma, Iota Sigma Pi, Sigma Delta Epsilon. (pres. Omicron chpt. 1969-71). Bd. editors Jour. Nat. Cancer Inst., 1968—, asst. editor in chief, 1971—. Contbr. profl. jours. Home: 5309 McKinley St Bethesda MD 20014 Office: Nat Cancer Inst Nat Inst Health Bethesda MD 20014

WEISEL, MARY RUTH, physician; b. Fairbury, Neb., Oct. 7, 1935; d. Benjamin Oscar and Ruth Norma (Vanier) Weisel; A.B., U. Neb., 1958; M.D., U. Neb., 1961. Intern, Immanuel Hosp., Omaha, 1961; resident anesthesiology, U. Ia., 1962-65; practice medicine specializing in anesthesia. Mpls., 1967—; mem. staff Lutheran Deaconess Hosp.; instr. U. Ia. Med. Sch., 1965, asst. prof., 1966. Diplomate Am. Bd. Anesthesiology. Mem. A.M.A., Am. Soc. Anesthesiologists. Home: 500 Westwood Village St Paul MN 55113 Office: Metropolitan Medical Office Bldg Minneapolis MN 55404

WEISENBERGER, ELSIE JANET, librarian; b. Mission, Tex., Mar. 11, 1917; d. Conrad Joseph and Stella Jane (Stewart) Weisenberger; student U. Okla., 1941-42; B.S. in Edn., U. Ark., 1949; M.L.S., George Peabody Coll., 1952; postgrad. N. Tex. State U., 1969. Tchr., librarian, Hope, Ark., 1937-39; librarian Hempstead County, 1947-51, Hope, 1940-46; pub. librarian, North Little Rock, Ark., 1952-57; librarian Houston Ind. Sch. Dist., 1957—. Sec., Country Club Civic Club, 1970-71. Mem. Am. Assn. U. Women (dir. 1970-73), Am., Tex. (sec. sch. library sect. 1959-60), Teenage (dir., sponsor 1960-71) library assns., Tex. Tchrs. Assn. (dist. chmn. sch. library sect.), Houston Sch. Librarians Assn. (v.p. 1961-62), Wesleyan Service Guild (past pres.). Methodist (adminstrv. bd., chmn. commn. on missions). Home: 6257 Pinehurst St Houston TX 77023 Office: 520 Mercury Dr Houston TX 77029

WEISENBORN, CLARA E., columnist, state legislator; b. Dayton, O., Feb. 9, 1907; d. William J. and Edna E. (Hartung) Nies; student pub. schs.; m. Herbert E. Weisenborn, Aug. 23, 1923; children—Donald, Howard. Home and garden editor Jour.-Herald, 1943-74; also lectr. Mem. Ohio Ho. of Reps., 1953-66, Ohio Senate, 1966-74. Dir. New Bank; chmn. bd. Imperial Bank Vandalia. Mem. Ohio Comprehensive Health Planning Adv. Council. Mem. nat., state and county Women's Republican clubs. Mem. Mus. Natural History; mem. bd. Children's Med. Center, Ohio Soc. for Prevention of Blindness; vice chmn. nat. res. com. Nat. Legislative Service Com. Recipient Woman of Year award Bus. and Profl. Women's Club, 1966; Outstanding Service award Ohio Water Quality Assn., 1973; Eye Safety award Ohio Ophthomology Assn., 1973. Mem. Order Women Legislators (v.p. 1956-57, 59-62, pres. 1966-67), Ohio Newspaper Assn., Am. Bankers Assn. (intergovtl. relations com.), Bus. and Profl. Women's Club, Nat. Garden Writers Assn., Am. Hort. Soc., Ohio Newspaper Assn., Delta Kappa Gamma (hon.). Lutheran. Mem. Order Eastern Star. Clubs: Altrusa (pres. Dayton, dist. vice gov.), Women's Republican, Nat. W. Pop. Home: 4940 Chambersburg St Dayton OH 45424 Office: Journal Herald Dayton OH

WEISENSEL, M. JOAN, hotel, restaurant exec.; b. Madison, Wis., Apr. 21, 1943; d. Arthur J. and Mary Pauline (Doyle) Weisensel; student Madison Bus. Coll., 1961-63, Am. Hotel-Motel Assn. Ednl. Inst., 1963-64. Sec., Parkway Inns, Inc., Madison, 1962-65, Green Bay, Wis., 1965-66, Des Moines, 1966, Cedar Rapids, Ia., 1967-69; room mgr. Pfister Hotel and Tower, Milw., 1969; gen. mgr. Dartmoor Motor Inn, Fond du Lac, Wis., 1969-74, Dartford Inn, Green Lake, Wis., 1969-74, Holiday Inn, Fond du Lac, 1974—. Chmn. Convention and Tourist Com., Fond du Lac, 1973-74. Mem. Fond du Lac Area Assn. Commerce (bd. dirs. 1973-74), Fond du Lac Area Innkeepers Assn. (pres. 1972-73), Wis. Restaurant Assn., Wis. Innkeepers Assn., Nat. Secs. Assn. Home: 48 Pioneer Ct Fond du Lac WI 54935 Office: Holiday Inn Hwy 151 Fond du Lac WI 54935

WEISFELD, ZELMA HOPE, educator, costume designer; b. Phila., Oct. 9, 1931; d. Nathan and Stella (Ritchie) Weisfeld; A.B., Temple U., 1953; M.F.A., Yale, 1956. Costumer Yale Sch. Drama, New Haven, Conn., 1956-58; costume designer Pitts. Playhouse, 1958-60; prof. theatre U. Mich., Ann Arbor, 1960—. Free lance costume designer, 1956—. Mem. exec. com., scholarship com. Founders Soc. Kennedy Center, U. Mich., Ann Arbor, 1970—, chmn. theatre, 1971. Faculty Research fellow U. Mich., 1966. Mem. Am. Theatre Assn., Costume Soc. Gt. Britain, U.S. Inst. Theatre Tech., Am. Nat. Theatre and Acad., United Scenic Artists, Am., Mich. speech assns., English Speaking Union, Zonta. Clubs: Women's Research, Faculty Women. Home: 1716 Charlton Ann Arbor MI 48103 Office: Dept Speech Communication and Theatre Univ of Michigan Ann Arbor MI 48104

WEISS, ANN LIZETTE HOPKINS, govt. ofcl.; b. Boston, July 15, 1934; d. Walter Francis and Cleo (Talbott) Hopkins; B.S. cum laude, Boston U., 1956; M. Pub. Adminstrn., Cal. State U. at Hayward, 1969; m. Roger Herbert Weiss, May 26, 1960 (div. 1974). Asst. buyer J.L. Hudsons, Detroit, 1956-57; acting buyer Fair Store, Chgo., 1957-59; asst. buyer Donaldsons, Mpls., 1959-60; dir. pub. affairs Joseph Magnins, San Francisco, 1962-64; dir pub. affairs Assn. Bay Area Govts., Berkeley, Cal., 1969—. Guest lectr. regional governance Golden Gate U., San Francisco, 1972—, Cal. State U., Hayward, 1969—, J.F. Kennedy U., Martinez, Cal., 1973—, Laney Jr. Coll., Oakland, Cal., 1969—, San Jose State U., 1972—, Fed. Exec. Tng. Seminar, Berkeley, Cal., 1974—. League rep., citizens adv. com. Contra Costa County (Cal.) Land Use and Transp. Study Commn., Martinez, 1968-69. Area chmn. Lafayette (Cal.) Incorp. Election, 1968. Mem. Diablo Valley League Women Voters (bd. dirs. 1966-68), Nat. Orgn. for Women, Pub. Relations Soc. Am., Am. Soc. Pub. Adminstrn. (chpt. pres. 1974-75, vice chmn. nat. task force on affirmative action 1974-75). Home: 1372 Henry St Berkeley CA 94709 Office: Hotel Claremont Berkeley CA 94705

WEISS, ANNE MACDONALD, lawyer; b. Parrish, Ala., Sept. 12, 1919; d. Daniel and Nettie Stein (Stith) MacDonald; student Birmingham-So. Coll., 1935-37; A.B., U. Ala., 1939; LL.B., Jones Law Sch., Montgomery, Ala., 1971; m. Lucius Haney, Apr. 3, 1943 (div. Apr. 1963); children—Larry Dean, Barbara Lynn McClure; m. 2d, Sanford Dorf Weiss, Apr. 27, 1968 (div. Oct. 1973). With copy desk Birmingham (Ala.) News, 1944; editorial asst., asst. editor, asso. editor Progressive Farmer mag., Birmingham, 1950-66; exec. editor Fuller & Dees Marketing Group, Montgomery, Ala., 1966-69; admitted to Ala. bar, 1972; with law office Sanford Weiss, 1969-72, partner, 1972; pvt. practice, Montgomery, 1973—. Pres., Flushing (N.Y.) Community Chorus, 1949. Mem. Am., Ala. (pub. relations com.) bar assns., Am. Assn. U. Women (legislative chmn. Montgomery br. 1972—), Ala. Trial Lawyers Assn., Assn. Trial Lawyers Am., Mensa, Theta Sigma Phi (pres. Birmingham chpt. 1964), Phi Mu. Author: (with L.A. Niven) The Rose Book, 1957. Editor: The Livestock Book, 1958; The Pasture Book, 1962. Home: 615 Hubbard St Montgomery AL 36106 Office: 138 Adams Av Montgomery AL 36104

WEISS, ANNE SHAMES, statistician; b. N.Y.C., Nov. 25, 1913; d. Max and Lena (Pomerantz) Shames; B.A., Hunter Coll., 1937; M.A. (Hebrew Tech. scholar), Columbia, 1941; m. David L. Goldin, Apr. 11, 1943 (dec. Oct. 1961); 1 dau., Joan Ellen (Mrs. Berkowitz); m. 2d, Alfred Weiss, July 18, 1972. Systems analyst Maurice R. Scharff, 1938-42; price economist OPA, 1943-47; research analyst Jewish Theol. Sem., 1956-58; sr. research analyst N.Y. Workmen's Compensation Bd., 1958—. Vol. tutor Hudson Guild Neighborhood House, 1965-67. Mem. Women's League for Israel, U.S. Servas, Am. Statis. Assn. (chmn. social statistics sect. N.Y. Area chpt. 1971-74), Met. Econ. Assn., Phi Beta Kappa, Pi Mu Epsilon. Home: 75 Henry St Brooklyn NY 11201 Office: Two World Trade Center New York City NY 10047

WEISS, BARBARA BARNETT (MRS. PAUL J. WEISS, JR.), counselor; b. Gary, Ind., Sept. 1, 1928; d. Richard Parker and Vivian Lucille (Allison) Barnett; B.A., U. Mich., 1951; M.Ed., U. N.C., 1968; m. Paul J. Weiss, Jr., June 27, 1948; children—Paul J. III, Jane Allison, Richard Barnett, Mary Louise. Counselor, Continuing Edn. Guidance Center for Women, Greensboro, N.C., 1969-72; ednl. planning and career guidance counselor, Greensboro, 1972—. Counselor Office for Adult Students, U. N.C., Greensboro, 1973—; cons. Women's Guidance Program, YWCA, Greensboro, 1972—; counselor Job Corps, Greensboro. Bd. dirs. Ministry for Social Change, Greensboro, 1972—, Parent Coop. Child Care Center for Student Mothers, Greensboro, 1969-72. Mem. Am. Personnel and Guidance Assn., Nat. Vocational Guidance Assn., Adult Student Personnel Assn., N.C. Family Life Council, N.C. Group Behavior Soc., Alumni Assn., Kappa Kappa Gamma. Democrat. Presbyn. Home: 2406 Hawthorne St Greensboro NC 27408 Office: Adult Student Office 208 Administration Bldg Univ of North Carolina Greensboro NC

WEISS, ETHEL, psychologist, educator; b. N.Y.C., Apr. 18, 1934; d. Samuel Benzon and Shirley (Kaplan) Weiss; B.A., Bklyn. Coll., 1956; M.A., New Sch. for Social Research, 1958, Ph.D., 1963; m. James Shed, Sept. 26, 1970; 1 dau., Melanie Frances. Asso. prof. Bard Coll., Annandale, N.Y., 1962-69; asso. prof. psychology City Univ. N.Y., N.Y.C., 1969—, dep. chmn. Sch.Gen. Studies. Cons. Nat. Assn. to Aid Fat Americans. Mem. Am. Psychol. Assn., Psychonomic Soc., Sigma Xi. Asso. editor; Development in High School Psychology, 1974. Home: 215 W 88th St New York City NY 10024 Office: City College New York 138 and Convent Sts New York NY 10031

WEISS, EVE, charitable orgn. exec.; b. N.Y.C., May 15, 1930; d. Irving David and Beatrice (Krauthamer) Sapir; B.A., N.Y. U., 1949, LL.B., J.D., 1962; m. Gustave Weiss, Mar. 18, 1951; children—Jonathan, Robin, Ricky. Admitted to N.Y. bar, 1952; mem. firm Weiss & Weiss, N.Y.C., 1952-66; dir. vol. services Albert Einstein Coll. Hosp., 1966-68; regional dir. Am. Jewish Congress, 1968-70; nat. dir. women's div. United Jewish Appeal, N.Y.C., 1970—. Mem. Bd. Higher Edn., City U. N.Y., 1970-74. Mem. Queens County Democratic Com., 1966-68. Bd. dirs. Futures for Children, Washington, Queens Council Arts, Am. Friends Haifa U.; mem. Five Towns Coll. Council, N. Woodmere, N.Y. Recipient certificate achievement Northeastern U., 1967; Seminar for World Jewish Service award Hebrew U., 1970. Mem. N.E. Queens Council Schs. (pres. 1965-68), Women's League Israel. Home: 47-43 Utopia Pky Flushing NY 11358 Office: 1290 Av Americas New York City NY 10019

WEISS, FLORENCE, research co. exec.; b. N.Y.C., Nov. 8, 1938; d. Jules J. and Pearl (Finklestein) Weiss; student (Woodrow Wilson fellow), Columbia U., 1959-60; B.A. magna cum laude, Syracuse U., 1959. Econ. research asst. Nat. Econ. Research Assos., N.Y.C., 1960-63, econ. analyst, 1964-68, supr. research, 1968-71, asst. v.p., 1971-73, v.p., 1973—. Mem. Am. Econ. Assn. (N.Y. coordinator com. on status women in econs. profession), Nat. Assn. Bus. Economists, Phi Beta Kappa, Phi Kappa Phi. Home: 101 W 12th St New York City NY 10011 Office: National Economic Research Assos 80 Broad St New York City NY 10004

WEISS, GRACE MAUDE (MRS. ROGER WILLIAM WEISS), curator; b. Gordon, Neb., Aug. 22, 1902; d. Napoleon and Mary Lee (Clark) Hively; grad. high sch.; m. Roger William Weiss, Oct. 21, 1924; 1 son, Roger Lee. Asst. librarian Alder Pub. Library, Ainsworth, Neb., 1922-45, librarian, 1945-67; sec. Ainsworth Park Homes, 1968-70; asst. curator Sellors Meml. Cabin, Ainsworth, 1967—. Committee woman Ainsworth Community Improvement, 1963—, co-chmn., 1971. Recipient Knights of AK-Sar-Ben State Good Neighbor award, Omaha, 1967. Conglist. Clubs: Garden (pres. 1953); Woman's (pres. Ainsworth 1969-70) Author: Along Pioneer Trails, 1967. Contbr. articles to profl. jours. Home: 565 N Oak St Ainsworth NE 69210 Office: Sellors Meml Cabin Ainsworth NE 69210

WEISS, JOAN GRACE TALMAGE, author, educator; b. South Pasadena, Cal., Nov. 7, 1928; d. Mason Arthur and Grace (Kalina) Talmage; student Pasadena Jr. Coll., 1946; A.A., U. Cal. at Berkeley, 1947; B.A. with honors, Cal. State Poly. Coll., Pomona, 1971; M.A. in English, Cal. State U. at Los Angeles, 1973; m. Robert E. Weiss, Apr. 19, 1947, (div.); children—Lorraine Joan, Kenneth Robert, Nancy Grace. Free lance writer, 1951—; instr. children's lit. Cal. State U. at Fullerton, 1973—, Mt. San Antonio Jr. Coll., 1973—. Mem. Cal. Writers Guild, Citrus Valley Lawyers' Wives. Republican. Author: Kenny and his Animal Friends, 1965; Danny, the Dory Boy, 1966; Lorrie, The Lemonade Lady, 1966; (with Dottie Waltees) The Selling Power of A Women, 1962. Asso. editor: Orange County Illustrated Mag., 1963-65. Home: 19750 Golden Bough Dr Covina CA 91724 also 4900 River Av Newport Beach CA 92660

WEISS, MADGE WEISBERGER (MRS. ANDREW B. WEISS), occupational therapist; b. Jersey City, Apr. 6, 1943; d. Phillip S. and Faye (Rapoport) Weisberger; B.A. in Psychology, Douglass Coll., 1963; certificate in Occupational Therapy, Columbia, 1965; m. Andrew B. Weiss, June 14, 1964; children—Adam Matthew, Jennifer Mara. Staff therapist Kenny Rehab. Inst., Mpls., 1965-66, U. Ia. Hosp. Sch. for Handicapped Children, Iowa City, 1966-68, sr. research asso. div. hand surgery U. Ia. Hosps., 1968-70, cons. to research project, 1970-73; asst. prof. occupational therapy U. Ala., Birmingham, 1973—. Mem. Am., Miss. occupational therapy assns. Contbr. articles to profl. publs. Home: 3636 Crestside Rd Birmingham AL 35223 Office: Dept Occupational Therapy U Ala Birmingham AL 35294

WEISS, MARJORIE ANN, lawyer; b. Phila., Apr. 24, 1945; d. Albert and Selma (Weinberg) Weiss; B.A., Pa. State U., 1967; J.D., Villanova U., 1970. Admitted to Pa. bar, 1970, since practiced in Phila.; house counsel Phila. br., Reliance Ins. Co., 1970—, def. of civil litigation. Vol. for McGovern for Pres., 1972, Good Judges for Phila., 1973. Mem. Phila. Bar Assn., Pa. Def. Inst. Office: 4 Penn Center Plaza Philadelphia PA 19103

WEISS, RENEE KAROL (MRS. THEODORE WEISS), editor, author; b. Allentown, Pa., Sept. 11, 1923; d. Abraham S. and Betty (Levitt) Karol; A.B., Bard Coll., 1951; m. Theodore Weiss, July 6, 1941. Co-editor, bus. mgr. Quar. Rev. of Lit., Princeton, N.J., 1945—. Violinist, N.C. State Symphony, 1942-45, Oxford U. (Eng.) Symphony Orch., 1953-54, Woodstock String Quartet, 1956-60, Hudson Valley Philharmonic Orch., 1960-66, Hudson Valley String Quartet Children's Concerts, 1965. Author children's books: To Win a Race, 1966; A Paper Zoo, 1968; The Bird from the Sea, 1970. Home: 26 Haslet Av Princeton NJ 08540

WEISS, RITA MILDRED SHAPIRO (MRS. LAWRENCE G. WEISS), educator; b. Newark, Jan. 5, 1922; d. Joseph and Dorothy (Hochberg) Shapiro; student N.J. State Tchrs. Coll. at Newark, 1939-41; B.S., Simmons Coll., 1945; M.A., U. Colo., 1957, Ph.D., 1967; m. Lawrence G. Weiss, June 15, 1942; children—Carolyn Judith, Jonathan Lawrence. Speech pathologist Laradon Hall Sch. for Exceptional Children, Denver, 1956-58; speech correctionist Boulder (Colo.) County Schs., 1958-61; instr., supr. Speech and Hearing Clinic, Dept. Speech and Drama, U. Colo., 1962-67, asst. prof., 1968-70, asso. prof. dept. speech pathology and audiology, 1970—, mem. faculty council, 1974—. Project dir. Inclass Reactive Lang. Therapy Program, 1974—. Bd. dirs. Boulder Day Nursery, 1974—. Recipient Teaching Recognition award U. Colo., 1969, Outstanding Educator Am. award, 1970. Mem. Am., Colo. speech and hearing assns., Am. Assn. on Mental Deficiency, Council on Exceptional Children. Home: 801 Euclid Av Boulder CO 80302

WEISS, SHIRLEY F. (MRS. CHARLES M. WEISS), educator, economist, city planner; b. N.Y.C.; d. Max and Vera (Hendel) Friedlander; B.A., Douglass Coll., Rutgers U., 1942; postgrad. Johns Hopkins, 1948-50; M. Regional Planning, U. N.C., 1958; Ph.D., Duke, 1973; m. Charles M. Weiss, June 7, 1942. Asso. research dir. Center for Urban and Regional Studies, U. N.C., Chapel Hill, 1957—, lectr. planning, 1958-65, asso. prof. planning, 1965-73, prof. planning, 1973—; research asso. Inst. for Research in Social Sci., U. N.C., 1957-73, research prof., 1973—. Mem. Am. Inst. Planners, Am. Econ. Assn., Regional Sci. Assn., Am. Soc. Planning Ofcls., Interamerican Planning Soc., Town and Country Planning Assn. (Eng.), Am. Statis. Assn., Royal Econ. Soc. (Eng.), Am. Assn. U. Profs., Phi Beta Kappa. Author, editor: Urban Growth Dynamics in a Regional Cluster of Cities, 1962; New Community Development: Planning Process, Implementation and Emerging Social Concerns, Vols. 1, 2, 1971; New Town Development in the United States: Experiment in Private Entrepreneurship, 1973. Home: PO Box 1368 155 Hamilton Rd Chapel Hill NC 27514

WEISSLEDER, CLAUDETTE A. PATRIZIO, educator; b. Nesquehoning, Pa., July 12, 1916; d. Eugene and Anna Marie (Santore) Patrizio; B.S., Jersey City State Coll., 1958, M.A., 1961, student, 1954-58; m. Frederick Arno Weissleder, Oct. 12, 1946 (separated Apr. 1958). Tchr. Adult Edn., Jersey City Bd. Edn., 1963-64; bookkeeper Colgate Palmolive Co., Jersey City, 1936-48; bookkeeper Provident Inst. for Savings, Jersey City, 1948-52; sec., mgr. Denman Rubber Co., N.Y.C., 1952; tchr. elementary sch. Jersey City, 1958-66; prof. elementary edn. Jersey City State Coll., 1966—. Bd. dirs. Pavonia council Girl Scouts U.S.A., 1972—. Recipient Woman of Achievement award, 1968, Distinguished Service award Jersey City State Coll., 1968. Mem. Am. Assn. U. Profs. (membership chmn. 1970), Am. Assn. U. Women (editor directory Coll. Club N.J. 1971, implementation chmn.-edn. 1971), Am. Assn. U. Women, Bus. and Profl. Womens Club (treas. 1950-54), Nat. Soc. for Study of Edn., Hudson County Edn. Assn. (v.p. 1964-66, treas. 1962-64), N.E.A., N.J. Edn. Assn. (higher edn. com. 1969-70, election com. 1973-74), Jersey City State Coll. Faculty Assn. (treas. 1966-70, 2d v.p. 1972), N.J. Council Social Studies (asst. treas. 1974—), Internat. Platform Assn., N.J. Assn. Student Teaching, Jersey City State Coll. Alumni Assn. (pres. 1965-66), Jersey City Tchrs. Club (v.p. 1964-66), League Women Voters, Kappa Delta Pi (co-counselor br. 1968—). Home: RD 1 Box 101D Neshanic NJ 08853

WEISSMAN, BARBARA NANCY WARREN (MRS. IRVING LOUIS WEISSMAN), radiologist; b. N.Y.C., Oct. 22, 1944; d. Morris and Lillian Geraldine (Zam) Warren; B.A., Queens Coll., 1965; postgrad. State U. N.Y. Bklyn., 1965-67; M.D., Tufts U., 1969; m. Irving Louis Weissman, June 19, 1966. Intern, St. Elizabeth's Hosp., Brighton, Mass., 1969-70; radiology resident Peter Bent Brigham Hosp., Boston, 1970-73, radiologist, 1973—; clin. fellow radiology Harvard Med. Sch., 1970-73, instr. radiology, 1973—. Home: 20 Gordon Rd Waban MA 02168

WEISSMAN, MYRNA DOREEN MILGRAM (MRS. SHERMAN WEISSMAN), educator; b. Boston; d. Samuel and Jeanette (Berger) Milgram; B.A., Brandeis U.; M.S., U. Pa.; Ph.D. in Epidemiology, Yale, 1974; m. Sherman Weissman; children—Susan, Judith, Sharon, Jonathan. Mem. faculty Yale U. Sch. Medicine, New Haven, Conn., 1967—, asst. prof. psychiatry, 1971—, dir. depression research unit, 1972—. Recipient Merit award NIH, 1967, grants Nat. Inst. Mental Health, 1970—. Mem. A.A.A.S., Am. Assn. Orthopsychiatry, Nat. Assn. Pub. Health. Author: The Depressed Woman: A Study of Social Relationships, 1974. Contbr. articles to profl. jours. Home: 459 St Ronan St New Haven CT 06511

WEISSMAN, SUSE, librarian; b. Karlsruhe, Germany, Aug. 7, 1927; d. Uscher and Rosa (Bierig) Kattler; came to U.S., 1937, naturalized, 1945; A.B. with honors, Hunter Coll., 1949; M.L.S., Columbia, 1964; m. Aaron Weissman, Jan. 1, 1948; children—Daniel, Terry, David. Children's librarian N.Y. Pub. Library, 1964-67; dir. Brunswick (Me.) Pub. Library, 1967—. Mem. Me. Library Assn., Phi Beta Mu. Home: 46 Stanwood St Brunswick ME 04011 Office: Capt John Curtis Memorial Library Brunswick ME 04011

WEISS-SCHWARTZ, SANDRA MARILYN (MRS. IRVING SCHWARTZ), physician; b. N.Y.C., May 2, 1935; d. Max Irwin and Pearl (Lefenfeld) Weiss; B.S. magna cum laude, Queens Coll., 1956; M.D., Albert Einstein Coll. Medicine, 1960; m. Irving Schwartz, May 15, 1960; children—Michael, David, Melody, Andree, Joyce, Barbara, Marion. Intern pediatrics N.Y. U. Med. Center, Bellevue Hosp., N.Y.C., 1960-61; asst. in Internal medicine, Livingston, N.J., 1968-71; resident psychiatry N.Y. Med. Coll., Met. Hosp. Center, N.Y.C., 1972—. Mem. Townwide Com. on Drugs, Livingston, 1971-72; mem. Bd. Edn. Revision Com., Drug Abuse Curriculum, 1971; mem. nursery and grade sch. com. YM-YWHA of Essex County, 1966-72. Leopold Schepp Found. scholar, 1956-60, Endl. Found. for Jewish Girls scholar, 1956-60. Mem. N.J. Med. Women's Assn. (corr. sec. 1971), A.M.A., Am. Med. Women's Assn., Essex County Med. Soc., Am. Assn. U. Women, Nat. Council Jewish Women, Phi Beta Kappa. Democrat. Mem. Jewish religion (adult edn. com. temple 1971-72). Mem. B'nai B'rith. Contbr. articles to profl. jours. Office: 131 E Mount Pleasant Av Livingston NJ 07039

WEISZ, MARTHA, psychologist; b. Budapest, Hungary, Nov. 4, 1913; d. Jeno M. and Irene (Silberman) Stamberger; came to U.S., 1940; B.A., Rutgers U., 1956, M.Ed., 1959; m. Hugo Weisz, Oct. 11, 1936. With Weisz's Fabrics, New Brunswick, N.J., 1945-58; sch. psychologist New Brunswick Bd. Edn., 1958—. Cons., Endl. Services for Sch. Age Parents. Mem. Nat., N.J. edn. assns., Am., N.J. psychol. assns., N.J., Middlesex County (pres. 1962-63) sch. psychologists assns., N.J. Assn. for Learning Disabled Children. Home: 311 Donaldson St Highland Park NJ 08904 Office: 66 Bartlett St New Brunswick NJ 08901

WEKSLER, BABETTE BARBASH (MRS. MARC E. WEKSLER), physician; b. N.Y.C., Jan. 18, 1937; d. Philip and Roslyn (Weichsel) Barbash; B.A., Swarthmore, 1958; M.D., Columbia, 1963; m. Marc E. Weksler, 1958; children—David, Jennifer. Intern, Bronx Municipal Hosp. Center, N.Y.C., 1963-64; resident internal medicine Georgetown U. Hosp., Washington, 1965-67; fellow St. Mary's Hosp. Med. Sch., London, Eng., 1967-68; asst. prof. medicine Cornell U. Med. Coll., N.Y.C., 1970—; mem. staff N.Y. Hosp., N.Y.C. Am. Cancer Soc. clin. fellow, 1968-69, NIH spl. fellow, 1970-72. Diplomate Am. Bd. Internal Medicine, subsplty. bd. hematology. Mem. Am. Soc. Hematology, Am. Fedn. Clin. Research, Phi Beta Kappa, Alpha Omega Alpha. Home: 1 Sussex Rd Tenafly NJ 07670 Office: Cornell U Med Coll 1300 York Av New York City NY 10021

WELBORN, JUNE RHOADS, banker; b. Jonesboro, Ark., Mar. 24, 1925; d. Edward Curtis and Verda (Rhoads) Welborn; student Union U. (Jackson, Tenn.), 1943-46. With The Planters Bank, Osceola, Ark., 1946—, asst. cashier, 1952, asst. v.p., 1966-72, v.p., cashier, 1972-74, v.p., 1974—. Treas. Osceola Goodfellows, 1964—; mem. adv. com. City Osceola, 1968—, chmn., 1973—. Mem. Ark. Jr. Bankers Assn. (sec. 1970), Chi Omega. Republican. Baptist. Club: Riverlawn Country (Osceola). Home: 807 W Semmes St Osceola AR 72370 Office: PO Box 407 Osceola AR 72370

WELCH, DALE THOMPSON (MRS. SAMUEL HENRY WELCH), librarian; b. York, Ala., Jan. 3, 1925; d. Bryant Jarman and Ethel Dale (Brandon) Thompson; student Belhaven Coll., 1942-44; B.A., U. Ala., 1946, M.A., 1968; m. Samuel Henry Welch, June 21, 1947; children—Samuel Henry, Elizabeth Dale. Instr., Campbellsville (Ky.) Coll., 1947-48; asst. librarian West Ga. Coll., Carrollton, 1948-50; librarian, Cove Elementary Sch., 1956-58; librarian Monroe County High Sch., 1959-67; head librarian Patrick Henry State Jr. Coll., Monroeville, Ala., 1967—. Mem. N.E.A., Ala. Edn. Assn., Ala.

Library Assn., Ala. Jr. Coll. Library Assn., Twentieth Century Study Club (pres. 1964-65 73-74). Baptist. Home: 511 Fore Av Monroeville AL 36460

WELCH, MARGARET WADE (MRS. JAMES A. WELCH), real estate exec.; b. Bronxville, N.Y., June 19, 1926; d. Stuart Adolph and Genevieve Elizabeth (Meehan) Wade; B.A., Trinity Coll., 1948; m. James Arthur Welch, Aug. 27, 1949; 1 dau., Elizabeth Margaret. Vice pres. Baer & Welch, Properties, Inc., Canton, Conn., 1967—. Mem. Conn. Sec. State's Steering Com. on Voting Rights, 1971-73; mem. Conn. Citizens Com. for Revenue Sharing, 1971—; pres. Friends Conn. Pub. TV, 1974—. Bd. dirs. League Women Voters, Simsbury, Conn., 1959-63, pres., 1961-63; bd. dirs. League Women Voters Conn., 1964-73, pres., 1971-73; trustee Conn. Pub. Expenditure Council, 1971-72, 72-73, Mary Morrison Internship Conn. Coll., 1971—; bd. dirs. Conn. Citizens for Jud. Modernization, 1971—. Mem. Simsbury Hist. Soc., Newington Children's Hosp. Aux. Roman Catholic (mem. Rosary Guild 1955—). Club: Simsbury Garden. Home: 791 Prospect Av Apt A3 West Hartford CT 06105

WELCH, MARY LOUISE (MRS. RALPH E. WELCH), motel adminstr.; b. Wellsville, O., Apr. 18, 1919; d. Luther and Louise (Marsden) Zearley; certificate Ohio Valley Bus. Coll., 1939; m. Ralph E. Welch, May 3, 1938; children—Mary (Mrs. James D. Elliott), Bonnie (Mrs. Charles A. Deshler), William D. Ct. stenographer, Lisbon, O., 1938-42; legal sec. to atty., Wellsville, 1942-44; insp. Crucible Steel Co., Midland, Pa., 1945-46; tool designer, tool maker Sterling China Co., East Liverpool, O., 1948-70; tax cons., East Liverpool, 1950-70; motel mgr. 12 Oaks Motel, Nashville, 1970—. City chmn. Heart Fund, Wellsville, 1960-70. Mem. Am., Tenn., Nashville hotel and motel assns., Nashville Area C. of C. Republican. Presbyn. Address: 656 W Iris Dr Nashville TN 37204

WELCH, MARY SCOTT STEWART (MRS. BARRETT FARLEY WELCH), writer; b. Chgo.; d. William Scott and Myrtle (Ferrin) Stewart; A.B., U. Ill., 1940; m. Barrett Farley Welch, Mar. 23, 1943; children—Farley, Laura, Margaret, Mary Barrett. Editor, Homemaker's Digest, 1968; columnist Seventeen mag., 1963-64; former food editor Glamour mag., entertainment editor Look mag., asso. editor Pageant mag.; past West Coast editor Esquire and Coronet mag.; free lance writer articles for women various nat. mags. including Glamour, Redbook, Woman's Day, Ladies Home Jour., McCalls, 1952—; columnist Vogue mag., 1972. Served as ensign WAVES, 1942-43. Mem. Soc. Mag. Writers, Child Study Assn., Am., N.Y. civil liberties unions, Wilderness Soc., Nat. Orgn. Women (coordinator rape prevention com.), Sierra Club, Phi Beta Kappa, Kappa Kappa Gamma. Author: Your First Hundred Meals; Handbook for Hosts; Esquire Etiquette; Esquire Cookbook; Art of Keeping Fit; What Every Young Man Should Know; Esquire Party Book; Seventeen Guide to Travel; The Family Wilderness Handbook. Address: South Rd Oyster Bay Cove NY 11771 also 55 Park Av New York City NY 10016

WELCH, NANCY LEE TURNER (MRS. CHARLES HILL WELCH), interior designer, TV show hostess; b. Nashville, July 25, 1941; d. Fred Phillips and Alice (Archambeau) Turner; B.S., Fla. State U., 1963; m. Charles Hill Welch, Sept. 7, 1963; children—Charles Turner, Nelson Hill. Tchr. home econs. Winthrop Coll. Tng. Sch., Rock Hill, S.C., 1963-65; interior designer Earl Jackson Carpet & Furniture Co., Rock Hill, 1965-66; writer newspaper article Furniture Tips by Nancy, 1965-66; hostess daily television program for women WBTV-TV, Florence, S.C., 1965-66; tchr. interior design Spartanburg Tech. Ednl. Center, 1967-69; lectr.-demonstrator Am. Textile Mfg. Inst., 1967-70; owner Nancy Welch Interiors, Inc., Spartanburg, S.C., 1967—; hostess Nancy Welch Show, WSPA-TV, 1967—. Recipient LuLu award for outstanding coverage of Men's Fashions for 1972. Mem. Am. Women in Radio and Television, Fla. State U. Alumni Assn., Zeta Tau Alpha. Presbyn. Author: The Nancy Welch Cookbook, 1967; The New Nancy Welch Cookbook, 1973. Home: 101 Summit Dr Greer SC 29651 Office: 123 N Converse St Spartanburg SC 29301

WELCOME, VERDA FREEMAN, state senator; b. Lake Lure, N.C.; d. John Nuborn and Docia (Proctor) Freeman; diploma Coppin State Coll., 1932; B.S., Morgan State Coll., 1939; M.A., N.Y. U., 1943; postgrad. Columbia, 1943-44; m. Henry C. Welcome, Dec. 21, 1935; 1 dau., Mary Sue. Tchr. pub. schs., Balt., 1934-45; mem. Md. Ho. Dels., 1959-62; mem. Md. Senate, 1963—, mem. finance com., vice chmn. corrections com.; mem. bd. Advance Fed. Savs. & Loan Assn., Balt., 1963—. Mem. Md. Commn. on Status of Women. Bd. dirs. Provident Hosp. Recipient World's Fair Citizenship award, Medgar Evers award, Capital Press Club award, 1966. Mem. League Women Voters, Internat. League for Peace and Freedom, Md. Hist. Soc., Nat. Order Women Legislators, N.A.A.C.P. (life), Nat. Council Negro Women (life), Delta Sigma Theta. Home: 2101 Liberty Heights Av Baltimore MD 21217 Office: State House Anapolis MD 21401

WELDY, NORMA JEAN, educator; b. Bremen, Ind., Aug. 26, 1929; d. Eldon J. and Lucile (Martin) Weldy; diploma LaJunta Mennonite Sch. Nursing, 1954; B.S., Goshen Coll., 1954; M.S., U. Colo., 1962. Staff nurse La Junta Mennonite Hosp., 1954, NIH, Bethesda, Md., 1956-57; instr. nursing LaJunta Mennonite Sch. Nursing, 1954-56; staff nurse Elkhart (Ind.) Gen. Hosp., 1957-58, charge nurse, 1958, head nurse, 1958-60; asst. prof. nursing Goshen (Ind.) Coll., 1960-73, asso. prof., 1973—. Nurse in spl. units Cedars-Sinai Med. Center, Los Angeles, 1971-72. Bd. dirs. Am. Cancer Soc., Elkhart, Ind. Mem. Nat. League Nursing, Am. Nurses' Assn. (dist. pres. 1960-61). Mennonite. Author: Body Fluids and Electrolytes: A Programmed Presentation, 1972. Home: 1601 S 8th St Goshen IN 46526

WELGOSS, BETTY (MRS. PETER L. WELGOSS), retail store exec.; b. Wilmore, Pa., Dec. 18, 1919; d. Wasyl and Tanka (Pasko) Durvetsky; student pub. schs.; m. Peter L. Welgoss, Oct. 4, 1941; children—Thomas Peter, Mary Ann, Barbara Jean. Treas., buyer, pres., owner Welgoss Tot Shop, Auburn, N.Y., 1949—; owner, operator Hislop's Toy and Baby Funiture, Auburn, 1951-57. Charter mem. Ann. Inst. Community Leaders sponsored by N.Y. State Coll. Home Econs., Cornell U., Ithaca, N.Y. Mem. East High Sch. P.T.A., Cayuga County Extension Service Assn. (4-H Club dept.), Zonta Internat.(pres. Auburn club 1961-62), Internat. Platform Assn., Acad. Polit. Sci. Contbr. articles to trade publ. Home: 15 Water St Auburn NY 13021

WELKE, JUDITH LYNN MCCLENAHEN (MRS. ROBERT JOSEPH WELKE), camp exec.; b. Wyandotte, Mich., Aug. 11, 1936; d. Lee Stuart and Ruth (Lerew) McClenahen; student U. Mich., 1954-55, Adrian Coll., 1960-61; B.A. (Weber Fisher scholar), Siena Heights Coll., 1973; m. Robert Joseph Welke, Dec. 28, 1954; children—David, Kimberly, Roberta. Co-owner, dir. Camp Sequoia, Adrian, Mich., 1955—, Sequoia Campground, 1970—. Instr. first aid, water safety A.R.C., Adrian, 1972—. Recipient Regents Alumni Honor award U. Mich., 1954-55. Mem. Am. Camping Assn. Episcopalian. Home: 365 Helme St Adrian MI 49221 Office: 2675 Gady Rd Adrian MI 49221

WELKER, DENISE GIBSON (MRS. RONALD EDWARD WELKER), editor; b. Huntington, W. Va., Aug. 12, 1950; d. Charles Dennis and Rachel Hope (Qualls) Gibson; A.B. magna cum laude, Marshall U., 1972, postgrad., 1973—; m. Ronald Edward Welker, Sept. 1, 1972. Staff reporter Huntington Herald-Dispatch, 1972-73; asso. editor Inco News, Huntington Alloy Products div. Internat. Nickel Co., Huntington, 1972—. Mem. Women in Communications, Sigma Delta Chi. Republican. Home: 1568 Main St Barboursville WV 25504 Office: Huntington Alloy Products Division Huntington WV 25720

WELKER, DORIS MAY, catalog librarian; b. Cleve., Feb. 22, 1919; d. Charles Eugene and Myrtle May (Robbins) Welker; B.A., Youngstown State U., 1942, B.Mus., 1943; M.A., U. Denver, 1961. Tchr. music pub. schs., E. Palestine and Youngstown, O., 1943-59; librarian jr. high sch., Youngstown, 1959-63; catalog librarian Kent State U., 1963-66, Shaker Heights (O.) Sch. Dist., 1966—. Mem. N.E.A., Am. (mem. com. cataloging children's materials 1972-74), Ohio (library devel. plan com. 1972—), (exec. com. div. V 1973) library assns., Ohio Assn. Sch. Librarians, No. Ohio Tech. Services Librarians (sec. 1973-74), Delta Kappa Gamma (scholarship 1960), Sigma Alpha Iota. Home: 15500 Van Aken Blvd Shaker Heights OH 44120 Office: 15600 Parkland Av Shaker Heights OH 44120

WELKOWITZ, JOAN, psychologist, educator; b. N.Y.C., Apr. 17, 1929; d. Abraham J. and Ray B. (Young) Horowitz; B.A., Queens Coll., 1949; M.A., U. Ill., 1953; Ph.D., Columbia, 1959; m. Walter Welkowitz, June 17, 1951; children—David, Larry, Julie. With dept. child psychiatry Mt. Sinai Hosp., N.Y.C., 1959-61; prof. psychology N.Y. U., 1963—. Mem. Am. Psychol. Assn., Soc. Psychotherapy Research, Harry Stack Sullivan Soc. Author: Introductory Statistics for the Behavioral Sciences, 1970. Home: 138 Highland Av Metuchen NJ 08840 Office: NY U Dept Psychology 4 Washington Pl New York City NY 10003

WELLEMEYER, JANE ELIZABETH (MRS. FRANK ROSS DELUCA), pediatrician; b. Modesto, Cal., Dec. 12, 1925; d. Ernst Edward and Myrtle (Schultz) Wellemeyer; A.B., U. Cal. at Berkeley, 1946; M.D., U. Cal. at San Francisco, 1950; m. Frank Ross Deluca, July 11, 1953; children—Alex Frank, Edward Ernst. Intern, Harlem Hosp., N.Y.C., 1950-51; pediatric intern Bellevue Hosp., N.Y.C., 1951-52; resident N.Y. Hosp., N.Y.C., 1952-53; practice medicine, specializing in pediatrics, Bronx, N.Y. 1953—; pediatrician Montefiore Med. Group, 1953—; adj. attending pediatrician Montefiore Hosp.; asst. clin. prof. Albert Einstein Sch. Medicine, 1968—; dir. Pre-sch. Health Screening Project South-East Bronx, 1972—. Diplomate Am. Bd. Pediatrics. Presbyn. (elder). Home: 4619 Douglas Av Bronx NY 10471 Office: 3455 Steuben Av Bronx NY 10467

WELLER, MARGARET PIERCE (MRS. JAMES J. WELLER), social worker; b. Lewiston, Me., Feb. 12, 1931; d. Greely C. and Alice (Mayo) Pierce; B.A., Colby Coll., 1952; M.S.W., U. Pa., 1958; m. James J. Weller, Oct. 19, 1956; children—James J. Jr., Mary Alice. Sec. to chr. pub. relations dept. Assn. Better Bus. Burs. N.Y.C., 1952; asst. dir. pub. relations dept. Welcome Wagon Inc., N.Y.C., 1953; caseworker Dept. Pub. Welfare, Dover, Del., 1954-57; sr. caseworker Caroline County Welfare Dept., Denton, Md., 1958-60; chief Cath. Social Services, Dover, 1959—; mem. faculty U. Del., extension dept. 1969—. Mem. Kent County Community Action Bd. Advisers, 1966-71, Del. Rural Housing Com., 1969-71, adv. com. Mental Hygiene Commr. Del., 1968—, Kent County Day Care Adv. Com., 1967-70; mem. Kent County Health Services Adv. Com.; mem. Del. Adv. Council on Alcoholism, 1972—; co-chmn. Kent County Inter Agy. Council, 1971—; chmn. Kent County Community Conf. for White House Conf. on Aging, 1971; mem. adv. bd. com. Big Brothers, 1970—. Mem. Nat. Assn. Social Workers, Acad. Certified Social Workers, Phi Beta Kappa. Roman Catholic (mem. parish council 1968-70). Clubs: Milford Duplicate Bridge, Milford Square Dance. Home: 905 S Dupont Blvd Milford DE 19963 Office: 42 Kings Highway East Dover DE 19901

WELLINGTON, FLORA HERMAN, librarian; b. St. Louis, Apr. 13, 1920; d. George Grover and Grace Douglas (Everett) Herman; B.S., Coll. William and Mary, 1941; B.S. in L.S., U. N.C., 1950; m. Charles William Wellington, Jan. 2, 1960 (div. Feb. 1963); 1 dau., Sandra Ann. Librarian Naval Med. Center, Guam, 1947-49; intern Tulane U. Sch. Medicine Library, New Orleans, 1950-51; cataloger U. Tenn. Coll. Medicine Library, Memphis, 1951-53; librarian Fla. State Bd. Health, Jacksonville, 1954-55; librarian periodicals and asst. prof. U. Miami (Fla.) Sch. Medicine Library, 1956-61, acting librarian and asst. prof., 1961-63, asso. librarian, 1963—, asso. prof., 1970—. Tchr., Norfolk (Va.) Pub. Schs., 1941-42; cons. St. Vincents Hosp. Med. Library, Jacksonville, 1955. Mem. Dade County (pres. 1961-62), Med. (chmn. subcom. internship 1956-57, sec.-treas. So. regional group 1964-65), Fla. Library assns., Spl. Libraries Assn. Republican. Methodist. Home: 3120 S W 27th St Miami FL 33133 Office: University of Miami Medical Library PO Box 520875 Biscayne Annex Miami FL 33152

WELLINGTON, JEAN WILLETT (MRS. C. BURLEIGH WELLINGTON), educator; b. Lynn, Mass.; d. Harold P. and Jeanette (Shrum) Willett; student Ind. U., 1939-40, Simmons Coll., 1940-41; A.B., Boston U., 1945; M.A., Tufts U., 1947; Ed. D., Columbia, 1951; m. C. Burleigh Wellington, May 1, 1943; children—Leigh, Beth. Tchr., guidance So. Sem. Jr. Coll., Buena Vista, Va. 1947-49; counselor U. N.H., Durham, 1951-52; asso. prof. in charge counselor edn. Tufts U., Medford, Mass., 1952—; Eastern Middlesex Guidance Center, Melrose, Mass., 1966—. Cons. pub. schs., North Reading, Mass. Mem. Am., Mass. psychol. assns., Am. Personnel and Guidance Assn. Author: (with C.B. Wellington) Teaching for Critical Thinking, 1960; (with C.B. Wellington) Help Your Child Prepare for College, 1962; (with C.B. Wellington) The Under-achiever, Challenges & Guidelines, 1965. Home: 50 Gleason Rd Reading MA 01867 Office: Lincoln Filene Center Tufts U Medford MA 02155

WELLINGTON, MARIE ADELE ZEILSTRA (MRS. JOHN ADAM WELLINGTON), educator; b. Chicago Heights, Ill., Aug. 11, 1924; d. Gerald and Marie Antoinette (Michaud) Zeilstra; A.B., St. Mary-of-the-Woods Coll., 1946; M.A., Northwestern U., 1949; Ph.D., 1951; m. John Adam Wellington, June 19, 1948; 1 dau., Marie Annette. Instr. Spanish, U. Ill., Chgo., 1946-47; instr. Mundelein Coll., Chgo., 1948-49; asst. prof. Elmhurst (Ill.) Coll., 1954-57, asso. prof., 1958-61, prof., chmn. dept. Spanish and Italian, 1962—, dir. Lang. Lab., 1962-64. Univ. fellow Northwestern U., 1949-51; Fulbright grantee to Italy, 1951; Alumni Study grantee for Italy, Elmhurst Coll., summer 1963. Mem. Modern Lang. Assn. Am. (conf. sec. 1970—, editor conf. papers 1969—, chmn. sect. 1971), Midwest Modern Lang. Assn., Am. Assn. Tchrs. Spanish and Portuguese, Am. Assn. Tchr. Italian, Paul Claudel Soc. Am., Renaissance Soc. Am., Ill. Modern Lang. Tchrs. Assn., Phi Sigma Iota (past pres.). Contbr. articles to tech. jours. Home: 130 Cottage Hill Av Elmhurst IL 60126

WELLMAN, MARY MCDONALD, broadcasting exec.; b. Mpls., Nov. 20, 1930; d. Stanley Lawrence and Mary (Reau) McDonald; B.A., Marquette U., 1952; m. Arthur David Wellman, Oct. 7, 1950; children—Kathleen, Thomas, Michael, Joseph, Mary. Asst. promotion dir. WWL-TV, New Orleans, 1966-70, promotion and pub. affairs dir. WWL AM-FM-TV, 1970—. Mem. Delta Zeta. Home: 6367 Canal Blvd New Orleans LA 70124 Office: 1024 N Rampart St New Orleans LA 70116

WELLS, BARBARA JANE, coll. dean; b. Cleve., Aug. 2, 1918; d. Guy McNeill and Berlynn (Kramer) Wells; B.A., Oberlin Coll., 1940; M.A., N.Y. U., 1957, Ph.D., 1963. Sec. coll. council Douglass Coll., Rutgers U., 1956-60; asst. prof. govt. Skidmore Coll., 1960-64; asso. prof. govt. Mills Coll., 1964-68; dean Thomas More Coll., Fordham U., 1968-72; dean faculty Vassar Coll., 1972—; mem. N.Y. State-Middle Eastern seminar Columbia, summer 1963; instr. Peace Corps, Dartmouth, summers 1964, 65. Bd. dirs. UN Assn. Alameda County, Cal., 1966-67, St. Francis Hosp., 1973—, Culinary Inst. Am., 1973—. Recipient Founders Day award N.Y. U., 1964. Mem. Am. Civil Liberties Union, Am. Polit. Sci. Assn., Am. Assn. U. Profs., Internat. Studies Assn. Address: Vassar College Poughkeepsie NY 12601

WELLS, BETTY CHILDS (MRS. GEORGE E. WELLS, JR.), artist; b. Balt., Dec. 7, 1926; d. William Melville and Elizabeth (Norris) Childs; diploma Fine Arts (Merit scholar), Md. Inst. Art, 1948, postgrad. (fine arts scholar), 1948-49; m. George E. Wells, Jr., June 14, 1947; children—George E., William H., John B. Illustrator various publs., 1944-59; exhibited one-woman shows including Internat. Gallery, Balt., 1965, Hartford Jr. Coll., 1973, Balt. Mus. Art Downtown, 1974; exhibited in group shows N.Y. Soc. Illustrators, 1948, Audubon Artists Ann., N.Y.C., 1965, Balt. Mus. Art, 1964, 67, Easton Acad. Arts, 1966, Peale Mus., 1959, 62-64; included in permanent collection New Zealand Nat. Art gallery, Peale Mus., Md. Instr. Md. Inst. Art, 1946-48; art cons.; courtroom illustrator for WBAL-TV, Washington Post, WTOP-TV, 1970-73; sketch artist NBC-TV, 1973—; executed murals for several pub; schs., recreation center, Balt., 1972-74. Mem. steering com. Shaefer for Mayor Balt., 1971, chmn. Mayor Schaefer's Inauguration Ceremonies, 1971. Bd. dirs. Mayor's Adv. Com. on Art and Culture, 1974. Recipient prizes including Best in show award Easton Acad. Arts, 1966. Grand prize Balt. Outdoor Art Festival, 1967; Md. Arts Council Traveling Exhbn., 1968-69. Mem. Artists Equity Assn. (chpt. pres. 1966-68). Home: 727 Nottingham Rd Baltimore MD 21229

WELLS, CAROLYN DIXON (MRS. PHILLIP EDWIN WELLS), educator; b. Dallas, Aug. 6, 1929; d. Roy Eliot and Eva Earl (Young) Dixon; B.S. in Psychology, Howard U., 1949, M.S., 1951; Ph.D., U. Tex. at Austin, 1971; m. Phillip Edwin Wells, Dec. 28, 1953. Clk., U.S. Govt., Washington, 1949-52; instr. Tex. So. U., Houston, 1952-71, asso. prof. psychology, 1971—; pvt. practice as psychologist, Houston, 1953—. Cons. Houston Ind. Sch. Dist., 1966. Active YWCA, United Negro Coll. Fund, March of Dimes. NSF Fellow, 1965; Ford Found. fellow, 1968-69. Mem. Am., S.W., Houston psychol. assns., Alpha Kappa Alpha. Democrat. Epsicopalian. Contbr. articles to profl. jours. Home: 3726 Eagle St Houston TX 77004

WELLS, CLAUDIA LOUISE CLARKE (MRS. JOHN KENDRICK WELLS III), artist, educator; b. Columbia, S.C., Apr. 5, 1943; d. Albert Bond and Claudia Nancy (McCain) Clarke; B.A., Furman U., 1965; M.F.A., Ohio U., 1967; m. John Kendrick Wells, III, Apr. 22, 1972. One-woman shows at Ky. So. Coll., Louisville, 1968, WHAS Gallery, Louisville, 1969; exhibited in group shows Ohio U., Athens, 1967, Nazareth Coll., Bardstown, Ky., 1968, U. Louisville, 1968, Furman U., Greenville, S.C., 1972, J.B. Speed Mus., Louisville, 1972. Instr. Ky. So. Coll., 1967-69, Louisville Sch. Art, 1970; asst. dir. Jr. Art Gallery, Inc., Louisville, 1969—. Co-chmn. Crafts Biennial, Louisville, 1971. Democratic precinct committeewoman, 1968. Mem. Art Center Assn. (dir. 1970-71), Coll. Art Assn., Phi Sigma Iota, Kappa Delta Epsilon. Baptist. Club: Arts (dir. 1971). Illustrator: A Seed Planted in the Hills (Claud N. McCain), 1973. Home: 7004 Springdale Rd Louisville KY 40222 Office: 301 West York St Louisville KY 40203

WELLS, DOROTHY VIOLA, librarian; b. Boulder, Colo., Feb. 6, 1916; d. Harold Merton and Laura Belle (McCardie) Wells; A.B., U. Wyo., 1938; B.S. in L.S., U. Ill., 1939. Asst. librarian (documents), Fort Hays (Kan.) State Coll., 1939-42; librarian Bur. Govtl. Research Library, U. Cal. at Los Angeles 1942-52, librarian bur. govtl. research John Randolph Haynes & Dora Haynes Found. collection. librarian Inst. Govt. Pub. Affairs Reading Room, 1962-70, asst. dept. head for tech. processes, local documents librarian Pub. Affairs Service, 1971—. Mem. Spl. Libraries Assn., Council Planning Librarians, Internat. City Mgmt. Assn., Western Govtl. Research Assn., Pi Gamma Mu. Office: Public Affairs Service URLU Cal at Los Angeles 405 Hilgard Av Los Angeles CA 90024

WELLS, ELSIE MARGARET KELLER (MRS. HOWARD G. WELLS), realtor; b. Cleve., Mar. 10, 1907; d. William E. and Amelia (Lauter) Keller; student Cleve. Inst. Music, 1941-43; Western Res. U., 1943-60; m. Howard G. Wells, Mar. 18, 1927; children—Evelyn L. (Mrs. Robert L. Rogge), Mildred E. (Mrs. Harold R. Belton), Howard G. and Richard G. (twins). Pvt. tchr. piano, 1930-40; sales lady, 1936-40; in real estate, 1953—, with Paragon Realty, Inc., 1953, 57, Kilburn-Lindsay, 1954; with Cy Burns Realty, Inc., Cleve. and Lakewood, O., 1959-64; owner Elsie Wells Realty, Lakewood, 1964—. Asst. leader Girl Scouts U.S.A., Cleve., 1930-40; mem. com. P.T.A., Cleve., 1934-62; sec. West Cleve. Round Table, 1960-61, 1966, 67-68. Mem. Nat. Assn. Real Estate Bds. (Nat. Inst., Internat. Traders Club, sec. women's council on nat., Ohio and Cleve. level), Cleve. Real Estate Bd., Nat. Brokers Council, Am. Inst. Parliamentarians, Nat. Assn. Parliamentarians. Club: Cleveland Real Estate Traders (sec. 1954-64, 66, v.p. 1968). Address: 1335 Warren Rd Lakewood OH 44107

WELLS, FAY GILLIS (MRS. LINTON WELLS), writer, broadcaster; b. Mpls., Oct. 15, 1908; d. Julius Howells and Minne (Shafer) Gillis; student Mich. State Coll., 1925-28; m. Linton Wells, Apr. 1, 1935; 1 son, Linton II. Saleswoman-pilot Curtiss Flying Service, N.Y.C., 1929-30; free-lance reporter, Russia and Far East, 1930-34, N.Y. Herald Tribune, Ethiopia, 1935-36; free-lance writing and broadcasting, Europe, Africa, Latin Am., 1936-42; dept. chief U.S. Govt. Mission, Portuguese W. Africa, 1942-46; interior design asso., N.Y.C., 1958-61; syndicated boating columnist N.Y. Herald Tribune Syndicate, 1960-62; White House corr. Storer Broadcasting Co., Washington, 1964—. Recipient CBS Charlotte Fried Meml. award, 1972. Mem. Am. Women in Radio and Television, Nat. League Am. Penwomen, Aviation/Space Writers Assn., Radio and Television Corrs. Assn., Am. Newspaper Women's Club, 99s Inc. (charter). White House Corrs. Assn. Clubs: Washington Press, Overseas Press Club (founder), Caterpillar, Ox-5. Home: 2601 Woodley Pl NW Washington DC 20008 Office: 1725 K St NW Washington DC 20006

WELLS, HARRIET, physician; b. Fairlawn, N.J., Mar. 7, 1933; d. Byron Garrett and Katherine (Raynes) Van Horne; student Columbia, 1959, Pratt Inst., 1951-55; M.D., Boston U., 1963; m. Allan Wells, June 23, 1957; children—Natalie, Wendy. Intern, Jefferson Med. Coll. Hosp., Phila., 1964-65, resident psychiatry, 1966-69; practice medicine, specializing in psychiatry Inst. Pa. Hosp., Phila., 1969—. Mem. Am. Soc. Adolescent Psychiatry, Phila. Soc. Adolescent Psychiatry (sec.-treas. 1971—), Am. Psychiat. Soc. Home: 1001 City

Line Av Philadelphia PA 19151 Office: 111 N 49th St Philadelphia PA 19139

WELLS, HELEN, author; b. Danville, Ill., Mar. 29, 1910; d. Henry and Henrietta (Basch) Weinstock; student Art Students League, Columbia U. Extension, 1926-28; B.S., N.Y. U., 1934; diploma Programming and Systems Inst., N.Y.C., 1969. Columnist, The Third Degree. Bd. dirs. Mystery Writers Am., 1970—, nat. sec., 1972-74. Author: (childrens books) Cherry Ames series, 1943—, Vicki Barr series, 1947—; The Girl in the White Coat, 1953; A Flair for People, 1955; Polly French of Whitford High, 1955, Polly French Takes Charge, 1955; Polly French and the Suprising Stranger, 1956; Introducing Patti Lewis, 1956; A City for Jean, 1956; Escape by Night, 1953; Adam Gimbel, Pioneer Trader, 1955; Barnum, Showman of America, 1957; Mystery in The Doctor's Office, 1967; Ski Nurse Mystery, 1968; Doctor Betty, 1969; also writer mag. short stories, radio Mem. Authors Guild, Mystery Writers of Am. (sec. 1970-74). Home: 345 E 57th St New York City NY 10022

WELLS, HELEN LAVERNE, educator; b. Springdale, Ark., Mar. 9, 1923; d. Norman Melville and Lillie (Riley) Wells; B.S., U. Ark., 1943, M.S., 1952, B.A., 1961; Ph.D., Cornell U., 1958. Food insp. U.S. Dept. Agr., 1943-45; with Agrl. Extension Service, U. Ark., 1945-52; resident staff U. Ark., 1952-55; research asst. Cornell U., 1956-58; asso. prof., resident staff U. Nev., 1958-63; asso. prof. Ore. State U., 1963-66; cons. Ford Found. and Ia. State U. joint project U. Baroda (India), 1966-68; asso. prof. housing and mgmt. Ia. State U., Ames, 1968-73; housing specialist, extension div. Va. Poly. Inst. and State U., Blacksburg, 1973—. Mem. Am. Assn. U. Women (pres. Reno br. 1961-62, 65-66, auditor Ames br. 1970-71), Internat. Assn. Housing Sci., Am. Home Econs. Assn., Pi Lambda Theta, Gamma Sigma Delta, Omicron Nu, Epsilon Sigma Phi. Home: 423 Ridgeview Dr SE Blacksburg VA 24060

WELLS, JOAN ALTHEA CLARK, state ofcl.; b. Drexel Hill, Pa.; d. Russell S. and Althea (Ottenbacher) Clark; B.A., Vassar Coll., 1951; m. H. Eugene Wells, June 11, 1951 (div. Sept. 1966); children—B. Christine, Robert E., Joan Marie, Russell E. Applied sci. programmer Dept. Pub. Works, State of Cal., Sacramento, 1960-64, supr. applied sci. programming, 1964-66, data processing mgr. I, 1966-71; sr. data processing systems analyst Cal. Dept. Finance, 1971—. Mem. faculty Am. River Coll., Sacramento, 1969—. Mem. Sacramento Statis. Assn. (councillor, treas.). Home: 1217 Mariemont Av Sacramento CA 95825 Office: 1025 P St Sacramento CA 95808

WELLS, LIDA WILSON (MRS. J. WILLIAM WELLS), real estate agt.; b. Pocomoke City, Md., Sept. 8, 1923; d. William Coulbourne and Emma (Stephens) Wilson; student Salisbury State Coll., 1941-42; A.A., U. Del., postgrad., 1973—; m. J. William Wells, June 20, 1946; 1 son, Joseph William. Sec., Masten Trucking Co., Milford, Del., 1940-48; bookkeeper J. William Wells Real Estate & Ins. Co., Milford, 1948—, salesman, 1973—. Chmn., Milford Meml. Hosp. Gift Shop, 1964-66; librarian Wright Meml. Library, Milford, 1966—; chmn. Holzmueller Gallery, Milford, 1968—; sec. Mispillion Asso., Milford, 1972—. Bd. dirs. Grand Opera Steering Com., Wilmington, Del., 1971-72. Mem. Sussex County Arts Council (dir., pres. 1969-70), Kent County Bd. Realtors, Women's Council Realtors. Methodist. Home: 311 Hall Pl Milford DE 19963 Office: 10 NW Front St Milford DE 19963

WELLS, LORRAINE ROSEMARY SIPLON (MRS. WARREN F. WELLS), educator, writer; b. Charles City, Ia., Dec. 12, 1930; d. Joseph J. and Emma (Wogsland) Siplon; B.A., U. No. Ia., 1951, M.A., 1953; postgrad. U. Ia., 1951, Chgo. Tchrs. Coll. N., 1963, Art Inst. Chgo., 1965; Ph.D., Northwestern U., 1973; m. Warren F. Wells, Nov. 23, 1950; children—Wendy Rose, Jeffrey Joe, Jerrold Patrick. Tchr., Clear Lake (Ia.) Consol. Schs., 1951-52; self employed, 1954-63; tchr. Roycemore Sch., Evanston, Ill., 1963-65; instr. humanities Kendall Coll., Evanston, 1965-69; writer Hallmark Edn. Systems, Chgo., 1969-70. Lectr. English, Northwestern U. Dental Sch., Chgo., 1967—; prin. 2d violin sect., bd. dirs., past personnel mgr. Evanston Symphony Orch., 1961—; organizer Savoy-Aires, opera co., 1964, bd. dirs., 1964—; first violinist YMCA Brillantine Show Group of Evanston, 1965-70; dir. children's choir Covenent Meth. Ch., Winnetka, Ill., 1968-73. Mem. Modern Lang. Assn., Ill. Assn. Tchrs. English, Nat. Council Tchrs. English Am. Assn. U. Profs., Conf. Coll. Composition and Communications, Internat. reading assns., Internat. Platform Assn., Tchrs. Linguistic Assn. (pres. 1963-64), Chgo. Art Inst., Nat. Soc. for Programmed Instrn., Coll. English Assn., N.E.A., Council for Exceptional Children, Div. for Children with Learning Disabilities, Sigma Alpha Iota, Methodist (choir mem., soloist). Author: English Writing Patterns, Books 11, 12, 1968; Food, Life, Colorful Meal Planning, The Exchange Pantry, 1970. Contbr. to profl. jours. Home: 1219 Scott St Winnetka IL 60093 Office: Northwestern U Chicago Campus 311 E Chicago Av Chicago IL 60611

WELLS, MARGARET STAGGERS (MRS. HAWEY A. WELLS, JR.), physician; b. Patuxent Naval Air Base, Jan. 12, 1945; d. Harley O. and Mary Veronica (Casey) Staggers; M.D., W. Va. U., 1969; m. Hawey A. Wells, Jr., June 8, 1960; 1 son, Hawey A. III. Intern, W. Va. U. Med. Center, 1969-70; dir. family planning So. W.Va. Regional Health Council Bluefield, 1970-71; dir. med. edn. Princeton (W.Va.) Community Hosp., 1971—, sec. med. staff, 1972—. Mem. A.M.A., Am. Acad. Family Physicians, Kappa Delta. Democrat. Home: Box 726 Athens WV 24712 Office: Route 1 Box 114 D Princeton WV 24710

WELLS, MARJORIE MARIE (MRS. MARK A. WELLS), publisher; b. Sayre, Okla., June 26, 1919; d. C. Lloyd and Anna Marie (Chapman) Clearman; grad. Sawyer Sch. Bus., 1939; m. Mark A. Wells, Sept. 21, 1940 (dec. Aug. 1970); children—Barbara May Mannell, William Mark, John Stuart. Owner, pub. Ins. Jour. Inc., Los Angeles, 1935—. Legal sec. Hindman & Davis, Los Angeles, 1939-40. Mem. Western Pubs. Assn. Mem. Order of Eastern Star. Clubs: Woodland Hills Country, Oakmont Country. Home: 858 N Poinsettia Pl Los Angeles CA 90036 Office: 3200 Wilshire Blvd 805 Los Angeles CA 90010

WELLS, PHYLLIS EVELYN, hosp. exec.; b. Oakshela, Sask., Can., Oct. 21, 1931; d. Reinhold and Sophie (Gerhardt) Frier; R.N., Regina Gen. Hosp., 1953; student U. Man., evenings 1966-67, U. Alta., 1967-70; m. William Wells, Oct. 3, 1959 (div. 1969); children—Aubrey, Chris. Tchr., Bradley Pub. Sch., Oakshela, Sask., Can., 1949-50, successively nurse, nursing arts instr., central supply head nurse Regina Gen. Hosp., 1953-57; supr. central supply room Winnipeg Gen. Hosp., 1957-59; charge nurse central supply room and emergency room Bethesda Hosp., Steinbach, Man., Can., 1964-67; dir. central supply dept. Edmonton (Alta.) Gen. Hosp., 1968—; cons. in field. Participant, coordinator Y-Neighbors, YWCA study group for young mothers, 1962-64, 67-68, summer camp nurse, 1968, 71-73. Trustee Hastings Lutheran Bible Camp, Alta., 1973-74. Mem. Alta. Assn. Hosp. Central Service (sec. 1971-74). Lutheran (edn. sec. ch. women 1973-74, Sunday sch. tchr. 1967-73). Author articles in field. Home: Sherwood Park AB Canada Office: 11111 Jasper Av Edmonton AB T5K 0L4 Canada

WELLS, SANDRA O'SHEA, journalist; b. Huntington, W.Va., Jan. 8, 1942; s. Harold Kenneth and Lois Eileen (Davis) O'Shea; B.S. cum laude, Marshall U., 1963; m. Daniel Bundy Wells, Aug. 21, 1965; children—Shannon O'Shea, Shea Davis. Fashion editor, reporter Charleston (W.Va.) Gazette, 1963—. Home: 1911 Huber Rd Charleston WV 25314 Office: 1001 Virginia St E Charleston WV 25330

WELLS, SHIRLEY FAY, banker; b. Norton, Va., Aug. 5, 1938; d. Ray E. and Delsie (Sturgill) Wells; grad. Nat. Trust. Sch., Northwestern U., 1968. With Wise County Nat. Bank, Norton, 1960—, asst. trust officer, 1964-72, trust officer, 1972—, also sec. to bd., 1964—. Mem. Nat. Assn. Bank Women, Inc. (past group chmn.), Bank Women's Club S.W. Va. (past pres.). Baptist. Home: Route 1 Box 1117 Norton VA 24273 Office: 702 Park Av Norton VA 24273

WELLS, SUSAN LOUISE GRUNWALD (MRS. RONALD BRUCE WELLS), land devel. co. exec.; b. Culver City, Cal., Feb. 1, 1947; d. Otto Antone and Genevieve Florence (Lindsay) G.; B.A. in Journalism (Hazel Flynn Meml. scholar), Pepperdine Coll., 1967; m. Ronald Bruce Wells, Sept. 13, 1969. Asst. pub. relations Hollywood Presbyn. Hosp., Los Angeles, 1967; editor So. Cal. Bus., Los Angeles, 1968-70; editorial cons. Len Hansen & Co., San Diego, 1971; dir. advt. and pub. relations Rancho Bernardo, San Diego, 1972—. Intern instr. San Diego State Sch. Journalism, 1973. Vol. media contact United Way, San Diego, 1973; mem. publicity com. San Diego Symphony Concert on Greens, 1972-73. Recipient All-Am. Award Internat. Coll. Press Assn., 1967. Named Outstanding Journalist Culver City Star News, 1964. Mem. Women in Communications (chpt. bd. dirs. 1972-73), San Diego Pub. Relations Club, San Diego Press Club, Children's Aux. Health Center, Theta Sigma Phi. Republican. Book reviewer Copley News Service, 1972—. Home: 15115 Calle Juanito San Diego CA 92129 Office: 17090 Bernardo Center Dr San Diego CA 92128

WELS, MARGUERITE SAMET (MRS. RICHARD H. WELS), interior decorator; b. N.Y.C.; d. Max and Bertha (Levine) Samet; student N.Y. U., 1937, N.Y. Sch. Interior Design, 1938-41; m. Richard H. Wels, Dec. 12, 1954; children—Susan Rebecca, Amy Elizabeth. Interior decorator—Marguerite Samet, N.Y.C., 1946-60; interior decorator, head Marguerite Samet Assos., 1960—; co-ordinator U.S. Army Spl. Services, 1942-46; cons. United Bowling Centers, Inc., Interboro Gen. Hosp. Active in William Alanson White Inst. of Psychiatry, Psychoanalysis and Psychology, Am. Jewish Com., Islands Research Found.; program chmn. Jewish Mus. Mem. Am. Inst. Interior Designers, Democratic Women's Workshop. Jewish religion. Club: Women's City. Home: 911 Park Av New York City NY 10021 Office: 75 E 55th St New York City NY 10021

WELSH, HELEN CLEMENTINE, librarian; b. Albany, N.Y., June 20, 1907; d. Edward and Helen (Maguire) Welsh; A.B. cum laude, Coll. St. Rose, 1931; B.S., Columbia, 1934; M.A., N.Y. State Coll. Tchrs., 1943; M.S. in L.S., Columbia, 1949. Library asst. N.Y. State Library, Albany, 1925-32; asst. librarian Albany High Sch., 1932-34; librarian Schuyler High Sch., Albany, 1934-55, North High Sch., Valley Stream, L.I., N.Y., 1955-59, Sr. High Sch., Seaford, N.Y., 1959-67; librarian Profl. Library and Instructional Materials Center, 1967-69, dir. libraries, 1969—; asso. prof. dept. librarianship N.Y. State Coll. Tchrs. 1945-62; library cons., also organizer, 1962—; instr. library sci. Coll. St. Rose, 1934-36, 54, Marywood Coll., Scranton, Pa., 1944. Chmn. photography Albany Tulip Festival, 1953-54, 58. Recipient Distinguished Alumni award Coll. St. Rose, 1973. Fellow Inst. Amateur Cinematographers (Gt. Britain), Amateur Cinema League, N.Y. (asso.), Photog. Soc. Am. (editor of Cine Reporter 1966-70); mem. Internat. Fedn. Catholic Alumni (first regent Albany Circle, 1938-40); N.Y. Library Assn. (pres. sch. libraries section 1955), Amateur Motion Picture Soc. Albany, Cath. Library Assn., Metropolitan Motion Picture Club N.Y. (dir.), Delta Epsilon Sigma. Author articles in field. Home: 44 Parkwood St Albany NY 12208 also 315 Atlantic Av East Rockaway NY 11518 Office: 2174 Jackson Av Seaford NY 11783

WELSH, LORRAINE THOMAS (MRS. LAURENCE T. WELSH), journalist; b. Bklyn., Aug. 4, 1928; d. Joseph and Marie Letitia (Stengle) Thomas; B.S. in Journalism, Boston U., 1950; m. Laurence T. Welsh, Sept. 20, 1952. Corr. Needham (Mass.) Chronicle, 1946-52; press rep. United Community Services of Met. Boston, 1952-54; press dir. United Fund. Greater Boston, 1958; news asso. Mus. Sci., Boston, 1958-66, dir. publs., 1968—. Mem. New Eng. Bus. Communicators (treas. 1965-66, dir. 1966—), Internat. Council Indsl. Editors (nat. affairs dir. 1964-65), Alpha Delta Pi. Home: 42 Gayland Rd Needham MA 02192 Office: Museum of Science Science Park Boston MA 02114

WELTMER, L. GRACE (MRS. W. W. WELTMER), librarian; b. Milw., Dec. 2, 1908; d. Herman Charles and Alice Gertrude (Fast) Mueller; B.Ed., Milw. State Tchrs. Coll., 1932; M.L.S., U. Wis., 1959; postgrad. McGill U., Cataloging Inst., 1960; m. W. W. Weltmer, Nov. 29, 1934; children—Gretel Si, Heidi Jo (Mrs. David B. Pierpont). Mem. staff Milw. Pub. Library, 1928-29; tchr. art edn., librarian Milw. High Schs., part time, 1932-56, full time, 1956-58; instr. U. Wis. at Milw., 1958-61; head tech. service Chapman Meml. Library Milw. Downer Coll., 1963-64; dir. library and learning resources Spencerian Coll., Milw., 1965-73, organized library technician's program, 1969. Established library John Marshall High Sch., Milw., 1961. Active Milw. County chpt. Girl Scouts Am., 1941-45; A.R.C. Gray Lady, 1953-56. Mem. Am. Assn. U. Profs., A.L.A., Wis. Library Assn., U. Wis. Library Sch. Alumni. Republican. Club: Allis Chalmers Sketch (Milw.). Home: 6177 Washington Circle Wauwatosa WI 53213

WENBERG, LOUISE BRUSE, librarian; b. Chgo., Sept. 11, 1924; d. Gustav F. and Hulda Elvira (Lindberg) Bruse; student Ind. U., 1942-43; B.A., U. Wash., 1947, B.A. in Librarianship, 1949, postgrad., 1956—; m. Johan Barstad Wenberg, Sept. 12, 1948 (dec. Oct. 25, 1970). Statistician, Sears Roebuck & Co., Seattle, 1946-48, Alaska Dept. Health, Anchorage, 1954-55; children's librarian King County (Wash.) and Tacoma pub. libraries, 1949-51; reference and circulation librarian Portland State Coll., 1951-52; tchr., elementary grade, sr. high sch. librarian, Oregon City, Ore., 1952-54; jr. high sch. librarian Issaquah (Wash.) Sch. Dist., 1957—. Founder, U. Wash. Sch. Medicine Class of 1950 Meml. Loan Fund, 1970. Mem. Am., Wash. library assns., Am., Wash. (pres. 1974—) assns. sch. librarians, N.E.A., Wash. Edn. Assn., Phrateres Internat., Mountaineers, Olympic Park Assos., Audubon Soc., Am. Civil Liberties Union, Swedish Cultural Soc., Sea-Belles, Toastmistress Internat., Pi Lambda Theta. Unitarian. Contbr. articles to profl. pubs. Home: 5360 232d Av SE Issaquah WA 98027 Office: PO Box L Issaquah WA 98027

WENCK, DOROTHY ANN (MRS. GEORGE JAMES WENCK), home economist; b. Watertown, Wis., Aug. 28, 1927; d. Carl August and Grace May (Hildemann) Semrich; B.S. with high honors, U. Wis., 1949; M.A., Chapman Coll., 1966; postgrad. Cal. State U., Long Beach, U. Cal. at Irvine; m. George James Wenck, June 25, 1949; children—James Carl, Mary Ellen. Tchr. home econs., high sch., Stevens Point, Wis., 1949-51; home service rep. So. Union Gas Co., Austin, Tex., 1951-52; tchr. home econs. Chapman Coll., Orange, Cal., 1962-63; home adv. adult consumer edn. U. Cal., Coop. Extension Service, Anaheim, 1963—; writer, specialist consumer edn. materials project Consumers Union, Mount Vernon, N.Y., 1971-73; coordinator, lectr. U. Cal. at Irvine extension, 1972-74; free lance writer. Mem. adv. com. 4th Dist. P.T.A., Orange County, Cal., 1967-74, Saddleback Jr. Coll., Orange County, 1969-73, home econs. dept. Orange Coast Coll., 1971-74, family and consumer studies Santa Ana Coll., 1971-74. Bd. dirs. Orange County Heart Assn., 1970-71. Mem. Cal. Home Econs. Assn. (pres. Orange dist. 1969-70, counselor 1970-72), Orange County Nutrition Council; hon. life mem. Cal. Congress Parents and Tchrs. Asst. editor Cal. Home Economist, 1968-74. Contbr. articles to profl. jours. Home: 15712 Pacific St Tustin CA 92680 Office: 1000 S Harbor Blvd Anaheim CA 92805

WENDEL, FAYE F., truck mfg. co. exec.; b. Newark, Sept. 16, 1928; d. John Thomas and Sara Rose (Agliozzo) Fiorenza; m. Daniel C. Wendel, Nov. 26, 1949; children—Catherine C., Daniel C. III, Wayne J. Sec., P. Ballantine & Sons, Newark, 1946-49; head hostess, asst. to mgr. Bambergers-Carriage House Restaurant, 1971-74; sec. Peter Wendel & Sons, Inc., Irvington, N.J., 1971—. Tchrs. aide St. Ann Sch.; asst. treas. Ladies Aux. St. Rose of Lima Ch., 1963. Mem. Short Hills Assn., Twig Group of Overlook Hosp., Rotary Assn. Clubs: Republican, Short Hills Racquet. Home: 33 Quaker Rd Short Hills NJ 07078 Office: 464 Coit St Irvington NJ 07111

WENDELBURG, NORMA RUTH, educator, composer, pianist; b. Stafford, Kan.; d. Henry and Anna (Moeckel) Wendelburg; Mus.B., Bethany Coll., 1943; Mus.M., U. Mich., 1947; Mus.M., Eastman Sch. Music, 1951, postgrad., 1964-65, 66-67, Ph.D. in Composition, 1969; postgrad. Mozarteum, 1953-54, Vienna Acad. Music, 1955. Asst. prof. music edn., piano Wayne (Neb.) State Coll., 1947-50, Bethany Coll., Lindsborg, Kan., 1952-53, State Coll., Cedar Falls, Ia., 1956-58; asst. prof. composition, theory, piano Hardin-Simmons U., Abilene, Tex., 1958-66, chmn. grad. com. Sch. Music, 1960-66, founder ann. univ. festival contemporary music, 1959, chmn., 1959—; research asst. to dir. grad. studies Eastman Sch. Music, 1966-67; former asso. prof., chmn. dept. theory, composition Southwest Tex. State U.; now asso. prof. piano and composition, chmn. piano dept. Dallas Bapt. Coll.; appeared as pianist various solo recitals, festivals. Composition scholar Composers' Conf. Middlebury (Vt.), 1950, Berkshire Center, 1953; Fulbright award, 1953-55; Residence fellow Huntington Hartford Found., 1955-56, 58, 61; MacDowell Colony, 1958, 60, 70. Mem. Music Tchrs. Nat. Conf., Am. Music Center, MacDowell Colonists, Am. Soc. Univ. Composers, Sigma Alpha Iota. Composer numerous works including Symphony, 1967, Suite for Violin and Piano, 1965, Triptych Orch., 1963. Address: PO Box 21206 Dallas TX 75211

WENDELKEN, EVA MAE (MRS. HENRY HOMES WENDELKEN), life ins. underwriter; b. Independence, La., June 18, 1912; d. Henry Louis and Johnnie Aileen (Warren) Nelson; certificate S.E. La. U., 1930; student La. State U., 1934-39, Tulane U., 1942-43; m. Henry Holmes Wendelken, Oct. 7, 1937; children—Linda R., Janice A. Tchr. elementary sch., Independence, La., 1930-31, Natalbany, La., 1931-42; life ins. field underwriter, New Orleans, 1944-45, Hammond, La., 1945—. Bd. dirs. United Givers' Fund, 1964-65; Southeastern Devel. Found., 1971-73. Recipient Nat. Quality award Nat. Assn. Life Underwriters, 1951-73. Mem. Baton Rouge Assn. Life Underwriters, Hammond C. of C. (publicity dir. 1951-54), Southeastern La. Univ. Alumni Assn. (sec. 1957-58), Women Leaders Round Table, D.A.R. (chpt. regent 1965-67, state honor roll chmn. 1967-70). Baptist (Sunday sch. tchr. 1948-70). Home: 400 Sanders Av Hammond LA 70401 Office: 1003 S Cypress St Hammond LA 70401

WENDER, RUTH MIRIAM (MRS. SIMON HAROLD WENDER), library adminstr.; b. Laurel, Miss., May 27, 1919; d. Sol Louis and Bessie Marian (Mindel) Wisenberg; B.A. with distinction, Rice U., 1939; M.L.S., U. Okla., 1968; m. Simon Harold Wender, Sept. 6, 1942; children—Joseph H., Barbara (Mrs. Fred D. Rothlein), Sheryl Ann. Instr. med. library scis. U. Okla., Oklahoma City, 1968-71, asst. prof. med. library scis., interlibrary loan librarian Health Scis. Center, 1968-70, coordinator regional library services, 1970—, asst. dir. Library for Regional Library Services, 1972—. Cons. Okla. Hosp. Libraries, 1970—. Mem. Med. (chmn. South Central Regional group 1974-75), Okla. (chmn. reference div. 1970-71, chmn. coll. div. 1974-75, mem. program com. 1970, 75), Spl. (pub. relations chmn. 1971-72) library assns., Beta Phi Mu, Pi Delta Phi, Phi Beta Kappa. Editor Infor-Med., 1970—. Contbr. articles on library sci. to profl. jours. Home: 2614 Meadowbrook Norman OK 73069 Office: 801 NE PO Box 26901 Oklahoma City OK 73190

WENDLER, ANN WEST (MRS. KENNETH S. WENDLER, JR.), constrn. co. exec.; b. Hillsboro, Tex., July 10, 1930; d. Guy Carney and Nellie Mae (Brooks) West; student U. Tex., Austin Adult Evening Sch., 1949-51; m. Kenneth S. Wendler, Jr., July 17, 1951; children—Mark W., Kim, Katheryn, Kris, Kena. Office sec. Bd. Nurse Examiners State Tex., Austin, 1948-52; new accounts officer, exchange dept. teller Tex. State Bank, Austin, 1953-55; exec. sec. U. Tex. Endowment Office, Austin, 1955-56; office sec. Brown Securities Corp. subsidiary Brown & Root, Inc., Austin, 1956-59; co-owner, sec., treas., dir. Anken Constrn. Co., Inc., Austin, 1965—; co-owner W W Bldg. Co., 1967—. Area team capt. KLRN Nat. Ednl. TV Fund Raising campaign, 1973; chmn. Bldg. Austin With Pride campaign, 1973. Mem. Nat. Assn. Women in Constrn. (chpt. pres. 1971, chpt. bd. dirs. 1969-73, nat. profl. edn. com. 1972, nat. bd. dirs. 1974-75), Austin C. of C. Club: South Austin Civic. Home: 4703 Arapahoe Pass Austin TX 78745 Office: 2130 Goodrich St Austin TX 78704

WENGER, NANETTE KASS (MRS. JULIUS WENGER), physician; b. N.Y.C., Sept. 3, 1930; d. Aaron Z. and Edith (Malkin) Kass; B.A., Hunter Coll., 1951; M.D., Harvard, 1954; m. Julius Wenger, Dec. 8, 1957; children—Deborah Anne, Judith Carolyn, Beth Suzanne. Intern, Mt. Sinai Hosp., N.Y.C., 1954-55, resident in medicine, 1955-56; chief resident cardiology, 1956-57; sr. resident in medicine Grady Meml. Hosp., 1958, fellow cardiology Ga. Heart Assn., Emory U. Sch. of Medicine, Grady Meml. Hosp., 1958-59; instr., asso. medicine Emory U. Sch. Medicine and Emory U. Sch. Dentistry, 1959-64; dir. cardiac clinics Grady Meml. Hosp., 1960—; asst. prof. medicine Emory U. Sch. Medicine and Emory U. Sch. Dentistry, 1964-68, asso. prof., 1968-71, prof. medicine (cardiology), 1971—. Mem. Nat. Thrombosis Adv. Council, 1971—; cons. internat. div. Social and Rehab. Services, Dept. Health, Edn. and Welfare, 1970—; mem. heart panel Nat. Heart and Lung Inst., 1972—. Past pres. Szold Group, Hadassah; bd. dirs. Atlanta Jewish Community Center, Jewish Children's Service, Brandeis U. Women's Com.; bd. dirs., pres. Atlanta Bur. Jewish Edn. Named Atlanta Woman of Year in Medicine, 1972; named to Hunter Coll. Hall Fame, 1971. Fellow Am. Coll. Cardiology, Council Clin. Cardiology, Am. Heart Assn. (chmn. rehab. com.); mem. Atlanta Clin. Soc., Atlanta Alumnae Group (founder, treas.), Phi Sigma Sigma. Editor: Electrocardiographic Interpretation, 1963; asst. editor The Heart, 1966, 70, 74; mem. editorial bd. Blakiston's New Gould Medical Dictionary. Contbr. articles in field to profl. jours. Home: 864 Somerset Dr NW Atlanta GA 30327 Office: Emory U School Medicine 69 Butler St SE Atlanta GA 30303

WENGLER, DIANE KIRK (MRS. VANCE W. WENGLER), journalist; b. Oakland, Cal., Apr. 3, 1945; d. Earl Leroy and Mary Ann (Haines) Kirk; B.S. with honors, U. Kan., 1967, M.S., 1968; m. Vance W. Wengler, July 30, 1965. Reporter, edn. editor, feature writer Topeka Capital-Jour., 1968-72; reporter, edn. writer, feature writer Colorado Springs (Colo.) Sun Newspaper, 1972—. Mem. bd. Performing Arts for Youth Orgn., 1972—; mem. Symphony Guild, 1973—, Friends of Opera, 1973—. Bd. dirs. Va. Neal Blue Resource Center for Colo. Women. Mem. Women in Communications, Colo. Press Women, Colorado Springs Press Club, Sigma Delta Chi, Theta Sigma Phi, Pi Lambda Theta, Kappa Alpha Theta. Democrat. Home: 717 Polaris Dr Colorado Springs CO 80906 Office: 102 W Colorado Av Colorado Springs CO 80901

WENINGER, PATRICIA (MRS. GEORGE J. WENINGER), banker; b. Vancouver, Wash., Dec. 17, 1925; d. George E. and Margaret (Hills) Kidwell; grad. pub. high sch.; m. George J. Weninger, Sept. 13, 1945; 1 dau., Dianne. With Fidelity Mut. Savs. Bank, Spokane, Wash., 1962—, br. loan officer, 1970-72, asst. v.p. loan dept., 1972—. Instr. banking Spokane Community Coll., 1971—, also mem. mid-mgmt. adv. com. Mem. Nat. Assn. Bank Women (nat. bd. dirs., v.p. 1974—), Zonta Internat. (treas. 1970, bd. dirs.; chmn. Expo '74 com.). Home: W 3342 Bruce St Spokane WA 99208 Office: W 524 Riverside St Spokane WA 99201

WENNERSTROM, MARY HANNAH, educator; b. Grand Rapids, Mich., Dec. 12, 1939; d. Walter William and Marie (Switzer) Wennerstom; B.Mus. with highest honors, Ind. U., 1961, Mus. M. with high honors, 1963, Ph.D., 1967. Lectr. music theory Ind. U., Bloomington, 1964-67, asst. prof. music theory, 1967-71, asso. prof., 1971—, sec. dept., 1964—, mem. All-U. Faculty Council, 1969—, sec. Student Affairs Com., 1969—. Chmn., Ind. U. United Fund, 1965. Recipient Susan Butler award, 1961. Kappa Kappa Kappa fellow, 1962. Mem. Am. Assn. U. Profs., Coll. Music Soc., Am. Musicological Soc., Music Panhellenic Assn., Pi Kappa Lambda (chpt. pres. 1971—), Sigma Alpha Iota. Methodist. Author: Parametric Analysis of Contemporary Musical Form, 1967; Anthology of 20th Century Music, 1969; Veracini Violin Sonatas (edit. figured bass realization), 1972. Compositions for piano, voice, chorus, winds. Home: 942 F Maxwell Terrace Bloomington IN 47401

WENNHOLD, ANN GERTRUDE RUHMANN (MRS. PHIL EUGENE WENNHOLD), physician; b. Bklyn., June 12, 1932; d. Warren Howard and Gertrude Ann (Oldis) Ruhmann; B.A. Seton Hill Coll., 1954; M.D. (Tobacco Industries fellow., Josiah Macy Found. fellow), State U. N.Y., 1958; m. Phil Eugene Wennhold, Apr. 8, 1967; children—Kim, B.J. Intern, N.C. Meml. Hosp., Chapel Hill, 1958-59; resident U. Utah Hosps., Salt Lake City, 1959-60, research scientist, dept. anatomy U. Utah, 1960-67, research scientist, dept. medicine, 1967—, instr. dept. anatomy, 1965-69, asst. research prof. dept. anatomy, 1969-74, asso. research prof., 1974—. USPHS research fellow, 1961-63. Mem. Endocrine Soc., Western Soc. Clin. Research, Am. Fedn. Clin. Research, Kappa Gamma Pi, Alpha Lambda Delta. Club: Wasatch Mountain, (Salt Lake City). Contbr. articles to profl. jours. Home: 2180 Belaire Dr Salt Lake City UT 84109 Office: 401 12th Av Salt Lake City UT 84103

WENSEL, LOUISE OFTEDAL, physician; b. Fargo, N.D.; d. Sverre John and Agnes (Holland) Oftedal; B.A., Wellesley Coll., 1939; M.D., George Washington U., 1949; children-Bertram, Olinda, David, Pamela, Theodore. Intern St. Elizabeth's Hosp., Washington, 1949-50; resident Camarillo (Cal.) State Hosp., 1965-66, Johns Hopkins Hosp., 1970-72; pvt. practice gen. medicine, LaMesa, Cal., 1950-52, Washington, 1952-54, Fisherville, Va., 1954-59; pvt. practice psychiatry, Norwalk, Cal., 1959-61, Gainesville, Fla., 1961-64, Tucson, 1966-69, Washington, 1969—; instr. psychiatry Johns Hopkins Med. Sch., 1972—; dir. Washington Acupuncture Center, 1973—; pres. Acupuncture Inst., D.C., 1973—; psychiatrist U. Fla., 1961-64, U. Ariz., 1966-68; cons. VA, Tucson, 1966-69. Mem. Am. Psychiat. Assn., A.M.A., Am. Coll. Health Assn., Am. Geriatric Soc., Am. Pub. Health Assn. Office: 1717 Massachusetts Av NW Washington DC 20036

WENTEN, RUTH POLLINGER (MRS. WOLFGANG CARL WENTEN), media specialist; b. Bklyn., Apr. 28, 1917; d. Henry Joseph and Sadie (Markowitz) Pollinger; B.E., Central Conn. State Coll., 1937; M.L.S., So. Conn. State Coll., 1964; m. Wolfgang Carl Wenten, Nov. 3, 1940; children—David Paul, Robert Peter. Librarian Bridgeport (Conn.) Pub. Library, 1938-42; tchr. Fairfield, Conn., 1954-61; librarian Fairfield Bd. of Edn., 1961—. Active Fairfield Democratic Women's Orgn., 1971—. Mem. Fairfield Hist. Soc. (council mem. 1967—; editor newsletter 1967—), Conn. Sch. Library Assn. (exec. bd. 1969-70, scholarship com.), Nat., Conn., Fairfield edn. assns., A.L.A., Park Av. Temple Library Com., Delta Kappa Gamma. Reviewer, Scholastic Tchr. Mag., 1966—, Previews Mag. Home: 283 High Ridge Rd Fairfield CT 06430 Office: Board of Education Fairfield CT 06430

WENTWORTH, ELIZABETH CATRON, educator; b. Ft. Leavenworth, Kan., June 10, 1916; d. Thomas Benton and Marjorie Hartwell (Knight) Catron; B.A., Occidental Coll., 1952; M.A., U. So. Cal., 1954, Ph.D., 1959; children—Marjorie (Mrs. H.D. Mosier), John. Mem. faculty Occidental Coll., 1954-60, Goucher Coll., 1960-61; engr. Bendix Corp., Balt., 1961-66; asst. dean Grad. Sch., Princeton, 1966-69; prof. philosophy Sweet Briar (Va.) Coll., 1969—. Mem. Am. Philos. Assn. Home: PO Box 576 Amherst VA 24521 Office: Sweet Briar Coll Sweet Briar VA 24595

WENTZ, EVELYN ELIZABETH, artist; b. nr. Risingsun, O., July 28, 1915; d. Alfred H. and Edna Mae (Roush) Shultz; studied art under Carl Gaertner, 1949; student (scholar Art Interests, Inc., 1951, 52, 54) Toledo Mus. Art, 1949-54; m. Paul L. Wentz, Dec. 24, 1933; children—Betty (Mrs. John Franklin Haley), Paula Kay (Mrs. Jerry Joe Leeson), Karen Sue (Mrs. Charles Dee Wilson), Craig V., Paul Eric. One man shows Toledo Mus. Art, 1952, Town Gallery, Toledo, 1954, Butler Inst. Am. Art, Youngstown, O., 1955, Ill. State Mus., Springfield, 1957, Davenport (Ia.) Municipal Art Gallery, 1959, Sienna Heights Coll., Adrian, Mich., 1961, Laura Musser Art Gallery, 1966, Toledo Mus. Art, 1967, Siena Heights Coll., Adrian, Mich., 1968, Zanesville (O.) Art Inst., 1969, Point Place Library Gallery, Toledo, 1970, McInnis Gallery, Toledo, 1970, Kaubisch Meml. Library, Gostoria, O., 1971, 72; exhibited in group shows including Pa. Acad. Fine Arts, Phila., U.S. Nat. Mus., Washington, Ill. State Mus., Springfield, N.A.D., N.Y.C. Boston Mus. Fine Arts, Riverside Mus., N.Y.C., Wadsworth Athenium, Hartford, Cleve. Mus. Art, Columbus Gallery Fine Art, Dayton Art Inst., Mus. Fine Arts, Springfield, Mass., Jersey City Mus., Uneo Park Municipal Mus. Art, Tokyo, Japan; paintings in 3 Am. touring exhbns., 1958-59; numerous invitational exhbns.; fgn. exhibits at Kunst Mus., Bern, Switzerland. Ciano Gallery, Lugano, Switzerland, Museo Nacional de Bellas Artes, Buenos Aires, Mus. Modern, Art, Rio de Janeiro, Royal Scottish Acad. Galleries, Royal Birmingham Artists Galleries, Prospectus 68 Expn., Monte Carlo, Monaco, Expn. Internationale, Charleroi, Belgium; represented in permanent collections Everson Mus. Art., Syracuse, N.Y., Fairleigh Dickenson U., Bluffton (O.) Coll., Ill. State Mus., Butler Inst. Am. Art, Toledo Fedn. Art Socs., Toledo Mus. Art, State Tchrs. Coll., Indiana, Pa., Davenport (Ia.) Municipal Art Gallery, Art Interests, Inc., Municipal Glicenstein Mus., Safad, Israel, Art Gallery and Regional Museum, Aberdeen, Scotland, Dept. State, Washington, Olivet-Nazarene Coll., Laura Musser Art Gallery and Mus., Zanesville (O.) Art Inst., Tri-County Nat. Bank, Findlay, O., Kaubisch Meml. Library, Fostoria Corp., and numerous pvt. collections; touring exhbns. Veracruz, Mexico City, and others. Recipient numerous prizes, 1949—, including 2d prize for watercolor 16th Ann. New Year Show, Butler Inst. Am. Art, 1951; Grumbacher award and hon. mention Fla. Internat. Exhbn., Lakeland, 1952; 1st award for gouache Fostoria (O.) Art Exhbn., 1952; Best Woman Artist award 28th Ohio Watercolor Circuit Exhbn., 1952; purchase award, hon. mention, enamel on metal 36th Toledo Area Ann., Mus. Art Toledo, 1954; 1st award enamel on metal Port Clinton Area Mid Winter Exhbn., 1957; honorable mention, 15th Nat. Ceramic Exhbn., 1960; hon. mention enamel on metal Regional Craft Bieenial, J.B. Speed Art Mus., Louisville, 1968. Fellow Internat. Inst. Arts and Letters (life); mem. World Crafts Council, Am. Craftsmen's Council N.Y., Ohio Designer Craftsmen, Painters and Sculptors Soc. N.J., Knickerbocker Artists, Ala., Ohio watercolor socs., Studio Guild, Washington Water Color Club, Nat. Assn. Women Artists, Nat. Smithsonian Asso. (charter), Am. Foundrymen's Soc., Internat. Arts Guild, Fostoria Art League (life), Centro Studi E Scambi Internazionali (internat. com.), Accademia Internazionale Leonardo da Vinci (hon.). Home and studio: 1733 North Countyline St Fostoria OH 44830

WENZEL, BERNICE MARTHA (MRS. WENDELL E. JEFFREY), educator; b. Bridgeport, Conn., June 22, 1921; d. Edward August and Gertrude (Card) Wenzel; A.B., Beaver Coll., 1942; A.M., Columbia, 1943, Ph.D., 1948; m. Wendell E. Jeffrey, June 14, 1952. Instr. Newcomb Coll. Tulane, 1945-46; instr. Barnard Coll., 1946-50, asst. prof. psychology, 1950-55; asst. research physiologist U. Cal. at Los Angeles Sch. medicine, 1957-1959, asst. prof., 1959-61, asso. prof., 1961-69, prof., 1969—, prof. psychiatry, 1971—, vice chmn. dept. physiology, 1971-73, asst. dean for ednl. research, 1974—. Mem. A.A.A.S., Am. Physiol. Soc., Am., Western psychol. assns., Am. Psychosomatic Soc., Internat. Brain Research Orgn., Neurosci. Soc., Internat. Soc. for Psychoneuroendocrinology, Soc. for Psychophysiol. Research. Contbr. articles to profl. jours. Home: 3334 Scadlock Lane Sherman Oaks CA 91403 Office: Dept Physiology Sch Medicine U Cal Los Angeles CA 90024

WENZEL, GLADYS LOREE, city ofcl.; b. Nebraska City, Neb., July 16, 1919; d. George William and Hazel Minnie (McAllister) Wenzel; student pub. schs. Sec., bookkeeper Jones Produce, Nebraska City, 1938-42, Ocoma Foods Co., 1942-70; city clk., treas. Nebraska City, 1970—. Mem. C. of C. (charter mem. women's div.; pres. 1953-54), Otoe County Hist. Soc. (pres. 1973-74). Presbyn. (bd. trustees 1973—). Home: 816 2d Av Nebraska City NE 68410 Office: 1409 Central Nebraska City NE 68410

WENZEL, SISTER KRISTEN, educator; b. Washington, Mar. 30, 1939; d. George and Ruth (Remon) Wenzel; B.A., Coll. New Rochelle, 1961; M.A. (scholar), Cath. U. Am., 1966, Ph.D. (scholar), 1970. Instr. sociology Coll. New Rochelle, (N.Y.), 1967-69, mem. Campus Ministry Team, 1971-74, asst. prof. sociology, 1971—, dir. women's studies program, 1973—; research asso., dir. undergrad. field experience demonstration project, div. spl. projects and research Council on Social Work Edn., N.Y.C., N.Y., 1969-71. Chairperson N.Y. chpt. Nat. Assembly Women Religious, Archdiocese N.Y., 1972—, chairperson conv., 1973, mem. nat. exec. bd., 1973—. Ursuline Sisters rep. Sisters' Council Archdiocese N.Y., N.Y.C., 1971-72; mem. adv. bd. Clergy Report, 1972—. Recipient grants Nat. Inst. Mental Health, 1968, Council on Social Work Edn., 1968. Mem. Am. Sociol. Assn., Am. Assn. U. Profs., Assn. for Sociology Religion, Soc. for Sci. Study Religion, Ursuline Sisters of Roman Union (chpt. del. 1970-71, chairperson task force edn. 1970-71), Alpha Kappa Delta. Author: Clergymen's Attitudes Toward Black Africa, 1971; Curriculum Guides for Undergraduate Field Instruction Programs, 1972; Undergraduate Field Instruction Programs—Correct Issues and Predictions, 1972. Home: 2401 E Tremont Av Bronx NY 10461 Office: Coll of New Rochelle New Rochelle NY 10801

WERA, ANNE REGINA, educator; b. Winona, Minn., June 1, 1936; d. Bernard S. and Alvina (Konter) Wera; B.A., Viterbo Coll., LaCrosse, Wis., 1958; M.Mus., MacPhail Coll., U. Minn., 1960; postgrad., U. Ia., 1968; M.A. in Adminstrn Edn., Loras Coll., 1972; D.Arts, Nat. Christian U., 1974. Orchestral instr. Logan Jr. High Sch., LaCrosse, Wis., 1958-60; supr. instrumental music, LaCrosse, Wis., 1960-64; grad. asst. U. Ia., 1964-65; instr. music edn. U. Nev., 1965, State U. Wis., Whitewater, 1966; asst. prof. music edn. State U. Wis., River Falls, 1966-67; instrumental music instr. Dubuque, Ia., 1967-68, music specialist, 1968-74; instr. organ and piano Loras Coll., Dubuque, 1972—; music adminstr.-coordinator Electronic Music Lab., 1971-74, Piano and Organ Lab. for the Blind, 1972—. Mem. Am. Assn. U. Profs., Mus. Educators Nat. Conf., Nat. Organists Guild, Music Tchrs. Nat. Assn., Wis., Ia. edn. assns., Wis. Music Tchrs. Assn., Wis. Mus. Educators Conf., Am. Assn. U. Women, Dubuque Community Schs. Assn., Women Band Dirs. Nat. Orgn. Contbr. articles to profl. jours. Home: 229 Ash St Onalaska WI 54650 Office: 2688 Marywood Dr Dubuque IA 52001

WERDEGAR, KATHRYN MICKLE (MRS. DAVID WERDEGAR), lawyer; b. San Francisco, Apr. 5, 1936; d. Benjamin Christy and Kathryn Marie (Clark) Mickle; student Wellesley Coll., 1954-55; A.B., U. Cal. at Berkeley, 1957; J.D. with distinction, George Washington U., 1962; m. David Werdegar, Sept. 1, 1961; children—Maurice Clark, Matthew Mickle. Admitted to Cal. bar, 1964; staff atty. Civil Rights Div., U.S. Dept. Justice, Washington, 1962-63; spl. cons. Cal. Commn. on Mental Retardation, Sacramento, 1963-64; asso. Center for Study of Law and Society, Berkeley, 1965-67; mem. staff misdemeanor benchbook project, Cal. Coll. Trial Judges, Berkeley, 1968-70; staff atty. Cal. Continuing Edn. of Bar, Berkeley, 1971—. Cons. to dir. planning Cal. Dept. Mental Hygiene, 1964-65. Mem. State Bar Cal. (ex-officio mem. com. criminal law and procedure 1974—), San Francisco Bar Assn., Order of Coif. Editor: Bench Book: Misdemeanor Procedure, 1971, rev. edit., 1975. Office: 2150 Shattuck Av Berkeley CA 94704

WERKLEY, CAROLINE ELSEA (MRS. JOHN G. WERKLEY), librarian; b. Clinton, Mo.; d. Luther Martin and Caroline Eleanor (Hutton) Elsea; student Moberly Jr. Coll., 1931-33; B.J., U. Mo., 1933-35; M.L.S., L.I. U., 1965; m. John G. Werkley, June 7, 1938 (dec. July 1949); 1 son, Christopher. Reporter, Moberly (Mo.) Monitor-Index, 1935-38; research librarian, dept. anthropology U. Pa., Phila., 1965—. Mem. A.L.A. Author: Mister Carnegie's Library, 1970. Contbr. articles to popular and profl. jours. Home: Wyndon Apartments Lancaster Av Wynnewood PA 19096 Office: Department of Anthropology University Museum Philadelphia PA 19104

WERLEY, HARRIET HELEN, coll. dean; b. Berks County, Pa., Oct. 12, 1914; d. Thomas G. and Cora M. (Hein) W.; diploma in nursing, Jefferson Med. Coll. Hosp., Phila., 1941; B.S. in Nursing Edn., U. Cal. at Berkeley, 1948; M.A. in nursing adminstrn., Columbia, 1951; Ph.D. in Psychology (NIH research fellow), U. Utah, 1969. Nurse, Jefferson Med. Coll. Hosp., 1940-41, commd. lt. Nurse Corps, U.S. Army, 1941, nurse to chief nurse, 1941-46, discharged, 1946, recommd., 1948, asst. chief nurse, then chief nurse Camp Stoneman, Cal., 1948-50, career planning officer Nurse Corps, Office of Surgeon Gen., 1951-55, nursing cons. dept. of atomic casualties studies, coordinator nursing activities, chief dept. nursing research, Walter Reed Army Inst. of Research, 1955-62, chief nurse 8th U.S. Army, Korea, 1962-63, ret. lt. col., 1964; dir. Center for Health Research, Wayne State U., 1969-73; asso. dean research Coll. Nursing U. Ill. Med. Center, Chgo., 1974—. Decorated Army Commendation medal, Legion of Merit; recipient Pfizer award of merit for U.S. Civil Def. Council, 1960, Fed. Nursing Service award, 1961, others. Charter fellow Am. Acad. Nursing; mem. A.A.A.S., Am. Nurses Assn., Am. Psychol. Assn., Am. Pub. Health Assn., Assn. Mil. Surgeons U.S., Nat. League for Nursing, Royal Soc. Health. Contbr. articles to profl. jours. Home: 1350 S Elizabeth St Lombard IL 60148 Office: U Ill Med Center Chicago IL 60612

WERNER, EMMY ELISABETH, child psychologist, educator; b. Eltville, Germany, May 26, 1929; d. Peter Josef and Liesel (Kunz) Werner; B.S., Johannes Gutenberg U. (Germany), 1950; M.A., U. Neb., 1952, Ph.D., 1955; postgrad. U. Cal. at Berkeley, 1953-54. Came to U.S., 1950, naturalized, 1962. Research asso. Inst. Child Welfare, U. Minn., 1956-59; vis. scientist NIH, 1959-62; from asst. prof. to prof. human devel. U. Cal. at Davis, 1962—. Cons. UNICEF, 1968-72, Dept. Health, Edn. and Welfare, 1967-71, Office of Child Devel., 1972—. Recipient Elsie Worcester Meml. award U. Neb., 1972. Mem. Am. Psychol. Assn., Soc. for Research in Child Devel. Sr. author: The Children of Kauai. Contbr. articles to profl. jours. Office: 209 Walker Hall U Cal Davis CA 94704

WERNER, ESTHER ELDORA BALLMANN (MRS. ELMER EDWARD WERNER), city ofcl.; b. Riesel, Tex., Sept. 20, 1915; d. Edwin Albert and Minnie (Matthys) Ballmann; student Blinn Jr. Coll., 1939-40; m. Elmer Edward Werner, Sept. 14, 1941; 1 dau., Margaret Elaine. Asst. cashier First State Bank, Riesel, Tex., 1940-54; city sec., tax assessor and collector City of Mart, Tex., 1966—. Income tax cons., 1945-73. Active Mart P.T.A., 1957-69, pres., 1964; sec. Mart Jr. Garden Club, 1966, treas., 1965. Lutheran (Sunday sch. tchr. 1928-68, zone pres. 1953-57). Home: 1511 Texas St Mart TX 76664 Office: 112 N Commerce St Mart TX 76664

WERNER, SISTER MARIA ASSUNTA, educator; b. Chgo., Jan. 4, 1916; d. Adolph Joseph and Mary Ann (Szudarski) Werner; B.A., Saint Mary's Coll., 1949, M.A., 1950, Ph.D., 1955; postgrad. Laval U., Ind. U., Catholic U. Am. Tchr. Saint Mary's Sch., Woodstock, Ill., 1939, Saint Mary's High Sch., Michigan City, Ind., 1939-41, St. Joseph's Acad., South Bend, Ind., 1941-42, 43-47, Saint Patrick's Sch., 1942-43; instr. Saint Mary's Coll., Notre Dame, Ind., 1949; tchr., dean girls Saint Mary's Acad., South Bend, Ind., 1949-53; instr., asst. prof., asso. prof. Saint Mary's Coll., Notre Dame, Ind., 1953-63, prof. theology, 1963—, dean freshmen, dir. admissions, 1955-56, registrar, 1959-61, v.p., 1965-67, chmn. dept. theology, 1961-65, 68-70; mem. exec. staff U.S. Cath. Mission Council, Washington, 1970-72. Vis. prof. Stonehill Coll., N. Easton, Mass., 1967-68. Mem. College Theol. Soc. (regional sec. 1962-66), Religious Edn. Assn., Catholic Biblical Assn., Am. Acad. Religion, Am. Soc. Christian Ethics. Contbr. articles in field to profl. jours. Address: Saint Mary's Coll Notre Dame IN 46556

WERNER, SISTER MARIJANE, educator; b. Doylestown, O., May 4, 1918; d. John Martin and Louise Catherine (Remark) Werner; A.B., U. Akron, 1946, M.Ed., 1955; Ph.D., Boston Coll., 1968. Research asso. U.S. Office Edn. Title I Elementary and Secondary Edn. Act Project, Chestnut Hill, Mass., 1965-66; asso. prof. dept. elementary edn. Kent (O.) State U., 1968—, co-dir. math. edn. program, 1968—. Cons. math. Cuyahoga County Sch. System, 1971-72, Patchogue-Medford Pub. Schs., 1970—. NSF fellow., 1964-65, summers 1958-60. Mem. Assn. for Supervision and Curriculum Devel., Nat., Ohio councils tchrs. math. Author: Teaching the Set of Integers to Elementary School Children, 1973. Contbr. articles to profl. jour. Home: 3393 Pendleton St Cuyahoga Falls OH 44221

WERNIG, STEPHANIE RAE, coll. adminstr.; b. Akron, O., Aug. 25, 1946; d. Raymond Rudolph and Martha (Gardner) Wernig; B.A., St. Mary's Coll., 1968; M.A., U. Denver, 1970. Hall dir. Loretto Heights Coll., Denver, 1968-70; dir. student affairs St. Joseph Coll., West Hartford, Conn., 1970-74, asst. to v.p. for student affairs St. Mary's Coll., Notre Dame, Ind., 1974—. Mem. Nat. Assn. Women Deans and Counselors, Nat. Assn. Student Personnel Adminstrs. (adv. bd. 1970-72), Conn. Women Deans and Counselors (v.p. 1973-74), Am. Assn. Higher Edn., Kappa Delta Pi. Home: 1651 Turtle Creek S Dr South Bend IN 46637 Office: St Mary's Coll Notre Dame IN 46556

WERTENBAKER, LAEL TUCKER (MRS. BRAMWELL FLETCHER), author; b. Bradford, Pa., Mar. 28, 1909; d. Royal K. and Juliet (Luttrell) Tucker; student U. Louisville, 1927; m. Charles Christian Wertenbaker, Sept. 1942 (dec. Jan. 1955); children—Christian Tucker, Timberlake; m. 2d, Bramwell Fletcher, Sept. 1970. Treas., road sec. Theatre Guild, Inc., N.Y.C., 1929-38; fortune researcher Time, Inc., N.Y.C., Time reporter, Wash. fgn. corr. Berlin, 1940-41, London, 1941-42, war corr. ETO, 1944-46, Paris Bur. Time-Life, 1946-47; time stringer St. Jean de Luz, France, 1947-55; free-lance writer, 1955—; author: (novels) Lament for Four Virgins, 1950; Festival, 1954; The Eye of the Lion, 1964; The Afternoon Women, 1966; (non-fiction) Death of a Man, 1957; Mister Junior, 1958; The Magic of Light, 1972; (juveniles) Mercy Percy, 1960; Tip and Dip, 1961; Rhyming Word Games, 1964; The World of Picasso, 1968; Unbidden Guests, 1970. Vis. prof. Boston U. Trustee Nat. Repertory Theatre; dir. MacDowell Assn., Monadnock Music. Clubs: Overseas Press, P.E.N. Home: RD Marlborough NH 03455

WERTHEIMER, LINDA RAE ACKERMAN (MRS. JACK WERTHEIMER, JR.), lawyer; b. McKeesport, Pa., May 22, 1940; d. Louis Joseph and Rose (Sanders) Ackerman; student Harvard, 1960; B.S. cum laude, U. Pitts., 1962; LL.B., So. Meth. U. Law Sch., 1966; m. Jack Wertheimer, Jr., Mar. 22, 1964; children—Dana Michele, David Bradley. Admitted to Tex. bar, 1965; law clk. to judge Irving L. Goldberg U.S. Ct. Appeals, 5th Circuit, 1966-67; asso. firm Geary, Bruce, Barron & Stahl, Dallas, 1969-73, Hewett Johnson Swanson & Barbee, Dallas, 1973—. Bd. dirs. Am. Jewish Com., Dallas, 1968-70, chmn. program series, 1969. Mem. Am., Dallas Jr., Dallas (mem. com. 1971-73) bar assns., State Bar Tex., Nat. Assn. Women Lawyers; Home: 11706 El Hara Circle Dallas TX 75230 Office: Hewett Johnson Swanson & Barbee 9th Floor 211 N Ervay Bldg Dallas TX 75201

WERTZ, MILDRED MARIE BEARD, educator; b. Cape Girardeau, Mo., Sept. 19, 1916; d. William Wallace and Mary Mildred (Rector) Beard; B.S., S.E. Mo. State Coll., 1937; M.A., U. Mo., 1945; postgrad. Pa. State U., 1948-49, So. Ill. U., 1962-63; m. Ray Cash Fee, Apr. 20, 1941 (killed in action 1945); m. 2d, Francis Dominic Wertz, June 7, 1947 (div. 1957); 1 dau., Mary Frances. Tchr. jr. high sch. English, Washington Sch., Cape Girardeau, Mo., 1937-41; tchr. speech and drama Norfolk (Neb.) Jr. Coll. and High Sch., 1945-46; instr. pub. speaking and radio speech Pa. State U., University Park, 1946-49; tchr. high sch. English, Sherwood Forest Sch., Sandy Spring,

Md., 1949-50; speech therapist Norfolk (Va.) City Schs., 1955-62, supr. speech hearing services, 1963-70; asso. prof. speech pathology Norfolk State Coll., 1970—. Part time instr. speech Norfolk div. Coll. William and Mary, 1956-62, Old Dominion U., 1963—; part-time faculty U. Va., 1964-65, Norfolk div. Va. State Coll., 1966-67. Bd. dirs. United Cerebral Palsy Met. Hampton Roads. Fellow Speech and Hearing Assn. Va. (pres. 1967-68); mem. Am. Speech and Hearing Assn., Speech Communication Assn., So. Speech Communication Assn. Home: 2312 Indian Hill Rd Virginia Beach VA 23455 Office: 2401 Corprew Av Norfolk VA 23504

WERTZ, VIRGINIA LORYMA, library ofcl.; b. Washington, Aug. 21, 1933; d. Melvin Moore and Ruth Belle (Johnson) Wertz; A.A., Am. U., 1958, B.A., 1961. Clk., C & P Telephone Co., Washington, 1951-62, Lord & Taylor, Washington, 1962-63; with D.C. Pub. Library, Washington, 1963—, supr. circulation, 1964—. Mem. Women in Communications, The Writer's League. Democrat. Episcopalian. Mem. Order Eastern Star.

WESLEY, GLORIA MAY WALKER (MRS. CLEO WESLEY), social worker; b. Rochester, N.Y., May 21, 1928; d. Spencer Malcolm and Blossom (Pye) Walker; B.A., Fisk U., 1950; M.S.W., Loyola U., 1959; m. Cleo Wesley, Feb. 11, 1961; children—Eric Jerome, Lia Cherise. Girls counselor Lake County Children's Home, Gary, Ind., 1952-53; social worker Lake County Dept. Pub. Welfare, Child Placement and Family Service, 1953-60, Schs. City Gary, 1960-70, Lake County Assn. Retarded Children, 1963, Norman Beatty Hosp., Westville, Ind., 1964, Lake County Mental Health Clinic, Gary, 1965; coordinator social services and day care Gary Income Maintenance Expt., Ind. U. N.W., Gary, 1970—; pvt. practice social work, Gary, 1962—; fieldwork supr. undergrad. students in social work Valparaiso U., 1963—, prof. social work dept., 1970—; interim dir. Campbell Friendship House, 1969. Social work cons. Planned Parenthood Assn. N.W. Ind., Gary, 1969—; cons. Green's Geriatric Health Center, Gary, 1969—, cons., resource person Maternal and Child Health Project for Model Cities program Gary, 1968—. With Semanon Civic and Social Clubs, Gary, 1960-68, treas., 1965-66; pres. County and Municipal Employees, Gary, 1956-58; sponsor St. Timothy Community Chs. Youth Usher Bd., 1963-65. Mem. Nat. Assn. Social Workers (chmn. nominating com. 1967-68, budget com. 1968-69), Internat., Tri-State assns. pupil personnel workers, Ind. State Conf. Social Welfare (program chmn. 1964-65, membership chmn. 1963-64). Home: 3373 W 20th Pl Gary IN 46404 Office: 3383 Broadway Gary IN 46409

WESLEY, SANDRA LOUISE, journalist; b. Buffalo, Aug. 2, 1939; d. Charles Joseph and Marguerite Georgina (Schmidt) Wesley; Ph.B., U. Detroit, 1962. Womens editor Boca Raton (Fla.) News, 1963-70; feature writer Palm Beach (Fla.) Post, 1970—. Recipient J. C. Penney-U. Mo. Journalist awards for excellence of women's pages, 1967, 69, 70; Dorothy Dawe award for reporting home furnishings, 1973. Mem. Women in Communications. Club: Florida Press (West Palm Beach). Home: 961 W Royal Palm Rd Boca Raton FL 33432 Office: 2751 S Dixie Hwy West Palm Beach FL 33405

WESS, GRACE IRENE BROWN (MRS. OTTO FRANCIS WESS), estimator, stables owner; b. Youngstown, O., May 13, 1925; d. Floyd Raymond and Ruth (Walter) Brown; student Bliss Bus. Coll., 1942-43; LL.B., LaSalle U., 1952; grad. nurse's tng. Youngstown Hosp. Assn., 1974; m. Otto Francis Wess, June 11, 1949 (dec. Mar. 1969); children—Raymond Francis, Shannon Grace (Mrs. W. Robert Weikart), Colleen Melody (Mrs. Dennis G. Bloomingdale), Honey Lucile, Alyson Rae. Nurse's aid St. Elizabeth Hosp., Youngstown, O., 1938-42; traffic clk. B.F. Goodrich Co., Akron, O., 1942-43; rate clk., traffic dept. Gen. Fireproofing Co., Youngstown, O., 1947-49; pres., co-owner Jewels by Lady Grace, Detroit, 1949-63, Grayce's Treasure Chests, Youngstown, O., 1949-63, Grayce's Medicine Chests, Youngstown, 1949-63; indsl., comml. bldg. estimator Ben Rudick & Son, Inc., Youngstown, O., 1963-71; free lance estimator, North Lima, O., 1971—; newspaper columnist, various newspapers, 1963-68; nurse, 1974—. Owner, Grace Wess Stables, Inc., Canfield, O., 1949—. Democratic candidate for Mahoning County commr., 1973. Served with WAVES, 1943-47. Mem. Am. Bus. Womens Assn. (pres. 1969-70), Youngstown Bus. and Profl. Womens Club, U.S. Trotting Assn., Canfield Harness Horsemens Assn., Ohio Harness Horsemens Assn., Am. Legion, V.F.W., Defense Supply Assn., McGuffey Meml. Assn., Women in Constrn., Constrn. Specifications Inst., Home and Sch. Assn., St. Charles Altar and Rosary Soc., Mahoning County Agrl. Soc., Youngstown Playhouse. Democrat. Roman Catholic. Home: 9525 Woodworth Rd North Lima OH 44452 Office: Box 37 North Lima OH 44452

WESSEL, HELEN ANN MUELLER, educator; b. Cin., July 4, 1925; d. Jacob C. and Helen (Maier) Mueller; B.S., U. Cin., 1948, B.S., 1955, D.Ed., 1964; M.Ed., Harvard, 1959; m. Robert Hoover Wessel, July 26, 1952. Asst. display mgr. Jenny, Inc., Cin., 1948-54; art tchr. Wyoming (O.) schs., 1955-56; art supr. Swampscott (Mass.) city schs., 1956-57; art tchr. Princeton city schs., Springdale, O., 1957-59; asst. prof. art U. Cin., 1959-65, asso. prof., 1965-71, prof., 1971—. Jury chmn. Women's Art Club Cin., 1965. Mem. Nat., Ohio (sec. 1971—) art edn. assns., Western Arts Assn., Am. Assn. U. Profs., Delta Phi Delta, Alpha Delta Pi. Republican. Home: 2106 Columbia Pkwy Cincinnati OH 45202

WESSEL, HELEN SYLVIA (MRS. WALTER WESTON WESSEL), pub. co. exec., author; b. San Anselmo, Cal., Jan. 9, 1924; d. John Albert and Laura Gertrude (Hammerli) Strain; B.A. cum laude, Sioux Falls Coll., 1960; postgrad. U. Minn., 1964-65; m. Walter Weston Wessel, June 22, 1945; children—Margaret (Mrs. James Wilke), Sharyl, Deborah, Dorothy, Daniel, Donald. Pres., Bookmates Inc., Pubs. and Distributors, Ossian, Ind., 1970—, also Bookmates Internat., Inc., Orange, Cal., 1970—. Pres. Internat. Childbirth Edn. Assn., 1964-66. Mem. Equipo Médico de Estudios Psicofísicos de Analgesia Obstétrica, Bogotá, Colombia (hon.). Author: Natural Childbirth and the Family, 1963, rev. edit., 1973; (with Neil and Peggy Verwey) Voice of Joy, 1973. Editor: (with Harlan F. Ellis) Childbirth Without Fear, 4th edit., 1972. Home and office: 3905 Rolling Hills Rd St Paul MN 55112

WESSLER, CAROL RUTH, librarian; b. Sheboygan, Wis., Mar. 30, 1933; d. Edward Henry and Elsie Frieda (Candler) Wessler; B.S., U. Wis., 1955; M.S., U. Ill., 1962. Kindergarten tchr. Long Beach (Cal.) Unified Sch. Dist., 1955-58, Sheboygan, 1958-61; reference librarian Wis. Valley Library Service, Wausau, 1962—. Bd. dirs. Wausau Community Concerts, 1966-71; bd. dirs. Ecumenical Lay Acad., 1971—, treas., 1972—. Mem. Am., Wis. (chmn. reference sect. 1966-67, sec. 1970-71) library assns., Wis. Valley Library Conf. (chmn. 1970-71), Common Cause (dist. chairperson 1973—). Presbyn. Home: 500 E Thomas St Wausau WI 54401 Office: 400 1st St Wausau WI 54401

WESSON, KAREN MCNEIL, veterinarian; b. Newton, Mass., June 6, 1941; d. Willard Francis and Susan (Young) McNeil; student Mt. Holyoke Coll., 1959-61; B.S., U. Ill., 1964, D.V.M., 1966; m. Joel Keith Wesson, Apr. 24, 1965; children—Wendy Yvonne, Jennifer Sue, Jeffrey Keith, Joshua Stephen. Veterinarian, Bellingham, Mass., 1966-67, Princeton, Ill., 1967-68; supervisory vet. med. officer U.S. Dept. Agr., Sterling, Ill., 1968—, also vet. recruiter. Mem. Women's Vet. Med. Assn., Am., Ill. Vet. med. assns., Nat. Assn. Fed. Veterinarians (v.p. Central Ill. chpt.). Home: Rural Route 1 Leland IL 60531 Office: PO Box D Sterling IL 61081

WEST, ALMA BROGWELL, librarian; b. Pitts., Sept. 1, 1910; d. Robert Henry and Henrietta Holmes (Billups) Brogwell; B.A., U. Pitts., 1928; B.S. in Library Sci., Hampton (Va.) Library Sch., 1936; m. Francis Montell West, June 17, 1928. Librarian, West Ky. State U., Paducah, 1936-38, Grambling (La.) Coll., 1940-44; br. librarian Carnegie Library, Pitts., 1945; staff librarian U.S. Dept. Commerce, 1946—, cataloger, 1946-54, reference librarian, 1954-63, supr. acquisitions, 1963—. Recipient Bronze medal Dept. Commerce, 1971. Mem. N.A.A.C.P., Urban League, Delta Sigma Theta. Mem. Atonement P.E. Ch. Home: 11512 Old Fort Rd SE Washington DC 20022 Office: 8060 13th St Silver Spring MD 20910

WEST, ANITA S. WOLFE (MRS. DAVID LEE WEST), mathematician; b. N.Y.C., Oct. 21, 1930; d. Bert S. and Dorothy (Sanders) Wolfe; B.S., U. Denver, 1960, M.S., 1962, Ph.D., 1969; m. David Lee West, Feb. 18, 1955; children—David Russell, Laurie Diane. Research asso. Tchrs. Coll. Columbia, 1949-51; engr. Martin Marrietta, Denver, 1960-64; research mathematician U. Denver Research Inst., 1964—. Tchr., U. Denver, Arapahoe Community Coll., 1970-71; cons. State Colo., 1970, 74, Eastman Kodak Corp., 1974. Grantee Law Enforcement Assistance Adminstrn., 1970, Office Naval Research, 1972-73, USAF, 1971-74. Mem. Nat. Council Tchrs. Math., Sigma Xi (chpt. v.p. 1972-73, pres. 1974-75). Contbr. articles to profl. jours. Home: 3856 S Holly St Denver CO 80237 Office: U Denver Research Inst University Park Denver CO 80210

WEST, ANN, physician; b. Richland Springs, Tex.; d. William Jackson and Iona Jane (Carter) West; student Baylor U., 1924, Tex. Tech., 1925; M.D., Baylor Med. Coll., 1930. Intern, Baylor Hosp., Dallas, 1930-31; gen. practice Lynn County, Tex., 1932-36, Dallas, 1936—; mem. staff Baylor, Parkland hosps.; clin. asst. prof. internal medicine Southwestern Med. Sch. U. Tex., Dallas. Executrix Lynn West Estate. Active Red Cross, Ark., Miss. flood relief, 1937. Club: Pilot (Dallas). Baptist. Republican. Home: 6620 Yosemite Dallas TX 75214 Office: 808 Med Art Dallas TX 75201

WEST, BARBARA GENE HILLMAN (MRS. USHER WEST), ednl. adminstr.; b. Silver City, Utah, Apr. 22, 1923; d. Eugene V. and Naoma (Ellsworth) Hillman; B.S., U. Utah, 1945, M.S., 1954, Ed.D., 1964; m. Usher West, May 20, 1944; children—Rebecca (Mrs. Dennis Simpson), Gregory, Nathan, Patricia. Tchr. East High Sch., Salt Lake City, 1945-51; tchr.'s adminstr. U. Utah, Salt Lake City, 1952—. Cons. elementary phys. edn. Bd. dirs. P.T.A., Salt Lake City, parliamentarian, 1970-71, recreation chmn., 1968-70. Mem. Am. (honor award 1973), Utah (pres. 1960-61) assns. for health, phys. edn. and recreation, Western Soc. Phys. Edn. Coll. Women, Am. Assn. Univ. Profs. (sec. 1972), U. Utah Faculty Club. Mem. Ch. of Jesus Christ of Latter Day Saints. Home: 3339 Joyce Dr Salt Lake City UT 84109 Office: HPRW 239 Univ of Utah Salt Lake City UT 84112

WEST, BETH INEZ, editor; b. San Antonio, Feb. 23, 1945; d. Robert Lee and Bernice Inez (King) West; B.J., U. Tex., 1966; M.Liberal Arts, So. Meth. U., 1973. Asst. editor So. Union Gas Co., Dallas, 1968-71, publs. editor, 1971—. Recipient Katie award Press Club Dallas, 1972, award of excellence Women in Communications, 1972, 73. Mem. Women in Communications, Internat. Assn. Bus. Communicators (v.p. publicity 1973, v.p. programs 1974, mem. com. 1973-74). Home: 5032 Matilda Dallas TX 75206 Office: 1433 Fidelity Union Tower Dallas TX 75201

WEST, CARLA LANE (MRS. SAMUEL G. WEST), hosp. adminstr.; b. Plentywood, Mont., July 11, 1945; d. Waldemar W. and Cora Louise (Angvick) Lane; grad. high sch.; m. Samuel G. West, Apr. 21, 1973. Legal sec. John B. Driver, atty., Marshall, Ark., 1961-63; key punch operator Summerfield Chevrolet Co., Flint, Mich., 1964-66; profl. photographer Cora's Photos, Marshall, 1967-68; adminstrv. asst. Van Buren County Meml. Hosp. and Nursing Home, Clinton, Ark., 1969, adminstr., 1969-74. Coordinator, cons. Cleveland County Meml. Hosp. and Nursing Home, Rison, Ark., 1971-74. Pres. Tri-County Econ. Devel. Council, 1971. Recipient Boss of Year award Clinton Jr. C. of C., 1971. Mem. Ark., N.Central Ark. (sec. 1972) hosp. assns. Home: PO Box 395 Leslie AR 72645 Office: PO Box 206 Clinton AR 72031

WEST, ELINOR JANE MADDOCK (MRS. LOWREN WEST), educator; b. Denver, Sept. 3, 1927; d. Edward G. and Mildred Marie (Menzel) Maddock; diploma Pratt Inst., 1947; B.S., Columbia, 1954, M.A., 1955, Ph.D., 1967; m. Lowren West, July 2, 1948; 1 son, Loren Arthur. Preceptor, Columbia, 1963-64; instr. Sarah Lawrence Coll., 1965-66, Rutgers U., 1966-67; asst. prof. philosophy L.I. U., Bklyn., 1967-71, asso. prof., 1971—; vis. asst. prof. philosophy Queens Coll., Flushing, N.Y., 1972-73. Mem. L.I. Philos. Soc., Am. Philos. Assn. Home: 300 Riverside Dr New York City NY 10025 Office: Long Island University Brooklyn NY 11201

WEST, IRMA, physician; b. Hespeler, Ont., Can.; d. Frank A. and Vera (Alderson) Calvert; A.B., Williamette U., 1943; M.D., Woman's Med. Coll., 1947; M. P.H., U. Cal. at Berkeley, 1953; m. Ernest West, Oct. 17, 1948 (div.); 1 son, Michael. Intern St. Joseph's Hosp., San Francisco, 1947-48; with Cal. Pub. Health, 1951—, med. officer, 1951-58, acting chief Bur. Occupational Health, Cal. Pub. Health Dept., 1958-60, cons. occupational medicine, 1960-68, coordinator injury control project, 1968-70, head kidney disease program, 1970—, asst. chief (med.) Bur. Adult Health and Chronic Disease, 1972-73, chief standards devel. sect., 1973; cons. occupational medicine Occupational Health sect. Cal. Dept. Health, Sacramento, 1973—. Diplomate Am. Bd. Preventive Medicine, Mem. Cal., Sacramento County med. assns., Am. Coll. Preventive Medicine, A.M.A., Am. Pub. Health Assn., Delta Omega. Home: 8428 Citadel Way Sacramento CA 95826 Office: 714 P St Sacramento CA 95814

WEST, KATHRYN LOUISE (MRS. LOUIS J. WEST), research psychologist; b. Fort Madison, Ia., Oct. 18, 1923; d. Rollin James and Harriet Elizabeth Dorothea (Diedrich) Hopkirk; student State U. Ia., 1941-44; B.A. summa cum laude, U. Minn., 1946, Ph.D., 1966; m. Louis Jolyon West, Apr. 29, 1944; children—Anne Kathryn, Mary Elizabeth, John Stuart. Researcher, tchr. dept. psychology U. Minn., 1946-49; testing and guidance counselor Casady Sch., Oklahoma City, 1958-66; tchr., researcher dept. psychiatry, neurology and behavioral scis. U. Okla. Med. Center, 1958-69; research psychologist U. Cal. at Los Angeles, 1969—. Nat. Inst. Child Health and Human Devel. postdoctoral fellow U. Cal. at Berkeley, 1966-67; Nat. Inst. Mental Health spl. research fellow U. Cal. at Los Angeles, 1970-71. Mem. Am., Western, Southwestern psychol. assns., Soc. for Research in Child Devel. Democrat. Contbr. articles to profl. jours., chpts. to books. Home: 207 N Glenroy Av Los Angeles CA 90049

WEST, LOIS (MRS. JOHN C. WEST), wife of gov. of S.C.; m. John C. West, Aug. 29, 1948; children—John Carl, Douglas Allen, Shelton Anne. Address: PO Drawer 100 Camden SC 29020

WEST, MARALYN H., educator; b. Lima, O., Mar. 13, 1928; d. Harold McDonald and Elaine A. (Ruck) West; B.S., Bowling Green State U., 1954; M.Edn., Cleve. State U., 1972. Tchr. phys. edn. John Adams High Sch., Cleve., 1954, Central Jr. High Sch., Cleve., 1955-56; head dept. phys. edn. John Hay High Sch., Cleve., 1956-69, adminstrv. asst., 1969-72, asst. prin., 1972-73; asst. prin. Collinwood High Sch., 1973—. Mgr. U.S. Women's Track and Field Team, Pan Am. Games, 1959; team mgr., 1965; field events referee U.S. Olympic Track and Field Trials for Women, 1964—; sec. women's track and field com. U.S. Olympic Com., 1965—; women's track and field chmn. Lake Erie Assn. Amateur Athletic Union, 1959-70, also mem. nat. com., 1959—, nat. chmn. rules com., 1964-70, mem. nat. track and field records com., 1964-70, mem. Lake Erie basketball com., 1964-70, chmn. women's track and field finance com., 1971—, mem. women's track and field internat. com., 1971—, mgr. Women's jr. track and field European team, 1973—, designed Amateur Athletic Union women's track and field emblem, 1972; nat. track and field chmn. Div. for Girls' and Women's Sports, 1960-64; supr. Girls Jr. Olympics, Cleve., 1957-62; mgr., asst. coach Cleve. div., Recreation Girls Track and Field Team, 1956-70; mgr. U.S. Women's Track and Field team, 1966—; mgr. U.S. Olympic Women's track and field team Mexico City, 1968; mem. women's adv. com. City of Cleve. Recreation Dept., 1961-70; author, dir., editor track and field instrnl. movie Girls on the Move, 1969. Recipient Master Teaching award Martha Holden Jennings Found., 1967. Mem. A.A.H.P.E.R. (nat. chmn. girls track and field 1960-64), Ohio Assn. for Health, Phys. Edn. and Recreation (state chmn. girls track and field 1959-64), Cleve. Bd. Women's Ofcls. (women's track and field chmn. 1958—), Ohio High Sch. Athletic Assn. (chmn. girls track and field adv. com. 1973—), Cleve. Women's Phys. Edn. Assn. (sec. 1962-64, v.p. 1964-65, membership chmn. 1965-67), Northeastern Ohio Tchrs. Assn. (chmn. 1962), Women's Nat. Ofcls. Rating Commn., Ohio Edn. Assn., N.E.A. (mem. nat. com. operational fitness 1960-63). Editor: Track and Field Guide, 1960-64. Home: 18700 Shawnee Av Cleveland OH 44119

WEST, MARGARET L., advt. exec.; b. Lincoln, Neb., Aug. 9, 1928; d. Granville F. and Catherine (Flau) West; student Neb. Wesleyan U., 1945-46. Mem. advt. staff Omaha World-Herald, 1946-48, J. L. Brandeis Dept. Store, 1948-49; advt. mgr. Philips Dept. Store, 1949-69, advt. and promotion dir. Young Quinlan Co., Mpls., 1969-74; advt. and marketing mgr. Dewitt Drug & Beauty Products, Inc., Greenville, S.C., 1974—. Lectr. seminars advt. staff Omaha Sun Newspapers, 1956—. Dir. Philips Employees Credit Union, 1961-63, pres., 1966-68. Mem. publicity com. YWCA, 1961; mem. Downtown Council Promotional Steering Com. Trustee Woodson Center Assn., 1961, chmn. pub. relations com., 1961-69. Mem. Omaha Advt. Club (Advt. Woman of Year 1960, dir., chmn. edn. com. 1961-69), Omaha Urban League Guild, C. of C. (pres. women's div. 1963-64, dir. 1963-64, mem. community devel. com. 1962-69), Greater Mpls. C. of C. (mem. Women's div.), Advt. Club Minn. Club: Omaha Sports (dir. 1962). Home: 2207 Wade Hampton Blvd #B-307 Greenville SC 29607 Office: Dewitt Drug & Beauty Products Inc PO Box 6827 Greenville SC 29606

WEST, MARGARET LILA WALKER (MRS. VICTOR ROYCE WEST), ednl. adminstr.; b. Gibbon, Neb., Aug. 28, 1905; d. James George and Niema Sybil (Converse) Walker; B.A., U. Neb., 1934; student U. Heidelberg (Germany), 1930-32, 35-36; postgrad. U. Minn., 1948-49, U. Ill., 1952; M.Ed., Nat. Coll. Edn., 1965; m. Victor Royce West, June 3, 1930; children—Sybel (Mrs. Thomas Hughes Kimmel), Vicki. Tchr. Gibbon (Neb.) Elementary Sch., 1926-30; tchr. German and Latin Omaha Central High Sch., 1938-40; prin., tchr. Sheltering Arms Hosp. Sch. for Polio Patients, Mpls., 1948-51; supervisory tchr. educable mentally handicapped Evanston (Ill.) Twp. High Sch., 1951-70; supr. student tchrs. in spl. edn. Ill. State U., Normal, 1972—. Bd. dirs. YWCA, Omaha, 1938-40, Evanston, 1965-67, North Shore Assn. for Retarded Children and Shore Tng. Center, Evanston, 1965-67. Am. Assn. Mental Deficiency fellow, 1967. Mem. Internat., Ill. (sec. 1956-58, bd. dirs. 1956-61, chpt. pres. 1960) councils for exceptional children, Am. Assn. Mental Deficiency, Am. Assn. U. Women, Gamma Phi Beta (province dir. 1939-41), Delta Kappa Gamma. Methodist. Home: 9310 Lincolnwood Dr Evanston IL 60203

WEST, NANCY RUTH (MRS. DAVID WILLIAM WEST), profl. assn. exec.; b. Blackwell, Okla., June 13, 1933; d. Everett Marian and Veronica (Kort) Brazelton; B.S., Mt. St. Scholastica Coll., 1955; postgrad. U. Md., 1964-65, U. Ariz., 1968-69; m. David William West, Apr. 17, 1970; children—Leann, Thaddeus; children by previous marriage—John, Michael, Seanna, Maureen, Partick, Mary. Asst. home agt. Okla. State U. Agrl. Extension Service, Fairview, 1955-56; home economist marketing div. Kan. Bd. Agr., Topeka, 1956-57; exec. dir. Dairy Council of Ariz., 1966—. Asst. prof., techniques in nutrition edn. Phoenix Coll., 1971; chmn. Ariz. Nutrition Council Task Force III, 1970-71; pres. Nutrition Council Ariz., 1972-73; participant White House Conf. Food, Nutrition and Health, 1969; mem. ad hoc adv. com. Ariz. House Bill 103, 1970-71; mem. adv. com. Am. Dietetic Assn. Pub. Relations Com., 1970-72; mem. adv. com., nutrition sect. Ariz. Dept. Health, 1973; adv. bd. United Dairy Industry Assn. Mem. New School Bldg. Com., Kiva Sch., Paradise Valley, Ariz., 1971. Recipient outstanding community service award Central Ariz. Dental Soc., 1968, appreciation award Ariz. Dietetic Assn., 1970. Mem. Am., Ariz. (chmn. pub. relations 1971-72, bd. dirs. 1971) home econs. assns. Republican. Home: 8005 N Coconino Rd Paradise Valley AZ 85253 Office: 3737 E Indian School Rd Phoenix AZ 85018

WEST, REBECCA (CICILY ISABEL FAIRFIELD), novelist; b. Edinburgh, Scotland, Dec. 21, 1892; d. Charles and Isabella Campbell (MacKenzie) Fairfield; grad. George Watson's Ladies Coll., Edinburgh; Litt.D., N.Y. U., 1965; m. Henry Maxwell Andrews, Nov. 1, 1930 (dec. 1968). Began as reviewer Free-women, 1911; joined staff of Clarion as polit. writer, 1912. Author: Henry James, 1916; The Return of the Soldier, 1918; The Judge, 1922; The Strange Necessity, 1928; Harriet Hume, 1929; St. Augustine, 1930; D. H. Lawrence, an Elegy, 1930; Ending in Earnest, 1932; The Rake's Progress, 1934; The Harsh Voice, 1935; The Thinking Reed, 1936; Black Lamb and Grey Falcon, 1941; The Meaning of Treason, 1947; A Train of Powder, 1955; The Fountain Overflows, 1957; The Court and the Castle, 1957; The Vassall Affair, 1963; The New Meaning of Treason, 1964; The Birds Fall Down, 1966. Decorated comdr. Order Brit. Empire, chevalier Legion Honor, 1957, dame comdr. Brit. Empire, 1959; recipient A. C. Benson Silver medal, 1966. Fellow Royal Soc. Lit.; mem. Am. Acad. Arts and Scis. Address: McMillans Little Essex St London WC 2 England

WEST, SANDRA ARLINE, city ofcl.; b. Detroit, Sept. 15, 1940; d. Walter Ernest and Arlie (Thomas) West; B.A. in Journalism (David Wilkie scholar, Inez Robb scholar), Wayne State U., 1963. Classified ad writer Detroit Free Press, 1963-66; feature writer Gary (Ind.) Post-Tribune, 1966; reporter U.P.I., Detroit, 1966-67; publicist City Detroit Dept. Report and Information Com., 1967-73, supervising publicist, 1973—. Mem. Mayor's Com. to keep Detroit Beautiful, 1968—; pub. relations rep. Detroit Hist. Soc., 1968-70. Mem. Women in Communications, Detroit Press Club. Episcopalian. Office: City County Bldg Detroit MI 48226

WEST, VIRGINIA SOUTH, city ofcl.; b. nr. Fayette, Ala., Aug. 22, 1920; d. William Andrew and Lucy Jane (South) West; B.S., Auburn U., 1941. Project auditor Coosa River Valley Def. Housing Authority, Ala., 1941-43; sec.-accountant Housing Authority of City of Childersburg and Sylacauga (Ala.) Housing Authority, 1943; housing mgr. Sylacauga Housing Authority, 1943-49, exec. dir., 1949—; coordinator Sylacauga's Workable Program for Community Improvement, 1957-69, dir. area community action agy., 1968-73. Worker community drives United Givers, A.R.C., Heart Fund, Cancer Crusade; county chmn. Crusade for Children, S. Talladega County, 1948; sec. Literacy Council Sylacauga, 1960-61; sec. Citizens Adv. Com., 1963-69; sec. Talladega County chpt. Ala. Soc. for Crippled Children and Adults, 1960-62, dir., 1966—. Recipient award Sylacauga Park and Recreation Bd., 1966. Mem. Southeastern Regional Council Nat. Assn. Housing and Redevel. Ofcls. (divisional v.p. housing div. 1966-67, sec.-treas. 1967-68, chmn. in-service tng. inst. 1967-69, v.p. renewal div. 1968-69, edn. com. chmn. 1968-69, pres. 1970-71, mem. exec. com. 1966—), Nat. Assn. Housing and Redevel. Ofcls. (exec. com. 1970—, v.p. housing div. 1973—), Nat. Housing Conf., Ala. Assn. Housing Authorities (exec. com. 1959-62, v.p. 1962-63, pres. 1963-64), Bus. and Profl. Women's Club (past pres.), Am. Assn. U. Women, Alpha Omicron Pi. Democrat. Mem. Ch. of Christ. Clubs: Pilot (past dir., treas. 1972—), Sylacauga Garden (past pres.), Alabama Garden (rec. sec. 1959-61). Home: 201 W Walnut St Sylacauga AL 35150 Office: PO Box 539 Sylacauga AL 35150

WESTCAMP, LILA BURNADEAN, banker; b. Ft. Smith, Ark., Dec. 8, 1926; d. Henry Horton and Florence (Moody) Bivins; Cert. Am. Inst Banking, 1969; m. William Charles Westcamp, Dec. 2, 1944; children—William Henry, Robert Charles. Teller First Nat. Bank of So. Md., Andrews AFB, Md., 1949-57; bank teller drafts and collections City Nat. Bank, Ft. Smith, Ark., 1957-62, supr. gen. ledger, 1962-66, asst. auditor, 1966-68, auditor, 1968—. Mem. Am. Inst. Banking (pres. Ft. Smith chpt. 1970-71), Credit Womens Internat. (pres. 1966). Home: Rt 1 Box 328 Fort Smith AR 72901 Office: City Nat Bank 1222 Rogers Av Fort Smith AR 72901

WESTERFELD, NANCY VIRGINIA WALNEY (MRS. MAURICE URBAN WESTERFELD), judge; b. Dallas, Jan. 15, 1928; d. Edward and Lena (Formann) Walney; B.A., U. Houston, 1949, LL.B., 1950; postgrad. U. Mex., summers 1945, 46, 47; m. Maurice Urban Westerfeld, Nov. 15, 1950; children—Maurice E., Nina Ann. Missy Beth. File research Fulbright, Crooker, Freeman & Bates, Houston, 1949-50; admitted to Tex. bar, 1955; gen. pvt. practice law, Houston, 1954—; mem. firm Westerfeld & Westerfeld, Houston; judge Justice Ct., Precinct 5, Harris County, Tex. Legal adviser pre-release program Goree Prison for Women; mem. State Bar Tex. PEER teaching team in domestic relations, chmn. Houston Bar juvenile delinquency com. State Bar Tex. Bd. dirs. Houston Legal Found., Tb and Lung Assn., Hope Center for Youth. Mem. Am., Houston (mem. domestic relations, juvenile, land, trust and probate coms., v.p.) bar assns., U. Houston Law Alumni (bd. dirs.), Nat. Platform Assn., Am. Assn. U. Women, Nat. Assn. Women Lawyers, Bus. and Profl. Women's Club, Altrusa, Kappa Beta Pi. Office: 6510 S Rice Av Houston TX 77401

WESTERHAUS, CATHERINE FRANCES (MRS. GEORGE H. WESTERHAUS), social worker; b. Corydon, Ind., Oct. 13, 1910; d. Anthony J. and Permelia Ann (Mathes) Kannapel; B. Music Edn., Kan. U., 1934; M.S.W., Loyola U., Chgo., 1949; m. George H. Westerhaus, Apr. 15, 1950. Social worker Harvey County Welfare Dept., Newton, Kan., 1934-38, 40-74, welfare dir., 1941-74; adult services supr., regional office Dept. Social and Rehab. Services, Wichita, Kan., 1974—; social worker Lyon County Welfare Dept., Emporia, Kan., 1938-39. Mem. adv. com. Sch. Social Work, Kan. U., Lawrence, 1966—; mem. adv. com. to homemaker service demonstration project, dept. family econs. Kan. State U., Manhattan, 1968-71. Served with USNR, 1945-46. Mem. Acad. Certified Social Workers, Kan. Conf. Social Workers, Am. Legion (dist. child welfare chmn. 1964-71), Daus. Isabella (regent 1966, 67). Home: 613 N Plum St Newton KS 67114 Office: 155 S Hydraulic Wichita KS 67211

WESTERMAN, CAROLE JOAN, psychologist; b. Phila., Oct. 20, 1937; d. Albert John and Melva Grace (Kuhn) Westerman; B.A., Bucknell U., 1959; M.S. in Edn., U. Pa., 1963, Ed.D., 1973. Tchr., counselor Haverford (Pa.) Twp. Sch. Dist., 1959-65; asst. prof., counselor N.Y. State Coll. Home Econs., Cornell U., Ithaca, 1965-68; counseling psychologist U. Pa., Phila., 1968—. Recipient Outstanding Service award Bd. Sch. Dirs., Haverford Twp., 1962; Nat. Def. Edn. Act Inst. fellow, 1963. Mem. Am., Eastern psychol. assns., Am., Pa. personnel and guidance assns. Home: 1030 Mason Av Drexel Hill PA 19026 Office: 3812 Walnut St Philadelphia PA 19174

WESTERMAN, SUSAN JANE SWARTZ (MRS. PETER WESTERMAN), lawyer; b. Lansing, Mich., Aug. 6, 1943; d. Howard Calvin and Cora Adelade (Walcutt) Swartz; B.A. cum laude, Mich. State U., 1964; J.D., U. Mich., 1970; m. Peter Westerman, Dec. 30, 1967. Admitted to Mich. bar, 1970; asso. Hooper, Hathaway, Fichera, Price & Davis, Ann Arbor, Mich., 1970-74, Dykema, Gossett, Spencer & Trigg, 1974—. Mem. League Women Voters, Am. Assn. U. Women. Home: 2058 Ascot Rd Ann Arbor MI 48103 Office: 610 City Center Bldg Ann Arbor MI 48108

WESTERVELT, ESTHER JULIA MANNING (MRS. ANDREW CASTLE WESTERVELT), educator; b. N.Y.C.; d. Hiram Terry and Emma (Wilson) Manning; B.A., Vassar Coll., 1935; M.A., Tchrs. Coll., Columbia, 1956; Ed.D., Columbia, 1961; m. Ira Hart Koenig, 1937 (div. 1939); m. 2d, Marvin Rothfielder, 1942 (div. 1944); 1 son, John Terry; m. 3d, Harold E. Shively, Oct. 24, 1944 (div. June 1961); children—Bonnie, Robin, Julie; m. 4th, Andrew Castle Westervelt, July 3, 1961. Exec. dir. Orange County Council Community Services, 1953-60; instr., research asso. Tchrs. Coll., Columbia, 1961-63, asst. prof. edn., 1964-67, adj. asso. prof. edn., 1967-69; dir. N.Y. State Guidance Center for Women, Suffern, N.Y., 1966-68, dir. research, 1969-70; exec. co-dir. Nat. Coalition for Research on Women's Edn. and Devel., State U. N.Y. at Stony Brook, 1970-72; holder alumnae endowed chair, dir. instl. studies Simmons Coll., Boston, 1973—. Lectr., cons., workshop leader to numerous colls., univs., and orgns. Mem. com. on home and community Pres.'s Commn. on Status of Women, 1962-63; mem. Woman's Council of N.Y. State Dept. Commerce Women's Program, 1963—, co-chmn. com. on edn., 1964—. Bd. dirs. Orange County Council for Community Services, Inc. Served with WAFS, 1942-44. Fellow Assn. for Applied Anthropology; mem. Am. Assn. U. Women, Am. Ednl. Research Assn., Am. Personnel and Guidance Assn. (mem. finance com. 1963-65), Nat. Vocational Guidance Assn. (commn. on occupational status of women 1969—), Nat. Assn. Women Deans and Counselors, Am. Assn. for Higher Edn., Am. Coll. Personnel Assn., N.E.A., Internat. Oceanographic Found., League Women Voters, Am. Civil Liberties Union, Nat. Council Negro Women, Nat. Council on Day Care of Children, Nat. Council on Family Relations, Pi Lambda Theta, Kappa Delta Pi. Author: (with D.A. Fixter) Women's Higher and Continuing Education, 1971. Editor: (with Esther Lloyd-Jones) Behavioral Science and Guidance: Perspectives and Proposals, 1963. Contbr. to books, also articles to profl. jours. Home: Breeze Valley Fam RD 1 Goshen NY 10924 also Yam Seed Newcastle Nevis West Indies

WESTERVELT, VIRGINIA VEEDER (MRS. RALPH V. WESTERVELT), educator, writer; b. Schenectady; d. Eugene W. and Millicent (Winton) Veeder; student Pomona Coll., 1931-33; A.B., Wellesley Coll., 1935; postgrad. summers Central Sch. Speech and Drama, London, Eng., 1935, Columbia, 1954, N.Y.U., 1940; M.A., Syracuse U., 1960; m. Ralph V. Westervelt, Sept. 1, 1936; children—Dirck Eugene, Deidre Virginia. Exec. trainee Jordan Marsh Co., Boston, 1935-36; tchr. Brown Sch., Schenectady, 1938-40; coordinator distributive edn. Nott Terrace High Sch., Schenectady, 1952-53; tchr. English, Mt. Pleasant High Sch., Schenectady, 1957, New Hartford (N.Y.) High Sch., 1958-68; prof. English dept. U. Redlands (Cal.), 1969-73, Crafton Hills Coll., 1973—. Cons. leadership confs., writers cons., 1950—; speaker to various orgns., 1958—; tchr. lit. extension courses Ithaca (N.Y.) Coll., 1962-68. Mem. Claverack Players Little Theater Group, Women's Civic Chorus, Women of Rotary, Schenectady Choral Soc.; mem. Luth. Commn. on Ch. Papers, 1962-66. Recipient Achievement award Pen Women, 1970. Am. Newspaper Pubs. Assn. grantee, 1960. Mem. Nat. League Am. Pen Women (sec. 1965, pres. 1968-70), Am. Assn. U. Women (leader lit. study group Schenectady 1954-55, Redlands 1967-69, leader creative writing group 1957-58, historian 1971-72, Community Service award 1958), Quill and Scroll, P.E.O. Lutheran (pres. ch. women 1970-72). Clubs: Wellesley (sec. Schenectady 1939-40). Author: Getting Along in the Teen-Age World, 1957; Choosing a Career in a Changing World, 1960; The World Was Its Laboratory: The Story of Dr. Willis Rodney Whitney, 1964; Incredible Man of Science: Irving Langmuir, 1968 (trans. into Burmese). Contbr. articles and stories to Am. Girl, Am. Mercury, Nature, Christian Sci. Monitor, N.Y. Times, Modern Maturity, Wilderness Camping, many others. Home: 1050 Bermuda Dr Redlands CA 92373

WESTHEAD, ELEANORE CLAIRE, educator; b. Phila., Nov. 7, 1935; d. Edward W. and Eleanore (Ritchie) Westhead; A.B., Cath. U. Am., 1956; M.Ed., Temple U., 1961; Ph.D., Syracuse U., 1965. Tchr., Devereux Schs., Devon, Pa., 1957-58; spl. class tchr. Phila. Pub. Schs., 1958-61; instr. spl. edn., rehab. Syracuse U., 1963-65; asst. prof. dept. spl. edn. Sch. Edn., U. Va., Charlottesville, 1965-69, asso. prof., 1969—. Cons. Neighborhood Youth Corps, 1966, 67, CAO, Charlottesville. Mem. Council for Exceptional Children (state rep. Div. Children with Learning Disabilities 1968-71, mem. nat. bd. at large 1972; del. tchr. edn. div.; mem. Council for Children with Behavioral Disorders 1968—), Am. Assn. Mental Deficiency (regional panel chmn. 1969), Orton Soc., Am. Assn. U. Profs., Assn. for Children with Learning Disabilities (pres. Va. assn. 1970-72, edn. adviser 1968-70, 74—). Contbr. articles to ednl. jours. Home: 2627 Jefferson Park Circle Charlottesville VA 22903

WESTHEIMER, RUTH KAROLA (MRS. MANFRED WESTHEIMER), educator; b. Wiesenfeld, Germany, June 4, 1928; d. Julius and Irma (Hanauer) Siegel; diploma, Tchrs. Sem., Jerusalem, 1950; B.A., Sorbonne, Paris, 1956; M.A., New Sch. for Social Research, 1959; Ed.D., Columbia, 1970; m. Manfred Westheimer, Dec. 10, 1961; children—Miriam, Joel. Came to U.S., 1956, naturalized, 1962. Dir., tchr. kindergarten in Paris and Israel, 1951-56; project dir. Planned Parenthood of N.Y.C., 1967-70; lectr. Tchrs. Coll., Columbia, 1970—; asso. prof. Lehman Coll., City U. N.Y., 1971—, mem. com. on research and grants Ednl. Forum, chmn. workshops, lectures. Mem. Sch. Adv. Bd., Bronx, N.Y., 1972-73. Mem. exec. bd. YM and YWHA of Washington Heights and Inwood. Recipient Faculty Research award City U. N.Y., 1973, 74. Mem. Am. Orthopsychiat. Assn., Am. Sociol. Assn., Soc. for Study Social Problems, Am. Pub. Health Assn., Nat. Council Family Relations, Kappa Delta Pi. Mem. B'nai B'rith. Contbr. articles profl. jours. Home: 900 W 190th St New York City NY 10040 Office: Lehman Coll City U NY Bronx NY 10468

WESTIN, JEANE EDDY (MRS. GENE THEODORE WESTIN), writer; b. Oklahoma City, July 3, 1931; d. Henry Franklin and Anna Blanche (Barnes) Eddy; student Fairmont State Coll., 1957, Am. River Coll., 1960-61, 70-73; m. Gene Theodore Westin, Apr. 28, 1962; 1 dau., Cara Marlene. Dir. information services Animal Protection Inst., Sacramento, 1968-70; advt. copywriter Schwalbe & Asso., San Francisco, 1970-72; asso. BPM Assos., Sacramento, 1972—; non-fiction writer contbr. to Parade, Woman's Day, Coronet, Pageant, True, Modern Maturity, PTA mag., Weight Watchers, Christian Sci. Monitor, TWA Ambassador, Westways and Discovery, 1970—. Media cons. Com. to End Violence Against the Next Generation, Berkeley, 1973—, Animal Protection Inst. Am., Sacramento, 1972—. Mem. Young Democrats, Chgo., 1960, Sacramento, 1961-62. Served with WAC, 1951-57. Mem. Cal. Writers Club, Soc. Mag. Writers. Address: 6456 Fordham Way Sacramento CA 95831

WESTLING, JEANINE NELSON (MRS. OREN N. WESTLING), govt. ofcl.; b. Mpls., Nov. 18, 1934; d. Stanley C. and Evelyn R. (Johnson) Nelson; student U. Minn., 1952-56; m. Oren N. Westling, Aug. 20, 1960. Copywriter, Montgomery Ward, St. Paul, 1957; editor Minn. Farm Bur., St. Paul, 1957; pub. relations asst. N. Central Airlines, Mpls., 1958-60; editorial asst. Mpls. C. of C., 1960-62; editor Greater Mpls., 1962-65; pub. relations dir. Met. Area Safety Council, Mpls., 1965-71; pub. information dir. Hennepin County Alcohol Safety Action Project, Mpls., 1971—. Chmn., Bloomington (Minn.) Republican party, 1960, Young Rep. League, 1958; dir. Hennepin County Young Rep. League, 1958-60, sec., 1958. Mem. Pub. Relations Soc. Am., Internat. Assn. Bus. Communicators, Mpls. Soc. Fine Arts, Walker Art Center, Minn. Orchestral Assn., Gamma Omicron Beta. Episcopalian. Home: 6620 Pawnee Rd Edina MN 55435 Office: 625 2d Av S Minneapolis MN 55402

WESTLUND, RUTH ELFRIEDA, educator, counselor; b. Mpls., July 15, 1916; d. Nathaniel and Alfrida (Peterson) Westlund; B.S., U. Minn., 1938, M.A., 1940, Ph.D., 1959. Head resident, asst. psychologist Coll. Wooster, O., 1939-42; hall counselor Stephens Coll., 1942-43; dir. govt. residence hall Fed. Works Agy.-Pub. Bldg. Adminstrn., 1943-50; counselor for women N.M. State U., 1950-52, Bemidji State Coll., 1952-53; instr. U. Minn., 1953-59; asso. dean women, prof. edn., No. Ill. U., DeKalb, 1959-72, counselor Coll. Bus., 1972—. Mem. Am. Assn. U. Women (br. pres. 1963-65), Am. Psychol. Assn., Am., Ill. personnel and guidance assns., Nat., Ill. (treas. 1970-72) assns. women deans and counselors, N.E.A., Ill. Edn. Assn., Delta Kappa Gamma. Home: 1117 Holmes Pl DeKalb IL 60115

WESTMORELAND, BARBARA F., physician; b. N.Y.C., July 22, 1940; d. Robert Edward and Wanda (Zabawski) Westmoreland; B.S. in Chemistry, Mary Washington Coll., 1961; M.D., U. Va., 1965. Med. intern Vanderbilt U. Hosp., 1965-66; asst. resident neurology U. Va. Hosp., 1966-67; research fellow U. Va., 1968, sr. resident neurology, 1969-70; fellow in electroencephalography Mayo Grad. Sch. Medicine, Rochester, Minn., 1970-72; asso. cons. in electroencephalography Mayo Clinic, 1970-73, cons., 1973—; asst. prof. neurology Mayo Med. Sch., 1973—. Recipient Colgate Darden award Mary Washington Coll., 1961. Diplomate Am. Bd. Psychiatry and Neurology. Mem. A.M.A., Am. Epilepsy Soc., Am. Acad. Neurology, Am. EEG Soc., Sigma Xi, Alpha Omega Alpha, Chi Beta Phi, Alpha Phi Sigma, Phi Sigma Iota. Address: 200 1st St SW Rochester MN 55901

WESTMORELAND, CAROL SLATER (MRS. CORLEY B. WESTMORELAND), educator; b. Ogden, Utah, Jan. 25, 1931; d. Horace Horatio and Gladys (Shaw) Slater; A.S., Weber State Coll., 1951; B.S., Utah State U., 1953, M.S., 1963; m. Corley B. Westmoreland, Dec. 18, 1955 (div. Dec. 1970). Tchr. pub. schs., Tooele, Utah, 1953-55; instr. Weber State Coll., Ogden, 1955-62, asst. prof., 1963-68, asso. prof., 1968—, head women's phys. edn., 1966—, dir. intramural sports, 1955-64, dir. extramural sports, 1964-70. Active Ogden chpt. A.R.C. Mem. A.A.H.P.E.R., Utah Edn. Assn., Utah Assn. for Health, Phys. Edn. and Recreation, Western Soc. Phys. Edn. for Coll. Women, Div. Girls' and Women's Sports (state chmn. 1965-66), N.C. Bus. Edn. Assn., N.C. Bus. Tchrs. Assn., Cardinal Key, Chi Omega, Phi Kappa Phi. Mem. Ch. Jesus Christ of Latter-day Saints. Home: 3507 Fowler Av Ogden UT 84403

WESTMORELAND, CAROLYN REBECCA, coll. pres.; b. Walkertown, N.C.; d. Moses Martin and Cynthia Elizabeth (Morris) Westmoreland; student Women's Female Coll. (now U. N.C.); grad. Draughon Bus. Coll. Sec. to pres. Draughon Bus. Coll., Winston-Salem, N.C., 1928-30, partner in coll., sec.-treas., 1930-60, owner, pres., 1960—. Mem. Nat., N.C. bus. edn. assns., Winston-Salem C. of C., Retail Mchts. Assn., Better Bus. Bur. (charter), N.C. Assn. Bus. Colls. (Distinguished Service award 1973), Southeastern Bus. Coll. Assn. (Outstanding Service award 1964), Woman's Soc. Christian Service (charter, past pres.), Methodist (charter Woman's United Women, Women Soc. Christian Service, past supt. youth dept., mem. ofcl. bd., sec. adminstrv. bd., chmn. Commn. on Edn. 1960—). Club: Stateman's (Winston-Salem, charter) Home: 4580 Old Belews Creek Rd Winston-Salem NC 27102 Office: 632 W 4th St Winston-Salem NC 27102

WESTON, ANE LEE KAUFMAN, ednl. adminstr.; b. Chgo.; d. Israel I. and Fannie (Berman) Kaufman; B.A. (scholarship 1954-55), Northwestern U., 1955, M.A., 1968 div. Indsl. psychologist Daniel D. Howard Assos., Chgo., 1955-56; dir. admissions Pestalozzi Froebel Tchrs. Coll., Chgo., 1959-68, dean of students, 1969-71, instr. psychology, 1969-71; dean students, instr. psychology Nat. Coll. Edn. Urban Campus, 1971—. Mem. Ill. Assn. Tchr. Edn. in Pvt. Colls. (sec. 1962-74, pres. 1974—), Am. Assn. U. Women (mem. social com. 1969-73), Am., Ill. personnel and guidance assns., Am., Ill. assns. coll. admission counselors, Ill. Assn. Sch., Coll. and Univ. Staffing, Am., Ill. assns. collegiate registrars and admissions officers, Pi Lambda Theta. Home: 720 Gordon Terrace Chicago IL 60613

WESTON, ELIZABETH STEWART, mag. editor; b. Chgo.; d. Stewart and Doris (Templeton) Weston; student Vassar Coll.; A.B., U. Chgo.; m. Jefferson Berryman, Jan. 8, 1949 (div. Sept. 1958). Features editor Glamour mag., N.Y.C., 1945-51; chief staff writer Good Housekeeping mag., N.Y.C., 1951-58; asst. to editor McCall's mag., N.Y.C., 1958-61, mng. editor, 1961-63, exec. editor, 1963-70; mng. editor Harper's Bazaar, 1970—. Mem. Fashion Group, N.Y. Travel Writers Assn. Republican. Episcopalian. Home: 225 E 46th St New York City NY 10017 Office: Harper's Bazaar 717 Fifth Av New York City NY 10022

WESTON, FRANCES PARKHURST MORRISON (MRS. HERMAN ELMER WESTON), assn. exec.; b. Berkeley, Cal., Nov. 3, 1907; d. Frank William and Alice Lackey (Parkis) Morrison; A.B., Wellesley Coll., 1928; M.S., Simmons Coll., 1931; postgrad. U. Chgo., 1937; m. Herman Elmer Weston, June 17, 1939; children—William Wheelock, Joseph Amory, Sarah Anne. Tchr. chemistry and math. Buffalo Sem., 1928-30; sr. exec. Jordan Marsh Co., Boston, 1931-32; social worker Childrens Aid Vt., 1934-39; financial rep. New Eng. Kurn Hattin Homes, Westminster, Vt., 1949—. Curator, Saxtons River (Vt.) Hist. Soc., 1968—. Bd. dirs. Fall Mountain (Vt.) YMCA, 1968-71, 72-74; bd. trustees John Strong Mansion, Addison, Vt., 1953—. Mem. Daus. Founders and Patriots Am. (nat. pres. 1973—, nat. treas. 1969-73), D.A.R. (regent Vt. 1956-59), Daus. Am. Colonists (regent Me. 1967-70), Nat. Soc. New Eng. Women (3d v.p. gen. 1962-65), Huguenot Soc. Vt. (recording sec. 1964-74), Nat. Soc. Dames Ct. Honor (nat. trustee 1973-75). Home: Box 216 Saxtons River VT 05154 Office: New England Kurn Hattin Homes Westminister VT 05158

WESTON, KATHLEEN ESTHER SHINGLER (MRS. JEAN K. WESTON), physician; b. Kenton, Mich., Mar. 26, 1907; d. William H. and Ednah (Lewis) Shingler; A.B., No. Mich. Coll., 1929; M.A., U. Mich., 1933; M.D., Temple U., 1951; m. Jean K. Weston, Sept. 23, 1933; children—John Lowe, Susan Margo. Tchr. biology Munising (Mich.) High Sch., 1929-33, U. Mich. Hosp., 1933-37; instr. Temple U., 1937-51; pathologist-toxicologist Parke Davis & Co., Detroit, 1952-61; dir. toxicology Burroughs-Wellcome Co., Tuckahoe, N.Y., 1961-63; chief div. toxicology Brookdale Hosp. Center, Bklyn., 1963-67; sec.-treas. Weston Research Labs., Inc., Purcellville, 1967—; cons. toxicologist, Purcellville, Va., 1967—; cons. dept. drugs A.M.A., Chgo., 1968—, Nat. Library Medicine, 1968—; mem. staff George Washington Sch. Medicine, Washington, 1972—. Mem. Am. Med. Women's Assn. (br. pres. 1959-61), Internat. Acad. Pathology, Electron Microscope Soc. N.Y., Drug Information Assn., A.A.A.S., Soc. Toxicology, Sigma Xi. Author articles pub. in profl. jours. Address: RFD 1 Box 33 Purcellville VA 22132

WESTOVER, DOROTHY WALLACE, lawyer; b. Atlanta, Mar. 24, 1924; d. Harry Clay and Helen Louise (Equen) Westover; B.A., U. Miss., 1945; LL.B., Southwestern U., 1963; m. John Allen Wallace, July 7, 1950; children—Helen Elizabeth, John Westover, Harry Allan. Admitted to Cal. bar, 1964; asst. U.S. atty. Central Dist. Cal., Los Angeles, 1964-67; sr. atty. Office Chief Counsel Western region IRS, Los Angeles br., 1967—. Mem. Am., Los Angeles County bar assns., Am. Judicature Soc., Lawyers Club Los Angeles, Women Lawyers Assn. (dir. 1966, 70), Fed. Bar Assn. Los Angeles (v.p. 1973), Phi Delta Delta (chpt. pres. 1972), Chi Omega, Phi Alpha Delta. Episcopalian. Home: 2700 Monterey Rd San Marino CA 91108 Office: 300 N Los Angeles Los Angeles CA 90012

WESTPHAL, BARBARA OSBORNE (MRS. HENRY J. WESTPHAL), librarian, educator, author; b. San Fernando, Cal., Jan. 31, 1907; d. Howard Edgerly and Jessie (Barber) Osborne; B.A., Pacific Union Coll., 1933; M.A., San Jose State Coll., 1968; m. Henry J. Westphal, July 11, 1927; children—Halcyon Alicia (Mrs. Keith Alden Rhodes), Arthur Eugene, Melbert Chester. Tchr., English, S.Am., 1941-44; tchr. Spanish, Cal., Mich., 1944-48, Tex., 1964-66; librarian Sonora Union High Sch., 1967-72. Mem. Audubon Soc. Author: A Bride on the Amazon, 1948; Gold, Silver, and Spice, 1951; Mexican Nuggets, 1956; Ana Stahl of the Andes and Amazon, 1960; These Fords Still Run, 1962; John The Intrepid, 1968; Crazy Pigs and Other Bible Stories, 1968. Asst. editor The Messenger, 1954-58. Contbr. articles to ch. papers, nature mags. Home: 482 N Snell Sonora CA 95370

WESTRA, DOROTHY LOUISE, educator, musician; b. Paterson, N.J., Dec. 18, 1910; d. Michael Louis and Rachel (Van der Wall) Westra; student Inst. Mus. Art, 1928; B.S., Columbia, 1934; diploma in singing Julliard Sch., 1935, postgrad. diploma in singing, 1937; M.Sacred Music, Union Theol. Sem., 1936; postgrad. Oxford U., 1962-63. Supr. music, Midland Park, N.J., 1933-35, instr. Bennington (Vt.) Coll., 1939-40, U. Del., Newark, 1943-44, Bard Coll., Annandale-on-Hudson, N.Y., 1945-47, asst. prof. U. Redlands (Cal.), 1947-51; instr. U. Minn., Mpls., 1955-56; asso. prof. U. Cal. at Santa Barbara, 1956, now prof. Singer radio concerts, church, oratorio, N.Y.C., 1936-41, concerts, opera, radio, Europe, 1951-55; choral arranger. Dir., Children's Choral Festival, Santa Barbara, 1962, 66; organist Youth Choral Festival, Santa Barbara, 1961, 65, 66, Oxnard, 1966; East Asian tour for State Dept. as conductor for U. Cal. at Santa Barbara Chamber Singers, 1968, 70, 73, European and Canadian tours, 1973. Mem. bd. Crestline Improvement Assn. Mem. League Women Voters, UN Assn. U.S.A., Choristers Guild (pres. 1963), Choral Condrs. Guild (pres. 1961), Am. Guild Organists, Am. Assn. U. Profs. (2d v.p. U. Cal. Santa Barbara chpt.). Democrat. Episcopalian (organist-choir dir.). Compositions include: Jesus Christ is Born Today, Benediction, A Babe is Born in Bethlehem, Prayer of St. Richard of Chichester, Medieval Carol Cycle, 1973. Home: 1123 Crestline Dr Santa Barbara CA 93105

WESTWATER, ANGELA KING, editor; b. Columbus, O., July 6, 1942; d. William K. and Shirle J. (Nesbitt) Westwater; B.A., Smith Coll., 1964; M.A. (Jr. fellow 1966-67), N.Y. U., 1967. Asst. to dir. Center for Internat. Studies, N.Y. U., N.Y.C., 1967-68, asst. dir., 1968; research asso. Inst. of Govt., U. Ga., Athens, 1969-71; mng. editor Artforum Mag., N.Y.C., 1972—. Editor Ga. Govt. Rev., 1969-71. Contbr. articles to various publs. Home: 2 Horatio St New York City NY 10014 Office: Artforum 667 Madison Av New York City NY 10021

WESTWOOD, JEAN MILES (MRS. RICHARD ELWYN WESTWOOD), chmn. Democratic Nat. Com., bus. exec.; b. Price, Utah, Nov. 22, 1923; d. Francis Marion and Nettie (Potter) Miles; m. Richard Elwyn Westwood, Sept. 6, 1941; children—Richard Elwyn, Beth (Mrs. Vernon S. Davies). Prodn. control Consol. Vultee Aircraft, 1943-45; partner Westwood Mink Farm, 1946—, Westwood Enterprises, 1960—; treas. Westwood Constrn. Inc., 1971-72; staff mem. former Congressman David S. King, 1964-67. Del., Dem. Nat. Conv., 1964, 68; mem. Dem. Platform Com., 1968; Dem. nat. committeewoman from Utah, 1967—; mem. exec. com. Dem. Nat. Com., 1967-73; chmn. Dem. Nat. Com., 1972—; co-chmn. Western States Dem. Conf., 1968-71; nat. co-chmn. Citizens for McGovern Nat., 1971-72; treas. Dem. Charter Commn., 1973—. Mem. Am. Civil Liberties Union, N.A.A.C.P., Emba Mink Breeders Assn., Great Lakes Mink Breeders Assn. (recipient special award), Beta Sigma Phi. Mem. Ch. of Jesus Christ of Latter Day Saints. Clubs: Alpine Country, Ambassador. Home: 1624 W 8600 S West Jordan UT 84084 Office: 363 E Second S Salt Lake City UT 84111

WETMORE, ROSAMOND BAYNE (MRS. THOMAS HALL WETMORE), educator, librarian; b. Middlesboro, Ky., Nov. 1, 1914; d. Herbert Elias and Almeda (Mason) Bayne; student Lincoln Meml. U., 1932-34; A.B., Earlham Coll., 1936; B.L.S., Columbia, 1940; M.A. in History, Ball State U., 1957; m. Thomas Hall Wetmore, July 5, 1941; children—Stephen Bayne, Allyn Christophers. Reference librarian Earlham Coll., Richmond, Ind., 1936-37; librarian Lloyd High Sch., Erlanger, Ky., 1937-40, Beachwood Sch., Ft. Mitchell, Ky., 1940-41; asst. cataloging Library Ball State U., Muncie, Ind., 1946-68, asst. prof. library sci., 1968-71, asso. prof., 1971—. Mem. Am., Ind. (chmn. tech. services roundtable 1973) library assns., Assn. Accredited Library Schs., Ohio Valley Regional Group of Tech. Librarians (sec. 1959-60, vice chmn. 1960-61, chmn. 1961-62), Am. Assn. U. Women, Tau Kappa Alpha. Methodist. Author: The Organization of Library Collections, 1966, rev. edits., 1969, 72. Editor: Ball State University Library Science Lectures, vol. 1, 1973. Home: 1501 Riverside Muncie IN 47303 Office: Dept of Library Science Ball State Univ Muncie IN 47303

WETMORE, SUSAN, editor; b. Salt Lake City, Jan. 14, 1946; d. Carl Frederick and Hanna (Ivory) Wetmore; student U. Utah, 1964-66, 73—. Illustrator, Utah State Hwy. Dept., Salt Lake City, 1963; free lance artist, Salt Lake City, 1963-65; regional editor TV Guide mag., Salt Lake City, 1965—. Recipient 2d pl. prize for landscape oil painting Utah County Art Fair, 1964. Mem. Another Mother for Peace. Home: 1675 Roosevelt Av Salt Lake City UT 84105 Office: 136 E South Temple Salt Lake City UT 84111

WETTENSTEIN, BEVERLY A., editor; b. Bridgeport, Conn.; d. Milton and Sylvia (Gordon) Wettenstein; B.S. in Journalism, Temple U. Promotional asst. Look mag., N.Y.C., 1964-65; promotional copywriter Good Housekeeping mag., N.Y.C., 1965-67; promotion mgr. N.Y. Conv. and Visitors Bur., N.Y.C., 1967-68; co-editor The Complete New Yorker, David McKay Co., N.Y.C., 1972; reporter L.I. Newsday, Garden City, N.Y., 1972; dir. advt. and pub. relations N.Y. Hilton, N.Y.C., 1973-74; editor Puerto Rico mag., N.Y.C., 1974—. Pub. relations cons. Internat. Student Travel Conf., N.Y. and London, 1968-73; pub. information officer World Campus Afloat, Chapman Coll., 1970. Mem. Women in Communications, Nat. Acad. TV Arts and Scis., Am. Women in Radio and TV. Contbg. editor: New York at a Glance, 1971. Office: 1335 Av of Americas Rockefeller Center New York City NY

WETTSTEIN, MARTHA, religious orgn. exec.; b. Markinch, Sask., Can., Oct. 21, 1918; d. Lorenz and Emma (Wirth) Blaser; R.N., Regina (Sask.) Gen. Hosp., 1941; grad. Luther Coll., 1937; m. John Wettstein, Jan. 31, 1942; children—Karl, Joan (Mrs. O.W. Sherritt), Lorne, Margaret (Mrs. E.J. Gaschler). Adminstr., Regina (Sask.) Luth. Home for Aged, 1964—; organizer aux. council Sask. Assn. Spl. Care Homes, 1967, exec. mem., 1968—, pres., 1972—. Pres., chmn. social concerns div. Luth. Ch. Women Central Can. Home: 12 Academy Park Rd Regina SK Canada Office: 200-2505 11th Av Regina SK Canada

WETZEL, RITA JEANNE, psychologist; b. Waukegan, Ill.; d. William Byron and Cecelia (Mahoney) Wetzel; B.A., Lake Forest Coll., 1949; M.A., MacMurray Coll. for Women, 1951; Ph.D., Fla. State U., 1962. Psychology intern Fla. State Hosp., 1950-51; psychologist Los Angeles Juvenile Hall Clinic, 1951-53; resident counselor Tex. Tech Coll., 1953-54; cons. psychologist Neurol. Hosp., Kansas City, Mo., 1954-59, dir. dept. psychology, 1955-59; asst. marriage counseling dept. Fla. State U., 1959-62; cons. Cath. Charities, Kansas City, Kan., Ralph Alcoholic Clin., Kansas City, Mo.; marriage and family counselor; chief psychologist Mental Health Clinic, Jacksonville, Fla., 1968-69, chief div. In-service Edn. and Profl. Services, 1969-71; community cons., 1972—. Faculty mem. Donnelly Coll., also Avila Coll., Kansas City, Kan. until 1968; lectr. Jacksonville U., 1969-72. Lt. comdr. USCG Res., active duty, 1973—. Recipient EVE award Fla. Times Union, 1970, 71. Mem. Am. Assn. Marriage Counselors, Nat. Council Family Relations, Am., Southwestern psychol. assns., Alpha Delta Kappa. Club: Sports Car of Am. Home: 14660 Stacey Rd Jacksonville Beach FL 32250

WEXLER, JACQUELINE GRENNAN, coll. pres.; B.A., Webster Coll.; M.A., U. Notre Dame; postgrad. St. Louis U.; m. Paul Wexler, 1969. Pres., Webster Coll., Webster Groves, Mo., 1965-69; v.p., dir. Internat. U. Studies Acad. for Ednl. Devel., N.Y.C., 1969-70; pres. Hunter Coll., N.Y.C., 1970—. Author: Where Am I Going, 1968. Home: Tenafly NJ Office: Hunter Coll 695 Park Av New York City NY 10021

WEYBRIGHT, JEANNINE FRANCES (MRS. WINFORD J. WEYBRIGHT), newspaper exec.; b. Centralia, Wash., Aug. 1, 1931; d. Arthur Francis and Edna Ellen (Goff) Ipe; student Centralia Coll., 1949-51, LaSalle Extension U., 1963-66; m. Winford J. Weybright, Mar. 30, 1964; children—Jacqueline (Mrs. Thomas Westfall), Carol (Mrs. Roy Short), Teresa (Mrs. Patrick Finnegan). Self-employed inlogging industry and retail business, 1953-62; with The Dalles (Ore.) Chronicle, 1965—, bookkeeper, 1965-68, credit mgr., mgr. bus. office, 1968—. Mem. City Beautification Com., 1971-73; chmn. Park Arboretum Com., 1971-73; service club liaison Community Attention, Inc., 1971—; chmn. Service Clubs Coordinating Council. Bd. dirs. Wasco County Vols. Mem. Internat. Consumer Credit Union, Credit Women Internat. (edn. chmn. 1971-73, pres. 1973-74). Democrat. Baptist. Clubs: Soroptimist (pres. 1971-73), Toastmistress (The Dalles), Rebekah. Home: 3245 W 7th St The Dalles OR 97058 Office: 414 Federal St The Dalles OR 97058

WHALEN, JOAN MARIE, banker; b. Scranton, Pa., Sept. 19, 1922; d. William M. and Alice (McCarthy) Whalen; pre-standard certificate Am. Inst. Banking, 1956, standard certificate, 1958, grad. certificate, 1961; grad. Virginia-Maryland Bankers Sch. Bank Mgmt. U. Va., 1966. With Suburban Trust Co., Bethesda, Md., 1951—, asst. br. mgr., 1960-70, asst. treas., 1962-69, br. mgr., Chevy Chase, Md., 1970—, asst. v.p., 1969—. Mem. Nat. Assn. Bank Women (chmn. Met. Md. group 1972), Bethesda, Chevy Chase C. of C. (treas, 1968-70). Roman Catholic. Club: Bank Women's of Washington (corr. sec. 1959-60, treas. 1961-62, bd. govs. 1964-65). Home: 4800 Chevy Chase Dr Chevy Chase MD 20015 Office: Suburban Trust Co 4411 S Park Av Chevy Chase MD 20015

WHALEN, JULIA MARY, film co. exec.; b. N.Y.C., Oct. 13, 1933; d. Myles Vincent and Julia A. (Quinn) Whalen; A.B., Coll. New Rochelle, 1955; M.A., Columbia, 1960. Sec., administrv. asst., copywriter J. Walter Thompson Co., N.Y.C., 1955-57; prodn. mgr. Kim & Gifford Prodns., N.Y.C., 1958—. Recipient Ursula Lauris citation Coll. New Rochelle, 1965. Mem. Coll. New Rochelle Alumnae Assn. (dir. 1958-62). Home: 525 W 238th St New York City NY 10463 Office: 342 Madison Av New York City NY 10017

WHALEN, LUCILLE, educator; b. Los Angeles, July 26, 1925; d. Edward Cleveland and Mary Lucille (Perrault) Whalen; B.A., Immaculate Heart Coll., 1949; M.S. in L.S., Cath. U. Am., 1955; D.L.S., Columbia, 1965. Tchr. various schs., 1945-52; reference librarian, library sci. tchr. Immaculate Heart Coll., Los Angeles, 1954-58, dean Sch. Library Sci., 1958-60, 65-70; asso. dean Sch. Library and Information Sci., State U. N.Y. at Albany, 1971—. Dir. U.S. Office Edn. Insts. for Librarians, 1968-69. Mem. A.L.A., N.Y. Library Assn., Am. Soc. Information Sci., Spl. Libraries Assn., Am. Civil Liberties Union, Center for Study Democratic Instns. Democrat. Roman Catholic. Home: 51-4 Woodlake Rd Albany NY 12203

WHALEN, MARY O'LEARY (MRS. WILLIAM P. WHALEN), artist; b. Ireland; d. Edward Magawly and Agnes (Manning) Banon; student Manhattanville Coll. Sacred Heart, 1940; m. William P. Whalen, Oct. 28, 1938; 1 dau., Mary Elizabeth. Artist, 1962—; exhibited in group shows Women's Nat. Republican Club, Parrish Art Mus., others. Vice chmn. Internat. Ball, N.Y.C., 1963, 64, 65, 67, 68; co-chmn. Candlelight Ball, N.Y., 1960; com. mem. Gothams, Inc., 1955—; publs. chmn. Manhattanville Coll. Alumnae Rev. 1960-63, editorial staff, 1963—. Bd. dirs. Manhattanville Coll. of Sacred Heart. Mem. art com., membership com. Women's Nat. Republican Club, 1969—. Mem. N.Y. Acad. Scis. (sec. bd. women's aux. 1970-71). Met. Mus. N.Y.C., Parrish Art Mus. Southampton (N.Y.), Hort. Soc. N.Y., Alumnae Assn. Manhattanville Coll., Ladies of Charity, Internat. Platform Assn., Friends of Whitney Mus. Home: Longwood 5IE 11811 Av of PGA Palm Beach Gardens FL 33403

WHALEN, PATRICIA ELEANOR, rehab. counselor; b. Mpls., Jan. 13, 1934; d. Joseph Willis and Eleanor (Annett) Whalen; B.B.A. with distinction, U. Minn., 1958, M.A., 1966. Rehab. counselor State Minn., Div. Vocational Rehab., Mpls., 1960-64; vocational adjustment coordinator Mpls. Pub. Schs., 1964—. Mem. Mpls. Area Council on Employment of Handicapped, 1965-72, sec.-treas., 1967; mem. Minn. Rehab. Counselor Joint Certification Bd., 1972—, Commn. on Rehab. Counselor Certification, 1973—. Recipient Elkins award, Counselor of the Year, State of Minn., 1969. Mem. Am., Minn. (sec. 1972-74) personnel and guidance assns., Nat., Minn. (Pres. 1969-70) rehab. counseling assns., Rehab. Counseling Assn. Minn. (dir. 1969-70), Twin City Vocational Guidance Assn. (dir. 1968-70), Phi Delta. Home: 8109 Toledo Av N Minneapolis MN 55443 Office: 807 NE Broadway Minneapolis MN 55413

WHALING, ANNE, educator; b. Houston, Mar. 30, 1914; d. Horace Morland and Annie Byrd (Ward) Whaling; B.A., So. Meth. U., 1933, M.A., 1934; Ph.D., Yale, 1946. Cataloger, specialist in music, fgn. langs., So. Meth. U., 1947-55; tchr., English dept. Arlington State Coll., 1955, instr., 1955-57, assistant professor, 1957-60, associate professor English, 1960-67, asso. prof. English, U. Tex., Arlington, 1967-71, prof. English, 1971—. Program annotator for chamber music series Dallas Mus. Fine Arts, 1956-61. Mem. bd. dirs. Dallas Chamber Music Soc., 1954—. Recipient Decima Lantern award So. Meth. U., 1933; Woman of Achievement award So. Meth. U. Alumni Assn., 1968. Mem. Am. Studies Assn. of Tex. (mem. steering com. 1956—, councilor 1961-62), Modern Lang. Assn., Music Library Assn., Am. Assn. U. Women (chmn. fellowship com. Dallas br. 1959-64), South Central Modern Language Assn., The Malone Soc., Phi Beta Kappa. Methodist. Home: 3320 Daniels Av Dallas TX 75205 Office: U Tex Arlington TX 76010

WHAM, DOROTHY STONECIPHER (MRS. ROBERT S. WHAM), govt. ofcl.; b. Centralia, Ill., Jan. 5, 1925; d. Ernest Joseph and Thelma (Shafer) Stonecipher; A.B. with honors, MacMurray Coll., 1946; A.M., U. Ill., 1949; m. Robert S. Wham, Jan. 26, 1947; children—Nancy (Mrs. Rohn L. Michell), Jeanne, Robert II. Mem. staff counselling bur. U. Ill., Champaign-Urbana, 1947-49; program dir. Colo./Wyo. ACTION, Denver, 1972—, also fed. women's program coordinator, region VIII. Mem. adv. com. on integration Denver Sch. Bd., 1965-67; active P.T.A. Thomas Jefferson Sch., Denver, 1968-72; commr. Colo. Civil Rights Com., 1972—; mem. Colo. Commn. on Status of Women. Republican precinct committeewomen, 1960-72. Mem. Am. Psychol. Assn. Methodist. Home: 2790 S High St Denver CO 80210 Office: 1050 17th St Denver CO 80202

WHAPLES, MIRIAM KARPILOW, educator; b. Bridgeport, Conn., Dec. 16, 1929; d. Samuel and Mollie (Micklin) Karpilow; B.A., Ind. U., 1950. Mus.M., 1954, Ph.D., 1958; m. George Whaples, Aug. 24, 1949; children—Tamar (Mrs. Charles Friedman), Barbara, Jonathan. Instr., then asst. prof. Western Md. Coll., Westminster, 1960-66; faculty U. Mass., Amherst, 1966—, asso. prof. music, 1972—. Performances as pianist and harpsicordist. Mem. Am., Internat. musicol. socs., Soc. Ethnomusicology, Am. Assn. U. Profs., Phi Beta Kappa. Contbr. to profl. jours. Home: 169 Northampton Rd Amherst MA 01002

WHARRY, RHODA ELIZABETH, educator; b. Charleston, Mo., July 3, 1917; d. John Paul and Louise Casey (Bransford) Wharry; B.S., U. Ark., 1939; M.A., Memphis State U., 1953; Ph.D., Purdue U., 1969; m. Michael H. Emmick, Nov. 3, 1950 (div. May 1960); 1 son, John Paul Wharry II. Service club dir. U.S.O., 1942-48; dir. service clubs USARL, Anchorage, 1949-52; dir. Lions Inst. for Visually Handicapped Children, Memphis, 1954-57; research asst. social psychology Rice U., Houston, 1960-61; tchr. minimally brain-damaged children Houston Ind. Sch. Dist., 1961-64; acting dir. reading clinic Purdue U., Lafayette, Ind., 1965-67, coordinator remedial academics, achievement center for children, 1966-67; asso. prof. developmental learning U. Ala., Huntsville, 1967—, chmn. developmental learning program, 1974—. Project dir., ednl. cons. Huntsville Achievement Sch., 1967—. Mem. Ala. Gov.'s Com. for Employment Handicapped; adv. bd. Ala. chpt. Assn. Children with Learning Disabilities. Recipient scholarship Delta Gamma, 1954, Lions Club, 1956. Mem. Nat., Ala. edn. assns., Council Exceptional Children, Assn. Children with Learning Disabilities, Jean Piaget Soc. (charter), Kappa Delta Pi, Delta Gamma. Home: 615 Hemlock Dr SE Huntsville AL 35803

WHARTENBY, CATHERINE ENGLISH (MRS. CHARLES ALFRED WHARTENBY), ins. co. cons.; b. Wellsboro, Pa., June 30, 1920; d. Robert Deane and Elizabeth Perpetua (Dwyer) English; B.S., Mansfield State Coll., 1941; J.D., Golden Gate Coll., 1968; m. Charles Alfred Whartenby, Feb. 9, 1946. Office employee Refractory Mica Products, Inc., Newark, 1941; clk., legal dept. 9th Service Command, Presidio of San Francisco, 1942-44; office sec., office mgr. Research Inst. Am., San Francisco, 1945-54; office sec. Conn. Gen. Life Ins. Co., San Francisco, 1954-62, asst. mgr., 1962-72, regional design cons. estate and bus. planning, No. Cal., 1973—; admitted to Cal. bar, 1969. Lectr. pension courses Am. Coll. Life Underwriters, 1969-71, instr. advanced estate planning course, 1973-74. Mem. Am. (mem. com. on pension and profit-sharing trusts, real property, probate and trust law sect. 1972-74), San Francisco bar assns., State Bar Cal., San Francisco Estate Planning Council, Am. Soc. C.L.U.s, Queens Bench. Club: Commonwealth (San Francisco). Home: 40 Corte Alegre Millbrae CA 94030 Office: 155 Bovet Rd Suite 303 San Mateo CA 94402

WHARTON, BETTY ANN (MRS. JOHN FRANKLIN WHARTON), librarian; b. Pasadena, Cal., June 26, 1911; d. Edward Dyer and Leila Cunard (Von Ache) Jenks; student Pasadena Playhouse Coll. Theatre Arts, 1929-31, Columbia Sch. Library Service, 1961-63; m. Carl Edgar Fisher, Jan. 11, 1936 (div. 1947); 1 dau., Judith Kathleen (Mrs. Martyn Douglas Greenacre); m. 2d, John Franklin Wharton, Aug. 30, 1949. Actress, appearing as Mary Mason, 1928-49; motion picture actress R.K.O., Twentieth Century Fox, 1931-33; appeared in Broadway prodns., featured actress in Brother Rat, The Schoolhouse on the Lot, The Primrose Path, Charley's Aunt, Cafe Crown, others, 1934-42; radio actress, appeared on NBC, CBS, starred in Maudie's Diary, 1938-49; research librarian theatre collection N.Y. Pub. Library, N.Y.C., 1963—. Mem. Theatre Library Assn. (exec. bd.), Am. Soc. Theatre Research, Internat. Congress Theatre Research (sec. exec. bd.), Internat. Fedn. Theatre Research. Home: 141 E 72d St New York City NY 10021 Office: Performing Arts Research Center 111 Amsterdam Av New York City NY 10023

WHARTON, CAROLYN ANN, educator; b. Michigan City, Ind., June 29, 1936; d. Clark Talmadge and Dorothy Ruth (Harris) Teel; B.S. in Speech Edn., Bob Jones U., 1958; M.S. in Journalism, Ohio U., 1967; m. Thomas James Wharton, July 1, 1972; children—Thomas, Annette, Lisa, Sheila. Tchr., Wooster (O.) High Sch., 1958-66; asso. prof. journalism Grace Coll., Winona Lake, Ind., 1967-72, part-time, 1972—; prof. journalism Bethel Coll., Mishawaka, Ind., 1973-74; free-lance manuscript editor Moody Press, Chgo.; free lance writer. Newspaper fund fellow Syracuse U., 1964. Mem. Women in Communication, Kappa Tau Alpha. Republican. Mem. Brethren Ch. Home: 904 Park Av Winona Lake IN 46590

WHATLEY, JACQUELINE BELTRAM (MRS. JOHN W. WHATLEY), lawyer; b. West Orange, N.J., Sept. 26, 1944; d. Quirino R. and Eliane (Gruet) Beltram; B.A., U. Tampa, 1966; J.D., Stetson U., 1969; m. John W. Whatley, June 25, 1966. Admitted to Fla. bar, 1969, Alaska bar, 1971; practiced in Anchorage, 1971-73; mem. firms Gibbons, Tucker, McEwen, Smith, Cofer & Taub, Tampa, Fla., 1969-71, 1973—; dir. Fla. Investment and Devel. Corp. Arbitrator Am. Can Co., Continental Can Co., United Steelworkers Am., Tampa, 1974—. Mem. Am., Alaska, Fla., Tampa-Hillsborough County, Anchorage bar assns., Nu Beta Epsilon, Delta Phi Epsilon, Phi Alpha Theta. Home: PO Box 17595 Tampa FL 33614 Office: 606 Madison St Tampa FL 33601

WHEADON, ROSETTA FAY DAWKINS (MRS. AQUILLA WENDELL WHEADON), coll. dean; b. East St. Louis, Ill., Dec. 27, 1934; d. Roosevelt and Wilma (Agnew) Dawkins; B.S., Ill. State U., 1956; M.Ed., U. Ill., 1960; postgrad. U. Heidelberg, 1963-64; Ph.D., St. Louis U., 1968; postgrad. George Williams Coll., Inst. Urban Sociology, 1969; m. Aquilla Wendell Wheadon, Aug. 13, 1960; 1 son, Michael Wendell. Summer high sch. tchr., Kansas City, Kan., 1952-55, St. Louis, 1955-67; dir. Stix Baer & Fuller program St. Louis Bd. Edn., 1967-69; asst. to exec. sec. Ill. Jr. Coll. Bd. for State Community Coll., East St. Louis, Ill., 1969-70; dean instructional services State Community Coll., East St. Louis, Ill., 1970—. Lectr., Maryville Coll. Sacred Heart, St. Louis, 1968-70; cons. So. Ill. U., Ill. Jr. Coll. Bd., 1970-71. Mem. Ill. Vocational Adv. Bd., 1968-69; mem. Ill. Bd. Vocational Edn. and Rehab., 1969; mem. nomination com. Danforth Found., 1972, 74. Bd. dirs. East West Gateway Coordinating Council. Recipient Outstanding Woman in Edn. award East St. Louis Monitor, 1970, Service to Youth of Metro-East award Bapt. Gen. State Conv., 1973. Mem. Am. Assn. U. Adminstrs., Am. Assn. Community and Jr. Colls., Am. Assn. Higher Edn., Ill. Adminstrs. Assn., Alpha Kappa Alpha. Mem. Order Eastern Star. Home: 2600 St Louis Av East St Louis IL 62205

WHEAT, HELEN FITCH, librarian; b. Pilot Point, Tex., Nov. 12, 1920; d. Victor Bell and Carmen Georgia (DeSpain) Fitch; B.A., N. Tex. State U., 1942; M.L.S., George Peabody Coll., 1958; m. John Henry Wheat, July 27, 1947 (div.); children—Rebecca Marie, John Henry, Mark Edward. Librarian, Perryton (Tex.) High Sch., 1942-43; airway traffic controller CAA, Washington, 1943-45; layout artist Taylor Pub. Co., Dallas, 1946-47; librarian Farmersville High Sch. (Tex.), 1947-48, Rice U., Houston, 1948-52; librarian Sam Houston State U., Huntsville, Tex., 1957—. Cons. library tech. processes and automation. Co-founder movement to obtain pub. library for Huntsville, 1964; resource person 1st Gov.'s Conf. on Libraries, 1966. Mem. A.L.A., Tex. Library Assn., Am. Assn. Univ. Profs., Tex. Assn. Coll. Tchrs., Univ. Women's Book Discussion Group, Huntsville Study Club (pres. 1965-66), P.T.A., Kappa Delta. Democrat. Methodist. Home: 2125 Av P Huntsville TX 77340

WHEATLEY, MILDRED AMANDA, coll. adminstr.; b. Washington, Apr. 16, 1917; d. Elmer C. and Mildred Cecelia (Middleton) Wheatley; B.A., Western Md. Coll., 1938; M.Ed., U. Wash., 1947; postgrad. U. Mo., U. Wis., Cath. U. Am., also various workshops. Faculty, East Stroudsburg (Pa.) State Coll., 1953—, exec. asso. dean students 1972—. Faculty, U. Balt., Bridgewater Coll., Stephens Coll. Served with WAVES, 1943-45. Mem. Nat., Pa. assns. women deans and counselors, Pa. Assn. State Coll. and Univ. Faculties, Comparative Edn. Soc., N.E.A., Am. Antiques Assn., Nat. Assn. Higher Edn. Home: 8811 Old Branch Av Clinton MD 20135 Office: Box 35 East Stroudsburg State College East Stroudsburg PA 18301

WHEATON, ELIZABETH LEE, educator; b. Sherman, Tex.; d. Percival King and Minerva Fay (Ratzel) Fulton; student Rice Inst., 1920-21, San Angelo Coll., 1949-51; certificate, S.W. Tex. State Coll., 1922, Kansas City-Horner Conservatory, 1929; B.S., McMurray Coll, 1952; postgrad. A. and I. Coll., 1953-54; m. Grant Wiltsie Wheaton, Dec. 23, 1923. Tchr. pub. schs., Texas City, Tex., 1922-24; pvt. tchr. speech, 1922-29, voice and speech, 1929-47; reporter, society editor Texas City Sun, 1930-36; corr. Galveston (Tex.) News, 1934; dir. The Texas City Hour, radio KGBC, 1947; elementary tchr. La Feria (Tex.) Pub. Schs., 1952—; pvt. tchr. voice, speech, 1956-57; originator, writer, dir., master of Story Book Time TV series, KRGV-TV, 1957; mem. staff S.W. Writers Conf., Corpus Christi, Tex., 1954—. Mem. Composers, Authors and Artists of Am. (pres. Rio Grande chpt., mem. nat. pub. com. 1960), Tex. Woman's Press Assn., Tex. State Tchrs. Assn., Tex. Poetry Soc. (charter mem., sec. chpt. 1970—), Tex. Inst. Letters, Am. Legion Aux. (past pres. units Texas City, San Angelo, La Feria; Tex. state dept. music chmn. 1960, past pres.'s parley), Nat. Soc. D.A.R. (chpt. edn. com.), Lower Rio Grande Valley Hist. Soc., Community Concert Assn. (bd. dirs. Harlingen chpt., chmn. La Feria com. 1961-62), Rio Grande Valley Internat. Music Festival (sponsor 1961-62), Am. Budgerigar Soc., Tex. Bird Breeders and Fanciers Assn., Tex. Southmost Bird Assn. (sec. 1962-64), Tip-O-Tex. Exhbn. Budgerigar Soc., Delta Kappa Gamma (chpt. publicity com.). Mem. Order Eastern Star. Clubs: P.M., LaFeria Garden. Author: Mr. George's Joint, 1941; Texas City Remembers, 1948; also poems, articles, reviews in various mags., newspapers. Home: N Beddoes Rd and Expwy Hwy 83 PO Box 1026 La Feria TX 78559 Office: Lee Sch La Feria TX 78559

WHEDON, PEGGY (MRS. G. DONALD WHEDON), TV producer; b. N.Y.C.; d. Henry and Anna (Nickel) Brunssen; student U. Rochester, 3 years; m. G. Donald Whedon, May 12, 1942; children—Karen, David. Writer weekly radio program ABC, N.Y.C., 1948-50; asst. producer Kate Smith TV Show, NBC-TV, N.Y.C., 1950-52, Coll. News Conf. ABC-TV and Radio, Washington, 1952-60; producer Issues and Answers, ABC-TV and Radio, 1960—, also corr. ABC-TV and Radio; producer From The Capital, ABC Radio, 1962-69; commentator Flair Reports, ABC Radio, 1962-64. Recipient Spl. award Nat. Conf. Christians and Jews, 1968; nominated Emmy award TV Acad. Arts and Scis., 1968. Mem. White House Corrs. Assn., TV and Radio Corrs. Assn., Am. Women in Radio and Television. Clubs: Am. Newspaper Women's, Washington Press. Home: 5605 Sonoma Rd Bethesda MD 20034 Office: ABC News Bur 1124 Connecticut Av NW Washington DC 20036

WHEELER, ARLINE ZILPHA FRANK (MRS. DOCK WHEELER), ret. educator; b. Sapulpa, Okla., July 16, 1908; d. Wiley C. and Rosa E. (Fuqua) Frank; B.S. in Edn., S.W. State Coll., Mo., 1948; M.S., U. Kan., 1954; diploma Advanced Study in Vocational Counselor Edn., U. Ark., 1964; m. Dock Wheeler, Feb. 26, 1927. Tchr. pub. schs., Ozark County, Mo., 1936-42; tchr. social studies high sch., Gainesville, Mo., 1942-48; tchr. social studies high sch. Bur. Indian Affairs, Haskell Inst., Lawrence, Kan., 1948-53, tchr., counselor Haskell All Am. Indian Jr. Coll. (formerly Haskell Inst.), 1963-71; tchr., adviser Stewart (Nev.) Indian Sch., 1953-54, Steamboat Boarding Sch., Ganado, Ariz., 1954-55, Cheyenne River Boarding Sch., Cheyenne Agy. S.D., 1957-60; prin. Klagetoh Community Boarding Sch., Ganado, 1955-57; prin., tchr. Dilcon Trailer Sch. (Ariz.) and Coal Mine Mesa, 1960-62; head dept. guidance Tuba City Boarding Sch. (Ariz.), 1962-63; engaged in cattle bus., 1971—. Chmn., Klagetoh chpt. A.R.C., 1955-57; chmn. Ft. Defiance Sub-Agy. Safety Com., 1955-57. Recipient Meritorious Service award Haskell Indian Jr. Coll., 1971, Superior Service award Fed. Bur. Indian Affairs, 1971. Mem. Internat. Platform Assn., Am. Personnel and Guidance Assn. Democrat. Mem. Christian Ch. Mem. Order Eastern Star, White Shrine. Home: Rural Route 2 Rogers AR 72756

WHEELER, CHRISTINE (MRS. JOHN RALPH WHEELER), newspaperwoman; b. Sadieville, Ky., Apr. 4, 1923; d. Luther Hall and Ura Ellen (Wilson) Gillispie; grad. high sch.; m. John Ralph Wheeler, Feb. 6, 1945; 1 son, Michael Lee. Secretarial position John Hancock Life Ins. Co., Hamilton, O., 1941-45; ch. sec. Park Av. United Meth. Ch., Hamilton, 1959-65; with Jour. News, Hamilton, 1966—, reporter, 1966—, food editor, 1969—. Mem. City of Hamilton Pub. Health Adv. Bd., 1971—. Home: 685 Franklin St Hamilton OH 45013 Office: Court and Journal Sq Hamilton OH 45012

WHEELER, DOROTHY ANN (MRS. ROGER EUGENE WHEELER), pub. relations exec.; b. Brookings, S.D., Apr. 17, 1923; d. James and Zeta (Forsee) Salisbury; student Bowling Green State U., 1941-42; m. Roger Eugene Wheeler, Jan. 29, 1943; children—James F., Sandra (Mrs. Robert Heinemann). Nat. pres. Res. Officers Assn. Ladies Clubs of U.S.A., Washington, 1956-57, 57-58, exec. sec., 1958-63; coordinator vols. Cafritz Meml. Hosp., Washington, 1963-69, dir. pub. relations, 1969—, dir. personnel, 1973—. Dir. Greenbelt Consumer Services, 1964-68, 72—, corporate sec., 1964-68. Bd. dirs. Greater S.E. Washington Hosp. Found. Home: 4812 Maury Lane Alexandria VA 22304 Office: Southern Av Washington DC 20020

WHEELER, EVA FLOY SMITH (MRS. SHERMAN SHAW WHEELER), ch. worker, author; b. Cestos, Okla., May 12, 1900; d. Samuel Theodore and Lillie May (Ausman) Smith; B.S., Colo. State U., 1922; M.A., U. Wyo., 1927; m. Sherman Shaw Wheeler, Aug. 26, 1925; children—Marilyn Margaret (Mrs. Edward Culver McKim), Robert Roderick, William Warren, Gerald Gilbert. Tchr. pub. schs. Ottawa County, Kan., 1917-19; 4-H club leader, nutrition specialist Colo. State U. Extension Service, 1922-25; tchr. pub. schs. Albany County, Wyo., 1944-45; radio commentator Sta. KZIX, Ft. Collins, Colo., 1959. Pres., Colo. United Ch. Women, 1958-61; mem. bd., 1961-66, nat. bd. dirs., 1958-64; mem. state bd. Colo. Council Chs., 1958-61; hon. mem. Nat. Missions Bd., trustee United Presbyn. Ch.; mem. women's planning com. Internat. Christian U.; mem. Coterie, Morning Garden Club; mem. Continuing Nat. Fellowship Ch. Women United, 1967—; pres. Raleigh Council Ch. Women United, 1969-74; legislative chmn. Ch. Women United N.C., 1970-73, hon. life mem., 1974—; chmn. Raleigh chpt. UNICEF, 1971-74, Raleigh Adult Sch. Lunch Program, 1973—; treas. Meals on Wheels of Wake County, Inc., 1974—. Mem. Am. Assn. for UN (pres. Laramie, Wyo. chpt.), Ft. Collins Woman's Clubs, Colo. State U. Women, Searchlight, Book Rev. Mem. Am. Home Econs. Assn., Omicron Nu, Pi Kappa Delta, Alpha Epsilon, Epsilon Sigma Omicron. Clubs: Colo. and Gen. Fedn. Women's (Colo. chmn. conservation 1959-60, Far East and Asia chmn. 1960-62, Am. div. chmn. 1962-64, family dir. chmn., 1964-66), N.C. State University Woman's, Raleigh Womans', Raleigh Garden; Ft. Collins Garden (sec. parliamentarian 1953-61, pres. 1962). Author: Wyoming Writers, 1940; also articles for mags. Home: 5002 Wickham Rd Raleigh NC 27606

WHEELER, EVANNE, librarian; b. Chgo., Mar. 20, 1916; d. Claude DeHaven and Eva C. (Toresen) Wheeler; B.A., Long Beach State Coll., 1951; B.L.S., U. Cal., 1952. Martinez br. librarian Contra Costa County, Cal., 1952-57; project librarian Amador-Stockton Fed. Demonstration, Jackson, Cal., 1957-59; Amador County librarian, Jackson, Cal., 1959-64; Humboldt County librarian, Eureka, Cal., 1964—; dir. Humboldt County Employees Fed. Credit Union, 1966—. Mem. Am., Cal. (exec. bd. 1969-70, councillor at large 1973-75) library assns., Cal. Credit Union Leagues (pres. chpt. 1970-71). Home: 2525 Pine St Eureka CA 95501 Office: 636 F St Eureka CA 95501

WHEELER, GERRIDEE STENEHJEM, Republican nat. committeewoman; b. Arnegard, N.D., May 29, 1927; d. Martin S. and Emma (Bjornstad) S.; A.A., Stephens Coll.; B.A., U. N.D.; m. Ronald Wheeler, Sept. 5, 1948; children—Mary Beth (Mrs. Penn Brandborg), Kim (Mrs. Dennis Collins), Lisa (Mrs. Steven DeLapp), Jennifer, Jo Ann, Pamela, Kathy, Fredrick. Legislative chmn. N.D. Mental Health Assn., 1965, pres., 1965-70; pres. Bismarck (N.D.) Regional Mental Health Assn., 1966; mem. pub. policy com. Nat. Assn. Mental Health, 1969-72, exec. com., 1971-74, regional v.p., 1972-73, com. community mental health centers, 1972; mem. Nat. Adv. Council Comprehensive Health Planning and Program Devel. Mem. Republican nat. com. for N.D., 1972—; del. Rep. nat. conv., 1972; chmn. N.D. Delegation Women's Conf.; mem. N.D. platform com. Chmn. bd. dirs. Meml. Mental Health and Retardation center, 1966-70; bd. dirs. Area Social Service Center, Bismarck. Named Pub. Health Worker of Year N.D. Pub. Health Assn., 1966, Woman of Decade N.D. Mental Health Assn., 1970; N.D. Girls' State named in her honor. Mem. U. N.D. Alumni Assn., N.D. Women's Coalition, Nat. Women's Polit. Caucus, N.D. Council Edn. (pres. 1971—), Kappa Alpha Theta. Lutheran. Club: Fortnightly (past pres.). Home: 1231 E Highland Acres Rd Bismarck ND 58501

WHEELER, HELEN JEAN BUTRIM, phys. therapy dir.; b. Rochester, N.Y.; d. Vincent J. and Johanna (Adamitis) Butrim; R.N., St. Mary's Hosp., Rochester, 1938; diploma Northwestern U., 1945; m. Rodney S. Wheeler, Feb. 19, 1947; children—Christopher S., Douglas B. Nurse St. Mary's Hosp., 1938-44; phys. therapist, Palm Beach, Fla., 1945-46; dep. chief nursing Sister's Hosp., Santa Maria, Cal., 1958-61; dir. phys. therapy dept. Crestwood Hosp., Huntsville, Ala., 1966—. Mem. Am. Phys. Therapy Assn., Am. Registry Phys. Therapists. Home: 3117 McDow Av Huntsville AL 35805 Office: 4411 McAllister Dr Huntsville AL 35805

WHEELER, HELEN RIPPIER, educator, media cons., librarian, women's studies counselor; b. N.Y.C.; B.A., Barnard Coll., 1950; certificate U. San Carlos, Guatemala, summer 1949; M.S., Sch. Library Service Columbia U., 1951; M.A., U. Chgo., 1954; Ed.D., Columbia U. Tchrs. Coll., 1964; postdoctoral U. Cal., 1968 certificate tng. program in affirmative action, 1974. Library dir. Hicksville (N.Y.) Pub. Library, 1951-53; asst. librarian U. Chgo. Lab. Sch., 1953-55; head tchr.-librarian Waller High Sch., Chgo., 1955-56; librarian Agnes Russell Center, Columbia U. Tchrs. Coll., 1956-58; asst. br. librarian, audio-visual coordinator Chgo. City Colls. (formerly Chgo. City Jr. Coll.), 1958-59, br. head librarian, audio-visual coordinator, 1959-62; Latin-Am. library specialist Columbia U., N.Y.C., 1962-64; adj. asst. prof. Drexel U. Grad. Library Sch., Phila., 1964-65; asso. prof., cons. community coll. system U. Hawaii Grad. Sch. Library Studies, Honolulu, 1965-66; asso. prof. dept. library sci. Ind. State U., Terre Haute, 1966-68; asso. prof. dept. library sci. St. John's U., Jamaica, N.Y., 1968-69; cons., 1969-71; asso. prof. La. State U. Sch. Library Sci., 1971-73. Mem. Task Force on Status Women in Librarianship, Action Council Social Responsibilities Round Table. Recipient LeRoy C. Merritt Humanitarian Fund award, 1974. Mem. A.L.A. (council 1973—, internat. relations com. 1974—), Assn. Coll. and Research Libraries (bibliographic com. jr. colls. sect. 1965-69), Assn. for Ednl. Communications and Tech., Spl. Libraries Assn. (dir. La. 1973—), Am. Assn. U. Profs., Social Responsibilities Round table (action council 1972-74, sec.-treas. 1974—), Nat. Orgn. for Women (treas. Baton Rouge 1972-73), Pi Lambda Theta. Author: Community College Library: A Plan for Action, 1965; Basic Book Collection for the Community College Library, 1968; Womanhood Media, 1972, Supplement, 1974; Learning the Library Media Package, 1975. Mem. editorial bd. Women Studies Abstracts. Contbr. to books, also articles and book revs. to social sci. periodicals. Home: 7940 Jefferson Hwy Baton Rouge LA 70809

WHEELER, JO FULLERTON (MRS. JOHN R. WHEELER), educator, polit. orgn. exec.; b. Blytheville, Ark., Mar. 20, 1936; d. John Odell and Edna Ethyl (Evans) Fullerton; B.S. in Edn., U. Ark., 1956, Ph.D. candidate, 1965-68; M.S. in Edn., Ark. State U., 1958; m. John Randall Wheeler, Dec. 22, 1955; children—John Randall, Scott Andrew. Tchr. elementary grades South Sch., Jonesboro, Ark., 1957-60, 61-63, 65-67, 68-69; Ark. coordinator Head Start Evaluation, Stanford Research Inst., 1970-71, Follow Through Evaluation, 1973; counselor middle sch. Trumann (Ark.) Middle Sch., 1974-75. Sec. Ark. League Women Voters, 1959-61, treas., 1969-71, pres., 1971-73; bd. mem. Jonesboro League Women Voters, 1959-63, 68-70, pres., 1963-65, 70-71; chmn. legislative task force Gov.'s Commn. on Status Women, 1971-73. Named Jonesboro Woman of Yr. Jaycees, 1970. Mem. Am. Assn. U. Women (bd. mem. Jonesboro br. 1959-62), Delta Kappa Gamma (1st v.p. 1968-70), Kappa Delta Pi, Delta Gamma (state recommendation chmn. 1957-61). Baptist. Home: 1106 Shenandoah Ct Jonesboro AR 72401

WHEELER, LINDA CLAIRE, news photographer; b. North Adams, Mass., Aug. 10, 1944; d. Halford Eugene and Evelyn (Balcolm) Wheeler; B.A. in Journalism, Ohio State U., 1967. News photographer Washington Post, 1968—; lectr. in field. Recipient photography awards Washington-Balt. Newspaper Guild, 1973; White House News Photographers Assn. award, 1969, 73, 75. Home: 1708 Q St NW Washington DC 20009 Office: Washington Post 1150 15th St NW Washington DC 20071

WHEELER, LOUISE HAESELER, educator; b. Springfield, O., Mar. 10, 1919; d. Walter E. and Erna (Haeseler) Wheeler; B.S., Wittenberg U., 1940; M.A., Ohio State U., 1946; postgrad. U. Pitts., 1948, N.Y.U., 1951, U. Colo., 1960, U. Dayton, 1962, U. N.D., 1969, 70. Tchr. Lostcreek Twp. High Sch., Casstown, O., 1940-42, German Local High Sch., Lawrenceville, O., 1942-46; exec. sec. Standard Register Co., Dayton, O., 1946-47; tchr. London (O.) High Sch., 1947; supervising tchr. bus. edn. Kent (O.) State U. Sch., 1947-48; instr. secretarial sci. Coll. Bus. Adminstrn., Kent State U., 1948-49, acting head dept. secretarial sci., 1948-49, asst. prof. secretarial sci., 1949-53, asso. prof. secretarial sci., 1953-59, asso. prof. office adminstrn., 1959-70, asso. prof. bus. edn., 1970—, dir. ann. workshops for ednl. secs., 1949-67. Advt. mgr. Ohio Bus. Tchr., 1960-65. Mem. Ohio Bus. Tchrs. Assn. (v.p. 1966-67, pres. 1967-68), Nat., North Central, Tri-State bus. edn. assns., Akron Area, Cleve. Area bus. tchrs. assns., Delta Kappa Gamma, Alpha Delta Pi, Delta Pi Epsilon, Pi Omega Pi, Kappa Delta Pi, Phi Gamma Nu (adviser 1951-69). Mem. Order Eastern Star. Author: (with others) Diatype, 2 vols., 1970. Contbr. articles to profl. jours. Home: 1333 S Lincoln St Kent OH 44240

WHEELER, MARGARET FRANCES, educator; b. Chattanooga, Nov. 20, 1918; d. Martin Luther and Ethel (Bowman) Wheeler; R.N., Baroness Erlanger Hosp. Sch. Nursing, 1940; student U. Chattanooga, 1940-41; A.B., Tusculum Coll., 1944; M.A. in Biol. and Phys. Nursing, Columbia, 1948, M.A. in Botany, 1955; grad. in botany U. Cal., Berkeley, 1965. Head nurse emergency Baroness Erlanger Hosp., 1940-41, sci. instr. Sch. Nursing, 1943-44, 46; asst. sch. nurse Tusculum Coll., 1941-43; asst. in microbiology Columbia Tchrs. Coll., 1948; asst. prof. nursing edn. Rutgers, The State U. N.J. Newark, 1948-58, asst. prof. biology, 1959-62, asso. prof. microbiology, 1962—. NSF Found. research participant Ind. U., summer 1964. Served with USNR, 1944-46. Mem. Am. Soc. Microbiology, Theobald Smith Soc., A.A.A.S., Am. Assn. U. Profs., Am. N.J. State nurses assns., Nat., N.J. leagues nursing. Author: (with Wesley A. Volk) Basic Microbiology, 1964, 3d edit., 1973, Instructor's Manual, 1973. Home: 372 Mt Prospect Av Newark NJ 07104

WHEELER, MARY ANN CORKINS, assn. exec., puppeteer; b. Portland, Ore., Jan. 22, 1924; d. Vernon Granding and Marian (Robertson) Corkins; student (scholar) Linfield Coll., 1942-43; B.A. (scholar), U. Wash., 1947; postgrad. U. Wash., 1947-49, Auerswald's Accounting and Secretarial Sch., Inc., 1958; m. Alfred W. Wheeler, Nov. 22, 1951 (div. Apr. 1956). Theatre asst., asst. dir. Children's Theater, properties mgr., U. Wash. Sch. Drama, 1943-49; various positions, 1949-51; sec. Am. Friends Service Com., 1951-52; spl. services sec. VA Hosp., 1952-53; prodn. and program asst. KVEC-TV, San Luis Obispo, Cal., 1953-55; various secretarial and statis. positions, 1955-64; sec. Benson & McLaughlin, C.P.A.'s, Seattle, 1964—; nat. exec. sec. Zeta Phi Eta Hdqrs., Seattle, 1965-70. Puppeteer, U. Wash. Puppeteers, 1943-49, Valentinetti Puppeteers, 1944-60, Corky, The Puppeteer, 1960—. Recipient Nat. Distinguished Service award Zeta Phi Eta, 1969. Mem. Union Internationale des Marionettes, Puppeteers of Am. (pres. Seattle guild 1963-64), Zeta Phi Eta (Seattle alumnae pres. 1950-51, nat. dir. mems.-at-large 1971—), Kappa Alpha Phi. Episcopalian. Address: PO Box 1236 Seattle WA 98111

WHEELER, MARY F. (MRS. RONALD W. WHEELER, JR.), educator; b. Bloomington, Ind., Feb. 27, 1919; d. Claude Elmer and Cordelia (Jones) Cogswell; B.S., Tex. Christian U., 1938, postgrad., 1940-41; M.A., East Texas State Univ., 1963, Ph.D., 1969; m. Ronald W. Wheeler, Jr., Aug. 5, 1938; children—Wendelyn Florence (Mrs. Edwin Donnell White) (dec.), Marilyn Anne (Mrs. Jon David Kindred), Gregg Alan, Carol Kay (Mrs. Thomas Ross Johnson), Ronald Scott. With Frederick Broadcasting Co., radio sta. KTAT, 1948-62, program dir., women's editor 1948-62, acting mgr., 1950-51, 61-62, bus. mgr., 1956-62; instrnl. specialist audio-visual edn. East Tex. State U., 1966-68, dir. ednl. TV services, asst. prof. audio-visual edn., 1969-73, asso. prof., 1973—, mem. faculty senate, 1973—, mem. exec. com., 1974—. Pres. Teen Town Adult Council, 1955-57; dir. Tillman County Day Nursery Bd., 1958-60. Mem. U. Dames-Faculty Wives (pres. 1963-64), Philharmonic Music Club (pres. 1957-58), Okla. Fedn. Music Clubs, Past Pres.'s Assembly C. of C., Am., Southwestern, Tex. psychol. assns., Tex. Personnel and Guidance Assn., N.E.A., Tex. Assn. Coll. Tchrs., Tex. Ednl. Television Assn. (sec.-treas. 1972-73, v.p. 1973-74, pres. 1974-75), Nat. Assn. Ednl. Broadcasters, Tex. Assn. Ednl. Tech. (v.p. 1972-73), Assn. Ednl. Communications and Tech., Mortar Board, Psi Chi. Mem. Christian Ch. Clubs: Psychology (corr. sec. 1963-65); Afflatus Culture (rec. sec. 1965-67, pres. 1969-71), Webb Hill Country, Sand Hills Golf and Country. Home: 2810 Tanglewood Dr Commerce TX 75428 Office: Ednl Media and Tech Center East Tex State U Commerce TX 75428

WHEELER, MARY FRANCES, educator; b. Chgo., Mar. 16, 1913; d. Francis L. and Mary (West) Wheeler; A.B., U. Mo., 1935, B.S. in Edn., 1937; M.A., Tchrs. Coll., Columbia, 1952; postgrad. U. Wis., 1945-47. Tchr. pub. schs., Salisbury, Mo., 1936-37, Clifton Hill, Mo., 1937-38, Maplewood, Mo., 1938-46, Madison, Wis., 1946-52; counselor, Webster Groves, Mo., 1957-68; dean women Neb. State Tchrs. Coll., Chadron, 1952-53; head resident counselor So. Ill. U., 1953-55; dir. residence Wayland Acad., Beaver Dam, Wis., 1955-56; asst. dean students MacMurray Coll., Jacksonville, Ill., 1955-57; counselor Pompano Beach (Fla.) Jr. High, 1968-69, Parkway East Jr. High Sch., Creve Coeur, Mo., 1969—. Mem. Mo. (pres.), Nat. (chmn. jr. high sch. sect. 1967—) assns. women deans and counselors, Mo. Tchrs. Assn., Pkwy. Ind. Tchrs. Assn. (exec. bd. 1973-74), Delta Gamma. Democrat. Presbyn. Home: 13527 Coliseum Dr Chesterfield MO 63017 Office: 181 Coeur de Ville Dr Creve Coeur MO 63141

WHEELER, RUTH HOOK (MRS. OTIS LAWRENCE WHEELER), educator; b. Stryker, O., Feb. 6, 1914; d. Firm and Pauline (Bringolf) Hook; B.S., Ohio State U., 1936, M.A., 1937; postgrad. Nazareth Coll., 1957-58, Toledo U., 1960; m. Otis Lawrence Wheeler, May 26, 1946; children—Maureen Jill, Alfred Hook. Instr., Ohio State U., Columbus, 1937-41, asst. prof., 1962-70, asso. prof. phys. edn., 1970—. Served to 1st lt. Phys. Therapy Corp, AUS, 1941-45. Mem. Women's Overseas League. Mem. Order Eastern Star. Author: (with Agnes Hooley) Physical Education for the Handicapped, 1969. Contbr. articles to profl. jours. Home: 3435 Inverness Way Columbus OH 43221

WHEELER, ZONA LORRAINE, advt. designer, painter; b. Lindsborg, Kan.; d. Carl Wheeler and Caroline (Carls) Wheeler; B.F.A., Bethany Coll., 1932; postgrad. Am. Acad. Art, Chgo., Wichita (Kan.) Art Assn. Sch. Graphics designer, illustrator, sr. art dir. McCormick Armstrong Co., Wichita; exhibited in one man shows Wichita Art Assn. Gallery, 1948, 70, Mustum Mus., Racine, Wis., 1952, Rutgers U., 1953; acryloprints Kans. Fedn. Art, 1970—, Oklahoma City Art Center, 1970—; exhibited in group shows at Kansas City Art Inst., Asso. Am. Artists Galleries, N.Y.C., also shows in Boston, Denver, Eng. at Rugby, Derbyshire and Lincolnshire; exhibited at Kansas City Art Dirs. Show (award 1969), most recently at N.Y. Art Dirs. Club Show, 1965, Tulsa Art Dirs. Show (award 1970, 73); represented in permanent collections at Wichita Art Assn. Galleries, Wichita Mus., Bethany Coll., Lindsborg, Kan., Kan. State Coll. and others. Recipient purchase prize Prairie Water Color Club, 1946, 50; Natfzger award, Wichita, 1947 and others. Fellow Internat. Inst. Arts and Letters; mem. Wichita Artists Guild, Wichita Art Assn., Nat. League Am. Pen Women, Prairie Water-Color Painters, Nat. Soc. Mural Painters. Club: Altrusa. Home: 230 S Belmont St Wichita KS 67218 Office: 1501 E Douglas St Wichita KS 67201

WHELAN, CRYSTLE JANE, educator; b. Muncie, Ind., Aug. 4, 1912; d. Walter Oliver and Eva (Poole) Moore; B.S., Ball. State Tchrs. Coll., 1933, M.A., 1940, postgrad., 1955-60; postgrad. George Washington U., 1933, U. Cin., 1935-36, Ohio State U., 1956; m. Fred D. Whelan, Oct. 19, 1946; 1 son, Joseph F. Legal and govt. sec., 1933-38; editorialist South-Western Pub. Co., 1938-43; tech. writer, pub. relations asst. Wright Field, O., 1943-44; advt. copywriter, 1945-52; tchr., 1952-55; mem. faculty Ball State U., Muncie, Ind., 1955—, spl. asst. prof. bus. edn. and office adminstrn., 1969—. Fellow Direct Mail Advt. Assn.; mem. Am. Bus. Communications Assn.,

Women in Communications, P.E.O., Pi Lambda Theta, Delta Pi Epsilon. Editor: Ball State Jour. for Bus. Educators, Publs. Bur. Bus. Research Coll. Bus. Ball State U. Home: 14 Kimberly St Muncie IN 47304

WHIDDEN, HELEN LOUISE, educator; b. East Brewster, Mass., Dec. 6, 1907; d. Creighton Percy and Louise Ann (Bourne) Whidden; A.B. Wellesley Coll., 1929; A.M., Smith Coll. 1937; Ph.D. (Horton-Hallowell alumnae fellow), U. Mass., 1952. Instr. chemistry Hood Coll., Frederick, Md., 1929-35; research asst. Harvard Med. Sch., Boston, 1937-41; instr. chemistry Randolph-Macon Woman's Coll., Lynchburg, Va., 1941-46, asst. prof., 1946-49, asso. prof., 1949-56, prof., 1956—, Fernando W. Martin prof., chmn. dept. 1963—. Tech. adviser chemistry sect., Babcock & Wilcox Co., Lynchburg, 1957-59; chem. tchr. Seven Hills Sch., Lynchburg, 1964—; dir. NSF Inst. for High Sch. Tchrs. of Math. and Sci., Randolph-Macon Woman's Coll., 1961-73. Fellow Am. Inst. Chemists; mem. Am. Soc. (Va. Blue Ridge sect. chmn.), A.A.A.S., Va. Acad. Sci., Nat. Sci. Tchrs. Assn., Sigma Xi (pres. Lynchburg). Club: Altrusa Internat. (Lynchburg pres. 1972-74). Home: 4928 Old Boonsboro Rd Lynchburg VA 24503 Office: Randolph-Macon Woman's Coll 2500 Rivermont Av Lynchburg VA 24504

WHIDDEN, MARY BESS, educator; b. San Angelo, Tex., Aug. 14, 1936; d. J. Edgar and Bess (Mullican) Whidden; B.A., U. Tex., Austin, 1957; M.A., U. N.C., 1959; Ph.D., U. Tex., Austin, 1965. Spl. instr. English U. Tex., Austin, 1962-63; asso. prof. U. N.M., Albuquerque, 1963—, dir. undergrad. studies dept. English, 1973—. Woodrow Wilson fellow, Mem. Modern Lang. Assn., Phi Beta Kappa, Phi Kappa Phi. Democrat. Home: PO Box 3202 San Angelo TX 76901

WHIPPLE, GLADYS ELAINE RUSSELL (MRS. GERALD H. WHIPPLE), physician; b. Stockton, Cal., Aug. 29, 1924; d. Robert G. and Dorothy A. (Kroninger) Russell; B.A., U. Cal., Berkeley, 1945; M.D., U. Cal., San Francisco, 1948; m. Gerald H. Whipple, Dec. 27, 1947; children—Erica, Edgar, Howard, Herric, Heather. Resident in psychiatry Foxborough State Hosp., 1955-57, Mass. Mental Health Center, Boston, 1957-58; sr. physician Foxborough State Hosp., 1958-59, dir. psychiatry, 1959-61; dir. Brookline Mental Health Center, 1961-67; children's unit fellow Mass. Mental Health Center, 1967-68; cons. Mass. Rehabln. Commn., 1959-65, chief psychiatric cons., 1965-68; cons. psychiatrist student health service U. Cal. at Riverside, 1969-72; psychiat. cons. Community Services div. Cal. Bur. Social Work, 1970-72; pvt. practice Cook Psychiat. Med. Group; mem. staff Riverside Gen. Hosp. Diplomate Am. Bd. Psychiatry and Neurology. Mem. Am. Psychiat. Assn., So. Cal. Psychiat. Soc. (pres. Inland chpt. 1973-74), Am., Cal., Riverside County med. assns. Office: 3777 Tibbetts St Riverside CA 92506

WHIPPLE, MAURINE, lectr., author; b. St. George, Utah; d. Charles and Annie (McAllister) Whipple; A.B., U. Utah, 1930; student U. Cal. at Los Angeles, 1927. Contbr. Life Mag., Look Mag., Collier's Mag., Sat. Eve. Post, 1945-52; lectr. Nat. Lecture Bur., 1941-45; lectr. Roman Forum, U. Cal. at Los Angeles, 1942, 1943; lectr. Coll. So. Utah at Cedar City, 1964, 70, 71, U. Nev. at Reno, 1966. Mem. Desert Protective Assn., Internat. Platform Assn. (lectr. Washington 1966), Chi Delta Phi. Author: Giant Joshua, 1942; This is the Place: Utah, 1945. Contbr. articles to popular mags., newspapers. Home: 410 W 600 N St George UT 84770

WHISENHUNT, MARGARET JEAN, clin. psychologist; b. Hamlet, N.C., Oct. 22, 1944; d. Robert Eugene and Edith Iola (Leonard) Whisenhunt; B.A., E. Carolina Coll., 1965, M.A., 1969. Clin. psychologist, mental health div. So. W.Va. Regional Health Council, Beckley, 1968, Southeastern Mental Health Center, Wilmington, N.C., 1971—. Extension instr. psychology E. Carolina U., 1972-73. Adv. bd. New Hanover County Advancement Center, Wilmington, 1971-72. Mem. Am., N.C. psychol. assns. Home: Route 3 Box 4 Leland NC 28451 Office: PO Box 1016 Southport NC 28461

WHITACRE, AGNES LUCILE FINCH (MRS. BENNIE B. WHITACRE), poet, civic worker; b. Howard County, nr. Kokomo, Ind., Apr. 5, 1911; d. Ernest Vernon and Zella Pearl (Simpson) Finch; student Ind. U., 1950-51; studying oil painting Hazel McMinn Studio, 1969—; m. Bennie B. Whitacre, June 2, 1929; children—Richard B., Nancy Joann (Mrs. Richard E. Obermeyer), Robert V. Pres. Parent-Tchrs. Ervin Elementary Sch., 1948-50, Northwestern High Sch., 1961-62; gen. sec. Youth Temperance Council Ind., 1953-57; encampment dir. Youth Temperance Council Ind., 1953-57; state pub. relations dir. Woman's Christian Temperance Union, 1960-63, state promotion sec., 1963-68, state pres., 1968—, mem. nat. finance bd., 1970—. Mem. Kokomo Poetry Circle (sec. 1969—), World Poetry Club, Greater Kokomo Assn. Chs. of Howard County (mem. council ministries 1968-72). Methodist (dist. pres. Women's Soc. Christian Service 1945-47, mem. nat. ofcl. bd. 1968-73, mem. nat. budget com. 1970-73; evangelism, membership chmn. work area 1967-72). Author: He Touched Me, 1972; also numerous poems and short stories in various publs. Editor: Indiana Memo, 1953-57. Address: Route 1 Box 317 Kokomo IN 46901

WHITAKER, REGINA LYDIA (MRS. PAUL WILLIAM JOHNS), lawyer; b. El Paso, Tex., Feb. 9, 1927; d. Reginald and Katharine Mary (Trippe) Whitaker; B.S., U. Miami, 1948; J.D., 1953; postgrad., Garland County Community Coll., 1973—; m. Paul William Johns, June 10, 1962 (dec.). Admitted to Fla. bar, 1953, Ark. bar, 1957, U.S. Supreme Court, 1970; mem. firm Marlow, Sinnamon & Marlow, Miami, Fla., 1953-57; individual practice, Hot Springs, Ark., 1957-63; law clk. Ark. Supreme Ct., Little Rock, 1963-72; claims atty. Ark. Hwy. Dept., Little Rock, 1972—. Atty., dir. Lakewood Convalescent Home, Hot Springs, Ark., 1959—. Vice pres. Ouachita council Girl Scouts U.S.A., 1960-66; mem. Ark. Assn. Community Theaters, 1962-63. Bd. dirs. Garland County United Fund, 1958-62, Community Players of Hot Springs, 1959-61; bd. govs. Hot Springs Showmen's Assn., 1962—. Mem. Ark. (mem. environmental com. 1972—), Garland County (sec., treas. 1959—) bar assns., Fla. bar, Ark. Assn. Women Lawyers, Am. Assn. U. Women (pres. 1967-69), Women's C. of C. Hot Springs (legislative chmn. 1968—), D.A.R. (Americanization chmn. 1969—), Sigma Kappa, Nu Beta Epsilon. Episcopalian. Club: Altrusa (pres. 1972-73) (Hot Springs, Ark.). Home: 1003 2d St Hot Springs AR 71901 Office: 9500 New Benton Hwy Little Rock AR 72203

WHITAKER, ROSE MARIE PEARCE (MRS. JAMES WESLEY WHITAKER), home economist; b. Baton Rouge, Apr. 22, 1940; d. Edward Joseph and Myra (Osgood) Pearce; B.S. in Vocational Home Econ. Edn., La. State U., 1962, M.S. in Coop. Extension Edn., 1966; m. James Wesley Whitaker, Dec. 14, 1966. Asst. home demonstration agt. St. Mary Parish, La., 1962-63; home demonstration agt. Iberville Parish, La., 1964-65, 68—, Assumption Parish, La., 1966-67; condr. weekly TV program Sewing Segment, Midday in La., sta. WBRZ-TV, Baton Rouge. Wardrobe chmn. Little Theatre, Plaquemine, La., 1969; chmn. youth devel. project Service League, Plaquemine, 1971—, rec. sec., 1972-73; chmn. edn., internat. relations com. Pilot Internat., 1971-72, pres., Denham Springs, 1973-74; mem. Iberville Parish Rural Devel. Com., Iberville Parish Bicentennial Com.; active Headstart Parents, Plaquemine, Girl Scouts U.S., A.R.C. Mem. La. (1st v.p. 1972-73), Nat. assns. extension home economists, Am. Home Econ. Assn., La. State U. Alumni Fedn., Phi Upsilon Omicron, Delta Zeta. Baptist. Mem. Order Eastern Star. Home: PO Box 212 Plaquemine LA 70764 Office: PO Box 677 Plaquemine LA 70764

WHITCOMB, KAY, artist-craftsman; b. Arlington, Mass., May 20, 1921; d. Herbert Hartwell and Mildred (Carr) Whitcomb; student R.I. Sch. Design, 1939-40, 41-42, Cambridge Sch. Art, 1940-41; apprenticed Doris Hall Enamels, 1946-47; m. Michael John Keith, July 11, 1951 (div. Oct. 1956); children—Richard Yankel, Deborah Nickerson. One man shows at Whistler Mus., Lowell, Mass., La Jolla (Cal.) Mus. Art, Positano (Italy) Art Workshop, Laguna Beach Mus. Art, 1971, Galeria del Sol, Santa Barbara, Cal., 1971, Am. Library, Brussels, Belgium, 1972, Ville de Grosselies, Belgium, 1972, Esther Lewittes Gallery, Los Angeles, 1973; exhibited in group shows San Diego Fine Arts Gallery, Denver Mus., Wichita (Kan.) Art Assn., Pasadena (Cal.) Mus., La Jolla Mus. Art, Everson Mus., Syracuse, N.Y., Walker Art Center, Mpls., Enamels 70, St. Louis, Internat. Kunsthandwerke Exhbn., Stuttgart, Germany, 1969, Bloomfield, Birmingham, Mich., many others; internationally represented in pvt. collections; first Am. to enamel at Gustavsberg Enamel Fabriker, Sweden, 1969; artist in residence Crahait Emailleries, Belgium, 2 months annually, 1970—; tchr. enameling La Jolla Art Center, Cal., 1956-59; juror and lectr. enamels, crafts, primitive design. Pres. Women's Com. La Jolla Civic Orch., 1963-64. Mem. San Diego Art Guild (pres. 1968-69), Allied Craftsmen (corr. sec. 1966-67, v.p. 1972-73), So. Cal. Designer-Craftsmen (mem. bd. 1962-63), World Craft Council, Soc. Arts and Crafts Boston, Am. Crafts Council, N.Y. Home: 1631 Mimulas Way La Jolla CA 92037

WHITE, ALICE PATRICIA, educator; b. Buffalo, Sept. 21, 1934; d. Vincent Sanford and Sara Virginia (Phelan) White; B.A., Rosary Hill Coll., 1955; M.S., State U. N.Y., 1958, Spl. Edn., 1961; postgrad. Canisius Coll., 1958-59, State U. N.Y. at Buffalo, 1965-67. Tchr., West Seneca (N.Y.) Central Sch., 1955-61, Bd. Coop. Ednl. Services, Erie County, 1961-66; dir. edn. Erie County chpt. Assn. for Retarded Children, Buffalo, 1966-71; coordinator spl. edn. Westwood (N.J.) Regional Sch., 1971-72; program dir. mental retardation services Cameron-Elk-McKean-Potter Counties Mental Health/Mental Retardation/Drug and Alcohol Program, Bradford, Pa., 1972—. Mem. Am. Assn. Mental Deficiency, Council for Exceptional Children (chpt. pres. 1961-64), N.Y. State (del. 1961-65), West Seneca (del. 1960-61) tchrs. assns., Erie County Edn. Assn. (sec. 1964-65), Rosary Hill Alumnae Assn. Home: 52 Summer St Bradford PA 16701 Office: 54 Boylston St Bradford PA 16701

WHITE, ANITA CAROLINE (MRS. PHILIP WHITE), ednl. adminstr.; b. Boston; d. Fred and Mary (Hill) White; B.A., Emerson Coll., 1950, M.A., 1951; M.F.A., Yale, 1957; Ph.D., N.Y. U., 1970; m. Philip White. Instr., Emerson Coll., 1950; dir. Conn. Exptl. Opera Co., 1954; tchr. Brearley Sch. for Girls, 1957; supr. Clarkstown High Sch. S., W.Nyack, N.Y., 1971—. Ednl. research cons. Recipient Founder's Day award N.Y. U., 1971. Author: H.T.P. and the Actor, 1957; Auline, Play for Opera, 1963; Tommaso Salvini: 19th Century Actor, 1970; Thunder Over Heaven, 1971. Home: PO Box 155 Cornwall NY 12518 Office: Clarkstown High Sch S West Nyack NY 10994

WHITE, ANN KAUFMAN (MRS. LAWRENCE WHITE), performing arts specialist; b. N.Y.C., Aug. 4, 1916; d. Joseph and Mary (Elcovitz) Kaufman; student Coll. City N.Y., 1935-37; m. Lawrence White, Dec. 3, 1939; children—Philip, Renee, Kenneth, Charles. Appeared in blackouts, skits, sketches U.S.O., N.Y.C., 1940-45; actress appearing at various resort hotels, 1945-50; pres. Actors Playhouse, N.Y.C., 1951-53, Meadowbrook Players, East Meadows, N.Y., 1957-60; co-founder Repertory Theatre of L.I., 1964-67; drama critic Griscom Corp., 1964-65; columnist L.I. Living Publs., 1965-67; performing arts specialist, supr. recreation handicapped unit Nassau County Dept. Recreation and Parks, 1967—; columnist Bethpage Tribune, 1967—; asso. prof. Ind. No. U. Grad. Sch. Human Relations, 1972—. Appeared in leading role The Days Between, N.Y.C., 1966, film documentary The Rat Race, 1972; cons., artists rep., 1968—; lectr. poetry therapy, theatre and the community; free-lance writer, 1960—. Drama workshop dir. Topic House, Nassau County drug addiction center, Nassau County Children's Shelter, sr. citizens groups; poetry therapy workshop dir., day hosp. patients, mental health clinic Meadowbrook Hosp., East Meadow, 1969-70; poetry therapist Bd. Coop. Ednl. Services, Hicksville, N.Y., Jones Inst., Hicksville; dir. Spotlight Players, blind theatre co. Trustee Lyric Theatre N.Y. Mem. Civil Service Employers Assn., Assn. for Poetry Therapy (v.p.), Nassau County Recreation, Park and Conservation Assn. Author: Poetry of the People. Home: 22 Greenvale Lane Levittown NY 11756 Office: Nassau County Dept Recreation and Parks Special Activities Center Eisenhower Park East Meadow NY 11554

WHITE, ARTIE MAE (MRS. THOMAS WHITE, JR.), civic worker; b. Caspiana, La., Mar. 7, 1926; d. Liner and Mary (Bates) Hudson; Gen. Ednl. Devel., Union Bapt. Sem., 1958, certificate in Communicable Health Diseases, 1971; m. Thomas White, Jr., July 24, 1948; children—Jackie Lynne, Cynthia Gale, Milford Alex, Lonnie Lee, Johnny Lee. Supr. park and recreation Harris County, Houston, 1970-71; tchr. aide Settegast Learning Center, 1970-71; with Community Health Center, Harris County Hosp. Dist., 1971-73. Mem. Neighborhood Council, 1968—; v.p. Community Action Assn., 1971; v.p. Settegast Civic Club, 1968; asst. sec. North Forest Bd. Edn., 1972, sec., 1973, now v.p.; mem. Band Boosters Club; active Am. Cancer Soc., United Fund, Sickle Cell Anemia drives. Recipient Merit certificate Barbara Jordan Voters Registration, 1968. Mem. Nat. Sch. Bd. Assn., N.A.A.C.P., Nurse Corps, Ind. Union Colored Laborers. Baptist. Home: 7968 Cinderella Houston TX 77028

WHITE, BARBARA A. GAZIN (MRS. JOHN AARON WHITE), librarian; b. Chgo., July 31, 1922; d. Charles Edward and Barbara (Kuda) Gazin; B.A., DePaul U., 1944; student Loyola Law Sch., Los Angeles, 1946-47; J.D., Loyola Law Sch., Chgo., 1949; M.S. in L.S., Fla. State U., 1963; m. John Aaron White, Dec. 27, 1968. Asst. librarian Covington & Burling, Washington, 1963-65; law librarian Nev. State Library, Carson City, 1966-73, Nev. Supreme Ct., Carson City, 1973—. Mem. Am. Assn. of Law Libraries (sec.-treas. Western-Pacific chpt. 1968—), Beta Phi Mu. Home: 1909 N Peters St Carson City NV 89701 Office: Supreme Court Bldg Carson City NV 89701

WHITE, BARBARA ANN LYON (MRS. FREDERIC L. WHITE), insect control corp. exec.; b. Bklyn., Nov. 28, 1938; d. William Randolph and Sonja (Kowha) Lyon; grad. high sch.; m. Frederic Louis White, Dec. 31, 1972. Exec. sec. Sperry Gyroscope Co., Great Neck, N.Y., 1959-61; with Detjen Corp., Clinton Corners, N.Y., 1961—, dir. pub. relations, 1970—; with Nat. Assn. Insect Electrocutors Mfrs., Clinton Corners, 1962—, exec. sec., 1968—. Sec. The Franklin D. Roosevelt Philatelic Soc., Hyde Park, N.Y., 1965—; editor Numismatic Information Service, Pleasant Valley, N.Y., 1962—. Mem. Am. Numismatic Assn. Contbr. articles to profl. jours. Home: Rossway Rd Pleasant Valley NY 12569 Office: Salt Point Turnpike Clinton Corners NY 12514

WHITE, BERTHA MARGARETHE ROTHE, librarian; b. Syracuse, N.Y., Mar. 26, 1915; d. Oscar Charles Andrew and Cora Fredericka (Fahrenwald) Rothe; A.B. cum laude, Syracuse U., 1934, A.M., 1935, B.S. in L.S., 1940; J.D., George Washington U., 1948, LL.M., 1956; m. Kermit D. White, May 4, 1962. Instr., Auburn (N.Y.) Collegiate Center, 1936-37; substitute tchr. Syracuse pub. schs., 1937-38; tchr. English, librarian Central Sch., Richmondville, N.Y., 1938-40; librarian Central Sch., Ovid, N.Y., 1940-41; library asst. Syracuse Pub. Library, 1941-43; cataloger State Dept. Library, Washington, 1943-45; cataloger, reviser Library of Congress, 1945-48, U.S. Army Map Service, 1948; reference librarian Dept. Justice, 1948-50; law librarian HHFA, 1950-53, George Washington U. Law Library, 1953-60, Social Security Adminstrn., 1960-62; mem. staff Los Angeles County Law Library, 1962—, head reference librarian, 1973—. Admitted to D.C. bar, 1948; cons. Nat. Conf. Met. Cts., 1972-73. Pres., Law Librarians Soc. Washington, 1956-58. Mem. Am., So. Cal. (pres. 1966-68) assns. law libraries, Phi Beta Kappa, Phi Kappa Phi, Pi Lambda Theta, Phi Gamma Phi. Author: Daniel Webster Reader, 1956; Biographical Directory of Law Libraries in the U.S. and Canada, 1964; The Law of Buying and Selling, 1968; Crimes and Penalties, 1970. Indexer, contbr. to profl. jours. Home: 7125 Sunnybrae Av Canoga Park CA 91306 Office: 301 W 1st St Los Angeles CA 90012

WHITE, BEVERLY JANE HIXSON, physician; b. Seattle, Oct. 9, 1938; d. George Wellington and Ada (Carter) Hixson; M.D., U. Wash., 1963; children—Mary, Tom. Intern Phila. Gen. Hosp., 1963-64; research fellow dept. obstetrics and gynecology and Cardiovascular Research Inst., U. Cal. at San Francisco 1964-65; staff fellow NIH, Bethesda, Md., 1965-67, sr. staff fellow and attending physician Nat. Inst. Arthritis, Metabolism and Digestive Diseases, 1969—; resident U. Wash., 1967-69. Recipient Mosby Book award C.V. Mosby Co., 1963, Matrix Table award U. Wash., 1963, Reuben award Am. Soc. Study Sterility, 1964. Fellow Am. Acad. Pediatrics; mem. Am. Women's Med. Assn., Reticuloendothelial Soc., Found. for Advanced Edn. in Scis., Internat. Dermatoglyphics Assn., Alpha Epsilon Delta. Contbr. to profl. jours. Home: 9509 Edgeley Rd Bethesda MD 20014 Office: Rm 9D-08 Bldg 10 Nat Inst Arthritis Metabolism and Digestive Diseases NIH Bethesda MD 20014

WHITE, BEVERLY JEAN LARSON (MRS. MARION FLOYD WHITE), state legislator; b. Salt Lake City, Sept. 28, 1928; d. Gustave Rudolf and Helene (Sterzer) Larson; grad. high sch.; m. Marion Floyd White, Apr. 8, 1947; children—Susie (Mrs. John Morris), Douglas Floyd, Robyn Ann (Mrs. James Bauder), David Scott, Wendy Jo. Bookkeeper, Tooele County (Utah) Clk., 1960—; mem. Utah State Bd., Corrections, 1964-70; adv. mem. Halfway House, 1968—; vice chmn. Mental Health Adv. Council, 1972—; mem. Utah Ho. of Reps., 1972—. Pres., Women's Democratic Club, 1957-58; vice-chairlady Democratic party Tooele County, 1959—; sec. Democratic party Utah State, 1971—. Mem. Order Women Legislators (nat. treas. 1973-74). Mem. Ch. of Jesus Christ of Latter-day Saints. Club: Tooele Woman's (treas. 1972-74). Home: 122 Russell Av Tooele UT 84074 Office: 47 S Main St Tooele UT 84074

WHITE, CAROL MAE, pub. relations exec.; b. Davenport, Ia., May 4, 1947; d. Hersel Francis and Eula Fern (Bultemeier) White; B.A., Drake U., 1969; postgrad. Syracuse U., 1969-70. Staff writer women's news Post Standard, Syracuse, N.Y., 1969-70; editorial asst., staff writer Now Mag., Dallas, 1971; editorial asst. S.W. Scene mag., Dallas Morning News, 1971-72; pub. relations asst., asst. editor Baylor Progress, Baylor U. Med. Center, Dallas, 1972-74; dir. pub. relations Ft. Worth Osteo. Hosp., 1974—. Leader, Tejas Girl Scout council, Plano, Tex., 1973-74. Mem. Internat. Assn. Bus. Communicators, Tex. Hosp. Assn., Tex. Soc. Hosp. Pub. Relations, Women in Communications, Inc. Home: 3911 Ranch Estates Dr Plano TX 75074 Office: 1000 Montgomery St Fort Worth TX 76107

WHITE, CAROLINE TAYLOR (MRS. WILLIAM CRAWFORD WHITE), civic worker; b. Wilmette, Ill., Nov. 25, 1893; d. Thomas Herbert and Jettie Edgerton (Hurlbut) Taylor; A.B., Wellesley Coll., 1915, M.Humane Arts, (hon.), 1950; m. William Crawford White, June 1, 1917; children—Thomas Taylor, Mary Lavell (Mrs. John Lawrence Fearey), Norval Crawford. Co-chmn. region 14 Wellesley 75th anniversary drive, 1947-50; v.p. Community Council Greater N.Y. Bd. dirs. Nat. YWCA, 1939-60, sec., 1940-46, chmn. Central br. N.Y.C., 1941-47, pres. bd. dirs. YWCA of N.Y.C., 1948-54; trustee Cyrenius Booth Library, Newtown, Conn., 1964-70, Congl. Ch., Newtown, 1965-70, Danbury (Conn.) Hosp., 1967-70. Mem. Wellesley Coll. Alumnae Assn. (v.p. 1946-48, pres. 1949-52), Hist. Soc. Newtown (pres. 1963-66). Democrat. Presbyn. (elder, pres. women's assn. 1932-34, mem. bd., exec. com. bd. nat. missions 1943-49). Clubs: Cosmopolitan, Wellesley (pres. 1928-30) (N.Y.C.) Home: 201 W Evergreen Av Philadelphia PA 19118

WHITE, CATHERINE DURKIN, social worker; b. Syracuse, N.Y.; d. John and Mary Ellen (McKeon) Durkin; B.S., Syracuse U., 1936; 1 son, Joseph Durkin. Social worker Ontario County Social Service, Geneva, N.Y., 1957—. Commr. health City of Geneva, 1957—; mem. mayor's exec. council, 1970—; exec. council on aid to handicapped, 1970—. Mem. exec. bd. United Negro Coll. Fund; pub. relations bd. Geneva Gen. Hosp.; mem. exec. com. Fed. Manpower Devel. and Tng. Program; chmn. publicity Coast Guard Aux. Mem. Syracuse U. Alumni Assn. (nat. dir. 1959-62), Geneva Gen. Hosp. Aux. (pres. 1959-60, v.p. pub. relations bd.), C. of C. (mem. speakers bur. 1959-60, 62-63), Syracuse University Alumni Assn. Geneva (pres. 1957), Internat. Platform Assn. Roman Catholic. Home: 488 Main St S Geneva NY 14456 Office: 120 N Main St Canandaigua NY 14424

WHITE, CATHERINE KILMURRAY, lawyer; b. Pikesville, Md., Apr. 19, 1930; d. Martin Francis and Catherine (McGrath) Kilmurray; B.A., U. Md., 1954; J.D., Columbia, 1969; 1 dau., Catherine Elizabeth. Sch. tchr., Prince George County, Md., also Tacoma, Wash., 1954-59; admitted to N.J. bar, 1969; pvt. practice, Plainfield, 1969-73; mem. firm Mutnick, Gast & White, Plainfield, 1973—. Pres. W.Va. Citizens-Consumers League, 1961-65, Kanawha Valley Human Relations Com., 1963-65; mem. Plainfield Human Relations Commn., 1966-68, Plainfield Charter Revision Study Com., 1971-72. Del. Democratic Nat. Conv., 1968, chmn. Union County (N.J.) Dem. credential com., 1972—. Mem. N.J., Plainfield bar assns., Columbia Law Sch. Alumni Assn., Women's Polit. Caucus (v.p. N.J. 1973, county v.p. 1972). Home: 1145 Woodland Av Plainfield NJ 07060 Office: 127 Watchung Av Plainfield NJ 07061

WHITE, CHARLOTTE VAN NOPPEN (MRS. WILLIAM DABNEY WHITE), educator; b. Greensboro, N.C., Mar. 13, 1908; d. Charles Leonard and Addie (Donnell) Van Noppen; A.B., U. N.C., 1930; M.A., U. Ala. 1961; postgrad. U. Mich., 1941, Pa. State U., 1954; m. William Dabney White, Nov. 19, 1941; Tchr. pub. schs., Rowan County, N.C., 1930-31, Graham, N.C., 1931-33, Greensboro, N.C., 1933-35; dir. Children's Little Theater, Greensboro, 1936-40; pvt. practice as speech therapist, Greensboro, N.C., 1941-42, Durham, N.C., 1951-54; speech therapist Cerebral Palsy Sch., Greensboro, 1954-60; owner, operator Greensboro Reading and Speech Center, 1961—; dir. Reading and Study Center, Inc.; instr. Greensboro Coll., 1955-58, U. N.C., 1954, 1959; originator 8 Fun and Phonics games for teaching remedial reading. Bd. dirs. PATH (Progressive Advancement Through Hearing) Sch., Greensboro. Mem. N.C. Speech Assn., Delta Kappa Gamma. Democrat. Presbyn. Home: 302 Woodlawn Av Greensboro NC 27401

WHITE, CRETHIE STOREY (MRS. LENSIE EDWARD WHITE), counselor; b. Seaboard, N.C., Nov. 29, 1931; d. Henry Clinton and Mattie Ruth (Sykes) Storey; B.S. in English and Sci. (Univ. scholar, Prospective Tchrs. scholar), E. Carolina U., 1963, M.A. in Counseling, 1966; m. Lensie Edward White, Dec. 23, 1948;

children—Ellen (Mrs. Edward M. Alderman, Jr.), Evelyn Kaye (Mrs. Robert E. Bunch), Susan (Mrs. Garland Rhea Butler). Tchr., West Bertie High Sch., Lewiston, N.C., 1962-63, Bertie Sr. High Sch., 1963-64; counselor Scotland Neck (N.C.) High Sch., 1964-65, Robersonville (N.C.) High Sch., 1966-69, Martin Tech. Inst., Williamston, N.C., 1969—. Trustee, sec. Bertie Acad., 1968-72. Mem. Student Nat. Edn. Assn., N.C. Personnel and Guidance Assn., Phi Theta Kappa. Republican. Baptist. Home: Route 2 Box 108 Aulander NC 27805 Office: PO Drawer 866 Williamston NC 27892

WHITE, DARE LAMBERTON (MRS. WILLIAM FRANCIS WHITE), pub. co. exec.; b. Winona, Minn., July 23, 1927; d. Henry McClelland and Gretchen (Leicht) Lamberton; B.A. cum laude, Vassar Coll., 1949; m. William Francis White, July 8, 1950; children—Angus, Dana, Andrea. With Rep. and Herald Pub. Co., Winona, Minn., 1961—, v.p., 1961—. Chmn. motor corps A.R.C., Winona, 1950-70; bd. mem. Community Meml. Hosp. Aux., 1957, 58, 66—, chmn. fund raising com., 1966, editor bull., 1967-73; vol. worker Catherine Allison Library, Winona, 1954-60. Bd. dirs. Tyrone Guthrie Theatre Found., Mpls., 1963-71. Mem. Am. Assn. U. Women, League Women Voters, Women's Art Class (pres. 1969-70), Women's Golf Assn. (pres. 1958), Winona County Hist. Soc. Episcopalian. Clubs: Winona Saddle and Bridle (bd. mem.), Ruskin Study (historian 1969-72, v.p. 1972-74, pres. 1974—), Shattuck School Mothers, Minn.-Dakota Vassar, Winona Country. Compiler, editor: Reflections and Recipes of the Casual Observer, 1966. Home: Drumnadrochit Box 70 Winona MN 55987 Office: 601 Franklin St Winona MN 55987

WHITE, DELILAH TEDDLIE, psychologist; b. Stephenville, Tex., Oct. 3, 1903; d. James Luke and Willie Lula (Oakes) Teddlie; B.S., U. Cin., 1934, M.A., 1946; divorced; 1 dau., Margaret. Sch. psychologist, Evanston, Ill., 1947-49; psychologist State of Ill., 1949-51; psychologist Levinson Center Mentally Handicapped Children, Chgo., 1951—, adminstrv. dir., chief psychologist, 1965—. Pvt. practice, psychology, 1951—; instr. U. Chgo. Downtown Center, 1955-61, Nat. Coll. Edn., Evanston, 1953-60. Mem. adv. bd. Lambs, Inc., Mongoloid Devel. Council. Fellow Am. Assn. Mental Deficiency; mem. A.A.A.S., Am. Psychol. Assn. Contbr. to profl. jours. Home: 300 N State St Chicago IL 60610 Office: Levinson Center 1850 W Harrison St Chicago IL 60612

WHITE, DORIS ANNE, artist; b. Eau Claire, Wis.; d. William I. and Mary (Dietz) White; grad. Art Inst. Chgo., 1950. Exhibited in one-man shows at IFA Galleries, Washington, Berestrum Art Center & Mus., Neenah, Wis., Adelle Rosenberg Gallery, Chgo., Susan Kohn Gallery, St. Paul, Bradley Gallery, Milw.; exhibited in group shows at Ill. Mus., Springfield, 1963, Art Alliance, Phila., 1963, Mus. Modern Art, N.Y.C., 1967, Pa. Acad. Fine Arts, Phila., 1963, 64, 66, Art Inst., Chgo., 1963, Met. Mus., 1966, N.A.D., N.Y.C., 1962, 63, 64, 65, 67, Butler Inst. Am. Art, Youngstown, O., 1960, 61, 63, 64, 65, Smithsonian Instn., Washington, 1960, Walker Art Center, Mpls., 1963, 64, Madison (Wis.) Salon Art, 1958-63, 64, Spanish Internat. Pavilion, St. Louis, 1969, Utah State U., Logan, 1969, 70, Cleve. Inst. Art, Miami (Fla.) U., Chautauqua (N.Y.) Art Assn., Soc. Four Arts, Palm Beach, Fla., Instituto de arte de Mexico, others; represented in permanent collections Butler Inst. Am. Art, Walker Art Center, Milw. Art Center. Recipient numerous art awards including Grand award, 1963, Grumbacker award, 1965, Paul Remmy award, 1964 (all Am. Watercolor Soc.); Ranger Fund Purchase award, Obrig award (both N.A.D.); Medal of Honor Knickerbocker Artists, 1963; Four Arts award Soc. of Four Arts, Palm Beach, 1963; RCA Victor Purchase award Lowe Gallery, Coral Gables, Fla., 1963; purchase awards Walker Art Center Biennial, Mpls., 1962, Butler Inst. Am. Art, 1960, 61; Gimbel award Milw. Art Center, 1961; M.L. Jarrott Art Scholarship, Nat. League Am. PenWomen, 1960; First Purchase award Union League Club of Chgo., 1962; Purchase award Springfield (Mo.) Mus., 1964, U.N.D., Grand Forks. Mem. Nat. Acad. Design, Am., Cal. watercolor socs., Phila. Watercolor Club. Home: Route 1 Jackson WI 53037

WHITE, DORIS JEAN WESTBROOK (MRS. JOHN HOYT WHITE), savs. and loan exec.; b. Fyffe, Ala., Nov. 22, 1933; d. Herbert Bud and Vada (Blackwell) Westbrook; attended Chattanooga Bus. Inst., 1955-56, U. Chattanooga, 1959-60; m. John Hoyt White, Sept. 16, 1950. Sec. to wool buyer Peerless Woolen Mills, Rossville, Ga., 1951-62, exec. sec. to pres., mem. exec. com. Quilted Textiles, Inc., Rossville, 1962-67; corporate sec. Interstate Textile Industries, Inc., Chattanooga, 1967; sec. to pres., savs. counselor Rossville Fed. Savs. & Loan Assn., 1968-72, asst. treas., 1972—. Gen. chmn. Little Miss Rossville contest, 1964, 68; hostess Ga. Governor's Mansion, 1972—. Mem. com. to study Rossville City Charter Revision, 1969. Bd. dirs. Girls Club of Rossville (pres., chmn. bd. 1968-71); adv. council vocational office tng. Rossville High Sch. Mem. Rossville Bus. and Profl. Women (2d v.p. 1965-66, 1st v.p. 1966-67, pres. 1967-68, award 1972), Ga. Fedn. Bus. and Profl. Women (chmn. personal devel. 1969-70; pub. relations com., chmn. dist. III nominating com. 1971-72; Woman of Achievement 1972). Baptist. Home: 214 Jomah Dr Rossville GA 30741 Office: Rossville Fed Savs & Loan Assn 403 Chickamauga Av Rossville GA 30741

WHITE, ELIZABETH DORIS, economist; b. Vallejo, Cal., Dec. 15, 1923; d. Forrest Russell and Evelyn (Finne) White; B.S., U. Cal., 1961, M.S., 1962; Ph.D., U. Ill., 1966. Clk., Mare Island Naval Shipyard, Vallejo, 1941-42, 48-51, Benicia (Cal.) Arsenal, 1942-47; bookkeeper Vallejo City Hall, 1947-48; communications supr. State Dept., Washington, 1951-58; research asst. econs. dept. U. Ill., Urbana, 1962-66; agrl. economist U.S. Dept. Agr., Albany, Cal., 1966—. Mem. Am. Marketing Assn., No. Cal. Inst. Food Technologists, Phi Kappa Phi, Gamma Sigma Delta. Episcopalian. Contbr. articles to profl. jours. Home: 401 Stannage St Apt 17 Albany CA 94706 Office: 800 Buchanan St Albany CA 94710

WHITE, ELIZABETH HARRIS, librarian; b. Fort Valley, Ga., Apr. 14, 1933; d. Willis and Lucile (Gilbert) Harris; B.S., Fort Valley State Coll., 1954; M.S. in L.S., Atlanta U., 1970; m. Johnny Miller White, Feb. 24, 1956; children—Shari Venise, Valerie Denise. Tchr. Monitor High Sch., Fitzgerald, Ga., 1954-56; tchr. Am. Dependent Sch., Regensburg, Germany, 1956-57; tchr. Booker High Sch., Barnesville, Ga., 1961-65; librarian Byron Sch., Fort Valley, Ga., 1965-72. Girl Scout leader, 1969-72. Baptist. Home: 520 Lawn St Fort Valley GA 31030

WHITE, ETHYLE HERMAN (MRS. S. ROY WHITE), artist; b. San Antonio, Apr. 10, 1904; d. Ferdinand and Minnie (Simmang) Herman; ed. pvt. schs., instrs.; m. S. Roy White, Mar. 23, 1924; children—De Lois Eileen (Mrs. William Marion Mohrle), Patsyruth (Mrs. Henry Wheeler). Exhibited in numerous one-man, group shows, Tex.; represented in pub. collections in U.S., pvt. collections in Switzerland, Germany, Sweden. Regional dir. Tex. Fine Arts Assn., 1948-61; del. Internat. Com. Centro Studi E Scambi Internazionali, 1961. Mem. Anahuac (Tex.) Fine Arts Group, San Antonio, Beaumont, Galveston, Houston Art leagues, Daus. Republic Tex., Nat. League Am. Pen Women, U.D.C., Lone Star Art Guild, Tex. Poetry Soc. (councilor), Internat. Arts Guild, Sumi-e Soc. Am., Southwestern Water Color Soc. Episcopalian. Mem. Order Eastern Star. Clubs: Book Trailers (Gulf Coast Area, Tex.); Fine Arts (Anahuac); Artist and Craftsmen (Dallas); Conservative Arts (Houston); Nat. Writers. Author Poet's Hour, 1967. Illustrator: Arabella, 1954. Home: Anchor Ranch Anahuac TX 77514

WHITE, EULA TOAL (MRS. LEROY J. WHITE), librarian educator; b. Albuquerque, July 24, 1917; d. Harvey Coleman and Bessie (Brierley) Toal; B.S. in Edn., Geneseo State Tchrs. Coll. (now State U. N.Y. at Geneseo), 1939; A.M. in L.S., U. Mich., 1952; m. LeRoy J. White, Dec. 12, 1952; 1 dau., Deborah Jane. Librarian Phelps (N.Y.) Central Sch., 1939-42; owner, prin. Toal's Store, Conesus Lake, N.Y., 1947-61; asso. prof. Sch. Library and Information Sci., State U. N.Y. at Geneseo, 1961—. Mem. bd. edn. Geneseo Central Sch. Dist., 1965-70. Served to 1st lt. WAC, 1943-47; PTO. Mem. Am., N.Y. library assns., Assn. Am. Library Schs., Assn. Edn. Communications and Tech., N.Y. State Tchrs. Assn., N.E.A. Faculty Assn. (sec.). Presbyn. (elder). Club: Livingston Country (Geneseo). Contbr. articles to profl. jours. Home: 108 Center St Geneseo NY 14454

WHITE, GLADYS BROOKS (MRS. C. B. WHITE), home economist; b. Richmond County, N.C., July 30, 1918; d. John Bunyon and Hattie Trithenia (Morgan) Brooks; B.S. in Home Econs., High Point Coll., 1942; postgrad. U. N.C. at Greensboro, 1959, 72, N.C. State U., 1963, 69, East Carolina U., 1955; m. Myron Roberts, Mar. 9, 1945 (dec. Dec. 1960); children—Myron, Joseph; m. 2d, Cotter Bright White, Jan. 15, 1967. Mem. Pamlico County (N.C.) Bd. Edn., 1942-61; mem. staff N.C. State U. Extension Service at Bayboro, 1961-67, Edenton, 1967—; home econs. extension agt., 1944-47, 60—. Sub.-dist. sec. Women's Soc. Christian Service, 1970—; chmn. rural fund Heart Fund Chowan County, 1968-73. Recipient Distinguished Service award Nat. Extension Agts. Assn., 1971. Mem. Bus. and Profl. Women (Edenton), Nat. Assn. Extension 4-H Agts., Delta Kappa Gamma. Home: Box 217 Tyner NC 27980 Office: Box 519 Edenton NC 27932

WHITE, GOLDIE SARAH PEARL, nurse; b. St. John's, Nfld., Can., July 16, 1938; d. Joseph Arthur Stanley and Marguerite (Parsons) Bath; student Grace Gen. Hosp., St. John's, 1956-59; m. Joseph Freeman White, Sept. 10, 1964; children—Fletcher Bath, Tyler Joseph. Tchr. elementary sch., Dover, Nfld., 1955-56; staff nurse Cottage Hosp., Channel, Nfld., 1959-60, Yellowknife, N.W.T., 1960-61; nurse in nursing stas., N.W.T., 1961-65; head nurse, Twillingate, Nfld., 1965-66; pub. health nurse, St. John's, 1966-68; dir. nursing Notre Dame Bay Meml. Hosp., Twillingate, 1968—. Mem. Nfld., B.C., Canadian assns. registered nurses (mem. council, pres. Triple Island chpt.), Canadian Nurses Found., Canadian Heart Found., Nfld. Tb and Respiratory Disease Assn., Nfld. Health Service Execs., TOPS. Home: PO Box 144 Durrell Twillingate NF Canada Office: Notre Dame Bay Meml Hosp Twillingate NF Canada

WHITE, HARRIET ELIZABETH, intergroup relations specialist; b. Hillsdale, N.J., Feb. 13, 1920; d. Albert T. and Laura C. (Price) White; A.B., Bates Coll., 1941; M.A., Ohio U., 1943. Indsl. relations aide Eastman Kodak Co., 1943-44; asst. house dir., employee counselor U.S. Govt., 1944-46; asst. dean of women Bucknell U., 1946-47; instr. edn. Ind. U., 1947-49; young adult program dir. Young Women's Christian Assn., Detroit, 1949-51, dir. Woodlawn Center YWCA, Chgo., 1951-56; program dir. Nat. Conf. Christians and Jews, Chgo., 1956-68; pub. relations supr. Ill. Bell Telephone Co., 1968-70, dist. staff supr. equal employment opportunity, 1970—; community relations coordinator Chgo. Police Dept., 1965-66. Mem. Met. bd. dirs. Chgo. YWCA, 1971—. Recipient Good Am. award Chgo. Com. of One Hundred, 1962. Mem. Acad. Certified Social Workers, Nat. Assn. Social Workers, Nat. Orgn. for Women, Delta Sigma Rho. Club: Executives (Chgo.). Home: 1660 N LaSalle St Chicago IL 60614 Office: 225 W Randolph St Chicago IL 60606

WHITE, HEDY KELLER (MRS. DEAN CASEY WHITE), pub. relations cons.; b. N.Y.C.; d. Maurice V. and Mollie (Sloane) Keller; grad. 1st Nat. U., 1938; m. Dean Casey White, Mar. 31, 1940. Sr. editor Our Pet World, N.Y.C., 1938—; treas., Pet Health, N.Y.C., 1940-68; sr. editor Pet Digest, 1965—; asso. pub. relations cons. Dean White Assos., N.Y.C., 1935—; free lance writer, 1935—. Mem. Met. Better Bus. Bur. Bd. dirs. League for Another Chance, Inc., 1960—, Employ the Handicapped League, 1954—, Greenwich Village Humane League, 1958—; founder, dir. Inst. Human-Animal Relationship, 1940—. Presbyn. (sec., treas.). Clubs: Overseas Press; Publicity (N.Y.C.). Contbr. articles pub. in leading mags. Home: 312 W 73d St New York City NY 10023 Office: 54 W 40th St New York City NY 10018

WHITE, HELEN BAKER (MRS. WARREN EUGENE WHITE), educator; b. Alicia, Ark., Sept. 14, 1932; d. William Edward and Alma Rita (Nicholson) Baker; B.S., Middle Tenn. State U., 1967, M.A., 1970, postgrad., 1972—; m. Warren Eugene White, Nov. 20, 1953; children—James Warren, Lora Margaret. Instr. speech Motlow State Community Coll., Tullahoma, Tenn., 1970—, dir. forensics, 1971—. Mem. Am., Tenn. Intercollegiate (pres. 1972-73) forensic assns., Speech, So. Speech communication assns., Tenn. Speech Assn. (mem. research and publ. com. 1973-74), Am. Assn. Univ. Profs., Kappa Delta Pi, Phi Sigma Beta, Phi Gamma Mu, Phi Rho Pi. Mem. Christian Ch. (chmn. Christian edn. 1969-70). Club: Texas A. & M. Aero. Engring. Wives (pres. 1957-58). Home: 1511 Diana Murfreesboro TN 37110 Office: Motlow State Community College Tullahoma TN 37388

WHITE, HELEN MAE MCKOWN (MRS. ERMAN B. WHITE), oilwell drilling contractor; b. Rich Hill, Mo., Apr. 5, 1915; d. Robert Lee and Ethel Elsie (Wilcox) McKown; student pub. schs.; m. Erman B. White, June 5, 1933 (dec.); children—William Earl, Thomas Dale. Vice pres. White & Ellis Drilling, Inc., El Dorado, Kan., 1948-59, pres., 1959—. Mem. El Dorado City Planning Commn., 1971—. Dir. Four Seasons Nursing Home, 1965-69. Mem. El Dorado C. of C. (dir.), Bus. and Profl. Women's Club (treas. 1961), Oil Secs. (v.p. 1967), Logopedics Aux. (pres. 1972). Clubs: El Dorado Country (dir. 1969-70), El Dorado Soroptomist (pres. 1965). Home: 1625 Pennsylvania St El Dorado KS 67042 Office: 1614 W 6th St El Dorado KS 67042

WHITE, HELYN (LYN) HILL, pub. co. exec.; b. Marquez, Tex.; d. Arthur Ray and Mary Elizabeth (Rankin) Hill; student U. Tex., 1928-29; m. Jules White, 1931 (div. 1939). Broadcaster, writer KRRC, KTRH, KXYZ, Houston, 1930-36; writer Houston Post, Dallas, 1930-36; columnist, feature writer San Francisco Chronicle, 1940-43; writer, broadcaster KQW, San Francisco, 1940-42; dir. book advt. N.Y. Post, 1943-49; advt. dir. United Nations World, N.Y.C., 1950-52; mgr. advt. devel. Saturday Review, N.Y.C., 1960-72; v.p., asso. pub. Saturday Review/World, N.Y.C., 1972—. Recipient Brown Freshman Math prize U. Tex., 1928. Mem. Am. Advt. Fedn., Advt. Women N.Y. Democrat. Baptist. Club: Texas (N.Y.C.). Home: 155 E 52d St New York City NY 10022 Office: 488 Madison Av New York City NY 10022

WHITE, JACQUELINE BANYAN WHITESIDE (MRS. WILLIAM L. WHITE), veterinarian; b. Hempstead, N.Y., Oct. 20, 1928; d. John and Margaret (LeGoza) Bryan; B.S. (univ. scholar), Mich. State U., 1951; postgrad., Clark U., 1954-57; B.S. in Vet. Sci., Mich. State U., 1962, D.V.M., 1963; m. William L. White, June 3, 1973. Lectr., tchr. Mass. Audubon Soc., Worchester, 1951-56; tchr. Wachusett High Sch., Holden, Mass., 1956-58; mem. staff hip displasia project U. Minn., Mpls., 1963-64; individual practice vet. medicine, San Bruno and Colma (both Cal.), 1964-67, Yountville, Cal., 1968—. Mem. Am., Cal., Napa-Solano (pres. 1972-73) vet. med. assns. Address: Box 2556 Yountville CA 94599

WHITE, JANE CARROLL (MRS. KEVIN JOSEPH WHITE), computer programmer; b. Durham, N.C., July 30, 1939; d. Hardy Abram and Mary Helen (Bailey) Carroll; B.S., Guilford Coll., 1961; A.M., Duke, 1963; m. Kevin Joseph White, June 18, 1966; children—Hilary Carroll, Brian Kevin, Alison Jane. Instr. math. U. N.C., Greensboro, 1963-66; part-time lectr. math. Goucher Coll., Towson, Md., 1966-69; asst. Computer Center, computer programmer Goucher Coll., Towson, 1969—. Methodist. Home: 406 Fowler Ct Joppa MD 21085 Office: Computer Center Goucher Coll Towson MD 21204

WHITE, JANE NEAL, librarian; b. Portland, Me., May 4, 1918; d. Charles McKendre and Anna (Bottorrff) Neal; A.B., U. Ky., 1964, M.S. in L.S., 1965; m. Winston Winn White, Aug. 8, 1941; children—C. Allen, Cheryl LeFever, Dale, Keith. Librarian Coll. Edn. Library, U. Ky., Lexington, 1965—. Mem. Ky., Southeastern library assns., Kappa Delta Pi. Mem. Christian Ch. Home: Greenbriar Rd Lexington KY 40506 Office: 205 Dickey Hall Univ Ky Lexington KY 40506

WHITE, JEAN CHRISTENSEN, polit. worker; b. Franksville, Wis., Aug. 19, 1934; d. Norman W. and Esther C. (Hansen) Christensen; B.S., Northwestern U., 1956; m. Robert Cecil White, June 16, 1956; children—Douglas Hunter, Carol Andersen. Staff asst. community relations dept. Ford Motor Co., 1956-58; exec. sec. Republican Central Com. San Diego County, Cal., 1964-66, exec. dir., 1966; campaign coordinator, dist. office mgr. Assemblyman Pete Wilson, 1966-68; campaign coordinator Pete Wilson for Mayor, 1971; campaign cons. Ron Del Principe for Assembly Com., 1972; San Diego County coordinator Houston Flournoy for Gov. Com., 1973-74. Fund-raiser Combined Arts and Edn. Council San Diego County, 1972-73; mem. steering com. Globe Guilders, 1971-74; press chmn. Shakespeare Festival Commn., 1971-72; mem. Mayor's Com. on Status of Women, 1973. Dir. Republican Assos., 1973; 1st vice-chmn. Rep. Central Com. San Diego County, 1973-75. Mem. Women in Communications, Alpha Omicron Pi. Home: 3151 Fryden Ct San Diego CA 92117

WHITE, JOYCE LOUISE, librarian; b. Phila., June 7, 1927; d. George William and Louisa (Adams) White; B.A., U. Pa., 1949; M.L.S., Drexel U., 1963. With U. Pa. Library, Phila., 1949—, with serials dept., 1949-52, acquisitions dept., 1954-56, librarian Penniman Library Edn., 1957—; mem. library exchange U. London, 1952-53. Cons., Van Guard Sch., Montgomery County, Pa., 1966-67; dir. Drexel Workshop for Ch. Librarians, 1962-66. Mem. Am., Church and Synagogue (exec. sec. 1970-71), Am. Theol. library assns. Episcopalian. Editor: Church Library Guide, 1963; Directory of Church and Synagogue Libraries in Maryland, 1973; guest editor Church and Synagogue Libraries, spl. issue Drexel Library Quar. 1970; joint editor Thomas Woody Bibliography. Home: 3414 Baring St Philadelphia PA 19104 Office: 36th and Walnut Sts Philadelphia PA 19104

WHITE, JUANITA GREER (MRS. THOMAS SHERMAN WHITE), univ. regent, legislator, educator; b. Atlanta, Nov. 19, 1905; d. Harry Goldsmith and Cleio E. (Greer) Greer; A.B., Agnes Scott Coll., 1926; Ph.D., Johns Hopkins U., 1929; m. Thomas Sherman White, June 6, 1935; 1 dau., Sally M. (Mrs. Paul Bu Falry). Prof. biology and chemistry, chmn. dept. sci. Mary Baldwin Coll., 1930-35; instr. anatomy, physiology Bennett Jr. Coll., 1935-38; research chemist Bell Labs., Murray Hill, N.J., 1943, De Luxe Labs., 20th Century-Fox Film Corp., N.Y.C., 43-46; instr. chemistry Hunter Coll. of City of N.Y., Sch. of Gen. Studies, 1943-44, 49-51; asso. prof. sci. Willimantic (Conn.) State Tchrs. Coll., 1951-52. Legislator, Nev. Assembly, 1970-72. Mem. exec. bd. A.R.C., Dutchess County, N.Y., 1940-44, Millbrook (N.Y.) Vis. Nurse Com., 1938-44, 46-50; mem. Nev. Gov.'s Com. on Aging, 1959-66; del. White House Conf. on Aging, 1961; mem. Nev. Gov.'s Com. on Med. Edn., 1963-64; edn. chmn. Nev. Gov.'s Commn. on Status of Women, 1963-66; dir. Nev. Tb and Respiratory Health Assn., 1963-73, pres., 1972-73; Nev. commr. Western Interstate Commn. Higher Edn., 1965-74, mem. exec. com., 1965-74; adv. com. Nat. Defense for Lang. Centers U.S. Office Edn., 1966-67; adv. com. S.W. Regional Lab. Edn. Research, 1967—; Nev. Higher Edn. Commn., 1963-69, Nev. Edn. Commn., 1965, Clark County Health Planning Council, 1972—; mem. Nev. adv. com. Rural Devel. Program, 1973-74. Regent U. Nev., 1963-71; trustee Nevada So. Univ. Land Found., 1966—. Recipient Distinguished Nevadan award U. Nev., 1972. Mem. Am. Assn. U. Women (dir. Nev. state div. 1957-67, state pres. 1963-65, nat. com. on social and econ. issues 1961-63, mem. internat. fellowships award com. 1964-73, chmn. internat. awards com. 1967-73, mem. edn. found. 1967-71), Phi Beta Kappa, Sigma Xi, Beta Sigma Phi (hon.). Republican. Episcopalian. Home: 639 Av I Boulder City NV 89005 Office: 509 Av C Boulder City NV 89005

WHITE, JUDITH KAUFMAN (MRS. JACK KAYLIN WHITE), artist; b. Youngstown, O., Sept. 23, 1935; d. Herman Benjamin and Ida (Snewind) Kaufman; A.A., Stephens Coll., 1955; B.S., Ohio State U., 1958; m. Jack Kaylin White, Mar. 15, 1957; children—Dana Alison, Mark Kaylin. Occupational therapist Crippled Children's Hosp., Memphis, 1958-59; sec., dir. Comsec, Inc., 1970-72; exhibited in group shows Schumacher Gallery, Capital U., O., Huntington, Gallery, Columbus, O., San Diego Art Inst.; docent LaJolla Contemporary Mus. Art, 1968-73. Area chmn. Heart Fund, Bexley, O., 1968-73; vol. occupational therapy Children's Hosp., Columbus, O., 1972-73. Mem. Occupational Therapy Assn., Central Ohio Watercolor Soc., Bexley Area Art Guild (treas. 1973), San Diego Art Inst., Columbus Fine Art Gallery. Club: Country (LaJolla). Home: 2954 Woodford Dr La Jolla CA 92037

WHITE, KATHARINE ELKUS, state ofcl.; b. N.Y.C., Nov. 25, 1906; d. Abram I. and Gertrude (Hess) Elkus; A.B., Vassar Coll., 1928; LL.D. (hon.), Douglass Coll., 1967; m. Arthur J. White, Oct. 3, 1929; children—Lawrence E., Frances E. (Mrs. John H. Cohen Jr.). Mayor Redbank, N.J., 1951-57; commr. N.J. Hwy. Authority, 1954—, chmn., 1955-64; acting treas. N.J., 1961; U.S. ambassador to Denmark, 1964-68. Mem. Ann. Assay Coin Comm., 1937, 50; chmn. adv. council President's Com. Traffic Safety, 1963-64. Chmn. Monmouth County (N.J.) Heart Fund drive, 1951, Monmouth Country Negro Coll. Fund drive, 1956. Dem. state committeewoman, Monmouth County, 1940-64; vice chmn. Dem. Com. N.J., 1954-64; del.-at-large Dem. Nat. Conv., 1944, 48, 52, 56, 60; candidate for U.S. Ho. of Reps., 1960. Trustee Red Bank Community YMCA, Monmouth County Orgn. Social Service, Monmouth County Welfare Council; pres. bd. mgrs. N.J. State Hosp., Marlboro, 1954-64; bd. govs. Rutgers U. Mem. Am. Assn. U. Women (treas. 1950-53), Alumnae Assn. Vassar Coll. (treas. 1949-52), Consumers League N.J., Internat. Fedn. U. Women (asst. hon. treas., 1959-64), Gen. Fedn. Women's Clubs; Bus. and Profl. Women's Club, Nat. Consumers League. Home: Elkridge Harding Rd Red Bank NJ 07701

WHITE, KATHLEEN MALLEY (MRS. RICHARD F. WHITE, JR.), educator; b. Boston, Aug. 28, 1940; d. Edward William and Barbara (Beyer) Malley; B.A., Swarthmore Coll., 1962; Ed.M., Boston

U., 1967, Ed.D. (U.S. Office Edn. fellow), 1970; m. Richard F. White, Jr., Apr. 10, 1964. Spl. class tchr. for educable retarded Dearborn Sch., Roxbury, Mass., 1963-64; co-dir. summer recreational program for retarded Peabody Sch., Newton, Mass., 1963-64; spl. class tchr. Manzanita Sch., Oakland, Cal., 1964-65; sr. clinician, parent counselor, instr. Boston U. Psychoednl. Clinic, 1967-68. lectr. psychology dept., 1970-72, asst. prof., 1972—. Trustee Paracure, Newton, Mass. Recipient 3d prize, Kennedy Found. Student awards in mental retardation, 1968, grant U.S. Office Edn., 1971-72, grant Grad. Sch. Boston U., 1973. Mem. Am. Psychol. Assn., Soc. Research Child Devel., Soc. Psychol. Study Social Issues, A.A.A.S., Am. Assn. Mental Deficiency, Council Exceptional Children, Am. Assn. Univ. Profs. Home: 12 Sylvester Dr Framingham MA 01701 Office: 64 Cummington St Boston MA 02215

WHITE, LEONE ALICE (MRS. PETER ELLSWORTH WHITE), accountant; b. Bengough, Sask., Can., July 18, 1932; d. John Nick and Elizabeth Rose (Schuck) Ortman; student Vancouver Bus. Coll., 1951; m. Peter Ellsworth White, July 1, 1957; children—Cindy Anne, Peter Russell, W.H. Boyce. Bookkeeper, Canadian Linen, Vancouver, B.S., 1951-54, Canadian Fairbanks Morse, Vancouver, 1954-56; accountant Holman's Dept. Store, Summerside, P.E.I., Can., 1966-68; accountant Prince County Hosp., Summerside, from 1969, now comptroller. Home: Wilmot Valley Rural Route 4 Kensington PE Canada Office: Prince County Hosp Beattie St Summerside PE Canada

WHITE, LORETTA, actress, author; b. Battle Creek, Mich., Dec. 20, 1912; d. Thomas Cauthorne and Loretta (Boro) White; B.S., Northwestern U., 1934, postgrad. in journalism, 1946; m. Charles Peter Jaeger, June 12, 1937 (div. Apr. 1944); 1 son, Peter Cauthorne Jaeger. Power's model, 1934-35; with Edgar Bergen's theater act, 1935-36; actress radio soap operas, Chgo., N.Y.C., 1936-39; actress summer stock, Woodstock, N.Y., 1940; feature article free lance writer, Chgo. Tribune, 1948-65; author interior decorating articles, Chgo. Tribune and women's mags., 1949-50; star of Homecooking daily TV show, NBC, Chgo., 1952-54; TV actress and TV commercial spokeswoman, 1954—; motion picture actress The Group, 1965, Seven Ups, 1974. Mem. Woman's Adv. Bd., Lanolin Plus Co., 1960—. Precinct chairwoman Woman's Republican Club, 1947. Recipient 1st prize award Chgo. Book Clinic, 1959. Mem. Am. Women of Radio and TV, Screen Actor's Guild, Am. Fedn. TV Artists, Zonta Internat., Kappa Kappa Gamma. Christian Scientist. Author: The Good Egg Cookbook, 1959, 66. Home: Windcrest Rd Rye NY 10580

WHITE, MARGARET (MRS. LUKE WHITE), educator; b. Culver, Ind.; d. Jerome Herman and Bertha (Fechner) Zechiel; student Heidelberg Coll., 1932-34; A.B., Ind. U., 1936; M.A., U. Ill. 1957, Ph.D. in English, 1971; m. Luke White, June 24, 1937; children—Barbara Ann (Mrs. Frank Loda), Mary Patricia (Mrs. M. Miyagi), Kipling Nels. Tchr. Latham (Ill.) High Sch., 1936-37, Covington High Sch., 1959-60, U. Ill., 1962-63, Perrysville High Sch., 1963-64, U. Ill., 1964-66. Trustee Purdue U., 1964-67, 67-70. Mem. Am. Assn. U. Women (co-founder, first pres. Veedersburg-Covington br.), Pi Beta Phi, Pi Lambda Theta, Psi Iota Xi. Democrat. Christian Scientist. Club: Fountain County Fedn. Women's (past pres.).Home: 702 Sixth St Covington IN 47932

WHITE, MARGUERITE GREENE (MRS. NEWTON HESTON WHITE), photographer, artist; b. Middletown, N.Y., May 26, 1889; d. Zophar Ketchum and Jennie Blanche (Preston) Greene; pvt. study with John Gould, Colton Waugh, Homer Davison; m. Newton Heston White, May 12, 1923; children—Patricia (Mrs. Harold Davidson), Newton Preston (dec.). Mgr., Branch Studio, N.Y.C., 1912-23; free lance portrait photographer and artist, 1926-36; exhibited in one-man shows East Orange and Montclair, N.J., Lakeville, Conn., Ft. Wayne, Warsaw, Logansport, Indpls., South Bend and Culver, Ind., Batavia, N.Y., and Canton, O. Pres., Washingtonville (N.Y.) P.T.A., 1935-36. Recipient several awards. Fellow Am. Artists Profl. League (organizer Ohio chpt.); mem. No. Ind. Artists, State Arts Commn. Clubs: Ind. Fedn. Art (South Bend). Died June 19, 1974. Home: 531 Beach Rd Sarasota FL 33581

WHITE, MARIBELL JOAN, occupational therapist, health service adminstr.; b. Independence, Kan., Apr. 8, 1927; d. William Nathan and Winifred Irene (Compton) White; student nursing Mercy Hosp., Independence, 1949; B.S. in Home Econs., Occupational Therapy, Colo. State U., 1952. Instr. occupational therapy State Hosp. Sch. Nursing, Jacksonville, Ill., 1953-54; dir. occupational therapy Am. Legion Hosp., Battle Creek, Mich., 1954-59; occupational therapist Inst. Logopedics, Wichita, Kan., 1959-60; night charge nurse psychiatry Wesley Med. Center, Wichita, 1960-63; dir. grants and research Frankfort (Ky.) State Hosp. and Sch., 1963-72; dir. occupational therapy, staff devel. and tng. Dept. Human Resources, Diagnostic and Evaluation Service, Frankfort, 1972—, chmn. research com. diagnostic and evaluation service, 1973—. Recipient Gov.'s Ky. Col. award, 1971. Mem. Am. Assn. for Mental Deficiency (chmn. gen. sect. 1970-71), Am., Ky. occupational therapy assns., Bus. and Profl. Women's Club (Woodford County chpt. 1974—). Episcopalian. Home: 319 Amsden Av Versailles KY 40383 Office: Diagnostic and Evaluation Service Glenns Creek Rd Frankfort KY 40601

WHITE, MARJORIE GRANT POHL, columnist; b. Redlands, Cal., Aug. 5; d. Egmont Sidney and Kate (Grant) Pohl; B.A., Mills Coll., 1932, tchrs. certificate, 1933; m. T. Robert White, Mar. 18, 1967. Social worker San Bernardino and Riverside Counties, Cal., 1933-38; publicity writer, jr. hostess Desert Inn, Palm Springs, Cal., 1938-39; gasoline contractor, operator Palm Springs Airport, 1940-43; air traffic controller CAA, Oakland, Cal., and Santa Monica, Cal., 1942-43; mem. staff Air Transport Command USAF, Palm Springs, 1943-46; columnist, gen. news writer Palm Springs Limelight and News, 1940-50; owner, operator Publicity by Pohl, 1940-70; columnist Los Angeles Examiner, 1939-62, Los Angeles Herald-Examiner, 1962—. Mem. Freedoms Found. Hist. Soc. Palm Springs, Palm Springs Desert Mus. Clubs: Desert Press, Racquet, Desert Riders (Palm Springs); Balboa Bay (Newport Beach, Cal.); Mt. Kenya Safari (Kenya); Silver Gate Yacht (San Diego). Contbr. articles, features to newspapers. Address: 245 W El Portal St Palm Springs CA 92262

WHITE, MARTHA EDNA (MRS. BOYD A. WHITE), physician; b. Stafford, Kan., Oct. 31, 1888; d. Robert McCain Cavett and Martha (Hindman) Wallace; B.S. Ottawa U. (Kan.), 1910; M.D., Boston U., 1915; Dr. Therapy (hon.), Am. Inst. Homeopathy, 1970; m. Boyd Alcorn White, Nov. 30, 1939; 1 adopted dau., May Li. Mem. Presbyn. med. mission to China, 1917-38, also staff mem. leper hosp.; practice gen. medicine, Kansas City, Mo., 1939-48, Hot Springs, Truth or Consequence, N.M., 1949—; built Dr. Edna W. White Clinic, Truth or Consequence, 1951. Recipient certificate of achievement Am. Assn. Med. Phys. Research, 1961. Mem. Medico-Phys. Research Soc., Am. Inst Homeopathy (senate of srs.), Am. Massage and Therapy Assn. Author: The Science of Anatomical Alignment of the Human Machine, 1959; Amazing System of Body Alignment, 1972. Home and office: Mims and Austin Sts Truth or Consequences NM 87901

WHITE, MARY FRANCES, educator; b. Connersville, Ind., Nov. 13, 1907; d. Alfred E. and Anna E. (Munns) White; B.S., Kan. State U., 1928, M.S., 1930; Ph.D., U. Denver, 1955. English tchr. Corning (Kan.) High Sch., 1928-29, Harper (Kan.) High Sch., 1930-34, Bartlesville (Okla.) High Sch., 1934-44; with U.S. Army Signal Corps, 1944-45; supr. personnel services personnel dept. Navy Dept., Taylor Model Basin, 1945-47; asso. prof. English, Kan. State U., Manhattan, 1947—. Trustee Delta Kappa Gamma Ednl. Found. Mem. Nat. Council Tchrs. English, Am. Assn. U. Women, Kan. Assn. Tchrs. English (pres. 1968-70), Kan. Council Women (sec. 1970-72, 2d v.p. 1972-74, 1st v.p. 1974—), Meml. Hosp. Aux., P.E.O., Mortar Bd., Delta Kappa Gamma (internat. 1st v.p. 1968-70, internat. pres. 1970-72), Kappa Kappa Gamma, Phi Kappa Phi (sec. 1970-71). Republican. Presbyn. Home: 1743 Fairchild St Manhattan KS 66502

WHITE, MARY LOU, educator; b. Seattle, July 11, 1922; d. George Washington and Mary Alice (McCorquodale) White; B.S., Ore. State Coll., 1946; M.S., Wash. State Coll., 1953; D.Ed., U. Ore., 1974. Instr. girls' phys. edn. St. Helens (Ore.) High Sch., 1946-48; instr., dir. women's phys. edn. Clark Coll., Vancouver, Wash., 1949-61; prof., head dept. women's phys. edn. Cal. Poly. State U., San Luis Obispo, 1961—; dir. sports clinics and workshops in Ore., Wash., Cal., 1950—; mgr. Cal. Phys. Edn. Workshop, 1967. Chmn. Girls' and Women's Sports Officiating Bd., 1955, sec., sports chmn. volleyball and basketball, 1949-66. Inland Empire women's handicap foil champion, 1959; Inland Empire women's open foil champion, 1958, 59; hon. basketball ofcl. Recipient Outstanding Educator Am. award, 1974. Mem. Am., Cal. assns. health, phys. edn. and recreation, Nat. Assn. Phys. Edn. for Coll. Women, Western Soc. Phys. Edn. for Coll. Women, Amateur Fencers League Am., Parthenia, Pi Lambda Theta. Author surveys, studies. Home: 395 Montecito Dr Cayucos CA 93430 Office: Cal Poly State Univ San Luis Obispo CA 93407

WHITE, MURIEL RAMONA RADECKI (MRS. BOB WHITE), graphic arts designer; b. Chgo., Aug. 8, 1935; d. Fred John and Mary (Kukielka) Radecki; student Chgo. Art Inst., 1956-57, Roosevelt U., 1957-59, Chgo. Conservatory Music, 1956-64, Inst. Design, 1965-66; m. Bob White, July 20, 1959. Sec., personnel interviewing Hart, Schaffner & Marx, Chgo., 1953-57; comml. artist Karzen & Assos., Chgo., 1957-60; graphical arts designer Portland Cement Assn., Chgo., 1960-64; designer H.B. Smith & Assos., Chgo., 1964-68. Advt. dir. Visual Arts Bulletin, 1964-68, treas., 1967-68; art dir. Art Scene Mag., 1967-69; free lance designer and art dir., 1969—. Mem. Artists Guild Chgo. (mem. council 1964-66, sec. 1966). Home: 732 W Belden Av Chicago IL 60614

WHITE, MYRA GOLDSTEIN (MRS. ALVIN M. WHITE), librarian; b. N.Y.C., June 17, 1926; d. Louis and Elsie (Horwitz) Goldstein; A.B., Bklyn. Coll., 1949; certificate Eastern and Russian Lang. Sch., U. Cal. at Berkeley, 1950; M.S. in L.S., U. So. Cal., 1965; m. Alvin M. White, Dec. 4, 1946; children—Louis, Michael. Instr. Russian, Coll. of Notre Dame, Belmont, Cal., 1959; librarian, Council on Library Resources Study, Feasibility of Coll.-Industry Information Center, Claremont (Cal.) Colls., 1963-64; Russian cataloger U. Cal. at Riverside, 1964-65; librarian Rancho Santa Ana Botanic Garden, Claremont, Cal., 1965-68; document cataloger Stanford U., 1968; head bibliography, sci. bibliographer Honnold Library, Claremont (Cal.) Coll., 1969—. Mem. Am. (sec.-treas. So. Cal. tech. processes group 1973-74, v.p., pres. elect 1974-75) Cal. (mem. council) library assns., Beta Phi Mu. Contbr. math. translations to Russian-English books, 1956—. Home: 934 Harvard Av Claremont CA 91711 Office: 8th and Dartmouth Sts Claremont CA 91711

WHITE, MYRTLE THEO LEMON, city ofcl.; b. Buford, Ark., Sept. 15, 1908; d. John David and Rosa Avo (Lee) Lemon; student Browns Peoria Sch. Bus., 1960; m. Herschel N. White, Apr. 28, 1941; children—J. Loretta Chatfield, John W., Robert E. Clk., State Hosp., Peoria, Ill., 1932-41; village clk. Creve Coeur, Ill., 1965—. Pres., P.T.A., 1955-56. Precinct committeewoman Democratic party, 1960. Mem. V.F.W. Aux. (pres. 1970-71). Methodist. Mem. Order Eastern Star. Club: Woman's (Creve Coeur, Ill.). Home: 126 Margaret Dr Creve Coeur IL 61611 Office: 101 N Thorncrest St Creve Coeur IL 61611

WHITE, NANCY (MRS. RALPH DELAHAYE PAINE, JR.), fashion dir.; b. Bklyn., July 25, 1916; d. Thomas J. and Virginia (Gillette) White; student pvt. schs.; m. Ralph Delahaye Paine, Jr., July 25, 1947; children—Gillette Dauphinot (Mrs. William Scott Piper III), Katharine Delahaye Paine. Fashion editor Pictorial Rev. mag., 1936-40; asst. fashion editor Good Housekeeping mag., 1940-47, fashion editor, 1947-57; asst. editor Harper's Bazaar, N.Y.C., 1957-58, editor-in-chief, 1958-71; fashion dir. Bergdorf Goodman, N.Y.C., 1972—. Decorated knight Order Merit (Italy), Silver medal Merit (Spain); recipient N.Y. Designers award. Mem. Fashion Group (past pres.). Clubs: Cosmopolitan, River (N.Y.C.). Home: Judd Rd Easton CT 04625 Office: 754 Fifth Av New York City NY 10019

WHITE, NEVA LOIS, librarian; b. Newton, Kan., Dec. 14, 1915; d. Elmer J. and Sadie (Byler) White; B.A., Goshen Coll., 1944; A.B. in Library Sci., U. Mich., 1946, postgrad., 1946. Librarian Goshen (Ind.) Coll., 1944-49; relief worker, tchr. English, Hong Kong, 1950-52; librarian St. Mary's Hosp. Library, Wausau, Wis., 1953; asst. librarian Marquette U., Milw., 1954-59; library adviser to Kabul (Afghanistan) U., 1959-66; librarian Kan. State U., Manhattan, 1966—. Mem. Am. Assn. U. Women, Book reviewer Library Jour., 1954—. Contbr. articles, book reviews to publs. Home: 2465 Vaughn St Manhattan KS 66502

WHITE, ONNA (MRS. LARRY DOUGLAS), choreographer; b. N.S., Can.; naturalized; m. Larry Douglas. Profl. debut San Francisco Opera Ballet; N.Y.C. debut in Finian's Rainbow; formerly modern and ballet dancer, asst. choregrapher various shows, choreographer stage show Fanny, London, also Carmen Jones, The Music Man, N.Y.C., Hot Spot, Half a Sixpence, 1965, Bye Bye, Birdie (film), Oliver (spl. Oscar) (film), 1968. Home: 19 Hamilton Terrace New York City NY 10031

WHITE, OPAL HINSEY, educator; b. Osceola, Ia., Jan. 29, 1915; d. Charles William and Rosa (Ehret) Hinsey; B.S., U. Colo., 1951; M.P.H., U. Minn., 1955; D.Nursing Sci., Boston U., 1969; 1 dau., Janice Sue (Mrs. Elmer Joseph Gable. Head nurse Presbyn. Hosp., Denver, 1939-44; clinic nurse Farm Labor Camp, Ft. Lupton, Colo., 1944-47; asst. supr. Weld County Health Dept., Greeley, Colo., 1948-49; supr. nurse Mesa County Health Dept., Grand Junction, Colo., 1951-53; asso. prof. U. Colo., 1955-66; prof. psychiat. nursing Tex. Woman's U., Dallas, 1967—, acting dean Coll. Nursing, 1972-73. Ednl. grantee Nat. Inst. Mental Health, 1953-55, 57-61. Fellow Am. Pub. Health Assn.; mem. Am. Nurses Assn., Nat. League Nursing, Am. Group Psychotherapy Assn., D.A.R., Sigma Theta Tau. Democrat. Conglist. Home: 10723 Villager Rd Dallas TX 75230 Office: 1810 Inwood Rd Dallas TX 75235

WHITE, PATRICIA SMITH, extension home economist; b. Greenville, R.I., Dec. 13, 1928; d. Ernest Leslie and Ruth (Leathers) Smith; B.S. in Textiles, Clothing and Related Arts, U. R.I., 1950; M.S. in Community Devel., U. Md., 1970, postgrad., 1970—; m. Winfield Horace White III, June 21, 1949 (div. July 1969); children—Cynthia Ellen, Deborah (dec.), Brian Winfield. Textile research technician Gillette Research Inst., Rockville, Md., 1965-67; extension home economist U. Md. Coop. Extension Service, College Park, 1967—, Anne Arundel County, Annapolis, Md., 1967-69, Prince George's County, Upper Marlboro, Md., 1969—; supervising agt. expanded food and nutrition edn. program U.S. Dept. Agr., Upper Marlboro, 1969—, also for Balt., 1971-72. Cons., Tuskegee Nat. Alumni Housing Found., 1970—. Mem. steering com. Common Cause, Montgomery County, 1972—. Bd. dirs. Community Action Agy.; pres. bd. Citizens against Rural Poverty in Prince George's County. U. Md. Coop. Extension Service fellow, 1970-71. Mem. Am., Md. home econ. assns., Nat., Md. assns. extension home economists, Met. Extension Com., Inst. Child Study Grad. Student Assn., Internat. Platform Assn., Speakers Bur. U. Md., Epsilon Sigma Phi. Democrat. Unitarian. Club: Unitarian Caring Singles (Rockville). Home: 4533 N Chelsea Lane Bethesda MD 20014 Office: 15209 Main St Upper Marlboro MD 20870

WHITE, RUTH ANN (MRS. THOMAS RAY WHITE), univ. adminstr.; b. Smith County, Tex., July 24, 1934; d. Robert Herschel and Minnie Ruth (Howell) Moore; B.S., East Tex. State U., 1955, M.Ed., 1956, Ph.D., 1970; m. Thomas Ray White, June 15, 1957 (dec. Dec. 1964); children—Robert Bruce, Anna Marie. Counselor, tchr. San Angelo (Tex.) Ind. Schs., 1956-58; counselor Harlingen (Tex.) Ind. Schs., 1958-61; tchr. dept. student personnel and guidance East Tex. State U., Commerce, 1967-73, v.p. student affairs, 1973—. Bd. dirs. Hunt County Mental Health Assn., 1972-74, sec., 1973-74; bd. dirs. Truax Scholarship Found. Mem. Am., Tex. (sec.) personnel and guidance assns., Student Personnel Assn. for Tchr. Edn., Nat. Council Adminstrv. Women in Edn., Am. Psychol. Assn., Nat., Tex. assns. student personnel adminstrs., Nat. Assn. Women Deans, Adminstrs. and Counselors, Psi Chi, Delta Kappa Gamma, Kappa Delta Pi. Home: 113 Royal Lane Commerce TX 75428

WHITE, RUTH BEELER, pub. relations exec.; b. Cabool, Mo.; d. James Walter and Myrtle (Forrester) Beeler; B.J., U. Mo., 1937; M.A., Washington U. St. Louis, 1947; Ph.D., Columbia U., 1966; m. Buel White, Dec. 23, 1939 (div. Sept. 1951); 1 son, Buel. Woman's editor Springfield (Mo.) Newspapers, Inc., 1937-41; news copy editor St. Louis Globe-Democrat, 1943-46; staff exec. Nat. Fedn. Bus. and Profl. Women's Clubs, Inc., 1949-53; copy editor House and Garden Mag., 1953; community cons. Health Ins. Plan of Greater N.Y., 1954-56; pub. relations cons. McCann-Erickson, Inc., 1957-58; dir. women's program div. Am. Petroleum Inst., 1958-63; pub. relations counsel, 1964-67; pub. relations dir. Leake and Watts, Inc., Yonkers, N.Y., 1967-72; spl. asst. for consumer programs Food and Drug Adminstrn., Washington, 1972—. Cons. Gen. Fedn. Women's Clubs, 1958-64; exec. com. Council Nat. Orgns. for Adult Edn., 1962-64. Mem. council consultants President's Com. on Traffic Safety, 1962-64. Mem. Pub. Relations Soc. Am., Am. Mgmt. Assn., English Grad. Union, Gamma Alpha Chi. Home: 3508 Leland St Chevy Chase MD 20015 Office: 5600 Fishers Lane Parklawn Bldg Rockville MD 20852

WHITE, RUTH MARGARET, librarian; b. Ludlow, Ky., Sept. 7, 1914; d. Carl H. and Mary Ethel (Irvin) White; B.S., Ohio State U., 1935; B.S., Western Res. U., 1938; A.M., U. Chgo., 1963. Librarian various schs., 1938-43; asst. buyer T.A. Chapman Co., 1946-47; librarian Chula Vista (Cal.) Pub. Library, 1947-51, U.S. Army spl. services libraries, Tokyo, Japan, 1951-53, Chippewa Falls (Wis.) Pub. Library, 1954-55, Detroit Pub. Library, 1955-58; asst. to exec. sec. Pub. Library Assn., Chgo., 1958-62; hdqrs. librarian A.L.A., 1963-68, exec. sec. Adult Services div., also Reference Service div., 1968-70; lectr. dept. library sci. No. Ill. U., 1971; asst. library dir. Pasadena (Cal.) Pub. Library, 1971-74, coordinator tech. services, 1974—. Served to lt. comdr. USCGR, 1943-45, now capt. Mem. Cal. Library Assn., Spl. Libraries Assn., A.L.A., Pub. Library Execs. Assn. So. Cal. (pres. 1974), Res. Officers Assn., Beta Phi Mu, Pi Lambda Theta. Presbyn. Club: Zonta (treas. 1973-74). Author: The School Housed Public Library. Home: 429 S Madison Av Pasadena CA 91106

WHITE, RUTH MIRIAM WEIHS (MRS. PAUL WHITE), trade and finance co. exec.; b. Vienna, Austria; d. Hugo and Ilka (Herzog) Weihs; came to U.S., 1947, naturalized, 1952; B.A. in Bus. Adminstrn., St. John's U., Shanghai, China, 1947; postgrad. N.Y.U., Coll. City N.Y.; m. Paul White, Sept. 18, 1949. Exec. sec. to chmn. bd. Pan Am. Trade Devel. Corp., N.Y.C., 1947-49, mgr., 1949-53, asst. v.p., 1953-58, v.p., 1958—; pres. Indsl. Crystal Corp. Office: 2 Park Av New York City NY 10016

WHITE, RUTH O'BRIEN (MRS. WALLACE BEASLEY WHITE), civic worker; b. N.Y.C., Dec. 20, 1909; d. Francis Athos and Caroline Rebecca (Young) O'Brien; student Miss Mason's School, Packer Collegiate Inst., 1921-27, N.Y. Sch. Fine and Applied Art, 1927-30; m. Wallace Beasley White, June 5, 1931; 1 son, John Wallace. Bd. mgrs., exec. com. Bklyn. Thoracic Hosp., 1940-48, trustee, 1948-57, pres. women's aux., 1956-57; mem. women's exec. bd. Bklyn. Hosp., 1957—, v.p., 1967-70, chmn. med. social service com., 1962-67, chmn. legislation com., 1971—, asst. treas., 1972—; dir. at large Nat. Tb Assn., 1949-57, 60—, sec. bd. dirs., exec. com., 1957-60, sec. pro tem, 1961-62, chmn. ann. meeting program com. 1973; del. Nat. Social Welfare Assembly, mem. com. vols. 1963-68, program com., 1964-67; bd. dirs., exec. com. Bklyn. Tb and Health Assn., 1946—, v.p., 1957-60, pres., 1960-62, sec., 1966—; del. N.E. Tb Conf., 1960—, pres.-elect, 1961-62; mem. council Tb Assns. N.Y., 1964-67; mem. Bklyn. Action Clean Air Com., 1965—; mem. at large women's com. Bklyn. Philharmonia, 1960-61, v.p., 1962; mem. adv. com. N.Y. State Bd. Edn. Div. Vocational Rehab., 1954-57; council mem. Tb Assns. Greater N.Y.; mem. joint com. on Tb Council Tb Assns. Greater N.Y. and Interdepartmental Health Council; del. council Tb and Respiratory Disease Assns. N.Y. State, 1971-73, vice chmn., 1973—; chmn. med. social service com. United Hosp. Fund Bklyn., 1949-53, women's exec. com., 1962-66, vice chmn. com. on legislation, 1969—; mem. social service com. Cancer Care Inc., 1966—, pub. relations com., 1969—, affiliate and contbg. groups com. cancer care, 1973—; vice chmn. Med. Social Services City Wide, 1959-62, chmn., 1962-66; group leader The Bklyn. Hosp. women's div. United Hosp. Fund Campaign, 1957-62, vice chmn., 1961-62; hon. life mem. N.H. Tb and Health Assn.; pres. North Eastern Tb Conf., 1962-63. Recipient Key to City of Manchester, 1961. Conglist. (mem. choir, deaconess, financial sec.). Club: Urban; Brooklyn Museum; Mardi; Dorchester Masquers. Home: 651 Marlboro Ct Brooklyn NY 11230

WHITE, RUTH S., record co. exec.; b. Pitts., Sept. 1, 1925; d. Leon H. and Rose (Stevenson) White; B.A. Music Composition, B.A. piano, Carnegie Inst. Tech., 1948, M.F.A., 1949. Supr., U. Cal. at Los Angeles Lab. Sch., 1951-59; composer-producer, pres. Rhythms Prodns. Records, Los Angeles, 1955—; v.p. Cheviot Corp., Los Angeles, 1961—; nat. v.p. Nat. Assn. Rec. Arts and Scis. Inst., 1974—; co-founder Electronic Music Assn., 1968. Nat. trustee Rec. Acad. Huntington Hartford Found. fellow, 1965. Mem. Nat. Assn. Am. Composers and Condrs., Am. Fedn. Musicians, A.S.C.A.P., Audio Engring. Soc., Music Educators Nat. Conf., Sigma Alpha Iota. Author: Mr. Windbag Stories. Composer: Pinions, Seven Trumps from the Tarot Cards, Flowers of Evil, Short Circuits. Office: Whitney Bldg Box 34485 Los Angeles CA 90034

WHITE, RUTH WILLIAMS, educator; b. Jericho, Vt., May 8, 1920; d. Theodore Bailey and Helen (Cashmore) Williams; A.B., U. Vt., 1940; M.S. in L.S., Simmons Coll., 1956; Ph.D. (fellow), U. So. Miss., 1963; m. Floyd Leon White, Jan. 2, 1943 (div. Sept. 1954); 1 dau., Carol Ann. Library asst. U. Vt., Burlington, 1953-55; head librarian West Springfield (Mass.) High Sch., 1956-59; librarian Graham-Eckes Sch., Palm Beach, Fla., 1959-60; head librarian Brevard Jr. Coll., Cocoa, Fla., 1960-62; asso. prof. library sci. U. So. Miss., Hattiesburg, 1963-64; prof., chmn. dept. library edn. U. Ga., Athens, 1964—. Cons. Xerox Corp., 1971—. Publicity chmn. Ga. Children's Book award U. Ga. Coll. Edn., 1969—. Mem. library staff Library 21, Seattle World's Fair, 1962; named Woman of Year in Edn., Athens Bus. and Profl. Women, 1968. Mem. Am., Southeastern, Ga., Fla. library assns., Am. Assn. U. Women (pres. Athens br.), Ga. Assn. Educators (pres. library dept.), Phi Beta Kappa, Kappa Delta Pi, Beta Phi Mu. Mem. Order Eastern Star. Club: Altrusa. Home: 109 Westchester Circle 7 Athens GA 30601

WHITE, SALLY BLANCHE FOX (MRS. JOSEPH A. WHITE), fashion promotion exec.; b. Waxahachie, Tex.; d. J. Gilbert and Nelia A. (Carter) Fox; B.J., U. Tex., 1946; postgrad. Allied Stores Exec. Tng., 1946, U. Mexico, 1945, Sheil Sch., Chgo., 1954, Dallas Sch. Comml. Art, 1956, Va. Commonwealth U., 1967; m. Joseph A. White, Dec. 25, 1947; 1 son, Clair Fox. Advt. mgr. Daily Texan, Austin, Tex., 1944-46; fashion copy-writer Joske's, San Antonio, 1946; Women's editor KGKL, San Angelo, 1947; advt. mgr. Meacham's, Fort Worth, 1948-49; retail promotion account mgr. The Merchandising Group, Inc., N.Y.C., 1949-68, spl. fiber cons. Du Pont Textile Fibers div., 1968-72; pub. relations mgr. Neiman-Marcus, Atlanta, 1972—. Free lance fashion commentator; spl. admissions counselor William Woods Coll., Fulton, Mo., 1960—. Publicity chmn. women's div. United Fund, Richmond, Va., 1967-68. Recipient Service award Fashion Group, Atlanta, 1967. Mem. Fashion Group Inc. (regional dir. 1959), Am. Assn. U. Women, Atlanta Art Assn., Bus. and Profl. Womens Assn., Alumnae Council Women's Colls., Women's C. of C. Atlanta, High Mus. Art, Mortar Bd., Theta Sigma Phi (chpt. pres. 1949-50). Club: Atlanta Press. Address: 6410 Colewood Ct NW Atlanta GA 30328 Office: Neiman-Marcus Lenox Sq Atlanta GA 30326

WHITE, VIRGINIA BETTS, pub. relations exec.; b. St. Louis, Dec. 29, 1918; d. Benjamin Earl and Hazel Catharine (Deffry) Betts; A.B., Washington U., St. Louis, 1940; m. Buel White, Jan. 29, 1953 (dec.). Dir., News Bur., editor Alumni mag. Washington U., 1941-58; dir. spl. pub. relations St. Louis U., 1959-62; editor womens news St. Louis Post-Dispatch, 1962-65; pub. relations dir. St. Louis Pub. Library, 1965-69; account exec. Gardner Hausman Pub. Relations, 1969-72; pub. relations dir. Met. St. Louis YMCA, 1973—. Mem. Advt. Women St. Louis, Mo. Press Women, Foremost Women in Communications, Women in Communications. Home: 7736 Blackberry Lane University City MO 63130 Office: 1528 Locust St St Louis MO 63103

WHITE, VIRGINIA TAFFINDER (MRS. JAMES A. WHITE), educator; b. Fairlee, Tex., Sept. 4, 1917; d. James Roy Taffinder and Irene (Gibson) Taffinder Mehlhoff; student La. Tech., 1934-35, La. State U., 1935-36, West Tex. State Coll., 1944-45; B.S., U. Wash., 1956, Ph.D., 1972; M.A. Teaching, Seattle U., 1964; postgrad. Yale, 1966; m. James A. White, Mar. 31, 1950; children—Gerald Gibson Wernli, Judith Wernli. Chemist Albers Milling Co. Control Research Lab., Seattle, 1945-50; tchr., chmn. math. dept. Lake Washington High Sch., Kirkland, Wash., 1956-72; tchr. math., area leader math./sci. Juanita High Sch., Kirkland, 1972—. Cons. Ency Brit. Press, 1964-65; editorial cons. John Wiley & Sons, Inc., 1965-67. NSF grantee, 1959, 61, 62, 63, 64; Nat. Def. Edn. Act grantee, 1969. Mem. Am. Math. Soc., Math. Assn. Am., Nat. Council Tchrs. Math. (nat. conv. speaker 1964-68), Puget Sound Math. Council, Wash. State Math. Council (pres. 1968-70, mem. exec. bd. 1970-72), Nat., Wash., Lake Washington edn. assns., Fibonnacci Soc. Republican. Baptist. Home: 1846 W Lake Sammamish SE Bellevue WA 98008 Office: 10604 NE 132d St Kirkland WA 98033

WHITE, VIVIAN PLEAS (MRS. LLOYD DEAN WHITE), publisher; b. Kansas City, Kan., Mar. 22, 1940; d. Thomas Lewis and Elberta Mae (Cummings) Pleas; grad. high sch., 1958; m. Lloyd Dean White, June 8, 1958; children—Lisa, Lloyd, Dana, Jill. Various clerical positions Kansas City, Kan. and Kansas City, Mo., 1956-62; owner, pub. Unique, Kansas City, Mo., 1971—. Mem. adv. bd. Mid-Continent Regional Ednl. Lab. Bd. dirs. Shawnee Mission Fair Housing Council, 1970-71, Linwood-Paseo YMCA, 1974—. Mem. Media Women, Advt. and Sales Execs. Club. Republican. Baptist. Club: Jack and Jill of America. Home: 5506 W 78th Terrace Prairie Village KS 66208 Office: PO Box 11386 Kansas City MO 64112

WHITE, WINIFRED DEMAREST (MRS. HERBERT A. WHITE), ret. assn. exec., editor; b. N.Y.C.; d. Peter Edward and Margaret (McLaughlin) Demarest; A.B., Coll. New Rochelle, 1914; postgrad. in journalism Columbia Extension, 1916-18; m. Joseph S. Gifford, Aug. 29, 1925 (dec. Feb. 1948); m. 2d, Herbert A. White, Nov. 14, 1964 (dec. Oct. 1972). Tchr. English, speech Bryant High Sch., N.Y.C., 1914-17; asst. to bursar Rockefeller Inst. for Med. Research, 1917-26; asst. editor, asst. to exec. sec. Am. Inst. Mining, Metall. and Petroleum Engrs., N.Y.C., 1947-59, editor, 1960—; exec. sec. Soc. Women Engrs., N.Y.C., 1961-73, asso. life mem., 1973—; freelance editor miscellaneous papers, 1959—. Recipient Ursula Laurus citation Coll. of New Rochelle, 1974. Editor: Ironmaking Proceedings, Open Hearth Proceedings, Honors Book, 1950-63, Proceedings Conf. on Women, 1971. Home: 12 E 97th St New York City NY 10029

WHITEAKER, BETTYE MCINTOSH, dentist; b. Newbern, Tenn., Feb. 17, 1933; d. Claude L. and Bettye (Flack) McIntosh; student U. Tenn., 1951-53; B.S., Union U. (Jackson, Tenn.), 1955; M.S., Okla. State U., 1958; D.D.S., Baylor U., 1968, M.S. in Dentistry, 1970; m. Kermit Eugene Whiteaker, Mar. 28, 1959. Tchr. biology Union City (Tenn.) High Sch., 1955-57; instr. biology East Tex. State U., Commerce, 1958-59, Kilgore (Tex.) Coll., 1959-64, Tex. Wesleyan U., Fort Worth, 1964; practice gen. dentistry, Hurst, Tex., 1968-70; practice dentistry, specializing in periodontics, Dallas, 1970—; vis. prof. periodontics Tarrant County Jr. Coll., Fort Worth, 1971. Bd. dirs. Vis. Nurse Assn., Dallas. NSF grantee, 1957; teaching fellow, 1969; recipient Tex. Acad. Gen. Dentistry award, 1968, Gold medal highest scholastic achievement Baylor U., 1968. Mem. Am. Acad. Periodontology, Am., Tex. dental assns., Dallas County Dental Soc. (health and sci. com. 1974—, chmn. ltd. attendance clinics 1973-74), Am. Assn. Preventive Dentistry, Am. Soc. Clin. Hypnosis, Oak Cliff Dental Study Club (lectr. 1971), Oak Cliff C. of C. (mem. exec. com. of 100), Omicron Kappa Upsilon, Upsilon Alpha Lambda. Baptist. Home: 1650 Cedar Hill Av Dallas TX 75208 Office: 801 N Zang Bldg Dallas TX 75208

WHITEHEAD, SISTER ALICE VIRGINIA, librarian; b. Chgo., Apr. 3, 1913; d. Thomas Francis and Alice (Gaynor) Whitehead; B.A., DePaul U., 1944; M.A. in Library Sci., Rosary Coll., 1953; M.A., U. Notre Dame, 1963. Tchr., librarian elementary and secondary schs., Chgo., 1934-44, 51-57, 61-65, Sault Ste. Marie, Mich., 1944-51, 65-69, Wheaton, Ill., 1957-61, 69-70; library cons. Inst. Blessed Virgin Mary, 1967-70; off-campus librarian St. Procopius Coll., Lisle, Ill., 1960-69; dir. Presentation Coll. Library, Aberdeen, S.D., 1970—. Mem. planning com. Sault Ste. Marie Edn. Plaza, 1967; bldg. cons. Sault Ste. Marie Pub. Library, 1971. Trustee Sault Ste. Marie Pub. Library, 1967-69, Tri-County Libraries, Upper Peninsula, Mich., 1968-69. Recipient Scholarship, Internat. Fedn. Cath. Alumnae, 1934-36, Nat. award 3M Co., 1963. Mem. Am., Catholic, S.D. library assns., Inst. Blessed Virgin Mary. Address: Presentation College 1500 N Main St Aberdeen SD 57401

WHITEHEAD, MARION E. STAUFFER (MRS. EDWIN ROBERT WHITEHEAD), educator; b. Landisville, Pa.; d. Samuel R. and Minnie B. (Eicker) Stauffer; certificate Millersville State Tchrs. Coll., 1927; B.S., U. Pitts., 1935; M.Ed., Chgo. Tchrs. Coll., 1960; m. Edwin Robert Whitehead, Sept. 1, 1934; children—Lance Dawson, Robert Keith. Tchr. pub. schs., Manheim Twp., Lancaster, Pa., 1924-26, Derry Twp., Hershey, Pa., 1927-30; tchr. mentally handicapped children pub. schs., Verona, N.J., 1930-34, Dist. No. 103, Cook County, Ill., 1953-59, Dist. No. 95, 1959-67; tchr. remedial basic edn. to adults in industry, 1967—; tape-recording for Ednl. Taping for Blind. Mem. bd. Brookfield Community Fund; trustee West Suburban Symphony Orch. Assn. Recipient Service to Youth award YMCA. Mem. N.E.A., Ill. Edn. Assn., Am. Assn. U. Women, Council for Exceptional Children, Nat., Ill., West Suburban Homemaker (service com.), P.E.O., Delta Kappa Gamma. Methodist. Home: 2640 Kohler Dr Boulder CO 80303

WHITEHEAD, OLIVE FRANCESE, librarian; b. Washington, Conn., Nov. 18, 1916; d. Philemon Beecher and Alice Lois (Hall) Whitehead; B.S., Westminster Coll., 1939; B.S. in L.S., Drexel U., 1941. Asst. librarian Hercules Powder Co., Wilmington, Del., 1941-47; librarian, research lab. Am. Sugar Refining Co., Phila., 1947-58; asst. librarian RCA Corp., Camden, N.J., 1958-69, librarian, 1969—. Mem. Spl. Libraries Assn. (recipient Achievement award Phila. chpt. 1970, pres. elect 1973-74), A.L.A., Am. Soc. Information Sci. Home: 204 S 42d St Philadelphia PA 19104 Office: RCA Govt Communications Library Bldg 10-6-5 Camden NJ 08102

WHITEHILL, MARGARET EMILY, librarian; b. Lander, Wyo., Feb. 3, 1935; s. Benjamin Milikin and Leona (Wendt) Whitehill; B.A., U. Minn., 1957, M.S. in L.S. (H.M. Wilson scholar), 1958, B.S., 1959. Librarian U. Minn. elementary lab. sch., Mpls., 1958-59; librarian, U.S. Army, Crailsheim, Germany, 1959-61; reference asst. U. Pitts. library, 1962-63; reference and young adult librarian Pub. Library, Tucson, 1964; pub. services librarian Juanita Coll. Library, Huntingdon, Pa., 1965-66; librarian Camp S.D. Butler, U.S. Marine Corps, Okinawa, 1966-68, Air Force library, Udorn, Thailand, 1968-71, Langley AFB library, Va., 1971—. Mem. Am. Library Assn., D.A.R., League Women Voters. Lutheran. Home: 313 Rudisill Rd Hampton VA 23369 Office: Base Library Langley AFB VA 23665

WHITEHURST, KETURAH ELISABETH, educator; b. Marianna, Fla.; d. Raymond Witherspoon and Laura (Robinson) Whitehurst; A.B., Howard U., 1932, M.S., 1934; A.M., Radcliffe Coll., 1946, Ph.D., 1953. Asst. prof. psychology, dean women Fla. A. and M. coll., 1934-44; prof., head dept. English, Albany (Ga.) State Coll., 1946-47; asso. prof. psychology Va. State Coll., Petersburg, 1949-54, prof., head dept. psychology, 1958—, co-dir. Children's House program, mem. adv. bd. sickle cell anemia project; prof. psychology, dir. children's sch. Fisk U., 1954-58; lectr. child growth and devel. Meharry Med. Sch., 1954-58. Pres., Vol. Services Council Petersburg (Va.) Tng. Sch., 1962-74; mem. adv. bd. Ednl. Therapy Center, Richmond, Va., 1950—, Learning Disabilities Center, Chesterfield County, Va., 1968-70; mem. evaluation and research com. Va. Dept. Mental Hygiene and Hosps., 1970-72. Mem. bd. Chesterfield Mental Health and Mental Retardation Services, Center, 1972—. Mem. Am., Southeastern psychol. assns., A.A.A.S., Council Exceptional Children, Am. Assn. U. Profs., Am. Assn. U. Women, Zeta Phi Beta. Home: 19205 Woodpecker Rd Ettrick VA 23803

WHITENACK, DOROTHY SPELMAN, physician; b. Cleve., July 3, 1937; d. Gordon and Kathleen (MacLaury) Spelman; B.A., Oberlin Coll., 1957; M.D., Western Res. U., 1961; m. David Charles Whitenack, Apr. 6, 1959 (div. Jan. 1970); children—Kathryn, Anne. Intern Kaiser Found Hosp., San Francisco, 1961-62, resident, 1965-66; resident Children's Hosp., Pitts., 1966-67; practice medicine specializing in pediatrics, Pitts., 1967—; med. dir. Home for Crippled Children, Pitts., 1971—; mem. staff Children's Hosp. Pitts.; clin. asst. prof. Med. Sch., U. Pitts., 1973—. Fellow Am. Acad. Pediatrics; mem. Pitts. Pediatric Soc., Phi Beta Kappa. Home: 618 Bellefonte St Pittsburgh PA 15232 Office: 1426 Denniston Av Pittsburgh PA 15217

WHITE-WARE, GRACE ELIZABETH, educator; b. St. Louis, Oct. 5, 1921; d. James Eathel, Sr. and Madree (Penn) White; B.A. in Edn., H.B. Stowe Tchrs. Coll., 1943; divorced; 1 son, James Otis II. Mgr. advt. Superior Press, St. Louis, 1935-39; tri-owner, v.p. Carolina Oil Co., St. Louis, 1938-42; with pub. relations Triangle Press, St. Louis, 1939-47, sales promotion, 1939-47; account supr. overtime payroll Bell Tel. Labs., Inc., N.Y.C., 1943-46; tchr. Dunbar Elementary Sch., St. Louis, 1946-47, Newberry Elementary Sch., St. Louis, 1949, Betsy Ross Elementary Sch., Chgo., 1951, Lincoln Sch., Richmond, Mo., 1951, Dunbar Sch., Kinlock, Mo., 1952, Gladstone Elementary Sch., Cleve., 1954-61, Quincy Elementary Sch., Cleve., 1961—, head tchr. Head Start program, 1965; adult edn. tchr. Cleve. Bd. Edn., 1965—; tchr. TV Tonight Sch., lessons for adults, Cleve., 1972; tri-owner, v.p., social editor Style mag., St. Louis, 1947-49; owner/mgr. Wentworth Record Distbrs., Chgo., 1947-51; supr. accounts receivable div. Spiegel, Inc., Chgo., 1947-52; radio panelist Calling All Americans, Cleve., 1957-58; sec. bd. dirs. Hough Pub. Co., also Hough Area Devel. Corp., Cleve., 1968-69. Mem. child devel. parent bd. Greater Cleve. Neighborhood Centers Assn.; mem. fund raising com. Food First Program, co.-chmn. woman's aux. Black Econ. Union, Cleve.; vice chmn. Cleve. com. Youth for Understanding Teenage Program; mem. Cleve. Council Human Relations; mem. Cleve. chpt. Congress Racial Equality; charter mem., financial sec. Tots and Teens, Inc.; treas. Jr. Women's Civic League; mem. Cleve. bd. Afro-Am. Cultural and Hist. Soc.; women's aux. bd. Talbert Clinic and Day Care Center, Cleve.; adv. bd. Langston Hughes Library; mem. Forest City Hosp. Aux. Bd., also Women's Aux. Com. Forest City Hosp.; scholarship com. Women's Allied Arts Assn. Greater Cleve., 1972-74. Named Most Outstanding Vol. of Year, N.Y. Fedn. Settlements, 1944, Leading Tchr. of Community, Cleve. Call and Post, weekly newspaper, 1958; recipient Martha Holden Jennings scholar award Martha Holden Jennings Found., Cleve., 1966-67, Spl. Outstanding Tchrs. award, 1973; Outstanding Service award Black Econ. Union, 1970; certificate appreciation City Cleve., 1973. Mem. Ohio, Cleve. edn. assns., Nat. Assn. Pub. Sch. Adult Edn., N.A.A.C.P., Phillis Wheatley Assn., Moreland Community Assn., Nat. Council Negro Women, Phi Delta Kappa (1st v.p. Cleve. 1971-73), Delta Sigma Theta (pres. Cleve. 1969-73). Democrat. Club: Novelette Bridge (pres. Cleve. 1973—). Home: 14701 Milverton Rd Cleveland OH 44120

WHITFORD, RUTH HORTON, educator; b. Ancramdale, N.Y., June 3, 1918; d. Ira Clifton and Clara Emmaline (Borland) Whitford; A.B., Wilson Coll., 1941; B.S., Columbia, 1945, M.S., 1950; Ph.D., N.Y. U., 1968; postgrad. (Am. Assn. Theol. Schs. fellow), Oxford (Eng.) U., 1968. Tchr. English, high sch., Pine Bush, N.Y., 1942-44; librarian N.Y. Theol. Sem., N.Y.C., 1947-70, prof. theology and lit., 1965-70; prof. English, Palm Beach Atlantic Coll., West Palm Beach, Fla., 1971—, chmn. dept. English, 1973—. Ednl. cons. Isabella Thoburn Coll., Lucknow, India, 1962. Mem. Modern Lang. Assn., Soc. for Arts, Religion and Contemporary Culture. Methodist. Author: T.S. Eliot's The Wasteland, Ash Wednesday, Four Quartets: Introducation and Commentary, 1969. Home: 730 NW 4th Court Boca Raton FL 33432 Office: 1101 S Olive West Palm Beach FL 33401

WHITING, ANITA, child psychologist; b. San Mateo, Cal., Oct. 13, 1928; d. Harris Murdock and Anita Eleanora (Sudden) Whiting; B.A., Stanford, 1951; M.A., Claremont (Cal.) Grad. Sch., 1963, Ph.D., 1969. Child psychologist for children with learning disabilities and for aurally handicaps Covina Valley United Sch. Dist., 1964—; vis. summer prof. Claremont Grad. Sch., 1970, 71. Trustee Hear Center; bd. dirs. Perceptual Learning Center. Mem. Am., Interam., Western psychol. assns., Soc. for Research in Child Devel., Cal. Assn. Neurologically Handicapped Children, Nat. Assn. Sch. Psychologists, Phi Lambda Theta. Republican. Episcopalian. Contbr. articles to profl. jours. Home: 428 Champlain Dr Claremont CA 91711 Office: 519 E Badillo St Covina CA 91722

WHITING, ELEANOR MARJORIE, librarian; b. Virginia, Minn.; d. Warren Studley and Matilda Johanna (Peterson) Whiting; B.E., State Tchrs. Coll., St. Cloud, Minn., 1933; B.L.S. with distinction, U. Minn., 1939. Library asst. Documents Library, U.S. Govt. Printing Office, Washington, 1942-44; cataloger Nat. Bur. Standards Library, Gaithersburg, Md., 1944-46; cataloger Dept. Health, Edn. and Welfare, Washington, 1946—, 1946-69, reference librarian, 1970—. Mem. A.L.A., D.C. Library Assn. (treas. 1966-68), Potomac Tech. Processing Librarians. Home: 1725 17th St NW Washington DC 20009 Office: 330 Independence Av SW Washington DC 20201

WHITING, HELEN CAROLYN, librarian; b. York, N.D., Jan. 2, 1915; d. Henry Bernhardt and Louise (Kowalke) Butke; B.A. cum laude, Carleton Coll., 1936; Library degree Winona State Coll., 1956; m. Edwin D. Whiting, Oct. 6, 1939; children—Don F., Nancy (Mrs. Alan E. Comer). Tchr. pub. high schs. N.D., 1936-37, Minn., 1937-40, 53-54; instr. English, Winona (Minn.) State Coll., 1954-55; librarian Winona pub. schs., 1956-67, Swedish Hosp. Sch. Nursing, Mpls., 1968-73, Edn. unit Met. Med. Center, Mpls., 1973—. Mem. Minn. Adv. Com. for Pub. Sch. Libraries, 1964-66; sec. Winona Council Social Agys., 1962-64. Mem. Winona (pres. 1956-58), Minn., Nat. edn. assns., Minn. Assn. Sch. Librarians (pres. 1964-66, chmn. state conv. 1966), Carleton Coll. Alumni Assn. (sec.), Am. Assn. Sch. Librarians, Am. Library Assn., Am. Assn. U. Women, Nat. League Nursing, Minn. Assn. Med. and Hosp. Librarians, Twin City Biomed. Consortium, Delta Kappa Gamma (pres. Omicron chpt. 1973-75). Lutheran. Home: 1620 Yosemite Av N Golden Valley MN 55422 Office: 700 10th Av S Minneapolis MN 55415

WHITING, HELEN HEDRICK, nurse; b. Lowell, Mass., Apr. 22, 1916; d. Clifton Fletcher and Mabelle Marsden (Grover) Hedrick; grad. Tewksbury (Mass.) Hosp. Sch. Practical Nursing, 1958; m. Kenneth Eugene Whiting, Nov. 14, 1932; children—Paul (dec.), Richard, Philip, Ronald, Linda (Mrs. Frederick W. Gawlik, Jr.). Staff nurse Tewksbury State Hosp., 1959—. Leader workshops and confs., speaker in field. Mem. bd. mgrs. Mass. Congress P.T.A., 1956-73; pres. Mass. P.T.A., 1970-72; mem. bd. Nat. P.T.A., 1970-72; editor Mass. P.T.A. Bull., 1970-72; active Girls Scouts U.S.A., mem. Citizens Adv. Com., Lowell, Mass., 1960-65. Mem. Licensed Practical Nurses Mass. (sec. 1967-69, pres. 1969-71), Tewksbury Hosp. Practical Nurses Alumnae Soc. treas. 1962-64, pres. 1964-65), Nat., Mass. P.T.A.'s, D.A.R. Home: 128 3d St Lowell MA 01850

WHITING, RAGNHILD, physiotherapist; b. Grefsen, Aker, Oslo, Norway, May 20, 1912; d. Carl Oscar and Borghild (Naess) Almqvist; diploma physiotherapy and gymnastics, Oslo Othopediske Mediko Mekaniske Skole, 1932; grad. student McGill U., 1962-63; m. Harold J. Whiting, Oct. 16, 1934; children—Kari (Mrs. Colin Morris), Joan (Mrs. Ronald J. Gaunce). Immigrated to Can., 1927, naturalized, 1934. Organizer, dir. physiotherapy dept. Smith Clinic, Hawkesbury, Ont., Can., 1964-66, Alexandra Hosp., Ingersoll, Ont., 1966-73; physiotherapist Windsor (Ont.) Western Hosp. Center, 1973—. Active United Community Services, Ingersoll, Ont. Mem. Ont. Hosp. Assn. (sec. rehab. com. 1972-73), Canadian, Ont. physiotherapy assns. also 114 Holcroft St W Ingersoll ON N5C 2B8 Canada Office: Windsor Western Hosp Centre Prince St Windsor ON Canada

WHITING, THELMA PACKARD, newspaper editor; b. Springfield, Mass., June 12, 1925; d. George Otis and Edith (Snyder) Packard; grad. Williamsburg High Sch., 1942; student Famous Writers Sch., Conn., 1968; 1 dau., Laurie Anne. Govt. reporter Daily Hampshire Gazette, Northampton, Mass., 1968—, suburban editor, 1972—. Sec., Cummington Hist. Commn., 1967—; mem. Cummington Finance Com., 1958-63, 73-74, Bd. of Health, 1960-63; mem. Regional Sch. Bldg. Com., 1963-69; chmn. Republican Town Com., 1952-60; town auditor, Cummington, 1959. Mem. Hillside Agrl. Soc. (sec. 1957 treas. 1956). Editor: Only One Cummington, 1974. Home: Thayer Corner Rd Cummington MA 01026 Office: Armory St Northampton MA 01060

WHITLEY, EDYTHE JOHNS RUCKER (MRS. ALBERT BOYD WHITLEY), genealogist, historian; b. nr. Christiana, Tenn., Nov. 3, 1900; d. Arch Edmondson and Clara Gibson (Johns) Rucker; student Middle Tenn. Tchrs. Coll., 1916-18, Draughons Bus. Coll., 1918, Blackstone Coll. of Law, 1930-31, Internat. U., 1929; m. Albert Boyd Whitley, June 25, 1919 (dec. June 1932); children—Sarah Frances (Mrs. Jack J. Dillon), Mary Anderson (Mrs. Harold George Hopton, Jr.), Lillian Boyd (Mrs. Lillian Schaefer). Genealogist, historian So. families, pvt. collection; profl. geneal., legal research, 1919—; certificate Nat. Geneal. Soc., 1935; sec. Tenn. Railroad Pensioners, 1947-60; mem. geneal. coms. Nat. Soc. D.A.R., 1930—, nat. vice chairwoman geneal. records com. 1971—; exec. sec. Andrew Jackson chpt. S.A.R., 1972—. Mem. Metro Govt. and Davidson County Pub. Records Commn., 1968—. Mem. Davidson County Women's Democratic Club, 1920-50; active in A.R.C., various civic drives. Mem. Sam Davis Meml. Assn., D.A.R. (regent 1939-41, 55-57, registrar Tenn. Soc. 1959-62, 2d vice regent 1962-65, nat. chmn. lineage research com. 1962-65, parliamentarian Tenn. 1969-71, nat. vice chmn. transp. 1968-71, state chairwoman geneal. records 1971—), U.S. Daus. War 1812 (organizer, pres. Nickajack chpt., chaplain Tenn. Soc. 1967-70), Magna Charta Dames (1st v.p. 1966-73, regent 1973—), Ladies Hermitage Assn., Tenn. Hist. Soc., Nat. Assn. of Nat. Officers D.A.R., Tenn. State Officers Club D.A.R. (rec. sec. Chmn's Club 1972—), Huguenot Soc. Tenn., Assn. Preservation Va. Antiquity, Tenn. Bot. Gardens and Fine Arts Center, Va. Assn., Cheekwood, Children Am. Revolution (sr. corr. sec. Tenn. soc. 13 years, past sr. pres. Adventure soc.). Mem. Ch. of Christ. Mem. Order Eastern Star; White Shrine. Author: Rucker's and Connections, 1927; Sam Davis Confederate Hero, 1947; Roster of Tennessee Daughters of American Revolution and Revolutionary Soldiers 1894-1960, 1960, vol. 2, 1960-70; Tennessee Genealogical Records Davidson County Pioneers, 1965; Tennessee Genealogical Records Overton County Tenn., 1966; Kith and Kin of Our President—Lyndon Baines Johnson, 1967; Tennessee Genealogical

Records, Henry County, 1968; Sam Davis, Hero of the Confederacy and Coleman's Scouts, 1971; many others. Compiler Forgotten Heroes and Heroines; frequent contbr. Tenn. Valley Hist. Quar.; hist. art adviser History of the American Revolution (record album), 1972. Home: 1604 S Observatory Dr Nashville TN 37215

WHITLOCK, MRS. DOUGLAS (JUDY) (MARY ELLEN JENKINS WHITLOCK), social worker; b. Brownville, Neb., Sept. 3, 1906; d. John Crisler and Mabel (Sapp) Jenkins; student Sullins Coll., 1923-24, Ferris Inst., 1924—; A.B., Ind. U., 1927; m. Douglas Whitlock, June 18, 1929; children—Douglas Whitlock II, Marilyn (Mrs. Robert E. Long), Sandra (Mrs. Theodore G. Driscoll, Jr.). Case worker Children's Aid Soc., Detroit, 1927-28, head of adoption dept., 1928-29; case supr. Asso. Charities Washington, 1929-32. Mem. Women's Inaugural Com., Washington, 1953, 57. Chmn. women's com. Devereux Found., Devon, Pa., 1959-61. Mem. League Rep. Women, Nat. Fedn. Rep. Women, Family Service Assn. of Am., Goodwill Industries Assn., Mental Health Assn., Vis. Nurse Assn. Trustee Family and Child Services, Washington, 1951-65, 1st v.p., 1962-65; v.p. Episcopal Ch. Women of Washington, 1963-69, pres., 1969-72. Recipient award Alpha Omicron Pi, 1963; award Episcopal Diocese Washington, 1972. Mem. Ind. Soc. of Washington (mem. exec. bd. 1932—; recipient award 1962), Indiana U. Alumni Assn., Alpha Omicron Pi. Republican. Episcopalian (vestrywoman 1968-71, 74—). Clubs: Little Garden (pres. 1938-40), Wednesday (pres. 1940-42) (Sandy Spring, Md.); International Neighbors (1st pres. 1956-58)) (Washington); Women of St. Thomas (pres. 1960-62). Home: 2550 Massachusetts Av NW Washington DC 20008

WHITLOW, ETHOLENE RAMSEY (MRS. HOMER P. WHITLOW), educator; b. Franklin County, Va., Aug. 6, 1910; d. Benjamin F. and Lillie (Hodges) Ramsey; ed. Coll. William and Mary; m. Homer P. Whitlow, Jan. 21, 1933; children—Berger M., Benjamin H., Mary Sue (Mrs. Arthur P. Burgess), D. Ramsey. Tchr., Snow Creek Sch., Martinsville, Va., 1948-58, prin., 1959-67; tchr. Sontag Elementary Sch. Franklin County, Va., 1967-72; dir. Continuing Edn. Media Center, Franklin County Pub. Schs., 1972—. Mem. Va., Franklin County (v.p. 1962-64) edn. assns., N.E.A., Franklin County Artist Guild, Ferrum (Va.) Jr. Coll. Alumni Assn. (dir. 1967—). Methodist. Home: RFD 2 Rocky Mount VA 24151

WHITLOW, SHARON LEE, city ofcl.; b. Concord, N.H., Dec. 21, 1946; d. Robert Edward and Frances Eleanor (Horne) Hobart; B.A. cum laude, Central Mich. U., 1969; M.A. in Polit. Sci., U. Conn., 1971; m. David A. Whitlow. Dir. research Colo. Municipal League, Wheat Ridge, 1971; adminstrv. asst. Town Vail, Colo., 1971-72; personnel asst. City Boulder, Colo., 1972, asst. personnel dir., 1973—. Co-chmn. Boulder (Colo.) Jobs Vets. Task Force, 1973. Mem. Internat. City Mgmt. Assn., Young Profls. Task Force, Municipal Mgmt. Asst's. Assn. (v.p. 1973), Am. Soc. Pub. Adminstrn., Western Govtl. Research Assn., Pi Sigma Alpha. Home: 3250 O'Neal Circle #20-F Boulder CO 80301 Office: PO Box 791 Boulder CO 80302

WHITMAN, JANE S., lawyer; b. Atlanta, Feb. 6, 1929; B.A., William Smith Coll., 1949; J.D., U. Mich., 1952. Admitted to Ill. bar, 1952; since practiced in Chgo.; mem. firm McDermott, Will & Emery. Mem. Am., Chgo., Ill. State bar assns., Women's Bar Assn. Ill., Phi Beta Kappa. Office: 111 W Monroe St Chicago IL 60603*

WHITMAN, (MARGARET) JANICE (MRS. DONALD EUGENE WHITMAN), librarian; b. Kansas City, Mo., Dec. 31, 1931; d. Ray Cecil and Agnes Lyle (Burney) Elkinton; B.S., Sterling Coll., 1954; postgrad., Kan. State U., 1954, 61, 62; M.S. in Librarianship, Kan. State Tchrs. Coll., 1965; m. Donald Eugene Whitman, June 2, 1951; children—Neil Allen, Cheryl Lynn. Tchr., Auburn High Sch., 1954-57; instr. nurse's chemistry Washburn U., 1957-59; reader's adviser Topeka Pub. Library, 1959; tchr. Berryton High Sch., 1959-62; librarian Shawnee Heights High Sch., 1962-67; library coordinator Shawnee Heights, Tecumseh, Kan., 1967—. Mem. N.E.A. (life), Kan. Edn. Assn., Kan. Assn. Sch. Librarians (dist. dir.), A.L.A., Shawnee Heights Edn. Assn., Alpha Delta Kappa. Home: 5530 W 15th Topeka KS 66604 Office: Route 1 Tecumseh KS 66542

WHITMAN, RUTH BASHEIN (MRS. MORTON SACKS), poet; b. N.Y.C., May 28, 1922; d. Meyer David and Martha (Sherman) Bashein; B.A. magna cum laude, Radcliffe Coll., 1944; m. Cedric Whitman, Oct. 13, 1941 (div. Nov. 1958); children—Rachel, Leda; m. 2d, Firman Houghton, July 23, 1959 (div. Apr. 1964); 1 son, David; m. 3d, Morton Sacks, Oct. 6, 1966. Research asst. Dr. MacKinley Helm, Boston, 1941-42; ednl. editor Houghton Mifflin, Boston, 1944-45; free-lance editor Harvard Press, Cambridge, Mass.; 1945-59; poetry editor mag. Audience, Cambridge, 1957-63; editorial sec. J.P. Marquand, Cambridge, 1958-59; dir. poetry Workshop, Cambridge Center for Adult Edn.; instr. poetry seminars, Radcliffe, 1969—, fellow Radcliffe Inst., 1968-70; dir. Mass. poetry writing program Mass. Council on Arts. Translator: (with others) Selected Poems of Alain Bosquet, 1963; Anthology of Modern Yiddish Poetry, 1967. Author: Blood and Milk Poems, 1963, Apples and Barns, 1963, Dead Center, 1963, The Marriage Wig, 1964, The Act of Bread, 1964; The Passion of Lizzie Borden: New and Selected Poems, 1973. Editor: The Selected Poems of Jacob Glatstein, 1972. Recipient Reynolds Lyric award Poetry Soc. Am., 1962, Jennie Tane award Mass. Rev., 1963; MacDowell Colony fellow, 1962, 64, 72, 73; Alice Fay di Castaghola award; Guiness Internat. Poetry Competition award, 1973; William Marion Reedy award, 1974. Mem. Poetry Soc. Authors Guild, Am., Phi Beta Kappa. Club: New England Poetry (Boston). Home and office: 70 Williston Rd Brookline MA 02146

WHITMARSH, LEONA ELAIN, hosp. supt.; b. Wainwright, Alta., Can., Sept. 3, 1919; d. George Charles and Edith Alice (Lowe) Boyd; R.N., Misericordia Hosp. Sch. Nursing, 1941; m. Elmer Henry Whitmarsh, Sept. 13, 1941; 1 son, Randolph Ruggless. Spl. duty nurse, Edmonton, Alta., 1941-43; gen. duty nurse Claresholm and Drumheller, Alta., 1943-45; maternity and operating room nurse Camrose Municipal Hosp., 1946-47; owner, supt. Carlsbad Pvt. Hosp., Vancouver, B.C., 1956—. Hon. instructress U. B.C. Mem. Registered Nurses Assn. B.C., Pvt. Hosp. Assn. Mem. Order Forresters. Address: 1901 Ocean Park Dr Surey BC V4A 3M2 Canada

WHITMIRE, CARRIE ELLA, research scientist; b. Electra, Tex., Oct. 17, 1926; d. Bernard Lyle and Fannie P. (Williams) Whitmire; B.A., U. Tex., 1946; M.A., U. Kan., 1953, Ph.D., 1955. Virologist, Ortho Research Found., Raritan, N.J., 1955-61, Merck Sharp & Dohme Pharm. Co., West Point, Pa., 1961-64; tech. asst. to plant mgr. Winthrop Labs., Rensselaer, N.Y., 1964-67; project dir. viral and chem. oncology research, head dept. exptl. oncology Microbiol. Assos., Bethesda, Md., 1967—. Mem. Am. Soc. Microbiologists, Am. Assn. Cancer Research, Am. Soc. Cell Biology, Internat. Assn. for Comparative Research on Leukemia and Related Diseases, Tissue Culture Assn., A.A.A.S., Soc. Exptl. Biology and Medicine, Sigma Xi, Phi Sigma. Home: 10636 Montrose Av Bethesda MD 20014 Office: Microbiological Assos 4733 Bethesda Av Bethesda MD 20014

WHITMORE, BERTHA HARPER (MRS. EDWARD HUGH WHITMORE), educator; b. Penfield, Ill., June 21, 1923; d. Edward and Lula Josephine (Holt) Harper; B.S., Ill. State U., 1945; M.S., U. Ill., 1946; postgrad., George Peabody Coll. for Tchrs., 1947, Ohio State U., 1951-53; m. Edward Hugh Whitmore, June 11, 1949; children—Stephen Harper, Ann Elizabeth. Instr. math. Metamora (Ill.) Twp. High Sch., 1945; sci. instr. Hall Twp. High Sch., Spring Valley, Ill., 1946-47; instr. phys. scis. Ill. State U., Normal, 1947-51; instr. chemistry West Sr. High Sch., Columbus, O., 1951-54; instr. sci. Mt. Pleasant (Mich.) Jr. High Sch., 1966—, chmn. dept. sci., 1968—. Cons. Gifted Child Program, San Bruno, Cal., 1960-65. Pres. Lab. Sch. P.T.A., Mt. Pleasant, 1966-67, Crestmoor P.T.A., San Bruno, 1961-62; chmn. March of Dimes, San Bruno, 1960-65, City Book Fair, San Bruno, 1961-63; sec. Com. for Better Schs., San Bruno, 1963; chmn. Profl. Study Com., Mt. Pleasant pub. schs., 1970-73. Recipient Outstanding Sci. Tchr. award Ohio Acad. Sci., 1954. Mem. Nat., Ohio, Mich. sci. tchrs. assns., Ill. Chemistry Tchrs. Assn. (v.p. 1948), Nat., Mich., edn. assns., Nat., Cal. congresses parents and tchrs. (hon. life), Kappa Delta Phi, Kappa Mu Epsilon, Kappa Delta Epsilon, Delta Kappa Gamma. Asst. editor Sci. Tchr., 1948-50. Home: 1105 N Fairfield Mount Pleasant MI Office: 440 S Bradley Rd Mount Pleasant MI 48858

WHITMORE, DOROTHY GATES (MRS. JOSEPH BOND WHITMORE), educator; b. Calgary, Alta., Can. (parents Am. citizens); d. George Ward and LaVerna (Hough) Gates; B.A., Western Wash. Coll., 1941; M.Ed., U. Ore., 1952; Ed.D., U. Colo., 1969; m. Joseph Bond Whitmore, Nov. 17, 1945; children—Mary Marilla (Mrs. Bruce Core), Joseph Bond (dec.), Dorothy Jane (Mrs. Neal Penney), David Craig, Elizabeth Kathryn, Jay Reed. Tchr. elementary sch., Wash., 1941; psychometrist U. Colo., 1956-57; guidance counselor Anchorage Sch. Dist., 1957-66; tchr. Head Start, Village of Hoonah, Alaska, 1965; asso. prof. psychology, edn., dean of students, dir. admissions Alaska Meth. U., Anchorage, 1966-69, dean students, dir. admissions, asso. prof. psychology, 1969-70, prof. psychology, edn., 1971—, coordinator coop. edn., 1974—. Counselor, VA, Anchorage, 1967-70; vis. lectr. North Shore Tchrs. Coll., Auckland, New Zealand, 1970-71; mem. Alaska Tchr. Evaluation Certification Adv. Bd. Served with USNR, 1942-46. Mem. Am., Alaska personnel and guidance assns., Am. Sch. Counselors Assn., Am. Coll. Personnel Assn., Nat. Vocational Guidance Assn., Assn. Measurement and Evaluation in Guidance Am. Psychol. Assn., Student Personnel Assn. for Tchr. Edn., Assn. Counselor Edn. and Supervision, Coll. Health Assn., Am. Assn. U. Women, Pi Lambda Theta, Delta Kappa Gamma. Home: Alaska Methodist Univ Anchorage AK 99504

WHITMORE, JANET JACOBSON, physician; b. Oak Park, Ill., July 8, 1925; d. Roland A. and Janet (Taylor) Jacobson; B.S., U. Wis., 1945, M.D., 1948; children—James McClellan, Steven Taylor. Intern, Med. Coll. Va., Richmond, 1948-49; fellow pathology U. Wis., Madison, 1949-50, physician Student Health Service, 1950-51, resident in internal medicine, 1951-52, instr. internal medicine, 1952-53; practice medicine specializing in internal medicine, Terre Haute, Ind., 1954-55; physician Winnebago (Wis.) State Hosp., 1957-59, physician, acting clin. dir. medicine and surgery No. State Hosp., Sedro Woolley, Wash., 1959-64; advanced trainee phys. medicine and rehab. U. Wash. Hosp., Seattle, 1964-66; chief phys. medicine and rehab. King County Hosp., Seattle, 1966-70; instr. dept. phys. medicine and rehab. U. Wash., 1966-68, asst. prof., 1968-70; asso. prof. preventive medicine and community health and medicine U. Rochester Sch. Medicine, 1970—; head rehab. service Monroe Community Hosp., Rochester, N.Y., 1970—. Diplomate Am. Bd. Phys. Medicine and Rehab. Mem. Am. Geriatric Soc., Gerontol. Soc., Am. Congress Phys. Medicine and Rehab., Am. Acad. Phys. Medicine and Rehab., Assn. Acad. Physiatrists, Alpha Omega Alpha, Sigma Kappa, Alpha Epsilon Iota. Home: 207 Roby Dr Rochester NY 14618 Office: 435 E Henrietta Rd Rochester NY 14620

WHITMORE, LENORE KRUMRINE (MRS. HARRY E. WHITMORE), artist, banker; b. Lemont, Pa., Aug. 9, 1920; d. Daniel Adam and Mary (Payne) Krumrine; B.S., Pa. State U., 1942; postgrad. Herron Sch. Art, Ind. U., 1962-64; m. Harry E. Whitmore, Nov. 4, 1942; children—Mary W. (Mrs. Frederick E. Schenfele), Harry B. Tech. asst. Manhattan Project, Control Lab., Oak Ridge, 1943-53; loan officer Citizens 1st Nat. Bank of N.J., Ridgewood, 1969—. One-woman shows at Provincetown (Mass.) Art Gallery, 1967, Cottage Gallery, Ridgewood, 1968; exhibited in numerous group shows, including Indpls. Art League, 1960, Tippecanoe Regional, 1964, Herron Mus., 1964. Eastern Mich. Nat., 1968, Knickerbocker Artists, 1970, Nat. Soc. Painters in Casein, 1970, Audubon Artists, 1968, 70, Modern Artists Guild, N.J., 1971, 72, 73; prof. Ridgewood Sch. Art, 1969-71. Pres., Indpls. Art League Found., 1959-63; mem. Ind. Gov.'s Com. for Sr. Citizens Activity. Recipient Achievement citation Manhattan Project, 1944, Motorola Nat. Arts Exhibits award, 1961, 62, Mark A. Brown award, 1963, Hoosier Salon award, 1963, Permanent Pigments award N.J. Painters and Sculptors Soc., 1968, Pen and Brush Profl. award Pen and Brush Club, N.Y.C., 1972. Mem. Modern Artists Guild (corr. sec. 1973-74), Ind. Artists (sec. 1964-65), Pen and Brush Club (mem. nominations com. 1973), Gamma Phi Beta. Home: PO Box 802 203 Oak St Ridgewood NJ 07451 Office: 54 E Ridgewood Av Ridgewood NJ 07450

WHITMOYER, CAROL BEITZEL (MRS. THEODORE FRED WHITMOYER), veterinarian; b. Milw., Aug. 2, 1932; d. Horace Clifton and Helen Caroline (Brien) Beitzel; B.S., Mich. State U., 1954, D.V.M., 1956; m. Theodore Fred Whitmoyer, Aug. 25, 1956; children—Paul Thomas, Daniel Stephen. With Small Animal Hosp., Milw., summer 1956; practice vet. medicine, Vernal, Utah, 1961-62, Boulder City, Nev., 1962—. Boulder City rep. Clark County Dist. Bd. Health, 1962—, sec., 1971-73; mem. Air Pollution Control Com., 1964—. Mem. Am., Nev., Clark County (pres. 1973), Women's, Intermountain vet. med. assns., Am. Animal Hosp. Assn. (asso.), Boulder City Hosp. Aux., Boulder City Firefighters Aux. Mem. Community Ch. Home: 609 Northridge Dr Boulder City NV 89005 Office: 1252 Wyoming St Boulder City NV 89005

WHITNEY, BARBARA CLAY, real estate broker; b. Grand Rapids, Mich., July 16, 1912; d. Carl Henry and Marion Vollam (Hall) Clay; student Munson Coll., 1929-30; m. R.V. Whitney, Mar. 21, 1921 (div. 1951); children—David Clay, Brian Clyde, James Kimball. Real estate sales Ted Kink Realty, La Mesa, Cal., 1953-55; real estate broker Barbara C. Whitney, Realtor, La Mesa, 1955—. Mem. La Mesa Bd. Realtors, Nat. Assn. Real Estate Bds., Mensa. Club: Exchange. Home: 8074 Lemon Av La Mesa CA 92041 Office: 8045 La Mesa Blvd La Mesa CA 92041

WHITNEY, MRS. CORNELIUS VANDERBILT (MARY HOSFORD), author; b. Kansas City, Mo., Dec. 24, 1925; d. Harry Robert and Marrie (Carr) Schroeder; student U. Ia., 1942-43; m. Frank Hobbs Hosford, Jan. 27, 1948 (div. July 1957); children—Marion Louise Frank Hobbs, Henry Deere, Heather Ann; m. 2d, Cornelius Vanderbilt Whitney, Jan. 24, 1958; 1 dau., Cornelia. Employed as announcer, continuity director radio sta. KCKN, Kansas City, Mo., 1943-45; realtor Ed Post Realty Co., Phoenix, 1956—; paintings exhibited Palm Beach Gallery, 1966, Wally F. Gallery, N.Y., 1966, Findlay Gallery, Palm Beach, 1967, 68. Bd. dirs. Mountain Laurel Festival Pineville, Ky.; mem. bicentennial com. Ky., 1972—; com. mem. Jimmy McHugh's charities, Inc.; bd. mem. St. John's Hosp., Los Angeles; bd. dirs. Sayre Sch. Decorated Order of Isabella Catolica (Spain), 1972. Life mem. Bklyn. Mus., Met. Mus., Whitney Mus. (all N.Y.), Buffalo Bill and Whitney Gallery Western Art, Cody, Wyo.; mem. Historic St. Augustine Preservation Bd., Woman's Symphony League, Kappa Alpha Theta. Episcopalian. Club: Women's (life mem.) (Greenwich, Conn.). Appeared in motion picture Missouri Traveler. Author: Missouri Traveler Cookbook, 1958; column, One Cook's Tour. Home: 834 Fifth Av New York City NY 10021 also Whitney House Bryan Station Rd Lexington KY 40505 also Cady Hill House Saratoga Springs NY 12866 also Deerlands Whitney Park Long Lake NY 12847

WHITNEY, ELLEN MEREDITH (MRS. FRANCIS A. WHITNEY), editor; b. Evanston, Ill., Mar. 13, 1920; d. Clyde Harold and Grace Irene (Whitehurst) Todd; B.E., So. Ill. Normal U., 1941; m. Francis A. Whitney, Aug. 9, 1940; 1 son, Blair. Publicity dir. So. Ill. Normal U., Carbondale, 1939-41; research asst. in publs. Ia. Child Welfare Research Sta., U. Ia., Iowa City, 1941-42; reporter Internat. News Service, Springfield, Ill., 1943-44; manuscript asst. Ill. State Hist. Library, Springfield, 1947-48, hist. research editor, 1948-63, 1967—; tchr. Feitshans High Sch., Springfield, 1963-67. Mem. Am. Civil Liberties Union. Mem. Am. Assn. State and Local History. Democrat. Editor: The Black Hawk War, 1831-32, Vol. I, 1970, Vol. 2, 1973. Asso. editor Jour. Ill. State Hist. Soc., 1958-63, 67—, editor, 1970—. Home: 1713 W Jackson St Springfield IL 62704 Office: Old State Capitol Springfield IL 62706

WHITNEY, (EVELYN) VIRGINIA PHILLIPS (MRS. RAYMOND L. WHITNEY), librarian; b. Medford, Mass., Dec. 1, 1914; d. Hervey Barnard and Wilhelmine (Richert) Phillips; B.S., Middlebury Coll., 1936; M.L.S., Rutgers U., 1962; m. Raymond Lawrence Whitney, May 27, 1939 (dec. 1971); children—Michele, Lawrence Phillips, Patricia. Library asst. East Orange (N.J.) Pub. Library, 1955-62; librarian Urban Studies Center, Rutgers U., New Brunswick, N.J., 1962-67, Douglass Coll. Library, 1967-69, asso. librarian for pub. services Rutgers U., 1969-71, univ. librarian, 1971—. Asst. dir. Vol. Urban Agts. Program, Urban Studies Center, 1964-66, dir., 1966-67; instr. Grad. Sch. Library Service, 1965-70; mem. nat. adv. council Nat. Agrl. Library, 1971-72; mem. commn. on access to resources Assn. Research Libraries, 1972—, bd. dirs., 1973—; bd. dirs. Center for Research Libraries, 1973—; mem. vis. com. for libraries Mass. Inst. Tech., 1973—; adv. council Princeton U. Library, 1973—; chmn. Middle Atlantic Research Library Information Network, 1973-74. Mem. A.L.A. (exec. com. circulation services sect. 1973—, mem. council 1974—), N.J. Library Assn. (exec. bd. 1971—), Am. Assn. U. Profs., Alumni Assn. Rutgers Grad. Sch. Library Service (pres. 1964-65). Home: 10 Landing Lane New Brunswick NJ 08901 Office: Library Rutgers U New Brunswick NJ 08901

WHITNEY, JANE BRYAN (MRS. RODGER FRANKLIN WHITNEY), savings and loan exec.; b. Dallas, May 28, 1948; d. Lewis Calvin and Lucy Jane (Nunn) Bryan; student Vanderbilt-in-France, Aix-en-Provence, 1969; B.A., So. Meth. U., 1970, M.L.A. (scholarship), 1974; m. Rodger Franklin Whitney, Aug. 11, 1973. Counselor, fencing instr. Brush Ranch Camp for Boys and Girls, Tererro, N.M., 1965-67; pub. relations asst. Pierce Allman Assos., Dallas, 1970; writer Sports Underwriters, 1970; pub. relations dir., dist. dir. Dallas County Camp Fire Girls, 1970-71; adminstrv. supr., legal librarian Jenkens, Spradley & Gilchrist, Dallas, 1971-73; asst. to v.p. marketing Dallas Fed. Savs. & Loan Assn., 1973—. Mem. Dallas Advt. League, Mortar Bd., Kappa Tau Alpha, Women in Communications, Pi Beta Phi. Methodist. Editor: So. Meth. U. Rotunda, 1970. Home: Box 471 So Meth U Dallas TX 75275 Office: 1505 Elm St Dallas TX 75201

WHITNEY, JANE ERDMANN (MRS. MORGAN WHITNEY), civic worker; b. N.Y.C., July 13, 1910; d. John Frederick and Georgiana (Wright) Erdmann; student The Spence Sch., N.Y.C.; grad. Nightengale Bamford, N.Y.C.; m. William Lafayette Burton II, 1934 (dec. 1957); children—Beverly Ann, William Lafayette III; m. 2d, Francisco Aurelio Gonzalez, Aug. 13, 1959 (div. Oct. 1964); m. 3d, Morgan Whitney, July 12, 1966. Com. work for numerous Charities; mem. Nat. Watershed Congress, 1963-65. Pub. relations work women's br. Navy League, N.Y.C., mem. women's aux. com. World War II, adv. mem. Home for N.Y. Aged and Indigent Females; com. mem. St. Barnabas House, 1962-65; women's aux. bd. William Waldo Burton Meml. Home, New Orleans; mem. bd. Christian Women's Exchange Herman-Grima House; mem. bd. Friends of the Cabildo, New Orleans. Fellow Royal Hort. Soc. Eng., La. Landmarks (mem. bd.); mem. Hort. Soc. N.Y., English-Speaking Union, N.Y. Bot. Garden Assos. (native plant garden vol.), D.A.R., Colonial Dames Am. Republican. Episcopalian. Clubs: Colony, Garden of Am. (vice chmn. conservation 1962-65); Women Flyfishers (charter mem.); Maidstone of East Hampton; Devon Yacht (Amagansett, L.I.). Address: 31 East 79th New York City NY 10021 also 1720 Valmont St New Orleans LA 70115 also PO Box 1226 Slidell LA 70456

WHITNEY, PHYLLIS AYAME, author; b. Yokohama, Japan, Sept. 9, 1903; d. Charles J. and Lillian (Mandeville) Whitney; grad. high sch., Chgo.; m. George A. Garner, July 2, 1925; 1 dau., Georgia; m. 2d, Lovell F. Jahnke, 1950. Instr. dancing, San Antonio, 1 yr.; sold first story to Chgo. Daily News; later wrote for pulp mags.; now specialist in juvenile writing; instr. juvenile fiction writing Northwestern U., 1945; children's book editor Chgo. Sun, 1942-46, Phila. Inquirer, 1947-48; instr. juvenile fiction writing N.Y.U., 1948-58; leader of juvenile fiction workshop Writer's Conf. Syracuse U., 1960. Recipient Friends of Lit. award for contbns. to children's lit., 1943. Pres. Authors Round Table, 1943, 44; pres. exec. bd. Fifth Ann. Writers Conf., Northwestern U., 1944. Author: A Place for Ann, 1941; A Star for Ginny, 1942; A Window for Julie, 1943; Red Is for Murder (mystery novel for adults), 1943; The Silver Inkwell, 1945; Willow Hill (Reynal and Hitchcock prize), 1947; Writing Juvenile Fiction, 1947; Ever After, 1948; Mystery of the Gulls, 1949; Linda's Homecoming, 1950; The Island of Dark Woods, 1951; Love Me, Love Me Not, 1952; Step to the Music, 1953; A Long Time Coming, 1954; Mystery of the Black Diamonds, 1954; The Quicksilver Pool, 1955; Mystery on the Isle of Skye, 1955; The Fire and The Gold (Jr. Lit. Guild), 1956; The Highest Dream (Jr. Lit. Guild), 1956; The Trembling Hills (Peoples Book Club), 1956; Skye Cameron, 1957; Mystery of the Green Cat (Jr. Lit. Guild), 1957; Secret of the Samurai Sword (Jr. Lit. Guild), 1958; The Moonflower, 1958; Creole Holiday (Jr. Lit. Guild), 1959; Thunder Heights, 1960; Mystery of the Haunted Pool (Edgar award Mystery Writers Am., Jr. Lit. Guild; also Sequoyah award Okla. 1963), 1960; Blue Fire, 1961; Secret of the Tigers Eye, 1961 (award Mystery Writers of Am.; Jr. Lit. Guild); Window on the Square, 1962; Mystery of the Golden Horn, 1962 (Jr. Lit. Guild); Seven Tears for Apollo, 1963; Mystery of the Hidden Hand (Edgar award Mystery writers of Am. and Jr. Lit. Guild), Black Amber, 1964; Secret of the Emerald Star, 1964; Sea Jade, 1965; Mystery of the Angry Idol, 1965; Columbella, 1966; Secret of the Spotted Shell, 1967; Silverhill, 1967; Mystery of the Strange Traveler, 1967; Hunter's Queen, 1968; Secret of Goblin Glen, 1968. Address: Rural Route 3 Box 202 Sussex NJ 07461

WHITNEY, RUTH REINKE, mag. editor; b. Oshkosh, Wis., July 23, 1928; d. Leonard G. and Helen (Diestler) Reinke; B.A., Northwestern U., 1949; m. Daniel A. Whitney, Nov. 19, 1949; 1 son, Philip. Copywriter edn. dept. circulation div. Time, Inc., 1949-53; editor-in-chief Better Living mag., 1953-56; asso. editor Seventeen magazine, 1956-62, exec. editor, 1962-67; editor-in-chief Glamour mag., 1967—. Mem. Fashion Group, Am. Soc. Mag. Editors, Alpha Chi Omega. Home: Riverview Rd Irvington-on-Hudson NY 10533 Office: 420 Lexington Av New York City NY 10016

WHITSON, KARIN KAY STORK (MRS. CHARLES MERRITT WHITSON), coll. dean; b. Dolores, Colo., Feb. 20, 1942; d. Chester Nimra Stork and Charlen Grace (Welkal) Stork Bour; B.A., Mary Hardin-Baylor Coll., 1964; M.Ed., Sam Houston State U., 1971; postgrad. Tex. A. and M. U., 1974—; m. Charles Merritt Whitson, Nov. 22, 1972. Exec. sec. Baptist Gen. Conv. of Tex., Dallas, 1964-65; tchr. English Edgemere Elementary Sch., El Paso, 1965-66, Killeen (Tex.) High Sch., 1966-67; adminstrv. asst. to pres. student enlistment Mary Hardin-Baylor Coll., Belton, Tex., 1968-69; asst. to dean women Sam Houston State U., Huntsville, Tex., 1969-71, asst. to dean students, 1971—, facilitator Quality of Life Conf., 1973, 74. Initiator, producer Miss Sam Houston State Pageant, Huntsville, 1973; program coordinator First Panhellenic Workshop for Tex. Colls., Huntsville, 1973; vol., supr. Huntsville Crisis Hotline, 1972-73. Mem. Nat. (campus membership rep. 1973—), Tex. (chmn. membership com. 1973—) assns. women deans, adminstrs. and counselors, Am. Assn. Univ. Women, League Women Voters (sec. 1974—), Tex. Assn. Student Personnel Adminstrs., So. Coll. Personnel Assn., Alpha Lambda Delta. Mem. Christian Ch. Home: 1602 Southwest Pkwy Apt 805 College Station TX 77840

WHITTAKER, ALMA TEELE (MRS. VIRGIL G. WHITTAKER), assn. adminstr.; b. Richmond, Va., Mar. 31, 1916; d. Joseph C. and Bessie L. (Scott) Teele; B.A., Va. Union U., 1935; postgrad. Temple U., 1944-45, Columbia, 1954, N.Y. U., 1959, York Coll., 1971-73; m. Virgil G. Whittaker, Mar. 22, 1949; 1 son by previous marriage, Sylvester E. Dance. Tchr. nursery sch., Richmond, 1939-41; supr. statis. div. U.S. Signal Corps, Phila., 1942-49; supr. displaced persons div. Ch. World Service, N.Y.C., 1949-52; librarian Nat. Social Welfare Assembly, N.Y.C., 1952-62; mgmt. cons. Investors Planning Corp., N.Y.C., 1962-66; asso. dir. Jamaica (N.Y.) Community Corp., 1966-69; field rep. N.Y. State div. Human Rights, N.Y.C., 1969-70; exec. dir. Queens YWCA, Jamaica, 1970—. Bd. dirs. Queens Child Guidance Corp., Nat. Conf. Christians and Jews, Queens Tb Assn. Sec., Queens County Republican Exec. Com., 1968-70. Recipient Community Service award United Democrats, 1970; Achievement award 26th Assembly Dist. Republican Club, 1970. Mem. Jamaica N.A.A.C.P. (edn. chmn. 1955-59, Achievement award 1970), Queens Urban League (housing chmn. 1961-62), Nat. Assn. Media Women, Nat. Assn. Negro Bus. and Profl. Women's Clubs (Sojourner Truth award 1971), Va. Union U. Alumni Assn. Republican (sec. Queens county exec. com. 1968-70). Conglist. Home: 111-31 144th St Jamaica NY 11435 Office: 118-44 Merrick Blvd Jamaica NY 11434

WHITTAKER, JEANNE EVANS, journalist; b. Detroit, Jan. 1, 1934; d. Alfred Heacock and Margaret Elizabeth (Evans) Whittaker; student Northwestern U., 1952-53; B.A. in History, U. Mich. at Ann Arbor, 1956; m. Charles M. Hines, Sept. 29, 1962 (div. 1969); children—Charles Martin III, Margaret Helen. With Am. Nat. Red Cross, Korea, 1956-57, France, 1958-60; dir. Jr. Red Cross for Bexar County chpt. A.R.C., 1960-62; asst. dir. Jr. Red Cross S.E. Mich. chpt. A.R.C., Detroit, 1968-69; soc. editor Detroit Free Press, 1969—. Mem. Sigma Gamma Assn.; founder, sponsor United Community Services Agy. Detroit Orthopaedic Clinic. Mem. Washington Press Club, Soc. Am. Social Scribes, Mich. Women's Press Club, Sigma Delta Chi, Sigma Gamma. Home: 17000 Maumee Av Grosse Pointe MI 48230 Office: 321 W Lafayette Detroit MI 48231

WHITTAKER, JUDITH CAMERON (MRS. KENT E. WHITTAKER), lawyer; b. N.Y.C., June 12, 1938; d. Thomas MacDonald and Mindel (Wallman) Cameron; B.A. magna cum laude, Pembroke Coll., 1959; postgrad. U. Mich., 1959-60; J.D., U. Mo., 1963; m. Kent E. Whittaker, Jan. 30, 1960; children—Charles Evans II, Catherine Cameron. Tchr. sixth grade Hartman Sch., Kansas City, Mo., 1961-62; admitted to Mo. bar, 1963, practiced in Kansas City, 1963—; partner Sheffrey, Ryder, Skeer, Kansas City, 1963-72; asst. gen. counsel Hallmark Cards, Inc., Kansas City, 1972—. Pres. bd. dirs. Legal Aid, Kansas City, Mo. Mem. Am., Mo., Kansas City bar assns., Lawyers Assn. Home: 838 West 52 Terrace Kansas City MO 64112 Office: 25th McGee Kansas City MO 64108

WHITTED, MILDRED MASON (MRS. JACK J. WHITTED), educator; b. Shuqualak, Miss., Sept. 11, 1929; d. Will and Lillie Maude (Brookshire) Mason; B.S., Ill. State U., 1952; M.S. in Edn., U. Ill., 1960; Ed.D., Ind. U., 1969; m. Jack J. Whitted, Aug. 19, 1956. Sec., stenographer St. Louis Adminstrn. Center, 1948-49; elementary tchr. Kansas City, Kan., East St. Louis, Ill., 1952-60; tchr. E. St. Louis Sr. High Sch., 1960-66; faculty Forest Park Community Coll., St. Louis, 1967—, prof. bus. edn. 1974—. Asst. prof. edn. U. Mo., St. Louis, 1972-73; dir. Project Operation Consumer Insight, 1971-72; bi-weekly columnist Consumer Hints, East St. Louis Crusader, Consumer Insights, St. Louis Argus, 1972—; mem. consumer product safety commn. Nat. Flammable Fabrics Act Nat. Adv. Bd. Chmn. bus. adv. com. St. Louis Cath. Archdiocese, 1972-74; v.p. University City (Mo.) Charter Assn., 1969-73. Vice pres. Creve-Coeur Democratic Club, 1970—; mem. St. Louis Polit. Womens Caucus, 1972—. Recipient Citation for devotion, encouragement and contbn. to improvement youth Jack and Jill Club Am., 1964. Mem. Internat. Platform Assn., Iota Phi Lambda, Kappa Delta Pi, Delta Pi Epsilon, Pi Lambda Theta, Alpha Kappa Alpha. Club: Les Finessers Bridge (University City). Home: 8140 Tulane St University City MO 63130 Office: Forest Park Community Coll 5600 Oakland St Louis MO 63110

WHITTEMORE, ALICE SEGERS, educator; b. N.Y.C., July 5, 1936; d. George A. and Margaret A. (Walsh) Segers; B.S. magna cum laude, Marymount Coll., 1958; M.A., Hunter Coll., 1964; Ph.D. (NSF fellow, Univ. fellow), City U. N.Y., 1967; m. William Whittemore, Sept. 6, 1958 (div. Apr. 1966); children—Margot, Gayle. Asst. prof. math. Hunter Coll., N.Y.C., 1967-72, asso. prof., 1972—; adj. asso. prof. environmental medicine N.Y. U. Med. Center, 1974—. Recipient Excellence in Teaching award City U. N.Y., 1974. Mem. A.A.A.S., Math. Assn. Am., Am. Math. Soc., N.Y. Acad. Sci., Sigma Xi. Home: 400 E 85th St New York City NY 10028

WHITTEN, MARY EVELYN, educator; b. Waskom, Tex., Aug. 23, 1922; d. Thomas Frank and Margaret Nellie (Huskey) Whitten; B.A., East Tex. State U., 1947; M.A., U. Tex., 1949, Ph.D., 1956; postgrad. U. Tenn., 1951-53. Tchr., Luling (Tex.) High Sch., 1948-49; supr. English, Central State Coll., Edmond, Okla., 1949-51; instr. English, U. Tenn., Knoxville, 1952-53, U. Tex. at Austin, 1956-57; prof. English, North Tex. State U., Denton, 1957—. Bd. dirs. Denton Humane Soc. Mem. Internat. Platform Assn., Am. Assn. U. Profs., Nat. Council Tchrs. English, Tex. Assn. Coll. Tchrs. Author: Creative Pattern Practice, 1966, rev. edit., 1975; Decisions, Decisions: Style in Writing, 1971; (with John E. Warriner) English Grammar and Compositions, Course Three, 1973; (with Alton C. Morris et al) College English, rev. edit., 1973; (with John E. Warriner et al) English Workshop Series, 1973; (with John C. Hodges) The Harbrace College Handbook, rev. edit., 1972. Home: 528 Headlee Lane Denton TX 76201

WHITTON, GLADYS PIPER, psychologist; b. Biloxi, Miss., July 26; d. Albert Francis and Mary May (Stille) Piper; A.A., Los Angeles City Coll., 1947; B.A. summa cum laude, Cal. State U. at Los Angeles, 1950, M.S., 1964; postgrad. U. So. Cal., summer 1969. From asst. prof. to prof. dept. psychology Cal. State U. at Los Angeles, 1949-50, sec. to v.p., 1952-54; instr. psychology Citrus Jr. Coll., 1960-61; tchr., psychologist, West Covina, S.D., 1960-64; tchr., LaPuente, S.D., 1962-64; psychologist Ontario (S.D.) Sch. Neurologically Handicapped Children, 1964-65; cons. Claremont (Cal.) Family Service, 1968-69; clin. psychologist, cons., family service and marriage counselor, Covina, Cal., 1969—; numerous TV and lecture appearances. Mem. Am., Western psychol. assns., A.A.A.S., Cal. Assn. Sch. Psychologists, Assn. Aviation Psychologists, Assn. Women Psychologists, Cal. State U. Alumni Assn. Contbr. articles to profl. jours. Home: 151 S Waterbury Av Covina CA 91722

WHITTY, GAIL ARLENE (MRS. MICHAEL D. WHITTY), pub. relations exec., city ofcl.; b. Buffalo, Feb. 8, 1947; d. Marvin and Miriam (Wernick) Gross; B.S., Syracuse U., 1968; M.A., Wayne State U., 1970; m. Michael D. Whitty, June 1, 1969. Instr. consumer edn. Wayne State U., Detroit, 1970; publicist, City of Detroit, 1971—. Mem. Women in Communications, Nat. Orgn. for Women (newsletter editor Detroit 1973—). Home: 924 E Lafayette Detroit MI 48207 Office: City County Bldg Detroit MI 48226

WHITWORTH, KATHRYNNE ANN, profl. golfer; b. Monahans, Tex., Sept. 27, 1939; d. Morris Clark and Dama Ann (Robinson) Whitworth; student Odessa Jr. Coll., 1957. Mem. Ladies Profl. Golf Tour, 1959—; winner various championships, 1965-71; winner Vare Scoring Trophy, 1965-67, 69, 71, 72. Named Woman Athlete of Year, A.P., 1965, 66; Player of Year Ladies Profl. Golf Assn., 1966-69, 71-73. Mem. Ladies Profl. Golf Assn. (pres. 1967, 68, 70). Address: 618 Ridgedale St Richardson TX 75080

WHITWORTH, PAULETTE C. (MRS. DAVID KERR WHITWORTH), banker; b. Indpls., Jan. 8, 1929; d. Robert E. and Jessie (Gibbs) White; student Murray State U., 1948-51; m. David Kerr Whitworth, Aug. 22, 1952. Teller First Bank & Trust Co., Cairo, Ill., 1951-55, Bank of Commerce & Trusts, Richmond, Va., 1955-58; utility teller State Palnters Bank Commerce & Trusts, Richmond, 1958-60; receptionist Ind. Nat. Bank, Indpls., 1961-62; v.p. First Am. Nat. Bank, Nashville, 1963-72, v.p., head specialized services div., 1963—. Capt. Heart Fund dr., Nashville, 1969-70; capt. fund dr. Am. Cancer Soc., Nashville, 1969-70; mem. adv. council practicing mgmt. profram Grad. Sch. Mgmt., Vanderbilt U., Nashville, 1970-72. Bd. dirs. Cheekwood (Tenn.) chpt. A.R.C., Women's Civic Forum, Nashville. Named Outstanding Woman Year, Nashville Jr. C. of C., 1970. Mem. Am. Bus. Women's Assn. (named Nat. Am. Bus. Woman Year 1969), Nashville C. of C., Bus. and Profl. Women's Assn. (named Woman Year 1969), Nat. Assn. Bank Women Inc. Republican. Episcopalian. Clubs: Junior Women's (Nashville); Altrusa (v.p. 1970-71). Home: 174 Lelawood Circle Nashville TN 37209 Office: 326 Union St Nashville TN 37237

WHYARD, FLORENCE ESTHER ELLIOTT (MRS. JAMES HERBERT WHYARD), editor; b. London, Ont., Can., Jan. 13, 1917; d. William Edmund and Henriette Pearl (Shafer) Elliott; B.A., U. Western Ont., 1938; m. James Herbert Whyard, July 22, 1944; children—Mary Ellen, Judith (Mrs. John Nels Anton), William Elliott. Sec., London (Ont.) Flying Club, 1939-40; dir. pub. relations U. Western Ont. (Can.), London, 1938-39; staff writer Johnston, Everson Charlesworth, Toronto, Ont., 1940-41; asso. editor Ft. Erie (Ont.) Times-Rev., 1941-43; free-lance writer-broadcaster, Yellowknife, N.W.T., Can., 1945-54, Whitehorse, Yukon Ty., Can., 1954-64; editor Whitehorse Star, 1964-71; Canadian editor Alaska Northwest Pub. Co., Whitehorse, 1971-74. Sec. U. Can. North, 1971-73; hon. v.p. Whitehorse br. Canadian Red Cross, 1970—. Bd. dirs. Yukon Visitors Assn., 1973—, YWCA, Whitehorse, 1971-73. Served to lt. WRCNS, 1943-45. Mem. Whitehorse C. of C. (dir. 1970-74), Bus. and Profl. Women's Club (v.p.), Kappa Alpha Theta. Progressive Conservative. Mem. Anglican Ch. (life mem., mem. exec. com. Diocese of Yukon 1961-74). Home: 89 Sunset Dr Whitehorse YT Canada

WHYTE, HELENA DAVISON, govt. ofcl., ednl. adminstr.; b. Halifax, N.S., Can., Nov. 8, 1928; d. Ralph Evans and Edith Verna (Davison) Marshall; B.A., Acadia U., 1949; m. Robert Allison Whyte, July 2, 1949 (dec. Mar. 1967); children—Sheila, Margaret. Pub. relations officer Dept. Adult Edn., Halifax, 1967-72, N.S. Communications Centre, 1972; tng. officer Dept. Municipal, Halifax, 1972—. Cons. to Nat. Home Economists; lectr. in communications, parliamentary procedures, 1969—. Recipient Pub. Relations prize Kings U., 1968; Presidents medal Canadian Pub. Relations Soc., 1973. Mem. Canadian Assn. for Adult Edn. (v.p. 1969-70), Continuous Learning Assn. N.S. (pres. 1970-72), Atlantic Pub. Relations Soc. (v.p. 1971—), Canadian Bldg. Officials Adv. Council. Home: 1755 Beech Halifax NS Canada Office: 1649 Hollis Halifax NS Canada

WIBERG, RUTH ELOISE LOWE (MRS. JOHN THEODORE WIBERG), author; b. Connersville, Ind.; d. Frank Curtis and Louise (Barrows) Lowe; student U. Denver; m. John Theodore Wiberg, Dec. 24, 1938; children—John Lawrence, Curtis Paul. Ednl. sec. Denver pub. schs., 1956-67; lectr. Community Coll. Denver, 1972-73, Friends of Denver Pub. Library, 1972—, Historic Denver, Inc., 1974—. Mem. Colo. Authors League (sec. 1969-70, 71-72), Nat. League Am. Pen Women (br. sec. 1968-70, v.p. 1970-72, 74-75). Contbr. articles popular mags. including Redbook, Parents, Am. Home, Christian Home, Together, My Baby, Empire, Contemporary. Home: 2800 Vrain St Denver CO 80212

WIBLE, MARY GRACE, painter, educator; b. Three Springs, Pa.; d. Frank and Luetta (Kirkpatrick) Wible; B.S., Pa. State U., 1938, M.Ed., 1942. Supr. art edn., State Coll., Pa., 1938-42; supr. art, Bradford, Pa., 1942-46; asst. prof. art LockHaven (Pa.) State Coll., 1946-54; asso. prof. art Kutztown (Pa.) State Coll., 1954-68; one-man shows Sheradin Studio Gallery, 1962, 69, LockHaven State Coll., 1961, 68, Sloan Gallery, 1968, Art Alliance Gallery, Reading, Pa., 1970, 72; tchr. Stone Mill Art Colony, Topton, Pa., 1969—. Mem. N.E.A., Parkland Art League, Am. Assn. U. Women, Reading, Lehigh art alliances, Am. Watercolor Soc., Berks Art Alliance (pres.), Delta Kappa Gamma. Episcopalian. Contbr. articles to mags. Address: 315 Wenz St Kutztown PA 19530

WICK, CAROL ANN MELLEN (MRS. LELAND HALL WICK), occupational therapist; b. Orange, N.J., Dec. 12, 1936; d. Earl Rufus and Isabel Pearl (Holloway) Mellen; B.S., Columbia, 1961; postgrad. N.Y. U., 1969—; m. Leland Hall Wick, May 25, 1974. Staff occupational therapist Meadowbrook Hosp., Hempstead, N.Y., 1961-62; sr. occupational therapist N.J. Orthopaedic Hosp., 1962-66, Easter Seal Center, Morris Plains, N.J., 1966-68; dir. occupational therapy John E. Runnells Hosp., Berkeley Heights, N.J., 1969-71; registered occupational therapist Robert E. Wood Johnson Meml. Hosp. of John F. Kennedy Community Hosp., Edison, N.J., 1971-74, sr. occupational therapist, 1974—. Mem. Am., N.J. occupational therapy assns. Home: 393 Wyoming Av Millburn NJ 07041 Office: Robert E Wood Johnson Memorial Hospital Edison NJ 08817

WICK, HILDA WINIFRED MARSH (MRS. LAWRENCE BERNARD WICK), librarian; b. River Rouge, Mich., May 3, 1923; d. William Henry and Elizabeth Ann (Bates) Marsh; A.B., U. Mich., 1943, A.B. in Library Sci., 1944, A.M., 1947; m. Lawrence Bernard Wick, Sept. 20, 1946; children—Marcia Anne (Mrs. Moore Meigs Davock), William David. Asst. librarian Shaw High Sch. br. East Cleveland Pub. Library, 1944-45; library service fellow U. Mich. Gen. Library, 1945-47; head circulation Cedar Rapids (Ia.) Pub. Library, 1950; reference asst. Hild br. Chgo. Pub. Library, 1953, head librarian Norwood Park br. 1954; instr. English, Drury Coll., 1958-60; head Bookmobile div. Delaware County (O.) Dist. Library, 1960-62; asst. reference librarian Ohio Wesleyan U., Delaware, O., 1962-68, head reference librarian, 1968—, asst. prof., 1962—. Mem. Affirmative Action Council. Bd. dirs. Des Plaines (Ill.) Pub. Library, 1955-58, Mem. Am., Ohio (sec. coll. and univ. roundtable 1971) library assns., Am. Assn. U. Profs., Midwest Acad. Librarians Conf. Club: University Women's (Ohio Wesleyan U.); Faculty (v.p., pres. elect 1971—). Home: 119 Troy Rd Delaware OH 43015 Office: Beeghly Library Ohio Wesleyan U Delaware OH 43015

WICKENDEN, BARBARA LYDDON HORNER (MRS. HERBERT R. WICKENDEN), ednl. cons.; b. Rockford, Ill., May 7, 1925; d. Forrest A. and Elva (Olander) Lyddon; B.S., Purdue U., 1947; M.S., Akron U., 1968; children—Robert A. II, Hollace Anne, Charles O.; m. 2d, Herbert R. Wickenden. Sec.-treas. ESTI, Inc., Stow, O., 1960-65; v.p. Invlux Corp., 1962-65; pres. Learning Center, Inc., Stow, 1965—; cons. Massillon, Chardon and Ritman (O.) schs., 1966—. Ency. Britannica, 1969-72. Pres. Silver Lake (O.) Republican Club, 1962-64. Mem. Delta Kappa Gamma, Pi Lambda Delta, Delta Gamma. Author books, films, tapes, puzzles and games for Ency. Britannica, also manuals, study cards for Holt, Rinehart & Winston Corp. and workbook series for Ideal Sch. Supply Co., primary reading program for Westinghouse Learning Corp., math. readiness program for Modern Curriculum Press, social studies program for Villa Press. Home: 2845 Kent Rd Stow OH 44224 Office: 3727 Darrow St Stow OH 44224

WICKENDEN, ELIZABETH (MRS. ARTHUR E. GOLDSCHMIDT), educator; b. Madison, Wis., May 8, 1909; d. William F. and Marion (Lamb) Wickenden; B.A., Vassar Coll., 1931; m. Arthur Goldschmidt, May 27, 1933; children—Arthur, Ann (Mrs. Raymond Richardson), Jean (Mrs. J. M. Kempton, Jr.) (dec.). With Emergency Exchange Assn., N.Y.C., 1932-33, fed. Emergency Relief Adminstrn., 1933-35; asst. to dep. adminstr. WPA, 1935-38, Nat. Youth Adminstrn., 1939-40; spl. asst. Office Defense Health and Welfare Services, 1940-41; Washington rep. Am. Pub. Welfare Assn., 1941-51; prof. urban studies City U. N.Y., N.Y.C., 1959—. Cons. nat. welfare orgns., 1951—, Welfare Adminstrn., 1964-68, Bur. Social Affairs U.N., 1962-65, Yale Law Sch., 1963; cons. Nat. Assembly Nat. Vol. Health and Social Welfare Orgns., also Children's Def. Fund; cons. to project on social welfare law Hays Center, N.Y. U. Law Sch., 1965-67; social policy cons. nat. bd. dirs. YWCA, 1960-69; research asso. Florence Heller Grad. Sch. for Advanced Studies in Social Welfare, Brandeis U., 1960-65; mem. nat. adv. com. to legal service program Office Econ. Opportunity, 1965—; mem. Adv. Council on Pub. Welfare, 1965-66; dir. Project on Pub. Services for Families and Children, N.Y. sch. Social Work, 1960-61; mem. Kennedy Task Force on Health and Social Security Legislation, 1960-61; v.p. Citizens Crusade Against Poverty, 1965-66; mem. Citizens Adv. Council on Status of Women, 1965-68. Recipient awards Nat. Conf. Social Work, 1955; Michael Schwerner Meml. Fund, 1967; W. S. Terry Jr. Meml. award Am. Pub. Welfare Assn., 1967. Home: 544 E 86th St New York City NY 10028

WICKENKAMP, SISTER MARY SUZANNE, hosp. adminstr.; b. Keokuk County, Ia., Jan. 15, 1921; d. Harry and Zelda (Ollinger) Wickenkamp; B.S., Marycrest Coll., Davenport, Ia., 1946; M.S., Marquette U., 1951. Joined Sister of Humility of Mary, 1943; mem. staff St. Joseph's Hosp., Ottumwa, Ia., 1942—, dir. nursing service, 1951-72, adminstr., 1972—, also mem. bd. dirs. Mem. gen. council and cabinet advisers, chmn. finance com. Sisters Humility of Mary; mem. Ia. Bd. Nursing, 1965—, vice chmn., 1970—. Mem. Am. Nurses Assn., Assn. Retarded Children. Address: 312 E Alta Vista Ottumwa IA 52501

WICKENS, ARYNESS JOY (MRS. D.L. WICKENS), ret. govt. ofcl., statistician; b. Bellingham, Wash., Jan. 5, 1901; d. Oliver H. and Elizabeth (Chapman) Joy; A.B., U. Wash., 1922; A.M., U. Chgo., 1924; m. David L. Wickens, June 29, 1935 (dec.); children—David Elder (dec.), Donaldson Vickers. Asst. prof. econs. Mt. Holyoke Coll., 1924-28; research asst. div. research and statistics Fed. Res. Bd., Washington, 1928-33, chief statistician, office econ. adviser Nat. Emergency Council, 1934-35; chief economist U.S. Central Statis. Bd., Washington, 1935-37; asst. to commr. Bur. Labor Statistics, Dept. of Labor, Washington, 1938-40, chief prices and cost of living br., 1940-45, asst. commr. for program operations, 1945-49, became dep. commr. of bur., 1949; dep. asst. sec. of labor for manpower and employment, 1956-59, econ. adviser to sec. of labor, 1959-62, consumer program adviser, 1962-66, spl. asst. to the asst. sec. for Manpower, 1967-68; dir. manpower mgmt. data systems Manpower Adminstrn., 1968-70, cons., 1970-71; pvt. cons., 1971—. Dir. Washington & Lee Savs. and Loan, McLean, Va., 1966—. Adviser U.S. delegation Inter-Am. Statis. Inst., 1947; adviser to U.S. delegation Internat. Labor Conf., 1947, 48; mem. U.S. delegation to UN Econ. and Social Council, 1951, 52, 60, 61; mem. Consumer Standards Bd., 1963-66; mem. consumer council Am. Nat. Standards Inst., 1966-69, 70—, dir., 1967-69. Recipient Distinguished Service award Dept. Labor, 1955; Civil Service Career award; Fed. Women's award, 1961. Fellow Am. Statis. Assn. (pres. 1952); mem. Am. Econ. Assn., Nat. Economists Club, Phi Beta Kappa, Kappa Kappa Gamma. Contbr. articles to profl. jours. Home: 2210 Hunter Mill Rd Vienna VA 22180

WICKER, IREENE, writer, singer, entertainer radio and TV; b. Quincy, Ill.; d. Kenner and Margaret (Hunsaker) Seaton; student U. Ill., 1 yr.; student Goodman Theatre Sch., Art Inst. Chgo., 1927-30; m. Walter Charles Wicker; children—Walter Charles, Nancy; m. 2d, Victor Hammer, Jan. 11, 1941. Began as actress in stock company at 12; appeared Goodman Theatre, Chgo., 1929-30; mem. dramatic staff Columbia Broadcasting Co., 1930-31; played in Painted Dreams, Harold Teen, Today's Children, Song of the City, Judy and Jane, Inner Sanctum, NBC Great Plays; originator, writer, performer Singing Lady radio and TV program; Sunday dramatic program Ireene Wicker's Music Plays, NBC and Mutual radio and TV network; also co-dir. Merry-Go-Round Children's Theatre; worked with profl. children on ABC-TV, 1951-54; weekly radio program WNYC, N.Y., 1959—; with Shakespearean group Am. Theatre Wing with Stella Adler and Joseph Kramm, 1955-56; dir. Children's Radio for C.D.V.O. Presbyn. Recipient highest honors 5 years in succession, for children's programs, by radio editors poll, conducted by N.Y. World Telegram; award for distinguished service to radio, by poll of Radio Star Mag.; award Radio Guide mag. for leading children's program, 4 yrs. in succession; Peabody award for children's radio program, 1961. Records made by Decca, Victor, Mercury, others; song books and plays pub. by Irving Berlin, Inc.; records and cassette library of dramatized mus. stories for children on Simon Sez label. Mem. Nat. League Am. Pen Women. Author: Young Music Makers; Young

Master Artists; The Little Hunchback Horse; other books, plays and songs for children; 4 books and albums for Regal and De Luxe recording. Made 12 Golden Book Records. Albums of childrens stories with songs, tape cassettes for children's libraries. Home: 781 Fifth Av New York City NY 10022 Office: 667 Madison Av New York City NY 10021

WICKHAM, MYRTICE M. (MRS. G. DORRANCE WICKHAM), librarian; b. Denison, Tex., Apr. 19, 1901; d. Herman E. and Lucy (Haskell) Morris; A.B., Baylor U., 1923; B.S., Columbia, 1927; postgrad. U. Del., 1952-56, Rutgers U., 1959; m. G. Dorrance Wickham, June 30, 1928; children—Robert, Francis Chandler. Librarian Carnegie Pub. Library, Sherman, Tex., 1923-26; reference librarian Pub. Library, Boise, Ida., 1927-29; library cons. Mt. Pleasant Spl. Sch. Dist., Wilmington, Del., 1952-58, coordinator of library services, 1958-71; library cons. Del. Dept. Pub. Instruction, 1971-73. Mem. Del. (pres.), Am. (mem. Newbery Caldecott awards com. of children's div.), library assns., Assn. for Ednl. Communications and Tech., Del. Instructional Materials Assn., Archaeol. Soc. Del., Brandywine Valley Assn., Hist. Soc. Del., Nat. Assn. Ret. Tchrs., Delta Kappa Gamma. Conglist. Home: 1100 Brandywine Blvd Wilmington DE 19809

WICKS, MURIEL PUTSCH, dentist; b. Mountainair, N.M., Sept. 23, 1913; d. Llewellyn J. and Edna (Calkins) Putsch; B.A., U. Ariz., 1935; D.D.S., Emory U., 1946; m. Edwin O. Wicks, Aug. 5, 1934 (div. Feb. 1962); children—Gail (Mrs. David Taylor), Karen (Mrs. Rod Stark), Rolf, Dane. Pvt. practice dentistry, Elgin, N.D., 1947-50, Valley City, N.D., 1954—. Mem. State bd. dental examiners, N.D., 1968—, sec.-treas., now pres. Del. N.D. Constl. Conv., 1971-72. Mem. Am. Dental Assn., Am. Pub. Health Assn., Royal Soc. Health, Am. Assn. U. Women (br. pres. 1956-58, state chmn. higher edn. 1959-60, mem. state by-laws com. 1963-66, finance com. 1966—), Flying Dentists (charter), Phi Beta Kappa, Phi Kappa Phi, Omicron Kappa Upsilon. Clubs: Fine Arts (treas. 1964-66), Zonta (pres. 1957-58, 65-67). Home: 1230 Central Av N Valley City ND 58072 Office: Box 150 Valley City ND 58072

WIDDER, BARBARA DIAMOND, clin. psychologist; b. N.Y.C., Jan. 11, 1931; d. Max and Mae (Hanauer) Diamond; B.A., N.Y. U., 1952, M.A., 1955; m. Bertram N. Widder, Sept. 6, 1953; children—Helen Beth, Russell Paul. Sch. psychologist Del. Dept. Pub. Instrn., 1955-67; clin. psychologist div. pub. health Del. Dept. Health and Social Services, Dover, 1967—, mem. exec. com. div. social services Del. adv. com. family services, 1971-73. Mem. Am., Del. (chmn. publicity 1967) psychol. assns., Del. Sch. Psychologists Assn., Am. Assn. U. Women (chmn. fed. legislation 1974—), Phi Beta Kappa. Home: 4 Woods Dr Dover DE 19901 Office: Office Psychol Services Cooper Meml Bldg Federal and Water Sts Dover DE 19901

WIDGER, JEAN INGLIS, educator; b. Charleston, Ill., Mar. 13, 1914; d. Howard DeForest and Ruby Lois (Carpenter) Widger; B.S., U. Ill., 1937. Lab. technologist City Hosp., Winston-Salem, N.C., 1937-38; lab. and x-ray technologist Holden Hosp., Carbondale, Ill., 1938-39, Ryburn Hosp., Ottowa, Ill., 1939-41, to Dr. E.J. O'Brien, Detroit, 1941-43; chief x-ray technologist to Dr. A.R. Bloom, Detroit, 1943-48, to Dr. Robert K. Dixon, Detroit, 1948-57; adminstrv. asst. Wayne State U., 1957—. Mem. Am. Registry Radiologic Technologists, Am. (Jerman meml. lectr. 1969), Mich., Detroit (sec.-treas. 1947-50, pres. 1950-51, 56-57) socs. radiologic technologists, Am. Med. Writers Assn., Ednl. Press Assn. Editor Radiologic Tech., 1956—, Grad. Comment (Wayne State U.), 1958-69. Home: 8100 E Jefferson Av Detroit MI 48214

WIDGERY, JEANNE-ANNA AYRES (MRS. ROLANDE CARPENTER WIDGERY), educator, author; b. Upland, Pa., May 18, 1920; d. Eugene Edmond and Carol (Meeser) Ayres; B.A., Chatham Coll., 1941; A.M., Radcliffe Coll., 1946; m. Rolande Carpenter Widgery, Mar 29, 1948; children—Carolyn Gail, Catherine Darcy, Claudia Joan. Instr. English, Chatham Coll., Pitts., 1947-50; dir. drama, tchr. speech Ellis Sch., Pitts., 1957-60; chmn. English dept. Winchester-Thurston Sch., Pitts., 1960—. Mem. Nat. Council English Tchrs. Author: (under pen name Jan Widgery) The Adversary, 1966; Trumpet at the Gates, 1970. Home: 2721 Oak Hill Dr Allison Park PA 15101 Office: 555 Morewood Av Pittsburgh PA 15213

WIDIGER, JAN STRASZHEIM, pub. relations cons.; b. Columbus, O., Apr. 16, 1929; d. Robert E. and Clara Belle (Shepherd) Straszheim; B.S., Purdue U., 1949; M.B.A., Ind. U., 1953; m. Almar Widiger, Sept. 7, 1957. Publicist pub. relations dept. The Dow Chem. Co., 1953-58; partner Promotive Arts, pub. relations agy., 1958-60, owner, 1960—. Mem. Midland Theatre Guild, Am. Women in Radio and Television, Inc., Purdue U. (life mem.), Ind. U. (life) alumni assns., Am. Marketing Assn. (sec. Saginaw Valley chpt. 1968-69, mem. bd. 1969-70, v.p. 1970-71, pres. chpt. 1971-73), Women in Communications. Methodist. Clubs: Midland Ski; Zonta of Midland (treas., 1962-63, 69-71, v.p., 1963-65, pres. 1965-67, dist. pub. relations chmn. 1969-70). Address: 701 Coolidge Dr Midland MI 48640

WIDMANN, FRANCES KING, med. educator; b. Boston, July 23, 1935; d. Lester Snow and Marjorie Clara (Meehan) King; B.A. magna cum laude, Swarthmore Coll., 1956; M.D., Western Res. U., 1960; m. Donald Eric Widmann, June 29, 1958; children—Jennifer Nicole, Allison King. Intern Cleve. Met. Gen. Hosp., 1960-61; resident pathology U. N.C., Chapel Hill, 1961-64; resident pathology Norfolk (Va.) Gen. Hosp., 1964-65, staff pathologist, 1965-66; instr. pathology U. N.C., 1966-68, asst. prof., 1968-70; asst. prof. Duke, 1971-73, asso. prof., 1973—, asso. dir. Sch. Med. Tech., 1971-72, dir., 1972—. Asst. dir labs. Durham VA Hosp., 1972—. Bd. dirs. Am. Assn. Blood Banks, 1973—. Dilpomate Am. Bd. Pathology. Author: Clinical Interpretation of Laboratory Tests, 7th edit., 1973. Home: 1504 Cumberland Rd Chapel Hill NC 27514 Office: Dept Pathology Med Sch Duke U Durham NC 27710

WIDMER, EMMY LOUISE, educator; b. Frankfurt/Main, Germany, Dec. 25, 1925; d. George and Magdalena (Schmidt) Numrich; brought to U.S., 1927, naturalized, 1932; A.B., Washington Sq. Coll., 1947; M.S., U. State N.Y., 1952; Ed.D., N.Y. U., 1963. Tchr. pub. schs., Rochester, N.Y., 1949-51, Riverdale, N.Y., 1957-58, East Stroudsburg, Pa., 1958-59; demonstration tchr., asst. prof. East Stroundsburg State Coll., 1959-62; asst. prof. Temple U., Phila., 1963-65; asso. prof. U. Miami, Coral Gables, Fla., 1965-67; prof., coordinator early childhood edn. Fla. Atlantic U., Boca Raton, 1967—, chmn. faculty Coll. Edn., 1974—; vis. prof. N.Y. U., 1962-63, Barry Coll., 1966—. Cons. Headstart and migrant programs, day care programs, in-service tchr. edn. pub. and pvt. sch. programs; mem. early childhood adv. bd. Gen. Learning Corp.; mem. adv. com. on early childhood edn., also migrant edn. Fla. Dept. Edn., 1966—; del., mem. ad hoc adv. com. White House Conf. on Children, 1970; mem. Fla. Task Force on Early Childhood Edn.; chmn. Early Childhood Devel. Council Fla. Bd. dirs., mem. exec. bd. Community Coordinated Child Care Services of Palm Beach County. Mem. Assn. Childhood Edn. Internat., Nat. Assn. for Edn. of Young Children, Am. Assn. Elementary-Kindergarten-Nursery Edn., Day Care Assn., Internat. Platform Assn., Kappa Delta Pi. Soroptimist. Author: The Critical Years, Early Childhood Education at the Crossroads, 1970. Contbr. to Fla. and Ga. State Depts. Kindergarten Handbooks, chpts. to The Social Foundations of Education (D. Westby-Gibson), Early Childhood Education Rediscovered (J. Frost). Home: 1910 S Ocean Blvd Delray Beach FL 33444 Office: Fla Atlantic U Coll Edn Boca Raton FL 33432

WIDULE, CAROL JUNE, educator; b. Chgo., Jan. 4, 1930; d. Walter E. and Pauline (Siegert) Widule; B.S., Monmouth Coll., 1952; M.S., MacMurray Coll., 1953; Ph.D., U. Wis., 1966. Asst. prof. Monmouth Coll., 1953-61; research asst., instr. U. Wis., Madison, 1961-65; mem. faculty Purdue U., West Lafayette, Ind., 1965—; asst. prof. phys. edn., 1965-70, asso. prof. phys. edn., 1970—. Mem. Am. Coll. Sports Medicine, A.A.H.P.E.R. (editor kinesiology review 1969-73), Am. Ednl. Research Assn., Nat., Midwest Assn. phys. edn. coll. women, Ind. Assn. Health, Phys. Edn. and Recreation, Kappa Delta, Sigma Xi. Contbr. articles to publs. Home: 120 Foster Dr West Lafayette IN 47906

WIEDEL, ANN ELIZABETH, librarian; b. Los Angeles, Mar. 14, 1944; d. Arthur John and Helen (Conaway) Wiedel; B.A., Immaculate Heart Coll., 1966; M.S. in L.S., U. So. Cal., 1967. Cataloguer WED Enterprises, Inc., Glendale, Cal., 1967-70; librarian, cataloguer Security Pacific Nat. Bank, Los Angeles, 1970—. Cons. Univ. Ch. of Our Saviour, U. So. Cal., 1967—. Bd. dirs. Hist. Soc. Centinela Valley, 1972—. Mem. Am. Inst. Banking, Spl. Libraries Assn., Cal. Library Assn., Libraria Sodalitas (U. So. Cal.), Catholic Alumni Club Los Angeles, Phi Delta Gamma. Home: 10702 8th Pl Inglewood CA 90303 Office: PO Box 2097 Terminal Annex Los Angeles CA 90051

WIEDEMANN, GLADYS H. GARDNER (MRS. KARL T. WIEDEMANN), fuel co. bus. exec.; b. Mpls.; d. Charles Henry and Delia Margaret (Blair) Gardner; student Minn. U., 1945-47, Wichita U., 1958-59; m. Karl T. Wiedemann, July 22, 1950 (dec. Jan. 1961). Sec., Pioneer Rim & Wheel Co., Mpls., 1925-35, Socony-Vacuum Oil Co., St. Paul, 1935-42, Rosemount War Plant, Minn., 1942-44, Tankar Gas, Inc., Mpls., 1944-50; v.p. Beaumont Petroleum Co., El Dorado, Kan., 1950-61, pres., 1961—; pres. K.T. Wiedemann Trust Co., El Dorado, 1961—, trustee, 1962—. Mem. research bd. Wesley Med. Center, Wichita, Kan., 1966—; mem. research bd., student nurse com. Wesley Hosp.; adv. bd. Wichita YWCA, 1968—; v.p. Wichita Symphony Inc.; pres. K.T. Wiedemann Found., Wichita; patron Wichita area Girl Scouts U.S.A. Bd. dirs. Friends U.; mem. bd. Crime Commn., Salvation Army, Booth Meml. Hosp. Mem. Wichita Art Assn. (exec. bd., vice chmn., hon. dir.), Women's Aux. Wichita Logopedics (dir.), Wichita Petroleum Club, Wichita Hist. Mus. Assn., Mu Phi Epsilon. Presbyn. (trustee ch.). Clubs: Soroptimist, 20th Century, Garden, Saturday Music, Helianthus, Organ Aires, Wichita, Plaza, Wichita Country (all Wichita); Minneapolis Athletic. Home: 8615 Shannon Way Wichita KS 67206 also 4200 Estero Blvd Fort Myers Beach FL 33931 Office: 1515 W 6th St El Dorado KS 67042

WIEDERHOLT, MARIE FRANCES, educator; b. Conception, Mo., Aug. 26, 1927; d. Valentine George and Mary (Bliley) Wiederholt; B.A. in History, St. Louis U., 1958, M.A. in Philosophy, 1971; M.A. in Ednl. Adminstrn., St. Xavier Coll., (Chgo.), 1971. Joined Sisters of Most Precious Blood, 1948; tchr. diocesan elementary schs., St. Louis, 1949-59, Conception, Mo., 1959-61, Florissant, Mo., 1961-64; cons. Diocesan Sch. Office, St. Louis, 1965-67; prof. philosophy, head dept. philosophy and theology St. Mary's Coll. of O'Fallon (Mo.), 1968—, also tchr. psychology. Mem. Am. Catholic Philos. Assn., Nat. Cath. Ednl. Assn. Home: 204 N Main St O'Fallon MO 63366 Office: 200 N Main St O'Fallon MO 63366

WIEGAND, JANE SHUTTLEWORTH, city atty.; b. Cin., Oct. 9, 1938; d. Washburn Finley and Catherine Agnes (Ceygan) Shuttleworth; B.A. (Alumni scholar), U. Cal. at Berkeley, 1960; J.D. cum laude, U. San Diego, 1971; m. Jeffery Wiegand, Apr. 30, 1961; children—Thomas Jeffery, Gregory Shuttleworth. Instr. U. del Valle, Columbia, 1960-61, U. Mayor de San Simon, Bolivia, 1963; admitted to Cal. bar, 1971; dep. city atty., San Diego, 1971—. Teaching fellow USIA, 1960. Mem. Commn. of Californias, 1973—. Recipient Most Valuable Woman Student Regional award Elks Club W., Covina, Cal., 1958. Republican. Lead article editor U. San Diego Law Rev., 1969-70. Contbr. to profl. jours. Home: Box 961 Rancho Santa Fe CA 92067 Office: 202 W C St San Diego CA 92102

WIEGERS, ELIZABETH COLWILL (MRS. GEORGE A. WIEGERS), pub. cons.; b. Balt., May 29, 1937; d. Edward P. and Elizabeth (Tunis) Colwill; B.A. cum laude, Sweet Briar Coll., 1959; m. George A. Wiegers, Oct. 30, 1965; 1 son, Edward Alexander. With Time, Inc., 1960—, sec. books dept. Life Mag., 1960-62, mgr. direct mail Life Books, 1962-63, Time-Life Books, 1966-67, asst. gen. mgr. Time-Life Internat., Amsterdam, Netherlands, 1964, asst. to bus. mgr. Time-Life Books, N.Y.C., 1965-66, cons. direct mail, pub. Time-Life, 1967—; cons. direct mail, pub. Erica Wilson Crewel Work, Apollo Mag., Mus. Natural History, Met. Mus. Art, 1967—. Mem. Phi Beta Kappa. Home: 134 E 80th St New York City NY 10021

WIEGERS, IRENE CALDWELL (MRS. HOWARD LYLE WIEGERS), ednl. adminstr.; b. Long Pine, Neb., Dec. 30, 1915; d. William Elmer and Amanda Mae (Butler) Caldwell; B.S., Neb. Wesleyan U., 1937; M.Ed., U. Neb., 1968; m. Howard Lyle Wiegers, Oct. 17, 1941; children—Jo Anne (Mrs. Gordon Lee Bair), John Howard. Asst. registrar Neb. Wesleyan U., Lincoln, 1963-64, registrar, 1964—. Mem. Am., Neb. (sec. 1967-70, pres. 1971-72) assns. collegiate registrars and admissions officers, Am. Assn. Univ. Women (treas. Lincoln br. 1973-74), P.E.O., Delta Zeta. Methodist (dean Neb. Sch. Missions 1964, 68). Home: Route 3 Lincoln NE 68507 Office: Nebraska Wesleyan Univ Lincoln NE 68504

WIELAND, PEG DOODY MAST, economist, editor; b. Kattowitz, Germany; d. Paul and Lucy (Olbrich) Mast; dipl. rer. pol. Berlin (Germany) U.; M.A., New Sch. for Social Research, 1960, postgrad., 1964-68. Came to U.S., 1954, naturalized, 1959. Researcher, tng. officer U.S. Forces, Garmisch, Germany, 1948-54; research asst. Milbank Meml. Fund, N.Y.C., 1954-58; economic analyst, mng. editor Chase Manhattan Fgn. Trade Service publ. The Chase Manhattan Bank N.A., N.Y.C., 1958-68, research economist, editor Chase Manhattan Guide for Exporters, 1968-70, bank officer, 1970—. Mem. Internat. Platform Assn., New Sch. Alumni Assn. (exec. com.). Office: Chase Manhattan Bank 1 Chase Manhattan Plaza New York City NY 10015

WIENER, JUNE WASSER (MRS. STEPHEN N. WIENER), lawyer; b. Brookline, Mass., June 14, 1932; d. Samuel and Lena (Karelitz) Wasser; A.B., Bryn Mawr Coll., 1953; J.D. summa cum laude, Cleve.-Marshall Law Sch., 1965; m. Stephen N. Wiener, Aug. 24, 1952; children—Clifford Michael, Andrew Robert. Admitted to Ohio bar, 1965; mem. firm Benesch, Friedlander, Mendelson & Coplan, Cleve., 1965-73; research dir. Metzenbaum for U.S. Senate Campaign, 1974—; lectr. in law Case Western Res. Law Sch., 1967-69; instr. law for women Cleve. Coll. Mem. community relations com. Jewish Community Fedn. Cleve. Mem. Am., Ohio, Cuyahoga County, Cleve. bar assns. Jewish religion. Club: Bryn Mawr (treas. 1963-65) (Cleve.). Office: 1525 Investment Plaza Cleveland OH 44114

WIENKE, MARY JANE CARTER (MRS. RAYMOND C. WIENKE), govt. ofcl.; b. Homer, Ill., Feb. 3, 1918; d. Walter V. and Edna Mae (Dickson) Carter; grad. Inst. Applied Sci., 1961; m. Raymond C. Wienke, Oct. 12, 1940; children—Ronald C., Richard C. Dep. sheriff Mohave County Sheriff's Office, Kingman, Ariz., 1950-63, chief civil dep., 1953-63; security Ford Motor Co., Ariz. Proving Ground, Yucca, 1963-64; clk. Mohave County Atty., Kingman, 1964-65; clk. Superior Ct., Mohave County, 1966—. Mem. Job Corps Community Relations Com., 1966-68, treas., 1967-68. Cub scout den-mother Boy Scouts of Am., 1952-54; pres. Mohave County Democratic Womens Club, 1960-62, treas., 1966-67; pres. Ariz. Fedn. Democratic Womens Clubs, 1967-68; pres. Women's Soc. Christian Service, 1954-56. Bd. dirs. Mohave Mental Health Clinic. Mem. Nat. Sheriffs Assn., Ariz. Pub. Employees Assn., Ariz. Assn. Clks. of Superior Ct. (v.p. 1971-72, pres. 1972-73), Ariz. Assn. Counties (Mohave County coordinator), Nat. Assn. Counties, Nat. Assn. for Ct. Adminstrn., Internat. Assn. Clks., Recorders, Election Ofcls. and Treasurers, Nat. Assn. Recorders and Clks., Bus. and Profl. Womens Club (dir. 1964-65), Kingman C. of C., Federated Womens Clubs. Methodist. Mem. Order Eastern Star (past matron). Club: Toastmistress (pres. 1965). Home: 132 E Oak St Kingman AZ 86401 Office: Courthouse Kingman AZ 86401

WIER, ESTER ALBERTI (MRS. HENRY R. WIER), author; b. Seattle, Oct. 17, 1910; d. Robert Armenio and Lydea (Harshbarger) Alberti; m. Henry Robert Wier, Oct. 29, 1934; children—David Anthony, Susan (Mrs. John Andrew Zoltewicz). Author: Gift of the Mountains, 1963; Loner, 1963; Rumptydoolers, 1964; Easy Does It, 1965; Barrel, 1966; Space Hut, 1967; Wind Chasers, 1967; Winners, 1968; Action at Paradise Marsh, 1968; Long Year, 1969; Straggler: Adventures of a Sea Bird, 1970; White Oak, 1971; Partner, 1972; The Hunting Trail, 1974. Lectr. book fairs. Mem. Authors Guild. Home: 2534 SW 14th Dr Gainesville FL 32608

WIERUM, ANN ROBINSON, librarian; b. Boston, Aug. 27, 1929; d. Richard Francis and Mildred (Robinson) Wierum; B.A. magna cum laude, Radcliffe Coll., 1950; M.A., U. B.C. (Vancouver, Can.), 1967, B.L.S., 1968. Editorial and research asst. project Letters Theodore Roosevelt, Mass. Inst. Tech., Cambridge, 1951-53; asst. to dir. Atlantic Monthly Press, Boston, 1954-60; librarian Washington State U., Pullman, 1968-70, chief humanities library, 1970—. Recipient Ruth Cameron medal librarianship, U. B.C., 1968. Fulbright scholar, 1953-54. Mem. Wash., Pacific Northwest library assns., Am. Assn. U. Profs., Modern Lang. Assn., Sierra Club (mem. exec. com. Palouse group 1971-72), Alpine Club of Can. Home: 5 NW 1335 Deane St Pullman WA 99163 Office: Humanities Library Washington State Univ Pullman WA 99163

WIERZBICKI, SISTER MARY LUCINA, hosp. adminstr.; b. Milw., Nov. 6, 1920; d. Michael J. and Louise C. (Walczak) Wierzbicki; B.S., Marquette U., 1953; M.P.H., Yale, 1970. Joined Sisters of Sorrowful Mother, 1940; lab. supr. St. John's Hosp., Tulsa, 1952-66; office supr. St. Clare's Hosp., Denville, N.J., 1966-68; adminstr. St. Mary's Hosp., Rhinelander, Wis., 1970—. Bd. dirs. Sacred Heart Hosp., Tomahawk, Wis., St. Michael's Hosps., Stevens Point, Wis., Conf. Cath. Hosp. Wis. Mem. Am. Coll. Hosp. Adminstrs., Wis. Hosp. Assn. (pres. N. Central hosp. dirs. 1974-75). Address: 1044 Kabel Av Rhinelander WI 54501

WIESE, MARION BERNICE, ednl. adminstr.; b. San Francisco, Apr. 18, 1905; d. George M. and Mary (Todd) Wiese; A.B., Goucher Coll., 1926; M.A., Duke, 1929; B.S. in L.S., Columbia, 1948. Jr. high sch. tchr. English, Balt. Pub. Schs., 1926-28, jr. high sch. librarian, 1935-38, sr. high sch. librarian, 1938-46, dir. library services, 1946-68; Fulbright Hays grant as sch. library cons. to Ministry of Edn., Malaysia, 1964-65; Fulbright Hays grant as lectr. library sci. Tchrs. Tng. Coll., Singapore, 1968-69; tchr. history Tubman High Sch., Augusta, Ga., 1929-35; summer tchr. library sci. Johns Hopkins Balt., 1950, U. Del., Newark, 1951-53, State U. N.Y., Geneseo, 1957, Drexel Inst. Tech. Library Sch., Phila., 1960; Sch. library cons., 1970—. Mem. Am. (adv. com. library tech. project 1959-63, sec. bldgs. and equipment sect.), Md. (sec. 1946-48) library assns., N.E.A., Assn. Supervision and Curriculum Devel., Assn. Sch. Librarians Md. (treas., pres. 1942), Am. Assn. Sch. Librarians (mem. nominating com., com. planning sch. library, 2d v.p. 1962-63). Editor Internat. Assn. Sch. Librarianship Newsletter, 1971—. Author: School Libraries and School Librarianship, 1971. Contbr. profl. jours. Home: 58 Hamill Ct Village of Cross Keys Baltimore MD 21210

WIESER, JEANETTE MARIAN, educator; b. Fredericksburg, Tex., Apr. 4, 1928; d. Joseph Benedict and Estella Emily (Hahn) Wieser; B.S. in Phys. Edn., S.W. Tex. State Tchrs. Coll., San Marcos, 1947, M.A. in Adminstrv. Edn., 1949; postgrad. Coll. of The Pacific, 1957, U. Cal. at Los Angeles, 1958-59, U. Tex., Austin, 1963, Tex. Women's U., Denton, 1963, Tex. A. and M. U., 1967, U. So. Cal. at Wellesley, 1969. Tchr. phys. edn. high schs. in Gonzales, Tex., 1947-49, San Antonio, 1950-51, Pearsall, Tex., 1951-52; tchr. health and phys. edn. Tex. A. and I. U., Kingsville, 1952-58; grad. asst. elementary phys. edn. and badminton U. Cal. at Los Angeles, 1958-59; tchr. health and phys. edn. Sam Houston State U., Huntsville, Tex., 1959—. Chmn. S. Tex. Bd. Ofcls. for Women, Kingsville, 1956-57, S.E., Tex. Bd. Ofcls. Women's Sports, Huntsville, 1959—. Mem. Am. (hon. ofcl.), Tex. (chmn. profl. sect. 1975-76) assns. health, phys. edn. and recreation, So. Assn. Phys. Edn. Coll. Women (editor newsletter 1969-71, chmn. div. girls and women's sports Tex. 1965-66, chmn. internat. relations com. 1964-66), Am. Assn. U. Women, Tex. Assn. Intercollegiate Athletics for Women (v.p. finances 1975-76). Co-author: Physical Education Handbook for Elementary Teaching, 1957; A Children's Book of Rhymes and Games, 1960. Home: 2001 19th St Huntsville TX 77340

WIG, PRISCILLA PORTER, cons.; b. Gainesville, Fla., Dec. 22, 1945; d. Ralpha Elma and Alma Pope (Conyers) Porter; B.S. in Math., U. Fla., 1967; M. Exptl. Statistics, N.C. State U., 1970; m. M.K. Wig, June 24, 1972. Field statistician U.S. Bur. Census, 1970; with Gen. Electric Co., Louisville, 1970—, cons. specialist mgmt. sci. techniques, 1973—. Mem. Am. Statis. Assn., Phi Mu (chpt. pres. 1967). Home: 8210 Paddington Dr Louisville KY 40222

WIGDERSON, DOROTHY MARKS (MRS. HENRY WIGDERSON), ednl. adminstr.; b. N.Y.C., Mar. 19, 1912; d. Oscar and Rose (Till) Marks; B.A., N.Y. U., 1932; M.A., Columbia, 1937; Ed.D., 1971; m. Henry Wigderson, Dec. 17, 1937; children—Jonathan, Seth, Katherine Ann. Tchr. pub. high schs., N.Y.C., 1932-49; dir. religious edn. Am. Ethical Union, N.Y.C., 1960-62; exec. dir. League for Parent Edn., N.Y.C., 1970—. Family and marriage counselor, N.Y.C., 1963—; asso. Sex Information and Edn. Council U.S. Vol. Family Life Edn. for Head Start Program, N.Y.C., 1972—. Mem. Am., N.Y. (corr. sec. 1973) assns. marriage and family counselors.

WIGDOR, BLOSSOM TEMKIN, psychologist; b. Montreal, Que., Can.; d. Solomon and Olga (Gilels) Temkin; B.A., McGill U., 1945, Ph.D., 1952; M.A., U. Toronto, 1946; m. Leon M. Wigdor, May 31, 1945; 1 son, Ernest Mitchell. Psychologist, Sunnybrook Vets. Hosp., Toronto, Ont., Can., 1946-47, St. Annes Vets. Hosp., Queen Mary's Vet. Hosp., Montreal, 1947-62, head dept. psychology, 1962—; mem.

faculty McGill U., Montreal, 1952—, asst. prof. psychology, 1958-71, asso. prof., 1972—. Cons. Maimonides Home and Hosp. for Aged, 1956-68; cons. to dir. gen. treatment services Dept. Vets. Affairs, Ottawa, 1969—; sr. cons. sub dept. psychology Queen Elizabeth Hosp., Montreal, 1968—; mem. Sci. Council Can., 1973—. Fellow Soc. Projective Techniques and Personality Assessment; mem. Am., Canadian, Eastern psychol. assns., Corp. Psychologists Province Que., Gerontol. Soc., Delta Phi Epsilon. Contbr. articles to profl. jours. Home: 503 Roslyn Av Montreal PQ Canada Office: Queen Mary Vets Hosp 4565 Queen Mary Rd Montreal PQ Canada

WIGGINS, DOLORES RUTH, hosp. adminstr.; b. Oklahoma City, Jan. 5, 1935; d. Albert Bryan and Rilla Cue (Reeves) Davis; student corr. course Am. Med. Record Assn., 1964-66, Okla. U., 1969-70, Oscar Rose Jr. Coll., 1972—; m. James E. Wiggins, Sept. 20, 1952; 1 son, James Donald. Sec. to pres. LeFevre Chem. Co., Oklahoma City, 1954-55; mem. staff Coyne Campbell Hosp., Spencer, Okla., 1957—, acting adminstr., 1970, adminstr., 1970—. Sec. Okla. Psychiat. Found., 1970—. Mem. Am. Med. Record Assn., Okla. Med. Record Assn. (past mem. exec. com.), Oklahoma City Area Hosp. Council (exec. com.). Club: Encore Toastmistress (Oklahoma City). Home: 7837 NE 10th Apt 165 Midwest City OK 73110 Office: 2601 Spencer Rd Spencer OK 73084

WIGGINS, EMILIE VERNE, librarian; b. Richmond, Ky., July 29, 1917; d. Ernst Theodore and Elsie Josephine (Gabany) Wiggins; A.B. with highest honors, Eastern Ky. State Tchrs. Coll., 1938; B.S. in Library Sci. with honors, U. Mich., 1947; postgrad. U. Cin., 1940-41. Tchr., Latin, English, Lynch High Sch., 1938-40; tchr. French, English, Rushville (O.) High Sch., 1942; library asst. Eastern Ky. State Tchrs. Coll., 1934-38, U. Cin. and U. Mich., 1945-47; mem. staff Nat. Library Medicine, Bethesda, Md., 1948—, cataloger, 1947-50, reviser, 1950-62, head catalog sect., 1962—. Sec. Columbia Heights Boys Club, Washington, 1960-69. Recipient Margaret Mann award U. Mich. at Ann Arbor, 1947. Mem. A.L.A., Med. Library Assn. (speaker ann. meetings), Mich. U. Alumnae Assn. (pres. Washington 1951), Bus. and Profl. Women (pres. Washington, 1964-66). Home: 2950 Newark St Washington DC 20008 Office: Nat Library Medicine 8600 Rockville Pike Bethesda MD 20014

WIGGINS, LORNA ANICE, librarian; b. Birmingham, Dec. 17, 1930; d. Matthew Edwin and Lelia Katherine (Harper) Wiggins; B.A., Agnes Scott Coll., 1952; M.L.S., Emory U., 1956. Reference librarian Biomed. Library, U. Cal., Los Angeles, 1957-60; med. librarian U. Ala. Med. Center Library, Birmingham, 1960-61; sci. tech., data processing librarian Ga. Inst. Tech., Atlanta, 1961-65; dir. library Birmingham So. Coll., 1965-68; head, acquisitions div. Auburn (Ala.) U. Library, 1968—. Mem. Southeastern (sec. coll.-univ. sect.), Ala. library assns., Audubon Soc. Home: 217 Kimberly Dr Auburn AL 36830 Office: Auburn U Library Auburn AL 36830

WIGGINS, MARTHA ELIZABETH DAVIS, assn. exec.; b. Denver, Tenn., Sept. 4, 1914; d. John Alfred and Effie Estelle (Patterson) Davis; student Falls Bus. Coll., Nashville, 1946, Watkins Inst., Nashville, 1955; m. John Herman Wiggins, May 4, 1935 (dec. 1937); 1 dau., Marion Elizabeth (Mrs. Bill Cobble). Civilian service with USAAF, 1942-45; with Am. Bible Soc., Nashville, 1947-51; with Nashville YMCA, 1951—, supr. secretarial div., 1972—. Recipient Civilian Service award USAAF, 1944. Mem. Am., Tenn. assns. profl. dirs. Democrat. Methodist. Home: 120 Two Valley Rd Hendersonville TN 37075 Office: 1000 Church St Nashville TN 37203

WIGHTMAN, BETTY JEAN LYON, assn. exec.; b. Des Moines, Apr. 21, 1922; d. James Everett and Pearl Ione (Eastman) Lyon; grad. high sch.; m. Carl Franklin Wightman, Feb. 21, 1942; children—Carl Franklin III, Denise (Mrs. Monte C. Sims). Membership dir. YMCA, Terre Haute, Ind., 1954—. Mem. Beta Sigma Phi. Home: 121 Monroe Blvd Terre Haute IN 47807 Office: 200 S 6th St Terre Haute IN 47807

WIGHTMAN, DORRIS ODOM, librarian; b. Jasper, Ala., July 20, 1921; d. Ira Lewis and Dorris Juanita (Hamilton) Odom; B.S., Auburn U., M.L.S., Peabody Coll., D.Sc. in Edn., U. Ga.; divorced; children—William Edgar Bagley, Ann (Mrs. James Anthony DeBortoli), Jean (Mrs. Leonard Dale Taylor), Mary Beth Bagley. Tchr., librarian Lee County High Sch., Leesburg, Ga., 1967-70; library dir. Kinchafoonee Regional Library, Dawson, Ga., 1970—. Mem. Am., Ga., Southeastern library assns., D.A.R., Alpha Delta Pi, Alpha Delta Kappa. Home: 2108 Robin Hood Rd Albany GA 31707 Office: Main St Dawson GA 31742

WILBANKS, ELIZABETH JOHNSON (MRS. SIMEON SEALY), lawyer; b. Clanton, Ala., Dec. 2, 1913; d. Napoleon Strock and Escharles (Stewart) Johnson; B.A., U. Ala., 1934, LL.B., 1936; student U. Madrid; m. Simeon Sealy Wilbanks, Feb. 15, 1936; children—Nancy (Mrs. Fred Wilson Sellers), Amelia, Simeon Sealy, Alice. Admitted to Ala. bar, 1936; mem. firm Wilbanks, Wilbanks & Dillon, 1936-71. Bd. dirs. Horseshoe Bend Regional Library, 1946-54, 66—; trial counsel C. of Ga. Ry., 1964-71; tchr. law Alexander City State Jr. Coll., chmn. membership com. Joint Legislative Council Ala., 1954-56; div. counsel So. Ry. System, 1959-71; mem. adv. council Small Bus. Adminstrn., 1964-67. Dir. City Bank Goodwater, Ala., 1955—, City Bank Tuskegee, 1967—, City Bank Roanoke, 1967—, Covington County Bank, Andalusia, 1969—, City Bank of Lineville, 1968—, Citibanc Group, Inc., 1973—. Sec. Tallapoosa County Dem. Exec. Com., 1942-70. Mem. Ala. Women Lawyers Assn. (pres. 1943-45, 46, 56—), C. of C. (dir. 1957-59), Nat. Assn. Women Lawyers, Nat. Orgn. Women. Methodist. Home: 102 Maplewood Lane Alexander City AL 35010 Office: 116 S Main St Alexander City AL 35010

WILBER, EDNA MAE BENNETT (MRS. DELBERT QUENTIN WILBER), pub. relations exec.; b. Del Rio, Tex., Jan. 29, 1925; d. Posey Archibald and Carrie Belva (Broadnay) Bennett; student San Antonio Jr. Coll., 1942-43, U. Tex., 1942-43; m. Delbert Quentin Wilber, Dec. 21, 1943; children—Delbert Quentin, Richard A., Cynthia Jan, Mary Lynn, Robert J. Reporter, KMOX Radio, St. Louis, 1960-67; dir. spl. events and promotions Cardinals, St. Louis, 1967-68; dir. pub. relations Jewish Hosp., St. Louis, 1968-69, St. Louis Challenge, 1969-71; dir. pub. information Mayor's Office, St. Louis, 1969-71; pres. Taffy Wilber & Assos., Inc., St. Louis, 1971—. Cons. Federalism '76, 1973-74, Tex. Forums, 1973-74; co-dir., tchr. System and Student, Bicentennial Youth Study Pilot Program, 1973—; pres., co-founder Pinch-Hitters, 1963. Mem. Pub. Relations Soc. Am., Women in Communications, St. Louis Press Club, St. Louis Ambassadors. Club: Nat. Fashion Group (St. Louis). Home: 513 Woodleaf Ct Kirkwood MO 63122 Office: 212 N Kingshighway St Louis MO 63108

WILBER, LAURA ANN, audiologist, educator; b. Memphis, May 26, 1934; d. Leon Austin and Ivah Edith (Ostrander) Wilber; B.S. in Speech Correction, U. So. Miss., 1955; M.S. in Deaf Edn. (grad. fellow), Gallaudet Coll., 1958; Ph.D. in Audiology (grad. fellow), Northwestern U., 1964. Tchr. hard of hearing and deaf McKinley Elementary Sch., Bakersfield, Cal., 1955-57; speech therapist, coordinator spl. edn. U.S. Army Dependent Sch. System, Heidelberg, Germany, 1957-61; audiology research asst. Northwestern U., Evanston, Ill., 1961-64; asst. research audiologist U. Cal. at Los Angeles, 1964-70; dir. Audiology Clinic, U. Cal. at Los Angeles Hosp., 1968-69; asso. prof. dept. otorhinolaryngology, dir. hearing and speech services Albert Einstein Coll. Medicine, Bronx, N.Y., 1970—, asst. profl. dept. rehab. medicine, 1971—. Lectr., mem. faculty Cal. State U., Los Angeles, U. So. Cal., 1964-71. Mem. working groups Am. Nat. Standards Inst., 1970—; noise expert N.Y.C. Environmental Control Bd., 1972—, mem. steering com. on noise subcom., 1971—; U.S. rep. working groups on techniques for audiometry and threshold of hearing Internat. Standards Orgn., 1973—; chmn. Clinic Sch.-Council of N.Y., 1972-73. Mem. Am. (com. on audiologic standards 1971—, subcom. on electroacoustic characteristics 1973—), N.Y. State (chmn. com. on standards in speech pathology and audiology 1972—, mem. noise com. 1971—), Cal. speech and hearing assns., Acoustical Soc. Am., N.Y. Audiology Study Group (chmn. 1973-74), Dirs. Hosp. Speech and Hearing Programs Assn., Soc. for Ear, Nose and Throat Advances in Children, Am. Civil Liberties Assn. Contbr. articles to profl. publs., also chpts. to books. Home: 111 N 3d Av Mt Vernon NY 10550 Office: 1300 Morris Park Av Bronx NY 10461

WILBER, MARGIE ROBINSON, editor; b. Florence, S.C., Apr. 13, 1920; d. Mack Donald and Bessie (Wright) Robinson; A.B., S.C. State Coll., 1942; student Am. U., 1954-55, George Washington U., 1955-58, Dept. Agr. Grad. Sch., 1961, 62, 65, 66; divorced; children—Norman L., Reginald G. Elementary sch. tchr., Marion, S.C., 1942-44; with State Dept., Washington, 1945—, editor, since 1962—, Founder, exec. dir., pres. Crime Stoppers Club, Inc., since 1967—. Mem. Woman's Nat. Democratic Club. Bd. dirs. D.C. Women's Comm. Crime Prevention. Recipient Community Service award Boys Club Greater Washington, 1968; commendation from President Nixon, 1970, Sigma Gamma Rho, 1971; Action Fed. Employee Distinguished Vol. Service award, 1973; award Iota Chi Lambda, 1973. Mem. Washington Urban League, Southeast Civic Assn., Capitol Hill Community Council, D.C. Fedn. Bus. and Profl. Women's Clubs, Delta Sigma Theta. Composer: D.C.—Tribute to Nation's Capital, 1971; We Are Future America, 1972; Safe for the Children, 1972. Home: 1366 South Carolina Av SE Washington DC 20003 Office: Dept State 21st and Virginia Av NW Washington DC 20520

WILBORN, ETHEL BALL, realtor; b. nr. Anniston, Ala., Aug. 30, 1913; d. Floyd and Mattie (Owens) Ball; student DeKalb County Sch., Ft. Payne, Ala., 1919-20; m. D. H. Wilborn, Feb. 23, 1929 (div. May 1963); children—Leroy F., Walden J., Olene (Mrs. Terry Ray), Dixie (Mrs. Elton Wisham), Jerrie (Mrs. Roland Ray). Real estate saleswoman T.E. Bazemore & Co., Anniston, Ala., 1956; real estate broker Wilborn Realty Co., Anniston, 1957; home builder, contractor Cheaha Acres Jo-Dell Sub-Div., Oxford, Ala., 1957—; developer Scenic Heights Sub-Div., Oxford, 1965—, Wilborn Park Heights Sub-Div., 1968, Joyview Heights, 1969; v.p. Jeray Investments, Anniston, 1967—; sec.-treas. Tirobi Inc., Anniston, 1967—, Dutch's Village Inc., Anniston, 1968—; owner Colonial Village Apts. Mem. Anniston Real Estate Bd. (hospitality chmn. 1963-67, membership chmn. 1968-69), Nat. Inst. Real Estate Bds., Anniston C. of C. Home: 22 Mont Camille Anniston AL 36201 Office: 1629 Wilmer Av Anniston AL 36201

WILBUR, HELEN JULIA (MRS. DONALD I. WILBUR), artist; b. Springfield, O., Feb. 28, 1913; d. William W. and Adele (Baer) Tokoph; student Diedenhofen Studios Art, 1929-30, Chgo. Art Inst., 1930-32, U. Chgo., 1934-35, Northwestern U., 1935-36; m. Donald Irving Wilbur, July 8, 1939; children—Ronald Irving, Joyce Lee (Mrs. David Doherty), Richard Dale. Exhibited in one-man shows including Goldenwest Art Gallery, Garden Grove, Cal., 1962, Bowers Mus., Santa Ana, Cal., 1964, Anaheim (Cal.) Ebell Club, 1969, Laguna Beach (Cal.) Art Gallery, 1968; exhibited in group shows at Pacific Coast Club, Long Beach, Cal., 1969, Salt Palace, Salt Lake City, 1969, Americana Traveling Art Show, Mont., 1970, others; represented in permanent collections at YMCA, Anaheim, Anaheim Ebell Club, various pvt. collections. Ordained to ministry Ch. of Scientology, 1957. Mem. exec. panel Cal. State Fair (South), 1967-70; judge 5th Annual Fest. Arts Orange County (Cal.), 1971, others. Recipient 1st place prize for Cal., Nat. League Pen Women, 1969; 1st place prizes in poetry and in essays, Festival Arts, Fullerton, Cal., 1970. Mem. Internat. Platform Assn., Am. Inst. Fine Arts, Nat. League Am. Pen Women (founding pres. Orange County chpt. 1970, recipient Woman of Achievement plaque 1972). Club: Ebell (Anaheim). Address: 17820 110th Av SE Renton WA 98055

WILCOX, BEATRICE PAULINE (MRS. THEODORE HERBERT WILCOX), curator; b. Portland, Ore., May 7, 1913; d. Samuel Leland and Emma (Edwards) Eddy; student Multonomah Jr. Coll., 1936-37; m. Theodore Herbert Wilcox, Oct. 4, 1946; 1 dau., Amanda Jane. Propr., Beach Shop, Newport, Ore., 1946-49; night supr. Pacific Communities Hosp., Newport, 1954-56; with Lincoln County Hist. Mus., Newport, 1967—, curator, dir., 1971—. 4-H Club leader, Newport, 1961-66; mother adviser Order Rainbow for Girls, Newport, 1964-65. Mem. Central Lincoln Republican Women, 1970—. Mem. Am. Assn. for State and Local History, Am. Assn. Museums, D.A.R. (treas. 1970-71). Presbyn. Mem. Order Eastern Star (past matron). Office: 579 S W 9th Newport OR 97365

WILCOX, ELEANOR REINDOLLAR (MRS. GEORGE C. WILCOX, JR.), author; b. Balt., Feb. 23, 1915; d. William Larmour and Marcella (Atkinson) Reindollar; student Md. Inst. Art, 1931-36, Johns Hopkins, 1934, Loyola Coll., summer 1957; m. George C. Wilcox, Jr., June 24, 1944; children—George Reindollar, David William. With exhibits dept. Enoch Pratt Free Library, 1937-41; staff artist, lectr. asso. curator Am. anthropology, curator film library Md. Acad. Scis., 1941-46; librarian Park Sch., 1954-56, secretarial asst., receptionist, 1956-67; free-lance writer, artist; partner Wilcox & Wilcox Indsl. Illustrators, 1967—; exhibited paintings Pikesville Library, 1955. Bd. dirs. St. Mark's Early Childhood Learning Center. Mem. Archaeol. Soc. Md. (editor newsletter), Nat. Geog. Soc., Md. Ornithol. Soc., Dorchester Community Assn. Methodist. Club: Mountain (Md.). Author: The Cornhusk Doll, 1956 (Dodd, Mead Librarian's award 1955); Mr. Slims' Argosy, 1958; (with George C. Wilcox, Jr.) Guard the North Gate. Contbr. numerous poems, articles to Balt. Sun papers, also Gardens, Houses and People, Balt., 1951—. Address: 4006 Liberty Heights Av Baltimore MD 21207

WILCOX, ELNORA BALTHROP, educator; b. Nashville, June 15, 1912; d. John Edgar and Sallie Theo (Cleveland) Balthrop; A.B., Tex. Wesleyan Coll., 1935; M.A., Tex. Christian U., 1942, postgrad., 1970; postgrad. Southwestern La. State Coll., 1964, So. Meth. U., 1970; m. Glenn M. Wilcox, June 7, 1946; children—Carol Page, Neil. Tchr. Ft. Worth pub. schs., 1935-41; mem. faculty Tex. Wesleyan Coll., 1941-46, 54—, now asst. prof. sci. Recipient Golden Rule award Tex. Wesleyan Coll. Students, 1958, 61, 65; named Alumna of Yr., Tex. Wesleyan Coll. Alumni Assn., 1966, Outstanding Educator, Tex. Wesleyan Coll., 1972. Club: Faculty Women's of Tex. Wesleyan College. Methodist (tchr. ch. sch. 1965—). Home: 4128 Av G Fort Worth TX 76105

WILCOX, FRANCES SMILEY (MRS. COURTENAY QUAYLE WILCOX), club woman; b. Athens, Ala., June 7, 1908; d. Herschel Harvey and Margaret (Anderson) Smiley; B.A., U. Neb., 1930; m. Courtenay Quayle Wilcox, Oct. 12, 1944; 1 dau., Margaret Allie Dora. Exhibited photography Sweatman Art Meml., 1968, Black Hills State Coll., 1969. Mem. D.A.R. (S.D. 1938—, state regent 1962-64, v.p. gen. nat. soc. 1964-65, 65-66, nat. vice chmn. mag. 1965-68, nat. vice chmn. Am. Indians 1968-72, nat. vice chmn. for vets. service 1972-74), D.A.R. State Vice Regents (life), Nat. Vice Regents Club (sec. 1960-61, pres. 1961-62), Children Am. Revolution (sr. nat. chmn. Am. Indians 1965-66, sr. pres. S.D. 1971—, sr. nat. officers club), Gen. Fedn. Womens' Clubs S.D. (lit. drama chmn. dist. I, 1956-64, state lit. and drama chmn. 1964-68, dist. 1, 2d v.p. 1967-69), S.D. Federated Woman's Clubs (dist. pres. 1969-71), Am. Contract Bridge League (certified dir. 1969), Am. Assn. U. Women, Black Hills Art Assn. (reporter, pres. 1966), Chi Omega. Dist. chmn. Black Hills council Girl Scouts U.S.A., 1959-61, bd. dirs., 1961-64, council rep., 1966—, del. nat. conv., 1969, mem. program com., 1962—. Recipient awards S.D. State Fair, 1966-72, Dakota Artist Guild, 1967, Black Hills Art, Assn. Internat. Show, 1964-73. Methodist (sec. ofcl. bd. 1956-59), Rebekah. Clubs: Northern Hills Duplicate (sec. 1964-68), Mile Hi Duplicate (sec. 1966—), Woman's of Lead (pres. 1964-65, 68-69). Home: 12 Parkdale St Lead SD 57754

WILCOX, LESLIE LOUISE COLEMAN, lawyer; b. Oakland, Cal., Mar. 25, 1945; d. Ralph Leslie and Wilda Louise (Cramer) Coleman; A.B. in Math., U. So. Cal., 1968, LL.B., 1968. Admitted to Cal. bar, 1969; atty. procurement law Dept. Navy, Washington, 1968-70; atty. gen. and civilian law U.S. Gen. Accounting Office, Washington, 1970—. Active Am. U. Symphony. Mem. Cal. Bar Assn., Mortar Bd. Home: 3800 N 23d St Arlington VA 22207 Office: 441 G St NW Washington DC 20549

WILCOX, MARY ELIZABETH, econ. research cons.; b. Fall River, Mass.; d. Philander F. and Elizabeth (Leary) Wilcox; B.B.A., Boston U., 1924, M.B.A., 1939; postgrad. Harvard, 1943, 44. Accountant Patterson, Teele & Dennis, C.P.A.'s, Boston, 1922-28; accountant, tax text editor Klein, Hinds & Fink, C.P.A.'s, N.Y.C., 1930-33; asst. dir., dir. research statistics Mass. div. Employment Security, Boston, 1937-61; research asso. Northeastern U., Boston, 1961-62; cons. manpower skills survey Boston Coll., 1963-64; labor economist Bur. Employment Security, U.S. Dept. Labor, Washington, 1965-66; research asso. Cambridge (Mass.) Center Social Studies, 1966-71. Mem. Am. Assn. U. Women, League Women Voters, Am. Statis. Assn., Am. Inst. C.P.A.'s, Indsl. Relations Research Assn., Mass. Soc. C.P.A.'s, Beta Gamma Sigma. Clubs: Boston University Graduates; Soroptimist (past pres.) (Boston). Address: 1282 Anthony Rd Portsmouth RI 02871

WILCOX, OMA ELLISON (MRS. GEORGE BENJAMIN WILCOX), civic worker; b. Layton, Utah, Apr. 20, 1909; d. Laurence Ephraim and Catherine (Adams) Ellison; student Utah State U., 1927-28; m. George Benjamin Wilcox, Apr. 12, 1936; 1 dau., Catherine Ellison (Mrs. Gibbs Morgan Smith). Bookkeeper, teller First Nat. Bank, Layton, 1931-39, sec., 1962—; dir. Farmers Union Dept. Store, Layton, 1949-50; dir. Farmers Union Corp., 1965—; substitute tchr. schs. nr. Anthony, N.M.-Tex., 1944-45. Home service case worker A.R.C., 1949-53, chmn. fund drive, 1954, bd. dirs. Bonneville chpt. pres. Layton Elementary Sch. P.T.A., 1950-51; v.p. Davis County P.T.A., 1956-57, pres., 1957-58; organizer Layton Art Guild, 1956; chmn. Layton Library Com., 1957-59; chmn. judiciary com. Women's State Legislative Council Utah, 1957-59, v.p., 1959-61, pres. 1961-63, parliamentarian, 1965-67; mem. Layton City Council, 1961-69; mem. Utah Gov.'s Americanism Com., 1961-62; mem. Verdeland Park Devel. Com., 1962-69; chmn. Am. Cancer Soc. drive, North Davis County, 1962; v.p. North Davis Assn. Retarded Children, 1965-67, pres., 1967—; mem. Utah Adv. Com. for Handicapped Children, 1972-73; mem. Utah Adv. Com. on Designing Edn. for Future; mem. com. Utah Heritage Found., 1966-73, trustee, 1973—; mem. Devereaux House Restoration Com., 1970; chmn. Layton City Beautification Com., 1970-72; mem. budget com. Davis County Community Services Council, 1970-71; chmn. bd. dirs. Lion House Social Centre. Precinct vice-chmn. Republican Party, 1956-58, Davis County vice-chmn., 1956-58, mem. state central com., 1956-65, state vice chmn., 1965-65; regional dir. Davis County Rep. Com., 1971—; alternate del. Rep. Nat. Conv., 1960, del., 1964; mem. resolutions com. 1964 conv.; bd. dirs. Salt Lake Women's Rep. Club, 1964-65, parliamentarian, 1965-67. Bd. dirs. United Fund No. Utah, Pro-Utah, Davis County Assn. for Retarded Children; mem. bd. Utah Friends of Library, 1972—, vice chmn., 1973—; vice chmn. Utah Div. Family Services Bd.; trustee Weber State Coll. Recipient award for one of outstanding women Davis County, 1961; Home Town Builders award Eagles Club, 1970; named Outstanding Club Woman Davis County, 1963; Man of Year, Phi Delta Kappa. Mem. Federated Womens Clubs (past pres., com. chmn. Davis dist.), Delta Kappa Gamma. Mem. Ch. of Jesus Christ of Latter-day Saints. Clubs: Bay View Literary (past pres.); Belletristic Literary (Layton); Authors (v.p. 1968-69, pres. 1969-70, program chmn. 1972-73), Forum (Salt Lake City). Home: 1877 Gentile St Layton UT 84041

WILCOX, PATRICIA KEELAN (MRS. FORREST EUGENE WILCOX), journalist; b. Boston, Apr. 30, 1920; d. Edward Joseph and Ethel Josephine (Pattison) Keelan Jr.; B.A., Wheaton Coll., 1941; M.A., Boston U., 1947; m. Forrest Eugene Wilcox, July 4, 1949; children—Katharine, Kent Forrest, Dana Allison, Pattison (Mrs. Daniel Von Feldt). Reporter, feature editor Tribune Publs., Boston, 1941-43, 47-49; reporter Jefferson County Sentinel, Lakewood, Colo., 1954-70; columnist Lakewood (Colo.) Sentinel, 1970—. Vol. probation counselor Jefferson County cts., 1967-70; vol. counselor Lakewood Municipal Cts., 1971—; Brownie troop day camp leader, 1957-59; mem. Lakewood Centennial-Bicentennial Commn., 1974—. Served with WAC, 1943-46; ETO. Recipient numerous writings awards. Mem. Women in Communications, Colo. (editor Bull. 1963-65), Nat. Fedn. (awards 1963-70) press women, Women's Overseas Service League, Am. Legion (historian 1959, adj. 1960), Denver Women's Press Club, Theta Sigma Phi. Home: 130 S Benton St Lakewood CO 80226 Office: 8885 W 14th Av Lakewood CO 80115

WILCOX, RUTH ALICE, educator; b. Chgo., June 6, 1905; d. Charles Elliott and Eva May (Rossman) Wilcox; B.A., Dakota Wesleyan U., 1927; M.A., Northwestern U., 1940; diploma for dean students Columbia Tchrs. Coll., 1958. High sch. tchr. in S.D., 1927-43; instr., dean women Dakota Wesleyan U., 1943-46; prof. speech and drama Marietta (O.) Coll., 1946—, dean women, 1947-70. Named Ohio Tchr. of Year, Ohio Speech Assn., 1972; recipient Communications award Ohio U., 1973. Mem. Nat. (parliamentarian), Ohio (pres. 1962-64) assns. deans women, Am. Assn. Univ. Women (v.p. Marietta 1971—), Pi Kappa Delta (past regional gov.), Delta Kappa Gamma. Methodist (lay speaker). Co-author: Teaching Speech in High Schools, 1953. Home: 503 College St Marietta OH 45750

WILCOX, VIRGINIA LEE, librarian; b. Portsmouth, O., Nov. 28, 1911; d. Ira Lloyd and Sallye (Foley) Wilcox; diploma Averett Coll., Danville, Va., 1934; A.B. and diploma in Library Sci., U. Denver, 1937, M.A., 1953. Librarian Colo. Fuel & Iron Corp., Pueblo, 1937-40; with Colo. Sch. Mines, 1940-42, 46—, successively asst. librarian, acting librarian, 1940-42, 46-55, 55-56, librarian, 1956—;

librarian Army AFB Library and Tech. Library, La Junta, Colo., 1943-45; army librarian Base Library, Rheims, France, 1945, area librarian, hdqrs. Rheims, 1945-46. Campus chmn. United Fund drives, 1957-64. Vice chmn. Council Librarians Assn. State Instns. Higher Edn. Colo., 1962-64, chmn., 1964-66. Mem. Spl. Libraries Assn. (pres. Colo. 1956-57, chmn. petroleum sect. 1965, 1966), Am., Colo. State (scholarship-loan fund com. chmn. 1957-59; chmn. No. dist. 1961-62), Mountain-Plains library assns., Bibliog. Center for Research Rocky Mountain Region (exec. com. 1955-56, chmn. exec. com. 1959-60), Colo. Hist. Soc., The Westerners, Denver Posse, Am. Soc. Engring. Edn. (sec. sch. libraries div. 1967-68, chmn. Rocky Mountain sect. 1966-67), P.E.O. Republican. Club: Faculty Women's (v.p. 1963-64). Author: Colorado: A Bibliography of Its Literature, 1858-1952, 1954; Index to The Westerners Brand Books, all Posses, 1955. Address: 1100 Zinnia Ashwood Park Golden CO 80401

WILCOX, WILHELMENIA LINDSAY (MRS. CLINTON LEWIS WILCOX, JR.), univ. dean; b. Chesterfield, S.C.; d. Samuel Julius and Margaret McLean (Edwards) McLean; B.S., Agrl. and Tech. State U., 1966; M.A., Appalacian State U., 1971; M.Ed., U. N.C., 1974; m. Clinton Lewis Wilcox, Jr., Dec. 27, 1967; 1 son, Clinton Lewis III. Tchr., Headstart Fed. Program, Charlotte, N.C., 1965-66; tchr. Charlotte-Mecklenburg Sch. System, 1967-71; dean women Johnson C. Smith U., Charlotte, 1971—. Mem. Am. Assn. Univ. Women (1st v.p. 1972-74). A.A.H.P.E.R., N.C. Assn. Women Deans and Counselors, N.C. Coll. Personnel Assn., Delta Sigma Theta. Home: 4312 Hidden Valley Rd Charlotte NC 28213 Office: 100 Beatties Ford Rd Charlotte NC 28216

WILCOX, ZELMA PEARL, stockyard exec.; b. Auglaize County, O., Dec. 3, 1910; d. Riley Andrew and Della Nella (Ellison) Gullett; grad. high sch.; m. Robert Wilcox, Aug. 30, 1932 (dec. Nov. 1970); children—Linda Jane (Mrs. Raymond Davis), Karen Sue (Mrs. Norman Lane Stauffer), Robert David, Douglas Earl. Owner Waynesfield (O.) Stock Yards, 1970—. Republican. Methodist (chmn. social concerns 1971—). Home: 208 N Westminister St Waynesfield OH 45896 Office: 504 N Westminister St Waynesfield OH 45896

WILD, LOIS MARJORIE TRUAX (MRS. NORMAN RUSSELL WILD), civic worker; b. Nashua, N.H., Mar. 22, 1922; d. James Abram and Hazel Ferne (Mercer) Truax; student Simmons Coll., 1939-40, Andover Inst. Bus., 1940-42; m. Norman Russell Wild, June 11, 1960; 1 son, James Mercer. Exec. sec. wood preserving div. Kopper Co., Nashua, N.H., 1942-55; adminstrv. sec. Sanders Assos., Inc., Nashua, 1956-60. Den mother Pack 7 Cub Scouts Am., Nashua, 1960-65; co-chmn. annual radio auction March of Dimes, Nashua, 1960-67; state chmn. N.H. chpt. Multiple Sclerosis Soc., Laconia, N.H., 1972—. Mem. Order Eastern Star (worthy matron 1951, grand rep. 1951-52), Order of White Shrine of Jerusalem (high priestess 1952-53, supreme dep. 1954-55), Order of Rebekahs (noble grand 1950). Home: Governor's Island RFD #5 Laconia NH 03246 also 4126 Voorne St Sarasota FL 33580

WILD, MARGARET MARY LAMBUR (MRS. W. LYDON WILD), civic worker; b. Chgo.; d. George E. and Mary (McQuaid) Lambur; grad. Chgo. Tchrs. Coll., 1932; m. W. Lydon Wild, Feb. 13, 1937; 1 dau., Margery Ann (Mrs. Homer J. Livingston, Jr.). Tchr. pub. schs., Chgo., 1932-36. Past pres. Chgo. Heart Woman's Council; founder, past pres. Marillac Woman's Bd., also founder, past pres. DePaul U. Women's Bd., 1963—; mem. 1st adv. council, bd. educators DePaul U.; founder, pres. woman's bd. Mundelein Coll., 1968—; mem. Chgo. Bd. Edn., 1964—; past pres., mem. exec. bd. Misericordia Home; pres. Ill. Club for Catholic Women, 1958—; mem. adv. council St. Joseph's Hosp., 1964. Co-chmn. Ill. Citizens for Kennedy-Johnson, 1960. Bd. dirs. Mercy Hosp.; bd. dirs. Am. Cancer Soc., past chmn. women's bd.; bd. dirs. Arthritis and Rheumatism Found., Chgo. Mental Health Soc.; mem. Women's bd. Chgo. Boys Club, 1972—; chmn. Community and Auction campaign Ednl. TV sta. WTTW. Recipient Almoner award, 1960, VIP in Chgo. award, 1962, citation DePaul U. Women's Bd., 1965, Am. Cancer Soc. award, 1968, Distinguished Philanthropic award Nat. Jewish Hosp., 1969, Loyola Founders Day Civic award, 1970; Chgo. medal of merit for civic contbns., 1972; named Man of Year Chgo. Conv. Bur., 1965. Roman Catholic. Address: 7006 S Bennett St Chicago IL 60649

WILD, RUTH FRIEDA ELIZABETH SCHAADT (MRS. ANTON JOSEPH WILD), packaging machinery co. exec.; b. Baden, Germany, Jan. 22, 1923; d. Adolf and Frieda (Pfeiffer) Schaadt; came to U.S., 1925, naturalized, 1944; student pub. schs.; m. Anton Joseph Wild, Apr. 28, 1945; children—William Karl, Susan Joyce. Solderer, Forstner Chain Co., Irvington, N.J., 1941-45; disbursing office Dept. Navy, Norfolk, Va., 1945-46; sec.-treas. Wild & Schulze, Inc., Kenilworth, N.J., 1958—. Mem. Am. Legion Aux. Presbyn. (Sunday sch. tchr. 1955-58). Clubs: Bavarian; Maplewood Country (bowling chmn.). Home: 310 Springfield Av Westfield NJ 07090 Office: 835 Fairfield Av Kenilworth NJ 07033

WILDE, MARY LEE LIPPERT (MRS. REDGE ARTHUR WILDE), occupational therapist; b. Youngstown, O., Oct. 17, 1948; d. John Leon and Martha Lee (Bratcher) Lippert; B.S., Ohio State U., 1970, postgrad., 1970—; m. Redge Arthur Wilde, July 11, 1970. Occupational therapist Neil Av. Sch., Columbus Pub. Schs. (O.), 1970-73, chmn., 1971-72, coordinator occupational therapy and phys. therapy dept., 1971-72; occupational therapist Ohio Sch. for Deaf, Columbus, 1973—. Mem. clin. faculty occupational therapy dept. Ohio State U., 1973, mem., sec., clin. council, 1971-73; judge high sch. and collegiate gymnastics competition, 1970—. Mem. World Fedn. Occupational Therapy, Council Exceptional Children, Am., Ohio, Columbus (chmn. developmental disabilities spl. interest group 1973—) occupational therapy assns., Kappa Delta. Home: Apt 206 60 E Norwich St Columbus OH 43201 Office: 500 Morse Rd Columbus OH 45214

WILDE, PATRICIA LORRAIN-ANN (MRS. GEORGE BARDYGUINE), dancer; b. Ottawa, Ont., Can.; d. John Herbert and Eileen (Simpson) White; student Am. Sch. Ballet, N.Y.C., 1943; m. George Bardyguine, Dec. 14, 1953. Came to U.S., 1943, naturalized, 1957. Dancer with Marquis de Quevas Ballet Internat., 1944, Ballet Russe de Monte Carlo, 1945-49, Roland Petit Ballet de Paris, 1949, Met. Ballet, Eng., 1949; prin. dancer N.Y.C. Ballet, 1950-65, regional rep., tchr. Sch. Am. Ballet, 1964—; dir. Sch. Ballet, Harkness House for Ballet, Arts; tchr., rehearsal dir. Am. Ballet Theatre Co. and Sch., 1969—; prof. dance State U. N.Y. at Purchase. Recipient award Dance Educators Am., 1957. Mem. A.F.T.R.A., Am. Guild Mus. Artists, Nat. Assn. for Regional Ballet (dir.). Choreographer: Palio, A Festival in Siena, 1964; At the Ball (commd. by N.Y. Philharmonic Orch.), 1965.

WILDER, ANNETTE BEDFORD (MRS. EUGENE WILDER), librarian; b. Natchez, Miss.; d. George Madison and Ella (Ford) Bedford; B.A., Miss. Woman's Coll., 1929; postgrad. Tulane U., 1932, U. So. Miss., 1940; M.L.S., Peabody Library Sch., 1948; m. Eugene Wilder, July 10, 1919; 1 son, Eugene. Instr. French and Spanish U. So. Miss., 1928-33, librarian Demonstration Sch., 1940-55, acquisitions librarian, asst. prof. library sci., 1955-60, reference librarian, 1960-64, reference librarian, asso. prof., 1964—. Pres., Hattiesburg Music Club, 1927-28; chmn. bd. dirs. Hattiesburg Civic Music Assn., 1927-29; v.p. Original Home and Garden Club, 1938-39; pres. Hattiesburg High Sch. P.T.A., 1938-39; bd. dirs. Garden Clubs of Miss., 1938-42; sec. bd. dirs. Hattiesburg Community Chest, 1942-43; chmn. bd. dirs. Hattiesburg council Girl Scouts Am., 1942; with Canteen Corps, A.R.C., 1942-45; pres. Womans Club, 1954-55; trustee Hattiesburg Pub. Library, 1955—, chmn., 1958-61; bd. dirs. Miss. dist. YWCA, 1956-60, Hattiesburg br. Am. Assn. U. Women Scholarship Fund, 1953. Mem. Am., Southeastern, Miss. library assns., D.A.R. (regent John Rolfe chpt., 1955-57, registrar Norvell Robertson chpt., 1961—), Daus. Am. Colonists (state regent, 1964-67, So. regional chmn., 1967—), Daus. Founders and Patriots Am. (state sec. 1957-60, state registrar 1970—), Magna Charta Dames, Order Americans of Armorial Ancestry, Order 1st Families of Miss., Colonial Dames Am., Delta Kappa Gamma (chpt. pres. 1968-70), Sigma Delta Pi, Pi Delta Phi, Kappa Delta Pi. Baptist. Address: 902 W Pine Hattiesburg MS 39401

WILDER, FREDERICA W., ret. sch. adminstr.; b. Courtland, Ariz., July 23, 1909; d. Frederick William and Anna (Royer) Wilder; B.A., U. Ariz., 1929; M.A., Columbia, 1950. Tchr. pub. schs., Douglas, Ariz., 1929-37; mem. teaching, adminstrv. staffs Tucson pub. schs., 1937-74, asst. supt. elementary edn., 1965-71, asst. supt. ednl. programs, 1971-74. Mem. adv. bd. family, child care div. Tucson Community Council, 1969-71; mem. Prevention Drug Abuse Coalition, 1970-71; dist. chmn. United Way campaign, 1973. Served with Women's Res., USMCR, 1943-46. Recipient Distinguished Citizen's award U. Ariz. Alumni Assn., 1974. Mem. Nat., Ariz., Tucson edn. assns., Ariz. Assn. Elementary Sch. Adminstrs. (pres. 1959-60), Internat. Comparative Edn. Soc., Assn. Supervision and Curriculum Devel., Nat. Assn. Elementary Sch. Prins., Nat. Council Adminstrv. Women in Edn., P.T.A. (hon. life), Pi Beta Phi. Club: Altrusa of Tucson (past pres. club; trustee spl. funds 1971—). Home: 4417 La Jolla Circle Tucson AZ 85711

WILDER, JOAN KATHLEEN, educator; b. Detroit, Dec. 1, 1932; d. John E. and Marie L. (Reynolds) Wilder; B.S. magna cum laude, U. Detroit, 1955, M.A., 1962; Ph.D., U. Wis., 1970. Tchr. Detroit pub. schs., 1955-59, critic tchr., 1958-59; tchr. Detroit parochial schs., 1959-62; recreation dir. City of Detroit, 1954-59; faculty U. Detroit, 1962—, now prof. edn.; teaching asst. U. Wis., 1964. Mem. Soc. Profs. Edn., History of Edn. Soc., Am. Ednl. Studies Assn., Nat. Humanities Assn., Pi Lambda Theta, Alpha Sigma Lambda. Author: Plan Book for Beginning Teachers, 1962. Office: U Detroit 4001 W McNichols Detroit MI 48221

WILDER, LESLIE JANE, editor; b. Gloucester, Mass., Oct. 10, 1934; d. Earle Forrest and Hildur Geraldine (Wester) Wilder; B.A., U. Mass., 1956. Copywriter, Radio Sta. WPOR, Portland, Me., 1957-58; traffic mgr. WGAN-TV, Portland, 1958-62; pub. information writer Peace Corps, Washington, 1963-66; writer, editor U.S. Dept. Commerce, Washington, 1966—. Sec., Foggy Bottom Assn., Washington, 1970-71, editor newspaper, 1970-72. Recipient Spl. Achievement award U.S. Dept. Commerce, 1972. Mem. Women in Communications, Am. Newspaper Women's Club. Home: 940 25th St NW Apt 816S Washington DC 20037 Office: US Dept Commerce Washington DC 20230

WILDER, MARION BURT (MRS. RICHARD BETHELL WILDER), civic worker; b. N.Y.C.; d. George Frederick and Grace (Knight) Burt; student pvt. schs.; m. John Williams Morgan; 1 son, George Frederick; m. Richard Bethell Wilder, Oct. 27, 1972. Vice pres. Internat. Garden Club, Pelham, N.Y., 1961—; hon. pres. women's com. Judson Health Center, 1949—, bd. govs., 1946-60, hon. life mem. bd. govs.; bd. dirs. Samaritan Home for Aged, 1950-58; bd. govs. N.Y. Women's Bible Soc., 1947-57. Mem. Nat. Inst. Social Scis., Nat. Soc. Colonial Dames, Nat. Trust for Historic Preservation, Am. Fedn. Arts, Huguenot Soc. Am., Soc. Daus. Holland Dames (bd. govs.). Soc. of Four Arts. Clubs: Colony (N.Y.C.); Bath and Tennis, Everglades (Palm Beach, Fla.). Episcopalian. Home: 30 E 65th St New York City NY 10021 also 389 S Lake Dr Palm Beach FL 33480 and Twin Brooks Kent CT 06757

WILDER, MARY ANN HACKETT (MRS. CHARLES WILDER), educator; b. Phila.; d. William Gorden and Cornelia (Johnson) Hackett; R.N., Lincoln Sch. for Nurses, 1939; B.S., N.Y.U., 1945, M.A., 1947, M.Pub. Adminstrn., 1974; profl. certificate in guidance, counseling, adminstrn. Bklyn. Coll., 1955; postgrad. Nat. Def. Edn. Act Guidance and Counseling Inst., 1963-64; m. Charles Wilder, July 29, 1937 (dec. Jan. 1961); children—Richard Christopher II, Agnes Cornelia. Pub. health nurse Bklyn. Vis. Nurse Assn., 1942-45; gen. duty nurse Cumberland Hosp., 1939-42; tchr. nurse edn. Yorkville High Sch., Manhattan, N.Y., 1947-66; counselor Day High Sch., N.Y.C., 1966-72, James Madison High Sch., Bklyn., 1966-72; counselor educator City U. N.Y. Grad. Sch. Guidance and Counseling, 1972—. Interviewer, tester Early Developmental Childhood Program, N.Y. Med. Coll., N.Y.C., 1964. Instr. A.R.C., Bklyn. chpt., 1945-53; jr. coordinator high sch. A.R.C., 1950-56; asst. examiner Bd. Edn., N.Y.C., 1950—; counselor Bklyn. Adult Tng. Center, Manpower Developmental Tng. Program, 1965; mem. exec. bd. Cath. Interracial Council, 1962-65; mem. L.I. Coordinator Council Voter Registration, 1962-63; pres. Nassau chpt. Jack and Jill of Am. Corp., 1962-65. Recipient Service Pin, A.R.C., Mem. Pub. Health Nurses Assn., Jack and Jill Nat. Found., Am. Personnel and Guidance Assn., Ednl. and Vocational Counselor's Assn., Key Women Am., Inc., City Wide Orgn. Health Services, Kappa Delta Pi, Pi Lambda Theta. Club: Newman (coordinator for high sch. 1949-66) (N.Y.C.). Author: (with Marguerite C. Holmes) Practical Nursing Examination Review Book, 1965, rev. edit., 1968. Home: 34 Forest Av Freeport NY 11520 Office: 3787 Bedford Av Brooklyn NY 11229

WILDERMAN, ANN MCPHERSON, educator; b. Knoxville, Tenn., June 6, 1935; d. Ben Hill and Dorothy Dee (Horne) McPherson; B.S., U. Tenn., 1958, M.S., 1961, Ed.D., 1967; married. Elementary tchr., Oak Ridge, 1958-67; vis. prof. U. Tenn., 1969-70, U. Del., 1973; prof. elementary edn. Temple U., Phila., 1967—; math. cons. Tenn., Va., Ga., Ky., Pa., N.J., N.H., Conn. Mem. N.E.A., Nat. Council Tchrs. Math., Am. Assn. Colls. of Tchr. Edn., Am. Ednl. Research Assn., Pa. Edn. Assn., Delta Kappa Gamma. Author: Metric Measurement Simplified, 1974; Mathematics Card Games, 1974. Editor, contbr. articles profl. jours. Home: 200 Jupiter Rd Newark DE 19711

WILDMAN, AUDREY MARIE, psychologist; b. Chgo., Oct. 3, 1920; d. John Murray and Muriel Grace (Camp) Long; B.A., Central Wash. State Coll., Ellensburg, 1954, M.Ed., 1957; postgrad. Western Wash. Coll., 1962, U. Utah, 1963, U. Cal. at Santa Cruz, 1968-69, Cal. State U. at San Jose, 1968-69, Pepperdine Coll., 1969. Tchr., Weston (Ore.) High Sch., 1954-55; tchr. adult edn. classes in psychology, Moses Lake, Wash., 1955-57; counselor Moses Lake Jr. High Sch., 1955-57; tchr. Longview (Wash.) Jr. Coll., 1957-58; sch. psychologist pub. schs., Longview, 1957-61, Tri-Cities Spl. Edn. Dept., Richland, Wash., 1961-64, Monterey County Office Edn., Salinas, Cal., 1965—. Mem. Am., Cal., Western Regional, Monterey Bay psychol. assns., Cal. Sch. Psychologists and Psychometrists Assn., Assn. Cal. Sch. Adminstrs. Home: 25262 Flanders Dr Carmel CA 93921 Office: Monterey County Office Edn Blanco Rd Salinas CA 93901

WILES, MARGARET CHIPMAN, accountant; b. Hays, N.C., Sept. 15, 1921; d. Thomas Luther and Lura Ellen (Wiles) Chipman; grad. Chillicothe Bus. Coll., 1953; m. John Dale Wiles, Sept. 3, 1938 (div. Jan. 1967); children—John Kenneth, Randall Craig. Secretarial position Ohio Valley Baking Co., Chillicothe, O., 1953-54; accountant, purchasing agt. Chipman Furniture Co., North Wilkesboro, N.C., 1959-61; accountant, sec. Wilkes YMCA, North Wilkesboro, 1961—. Treas. Mountain View Sch. P.T.A., 1963; collector Wilkes United Fund, 1963-73; sec., reporter Wilkes YMCA Women's Bowling League, 1964-72; residential capt. Cancer Fund, 1972; chmn. concessions com., mem. finance com. Wilkes Jr. Miss Pageant, 1973. Mem. Grange (mem. youth com. 1958-59). Baptist (pres. Bapt. Community Service Club 1964-65). Home: Route 1 Box 151 Hays NC 28635 Office: PO Box 846 North Wilkesboro NC 28659

WILEY, BONNIE JEANNE, taxonomic mycologist; b. Moline, Ill., Oct. 16, 1937; d. Thomas Laverne and Gladys Jeane (Mayne) Wiley; B.S. in Edn., Western Ill. U., 1959; M.S., Kan. State U., 1963. Research microbiologist U.S. Army Natick (Mass.) Labs., 1963—. Mem. Mycological Soc. Am., Bot. Soc. Am., Brit. Mycological Soc., Am. Inst. Biol. Scis., Sigma Xi, Kappa Delta Pi, Sigma Zeta, Beta Beta Beta. Basic research and publs. in morphology, cytology and physiology of fungi. Office: US Army Natick Labs Natick MA 01760

WILEY, KATHERINE HOYT, educator; b. Mpls.; d. Alfred E. and Grace (Hoyt) Wiley; B.A., Los Angeles Coll., 1960; M.A., San Francisco State Coll., 1966; m. Ernest Salomon, Aug. 16, 1947 (div. June 1962). Legal sec. to Justice Marshall F. McComb, 1928-43; actress films, radio, tv, 1944-54; sec. to U.S. Consul Gen., Shanghai, China, 1932-33; with Cal. State Coll. system, 1954—, adminstrv. asst. to chmn. div. psychology, ednl. health scis. and phys. edn. Sonoma State Coll., 1968-70, asso. prof. psychology and expressive arts, dir. advising, 1970—. Mem. Am. Assn. U. Women, Assn. Cal. State Coll. Profs., Rec. for Blind, Alpha Phi, Pi Lambda Theta. Democrat. Home: 3032 Yulupa Av Santa Rosa CA 95405 Office: 1801 E Cotati Av Rohnert Park CA 94928

WILEY, MARY ALICE, assn. exec.; b. San Pedro, Cal., Nov. 29, 1941; d. George Asa and Dorothy Lucille (Crostic) Kuehne; A.A., Harbor Coll., 1961; m. Michael David Wiley, Dec. 16, 1961; children—David Michael II, Heather Jane. Sec. to plant mgr. Reynolds Metals Co., Torrance, Cal., 1961; sec. dept. zoology U. Wash., Seattle, 1962-67; bus. mgr. Am. Soc. Zoologists, Thousand Oaks, Cal., 1967—. Democrat. Methodist. Home: 10881 Citrus Dr Moorpark CA 93021 Office: Box 2739 Cal Luth Coll Thousand Oaks CA 91360

WILEY, MICHELE MARY (MRS. HARRY JAMES WILEY), coll. adminstr.; b. Boston, Feb. 21, 1944; d. Hal and Naomi Audrey (Schoville) Weiss; B.S., U. Wis., 1966; postgrad. Northwestern U., 1966-67; m. Harry James Wiley, Dec. 13, 1968. Pub. safety specialist writer, dept. pub. information Nat. Safety Council, Chgo., 1966-68; writer information office Nixon-Agnew Com., N.Y.C., 1968; communicator Office of Communications, Portland (Ore.) State U., 1968—. Bd. dirs. Monday through Friday Bd., 1972-73. Presidential citation for loyal service and spl. contbn. Ore. Assn. Editors and Communicators, 1973. Mem. Women in Communications (treas. 1973-74, pres. elect 1974-75), Ore. Assn. Editors and Communicators (workshop coordinator 1973-74), Pub. Relations Roundtable, Pi Beta Phi. Club: Metro Women's (dir. 1972-74) (Portland, Ore.). Home: 8545 SW Fairway Dr Portland OR 87225

WILEY, NAN HEILEMANN (MRS. VERYL OTIS WILEY), food writer; b. Forest Park, Ill.; d. Henry R. and Edith (Kunz) Hellemann; student Chgo. Acad. Fine Arts, 1922; m. Veryl Otis Wiley, July 30, 1924; children—Jayne (Mrs. Paul A. Dodder), John Kendall. Dir. Happy Kitchen radio, TV shows sta. KMBC, Kansas City, Mo., 1950-53; writer retail fashion advt., 1953-58; food cons. Safeway Stores, Inc., Kansas City, 1958-62; columnist foods dept. Kansas City Star, 1962-67; syndicated food columist Let's Ask the Cook, Register-Tribune Syndicate, Des Moines, 1967—. Named nat. contest winner women's new radio shows, Billboard Mag., 1949. Author: Let's Ask the Cook, 1970; (cookbook) The Best of Let's Ask the Cook, 1973. Home: 8101 E 87th Kansas City MO 64138 Office: Register-Tribune Syndicate Des Moines IA 50304

WILHELM, MARY LOU, librarian; b. Custer, S.D., Sept. 27, 1937; d. John Albert and Mary (Koch) W.; B.S., Concordia Tchrs. Coll., 1960; M.S., U. So. Cal., 1966. Catalog-reference librarian San Marino (Cal.) Pub. Library, 1964-66; librarian Orange Coast Coll. Library, Costa Mesa, Cal., 1966-67, library dir., 1967—. Mem. Cal., Orange County library assns., Cal. Jr. Coll. Assn. Home: 23481 Los Adornos St Laguna Hills CA 92653 Office: 2701 Fairview Rd Costa Mesa CA 92626

WILHELM, MURIEL L., ednl. adminstr.; b. Elizabeth, N.J., Jan. 6, 1922; d. William Carroll and Leona (Kempe) Wilhelm; B.S., Russell Sage Coll., 1943; M.A., Columbia, 1961, profl. diploma, 1964. Tchr. phys. edn. Windham (N.Y.) Central Sch., 1943-44; successively service rep., chief clk., asst. staff supr. N.J. Bell Telephone Co., Elizabeth, 1946-61; asst. registrar, asst. dir. admissions Newark State Coll., 1961-66; registrar Middlesex County Coll., 1966-69; coordinator ind. study program State U. N.Y.-Empire State Coll., 1969-72, coll. registrar, 1972—. Active United Fund, March of Dimes. Served with Women's Res., USMC, 1944-46. Mem. Am. Assn. Collegiate Registrars and Admissions Officers, Russell Sage Coll. Alumnae Assn. (pres. 1971—), Kappa Delta Pi, Pi Lambda Theta. Office: 2 Union Av Saratoga Springs NY 12866

WILHELM, ROWENA MAY (MRS. ROSS JOHNSTON WILHELM), educator; b. Independence, Mo., July 7, 1917; d. Alvin Roderick and Clara Anderson (Bradbury) May; B.A., Washburn U., 1939; M.A., U. Mich., 1962, Ed.S., 1970, Ph.D. in Ednl. Psychology, 1971; m. Ross Johnston Wilhelm, Jan. 3, 1944; 1 son, Peter Bradbury. Student therapist Menninger Clinic, Topeka, 1939-41; asst. dir. occupational therapy Cherokee (Ia.) State Hosp., 1941-43; recreational dir. A.R.C., St. Louis, 1943-45; occupational therapist Ann Arbor (Mich.) Sch., 1949-50, 54-56; asst. psychologist Reading and Learning Skills Center U. Mich., Ann Arbor, 1962-70, chief, 1971—. Cons. in field; mem. editorial adv. bd. Nat. Reading Conf., 1974-75. Mem. Internat., Southeastern Mich. (pres. 1970), Mich., North Central reading assns., Washtenaw Reading Council, Am., Mich. psychol. assns., Kappa Alpha Theta, Pi Gamma Mu, Phi Delta Kappa. Club: Women's City (Ann Arbor). Home: 710 Greenhill Dr Ann Arbor MI 48104

WILHELMI, KRISTINE MARIE, theater ofcl.; b. Burlington, Wis., Jan. 5, 1948; d. Elmer Herman and Jean Helen (Tomlinson) Ebert; grad. high sch.; m. Jeffrey Allen Wilhelmi, Oct. 2, 1970. Soc. editor Pictorial News-Advertiser, Burlington, 1965-66; reporter-photographer Racine (Wis.) Jour. Time, 1970-73; prodn. chmn. Haylofter's, Inc., theatre, 1973—. Mem. Burlington Bd. Zoning Appeals. Sec., publicity chmn. Wis. Fedn. Young Republicans, 1968—. Named Miss Wis. Young Rep., 1968. Mem. Women in Communications (chpt. pres. 1969-70), Bus. and Profl. Women's Club (chpt. sec. 1973). Home: 449 Summit Av Burlington WI 53105 Office: 189 W Chestnut St Burlington WI 53105

WILHELMI, SISTER MARY MARCIA, hosp. adminstr.; b. Seney, Ia., Oct. 10, 1921; d. Frank Joseph and Mary Frances (Block) Wilhelmi; R.N., St. Joseph Mercy Coll. Nursing, 1945; B.S., Mercy Coll. Detroit, 1959; M.H.A., U. Mich., 1962. Joined Religious Sisters Mercy, 1939; nursing supr. St. Joseph Mercy Hosp., Sioux City, Ia., 1945-47, 53-58, St. Joseph Mercy Hosp., Dubuque, Ia., 1947-48, Leila Hosp., Battle Creek, Mich., 1948-53; nursing supr. St. Joseph Mercy Hosp., Ft. Dodge, Ia., 1958-62, adminstr., 1974—; asst. adminstr. St. Mary's Hosp., Grand Rapids, Mich., 1962-64; adminstr. Mercy Community Hosp., Manistee, Mich., 1964-67, St. Joseph Mercy Hosp., Waverly, Ia., 1967-71, Our Lady Mercy Hosp., Dyer, Ind., 1971-73. Pres. Sisters Mercy of Hammond, Inc., 1972—. Pres. Local Dist. Planning, 1972-73; sec. Hosp. Community Devel. Com., 1965-66. Address: Our Lady of Mercy Hospital Lincoln Hwy 30 Dyer IN 46311

WILKE, IRENE MARGARET, civic worker; b. Waco, Neb., Nov. 13, 1911; d. George F. and Anna Louise (Barth) Snyder; student Kearney Coll., 1928-72; m. Leonard H. Wilke, Dec. 28, 1931 (dec. 1970); children—Loren A., Lloyd A. Tchr., York County, Neb., 1929-30. Pres. local Girl Scout Council, 1964-66; sec. Grand Island Unit Parliamentarian, 1973-74; pres. Am. Legion Aux., 1969-70; policy adv. council bd. Am. Cancer Soc. Mem. Ravenna (Neb.) Housing Authority Bd., 1966—. Recipient Thanks badge Girl Scouts Am., 1965; Good Neighbor award Aksarben, 1969; named Outstanding Citizen Ravenna, 1970. Mem. Nat. Assn. Parliamentarians, Fed. Woman's Club (pres. Neb. dist. 6 1968-70), Fed. Garden Club. Lutheran (Sunday sch. tchr.). Address: 313 Buell Av Ravenna NE 68869

WILKE, MARION FLORENCE (MRS. RICHARD ERWIN WILKE), newspaperwoman; b. Watertown, Wis., May 11, 1932; d. Theodore Christian and Florence (Schroeder) Voigt; B.A., U. Wis., 1954; M.A., Rockford Coll., 1968; m. Richard Erwin Wilke, Dec. 16, 1955; children—Susan, Theodore, Julia. Society editor Dubuque (Ia.) Telegraph-Herald, 1954-55; with Rockford (Ill.) Morning Star and Register-Republic, 1955—, family page editor, 1970-72, editorial writer, 1972—, editor editorial pages, 1973—. Second v.p. Rock River Valley council Girl Scouts U.S.A. Lutheran. Home: 2630 Craig Hill Dr Rockford IL 61109 Office: 97 E State St Rockford IL 61104

WILKES, ANNE PALMER (MRS. GEORGE RUSSELL WILKES), artist; b. Clinton, Ia., Feb. 22, 1923; d. Charles Fremont and Mary Edna (Mitchell) McConnell; student Chgo. Art Inst., 1938-40; pvt. study with various artists, 1950-70; m. George Russell Wilkes, Feb. 22, 1944; children—George Russell, Christopher John, Barton Charles. Art tchr. South Colonie (N.Y.) Sch. System, 1970-74; exhibited group shows Albany (N.Y.) Inst. History and Art, Albany Art Gallery, N.Y. State Capital Shows, Albany Artist Group Ann. Juried Shows, numerous invitational area exhibits, 1955—; represented in numerous pvt. collections; instr. adult edn. fine art Colonie, N.Y., 1970-73. Pres. Sch. 26 P.T.A., Albany, N.Y., 1951-53, Westland Hills Little League, Albany, N.Y., 1955. Served with WAVES, 1942-44. Mem. N.Y. State Tchrs. Assn., Albany Artist Group (dir. 1970-72). Lutheran. Home: 30 Danker Av Albany NY 12206

WILKES, CHERYL WHELCHEL (MRS. JAMES BURPEE WILKES), coll. adminstr.; b. Alma, Ga., July 20, 1944; d. John Davis and Charnell (Ramsey) Whelchel; A.B. cum laude, U. Ga., 1966, M.A., 1968; m. James Burpee Wilkes, Sept. 10, 1967; 1 son, John William. Research asst. Inst. Govt., Athens, Ga., 1966-67; asso. editor Naval Weapons Evaluation Facility, Albuquerque, 1968-69; dir. student financial aid and career planning and placement Augusta (Ga.) Coll., 1969—, instr. journalism, 1971—. Vice pres. Augusta Panhellenic Council, 1972-73. Bd. dirs., v.p. Augusta (Ga.) Met. YWCA. Mem. Nat., So., Ga. assns. student financial aid adminstrs., Ga., So. coll. placement councils, Ga. Assn. Women Deans, Adminstrs. and Counselors, Jr. League Augusta (provisional), Mortar Bd., Phi Beta Kappa, Phi Kappa Phi, Phi Mu. Home: 750 Malvern Lane Augusta GA 30904 Office: 2500 Walton Way Augusta GA 30904

WILKES, MARGARET LEE (MRS. HILBERT GARRISON WILKES), vol. ch. worker; b. Taft, Cal., July 4, 1916; d. Mervyn Jefferson and Jennie Maude (Renfro) Boggs; student Long Beach Jr. Coll., 1934-35, U. Cal., Berkeley, 1936-37; m. Hilbert Garrison; children—Russell Mervyn, Timothy Northcutt. Pres., North Hollywood Ch. Women United, 1950; chmn. bd., pres. congregation North Hollywood First Christian Ch., 1958; chmn. bd., moderator Christian Ch. in So. Cal.-So. Nev., 1967-70; first vice-moderator Christian Ch. (Disciples of Christ) in U.S. and Can., 1971-73, also mem. gen. bd., bd. higher edn., former mem. bd. unified promotion, mem. delegation to Consultation on Ch. Union. Fraternal visitor from Christian Ch. to Asia, 1972. Formerly active North Hollywood P.T.A., Boy Scouts Am., Am. Field Service; mem. Sierra Club, North Hollywood YMCA. Former mem. bd. dirs. Disciples Sem. Found., Internat. Christian Scholarship Found., Pacific S.W. Conf. on World Christian Mission; bd. dirs. Disciples Homes Corp., Council on Christian Unity. Mem. Lake County, Mo. hist. socs., Cal. Alumni Assn. U. Cal. (life), Am. Bonsai Soc. Mem. Disciples of Christ (life patron). Republican. Address: 4363 Lemp Av North Hollywood CA 91604*

WILKES, MARGIE LOUISE, city ofcl.; b. Stoneburg, Tex., Apr. 1, 1933; d. Floyd Matthew and Frances Elizabeth (Faulkner) Segler; student Southwestern Union Coll., Keene, Tex., 1953-54; m. Harold Eugene Wilkes, Jan. 27, 1957; children—Julie Ann, Charles Eugene, David Alan, Terry Wayne. With Pitts. Testing Labs., Baton Rouge, 1954-57, Bell Helicopter Co., Ft. Worth, 1957-67, 70; finance officer, tax assessor/collector City of Keene (Tex.), 1970—. Mem. Tex. Assn. Assessing Officers, Finance Officers Assn. U.S. and Can. Home: 317 S Fairview St Keene TX 76059 Office: 100 N Mockingbird St Keene TX 76059

WILKEY, LUCILLE VIVIEN, realtor, pianist, composer; b. Yeddo, Ind.; d. Elmer Sylvester and Madge (Dunn) Wilkey; A.B., U. Ill., 1919; postgrad. Ind. U., De Pauw U., Brenau Coll. Tchr. French, Spanish Ohio U., 1920-21, Ariz. State Coll., 1921-22; tchr. adult edn., Long Beach, Cal., 1926-35; real estate broker Lucille V. Wilkey Firm, Long Beach, 1943—; composer ballads including Another Day, 1942, Spring's Again in the Heart of Me, 1948. Capt. Community Chest, Long Beach, 1957-58, A.R.C., Long Beach, 1958-74, Heart Assn., Long Beach, 1963-64. Active Council Republican Women. Bd. dirs. Long Beach Symphony, 1964-65, Long Beach Council Music, 1964-65. Medalist Eisteddfod piano open, Los Angeles, 1925, Long Beach, 1926; recipient City of Hope award, 1960, Community Chest award, 1960. Mem. Long Beach Art Assn. (dir. 1945-46), So. Cal. Opera Guild, D.A.R., Ret. Tchrs. Club (dir. 1964-65, 74), Am. Bus. Women's Assn. (dir. 1964-65, 74), Long Beach Realty Bd., Gamma Pi Gamma (charter), Alpha Chi Omega. Methodist. Club: Musical Arts (pres. 1943-44, 64-65). Home: 2230 Pasadena Av Long Beach CA 90806 Office: 2387 Atlantic Av Long Beach CA 90807

WILKIE, HARRIET DOROTHY SMITH (MRS. GEORGE DWIGHT WILKIE), artist; b. Boston, July 15, 1919; s. Lewis Elba and Edith May (Allen) Smith; grad. Kents Bus. Sch., Auburn, N.Y., 1938; student Cayuga Mus. History and Art, Auburn, 1947-50, 52-56; m. George Dwight Wilkie, Jan. 16, 1945; children—Susan Ann, Patricia Jean. Free-lance art work, 1956—; oil portraits include Mrs. Kenney, Mrs. Belmont, Mrs. Kitchens, Sherif Hussein Ben Ahmid and others; one-man show Cayuga Mus. of History and Art, 1961; exhibited in group shows at Everson Mus., Syracuse, Bible House, N.Y.C., Mpls., N.Y. State Capitol, Albany, N.Y. Telephone Bldg., Syracuse, N.Y. State Fair, 1974, others; represented in permanent collection Grumbacher Pallette Collection, Marine Midland Collection; instr. youth div. art classes Cayuga Mus. History and Art, 1960; with marketing dept. Marine Midland Bank-Central, Syracuse, 1966—. Recipient award for collage, indsl. art show, Syracuse, 1974. Mem. Asso. Artists Syracuse, Finger Lakes Art Retreat Assn., Baldwinsville Art Guild, Am. Harp Soc., Syracuse Bus. and Profl. Women. Presbyn. Club: Daubers of Auburn (N.Y.) (past pres., v.p. and program chmn.). Home: Village Green E83 Baldwinsville NY 13027

WILKIN, KAREN LINDA KISSIN (MRS. RICHARD LEIGH WILKIN), art gallery ofcl.; b. N.Y.C., Dec. 6, 1940; d. Milton and Jean (Gurkin) Kissin; B.A. cum laude, Barnard Coll., 1962; M.F.A. (Murray fellow, Brevoort-Eickemeyer fellow), Columbia, 1963; m. Richard Leigh Wilkin, Aug. 11, 1966. Chief curator Edmonton (Alta.) Art Gallery, 1971—. Writer art criticism, 1971. Fulbright fellow, 1964-65; Hon. Woodrow Wilson fellow. Home: 9831 87th Av Edmonton AB Canada Office: Edmonton Art Gallery 2 Churchill Sq Edmonton AB Canada

WILKINS, ALICE LINA, librarian; b. Fillmore, N.Y., May 4, 1939; d. John Marshall and Lila (Scarborough) Andrews; B.A., Houghton Coll., 1960; M.S. in Library Sci., Columbia, 1962; m. David Bruce Wilkins, Aug. 26, 1961; children—Julie Renee, Melissa Lynne. Asst. librarian U.S. Steel Corp., N.Y.C., 1960-62; cataloger Fairleigh-Dickinson U., Madison, N.J., 1963-65; catalog librarian Joint Univ. Libraries, Nashville, 1965-67; tech. services librarian Kings Co., Briarcliff Manor, N.Y., 1967—; cons. tech. services Briarcliff Coll., Briarcliff Manor, N.Y., 1968—. Mem. Am., N.Y. State, Westchester library assns. Contbr. to profl. jours. Home: 48 McKeel Av Tarrytown NY 10591 Office: The King's Coll. Library Briarcliff Manor NY 10510

WILKINS, CAROLINE HANKE, polit. party ofcl.; b. Corpus Christi, Tex., May 12, 1937; d. Louis Allen and Agnes Jean (Guckian) Hanke; B.A., U. Tex., 1961; M.A. magna cum laude, U. Americas; m. Billy Hughel Wilkins, Aug. 31, 1957; 1 son, Brian Hughel. Instr. history Ore. State U., 1967-68. Democratic precinct committeewoman, 1964—; del. Ore. Dem. Conv., 1966, 68, 70, 72, 74, Dem. vice chmn. 1st Congl. Dist., 1966-68, Dem. vice chmn. Benton County, 1966-70; mem. platform and resolutions com., mem. credentials com., sects. chmn. resources com. Ore. Pre-primary, 1968; vice chmn. Dem. Party Ore., 1968-69, Dem. elector, 1968, mem. credentials com. state conv., 1968; Ore. Dem. chmn., 1969—; mem. exec. com. Western States Dem. Conf., 1970-72; mem. arrangements com. Nat. Dem. Conv., 1972; vice chmn. Dem. Nat. Com., 1972—; mem. Dem. Nat. Charter Commn., 1972—; del. from Ore. Dem. Nat. Conf., 1974. Named Woman of Achievement Ore. State U., 1973. Mem. Assn. State Dem. Chmn. (v.p. 1970-73). Home: 3311 NW Roosevelt St Corvallis OR 97330 Office: Box 189 Corvallis OR 97330

WILKINS, JANET ROSEMARY, profl. assn. exec.; b. N.Y.C., Oct. 30, 1917; d. Harvey and Jeannette (Symes) Wilkins; B.S. magna cum laude, N.Y. U., 1939, postgrad., 1944-46. Security analyst Mfrs. Hanover Trust bank, N.Y.C., 1942-51; research economist Am. Can Co., N.Y.C., 1951-54; producer audio-visual programs Nat. Assn. Mfrs., 1954-63; free lance writer First Nat. City Bank, N.Y.C., 1963-64; recruitment specialist Girl Scouts U.S., N.Y.C., 1964-66; mgr. econ. analysis and long range planning MacManus, John & Adams, advt. agy., N.Y.C., 1966-67; dir. membership Nat. League Nursing, 1967—. Photographer; lectr. on travel and audio-visual techniques at clubs and workshops; tchr. photography and audio-visual techniques Bronxville Adult Sch., 1973-74. Trustee Westchester County Hist. Soc. Mem. Nat. Visual Presentation Assn. (dir. 1958-64), Com. on Internat. Non-Theatrical Events (dir. 1961-65), Am. Assn. U. Women, Bronxville League Women Voters, Photog. Soc. Am. (recipient APSA award for service 1971), Beta Gamma Sigma, Mu Gamma Tau. Episcopalian. Clubs: Bronxville Camera (founder, past pres.), Bronxville Field. Home: 3 Alden Pl Bronxville NY 10708 Office: 10 Columbus Circle New York City NY 10019

WILKINS, LILLIAN CARLET LINDSAY (MRS. WILLIAM REGINALD WILKINS), banker; b. Dare, Va., Dec. 21, 1911; d. Charles Victor and Della (Crockett) Lindsay; student Coll. William and Mary, 1929-30; m. William Reginald Wilkins, May 22, 1943. Office mgr., store and office trainer Montgomery Ward & Co., Newport News, Va., 1937-46; office mgr., cashier Terminal Stockyard Co. and Levinson Livestock Co., Newport News, 1946-56; credit mgr., cashier Benel Corp., Newport News, 1952-56; mgr. mortgage loan dept. United Va. Bank Williamsburg (formerly Peninsula Bank & Trust Co.), Williamsburg, Va., 1956-59, asst. treas., 1959—, asst. v.p., 1959-62, asst. sec., 1960—, v.p., 1962—. Treas., Williamsburg Cancer Crusade, 1960-61; treas. Williamsburg Area Recreational Assn., 1963-64. Mem. Nat. Assn. Bank Women (regional v.p. 1962-63, treas. 1964-66, nat. v.p. 1966-67, pres. 1967-68), Bus. and Profl. Women's Club (treas. Williamsburg 1964-65, 1st v.p. 1965-66, pres. 1966-67), Am. Bankers Assn. (exec. com. 1968-69). Methodist. Mem. Order Eastern Star. Clubs: Soroptimist (pres. 1962-63); Newport News Woman's. Home: 107 Hermitage Rd Williamsburg VA 23185 Office: Duke of Gloucester St Williamsburg VA 23185

WILKINS, MARGARET EVA RICHARDSON (MRS. DONALD BRUCE WILKINS), artist; b. Covington, Va., Apr. 11, 1927; d. James Wallace and Blanche (Walthall) Richardson; student Livingstone Acad. Dress Design, 1945-46, George Washington U., 1946-47, Famous Artists Sch., 1961-65; m. Donald Bruce Wilkins, June 12, 1948; children—Donald Bruce (dec.), Janice Leslie, Diane Louise. Sec. various govt. agys., pvt. industry, 1947-52; editor-in-chief Survey, Manhasset, N.Y., 1967-69; now portrait artist specializing in dogs. Guest lectr. Manhasset High Sch., 1972. Sec. North Park Civic Assn., Roslyn, 1957-59. Publicity chmn. Manhasset br. Am. Cancer Soc., 1971. Mem. U.D.C. (chpt. pres. 1967-71, chpt. treas. 1971—, N.Y. div. rec. sec. 1964-70, 3d v.p. 1970—), Manhasset Art Assn., Creative Artists League Nassau County, Suffolk County Art League. Club: Strathmore-Vanderbilt Women's (publicity chmn. 1967-69, corr. sec. 1970-71). Home: Apt F-2 3000 Ford Rd Bristol PA 19007

WILKINS, MARY LOUISE HUISKAMP CALHOUN (MRS. LEON R. WILKINS), author; b. Keokuk, Ia., Aug. 3, 1926; d. William Clark and Louisa (Waples) Huiskamp; B.A., U. Ia., 1948; m. James Franklin Calhoun, Sept. 3, 1948 (dec. Aug. 1961); children—Michael H., Gregory J.; m. 2d, Leon R. Wilkins, Nov. 1962. Newspaper reporter Omaha World Herald, Gresham (Ore.), Outlook, 1947-49. Past trustee Mt. Vernon (Wash.) Pub. Library, Rangely (Colo.) Library Bd. Mem. Rangely Friends of Library (pres. 1964-65), Authors Guild Am. Episcopalian (trustee Diocese Colo.). Author: Making the Mississippi Shout, 1957; The Sweet Patootie Doll, 1957; Wobble the Witch Cat, 1958; Katie John, 1960; Cowboy Cal and the Outlaw, 1961; The Hungry Leprechaun, 1962; The Witch of Hissing Hill, 1964; The House of Thirty Cats, 1965; The Thieving Dwarfs, 1967; The Runaway Brownie, 1967; The Last Two Elves in Denmark, 1968; The Goblin Under the Stairs, 1968; Magic in the Alley, 1970; White Witch of Kynance, 1970; Mermaid of Storms, 1970; It's Getting Beautiful Now, 1971; The Flower Mother, 1972; Mrs. Dog's Own House, 1972; The Battle of Reuben Robin and Kite Uncle John, 1973; The Horse Comes First, 1974; many others. Home: St Paul's Ch Steamboat Springs CO 80477 Office: Box 722 Steamboat Springs CO 80477

WILKINS, MIRA (MRS. GEORGE B. SIMMONS), historian, educator; b. N.Y.C., June 1, 1931; B.A., Radcliffe Coll., 1953; Ph.D., Newnham Coll., Cambridge U., 1957; m. George B. Simmons, June 15, 1968. Supr. Am. history Corpus Christi Coll., Cambridge U., 1956-57; researcher Weyerhaeuser history Columbia, 1957-58, Lectr. Am. history, gen. studies, 1958, researcher Ford Motor Co. history, 1958-60, co-dir. Ford Overseas Project, 1960-62, dir. Project in History Am. Bus. Overseas, Grad. Sch. Bus., 1962-66, adj. asst. prof. bus. Grad. Sch. Bus., 1964-66; asso. prof. history and indsl. adminstrn. Union Coll., 1966-68; lectr. in history Smith Coll. Dept. History, 1968-70; part-time instr. modern European history Wayne State U., 1958-59; part-time lectr. dept. econs. U. Mass., Amherst, 1972; adj. prof. Union Coll., 1972; prof. dept. econs. Fla. Internat. U., Miami, 1974—; prin. investigator State Fla. grant investigate non-U.S. multinat. corps. on Fla. resources, 1975—. Mem. Am. Hist. Assn. Author: (with Frank Ernest Hill) American Business Abroad: Ford on Six Continents, 1964; The Emergence of Multinational Enterprise: American Business Abroad from the Colonial Era to 1914, 1970; The Maturing of Multinational Enterprise: American Business Abroad from 1914 to 1970, 1974. Cons., contbr. Harper Ency. the Modern World, 1970. Mem. editorial adv. bd. Business History Review, 1971-74. Contbr. to various publs. Home: 40 Prospect Dr Coral Gables FL 33133 Office: Dept Econs Fla Internat Univ Tamiami Trail Miami FL 33144

WILKINS, PHOEBE ELEANOR, educator; b. Alto Pass, Ill., Apr. 24, 1921; d. Roy and Bertha (Alvis) Wilkins; A.B., MacMurray Coll., 1943; M.S., So. Ill. U., 1950; Ph.D., U. Ia., 1966. Tchr., Alto Pass (Ill.) High Sch., 1943-48; grad. asst., instr. So. Ill. U., 1950; faculty, mem. adminstrv. staff MacMurray Coll., Jacksonville, Ill., 1950—, prof. edn., dir. counseling, 1969—. Psychol. test cons. Jacksonville Pub. Schs., intermittantly 1950-68; psychol. cons. various small industries Jacksonville area. Mem. Am., Ill. psychol. assns., Am., Ill. personnel and guidance assns., Am., Ill. coll. personnel assns., Assn. for Measurement in Evaluation in Guidance, Nat. Council on Measurement in Edn. Home: 404 Lake St Jacksonville IL 62650

WILKINS, RUTH LOIS, mus. curator; b. Boston, Nov. 20, 1926; d. Abraham and Harriett Olive Strauss; B.A., Wellesley Coll., 1948; children—Peter Dana, Michael Paul. Adminstrv. Asst. Everson Mus. of Art, Syracuse, N.Y., 1959-65, curator of collections, 1966-70; cons. Mus. of Am. China Trade, Milton, Mass., 1971; curator edn. Kimbell Art Mus., Fort Worth, 1971—. Named Post Standard Woman of Achievement in Arts, 1968. Co-author: China Trade Silver, 1971. Editor: American Painting from 1830, 1965; Chinese Art from the Cloud Wampler and Other Collections, 1968; Everson Dedication, 1968; American Ship Portraits and Marine Painting, 1970; What Is an Art Museum?, 1970. Contbr. Kimbell Art Museum Catalogue of the Collection, 1972; reporter Council on Museums and Edn. in Visual Arts, N.Y., 1973. Home: 308 Ridglea Village 6035 Westridge Lane Fort Worth TX 76116 Office: Kimbell Art Museum Will Rogers Rd W Fort Worth TX 76107

WILKINSON, ANNA MARY FITTS, elementary sch. adminstr.; b. Upland, Pa., Oct. 2, 1925; d. Frank and Mary Alberta (Thatcher) Fitts; A.B., Swarthmore Coll., 1946; m. Peter Barr Wilkinson, June 18, 1949; children—Ellen, T. Gregg, G. Geoffrey. Elementary pub. sch. tchr., West Chester, Pa., 1960-66; tchr. Wilmington (Del.) Friends Sch., 1966-71; prin. Lansdowne (Pa.) Friends Sch., 1971—. Meeting recorder Willistown (Pa.) Monthly Meeting, Religious Soc. Friends, 1960—; mem. com. on edn. Phila. Yearly Meeting, 1971—; exec. com. Friends Council Edn. Trustee Friends Central Sch. Home: 29 Chetwynd Rd Paoli PA 19301 Office: 110 N Lansdowne Av Lansdowne PA 19050

WILKINSON, CAROL LEHMANN ELLSWORTH (MRS. DONALD P. WILKINSON), mathematician; b. Seattle, Jan. 11, 1930; d. Arthur I. and Elise (Lehmann) Ellsworth; student Reed Coll., 1947-49; B.A., U. So. Cal., 1969; children—Clay Scott, Paul Fraser; m. 2d, Donald P. Wilkinson, June 26, 1971. Mathematician Boeing Airplane Co., Seattle, 1949-50, Hughes Aircraft Co., Culver City, Cal., 1951-53; mathematician North Am. Aviation, El Segundo, Cal., 1953-54; mem. tech. staff Hughes Aircraft Co., Culver City, 1955-63, head reliability analysis group for the research and devel. div., 1963-66, staff engr., 1966-73, sr. scientist, 1973—. Mem. Am. Soc. for Quality Control, Am. Statistical Assn. Methodist. Home: 5423 W 141st St Hawthorne CA 90250 Office: Hughes Aircraft Co Culver City CA 90230

WILKINSON, CAROLYN JANE, med. educator; b. Clarksburg, W.Va., Aug. 30, 1935; d. Bernard Waldo and Ollie Lewis (Connor) Wilkinson; B.A., Wellesley Coll., 1957; M.D., Med. Coll. Va., 1961. Intern Jefferson Hosp., Phila., 1961-62; resident anesthesiology U. Pa. Hosp., 1962-64; fellow anesthesiology Bispebjerg Hosp., Copenhagen, Denmark, 1965; instr. surgery U. W.Va. Med. Sch., 1964-65; asso. in anesthesia Northwestern U., Evanston, Ill., 1966-70, asst. prof. anesthesiology Med. Sch., 1970—. Diplomate Am. Bd. Anesthesiology. Mem. A.M.A., Ill., Chgo. med. socs., Am., Ill. socs. anesthesiologists. Club: Wellesley (Chgo.). Co-inventor Kamen-Wilkinson cuff for prevention of tracheal damage during long term endotracheal intubations. Home: 910 Lake Shore Dr Chicago IL 60611

WILKINSON, DORIS YVONNE, educator; b. Lexington, Ky.; d. Howard Thomas and Regina Lavonne (Cowherd) Wilkinson; B.A., U. Ky., 1958; M.A., Case Western Res. U., 1960, Ph.D., 1968. Asst. prof. sociology U. Ky., 1967-70; asso. prof. Macalester Coll., St. Paul, 1970—. Asst. prof. Columbia, summer 1969; vis. asso. prof. U. Conn., 1973-74. Named Alpha Kappa Delta Outstanding Grad. Student, 1964, Outstanding Woman Faculty Mem., U. Ky., 1969; Woodrow Wilson fellow, 1959-61, Nat. Inst. Mental Health fellow, 1963-66. Mem. Am. Sociol. Assn., Midwest Sociol. Soc., Am. Assn. U. Profs. (co-chairperson Macalester Coll. 1971-72), Am. Med. Writers Assn., Soc. Women Sociologists, Am. Orthopsychiat. Assn. Editor: Black Revolt, 1969; Social Structure and Assassination; Black Male/White Female, 1973. Contbr. to profl. publs.

WILKINSON, HILDEGARDE R.J., physician; b. St. James, Mich., July 6, 1903; d. Allan Marshall and Ada (Blodgett) Wilkinson; B.A., U. So. Cal., 1926, M.D., 1942; R.N., Cal. Lutheran Hosp., Los Angeles, 1932. Intern, Los Angeles County Gen. Hosp., 1941-42, resident, 1942-45; practice medicine, specializing in gynecology, Glendale, Cal., 1945—; mem. staff Glendale Meml. Hosp., chief staff, 1970. Diplomate Am. Bd. Obstetrics and Gynecology, Am. Bd. Surgery. Mem. Phi Beta Kappa, Delta Zeta. Methodist. Club: Altrusa Internat. (Glendale). Office: 655 N Central Av Glendale CA 91203

WILKINSON, JUNE ROSE, actress; b. Eastbourne, Eng.; d. Robert Peckett and Lily (Curryer) Wilkinson; student Carlisle Sch. for Girls, Sussex Sch. Dancing; m. Dan Pastorini, June 1, 1973. Appeared in Pajama Tops on Broadway at Winter Garden, 1963; appeared with Nat. Touring Co. in Pajama Tops, 1964, Any Wednesday, 1965-66, Come Blow Your Horn, 1968-69; toured with Louis Jourdan in Marriage Go Round, 1971, 10 Day Mistress, 1972-73, with Jackie Coogan in Mr. and Mrs. 1974. Home: 8310 Grandview Dr Hollywood CA 90046 Office: 449 S Beverly Dr Beverly Hills CA 90212

WILKINSON, LUANA WARREN, hosp. adminstr.; b. Sidney, Mont., Sept. 20, 1915; d. DeWitt Cregier and Anna Marie (Beck) Warren; B.A. magna cum laude, U. Mont., 1938; m. William Ross Wilkinson, May 13, 1938; children—Noreen Ann (Mrs. Richard Mulligan), Warren Harvey, Steven Paul. Bookkeeper Waterville Hardware and Douglas County Realty Co., Waterville, Wash., 1953-66; mem. staff Douglas County Meml. Hosp., Waterville, 1953—, adminstr., 1965-66, 69—. Chmn. Douglas County chpt. A.R.C., 1964; pres. Waterville P.T.A., 1953. Episcopalian. Mem. Order Eastern Star (past worthy matron). Home: 211 W Walnut St Waterville WA 98858 Office: 107 W Chelan St Waterville WA 98858

WILKINSON, NANA MIRIAM SLATEN (MRS. WESLEY O. WILKINSON), realtor; b. Dahlgren, Ill., June 8, 1912; d. John R. and Fleta E. (Berry) Slaten; student Carthage Coll., 1930-32; m. Wesley Owen Wilkinson, Feb. 14, 1945. Sec. pres.' office DePauw U., Greencastle, Ind., 1935-37; exec. sec. to v.p. Beach & Arthur Paper Co., Indiana, Pa. and N.Y.C., 1937-45; broker Henry B. Trachy Real Estate Agy., Franklin, N.H., 1970—; mem. 3d Dist. Belknap County N.H. Ho. of Reps., 1970-73. Mem. N.H. Fedn. Garden Clubs, 1957—, 1st v.p., 1966-67, state pres., 1967-69, legislative chmn., 1971-74, editor Lilac Letter, 1969-71; mem. Nat. Council State Garden Clubs, 1957—, treas. New Eng. region Symposium, 1969-71, chmn. New Eng. Regional Youth activities, 1969-71, mem. nominating com. New Eng. region 1971—, life mem., 1969—; pres. Tiltor-Northfield Woman's Club, 1953-55; pres. Tilton Garden Club, 1959-61, now life mem.; mem. Tilton Park Commn., 1963—; mem. Tilton Planning Bd., 1969-70; mem. Flood Plains Commn. N.H., 1972-74; treas. Tilton Republican Com., 1958—. Trustee Arthur S. Brown Found. Recipient Presdl. citation N.H. Fedn. Garden Clubs, 1970, 73, Order Purple Finch for outstanding woman, 1970. Mem. Nat. Assn. Real Estate Brokers, Lakes Region Bd. Realtors, Nat. Wildlife Fedn., Audubon Soc. N.H., Nat. Resources Council N.H., Tilton Woman's Club, Nat. Assn. Parliamentarians, Mass. Horticulture Soc., Soc. for Protection N.H. Forests, Nat. Assn. Women Legislators. Conglist. (pres. Ladies' Circle 1961-62, 70-71; chmn. music com. 1971—; trustee (1st woman 1965-70). Home: Calef Hill Rd Tilton NH 03276 Office: 395 Central St Franklin NH 03235

WILKINSON, SYLVIA, author; b. Durham, N.C., Apr. 3, 1940; d. Thomas Noell and Peggy (George) Wilkinson; B.A., U. N.C., 1962; M.A., Hollins Coll., 1963; postgrad. Stanford, 1965-66. Instr. English, art, drama U. N.C., Asheville, 1963-65; instr. English, Coll. William and Mary, Williamsburg, Va., 1966-67; creative writing dept., U. N.C., Chapel Hill, 1967-70; mem. pub. relations com. Sports Car Club Am., 1970—; tchr. Learning Inst. N.C., 1968-69; writer in-residence Hollins Coll., 1969, Poetry in the Schs., Va., 1972-74, N.C., 1972; writer-in residence Sweet Briar Coll., 1973, 74—, KCRCHE, Kansas City, 1974. Named one of Outstanding Young Women Am., 1965; Wallace Stegner creative writing fellow, 1965-66; recipient Mademoiselle Merit award, 1966; Sir Walter Raleigh award, 1968; Durham, Eastern N.C. women's tennis championships. Nat. Endowment for Arts grantee, 1973-74. Author: Moss on the North Side (Eugene Saxton Meml. Trust grant, 1964); A Killing Frost, 1967; Cale, 1970; The Stainless Steel Carrot, An Auto Racing Odyssey, 1973. Editor: CHANGE, 1971. Contbr. various lit. jours. Home: 109 Williams St University Heights Chapel Hill NC 27514 also 1613 Kent St Durham NC 27707 Office: care Houghton Mifflin & Co 2 Park St Boston MA 02107

WILKOWSKI, JEAN MARY, fgn. service officer; b. Wis., Aug. 28, 1919; B.A., St. Mary-of-Woods Coll., 1941; M.A., U. Wis., 1944; postgrad. U. Habana, 1944. Publicity dir. Barry Coll., 1941-43; agrl. reporter U. Wis., 1943; joined Fgn. Service, Dept. State, 1943; vice consul, Port-of-Spain, 1944-46, Bogota, 1946-48, Milan, Italy, 1948-51; assigned Dept. State, 1951, inter-agy. exchange program Dept. Commerce, 1951-53; vice consul, Paris, France, 1953-54, sec., consul, 1954-56; econ. study U. Cal. at Berkeley, 1956-57; Spanish lang. era tng. Fgn. Service Inst., 1957; 2d sec., Santiago, Chile, 1957-60; internat. economist Dept. State, 1960-62; assigned to Sr. Seminar Fgn. Policy, Fgn. Service Inst., 1962-63; 1st sec. Am. embassy, Rome, Italy, 1963-66; dep. chief mission, Tegucigalpa, Honduras, 1966-70; counselor for comml. affairs, Rome, 1970-71, minister-counselor econ. affairs, 1971-72; ambassador to Zambia, Lusaka, 1972—. Address: Care Dept of State Washington DC

WILL, KATHY JO, ednl. adminstr.; b. Evansville, Ind., June 30, 1947; d. Urban Henry and Betty Mae (Goebel) Will; B.A., Ind. State U., 1969; M.A., Ball State U., 1972. Advt. saleswoman Evansville Printing Corp., 1967-69; sec. to pres. Ind. State U., Evansville, 1969, asst. to pres., 1970—. Publicity chmn. for Miss Freedom Festival, Evansville, 1971—. Mem. Ind. Coll. Public Relations Assn. (sec.-treas. 1972-73, 73-74). Roman Catholic. Home: Rural Route 4 Evansville IN 47712

WILLARD, ANN MADELEINE, pub. relations ofcl.; b. Knoxville, Tenn., Feb. 6, 1923; d. James Edward and Helen Claire (Ashe) Willard; A.B., Webster Coll., 1945; M.A., U. Notre Dame, 1958; postgrad. St. Louis U., 1949, Laval U., 1961, 63-64, U. Wis., 1967. Joined Sisters of Loretto; instr., Loretto High Sch., Louisville, 1948-56, prin., 1960-61; instr. speech Loretto Heights Coll., Denver, 1956-59, dean students, 1957-59, chmn. theatre dept., 1965-69, dir. pub. relations, 1969-71, dir. adult extension courses, 1967-68; instr. St. Patrick High Sch., Kankakee, Ill., 1959-60, Nerinx Hall, St. Louis, 1961-65; dir. pub. relations St. Mary's Acad., Englewood, Colo., 1971—, dir. devel., 1974—. Cons., bd. dirs. Catholic Ednl. Guild Film Festival, Denver, 1967-69. Mem. Pub. Relations Soc. Am., Am. Film Assn. Democrat. Roman Catholic. Author, producer, dir. Readers Theatre, 1968. Address: 4545 S University Blvd Denver CO 80110

WILLARD, ANNE OLDHAM, phys. therapist; b. Cleve., Aug. 4, 1916; d. John Lorraine and Olga Caroline (Wellington) Oldham; B.A., Rollins Coll., 1940; postgrad. U. Wis., 1942-44, U. Pa., 1959; m. Leland Henry Willard, June 8, 1945 (dec. Nov. 1960); children—Dorothy Ann, Byron Keith, David. Phys. therapist Dr. Charles Graybill Meml. Hosp., Lawton, Okla., 1951-53, State Ala., Gadsden, Ala., 1954-57; chief phys. therapist Crippled Children's Soc., Ft. Worth, 1957-60; pvt. practice phys. therapy, Mineral Wells, Tex., 1960-61; head phys. therapist Flow Meml. Hosp., Denton, Tex., 1961-71; chief phys. therapy Collin Meml. Hosp., McKinney, Tex., 1971—. Served to 1st lt. AUS, 1940-46. Mem. Nat. Wildlife Fedn., McKinney Human Soc., Internat. Platform Assn., McKinney Bus. and Profl. Women's Club, Alpha Phi. Episcopalian. Mem. Order Eastern Star (officer Denton). Office: PO Box 703 McKinney TX 75069

WILLARD, ISABEL BREWSTER SIMS, oil co. exec.; b. Spartanburg, S.C. Dec. 29, 1910; d. Benjamin Franklin and Helen Gertrude (Knight) Sims; B.A., Converse Coll., 1932; m. William Grant Willard, Mar. 19, 1935; children—William Grant III, Benjamin Sims. Dir. Willard Oil Co., Spartanburg, 1958—, mem. exec. com., 1967-70, dir. beautification, recreation and health, 1969—. Head Travellers Aid vols., also Travellers Aid, 1943-50, mem. adv. com., 1968-70; mem. Jr. League, Spartanburg, 1940-50, bd. dirs., 1943-44; sec., v.p. Ga. Cleveland Home for Old Ladies, Spartanburg, S.C., 1956—; mem. regional task force Appalachian Council of Govts., Greenville, S.C., 1974—. Mem. bd. regents S.C., Gunston Hall, Mus. House and Plantation, Lorton, Va.; mem. alumnae council Converse Coll., 1973—. Mem. Nat. Soc. Colonial Dames Am. (mem. S.C. bd. dirs. 1959—, chmn. Spartanburg com. 1958-59), The Assembly (pres. 1958-59). Clubs: Country, Piedmont (both Spartanburg). Home: 2 Woodburn Rd Spartanburg SC 29302 Office: 2024 Howard St Spartanburg SC 29303

WILLARD, NANCY MARGARET (MRS. ERIC LINDBLOOM), author; b. Ann Arbor, Mich., June 26, 1936; d. Hobart Hurd and Margaret (Sheppard) Willard; B.A., U. Mich., 1958, Ph.D., 1963; M.A., Stanford, 1960; m. Eric Lindbloom, Aug. 15, 1964; 1 son, James Anatole. Lectr. dept. English, Vassar Coll., 1965—; author: (poems) In His Country, 1966, A New Herbal, 1968, Nineteen Masks for the Naked Poet, 1971; The Carpenter of the Sun, 1974; (stories) The Lively Anatomy of God, 1967, The Childhood of the Magician, 1973; (juvenile) The Merry History of a Christmas Pie, 1974, Sailing to Cythera, 1974; (criticism) Testimony of the Invisible Man, 1970. Recipient Hopwood awards U. Mich., 1954, 55, 56, 57, 58; Devins Poetry award U. Mo. Press, 1967. Mem. Phi Beta Kappa, Phi Kappa Phi. Home: 133 College Av Poughkeepsie NY 12603

WILLARD, SHIRLEY ANN, editor; b. Morocco, Ind., Sept, 28, 1936; d. Charlie Ernest and Maye Elizabeth (Nicewander) Ogle; B.A. Tri Kappa scholar, Coll. scholar, 1955, Manchester (Ind.) Coll., 1959; postgrad. Va. State Coll., 1962, Ind. Language Program scholar, 1963. U. Ariz. in Guadalaj, Mexico, 1963; M.A., Ball State U., 1966; m. Willis Dean Willard, June 5, 1964; children—Thomas Jefferson, Doyle Allen, William Joseph. Tchr. Spanish, English and social studies Rockcreek Sch., Bluffton, Ind., 1959-60, Kewanna (Ind.) High Sch., 1960-67, N. Miami High Sch., Denver, Ind., 1968-73; sec. Fulton County Hist. Soc., Rochester, Ind., 1962-63; pres., 1971—; editor soc. quar., 1971—. Active local Cub Scouts, 1967-69; vol. Proverty Program, 1966-67; founder, sponsor Spanish Club, Kewanna High Sch., 1961-67; sponsor Spanish Club, N. Miami High Sch., 1968-73. Mem. Ind. Tchrs. Assn., Am. Assn. Tchrs. Spanish and Portuguese, N.E.A., Classroom Tchrs. Assn. Editor: Fulton County Folks, 1974. Author history of county railroad and depot museum, arranged and opened county museum, 1972. Address: Route 1 Box 130 Rochester IN 46975

WILLE, BERNILDA STUCKEY (MRS. DICK WILLE), banker; b. Wauzeka, Wis., Nov. 16, 1920; s. Fred W. and Lena (Sander) Stuckey; grad. Internat. Accountants Soc., Chgo., 1955; student Am. Inst. Banking, Chgo., 1958-63, 70—; grad. Nat. Assn. Bank Auditors and Controllers Banking Sch., U. Wis., 1967, Nat. Trust Sch., Northwestern U., 1970; m. Dick Wille, Nov. 16, 1940; children—Walter, Richard, Jean (Mrs. Paul Rasmussen). With Bremen Bank & Trust Co. (formerly Bremen State Bank), Tinley Park, Ill., 1955—, asst. cashier, 1961-66, controller, 1966-68, cashier, 1968-71, v.p. finance, asst. trust officer, 1971—. 4-H leader, 1945-48; mem. Home Bur., 1942-57, chmn., 1951-52; Cook County camp counselor, 1954-55. Recipient Honor award Chgo. Clearing House Assn., 1963, Hon. resolution from Bremen Bank Dirs., 1964; named State Outstanding 4-H Mem., 1940. Mem. Bank Adminstrn. Inst. (dir. Sauk Trail chpt. 1965), Nat. Assn. Bank Women (Ill. membership chmn. 71), Nat. Orgn. Women. Lutheran. Home: 6540 W 174th St Tinley Park IL 60477 Office: 17500 Oak Park Av Tinley Park IL 60477

WILLENBERG, NORMA FAYE, realtor; b. Fritch, Tex., Dec. 31, 1931; d. William Guy and Cora Audria (Stroud) Sallis; student Southwestern Coll., 1968-71; m. Raymond F. Willenberg, Aug. 10, 1950; children—Raymond F., Guy Louis, Renee Faye. With Chula Vista Realty (Cal.), 1968-69, Jim Lay Realty, Chula Vista, 1969-71; owner Willenberg Realty, Chula Vista, 1971—. Active P.T.A., Little League. Mem. Nat. Fedn. Ind. Bus., Nat. Assn. Female Execs., Nat. Inst. Real Estate Brokers, Nat. Assn. Real Estate Bds., Cal. Real Estate Assn., South San Diego Bay Cities Bd. Realtors (membership, multiple listing, savs. and loan coms.), Chula Vista C. of C., Nat. Assn. Tri-T Soc. (dir.). Mem. Pentacostal Ch. Home: 602 Myra Av Chula Vista CA 92010 Office: 733 3d Av Chula Vista CA 92010

WILLENS, DORIS, pub. relations exec.; b. N.Y.C.; d. Sam and Bertha (Heskin) Willens; B.A., U. Cal. at Los Angeles, 1945; M.S., Columbia, 1947; m. Milton Lewis Kaplan, May 26, 1949 (dec.); children—Jeffrey M., Andrew L., Dan H. Reporter, Mpls. Tribune, 1948-49; reporter Editor and Pub. mag., N.Y.C., 1949-50; freelance writer, London, Eng., 1950-55; columnist N.Y. Jour.-Am., 1957-61; pub. relations exec. Grey Advt., N.Y.C., 1961-63; reporter, copy editor Washington Post, 1963-66; dir. pub. relations Doyle Dane Bernbach, Inc., N.Y.C., 1966—. Mem. Pub. Relations Soc. Am., Broadcast Music, Inc. Mem. Babysitters, performer-songwriting group, recs. for Vanguard, 1958, 60, 64, 68; lyricist numerous pub. childrens songs. Home: 64 Edgecliff Terrace Yonkers NY 10705 Office: 20 W 43d St New York City NY 10036

WILLERDING, MARGARET FRANCES, educator; b. St. Louis, Apr. 26, 1919; d. Herman J. and Mildred F. (Icenhower) Willerding; A.B., Harris Tchrs. Coll., 1940; M.A., St. Louis U., 1943, Ph.D., 1947. Tchr. pub. schs., St. Louis, 1940-46; instr. math. Washington U., St. Louis, 1947-48; asst. prof. Harris Tchrs. Coll., St. Louis, 1948-56; mem. faculty San Diego State Coll., 1956—, asso. prof., 1959-65, prof., 1966—. Mem. Nat. Council Tchrs. Math., Assn. Tchrs. Sci. and Math., Am. Math. Soc., Math. Assn. Am., Greater San Diego Math. Council (dir. 1963-65), Sigma Xi, Pi Mu Epsilon. Author: Intermediate Algebra, 1969; Elementary Mathematics, 1971; College Algebra, 1971; College Algebra and Trigonometry, 1971; Arithmetic, 1968; Probability: The Science of Chance, 1969; Mathematics Around the Clock, 1969; Mathematical Concepts, 1967; From Fingers to Computers, 1969; Probability Primer, 1968; Mathematics: The Alphabet of Science, 1972; A First Course in College Mathematics, 1973; Mathematics Worktext, 1973. Home: 10241 Vivera Dr La Mesa CA 92041 Office: Dept Math San Diego State College San Diego CA 92041

WILLETT, PATRICIA ANNE, municipal judge; b. Elizabeth, N.J., Oct. 1, 1935; d. Andrew Charles and Alma Elizabeth (Lieber) Eckels; A.A., Centenary Coll. Women, Hackettstown, N.J., 1955; grad. Am. Bar Assn. Traffic Ct. Inst., 1971, Youth Devel. Delinquency Inst., 1971, Nat. Inst. Corrections, 1972; m. Charles F. Willett, Aug. 30, 1957; 1 son, Yeulin V. II; stepdau., Allison Griffith. Asst. personnel mgr. Sears, Roebuck & Co., Asbury Park, N.J., summer 1956; dir. spl. activities Koos Bros., Rahway, N.J., 1956-57; municipal ct. judge, Delta, Colo., 1967—; city and county election judge, absentee judge. Mem. Colo. Commn. Status Women; Colo. chmn. juvenile protection P.T.A.; mem. Colo. Adv. Commn. Health Occupations; chmn. region 10 Alcohol and Drug Abuse Task Force; mem. Keep Colo. Beautiful; vice chmn. Colo. Hwy. Safety Adv. Commn.; chmn. region 10 Div. Criminal Justice, 1971—, Youth Devel. Delinquency Prevention Program, 1971—. Pres. Delta County Republican Women, 1968; vice chairwoman 4th Congl. Dist., 1970; mem. Gossard for Congress Com., 1970. Recipient Good Citizenship award D.A.R., 1949. Mem. Colo. Municipal Judges Assn. (sec.-treas. 1970—), Colo. Safety Assn., Bus. and Profl. Women's Club, Jr. League of Elizabeth and Cranford, Toastmistress Club, Sweet Adelines. Episcopalian (edn. chmn. 1966, pres. St. Luke's Guild 1964). Mem. Order Eastern Star. Home: 509 Leon St Delta CO 81416 Office: PO Box 19 Delta CO 81416

WILLETT, ROSLYN LEONORE, marketing, communications and food service cons.; b. N.Y.C., Oct. 18, 1924; d. Edward and Celia (Stickler) Sternberg; B.A., Hunter Coll., 1944; student Tchrs. Coll., Columbia, 1944-45, N.Y. U., 1947-48, 51-52, Coll. City N.Y., 1947-48; m. Edward Willett, June 8, 1949; 1 son, Jonathan Stanley. Head tech. service and devel., food products Stein, Hall & Co., N.Y.C., 1944-48; editor McGraw-Hill Pub. Co., Laurel Publns., others, 1949-54; head instl. and bus. press dept. Farley Manning Assos., N.Y.C., 1954-58; propr. Roslyn Willett Assos., N.Y.C., 1959—. Lectr. Columbia Sch. Pub. Health, 1971—, N.Y. U. Sch. Bus., 1969-71; tchr. Hunter Coll., 1955-56. Seminar del. White House Conf. Food, Nutrition and Health, 1969. Organizer Nat. Women's Polit. Caucus, 1971—; chairwoman Women's Polit. Caucus, Inc., 1971-73; chairwoman 1st women candidates workshops for polit. candidates, N.Y., N.J., Conn., 1971, 72. Bd. dirs. Women Studies Abstracts, Internat. Soc. Food Service Cons. Recipient award Nat. Restaurant Assn., 1968-69, 70-71. Mem. Inst. Food Technologists, Am. Marketing Assn., Nat. Orgn. for Women (dir. Image of Women program), N.Y. Film Council, Am. Home Econs. Assn., Am. Acad. Polit. and Social Scis., Hunter Coll. Alumni Assn. (dir.). Club: Publicity. Contbr. profl. publs. Office: 441 West End Av New York City NY 10024

WILLEY, MIRIAM SHOWALTER, educator; b. Kokomo, Ind., Oct. 13, 1929; d. Edward Haldeman and Ethel May (Duce) Showalter; B.A., U. Ia., 1951, M.A., 1954, Ph.D., 1958; advanced certificate U. London (Eng.), 1953; m. Lawrence Vernon Willey, Jr., Oct. 5, 1968. Spl. edn. tchr. pub. schs., Iowa City, 1951-52; residence dir. Children's Service Center, Wilkes Barre, Pa., 1954-55; asst. prof. psychology and edn. Ia. State Tchrs. Coll., Cedar Falls, 1958-59; asso. dir. tumor registry Ia. State U. Hosp., Iowa City, 1959-61; school psychologist pub. schools, also asst. prof. edn. Drake U., Des Moines, 1961-62; school psychologist Niles Twp. Sch. System, Skokie, 1962-63; senior project dir. materials evaluation Sci. Research Assos., Chgo., 1963-65, pre-school editor, 1965-67, mgr. evaluation and tng. Computer-Related Instructional System Dept., 1967-68; dir. office med. edn. Howard U., Washington, 1973—. Mem. Am. Psychol. Assn., Am. Edn. Research Assn., Am. Soc. Cybernetics, Nat. Council Measurement in Edn. Home: 2812 29th Pl NW Washington DC 20008 Office: 520 W St NW Washington DC 20059

WILLEY, RUTH LIPPITT (MRS. ROBERT B. WILLEY), educator; b. North Kingstown, R.I., May 11, 1928; d. Gorton Thayer and Katharine (Lindsay) Lippitt; B.A., Wellesley Coll., 1950; Ph.D., Radcliffe Coll., 1956; m. Robert Bruce Willey, Feb. 14, 1956. Docent, Peabody Mus., Yale, 1950-52; teaching fellow Harvard, 1952-56; instr. Wellesley (Mass.) Coll., 1956-57; histologist Triarch Products Co., Ripon, Wis., 1959-61; asst. prof. Ripon Coll., Wis., 1961-63; asst. prof. dept. biol. sci., U. Ill. at Chgo., 1965-71, asso. prof., 1971—. Mem. research staff Rocky Mountain Biol. Lab., Gothic, Colo., 1958—. NSF grantee, 1964-66, 72—, U. Ill. Grad. Research Bd. grantee, 1967-72, Sigma Xi grantee, 1953, 69. Mem. Am. Micros. Soc. (bd. reviewers), A.A.A.S., Am. Soc. Profl. Microscopists (charter), Entomol. Soc. Am., Am. Inst. Biol. Scis., Micros. Soc. Ill., Ill. Acad. Scis., The Nature Conservancy, Societas Internationalis Odonatologica, Soc. of Odonatology in Tokyo, Am. Women in Sci., Phycological Soc. Am., Sigma Xi. Author: Microtechniques, 1971. Contbr. articles to profl. jours. Office: Dept Biol Scis Univ Ill Box 4348 Chicago IL 60680

WILLEY, SHIRLEY FAYE (MRS. RICHARD WARREN WILLEY), antique dealer; b. Dawson, N.D., Aug. 5, 1933; d. Fern Clifford and Bessie Christine (Nord) Werner; student Pierce Coll., 1952, U. Cal. Los Angeles, 1961; m. Richard Warren Willey, Feb. 25, 1967. Resident adminstr. Arrowhead Residential Mgmt., Denver; communications cons. Fairmont Hotel, San Francisco and Dallas, 1968-70, Beverly Hilton Hotel, Beverly Hills, Cal., 1964-67; chief communications Better 'n Nothing TV show, Grass Valley, Cal., 1968-69. Mgr. antique show for theatre restoration benefit, 1969; chmn. Nevada County chpt. Heart Assn., 1971—. Bd. dirs. Nevada County Liberal Arts Commn., cons., 1969-71. Recipient Meritorious service award Am. Heart Assn., 1971. Mem. Ch. of Religious Sci. (dir. 1967).

WILLHAM, HAYES ELLEN, coll. dean, educator; b. Perryville, Ky., Aug. 7, 1922; d. Henry Gabhart and Myrtie Givens (Overstreet) Willham; B.S., Eastern Ky. U., 1949; M.A., 1950. Asst. prof. health and phys. edn. Middle Ga. Coll., 1950-60, chmn. health and phys. edn. for women, infirmary dir., 1950-52, asso. prof., 1960—, dean of women, dir. student health services, 1966—. Acting chmn. Bleckley County chpt. A.R.C., 1971-73, chmn. blood program, 1971. Grad. Teaching fellow Eastern Ky. U., 1949-50. Mem. Nat., Ga. assns. women deans, adminstrs. and counselors, Ga. Assn. Educators (pres. Middle Ga. Coll. chpt. 1964), Wesleyan Service Guild (v.p. 1954), pres. 1958), Ga. Assn. Higher Edn., Kappa Delta Pi. Methodist (Sunday sch. tchr.). Home: Route 2 Cochran GA 31014 Office: Middle Georgia College Cochran GA 31014

WILLIAMS, ALENE ELLIOTT, city govt. ofcl.; b. Windom, Tex., Dec. 2, 1911; d. Commodore Edison and Mattie Edna (Caffee) Elliott; student Draughon Bus. Coll., 1930; m. Clarence James Williams, Dec. 24, 1937; children—James Elliott. City sec., tax assessor, collector, O'Donnell, Tex., 1967—, also municipal judge, civil def. dir. Past pres. Tahoka (Tex.) Garden Club, Draw (Tex.) Home Demonstration Club. Mem. Tex. Assessing Officers, Tex. Assn. City Secs., Dawson County and Lynn County Art Assn. Democrat. Methodist. Home: 504 S 12th St O'Donnell TX 79351 Office: 615 8th St O'Donnell TX 79351

WILLIAMS, ALMA WESTINE STONE (MRS. RUSSELL EUGENE WILLIAMS), educator; b. Athens, Ga.; d. Percy Hunter and Estelle (Price) Stone; A.B., Spelman Coll., 1940; M.A., Atlanta U., 1942; postgrad. Black Mountain Coll., 1944, Juilliard Sch. Music, 1945-46, U. N.C., 1961; Mus.M., U. Md., 1966; m. Russell Eugene Williams, July 16, 1947 (dec. Oct. 1961); children—Estelle Harriet, Russell Eugene, Julian Marshall, Kenneth VanHunter, Percy Vandella. Instr. Penn Sch., Frogmore, S.C., 1942-43; mem. faculty Fort Valley State Coll., 1943-48; Instr. pub. schs., Lansing, Mich., 1956-58; mem. faculty S.C. State Coll., Orangeburg, 1961-68, asst. prof. English, 1963-68; asst. prof. humanities Savannah (Ga.) State Coll., 1968—. Concert pianist, 1940. Active Muscular Dystrophy Assn. Mem. Coll. Lang. Assn., Council on Human Relations, Music Educators Nat. Conf., Nat. Guild Piano Tchrs., Internat. Platform Assn., Juilliard Alumni Assn., Nat. Council Tchrs. English, Savannah Concert Assn., Savannah Spelman Club (pres.). Mem. Ch. of Covenant. Home: 2214 Bartlett Dr Savannah GA 31404

WILLIAMS, ANN CRAIG (MRS. GORDON TOWNLEY WILLIAMS, JR.), distbg. co. exec.; b. Ridgewood, N.J., Jan. 14, 1927; d. Arthur Hegeman and Dorothy (Boreham) Craig; certificate Mary Baldwin Coll., 1947; m. Gordon Townley Williams, Jr., June 11, 1948; children—Walter J., Elizabeth (Mrs. David J. Neer), Gordon C. Sec. sch. dept. Conde Nast Publs., Inc., N.Y.C., 1947-48; sec. Stihl Am., Inc., Oakland, N.J., 1962—; pres. E.A. McQuade Travel Agy., Ft. Lauderdale, 1974—. Vol. Valley Hosp., Ridgewood, N.J., 1970—. Clubs: Woman's of Ridgewood, Coll. of Ridgewood. Home: 333 Godwin Av Ridgewood NJ 07450 Office: 107 Bauer Dr Oakland NJ 07436

WILLIAMS, ANNIE LEE MARSHALL (MRS. WILLOUGHBY C. WILLIAMS), editor; b. Graham, Tex., Aug. 30, 1912; d. Charles Fay and Gladys (Burns) Marshall; B.J., U. Tex., 1934; m. Robert G. Shelton, May 20, 1938 (dec. Oct. 1942); children—Linda (Mrs. James A. Pack), Cezanne (Mrs. Charles D. McCullough); m. 2d, Willoughby C. Williams, June 1, 1951 (dec. June 1959). Reporter, woman's editor Graham Leader, 1933-37, Wichita Falls (Tex.) Record News, 1937-40; with other papers, 1941-44; news writer News Service, U. Tex., 1944-49; pub. relations dir. Wharton County Jr. Coll., Wharton, Tex., 1949-61; woman's editor Wichita Falls Times and Record News, 1961—. Mem. Woman's Forum (life), Symphony Women's League, W.F. Mus. and Art Center, Tex. Press Women, Women in Communication, P.E.O. Presbyn. (elder 1973—). Author: History Wharton County, 1964. Home: 2410 Cambridge St Wichita Falls TX 76308 Office: 1301 Lamar St Wichita Falls TX 76307

WILLIAMS, BARBARA JEAN, librarian; b. Union, S.C., Aug. 17, 1934; d. Ernest Nesbitt and Johncie (Sartor) Williams; B.A. with honors, Bennett Coll., 1955; M.S. in L.S., U. Ill., 1956, postgrad., summer 1958, U. N.C., summer 1961, Atlanta U., summer 1965, Rutgers U., 1971-73. Mem. library staff S.C. State Coll., Orangeburg, 1956—, reference and documents librarian, 1958-62, head librarian, 1962—. Tchr. Inst. Tng. Para-profl. Librarians, Voorhees Coll., Denmark, S.C., 1971—. Evaluator So. Assn. Colls., 1969—. Membership chmn. Orangeburg br. N.A.A.C.P., 1971. Sec. treas. Suburban I Precinct Orangeburg County Democratic Com., 1968—. Mem. Am. (Black Caucus steering com. 1971-73), Southeastern, S.C. (chmn. coll. sect. 1969-71) library assns., Nat. Assn. Coll. Women, Am. Soc. Information Sci., Alpha Kappa Mu, Delta Sigma Theta (South Atlantic regional dir. 1968-70, mem. nat. com. on constn. and by-laws 1971—). Club: Thirteen Hearts Bridge (Orangeburg). Home: Box 1565 South Carolina State Coll Orangeburg SC 29115 Office: Miller F Whittaker Library South Carolina State Coll Orangeburg SC 29115

WILLIAMS, BEATRICE LENORA, senatorial asst.; b. Larned, Kan., Oct. 28, 1911; d. Henry Joseph and Albessie Ann (Robinson) Jacquart; A.B., Ft. Hays (Kan.) State Coll., 1935; m. James Alfred Williams, Dec. 26, 1969. Editor Johnson (Kan.) Pioneer, 1933, Plains (Kan.) Jour., 1935-37, Ulysses (Kan.) News, 1937-42, Satanta (Kan.) Chief, 1946-67; Western Kan. asst. to U.S. Senator Robert Dole, 1967-73. Mem. Kan. Ho. of Reps. from 121st Dist., 1957-66. Div. chmn. Dodge City United Fund, 1973; county chmn. Kan. Crippled Children's Soc., 1974—; mem. adv. com. Kan. chpt. Nat. Easter Seal Soc., 1974—. Trustee Dodge City Library, 1969—, Ft. Hays Endowment, 1966—; bd. dirs. Valley Hope Alcoholic Treatment Center, Norton, Kan., 1966—. Served to capt. WAC, 1943-46. Recipient Distinguished Alumnae award Ft. Hays State Coll., 1966; Distinguished Citizen award Satanta C. of C., 1967; award Kan. Mental Health Assn., 1964; Honor award Valley Hope Alcoholic Treatment Center, 1970; Thanks award Girl Scouts, 1972. Mem. Dodge City Women's C. of C. (dir.), P.E.O., Philomath Study Club, Kappa Alpha Theta. Republican. Mem. Christian Ch. Mem. Order Eastern Star. Club: Dodge City Country. Address: 504 El Trigo St Dodge City KS 67801

WILLIAMS, BETTY KATHLEEN TARAZANO GARDNER (MRS. DAVID J. WILLIAMS), ednl. adminstr.; b. Rochester, Pa., Sept. 9, 1932; d. Charles and Ethyln Ruth (Lambert) Tarazano; B.S., Edinboro State Coll., 1954; postgrad. Geneva Coll., 1957-58; M. Ed., U. Pitts., 1970; m. Henry Albert Gardner, Jr., Dec. 27, 1953 (div. Jan. 1968); children—Elizabeth Ann, Trilby Lee; m. 2d, David J. Williams, Aug. 26, 1968 (dec. June 1973). Art tchr. Rochester area Sch. Dist., 1954; tchr. art, mech. drawing Monaca (Pa.) Sch. Dist., 1955-70; dir. urban center Community Coll. of Beaver County, Monaca, 1970-72, dean acad. services, 1973—. Sec., Rochester Planning and Zoning Commn., 1960-72; mem. legislation adv. com. Pa. Bd. Edn., 1967-68; mem. adv. bd. on quality edn. assessment Pa. Dept. Pub. Instrn., 1968; mem. edn. adv. com. Rochester Area Sch. Dist., 1966-67; charter mem., dir. Chippewa Playhouse, Beaver, Pa., 1960-61, sec., 1961; charter mem., dir. Regent Theatre, Beaver Falls, 1961-62, v.p., 1961; mem. Beaver County Human Service Forum, 1970—; mem. task force on revision master plan higher edn. Pa. State Bd. Edn., 1969-70; mem. Beaver-Butler-Lawrence Counties Comprehensive Health Plan, 1973—. Bd. dirs. Children's Aid and Family Services of Beaver County, Pa. League for Consumer Protection. Named one of Outstanding Young Women in Am. leaders of women's orgns., 1965. Mem. Pa. State Art Edn. Assn. (sec. 1970-72), Nat. Council on Community Services (charter) Beaver County Art Tchrs. Assn. (v.p. 1967-68), Pa. Planning Assn., Pa. Fedn. Women's Clubs (state bd. 1964—). Lutheran. Home: 482 E Washington St Rochester PA 15074

WILLIAMS, CAROL FRANCES (MRS. FREDERICK DURHAM PETERSON), physician; b. Chattanooga, Sept. 13, 1931; d. Daniel Newton and Frances Allison (Blair) Williams; student Vanderbilt U., 1949-51; B.A., U. Tenn., 1953, M.D., 1955; m. Frederick Durham Peterson, Jan. 21, 1961. Intern Bapt. Meml. Hosp., Memphis, 1956; resident in obstetrics and gynecology Barnes and Allied Hosp., St. Louis, 1957-60; Am. Cancer Soc. advanced clin. fellow Washington U., St. Louis, 1960-63, instr. obstetrics and gynecology, 1963-65, asst. prof. clin. obstetrics and gynecology, 1965—; practice medicine specializing in obstetrics and gynecology, St. Louis, 1961—; chief dept. obstetrics, gynecology St. Luke's Hosp., St. Louis, 1968—. Diplomate Am. Bd. Obstetrics and Gynecology. Mem. Am. Coll. Obstetricians and Gynecologists, A.M.A., Central Assn. Obstetricians and Gynecologists. Episcopalian. Home: 14 Berkley Lane St Louis MO 63124 Office: 5505 Delmar Blvd St Louis MO 63112

WILLIAMS, CAROLINE JANE (MRS. FENWICK TATTNALL NICHOLS), physician; b. Ramer, Ala. Sept. 13, 1918; d. Peyton Ward and Evelyn (Waller) Williams; A.B., U. Ala., 1937: M.D., Vanderbilt U., 1941; m. Fenwick Tattnall Nichols, Oct. 24, 1944; children—Fenwick Tattnall III, Edith Caroline, William Ward. Intern, Mass. Meml. Hosp., Boston, 1941-42; resident Univ. Hosps., Augusta, Ga., 1942-44; mem. staff Roberts Meml. Clinic, Atlanta, 1944-46; fellow cardiology Grady Hosp., Atlanta, 1947-48, fellow biochemistry, 1948-49; med. supt. Savannah TB Sanitarium, 1952-54; cardiologist VA, Savannah, 1954-57; internist cons. Div. Vocational Rehab., Savannah, 1955—; practice medicine, specializing in internal medicine, Savannah, 1970—; staff Meml. Med. Center, Savannah; cons. Savannah Heart Clinic. Mem. Chatham-Savannah Health Council, 1949-53; pres. Chatham-Savannah Tb and Health Assn., 1955-56; pres. 1st Dist. Heart Assn., 1966; chmn. Combined Pub. Health Nursing Services, 1969—. Named Mother of Year for Greater Savannah, Savannah C. of C., 1959; recipient award for service to mankind Sertoma Club, 1968; Profl. Achievement award Ga. Rehab. Assn., 1973. Mem. A.M.A., Med. Assn. Ga., Ga. Med. Soc. Episcopalian. Home: 5727 Sweetbriar Circle Savannah GA 31406 Office: 12 Med Arts Center Savannah GA 31405

WILLIAMS, CAROLYN LEE (MRS. SIDNEY B. WILLIAMS, JR.), lawyer, state ofcl.; b. Washington, Nov. 22, 1943; d. Shelly and Flordella Louise (Brown) Hickson; B.A., George Washington U., 1964, J.D. cum laude, 1968; m. Sidney B. Williams, Jr., June 8, 1968; children—Martin Sidney, Christopher Daniel. Admitted to Mich. bar, 1968; asso. mem. firm Crum & Allen, Kalamazoo, 1968-69, Stapleton, Adams, Burgie, Kidston & Crocker, Kalamazoo, 1969-71; hearing examiner Mich. Dept. social services, Kalamazoo, 1972—. Social sci. research analyst U.S. Labor Dept., Washington, 1964-68; tchr. Nazareth Coll., Kalamazoo, 1971, Kalamazoo Coll., 1973. Mem. Kalamazoo Implementation Commn., 1970-72, Citizens Probation Authority, 1972—, Kalamazoo County Human Services Commn., 1974—; treas. Kalamazoo United Way, 1971-72. Bd. dirs. Kalamazoo Community Services Council, 1968-70. Mem. Am., Kalamazoo County, Mich. bar assns. Home: 7640 Ravenswood Dr Portage MI 49081 Office: 350 S Burdick St Kalamazoo MI 49006

WILLIAMS, CATHARINE MELISSA, educator; b. West Mansfield, O.; d. Horton Blake and Frances (Roling) Williams; B.S., Ohio State U., 1924, M.A., 1927, Ph.D., 1947. Dir., Noble County Normal Sch., 1924-28; demonstration tchr. Bowling Green (O.) State U., 1928-30; instr., tchr. Ohio State U., Columbus, 1930-55, asst. prof., 1955-62, asso. prof., 1962-73, emeritus, 1973—. Vis. prof. summer programs U. Mich., 1936, 38, U. Fla., 1955. Mem. Assn. Supervision and Curriculum Devel., Am. Assn. Ednl. Communication and Tech., Nat. Soc. Study Edn., Am. Assn. U. Women, Delta Kappa Gamma, Pi Lambda Theta. Democrat. Conglist. Author: Sources of Teaching Materials, 4th edit., 1970; Learning From Pictures, 1963, rev. edit., 1968; (with Collins W. Burnett) The Teen Tutor and Learning, 1969; (with I. Keith Tyler) Educational Communication in a Revolutionary Age, 1973; Community Resources for Learning, 1974. Home: 1889 Andover Rd Columbus OH 43212

WILLIAMS, CATHERINE POLK, assn. exec.; b. Concord, N.C., May 18, 1944; d. Homer and Ethel (Davis) Polk; B.A., Johnson C. Smith U., 1966; m. Franklin Eugene Williams, Oct. 1, 1966 (div. Sept. 1972). Tchr., Morningside Elementary Sch., Statesville, N.C., 1966-67, Roosevelt Elementary Sch., Clover, S.C., 1967-68; program dir. McCrorey Br. YMCA, Charlotte, N.C., 1969—. Pres., Mecklenburg County chpt. Les Premiere Femmes, Inc., 1970—. Bd. dirs. Nat. Conf. Christians and Jews. Named First Lady of Year, Mecklenburg Chpt. Les Premieres Femmes, 1973. Mem. Bus. Women's Assn., Assn. Profl. Dirs., Phi Delta Kappa. Mem. Elks of World. Home: 1608 Rose Tree Ct Charlotte NC 28213 Office: 3801 Beatties Ford Rd Charlotte NC 28216

WILLIAMS, CHARLOTTE EVELYN FORRESTER (MRS. WALKER ALONZO WILLIAMS), civic worker; b. Kansas City, Mo., Aug. 7, 1905; d. John Dougal and Georgia (Lowerre) Forrester; student U. Kan., 1924-25; m. Walker Alonzo Williams, Sept. 25, 1926; children—Walker Forrester, John Haviland. Trustee, Detroit Grand Opera Assn., 1960—, dir., 1955-60; chmn. Grinnell Opera Scholarship, 1959-65; founder, dir., chmn. adv. bd. Cranbrook Music Guild, Inc., 1952-59, life mem., 1952—; dir. St. Peters Home for Boys, Detroit, 1951-53, Detroit Opera Theater, 1959-61, Severo Ballet, 1959-61; Detroit dist. chmn. Met. Opera Regional Auditions, 1959-65; sponsor Opera Guild Ft. Lauderdale (Fla.); patron mem. Asol. Festival Theatre Assn., Sarasota, Fla.; trustee Detroit Grand Opera Assn. Mem. Central Opera Service N.Y.C., Debbie-Rand Meml. Service League (life), Fla. Atlantic Music Guild, D.A.R., P.E.O. Mem. Order Eastern Star. Club: Music Study (Boca Raton, Fla.). Home: 1355 Fan Palm Rd Boca Raton FL 33432

WILLIAMS, CLARICA, librarian, educator; b. Meta, Ky., Feb. 5, 1911; d. Hiram and Reta (Phillips) Williams; student Pikeville Jr. Coll., 1931-33; A.B., Eastern Ky. U., 1936; B.S. in L.S., U. Ky., 1946; M.A., Peabody Coll. for Tchrs., 1957. Tchr., librarian Pike County Pub. Schs., Pikeville, Ky., 1930-50; librarian Lab. Sch., Morehead State U. (Ky.), 1950-58, asso. prof. L.S., 1968—. Treas. League Women Voters Rowan County, Ky., 1970—; mem. Ky. Hist. Soc., 1968—. Mem. Am., Southeastern, Ky. (pres. 1954) library assns., N.E.A., Am. Assn. U. Profs., Am. Assn. U. Women (pres. Ky. 1966-68), Beta Phi Mu, Kappa Delta Pi, Delta Kappa Gamma. Home: 309 Knapp St Morehead KY 40351 Office: 502 Sch Edn Morehead State U Morehead KY 40531

WILLIAMS, DOROTHY EULALIA, librarian; b. Patton, Pa., July 29, 1902; d. Fred and Martha Marcella (Gunsallus) Williams; student Ind. State U., 1920-22; B.A., Pa. State U., 1930, M.Ed., 1940; B.S. library sci. magna cum laude, Syracuse U., 1943. Elementary tchr. Cooper Twp., Pa., 1922-25; secondary tchr. Canoe Twp., Pa., 1925-30; elementary tchr., prin., Jeannette, Pa., 1930-35; secondary tchr., librarian, audio-visual dir. Clearfield (Pa.) Pub. Schs., 1935-72; librarian, Clearfield County, 1972; adminstr. Non Pub. Sch. Dept., Philipsburg, Pa., 1972—. Mem. Pa. Edn. Assn. (state exec. council 1945-47), N.E.A., A.L.A., Assn. Ednl. Communication and Tech., Bus. and Profl. Womens Club, Pi Lambda Theta, Delta Kappa Gamma. Methodist. Home: 902 Cemetery Rd Clearfield PA 16830 Office: Central Intermediate Unit RD 1 Radio Park Philipsburg PA 16866

WILLIAMS, DOROTHY FRANCES, educator; b. Brookline, Mass., Aug. 23, 1918; d. John Joseph and Gertrude (Riley) Williams; student Lasell Jr. Coll., 1938-39; B.S., Simmons Coll., 1941; postgrad. Providence Coll., 1953-56; M.S., Boston U., 1967. Mem. personnel dept. Am. Optical Co., Boston, 1942-43; news editor Raytheon News, Raytheon Mfg. Co., Newton, Mass., 1943-45; editor Hammett Herald, J.L. Hammett Co., Cambridge, Mass., 1945-46; editor Your Home mag., Boston, 1946-50; chmn. dept. communications, prof. pub., mng. editor Simmons Rev., Simmons Coll., Boston, 1947—. Communications cons. labor, mgmt., alumni publs., writer-editor; dir. editorial graphic arts workshops; adviser Leadership Tng. Inst., U.S. Office of Edn. Mem. corp. Editorial Projects for Edn. Balt. Recipient Am. Alumni Council award for editorial achievement, 1948-73; Internat. Council Indsl. Editors, New Eng. Bus. Communicators, Am. Coll. Pub. Relations Assn. awards for editorial excellence; Am. Graphic Arts Inst. award for excellence in graphic arts in Simmons Rev. Mem. Mass. Indsl. Editors Assn. (treas. 1945-47), Nat. Conf. internat. Council Indsl. Editors (edn. coordinator 1967), Am. Alumni Council (mag. chmn. dist. I conf. 1964, dir. communicators insts. 1964-74), Advt. Club Greater Boston, Am. Advt. Fedn., New Eng. Assn., Colls. and Secondary Schs. (editorial bd.), Assn. for Edn. in Jour. Author: The Labor Press in Profile, 1964; A Primer for the Graphically Illiterate, 1966; The Day A Lincoln Was Saved, 1963. Home: 84 Davis Av Brookline MA 02146 Office: Simmons Coll 300 The Fenway Boston MA 02115

WILLIAMS, DOROTHY JUNE (MRS. JOHN THOMAS WILLIAMS), mus. ofcl.; b. Greenfield, Ind., Oct. 26, 1908; d. Omer Stokes and Ellis June (Rock) Jackson; student Butler U., Indpls., 1925-27; A.B., Ind. U., 1929; postgrad. U. Md., 1930; m. John Thomas Williams, Sept. 6, 1934; children—Rosemary (Mrs. Robert D. Lewis), Diana (Mrs. Gunnar Hansen), Elise (Mrs. Allen Teagle), Omer S.J., Thomas E.Q., Daniel Matthew. Tchr. high sch. English, Austin, Ind., Greenfield and Hancock County schs., 1931-34; hostess, bus. mgr., writer weekly newspaper James Whitcomb Riley Home, Greenfield, 1958—. Pres. P.T.A., 1948-49, Greenfield Womans Club, 1950, Gradatim Club, 1951; Hancock County chmn. Ind. Sesquicentennial, 1966; gen. co-chmn. Riley Festival, 1971, bd. dirs., 1973—. Pres., Hancock County Womens Democratic Club, 1948. Mem. Christian Womens Fellowship (pres. 1961-63), Soc. Ind. Pioneers, Ind. Mus. Soc., Ind., Hancock County (pres. 1969-71) hist. socs., D.A.R., Phi Beta Kappa, Kappa Alpha Theta, Tri Kappa, Theta Sigma Phi. Mem. Christian Ch. Writer column for Hancock County Jour.-Democrat, 1958-74; writer series A Backward Glance in county papers, 1972-74. Editor The Log Chain, 1974. Home: 216 W 5th St Greenfield IN 46140 Office: 250 W Main St Greenfield IN 46140

WILLIAMS, E. VIRGINIA, ballerina; b. Melrose, Mass.; d. Charles F. and Mary Virginia (Evitts) Williams; ballet pupil of Geraldine Cragin, then Dana Sieveling; also student piano, drama and art; m. Herbert T. Hobbs, June 29, 1958; 1 dau., Carla. Profl. dancer in concert groups and opera ballet; tchr. ballet; choreographer; dir. New Eng. Civic Ballet Co., 1958—; now artistic dir. Boston Ballet Co.; dir. Boston Sch. Ballet. Mem. Dance Tchr.'s Club Boston (past pres.; hon. citation). Office: 614 Main St Boston MA 02138

WILLIAMS, ELEANOR VICTORIA TUBBS, coll. adminstr.; b. Westfield, Ala., Jan. 12, 1946; d. Charlie and Sara Evalena (Cody) Tubbs; A.B., Spelman Coll., Atlanta, 1967; M.S., Ind. U., 1968, Ed.D., 1972; m. Darnell Duprie Williams, June 1, 1968 (div. Dec. 1972); 1 dau., Victoria Darnell. Asst. dir. Reading and Study Skills Center, Ind. U., Bloomington, 1968-74, coordinator minority student services, 1972-74, instr. Coll. Arts and Scis., 1970-74, faculty adviser Univ. div., 1969-74, sec.-treas., 1969-72, chmn., 1972-73, adv. com. 1973-74, black faculty and staff, adv. com. to vice-chancellor Afro-Am. affairs, 1971-73, Latino affairs, 1972-74, womens affairs, 1973-74, chief resource adviser to groups program, 1972-73; asso. dean students, asst. prof. edn. Spelman Coll., Atlanta, 1974—. Recipient certificate of Merit for outstanding service in recreation Birmingham Bd. Edn., 1965, Pi Lambda Sigma award merit for outstanding service Daniel Payne Coll., Birmingham, 1973. Mem. Nat. Assn. Student Personnel Adminstrs., Nat. Assn. Women Deans and Counselors, Am. Assn. Higher Edn., Am. Assn. Univ. Women, Ind. U. Alumni Assn. Club: Spelman College Alumni. Author: Institutional Changes as a Result of the Groups Program at Indiana University, Bloomington, 1968-71; Directory of Student Services for Minority Students, 1973. Editor Black Faculty and Staff Directory, 1970-73, Black Faculty and Staff Newsletter, 1973. Home: 4070 Valley Brook Terrace College Park GA 30337 Office: 350 Spelman Lane SW Spelman College Atlanta GA 30314

WILLIAMS, ELISABETH SIMS GREEN (MRS. WALTER A. WILLIAMS), educator; b. Ocala, Fla.; d. Louen Newton and Edna (Sims) Green; B.S., Fla. State U., 1936; postgrad. Columbia, 1936-39; U. Frankfurt, Germany, 1948, San Francisco State U., 1951, U. Ga., Summer 1955, U. Hawaii, 1960, U. Ky., 1961, Pikeville (Ky.) Coll., 1962, U. So. Fla., 1971, Rollins Coll., 1971, Fla. Technol. U., 1971; m. Walter A. Williams, Nov. 13, 1948; 1 dau., Roberta Sims. Elementary sch. tchr., Avon Park, Fla., 1936-41; Civil Service worker with U.S. Army, 1941-42; exec. sec. Juvenile Protective Assn., Jacksonville, Fla., 1942-44; dir. A.R.C. Club, Eng., Germany, club dir. U.S. Spl. Services, instr. troops U.S. Army Troops Information Edn., Bremerhaven, Germany, 1948-50; tchr. pub. schs., Pittsburg, Cal., 1950-51, Arlington, Va., 1954-56, Washington, Ga., 1956-61; tchr. Howard Jr. High Sch., Orlando, 1962-66; tchr. English, Edgewater High Sch., Orlando, 1966—, pub. relations chmn., 1971—, sponsor TRI-Hi-Y, 1970—; attended Internat. Classroom Tchrs. Assn., New Delhi, India, conf. participant, Honolulu, Normal U., Ill.; European tour condr. Orange County Classroom Tchr.'s Assn., 1967, Fgn. Lang. League, 1968. Pres. Wesleyan Service Guild, 1959-61; pres. P.T.A., Washington, Ga., 1960. Recipient Service award A.R.C., 1946. Ky. Col. Mem. Am. Assn. U. Women (state pres. 1968-70, state dir. 1971-72, 1st v.p. br. 1971-72, state cons. 1971—), N.E.A. (past del., state v.p.), Classroom Tchrs. Assn. Ga. (past chmn.), D.A.R. (regent Orlando chpt. 1970-72, dir. Orlando chpt. 1972—), Fla. Edn. Assn., Nat. Council Tchrs. English (1st v.p. Orange County 1972-73, pres. 1973-74), Nat., Fla., Central Fla. (1st v.p. 1973—) parliamentarian assns., Central Fla. Execs. Club, Daus. Am. Colonies, U.D.C., Internat. Platform Assn., Nat. Trust for Historic Preservation, Womans Soc. Christian Service (life mem.), Central Fla. Symphony Assn. (mem. women's com.), Friends of Library, Delta Kappa Gamma (pres. Beta Tau chpt. 1969-72, mem. Orange/Osceola counties coordinating council 1969-72, pres. council 1972—), Zeta Tau Alpha. Club: Sorosis (Orlando). Methodist (pres. Circle 13, 1974—). Home: 1849 Oak Lane Orlando FL 32803 Office: 3100 Edgewater Dr Orlando FL 32804

WILLIAMS, ELIZABETH PARKER, custom transformer co. exec.; b. Houston, Dec. 29, 1919; d. Gaines Foster and Bonnie Belle (Crain) Parker; certificate dental hygiene Baylor U., 1954; B.S., U. Houston, 1960; m. Harold Russell Williams, July 28, 1955. Dental asst., 1935-51; dental hygienist, 1951-67; owner, gen. mgr. owner Houston Transformer Co., 1970—. Mem. Order Eastern Star (past matron). Mem. Christian Ch. (past del.). Home: 10810 Moonlight Dr Houston TX 77035 Office: 6115 Hillcrest Houston TX 77036

WILLIAMS, ELMA, pub. relations exec.; b. Carroll County, Va.; d. Preston and Macy (Goad) Williams; A.B. with spl. honors, George Washington U., 1953; M.A. in Pub. Adminstrn., Am. U., 1961. Asst. program dir., asst. dir. operations WTOP, CBS-Radio and TV, 1947-51; mem. pub. relations staff George Washington U., 1951-52; registrar Washington Sch. for Secs., 1953; exec. sec. Joint Econ. com. of U.S. Congress, 1956-59; legislative information specialist N.E.A., 1960— (all Washington). Sec., Kenwood Beach Assn., 1973—. Bd. dirs. N.E.A. Employees Fed. Credit Union, 1973—. Recipient Alumni Service award George Washington U., 1970. Mem. Am. Assn. U. Women (br. publicity chmn. 1956-59), Am. Newspaper Women's Club, N.E.A. (life), Columbian Women George Washington U. (pres. 1965-67), George Washington U. Alumni Assn. (dir. 1965-67, 69-70), Edn. Writers Assn., Ednl. Press Assn., Women's Joint Congl. Com. (chmn. 1974—), 1974—), Phi Delta Gamma (chpt. pres. 1973-74), Pi Sigma Alpha. Club: White Sands Country. Home: 4000 Cathedral Av NW Washington DC 20016 Office: Div Govt Relations NEA 1201 16th St NW Washington DC 20036

WILLIAMS, FRANCES MARION, librarian; b. Elkton, Ky., Nov. 7, 1919; d. John N. and Marion (Trabue) W.; A.B., Transylvania U., 1942; postgrad. Austin Peay State U., Western Ky. U., George Peabody Coll. for Tchrs. Librarian, Todd County High Sch., Elkton, 1950-63, Todd County Central High Sch., 1963—. Mem. Ky. Assn. High Sch. Librarians, N.E.A., Ky. Hist. Soc., Phi Mu. Author: The Story of Todd County, 1820-1970, 1972; A Mother Goose History for Grown-Ups and Children, 1974. Office: Todd County Central High Sch Library Elkton KY 42220

WILLIAMS, FREDERICA FULLERTON, educator; b. Birmingham, Ala., Sept. 23, 1926; d. Rudolph Maurice and Naomia (Pharris) Patton; B.A., Ala. State U., 1953; M.A., Columbia, 1960; postgrad. Syracuse U., Auburn U.; m. Charles Mason Fullerton, Apr. 4, 1946; children—Charles Maurice, Frederiç Lynn. Tchr., Birmingham Bd. Edn., 1953-63; instr. Tuskegee Inst., 1963-66, dir. reading clinic, 1966—. Reading cons., 1966—. Pres. Plains Reading Council, 1973-74. Mem. Nat. Assn. Coll. Women, Nat. Reading Conf., Coll., Internat., Ala. reading assns. Roman Catholic. Home: 307 Barrow St Tuskegee AL 36088

WILLIAMS, GENEVA MARIE TAYLOR, educator, librarian; b. Pocasset, Okla., Mar. 27, 1923; d. Thomas Herman and Nellie Ruth (Owen) Taylor; B.S. in Elementary Edn. and Spanish magna cum laude, Okla. Coll. Women, Chickasha, 1962; M.L.S., U. Okla. at Norman, 1965; m. Jerry Dalton Williams, Mar. 10, 1949 (div.); children—Valerie (Mrs. Fred Schmalz), Thomas D., David B. Tchr. Spanish, Chickasha (Okla.) High Sch., 1962-65; children's librarian Oklahoma City Pub. Library, 1964-65; reference and inter library loan librarian, asst. prof. library sci. Western State Coll., Gunnison, Colo., 1965—. Mem. Colo. (pres. elect coll. and univ. div. 1974), Mountain Plains library assns., Colo. Assn. Sch. Librarians, Nat., Colo. (sec., treas. Western State Coll. chpt. 1972-74) edn. assns., Am. Assn. U. Profs. (past pres., sec. Western State Coll.), Okla. Seqouyah Com., Pi Gamma Mu, Alpha Lambda Delta. Club: Gunnison Valley Naturalists. Home: 11 Floresta St Gunnison CO 81230

WILLIAMS, GERTRUDE JOANNE, psychologist; b. Boston, June 8, 1927; d. Barnet and Belle (Thorner) Rubin; A.B., U. Cal. at Los Angeles, 1948; A.M., U. So. Cal., 1951; Ph.D., Washington U., St. Louis, 1958. Trainee, Cal. Jr. Republic, 1951-52; extern San Diego Mental Hygiene Clinic, San Diego Hosp. Psychiat. Unit, 1952-53; intern, staff psychologist U. Neb. Med. Sch., also Norfolk State Hosp.; clin. psychology intern VA, St. Louis, 1954-55; testing, clin. asst. psychology dept. Washington U., 1955-56, grad. instr., 1956-57, research asst., research fellow Med. Sch., 1956-58; chief psychologist, research dir. psychiat. child guidance sect. St. Louis Municipal Div. Health, 1958-68, dir., 1968-69; professorial lectr. (asso. prof.) St. Louis U., 1965-69; pvt. practice clin. and cons. psychology, 1969—. Exec. com. Nat. Council Grad. Edn. in Psychology, Fellow Am. Psychol. Assn. (mem. exec. com., sect. on clin. child psychology), Mo. Psychol. Assn.; mem. Am. Assn. U. Profs., Sigma Xi, Psi Chi. Editor Jour. Clin. Child Psychology; editorial bd. Profl. Psychology. Contbr. articles to profl. jours. Home: 6458 Lloyd Av St Louis MO 63139 Office: 111 S Meramec Av Clayton MO 63105

WILLIAMS, GWENDOLYN, librarian; b. Mobile, Ala., June 16, 1934; d. Carl C. and Dorothy (Parker) Williams; B.S. in Secondary Edn., Ala. State Coll., 1956; m. Edmund G. Jones, June 7, 1958 (div. June 1961); 1 son, Durwyn. Founder, head librarian Hogan Pub. Library, Prichard, Ala., 1956—; librarian Mobile County Tng. Sch., Plateau, Ala., 1958. Mem. library tech. asst. adv. com. Bishop Jr. Coll., Mobile, 1972—. Mem. Bay Area, Ala. library assns., A.L.A., N.A.A.C.P., Nat. Council Negro Women, Delta Sigma Theta. Roman Catholic. Club: Civic (Prichard). Home: 503 Snyder Dr Prichard AL 36610 Office: 523 W Clark Av Prichard AL 36610

WILLIAMS, HATTIE ROSE, educator; b. Greenwood, Miss., May 10, 1944; d. Leroy and Tennessee (Mayfield) Williams; student Knoxville Coll., 1963-64; B.S. in Edn., Ind. Central Coll., 1967; M.Ed., Ohio U., 1968; Ph.D. (Advance Study fellow), Ohio State U., 1973. Tchr. elementary schs., Indpls., 1965-67; dormitory dir. Ohio U., Athens, 1967-68; systems engr. IBM, Columbus, O., 1968-69; reseading specialist Columbus schs., 1969-70; dormitory dir. Ohio State U., Columbus, 1970-71, instr., 1972, counseling psychologist, 1972, grad. adminstrv. asso. dept. Black Studies, 1973; asst. prof. edn. Colgate U., Hamilton, N.Y., 1973—. Cons. minority edn. Ford Found. Grad. research fellow Nigerian Inst. Social and Econ. Research U. Ibadan, 1972; Ohio State U. grantee study in Nigeria, 1971; Colgate U. Research Study grantee, 1973-74. Mem. Am. Personnel and Guidance Assn. (non-white concerns div.), Internat. Assn. Ednl. and Vocational Guidance, League Women Voters, Pi Lambda Theta, Phi Delta Kappa, Alpha Kappa Alpha. Home: 4 W Pleasant St Hamilton NY 13346

WILLIAMS, HUBERTIEN HELEN RAPP (MRS. JOHN HENRY WILLIAMS), educator; b. St. Paul, Dec. 9, 1927; d. Edward William and Hubertien (Gerard) Rapp; R.N., Springfield (O.) City Hosp. Sch. Nursing, 1949; B.A. in Edn., U. N.M., 1962, M.A. (Ford Found. fellow 1962), 1963; Ph.D. (Nat. Def. Edn. Act fellow 1962-65), Bowling Green State U., 1968; m. John Henry Williams, Sept. 19, 1949; children—Richard Dale, John David, Hubertien Helen, Elizabeth Marie. Sec., liaison office Wright Patterson AFB, O., 1944-45; nurse Springfield (O.) City Hosp., 1949; sec. to gen. USAF, Europe, 1950-51; asst. prof. English, U. Chattanooga, 1965-70; asso. prof. Appalachian State U., Boone, N.C., 1970-74, prof. English, 1974—. Chmn. sychronized swimming N.M. Amateur Athletic Union, 1956-58; v.p. Duke City Aquatics Clubs, 1956-59. Nat. Endowment Humanities fellow, 1974; Outward Bound Lily Found. fellow, 1973-74. Mem. Modern Lang. Assn., South Atlantic Modern Lang. Assn., Tenn. Philol. Assn. East Tenn. Edn. Assn. (chmn. English 1966-67), Phi Kappa Phi, Phi Sigma Tau, Pi Lambda Theta. Episcopalian. Home: Route 1 Box 90H Boone NC 28607

WILLIAMS, JEAN RATLIFF, physician; b. Mt. Sterling, Ky., Sept. 7, 1929; d. Byram N. and Virginia (Wilson) Ratliff; student Ward-Belmont Jr. Coll., 1946-48; B.A. cum laude, Vanderbilt U., 1950; M.D., U. Louisville, 1954; m. Donald Joseph Williams, July 5, 1955; children—Robert, Susan, J. Russell. Intern D.C. Gen. Hosp., 1954-55; resident Children's Hosp., Louisville, 1955-56; health officer Ky. Dept. Pub. Health, La Grange, 1956-62; health officer Colo. Dept. Pub. Health, Trinidad, 1963-69; practice medicine, specializing in pub. health; mem. staff Colo. State Hosp., Pueblo, 1969—. Mem. Am. Assn. U. Women, Altrusa Internat., Alpha Omega Alpha. Home: 1415 Constitution St Pueblo CO 81001 Office: Colo State Hosp Pueblo CO 81003

WILLIAMS, JEAN WEBB (MRS. PETER A. WILLIAMS), univ. adminstr.; b. Camillus, N.Y., Oct. 4, 1927; d. Orville Downing and Jean Inglis-Steel (Shaw) Webb; B.S., Syracuse U., 1949; M.A., Union Coll., Schenectady, 1970; m. Peter A. Williams, Oct. 20, 1951; children—Laurie, Heather. Asst. home demonstration agt., Delaware County, 1949-50; home demonstration agt., Schoharie County, 1950-62; acting dir. Schoharie County Community Action Program, 1966; countryside speaker Farm Paper of the Air, WGY, Schenectady, 1967-69; asst. to pres., dir. pub. relations State U. N.Y., Agrl. and Tech. Coll. at Cobleskill, 1970—. Played feature role in documentary film I Open the Door, 1956; writer weekly column Fact and Fancy for local newspaper. Active campaign to rename N.Y. Route 30 Timothy Murphy Trail. Pres. Cobleskill Garden Club, 1962-63; sec., bd. dirs. Schoharie County Mental Health Bd., Community Hosp. of Schoharie County; bd. dirs. Schoharie County Devel. Corp., Schoharie County Community Action Program, 1967-71; mem. exec. com. State U. N.Y. Pub. Relations Council, 1973. Recipient Nat. Distinguished Service award for home demonstration work, Chgo., 1960. Mem. N.Y. State Home Demonstration Agts. Assn. (pres. 1956-57), Cobleskill Bus. and Profl. Womens Club (past pres., Women of Year 1955, 66), Epsilon Sigma Phi. Methodist. Author: Schoharie's Man of Might, 1968. Contbr. articles profl. publs. Home: Shad Point Cobleskill NY 12043

WILLIAMS, JEANETTE K. (MRS. DAVID H. WILLIAMS), city ofcl.; b. Seattle, June 11, 1917; d. Louis Herman and Olga Nilovna (Krelova) Klemptner; B.A. interior design, U. Wash., 1937; Mus.B. violin, Am. Conservatory Music, 1938, Mus.B., 1939, diploma in composition, 1940; m. David Houston Williams, Aug. 8, 1942; children—Patricia Ellen (Mrs. Konstantinos Kraniotis), George Frederick. Violinist, del. King County Dem. Exec. Bd., 1960; vice chmn. Dem. Central Com. King County, 1961-62, chmn., 1963-64, 65-66, 67-68; mem. exec. bd. Wash. Dem. Com., 1967-68, 69-70; councilwoman Seattle, 1969—. Del. Dem. Nat. Conv., 1964, 68, mem. platform com., 1964, 68; chmn. pub. relations Washington Fedn. Dem. Women's Clubs; mem. Urban League, League Women Voters, City Wide Democratic Women, Nat. Orgn. Women, Mcpl. League. Recipient Composition award 1939. Mem. Musicians Union (life), Bus. and Profl. Women, Sigma Alpha Iota, Phi Mu. Democrat. Composer. Home: 7132 58th Av NE Seattle WA 98115 Office: Municipal Bldg Seattle WA 98104

WILLIAMS, JEANNE FREEMAN (MRS. JOHN HOWARD WILLIAMS), educator; b. Providence, Feb. 9, 1924; d. Albert M. and Helen (Bishop) Freeman; B.S., U. R.I., 1944; M.S., N.C. State U., 1946; m. John Howard Williams, May 28, 1947; children—Deborah (Mrs. Raymond Clyde Ball), John Bradford, Ross Freeman. Research instr. exptl. statistics N.C. State U., Raleigh, 1944-46; biometrician Office Fgn. Agrl. Relations, U.S. Dept. Agr., Washington, 1947; instr. math. U. Conn., New London, 1947-48; asso. prof. statistics Elon (N.C.) Coll., 1957—, chmn. dept. bus. adminstrn. and accounting, 1961-71. Mem. Community Council of Alamance County, 1964—; chmn. health information and edn. com. Alamance County Health Planning Adv. Council, 1971-73, chmn. council, 1973-75; editor Alamance County Health Services, 1972, organizer information center, 1973; active Girl Scouts U.S. Mem. Am. Statis Assn., Am. Assn. U. Women (pres. N.C. 1969-70, pres. Alamance 1971-73), Pi Gamma Mu. Mem. United Ch. of Christ (chmn. bd. Christian edn. 1968-72). Home: 2209 Walker Av Burlington NC 27215 Office: Box 2158 Elon Coll Elon College NC 27244

WILLIAMS, JEANNINE CLAIRE, physician; b. Pontotoc, Miss., Jan. 2, 1936; d. John Frank and Ione (Babbitt) Williams; B.A., Baylor U., 1956; M.D., Johns Hopkins U., 1961. Intern Parkland Meml. Hosp., Dallas, 1962-63, resident, 1962-63; sr. med. resident Cornell div. Bellevue Hosp., N.Y.C., 1963-64; fellow med. oncology and hematology Meml. Hosp., N.Y.C., 1964-66; Sloan-Kettering Inst. research fellow, 1965-66; practice medicine, specializing in hematology, N.Y.C., 1966—; adj. physician Montefiore Hosp., Bronx, 1970—; vis. physician Morrisania Hosp., Bronx, N.Y., asst. head hematology, 1966—; instr. medicine Coll. Medicine, Cornell U., N.Y.C., 1964-66; instr. Albert Einstein Coll. Medicine, Bronx, 1967-70, asst. prof., 1970—. Vis. physician Montefiore-Morrisania Affiliation, Bronx, 1970—. Diplomate Am. Bd. Internal Medicine. Fellow A.C.P.; mem. N.Y. Acad. Scis., Soc. Study Blood, Am. Soc. Hematology. Home: 345 E 68th St New York City NY 10021 Office: 168th St and Gerard Av Bronx NY 10452

WILLIAMS, JOANNA POZZI, psychologist, educator; b. Providence, June 9, 1935; d. Angelo J. and Sylvia (Colicci) Pozzi; A.B., Brown U., 1955; Ed.M., Harvard, 1956; postgrad. U. Paris (France), 1956-57; M.S., Yale, 1959, Ph.D., 1961; M.A. (hon.) U. Pa., 1972. From lectr. to prof. psychology U. Pa., Phila., 1961—. Vis. prof. psychology and edn. Tchrs. Coll., Columbia, 1971—. Fulbright scholar, 1956-57; recipient Lindback award for distinguished teaching U. Pa., 1965. Fellow Am. Psychol. Assn.; mem. Am. Ednl. Research Assn. Editor: (with Harry Levin) Basic Studies on Reading, 1970. Editor Jour. Ednl. Psychology, 1973—. Office: Box 51 Tchrs Coll Columbia U New York City NY 10027

WILLIAMS, JOY ELIZABETH PORTER (MRS. AUGUSTUS K. WILLIAMS), educator; b. Blackshear, Ga., June 12, 1929; d. Justus J. and Elsie (Norton) Porter; B.S., U. Ga., 1950, M.S., 1958, Ph.D., 1961; m. Bruce Eller, Sept. 22, 1949 (div. 1953); m. 2d, Augustus K. Williams, Dec. 30, 1959; children—Bruce Edwin, Kenneth Porter. Tchr. pub. schs., Blackshear, 1952-57; post-doctoral fellow Oak Ridge Nat. Lab., 1961-63; research asso. dept. microbiology U. Ga., Athens, 1963-66, asst. prof., 1966-68, mgr. Biol. Automated Information Computer Center, 1968-70, asst. dir. honors program, also asst. prof. sci. edn., 1970—. Mem. Nat. Collegiate Honors Council, So. Regional Honors Council (exec. sec.-treas. 1973—), Am. Assn. U. Women, Am. Soc. for Microbiology, N.Y. Acad. Sci., A.A.A.S., Sigma Xi, Phi Kappa Phi. Contbr. articles in field to profl. jours. Home: 235 Stoneland St Athens GA 30601

WILLIAMS, KATHRYN VINSON (MRS. BLENUS WILLIAMS), educator; b. Cordele, Ga., Mar. 23, 1911; d. Edward Augustus and Laura Cordelia (Scott) Vinson; B.A., Ga. State Coll. Women, 1932; M.A., Rollins Coll., 1966; m. Blenus Williams, Apr. 16, 1933; children—Edward Vinson, Melissa Jane (Mrs. Arthur Sanford Kirkindall). Tchr. French, English, Candler County High Sch., Metter, Ga., 1932-33; asst. prof. English, Coll. Orlando (Fla.), 1966-71; adj. instr. English, Fla. Tech. U., Orlando, 1969-71; add. instr. humanities Valencia Community Coll., Orlando, 1971—. Lectr. various civic, cultural groups. Mem. Am. Assn. U. Women, Nat. Council Tchrs. English, Hist. Soc. Orange County, Orlando Art Assn. (sec. 1938-40), Artists League Orange County, Antiquarian Soc. Orange County (lt. gov. 1948-55), Delta Kappa Gamma. Author: The Luck of the Golden Cross, 1960; Run With the Ring, 1965. Home: 844 Kenilworth Terrace Orlando FL 32803

WILLIAMS, LEAH MILDRED, physician; b. Union, W.Va., Apr. 8, 1917; d. Raymond and Golda (Carlisle) Williams; B.S., Marshall Coll., 1943; M.D., Med. Coll. Va., 1947. Intern, Med. Coll., Va. Hosp., Richmond, 1947-48; health service tchr. U. Ill., Champaign, 1948-49; gen. practice medicine, Charlestown, W.Va., 1949—; mem. staff Charlestown Gen. Hosp., Ransom, W.Va. Coroner Jefferson County, W.Va. 1954—; chmn. Bd. Health, Jefferson County, 1957—; mem. Health Adv. Bd., Jefferson County, 1956—; dir. Sabin Oral Vacine Program Jefferson County. Mem. Eastern Panbansee Med. Soc. Home: 115 W Congress St Charles Town WV 25414

WILLIAMS, LELIA ERNESTINE, librarian; b. Mathews, Va.; d. George L. and Sarah (Brooks) Williams; B.S., Hampton Inst., 1940; B.S. in L.S., Simmons Coll., 1949; M.S., Columbia, 1960. Tchr., Thomas Hunter High Sch., Mathews, 1935-48, also librarian, 1937-48; mem. library staff, faculty Norfolk (Va.) State Coll., 1949—, became reference librarian, 1962, now head librarian, also asso. prof. library sci., 1969—. Mem. Am., Va. library assns., N.E.A., N.A.A.C.P., Am. Assn. U. Profs. Baptist. Home: 2835 E Princess Anne Rd Norfolk VA 23504 Office: Norfolk State Coll Norfolk VA 23504

WILLIAMS, LORETTA ANN, pub. relations ofcl.; b. Oklahoma City, Dec. 11, 1936; d. Delbert Newton and Myra (Qualls) Williams; student Cameron Jr. Coll., 1957-58, Okla. Coll. Women, 1958-59; B.A., U. Okla., 1961. Asst. to supr. promotion WKY-TV, Oklahoma City, 1965-66; asst. to advt. mgr. Montgomery Ward Co., 1966; asst. to dir. pub. information Oklahoma City U., 1967, dir. pub. relations, 1967-72, dir. pub. information, 1972; publicity dir. Lyric Theatre of Okla., Inc., 1968-72; dir. pub. relations Oklahoma City Symphony Orch., 1972-74; pub. relations account exec., writer Ackerman Inc., Oklahoma City, 1974—; master of ceremonies, singer The Loretta Show, TV show, Lawton, Okla., 1955; profl. singer, 1955-62. Vol. publicity worker Campus Crusade for Christ, 1967; mem. Okla. City Christian Bus. and Profl. Women's Council, 1964-70, contact chmn., 1964-65, music chmn., 1965-67, hostess co-chmn., 1967-68, music chmn., 1969-70. Home: 1844 NW 23d St Oklahoma City OK 73106 Office: Ackerman Inc 5708 N Mosteller Dr Oklahoma City OK 73112

WILLIAMS, MADELINE CRIMMINS (MRS. MACK H. WILLIAMS), newspaperwoman; b. Fort Worth, Dec. 29, 1915; d. Fred Thomas and Madeline Adelaide (Tolksdorf) Crimmins; B.S., U. Tex., 1937; m. Mack H. Williams, Sept. 17, 1947; 1 son, Thomas Joseph. With Fort Worth Star Telegram, 1943-50; with Fort Worth Press, 1956-57; with Dallas Times Herald, 1953-60; with Denton (Tex.) Record Chronicle, 1952-53; founder Tex. Beverage News, Fort Worth, 1958—, mng. editor, 1958-71; founder and mng. editor The Texas Price Book, Fort Worth, 1961-71; mng. editor, co-publisher The News-Tribune, Fort Worth, 1971—. Named Industry Woman of Year, Alcoholic Beverage Industry, 1965. Mem. Theta Sigma Phi. Home: 3901 Meadowbrook St Fort Worth TX 76103 Office: 411 W 7th St Fort Worth TX 76102

WILLIAMS, MADELYN CLAIRE, educator; b. Oakland, Cal.; d. Madison Lafayette and Carolyn Helena (Plath) Williams; B.S., U. Cal. at Berkeley, 1954; M.A. (Grad. Tuition scholar), Mich. State U., 1963. Tchr. Thomas Downey High Sch., Modesto, Cal., 1954-56; home adviser agr. extension U. Cal. at Modesto, 1956-64; extension specialist clothing, textiles U. Cal. Statewide, Davis, 1964—, instr. dept. consumer scis., 1967-68; instr. Eastern N.M. State U., 1969, Santa Rosa Jr. Coll., 1970. Vice chmn. Cal. Liaison Council Home Econs., 1971-75; tech. cons. Jour. Home Econs., 1973-75. Mem. Am., Cal. (pres. Bay dist. 1961-62) home econs. assns., Academic Staff Orgn. (sec. 1971-72), Fashion Group San Francisco. Writer innumerable extension pamphlets. Office: 160 Everson Hall U Cal at Davis Davis CA 95616

WILLIAMS, MARGARET PEEL (MRS. EDWARD LEROY WILLIAMS), librarian; b. Zetto, Ga., Nov. 18, 1912; d. Henry Charleton and Ruth Adele (Kelly) Poindexter; A.B., Ala. Coll., 1933; M.A., Florence State Coll., 1960; m. Edward LeRoy Williams, Oct. 15, 1937; children—Lillian (Mrs. J.B. Mansell), Heather (Mrs. William Foote), Henry C., Albert P. Tchr., librarian Russellville (Ala.) City Schs., 1933-37, tchr. history, 1949-55; social worker Fed. Govt., 1937-43; librarian Ala. Coll., summers 1962, 63, librarian instr. in workshop, 1963-68; instr. Jacksonville (Ala.) State U., also librarian, 1968—. Pres., P.T.A., Russellville, 1944-45, Jacksonville, 1966. Mem. Ala., Southeastern library assns., Am. Assn. U. Women (v.p. 1966-67), Alpha Beta Alpha. Home: 518 10th Av Jacksonville AL 36265 Office: Houston Cole Library Jacksonville State U Jacksonville AL 36265

WILLIAMS, MARGUERITE LUCILLE STEELE, physician; b. Battle Creek, Mich., Jan. 28, 1902; d. Harvey Bowman and Rhoda (Paustian) Steele; B.S., Union Coll., 1930; M.D., Coll. Med. Evangelists, 1932; student U. Pa., 1942-43; m. Roy Oliver Williams, Jan. 1, 1924; foster-children—Margaret Littlefield (Mrs. Paul Almer Davis), June Skinner (Mrs. Bill Jacobs). Intern Loma Linda (Cal.) Sanitarium and Hosp., 1931-32; gen. practice medicine, Tucson, 1932-42, specializing in internal medicine, 1943—; mem. staff Tucson Med. Center, St. Mary's, Pima County, St. Joseph's, M.J.L. Meml. hosps.; instr. sch. nursing St. Mary's Hosp., 1938-40; chief Tb service Pima County Hosp., 1938. Mem. adv. com. Pima County Mental Health Assn., 1955-57; dir. Tucson YWCA, 1961-63; chmn. Med. Forum Tucson, 1951-60; mem. Ariz. gov.'s com. on Aging for White House Conf., 1961. Fellow Internat. Coll. Angiology; mem. Am., Ariz. Diabetes assns., Pima County (chmn. diabetes com. 1955-65), Coconino med. socs., Ariz. chmn. diabetes sect. 1966, 67) med. assns., Ariz. Soc. Internists, Am. Med. Women's Assn. Med. Women's Internat. Assn., Alumni Assn. Loma Linda U., Bus. and Profl. Women's Club, Ariz. Fedn. Women's Clubs (dir. 1958-60, 62-64, state chmn. community affairs, community achievement contest chmn. 1958-60, chmn. edn. dept. 1962-64, chmn. leadership devel. div. 1964-66), Gen. Fedn. Women's Clubs, Am. Soc. Internal Medicine. Seventh-day Adventist (health edn. sec.). Clubs: Presidents', Woman's (pres. 1957-58) (Tucson). Address: Hwy 89A Soldier Pass Rd Drawer 1328 Sedona AZ 86336

WILLIAMS, MARIE HELENE, librarian; b. New Haven, Dec. 17, 1923; d. George Wilfred and Marie (Le Roi) Stumberg; B.A., U. Tex., 1944; M.L.S., Columbia, 1948; m. Roger John Williams, Jr., Sept. 7, 1946; children—Robert George, Thomas Roger, Kenneth John. Children's librarian Arnett br. Rochester (N.Y.) Pub. Library, 1948-50; librarian Strongsville Elementary Sch., Strongsville, O., 1954-56; librarian Washington Sch., Westfield, N.J., 1968-69, Grant Elementary Sch., Westfield, 1969—. Active P.T.A., 1960-61; treas. YWCA, Westfield, 1963—. Served with WAVES, 1944-46. Mem. A.L.A., Alpha Phi. Democrat. Episcopalian. Club: College (Westfield). Home: 425 Topping Hill Rd Westfield NJ 07090 Office: 550 E Broad St Westfield NJ 07090

WILLIAMS, MARILYN SIMPSON (MRS. BENJAMIN B. WILLIAMS, II), librarian, govt. ofcl.; b. Nashville, Feb. 14, 1928; d. Julian B. and Addie Little (Moores) Simpson; B.A., Mary Baldwin Coll., 1950; M.A. in L.S., George Peabody Coll., 1951; grad. Air Force Mgmt. Sch., 1957; m. Benjamin B. Williams II, June 3, 1953; children—Julianne Moores, Benjamin Buford III, Randall Simpson, Marilyn McCallum. Asst. reference librarian, acting head circulation library Baylor U., Waco, Tex., 1951-52; head librarian Martin Coll., Pulaski, Tenn., 1952-53; asst. periodicals librarian Air U. Library, Maxwell AFB, Montgomery, Ala., 1953-54, chief authority sect., 1954-58, asst. bibliographer Squadron Officer Sch., 1958-60; bibliographer CED and Chaplains' Writers Bd., 1960-62, bibliographer Air Command and Staff Coll., 1962-72, chief reference librarian Air U. Library, 1972—. Mem. Res. Officers Assn. Ladies (chpt. treas., state pres. 1971-72, Spl. Libraries Assn., Ala. Library Assn. Episcopalian. Home: 3813 Marie Cook Dr Montgomery AL 36109 Office: Air University Library Maxwell AFB AL 36112

WILLIAMS, MARION, gospel singer; b. Miami, Fla., Aug. 29, 1927. Joined Clara Ward Singers, 1947, lead singer, 1947-58; formed group Stars of Faith, 1958; star Black Nativity, U.S., Europe, 1961-65; concertized, U.S., Europe; recs. Epic, Savoy. Address: 1020 W Columbia Av Philadelphia PA 19122

WILLIAMS, MARJORIE J. DIX (MRS. BILL HENRY WILLIAMS), physician; b. Calcutta, India; d. Alfred Norman and Catherine (Bagshawe) Dix; M.B., Ch.B., U. Bristol (Eng.), 1944; m. Bill H. Williams, Feb. 4, 1943; 1 son, Robert James. Came to U.S., 1945, naturalized, 1948. Intern, Queen Elizabeth Hosp., Birmingham, Eng., 1944; successively asst. pathology U. Bristol, also Tulane U. Med. Sch., then pathologist St. John's Hosp., Joplin, Mo., 1944-48; with VA, 1949—, dep. dir. pathology and allied scis. service, 1962-63, dir., 1963—; asst. clin. prof. George Washington U. Med. Sch., 1963. Organizer chmn. Interagy. Com. Lab. Medicine; cons. NIH, Armed Forces Inst. Pathology; mem. com. on pathology NRC-Nat. Acad. Scis. Recipient Nat. Civil Service award, 1965, 67, Fed. Woman's award, 1967; Stitt award Assn. Mil. Surgeons U.S., 1972. Diplomate Am. Bd. Pathology. Fellow Coll. Am. Pathologists (bd. govs., chmn. com. on lab. mgmt. and planning), Am. Soc. Clin. Pathologists, Royal Soc. Medicine; mem. Royal Coll. Surgeons, Internat. Acad. Pathology, Am. Assn. Pathologists and Bacteriologists, Path. Soc. Great Britain and Ireland, A.M.A., Am. Assn. U. Women. Contbr. numerous articles to profl. jours. Editorial bd. Jour. Med. Edn. Address: Dept Medicine and Surgery Vet Adminstrn Bldg Vermont at H St Washington DC 20420

WILLIAMS, MARTHA ELAINE, educator; b. New Kensington, Pa., Aug. 20, 1931; d. James Halden and Martha (Wallace) Williams; B.S., Coll. William and Mary, 1953; M.A., Bryn Mawr Coll., 1955, Ph.D., 1959; postgrad. U. Basle (Switzerland), 1957-58; m. Donald G.G. Kerr, Aug. 26, 1961. Mem. faculty dept. philosophy U. Western Ont., London, Can., 1959—, asst. prof., 1963-71, asso. prof., 1971—; exhibited works Glen Gallery, London, Ont., 1969—. Mem. Mind Assn., Am., Canadian philos. assns., Internat. Fedn. U. Women (panel experts), Phi Beta Kappa. Contbr. to profl. jours. Home: 29 Benson Crescent London ON N5X 2B1 Canada Office: Talbot Coll Univ Western Ont London ON Canada

WILLIAMS, MARTHA PIERCE (MRS. WILLIS LUKE WILLIAMS), coll. adminstr.; b. Martin, Tenn., Mar. 25, 1928; d. L.T. Fuller and Attie Beatrice (Gardiner) Pierce; A.A., U. Tenn. Jr. Coll., 1947; B.S., U. Tenn., 1960, M.S., 1969; m. Willis Luke Williams, Sept. 14, 1950 (dec. Sept. 1972). Sec., Pet Milk Co., Martin, 1947-57; sec. U. Tenn., Martin, 1957-63, asst. registrar, 1963-69, registrar, 1969—. Mem. Am., Tenn. (sec. 1972) assns. coll. registrars and admissions officers, Am. Assn. U. Women (sec. 1963), Nocturnal Music Guild, Phi Kappa Phi. Republican. Methodist. Clubs: Martin Garden; Faculty Women's. Home: Rural Route 1 Martin TN 38237

WILLIAMS, MARY BEARDEN, educator; b. Lexington, Ky., Aug. 29, 1936; d. Edwin Gantt and Walter Harnesberger (Dallas) Williams; B.A., Reed Coll., 1958; M.A., U. Pa., 1961; Diplomate Imperial Coll., 1967; Ph.D. (USPHS fellow), U. London (Eng.), 1967. Instr. Agnes Scott Coll., Decatur, Ga., 1960-61; research asso. U. Tex., M.D. Anderson Hosp., Houston, 1963-64; asst. prof. N.C. State U., Raleigh, 1967-73; vis. asst. prof. Ind. U., Bloomington, 1973-74; asst. prof. Ohio State U., Columbus, 1974—. Mem. Soc. for Study of Evolution, Am. Soc. Naturalists, Am. Math. Soc., Math. Assn. Am., A.A.A.S., Philosophy of Sci. Assn., Soc. of Systematic Zoology. Home: 4695 Greentree Ct Columbus OH 43220

WILLIAMS, MARY ELIZABETH, educator; b. Augusta, Ky., Nov. 30, 1909; d. Thomas Sanford and Effie (Nickel) Williams; student Randolph-Macon Woman's Coll., 1928-30; A.B., Radcliffe Coll., 1933; M.A., U. Ky., 1936. Tchr. pub. schs., Ashland, Ky., 1936-41; instr. math. Ashland Jr. Coll., 1941-42; instr. Marshall Coll., Huntington, W. Va., 1942, asst. prof., 1942-46; asst. prof. Skidmore Coll., Saratoga Springs, N.Y., 1946-49, asso. prof., 1949-57, prof., 1957—, chmn. dept., 1946-73. Partner Saratoga Travel Bur., 1958—. Mem. Am. Math. Soc., Math. Assn. Am., Am. Assn. U. Women, Republican. Mem. Christian Ch. Contbr. to profl. jours. Home: 15 Ten Springs Dr Saratoga Springs NY 12866 Office: Dept Math Skidmore Coll Saratoga Springs NY 12866

WILLIAMS, MARY GOSHORN (MRS. CHARLES C. WILLIAMS), psychologist; b. Kansas City, Mo., Aug. 1, 1917; d. John Franklin and Myrtle Ann (Newman) Goshorn; A.A., Chevy Chase Coll., 1936; A.B., U. Kan., 1938, M.A., 1939, Ph.D., 1958; m. Charles C. Williams, Sept. 2, 1937; children—Kathryn William (Mrs. Richard Harvey Sargent), Geoffrey John. With psychiat. unit Jackson County Juvenile Ct., Kansas City, Mo., 1948-52; with neuropsychiat. unit Alfred Banjemin Dispensary, Kansas City, Mo., 1952-55; psychologist Florence Crittenton Home, Kansas City, 1955-59, Menorah Med. Center, Kansas City, 1959-65; individual practice as psychologist, Kansas City, 1965-73; psychologist Four County Mental Health Center, Independence, Kan., 1973—. Mem. Am. Psychol. Assn., Am. Sociol. Assn., Am. Group Psychotherapy Assn., Am. Assn. U. Women, Women's Polit. Caucus. Home: 2311 Gary Av Independence KS 67301 Office: 610 Professional Bldg Independence KS 67301

WILLIAMS, MARY HELEN MEWSHAW (MRS. JAMES H. WILLIAMS), hosp. adminstr.; b. Loraine, Tex., Aug. 18, 1922; d. Robert Lee and Dell (Spenser) Mewshaw; B.S., Baylor U., 1946; M.D., U. Tex., 1946; m. James H. Williams, Aug. 31, 1946; children—James, Eddie, Nancy. Intern, Brackenridge Hosp., Austin, Tex., 1946; asst. prof. biology Union U., Jackson, Tenn., 1947-48; physician Red Cross Blood Center, Nashville, 1948-50, Columbia, S.C., 1953-54; staff physician Central State Hosp., Nashville, 1956-58, Fla. State Hosp., Chattahoochee, Fla., 1958-61; sr. physician Bur. Alcoholic Rehab., Avon Park, Fla., 1961-67, med. dir., 1967—; med. dir. Fla. Alcoholism Treatment and Research Center, Avon Park, Fla., 1967—. Mem. Am., Fla. med. assns., Highlands County Med. Soc. (sec.-treas. 1963-64, 68-69), N. Am. Assn. Alcoholism Programs, Soc. for Study Social Problems, Nat. Rehab. Assn. Contbr. articles to profl. pubs. Home: 91 E Kendall Blvd Avon Park FL 33825 Office: PO Box 1147 Avon Park FL 33825

WILLIAMS, MARY MARGARET LAHIFF (MRS. JOHN ROBERT WILLIAMS, JR.), park ranger; b. Buffalo, Apr. 1, 1943; d. John Vincent and Mildred Beatrice (Kelly) Lahiff; B.A., Rosary Hill Coll., 1964; M.A., U. Conn., 1965; m. John Robert Williams, Jr., Nov. 30, 1968; 1 dau., Meghan Maureen. Tchr., Chappaqua (N.Y.) Pub. Schs., 1965-68; park ranger, technician, historian, Fort Davis, Tex., 1969—. Regional mem. Students Toward Environmental Participation team Nat. Park Service, 1972—. Active Permian Basin Mus. Inst. Summer grantee U. Dublin, Ireland, 1963, Columbia, 1966. Mem. U.S. Border Patrol Recreation Assn., Fort Davis Hist. Soc., Pi Gamma Mu, Phi Alpha Theta. Roman Catholic. Home: PO Box 830 620 N Summer St Marfa TX 79843 Office: PO Box 1456 Fort Davis TX 79734

WILLIAMS, MARY TULLOH, extension agt.; b. South Boston, Va., Sept. 29, 1923; d. Edward Lewis and Lillian (Carter) Tulloh; student Ferrum Jr. Coll., 1941-42; B.S., Va. Poly. Inst. and State U., 1945; m. Richard Ellis Williams, Nov. 29, 1947; children—Helen Carter, Elizabeth Ann. With Va. Extension Service, Va. Poly. Inst. and State U., 1945—, home demonstration agt., Blacksburg, 1945-52, extension agt., Amelia, Va., 1953—. Mem. Amelia County Beautification Com., 1969-72. Bd. dirs. James L. Hamner Pub. Library, Amelia County, 4-H Camp Farrar, Virginia Beach, Va. Mem. Va. Assn. Extension Home Econ. (pres. 1966-67), Nat. Assn. Extension Home Econ., Va., Am. home econ. assns., Amelia Home Demonstration Club, Delta Kappa Gamma, Phi Upsilon Omicron. Club: Bridge (Mannboro, Va.). Home: Rte 2 Box 5 Amelia VA 23002 Office: PO Box 235 Amelia VA 23002

WILLIAMS, MARY WENDY RABLAH, educator; b. London, Eng., Oct. 15, 1932; d. George Val and Enid (Suthons) Rablah; B.S., U. London, 1955, Ph.D., 1960; m. Ian Ronald Williams, July 19, 1958 (div.); 1 dau., Sally Ann. Came to U.S., 1960, naturalized, 1972. Asst. lectr. U. London, 1955-59, lectr., 1959-60; asst. prof. physics La. State U., New Orleans, 1960-65; asst. prof. physics U. Tenn., Knoxville, 1965-72; cons. Oak Ridge Nat. Lab., 1965-72, research worker, 1972—. Mem. Am. Phys. Soc., Am. Assn. U. Profs., Sigma Xi. Episcopalian. Author: (with I. R. Williams) Basic Nuclear Physics, 1962. Home: 117 W Vanderbilt Dr Oak Ridge TN 37830 Office: Health Physics Div Oak Ridge Nat Lab Oak Ridge TN 37830

WILLIAMS, MAUDE ELLA GRIFFIN (MRS. EDGAR M. WILLIAMS), social worker; b. Balt., Oct. 3, 1906; d. Wade Hamilton and Mamye Frances (Jones) Griffin; A.B., Morgan State Coll., 1926; M.S., Cath. U., 1942; M.S.W., U. Pa., 1947; m. Edgar M. Williams, June 12, 1935. Caseworker, supr. Dept. Social Services, 1934-42; supr. childrens div., 1944-66; probation officer Juvenile Ct., Balt., 1942-44; dir. Emergency Services Center, 1966-68; family counselor in pvt. agy., Balt., 1968—. Third v.p. Balt. Urban League, 1950; mem. Mayor's Adv. Com. to Vol. Program, Dept. Social Services, 1969-70. Bd. dirs., cons. to social service dept., chmn. social service com. Keswick Home, Balt., 1973—; bd. dirs. Balt. Sickle Cell Anemia Com. Recipient Eliza Jane Cummings award for outstanding work in sociology, 1926; award Dept. Social Services Balt., 1968, Honored and Outstanding Citizen award Balt., 1969; named Guild Woman of Month, Wesleyan Service Guild, 1954, recognition award, 1972. Mem. Nat. Assn. Social Workers, Md. Conf. Welfare, Am. Legion Aux., Otto Bank Assn., N.A.A.C.P., Wesleyan Service Guild (past pres.), Delta Sigma Theta. Home: 603 Rosedale St Baltimore MD 21216

WILLIAMS, MELBA RUTH (MRS. HARRY BIXLER WILLIAMS, JR.), personnel specialist; b. Cullman, Ala., Feb. 28, 1921; d. William Claiborne and Rebecca Elizabeth (McGill) Jones; B.S. summa cum laude, Ala. Coll., 1942; postgrad. U. N.C., 1946-47; m. Harry Bixler Williams, Jr., Oct. 21, 1944; children—Harry Bixler III, Randolph Claiborne. Personnel officer, research asso. TVA, 1944-46; tchr. DeKalb County, Ga., 1949-50; asst. dir. pub. relations Presbyn. Ch. U.S., 1950-52; researcher Atlanta Area Met. Planning Com., 1961-62, Bell & Stanton Pub. Relations, Atlanta, 1965-66; cons. Ga. sec. state, 1967-68; local govt. tng. specialist Inst. Govt., U. Ga., 1968-70; personnel cons. Ga. Municipal Assn., 1970-72; personnel specialist Ga. Municipal Assn. and Assn. County Coms. Ga., Atlanta, 1972—. Mem. Montgomery County (Md.) Personnel Bd., 1958-59, Ga. Commn. on Status of Women, 1964-73; mem. Ga. Election Bd., 1964—, vice chmn., 1964-70; chmn. Joint House-Senate Election Laws Study Com., 1967, sec., 1966-69. Precinct vice chmn. Montgomery County Democratic party, 1958-59; sec., vice chmn. DeKalb County Dem. Exec. Com., 1962-68; del., mem. credentials com. Dem. Nat. Conv., 1964, del., 1968; vice chmn. Clarke County (Ga.) Dem. Exec. Com., 1970—; finance chmn. 10th Dist. Ga. Dem. Orgn., 1971—. Mem. Pub. Adminstrn. Assn., Internat. Pub. Mgmt. Assn., Ga. Fedn. Womens Clubs (legislative chmn. 1966-68). Author: Handbook for Georgia Voter Registrars, 1968; Handbook for Georgia Election Officials, 1968; Handbook for Georgia Minicipal Election Officials, 1969; A Guide to the Development and Establishment of An Effective Personnel Management System, 1971. Home: 620 Forest Rd Athens GA 30601 Office: 220 10 Pryor St Bldg Atlanta GA 30303

WILLIAMS, MIMA ANN, educator; b. Brownwood, Tex., Jan. 18, 1914; d. Ben Franklin and Jennie (Huffman) Williams; B.A., Daniel Baker Coll., 1935, B.S. in Edn., 1936; M.A., U. Tex., 1940; certificate U. London, 1955, U. Edinburgh (Scotland), summer 1966. Tchr. Midway High Sch., Eldorado, Okla., 1935-36, Star (Tex.) High Sch., 1936-38; head English dept. Eden (Tex.) High Sch., 1938-43, 45-46; tchr. Austin (Tex.) High Sch., 1946; asst. prof. English, Abilene (Tex.) Christian Coll., 1947-62, asso. prof. English, 1962—; guest lectr. Am. lit. Ibaraki State U., Mito, Japan, summer 1963; cons. workshop for Japanese tchrs. English at Ibaraki Christian Coll.; cons., tchr., linguistics Tex. Edn. Agy., 1965-66, also for Region XIV Edn. Center, 1968; conducted linguistic workshop Wayland Baptist Coll., 1967. Mem. Tex. joint English com. for sch. and coll., 1957-58; gen. chmn. Dist. VII English Workshop, 1957-58. Served with WAVES, 1943-45. Mem. Am. Assn. U. Women (local pres. 1968-70, sec. 1957-59, scholarship award 1955, implementation chmn. 1964-65, corporate del., liaison officer 1965-68, 70—), Coll. English Assn. (sec.-treas. Tex. div. 1954, treas. 1974), Tex. Conf. Coll. Tchrs. English, (mem. com. on professions 1961—, chmn. com. on standards and accreditation 1970—), Nat. Council Tchrs. English (curriculum bull. com. 1973—, judge for achievement awards 1972—), South-Central Modern Lang. Assn., Oilbelt English Tchrs. (v.p. 1962), Tex. Council Tchrs. English, Bus. and Profl. Women's Club (sec. 1961-62), Sigma Tau Delta, Alpha Psi Omega, Delta Kappa Gamma (local sec. 1949-51, chpt. pres. 1962-64, chmn. coordinating council 1964-66). Contbr. jours. in field. Home: 526 East North 18th St Abilene TX 79601

WILLIAMS, MINNA, lawyer; b. Aarhus, Denmark, Oct. 5, 1939; d. Thomas Oliver Abye Gaarn and Gerda Rasmine (Hemmingsen) Larsen; D. Law, U. Copenhagen (Denmark), 1967; certificate (fgn. exchange student scholar), Lake Erie (O.) Coll., 1962; m. Bartley C. Williams, Oct. 17, 1967; 1 dau., Cristina Conroy. Came to U.S., 1967, naturalized, 1971. Law student Ministry of Greenland, Copenhagen, 1964-66; admitted to Danish bar, 1967, Cal. bar, 1972; atty. County Counsel's Office, Copenhagen, 1967; atty. U.S. Army Corps Engrs., Sacramento, 1972—. Mem. Cal., Danish bar assns., Internat. Fellowship Reconciliation (co-founder, sec. subcom. internat. com. of conscience on Vietnam 1964-67). Author law outlines, translator. Home: 1323 Buchanan St Marysville CA 95901 Office: 650 Capitol Mall Sacramento CA 95814

WILLIAMS, MINNIE BROWN JOHNSON (MRS. REDMOND J. WILLIAMS), univ. adminstr.; b. Falkland, N.C., Apr. 18, 1945; d. Spellman and Clara Marie (Williams) Johnson; B.S. in Elementary Edn., Elizabeth City State U., 1967; postgrad. E. Carolina U.; m. Redmond J. Williams, Oct. 24, 1967; children—Clarence Purcell, Redmont Julius. 5th grade tchr. Fillmore Elementary Sch., Washington, 1967-68, Neval Thomas Elementary Sch., Washington, 1969; propr. Platter House Carryout, Washington, 1970; residence adminstr. women E. Carolina U., Greenville, N.C., 1971—. Ednl. specialist D.C. Bd. Edn., Camp Meadow, Catoctin Mountains, Thurmont, Md., summer 1970. Mem. Nat., N.C. assns. women deans and counselors. Home: 303 Elizabeth St Greenville NC 27834

WILLIAMS, MONA GOODWYN (MRS. HENRY MEADE WILLIAMS), author; b. Rutland, Vt., Mar. 26, 1908; d. Wirt and Annable (Trask) Goodwyn; student pvt. schs.; m. Henry Meade Williams, Dec. 24, 1929; children—Karen (Mrs. Ben Lyon), Christopher, Lacy (Mrs. John Faia III). Author: Here Are My Children, 1932; Bright is the Morning, 1934; The Marriage, 1958; Hot Breath of Heaven, 1961; The Company Girls, 1965; Voices in the Dark, 1968; Celia, 1968; Movie Woman's World, 1955. Home: Box 2133 Carmel CA 93921

WILLIAMS, MONICA DONNELLY (MRS. BERNARD G. WILLIAMS), nursing adminstr.; b. N.Y.C., July 21, 1946; d. Francis Joseph and Monica Joan (McMahon) Donnelly; B.A. in French, Manhattanville Coll. of Sacred Heart, 1968; M.A. in French (Univ. fellow), Tufts U., 1969; B.S. in Nursing, Columbia, 1971; m. Bernard G. Williams, Aug. 19, 1972. Staff nurse, head nurse Vanderbilt Clinic, Columbia-Presbyn. Med. Centre, N.Y.C., 1971-72; dir. inservice edn. John T. Mather Meml. Hosp., Port Jefferson, N.Y., 1972—. Attaché, Costa Rican Mission to UN, 1971-72. Mem. Modern Lang. Assn., Am. Nurses Assn., Suffolk County Inservice Council (sec. 1973-74), Sigma Theta Tau. Roman Catholic. Home: 645-21 Belle Terre Rd Port Jefferson NY 11777 Office: Dept Nursing John T Mather Hosp North Country Rd Port Jefferson NY 11777

WILLIAMS, NANCY ANN, hosp. adminstr.; b. Decatur, Ill., Apr. 28, 1931; d. Herbert E. and Gertrude C. (Maxwell) Williams; B.S., U. Ill., 1954; M.B.A., George Washington U., 1968. Asst. dir. occupational therapy Cook County Hosp., Chgo., 1954-56; occupational therapist Michael Reese Hosp., Chgo., 1956-58; dir. occupational therapy Schawb Rehab. Center, Chgo., 1958-66; adminstrv. coordinator Milw. County Mental Health Center, 1969—. Instr. occupational therapy U. Ill., 1965-66. Mem. Am. Coll. Hosp. Adminstrs., Am. Occupational Therapy Assn. Home: 10141 W Forest Home Hales Corners WI 53130 Office: 9191 Watertown Plank Milwaukee WI 53226

WILLIAMS, NANCY MCGIONE, wife of U.S. senator; m. Harrison A. Williams, Feb. 14, 1948; children—Nancy, Peter, Wendy, Jonathan, Nina. Wife of U.S. Senator from N.J. Address: 231 Elizabeth Av Westfield NJ 07090*

WILLIAMS, NAOMI SAUNDERS, librarian; b. Texarkana, Tex.; d. Jeremiah P. and Lena G. (Munford) Williams; student Crane Jr. Coll., Chgo., 1929. U. Chgo., 1934; m. Vernon Bernard Williams, Jr., June 5, 1929; 1 son, Vernon Bernard, III. Asst. to med. social worker Chgo. Relief Adminstrn., 1935-37; jr. asst. librarian Englewood High Sch., 1937; library asst. Woodlawn Regional Library, 1952-61, head asst. Chatham Br. Library, 1961-62, librarian, 1968—; librarian Altgeld Gardens Sub-Br., 1962—; head asst. librarian Pullman Br. Library, Chgo., Dr. Martin Luther King Jr. br. library, 1968-70, librarian Hiram Kelly br., 1970—. Mem. center com., bd. dirs. Woodlawn YWCA. Mem. A.L.A., Ill. Library Assn., N.A.A.C.P., Chgo. Library Staff Assn. (council mem. 1942-43, 56-57), Chgo. Library Club, Internat. Visitors Center Chgo., Women's Aux. Chatham Lions Club (pres. 1969—), Art Inst. Chgo. Sigma Lambda Sigma. Conglist. Editorial bd. Staff News, Chgo. Pub. Library, 1948-52. Home: 3001 S Michigan Av Chicago IL 60616 Office: 6151 S Normal Blvd Chicago IL 60621

WILLIAMS, NELLIE CAPITOLA, assn. adminstr.; b. Atlanta, May 7, 1943; d. Handy Garfield and Nellie Bell (Gardner) Williams; B.S. in Math., Bethune-Cookman Coll., 1963. Counselor, Mercer Coll., Trenton, N.J., 1969-70; dean students Job Corps, N.J., Edison, 1970-71; mgr. residential programs RCA Service Co., Drums, Pa., 1971-72; dir. Tidewater (Va.) Job Corps Center, 1972-73; asso. planning and evaluation Stop Orgn., Norfolk, Va., 1973—. Cons. Dynacom., Inc., Norfolk, 1973-74. Mem. Nat. Assn. Women Deans, Adminstrs. and Counselors, Nat. Assn. Community Devel., Communities in Action Together, Alpha Kappa Alpha. Democrat. Methodist. Home: 529 Fountain Lake Dr Virginia Beach VA 23451 Office: 101 Mount Pleasant Rd Chesapeake VA 23320

WILLIAMS, PAT PARKER, radio sta. exec., composer; b. Berkeley, Cal., Jan. 27, 1923; d. George and Mildred (Johnston) Parker; student Sullins Jr. Coll., 1940-41; Mus.B., U. Miss., 1943; m. Grayson Headley, Dec. 30, 1946 (dec. 1961); m. 2d, M. Lee Williams, Dec. 18, 1964 (div.); 1 son, Philip Lee. Women's dir. radio sta. WNNT, Warsaw, Va., commentator daily women's program, Chat with Pat, 1952-60, now owner, pres. radio station WNNT AM-FM; asst. soc. editor Jackson Daily News, 1943-44. Composer: concerto for piano and orch., Rhapsody of Youth, performed by Nat. Air Force Symphony, Washington, Lisner Auditorium, 1947, guest pianist with Nat. Air Force Symphony, 1964; (song) Cotton Picking Blues, featured in several musicals in Miss., Washington; (song) Maid of Cotton, used as theme song Nat. Cotton Council, 1945-51; (song) Lucky X, ofcl. song Chi Omega. Chmn., Red Cross water safety program, Lancaster County, Va., 1950-56; mem. exec. com. Jr. Assembly, Washington; jr. chmn. Home Hospitality Com., Washington, 1943-46; also UN Club activities, Washington, 1943-48. Mem. Am. Women in Radio and Television (dir. Va. 1962-65), Nat. Soc. Arts and Letters (music chmn. Washington chpt. 1964-65), Va. Assn. Broadcasters, Internat. Platform Assn., Salvation Army Aux., Nat. Assn. Am. Composers and Conductors, Women's Com. for Nat. Symphony Orch., Chi Omega, Delta Beta Sigma, Sigma Alpha Iota, Alpha Psi Omega. Episcopalian. Clubs: Friday Morning Music; Debutante of Miss., Women's (chmn. music div. Lancaster County, Va. 1956-60); Washington; Kenwood Golf and Country; Kenwood Garden; Tides Inn Chesapeake; Indian Creek Yacht and Country, Windmill Point Yacht. Home: 6211 Garnett Dr Chevy Chase MD 20015 also Lavendar Landing Box 33 Irvington VA 22480 Office: Radio Sta WNNT Warsaw VA 22572

WILLIAMS, PATRICIA ANN (MRS. PAUL WYMAN WILLIAMS), mus. ofcl., educator; b. Sterling, Colo., Nov. 18, 1947; d. Donald Edward and Harriett Lucille (Rolph) McAlister; B.A. in Anthropology, U. N.M., 1970; m. Paul Wyman Williams, Dec. 2, 1972. Curator edn. Sanford Mus., Cherokee, Ia., 1970, adminstrv. asst., 1971—. Tchr. Cherokee Community Schs., 1973—. Mem. Ia. (v.p.), N.W. Ia. (asst. editor Newsletter) archeol. socs., Cherokee County Hist. Soc. (newsletter editor, co-chmn. geneal. com.). Contbr. articles to profl. jours. Home: 719 N 2d St Cherokee IA 51012 Office: 117 E Willow St Cherokee IA 51012

WILLIAMS, PATRICIA GABRIEL (MRS. LUCIUS WILLIAMS, JR.), coll. counselor; b. Thomasville, Ga., Oct. 4, 1946; d. Edward and Tiney (Reynolds) Gabriel; student Rutgers U., 1967; B.S. in Psychology, Morgan State Coll., 1968; M.A. in Psychology, Montclair State Coll., 1970; m. Lucius Williams, Jr., Mar. 25, 1972. Resident adviser Job Corps for Women, Jersey City, 1968; grad. asst. Montclair State Coll. Urban Inst., Upper Montclair, N.J., 1968-69, staff asst. housing, 1969-70; counselor Essex County Coll., Newark, 1970—, adj. prof. psychology, 1972-73. Coordinator counseling Equal Opportunity Fund, 1971—, mem. adv. bd., 1971—; mem. Bertha Buckman Scholarship Fund, 1970—; supr. Youth in Action Orgn., 1972—. Bd. trustees Leaguers, Newark. Named Outstanding Educator of Am., 1973. Mem. Am. Personnel and Guidance Assn., Nat. Assn. Women Deans and Counselors. Office: 31 Clinton St Newark NJ 07102

WILLIAMS, PAULINE BOLTON, civic worker; b. Cleve., Apr. 2, 1924; d. Irving Castle and Rachel Katherine (Wilson) Bolton; diploma Ethel Walker Sch., 1942, Sarah Lawrence Coll., 1946; m. David Rogerson Williams, Jr., May 28, 1944; children—Pauline B. (Mrs. Gerard E. d'Aquin), David Rogerson III, Rachel K. Treas. Rainbow Hosp., Cleve., 1965-66, trustee, 1949—; trustee Cleve. Zoo, 1966-68; mem. exec. com. Garden Club Cleve., 1962-64, Recreation League

Cleve., 1963-65. Club: Colony (N.Y.C.). Home: Oak Bar Ranch Route 82 Nogales AZ 85621 also 53 E 66th St New York City NY 10021

WILLIAMS, PETRA, interior designer; b. Poughkeepsie, N.Y., Sept. 2, 1913; d. Grover Henry and Mayme Nickerson (Bullock) Schatz; A.B., Skidmore Coll., 1936; LL.D., Fordham U., 1940; m. J. Calvert Williams, Nov. 26, 1946; children—Miranda (Mrs. Gordon Pratt), Frederica, Valerie. Founder, Fountain House, Phoenix, 1953, Fountain House East, Jeffersontown, Ky., 1966. Past pres. Meml. Hosp. Aux., Phoenix, Heard Mus. Guild, Phoenix. Bd. dirs. Ky. Humane Soc. Mem. Nat. Soc. Interior Designers (nat. dir. for Ariz. 1957-58, Ky. 1968, pres. Ky. 1967-68), Nat. Assn. Dealers in Antiques (dir., nat. chmn. legislation), Jeffersontown C. of C. (dir.), D.A.R., Ky. Hist. Soc., Nat. Orgn. Women (legislative coordinator Ky.), Antique Appraisal Soc. Am. Mem. Soc. Friends. Club: Filson. Author: Flow Blue China, An Aid to Identification, 1971; Flow Blue China II, 1973. Home: 4906 Chenoweth Run Rd Jeffersontown KY 40299 Office: 10412 Walterson Trail Jeffersontown KY 40299

WILLIAMS, RACHAEL VIENNA, aviation sch. adminstr.; b. Waterbury, Conn., June 13, 1918; d. Samuel Parmalee and Leonie (Brown) Williams; grad. Pine Manor Jr. Coll., 1938; student U. Conn., 1957-58; grad. Simsbury (Conn.) Flight Sch., 1944. Head, A.R.C. Motor Corps, 1939-43; clearance officer FAA, 1943-45; co-operator Oak Bluffs (Mass.) Airport, Trade Wind Flying Service, Martha's Vineyard, Mass., 1947-54; mgr. Amerind Found., Dragoon, Ariz., 1959-60; mgr. Martha's Vineyard Shipyard, marine store, Vineyard Haven, Mass., 1960-65, dir., 1949-54; dir. Trade Wind Flying Service, 1947—; sec.-treas., dir. East Chop Yacht Club, Oak Bluffs, 1969—. Mem. Finance Com. Oak Bluffs, 1973—. Mem. 99's (pres. Conn. chpt. 1946-47), Jr. League Waterbury, Grange. Club: Madison Beach Yacht. Home: Winemack Oak Bluffs MA 02557 Office: Box 525 Oak Bluffs MA 02557

WILLIAMS, ROBERTA LOUISE, mus. ofcl.; b. Louisville, July 10, 1943; d. James and Johnnie Roberta (Drake) Williams; B.S. in Art Edn., U. Louisville, 1965. Tchr., Jr. Art Gallery, Louisville, part-time 1961-65, asst. dir., 1965-69, exec. dir., 1969—. Mem. Am. Assn. Museums, Ky. Art Edn. Assn., Louisville Art Center Assn., Kappa Delta Pi. Home: 2117 Magazine St Louisville KY 40211 Office: 301 York St Louisville KY 40203

WILLIAMS, SALLY JANE ROBINSON (MRS. JOHN F. WILLIAMS), nurse; b. Detroit, Nov. 20, 1926; d. Edward Leslie and Lucile (Ford) Robinson; R.N., Harper Hosp. Sch. Nursing, 1947; B.S., Cal. State U. at Long Beach, 1956, M.A., 1959; m. John Tilman Williams, Aug. 23, 1947; children—Leslie Ann, Martha Lou (Mrs. James G. Hitchcock). Dir. nursing Ingham County Hosp., Lansing, Mich., 1950-51; sch. nurse Little Lake City Sch. Dist., Santa Fe Springs, Cal., 1952-61; sch. nurse Anaheim (Cal.) Union High Sch. Dist., 1961-65, cons. family life and sex edn., 1965-69; sch. nurse Savanna High Sch., Anaheim, 1969—; instr. U. Cal. at Riverside, 1969—; instr. U. Cal. at Irvine, 1970—; editor Cal. Sch. Nurses Orgn. Newsletter, 1962-69. Mem. Cal. Sch. Health Assn. (rec. sec. 1957-61), N.E.A. (pres. dept. sch. nurses 1969-70), Am. Sch. Health Assn., Am. Pub. Health Assn., Anaheim Secondary Tchrs. Assn. Author: Family Life and Sex Education, K-12, 1969; (with Esther D. Schulz) Family Life and Sex Education: Curriculum and Instruction, 1969. Contbr. articles to profl. jours. Home: 13251 Safford St Garden Grove CA 92643 Office: Savanna High Sch 301 N Gilbert St Anaheim CA 92801

WILLIAMS, SHIRLEY MALINDA WARRICK, journalist; b. Birmingham, Ala., Jan. 6, 1947; d. William Donald and Alice Athelene (Royston) Warrick; B.S., U. So. Miss., 1969; M.A., N. Tex. State U., Denton, 1973; m. Richard Harold Williams, June 2, 1973. Travel columnist Shades Valley Sun, Birmingham, 1969; writer women's dept. Birmingham Post-Herald, 1969-70; music sch. reporter pub. information office N. Tex. State U., 1970-71; asst. ednl. services dept. Memphis Comml. Appeal, 1971—. Instr. journalism Memphis State U., 1973—. Mem. Fedn. Republican Women. Recipient Writer's award Pub. Relations Soc. Am. Mem. Women in Communications (student liaison chmn.), Sigma Delta Chi, Delta Delta Delta. Baptist. Author: A Study of Thirty Newspaper in the Classroom Programs, 1973. Home: 1505 Central Av Memphis TN 38104 Office: 495 Union St Memphis TN 38104

WILLIAMS, VIRA KENNEDY (MRS. MATTHEW ALBERT WILLIAMS), city ofcl.; b. Hartford, Conn., July 24, 1928; d. Charles Leonard and Maude Gladys (Warring) Kennedy; B.S., Bennet Coll., 1949; certificate med. technology Boston U. Sch. Medicine, 1951; M.S., U. So. Cal., 1961; m. Mathew Albert Williams, June 19, 1955; children—Linda Miyoko, Nanci Jean, Pamela Lynn. Med. technologist Free Hosp. for Women, Brookline, Mass., 1951-52; research asst. Howard U. Med. Sch., Washington, 1952-55; med. technician Guadalupe Clinic, San Diego, 1955-56; tchr. pub. schs. Los Angeles, 1959-60, substitute, San Diego, 1960-61; mem. adv. bd. San Diego Volunteer Bur., 1963-68; mem. Los Munecas Aux. to Children Home Soc., 1962—; mem. adv. bd. City Schs. Health Occupations, 1969—, also Health Services; chmn. Health Career Clubs, 1967-68; dir. med. careers Women's Aux. to San Diego County Med. Soc., 1968-69; med. edn. chmn. Women's Aux. S.D. County Med. Soc., 1969—; v.p. San Diego Civil Service Commn., 1971-73, pres., 1974—. Mem. Am. Freedoms Found. Valley Forge, 1971—; student lectures coordinator San Diego Opera Guild, 1969-72. Bd. dirs. Salvation Army Door of Hope, 1973—; trustee Children's Health Center, 1973—. Named San Diego Woman of Distinction, Women, Inc., 1969, San Diego Woman of Valour, Temple Beth Israel Sisterhood, 1970, San Diego Woman of Elegance, Salvation Army Aux., 1971. Mem. Alumni Assn. Edn. U. So. Cal., Intergovtl. Personnel Mgmt. Assn. (affirmative action com.). Democrat. Presbyn. Home: 5740 Daffodil Lane San Diego CA 92120 Office: City Adminstrn Bldg Civil Service Dept San Diego CA 92101

WILLIAMS, WILMA CODE, real estate broker; b. Mpls., May 20, 1912; d. William Andrew and Della Grace (Burnell) Simpson; grad. high sch.; m. Russell E. Code, Jan. 10, 1931 (div. Mar. 1968); children—John E., Judith (Mrs. Robert H. Flanegin); m. 2d, Winston C. Williams, Feb. 27, 1970. Saleslady, L.S. Donaldson Dept. Store, Mpls., 1935-42; asst. sportswear buyer Bon March'e Seattle, 1942-43; buyer, mgr. Anticipation Shop, Beverly Hills, Cal., 1948-53; buyer Sears Roebuck, Hollywood, also Glendale, Cal., 1953-58; with Jack Holt Realty Glendale, 1958-62; v.p., sec. Win-Code Realty, Inc., Glendale, Cal., 1963—. First v.p. Glendale (Cal.) Rep. Federated Study Club, 1973—. Bd. govs., mem. women's com. Glendale Symphony. Mem. Glendale C. of C., Glendale Multiple Listings Assn. (dir. 1963-65, 74), Women's Council Real Estate Bds. (chpt. pres. 1964). Mem. Assn. Religious Sci. Ch. Home: 1515 El Miradero Glendale CA 91201 Office: 1629 W Glenoaks Blvd Glendale CA 91201

WILLIAMS, ZEANETTE MOORE (MRS. RALPH L. WILLIAMS), hosp. exec.; b. Los Angeles, Mar, 8, 1921; d. John Lawson and Alice Flora (Lynn) Moore; B.A., Occidental Coll., 1942; children—Leslie (Mrs. Frank Armstrong), John Roberts, James Roberts; m. 2d, Ralph L. Williams, May 8, 1970. With editorial dept. Los Angeles Times, 1940-52; free-lance publicity work, Los Angeles, 1952-58; pub. relations dir. Children's Hosp. Med. Center, Oakland, 1962-67, Alta Bates Hosp., Berkeley, 1967—. Press sec. Mrs. Barry Goldwater, Republican Nat. Conv., 1964. Mem. Am. Soc. Hosp. Pub. Relations (dir. 1973-74), Hosp. Pub. Relations Assn. No. Cal. (pres. 1972-73). Home: 1477 A Pico Ct Walnut Creek CA 94596 Office: Alta Bates Hosp Webster and Colby Sts Berkeley CA 94705

WILLIAMSON, ALIX B. (MRS. JOSEPH A. LIPPMAN), publicist; b. N.Y.C.; d. Victor William and Marion (Schlang) Williamson; B.A., Hunter Coll., 1935; m. Joseph A. Lippman, June 1, 1947; 1 dau., Victoria Alexandra. Publicist, specializing in promotional campaigns for concert and opera artists, 1938—; publicity dir. Stadium Concerts, N.Y.C., 1950-64; Author: Mother Is Minnie, 1960. Contbr. to mags. including Reader's Digest, Good Housekeeping, Vogue, Better Homes and Gardens. Office: 1860 Broadway New York City NY 10023

WILLIAMSON, BERNICE LINDERMAN (MRS. CHARLES T. WILLIAMSON), coll. adminstr.; b. Palmer, Neb., Sept. 20, 1912; d. Charles R. and Elsie (Davis) Linderman; A.A., Stephens Coll., 1932; B.S., U. Mo., 1952, M.Ed., 1955, postgrad. 1963, Northwestern U., summer 1936; m. Charles T. Williamson, June 30, 1938. Residence counselor Stephens Coll., Columbia, Mo., 1933-38, asst. in psychology dept., 1941-43, counselor counseling services, 1943-71, asst. dir., 1956-71, asst. to pres., 1971-74, exec. asst. to pres., 1974—. Bd. dirs. Boone County Assn. Mental Health, 1964-69; v.p. Mental Health Assn., 1967-69. Mem. Am. Personnel and Guidance Assn., Am. Coll. Personnel Assn. (chmn. student health commn. 1965-67), Nat. Vocational Guidance Assn., Mo. Psychol. Assn. (asso.), Am. Assn. U. Profs. (asso.), Am. Assn. for Higher Edn., English Speaking Union, Pi Lambda Theta. Home: 1413 Anthony St Columbia MO 65201 Office: Stephens Coll Columbia MO 65201

WILLIAMSON, BETTY JAYNE HUGHES (MRS. JOSEPH ROBERT WILLIAMSON), systems design cons.; b. New Brunswick, N.J., May 29, 1941; d. Ronald Clyde and Esther (Wenzel) Hughes; B.S., Mich. State U., 1963; A.D.A., Duke U. Med. Center, 1964; m. Joseph Robert Williamson, June 3, 1972. Therapeutic dietitian Lankenau Hosp., Phila., 1964-65, asst. chief dietitian, 1965-66, chief dietitian, 1966-68; administrv. dietitian Hahnemann Med. Coll. and Hosp., Phila., 1968-72; asso.-facilities planning E.F. Johnson Co., Inc., Phila., 1972—; cons. Community Meml. Hosp., West Grove, Pa. The Larchwood Sch., Phila. Mem. Am., Pa., Phila. (nominating chmn. 1973-74, sec. 1969-71, pres. 1972-73) dietetic assns., Pi Beta Phi. Republican. Mem. United Ch. Christ. Contbr. to Cyclopedia of Medicine, also jours. in field. Home: 274 Iven Av St Davids PA 19087 Office: 613 W Cheltenham Av Philadelphia PA 19126

WILLIAMSON, DOROTHY LOUISE DAVIDSON, toy mfg. co. exec.; b. Seminole, Okla., Jan. 27, 1930; d. Otis E. and Fredonia E. (Kohlhorst) Davidson; grad. high sch.; m. Quentin Oscar Williamson, June 5, 1949; children—Carol (Mrs. Samuel Marvin Miller), Linda (Mrs. Earl Floyd Hicks). Vice pres. Superior Insulation and Weather Strip, Tulsa, 1947-54; bookkeeper Nu-Cushion Products Co., Keene, Tex., 1957-74, mgr., 1969-74, v.p., gen. mgr., 1974—. Home: Route 2 Box 63 Bowie TX 76230 Office: 425 College Av Box 347 Keene TX 76059

WILLIAMSON, ELECTA JANE, educator; b. Blanchester, O., Nov. 29, 1920; d. Thomas Alexander and Gelnna May (Smith) Williamson; B.S., U. Md., 1943; M.A., N.Y. U., 1947; Ed.D., Northwestern Colo. U., 1959. Tchr. Eastern High Sch., Washington, 1943-45, Blanchester Pub. Schs., 1945-47, Wyo. Pub. Schs., 1945-48; asst. prof. edn. Morehead (Ky.) State U., 1960-63, counsellor, 1963-64; prof. edn. Pacific Luth. U., Tacoma, Wash., 1964—; Fulbright exchange tchr. Fakenham Grammar Sch., Eng., 1953-54. cons. Head Start, 1966—; cons. day care, 1969—. Recipient Distinguished Tchr. award Wash. State Auto Dealers Assn., 1970. Mem. Kappa Delta Phi, Phi Lambda Theta. Mem. Order Eastern Star. Home: PO Box 44054 Tacoma WA 98444

WILLIAMSON, ELLEN DOUGLAS, author; b. Cedar Rapids, Ia., Oct. 31, 1905; d. George Bruce and Irene (Hazeltine) Douglas; grad. Spence Sch., N.Y.C., 1923; B.A. cum laude, Vassar Coll., 1927; m. George J. Jaeger, 1931 (dec. 1937), 1 dau., Margaret Douglas (Mrs. Nathaniel Litt); m. 2d, Gregory Williamson, June 28, 1939. Dir. Hazeltine & Perkins Drug Co., Grand Rapids, Mich., 1940-58. First pres. Cedar Rapids Jr. League, 1928-31. Trustee Coe Coll., Cedar Rapids; mem. nat. bd. Plays for Living. Mem. Author's League, Midwest Author's League. Republican. Presbyn. Author: Moon of Violence, 1960; Wall Street Made Easy, 1965; Spend Yourself Rich, 1970. Address: 100 Battle Rd Princeton NJ 08540

WILLIAMSON, JANE LOUISE, veterinarian; b. Jersey City, Sept. 30, 1925; d. George Parke and Eunice (Bush) Williamson; D.V.M., Cornell U., 1949. Asso., Dr. Robert Ticehurst, Red Bank, N.J., 1949-50; veterinarian staff Am. Soc. Prevention Cruelty to Animals, N.Y.C., 1950-53; individual practice vet. medicine, Fair Lawn, N.J., 1953—. Merit badge counselor Fair Lawn council Boy Scouts Am., 1965-66. Mem. Women's (Eastern v.p.), No. N.J. vet. med. assns. (pres., chmn. state ethics com.). Mem. Community Ch. Club: Cornell Women's of Bergen County. Home: 3-15 Saddle River Rd Fair Lawn NJ 07410 Office: 3-21 Saddle River Rd Fair Lawn NJ 07410

WILLIAMSON, JUANITA VIRGINIA, educator; b. Shelby, Miss.; d. John Morris and Alice (McAllister) Williamson; B.A., LeMoyne Coll., 1938; M.A., Atlanta U., 1940; Ph.D., U. Mich., 1961. Tchr. pub. schs., Memphis, 1940-46; instr. English, LeMoyne Coll., Memphis, 1946-53, prof. English, 1953—; vis. prof. English and linguistics Ball State U., 1962-63; vis. prof. U. Wis.-Milw., 1971, U. Tenn., 1973; cons. Bd. dirs. Bethlehem Center, 1964-68, mem. Tenn. Council on Human Relations, 1962—; exec. com. Conf. Coll. Composition and Communication. Gen. Edn. Bd. fellow, 1949-51; Ford Found. Fellow, 1954-55; Am. Council Learned Socs. grantee, summer 1951; United Negro Coll. Fund fellow, 1960; U.S. Office Edn. grantee; Amistad Found. grantee. Mem. Linguistic Soc. Am., Am. Assn. U. Profs., Modern Lang. Assn., (del. assembly), Coll. Lang. Assn., Nat. Council Tchrs. English, Conf. Coll. Composition, Am. Dialect Soc. (exec. com.), Am. Assn. U. Women, Phi Lambda Theta, Delta Sigma Theta. Conglist. Author: A Phonological and Morphological Study of the Speech of the Negro of Memphis, 1970. Co-editor: A Various Language, 1971. editorial bd. Am. Speech, Coll. Composition and Communication. Contbr. articles to profl. jours. Research in the area Negro speech. Home: 1217 Cannon St Memphis TN 38106

WILLIAMSON, MARGARET MADISON (MRS. NATHANIEL HOWARD WILLIAMSON), librarian; b. Washington, June 26, 1935; d. George William and Myrtle (Reed) Madison; B.A. in English, U. Md., 1957; M.S. in L.S., Columbia, 1965; m. Nathaniel Howard Williamson, Aug. 17, 1965. Classification record asst. Library of Congress, Washington, 1957-64; asst. catalog librarian U. Houston Libraries, 1965-67, catalog librarian, 1967-74, serials editor, 1974—. Instr. exercise class Houston YWCA, 1970—. Mem. A.L.A., Tex. Library Assn., Nat. Geog. Soc., Spl. Libraries Assn., Mensa; Beta Phi Mu. Home: 10008 Bob White St Houston TX 77035

WILLIAMSON, MARY ELLEN, educator; b. Kansas City, Mo., Apr. 24, 1924; d. Elmer Clay and Ruth (Peterman) Williamson; B.J., U. Mo., 1947, Ph.D., 1973; M.A., Columbia, 1951. Pub. relations dir. Kansas City Tb Soc., 1947-50; asst. editor N.E.A., Washington, 1951-52; promotion and pub. affairs dir. Radio Sta. KXOK, St. Louis, 1952-55; cons. Jean Sullivan Advt. Agy., Omaha, 1955-68; asst. prof., dept. speech U. Neb., Omaha, 1969—. Mem. Internat. Communication Assn., Assn. for Edn. in Journalism, Omaha Press Club, Quota Club Internat., Nat. Orgn. for Women, Alpha Chi Omega, Alpha Psi Omega, Kappa Tau Alpha. Clubs: Field (Omaha); Ak-Sar-Ben Curling. Home: 5217 Mason St Omaha NE 68106 Office: Box 688 Downtown Sta Omaha NE 68101

WILLIAMSON, SANDRA DIANNE KILGORE, utility exec.; b. Ruston, La., May 12, 1948; d. James Henry and Margie Merle (Simmons) Kilgore; B.S. magna cum laude, La. Tech. U., 1969, M.B.A., 1971; m. Robert Lee Williamson, Dec. 8, 1973. Sec. to dean women La. Tech. U., Ruston, 1971-72, coordinator women's housing, 1972-73; exec. sec. Ark. La. Gas Co., Shreveport, La., 1974—. Mem. Nat. Assn. Women's Deans and Counselors, Nat. Collegiate Assn. Secs., Cwens, Phi Kappa Phi, Omicron Delta Epsilon, Beta Gamma Sigma. Baptist. Home: PO Box 338 Mooringsport LA 71060

WILLIAMSON, SUE DODDS, antique dealer; b. Clarksburg, W.Va., Apr. 29, 1935; d. Okey Lee and Edna Elizabeth (Corder) Brown; B.S. cum laude, W.Va. U., 1957; postgrad. U. Md., 1960-63; m. Hal Whitney Williamson, Aug. 20, 1960. Tchr., Prince Georges Bd. Edn., 1957-64; owner Williamsons Antiques, New Market, Md., 1966—. Lectr., Hood Coll., Frederick, Md., Carroll County Bd. Recreation. Sec., Williamsburg Village Civic Assn., 1965; co-chmn. Planned Parenthood Montgomery County, 1965-66. Town clk., New Market, 1969—. Mem. Nat. Assn. Dealers in Antiques (state membership chmn. 1970-72), New Market Antique Dealers Assn. (pres. 1970), Olney C. of C., Mortar Bd. (editor 1957), Chi Omega. Methodist. Contbr. articles to profl. jours. Address: PO Box 33 20 W Main St New Market MD 21774

WILLIAMSON, SUSAN, coll. dean; b. Boston, Dec. 29, 1936; d. Richard Phillip and Mary (McCarthy) Williamson; A.B., Radcliffe Coll., 1958; M.A., Brandeis U., 1961, Ph.D., 1963; Instr., Cardinal Cushing Coll., Brookline, Mass., 1962-63, lectr., 1964-65, 71-72; asst. prof. Boston Coll., Chestnut Hill, Mass., 1963-64, Regis Coll., Weston, Mass., 1965-67, asso. prof. math., 1967-71, prof., 1971—, acad. dean, 1973—. Mem. Am. Assn. U. Profs., Am. Math. Soc., Assn. for Women in Math., Math. Assn. Am. Contbr. articles to profl. jours. Home: 37 Hagen Rd Newton Centre MA 02159 Office: Wellesley St Weston MA 02193

WILLIFORD, CYNTHIA VERNELL WILLIAMS, educator; b. Seneca, S.C., Mar. 14, 1917; d. Nathaniel and Lula (Majors) Williams; B.S. in Home Econs., S.C. State Coll., 1939; M.S., Mich. State U., 1963; m. Preston Williford, Sept. 2, 1949. Tchr. pub. schs. Liberty, S.C., 1939-41, Lancaster, S.C., 1941-44; mem. staff extension home econs. programs Clemson (S.C.) U., 1944—, asso. home economist Anderson County, 1947-72, asst. prof. home econs., asst. to state leader extension programs home econs. Coop. Extension Service, 1972—. Mem. Wesleyan Service Guild, 1969—. Recipient Home Demonstration Agts. Distinguished Service award Nat. Negro Home Demonstration Agts. Assn., 1964. Mem. Palmette (past pres.), Nat. Negro (past pres.) home demonstration agts. assns., Am., S.C. home econs. assns., S.C., Am. assns. extension home economists, Womens Soc. Christian Service, Zonta Internat., Alpha Kappa Alpha, Epsilon Sigma Phi. Methodist. Club: Wives (Anderson). Address: 222 Hill Crest Anderson SC 29621

WILLIFORD, MIRIAM, historian, coll. adminstr.; b. Rock Hill, S.C., Mar. 26, 1926; d. Samuel Elliott and Lillie (Parrish) Williford; B.A., Winthrop Coll., 1945; M.A., U. N.C., 1950; Ph.D., Tulane U., 1963. Social studies tchr. Cambridge (Md.) High Sch., 1945-47; supr. social studies Winthrop Tng. Sch., Winthrop Coll., Rock Hill, S.C., 1947-62, asso. prof. history Winthrop Coll., 1963-68, prof., 1968—, chmn. Latin Am. area studies, 1964—, dir. pub. service, 1973—. Mem. steering com. Consortium of Latin Am. Studies Programs. Orgn. Am. States Research fellow, 1962, Ford Found. Humanities fellow, 1964-65. Mem. Am., So. hist. assns., Conf. Latin Am. History, Latin Am. Studies Assn., Audubon Soc., Phi Kappa Phi, Phi Alpha Theta, Sigma Delta Pi. Author: Las Luces y La Civilization: The Social Reform of Mariano Galvez, 1969. Contbr. articles to profl. jours. Home: Route 8 Box 86 Rock Hill SC 29730

WILLIG, NANCY TOBIN, art critic; b. N.Y.C., Aug. 31, 1943; d. Robert and Sylvia (Moscowitz) Tobin; B.F.A., Syracuse U., 1965; m. Ronald Willig, Nov. 25, 1966; children—H. Jason, Daniel Tobin. Asst. editor, art dir. Buffalo Mag., 1965-69, art dir., 1969-74; art critic Buffalo Courier Express, 1971—, book reviewer, 1972—. Guest lectr. State U. N.Y. at Buffalo, 1973. Mem. Art Dirs. Club Buffalo (dir. 1968-70, sec. 1969-70), Am. Newspaper Guild, Patteran Artists (hon.). Contbr. to various publs. Home: 497 Sprucewood Terrace Williamsville NY 14221 Office: Buffalo Courier Express Buffalo NY 14240

WILLINGHAM, MARY MAXINE, fashion retailer; b. Childress, Tex., Sept. 12, 1928; d. Charles Bryan and Mary (Bohannon) McCollum; B.A., Tex. Tech. U., 1949; m. Welborn Kiefer Willingham, Aug. 14, 1950; children—Sharon, Douglas, Sheila. Interviewer Univ. Placement Service, Tex. Tech. U., Lubbock, 1964-69; owner, mgr., buyer Maxine's Accent, Lubbock, 1969—. Leader Campfire Girls, Lubbock, 1964-65; sec. Community Theatre, Lubbock, 1962-64. Named Outstanding Mcht., Fashion Retailor mag., 1971. Mem. Am. Bus. Women's Club. Democrat. Home: 1605 56th St Lubbock TX 79412 Office: 8 Briercroft Center Lubbock TX 79412

WILLIS, BRONNA YVONNE, coll. dean; b. Morehead City, N.C., May 18, 1940; d. Henry Delance and Olga Elberta (Lewis) Willis; B.A., Woman's Coll. U. N.C., 1962; M.S., Ind. U., 1969. Caseworker Dept. Pub. Welfare, Rockingham County, N.C., 1962-64, A.R.C., Maxwell Air Force Base Hosp., Montgomery, Ala., 1964-65; asst. to dean of students Agnes Scott Coll., Decatur, Ga., 1965-68; asst. dean of women U. S.C., Columbia, 1969-71; dean of students Randolph-Macon Woman's Coll., Lynchburg, Va., 1971—. Mem. Lynchburg City Republican Com., 1971-72. Mem. Nat., Regional assns. women deans and counselors. Club: Altrusa of Lynchburg. Home: 305 Rowland Dr Lynchburg VA 24503 Office: Randolph Macon Woman's College Lynchburg VA 24504

WILLIS, CONSTANCE LAURICELLA (MRS. HARRY N. WILLIS), librarian; b. Somerville, Mass., Nov. 6, 1912; d. John and Ida (Bianconi) Lauricella; B.S., Simmons Coll., 1935, M.S., 1967; m. Harry Nelson Willis, Aug. 18, 1940 (dec.); children—Stephen John, Douglas James, Paul Richard. Asst. research librarian Arthur D. Little, Inc., 1936-39; reference librarian Mitre Corp., Bedford, Mass., 1960-64; circulation librarian Malden (Mass.) Pub. Library, 1961-64; head librarian Saugus (Mass.) Pub. Library, 1964—; book reviewer, lectr. Mem. A.L.A., Greater Boston Pub. Library Adminstrs., North Shore Library Club (sec. 1965-67), New Eng., Mass. library assns., Mass. Library Adminstrs. Assn., Saugus Hist. Soc., Simmons

Alumnae Assn. Episcopalian. Home: 14 Clayton St Malden MA 02148 Office: Saugus Public Library 295 Central St Saugus MA 01906

WILLIS, CORINNE DENNENY (MRS. NORMAN WILLIS), librarian; b. Buffalo, Apr. 23, 1907; d. Edward James and Cora (Schwarz) Denneny; B.A., D'Youville Coll., 1928; M.A., St. Louis U., 1930; m. Norman Willis, Oct. 14, 1944; 1 son, Peter Denneny. Tchr. pub. high schs., Buffalo, 1930-50, librarian, 1950—. Mem. Kappa Gamma Pi. Author: The Ivory Cage, 1966; Boy Minus Girl, 1967; Tilli, 1969. Home: 3052 Eggert Rd Tonawanda NY 14150

WILLIS, DIANE JANICE, clin. and pediatric psychologist; b. Tahlequah, Okla., May 9, 1937; d. William Pascal and Zelma Marie (Bynum) Willis; B.S. in Biology, Northeastern State Coll., Tahlequah, 1960; M.A. in Psychology, George Peabody Coll., 1965; Ph.D. in Exptl. Psychology, U. Okla., 1970. Intern clin. psychology U. Okla. Med. Center, 1969-71; med. technologist Am. Soc. Clin. Pathologists, 1960-64; research asst. neuropsychology lab. U. Okla. Med. Center, 1965-66, staff psychologist Child Study Center, 1967-69; staff psychologist dept. communication disorders and dept. pediatrics U. Okla. Health Scis. Center, 1966-67, chief clin. psychologist, 1971-74, asst. dir. pediatric psychology, coordinator in-patient psychol. services, also chief pediatric psychol. services Children's Hosp., 1974—, asst. prof. child and med. psychology, 1971—; cons. in field. Co-chmn. Democratic Com. Cleveland County, Okla., 1972-74, precinct chmn., 1972-73. Mem. Am., Southwest, Okla. psychol. assns., Soc. Pediatric Psychology (council rep. 1972-75, editor newsletter 1973—), Okla. Assn. Children With Learning Disabilities (adv. bd. 1972-76), Soc. Research Child Devel., Council Exceptional Children, Am. Soc. Clin. Pathologists, Okla. Council Hearing Impaired (chmn. pub. relations and publicity 1973-74), Alpha Sigma Alpha. Baptist. Contbr. profl. publns. Home: 1132 W Brooks St Norman OK 73069

WILLIS, JANE MARLOW, newspaper editor; b. Brandenburg, Ky., Mar. 8, 1942; d. James Mercer and Thelma (Marlow) Willis; B.A., So. Meth. U., 1964; postgrad. (Mark Ethridge fellow), U. N.C., 1966. Mem. staff Meade County Messenger, Brandenburg, 1964—, editor, 1966—. Former den mother local Cub Scouts; mem. drive com. Patton Museum Fund, 1965; mem. local com. Ky. Bicentennial, 1973; patron Pioneer Playhouse, Danville, Ky., 1972. Mem. Ky., Western Ky. (pres. 1971) press assns., Nat. Newspaper Assn., Sigma Delta Chi. Democrat. Methodist. Home: 321 Main St Brandenburg KY 40108 Office: Box 612 Brandenburg KY 40108

WILLIS, JO ANN (MRS. JAMES D. WILLIS), coll. dean.; b. Portland, Ore., Nov. 1, 1944; d. Alvin and Lydia (Obermiller) Williams; A.B., Northwest Nazarene Coll., 1965; M.A., U. Mo. at Kansas City, 1970; postgrad. Ore. State U.; m. James D. Willis, Aug. 1, 1964; children—Lori Ann, James Robert. Tchr. Roosevelt High Sch., Portland, Ore., 1965-66; asst. dean of Women Northwest Nazarene Coll., Nampa, Ida., 1968-70, dean of women, 1970—. Home: 824 Elder St Nampa ID 83651 Office: Northwest Nazarene College Box H Nampa ID 83651

WILLIS, JUDITH LAURA LEVINE, editor; b. Bklyn., May 24, 1941; d. Abraham Solomon and Ida (Erdberg) Levine; B.S. in Journalism, Ohio U., 1963; m. Ronald J. Willis, May 2, 1965; 1 dau., Heidi Ruth. Reporter, Trenton (N.J.) Times, 1963-64; asso. editor Met. Restaurant News, N.Y.C., 1964-65; information specialist Nat. Clearinghouse for Smoking and Health, USPHS, Washington, 1965-67; owner, sr. editor Judith Willis, The Traveling Editor, cons. services, Arlington, Va., 1967—. Mem. Women in Communications, Nat. Orgn. for Women. Book editor, editor, cons. editor Woodwind arts paper, Washington, 1971—. Office: 405 S Garfield St Arlington VA 22204

WILLIS, KATHRYN SETZER (MRS. JOHN KELVER WILLIS), radio broadcaster; b. Johnson City, Tenn., May 14, 1922; d. Glenn Warner and Kate (Ross) Setzer; grad. Pasadena Playhouse Sch. Theatre, 1942; m. John Kelver Willis, Mar. 12, 1945; children—John Kelver, Katy Glenn. Hostess, Half-Hour Show, NBC Shortwave Radio, N.Y.C., 1942-43; actress Broadway prodn. Winged Victory, 1943, Chgo. Co. Three's A Family, 1944; staff announcer WKPT Radio, Kingsport, Tenn., 1945; hostess half-hour WJHL radio show Women's Interest, Johnson City, Tenn., 1950—. Chmn. communications panel Tenn. Arts Commn., 1970. Mem. Am. Women in Radio and Television. Club: Junior Service League (Johnson City). Author: Kathryn Willis Cookbook, 1971. Home: 1807 New Haven Dr Johnson City TN 37601 Office: 137 W Main St Johnson City TN 37601

WILLIS, KATHRYN W., physician; b. Haslet, Tex., Nov. 26, 1922; d. Joseph Clifton and Ella (Long) Willis; A.S., Arlington State Coll., 1941; M.D. (pre-doctorate fellow, 1949-51), U. Tex., 1951. Intern Univ. Hosp., Med. Coll. Ala., Birmingham, 1951-52, fellow in internal medicine, 1952-53; resident Children's Med. Center, Dallas, 1953-55, fellow pediatric cardiology, 1955-57; practice medicine specializing in pediatrics, cardiology, Dallas, 1957—; mem. staff Children's Med. Center, Children's Hosp., both Dallas; mem. faculty Southwestern Med. Sch., U. Tex. at Dallas, 1957—, clin. asst. prof. pediatrics, 1959-71, clin. asso. prof., 1971—. Cons. pediatric cardiology Regional Heart Program, Tex. Health Dept., 1958—. Am. Heart Assn. postdoctoral fellow, 1952-53. Mem. Am. Acad. Pediatrics, A.M.A., Tex. Med. Assn., Dallas County Med. Soc., Dallas So. Clin. Soc., Tex. Pediatric Soc. Home: Box 27 Itasca TX 76055 Office: 1935 Amelia St Dallas TX 75235

WILLIS, MARGARET FRISTOE, librarian; b. St. Louis, Apr. 7, 1906; d. Prior Fristoe and Elva (Moss) Willis; B.A., Washington U., 1928; postgrad. St. Louis Library Sch., 1929, U. Mo., 1937, Ariz. State Coll., 1950. Asst. St. Louis Pub. Library, 1928-37; asst. The Booklist, A.L.A., 1937-42; hosp. librarian Jefferson Barracks, Mo., 1942-44; head circulation dept. Louisville Free Pub. Library, 1944-55; coordinator Library Extension Div., Frankfort, Ky., 1955-57, dir., 1957-62; state librarian Ky. Dept. of Libraries, 1962—. Sec. Ky. Bookmobile Project, 1953-55. Del. White House Conf. on Children and Youth. Mem. Am. Assn. U. Women, A.L.A. (council mem. 1956—), Southeastern (mem. exec. bd. 1960—), Ky. (state pres. 1954) library assn. Club: Arts (Louisville); Altrusa (Frankfort, Ky.). Author: Adult Study Camps, 1952. Home: 130 W State St Frankfort KY 40601 Office: Dept Libraries Frankfort KY 40601

WILLIS, MARILYN, univ. librarian; b. Magnolia, Ark., Mar. 10, 1933; d. Louie Marshall and Mary Eleanor (Casey) Willis; student La. Poly. Inst., 1951-54; Mus.B., La. State U., 1955, M.S., 1966. Writer commls., appeared on childrens daytime show WBRZ-TV, Baton Rouge, 1955-57; engring. sec. Wyandotte Chems. Corp., Baton Rouge, 1957-65; acquisitions and serials librarian La. State U., Shreveport, 1967-69, serials librarian Sch. Medicine, 1969—. Mem. La. Library Assn., Med. Library Assn., Delta Kappa Gamma. Democrat. Mem. Christian Ch. Club: Am. Contract Bridge League. Home: 2524 Sheri Lane Shreveport LA 71109

WILLIS, PHYLLIDA MAVE, educator; b. Wallington, Eng., Mar. 11, 1918; d. Charles Benneworth and Amy (Sellers) Willis; came to U.S., 1927, naturalized, 1933; A.B. summa cum laude, Mt. Holyoke Coll., 1938; A.M., Smith Coll., 1940; Ph.D., Columbia, 1946. Teaching fellow Smith Coll., 1938-40; sci. tchr. Knox Sch., Cooperstown, N.Y., 1940-42; univ. fellow Columbia, 1944-45; instr. chemistry Wellesley (Mass.) Coll., 1946-49, asst. prof., 1949-54; asso. prof., head dept. chemistry Newcomb Coll., Tulane U., New Orleans, 1954-60; Whitaker prof. chemistry, chmn. dept. phys. scis. and math. Hood Coll., Frederick, Md., 1960—. Sarah Berliner fellow Phys. Chemistry Lab., Oxford (Eng.) U., 1951-52; NSF Faculty fellow U. Minn., 1958. Fellow A.A.A.S.; mem. Research Soc. Am., Am. Assn. U. Profs., Am. Chem. Soc., Am. Assn. Physics Tchrs., Middle Atlantic Assn. Liberal Arts Chemistry Tchrs. (pres. 1972), Phi Beta Kappa, Sigma Xi. Presbyn. Clubs: Ladies Alpine (London); Appalachian Mountain (Boston), Potomac Appalachian Trail (Washington). Address: 805 Wilson Pl Frederick MD 21701

WILLMAN, CAROL ELSIE, educator; b. St. Louis, Jan. 16, 1934; d. Julius Carl and Johanna Henrietta (Strassner) Willman; A.B., Harris Tchrs. Coll., 1955; A.M., U. Mich., 1960, Ph.D. (Regents scholar, Fed. Govt. Spl. Edn. fellow), 1966. Tchr. pub. schs., St. Louis, 1955-56; spl. tchr. orthopedically handicapped Michael Sch., St. Louis, 1956-62, spl. tchr. multiple handicapped, 1962-64; founder, dir. tchr. tng. program in spl. edn. Harris Tchrs. Coll., St. Louis, 1965—, asso. prof. spl. edn., 1972—, chmn. urban edn. spl. edn. dept., 1973—; inservice tng. workshops for spl. edn. tchrs. St. Louis Bd. Edn., 1970—. Chmn. Harold C. Smith-Luch C. Elliott Meml. Fund, 1967—. Bd. dirs. Glennon Day Care Center. Mo. Soc. for Crippled Children scholar 1957; named Outstanding Young Woman of Yr., St. Louis Jr. C. of C., 1963. Mem. N.E.A., Mo., St. Louis (dir. 1967-69) tchrs. assns., Council for Exceptional Children (St. Louis area pres. 1963-64, state dir. 1968-71, state pres. 1973), Beta Beta Beta, Sigma Tau Delta, Pi Lambda Theta, Kappa Delta Pi, Phi Kappa Phi, Alpha Delta Kappa, Delta Kappa Gamma. Home: 4933 Finkman St St Louis MO 63109 Office: Harris Tchrs Coll 3026 Laclede St St Louis MO 63103

WILLMAN, MARY EVELYN, musician; b. Galveston, Tex., Nov. 8, 1938; d. Albert Gilbert and Elizabeth Mary (Lege) Collier; B.S. in Music (scholar), Larmar U., 1960; certificate educable mentally retarded Dominican Coll., 1969; m. John Charles Willman, Dec. 26, 1969; children—Andrew James, Eric John. Flutist, Beaumont (Tex.) Symphony, 1958-60; music tchr. Austin Ind. Sch. Dist., 1960-62; music tchr. Houston Ind. Sch. Dist., 1966-68, tchr. educable mentally retarded, 1968-70, tchr. Lamar Consol. Inds. Sch. Dist., Rosenberg, Tex., 1970-72; pvt. flute tchr., Houston, 1966—. Pres. United Ch. Women El Campo, Tex., 1962-63, LaLeche League, 1972-73, Houston Orgn. Parent Edn., 1972-74, Sutton Elementary Sch. Parent Tchrs. Orgn., 1970-74; den mother Cub Scouts, 1972-73. Music scholarship E. Tex. State Coll., 1956-58; Canterbury scholar, 1959. Democrat. Episcopalian. Club: Servetus (Houston). Address: 7809 Albacore Dr Houston TX 77036

WILLNER, ANN RUTH, polit. scientist, educator; b. N.Y.C.; d. Norbert and Bella (Richman) Willner; B.A., Hunter Coll., 1945; M.A., Yale, 1946; Ph.D., U. Chgo., 1961. Adviser, Govt. Indonesia, 1952-54; research asso. Center for Econ. Devel. and Cultural Change. U. Chgo., 1954-57, lectr., 1946-47, research asso., 1961-62; fgn. affairs analyst for Asian affairs Library Congress, 1960-61; asst. prof. State U. N.Y., Binghamton, 1962-63; postdoctoral research fellow Yale, 1963-64; research asso. Center Internat. Studies, Princeton, 1964-69; asso. prof. polit. sci. U. Kan., Lawrence, 1969-70, prof., 1970—. Mem. Am. Polit. Sci. Assn., Assn. for Asian Studies, Internat. Studies Assn. Author: The Neotraditional Accomodation to Political Independence, 1966; Charismatic Political Leadership, 1968. Home: 2112 Terrace Rd Lawrence KS 66044

WILLNER, FRAN CHARIN (MRS. MILTON M. WILLNER), artist; b. Newark, May 4, 1918; d. Morris and Alice (Kriegman) Charin; Asso. degree Am. Sch. Design, 1936-40; student Newark Sch. Fine and Indsl. Arts, 1955-56, Fairleigh Dickinson U., 1963; m. Milton H. Willner, Sept. 14, 1941; children—Andrew, Neil, Terry Tainow. One-woman shows at Newark State Coll., Newark Main Library, 1973, Newark Mus., 1974; exhibited in group shows at N.J. State Mus., Trenton, Montclair Art Mus., Morris Mus. Arts and Scis., Morristown, N.J.; represented in permanent collections Contemporary Art N.J., Bambergers, Newark, N.Y. Med. Coll.; mem. Atelier 3 graphic studio. Mem. Nat. Assn. Women Artists, Artists Equity, Print Club Phila. Contbr. to book Contemporary Decoupage (Thelma Newman). Home: 492 Summit Av Maplewood NJ 07040

WILLOCK, MARCELLE MONICA, physician; b. Georgetown, Guyana, Mar. 30, 1938; d. George and Renee (Dumaneir) Willock; brought to U.S., 1954, naturalized 1969; A.B., Coll. New Rochelle, 1958; M.D., Howard U., 1962. Intern Kings County Hosp., Bklyn., 1962-63; resident Presbyn. Hosp., N.Y.C., 1963-65; practice medicine, specializing in anesthesiology, N.Y.C., 1965—; mem. staff Univ. Hosp.; asst. prof. anesthesiology Med. Center, N.Y. U., 1968-73, asso. prof. anesthesia, 1973—; asst. med. examiner Office Chief Med. Examiner N.Y.C., 1966—; asso. dir. dept. anesthesiology Bellevue Hosp. Center, 1973—. Pres. Louis and Martha Deveaux Found., Panama City, Panama, 1966—. Diplomate Am. Bd. Anesthesiology. Mem. Am. Soc. Anesthesiologists, New York County Med. Soc. Home: 473 West End Av New York City NY 10024 Office: 560 1st Av New York City NY 10016

WILLOUGHBY, AVALEE, educator; b. McComb, Miss.; d. John Cletus and Vertner (Tynes) Willoughby; B.S., La. State U., 1942; M.A., U. Fla., 1956; Ed.D., U. Ala., 1972. Tchr. phys. edn. Southwest Miss. Jr. Coll., Summitt, 1944-51; phys. dir. YMCA, Birmingham, Ala., 1952-55; instr. phys. edn. U. Md., College Park, 1956-58; asst. prof., chmn. div. health, phys. edn. and recreation Samford U., Birmingham, 1958—; also rehab. work with handicapped. Extensive work Aquatics, A.R.C.; mem. Gov.'s Commn. on Phys. Fitness. Named to Sports Hall Fame, S.W. Miss. Jr. Coll., 1972. Fellow A.A.H.P.E.R.; mem. N.E.A., Ala. Assn. Health, Phys. Edn. and Recreation (pres. 1973-74), Am. Assn. U. Profs., Phi Kappa Phi, Delta Kappa Gamma; Kappa Delta Pi. Methodist. Club: Soroptimist. Home: 1841 Burning Tree Circle Birmingham AL 35226

WILLOUGHBY, FRANCES LOIS, psychiatrist, educator; b. Harrisburg, Pa., July 1, 1905; d. Frank Faul and Annie (Smith) Willoughby; A.B., Dickinson Coll., 1927; M.D., U. Ark., 1938. Tchr. Cramer Jr. High Sch., Camden, N.J., 1927-28, Jr. High Sch., Shippensburg, Pa., 1929-31; sec. First Meth. Ch., Camden, N.J., 1928-29; intern St. Lawrence Hosp., Lansing, Mich., 1938-39; resident Traverse City State Hosp., 1939-42, in charge women's receiving service, 1942-44; with M.C., USNR, 1944-48, USN, 1948-64, advanced through grades to capt., 1955, ret., 1964; practice medicine specializing in psychiatry, Glassboro, N.J., 1965—; mem. staff Underwood Meml. Hosp., Woodbury, N.J. Recipient Alumni citation Dickinson Coll., 1948. Diplomate Am. Bd. Psychiatry and Neurology. Fellow Am. Psychiat. Assn., A.A.A.S.; mem. Royal Soc. Health, A.M.A., Am. Assn. U. Women, Am. Med. Women's Assn. (life), U. Pa. Mus., Gloucester County (N.J.) Hist. Soc., Ocean City (N.J.) Hist. Mus., Little Rock Natural and Historic Soc. Methodist. Home: 414 W Holly Av Pitman NJ 08071 Office: Route 1 Box 405 Glassboro-Richwood Rd Glassboro NJ 08028

WILLOUGHBY, SARAH MARGARET CLAYPOOL, educator; b. Bowling Green, Ky.; d. Austin Burrell and Minerva (Renfrow) Claypool; B.S., Western Ky. U., 1938; Ph.D., Purdue U., 1950; m. John Richard Evans II, Aug. 30, 1938 (dec. Dec. 1942); 1 son, Richard Claypool; m. 2d, O. Glenn Willoughby, June 18, 1948 (div. Aug. 1956); children—Sarah Peyton, Stephen Burrell. Chemist, Devoe-Raynolds, Inc., Louisville, 1941-43; jr. engr. Curtiss-Wright Corp., Louisville, 1943-44; research fellow Purdue U. Sch. Chem. Engring., West Lafayette, Ind., 1946-50; research chemist Monsanto Chem. Co., Boston, 1950-51; asst. prof. chemistry U. Tex., Arlington, 1954-55; asso. prof., 1955—. Profl. engr., Ind., Tex. Fellow Am. Inst. Chemists; mem. Am. Chem. Soc. (sect. sec.-dir. 1967-68), Soc. Women Engrs., Tex. Acad. Sci., Colonial Dames of Am., Magna Charta Dames (chpt. v.p. 1970—), Descs. of Knights of Garter, Ams. of Royal Descent, Plantagenet Soc., D.A.R. (chpt. regent 1967-69, state bicentennial chmn. 1969-70), Children of Am. Revolution (sr. state pres. 1969-71), Sigma Xi (pres. U. Tex. club, 1966-68), Alpha Chi Omega. Presbyn. Club: Arlington Womens. Home: 1630 Pecan Park Dr Arlington TX 76012

WILLOW, SISTER MARY BONITA, coll. pres.; b. Chgo., Oct. 13, 1912; d. Martin and Julia (Skora) Willow; A.B., Loyola U., 1949, M.Ed., 1956, Ed.D., 1961. Instr., Felician Coll., 1956-62, registrar, 1957-63; pres., dean Felician Coll., Chgo., 1963—. Lectr. Loyola U., Chgo., 1961-62, 66-67. Chmn. Cal. Scholarship Fedn., 1950-55. Bd. dirs. juvenile welfare program, Back of Yards Neighborhood Council, St. Mary's Hosp., Centralia, Ill., St. Francis Hosp., Milw. Recipient Summer Grant, Kellogg Found. Jr. Coll. Community Inst., 1962. Certificate of Appreciation, Jr. Coll. Student Personnel Assn., 1964. Mem. Am. Assn. Jr. Colls., Assn. Higher Edn., Nat. Cath. Ednl. Assn., N.E.A., Nat. Assn. Women Deans and Counselors, Nat. Assn. Supervision and Curriculum, Nat. Council Ind. Jr. Colls. Author: Student Handbook, 1972; Faculty Handbook, 1972; Institutional Study, 1972. Home: 3800 W Peterson St Chicago IL 60659

WILLOW, SISTER MARY BONITA, ednl. adminstr.; b. Chgo., Oct. 13, 1912; d. Martin and Julia (Skora) Willow; B.A., Loyola U., 1949, M.Ed., 1956; Ed.D., 1961. Instr. Felician Coll., Chgo., 1956-62, registrar, 1957-63, pres., 1963—; instr. Loyola U., Chgo., 1961-62, 1966-67. Chmn. Cal. Scholarship Fedn., Pomona, 1953-55. Bd. dirs. Juvenile Welfare Program, Chgo., 1970—; bd. dirs. St. Mary's Hosp., Centralia, Ill., 1963—, St. Francis Hosp., Milw., 1963—. Recipient Summer grant Kellog Found. for Jr. Coll., 1962—. Mem. Am. Assn. Jr. Colls., Assn. for Higher Edn., N.E.A., Nat. Assn. Women Deans and Counselors, Nat. Assn. Supervision and Curriculum, Nat. Cath. Edn. Assn. Home: 3800 Peterson Av Chicago IL 60659 Office: Felician Coll Chicago IL 60659

WILLS, ISABEL HAYES, ednl. counselor; b. Pitts., Aug. 6, 1917; d. Stephen Q. and Helen Grace (Buck) Hayes; B.S., U. Pitts., 1942; postgrad. Western Res. U., 1947; M.S., U. Miami, 1955, postgrad., 1958-60. Tchr. pre-sch. deaf, Miami, Fla., 1947-49; tchr. Kindergarten, Miami, 1950-57; psychometrist psychology dept. U. Miami, 1955-58, instr. adult remedial reading, 1960-61; acad. dir. Coral Gables Reading Acad., 1962; pvt. practice as evaluator, Miami, 1962-66; dir. evaluation dept. McGlannon Sch., 1966-67; diagnostic dir. Ednl. Guidance Services, Inc., Miami, 1967—. Guest lectr. various univs., 1964—, instr. learning disability inst., 1969. Supt., Dade County Youth Fair Assn., 1972—. Mem. Council Exceptional Children, Nat. Assn. Sch. Psychologists, Assn. Children with Learning Disabilities, Am. Psychol. Assn., Psi Chi. Co-author various worktexts, books, articles. Contbg. editor Acad. Therapy, 1968—. Home: 9360 SW 66th St Miami FL 33143 Office: PO Box 7251 Ludlam Br Miami FL 33155

WILLS, NOREEN RENKER (MRS. JON FRANKLIN WILLS), pub. relations exec.; b. Cleve., Jan. 16, 1949; d. Lee Franklin and Dorothy (Sherley) Renker; B.S. summa cum laude, Ohio U., 1970; m. Jon Franklin Wills, June 14, 1970. Program asso. Tb Soc. Columbus and Franklin County, 1971-72, pub. relations dir., 1972-73; pub. information specialist Ohio Environmental Protection Agy., Columbus, 1973—. Mem. Sigma Delta Chi, Theta Sigma Phi, Chi Omega. Democrat. Lutheran. Home: 3755 Wenwood Dr Columbus OH 43220 Office: 361 E Broad St Columbus OH 43216

WILLSON, MARY FRANCES (MRS. R.A. VON NEUMANN), educator; b. Madison, Wis., July 28, 1938; d. Gordon L. and Sarah (Loomans) Willson; B.A., Grinnell Coll., 1960; Ph.D., U. Wash., 1964; m. R.A. von Neumann, May 24, 1972. Asst. prof. dept. zoology U. Ill., Urbana, 1965-71, asso. prof., 1971—. Mem. Am., Brit. ornithologists unions, Am. Soc. Naturalists, Ecol. Soc. Am., British Ecol. Soc., Soc. Study Evolution, Cooper Ornithol. Soc. Research in avian and plant ecology. Home: Route 1 St Joseph IL 61873 Office: Dept Ecology Ethology and Evolution Vivarium Bldg U Ill Champaign IL 61820

WILNER, MARIE SPRING, painter; b. Paris, France, July 24, 1910; d. Joseph and Helene Spring; came to U.S., 1915, naturalized, 1920; B.A., Hunter Coll., 1927; m. Joseph Walter Wilner, Sept. 4, 1926; children—Helene Victoria, Harvey I., George Dubar. Exhibited one-man shows Gallery 21, 1959, Bodley Gallery, N.Y.C., 1960, Galeries Raymond Duncan, Paris, 1961, 63, 65, 67-69, Jason Gallery, N.Y.C., 1963, Bridgeport (Conn.) Mus. Art, 1962, Evansville (Ind.) Mus., 1964, Irving Gallery, Milw., 1964, Sheldon Swope Gallery, 1965, Pietrantonio Gallery, N.Y.C., 1966, 68, 69, Oliva Gallery, South Hampton, N.Y., 1966, N.Y. U., 1966, La Salle Coll., Phila., 1966-68, U. Del., 1966, Dickson Gallery, Washington, 1968-69, Bohmann's Gallery, Stockholm, Sweden, 1968, Rioboo Nueva Gallery, Buenos Aires, Argentina, 1969, Tweed Gallery, U. Minn., 1969, Karelon Gallery, Provincetown, N.Y., 1970, Galerie fur Zeitgenossische Kunst, Hamburg (Germany) U., 1971, Musee d'Art Moderne, Paris, 1972, Charleroi, Belgium, 1972, Nat. Mus. Arts and Sports, N.Y.C., 1971, Lehigh U., 1972, Galerie Rene Borel, Deauville, France, 1972, La Traboule, Lyon, 1972, Musee de Lyon, Musee d'Art Moderne, Paris, Salon d'Ete, France, Salon d'Automne, France, Salon de l'Ecole de Paris, Salon de Thomas, Salon des Artistes, Paris, Palais de Beaux Arts, Rome, Societe de la Palmes d'Or, Monaco, 1972, 73; others; works included traveling shows; works represented permanent collections Tweed Gallery, Community Coll. N.Y., LaSalle Coll., Evansville Mus., Art Inst. Richmond (Ind.), Norfolk (Va.) Mus. Art, Seton Hall U. Mus., N.Y. U., Fla. So. Coll., Ga. Mus. Art, St. Vincent Coll., Latrobe, Pa., Mus. Ala., Emily Lowe Mus., Bat Yam Mus., Israel, Safad Mus., Israel, Muss d'Angouleme, France, Musee de Cognac, France, S.I. Mus., Musee des Beaux Arts de Montbard. Sec., treas. Rosemarie Holding Inc., N.Y.C. Recipient Gold medal Am. Artist Profl. League, 1965, Grumbacher Purchase prize, 1966; Bronze medal Gran Prix Internationale de Peintures et Scalptures du Pays Noir, Charleroi, Belgium; 1972; named chevalier Societe d'Encouragement au Prog, 1969, chevalier 4th grade Merite Belgo-Hispanique, 1973. Fellow Royal Soc. Art, Nat. Assn. Women Artists (chmn. jury award 1966—, chmn. traveling oil show), Artists Equity Assn. (dir.); mem. Nat. Soc. Arts and Letters, Internat. Arts Guild, Intercontinental Biog. Assn. Address: 77 7th Av New York City NY 10011

WILSON, ALICE SHERMAN (MRS. JAMES T. WILSON), civic worker; b. Stratford, Conn., Dec. 22, 1905; d. John and Agnes (Anderson) Wallin; student Smith-Froebel Kindergarten Training Sch., 1925-27, Booth & Bayliss Commercial Sch., 1930-31, Merrill Bus. Sch., 1946-47; m. James T. Wilson, May 19, 1956. Library asst. Bridgeport (Conn.) Pub. Library, 1927-42; priorities clk. United Aircraft Corp., Change Vought Aircraft div., Stratford, Conn., 1942-45; priorities and asst. purchasing agt. Bead Chain Mfg. Co., Bridgeport, Conn., 1945-51; accounts receivable dept. Getman & Judd Lumber Co., Stamford, Conn., 1951-52; tech. librarian Remington Rand Inc. Lab. Advanced Research, South Norwalk, Conn., 1952-56. Mem. Steamship Hist. Soc., Am., Inc. (librarian, sec., dir.), Spl. Libraries Assn. Club: Castle Manor Garden (pres. 1964-66) (S.I., N.Y.). Home: 414 Pelton Av Staten Island NY 10310

WILSON, ANNE CHAPMAN, real estate co. exec.; b. St. Louis, Aug. 24, 1929; d. Thomas Howard and Gean Warren (La Mont) Chapman; student U. Miami (Fla.), 1947-48; m. Frank G. Wilson, Sept. 3, 1947 (div. Apr. 1964); children—Rebecca (Mrs. Thomas K. McLaughlin, Jr.), F. Gavin, Dwight C. Circulation mgr. I.S.M. Pub. Co., Coral Gables, Fla., 1965-69; asst. to dir. Miami (Fla.) Art Center, 1969-72; sales mgr. Stadler Assos., Inc., Coral Gables, 1972—. Chairperson Dade County Commn. on the Status of Women, 1972-73. Chairwoman Dade County Republican Com., 1968-70; vice chairwoman Dade County Rep. Com., 1966-68; del. Rep. Nat. Conv., 1968. Bd. dirs. South Fla. Muscular Dystrophy Assn. Mem. Nat. Inst. Real Estate Brokers. Presbyn. Home: 3710 Battersea Rd Miami FL 33133 Office: 375 Miracle Mile Coral Gables FL 33134

WILSON, AUDREY LAGERQUIST (MRS. GEORGE BUTTEMILLER), radiologist; b. Chgo., Dec. 5, 1913; d. Axel Karl Martin and Amanda Ida (Fogelberg) Lagerquist; M.B., Northwestern U., 1941, M.D., 1942; m. George Buttemiller, Oct. 23, 1971; children by previous marriage—Jeremy Wilson, Peter Wilson, Jonathan Wilson. Intern Cook County Hosp., Chgo., 1941-42; resident Research and Ednl. Hosps., U. Ill. at Chgo., 1942-45, clin. asst. radiologist, 1944-46; asst. prof. radiology U. Ill. at Chgo., 1946-60; radiologist Lake Forest (Ill.) Hosp., 1948-60, Condell Hosp., Libertyville, Ill., 1968-71; practice medicine specializing in radiology, Lake Forest, Ill., 1948-60, Libertyville, 1948-71, Waukegan, Ill., 1960—; mem. staff Physicians and Surgeons X-Ray and Clin. Lab., Waukegan. Vice pres. Am. Women's Vol. Services, 1969—. Diplomate Am. Bd. Radiology. Mem. Am. Coll. Radiology, A.M.A. Club: Knollwood (Lake Forest, Ill.). Home: 1577 N Green Bay Rd Lake Forest IL 60045 Office: 1616 W Grand Av Waukegan IL 60085

WILSON, BARBARA CLAIRE, child neuropsychologist; b. N.Y.C., Feb. 13, 1928; d. Herb and Marion (Bennin) Brookman; B.A., Bklyn. Coll., 1949; Ph.D., N.Y. U., 1964; m. James J. Wilson, June 19, 1959. Field psychologist Ia. Dept. Spl. Edn., Des Moines, 1949-51; social worker Family Service, Des Moines, 1951-54; med. social worker Meml. Center Cancer and Allied Diseases, N.Y.C., 1954-57; research asso. N.J. Neuropsychiatric Inst., Princeton, 1958-60; research asso. children's rehab. unit N.Y. U. Med. Center, N.Y.C., 1960-68; chief psychologist children's unit St. Agnes Hosp., White Plains, N.Y., 1968-71; coordinator psycho-social services United Cerebral Palsy Assn. Nassau County (N.Y.) Pub. Aid, 1971-72; chief child psychology North Shore U. Hosp., Manhassett, N.Y., 1972—. Research asso. Dept. of Neurology Albert Einstein Coll. Med., N.Y.C., 1970-74; asst. clin. prof. psychology Coll. Medicine Cornell U., N.Y.C., 1972. Office of Vocational Rehab. grantee, 1959-61; Nat. United Cerebral Palsy Assn. grantee, 1962-68; Assn. for Aid Crippled Children grantee, 1965-68; Nat. Inst. Neurol. Disease and Stroke-NIH grantee, 1967-68; Office of Edn. grantee, 1973—. Mem. Am., Eastern psychol. assns., Am. Assn. Behavior Therapy, Internat. Neuropsychol. Soc., Am. Acad. Cerebral Palsy, Am. Assn. Mental Retardation, Council Exceptional Children, Sigma Xi. Mem. editorial bd. Jour. of Communications Disorders, 1970—. Contbr. articles to profl. jours. Office: North Shore Univ Hosp Dept Child Psychiatry 400 Community Dr Manhasset NY 11031

WILSON, BEATRICE FISCHER MEYER (MRS. HENRY M. WILSON), civic worker; b. Bklyn., Mar. 5, 1915; d. Bernhard Ditlip and Henrietta (Schaffer) Meyer; A.B., Vassar Coll., 1936; postgrad. Columbia; m. Henry Mayer Wilson, Nov. 20, 1947; children—Beatrice Anne, William Boyd. Sec. of vols. N.Y. Hosp., Cornell Med. Center, N.Y.C., 1936-41; dir. central vol. bur. Bklyn. Jr. League, 1941; employment and personnel asst. R.H. Macys & Co., N.Y.C., 1942-44; personnel dir. Davison's, Atlanta, 1944-47; mgmt. counselor, employee relations Bowery Savs. Bank, N.Y.C., 1947-52; cons. employee relations various industries, 1952-60; mgr. employment services Allied Chem. Corp., Morristown, N.J., 1972-73; v.p. Home crafters, Inc., 1973-74. Chmn. home service Madison (N.J.) Chatham A.R.C., 1947-49; mem. Bd. Edn., Madison, 1962-67, v.p., 1967-70, pres., 1970-71; vol. Morristown (N.J.) Meml. Hosp., 1968—. Bd. dirs. Madison-Chatham Adult Sch., 1972—, chmn., 1974-75. Mem. Am. Assn. U. Women. Presbyn. Club: Vassar (pres. Summit (N.J.) area 1950-52). Home: 12 Holden Lane Madison NJ 07940

WILSON, BEATRICE KRUGER (MRS. N. LELAND WILSON, JR.), apparel designer, apparel product co. exec.; b. Phila., June 6, 1925; d. August Frank and Elizabeth Anne (Lambert) Kruger; grad. Moore Coll. of Art, Phila., 1946; m. N. Leland Wilson, Jr., Sept. 28, 1963; 1 son, Jeffrey Scott Thielen; stepsons—J. Michael, N. Leland III. Asst. fashion coordinator N. Snellenburg Co., Dept. Store, Phila., 1946; tchr. Moore Coll. Art, Phila., 1947-48; designer Rosenau Bros., Inc., Phila., 1954-57, asst. to design dir., 1957-68, v.p., 1968—. Free lance designer, 1946-48. Mem. Phila. Fashion Group, treas., 1970-71. Home: 756 St Georges Rd Philadelphia PA 19119 Office: Fox St and Roberts Av Philadelphia PA 19129

WILSON, BETTY REINHARDT, nurse; b. Little Rock, Sept. 11, 1927; d. Herbert Paul and Cleffie Ritchie (Brewer) Reinhardt; R.N., St. Vincent Infirmary, Little Rock, 1948; m. Frank William Wilson, Sept. 17, 1948; children—Carolyn Lee, Frank William, James Paul. Staff nurse Greenville (S.C.) Gen. Hosp., 1948, St. Vincent Infirmary, 1949-50; office nurse, 1948-49, 50-68; dir. nursing Alexander unit Ark. Children's Colony, 1968—. Pres. Asso. Women for Harding Coll., 1970-71; pres. Meadowcliff Elementary Sch. P.T.A., Little Rock, 1958-59; ofcl. judge, chaperon Ark. Jr. Miss Pageant, 1957—; mem. ofcl. staff Ark. Youth Council, 1957—. Mem. Am. Assn. Mental Deficiency (nurse chmn. region 5, 1970—), Ark. Nurses Assn. (membership chmn.), Ark. Pub. Employees Assn., Assn. Retarded Children, Beta Sigma Phi (treas. 1970). Mem. Ch. of Christ. Club: Meadowcliff Garden (pres. 1957-58, 71-72). Home: PO Box 1454 Little Rock AR 72203 Office: Ark Children's Colony Alexander AR 72002

WILSON, CAROL GREEN (MRS. GEORGE OSBORNE WILSON), editor, author; b. Livingston, Mont., Apr. 16, 1892; d. Dennis Stephen and May (Staats) Green; A.B., Stanford, 1914; m. George Osborne Wilson, Oct. 14, 1914; children—George Osborne, Lloyd Macy, Waldron Edward. Editor, Stanford Alumni Mag., 1918-21, 28-35, dir. pub. relations Stanford U., 1934, editor Half Century Notes, Stanford Almanac, 1964—. Mem. archives adv. council region 9, Nat. Archives, 1971—. Mem. women's planning com. Japan Internat. Christian U., 1957—. Mem. nat. council Nat. Republican Club N.Y., 1965. Recipient award of merit Cal. Hist. Soc., 1966. Mem. Nat. Soc. Colonial Dames Am. (chmn. Cal. com. geneal. information service 1968), Soc. Mayflower Descendants, Cal. Writers Club, Women in Communication, Cap and Gown, Phi Beta Kappa, Kappa Alpha Theta (nat. historian 1953—). Republican. Conglist. Clubs: Metropolitan, Century (pres. 1959-61). Author: Chinatown Quest, 1931, rev. edit., 1950, Centennial edit., 1974; California Yankee, 1946; Gump's Treasure Trade, 1949, rev. edit., 1966; Alice Eastwood's Wonderland, 1956; We Who Wear Kites, 1956; Arthur Fielder—Music for the Millions, 1968; Herbert Hoover—A Challenge for Today, 1968; From Mayflower to Clippers, 1968. Home: 1880 Jackson St San Francisco CA 94109

WILSON, CATHERINE MARIE, physician; b. Takoma Park, Md., Jan. 22, 1938; d. Edward Amos and Lotty (Millard) Wilson; B.A., Columbia Union Coll., 1959; M.D., Loma Linda U., 1963. Intern Washington Sanitarium and Hosp., 1963-64; resident U. Md. Hosp., Balt., 1964-68; practice medicine, specializing in obstetrics and gynecology, Asheville, N.C., 1968—; mem. staff Meml. Mission Hosp., St. Joseph's Hosp. Mem. Am. Coll. Obstetricians and Gynecologists, N.C., Buncombe County med. socs., Asheville C. of C. Home: 24 Amherst Rd Asheville NC 28803 Office: 675 Biltmore Av Asheville NC 28803

WILSON, CORINNE GREEN, educator; b. Muskogee, Okla., July 21, 1924; d. Benjamin Franklin and Julia (Allen) Green; A.B., Rockford Coll., 1943; Ph.D. (Teaching fellow 1943-47), U. N.C., 1947, B.S. in Library Sci., 1951; m. Robert Monroe Wilson, May 16, 1953 (dec. Mar. 1957). Instr. U. N.C. at Chapel Hill, 1947-48; asst. prof. classics Queens Coll., Charlotte, N.C., 1948-50; reference librarian La. State U., Baton Rouge, 1951-52; acting prof. classics Hollins Coll., Roanoke, Va., 1960; programmer Center for Programmed Instrn., N.Y.C., 1961-62; librarian, asst. prof. classics New Coll., Sarasota, Fla., 1963-67, librarian, asso. prof., 1967—. Bd. dirs. Friends Library, Sarasota Pub. Library, 1958-60, Jr. Welfare League Sarasota, 1958—; founding dir. League Women Voters, Sarasota, 1961-63. Mem. Am. Philol. Assn., Am., Fla. library assns., Women's Library Assn. New Coll. (dir.), Am. Assn. U. Women. Democrat. Episcopalian. Home: 2300 Mietaw Dr Sarasota FL 33579 Office: Box 1898 Sarasota FL 33578

WILSON, DAGMAR (MRS. CHRISTOPHER BERNARD WILSON), artist, illustrator; b. N.Y.C., Jan. 25, 1916; d. Cesar Victor and Marion (Ballin) Saerchinger; Fine Arts diploma, Slade Sch., Univ. Coll., London, Eng., 1936; m. Christopher Bernard Wilson, Aug. 24, 1939; children—Sally Marion (Mrs. Paul Bartholemew Bortz), Anna Clare, Jessica. Art tchr. Burgess Hill Sch. London, 1936-39; asst. art tchr. Lincoln Sch., Tchrs. Coll., N.Y.C., 1940-41; graphic artist, co-ordinator inter-Am. affairs U.S. Govt., Washington, 1943-46; free-lance artist, illustrator, Washington, 1946—; stage designer Dance Theatre of Washington, 1950—. Founder Action Com. for D.C. Sch. Libraries, 1958, Women Strike for Peace Movement, 1961. Recipient Gold medal Art Dirs. Club of Washington, 1955, Statue of Liberty award Women for Legislative Action, 1962, Janice Holland award Women Strike for Peace, 1962. Mem. Children's Book Guild of Washington (program chmn. 1958-59) Illustrator: While Susie Sleeps, 1948; Berlitz French for Children, 1961; Let's Hear a Story, 1961; Poems to Read to the Very Young, 1961; others. Address: 1406 29th St Washington DC 20007

WILSON, DOROTHY MARIE, newspaper editor; b. Ohio County, Ky., July 23, 1922; d. Lonnie Edison and Marie (Keown) Daugherty; student Bryant Stratton Bus. Coll., Louisville, 1941-42; m. Aubrey C. Wilson, June 29, 1943; children—Aubrey C., Nedra (Mrs. Harold Morrison). Office mgr., bookkeeper Ohio County Messenger, Beaver Dam, Ky., 1942-43, 44-45; receptionist, bookkeeper, Ft. Smithian, Ft. Smith, Ark., 1943-44; asso. editor Progress newspaper, Cave City, Ky., 1946—, owner, editor, 1968—; editor, partner Hart County News, Munfordville, Ky., 1949-68, Hart County Herald, Horse Cave, Ky., 1965-68; operator Dairy Freeze, Munfordville, 1957—; partner, bookkeeper Wilson Enterprises, Cave City, 1967—. Active numerous local fund drives. Named Women of Achievement, Barren County, Glasgow, Ky., 1973. Mem. Cave City Bus. and Profl. Women's Club (charter, pres. 1972-73, Ky. chmn. pub. relations 1973-74, Woman of Year award 1971), Am. Legion Aux., Dale Carnegie Alumni Assn., Nat. Newspaper Assn., Ky. Press Assn. Baptist (tchr.). Clubs: Junior Woman's (charter), Younger Woman's (Cave City). Mem. Order Eastern Star (sec.). Home: 609 E Broadway Cave City KY 42127 Office: PO Box 546 Cave City KY 42127

WILSON, DOROTHY SIMPSON, librarian; b. Columbus, O., Mar. 7, 1907; d. Robert Harris and Cora (Coleman) Simpson; A.B., Ohio State U., 1928; M.L.S., Pratt Inst., 1965; m. John Larimer Wilson, Sept. 4, 1928; children—Coralyn (Mrs. Tom Black), Robert Frazer, Wylie (Mrs. Robert Thorne), Sandra (Mrs. Michael Gyamerah), Jennifer (Mrs. M.S. Baloch). With Columbus Pub. Library, 1946—, asst. librarian br. head, 1957-65, reference div. main library, 1966-67, head fine arts div. main library, 1967—. Mem. Am., Ohio, Franklin County library assns., League Women Voters, Sigma Kappa. Unitarian. Home: 115 W Tompkins St Columbus OH 43202 Office: 96 S Grant Av Columbus OH 43215

WILSON, ELLEN JANET CAMERON (MRS. WILLIAM E. WILSON), author; b. Allegheny, Pa.; d. Henry Nesmith and Belle (Morgan) Cameron; A.B., Ohio Wesleyan U., 1924; M.A., Radcliffe Coll., 1927; postgrad. Sch. for Fgn. Students U. Aix-Marseilles (France), 1956; m. William Edward Wilson, June 29, 1929; children—William Edward III, Henry Cameron, Douglas Cook. Author: Ernie Pyle, 1955; Annie Oakley, 1958; Robert Frost, 1967; (with Nan Agle) Three Boys series, 1951-68; American Painter in Paris: Life of Mary Cassatt, 1971; They Named Me Gertrude Stein, 1973. Tchr. English R.I. Sch. Design, Providence, 1931-33; Katherine Gibbs Sch., 1935-38; book reviewer Providence Jour., 1951—, Louisville Courier Jour., 1963—; tchr. children's lit. Ind. U. at Bloomington, 1954—; mem. staff writer's conf. U. Colo., 1966. Recipient Ind. Authors' Day award, 1972. Mem. Nat. Soc. Arts and Letters, Kappa Alpha Theta, Theta Sigma Phi. Democrat. Methodist. Home: 1326 Pickwick Pl Bloomington IN 47401

WILSON, EVELYN HODES (MRS. ARMIN G. WILSON), univ. adminstr.; b. Phila., Oct. 8, 1921; d. Morris and Anne (Jacobsen) Hodes; A.B., Bryn Mawr Coll., 1942; A.M., Radcliffe Coll., 1944, Ph.D., 1946; m. Armin G. Wilson, June 5, 1943; children—Jonathan, Robert. Research chemist Merck & Co., Rahway, N.J., 1946-53, Johnson & Johnson, New Brunswick, N.J., 1953-59; chemistry lectr. Westfield (N.J.) High Sch., 1959-65; head sci. dept. New Brunswick schs., 1965-67; asso. prof. sci. edn. Rutgers U., New Brunswick, 1967-72, prof. sci. edn., dir. univ. planning and budget, 1972—. Mem. N.Y. Acad. Scis., Am. Chem. Soc., Am. Assn. U. Profs., Nat. Sci. Tchrs. Assn., League Women Voters, Sigma Xi, Phi Beta Kappa. Contbr. articles on organic chemistry and sci. edn. to profl. jours. Home: 249 Harrison Av Highland Park NJ 08904 Office: Rutgers Univ New Brunswick NJ 08903

WILSON, FLORABELLE (MRS. JOHN A. WILSON), librarian; b. Indpls., Jan. 12, 1927; d. James Samuel and Hattie Virginia (Hollis) Williams; B.S. in Edn., Ind. Central Coll., 1949; M.L.S., Ind. U., 1961; m. John A. Wilson, Mar. 28, 1964. Tchr. elementary pub. schs., Indpls., 1949-57; asst. librarian Ind. Central Coll. Library, Indpls., 1957-70, librarian, 1970—. Mem. A.L.A., Ind. Library Assn., N.A.A.C.P., Beta Phi Mu. Presbyn. Home: 5344 N Kenwood Av Indianapolis IN 46208 Office: 1400 E Hanna Av Indianapolis IN 46227

WILSON, FRANCES HELEN, occupational therapist; b. Pitts., Oct. 17, 1929; d. J. Vernon and Margaret Hassler (Prugh) Wilson; B.A., Conn. Coll., 1951; advanced standing certificate Columbia Sch. Occupational Therapy, 1953. Therapist, Washington County Soc. Crippled Children and Adults, Washington, Pa., 1953-54; staff therapist Oakland VA Hosp., U. Pitts., 1955-66; supr. occupational therapy Aspinwall VA Hosp., Pitts., 1966-74, Oakland VA Hosp., Pitts., 1974—. Active Jr. League Pitts., Inc. Mem. Western Pa. Occupational Therapy Assn. (treas. 1967-69). Republican. Presbyn. Clubs: Connecticut College (treas. 1971—), Twentieth Century (Pitts.). Home: 14 Devon Lane Ben Avon Heights Pittsburgh PA 15202 Office: University Dr Pittsburgh PA 15240

WILSON, FREDERICKA READEN (MRS. JESSE MYLES WILSON, SR.), civic worker; b. Charleston, S.C., Aug. 26, 1924; d. Frederick and Christina Dorothea (Claussen) Readen; grad. Dickenson Secretarial Sch., Columbia, S.C., 1942; m. Jesse Myles Wilson, Sr., Aug. 21, 1948; children—Johanna Marie, Jesse Myles. Sec. Motor Supply Co., auto parts supplies, Columbia, 1942-46; sec., bookkeeper Standard Parts Co., Columbia, 1946-50, Spartanburg, S.C., 1950-52. Unit pres. Am. Cancer Soc., Spartanburg, 1970-72, Appalachia region dir., 1971-73, S.C. div. bd., 1968-70, 71-73; pres. Piedmont Pharm. Aux., Spartanburg, 1950-52; pres. Coop. Sch. PTA 1961-63, pres. council 7, 1963-65, dist. pres., 1965-68; v.p. State PTA 1968; pres. S.C. Congress Parents and Tchrs., 1968-71, life mem.; pres. Ch. Women United, 1961-65, life mem.; pres. S.C. chpt. Lutheran Sem. Aux., 1973-75; sec., chmn. publicity East Piedmont Dist. Garden Clubs, 1973-75; 2d v.p. Spartanburg Garden Council, 1973-75. Lutheran (vice chmn. council 1960-63, 73-76, dir. kindergarten 1959-63; v.p. theol. sem. aux. 1970-72; sec. S.C. synod ch. vocations 1971—). Mem. Nat. Congress PTA (life). Club: Tulip Garden (v.p. 1971-74, pres. 1974-75). Home: 247 Cedar Spring Rd Spartanburg SC 29302

WILSON, GERALDINE O'CONNOR (MRS. RICHARD THOMAS WILSON), psychologist; b. Hartford, Conn., Oct. 18, 1933; d. Dennis Paul and Florence Marguerite (Sheehan) O'Connor; B.A., Marymount Coll., 1955; M.S., So. Conn. State Coll., 1971, postgrad., 1971—; m. Richard Thomas Wilson, Apr. 12, 1958; children—Susan, Deirdre, Moira Carey, Megan Abigail. Social worker Southbury (Conn.) Tng. Sch., 1956-58; psychol. examiner Waterbury (Conn.) Sch. System, 1971-72; sch. psychologist Brookfield (Conn.) Schs., 1972—. Pres., Parent Tchr. Orgn., 1967-68. Mem. town com. Democratic party Southbury, 1968—, del. state conv., 1970, 72. Bd. govs. Noroton Sch., Darien, Conn. Mem. Nat. Conn. assns. sch. psychologists. Roman Catholic. Home: Southbury Tng Sch Southbury CT 06488 Office: Huckleberry Hill Sch White Turkey Rd Brookfield CT 06804

WILSON, GLENNA LOUISE GERMANN, editor; b. Manhattan, Kan., May 2, 1923; d. G.F. and Blanche Isabel (Clark) Germann; B.S. cum laude in Home Econs. and Journalism, Kan. State U., 1968, postgrad. journalism, 1969—; m. W. John Wilson, Aug. 2, 1947; children—John F., Stanley, Ronald. Rural sch. tchr., Kan., 1940-48; prodn. editor Kan. 4-H Jour., Manhattan, 1970—. Mem. Riley County Welfare Adv. Com., 1966-72; publicity chmn. Riley County Bloodmobile, 1972-73. Democratic precinct committeewoman, 1966-68. Mem. Women in Communications (chpt. pres. 1969-70), Phi Kappa Phi, Omicron Nu. Presbyn. Home: Route 3 Box 180 Manhattan KS 66502 Office: Umberger Hall Kan State U Manhattan KS 66506

WILSON, GLORIA SCOTT (MRS. EDWIN ROWE WILSON), radio-TV broadcasting co. exec.; b. St. Petersburg, Fla., Feb. 3, 1929; d. Frederick Martin and Florence Hannah (Cook) Scott; A.A., Stephens Coll., 1947; B.S., Northwestern U., 1949; m. Edwin Rowe Wilson, Sept. 2, 1950. Copy writer radio stat. WUSN, Charleston, S.C., 1951-53, copy chief TV sta. WUSN, 1957-59; copy chief radio sta. WCSC, Charleston, 1959-70, promotion mgr., 1970—. Mem. Am. Assn. U. Women (pres. Charleston chpt. 1968-70, S.C. sec. 1972-74), Am. Women in Radio and TV (S.C. v.p. 1968-69), Am. Contract Bridge League. Episcopalian. Home: 59 S Concord Charleston SC 29401 Office: PO Box 186 Charleston SC 29402

WILSON, GRACE ELIZABETH, ednl. adminstr.; b. Waco, Tex., Feb. 14, 1922; d. Robert Alexander and Sadye (Grace) Wilson; B.A., Baylor U., 1940, M.A., 1941; Ed.D., U. Va., 1955; postgrad. summer and extension courses Tchrs. Coll., Columbia, So. Methodist U., Memphis State U. Instr., Baylor U., summer 1941; clerical worker Tex. Power and Light Co., Dallas, 1941-42; sec. to prin., tchr. English, Highland Park Jr. High Sch., 1942-43; sec. to prin., tchr. English Highland Park Sr. High Sch., 1943-44, tchr., 1944-53, 54-56; clin. asst. McGuffey Reading Clinic, U. Va., Charlottesville, 1953-54; counselor, tchr. English Alex W. Spence Jr. High Sch., Dallas, 1956-57; secondary English cons. Dallas Ind. Sch. Dist., 1957-71, coordinator curriculum devel., 1971-72, coordinator curriculum devel. career edn., 1972-73, program facilitator secondary reading, 1973—; tchr. English Dallas Coll., 1947-48, So. Meth. U., 1956; mem. woman's adv. com. ednl. TV station KERA; mem. Tex. Textbook Com., 1965, Tex. Commn. on Study Instrnl. Resources, 1971-72, Tex. Bd. Examiners for Tchr. Edn., 1973—. Mem. N.E.A., Tex. Tchrs. Assn., Dallas Sch. Adminstrs. Assn., Nat. (dir., com. chmn. editorial chmn. for publ. composition Situations, 1966), Tex. (liaison officer 1967—, v.p. 1971-73, pres. 1972-74), Greater Dallas councils tchrs. English, Internat. Reading Assn., Tex. Assn. Improvement Reading (area v.p. 1956-57), Assn. Supervision and Curriculum Devel., Tex. Assn. Supervision and Curriculum Devel., Internat. Platform Assn., Delta Kappa Gamma. Baptist. Contbr. articles to edn. jours. Home: 6036 Birchbrook Dr Dallas TX 75206 Office: 3700 Ross Av Dallas TX 75204

WILSON, HAZEL HUTCHINS (MRS. WILLIAM JEROME WILSON), author; b. Portland, Me.; d. Fred Linwood and Emma (Jones) Mutchins; A.B., Bates Coll., 1919, M.A. (hon.), 1956; B.S., Simmons Coll., 1920; m. William Jerome Wilson, Sept. 16, 1930; (dec. Oct. 1963); 1 son, Jerome Linwood. Librarian, Me., 1920-23, Mo., 1923-26, Paris, France, 1926-28, Mass., 1928-29, Denver, 1929-30. Spl. lectr. George Washington U., Washington, 1959-66; children's book reviewer Washington Sunday Star, 1963-72; reviewer Parents' Mag., 1969-72; lectr. writer's conf. Georgetown U., 1965-70. Recipient Boys' Club award, 1951, Ohioana award Ohioana Library, 1949; Thomas Edison award Thomas Edison Found., 1956, Cumberland County 200th Anniversary award Cumberland County, 1960. Mem. Children's Book Guild (pres. 1970-71), Am. Newspaper Women's Club, Washington Bookseller's Assn., Women in Communication, Authors Guild, Inc. Author numerous children's books, including: His Indian Brother; The Little Marquise, 1957; Tall

Ships, 1959; Jerry's Charge Account, 1960; Herbert's Homework, 1960; The Seine: River of Paris, 1962; The Last Queen of Hawaii, 1963; Herbert's Space Trip, 1965; The Years Between, 1969; Herbert's Stilts, 1972. Address: 4912 Berkley St Washington DC 20016

WILSON, HELEN AREHART, assn. exec.; b. Marshall, Mo., Apr. 27, 1918; d. Robert Patterson Clark and Helen Taylor (Arehart) Wilson; B.S. in Edn., U. Mo., 1940; M.A., U. Colo., 1941. Dir. personnel and tng. Rothschild's, Kansas City, Mo., 1954-58; pub. affairs specialist Girl Scouts U.S.A., Washington, 1960—. Mem. nat. adv. council President's Com. for Employer Support of Guard and Res., 1972-74. Served to lt. col. USMCR, 1943-46, 50-54; col. Res. Mem. Pub. Relations Soc. Am., Mo. Soc., Kappa Kappa Gamma. Democrat. Methodist. Contbg. author: History of the Marine Corps Reserve, 1966. Home: 4921 Seminary Rd Alexandria VA 22311 Office: 2000 L St NW Washington DC 20036

WILSON, HELEN ELIZABETH, educator; b. Battle Creek, Mich., Mar. 14, 1916; d. Everett F. and Ruth B. (Fisher) Wilson; B.A., Mich. State U., 1938; M.A., U. Denver, 1950; Ph.D., U. Utah, 1958. Rehab. dir. State and County Tb Assn., Lansing, Mich., Columbus, O., Seattle, Denver, 1939-48; psychologist State Mental Hygiene Clinic, Billings, Mont., 1950-54, clin. psychologist, 1956-61; prof. psychology Eastern Mont. Coll., Billings, 1961—, head psychology dept., 1972—, bd. dirs. Ednl. Found., 1968-73, v.p., 1969-70, pres., 1970-71. Cons. psychologist Mont. State Hosp., 1958-59, Herrod Aviation Co., Billings, 1964-66; mem. Mont. Bd. Psychologist Examiners. Bd. dirs. Yellowstone County Tb Assn., 1970-71. Mem. Mont. Psychol. Assn. (chmn. bd. examiners 1965-71), Am. (mem. council reps. 1968-71), Rocky Mountain (treas. 1965-67, pres. 1972-73) psychol. assns. Club: Zonta (dir. 1966-68). Home: 4009 Bench Blvd Billings MT 59101

WILSON, HELEN PAXTON GIBBENS (MRS. ROBERT FLOYD WILSON), educator; b. Bloomington, Ill., Dec. 16, 1919; d. George Noble and Arlie Lorraine (Shinkle) Paxton; A.A., Monticello Coll., 1939; B.A., Vanderbilt U., 1941, B.L.S. with distinction, U. Okla., 1963, M.A. (Kingfisher fellow), 1968, Ph.D., 1970; m. Robert Floyd Wilson, Aug. 10, 1971; children by previous marriage—William Paxton Gibbens, Robert M. Gibbens, Everett N. Gibbens. Analytical chemist Campbell-Taggert Research Co., Kansas City, Mo., 1942-43; instr. philosophy U. Okla., Norman, 1964-67, faculty adviser Coll. Continuing Edn., 1969—; chmn. dept. philosophy N.M. Highlands U., Las Vegas, 1967—; field faculty Goddard Coll., Plainfield, Vt., 1970—; vis. staff mem. U. Cal., Los Alamos Sci. Lab., 1974—. Pres., dir. Jr. Scientific Research Labs., 1957-61. Bd. dirs. Okla. Sci. and Arts Found., 1960; bd. dirs. P.T.A., 1950-61, pres. 1953-54. Recipient Outstanding Educators Am. award, 1972. Mem. West Tex.-N.M. Philos. Soc. (pres. 1971-72), Am. Chem. Soc., Am., Southwestern philos. assns., Philosophy of Sci. Assn. Contbr. articles to profl. jours. Home: Box 7 Glorieta NM 87535 Office: New Mexico Highlands Univ Dept Philosophy Las Vegas NM 87701

WILSON, JANE, artist; b. Seymour, Ia., Apr. 29, 1924; d. Wayne and Cleone (Marquis) Wilson; B.A., U. Ia., 1945, M.A., 1947; m. John Gruen, Mar. 28, 1948; 1 dau., Julia. One-man shows include Hansa Gallery, N.Y.C., 1953, 55, 57. Stuttman Gallery, N.Y.C., 1958, 59, Tibor de Nagy Gallery, N.Y.C., 1960-66, Graham Gallery, N.Y.C., 1968, 69; rep. permanent collections Mus. Modern Art Whitney Mus., Wadsworth Atheneum, Herron Art Mus., N.Y.U., Rockefeller Inst. Recipient Ingram-Merrill grant, 1963, Louis Comfort Tiffanv grant, 1967. Mem. Phi Beta Kappa. Address: 317 E 19th St New York City NY 10024

WILSON, JANE BLISS, library cons.; b. Durham, N.C., Feb. 24, 1914; d. Robert North and Saza Hendrick (Peck) Wilson; A.B., Duke, 1934, M.A., 1947; A.B. in L.S., U. N.C., 1937. Childrens librarian Detroit Pub. Library, 1937-40, Durham Pub. Library, 1940-41, Olivia Raney Library, Raleigh, 1941-43; head sch. librarian R.J. Reynolds High Sch., Winston-Salem, N.C., 1944-46; library supr. Durham Pub. Schs., 1946-58, dir. sch. libraries, 1958-68; cons. childrens library services Dept. Cultural Resources, N.C. State Govt., Raleigh, 1968—. Vis. prof. Duke, U. N.C., Chapel Hill, U. Md., College Park, U. Ky.; producer first children's radio program in N.C., WDNC, Durham, 1934, first ednl. TV program for children WUNC-TV, Chapel Hill, 1952; cons. H.W. Wilson Cos. Childrens Catalog, 1966—. Mem. N.C. Gov.'s Commn. on Library Resources, 1964-65. Mem. Am. (chmn.), Southeastern N.C. (pres. 1950-53) library assns., Delta Kappa Gamma. Democrat. Episcopalian. Home: Route 6 Box 133 Farrington Rd Chapel Hill NC 27514 Office: 109 E Jones St Raleigh NC 27611

WILSON, JANICE LEE DEPPE (MRS. JOHN ATKINS WILSON), jewelry mfg. co. owner; b. Cedar Falls, Ia., Feb. 2, 1939; d. Ralph William and Helen Margaret (Bayne) Deppe; student U. N.H., 1964-72; m. John Atkins Wilson, June 15, 1958; children—John, Sandra. Owner, Jewelry by Janice, Durham, N.H., 1968—. Head conf. bookings hotel New Eng. Center Continuing Edn., Durham, N.H., 1973—. Mem. League N.H. Craftsmen. Jewelers Guild N.H., Durham Art Assn. (v.p. 1973-74). Club: Chatham (Mass.) Yacht (mem. exec. com., sec. 1970—). Home: 48 Mill Rd Durham NH 03824 Office: Strafford Av Durham NH 03824

WILSON, JEAN SMOLLEN, lawyer; b. Richton, Miss., Dec. 29, 1917; d. Lemuel Albert and Josie (Smollen) Wilson; J.D., U. Miss., 1949. Served with WAC, 1942-46; admitted to Miss. bar, 1949; commd. 1st lt. USAF, 1949, advanced through grades to lt. col., 1958; judge adv. officer U.S. Air Force, 1949-50; spl. investigations staff officer, Washington, Germany, 1950-56; ednl. staff officer Air U., Maxwell AFB, Ala., 1957-61; dep. dir. women in Air Force, Hdqrs. USAF Washington, 1961-64, planning and programming officer Aerospace Studies Inst., 1964-69, ret.; spl. asst. to asso. dir. Miss. Research and Devel. Center, Jackson, 1969; practiced in Gulfport, Miss. 1970—; now with firm Boyce Holleman. Bd. dirs., 1st v.p. Gulf Coast Assn. for Mental Health; v.p., bd. dirs. Moore Community House, Inc. Mem. State Bar, Am. Assn. U. Women (1st v.p. Montgomery br. 1967-69, sec. Gulfport br. 1970-71, 1st v.p. Gulfport br. 1972—). Methodist (chmn. adminstrv. bd. 1974—). Clubs: Richton Woman's (hon.); Soroptimist (pres. Montgomery, Ala., 1960, UNESCO chmn. South Atlantic region 1964). Home: 2-G Edgewater Gardens Biloxi MS 39531 Office: Boyce Holleman Gulfport MS 39501

WILSON, JESSIE ELIZABETH, librarian; b. Keysville, Va., June 20, 1926; d. Clarence Veasy and Violet (Gray) Wilson; student Va. State Coll., 1943-44; B.A., Va. Union U., 1947; B.S. in Library Sci., Atlanta U., 1948; postgrad. U. Md., 1959-62; M. Liberal Arts, Johns Hopkins U., 1968. Library asst. Army library, Pentagon, Washington, 1951-52; hosp. br. librarian Post Library, Fort Devens, Mass., 1952-54; asst. reference librarian Va. State Coll., Petersburg, 1954-58; sch. librarian Bates High Sch., Annapolis, Md. 1958-63, Cockran Jr. High Sch., Glen Burnie, Md., 1963-64; mng. librarian Library Processing Center, Bd. Edn. Annapolis, 1964—. Mem. Nat. Council Negro Women, N.A.A.C.P., Y.W.C.A., Mem. Md. Library Assn., Edn. Media Assn. Md., Md. State Tchrs. Assn., Tchrs. Assn. Anne Arundel County, Assn. Edn. Leaders, N.E.A., Delta Sigma Theta. Democrat. Baptist. Club: Girl Friends, Inc. Home: 7901 13th St NW Washington DC 20012 Office: 27 Chinquapin Round Rd Annapolis MD 21401

WILSON, JOYCE RICHARDSON, editor; b. N.Y.C., Nov. 21, 1926; d. Wiley M. and Inez (Richardson) Wilson; B.A., Goddard Coll., 1948. Profl. mag. photographer, photographs pub. in mags., including Time, Life, Fortune, Ladies Home Jour., many garden books, 1960-71; sr. editor textbook div., div. urban edn. Harcourt Brace Jovanovich, Inc., San Francisco, 1971—. Mem. Profl. Photographers No. Cal. Contbr. mystery stories to various mags. Home: PO Box 690 Mill Valley CA 94941 Office: Harcourt Brace Jovanovich Bldg Polk and Geary Sts San Francisco CA 94109

WILSON, JUDITH, educator; b. Columbus, O., July 6, 1936; d. Fred Edson and Helen (Stroupe) Wilson; B.S., U. Md., 1958; M.S., Pa. State U., 1962; postgrad. U. So. Cal., 1966; Ph.D., U. Minn., 1972. Tchr., Broome Jr. High Sch., Rockville, Md., 1958-61; grad. asst. Pa. State U., University Park, 1961-62; instr. Carleton Coll., Northfield, Minn., 1962-66; asst. prof. health, phys. edn. U. Wis., River Falls, 1966-73, asso. prof., 1973—. Mem. Am., Midwest, Wis. assns. health, phys. edn. and recreation, Am. Acad. Sports Medicine, Minn. Bd. Women Ofcls. (chmn. 1968-69), Nat. Assn. Phys. Edn. for Coll. Women, Kappa Alpha Theta. Home: 1117 Summit Av Mahtomedi MN 55115 Office: Phys Edn Dept U Wis River Falls WI 54022

WILSON, JULIANA DAVIS, lawyer; b. Jacksonville, Fla., June 16, 1921; d. Chaires Bowman and Alice Gwenn (Dancy) Davis; B.S. in Edn., Fla. State Coll. Women, 1942; LL.B., J.D., U. N.C., 1950; m. Thomas Stanton Wilson, May 19, 1945; children—Dale Brent, Diana Lynn. Admitted to Alaska bar, 1951; asso. J.L. McCarrey, Jr., Anchorage, 1950-52; pvt. practice, Anchorage, 1952-54; partner with T. Stanton Wilson, Anchorage, Alaska, 1954—. Served with WAVES, 1944-45. Mem. Am. Legion. Club: Quota (pres. Anchorage 1958-60). Home: 1615 Birchwood St Anchorage AK 99501 Office: 360 K St Anchorage AK 99501

WILSON, KATHERINE SCHMITKONS, biologist; b. Lorain, O., Jan. 22, 1913; d. H. William and Katherine (Bauman) S.; A.B., Oberlin Coll., 1933; postgrad. U. Colo., 1934; M.S., Northwestern U., 1935; postgrad. U. Chgo., 1939; Ph.D., Yale, 1944; m. George Edward Woodin, Nov. 23, 1961. Instr. biology Muskingum Coll., New Concord, O., 1935-41, Day Sch., New Haven, 1941-42; researcher biology Yale, 1941-53, instr., 1953-56; biologist div. research grants NIH, Bethesda, Md., 1956-62, scientist-adminstr., 1962—. Seessel research fellow Yale, 1948-49, Organon fellow, 1949-50. Fellow A.A.A.S., N.Y. Acad. Scis.; mem. Genetics Soc. Am., Bot. Soc. Am., Sigma Xi, Sigma Delta Epsilon. Conglist. Co-author: Botany-Principles and Problems, 6th edit., 1963; Manual of Botany, 6th edit., 1963. Contbr. to profl. jours. Home: 2725 29th St NW Washington DC 20008 Office: Div Research Grants Nat Insts Health Bethesda MD 20014

WILSON, LAVERNE (MRS. KENNETH WILSON), realtor; b. Rocklin, Cal., Jan. 29, 1913; d. Thomas and Lottie (Gannon) Shaves; R.N., Mercy Coll., 1934; m. Kenneth Wilson, July 16, 1935; 1 dau., Monte. Salesman, broker, mem. pres.'s club Fox and Carskadon, Menlo Park, Cal., 1960—. First recipient Million Dollar Club Lifetime award Menlo-Atherton Bd. Realtors, 1962. Home: PO Box 7123 Menlo Park CA 94025 Office: 611 Santa Cruz Av Menlo Park CA 94025

WILSON, LEONA ELIZABETH, educator; b. Almira, Wash., Apr. 22, 1925; d. Alonzo Canada and Margaret Ruth (Russell) Wilson; B.A., Wash. State U., 1955; M.S., Purdue U., 1958; postgrad. various univs. and colls. Asst. bookkeeper Ken Bush & Co., Spokane, 1943-44; tchr. in Deary, Worley and Ruebens, Idaho, 1943-50; sec. Wash. State U., Pullman, 1950-52; tchr., Colfax, Wash., 1955-57; counselor U. Cal. at Berkeley Sch. Edn., 1958-59; dean girls, counselor, Monteca and Ceres, Cal., 1959-63; tchr., counselor spl. edn., Union City, Cal., 1964-67, tchr. spl. edn., 1967—. Mem. N.E.A., Cal. Tchrs. Assn., Am. Assn. Personnel and Guidance, Nat. Vocational Guidance Assn., Am. Sch. Counselors Assn., Women's Deans and Counselors Assn., Am. Assn. Mental Deficiency, Pi Lambda Theta, Beta Sigma Phi. Home: PO Box 514 Union City CA 94587 Office: 33480 Western Blvd Union City CA 94578

WILSON, LOIS FAIR (MRS. HERBERT B. WILSON), ednl. adminstr; b. Redlands, Cal., Mar. 17, 1924; d. James Albert and Emma (Lederer) Fair; B.A., U. Redlands, 1945; M.S., U. So. Cal., 1954; Ed.D., U. Ariz., 1972; m. Herbert B. Wilson, Feb. 20, 1964. Curriculum cons. San Bernardino County (Cal.) Schs., 1951-61; asst. prof. U. Redlands (Cal.), 1961-64; pre-sch. tchr. Tucson Easter Seal Soc., 1964-65; program asst. Tucson Sch. Dist. 1, 1965-71, curriculum coordinator, elementary dept., 1972—; lectr. Coll. Edn., U. Ariz., 1972-73. Mem. Assn. Childhood Edn. Internat. (publs. com. 1969-72), Assn. for Edn. of Young Children, Am. Assn. Elementary-Kindergarten-Nursery Educators, Nat. Council Tchrs. English, Internat. Reading Assn., Delta Kappa Gamma, Pi Lambda Theta, Delta Kappa Pi. Home: 6451 N Camino Libby Tucson AZ 85718 Office: 1010 E 10th St Tucson AZ 85717

WILSON, LOIS J., edn. adminstr.; b. Batavia, N.Y., Dec. 1, 1936; d. Hugh M. and Margaret (Northrup) Wilson; A.B. magna cum laude, Elmira Coll., 1958; M.A., Cornell U., 1961. Pub. adminstrn. intern N.Y. State Assembly, Office Legislative Research, Albany, 1960-61, research asst., 1961-62, research analyst, 1962, sr. research analyst, 1962-63, asst. to dir., 1963-65; asst. dir. studies N.Y. State Tchrs. Assn., Albany, 1965-67, dir. studies, 1967-71, asst. exec. sec. studies and profl. services, 1971-73; dep. sec. to gov. N.Y., 1973—. N.Y. State commr. Edn. Commn. States, 1974—. Mem. Am. Assn. U. Women, Am. Soc. Pub. Adminstrn., N.E.A. (chmn. human relations council 1972-73), Urban League Albany, Am. Civil Liberties Union, N.Y. State Congress Parents and Tchrs. (life), Elmira Coll. Alumni Assn. (exec. bd. 1964-65), Bus. and Profl. Women, Zonta, Phi Beta Kappa. Home: 761 A Madison Av Albany NY 12208 Office: State Capitol Albany NY 12224

WILSON, LORRAINE NUALA MARY (MRS. LYNDELL FREDRIC WILSON), dietician; b. No. Ireland, Feb. 11, 1944; d. Leslie and Esther Jane (McCahon) Smitten; B.H.E. (Canadian Dietetic Assn. scholar), U. B.C. (Can.), 1965; m. Lyndell Fredric Wilson, May 8, 1965; children—Shaun Durand, Steven Darren. Chief dietician Powell River (B.C.) Gen. Hosp., 1966—. Cons. Olive Devaud Home, Powell River. Mem. Canadian Dietetic Assn., Beta Sigma Phi. Home: 7137 Kemano St Powell River BC Canada Office: 5871 Arbutus St Powell River BC Canada

WILSON, MABEL FLOREY (MRS. WILLIAM JOHN WILSON), scientist; b. Omaha, Mar. 17, 1906; d. Louis Byron and Cora Belle (Walker) Florey; B.S. magna cum laude, Buena Vista Coll. 1927; M.S., Mich. State U., 1930, Ph.D., 1937; m. William John Wilson, July 1, 1929; children—Jack Ross, Joan (Mrs. Alan C. Rice). Tchr. high schs., Titonka, Ia., 1927-28, Barnum, Ia., 1928-29; grad. asst. Mich. State U., East Lansing, 1935-37; chemist-spectroscopist Burgess Labs., Madison, Wis., 1937-38; instrumental analytical chemist Diamond Alkali Co., Painesville, O., 1938-52; group leader, instrumental analytical chemist Air Reduction Research Lab., Murray Hill, N.J., 1952-61; group leader, instrumental analytical chemist plastics research div. Allied Chem. Corp., Morristown, N.J., 1961-66, research asso., 1966-70; in charge instrumental analysis, lab. Office of N.J. State Med. Examiner, Newark, 1970-72, forensic spectroscopist, 1972—. Fellow Am. Inst. Chemists, Am. Soc. Testing and Materials (recipient award of merit 1971) (editor E-2 newsletter 1966—); mem. Am. Chem. Soc., Soc. for Applied Spectroscopy, Sigma Xi, Sigma Pi Sigma. Home: 767 Springfield Av Summit NJ 07901

WILSON, MABEL PONDER (MRS. OTHA BERNON WILSON), educator; b. Decatur, Ala., May 14, 1907; d. Thomas Reese and Mary Ann (Breedlove) Ponder; A.B., Brimingham-So. Coll., 1928; m. Otha Bernon Wilson, Sept. 18, 1936; 1 son, Joseph Wheeler II. Classroom tchr. Gorgas Elementary Sch., Birmingham, Ala., 1928-36, 43-55, prin., 1955-67. Mem. Nat., Ala. edn. assns., Birmingham Tchrs. Assn., Birmingham Prins. Assn., D.A.R. (regent gen. Sumter chpt. 1966-68, pres. Jefferson County regents council 1967-68, dir. dist. IV, 1971—, chmn. Am. Hist. Month, Ala. Soc. 1970—, nat. resolutions com. 1973, chmn. com. to compile Some Early Ala. Chs. 1973), U.S. Daus. 1812 (charter chpt.), Ala. Geneal. Soc., Daus. Am. Colonists, Arlington Hist. Soc., Ala. Hist. Assn., Delta Kappa Gamma, Kappa Delta Epsilon. Presbyn. Home: 1701 Fourth Terrace W Birmingham AL 35208

WILSON, MARGARET BERENICE BUSH, lawyer; b. St. Louis, Jan. 30, 1919; d. James Thomas and Margaret Berenice (Casey) Bush; B.A. cum laude, Talladega Coll., 1940; LL.B., Lincoln U. Sch. Law, 1943; m. Robert E. Wilson, Jr., Mar. 19, 1944 (div. Mar. 1968); 1 son, Robert Edmund III. Admitted to Mo. bar, 1943, Ill. bar, 1947, Supreme Ct. U.S., 1966; U.S. atty. legal div. Rural Electrification Adminstrn., U.S. Dept. Agr., St. Louis, 1943-45; practiced in St. Louis, 1947-65, 72—, asst. atty. gen. State Mo., 1961-62; legal services specialist State Mo., 1965-67; adminstr. Mo. Com. Service and Continuing Edn., 1967-68; dep. dir. acting dir. St. Louis Model City Program, 1968-69; asst. dir. St. Louis Lawyers for Housing, 1969-72. Instr. civil procedure Council on Legal Edn. Opportunities Inst., St. Louis U., Sch. Law, 1973—. Vice-chmn. Land Reutilization Authority, City St. Louis, 1973; mem. Mo. Council on Criminal Justice, 1972—. Treas. N.A.A.C.P. Nat. Housing Corp., Arts and Edn. Council, St. Louis, Health and Welfare Council, St. Louis. Juliette Derricotte fellow, 1939-40; recipient Bishop's award Episcopal Diocese Mo., 1963. Mem. N.A.A.C.P. (nat. bd. mem. 1963—), Lawyers Assn., Am., Mo., Mound City, St. Louis bar assns., Alpha Kappa Alpha. Episcopalian. Home: 4200 W Page Blvd St Louis MO 63113 Office: 4054 Lindell Blvd Suite 100 St Louis MO 63108

WILSON, MARGARET DAULER (MRS. EMMETT WILSON, JR.), educator; b. Pitts., Jan. 29, 1939; d. Lee Van Voorhis and Margaret (Hodge) Dauler; A.B., Vassar Coll., 1960; M.A., Harvard, 1963, Ph.D., 1965; postgrad. Oxford (Eng.) U., 1963-64; m. Emmett Wilson, Jr., June 12, 1962. Teaching fellow Harvard, 1962-63, 64-65; asst. prof. philosophy Columbia, N.Y.C., 1965-67; asst. prof. Rockefeller U., 1967-70; vis. asst. prof. philosophy Barnard Coll., part-time 1969-70; asso. prof. philosophy Princeton, 1970—; visitor Inst. Advanced Study, 1973. Woodrow Wilson fellow, 1960-61. Mem. Am. Philos. Assn. (chmn. subcom. on status of women in the profession 1969-71, Eastern div. exec. com. 1973—), Am. Assn. U. Profs., Gottfried-Wilhelm-Leibniz Gesellschaft, Soc. for Philosophy and Pub. Affairs, Phi Beta Kappa. Editor: The Essential Descartes, 1969; editorial bd. Archiv fur Geschichte der Philosophie, 1973—. Home: River Rd RD 2 Belle Mead NJ 08502 Office: Dept Philosophy Princeton U Princeton NJ 08540

WILSON, MARGARET EILEEN, educator; b. Kansas City, Mo.; d. Edward Leslie and Bertha (Coe) Wilson; B.S., U. Ark., 1944, M.S., 1949; Ph.D., State U. Ia., 1960. Recreation dir. Pine Bluff (Ark.) Arsenal Housing Project, 1944; instr. Central High Sch., Muskogee, Okla., 1945-48; grad. asst. U. Ark., 1948-49; instr. Fayetteville (Ark.) High Sch., 1949-52; instr. to asst. prof. Ark. Poly. Coll., 1952-57; grad. asst. State U. Ia., 1957-59; asso. prof., women's dir. phys. edn. Ark. Poly. Coll., 1959-65; prof. Tex. Tech. U., 1965—, chmn. dept. health, phys. edn. and recreation for women, 1967—. Basketball staff 4th Nat. Inst. on Girls Sports, 1966; cons. basketball workshop State Coll. of Cortland (N.Y.), 1967; sec. Dist. XVII of Gov.'s Regional Adv. Council on Lifetime Sports, 1969-70; women's basketball chmn. Region 12 of Amateur Athletic Union, 1967-69; sec.-treas. DGWS-Amateur Athletic Union Basketball rules com., 1970-71, mem. 1968-71; dirs.' rep. Tex. Commn. on Intercollegiate Athletics for women, 1970-72. Mem. com. med. and pub. edn. W. Tex. Tb and Respiratory Disease Assn., 1968-70. Mem. Am. (sec. measurement sect. 1971-72, mem. rep. assembly 1973-74), Tex. (auditing com. 1970-73, dist. 13 rep., chmn. measurement and evaluation sect. 1973-74) assns. health, phys. edn. and recreation, W. Tex. Bd. Women Ofcls. (chmn. 1968-70), Nat., So. (mem. internat. relations com. 1972—) assns. phys. edn. for coll. Women, Tex. Assn. Coll. Tchrs., Am. Assn. U. Profs. (chpt. sec. 1972-73, v.p. 1973-74), Mortar Board (sponsor Forum chpt. 1972—), Pi Lambda Theta, Delta Kappa Gamma (chpt. pres. 1972—), Delta Psi Kappa, Delta Gamma. Democrat. Presbyn. Home: 5411 46th St Lubbock TX 79414 Office: Texas Tech University Lubbock TX 79409

WILSON, MARILYN ANN (MRS. ROY THOMAS WILSON), psychologist; b. Great Falls, Mont., Apr. 13, 1946; d. George Joseph and Mary (Bacha) Sechena; B.A., Coll. Great Falls, 1967; M.A., Pepperdine Coll., 1969; m. Roy Thomas Wilson, July 27, 1969. Psychologist, Community Mental Health Center, Spokane, Wash., 1970—. Active Gardena (Cal.) Youth Counseling Service, 1968-69, recipient Service award, 1968-69. Mem. Am. Psychol. Assn., Psi Chi. Club: Doberman Pinscher of Greater Spokane (sec. 1974). Home: N 5644 Drumheller Spokane WA 99208 Office: S 107 Division Spokane WA 99201

WILSON, MARJORIE GRACE PRICE (MRS. LYNN MINFORD WILSON), physician; b. Pitts.; d. Robert John and Grace (McMillen) Price; student Bryn Mawr Coll., 1942-45; M.D., U. Pitts., 1949; m. Lynn Minford Wilson, Sept. 15, 1951; children—Lynn Deyo, Liza Price. Intern, U. Pitts. Med. Center Hosps., 1949-50; resident Childrens Hosp. and U. Pitts, Sch. Medicine, 1950-51; resident U. Miami Sch. Medicine and Jackson Meml. Hosp., 1954-56; chief contractural research sect. Research and Edn. Service VA Central Office, 1952-53, chief residency and intership div. Edn. Service Office Research and Edn., 1956, chief profl. tng. div., 1956-60, asst. dir., 1960; chief tng. br. extramural programs Nat. Inst. Arthritis and Metabolic Diseases NIH, 1960-63, asst. to asso. dir. tng. Office of Dir. NIH, 1963-64, asso. dir. extramural programs Nat. Library Medicine, 1964-67, asso. dir. program devel. Office Program Planning and Evaluation, 1967-69, asst. dir. program planning and evaluation NIH, 1969-70; dir. dept. institutional devel. Assn. Am. Med. Colls., 1970—. Mem. Assn. Am. Med. Colls., Am. Fedn. Clin. Research, Am. Med. Womens Assn., A.A.A.S. Contbr. articles profl. jours. Home: 6913 Bradley Blvd Bethesda MD 20034 Office: 1 DuPont Circle Washington DC 20036

WILSON, MARJORIE MONTAGUE (MRS. WESLEY MCCOOL WILSON), physician; b. Sweetwater, Tex., Nov. 23, 1920; d. Harley Howard and Rebecca (Wilder) Montague; B.A., Colo. State Coll., 1942; M.D., U. Chgo., 1953; M.S., U. Wash., 1969;

student U. Chile, Santiago, 1947-49; m. Wesley McCool Wilson, Sept. 7, 1957; children—Larry Arthur, Bruce Alan. Intern King County Hosps., Seattle, 1953-54; practice medicine Group Health Coop. of Puget Sound, Seattle, 1954-58; hosp. epidemiologist U. Wash. Hosp., Seattle, 1964-67; postdoctoral fellow dept. preventive medicine U. Wash., 1967-69; asst. pub. health officer, Yakima, Wash., 1970-71; physician Farm Workers Family Health Center, Toppenish, Wash., 1971; community health physician, Yakima, 1971-72; med. dir. Southeast Yakima Community Center, 1972—. Mem. Am. Pub. Health Assn., Soc. for Epidemoil. Research, Yakima County Med. Soc., League Women Voters, Alpha Omega Alpha. Home: 1403 S 1st Av Yakima WA 98902 Office: 1211 S 7th St Yakima WA 98901

WILSON, MARY FLORENCE, librarian; b. Lancaster, Pa.; d. Col. William B. and Sarah A. (Urich) Wilson; student Gibson's Coll. Prep., Phila., Drexel Inst., U. of Pa. Extension, Columbia; student Drexel Inst. Library Sch., 1909, LL.D., 1942. With Columbia U. Library, 1909-17; organized various libraries, English, Dramatic, Map and Natural Scis., and Library for the Nat. Com. for Mental Hygiene; instr. in cataloging and classification and librarian natural scis., 1913-17; with U.S. Govt. Inquiry on Peace Terms, N.Y.C., and organized library for the Peace Conf., 1917-18; mem. Am. Commn. to Negotiate Peace, Paris, 1918-19; librarian League of Nations Geneva, Switzerland, 1919-27; ednl. work with European Centre, Carnegie Endowment, 1927-30. Represented secretariat of League of Nations at Internat. Women's Suffrage Alliance, Geneva, June 1920, and Internat. Assn. U. Women, Paris, 1922; ednl. survey for Carnegie Endowment to Egypt. Syria, Turkey and Greece, spring and summer 1927; prof. Ecole de Bibliothecaires, Paris, 1926-28; work for refugees in France with Comite American de Secours Civil, 1940—. Episcopalian. Clubs: Chilton (Boston); Union Interalliee (Paris); Golf, (Lausanne). Author: The Covenant of the League of Nations (documentary history); Near East Survey; History of the League of Nations Library; also articles in mags. and newspapers. Home: 80 Av de Sully La Tour de Peilz 1814 Switzerland

WILSON, MIRIAM GEISENDORFER (MRS. HOWARD GENE WILSON), physician; b. Yakima, Wash.; B.S., U. Wash., 1944, M.S., 1945; M.D. U. Cal. at San Francisco, 1950. Prof. pediatrics U. So. Cal. Med. Sch., also dir. Cytogenetics lab. of Genetics div. Pediatric Dept. Mem. Pres.'s Com. on Mental Retardation. Diplomate Am. Bd. Pediatrics. Fellow Am. Pub. Health Assn.; mem. Am. Soc. Human Genetics, Am. Acad. Pediatrics, Los Angeles Pediatric Soc., Western Soc. for Pediatric Research, Phi Beta Kappa, Sigma Xi. Contbr. profl. jours. Home: 2050 Mandeville Canyon Los Angeles CA 90049 Office: Dept Pediatrics U So Cal Los Angeles CA 90033

WILSON, NORMA JEANNE, occupational therapist; b. Saginaw, Mich., July 28, 1921; d. George Henry and Elsie Helen (Boerema) Wilson; B.S. in Elementary Edn., Western Mich. Coll. Edn., 1943; certificate in Occupational Therapy, U. So. Cal., 1953. Tchr. elementary sch. Redford Twp., Mich., 1943-45, Lansing, Mich., 1945-49, Long Beach, Cal., 1949-51; occupational therapist Crippled Children's Services, Paramount, Cal., 1953-55, Long Beach, 1955-59, Cal. Elks Maj. Project, Redding Cal., 1959-69, Home de Réadaptation, Huémoz, Switzerland, 1969-70, Cal.-Hawaii Elks Maj. Project, Fresno, Cal., 1970—. Mem. Am. No. Cal. Occupational Therapy assns., Christian Women's Council (lit. chmn. 1972-74). Address: Travelodge Mobile Home Park 1724 N Minnewawa Space 164 Clovis CA 93612

WILSON, PATRICIA BOYD (MRS. ROBERT WILSON), journalist, ednl. adminstr.; b. Everett, Wash., Oct. 22, 1911; d. John and Addie Alberta (Foss) Boyd; B.S., N.Y. U., 1943; M.S., Columbia, 1944; m. Robert Wilson, Jan. 18, 1952. By-line on art Christian Sci. Monitor, Boston, 1962—. Cons. pilot project M.W. Smith Found., Mobile, Ala.; also dean edn. Mobile Art Gallery. Home: West Point Sebasco Estates ME 04565

WILSON, PHYLLIS STARR (MRS. HUGH H. WILSON), editor; b. New Orleans, Feb. 11, 1928; d. Daniel David and Anita (Garripy) Starr; B.A. in English, Tulane U., 1949; m. Hugh Hamilton Wilson, Dec. 24, 1958. Receptionist, asst. Coca-Cola Co. house organ, New Orleans, 1949; sec., editor Weird Tales mag., N.Y.C., 1950; sec. Conde Nast Publs., N.Y.C., 1951-55, researcher, writer Vogue mag., 1955-62, writer Glamour mag., 1962-67, sr. editor copy and features, 1967-71, mng. editor, 1971—; also free-lance editor, writer. Recipient J. C. Penny and U. Mo. journalism award for med. article, 1969. Mem. Am. Soc. Mag. Editors. Democrat. Editor, researcher The Artist in His Studio (Alexander Liberman), 1960; Moments Preserved (Irving Penn), 1960; editor Glamour's Health and Beauty Book, 1972. Home: 242 W 12th St New York City NY 10014 Office: 350 Madison Av New York City NY 10017

WILSON, ROSLYNNE VALERIE, mus. curator; b. Elizabeth, N.J., Feb. 3, 1944; d. Lenward Delmas and Eulalie Josephine (Zeff) Wilson; diploma Northrop Collegiate Sch., 1962; B.A., Skidmore Coll., 1966; M.A., Case Western Res. U., 1969. Photograph librarian Cleve. Mus. Art, 1968-69; edn. dept. lectr., creative class instr. Cleve. Mus. Art, 1966-69; asst. curator edn. Cin. Art Mus., 1969, asso. curator edn., 1970-73, curator edn., 1973—. Lectr. for Jr. League Cin. Docent Tng. Course, 1973—; cons. several bds. edn. Cin. area, 1970—. Mem. Coll. Art Assn., Am. Assn. Museums, Archeol. Soc. Am., Nat. Art Edn. Assn., Ohio Art Edn. Assn., Skidmore College Alumnae Club Cin. and Dayton (pres. 1969-73), Jr. League Cin. (provisional). Episcopalian (cons. youth program and Sunday Sch. tchrs. tng. 1970-73, cons. musica sacra 1969-73). Home: 8480 Blome Rd Cincinnati OH 45243 Office: Cin Art Mus Eden Park Cincinnati OH 45202

WILSON, RUTH ELISE (MRS. NATHAN R. WILSON), civic worker; b. Greenville, Miss., May 5, 1920; d. James and Hattie (Mack) Carter; student Crane Jr. Coll., Chgo., 1957, Loop Jr. Coll. Chgo., 1964; m. Nathan R. Wilson, Dec. 28, 1938; children—Donald, Rita, Claude, Linda, Natalie, Rhonda, Lawrence Wilson. Clk., U.S. Treasury Dept., Chgo., 1957-65; procurement clk., typist Gen. Services Adminstrn., Chgo., 1965-68; Stenographer U.S. Probate Ct., Chgo., 1968—. Co-chmn. Crusade of Mercy, Lawndale area, Chgo., 1958-59; sec. Block Club, 1962; active United Negro College Fund drive, 1965; founder Ladies Aux. Greater Lawndale Conservation Commn., Chgo., pres., 1958-59; v.p., bd. dirs. Greater Lawndale Conservation Commn., 1959; cons. bd. dirs. Chgo. Urban League, 1968—, pres. women's div., 1968—; treas. women's div., 1971— bd. dirs. Citizens for Day Care, Inc., 1968—. Roman Catholic (pres. altar and rosary soc., 1963, pres. Mother's Club, 1964-66). Home: 8801 S Ridgeland Av Chicago IL 60617 Office: US Dist Ct Probation Office Chicago IL 60604

WILSON, RUTH MARIAN, educator; b. Colo., Sept. 18, 1910; d. Raymond C. and Emma (Ericson) Wilson; B.S., U. Utah, 1931; M.S., U. Wis., 1936; postgrad. U. Cal. at Berkeley, N.Y.U. Phys. edn. tchr. elementary schs., Salt Lake City, 1931-35; faculty U. Wash., Seattle, 1936—, chmn. dept. for women Sch. Phys. and Health Edn., 1947-66, prof., 1966—. Mem. hobby sch. bd. Seattle YMCA, 1947-51. Bd. dirs. Seven Oaks Homeowners Assn., Rancho Bernardo, San Diego, 1973-75, 2d v.p., 1974. Recipient Honor award Wash. Assn. Health, Phys. Edn. and Recreation, 1969. Amy Morris Homans scholar Wellesley Coll. 1962. Fellow Am. Acad. Phys. Edn. (pres. 1970-71, exec. com. 1969-72), A.A.H.P.E.R. (treas. N.W. dist. 1939-41, pres. 1958-60, honor fellow award 1958, honor award N.W. dist. 1963); mem. Nat. Assn. Phys. Edn. Coll. Women (pres. 1955-57), Western Soc. Phys. Edn. Coll. Women (pres. 1951-53, exec. bd. 1967-69), King County (pres. 1939-40), Utah (sec.-treas. 1932-34) health and phys. edn. assns., Am. Assn. U. Women, P.E.O., Delta Zeta, Phi Delta Pi. Author: Folk Dance Syllabus, 1954; (with Marion R. Broer) Handbook of Marching Tactics, 1956, Fundamentals of Marching. 1965; Assessing Competency in Physical Education Activities, 1966. Address: U Wash Seattle WA 98115

WILSON, STEPHANY SUE, research center ofcl.; b. Flint, Mich., Aug. 8, 1942; d. Bill R. and Jewell L. (Crawford) Crow; B.A. with distinction, U. N.M., 1964; m. Thomas E. Wilson, Aug. 25, 1962; 1 dau., Lauren Ann. Soc. editor, reporter Calsbad (N.M.) Current Argus, 1961-62, 62; reporter Albuquerque Tribune, 1963, 64-65; information dir. Presbyn. Hosp. Center, Albuquerque, 1965-67; tech. editor Dikewood Corp., Albuquerque, 1967-69; cons. writing, editing, pub. relations, Albuquerque, 1969-72; community research specialist criminal justice program U. N.M., Albuquerque, 1972-73, grant adminstr. Cancer Research and Treatment Center, 1973—. Vol. worker Albuquerque Task Force on Victims of Sex Crimes. Author, editor numerous reports and publs. Home: 1612 Haines Pl NE Albuquerque NM 87112 Office: Cancer Research and Treatment Center U NM Albuquerque NM 87131

WILSON, THEODORA NADELSTEIN, journalist; b. Bklyn., May 22; d. Adolph and Rebecca Nadelstein; B.A. summa cum laude, U. Ky.; m. William Robert Wilson; 1 son, Delph Robert. Tri-state editor Evansville (Ind.) Press; reporter, editor Richmond (Va.) News Leader; writer A.P., Phila.; reporter, writer Phila. Bull.; reporter, writer, editorial dept. N.Y. Daily News, N.Y.C., 1952—. Recipient Page One awards N.Y. Newspaper Guild, 1958, 66, Pioneer Reporting in Welfare award N.Y. Senate and Assembly, 1963. Mem. Women in Communications, Silurians (award 1967), N.Y. Press Club, Wash. Press Club, N.Y. Newswomen's Club (awards 1961-72), Overseas Press Club, Phi Beta Kappa, Theta Sigma Phi (award 1969). Home: 21 Chittenden Av New York City NY 10033 Office: The News 220 E 42nd St New York City NY 10017

WILSON, YVONNA A., univ. dean; b. Batesville, Ark., Nov. 18, 1932; d. George Albert and Lorena (Weaver) Wilson; B.A., Ark. Coll., 1953; M.Ed., U. Ark., 1965; student Kan. State Tchrs. Coll., 1965-68. Tchr. pub. sch., Blytheville, Ark., 1953-57; admissions counselor Ark. Coll., Batesville, 1957-64; asst. dean women Kan. State Tchrs. Coll., Emporia, 1965-68; dean women Mo. So. Coll., Joplin, 1968-71; dean of women Southwest Mo. State U., Springfield, 1971—. Bd. dirs. Wesley Found., 1st United Meth. Ch., Emporia, Kan., 1966-68. Mem. Kan. Assn. Women Deans and Counselors (treas. 1966-68), Nat. Assn. Women Deans and Counselors, Am. Assn. U. Women (corr. sec. br. 1966-68), Mo. State Tchrs. Assn., Mo. So. Coll. Faculty Assn. (treas. 1968-69), Independence County Hist. Soc., Nat. Assn. Jr. Colls., Mo. Women in Traffic Safety, Central Kan. Ark. Alumni Assn. (sec.-treas. 1965-66), U. Ark. Alumni Assn., Greene County Mental Health Assn., Altrusa Internat., Cardinal Key, Kappa Kappa Alpha. Methodist (adminstrv. bd. 1968-71). Home: 2154 S Fairway Terrace Springfield MO 65804

WIMBERLY, SARAH JEANET, educator; b. El Dorado, Ark., June 10, 1927; d. Ross W. and Grace P. (Haynie) Wimberly; B.A., Southwestern Assemblies of God Coll., 1948; B.S., John Brown U., 1949; B.A., La. Poly Inst., 1960; M.Ed., La. State U., 1962; postgrad. Auburn U., 1963—. Tchr. pub. schs., Sabine Parish, La., 1948-51; tchr. Canyonville (Ore.) Bible Acad., 1951-52; missionary tchr. Assemblies of God, Liberia and Nigeria, West Africa, 1952-59; tchr. pub. schs., Morehouse Parish, La., 1960-62; librarian Bastrop (La.) High Sch., 1962-72, head librarian, 1968-72; asst. prof. library sci. Coll. Edn., La. Tech. U., Ruston, 1972—; instr. Coll. Edn., Auburn (Ala.) U., 1967-70. Mem. La. Tchrs. Assn., La. Assn. Higher Edn., La. Assn. Tchr. Educators, Am. Assn. U. Women, Southwestern, La. library assns., La. Assn. Sch. Librarians, Alpha Beta Alpha, Kappa Kappa Iota. Mem. Assemblies of God. Home: 126 Haynie Av Bastrop LA 71220 Office: Coll Edn La Tech Univ Ruston LA 71270

WIMMER, ELIZABETH JANE, pub. relations exec.; b. Duluth, Minn., Nov. 15, 1921; d. Thomas Elmer and Mercedes Hyacinth (Cashin) Wimmer; A.A., U. Wis., 1944; B.J., U. Mo., 1949. Women's editor South Bay Daily Breeze, Torrance, Cal., 1950-54, reporter-photographer, 1954-57, city editor, 1957-58, news editor, 1958-63; copy editor San Diego Union, 1963-67; corr. Los Angeles bur. Copley News Service, 1967-68; pub. information specialist Los Angeles Dept. Water and Power, 1968—. Publicity chmn. Redondo Beach March of Dimes, 1955-63. Served with USMC Women Res., 1945-46. Mem. Am. Women in Radio and TV (chpt. chmn. pub. affairs 1973-74), Nat. Fedn. Press Women, Cal. Press Women (dist. pres. 1971-72, state v.p. 1971-72), Women in Communications, Greater Los Angeles Press Club, World Affairs Council. Home: 1828 Wayne Av South Pasadena CA 91030 Office: 111 N Hope St Los Angeles CA 90051

WIMMER, KATHERINE, educator, med. librarian; b. Spokane, Wash.; d. Joseph and Laura (Courtenay) Wimmer; B.A., Whitman Coll., 1945; M.Ed., De Paul U., 1955; M.A. in Library Sci., Rosary Coll., 1972. Ednl. therapist Inst. for Juvenile Research, Chgo., 1947-50; remedial tchr. Day Sch., Chgo., 1950-55; elementary tchr. Inst. for Juvenile Research, Chgo., 1955-56, prin. Healy Sch., 1956-68; dir. spl. edn. John J. Madden Center, Maywood, Ill., 1968-70; med. librarian St. Joseph's Hosp., Chgo., 1972—. Mem. adv. bd. Chgo. chpt. Council for Exceptional Children, 1963-69, chpt. treas., 1965-67. Fellow Am. Orthopsychiat. Assn.; mem. Beta Phi Mu. Home: 316 W Barry St Chicago IL 60657 Office: 2900 N Lake Shore Chicago IL 60657

WINAKOR, BESS RUTH, journalist; b. Springfield, Ill., Mar. 17, 1942; d. Arthur H. and Annette (Wright) Winakor; B.A., Northwestern U., 1963, M.S. in Journalism, 1964. Interviewer Creative Research Workshop of Leo Burnett Co., Chgo., 1963-64; research analyst Post-Keyes-Gardner Advt., Chgo., 1964-65; account exec. Daniel J. Edelman & Assos., Chgo., 1965-67; Chgo. corr. Fairchild Publs. Women's Wear Daily, also broadcaster Capital Cities Broadcast, 1967-74; feature writer Chgo. Sun-Times, 1974—. Mem. Am. Home Econs. Assn., Home Economists in Bus., Chgo. Council Fgn. Relations, Women in Communications. Home: 1150 N Lake Shore Dr Chicago IL 60611 Office: 401 N Wabash Av Chicago IL 60611

WINCHELL, CAROL ANN (MRS. JAMES F. WINCHELL), librarian; b. Columbus, O., July 16, 1936; d. Homer S. and Helen Mary (Stultz) French; B.M., Ohio State U., 1958, M.A., 1960; M.S. in L.S., Case Western Res. U., 1964; m. James F. Winchell, July 1963; 1 son, Philip. Reference librarian Ohio State U. Libraries, Columbus, 1964—. Mem. A.L.A., Ohio Library Assn., Am. Assn. U. Women, Am. Assn. Univ. Profs. Methodist. Author: Pathfinder Bibliography, 1974; The Hyperkinetic Child: A Bibliography of Medical, Educational and Behavioral Studies, 1975. Editor: Pathfinder Bibliography, 1974. Home: 3840 Schirtzinger Columbus OH 43220 Office: 1858 Neil Av Columbus OH 43210

WINCHESTER, ALMA ELIZABETH TATSCH (MRS. CLARENCE FLOYD WINCHESTER), civic worker, radio writer and broadcaster; b. Fredericksburg, Tex.; d. Otto August and Meta (Hohenberger) Tatsch; student Am. Conservatory Music (Chgo.), 1937-38; m. Clarence Floyd Winchester, Sept. 25, 1943. Singer Chgo. Civic Opera Jr. Chorus, 1937-38; writer radio script Evans Fur Co., Chgo., 1941-42; writer Radio Sta. KTSA, San Antonio, 1942-43; womens dir., writer, broadcaster Radio Sta. KNOE, Monroe, La., 1944-45; writer, music lead ins Boyce Smith Show, Sta. WGN, Chgo., 1944; womens dir., writer, broadcaster Radio Sta. WGGG, Gainesville, Fla., 1948-49; pub. relations Stokeley-Van Camp, Inc., Washington, 1954-55. Mem. Salvation Army Aux., Washington; mem. women's bd. Providence Hosp., Washington; Pan-Am. liaison com. Womens Orgns., Washington; mem. Womens Internat. Religious Fellowship in cooperation with UNESCO, UNICEF, Schs., embassies; pres. City of Hope Med. Research chpt. 56, Washington. Mem. Internat. Platform Assn., Los Picaros (hon.), Howard University Faculty Wives. Mem. Christian Ch. Home: 2124 Sudbury Pl Washington DC 20012

WINCHESTER, LUCY ALEXANDER, White House social sec.; b. Lexington, Ky., Jan. 11, 1937; d. James Holloway and Lucy (Moulthrop) Alexander; B.A., U. Ky., 1960; student art history, Florence, Italy, also Nat. Acad. Sch., N.Y.C.; divorced, 1 dau., Lucy Alexander. With Protocol Office, U.S. mission to UN, 1960; guide UN Hdqrs., 1961-62; owner/mgr. Alexander Farms, 1962-69; social sec. White House, 1969—. Mem. Jr. League. Republican. Club: Iroquois Hunt. Office: The White House Washington DC 20500

WINCHESTER, VERA HILLMAN (MRS. ALFRED SMITH WINCHESTER), artist; b. London, Eng., Feb. 11, 1904; d. Joseph Elliot and Annie Murray (Frier) Hillman; came to U.S., 1906, naturalized, 1925; B.S., N.Y. U., 1940, postgrad. 1944; m. Alfred Smith Winchester, Oct. 25, 1924; 1 dau., Marian (Mrs. Robert L. Andersen). Exhibited in one-man shows Met. Savs. Bank, Bklyn., 1969, Summa Gallery, Bklyn., 1970, Hamilton Fed. Savs. Bank, Bklyn., 1971; exhibited in group shows Bklyn. Mus., Bklyn. Heights Promenade Art Show, 1967-74, Am. Artists Profl. League, 1967-73, Grand Nat. Art Show, Bklyn. All Community Artists, 1973, Union Ch., Bklyn., 1968-74; represented in permanent collections, St. Patrick's Ch. rectory, Bklyn. Tchr., Lafayette High Sch., Bklyn., 1939-66, vocational guidance counsellor, 1956-66. Mem. Am. Artists Profl. League, All Community Artists, Bklyn. Woman's Club (treas. 1971-74, chmn. way and means com. 1966-72), Morning Choral Club, Christian Scientist (chmn. bd. trustees 1954-57). Club: Salmagundi (N.Y.C.). Home and studio: 9801 Shore Rd Brooklyn NY 11209

WINCKLER, SUE (MRS. DONAL WINCKLER), systems engr.; b. Lowville, N.Y., Dec. 20, 1942; d. Bernard J. and Jane (Klett) Cassidy; B.S. magna cum laude, State U. N.Y. at Plattsburgh, 1964; M.S. (NSF fellow), U. Ore., 1968; m. Donal Winckler Aug. 22, 1970; children—Nancy, Lynn, David. Tchr. math. Glens Falls (N.Y.) High Sch., 1964-66, Hadley-Luzerne Central Sch., Lake Luzerne, N.Y., 1966-67; systems engr. IBM, Utica, N.Y., 1969—. Mem. Nat. Assn. Accountants, Math. Assn. Am., Soc. for Indsl. and Applied Math., Kappa Delta Pi. Home: 7777 Soule Rd Rural Route 4 Rome NY 13440 Office: 1427 Genesee St Utica NY 13501

WINDELBORN, PATRICIA ANN, assn. adminstr.; b. Elgin, Ill., Nov. 13, 1946; d. Robert Lysle and Virginia Irene (Davis) Helm; grad. high sch.; m. Martin L. Windelborn, Apr. 27, 1968. Mem. staff Elgin YMCA, 1963-74, adminstrv. asst. to exec. v.p., 1973-74; adminstrv. sec. to the v.p. bus. and finance Elgin Community Coll., 1974—. Recipient certificate for scholastic achievement Rotary Club Elgin, 1964. Mem. Beta Sigma Phi (pres. Eta Lambda chpt. 1965-66, 66-67, rec. sec. 1967-68, sec. city council 1968-69, pres. council 1972-73, named princess 1967). Home: 659 Wright Av Elgin IL 60120 Office: 111 N Channing St Elgin IL 60120

WINDHAM, EULA HEARD, librarian; b. Tifton, Ga., Feb. 3; d. William Guy and Eula Beall (Wilson) Windham; A.B., Ga. Coll., 1940; M.R.E., So. Baptist Sem., 1950; M.L.S., Emory U., 1956. Tchr. Tifton (Ga.) pub. schs., 1941-44; state jr. leader Ga. Baptist Conv., Sunday Sch. Dept., Atlanta, 1947-55; reference librarian Harden Simmons U., Abilene, Tex., 1957-59, asst. librarian, 1960-61; librarian Middle Ga. Coll., Cochran, Ga., 1961—. Mem. Southeastern, Am. (state chmn. jr. coll. sec. 1969—), Ga. (chmn. resources and tech. services 1963-65) library assns., Ga. Assn. Jr. Colls. (library chmn. 1965, 69). Baptist (adult Sunday sch. tchr. 1961—). Club: Cochran Woman's. Compiler: Sanford Library Handbook, 1961, Roberts Library Handbook, 1965, rev. edit., 1973. Home: Route 3 Box 299 Cochran GA 31014 Office: Middle Georgia College Roberts Library Cochran GA 31014

WINDHORST, DOROTHY BAKER, physician; b. Pawhuska, Okla., Mar. 25, 1928; d. Wilbur Gerald and Eunice Elizabeth (Morton) Baker; B.A. with honors (Marshall Field & Co. scholar), U. Chgo., 1948, B.S., 1954, M.D. with honors in Pathology, 1954; m. Richard Windhorst, Mar. 25, 1950 (div. Jan. 1967); children—Nancy Lorraine, Anne Louise. Intern, Presbyn. Hosp., Chgo., 1954-55; resident dermatology U. Chgo., 1955-58; clin. asst. prof. dermatology Washington U., St. Louis, 1958-62; practice medicine, specializing in dermatology, St. Louis, 1958-62; physician venereal disease clinic, health dept. St. Louis County, Mo., 1959-62; asst. prof. dermatology U. Minn., Mpls., 1962-65, asst. prof. pediatrics, 1965-68; asst. prof. dermatology U. Chgo., 1968-71, asso. prof., 1971-73; on leave to Nat. Cancer Inst., 1972-73; med. officer NIH, 1972—. Mem. task force Nat. Program for Dermatology, 1970—; mem. dermatology tng. grants com. Nat. Inst. Arthritis and Metabolic Disease, 1971-73. Recipient Spl. fellowship award Nat. Inst. Arthritis and Metabolic Diseases, 1965-67; faculty scholar award Am. Cancer Soc., 1967-69. Mem. Am. Acad. Dermatology, A.A.A.S., Chgo. Soc. Immunology, Chgo. Dermatological Soc., Soc. Investigative Dermatology, Central Soc. Clin. Research, Am. Fedn. Clin. Research, Am. Assn. Immunologists. Contbr. to publs. in field. Home: 8804 Garfield St Bethesda MD 20034 Office: Immunology Branch National Cancer Institute Bethesda MD 20014

WINDSOR, ELIZABETH ARNOLD, ret. librarian; b. Austin, Tex., June 20, 1909; d. Phineas Lawrence and Margaret (Boynton) Windsor; B.A. in History, U. Ill., 1931, B.S. in L.S., 1932, M.S., 1938. Librarian Charleston (Ill.) Pub. Library, 1932-35, Rochelle (Ill.) Pub. Library, 1935-37; asst. reference librarian Muskegon (Mich.) Pub. Library, 1938-40; reference librarian Coe Coll., Cedar Rapids, Ia., 1940-42, head librarian, 1942-54; head reference dept. Ia. State U. Sci. and Tech., Ames, 1954-74. Mem. A.L.A. (council 1958-62), Ia. Library Assn. (dir. 1966-67), Assn. Coll. Research Librarians (sec. agrl. and biol. sect. 1971-72), Am. Assn. U. Women (pres. br. 1968-70), Phi Beta Kappa, Phi Kappa Phi, Delta Kappa Gamma, Phi Mu. Mem. P.E.O. Home: 2004 McCarthy Rd Ames IA 50010 Office: Iowa State U Library Ames IA 50010

WINER, RACHEL KOLODIZ (MRS. MOSES WINER), state ofcl.; b. Chelsea, Mass.; d. Nathan and Ida (Chizik) Kolodiz; B.S., State Tchrs. Coll., Hyannis, Mass., 1942; A.M., Boston U., 1958, Ed.D., 1974; m. Moses Winer, Nov. 14, 1942. Tchr. pub. schs. East Bridgewater, Mass., 1942-43, Holliston, Mass., 1958-59; med. technologist U.S. Civil Service, Columbia, S.C., 1943-45; head clin. and X-ray labs. Jewish Meml. Hosp., Boston, 1947-57; instr. biochemistry Garland Jr. Coll., 1959-65, chmn. dept. sci., 1966-68; sci. coordinator, instr. dept. health, hosps. Boston City Hosp. Sch. Nursing, 1968-71; chief health occupations edn. Dept. Edn., Commonwealth of Mass., 1971—. Mem. Nat. Sci. Tchrs. Assn., New Eng. Assn. Chemistry Tchrs. (N.S.F. selection grant chmn. 1966), Nat. Assn. Biology Tchrs., A.A.A.S., Am. Soc. Radiologic Technologists, Nat. Faculty Assn. Community and Jr. Colls. (charter). Home: 226 Grove St Chestnut Hill MA 02167 Office: 182 Tremont St Boston MA 02111

WING, ANNE MARIE HINSHAW (MRS. LEONARD WILLIAM WING), writer, artist, naturalist; b. Chgo., Oct. 28, 1901; d. William Wade and Anna T. (Williams) Hinshaw; A.B., U. Mich., 1923, M.A., in English and Journalism, 1928, M. in Landscape design, 1937, life certification edn., 1929; m. Leonard W. Wing, Mar. 18, 1936; children—William Hinshaw, Thomas Leonard Hinshaw, Anne (Mrs. Robert Bruce Petters), George Clyde. Author, illustrator nature conservation articles, Ypsilanti (Mich.) Press, 1957, Ann Arbor (Mich.). News, series 1958-64, various other newspapers, mags., etc. Chmn., Ann Arbor Garden Club conservation com., Washtenaw Roadside Council, Ann Arbor, 1931-35; landscape architect asst. PWA, Detroit, 1935-36; mem. Superior Twp. (Mich.) Citizens' Adv. Com., 1967; pres. Superior Twp. Civic Assn., 1959. Mem. D.A.R., P.E.O., Nat. League Am. Penwomen, Ann Arbor Art Assn., Nat., Mich. Audubon socs., Am. Ornithologists Union, U. Mich. Alumni Assn., Internat. Platform Assn., A.A.A.S., Am. Forestry Assn., Enact Ecology Center, Assn. Interpretive Naturalists, Sierra Club, Mich., Washtenaw hist. socs., Alpha Phi. Clubs: Ann Arbor Women's City, Ann Arbor Garden. Research and publs. on musical aspects of bird song. Home: 2129 Medford Rd Ann Arbor MI 48104

WING, KYLENE SCARBOROUGH (MRS. ROBERT L. WING), columnist; b. Charlotte, N.C.; d. Kyle and Tomi (Riggs) Scarborough; student grad. Stevens Schs. for Models, 1946-47, Ben Bard Acad. Theatre, Hollywood, Cal., 1952, Nat. Acad. Broadcasting Washington, 1957, U. Cal. at Los Angeles Extension, 1965; m. Robert L. Wing, Jan. 16, 1943; children—Susan, Jayme. Columnist, Kylene's Kalifornia Kapers, Inverness, Fla., 1965-66, Kylene's Kontinental Kapers, Berlin, Germany, 1966-68, Founder patron Huntington Hartford Theatre. Mem. Soc. Motion Picture and Television Engrs., Greater Los Angles Press Club, Arcs, Antons, Japan Am. Soc. Presbyn. Clubs: German American Women's, American Women's, American Yacht (all Berlin). Address: 3405 Blair Dr Hollywood CA 90028 also Box 362 Inverness FL 32650

WINGATE, ISABEL BARNUM (MRS. JOHN WILLIAMS), educator; b. Danbury, Conn., Oct. 12, 1901; d. Starr Clifford and Emma Louise (Lyon) Barnum; A.B., Radcliffe Coll., 1923; M.S., N.Y. U., 1925; Ph.D., Yeshiva University, 1961; m. John Williams Wingate, June 22, 1925; children—Elaine Louise (Mrs. Conway), John Barnum. Research fellow N.Y. U. Sch. Retailing, 1924-25, instr. retailing, 1926-33, asst. prof. retailing, coordinator, 1934-46, asso. prof., 1947-61, prof. retailing, 1961-64, prof. retail mgmt., 1964-68, prof. emeritus, 1968—; lectr. Parson Sch. Design, 1965-66, Traphagen Sch. Fashion, 1967-68. Textile cons. Mem. gen. assembly YMCA of Greater N.Y., 1953-59, bd. mgrs. Intercollegiate br., 1956-64, sec. com. campus work bd. dirs.; chmn. interfaith council N.Y.U., 1962-64, mem., 1965-68, trustee U. Christian Found., 1960-68, mem. N.Y. U. Senate (first woman member). Recipient N.Y. U. Service citation, 1955, Gold medallion Alumni Fedn. N.Y. U., 1961, Scroll Acknowledgement Bur. Bus. and Distributive Edn., N.Y.C., Bd. Edn., 1964, N.Y. Times certificate, 1966, Achievement award N.Y. U. Retailing Assn. Alumni, 1968, Gold Key for service N.Y. U. School Edn., 1968. Mem. Am. Assn. Textile Chemists and Colorists, Spiritual Frontiers Fellowship, Assn. Research and Enlightenment, Inst. Ret. Profls., Asso. Harvard Alumni. Am. Soc. Psychical Research, Eta Mu Pi. Author: Textile Fabrics and Their Selection, 5th edit., 1964, 6th edit., 1970; (with Karen Gillespie) Know Your Merchandise, 3d edit., 1964; Textiles: From Source to Consumer, Parts I-IV, 1971-74. Contbg. author yearbook, ednl. and trade jours.; co-author several textbooks and lab. manuals. Editor Fairchild's Dictionary of Textiles, 1967. Home: Box 432 Hewitt NJ 07421

WINGFIELD, MRS. JOSIEPHINE B., librarian; b. Lynchburg, Va., Jan. 12, 1915; d. Lemuel and Irene May (Sale) Bennington; A.B. cum laude, Randolph-Macon Woman's Coll., 1934; student Va. Comml. Coll., 1941; m. Joseph Elmo Wingfield, Nov. 6, 1941. With Jones Meml. Library, Lynchburg, 1936—, successively library asst., 1936-41, sec. to head librarian, 1941-47, asst. librarian, 1947-55, head librarian, 1956—. Mem. Va., Southeastern library assns., Anns. Preservation Va. Antiquities, Nat. Honor Soc. Mem. Christian Ch. Home: 1807 Richmond Av Lynchburg VA 24502 Office: 434 Rivermont Av Lynchburg VA 24504

WINICK, VETA LOIS EDELSTEIN (MRS. DARVIN WINICK), polit. orgn. exec.; b. Boston, May 28, 1931; d. Samuel and Sadye (Sharansky) Edelstein; grad. high sch.; m. Darvin Winick, Aug. 19, 1951; children—Mitchel, Mara Beth, Seth. Pres. League Women Voters Dickinson (Tex.), 1964-66; v.p. League Women Voters Tex., 1967-70, pres., 1970—; nat. orgn. com. for League Women Voters U.S., 1971-72, nat. budget com., 1973-74. Profl. artist, 1960—. Mem. Tex. Adv. Com. Adult and Continuing Edn., 1973—, Tex. Adv. Com. for Constnl. Revision, 1973—; mem. Gov. Tex.'s Com. Criminal Justice Standards Goals, 1974—. Bd. dirs. United Fund Galveston County, Tex., 1966, Clear Creek Art League, 1971—, Citizens for Tex., 1971—, League Women Voters Tex. Edn. Fund, 1969—. Named Woman of Yr. C. of C., 1969. Home: Route 2 Box 81 Dickinson TX 77539 Office: Dickinson Plaza Center Dickinson TX 77539

WINKLE, BARBARA SUE ALLEN (MRS. KENNETH WAYNE WINKLE), editor; b. Fort Worth, Nov. 14, 1948; d. James C. and F. Opal (Wheeler) Allen; A.A., Tarrant County Jr. Coll., 1969; B.S., Tex. Christian U., 1971; m. Kenneth Wayne Winkle, Aug. 25, 1972; 1 dau., Bridget Suzanne. Advt. mgr. Tarrant County Jr. Coll., 1968-71; layout artist Galaxy Press, Dallas, 1971; asst. editor Fort Worth mag. Ft. Worth C. of C., 1971, editor, 1971—. Mem. Press Club, Women in Communications, Sigma Delta Chi. Home: 5617 Starlight Fort Worth TX 76117 Office: 700 Throckmorton St Fort Worth TX 76102

WINKLER, HELEN HUTULA (MRS. WILLIAMS POWELL), physician; b. Covington, Mich., Jan. 20, 1939; d. Charles August and Dagmar (Kaura) Hutula; student Mich. Technol. U., 1956-57; B.A., Mich. State U., 1959; M.D., Wayne State U., 1963; m. Williams Powell, Mar. 1, 1968; children—Tanya Marie, Michael Randall. Intern Wayne County Gen. Hosp., Detroit, 1963-64; instr. Wayne State U. Coll. Medicine, Detroit, 1964-65; resident internal medicine Henry Ford Hosp., Detroit, 1965-68, now mem. staff; practice medicine specializing in internal medicine, Detroit, 1968—; staff physician Blain Clinic, Detroit, 1969-70. Diplomate Am. Bd. Internal Medicine. Mem. A.M.A., Mich., Wayne County med. socs., A.C.P., Am. Women's Med. Assn., Mich. Heart Assn., Alpha Omega Alpha. Home: 445 Neff Rd Grosse Pointe MI 48230 Office: 15618 E Warren St Detroit MI 48224

WINKLEY, CAROL M. KESLINGER (MRS. EVERETT G. WINKLEY), educator; b. Aurora, Ill., Mar. 4, 1917; d. Charles W. and Jennie (Johnson) Keslinger; B.S., No. Ill. State Tchrs. Coll., 1948; M.Ed., U. Colo., 1953; Ph.D., U. Chgo., 1965; m. Everett G. Winkley, July 10, 1937; 1 son, Donald C. Tchr., LaFox (Ill.) Sch., 1935-37, Stewart Sch., Elburn, Ill., 1941-42, Elburn Elementary Sch., 1942-45, Greenman Sch., Aurora, 1945-57; instr. Aurora Coll., 1958-64; reading cons. Aurora Pub. Schs., Aurora, 1957-65; prof. edn. No. Ill. U., DeKalb, Ill., 1965—. Adv., No. Ill. Reading Council, 1965—. Mem. Internat. Reading Assn. (state chmn. 1966—), Am. Ednl. Research Assn., Nat. Council Tchrs. English, N.E.A., Ill. Edn. Assn., Nat. Soc. for Study of Edn., Ill. Reading Council, Pi Lambda Theta. Contbr. articles to profl. jours. Home: 125 Forsythe Lane DeKalb IL 60115

WINN, ELIZABETH ANN (MRS. CARL E. WINN), banker; b. Paris, Ark., Sept. 3, 1917; d. Joseph Pendelton and Elsie (Vaughn) Watson; student So. Methodist U., 1964-66; m. Carl E. Winn, Aug. 3, 1935; 1 son, Robert Joseph. Credit clk. Bank America, Wilmington, Cal., 1953-55; asst. v.p. City Nat. Bank, Fort Smith, Ark., 1955-74, v.p., 1974—. Asso. trustee Sparks Regional Med. Center, Fort Smith; bd. dirs. Y.W.C.A., Fort Smith, 1965—, March Dimes, Fort Smith. Mem. Nat. Assn. Bank Women, Credit Women Internat. (past dist. pres.), Bus. and Profl. Women's Club. Methodist. Club: Zonta (pres. 1972-73) (Fort Smith). Home: 2025 N 52d St Fort Smith AR 72901 Office: 1222 Rogers Av Fort Smith AR 72901

WINN, ELLENE, lawyer; b. Clayton, Ala.; B.A. magna cum laude, Agnes Scott Coll., 1931; M.A., Radcliffe Coll., 1932; LL.B., Birmingham Sch. Law, 1941. Admitted to Ala. bar, 1941; mem. firm Bradley, Arant, Rose & White, Birmingham, Ala. Exec. bd. Ala. Opera Assn; trustee Birmingham Civic Opera Assn., Birmingham Music Club. Mem. Am., Birmingham bar assns., Ala. State Bar. Office: Brown-Marx Bldg Birmingham AL 35203

WINN, HELEN HARTMANN (MRS. BURKHARD DANIEL WINN), librarian, educator; b. Houghton, N.Y., Aug. 21, 1916; d. Arthur and Claire Marie (Tucker) Hartmann; B.A., Barnard Coll., 1937; M.A., Columbia, 1954, M.S., 1957; m. Burkhard Daniel Winn, July 2, 1938; children—Claire Marie (Mrs. Thomas Carlyle Marshall), Gregory Francis Tucker. Tchr. English, Oradell (N.J.) Jr. High Sch., 1954-56; librarian River Dell Jr. High Sch., 1956-58, River Dell Sr. High Sch., 1958-61; dir. River Dell Media Centers, 1961—; dir. Center for Promotion of Humanities, 1966-69; chmn. River Dell Humanities Dept., 1967-71, 74-75. Trustee, River Dell Adult Edn. Center; mem. exec. com. Project Impact, N.J. Cultural Council. Recipient awards for excellence Rutgers Sch. Bd. Publs. Assn., 1960-63. Elementary and Secondary Edn. Act Title III fed. grantee, 1966-69; John Hay fellow Williams Coll., 1965. Mem. N.E.A., A.L.A., N.J. Edn. Assn., Bergen County Sch. Librarians Assn. (pres. 1960-62), Nat. Assn. for Humanities Edn., Am. Assn. U. Women. Editor: Regional Bd. Edn. Newsletter, 1958-67. Contbr. articles to profl. jours. Home: 248 Country Club Dr Oradell NJ 07649 Office: Pyle St Oradell NJ 07649

WINN, JOAN TARPLEY (MRS. ELBERT T. WINN), lawyer; b. Dallas, Apr. 11, 1942; d. Zollie Scott and Lola (Williams) Tarpley; B.A. cum laude, Dillard U., 1962; J.D., So. Meth. U., 1968; m. Elbert T. Winn, Aug. 25, 1966; 1 son, Elbert Ikoyi. Admitted to Tex. bar, 1968; mem. firm Durham & Winn, Dallas, 1968-70; trial atty. U.S. Dept. of Labor, Dallas, 1970-73; asst. regional appeals examiner U.S. Civil Service Commn., Dallas, 1973—. Bd. dir. Dallas Family Guidance Center, 1972—. Mem. State Bar Tex., Dallas, Fed. bar assns., J.L. Turner Legal Soc., Order of the Coif, Dallas Urban League Guild, Delta Sigma Theta. Club: Zonta Internat. (Dallas). Home: 5527 Williamstown Rd Dallas TX 75230 Office: 4C59 1100 Commerce St Dallas TX 75201

WINNABERG, JOSEPHINE MARIE, sch. librarian; b. Kendallville, Ia., July 7, 1927; d. George and Gusta (Moe) Winnaberg; B.A., Luther Coll., Decorah, Ia., 1950; M.S. in L.S., U. Ill., 1960; postgrad. U. No. Ia., Cedar Falls, summers 1970-71. Elementary rural sch. tchr., Howard County, Ia., 1950-52; elementary tchr., Calmar, Ia., 1953-55, Mason City, Ia., 1955-58; sch. librarian, Minn., 1959-61; cataloger Luther Coll., 1961-65; reference librarian, Rochester, Minn., 1965-66; elementary library supr. Howard-Winneshiek Sch. Dist., 1966-69; librarian, audio visual coordinator Crestwood Jr. High Sch., Cresco, Ia., 1969—. Mem. Nat., Ia., Howard Winneshiek edn. assns. Home: Route 1 Cresco IA 52136

WINNIE, THELMA LORRAINE, editor; b. San Francisco, Feb. 7, 1924; d. Byron H. and Vale B. (Davis) Smith; student Multnomah Coll., Portland, Ore., 1952, 53, Coll. of Marin, 1959; m. E. Jasper Winnie, Dec. 30, 1956; children—Linda V. (Mrs. Thomas Edgeworth); stepchildren—Charlisle J., Melvin M. Editor, Western Collector mag., San Francisco, 1963-66, asso. exec. editor, 1966-70; editor Profl. Publs., Desert Research Inst. U. of Nev., 1968-72; publs. mgr. Bently Nev. Corp., Minden, 1972—; v.p., dir. Western World Publs. (San Francisco), 1966-67. Activities chmn. Sierra Arts Found., Reno, 1971-72. Mem. Nat. League Am. Pen Women (v.p. Reno), Theta Sigma Phi. Asso. editor: Archeological Survey in Eastern Nevada (Don D. Fowler), 1966; Archaeology of Newark Cave, White Pine County, Nevada (Fowler), 1968; Great Basin Anthropology, a Bibliography (Catherine S.Fowler), 1970; The Asian in the West (Stanford M. Lyman), 1970. Home: 128 Lake Glen Dr Carson City NV 89701 Office: PO Box 157 Minden NV 89423

WINSCOTT, REBECCA JANE (MRS. CHARLES JOHN WINSCOTT), therapist; b. Zanesville, O., Mar. 4, 1942; d. Frank S. and Pauline Phyllis (Brookover) Davidson; B.S., Ohio State U., 1965; student Famous Artists' Sch., 1969—; m. Charles John Winscott, Sept. 2, 1966; children—Kevin Michael, Kimberly Michelle. Staff occupational therapist Sarasota (Fla.) Meml. Hosp., 1965-67; occupational therapy cons. Hillhaven Nursing Home, Sarasota, 1967, Newark Convalescent & Nursing Inn (O.), 1970, Coastal Carolina Community Coll., Jacksonville, N.C., 1971; individual practice occupational therapy, Parris Island, S.C., 1972-73. Vol., Navy Relief Soc., 1972-73, recipient 100 and 300 hr. awards; vol. swimming instr. A.R.C., 1973; sec.-treas. Beaufort Marine Swim Team, 1972. Mem. Am. Occupational Therapy Assn. (Fla. recruitment publicity rep. 1967), Beaufort Art Assn., Phi Mu. Democrat. Baptist. Mem. Order Eastern Star. Home: T 100 Argonne Trailer Park Parris Island SC 29905 Office: 415 Hudson Av Newark OH 43055

WINSLOW, GAIL HAMILTON (MRS. ROBERT NEVILLE GINSBURGH), investment banker; b. Balt., Dec. 2, 1929; d. Allyn Gorman and Carolyn (Myers) Whitehead; student Radcliffe Coll., 1947-49, N.Y. Inst. Finance, 1956-58; m. Alan Francis Winslow, Jr., Mar. 13, 1949, (div. Feb. 1956); children—Alan Francis III, William Castle, Rosamond Castle (dec.); m. 2d Robert Neville Ginsburgh, Apr. 4, 1959; stepchildren—Robert, Charles; children—Carolyn, Anne. Editorial asst. Swen Publs., Hong Kong, Manila, 1950-52; English, journalism tchr. The Am. Sch., Manila, 1951-52; polio and cancer research Microbiol. Assn., Bethesda, Md., 1953-55; registered rep. N.Y. Stock Exchange, 1956—; stock broker, 1956—; gen. partner Ferris & Company, 1965-71; sr. v.p., dir. Ferris & Co., Inc., 1971—. Bd. dirs. Met. Washington YMCA. Asso. mem. N.Y. Stock Exchange, Investment Bankers Assn. Inst., Washington Bd. Trade, Am. Assn. Financial Analysts. Episcopalian (mem. vestry). Clubs: Army Navy, Kenwood Country, Radcliffe, Internat. (Washington). Home: 5500 Newington Rd Washington DC 20016 Office: 1720 Eye St NW Washington DC 20006

WINSTEAD, MAMIE HENEGER, librarian; b. Knoxville, Tenn.; d. William Daniel and Bridget (Foley) W.; student pvt. schs. Law Librarian Supreme Ct., Knoxville, 1938—. Mem. Am. Assn, Law Librarians, Am. Orchid Soc., U.D.C. Roman Catholic. Democrat. Home: 1917 Bethel Av SE Knoxville TN 37915 Office: 719 Locust St Knoxville TN 37902

WINSTON, SANDRA ANNE, occupational therapist; b. Gainesville, Fla., June 30, 1941; d. Fred H. and Annita J. (Jones) Winston; B.A. in English, U. Fla., 1963, B.S. in Occupational Therapy, 1965. Occupational therapist Baptist Hosp., Pensacola, Fla., 1966-71; chief occupational therapy VA Hosp., Lake City, Fla., 1971—. Mem. Am., Fla. occupational therapy assns., Am. Assn. Univ. Women. Home: Apt G-1 2620 S Marion Lake City FL 32055 Office: Veteran's Administration Hospital Lake City FL

WINSTON, SARA STEINBERG (MRS. WILLIAM WEINSTEIN), artist; b. N.Y.C.; d. Jacob and Lena (Brief) Steinberg; student Newark State Tchrs. Coll., 1920-22, Columbia, 1922-24, with W. Hayter, Paris 1954-55, Hans Hofman, N.Y.C., 1955-57; m. William Weinstein, Oct. 4, 1930 (dec. Nov. 1958); 1 son, Lawrence. Exhibited one-woman show Jayson Gallery, N.Y.C., also 78 one-woman shows in museums and colls., U.S., Europe, Mexico; exhibited in group shows Bklyn. Mus., 1957, Pa. Acad. Fine Arts, 1957, Smithsonian Inst., 1956; Soc. Am. Graphic Artists, N.Y.C., 1956, Athens, Greece, 1958; Newark Mus., Jersey City Mus., N.W. Printmakers 29th Internat., others; represented in permanent collections Norfolk (Va.) Mus., Jersey City Mus., Jersey City State Coll., many pvt. collections. Tchr., Newark schs., 1935-46, N.Y.C. schs., 1960—, spl. work with retarded children Sch. for Exceptional Children, Newark, 1957. Pres., Sharey Tefilo, East Orange, N.J., 1940-42. Recipient 1st prize oil Maplewood Meml. Library, 1956; graphics prizes Montclair Mus., 1957, Maplewood-South Orange Art Gallery, 1958; oil and graphics prize Painter and Sculptors Soc. N.J., City Mus., 1960. Mem. Artists Equity N.Y., Audubon Soc., Sculptors and Painters N.J., Nat. Assn. Women Artists (Eve Clendenin prize graphics, 20 other prizes; chmn. membership jury 1973), Hunterdon Art Center, Art Students League (life). Address: 1 Sheridan Sq New York City NY 10014

WINSTON, SARAH, author; b. N.Y.C., Dec. 15, 1912; d. Henry and Esther (Lorenz) Rosenblum; student N.Y. U., 1930-31; student Barnes Found., Merion, Pa., 1966-67, mem. research seminar philosophy and appreciation of art, 1966—; m. Keith Winston, June 11, 1932 (dec. 1970); children—Neil, David. Free-lance writer, 1948—. Mem. League Women Voters (chmn. pub. relations 1950-51), Friends of Barnes Found. Author (all rec. on Talking Books): And Always Tomorrow (1st prize Nat. League Am. Pen Women), 1963; Our Son, Ken, 2d edit., 1970; Everything Happens for the Best (1st prize Nat. League Am. Pen Women, 2d edit. 1970). Address: 1838 Rose Tree Lane Havertown PA 19083

WINTER, CLOTILDA CLARICE, educator; b. Port Arthur, Tex., May 17, 1916; d. Claude Coleman and Etta Anna (Pickett) Winter; student Lamar Jr. Coll., 1934-36; B.S., Southwest Tex. State Coll., 1941; M.Ed., U. Tex., 1946, Ed.D., 1957. Elementary tchr. Cove Ind. Sch. Dist., Orange, Tex., 1936-42, Orange (Tex.) Ind. Sch. Dist., 1942-46, U. Lab. Sch., Austin, Tex., 1946-58; head tchr. Minnie G. Dill Sch., Austin, Tex., 1954-58; prof. edn. Tex. Christian U., Ft. Worth, 1958—. Cons. with various pub. sch. systems in Tex. Mem. N.E.A., Tex. Tchrs. Assn., Assn. Childhood Edn. Internat., Am. Edn. Research Assn., Assn. Supr. Curriculum Devel., Nat. Council Tchrs. English, Nat. Council Social Studies, Alpha Chi, Pi Gamma Mu, Pi Lambda Theta, Kappa Delta Pi, Delta Kappa Gamma. Methodist (mem. bd. of stewards 1954-58). Contbr. articles in field to profl. jours. Home: 3204 University Dr Fort Worth TX 76109 Office: Texas Christian University School of Education Fort Worth TX 76129

WINTER, JANE ANN, pub. exec.; b. N.Y.C., Oct. 13, 1926; d. Frank F. and Alice (Kretz) Hendrickson; student pub. schs.; m. Donald J. Winter, Sept. 7, 1946 (div. Aug. 1962); children—Donald J., Robert W. Photo tintist Jean Sardou Studio, Hempstead, N.Y., 1943-44; clk.-typist World Conv. Dates, N.Y.C., 1944, various positions, Bklyn., Hempstead, N.Y., 1946-62, pub., 1962-74; model Harry Conover, N.Y.C., 1945-46; dir., treas. Hendrickson Pub. Co., Inc., Hempstead, 1959-74, pres., 1962-74; now bus. mgr. Chmn. parent edn. P.T.A., 1956, community council del., 1957; active Little League, 1956-60. Mem. Hotel Sales Mgmt. Assn. (sec. N.Y.C. chpt. 1966), Am. Hotel and Motel Assn., Am., N.Y. socs. assn. execs., U.S. Amateur Ballroom Dancers Assn. Episcopalian. Home: 208 Gruber Ct West Hempstead NY 11552 Office: 91 N Franklin St Hempstead NY 11550

WINTER, MADELINE FIELD (MRS. JAMES EMORY WINTER, JR.), librarian; b. Lanesboro, Mass., May 25, 1922; d. George Allen and Edith May (Young) Field; student Bishop Meml. Tng. Sch. for Nurses, 1940, Berkshire Bus. Coll., 1942; m. James Emory Winter, Jr., Apr. 19, 1947; 1 son, Douglas Paul. Customer services First Agrl. Nat. Bank, Pittsfield, Mass., 1943-67; librarian, garden editor Berkshire Eagle, Pittsfield, 1967—. Sec., Richmond Republican Town Com., 1955-68, chmn., 1968—; mem. Berkshire County Rep. Assn., 1968—; del. Mass. Rep. State Conv., 1967, 71; mem. Rep. Club Mass. Named So. Berkshire County Republican Woman of Year, Berkshire County Rep. Assn., 1973. Mem. Garden Writers Assn. Am., Berkshire Med. Center Aux. Conglist. Home: Dublin Rd Richmond MA 01254 Office: 33 Eagle St Pittsfield MA 01201

WINTER, SISTER MIRIAM THERESE, composer; b. Passaic, N.J., June 14, 1938; d. Mathias William and Irene Theresa (Marton) Winter; student Trinity Coll., 1959-61; Mus. B., Cath. U., 1964. Joined Soc. Cath. Med. Missionaries, 1955, coordinator pub. relations in U.S., 1966-70, toured African instns., 1970-71, editor Med. Missionary 1965-71. Mem. A.S.C.A.P., Composers Forum for Cath. Worship, Phi Beta Kappa. Co-author If It Matters, 1967. Composer: (albums) Joy Is Like the Rain, 1966, I Know The Secret, 1967, Mass of A Pilgrim People, 1967, Knock Knock, 1968, Seasons, 1969, In Love, 1971, RSVP, 1971, Songs of Promise, 1971, Gold, Incense and Myrrh, 1972. Address: 8400 Pine Rd Philadelphia PA 19111

WINTER, RUTH GROSMAN (MRS. ARTHUR WINTER), writer; b. Newark, May 29, 1930; d. Robert Delmas and Rose (Rich) Grosman; B.A., Upsala Coll., 1951; m. Arthur Winter, June 16, 1955; children—Robin, Craig, Grant. Gen. assignment Newark Star Ledger, 1951-55, sci. editor, 1956—; with Houston Press, 1955-56; syndicated columnist Los Angeles Times Syndicate; contbr. to consumer mags.;

instr. St. Peters Coll., Jersey City. Recipient award of merit Am. Dental Assn., 1966, Cecil award Arthritis Found., 1967, Am. Soc. Anesthesiologists award, 1969; named Alumnus of Year, Upsala Coll., 1971, Woman of Year, N.J. Daily Newspaper Women, 1971. Mem. Soc. Mag. Writers, Authors League, Nat. Assn. Sci. Writers, Am. Med. Writers Assn., Overseas Press Club, N.J. Daily Newspaper Women (award 1959, 63). Author: Poisons in Your Food, 1969; How to Reduce Your Medical Bills, 1970; A Consumers Dictionary of Food Additives, 1972; Vitamin E: The Miracle Worker, 1972; So You Have Sinus Trouble, 1973; Ageless Aging, 1973; A Consumers Dictionary of Cosmetic Ingredients, 1974; So You Have a Pain in the Neck, 1974. Address: 44 Holly Dr Short Hills NJ 07078

WINTERROSE, HAZEL GENEVA, educator; b. Heber City, Utah, June 12, 1923; d. John G. and LaPreal (Mitchell) Winterrose; B.S., Brigham Young U., 1948, M.S., 1951; postgrad. U. Southern Cal., 1956-57; Ed.D., Utah State U., 1968. Elementary tchr., sch. librarian Gregory Heights Elementary Sch., Portland, Ore., 1951-55; counselor Ogden (Utah) High Sch., 1955-56; grade level counselor, social studies tchr. Hosler Jr. High, Lynwood, Cal., 1957-60; counselor to women, tchr., and student tchr. supr. Ch. Coll. of Hawaii, Laie, 1960-66; asso. prof. edn. Brigham Young U., Provo, Utah, 1967—. Asst. dir., univ. coordinator Career Opportunity Project San Juan Sch. Dist., Blanding, Utah, 1970—. Mem. Am. Assn. U. Women (pres. 1971-72), Assn. Childhood Edn. Internat. (v.p. 1971—), Brigham Young U. Edn. Assn. (treas. 1969—), Nat. Council Social Studies, Delta Kappa Gamma, Pi Lambda Theta. Home: 160 S Westwood Dr Orem UT 84057

WINTERS, ALICE GRAHAM BUTLER (MRS. CARL S. WINTERS), civic worker; b. Linton, Ind., July 5, 1907; d. William Austin and Mary (Inman) Butler; A.B., Franklin Coll., 1932; spl. student U. Rochester, 1929-30, Colgate-Rochester Div. Sch., 1929-30; m. Carl S. Winters, May 23, 1925; children—Barbara (Mrs. Robert Kane), Janet (Mrs. Ralph Kuzmic), Linda (Mrs. Allen F. Jones). Minster junior church, Jackson, Mich., 1931-39, 1st Bapt. Ch. Oak Park, Ill., 1939-59; lectr. Adult Edn. Council Chgo.; also free-lance writer. Organizer, pres. Jackson (Mich.) Peace Council, 1933-35; pres. Jackson County League Women Voters, 1935, Chgo. Drama League, 1948-50, Chgo. Mission Union, 1956-60; treas. Art Assos. Oak Park, 1961-64; pres. Infant Welfare Soc., 1960-62; mem. Com. of 100, Nat. Council of Churches, 1963—; bd. dirs. Woman's Bd. Salvation Army, Chgo., 1960—, pres. bd., 1969—; bd. dirs. Women's Bd. Mental Health Assn., Chgo.; bd. dirs. Maywood (Ill.) Home and Hosp., 1940-62, v.p. bd., 1958-62; mem. woman's bd. Christian U. of Tokyo, 1963—. Mem. Delta Zeta, Beta Sigma Phi Kappa Delta. Clubs: Conference Club Presidents (bd. dirs. 1962—, chmn. pub. relations, sec.); 19th Century Woman's; Garden; Chautauqua (N.Y.) Women's; Oak Park Country; Zonta. Home: 404 N East Av Oak Park IL 60602 also Packard Manor Chautauqua NY 14722

WINTERS, ANN ELOISE, journalist; b. Columbus, O., Aug. 16, 1946; d. Philip E. and Eloise M. (Lichty) Winters; student Miami U., 1964-66, U. Cin., 1972; m. L. Jack Hicks, Nov. 9, 1974. Column researcher Cin. Enquirer, 1966—. Mem. Women in Communications (v.p. programs Cin. chpt. 1973-74, v.p. projects 1974-75). Home: 29 Avenel Place Fort Thomas KY 41075 Office: 617 Vine St Cincinnati OH 45201

WINTERS, BARBARA JO, musician; b. Salt Lake City; d. Louis McClain and Gwendolyn (Bradley) Winters; A.B. cum laude, U. Cal. at Los Angeles, 1960, postgrad., 1961; postgrad. Yale, 1960. Mem. oboe sect. Pasadena (Cal.) Symphony, 1958-60, Los Angeles Phil., 1961—. Recordings movie, TV sound tracks. Mem. Mu Phi Epsilon. Home: 633 S Barrington Los Angeles CA 90049 Office: 135 N Grand Av Los Angeles CA 90049

WINTERS, DENNY, artist; b. Grand Rapids, Mich., 1909; d. James Henry Sonke and Eva May (Taylor) Sonke; student Chgo. Acad. Fine Arts, Chgo. Art Inst.; m. Herman Joseph Cherry, Sept. 20, 1940; m. 2d Lew Dietz, 1951. Work exhibited Mus. Modern Art, Carnegie Mus., Pa. Acad. Fine Arts, Chgo. Art Inst., San Francisco (Cal.) Mus., Nat. Acad. show, 1968, Nat. Acad. Art, 1970-72; one-man Levitt shows Los Angeles Mus., San Francisco Mus., Mortimer Levitt Gallery, N.Y.C., Frank Rehn Gallery, 1948-57, 61, Wiscasset (Me.) Mus., 1961, Rehn Gallery, 1953, 57, 63, U. Me., 1959, 65, C. of C. Northeast Harbor, Me., 1960, 62, Phila. Art Alliance, 1964, Bowdoin Coll., 1968, Rehn Gallery, N.Y.C., 1971, 72, Grand Rapids Mus. Art, 1971, Kalamazoo Inst. Art, 1971, tchr. Camden (Me.) Extension; traveled, painted in France, Italy, 1949. Awarded first prize for prints San Francisco Mus., 1941, first prize for oils Denver Mus., 1940; Purchase prize Butler Inst. Am. Art, 1964; recipient Guggenheim fellowship, 1948. Member Me. Coast Artists Maine Hist. Soc. Illustrator; Full Fathom Five (by Lew Dietz), Wilderness River (by Lew Dietz). Address: Rockport ME 04856

WINTERS, RITA JO, journalist; b. Delaware County, Ind., Jan. 12, 1932; d. George Leo and Enid Anita (Bell) Affert; student Ball State U., 1949-51; student leadership and workshops, 1950—, Inst. Safety Council Adminstrn., 1961; m. Allen Leroy Winters, Nov. 24, 1957; children—Kimberly Ann, Jon Sterling. Farm editor monthly Farm News, 1957-66; engaged in pub. relations and advt., 1957-66; woman's editor sta. WLBC AM-TV, Muncie, Ind., 1966-70; feature writer, author daily column Muncie (Ind.) Newspapers Inc., 1971—. Chairwoman Delaware County Farm Bur. Pub. Relations, 1968-74; exec. sec. Delaware County Safety Council, 1961-62, chmn. bd., 1964; hon. adviser Delaware County Farm Bur. Rural Youth; mem. E.K. Keesling living meml. scholarship com. Center Sch. Alumni Assn., 1963-71. Pres. Delaware County Republican Women, 1973. Recipient 9 Ind. and nat. writing awards for radio and TV continuity and advt., 6 Ind. writing awards for newspaper features; Community Service award Delaware County Safety Council, 1968; named Broadcast Woman of Yr. for Muncie, 1969-70. Mem. Women in Communications (pres. 1974-75), Nat. Fedn. Press Women, Women's Press Club Ind., Women in Communications, Altrusa Club Muncie (chmn. ways and means 1972, dir. 1974-76), Am. Antiques and Crafts Soc., Delta Zeta (alumnae pres. 1965-66, adviser to top Delta Zeta chpt. 1968). Methodist. Home: 218 S Cole Av Muncie IN 47303 Office: PO Box 2408 125 S High St Muncie IN 47302

WINTERSON, HELEN JANE, educator; b. Omaha, July 10, 1937; d. George McPherson and Helen Julia (Patach) Winterson; B.A., Duchesne Coll., 1958; postgrad. Washington U., St. Louis, 1965-66; M.S., U. Mo. at St. Louis, 1969; postgrad. Colo. State U., 1971; R.N., Maryville Coll., 1974. Instr., Republic (Mo.) High Sch., 1959-60; instr. sci. Villa Duchesne Acad. Sacred Heart, 1960-65; instr., asst. to dean Maryville Coll., St. Louis, 1965-68, counselor, 1969-72, asst. prof. biology, 1969—, dir. student financial aid, 1972—; title III grant coordinator Maryville Coll.-Fontbonne Coll. Consortium, 1968-69. Mem. staff Jewish Hosp. St. Louis, 1973-74, DePaul Hosp., 1973-74, St. John's Mercy Med. Center, 1973-74; sci. fair judge Post Dispatch, 1970—. Vol. counselor Good Shepherd Camp, 1964-65; vol. tutor Children's Hosp., 1958-73. Mem. Nat., Mo. assns. student financial aid adminstrs., Nat. Sci. Tchrs. Assn., Am. Personnel and Guidance Assn., Mid-West Biol. Assn., U. Mo. (mem. scholarship com. 1971—), Maryville Coll. alumni assns. Home: 2039 N Geyer Rd St Louis MO 63131

WINTHROP, EMILIE ANN KOSTITCH (MRS. WILLIAM KENDAL CUTHBERT), interior designer; b. Denver; s. Theodore S. and Florence (Engelbach) Kostitch; student Pomona Coll., 1949-50; grad. Persons Sch. Design, N.Y. and Paris, France, 1953; m. Robert W. Caulfield, Mar. 4, 1955 (dec. May 1961); 1 dau., Emilie Florence; m. 2d, William Kendal Cuthbert, June 7, 1968. Asst. to dir. Joslyn Meml. Art Mus., Omaha, 1950; asst. Guy Brink, A.I.D., Pasadena, Cal., 1953-54; interior designer Emilie Winthrop, South Pasadena, Cal., 1955-60, J.W. Robinson, Pasadena, 1961-62; asso. designer Gerald Jerome, A.I.D., Inc., San Diego, 1961-65; pres. Emilie Winthrop, A.I.D., interior design, La Jolla, Cal., 1965—. Mem. Ams. Inst. Interior Designers. Office: PO Box 9514 San Diego CA 92109

WINTON, JANIN, educator; b. San Francisco, Jan. 19, 1929; d. Richard C. and Jeanne (Gustin) Winton; A.A., Coll. Marin, 1948; B.A., Cal. State Coll. at Long Beach, 1956, M.A., 1958. Dir. recreation City of San Anselmo (Cal.), 1947, City San Rafael (Cal.) 1948; various secretarial and personnel supervisory positions, San Francisco and Honolulu, 1948-54; asst. prof. phys. edn. Chapman Coll., Orange Cal., 1956-58; tchr., counselor Mayfair High Sch., Bellflower, Cal., 1958-61; counselor, psychometrist Long Beach City Coll., 1961-62; asst. dean women Long Beach State Coll., 1962-64; dir. women's activities, counselor W. Valley Coll., Campbell, Cal., 1964-68, counselor, psychometrist, 1968—. Named Outstanding Alumna, Long Beach State Coll., 1963, Citizen of Year, Campbell Police Dept., 1968, Woman of Year, Los Gatos Bus. and Profl. Club, 1971; recipient numerous other awards for achievement, 1963-68. Mem. Cal. Assn. Women Adminstrs. and Counselors (chmn. jr. coll. div. No. region 1966-68, chmn. No. region 1968-70, mem. Cal. exec. bd. 1966-72, state v.p. 1970-72, Cal. membership chmn., also rep. nat. orgn. 1968-70), Nat. Assn. Women Deans and Counselors, Am., Cal. personnel and guidance assns., Am. Assn. U. Women, Am. Coll. Personnel Assn., Nat. Vocational Guidance Assn., Nat. Bus. and Profl. Women's Assn., Cal. State U. at Long Beach Alumni Assn. (life), Cal. Bus. and Profl. Women (v.p. 1968-69, pres. 1969-70), Delta Kappa Gamma. Clubs: Nat. Bowling; Cal. 600 Bowling. Home: 502 Playa Blvd La Selva Beach CA 95076 Office: West Valley Coll 14000 Fruitvale Av Saratoga CA 95070

WIRSIG, MRS. WOODROW (JANE DEALY WIRSIG), writer, editor; b. Boston, Aug. 22, 1919; d. James Bond and Anna B. (McQuillen) Dealy; B.A., Vassar Coll., 1941; M.S. (Vassar Coll. fellow 1941-42), Columbia, 1942; m. Woodrow Wirsig, Dec. 11, 1942; children—Alan Robert, Guy Rodney, Paul Harold. Network radio newswriter CBS, 1942-43; free lance writer articles, short stories various mags., 1942—; editor Vassar Alumnae mag., 1952-53; editor, rewriter Companion in Paris, Woman's Home Companion, 1953-56; editor Wirsig, Gordon & O'Connor, Inc., Princeton, N.J., 1956-58; editorial cons. Ednl. Testing Service, Princeton, 1957-60, dir. publs., 1960-70, exec. dir. information services and publs., 1971-74, sec. corp., 1974—. Mem. Am. Assn. Higher Edn., Phi Beta Kappa. Club: Vassar (Central N.J. v.p. 1955-57). Home: 25 Gordon Way Princeton NJ 08540 Office: Ednl Testing Service Princeton NJ 08540

WIRT, JUTTA ELISABETH HENRIETTA AUGUSTA GRUNEWALD, fashion exec.; b. Dresden, Saxony, Germany, Sept. 7, 1928; d. Carl and Elisabeth (Wiegand) Grunewald; A.B., Inst. Fashion Design U. Munich, West Germany, 1959; m. Charles Alvin Wirt, Mar. 22, 1947; children—Pamela Faye, Adrienne Lee. Came to U.S., 1947, naturalized, 1950. Fashion coordinator The Model, Leavenworth, Kan., 1959-63; asst. buyer Hecht's, Washington, 1963-64; buyer Hanna's, Newport News, Va., 1964-65, Hayman's, Alexandria, Va., 1965-67; better dress buyer, retail exec. Raleigh's, 10 stores Washington met. area, 1967—. Clubs: International Fashion Group, Army and Navy Country and Town (Washington). Home: 929 6th St SW Washington DC 20024 Office: 1133 Connecticut Av NW Washington DC 20036

WIRTH, MARIAN PURSE (MRS. KARL W. WIRTH), educator; b. Pitts., Aug. 28, 1924; s. Henry and Marian (Lewis) Purse; B.A. summa cum laude, Central State Coll., 1966, M.Teaching, 1969; postgrad. U. Tex., 1970-71; Ed.D., U. Tulsa, 1973; m. Karl W. Wirth, July 17, 1943; children—Martin E., Deborah (Mrs. Wendell Routan). Tchr., Oklahoma City Schs., 1966-68; reading specialist Los Angeles City Schs., 1968-69; dean women Connors State Coll., 1969-73; prof. Central State Coll. Sch. Edn., Edmond, Okla., 1973—. Active Camp Fire Girls. Mem. Higher Edn. Alumni Council, N.E.A., Internat. Reading Assn., Jr. Coll. Affiliates, Kappa Kappa Iota, Kappa Delta Pi. Home: 1804 Kickingbird Rd Edmond OK 73034

WIRTH, MARY TOWN, pub. relations exec.; b. Utica, N.Y., Jan. 17, 1937; d. George Hendrick and Cecilia Katherine (McDermott) Town; B.S. in Biology, Le Moyne Coll., 1958; postgrad. Charles Morris Price Sch. Advt. and Journalism, Phila., 1968, N.Y. U., also New Sch. for Social Research, 1970-71; m. Roger A. Wirth, May 27, 1972. Adminstrv. asst. Holy Family Hosp., Rawalpindi, Pakistan, 1962-65; pub. relations writer Med. Mission Sisters, Phila., 1965-69; pub. relations asso. N.Y. Lung Assn., 1969-71; pub. relations dir. Manhattan Eye, Ear and Throat Hosp., N.Y.C., 1971—. Recipient Pub. Relations award Am. Lung Assn., 1971. Mem. Community Agencies Pub. Relations Assn. (treas. 1971-74), Women in Communications. Home: 3777 Independence Av Bronx NY 10463 Office: 210 E 64th St New York City NY 10021

WIRTZ, VIRGINIA WADSWORTH (MRS. ARTHUR M. WIRTZ), civic worker; b. Cleve., Jan. 30, 1903; d. Charles and Anna (Doyle) Wadsworth; grad. Frank W. Parker Sch., 1920; student U. Colo., 1920-21; B.S., Northwestern U., 1924; m. Arthur Michael Wirtz, March 1, 1926; children—Cynthia (Mrs. Wirtz MacArthur), William Wadsworth, Arthur Michael, Jr., Elizabeth Virginia (Mrs. Donald Huerman), Mem. Presbyn. St. Luke's Hosp. Women's Bd., 1926—; trustee Ill. Children's Home and Aid Soc., Am. Opera Soc., Bd.; mem. Women's Council Chgo. Heart Assn., Women's bd. U.S.O., Chgo.; sec. Chgo. br. English Speaking Union; bd. govs. Chgo. Symphony, McCormick Theol. Sem. Presbyn. Mem. Mortar Bd., Pi Beta Phi. Clubs: Women's Athletic, Saddle and Cycle, Racquet, Arts. Home: 1420 Lake Shore Dr Chicago IL 60610

WISDOM, ALINE CROWLEY GRAF (MRS. CLYDE WISDOM), coll. librarian; b. Mulberry, Ark., Nov. 6, 1917; d. Charlie Edward and Nellie (Fisher) Graf; B.A., Coll. Ozarks, 1938; M.Ed., U. Ark., 1948; M.L.S., U. Denver, 1963; m. Monte Roe Crowley, Feb. 11, 1939 (dec. Mar. 1961); 1 dau., Edwina Joyce Hain; m. 2d, Clyde Wisdom, Nov. 28, 1963. Tchr., librarian Pleasant View High Sch., Mulberry, 1939-42, Mulberry High Sch., 1942-53, Bear Creek High Sch., Jefferson County Schs., Lakewood, Colo., 1953-54; head librarian Citrus Jr. Coll., Azusa, Cal., 1954—. Chief exec. officer San Gabriel Community Coll. Library Coop., 1973—. Bd. dirs. Crawford County Hosp., Van Buren, Ark., 1949-53; trustee, pres. Glendora Library. Mem. N.E.A., Am., Cal. library assns., Cal. Tchrs. Assn. Author: Introduction to Libraries and Library Services, 1974. Home: 558 N Vista Bonita Glendora CA 91740 Office: 18824 E Foothill St Azusa CA 91702

WISE, BETTY JEAN DAVIS (MRS. EUGENE EDWARD WISE, JR.), social worker; b. Covington, Ky., Apr. 27, 1932; d. John Henry and Anna (Asher) Davis; B.S., Central State Coll. (O.), 1954; M.S. in Social Work, U. Conn., 1956; m. Eugene Edward Wise, Jr., Dec. 18, 1955; children—Eugene Edward III, Lauren Ann, Roland Walter. Tchr. Hamilton South elementary sch., 1966-69; asst. dean of students for women Wilmington (O.) Coll., 1969-71; counselor Counseling Center, Yochum Hall, Capital U., Columbus, O., 1972—, fgn. student adviser, 1973—; an incorporator, dir. Attention to Neglected Diseases, Inc., Columbus, O., 1971—; trustee Children's Mental Health Center, Inc. Dir. social services dept. Catherine Booth Maternity Home and Hosp., Cin., 1958-59, psychiat. social worker, Spokane, 1959-60; case analyst for study Wash. State Dept. of Pub. Assistance, Greenleigh Assos., Inc., Spokane, 1964; adult edn. instr. USAF, Fairchild AFB, Wash., 1962-64. Mem. Royal Soc. Health (London, Eng.), Nat. Assn. Social Workers, Assn. Certified Social Workers, Nat., Ohio assns. women adminstr. deans and counselors, Am. Assn. Higher Edn., Nat. Assn. for Student Affairs, Nat. Council Negro Women (life), Franklin City Mental Health Assn., Alpha Kappa Alpha. Democrat. Baptist. Home: 2650 Halleck Dr Columbus OH 43209 Office: Yochum Hall Capital U Columbus OH 43209

WISE, GLADYS E. DICKERSON (MRS. H. GRADY WISE), govt. ofcl.; b. Bronson, Tex.; d. Samuel E. and Emma Davis (Avera) Dickerson; B.S., Sam Houston State U., 1944; postgrad. George Washington U., 1959, Am. U., 1972—; m. H. Grady Wise, July 29, 1945. Spl. asst. Pub. Information Div., Office of Sec. Air Force, USAF, Washington, 1960—. Contbg. editor Airport World Mag., 1968-74, Popular Aviation mag., 1967-68, Pilot mag., 1973—. Mem. Am. Newspaper Womens Club (bd. 1969-70), Ninety Nines (chpt. bd. 1968-69, chpt. chmn. 1974—), Avian Space Writers Assn., Aircraft Owners and Pilots Assn. Contbr. articles to Air Force and Space Digest, Res. Officers Assn. mag., others. Home: 3810 Sulgrave Dr Alexandria VA 22309 Office: Hq USAF Sec of Air Force Office of Information Washington DC 20330

WISE, JUDITH ELAINE, counselor; b. Sturgis, Mich., July 29, 1938; d. Urban R. and Nell (Leestma) Wise; B.A., Western Mich. U., 1961, M.A., 1967. Tchr., Godwin Heights Pub. Schs., Wyoming, Mich., 1961-67; head resident, asst. dean students U. Wis., Oshkosh, 1967-69; asst. dean student life Ind. State U., Terre Haute, Ind., 1969-73; asst. dir. residence life Ohio U., Athens, 1973-74; counselor Women's Resource Center, Grand Rapids, Mich., 1974—. Mem. Vigo County Coordinating Council, 1971-73; mem. United Appeal Allocations Bds., 1972-73; mem. Vigo County Com. on Drug Abuse, 1971-73. Mem. Nat., Mich. assns. women deans, adminstrs. and counselors, Altrusa. Home: 2626 McKee SW Wyoming MI 49509

WISEHEART, DOROTHY A. (MRS. MALCOLM BOYD WISEHEART), business exec., club woman; b. N.Y.C., July 31, 1908; d. William K. and Maude (Bell) Allen; A.B. cum laude, Allegheny Coll., 1930; M.A., Barry Coll., Miami, 1964; m. Malcolm Boyd Wiseheart, May 21, 1934 (dec. Jan. 1972); children—Marilyn Joy (Mrs. Richard Lee Little), Carolyn Boyd (Mrs. George Hector Fanjoy Milne), Malcolm Boyd, Elizabeth Gay (Mrs. Michael George Joyce). Vice pres. West Kingsway Corp., Inc., 1950—, Dade Frutkoff, Inc., 1952—; staff writer Abstracts of English Studies jour., 1966-70; v.p. Wiseheart Found., Inc., 1958-61, pres., 1972—. Recipient Distinguished Service citation Am. Cancer Soc., Inc., 1957. Mem. Nat. Assn. Parliamentarians, Miami Parliamentary Law Unit (rec. sec. 1966), Phi Beta Kappa, Lambda Iota Tau, Kappa Kappa Gamma, Phi Sigma Iota. Republican. Presbyn. Clubs: Miami Beach Garden (historian 1946, rec. sec. 1960-); Miami Shores Country. Home: 430 NE 101st St Miami FL 33138 Office: Wiseheart Found Forte Plaza 1401 Brickell Av Miami FL 33131

WISEMAN, MILLIE GARLAND (MRS. ROBERT NOYLES WISEMAN), coll. adminstr.; b. Crossnore, N.C., July 7, 1939; d. Zack and Villa (Biggs) Garland; bus. certificate Caldwell Tech., 1971; m. Robert Noyles Wiseman, Jan. 19, 1961; 1 dau., Robin Villa. Sec. to registrar Lees-McRae Coll., Banner Elk, N.C., 1959-62, sec. dir. to admissions, dean students, asst. registrar, 1962-63, registrar, 1964—. Recipient Order of Tower award, Spl. award We Care Fund, Lees-McRae Coll., 1973. Mem. Am., Carolinas assns. collegiate registrars and admissions officers. Club: Presidents. Home: Route 2 Box 7 Newland NC 28657 Office: PO Box 278 Banner Elk NC 28605

WISHERT, HAZEL ONITA FERGUSON (MRS. TONY B. WISHERT), purchasing exec.; b. Emenence, Mo.; d. Benjeman Franklin and Vada (Smith) Ferguson; student Washburn U., 1960-62; m. Tony B. Wishert, Dec. 28, 1946; 1 son, Jeffrey Bryant. Insp., Adjustable Cap Co., St. Louis, 1939-42; asst. buyer-mdse. trainee Garlands, St. Louis, 1943-45; buyer children's sportswear Palace, Topeka, 1945-50, buyer coats, suits, dresses, 1965-71; buyer, merchandiser dresses Palace Clothing Co., Topeka, Kansas City, Mo., St. Joseph, Mo., 1971-73, mgr., Prairie Village, Kan., 1973—. Mem. Prairie Village Mchts. Assn., Am. Bus. Women Assn., Topeka C. of C., Kappa Sigma Mothers Club, Altrusa. Democrat. Presbyn. (womens club v.p. 1958-59). Home: 1732 Amhurst Rd Topeka KS 66604 Office: 10 On The Mall Prairie Village KS 66208

WISSMANN, RUTH HELEN LESLIE, author; b. Lima, O., May 29, 1916; d. Lowell Clement and Lucille Marguerite (Welch) Leslie; ed. Student's Sch. Art, Denver, 1932-34; student Pasadena Sch. Fine Arts, 1942-44; m. Milton Harold Wissmann, May 9, 1938; children—Ruth Ann (Mrs. Richard Harold Shellhart), Gary Leslie. Author: The Summer Ballet Mystery, 1962; Scuba Divers Mystery, 1966; Katy Kelly of Cripple Creek, 1968; Desert of Darkness, 1972; The Shadow of Sheila Ann, 1974; Claws of the Crow, 1974; To Hang A Witch, 1974. Recipient award Dodd, Mead, 1962. Mem. Cal. Writer's Guild, So. Cal. Council on Lit. for Children and Young People, Martha Kinney Cooper Ohioana Library Assn. for Writers and Composers. Home: 620 Sierra Madre Blvd San Marino CA 91108

WISTED, BEATRICE ELEANOR (MRS. MORELL WISTED), court reporter; b. Barnesville, Minn., Oct. 29, 1923; d. Laures and Anna J. Olson; student Detroit Lakes Bus. Coll., 1941-42; m. Morell Wisted, May 22, 1946; children—Bruce, Craig, Janice, Ronald. With Becker County (Minn.) Attys. Office, Judge Fred Dennis Office and T.F. Telander, Minn. parole agt., 1943-49; free lance ct. reporter, 12 counties in Western Minn., 1963—; reporter for Upper Midwest Research and Devel. on Hill Found. grant, 1967-69; mgr. real estate properties. Mgr., leader musicians trio working in pvt. clubs and supper clubs No. Minn., 1942—; bus. agt. Musicians Union Locals 382 and 434, Detroit Lakes, 1942-49; organist Frazee and Detroit Lakes Lutheran Chs., 1942-45; tchr. classes in piano and electric organ, 1943-66. Sec. Detroit Lakes Concert Assn., 1946-50; pres., Lincoln Grade, Jr. High and Sr. High P.T.A.'s, 1955-59; Spl. Day com. chmn. Detroit Lakes Centennial and banquet, 1971. Dist. treas. 7th Congl. Minn. Democratic Farmer Labor Party, 1965—. Mem. Detroit Lakes Bus. and Profl. Womens Club (pres. 1948-50, chmn. legis. com. 1973). Home: 1302 Roosevelt Av S Detroit Lakes MN 56501

WITCOVER, CHRISTINE ANN, lawyer; b. Washington, May 23, 1947; d. Henry Wallace and Kate Dean (Briggs) Witcover; B.A. cum laude, Sweet Briar Coll., 1968; J.D., Duke, 1971. Admitted to N.C. bar, 1971; asso. atty. gen. for N.C., Raleigh, 1971-73; asst. U.S. atty.

Eastern dist. N.C., Raleigh, 1973—. Research asst. Dean F. Hodge O'Neal, summer 1970. Mem. Am., N.C., Wake County bar assns., Raleigh Spinsters, Phi Beta Kappa, Phi Alpha Delta. Republican. Mem. editorial staff Duke Law Jour., 1970-71. Home: 3030 Spanish Ct Raleigh NC 27607 Office: Federal Bldg Raleigh NC 27611

WITHERSPOON, FREDDA LILLY, educator; b. Houston; d. Fred D. and Vanita E. (Meredith) Lilly; A.B., Bishop Coll.; M.S.W., Washington U., 1949, M.A. in Guidance and Counseling, 1954; Ph.D., St. Louis U., 1965; m. Robert L. Witherspoon; children—Robert L., Vanita. Social worker, supr. St. Louis City Welfare Office, Homer G. Phillips Hosp., 1943-50; tchr. English, guidance counselor St. Louis Pub. Schs., 1950-65; prof. student personnel services Forest Park Community Coll., St. Louis, 1965—; cons. Ednl. Testing Service, Princeton, N.J., Head Start program, 1965-68; counseling cons. St. Louis Job Corps Center for Women, 1966-68. Organizer teenage service guild Annie Malone Children's Home, 1964; v.p. St. Louis chpt. N.A.A.C.P., 1969—, pres. Mo. chpt., 1973—; mem. Challenge of 70's Crime Commn., 1970—; mem. adv. council Central Inst. for Deaf; dir. teens fund drive March of Dimes, 1960-72, Lily Day drive for Crippled Children, 1966-72; chpt. chmn., mem. speakers bur. United Fund, 1969—. Bd. dirs. children's services City of St. Louis, Urban League, Met. YWCA, N.A.A.C.P., Social Health Assn., St. Louis Heart Assn., Girl Scouts. Named woman of Year, Greyhound Bus Corp., 1967, St. Louis Argus, 1968, Iota Phi Lambda; named Outstanding Woman of Achievement, Globe Dem., 1970, Outstanding Educator of Am., 1971, Nat. Top Lady Distinction, 1974; recipient Negro History award, 1971. Mem. Am. Personnel and Guidance Assn., Am. Assn. U. Profs., Am. Assn. U. Women, Nat. Assn. Women Deans and Counselors, Am. Sch. Counselors Assn., Am. Vocational Guidance Assn., Assn. Measurement and Evaluation in Guidance, Nat. Assn. Jr. Colls., Nat. Faculty Assn. Jr. Colls., League Women Voters, Nat. Council Negro Women, Mo. Assn. Social Welfare, Jack and Jill, Mound City (pres. 1946-49), Nat. (pres. 1950) bar auxs., Kappa Delta Pi, Iota Phi Lambda, Sigma Gamma Rho. Research on high sch. drop outs with police records, uses of group guidance techniques in jr. colls. Home: 20 Lewis Pl St Louis MO 63113

WITHERSPOON, HELEN ADELE, lawyer; b. Jackson, O., Aug. 24, 1912; d. Jay Bert and Orpha Mae (Halterman) Witherspoon; B.S. in Edn., Ohio State U., 1935. M.A. in Psychology, 1937; LL.B., U. Cin., 1939. Admitted to Ohio bar, 1939; atty. Ohio Div. Securities, 1940-44; corp. counsel to sec. state Ohio, 1944-47; pvt. practice, Columbus, 1947—. Mem. Am., Ohio, Columbus bar assns., Nat. Assn. Women Lawyers, Pilot Club Internat. Republican. Methodist. Mason. Club: Clintonville (O.) Women's; North Broadway Camera (Columbus). Home: 969 Meeklynn Dr Worthington OH 43085 Office: 83 S High St Columbus OH 43215

WITHERSPOON, MRS. JAMES W. (ELIZABETH WITHERSPOON), ins.-abstract operator; b. Friona, Tex., July 3, 1917; d. James Walter and Cora Mae (Davis) Spradley; student Mary Hardin-Baylor Coll., 1936-37; m. James W. Witherspoon, Feb. 14, 1959; children—Jane (Mrs. D. L. Smith, Jr.), Irene (Mrs. Calvin Couch). Owner-operator Hereford Ins. Agy., 1942-70. Deaf Smith County Abstract Co., 1942-70. Deaf Smith dep. county clk., 1939-41. Mem. Bus. and Profl. Women's Club, C. of C., Wives Club of Legal Profession. Democrat. Clubs: Calliopian, Hereford (Tex.) Country; Amarillo (Tex.). Home: 1712 Plains Hereford TX 79045

WITHINGTON, LUCILE FRANCES, rehab. counselor; b. Cambridge, Mass., June 24, 1933; d. Nelson Eugene and Frances (Knowles) Withington; B.A., Middlebury Coll., 1955; M.S., San Francisco State Coll., 1966. Camp counselor, pvt. and Girl Scout camps, summers, 1949-54; certified skiing instr., North Conway, N.H., 1956-57, Squaw Valley, Cal., 1959-66; airline hostess Trans World Airlines, 1957-59; med. recreation worker A.R.C., Letterman Gen. Hosp., 121st Evacuation Hosp., Korea, 1960-62, staff recreation worker, Tachikawa (Japan) USAF Hosp., 1962-65; residential worker, counselor mentally ill juvenile delinquents Marin County (Cal.) Probation Dept., 1966; vocational rehab. counselor Cal. Dept. Vocational Rehab., Oakland, 1966-72, San Bruno, 1972—. Water safety instr. A.R.C., 1951-71, first aid instr., 1952—; vol. Ski Patrol, 1952-55, Nat. Patrol, 1955—, now chmn. ski proficiency Alpine Meadows Vol. Ski Patrol-Farwest Div. Recipient Distinguished Service award V.F.W., Japan, 1963. Mem. Am., Cal. personnel and guidance assns., Nat. Rehab. Counseling Assn., Profl. Ski Instrs. Assn., Soc. Mayflower Descs., Kappa Kappa Gamma. Episcopalian. Club: Royal Norwegian Yacht (hon.). Inventor bathroom scale attachment for weighing people in wheelchairs. Home: 568 Panoramic Hwy Mill Valley CA 94941 Office: Cal Dept Rehab 600 El Camino Real San Bruno CA 94066

WITHROW, JACKIE NEUBERT (MRS. WILLIAM WILSON WITHROW), state legislator; b. Mabscott, W.Va.; d. Charles Frank and Willie (Flanagan) Neubert; grad. high sch.; m. William Wilson Withrow, Apr. 20, 1942. Mem. W.Va. Ho. Dels., 1960—. Pres., Raleigh County Young Democrat Club, 1956-58. Mem. Raleigh County Park Bd., 1960—, W.Va. Gov.'s Commn. on the Handicapped, 1961—, Gov.'s Adv. Com. on Mental Health, 1961—, Gov.'s Commn. on the Status of Women, 1964—, Gov.'s Progress Corps., 1965—; legislative chmn. Gen. Fedn. Women's Clubs W.Va., 1962-64; co-chmn. state adv. council Mental Retardation Facilities and Community Mental Health Centers Constrn. Program, 1965—; tchr. Sunday sch. Friendship Baptist Ch., 1945—, sponsor Bapt. Youth Tng., 1945—, choir leader, 1959—; gen. Progress Corps State of W.Va.; mem. Beckley Child Care Aux., 1961—; mem. W.Va. Adv. Council Deaf and Blind, 1972—; exec. com. W.Va. Planning Commn. for Nursing, 1972—; pres. Adv. Council Appalachian Regional Hosp., 1971—; chmn. mental health com. W.Va. Gov.'s Adv. Council Health Planning, 1970—. Bd. dirs. Sophia (W.Va.) Vol. Fire Dept., 1965—, Mental Health Assn. Raleigh County, 1959—, Sophia High Sch. Scholarship Fund; bd. dirs. W.Va. Mental Health Assn., v.p., 1967. Recipient award for greatest contbn. in civic affairs in Raleigh County, Beckley Post Herald, 1959; named W.Va. State Dem. Woman of Year, 1963; recipient merit citation Beckley Bus. and Profl. Woman's Club, 1965; numerous other citations; named Ky. Col., 1964. Hon. mem. Jr. Historians Soc., Woodrow Wilson High Sch., Rhododendron Girls State; mem. Nat. Order Women Legislators, Beckley Bus. amd Profl. Women's Club (legislative chmn. 1967-68), Am. Legion Aux., V.F.W. Aux. Mem. Order Eastern Star. Club: Gulf Womans (pres. 1958-60). Home: 1301 Maxwell Hill Rd Beckley WV 25801

WITKIN, BELLE RUTH CLAYMAN, educator; b. Seattle; d. Samuel and Lena (Eichenwald) Clayman; B.A., U. Puget Sound, 1939; M.A., U. Wash., 1951; Ph.D., 1962; m. Joseph J. Witkin, Jan. 8, 1944; 1 dau., Sheryl Marie Chambers. High sch. tchr., Gig Harbor, Wash., 1940-43; newspaper reporter Tacoma News Tribune, 1943-44; U.S. Army clk., Riverside, Cal., 1944-45; newspaper feature writer Brownwood (Tex.) News Tribune, 1945; tchr. Vero Beach, 1945; teaching fellow, instr., lectr. U. Wash., Seattle, 1948-60; speech cons. King County (Wash.) Schs. Office, 1960-66; program research and evaluation specialist Alameda County Title III PACE Center, 1966-69, dir., 1969-70; dir. auditory perceptual tng. project Alameda County Sch. Dept., 1970-73, coordinator research and evaluation, 1973—. Mem. Am. Speech and Hearing Assn., Speech Communication Assn. (com. curricula certification 1966-67), Western Speech Communication Assn. (speech correction-audiology councilor 1965-66), Wash. State (pres. 1964-65) Cal. (v.p. ednl. policies) speech assns., Wash. Speech and Hearing Assn., N.E.A., Am., Cal. ednl. research assns., Cal. Adv. Council Ednl. Research, Cal. Tchrs. Assn., Beta Sigma Phi, Zeta Phi Eta, Mu Sigma Delta. Author: (monographs) Fault Tree Analysis: A Research Tool for Educational Planning, 1968, Management Information Systems, 1971; chpt. in Listening: Readings, Vol. 2, 1971. Editor: Composite Auditory Perceptual Test, 1973; Auditory Perceptual Training Program, 1973. Home: 1450 Avila Ct Hayward CA 94544 Office: 685 A St Hayward CA 94541

WITKIN, MILDRED HOPE FISHER (MRS. GEORGE JOSEPH WITKIN), psychologist, educator; b. N.Y.C.; d. Samuel and Sadie (Goldschmidt) Fisher; A.B., Hunter Coll., 1940; M.A., Columbia, 1968; Ph.D., N.Y. U., 1973; m. George Joseph Witkin, June 22, 1940; children—Georgia Hope (Mrs. Jerry Lanoil), Roy Thomas. Head counselor Camp White Lake, Camp Emanuel, Long Beach, N.J., 1939-40; dir., group leader Follow-up program Jewish Vacation Assn., N.Y.C., 1940-42; investigator N.Y.C. Housing Authority, 1943-45; grad. intern, student personnel adminstr. Montclair State Coll., Upper Montclair, N.J., 1967-68; mem., lectr. Creative Problem-Solving Inst., U. Buffalo, 1968; counselor Fairleigh Dickinson U., Teaneck, N.J., 1968, dir. counseling services, 1969—, supr. counselor tng., 1970—; attending psychologist N.Y. Hosp., Payne Whitney Clinic, 1973—; cons. City N.Y. counselor edn. tng. program Bd. Edn., 1971—, health information systems, 1972—. Tchr. econs. and polit. sci. Hunter Coll. High Sch., 1940; lectr., workshop leader numerous colls., orgns.; judge essays on good citizenship, 1955; exhibited in group shows at Scarsdale (N.Y.) Art Show, 1959, Red Shutter Art Studio, Long Beach, 1968. P.T.A. rep. to City Council, Yonkers, N.Y., 1953-55, edn. legislation chmn., 1955; publicity chmn. United Jewish Appeal, Scarsdale, 1959-65; Scarsdale chmn. mothers com. Boy Scouts Am., 1961-64; mem. Morrow Assn. on Correction N.J., 1969—. Bd. dirs. Girl Scouts Am., Yonkers, 1954-56. Recipient Bronze pin for services Hunter Coll., 1940; Gold Pin award P.T.A., Yonkers, 1955; United Jewish Appeal plaque, 1962. Mem. Am. Assn. U. Women, Am. Coll. Personnel Assn., Nat. Assn. Women Deans and Counselors, Nat. Assn. Student Personnel Adminstrs., N.J., N.Y. State Am. psychol. assns., Ackerman Family Inst., Am., N.J. personnel and guidance assns., Creative Edn. Found., Am. Assn. for Higher Edn., Assn. for Counselor Supervision and Edn., League Women Voters, Profl. Women's Caucus, Pi Lambda Theta, Kappa Delta Pi, Alpha Chi Alpha. Contbr. articles to profl. jours. Home: 35 Park Av New York City NY 10016 also 9 Sturges Commons Westport CT 06880 Office: Fairleigh Dickinson U Teaneck NJ 07666

WITKOV, BARBARA DINAH (MRS. HYMAN WITKOV), social worker, marital counselor; b. Lowell, Mass., Dec. 1931; d. Bernard Mathew and Anna (Gardner) Ritter; student Smith Coll., 1949-50; B.A., McGill U., 1954, M.S.W., 1963, advanced diploma in clin. practice, 1970; m. Hyman Witkov, July 30, 1950; children—Brian, Jeffrey. Caseworker Family Service Assn., Montreal, Que., Can., 1963-67, Marriage Counseling Center Mental Hygiene Inst., Montreal, 1967-68; sr. caseworker, field supr. Cath. Family and Children's Service, Montreal, 1961-70; caseworker Allan Meml. Hosp., Montreal, 1969-70; psychotherapist, Montreal, 1970-72; sr. supr., sr. clinician, marital cons. Jewish Family and Children's Services, Montreal, from 1972; pvt. practice as marriage and family counselor, Montreal, 1974—. Prof. in field U. Montreal, 1972—; cons. Eastern Region Conservative Synagogues Am. Mem. Corp. Profl. Social Workers of Que., Canadian, Nat. assns. social workers, Am. Assn. Marriage and Family Counselors, Am. Group Psychotherapy Assn. (asso.), Canadian Guidance and Counseling Assn. Canadian Psychiat. Assn. (affiliate), Acad. Psychosomatic Medicine, Am. Assn. Sex Educators and Counselors, Assn. Couples for Marital Enrichment. Home: 530 Victoria Av Westmount Montreal PQ H3G 1L2 Canada Office: Suite 715 1538 Sherbrooke St West Medical Arts Bldg Montreal PQ Canada

WITSIL, ELIZABETH SMITH ALISON (MRS. WALTER EARLE WITSIL), social worker; b. Wilmington, Del., Sept. 13, 1909; d. Alexander and Katharine Anna (Smith) Alison; A.B., Wilson Coll., 1931; postgrad. Columbia, 1934-36; m. Walter Earle Witsil, Aug. 27, 1938 (dec. Feb. 1964); 1 dau., Adah Elizabeth (Mrs. James Girard Unger); step-children—Walter Earle, Sarah Virginia (Mrs. Sherman C. Lloyd, Jr.). Accounting clk. Remington Rand, Inc., Bridgeport, Conn., 1932-33; social case-worker Bridgeport Br.-New Eng. Home for Little Wanderers, 1933-36; social case worker Conn. Childrens Aid Soc., Danbury, 1936-38; dir. membership, pub. relations and publicity YWCA, Bridgeport, 1964—. Mem. Bd. Finance, Fairfield, Conn., 1955—; mem. Fairfield Rep. Town Meeting, 1947-55. Pres. bd. mgrs. Woodfield Maternity Home and Adoption Service, Bridgeport, 1954-57, mem. corp.; bd. dirs. Vis. Nurse Assn. Bridgeport, United Fund Council Eastern Fairfield County, Bridgeport Council Ch. Women, Child Guidance Center of Bridgeport, Conn. Conf. Social Work, Mountain Grove Cemetery Assn., Bridgeport; bd. assos. U. Bridgeport. Mem. Republican Women's Assn. Fairfield. Mem. Am. Assn. U. Women, League Women Voters, D.A.R., Bridgeport Hosp. Aux. (pres. 1961-63). Presbyn. (trustee, elder). Clubs: Contemporary (sec. 1957-64, Wilson College. Home: 318 Buena Vista Rd Fairfield CT 06432 Office: 968 Fairfield Av Bridgeport CT 06604

WITT, DRENDA GAY WILLIAMS, newspaper editor; b. Abilene, Tex., Aug. 11, 1948; d. William Joseph and Norma Pauline (Herrington) Williams; B.S. with honors, E. Tex. State U., 1970; m. John Charles Witt, May 6, 1972. Mem. staff Ft. Worth Press, 1970—, women's news editor, 1971—. Mem. Women in Communications, Sigma Delta Chi. Home: 135 Manchester Euless TX 76039 Office: Fort Worth Press 5th and Jones Sts Fort Worth TX 76102

WITT, MARGARET ABBOTT, educator; b. Hudson, Mass., Dec. 8, 1911; d. Charles Madison and Agnes (Abbott); A.B. cum laude, Middlebury Coll., 1932; B.S., Simmons Coll., 1933; M.A., U. Omaha, 1961. Sec., research asst. Harvard Bus. Sch., Boston, 1937-43; sec., pres.'s office Harvard, 1943-44, asst. to counselor for vets., 1944-53; office mgr. Heart Fund, Los Angeles, 1953-54; asst. to pres. Pacific Oaks Coll., Pasadena, 1954-63; mem. faculty, dir. alumnae relations Stephens Coll., Columbia, Mo., 1963-74, asst. to v.p. devel., 1974—. Mem. Am. Coll. Personnel Assn. (com. on continuing edn. of the adult 1965-68), Am. Assn. U. Women (br. treas. 1974—), Nat. Audubon Soc., League Women Voters. Club: Quota (dir. 1966-67, 71-72, 73-74, 1st v.p. 1974—) (Columbia, Mo.). Home: 1701 Cliff Dr Columbia MO 65201

WITT, MARY, educator; b. nr. Humboldt, Tenn.; d. John N. and Sammie (Richardson) Witt; B.S., Memphis State Tchrs. Coll., 1938; M.A., George Peabody Coll., 1942, Ed.D., 1954; postgrad. U. N.C., 1945-47, Fla. State U. 1946-52. Tchr. elementary grades Gibson County, Tenn., 1924-27; elementary prin. Meth. Children's Home, Ruston, La., 1927-43; tchr. Ruston High Sch., 1943-46; tchr. lab. sch. Ga. State Coll. for Women, Milledgeville, 1946-48; faculty Fla. State U., 1948-65; on leave with AID program in Colombia, 1961-63; prof. Memphis State U., 1965—. Mem. Am. Assn. U. Women, Delta Kappa Gamma, Kappa Delta Pi, Pi Gamma Mu. Author: Tennesseans, 1972. Contbr. articles to prof. jours. Home: 237 S Holmes St Memphis TN 38111

WITTE, HAZEL, artist; b. Bklyn., Feb. 27, 1917; d. George and Celia (Lessler) Reilly; student Hunter Coll., 1935, Design Lab., 1939, Bklyn. Mus., 1942, Ruth Leaf Graphics Studio, 1965; m. Arnold Witte, Dec. 31, 1939; 1 dau., Arnel (Mrs. Spencer Leitman). Art tchr. jr. high sch., Munford, Ala., 1943; post artist Ft. McClellan, Ala., 1944-45; fashion illustrator, fabric designer, 1946-54; painter in oils and watercolor, printmaker, 1954—; artist-in-residence Inst. Man and Sci., Rensselaerville, N.Y., 1967; exhbns. include Nat. Acad., Nat. Assn. Women Artists, Audubon Artists and Nat. Arts Club annuals, U.S. State Dept. Internat. Traveling Exhibit, Pratt Internat. Miniature Graphic Exhibit; exhbn. color etching, silver and gold jewelry incorporating ancient Egyptian beads shown jointly with ancient Egyptian sculpture from collection Met. Mus. Art at C.W. Post Coll., 1967; represented in Am. and European pvt. and pub. collections. Recipient purchase award Hofstra U., 1966, Albany Inst. Art and History, 1968; Donna Miller award Nat. Assn. Women Artists, 1971, S.M. Hollander meml. award, 1973. Mem. Nat. Assn. Women Artists (bd. dirs., chmn. traveling graphics 1969-71), Boston Printmakers, Print Club Albany, Profl. Artists Guild. Address: 136 Milburn St Rockville Centre NY 11570

WITTE, SISTER MARIE BERNARD, educator; b. Richmond, Ind.; d. William and Mary (Horstman) Witte; B.A., Marian Coll., 1941; M.S., Fordham U., 1945, Ph.D., 1947, Prof., chmn. dept. biology Marian Coll., Indpls., 1951—. Mem. Ind. Coll. Biology Tchrs. Assn. (pres. 1971-72), Am. Inst. Biol. Sci., Ind. Acad. Sci., Assn. Midwest Biology Tchrs., Nat. Assn. Tchrs. Biology. Address: 3200 Cold Spring Rd Indianapolis IN 46222

WITTELS, MARTHA SZERLIP (MRS. BENJAMIN WITTELS), sculptor; b. Newark, Apr. 12, 1930; d. Leopold and Eva (Dvorken) Szerlip; B.A., Smith Coll., 1952; M.A., Harvard, 1954; m. Benjamin Wittels, Dec. 3, 1955; children—Evan, Daniel. Exhibited one man show Art Gallery, Chapel Hill, N.C., 1974; exhibited sculpture in shows at N.C. State Mus., Lever House, N.Y.C., Am. Acad., N.Y.C., Allied Arts, Durham, N.C.; permanent works at Duke U., Yates Bapt. Ch., Durham, N.C., Friends Sch., Durham, Learning Insts. of N.C. Child Devel. Center, Greensboro, N.C.; pvt. tchr. sculpture, 1962—; playground designer, including work for handicapped children, 1963—; designed sand area for Duke Meml. Methodist Ch., 1970; cons. custom designed playgrounds and equipment, 1964—; tchr. sculpture Allied Arts Center, Durham, 1970—. Recipient 2d prize Durham Art Guild Show, 1972. Mem. Nat. Assn. Women Artists, Sigma Xi. Author, illustrator: A Small World of Play and Learning, 1970; illustrator: Instinct is a Cheshire Cat (by Peter Klopfer), 1972. Custom designed sculpture used for therapy and edn. of handicapped children N.C. Cerebral Palsy Hosp., 1966-67. Address: 2308 Prince St Durham NC 27707

WITTEN, KATHLEEN BODINE RUBICAM, librarian; d.; Raymond and Regina (McCloskey) Rubicam; B.A., Vassar, 1939; M.S., Columbia, 1955; m. John D. Witten, June 14, 1941 (dec.); children—Anne Rubicam, John McKenzie, M. Wray. Research asst. Audience Research Inst., Princeton, N.J., 1940; circulation asst. Hartford (Conn.) Pub. Library, 1952-54; reference librarian Wesleyan U. Library, 1955-64; acquisitions librarian, bibliographer Sarah Lawrence Coll. Library, 1964-68; asso. dir. Library State U. N.Y., Purchase, N.Y., 1968—. Mem. A.L.A., N.Y. Library Assn., Am. Assn. Univ. Profs., Jr. League Bronxville, League Women Voters. Home: 4 Merestone Terrace Bronxville NY 10708 Office: State University of New York Purchase NY 10577

WITTENBERG, ELEANOR EULALA, librarian; b. Falls City, Neb., July 24, 1920; d. Frederick Rufus and Mary Eulala (Kilbury) Marsh; B.S. in Edn., Kan. State Tchrs. Coll., 1947; m. David F. Wittenberg, Oct. 11, 1952 (div. Dec. 1969); children—Stephanie Karen, Janis Carol, Laurel Anne. Tchr. rural schs., Cowley County, Kan., 1940-43; with G&S Tool Co., Wichita, Kan., 1944-45; children's librarian Whiting (Ind.) Pub. Library, 1947-51, cataloger, 1960-65, asst. librarian, 1965-69, head librarian, 1969—; librarian Army Spl. Services in Germany, 1951-54. Home: 3215 Glenwood St Highland IN 46322 Office: 1735 Oliver St Whiting IN 46394

WITTENMYER, MARY OLETA HAMILTON (MRS. RALPH W. WITTENMYER), librarian; b. Bowie, Tex., July 20, 1920; d. P. A. and Bess (Worley) Hamilton; student Cameron Jr. Coll., 1938-39; B.A. with honors, N. Tex. State U., 1954; M.L.S., Tex. Woman's U., 1960; m. Ralph W. Wittenmyer, June 22, 1941 (dec. Apr. 1945); 1 son, Eugene Lynn. Asst. reference librarian N. Tex. State U., Denton, 1954-63; asst. librarian Northeast La. State Coll., Monroe, 1963-65; serials librarian Tex. Christian U., Ft. Worth, 1965—. Librarian Parkview Bapt. Ch., Monroe, 1963-65. Mem. A.L.A., Tex., Southwestern library assns., Bus. and Profl. Women's Club (sec. 1961), Am. Assn. U. Women, Alpha Chi, Alpha Lambda Sigma, Alpha Beta Alpha. Baptist. Editor: A Union List of Newspapers in the Fort Worth Dallas Major Resource Centers, 1969. Office: Mary Couts Burnet Library Tex Christian U Fort Worth TX 76129

WITTNER, ASTA JUDITH, physician; b. Bklyn., 1902; d. Charles and Fannie (Gredinger) Wittner; ed. Adelphi Coll.; M.D., L.I. Coll. (now Med. Coll. State U. N.Y.), 1926. Intern Women's Hosp., Phila., 1928, resident obstetrics, 1928; resident Booth Meml. Hosp., N.Y.C., 1928-32; clinician gynecology Cornell U. Clinic, N.Y.C., 1930-32; cons. obstetrics and gynecology, dir. cytogenetics lab. N.Y. Infirmary, 1932-43; mem. attending staff Strang Clinic and Meml. Hosp., N.Y.C., 1961-68; dir. obstetrics and gynecology Strang Therapy dept. N.Y. Infirmary, 1961-68, cons., 1968—; instr. Women's Med. Coll. Pa., 1928. Diplomate Am. Bd. Obstetrics and Gynecology. Mem. A.M.A., Internat. Fertility Assn., Am. Med. Women's Assn., Am. Fertility Soc. Home: 3725 S Ocean Dr Hollywood FL 33020 Office: 150 E 37th St New York City NY 10016

WOELLHOF, ELDENE COOK (MRS. LAWRENCE R. WOELLHOF), psychologist; b. Rock Creek, O., June 16, 1924; d. Edward E. and A. Myrtle (Oliver) Cook; B.S., N.Y. State Coll. for Tchrs. at Buffalo, 1945; M.Ed., Miami U., Oxford, O., 1954; Ph.D., Fla. State U., 1961; m. Charles E. Moulton, 1945 (div. 1957); m. 2d, Lawrence R. Woellhof, Sept. 21, 1962; 1 son, Jeffrey Ray. Tchr. home econs. pub. schs., Springville, N.Y., Hamilton, O., Westfield, N.Y., Alton, Ill., 1945-57; head home econs. dept. Ribault High Sch., Jacksonville, Fla., 1957-59; asst. prof. Grad. Sch. Edn., Kan. State Tchrs. Coll., 1961-63; chief psychologist Kan. Neurol. Inst., Topeka, 1963-72, Topeka State Hosp., 1972—; instr. U. Kan., 1965, adj. asso. prof. psychology, 1970—; lectr. Washburn U., Topeka, 1967. Adv. council Shawnee Community Mental Health Corp., 1967-71, sec., 1967-68; mental retardation planning State of Kan. Task Force III, 1964-65; mem. State of Kan. Research Com., 1968—. Fellow Kan. Psychol. Assn.; mem. Am. Psychol. Assn., Nat., Kan., Topeka assns. for retarded children, Delta Pi Epsilon. Home: 4432 Twilight Dr Topeka KS 66614 Office: 2700 W 6th St Topeka KS 66606

WOERNER, LAUREL JEAN NICHOLS (MRS. THOMAS EDWIN WOERNER), physician; b. Monroe County, Ind., Apr. 22, 1924; d. Richard Glenn and Ralva Adeline (Byers) Nichols; M.D., Ind. U., 1962; m. Thomas Edwin Woerner, Nov. 7, 1965; children from previous marriage—Alan J. Stanley, Sali Jean Stanley, Joni Kim Stanley; stepchildren—Kurt David, Theresa Lynn, Frederick

Norman. Intern, St. Vincent's Hosp., Indpls., 1962-63; resident, 1963-66; resident Univ. Hosp., 1963-66; resident Marion County Hosp., Indpls., 1963-66, staff physician, pulmonary disease, 1966-71; with Woerner & Woerner, M.D.'s, Inc., Indpls., 1971—; mem. staffs St. Vincent Hosp., Winona Hosp., Indpls., Methodist Hosp., Indpls. Home: Rural Route 2 Zionsville IN 46077 Office: 8402 Harcourt Rd Indianapolis IN 46260

WOFFORD, GRACE KIRK (MRS. GEORGE CONGER WOFFORD), govt. ofcl.; b. Grenada, Miss., Dec. 9, 1914; d. William Hester and Ella Inez (Jones) Kirk; student Grenada Jr. Coll., 1932; B.A., Blue Mountain Coll., 1934; postgrad. U. Chgo., 1936-37, U. Miss., 1937; m. George Conger Wofford, Aug. 6, 1939; children—Martha Kirk (Mrs. John R. Pleasant, Jr.), Susan Elizabeth (Mrs. Riley H. Lunn), Alice Louise (Mrs. Charles R. Hallford), Sarah Margaret. High sch. tchr., Ripley, Miss., 1934-36, Louisville, Miss., 1937-39, Cleveland, Miss., 1965-66; mgr. central warehouse Miss. Dept. Pub. Welfare, U.S. Dept. Agr., Drew, 1966-74; journalist Sunflower County News, Drew, 1966; columnist Drew Leader and Ruleville Record, 1968-70; freelance feature writer, photographer. Leader, Girl Scouts U.S.A., Drew, 1951-72, neighborhood chmn. 1951—. Recipient Woman of Achievement award Bus. and Profl. Woman's Club, 1969. Mem. Nat. League Am. Pen Women (pres. Delta br. 1956-58, state pres. 1958-60, 70-72, mem. nat. letters bd. 1973-74, nat. corr. sec. 1974-76), Woman's Soc. Christian Service (pres. 1951-52, sub. dist. pres. 1952-54, dist. rec. sec. 1954-58), Miss. Poetry Soc., Blue Mountain Coll. Alumni Assn. (nat. alumni bd. 1960-64, v.p. 1972-74). Methodist (mem. adminstrv. bd. 1956—). Author: Lyric Poems, 1964. Contbr. poetry to numerous anthologies. Home: 123 N 3d St Drew MS 38737 Office: Box 188 Drew MS 38737

WOHLER, MILLY MARTHA WILSON (MRS. BENJAMIN OTTO WOHLER), journalist; b. Eugene, Ore., Jan. 19, 1922; d. Andrew Symington and Geneva Lucretia (Bailey) Wilson; B.S., U. Ore., 1943; m. Benjamin Otto Wohler, Aug. 5, 1945; children—Jeffery, John. Reporter, San Francisco Call-Bull., 1943-45; display advt. Pensacola News-Jour., 1945-47; travel writer, reporter The Oregonian, Portland, Ore., 1960—. Mem. League Women Voters (bd. dirs. 1958-59), Phi Beta Kappa, Theta Sigma Phi, Sigma Delta Chi. Home: 3522 NE Cadet Av Portland OR 97220 Office: 1320 SW Broadway Portland OR 97201

WOJCIECHOWSKA, MAIA TERESA (MRS. RICHARD LARKIN), author; b. Warsaw, Poland, Aug. 7, 1927; d. Zygmunt and Zofia (Rudakowska) Wojciechowski; came to U.S., 1942, naturalized, 1950; student Immaculate Heart Coll., Hollywood, Cal., 1945-46; m. Selden Rodman, Dec. 10, 1950 (div.); 1 dau., Oriana; m. 2d, Richard Larkin, Jan. 9, 1972. Asst. editor labor paper RWDSU Record, 1959, trade mag. Am. Hairdresser, 1960; translator Radio Free Europe, 1950; publicity dir. Hawthorn Books, 1961-62. Mem. Polish Inst. Art and Scis., Pen Club, Authors' Guild, U.S. Lawn Tennis Assn. Democrat. Roman Catholic. Author: (juveniles) Market Day for Ti Andre, 1952; Shadow of a Bull (John Newbery award), 1964; Odyssey of a Courage, 1965; A Kingdom in a Horse, 1965; The Hollywood Kid, 1966; Hey, What's Wrong with This One, 1967; A Single Light, 1968; Tuned Out, 1968; Don't Play Dead Until You Have To, 1970; The Rotten Years, 1971; The Life and Death of a Brave Bull, 1972; Through the Broken Mirror with Alice, 1972; Till the Break of Day, 1972; Winter Tales from Poland, 1973; also mag. writer, reviewer; translator from Polish. Home: 659 Valley Rd Oakland NJ 07436

WOJINSKI, SISTER REGINA MARGARET, printmaker, educator; b. Detroit, June 30, 1910; d. Stanley Francis and Anna Rose (Zackrewski) Wojinski; B.A., Siena Heights Coll., 1940; M.A., De Paul U., Detroit, 1951; M.F.A., U. So. Cal., 1967; postgrad. Stephen F. Austin State U., 1969, Trinity Coll., 1970. Joined Dominican Sisters, 1927; tchr. primary grades schs., Oak Park, Ill., 1930-40, Dearborn, Mich., 1940-44, Las Vegas, tchr. Nev., 1972—, elementary schs., Chgo., 1944-48, jr. high sch., Detroit, 1948-52, high sch., Santa Cruz, Cal., 1950-60, Oakland, Cal., 1960-65; instr. art U. Las Vegas, Nev., 1972—. One-woman shows of prints at Rochester (N.Y.) Festival Religious Arts, 1964, Siera Heights Coll., 1967, U. Tex. Med. Center, 1971, Incarnate Word Coll., 1971, St. Mary's U., San Antonio, 1971; represented in permanent collections at U. Tex. at Austin, John Fisher U., Rochester. Chmn. for art tchrs., Cath. High Sch., Oakland, Cal., 1952-60; Newman chaplain asst. Stephen F. Austin State U., 1968-69. Recipient Nat. Print award Rochester Festival of Religious Art, 1964. Author: Reading Readiness Text for Preprimer; Work for Reading Readiness; Color Surprises. Home: 5779 Madera Circle Las Vegas NV 89119 Office: St Joseph Sch 1300 Bridger Sch Las Vegas NV 89101

WOJNICH, ELEANOR MAE BENSON (MRS. WILLIAM WOJNICH), photojournalist; b. Louisville, July 7, 1917; d. Andy T. and Jennie Mae (Venable) Benson; A.B., Allegheny Coll., 1939; postgrad. Boston U., 1947; M.Ed., U. Ark., 1967; m. William Wojnich, June 20, 1946. Social worker Pitts. Assn. for Improvement of Poor, 1940-43; counselor Fla. Employment Service, Miami, 1950-54; asst. dir. Mpls. council Camp Fire Girls, 1954-57; case worker Minn. Div. Child Welfare, St. Paul, 1957-60, University Mound Sch., San Francisco, 1961-63; social worker Ark. Rehab. Services, Little Rock, 1966-67; counselor Minn. Div. Vocational Rehab., St. Paul, 1967-69; counselor, tchr. Berryville (Ark.) High Sch., 1970-73; photojournalist, 1973—. Served as 1st lt. WAC, 1943-46. Mem. Internat. Platform Assn., Am. Assn. U. Women, Am. Personnel and Guidance Assn., Photog. Soc. Am. Home: Box 112 Index WA 98256

WOJTAS, SISTER JEAN MARIE, educator; b. Grand Rapids, Mich., June 29, 1941; d. Carl Michael and Lottie Rose (Bartnik) Wojtas; B.A., Madonna Coll., Livonia, Mich., 1968; M.A., Eastern Mich. U., 1974. Receptionist, sec. Rex Sewing Center, Grand Rapids, 1959-60; joined Order of Felician Sisters, 1960; tchr. Cath. schs., Mich., 1962—, St. John's Sch., Wyoming, Mich., 1972-73; tchr. mentally handicapped St. Joseph Home for Dependent Children, Jackson, Mich., 1973-74, St. Mel Sch., Dearborn, Mich., 1974—. Condr. art workshop for spl. edn. tchrs., Flint, Mich., 1970, children's liturgies workshop for religious tchrs. in Grand Rapids, Portland and Holland, Mich., 1973. Kennedy scholar, 1971-72; Alhambra scholar, 1972-73; United Comml. Travelers of Am. scholar, 1973-74. Mem. Am. Assn. Mental Deficiency, Nat. Cath. Ednl. Assn.

WOLANIN, SOPHIE MAE, credit corp. exec., civic worker; b. Alton, Ill., June 11, 1915; d. Stephen and Mary (Fijalka) Wolanin; student Pa. State Coll., 1943-44; certificate secretarial sci. U. S.C., 1946; B.S. in Bus. Adminstrn. cum laude, 1948; Ph.D. (hon.), Colo. State Christian Coll., 1972. Clk., stenographer, sec. Mercer County (Pa.) Tax Collector's Office, Sharon, 1932-34; receptionist, social sec., nurse-technician to Dr., N.Y.C., 1934-37; coil winder, assembler Westinghouse Electric Corp., Sharon, 1937-39, duplicator operator, typist, stenographer, 1939-44, confidential sec., Pitts., 1949-54, exec. sec., charter mem. Westinghouse Credit Corp., 1954-72, sr. sec., 1972—; reporter WCC News, 1967-68, asst. editor, 1968-71, asso. editor, 1971—; student office sec. to dean U. S.C. Sch. Commerce, 1944-46, instr. math., bus. adminstrn., secretarial sci., 1946-48. Publicity and pub. relations chmn., corr. sec. South Oakland Rehab. Council, 1967-69; mem. nat. voter adv. bd. Am. Security Council. Named to Woman's Hall Fame, Seneca Falls, N.Y., recipient various 1st prize awards Allegheny County Fair, gold plaque Westinghouse Credit Corp., 1968, citation Congl. Record, 1969, TWA, 1969, Community Leaders Am. Plaque, 1971-74, numerous other plaques and certificates. Fellow Intercontinental Biog. Assn. (life); mem. Allegheny County Scholarship Assn. (life), Allegheny County League Women Voters, Am. Judicature Soc., Am. Assn. U. Women (life), Internat. Fedn. U. Women, Am. Mus. Natural History, (asso.), N.E. Historic Geneal. Soc., Internat. Platform Assn., Nat. Hist. Soc. of Gettysburg (founding), Nat. Trust Hist. Preservation, U. S.C. Alumni Assn. Ednl. Found. (gen. chmn. Tri-State area 1959, Pa. state fund chmn. 1967-68, pres.'s council 1972—), Smithsonian Assos. (charter), UN Assn. U.S., Am. Bible Soc., Hypatian Lit. Soc., Acad. Polit. Sci. (Columbia), Societe Commemorative de Femmes Celebres, Bus. and Profl. Women's Club Pitts. (dir. 1963—, editor Bull. 1963-65, treas. 1965-66, historian 1969-70, pub. relations 1971-73, Woman of the Year Award, 1972), Liturgical Conf. N. Am. (life), Am. Counselors Soc. (life), Am. Hort. Soc., Westinghouse Vet. Employees Assn., Am. Acad. Social and Polit. Sci., Mercer County Hist. Soc. (life), Nat., Pa. (key club) fedns. bus. and profl. women's clubs, St. Paul's Cathedral Altar Soc. Republican. Roman Catholic. Clubs: Jonathan Maxcy of U. S.C. (charter), University Catholic of Pitts., College of Sharon. Contbr. articles to newspapers. Home: 232 Meyran Av Pittsburgh PA 15213 Office: 3 Gateway Center (23 South) Pittsburgh PA 15222

WOLANSKE, ANN CHRISTINE CEA, physician; b. N.Y.C., June 25, 1941; d. Nicholas Stephen and Alice (Roman) Cea; B.A., Northwestern U., 1963; M.D., Boston U., 1967; m. Stephen Donnis Wolanske, Aug. 22, 1964; children—Stephen Nicholas, Kristen Ann, Douglas Charles. Intern Lenox Hill Hosp., N.Y.C., 1967-68; radiology resident Bronx Municipal Hosp. Center, N.Y.C., 1968-71; practice medicine specializing in radiology; asst. prof. George Washington U. Hosp., 1972—; attending physician nuclear medicine, instr. gen. diagnostic radiology Albert Einstein Coll. Medicine, N.Y.C., 1971-72; now asst. prof. N.Y. Med. Coll.-Grass lands Hosp. Mem. P.T.A. NIH grantee, 1964-65. Diplomate Am. Bd. Nuclear Medicine, Am. Bd. Radiology. Mem. Am. Coll. Radiology, Soc. Nuclear Medicine, Gamma Phi Beta. Roman Catholic. Home: Rogers Dr Greenwich CT 06830

WOLCHANSKY, DOROTHY LOUISE LAVES, editor; b. Tyler, Tex., Feb. 24, 1942; d. Abe and Grace (Luskey) Laves; B.J., B.A., tchr.'s certificate, U. Tex. at Austin, 1963; m. Lee M. Wolchansky, Aug. 23, 1964; children—Michelle Lynn, Sandi Ilene, Howard Nathan. Reporter, Grand Prairie (Tex.) News Texan, summer 1963; editor Family Security Co. Am., Ft. Worth, 1963-64; office mgr., interim exec. sec. Women in Communications, Austin, Tex., 1964-66; free-lance writer, 1966-71; sec., researcher Goals for Dallas, 1967-71; editor Roderunner publ. of Rodeways Inns Am., Dallas, 1971-74, Innside Rodeway, 1974—. Mem. Women in Communications, Internat. Assn. Bus. Communicators, Nat. Assn. Parliamentarians, Dallas Forum Parliamentary Law, Nat. Council Jewish Women, B'nai B'rith Women (pres. Starlight chpt. 1973-74), Gamma Alpha Chi. Co-author bibliography for indsl. publs. Home: 3252 Galahad Dr Dallas TX 75229 Office: PO Box 34736 2880 LBJ Freeway Dallas TX 75234

WOLCOTT, DOROTHEA KATHRYN, educator; b. Newton Falls, O., Apr. 23, 1908; d. Orvis Orlando and Carrie Maria (Maltbie) Wolcott; A.B., Asbury Coll., 1930; M.A., Ohio State U., 1944; Ph.D., Northwestern U., 1957. Tchr., Gettysburg, O., 1930-35, Findlay, O., 1935-39; dir. religious edn. Cin. Council Chs., 1939-44; state supr. weekday religious edn. Ohio Council Chs., Columbus, 1944-48; prof. elementary edn. and religious edn. Findlay Coll., 1948-64; prof. religious edn. St. Paul Sch. Theology, Kansas City, Mo., 1965—; summer prof. Oberlin Grad. Sch. Theology, 1946, 52, 56, Garrett Theol. Sem., 1950, 54, 55, 56, 57; United Meth. seminar leader Albion (Mich.) Coll., 1967; curriculum writer for Meth. Ch. Mem. Assn. Childhood Edn. Internat. (dir.), Assn. Profs. and Researchers in Religious Edn., Am. Assn. U. Women (named Woman of Year 1971). Club: Altrusa (pres. Kansas City). Author: Strangely Warm, 1971. Home: 2823 Berry Lane Independence MO 64057 Office: 5123 Truman Rd Kansas City MO 64127

WOLD, BEVERLEY MARY, therapist; b. Moore, Ida., Aug. 4, 1919; d. Harvey Douglas and Mary Brewer (Shelley) Jones; B.A., U. Redlands, 1942; certificate in Occupational Therapy, Columbia, 1946, postgrad., 1953; postgrad. U. Cal. Extension at Riverside, 1967-70; m. Robert R. Wold, Apr. 26, 1957; children—Larry D., Eugene N. Occupational therapist Shriner's Hosp. Crippled Children, San Francisco, 1946, Hosp. for Spl. Surgery, N.Y.C., 1947-48; dir. occupational therapy dept. Roosevelt Hosp., N.Y.C., 1948-50; occupational therapist Sunshine Sch. for Cerebral Palsy Children, Riverside, Cal., 1950-54; recreational dir. U.S. Spl. Services, Germany, 1954-56; therapist Elks Mobile Unit, Riverside and San Bernardino counties, Cal., 1956-57; tchr. Sunshine Sch. for Orthopedically Handicapped Children, Riverside, 1957-58; dir. occupational therapy Riverside Gen. Hosp. (Cal.), 1958-67, initiator spl. tng. program for vol. occupational therapy aides, 1962-67; tchr. spl. edn. Riverside County schs., 1967-70; dir. edn., tchr. Coronita Sch. for Educationally Handicapped Children, Riverside, 1971-72; occupational therapist various convalescent homes for geriatrics, Hemet, Cal., 1972-73; occupational therapist cons., therapist Meadowbrook Convalescent Hosp. and Ret. Homes, Hemet, 1973—, also geriatric restorative care cons. rehab. services, Santa Monica, Cal., 1973—. Participant, condr. various rehab. workshops for students, profl. and civic groups, Riverside, Cal., 1958-70; instr. occupational therapy theory and pediatrics dept. occupational therapy Loma Linda U. Med. Sch., 1961, 62. Asso., Idyllwild Sch. Music and Arts, 1970—; mem. Mt. San Jacinto Coll. Patron's Assn., 1972—. Recipient Am. award Outstanding Therapist So. Cal. Occupational Therapy Assn., 1954, various awards in photog. contests. Mem. World Fedn. Occupational Therapists, Nat., So. Cal. occupational therapy assns., Cal. Human Health Services, local assns. mental health, mentally retarded children, Internat. Relations Club, Inland U. Council World Affairs, Beta Sigma Phi. Club: Sierra (exec. com. San Gorgonio chpt. 1964-66). Address: Arroyo Fairways #64 42751 E Florida Av Hemet CA 92343

WOLF, KATIE LOUISE, Dem. nat. committeewoman; b. Wolcott, Ind., July 9, 1925; d. John H. and Helen (Brtulag) Munsterman; ed. Ind. Bus. Coll., 1943-44; m. Charles W. Wolf, Dec. 2, 1945; children—Mark, Marcia. Registration officer White County, Ind., 1960; mgr. White County License Bur., 1960-68. Vice chmn. White County Dem. Com., 1960-64; vice chmn. 2d Congl. Dist. Dem. Com., 1964-68; mem. Dem. Nat. Com., 1968—. Chmn., Ind. Assn. for Retarded Children; chmn. legislative com. White County Mental Health Assn.; mem. Ind. State Mental Health Assn. Mem. Bus. and Profl. Women's Club, Kappa Kappa Sigma. Home: Box 121 Reynolds IN 47980*

WOLF, MARJORIE HARRIS, public relations exec.; b. Phila., Feb. 25, 1916; d. Richard and Helen (Cathcart) Harris; Tyler Sch. Fine Arts, Temple U., 1936-39, Barnes Found., Phila., 1938-39, U. Pa., 1940; m. Horace Gard Wolf, June 22, 1946; children—Carol Elizabeth, Jeanne Louise. Bd. dirs. Montgomery County chpt. Pa. Assn. Retarded Children, 1951-55, Fund drive activities coordinator, 1954-64; writer pub. information for Montgomery County commnrs., 1964-65; dir. pub. relations, Pa. Hosp., Phila., 1965-66, Phila. chpt. Girls Scouts U.S.A., 1967-71; pub. information officer Pennhurst State Hosp., Spring City, Pa., 1971-73; partner Conv. Coordinators, services for convs., Phila., 1973—. Pres. Parent Staff Assn., Elwyn (Pa.) Inst., 1970-73, now mem. bd. dirs.; participant 1st White House Conf. Mental Retardation, 1963. Mem. Women in Communication, Phila. Pub. Relations Assn., Pa. Assn. Retarded Children, Pa. Acad. Fine Arts, Acad. Natural Scis., Woodmere Art Gallery. Contbr. articles on health services to profl. publs. Painting exhibited, Phila., N.Y.C., other area group shows, 1945—. Address: 296 Schooners Mews 1027 Valley Forge Rd Devon PA 19333

WOLF, RUTH SCRIVEN (MRS. ROBERT E. WOLF), civic worker; b. N.Y.C., Mar. 22, 1923; d. William Henry and Ada Mabel (Piers) Scriven; student Hunter Coll., 1940-41; R.N., N.Y. U., 1945; postgrad. Syracuse U., 1946-47; m. Robert E. Wolf, June 9, 1944; children—James T., Glenn J., Nancy Joan, Richard Lewis. Tchr. surg. nursing U. Hosp., 1948-51; mem. League Women Voters, Prince George's Country, Md., 1953—, bd. dirs. local league, 1955-59, pres., 1959-62; chmn. Com. on Hosp. and Health Facility Needs Prince George's Health Study Council, 1964-66; mem. Health Planning Adv. Com., 1967; mem. County Constn. Adv. Com., 1967-68; area v.p. County Council P.T.A.'s, 1965-67, 1st v.p., 1967-68, pres., 1967-68, Bd. Edn. rep., 1968—; mem. Prince George's County Bd. Edn., 1968-74, pres., 1970-71. Home: 5824 Carlyle St Cheverly MD 20785

WOLF, SALLY, publisher; b. Poland, July 4, 1915; d. Abraham and Anna (Ribnick) Ruzansky; m. Joseph Wolf, Oct. 13, 1935; children—Evelyn (Mrs. Michael Rokito), Gilda (Mrs. Richard Schwartz). Came to U.S., naturalized, 1929. Co-owner J&W Newsprinters Inc., Bklyn., 1949—, Gerry Press, Bklyn., 1961—; co-pub. Jewish Jour., Bklyn., 1971—; co-owner Internat. Newsprinting Co., 1972—, Roosevelt Raceway Thoroughbreds, 1970—. Co-sponsor K.P. Boys Camp; charter mem. Leukemia Soc. Home: 79-25 150th St Flushing NY 11367 Office: 1305 44th Av Queens NY 11367

WOLFE, BETTY HOOVER, lawyer; b. Halifax, Pa., Jan. 8, 1934; d. Charles Herbert and Mary May (Hoffman) Hoover; B.S., Bloomsburg State Coll., 1954; M.A. in L.S., Peabody Coll., 1957; J.D., U. Cal. at Davis, 1971; m. Stephen Landis Wolfe, Dec. 19, 1953; children—Andrea, Eric. Reference librarian Columbus (O.) Pub. Library, 1958-59; catalog librarian Enoch Pratt Free Library, Balt., 1960-62, U. Cal. at Davis, 1964-68; admitted to Cal. bar, 1972; law clk. to U.S. Dist. Ct. judge, Sacramento, 1971-74; asst. U.S. atty., 1974—. Asso. editor U. Cal. at Davis Law Rev., 1970-71. Home: 1133 Dartmouth Pl Davis CA 95616 Office: 650 Capitol Mall Sacramento CA 95814

WOLFE, ETHEL MARSH (MRS. GLENN FRANKLIN WOLFE), vocational counselor; b. Moundsville, W.Va., Apr. 13, 1909; d. Charles and Annie (Wild) Marsh; A.B., W.Va. U., 1933; M.A., 1968; postgrad. U. Md., 1964, U. Pitts., 1965, Columbia, 1966; m. Glenn Franklin Wolfe, Apr. 21, 1935; children—Margaret Ann (Mrs. Robert O. Hill), Nancy Louise (Mrs. Robert J. Sweeney). Tchr., Warwood High Sch., Wheeling, W.Va., 1933-35, Webster Jr. High Sch., Wheeling, 1955-56; employment security counselor vocational W.Va. Dept. Employment Security, Wheeling, 1957-64; counseling supr. Youth Opportunity Center, Wheeling, 1965-66; counseling supr. Employment Opportunity Center, Wheeling, 1966-73. Mem. Am., W.Va. personnel and guidance assns., Ohio Valley Profl. Service Assn., Phi Beta Kappa, Alpha Xi Delta Alumni (pres. 1966-67). Republican. Episcopalian. Home: 1727 Cullman Av SW Port Charlotte FL 33952

WOLFE, EVELYN ELAINE (RINNA), educator; b. Bklyn., May 2, 1925; d. Henry and Pauline (Tabb) Wolfe; B.B.A. in Retailing, Bklyn. Coll. and Coll. City N.Y., 1957; M.A. in Creative Arts, San Francisco State U., 1966. Buyer, Rayless & Charles Store Corp., N.Y.C., 1944-59; tchr., Lompoc, Cal., 1959-60, Mt. Diablo, Cal., 1960-66, Danville, Cal., 1967-69, Berkeley, Cal., 1969-74; lectr. edn. U. Cal. at Berkeley, 1967—. Cons., sch. dists. in Cal. Berkeley Pub. Schs. grantee, 1969-70, Point Found. San Francisco fellow, 1973. Mem. Cal. Writer's Club. Home: 256 Fairlawn Dr Berkeley CA 94708 Office: 1414 Walnut St Berkeley CA 94707

WOLFE, HELEN BICKEL, educator; b. Buffalo, Jan. 25, 1934; d. Thomas W. and M. Helen (McIntyre) Bickel; B.S., State U. N.Y. Coll. at Buffalo, 1955; M.S., Cornell U., 1961; Ed.D., State U. N.Y. at Albany, 1968; m. Charles E. Wolfe, Sept. 13, 1968. Home econs. tchr. Kenmore (N.Y.) Pub. Schs., 1955-61, guidance counselor, 1962-65; guidance asst. bur. guidance N.Y. State Edn. Dept., 1966-67, research asso., 1967-69, chief bur. research higher and profl. edn., 1969-72, chief dept. programs evaluation, 1972-73, prin. ednl. evaluator Office Edn. Performance Rev., 1973—. Pres. council of Women N.Y. State Edn. Dept.; Mem. Women's Task Force Empire State Coll. Bd. dirs. St. Peter's Hosp. Gen. Electric Co. Guidance fellow, 1964. Mem. N.Y. State, Capital Dist. personnel and guidance assns., Am. Edn. Research Assn., N.Y. State Ednl. Research Assn., Erie County Home Econs. Assn. (pres. 1958), Psi Chi, Phi Delta Kappa. Club: Cornell (v.p. 1964 Buffalo). Contbr. articles to profl. jours. Home: 153 S Manning Blvd Albany NY 12208 Office: Executive Chamber State Capitol Albany NY 12224

WOLFE, HILDRED WEXLER, educator; b. Piney Flats, Tenn., Nov. 26, 1918; d. Samuel Robert and Nan Elizabeth (Wexler) Wolfe; B.S., E. Tenn. State U., 1940; M.A., Columbia, 1941, postgrad., 1951-53. Faculty, E. Tenn. State U., Johnson City, 1941-43, Greensboro (N.C.) Coll., 1943-48, U. Ga., Atlanta, 1948-53; tchr. phys. edn., head womens dept. No. State Coll., Aberdeen, S.D., 1953—. Mem. Am., S.D. (pres., sec.-treas. coll. div.) assns. health, phys. edn. and recreation, Kappa Delta Pi. Mem. Order Eastern Star. Club: Zonta (v.p., treas. Aberdeen). Home: 1105 N 4th St Aberdeen SD 57401

WOLFE, JEAN ELIZABETH, med. artist; b. Newark, Oct. 3, 1925; d. Arthur Howard and Ethel (Harper) Wolfe; B.S., Russell Sage Coll., 1947; student Pratt Inst., 1949-50; diploma U. Rochester Sch. Medicine and Dentistry, 1955; M.F.A. (W.B. Saunders fellow 1955-56), U. Pa., 1973. Exhibitor, Pratt Inst. Galleries, Bklyn., 1958, N.Y. Med. Coll., 1958, Assn. Med. Illustrators, 1961-70, A.M.A., N.Y.C., 1965, Phila., 1965, Am. Coll. Surgeons Atlantic City, 1965, Research Study Club Los Angeles, 1966, Phila. Art Alliance, 1967, U. Pa. Optholmol. Soc., 1967-68, Cayuga Mus. History and Art, 1968, Pensacola Art Center, 1969, FAA Aero. Center, Okla., 1970, Scheie Eye Inst., 1972—; illustrations in med. books, jours., pharm. house pubs.; instr. Pembroke Coll. Brown U., 1947-49; mem. faculty Kimberley Sch., Upper Montclair, N.J., 1950-52; free lance med. illustration Studio N.Y. Med. Coll., 1956-60; instr. Pratt Inst., 1958-59; asso. in med. illustration in ophthalmology U. Pa. Sch. Medicine, 1960-72, research asst. prof. med. art, 1972—; guest lectr. Johns Hopkins Med. Sch., 1973, NIH; guest artist U.S. Air Force Acad., 1971. Recipient Merit certificate A.M.A.; Appreciation certificate A.C.S.; 1st prize Pensacola Art Center and Am. Heart Assn., 1969. Mem. Phila. Art Alliance, Assn. Med. Illustrators (bd. govs. 1970—, vice chmn. bd. 1973-74, chmn. nominating com. 1972-73, Ralph Sweet, Tom Jones awards), Soc. Illustrators N.Y.

Phila. Mus. Art, Am. Assn. U. Profs., Internat. Platform Assn., Marquis Biog. Library Soc. Presbyn. Club: Appalachian Mountain. Contbg. illustrator: Adler's Textbook of Ophthalmology (Scheie and Albert), 8th edit. Home: 7 Devon Rd Malvern PA 19355 Office: Hosp U Pa Gates Bldg Philadelphia PA 19104

WOLFE, JOSEPHINE BRACE, educator; b. Columbia Cross Roads, Pa., Dec. 11, 1917; d. Lloyd Churchill and Martha (Brace) W.; B.S., Pa. State U., 1942; Ed.M., Temple U., 1947, postgrad. 1945-49; postgrad. Tchrs. Coll., Columbia, 1952-56. Tchr. pub. schs. rural areas, Pa., 1936-38; asst. prin. pub. schs., Towanda, Pa., 1938-42, prin., Camp Hill, Pa., 1942-45; supr., dir. Reading Clinic Lab. Sch., Temple U., Phila., 1945-46; reading cons. jr. high sch., Upper Darby, Pa., 1947-49; reading cons., dir. City-Wide Reading Clinic, Springfield, Mass., 1947-49; asst. mng. editor Am. Edn. Press, Columbus, O., 1949-50; supr. elementary edn., Springfield, Pa., 1950-55, Gary, Ind., 1956-60; dir. research projects in reading, also in charge higher edn. in reading Dept. Pub. Instrn., Harrisburg, Pa., 1960-62; mem. faculty Tchs. Coll., Temple U., Phila., 1950-51, Portland (Ore.) State Extension Center, summer 1954, State Coll. Wash., Pullman, summer 1955; asso. prof. edn. Rutgers U., New Brunswick, N.J., 1960-62; dir. lang. arts research Beaver Coll., Glenside, Pa., 1964-66, Grad. Sch. U. Scranton, Pa., 1966—. Cons. Ednl. Research Council Am., 1970—. Lectr., cons., condr. workshops in reading and English, U.S., Eng., Can., 1950—; mem. English Tchr. Preparation Study, U.S. Office Edn., 1965—. Mem. Pa. Ednl. Research Assn. (state chmn. orgn. com., 1960—), Assn. for Supervision and Curriculum Devel. Nat. Elementary Prins., Assn. Am. Sch. Adminstrs., Nat. Council Tchrs. of English, Nat. Soc. for Study Edn., M.M.S., Internat. Reading Assn., Assn. Am. Childhood Ednl. Internat., N.E.A., Am. Research Assn., Nat. Conf. Research in English., Coll. Reading Assn. Author: (with Thomas Ryan and Adele J. Wright) English—Your Language, 1963, 65, 66; A Dictionary of Basic Words, 1970; Merrill Phonics Skillerts, 1972. Editorial dir. Book Pubs. Projects, Inc., 1964—. Contbr. numerous articles in field of English and reading to profl. bulls and chpts. in books. Home: Beaver Hill Apts Jenkintown PA 19046 Office: Grad Sch Edn U Scranton Scranton PA 18510

WOLFE, MARY-LOU (MRS. F. JAMES WOLFE), banker; b. South Bend, Ind., Jan. 28, 1927; d. William O. and Myrtle (Hentschel) Harding; grad. pub. schs.; student Am. Inst. Banking; m. Forrest James Wolfe, Nov. 18, 1960; 1 dau., Linda L. Williams. With Am. Nat. Bank & Trust Co., South Bend, 1946—, temporary supr. personnel and payroll depts., 1967, trust asst., 1963-68, asst. sec., 1968-69, asst. trust officer, 1969-72, trust officer, asst. sec., 1972—. Home: 17147 Hagey St Granger IN 46530 Office: 101 N Main St South Bend IN 46601

WOLFE, NANCY JEAN BEALS (MRS. DONALD H. WOLFE), city ofcl.; b. Fargo, May 20, 1933; d. Albert Percy and Vina Beatrice (Rugg) Beals; B.S. in Speech, U. Vt., 1954; M.S. in Theatre, So. Ill. U., 1960; m. Donald H. Wolfe, Aug. 9, 1962; 1 dau., Alison Lee. State polit. reporter Burlington (Vt.) Free Press., 1960-62; dir. English dept. Oletha (Colo.) High Sch., 1962-63; mng. editor Montpelier (Vt.) Monitor, 1963-64; dir. information Montpelier Pub. Sch. System, 1964-65; instr. Ithaca (N.Y.) Coll., 1965-68; city govt. reporter Twin City Sentinel, Winston-Salem, N.C., 1969; dir. pub. relations City Winston-Salem, 1969—. Dir. speech/theatre Montpelier and Shelburne (Vt.) High schs., 1954-58. Bd. dirs. Little Theatre Winston-Salem. Vice pres. United Fund Forsyth County, 1973—; Winston-Salem/Forsyth County Bicentennial Commn., 1973—; mem. pub. relations com. arts council Forsyth County Adv. Bd., 1969-73. Mem. Pub. Relations Soc. Am. (mem. govt. sect. bd. dirs. exec. bd. 1971-73, sect. vice chmn. 1973-74, state bd. dirs.), Internat. City Mgmt. Assn. (chmn. Mpls. conv. 1972). Home: 1023 Willowlake Rd Winston-Salem NC 27106 Office: PO Box 2511 Winston-Salem NC 27102

WOLFERS, ELSIE ELIZABETH GUTTMANN (MRS. PHILIP M. WOLFERS), civic worker; b. N.Y.C., Feb. 7, 1906; d. Alexander and Rose (Kohn) Guttmann; student Washington Irving Art Sch., 1920-23, N.Y. Bus. Sch., 1923, McDowell Sch. Design, 1937, N.Y. Sch. Drama and Radio, 1939, U. Pitts., 1952-54, Carnegie Inst., 1949, 63; m. Philip M. Wolfers, Sept. 26, 1926; children—Harvey Philip, Daryle, Faith (Mrs. Fredric Seil), June Heather (Mrs. Philip Green), Alfred Belmont. Sec., med. asst. to dr. N.Y.C., 1923-26; tchr., drama, Long Beach, L.I., N.Y., 1934-36, creative dramatics, Pitts., 1951-54, crafts and basic design, 1966-67; pvt. practice interior decorating, Hollywood, Cal., 1928-30, Pitts., 1953—; columnist Mt. Lebanon News, 1950-54, Spire, 1965-68. Chmn., Cultural Com., L.I., 1933-34; dir. Community Arts, Long Beach, 1934-35; founder, dir. Dads Club, Long Beach, 1934-35; dir., producer Mt. Lebanon Players, Pitts., 1949-56; mem. various coms. Music for Mt. Lebanon, 1957-58; organizer, player Little Lake Theatre, Pitts., 1950-56; active fund drives Red Feather Agy., 1949-51, A.R.C., 1966; presented travelogues Carnegie Inst., 1954; pres., bd. dirs. Childrens' Civic Theater Soc., Pitts., 1950-54; chmn. creative workshop, Pitts., 1955-64; writer, producer, performer, mem. altruistic com. Tuesday Mus. Club, Pitts., 1955-64; active Boy Scouts Am., 1950-54; founder, dir. Teach, 1969—; active numerous fund raising projects for various charities. Bd. dirs. Hill City, Pitts. Recipient award Pa. Fedn. of Women's Clubs; named hon. 1st lt. Police Force N.Y.C., 1924, hon. mem. med. bd. 1923. Mem. Nat. League Am. Pen Women (regional chmn. Mid-Atlantic States 1960, 68-69, br. pres. 1960-62, state pres. 1963-65, nat. regional chmn. 1968-72, nat. 3d v.p. 1972—, nat. dir., nat. workshop chmn.), Poetry Soc. City Pitts., Women's Club City Pitts. (drama chmn., dir., past pres.). Author: History Silver Fox Breeding in the United States, 1926. Address: 97 Wessex Way San Carlos CA 94070

WOLFF, ALICE ECKSTEIN (MRS. WERNER WOLFF), editor; b. N.Y.C., Oct. 27, 1914; d. Henry Joseph and Alice P. (Raphael) Eckstein; B.A. cum laude, Smith Coll., 1936; m. Werner Wolff, Sept. 21, 1941; children—Steven, Mark H. Asso., Virginia Kirkus, 1936-45; partner Kirkus Service, 1945-62; pres., editor Kirkus Reviews, N.Y.C., 1962—. Mem. League Women Voters, Smith Coll. Alumni Assn. Democrat. Home: 397 Bleecker St New York City NY 10014 Office: 60 W 13th St New York City NY 10011

WOLFF, GERRY PAULA, city and regional planner; b. San Francisco, Nov. 18, 1933; d. Henry Norbert and Dorothy (Stone) Wolff; B.S. in Landscape Architecture, U. Cal. at Berkeley, 1956, grad. student city and regional planning, 1960-61; grad. student city planning and architecture U. Pa., 1963-64, 65-66. With Santa Cruz (Cal.) County Planning Dept., 1958-60, Santa Clara (Cal.) County Planning Dept., 1961-63, Phila. Planning Dept., 1965, San Mateo (Cal.) County Planning Dept., 1966-68, Los Gatos (Cal.) Planning Dept., 1969-71, Mountain View (Cal.) Planning Dept., 1971; cons., 1972-73; with Wilsey and Ham, planning, architecture, engring., surveying and landscape architecture, Foster City, Cal., 1973—. Mem. Am. Inst. Planners. Home: 472 Selby Lane Atherton CA 94025 Office: 1035 E Hillsdale Blvd Foster City CA 94404

WOLFF, JANE APPLE, data processing cons.; b. Hazleton, Pa., May 28, 1935; d. Milton Weill and Hilda Bertha (Honig) Apple; B.A. in Math., Cornell U., 1956; B.Mech. Engring., N.Y. U., 1964; m. Arnold Jerome Wolff, Sept. 3, 1961; 1 dau., Juliann. Programmer, Ind. News Co., N.Y.C., 1964-67; systems analyst Chase Manhattan Bank, N.Y.C., 1967-68; electronic data processing cons. Cottage Industries Unltd., Bklyn., 1969—. Mem. Soc. Women Engrs. Address: 95 Joralemon St Brooklyn NY 11201

WOLFF, MARIANNE (MRS. HERBERT SCHAINHOLZ), pathologist; b. Berlin, Germany; d. Joe and Hedy (Wolff) Wolff; B.A., Hunter Coll., 1948; M.D., Columbia, 1952; m. Herbert Schainholz, June 8, 1952; children—Jay David, Daniel Curtis. Came to U.S., 1945; naturalized, 1945. Intern, Presbyn. Hosp., N.Y.C., 1952-53; resident Mt. Sinai Hosp., N.Y.C., 1953-54, St. Luke's Hosp., N.Y.C., 1954-56, Presbyn. Hosp., 1956-57; asst. pathologist Roosevelt Hosp., N.Y.C., 1957-60, asso. pathologist, 1960-68; asst. surg. pathologist Presbyn. Hosp., 1968-70, asso. surg. pathologist, 1971—; asso. in pathology Columbia, 1960-68, asst. prof., 1968-70, asso. prof., 1970—. Recipient Annual Citation Women's Med. Assn. N.Y.C., 1952. Diplomate Nat. Bd. Med. Examiners, Am. Bd. Pathology. Mem. Phi Beta Kappa, Phi Sigma, Alpha Omega Alpha. Home: 316 Locust St Teaneck NJ 07666 Office: Dept Surg Pathology Coll Physicians Surgeons Columbia 630 W 168th St New York City NY 10032

WOLFF, MARY ROSAMOND KATZ (MRS. SAMUEL U. WOLFF), bus. exec.; b. Florissant, Mo., June 16, 1901; d. Morris and Sarah (Levinson) Katz; grad. Blackburn U., 1922; A.B., Washington U., 1925; m. Samuel U. Wolff, June 16, 1933; 1 dau., Rita Rae (Mrs. Robert S. Wolff). Mgr., Katz Dept. Store, Benld, Ill., 1925-34; investment, mng. real estate, St. Louis, 1935—; owner Mary R. Wolff Real Estate Mgmt., St. Louis, 1941—; pres. Amherst-Barnard Apts. Corp., Embassy Apts. Corps., Gotham Apts. Corp., Hampden Hall Corp., Harlan Ct. Apts. Corp., M.R.W. Sales Corp., Mary R. Wolff Mgmt. Corp., Randolph Apts. Corp., Saun Hotel Corp.; dir. Fidelity Bank & Trust Co. of Creve Coeur (Mo.). Mem. Am. Assn. U. Women, St. Louis Restaurant Assn., Mo., Am. hotel assns., Real Estate Bd. Met. St. Louis, Nat. Apt. Assn., Women's Assn. St. Louis Symphony, Mo. Hist. Soc., St. Louis Art Mus., Internat. Platform Assn., League Women Voters, C. of C., Better Bus. Bur. Greater St. Louis, Central West End Assn. (dir.), Alumni Assn. Washington U., Women's Soc. Washington U., Jewish Hosp. Aux. Mem. Order Eastern Star, Hadassah. Address: 1919 S Grand Blvd St Louis MO 63104

WOLFF, MILLIE BENDER, author, civic worker; b. Mt. Pleasant, Pa.; d. Ben and Ruth (Murstein) Bender; student Ohio State U., 1936-37, Akron U., 1940-41, Washington U., 1958-60 children—Mack Bender Shaw, Henry Stephen Shaw, Alvin Wolff. TV chmn., pub. relations chmn., v.p. Akron League Women Voters, 1946-54; community relations dir. Family Service Soc., Akron, 1954-55; author column Family Counselor, Akron Beacon Jour., 1955; dir. spl. events GEM Internat., 1961; tv, radio chmn. Leagues Women Voters Met. St. Louis, 1956-63; bd. dirs. League Women Voters Mo., 1964; dir. People's Art Center, 1958-61, JCCA, 1956—; author-free lance acticles. Pub. realtions dir. Gateway Theatre, 1964—, Loretto-Hilton Theatre, 1969-71; pub. relations cons., also producer Armchair Critic, Edn. Council Greater St. Louis. Bd. dirs. Friends of McDonnell Planetarium. Mem. St. Louis Writer's Guild, Nat. Fedn. Press Women, Writer's Guild Am., Theta Sigma Phi. Home: 10374 Chimney Rock St Louis MO 63141

WOLFF, MIRIAM E., lawyer, port dir.; b. Portland, Ore.; d. Leon and Rose (Hochberg) Wolff; A.B., Stanford, 1937, LL.B., 1940. Admitted to Cal. bar, 1940; practiced in Los Angeles, 1942; atty. Dept. Employment, Sacramento, 1942-43; chief research atty. Dist. Ct. Appeals, San Francisco, 1944-45; dep. atty. gen. State of Cal., 1945-68; chief counsel San Francisco Port Commn., 1968-70; port dir., San Francisco, 1970—. Chmn. bd. visitors, exec. com. Stanford. Mem. Internat., Am. (dir.) Cal. (past pres.), Pacific Coast (v.p.) assns. port authorities, Am., Cal., San Francisco bar assns., Queen's Bench, Stanford Law Soc., Stanford Alumni Soc., San Francisco C. of C., Cal. Council Internat. Trade, Nat. Def. Transp. Assn. (dir.), Marine Exchange (v.p.). Clubs: Zonta (pres. San Francisco 1955; area dir. No. Cal. 1956-59, Women's City (past dir.)., Propeller; World Trade; Stock Exchange. Home: 25623 Elena Rd Los Altos Hills CA 94022 Office: World Trade Center Ferry Bldg San Francisco CA 94111

WOLFHAGEN, HELEN JANE (MRS. JAMES LANGDON WOLFHAGEN), educator; b. Salem, Ore., July 28, 1921; d. Thomas and Mary Lydia (Cone) Acheson; B.S., Willamette U., 1942; Ph.D., U. Cal. at Berkeley, 1949; m. James Langdon Wolfhagen, Jan. 23, 1948; children—Carl Frederick, Margaret Jo, Roger Charles. Chemist gen. research dept. Hercules Powder Co., Wilmington, Del., 1942-44; control chemist Pabco Paint Co., Emeryville, Cal., 1945-49; instr. Whitworth Coll., Spokane, 1949-52; instr. chemistry dept. U. Me., Orono, 1964-71, lectr., 1971—. Mem. New Eng. Assn. Chemistry Tchrs., Am. Chem. Soc., Sigma Xi. Home: 18 Grove St Orono ME 04473

WOLFORD, HELEN MOORE, civic worker; b. Indio, Cal., Sept. 30; d. John Clayton and Margaret (McGregor) Moore; student U. Cal., 1941-43, Harvard, 1947, U. Cal. at Los Angeles, 1956; m. Richard H. Wolford, Feb. 13, 1943; children—Richard George, Felicia Jane, Peter Arlington. Dir. Harvard Law Sch. Nursery, 1946-48; mem. capital funds com. Children's Hosp., 1957-60, mem. doll fair com., 1956-66; pres. Cal. Jr. Programs, 1959-61, U. Cal. at Los Angeles Art Council, 1967-68; chmn. Hollywood Bowl Vols., 1967-69; v.p. So. Cal. Symphony-Hollywood Bowl Assn., 1967-69; pres. Blue Ribbon 400, Music Center, 1969-74, v.p. performing arts council, 1974. Recipient Distinguished Service award U. Cal. at Los Angeles, 1966; named Woman of Year, Los Angeles Times, 1970. Home: 2201 LaMesa Dr Santa Monica CA 90402

WOLFSON, FRANCES LOUISE, artist; b. Pensacola, Fla., Dec. 16, 1906; d. Adolph and Theresa (Frohlichstein) Cohen; student Gesu Convent (Miami); m. Mitchell Wolfson, Jan. 27, 1926; children—Louis II, Frances (Mrs. Elton Cary), Mitchell, Jr. One man shows, U. N.C., Mayfair Art Theatre, Miami, Jordan Marsh Galleries, Miami, Twin Theatres-Dadeland, South Miami, Martello Gallery, Key West, Internat. City Bank, New Orleans, USIA-sponsored tour, Singapore, Hong Kong, South Vietnam, and others; exhibited group shows; also represented permanent collections. Adviser Beaux Arts of Joe and Emily Lowe Art Galleries. Dir. Wometco Enterprises, Inc. Former pres. Symphony Club Miami; acting chmn. Ad Hoc Com. Miami Beach Performing Arts Center; founding chmn. internat. welcoming com. U.S. State Dept.; pres. council internat. visitors, Washington, now chmn. bd. dirs.; chmn. endowment fund com. Greater Miami Philharmonic Soc., now bd. dirs.; active council Girl Scouts, Miami Beach; mem. women's com. Big Bros. Greater Miami; bd. dirs. Horseman's Benevolent and Protective Assn., Mental Health Assn. Dade County, Coral Gables People-to-People Program, Seacamp youth camp, women's guild U. Miami; mem. ladies aux. Isabella McCosh Infirmary, Lawrenceville, N.J., Combined Jewish Appeal; life mem. women's com. Variety Children's Hosp.; charter life mem. women's aux. Mt. Sinai Hosp., Children's Center, Jewish Home Aged; mem. Community TV Found., Civic League Miami Beach, Vancouver Art Gallery Assn., Key West Art and Hist. Soc., Fla. Audubon Soc., Mus. Sci. and Natural History, Nat. Trust Historic Preservation, Asheville (N.C.) Art Mus., Miami Mus. Modern Art, Miami Civic Music Assn., Opera Guild Greater Miami, Asia Soc., Inc., Artists Equity Assn., Temple Israel Sisterhood; patron mem. Asso. Artists N.C., Inc. Bd. dirs. Beautification Com. Greater Miami; trustee Miami Art Center. Recipient several civic awards, including greatest service award Symphony Club, 1955, Community Headliner award Theta Sigma Phi journalism sorority, 1960, appreciation award Gov. Claude Kirk of Fla., 1968. Mem. Daus. Confederacy, Am., Southeastern orchid socs., Fla. Horse Council. Clubs: Harmonie, Princeton (N.Y.C.); Key Westers, Miami Music, Miami, Palm Bay, Beaver Lake Women's Golf Assn., Mt. Sinai Garden, Vizcayans, Westview Country, Beaverdam Garden, Westview Women's Golf Assn.; Jockey (Miami); Golden Hills Golf and Turf (Ocala, Fla.); Country, Beaver Lake Golf, Quota (hon.) (Asheville, N.C.). Co-restorer Audubon House, Key West, Fla. Home: 5030 N Bay Rd Miami Beach FL 33140 Office: 306 N Miami Av Miami FL 33128

WOLGAST, ELIZABETH HANKINS (MRS. RICHARD CARL WOLGAST), educator; b. Dunnellen, N.J., Feb. 27, 1929; d. Francis William and Evelyn C. (Call) Hankins; B.A., Cornell U., 1950, M.A., 1952; Ph.D., U. Wash., 1955; m. Richard Carl Wolgast, June 26, 1949; children—Stephen, Johanna. Asst. in econ. research Survey Center, U. Mich., 1956-58; vis. prof. U. Cal. at Davis, 1966-67; prof. philosophy Cal. State U., Hayward, 1968—. Am. Assn. U. Women fellow, 1958-59, Am. Council Learned Socs. fellow, 1970-71. Mem. Am. Philos. Assn., Am. Friends Service Com. No. Cal. Mem. Soc. of Friends. Contbr. articles to profl. jours. Home: 1536 Olympus Av Berkeley CA 94708 Office: Hillary St Hayward CA 94542

WOLKOMIR, JOYCE MARY (MRS. RICHARD WOLKOMIR), ednl. adminstr.; b. Canandaigua, N.Y., July 20, 1942; d. Arthur Fred and Ruth Mary (Hogle) Rogers; B.A., Syracuse U., 1964; m. Richard Wolkomir, June 19, 1964. Editorial asst. United Ch. Women mag., N.Y.C., 1964-65; writer Scholastic mag., N.Y.C., 1965-66; tchr. English, Montpelier (Vt.) High Sch., 1967-68; information specialist Montpelier Pub. Sch. System, 1968—. Mem. Montpelier Edn. Adv. Com., 1969-72. Mem. Theta Sigma Phi. Editor: Edn. Reporter, Vt. Dept. Edn., 1967; coordinator Montpelier Ann. Report, 1968-73. Contbr. articles to Christian Sci. Monitor. Home: Calais Stage Montpelier VT 05602 Office: 152 Main St Montpelier VT 05602

WOLKSTEIN, DIANE, educator, storyteller; b. N.Y.C., Nov. 11, 1942; d. Harry William and Ruth (Barenboim) Wolkstein; B.A., Smith Coll., 1964; M.A., Bank St. Coll. Edn., 1967; m. Bernard Zucker, Sept. 7, 1969; 1 dau., Rachel Cloudstone. Ofcl. storyteller for N.Y.C., 1967—; storyteller radio program Stories from Many Lands, WNYC-FM, 1967—; grad. tchr. children's lit. Bank St. Coll., N.Y.C., 1969—. Lectr. on storytelling at colls., secondary schs., elementary schs. Marshall grantee to study Hans Christian Andersen, 1969. Author: 8,000 Stones, 1971; The Cool Ride in the Sky, 1972; Lazy Stories, 1974; (records) Tales of the Hopi Indians, 1972, California Fairy Tales, 1972, Eskimo Stories: Tales of Magic, 1974. Office: WNYC Radio Municipal Bldg New York City NY 10007

WOLLER, OLGA, author; b. Zidani Most, Yugoslavia; d. Ivan and Josephine V. (Stockel) Malgaj; student Acad. Fine Arts, Vienna, Austria; m. Rudolph Weigner 1918; children—Raoul M., Madeleine R. (Mrs. John T. Taeni); m. 2d, Franz H. Woller, Apr. 14, 1934. Author: Sex Alarm, 1946; Strange Conflict, 1955; The Heartbeat of Rome (hist. novel); Foolish, But Oh So Sweet, 1963; The Eccentric Loves of Elagabal (hist. novel), 1964; Poems, 1974. Composer songs: There Will Be Sunday; No, No Johnny, Let It Be. Home: 101 Greenway N Forest Hills NY 11375 also Pinehurst NC 28374

WOLMAN, AGATHA STRATES (MRS. WILLIAM WOLMAN), govt. ofcl.; b. Boston, July 16, 1933; d. Manassis and Rose (Papagelis) Strates; B.A., George Washington U., 1956, M.S., 1971; m. William Wolman, Feb. 14, 1967; 1 dau., Elaine. Statistician, Dept. Navy, Washington, 1954-61; group chief Dept. Army, Washington, 1961—. Mem. Am. Statis. Assn., Inst. Math. Statistics, Assn. Computing Machinery. Office: 8120 Woodmont Av Bethesda MD 20014

WOLPE, CLAIRE FOX (MRS. ARTHUR S. WOLPE), civic worker, psychiat. social worker; b. N.Y.C., June 24, 1909; d. David and Pauline (Hirsch) Fox; A.B., Mills Coll., 1930; M.A., U. So. Cal., 1936, M.S.W., 1965; student Smith Coll., summer 1931; postgrad. Columbia, summer 1963, U. Mexico City, summer 1964; Ph.D., Marquette U., 1970; m. Arthur S. Wolpe, Dec. 25, 1932 (dec. Mar. 1962); children—Ruth (Mrs. Roy Rose), Sheri (Mrs. Jerome Langer). Student advisor Jewish student orgn. U. Cal. at Los Angeles, 1931-33; with Travelers Aid, Los Angeles, 1934; med. social work Los Angeles County Gen. Hosp., 1934-38; with USPHS, 1938; social worker Los Angeles County Health Dept., 1938-39; psychiat. social worker Gateways Psychiat. Hosp., Los Angeles, 1962-63, 65-66; exec. dir. Bay Cities Mental Health Center, Los Angeles, 1966-68. Mem. Mayors Com. on Civil Def. 1950-52, Wilshire Coordinating Council, 1954-58; leader Girl Scouts U.S.A., 1954-58; mem. regional bd. Nat. Conf. Christians and Jews, 1951-55. Bd. dirs. So. Cal. Mental Health Assn., 1955-58, Los Angeles chpt. A.R.C., 1951-53, Community Relations Conf. So. Cal., 1950-60, Los Angeles Jewish Fedn. Council, 1952-58, B'nai B'rith Anti-Defamation League, 1973—, Hillel Assn., 1973—. Fellow Soc. Clin. Social Workers; mem. Nat. Assn. Social Workers, Psychotherapy Assn. So. Cal. (dir. 1967—), Cal. Marriage Counseling Assn., Am. Group Psychotherapy Assn., Los Angeles Transactural Analysis Soc. (sec.-treas. 1966-68), Psi Chi. Jewish religion. Mem. B'nai B'rith. Home: 234 S Orange Dr Los Angeles CA 90036 Office: 11601 Santa Monica Blvd Los Angeles CA 90025

WOLSK, VIVIEN NANCY, clin. psychologist; b. N.Y.C., Oct. 10, 1940; d. Paul Benjamin and Stella (Zucker) Deutsch; B.A., Barnard Coll., 1962; Ph.D., Adelphi U., 1970; m. Paul M. Wolsk, Sept. 8, 1963; children—Daniel, Jennifer, Matthew. Asst. psychologist VA Hosp., Northport, N.Y., 1963-64, N.Y.C., 1964-66; psychotherapist Lincoln Inst. for Psychotherapy, N.Y.C., 1969—; individual practice clin. psychology, N.Y.C., 1972—; research psychologist Child Devel. Center, N.Y.C., 1973—. Adj. prof. psychology John Jay Coll., N.Y.C., 1973. Mem. Am. Psychol. Assn. Home: 73 Perry St New York City NY 10014 Office: 1700 Broadway New York City NY 10019

WOLTER, BEVERLY ELAINE, pub. relations exec.; b. Norfolk, Neb., Jan. 28, 1927; d. F. William E. and Madeline Louise (Welge) Wolter; student Valparaiso U., 1943-45; B.J., U. Mo., 1947. Women's editor, reporter Baron Rouge State-Times and Morning Advocate, 1947-55; reporter Columbus (O.) Citizen, 1956; arts editor Winston-Salem (N.C.) Jour. and Sentinel, 1956-70; pub. information dir. N.C. Mus. Art and Dept. Cultural Resources, Raleigh, 1971—. Reid Found. fellow, 1955. Mem. Am. Assn. Museums, Music Critics Assn. (pres. 1967-68), N.C. Presswomen (pres. 1967-68), Am. Civil Liberties Union. Democrat. Lutheran. Home: 2321 Byrd St Raleigh NC 27608 Office: NC Dept Cultural Resources Raleigh NC 27611

WOMACH, EMILY HITCH (MRS. WILLIAM SCOTT WOMACH), state ofcl., banker; b. Laurel, Del., Jan. 27, 1927; d. Elon G. and Jennie (Neal) Hitch; grad. Sch. Financial Pub. Relations Northwestern U., 1957; pre-standard certificate Am. Inst. Banking, 1953, standard, 1958, grad., 1958; grad. Stonier Sch. Banking, Rutgers U., 1968; m. William Scott Womach, Mar. 13, 1943; 1 son, William Richard. With Sussex Trust Co., Laurel, Del., 1945-68 beginning as bookkeeper, successively proof operator, with trust dept., teller, asst.

sec., sec., 1954-56, former v.p., sec., in charge advt., pub. relations and personnel; adminstrv. asst. to Gov. Terry, Del., 1968-69; treas. State of Del., 1971-73, dir. Div. of Treasury, Dept. Finance, 1971-73; v.p. Farmers Bank of State of Del., Wilmington, 1973—. Cons. Womach Enterprises, 1969—; pub. speaker. Mem. Del. Bank Adv. Bd., 1963-71; bd. mgrs. Wilmington Savs. Fund Soc., 1970—. Charter mem. Del. Council for Women, 1971-74; chmn. Del. Heart Fund Drive, 1972. Bd. dirs., v.p., mem. exec. com. Del. div. Am. Cancer Soc., 1959-71; mem. exec. com., Delmarva Poultry Industry, Inc., 1964-69, achievement award, 1967; treas. Laurel chpt. Muscular Dystrophy Assn., 1958-64; mem. Del. Small Bus. Advisory Council, 1965-67, Laurel Planning Commn., 1965-71, Sussex County Overall Econ. Devel. Com., 1967-71. Trustee Wesley Coll., Dover, Del., 1973—, Peninsula Ann. Conf., United Meth. Ch., 1973—. Recipient Outstanding Woman Who Works award Downtown Assn. Memphis, 1964; named Outstanding Citizen Laurel, Laurel C. of C., 1965; award of merit in bus. Del. Fedn. Bus. Profl. Women, 1966. Mem. Nat. Assn. Bank Women (nat. chmn. revisions com. 1961-62, nat. v.p. 1962-63, nat. pres. 1963-64), Am. Inst. Banking (past pres. Sussex chpt.), Internat. Platform Assn., Rehoboth Art League, Del. (chmn. pub. relations com. 1959-63, mem. pub. relations com.), Am. (mem. com. savs. promotion savs. div. 1964-67, mem. exec. com. savs. div. 1966-67) bankers assns., Del. C. of C. (Marvel Cup 1968), Am. Acad. Polit. and Social Sci., Del. Fedn. Bus. and Profl. Women's Clubs, Northeastern Indsl. Developers Assn., Bank Marketing and Pub. Relations Assn. (membership chmn. Del. 1961-63), Laurel League Women Voters (chmn. budget com., auditor), Laurel Bus. and Profl. Women's Club (past pres.), Delta Kappa Sigma (hon. Beta chpt.). Methodist (mem. choir, commn. on edn.). Mem. Order Eastern Star. Home: RD 2 Box 140 Middletown DE 19709 Office: Farmers Bank of Del 10th and Market Sts Wilmington DE 19899

WOMACH, MILDRED KATHERINE, county govt. ofcl.; b. Ritzville, Wash., July 19, 1915; d. Isaac Newton and Emma (Anderson) Womach; grad. high sch. Sec. to Adams County (Wash.) supt. schs., 1944-48, to Adams County extension agt., 1948-50; dep. clk. Adams County, 1950-55; clk. superior ct. Adams County, 1955—. Gen. mgr. Family Concerts, Ritzville, 1971—. Committeewoman Adams County Republican Party. Trustee Spokane Symphony Assn. Mem. Wash. Assn. County Clks. (past pres.), Wash. Assn. County Ofcls. (past trustee), Spokane Civic Theatre Assn., Adams County Hist. Soc. Mem. Rebekah. Clubs: Ritzville Women's Republican, Grand's (past noble) (Ritzville). Home: 516 W Main Av Ritzville WA 99169 Office: 210 W Broadway Ritzville WA 99169

WOMACK, NELLEEN RUTH (MRS. AARON M. WOMACK, JR.), librarian; b. Henry Grove, Tex., Jan. 13, 1926; d. George Henry and Nellie (Kirkpatrick) Stroud; student North Tex. State U., 1943-44; B.S. in Edn., East Tex. State U., 1957, M.Ed., 1960, M.L.S., 1967; postgrad., Tex. Women's U., 1965-66; m. Aaron M. Womack, Jr., July 20, 1944; 1 son, Robert Henry. Tchr. pub. elementary schs., Mesquite, Tex. 1957-60, librarian, 1959-60; head librarian Garland (Tex.) High Sch., 1960-63; head librarian Mesquite Pub. Library, 1963—. Chmn. March Dimes, Mesquite, 1967-68. Mem. Tex. Municipal (past pres.), Dallas Met. (past pres.) librarians assns., A.L.A., Dallas County, Tex., Southwest library assns., Bus. and Profl. Women's Club (pres. 1966-67), Mesquite C. of C., Am. Assn. U. Women. Clubs: Mesquite Woman's, Altrusa (pres. 1970-72, recipient Outstanding Performance award 1971) (Mesquite). Home: 520 Kathy Dr Mesquite TX 75149 Office: 300 Grubb Dr Mesquite TX 75149

WONENBURGER, MARIA JOSEFA, educator; b. La Coruna, Spain, July 19, 1927; d. Julio and Amparo (Planells) Wonenburger; Lda. en Matematicas, U. Madrid, 1950, Dr. en Matematicas, 1960; Ph.D., Yale, 1957. Came to U.S., 1966. Nat. Research Council of Can. fellow Queens U., Kingston, Ont., 1960-62; asst. prof. Toronto (Ont.) U., 1962-65, asso. prof., 1965-66; prof. State U. N.Y. at Buffalo, 1966-67; prof. math. Ind. U., Bloomington, 1967—. Mem. Am. Math. Soc., Math. Assn. Am., Canadian Math. Congress. Home: 413 S Henderson St Bloomington IN 47401

WONG, ANNETTE SHUEYEE JANN (MRS. DANIEL SOONG), educator; b. Canton, China, Apr. 22, 1941; d. Joe-Wai and Wah-Lee (Ko) Jann; came to U.S., 1956, naturalized, 1961; B.A., State U. San Francisco, 1964, teaching credential, 1966, M.A., 1971; m. Daniel Song, Aug. 24, 1968; children—Terrelea, Justin. Typist, Marine Office Am., San Francisco, 1962-65; tchr. mentally retarded children San Francisco Unified Sch. Dist., 1966-71, lang. tchr., 1971—. Internat. Inst. grantee, 1961; Nat. Def. Edn. Act fellow State U. San Francisco, 1965. Home: 2344 Shannon Dr S San Francisco CA 94080 Office: 2190 Powell St San Francisco CA 94133

WONG, GWENDOLYN JEAN, occupational therapist; b. Marks, Miss., July 25, 1948; d. George H. and Rose (Chin) Wong; B.S., U. Ill., 1970. Occupational therapist McAuley Neuropsychiat. Inst., St. Mary's Hosp., San Francisco, 1970-71, Contra Costa County Hosp., Martinez, Cal., 1972, Child Devel. Center Children's Hosp., San Francisco, 1972—. Mem. Am. Occupational Therapy Assn. Home: 1344 Jackson St No 113 San Francisco CA 94109 Office: 3700 California St San Francisco CA 94118

WONG, HELEN LAU, coll. librarian; b. Canton, China, Sept. 12, 1919; d. Fu-Yao and Wai-Chong (Ho) Lau; A.B., Nat. Sun Yat-Sen U., 1944; M.A. in L.S., U. Mich., 1959; m. Wong Yau-Tai, Aug. 15, 1944; children—Mimi, Jane, Nancy. Came to U.S., 1956, naturalized, 1961. Cataloger, USIS Library, Honk Kong, 1950-56, Grand Rapids (Mich.) Pub. Library, 1956-58, 59-62, Asia Library, U. Mich., 1962-63; spl. materials librarian Grand Valley State Coll., Allendale, Mich., 1963—. Lectr. on China, 1964—. Mem. A.L.A., Mid-West Chinese Am. Assn., Grand Rapids Librarian Club. Mem. Liberal Ch. Home: 1486 Burke St NE Grand Rapids MI 49505 Office: Grand Valley State Colls Allendale MI 49401

WONG, NANYING STELLA (MRS. KEM LEE), artist; b. Oakland, Cal., Mar. 30, 1919; d. Albert Loy and Violet Gwei-Sung (Jung) Wong; student U. Cal., 1933; B.A., Cal. Coll. Arts and Crafts, 1935; postgrad. Mills Coll., Oakland, 1938, Cornell U., 1939, Mexico City Coll., 1951; m. Kem K. Lee, Oct. 27, 1949; 1 son, Colin Loy. Art instr. Oakland Pub. Schs., Durant, Castlemont High, Oakland YWCA, 1936-38; free lance artist, designer, lectr., 1940-50; illustrated talks on Chinese art and culture at Town Hall, San Francisco; illustrated book revs. Kahn's Rotunda Gallery, Oakland; exhibited Contemporary Masters' Exhbn., Golden Gate Internat. Exhbn., 1939-40; exhibited in one man and group shows at Gumps and Paul Elder galleries, San Francisco Mus. Art, DeYoung, Los Angeles and N.Y.C. museums and galleries; slide lectures and photo exhbns. on China Today at U. Cal. Art Mus., U. Cal., Davis, San Francisco State U., San Jose State Coll. and pub. orgns.; executed murals San Francisco Bakery, Oakland Furrier Salons; designer store fronts, cornucopias, free-standing signs, jewelry, fashions, mag. illustrations in Cal. and N.Y. Dir. pub. relations, programs, exhbns. at Golden Pacific Restaurant and Art Gallery, El Cerrito, 1969-72; program chmn., coordinator Three Generations of Chinese: East and West exhbn. at Oakland Mus., 1973; delivered seminars on human story of Chinese-Ams. in Sunnyvale and Berkeley schs.; poet-dramatist at Zellerbach Playhouse, 1972; cultural dir. Plum Blossom Studio, Berkeley, 1974—. Civic art commr., Berkeley, 1969—; organizer, dir. Ann. Fortune Cookie Verse Contest, 1969—. Recipient numerous art and lit. awards including Bay Area Art Lovers Assn. Honored Artist award, 1941. Grantee Berkeley Art Commn., 1973, 74. Mem. Cal. Writers, Ina Coolbrith Circle Poets, Cal. Fedn. Chaparral Poets, Margaret Shedd Writers Group, Chinese Culture Found. San Francisco, Chinese Hist. Soc. Am., Alameda Poets (dir., v.p. 1975—), Pacific Assn. of Arts (pres. 1970-71, 73—), San Francisco Soc. Women Artists, Internat. Platform Assn. Author: Henry: An Anthology by World Poets, 1970; Here Today: San Francisco's Architectural Heritage, 1970; Asian Women, 1971; Peace and Pieces: Anthology of Contemporary American Poetry, 1973; Number, 1970. Ting: The Caldron, Chinese Art and Identity in San Francisco, 1970. Columnist newspaper Chinese World News, 1964-66; contbr. to numerous mags. Address: 1537 Comstock Ct Berkeley CA 94703

WONG, RUTH (MRS. MELVIN LYON), psychiatrist; b. Sacramento, May 31, 1920; d. Ying Chun and May Yuk (Gee) Wong; B.S., U. Nev., 1943; M.D., Med. Coll. Pa., 1947; m. Melvin Lyon, Apr. 25, 1952. Practice medicine, specializing in child psychiatry, Paterson, N.J., 1950-67; psychiat. tng. Roosevelt Hosp., St. Vincent's Hosp., Jewish Bd. Guardians, N.Y.C., 1967-71; psychiat. cons. Demonstration Project in Sch. Health, N.Y.C., 1971-72; staff psychiatrist Roosevelt Hosp., N.Y.C., 1971—; asst. prof. Rutgers Med. Sch., New Brunswick, N.J., 1972—. Home: 225 E 30th St Paterson NJ 07514

WOOD, BERNICE ERMINE (MRS. RICHARD CLARK WOOD), realtor; b. Clay County, Ill, Feb. 19, 1926; d. Solomon and Leora Agnes (Travis) Ross; student So. Ill. U., 1962-64; B.A., McKendree Coll., 1965; postgrad. Eastern Ill. U., 1966; m. Richard Clark Wood, Feb. 21, 1945; 1 son, Jerry Lynn. Tchr. remedial reading Clay County Schs., 1965-66; co-owner, v.p. Clark Wood Constrn., Inc., Flora, Ill., 1967—; pres., owner Ermine Enterprises, Inc., Flora, 1967—. Mem. ladies adv. bd. I.O.O.F. Home, Mattoon, Ill., 1967-72, chmn., 1971-72. Mem. Nat. Assn. Real Estate Bds. Egyptian Bd. Realtors, Egyptian Realtors Assn. (budget and finance com. 1971), Ill. Fedn. Women's Clubs (dist. pres. 1966-68, state v.p. 1968-70, state sec. 1970, past state meml. chmn.), Ill. Fedn. Bus. and Profl. Womens Clubs, Flora Bus. and Profl. Women's Club (pres. 1971-72), Weaver McKendree Alumni Assn. (sec.-treas. 1972, 73), Flora C. of C., Wabash Valley Assn. Rebekah (dist. pres. 1961-62, state warden 1973—, past state trustee). Home: 755 E 3d St Flora IL 62839 Office: 847 E North Av Flora IL 62839

WOOD, CLARA REBECCA CHALOUPKA, educator, clergyman; b. Yale, Ia., Aug. 10, 1917; d. Frank and Mary Elizabeth (Greenawalt) Chaloupka; student Ia. State Coll., 1934-35; A.B., Manchester Coll., 1940; B.D., Yale, 1945, M.A., 1946; Th.D., Pacific Sch. Religion, 1959; m. Bruce K. Wood, June 13, 1940; children—Loretta Jean, Roger Bruce, Carol Rebecca, Marvin Chaloupka. Elementary tchr., Guthrie County, Ia., 1935-37; summer pastor Ch. of Brethren, Arriba, Colo., 1939, 40; tchr., prin. high sch., Kellerton, Ka., 1940-41; high sch. tchr., librarian, Silver Lake, Ind., 1941-42; tchr. Chester Twp. High Sch., North Manchester, Ind., 1942-43; dir. Brethren Service in Poland, 1946-49; prof., co-dir. sch. religion Mont. State U., 1950-54; pastor Oakland (Cal.) Ch. of Brethren, 1956-58; prof. Lewis and Clark Coll., Portland, Ore., 1960-61; tchr. Oakland Unified Sch. Dist., also evening instr. Diablo Valley Coll., 1962-64; prof. dept. philosophy and humanities, former dept. chmn. Diablo Valley Coll., Pleasant Hill, Cal., 1964—. Interim pastor San Francisco Ch. of Brethren, 1961, Fruitvale United Ch. Christ, Oakland, 1962, Hayward (Cal.) United Ch. Christ, 1963. Active P.T.A., Girl Scouts, Boy Scouts Am. Bd. dirs. San Francisco Coll. Opera Assn. Mem. Nat. Assn. Humanities Edn. (pres. Western region 1973, com. mem. 1971-72), Internat. Assn. Women Ministers (v.p. 1952-53, pres. 1953-55), Cal. Tchrs. Assn., Nat. Orgn. Women, Cal. Humanities Assn., Faculty Assn. Cal. Community Colls., Classical Alliance Western States, Am. Assn. Univ. Women, San Francisco Opera Guild. Author: (with Herman H. Chrisman) Supplementary Readings for the General Course in Humanities, 1965, Readings in the Humanities, 2d edit., 1971. Home: 1011 Villa Nueva El Cerrito CA 94530 Office: Diablo Valley College Pleasant Hill CA 94523

WOOD, DOLORES MARIE JEMIONEK, ednl. adminstr.; b. Phila., Aug. 13, 1937; d. Felix and Laura (Ziembicki) Jemionek; B.S., Villanova U., 1961, M.A., 1965; m. John F. Wood, Feb. 14, 1973. Tchr., St. Mary's Elementary Sch., Conshohocken, Pa., 1955-62; tchr. social studies John W. Hallahan Cath. Girls' High Sch., 1962-66; guidance counselor Acad. Notre Dame de Namur, Villanova, Pa., 1966—, vice prin., 1967—, dean students, 1968-70, acad. dean, 1969-70. Mem. Phila. Archdiocesan Guidance Com., 1966—; lectr. Rosemont Coll., 1967, 68; mem. conv. planning com. Nat. Catholic Guidance Conf., 1971, sec., 1972—. Troop leader Girl Scouts U.S.A., Conshohocken, 1955-72, neighborhood organizer, 1965-72; asst. to dir. Camp Overbrook, Phila., summers, 1968-71. Trustee Conshohocken Free Library. Mem. Am. Personnel and Guidance Assn., Am., Pa. sch. counselors assns., Ind. Sch. Tchrs. Assn. (exec. com. 1967-73), Delaware County Counselors Assn., Middle States Council Social Studies. Home: Woodstar Radnor PA 19087 Office: 560 Sproul Rd Villanova PA 19085

WOOD, (DOROTHY) HELEN PATTON, educator; b. Nixon, Tex., Dec. 26, 1918; d. Reginald William and Winnie Davis (Jordan) Patton; B.A., U. Tex., 1940; M.Ed., Our Lady of the Lake Coll., 1955, counselor certificate, 1966; m. Frank Lee Wood, Jr., Sept. 10, 1940 (div. June 1953); children—Carole (Mrs. Carole Debney), Andrea (Mrs. John Franklin Glodt). Elementary tchr., 1952-59; reading specialist, counselor San Antonio Coll., 1959-66; reading specialist edn. dept. Trinity U., San Antonio, 1966—. Mem. women's com. San Antonio Symphony, 1960—. Mem. Am., Tex. personnel and guidance assns., Nat. Reading Conf., Internat. Reading Assn., San Antonio Women Deans and Counselors, Zeta Tau Alpha. Mem. Christian Ch. Home: 634 Mandalay Dr E San Antonio TX 78212

WOOD, ELEANOR NORTON (MRS. NATHANIEL F. WOOD), state ofcl.; b. Cambridge, Mass., June 24, 1925; d. Curtis Elliott and Florence (Bell) Norton; B.A. cum laude (tuition scholar), Syracuse U., 1946; postgrad. U. Minn., 1947-48, Pasadena City Coll., 1956-62, U. Cal. at Los Angeles, 1963-64; m. Nathaniel F. Wood, Dec. 14, 1945; children—Gary Nathaniel, Janet. Editorial staff Milw. Jour., 1942, Sports Afield, Mpls., 1948; advt. copywriter Sears Roebuck, Powers Dept. Store, Mpls., 1951; with various weekly and daily newspapers, 1951-57; editorial staff Monrovia (Cal.) Daily News Post, 1957-58; tech. editor Consol. Electrodynamics, 1958-60; dir. Norton Wood Editorial Service, 1960-65; information officer Div. Hwys., State Cal., Los Angeles, 1965—. Tchr., cons., Bates Advt., Publs. and Tech. Communications Inst., 1960-61; lang. tutor Internat. Inst. Los Angeles, 1956-58. Active P.T.A. Served with WAVES, 1945-46. Recipient Bronze Medal for editorial excellence State Cal., 1962, Merit award Cal. State Service, 1971. Mem. Soc. Tech. Writers and Pubs. (area sec. 1960), Los Angeles Press Club, Delta Gamma, Theta Sigma Phi. Presbyn. Clubs: Mensa, Athletic (Los Angeles); Golf, Bridge (Pasadena). Feature columnist Sierra Madre (Cal.) News, 1956-60; feature writer Pasadena Times, 1961-62; editor Interchange, 1970—. Intercom, 1973—. Contbr. articles to profl. jours. Home: 1430 Tropical Av Pasadena CA 91107 Office: 120 S Spring St Los Angeles CA 90012

WOOD, EVA RUTH MCBEE (MRS. JESS D. WOOD), state ofcl.; b. Trenton, Neb.; d. John Franklin and Eva (Morrison) McBee; diploma LaSalle Extension U., 1962; grad. Concordia Bus. Coll., 1927; m. Jess D. Wood, Jan. 6, 1931 (dec. 1969); children—William J., Earl J. (dec.). Bookkeeper, Kugler Oil Co., Culbertson, Neb., 1928-29; account clk. Omaha Cold Storage Co., McCook, Neb., 1930, Winner, S.D., 1931-32; accountant A. & M. Oil Co., Culbertson, Neb., 1934-57; chief fiscal officer Neb. Dept. Motor Vehicles, 1957—. Dir. Lincoln Lancaster Hist. Soc., 1967—. Mem. Am. Inst. C.P.A.'s, Am. Neb. Soc. C.P.A.'s, V.F.W. Aux. (past sec.), Am. Legion Aux., Daus. Union Vets. (pres. 1972), Neb. State, Lincoln Lancaster hist. socs. Home: 901 F St Lincoln NE 68508 Office: State Capitol Lincoln NE 68509

WOOD, FRANCES, educator; b. Bristow, Okla., June 11, 1926; d. Lea Audos and Vera (Thompson) Wood; B.S., Okla. State U., 1947, M.S., 1948; Ed.D., U. Houston, 1965. Tchr. corrective phys. edn. Tulsa pub. schs., 1948, Roosevelt Jr. High Sch., Tulsa, 1948; asst. prof. phys. edn. Okla. State U., Stillwater, 1948-52; instr. phys. edn. U. Ark., Fayetteville, 1952-58, asst. prof., 1958-65, asso. prof., 1966-72, prof., 1972—. Bd. dirs. Washington County Sch. for Retarded Children, 1964-68. Mem. Am., Ark. assns. health, phys. edn. and recreation, Internat. Fedn. Phys. Edn., Am. Assn. U. Profs., Nat., So. assns. phys. edn. for coll. women, Ark. Edn. Assn., Kappa Delta Pi, Sigma Sigma Psi. Democrat. Methodist. Home: 1627 Wedington Dr Fayetteville AR 72701 Office: U Ark Fayetteville AR 72701

WOOD, FREDA BUSHMAN (MRS. JOSEPH HERBERT WOOD), state ofcl.; b. Salt Lake City, Oct. 27, 1911; d. Gustave Fred and Freda (Hertel) Bushman; student Salt Lake Bus. Coll., 1926-27; certificate Inst. Govt., U. Utah, 1959; m. Joseph Herbert Wood, Nov. 28, 1929; children—Jack Bushman, Patricia Jean (Mrs. William C. Petersen), William Joseph. Councilwoman finance dept. North Salt Lake, Utah, 1950-62, planning commn., 1950-56, recorder, 1950-60; charter trustee South Davis County Sewer Improvement Dist., Woods Cross, Utah, 1959, clk. treas., 1959-74; mem. bd. Utah State Retirement System, 1966—, mem. investment com., 1967—, v.p., 1973. Partner Orchard Village Enterprise, North Salt Lake, 1973. Vice pres. Soc. Multiple Handicapped Children, 1956-59; active P.T.A., 1937-49. Del. to Internat. Union of Local Authorities, Washington, 1961, Brussels, Belgium, 1963; county and state democratic del., 1952—; del. Utah State Women's Legislative Council, 1958—. Bd. dirs. South Davis Youth Center, 1955-57. Mem. Utah League of Cities and Towns (dir. 1958-59), Utah Pub. Employees Service Assn., Nat. Inst. Municipal Clks. Assn. (sec. Utah chpt. 1957). Mem. Ch. of Jesus Christ of Latter-day Saints. Club: Garden Bouquet, Jane Jefferson (charter pres. 1956-57, parliamentarian, auditor 1957-68). Home: 56 South Main North Salt Lake UT 84054

WOOD, GLADYS CROWTHER (MRS. NEWELL E. WOOD), writer, educator, civic worker; b. Sanborn, N.D., Aug. 12, 1921; d. Charles Kershaw and Blanche (Kee) Crowther; student Valley City State Tchrs. Coll., 1939-41; B.A., U. Minn., 1943; M.S., San Jose State Coll., 1972; m. Newell E. Wood, June 13, 1943; children—Terry Newell, Lani Carol, Brian Robert, Kevin Charles. City desk, gen. assignment reporter St. Paul Pioneer Press-Dispatch, 1943-45; temporary editor J. C. Penney Co. house organ, N.Y.C., 1945, asst. editor, 1946; editor Army newspaper Camp Robinson, Ark., 1946; free lance reporter St. Paul, Livermore, Cal., San Jose Cal., 1946—; English lay reader Los Gatos Union High Sch. Dist., 1961-63; tchr. English, journalism Willow Glen High Sch., San Jose Unified Sch. Dist., 1968—. Cellist Los Gatos-Saratoga Symphony, 1963—; mem. Citizens Com. for Adult Edn., Los Gatos Union High Sch. Dist. Adult Sch. Program, 1963. troop leader Santa Clara County council Girl Scouts U.S.A., 1956-63; den mother Cub Scouts Am., 1962-63. Bd. dirs. Saratoga P.T.A., 1956-66, Vis. Nurse Assn. Inc., 1963-65. Mem. League Women Voters, Santa Clara County Med. Soc. Woman's Aux. (dist. pres. 1962-63, county pres. 1964-65), Cal. Tchrs. Assn., Am. Assn. U. Women, Theta Sigma Phi, Alpha Omicron Pi. Home: 14161 Douglas Lane Saratoga CA 95070

WOOD, ISABELLE LUCILLE (MRS. ARTHUR GEORGE WOOD), nurse; b. Strathclair, Man., Can., Apr. 9, 1924; d. Alexander Hugh and Margaret Maud (MacDonald) McKerchar; Nursing diploma Winnipeg Gen. Hosp., 1946; Supervisory Mgmt. certificate Brandon U., 1970; m. Arthur George Wood, Oct. 16, 1948; children—Linda Lucille (Mrs. Alfred Sterling Eastcott), Gweneth May, Joan Marie, Richard Harold. Gen. duty nurse Shoal Lake (Man.) Dist. Hosp., 1946—. Mem. Shoal Lake Dist. Registered Nurses Assn. (pres.), Shoal Lake Dist. Hosp. Nursing Staff Assn. (treas.). Anglican (past pres. womens aux.). Home: Shoal Lake MB Canada Office: Shoal Lake Dist Hosp Shoal Lake MB Canada

WOOD, JANICE MARIE EBERT, psychologist; b. Hamburg, Ia., Sept. 20, 1928; d. Henry Chris and Clara Anna (Hirz) Ebert; B.S., U. Neb. at Omaha, 1956, M.A., 1960; m. Norman Wood, May 5, 1973. Psychologist Ia. Sch. Deaf, Council Bluffs, 1959—. Mem. Nat. Assn. Sch. Psychologists, Conv. Am. Instructors Deaf, Alexander Graham Bell Assn. Deaf. Lutheran. Home: 1707 Washington St Bellevue NE 68005 Office: Ia Sch Deaf Council Bluffs IA 51501

WOOD, JUNE POPHAM (MRS. GLEN NORRIS WOOD), educator; b. Houston, Nov. 27, 1920; d. Jesse Lee and Esther Bailey (Brown) Popham; student Sophie Newcomb Coll., 1936, Tex. Christian U., summer 1936; B.A., Baylor U., 1941; M.A., U. Houston, 1958; m. Glen Norris Wood, Aug. 15, 1942; children—Esther Wood (Mrs. Robert Carter Wilson), Glen Norris. Asst. prof. math. U. Houston, 1947-60; prof., chmn. dept. math. South Tex. Jr. Coll., Houston, 1960—. Mem. Com. on Undergrad. Program in Math., 1971—, mem. panel on two-year colls., 1970-73. Sect. chmn. Houston Symphony Soc., 1958; leader Girl Scouts, 1950-51; chmn. March of Dimes, City of Bunker Hill, 1960. Named Outstanding Tchr., Tex. Assn. Jr. Colls., 1970. Mem. Math. Assn. Am. (mem. com. on two yr. colls. 1972-75, mem. Tex. exec. council 1972—, 2d v.p. 1973—), Tex. Assn. Jr. Coll., South Tex. Jr. Coll. Faculty Assn. (pres. 1967), Alpha Chi. Episcopalian. Author: Introductory Algebra, 1969; A First Course in Algebra, 1971; (with David Outcalt) A Second Course in Algebra, 1974. Editorial bd. Two-Year Coll. Math. Jour., 1972—, book rev. editor, 1974—. Home: 10 Carolane Trail Houston TX 77024

WOOD, K. COLLET-ROSE, social worker; b. Chgo., Apr. 22, 1905; d. F. William and Sine Caroline (Hansen) Collet; B.S., U. Minn., 1928; certificate Sch. Social Work, 1932; postgrad. U. So. Cal., 1938, U. Utah, 1940-41, U. Denver, 1945-46, 68, U. N.M., 1955-57, Brandeis U., 1966; m. Edward W. Peterson, June 1929 (div. 1935); m. 2d, E. A. Rose, Mar. 29, 1941 (dec. May 1948); m. 3d, Charles H. Wood, Dec. 10, 1953 (dec. 1965). Family case worker Family Welfare Soc., Duluth, 1929-30; welfare worker St. Louis County Child Welfare Bur., Virginia, Minn., 1930-32; supr. pub. assistance West End br. St. Louis County Poor Commn., Duluth, 1932-34; county dir. social services N.M. Emergency Relief Adminstrn., Raton, 1935-36; field rep. N.M. Dept. Pub. Welfare, Las Cruces, 1936-41; cons. hearing and vision conservation N.M. Dept. Pub. Health, Santa Fe, 1948-53; program coordinator N.M. Program in Aging, 1959-61; supr. program operations N.M. Dept. Pub. Welfare, 1960-62; supr. div. community services, 1962-63; supr. N.M. Unit on Aging; chief program on aging

N.M. Health and Social Services Dept., 1966-69; dir. N.M. Commn. on Aging, 1969—; supr. social service Japanese Assembly Center, Salinas, Cal., 1942; researcher N.M. Reorgn. Commn., 1951-52; posistion classification analyst U.S. War Dept., Salt Lake City, 1943-45. State dir. Spl. Joint Dept. Pub. Welfare-Am. Assn. U. Women Project in Aging, 1963-65. Mem. Acad. Certified Social Workers (charter mem.), Nat. Assn. Social Workers, Am. Pub. Welfare Assn., Gerontol. Soc., Am. Assn. U. Women, Santa Fe Woman's Club and Library Assn., League Women Voters. Episcopalian. Author: (with Dorothy Cline) Recreation Adminstration in New Mexico, 1948, also other publs. Home: 118 Valley Dr Santa Fe NM 87501 Office: 408 Galisteo St Santa Fe NM 87501

WOOD, KATHLEEN OLIVER, pub. relations ofcl., radio personality; b. Mt Kisco, N.Y., Sept. 17, 1921; d. Eli Leslie and Melba Antoinette (Gislason) Oliver; student Swarthmore Coll., 1938-39, Antioch Coll., 1940-41, U. N.M., 1949, Cleve. Coll., 1960-61; m. John Thornton Wood, June 19, 1941 (div. Nov. 1947); children—Mark Thornton, Jonna (Mrs. Roger Grim), Karen (Mrs. E. Grant Weston); m. 2d, Clifford Emanuel Huff, June 27, 1948 (div. Oct. 1955). Tech. sec. Gray Iron Founders Soc., Cleve., 1955-57; tchr. Whiting Bus. Coll., Cleve., 1957-62; editorial asst. Chem. Rubber Co., Cleve., 1966; editor, writer Jefferson Ency., World Pub. Co., Cleve., 1967-68; disc jockey, announcer WCLV, Cleve., 1968-69; asst. pub. relations dir., writer, editor Highlights newsletter Univ. Circle Inc., Cleve., 1971—; talk-show hostess, announcer WERE, Cleve., 1972-73. Active Cleve. Soc. for Blind. Mem. Internat. Assn. Bus. Communicators, AFTRA, Esperanto League N.Am., Esperanto Assn. Ohio, Espermenso, Mensa, Cleve. Cultural Garden Fedn., Zonta. Clubs: Press (Cleve.), Women's Advt., Early Settlers. Author: Greenwood, 1967. Editor, pub. Frog in the Milk Pan (Marie Wallace), 1963; editor Graffiti mag., Mensa Cleve., 1967, Office Gal mag., Cleve., 1962-63, Smorgasbrain mag., 1968—. Home: 3590 Silsby Rd University Heights OH 44118 Office: 10831 Magnolia Dr Cleveland OH 44106

WOOD, LISSIE CHARLOTTE, librarian; b. San Diego, Apr. 16, 1920; d. Frank and Bertha Olive (Steck) Miller; B.A., San Jose (Cal.) State U., 1963, M.S., 1968; grad. student U. Cal. at Santa Cruz, U. Santa Clara; m. Robert Beard Wood, Dec. 21, 1941; 1 dau., Lissie Ruth. Tech. librarian MMD div. Sylvania Elec. Products Co., Mountain View, Cal., 1958-63; librarian Leigh High Sch., San Jose, 1963—; instr. San Jose City Coll., 1969-71, Foothill Coll., Los Altos, Cal., 1972-73; rep. Campbell Edn. Assos., exec. bd., 1974-75. Participant 1st Nat. Def. Edn. Act inst. ednl. media specialists San Jose State U., summer 1965. Mem. Cal., (Santa Clara County (pres. 1969-70, assns. sch. librarians, Cal Tchrs. Assn. Baptist. Home: 1439 Essex Way San Jose CA 95117

WOOD, LYNDA MCKEE (MRS. J. LEE WOOD), editor; b. Alpena, Mich., Oct. 2, 1945; d. Frank McKee and Luana Mame (Mellon) Chambers; A.A., Amarillo Jr. Coll., 1965; B.A., Am. U., 1967; m. J. Lee Wood, Aug. 9, 1968. Editorial asst. Nat. Newspaper Assn., Washington, 1967-68; editorial asst. Signal mag., Washington, 1968-69; editor Plumbing, Heating and Cooling Reports, Washington, 1969; editor, co-pub. Skaneateles Press, Marcellus Observer, Skaneateles, N.Y., 1969—. Mem. Women in Communications, Soc. Bus. Women. Club: Garden (Skaneateles). Home: Sheldon Rd Skaneateles NY 13152 Office: 56 E Genesee St Skaneateles NY 13152

WOOD, MARTHA CROSIER, public relations cons.; b. Emporia, Kan., Dec. 29, 1937; d. Clayton Madison and N. Ferne (Crooks) Crosier; B.S. in Journalism, U. Kan., 1959, postgrad., 1959; m. James Campbell Wood, Jr., Aug. 19, 1961; children—Jamie Lizabeth, Mark Campbell. Mem. staff Topeka Daily Capitol, 1960; feature editor Olathe (Kan.) Daily News, 1960-62; free-lance writer, 1962-71; dir. pub. relations, spl. asst. to hosp. dir. Middlesex County Hosp., Waltham, Mass., 1970-73; free-lance writer, pub. relations cons., Lexington, Mass., 1973—. Lectr. Middlesex Community Coll., 1973—, Suffolk U., 1974; staff mem. writers confs. and clinics, 1968—. Mem. Lexington Cable TV Adv. Com., 1973—, Lexington Com. on Aging, 1972—. Mem. Lexington Town Meeting, 1973—. Bd. dirs. Art Work 200, Inc. Recipient 1st place, catalogue div. Eastern continental region Soc. Tech. Communication, 1973; Feature Writing award Kan. Press Assn., 1961, 62. Mem. Women in Communications (pres. Boston 1971-73, profl. adviser Boston U. 1973-74, bd. dirs. Washington chpt. 1965-66), Publicity Club, League Women Voters (v.p. Lexington 1971-73, bd. dirs. 1966-71), Friends of Recreation, Citizens for Lexington Conservation, Lexington Hist. Soc., Workshop '75, Delta Gamma (No. Va. Panhellenic rep. 1962-65). Lutheran (local pres. ch. women 1969-71). Author: Rehabilitation and Chronic Hospitals in Massachusetts, 1973. Editor: Look at Lexington Pub. Schs., 1970. Home: 51 Gleason Rd Lexington MA 02173

WOOD, MARY ELIZABETH TEMPLE (MRS. RICHARD K. WOOD), physician; b. Vineland, N.J., May 1, 1939; d. Richard Underhill and Edna (Wells) Temple; B.A., Earlham Coll., 1961; M.D., U. Wis., 1967; m. Richard Kilbon Wood, June 3, 1962; children—Barbara Ann, Deborah Elizabeth, Lisa. Intern Madison (Wis.) Gen. Hosp., 1968; resident U. Wis. Hosp., Madison, 1969; physician student health service U. Wis., Madison, 1968-69; practice gen. medicine, Gettysburg, Pa., 1969—; asst. dir. health service Gettysburg Coll., 1971—; mem. staff Annie Warner Hosp., Gettysburg, chief medicine, 1971—; physician Adams County Sheltered Workshop, 1969—, Adams County Day Care Center, 1970—, Adams County Family Planning Agy., 1972—. Trustee Adams County units A.R.C., Am. Cancer Soc. Mem. Am. Acad. Family Practice (asso.), A.M.A., Am. Trauma Soc. (founding mem.). Home: Route 1 Orrtanna PA 17353 Office: 571 W Middle St Gettysburg PA 17235

WOOD, MARY HAWES, journalist; b. New Orleans, Jan. 19, 1914; d. Robert E. Lee and Ida May (Thompson) Hawes; student Millersburg Female Coll.; m. Charles P. Wood, Jr., Jan. 31, 1934 (div. 1950); 1 dau., Sally (Mrs. Alexander Thomson III). Writer, publicist WLW, 1930s and 1940s; columnist Cin. Post, 1943—. Mem. Planned Parenthood, 1945—. Episcopalian. Author: Just Lucky I Guess, 1967. Home: 416 Riverside Dr Covington KY 41011 Office: Cin Post 800 Broadway Cincinnati OH 45202

WOOD, MARYLAIRD (LARRY) (MRS. BYRON WOOD), writer; b. Sandpoint, Ida.; d. Edward Hayes and Alice (McNeel) Small; B.A. magna cum laude, U. Wash., Seattle, 1938, M.A. with highest honors, 1940; postgrad. Stanford, 1941-42; postgrad. U. Cal. Berkeley, 1943-44, Certificate of Photography, 1971; postgrad. in journalism U. Wis., 1971-72, U. Ga., 1972-73; m. W. Byron Wood, Jan. 30, 1942; children—Mary, Marcia, Barry. By-line columnist Oakland (Cal.) Tribune, San Francisco Chronicle, 1946—; spl. corr. Western region Christian Sci. Monitor and CSM Syndicate, 1973—; free lance writer for various nat. mags. including Parents', Sports Illustrated, Am. Home, 1946—; dir. pub. relations No. Cal. Assn. Phi Beta Kappa, 1969—; vis. prof. journalism San Diego State U., 1974—. Pub. relations dir. YWCA, YM-YW U.S.O., Seattle, 1942-46, YWCA, Oakland, Cal., 1946-56, Children's Home Soc. Cal., 1946-56, Children's Med. Center No. Cal., 1946-70, Eastbay Regional Park Dist., 1946-58, Cal. Spring Garden Show, 1946-58, Girl Scouts U.S.A., Oakland, 1948-56; speaker for ednl. insts., profl. groups, 1946—; sec. Jr. Center of Arts, Oakland, 1952—; vol. pub. relations Am. Cancer Soc., YMCA, Oakland, 1946-52; pub. relations writer A.R.C., 1946-56, cons. Oakland Park Dept. Bd. dirs. Camp Fire Girls, Oakland, Joaquin Miller P.T.A., Oakland. Mem. Pub. Relations Soc. Am., Nat. Sch. Pub. Relations Assn., Environmental Cons. N.Am., Internat. Environmental Cons., Internat. Oceanographic Soc., Am. Assn. Edn. in Journalism (nat. mag. com. 1969—), U. Wash. Ocean Scis. Alumni Assn. (charter), Eastbay Women's Press Club, Cal. Writers' Club, San Francisco Press Club, Phi Beta Kappa (pub. relations dir. No. Cal. 1969—), Phi Beta Kappa Alumni, Mortar Bd., Women in Communication (Woman of Year, Eastbay 1952, regional pres. 1970-71), Chi Omega, Pi Lambda Theta, Sigma Delta Chi. Address: 6161 Castle Dr Oakland CA 94611

WOOD, MARYLEA HENDERSON (MRS. RICHARD GLEE WOOD), educator; b. Coleman, Tex., May 4, 1929; d. Clyde Michael and Audrey (Lane) Henderson; B.A., Howard Payne Coll., 1950; M.R.E., Southwestern Sem., 1952; Ed.D. (fellow), Tex. Tech. U., 1969; m. Richard Glee Wood, Dec. 18, 1954; children—Margaret Lane, Brenda, Donald, Kay. Tchr., Lubbock (Tex.) High Sch., 1963-65, Levelland (Tex.) High Sch., 1965-66; faculty South Plains Coll., Levelland, 1966-67, Campbellsville (Ky.) Coll., 1967-69, Sul Ross State U., Alpine, Tex., 1969-71; faculty Howard Payne Coll., Brownwood, Tex., 1971-73, asst. prof. sociology, 1971-73; asso. prof. edn. and psychology Grand Canyon Coll., Phoenix, 1973—. State youth dir. Bapt. Conv. Ill., 1952-55. Bd. dirs. Permiam Basin council Girl Scouts U.S.A., 1970-71. Recipient Tchr. of Yr. award Levelland High Sch., 1965, Citizen award Pilot Club, Alpine, 1970. Mem. Am. Assn. U. Women, Nat. Educators Fellowship (pres. Phoenix chpt.), Delta Kappa Gamma, Kappa Delta Pi. Author: Persons, Not Things, 1972. Home: 5052 N 35th Av Phoenix AZ 85017

WOOD, NANCY E(LIZABETH), educator; b. Martins Ferry, O.; d. Donald Sterret and Orne (Erwin) Wood; B.S., Ohio U., 1943, M.A., 1947; Ph.D., Northwestern U., 1952. Tchr., St. Clairsville High Sch., 1943-45, Ohio U., 1946-47, Bethany Col., 1947-48, Northwestern U., 1948-52; coordinator Clin. Services, also Lang Found., Cleve. Hearing & Speech Center, 1952, dir. lang. disorders sect., 1959-60; asso. prof. Western Res. U., 1952-60; specialist speech and hearing disorders U.S. Office of Edn., Washington, 1960-62; asst. chief research Neurol. and Sensory Disease Service Program, div. Chronic Diseases, USPHS, Washington, 1963-64; dir. research John Tracy Clinic, Los Angeles, 1964-65; prof. lang. pathology and otolaryngology U. So. Cal., Los Angeles, 1966-72, chmn. grad. program communicative disorders, 1972—. Fellow Internat. Council Women Psychologists, Am. Psychol. Assn., Soc. Research in Child Devel., Am. Speech and Hearing Assn. (mem. exec. com.); mem. Council Exceptional Children and Youth, Delta Kappa Gamma. Author: Language Disorders in Children; Delayed Speech and Language Development; Verbal Learning; also articles profl. jours. Office: U So Cal 734 W Adams Blvd Los Angeles CA 90007

WOOD, NANCY KATHRYN, author; b. Trenton, N.J., June 20, 1936; d. Harold William and Eleanor (Green) Clopp; student Bucknell U., 1955-56; m. Myron Wood, Mar. 1, 1961 (div. Oct., 1969); children—Karin, Christopher, Kathryn, India. Author: Little Wrangler, 1966; Colorado: Big Mountain County, 1968; The Last Five Dollar Baby, 1972; Hollering Sun, 1972; Clearcut: The Deforestation of America, 1972; In This Proud Land, 1973; Many Winters, 1974. Home and office: 825 Paseo St Colorado Springs CO 80907

WOOD, NANCY WINTRINGER, orgn. exec.; b. Montclair, N.J., June 1, 1941; d. John Wintringer and Letha (Morris) Wood; B.A. cum laude, Sweet Briar Coll., 1963; M.R.E., Princeton Theol. Sem., 1967. Women and girls dir., Buffalo YMCA, 1963-65; dir. religious edn. Wesley Ch. and Found., Urbana, Ill., 1967-69; program asso. U. Christian Movement, Cleve., 1969—. Mem. Phi Beta Kappa. Home: 1725 Compton Rd Cleveland OH 44118 Office: 11205 Euclid Av Cleveland OH 44106

WOOD, NORMA (WODE) (MRS. ROBERT D. WOOD), librarian; b. Borger, Tex., May 26, 1927; d. Herman Harvey and Charlotte (Jones) Wode; B.A. in L.S., U. Okla., 1948, B.A. in German, 1951; postgrad. U. Ill., summers 1967, 68, 70; m. Robert Dillon Wood, Mar. 26, 1949. Asst. librarian Doane Coll., Crete, Neb., 1948-50; night supr. loan desk U. Okla. Library, 1950-51; br. librarian Assn. Portland, (Ore.), 1951-52, cataloger, 1952-53; base librarian Vance AFB, Okla., 1953-54; head tech. processes Miss. Library Commn., Jackson, 1955-57; head tech. services dept. East Chgo. Pub. Library, (Ind.), 1957—. Guest lectr. Purdue U., Calumet Campus, 1968, U. Ind., Gary, 1969, 70, 71. Adv. com. Coop. Bibliog. Center for Ind. Libraries, 1973—. Mem. A.L.A. (life), Ind. Library Assn. (area rep. exec. com. tech. services roundtable 1973-74). Home: 5504 Wegg St East Chicago IN 46312 Office: 2401 E Columbus Dr East Chicago IN 46312

WOOD, PRISCILLA RINGSMUTH (MRS. JEFFERSON KEMP WOOD), realtor, civic worker; b. Mansfield, Ark., July 28, 1920; d. Francis Karel and Emelia (Cajak) Ringsmuth; grad. high sch.; m. Jefferson Kemp Wood, Dec. 3, 1944; 1 son, William James II. With Charlotte (N.C.) Observor, 1943-44; asso. W.C. McGee, Real Estate, Ft. Myers Beach, Fla., 1951-53, Scotti Realty, 1964-67, Will Hayes, Realtor, Ft. Myers Beach, 1967—; corporate sec. Growing Enterprises, Inc. Mem. Nat. Assn. Real Estate Bds., 1965—; sec. Ft. Myers Beach Bd. Realtors, 1967-68, com. chmn. assos. div., 1968, chmn. assos. div., 1971. Mem. Am. Legion Aux., 1951—, 1st v.p., chmn. community service, 1960—, pres., 1962-63, dist. treas., 1971, dist. chmn. fgn. affairs, 1972, dist. Poppy Day chmn., state vice chmn. community services, 1963-64, dist. fgn. affairs chmn., 1972; mem. Beach Improvement Assn., 1949—, 2d v.p., 1967—, hostess, recreation, taxation chmn., 1968-69; active mem. Community Orgns. Project, 1967—, sec., 1970-71, bd. dirs., 1971-72; mem. Beach Players, 1969—; dir., chmn. Ft. Myers Womans Bowling Assn., 1964—; v.p. Beach Rolling Waves Bowling League, 1960, team capt., 1960—, pres., 1961; bd. dirs., membership chmn. Edison Players, 1971-72; active mem. Lee Meml. Hosp. Aux. Bd. dirs. Lee County Tb and Health Assn. Recipient citations from dist., state and nat. levels for community service work Am. Legion Aux., Spl. award for community service state level, 1968, Woman of Year award, 1969; asso. of year award Fort Myers Beach Bd. Realtors, 1971. Home: PO Box 3082 Fort Myers Beach FL 33931 Office: 6051 Estero Blvd Fort Myers Beach FL 33931

WOOD, SARAH ANN, chem. co. exec.; b. Harvey, Ill., Apr. 8, 1936; d. Edgar DeBolt and Alice LaVerne (Harvey) McCollum; A.B. in Journalism, Ind. U., 1958; m. Kenneth Earl Wood, July 11, 1964. Prodn. mgr. Hosp. Topics mag., 1958-60; copywriter Montgomery Ward & Co., 1960-61; mng. editor Package Engring. mag., 1961-63; pub. relations asst. Velsicol Chem. Corp., 1965-69, pub. relations mgr., 1969—. Mem. Publicity Club Chgo. Home: Palatine IL Office: 341 E Ohio St Chicago IL 60611

WOOD, SARALUE, educator; b. Wehadkee, Ala., June 26, 1934; d. Tom Fuller and Sarah Bonceil (Huey) Wood; A.B. cum laude, Mercer U., 1955; M.S., U. Fla., 1959. Instr. math. Mercer U., Macon, Ga., 1956-57; teaching asst. physics U. Fla., Gainesville, 1955-56, 57-59; asst. prof. physics, Austin Peay State U., Clarksville, Tenn., 1959-66, asso. prof. physics, 1966—, acting chmn. dept., 1970-72, chmn. dept. physics, 1972—. Dir. Physics: The Program for Tchrs., 1970—. Research participant Oak Ridge Nat. Lab., summers, 1961, 62, U. Fla., summers, 1964, 65; research asso. U. Fla., summers, 1966, 67, 68. NSF research grantee, 1964, 67, Personal contract with Oak Ridge Asso. Univs., 1964, 67, 69, 71—. Fellow Tenn. Acad. Sci., A.A.A.S.; mem. Am. Assn. Physics Tchrs., Am. Phys. Soc., Tenn., Middle Tenn. edn. assns., C. of C., Bus. and Profl. Women's Club, Sigma Xi (asso.), Sigma Pi Sigma. Home: 112 8th St Clarksville TN 37040

WOOD, SUE ANN, journalist; b. Jefferson City, Mo., Nov. 5, 1930; d. William Benson and Glee (Cardwell) Wood; B.J., U. Mo., 1952; postgrad. (Rotary Internat. Found. fellow) U. Edinburgh, Scotland, 1952-53. Reporter, St. Petersburg (Fla.) Times, 1954-55; gen. assignment reporter, feature writer St. Louis Globe-Democrat, 1955—. Recipient Faculty-Alumni award U. Mo. Alumni, 1970. Mem. Press Club Met. St. Louis (sec., dir. 1961-63), U. Mo. Alumni Assn. (dir. 1971-74), Theta Sigma Phi (pres. 1960), Sigma Delta Chi (pres. 1973-74), Kappa Kappa Gamma. Republican. Methodist. Home: 400 Mansion House St Louis MO 63102 Office: 12th St at Delmar St Louis MO 63101

WOODALL, AVIE STELLA JAMES, author, historian; b. Hillsboro, Tex., Jan. 15, 1899; d. Leslie Christopher and Orena Belle (Malone) James; Corr. student Famous Writer's Sch., 1940-42, U. Tex., 1943-44; m. Warren Christopher Proctor, Jan. 20, 1920 (dec. Feb. 1923), children—Ruth (Mrs. Raymond P. James), Anna (Mrs. Jean D. Frost); m. 2d, Howard Woodall, Aug. 5, 1934 (dec. Apr. 1943); 1 dau., Clara Elizabeth (Mrs. Ben Urban) Sec. VA, Dallas, 1923-34; historian, Writer San Marcos Del Rio, and Laredo AFB, Tex., 1943-59; writer textbooks, San Antonio, 1959; free-lance writer and poet published in Christman Ideals, Poet, The Pen Woman, West Tex. Hist. Year Book, U. D.C. mag., Tex. Methodist, Travis Park News, Air Force Times, others. Dir. Beautify San Antonio Assn. 1968—, Recipient Council of Pres. award, Council Pres., 1971, 72, 73, award Tex. Fedn. Women's Clubs, 1971-72; named alternate poet laureate Tex., 1973. Mem. Poetry Soc. San Antonio (pres. 1968-74), Stella Woodall Poetry Soc. (chmn.), Armed Forces Writer's League (past pres.), Am. Poetry League (past nat. v.p.), Internat. Platform Assn., (mem. hospitality com.), Nat. League Am. Pen Women (pres. San Antonio br.), Nat. Assn. Ret. Fed. Employees (program chmn.) Nat. Soc. Arts and Letters (past 1st v.p.). Methodist. Club: Woman's (chmn. strategy bd. round table) (San Antonio). Author: Women of the Bible; Lectures of St. John; (poetry) Most Asked for Poems, 1969; Inspirational Poems, 1970; Golden Treasures, 1972; Adventures in Friendship, 1973. Editor, pub. San Antonio Poetry Mag. 1971—. Home: 3915 SW Military Dr San Antonio TX 78211

WOODARD, ELIZABETH DOROTHY (MRS. RICHARD CHARLES WOODARD), physician; b. Waverly, N.Y., Nov. 11, 1943; d. Charles Chauncey and Madeline Mary (Wells) Vanderpool; A.B., Syracuse U., 1964; M.D. (Grace Legendre fellow), State U. N.Y. at Syracuse, 1967; M.P.H. (USPHS trainee), U. Mich., 1969; m. Richard Charles Woodard, Sept. 10, 1965; 1 dau., Lisa Beth. Intern pediatrics U. Hosp., U. Mich. Med. Center, Ann Arbor, 1967-68; resident preventive medicine and pub. health N.Y. State Health Dept., Albany, 1969-71; asst. health officer Butte County Health Dept., Oroville, Cal., 1971-73; dep. dir. Monroe County Health Dept., Rochester, N.Y., 1973—. Mem. Am. Pub. Health Assn., Phi Beta Kappa, Alpha Omega Alpha, Delta Omega. Home: 528 Wintergreen Way Rochester NY 14618 Office: Monroe County Health Dept 111 Westfall Rd Rochester NY 14620

WOODARD, HELEN BOTKA, librarian; b. Scranton, Pa., July 28, 1912; d. Joseph and Julia (Ban) Botka; B.A., Hillsdale Coll., 1935; M.L.S., Rutgers State U., 1958; m. Howard Arthur Woodard, Aug. 1, 1940. Lab. technician Chance Vought div. United Aircraft Corp., Startford, Conn., 1942-48; with Newark Free Pub. Library, 1955—, sr. librarian, 1963-64, prin. and br. librarian librarian Roseville br., 1965—. Mem. adv. bd. YWCA, Roseville, 1966—. Mem. Weequahic Adult Sch. Bd., 1964-66. Mem. Am., N.J. library assns., Hillsdale Coll. Alumni Assn., Alumni Assn. Grad. Sch. Library Service Rutgers, N.Y. Parapsychology Forum. Baptist (primary Sunday sch. supt. 1965-68). Home: 94 Cedar Lake W Denville NJ 07834 Office: Roseville Br Library 99 5th St Newark NJ 07107

WOODBRIDGE, GENEVIEVE BLANCHE ROHRABACHER (MRS. HOWARD J. WOODBRIDGE), former mus. and planetarium exec.; b. Janesville, Ia.; d. Myron A. and Blanche L. (Newell) Rohrabacher; B.S. in Edn., U. Minn., 1929; m. Howard J. Woodbridge, Sept. 5, 1931 (dec. Jan. 1954). Tchr. jr. high sch., Elk River, Minn., 1930-31; dir. Mus. History and Sci. and Planetarium, Waterloo, Ia., 1955-73. Adv. bd. Renssalaer Russell House Restoration, 1964-65, 73—; sec. Black Hawk County (Ia.) Am. Bicentennial Commn., 1972-73; mem. U.I. Old Capitol Restoration Com. of Black Hawk County, 1973—; Mem. Am. Assn. U. Women, Am. Assn. Museums, Midwest Mus. Conf., Waterloo Arts Council (charter, sec.-treas. 1959-65), Cedar Valley Hist. Soc. (charter), D.A.R., Internat. Council Museums, Northeast Ia. (charter, historian 1971-73) geneal. socs., Waterloo C. of C. (awards com. 1972-73). Club: Altrusa (charter, dir. 1958-61, 69-72). Home: 1509 W 3d St Waterloo IA 50701

WOODBURY, DOROTHY JO FRENCH (MRS. JOHN EDWARD WOODBURY, JR.), judge; b. Salt Lake City; d. Frank Chauncey and Theo C. (Plambeck) French; student U. Colo., 1933-37; LL.B., Westminster Law Sch., Denver, 1943; LL.B., U. Denver, 1957, LL.D., 1971; m. John Edward Woodbury, Jr., Aug. 26, 1945; 1 son, John Edward III. Sec. to registrar Westminster Law Sch., 1941-43; admitted to Colo. bar, 1943; practiced in Denver, 1944-46, Lake City, 1947-67; asso. mem. firm Gabriel, Mills & Mills, 1944-46; pvt. practice, 1947-67; judge Municipal Corp. Ct., Andrews, Tex., 1967—; exhibited paintings art show Andrews, 1962; represented in permanent collections at Houston Humble Club Art League. Pres. Women of St. Matthias Episcopal Ch., 1961-63, treas., 1969; del. State Conv. Home Demonstration Orgn., Houston, 1957. Colo. state chmn. Nat. Womans Party, 1944-45; pres. Republican Women Andrews County, 1963-64. Mem. Bus. and Profl. Women Andrews (sec.), Andrews Art Guild (parliamentarian). Mem. Order Eastern Star. Home: 707 NW 10th St Andrews TX 79714 Office: City Hall NE First at Logsdon Andrews TX 79714

WOODDELL, SHIRLEY ELIZABETH, advt. exec.; b. Warwick, R.I., Mar. 2, 1924; d. Henry F. and Florence LaVerne (Winsor) Wooddell; B.S. in Art Edn., R.I. Sch. Design, 1945; extension student Brown U., 1946, R.I. Coll. Art tchr., Warwick, 1946-47, Providence, 1956-58; owner advt. agy. S.E. Wooddell Advt., Providence, 1953-56; copy chief Halladay Advt., East Providence, 1964—; owner Wooddell Typesetting Service, Warwick, 1972—. Mem. bus. and finance commn. Am. Bapt. Chs. R.I., 1971—. Bd. dirs. Narragansett council Camp Fire Girls, recipient Sebago award, 1973. Home: 104 Benedict Rd Warwick RI 02888 Office: 200 Amaral St East Providence RI 02914

WOODHAM, JEAN, sculptor; b. Midland Ala., Aug. 16, 1925; d. Marcus Morton and Alma (Clements) Woodham; B.A., Ala. Poly. Inst., 1946; student Sculpture Center, N.Y.C., 1946-49; (Kate Neal Kinley Meml. fellow), U. Ill., 1950; m. James Lee Caraway, Nov. 18, 1949 (div. 1968); children—Susan Melissa, Elizabeth Leigh. Exhibited one-man shows Auburn U., 1950, U. Ill., 1952, Silvermine Guild Of Artists, New Canaan, Conn., 1955, Davison Art Center Wesleyan U., Middletown, Conn., 1956, Stuttman Gallery, N.Y.C., 1959, Rive Gauche Gallery, Darien, Conn., 1962, 1966, New Canaan (Conn.) Library, 1963, Wilton (Conn.) Library, 1963, Mattatuck Mus., 1968, Fairfield U., 1970; exhibited group shows museums, galleries U.S., Argentina, Belgium, Brazil, Chile, Eng., Mexico; exhibited Gen. Foods, N.Y. World's Fair, 1964-65; represented in permanent collections Massillon (O.) Mus., Norfolk (Va.) Mus. Arts, Westport (Conn.) Permanent Collection; instr. sculpture Stamford (Conn.) Mus.; vis. asst. prof. art Auburn (Ala.) U., 1970-71, asso. prof. art, 1974—; participant Bd. Edn. Exhbns. N.Y.C. Bd. dirs. Rowayton Art Center. Recipient Naomi Lorne Meml. prize, Conn. Acad. Prize for Sculpture, Michael J. Salomone prize. Mem. Nat. Assn. Women Artists (chmn. sculpture 1965-66, medal of honor for sculpture 1974), Sculptors Guild (treas. 1960-65, exec. bd. N.Y.C. 1966—, sec. 1972-74), Audubon Artists (juror 1964), Artists Equity, Archtl. League N.Y. Archtl. commns. include welded bronze Menorah, Jewish Community Center, Harrison, N.Y.; welded bronze sculpture Ala. State Coll., Montgomery, Menorah for Temple Israel, Westport, Conn., 1966-68; 3 welded bronze fountain sculptures Flintkote Corporate Hdqrs. bldg., White Plains, N.Y., 3 welded bronze fountain sculptures Gen. Electric Credit Corp., Stamford; welded bronze fountain sculpture Gen. Telephone & Electronics Hdqrs. Bldg., Stamford; fountain sculpture Houston Center, Tex. Eastern Transmission. Home: 26 Pin Oak Lane Westport CT 06880

WOODHOUSE, MRS. CHASE GOING, economist; b. Victoria, B.C., Can.; d. Seymour and Harriet (Jackson) Going (parents Am. citizens); B.A., M.A., McGill U.; LL.D., Allegheny Coll., Alfred U., U. Hartford; 1 dau., Margaret (Mrs. John E. Becker). Formerly instr. to asso. prof. Smith Coll., sr. economist Bur. Home Econs., U.S. Dept. Agr.; personnel dir. Women's Coll., U. N.C., prof. econs. Conn. Coll.; elected sec. of State of Conn., 1940; mem. U.S. Congress, 2d dist. Conn., 1944-46, 48-50; asst. to dir. OPS, 1951-53. Planned Women's div. Office Mil. Govt. U.S. (Germany), 1947. Del. White House Conf. on Children and Youth, 1960; exec. com. Conn. Mental Health Assn., 1959-63, 1st v.p., 1963-65; mem. adv. council Conn. Bd. Mental Health, 1965-67; bd. dirs. Nat. Mental Health Assn., 1964-66; chmn. legislative com. State Mental Health Planning Project, 1963-65; mem. New Eng. Govs. Research Com., 1962-69; adv. council Conn. Dept. Community Affairs, 1967-72, Comprehensive Health Plan, 1968-72, Gov.'s Com. Libraries, Gov.'s Com. Br. of Univ., 1962; chmn. Gov.'s Com. on Status of Women, 1967; mem. State Adv. Com. Unemployment Compensation, 1962-65; exec. com. Council Services to Internat. Visitors, Washington, 1961-66; pres., 1965-66; mem. Gov.'s Clean Water Task Force, 1965-66, State Library Research Adv. Com., 1965-67; exec. com. Assn. Conn. Library Bds., 1965-67; mem. Sprague Town Zoning and Planning Commn., 1960-65, chmn. 1965-71; chmn. Sprague Community-Devel. Action Plan, 1968—; bd. dirs. S.E. Conn. Regional Planning Agy., 1963-73; mem. Conn. Com. on Housing in Optimum Environment, 1970-71, Gov.'s Com. on Environmental Policy, 1970-71, Conn. Permanent Commn. on Status Women, 1973—. Dir. women's div. Democratic Nat. Com., 1947; mem. Conn. Constl. Conv., 1965. Mem. exec. com. Conn.-Brazil Partners for Progress 1965—. Dir. Auerbach Service Bur. for Conn. Orgn., Beatrice Fox Auerbach Found., 1954—; mem. founders com. U. of Hartford. Recipient Distinguished Pub. Service award Conn. Bar Assn., 1973. Mem. bd. State Fedn. Zoning and Planning Agys. (1963-65), Pi Lambda Theta, Omicron Nu, Delta Kappa Gamma. Home: Falcon Farm RD 1 Box 413 Baltic CT 06330 Office: 956 Main St Hartford CT 06115

WOODLAND, DOROTHY JANE, ret. educator, univ. dean; b. Warren, O., Sept. 20, 1908; d. William Charles and Agnes (Blankenhorn) Woodland; B.S., Coll. Wooster, 1929; M.Sc., Ohio State U., 1930, Ph.D., 1932. Instr. Wellesley Coll., 1932-36, asst. prof. chemistry, 1936-38; asso. prof. Western Coll. Women, Oxford, O., 1938-44; prof. chemistry John Brown U., Siloam Springs, Ark., 1944-74, dean acad. faculty, 1947-48, asst. dean acad. affairs, 1948-74, prof. emeritus, 1974—. Mem. Am. Chem. Soc., Phi Beta Kappa, Sigma Xi, Theta Chi Delta. Presbyn. Home: 124 N Dogwood Siloam Springs AR 72761

WOODMAN, CORRINE NORMA, art center adminstr.; b. Portland, Ore., Dec. 5, 1926; d. Ernest Raymond and Lois Emma (Rawles) Sundberg; student art Ore. State U., 1960-61; m. M. Frank Woodman, Mar. 7, 1970; children by previous marriage—Nioma Marie (Mrs. Thomas Wood), Marlea Anne (Mrs. Merickel). Profl. vocalist, music librarian, comml. writer; dir. Corvallis (Ore.) Arts Center, 1967—, also life mem. Active Community Theatre, Univ. Theatre; pres. Good Samaritan Hosp. Aux. Home: 3207 NW Polk St Corvallis OR 97330 Office: 700 SW Madison St Corvallis OR 97330

WOODMAN, KATHLEEN IRENE, pub. relations dir.; b. Oak Park, Ill., Mar. 20, 1942; d. John A. and Ethel D. (Ballent) Woodman; B.S. in Journalism, No. Ill. U., 1964. Asst. mental health educator pub. relations Elgin (Ill.) State Hosp., 1964-68; client rep. FVT Communications Co., Elgin, 1968; dir. pub. relations Sch. Dist. U46, Elgin, 1968—. Speaker in field. Mem. Elgin Area C. of C. (sec. women's council), Ednl. Press Assn. Am. (coordinator protem), Nat. Sch. Pub. Relations Assn. (past sec., bd. dirs. Ill. chpt.). Editor: Sch. News Quar., 1968—. Home: 869 Carriage Way Elgin IL 60120 Office: Sch Dist U46 4 S Gifford St Elgin IL 60120

WOODRING, VIRGINIA JANE MCKEE (MRS. WILEY FLETCHER WOODRING), editor; b. Darrow, Okla., Sept. 13, 1914; d. William Clinton and Dora Gertrude (Rothwell) McKee; B.S., S.W. Mo. State U., 1945; M.A., Northwestern U., 1949; postgrad. U. Mo., 1949, 70-71, U. Minn., 1967; m. Wiley Fletcher Woodring, Apr. 18, 1936. Reporter, Mountain View Standard, 1930-32; elementary tchr. Howell County (Mo.), Texas County (Mo.) Schs., 1933-42; art cons. Cabool Consol. Schs., 1942-45; journalism tchr. Springfield (Mo.) Pub. Schs., 1945-56, journalism coordinator, 1956-73; editor Communication: Journalism Edn. Today, Springfield, Mo., 1967—. Journalism speaker, cons. Ind. U., 1963, U. Ia., 1972, U. Mo., 1967, 71, 73; cons. Journalism in Mass Media, Ginn & Co., 1970—. Mem. Goals of Springfield Com., 1971. Named Journalism Tchr. of Year, Nat. Newspaper Fund, 1969; recipient Medal of Merit Journalism Edn. Assn., 1967, Carl Towley award, 1972; Pioneer Journalism award Nat. Scholastic Press Assn., 1969; award Freedom Found., 1968; Golden Mike award Am. Legion Aux., 1967, Fellowship, Newspaper Fund, 1967. Mem. Journalism Edn. Assn. (mem. exec. bd. 1967—), Assn. Edn. Journalism (mem. financial structure com. 1972, TV commn. 1974), Mo. State Tchrs. Assn., Mo., Nat. press women, Springfield Press Club, Delta Kappa Gamma (pres. Epsilon chpt.). Republican. Episcopalian. Club: Soroptimist (Springfield). Author tchrs. manuals. Editor: Communication: Journalism Education Today. Home: 2642 S Edgewater Dr Springfield MO 65804 Office: 940 N Jefferson St Springfield MO 65802

WOODROW, JANE ZARTMAN (MRS. JOHN A. WOODROW), psychologist, health service adminstr.; b. Hartville, O., June 8, 1938; d. Edwin Jay and Mary Evelyn (Kile) Zartman; A.B., Heidelberg Coll., 1960; M.S., Ohio U., 1966, Ph.D., 1973; m. John A. Woodrow, Feb. 8, 1962. Staff psychologist Athens (O.) Mental Health Center, 1966-69; asst. dir. psychology, 1970-71; psychology dir. Community Mental Health Clinics, Gallipolis, O., 1972—. Cons., Western Dist. Guidance Center, Parkersburg, W.Va., 1972—. Mem. Athens Community Choir, 1972—. Mem. Am., Midwestern, Ohio, Southeastern Ohio psychol. assns., League Women Voters, Textile Arts Guild. Home: 204 West State Athens OH 45701 Office: Community Mental Health Clinic Spring Valley Plaza Gallipolis OH

WOODRUFF, FRIEDA WAGONER (MRS. D. STRATTON WOODRUFF, JR.), physician; b. Bryn Mawr, Pa., Apr. 6, 1930; d. George W. and Marjorie (Jefferies) Wagoner; grad. Baldwin Sch., 1947; A.B. in History cum laude, Bryn Mawr Coll., 1951; M.D., U. Pa., 1955; m. D. Stratton Woodruff, Jr., June 16, 1955; children—David S., George Wagoner. Intern Presbyn. Hosp., Phila., 1955-56; practice gen. medicine, Gladwyne, Pa., 1956—; physician Bryn Mawr Coll., 1957-68, dir. health service, 1969—; mem. staff Bryn Mawr Hosp. Mem. A.M.A., Pa., Montgomery County med. socs., Am. Acad. Family Physicians, Phila. Club Med. Women, Pa. Hort. Soc. Home: 121 Pennswood Rd Bryn Mawr PA 19010 Office: 949 Youngsford Rd Gladwyne PA 19035

WOODRUFF, JUDY CARLINE, TV news announcer; b. Tulsa, Nov. 20, 1946; d. William Henry and Anna Lee (Payne) Woodruff; student Meredith Coll., 1964-66; B.A., Duke U., 1968. Congl. intern U.S. Rep. Robert G. Stephens, summers 1966, 67; news sec. trainee, WQXI-TV, Atlanta, 1968-69, weekend weather girl, 1969; news reporter WAGA-TV, Atlanta, 1970—, noon news announcer, 1971—. Mem. Ga. Conservancy, 1969—; mem. Atlanta High Mus. Art, 1968—, steering com. Collectors, 1973—; exec. bd. Atlanta council Campfire Girls. Mem. Ga. Women's Polit. Caucus, 1972—. Recipient AP award, 1971. Mem. A.F.T.R.A., Nat. Acad. TV Arts and Scis. (gov., founding mem. Atlanta chpt.), C. of C., Alpha Delta Pi. Episcopalian. Home: 2243 Haven Ridge Dr NW Atlanta GA 30305 Office: 1551 Briarcliff Rd NE Atlanta GA 30318

WOODRUM, FRANCES LUCILLE, librarian; b. Springfield, Ill., Nov. 3, 1934; d. Earl Clifford and Lucille (Wiebking) W.; B.A., U. Ill., 1956, M.S. in L.S., 1957. Circulation asst. Lincoln Library, Springfield, 1957-58, asst. reference librarian, 1958-68, head circulation dept., 1968-70; dir. Jacksonville (Ill.) Pub. Library, 1970—. Mem. Am., Ill. library assns., Bus. and Profl. Women (pres.). Club: Altrusa of Jacksonville (v.p.). Home: 2 Alberta Lane Springfield IL 62704 Office: 201 W College St Jacksonville IL 62650

WOODS, BETTY LINDLEY, newspaper co. exec.; b. Wynne, Ark., Apr. 12, 1932; d. Jim and Effie Lea (Armstrong) Lindley; student Ark. State Coll., 1949-50, San Diego State Coll., 1951-52; m. William Franklin Woods, Apr. 3, 1952; children—Roxanne, Patti Lee, Billie Suzette. Bus. mgr., owner Herald Pub. Co., Hazen, Ark., 1953—. Recipient Sch. Bell award, 1972; Rice award, 1971; Centennial Service award, 1973. Mem. Alpha Gamma Delta. Methodist (youth coordinator and counselor, choir dir.). Home: PO Box 377 Hazen AR 72064

WOODS, DOROTHY LONGSTRETH, psychiatrist; b. Kansas City, Mo., July 23, 1928; d. Bevis and Mary (Shiras) Longstreth; B.S., U. Ariz., 1953; M.D., Duke U., 1957; postgrad. U. Okla., 1961-62; m. Alexander Hamilton Woods, Jan. 26, 1956 (div. Mar. 1965); children—Linda L., Andrea G. Neurology fellow Duke U. and VA Hosp., Durham, N.C., 1957-58; intern Med. Center, U. Okla., Oklahoma City, 1958-59, resident neurology, 1960-61; resident psychiatry Hawaii State Hosp., Kaneohe, 1964-65, Napa (Cal.) State Hosp., 1965-67; practice psychiatry, Napa, 1967-73, Seaside, Cal., 1973—; founder, mem. staff Our Family Inc., drug abuse program Napa State Hosp., 1968-73; cons. psychiatrist Oasis Center, Lafayette, Cal., 1973—. Mem. Internat. Transactional Analysis Assn., No. Cal., Am. pscyhiat. assns., Phi Beta Kappa, Phi Kappa Phi, Sigma Xi. Home: 1030 Pleasant Valley Rd Aptos CA 95003 Office: Monterey Bay Professional Bldg 668 Williams Seaside CA 93955

WOODS, SISTER FRANCES JEROME, educator; b. Guthrie, Okla., Jan. 4, 1913; d. Francis Michael and Catherine (Ryan) Woods; B.A., Our Lady of Lake Coll., 1940; M.A., Cath. U. Am., 1945, Ph.D., 1949. Joined Congregation of Divine Providence, 1931; tchr. elementary, secondary schs. Congregation of Divine Providence, Alexandria, La., Tulsa, Houston, San Antonio, 1932-44; faculty sociology Our Lady of Lake Coll., San Antonio, 1948-64, prof. sociology and social work, 1958-64, v.p. coll., 1964-67; prof. sociology Our Lady of the Lake Coll., San Antonio, 1970—, Piper prof., 1973; councilor Congregation of Divine Providence, Helotes, Tex., 1967-70. Cons. Kenwood Community Council, 1972-73, Outreach In-service Tng. Kerriville (Tex.) Dept. Mental Health and Mental Retardation, 1973. NIH Research grantee, 1962-65; Social Sci. Research Council research grantee, 1965. Mem. Am. Sociol. Assn., Assn. for Sociology of Religion (pres. 1961-62), Soc. for Sci. Study Religion, Nat. Council on Family Relations, Population Assn. Am., Am. Anthrop. Assn. Author: Cultural Values of American Ethnic Groups, 1956; The American Family System, 1959; Introductory Sociology, 1966; Marginality and Identity, 1972. Address: 411 SW 24th St San Antonio TX 78285

WOODS, GERALDINE PITTMAN, cons.; b. West Palm Beach, Fla.; d. Oscar and Susie (King) Pittman; student Talladega Coll., 1938-40; B.S. in Zoology, Howard U., 1942; M.A., Radcliffe Coll. and Harvard Biol. Lab., 1943, Ph.D. in Neuro-embryology, 1945; m. Dr. Robert I. Woods, Jan. 30, 1945; children—Jan, Jerri, Robert I. Instr. Howard U., Washington, 1945-46. Pres. Los Angeles chpt. Jack and Jill, 1954-56; pres. Aux. to Med., Dental and Pharm. Assn. of So. Cal., 1951-54, state pres., 1955; mem. Lulaby Guild Children's Home Soc.; past mem. local met. bd., chmn. pub. affairs com. YWCA; mem. nat. adv. council Gen. Med. Scis. Inst. NIH, 1964-68, cons., 1969—, mem. gen. research support adv. com., div. research resources, 1971—; mem. fgn. service officers selection bds. Dept. of State, 1967; nat. 1st v.p. Delta Sigma Theta, 1958-63, nat. pres., 1963-67, pres. Los Angeles Alumnae chpt., 1952-56; mem. League Women Voters, N.A.A.C.P. (life); men. nat. bd. Nat. Council Negro Women (life); mem. regional com. Girl Scouts U.S.A., 1969—; v.p. Community Relations Conf. So. Cal.; exec. com. Leadership Conf. Civil Rights; chmn. def. adv. com. Women in Services, 1968; mem. air pollution manpower devel. adv. com. Environmental Protection Agy., 1973—; trustee Howard U., Cal. Museum Found., Cal. Mus. Sci. and Industry. Named Woman of Yr., Zeta Phi Beta, 1954; Meritorious Achievement award Nat. Panhellenic Council, 1966; spl. awards presented by Iota Phi Lambda, Howard U. Alumni Assn., Nat. Assn. Colored Women, Pres. Johnson's Council on Youth Opportunity. Mem. Phi Beta Kappa. Conglist. Home: 12065 Rose Marie Lane Los Angeles CA 90049

WOODS, KATHRYN REID (MRS. BARRY MONTAGUE WOODS), curator; b. Hamilton, Ont., Can., Nov. 15, 1921; d. Arthur Victor and Sarah Elizabeth (Higgerson) Peacock; student McMaster U., Hamilton, 1941-42, York U., Toronto, 1973; m. Barry Montague Woods, Apr. 25, 1944; children—Donald, Barbara, Jayne (Mrs. Robert F. Andrews). Pres., Women's Com. Robert McLaughlin Gallery, Oshawa, Ont., Can., 1967-69, chmn. acquisition com., 1969-71, curator, 1970—, also cons. Mem. Canadian Mus. Assn. Author: A History of Painters Eleven, 1970, also catalogues Painters Eleven 1953-59, 1972, Franz Johnston, Frances-Anne Johnston, Paul Rodrik, 1972, Kazuo Nakamura, 1974. Home: 843 Glencairn St Oshawa ON L1J 5B3 Canada Office: Robert McLaughlin Gallery Civic Center Oshawa ON Canada

WOODS, LINNIE SKIPPER, med. record librarian; b. Bessemer, Ala., Dec. 4, 1927; d. Robert Lee and Annie Mae (Hood) Skipper; student U. Ala., 1955-57, U. Chgo., 1958; certificate as med. record librarian, Emory U., 1958; m. Clarence David Woods, Sept. 20, 1948; 1 dau., Angela Maria. Cons. librarian East End Meml. Hosp., Birmingham, 1955, chief librarian, 1962; coordinator patient services Center Devel. and Learning Disorders, U. Ala., Birmingham, 1969—; cons. Briarcliff Nursing Home, Alabaster, Ala., 1973-74, Shelby County Hosp., Alabaster, 1956-69. Recipient Humanitarian award East End Meml. Hosp., 1965. Mem. Ala. Assn. Med. Record Librarians, Am., Southeastern assns. record librarians, Birmingham Regional Assn. Librarians, Am. Assn. Mental Deficiency, Bus. and Profl. Women's Club. Baptist. Club: Pioneer Diners (Birmingham). Author: (coding manual) Conditions of Mentally Retarded, 1970; also articles. Home: 2141 Brookview Dr Birmingham AL 35226 Office: Center Devel and Learning Disorders 1720 7th Av S Birmingham AL 35233

WOODS, LUCY BROOKE (MRS. RICHARD LANE FRAUTSCHI), ednl. adminstr.; b. Richmond, Va., July 26, 1930; d. Edgar Colin Cooper and Mary Garnett (Stark) Woods; B.A. in Psychology, Mary Washington Coll., 1951; M.A. in English, U. Va., 1965; m. Richard Lane Frautschi, Nov. 17, 1973. Asst. dean women Coll. of William and Mary, Williamsburg, Va., 1960-62; head English dept. St. Catherine's Sch., Richmond, Va., 1962-66, Stuart Hall Sch., Staunton, Va., 1968-72; dir. student life Mary Baldwin Coll., Staunton, 1972-74. Dir., creator workshop in Children's Theatre, Staunton, 1972-74. Mem. Am. Assn. U. Women, Nat. Assn. Women Deans and Counselors. Home: Route 1 Box 126 C Port Matilda PA 16870

WOODS, MARGARET STAEGER, educator; b. Chehalis, Wash.; d. Carl P. and Olivia (Waring) Staeger; B.A., Wash. State U., 1932; M.Ed., U. Wash., 1954; m. Frederick Earl Woods, June 19, 1937; children—Frederick Waring, Pamela Fay (Mrs. Daryl F. Templeton). Tchr. langs. Chehalis (Wash.) High Sch., 1932-37; kindergarten tchr. Seattle Pub. Schs., 1955-56; lectr. U. Wash., Seattle, 1949-58; asso. prof. edn. Seattle Pacific Coll., 1958—. Lectr., dir. workshops on creative edn. throughout U.S., 1955—; founder, dir. pre-sch. program in creative dramatics Seattle pub. libraries, 1952—; dir. Children's World, Seattle World's Fair, 1962, N.Y. World's Fair, 1964, del. White House Conf. Children and Youth, 1960, 70. Chmn. creative arts Seattle P.T.A. Council, 1949-58. Bd. dirs. Group Homes, Inc. Recipient Nat. Woman of Yr. award Delta Zeta, 1967, Distinguished Service award Zeta Phi Eta, 1968. Mem. N.E.A. (life), Assn. Childhood Edn. Internat., Am. Assn. Elementary-Kindergarten-Nursery Educators (life mem., pres. 1969-70), Assn. Supervision and Curriculum Devel. (dir.-at-large 1969-72), Washington Congress P.T.A. (chmn. cultural arts 1959-62), Pi Lambda Theta (life). Author: Thinking, Feeling, Experiencing: Toward Realization of Full Potential, 1964, Wonderwork, 1970. Home: 10 Leisure St Coupeville WA 98239

WOODS, MARY HOUSTON, constrn. co. exec.; b. Clayton, Ga., Mar. 17, 1917; d. Charles Presley and Mary Grace (Jenkins) Houston; grad. high sch.; m. Russell E. Woods, Oct. 17, 1942 (dec. 1955); children—Donald Overton, Russell E., Antoinette (Mrs. Joseph P. Hix). Sec., Beck & Gregg Hardware Co., Atlanta, 1940-42; with C.E., Lawson Gen. Hosp., Atlanta, 1942-43, Office Def. Transp., Charlotte, N.C., also Atlanta, 1943-44; bookkeeper A.K. Adams & Co., Atlanta, 1948-50; sec. Wesley & Co., Inc., also Robert L. Mathews, gen. contractors, Atlanta, 1951-68, sec.-treas., part owner, 1969—. Served with WAC, 1945. Mem. Nat. Assn. Women in Constrn. (treas. Atlanta 1971-73). Home: 1466 Ryan St SW Atlanta GA 30310 Office: 285 Hunnicutt St NW Atlanta GA 30313

WOODS, PAGE BIRD (MRS. WILLIAM S.D. WOODS), author, artist; b. Columbia, Mo., Apr. 26, 1906; d. Robert Montgomery and Caroline (Reid) Bird; B.A., Sweet Briar Coll., 1928; m. William S.D. Woods, Apr. 17, 1929 (dec. 1971); children—William S.D., Montgomery Bird. Artist, flower arranger, sculptor, ceramacist, designer; works exhibited Va., Conn.; poet, works pub. coll. and club mags., yearbooks. Dir. Va. Soc. N.Y., 1930-37; speaker So. Woman's Ednl. Alliance; mem. Mus. Fine Arts, Valentine Mus., Richmond Symphony Soc.; v.p., dir. Brookfield Home for Girls, 1938-47. Mem. Greater N.Y. Sweet Briar Alumnae Assn. (pres. 1932-36), Richmond Woman's Exchange (pres.), Garden Club Va., Poetry Soc. Va., Acad. Am. Poets, Franklin Mint Collectors Soc., Internat. Platform Assn. Episcopalian. Clubs: Philadelphia Quarry (1st v.p., dir.), Three Chopt Garden (pres.), Tuckahoe Woman's. Author: (self-illustrated collection poems) Velvet Hours, 1970. Home: 204 Ampthill Rd Richmond VA 23226

WOODS, ROSE MARY, exec. sec. to Pres.; b. Sebring, O.; d. Thomas M. and Mary (Maley) Woods; grad. high sch. Sebring; D.H.L., Pfeiffer Coll., 1971. Mem. staff Office of Censorship, Washington, 1943-45, Surplus Property Bd., 1945; sec. to pres. Internat. Tng. Adminstrn., Washington, 1945-47, staff select com. fgn. aid. U.S. Ho. of Reps., 1947-48; sec. Fgn. Service Ednl. Found., Washington, 1947-51; exec. sec. to Senator and later Vice-Pres. Richard M. Nixon, 1951-61, to law firm Adams, Duque & Hazeltine, Los Angeles, 1961-63, and firm Nixon, Mudge, Rose, Guthrie, Alexander & Mitchell, N.Y.C., 1963-68, to Pres. Nixon, 1969—. Named one of 10 women of year Los Angeles Times, 1961, one of 75 most important women in Am., Ladies Home Jour., 1971. Home: 2500 Virginia Av NW Washington DC 20037 Office: White House Washington DC 20500

WOODSIDE, NINA L. BENCICH (MRS. BYRON CROSBY WOODSIDE), physician; b. Washington, June 1, 1931; d. Peter and Sarah (Peltz) Bencich; B.S., George Washington U., 1953; M.D., Womans Med. Coll., Pa., 1957; M.P.H., Johns Hopkins, 1963; m. Byron Crosby Woodside, Oct. 8, 1955; children—David Byron, Andrew Bencich, Steven Peter, Anne Nina, Kevin Nicolas, Jason Scott. Intern Hosp. Woman's Med. Coll. Pa., 1957-58; resident D.C. Pub. Health Dept., 1966-68; practice medicine, specializing in pub. health; clinician Fairfax (Va.) County Health Dept., 1958, asst. health officer, 1959-62, dir. div. adult health services, 1963; clinician Arlington (Va.) Health Dept., summer 1958; lectr. pub. health sci. Georgetown U. Sch. Nursing, 1963-64; chief Bur. Chronic Disease Control, Dept. Pub. Health, Washington, 1964-68, asso. dir. planning and research, 1968—, acting dep. dir., 1970; asso. coordinator Met. Washington Regional Med. Program, 1971-72; asso. prof. health care adminstrn. George Washington U., 1971-73; dir. Center for Women in Medicine, Med. Coll. Pa., Phila., 1973—. Mem. Sec. HEW's Adv. Com. on Rights and Responsibilities of Women, 1972—. Bd. dirs. Am. Cancer Soc., Washington, 1969. Mem. A.M.A., Va., Prince William

County med. socs., Am., D.C. pub. health assns., Womans Med. Coll. Alumni Assn., Johns Hopkins Alumni Assn. Home: 4114 Sudley Rd Haymarket VA 22069 Office: Medical College of Pa Philadelphia PA 19129

WOODUL, DOLLIE ROBBINS (MRS. JOSEPH ROSS WOODUL), dentist; b. Riviera, Tex., Nov. 3; d. Wilson Lawrence and Josephine Olivia (Chaffin) Robbins; B.S., Tex. Coll. Arts and Industries, 1935; D.D.S., Baylor U., 1954; m. Joseph Ross Woodul, July 8, 1939; children—Patricia Ross (Mrs. John W. Johnston), Joseph Richard. Tchr., 1935-39; practice dentistry, specializing in pedodontics, Dallas, 1954—. Clinic instr. Baylor U. Coll. Dentistry, Dallas. Trustee Gillette Hayden Found., Altrusa Meml. Found. Fellow Am. Coll. Dentists; mem. Assn. Am. Women Dentists (pres. 1963), Am. Dental Assn., Am. Academy Pedodontics, Am. Soc. Dentistry for Children, Tex., Dallas County dental assns., Am., Tex., Dallas County dental assns. women's auxs., Upsilon Alpha (grand pres. 1968-70), Omicron Kappa Upsilon. Mem. Order Eastern Star, Altrusa Club (Woman of Year 1963, pres. 1969). Home: 7003 Wabash Circle Dallas TX 75214 Office: 6115 LaVista St Dallas TX 75214

WOODWARD, EDITH STEPHENS (MRS. ERNEST BURTON WOODWARD), librarian; b. Kiowa, Kan., June 4, 1917; d. Jesse Sanford and Nola Dale (Hutchison) Stephens; B.A. with distinction, George Washington U., 1946; M.A. in Library Sci., U. Mich., 1958; m. Ernest Burton Woodward, Apr. 25, 1943. Tchr. rural sch. Lake City, Kan., 1936-39; classifier FBI, 1941-45; asst. librarian Columbus (O.) Pub. Library, 1947-57, head Linden Br., 1955-57; head documents div. State Library of Ohio, 1957-69; research librarian Ohio Legislative Service Commn., 1969— (both Columbus). Mem. Spl. Library Assn. (treas. Dayton chpt. 1969-70, pres. 1973-74), Ohio Regional Assn. Law Librarians, Franklin County Library Assn. (v.p. 1959-60, 71-72, treas. 1962-64), Pi Lambda Theta, Beta Phi Mu. Lutheran. Home: 4160 Lyon Dr Columbus OH 43220 Office: Ohio Legislative Service Commn State House Columbus OH 43215

WOODWARD, GRACE STEELE, author; b. Joplin, Mo., Sept. 14, 1899; d. John Thomas and Dora (Simms) Steele; student U. Mo., 1917, U. Okla., 1918, Columbia, 1919-20; m. Guy H. Woodward, Sept. 8, 1920; children—John A., Robert L. Author: The Man Who Conquered Pain: A Biography of William Thomas Green Morton, 1962; The Cherokees, 1963; Pocahontas, 1969; Secret of Sherwood Forest, 1973. Named to Okla. Hall of Fame, 1968. Mem. Inst. Am. History and Art, Assn. Preservation Va. Antiquities, Daus. Am. Colonists, D.A.R., Okla. Heritage Soc. (dir.), Tuesday Writers, Delta Sigma Phi. Home: 3618 S Atlanta Av Tulsa OK 74105

WOODWARD, JULIE VIOLA BESTOR, realtor; b. Washington; d. Armond Dudley and Viola Estelle (Jones) Bestor; m. Julie Viola Bestor, Jan. 19, 1947; children—Jacqueline Joy Sperry (Mrs. Ronald Loren Wilkes), Lee Anna (Mrs. Malvern Stevens), Carolyn Frances (Mrs. Pryon Scott McMillen), George William. Operator Pacific Telephone Co., Los Angeles; mem. staff Bur. Internat. Revenue, 1942-46; dental asst., Los Angeles, 1946; realtor Julie V. Woodward, Realtor, Tujunga, Cal., 1948—; owner Julie & Jack, 1968—. Mem. Los Angelnas Vol. Group for City Los Angeles, 1971. Mem. Los Angeles Realty Bd., The American, Bell Assn. So. Cal., Campanology. Club: Altrusa (Tujunga). Home: 73071/2 Foothill Blvd Tujunga CA 91042 Office: 7307 Foothill Blvd Tujunga CA 91042

WOODWARD, SISTER MARY IRENE, coll. pres.; b. Laramie, Wyo., Apr. 18, 1933; d. Richard Joseph and Mary Irene (Campbell) Woodward; B.A., U. So. Cal., 1961; M.A. with distinction, Cath. U. Am., 1963, Ph.D. with distinction, 1966. Joined Sisters of Holy Names; music tchr. St. Elizabeth Sch., Altadena, Cal., 1954-58, Ramona Convent High Sch., Alhambra, Cal., 1958-61; asst. prof. philosophy Holy Names Coll., Oakland, Cal., 1963-72, pres., 1972—. Mem. nat. adv. council Danforth Found. Asso. Program. Sect. chmn. United Bay Area Crusade, 1973—. Danforth asso., 1968—; Inst. Ednl. Mgmt., Harvard Bus. Sch. grantee, 1973. Mem. Am. Cath. Philos. Soc., Metaphys. Soc. Am., Assn. Ind. Cal. Colls. and Univs. (trustee), Ind. Colls. No. Cal. (sec.-treas. 1974—), Oakland Mus. Assn., Nat. Cath. Edn. Assn., Oakland C. of C. (edn. com.). Address: Holy Names Coll Oakland CA 94619

WOODWARD, SHARON LEE, advt. copywriter; b. Indpls., Jan. 22, 1948; d. David Franklin and Phyllis Marie (Ridgeway) Woodward; A.B. in Journalism, Ind. U., 1971. Pub. relations with Ind. State Fair, 1970; advt. copywriter L.S. Ayres and Co., Indpls., 1972—. Mem. Women in Communications. Club: Ind. University Women's (Indpls.). Home: 2519 Debonair Terrace Indianapolis IN 46224 Office: 1 W Washington St Indianapolis IN 46204

WOODWORTH, BETTY, newspaper editor; b. Ft. Collins, Colo., Oct. 15, 1914; d. Edward James and Ethel (Avery) Woodworth; B.A., U. Mich., 1937. With Downers Grove (Ill.) Jour., 1938-41, asst. editor, 1940-41; with Chgo. chpt. A.R.C., 1942; with Ft. Collins Coloradoan, 1943—, women's news editor, 1949—. Mem. Ft. Collins Landmark Preservation Commn., 1966-67. Recipient award N. Am. Indian Women's Assn., 1971. Mem. P.E.O., Am. Civil Liberties Union, Women in Communication, Delta Delta Delta. Home: 637 Del Norte Pl Fort Collins CO 80521 Office: 145 E Mountain Av Fort Collins CO 80521

WOODY, REGINA J(ONES), ballerina, author; b. Boston, Jan. 4, 1894; d. Lewis Llewellyn and Regina M. (Lichtenstein) Jones; student pvt. schs.; m. McIver Woody, May 1, 1918; children—McIver Wallace, Regina Llewellyn, Jean Butler, Emma McIver (Mrs. James M. Sowa). Author: Stars Came Down, 1945; Starlight, 1946; Boarding School, 1949; Student Dancer, 1951; Ballet in the Barn, 1952; Almena's Dogs, 1954; Young Dancer's Career Book, 1958; Dancing for Joy, 1959; Time to Dance, 1962; Widsom To Know, 1964; Summer of Decision, 1966, TV Dancer, 1966; One Day at a Time, 1968; The Young Medics, 1968; Dance To A Lonely Tune, 1970; Second Sight for Tommy, 1972; Schoolgirl Ballerina; Teenage Ballerinas; also numerous articles, short stories pub. in popular mags.; tchr. juvenile writing N.Y.U., 1946-50; editor young dancer sect. Dance Mag., 1951-61; jr. dance notator Dance Notation Record, 1958-60. Mem. A.L.A., D.A.R., Soc. Descs. of Colonial Clergy, Am. Camellia Soc. Republican. Club: Author's League. Home: 440 Westminster Av Elizabeth NJ 07208

WOOL, MURIEL BEZINSKY, labor economist; b. Bklyn., Dec. 7, 1920; d. Benjamin and Theresa A. (Von Newmann) Bezinsky; student Coll. City N.Y., 1937-40, Am. U., 1942-45; m. Dr. Harold Wool, July 6, 1941; children—Carolyn Diane, Barbara Ellen, Pamela Susan. Adminstr. Interuniv. Consortium for Peace Corps of Am. U., 1962-63; labor economist Women's Bur. of U.S. Dept. Labor, Washington, 1963-69, Office of Finance/Mgmt. Information Systems, 1969-72, Bur. Labor Statistics, 1972—; owner Muriel B. Wool Interiors; cons. on color and sound on productivity. Active charity fund drives, P.T.A. Recipient group honor award for outstanding services, U.S. Dept. labor, 1964. Mem. Am. Econ. Assn., Indsl. Relations Assn., Am. Statis. Assn., Internat. Assn. Personnel in Employment Security, Exec. Com. Profl. Women, Soc. Govt. Economists (publicity chmn.), Group Health Assn. (vice chmn. mem. adv. council). Mem. B'nai B'rith. Home: 6716 Brigadoon Dr Bethesda MD 20034 Office: 1111 20th St N W Washington DC 20210

WOOLDRIDGE, ELIZABETH TAYLOR (MRS. EDWARD MANSFIELD WOOLDRIDGE), educator; b. Salem, Ky., Sept. 6, 1908; d. Frank Park and Lillie M. (Hord) Taylor; A.B., Murray State U., 1931; M.A., George Peabody Coll., 1941; Ph.D., U. Neb., 1964; student U. Colo., 1957-58; m. Edward Mansfield Wooldridge, July 25, 1937 (dec. Aug. 1937); 1 son, David Mansfield. Tchr., Salem (Ky.) High Sch., 1928-29, 36-42, West Carroll Parish Schs., Pioneer, La., 1942-45, Wayne (Neb.) High Sch., 1945-46; asso. prof. mathematics Neb. State Coll., Wayne, 1946-62; prof. math. Florence State U., Ala., 1962—; grad. asst. U. Neb., 1958-59. Mem. N.E.A., Ala. Edn. Assn., Nat. Council Tchrs. Math., Ala. Assn. Coll. Tchrs. Math., Delta Kappa Gamma, Kappa Mu Epsilon (nat. sec.), Pi Lambda Theta, Phi Kappa Phi. Baptist. Author: (with Lula Way) Let's Play 'Rithmetic, 1959. Home: 1550 Helton Dr Florence AL 35630

WOOLEY, SUSAN CLARK (MRS. ORLAND WAYNE WOOLEY), educator, clin. psychologist; b. Rochester, N.Y., Aug. 9, 1941; d. Leland Charles and Eleanor Wilbur (Wyckoff) Clark, Jr.; B.A. in Philosophy, Antioch Coll., 1964; Ph.D. in Clin. Psychology (USPHS fellow), U. Ill., 1969; m. Orland Wayne Wooley, Sept. 4, 1965. Asst. prof. counseling service U. Ill., Urbana, 1969; asst. prof. U. Cin. Coll. Medicine, Cin., 1969-73, asso. prof., 1974—, asso. dir. psychosomatic unit, 1973—. Recipient Nat. Inst. Mental Health grant, 1970, 1971—. Mem. Am. Psychol. Assn. Contbr. articles to profl. jours. Home: 3831 Middleton Av Cincinnati OH 45220 Office: Psychiatry Dept University of Cincinnati College Medicine Cincinnati OH 45267

WOOLF, LENORE ADELE, writer; b. St. Louis, Sept. 11, 1920; d. Sam and Mary (Stockman) Shurman; student U. Wis., 1938-41, U. Okla., 1951-53; m. Raleigh Woolf, Oct. 4, 1941; children—Steven M., Thomas E. Writer, Milw. Repertory Theatre, 1961-68, also dir.; writer/editor Milw. County Hist. Soc., 1968-73; mem. Mayor Milw. Com. on Arts. Bd. dirs. Shorewood Library. Seminar grantee Am. Assn. Local History, 1969. Mem. Writer's Guild Am. Author: In Time of Trouble, 1965; In Spring, Everything is New Except Me, 1969; (book and lyrics) Ticket to Chautauqua, 1962; also articles. Address: 5129 N Kimbark Pl Milwaukee WI 53217

WOOLFOLK, ASA JEAN, life ins. co. exec.; b. Little Rock, Jan. 3, 1921; d. Asa Lucian and Jennie (Wright) Woolfolk; student Little Rock Jr. Coll., 1938-40; B.S. in Bus. Adminstrn. with high honors, U. Ark., 1942; LL.B., Ark. Law Sch., 1948, LL.D., Phillips U., Eureka Coll., 1972. Actuarial clk. Union Life Ins. Co., Little Rock, 1942-48, asst. sec., 1948-55; sec.-treas., dir. Am. Found. Life Ins. Co., Little Rock, 1955-68, v.p., sec.-treas., dir., 1968-72, v.p., sec., dir., 1972—; v.p., dir. Am. Found. Mortgage & Realty Co., Little Rock, 1973—. Trustee Jarvis Christian Coll., Disciples Div. House, U. Chgo. Mem. Nat. Assn. Women Lawyers, Ins., Accounting and Statis. Assn. (pres. 1963-64), Am. Soc. C.L.U.'s, L.R. Chamber Music Soc. (pres. 1972-73), Ark. Bar Assn., Mortar Board, Phi Theta Kappa (nat. treas. 1942-56), Beta Gamma Sigma, Delta Delta Delta. Mem. Christian Ch. (moderator 1973—). Club: Altrusa (Little Rock). Home: 470 Ridgeway Little Rock AR 72205 Office: 1020 W 4th St Little Rock AR 72201

WOOLFOLK, MARGARET ELIZABETH, editor; b. Little Rock, Sept. 3, 1917; d. Robert Lee and Claudine (Jamison) Woolfolk; student U. Tenn., 1955, Memphis State U., 1958. Asso. editor Crittenden County Times, West Memphis, Ark., 1936-42, 45-50, editor, 1950-60; radio operator Chgo. and So. Air Lines, 1942-45, link trainer operator, 1945; asso. editor West Memphis News, 1950; editor, gen. mgr. Evening Times-Crittenden Pub. Co., West Memphis, 1957—. Vice-chmn. Crittenden County Democratic Central Com., 1964—; mem. Crittenden County Library Commn. Trustee Crittenden Meml. Hosp., West Memphis, 1966-68. Recipient Good Citizen award D.A.R., 1936, Woman of Achievement award Ark. Press Women, 1957-67, 71, Best Daily Editor award Nat. Fedn. Press Women, 1960, 66, 73, Outstanding Service award Marion-West Memphis post V.F.W., 1969, Outstanding Service award Am. Legion, 1969; named Boss of Year, West Memphis Jr. C. of C., 1968. Mem. Nat. Fedn. Press Women (dist. dir. 1968-70), Ark. Press Women (pres. 1955), West Memphis C. of C. (dir.), Theta Sigma Phi, Sigma Delta Chi. Home: 155 Hwy 77 Marion AR 72364 Office: 111 E Bond St West Memphis AR 72301

WOOLFOLK, MARY ANNIE, educator; b. Richmond, Va., May 30, 1920; d. Maurice Linwood and Mary Jane (Johnson) Liggins; B.A., Va. Union U., 1942; M.Ed., U. Del., 1960; m. John Henry Woolfolk, June 23, 1945; children—John Harvey, Gerald Alexis, Ronald Oliver. Tchr., Branch Fork, Va., 1942-43, Granite Springs, Va., 1943-47; social worker Del. Dept. Pub. Welfare, 1958-63; tchr. New Castle (Del.) Sch. Dist., 1963-64, Stanton Sch. Dist., Wilmington, Del., 1964—. Coordinating tchr. Meadowood Sch., Wilmington, 1968-71, dir. summer sch. program, 1968-69. Chmn. Del. P.T.A. Assn. Exceptional Children, 1968-73; pres. Del. Council Exceptional Children, 1968-69; rep. Coordinating Council Handicapped of Del., 1968-69; sec. Hockessin (Del.) Community Center, 1973; founder Hockessin Mother's Club, 1962; mem. Hockessin Inter-Ch. Assn., 1968—. Bd. dirs. United Cerebral Palsy. Mem. Am. Assn. Mental Deficiency, Del. Assn. Retarded Children, Council Exceptional Children, N.E.A., Sigma Gamma Rho, Delta Kappa Gamma. Democrat. Methodist (treas. chapel, mem. stewardness bd.). Club: Coronet (past pres. Hockessin, Del.). Home: Route 1 Box 260 Hockessin DE 19707 Office: 55A S Meadowood Dr Newark DE 19711

WOOLLEY, CATHERINE (JANE THAYER), author; b. Chgo., Aug. 11, 1904; d. Edward Mott and Anna L. (Thayer) Woolley; A.B., U. Cal. at Los Angeles, 1927. Advt. copywriter Am. Radiator Co., 1927-31; free-lance writer, 1931-33; copywriter, editor house organ Am. Radiator & Standard San. Corp., 1933-40; desk editor Archtl. Record, 1940-42; prodn. editor SAE Jour., 1942-43; pub. relations writer N.A.M., 1943-47 (all N.Y.C.). Instr. juvenile writing Cape Cod Writers Conference, 1965, 66. Mem. Passaic Bd. Edn., 1953-56, Passaic Redevel. Agy., 1952-53. Mem. Authors League Am., League Women Voters (pres. Passaic 1950-53), Kenilworth Soc. Democrat. Club: Women's College (Passaic). Author juvenile books (under name Catherine Woolley); I Like Trains, rev., 1965; Two Hundred Pennies, 1947; Ginnie and Geneva, 1948; David's Railroad, 1949; Schoolroom Zoo, 1950; Railroad Cowboy, 1951; Ginnie Joins In, 1951; David's Hundred Dollars, 1952; Lunch for Lennie, 1952 (pub. as L'Incontentabile Gigi in Italy); The Little Car that Wanted a Garage, 1952; The Animal Train and Other Stories, 1953; Holiday on Wheels, 1953; Ginnie and the New Girl, 1954; Ellie's Problem Dog, 1955; A Room for Cathy, 1956; Ginnie and the Mystery House, 1957; Miss Cathy Leonard, 1958; David's Campaign Buttons, 1959; Ginnie and the Mystery Doll, 1960; Cathy Leonard Calling, 1961; Look Alive, Libby!, 1962; Ginnie and Her Juniors, published 1963; Cathy's Little Sister, 1964; Libby Looks for s Spy, 1965; The Shiny Red Rubber Boots, 1965; Ginnie and the Cooking Contest, 1966; Ginnie and the Wedding Bells, 1967; Chris in Trouble, 1968; Ginnie and the Mystery Cat, 1969; Libby's Uninvited Guest, 1970; Cathy and the Beautiful People, 1971; Cathy Uncovers a Secret, 1972; Ginnie and the Mystery Light, 1973; Libby Shadows a Lady, 1974; (under name Jane Thayer) The Horse with the Easter Bonnet, 1953; The Popcorn Dragon, 1953; Where's Andy?, 1954; Mrs. Perrywinkle's Pets, 1955; Sandy and the Seventeen Balloons, 1955; The Chicken in the Tunnel, 1956; The Outside Cat, 1957 (English edit. 1958); Charley and the New Car, 1957; Funny Stories To Read Aloud, 1958; Andy Wouldn't Talk, 1958; The Puppy Who Wanted a Boy, 1958; The Second-Story Giraffe, 1959; Little Monkey, 1959; Andy and His Fine Friends, 1960; The Pussy Who Went To the Moon, 1960 (English edit. 1961); A Little Dog Called Kitty, 1961; The Blueberry Pie Elf, 1961 (English edit. 1962); Andy's Square Blue Animal, 1962; Gus Was a Friendly Ghost, 1962; A Drink for Little Red Diker, 1963; Andy and the Runaway Horse, 1963; Quiet on Account of Dinosaur, 1964 (English edit. 1965); Emerald Enjoyed the Moonlight, 1964 (English edition, 1965); The Bunny in the Honeysuckle Patch, 1965; Part-Time Dog, 1965; The Light Hearted Wolf, 1966; What's a Ghost Going to Do?, 1966; The Cat that Joined the Club, 1967; Rockets Don't Go To Chicago, Andy, 1967; A Contrary Little Quail, 1968; Little Mr. Greenthumb, 1968; Andy and Mr. Cunningham, 1969; Curious, Furious Chipmunk, 1969; Im Not a Cat, Said Emerald, 1970; Gus Was A Christmas Ghost, 1970; Mr. Turtle's Magic Glasses, 1971; Timothy And Madam Mouse, 1971; Gus And The Baby Ghost, 1972; The Little House, 1972; Andy and the Wild Worm, 1973; Gus Was a Mexican Ghost, 1974. Contbr. stories to juvenile anthologies, sch. readers, juvenile mags. Home: Higgins Hollow Rd Truro MA 02666

WOOLLEY, DONNA RYDELL (MRS. HAROLD WOOLLEY), lumber co. exec.; b. Drain, Ore., Jan. 3, 1926; d. Chester Arthur and Mona B. (Cheever) Rydell; m. Harold Woolley, Dec. 27, 1952; children—Daniel, Debra, Donald. Sec., No. Life Ins. Co., Eugene, Ore., 1943; bookkeeper Smith River Lumber Co., Drain, 1944; bookkeeper Woolley Logging Co., Drain, 1944, exec. Woolley Enterprises, 1970—. Mem. Douglas County Budget Commn., Roseburg, Ore., 1971—; mem. Drain Sch. Bd., 1967—. Mem. Sunnydale Grange, Pacific Internat., Amateur trapshooting assns. Mem. Rebekah Lodge. Home: PO Box 43 Drain OR 97435 Office: Woolley Enterprises Inc Box 43 Drain OR 97435

WOOLMAN, BERTHA ALICE (MRS. MILTON H. WOOLMAN), ret. librarian; b. Ponca City, Okla., Dec. 11, 1907; d. Robert Barclay and Sarah (Whitehead) Overman; A.B., Southwestern Coll. (Winfield, Kan.), 1930; M.A., U. Wichita, 1955; m. Milton Henry Woolman, Nov. 5, 1932; children—Nancy (dec.), Neil Arlen, Patricia (Mrs. Leslie Litsey), Gail. Tchr. Cowley County Rural Elementary Sch., Kan., 1926-28, Maize (Kan.) High Sch., 1930-32; elementary sch. librarian, Wichita, Kan., 1949-66; librarian Cocopah and Kiva Elementary Sch., Scottsdale, Ariz., 1966-72. Elementary sch. library cons., Wichita, 1954-59. Mem. Nat., Ariz. ret. tchrs. assns., A.L.A., Ariz. Sch. Library Assn. Home: 3917 W McLellan Blvd Phoenix AZ 85019

WOOLRICH, AVIS MAXINE, univ. dean; b. Knoxville, Tenn., Feb. 3, 1918; d. Willis Raymond and Neena (Myhere) Woolrich; B.S., U. Tex., 1938; M.S., U. Tenn., 1942; postgrad. Am. U., 1957-63. High sch. tchr., Tex., 1938-41; instr. Morehead (Ky.) State Coll., 1942-44, U. Me., Orono, 1944-46; research housing specialist U.S. Dept. Agr., Beltsville, Md., 1946-65; prof., head dept. consumer scis. and housing Colo. State U., Ft. Collins, 1965-71, asso. dean Coll. Home Econs., 1971—. Recipient certificate of merit U.S. Dept. Agr., 1965. Mem. Am. Colo. home econs. assns., Soroptomist, Am. Assn. Housing Educators, Soroptomist Internat., Sigma Xi, Omicron Nu, Delta Delta Delta. Democrat. Methodist. Research and numerous publs. on human requirements for housing. Home: 3625 Terry Ridge Rd Fort Collins CO 80521

WOOLSTON, MAXINE YAPLE (MRS. WILLIAM JENKS WOOLSTON), economist, author; b. El Dorado, Mo., Sept. 16, 1911; d. Arthur Algernon and Alma Lee (Burner) Yaple; A.B., Stanford, 1933, M.A. in History, 1934; Ph.D., in Econs., Harvard, 1939; postgrad. London (Eng.) Sch. Econs., 1936; m. William Jenks Woolston, Mar. 10, 1944; children—William Pratt, Joseph Longstreth. Instr. econs. Tufts Coll., Medford, Mass., 1938, Sarah Lawrence Coll., Bronxville, N.Y., 1939; asst. prof. econs. Vassar Coll., Poughkeepsie, N.Y., 1940-41; div. chief OPA and Fgn. Econ. Adminstrn., Washington, 1942-45; dir. social studies Am. Assn. Univ. Women, Washington, 1945-46; chief economist Phila. Planning Commn., 1946-48; lectr. econs. Bryn Mawr (Pa.) Coll., 1949-59, Haverford (Pa.) Coll., 1956-57, Swathmore (Pa.) Coll., 1957-59; div. chief, div. internat. relations, women's bur. U.S. Labor Dept., Washington, 1969-72; cons. bus. and govt., 1972—. Mem. Phila. Fellowship Com. Bd. dirs. Phila. Met. YWCA, Med. Coll. of Phila. Recipient Caroline I. Wilby prize Radcliffe Coll., 1940. Mem. Am. Econ. Assn., Am. Statis. Assn., Am. Inst. Planning Ofcls., Phila. Assn. Univ. Women (past dir.), Phi Beta Kappa. Mem. Soc. of Friends. Author: American Economic Program for American Democracy, 1939; Structure of the Nazi Economy, 1941; La Economic National Socialists, 1941; Economic Base of Philadelphia, 1948; Basic Information on the American Economy, 1957; Charlotte Atlee, Mission to India, 1974. Home: 2166 Harts Lane RD Conshohocken PA 19428

WOOTEN, EDNA PLOCK, educator; b. Columbus, O., Sept. 12, 1923; d. William Edward and Margaret May (Webster) Plock; B.Sc., Ohio State U., 1945, M.A., 1946, Ph.D., 1961; m. Edward Leon Wooten, Mar. 18, 1951 (div. Dec. 1958); children—Margaret Susan, Barbara Jane. Asst. prof. Ariz. State U., Tempe, 1946-49; tchr. Phoenix Union High Sch., 1958-60; asso. prof. Ohio State U., Columbus, 1961-65; prof. anatomy U. Ore., Eugene, 1965—, acting chmn. women's phys. edn. dept., 1966-68. Cons. phys. edn. for exceptional child, state dept. and local pub. and spl. schs., 1966-73. Bd. dirs. Serenety Lane. Recipient Service award Camp Fire Girls, 1972. Fellow Am. Coll. Sports Medicine (trustee); mem. Council Exceptional Children, Am. Assn. Mental Deficiency, Am., Ore. assns. health, phys. edn. and recreation, Nat., Western assns. phys. edn. coll. women. Author: Structural Kinesiology, 1973. Home: 635 W 27th Pl Eugene OR 97405

WOOTEN, MILDRED CROZIER (MRS. DAN J. WOOTEN), librarian; b. Winnfield, La., Oct. 3, 1910; d. Valentine Barrett and Marie Gertrude (Milburn) Crozier; B.A., La. State Normal Coll., 1929; B.L.S., La. State U., 1940; m. Dan J. Wooten, Nov. 28, 1951; children—Robert H., Timothy D. Tchr. English, Eunice (La.) High Sch., 1930-41, librarian, 1941—; librarian Loyola U., New Orleans, summers 1932-33. Bd. dirs. La. State U. Friends of Library. Recipient Modisette awards for outstanding library service in secondary schs. in La., 1957, 70. Mem. La. Assn. Sch. Librarians (pres.), La. State U. Alumni Assn. (sec. St. Landry Parish), Order Blue Violet, Alpha Phi Gamma, Delta Kappa Gamma. Democrat. Roman Catholic. Home: 601 W Oak St Eunice LA 70535 Office: Charlotte St Eunice LA 70535

WOOTEN, SYLVIA WOOD (MRS. HOLLOWAY WOOTEN), pediatrician; b. Balt., May 21, 1941; d. John Teaveious and Marion Adlena (Miller) Wood; B.S. (William Deiches Fund grantee), Morgan State Coll., 1963; M.D., (Med. Alumni scholar), Howard U., 1967; m. Holloway Wooten, June 27, 1970; 1 son, Eric Robin. Intern, S.I. (N.Y.) Hosp., 1967-68; resident pediatrics Children's Hosp. of D.C.,

Washington, 1968-70, clin. pediatrician Comprehensive Health Care Clinic, 1970-73; med. dir. sickle cell screening and edn. clinic Dept. Human Resources, 1973-74; chief, pediatrician S.W. Neighborhood Health Center, Washington, 1974—; clin. instr. child health devel. (pediatrics) George Washington U. Sch. Medicine, Washington, 1971-73, asst. prof., 1973—. Recipient Trusteeship award Morgan State Coll., 1959-62, William Naylor award, 1962-63; recipient Anna Bartchs Dunne award for women med. students Howard U. Sch. Medicine, 1965. Mem. Promethean Kappa Tau, Beta Kappa Chi, Alpha Kappa Mu. Democrat. Home: 1320 Hemlock St NW Washington DC 20012 Office: 850 Delaware Av SW Washington DC 20003

WOOTTON, ETNA ELENA, dietitian; b. Tarlac, P.I., Oct. 3, 1941; d. Severino and Asuncion (Padilla) Empaynado; B.S. in Home Econs., Holy Spirit Coll., P.I., 1961; diploma dietetics, Good Samaritan Hosp., Cin., 1965; m. Arthur Heath Wootton, Sept. 6, 1969. Came to U.S., 1964, naturalized, 1972. Therapeutic dietitian St. Elizabeth Hosp., Youngstown, O., 1965-66; asst. main kitchen dietitian Union Meml. Hosp., Balt., 1966-67; therapeutic dietitian Civic Hosp., Ottawa, Ont., Can., 1967-68; travelling dietitian Beaver Food Service Ltd., London, Ont., Can., 1968-70; asst. food service St. Thomas (Ont.) Psychiat. Hosp., 1970-73, food service adminstr., 1973—. Mem. Am., Canadian, Ont. (liaison officer region 1) dietetic assns. Home: 111 Lawrence Av St Thomas ON Canada Office: Box 2004 St Thomas ON Canada

WOOTTON, JANE PENDLETON, physician; b. Cuckoo, Va., Apr. 21, 1939; d. Eugene Barbour and Mildred (McLean) Pendleton, Jr.; B.A., Salem Coll., 1961; M.D. (Nat. Found., Polio Found. scholar, Joseph Collins Found. scholar), Med. Coll. Va., 1965; m. Percy Wootton, June 16, 1962; children—Jane Meredith, Madison Pendleton. Intern Med. Coll. Va., 1965-66, pulmonary fellow, 1966-67; practice medicine, specializing in internal medicine, Richmond, Va., 1972—; physician med. clinic City Health Dept., Richmond, 1972—; mem. courtesy staff Richmond Hosp.; mem. staff Johnston Willis Hosp. lectr. advanced phys. edn. U. Richmond, 1971. Mem. woman's com. Richmond Symphony, 1967—, Va. Mus. Fine Arts; co-chmn. fund dr. Am. Cancer Soc., Richmond, 1970, bd. dirs., 1967-72. Mem. A.M.A., Med. Soc. Va., Johnston Willis Hosp. Aux. (pres.), Women's Aux. Richmond Acad. Medicine, Am. Assn. U. Women, Am., Richmond Area heart assns., Richmond Acad. Medicine, Ikebana Internat. Mem. Christian Ch. (v.p. women's fellowship 1970-71). Clubs: The Country of Virginia, Glenbernie Garden (both Richmond). Home: 509 Tuckahoe Blvd Richmond VA 23226 Office: City Health Dept 1312 Bainbridge St Richmond VA 23113

WORDEN, KATHARINE COLE, sculptor; b. N.Y.C., May 4, 1925; d. Philip Gillette and Katharine (Pyle) Cole; student Potters Sch., Tucson, 1940-42, Sarah Lawrence Coll., 1942-44; m. Frederic G. Worden, Jan. 8, 1944; children—Rick, Dwight, Philip, Barbara, Katharine. Sculptor, works exhibited Royce Galleries, Galerie Francoise Besnard (Paris), Cooling Gallery (London), Galerie Schumacher (Munich), Selected Artists Gallery, N.Y.C.; works permanently exhibited Royce Galleries, Gilcrease Mus. (Tulsa), Galerie des Capucines (Paris), pvt. collections Grand Palais (Paris), Dakar and Bathurst, Africa. Occupational thrapist psychopathic ward Los Angeles County Gen. Hosp., 1953-57; headstart vol., Watts, Cal., 1965-67; tchr. sculpture Watts Towers Art Center, 1967-69; participant White House Women Doers Luncheon meeting, 1968; dir. Cambridgeport Problem Center, Cambridge, Mass., 1963-70. Trustee Communication Research Inst., Miami, Fla., 1960-69, chmn. bd., 1966-69. Mem. Common Cause (Mass. adv. bd. 1971-72), Mass. Civil Liberties Union (exec. bd. 1973-74). Home: 45 Hilltop Rd Weston MA 02193

WORELL, JUDITH PAULA, psychologist, educator; b. N.Y.C., May 9, 1928; d. Moses and Dorothy (Goldbaum) Goldfarb; B.A. in Psychology, Queens Coll., 1950; M.A. in Clin. Psychology, Ohio State U., 1952, Ph.D. in Child Clin. Psychology, 1954; m. Leonard Worell (div. Jan. 1974); children—Amy, Beth, Wendy. Instr., Portland (Ore.) State Coll., 1954-55; research asso. Ia. Psychopathic Hosp., Iowa City, 1957-59; asst. prof. psychology Okla. State U., 1960-66; asso. prof., dept. edni. psychology and counseling U. Ky., Lexington, 1969—. Cons., Payne County Mental Health Center, Okla., 1960-62, Ky. Dept. Mental Health, Lexington, 1967-69, Dale Farabee Re-edn. sch., Lexington, 1972—, Ky. Dept. Human Resources, Lexington, 1974—. NIH Research grantee, 1960-63, 63-67, Ky. Research Found. grantee, 1970, 73, 74. Mem. Am., Southeastern (chmn. research awards com. 1973—), Ky. (chmn. dir. com. 1973-74) psychol. assns., Am. Women in Psychology (chmn. feminist therapy com. 1973—), Council for Exceptional Children, Council for Children with Behavior Disorders, Am. Ednl. Research Assn., Soc. for Research in Child Devel., Am. Assn. Univ. Profs. (chmn. com. on women 1973—). Author: (with C.M. Nelson) Managing Instructional problems, 1974. Cons. editor Jour. Cons. and Clin. Psychology, 1974—. Contbr. articles on clin. and ednl. psychology to profl. jours. Home: 1243 Cross Keys Rd Lexington KY 40504 Office: Dept Educational Psychology Univ of Kentucky Lexington KY 40506

WORLEY, JUNE MARIE, educator; b. West Palm Beach, Fla., May 22, 1934; d. Milton Dayton and Della Marie (Ross) Worley; B.S., Phillips U., 1956; M.S., Okla. State U., 1958; postgrad. U. Minn., 1966, U. Ore., 1968, Springfield Coll., 1970-72. Instr. phys. edn. Phillips U., Enid, Okla., 1956-59, asst. prof., 1959-61, asso. prof., 1961-72, dir. women's phys. edn. program, 1972—. Mem. Am., Okla. assns. health, phys. edn. and recreation, Assn. intercollegiate Athletics for Women, Altrusa (pres. Enid 1966, dir. 1974-75). Home: 1621 E Maine St Enid OK 73701

WORRALL, OLGA NATHALIE RIPICH (MRS. AMBROSE ALEXANDER WORRALL), designer, papapsychologist; b. Cleve., Nov. 30, 1906; d. John Gabriel and Elizabeth (Karanczay) Ripich; grad. Cleve. Bus. U., 1925, Cleve. Comml. Sch., 1927; m. Ambrose Alexander Worrall, June 7, 1928; children—Ambrose K., Alexander M. (dec.). Tchr., Cleve. Comml. Sch., 1927; comml. tchr. Balt. Sr. High Schs., 1942-50; inventor-designer, sr. v.p. K & W Enterprises, Inc., Balt., 1964—. Asso. dir. New Life Clinic, Meth. Ch., Balt., 1950—; cons. Research in Spiritual Healing-Sci. of Mind Inst.; internat. lectr. parapsychology and unconventional healing. Mem. Chs. Fellowship for Psychical Studies (London, Eng.), Spiritual Frontiers Fellowship, Am. Soc. Psychical Research, Acad. Parapsychology and Medicine, Internat. Platform Assn. Methodist, also mem. Russian Orthodox Ch. Author: How to Start a Healing Service, 1957; The Gift of Healing, 1965; (with others) Miracle Healers of Maryland, Your Power to Heal, 1972; A Healing Service Manual; (with husband) Explore Your Psychic World; articles in various mags. Home: 1208 Havenwood Rd Baltimore MD 21218

WORRELL, AUDREY FRANCES MARTINY (MRS. RICHARD V. WORRELL), physician; b. Phila., Aug. 12, 1935; d. Francis A. and Dorothy (Rawley) Martiny; student Fisk U., Whittier Coll., 1953-56; M.D., Meharry Med. Coll., 1960; m. Richard V. Worrell, June 14, 1958; children—Philip Vernon, Amy Elizabeth. Intern, Misericordia Hosp., Phila., 1960-61; resident psychiatry E. J. Meyer Meml. Hosp., Buffalo, 1961-63; resident Buffalo State Hosp., 1963-64, staff psychiatrist, 1964-65; staff psychiatrist Buffalo Children's Hosp., 1964-65; chief psychiatrist Haverford (Pa.) State Hosp., 1965-68; asst. prof. psychiatry U. Pa., Phila., 1967; asst. prof. psychiatry U. Conn. Med. Sch., Hartford, 1968-71; chief Erie County unit Buffalo State Hosp., 1971-74; clin. asst. prof. psychiatry State U. N.Y. at Buffalo Sch. Medicine, 1971-74; dir. ambulatory psychiat. services Capitol Region Mental Health Center, Hartford, Conn., 1974—; asst. prof. psychiatry U. Conn. Sch. Medicine, 1974—. Vice chmn. Erie County Mental Health Bd., 1971. Mem. Am., Conn. psychiat. socs. Home: 39 Midlands Dr West Hartford CT 06107 Office: U Conn Health Center Farmington CT 06032

WORRELL, ELIZABETH, educator; b. Mexico, Mo., May 7, 1905; d. Robert Deaton and Jennie Lee (Hitt) Worrell; A.A., Hardin Coll., 1922; B.S., U. Mo., 1926; M.A., Northwestern U., 1931, Ph.D., 1954. Instr. speech Hardin Coll., Mexico, 1926-30, Central Methodist Coll., Fayette, Mo., 1930-42, instr. speech William Woods Coll., Fulton, Mo., 1945-47; mem. faculty Northeast Mo. State U., Kirksville, 1947-70, prof. speech emeritus, 1970—. Vis. prof. U. Mo., 1970-72, U. Ariz., 1972, 73. Served to 1st. lt. USMCR, 1942-45. Mem. Speech Communications Assn., Central States Speech Assn., Am. Assn. Univ. Profs., Kappa Alpha Theta. Democrat. Contbr. articles to profl. jours. Home: Manor House 306 Mitt St Columbia MO 65201

WORRELL, MARY THORA LEWIS, pub. affairs exec.; b. Montreal, Que., Can., July 8, 1932; d. Samuel Reinhardt and Rose Elizabeth (St. Louis) Lewis; B.A., Sir George Williams U., Montreal, 1957; m. Henry G. Worrell, July 18, 1953 (div.); children—Deborah Anne, H. Gregory, John Craig. Sec. to dean medicine McGill U., Montreal, 1950-51; sec. to headmaster Sir George Williams U., 1951-55, lectr., 1963-74; mgr. information services Descon/Concordia Systems, Ltd., 1970-71; information specialist Alcan Aluminium Ltd., Montreal, 1973-74; mgr. pub. affairs research B.F. Goodrich Co., Akron, O., 1974—. Chmn. human rights panel Action Can. Conv., 1971; panelist seminar human rights Nat. Parliamentary Prayer Breakfast, Ottawa, Ont., Can., 1972. Former trustee Pointe Claire (Que.) Municipal Library. Mem. Am. Soc. Information Sci. (pub. affairs com.). Home: 3631 Kenwood Dr Uniontown OH 44685 Office: BF Goodrich Co 500 S Main St Akron OH 44318

WORSHAM, CLARA BELL TERRY (MRS. JOHN HOWARD WORSHAM, SR.), hotel exec.; b. Billings, Okla., Dec. 28, 1914; d. Boyd Calvin and Isabelle (Caskey) Terry; student Geneva Coll., 1932-33; m. John Howard Worsham, Sr., Jan. 13, 1937; children—John Howard, Joseph Terry, Susan Ammorette (Mrs. Robert H. Henderson). Sec., John G. Baker & Campbell Thornal, attys., Orlando, Fla., 1933-43; exec. sec. Finley M. Hamilton, pres. Hilton Inns, Orlando, Fla., 1963—; sec., dir. Trubuilt, Inc., Central Fla. Motels, Inc., World Wide Inns, Inc., Global Motor Inns, Inc. Mem. Nat. Secs. Assn. Democrat. Presbyn. Home: Route 3 Box 340 Orlando FL 32811 Office: 3200 W Colonial St Orlando FL 32808

WORTH, HELEN, food authority; b. Cleve., July 17, 1913; d. Carol and Birdie (Stone) Levison; B.A., U. Mich., 1935; m. Monroe Worth, 1936 (div. 1946). Editor house organ, copywriter Scheel Advt. Agy., Cleve., 1943-45; dir. Helen Work Cooking Sch., N.Y.C., 1948—; moderator Shopper's Matinee, Dumont TV, N.Y.C., 1950; syndicated columnist, 1949-60; lectr., food cons., 1955—. Judge profl. chef's competition, Israel, 1967. Author: Down-on-the-Farm Cook Book, 1943; Shrimp Cookery, 1952; Cooking without Recipes, 1965; Hostess without Help, 1971 (Outstanding Cook Book award 1972); DamnYankee in a Southern Kitchen, 1973. Food editor Girl Talk mag., 1970—. Contbr. articles to mags. Creator Brown-Quick precooking aid. Address: 106 E 31st St New York City NY 10016

WORTSMAN, JOAN MARY SMITH (MRS. LESTER WORTSMAN), art gallery exec.; b. Mpls., Dec. 8, 1933; d. James A. and Frances H. (Schmidt) Smith; B.A., U. Minn., 1957; m. Lester Wortsman, Mar. 15, 1961. With Maxwell Galleries, San Francisco, 1956-73, dir. exhbns., 1970-73; partner, adminstr. Wortsman-Rose Galleries, Inc., San Francisco, 1973—. Home: 50 Seafirth Rd Tiburon CA 94920 Office: 575 Sutter St San Francisco CA 94102

WOSEPKA, ELIZABETH BEYLER, editor, reporter; b. Madison, Wis., July 14, 1947; d. William George and Evelyn Anna (Derleth) Beyler; B.A., U. Wis., 1969; m. Raymond W. Wosepka, Aug. 2, 1974. News editor, continuity writer Badger Broadcasting Co., radio sta. WIBA, Madison, Wis., 1968-69, news reporter, 1969—. Named Radio Newsman of Year, Madison Press Club, 1971. Mem. Women in Communications (pres. chpt. 1972-73). Club: Madison Press (dir. 1972). Home: 3024 Churchill Dr Madison WI 53713 Office: PO Box 99 Madison WI 53701

WOY, SARA GERMON (MRS. JAMES BAYLY WOY), librarian; b. Wellsburg, W.Va., Dec 25, 1925; d. Wesley Marion and Bertha (Croston) Germon; A.B., Bethany Coll., 1947; postgrad. Carnegie Inst. Tech., 1951; m. James Bayly Woy, Mar. 14, 1953; children—Susan Kate, Patricia-Ruth, Jeffrey Bayly. Tchr., librarian Cross Creek Pub. Sch., Wintersville, O., 1947-50; young adult librarian Bklyn. Pub. Library, 1951-53; asst. coordinator office work with young adults Free Library Phila., 1954-61, asst. coordinator office work with adults and young adults, 1961-65; librarian Germantown Friends Sch., Phila., 1965-70; head Friends Free Library of Phila., 1970—. Mem. A.L.A. (council 1961-65), Pa. Library Assn. Home: 405 W Stafford St Philadelphia PA 19144 Office: 5418 Germantown Av Philadelphia PA 19144

WOYSKI, MARGARET W. SKILLMAN (MRS. MARK M. WOYSKI), educator; b. West Chester, Pa., July 26, 1921; d. Willis R. and Clara (Howson) Skillman; B.A., Wellesley Coll., 1943; M.S., U. Minn., 1945, Ph.D., 1946; m. Mark M. Woyski, June 19, 1948; children—Nancy Elizabeth, William Bruno, Ronald David, Wendelin Jane. Teaching asst., instr. U. Minn., Mpls., 1943-46; research asst. Minn. Geol. Survey, Mpls., summers, 1944-46; geologist Mo. Geol. Survey and Water Resources, Rolla, Mo., 1946-48; instr. U. Wis., Madison, 1948-51; lectr. geology Cal. State Coll., Long Beach, 1963-66, prof. earth sci., Fullerton, 1966—, dept. chmn., 1973—. Troop leader, day camp dir. Du Page County Council, Girl Scouts of Am., Ill., 1954-63. Mem. Mineralogical Soc. Am., Geol. Soc. Am., Nat. Assn. Geology Tchrs., So. Coast Geol. Soc., Phi Beta Kappa, Sigma Xi. Contbr. articles in field to profl. jours. Home: 1843 Kashlan Rd LaHabra CA 90631 Office: Cal State U Fullerton CA 92634

WOZENCRAFT, MARIAN, educator; b. McConnelsville, O.; d. John George and Marian (Leitch) Wozencraft; B.A., U. Chgo., 1941; M.A., U. Ill., 1950; Ph.D., Case-Western Res. U., 1957. Elementary tchr. Dupage County, (Ill.) pub. schs., 1937-41; cost engr. Johns-Manville Co., Waukegan, Ill., 1942-49; elementary supr. Paris (Ill.) pub. schs., 1950-51; instr. Ind. State Tchrs. Coll., 1951-52; asst. prof. Fenn Coll. (now Cleve. State U.), 1952-59; prof. N.Y. State U. Coll., Geneseo, 1959—. Guest lectr. Eastern Ill. U., 1969-70, 71-72, Northeastern Ill. U., 1971. Mem. Am. Assn. U. Profs., Internat. Reading Assn., Nat. Council Tchrs. English (nat. com. jr. memberships 1960-63), Am. Assn. U. Women (legislative chmn. Geneseo br.), Kappa Delta Pi. Contbr. articles to profl. jours. Home: 1219 Monroe St Charleston IL 61920 also 28 Court St Geneseo NY 14454

WRAY, CLAIRE FRANCES LEEDS (MRS. WILSON J. WRAY), pub. relations cons.; b. San Francisco, Mar. 13, 1923; d. Roy Maxwell and Marie (Coops) Leeds; A.B. in Polit. Sci., U. Cal. at Berkeley, 1945; m. Wilson J. Wray, July 21, 1961. Feature writer, reporter San Francisco Examiner, 1944-66, spl. feature writer, 1966-67; nat. dir. publicity, pub. relations, ann. conf. A.L.A., San Francisco, 1967; pub. information dir. Irwin Meml. Blood Bank of San Francisco Med. Soc., 1967-71; freelance com. pub. relations, 1971-73; coordinator publicity Concours d'Elegance, Silverado Country Club, Napa, 1972-73; editor Hosps. and Clinics newsletter U. Cal. San Francisco Med. Center, 1972-73; editor newsletter San Francisco Gen. Hosp., 1972—; editor Reciprocity newsletter nat. clearinghouse program Am. Assn. Blood Banks, San Francisco, 1973—. Instr. publicity, pub. relations YWCA, San Francisco, 1963-66; vice chmn. com. on pub. relations and information Am. Assn. Blood Banks, chmn. ad hoc com. on pub. sch. edn. programs, 1971-73. Coordinator women's activities Alioto for Mayor Com., San Francisco, 1967; publicity chmn. San Francisco Women's Com. to Re-elect Gov. Brown, 1966. Bd. dirs. Vol. Bur. San Francisco, 1967-70, Columbia Park Boys Club Aux., Aux. to San Francisco Gen. Hosp. Mem. Friends San Francisco Library, San Francisco-Oakland Newspaper Guild. Democrat. Home: 4124 21st St San Francisco CA 94114

WREN, SUSAN BOND, realtor; b. New Orleans, May 4, 1940; d. Hayden Wilson and Jessica Marjory (Schmidt) Wren, Jr.; grad. Cottey Jr. Coll., 1959; B.S., U. So. Miss., 1961. Tng. supr. D.H. Holmes Co., Ltd., New Orleans, 1961-64; realtor Bond Inc., New Orleans, 1964—. Mem. Nat. Assn. Real Estate Bds., Nat. Inst. Real Estate Brokers, Soc. Real Estate Appraisers (asso. mem.), Orleans, Jefferson bd. realtors, Hall Group, New Orleans Garden Soc., Chi Omega Alumnae Assn. Home: 2219 Neyrey Dr Metairie LA 70001 also 929 Bourbon St New Orleans LA 70016 also 1949 Veterans Memorial Blvd New Orleans LA 70005

WRIGHT, ALMA MCINTYRE, mag. editor; b. Knoxville, Tenn., July 31, 1909; d. William Mobry and Theresa (Biagiotti) McIntyre; B.S. in Edn., U. Tenn., 1932; m. Robert Oliver Wright, Feb. 17, 1931; 1 son, Robert Oliver. Writer stories, articles on African violets, house plants, 1947—; editor African Violet Mag., 1947-63, The Master List of African Violets, 1962, GSN (Gesneriad-Saintpaulia News), 1963—, publs. of Saintpaulia Internat., 1963 (rec. sec. 1963), Am. Gerneria Soc., Inc., 1963; exec. dir. the African Violet Soc. of Am., Inc., 1960-63; pres. Indoor Gardener Pub. Co., Inc., 1963—. Mem. Am. Hort. Soc., Inc. (hon. v.p. 1954), African Violet Soc. of Am., Inc., (hon. life mem., rec. sec., 1946-48, nat. pres. 1948-49, membership sec. 1953-63). Home: 4752 Calumet Dr Knoxville TN 37919 Office: 1800-1802 Grand Av Knoxville TN 37901

WRIGHT, ANN KATHERINE FOLLINGER, social worker; b. Fort Wayne, Ind., Feb. 17, 1927; d. Alfred Martin and Margery (Moon) Follinger; student U. Mich.; B.A., Chapman Coll., 1966; M.S.W., San Diego State Coll., 1969; m. Dudley K. Wright, Sept. 24, 1947 (div. Oct. 1967); children—Margery Ann (Mrs. Howard J. Barnhorst II), Dudley K., Joan Chisholm, Pauline Clarissa, Stacey Elizabeth. Social worker Bur. Social Work, Santa Ana, Cal., 1966-67; asso. dir. Vista Assos., San Diego, 1968; social worker San Diego County Dept. Pub. Welfare, San Diego, 1969-71; Youth Service Bur., San Diego, 1971-73; supr. child protective services San Diego County Dept. Pub. Welfare, 1973—. Instr. social work Chapman Coll., 1973—. Asso. mem. St. Stephen's Group Home, San Diego, 1969-71; sec. San Diego Youth Services; mem. Community Congress San Diego, Comprehensive Health Planning Assn.; bd. dirs. In-Between, San Diego. Mem. Nat. Assn. Social Workers, Delta Delta Delta. Episcopalian. Home: 2323 Caminito Mira San Diego CA 92107 Office: 7947 Mission Center Ct San Diego CA 92108

WRIGHT, BETH JAMES (MRS. HAROLD B. WRIGHT), judge; b. Madison, Wis., Aug. 23, 1908; d. A. Earl and Ruth (Varney) James; A.B. with honors, Wellesley Coll., 1929; M.A., Radcliffe Coll.; postgrad. Columbia, 1937-39; LL.B., So. Meth. U., 1940; m. Harold B. Wright, Sept. 2, 1939; children—Ellen (Mrs. David Britton), Judith (Mrs. Alan Mason), Arthur James. Tchr., Dallas Ind. Sch. Dist., 1949-53; admitted to Tex bar, 1941; atty. Dallas County Probate Ct., 1955-56; asst. dist. atty. Dallas County Dist. Atty's. Office, 1956-57; judge Ct. Domestic Relations, Dallas County, Tex., 1957—. Mem. Nat. Assn. Women Lawyers, Am. Judicature Soc., Am., Tex. (dir. family law sect. 1966-67), Dallas bar assns., Bus. and Profl. Women Dallas, Kappa Beta Pi. Home: 1222 Commerce St Dallas TX 75202 Office: Ct Domestic Relations Courthouse Dallas TX 75202

WRIGHT, BETTY RHOADS (MRS. FRANK LESTER WRIGHT), soc. adminstr.; b. Asheville, N.C., Oct. 26, 1924; d. Edward M. and Gladys (Buckner) Rhoads; m. Frank Lester Wright, Mar. 6, 1949. Asst. promotion mgr. U.S. News & World Report, Washington, 1946-53; exec. dir. Alexandria (Va.) YWCA, 1962-63; membership dir. Nat. Hist. Soc., Harrisburg, Pa., 1963—; dir. Am. promotion Brit. History Illustrated mag., London, Eng., 1973—. Free lance writer, cons. on pub., pub. relations, 1953—. Bd. dirs. Alexandria Bi-Centennial Commn.; trustee Historic Alexandria Found. Mem. Am. Assn. for State and Local History, Early Am. Soc. (v.p. 1972—), Assos. Nat. Archives. Asst. editor Early Am. Life mag., 1972—. Home: 212 S Fairfax St Alexandria VA 22314 Office: 1001 Connecticut Av NW Washington DC 20036

WRIGHT, CHARLOTTE LEE, orgn. exec.; b. Charleston, W.Va., Nov. 7, 1947; d. Wilson Marshall and Henrietta Charlotte (Fritz) Smith; summer student E. Tex. State U., 1968, Rollins Coll. Verano Espanol, Madrid, Spain, 1969; B.J., U. Tex., 1970; m. Carroll Edward Wright, Aug. 29, 1970. Asso. news editor Daily Texan, U. Tex., Austin, 1968-69; mem. staff Herald Banner, Greenville, Tex., summers 1967-70; editor asst. Studies in English Lit. jour., Houston, 1970-72; pub. relations dir. Dayton Area chpt. A.R.C., 1972—. Will H. Mays scholar, 1969. Mem. Women in Communications (sec. 1969-70, 73-74), Dayton Advt. Club, Kappa Tau Alpha. Home: 5730 Saranac Dr Columbus OH 43227 Office: 370 W 1st St Dayton OH 45402

WRIGHT, CLEO ALVA BUCKNER (MRS. MERRILL CLAIR WRIGHT), civic worker; b. Bertram, Tex.; d. Ira Arthur and Vonnie (Ross) Buckner; B.A. (scholar 1947-51), U. Houston, 1951; m. Merrill Clair Wright, Apr. 23, 1938. Vice pres. Wright Light, Inc., Houston, 1950-67. Vol. worker hosp. and recreation corps A.R.C., Atlanta, 1942-43, Houston, 1946-48; charter founder sec. Elva A. Wright Aux. to City Tb Hosp., Houston, 1950-52, pres., 1952-53, bd. dirs. 1950-60; mem. Past Pres.'s Bd. Hosp. Auxs., 1950—; sec. Glenbrook Valley Civic Club, 1972—. Mem. Nat. Hist. Soc. (charter founding mem.), Houston Turn Verein Ladies Aux. (historian 1965-66, 68-70), Woman of Rotary (vol. and publicity chmn. 1964-65), Turn Verein Ladies Bowling Assn. (pres. 1962-64), Theta Sigma Phi (v.p. 1966-67), Phi Kappa Phi, Gamma Delta Chi. Club: Caprice Dance (sec. 1970-71). Home: 8102 Colgate St Houston TX 77017

WRIGHT, DOROTHY MARIE (MRS. JOHN WEBB WRIGHT), librarian; b. Roswell, N.M., Sept. 18, 1922; d. William August and Ollie Otelia (Conn) Hoffman; student Eastern N.M. U., 1939-41, N.M. State U., 1941-42; B.A., U. Denver, 1943; postgrad. U. Tex., 1955, Odessa Coll., 1956; M.L.S. (Nat. Def. Edn. Act Inst. grantee), Tex. Womans U., 1970; m. John Webb Wright, Apr. 18, 1945; children—John David, Gary Hoffman, Barbara Ann. Childrens librarian Sioux Falls Pub. Library, 1943-44, Enoch Pratt Free Library, Balt., 1944, Midland (Tex.) Pub. Library, 1945; librarian Hays and Burnet Elementary Schs., Odessa, Tex., 1957—. Mem. Am., Tex. library assns., Tex. Assn. Sch. Librarians, Tex. Tchrs. Assn. (dist. sec.-treas. library sect. 1971), Tex. Classroom Tchrs. Assn., N.E.A., P.E.O. (chpt. pres. 1970), Permian Basin Geneal. Soc. Methodist. Home: 3600 Springdale St Odessa TX 79762 Office: PO Box 3912 Odessa TX 79760

WRIGHT, DOROTHY VIRGINIA GAY (MRS. RUSSELL M. WRIGHT), corp. exec.; b. Des Moines, Dec. 4, 1906; d. Charles L. and Eleanor (Thackston) Gay; Drake U., 1929; m. Russell M. Wright, June 5, 1929; children—Richard Alexander, Dorothy Gay (Mrs. Luis F. Vela), Katherine Sue (Mrs. Jan Willioughby). Dir., treas. Machete Nile Corp. British Honduras Central Am., 1964-70; sec., treas., dir. Richard Wright Corp., Delray Beach, Fla.; owner, dir. Wright by the Sea, Delray Beach; sec., photographer med. com. Internat. Fedn. Weightlifting. Mem. Nat., Mich. (counselor 1963) rehab. assns. Home: Wright By the Sea Delray Beach FL 33444 also Vztop Mountain Highlands NC Office: 1901 S Ocean Blvd Delray Beach FL 33444

WRIGHT, ELEANOR BUMGARDNER (MRS. FRANK S. WRIGHT), former govt. ofcl.; b. Peoria, Ill., Mar. 4, 1900; d. Harry Daniel and Ella (Hartnett) Bumgardner; student U. Detroit, 1919-20, Detroit Tchrs. Coll., 1921, U. Mich., 1922-24; m. Frank Sumner Wright, Dec. 29, 1966. Exec. sec. Detroit Edison Co., 1927-28; exec. sec., v.p. Union Guardian Trust Co., Detroit, 1929-32; exec. sec. to Frank Murphy, Mayor Detroit, Gov. Gen. and High Commr. to Philippines, 1933-36, Gov. Mich., 1937-38, then U.S. Supreme Ct. Justice, Washington, 1939-49; floating exec. sec. U.S. Supreme Ct., Washington, 1949-61; asst. to Eunice Shriver on Pres. Kennedy's Panel on Mental Retardation, 1962; asst., companion to Jeane Dixon, 1963-66; lectr. secretarial classes, 1961-66. Recipient prize for article Profl. Writers Contest, 1964. Mem. Profl. Writers Club, Nat. League Am. Pen Women, Writers League (pres. 1965-66), Palm Beach Quills, Women in Communication, Mich. State Club. Republican. Contbr. numerous articles to profl. jours. Address: 701 Trianon 1200 S Flagler Dr West Palm Beach FL 33401

WRIGHT, ELEANOR STRAUB (MRS. JAMES A. WRIGHT), editor; b. St. Louis, June 25, 1923; d. Charles H. and Edna C. (Schulz) Straub; A.A., Monticello Coll., 1943; B.S., M.S., Northwestern U., 1945; m. James A. Wright, June 21, 1947; children—Carolyn (Mrs. Tommy Whitton), Elizabeth Ann. Soc. reporter St. Louis Post-Dispatch, 1945-47; publicity, field worker Trenton (N.J.) Community Chest, 1947-50; weekly columnist Webster Advertiser, 1960-65; asso. editor Barks Publs., Inc., St. Louis, Chgo., 1964-73; editor Unicorn, Theta Xi Frat., Webster Groves, Mo., 1973—; asst. editor St. Louis County Observer, 1973—. Area rep. Am. Field Service Internat. Scholarships, 1971—; leader St. Louis council Girl Scouts U.S.A., 1956-61, mem. bd., 1960-64. Mem. Women in Communication. Presbyn. Asst. editor Elec. Apparatus Mag., 1964-71. Home: 550 Lee Av Webster Groves MO 63119

WRIGHT, ESTELLA VIOLA HARRISON (MRS. WILLIAM M. WRIGHT), sculptor; b. Riceville, Ga.; d. Elijah and Elicia (Butler) Harrison; student Art Student's League, 1937, 48-50, (scholar) Newark Mus., 1961, summer 1962, Nat. Acad. Sch. Fine Arts, 1962, Nat. Acad. Design, fall 1962; m. William M. Wright, Apr. 24, 1928 (dec. Feb. 1936). One-man shows at various banks, also Scott's Auditorium; exhibited in group shows at Artists of Am. at Master Inst., 1941, Audubon Artists Ann., 1942, N.A.D., 1962, Art Exhbn. Springfield (Mass.), 1962, Countee Cullen Pub. Library, 1963, others; life-size works various persons, including George Washington Carver, Thomas Bethune, also portrait busts; represented in permanent collections. Gray Lady, Harlem Hosp., N.Y.C., 1951—. Recipient certificate of pub. service State of N.Y., 1958, citation for meritorious service Bklyn. Women's Council, 1963. Mem. Art Student's League (life), John Brown Meml. Assn., Rosicrucian Anthrosophic League Sch. Philosophy. Address: 226 W 138th St New York City NY 10030

WRIGHT, HELEN DALE (MRS. CARROLL JOSEPH WRIGHT, JR.), Clin. psychologist; b. Tylertown, Miss., Sept. 26, 1926; d. William Henry and Frances Pauline (White) Armstrong; B.A., Miss. Coll., 1946; M.A., U. Louisville, 1955; postgrad. Wayne State U., 1957-58; Ph.D. (USPHS fellow), U. Cal at Los Angeles, 1966; m. Carroll Joseph Wright, Jr., Aug. 25, 1951; children—William Douglas, Debora Dawn. Teaching fellow Wayne State U., Detroit, 1957-58; clin. psychology fellow Neuropsychiat. Inst. U. Cal. at Los Angeles Center for Health Scis., 1965-66; lectr. psychology dept. U. Cal at Los Angeles, summer 1966, asst. prof. in residence, 1966-67; dir. Asso. Marriage Counselors, Encino, Cal., 1970—. Instr. psychology U. Cal at Los Angeles Extension, 1971. Mem. Am. Psychol. Assn., Sigma Xi, Psi Chi. Contbr. articles to profl. jours. Home: 4901 Gaviota Encino CA 91436 Office: 15840 Ventura Blvd Encino CA 91436

WRIGHT, HELEN JOHN, extension home economist; b. Lenoir, N.C., Apr. 9, 1914; d. Thomas Alexander and Harriet (Harkey) Wright; student Baylor U., 1931-32; B.S. in Sci. and Home Econ., Queens Coll., 1937; postgrad. Colo. State U., 1966, Ariz. U., 1967, Kan. State U., 1971. With extension service N.C., 1938-60, Extension home economist N.C. State U., Charlotte, N.C., 1938-60; food and nutrition cons. South and West Cafeterias, Charlotte, 1960-61; home economist extension service Elko, Nev., 1963-66; home economist Lander, Wyo., 1966—. Mem. Altrusa Club, Charlotte, 1966—. Mem. Nat. Home Econ. Assn., Nat. Extension Home Economists Assn., Nat. Assn. Home Econs., Am. Assn. U. Women, Wind River Artists Guild, Epsilon Sigma Phi, Kappa Delta, Alpha Kappa Gamma. Mem. White Shrine Jerusalem, Order Eastern Star. Home: 1395 Hillcrest Dr Lander WY 82520 Office: County Court House Lander WY 82520 also Box 248 Fort Washakie WY 82514

WRIGHT, HELEN KENNEDY (MRS. SAMUEL A. WRIGHT), editor; b. Indpls., Sept. 23, 1927; d. William Henry and Ida Louise (Crosby) Kennedy; B.A., Butler U., 1945, M.S., 1950; M.S., Columbia, 1952; m. Samuel A. Wright, Sept. 5, 1970; 1 son, Carl F. Prince II. Reference librarian N.Y. Pub. Library, N.Y.C., 1952-53, Bklyn. Pub. Library, 1953-54; cataloger U. Utah, 1954-57; librarian Chgo. Pub. Library; asst. dir. pub. dept. A.L.A., Chgo., 1958—, now subscription books coordinator. Mem. Phi Kappa Phi, Kappa Delta Phi, Sigma Gamma Rho. Roman Catholic. Home: 1138 W 111th St Chicago IL 60643 Office: 50 E Huron Chicago IL 60611

WRIGHT, HELEN MITCHELL PATTON (MRS. J. SKELLY WRIGHT), civic worker; b. Washington, Jan. 15, 1919; d. Raymond Stanton and Virginia (Mitchell) Patton; student Sweet Briar Coll., 1936-38; m. J(ames) Skelly Wright, Feb. 1, 1945; 1 son, James Skelly. Tchr., Washington Sch. for Secretaries, N.Y.C., 1939-40; sec. White House, Washington, 1941-43; sec. to minister econ. warfare Am. embassy, London, Eng., 1943-45; asst. to exec. dir. Senate AEC, U.S. Capitol, Washington, 1946-47. Vice pres. United Fund, New Orleans, 1960-62, Dept. Pub. Welfare, New Orleans, 1954-62, Milne Asylum for Destitute Orphan Boys, 1958-62; mem. Social Welfare Planning Council, New Orleans, 1954-60; v.p. La. Assn. Mental Health, 1960-62. Bd. dirs. Washington Health and Welfare Council, 1962-64, D.C. Assn. Mental Health, 1962-72, Hillcrest Childrens Center, 1963-69; dir.-at-large Nat. Assn. Mental Health, 1962-68, 69—, sec., 1968-70, v.p., 1970-71, pres., 1972-73; mem. adv. council Nat. Inst. Mental Health, 1971—; mem. commn. on mentally disabled Am. Bar Assn., 1973-74. Home: 5317 Blackistone Washington DC 20016

WRIGHT, IRENE KUHN (MRS. HERBERT G. WRIGHT), banker, artist; b. Shreveport, Pa., May 26, 1917; d. John and Susie (Phillips) Kuhn; B.S., Centenary Coll. La., 1938; m. Herbert G. Wright, Nov. 21, 1951 (dec. 1969). With First Nat. Bank of Shreveport, 1941—, asst. trust officer, 1951-57, trust officer, 1957-72, v.p., trust officer, 1972—; one-artist exhibit Centenary Coll., 1973; exhibited in numerous group shows, area shows, travelling shows. Recipient various art awards. Mem. Nat. Assn. Bank Women (chmn. La. group 1956), So. Intercoll. Math. Assn., Hoover Watercolor Soc. (pres. 1972-73), Alpha Chi, Alpha Xi Delta. Home: 809 Camilla Dr Shreveport LA 71104 Office: First Nat Bank of Shreveport PO Box 1116 Shreveport LA 71154

WRIGHT, JANE COOKE (MRS. DAVID D. JONES JR.), physician; b. N.Y.C., Nov. 30, 1919; d. Louis T. and Corinne (Cooke) Wright; A.B., Smith Coll., 1942; M.D., N.Y. Med. Coll., 1945; D.Sc., Woman's Med. Coll., 1965; Sc.D., Denison U., 1971; m. David D. Jones, July 27, 1947; children—Jane, Alison. Intern Bellevue Hosp. 4th Med. Div., 1945-46, asst. resident internal medicine, 1946; resident Harlem Hosp., 1947, chief resident, 1948, clin. asst. vis. physician, 1949, asst. vis. physician medicine, 1949-55; sch. physician N.Y.C. Dept. Health, 1949; clinician Cancer Research Found. Harlem Hosp., 1949-52, dir., 1952-55; asst. vis. physician Bellevue Hosp. 4th Surg. Div., 1955-60, asso. vis. physician, 1960-67; instr. research surgery postgrad. surgery dept. N.Y.U.-Bellevue Med. Center, 1955, asst. prof., 1956-67, dir. cancer chemotherapy service, 1955-67; adj. asso. prof. research surgery N.Y.U., 1961-67; prof. surgery, asso. dean N.Y. Med. Coll., 1967—; asst. attending physician U. Hosp., 1956—; cons. in oncology Wyckoff Heights Hosp., 1969—, Blvd. Hosp., 1963—; courtesy staff Midtown Hosp., 1962—; attending in surgery Flower-Fifth Av. Hosps., 1967—, Met. Hosp., 1967—, Bird S. Coler Meml. Hosp., 1967—; cons. dept. medicine St. Vincent's Hosp., 1966—. Bd. dirs. Medico-Care, N.Y. Cancer Soc., pres., 1970-71; bd. dirs. N.Y.C. div. Am. Cancer Soc., 1962—; mem. Manhattan Council State Commn. Human Rights; mem. President's Commn. Heart Disease, Cancer and Stroke; mem. Nat. Cancer Adv. Council, 1966-70; cons. Nat. Inst. Gen. Med. Scis., 1973—. Vice pres. African Research Found.; trustee Smith Coll., 1970—. Recipient Mademoiselle award, 1952; Spirit of Achievement award Albert Einstein Sch. Medicine, 1965; Smith medal Smith Coll., 1968; Outstanding Am. Woman award Am. Mothers Com., 1970. Mem. Am. Assn. Clin. Onocology, A.A.A.S., N.Y. County Med. Assn., Manhattan Central Med. Soc., Nat. Med. Assn., N.Y. Acad. Scis,, Contin Soc., N.Y. Cancer Soc., UN Assn. of U.S.A., Am. Assn. Cancer Research (dir. 1971—). Author numerous articles in field. Office: NY Med Coll Fifth Av at 106th St New York City NY 10029

WRIGHT, JANE ELIZABETH, librarian; b. Anderson, S.C., Dec. 21, 1918; d. Alvin McLenna and Elisabeth (Robertson) Wright; A.B., Winthrop Coll., 1940; B.S. in L.S., U. N.C., 1950; M.S., Columbia, 1959. Tchr. pub. schs., Anderson, 1940-44; clk. Shell Oil Co., N.Y.C., 1944-45; transit clk. Carolina Nat. Bank, Anderson, 1945-46; librarian Boys' High Sch., Anderson, 1946-50; asst. librarian Poly. High Sch., Long Beach, Cal., 1950-51; instr. Winthrop Coll., Rock Hill, S.C., 1951-59, asst. prof. Winthrop Coll., 1959-67; grad. asst. Sch. Library Service, Columbia U., 1958-59; asst. prof. Furman U., Greenville, S.C., 1967-70, asso. prof., 1970-73; librarian Brevard (N.C.) Coll., 1973—; vis. asst. prof. Sch. Library Sci., U. N.C. summers, 1961-66, U. Washington, summer 1961, Columbia, 1968, U. N.C., Greensboro, summer 1969; vis. asso. prof. Appalachian State U., summer 1971; mem. editorial bd. E.M. Hale Pub. Co., 1969-72. Recipient Grolier Americana scholarship, Sch. of Library Service, Columbia U., 1957. Mem. Assn. Am. Library Schs., A.L.A. (council 1972-73), Am. Assn. Sch. Librarians, S.C. Edn. Assn., S.C. (treas. 1961-62), N.C., Southeastern library assns., Altrusa (pres. Greenville 1972-73), Beta Phi Mu, Delta Kappa Gamma. Home: Box 1183 Brevard NC 28712

WRIGHT, JANE ELIZABETH, univ. librarian; b. Fulton, N.Y., Apr. 20, 1927; d. William Robertson and Genevieve Agnes (McCormick) Wright; B.E., State U. Coll. at Oswego, 1948, M.S., 1955; M.S. in L.S., Syracuse U., 1955. Tchr., Lowville Acad., 1948-49, Oswego (N.Y.) City Sch. Dist., 1949-54; childrens librarian Rochester Pub. Library, 1955-61; periodicals librarian State U. Coll. at Oswego, 1961-70, head tech. services, 1970-74, head periodicals dept., profl. studies area of collection devel. unit, 1974—. Mem. Am., N.Y. State library assns., State U. N.Y. Librarians Assn., Kappa Delta Pi, Phi Beta Mu, Delta Kappa Gamma. Club: Philomelian Alumnae. Home: 42 Lincoln Av Oswego NY 13126

WRIGHT, KATHERINE SETTLE (MRS. FRED BOYER WRIGHT, JR.), lawyer; b. Roanoke, Va., Aug. 8, 1926; d. Byron Wheeler and Katherine Haller (Henson) Settle; A.B., Coll. William and Mary, 1947; LL.B., U. N.C., 1949; LL.M., Tulane U., 1957; m. Fred Boyer Wright, Jr., Sept. 4, 1948; children—Amanda Lois, Katherine Irene. Admitted to Va. bar, 1948, Ill. bar, 1950, La. bar, 1961, N.C. bar, 1969; clk., asso. Sonnenschein, Berkson, Lautmann, Levinson & Morse, 1949-51; asso. Defrees, Fiske, O'Brien & Thomson, 1951-53; asso., mem. firm Pilie, Pilie & Landry, 1963-67; mem. firms Nelson, Ormond & Nelson, 1967-68, Manning, Allen & Hudson, Chapel Hill, N.C., 1973-74, Allen, Hudson & Wright, 1974—; pvt. practice New Orleans, Chapel Hill, 1961-63, 69-73. Research asst. trust code project La. Law Inst., 1959-61. Mem. Com. for Equal Rights Amendment, N.C. Women's Polit. Caucus, 1973—; mem. citizens adv. com. New Orleans Child Welfare Dept., 1967-68; mem. profl. adv. bd. Durham-Chapel Hill chpt. Parents Without Partners, 1973—. Election judge Democratic party, 1953. Bd. dirs. Save our Schs. Mem. Nat. Assn. Women Lawyers, N.C. State Bar, Women's Bar Ill. (treas. 1953-54), Order of Coif, Phi Beta Kappa, Kappa Delta. Episcopalian. Asst. editor: Forrester, Cases on Constitutional Law, 1958. Home: Buttons Lane Chapel Hill NC 27514 Office: 123 W Franklin St Chapel Hill NC 27514

WRIGHT, KATIE HARPER, ednl. adminstr.; b. Crawfordsville, Ark., Oct. 5, 1923; d. James Hale and Connie Mary (Locke) Harper; B.A., U. Ill., 1944; M.Ed., 1959; postgrad. So. Ill. U., 1962-73; m. Marvin Wright, Mar. 21, 1952; 1 dau., Virginia (Mrs. Ed Jordan). Elementary and spl. edn. tchr. East St. Louis (Ill.) Pub. Schs., 1944-65, dir. Dist. 189 Instructional Materials Program, 1965-71, dir. spl. edn. Dists. 188, 189, 1971—. Cons. to numerous workshops, seminars in field; mem. Ill. Commn. on Children, 1973—; mem. Ill. Assn. Spl. Educators Bd., 1974—; mem. Pub. Library Children's Services Task Force, 1973—. Pres. bd. dirs. St. Clair Community Mental Health Center, 1970-72; bd. dirs. Tri-County Health and Welfare Council, 1960—; pres. bd. trustees East St. Louis Pub. Library, 1972—. Recipient Lamp of Learning award East St. Louis Jr. Wednesday Club, 1965; Outstanding Working Woman award Downtown St. Louis, Inc., 1967; Ill. State citation for ednl. document Love is Not Enough, 1974; Model Cities grantee for spl. edn., 1972-74. Mem. Am. Libraries Trustees Assn. (nat. membership chmn.), Mensa, Top Ladies of Distinction, Delta Sigma Theta Sorority (chpt. pres. 1970-72), Kappa Delta Pi (pres. So. Ill. U. chpt.). Republican. Mem. African Episcopal Zion Ch. Club: East St. Louis Women's (pres.). Contbr. articles to profl. jours. Home: 733 North 40th St East St Louis IL 62205 Office: 231 N 10th St East St Louis IL 62201

WRIGHT, LILYAN BOYD, educator; b. Upland, Pa., May 11, 1920; d. Albert Verlenden and Mabel (Warburton) Boyd; B.S., Temple U., 1942, M.Ed., 1946; Ed.D., Rutgers U., 1972; m. Richard P. Wright, Oct. 23, 1942; 1 dau., Nicki Warburton (Mrs. Arthur Scott Vanek). Tchr. health and phys. edn. Woodbury (N.J.) High Sch., 1942-43, Glen-Nor High Sch., Glenolden, Pa., 1944-46, Chester (Pa.) High Sch., 1946-54; chmn. women's dept. health and phys, edn. Union (N,J.) High Sch., 1954-61; with Trenton State Coll., 1961—, head women's program health and phys. edn., 1967—. Mem. N.J. State Com. Div. Girls and Women's Sports, 1958—. Active Chester United Fund; water safety, first aid instr. A.R.C. Scholarship in her honor N.J. Athletic Assn. Girls, 1971. Mem. Am. (chmn. Eastern dist. assn. div. girls and women's sports), N.J. (pres. 1974—, v.p. phys. edn., Distinguished Service and Leadership award 1969), assns. health, phys. edn. and recreation, N.J. Women's Lacrosse Assn. (umpiring chmn. 1972—), Am. Assn. Sch. Adminstrs., Nat., Eastern assns. phys. edn. coll. women, Am. Assn. U. Profs., North Jersey, Central Jersey bds. women's ofcls., Am., Pa. (v.p. 1953-54), Chester (pres. 1949-54) fedns. tchrs., U.S. (exec. com.), North Jersey (past pres.) field hockey assns., Kappa Delta Epsilon, Delta Psi Kappa (past pres. Phila. alumni chpt.), Kappa Delta Pi. Episcopalian. Home: 260 Green Valley Rd Langhorne PA 19047 Office: Trenton State College Trenton NJ 08625

WRIGHT, LUCY MAE MARABLE (MRS. WILLIAM F. WRIGHT), city ofcl.; b. Nashville, Jan. 3, 1920; d. Robert Lee and Sarah Elizabeth (Wylie) Marable; student Ward Belmont Coll., 1936-37, Watkins Bus. Sch., 1940-41; m. William F. Wright, Jan. 21, 1937; 1 son, Robert Marable. Account clk. Vultee Aircraft Corp., Nashville, 1941-46; accounts payable clk., City of Richland Hills, Tex., 1954-62, sec., treas., assessor-collector, 1962—. Mem. Municipal Finance Officers Assn., Tex. Assn. Assessing Officers, Assn. City Clks. Tex. Home: 7274 Hardisty St Fort Worth TX 76118 Office: 3201 Diana Dr Fort Worth TX 76118

WRIGHT, MARGARET RUTH, zoologist, educator; b. Rochester, N.Y., Mar. 24, 1913; d. Adelbert Frank and Ethal (Potter) Wright; A.B., U. Rochester, 1934, M.S., 1938; Ph.D., Yale, 1946. Instr. zoology Middlebury (Vt.) Coll., 1943-46; instr. zoology Vassar Coll., 1946-48, asst. prof., 1948-53, asso. prof., 1953-59, prof., 1959—. Mem. A.A.A.S., Am. Soc. Zoologists, N.Y. Acad. Scis., Am. Inst. Biol. Scis., Am. Assn. U. Profs., Ecol. Soc. Am., Sigma Xi. Contbr. articles to profl. jours. Home: 47 Marian Av Poughkeepsie NY 12601

WRIGHT, MARGUERITE WITTWER (MRS. THOMAS GREER WRIGHT), govt. ofcl.; b. Scharnachthal, Switzerland, Feb. 19, 1926; d. Jacob and Madeleine (Hari) Wittwer; came to U.S., 1930, naturalized, 1948; B.A., U. Ore., 1947; m. Thomas Greer Wright, June 14, 1946; children—Suzanne Katherine, Patricia Madeleine, Sarah Elizabeth, Jeanne Marguerite. Women's editor Capital Press, Salem, Ore., 1963-65; asst. publs. editor Ore. Dept. Edn., Salem, part-time, 1965; instr. journalism Ore. Coll. Edn., Monmouth, part-time, 1965; health educator Marion County Health Dept., Salem, 1965-66; community organizer Mid-Williamette Valley Community Action Program, Salem, 1966-69; dir. publs.-information services Ore. Bd. Edn. 1970-73; adminstrv. asst. to majority leader Ore. Ho. of Reps., 1973—. Charter mem. Salem Area Human Relations Commn., 1964-67; mem. Ore. Civil Rights Adv. Com., 1965-69, Ore. Small Bus. Adv. Council, 1965-66; mem. County Budget Adv. Com., 1967; v.p. Marion County Health Council, 1967. A founder, pres. Salem Jane Jefferson Democratic Club, 1957; pres. Marion County Dem. Club, 1964; mem. Ore. Dem. Central Com., 1964. Bd. dirs. Salem Art Assn., 1963-66, Pentacle Theatre, Salem, 1967-68. Recipient Distinguished Service award City of Salem, 1966; Woman of Achievement award Theta Sigma Phi; Rural Service award U.S. Office Econ. Opportunity, 1968. Mem. Mortar Bd., Theta Sigma Phi, Sigma Kappa. Presbyn. (deacon 1967—). Home: 6914 SW Burlingame Av Portland OR 97219 Office: 106 State Capitol Bldg Salem OR 97310

WRIGHT, MARY JEAN, educator; b. Strathroy, Ont., Can., May 20, 1915; d. Ernest Joel and Mary Jean (Clark) Wright; B.A., U. Western Ont., 1939; M.A., U. Toronto, 1940, Ph.D., 1949. Psychologist, Protestant Children's Village, Ottawa, 1941-42; instr. Garrison-Lane Nursery Tng. Sch., Birmingham, Eng., 1942-44; psychologist Mental Health Clinic, Hamilton, Ont., 1944-45; instr. Inst. Child Study, U. Toronto, Ont., 1945-46; asst. prof. U. Western Ont., London, 1946-55, asso. prof., 1955-62, prof., 1962—, chmn. dept. psychology Middlesex Coll., 1960-63, chmn. dept. psychology, 1963-70, dir. univ. lab. presch., 1973—. Sec., E.J. Wright Central and affiliated cos., Strathroy, 1956—. Mem. adv. bd. London Children's Psychiat. Research Inst., 1966-70; chmn. Ont. Bd. Examiners in Psychology, 1973-74. Mem. Am., Eastern, Canadian (dir., pres. 1968-69), Ont. (dir. 1950-53, pres. 1950-51) psychol. assns., Canadian Com. on Early Childhood, Nursery Edn. Assn. Ont. (dir. 1956-60, chmn. certification bd. 1964-66), Canadian Assn. U. Profs., Soc. for Research in Child Devel., Gamma Phi Beta. Mem. Anglican Ch. Home: 1032 Western Rd London N6G 1G4 ON Canada

WRIGHT, MARY RUTH (MRS. WILLIAM KEMP WRIGHT), psychologist; b. St. Louis, Apr. 2, 1922; d. Leon Carl and Gwendolyn (Travis) Brown; R.N., Washington U., St. Louis, 1944; B.S., U. Houston, 1966, M.A., 1967; m. William Kemp Wright, Feb. 10, 1945; children—Gwendolyn, Veronica, Victoria, Jennifer. Instr. surgery Washington U. Sch. Nursing, 1944-45; instr. pediatrics Childrens Meml. Hosp., Chgo., 1945-46; teaching fellow U. Houston, 1965-66; instr. S. Tex. Jr. Coll., Houston, 1967-70; mental health cons. St. Joseph Mental Hosp., Houston, 1966-67; staff psychol. services Almeda Clinic, Houston, 1966-70; pvt. practice marriage and family counselor, Houston, 1970—; research asso. William Kemp Wright, 1970—; psychologist Vasectomy Clinic, City of Houston Health Dept., 1971—. Panelist, Pan Am. Congress Otorhinolaryngology and Bronchoesophogology, Panama, 1973, Ann. Meeting Am. Acad. Facial Plastic and Reconstructive Surgery, St. Louis, 1974. Instr. U.S. Cadet Nurse Corps, USPHS, 1944, recipient Spl. award Security Agy. Mem. Am. Psychol. Assn., Am. Assn. Marriage and Family Counselors, Am. Assn. Sex Educators and Counselors, Internat. Council Psychologists, Nat. Council Family Relations, Nat. Assn. Social Workers, Mental Health Assn. Houston and Harris County (dir.). Contbr. articles profl. jours. Home: 3671 Del Monte St Houston TX 77019 Office: 508 Hermann Profl Bldg Houston TX 77025

WRIGHT, MATTIE K., govt. ofcl.; b. Savannah, Ga., Nov. 7, 1923; d. Joseph William and Mattie (Simkins) Handy; student Herzl Jr. City Coll., Chgo., 1940-43; B.A., Roosevelt U., Chgo., 1947; M.S.W., Loyola U., Chgo., 1949; m. William Earl Wright, 1954 (dec.); 1 dau., Pamela Y. (Mrs. Peter Woolfolk). Psychiat. social worker Ill. Dept. Mental Health, Chgo., 1949-52; social worker Family Service Bur., United Charities Chgo., 1952-58; social worker, supr. West Side VA

Hosp., Chgo., 1958-63; dir. Community Services Project for Unwed Pregnant Adolescents, Chgo. Bd. Health, 1963-66; dir. Crittenton Comprehensive Care Centers, Florence Crittenton Assn. Am., Chgo., 1966-73; spl. asst. to adminstr. Health Services and Mental Health Adminstrn., Dept. Health, Edn. and Welfare, Rockville, Md., 1972-73, dir. equal employment opportunity Office Asst. Sec. Health, Pub. Health Services, 1973—. Bd. dirs. Chgo. United Cerebral Palsy, Friends of Chgo. Pub. Library. Recipient Meritorious Service award Chgo. City Coll., Amundsen-Mayfair Campus, 1969; named One of Chgo.'s Outstanding Progressive Women, 1967. Mem. Nat. Assn. Social Workers, Am. Acad. Certified Social Workers, Nat. Council on Illegitimacy (past vice chmn. Chgo. chpt.), Am. Orthopsychiat. Assn. (nat. conf. social welfare), Urban League, N.A.A.C.P., Alpha Gamma Pi. Home: Highland House W 4450 S Park Av Chevy Chase MD 20015 Office: 5600 Fishers Lane Rockville MD 20852

WRIGHT, MURIEL HAZEL, social scientist; b. Lehigh, Indian Ty.; d. Eliphalet Nott and Ida Belle (Richards) Wright; grad. E. Central State Normal, Ada, Okla., 1912; postgrad. Barnard Coll., Columbia, 1916-17; L.H.D., Oklahoma City U., 1964. High sch. and elementary sch. tchr., Johnston and Coal Counties, Okla., 1912-24; mem., sec. Choctaw Adv. Council, 1934-44; researcher, writer articles Okla. Hist. Soc., 1924-73, editor The Chronicles of Okla., 1943-73. Mem. hist. adv. panel Gov.'s Council for Cultural Devel., 1964-73; mem. Okla. bd. geog. names Okla. Geol. Survey, 1965. Recipient Distinguished Service citation U. Okla., 1948; named Woman of Yr., Oklahoma City Bus. and Profl. Women, 1951; named to Okla. Hall of Fame, 1940; Matrix award Theta Sigma Phi, 1941; award for contbn. to youth Campfire Girls, 1968; named Outstanding Indian Woman, Nat. Am. Indian Women's Assn, 1971; certificate of appreciation for vol. service White House, 1971. Mem. Okla. Poetry Soc., Okla. Writers Assn. (hon.), Nat. League Am. Pen Women (pres. Okla. City br. 1962-64), Orgn. Am. Historians, Okla. City Civil War Round Table (pres. 1963-64), MacDowell Colony of Fellows, Am. Assn. State and Local History, So. Hist. Assn., Soc. Mayflower Descs., U.D.C., Daus. Am. Revolution, Colonial Dames XVII Century, Okla. Hist. Soc. (hon. life), Okla. Heritage Assn., Alpha Gamma Delta, Delta Kappa Gamma (hon.). Presbyn. Clubs: Red Bud, Women's Dinner, Nat. Hall of Fame for Famous Am. Indians (pres.). Author: A Guide to the Indian Tribes of Oklahoma, 1951; The Story of Oklahoma, 1929; Our Oklahoma, 1939; The Oklahoma History, 1955; (with J. B. Thoburn) Oklahoma: A History of the State and Its People, 1929; (with George H. Shirk) The Rambler in Oklahoma, 1955, Oklahoma Mark of Heritage, 1958, 74; (with Dr. Le Roy H. Fischer) Civil War Sites in Oklahoma, 1968. Office: Okla Hist Soc Hist Bldg Oklahoma City OK 73105

WRIGHT, NATHALIA, educator; b. Athens, Ga., Mar. 29, 1913; d. Hilliard Carlisle and Elizabeth (MacNeal) Wright; B.A., Maryville Coll., 1933; M.A., Yale, 1938, Ph.D., 1949. Instr. Maryville Coll., 1934-35, 41-47, asst. in library, 1940-43, asst. librarian, 1943-48; asst. prof. U. Tenn., 1949-55, asso. prof., 1955-62, prof., 1962—. Recipient Willis Tew prize Yale, 1936, Albert Stanburrough Cook prize in poetry, 1937. Guggenheim fellow 1953; Am. Philos. Soc. grantee, 1952; Am. Assn. U. Women fellow, 1959. Mem. Modern Lang. Assn. (adv. council Am. lit. sect. 1973—, editorial com. publs. 1970—), Melville Soc., Internat. Assn. U. Profs. English, Am. Soc. Learned Socs. (dir.), Phi Beta Kappa, Phi Kappa Phi. Author: The Inner Room, 1938; Melville's Use of the Bible, 1949; Horatio Greenough, The First American Sculptor, 1963; American Novelists in Italy: Allston to James, 1965; (with Harold Orton) Questionaire for the Investigation of Regional American English, 1972; also articles in scholarly jours. Introduction: Horatio Greenough, The Travels, Observations, and Experience of a Yankee Stonecutter, 1958; John Galt, The Life of Benjamin West, 1959; Washington Allston, Lectures on Art and Poems, and Monaldi, 1967; Mary Noailles Murfree, In The Tennessee Mountains, 1970. Editor: Washington Irving Journals and Notebooks, Vol. I, 1803-1806, 1969; The Letters of Horatio Greenough, 1972. Editorial bd. Publ. Modern Lang. Assn., 1970—. Home: 713 Court St Maryville TN 37801

WRIGHT, PAULINE REYNOLDS (MRS. S. EARL WRIGHT), lawyer; b. New Berlin, Ill., June 30, 1924; d. William Andrew and Ellen (Frogge) Pogue; LL.M., Van Norman U., 1968; m. S. Earl Wright, Feb. 25, 1972. Exec. sec. Electro-Mech. Research, Inc., 1957-66; admitted to Cal. bar, 1969; partner firm Wright & Wright, Los Angeles, 1972—. Mem. Am., Los Angeles County, Lawyer-Pilot, Women-Lawyers bar assns. Home: 2137 Buenos Aires Dr Covina CA 91722

WRIGHT, SARAH E., author. Cons. N.Y. State Council Arts, Creative Artists Pub. Service Program. Fellow MacDowell Colony; mem. P.E.N., Authors Guild, Inc., Authors League Am. Author: This Child's Gonna Live, 1969. Address: care Dell Publishing Co Inc 750 3d Av New York City NY 10017

WRIGHT, WILLIE RUTH, coll. dean; b. Cherokee County, Ala., May 18, 1934; d. Mark and Glennie Aronia (Booker) Wright; B.S., Ala. State U., 1968, M.Ed., 1970; postgrad. Atlanta U., summer 1969; m. A.J. Lindsey, Oct. 18, 1953 (div. Jan. 1956); 1 dau., Sara Joyce Lindsey. Dormitory dir. Ala. State U., Montgomery, 1968-70; Freshmen counselor Miles Coll., Birmingham, Ala., 1971, dir. women affairs, 1972, dir. student life and devel., 1973—, instr. edn., 1970—; instr. edn. Ala. State U., Montgomery, 1969-70. Mem. Nat. Assn. Women Deans, Adminstrs. and Counselors, P.T.A., Order Eastern Star. Democrat. Methodist. Club: Progressive Women Guild Service (sec. 1956-58). Home: 5705 Av H Fairfield AL 35264 Office: 5500 Av G Birmingham AL 35208

WRIGLEY, ELIZABETH SPRINGER (MRS. OLIVER K. WRIGLEY), found. exec.; b. Pitts., Oct. 4, 1915; d. Charles Woodward and Sarah Maria (Roberts) Springer; B.A., U. Pitts., 1935; B.S., Carnegie Inst. Tech., 1936; m. Oliver Kenneth Wrigley, June 16, 1936. Procedure analyst U.S. Steel Corp., Pitts., 1941-43; Research asst. The Francis Bacon Found., Inc., Los Angeles, 1944, exec., 1945-50, trustee, 1950—, dir. research, 1951-53, pres., 1954—. Mem. Renaissance Soc. Am., Modern Humanities Research Assn., Am. Cryptogram Assn., Alpha Delta Pi. Presbyn. Mem. Order Eastern Star, Damascus Shrine. Editor: The Skeleton Text of the Shakespeare Folio L.A. (by W. C. Arensberg), 1952; (with David W. Davies) A Concordance to the Essays of Francis Bacon, 1973. Compiler: Short Title Catalogue Numbers in the Library of the Francis Bacon Foundation, 1958, supplement, 1967; compiler, pub. Wing Numbers in the Francis Bacon Library, 1959. Home: 4805 N Pal Mal Av Temple City CA 91780 Office: 655 N Dartmouth Av Claremont CA 91711

WU, DOROTHEA WAN LIEN, librarian; b. Peking, China, July 19, 1927; d. Hsien and Daisy Ts'ai Yun (Yen) Wu; student Cath. U., Peking, 1944-46; B.A., Yenching U., Peking, 1948; postgrad. U. Cal. at Berkeley, summer 1949; postgrad. Sch. Library Service U. Ala., 1949-50; M.S., Simmons Coll. Sch. Library Sci., 1951. Came to U.S., 1949, naturalized, 1965. Chinese cataloger Harvard-Yenching Library, Cambridge, Mass., 1951-58; asst. music dept. Chgo. Pub. Library, 1958-60; asst. head art and music div. Queens Borough Pub. Library, Jamaica, N.Y., 1960-65, 66-68, head picture div., 1965-66, head art and music div., 1968—. Mem. Met. Mus. Art, 1961—, Mus. Modern Art, 1963—, Friends of City Center, 1961—, Friends of Am. Ballet, 1971—. Mem. Joffrey Circle, A.L.A., Internat. Assn. Music Libraries, Music Library Assn., N.Y. Library Club, Assn. Recorded Sound Collections. Home: 110-45 71st Rd Forest Hills NY 11375 Office: Art and Music Div Library 89-11 Merrick Blvd Jamaica NY 11432

WU, ELLEN CHI-LAN LEM (MRS. HOSEAH WU), chemist; b. Shanghai, China; d. Frank Y. and Yau-ho (Choi) Lem; came to U.S., 1950; B.A., Carleton Coll., 1954; Ph.D., U. Minn., 1962; m. Hoseah Wu, June 26, 1954; children—Bithiah Grace, Persis Ann. Naturalized Am. citizen, 1972. Sr. research chemist Mobil Research & Devel. Corp., Pauisboro, N.J., 1962-71, research asso., 1971—. Mem. Am. Chem. Soc., Phi Beta Kappa, Sigma Xi (local treas. 1966-67), Iota Sigma Pi, Sigma Delta Epsilon. Club: Catalysis (Phila.), Contbr. articles to profl. jours. Home: 1203 Woodruff Rd Glassboro NJ 08028 Office: care Mobil Research & Devel Corp Paulsboro NJ 08066

WU, HELEN (MRS. SHIH-CHI WU), real estate broker; b. Anking, China, Apr. 7, 1919; d. Chi-Hua and Dee-Hua (Hueng) Yuen; B.A., ChungKing China Central Polit. Inst., 1942; M.A., Columbia U., 1949; m. Shih-Chi Wu, Oct. 10, 1946; children—Ying-Ying, Winston, Mona. Came to U.S., 1945, naturalized, 1955. Payroll clk. Pacific Ship Repair, San Francisco, 1957-63; real estate salesman George O'Niel Co., San Francisco, 1963-66; real estate broker Pacifisia Investment & Realty Co., San Francisco, 1966—. Home: 5429 Anza St San Francisco CA 94121 Office: 4827 Geary Blvd San Francisco CA 94118

WU, YING-CHU LIN (MRS. JAIN-MING WU), aero. engr., educator; b. Peking, China, June 23, 1932; d. Chi-yu and K.C. (Kung) Lin; came to U.S., 1957; B.S. in Mech. Engring., Nat. Taiwan U., 1955; M.S. in Aero. Engring., Ohio State U., 1959; Ph.D. in Aeros., Cal. Inst. Tech., 1963; m. Jain-Ming Wu, June 13, 1959; children—Ernest, Albert, Karen. Engr. Taiwan Hwy. Bur., Taipei, Taiwan, 1955-56; teaching asst. Nat. Taiwan U., 1956-57; research asst. Ohio State U., 1957-58, Cal. Inst. Tech., 1959-62; sr. engr. Electro-Optical Systems, Inc., Pasadena, Cal., 1963-65; asst. prof. U. Tenn. Space Inst., Tullahoma, 1965-67, asso. prof., 1967-73, prof., 1973—. Amelia Earhart scholar, 1958, 59, 62. Mem. Am. Inst. Aeros. and Astronautics (plasmadynamics com., Booster award Tenn. sect., 1968), Sigma Xi (sec. U. Tenn. Space Inst. Club 1973—). Home: 111 Lakewood Dr Tullahoma TN 37388 Office: U Tenn Space Inst Tullahoma TN 37388

WUERFEL, ESTHER LEE MILLER (MRS. RICHARD KARL WUERFEL), civic worker; b. Los Angeles, Mar. 27, 1911; d. Leonard Darvin and Cora Fern (Rawdon) Miller; B.F.A., Eastern Mich. U., 1932; m. Richard Karl Wuerfel, Oct. 13, 1934; children—Judith Ann (Mrs. Raymond Gordon), Nancy Kay, Randall. Sch. tchr., Flint, Mich., 1932-35; service rep., personnel Mich. Bell Telephone Co., Detroit, 1935-43; memb. Bd. Edn., Balt., 1956-60, 68—. Chmn. Senatorial Scholarships, 1968, State P.T.A. Scholarship Bd., 1969-71. Pres., Republican Women Baltimore County, 1953-56; mem. Spl. Com. to Elect Spiro Agnew to County Exec. and Gov., 1962-68. Pres. P.T.A. Council Baltimore County, 1964-68; trustee Community Colls. Baltimore County. Recipient award for work in community colls., 1972. Life mem. Md. P.T.A., Nat. P.T.A. Methodist. Home: 103 S Rolling Rd Baltimore MD 21228

WUKASCH, DORIS LUCILLE STORK, educator, counselor; b. Somerville, Tex., Dec. 30, 1924; d. Edwin William and Clara Rofine (Fuchs) Stork; B.A. with high honors, U. Tex., 1944, M.Ed., 1969; m. Joe Eugene Wukasch, July 7, 1945 (div. 1971); children—Linda (Mrs. Hugh J. Williamson), Susan, Jean (Mrs. Richard P. Mihalik), Jonathan. Chemist Tex. Dept. Health, Austin, 1944-45; microbiologist Terrell Labs., Ft. Worth, 1946-47; exec. sec. Wukasch Architects and Engrs., Austin, 1954-66; editorial asst. Steck-Vaughn Pubs., Austin, 1966; rehab caseworker, job counselor Mary Lee Sch., Austin, 1969-70; spl. tchr. career edn. Austin Ind. Sch. Dist., 1970—. Instr. A.R.C., 1972—; vol. tchr. Austin State Sch., 1958-68. Area chmn. Am. Cancer Soc., 1970; mem. Women's Archtl. Guild, 1954-71, pres., 1964; mem. Tex. Fine Arts Assn., 1960—, Smithsonian Assos., 1972—, Wycliffe Assos., 1973—. Dept. Health, Edn. and Welfare grantee, 1968-69. Mem. Austin Mental Health Assn., Nat. Rehab. Counselors Assn., Nat., Tex. State tchrs. assn., Am. Judicature Soc., Austin Heritage Soc., Christian Bus. and Profl. Women's Council, Nat. Orgn. Women, Phi Beta Kappa. Lutheran. Contbr. poems and articles to mags. and newspapers. Home: 2500 Inwood Place Austin TX 78703 Office: 6100 Guadalupe Austin TX 78752

WULFECK, DOROTHY FORD, editor, genealogist; b. Bowling Green, Ky., July 2, 1897; d. Joseph William and Virginia Lois (Wilcoxson) Ford; B.A., Brenau Coll., 1917; B.C.S., Coll. Commerce, Bowling Green, Ky., 1918; M.A., Vanderbilt U., 1927, Yale U., 1940; m. Wallace Howard Wulfeck, June 24, 1922; 1 son, Joseph Wallace. Instr. Coll. of Commerce, Bowling Green, Ky., 1923-26; head dept. Larson Coll., New Haven, Conn., 1934-38; genealogy editor, Virginia Gazette, Williamsburg, Va., 1956—. Mgr. Vets. Information Center, Naugatuck, Conn., 1944-60. Mem. Gov.'s Com. for Employment of the Handicapped, 1950-60; chmn. mayor's Environmental Adv. Com., Naugatuck, 1971-72. Mem. Am. Assn. U. Women, Ky., Naugatuck hist. socs., D.A.R. Conglist. Author: Wicoxson and Allied Families, 1958; Culpepper County, Virginia Will Books B and C, 1965; Marriages of Some Virginia Residents, 1607-1800, 7 vols., 1961-67; Connecticut Trips-What, When, Where, 1971; numerous other books in genealogy, 1959—. Address: 51 Park Av Naugatuck CT 06770

WULP, PATRICIA, ednl. adminstr., counselor; b. Ann Arbor, Mich., Jan. 30, 1929; d. George Adolph and Dorothy (Jeffrey) Wulp; B.A., Middlebury Coll., 1950; M.S. in Social Work, Simmons Coll., 1958. Field sec. League Women Voters N.Y.C., 1950-53; program sec. Service Bur. for Women's Orgns., Hartford, Conn., 1953-56; med. social work supr. U. Hosps. of Cleve., 1958-62; dir. Latin Am. programs, asst. dir. Overseas Edn. Fund, League Women Voters, Washington, 1962-68; asst. dir., counselor Center for Continuing Edn. of Women, U. Mich. Ann Arbor, 1968—. Mem. Nat. Assn. Social Workers (com. 1969—), League of Women Voters. Home: 2113 Medford Rd Ann Arbor MI 48104

WUNDERMAN, LILJAN DARCOURT (MRS. LESTER WUNDERMAN), artist; b. Winnipeg, Man., Can., Jan. 22, 1921; d. Rene Wegbecher and Georgette (Guionet) Darcourt; came to U.S., 1933, naturalized, 1943; student Otis Art Inst., 1939-43, Reuben Tam, Bklyn. Mus. Art Sch., 1957; m. Lester Wunderman, June 14, 1947 (div.); children—Marc George, Karen Renee. One man shows, Pasadena (Cal.) Mus., 1944, U. S.C., 1965, Mansfield (O.) Fine Art Guild, 1965, U. Wis., 1965, U. Me., 1965, Tweed Gallery, Duluth, Minn., 1966, Kan. State U., 1966, Gastine Gallery, Hollywood, Cal., 1944, Roko Gallery, N.Y.C., 1963, 66, 68, 70, 73, Easthampton (L.I., N.Y.) Guild Gallery, 1966; exhibited group shows U.S. and abroad, 1942—, including Laguna Nat. Print and Drawing Exhbns., Laguna Beach, Cal., 1944-47, Los Angeles County Mus., 1944, Bklyn. Mus. Painting Exhbn., 1959, Artists Gallery, N.Y.C., 1960, Provincetown (Mass.) Art Assn., 1961-67, Pan-Pacific Exhbn. Young Painters, Osaka, Tokyo, Japan, 1962, Butler Inst., Youngstown, O., 1962-63, Museo de Bellas Artes, Buenos Aires, 1963, Pa. Acad. Fine Arts, Phila., 1963, Phila. Mus. Art Lending Collection, 1965; represented in permanent collections Loeb Collection, N.Y. U., N.Y.C., Norfolk Mus., U. S.C., Columbia, Post Coll., L.I., Harry N. Abrams, Ebasco Industries, N.Y.C., Intra-Media Inc., N.Y.C., White Weld Inc., N.Y.C., Pubaid S.A., London, Eng. Franklin Nat. Bank, N.Y.C., others. Recipient Ohashi award Pan-Pacific Exhbn., 1962; Marcia Brady Tucker award Nat. Assn. Women Artists, 1963, Medal of Honor, 1966; one-man show award Easthampton Guild Hall, 1964; Emily Lowe award Eggleston Gallery, N.Y.C., 1965. Mem. Internat. Platform Assn. Home: 131 E 19th St New York City NY 10003 Studio: 752 Broadway New York City NY 10003

WUNNICKE, ESTHER CRANE, lawyer; b. Kline, Colo., Mar. 15, 1922; d. James Harfield and Bessie Gertrude (Harris) Crane; A.B., George Washington U., 1949, J.D., 1950; M.Ed., Adams State Coll., 1958; m. William Charles Wunnicke, Apr. 29, 1959; children—W. Paul, Amy Margaret. Admitted to N.M. bar, 1950, Alaska bar, 1972; with firm Crane & Koogler, Aztec, N.M., 1950-57; atty. advisor Fed. Field Com., Alaska, 1966-71; asst. atty. gen. Alaska, 1971-72; co-counsel Fed.-State Land Use Planning Commn., Anchorage, 1972—. Mem. Anchorage Human Relations Commn., 1968-71. Councilman Aztec, 1952-56. Mem. Am., Alaska, N.M. bar assns. Author: (with R.D. Arnold) Alaska Natives and Federal Hire, 1967; Alaska Natives and the Land, 1969; Legal Framework for Alaska Fisheries, 1972. Home: 1406 Sunrise Dr Anchorage AK 99504 Office: 733 W 4th Av Anchorage AK 99501

WURLITZER, ANNA LEE (MRS. REMBERT WURLITZER), stringed instrument co. exec.; b. Jeffersonville, O., July 29, 1912; d. Herbert Leroy and Altha Amanda (Paullin) Little; B.S., Ohio State U., 1934; m. Rembert Wurlitzer, Oct. 20, 1935 (dec. 1963). Pres. Rembert Wurlitzer, Inc., N.Y.C., 1963—. Bd. dirs. House of Holy Comforter, N.Y.C. Mem. Soc. for Strings (dir 1963). Club: Colony (N.Y.C.). Author: The Hottinger Collection 1964. Home: 910 Park Av New York City NY 10021 Office: 16 W 61st St New York City NY 10023

WURSTER, MARGUERITE RAY SMITH, librarian; b. Ocala, Fla., Sept. 7, 1916; d. William Edward and Inez (Ray) Smith; B.A., U. Fla., 1963; M.A., U. South Fla., 1972; m. Hal Crockett Batey, Jr., Feb. 20, 1933 (div. June 1948); children—Hal Smith, Marilyn (Mrs. James Lynn Holeman), Diana Ed (Mrs. David Miller Pettengill); m. 2d, Robert Frederick Wurster, June 6, 1965. Library asst., library U. Fla., 1952-58; librarian, div. plant industry Fla. Dept. Agr., Gainesville. 1958-63; asst. to dir. library Fla. Inst. for Continuing U. Studies, Gainesville, 1963-65; asst. dir. Extension Library, U. South Fla., Bay Campus, St. Petersburg, 1965-71; asst. dir. State Univ. System of Fla., Extension Library, 1971—. Mem. Spl. Librarian Assn. (pres. Fla. chpt. 1970-71), Fla., Southeastern library assns., D.A.R., Y.W.C.A., Kappa Delta Pi, Delta Kappa Gamma. Methodist. Club: University South Florida Women's. Home: 6514 27th Av N St Petersburg FL 33710 Office: State U System Fla Extension Library 1011 1st Av N St Petersburg FL 33705

WURSTER, MARION V., assn. exec.; b. Hudson, N.Y., Feb. 13, 1919; d. Fred Michael and Gertrude (Sausbier) Wurster; B.A., Syracuse U., 1941; M.A., Northwestern U., 1948; student U. Fribourg (Switzerland), 1949. Tchr., Dexter (N.Y.) High Sch., 1941; counselor freshmen women Northwestern U., Evanston, Ill., 1942-43; group worker, dir. childrens theater Olivet Inst., Chgo., 1943-47; asst. dir. Neighborhood House, Salt Lake City, 1947-50; field instr. Sch. Social Work, U. Ia., Iowa City, 1950-52; cons., coordinator of instns. State of Ill., Chgo., 1952-62; regional cons. Am. Found. for the Blind, N.Y.C., 1962-67, dir. program devel. div., 1967—; staff asso. Commn. on Standards and Accreditation Services for the Blind, N.Y.C., 1964-66. Mem. Nat. Assn. Social Workers, Acad. Certified Social Workers, Am. Assn. U. Profs., Nat. Conf. Social Welfare, Am. Assn. U. Women, Nat. Recreation and Park Assn., Council for Exceptional Children, N.Y. State Certified Social Workers, Am. Assn. Workers for Blind, Assn. for Edn. Visually Handicapped. Home: 335 E 51st St New York City NY 10022 Office: 15 W 16th St New York City NY 10011

WYATT, DOROTHEA EDITH, educator; b. San Francisco, July 25, 1909; d. Thomas Grant and Mary Elizabeth (Healey) Wyatt; A.B., Stanford, 1930, M.A., 1931, Ph.D., 1936. Acting instr. history Stanford, 1936-37; tutor Am. history, head house Radcliffe Coll., Cambridge, Mass., 1937-39; instr. history and polit. sci. Milw.-Downer Coll., 1939-40; mem. faculty Goucher Coll., Towson, Md., 1940-52; dean women, prof. history Coll. William and Mary, Williamsburg, Va., 1952-56; prof. Am. history U. Mich. at Flint, 1956—, chmn. dept. history, 1965-70; vis. prof. McCoy Coll. Johns Hopkins, 1947-52. Mem. Genesee County Library Bd. and Mid.-Mich. Library Coop. Bds. Served to lt., USCG Women's Res., 1942-45. Recipient Outstanding Professorship award U. Mich. at Flint, 1973-74. Mem. Am. Hist. Assn., Am. Assn. U. Women, Am. Assn. U. Profs., Zonta (dir. 1972-74). Club: Flint Golf. Author: (with Anne Gary Pannell) Julia S. Tutwiler and Social Progress in Alabama, 1961. Home: 1901 Woodslea Dr Flint MI 48507

WYATT, FREDERICA CHARLOTTE, mayor; b. Kimble County, Tex., July 2, 1930; d. John Matt and Bessie Lee (Allsup) Burt; grad. high sch.; m. Chevis Reginald Wyatt, Jan. 29, 1955. With Randolph Abstract Co., Junction, Tex., 1947-50, Cummins Ins. Agy., Junction, 1950-55; mem. staff City of Junction, 1955-67, mayor, 1972—. Corr. San Antonio Express, 1971—, also writer feature articles Junction Eagle. Sec.-reporter Kimble County Hist. Survey Com., 1963-73; co-chmn. Kimble County Centennial Commn., 1973—. Pres. Am. Legion Aux., Junction, 1962-63, Junction Firemen's Aux., 1968-69, Junction Band Boosters, 1972-73; mem. Junction Community Action Council. Named Mrs. Kimble County Citizen, 1967. Mem. Kimble County Hist. Assn. (pres. 1972-73), D.A.R. (regent Chanes chpt. 1973-74), Daus. of 1812, Bus. and Profl. Women's Club (pres. Kimble County 1962-63). Democrat. Mem. Ch. of Christ. Home: PO Box 271 Junction TX 76849 Office: 102 N 5th St Junction TX 76849

WYATT, LOIS CAROLYN, physician; b. Rock Port, Mo., Oct. 5, 1905; d. Dean Trimble and Evangeline (McKillop) Wyatt; A.B., U. Mo., 1925; M.D., U. Chgo., 1931; m. George W. Schmick, Dec. 26, 1935 (div. 1945); children—Loie Lee (Mrs. John William Riehl), Lynn Georgiana (Mrs. Frederick G. Reynolds). Intern Los Angeles County Gen. Hosp., 1931-32; resident Los Angeles City Maternity Service, also Hillcrest Sanitarium, La Crescenta, Cal., 1932-33; gen. practice, Simi, also Moorpark, Cal., 1933-36, Kirkwood, Mo., 1936—. Sch. physician St. Louis pub. schs., 1960-62; chief sec. obstetrics, gynecology, Park Lane Hosp., 1963-64; chief staff, Sunset Hosp., 1965; clin. instr. U. Mo. Med. Sch., 1965—; preceptor St. Louis U. Sch. Medicine, 1971—. Mem. Kirkwood health and welfare com., 1960-64; mem. council Vis. Nurses Assn., St. Louis, 1963 mem. med. adv. bd., 1963-70; mem. council on continuing edn. in mental health St. Louis U., 1963-70; chmn. com. on med. assts. and secs. curriculum Forest Park Community Coll., 1966—, chief med. adviser, 1972—. Fellow Am. Acad. Family Physicians; mem. St. Louis County, Mo. State med. assns., A.M.A., Am. Assn. Physicians and Surgeons, Mo. (sec.-treas. 1967-70, v.p. 1970-72, pres.-elect 1973-74), St. Louis (charter, pres. 1962-63, editor newsletter 1968—) acads. family physicians, Airplane Owners and Pilots Assn., Flying Physicians Assn. Republican. Meth. Home: 402 Fairwood Lane Kirkwood MO 63122 Office: 103 N Taylor St Kirkwood MO 63122

WYATT, PHILLIPA, advt. agy. owner; b. Anderson, Ind.; d. Harold H. and Hilda W. (Keen) Wyatt; B.S., Ind. U., Dir. radio-TV advt. William H. Block Co., Indpls., 1952-54; sr. writer-producer WFBM-AM, WFBM-TV, Indpls., 1954-55; v.p. Tevie Jacobs Advt. Agy., Indpls., 1955-57; owner, pres. Wyatt Advt. Agy., Indpls., 1957—. Mem. bd. mgmt. Central YMCA, 1971. Recipient Direct Mail Advt. award Am. Indpls. Bankers Assn., 1964; named Indpls. Advt. Woman of Year, Advt. Club Indpls., 1960. Mem. Sales and Marketing Execs. Internat., Women in Communications, Ind. Fedn. Advt. Agys., Indpls. Advt. Club, Internat. Platform Assn., Sigma Kappa. Lutheran. Home: 3819 Rue Delacroix Indianapolis IN 46220 Office: 108 E Washington St 12th Floor Indianapolis IN 46204

WYCKOFF, EDITH HAY (MRS. WILLIAM LEROY WYCKOFF), editor; b. Pitts., Dec. 28, 1916; d. Thomas Robson and Helen Goldsmith (Goldsmith) Hay; student Hofstra U., 1935; m. James Byrd Anderson, Jr., Nov. 24, 1944 (div. 1947); m. 2d, William LeRoy Wyckoff, Dec. 10, 1949 (dec.). Reporter, North Shore Daily Jour., Flushing, N.Y., 1935-38, Star Jour., 1938-39, L.I. Star, also Nassau Jour., Long Island City, Newsday, Garden City (all L.I.), 1940-45; editor, pub. founder Locust Valley (N.Y.). Leader, also pres. Locust Valley Pub. Co., Inc., 1946—; owner Matinecock Printing Co., Locust Valley, 1967—. Author: Editing and Producing the Small Publication, 1956. Home: Box 468 Locust Valley NY 11560 Office: 160 Birch Hill Rd Locust Valley NY 11560

WYCKOFF, SYLVIA SPENCER, educator; b. Pitts., Nov. 14, 1915; d. Lynn Boyd and Bess Jeannette (Hohes) Wyckoff; B.F.A., Syracuse U., 1937, M.F.A., 1944. Tchr. pub. schs. N.Y. State, 1937-42; faculty Syracuse (N.Y.) U., 1942—, prof. art Coll. Visual and Performing Arts, 1971—, resident chmn. Syracuse in London program, 1972-73, chmn. dept. core programs Coll. Visual and Performing Arts, 1973—. Two-man exhibits Cortland (N.Y.) Asso. Artists, Syracuse, May Meml. Gallery, Syracuse, Oneida (N.Y.) Gallery; exhibited in group shows at Nat. Assn. Women Artists, N.Y.C., Nat. League Am. Pen Women, Washington; represented in permanent collections Marine Midland Bank, WSYR-Radio. Recipient 1st prize watercolor Syracuse Regional Show, 1943, Onondaga Hist. Soc., 1945; League prize for watercolor Nat. League Am. Pen Women Nat. Show, 1945; Gordon Steele award for painting Asso. Artists Show, 1968. Mem. Alpha Xi Delta, Eta Pi Upsilon. Presbyn. Home: 2 Seminary St Cazenovia NY 13035

WYLDER, KAY ERMINA GANTENBEIN (MRS. WILLIAM THOMAS WYLDER), clothing retailor; b. Osceola, Wis., May 21, 1923; d. Walter Leslie and Florence (Sigmund) Gantenbein; grad. pub. high sch.; m. Herbert F. Berreau, June 23, 1945 (div. Sept. 1967); children—James A., Jo (Mrs. John Subik), Lea Reed; m. 2d, William Thomas Wylder, Oct. 17, 1967. Saleswoman fabrics dept. Donaldson's, Mpls., 1964-65; bridal cons. Dayton's, Mpls., 1965-68; buyer Blakleys, Taylorville, Ill., 1968, McCabes, Rock Island, Ill., 1968-71; mgr. women's apparel store The Front Porch, New Castle, Ind., 1971-73; asst. mgr. Carson Pirie Scott & Co., 1973; mgr. Profl. Uniforms, Inc., 1973—. Campaign chairwoman state legislator Bill Frenzel, U.S. Senate candidate Wheelock Whitney, Hennepin County (Minn.) supr. Rubin Lundquist, 1964; chmn. 2d ward Republican Com. Crystal, Minn., 1962-66; chmn. campaign Barry Goldwater for Pres., 30th dist. Minn., 1964. Methodist. Home: 1710 Plymouth St New Castle IN 47362 Office: 1326 Broad St New Castle IN 47362

WYLE, MARTHA PRUDENCE HARPER (MRS. EWART HERBERT WYLE), educator; b. Independence, Mo., June 7, 1932; d. Lyndon Wesley and Helen (Smith) Harper; B.S., Kan. U., 1954; student Lexington Theol. Sem., 1957; m. Ewart Herbert Wyle, June 12, 1959. Dir. Christian edn. Country Club Christian Ch., Kansas City, Mo., 1954-59, Torrey Pines Christian, Ch., La Jolla, Cal., 1959—. Dir. Christian edn. and music. Girl Scouts U.S.; mem. Freedoms Found., 1967—. Bd. govs. Chapman Coll. Mem. Assn. Christian Ch. Educators, Delta Gamma, P.E.O. (pres. 1965-67). Club: La Jolla Beach and Tennis. Home: 8850 La Jolla Scenic Dr N La Jolla CA 92037 Office: 8320 La Jolla Scenic Dr N La Jolla CA 92037

WYMAN, LOTTE ANN NOVAK (MRS. RALPH M. WYMAN), civic worker; b. Vienna, Austria, Aug. 15, 1925; d. Josef and Hertha (Wallnstorfer) Novak; B.A., Barnard Coll., 1947; 1 dau., Leslie Andrea. Grey Lady, A.R.C., 1947-55; treas. Women's Assn. First Presbyn. Ch., Greenwich, Conn., 1963-65; mem. bd. Sunny Hill Sch. for Phys. and Emotionally Handicapped Children, Greenwich, 1972—; mem. bd. YWCA, Greenwich, 1963—, chmn. world fellowship, 1965, mem. bldg. com., 1965-70, pres., 1967-70; bd. dirs. Drug Liberation Program of Greater Stamford, 1970—, Community Chest, Greenwich, 1967-70, Community Council Greenwich, 1970—; bd. dirs., v.p. Turtle Bay Music Sch., N.Y.C., 1970—. Mem. N.Y. Zool. Soc., Ch. Women United (v.p. 1971-72). Republican. Presbyn. Clubs: Greenwich Country Burning Tree Country (Greenwich); Stratton Mountain (Vt.) Country. Home: Baldwin Farms North Greenwich CT 06830

WYND, GLADYS BUEHLER (MRS. FREDERICK LYLE WYND), lawyer; b. Ritzville, Wash., Aug. 14, 1906; d. George Adam and Ethel Wynn (Kaufman) Buehler; B.A., U. Ore., 1926, M.A., 1928; m. Howard D. Stabler, June 14, 1930 (dec. Mar. 1963); m. Frederick Lyle Wynd, Jan. 6, 1968. High sch. math. tchr., Juneau, Alaska, 1928-30; admitted to Alaska bar, 1951; practiced in Juneau, 1951-67; mem. firms Stabler & Stabler, 1951-63, Stabler, Gregg & Meuwissen, 1963-65, Stabler, Gregg & Kohls, 1966, Stabler, Gregg, Kohls, & Shulz, 1967. Mem. Order Eastern Star. Club: Quota (Juneau, Alaska). Home: 4800 Whiteaker St Eugene OR 97405

WYNHOFF, JULIANNE, home economist; b. Racine, Wis., Aug. 12, 1948; d. Bernard Joseph and Velma (Schowalter) Wynhoff; B.S. in Home Econ. Journalism, U. Wis.-Madison, 1971. Pub. relations intern Oscar Mayer & Co., Madison, 1970; retail account exec. Madison Newspapers, 1971-72; home economist consumer information Am. Dairy Assn. Wis., Madison, 1972-74; an organizer, v.p. assn.'s advt. agy. M.A.P. Agy., 1972-74; prin. Creative Food Cons., Breckenridge, Colo., 1974—. Mem. Am. Home Econs. Assn., Home Economists in Bus., U. Wis. Home Econs. Alumni Assn., Women in Communications (sec. Madison chpt. 1972, del. ann. meeting 1973), Nat. Orgn. for Women. Home and office: PO Box 817 Breckenridge CO 80424

WYNKOOP, MILDRED BANGS, educator; b. Seattle, Sept. 1905; d. Carl Oliver and Mery (Dupertuis) Bangs; A.B., Pasadena Coll., 1931, Th.B., 1933; M.Div., Western Evang. Sem., 1952; M.S., U. Ore., 1953; Th.D., No. Baptist Theol. Sem., Chgo., 1955; m. Ralph Carl Wynkoop, Dec. 27, 1928. Chmn. dept. theology Western Evang. Sem., Portland, Ore., 1955-60; vis. prof. theology colls. supported by Oriental Missionary Soc. in Korea, Hong Kong, Taiwan and Japan, 1960; tchr., dean Nazarene Japan Coll., Tokyo, 1961-63; pres. Japan Nazarene Sem., Chiba, 1963-66; vis. prof. theology Nazarene Theol. Sem., Kansas City, Mo., 1967; prof., head religion/philosophy dept. Trevecca Nazarene Coll., Nashville, 1968-69, prof., head dept. missiology and human services, 1969—. Mem. Soc. Bibl. Lit., Am. Ch. History Soc., Am. Catholic Hist. Soc., Wesleyan Theol. Sec. (pres.). Author: Foundations of Wesleyan Arminianism, 1967; John Wesley, Christian Revolutionary, 1970; Theology of Love-dynamic of Wesleyanism, 1972. Home: 4817 Merrill Lane Nashville TN 37211

WYNN, JOAN LEVENTHAL, mag. editor; b. N.Y.C., 1941; d. Jack and Rose (Binder) Leventhal; grad. cum laude, Conn. Coll. Women, 1962; m. Richard Wynn; 1 son, Andrew Michael. With Community Progress, New Haven, 1963, New Haven Redevel., 1962-63; various editorial positions Seventeen mag., N.Y.C., 1963-67; editor-in-chief Ingenue mag., N.Y.C., 1967—. Home: 25 Chapel Pl Great Neck NY 11021 Office: 750 3d Av New York City NY 10017*

WYNNE, MARIAN PATRICIA, journalist; b. N.Y.C., Aug. 23, 1936; d. Louis and Sara Pauline (Ingber) Feit; A.A., U. Fla., 1956; B.A. in Journalism, U. Miami, 1958; m. Sheldon Wynne, June 14, 1959 (dec. Sept. 1963); children—Susan, Robert. Reporter, Hollywood (Fla.) Sun-Tattler, 1958-59, Coral Gables Times Guide, 1963-69, Miami News, 1969-70; writer Miami Beach (Fla.) Tourist Devel. Authority, 1972—. Tchr. creative writing Palmetto Community Sch., 1972, U. Miami Adult Edn., summer 1973. U.S. Dept. Health, Edn. and Welfare fellow, 1970-72. Diplomate U. Miami, 1972. Mem. Women in Communications, Sigma Delta Chi. Home: 9240 SW 58 Terrace Miami FL 33173 Office: 555 17th St Miami Beach FL 33139

WYNNE, MARIGAIL, physician; b. Houston, Nov. 26, 1942; d. Hugh Richard and Margaret (Adair) Wynne; A.B. in Psychology, U. Rochester, 1964; M.D., Duke U., 1968. Intern Med. Coll. Va., Richmond, 1968-69, resident, 1969-72; founder, med. dir. Fulton Med. Center, Richmond, 1972—; mem. staff Hosp. Med. Coll. Va., Richmond. Recipient Upjohn award community medicine, 1967. Mem. Alpha Omega Alpha. Episcopalian. Home: 2401 Hanover Av Richmond VA 23220 Office: 1009 Denny St Richmond VA 23231

WYSE, LOIS HELENE (MRS. MARC ALLEN WYSE), advt. exec., publisher, author; b. Cleve.; d. Roy B. and Rose (Schwartz) Wohlgemuth; m. Marc Allen Wyse; children—Katherine, Robert. Vice pres. Wyse Advt., 1951—; pres. Garret Press, 1970—. Record albums: I Don't Want To Go to Bed; Love Poems for the Very Married, I Love You Better Now. Author: I Don't Want To Go to Bed Book for Boys, 1963; I Don't Want to Go to Bed Book for Girls, 1963; The Absolute Truth About Marriage, 1964; What Kind of Girl Are You Anyway?, 1965; P.S. Happy Anniversary, 1966; Help I Am the Mother of a Teen-Age Girl, (with Joan Javits) The Compleat Child, 1966; Two Turtles, A Guppy and Aunt Edna, 1967; I Wish Everyday Were My Birthday, 1967; Grandfathers Are to Love, 1967; Grandmothers Are to Love, 1967; Love Poems for the Very Married, 1967; Are You Sure You Love Me?, 1969; I Love You Better Now, 1970; Mrs. Success, 1970; Little Volumes of Love (series of 12), 1971; (calendar) A Year of Love, 1971, 72; A Weeping Eye Can Never See, 1972; Love Lines (series of 6), 1972; Lovetalk, 1973. Home: 3126 Bremerton Rd Pepper Pike OH 44124 Office: 2800 Euclid Av Cleveland OH 44115 also 78 E 56th St New York City NY 10022

WYSE, OLIVE GERTRUDE, educator; b. Wayland, Ia., Mar. 9, 1906; d. Amos and Luvina (Gerig) Wyse; student Ia. Wesleyan Coll., 1922-24; B.A., Goshen Coll., 1926; M.S., State U. Ia., 1933; Ed.D., Columbia, 1946; postgrad. U. Chgo., 1936, Harvard Sch. Pub. Health, 1964. Instr. Goshen (Ind.) Acad., 1926-32; mem. faculty Goshen Coll., 1926—, chmn. dept. home econs., 1933—, prof. home econs., 1946—. Participant workshop tchrs. in ch. related schs. P.R. Dominican Republic, 1964; cons. home econs. Asso. Colls. Central Kans., 1968. Mem. Am. (accreditation com., 1961-68), Ind. (chmn.) coll. and univ. sect., 1960-62; award certificate of distinguished service 1969) home econ. assns., A.A.A.S., Am. Assn. U. Women, Nat. Council Adminstrs. Home Econs. (proceedings chmn., 1967, v.p., 1970-72), Nat. Council Family Relations, Foods and Nutrition Conf. (sec. north central region, 1955-57), Omicron Nu, Pi Lambda Theta, Kappa Delta Pi. Home: 1804 S 12th St Goshen IN 46526

WYSOCKI, MIRIAM SANTISTEBAN, physician; b. Mayaguez, P.R., Mar. 4, 1933; d. Angel and Dalila (Irizarry) Santisteban; M.D., U. P.R. (San Juan), 1960; m. Louis E. Wysocki, Jan. 28, 1964; children—Louis Alan, Lisa Ann. Intern Episcopal Hosp., Phila., 1960-61; resident Woman's Med. Coll. Hosp., Phila., 1961-65; practice medicine, specializing in obstetrics and gynecology, Garden Grove, Cal., 1965—; mem. staff West Anaheim (Cal.) Community Hosp., Garden Park Hosp., Anaheim Gen. Hosp., all Anaheim, Huntington Beach (Cal.) Intercommunity Hosp., Palm Harbor Hosp., Garden Grove, Westminster (Cal.) Hosp., Long Beach (Cal.) Community Hosp., Fountain Valley Community Hosp.; chief obstetrics, gynecology dept. West Anaheim Community Hosp., 1968-69, 72—. Mem. A.M.A., Orange County, Am. Women's med. assns. Home: 10041 Sycamore St Villa Park CA 92667 Office: 9872 Chapman Av Garden Grove CA 92641

WYSS, NORMA ROSE TOPPING (MRS. WERNER O. WYSS), state ofcl.; b. Wautoma, Wis., Jan. 7, 1919; d. Eugene Leonard and Sylvia Maude (Attoe) Topping; B.A., Fla. State U., 1949, M.S., 1960; postgrad. U. Md., 1963-64; m. Werner O. Wyss, July 25, 1940. Mem. faculty Hoeft Sch., Berlin, Wis., 1939-40, Pensacola (Fla.) Bd. Pub. Instrn., 1946-66; counseling supr. dept. commerce Fla. Employment Service, Pensacola, 1966—. Program chmn. Indsl. Mgmt. Assn. Greater Pensacola, 1969-70. Mem. Internat. Assn. Personnel Employment Services, C. of C., Fla. State Employees Assn. (pres. chpt. 1971-72), Altrusa (dir.), Kappa Delta Pi, Phi Sigma Alpha (v.p. 1969-70), Alpha Delta Kappa (charter; 1st pres.). Lutheran (mem. altar com. 1954-70). Home: 1100 Patton Dr Warrington FL 32507 Office: 236 W Garden St Pensacola FL 32502

WYZANSKI, GISELA WARBURG (MRS. CHARLES E. WYZANSKI JR.), civic worker; b. Hamburg, Germany, May 5, 1912; d. Max M. and Alice (Magnus) Warburg; student Hamburg U., 1931, London Sch. Econs., 1931-32, Oxford (Eng.) U., 1932; m. Charles E. Wyzanski, Jr., July 23, 1943; children—Charles Max, Anita Henrietta. Came to U.S., 1938, naturalized, 1943. Nat. chmn. Youth Aliyah; nat. bd. mem. Hadassah, 1940-60, 70—, nat. asso. bd., 1960—, pres. Boston chpt., 1963-64; bd. dirs. Window Shop Inc., Cambridge, Mass.; exec. com. Fellowship in Israel for Arab-Jewish Youth, Inc. Bd. dirs. Boston council Girl Scouts U.S.A., 1945-50; overseer Shady Hill Sch., 1956-59. Dir. World Affairs Council; chmn. vols. UNICEF, Cambridge, 1966, 67, Boston, 1968, greeting card chmn., Eastern Mass., 1969—; nat. chmn. Hadassah for Israel's Nat. Inst. for Behavorial Scis., 1970—. Home: 39 Fayerweather St Cambridge MA 02138

XINOS, SUZANNE MARIE, lawyer; b. Chgo., Aug. 21, 1938; d. Walter and Pearl (Podlesna) Kohut; B.S., No. Ill. U., 1959, M.A., 1960; J.D., John Marshall Law Sch., 1966; m. Constantine P. Xinos, Oct. 7, 1972. Admitted to Ill. bar, 1966; pvt. practice law specializing in estate and family law, Chgo., 1966—; partner law firm Xinos & Xinos, Ltd., Chgo., 1966—; pub. defender Cook County, Appellate div., supr. criminal appeals, 1967—. Instr., Elmhurst Coll., 1962-66, Loyola U., 1967-68. Vol. worker for judges seeking to retain judgeships, prospective judges seeking judgeships, 1963—. Mayor of City Chgo. scholar, 1956-60; Am. Assn. U. Women scholar, 1959-60. Mem. Am., Ill. State bar assns., Assn. Def. Lawyers, Sigma Alpha Eta, Sigma Tau Delta. Contbr. poetry, creative writing to periodicals, mags. Home: 149 Briarwood N Oak Brook IL 60521 Office: 35 E Wacker Dr Chicago IL 60602

YACAVONE, MURIEL TAUL, state legislator; b. Hartford, Conn., May 26, 1920; d. William McClellan and Elizabeth (Griffing) Taul; grad. high sch.; m. John Peter Yacavone, Jan. 19, 1944 (dec.); children—John Peter, Mark Philip, Teresa Jane, Elizabeth Rose. Health commr. Town of East Hartford Bd., 1962-63; mem. East Hartford Econ. Opportunity Commn., 1964-65; chmn. East Hartford Community Council on Youth, 1965-68; justice of peace, 1968-70; mem. Drug Adv. Council, State of Conn., 1969-73; mem. Conn. Ho. of Reps., 1971—. Served with USMCR, 1943-45. Mem. Nat. Order Women Legislators, League Women Voters of East Hartford, Democratic Womens Club of East Hartford, Conn. (dir.), Hartford County (dir.) fedns. Dem. womens clubs, Women Marines Assn. (sec. Nutmeg chpt.). Roman Catholic. Home: 176 Wakefield Circle East Hartford CT 06118 Office: The Capitol Hartford CT 06115

YAFFE, SILVIA FISHBEIN (MRS. JOSEPH X. YAFFE), psychologist; b. Phila.; d. Herman and Rose (Fishbaum) Fishbein; A.B., Temple U., 1940, M.A., 1942; m. Joseph X. Yaffe, July 21, 1940; children—Roy, Peter M., Lisa Jo. Clin. asst., psychology dept. Temple U., 1940-42; psychologist York House, Phila., 1963—; research asso. Phila. Geriatric Center, 1965, dir. health maintenance project, 1963—, dir. nat. study housing for elderly, 1973—. Pres., M.M. Fuhrman Charities, 1942-43, hon. dir., 1943—, mem. admissions com. Fuhrman Clinic Sch., 1956—. Mem. Am., Pa. psychol. assns., Gerontol. Soc., A.A.A.S., Am. Acad. Polit. and Social Sci. Home: 1006 Arboretum Rd Wyncote PA 19095 Office: Phila Geriatric Center 5301 Old York Rd Philadelphia PA 19141

YAFFEE, RUTH POWERS (MRS. I. SANFORD YAFFE), educator; b. Duluth, Minn., June 4, 1927; d. Elbert and Cleo Lorraine (deVore) Powers; B.A. summa cum laude, Macalester, Coll., 1948; Ph.D. in Phys. Chemistry, Ia. State U., 1951; m. I. Sanford Yaffe, Dec. 26, 1950 (dec. May 1961); children—Patricia Leslie, Laurence Gregory. Research fellow Ames (Ia.) Lab., U.S. AEC, 1948-51, fellow, 1951-52; chemist Oak Ridge Nat. Lab., 1952-53; instr. U. Tenn., 1955-56; asst. prof. San Jose State U., 1957-62, asso. prof., 1962-66, prof. chemistry, 1966—, radiation safety officer, 1960—, nuclear sci. area adminstr., 1972—. Active Girl Scouts U.S., Boy Scouts Am. Named Woman of Year in Edn., Los Angeles Mus. Sci. and Industry, 1972, San Jose Mercury News, 1972. Mem. Am. Chem. Soc., Health Physics Soc., A.A.A.S., Cal. Chemistry Tchrs. Assn., Sigma Xi. Author: (with G.L. Helgeson) Practical Health Physics, 1966; A Laboratory Manual for General College Chemistry, 1965. Contbr. articles to profl. jours. Home: 1481 Elnora Ct Los Altos CA 94022 Office: Dept Chemistry San Jose State U San Jose CA 95192

YAGELLO, VIRGINIA ELIZABETH, librarian; b. Cleve., Sept. 10, 1919; d. John Adolph and Louise Sophy (Midura) Yagello; A.B., Western Res. U. (now Case Western Res. U.), 1944; M.L.S., Carnegie Tech. Library Sch., 1950. Young adult librarian, Enoch Pratt Free Library, Balt., 1950-54; librarian U.S. Army Europe Spl. Services, France, Germany, Italy, 1954-59, command librarian Hdqrs. So. European Task Force, 1959-61; asst. to supr. dept. libraries Ohio State U., Columbus, 1961-63, head chemistry and physics libraries, asst. prof. library adminstrn., 1967-72, asso. prof., 1972—. Mem. Spl. Libraries Assn. (chpt. pres. 1971-72, chmn. chemistry div. 1974—), Am. Soc. Information Sci. (chmn. membership and nominating com., 1970-71), Franklin County Library Assn. (v.p. 1970-71). Contbr. to publs. in field. Home: 3677 N High St Columbus OH 43214 Office: 140 W 18th Av Columbus OH 43210

YAGER, ANNETTA TONI, assn. exec.; b. Washington, Mar. 18, 1937; d. David and Jean (Tash) Yager; student Montgomery Jr. Coll., 1955-56, Am. U., 1956-58, U. Va., 1958-62, George Washington U., 1961-64. Mem. Am. U. Players, 1956-57; engr., disc jockey Radio Sta. WAMU, Am. U., Washington, 1956-57; mem. Chevy Chase Community Players, 1959—; pres. Adventure Theatre, Montgomery County, Md., 1972—; mem. George Washington U. Players, 1962-65; corr. sec. D.C. Recreation & Park Soc., 1966-67; v.p. D.C. dist. Am. Ednl. Theatre Assn., Washington, 1966-67, pres., 1967-68, regional gov. Children's Theatre Conf., 1966-72, nat. local arrangements chmn. conv., Washington, 1970; asst. chief music and theatre Schofield Barracks, Hawaii, 1972—; dir. numerous prodns. Camp Louise, also D.C. Recreation Dept., 1956-72, including The Diary of Anne Frank, 1958, The Miracle Worker, 1960, Auntie Mame, 1959, Taming of the Shrew, 1962, The Farewell Supper, 1960, Take Her, She's Mine, 1965, Beauty & the Beast, 1967; lighting design, set constrn. numerous prodns. Shakespeare Summer Festival, Am. Light Opera Co.; head drama dept., asst. adminstr. Camp Louise, Cascade, Md., summers 1956-62; bus. mgr. The Georgetowners touring Europe entertaining U.S. soldiers, 1969. Home: 95-235 Waimakua Dr Wahiawa HI 96786 Office: USASCH Recreation Services Div Schofield Barracks HI

YAGER, WINNIFRED LOUISE COLLER (MRS. MARSHALL PORTER YAGER), assn. exec.; b. Claremore, Okla., May 8, 1908; d. Francis Norman and Daisy Dean (Skelly) Coller; grad. high sch.; m. Marshall Porter Yager, May 2, 1927. With Mullens Ins., Bristow, Okla., 1946-47; editor Bristow News and Record-Citizen, 1950-62; free-lance writer, 1960-64; sec. Bristow C. of C., 1964-70, mgr., 1970—. Mem. Positive Action Com. Econ. Devel. Adminstrn., 1971—; sec. Bristow City Planning Commn. 1973—; sec. Bristow Indsl. Authority; chmn. B & PW Museum Com. Mem. adv. bd. Salvation Army, 1952—; bd. dirs. New Hope Villa, Bristow, Okla. div. Am. Cancer Soc. Recipient awards Freedom's Found., 1961, Bristow Sch. Bd., 1962, Future Tchrs. Am., 1955, Okla. Coll. Women, Chickasha, 1961, numerous others. Mem. Okla. C. of C., Okla. C. of C. Execs., Bristow Area Arts Assn., Bus. and Profl. Women's Club (past sec., publicity chmn., museum com.). Presbyn. (deacon). Home: 306 W 10th Bristow OK 74010 Office: 121 N Main Bristow OK 74010

YAHRAES, MARJORIE ASHWORTH, editor; b. Ocala, Fla., May 29, 1916; d. Arthur Elmer and May Lyndon Ashwoth; A.B., Barnard Coll., 1938; certificate in French civilization, Sorbonne, U. Paris, 1939; 1 son, Richard Michael. Woman's editor Easton (Pa.) Free Press, 1940; free lance writer, corr. McGraw Hill, Newsweek, Mexico City, 1945; writer U.S. Mil. Govt., Germany, 1947; editor USIA, Washington, 1952—. Exhibited group and one person shows, Washington, Del., N.Y. Recipient painting awards. Mem. Washington Press Club, Washington Newspaper Women's Club. Home: 613 E St SE Washington DC 20003 Office: 1776 Pennsylvania Av NW Washington DC 20547

YAKOBSON, HELEN JAMES BATES (MRS. SERGIUS YAKOBSON), educator; b. St Petersburg, Russia; d. Alexander and Zinaida (Volkov) James; B.S., U. Harbin Law Sch., China, 1935; m. Abraham Bates, Mar. 21, 1937 (div. 1950); 1 dau., Natalie; m. 2d, Sergius Yakobson, Sept. 23, 1951; 1 son, Dennis. Came to U.S., 1938, naturalized, 1941. Tchr. Russian lang. and lit. Tientsin (China) High Sch., 1936; pvt. tutor Russian lang., N.Y.C., 1939-46; script writer, announcer, information specialists State Dept. Voice of Am., 1947-50;

lectr. Russian lang. George Washington U., Washington, 1951-53, asst. prof., 1953-60, asso. prof., 1960-64, prof., 1964—, exec. officer dept. Slavic langs. and lits., 1953-60, chmn. dept. Slavic and Oriental langs. and lits., 1960-69. Adviser, Russian Studies Center for Secondary Schs., Choate Sch., 1962—; guest speaker U. Sydney Sch. Edn., 1960, U. Melborne, 1960, New South Wales Dept. Edn., 1960. Recipient Nat. Fgn. Lang. Achievement award Nat. Fedn. Modern Lang. Tchrs. Assn., 1965, Outstanding Prof. award George Washington U., 1966. Mem. Am. Assn. Tchrs. Slavic and East European Langs. (pres. 1961-63, historian 1965) Nat. Slavic Honor Soc. (v.p. 1965, pres. 1970—), Am. Assn. Advancement Slavic Studies, Modern Lang. Assn., N.E.A. (dir. dept. fgn. langs.), Am. Assn. U. Profs., Greater Washington Assn. Tchrs. Fgn. Langs. (pres. 1967-68). Author: TV Guide: Parts I and II, 1958-59; Beginners Book in Russian, 1959; Guide to Conversational Russian, 1960; New Russian Reader, 1960; (with Andre von Gronicka) Essentials of Russian, 1948; Conversational Russian, An Intermediate Course, 1965; Russian Reading; Past and Present, 1967. Contbr. articles to profl. jours. Office: Slavic Lang Dept George Washington U Washington DC 20006

YALOW, ROSALYN SUSSMAN (MRS. AARON YALOW), physicist; b. N.Y.C., July 19, 1921; d. Simon and Clara (Zipper) Sussman; A.B., Hunter Coll., 1941; M.S., U. Ill., 1942, Ph.D., 1945; m. Aaron Yalow, June 6, 1943; children—Benjamin, Elanna. Research and devel. electronics physicist Fed. Telecommunication Lab., N.Y.C., 1945-46; lectr., temporary asst. prof. physics Hunter Coll., N.Y.C., 1946-50; physicist, asst. chief radioisotope service VA Hosp., Bronx, N.Y.C., 1950-68, acting chief, 1968-70, chief Radioimmunoassay Reference Library, 1969—, chief nuclear medicine service, 1970—; sr. med. investigator VA, 1972—; research prof. Mt. Sinai Sch. Medicine, 1968—. Recipient William S. Middleton Med. Research award VA, 1960; Fed. Woman's award for fed. govt. service, 1961; Eli Lilly award Am. Diabetes Assn., 1961; Van Slyke award Am. Assn. Clin. Chemists, 1968; award for distinguished contbns. in sci. as related to medicine A.C.P., 1971; Harvey Soc., 1966; Internat. award Gairdner Found., 1971; Dickson prize U. Pitts., 1971; Howard Taylor Ricketts award U. Chgo., 1971. Diplomate Am. Bd. Radiology. Fellow Am. Coll. Radiology (asso.), N.Y. Acad. Sci., Clin. Soc. N.Y. (hon.), New Eng. diabetes assns. mem. Am. Phys. Soc., Am. Assn. Physics Tchrs., Radiation Research Soc., Am. Assn. Physicists in Medicine, Biophys. Soc., Endocrine Soc. (recipient Koch award 1972), Phi Beta Kappa, Sigma Xi, Sigma Pi Sigma, Pi Mu Epsilon, Sigma Delta Epsilon. Home: 3242 Tibbett Av New York City NY 10463 Office: 130 W Kingsbridge Rd New York City NY 10468

YAMADA, ANNIE HANAKO KANESHIRO, educator; b. Honolulu, July 7, 1930; d. Seimatsu and Naye (Nakahara) Kaneshiro; B.A., Carleton Coll., 1952; postgrad. So. Ore. Coll., 1953-54; M.Ed., U. Hawaii, 1968; 1 dau., Annette; m. 2d, William Yuuji Yamada, May 3, 1974; adopted children—Grant, Marc, Guy, Dan. Elementary tchr. dept. edn., Honolulu, 1954-58, Wiseburn Sch. Dist., Hawthorne, Cal., 1958-60, dept. edn., Honolulu, 1960-67; counselor U. Hawaii, Honolulu Community Coll., 1968—, supr. student tchrs., dept. edn., 1961-64. Mem. Coll. and U. Profl. Assn. (sec. 1972-73), N.E.A., Hawaii Fedn. Coll. Tchrs. (chpt. sec. 1973-74), Hawaii Personnel and Guidance Assn., Hawaii Edn. Assn. Conglist. Home: 46-278 Kalua Pl Honolulu HI 96744 Office: 874 Dillingham Blvd Honolulu HI 96817

YAMAMOTO, TOSHIKO TOSHI, state ofcl.; b. Seattle, Dec. 1, 1915; d. Mokuji and Tome (Watanabe) Yasutake; grad. Am. Barber Coll., 1953, Hollywood Barber Coll., 1970; m. George Masashi Yamamoto, Aug. 19, 1943. With Columbia River Mercantile, Longview, Wash., 1938-41; receptionist to doctor, Los Angeles, 1941-42; with Bullock's, Los Angeles, 1947-55; founder, owner Toshi's Barber Shop and Gift Shop, Los Angeles, 1955-70; v.p. Cal. Bd. Barber Examiners, 1971-72, state barber examiner, field rep., 1972—. Mem. women's adv. com. office Equal Opportunity, 1970-72. Mem. Cal. Republican Central Com., 1967—, sec. nationalities com., 1967-69, exec. com., 1969-71; Western regional chairwoman heritage group div. Rep. Nat. Com., 1973—. Bd. dirs. Nat. Center Vol. Action, 1970-71. Mem. Am. of Japanese Ancestry Republicans (founder, pres. 1969-70, adviser 1970—), Japanese Am. Citizens League, Japan Am. Soc. So. Cal., Nat. Fedn. Bus. and Profl. Women's Clubs, Nat. Fedn. Rep. Women, Los Angeles Area C. of C. Women's Div. Club: Nisei Women's Golf So. Cal. (charter). Address: 253 S Gerhart Av Los Angeles CA 90022

YAMASHITA, ELIZABETH SWAYNE (MRS. DONALD M. YAMASHITA), educator; b. Australia; B.S. in Econs., U. Sydney, 1949; M.S., Northwestern U., 1959, Ph.D., 1969; m. Donald M. Yamashita, 1969. Came to U.S., 1957. Financial writer Financial Rev., Sydney, Australia, 1951-57; reporter Fortune Mag., N.Y.C., 1960-63; asso. prof. Sch. Journalism, Northwestern U., Evanston, Ill., 1963—. Mem. Women in Communications, Assn. for Edn. Journalism, Am. Assn. U. Profs. (chpt. pres.), Soc. Profl. Journalists. Office: Sch Journalism Northwestern U Evanston IL 60201

YANCEY, ELISE KILPATRICK (MRS. KERMIT CECIL YANCEY SR.), educator; b. Altoona, Ala., Aug. 14, 1918; d. Charles Allen and Martha Idell (Camp) Kilpatrick; A.B., Athens Coll., 1938; M.S., Auburn U., 1960, Specialist in Math, 1967; postgrad. U. Ala., 1967-68, Miss. State U., 1968-69; m. Kermit Cecil Yancey, Sr., Sept. 30, 1938; children—William Charles, Martha (Mrs. James Garner), Kermit Cecil. Chmn. math. dept., leader of county math-in-service program Etowan County High Sch., Altalla, Ala., 1960-65; chmm. math. dept., chmn. div. of computer sci., engring., electronics and math. Gadsen (Ala.) State Jr. Coll., 1969—. Mem. Nat. Classroom Tchrs. Math., Am. Assn. U. Women, Math. Assn. Am., Ala. Coll. Tchrs. Math., Nat., Ala. edn. assns., Kappa Mu Epsilon. Democrat. Baptist (ch. treas. 1971-72, financial sec. 1968-72). Home: Rural Route 1 Altoona AL 35952 Office: 213 Naylor Hall Gadsen AL 35901

YANDELL, KATHRYN MAUDINE, educator; b. Houston, May 2, 1938; d. Eunice Clyde and Grace Emogene (Roquemore) Yandell; A.A., Lee Coll., Baytown, Tex., 1958; B.S., Tex. Woman's U., Denton, 1960, M.A., 1965, postgrad., 1971-72; postgrad. U. Tex. at Austin, 1973-74. Tchr. phys. edn. Staunton (Va.) City Schs., 1960-62; prof. phys. edn. Tex. Lutheran Coll., Seguin, 1962—, now dept. chmn. Vol. A.R.C. Safety Services, Am. Cancer Soc. Recipient Faculty Growth awards Am. Lutheran Ch., 1972, 73, 74. Mem. Am., Tex. (sect. chmn. 1969-70) assns. health phys. edn. and recreation, Nat., So. assns. phys. edn. for coll. women, Nat. Intramural Sports Council. Home: PO Box 84 Seguin TX 78155

YANDRE, ANN B. MILLER (MRS. E. W. YANDRE), lawyer; b. Chattanooga, Dec. 22, 1897; d. Jeremiah T. and Rachel E. (Callahan) Miller; student Tampa U., Wash. Coll. Law, Am. Inst. Banking, 1938-48; m. Richard D. Morales, June 29, 1921 (dec. 1931); m. 2d, Edward W. Yandre, Mar. 4, 1954 (dec. Sept. 1967). Admitted to Fla. bar, 1946; asso. with husband in gen. practice law, Tampa, Fla., 1921-31; asso. with firm Lewis H. Hill, Jr. & Robert D. Hill, attys., Tampa, 1931-37; legal sec., office (mgr.) trust dept. Exchange Nat. Bank Tampa (Fla.), 1938-48; pvt. practice law, Tampa Orlando, Fla., 1948—. Mem. Am., Hillsborough and Orange Counties bar assns., Estate Planning Council Tampa (treas.), Central Fla. Estate Planning Council, Nat. (S.E. regional dir. 1962—), Fla. (sec., v.p., dir., past pres.) assns. women lawyers, Am. Inst. Banking (pres. Tampa chpt., 1946—), U.S. Council Bus. and Financial Cons. (asso. counsel). Phi Delta Delta. Presbyn. Clubs: Tampa (Fla.) Yacht and Country; Orlando Country, Dubsdread Country (Orlando, Fla.). Address: 2426 Sunset Dr Tampa FL 33609

YANG, DOROTHY CHUAN-YING, physician; b. Shanghai, China; d. Lin-Chi and Ruth (Wong) Yang; student Hong Kong U., 1937-42; M.D., St. John's U., Shanghai, 1945; M.S., N.Y. Med. Coll., 1950; m. Swee Chee Wong, Feb. 9, 1942 (div.); children—Ruth C., James C. Came to U.S., 1946, naturalized, 1962. Rotating intern St. Lukes Hosp., Shanghai, 1944-45; med. resident Govt. Hosp., Tenchi, China, 1945-46; resident pediatrics Childrens Center, N.Y.C., 1947-48; asst. resident pediatrics New Eng. Hosp. for Women and Children, Boston, 1948-49, Syracuse (N.Y.) Med. Center, 1949-50; resident neurology Hosp. of U. Pa., Phila., 1960-61, fellow neurology, 1962-63; fellow pediatric neurology Childrens Hosp., Phila., 1961-62; neurology tng. NIH, 1960-63; teaching, research fellow N.Y. Med. Coll., 1950-52, instr. pediatrics, 1952-54, asso. pediatrics, 1954-55, asst. clin. prof., 1955-56, asst. prof., 1956-60, coordinator jr. pediatrics, 1956-60, asso. prof., 1964-68, asst. prof. neurology, 1966-68, chief sect. pediatric neurology dept., 1968; instr. neurology Hosp. U. Pa., 1963-64; pediatrician on collaborative study neurol. diseases and blindness NIH, 1957-60, pediatric neurologist, 1964-68; asso. dir. Childrens Center for Developmental Disorders, L.I. Coll. Hosp., 1969, attending pediatric neurologist, 1969—, chief pediatric neurology clinic, 1969, dir. Seizure Clinic, 1969—; asst. pediatrician Flower and Fifth Av. Hosp., N.Y.C., 1954-60, chief Pediatric Clinic, 1955-60, asso. attending pediatrician, 1964-68, asst. attending neurologist, 1966-68; vis. asst. pediatrician Met. Hosp., 1958-60, asso. attending pediatrician, 1964-68, asst. attending neurologist, 1966-68, chief Child Devel. Clinic, 1966-68; attending pediatric neurologist Prospect Hts. Hosp., Bklyn., 1969—; asso.-vis. pediatrician Kings County Hosp. Center, 1971—; cons. pediatric neurology St. John's Episcopal Hosp., Bklyn., 1972—. Diplomate Nat. Bd. Med. Examiners, Am. Bd. Pediatrics. Fellow Am. Acad. Pediatrics; mem. Am. Acad. Neurology, A.M.A., Am. Chinese Med. Assn., Child Neurology Soc., Am. Med. Electroencephalographic Assn. Contbr. articles profl. jours. Home: 1801 John F Kennedy Blvd Philadelphia PA 19103 Office: 340 Henry St Brooklyn NY 11201

YANIZ, LILLIAN (MRS. ROBERT DEMME), hotel sales exec.; b. Havana, Cuba; d. Enrique and Elodia (Norona) Yaniz; student pvt., parochial schs.; m. G. B. May, (dec. June 1960); children—Sheryl Ann, George B.; m. 2d, Robert Demme, May 20, 1965. Sales rep. Allied Travel, Miami, Fla., 1954-61; sales dir. Roney Plaza Hotel, Miami Beach, Fla., 1961-66; dir. sales Hotel Sheraton Four Ambassadors, Miami, 1966-68, dir. sales, 1972—; sales mgr. Hollywood (Fla.) Beach Hotel, 1968-69; sales exec. Eden Roc Hotel, Miami Beach, Fla., 1970-72. Dist. chmn. Muscular Dystrophy Assn., Dade County, Fla. Mem. Hotel Sales Mgrs. Assn., Confederacion de Organizaciones Turisticas de la America Latina. Home: 2121 N Bayshore Dr Miami FL 33137

YANKE, ELIZA BELLE, physician; b. Collins, Ky., July 4, 1939; d. Lee and Evelyn Joyce (Potter) Compton; B.A., Pikeville Coll., 1961; M.D., U. Louisville, 1965; m. August Frank Yanke, July 2, 1966; children—Christopher, Elizabeth, Patrick. Intern Highland Alameda County Hosp., Oakland, Cal., 1965-66; asso. Kaiser Permanente Med. Group, Hayward, Cal., 1966-70, partner, 1970—; mem. staff Kaiser Hosp. Mem. Am. Coll. Emergency Physicians. Home: 31 Cherry Hills Ct Alamo CA 94507 Office: 1425 S Main St Walnut Creek CA 94596

YANKEY, MARGARET WEIR (MRS. MICHAEL UNDREA YANKEY), editor; b. Barstow, Cal., July 12, 1946; d. Allison Bradley and Margaret Mary (Gerwitz) Weir; B.S. in Tech. Journalism, Ia. State U., 1968; postgrad., U. Ia., 1969-70; m. Michael Undrea Yankey, Sept. 8, 1967. Copy editor Des Moines Register, 1968-69; editor Cedar Rapids (Ia.) Gazette, 1969-72; artist Nat. Investors Life Ins. Co., Little Rock, 1973-74; writer World Changers, Inc., 1974—. Recipient Dorothy Dawe award Am. Furniture Mart, 1971, 73. Mem. Nat. Assn. Real Estate Editors, Sigma Delta Chi, Beta Sigma Phi. Home: 7018 E 71st Pl Tulsa OK 74133 Office: 314 W 2d St Tulsa OK 74105

YANTIS, ETHEL MAY BEATY (MRS. NORVAL K. YANTIS), ednl. adminstr.; b. nr. Howard, Kan., Oct. 1, 1903; d. John S. and Margaret (Patterson) Beaty; B.A., Southwestern Coll., 1959; m. Norval K. Yantis, Apr. 4, 1923; children—John, Sharolyn Kay (Mrs. Robert Lager). Tchr. elementary schs., Elk County, Kan., 1922-56, supt. schs., 1956-68, dir. sch. dist., dir. fed. projects, 1965-70. Mem. adoption com. Kan. State Reading Circle, 1960-61. Named Kan. Master Tchr., Kan. State Tchrs. Coll., 1965. Mem. S.E. Kan. (pres. 1964-67), Kan. Past (sec.-treas. 1969) county supts. assns., Howard C. of C., N.E.A., Kan. State Tchrs. Assn., Elk County Edn. Assn., P.E.O. (chpt. pres. 1964-66), Delta Kappa Gamma. Republican. Methodist (Sunday Sch. supt. 1940-50). Address: 853 Jefferson St Howard KS 67349

YAP, VIOLET YEE (MRS. PETER J. YAP), real estate broker; b. Honolulu; d. Yee Yap and Yee Chun Shee; B.A., U. Hawaii, 1933; M.A., Columbia, 1941; m. Peter J. Yap, Sept. 4, 1938. Real estate salesman, Cal., 1951, Hawaii, 1965-68; broker Violet Yap, Realtor, Honolulu, 1968—; dir. Investment Group, Realtors, 1969. Mem. Honolulu Bd. Realtors. Mem. Gov.'s Art Commn., 1961; dir. Hawaii Chinese Civic Assn., 1964; Art Center dir. Honolulu Advertiser Contemporary Arts Center of Hawaii, 1960-70. Recipient hon. award for meritorious service and ability in field real estate investment counseling, 1972. Mem. Nat. Inst. Real Estate Brokers, Nat. Assn. Real Estate Bds. Office: Kahala Mall Office Tower 4211 Waialae Av Honolulu HI 96816

YAPP, BETTY JEAN, health service adminstr.; b. Manhattan, Kan., May 5, 1924; d. Rockford Glenn and Lena I. (Topliff) Yapp; B.S., Kan. State U., 1946; M.S., U. Neb., 1957. Dir. dietary dept. Mary Lanning Hosp., Hastings, Neb., 1947-53; dir. of dietary dept. Lincoln (Neb.) Gen. Hosp., 1953-74, adminstrv. asst., 1974—, preceptor food service supr. course, 1952-56. Dietary cons. for Haccepette Med. Center, Ankara, Turkey, 1965-68; asst. prof. Sch. Home Econs., U. Neb., Lincoln, 1970—. Recipient Outstanding Neb. Dieticians award, 1973. Mem. Am. Soc. Hosp. Food Service Adminstrn., Am. (dietetic internship bd. 1973—), Neb. (pres. 1953-54), Lincoln (pres. 1956) dietetics assns., Am. (mem. legislative com. 1972-74), Neb. (pres. 1962-64) home econs. assns., Beta Sigma Phi, Omicron Nu. Club: Altrusa Internat. (pres. Lincoln 1967-68). Home: 3520 South 31 St Lincoln NE 68502 Office: 2300 South 16 Lincoln NE 68502

YARBOROUGH, BETTY HATHAWAY, educator; b. Portsmouth, Va.; d. Joseph Samuel and Isabelle (Rountree) Hathaway; student Coll. William and Mary, 1945-46, M.A. in Guidance, 1955, postgrad. 1956-57; B.A. in English, Edn., Duke, 1948; postgrad. U. Miami (Fla.), 1960, Richmond Profl. Inst., 1963; diploma Edn., U. Va., 1959, Ed.D., 1964; m. Frank Graham Yarborough, July 3, 1949 (div.). Tchr., Cradock High Sch., Portsmouth, 1948-56, head English dept. 1951-56; supr. lang. arts Norfolk County (Va.) Pub. Schs., 1956-57, supr. high schs., dir. developmental reading program, 1957-66; dir. lang. arts Chesapeake (Va.) Pub. Schs., 1966-72. Extension instr. Coll. William and Mary, 1957-67, Hampton Roads Center U. Va., 1965-73; vis. instr., asst. reading clinic dir. U. Va., 1959-62; vis. instr. Mich. State U., 1965; vis. instr. Old Dominion U., Norfolk, Va., 1967-72, prof. elementary edn., 1972—; diagnostician Psychiat. Assos., Ltd., Portsmouth, Va., 1972—; tchr. adult reading improvement course Norfolk Newspapers, Inc., also Armed Forces Staff Coll., Norfolk; project dir. demonstration primary sch. in Chesapeake, 1967-72; dir. diagnostic reading centers, Chesapeake, 1966-72. Reading cons. Spong Commn., 1960; dir. workshops, participant tchr. tng. programs Va., N.C., S.C. schs.; chmn. task force reading Regional Edn. Lab. of Carolinas and Va., 1966-67; research English, fgn. lang. instrn. Recipient Ullin W. Leavell award contbn. reading instrn. U. Va., 1967; Outstanding Civic Achievement award Chesapeake C. of C., 1965. Mem. Va. Edn. Assn. (state com. tchr. edn., profl. standards, 1961), Am. Edn. Research Assn., Am. Psychol. Assn., Nat. Council Measurement Edn., Va. Assn. Tchrs. English (sec., treas. 1960-62), Nat. Council Tchrs. English (participant convs. 1960, 62, chmn. composition inst. 1965), Internat. (participant conv. 1966, 70, 71, 73, com. chmn. 1970), Coll. (participant convs. 1969, 70, 73), Va. (pres. 1968-69) reading assns., Nat. Assn. Edn. Young Children, Assn. Childhood Edn. Internat., Va. Ednl. Research Assn. (pres. 1972), Nat. Reading Conf., S. Atlantic Philosophy Edn. Assn., Modern Lang. Assn., Nat. Conf. Research in English (asso.), Council for Exception Children, Nat. Assn. Elementary Sch. Prins., Kappa Delta Pi, Theta Alpha Phi, Delta Kappa Gamma. Presbyn. Club: Sigma Kappa. Author: Teaching English to Slow Learners, 1962; Guidelines for Improving Spelling Instruction, 1964; Sound and Sense in Spelling textbooks series, 1964, rev. edit., 1968; On Wings of Words, 1970; Reading in Virginia: Innovative and Research Programs 1970-72, 1972. Editor: Chesapeake Schools at Work. Contbr. to Ency. Edn., also articles profl. jours. Home: 3008 Ferguson Dr Portsmouth VA 23703 Office: Hampton Blvd PO Box 6173 Norfolk VA 23508

YARBOROUGH, JEAN SMITH, city ofcl.; b. Waco, Tex., Feb. 15, 1944; d. John Hugh and Ida Maude (Smitham) Smith; B.A., N. Tex. State U., Denton, 1973; m. Charles David Yarborough, Apr. 8, 1966; children—Vicki Lynn, Charla Jane, Donna Jean. Mem. Bedford (Tex.) City Council, 1972—. Troop leader Richland Hills (Tex.) Girl Scouts, 1968-69; v.p. Haltom City (Tex.) Jaycees Wives, 1970; chmn. publs. Tarrant County League Women Voters, 1972, chairperson services to children and youth, 1973-74; sec. Bedford Park and Recreation Bd., 1971-72; citizen mem. Friends of Channel 13 Pub. TV, 1971—; dir. publs. Women's Place, 1974—. Mem. N. Central Tex. Ecol. Coalition, Tex. Municipal League, N. Tex. State U. Alumni Assn., Nat. League Cities, Nat. Worldlife Fedn., Stonegate Elementary Sch. P.T.A., Concerned Citizens for Conservation (pres. 1971-72). Democrat. Co-editor, pub. Yarborough Family mag., 1967-69. Address: 720 Rankin Rd Redford TX 76021

YARBROUGH, KAREN MARGUERITE, geneticist, educator; b. Memphis, Mar. 4, 1938; d. David Williamson and Cleo Marguerite (Hartsfield) Yarbrough; student Perkinston Jr. Coll., 1956-58; B.S. (John Rust Trust scholar), Miss. State U., 1961, M.S., 1963; Ph.D., N.C. State U., 1967. Research asst. Miss. State U., 1961-63, N.C. State U., 1963-67; asst. prof. U. So. Miss., Hattiesburg, 1967-70, asso. prof., 1970-72, asso. prof., dir. Inst. of Genetics, 1972—. Genetic cons. Ellisville State Sch. Nat. Inst. Mental Health grantee, 1972-73. Mem. N.Y., Miss. acads. sci., Genetics Soc. Am., Am. Soc. Human Genetics, Sigma Xi, Phi Sigma, Delta Kappa Gamma, Phi Theta Kappa, Zeta Tau Alpha. Democrat. Baptist. Contbr. articles to profl. jours. Home: Route 10 Box 152A Hattiesburg MS 39401

YARGER, MARGUERITE SCOTT (MRS. DONALD EUGENE YARGER), cultural activities coordinator; b. Hastings, Mich., Dec. 26, 1927; b. Leon Lake and Madelene Emily (Bull) Scott; grad. high sch.; m. Donald Eugene Yarger, Oct. 24, 1946; children—Charles Kent, Michele (Mrs. Gregory Abbey). Office mgr. Battle Creek Box Co. (Mich.), 1946-52; coordinator cultural activities Kellogg Community Coll. and Battle Creek Community United Arts Council, 1966—. Sec., Calhoun County Republican Com., 1958-64; charter mem. Battle Creek City Canvassing Bd., 1964—. Club: Altrusa (dir.). Home: 40 Stuart Blvd Battle Creek MI 49017 Office: 450 North Av Battle Creek MI 49016

YARKONI, GENYA, art mus. adminstr.; b. N.Y.C., Jan. 12, 1943; d. Alexander and Raya (Magid) Markon; student Bezalel Sch. Arts and Crafts, Jerusalem, 1962-63, Hebrew U. of Jerusalem, 1962-63; B.S., Skidmore Coll., 1964; postgrad. City U. N.Y., 1964-66; m. Uriel Yarkoni, Apr. 27, 1968; children—Dov, Yaron. Asst. illustrations editor Ency. Judaica, Jerusalem, Israel, 1967-70; adminstrv. asst. Herbert F. Johnson Mus. Art, Ithaca, N.Y., 1971—. Home: 126 S Hill Terrace Ithaca NY 14850 Office Herbert F Johnson Mus Ithaca NY 14850

YARMON, BETTY GROSS (MRS. MORTON YARMON), writer, pub. relations exec.; b. Plainfield, N.J., Nov. 14; d. Samuel Harrison and Ruth (Livingston) Gross; student Los Angeles Jr. Coll., 1946-47; m. Morton Yarmon, Nov. 7, 1948. Dir. pub. relations and advt. Abe Schrader Corp., N.Y.C., 1952-72; dir. pub. relations and advt. Genesco Dress divs., 1972—; pres. Betty Yarmon Assos., Advt. and Pub. Relations dir. pub. relations and advt. Fair-Tex Mills, Inc., Rona, Adele Martin & Dalani Dresses; editor, co-founder, v.p. Pub. Relations Aids Pub. Co., N.Y.C., 1960—. Syndicated columnist Womens News Service div. United Features, N.Y.C., 1963—. Mem. Fashion Group. Author: How to Buy a House, 1966. Address: 35 Sutton Pl New York City NY 10022

YARNO, ELIZABETH FLORENCE (MRS. PHILIP L. YARNO), banker; b. Leadville, Colo., Aug. 1, 1915; d. David B. and Estella Miranda (Peterson) Cooperman; student U. Wash., 1932-34, Met. Bus. Coll., 1934-35; m. Philip L. Yarno, Apr. 1, 1939; children—Patricia (Mrs. John A. Richards), Nanci (Mrs. Arthur J. Leonard). Clk. Prudential Ins. Co., Seattle, 1935-39; with Seattle Trust & Savs. Bank, Burien, Wash., 1953-65, Seattle, 1965—, v.p., mgr. Arcade Plaza Office, 1971—. Mem. Am. Inst. Banking, Nat. Assn. Bank Women (mem. scholarship com. 1968-69), Matrix Table, Seattle C. of C. Clubs: Soroptimist (v.p. 1967-68). Home: 1616 SW 152d St Seattle WA 98166 Office: 1323-2nd Av Seattle WA 98101

YARVOTE, PATRICIA MCCAFFREY, physician; b. Paterson, N.J., Feb. 14, 1936; d. Evart and Loretta (McCaffrey) Yarvote; B.A., Rutgers U., 1956; M.D. cum laude, Woman's Med. Coll. Pa., 1960. Rotating intern, resident internal medicine St. Vincents Hosp., N.Y.C., 1960-64, now asst. attending physician; practice medicine, specializing in internal medicine, N.Y.C., 1964-66; staff physician A.T.&T., 1964-72; staff physician Exxon Corp., N.Y.C., 1972—; editor med. bull., 1974—; attending in adult and obstet. cardiac clinics St. Vincents Hosp. Task Force, Hosp. Information Systems. Lectr., Am. Coll. Cardiology, 1967-72. Diplomate Nat. Bd. Med. Examiners. Fellow Nat. Found.; mem. A.M.A., Am. Coll. Cardiology, Am. Occupational Med. Assn. (med. practice com.), A.C.P. Contbr. articles profl. jours.

YARYAN, RUBY BELL, psychologist; b. Toledo, Apr. 28, 1938; d. John Sturges and Susan Barrett (Bell) Yaryan; B.A. in Psychology (NSF fellow), Stanford, 1960; Ph.D. in Psychology, U. London, 1968;

m. John Frederick Buenz, Jr., Dec. 15, 1962 (div. Aug. 1967). Dir. communications research div. U. Cal. at San Francisco, 1963-67; reporter-analyst news KING-TV, Seattle, 1968-69, KIRO-TV, 1968-69; research dir. U. Radio and TV programs U. Cal., San Francisco, 1969-70; dir. interdept. council to coordinate all fed. juvenile delinquency programs, Washington, 1970-73; dir. evaluation Cal. Regional Med. Program, Oakland, 1974—. Cons., White House Conf. Children and Youth and Follow-Up, 1970-71, Dept. Health, Edn. and Welfare Task Force on Classifications of Exceptional Children, 1972-73, Cal. Council Criminal Justice, 1973-74; gov. Sci. Analysis Corp., San Francisco, 1969-70. Rotary Found. fellow, 1960-61; recipient Hon. Gold Key to State Capitol, Olympia, Wash., 1970. Mem. Nat. Adv. Commn. Criminal Justice, Standards and Goals, 1972-73; del. Nat. Conf. Criminal Justice, 1973. Mem. Am., Western, Cal. State Psychol. assns., Am. Ednl. Research Assn., Am. Assn. Pub. Opinion Research, Internat. Orgn. Study Group Tensions, Am. Fedn. TV and Radio Artists, Phi Beta Kappa. Contbr. articles to profl. jours. and chpts. to profl. books. Home: 160 Caldecott Lane Oakland CA 94618 Office: California Regional Medical Program 7700 Edgewater Dr Oakland CA 94621

YASAITIS, VIRGINIA D. DILTS (MRS. JOHN JOSEPH YASAITIS), educator; b. Scranton, Pa., Feb. 15, 1918; d. Carl Leland and Florence (Miller) Dilts; student Lake Erie Coll., 1935-37; A.B., U. Mich., 1939, M.A., 1951, Ph.D., 1970; m. John Joseph Yasaitis, July 12, 1941; children—John Allen, Mary Ann. Tchr. pub. schs., Saginaw, Mich., 1940-41; tchr., counselor Boys Republic, Farmington, Mich., 1941-42, Grosse Pointe, Mich., 1943-46; asst. prin. Lake Orion (Mich.) Jr. High Sch., 1954-57, counselor, 1957—; counselor, asso. prof. psychology Oakland Community Coll., Pontiac, Mich., 1969—; vis. prof. Oakland U., Rochester, Mich., 1972—; mem. adv. com. for counselor edn. Oakland U., 1971—. Mem. N.E.A., Mich., Lake Orion edn. assns., Oakland Area Counselors Assn., Orion Area Youth Guidance Assn. (pres. 1964-66), Am. Personnel and Guidance Assn., Am. Assn. U. Women, Ednl. Scis. Assn., Internat. Platform Assn., P.E.O., Delta Kappa Gamma (v.p. 1962-64). Home: 100 Baldwin Rd Clarkston MI 48016 Office: 485 Scripps Rd Lake Orion MI 48035

YASER, BETTY FRANCES SLADE (MRS. YASAR YASER), economist; b. Norfolk, Va., Sept. 23, 1939; d. Frank Moncure and Betty Irene (Knighton) Slade; B.S. in Fgn. Service, Georgetown U., 1961; Ph.D. in Econs. (Ford Found. fellow), Vanderbilt U., 1967; m. Yasar Yaser, Sept. 19, 1964; children—H. Kenan, H. Aylin. Instr. Vanderbilt U., 1963, Middle East Tech. U., Ankara, Turkey, 1964-66; adviser State Inst. Statistics, Ankara, 1966-68; econs. analyst AID, Ankara, 1968—; cons. Turkey Ministry Finance, 1971; instr. U. Md. extension Ankara. U.S. coordinator for CENTO, 1973. Mem. coms. Turkish-Am. Assn. Mem. Am. Econs. Assn., Soc. Internat. Devel. Author: An Analysis of the Financial System in Turkey 1949-1963, 1967; An Approach to a Flow of Funds Accounting System for Turkey, 1968; also articles. Address: Vali Dr Resit Cad 39/9 Ankara Turkey

YASINSKI, RHODA (MRS. VICTOR YASINSKI), nursing adminstr.; b. Regina, Sask., Can., Dec. 18, 1917; d. Victor Garfield and Sarah Christine (Wardrop) Ridley; R.N., Regina Gen. Hosp. Sch. Nursing, 1940; student Canadian Hosp. Assn., 1963; m. Victor Yasinski, July 17, 1943, (dec.); children—Tracey, Ruth (Mrs. Gregory Sinclair). Head nurse Regina Gen. Hosp., 1940-42, dir. inservice edn., 1942-43; evening and night supr. Deer Lodge Vets. Hosp., Winnipeg, Man., Can., 1952-55; head nurse Grace Gen. Hosp., Winnipeg, 1955-60, nursing service adminstr., 1960-69; dir. Heritage Lodge Personal Care Home, Winnipeg, 1969-71; nursing adminstr. Fred Douglas Lodge Personal Care Home, Winnipeg. 1971—. Mem. Man. Assn. Registered Nurses (chmn. nursing service com. 1964-66). Mem. United Ch. of Can. Home: 1712 Portage Av Winnipeg MB Canada Office: 1275 Burrows Av Winnipeg MB Canada

YAST, HELEN THERESE, librarian; b. Sturgis, Mich., Jan. 19, 1917; d. Charles J. and Elizabeth (Richards) Yast; A.B., Ind. U., 1937; M.A., Rosary Coll., 1967. Librarian, Rocky Mountain Lab., Hamilton, Mont., 1942-44, U.S. Navy, New Orleans, 1944-45, VA, Hines, Ill., 1946, Indpls., 1946-47; asst. librarian Am. Hosp. Assn., Chgo., 1947-53, librarian, 1954—. Recipient Exceptional Service award Assn. Hosp. and Instn. Libraries, 1967. Mem. A.L.A. (council 1967-71), Assn. Hosp. and Instn. Libraries (pres. 1959-60), Med. Library Assn. (treas. 1972-74), Spl. Libraries Assn., Phi Beta Kappa. Co-editor: Library Practice in Hospitals, 1972. Contbr. articles to profl. jours. Home: 703 N Marion St Oak Park IL 60302 Office: 840 N Lake Shore Dr Chicago IL 60611

YATER, RUTH MILLICENT BECKER (MRS. WALLACE MASON YATER), civic worker; b. Washington, Oct. 19, 1910; d. Edmund Henry and Daisy (Birkle) Becker; A.B., Vassar Coll., 1931; M.A., Am. U., 1939; postgrad. Cornell U., 1932; m. Wallace Mason Yater, Dec. 22, 1932; children—Millicent Y. Howard, Stephanie M., Wallace Mason, Camille F. (Mrs. Charles T. Stanley). Gen. asst. Waterbury Nat. Bank (Conn.), 1929; instr. arts and crafts Camp Andre, Briarcliff Manor, N.Y., 1930; tchr. jr. high sch., Washington, 1931-32. Trustee D.C. Pub. Library, 1960—, v.p. bd. trustees, 1970-71; trustee Barney Neighborhood House, Washington, 1955-65, pres. bd., 1961-64; mem. women's bd. Washington Hosp. Center, 1959—, Peirce Guild (adoption service), 1960-64, Georgetown U. Hosp., 1933—, pres. bd. 1942-44, D.C. Med. Soc. Aux., 1933—, So. Med. Assn., 1961—; mem. Women's Com. for Nat. Symphony Orch.; trustee Peirce-Warwick Adoption Service, 1964-69; mem. steering com. Internat. Visitors' Service Council, chmn., 1966-68; chmn. Mayor's Com. Internat. Visitors, Washington, 1969-70, mem. exec. com., 1969—. Mem. A.L.A., UN Assn. (dist. chmn. 1959-67, trustee 1959—), D.C. Library Assn., English-Speaking Union (trustee), Meridian House Internat. (trustee), Nat. Fedn. Settlements. Home: 4907 Indian Lane Washington DC 20016

YATES, BARBARA ANN, educator; b. Troy, N.Y., Oct. 14, 1933; d. John Gardinier and Marion Mercedes (Haines) Yates; A.B. with honors, U. Cal. at Berkeley, 1955, M.A. in Econs., 1956; postgrad. U. Paris (France), Sorbonne, 1961; Ph.D. in Comparative Edn. and History, Columbia, 1967. Cultural officer USIA, Phnom Penh, Cambodia, Djarkarta, Indonesia, Leopoldville, Belgian Congo, 1956-61; lectr. Bklyn. Coll., City U. N.Y., summer 1963, 65-66; asso. prof. comparative edn. U. Ill. at Champaign, 1966—, asso. dir. internat. programs and studies, 1966-72. U. Ill. summer faculty fellow, 1968, 69, U. Ill. Research Bd. grantee, 1970-73. Mem. Comparative and Internat. Edn. Soc. (sec., editor newsletter 1968-71), History of Edn. Soc. Contbr. articles to profl. publs. Office: Div Comparative Edn Ill Champaign IL 61820

YATES, EDITH OLIVE COE, club woman; b. McPherson, Kan., Dec. 31, 1890; d. James Buchanan and Christine Matilda (Aelmore) Coe; tchrs. certificate U. Tex., 1909; m. Calder Emmet Yates, Apr. 28, 1917 (dec. 1968); 1 dau., Mildred (Mrs. Herbert Aden Plummer). Auditor 4th dist. Tex. Fedn. Music Clubs, 1946; pres. Dept. Club, Port Arthur, Tex., 1940-41, Symphony Club, 1929-30, 44-45; pres. Country Club Aux., 1941-42; pres. Griffing Park Garden Club, 1954-55, treas. 1965; del. to 68th Continental Congress of D.A.R., Washington, 1959, historian, Port Arthur, 1965; 1st pres., past pres. Symphony Club, also treas. Recipient with Dau. of Outstanding Club Family award Tex. Fedn. Women's Clubs, 1958. Mem. Tex. Hist. Assn., Tex. Fedn. Women's Clubs (parliamentarian Magnolia dist. 1962-64, friendship com. 1964-66). Home: 4200 Griffing Dr Port Arthur TX 77640

YATES, HELEN EVA, author, lectr.; b. Omaha; d. Edward Truman and Christina (Chapp) Yates; student Girl's Collegiate Sch., Los Angeles, 1921, Art Inst., Chgo., 1922, Columbia, 1923. Editorial reader Sam Goldwyn, N.Y.C., 1923; promotion writer Chas. Schribners, 1924; editor-pub. New Orleans Life Mag., 1925; women's editor China Press, Shanghai, 1926; Dutch Govt. writer, Java, 1927; radio travel program KFRC, San Francisco, 1933; copywriter BBDO Agy., Los Angeles, 1940-41; writer Westfal Larson Line, S.A., 1941; writer around world Am. Pres. Line, 1950-51; staff lectr. Writers Conf. Cal. Western U., 1960, San Diego State Coll., 1963. Founder World-House, 1955. Mem. P.E.N., Authors League, Hollywood Fgn. Press, Internat. Platform Assn., World Craft Council. Author: Bali, Enchanted Isle, 1933; The World Is Your Oyster, 1939; Java Orchid 1945; How to Travel for Fun, 1950; Folk Art Guide, India Govt., 1951; Hong Kong Crafts, 1952; Shopping All Over the World, 1953; World House Party, The Story of Tante, 1966; Her Magic Island, 1972. Address: care Bertha Klausner Lit Agt 71 Park Av New York City NY 10016

YATES, MARY CAROLYN, univ. ofcl.; b. Knoxville, Tenn., June 29, 1948; d. James Turner and Carolyn Elizabeth (Deal) Yates; B.S., Va. Commonwealth U., 1970, M.Ed., 1972. Residence dir. Va. Commonwealth U., Richmond, 1970-71; residence dir., dir. student activities N.W. Mo. State U., Maryville, 1971-73; program adviser N. Tex. State U., Denton, 1973—. Mem. Assn. Coll. Unions Internat., North Central Tex. Assn. Student Personnel Adminstrs.

YATES, SUZANNE VAUGHENE, govt. ofcl.; b. Little Rock, May 10, 1926; d. Charles Bryan and Nell Edith (Kennerly) Yates; student Little Rock Jr. Coll., 1943-44, U. Ark., 1944-46; LL.B., Ark. Law Sch., 1950. Mem. staff VA Regional Office, Little Rock, 1946-57; admitted to Ark. bar, 19—; mem. staff VA Hosp., Little Rock, 1957—, supr., comdt. med. information sect., 1972—, also equal employment opportunity counselor. Mem. Third Order of Our Lady of Mt. Carmel, Roman Cath. Ch., 1952—, sec. Little Rock chpt., 1955-60. Mem. Nat. Assn. Med. Assts. Home: 89 W Windsor Dr Little Rock AR 72209 Office: 136D2 VA Hosp 300 E Roosevelt Rd Little Rock AR 72206

YAVELBERG, CHERYL PARSONS, advt. exec.; b. Lenoir, N.C., May 14, 1945; d. Winfred R. and Constance L. (Boggs) Parsons; student East Carolina U., 1963-67, Corcoran Sch. Art, 1973—; m. Arthur Howard Yavelberg, July 22, 1972. Caseworker, U.S. Senator Richard Russell-Ga., 1968-70; dir. traffic/prodn., account exec. Abramson/Himelfarb Advt., Washington, 1970-72; dir. traffic/prodn., buyer print media Denniberg Advt., Washington, 1972-73; account asst. Bill Hartman Advt., Miami, 1974—. Mem. Art League Alexandria (Va.), 1973. Mem. Washington Met. Prodn. Assos. (v.p. 1972). Home: 9390 SW 77th Av Miami FL 33156

YEAGER, HELEN FRIEDA, educator; b. Cin., Sept. 17, 1905; d. Frank Henry and Katherine Eva (Joest) Yeager; B.A., U. Cin., 1927; B.E., 1928, M.A., 1942; postgrad. Ohio U., summer 1953, U. Md., summer, 1948, Columbia U., summer 1946. Tchr. pub. schs., Cin. 1929-42, high sch. counselor, 1943-47, asst. prin., 1948-50, supr., 1950-68; asst. prof. soc. studies edn. U. Cin., 1970—; cons. Nat. Assessment of Edn. Progress. Mem., vol. worker Sch. Found., Cin., 1971-72. Bd. dirs. Nat. Council for the Social Studies, 1964-67, pres. Ohio council, 1963-64. Mem. Delta Kappa Gamma, Phi Mu. Presbyn. (deacon 1967-70). Clubs: U. Cin. Faculty, Woman's City (mem. courts com. 1969-72), Westwood Woman's (chmn. drama dept. 1972-74, corr. sec. 1974—), Cincinnati Woman's (leader Greek Circle 1973—). Author: (with Dorothy McClure Fraser) Under Freedom's Banner, 1964; The Adventure of America, 1964. Contbr. articles to profl. jours. Home: 3216 Hanna Av Cincinnati OH 45211

YEE, MARILYNN K., photojournalist; b. Sioux City, Ia., Jan. 31, 1950; d. Kee W. and Sylvia S. Yee; ed. U. Cal. at San Jose. Photographer, San Francisco Examiner, 1972; lab. technician Ventura County Star Free Press, 1973; photographer St. Louis Post Dispatch, 1974—. Freelance photojournalist A.P., U.P.I. Mem. Nat., Cal. press photographers assns. Home: 1010 Hi-Pointe Pl St Louis MO 63117 Office: St Louis Post Dispatch 900 N 12th St St Louis MO 63103

YEGLIN, DOROTHY JEAN, newspaper editor; b. Des Moines, Feb. 23; d. Oliver Howard and Ruby Winifred (Norman) Miller; B.S., Ia. State U., 1950; m. Harold Yeglin, July 25, 1962; children—Kent, Sara. Promotion coypwriter Meredith Pub. Co., Des Moines, 1951-52; editorial asst. Better Homes and Gardens, Des Moines, 1953-54; staff writer Mpls. Star and Tribune, 1955-58; staff writer Des Moines Register and Tribune, 1958-63, food editor, 1965—. Home: 5508 Westwood Dr Des Moines IA 50312 Office: 715 Locust St Des Moines IA 50309

YELL, PATRICIA MAUDE (MRS. RICHARD YELL), educator; b. Buffalo, Nov. 30, 1935; d. Glenn Frederick and Gladys Mae (Fix) Staffen; B.S. magna cum laude, State U. N.Y., 1957; M.A., George Peabody Coll., 1961, Ed.S. (NSF fellow), 1962, Ed.D. (U.S. Office of Edn. fellow), 1968; m. Richard Yell, Nov. 26, 1969; children—Jennifer Maude, David Andrew. Elementary tchr. Bay Rd. Elementary Sch., Webster, N.Y., 1957-60; day tchr. counselor, diagnostic tchr. N.C. Re-Education Center, Durham, N.C., 1962-64; teaching asst. Project Re-edn., George Peabody Coll., Nashville, 1966-67; co-dir. emotional disturbance program U. Conn., Storrs, 1967-70; dir. emotional disturbance program, asst. prof. edn. U. N.C., Chapel Hill, 1970—. Cons. for child advocacy program, Durham, N.C., 1969-70. Task force mem. Govs. Study Commn. on Emotional Disturbance, N.C., 1969-70; mem. exec. com. Orange County Mental Health Assn., 1971—. Mem. Assn. for Children with Learning Disabilities, Council for Exceptional Children, Internat. Reading Assn., Orton Soc., Kappa Delta Pi. Home: 328 Umstead Dr Chapel Hill NC 27514

YELLIN, CAROL LYNN GILMER (MRS. DAVID GILMER YELLIN), editor; b. Clinton, Okla., Mar. 3, 1920; d. Thomas Prather and Eulala (Rogers) Gilmer; student Okla. State U., 1937-39; B.S. in History with honors, Northwestern U., 1941, M.S. in Journalism cum laude, 1942; m. David Gilmer Yellin, Aug. 27, 1950; children—Charles Franklin, Thomas Gilmer, Douglas Simon, Emily Anne. Editorial asst. Reader's Digest, Pleasantville, N.Y., 1942-44, asso. editor, 1949-64; club staff asst. A.R.C., Hawaii, Saipan, Guam, 1945; asso. editor Coronet Mag., N.Y.C., 1946-49; freelance author, editor, edit. cons., Memphis, 1964—; contbr. several nat. mags.; edit. coordinator grant to Memphis Multi-Media Archival Project, Nat. Endowment Humanities, 1971-74; chmn. bd. dirs. Women in Cable, Inc., 1973— Chmn. bd. dirs. Shelby County Vol. Women's Roundtable, 1970-71; bd. dirs. YWCA, Memphis, 1971—, Memphis Little Theatre, 1965-68. Mem. Women in Communications, Chi Omega. Democrat. Unitarian. Author: (with Neil V. Sullivan and Thomas L. Maynard) Bound for Freedom, 1965. Address: 4241 Park Av Memphis TN 38117

YENGER, RUTH ALICE JACOBSEN, advt. exec.; b. West Branch, Ia., July 15, 1921; d. Jens Peter and Magda Elisa (Jensen) Jacobsen; student Am. Inst. Commerce, 1940; 1 son by previous marriage, Steven M. With L.W. Ramsey Advt. Agy., Davenport, Ia., 1952—, media asst., 1952-64, traffic mgr., 1964-71, prodn. mgr., 1971—, v.p., 1972—. Lutheran. Mem. Order Eastern Star, Order of the Amaranth (grand marshall Ia. ct. 1973-74), Daus. of Nile. Home: 728 24th St Bettendorf IA 52722 Office: 430 Union Arcade Davenport IA 52801

YENI-KOMSHIAN, GRACE HELEN, educator; b. Beirut, Lebanon, Jan. 29, 1936; came to U.S. 1958; d. Hovsep Aghek and Helen Marie (Krajian) Yeni-komshian; B.A., Am. U. of Beirut, 1957, postgrad. 1958; M.S., Cornell U., 1962; Ph.D., McGill U., 1965; Research asso. Center for Applied Linguistics, Washington, 1964-65; instr. in med. psychology Johns Hopkins U., Balt., 1966-68, NIH spl. postdoctoral fellow in auditory neurophysiology, 1969-71, instr. in otolaryngology, 1972, asst. prof., 1973—; instr. psychology U. Md., Balt., part-time 1971-73. Cons. Center for Applied Linguistics, Washington, 1965-66; cons. Ford Found., Manila, Phillipines, 1968. Mem. A.A.A.S., Am. Psychol. Assn., Acoutical Soc. Am., Soc. for Research in Child Devel. Contbr. articles to profl. jours. Research in speech perception and production, language and brain functions, Home: 1510 Park Av Baltimore MD 21217 Office: Johns Hopkins University School of Medicine 410 Traylor Bldg Baltimore MD 21205

YEUELL, EUGENIA OSBURN, librarian; b. Tuscaloosa, Ala., Oct. 12, 1932; d. Gladstone Horace and Eugenia (Osburn) Yeuell; B.S. in Edn., U. Ala., 1954, M.A. in L.S., 1958. Asst. librarian Westover Sch., Middlebury, Conn., 1954-56; army librarian European Command, 1956-57; head librarian med. nursing library Druid City Hosp., Tuscaloosa, Ala., 1957-58; head cataloger Nashua (N.H.) Pub. Library, 1958-60; asst. cataloger Amherst Coll., 1960-61; head librarian med. nursing library Norfolk (Va.) Gen. Hosp., 1961-62; head tech. processing Portsmouth (Va.) Pub. Library, 1962—; instr. U. Va., 1962. Mem. Am., New Eng., N.H., Ala., Southeastern, Va. library assns., Bus. and Profl. Women's Club, Delta Psi Omega, Alpha Psi Omega, Alpha Beta Alpha, Chi Omega. Presbyn. Club: Druid City (charter). Contbr. articles to profl. jours. Home: 3158 Havenwood Ct Portsmouth VA 23703 Office: 601 Court St Portsmouth VA 23704

YEVAK, MARIE ELIZABETH, educator; b. Bentleyville, Pa., Dec. 3, 1914; d. Michael and Sue (Kolesar) Yevak; A.B. cum laude, Wilson Coll., 1934; postgrad. Columbia, summers 1936-39, Temple U. summer 1954; Ed.D., U. Pa., 1963. Reading tchr. D.A. Harman Jr. High Sch., Hazleton, Pa., 1935-42; tchr. Latin and English, Hazleton High Sch., 1942-54; tchr. English, then guidance counselor P.S. duPont High Sch., Wilmington, Del., 1955-61; asst. dir. student personnel William Paterson Coll., Wayne, N.J., 1965-67, asso. prof. psychology 1967-71, chmn. student personnel services faculty, 1972—. Troop leader Anthracite council Girl Scouts U.S.A., 1938-45, camp dir., 1944-45; reading cons. YMCA, Wilmington Del., 1956, group leader, 1955-56. Trustee Catholic Family and Community Services, Paterson. Mem. Am. Assn. U. Women (Hazleton br. pres. 1942-43, Morristown br. area rep. edn. 1964-68, N.J. div. area rep. edn. 1968-72, v.p. 1972-73, dir. at large 1973-74, N.J. div. pres. 1974-76), Paterson State Coll. Faculty Assn. (v.p. 1968-70), Am. Assn. U. Profs., Delta Kappa Gamma (select recruitment chmn. 1963-65), Pi Lambda Theta. Home: 3 Shepard Pl Convent Station NJ 07961 Office: 300 Pompton Rd Wayne NJ 07470

YIN, FAY HOH, virologist; b. Peking, China, Mar. 10, 1932; d. Gunsun and Dorothy Tze (Kao) Hoh; came to U.S., 1951, naturalized, 1968; B.A., U. Wis., 1954, M.S., 1956, Ph.D., 1960; m. Theodore P. Yin, Jan. 24, 1959 (dec. Jan. 1970); children—Duncan A., Monona A. Grad. biophysicist virus lab. U. Cal. at Berkeley, 1956-57; postdoctoral trainee dept. biochemistry U. Wis., Madison, 1960-61; research asso. dept. pathology U. Pa., Phila., 1963-65; research chemist Central Research dept. E.I. duPont de Nemours & Co., Wilmington, Del., 1966—. Mem. Am. Soc. Microbiology. Home: 1804 Bellewood Rd Wilmington DE 19803 Office: Central Research Dept E I duPont de Nemours & Co Wilmington DE 19898

YINGLING, HARRIET ELIZABETH, educator; b. Muscatine, Ia., Sept. 7, 1910; d. Roy and Katherine Mary (Wippelhouser) Yingling; B.S., State U. Ia., 1932; M.A., 1940; Ed.D., N.Y. U., 1966. Instr. Ia. State Coll., Ames, 1934-35; tchr. pub. schs., Wheaton, Ill., 1935-38, Kenosha, Wis., 1938-44; asso. prof. phys. edn. Neb. State Coll., Kearney, 1944-63; asso. prof., chmn. women's phys. edn. dept. Frostburg (Md.) State Coll., 1962-67; prof., head women's phys. edn. dept. Eastern Ill. U., Charleston, 1967—. Mem. Nat. Assn. Phys. Edn. Coll. Women (dir. 1959-61), Am. Assn. Univ. Profs. (pres. Neb. chpt. 1962-63), Neb. (award 1956), Central Dist. (award 1959), Md. (pres. 1967-68) assns. health, phys. edn. and recreation, Delta Kappa Gamma. Home: 125 Tyler Charleston IL 61920 Office: Eastern Ill U Charleston IL 61920

YLISTO, INGRID PYLVAINEN (MRS. INTO P. YLISTO), educator; b. Kearsarge, Mich., Apr. 8, 1918; d. Paul and Hilda Katarina (Muskos) Pylvainen; M.A., State U. Ia., 1945; Ph.D., U. Mich., 1967; m. Into P. Ylisto, 1946; children—Andrew, Briita, Alexander. Tchr. Lab. Sch., State U. Ia., 1944-45; faculty U. Nev., 1961-63; prof. edn. Eastern Mich. U., Ypsilanti, 1964—. Dir., Nat. Def. Edn. Act Inst., 1967-68. Mem. N.E.A., Nat. Council Tchrs. English, Assn. Supervision and Curriculum Devel., Assn. Childhood Edn., Internat. Reading Assn., Pi Lambda Theta. Home: 424 N Huron St Ypsilanti MI 48197

YNTEMA, MARY KATHERINE, educator; b. Urbana, Ill., Jan. 20, 1928; d. Leonard F. and M. Jean (Busey) Yntema; B.A., Swarthmore Coll., 1950; postgrad. U. Wis., 1957, Mont. State U., 1959; A.M., U. Ill., 1961, Ph.D., 1965. Tchr. secondary sch. math. Am. Coll. Girls, Istanbul, Turkey, 1950-54, Columbus (O.) Sch. for Girls, 1954-57, Roundup (Mont.) High Sch., 1959-60; digital computer programmer Mass. Inst. Tech. Lincoln Lab., Lexington, 1957-58; asst. prof. math. U. Ill., Chgo. Circle, 1965-67; asst. prof. computer sci. Pa. State U., University Park, 1967-71; asso. prof. math. Sangamon State U., Springfield, Ill., 1971—. Mem. Am. Math. Soc., Math. Assn. Am., Assn. Computing Machinery, Am. Assn. U. Profs., Sigma Xi, Phi Kappa Phi, Pi Mu Epsilon, Sigma Delta Epsilon. Mem. Bahai Faith (past sec. local spiritual assembly, chmn., rec. sec., mem. Central states youth projects com., mem. dept. temple activities, mem. Ill. state goals com.). Home: 3204 St Francis Dr Springfield IL 62703

YOAKUM, ANNA MARGARET, chemist; b. Loudon, Tenn., Jan. 13, 1933; d. Hugh L. and Emily (Watkins) Yoakum; A.B., Maryville Coll., 1954; M.S., U. Fla., 1956, Ph.D., 1960. Chief chemist, lab. supr. Greenback Industries, Inc., 1956-59; research chemist Chemstrand Research Center, Inc., 1960-64; research staff Oak Ridge Nat. Lab., 1964-69, exec. v.p., lab. dir. Stewart Labs., Inc., Knoxville, 1969—. Fellow Am. Inst. Chemists; mem. Am. Chem. Soc., Am. Soc. for Testing and Materials, Soc. Applied Spectroscopy (sect. sec., treas. 1965-68), N.Y. Acad. Scis., Phi Beta Kappa, Sigma Xi, Phi Kappa Phi, Gamma Sigma Epsilon. Methodist. Club: Knoxville Executive. Home: 7844 Ramsgate Dr Knoxville TN 37919 Office: 820 Tulip Av Knoxville TN 37921

YOCHIM, CHARMAINE STANDER (MRS. DAVID A. YOCHIM), librarian; b. Saginaw, Mich., Sept. 23, 1940; d. Aaron Carl and Charlotte Rose (Hammeschmidt) Stander; student Northwestern U., 1958-60; B.A., U. Mich., 1962, M.A. in L.S., 1966; m. David A. Yochim, July 23, 1966; children—Joshua David, Catherine. Reference librarian Arlington County (Va.) Pub. Library, 1966-67; librarian Prince George's Community Coll., Largo, Md., 1967-71, head acquisitions, preparation and processing dept., 1971—. Mem. A.L.A., Assn. for Ednl. Communications and Tech., Md. Assn. Jr. Colls. (editor newsletter 1968-70), Md. Library Assn. (chmn. fed. relations com. 1972—), Beta Phi Mu, Phi Kappa Phi. Home: 209 8th St Washington DC 20003 Office: 301 Largo Rd Largo MD 20870

YOCHIM, LOUISE DUNN (MRS. MAURICE YOCHIM), artist, educator; b. Jitomir, Ukraine; d. Solomon and Gitil (Milstein) Dunn; came to U.S., 1924, naturalized, 1929; student U. Chgo., 1930-31, postgrad., 1956; B.Art Edn., Art Inst. Chgo., 1942, M.Art Edn., 1952; m. Maurice Yochim, June 19, 1932; 1 son, Jerome. Tchr., Longfellow Elementary Sch., Oak Park, Ill., 1932, Jr. Sch., Art Inst., Chgo., 1930-32; tchr. pub. elementary and high schs., Chgo., 1934-50; tchr. Chgo. Acad. Fine Arts, 1952, Chgo. Tchrs. Coll., 1952, 53, 60, Wright Jr. Coll., Chgo., 1952, 53; supr. art Chgo. Pub. Schs., 1950—; exhibited in group shows Art Inst. Chgo., 1935, 36, 42, Riverside Mus. (N.Y.), 1951, Asso. Artists Gallery, Chgo., 1953, Ill. State Mus., Springfield, 1959, 61, Butler Mus., Cleve., 1958, Des Moines Art Center, 1955, Renaissance Soc. U. Chgo., 1955-58, Cleve. Mus. Art, 1958, Northwestern U., 1963, Chgo. Tchrs. Coll. N., 1964, Covenant Club, 1964, Nat. Design Center, 1965, U. Club Chgo., 1966, 1st Fed. Gallery (Chgo.), 1960, McCormick Pl. Art Gallery, Chgo., 1963, Contemporary Art Gallery, Chgo., 1962, Library Congress, Washington, 1958, Asso. Artists Gallery, Washington, 1962, Terry Mus. Art (Fla.), 1961, A. Werbe Gallery, Detroit, 1961-68, and others. Art cons. Rand McNally Pubs., 1967, Ency. Brit., 1968. Recipient awards for painting and graphics, 1948, 53-55, 58, 59, 61. Mem. Chgo. Soc. Artists (pres. 1972-73), Renaissance Soc. Art U. Chgo., Nat. Art Edn. Assn., Western Arts Assn., Chgo. Tchrs. Union, Nat. Com. Art Edn., Designer Craftsmen Assos., Delta Kappa Gamma. Author: Building Human Relationships Through Art, 1954; Perceptual Growth in Creativity, 1967; also articles. Editor: Art in Action, 1970. Collaborator on film, Richard Hunt, Sculptor, 1970. Home: 9545 N Drake St Evanston IL 60203 Office: 228 N LaSalle St Chicago IL 60601

YOCKEY, CAROL COX (MRS. JAMES E. YOCKEY), advt. agy. exec.; b. Danville, Ill., Nov. 4, 1929; d. Norris Wayne and Hazel (Bennett) Cox; student Hammond Bus. Sch., 1948; m. James E. Yockey, Aug. 10, 1946; children—Pamela (Mrs. Charles E. Stevenson, Jr.), Keith, Christopher. Asso. news editor, producer own Talk Show, TV weather, radio features, television documentaries WFBC-TV, Greenville, S.C., 1960-68; account exec., dir. radio/TV, Lowe & Hall Advt., Inc., Greenville, 1968—. Active YWCA Y-Teens, Greenville Civic Chorale. Home: 109 Ashford Av Greenville SC 29609 Office: PO Box 1824 Greenville SC 29602

YOCUM, NORMA LENORE YOUNG (MRS. SAM A. YOCUM), civic worker; b. Redkey, Ind., Jan. 10, 1911; d. Fern Leigh and Mattie (Rathbun) Young; grad. Central Jr. Coll., 1930, Woodbury Bus. Coll., 1931; Ph.D. (hon.), Hamilton State U., 1973; m. Sam A. Yocum, Oct. 2, 1932; children—Virginia (Mrs. Clyde Fraser), Martha (Mrs. Edward White), Robert, Phyllis. (Mrs. Robert Frank). Mayor, City of Alhambra (Cal.), 1964-67. Pres. Sam Yocum, Inc., mfrs. office equipment, Alhambra, 1970-72. Organizing pres. Alhambra-San Gabriel Area Council Ch. Women, 1939-45; pres. Alhambra Coordinating Council, 1943-45, Los Angeles County Fedn. Community Coordinating Councils, 1950, Alhambra Pub. Library Bd., 1948-55, Cal. Library Trustee Assn., 1953-55; mem. Alhambra Planning Commn., 1959-61, Alhambra Recreation Commn., 1962; pres.-elect dist. bd. Am. Cancer Soc., 1972, chmn. lay speakers bur., 1971—; adviser Los Angeles County Youth Coordinating Councils, 1946-48; chmn. Los Angeles County Adv. Com. on Recreation, 1946-49; presiding clk. Alhambra Friends Ch., 1949-55, tchr. adult Ch. Sch. class, 1951-70; v.p. Cal. Bd. Friends Women, 1958-60; bd. stewardship and finance 5-Years Nat. Meeting of Friends; chmn. Cal. bd. stewardship and finance Cal. Yearly Meeting of Friends, 1962-64. Councilman, Alhambra, 1955-71; pres. D.A.V. Charities of West San Gabriel Valley, 1970—; chmn. office of vols. A.R.C., 1970-73; bd. dirs. Commn. on Aging of West San Gabriel Valley, 1966—. Republican candidate for state assembly, 1966, 68; sec. Cal. Rep. party convention, 1966, 68. Recipient Life Membership citation Los Angeles County Bd. Suprs., 1955, citation for service Cal. Library Assn., 1954; named Woman of Year, Alhambra Quota Club, 1958; named Woman Yr., B'nai B'rith, 1965; Woman Yr. Govt., Cal. Bus. and Profl. Women's Clubs, 1966; Mayor's award merit, Los Angeles County Bd. Suprs., 1966, others. Mem. Am. Bus. Women's Assn., Alhambra Hist. Soc. (founder, pres. 1965), Business and Profl. Women's Club. Republican. Clubs: Alhambra Round Table (community service chmn. 1951-64), Soroptimist (treas. 1958; pres. 1970) (Alhambra). Home: 1815 S 4th St Alhambra CA 91801 Office: 420 W Valley Blvd San Gabriel CA 91776

YODER, GLEE EVELYN GOUGHNOUR (MRS. R(ALPH) GORDON YODER), author; b. Elkhart, Ia., Sept. 15, 1916; d. Earl Miller and Mary Diane (Mathis) Goughnour; A.B. cum laude, McPherson (Kan.) Coll., 1938; m. R(alph) Gordon Yoder, Aug. 20, 1939; 1 dau., Marcia (Mrs. Dennis Emmert). Elementary sch. tchr., Kan., 1938-39; survey interviewer Young & Rubicam, Inc., Nampa, Ida., 1943, McPherson, Kan., 1953; adminstrv. asst. Ch. of Brethren, Western Region, McPherson, 1953-64, dir. children's work, 1948-58, adminstrv. asst. Kan. Dist., McPherson, 1964-67, area curriculum counselor for Mid-West, 1968—; prof. Christian edn. McPherson Coll., 1951-52, 53-54. Participant, Communications for Laity Conf., Lilly Endowment, U. Denver, summer 1969, 3d Theol. Conf., Bethany Theol. Sem., Oak Brook, Ill., summer 1969. Mem. McPherson City Parent-Tchrs.' Council, 1949-53, pres., 1953. Mem. Kan. Authors' Club, Nat. League Am. Pen Women, Inc. Author: The Church and Infants and Toddlers, 1966; Who Is God?, 1969; All That Is Within Me, 1970; The Christian Faces His World, 1970; The Gospel of Luke, 1971; Why Not Peace?, 1972; A World-Wide Fellowship, 1972; Take It From Here, 1973; Foundations for Life, 1973; Handle With Care, 1974; Christian Sign Language, 1974. also articles, pamphlets. Home: 6406 E 15th St Wichita KS 67206

YODER, HILDA (MRS. ALBERT FRANCIS GARROU), ednl. adminstr.; b. Hickory, N.C., Jan. 1, 1903; d. Ellis Hampton and Elizabeth (Frye) Whitener; B.S., Lenoir Rhyne Coll., 1924, L.H.D., 1955; M.A., Tchrs. Coll., Columbia, 1945; m. Luther Glenn Yoder, July 7, 1928 (dec. Oct. 1940); m. 2d, Albert Francis Garrou, Nov. 4, 1956. Tchr., supr. high sch., N.C., N.J., 1926-45; research anti-convulsive clinic psychiat. and neurol. dept. U. Va. Hosp., 1945-47; founder, dir. Yoder Sch., N.Y.C., 1949—; lectr. postgrad. Sch. Ophthalmology, N.Y.U., Bellevue Med. Center, 1950-53. Dir. Reading Clinic Inst. Ophthalmology, Columbia-Presbyn. Med. Center, 1950-56. Mem. Assn. Ind. Schs., D.A.R. Presbyn. Club: Woman's University (N.Y.C.). Home: Valdese NC 28690 Office: Yoder School 2 Hammarskjold Plaza New York City NY 10017

YOEMANS, DANNIELLE SUZETTE, occupational therapist; b. Brainerd, Minn., Dec. 7, 1947; d. John Albert and Edna Orvilla (Williams) Hayes; B.S., U. Minn., 1970; m. Thomas William Yoemans, Sept. 21, 1968; children—Brandon Thomas, Stephen Nicholas. Cons. occupational therapy research Lyngblomsten Center, St. Paul, 1970-73, St. Anthony Nursing Home, St. Paul, 1972-73; self-employed occupational therapist in community therapy and cons. services, Red Wing, Minn., 1974—. Mem. Am., Minn. assns. occupational therapy. Address: 1026 Lidberg St Red Wing MN 55066

YOHO, BETTY EILEEN, librarian; b. Warren, O.; d. Chester Earl and Nora Vienna (Bell) Cavender; B.A. with high honors, Ohio Wesleyan U., 1945; postgrad. Katharine Gibbs Sch., N.Y., 1947; M.S. in L.S., Drexel U., 1965. High sch. tchr., Ohio, 1945-47; sec. to pres. Warren Tool Corp., 1947-48; tchr. Drew Sch. for Girls, Carmel, N.Y., 1948-51; tchr., librarian Oakgrove Sch., Wilmington, Del., 1951-57; librarian Lombardy Sch., Wilmington, 1957—. Mem. A.L.A., Del. Sch. Library Assn. (pres.), Del. Library Assn. (treas.), N.E.A., Del. Edn. Assn., Phi Beta Kappa, Chi Omega, Kappa Delta Pi. Mem. Christian Ch. (sec.). Club: Racquets (sec.) (Wilmington). Home: 2300 Riddle Av Wilmington DE 19806 Office: 412 Foulk Rd Wilmington DE 19803

YOLKUT, ALINE SCHLESINGER, educator; b. Lyon, France, June 25, 1947; d. Charles and Marie (Wind) Schlesinger; came to U.S., 1953, naturalized, 1958; B.A., U. Ill., 1968, M.A., 1972; m. Morton F. Yolkut. High sch. English tchr. Ida Crown Jewish Acad., Chgo., 1968-69; instr. English lang. YMCA Community Coll., Chgo., 1969—. Home: 2650 Touhy Av Chicago IL 60645 Office: 211 W Wacker Dr Chicago IL 60606

YOLLES, TAMARATH KNIGIN (MRS. STANLEY FAUSST YOLLES), physician; b. Bklyn., Feb. 27, 1919; d. Max H. and Bessie (Krokoff) Knigin; A.B., Bklyn. Coll., 1939; M.D., N.Y. U., 1950; m. Stanley Fausst Yolles, Oct. 10, 1942; children—Melanie A., Jennifer C. Research asst. U. Minn., St. Paul, 1939-40; asst. parasitologist Army Med. Sch., Walter Reed Army Med. Hosp., Washington, 1941; parasitologist U.S.C.E., British Guiana, 1941-43; asso. dir. Area Lab. Trinidad Sector and Base Command, 1943-45; parasitologist Nat. Research Council Schistosomiasis Project, N.Y. U. Coll. Medicine, 1946-47; intern USPHS Hosp., S.I., N.Y., 1951-52; commd. surgeon USPHS, 1954, advanced through grades to asst. surgeon gen., 1970; dep. chief medicine Pub. Health Service Out-patient Clinic, Washington, 1959-61, health maintenance officer Office Surgeon Gen., 1961-64, dir. div. commd. personnel operations Office Sec. Health, Edn. and Welfare, Rockville, Md., 1968-71; asst. adminstr. for orgn. devel. Health Services and Mental Health Adminstrn., Rockville, 1971-72, cons. to adminstr., 1972-73; prof. clin. community medicine Sch. Medicine, State U. N.Y. at Stony Brook, 1972-73, prof. community medicine, 1973—. Mem. A.M.A., Am. Soc. Parasitologists, Am. Soc. Tropical Medicine (Medal of Freedom 1947), Alpha Omega Alpha. Home: 2 Soundview Ct Stony Brook NY 11790

YOLTON, JEAN MARY SEBASTIAN (MRS. JOHN WILLIAM YOLTON), librarian; b. Norwood, O., Mar. 22, 1924; d. Joseph and Mary Josephine (Lampe) Sebastian; B.A., U. Cin., 1945; M.A. in L.S., U. Cal. at Berkeley, 1947; m. John William Yolton, Sept. 5, 1945; children—Karin Frances (Mrs. Bryant Griffith), Pamela Holmes. Librarian I, Oakland Pub. Library, 1947-50; tchr. Mt. Vernon (O.) High Sch., 1958-60; serials cataloger U. Md., 1961-63; cataloger charge books-with-cards program Coop. Book Centre of Can., 1963-64; serials cataloger U. Toronto (Ont.) Library, 1964—. Democratic committeewoman, Princeton, N.J., 1953-55. Taft teaching fellow U. Cin., 1945-46. Mem. Am., Canadian (dir. serials workshop Ann. Conf., Regina, Sask. 1972). Club: University Womens (Toronto). Compiler: (with Anni Woodsworth) OCUL Union List of Microform Sets, 1972. Home: 18 Paulson Rd Toronto ON Canada Office: Serials Dept Robarts Library U Toronto Toronto ON Canada

YON, LINDA IDDINS (MRS. CHARLES LINDSAY YON), physician; b. Bellingham, Wash., Mar. 24, 1918; d. Bert R. and Margaret V. (Jennings) Iddins; student Maryville Coll., 1936-37, U. Tenn., 1938-39; D.O., Los Angeles Coll. Osteo. Physicians and Surgeons, 1943; M.D., U. Cal., 1962; m. Charles Lindsay Yon, Nov. 11, 1951; children—Stephen C., Sharon L., Jeffrey J. Intern, Los Angeles County Gen. Hosp., 1943-44; resident gynecology and gen. surgery Los Angeles Osteo. Physicians and Surgeons, 1947-48; practice medicine specializing in obstetrics and gynecology, in Big Bear Lake, Cal., 1944-47, Seattle, 1948-51; mem. staff Waldo Gen. Hosp., Seattle; staff physician Met. Life Ins. Co., 1963, asst. med. dir., 1964-70, apptd. officer, San Francisco, 1964. Project coordinator San Francisco Alliance for Health Care, 1970-71. Mem. Am., Cal., med. assns., Assn. Life Ins. Med. Dirs., Am. Pub. Health Assn., Am. Geratric Soc., San Francisco Med. Soc. (com. chmn. 1970-71), Alpha Delta Pi. Republican. Home: 78 Scenic Dr Orinda CA 94563

YOOS, IVY MORTON (MRS. ROY WILLIAM YOOS), museum curator; b. Achilles, Kan., June 17, 1895; d. Benjamin Franklin and Luella Susan (Hurst) Morton; grad. high sch.; m. Roy William Yoos, June 1, 1917; 1 son, Kenneth Morton. Tchr. country sch., 1914-15; clk. Dist. Ct., Rawlins County, Atwood, Kan., 1933-37; clk. Social Security Bd., Balt., 1938-46; dep. county clk. Rawlins County, Atwood, 1946-51, register of deeds Rawlins County, 1951-61; curator Rawlins County Mus., 1961—. Methodist. Mem. Order Eastern Star. Author: This Is My Life, 1970. Home: 700 Vine St Atwood KS 67730

YORBURG, BETTY (MRS. LEON YORBURG), educator; b. Chgo., Aug. 27, 1926; d. Max and Hannah (Bernstein) Gitelman; Ph.B., U. Chgo., 1945, M.A., 1948; Ph.D., New Sch. for Social Research, 1968; m. Leon Yorburg, June 23, 1946; children—Harriet, Robert. Instr., Coll. of New Rochelle, 1966-67; lectr. City Coll. and Grad. Center, City U. N.Y., 1967-69, asst. prof., 1969-73, asso. prof. sociology dept., 1973—. Research asst. Prof. Clifford Shaw, Chgo. Area Project, 1946-47. Mem. Am., Eastern sociol. assns. Author: Utopia and Reality, 1969; The Changing Family, 1973; Sexual Identity: Sex Roles and Social Change, 1974. Home: 1046 Clay Av Pelham Manor NY 10803 Office: Sociology Dept City U NY 133d and Convent Av New York City NY 10031

YORE, DOLORES LOUISE (MRS. EDWARD YORE), pub. relations exec.; b. Chgo., Aug. 17, 1921; d. William Joseph and Louise (Gehrig) Dressel; B.A., DePaul U., 1943; postgrad. Loyola U. Sch. Social Service, 1944-45; m. Edward Yore, Nov. 17, 1945; children—Gregory, William, Victoria (Mrs. Raymond Janutis), Douglas. Asst. supr. A.R.C., 1943-46; dir. pub. relations South Chicago Hosp., 1967-72, Palos Community Hosp., Palos Heights, Ill., 1972—. Bd. dirs. Riviera in Palos Improvement Assn. Mem. South Chicagoland Hosp. Pub. Relations Dirs. Assn. (treas. 1970-73), Am. Hosp. Assn. Pub. Relations Dirs., Chgo. Hosp. Council Pub. Relations Dirs., Womens Aux. Palos Community Hosp., Palos Bus. and Profl. Women's Club. Editor: Inside-South Chicago Community Hosp., 1967-72; Kaleidoscope-Englewood Hosp., 1972; Perspective and Chips and Chirps-Palos Community Hosp., 1972—; Riviera News, 1973—. Home: 10 Cour St Tropez Palos Hills IL 60465 Office: 123d and 80th Av Palos Heights IL 60463

YORK, GERTRUDE JAMES PUDIG (MRS. CHRISTOPHER LAFAYETTE YORK), librarian; b. Waco, Tex., July 30, 1915; d. Frank Louis and Gertrude (James) Pudig; A.B., Baylor U., 1936; A.B. in L.S., Emory U., 1939; m. Christopher LaFayette York, June 28, 1942. Librarian, Gladewater (Tex.) Jr. High Sch., 1939-43; staff mem. Waco Pub. Library, 1943-46; cataloger U. Tex. Library, Austin, 1946-50; librarian Belton (Tex.) High Sch., 1954—. Mem. N.E.A., Tex. Tchrs. Assn., Tex. Library Assn. Mem. Christian Ch. Home: 409 W 9th St Belton TX 76513 Office: Belton High Sch North Wall St Belton TX 76513

YORK, KAREN PORTUGAL (MRS. ARNOLD G. YORK), graphic artist; b. Mpls., May 22, 1943; d. Samuel William and Dorothy Dolores (Shapiro) Portugal; B.A. in Sociology, U. Cal., Los Angeles, 1965, M.A., 1968; m. Arnold G. York, Jan. 30, 1965; 1 son, Clayton Matthew. Social worker Jewish Centers Assn., Los Angeles, 1966; adminstr. Westside Therapy Center, 1968-69; free lance graphic artist, 1969-72; adminstr. poligraphics, Los Angeles, 1973-74; prodn. mgr. Furniture Marketing Concepts, advt. agy., 1974—. Cons. home health care of aged; ednl. cons. on aging Los Angeles City Coll. Mem. Cal. Children's Lobby, 1973. Recipient Health, Edn. and Welfare Edn. grant U. So. Cal., 1967, Graphic Arts student award, 1972; named Democratic Woman of Year for vol. activities, 1971-73. Mem. Am., So. Cal. occupational therapy assns. Jewish religion.

YORK, MARGARET RUTH ASHTON (MRS. GORDON C. YORK), occupational therapist; b. Reynoldsburg, O., June 9, 1911; d. George Edward and Mary Ruth (Abbott) Ashton; A.A., Los Angeles City Coll., 1933; postgrad. U. Cal. at Los Angeles, 1940; B.S., U. So. Cal., 1958, certificate occupational therapy, 1959; m. Edward T. Randall, Nov. 2, 1938 (dec. Mar. 1968); m. Gordon C. York, Mar. 26, 1973; 1 stepdau., Paulette Marie. Audio-visual specialist U. Cal. Extension, Los Angeles, 1940-56; registered occupational therapist Bur. Crippled Children Services, Schs. for Physically Handicapped, Cal. Dept. Pub. Health, El Monte, Burbank and Ontario, 1959-63; supervising occupational therapist Crippled Children Services, Orange County Health Dept., Santa Ana, Cal., 1963—. Hon. clin. faculty Sargent Coll. Allied Health Professions, Boston U., Sch. Allied Health Professions, Loma Linda U. Mem. Audio-Visual Assn. So. Cal. (v.p. 1955-56), So. Cal. (sec. 1960-61), Orange County (sec. 1969-70) occupational therapy assns. Episcopalian. Club: Pilot (v.p. 1955) (Westwood Village, Cal.). Home: 320-F Avenida Carmel Laguna Hills CA 92653 Office: PO Box 355 Santa Ana CA 92702

YORK, MILLIE, advt. exec.; b. N.Y.C., Mar. 21, 1929; d. Max and Sarah (Williamsburg) Yorkowitz; grad. high sch. With Altman Stoller Advt. Agy., N.Y.C., 1955-66; office mgr. Chalk, Nissen, Hanft, Inc., N.Y.C., 1968—. Free lance cons. for advt. accountants. Home: 405 W 23d St New York City NY 10011 Office: 645 Madison Av New York City NY 10022

YOSEPIAN, JANE MARIE, educator; b. Chgo.; d. Apkar and Helen (Harten) Yosepian; B.S., U. Ill., 1956; M.S., U. Utah, 1958; courses Colo. Coll., Arts Inst. Chgo., Ariz. State U., Conn. Coll. Instr. phys. edn. for women U. R.I., 1958-60, asst. prof., 1960—; named specialist in modern dance U.S. State Dept., 1965; cons. Bolivarian Games. Mem. Nat. Assn. for Armenian Studies and Research, Inc. Mem. Am., R.I. assns. for health, phys. edn. and recreation, Eastern Assn. Phys. Edn. for Coll. Women, Am. Assn. U. Profs., R.I. Div. Girls and Women's Sports, Amateur Fencer's League of Am. Producer: Plastic Body—a dance demonstration for high sch. and colleges. Home: 811 W Lawrence Av Chicago IL 60640 also 5745 E Camelback Rd Phoenix AZ 85018 Office: U RI Kingston RI 02881

YOSKEY, MARY ANN, educator; b. Waynesburg, Pa., Oct. 8, 1950; d. Walter John and Teresa Mary (Matergan) Yoskey; B.S. in Edn., California (Pa.) State Coll., 1971, M.A., 1974. Substitute tchr., 1972-73; tchr. Trinity Area Schs., Washington, Pa., 1973—. Mem. Speech Communication Assn., Nat. Council Tchrs. English, Alpha Xi Delta (treas. bldg. corp. California 1973—), Pi Kappa Delta. Roman Catholic. Home: Box 183 Marianna PA 15345 Office: Park Av Washington PA 15301

YOST, HELEN MARGUERITE, social worker; b. San Diego; d. Don M. and Susie Marguerite (Sims) Yost; A.A., Pasadena Jr. Coll., 1939; B.S., U. Cal. at Los Angeles, 1948, postgrad. Girls worker Pasadena Settlement Assn., 1948-52; worker with aux. Car Club groups Los Angeles YWCA, 1952-56; field service and community orgn. worker, dir. camping, supr. extension work, program coordinator, adminstrv. dept. head Cath. Youth Orgn., Los Angeles, 1956—. Dir., tchr. Pasadena Jarabe Club; tchr. folk dance at Insts. and Folk Dance Fedn. Workshops, 1948-62. Mem. steering com. Interfaith Coalition on Aging of So. Cal.; chmn. steering com. Los Angeles Archdiocesan Commn. on Cath. Camping. Served with USNR, 1943-45. Recipient award for outstanding work in community Los Angeles County Bd. Suprs., 1955; 1st Place in Press Book judging in So. Cal., 1969. Mem. Nat. Assn. Social Workers, Acad. Certified Social Workers, Am. Camping Assn. (chmn. Day Camp com., camp visitor for nat. pilot study, dir., past sec.), Kap and Bells, Delta Zeta, Phi Beta. Democrat. Roman Catholic. Home: 529 S Madison Av Pasadena CA 91101 Office: 1400 W 9th St Los Angeles CA 90015

YOST, NELLIE IRENE (MRS. DAVID HARRISON YOST), author; b. Sutherland, Neb., June 20, 1905; d. Albert Benton and Grace Bell (McCance) Snyder; grad. high sch.; m. David Harrison Yost, July 6, 1929; 1 son, Thomas Snyder. With Miller Dept. Store, Salem, Ore., 1927-29. Grand marshal Buffalo Bill Blowout, 1963; apptd. col. North Platte Cody Scouts, 1965; pres., bd. dirs. Neb. Hist. Soc.; chmn. museum com. Lincoln County Soc.; trustee Neb. Hist. Soc. Found. Recipient Eyes on Neb. award Neb. Optometric Soc., 1970. Mem. Neb. Writers Guild (pres. 1969-71, now dir.), Western Writers Am. (sec.-treas.), Nat., Neb. cowbelle assns., Western History Assn., North Platte Buffalo Bill Corral of The Westerners (sec. 1969-70), P.E.O., North Platte Federated Womans Club, Neb. Hist. Soc. (1st v.p.), Beta Sigma Phi (internat. hon. mem.; named 1st Lady of Yr. for North Platte 1972). Republican. Baptist. Club: North Platte Altrusa. Author: Pinnacle Jake, 1951; The West That Was, 1958; No Time On My Hands, 1963; Call of the Range, 1966; Boss Cowman (Spur award Western Writers Am.), 1969; Medicine Lodge, 1970. Home: 1505 W D St North Platte NE 69101 Office: care Dir Pub Relations U Neb Press 907 N 17th St Lincoln NE 68508

YOST, NOLA BELL, realtor; b. Windom, Tex., Nov. 28, 1929; d. Jacob Rector and Clara Rosetta (Wrinkle) Butler; grad. various real estate schs.; m. Eugene B. Yost, Dec. 14, 1951; 1 son, Roger Wayne. With firm Kane, Hall, Palmtag, realtors, Watsonville, Cal., 1969-71; propr. Nola Yost, realtor, Watsonville, 1971—. Trustee Alial Sch. Bd., Salinas, Cal., 1962-64. Mem. Watsonville Real Estate Bd. (dir. 1971—; award most sales on multiple listing 1972). Mem. Ch. of Christ. Address: PO Box 645 Watsonville CA 95670

YOUELL, ELIZABETH NOYES, real estate exec.; b. Pratt, W.Va., Apr. 27, 1915; d. Bradford Noyes and Kathleen Elizabeth (Veazey) Coleman; certificate proficiency real estate. Coll. of Desert, 29 Palms, Cal., 1972; m. Aaron Stockton Youell, Aug. 15, 1946 (dec. 1972); children—Sally Kathleen, Nancy Noyes. Statis. clk., sec. div. vital statistics W.Va. Dept. Health, 1934-44; IBM operator Eastern

Aircraft Co., Trenton, 1944-45; sec., bookkeeper, salesman Red Barn Realty, 29 Palms, 1964—, office mgr., 1973—, inc., 1974, sec.-treas., 1974—. Mem. Cal. Real Estate Assn. Home: 73983 Casita Dr Twentynine Palms CA 92277 Office: PO Box 427 Twentynine Palms CA 92277

YOUENS, CYNTHIA TANNER, educator; b. Columbus, Tex., Sept. 7, 1905; d. John Osborne and Phyrne (Claiborne) Tanner; B.S., U. Houston, 1951, M.Ed., 1953; m. Willis George Youens, Feb. 13, 1935; children—Phyrne (Mrs. Philip Bacon), Leonard Claiborne, John Tanner, Phillip Whitfield. Faculty mem. Alief (Tex.) Sch., 1951—, 4th grade tchr., 1954-66, 3d grade tchr., 1966—. Mem. Houston Mus. Fine Arts, P.T.A. Alief Sch. renamed Cynthia Youens Elementary Sch. in her honor, 1974. Mem. A.A.A.S., Tex. Tchrs. Assn., Internat. Platform Assn., Tex. State Hist. Assn., Women's Aux. Harris County Med. Soc., Kappa Delta Pi. Home: 19 West Lane Houston TX 77019 Office: Cynthia Youens Elementary Sch Alief TX 77411

YOUNG, ALICE BAUCOM (MRS. JOHN ALBERT YOUNG), librarian; b. Ellerbe, N.C., May 9, 1934; d. B. Duane and Bertha Virginia (Sinclair) Baucom; A.A., Gardner-Webb Jr. Coll., 1954; B.S., Appalachian State Tchrs. Coll., 1956; M.L.S., George Peabody Coll. for Tchrs., 1970; m. John Albert Young, Aug. 23, 1959; children—Jay, Allen. Asst. librarian Gardner-Webb Jr. Coll., 1956-59; library asst. Washington Meml. Lab., Macon, Ga., 1959-61, childrens librarian, 1961-66; head librarian Tift Coll., Forsyth, Ga., 1966—. Trustee, Monroe County Pub. Library. Mem. Ga., Southeastern library assns., Beta Phi Mu. Home: 267 Tift College Dr Forsyth GA 31029

YOUNG, AURELIA NORRIS (MRS. JACK HARVEY YOUNG), educator; b. Knottsville, Ky., Dec. 9, 1915; d. John Henry and Hilda (Stone) Norris; B.S., Wilberforce U., 1937; M.Mus. (Delta Sigma Theta grantee), Ind. U., 1955; Ph.D. (hon.), Campbell Coll., 1953; m. Jack Harvey Young, Sept. 4, 1938; children—Hilda Jeannette, Jack Harvey. Choral dir. Campbell Coll., 1937-41; band dir. Tougaloo Coll., 1943-47; asst. prof. music theory Jackson (Miss.) State Coll., 1947—. Appearances as duo piano team Norris and Young, 1964—. Mem. exec. bd. Miss. Human Relations Council, 1967—, Miss. Family Service Assn., 1968; mem. Miss. Instructional Television Lab. Adv. Tchrs., 1968. Recipient Distinguished Alumni award Ind. U., 1970. Mem. Am. Assn. U. Profs. (pres. Jackson State chpt. 1967—; pres. Miss. conf. 1969-71, nat. council 1971—), N.E.A., Com. Status of Women Acad. Profession, Panel Am. Women, Am. Assn. U. Women, Miss. Tchrs. Assn., League Women Voters, Delta Sigma Theta (Woman of Year Jackson chpt. 1957, exec. bd. 1964-67). Club: Jackson Links. Home: 3760 Brinkley Dr Jackson MS 39213

YOUNG, BEATRICE CARPENTER, state ofcl.; b. Phila., July 29, 1933; d. Alfred Barrett and Dorothy (Buzby) Carpenter; B.A., U. Chgo., 1960, M.A., 1964, now postgrad. 1 son, DuBois Douglass. Dir. edn. Ill. Commn. on Human Relations, 1965-70, exec. dir., Chgo. and Springfield, 1970-74; trainer-cons. ACTION, 1974—; instr. Northeastern Ill. U., Chgo., 1966-70. Recipient Superior Pub. Service award as outstanding profl. employee State of Ill., 1970. Contbr. articles to profl. jours. Home: 8668 S Kimbark Av Chicago IL 60619 Office: 1 N Wacker Dr Chicago IL 60606

YOUNG, BERNICE ELIZABETH, author; b. Cleve., Oct. 7, 1931; d. James Anthony and Josephine Juanita (Paige) Young; student Vassar Coll., 1949-51, Western Res. U., 1951-52. Dir. Beatles (U.S.A.) Ltd., 1964-67; protestant adviser, media adviser Girl Scouts Am., 1968; publicity chmn. St. Thomas Ch., N.Y.C., account exec. Addison, Goldstein & Walsh, N.Y.C., 1969-70; free-lance author, 1970—; author radio series You and Your Money, 1970. Bd. dirs. Sheltering Arms Childrens Service, Children's Day Care Center. Mem. Authors Guild, Authors League, Internat. Platform Assn., Joffrey Circle, Young Friends of City Center. Author: Harlem, The Story of a Changing Community, 1972; The Picture Story of Hank Aaron, 1974; The Picture Story of Frank Robinson, 1975; Great Tribes of Africa, 1976. Contbr. articles to jours., mags. Episcopalian (altar guild, acolyte). Address: 333 E 34th St New York City NY 10016

YOUNG, BILLIE, pub. co. exec., author; b. Bklyn., June 27, 1933; d. Albert and Reda (Bromberg) Young; student Bklyn. Coll., 1949-51, New Sch. Social Research, 1953-54; m. Simeon Paget, Jan. 2, 1959; children—Bruce, Richard, Dana, Laurie Lief, Kristie. Copywriter Camp Chem. Co., Bklyn., 1950-53; reporter Cowles Communications, Deer Park, N.Y., 1968-69; pres. Ashley Books, Inc., Port Washington, N.Y., 1970—; treas. Born Blessed Publs., Los Angeles, 1973—. Lectr., guest numerous TV talk shows; promoter books, cons. in field; free-lance writer. Dir. pub. relations Am. Repertory Theatre; active North Shore Community Arts Center, 1953-59, North Shore Hosp., 1958-63. Mem. A.L.A., Am. Booksellers Assn., Publishers Ad Club, Cancer Care, Com. Small Mag. Editors and Pubs. Author: The Naked Chef, 1971; Vive La Difference, 1975. Contbr. articles to newspapers, popular mags. Promoted Naked Came the Stranger as author, Penelope Ashe, 1969. Home: 14 Capi Lane Port Washington NY 11050 Office: Box 768 Port Washington NY 11050

YOUNG, CAROL ANN, educator; b. Fort Worth, Sept. 10, 1946; d. Travis Pinson and Marion Adelaide (Swor) Young; B.S., North Tex. State U., 1968, M.Ed., 1971; Spl. Edn. Certification, Tex. Woman's U., 1974; 1 son, David McKenzie Young. Tchr. math. Lewisville (Tex.) Middle Sch., 1968-70, Boswell High Sch., Saginaw, Tex., 1970-71; counselor, psychodiagnostician North Tex. State U. Counseling Center, Denton, 1971; tchr. Shady Oaks Sch., Fort Worth, 1973-74; psychol. asso., evaluator for work activity centers Tarrant County Mental Health and Mental Retardation, Richland Hills, Tex., 1974—, Psychodiagnostic cons Spl. Friends Sch., Hurst, Tex., 1973. Mem. Am. Psychol. Assn. (asso.), Tex. State Tchrs. Assn., Am. Legion Aux. Contbr. articles to profl. jours. Office: 7431-C Dogwood Park Richland Hills TX 76118

YOUNG, CECELIA ALCANTARA, physician; b. Rockaway Beach, N.Y., Oct. 5, 1932; d. Joseph Sylvester and Cecelia W. (Vollmer) Young; B.S., St. John's U.; M.D., N.Y. Med. Coll.; m. James W.G. Murray, June 23, 1966; children—Michael James, James Joseph. Intern, St. Vincent's Hosp., N.Y.C., 1959-60; resident Roosevelt Hosp., N.Y.C., 1960-61, St. Vincent's Hosp. N.Y.C., 1961-63; practice medicine, specializing in internal medicine, Stony Brook, N.Y., 1966—; attending staff St. Charles, Mather Meml. hosps., Port Jefferson, N.Y., St. John's, Smithtown hosps., Smithtown, N.Y.; asst. attending St. Vincent's Hosp., 1963-70; geratric care Little Sisters of Poor, N.Y.C., 1963-66, Mary Manning Walsh Home, N.Y.C., 1963-66, Village Nursing Home, N.Y.C., 1963-69. Mem. A.C.P. (asso.), Suffolk County, N.Y. State med. socs., Am. Soc. Internal Medicine, A.M.A., Suffolk County, Am. heart assns., Royal Soc. Medicine (affiliate), Am. Med. Women's Assn., Pan Am. Med. Soc. Home and Office: 60 Hastings Dr Stony Brook NY 11790

YOUNG, CHARLOTTE MARIE, nutritionist, educator; b. Mpls., Aug. 19, 1910; d. Will Morris and Charlotte (Webster) Young; B.S. with high distinction, U. Minn., 1935; M.S., Ia. State U., 1937, Ph.D., 1940; D.Sc. (hon.), Syracuse U., 1973. Grad. asst. U. Minn., Mpls. 1934-35, Ia. State U., Ames, 1936-40; dietetic intern U. Ind. Med. Center, Indpls., 1935-36; instr. Mich. State U., East Lansing, 1940-42; instr. med. nutrition Grad. Sch. Nutrition, Cornell U., Ithaca, N.Y., 1942-43, asst. prof., 1943-46, asso. prof., 1946-52, prof., 1952—, sec. Grad. Sch. Nutrition, 1952—, sec. Grad. Faculty, 1971—; Lydia J. Roberts lectr., P.R., 1972; nutrition cons. Gannett Med. Clinic; WHO cons. to INCAP in Guatemala, 1956, 57, 61, 66; USOM cons. to Nat. Inst. Nutrition, Peru, 1961-66; AID cons. Agarian U., La Molina, Peru, 1963. Recipient Centennial award Ia. State U., 1958, Outstanding Achievement award Bd. Regents U. Minn., 1959, Borden award for nutrition research Am. Home Econs. Assn., 1963, Distinguished Achievement citation Ia. State U., 1971. Diplomate Am. Bd. Nutrition. Fellow Am. Pub. Health Assn.; mem. Am. Dietetic Assn. (del., council mem., del.-at-large, coordinating cabinet mem., Cooper lectr. 1971, Marjorie Hulzier Copher award 1972), Am. Inst. Nutrition, Am. Soc. Clin. Nutrition, Am. Home Econs. Assn., Internat. Union Nutritional Scientists, Sigma Xi, Phi Kappa Phi (pres. Cornell U. 1960-61), Iota Sigma Pi, Omicron Nu (past nat. pres.). Republican. Episcopalian. Club: Zonta Internat. (Ithaca, N.Y.). Contbr. articles on human nutrition to profl. jours. Home: 110 Warren Rd Ithaca NY 14850

YOUNG, CHESLEY VIRGINIA BARNES (MRS. MORRIS N. YOUNG), author, civic worker; b. Hamburg, Ark., Sept. 7, 1919; d. Lewis Chesley and Winifred (Massey) Barnes; B.A., U. Ark., 1947; M.A., Columbia, 1951; m. Morris N. Young, Aug. 20, 1948; children—Cheryl Lesley (Mrs. Johan Uiling), Charles Chesley. Statistician, U.S. Civil Service, Washington, Cin., 1942; tchr. pub. schs. N.Y.C. Dept. Edn., 1954-67; treas. Gem Music Corp.; pres. Denton & Haskins Corp.; v.p. Intercollegiate Syndicate, Inc.; sec. Godell Music Corp. (all N.Y.C.). Pres. Women's Aux. N.Y. Polyclinic Hosp. and Med. Sch., 1969-72; mem. pres.'s council Finch Coll., 1967-69, mem. council Parents Assn., 1969-70. Served to capt. WAC, 1942-46. Mem. N.E.A., A.S.C.A.P., Nat., N.Y. State fedns. bus. and profl. women's clubs, Manhattan Bus. and Profl. Women's Club (pres. 1949-51), N.Y. Hort. Soc., U. Ark. Alumni Assn. Greater N.Y. (charter, vice regent N.Y. chpt.), D.A.R., Knights of Malta (Dame of Honour), Order of Lafayette, Pi Kappa, Zeta Tau Alpha, Kappa Delta Pi. Methodist. Clubs: Women's Nat. Republican, Women's City (N.Y.C.). Author: How to Read Faster and Remember More, 1965; Magic of a Mighty Memory, 1971. Editor: Magic Tricks (Wilfred Johnson), 1952; Card Tricks (Wilfred Johnson), 1952. Composer songs: Have You, 1949; Come On, Come to the Fair, 1963. Contbr. articles to mags., newspapers. Donor (with husband) magic libraries to Library of Congress, U. Tex., U. Cal. at Berkeley. Home: 270 Riverside Dr New York City NY 10025 Office: 2 Fifth Av New York City NY 10011

YOUNG, DOROTHY ANNE SMITH (MRS. JOSEPH CHARLES YOUNG), occupational therapist, psychologist; b. N.Y.C., July 16, 1937; d. John Walter and Anna (Gaydosh) Smith; B.S., Columbia, 1960; M.A., U. So. Cal., 1961; postgrad. Cal. Sch. Profl. Psychology, 1973—; m. Joseph Charles Young, July 14, 1962; children—Catherine, Patricia, John, Joanne. Therapist, Kings Park State Hosp., N.Y.C., 1960, Queen of Angels Hosp., Los Angeles, 1960-62, Community Hosp., Fresno, Cal., 1965-68; faculty San Jose State Coll., 1962-63, Fresno State Coll., 1969-70, Fresno City Coll., 1970—; therapist VA Hosp., Fresno, 1971-73. Mental health cons. Northside Psychiat. Hosp. Mem. Fresno Community Council, 1970—; mem. San Joaquin Mental Health Consortium. Bd. dirs. Newman Center, Fresno State Coll. Recipient Fed. Office Vocational Rehab. Traineeship award, 1960. Leopold Schepp scholar, 1957-59. Mem. Am., No. Cal. occupational therapy assns., Cal. Psychol. Assn., Nat. Rehab. Assn., Am. Assn. U. Women (dir. Fresno br.), Faculty Wives Fresno City Coll. (pres.). Roman Catholic. Home: 2608 E Fedora Av Fresno CA 93726

YOUNG, EDDIE MAE (MRS. JAMES ELDRIDGE YOUNG, JR.), librarian; b. New Orleans, Sept. 10, 1935; d. Eddie Riley and Clementine Theresa (Ricard) Wilson; B.S. cum laude, So. U., Baton Rouge, 1956; M.S. in L.S., Atlanta U., 1962; m. James Eldridge Young, Jr., Apr. 16, 1961; children—James Eldridge III, Adrienne, Darrin. Substitute tchr. Orleans Parish Sch. Bd., New Orleans, 1957-58; librarian St. Tammany Parish Sch. Bd., Slidel, La., 1958-59; asst. law librarian So. U. Law Sch., 1959-60; asst. librarian So. U., New Orleans, 1960-73, library dir., 1973—. Andrew Carnegie fellow, 1956-57. Mem. La. Library Assn., Conf. La. Colls. and Univs. (sec. library sect. 1973), Kappa Delta Pi, Delta Sigma Theta. Home: 4624 Lafon Dr New Orleans LA 70126 Office: 6400 Press Dr New Orleans LA 70126

YOUNG, EDITH JEANNE, assn. exec.; b. Akron, O., Mar. 24, 1922; d. Harley Grant and Lona Elizabeth (Taylor) Styer; student Bethany (W. Va.) Coll., 1940-42; student nursing, Buffalo Gen. Hosp., 1942-44; div.; children—Christopher Earl, Laurie Elizabeth. Certified aquatic dir. Phoenixville (Pa.) Area YMCA, 1971—, sr. dir. certification, 1974—. Water safety instr. A.R.C., 1943—. Mem. Zeta Tau Alpha. Home: 1100 Cherry St Phoenixville PA 19460 Office: 124 S Main St Phoenixville PA 19460

YOUNG, ELEANOR ANNE, nutritionist, educator; b. Houston, Oct. 8, 1925; d. Carl Buchannan and Eleanor (Hamilton) Young; B.A., Incarnate Word Coll., 1947; M.Ed., St. Louis U., 1955; Ph.D. in Nutrition, U. Wis., 1968. Sr. research asso. U. Tex. Med. Sch., 1968-71; asso. prof. foods and nutrition, dept. home econs. Incarnate Word Coll., San Antonio, 1970—, chmn. dept., 1968-71; asst. prof. sect. gastroenterology U. Tex. Med. Sch., San Antonio, 1971—. Mem. Am. Dietetics Assn., Am., Tex. (chmn. nutrition sect. 1972-73) pub. health assns., Am., Tex. home econs. assns., San Antonio (pres. elect 1973-74) Tex. dietetic assns., Tex. State Nutrition Council (chmn. research com. 1972-74), N.Y. Acad. Sci., A.A.A.S., Soc. for Nutrition Edn. Contbr. articles to profl. jours. Home: 4301 Broadway San Antonio TX 78209 Office: 7703 Floyd Curl Dr San Antonio TX 78284

YOUNG, ELEANOR ROBBINS (MRS. HERBERT YOUNG), author; b. Boston, May 8, 1918; d. John and Annie (Weinstein) Robbins; A.B., Radcliffe Coll., 1939; M.Ed., Boston U., 1960; m. Herbert Young, Jan. 25, 1942; 1 dau., Martha (Mrs. Peter Hasselbacher). Tchr., Burr Sch., Newton, Mass., 1959-66; editor, writer Ginn & Co., Lexington, Mass., 1966-69; free-lance writer, 1969—. Mem. Pi Lambda Theta. Author numerous books, including Basic Skills, 1972, Pearls, 1970, Venereal Disease, 1973, Fathers, Fathers, Fathers, 1971, Guide to Buying Pearls, 1972, Come Along to Greece, 1974, Basic Skills in Shopping, 1974, Basic Skills in Using Money, 1974, Mothers, Mothers, Mothers, 1971, Rice, 1971, Needlepoint, 1974, others. Home: 21 Jules Terrace Newton Center MA 02159

YOUNG, ELISE CLINARD (MRS. DONALD LEHMAN YOUNG), real estate broker; b. Winston-Salem, N.C., Jan. 9, 1914; d. Ralph Roland and Alice (Maxwell) Clinard; grad. high sch.; m. Donald Lehman Young, Apr. 30, 1938; children—Donna Elise (Mrs. J.A. Plotner), Ralph Arthur, Elise Marie. Real estate salesman, Palos Verdes Estates, Cal., 1959-69; owner Palos Verdes Realty Co., 1969—; pres. Redondo Blacksmith, Inc., Redondo Beach, Cal. Dir., Palos Verdes Estates Bd. Realtors, 1971-72. Scout leader, instr. leaders Boy Scouts Am. and Girl Scouts, 1946-64. Mem. D.A.R. (past regent), Colonial Dames XVII Century (state pres. 1970-72, nat. orgn. sec. 1971-73, nat. rec. sec. 1973—), Huguenots (state rec. sec. 1970-72), U.D.C. Home: 528 Paseo Del Mar Palos Verdes Estates CA 90274 Office: Box 1055 Palos Verdes Estates CA 90274

YOUNG, ERMA LORETTA, journalist; b. McFall, Mo.; d. James Andrew and Bettie Triphena (Abbott) Young; B.J., U. Mo., 1929, Sec. to pub., book reviewer St. Joseph News-Press, 1931-35, Sunday editor, 1935-36, reporter, 1936-44; city desk reporter Kansas City Star, 1944-50, asst. woman's editor, 1950-54, editor Women's News, 1954-69, spl. writer, cookbook editor Star Mag., 1970—; free lance writer. Mem. Kansas City Commn. Internat. Relations and Trade, 1959-61, Mo. Gov.'s Commn. on Status Women, 1964-67; adv. bd. George H. Nettleton Home, 1954-69; hon. mem. women's div. Kansas City Philharmonic, 1954-70; bd. dirs. Westwood Homes Assn., 1970-72. Recipient Women of Achievement Centennial award U. Mo., 1968; Matrix Table award Theta Sigma Phi, 1967. Mem. Am. Bus. Women's Assn. (hon.), Kansas City Women's C. of C. (hon.), U. Mo. Assn., La Causerie Francaise, Alliance Francaise, Women in Communication, Alpha Chi Omega. Republican. Presbyn. Home: 4966 Westwood Rd Kansas City MO 64112

YOUNG, GENEVIEVE LEMAN (MRS. GORDON PARKS), editor; b. Geneva, Switzerland, Sept. 25, 1930; d. Clarence Kuangson and Juliana Helen (Yen) Young; B.A., Wellesley Coll., 1952; m. Gordon Parks, Aug. 26, 1973. Asst. editor Harper & Row, Pubs., N.Y.C., 1960-62, editor, 1962-64, asst. mng. editor, 1964-66, mng. editor, 1966-70; exec. editor J.B. Lippincott Co., N.Y.C., 1970—, v.p., 1972—; v.p. Winger Enterprises, Inc. Mem. Assn. Am. Pubs. Home: 860 United Nations Plaza New York City NY 10017 Office: 521 Fifth Av New York City NY 10017

YOUNG, GWEN ALEEN IRWIN (MRS. JAMES GORDON YOUNG), educator; b. San Angelo, Tex., Oct. 18, 1922; d. Edwin Lewis and Gwendolyn Aleen (Reiley) Irwin; A.A., San Angelo Coll., 1944; B.S. cum laude, Ohio U., 1964, postgrad., 1966-67; postgrad. Miami U., 1970—, Marietta Coll., 1972-73; m. James Gordon Young, Aug. 1, 1944; children—Dennis James, F. Idelle (Mrs. George Sagan), Kevin Reiley. Recreation dir. Somerset (O.) Village, 1955-59; kindergarten tchr. Somerset Sch. Bd., 1958; tchr. Sheridan Jr. High Sch., Thornville, O., 1972—. Pres. womens com. Perry County Extension Adv. Com., 1948-49; 4-H adviser, Perry County, 1953-65; pres. Perry County Council Garden Clubs, 1954; pres. Somerset Child Conservation League Fedn., 1956-57; pres. Somerset P.T.A., 1952, 59, 71; sec. Perry County Community Study Com., 1973—. Pres., trustee Perry County Hist. Soc.; sec. Southeastern Ohio Library Bd.; trustee Perry County Library; bd. dirs. Somerset Sesquicentennial Named Mrs. Buckeye Child Conservation League, S.E. Ohio, 1956. Mem. Nat., Ohio, No. Local (pres. 1973) edn. assns., Delta Kappa Gamma. Home: Box Route 1 Somerset OH 43783 Office: Sheridan Jr High Sch Route 1 Thornville OH 43076

YOUNG, HELEN ELIZABETH MATTOX (MRS. M. NORVEL YOUNG), educator, editor; b. Bristow, Okla., Aug. 31, 1918; d. Perry and Irene (Young) Mattox; student Harding Coll., 1935-37; B.A., Pepperdine U., 1939; M.A., George Peabody Coll., 1942; m. M. Norvel Young, Aug. 31, 1939; children—Emily Mattox (Mrs. Steven Smith Lemley), Matt Norvel III, Marilyn Morrow, Sara Helen. Editor, Power for Today mag., Nashville, Tenn., 1955—; instr. home econs., sociology, religion Pepperdine U., Los Angeles, 1959—; lectr., marriage and family relations Christian Mental Health, 1949—. Ofcl. hostess Pres. Home, Pepperdine U., 1957-71, chancellor's residence, 1971—. Active Arcs, sci. scholarship funding group, Aware, women's ednl. encouragement group. Bd. dirs. Lubbock (Tex.) Library, 1955-57, Otis Art Inst., 1971—, Muses, Cal. Mus. Sci. and Industry, 1970, Pepperdine U., 1970—. Mem. Associated Women Pepperdine U. (founder 1958, pres. 1958-60), Am. Assn. U. Women, Los Angeles C. of C. (div. dir. 1967-70). Writer womens and teenagers mags. Home: 23200 Pacific Coast Hwy Malibu CA 90265

YOUNG, IRENE MARIE (MRS. FRANK DENNIS YOUNG), TV broadcaster; b. Los Angeles, Nov. 17, 1944; d. Glenn Gregory and Carol Geraldine (Barber) Herring; student Portland State Coll., 1962-63; m. Frank Dennis Young, Dec. 28, 1963; children—Glenn William, Stacy Katherine. Hostess, producer daily childrens TV show KKTV, Colorado Springs, Colo., 1967-68; hostess, producer daily TV show KOIN-TV, Portland, Ore., 1970—. Producer and performer of childrens shows for hosps., dependent homes and schs., also adult shows for charity functions, state and vet. hosps. Hon. mem. Ore. Mus. Sci. and Industry, 1971-72, Ore. Humane Soc., 1971. Recipient citation for meritorious pub. service Employment div. State of Ore., 1971, award for outstanding service Nat. Found., March of Dimes, 1972. Republican. Methodist. Home: 1820 SW 216th St Aloha OR 97005 Office: TV Station KOIN TV 140 SW Columbia St Portland OR 97201

YOUNG, JANET RANDALL (MRS. ROBERT WILLIAM YOUNG), author; b. Lancaster, Cal., Mar. 6, 1919; d. James Elisha and Blanche Pearl (Barrett) Randall; A.A., U. Cal. at Los Angeles, 1938; m. Robert William Young, Sept. 14, 1940 (dec. July 1969); children—Michael Jay, Timothy Robert, Gary Edward, Randi Roberta. Pub., La Verne (Cal.) Leader, 1942-44; mag. writer, 1950-58; author, Ferndale, Cal., 1958—. Mem. Nat. League Am. Pen Women, Western Writers Am., Kappa Delta. Democrat. Conglist. Author: Saddles for Breakfast, 1958; Across the Tracks, 1958; Pony Girl, 1963; Where Tomorrow, 1967; Island Ghost, 1970; To Save A Tree, 1971. Home: 460 Main St Ferndale CA 95536 Office: PO Box 607 Ferndale CA 95536

YOUNG, JEANE ANSLEY RIDGE, broadcasting exec.; b. Memphis, Jan. 7, 1930; d. Alfred George and L. Bernice (Aycock) Ridge; student Memphis State U., 1948-50, B.S., 1962; postgrad. U. Wis., 1962-65; m. Harl H. Young, Jr., Dec. 15, 1950 (div. Sept. 1959); children—Cynthia Ansley, Alfred Harl. Mng. editor Furniture and Woodworking, Memphis, 1959-62; with pub. relations U. Wis., Madison, 1962-65; prof. journalism U. Evansville (Ind.), 1965-67; community relations dir. WKNO-TV, Memphis, 1967-73; spl. instr. journalism dept. Memphis State U., 1968-73; dir. pub. information Pub. Broadcasting Service, Washington, 1973—. Bd. dirs. Memphis Heart Assn., 1970-73. Mem. Pub. Relations Soc. Am. (accredited), Nat. Assn. Ednl. Broadcasters, Wis. Acad. Arts, Scis. and Letters, Women in Communications. Home: 7371 Montcalm Dr McLean VA 22101 Office: 475 L'Enfant Plaza North SW Washington DC

YOUNG, KAREN SUE (MRS. JON NATHAN YOUNG), museum designer; b. Geneseo, Ill., Jan. 15, 1941; d. Kenneth Arthur and Sara Eleanor (Ball) Johnson; B.A., U. Ariz., 1969, M.A., 1971; m. Jon Nathan Young, June 5, 1961; children—Shawn Nathan, Kevin Leigh. Lab. dir. Archeol. Lab., Dept. Army, Ft. Huachuca, summer 1964; freelance sci. illustration for archeologists Mr. Watson Smith and Dr. Emil Haury, Tucson, 1966-71; curator of collections S.W. Archeol. Center, Globe, Ariz., 1967-71; curator of exhibits Ariz. Hist. Soc., Tucson, 1971—. Lab. dir. Summer-at-Taos Program, Ft. Burgwin Research Center, Ranchos de Taos, N.M., summers 1968-71. Am. Assn. for State and Local History scholar, 1973. Mem. Am. Anthrop. Assn., Am. Assn. for State and Local History, Am. Assn. Museums, Soc. for Am. Archeology, Ariz. Hist. Soc., Gila County Archeol. and

Hist. Soc., Kit Carson Meml. Found. Home: 6970 Camino Namara Tucson AZ 85715 Office: 949 E 2d St Tucson AZ 85719

YOUNG, LORYNNE ELLEN, editor; b. Huntington Park, Cal., Mar. 30, 1949; d. Roy O. and Doris Ellen (Smith) Young; student Biola Coll., 1968-70; B.A., Cal. State U. at Los Angeles, 1972. Reporter, Sun-Independent Newspaper, San Gabriel, Cal., 1971-72; reporter, sect. editor Inglewood (Cal.) Daily News, 1972-73; editor house organ Los Angeles Jr. C. of C., 1973—. Publicity dir. Simi Valley Citizens Econ. Devel. Commn., 1973. Bd. dirs. Los Angeles County Christian Endeavor. Recipient Cal. State U. at Los Angeles Alumni Departmental Honor award in journalism, 1972. Mem. Women in Communications, Sigma Delta Chi. Baptist. Mng. editor Cal. State U. at Los Angeles Times, 1971. Home: 5100 Woodman Apt 15 Sherman Oaks CA 91403 Office: 404 S Bixel St Los Angeles CA 90017

YOUNG, LOUISE GRAY (MRS. ANDREW TIPTON YOUNG), research scientist; b. Los Angeles, Oct. 4, 1935; d. Frank Elliot and Ruth Alice (Davis) Dillon; B.S., U. Cal. at Los Angeles, 1958, M.S., 1959; Ph.D., Cal. Inst. Tech., 1963; m. Bruce Everett Gray, Nov. 20, 1954 (div. Sept. 1959); children—Gregory Edward, Elizabeth Marie; m. 2d, Andrew Tipton Young, Dec. 14, 1968. Grad. research engr. U. Cal. at Los Angeles, 1957-59; research fellow Cal. Inst. Tech., 1959-63; sr. scientist Cal. Inst. Tech. Jet Propulsion Lab., 1963-73, mem. tech. staff, 1973; research scientist, physics dept. Tex. A. and M. U., College Station, 1974—. Cons. Douglas Aircraft, Santa Monica, Cal., 1963; asst. prof. engring. U. Cal. at Los Angeles, 1965-66. Mem. Optical Soc. Am., Am. Astron. Soc., Am. Meteorol. Soc., Sigma Xi, Phi Beta Kappa, Tau Beta Pi. Asso. editor Jour. Quantitative Spectroscopy and Radiative Transfer, 1969—; contbr. articles to profl. jours. Home: 1200 Holleman Dr College Station TX 77840

YOUNG, LOUISE KERN, newspaper editor; b. Nazareth, Pa., July 26, 1920; d. Andrew Griffith and Alma Amelia (Hoch) Kern; B.A., Ursinus Coll., 1941; m. Glenn Edgar Young, June 12, 1943; children—Andrew, Robert, Linda Louise, Glennys Jeanne. Pres., Trumbower Co., Nazareth, Pa., 1971—; editor Nazareth Item, 1964—. Mem. Am. Newspaper Publishers Assn., Omega Chi. Republican. Lutheran. Mem. Order Eastern Star. Club: Nazareth Sr. Woman's. Home: 340 S Broad St Nazareth PA 18064 Office: 46-48 S Main St Nazareth PA 18064

YOUNG, LYNN POVICH, mag. editor; b. Washington, June 4, 1943; d. Shirley Lewis and Ethyl (Friedman) Povich; B.A. in Modern European History, Vassar Coll., 1965; m. Jeffrey Alan Young, Jan. 21, 1968. Mem. staff Newsweek mag., N.Y.C., 1965—, asso. editor, 1971-74, gen. editor, 1974—, also editor Life/Style sect. Home: 56 W 12th St New York City NY 10011 Office: 444 Madison Av New York City NY 10022

YOUNG, MABLE REED (MRS. MARVIN P. YOUNG), educator; b. Dunbar, W.Va., Apr. 10, 1922; d. Roy and Blanche (Garrett) Reed; student Morris Harvey Coll., 1938; A.B., Glenville Coll., 1950; M.S., W.Va. U., 1953; postgrad. U. Fla., 1958; m. James R. Smith, Nov. 19, 1939 (dec. Apr. 1962); children—William Richard, Betty Jo (Mrs. Dan L. Johnson); m. 2d, Jerry E. Smith, Aug. 14, 1961 (dec. Aug. 1966); m. 3d, Marvin P. Young, Apr. 19, 1968. Clk. Cabin Creek Dist. Draft Bd., Charleston, W.Va., 1942; vital statistician Gilmer County, W.Va. 1948-50; tchr. Normantown (W.Va.) High Sch., 1950-55; tchr. trainer Glenville Coll., 1953-55; tchr. home econs. Largo (Fla.) Jr. High Sch., 1955-58, dean of girls, 1958-62, guidance counselor, 1962-68; evaluation co-ordinator fed. programs Manatee County (Fla.) Sch. Bd., 1969-72; ESEA program supr. Manatee County, 1973—. Home economist Pinellas County Water Conditioning Co., Largo, Fla., 1960-66, corp. sec., 1961-63, v.p., 1963-66. Mem. Fla., Manatee County, edn. assns. V.F.W. Aux., N.E.A., Internat. Reading Assn., Fla. Reading Council, Fla. Suprs. Assn., Omicron Nu, Kappa Delta Pi. Jehovah Witness. Mem. Order Eastern Star (worthy matron 1954-55). Clubs: Garden, Junior Woman's. Home: 1006 19th St W Bradenton FL 33505 Office: 215 Manatee Av W Bradenton FL 33505

YOUNG, MARGARET ALETHA MCMULLEN (MRS. HERBERT WILSON YOUNG), social worker; b. Vossburg, Miss., June 13, 1916; d. Grady Garland and Virgie Aletha (Moore) McMullen; B.A. cum laude, Columbia Bible Coll., 1949; grad. Massey Bus. Coll., 1958; M.S.W., Fla. State U., 1965; postgrad. Jacksonville U., 1961-62, Tulane U., 1967; m. Herbert Wilson Young, Aug. 19, 1959. Dir. Christian edn. Eau Claire Presbyn. Ch., Columbia, S.C., 1946-51; tchr. Massey Bus. Coll., Jacksonville, Fla., 1954-57, office mgr., 1957-59; social worker, unit supr. Fla. div. Family Services, St. Petersburg, 1960-66, dist. casework supr., 1966-71; social worker Project Playpen, Inc., 1971—. Mem. Acad. Certified Social Workers, Nat. Assn. Social Workers (pres. Tampa Bay chpt.), Fla. Assn. for Health and Social Services (pres. chpt. 1971), Fla. Assn. on Children Under Six, Clearwater Audubon Soc. Democrat. Presbyn. Rotary Ann (pres. 1970-71). Home: 330 Roebling Rd N Belleair Clearwater FL 33516 Office: 1250 1/2 Rogers St Clearwater FL 33516

YOUNG, MARGARET BUCKNER (MRS. WHITNEY M. YOUNG, JR.), civic worker, author; b. Campbellsville, Ky.; d. Frank W. and Eva (Carter) Buckner; B.A., Ky. State Coll., 1942; M.A., U. Minn., 1946; m. Whitney M. Young, Jr., Jan. 2, 1944 (dec. Mar. 1971); children—Marcia Elaine, Lauren Lee. Instr., Ky. State Coll., 1942-45; instr. edn. and psychology Spelman Coll., Atlanta, 1958-60. Dir. Philip Morris, Inc. Chmn. bd. Whitney M. Young, Jr. Meml. Found.; mem. pub. policy com., advt. council Rockefeller U. Council; mem. devel. com. UN Internat. Sch.; alternate rep. of U.S. delegation 28th Assembly of UN. Bd. dirs. Girl Scouts U.S., New Rochelle Vol. Bur.; trustee Blythedale Children's Hosp., Valhalla, N.Y. Author: The First Book of American Negroes, 1966; The Picture Life of Martin Luther King, Jr., 1968; The Picture Life of Ralph J. Bunche, 1968; Black American Leaders, 1969; The Picture Life of Thurgood Marshall, 1971; pub. affairs pamphlet. Home: 330 Oxford Rd New Rochelle NY 10804

YOUNG, MARGARET LABASH (MRS. HAROLD CHESTER YOUNG), editor; b. Bridgeport, Conn., Aug. 17, 1926; d. George and Mary (Feltovich) Labash; B.A., Cornell U., 1948; postgrad. Radcliffe Coll., 1953, U. Lausanne, Switzerland, 1955; M.A. in L.S., U. Mich., 1959; m. Harold Chester Young, June 7, 1958; children—Jeffery, Amy. Marketing grader Harvard Bus. Sch., Boston, 1949-52; tchr. sci. Willard Day Sch., Troy, N.Y., 1952-53; sales asst. Arthur D. Little, cons., Cambridge, 1953-57; reference librarian Cambridge (Mass.) Pub. Library, 1957-58, U. Mich. at Dearborn, 1959-62; editor library reference books Gale Research Co., Detroit, 1965—. Free-lance indexer Ford Motor Co., Dearborn, 1964-72. Mem. Spl. Libraries (editor Mich. chpt. bull. 1967-68), Am. Assn. U. Women, Beta Phi Mu. Editor: Directory of Special Libraries and Information Centers, 3d edit. Asso. editor: Library Of Congress and National Union Catalog Author Lists, 1942-62: A Master Cumulation, 1969-71. Home: 6 Clinton Lane Dearborn MI 48120 Office: Book Tower Detroit MI 48226

YOUNG, MARJORIE WILLIS (MRS. JAMES RUSSELL YOUNG), journalist; b. Mansfield, O.; d. John Edgar and Mary Adelle (Reiter) Willis; student Agr. Coll., Cornell U., 1924; student Art Students League, 1925-27, Cooper Union, 1925-27, Columbia, 1927, N.Y. U., 1943-44; student history Sorbonne, U. Paris (France), 1928-30, Japanese Lang. Sch., Tokyo, 1934-35; m. James Russell Young, Oct. 2, 1934; 1 son, Willis Patterson. Far Eastern columnist Internat. News Service, Tokyo, Japan, 1938-41; feature writer King Features Syndicate, Tokyo, Japan, 1939, Saturday Pictorial Rev., N.Y.C., 1941-45; lectr. Nat. Concert and Artists Corp., 1942-43; promotion dir. David McKay Pub. Co., 1945-48; mem. research dept. Believe It or Not, Wilmington, Del., 1946-48; feature editor, columnist The Sunday Star, 1946-48; feature writer Anderson Ind., Ind., 1949-73, Anderson Daily Mail, 1949-73, condr. travel radio program WAIM-WCAC-FM, 1973—; editor, pub. The Safety Jour., Anderson, 1953—; Fodor's tour guide, S.C., 1966-68; bd. dirs. Capito City Communications, Inc., Anderson County Hist. Soc.; trustee Anderson Heritage, Inc. Asst. tech. dir. Behind the Rising Sun, R.K.O., Hollywood, Cal., 1943; moderator Holiday Decorating, Sta. WAIM-TV, Anderson, 1953, How To Cut and Sew, 1954, Safety Program, 1953. Dir., Chinese War Orphans Relief, N.Y.C., 1941-45, S.C. 4-H Club TV Safety Program, Anderson, 1953; publicity dir. Del. Crusade for Children, Wilmington, 1948; publicity chmn. S.C. Indsl. Nurses Assn., Anderson, 1953-59. Recipient Distinguished Service award S.C. Occupational Safety Council, 1973. Mem. Far East Soc., Garden Writer's Assn., S.C. Recreation Soc. (v.p., program dir. 1954—), Am. Soc. Safety Engrs. (affiliate; pub. relations and achievement awards chmn. S.C. chpt.), Am. Women in Radio and TV, Am. Pen Women, D.A.R., Nat. Press Photog. Assn., Soc. Am. Travel Writers. Clubs: Overseas Press of Am. (N.Y.C.); Am. Newspaper Women's, Washington Press (Washington). Author: Decorating for Joyful Occasions, 1952; It's Time for Christmas Decorations, 1957. Editor: Textile Leaders of the South, 1964; Japanese-American Cook Book, 1972; asso. editor: The New South, ann. Home: 2003 Laurel Dr Anderson SC 29621 Office: Anderson Daily Mail Anderson SC 29621

YOUNG, MARY LYNN, psychologist; b. DuBois, Pa., Apr. 24, 1941; d. Fredrick Frick and Gertrude Cruzan (Carns) Young; student Smith Coll., 1959-60, Clark U., 1960-62; B.A., Ariz. State U., 1965, Ph.D., 1971. Postgrad. fellow Ind. U. Sch. Medicine, 1971-72, instr., 1972; instr. Glendale (Ariz.) Community Coll., 1969-71; research specialist State of Cal. Youth Authority, Stockton, 1973—. Adj. prof. U. of Pacific, 1973—; behavior modification cons. Santa Clara County Probation Dept., 1973-74; instr. Chapman Coll., 1974—. Mem. Am., Western psychol. assns., Am. Civil Liberties Union. Contbr. articles to profl. jours. Home: 3720 W Ben Holt Dr 9 Stockton CA 95207 Office: PO Box 6000 NCYC New Castle Rd Stockton CA 95206

YOUNG, NATHALIE M., psychologist; b. N.Y.C., Aug. 26, 1922; d. Benjamin and Charlotte (Ruschin) Marmolstein; B.A., N.Y. U., 1943; M.A., Columbia, 1945; m. Arthur Henry Young, Sept. 8, 1946; children—Victoria (Mrs. William M. Johnson), Arthur. Counseling psychologist Fedn. Employment and Guidance Service, 1945-51, Measurement and Evaluation Service, Nat. League Nursing, N.Y.C., 1944-64; co-dir. reading tchrs. workshop, psychologist reading clinic Grad. Sch. Edn., U. Bridgeport (Conn.), 1966—; counseling psychologist Bronx (N.Y.) Community Coll., 1966—. Sec., Friends of New Rochelle (N.Y.) Library. Fellow Am. Orthopsychiat. Assn.; mem. Am., N.Y. State, Westchester (sec., dir., editor publ.) psychol. assns., Am. Personnel and Guidance Assn., Pi Lambda Theta, Kappa Delta Pi. Home: 22 Bailey Pl New Rochelle NY 10801

YOUNG, OLIVIA RUDOLPH (MRS. GEORGE DEMMING YOUNG), author, educator; b. Lompoc, Cal., May 15, 1894; d. John Caspar and Nina Durand (Morehead) Rudolph; individual study in piano teaching, Berkeley, 1930-33; student U. Cal. Extension, 1950-54; m. George Demming Young, June 25, 1913 (dec. Aug. 1972); children—George Demming, Winifred Elizabeth (Mrs. Charles Washburn), Jean Lucille (Mrs. Robert Greenshield), William Morehead, Robert Neal, Marion Lenore. Organist, choir dir., Oakland, Cal., 1928-48; tchr. piano, Oakland, 1932-48; instr. adult edn. poetry workshop, Carmel, Santa Cruz, Cal., 1956-68; curator Santa Cruz Art League Galleries, 1964-69. Writer poetry, non-fiction, 1944—; poetry reader, lectr., 1958—; judge nat., Cal. poetry contests, 1955—. Recipient numerous awards for writing and poetry. Mem. Poetry Soc. Am. N.Y., Cal. Writers Club, Ina Coolbrith Circle, Cal. Fedn. Chaparral Poets, Santa Cruz Chaparral Poets (hon.). Author: Take The Dirt Road, 1960; The Honey and the Root, 1972. Contbr. poems and articles to anthologies, mags. including Good Housekeeping, Christian Sci. Monitor, Am. Bard, Poet Lore, State Chaparral Anthology, Ina Coolbrith Anthology. Home: 555 Crespi Dr #N304 Pacifica CA 94044

YOUNG, RUTH FORBES (MRS. ARTHUR MIDDLETON YOUNG), founder Internat. Peace Acad.; b. Milton, Mass., Oct. 4, 1903; d. Ralph Emerson and Elise (Cabot) Forbes; student Milton Acad., Art Students League, N.Y.C., also Colorossi, Paris, France, with Hans Hoffman, N.Y.C.; m. Arthur Middleton Young, June 25, 1948; children by previous marriage—Michael Ralph Paine, Cameron Forbes Paine. Founder, Internat. Peace Acad., N.Y.C., 1970, hon. chmn., 1971—. Mem. World Federalists U.S.A., 1959—, hon. v.p., 1966—; bd. dirs. Found. for Study of Consciousness, Phila., Berkeley, Cal. Club: Cosmopolitan (Phila.). Home: 1810 Delancey Pl Philadelphia PA 19103

YOUNG, RUTH LUBBE (MRS. ALFRED E. YOUNG), lawyer; b. McMinnville, Ore., Apr. 23, 1928; d. Fred Roy and Edna Margaret (McFarland) Lubbe; B.A., U. Wash., 1952; LL.B., U. Cal. at Berkeley, 1956; m. Alfred E. Young, Jan. 7, 1952; children—Samuel, Maggie, Juliet. Admitted to Cal. bar, 1957, practiced in Albany, 1959-68; mem. pub. defender staff Contra Costa County, Cal., 1968—, asst. supr. Richmond Office of Pub. Defender, 1972—. Mem. teaching staff Police Acad., Diablo Valley Community Coll., Concord, Cal. Mem. Albany Planning Commn., 1960-62; legislative chmn. Richmond Council P.T.A., 1967-68; mem. Cal. Gov.'s Women's Adv. Council Fair Employment Practice, 1964-65. Mem. Richmond Bar Assn. (dir., law day chmn. 1974), Queens Bench, Cal. Trial Attys. Assn., Pub. Defenders Assn. Club: Richmond Golf and Country. Home: 1313 Brewster Dr El Cerrito CA 94530 Office: 3811 Bissell Av Richmond CA 94805

YOUNG, SHARON CLAIRENE, educator; b. Elk City, Okla., Aug. 3, 1942; d. Clair E. and Eva Mae (Hamman) Young; B.S., Bethany Nazarene Coll., 1964; M.S., Okla. State U., 1965, Ph.D., 1969. Research asst. Okla. State U., Stillwater, 1965-68; asst. prof. biology Bethany (Okla.) Nazarene Coll., 1968-70, asso. prof., 1970-72, prof., 1973—. Mem. A.A.A.S., Sigma Xi. Mem. Ch. of Nazarene. Contbr. articles to profl. jours. Home: 8208 NW 27th St Bethany OK 73008

YOUNG, SUE MARIE (MRS. L.A. YOUNG, JR.), constrn. co. exec.; b. Safford, Ariz., Apr. 29, 1938; s. Almon Guy and Elizabeth (Layton) Anderson; B.S., Brigham Young U.; m. L.A. Young, Jr., June 24, 1959; children—Leland Anderson, Steven Archibald. Co-owner, sec.-treas. L.A. Young Sons, Inc., Richfield, Utah, 1963—; corporate officer Am. Bldg. Corp., Young, Inc., B.A.S.K. Co. Pres., Richfield Jr. Culture Club, 1965, Richfield P.T.A., 1973—; mem. dist. adv. council Small Bus. Adminstrn., 1973—. Precinct chmn. Richfield, 1970—. Officer, Sevier Valley Tech. Sch. Adv. Council, S. Central Utah Health Council. Mem. Utah Hist. Soc. Mem. Ch. of Jesus Christ of Latter-day Saints (pres. Young Womens Improvement Assn. 1965). Home: 245 N 5th West Richfield UT 84701 Office: Box 604 Richfield UT 84701

YOUNG, SYLVIA JEANNETTE, nursing adminstr.; b. Grand Falls, Nfld., Can., Jan. 26, 1935; d. Issac John and Jessie Caroline (Hynes) Budgell; R.N., St. John's (Nfld.) Sch. Nursing, 1956; m. Lloyd Young, Oct. 20, 1956; children—Barbara Ann, Juliette, Terri Lynn, Dana, Andrea, Christopher. Successively staff nurse hosps., Ont., supr. nursing office, in-service coordinator James Paton Meml. Hosp., Gander, Nfld., head nu- rse, supr., asst. dir., dir. nursing Western Meml. Hosp., Corner Brook, Nfld.; now dir. nursing Charles S. Curtis Meml. Hosp., Internat. Grenfell Assn., St. Anthony, Nfld.; also mem. liaison bd. Mem. Assn. Registered Nurses Nfld. (mem. nursing service com., mem. council, pres. St. Anthony chpt.). Capt. 3d St. Anthony Girl Guide Co., 1970-73. Mem. United Ch. Can. Home: PO Box 264 St Anthony NF AOK 450 Canada

YOUNG, VIRGINIA GARTON (MRS. RAYMOND ARTHUR YOUNG), civic worker; b. Mountain View, Mo., Jan. 16, 1919; d. Charles Clinton and Mattie Belle (Cartwright) Garton; student U. Mo., 1936-38; A.B., So. Mo. State U., 1939; M.L.S., U. Okla., 1940; m. Raymond Arthur Young, June 18, 1940; 1 son, David Bruce. Mem. library staff U. Mo., 1940, 42-44; librarian William Woods Coll., Fulton, Mo., 1941; guest lectr. Columbia, 1960, 67, Inst. Govt., U. N.C., 1968, Sch. Library Sci., U. Mo., 1971. Del. Internat. Fedn. Library Assns., 1965—; cons. Library Trustee Workshops, U. Colo., 1969. Mem. Citizens Com. on Reorgn. Mo. Legislature, 1973—; mem. Mo. Press Bar Commn., 1973—; vice chmn. Mo. Coordinating Bd. Higher Edn., 1974—. Bd. dirs. Friends U. Mo. Library, pres., 1964-66; pres. Columbia League Women Voters, 1943-44, bd. dirs., 1943-44, 68-69; bd. dirs. YWCA, 1953-56, Planned Parenthood, 1970—; mem. adv. com. U.S. Commr. Edn., Library Services br. Dept. Health, Edn. and Welfare; mem. def. adv. com. Women in the Services, Dept. Def., 1963-65; mem. exec. com. of bd. Nat. Book Com., 1967—; mem. vis. com. Case Western Res. U. Sch. Library Sci., 1969-71; trustee Columbia Pub. Library, 1950-53, 56-59, 62-65, pres., 1957-59, 62-64; pres. Mo. State Library Com., 1956-57. Recipient Outstanding Alumni award So. Mo. State U., 1965, certificate of Appreciation, Dept. Army, 1966, Distinguished Alumni award U. Mo., 1972, Civic award Alpha Kappa Psi, 1973. Ky. Col., Neb. Adm., Ark. Traveler. Mem. Am. (trustee citation of merit 1962), Mo. (Meritorious Achievement award 1956, pres. 1967-68) library assns., Am. Library Trustees Assn. (pres. 1959-61, dir. 1962—), Ninety- Niners, Mo. Acad. Squires. Club: Readers. Author: The Trustee of a Small Public Library, 1962; The Library Trustee: A Practical Guidebook, 1964, rev. edit., 1969. Contbr. articles library periodicals. Home: 10 E Parkway Dr Columbia MO 65201

YOUNG, VIRGINIA SHUMAN (MRS. GEORGE FENWICK YOUNG), mayor, constrn. co. exec., city ofcl.; b. Norfolk, Va., Sept. 16, 1917; d. Irving George and Myrtle (Tenbrook) Shuman; student pub. schs., Ft. Lauderdale, Fla.; m. George Fenwick Young, Mar. 27, 1937; children—George William, Nancy Anne Stayman, Catherine Reta, (Mrs. John H. Moore). Co-owner, George F. Young Bldg. Constrn. Co., Ft. Lauderdale, Fla. Chmn. bd. trustees Broward County Sch. System, 1953-57, mem. bd. pub. instrn., 1958-66, chmn. bd., 1961, 65; pres. Fla. Sch. Bd. Assn., 1965; camp dir. Girl Scouts Am., 1945-46; mem. Gov.'s Com. on Aging, Ft. Lauderdale, 1956, Citizens Tax Council, 1957, Gov.'s Conf. Edn., 1966; vice mayor of Ft. Lauderdale, 1971-72, mayor, 1973—. Mem. Nat. Sch. Bds. Assn. (legislative com.), Bus. and Profl. Woman's Club, League Women Voters, C. of C. (pres. women's div. 1969-71), Delta Kappa Gamma. Methodist. Clubs: Fort Lauderdale Woman's (pres. 1969-71). Soroptimist. Home: 1101 SE 7th St Fort Lauderdale FL 33301

YOUNGBLOOD, BETTYE SUE, educator; b. Powhatan, Ala., Dec. 6, 1926; d. O. H. and Theona (Snow) Youngblood; B.S., Auburn U., 1946; M.S., U. Ala., 1949, Ph.D., 1957. Tchr. West Jefferson High Sch., Quinton, Ala., 1946-50, 56-57; instr. in chemistry U. Miss., Oxford, 1950-52; asst. editor Chemical Abstracts, Columbus, O., 1957-59, asso. editor, 1959-62; asst. prof. chemistry Jacksonville (Ala.) State U., 1962-65, prof., 1965—. Mem. A.A.A.S., Am. Chem. Soc., Am. Inst. Chemists, Nat., Ala. edn. assns., Ala. Acad. Sci. Baptist. Mem. Order of Eastern Star. Home: 602 12th St Jacksonville AL 36265 Office: Jacksonville State University Jacksonville AL 36265

YOUNGBLOOD, ELAINE MICHELE (MRS. WILLIAM G. YOUNGBLOOD), lawyer; b. Schenectady, Jan. 9, 1944; d. Roy W. and Mary Louise (Read) Ortoleva; B.A., Wake Forest Coll., 1965; J.D., Albany Law Sch., 1969; m. William G. Youngblood, Feb. 14, 1970. Tchr., Annapolis (Md.) Jr. High Sch., 1965-66; admitted to Tex. bar, 1970; with firm McClure & Burch, Houston, 1972-74, Brown, Bradshaw & Plummer, 1974—; corp. adviser M.D.L. Corp., 1972, La-Rey Corp., 1973—. Mem. Com. for Women in Govt., Dallas, 1971. Mem. Am., Dallas, Houston bar assns., Tex. Trial Lawyers, Nat. Assn. Women Lawyers. Home: 7707 Braesview Lane Houston TX 77071 Office: 1212 Main St Houston TX 77002

YOUNGBLOOD, MARY JANE (MRS. MORRIS WILLIAM YOUNGBLOOD), retail co. exec., b. Johnstown, Pa., Sept. 8, 1926; d. William Peter and Mary Anna (McTigue) Burkhart; student Indian Capitol Vocational Tech. Sch., 1971-72; m. Morris William Youngblood, Jan. 26, 1947; children—Gwendolyn (Mrs. Gwen Harrington) and Lyndolyn (Mrs. Billy Frank Sherman) (twins). Civil service adminstr. Camp Gruber, Muskogee, Okla., 1947; cashier Tulsa Pub. Sch., 1958-65; bookkeeping asst. Triple S Corp, Muskogee, 1965-67, office mgr., 1967-72, adminstrv. asst. and buyer, and asst. to gen. mgr., 1972-73; adminstrv. asst. to mgr. Tumble In Discount, Muskogee, 1973—. Named Citizen of Day KBIX radio, 1973. Mem. Theresians Am. (trustee Muskogee chpt. 1965-66), Altar Soc. (pres. Muskogee chpt council 1972-73, parliamentarian 1973-74), Epsilon Sigma Alpha (parliamentarian 1972-73, pres. Alpha Theta chpt. 1971-72, v.p. 1970-71, named Outstanding Mem. of Yr. 1970-71). Home: 405 Crabtree Rd Muskogee OK 74401 Office: PO Box 1247 Muskogee OK 74401

YOUNGER, LORENE LANE (MRS. ELDRED W. YOUNGER), banker; b. Cookeville, Tenn., Jan. 17, 1929; d. Luther S. and Alba (Dailey) Lane; grad. high sch.; m. Eldred W. Younger, Dec. 4, 1948; 1 son, Joseph Kevin. Clk. Ideal Cleaners, Cookeville, 1947-49; sec. to plant mgr. Wilson Athletic Goods Mfg. Co., Cookeville, 1949-62; with First Nat. Bank, Cookeville, 1964—, asst. cashier, 1970—, asst. v.p., 1973—. Mem. Order Eastern Star. Home: 1250 Circle Dr Cookeville TN 38501 Office: 1 S Jefferson Av Cookeville TN 38501

YOUNGS, BETTY FERRELL (MRS. PAUL AUSTIN YOUNGS), author; b. Durham, N.C., Feb. 15, 1928; d. Rufus F. and Ora Ethel (Wallace) Ferrell; A.A., Mars Hill Coll., 1949; B.A., George Peabody Coll. for Tchrs., 1952; postgrad. Columbia, 1961; M.A., Ariz. State U., 1971; m. Paul Austin Youngs, Aug. 23, 1966; 1 stepson, Douglas Lee. Style editor, vocational guidance cons., editor vocational guidance materials Baptist Bd., Nashville, 1958-66; free lance writer, 1967—. Tchr. mag. article writing Glendale (Ariz.) Community Coll., 1972—, Ariz. State U., Tempe, 1974—. Mem. Women in Communications (exec. bd. Phoenix chpt.), Am. Vocational Edn. Research Assn., Phoenix Obs. Assn. Author: Let's Explore Jobs, 1971; What's Bugging You?, 1973. Columnist, Accent monthly. Contbr. articles to mags. Address: 6130 W Fairmount Av Phoenix AZ 85033

YOUNIS, ADELE LINDA, educator; b. N.Y.C.; d. Joseph and Sarah (Najjar) Younis; B.S., R.I., Coll., 1933; M.A., Boston U., 1943, Ph.D., 1961; student Brown U., 1948-49. Tchr. Fall River (Mass.) pub. schs., 1934-42; tchr. social sci. Case High Sch., Swansea, Mass., 1942-47; prof. lit. and history Bryant Coll., 1947-52; faculty dept. history Salem State Coll., 1956—, prof. history; cons. Inst. Higher Learning, Lima, Peru, Voice of Am., USIA; lectr. World Lebanese Union, 1968; radio lectr., Fall River, New Bedford, 1967; counsellor Arabic speaking Ams. Mem. Fall River (Mass.) Civic Council, 1950-56; alternate Am. Assn. for Middle East Studies in Fellowship award for overseas study, summer 1963. Mem. Am. Assn. U. Women (corr. sec. Fall River 1950-52, 1st v.p. Fall River 1952-54, pres. Fall River 1954-56, chmn. higher edn. Mass. div. 1958-61), Am., New Eng. hist. assns., Acad. Polit. Sci., Am. Acad. Polit. and Social Scis., Am. Judicature Soc., Phi Alpha Theta, Pi Gamma Mu. Contbr. articles in field to profl. jours., works on Arabic emigration to U.S., 1966, 72. Home: Apt 501 Park Towers 320 Lafayette St Salem MA 01970

YOUNKER, DONNA LEE, educator; b. Evanston, Ill., Feb. 7, 1932; d. Fred Lee and Florence (Jett) Younker; B.A., Baylor U., 1952; M.A., So. Meth. U., 1958; Ph.D., U. Tex., 1964. Vis. prof. Purdue U., Lafayette, Ind., 1964; faculty Central State U., Edmond, Okla., 1966—, asso. prof. philosophy of edn., 1966—, mem. faculty senate, 1971-72; tchr. Ind. Sch. Dist., Dallas, 1958-60; lectr. U. Tex., 1962-64. Fellow Philosophy of Edn. Soc.; mem. Southwestern Philosophy of Edn. Soc. (pres. 1971-72), History of Edn. Soc., Am. Ednl. Research Assn. Methodist. Home: 1404 Mockingbird Lane Edmond OK 73034

YOUNKIN, JOSEPHINE COLLINS, state legislator; b. Junction City, Kan., July 27, 1903; d. Joseph LaFayette and Agnes (Webster) Collins; grad. high sch.; m. Francis Earl Younkin, Nov. 21, 1923; children—Norma Jean (Mrs. Gayle Milligan), James Earl, David Joseph. Bookkeeper, clk., 1941-63. Precinct committeewomen, Democratic party, 1925-71; treas., Geary County, 1963-66, dep. treas., 1967-68; mem. Kan. Ho. of Reps., 1969—. Mem. Nat. Bus. and Profl. Women's Club, Geary County Bus. and Profl. Womens Club. Club: Pilot International (Junction City, Kan.). Address: 128 W Pine St Junction City KS 66441

YOUNTS, ELIZABETH MENDENHALL, broadcasting exec.; b. Winston-Salem, N.C., Oct. 19, 1922; d. Robah Kermit and Erma May (Teague) Mendenhall; Mus.B., U. Rochester (N.Y.), 1941; grad. fellow Juilliard Sch. Music, 1941-42; m. John Spurgeon Younts, Dec. 5, 1942; children—Sandra Louise, Millard Stephen, Gerlind Elizabeth. With music div. NBC, 1942-43; staff organist, pianist ABC, 1943-45; organist Arthur Godfrey program CBS, 1945; freelance organist NBC, 1945-46, also supper club entertainer, N.Y.C.; music and program dir. radio sta. WEEB, Southern Pines, N.C., 1947, sec., treas., 1948—, program dir., 1968—; v.p., sec. radio sta. WUSM, Havelock, N.C., 1962—. Mem. founding com. N.C. Sch. Arts, Winston-Salem, 1962. Mem. Nat., N.C. assns. broadcasters, Am. Women in Radio and TV, Moore Meml. Hosp. Aux., Moore County Hist. Assn., Sandhill Music Assn., N.C. Art Soc., N.C. Soc. Preservation Antiquities. Clubs: Sandhills Garden (pres. 1968-69) (Southern Pines); Country of N.C. (Pinehurst); Carolina Carribbean (Beech Mountain, N.C.). Home: 130 Bethesda Rd Southern Pines NC 28387 Office: Sta WEEB Midland Rd Southern Pines NC 28387

YOURCENAR, MARGUERITE, author; b. Brussels, Belgium, June 8, 1903; d. Michel de Crayencour and Fernande de Cartier de Marchienne (parents French citizens); ed. privately; Litt.D., Smith Coll., 1961; Bowdoin Coll., 1968. Naturalized Am. citizen. Lectr. univs. U.S. and Europe, 1940—. Author: (novels and short stories) Alexis ou le Traite du Vain Combad, 1929, 1971; La Nouvelle Eurydice, 1931; La Mort conduit l'Attelage, 1934; Denier du Reve, 1934, 2d version, 1959; Nouvelles Orientales, 1938, rev. edit., 1963; Le Coup de Grace, 1939, (English transl. 1957; Memoires d'Hadrien. 1951, English transl. 1954; L'Oeuvre au Noir, 1968; (essays) Pindare, 1932, Les Songes et les Sorts, 1938, Sous Benefice d'Inventaire, 1962; (plays) Electre ou la Chute des Masques, 1954, Le Mystere d'Alceste et Qui n'a pas son minotaure?, 1963; Theatre I: theatre II, 1971; Rendre a Cesar, (poems and press poems) Feux, 1936, Les Charites d'Alcippe, 1956; (articles) The Legend of Krishna, in Encounter, Dec. 1959, Humanism in Thomas Mann, in Partisan Rev. Anthology, 1962; (La Petite Sirene, Le Dialogue dans le Marieage, 1971; Discours de Reception a 'l Academie Royal Belge, 1971; Entretiens Radio phoniques, 1972. Translator into French: from English, The Waves (Virginia Woolf), 1937, 2d edit., 1957, What Maisie Knew (Henry James), 1947, Negro Spirituals, Fleuve Profond, Sombre Riviere, 1964, Poems (Hortense Flexner), 1969; from modern Greek, Poems (Constantin Cavafy), 1958; from ancient Greek, an anthology of poetry, La Couronne et la Lyre (in preparation). Recipient Prix Femina Vacaresco, 1952; Page One award Newspaper Guild N.Y., 1955; Prix Combat for Sous Benefice d'Inventaire and the ensemble of her work, 1963; Prix Femina for L'Oeuvre au Noir, 1968; decorated Legion of Honor, Order of Leopold. Mem. Academie Royale Belg, civil rights and conservation socs. Address: Petite Plaisance Northeast Harbor ME 04662

YOUTZ, DOROTHY JANE KEYSER (MRS. WAYNE EMERSON YOUTZ), med. cons.; b. Iowa City; d. Clarence William and Lillian (Mylius) Keyser; A.B., Wellesley Coll., 1941; postgrad. State U. Ia., 1945; m. Wayne Emerson Youtz, May 30, 1943; children—Saralinda Keyser (Mrs. Thomas Tai Ngok Woo), Gregory Keyser. Data processing systems rep. IBM, 1941-45; adminstrv. analyst USPHS, Chgo., 1945-49, chief records consultation unit Bur. State Services, Washington, 1949-53, prin. staff advisor for devel. joint USPHS Children's Bur. state plan, 1953-54, spl. staff asst. office chief div. Indian health, 1955-61; health program specialist Office Planning, D.C. Dept. Pub. Health, Washington, 1961-69; spl. asst. D.C. Dept. Human Resources, 1970-72; staff asso. Meml. Gen. Hosp., Elkins, W.Va., 1972. Mem. health com. Urban League, Washington, 1961-64; D.C. del. Health and Welfare Council, 1963-64. Bd. dirs. Health Facilities Planning Council, 1970-71. Recipient Superior Service award USPHS, 1961; Spl. Commendation for outstanding service D.C. City Council, 1970. Fellow Am. Pub. Health Assn.; mem. D.C. Pub. Health (charter, Leadership award 1972), Group Health Assn. (dir. 1969-72, 2d v.p. 1972—), League Women Voters (dir. Prince Georges County), Elkins Bus. and Profl. Women's Club: Episcopalian (ch. sch. tchr. 1959-70). Mem. Order Eastern Star. Contbr. articles to periodicals. Home: PO Box 971 Kelly Mountain Rd Elkins WV 26241

YU, DINAH TIHUA, pathologist; b. Shangtung, China, May 5, 1937; d. Wen Yuan and I Ting (Neih) Yu; M.B., Kaohsiung Med. Coll., Taiwan, 1960; Ph.D., U. Toronto (Can.), 1972. Immigrated to Can., 1969. Resident in medicine Kaohsiung Med. Coll. Hosp., 1960-62, resident in pathology, 1962-63; resident in pathology Beth Israel Hosp., 1963-67, clin. fellow in pathology, 1967-68; asst. pathologist St. Michael's Hosp., Toronto, 1972—; teaching fellow Harvard Med. Sch., 1965-68; lectr. U. Toronto Med. Sch., 1972—. Fellow Med. Research Council Can., 1968-72. Fellow Royal Coll. Phys. and Surg. Can. Research devel. animal model of human disease: hereditary fructose intolerance. Home: 120 Rosedale Valley Rd Toronto ON Canada Office: 30 Bond St Toronto ON Canada

YUDELL, CHARLOTTE D. (MRS. ALEXANDER RICHMAN), physician; b. N.Y.C.; d. Hyman and Jennie (Mendelson) Yudell; B.A., Hunter Coll., 1932; M.D., N.Y. Med. Coll., 1933, postgrad. 1953-55; m. Alexander Richman, June 11, 1933; children—Myra (Mrs. Allen J. Togut), Beverly (Mrs. Prutkin), Janice (Mrs. Gerald Sufrin), Lesley (Mrs. Kenneth Winaker). Intern, house physician Morrisania City Hosp., N.Y.C., 1933-35; resident Grasslands Hosp., Valhalla, N.Y., 1952-54; practice medicine, Bronx, N.Y., 1935-42, New Rochelle, N.Y., 1942-51, specializing in psychiatry, N.Y.C., 1953—; mem. staff Met. Hosp., N.Y.C.; instr. psychiatry N.Y. Med. Coll., 1953—. Mem. A.M.A., Am. Psychiatric Assn., Acad. Psychoanalysis, Soc. Med. Psychoanalysts. Jewish religion. Hadassah. Home: 47 E 88th St New York City NY 10028 Office: 1050 Fifth Av New York City NY 10028

YUDIN, CAROL GOLDFINGER (MRS. WILFRED YUDIN), artist, printmaker; b. Bklyn.; d. Henry and Esther (Berenson) Goldfinger; student Pratt Graphic Center, N.Y.C., 19—; m. Wilfred Yudin; children—Robert, Diane. Exhibited in one-man shows at St. Thomas Aquinas Coll., Sparkill, N.Y., 1973, Korby Gallery, Cedar Grove, N.J., 1973, Fla. So. Coll., 1973, Old Bergen Art Guild Nat. Tour Colls. and Mus., 1974; exhibited in group shows at N.J. State Mus., Trenton, 1969, 7th Triennial, Newark, 1971, Audubon Artists, N.Y.C., 1974, Jersey City Mus., 1974, Nat. Assn. Women Artists, N.Y.C., 1974; represented in collections at Trenton State Mus., N.J. Miniature Soc., Jersey City Mus., N.Y. State U. at Albert. Mem. Nat. Assn. Women Artists (graphic juror 1972-74), Painters and Sculptors Soc. N.J. (pres. 1970-73), Artists Equity of N.J., Hunterdon Art Center. Home: 490 Joralemon St Belleville NY 07109

YUEN, EUGENIA BROWN (MRS. GEORGE A.L. YUEN), performing arts adminstr.; b. Lexington, Ky., Sept. 9, 1924; d. Roy M. and Lona D. (Crough) Brown; B.A. in Art History, U. Hawaii, 1973; m. George A.L. Yuen, May 18, 1945; children—Lenora Mimi, Georgia Lynn, Laura Jean. Draftsman Ford Motor Co., Dearborn, Mich., 1943-45, N.Am. Aviation, Inglewood, Cal., 1945-47, with CAA, Honolulu, 1947-51; dir. The Dance Studio, Honolulu, 1967—. Mgr. Telford Smith Water Supply Co., Honolulu, 1975—. Leader Girl Scouts, 1960, 61, 62, 65, 66; membership com. YWCA; mem. Hawaii State Dance Council. Mem. C. of C., Women in Constrn. Episcopalian (treas. women's bd. 1970—). Club: Pan Hellenic (sec. 1950). Home: 3280 Pauma Place Honolulu HI 96822 Office: 1533A Kalani St Honolulu HI 96819

YUNCKER, BARBARA, sci. writer; b. Greencastle, Ind.; d. Truman George and Ethel (Claflin) Yuncker; A.B., DePauw U. Copyreader, Wall St. Jour.; various editing positions N.Y. Post; asst. dep. commnr. commerce, N.Y. State, 1956-57; medicine and sci. writer N.Y. Post, 1959—; med. columnist Good Housekeeping mag., 1963—. Recipient Page One award Newspaper Guild N.Y., 1961; Adolph Meyer award, 1961; Alumni citation DePauw U., 1963; Page One award Newspaper Women's Club N.Y., 1963, 68; Albert Lasker med. journalism award, 1967, 69. Mem. Newspaper Guild N.Y., Nat. Assn. Sci. Writers, Soc. Mag. Writers. Democrat. Contbr. articles to nat. mags. Home: 361 W 22d St New York City NY 10011 Office: 210 South St New York City NY 10002

ZABRISKIE, VIRGINIA M., art dealer; b. N.Y.C.; B.A., N.Y. U., 1950, M.A., 1952; married. Dir., Zabriskie Gallery, N.Y.C., 1955—. Mem. Art Dealers Assn. (dir.). Home: 400 E 57th St New York City NY 10019 Office: 29 W 57th St New York City NY 10019

ZACHERT, VIRGINIA, psychologist; b. Jacksonville, Ala., Mar. 1, 1920; d. Rev. R. E. and Cora H. (Massee) Zachert; student Norman Jr. Coll., 1937; A.B., Ga. State Woman's Coll., 1940; M.A., Emory U., 1947; Ph.D., Purdue U., 1949. Statistician, Davison-Paxon Co., Atlanta, 1941-44; research psychologist Mil. Contracts, Auburn Research Found., Ala. Poly. Inst.; indsl. and research psychologist Sturm & O'Brien, cons. engrs., 1958-59; research project dir. Western Design, Biloxi, Miss., 1960-61; self-employed cons. psychologist, Norman Park, Ga., 1961-71, Good Hope, Ga., 1971—; research asso. med. edn. Med. Coll. Ga., Augusta, 1964-66, asso. prof., 1966-70, prof., 1970—. Served as aerologist USN, 1944-46, aviation psychologist USAF 1949-54, mem. air tng. command adv. bd. 1967—. Diplomate Am. Bd. Profl. Psychology. Fellow Am. Psychol. Assn.; mem. Am. Statis. Assn., N.E.A., Nat. Soc. Programmed Instrn. (nat. sec. 1968, adv. bd. 1969-71), Sigma Xi. Baptist. Author programmed instrn. texts. Home: Route 1 Good Hope GA 30641 Office: Dept Obstetrics and Gynecology Med Coll GA Augusta GA 30902

ZACK, DONNA FRANCES, mag. editor; b. Uniontown, Pa., Aug. 26, 1939; d. Charles N. and Ella Grace (Broderick) Zack; B.S., U. Fla., 1960, M.A., 1966. Tchr. bus. edn. Duval County Schs., Jacksonville, Fla., 1960-67; asso. editor Jr. Sec. mag. McGraw-Hill Book Co., 1967-69, editor Today's Sec. mag., 1969-72, editor Gregg tests and awards program, 1971-72; mng. editor Conv., Meetings, Incentive World mags., N.Y.C., 1972-73; exec. editor Meetings and Convs. mag., 1973—. Cons. Office Edn.; speaker various orgns. and schs. Mem. Nat. Bus. Edn. Assn., N.Y. Bus. Press Editors (sec. 1969-71, dir. 1971-73), U. Fla. Alumni Assn. (v.p. alumna N.Y. chpt. 1968—), Delta Pi Epsilon. Home: 305 E 40th St New York City NY 10016 Office: 1 Park Av New York City NY 10016

ZACKS, AYALA, art patron; b. Jerusalem, Israel, Dec. 31. 1912; d. Samuel and Rachel (Berman) Bentovim; ed. Coll. Feminin de Bouffemont, Paris, 1929-30, Sorbonne, 1931-32, London Sch. Econs., 1933-34, Columbia and Mus. Modern Art, N.Y.C., 1951-53; LL.D., U. Toronto, 1971; m. Samuel J. Zacks, 1947 (dec. 1970). Bd. dirs. Am.-Israel Cultural Found., Art Gallery Ont.; hon. patron, Royal Ont. Mus., bd. govs. Internat. Council Museums Found., Weizmann Inst. Sci., Rehovot, Israel, Hebrew U., Jerusalem; mem. internat. council Mus. Modern Art, N.Y.C.; chmn. Henry Moore Sculpture Centre Com., Toronto; former pres. Nat. Youth Orch. Can. Served with French Resistance, 1940-45. Recipient Eleanor Roosevelt Humanities award, 1970, Order of Can., 1972. Jewish religion. Club; Oakdale Golf and Country (Toronto). Home: 400 Walmer Rd East Tower Penthouse 26 Toronto ON M5P 2X7 Canada

ZADIG, JEAN MACCUBREY, educator; b. Hartford, Conn., May 23, 1934; d. P. Kenton and Marion A. (Porter) MacCubrey; Mus.B., Boston U., 1956; M.Ed., Boston Coll., 1967, Ph.D. (U.S. Office of Edn. fellow), 1969; m. Alfred T.K. Zadig, June 5, 1971; children—Michael David, Andrew Kent. Tchr. St. Anne's Sch., Arlington Heights, Mass., 1956-61, tchr., dir. research with mentally retarded children, 1968-69; tchr. St. Francis High Sch., Upi, Cotabato, Philippines, 1962-66; dir. spl. edn. Developmental Evaluation Clinic, Children's Hosp. Med. Center, Boston, 1969—; asst. prof. Boston Coll. Grad. Sch. Arts and Scis., 1969—. Mem. Am. Psychol. Assn., Am. Assn. Mental Deficiency, Am. Assn. U. Profs., New Eng. Materials Instruction Center. Episcopalian. Home: 9 Staples St Melrose MA 02176 Office: 300 Longwood Av Boston MA 02115

ZAEHRINGER, MARY VERONICA, educator; b. Phila., May 27, 1911; d. Paul J. and Mary (Bolton) Zaehringer; B.S., Temple U., 1946; M.S., Cornell U., 1948, Ph.D., 1953. Grad. research asst. N.Y. Coll. Home Econs. at Cornell U., 1946-48, asst. foods research, 1951-53; instr. home econ. research Mont. State Coll., 1948-49, asst. prof., 1949-50; research prof., head dept. home econs. research U. Ida., 1953-72, research prof. food sci., 1972-73, research prof. dept. bacteriology and biochemistry, 1973—. Research fellow Inst. Storage and Processing of Agrl. Produce, Wageningen, Netherlands, 1967-68. Mem. Inst. Food Technologists, Am. Chem. Soc., Am. Assn. Cereal Chemistry, Potato Assn. Am., Ida. Acad. Sci., Am. Soc. Hort. Sci., Sigma Xi, Omicron Nu, Pi Lambda Sigma, Kappa Delta Epsilon. Contbr. articles to profl. jours., 1948—. Home: 614 Ash St Moscow ID 83843

ZAGAT, CORNELIA ERNST, civic worker; b. N.Y.C., Dec. 28, 1910; d. Bernard M.L. and Roberta Christine (Claus) Ernst; B.A., Vassar Coll., 1932; B.S. in L.S., Columbia, 1937; m. Eugene H. Zagat, June 12, 1935 (div. 1964); children—Eugene H., Cornelia (Mrs. Timothy B.B. Eland). Librarian, Stamford Hist. Soc. Bd. dirs. Child Study Assn. Am./Wel-Met, Inc., 1936—, mem. children's book com., 1936—; bd. dirs. Southwestern Conn. Mental Health Assn. Mem. Stamford (Conn.) Museum, Stamford Citizens for Conservation, Bartlett Arboretum, Women's Nat. Book Assn. Children's book reviewer mags., newspapers. Address: 1709 Newfield Av Stamford CT 06903

ZAGIER, HELENE JOHANNA DE BOEY (MRS. DAVID D. ZAGIER), psychiatrist, educator; b. London, Eng., Feb. 23, 1918; d. Adolf and Johanna (Sassen) de Boey; student Barnard Coll., 1936-38, N.Y.U., 1941-42; M.D., George Washington U., 1947; m. David D. Zagier, July 3, 1942; children—Vega Johanna, Don Bernard. Pediatrician U.S. Air Force Hosp., Tachikawa, Japan, 1952-54; resident Eastern State Hosp., Williamsburg, Va., 1955-56, Medfield (Mass.) State Hosp., 1956-57, Hawaii State Hosp., Kaneohe, 1957-58; dir. Mental Health Service Clinic, Kingsport, Tenn., 1958-59; chief outpatient clinic San Joaquin County Hosp., Stockton, Cal., 1959-65; mem. faculty Am. Coll. of Switzerland, Leysin, 1965—, coll. psychiat. cons., 1966—, prof. psychology, 1965-68; asso. dir. Cantonal Psychiat. Hosp., Valais, 1966-71. Mem. Am., Swiss psychiat. assns., Royal Coll. Psychiatrists (Eng.). Home: Villa Quand Meme aux Fontaines sur Monthey 1870 Switzerland Office: 16 Av de la Gare 1870 Monthey Switzerland

ZAGULA-MALLY, ZENONA WANDA, physician; b. Toronto, Ont., Can., Nov. 28, 1934 (came to U.S. 1966, naturalized 1972); d. Peter and Julia (Sarzynski) Zagula; M.D., U. Toronto, 1958; m. Gerhard Mally, June 27, 1964; children—Robert Stephan, Jennifer Yvonne. Rotating intern Toronto Gen. Hosp., 1958-59; med. intern Johns Hopkins Hosp., Balt., 1959-60; resident pathology Ont. Cancer Research Inst., Wellesley Hosp., Toronto, 1960-61; resident dermatology U. Pa. Hosp., Phila., 1961-64; med. research, clin. dermatology asst. La Foundation de Rothschild, Paris, France, 1964-66; asst. dermatologist Grad. Hosp. U. Pa., 1967-68; attending physician VA Hosp., Memphis, 1969-73; former mem. cons. staff St. Jude's Children's Research Hosp., Memphis; former mem. jr. staff Baptist Meml. Hosp., Memphis; now active staff Providence Hosp., Dr.'s Hosp.; practice medicine specializing in dermatology, Washington, 1973—; asst. prof. dermatology med. units, U. Tenn., Memphis, 1969-73; now active teaching staff Georgetown U.; spl. lectr. dermatology, George Washington U. Co-dir. skin cancer study project Memphis Regional Med. Program, 1969-71; prin. investigator skin cancer and skin lesion research project Clin. Research Center, Bowld Hosp., Memphis, 1970-73. Am. Cancer Soc. instl. grantee, 1970-71; cons. FDA, U. Md. Diplomate Am. Bd. Dermatology. Fellow Am. Acad. Dermatology; mem. Coll. Physicians and Surgeons of Ont., Am. Soc. Dermatologic Surgery, Am. Med. Women's Assn., Inc., Soc. Investigative Dermatology, Indsl. Med. Assn., Washington Soc. Dermatology, Am. Soc. Contemporary Medicine and Surgery, Med. Soc. D.C. Roman Catholic. Author: (with Edwin Sidi and Marc Hincky) Psoriasis, 1968. Contbr. to profl. jours. Home: 6300 Dahlonega Rd Washington DC 20006 Office: 1835 Eye St NW Suite 814 Washington DC 20006

ZAHM, BERNICE SCHULTZ (MRS. NATHAN R. ZAHM), ednl. adminstr.; b. Cleve., May 25, 1919; d. Sam and Lillian (Levin) Schultz; B.A., Ohio State U., 1941; M.A. in Ednl. Guidance, Cal. State Coll., Los Angeles; Ph.D. in Human Behavior, U.S. Internat. U., San Diego, 1972; m. Nathan R. Zahm, Aug. 6, 1939; children—Stephen, Barbara (Mrs. Thomas Hurwitz). Tchr. pub. schs., Los Angeles, 1952-53; pvt. remedial educator, 1953-56; founder Ednl. Guidance Center, Los Angeles, 1956; founder, dir. Zahm Sch., Los Angeles, 1957—. Speaker, lectr. profl. assns., 1965—; cons. to pvt. and pub. schs., 1965—. Recipient award for contbn. to remedial edn. County of Los Angeles, 1964. Mem. Am. Psychol. Assn., Nat., Cal. assns. sch. psychologists, Am. Personnel and Guidance Assn. Contbr. articles to profl. jours. Originator multilectic approach to edn. Address: 4422 Sherman Oaks Circle Sherman Oaks CA 91403

ZAHRADKA, LINDA LEE, educator; b. Pasadena, Cal., Dec. 1, 1942; d. Joseph A. and Libby L. (Link) Zahradka; B.A., U. So. Cal., 1965; M.S., 1967. Student counselor U. So. Cal. Sch. Edn., Los Angeles, 1966-71; tchr. pub. sch., San Gabriel Valley, Cal., 1971-73; tchr. Catholic Archdiocese Los Angeles, 1974—. Ednl. cons. Cal. Migrant Tchr. Corps and Vista program, 1969-71. Vol., Charity Clinic Med. Center, Los Angeles, 1958-64, Pacific State Hosp., Spadra, Cal., 1961-65. Mem. Am. Assn. Mental Deficiency, U. So. Cal. Student Tchrs. Assn. (pres. 1964), Exceptional Children's Found., Assn. for Women in Edn. (pres. 1972-73), U. So. Cal. Sch. Edn. Alumni Assn. (recipient Outstanding Leadership award 1963-65, dir. 1965—), Pi Lambda Theta (life), Chi Omega. Republican. Roman Catholic. Home: 1210 Huntington Dr San Marino CA 91108

ZAIKA, LAURA LARYSA, govt. chemist; b. Kharkow, Ukraine, June 23, 1938 (came to U.S. 1950, naturalized 1958); d. Peter and Lydia (Sherbak) Zaika; B.S., Drexel Inst. Tech., 1960; Ph.D., U. Pa., 1964. Research chemist U.S. Dept. Agr., Phila., 1964—. Mem. Am. Chem. Soc., Phi Kappa Phi, Sigma Xi. Home: 5023 N Rosehill St Philadelphia PA 19120 Office: Regional Research Center 600 E Mermaid Ln Philadelphia PA 19118

ZAISER, SALLY SOLEMMA VANN (MRS. FOSTER E. ZAISER), retail book co. exec.; b. Birmingham, Ala., Jan. 18, 1917; d. Carl Waldo and Einnan (Herndon) Vann; student Birmingham-So. Coll., 1933-36, Akron Coll. Bus., 1937; m. Foster E. Zaiser, Nov. 11, 1939. Accountant, A. Simionato, San Francisco, 1958-65; head accounting dept. Richard T. Clarke Co., San Francisco, 1966; accountant John Howell-Books, San Francisco, 1967-72, sec., treas., 1972—; sec. Great Eastern Mines, Inc., Albuquerque, 1969—. Braille transcriber for A.R.C., Kansas City, Mo. 1941-45; vol. worker A.R.C. Hosp. Program, Sao Paulo, Brazil, 1952. Mem. Book Club Cal., Cal. Hist. Soc., Theta Upsilon. Republican. Episcopalian. Home: 355 Serrano Dr San Francisco CA 94132 Office: 434 Post St San Francisco CA 94102

ZAJICEK, SARITA SOTO, educator; b. Austin, Tex.; B.A., U. Tex., 1937, M.A., 1937, Ph.D., 1949; postgrad. Columbia, summers 1957-60, 62, U. Miami, summer 1964. Tchr., supr. pub. schs., Austin, 1937-42; with Office Censorship, USN, 1942-44; payroll clk. Army Service Forces, summers 1944-45; asst. prof. Okla. Coll. for Women,

1944-46; instr. Spanish U. Tex., 1946-49; asst. prof. Spanish and edn. Tex. Christian U., 1949-51; mem. faculty Southwestern U., Georgetown, Tex., 1954-67, dir., supr. elementary student program, 1954-67; dir. elementary edn. program St. Mary's U., San Antonio, 1967—; dir. bi-lingual workshop for tchrs. Edgewood Ind. Sch. Dist., San Antonio, summer 1969; dir. bi-lingual workshop for tchrs. Edgewood, San Antonio, South San Antonio, Harlandale sch. dists., summer 1970; mem. Workshop for Consultants on Guided Edn., 1974. Carnegie Study grantee for research work, 1951. Mem. Am. Assn. U. Profs., Nat., Tex. assns. for supervision and curriculum devel., Nat., Tex. assns. for student teaching, N.E.A., Am. Assn. U. Women. Methodist (trustee ch.). Author: State Course of Study for the Teaching of Conversational Spanish in Grades One Through Eight, 1942. Editor: El Camino Real, 1954. Contbr. articles to profl. jours. Home: 937 Sutton Dr San Antonio TX 78228 Office: St Mary's U 2700 Cincinnati Av San Antonio TX 78284

ZALLEN, EUGENIA MALONE, nutritionist, educator; b. Camp Hill, Ala., July 18, 1932; d. Benjamin Floyd and Pauline Phillips (Kelly) Malone; B.S., Auburn U., 1953; M.S., Purdue U., 1960, Ph.D., U. Tenn., 1974; m. Harold Zallen, Aug. 23, 1959. Asso. adminstrv. dietitian Duke U. Med. Center, 1954-57; asst. chief dietitian Emory U. Hosp., Atlanta, 1957-58; instr. Auburn (Ala.) U., then asst. prof., 1962-66; asst. prof. U. Md., College Park, 1967-72; dir. sch. home econs. and asso. prof. home econs. U. Okla., Norman, 1974—. Mem. Arts and Humanities Council Stillwater, 1972-73. Mem. Am. Dietetic Assn., Am. Home Econs. Assn., Soc. for Nutrition Edn., Inst. Food Technologists, Mortar Bd., Phi Kappa Phi, Sigma Delta Epsilon Zeta Tau Alpha (recipient Certificate Achievement 19—). Baptist. Author: Food and Nutrition Manual, 1969. Home: PO Drawer 2790 Norman OK 73069 Office: School Home Economics University of Oklahoma 610 Elm St Norman OK 73069

ZAMACONA, JO ANN CAROL HAWLEY, librarian; b. Madison, Wis., Apr. 15, 1934; d. Forest Marvin and Hazel Rachel (Hartmann) Hawley; B.A., U. Wis., 1956, M.A. (Library Services and Constrn. Act grantee), 1965; m. Jorge Zamacona, July 28, 1956 (div. 1967); children—Jorge, Debora Jo. Librarian, Madison Pub. Library, 1965-66, br. librarian, 1967-72, supervising librarian, 1972—. Adminstr., Thompson State Camp Fund, 1969—; mem., co-founder Concerned Citizens for Prison Reform, 1971—. Mem. Wis. Gov.'s Task Force Citizen Study Com. on Offender Rehab., 1971-72. Mem. Wis. Library Assn. (dist. sec., treas. 1971-72), U. Wis. Alumni Assn. (alumni day chmn. 1968, 69, 70), Sigma Delta Pi, Sigma Kappa. Home: 4316 Hillcrest Circle Madison WI 53705 Office: 513 S Midvale Blvd Madison WI 53711

ZAND, CHARLENE ROOTH (MRS. ROBERT ZAND), speech pathologist; b. Chgo., June 10, 1930; d. George and Dorothy (Zaretsky) Rooth; B.S. in Speech, Northwestern U., 1951; M.A. in Edn., Coll. City N.Y., 1956; m. Robert Zand, June 14, 1952; children—Martin Stuart, Joel Raphael, Dina Jane. Speech therapist Ill. Children's Hosp. Sch., Chgo., 1951-52, Inst. Crippled and Disabled, N.Y.C., 1952-56, Parmenter Health Center, Wayland, Mass., 1958-62; psychologist Boston Neurol. Lab., 1958-62; cons. speech pathologist Lutheran Retirement Center, Ann Arbor, Mich., 1974—. Speech pathologist pvt. practice, Ann Arbor, 1971—. Chmn. Hebrew Gan Beth Israel Synagogue, Ann Arbor, 1966-73. B'nai B'rith Hillel Found. scholar, 1948-51. Mem. Am. Speech and Hearing Assn., Am. Psychol. Assn., Hadassah. Address: 2098 Yorktown Dr Ann Arbor MI 48105

ZANDLER, HELEN CATHERINE SCHERMULY (MRS. CLEMENT W. ZANDLER), social concerns exec.; b. Wichita, Kan., Jan. 18, 1922; d. Joseph John and Cecilia Marie (Switlik) Schermuly; B.A. cum laude in Journalism, Wichita State U., 1943; m. Clement W. Zandler, July 17, 1944; children—Kenneth, Donald, Paula (Mrs. Bill Betts), Pamela, Thomas, John, Michael. Editor Internal-External House Organ, pub. relations dir. Davis-Westholt Co., Wichita, 1943-47; columnist True Voice, Omaha, 1963-65. Pres. League Women Voters Phoenix, 1969-71; state pres. League Women Voters Ariz., 1971-73; v.p. Holy Cross Home and Sch. Assn., 1960-61, Catholic Social Service, Phoenix, 1971-72; pres. Mercy High Sch. Home and Sch., Omaha, 1965; pub. relations dir. Archdiocesan Council Cath. Women, 1963-65; program and resource dir. Phoenix Diocesan Human Devel. Commn., 1973—; v.p. Omaha Deanery Council Cath. Women, 1965; v.p. Urban League Guild, Omaha, 1963-64; mem. health services and facilities rev. com. Maricopa County Comprehensive Health Council. Recipient merit awards Southwestern Assn. Indsl. Editors, 1944, 45. Mem. Am. Assn. U. Women (v.p. Wichita 1944), Am. Arbitration Assn. (Phoenix adv. council), UN Assn. Greater Phoenix (pres. 1973), Mortar Bd. Alumnae (sec.-treas. 1963-65). Home: 7240 N 11th Av Phoenix AZ 85021 Office: 1825 W Northern Av Phoenix AZ 85021

ZANELLA, PATRICIA FAGAN (MRS. LOUIS JOSEPH ZANELLA), state agy. adminstr.; b. Providence, June 24, 1932; d. John Joseph and Florence Mildred (Seese) Fagan; A.B., U. R.I., 1954, M.S., 1968; postgrad. Kan. State U., 1956; m. Louis Joseph Zanella, Nov. 28, 1953; children—Deborah, Joanne, Stephen, Robert, Leslie, Carol, Patricia, Christine. Social worker R.I. Div. Pub. Assistance, 1960-65; project dir. Health, Edn. and Welfare funded Demonstration Project, R.I. Div. Retardation, Cranston, 1969-71, asso. adminstr. Joseph H. Ladd Sch., 1971-72, adminstr. Social and Developmental Service, 1972—. Dir. pub. welfare, Narragansett, R.I., 1968—; mem. R.I. Spl. Edn. Adv. Com., 1973—. Mem. Citizens Adv. Com., Narragansett, 1969. Bd. dirs. Moderate Income Housing Com., Narragansett. Mem. Am. Assn. for Mental Deficiency, Nat. Assn. for Retarded Children, Omicron Nu. Home: 83 Kingstown Rd Narragansett RI 02882 Office: 600 New London Av Cranston RI 02920

ZANETTA, POLLY NASH (MRS. RICHARD ANTHONY ZANETTA), educator; b. Corpus Christi, Tex., Aug. 9, 1945; d. John McElyea, Jr. and Pauline Ann (Fawcus) Nash; B.S., Murray (Ky.) State U., 1967, M.S., 1969; postgrad. U. Okla., summer 1973; m. Richard Anthony Zanetta, Sept. 2, 1968. Grad. asst. Murray State U., 1967-69, instr. speech communication dept., 1969-74; chmn. div. communication and arts East Ark. Community Coll., Forrest City, 1974—. Program dir., mem. exec. bd. United Campus Ministry; adviser Murray State U. Student Senate, 1971-74. Named Outstanding Woman Prof., Womens Student Govt. Assn., 1972. Mem. Ky. Assn. Communicative Arts, Central States Speech Assn., Speech Communication Assn., Pi Phi Delta, Alpha Sigma Alpha. Republican. Roman Catholic. Compiler, adapter scripts Mark Twain: An Evening of Social Comment, 1970; Thurber's World and Welcome to It, 1971; Poetry in Motion, 1973; Flowers for Algernon, 1973. Home: 430 Trenton Rd Forrest City AR 72335

ZANGWILL, ESTELLE PAULA RICHEST (MRS. DONALD P. ZANGWILL), speech pathologist; b. Pitts.; d. Joseph P. and Anne (Burckin) Richest; B.S., U. Pitts., 1950, M.S., 1963; m. Steven Osgood, June 7, 1948 (div. 1972); children—Linda Carole, Robert Alexander; m. 2d, Donald P. Zangwill, June 5, 1972. Speech pathologist Childrens Hosp., Pitts., 1960—, coordinator mutidisciplinary diagnostic program for lang. disturbed children, 1966-68. Mem. Allegheny Children and Youth Service Council. Bd. dirs. Pitts. chpt. World Federalist. Mem. Am., Pa. speech and hearing assns., Internat. Soc. Gen. Semantics, Internat. Platform Assn., Chartiers Mental Health and Mental Retardation Assn., Allegheny County Med. Soc. Aux., Womens Assn. Pitts. Symphony Soc. Home: 109 Oak Park Pl Pittsburgh PA 15243 Office: 125 DeSoto St Pittsburgh PA 15213

ZAPOLEON, MARGUERITE WYKOFF, cons., lectr., author; b. Cin., Aug. 18, 1907; d. Fred Clark and Elizabeth (Voth) Wykoff; B.A., engrng. degree, U. Cin., 1928; postgrad. Geneva Sch. Internat. Studies, 1927, N.Y. Sch. Social Work, 1928-29, London Sch. Econ. and Polit. Sci., 1932; M.A., Am. U., 1938; m. Louis B. Zapoleon, Oct. 2, 1937 (dec. Dec. 1969). Vocation counselor Cin. pub. schs., 1929-35; chief counseling div. D.C. Employment Center, 1935-39; specialist occupational information and guidance service U.S. Office Edn., 1939-43; tng. specialist Hdqrs. ASF, 1943-44; chief employment opportunities br. Women's Bur., Dept. Labor, 1944-51, spl. asst. occupational outlook service Bur. Labor Statistics, 1951-55, spl. asst. to dir. Women's Bur., 1955-60; cons. on labor econs. and vocational guidance, 1960—; lectr., workshop leader, instr. vocational guidance and occupational research colls., univs., Am. Assn. U. Women adult counseling project, 1965; adv. com., panel asso. Assn. Appraisers Earning Capacity, 1964-69; mem. Fla. Council Aging, 1973—; mem. tech. com. employment and retirement, recorder employment and retirement sect. White House Conf. Aging, 1971. Bd. dirs. Am. Soc. Econometric Appraisers, 1967-69. Mem. Nat. Vocational Guidance Assn. (trustee 1945-51), Council Guidance and Personnel Assn. (v.p. 1947-48), Alliance for Guidance Rural Youth (2d v.p. 1952-60), Am. Personnel and Guidance Assn. (del. to Assembly 1951-60), Am. Econ. Assn., Indsl. Relations Research Assn., Am. Ednl. Research Assns., Nat. Assn. Deans and Counselors of Women. Am. Assn. U. Woman, Nat. League Am. Pen Women, A.A.A.S., Am. Statis. Assn., Internat. Platform Assn., Gerontology Soc., Nature Conservancy (rec. sec. Fla. chpt.), Friends of Everglades (chmn. Broward County 1973—, Kappa Kappa Gamma (alumnae achievement award 1968. Presbyn. Author: (with Louise Moore) Reference and Related Information, Vocational Guidance for Girls and Women, 1941; Community Occupational Surveys, 1942; The College Girl Looks Ahead to Her Career Opportunities, 1956; Occupational Planning for Women, 1961; Girls and Their Futures, 1963; Economic Aspects of Counseling Mature women, 1966; also author of numerous govtl. pamphlets on occupations and vocational guidance edn. and tng. Editor: Vocational Guidance Quar., 1953-54. Contbr. articles to profl. jours. Home: 816 SE Riviera Isle Fort Lauderdale FL 33301

ZARATZIAN, VIRGINIA LOUISE, pharmacologist; b. Highland Park, Mich., Nov. 15, 1918; d. Vahan Oskihan and Makrouhie (Kevorkian) Zaratzian; student Highland Park Jr. Coll., 1937-39; B.S., U. Mich., 1942, B.S. in Pharmacy, 1946, M.S., 1949; Ph.D., Wayne State U., 1956. Research asso. U. Ill. Coll. Medicine, Chgo., 1956-59; acting chief pesticides sect., pharmacologist Food and Drug Adminstrn., Dept. Health, Edn., Welfare, Washington, 1959-61; acting chief pharm. sect., research pharmacologist Div. Air Pollution USPHS, Dept. Health, Edn., Welfare, Cin., 1961-63; chief pharmacology br. U.S. Environmental Hygiene Agy., Dept. of Def., Edgewood Arsenal, Md., 1963-66; pharmacologist pesticides regulation div. U.S. Dept. of Agr., Washington, 1966-68; pharmacologist psychopharmacology research br., div. extramural research programs Nat. Inst. Mental Health, Rockville, Md., 1968—. Asso. prof. pharmacology U. Cin., 1962-63; vis. prof. pharmacology and therapeutics Tex. Tech. U. Sch. Medicine, 1973—; cons. Adv. Center Toxicology, Nat. Acad. Scis., NRC, Washington, 1957-59. Mem. Soc. Toxicology, Am. Chem. Soc., A.A.A.S., Pan Am. Med. Assn. Council on Toxicology, Iota Sigma Pi, Rho Chi. Home: 19324 Frenchton Pl Gaithersburg MD 20760 Office: 5600 Fishers Lane Rockville MD 20852

ZARSKY, SANDRA MOSAK (MRS. EFRAIM ZARSKY), psychologist, health services adminstr.; b. Chgo., Dec. 14, 1941; d. Jacob Louis and Pearl (Ribaysen) Mosak; B.A., Yeshiva U., 1962; postgrad. 1965-66; M.A., City U. N.Y., 1965, postgrad., 1968-70; m. Efraim Zarsky, Aug. 23, 1966. Psychologist, Yonkers (N.Y.) Youth Bd., 1966-67; research asso. Speech Rehab. Inst., N.Y.C., 1967-68; psychologist prison mental health service Adolescent Reception and Detention Center, Rikers Island, N.Y.C., 1970—, adminstr., 1973—. Lectr. N.Y.C. Correctional Acad., 1972—; sec. local psychologists chpt. AFL-CIO, 1973—, del. N.Y. constl. conv., 1973. Mem. Am. Psychol. Assn. (asso.), Am. Assn. Correctional Psychologists. Office: New York City Prison Mental Health 11-11 Hazen St East Elmhurst NY 11370

ZATURENSKA, MARYA (MRS. HORACE V. GREGORY), poet, biographer; b. Kiev, Russia, Sept. 12, 1902 came to U.S. 1910, naturalized 1914; d. Abram and Johanna (Lubovska) Zaturensky; student (scholar), Valpararaiso U., 1921-23, U. Wis. Library Sch., 1925; m. Horace V. Gregory, Aug. 21, 1925; children—Joanna (Mrs. S. H. Zeigler), Patrick Bolton. Recipient Shelley award Poetry Soc. New Eng., 1935; Pulitzer prize in poetry, 1938; Guaranters award Poetry mag., also others. Author: (poetry) Threshold and Hearth. 1934, Cold Morning Sky, 1937, The Listening Landscape, 1941, The Golden Mirror, 1944, Selected Poems, 1954, Terraces of Light, 1960, Collected Poems, 1966, The Hidden Waterfall, 1974; (with husband) History of American Poetry Since 1900, 1946; The Mentor Book of Religious Poems, 1957, The Crystal Cabinet, 1962, The Silver Swan, 1966; (biography) Christina Rosetti: A Portrait with Background, 1949; also introductions to poetry vols. Editor: The Selected Poems of Christina Rossetti, 1970. Address: Palisades NY 10964

ZAVADA, MARY ROBERTA, editor; b. Passaic, N.J., Jan. 11, 1936; d. John Michael and Sophie Catherine (Majowicz) Zavada; A.B. magna cum laude (scholar), Coll. St. Elizabeth, 1957; M.A., DePaul U., 1959; post-grad. (English-Speaking Union grant) U London, 1962. Grad. asst. DePaul U., Chgo., 1957-58; feature writer United Press Internat., London, Eng., 1964; writer Honeywell, Inc., Newton Highlands, Mass., 1966-67; editor Sylvania Electronic Systems, Waltham, Mass., 1968-69; account exec. Anderson Assos., pub. relations and advt., Boston, Mass., 1969-70; editor Ednl. Testing Service, Princeton, N.J., 1971—. Tchr. Pilot Adult Career evening program Mass. Bay Community Coll., 1969-70, Univ. Coll., Northeastern U., 1967-70; communications cons. div. retardation R.I. Dept. Health, 1971-72. Mem. Bus. and Profl. Women's Club, Kappa Gamma Pi (2d nat. v.p. 1969-71). Democrat. Roman Catholic. Contbr. articles and short stories to various mags. and newspapers. Home: 161 Franklin Corner Rd Lawrenceville NJ 08648 Office: Ednl Testing Service Rosedale Rd Princeton NJ 08540

ZAYDON, JEMILLE ANN, educator; b. Peckville, Pa., Feb. 21, 1940; d. Joseph and Catherine Ann (Hazzouri) Zaydon; student Barry Coll. for Women, 1957-59; B.S., Marywood Coll., 1963, postgrad., 1964, 67; postgrad. Miami Dade Jr. Coll., 1964, U. Scranton, 1964, Newark State Coll., 1965, Temple U., 1969, 73, Wilkes Coll., 1974—. Tchr. St. Hugh Elementary Sch., Coconut Grove, Fla., 1963-64; Allapattah Elementary Sch., Miami, 1964-65, Columbus Elementary Sch., Westfield, N.J., 1965-66; communications instr. Keystone Job Corps, Drums, Pa., 1966-73; vol. instr. Keystone Rehab. Center, Scranton, Pa., 1970-71; curriculum cons. for mentally retarded, Vienna, Austria, 1974. Supr. recreation program, Hazleton, Pa., summer 1968; founder, adviser Keystone Kourier, 1967-69. Sec. Fedn. Youth, William W. Scranton, 1963; supr. students Heart Fund campaign, 1968-71; developer program mentally retarded Allied Services for Handicapped Scranton, 1973; active A.R.C., March of Dimes, Heart Fund, Leukemia and United Fund drives, also Sickle Cell Anemia Found. Bd. dirs. Michael F. Harrity Meml. Fund., 1969-73. Recipient Staff Mem. of Year award, Job Corps, 1969; Service scholarship, Barry Coll., 1958; Educators award Dade County, 1973. Mem. Nat., Pa. State edn. assns., Beta Lambda Tau, Sigma Tau Delta, Theta Chi Beta (charter pres. 1961-63), Lambda Iota Tau (life). Democrat. Roman Catholic (instr. Confraternity Christian Doctrine, 1956-71). Editor Lebanese Am. Jour., 1957-63. Home: 608 N Main Av Scranton PA 18504

ZEALBERG, CATHERINE LOUISE, librarian; b. Mahanoy City, Pa., Feb. 9, 1920; d. William Henry and Mary Louise (Hollerbach) Zealberg; B.S. in Edn., Kutztown (Pa.) State Tchrs. Coll., 1943; M.A., George Peabody Coll. Tchrs., 1947. High sch. librarian, Wellsboro, Pa., 1943-45; instr. library sci. Western Ill. State Coll., Macomb, 1947-48; head librarian Bloomsburg (Pa.) State Tchrs. Coll., 1948-51; librarian U.S. Army War Coll., Carlisle Barracks, Pa., 1951—. Mem. tng. com. Carlisle Barracks, 1970—, coordinator fed. women's program, 1973—. Bd. dirs. United Community Fund, 1970—, Def. Activities Fed. Credit Union, 1973—. Mem. Am. Assn. U. Women (pres. Carlisle br. 1958-60, rec. sec. Pa. div. 1962-65, dir. Carlisle 1968—), League Women Voters, Pa. Citizens Council, Harrisburg Diocesan Council Catholic Women (v.p. 1972—). Democrat. Home: 300 E St Carlisle PA 17013 Office: US Army War Coll Carlisle Barracks PA 17013

ZEBROWSKI, MARTHA MAY KADERLY (MRS. EDWARD ZEBROWSKI), librarian; b. Charlotte, N.C., Apr. 26, 1922; d. William Frederick and Martha Lavinia (Lewis) Kaderly; A.B., Mercer U., 1942; postgrad. Adrian Coll., 1959, Siena Hts. Coll., 1960-63, U. Mich., 1965; m. Edward Zebrowski, Aug. 26, 1943; 1 dau., Martha K. With U.S. Social Security Bd., Macon, Ga., 1943, U.S. War Dept., Deming, N.M., 1944, Wendover, Utah, 1945; sec. Willow Run (Mich.) Pub. Schs., 1954-56; jr. high sch. librarian Adrian (Mich.) Pub. Schs., 1960-65; librarian Edinboro (Pa.) State Coll., 1966—. Mem. Pa. Library Assn., Phi Mu. Home: PO Box 152 125 High St Edinboro PA 16412 Office: Hamilton Library Edinboro State Coll Edinboro PA 16412

ZEDDIES, RUTH JULIENE DENHAM (MRS. ZORN A. ZEDDIES), real estate broker; b. El Reno, Okla., Dec. 14, 1921; d. James Graham and Joy (Dunaway) Denham; student San Diego Bus. Coll., 1941, San Diego Beauty Coll., 1952, Deanza Coll., 1968, Grossmont Coll., 1971—; m. Zorn A. Zeddies, Feb. 24, 1941, also Jan. 29, 1971; m. 2d, Norville C. Miller, Feb. 8, 1944; children—Juleen (Mrs. Dennis Lee Monson), Kim Ivan, Kelly Joneen. Bus driver City of San Diego, 1943; saleswoman Kelly Miller Realty, San Diego, 1953-54; cosmotologist, owner Cut and Kurl Beauty Shop, Dighton, Kan., 1954-60, Comb and Kurl Beauty Shop, Santa Clara, Cal., 1960; co-owner Valley Realty, San Jose, Cal., 1960-71; owner Ruth Zeddies Realty, Santee, 1971—. Served with AUS, 1942-43. Mem. San Jose (membership com. 1968-69), El Cajon realty bds., Christian Profl. Women's Club, Pink Ladies Aux., Scottish Rite Women's Assn. Baptist (past supt. Sunday sch., deaconess). Mem. Order Eastern Star. Address: 9867 Via Rita Santee CA 92071

ZEHE, SISTER MARY MARGARET THERESE, ednl. adminstr.; b. Cleve., June 8, 1933; d. Herbert L. and Coletta M. (Schultheis) Zehe; B.A., Notre Dame Coll., 1961, M.B.A., U. Notre Dame, 1967. Joined Sisters of Notre Dame, 1951; instr. bus. edn. Our Lady of Lourdes High Sch., Cleve., 1954-60, John F. Kennedy High Sch., Warren, O., 1961-71; instr. bus. edn. Notre Dame Coll., Cleve., 1971-72, financial aid officer, 1971—, dir. instl. research 1971-72, dir. continuing edn., 1974—. Mem. Nat., Midwest assns. student financial aid adminstrs., Assn. Instl. Research. Address: Notre Dame Coll 4545 College Rd Cleveland OH 44121

ZEHNPFENNIG, GLADYS BURANDT (MRS. FRANK E. ZEHNPFENNIG), author; b. Watertown, S.D., Dec. 9, 1910; d. Adolph Henry and Ida (Baumann) Burandt; student S.D. State Coll.; m. Frank E. Zehnpfennig, Dec. 23, 1936; children—Theodore Francis, Gary Harold. Author: (novels) The Rock and the Sand, 1954; Search for Eden, 1955; Son of Nazareth, 1957; (biographies) Charles F. Kettering, Inventor and Idealist, 1962; Carl Sandburg, Poet and Patriot, 2d edit., 1974; Nathaniel Leverone, Pioneer in Automatic Merchandising, 1963; Harry A. Bullis, Champion American, 1964; Carlos P. Romulo, Defender of Freedom, 1965; Hubert H. Humphrey: Champion of Human Rights, 1966; Melvin J. Maas; Gallant Man of Action, 1967; Lawrence Welk: Champagne Music Man, 1968; Henry R. Luce, Tycoon of Journalism, 1969; Carl T. Rowan, Spokesman for Sanity, 1972; Ecology for Young People, 1972; Lawrence M. Brings, Book Publisher, 1973. Mem. Nat. League Am. Pen Women, Internat. Platform Assn., Delta Phi Lambda. Roman Catholic. Home: 75 Battle Creek Rd St Paul MN 55119

ZEIDERS, BARBARA, bus. exec.; b. Paterson, N.J., Mar. 23, 1930; d. E.P. and Cornelia (Van Der Vliet) Zeiders; B.S. with high honors in Library Sci., U. Ill., 1950. Head editing sect. Ill. Geol. Survey, Urbana, 1950-55; editing supr. coll. dept. McGraw-Hill Book Co., N.Y.C., 1956-59; head editing sect. Intersci. Publs., N.Y.C., 1959-61; mng. editor, prin. officer W.A. Benjamin, Inc., N.Y.C., 1961-64; pres. Sci. Bookcrafters, Hastings-on-Hudson, N.Y., 1964-72; pres. Service to Pubs., Lewisburg, Pa., 1972—. Home: Route 1 Winfield PA 17889 Office: 30 Brown St Lewisburg PA 17837

ZEIGLER, ELISABETH EBERHARD, judge; b. Los Angeles, Apr. 13, 1917; d. Ray Charles and Lucy (Dorival) Eberhard; A.B. magna cum laude, U. So. Cal., 1938, J.D., 1941; m. John H. Zeigler, Dec. 25, 1941. Admitted to Cal. bar, 1942; asst. to legal aide U.S. Naval Aid Sta., Seattle, 1942; enforcement atty. OPA, Seattle, 1943; mem. firm Eberhard & Zeigler, Los Angeles, 1943-49; apptd. judge Municipal Ct., Los Angeles, 1949, elected, 1956, 62, 68, presiding judge, 1959; assigned Superior Ct., Los Angeles County, 1953; apptd. judge Superior Ct. Los Angeles county, 1968-70, elected judge, 1970—. Chmn. Los Angeles County Municipal Ct. Judges Assn., 1962-63; mem. conf. Cal. judges, chmn. com. jud. ethics, 1962. Mem. Am., Los Angeles bar assns., Women Lawyer's Club, Nat. Bus. and Profl. Women, Los Angeles C. of C. (dir. women's div.), Legion Lex, Phi Beta Kappa, (pres. So. Cal. alumni 1972, 73), Alpha Delta Pi, Phi Delta Gamma (hon.), Phi Delta Delta, Phi Alpha Delta, Phi Kappa Phi, Delta Sigma Rho, Delta Kappa Gamma (hon.), Mortar Bd. Presbyn. (ruling elder; trustee). Clubs: Soroptimist (dir. found.), Ebell (Los Angeles.). Office: County Courthouse Los Angeles CA 90012

ZEIGLER, FRANCES T. MARBURG (MRS. SAMUEL J. ZEIGLER), club woman; b. nr. Falmouth, Va.; d. Edgar and Fanny (Moncure) Marburg; A.B., Vassar Coll., 1915; M.A., Radcliffe Coll., 1918; m. Samuel J. Zeigler, Sept. 18, 1915; children—Frances Landon (dec.), Samuel Howell, Edgar Landon. Newspaper woman Phila. Press, 1918-19; tchr. Sidwell Friends Sch., Washington, 1925-30; instr. pvt. schs., Pila. Devon Sch. for Girls, Agnes Irwin Sch., 1930-38; social worker Asso. Charities, Cambridge, 1916-18; White-Williams Found., Phila., 1932-33. Pres. Brit. War Relief, 1939-41, Am. Com.

for Russian War Relief, 1941-42; mem. woman's com. Nat. Symphony Orch. Mem. D.A.R. (dir. Army Navy chpt.), Nat. Soc. Colonial Dames, Huguenot Soc., Phi Beta Kappa. Episcopalian (mem. bd.). Clubs: National Democratic Woman's; Vassar; Radcliffe; Belle Haven Women's; Alexandria Woman's. Home: 4360 Ivymount Ct Annandale VA 22003

ZEILER, JEANNETTE TUCCI (MRS. LEONARD A. ZEILER), social worker; b. Syracuse, N.Y., Nov. 13, 1936; d. Angelo and Jennie Tucci; B.A. in Psychology, Syracuse U., 1958, M.S.W., 1964; m. Leonard A. Zeiler, Sept. 14, 1968. Jr. caseworker childrens div. Onondaga County Dept. Social Services, Syracuse, 1962-63, sr. caseworker, 1965-68, supr. homemaker service, 1968-70, supr. home services, day care, home finding, 1970—. Del. Nat. Child Welfare Conf., 1965; mem. program com. N.Y. State Welfare Conf., 1967; mem. planning com. N.Y. State Conf.-Council for Homemaker-Home Health Aides, 1969; chmn. Upstate N.Y. Homemaker Conf., 1969. Served to 1st lt. USMCR, 1958-61. Mem. Nat. Assn. Social Workers, Acad. Certified Social Workers. Home: 2499 Country Lane Baldwinsville NY 13027 Office: 600 S State St Syracuse NY 13202

ZEIS, SISTER RITA CELIA, psychotherapist, educator; b. St. Louis, Aug. 18, 1926; d. Frank Xavier and Mary Catherine (Brune) Zeis; B.S., Webster Coll., 1953; Ed.M., St. Louis U., 1957; Ph.D., Catholic U., 1964; postgrad. U. Notre Dame, U. Minn., U. Mo., U. Md. Joined Sch. Sisters Notre Dame, 1945; tchr. elementary sch., 1948-51; tchr. chemistry and guidance counseling Rosati-Kain High Sch., St. Louis, 1953-60; prof. psychology and edn. Notre Dame Coll., St. Louis, 1964—. Charter mem., team, mem. Traveling Workshops on Race Relations, 1965-68; cons. Sojourner Truth Home and Elementary Sch. NSF grantee, 1955, 59-60; Nat. Inst. Mental Health fellow, 1963-64; NSF Chataqua grantee, 1971, 72, 73. Mem. Am. Psychol. Assn., Psychologists Interested in Religious Issues, Soc. Encouragement Sci. Research, Sigma Xi, Psi Chi. Contbr. articles to profl. jours. Home: 320 E Ripa St St Louis MO 63125

ZEITNER, JUNE CULP (MRS. C. ALBERT ZEITNER), museum ofcl.; b. Bay City, Mich.; d. Vernon H. and Pearl (Ailes) Culp; B.S., No. State Coll., 1936; m. C. Albert Zeitner, June 25, 1941. Prin., Todd County High Sch., 1939-43, supt., 1945-46; dir., co-owner Zeitner Geol. Mus., Mission, S.D., 1950—; contbg. editor Earth Sci., 1962-67; contbg. editor Lapidary Jour., 1967—, columnist, 1970—. Continuing Edn. Center tchr. Pan Am. U., Edinburg, Tex., 1973—; lectr., judge Nat. Gem and Mineral Shows, 1962—; emcee Nat. Bull. Editors Breakfast, 1969-73. Publicity dir. Am. Fedn. Scholarship Found., 1971-73, elector, 1973. Mem. Am. (dir. 1968-69, publs. chmn. 1968—), Midwest (pres. 1968-69, hon. life mem., awards chmn. 1973) fedns. mineral. socs., Soc. Vertebrate Paleontology, Badlands, West River earth sci. socs., Sioux Empire Gem and Mineral Soc., Rio Grande Valley Mineral Soc. Methodist. Author: Midwest Gem Trails, 1956; Appalachian Mineral and Gem Trails, 1968; South Dakota, 1969; Southwest Mineral and Gem Trails, 1972. Contbr. chpts. to Agates of North America, 1965. Home: Box 69 Mission SD 57555 also 2205 S Hwy 281 Edinburg TX 78539

ZELENY, MARJORIE PFEIFFER (MRS. CHARLES ELLINGSON ZELENY), psychologist; b. Balt., Mar. 31, 1924; d. Lloyd Armitage and Mable (Willian) Pfeiffer; B.A., U. Md., 1947; M.S., U. Ill., 1949, postgrad., 1951-54; m. Charles Ellingson Zeleny, Dec. 11, 1950; children—Ann Douglas, Charles Timberlake. Vocational counseling psychologist VA, Balt., 1947-48; asst. U. Ill. at Urbana, 1948-50, research asso. Bur. Research, 1952-53; chief psychologist dept. neurology and psychiatry Ohio State U. Coll. Medicine, Columbus, 1950-51; research psychologist, cons., Tucson, Washington, 1954—. Mem. Am., D.C. psychol. assns., A.A.A.S., Soc. for Psychol. Study Social Issues, D.A.R., Mortar Bd., Delta Delta Delta, Sigma Delta Epsilon, Psi Chi, Sigma Tau Epsilon. Episcopalian. Home: 6825 Wemberly Way McLean VA 22101

ZELEZNOCK, JANET GARDNER, educator; b. Roanoke, Va., Feb. 25, 1933; d. George Shackford and Edna Elizabeth (Equi) Gardner; B.S., St. Francis Coll., 1956; NSF grantee Clark U., summer 1960; M.A., Duquesne U., 1964; m. Richard M. Zeleznock. Research chemist Dow Corning Corp., Midland, Mich., 1956-58; instr. math. St. Francis Coll., Loretto, Pa., 1958-61; asst. prof. math. La Roche Coll., Allison Park, Pa., 1964-67, Mary Washington Coll., Fredericksburg, Va., 1967—. Mem. Mary Washington Hosp. Aux. Mem. Math. Assn. Am., Nat. Council Tchrs. Math., Delta Epsilon Sigma. Roman Catholic. Home: 127 Bell Rd Fredericksburg VA 22401

ZELLERBACH, MERLA (MRS. FREDERICK ALLAN GOERNER), journalist; b. San Francisco, Aug. 27, 1930; d. Elliot Maurice and Lottie (Greenfield) Burstein; student Stanford, 1949-50; m. Frederick Allan Goerner, Jan. 4, 1968; 1 son, Gary Allen. Feature columnist San Francisco Chronicle, 1961—; television panelist ABC's game show Oh My Word, 1965-70; lectr. journalism Women in Media, Identity Crises, San Francisco, 1961—. Staff mem. Am. Friends Service Com., 1959; founder, pres. San Francisco Sponsors, 1960-61, Singles Orgn., 1966-67. Vice pres. San Francisco Women's Round Table; bd. dirs. Nat. Orgn. for Non-Parents. Queen of Mardi Gras, San Francisco, 1957. Club: Burke Tennis. Author: Love in a Dark House, 1961. Contbr. articles nat. mags. Home: 24 Presidio Terrace San Francisco CA 94118 Office: San Francisco Chronicle Fifth and Mission Sts San Francisco CA 94119

ZELLERS, THELMA FAYE, mcht.; b. Kingfisher, Okla., Sept. 26, 1911; d. Adam Ray and Ethel May (Batterton) Zellers; A.A., Cottey Coll., 1931; diploma Enid Bus. Coll., 1932; B.S., Central State U., Edmond, Okla., 1933; diploma in Jewelry Store Mgmt., N.Y. U., 1964. Tchr., Oilton (Okla.) High Sch., 1933-34; sch. tchr., Cushing, Okla., 1934-38; faculty Enid Bus. Coll., summers 1937; owner Zellers Jewelers, Guymon, Okla., 1948—. Bd. dirs. Okla. Arthritis Assn. Mem. Okla. Retail Jewelers Assn. (v.p., dir.), D.A.R. (rec. sec. Okla. 1968-70, state transp. chmn. 1970-72, nat. vice-chmn. patriot index com. 1968-74, organizing regent High Plains chpt. 1963), Am. Assn. U. Women (chpt. sec. 1971-72), Daus. Colonial Wars (state 3d v.p. 1968-71), Colonial Dames 17th Century (state v.p. Tulsa chpt. 1969-70), Magna Charta Dames, Ams. of Royal Descent, Phi Theta Kappa, Tau Theta Kappa. Republican. Mem. Christian Ch. Mem. Order Eastern Star. Home: 815 W 5th St Guymon OK 73942 Office: 415 N Main St Guymon OK 73942

ZELT, BEVERLY ANN, physician; b. Ft. Wayne, Ind., June 2, 1937; d. Rudolph F. and Martha (Fuchshuber) Zelt; A.B., Ball State Tchrs. Coll., 1959; M.D., Ind. U., 1963, M.Anesthesiology, 1969; m. Scott C. Yew, Sept. 15, 1962 (div. Mar. 1966); children—Kenneth Scott, Kristine Ann. Intern, Helene Fuld Hosp., Trenton, N.J., 1963-64; psychiatrist Madison (Ind.) State Hosp., 1964-66; resident Ind. U. Med. Center, Indpls., 1966-69; anesthesiologist Burns Clin. Med. Center, Petoskey, Mich., 1969—; med. dir. Sch. Inhalation Therapy, North Central Mich. Coll., Petoskey, 1969—, asst. prof., 1969—. Diplomate Am. Bd. Anesthesiologists. Mem. Am., Internat. socs. anesthesiologists, Audubon Soc., Sierra Club, Alpha Omega Alpha. Home: Box 117 Kilborn Dr Petoskey MI 49770 Office: Burns Clinic Med Center 560 W Mitchell St Petoskey MI 49770

ZEMAN, FRANCES JUNE, educator; b. Cleve., Mar. 5, 1925; d. Frank Joseph and Mary (Graham) Zeman; B.S., Western Res. U., 1946, M.S., 1957; Ph.D., Ohio State U., 1963. Hosp. dietitian Cleve. City Hosp., 1947-57; asst. prof. Kent (O.) State U., 1957-63; prof. dept. nutrition U. Cal. at Davis, 1963—. Home: 1102 Colby Dr Davis CA 95616

ZENAR, LINDA ALICE (MRS. WILLIAM JOHN BUX), educator; b. Ravenna, O., Sept. 17, 1947; d. Joseph and Virginia Alice (Cackowski) Zenar; B.S., Ohio State U., 1969, M.A. (Dept. Health, Edn. and Welfare grad. fellow), 1970; m. William John Bux, Feb. 13, 1971. Primary spl. edn. tchr. Kent (O.) City Pub. Schs., 1970-71; intermediate spl. edn. tchr. Harlandale Ind. Sch. Dist., San Antonio, 1971-72; intermediate spl. edn. tchr. Dept. Def. Overseas Dependent Schs., Okinawa, Japan, 1972-73, adult edn. tchr. math., English and govt., 1973, primary spl. edn. tchr., 1973—. Spl. edn. classroom demonstration tchr. Kent State U. Coll. Edn., 1970-71. Mem. Am. Assn. Mental Deficiency, Nat. Assn. for Retarded Children, Council for Exceptional Children, Mortar Bd., Pi Lambda Theta, Kappa Delta Pi. Home: 508 Roosevelt Av Kent OH 44240

ZENGER, DORIS BAKER (MRS. EDWIN L. SHERRILL, JR.), pediatrician; b. East Hampton, N.Y., Sept. 5, 1919; d. Joseph and Maude Sherrill (Bassett) Zenger; B.S., U. Ky., 1941; M.D., U. Mich., 1948; m. Edwin L. Sherrill, Jr., June 19, 1952; children—Edwin L. III, Linus Z. Intern, Madison (Wis.) Gen. Hosp., 1948-49; pediatric intern Bellevue Hosp., N.Y.C., 1949-50; asst. resident Willard Parker Hosp., N.Y.C., 1950; extern, outpatient dept. Boston Children's Hosp., 1951; practice medicine specializing in pediatrics, East Hampton, N.Y., 1951—; mem. staff Southampton Hosp. Mem. A.M.A., Suffolk County Med. Soc. Address: Box 789 Hither Lane East Hampton NY 11937

ZENICH, MARGRETT BARTON, librarian; b. Mead, Okla., Dec. 4, 1915; d. John Danridge and Inez (Hightower) Barton; student A. and M. Engring. Sch., 1943; B.A., Southeastern State Coll., 1938; postgrad. San Jose State Coll., 1947; B.S. in L.S., U. Okla., 1951; spl. student Tex. Western Coll., U. Tex., 1965; children by previous marriage—Ruth Ann Linder, Peter Barton Linder, Mary Antoinette Camillo. Tchr. Big Cabin, Okla., 1938-39; Carnegie br. librarian, pub. sch. library, Oklahoma City, 1946-51; spl. services librarian 4th Army White Sands Missile Range, 1951-55, chief tech. library br., 1955-68; chief Sci. and Tech. Information div. Office Chief Engrs., Washington, 1968—, also mgr. U.S. Army research project; tech. information support activities, 1962—. Mem. Adj. Gen.'s adv. com. librarian career program, 1964, Comdg. Gen.'s equal opportunity com., 1965, Task Force on Role of Library in Information Systems, Fed. Library Com.; army rep. Mil. Librarians Long Range Planning; career field program coordinator, 1966. Mem. Am. Ordnance Assn. (sec. Rio Grande chpt. 1963), Rio Grande Spl. Library Assn. (treas. 1957—, v.p. 1964-65, pres. 1966-67, adv. council 1964—), Am. Soc. Testing and Materials, A.L.A. (sec.-treas. documentation div. 1958-60; chmn. mil. librarians), Nat. Micro-film Assn., Humane Soc. (mem. El Paso County bd. dirs.), A.A.A.S., Am. Assn. U. Women. Baptist. Clubs: Garden, Gemcraftaer, and Explorer. Home: 4712 Poplar Dr Alexandria VA 22310 Office: Office Chief Engrs US Army Sci and Tech Information Div Washington DC 20314

ZENN, FAY MCWHORTER (MRS. PHILIP ZENN II), club woman; b. Roopville, Ga., Aug. 2, 1916; d. Lorenza B. and Agnes (Ward) McWhorter; R.N., Middle Ga. Hosp., 1937; B.B.A., U. Miami, Coral Gables, Fla., 1970; m. Philip Zenn II, Feb. 28, 1972; children by previous marriage—William McWhorter, Robert Holder. Supt. hosp., Bremen, Ga., 1938-39. Pres. Fla. Fedn. Garden Clubs, Inc., 1959-61; pres. Fla. chpt. 99's, 1944; editor Fla. Gardener, 1955-57; pres. Fla. Assn. Parliamentarians, 1961-63; past pres. Fla. Atlantic Music, Inc. Mem. Fla. Fedn. Garden Clubs, Nat. Council State Garden Clubs (life mem.; bd. dirs.), N. Broward Soc. of Symphony (life), Women's Aux. Oral Sch. of Ft. Lauderdale (life), Fort Lauderdale Ballet, Opera Guild Fort Lauderdale. Author: Program Patterns, 1958; The New Program Patterns, 1961; Public Relations and Publicity Pointers. Home: 1100 S Ocean Blvd Pompano Beach FL 33062

ZENO, PHYLLIS ANN WOLFE (MRS. NORMAN ZENO), editor; b. Cleve., Feb. 16, 1926; d. Oliver MacKenzie and Helen Virginia (Shipley) Wolfe; student U. Wis., 1944-45, Am. Theatre Wing, 1948; m. Thomas Williams, July 28, 1945 (div. Jan. 1958); children—Richard, Linda (Mrs. Harold Aber), Leslie; m. Norman Zeno, June 10, 1960. Editor, North Shore Club Life Mag., Manhasset, N.Y., 1971-74. Lyric and music writer for indsl. shows including Buick Announcement Show, 1972, 73, 74, Zenith, 1959-74, Admiral, 1965-74, DuPont, 1970-73. Mem. A.S.C.A.P., Cow Neck Hist. Soc. (trustee 1961-67), Alpha Chi Omega. Christian Scientist. Composer: This Is An Opening, 1967; Friends, Relative and Parents, 1969; That's A Very Good Sign, 1968; How Do You Open a Show, 1971; Bet You Never Guessed, 1970; We're Through, 1968; We Never Sing Openings, 1970. Home: 8834 Bay Pointe Dr Tampa FL 33615

ZENS, MILDRED IRENE LARSEN (MRS. CLARENCE MICHAEL ZENS), librarian; b. Racine, Wis., Sept. 14, 1917; d. Lars Anderson and Esther Bolette (Skow) Larsen; student Marquette U., 1936-38; B.A., Lawrence U., 1940; M.A., Catholic U., 1963; postgrad. U. Wis., 1941; m. Clarence Michael Zens, May 24, 1944; children—Michael Louis, Karen Larson. Tchr., librarian, Calumet, Mich., 1940-41; Frank McKee High Sch., Muskegon, Mich., 1941-43; reporter Jour. Times, Racine, 1944; librarian Am. Alumni Council, Washington, 1963-64; Gonzaga Coll. High Sch., Washington, 1964-74, Western High Sch., Washington, 1974—. Area dir. Girl Scout ann. cookie drive, 1958-59; dir. County Cub Scouts, 1955-56; organizer Friends of the Library, Fairfax City, Va., 1955-57. Mem. Am., D.C. (publicity dir., 1968-71), Catholic (area dir. 1967-72), library assns., D.C. Assn. Sch. Libraries, Am. Assn. U. Women, Sch. Libraries Assn. Home: 406 A St SE Washington DC 20003 Office: 35th and R St NW Washington DC 20007

ZERA, GRETCHEN FRIEDA SCHRAMM (MRS. STANLEY A. ZERA), social worker; b. Flint, Mich.; d. Charles F. and Pauline (Klemach) Schramm; B.A., Mich. State U., 1936; M.A., Mich. State U., 1962, M.S.W., 1965; student U. Mich., 1935-37; m. Stanley A. Zera, July 17, 1946; children—Stanley A., Paula M. Social worker Mich. Childrens Aid Soc., Flint, 1941-43, U.S. Navy, San Francisco, 1944-46, Whaley Home, Flint, Mich., 1946; girls probation officer Genesee County Probate Ct., Flint, 1958-61; sch. social worker Genesee Intermediate Sch. Dist., Flint, 1961-64, chief social worker, 1966—; sch. social worker Carman Sch. Dist., Flint, 1965-66. Field supr. Mich. State U. Sch. Social Work, 1969—, U. Mich. Sch. Social Work, 1972—. Mem. com. on unwed parents Council Social Agys., Flint, 1969—. Mem. Am. Orthopsychiat. Assn., Nat. Assn. Social Workers (br. sec. 1967), N.E.A., Mich., Genesee Intermediate edn. assns., Mich. Sch. Social Workers Assn. (treas. 1969), Pi Omicron. Baptist. Home: 1159 Maple Krest Dr Flint MI 48504 Office: 2413 W Maple Rd Flint MI 48507

ZIBBEL, FREDA WILHELMINIA (MRS. ARTHUR JOHN ZIBBEL), banker; b. Oak Harbor, O., Oct. 4, 1919; d. Charles Henry and Minnie Elizabeth (Miller) Miller; grad. high sch.; m. Arthur John Zibbel, May 30, 1941; children—Marjorie Ann, Charles John. With Nat. Bank of Oak Harbor, 1940-47, 61—, asst. v.p. 1967—, sec. bd. dirs., 1968—; sec. St. John's Evang. Luth. Ch., Oak Harbor, 1951-61. Mem. Am. Inst. Banking (chmn. women's chpt. 1968-70). Lutheran. Home: 248 E Water St Oak Harbor OH 43449 Office: 147 W Water St Oak Harbor OH 43449

ZIBILICH, BERNICE GOODMAN (MRS. ROBERT J. ZIBILICH), librarian; b. San Antonio; d. Benjamin and Fannie (Ludwig) Goodman; B.A. cum laude, Our Lady of the Lake Coll., 1941; M.A., 1947; m. Robert J. Zibilich, Dec. 20, 1952; children—Franz Ludwig, Gretchen Gwen. Library asst. New Orleans Pub. Library, 1945-46, librarian, 1947-61, head children's services, 1961—; prof. Children's lit. Delgado Coll., spring 1974; lectr. ednl. orgns. on library facilities and services. Coordinator U.S. State Dept. Open Door, 1966-69. Bd. dirs. Council of the Arts for Children, Puppet Playhouse. Recipient Community Vol. Service awards, 1967, 68, 69, 70; Outstanding Alumni award Our Lady of Lake Coll., 1969; Pub. Service award Assn. Childhood Edn. Internat., 1970, others. Mem. Am., Southwestern (publicity chmn., 1971-72), La. (pub. relations com., 1971-73), Catholic library assns., League of Women Voters. Clubs: New Orleans Library (sec. 1961-62, v.p., pres.-elect 1974—), Vista Shores Country (New Orleans). Home: 1350 Filmore Av New Orleans LA 70122 Office: 219 Loyola Av New Orleans LA 70140

ZICH, AMANDA QUACKENBUSH (MRS. GERALD ZICH), agr. editor; b. Hightstown, N.J., Oct. 23, 1920; d. Earl Culver and Alice Amanda (Castner) Quackenbush; student U. Del., 1939-40; Litt.B., Douglass Coll., 1942; m. Gerald Emil Zich, May 7, 1955. Copywriter N.J. Dept. Agr., Trenton, 1942-44; editor Conn. Agr. Expt. Sta., New Haven, 1944-55; with div. information N.J. Dept. Agr., Trenton, 1957—, sr. pub. information asst., 1968-70, head press and publ. sect., 1970-73, coordinator agrl. information, 1973—. Bucks county editor N.J. Farm and Garden Mag., 1956-57; information officer United Milk Producers, Trenton, 1956-57. Mem. Am. Assn. Agrl. Coll. Editors (nat. membership chmn. 1951-52), N.J. Agrl. Soc. Contbr. to newspapers, mags., profl. jours. Home: 76 Franklin Corner Rd Lawrenceville NJ 08648 Office: 1 Dept Agr Trenton NJ 08625

ZICK, GLENNA SCHOFIELD (MRS. CLARENCE A. ZICK), ins. assn. exec.; b. Teton, Ida., May 19, 1923; d. Leo H. and Hazel (Richman) Schofield; student LDS Bus. Coll., 1940; m. Clarence A. Zick, Jan. 22, 1946; children—Marilyn, Steven. Casualty underwriter Kolob Corp., Salt Lake City; office mgr. Seeley Co., Los Angeles; pvt. sec. Republic Indemnity; with Independent Ins. Agents & Brokers Assn., Los Angeles, 1967—, exec. dir., 1969—. Home: 1980 Cummings Dr Los Angeles CA 90027 Office: 1541 Wilshire Blvd Los Angeles CA 90017

ZIEGLER, CAROLYN HILLES (MRS. JOHN B. ZIEGLER), physician; b. Alliance, O., June 30, 1909; d. Ross P. and Effie M. (Hoiles) Hilles; A.B., Mt. Union Coll., 1930; M.S., Ohio State U., 1938, M.D., 1948; m. John B. Ziegler, Sept. 6, 1947. Intern, Mt. Carmel Hosp., Columbus, O., 1949-50; resident Univ. Hosps., Columbus, 1950-52; practice medicine, specializing in anesthesiology, Columbus, 1952; asst. dir. dept. anesthesia Ohio State U., 1952-59, instr. dept. surgery, 1952-53, asst. prof., 1953-57, asso. prof., 1957-59; dir. dept. anesthesia VA Hosp., Pitts., 1959-61; asst. prof. dept. surgery U. Pitts., 1959-61; chief anesthesia Meml. Hosp., Marysville, O., 1961—. Diplomate Am. Bd. Anesthesiology. Mem. Am. Soc. Anesthesiologists, Sigma Xi, Alpha Xi Delta. Contbr. articles profl. jours. Home: Route 4 Box 7 Marysville OH 43040 Office: 79 E State St Columbus OH 43215

ZIEGLER, LILLIAN LENORE (MRS. GEORGE ZIEGLER), newspaper editor; b. Sparland, Ill., Apr. 17, 1930; d. Clifford C. and Mary E. (Watkins) Gibbs; student Wesleyan U., 1949-50; m. George Ziegler, Jan. 5, 1951; children—Linda L., George Douglas. Head bookkeeper Watercott Dept. store, Henry, Ill., 1954-59; with Bradford (Ill.) Republican weekly newspaper, 1961-75, editor, mgr., 1966-75; editor Stark Co. News, Toulon, Ill., 1968-75, foreman advt. dept., 1966—. Del. to Nat. 4-H Club Congress, 1950. Mem. Bradford Woman's League (pres. 1963-64). Methodist. Home: 1130 Main Henry IL 61537 Office: 120 N Peoria Bradford IL 61421

ZIEGLER, LORENE ELIZABETH, ret. educator; b. Trenton, Ill., Jan. 13, 1909; d. Joseph and Ruby (Emig) Ziegler; B.Ed., Ill. State U., 1942; M.A., Northwestern U., 1947; Ed.D., Columbia, 1963. Tchr. rural sch., Trenton, 1927-31, Port Byron, Ill., 1932-33; tchr., prin. elementary sch., Breese, Ill., 1933-34, Rossville, Ill., 1934-42; tchr. Melrose Park (Ill.) Sch., 1942-47; supervising tchr. Lab Sch., Eastern Ill. U., Charleston, 1947-69, prof. edn., 1969-74. Mem. Assn. Tchr. Educators (state pres. 1963-64), Internat. Reading Assn., Nat. Council Tchrs. English, Kappa Delta Pi, Delta Kappa Gamma. Mem. United Ch. of Christ. Home: 1547 3d St Charleston IL 61920

ZIELINSKI, MARY VANDERMAN (MRS. JOHN M. ZIELINSKI), journalist; b. Willimantic, Conn., Aug. 22, 1943; d. William R. and Leona J. (Marrotte) Vanderman; B.S., Willimantic State Coll., 1963; M.A., U. Ia.; m. John M. Zielinski, Sept. 18, 1965; children—William R., Zane L. Grad. asst. U. Ia., 1965; reviewer, feature writer, city desk Jour. Co., Milw., 1966-67; legislative reporter, mag. writer The Times, Hartford, Conn., 1967-69; feature writer The Gazette, Cedar Rapids, Ia., 1969—. Co-dir. New Chautauqua, 1973. Mem. Ia. Press Photographers, Am. Assn. U. Women. Home: 105 B Av Kalona IA 52247 Office: Box C Kalona IA 52247

ZIEVERINK, SARA ELIZABETH, physician; b. Cin., Aug. 10, 1943; d. William Henry and Bessie (Donelan) Zieverink; B.S., Purdue U., 1965; M.D., Vanderbilt U., 1968. Intern in pathology Vanderbilt U. Hosp., Nashville, 1968-69; med. intern, Jewish Hosp., Cin., 1969-70, emergency room physician, 1970-72; resident psychiatry Washington U., St. Louis, 1972-73. Mem. Acad. Medicine Cin., Ohio State Med. Assn., Am. Coll. Emergency Physicians, Purdue, Vanderbilt alumni assns. Home: 3427 Locust Lane Cincinnati OH 45238

ZIFF, RUTH (MRS. SOLOMON ZIFF), advt. agy. exec.; b. N.Y.C., May 26, 1924; d. Herman and Lena (Medoff) Baron; B.A., Hunter Coll., 1944; M.A. (Acad. scholar), Columbia, 1948; Ph.D. candidate, City U. N.Y.; m. Solomon Ziff, Mar. 29, 1942; children—Charles Elliot, Ellen Barbara. Dir. psychol. barometer and link audit pub. attitudes Psychol. Corp., N.Y.C., 1944-49; v.p., mgr. research Benton & Bowles, Inc., N.Y.C., 1950—. Named Advt. Woman of Year, Am. Advt. Fedn., 1973. Mem. Advt. Women of New York (1st v.p. 1970), Am. Marketing Assn., Am. Assn. Pub. Opinion Research, Am. Psychol. Assn., Am. Sociol. Assn., Market Research Council, Phi Beta Kappa, Alpha Chi Alpha. Contbr. articles profl. jours. Home: 3 Valley Lane Chappaqua NY 10514 Office: 909 3d Av New York City NY 10022

ZILE, MAIJA HELENE (MRS. ZIGURDS L. ZILE), biochemist; b. Riga, Latvia, Aug. 3, 1929; d. Juris and Helene (Vitols) Vilums; came to U.S., 1949, naturalized, 1955; B.S., U. Md., 1954; M.S., U. Wis., 1956, Ph.D., 1959; m. Zigurds L. Zile, June 11, 1955; children—Mara, Anda, Inga. Postdoctoral fellow Enzyme Inst., U.

Wis., Madison, 1959; research fellow dept. biology Harvard, 1959-61; project asso. dept. biochemistry U. Wis., 1961—. Mem. Am. Nutrition Soc., Sigma Xi, Sigma Delta Epsilon. Contbr. articles to profl. jours. Home: 5101 Odana Rd Madison WI 53711 Office: Dept Biochemistry U Wis Madison WI 53706

ZILLY, MARY FRANCES ANNING (MRS. ROBERT ZILLY), polit. orgn. exec.; b. Aurora, Ill., Feb. 25, 1924; d. Francis Abner and Olga Mathilda (Olsen) Anning; student Knox Coll., 1941-43, U. Ill., 1943-44; m. Robert George Zilly, Oct. 2, 1943; children—Ann, Michael, James. Tchr. primary grades Pekin (Ill.) Community Schs., 1945-46; pres. League Women Voters, Batavia, Ill., 1953, St. Joseph, Mich., 1963-65; mem. state bd., 1965-68, mem. Neb. state bd., 1968-71, state pres., Lincoln, Neb., 1971—. Chairperson elect Citizen's Adv. Com. Dept. Rds. Mem. Pi Beta Phi. Conglist. (bd. deacons 1965-67). Home: 2525 Lafayette St Lincoln NE 68502 Office: 1614 N St Lincoln NE 68508

ZIMAN, ANNALEE, grievance adminstr.; b. Eugene, Ore., Nov. 25, 1943; d. Louis and Janice Julia (Wright) Ziman; B.A., Ariz. State U., 1966, M.A., 1969. Tchr. Phoenix Union High Sch., 1966-70; information specialist Nat. Edn. Assn. Profl. Rights and Responsibilities Commn., Washington, 1970-71; grievance adminstr., rep. for profs. and profls. State U. N.Y., Albany, 1972-73; negotiations specialist Thealan Assos., Inc., Albany, 1973—. Central regional dir. Ariz. Classroom Tchrs. Assn., 1969-70; negotiator Phoenix Union High Sch. Dist., 1968-70, N.Y. State United Tchrs. Assn., 1973; tchr. YW-YMCA experimental teen-age program, Washington, 1970-71. Mem. Rep. Educators in Politics, Nat. Council Tchrs. English, Nat. Edn. Profl. Staff Assn., N.E.A., Nat. Edn. Field Staff Assn., Nat. High Ed Staff Assn., Albany Panhellenic (del., publicity chmn. 1971—), Kappa Kappa Iota (sec. 1969-70), Alpha Sigma Alpha (pres. 1963-64). Home: 56-1 Woodlake Rd N Albany NY 12203 Office: 15 Computer Dr W Albany NY 12205

ZIMET, SARA FLORENCE GOODMAN (MRS. CARL NORMAN ZIMET), educator; b. Newark, July 26, 1929; d. Samuel Morris and Esther (Trop) Goodman; B.S., N.Y.U., 1950; M.A., Syracuse U., 1952; Ed.D., U. Denver, 1968; m. Carl Norman Zimet, June 4, 1950; children—Andrew Leon, Gregory David. Kindergarten tchr., North Syracuse, N.Y., 1950-52, Palo Alto (Cal.) Sch., 1953-54; instr. edn. So. Conn. State Coll., New Haven, 1963; lectr. edn. U. Denver, 1966-69, Temple Buell Coll., Denver, 1969; research asso. U. Colo. Med. Center, Denver, 1963-67, instr. psychiatry, 1967-70, asst. prof. psychiatry, research project dir., 1970-73, staff psychologist Day Care Center, 1973—. Nat. Inst. Mental Health research grantee, 1968; Nat. Inst. Edn. grantee, 1973. Mem. edn. com. Colo. Gov.'s Commn. on Status of Women, 1971-73. Mem. Soc. for Research in Child Devel., Delta Kappa Pi. Sr. author: A Teacher's Guide for Selecting Stories of Interest to Children, 1968. Editor: What Children Read in School: Critical Analyses of First Grade Reading Textbooks, 1972. Home: 4325 E 6th Avenue Pkwy Denver CO 80220

ZIMMER, LYNDA LOUISE, journalist; b. Tucson, May 8, 1946; d. Lloyd and Vivian (Dehn) Cuqua; B.A. in Journalism, U. Ariz., 1968; m. Robert Lee Zimmer, Sept. 12, 1969. Reporter, Ariz. Daily Star, Tucson, 1967-68; broadcast and news editor, corr. Asso. Press, Phoenix and Tucson, 1968-69; reporter Ark. Democrat, Little Rock, 1970—. Mem. Women in Communications, Sigma Delta Chi (dir. Little Rock chpt. 1972-74), Chi Omega. Home: 409 N Midland Av Little Rock AR 72205 Office: Capitol and Scott Sts Little Rock AR 72203

ZIMMER, SUZANNE CHASAN (MRS. BERNARD ZIMMER), social worker; b. Bronx, N.Y., Sept. 4, 1928; d. Nathan and Jennie (Cohen) Chasan; B.S., N.Y. U., 1949, M.A., 1952; m. Bernard Zimmer, Feb. 10, 1950; 1 dau., Susan. Dir., Fuld Neighborhood Nursery, Newark, 1951-55; exec. dir. Community Day Nursery, East Orange, N.J., 1957—. Project dir. Head Start Community Service Council of the Oranges, East Orange, 1965; mem. N.J. Bd. Pub. Welfare, 1966—, Eastern regional conf. Child Welfare League Am., 1966—; chmn. N.J. Day Care Adv. Com., 1963-66; chmn. Timothy J. Still program Upsala Coll., East Orange, 1971-74; day care cons. Essex County Council Jewish Women, 1970; pres. Day Care Coordinating Council Essex County, 1973—. Bd. dirs. (hon.) Fuld Neighborhood House. Mem. Nat. Assn. Social Workers. Home: 131 Sagamore Rd Millburn NJ 07041 Office: 38 Freeman Av East Orange NJ 07018

ZIMMERMAN, BARBARA ROLLINS (MRS. CHARLES VERNON ZIMMERMAN), speech therapist; b. Portsmouth, O., Oct. 6, 1933; d. Elbert Newton and Oda Marie (Phillips) Rollins; B.S., Bowling Green State U., 1954; M.S., Wayne State U., 1963; Ph.D., Ohio U., 1968; m. Charles Vernon Zimmerman, Sept. 15, 1953; children—Michael, Craig, Tad. Speech correctionist in Mich., 1957-58; elementary tchr. Army Sch. System, 1958-59; spl. edn. cooordinator in Mich., 1963-65; prof., dir. Speech and Hearing Center Western Ill. U., Macomb, 1968-73; dir. Regional Speech and Hearing Center, Shreveport, La., 1973—. Lang. cons. Peoria (Ill.) Evaluation Center. Mem. exec. bd. Heart Fund. Neurol. and Sensory Diseases Fed. grantee, 1966-68. Mem. Am., Ill. (chmn. editorial com.) speech and hearing assns., League Women Voters (exec. bd.), Phi Mu. Presbyn. (elder). Editor: Ill. Speech and Hearing Jour., 1971-73. Home: 7325 University Dr Shreveport LA 71105 Office: 3735 Blair St Shreveport LA 71104

ZIMMERMAN, DELILA MARCILEE VOJTA (MRS. ROBERT JOHN ZIMMERMAN), savs. and loan exec.; b. Falls City, Neb., Jan. 10, 1928; d. Henry and Opal Margaret (Goslen) Vojta; A.A., Mt. San Antonio Coll., 1961; B.S., Cal. State Coll., 1968; m. Robert John Zimmerman, July 9, 1949; children—Nancy Lee, Peggy Ann. Sec. escrow dept. Title Ins. & Trust Co., Los Angeles, 1946-53; asst. mgr. Pomona First Fed. Savs. & Loan Assn. (Cal.), 1953-73, asst. sec., 1962—, mgr. Alta Loma office, 1973—. Rec. sec. Pomona Community Coordinating Council; sec.-treas. Briney Water Group. Baptist. Club: Altrusa (pres. 1971-73, dir. 1973-74) (Pomona). Home: 4465 Briney Point Rd La Verne CA 91750 Office: 9634 Baseline Rd Alta Loma CA 91701

ZIMMERMAN, ELIZABETH THAYER, educator; b. Colorado Springs, Colo., Jan. 8, 1907; d. Harry Stanley and Mary Elizabeth (Brown) Thayer; B.A., U. Colo., 1928; m. Austin M. Zimmerman, Dec. 26, 1934; children—Edward Austin, John Jeffrey. Lectr. horticulture, botany, ecology Morton Arboretum, Lisle, Ill., 1956—, instr., 1961—. Rec. sec. Conservation Council Chgo., 1961—. Trustee Ill. chpt. Nature Conservancy, 1962—. Recipient Award for Horticulture, 1963, Conservation, 1965; Eloise Payne Luquer medal Garden Club Am., 1971. Mem. Chgo. Hort. Soc. (dir.), Delta Gamma. Home: Brae Burn Farm Barrington Hills PO Algonquin IL 60102

ZIMMERMAN, ELSBETH CLARE (BETTY), broadcasting co. exec.; b. Winnipeg, Man., Can.; d. W. Harry and Elizabeth (Gillies) Zimmerman; B.A., U. Man., 1945. Liaison officer internat. distbn. Nat. Film Bd. Can., 1947-51; producer, dir. Crawley Films, 1951-58; radio producer Canadian Broadcasting Corp., 1958-59; TV producer Canadian Broadcasting Corp., 1960-64, dir. overseas and fgn. relations, 1967—. Mem. Zonta Internat. Writer Children's plays. Home: 52 Alexander St Ottawa ON Canada Office: 1500 Bronson St Ottawa ON Canada

ZIMMERMAN, HELENE LORETTA, educator; b. Rochester, N.Y., Feb. 26, 1933; d. Henry Charles and Loretta (Hobert) Zimmerman; B.S., State U. N.Y. at Albany, 1953, M.S., 1959; Ph.D., (Delta Kappa Gamma grantee 1968), U. N.D., 1969. Tchr., chmn. bus. dept. Williamson Central Sch. (N.Y.), 1953-67; asst. prof. vocational edn. U. Ky., Lexington, 1969-70; asso. prof. bus. edn. Central Mich. U., Mt. Pleasant, 1970-74, prof., 1974—. Cons. pub. vocational schs. Mem. Internat. Soc. Bus. Edn., Nat., Mich., Catholic, North-Central bus. edn. assns., Eastern Bus. Tchrs. Assn., Bus. Tchrs. Assn. N.Y. State, Am. Vocational Assn. (mem. internat. edn. commn. bus. edn. individualized projects 1971-73), Am. Assn. U. Women, Delta Kappa Gamma (pres. chpt. 1974—), Delta Pi Epsilon, Pi Omega Pi. Club: Central Michigan University Faculty Women's (Mt. Pleasant). Editor Sincerely Yours jour. Bus. Tchrs. Assn. N.Y. State, 1964-67. Home: 1405 Lincoln Ct Mount Pleasant MI 48858 Office: Grawn 308 Central Mich Univ Mount Pleasant MI 48859

ZIMMERMAN, IRENE, librarian; b. Idana, Kan., Feb. 23, 1907; d. Harvey A. and Mary Catherine (Mechlin) Zimmerman; B.A., Coll. of Emporia, 1927; M.A. in Spanish, U. Chgo., 1937; M.A. in History, Columbia, 1938; M.A. in L.S., U. Mich., 1951, Ph.D. in L.S., 1956. Tchr., Spanish, history pub. high sch., Ray, Ariz., 1928-37, South Orange, N.J., 1938-39, Spokane, Wash., 1939-41, Teaneck, N.J., 1941-43; instr. Spanish, Latin Am. lit., Latin Am. history Colby Jr. Coll., New London, N.H., 1943-48; asst. prof. Spanish, Latin Am. lit. Bucknell U., Lewisburg, Pa., 1948-50; Latin Am. specialist dept. reference and bibliography U. Fla. Library at Gainesville, 1951-67, librarian in charge Latin Am. collection, 1967—; vis. lectr. Latin Am. bibliography U. Mich. at Ann Arbor, summer 1966. Mem. A.L.A., League Women Voters, (chmn. Fla. tax structure com. 1973-74, 2d v.p. 1973-74), Latin Am. Studies Assn., Assn. Caribbean U. and Research Inst. Librarians, Am. Assn. U. Women (chmn. legislative program com. 1970-72), Am. Assn. U. Profs. (sec. 1968-69), UN Assn. U.S.A. (sec. 1961, chmn. program 1963-64), S.E. Conf. Latin Am. Studies, Pi Kappa Delta, Pi Gamma Mu, Sigma Delta Pi, Phi Alpha Theta, Beta Phi Mu. Democrat. Author: A Guide to Current Latin American Periodicals: Humanities and Social Science, 1961; Current National Bibliographies of Latin America: A State of the Art Study, 1971. Contbr. articles to profl. jours. Home: 1126 NW 33rd AV Gainesville FL 32601

ZIMMERMAN, KATHLEEN MARIE (MRS. RALPH S. IWAMOTO), artist; b. Floral Park, N.Y.; d. Harold G. and Evelyn M. (Andrade) Zimmerman; student Art Students League, N.Y.C., 1942-44, Nat. Acad. Sch. Fine Arts, N.Y.C., 1944-47, 50-54; m. Ralph S. Iwamoto, Nov. 23, 1963. Exhibited in one-woman shows Westbeth Gallery, N.Y.C., 1973, 74; exhibited in group shows at Woodstock (N.Y.) Art Gallery, 1945, Nat. Arts Club, N.Y.C., 1948-56, Emily Lowe Award Show, 1951, Contemporary Arts Gallery, N.Y.C., 1952, 60, Allied Artists Ann., N.Y.C., 1956, Art USA, 1958, Village Art Center, 1956-61, ACA Gallery, 1958, 59, Studio Gallery, 1957-60, City Center Gallery, 1960, Janet Nessler Gallery, N.Y.C., 1961, Silvermine Guild, Conn., 1962, Pioneer Gallery, Cooperstown, N.Y., 1962, 63, Audubon Artists Anns., N.Y.C., 1963, 65, 68-74, N.A.D., 1969, Nat. Assn. Women Artists Anns., N.Y.C., 1957-74, Women Artists Award Winners show, N.Y.C., 1974; represented in permanent collections at Butler Art Inst., Youngstown, O., Sheldon Swope Art Gallery, Terre Haute, Ind., Lauren Rogers Mus. Art, Laurel, Miss., U. Wyo. Art Mus., Laramie, U. Miami Lowe Art Mus., Coral Gables, Fla., N.C. Mus. Art, Raleigh; tchr. drawing and painting Midtown Sch. Art, N.Y.C., 1947-52. John F. and Anna Lee Stacey scholar, 1954. Mem. Audubon Artists, Nat. Assn. Women Artists (prizes 1957, 63, 68, 71, 72). Illustrator: (with Ralph S. Iwamoto) Diet for a Small Planet, 1971. Home: 463 West St New York City NY 10014

ZIMMERMAN, LEILA MARTHA (MRS. EDWARD B. ZIMMERMAN), museum ofcl.; b. Three Springs, Pa., Feb. 17, 1913; d. James Blaine and Mabel Lucretia (Johnson) Staines; grad. high sch.; m. Edward B. Zimmerman, June 29, 1935; children—Frances Joanne Sollers, Leila Eleanor Cassatt, Janet Louise Rudy. Salesman, J.C. Penney Co., Huntingdon, Pa., 1955-56; dir. Swigart's Antique Car Mus., Huntingdon, 1956-74. Chmn. vols. J.C. Blair Meml. Hosp., 1954-55; pres. Huntingdon Music Club, 1962-64. Club: Huntingdon Garden. Home: 1410 Washington St Huntingdon PA 16652

ZIMMERMAN, MARILYN RUTH PFLEDERER (MRS. VERNON K. ZIMMERMAN), educator; b. Peoria, Ill., Mar. 15, 1929; d. Joseph William and Emma Irene (Laukhuf) Pflederer; B. in Music, Ill. Wesleyan U., 1951; M.S., U. Ill., 1955, Ed. D., 1963; m. Vernon K. Zimmerman, Dec. 16, 1967. Instr. Ill. Wesleyan U., Bloomington, 1955-56, So. Ill. U., Carbondale, 1956-59; instr. U. Ill., Urbana, 1959-64, vis. asso. prof., 1968-70; asso. prof. Northwestern U., Evanston, Ill., 1964-68; lectr. Ill. State U., Normal, 1970-71, Nat. Acad. Arts, Champaign, 1972—; ind. music edn. cons., lectr., Champaign, Ill., 1972—. Mem. Music Educators Nat. Conf., Music Edn. Research Council, (nat. coordinator 1969-72). Author: How Children Conceptually Organize Musical Sounds, 1968; pamphlet Musical Characteristics of Children, 1971. Address: 11 Carriage Pl Champaign IL 61820

ZIMMERMAN, MARY HELEN CAMPION, lawyer; b. St. Louis, July 22, 1901; d. George Henry and Mary (McNamara) Campion; J.D., DePaul U., 1926, L.H.D., 1971; LL.D., Assumption U., Windsor, Ont., Can., 1957; m. George Herbert Zimmerman, July 7, 1926; children—Doris (Mrs. Andrew Bato), Elaine (Mrs. Rankin Peck), Jessie (Mrs. John Daniel Hitchens), Georgia (Mrs. John J. Loftus), Louis. Admitted to Md. bar, 1927, Mich. bar, 1933; practice of law, Balt., 1927-28, Grosse Pointe, Mich. also Detroit, 1933—. Mem. tax com. Detroit Bd. Commerce, 1945-51. Mem. adv. bd. Marygrove Coll., Detroit, 1961-64. Fellow Am. Bar Found.; mem. Women's Assn. Detroit Symphony, League Cath. Women, Cath. Daus. Am., Nat. Assn. Women Lawyers (past pres.), Inter-Am. (mem. council 1951-63, dir. Found. 1957—), Internat. (dep. House of Deps., London, 1950, Madrid, 1952), Am. (resolutions com. 1952-55), Detroit bar assns., State Bar Mich. (chmn. com. cooperation with Inter-Am. Bar Assn. 1958-63; trustee State Bar Found. 1960—, pres. 1972-74), Am. Judicature Soc., Women Lawyers Assn., Mich. (past pres.), Internacional Federacion de Abogadas, Kappa Beta Pi (editor quarterly 1961-62). Republican. Roman Catholic. Clubs: Women's City (Detroit); Pardi (past pres.), Republican Women's (Grosse Pointe); Lawyers (Washington). Home: 125 Kenwood Rd Grosse Pointe Farms MI 48236

ZIMMERMAN, VEVA HAMPTON, psychiatrist; b. St. Louis, Mar. 6, 1937; d. Henry Eugene and Julia Veva (Gullatte) Hampton; A.B., Wellesley Coll., 1958; M.D., Tufts U., 1962; m. David Radoff Zimmerman, Oct. 12, 1966; children—Jacob Ben, Tobias Eli. Intern Bronx-Lebanon Med. Center, 1962-63; resident Bellevue N.Y.U. Med. Center, 1963-66; pvt. practice psychiatry, N.Y.C., 1966—; mem. staff Harlem Hosp., 1966-68, Washington Square campus N.Y.U., 1968—; clin. asst. prof. psychiatry N.Y.U., 1972—. Mem. Am. Psychiat. Assn. (Black psychiatrist caucus). Office: 12 E 87th St New York City NY 10028

ZIMMERMANN, BETTY LOUISE (MRS. ELWOOD HENRY ZIMMERMANN), occupational therapist; b. Vallonia, Ind., Apr. 29, 1920; d. John Gustave and Elizabeth Louise (Limbeck) Jeske; B.S., Milw.-Downer Coll., 1942, B.S. in Occupational Therapy, 1943; postgrad. Purdue U., Ft. Wayne, Ind., 1973; m. Elwood Henry Zimmermann, Oct. 8, 1944; children—John, Paul, Philip, Ruth. Asst. occupational therapist Toledo Soc. for Crippled Children, 1943; dir. occupational therapy Milw. Childrens Hosp., 1943-44, Parkview Meml. Hosp., Ft. Wayne, 1968—. Lectr., Purdue U.; high sch. career guidance work; tchr. deaf children in pub. sch. system. Mem. Am., Ind. occupational therapy assns. Lutheran. Home: 1928 Reed Rd Fort Wayne IN 46805 Office: 2200 Randalia St Fort Wayne IN 46805

ZIMMERMANN, CAROLINE, direct marketing advt. exec.; b. Amityville, N.Y., Oct. 19, 1944; d. H. Paul and Frances (Short) Zimmermann; B.A. in English, Ga. State U., 1966; m. Paul R. Tully, July 26, 1969. Fulfillment mgr. book club dept. Christian Herald Pub. Co., N.Y.C., 1966-68; v.p. William Steiner Assos., Inc., N.Y.C., 1968-72; pres. Direct Marketing Communications, Inc., N.Y.C., 1973—; partner Zimmermann & Tully Co., real estate holders, 1971—; speaker in field. Home: 34 W 88th St New York City NY 10024 Office: 35 W 88th St New York City NY 10024

ZIMMERMANN, DORIS F., librarian; b. North Hempstead, N.Y., July 6, 1914; d. G. Albert and Hilda (Bohnet) Zimmermann; A.B., Mt. Holyoke Coll., 1936; M.A., Columbia, 1938. Tchr. N.Y. Inst. Edn. Blind, 1936-38; files cataloger Cravath Swaine and Moore, N.Y.C., 1938-43; librarian Fed. Res. Bank, Phila., 1943-71, mgr. library services, 1972—. Mem. Spl. Libraries Assn., English Speaking Union, Acad. Natural Scis., Phi Beta Kappa. Mem. P.E. Ch. Author: Fed in Print. Editor Fed. Res. Bank Revs. Selected Subjects, 1950—. Home: 1218 Walnut St Philadelphia PA 19107 Office: Fed Res Bank Philadelphia PA 19105

ZIMNY, MARILYN LUCILE, anatomist, educator; b. Chgo., Dec. 12, 1927; d. John and Lucile Ruth (Andryske) Zimny; B.A., U. Ill., 1948; M.S., Loyola U., Chgo., 1951, Ph.D., 1954. Asst. prof. anatomy La. State U. Med. Center, New Orleans, 1954-59, asso. prof., 1959-64, prof., 1964—. NIH grantee, 1958-72, Arthritis Found. grantee, 1969-72, Schlieder Ednl. Found. grantee, 1972-75; recipient Distinguished Faculty Service award, 1969. Mem. Am. Assn. Anatomists, Am. Physiol. Soc., Orthopaedic Research Soc., Electron Microscopic Soc. Am., A.A.A.S., Omicron Kappa Upsilon. Home: 1106 Burgundy St New Orleans LA 70116

ZIMRING, LOIS EILEEN JACOBS, educator; b. Chgo., Nov. 19, 1923; d. Edward Lawrence and Lona (Bert) Jacobs; B.S., U. Chgo., 1945, M.S., 1949, Ph.D., 1964; m. Fred M. Zimring, Dec. 17, 1949 (div. Dec. 1961); 1 son, Craig Marshall. Instr., Morgan Park Jr. Coll., Chgo., 1949-51, U. Chgo., 1959-64; asst. prof. U. Minn. at Morris, 1964-66; asst. prof. Mich. State U., East Lansing, 1966-68, asso. prof. natural sci., 1968-72, prof., 1972—; research asst. Molecular Spectroscopic Research Lab., U. Chgo., 1945-48. Mem. Am. Chem. Soc., A.A.A.S., Am. Assn. U. Profs., Am. Civil Liberties Union, Phi Beta Kappa, Sigma Xi. Contbr. articles to profl. jours. Home: 1123 Abbott Rd East Lansing MI 48823

ZINBERG, DOROTHY SHORE, sociologist; b. Boston, Feb. 25, 1928; d. Ernest and Esther (Cohen) Shore; student U. Wis., 1945-47, U. Buffalo, 1947-48; B.A., Boston U., 1949, M.A. in Sociology, 1958; Ph.D. (Nat. Inst. Mental Health fellow and teaching fellow 1958-66), Harvard, 1966; m. Norman E. Zinberg, Apr. 4, 1956; children—Sarah, Anne. Technician in biochemistry Harvard Med. Sch., Cambridge, Mass., 1949-50, research asst. in biochemistry, 1952-56, teaching asst. in biochemistry, 1956-57; research chemist Lever Bros., Cambridge, 1950-52; research asso. Center for Research in Careers Grad. Sch. Edn. Harvard U., Cambridge, 1966-67; sr. research asso. Daniel Yankelovich, Inc. (N.Y.) and Cambridge Center for Research in Behavioral Scis., 1966-68; research sociologist dept. chemistry U. Coll. London, 1968-69; acting dean North House Radcliffe Coll., Cambridge, Mass., 1970; research sociologist U. Health Services dept. chemistry Harvard U., 1969-72; lectr. dept. sociology Harvard, 1972—, research asso. Program for Sci. and Internat. Affairs, 1973—; tutor Lowell House Harvard, 1970—; asso. North House Radcliffe Coll., 1970-72. Mem. adv. com. Office Scientific Personnel NRC, Washington, 1971—. Bd. dirs. Fine Arts Workship, Provincetown, Mass., 1970—; trustee Simon's Rock Early Coll., Gt. Barrington, Mass., 1971—, Buckingham Sch., Cambridge, 1971—. Mem. A.A.A.S. (com. on sci. freedom and responsibility 1972—, opportunities in sci.). NSF fellow U. Coll. London, 1968-69, Harvard U., 1969-70; recipient Nuffield Found. award U. Coll. London, 1971-72; awards Sloan Found., 1972-73 Ford Found., 1973-74. Home: 11 Scott St Cambridge MA 02138

ZINDLER, MILDRED, sculptor; b. Bklyn., Apr. 1, 1922; d. Irving and Mae (Luban) Zindler; A.B., Fla. State U., 1945; M.A., Columbia, 1956, Ed. D., 1959; student Corcoran Sch. Art, Washington, 1942-44, 49-50, Royal Acad. (Brussels), 1952. Faculty, Towson State Coll., Balt., 1956—, prof. art, 1960—; one-man shows Vertical Gallery, Living Arts Gallery, Johns Hopkins Med. Residence Hall, Cath. Center Gallery, Van Bokklen Gallery, Towson State Coll.; exhibited in group shows Riverside Mus., Nat. Arts Club (N.Y.), Corcoran Gallery, Norton Gallery (Palm Beach, Fla.), Peale Mus. and Mus. Modern Art (Balt.); represented in pvt. collections. Danforth Found. grantee, 1963. Mem. Md. Tchrs. Assn., Am. Assn. U. Profs., Artists Equity (corr. sec. 1965, chmn. publicity 1968). Home: 3916 Susamna Rd Randallstown MD 21133 Office: Towson State Coll Baltimore MD 21204

ZINGLER, GILBERTA HEID (MRS. ERVIN KENNETH ZINGLER), librarian; b. Indpls., Feb. 24, 1911; d. Charles Herbert and Emma (Donahue) Heid; A.B., Butler U., 1932; B.S. in L.S., U. Ill., 1935; m. Ervin Kenneth Zingler, Aug. 3, 1939. Asst. loan librarian Butler U., Indpls., 1932-34; asst. librarian George Washington High Sch., Indpls., 1935-36; asst. loan librarian U. Ill. at Urbana, 1936-39; asst. reference librarian La. State Library Commn., Baton Rouge, 1939-43; order librarian Methodist U., Dallas, 1943-53; catalog librarian Library Rice U., Houston, 1953-54, order librarian, 1954-57, head acquisitions, 1958—. Mem. A.L.A., La., Tex., Southwestern library assns., Houston Library Club, Phi Mu. Home: 1700 Herman Dr Houston TX 77004 Office: PO Box 1892 Houston TX 77001

ZINK, MARY STILLMAN, educator; b. Bridgeport, Conn., July 21, 1916; d. George Willard and Clara (Preston) Zink; A.B., Cornell U., 1938, Ph.D., 1960; M.A., Yale, 1955. Exec. dir. Girl Scout Councils, various locations, 1938-52; counselor for women, instr. social sci. Quinnipiac Coll., New Haven, 1952-54; dean women, asso. prof. edn. Elon (N.C.) Coll., 1954-56; house counselor Duke, 1956-58; research asst., acting supr. Univ. Testing & Counseling Bur., Cornell U., Ithaca, N.Y., 1958-60; dir. Univ. Testing Service, asso. dean women U. Me., Orono, 1960-62, dean women, 1962-69, prof. edn., 1962-71, dean freshman, 1969-71; prof. liberal studies, chmn. social scis. Husson Coll., Bangor, Me., 1971—. Mem. Def. Adv. Com. on Women in Service, 1969-71. Mem. Am. Assn. U. Women, (br. pres. 1966-68), Nat., Me. (pres. 1965-67) assns. women deans and counselors, Am. Personnel and Guidance Assn., Am. Psychol. Assn., Pi Lambda

Theta, Phi Kappa Phi (chpt. pres. 1966-68). Club: Zonta (pres. 1972-74). Home: 29 College Heights Orono ME 04473

ZINKE, MYRA ROSE, physician; b. Buffalo, Nov. 23, 1926; d. Herman Robert and Rose Elizabeth (Gaiser) Zinke; M.D., U. Buffalo, 1950 (div.); 1 son, Matthew Sokolowski. Intern Jersey City Med. Center, 1950-51, fellow, 1952-53, resident internal medicine, 1953-56, NIH trainee, 1956-58; practice medicine specializing in internal medicine, Matawan, N.J., 1959-64, Holmdel, N.J., 1964—; mem. staff Monmouth Med. Center, Long Branch, N.J., Riverview Hosp., Red Bank, Bayshore Community Hosp., Holmdel. Asst. clin. prof. internal medicine N.J. Coll. Medicine, Newark, 1965-73. Mem. med. adv. bd. Planned Parenthood, Monmouth County, N.J. Trustee Bayshore Community Hosp., Holmdel, 1972—. Diplomate Am. Bd. Internal Medicine. Fellow A.C.P. (life); mem. Am. Med. Women's Assn. (N.J. pres. 1971, treas. 1973—), Monmouth County Med. Soc. (pres. 1972-73). Address: 895 Holmdel Rd Holmdel NJ 07733

ZINN, NANCY ELAINE WHITTEN (MRS. WILLIAM MATTHEW ZINN), librarian; b. Oak Park, Ill., June 28, 1935; d. Francis Dwight and Fern Isobel (Johnston) Whitten; B.A., U. Del., 1957; M.A., Bryn Mawr Coll., 1959; M.S. in L.S., Drexel U., 1962; m. William Matthew Zinn, Mar. 29, 1969; 1 son, Matthew Dwight. Jr. reference librarian New Haven Pub. Library, 1959-60; USPHS grantee med. library internship program Emory U., Atlanta, 1962-63; librarian trainee Phila. Pub. Library, 1960-61; head reference and circulation dept. Coll. Physicians, Phila., 1963-65; asso. librarian history collection U. Cal. at San Francisco, 1966-74, librarian, 1974—, supr. archives, 1970—, lectr. hist. health scis., 1974—. Mem. Med. Library Assn. (chmn. membership com. 1966-69, internship com. 1971-72, hist. med. group 1970-72), Am. Assn. History Medicine, Manuscript Soc., Guild Bookworkers, Soc. Cal. Archivists, No. Cal. Med. Library Group (pres. 1970-71), Phi Kappa Phi, Beta Phi Mu. Home: 1410 21st Av San Francisco CA 94122

ZINN, VENITA FLOANN, educator; b. St. Marys, W.Va., May 24, 1933; d. Joseph Lealand and Gladys Elisabeth (Randolph) Vincent; B.A., Salem Coll., 1955; M.A., W.Va. U., 1966; m. William Frederick Zinn, Jan. 25, 1952; children—Martin Conrad, Leona Fredette, Franklin Eugene, Beatrice Alberta. Tchr., recreation dir. W.Va. Indsl. Home for Girls, 1957-63; mem. faculty Salem Coll., 1965—, now asso. prof., chmn. dept. oral communication. Mem. Laudati Soc. (pres. 1967-68). Baptist (tchr., youth leader, dir. Christian Edn.). Home: Route 3 Valley View Salem WV 26426

ZINNER, THELMA SCHWARTZ, lawyer; b. Chgo., Nov. 17, 1922; d. Ben Irving and Sara Ida (Rouske) Schwartz; student U. Ill. at Urbana, 1940; J.D., DePaul U., 1946; m. Leon Zinner, Apr. 27, 1942; children—Lynn (Mrs. Michael Schoenberger), Hollis Leslie. Admitted to Ill. bar, 1947; practiced in Chgo., 1947-49, 1950-52, Urbana, 1949, Biloxi, Miss., 1965—; McKoin, Zinner, Hawkins & Johnson, 1968-71, Zinner & Hawkins, 1971-73; master in chancery Harrison County, Miss., 1973—. Dir. Koockie Fashions, Inc., Ocean Springs, Miss., Coastal Motorcycle, Inc., Biloxi. Chmn. Miss. Gulf Coast chpt. A.R.C., 1968-71; chmn. Gulf Coast United Jewish Appeal, 1970—; chmn. Miss. Gulf Coast Help, Inc., 1971—; team cap. United Fund Drive, Biloxi, 1972-73. Bd. dirs. Gulf Coast Mental Health Center Initiation and Devel. Drug Project. Named Outstanding Citizen Jackson County Bus. and Profl. Women's Club, 1973. Mem. Nat. Assn. Women Lawyers, Miss., Harrison County, Ill. Biloxi (pres. 1972-73) bar assns., Nat. Council Jewish Women, Ocean Springs Intra Club Council. Jewish religion. Club: Gulf Hills Golf. Home: 45 Shore Dr Ocean Springs MS 39564 Office: 523 Lameuse St Biloxi MS 29533

ZINNES, HARRIET FICH, educator; b. Hyde Park, Mass., Apr. 18, 1919; d. Assir N. and Sara L. (Goldberg) F.; B.A., Hunter Coll., 1939; M.A., Bklyn. Coll., 1944; Ph.D., N.Y. U., 1953; m. Irving I. Zinnes, Sept. 24, 1943; children—Clifford, Alice. Editor publs. div. Raritan (N.J.) Arsenal, 1942-43; asso. editor Harper's Bazaar, 1944-46; tutor Hunter Coll., 1946-49; tutor Queen's Coll., 1949-53, asso. prof. English, 1962—; lectr. Rutgers U., 1961-62; art and lit. critic Weekly Tribune, Geneva, Switzerland, 1968-70; art critic Pictures on Exhibit, 1971—; vis. prof. Am. Lit. U. Geneva, 1969; poetry cons. Gt. Neck (N.Y.) Pub. Library. Resident fellow MacDowell Colony, Peterborough, N.H., 1972, 73. Mem. Am. Center P.E.N., Poetry Soc. Am., Acad. Am. Poets, English Grads. Assn. N.Y. U. Author: Waiting and Other Poems, 1964; An Eye for an I, 1966; I Wanted to See Something Flying. Contbr. articles and revs. to numerous mags. and jours., poems to mags. and anthologies. Home: 9 Cary Rd Great Neck NY 11021 Office: Dept English Queens Coll Flushing NY 11367

ZINOBER, JOAN WAGNER, health services adminstr., psychologist, educator; b. Los Angeles, July 30, 1944; d. Leonard I. and Maida Ruth (Prenn) Wagner; B.A. in Psychology, Mich. State U., 1965; M.A. in Child and Devel. Psychology, U. Conn., 1967, Ph.D. in Child and Devel. Psychology, 1970; m. Peter Wolfson Zinober, June 13, 1971. Asst. prof. ednl. psychology N.Y. U., N.Y.C., 1969-71; research coordinator Office Edn., U.S. Dept. Health, Edn. and Welfare, Washington, 1971-72; dir. research and evaluation Hillsborough Community Mental Health Center, Tampa, 1972—; clin asst. prof. psychiatry U.S. Fla., Tampa 1972—. Cons. community mental health evaluation, 1972—. USPHS fellow, 1968-69; N.Y. U. Office Ednl. Research Services grant, 1970-71, U.S. Office Edn. grant, 1965-68. Mem. Am., Fla. Psychol. assns., Hillsborough, Mental Health Assn., So. Regional Conf. Mental Health Statistics, Fla. Mental Health Consortium. Contbr. articles to profl. jours. Home: 2502 Sunset Dr Tampa FL 33609 Office: 5707 N 22d St Tampa FL 33610

ZION, LEELA CLARICE, educator; b. San Francisco, Nov. 4, 1929; d. Edwin Ray and Clarice (Davis) Zion; A.A., San Mateo Jr. Coll., 1948; B.A., Chico State Coll., 1950; M.A., Stanford, 1951; Ed.D., U. Cal. at Berkeley, 1963. Tchr. girls' phys. edn. San Juan Union High Sch., Fair Oaks, Cal., 1951-53; instr. health and phys. edn. Central Wash. Coll., Ellensburg, 1953-55; service club dir. U.S. Govt., Laon, France, 1955-58; lectr. health, phys. edn. and recreation Mills Coll., Oakland, Cal., 1958-59; prof. health and phys. edn. Humboldt State U., Arcata, Cal., 1959—, sec. gen. faculty, 1965-66, sec. acad. senate, 1969-70. Commr. Arcata Parks and Recreation Commn., 1967-71. Mem. A.A.H.P.E.R. (Cal.-N. chmn. girls and womens sports com. 1968-69), N.E.A., Am. Assn. U. Profs., No. Cal. Women's Intercollegiate Council (pres. 1969-70), Cal. Assn. Health, Phys. Edn. and Recreation (dist. chmn. div. girls and womens sports 1960-61), Cal. Tchrs. Assn., Cal. State Employees Assn., Assn. Cal. State Coll. Profs. Ednl. Research Assn. A.A.A.S., Western Soc. Phys. Edn. Coll. Women, Nat. Assn. Phys. Edn. Coll. Women, Internat. Acad. Aquatic Art, Internat. Soc. Gen. Semantics, Amateur Fencers League Am. Internat. Council Health, Phys. Edn. and Recreation, Delta Kappa Gamma. Contbr. chpt. to textbook. Home: 1570 Bayside Rd Arcata CA 95521

ZIPF, DOROTHY CHALLIS (MITZI) (MRS. WALTER ZIPF), reporter, editor; b. Omaha, July 13, 1899; d. William Allen and Jessie lileon (Jenkins) Challis; A.A., St. Joseph Jr. Coll., 1920; A.B., U. Ariz., 1935; m. Walter Henry Zipf, Aug. 23, 1942. Reporter Gazette, St. Joseph, Mo., 1920-21; news staff Phila. Daily News, 1925-26; editorial asst. System Mag. Bus., A. W. Shaw Co., Chgo., 1926-27; soc. editor, feature writer, Ariz. Republic, Mesa, free-lance publicity, pub. relations, 1927-41, book rev. editor, reporter, 1951-64; telegraph editor Douglas (Ariz.) Dispatch, 1941-45, Prescott (Ariz.) Courier, 1945-48; woman's editor Sun Valley Spur, Mesa, 1965—. Mem. Ariz. State Hist. Adv. Com., 1962—; adv. bd. Mesa Assn. for Retarded Children, 1957—, bd. dirs., 1966—; bd. mem. Mesa United Fund. Recipient Best Writer award Ariz. Newspaper Assn., 1964; Cultural Affairs award, Mesa C. of C., 1970; Mesa Woman of Year award, 1971. Mem. Mesa Fine Arts Assn. (dir.), Mesa Archeol. and Hist. Soc. (pres.), Ariz. Press Women, Nat. Fedn. Press Women, Mesa Bus. and Prof. Women's Club (Woman of Year 1956), M.M.S., Am. Assn. U. Women, Theta Sigma Phi. Episcopalian. Clubs: Superstition Kennel, Soroptimist (pres. 1961-62). Home: 112 E Marilyn Av Mesa AZ 85202 Office: 132 W 1st Av Mesa AZ 85202

ZIRKLE, VIRGINIA IRENE, home economist; b. Tippicanoe, Ind., Sept. 18, 1923; d. Paul and Gladys Fern (Galvert) Zirkle; B.Sc., Ohio State U., 1945; postgrad. U. Wis., 1952; M.A., Columbia U., 1959. Tchr., home econs. and English, Sugar Creek Sch., Vaughnsville, O., 1945-47; extension home economist, Ohio State U., Ottawa, 1947—. Bd. dirs. Tb and Health Assn., 1957-73, Putnam County Unit Am. Cancer Soc., 1964-73; 4H Camp Palmer, 1955-71. Horace B. Moses scholar, 1952; Pfizer fellow, 1958; recipient Distinguished Service award, Ohio State U. Sch. Home Econs., 1971. Mem. Nat. Assn. County Agrl. Agts. (chpt. exec. com., 1967-71), Ohio Coop. Extension Agts. Assn. (pres. 1973—), Nat. Assn. Extension Home Economists (dir., Distinguished Service award 1958), Ohio State U. Alumni Assn. (county chpt. 1st. v.p., 1969-72; pres. 1972), Am., Ohio, Allen County home econs. assns., Am. Cancer Soc., Epsilon Sigma Phi, Omicron Nu. Home: 1165 E 3d St Ottawa OH 45875 Office: 219 S Oak St Ottawa OH 45875

ZIRWES, ELIZABETH ANN, real estate broker; b. Burbank, Cal., Dec. 7, 1941; d. Franklin Theodore and Rachel Mary (Jaques) Zirwes; student Grossmont Coll., 1971-72, John Hancock Bus. Sch., St. Louis, 1963-64. Pub. relations St. Louis Globe Democrat newspaper, 1963-69; broker Service Realty, El Cajon, Cal., 1969—; sec.-treas. Delta San Diego, Inc.; artists mgr. Delta Prodns. Home and office: 224 S Orange St El Cajon CA 92020

ZISK, BETTY ANN HERSHBERGER (MRS. STANLEY H. ZISK), educator; b. Washington, Nov. 10, 1930; d. William Delmar and Mary (Martin) Hershberger; B.A., Swarthmore Coll., 1951; M.A., Haverford Coll., 1953; Ph.D., Stanford, 1964; m. Stanley H. Zisk, July 3, 1954; children—Jonathan Lee, Stephen Robert, Matthew Bruce. Research asst., editor Soc. of Friends Com. on Nat. Legislation, Washington, 1952-55; teaching asst., dept. polit. sci. Stanford U., 1960-63, acting asst. prof., 1964; asst. prof., dept. govt. Boston U., 1965-69, asso. prof., 1969-72, prof., 1972—. NSF grantee, 1969-73. Mem. Am., Midwest, New Eng. polit. sci. assns. Mem. Religious Soc. of Friends. Author: Local Interest Politics: A One-Way Street, 1972. Editorial bd. Midwest Jour. Polit. Sci., 1971-73, Am. Polit. Quar., 1972—, Social Sci. Quar., 1972—. Home: 9 Diana Lane Lexington MA 02173 Office: 232 Bay State Rd Boston MA 02215

ZISKIN, LEAH ZOOLE (MRS. MARVIN CARL ZISKIN), physician; b. Pottsville, Pa., Nov. 30, 1936; d. Charles Daniel and Bertha J. (Cohen) Zoole; A.B. summa cum laude, Temple U., 1958; M.D., 1962; m. Marvin Carl Ziskin, Aug. 14, 1960; children—Daniel, Alan, Jennie. Intern, Cooper Hosp. Camden, N.J., 1962-63; practice gen. medicine Cherry Hill, N.J., 1963-66; occupational medicine at Wright-Patterson AFB, Dayton, Ohio, 1966-68; pub. health physician, Camden, N.J., 1968-71; pub. health resident N.J. Dept. Health, 1971-74, chief communicable disease program, 1974—. Home: 900 Abington Rd Cherry Hill NJ 08034

ZISKIND, SYLVIA GOLDBERG (MRS. DAVID ZISKIND), educator; b. Phila., Jan. 12, 1906; d. Israel and Sara (Starkman) Goldberg; student Cumnock Coll., Los Angeles, 1925-27; B.A., U. Cal. at Berkeley, 1930; M.A., U. So. Cal., 1937; M.A. in L.S., Immaculate Heart Coll., 1962; m. David Ziskind, June 5, 1931; children—Ellen (Mrs. Robert Berg), Jane (Mrs. Raymond Carhart). Tchr. speech, drama, Washington, 1936-41; librarian Bellflower (Cal.) High Sch., 1949-62; lectr. Immaculate Heart Coll., Los Angeles, 1958-62, asst. prof. library sci., 1962-65, asso. prof., 1966-72, acting dean library sci., 1971-72; guest prof. Simmons Coll., summer, 1966, U. So. Cal., summers 1972-74; cons. sch. libraries; lectr. children's lit. Active Reading is Fundamental program, Los Angeles. Mem. Am. Assn. U. Profs., Am., Cal. (sect. pres. 1967) library assns., Cal. Assn. Sch. Libraries (sect. pres. 1959), So. Cal. Council Lit. for Children (v.p. 1968), Zeta Phi Eta. Author: Reference Readiness, 1971. Home: 2339 Silver Ridge Av Los Angeles CA 90039

ZISS, JUDITH SEPLOWITZ (MRS. ALEXANDER ZISS), lawyer; b. Bronx, N.Y., Sept. 17, 1943; d. Joseph and Mildred Seplowitz; B.A. magna cum laude, U. Pa., 1965; LL.B. cum laude, Columbia, 1968; m. Alexander Ziss, Mar. 15, 1971. Admitted to Conn. bar, 1968, N.Y. bar, 1974; atty. appellate sect. civil div. U.S. Dept Justice, Washington, 1968-71, atty. antitrust div., N.Y.C., 1972—. Mem. Fed. Bar Assn. (nat. dir. council younger lawyers 1970-71), Conn., N.Y. bar assns., Phi Beta Kappa. Home: 19-12 Greenwood Dr Fair Lawn NJ 07410 Office: 26 Federal Plaza New York City NY 10007

ZISSIS, CECELIA, univ. dean; b. Lebanon, Ind., Feb. 23, 1919; d. John and Georgia (Antonakous) Zissis; B.S., Purdue U., 1949, M.S., 1953; Ph.D., U. Mich., 1962. Producer-dir., radio sta. WBAA, Purdue U., Lafayette, Ind., 1949-50, asst. dean women, 1950-55, 57-68, asso. dean women, 1968—; dir. Span Plan program for women, 1970; univ. fellow, counseling lab. U. Mich., 1956-57. Mem. Nat., Ind. assns. women deans and counselors, Am. Personnel and Guidance Assn., Am. Coll. Personnel Assn., Nat. Vocational Guidance Assn., Am. Assn. U. Women (dir. 1973-75), Mortar Bd., Pi Lambda Theta. Home: 629 Rose St West Lafayette IN 47906

ZITIN, MARGO KAUFMAN (MRS. GILBERT N. ZITIN), advt. and pub. relations exec.; b. Indpls., Oct. 21, 1939; d. Ben and Helen (Hassan) Kaufman; A.B., Vassar Coll., 1960; postgrad. Bryn Mawr, U., 1963-64; m. William H. Maxman, Dec. 20, 1959 (div. Dec. 1969); children—Melissa Helen, William H., Abby Kaufman; m. Gilbert N. Zitin, May 21, 1971. Nat. pub. relations dir. Phila. Designers Show House, 1965-69; pub. relations asst. Advt. and Pub. Relations Dept., 1st Pa. Bank, Phila., 1969-71, editor First Word, 1969-71; dir. advt. and pub. relations Mgmt. Data Corp., Cherry Hill, N.J., 1971—. Mem. World Affairs Council Phila., 1965-68. Bd. dirs. Rodeph Shalom Nursery Sch., 1967-71. Clubs: Philadelphia Vassar (exec. bd. 1964-69); Philmont (Pa.) Country. Home: 225 McClenaghan Mill Rd Wynnewood PA 19096 Office: 26 Springdale Rd Cherry Hill NJ 08003

ZITTEL, MILDRED ADELINE, exporter; b. N.Y.C., Dec. 27, 1926; d. Walter William and Florence Marie (Lindeke) G.; student Emporia State Tchrs. Coll., 1946-47; m. Walter Robert Zittel, June 14, 1947; children—Walter David, Warren Arthur, Eric Gordon. Country elevator co-ordinator Garvey Grain, Inc., Wichita, Kan., 1966-68; export coordinator Garvey Internat., Inc., Wichita, 1969—. Mem. Am. Recorder Soc., Classic Guitar Soc., Cosmopals (pres. 1972). Episcopalian (choir mother 1958—). Home: 2163 Bella Vista St Wichita KS 67203 Office: 515 R H Garvey Bldg 300 W Douglas St Wichita KS 67202

ZMUDA, MARCIA LOUISE BLUMENFELD (MRS. RAYMOND ANTHONY ZMUDA, JR.), city ofcl.; b. Pitts., July 5, 1949; d. Adolph Meyers and Dorothy Marie (O'Brien) Blumenfeld; B.S. in Journalism (Pa. scholar), Ohio U., 1970; m. Raymond Anthony Zmuda, Jr., Sept. 30, 1972. Pub. relations intern Bethesda Hosp., Zanesville, O., 1969; jr. exec. publs. specialist Norfolk (Va.) Redevel. and Housing Authority, 1973—. Served as pub. affairs officer USNR, 1970-72, lt. (j.g.) Res., 1972—. Mem. Women in Communications, Sigma Delta Chi. Roman Catholic. Home: Park Towne Apts 4023-A Flowerfield Rd Norfolk VA 23518 Office: Box 968 Norfolk VA 23501

ZOBEL, LOUISE PURWIN (MRS. JEROME FREMONT ZOBEL), author, lectr.; b. Laredo, Tex., Jan. 10, 1922; d. Leo Max and Ethel Catherine (Levy) Purwin; B.A., Stanford, 1943, postgrad.; m. Jerome Fremont Zobel, Nov. 14, 1943; children—Lenore (Mrs. R. Thomas Harris), Janice, Robert, Audrey (Mrs. Todd Dollinger). Writer, editor United Press Bur., San Francisco, 1943; free lance mag. writer Palo Alto, Cal., 1942-45, 58—; lectr. writing subjects, history and travel subjects No. Cal., 1964—; tchr. mag. writing Foothill Community Coll., Los Altos, Cal., 1969—; editorial asst. Bull. Assn. Coll. Unions-Internat., Palo Alto, 1972-73; lectr., tchr. adult edn. travel programs No. Cal., 1973—; cruise enrichment travel lectr., tchr. writing Royal Viking Lines, 1974—. Resource person New Life Patterns for Women, YWCA, Palo Alto, 1966; chmn. Non-fiction Seminars, Cal. Writers Club Conf., Oakland, 1967. Mem. Cal. Writers Club (v.p. Peninsula br. 1970-71), Nat. League Am. Pen Women, Am. Assn. U. Women (1st v.p. charge program Palo Alto br. 1955-57, dir., publicity chmn.), Santa Clara County Med. Aux. (v.p. programs 1964-65, 70-71, publicity chmn.), Stanford Alumni Assn., Stanford Med. Faculty Wives, Women in Communications, Phi Beta Kappa, Sigma Delta Chi (award for scholarship in journalism 1943). Contbr. articles to mags. Address: 877 Northampton Dr Palo Alto CA 94303

ZOERB, VIRGINIA GLOVER (MRS. DELBERT M. ZOERB), newspaper editor; b. Youngstown, O., Sept. 13, 1920; d. Henry James and Hannah Myrll (Baker) Glover; B.S.J., Ohio U., 1942; m. Delbert Meredith Zoerb, July 1, 1949. With Youngstown Vindicator, 1942—, copy editor, 1943-70, women's page editor, 1971—. Mem. Nat. Panhellenic Editors Conf. (chmn. 1971). Women in Communications, Phi Mu (editor Aglaia, 1960—). Home: 114 Mill Run Dr Youngstown OH 44505 Office: The Vindicator Youngstown OH 44501

ZOESCH, MARIAN ROSE, occupational therapist; b. International Falls, Minn., Sept. 13, 1935; d. Walter Gustavus Joseph and Buelah Marian (Benson) Zoesch; B.S. in Occupational Therapy, U. Puget Sound, Tacoma, 1958. Occupational therapist VA Hosp., Muskogee, Okla., 1959-61, Eastern State Hosp., Medical Lake, Wash., 1962-71, Spokane Community Mental Health Center, 1971. Community mental health rep., mem. planning and evaluation com. Spokane Regional Agy. Aging, 1971—. Grantee workshops. Mem. Am., Wash. occupational therapy assns., Nat. Rehab. Assn. Lutheran (sec. Luth. Council Greater Spokane Area 1972—; parish life commn. Luth. Ch. Am. 1973—). Soroptimist, Toastmistress. Contbr. articles to jours. Home: 4828 N Cannon St Spokane WA 99208 Office: 107 S Division St Spokane WA 99202

ZOLBER, KATHLEEN KEEN (MRS. MELVIN L. ZOLBER), educator; b. Walla Walla, Wash., Dec. 9, 1916; d. Wildie H. and Alice (Johnson) Keen; B.S. in Foods and Nutrition, Walla Walla Coll., 1941; M.A., Wash. State U., 1961; Ph.D., U. Wis., 1968; m. Melvin L. Zolber, Sept. 19, 1937. Dir. food service Walla Walla Coll., 1941-50, mgr. coll store, 1951-59, asst. prof. food and nutrition, 1959-62, asso. prof., 1962-64; asso. prof. nutrition Loma Linda (Cal.) U., 1964-72, prof. nutrition, 1972—, dir. dietetic edn., 1967—. Mead Johnson grantee, 1965-67. Mem. Am. Dietetic Assn., Am. Pub. Health Assn., Am. Home Econs. Assn., Am. Mgmt. Assn., Am. Assn. U. Profs., Creative Edn. Found., Soc. Personnel Adminstrn., Omicron Nu. Mailing address: Box 981 Loma Linda CA 92354

ZOLOTOW, CHARLOTTE SHAPIRO, editor, author; b. Norfolk, Va., June 26, 1915; d. Louis J. and Ella F. (Bernstein) Shapiro; student U. Wis., 1933-36; m. Maurice Zolotow, Apr. 14, 1938 (div. 1969); children—Stephen, Ellen. Sr. editor children's book dept. Harper & Row, N.Y.C., 1938-44, sr. editor, 1962—; tchr. U. Colo. Writers Conf. on Children's Books, U. Ind. Writers Conf.; also lectr. childrens books. Author: The Park Book, 1944; Big Brother, 1960; The Sky Was Blue, 1963; The Magic Words, 1952; Indian Indian, 1952; The Bunny Who Found Easter, 1959; In My Garden, 1960; Not a Little Monkey, 1957; The Man With The Purple Eyes, 1961; Mr. Rabbit and the Lovely Present, 1962; The White Marble, 1963; A Rose, A Bridge and A Wild Black Horse, 1964; Someday, 1965; When I Have a Little Girl, 1965; If It Weren't for You, 1966; Big Sister, Little Sister, 1966; All That Sunlight, 1967; When I Have A Son, 1968; My Friend John, 1968; Summer Is, 1968; Some Things Go Together, 1969; The Hating Book, 1969; The New Friend, 1969; River Winding, 1970; Lateef and His World, 1970; Yani and His World, 1970; You and Me, 1971; Wake Up and Goodnight, 1971; William's Doll, 1972; Hold My Hand, 1972; The Beautiful Christmas Tree, 1972; Janey, 1973; My Grandson Lew, 1974; others. Recipient Harper gold medal for editorial excellence. Mem. Pen Soc., Authors League. Home: 29 Elm Pl Hastings on Hudson NY 10706 Office: Harper and Row 49 E 33d St New York City NY 10016

ZONERAICH, OLGA BELIS (MRS. SAMUEL ZONERAICH), physician; b. Harlau, Rumania, Jan. 4, 1926 (came to U.S., 1962, naturalized, 1967); d. Iancu and Laura (Leibovici) Belis; M.D., Sch. Medicine Iassy-U., 1951; student Med. Sch. State U. N.Y., 1965; m. Samuel Zoneraich, Jan. 5, 1947. Intern Univ. Hosp., Iassy, 1948-49, resident, 1949-50; intern Flushing (N.Y.) Hosp., 1962-63; resident VA Hosp., 1963-66; practice medicine specializing in cardiology Iassy Med. Sch., 1951-61, Paris, France, 1961-62; mem. staff L.I. Jewish Med. Center, Queens Hosp. Center, N.Y.C. Researcher Cardiographic Lab. Research Hosp., Queens, N.Y., 1966—; asso. prof. medicine State U. N.Y. at Stony Brook, 1972—. Fellow Am. Coll. Angiology.; mem. Harvey Soc., Queens County Med. Assn., A.M.A. Contbg. author: Vectorcardiography 2, 1971. Contbr. to profl. jours. Home: 69-43 Utopia Pkwy Flushing NY 11365

ZORNIG, PHYLLIS JUNE, investment co. exec.; b. Chgo., June 14, 1933; d. Elmer Bruce and Ethel Martha (Smith) Spielman; student Patricia Stevens Finishing Sch., 1950, Loop Jr. Coll., City Colls. of Chgo., 1970; div.; children—Charles William III, David Eugene. Showgirl, singer, chorus dancer, Chgo., 1952-55; receptionist Joy Recording Studios, Chgo., 1966; asst. dir.-producer Producers Corp. of Am. Indsl. Shows, 1966-67; mgmt. cons. Indsl. Systems Corp., 1967-69; exec. sec. Office of Planning, Research and Evaluation, Loop Jr. Coll., 1969-71; exec. sec. Dick Loew & Assos., Chgo., 1971-74; office adminstrn. mgr. Monex Internat. Ltd., Chgo., 1974—. Publicity chmn. Central P.T.A., Evanston, Ill., 1962-63; assn. sec. William B. Ogden P.T.A., Chgo., 1965-68; hospitality chmn. YWCA-Young Wives Club, 1963-64; house staff Old Town Players Community

Theatre, 1972—. Unitarian. Home: 11 E Elm St Chicago IL 60611 Office: 645 N Michigan Av Chicago IL 60611

ZORZOLI, ANITA, educator; b. N.Y.C., Dec. 27, 1917; A.B. Hunter Coll., 1938; A.M., Columbia, 1940; Ph.D.(fellow), N.Y.U., 1945. Asst. in zoology Columbia, 1940-42; asst. instr. biology N.Y.U., 1944-45; research asst. pathology Washington U. Sch. Medicine, St. Louis, 1945-46, instr. physiology and biochemistry Sch. Dentistry, 1940-49, research asso. pharmacology, 1948-49, asst. prof. physiology and biochemistry, 1948-52; asst. prof. physiology So. Ill. U., 1952-55; asso. prof. Vassar Coll., Poughkeepsie, N.Y., 1955-61, prof., 1961—, John Guy Vassar chair natural history, 1973—. Mem. corp. Marine Biol. Lab., Woods Hole, Mass. Fellow A.A.A.S., Am. Gerontology Soc. (v.p. 1965-66); mem. Am. Physiol. Soc., Zool. Soc. Am., Internat. Assn. Gerontology. Address: Dept Biology Vassar Coll Poughkeepsie NY 12601

ZUCKER, ADELE HABER (MRS. HENRY J. ZUCKER), journalist; b. Chambersburg, Pa., Apr. 7, 1932; d. Ira and Caroline (Reiner) Haber; B.S., Ohio U., 1954; m. Henry J. Zucker, Sept. 2, 1956; children—Clifford A., JoAnn Sue. Program editor TV Guide mag., Cleve., 1954-56; editor internal publ. Blue Cross of N.E. Ohio, Cleve., 1956-58; suburban reporter Cleve. Plain Dealer, 1967-74; Cleve. rep. for cotton promotions Nat. Cotton Council, N.Y.C., 1969-71; freelancer The Flappers, 1974—. Recipient citation for work in Northeastern Ohio Indsl. Editors Assn., 1958. Mem. Women in Communications, Womens Am. ORT (chpt. pres. 1973—), Hadassah, Parent Vol. Assn. for Retarded Children, Nat. Council Jewish Women. Home: 2461 Claver Rd University Heights OH 44118

ZUCKER, DEVRA HILL (MRS. IRWIN ZUCKER), author; b. Berkeley, Cal., Aug. 26; d. James J. and Giovanna Z. (Muzio) Bolton; student San Francisco City Coll., 1953, San Francisco State Coll., 1954-55, U. Cal. at Berkeley, 1956; m. Irwin Zucker, Sept. 1, 1957; children—Lori Brana, Judi Michele and Shari Lynne (twins). Columnist, So. Cal. Newspaper Pub. Co. Author: Three to Make Merry, 1961; You Better Believe It, 1962; My Name is Leona Gage, 1964. Contbr. articles to mags., newspapers. Home: 714 N Crescent Dr Beverly Hills CA 90210

ZUCKER, ISABEL SCHNAPPER (MRS. MYRON ZUCKER), hort. journalist; b. Phila.; d. Henry and Johanna (Neugass) Schnapper; B.S., Cornell U., 1926, postgrad., 1927-28; m. Myron Zucker, Jan. 28, 1929; children—Judith (Mrs. David Clark), Ralph, Jack. Owner flower shop Great Neck, N.Y., 1926-29, landscape firm, 1929-40; garden editor The Detroit Times, 1941-60; editor Question Box, Flower Grower Mag., 1961-62; dir. Nat. Garden Bur., Bloomfield Hills, Mich., 1962-72; tchr. counsellor Camp Pontiac, Mich. Conservation-Corrections Program, 1954—. Recipient plaque All Am. Selections, 1971; honor plaque award Am. Seed Trade Soc., 1958; named Garden Writer of the Year, Am. Assn. Nurserymen, 1964. Fellow Royal Hort. Soc. (Great Britain); mem. Garden Writers Assn. Am. (editor Bulletin 1949-69, pres. 1969-71), Am. (citation 1967), Mich. (medal 1966), Mass. hort. socs., Internat. Am. socs. hort. sci., Internat. Lilac Soc. (dir. 1972—). Author: Flowering Shrubs, 1966; Four Seasons of Fun for Youngsters, 1969. Home and office: 708 W Long Lake Rd Bloomfield Hills MI 48013

ZUCKER, MARJORIE BASS (MRS. HOWARD D. ZUCKER), physiologist, educator; b. N.Y.C.; d. Murray H. and Agnes (Naumburg) Bass; A.B., Vassar Coll., 1939; Ph.D., Columbia, 1944; student, Columbia U. Coll. Phys. and Surg., 1943-45; m. Howard D. Zucker, June 25, 1938; children—Andrew, Ellen, Joan, Barbara. Research asst. physiology Columbia U. Coll. Phys. and Surg., N.Y.C., 1945-49; asst. prof. physiology N.Y.U. Coll. Dentistry, 1949-54, asso. prof., 1954-55; asso. mem. Sloan-Kettering Inst. Cancer Research, N.Y.C., 1955-63; asso. prof. physiology Sloan-Kettering Div., Grad. Sch. Med. Sci., Cornell U. Med. Coll., N.Y.C., 1955-63; mem. grad. faculty N.Y.U., 1955, 63—, asso. prof. pathology, 1963-71, prof. pathology, 1971—; asst. research dir. Am. Nat. Red Cross Research Lab., N.Y.U. Med. Center; 1963-70; mem. NIH Hematology study sect., 1970-74. Fellow N.Y., Acad. Scis.; mem. Am. Physiol. Soc., Harvey Soc., Soc. Exptl. Biology and Medicine, Soc. Study of Blood, Internat. Soc. Hematology, Am. Soc. Hematology, Sigma Xi. Editor in hematology Proc. of Soc. Exptl. Biology and Medicine, 1960-65. Editorial bd. Transfusion, 1968—, Am. Jour. Physiology, 1969—, Thrombosis Diathesis Haemorrhagica, 1972—. Home: 333 Central Park W New York City NY 10025

ZUCKER, PHYLLIS ANN (MRS. JACK I. ZUCKER), occupational therapist; b. Columbus, O., Apr. 23, 1932; d. Joe and Sara (Koltun) Blane; B.S., Ohio State U., 1956; m. Jack I. Zucker, Sept. 19, 1954; children—Ralph, Miriam, Steven. Occupational therapist Highland View Hosp., Cleve., 1956, 65-66; chief occupational therapy Sunny Acres Hosp., Cleve. 1966-73; sr. occupational therapist in neurology VA Hosp., Wade Park, Cleve., 1974; pvt. practice, 1974—. Mem. adv. bd. occupational therapy asst. curriculum Cuyahoga Community Coll., 1971—. Mem. Am. Occupational Therapy Assn., Hadassah (group pres. 1965-66). Home: 2420 Fenwick Rd University Heights OH 44118

ZUCKERMAN, LINDA JANE, editor; b. Bklyn., Sept. 30, 1941; d. Benjamin Harry and Hildegarde (Kesilman) Zuckerman; B.A., Bklyn. Coll., City U. N.Y., 1963. Editor Springer Pub. Co., Inc., N.Y.C., 1965-67; asso. editor Four Winds Press div. Scholastic Mags., N.Y.C., 1967-72; asso. editor Viking Jr. Books, Viking Press, N.Y.C., 1972-73, editor, 1973—. Mem. Janus Chorale N.Y., Inc. (pres., gen. mgr. 1969—). Home: 113 Columbia Heights Brooklyn NY 11201 Office: Viking Press 625 Madison Av New York City NY 10022

ZUNIGHA, BENNIE JEAN, educator, home economist; b. Okemah, Okla., June 11, 1926; d. Benjamin Berry and Olive (Shumard) Benson; B.A., Okla. Baptist U., Shawnee, 1948; M.Ed., U. Okla., 1964; postgrad. U. No. Ariz., Flagstaff, 1966-67; postgrad. Indian housing and Indian sociology, Manitee Jr. Coll., Bradenton, Fla., 1971, edn. Indian youth, Northwestern U., Weatherford, Okla., 1972; m. Freeman Wilson Zunigha, Dec. 24, 1947; children—Merle Eugene, Michael Dale, Roger Lynn, Olivia Ann, Gayla Jo. Tchr. home econs. Tecumseh (Okla.) High Sch., 1951; elementary tchr. Rock Point Boarding Sch., Chinle, Ariz., 1963-64; tchr. home econs. Wingate Boarding Sch., Ft. Wingate, N.M., 1964-67; supr. home econs. and bus. dept. Wingate High Sch., 1968—; tchr., prin. Okla. Elementary Sch., Newkirk, 1960-63; active projects Bur. Indian Affairs, Navajo area high schs. Recipient spl. commendations for work with Indians. Mem. Nat. Soc. Study Edn., Delta Kappa Gamma (1st v.p. Upsilon chpt. 1969). Baptist. Home: 601 Cedar St Fort Wingate NM 87316

ZWART, ELIZABETH CLARKSON, columnist; b. Des Moines, Aug. 20, 1904; d. Joseph Stripe and Bertha (Clarkson) Zwart; grad. pvt. sch.; m. Donald J. Metcalf, Jan. 14, 1928; 1 dau., Elizabeth Clarkson. Reporter, woman's page editor Des Moines Capitol, 1924-26; woman's page editor Des Moines Tribune, 1927; book editor Des Moines Sunday Register, 1935-49; writer Front Row column Des Moines Tribune, Des Moines Sunday Register, 1931—. Home: 3221 Grand Av Des Moines IA 50312 Office: 715 Locust St Des Moines IA 50304